SCOTT

1996 Standard Postage Stamp Catalogue

ONE HUNDRED AND FIFTY-SECOND EDITION IN SIX VOLUMES

VOLUME 2

EUROPEAN COUNTRIES and COLONIES,
INDEPENDENT NATIONS of
AFRICA, ASIA, LATIN AMERICA

A-C

VICE PRESIDENT/PUBLISHER	Stuart J. Morrissey
EDITOR	James E. Kloetzel
ASSOCIATE EDITOR	William W. Cummings
VALUING EDITOR	Martin J. Frankevicz
NEW ISSUES EDITOR	David C. Akin
COMPUTER CONTROL COORDINATOR	Denise Oder
VALUING ANALYST	Jose R. Capote
EDITORIAL ASSISTANTS	Judith E. Bertrand, Beth Brown
CONTRIBUTING EDITOR	Joyce Nelson
ART/PRODUCTION DIRECTOR	Janine C. S. Apple
PRODUCTION COORDINATOR	Nancy S. Martin
PRODUCTION ARTIST	Meg Schultz
MARKETING/SALES DIRECTOR	William Fay
ADVERTISING	David Lodge
CIRCULATION/PRODUCT PROMOTION MANAGER	Tim Wagner

Scott Publishing Co.

911 Vandemark Road, Sidney, OH 45365

A division of AMOS PRESS, INC., publishers of *Linn's Stamp News, Coin World, Cars & Parts* magazine, *Moneycard Collector* and *The Sidney Daily News.*

Table of Contents

See Volume 1A for United States and affiliated territories, United Nations, Canada and British America.

See Volume 1B for the British Commonwealth of Nations other than British America.

See Volumes 3, 4 and 5 for nations of Africa, Asia, Europe, Latin America D-Z and their affiliated territories.

Copyright Notice

Trademark Notice

ISBN 0-89487-210-9

Library of Congress Card No. 2-3301

Scott Publishing Co.

911 VANDEMARK ROAD, SIDNEY, OHIO 45365 513-498-0802

SCOTT

Dear Catalogue User:

At the beginning of each year, we get together and ask ourselves a very basic question. Why should someone buy the next edition of the Scott Catalogue? After all, in many cases a catalogue user just spent $198 for the previous edition.

What have we changed, added or improved to earn your purchase of the 1996 catalogue?

There are indeed many, many changes and improvements. So numerous I'm almost not sure where to begin. In the past I've used an imaginary snappy reporter or energetic talk show host to ask a few questions. At a recent stamp show a wag collector asked if I was going to have a man from outer space do the honors this year. Not necessary. This time I'll just ask myself the questions.

However, before I get carried away, let me remind you that Volume 1 has split. Volume 1A contains United States, United Nations and British Commonwealth Countries of North and South America and the Caribbean. The balance of British Commonwealth countries can be found in Volume 1B.

In this volume we have totals for sets with three and four stamps. It is an ambitious project (trust me on this) and it is unclear how far we will get in the other volumes.

Tell us something out of the ordinary.

I'll tell you, but you won't believe it until you read it. ***And I dare you to read it.*** I'm talking about the completely revised and re-written catalogue introduction.

The new introduction is a pleasure to read and includes updated information on printing methods, separation methods and tagging.

Let's get down to the nitty gritty. Where is the action in Volume 2?

China. Imperial and Republican China show some strong increases. Scott 11, the 1885 3¢ perf 12 1/2 Dragon, rises to $60 unused, from $35 in the 1995 Volume 2. The 1897 Empress Dowager set, Scott 16n-24n, shows remarkable strength, particularly in the high values, with the 9¢, Scott 22n, doubling to $1,000 from $500. The $5 1912 Foochow issue, Scott 137, leaps to $2,500 unused, from $1,750. The 1928 Marshal Tso-lin set, Scott 276-279, climbs to $42 unused, from $37.30, and the 1933 Tan Yuan-chang set, Scott 326-330, increases to $55 unused, from $44.

In Republic of China, the issues of the 1950s do not show a great number of changes, but whatever does change is usually up. Most of the changes from this period are in the used column.

Starting about 1960, however, many unused sets show decreases. For example, the 1962 Emperor quartet, Scott 1355-1358, dips to $140.75 from $151.50, and the 1965 ICY set, Scott 1462-1463, drops to $5.70, from $9.

There are many increases in the Japanese Occupation issues. The Supeh 1941 overprints on watermarked 1940 stamps with secret marks, Scott 7N27-7N29, rise to $18.25 unused and used, from $13.75 unused and used.

In People's Republic of China, decreases predominate throughout, most noticeably in issues of the 1970s and 1980s. The issues of the early years of the Cultural Revolution, 1966-68, however, show more increases than decreases, while earlier issues show a fair mix of increases and decreases.

What about values for countries other than China?

Cambodia shows more than 550 value changes, all increases. For example, the 1956 Coronation set, Scott 53-58, jumps to $40.30 unused and used, from $28.95 used and unused.

Nineteenth century Brazil issues reflect many decreases. Scott 2, the 60r Bull's-eye, falls to $450 unused and $175 used, from $575 unused and $200 used; and the 1861 430r, Scott 40, dips to $175 unused and $90 used, from $225 unused and $125 used. The 1876-77 rouletted Dom Pedro issue, Scott 61-67, decreases to $343.50 unused and $82.45 used, from $380 unused and $95.95 used.

Most of the changes made in Austria are on back-of-the-book stamps. Never hinged semi-postal sets show some strength. The 1922 Musicians set, Scott B50-B56, rises to $47.50 from $37.50, and the 1931 Rotary Convention overprints, move to $340 from $275.

Algeria records more than 100 changes.

Are there any new listings for stamps in never-hinged condition?

The breakpoints for never hinged in Czechoslovakia's postage and postage due sections have been moved back. Values for never hinged now start with the 1928 Tenth Anniversary of Independence set, Scott 142-151 and the 1928 postage dues, Scott J58-J69.

What editorial improvements and revisions await catalogue users?

Three minors have been added to China's Meng Chang Japanese Occupation section. The new items, Scott 2N115b, 2N116b and 2N122a are 1945 surcharges on stamps with the 4mm type I overprints issued in 1941.

New information establishes the 1903 handstamped 10¢ Acknowledgment of Receipt stamp, listed in the 1995 catalogue as Antioquia Scott H3, as a national issue of Colombia, and brings about its renumbering as Colombia Scott H4.

Imperforate pairs of China's 1878 Large Dragon issue have been footnoted as they are proofs or unfinished stamps.

A number of double or inverted overprints in Angola have been footnoted as they were intentionally made.

Angola's 1962 and 1965 Postal Tax Due stamps also have been footnoted as they were used only for revenue purposes.

The red surcharge variety of Bolivia's 1924 15¢-on-22¢ has been footnoted as it is found jointly with black surcharges in blocks and probably is a trial impression.

Footnotes concerning the abundance of counterfeits of Belgium Scott B25-B30 have been strengthened.

Issue dates have been refined in Bolivia, Brazil, Burkina Faso, Burundi, Colombia and Costa Rica.

Anything else?

Renumberings affect many of Bulgaria's 1989 stamps and the following definitives: French Andorra's 1990-93 Arms, Armenia's 1992 set showing various subjects, Brazil's 1989-93 Flora set and Bulgaria's 1991-92 Farm Animals.

Happy Collecting!

Stuart Morrissey/Publisher

Acknowledgments

Our appreciation and gratitude go to the following individuals and organizations who have assisted us in preparing information included in the 1996 Scott Catalogues. Some helpers prefer anonymity. These individuals have generously shared their stamp knowledge with others through the medium of the Scott Catalogue.

Those who follow provided information that is in addition to the hundreds of dealer price lists and advertisements and scores of auction catalogues and realizations which were used in producing the Catalogue Values. It is from those noted here that we have been able to obtain information on items not normally seen in published lists and advertisements. Support from these people of course goes beyond data leading to Catalogue Values, for they also are key to editorial changes.

George F. Ackermann
A. R. Allison
B. J. Ammel
Mike Armus
Don Bakos
Jules K. Beck
Ron Bentley
Vladimir Berrio-Lemm
Kenneth R. Berry
John Birkinbine II
John R. Boker, Jr.
Jeff Brasor
George W. Brett
Roger Brody
William C. Brooks VI
Randall Brooksbank
Michael Bryne
A. Bryan Camarda
Nathan Carlin
Dr. Herman J. Cestero, Jr.
E. J. Chamberlin
Richard A. Champagne
Andrew Cronin
James A. Cross
William T. Crowe
Thomas De Luca
Dan Demetriade
Brian Dias
Harry Dober
Rich Drews
Bob Dumaine
William S. Dunn
Harry A. Eisenstein
J. A. Farrington
Leon Finik
Henry Fisher
William Fletcher
Joseph E. Foley
Marvin Frey
Richard Friedberg
Huguette Gagnon
D. Scott Gallagher
Eugene A. Garrett
Peter Georgiadis
Brian M. Green
Henry Hahn
Erich E. Hamm
Dr. James B. Helme
Clifford O. Herrick
Lee H. Hill, Jr.
Dr. Eugene Holmok
Rollin C. Huggins, Jr.
W. Wilson Hulme II
Clyde Jennings
Jack Jonza
Henry Karen
Stanford M. Katz
Dr. James Kerr

Charles F. Kezbers
William Langs
Ken Lawrence
Pedro Llach
William Thomas Lockard
David MacDonnell
Robert L. Markovits
F. Brian Marshall
Clyde R. Maxwell
Timothy M. McRee
Dr. Hector Mena
Giorgio Migliavacca
Jack Molesworth
William E. Mooz
Gary M. Morris
Peter Mosiondz, Jr.
Bruce M. Moyer
Jack Nalbandian
James Natale
Gregg Nelson
Robert Odenweller
Victor Ostolaza
Sheldon Paris
John E. Pearson
Donald J. Peterson
Vernon Pickering
Stanley M. Piller
Jon Rose
Frans H. A. Rummens
Richard H. Salz
Byron Sandfield
Jacques C. Schiff, Jr.
F. Burton Sellers
Richard Simchak
Dr. Hubert Skinner
Roger D. Skinner
Richard Stambaugh
R. J. Thoden
Scott Trepel
Ming W. Tsang
A. John Ultee
James O. Vadeboncoeur
William R. Wallace
Jerome S. Wagshal
Daniel C. Warren
Richard A. Washburn
Stephen S. Washburne
Giana Wayman
Larry S. Weiss
Nelson A. L. Weller
Hans A. Westphal
Ernest C. Wilkins
Greg Winston
Robert F. Yacano
Clarke Yarbrough
Val Zabijaka
Nathan Zankel

American Air Mail Society
Stephen Reinhard, PO Box 110,
Mineola, NY 11501

American Philatelic Society
PO Box 8000, State College, PA 16803

American Revenue Association
Bruce Miller, Suite 332,
701 South First Ave.,
Arcadia, CA 91006

American Stamp Dealers' Association
3 School St., Glen Cove, NY 11542

American Topical Association
PO Box 630, Johnstown, PA 15907

Booklet Collectors Club
James Natale, PO Box 2461,
Cinnaminson, NJ 08077-5461

Bureau Issues Association
George V.H. Godin, PO Box 23707,
Belleville, IL 62223

Confederate Stamp Alliance
Richard L. Calhoun,
1749 W. Golf Rd., Suite 366,
Mt. Prospect, IL 60056

Errors, Freaks, and Oddities Collectors Club
Jim McDevitt, 1903 Village Road West,
Norwood, MA 02062-2516

International Society of Worldwide Stamp Collectors
Carol Cervenka, Route 1 Box 69A,
Caddo Mills, TX 75135

Junior Philatelists of America
Sally Horn, PO Box 850,
Boalsburg, PA 16827-0850

No-Value-Identified Collectors Club
Albert Sauvanet, Le Clos Royal B,
Boulevard des Pas Enchantes,
44230 St. Sebastien-sur-Loire, France

Plate Number Coil Collectors Club
Joann Lenz, 37211 Alper Drive,
Sterling Heights, MI 48312-2203

Precancel Stamp Society
1750 Skippack Pk. #1603,
Center Square, PA 19422

Royal Philatelic Society
D. J. Springbett, 41 Devonshire Place,
London, U.K. W1N 1PE

Royal Philatelic Society of Canada
PO Box 929, Station Q,
Toronto ON, CANADA M4T 2P1

United Postal Stationery Society
Joann Thomas, PO Box 48,
Redlands, CA 92373

US Philatelic Classics Society
Patricia S. Walker, Briarwood,
Lisbon, MD 21765

US Possessions Philatelic Society
Charles A. Richmond, PO Box 26724,
Busch Finance Station,
Columbus, OH 43226

Society for the New Republics of the Former USSR (Armenia, etc.)
Michael Padwee, 163 Joralemon St.,
PO Box 1520,
Brooklyn, NY 11201-1520

American Belgian Philatelic Society
Kenneth L. Costilow,
621 Virginius Dr.,
Virginia Beach, VA 23452-4417

Belize Philatelic Study Circle
Charles R. Gambill, 730 Collingswood,
Corpus Christi, TX 78412

Bermuda Collectors Society
Thomas J. McMahon, 86 Nash Road,
Purdys, NY 10578

Brazil Philatelic Association
Kurt Ottenheimer,
462 West Walnut St.,
Long Beach, NY 11561

British Caribbean Philatelic Study Group
Gale J. Raymond, PO Box 35695,
Houston, TX 77235

British North America Philatelic Society
Jerome C. Jarnick, 108 Duncan Drive,
Troy, MI 48098

Burma Philatelic Study Circle
A. Meech, 7208 91st Ave.,
Edmonton, AB, CANADA T6B 0R8

Canal Zone Study Group
Richard H. Salz, 60 27th Ave.,
San Francisco, CA 94121

China Stamp Society
Paul H. Gault, 140 West 18th Ave.,
Columbus, OH 43210

COPAPHIL (Colombia & Panama)
PO Box 2245, El Cajon, CA 92021

Society of Costa Rica Collectors
Dr. Hector Mena, PO Box 14831,
Baton Rouge, LA 70808

Croatian Philatelic Society (Croatia and other Balkan areas)
Eck Spahich, 1512 Lancelot Rd.,
Borger, TX 79007

Cuban Philatelic Society of America
PO Box 450207,
Miami, FL 33245-0207

Society for Czechoslovak Philately
Robert T. Cossaboom, PO Box 332,
Scott AFB, IL 62225

Ethiopian Philatelic Society
Huguette Gagnon, PO Box 8110-45,
Blaine, WA 98230

Falkland Islands Philatelic Study Group
James Driscoll, PO Box 172,
South Dennis, NJ 08245

France & Colonies Philatelic Society
Walter Parshall, 103 Spruce St.,
Bloomfield, NJ 07003

Germany Philatelic Society
PO Box 779,
Arnold, MD 21012-4779

GDR Study Group of German Philatelic Society
Ken Lawrence, PO Box 8040,
State College, PA 16803-8040

Great Britain Collectors Club
Frank J. Koch, PO Box 309,
Batavia, OH 45103-0309

Hellenic Philatelic Society of America (Greece & related areas)
Dr. Nicholas Asimakopulos,
541 Cedar Hill Ave., Wyckoff, NJ 07481

International Society of Guatemala Collectors
Mrs. Mae Vignola, 105 22nd Ave.,
San Francisco, CA 94116

Haiti Philatelic Society
Dwight Bishop, 16434 Shamhart Dr.,
Granada Hills, CA 91344

Hong Kong Stamp Society
Dr. An-Min Chung, 120 Deerfield Rd.,
Broomall, PA 19008

Hong Kong Collectors Club
Nikolai Lau, 6021 Yonge Street #888,
North York, ON, CANADA M2M 3W2

Hungary Philatelic Society
Thomas Phillips, PO Box 1162,
Samp Mortar Sta., Fairfield, CT 06432

India Study Circle
John Warren, PO Box 70775,
Washington, DC 20024

Society of Indochina Philatelists
Paul Blake, 1466 Hamilton Way,
San Jose, CA 95125

Iran Philatelic Study Circle
A. John Ultee, 816 Gwynne Ave.,
Waynesboro, VA 22980

Eire Philatelic Association (Ireland)
Michael J. Conway, 74 Woodside Circle,
Fairfield, CT 06430

Society of Israel Philatelists
Howard D. Chapman,
28650 Settlers Lane,
Pepper Pike, OH 44124

Italy and Colonies Study Circle
David F. Emery, PO Box 86,
Philipsburg, NJ 08865

International Society for Japanese Philately
Kenneth Kamholz, PO Box 1283,
Haddonfield, NJ 08033

Korea Stamp Society
William A. Matthews, PO Box 15306,
Columbus, OH 43215

Latin American Philatelic Society
Piet Steen, PO Box 6420,
Hinton, AB, CANADA T7V 1X7

Liberian Philatelic Society
William Thomas Lockard, PO Box 267,
Wellston, OH 45692

Lithuanian Philatelic Society of New York
Vincent M. Alones, 217 McKee St.,
Floral Park, NY 11001-1314

Plebiscite-Memel-Saar Study Group
Clay Wallace, 158 Arapaho Circle,
San Ramon, CA 94583

Mexico-Elmhurst Philatelic Society International
William E. Shelton, PO Box 39838,
San Antonio, TX 78218

Nepal & Tibet Philatelic Study Group
Roger D. Skinner,
1020 Covington Road,
Los Altos, CA 94022

American Society of Netherlands Philately
Jan Enthoven,
W6428 Riverview Drive,
Onalaska, WI 54650

Nicaragua Study Group
Clyde R. Maxwell, Airport Plaza,
2041 Business Center Drive,
Suite 101, Irvine, CA 92715

Society of Australasian Specialists/Oceania
Henry Bateman, PO Box 4862,
Monroe, LA 71211

Orange Free State Study Circle
J. R. Stroud, 28 Oxford St.,
Burnham-on-sea,
Somerset, U.K. TA8 1LQ

International Philippine Philatelic Society
Eugene A. Garrett, 446 Stratford Ave.,
Elmhurst, IL 60126-4123

American Society of Polar Philatelists (Antarctic areas)
S.H. Jacobson, PO Box 945,
Skokie, IL 60077

Pitcairn Islands Study Group
Nelson A.L. Weller,
2940 Wesleyan Lane,
Winston-Salem, NC 27106

Polonus Philatelic Society (Poland)
864 N. Ashland Ave.,
Chicago, IL 60622

International Society for Portuguese Philately
Michael Bryne, Adirondack Stamps,
PO Box 13100,
Mexico Beach, FL 32410

Rhodesian Study Circle
William R. Wallace, PO Box 16381,
San Francisco, CA 94116

Romanian Chapter of Croatian Philatelic Society
Dan Demetriade, PO Box 10182,
Detroit, MI 48210

Rossica Society of Russian Philately
Gary Combs, 8241 Chalet Ct.,
Millersville, MD 21108

Canadian Society of Russian Philately
Andrew Cronin,
PO Box 5722, Station A,
Toronto, ON, CANADA M5W 1P2

Ryukyu Philatelic Specialist Society
Carmine J. DiVincenzo, PO Box 381,
Clayton, CA 94517-0381

St. Helena, Ascension & Tristan Society
Dr. Russell V. Skavaril,
222 East Torrance Road,
Columbus, OH 43214-3834

Associated Collectors of El Salvador
Jeff Brasor, 7365 NW 68th Way,
Pompano Beach, FL 33067-3918

Sarawak Specialists' Society
Art Bunce, PO Box 2516,
Escondido, CA 92033

Arabian Philatelic Association
ARAMCO Box 1929,
Dhahran 31311, SAUDI ARABIA

Scandinavia Collectors Club
Robert W. Lang, PO Box 125,
Newark, DE 19715-0125

Philatelic Society for Greater Southern Africa
William C. Brooks VI, PO Box 2698,
San Bernardino, CA 92406-2698

Slovakia Stamp Society
Jack Benchik, PO Box 555,
Notre Dame, IN 46556

Spanish Philatelic Society
Robert H. Penn, RD #3, Box 3349-1
Bangor, PA 18013

American Helvetia Philatelic Society (Switzerland, Liechtenstein)
Richard T. Hall, PO Box 666,
Manhattan Beach, CA 90267-0666

Society for Thai Philately
H.R. Blakeney, PO Box 25644,
Oklahoma City, OK 73125

Tonga/Tin Can Mail Study Circle
Tom Jackson, 121 Mullinger Ct. #1A,
Schaumburg, IL 60193

Turkey and Ottoman Philatelic Society
Gary F. Paiste, 4249 Berritt St.,
Fairfax, VA 22030

Tuvalu & Kiribati Philatelic Society
Frank Caprio, PO Box 218071,
Nashville, TN 37221

Ukrainian Philatelic & Numismatic Society
Val Zabijaka, PO Box 3711,
Silver Spring, MD 20918

United Nations Philatelists
Helen Benedict,
408 S. Orange Grove Blvd.,
Pasadena, CA 91105

Vatican Philatelic Society
Louis Padavan, PO Box 127,
Remsenburg, NY 11960

Yugoslavia Study Group
Michael Lenard, 1514 North 3rd Ave.,
Wausau, WI 54401

Catalogue Information

Catalogue Value

The Scott Catalogue value is a retail value; that is, an amount you could expect to pay for a stamp in a grade of Fine to Very Fine with no faults. Any exceptions to the grade valued will be noted in the text. The value listed for any given stamp is a reference that reflects recent actual dealer selling prices for that item.

Dealer retail price lists, public auction results, published prices in advertising and individual solicitation of retail prices from dealers, collectors and specialty organizations have been used in establishing the values found in this catalogue. Scott Publishing Co. values stamps, but Scott is not a company engaged in the business of buying and selling stamps as a dealer.

Use this catalogue as a guide for buying and selling. The actual price you pay for a stamp may be higher or lower than the catalogue value because of many different factors, including the amount of personal service a dealer offers, or increased or decreased interest in the country or topic represented by a stamp or set. An item may occasionally be offered at a lower price as a "loss leader," or as part of a special sale. You also may obtain an item inexpensively at public auction because of little interest at that time or as part of a large lot.

Copies of stamps that are of a lesser grade than Fine to Very Fine, or those with condition problems, trade at lower prices than those given in this catalogue. Stamps of exceptional quality in both grade and condition often command higher prices than those listed.

Values for pre-1900 unused issues are for stamps with at least most of their original gum. Later issues are assumed to have full original gum. From breakpoints in most countries' listings, stamps are valued as never hinged, due to the wide availability of stamps in that condition. These notations are prominently placed in the listings and in the counrty information preceding the listings. Some countries also feature listings with dual values for hinged and never-hinged stamps.

Grade

A stamp's grade and condition are crucial to its value. The accompanying illustrations show examples of Fine-Very Fine stamps from different time periods, along with examples of stamps in Fine and Very Fine grades as points of reference.

FINE stamps have designs that are noticeably off center on two sides. Imperforate stamps may have small margins, and earlier issues may show the design touching one edge of the stamp. For perforated stamps, perfs may barely clear the design on one side. Used stamps may have heavier than usual cancellations.

FINE-VERY FINE stamps may be somewhat off center on one side, or slightly off center on two sides. Imperforate stamps will have two margins of at least normal size, and the design will not touch any edge. For perforated stamps, the perfs are well clear of the design, but are still noticeably off center. *However, early issues of a country may be printed in such a way that the design naturally is very close to the edges.* Used stamps will not have a cancellation that detracts from the design. This is the grade used to establish Scott Catalogue values.

VERY FINE stamps may be slightly off center on one side, but the design will be well clear of the edge. The stamp will present a nice, balanced appearance. Imperforate stamps will have three normal-sized margins. Used stamps will have light or otherwise neat cancellations.

Condition

Grade addresses only centering and (for used stamps) cancellation. *Condition* refers to factors other than grade that affect a stamp's desirability.

Factors that can increase the value of a stamp include exceptionally wide margins, particularly fresh color, the presence of selvage, and plate or die varieties. Unusual cancels on used stamps (particularly those of the 19th century) can greatly enhance their value as well.

Factors other that faults that decrease the value of a stamp include loss of original gum, regumming, a hinge remnant or foreign object adhering to the gum, natural inclusions, straight edges, and markings or notations applied by collectors or dealers.

Faults include missing pieces, tears, pin or other holes, surface scuffs, thin spots, creases, toning, short or pulled perforations, clipped perforations, oxidation or other forms of color changelings, soiling, stains, and such man-made changes as reperforations or the chemical removal or lightening of a cancellation.

Scott Publishing Co. recognizes that there is no formally enforced grading scheme for postage stamps, and that the final price you pay or obtain for a stamp will be determined by individual agreement at the time of transaction.

Catalogue Listing Policy

It is the intent of Scott Publishing Co. to list all postage stamps of the world in the *Scott Standard Postage Stamp Catalogue.* The only strict criteria for listing is that stamps be decreed legal for postage by the issuing country. Whether the primary intent of issuing a given stamp or set was for sale to postal patrons or to stamp collectors is not part of our listing criteria. Scott's role is to provide basic comprehensive postage stamp information. It is up to each stamp collector to choose which items to include in a collection.

It is Scott's objective to seek reasons why a stamp should be listed, rather than why it should not. Nevertheless, there are certain types of items that will not be listed. These include the following:

1. Unissued items that are not officially distributed or released by the issuing postal authority. Even if such a stamp is "accidentally" distributed to the philatelic or even postal market, it remains unissued. If such items are officially issued at a later date by the country, they will be listed. Unissued items consist of those that have been printed and then held from sale for reasons such as change in government, errors found on stamps or something deemed objectionable about a stamp subject or design.

2. Stamps "issued" by non-existent postal entities or fantasy countries, such as Nagaland, Occusi-Ambeno, Staffa, Sedang, Torres Straits and others.

3. Semi-official or unofficial items not required for postage. Examples include items issued by private agencies for their own express services. When such items are required for delivery, or are valid as prepayment of postage, they are listed.

4. Local stamps issued for local use only. Postage stamps issued by governments specifically for "domestic" use, such as Haiti Scott 219-228, or the United States non-denominated stamps, are not considered to be locals, since they are valid for postage throughout the country of origin.

5. Items not valid for postal use. For example, a few countries have issued souvenir sheets that are not valid for postage. This area also includes a number of worldwide charity labels (some denominated) that do not pay postage.

6. Intentional varieties, such as imperforate stamps that look like their perforated counterparts and are issued in very small quantities. These are often controlled issues intended for speculation.

7. Items distributed by the issuing government only to a limited group, such as a stamp club or a single stamp dealer, and later brought to market at inflated prices. These items normally will be included in a footnote.

The fact that a stamp has been used successfully as postage, even on international mail, is not in itself sufficient proof that it was legitimately issued. Numerous examples of so-called stamps from non-existent countries are known to have been used to post letters that have successfully passed through the international mail system.

There are certain items that are subject to interpretation. When a stamp falls outside our specifications, it may be listed along with a cautionary footnote.

A number of factors are considered in our approach to analyzing how a stamp is listed. The following list of factors is presented to share with you, the catalogue user, the complexity of the listing process.

Additional printings — "Additional printings" of a previously issued stamp may range from an item that is totally different to cases where it is impossible to differentiate from the original. At least a minor number (a small-letter suffix) is assigned if there is a distinct change in stamp shade, noticeably redrawn design, or a significantly different perforation measurement. A major number (numeral or numeral and capital-letter combination) is assigned if the editors feel the "additional printing" is sufficiently different from the original that it constitutes a different issue.

Commemoratives — Where practical, commemoratives with the same theme are placed in a set. For example, the U.S. Civil War Centenniel set of 1961-65 and the Constitution Bicentennial series of 1989-90 appear as sets. Countries such as Japan and Korea issue such material on a regular basis, with an announced, or at least predictable, number of stamps known in advance. Occasionally, however, stamp sets that were released over a period of years have been separated. Appropriately placed footnotes will guide you to each set's continuation.

Definitive sets — Blocks of numbers generally have been reserved for definitive sets, based on previous experience with any given country. If a few more stamps were issued in a set than originally expected, they often have been inserted into the original set with a capital-letter suffix, such as U.S. Scott 1059A. If it appears that many more stamps than the originally allotted block will be released before the set is completed, a new block of numbers will be reserved, with the original one being closed off. In some cases, such as the British Machin Head series or the U.S. Transportation and Great Americans series, several blocks of numbers exist. Appropriately placed footnotes will guide you to each set's continuation.

New country — Membership in the Universal Postal Union is not a consideration for listing status or order of placement within the catalogue. The index will tell you in what volume or page number the listings begin.

"No release date" items — The amount of information available for any given stamp issue varies greatly from country to country and even from time to time. Extremely comprehensive information about new stamps is available from some countries well before the stamps are released. By contrast some countries do not provide information about stamps or release dates. Most countries, however, fall between these extremes. A country may provide denominations or subjects of stamps from upcoming issues that are not issued as planned. Sometimes, philatelic agencies, those private firms hired to represent countries, add these later-issued items to sets well after the formal release date. This time period can range from weeks to years. If these items were officially released by the country, they will be added to the appropriate spot in the set. In many cases, the specific release date of a stamp or set of stamps may never be known.

Overprints — The color of an overprint is always noted if it is other than black. Where more than one color of ink has been used on overprints of a single set, the color used is noted. Early overprint and surcharge illustrations were altered to prevent their use by forgers.

Se-tenants — Connected stamps of differing features (se-tenants) will be listed in the format most commonly collected. This includes pairs, blocks or larger multiples. Se-tenant units are not always symmetrical. An example is Australia Scott 508, which is a block of seven stamps. If the stamps are primarily collected as a unit, the major number may be assigned to the multiple, with minors going to each component stamp. In cases where continuous-design or other unit se-tenants will receive significant postal use, each stamp is given a major Scott number listing. This includes issues from the United States, Canada, Germany and Great Britain, for example.

Understanding the Listings

On the following page is an enlarged "typical" listing from this catalogue. Below are detailed explanations of each of the highlighted parts of the listing.

1 Scott number — Scott catalogue numbers are used to identify specific items when buying, selling or trading stamps. Each listed postage stamp from every country has a unique Scott catalogue number. Therefore, Germany Scott 99, for example, can only refer to a single stamp. Although the Scott catalogue usually lists stamps in chronological order by date of issue, there are exceptions. When a country has issued a set of stamps over a period of time, those stamps within the set are kept together without regard to date of issue. This follows the normal collecting approach of keeping stamps in their natural sets.

When a country issues a set of stamps over a period of time, a group of consecutive catalogue numbers is reserved for the stamps in that set, as issued. If that group of numbers proves to be too few, capital-letter suffixes, such as "A" or "B," may be added to existing numbers to create enough catalogue numbers to cover all items in the set. A capital-letter suffix indicates a major Scott catalogue number listing. Scott uses a suffix letter only once. Therefore, a catalogue number listing with a capital-letter prefix will not also be found with the same letter (lower case) used as a minor-letter listing. If there is a Scott 16A in a set, for example, there will not also be a Scott 16a.

Suffix letters are not cumulative. A minor variety of Scott 16A would be Scott 16b, not Scott 16Ab. Any exceptions, such as Great Britain Scott 358cp, are clearly indicated.

There are times when a reserved block of Scott catalogue numbers is too large for a set, leaving some numbers unused. Such gaps in the numbering sequence also occur when the catalogue editors move an item's listing elsewhere or have removed it entirely from the catalogue. Scott does not attempt to account for every possible number, but rather attempts to assure that each stamp is assigned its own number.

Scott numbers designating regular postage normally are only numerals. Scott numbers for other types of stamps, such as air post, semi-postal, postal tax, postage due, occupation and others have a prefix consisting of one or more capital letters or a combination of numerals and capital letters.

2 Illustration number — Illustration or design-type numbers are used to identify each catalogue illustration. For most sets, the lowest face-value stamp is shown. It then serves as an example of the basic design approach for other stamps not illustrated. Where more than one stamp use the same illustration number, but have differences in design, the design paragraph or the description line clearly indicates the design on each stamp not illustrated. Where there are both vertical and horizontal designs in a set, a single illustration may be used, with the exceptions noted in the design paragraph or description line.

When an illustration is followed by a lower-case letter in parentheses, such as "A2(b)," the trailing letter indicates which overprint or surcharge illustration applies.

Illustrations normally are 75 percent of the original size of the stamp. An effort has been made to note all illustrations not illustrated at that percentage. Virtually all souvenir sheet illustrations are reduced even more. Overprints and surcharges are shown at 100 percent of their original size, unless otherwise noted. In some cases, the illustration will be placed above the set, between listings or omitted completely. Overprint and surcharge illustrations are not placed in this catalogue for purposes of expertizing stamps.

3 Paper color — The color of a stamp's paper is noted in italic type when the paper used is not white.

4 Listing styles — There are two principal types of catalogue listings: major and minor.

Major listings are in a larger type style than minor listings. The catalogue number is a numeral that can be found with or without a capital-letter suffix, and with or without a prefix.

Minor listings are in a smaller type style and have a small-letter suffix or (if the listing immediately follows that of the major number) may show only the letter. These listings identify a variety of the major item. Examples include perforation, color, watermark or printing method differences, multiples (some souvenir sheets, booklet panes and se-tenant combinations), and singles of multiples.

Examples of major number listings include 16, 28A, B97, C13A, 10N5, and 10N6A. Examples of minor numbers are 16a and C13b.

5 Basic information about a stamp or set — Introducing each stamp issue is a small section (usually a line listing) of basic information about a stamp or set. This section normally includes the date of issue, method of printing, perforation, watermark and, sometimes, some additional information of note. *Printing method, perforation and watermark apply to the following sets until a change is noted.* Stamps created by overprinting or surcharging previous issues are assumed to have the same perforation, watermark and printing method as the original. Dates of issue are as precise as Scott is able to confirm and often reflect the dates on first-day covers, rather than the actual date of release.

6 Denomination — This normally refers to the face value of the stamp; that is, the cost of the unused stamp at the post office at the time of issue. When a denomination is shown in parentheses, it does not appear on the stamp. This includes the non-denominated stamps of the United States, Brazil and Great Britain, for example.

7 Color or other description — This area provides information to solidify identification of a stamp. In many recent cases, a description of the stamp design appears in this space, rather than a listing of colors.

8 Year of issue — In stamp sets that have been released in a period that spans more than a year, the number shown in parentheses is the year that stamp first appeared. Stamps without a date appeared during the first year of the issue. Dates are not always given for minor varieties.

9 Value unused and Value used — The Scott catalogue values are based on stamps that are in a grade of Fine-Very Fine unless stated otherwise. Unused values refer to items that have not seen postal, revenue or any other duty for which they were intended. Pre-1900 unused stamps that were issued with gum must have at least most of their original gum. Later issues are assumed to have full original gum. From breakpoints specified in most countries' listings, stamps are valued as never hinged. Stamps issued without gum are noted. Modern issues with PVA or other synthetic adhesives may appear ungummed. Self-adhesive stamps are valued as appearing undisturbed on their original backing paper. For a more detailed explanation of these values, please see the "Catalogue Value," "Condition" and "Understanding Valuing Notations" elsewhere in this introduction.

In some cases, where used stamps are more valuable than unused stamps, the value is for an example with a contemporaneous cancel, rather than a modern cancel or a smudge or other unclear marking. For those stamps that were released for postal and fiscal purposes, the used value represents a postally used stamp. Stamps with revenue cancels generally sell for less.

10 Changes in basic set information — Bold type is used to show any changes in the basic data given for a set of stamps. This includes perforation differences from one stamp to the next or a different paper, printing method or watermark.

11 Total value of a set — The total value of sets of three or more stamps issued after 1900 are shown. The set line also notes the range of Scott numbers and total number of stamps included in the grouping. *Set value* is the term used to indicate the value of a stamp set when its combined total is less than the sum of the individual stamps. This happens when some of the stamps in a set have the minimum catalogue value.

King George VI and Leopard — A6

King George VI — A7

1938-44 Engr. *Perf. 12½*

54	A6	½p green		15	15
54A	A6	½p dk brn ('42)		15	15
55	A6	1p dk brn		15	15
55A	A6	1p grn ('42)		15	15
56	A6	1½p dk car		45	75
56A	A6	1½p gray ('42)		15	15
57	A6	2p gray		55	22
57A	A6	2p dk car ('42)		15	15
58	A6	3p blue		18	15
59	A6	4p rose lil		18	18
60	A6	6p dk vio		22	22
61	A6	9p ol bis		38	75
62	A6	1sh org & blk		52	45

Typo.
Perf. 14
Chalky Paper

63	A7	2sh ultra & dl vio, *bl*		75	75
64	A7	2sh6p red & blk, *bl*		95	95
65	A7	5sh red & grn, *yel*		18.00	17.00
	a.	5sh dk red & dp grn, *yel* ('44)		37.50	20.00
66	A7	10sh red & grn, *grn*		14.00	12.00

Wmk. 3

67	A7	£1 blk & vio, *red*		18.00	17.00
		Nos. 54-67 (18)		55.08	51.32

1 SCOTT NUMBER

2 ILLUS. NUMBER

3 PAPER COLOR

4 LISTING STYLES — MAJORS, MINORS

5 BASIC INFORMATION ON STAMP OR SET

6 DENOMINATION

7 COLOR OR OTHER DESCRIPTION

8 YEAR OF ISSUE

9 CATALOGUE VALUES — UNUSED, USED

10 CHANGES IN BASIC SET INFORMATION

11 TOTAL VALUE OF SET

Special Notices

Classification of stamps

The *Scott Standard Postage Stamp Catalogue* lists stamps by country of issue. The next level of organization is a listing by section on the basis of the function of the stamps. The principal sections cover regular postage, semi-postal, air post, special delivery, registration, postage due and other categories. Except for regular postage, catalogue numbers for all sections include a prefix letter (or number-letter combination) denoting the class to which a given stamp belongs.

The following is a listing of the most commonly used catalogue prefixes.

Prefix....Category
C ....Air Post
M...........Military
P............Newspaper
N ....Occupation - Regular Issues
O ....Official
Q...........Parcel Post
J.............Postage Due
RA ....Postal Tax
B............Semi-Postal
E............Special Delivery
MR ....War Tax

Other prefixes used by more than one country include the following:
H ....Acknowledgment of Receipt
CO.........Air Post Official
CQ.........Air Post Parcel Post
RAC.......Air Post Postal Tax
CF..........Air Post Registration
CB ....Air Post Semi-Postal
CBO.......Air Post Semi-Postal Official
CE ....Air Post Special Delivery
EY..........Authorized Delivery
S ....Franchise
G ....Insured Letter
GY ....Marine Insurance
MC ....Military Air Post
MQ........Military Parcel Post
NC.........Occupation - Air Post
NO.........Occupation - Official
NJ ....Occupation - Postage Due
NRA.......Occupation - Postal Tax
NB ....Occupation - Semi-Postal
NE ....Occupation - Special Delivery
QY ....Parcel Post Authorized Delivery
AR ....Postal-fiscal
RAJ ....Postal Tax Due
RAB ....Postal Tax Semi-Postal
F............Registration
EB..........Semi-Postal Special Delivery
EO ....Special Delivery Official
QE ....Special Handling

New issue listings

Updates to this catalogue appear each month in the *Scott Stamp Monthly* magazine. Included in this update are additions to the listings of countries found in the *Scott Standard Postage Stamp Catalogue* and the *Specialized Catalogue of United States Stamps*, as well as corrections and updates to current editions of this catalogue.

From time to time there will be changes in the final listings of stamps from the *Scott Stamp Monthly* to the next edition of the catalogue. This occurs as more information about certain stamps or sets becomes available.

The catalogue update section of the *Scott Stamp Monthly* is the most timely presentation of this material available. Annual subscriptions to the *Scott Stamp Monthly* are available from Scott Publishing Co., Box 828, Sidney, OH 45365-0828.

Number changes

A listing of catalogue number changes from the previous edition of the catalogue appears at the back of each volume.

Understanding valuing notations

The *minimum catalogue value* of an individual stamp or set is 15 cents. This represents a portion of the costs incurred to a dealer when he prepares an individual stamp for resale. As a point of philatelic-economic fact, the lower the value shown for an item in this catalogue, the greater the percentage of that value is attributed to dealer mark up and profit margin. In many cases, such as the 15-cent minimum value, that price does not cover the labor or other costs involved with stocking it as an individual stamp. The sum of minimum values in a set does not properly represent the value of a complete set primarily composed of a number of minimum-value stamps, nor does the sum represent the actual value of a packet made up of minimum-value stamps. Thus a packet of 1,000 different common stamps — each of which has a catalogue value of 15 cents — normally sells for considerably less than 150 dollars!

The *absence of a retail value* for a stamp does not necessarily suggest that a stamp is scarce or rare. In the U.S. listings, a dash in the value column means that the stamp is known in a stated form or variety, but information is either lacking or insufficient for purposes of establishing a usable catalogue value.

Stamp values in *italics* generally refer to items that are difficult to value accurately. For expensive items, such as those priced at $1,000 or higher, a value in italics indicates that the affected item trades very seldom. For inexpensive items, a value in italics represents a warning. One example is a "blocked" issue where the issuing postal administration may have controlled one stamp in a set in an attempt to make the whole set more valuable. Another example is an item that sold at an extreme multiple of face value in the marketplace at the time of its issue.

One type of warning to collectors that appears in the catalogue is illustrated by a stamp that is valued considerably higher in used condition than it is as unused. In this case, collectors are cautioned to be certain the used version has a contemporaneous cancellation. The type of cancellation on a stamp can be an important factor in determining its sale price. Catalogue values do not apply to fiscal or telegraph cancels, unless otherwise noted.

Some countries have released back issues of stamps in canceled-to-order form, sometimes covering at much as a 10-year period. The Scott Catalogue values for used stamps reflect canceled-to-order material when such stamps are found to predominate in the marketplace for the issue involved. Notes frequently appear in the stamp listings to specify which items are valued as canceled-to-order, or if there is a premium for postally used examples.

Many countries sell canceled-to-order stamps at a marked reduction of face value. Countries that sell or have sold canceled-to-order stamps at *full* face value include Australia, Netherlands, France and Switzerland. It may be almost impossible to identify such stamps if the gum has been removed, because official government canceling devices are used. Postally used copies of these items on cover, however, are usually worth more than the canceled-to-order stamps with original gum.

Abbreviations

Scott Publishing Co. uses a consistent set of abbreviations throughout this catalogue to conserve space, while still providing necessary information.

COLOR ABBREVIATIONS

amb.....amber
anil.....aniline
ap.....apple
aqua.....aquamarine
az.....azure
bis.....bister
bl.....blue
bld.....blood
blk.....black
bril.....brilliant
brn.....brown
brnsh.....brownish
brnz.....bronze
brt.....bright
brnt.....burnt
car.....carmine
cer.....cerise
chlky.....chalky
cham.....chamois
chnt.....chestnut
choc.....chocolate
chr.....chrome
cit.....citron
cl.....claret
cob.....cobalt
cop.....copper
crim.....crimson
cr.....cream
dk.....dark
dl.....dull
dp.....deep
db.....drab
emer.....emerald
gldn.....golden
grysh.....grayish
grn.....green
grnsh.....greenish
hel.....heliotrope
hn.....henna
ind.....indigo
int.....intense
lav.....lavender
lem.....lemon
lil.....lilac
lt.....light
mag.....magenta
man.....manila
mar.....maroon
mv.....mauve
multi.....multicolored
mlky.....milky
myr.....myrtle
ol.....olive
olvn.....olivine
org.....orange
pck.....peacock
pnksh.....pinkish
Prus.....Prussian
pur.....purple
redsh.....reddish
res.....reseda
ros.....rosine
ryl.....royal
sal.....salmon
saph.....sapphire
scar.....scarlet
sep.....sepia
sien.....sienna
sil.....silver
sl.....slate
stl.....steel
turq.....turquoise
ultra.....ultramarine
Ven.....Venetian
ver.....vermilion
vio.....violet
yel.....yellow
yelsh.....yellowish

When no color is given for an overprint or surcharge, black is the color used. Abbreviations for colors used for overprints and surcharges include: "(B)" or "(Blk)," black; "(Bl)," blue; "(R)," red; and "(G)," green.

Additional abbreviations in this catalogue are shown below:

Adm. ....Administration
AFL ....American Federation of Labor
Anniv. ....Anniversary
APS ....American Philatelic Society
Assoc. ....Association
ASSR. ....Autonomous Soviet Socialist Republic
b. ....Born
BEP ....Bureau of Engraving and Printing
Bicent. ....Bicentennial
Bklt. ....Booklet
Brit. ....British
btwn. ....Between
Bur. ....Bureau
c. or ca. ....Circa
Cat. ....Catalogue
Cent. ....Centennial, century, centenary
CIO ....Congress of Industrial Organizations
Conf. ....Conference
Cong. ....Congress
Cpl. ....Corporal
CTO ....Canceled to order
d. ....Died
Dbl. ....Double
EKU ....Earliest known use
Engr. ....Engraved
Exhib. ....Exhibition
Expo. ....Exposition
Fed. ....Federation
GB ....Great Britain
Gen. ....General
GPO ....General post office
Horiz. ....Horizontal
Imperf. ....Imperforate
Impt. ....Imprint
Intl. ....International
Invtd. ....Inverted
L. ....Left
Lieut., lt. ....Lieutenant
Litho. ....Lithographed
LL ....Lower left
LR ....Lower right
mm ....Millimeter
Ms. ....Manuscript
Natl. ....National
No. ....Number
NY ....New York
NYC ....New York City
Ovpt. ....Overprint
Ovptd. ....Overprinted
P. ....Plate number
Perf. ....Perforated, perforation
Phil. ....Philatelic
Photo. ....Photogravure
PO ....Post office
Pr. ....Pair
P.R. ....Puerto Rico
Prec. ....Precancel, precanceled
Pres. ....President
PTT ....Post, Telephone and Telegraph
Rio ....Rio de Janeiro
Sgt. ....Sergeant
Soc. ....Society
Souv. ....Souvenir
SSR ....Soviet Socialist Republic, see ASSR
St. ....Saint, street
Surch. ....Surcharge
Typo. ....Typographed
UL ....Upper left
Unwmkd. ....Unwatermarked
UPU ....Universal Postal Union
UR ....Upper Right
US ....United States
USPOD ....United States Post Office Department
USSR ....Union of Soviet Socialist Republics
Vert. ....Vertical
VP ....Vice president
Wmk. ....Watermark
Wmkd. ....Watermarked
WWI ....World War I
WWII ....World War II

Examination

Scott Publishing Co. will not comment upon the genuineness, grade or condition of stamps, because of the time and responsibility involved. Rather, there are several expertizing groups that undertake this work for both collectors and dealers. Neither will Scott Publishing Co. appraise or identify philatelic material. The company cannot take responsibility for unsolicited stamps or covers sent by individuals.

How to order from your dealer

When ordering stamps from a dealer, it is not necessary to write the full description of a stamp as listed in this catalogue. All you need is the name of the country, the Scott catalogue number and whether the desired item is unused or used. For example, "Japan Scott 422 unused" is sufficient to identify the unused stamp of Japan listed as "422 A206 5y brown."

Basic Stamp Information

A stamp collector's knowledge of the combined elements that make a given stamp issue unique determines his or her ability to identify stamps. These elements include paper, watermark, method of separation, printing, design and gum. On the following pages each of these important areas is briefly described.

Paper

Paper is an organic material composed of a compacted weave of cellulose fibers and generally formed into sheets. Paper used to print stamps may be manufactured in sheets, or it may have been part of a large roll (called a web) before being cut to size. The fibers most often used to create paper on which stamps are printed include bark, wood, straw and certain grasses. In many cases, linen or cotton rags have been added for greater strength and durability. Grinding, bleaching, cooking and rinsing these raw fibers reduces them to a slushy pulp, referred to by paper makers as "stuff." Sizing and, sometimes, coloring matter is added to the pulp to make different types of finished paper.

After the stuff is prepared, it is poured onto sieve-like frames that allow the water to run off, while retaining the matted pulp. As fibers fall onto the screen and are held by gravity, they form a natural weave that will later hold the paper together. If the screen has metal bits that are formed into letters or images attached, it leaves slightly thinned areas on the paper. These are called watermarks.

When the stuff is almost dry, it is passed under pressure through smooth or engraved rollers - dandy rolls - or placed between cloth in a press to be flattened and dried.

Stamp paper falls broadly into two types: wove and laid. The nature of the surface of the frame onto which the pulp is first deposited causes the differences in appearance between the two. If the surface is smooth and even, the paper will be of fairly uniform texture throughout. This is known as *wove paper.* Early papermaking machines poured the pulp onto a continuously circulating web of felt, but modern machines feed the pulp onto a cloth-like screen made of closely interwoven fine wires. This paper, when held to a light, will show little dots or points very close together. The proper name for this is "wire wove," but the type is still considered wove. Any U.S. or British stamp printed after 1880 will serve as an example of wire wove paper.

Closely spaced parallel wires, with cross wires at wider intervals, make up the frames used for what is known as *laid paper.* A greater thickness of the pulp will settle between the wires. The paper, when held to a light, will show alternate light and dark lines. The spacing and the thickness of the lines may vary, but on any one sheet of paper they are all alike. See Russia Scott 31-38 for examples of laid paper.

Batonne, from the French word meaning "a staff," is a term used if the lines in the paper are spaced quite far apart, like the printed ruling on a writing tablet. Batonne paper may be either wove or laid. If laid, fine laid lines can be seen between the batons. The laid lines, which are a form of watermark, may be geometrical figures such as squares, diamonds, rectangles or wavy lines.

Quadrille is the term used when the lines in the paper form little squares. *Oblong quadrille* is the term used when rectangles, rather than squares, are formed. See Mexico-Guadalajara Scott 35-37 for examples of oblong quadrille paper.

Paper also is classified as thick or thin, hard or soft, and by color if dye is added during manufacture. Such colors may include yellowish, greenish, bluish and reddish.

Brief explanations of other types of paper used for printing stamps, as well as examples, follow.

Pelure — Pelure paper is a very thin, hard and often brittle paper that is sometimes bluish or grayish in appearance. See Serbia Scott 169-170.

Native — This is a term applied to handmade papers used to produce some of the early stamps of the Indian states. Stamps printed on native paper may be expected to display various natural inclusions that are normal and do not negatively affect value. Japanese paper, originally made of mulberry fibers and rice flour, is part of this group. See Japan Scott 1-18.

Manila — This type of paper is often used to make stamped envelopes and wrappers. It is a coarse-textured stock, usually smooth on one side and rough on the other. A variety of colors of manila paper exist, but the most common range is yellowish-brown.

Silk — Introduced by the British in 1847 as a safeguard against counterfeiting, silk paper contains bits of colored silk thread scattered throughout. The density of these fibers varies greatly and can include as few as one fiber per stamp or hundreds. U.S. revenue Scott R152 is a good example of an easy-to-identify silk paper stamp.

Silk-thread paper has uninterrupted threads of colored silk arranged so that one or more threads run through the stamp or postal stationery. See Great Britain Scott 5-6 and Switzerland Scott 14-19.

Granite — Filled with minute cloth or colored paper fibers of various colors and lengths, granite paper should not be confused with either type of silk paper. Austria Scott 172-175 and a number of Swiss stamps are examples of granite paper.

Chalky — A chalk-like substance coats the surface of chalky paper to discourage the cleaning and reuse of canceled stamps, as well as to provide a smoother, more acceptable printing surface. Because the designs of stamps printed on chalky paper are imprinted on what is often a water-soluble coating, any attempt to remove a cancellation will destroy the stamp. *Do not soak these stamps in any fluid.* To remove a stamp printed on chalky paper from an envelope, wet the paper from underneath the stamp until the gum dissolves enough to release the stamp from the paper. See St. Kitts-Nevis Scott 89-90 for examples of stamps printed on this type of chalky paper.

India — Another name for this paper, originally introduced from China about 1750, is "China Paper." It is a thin, opaque paper often used for plate and die proofs by many countries.

Double — In philately, the term double paper has two distinct meanings. The first is a two-ply paper, usually a combination of a thick and a thin sheet, joined during manufacture. This type was used experimentally as a means to discourage the reuse of stamps.

The design is printed on the thin paper. Any attempt to remove a cancellation would destroy the design. U.S. Scott 158 and other Banknote-era stamps exist on this form of double paper.

The second type of double paper occurs on a rotary press, when the end of one paper roll, or web, is affixed to the next roll to save time feeding the paper through the press. Stamp designs are printed over the joined paper and, if overlooked by inspectors, may get into post office stocks.

Goldbeater's Skin — This type of paper was used for the 1866 issue of Prussia, and was a tough, translucent paper. The design was printed in reverse on the back of the stamp, and the gum applied over the printing. It is impossible to remove stamps printed on this type of paper from the paper to which they are affixed without destroying the design.

Ribbed — Ribbed paper has an uneven, corrugated surface made by passing the paper through ridged rollers. This type exists on some copies of U.S. Scott 156-165.

Various other substances, or substrates, have been used for stamp manufacture, including wood, aluminum, copper, silver and gold foil, plastic, and silk and cotton fabrics.

Wove **Laid** **Granite**

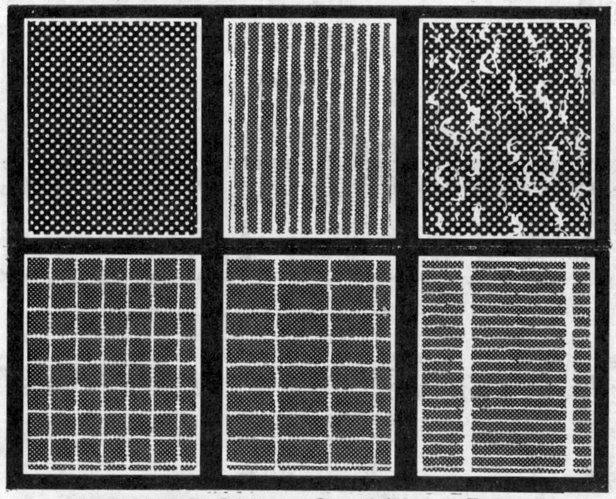

Quadrille **Oblong Quadrille** **Batonne**

Watermarks

Watermarks are an integral part of some papers. They are formed in the process of paper manufacture. Watermarks consist of small designs, formed of wire or cut from metal and soldered to the surface of the mold or, sometimes, on the dandy roll. The designs may be in the form of crowns, stars, anchors, letters or other characters or symbols. These pieces of metal - known in the paper-making industry as "bits" - impress a design into the paper. The design sometimes may be seen by holding the stamp to the light. Some are more easily seen with a watermark detector. This important tool is a small black tray into which a stamp is placed face down and dampened with a fast-evaporating watermark detection fluid that brings up the watermark image in the form of dark lines against a lighter background. These dark lines are the thinner areas of the paper known as the watermark. Some watermarks are extremely difficult to locate, due to either a faint impression, watermark location or the color of the stamp. There also are electric watermark detectors that come with plastic filter disks of various colors. The disks neutralize the color of the stamp, permitting the watermark to be seen more easily.

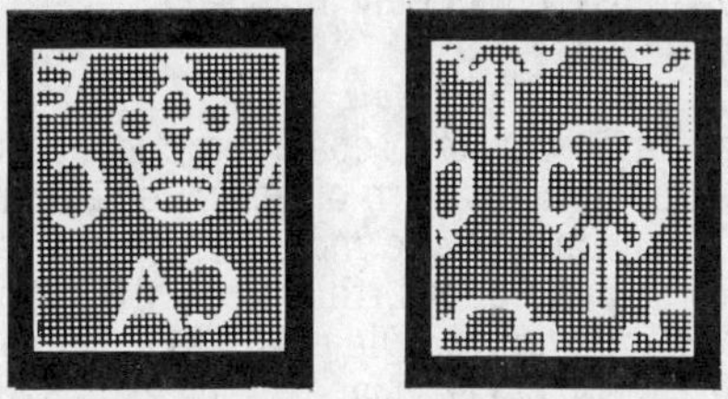

Multiple watermarks of Crown Agents and Burma

Watermarks of Uruguay, Vatican City and Jamaica

WARNING: Some inks used in the photogravure process dissolve in watermark fluids (Please see the section on Soluble Printing Inks). Also, see "chalky paper."

Watermarks may be found normal, reversed, inverted, reversed and inverted, sideways or diagonal, as seen from the back of the stamp. The relationship of watermark to stamp design depends on the position of the printing plates or how paper is fed through the press. On machine-made paper, watermarks normally are read from right to left. The design is repeated closely throughout the sheet in a "multiple-watermark design." In a "sheet watermark," the design appears only once on the sheet, but extends over many stamps. Individual stamps may carry only a small fraction or none of the watermark.

"Marginal watermarks" occur in the margins of sheets or panes of stamps. They occur on the outside border of paper (ostensibly outside the area where stamps are to be printed). A large row of letters may spell the name of the country or the manufacturer of the paper. Careless press feeding may cause parts of these letters to show on stamps of the outer row of a pane.

Soluble Printing Inks

WARNING: Most stamp colors are permanent; that is, they are not seriously affected by short-term exposure to light or water. Many colors, especially of modern inks, fade from excessive exposure to light. There are stamps printed with inks that dissolve easily in water or in fluids used to detect watermarks. Use of these inks was intentional to prevent the removal of cancellations. Water affects all aniline inks, those on so-called safety paper and some photogravure printings - all such inks are known as *fugitive colors. Removal from paper of such stamps requires care and alternatives to traditional soaking.*

Separation

"Separation" is the general term used to describe methods used to separate stamps. The three standard forms currently in use are perforating, rouletting and die-cutting. These methods are done during the stamp production process, after printing. Sometimes these methods are done on-press or sometimes as a separate step. The earliest issues, such as the 1840 Penny Black of Great Britain (Scott 1), did not have any means provided for separation. It was expected the stamps would be cut apart with scissors or folded and torn. These are examples of imperforate stamps. Many stamps were first issued in imperforate formats and were later issued with perforations. Therefore, care must be observed in buying single imperforate stamps to be certain they were issued imperforate and are not perforated copies that have been altered by having the perforations trimmed away. Stamps issued imperforate usually are valued as singles. However, imperforate varieties of normally perforated stamps should be collected in pairs or larger pieces as indisputable evidence of their imperforate character.

PERFORATION

The chief style of separation of stamps, and the one that is in almost universal use today, is perforating. By this process, paper between the stamps is cut away in a line of holes, usually round, leaving little bridges of paper between the stamps to hold them together. Some types of perforation, such as hyphen-hole perfs, can be confused with roulettes, but a close visual inspection reveals that paper has been removed. The little perforation bridges, which project from the stamp when it is torn from the pane, are called the teeth of the perforation.

As the size of the perforation is sometimes the only way to differentiate between two otherwise identical stamps, it is necessary to be able to accurately measure and describe them. This is done with a perforation gauge, usually a ruler-like device that has dots or graduated lines to show how many perforations may be counted in the space of two centimeters. Two centimeters is the space universally adopted in which to measure perforations.

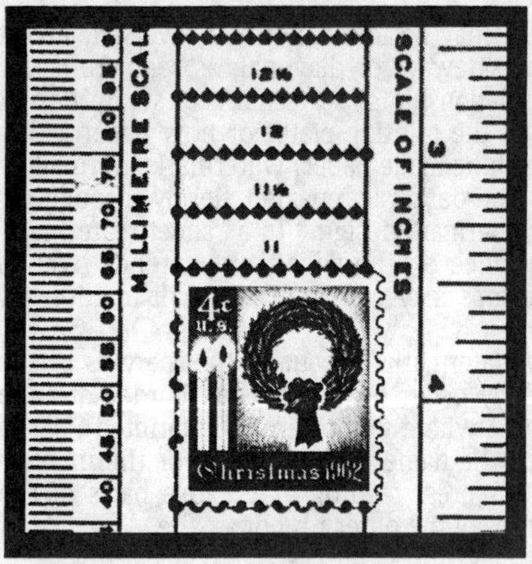

Perforation gauge

To measure a stamp, run it along the gauge until the dots on it fit exactly into the perforations of the stamp. If you are using a graduated-line perforation gauge, simply slide the stamp along the surface until the lines on the gauge perfectly project from the center of the bridges or holes. The number to the side of the line of dots or lines that fit the stamp's perforation is the measurement. For example, an "11" means that 11 perforations fit between two centimeters. The description of the stamp therefore is "perf. 11." If the gauge of the perforations on the top and bottom of a stamp differs from that on the sides, the result is what is known as *compound perforations.* In measuring compound perforations, the gauge at top and bottom is always given first, then the sides. Thus, a stamp that measures 11 at top and bottom and 10 1/2 at the sides is "perf. 11 x 10 1/2." See U.S. Scott 632-642 for examples of compound perforations.

Stamps also are known with perforations different on three or all four sides. Descriptions of such items are clockwise, beginning with the top of the stamp.

A perforation with small holes and teeth close together is a "fine perforation." One with large holes and teeth far apart is a "coarse perforation." Holes that are jagged, rather than clean-cut, are "rough perforations." *Blind perforations* are the slight impressions left by the perforating pins if they fail to puncture the paper. Multiples of stamps showing blind perforations may command a slight premium over normally perforated stamps.

The term *syncopated perfs* describes intentional irregularities in the perforations. The earliest form was used by the Netherlands from 1925-33, where holes were omitted to create distinctive patterns. Beginning in 1992, Great Britain has used an oval perforation to help prevent counterfeiting. Several other countries have started using the oval perfs.

A new type of perforation, still primarily used for postal stationery, is known as microperfs. Microperfs are tiny perforations (in some cases hundreds of holes per two centimeters) that allows items to be intentionally separated very easily, while not accidentally breaking apart as easily as standard perforations. These are not currently measured or differentiated by size, as are standard perforations.

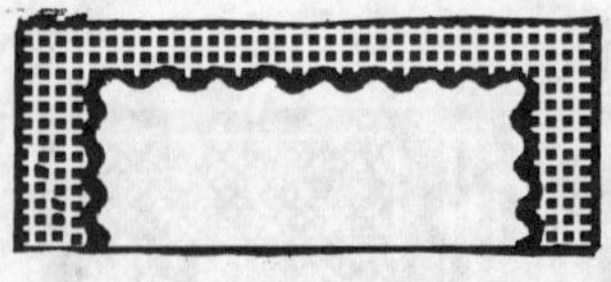

perce en arc

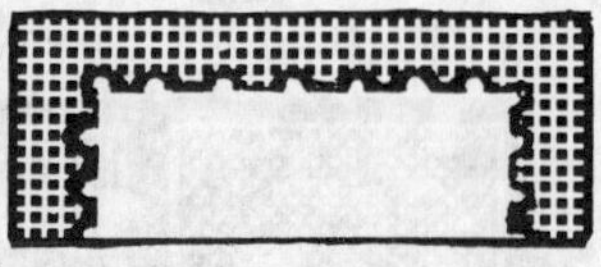

perce en lignes

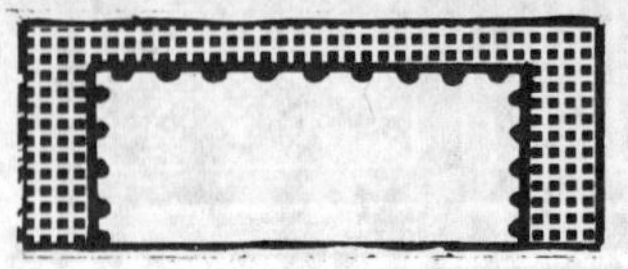

perce en points

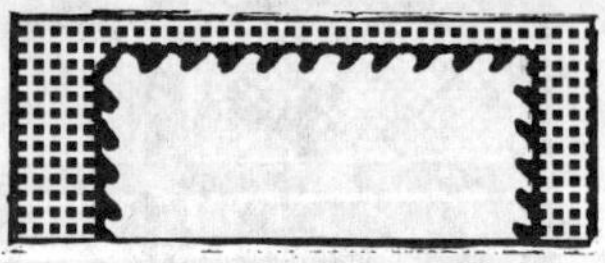

oblique roulette

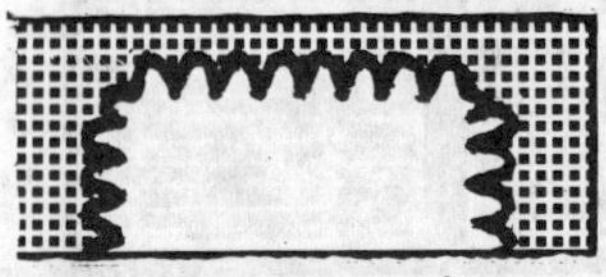

perce en scie

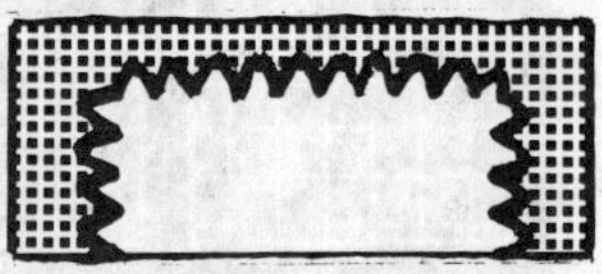

perce serpentin

ROULETTING

In rouletting, the stamp paper is cut partly or wholly through, with no paper removed. In perforating, some paper is removed. Rouletting derives its name from the French roulette, a spur-like wheel. As the wheel is rolled over the paper, each point makes a small cut. The number of cuts made in a two-centimeter space determines the gauge of the roulette, just as the number of perforations in two centimeters determines the gauge of the perforation.

The shape and arrangement of the teeth on the wheels varies. Various roulette types generally carry French names:

Perce en lignes - rouletted in lines. The paper receives short, straight cuts in lines. This is the most common type of rouletting. See Mexico Scott 500.

Perce en points - pin-rouletted. This differs from a small perforation because no paper is removed, although round, equidistant holes are pricked through the paper. See Mexico Scott 242-256.

Perce en arc and *perce en scie* - pierced in an arc or saw-toothed designs, forming half circles or small triangles. See Hanover (German States) Scott 25-29.

Perce en serpentin - serpentine roulettes. The cuts form a serpentine or wavy line. See Brunswick (German States) Scott 13-18.

Once again, no paper is removed by these processes, leaving the stamps easily separated, but closely attached.

DIE-CUTTING

The third major form of stamp separation is die-cutting. This is a method where a die in the pattern of separation is created that later cuts the stamp paper in a stroke motion. Although some standard stamps bear die-cut perforations, this process is primarily used for self-adhesive postage stamps. Die-cutting can appear in straight lines, such as U.S. Scott 2522, shapes, such as U.S. Scott 1551, or imitating the appearance of perforations, such as New Zealand Scott 935A and 935B.

Printing Processes

ENGRAVING (Intaglio, Line-engraving, Etching)

Master die - The initial operation in the process of line engraving is making the master die. The die is a small, flat block of softened steel upon which the stamp design is recess engraved in reverse.

Master die

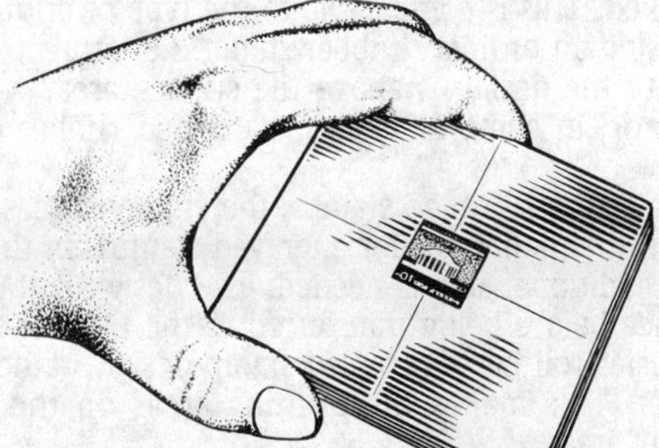

Photographic reduction of the original art is made to the appropriate size. It then serves as a tracing guide for the initial outline of the design. The engraver lightly traces the design on the steel with his graver, then slowly works the design until it is completed. At various points during the engraving process, the engraver hand-inks the die and makes an impression to check his progress. These are known as progressive die proofs. After completion of the engraving, the die is hardened to withstand the stress and pressures of later transfer operations.

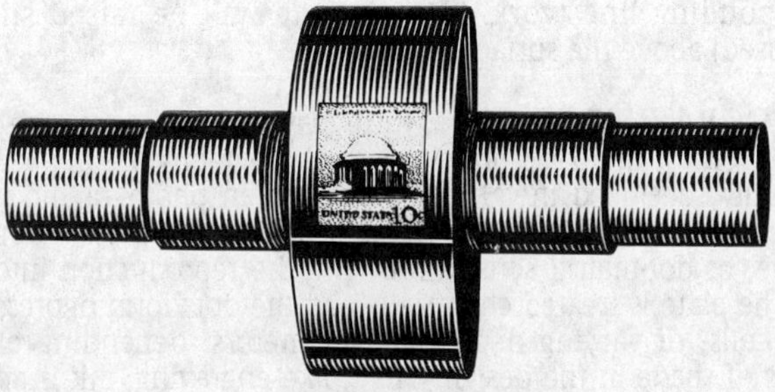

Transfer roll

Transfer roll — Next is production of the transfer roll that, as the name implies, is the medium used to transfer the subject from the master die to the printing plate. A blank roll of soft steel, mounted on a mandrel, is placed under the bearers of the transfer press to allow it to roll freely on its axis. The hardened die is placed on the bed of the press and the face of the transfer roll is applied to the die, under pressure. The bed or the roll is then rocked back and forth under increasing pressure, until the soft steel of the roll is forced into every engraved line of the die. The resulting impression on the roll is known as a "relief" or a "relief transfer." The engraved image is now positive in appearance and stands out from the steel. After the required number of reliefs are "rocked in," the soft steel transfer roll is hardened.

Different flaws may occur during the relief process. A defective relief may occur during the rocking in process because of a minute piece of foreign material lodging on the die, or some other cause. Imperfections in the steel of the transfer roll may result in a breaking away of parts of the design. This is known as a relief break, which will show up on finished stamps as small, unprinted areas. If a damaged relief remains in use, it will transfer a repeating defect to the plate. Deliberate alterations of reliefs sometimes occur. "Altered reliefs" designate these changed conditions.

Plate — The final step in pre-printing production is the making of the printing plate. A flat piece of soft steel replaces the die on the bed of the transfer press. One of the reliefs on the transfer roll is positioned over this soft steel. Position, or layout, dots determine the correct position on the plate. The dots have been lightly marked on the plate in advance. After the correct position of the relief is determined, the design is rocked in by following the same method used in making the transfer roll. The difference is that this time the image is being transferred from the transfer roll, rather than to it. Once the design is entered on the plate, it appears in reverse and is recessed. There are as many transfers entered on the plate as there are subjects printed on the sheet of stamps. It is during this process that double and shifted transfers occur, as well as re-entries. These are the result of improperly entered images that have not been properly burnished out prior to rocking in a new image.

Modern siderography processes, such as those used by the U.S. Bureau of Engraving and Printing, involve an automated form of rocking designs in on preformed cylindrical printing sleeves. The same process also allows for easier removal and re-entry of worn images right on the sleeve.

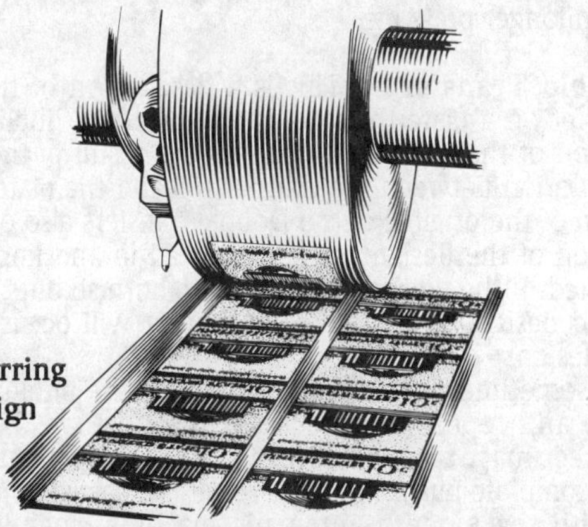

Transferring the design to the plate

Following the entering of the required transfers on the plate, the position dots, layout dots and lines, scratches and other markings generally are burnished out. Added at this time by the siderographer are any required *guide lines, plate numbers* or other *marginal markings.* The plate is then hand-inked and a proof impression is taken. This is known as a plate proof. If the impression is approved, the plate is machined for fitting onto the press, is hardened and sent to the plate vault ready for use.

On press, the plate is inked and the surface is automatically wiped clean, leaving ink only in the recessed lines. Paper is then forced under pressure into the engraved recessed lines, thereby receiving the ink. Thus, the ink lines on engraved stamps are slightly raised, and slight depressions (debossing) occur on the back of the stamp. Prior to the advent of modern high-speed presses and more advanced ink formulations, paper had to be dampened before receiving the ink. This sometimes led to uneven shrinkage by the time the stamps were perforated, resulting in improperly perforated stamps, or misperfs. Newer presses use drier paper, thus both *wet* and *dry printings* exist on some stamps.

Rotary Press — Until 1914, only flat plates were used to print engraved stamps. Rotary press printing was introduced in 1914, and slowly spread. Some countries still use flat-plate printing.

After approval of the plate proof, older *rotary press plates* require additional machining. They are curved to fit the press cylinder. "Gripper slots" are cut into the back of each plate to receive the "grippers," which hold the plate securely on the press. The plate is then hardened. Stamps printed from these bent rotary press plates are longer or wider than the same stamps printed from flat-plate presses. The stretching of the plate during the curving process is what causes this distortion.

Re-entry — To execute a re-entry on a flat plate, the transfer roll is re-applied to the plate, often at some time after its first use on the press. Worn-out designs can be resharpened by carefully burnishing out the original image and re-entering it from the transfer roll. If the original impression has not been sufficiently removed and the transfer roll is not precisely in line with the remaining impression, the resulting double transfer will make the re-entry obvious. If the registration is true, a re-entry may be difficult or impossible to distinguish. Sometimes a stamp printed from a successful re-entry is identified by having a much sharper and clearer impression than its neighbors. With the advent of rotary presses, post-press re-entries were not possible. After a plate was curved for the rotary press, it was impossible to make a re-entry. This is because the plate had already been bent once (with the design distorted).

However, with the introduction of the previously mentioned modern-style siderography machines, entries are made to the preformed cylindrical printing sleeve. Such sleeves are dechromed and softened. This allows individual images to be burnished out and reentered on the curved sleeve. The sleeve is then rechromed, resulting in longer press life.

Double Transfer — This is a description of the condition of a transfer on a plate that shows evidence of a duplication of all, or a portion of the design. It usually is the result of the changing of the registration between the transfer roll and the plate during the rocking in of the original entry. Double transfers also occur when only a portion of the design has been rocked in and improper positioning is noted. If the worker elected not to burnish out the partial or completed design, a strong double transfer will occur for part or all of the design.

It sometimes is necessary to remove the original transfer from a plate and repeat the process a second time. If the finished reworked image shows traces of the original impression, attributable to incomplete burnishing, the result is a partial double transfer.

With the modern automatic machines mentioned previously, double transfers are all but impossible to create. Those partially doubled images on stamps printed from such sleeves are more than likely re-entries, rather than true double transfers.

Re-engraved — Alterations to a stamp design are sometimes necessary after some stamps have been printed. In some cases, either the original die or the actual printing plate may have its "temper" drawn (softened), and the design will be re-cut. The resulting impressions from such a re-engraved die or plate may differ slightly from the original issue, and are known as "re-engraved." If the alteration was made to the master die, all future printings will be consistently different from the original. If alterations were made to the printing plate, each altered stamp on the plate will be slightly different from each other, allowing specialists to reconstruct a complete printing plate.

Dropped Transfers — If an impression from the transfer roll has not been properly placed, a dropped transfer may occur. The final stamp image will appear obviously out of line with its neighbors.

Short Transfer — Sometimes a transfer roll is not rocked its entire length when entering a transfer onto a plate. As a result, the finished transfer on the plate fails to show the complete design, and the finished stamp will have an incomplete design printed. This is known as a "short transfer." U.S. Scott No. 8 is a good example of a short transfer.

TYPOGRAPHY (Letterpress, Surface Printing, Flexography, Dry Offset, High Etch)

Although the word "Typography" is obsolete as a term describing a printing method, it was the accepted term throughout the first century of postage stamps. Therefore, appropriate Scott listings in this catalogue refer to typographed stamps. The current term for this form of printing, however, is "letterpress."

As it relates to the production of postage stamps, letterpress printing is the reverse of engraving. Rather than having recessed areas trap the ink and deposit it on paper, only the raised areas of the design are inked. This is comparable to the type of printing seen by inking and using an ordinary rubber stamp. Letterpress includes all printing where the design is above the surface area, whether it is wood, metal or, in some instances, hardened rubber or polymer plastic.

For most letterpress-printed stamps, the engraved master is made in much the same manner as for engraved stamps. In this instance, however, an additional step is needed. The design is transferred to another surface before being transferred to the transfer roll. In this way, the transfer roll has a recessed stamp design, rather than one done in relief. This makes the printing areas on the final plate raised, or relief areas.

For less-detailed stamps of the 19th century, the area on the die not used as a printing surface was cut away, leaving the surface area raised. The original die was then reproduced by stereotyping or electrotyping. The resulting electrotypes were assembled in the required number and format of the desired sheet of stamps. The plate used in printing the stamps was an electroplate of these assembled electrotypes.

Once the final letterpress plates are created, ink is applied to the raised surface and the pressure of the press transfers the ink impression to the paper. In contrast to engraving, the fine lines of letterpress are impressed on the surface of the stamp, leaving a debossed surface. When viewed from the back (as on a typewritten page), the corresponding line work on the stamp will be raised slightly (embossed) above the surface.

PHOTOGRAVURE (Gravure, Rotogravure, Heliogravure)

In this process, the basic principles of photography are applied to a chemically sensitized metal plate, rather than photographic paper. The design is transferred photographically to the plate through a halftone, or dot-matrix screen, breaking the reproduction into tiny dots. The plate is treated chemically and the dots form depressions, called cells, of varying depths and diameters, depending on the degrees of shade in the design. Then, like engraving, ink is applied to the plate and the surface is wiped clean. This leaves ink in the tiny cells that is lifted out and deposited on the paper when it is pressed against the plate.

Gravure is most often used for multicolored stamps, generally using the three primary colors (red, yellow and blue) and black. By varying the dot matrix pattern and density of these colors, virtually any color can be reproduced. A typical full-color gravure stamp will be created from four printing cylinders (one for each color). The original multicolored image will have been photographically separated into its component colors.

For examples of the first photogravure stamps printed (1914), see Bavaria Scott 94-114.

LITHOGRAPHY (Offset Lithography, Stone Lithography, Dilitho, Planography, Collotype)

The principle that oil and water do not mix is the basis for lithography. The stamp design is drawn by hand or transferred from engraving to the surface of a lithographic stone or metal plate in a greasy (oily) substance. This oily substance holds the ink, which will later be transferred to the paper. The stone (or plate) is wet with an acid fluid, causing it to repel the printing ink in all areas not covered by the greasy substance.

Transfer paper is used to transfer the design from the original stone or plate. A series of duplicate transfers are grouped and, in turn, transferred to the final printing plate.

Photolithography — The application of photographic processes to lithography. This process allows greater flexibility of design, related to use of halftone screens combined with line work. Unlike photogravure or engraving, this process can allow large, solid areas to be printed.

Offset — A refinement of the lithographic process. A rubber-covered blanket cylinder takes the impression from the inked lithographic plate. From the "blanket" the impression is *offset* or transferred to the paper. Greater flexibility and speed are the principal reasons offset printing has largely displaced lithography. The term "lithography" covers both processes, and results are almost identical.

EMBOSSED (Relief) Printing

Embossing, not considered one of the four main printing types, is a method in which the design first is sunk into the metal of the die. Printing is done against a yielding platen, such as leather or linoleum. The platen is forced into the depression of the die, thus forming the design on the paper in relief. This process is often used for metallic inks.

Embossing may be done without color (see Sardinia Scott 4-6); with color printed around the embossed area (see Great Britain Scott 5 and most U.S. envelopes); and with color in exact registration with the embossed subject (see Canada Scott 656-657).

COMBINATION PRINTINGS

Sometimes two or even three printing methods are combined in producing stamps. In these cases, such as Austria Scott 933, the stamp's dual printing technique can be determined by studying the individual characteristics of each printing type (intaglio and offset). A few stamps, such as Singapore Scott 684-684A, combine as many as three of the four major printing types (offset, intaglio and letterpress). When this is done it often indicates the incorporation of security devices against counterfeiting.

INK COLORS

Inks or colored papers used in stamp printing often are of mineral origin, although there are numerous examples of organic-based pigments. As a general rule, organic-based pigments are far more subject to varieties and change than those of mineral-based origin.

The appearance of any given color on a stamp may be affected by many aspects, including printing variations, light, color of paper, aging and chemical alterations.

Numerous printing variations may be observed. Heavier pressure or inking will cause a more intense color, while slight interruptions in the ink feed or lighter impressions will cause a lighter appearance. Stamps printed in the same color by water-based and solvent-based inks can differ significantly in appearance. This affects several stamps in the U.S. Prominent Americans series. Hand-mixed ink formulas (primarily from the 19th century) produced under different conditions (humidity and temperature) account for notable color variations in early printings of the same stamp (see U.S. Scott 248-250, 279B, for example). Different sources of pigment can also result in significant differences in color.

Light exposure and aging are closely related in the way they affect stamp color. Both eventually break down the ink and fade colors, so that a carefully kept stamp may differ significantly in color from an identical copy that has been exposed to light. If stamps are exposed to light either intentionally or accidentally, their colors can be faded or completely changed in some cases.

Papers of different quality and consistency used for the same stamp printing may affect color appearance. Most pelure papers, for example, show a richer color when compared with wove or laid papers. See Russia Scott 181a, for an example of this effect.

The very nature of the printing processes can cause a variety of differences in shades or hues of the same stamp. Some of these shades are scarcer than others, and are of particular interest to the advanced collector.

Luminescence

All forms of tagged stamps fall under the general category of luminescence. Within this broad category is fluorescence, dealing with forms of tagging visible under longwave ultraviolet light, and phosphorescence, which deals with tagging visible only under shortwave light. Phosphorescence leaves an afterglow and fluorescence does not. These treated stamps show up in a range of different colors when exposed to UV light. The differing wavelengths of the light activates the tagging material, making it glow in various colors that usually serve different mail processing purposes.

Intentional tagging is a post-World War II phenomenon, brought about by the increased literacy rate and rapidly growing mail volume. It was one of several answers to the problem of the need for more automated mail processes. Early tagged stamps served the purpose of triggering machines to separate different types of mail. A natural outgrowth was to also use the signal to trigger machines that faced all envelopes the same way and canceled them.

Tagged stamps come many different ways and in different forms. Some tagged stamps have luminescent shapes or images imprinted on them as a form of security device. Others have blocks (United States), stripes, frames (South Africa and Canada), overall coatings (United States), bars (Great Britain and Canada) and many other types. Some types of tagging are even mixed in with the pigmented printing ink (Australia Scott 366, Netherlands Scott 478 and U.S. Scott 1359 and 2443). Each form of tagging has a different purpose, some to give different machines different types of signals, and others as adaptive forms of technological growth.

The means of applying taggant to stamps differs as much as the intended purposes for the stamps. The most common form of tagging is a coating applied to the surface of the printed stamp. Since the taggant ink is frequently invisible except under UV light, it does not interfere with the appearance of the stamp. Another common application is the use of phosphored papers. In this case the paper itself either has a coating of taggant applied before the stamp is printed or has taggant applied during the papermaking process, incorporating it into the fibers. This is currently in use in the United States. A similar form is the application of a fluorescent coating either to the finished paper or during the papermaking process. This type of tagging has been extensively used by Australia and Germany.

Many countries now use tagging in various forms to either expedite mail handling or to serve as a printing security device against counterfeiting. Following the introduction of tagged stamps for public use in 1959 by Great Britain, other countries have steadily joined the parade. Among those are Germany (1961); Canada and Denmark (1962); United States, Australia, France and Switzerland (1963); Belgium and Japan (1966); Sweden and Norway (1967); Italy (1968); and Russia (1969). Since then, many other countries have begun using forms of tagging, including Brazil, China, Czechoslovakia, Hong Kong, Guatemala, Indonesia, Israel, Lithuania, Luxembourg, Netherlands, Penrhyn Islands, Portugal, St. Vincent, Singapore, South Africa, Spain and Sweden to name a few.

In some cases, including United States, Canada, Great Britain and Switzerland, stamps were released both with and without tagging. Many of these were released during each country's experimental period. Tagged and untagged versions are listed for the aforementioned countries and are noted in some other countries' listings. For at least a few stamps, the experimentally tagged version is worth far more than its untagged counterpart, such as the 1963 experimental tagged version of France Scott 1024.

In some cases luminescent varieties of stamps were inadvertently created. Several Russian stamps, for example, sport highly fluorescent ink that was not intended as a form of tagging. Older stamps, such as early U.S. postage dues, can be positively identified by the use of UV light, since the organic ink used has become slightly fluorescent over time. Other stamps, such as Austria Scott 70a-82a (varnish bars) and Obock Scott 46-64 (printed quadrille lines), have become fluorescent over time.

Various fluorescent substances have been added to paper to make it appear brighter. These optical brightners, as they are known, greatly affect the appearance of the stamp under UV light. The brightest of these is known as Hi-Brite paper. These paper varieties are beyond the scope of the Scott Catalogue.

Shortwave UV light also is used extensively in expertizing, since each form of paper has its own fluorescent characteristics that are impossible to perfectly match. It is therefore a simple matter to detect filled thins, added perforation teeth and other alterations that involve the addition of paper. UV light also is used to examine stamps that have had cancels chemically removed and for other purposes as well.

Gum

The gum on the back of a stamp may be shiny, dull, smooth, rough, dark, white, colored or tinted. It may be obvious or virtually impossible to distinguish, as on Canada Scott 453 or Rwanda Scott 287-294. Most stamp gumming adhesives use gum arabic or dextrine as a base. Certain polymers such as polyvinyl alcohol (PVA) have been used extensively since World War II. The PVA gum used by security printers Harrison and Sons since 1968 is dull-surfaced, slightly yellowish and almost invisible.

The *Scott Standard Postage Stamp Catalogue* does not list items by types of gum. The *Scott Specialized Catalogue of United States Stamps* does differentiate among some types of gum for certain issues.

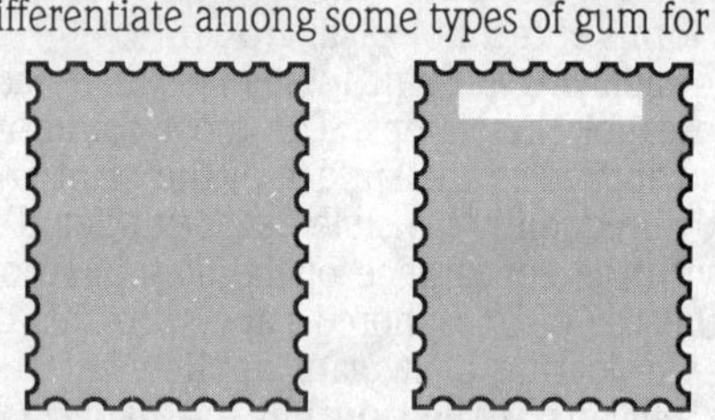

Never Hinged **Lightly Hinged**

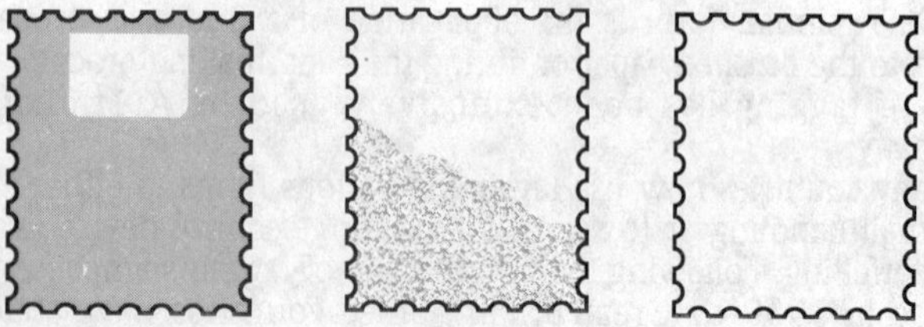

Original Gum **Part Gum** **No Gum/Regummed**

For purposes of determining the condition of an unused stamp, Scott Publishing Co. presents the following definitions (with accompanying illustrations): **Never Hinged (NH)** - Full original gum with no hinge mark or other blemish or disturbance. The presence of an expertizer's mark does not disqualify a stamp from this designation; **Lightly Hinged (LH)** - Full original gum with a light disturbance of the gum from the removal of a peelable hinge; **Original Gum (OG)** - Hinging and other disturbances should affect 20 percent or less of the original gum. **Part Gum (PG)** - Between 20 and 80 percent of the original gum remains. The stamp may have hinge remnants; **No Gum (NG) or Regummed (RE)** - A stamp with no gum or less than 20 percent of the original gum. A regummed stamp is considered the same as a stamp with none of its original gum for purposes of grading.

Reprints of stamps may have gum differing from the original issues. In addition, some countries have used different gum formulas for different seasons. These adhesives have different properties that may become more apparent over time.

Many stamps have been issued without gum, and the catalogue will note this fact. See United States Scott PR33-PR56. Sometimes, gum may have been removed to preserve the stamp. Germany Scott B68, for example, has a highly acidic gum that eventually destroys the stamps. This item is valued in the catalogue with gum removed.

Reprints and Reissues

These are impressions of stamps (usually obsolete) made from the original plates or stones. If they are valid for postage and reproduce obsolete issues (such as U.S.Scott 2875), the stamps are *reissues.* If they are from current issues, they are designated as *second, third,* etc., *printing.* If designated for a particular purpose, they are *special printings.*

Scott will list those reissues and reprints that are valid for postage if they differ significantly from the original printing.

When reprints are not valid for postage, but are made from original dies and plates by authorized persons, they are *official reprints. Private reprints* are made from original plates and dies by private hands. *Official reproductions* or imitations are made from new dies and plates by government authorization.

The U.S. government made official imitations of its first postage stamps in 1875. Produced were copies of the first two stamps (listed as Scott 3-4), reprints of the demonetized pre-1861 issues and reissues of the 1861 stamps, the 1869 stamps and the then-current 1875 denominations. An example of a private reprint is that of the New Haven, Conn., postmaster's provisional.

Most reprints differ slightly from the original stamp in some characteristic, such as gum, paper, perforation, color or watermark. Sometimes the details are followed so meticulously that only a student of that specific stamp is able to distinguish the reprint from the original.

Remainders and Canceled to Order

Some countries sell their stock of old stamps when a new issue replaces them. To avoid postal use, the *remainders* usually are canceled with a punch hole, a heavy line or bar, or a more-or-less regular-looking cancellation. The most famous merchant of remainders was Nicholas F. Seebeck. In the 1880s and 1890s, he arranged printing contracts between the Hamilton Bank Note Co., of which he was a director, and several Central and South American countries. The contracts provided that the plates and all remainders of the yearly issues became the property of Hamilton. Seebeck saw to it that ample stock remained. The "Seebecks," both remainders and reprints, were standard packet fillers for decades.

Some countries also issue stamps *canceled-to-order (CTO),* either in sheets with original gum or stuck onto pieces of paper or envelopes and canceled. Such CTO items generally are worth less than postally used stamps. In cases where the CTO material is far more prevalent in the marketplace than postally used examples, the catalogue value relates to the CTO examples, with postally used examples noted as premium items. Most CTOs can be detected by the presence of gum. However, as the CTO practice goes back at least to 1885, the gum inevitably has been soaked off some stamps so they could pass as postally used. The normally applied postmarks usually differ slightly from standard postmarks, and specialists are able to tell the difference. When applied individually to envelopes by philatelically minded persons, CTO material is known as *favor canceled* and generally sells at large discounts.

Cinderellas and Facsimiles

Cinderella is a catch-all term used by stamp collectors to describe phantoms, fantasies, bogus items, municipal issues, exhibition seals, local revenues, transportation stamps, labels, poster stamps and many other types of items. Some cinderella collectors include in their collections local postage issues, telegraph stamps, essays and proofs, forgeries and counterfeits.

A *fantasy* is an adhesive created for a nonexistent stamp-issuing authority. Fantasy items range from imaginary countries (Occusi-Ambeno, Kingdom of Sedang, Principality of Trinidad or Torres Straits), to non-existent locals (Winans City Post), or nonexistent transportation lines (McRobish & Co.'s Acapulco-San Francisco Line).

On the other hand, if the entity exists and could have issued stamps (but did not) or was known to have issued other stamps, the items are considered *bogus* stamps. These would include the Mormon postage stamps of Utah, S. Allan Taylor's Guatemala and Paraguay inventions, the propaganda issues for the South Moluccas and the adhesives of the Page & Keyes local post of Boston.

Phantoms is another term for both fantasy and bogus issues.

Facsimiles are copies or imitations made to represent original stamps, but which do not pretend to be originals. A catalogue illustration is such a facsimile. Illustrations from the Moens catalogue of the last century were occasionally colored and passed off as stamps. Since the beginning of stamp collecting, facsimiles have been made for collectors as space fillers or for reference. They often carry the word "facsimile," "falsch" (German), "sanko" or "mozo" (Japanese), or "faux" (French) overprinted on the face or stamped on the back. Unfortunately, over the years a number of these items have had fake cancels applied over the facsimile notation and have been passed off as genuine.

Forgeries and Counterfeits

Forgeries and counterfeits have been with philately virtually from the beginning of stamp production. Over time, the terminology for the two has been used interchangeably. Although both forgeries and counterfeits are reproductions of stamps, the purposes behind their creation differ considerably.

Among specialists there is an increasing movement to more specifically define such items. Although there is no universally accepted terminology, we feel the following definitions most closely mirror the items and their purposes as they are currently defined.

Forgeries (also often referred to as *Counterfeits*) are reproductions of genuine stamps that have been created to defraud collectors. Such spurious items first appeared on the market around 1860, and most old-time collections contain one or more. Many are crude and easily spotted, but some can deceive experts.

An important supplier of these early philatelic forgeries was the Hamburg printer Gebruder Spiro. Many others with reputations in this craft included S. Allan Taylor, George Hussey, James Chute, George Forune, Benjamin & Sarpy, Julius Goldner, E. Oneglia and L.H. Mercier. Among the noted 20th-century forgers were Francois Fournier, Jean Sperati and the prolific Raoul DeThuin.

Forgeries may be complete replications, or they may be genuine stamps altered to resemble a scarcer (and more valuable) type. Most forgeries, particularly those of rare stamps, are worth only a small fraction of the value of a genuine example, but a few types, created by some of the most notable forgers, such as Sperati, can be worth as much or more than the genuine. Fraudulently produced copies are known of most classic rarities and many medium-priced stamps.

In addition to rare stamps, large numbers of common 19th- and early 20th-century stamps were forged to supply stamps to the early packet trade. Many can still be easily found. Few new philatelic forgeries have appeared in recent decades. Successful imitation of well-engraved work is virtually impossible. It has proven far easier to produce a fake by altering a genuine stamp than to duplicate a stamp completely.

Counterfeit (also often referred to as *Postal Counterfeit* or *Postal Forgery*) is the term generally applied to reproductions of stamps that have been created to defraud the government of revenue. Such items usually are created at the time a stamp is current and, in some cases, are hard to detect. Because most counterfeits are seized when the perpetrator is captured, postal counterfeits, particularly used on cover, are usually worth much more than a genuine example to specialists. The first postal counterfeit was of Spain's 4-cuarto carmine of 1854 (the real one is Scott 25). Apparently, the counterfeiters were not satisfied with their first version, which is now very scarce, and they soon created an engraved counterfeit, which is common. Postal counterfeits quickly followed in Austria, Naples, Sardinia and the Roman States. They have since been created in many other countries as well, including the United States.

An infamous counterfeit to defraud the government is the 1-shilling Great Britain "Stock Exchange" forgery of 1872, used on telegraph forms at the exchange that year. The stamp escaped detection until a stamp dealer noticed it in 1898.

Fakes

Fakes are genuine stamps altered in some way to make them more desirable. One student of this part of stamp collecting has estimated that by the 1950s more than 30,000 varieties of fakes were known. That number has grown greatly since then. The widespread existence of fakes makes it important for stamp collectors to study their philatelic holdings and use relevant literature. Likewise, collectors should buy from reputable dealers who guarantee their stamps and make full and prompt refunds should a purchased item be declared faked or altered by some mutually agreed-upon authority. Because fakes always have some genuine characteristics, it is not always possible to obtain unanimous agreement among experts regarding specific items. These students may change their opinions as philatelic knowledge increases. More than 80 percent of all fakes on the philatelic market today are regummed, reperforated (or perforated for the first time), or bear forged overprints, surcharges or cancellations.

Stamps can be chemically treated to alter or eliminate colors. For example, a pale rose stamp can be re-colored to resemble a blue shade of high market value. In other cases, treated stamps can be made to resemble missing color varieties. Designs may be changed by painting, or a stroke or a dot added or bleached out to turn an ordinary variety into a seemingly scarcer stamp. Part of a stamp can be bleached and reprinted in a different version, achieving an inverted center or frame. Margins can be added or repairs done so deceptively that the stamps move from the "repaired" into the "fake" category.

Fakers have not left the backs of the stamps untouched either. They may create false watermarks, add fake grills or press out genuine grills. A thin India paper proof may be glued onto a thicker backing to create the appearance an issued stamp, or a proof printed on cardboard may be shaved down and perforated to resemble a stamp. Silk threads are impressed into paper and stamps have been split so that a rare paper variety is added to an otherwise inexpensive stamp. The most common treatment to the back of a stamp, however, is regumming.

Some in the business of faking stamps have openly advertised fool-proof application of "original gum" to stamps that lack it, although most publications now ban such ads from their pages. It is believed that very few early stamps have survived without being hinged. The large number of never-hinged examples of such earlier material offered for sale thus suggests the widespread extent of regumming activity. Regumming also may be used to hide repairs or thin spots. Dipping the stamp into watermark fluid, or examining it under longwave ultraviolet light often will reveal these flaws.

Fakers also tamper with separations. Ingenious ways to add margins are known. Perforated wide-margin stamps may be falsely represented as imperforate when trimmed. Reperforating is commonly done to create scarce coil or perforation varieties, and to eliminate the naturally occurring straight-edge stamps found in sheet margin positions of many earlier issues. Custom has made straight-edged stamps less desirable. Fakers have obliged by perforating straight-edged stamps so that many are now uncommon, if not rare.

Another fertile field for the faker is that of overprints, surcharges and cancellations. The forging of rare surcharges or overprints began in the 1880s or 1890s. These forgeries are sometimes difficult to detect, but experts have identified almost all. Occasionally, overprints or cancellations are removed to create non-overprinted stamps or seemingly unused items. This is most commonly done by removing a manuscript cancel to make a stamp resemble an unused example. "SPECIMEN" overprints may be removed by scraping and repainting to create non-overprinted varieties. Fakers use inexpensive revenues or pen-canceled stamps to generate unused stamps for further faking by adding other markings. The quartz lamp or UV lamp and a high-powered magnifying glass help to easily detect removed cancellations.

The bigger problem, however, is the addition of overprints, surcharges or cancellations - many with such precision that they are very difficult to ascertain. Plating of the stamps or the overprint can be an important method of detection.

Fake postmarks may range from many spurious fancy cancellations to a host of markings applied to transatlantic covers, to adding normally appearing postmarks to definitives of some countries with stamps that are valued far higher used than unused. With the increased popularity of cover collecting, and the widespread interest in postal history, a fertile new field for fakers has come about. Some have tried to create entire covers. Others specialize in adding stamps, tied by fake cancellations, to genuine stampless covers, or replacing less expensive or damaged stamps with more valuable ones. Detailed study of postal rates in effect at the time a cover in question was mailed, including the analysis of each handstamp used during the period, ink analysis and similar techniques, usually will unmask the fraud.

Restoration and Repairs

Scott Publishing Co. bases its catalogue values on stamps that are free of defects and otherwise meet the standards set forth earlier in this introduction. Most stamp collectors desire to have the finest copy of an item possible. Even within given grading categories there are variances. This leads to a controversial practice that is not defined in any universal manner: stamp *restoration.*

There are broad differences of opinion about what is permissible when it comes to restoration. Carefully applying a soft eraser to a stamp or cover to remove light soiling is one form of restoration, as is washing a stamp in mild soap and water to clean it. These are fairly accepted forms of restoration. More severe forms of restoration include pressing out creases or removing stains caused by tape. To what degree each of these is acceptable is dependent upon the individual situation. Further along the spectrum is the freshening of a stamp's color by removing oxide build-up or the effects of wax paper left next to stamps shipped to the tropics.

At some point in this spectrum the concept of *repair* replaces that of restoration. Repairs include filling thin spots, mending tears by reweaving or adding a missing perforation tooth. Regumming stamps may have been acceptable as a restoration or repair technique many decades ago, but today it is considered a form of fakery.

Restored stamps may or may not sell at a discount, and it is possible that the value of individual restored items may be enhanced over that of their pre-restoration state. Specific situations dictate the resultant value of such an item. Repaired stamps sell at substantial discounts from the value of sound stamps.

When the purchaser of an item has any reason to suspect that an item has been repaired, and the detection of such a repair is beyond his own ability, he should seek expert advice. There are services that specialize in giving such advice.

Terminology

Booklets — Many countries have issued stamps in small booklets for the convenience of users. This idea continues to become increasingly popular in many countries. Booklets have been issued in many sizes and forms, often with advertising on the covers, the panes of stamps or on the interleaving.

The panes used in booklets may be printed from special plates or made from regular sheets. All panes from booklets issued by the United States and many from those of other countries contain stamps that are straight edged on the sides, but perforated between. Others are distinguished by orientation of watermark or other identifying features. Any stamp-like unit in the pane, either printed or blank, that is not a postage stamp is considered to be a *label* in the catalogue listings.

Scott lists and values booklet panes only. Complete booklets are listed and valued in only a few cases, such as Grenada Scott 1055 and some forms of British prestige booklets. Individual booklet panes are listed only when they are not fashioned from existing sheet stamps and, therefore, are identifiable from their sheet stamp counterparts.

Panes usually do not have a used value assigned to them because there is little market activity for used booklet panes, even though many exist used and there is some demand for them.

Cancellations — The marks or obliterations put on stamps by postal authorities to show that they have performed service and to prevent their reuse are known as cancellations. If the marking is made with a pen, it is considered a "pen cancel." When the location of the post office appears in the marking, it is a "town cancellation." A "postmark" is technically any postal marking, but in practice the term generally is applied to a town cancellation with a date. When calling attention to a cause or celebration, the marking is known as a "slogan cancellation." Many other types and styles of cancellations exist, such as duplex, numerals, targets, fancy and others. See also "precancels," below.

Coil Stamps — These are stamps that are issued in rolls for use in dispensers, affixing and vending machines. Those coils of the United States, Canada, Sweden and some other countries are perforated horizontally or vertically only, with the outer edges imperforate. Coil stamps of some countries, such as Great Britain and Germany, are perforated on all four sides and may in some cases be distinguished from their sheet stamp counterparts by watermarks, counting numbers on the reverse or other means.

Covers — Entire envelopes, with or without adhesive postage stamps, that have passed through the mail and bear postal or other markings of philatelic interest are known as covers. Before the introduction of envelopes in about 1840, people folded letters and wrote the address on the outside. Some people covered their letters with an extra sheet of paper on the outside for the address, producing the term "cover." Used airletter sheets, stamped envelopes and other items of postal stationery also are considered covers.

Errors — Stamps that have some major, consistent unintentional deviation from the normal are considered errors. Errors include, but are not limited to, missing or wrong colors, wrong paper, wrong watermarks, inverted centers or frames on multicolor printing, inverted or missing surcharges or overprints, double impressions, missing perforations and others. Factually wrong or misspelled information, if it appears on all examples of a stamp, are not considered errors in the true sense of the word. They are errors of design. Inconsistent or randomly appearing items, such as misperfs or color shifts, are classified as freaks.

Overprints and Surcharges — Overprinting involves applying wording or design elements over an already existing stamp. Overprints can be used to alter the place of use (such as "Canal Zone" on U.S. stamps), to adapt them for a special purpose ("Porto" on Denmark's 1913-20 regular issues for use as postage due stamps, Scott J1-J7) or to commemorate a special occasion (United States Scott 647-648).

A *surcharge* is a form of overprint that changes or restates the face value of a stamp or piece of postal stationery.

Surcharges and overprints may be handstamped, typeset or, occasionally, lithographed or engraved. A few hand-written overprints and surcharges are known.

Precancels — Stamps that are canceled before they are placed in the mail are known as precancels. Precanceling usually is done to expedite the handling of large mailings and generally allow the affected mail pieces to skip certain phases of mail handling.

In the United States, precancellations generally identified the point of origin; that is, the city and state. This information appeared across the face of the stamp, usually centered between parallel lines. More recently, bureau precancels retained the parallel lines, but the city and state designations were dropped. Recent coils have a service inscription that is present on the original printing plate. These show the mail service paid for by the stamp. Since these stamps are not intended to receive further cancellations when used as intended, they are considered precancels. Such items often do not have parallel lines as part of the precancellation.

In France, the abbreviation *Affranchts* in a semicircle together with the word *Postes* is the general form of precancel in use. Belgian precancellations usually appear in a box in which the name of the city appears. Netherlands precancels have the name of the city enclosed between concentric circles, sometimes called a "lifesaver." Precancellations of other countries usually follow these patterns, but may be any arrangement of bars, boxes and city names.

Precancels are listed in the Scott catalogues only if the precancel changes the denomination (Belgium Scott 477-478); if the precanceled stamp is different from the non-precanceled version (such as untagged U.S. precancels); or if the stamp exists only precanceled (France Scott 1096-1099, U.S. Scott 2265).

Proofs and Essays — Proofs are impressions taken from an approved die, plate or stone in which the design and color are the same as the stamp issued to the public. Trial color proofs are impressions taken from approved dies, plates or stones in colors that vary from the final version. An essay is the impression of a design that differs in some way from the issued stamp. "Progressive die proofs" generally are considered to be essays.

Provisionals — These are stamps that are issued on short notice and intended for temporary use pending the arrival of regular issues. They usually are issued to meet such contingencies as changes in government or currency, shortage of necessary postage values or military occupation.

During the 1840s, postmasters in certain American cities issued stamps that were valid only at specific post offices. In 1861, postmasters of the Confederate States also issued stamps with limited validity. Both of these examples are known as "postmaster's provisionals."

Se-tenant — This term refers to an unsevered pair, strip or block of stamps that differ in design, denomination or overprint.

Unless the se-tenant item has a continuous design (see U.S. Scott 1451a, 1694a) the stamps do not have to be in the same order as shown in the catalogue (see U.S. Scott 2158a).

Specimens — The Universal Postal Union required member nations to send samples of all stamps they released into service to the International Bureau in Switzerland. Member nations of the UPU received these specimens as samples of what stamps were valid for postage. Many are overprinted, handstamped or initial-perforated "Specimen," "Canceled" or "Muestra." Some are marked with bars across the denominations (China-Taiwan), punched holes (Czechoslovakia) or back inscriptions (Mongolia).

Stamps distributed to government officials or for publicity purposes, and stamps submitted by private security printers for official approval, also may receive such defacements.

The previously described defacement markings prevent postal use, and all such items generally are known as "specimens."

Tete Beche — This term describes a pair of stamps in which one is upside down in relation to the other. Some of these are the result of intentional sheet arrangements, such as Morocco Scott B10-B11. Others occurred when one or more electrotypes accidentally were placed upside down on the plate, such as Colombia Scott 57a. Separation of the tete-beche stamps, of course, destroys the tete beche variety.

Currency Conversion

Country	Dollar	Pound	S Franc	Guilder	Yen	Lira	HK Dollar	D-Mark	Fr Franc	Cdn Dollar	Aust Dollar
Australia	1.311	2.089	1.028	0.7722	0.0132	0.0008	0.1694	0.8655	0.2495	0.9266	....
Canada	1.415	2.255	1.109	0.8334	0.0142	0.0009	0.1828	0.9340	0.2693	....	1.079
France	5.253	8.372	4.119	3.095	0.0528	0.0033	0.6787	3.468	....	3.713	4.007
Germany	1.514	2.414	1.188	0.8923	0.0152	0.0009	0.1957	....	0.2883	1.071	1.156
Hong Kong	7.739	12.33	6.069	4.559	0.0778	0.0048	....	5.109	1.473	5.471	5.904
Italy	1603.	2554.6	1256.9	944.27	16.115	....	207.11	1058.30	305.14	1133.02	1222.8
Japan	99.47	158.52	77.99	58.59	....	0.0621	12.852	65.669	18.935	70.307	75.879
Netherlands	1.698	2.705	1.331	....	0.0171	0.0011	0.2193	1.121	0.3231	1.199	1.295
Switzerland	1.275	2.032	....	0.7512	0.0128	0.0008	0.1648	0.8419	0.2428	0.9014	0.9728
U.K.	0.6275	....	0.4920	0.3696	0.0063	0.0004	0.0811	0.4143	0.1194	0.4435	0.4787
U.S.	....	1.594	0.7841	0.5891	0.0101	0.0006	0.1292	0.6602	0.1904	0.7068	0.7628

Country	Currency	U.S. $ Equiv.
Afghanistan	afghani	.00028
Albania	lek	.0099
Algeria	dinar	.0236
Andorra (French)	franc	.1904
Andorra (Spanish)	peseta	.0076
Angola	kwanza	.000002
Argentina	peso	1.00
Aruba	guilder	.5586
Austria	schilling	.0938
Belgium	franc	.032
Benin	Community of French Africa (CFA) franc	.0019
Bhutan	ngultrum	.032
Bolivia	boliviano	.211
Brazil	real	1.18
Bulgaria	lev	.015
Burkina Faso	CFA franc	.0019
Burundi	franc	.0041
Cameroun	CFA franc	.0019
Cape Verde	escudo	.012
Central African Republic	CFA franc	.0019
Chad	CFA franc	.0019
Chile	peso	.0025
China (Taiwan)	dollar	.038
China (People's Republic)	yuan	.1185
Colombia	peso	.0012
Comoro Islands	CFA franc	.0019
Congo	CFA franc	.0019
Costa Rica	colon	.0059
Czecho Republic	koruna	.036

Source: ***Wall Street Journal*** *Jan. 30, 1995. Figures reflect values as of Jan. 27, 1995.*

Colonies, Former Colonies, Offices, Territories Controlled by Parent States

Belgium

Belgian Congo
Ruanda-Urundi

Denmark

Danish West Indies
Faroe Islands
Greenland
Iceland

Finland

Aland Islands

France

COLONIES PAST AND PRESENT, CONTROLLED TERRITORIES

Afars & Issas, Territory of
Alaouites
Alexandretta
Algeria
Alsace & Lorraine
Ajouan
Annam & Tonkin
Benin
Cambodia (Khmer)
Cameroun
Castellorizo
Chad
Cilicia
Cochin China
Comoro Islands
Dahomey
Diego Suarez
Djibouti (Somali Coast)
Fezzan
French Congo
French Equatorial Africa
French Guiana
French Guinea
French India
French Morocco
French Polynesia (Oceania)
French Southern & Antarctic Territories
French Sudan
French West Africa
Gabon
Germany
Ghadames
Grand Comoro
Guadeloupe
Indo-China
Inini
Ivory Coast
Laos
Latakia
Lebanon
Madagascar
Martinique
Mauritania
Mayotte
Memel
Middle Congo
Moheli
New Caledonia
New Hebrides
Niger Territory
Nossi-Be
Obock
Reunion
Rouad, Ile
Ste.-Marie de Madagascar
St. Pierre & Miquelon
Senegal
Senegambia & Niger
Somali Coast
Syria
Tahiti
Togo
Tunisia
Ubangi-Shari
Upper Senegal & Niger
Upper Volta
Viet Nam
Wallis & Futuna Islands

POST OFFICES IN FOREIGN COUNTRIES

China
Crete
Egypt
Turkish Empire
Zanzibar

Germany

EARLY STATES

Baden
Bavaria
Bergedorf
Bremen
Brunswick
Hamburg
Hanover
Lubeck
Mecklenburg-Schwerin
Mecklenburg-Strelitz
Oldenburg
Prussia
Saxony
Schleswig-Holstein
Wurttemberg

FORMER COLONIES

Cameroun (Kamerun)
Caroline Islands
German East Africa
German New Guinea
German South-West Africa
Kiauchau
Mariana Islands
Marshall Islands
Samoa
Togo

Italy

EARLY STATES

Modena
Parma
Romagna
Roman States
Sardinia
Tuscany
Two Sicilies
 Naples
 Neapolitan Provinces
 Sicily

FORMER COLONIES, CONTROLLED TERRITORIES, OCCUPATION AREAS

Aegean Islands
 Calimno (Calino)
 Caso
 Cos (Coo)
 Karki (Carchi)
 Leros (Lero)
 Lipso
 Nisiros (Nisiro)
 Patmos (Patmo)
 Piscopi
 Rodi (Rhodes)
 Scarpanto
 Simi
 Stampalia
Castellorizo
Corfu
Cyrenaica
Eritrea
Ethiopia (Abyssinia)
Fiume
Ionian Islands
 Cephalonia
 Ithaca
 Paxos
Italian East Africa
Libya
Oltre Giuba
Saseno
Somalia (Italian Somaliland)
Tripolitania

POST OFFICES IN FOREIGN COUNTRIES

"ESTERO"*
Austria
China
 Peking
 Tientsin
Crete
Tripoli
Turkish Empire
 Constantinople
 Durazzo
 Janina
Jerusalem
Salonika
Scutari
Smyrna
Valona

*Stamps overprinted "ESTERO" were used in various parts of the world.

Netherlands

Aruba
Netherlands Antilles (Curacao)
Netherlands Indies
Netherlands New Guinea
Surinam (Dutch Guiana)

Portugal

COLONIES PAST AND PRESENT, CONTROLLED TERRITORIES

Angola
Angra
Azores
Cape Verde
Funchal
Horta
Inhambane
Kionga
Lourenco Marques
Macao
Madeira
Mozambique
Mozambique Co.
Nyassa
Ponta Delgada
Portuguese Africa
Portuguese Congo
Portuguese Guinea
Portuguese India
Quelimane
St. Thomas & Prince Islands
Tete
Timor
Zambezia

Russia

ALLIED TERRITORIES AND REPUBLICS, OCCUPATION AREAS

Armenia
Aunus (Olonets)
Azerbaijan
Batum
Estonia
Far Eastern Republic
Georgia
Karelia
Latvia
Lithuania
North Ingermanland
Ostland
Russian Turkestan
Siberia
South Russia
Tannu Tuva
Transcaucasian Fed. Republics
Ukraine
Wenden (Livonia)
Western Ukraine

Spain

COLONIES PAST AND PRESENT, CONTROLLED TERRITORIES

Aguera, La
Cape Juby
Cuba
Elobey, Annobon & Corisco
Fernando Po
Ifni
Mariana Islands
Philippines
Puerto Rico
Rio de Oro
Rio Muni
Spanish Guinea
Spanish Morocco
Spanish Sahara
Spanish West Africa

POST OFFICES IN FOREIGN COUNTRIES

Morocco
Tangier
Tetuan

Common Design Types

Pictured in this section are issues where one illustration has been used for a number of countries in the Catalogue. Not included in this section are overprinted stamps or those issues which are illustrated in each country.

EUROPA

Europa Issue, 1956

The design symbolizing the cooperation among the six countries comprising the Coal and Steel Community is illustrated in each country.

Belgium	496-497
France	805-806
Germany	748-749
Italy	715-716
Luxembourg	318-320
Netherlands	368-369

Europa Issue, 1958

"E" and Dove – CD1

European Postal Union at the service of European integration.

1958, Sept. 13

Belgium	527-528
France	889-890
Germany	790-791
Italy	750-751
Luxembourg	341-343
Netherlands	375-376
Saar	317-318

Europa Issue, 1959

6-Link Endless Chain – CD2

1959, Sept. 19

Belgium	536-537
France	929-930
Germany	805-806
Italy	791-792
Luxembourg	354-355
Netherlands	379-380

Europa Issue, 1960

19-Spoke Wheel – CD3

First anniversary of the establishment of C.E.P.T. (Conference Europeenne des Administrations des Postes et des Telecommunications.)

The spokes symbolize the 19 founding members of the Conference.

1960, Sept.

Belgium	553-554
Denmark	379
Finland	376-377
France	970-971
Germany	818-820
Great Britain	377-378
Greece	688
Iceland	327-328
Ireland	175-176
Italy	809-810
Luxembourg	374-375
Netherlands	385-386
Norway	387
Portugal	866-867
Spain	941-942
Sweden	562-563
Switzerland	400-401
Turkey	1493-1494

Europa Issue, 1961

19 Doves Flying as One – CD4

The 19 doves represent the 19 members of the Conference of European Postal and Telecommunications Administrations C.E.P.T.

1961-62

Belgium	572-573
Cyprus	201-203
France	1005-1006
Germany	844-845
Great Britain	383-384
Greece	718-719
Iceland	340-341
Italy	845-846
Luxembourg	382-383
Netherlands	387-388
Spain	1010-1011
Switzerland	410-411
Turkey	1518-1520

Europa Issue, 1962

Young Tree with 19 Leaves – CD5

The 19 leaves represent the 19 original members of C.E.P.T.

1962-63

Belgium	582-583
Cyprus	219-221
France	1045-1046
Germany	852-853
Greece	739-740
Iceland	348-349
Ireland	184-185
Italy	860-861
Luxembourg	386-387
Netherlands	394-395
Norway	414-415
Switzerland	416-417
Turkey	1553-1555

Europa Issue, 1963

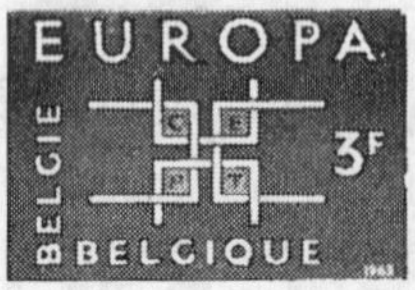

Stylized Links, Symbolizing Unity – CD6

1963, Sept.

Belgium	598-599
Cyprus	229-231
Finland	419
France	1074-1075
Germany	867-868
Greece	768-769
Iceland	357-358
Ireland	188-189
Italy	880-881
Luxembourg	403-404
Netherlands	416-417
Norway	441-442
Switzerland	429
Turkey	1602-1603

Europa Issue, 1964

Symbolic Daisy – CD7

5th anniversary of the establishment of C.E.P.T. The 22 petals of the flower symbolize the 22 members of the Conference.

1964, Sept.

Austria	738
Belgium	614-615
Cyprus	244-246
France	1109-1110
Germany	897-898
Greece	801-802
Iceland	367-368
Ireland	196-197
Italy	894-895
Luxembourg	411-412
Monaco	590-591
Netherlands	428-429
Norway	458
Portugal	931-933
Spain	1262-1263
Switzerland	438-439
Turkey	1628-1629

Europa Issue, 1965

Leaves and "Fruit" – CD8

1965

Belgium	636-637
Cyprus	262-264
Finland	437
France	1131-1132
Germany	934-935
Greece	833-834
Iceland	375-376
Ireland	204-205
Italy	915-916
Luxembourg	432-433
Monaco	616-617
Netherlands	438-439
Norway	475-476
Portugal	958-960
Switzerland	469
Turkey	1665-1666

Europa Issue, 1966

Symbolic Sailboat – CD9

1966, Sept.

Andorra, French	172
Belgium	675-676
Cyprus	275-277
France	1163-1164
Germany	963-964
Greece	862-863
Iceland	384-385
Ireland	216-217
Italy	942-943
Liechtenstein	415
Luxembourg	440-441
Monaco	639-640
Netherlands	441-442
Norway	496-497
Portugal	980-982
Switzerland	477-478
Turkey	1718-1719

Europa Issue, 1967

Cogwheels – CD10

1967

Andorra, French	174-175
Belgium	688-689
Cyprus	297-299
France	1178-1179
Greece	891-892
Germany	969-970
Iceland	389-390
Ireland	232-233
Italy	951-952
Liechtenstein	420
Luxembourg	449-450
Monaco	669-670
Netherlands	444-447
Norway	504-505
Portugal	994-996
Spain	1465-1466
Switzerland	482
Turkey	B120-B121

Europa Issue, 1968

Golden Key with C.E.P.T. Emblem CD11

1968

Andorra, French	182-183
Belgium	705-706
Cyprus	314-316
France	1209-1210
Germany	983-984
Greece	916-917
Iceland	395-396
Ireland	242-243
Italy	979-980
Liechtenstein	442
Luxembourg	466-467
Monaco	689-691
Netherlands	452-453
Portugal	1019-1021
San Marino	687
Spain	1526
Turkey	1775-1776

Europa Issue, 1969

"EUROPA" and "CEPT" – CD12

Tenth anniversary of C.E.P.T.

1969

Andorra, French	188-189
Austria	837
Belgium	718-719
Cyprus	326-328
Denmark	458
Finland	483
France	1245-1246
Germany	996-997
Great Britain	585
Greece	947-948
Iceland	406-407
Ireland	270-271

Italy 1000-1001
Liechtenstein 453
Luxembourg 474-475
Monaco 722-724
Netherlands 475-476
Norway 533-534
Portugal 1038-1040
San Marino 701-702
Spain 1567
Sweden 814-816
Switzerland 500-501
Turkey 1799-1800
Vatican 470-472
Yugoslavia 1003-1004

Europa Issue, 1970

Interwoven Threads CD13

1970

Andorra, French 196-197
Belgium 741-742
Cyprus 340-342
France 1271-1272
Germany 1018-1019
Greece 985, 987
Iceland 420-421
Ireland 279-281
Italy 1013-1014
Liechtenstein 470
Luxembourg 489-490
Monaco 768-770
Netherlands 483-484
Portugal 1060-1062
San Marino 729-730
Spain 1607
Switzerland 515-516
Turkey 1848-1849
Yugoslavia 1024-1025

Europa Issue, 1971

"Fraternity, Cooperation, Common Effort" – CD14

1971

Andorra, French 205-206
Belgium 803-804
Cyprus 365-367
Finland 504
France 1304
Germany 1064-1065
Greece 1029-1030
Iceland 429-430
Ireland 305-306
Italy 1038-1039
Liechtenstein 485
Luxembourg 500-501
Malta 425-427
Monaco 797-799
Netherlands 488-489
Portugal 1094-1096
San Marino 749-750
Spain 1675-1676
Switzerland 531-532
Turkey 1876-1877
Yugoslavia 1052-1053

Europa Issue, 1972

Sparkles, Symbolic of Communications CD15

1972

Andorra, French 210-211
Andorra, Spanish 62
Belgium 825-826
Cyprus 380-382
Finland 512-513
France 1341
Germany 1089-1090
Greece 1049-1050
Iceland 439-440
Ireland 316-317
Italy 1065-1066
Liechtenstein 504
Luxembourg 512-513
Malta 450-453
Monaco 831-832
Netherlands 494-495
Portugal 1141-1143
San Marino 771-772
Spain 1718
Switzerland 544-545
Turkey 1907-1908
Yugoslavia 1100-1101

Europa Issue, 1973

Post Horn and Arrows CD16

1973

Andorra, French 319-320
Andorra, Spanish 76
Belgium 839-840
Cyprus 396-398
Finland 526
France 1367
Germany 1114-1115
Greece 1090-1092
Iceland 447-448
Ireland 329-330
Italy 1108-1109
Liechtenstein 528-529
Luxembourg 523-524
Malta 469-471
Monaco 866-867
Netherlands 504-505
Norway 604-605
Portugal 1170-1172
San Marino 802-803
Spain 1753
Switzerland 580-581
Turkey 1935-1936
Yugoslavia 1138-1139

PORTUGAL & COLONIES

Vasco da Gama Issue

Fleet Departing – CD20

Fleet Arriving at Calicut – CD21

Embarking at Rastello – CD22

Muse of History – CD23

San Gabriel, da Gama and Camoens – CD24

Archangel Gabriel, the Patron Saint CD25

Flagshig San Gabriel CD26

Vasco da Gama CD27

Fourth centenary of Vasco da Gama's discovery of the route to India.

1898

Azores 93-100
Macao 67-74
Madeira 37-44
Portugal 147-154
Port. Africa 1-8
Port. india 189-196
Timor 45-52

Pombal Issue

POSTAL TAX

Marquis de Pombal CD28

Planning Reconstruction of Lisbon, 1755 CD29

Pombal Monument, Lisbon – CD30

Sebastiao Jose de Carvalho e Mello, Marquis de Pombal (1699-1782), statesman, rebuilt Lisbon after earthquake of 1755. Tax was for the erection of Pombal monument. Obligatory on all mail on certain days throughout the year.

1925

Angola RA1-RA3
Azores RA9-RA11
Cape Verde RA1-RA3
Macao RA1-RA3
Madeira RA1-RA3
Mozambique RA1-RA3
Portugal RA11-RA13
Port. Guinea RA1-RA3
Port. India RA1-RA3
St. Thomas & Prince Islands RA1-RA3
Timor RA1-RA3

Pombal Issue

POSTAL TAX DUES

CD31

CD32

CD33

1925

Angola RAJ1-RAJ3
Azores RAJ2-RAJ4
Cape Verde RAJ1-RAJ3
Macao RAJ1-RAJ3
Madeira RAJ1-RAJ3
Mozambique RAJ1-RAJ3
Portugal RAJ2-RAJ4
Port. Guinea RAJ1-RAJ3
Port. India RAJ1-RAJ3
St. Thomas & Prince Islands RAJ1-RAJ3
Timor RAJ1-RAJ3

Vasco da Gama CD34

Mousinho de Albuquerque CD35

Dam CD36

Prince Henry the Navigator – CD37

Affonso de Albuquerque CD38

Plane over Globe CD39

1938-39

Angola 274-291
Cape Verde 234-251
Macao 289-305
Mozambique 270-287
Port. Guinea 233-250
Port. India 439-453
St. Thomas & Prince Islands 302-319, 323-340
Timor 223-239

1938-39

Angola C1-C9
Cape Verde C1-C9

Macao	C7-C15
Mozambique	C1-C9
Port. Guinea	C1-C9
Port. India	C1-C8
St. Thomas & Prince Islands	C1-C18
Timor	C1-C9

Lady of Fatima Issue

Our Lady of the Rosary, Fatima, Portugal CD40

1948-49

Angola	315-318
Cape Verde	266
Macao	336
Mozambique	325-328
Port. Guinea	271
Port. India	480
St. Thomas & Prince Islands	351
Timor	254

A souvenir sheet of 9 stamps was issued in 1951 to mark the extension of the 1950 Holy Year. The sheet contains: Angola No. 316, Cape Verde No. 266, Macao No. 336, Mozambique No. 325, Portuguese Guinea No. 271, Portugese India Nos. 480, 485, St. Thomas & Prince Islands No. 351, Timor No. 254.

The sheet also contains a portrait of Pope Pius XII and is inscribed "Encerramento do Ano Santo, Fatima 1951." It was sold for 11 escudos.

Holy Year Issue

Church Bells and Dove CD41

Angel Holding Candelabra CD42

Holy Year, 1950.

1950-51

Angola	331-332
Cape Verde	268-269
Macao	339-340
Mozambique	330-331
Port. Guinea	273-274
Port. India	490-491, 496-503
St. Thomas & Prince Islands	353-354
Timor	258-259

A souvenir sheet of 8 stamps was issued in 1951 to mark the extension of the Holy Year. The sheet contains: Angola No. 331, Cape Verde No. 269, Macao No. 340, Mozambique No. 331, Portuguese Guinea No. 275, Portuguese India No. 490, St. Thomas & Prince Islands No. 354, Timor No. 258, some with colors changed. The sheet contains doves and is inscribed "Encerramento do Ano Santo, Fatima 1951." It was sold for 17 escudos.

Holy Year Conclusion Issue

Our Lady of Fatima CD43

Conclusion of Holy Year. Sheets contain alternate vertical rows of stamps and labels bearing quotation from Pope Pius XII, different for each colony.

1951

Angola	357
Cape Verde	270
Macao	352
Mozambique	356
Port. Guinea	275
Port. India	506
St. Thomas & Prince Islands	355
Timor	270

Medical Congress Issue

Medical Examination CD44

First National Congress of Tropical Medicine, Lisbon, 1952.

Each stamp has a different design.

1952

Angola	358
Cape Verde	287
Macao	364
Mozambique	359
Port. Guinea	276
Port. India	516
St. Thomas & Prince Islands	356
Timor	271

POSTAGE DUE STAMPS

CD45

1952

Angola	J37-J42
Cape Verde	J31-J36
Macao	J53-J58
Mozambique	J51-J56
Port. Guinea	J40-J45
Port. India	J47-J52
St. Thomas & Prince Islands	J52-J57
Timor	J31-J36

Sao Paulo Issue

Father Manuel de Nobrega and View of Sao Paulo – CD46

400th anniversary of the founding of Sao Paulo, Brazil.

1954

Angola	385
Cape Verde	297
Macao	382
Mozambique	395
Port. Guinea	291
Port. India	530
St. Thomas & Prince Islands	369
Timor	279

Tropical Medicine Congress Issue

Securidaca Longipedunculata – CD47

Sixth International Congress for Tropical Medicine and Malaria, Lisbon, Sept. 1958.

Each stamp shows a different plant.

1958

Angola	409
Cape Verde	303
Macao	392
Mozambique	404
Port. Guinea	295
Port. India	569
St. Thomas & Prince Islands	371
Timor	289

Sports Issue

Flying – CD48

Each stamp shows a different sport.

1962

Angola	433-438
Cape Verde	320-325
Macao	394-399
Mozambique	424-429
Port. Guinea	299-304
St. Thomas & Prince Islands	374-379
Timor	313-318

Anti-Malaria Issue

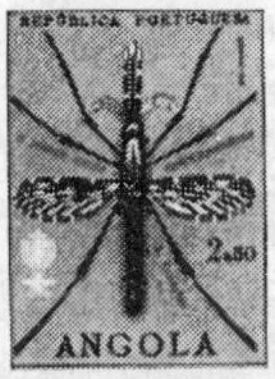

Anopheles Funestus and Malaria Eradication Symbol – CD49

World Health Organization drive to eradicate malaria.

1962

Angola	439
Cape Verde	326
Macao	400
Mozambique	430
Port. Guinea	305
St. Thomas & Prince Islands	380
Timor	319

Airline Anniversary Issue

Map of Africa, Super Constellation and Jet Liner – CD50

Tenth anniversary of Transportes Aereos Portugueses (TAP).

1963

Angola	490
Cape Verde	327
Mozambique	434
Port. Guinea	318
St. Thomas & Prince Islands	381

National Overseas Bank Issue

Antonio Teixeira de Sousa – CD51

Centenary of the National Overseas Bank of Portugal.

1964, May 16

Angola	509
Cape Verde	328
Port. Guinea	319
St. Thomas & Prince Islands	382
Timor	320

ITU Issue

ITU Emblem and St. Gabriel CD52

Centenary of the International Communications Union.

1965, May 17

Angola	511
Cape Verde	329
Macao	402
Mozambique	464
Port. Guinea	320
St. Thomas & Prince Islands	383
Timor	321

National Revolution Issue

St. Paul's Hospital, and Commercial and Industrial School – CD53

40th anniversary of the National Revolution.

Different buildings on each stamp.

1966, May 28

Angola	525
Cape Verde	338
Macao	403
Mozambique	465
Port. Guinea	329
St. Thomas & Prince Islands	392
Timor	322

Navy Club Issue

Mendes Barata and Cruiser Dom Carlos I – CD54

Centenary of Portugal's Navy Club.

Each stamp has a different design.

1967, Jan. 31

Angola	527-528
Cape Verde	339-340
Macao	412-413
Mozambique	478-479
Port. Guinea	330-331
St. Thomas & Prince Islands	393-394
Timor	323-324

Admiral Coutinho Issue

Admiral Gago Coutinho and his First Ship – CD55

Centenary of the birth of Admiral Carlos Viegas Gago Coutinho (1869-1959), explorer and aviation pioneer.

Each stamp has a different design.

1969, Feb. 17

Angola	547
Cape Verde	355
Macao	417
Mozambique	484
Port. Guinea	335
St. Thomas & Prince Islands	397
Timor	335

Administration Reform Issue

Luiz Augusto Rebello da Silva – CD56

Centenary of the administration reforms of the overseas territories.

1969, Sept. 25

Angola	549
Cape Verde	357
Macao	419
Mozambique	491
Port. Guinea	337
St. Thomas & Prince Islands	399
Timor	338

Marshal Carmona Issue

Marshal A.O. Carmona CD57

Birth centenary of Marshal Antonio Oscar Carmona de Fragoso (1869-1951), President of Portugal.

Each stamp has a different design.

1970, Nov. 15

Angola	563
Cape Verde	359
Macao	422
Mozambique	493
Port. Guinea	340
St. Thomas & Prince Islands	403
Timor	341

Olympic Games Issue

Racing Yachts and Olympic Emblem CD59

20th Olympic Games, Munich, Aug. 26-Sept. 11.

Each stamp shows a different sport.

1972, June 20

Angola	569
Cape Verde	361
Macao	426
Mozambique	504
Port. Guinea	342
St. Thomas & Prince Islands	408
Timor	343

Lisbon-Rio de Janeiro Flight Issue

"Santa Cruz" over Fernando de Noronha – CD60

50th anniversary of the Lisbon to Rio de Janeiro flight by Arturo de Sacadura and Coutinho, March 30-June 5, 1922.

Each stamp shows a different stage of the flight.

1972, Sept. 20

Angola	570
Cape Verde	362
Macao	427
Mozambique	505
Port. Guinea	343
St. Thomas & Prince Islands	409
Timor	344

WMO Centenary Issue

WMO Emblem – CD61

Centenary of international meterological cooperation.

1973, Dec. 15

Angola	571
Cape Verde	363
Macao	429
Mozambique	509
Port. Guinea	344
St. Thomas & Prince Islands	410
Timor	345

FRENCH COMMUNITY

Upper Volta can be found under Burkina Faso in Vol. 2

Colonial Exposition Issue

People of French Empire – CD70

Women's Heads – CD71

France Showing Way to Civilization CD72

"Colonial Commerce" – CD73

International Colonial Exposition, Paris 1931.

1931

Cameroun	213-216
Chad	60-63
Dahomey	97-100
Fr. Guiana	152-155
Fr. Guinea	116-119
Fr. India	100-103
Fr. Polynesia	76-79
Fr. Sudan	102-105
Gabon	120-123
Guadeloupe	138-141
Indo-China	140-142
Ivory Coast	92-95
Madagascar	169-172
Martinique	129-132
Mauritania	65-68
Middle Congo	61-64
New Caledonia	176-179
Niger	73-76
Reunion	122-125
St. Pierre & Miquelon	132-135
Senegal	138-141
Somali Coast	135-138
Togo	254-257
Ubangi-Shari	82-85
Upper Volta	66-69
Wallis & Futuna Isls.	85-88

Paris International Exposition Issue

Colonial Arts Exposition Issue

"Colonial Resources"

CD74 CD77

Overseas Commerce – CD75

Exposition Building and Women – CD76

"France and the Empire" – CD78

Cultural Treasures of the Colonies CD79

Souvenir sheets contain one imperf. stamp.

1937

Cameroun	217-222A
Dahomey	101-107
Fr. Equatorial Africa	27-32, 73
Fr. Guiana	162-168
Fr. Guinea	120-126
Fr. India	104-110
Fr. Polynesia	117-123
Fr. Sudan	106-112
Guadeloupe	148-154
Indo-China	193-199
Inini	41
Ivory Coast	152-158
Kwangchowan	132
Madagascar	191-197
Martinique	179-185
Mauritania	69-75
New Caledonia	208-214
Niger	72-83
Reunion	167-173
St. Pierre & Miquelon	165-171
Senegal	172-178
Somali Coast	139-145
Togo	258-264
Wallis & Futuna Isls.	89

Curie Issue

Pierre and Marie Curie – CD80

40th anniversary of the discovery of radium. The surtax was for the benefit of the International Union for the Control of Cancer.

1938

Cameroun	B1
Dahomey	B2
France	B76
Fr. Equatorial Africa	B1
Fr. Guiana	B3
Fr. Guinea	B2
Fr. India	B6
Fr. Polynesia	B5
Fr. Sudan	B1
Guadeloupe	B3
Indo-China	B14
Ivory Coast	B2
Madagascar	B2
Martinique	B2
Mauritania	B3
New Caledonia	B4
Niger	B1
Reunion	B4
St. Pierre & Miquelon	B3
Senegal	B3
Somali Coast	B2
Togo	B1

Caillie Issue

Rene Caille and Map of Northwestern Africa – CD81

Death centenary of Rene Caillie (1799-1838), French explorer.

All three denominations exist with colony name omitted.

1939

Dahomey	108-110
Fr. Guinea	161-163
Fr. Sudan	113-115
Ivory Coast	160-162
Mauritania	109-111
Niger	84-86
Senegal	188-190
Togo	265-267

New York World's Fair Issue

Natives and New York Skyline – CD82

1939

Cameroun	223-224
Dahomey	111-112
Fr. Equatorial Africa	78-79
Fr. Guiana	169-170
Fr. Guinea	164-165
Fr. India	111-112
Fr. Polynesia	124-125
Fr. Sudan	116-117
Guadeloupe	155-156
Indo-China	203-204
Inini	42-43
Ivory Coast	163-164
Kwangchowan	121-122
Madagascar	209-210
Martinique	186-187
Mauritania	112-113
New Caledonia	215-216
Niger	87-88
Reunion	174-175
St. Pierre & Miquelon	205-206
Senegal	191-192
Somali Coast	179-180
Togo	268-269
Wallis & Futuna Isls.	90-91

French Revolution Issue

Storming of the Bastille – CD83

150th anniversary of the French Revolution. The surtax was for the defense of the colonies.

1939

Cameroun	B2-B6
Dahomey	B3-B7
Fr. Equatorial Africa	B4-B8, CB1
Fr. Guiana	B4-B8, CB1
Fr. Guinea	B3-B7
Fr. India	B7-B11
Fr. Polynesia	B6-B10, CB1
Fr. Sudan	B2-B6
Guadeloupe	B4-B8
Indo-China	B15-B19, CB1
Inini	B1-B5
Ivory Coast	B3-B7
Kwangchowan	B1-B5
Madagascar	B3-B7, CB1
Martinique	B3-B7
Mauritania	B4-B8
New Caledonia	B5-B9, CB1
Niger	B2-B6
Reunion	B5-B9, CB1
St. Pierre & Miquelon	B4-B8
Senegal	B4-B8, CB1
Somali Coast	B3-B7
Togo	B2-B6
Wallis & Futuna Isls.	B1-B5

Plane over Coastal Area – CD85

All five denominations exist with colony name omitted.

1940

Dahomey	C1-C5
Fr. Guinea	C1-C5
Fr. Sudan	C1-C5
Ivory Coast	C1-C5
Mauritania	C1-C5
Niger	C1-C5
Senegal	C12-C16
Togo	C1-C5

Colonial Infantryman CD86

1941

Cameroun	B13B
Dahomey	B13
Fr. Equatorial Africa	B8B
Fr. Guiana	B10
Fr. Guinea	B13
Fr. India	B13
Fr. Polynesia	B12
Fr. Sudan	B12
Guadeloupe	B10
Indo-China	B19B
Inini	B7
Ivory Coast	B13
Kwangchowan	B7
Madagascar	B9
Martinique	B9
Mauritania	B14
New Caledonia	B11
Niger	B12
Reunion	B11
St. Pierre & Miquelon	B8B
Senegal	B14
Somali Coast	B9
Togo	B10B
Wallis & Futuna Isls.	B7

Cross of Lorraine and Four-motor Plane – CD87

1941-5

Cameroun	C1-C7
Fr. Equatorial Africa	C17-C23
Fr. Guiana	C9-C10
Fr. India	C1-C6
Fr. Polynesia	C3-C9
Fr. West Africa	C1-C3
Guadeloupe	C1-C2
Madagascar	C37-C43
Martinique	C1-C2
New Caledonia	C7-C13
Reunion	C18-C24
St. Pierre & Miquelon	C1-C7
Somali Coast	C1-C7

Transport Plane CD88

Caravan and Plane CD89

1942

Dahomey	C6-C13
Fr. Guinea	C6-C13
Fr. Sudan	C6-C13
Ivory Coast	C6-C13
Mauritania	C6-C13
Niger	C6-C13
Senegal	C17-C25
Togo	C6-C13

Red Cross Issue

Marianne CD90

The surtax was for the French Red Cross and national relief.

1944

Cameroun	B28
Fr. Equatorial Africa	B38
Fr. Guiana	B12
Fr. India	B14
Fr. Polynesia	B13
Fr. West Africa	B1
Guadeloupe	B12
Madagascar	B15
Martinique	B11
New Caledonia	B13
Reunion	B15
St. Pierre & Miquelon	B13
Somali Coast	B13
Wallis & Futuna Isls.	B9

Eboue Issue

Felix Eboue – CD91

Felix Eboue, first French colonial administrator to proclaim resistance to Germany after French surrender in World War II.

1945

Cameroun	296-297
Fr. Equatorial Africa	156-157
Fr. Guiana	171-172
Fr. India	210-211
Fr. Polynesia	150-151
Fr. West Africa	15-16
Guadeloupe	187-188
Madagascar	259-260
Martinique	196-197
New Caledonia	274-275
Reunion	238-239
St. Pierre & Miquelon	322-323
Somali Coast	238-239

Victory Issue

Victory – CD92

European victory of the Allied Nations in World War II.

1946, May 8

Cameroun	C8
Fr. Equatorial Africa	C24
Fr. Guiana	C11
Fr. India	C7
Fr. Polynesia	C10
Fr. West Africa	C4
Guadeloupe	C3
Indo-China	C19
Madagascar	C44
Martinique	C3
New Caledonia	C14
Reunion	C25
St. Pierre & Miquelon	C8
Somali Coast	C8
Wallis & Futuna Isls.	C1

Chad to Rhine Issue

Leclerc's Departure from Chad – CD93

Battle at Cufra Oasis – CD94

Tanks in Action, Mareth – CD95

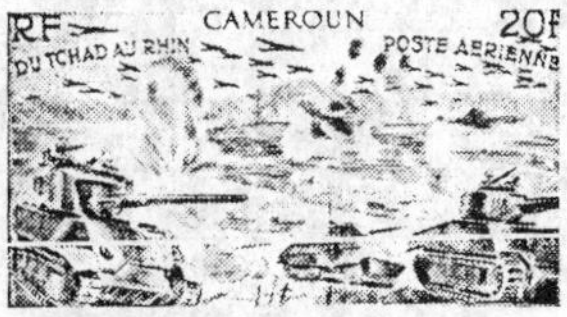

Normandy Invasion – CD96

Entering Paris – CD97

Liberation of Strasbourg – CD98

"Chad to the Rhine" march, 1942-44, by Gen. Jacques Leclerc's column, later French 2nd Armored Division.

1946, June 6

Cameroun	C9-C14
Fr. Equatorial Africa	C25-C30
Fr. Guiana	C12-C17
Fr. India	C8-C13
Fr. Polynesia	C11-C16
Fr. West Africa	C5-C10
Guadeloupe	C4-C9
Indo-China	C20-C25
Madagascar	C45-C50
Martinique	C4-C9
New Caledonia	C15-C20
Reunion	C26-C31
St. Pierre & Miquelon	C9-C14
Somali Coast	C9-C14
Wallis & Futuna Isls.	C2-C7

UPU Issue

French Colonials, Globe and Plane CD99

75th anniversary of the Universal Postal Union.

1949, July 4

Cameroun	C29
Fr. Equatorial Africa	C34
Fr. India	C17
Fr. Polynesia	C20
Fr. West Africa	C15
Indo-China	C26

Madagascar....C55
New Caledonia....C24
St. Pierre & Miquelon....C18
Somali Coast....C18
Togo....C18
Wallis & Futuna Isls....C10

Tropical Medicine Issue

Doctor Treating Infant – CD100

The surtax was for charitable work.

1950
Cameroun....B29
Fr. Equatorial Africa....B39
Fr. India....B15
Fr. Polynesia....B14
Fr. West Africa....B3
Madagascar....B17
New Caledonia....B14
St. Pierre & Miquelon....B14
Somali Coast....B14
Togo....B11

Military Medal Issue

Medal, Early Marine and Colonial Soldier – CD101

Centenary of the creation of the French Military Medal.

1952
Cameroun....332
Comoro Isls....39
Fr. Equatorial Africa....186
Fr. India....233
Fr. Polynesia....179
Fr. West Africa....57
Madagascar....286
New Caledonia....295
St. Pierre & Miquelon....345
Somali Coast....267
Togo....327
Wallis & Futuna Isls....149

Liberation Issue

Allied Landing, Victory Sign and Cross of Lorraine – CD102

10th anniversary of the liberation of France.

1954, June 6
Cameroun....C32
Comoro Isls....C4
Fr. Equatorial Africa....C38
Fr. India....C18
Fr. Polynesia....C23
Fr. West Africa....C17
Madagascar....C57
New Caledonia....C25
St. Pierre & Miquelon....C19
Somali Coast....C19
Togo....C19
Wallis & Futuna Isls....C11

FIDES Issue

Plowmen
CD103

Efforts of FIDES, the Economic and Social Development Fund for Overseas Possessions (Fonds d' Investissement pour le Developpement Economique et Social).

Each stamp has a different design.

1956
Cameroun....326-329
Comoro Isls....43
Fr. Polynesia....181
Madagascar....292-295
New Caledonia....303
Somali Coast....268
Togo....331

Flower Issue

Euadania
CD104

Each stamp shows a different flower.

1958-9
Cameroun....333
Comoro Isls....45
Fr. Equatorial Africa....200-201
Fr. Polynesia....192
Fr. So. & Antarctic Terr....11
Fr. West Africa....79-83
Madagascar....301-302
New Caledonia....304-305
St. Pierre & Miquelon....357
Somali Coast....270
Togo....348-349
Wallis & Futuna Isls....152

Human Rights Issue

Sun, Dove and U.N. Emblem – CD105

10th anniversary of the signing of the Universal Declaration of Human Rights.

1958
Comoro Isls....44
Fr. Equatorial Africa....202
Fr. Polynesia....191
Fr. West Africa....85
Madagascar....300
New Caledonia....306
St. Pierre & Miquelon....356
Somali Coast....274
Wallis & Futuna Isls....153

C.C.T.A. Issue

Map of Africa & Cogwheels – CD106

10th anniversary of the Commission for Technical Cooperation in Africa south of the Sahara.

1960
Cameroun....335
Cent. African Rep....3
Chad....66
Congo, P.R....90
Dahomey....138
Gabon....150
Ivory Coast....180
Madagascar....317
Mali....9
Mauritania....117
Niger....104
Upper Volta....89

Air Afrique Issue, 1961

Modern and Ancient Africa, Map and Planes – CD107

Founding of Air Afrique (African Airlines).

1961-62
Cameroun....C37
Cent. African Rep....C5
Chad....C7
Congo, P.R....C5
Dahomey....C17
Gabon....C5
Ivory Coast....C18
Mauritania....C17
Niger....C22
Senegal....C31
Upper Volta....C4

Anti-Malaria Issue

Malaria Eradication Emblem – CD108

World Health Organization drive to eradicate malaria.

1962, Apr. 7
Cameroun....B36
Cent. African Rep....B1
Chad....B1
Comoro Isls....B1
Congo, P.R....B3
Dahomey....B15
Gabon....B4
Ivory Coast....B15
Madagascar....B19
Mali....B1
Mauritania....B16
Niger....B14
Senegal....B16
Somali Coast....B15
Upper Volta....B1

Abidjan Games Issue

Relay Race – CD109

Abidjan Games, Ivory Coast, Dec. 24-31, 1961.

Each stamp shows a different sport.

1962
Chad....83-84
Cent. African Rep....19-20
Congo, P.R....103-104
Gabon....163-164
Niger....109-111
Upper Volta....103-105

African and Malagasy Union Issue

Flag of Union – CD110

First anniversary of the Union.

1962, Sept. 8
Cameroun....373
Cent. African Rep....21
Chad....85
Congo, P.R....105
Dahomey....155
Gabon....165
Ivory Coast....198
Madagascar....332
Mauritania....170
Niger....112
Senegal....211
Upper Volta....106

Telstar Issue

Telstar and Globe Showing Andover and Pleumeur-Bodou – CD111

First television connection of the United States and Europe through the Telstar satellite, July 11-12, 1962.

1962-63
Andorra, French....154
Comoro Isls....C7
Fr. Polynesia....C29
Fr. So. & Antarctic Terr....C5
New Caledonia....C33
Somali Coast....C31
St. Pierre & Miquelon....C26
Wallis & Futuna Isls....C17

Freedom From Hunger Issue

World Map and Wheat Emblem – CD112

United Nations Food and Agriculture Organization's "Freedom from Hunger" campaign.

1963, Mar. 21
Cameroun....B37-B38
Cent. African Rep....B2
Chad....B2
Congo, P.R....B4
Dahomey....B16
Gabon....B5
Ivory Coast....B16
Madagascar....B21
Mauritania....B17
Niger....B15
Senegal....B17
Upper Volta....B2

Red Cross Centenary Issue

Centenary Emblem – CD113

Centenary of the International Red Cross.

1963, Sept. 2

Comoro Isls.	55
Fr. Polynesia	205
New Caledonia	328
St. Pierre & Miquelon	367
Somali Coast	297
Wallis & Futuna Isls.	165

African Postal Union Issue

UAMPT Emblem, Radio Masts, Plane and Mail – CD114

Establishment of the African and Malagasy Posts and Telecommunications Union, UAMPT.

1963, Sept. 8

Cameroun	C47
Cent. African Rep.	C10
Chad	C9
Congo, P.R.	C13
Dahomey	C19
Gabon	C13
Ivory Coast	C25
Madagascar	C75
Mauritania	C22
Niger	C27
Rwanda	36
Senegal	C32
Upper Volta	C9

Air Afrique Issue, 1963

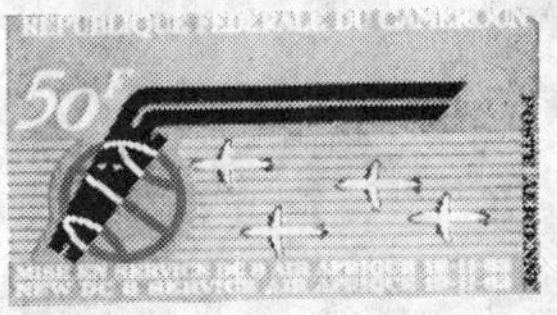

Symbols of Flight – CD115

First anniversary of Air Afrique and inauguration of DC-8 service.

1963, Nov. 19

Cameroun	C48
Chad	C10
Congo, P.R.	C14
Gabon	C18
Ivory Coast	C26
Mauritania	C26
Niger	C35
Senegal	C33

Europafrica Issue

Europe and Africa Linked – CD116

Signing of an economic agreement between the European Economic Community and the African and Malagasy Union, Yaounde, Cameroun, July 20, 1963.

1963-64

Cameroun	402
Chad	C11
Cent. African Rep.	C12
Congo, P.R.	C16
Gabon	C19
Ivory Coast	217
Niger	C43
Upper Volta	C11

Human Rights Issue

Scales of Justice and Globe – CD117

15th anniversary of the Universal Declaration of Human Rights.

1963, Dec. 10

Comoro Isls.	58
Fr. Polynesia	206
New Caledonia	329
St. Pierre & Miquelon	368
Somali Coast	300
Wallis & Futuna Isls.	166

PHILATEC Issue

Stamp Album, Champs Elysees Palace and Horses of Marly – CD118

"PHILATEC," International Philatelic and Postal Techniques Exhibition, Paris, June 5-21, 1964.

1963-64

Comoro Isls.	60
France	1078
Fr. Polynesia	207
New Caledonia	341
St. Pierre & Miquelon	369
Somali Coast	301
Wallis & Futuna Isls.	167

Cooperation Issue

Maps of France and Africa and Clasped Hands – CD119

Cooperation between France and the French-speaking countries of Africa and Madagascar.

1964

Cameroun	409-410
Cent. African Rep.	39
Chad	103
Congo, P.R.	121
Dahomey	193
France	1111
Gabon	175
Ivory Coast	221
Madagascar	360
Mauritania	181
Niger	143
Senegal	236
Togo	495

ITU Issue

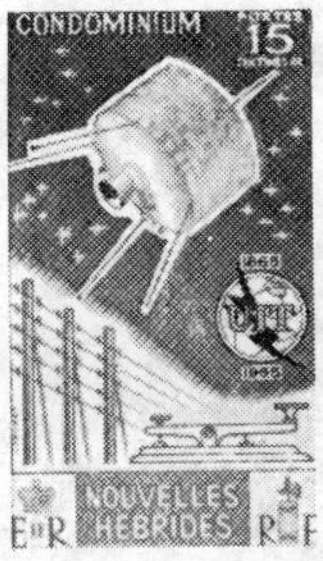

Telegraph, Syncom Satellite and ITU Emblem – CD120

Centenary of the International Telecommunication Union.

1965, May 17

Comoro Isls.	C14
Fr. Polynesia	C33
Fr. So. & Antarctic Terr.	C8
New Caledonia	C40
New Hebrides	124-125
St. Pierre & Miquelon	C29
Somali Coast	C36
Wallis & Futuna Isls.	C20

French Satellite A-1 Issue

Diamant Rocket and Launching Installation – CD121

Launching of France's first satellite, Nov. 26, 1965.

1965-66

Comoro Isls.	C15-C16
France	1137-1138
Fr. Polynesia	C40-C41
Fr. So. & Antarctic Terr.	C9-C10
New Caledonia	C44-C45
St. Pierre & Miquelon	C30-C31
Somali Coast	C39-C40
Wallis & Futuna Isls.	C22-C23

French Satellite D-1 Issue

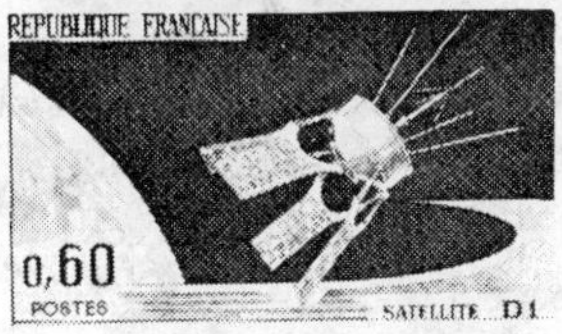

D-1 Satellite in Orbit – CD122

Launching of the D-1 satellite at Hammaguir, Algeria, Feb. 17, 1966.

1966

Comoro Isls.	C17
France	1148
Fr. Polynesia	C42
Fr. So. & Antarctic Terr.	C11
New Caledonia	C46
St. Pierre & Miquelon	C32
Somali Coast	C49
Wallis & Futuna Isls.	C24

Air Afrique Issue, 1966

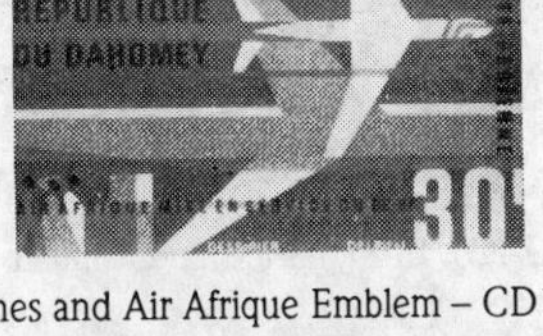

Planes and Air Afrique Emblem – CD123

Introduction of DC-8F planes by Air Afrique.

1966

Cameroun	C79
Cent. African Rep.	C35
Chad	C26
Congo, P.R.	C42
Dahomey	C42
Gabon	C47
Ivory Coast	C32
Mauritania	C57
Niger	C63
Senegal	C47
Togo	C54
Upper Volta	C31

African Postal Union, 1967

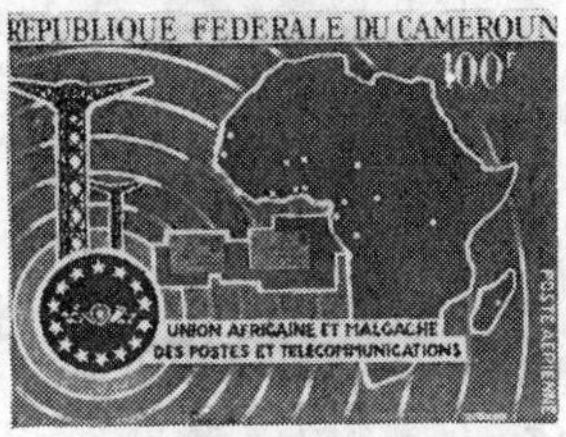

Telecommunications Symbols and Map of Africa – CD124

Fifth anniversary of the establishment of the African and Malagasy Union of Posts and Telecommunications, UAMPT.

1967

Cameroun	C90
Cent. African Rep.	C46
Chad	C37
Congo, P.R.	C57
Dahomey	C61
Gabon	C58
Ivory Coast	C34
Madagascar	C85
Mauritania	C65
Niger	C75
Rwanda	C1-C3
Senegal	C60
Togo	C81
Upper Volta	C50

Monetary Union Issue

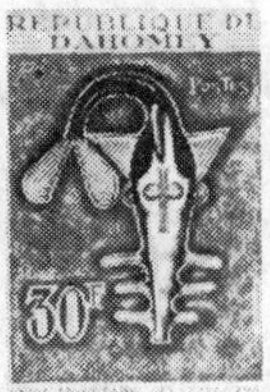

Gold Token of the Ashantis, 17-18th Centuries – CD125

Fifth anniversary of the West African Monetary Union.

1967, Nov. 4

Dahomey	244
Ivory Coast	259
Mauritania	238
Niger	204
Senegal	294
Togo	623
Upper Volta	181

WHO Anniversary Issue

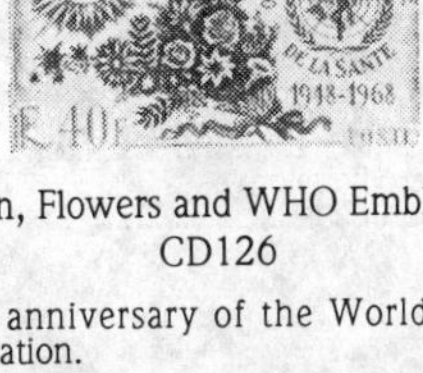

Sun, Flowers and WHO Emblem CD126

20th anniversary of the World Health Organization.

1968, May 4

Afars & Issas	317
Comoro Isls.	73
Fr. Polynesia	241-242

Fr. So. & Antarctic Terr. 31
New Caledonia 367
St. Pierre & Miquelon 377
Wallis & Futuna Isls. 169

Human Rights Year Issue

Human Rights Flame – CD127

International Human Rights Year.

1968, Aug. 10

Afars & Issas 322-323
Comoro Isls. 76
Fr. Polynesia 243-244
Fr. So. & Antarctic Terr. 32
New Caledonia 369
St. Pierre & Miquelon 382
Wallis & Futuna Isls. 170

2nd PHILEXAFRIQUE Issue

Gabon No. 131 and Industrial Plant CD128

Opening of PHILEXAFRIQUE, Abidjan, Feb. 14. Each stamp shows a local scene and stamp.

1969, Feb. 14

Cameroun C118
Cent. African Rep. C65
Chad C48
Congo, P.R. C77
Dahomey C94
Gabon C82
Ivory Coast C38-C40
Madagascar C92
Mali C65
Mauritania C80
Niger C104
Senegal C68
Togo C104
Upper Volta C62

Concorde Issue

Concorde in Flight – CD129

First flight of the prototpye Concorde super-sonic plane at Toulouse, Mar. 1, 1969.

1969

Afars & Issas C56
Comoro Isls. C29
France C42
Fr. Polynesia C50
Fr. So. & Antarctic Terr. C18
New Caledonia C63
St. Pierre & Miquelon C40
Wallis & Futuna Isls. C30

Development Bank Issue

Bank Emblem CD130

Fifth anniversary of the African Development Bank.

1969

Cameroun 499
Chad 217
Congo, P.R. 181-182
Ivory Coast 281
Mali 127-128
Mauritania 267
Niger 220
Senegal 317-318
Upper Volta 201

ILO Issue

ILO Headquarters, Geneva, and Emblem – CD131

50th anniversary of the International Labor Organization.

1969-70

Afars & Issas 337
Comoro Isls. 83
Fr. Polynesia 251-252
Fr. So. & Antarctic Terr. 35
New Caledonia 379
St. Pierre & Miquelon 396
Wallis & Futuna Isls. 172

ASECNA Issue

Map of Africa, Plane and Airport – CD132

10th anniversary of the Agency for the Security of Aerial Navigation in Africa and Madagascar (ASECNA, Agence pour la Securite de la Navigation Aerienne en Afrique et a Madagascar).

1969-70

Cameroun 500
Cent. African Rep. 119
Chad 222
Congo, P.R. 197
Dahomey 269
Gabon 260
Ivory Coast 287
Mali 130
Niger 221
Senegal 321
Upper Volta 204

U.P.U. Headquarters Issue

U.P.U. Headquarters and Emblem CD133

New Universal Postal Union headquarters, Bern, Switzerland.

1970

Afars & Issas 342
Algeria 443
Cameroun 503-504
Cent. African Rep. 125
Chad 225
Comoro Isls. 84
Congo, P.R. 216
Fr. Polynesia 261-262
Fr. So. & Antarctic Terr. 36
Gabon 258
Ivory Coast 295
Madagascar 444
Mali 134-135
Mauritania 283
New Caledonia 382
Niger 231-232
St. Pierre & Miquelon 397-398
Senegal 328-329
Tunisia 535
Wallis & Futuna Isls. 173

De Gaulle Issue

General de Gaulle 1940 – CD134

First anniversay of the death of Charles de Gaulle, (1890-1970), President of France.

1971-72

Afars & Issas 356-357
Comoro Isls. 104-105
France 1322-1325
Fr. Polynesia 270-271
Fr. So. & Antarctic Terr. 52-53
New Caledonia 393-394
Reunion 377, 380
St. Pierre & Miquelon 417-418
Wallis & Futuna Isls. 177-178

African Postal Union Issue, 1971

Carved Stool, UAMPT Building, Brazzaville, Congo – CD135

10th anniversary of the establishment of the African and Malagasy Posts and Telecommunications Union, UAMPT.

Each stamp has a different native design.

1971, Nov. 13

Cameroun C177
Cent. African Rep. C89
Chad C94
Congo, P.R. C136
Dahomey C146
Gabon C120
Ivory Coast C47
Mauritania C113
Niger C164
Rwanda C8
Senegal C105
Togo C166
Upper Volta C97

West African Monetary Union Issue

African Couple, City, Village and Commemorative Coin – CD136

10th anniversary of the West African Monetary Union.

1972, Nov. 2

Dahomey 300
Ivory Coast 331
Mauritania 299
Niger 258
Senegal 374
Togo 825
Upper Volta 280

African Postal Union Issue, 1973

Telecommunications Symbols and Map of Africa – CD137

11th anniversary of the African and Malagasy Posts and Telecommunications Union (UAMPT).

1973, Sept. 12

Cameroun 574
Cent. African Rep. 194
Chad 272
Congo, P.R. 289
Dahomey 311
Gabon 320
Ivory Coast 361
Madagascar 500
Mauritania 304
Niger 287
Rwanda 540
Senegal 393
Togo 849
Upper Volta 285

Philexafrique II — Essen Issue

Buffalo and Dahomey No. C33 – CD138

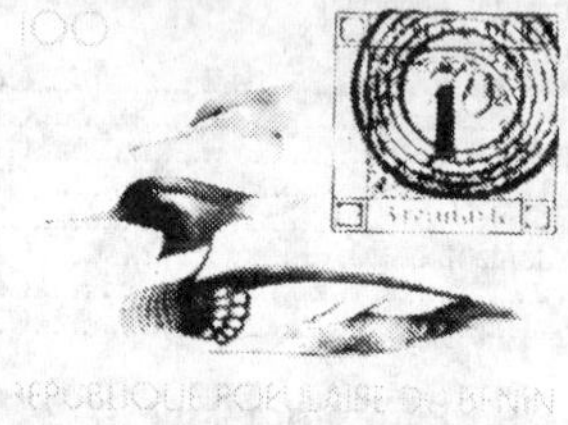

Wild Ducks and Baden No. 1 – CD139

Designs: Indigenous fauna, local and German stamps.

Types CD138-CD139 printed horizontally and vertically se-tenant in sheets of 10 (2x5). Label between horizontal pairs alternately commemoratives Philexafrique II, Libreville, Gabon, June 1978, and 2nd International Stamp Fair, Essen, Germany, Nov. 1-5.

1978-1979

Benin C285-C286
Central Africa C200-C201
Chad C238-C239
Congo Republic C245-C246
Djibouti C121-C122
Gabon C215-C216
Ivory Coast C64-C65
Mali C356-C357
Mauritania C185-C186
Niger C291-C292
Rwanda C12-C13
Senegal C146-C147
Togo C363-C364
Upper Volta C253-C254

ABU DHABI

LOCATION — Arabia, on Persian Gulf
GOVT. — Sheikdom under British protection
POP. — 25,000 (estimated)
CAPITAL — Abu Dhabi

Abu Dhabi is one of six Persian Gulf sheikdoms to join the United Arab Emirates, which proclaimed its independence Dec. 2, 1971. See United Arab Emirates.

100 Naye Paise = 1 Rupee
1000 Fils = 1 Dinar (1966)

Catalogue values for all unused stamps in this country are for Never Hinged items.

Sheik Shakbut bin Sultan — A1

Palace — A2

Designs: 40np, 50np, 75np, Gazelle. 5r, 10r, Oil rig and camels.

Perf. 14½

1964, Mar. 30 Photo. Unwmk.

1 A1 5np brt yel green 15 15
2 A1 15np brown 24 16
3 A1 20np brt ultra 30 20
4 A1 30np red orange 38 25
5 A1 40np brt violet 50 32
6 A1 50np brown olive 60 35
7 A1 75np gray 90 55

Engr. *Perf. 13x13½*

8 A2 1r light green 1.25 75
9 A2 2r black 3.00 1.75
10 A2 5r carmine rose 7.75 4.75
11 A2 10r dark blue 17.50 12.00
Nos. 1-11 (11) 32.57 21.23

For surcharges, see Nos. 15-25.

Falcon Perched on Wrist — A3

Designs: 40np, Falcon facing left. 2r, Falcon facing right.

1965, Mar. 30 Photo. *Perf. 14½*

12 A3 20np chlky blue & brn 1.50 50
13 A3 40np ultra & brown 3.00 1.75
14 A3 2r brt blue grn & gray brn 14.00 14.00
Nos. 12-14 (3) 18.50 16.25

Nos. 1-11 Surcharged

5Fils ٥ فلس
a

Fils فلس
b

100 Fils **١٠٠ فلس**
c

1966, Oct. 1 Photo. *Perf. 14½*

15 A1 (a) 5f on 5np 15 15
16 A1 (a) 15f on 15np 50 35
17 A1 (a) 20f on 20np 55 50
18 A1 (a) 30f on 30np 80 60
19 A1 (b) 40f on 40np 1.40 85
20 A1 (b) 50f on 50np 6.50 8.25
21 A1 (b) 75f on 75np 8.00 8.25

Engr.

Perf. 13x13½

22 A2 (c) 100f on 1r 8.00 5.50
23 A2 (c) 200f on 2r 17.50 11.00
24 A2 (c) 500f on 5r 37.50 40.00
25 A2 (c) 1d on 10r 80.00 92.50
Nos. 15-25 (11) 160.90 167.95

Overprint on #25 has "1 Dinar" on 1 line and 3 bars through old denomination.

Sheik Zaid bin Sultan al Nahayan
A4 A6

Dorcas Gazelle — A5

Designs: 5f, 15f, 20f, 35f, Crossed flags of Abu Dhabi. 200f, Falcon. 500f, 1d, Palace.

Engr.; Flags Litho.

1967, Apr. 1 *Perf. 13x13½*

26 A4 5f dull grn & red 15 15
27 A4 15f dk brown & red 30 20
28 A4 20f dk blue & red 38 25
29 A4 35f purple & red 65 45

Engr.

30 A4 40f green 75 55
31 A4 50f brown 1.00 70
32 A4 60f blue 1.40 80
33 A4 100f car rose 2.25 1.50

Litho.

34 A5 125f green & brn ol 2.75 1.90
35 A5 200f sky blue & brn 4.50 3.00
36 A5 500f org & brt pur 12.00 7.50
37 A5 1d green & vio bl 25.00 15.00
Nos. 26-37 (12) 51.13 32.00

In 1969, the 15f was surcharged "25" in Arabic in black with a numbering machine.

1967, Aug. 6 Photo. *Perf. 14½x14*

38 A6 40f Prussian green 1.25 1.10
39 A6 50f brown 1.25 75
40 A6 60f blue 2.00 1.00
41 A6 100f carmine rose 3.75 1.90
Nos. 38-41 (4) 8.25 4.75

Human Rights Flame and Sheik Zaid A6a

Perf. 14½x14

1968, Apr. 1 Photo. Unwmk.

Emblem in Red and Green

42 A6a 35f peacock bl & gold 1.10 60
43 A6a 60f dk blue & gold 1.75 75
44 A6a 150f dk brown & gold 4.50 1.75
Nos. 42-44 (3) 7.35 3.10

International Human Rights Year.

Sheik Zaid and Coat of Arms A7

Perf. 14x14½

1968, Aug. 6 Photo. Unwmk.

45 A7 5f green, sil, red & blk 42 15
46 A7 10f brn org, sil, red & blk 60 22
47 A7 100f lilac, gold, red & blk 3.75 1.50
48 A7 125f lt blue, gold, red & blk 5.50 2.25
Nos. 45-48 (4) 10.27 4.12

Accession of Sheik Zaid, 2nd anniversary.

Abu Dhabi Airport A8

Designs: 5f, Buildings under construction and earth-moving equipment. 35f, New bridge and falcon. Each stamp shows different portrait of Sheik Zaid.

Perf. 12, 12½x13 (10f)

1969, Mar. 28 Litho.

Size: 5f, 35f, 59x34mm

49 A8 5f multicolored 1.00 25
50 A8 10f multicolored 1.50 60
51 A8 35f multicolored 6.00 2.50
Nos. 49-51 (3) 8.50 3.35

Issued to publicize progress made in Abu Dhabi during preceding 2 years.

Sheik Zaid and Abu Dhabi Petroleum Co. — A9

Designs: 60f, Abu Dhabi Marine Areas drilling platform and helicopter. 125f, Zakum Field separator at night. 200f, Tank farm.

1969, Aug. 6 Litho. *Perf. 14x13½*

52 A9 35f olive grn & multi 65 25
53 A9 60f yel brown & multi 1.25 55
54 A9 125f multicolored 2.75 1.10
55 A9 200f red brown & multi 5.00 2.00
Nos. 52-55 (4) 9.65 3.90

Accession of Sheik Zaid, 3rd anniversary.

Sheik Zaid — A10

Sheik Zaid and Stallion A11

Designs: 5f, 25f, 60f, 90f, Oval frame around portrait. 150f, Gazelle and Sheik. 500f, Fort Jahili and Sheik. 1d, Grand Mosque and Sheik.

1970-71 Litho. *Perf. 14*

56 A10 5f lt green & multi 15 15
57 A10 10f bister & multi 28 15
58 A10 25f lilac & multi 55 18
59 A10 35f violet & multi 90 25
60 A10 50f sepia & multi 1.25 35
61 A10 60f violet & multi 1.50 40
62 A10 70f rose red & multi 2.00 50
63 A10 90f car rose & multi 2.25 60
64 A11 125f multi ('71) 3.00 85
65 A11 150f multi ('71) 3.50 1.00
66 A11 500f multi ('71) 11.00 3.50
67 A11 1d multi ('71) 22.50 6.50
Nos. 56-67 (12) 48.88 14.43

For surcharge, see No. 80.

Sheik Zaid and Mt. Fuji — A12

1970, Aug. Litho. *Perf. 13½x13*

68 A12 25f multicolored 1.65 90
69 A12 35f multicolored 2.00 1.25
70 A12 60f multicolored 3.75 1.75
Nos. 68-70 (3) 7.40 3.90

Issued to publicize EXPO '70 International Exhibition, Osaka, Japan, Mar. 15-Sept. 13.

Abu Dhabi Airport A13

Designs: 60f, Airport entrance. 150f, Aerial view of Abu Dhabi Town, vert.

Perf. 14x13½, 13½x14

1970, Sept. 22 Litho.

71 A13 25f multicolored 1.25 50
72 A13 60f multicolored 4.00 1.25
73 A13 150f multicolored 7.25 3.00
Nos. 71-73 (3) 12.50 4.75

Accession of Sheik Zaid, 4th anniversary.

Gamal Abdel Nasser — A14

1971, May 3 Litho. *Perf. 14*

74 A14 25f deep rose & blk 2.75 2.00
75 A14 35f rose violet & blk 4.00 3.00

In memory of Gamal Abdel Nasser (1918-1970), President of UAR.

Scout Cars — A15

Designs: 60f, Patrol boat. 125f, Armored car in desert. 150f, Meteor jet fighters.

1971, Aug. 6 Litho. *Perf. 13*

76 A15 35f multicolored 1.50 1.00
77 A15 60f multicolored 2.25 1.50
78 A15 125f multicolored 3.25 2.25
79 A15 150f multicolored 3.50 3.00
Nos. 76-79 (4) 10.50 7.75

Accession of Sheik Zaid, 5th anniversary.

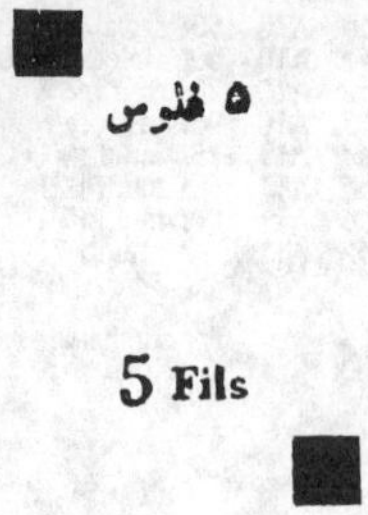

No. 60 Surcharged in Green

1971, Dec. 8 *Perf. 14*

80 A10 5f on 50f multi *45.00 30.00*

Dome of the Rock, Jerusalem — A16

Designs: Different views of Dome of the Rock.

1972, June 3 *Perf. 13*

81 A16 35f lt violet & multi 5.50 1.90
82 A16 60f lt violet & multi 8.25 2.50
83 A16 125f lilac & multi 15.00 5.25
Nos. 81-83 (3) 28.75 9.65

Nos. 80-83 were issued after Abu Dhabi joined the United Arab Emirates Dec. 2, 1971. Stamps of UAE replaced those of Abu Dhabi. UAE Nos. 1-12 were used only in Abu Dhabi except the 10f and 25f which were issued later in Dubai and Sharjah.

AFARS AND ISSAS

French Territory of the

LOCATION — East Africa
GOVT. — French Overseas Territory
AREA — 8,880 sq. mi.
POP. — 150,000 (est. 1974)
CAPITAL — Djibouti (Jibuti)

The French overseas territory of Somali Coast was renamed the French Territory of the Afars and Issas in 1967. It became the Djibouti Republic. (which see) on June 27, 1977.

100 Centimes = 1 Franc

Catalogue values for all unused stamps in this country are for Never Hinged items.

Imperforates

Most stamps of Afars and Issas exist imperforate in issued and trial colors, and also in small presentation sheets in issued colors.

Grayheaded Kingfisher A48

Designs: 15fr, Oystercatcher. 50fr, Greenshanks. 55fr, Abyssinian roller. 60fr, Ground squirrel, vert.

1967 Engr. Unwmk. *Perf. 13*

310 A48 10fr brt bl, gray grn & blk 1.25 1.10
311 A48 15fr dk brn, bl, ol & ocher 2.00 1.75
312 A48 50fr blk, sl grn & brn 7.75 4.00
313 A48 55fr vio, brt bl & gray grn 9.50 5.00
314 A48 60fr ocher, brt grn & sl grn 13.00 8.00
Nos. 310-314 (5) 33.50 19.85

Dates of Issue: 10fr, 55fr, Aug. 21; 15fr, 50fr, 60fr, Sept. 25. See No. C50.

Soccer — A49

1967, Dec. 18 Engr. *Perf. 13*

315 A49 25fr shown 1.50 1.00
316 A49 30fr Basketball 2.00 1.75

WHO Anniversary Issue
Common Design Type

1968, May 4 Engr. *Perf. 13*

317 CD126 15fr multi 1.10 75

20th anniv. of WHO.

Damerdjog Fortress — A50

Administration Buildings: 25fr, Ali Adde. 30fr, Dorra. 40fr, Assamo.

1968, May 17 Engr. *Perf. 13*

318 A50 20fr sl, brn & emer 90 50
319 A50 25fr brt grn, bl & brn 95 50
320 A50 30fr brn ol, brn org & sl 1.10 75
321 A50 40fr brn ol, sl & brt grn 2.00 1.50
Nos. 318-321 (4) 4.95 3.25

Common Design Types
Pictured in section at front of book.

Human Rights Year Issue
Common Design Type

1968, Aug. 10 Engr. *Perf. 13*

322 CD127 10fr pur, ver & org 75 60
323 CD127 70fr grn, pur & org 1.50 1.10

International Human Rights Year.

Radio-television Station, Djibouti — A52

High Commission Palace, Djibouti — A53

Designs: 2fr, Justice Building. 5fr, Chamber of Deputies. 8fr, Great Mosque. 15fr, Monument of Free French Forces (vert.). 40fr, Djibouti Post Office. 70fr, Residence of Gov. Léonce Lagarde at Obock. No. 332, Djibouti Harbormaster's Building. No. 333, Control tower, Djibouti Airport.

1968-70 Engr. *Perf. 13*

324 A52 1fr dk red, sky bl & ind ('69) 20 15
325 A52 2fr grn, bl & ind ('69) 20 15
326 A52 5fr brn, sky bl & grn ('69) 28 20
327 A52 8fr choc, emer & gray ('69) 32 20
328 A52 15fr grn, sky bl & yel brn ('69) 2.25 1.75
329 A52 40fr grn, brn & sl ('70) 1.50 85
330 A53 60fr multi 1.75 1.40
331 A53 70fr dl grn, gray & ol bis ('69) 2.25 1.75
332 A53 85fr multi ('69) 3.00 2.00
333 A52 85fr dk grn, bl & gray ('70) 3.50 2.25
Nos. 324-333 (10) 15.25 10.70

Locust — A54

Designs: 50fr, Pest control by helicopter. 55fr, Pest control by plane.

1969, Oct. 6 Engr. *Perf. 13*

334 A54 15fr brn, grn & slate 1.10 65
335 A54 50fr dk grn, bl & ol brn 1.75 1.00
336 A54 55fr red brn, bl & brn 2.25 1.75
Nos. 334-336 (3) 5.10 3.40

Campaign against locusts.

ILO Issue
Common Design Type

1969, Nov. 24 Engr. *Perf. 13*

337 CD131 30fr org, gray & lil 1.25 80

Afar Dagger in Ornamental Scabbard A56

1970, Apr. 3 Engr. *Perf. 13*

338 A56 10fr yel grn, dk grn & org brn 50 25
339 A56 15fr yel grn, bl & org brn 60 25
340 A56 20fr yel grn, red & org brn 65 40
341 A56 25fr yel grn, plum & org brn 1.10 40
Nos. 338-341 (4) 2.85 1.30

See No. 364.

UPU Headquarters Issue
Common Design Type

1970, May 20 Engr. *Perf. 13*

342 CD133 25fr brn, brt grn & choc 1.00 60

Trapshooting A57

Motorboats A58

Designs: 50fr, Steeplechase. 55fr, Sailboat, vert. 60fr, Equestrians.

1970 Engr. *Perf. 13*

343 A57 30fr dp brn, yel grn & brt bl 1.40 1.00
344 A58 48fr bl & multi 1.50 80
345 A58 50fr cop red, bl & pur 1.75 1.10
346 A58 55fr red brn, bl & ol 1.50 1.00
347 A58 60fr ol, blk & red brn 2.25 1.75
Nos. 343-347 (5) 8.40 5.65

Issue dates: 30fr, June 5; 48fr, Oct. 9; 50fr, 60fr, Nov. 6.

Automatic Ferry, Tadjourah A59

1970, Nov. 25

348 A59 48fr blue, brn & grn 1.40 75

Volcanic Geode — A60

Diabase and Chrysolite A61

Designs: 10fr, Doleritic basalt. 15fr, Olivine basalt.

1971 Photo. *Perf. 13*

349 A61 10fr blk & multi 40 35
350 A61 15fr blk & multi 50 35
351 A60 25fr blk, crim & brn 1.10 80
352 A61 40fr blk & multi 2.00 1.40
Nos. 349-352 (4) 4.00 2.90

Issue dates: 10fr, Nov. 22; 15fr, Oct. 8; 25fr, Apr. 26; 40fr, Jan. 25.

Manta Ray — A62

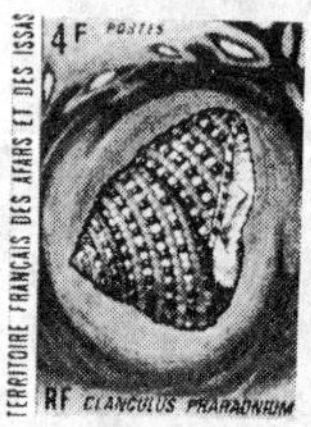

Strawberry Top — A63

Fishes: 5fr, Dolphinfish. 9fr, Smalltooth sawfish.

1971, July 1 Photo. *Perf. 12x12½*

353 A62 4fr green & multi 45 25
354 A62 5fr blue & multi 45 25
355 A62 9fr red & multi 75 55
Nos. 353-355 (3) 1.65 1.05

See No. C60.

De Gaulle Issue
Common Design Type

Designs: 60fr, Gen. Charles de Gaulle, 1940. 85fr, Pres. de Gaulle, 1970.

1971, Nov. 9 Engr. *Perf. 13*

356 CD134 60fr dk vio bl & blk 1.50 1.25
357 CD134 85fr dk vio bl & blk 2.00 1.25

1972, Mar. 8 Photo. *Perf. 12½x13*

Shells: 9fr, Cypraea pantherina. 20fr, Bullmouth helmet. 50fr, Ethiopian volute.

358 A63 4fr ol & multi 32 22
359 A63 9fr dk bl & multi 42 40
360 A63 20fr dp grn & multi 1.00 55
361 A63 50fr dp cl & multi 2.00 1.00
Nos. 358-361 (4) 3.74 2.17

Shepherd — A64

Design: 10fr, Dromedary breeding.

1973, Apr. 11 Photo. *Perf. 13*

362 A64 9fr bl & multi 50 30
363 A64 10fr bl & multi 50 30

Afar Dagger — A65

1974, Jan. 29 Engr. *Perf. 13*

364 A65 30fr sl grn & dk brn 1.10 65

For surcharge see No. 379.

Flamingos, Lake Abbe — A66

Designs: Flamingos and different views of Lake Abbe.

1974, Feb. 22 Photo. *Perf. 13*
370 A66 5fr multi 28 20
371 A66 15fr multi 50 22
372 A66 50fr multi 1.50 75
Nos. 370-372 (3) 2.28 1.17

Soccer Ball — A67

1974, May 24 Engr. *Perf. 13*
373 A67 25fr blk & emer 1.25 80

World Cup Soccer Championship, Munich, June 13-July 7.

Letters Around UPU Emblem A68

Oleo Chrysophylla A69

1974, Oct. 9 Engr. *Perf. 13*
374 A68 20fr multi 1.10 60
375 A68 100fr multi 2.75 2.25

Centenary of Universal Postal Union.

1974, Nov. 22 Photo.
376 A69 10fr *shown* 35 28
377 A69 15fr *Ficus species* 50 40
378 A69 20fr *Solanum adoense* 1.10 80
Nos. 376-378 (3) 1.95 1.48

Day Primary Forest.

No. 364 Surcharged with New Value and Two Bars in Red

1975, Jan. 1 Engr. *Perf. 13*
379 A65 40fr on 30fr multi 1.50 90

Treasury — A70

Design: 25fr, Government buildings.

1975, Jan. 7 Engr. *Perf. 13*
380 A70 8fr bl, gray & red 40 28
381 A70 25fr red, bl & ind 75 60

Ranella Spinosa — A71

Sea Shells: No. 382, Darioconus textile. No. 383, Murex palmarosa. 10fr, Conus sumatrensis. 15fr, Cypraea pulchra. No. 386, 45fr, Murex scolopax. No. 387, Cypraea exhusta. 55fr, Cypraea erythraensis. 60fr, Conus taeniatus.

1975-76 Engr. *Perf. 13*
382 A71 5fr bl grn & brn 38 20
383 A71 5fr bl & multi ('76) 28 15
384 A71 10fr lil, blk & brn 40 28
385 A71 15fr bl, indigo & brn 75 38
386 A71 20fr pur & lt brn 1.10 75
387 A71 20fr brt grn & multi ('76) 38 22
388 A71 40fr grn & brn 2.00 1.00
389 A71 45fr grn, bl & bis 1.75 1.00
390 A71 55fr turq & multi ('76) 1.10 75
391 A71 60fr buff & sepia ('76) 2.00 1.10
Nos. 382-391 (10) 10.14 5.83

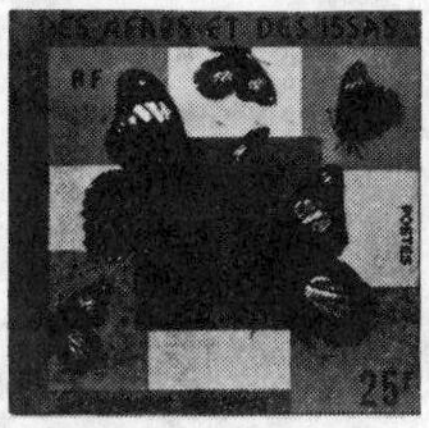

Hypolimnas Misippus A72

Butterflies: 40fr, Papilio nireus. 50fr, Acraea anemosa. 65fr, Holocerina smilax menieri. 70fr, Papilio demodocus. No. 397, Papilio dardanus. No. 398, Balachowsky gonimbrasca. 150fr, Vanessa cardui.

1975-76 Photo. *Perf. 13*
392 A72 25fr emer & multi 1.00 75
393 A72 40fr yel & multi 1.10 75
394 A72 50fr ultra & multi ('76) 1.40 1.00
395 A72 65fr ol & multi ('76) 1.75 1.00
396 A72 70fr vio & multi 2.25 2.00
397 A72 100fr bl & multi 3.00 2.00
398 A72 100fr Prus bl & multi ('76) 2.25 1.75
399 A72 150fr grn & multi ('76) 3.00 2.00
Nos. 392-399 (8) 15.75 11.25

Mongoose — A73

Animals: 10fr, Hyena. No. 401, Catarrhine monkeys, vert. No. 402, Wild ass, vert. 30fr, Antelope. 60fr, Porcupines, vert. 70fr, Skunks. 200fr, Aardvarks.

Perf. 13x12½, 12½x13
1975-76 Photo.
400 A73 10fr lt vio & multi ('76) 28 20
401 A73 15fr yel grn & multi 60 38
402 A73 15fr grn & multi ('76) 40 28
403 A73 30fr bl & multi ('76) 65 50
404 A73 50fr dp org & multi 1.75 1.00
405 A73 60fr yel brn & multi 2.00 1.25
406 A73 70fr blk & brn 3.00 1.75
407 A73 200fr bl gray & multi 4.00 3.00
Nos. 400-407 (8) 12.68 8.36

Pin-tailed Whydah — A74

Palms — A75

Birds: 25fr, Rose-ringed parakeet. 50fr, Variable sunbird. 60fr, Purple heron. No. 417, Hammerhead. No. 418, Turtle dove. 300fr, African spoonbill.

1975-76 Photo. *Perf. 12½x13*
413 A74 20fr lil, blk & org 65 50
414 A74 25fr car rose & multi ('76) 65 28
415 A74 50fr bl & multi 1.40 85
416 A74 60fr multi 2.00 1.10
417 A74 100fr lt grn & multi 2.50 1.75
418 A74 100fr lt yel & multi ('76) 2.00 1.40
419 A74 300fr multi ('76) 5.50 3.75
Nos. 413-419 (7) 14.70 9.63

1975, Dec. 19 Engr. *Perf. 13*
421 A75 20fr brt bl & multi 50 28

Satellite and Alexander Graham Bell — A76

1976, Mar. 10 Engr. *Perf. 13*
422 A76 200fr dp bl, org & sl grn 3.00 2.00

Centenary of the first telephone call by Alexander Graham Bell, Mar. 10, 1876.

Basketball A77

1976, July 7 Litho. *Perf. 12½*
423 A77 10fr shown 26 15
424 A77 15fr Bicycling 55 30
425 A77 40fr Soccer 1.00 70
426 A77 60fr Running 1.65 1.10
Nos. 423-426 (4) 3.46 2.25

21st Olympic Games, Montreal, Canada, July 17-Aug. 1.

Turkeyfish — A78

1976, Aug. 10 Photo. *Perf. 13x13½*
428 A78 45fr bl & multi 1.40 1.00

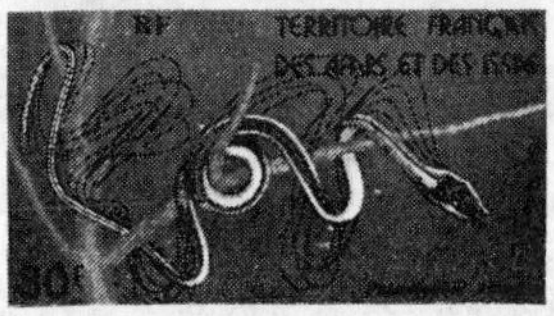

Psammophis Elegans — A79

Design: 70fr, Naja nigricollis, vert.

Perf. 13x13½, 13½x13
1976, Sept. 27 Photo.
430 A79 70fr ocher & multi 1.75 1.50
431 A79 80fr emer & multi 2.00 1.75

Motorcyclist — A80

1977, Jan. 27 Litho. *Perf. 12x12½*
432 A80 200fr multi 3.75 2.75

Moto-Cross motorcycle race.

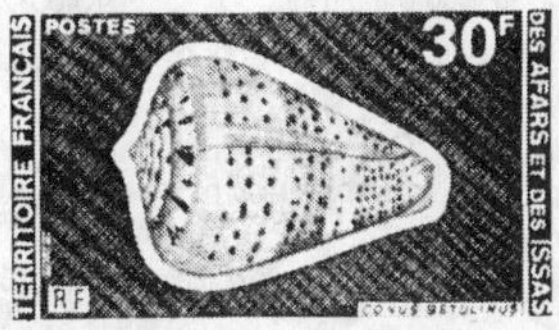

Conus Betulinus — A81

Sea Shells: 5fr, Cyprea tigris. 70fr, Conus striatus. 85fr, Cyprea mauritiana.

1977 Engr. *Perf. 13*
433 A81 5fr multi 45 28
434 A81 30fr multi 60 38
435 A81 70fr multi 2.25 1.10
436 A81 85fr multi 3.25 2.00
Nos. 433-436 (4) 6.55 3.76

Gaterin Gaterinus A82

1977, Apr. 15 Photo. *Perf. 13x12½*
437 A82 15fr shown 55 28
438 A82 65fr Barracudas 1.50 80

Stamps of the French Territory of the Afars and Issas were replaced in 1977 by those of the Republic of Djibouti.

AIR POST STAMPS

Tawny Eagles AP16

Parachutists AP17

Unwmk.

1967, Aug. 21 Engr. *Perf. 13*
C50 AP16 200fr multi 12.00 7.50

1968 Engr. *Perf. 13*

Design: 85fr, Water skier and skin diver.

C51 AP17 48fr brn ol, Prus bl & brn 2.75 1.50
C52 AP17 85fr dk brn, ol & Prus bl 3.50 2.25

Issue dates: 48fr, Jan. 5; 85fr, Mar. 15.

Aerial Map of the Territory — AP18

1968, Nov. 15 Engr. *Perf. 13*

C53	AP18 500fr bl, dk brn & ocher	26.00	8.00

Buildings Type of Regular Issue

Designs: 100fr, Cathedral, vert. 200fr, Sayed Hassan Mosque, vert.

1969 Engr. *Perf. 13*

C54	A53 100fr multi	2.50	1.25
C55	A53 200fr multi	5.00	2.75

Issue dates: 100fr, Apr. 4; 200fr, May 8.

Concorde Issue
Common Design Type

1969, Apr. 17

C56	CD129 100fr org red & olive	17.50	10.00

Arta Ionospheric Station — AP19

Japanese Sword Guard, Fish Design — AP20

1970, May 8 Engr. *Perf. 13*

C57	AP19 70fr multi	2.50	2.00

Gold embossed

1970, Sept. 29 *Perf. 12½*

Design: 200fr, Japanese sword guard, horse design.

C58	AP20 100fr multi	7.50	5.00
C59	AP20 200fr multi	9.50	5.50

EXPO '70 International Exposition, Osaka, Japan, Mar. 15-Sept. 13.

Parrotfish AP21

1971, July 1 Photo. *Perf. 12½*

C60	AP21 30fr blk & multi	2.00	1.75

Djibouti Harbor AP22

1971, Nov. 26

C61	AP22 100fr bl & multi	3.25	2.00

New Djibouti harbor.

Lichtenstein's Sandgrouse AP23

Running, Olympic Rings AP24

Birds: 49fr, Hoopoe. 66fr, Great snipe. 500fr, Tawny-breasted francolin.

1972 Photo. *Perf. 12½x13*

C62	AP23 30fr multi	1.90	1.40
C63	AP23 49fr multi	2.75	2.50
C64	AP23 66fr bl & multi	3.75	2.50
C65	AP23 500fr multi	17.50	8.00
	Nos. C62-C65 (4)	25.90	14.40

Issue dates: #C65, Nov. 3, others Apr. 21.

1972, June 8 Engr. *Perf. 13*

Designs (Olympic Rings and): 10fr, Basketball. 55fr, Swimming, horiz. 60fr, Olympic torch and Greek frieze, horiz.

C66	AP24 5fr multi	30	20
C67	AP24 10fr multi	38	20
C68	AP24 55fr multi	1.40	75
C69	AP24 60fr multi	1.90	90
	Nos. C66-C69 (4)	3.98	2.05

20th Olympic Games, Munich, Aug. 26-Sept. 11.

Louis Pasteur — AP25

Design: 100fr, Albert Calmette and C. Guérin.

1972, Oct. 5 Engr. *Perf. 13*

C70	AP25 20fr multi	80	50
C71	AP25 100fr multi	3.00	2.25

Pasteur, Calmette, Guerin, chemists and bacteriologists, benefactors of mankind.

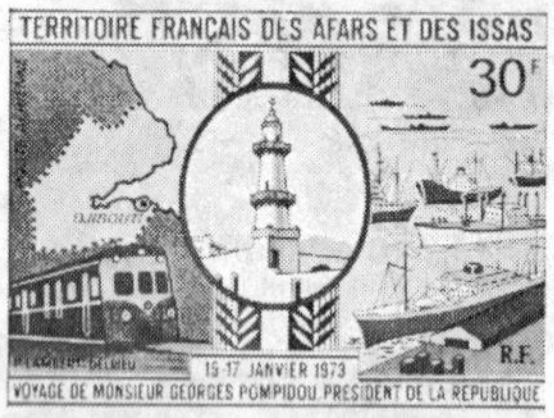

Map and Views of Territory — AP26

Design: 200fr, Woman and Mosque of Djibouti, vert.

1973, Jan. 15 Photo. *Perf. 13*

C72	AP26 30fr brn & multi	3.25	2.75
C73	AP26 200fr multi	7.25	5.75

Visit of Pres. Georges Pompidou of France, Jan. 15-17.

Oryx AP27

1973, Feb. 26 Photo. *Perf. 13x12½*

C74	AP27 30fr shown	1.00	75
C75	AP27 50fr Dik-dik	1.75	1.00
C76	AP27 66fr Caracal	2.50	2.00
	Nos. C74-C76 (3)	5.25	3.75

See Nos. C94-C96.

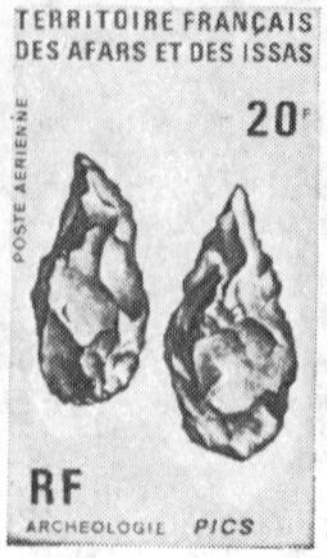

Celts — AP28

Designs: Various pre-historic flint tools. 40fr, 60fr, horiz.

1973 *Perf. 13*

C77	AP28 20fr yel grn, blk & brn	1.50	1.10
C78	AP28 40fr yel & multi	1.50	1.10
C79	AP28 49fr lil & multi	2.50	1.75
C80	AP28 60fr bl & multi	2.50	1.75
	Nos. C77-C80 (4)	8.00	5.70

Issued: 20fr, 49fr, Mar. 16; 40fr, 60fr, Sept. 7.

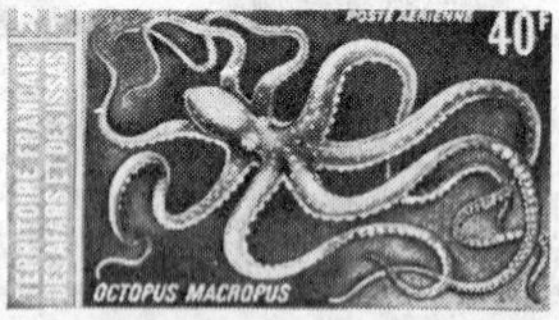

Octopus — AP29

1973, Mar. 16

C81	AP29 40fr shown	1.50	80
C82	AP29 60fr Dugong	2.75	1.75

Copernicus — AP30

Baboons — AP31

Designs: 8fr, Nicolaus Copernicus, Polish astronomer. 9fr, William C. Roentgen, physicist, X-ray discoverer. No. C85, Edward Jenner, physician, discoverer of vaccination. No. C86, Marie Curie, discoverer of radium and polonium. 49fr, Robert Koch, physician and bacteriologist. 50fr, Clement Ader (1841-1925), French aviation pioneer. 55fr, Guglielmo Marconi, Italian electrical engineer, inventor. 85fr, Moliere, French playwright. 100fr, Henri Farman (1874-1937), French aviation pioneer. 150fr, Andre-Marie Ampere (1775-1836), French physicist. 250fr, Michelangelo Buonarroti (1475-1564), Italian sculptor, painter and architect.

1973-75 Engr. *Perf. 13*

C83	AP30 8fr multi	50	28
C84	AP30 9fr multi	40	28
C85	AP30 10fr multi	40	28
C86	AP30 10fr multi	50	28
C87	AP30 49fr multi	2.50	1.75
C88	AP30 50fr multi	2.00	1.40
C89	AP30 55fr multi	1.75	1.40
C90	AP30 85fr multi	3.50	2.25
C91	AP30 100fr multi	3.25	2.75
C92	AP30 150fr multi	3.25	2.75
C93	AP30 250fr multi	5.50	4.00
	Nos. C83-C93 (11)	23.55	17.42

Issue dates: 8fr, 85fr, May 9, 1973. 9fr, No. C85, 49fr, Oct. 12, 1973. 100fr, Jan. 29, 1974. 55fr, Mar. 22, 1974. No. C86, Aug. 23, 1974. 150fr, July 24, 1975. 250fr, June 26, 1975. 50fr, Sept. 25, 1975.

Perf. 12½x13, 13x12½

1973, Dec. 12 Photo.

C94	AP31 20fr shown	80	60
C95	AP31 50fr Genets, horiz.	1.75	80
C96	AP31 66fr Hares	2.75	1.75
	Nos. C94-C96 (3)	5.30	3.15

Spearfishing — AP32

1974, Apr. 14 Engr. *Perf. 13*

C97	AP32 200fr multi	5.00	4.25

No. C97 was prepared for release in Nov. 1972, for the 3rd Underwater Spearfishing Contest in the Red Sea. Dates were obliterated with a rectangle and the stamp was not issued without this obliteration.

Rock Carvings, Balho — AP33

1974, Apr. 26

C98	AP33 200fr car & slate	6.25	4.25

Lake Assal AP34

Designs (Lake Assal): 50fr, Rock formations on shore. 85fr, Crystallized wood.

1974, Oct. 25 Photo. *Perf. 13*

C99	AP34 49fr multi	1.00	80
C100	AP34 50fr multi	1.25	1.00
C101	AP34 85fr multi	2.25	2.00
	Nos. C99-C101 (3)	4.50	3.80

Guinea Dove — AP35

1975, May 23 Photo. *Perf. 13*

C102	AP35 500fr multi	11.00	6.00

Djibouti Airport — AP36

1977, Mar. 1 Litho. *Perf. 12*

C103	AP36 500fr multi	9.00	7.50

Opening of new Djibouti Airport.

Thomas A. Edison and Phonograph — AP37

Design: 75fr, Alexander Volta, electric train, lines and light bulb.

1977, May 5 Engr. *Perf. 13*

C104	AP37	55fr multi	2.00	1.40
C105	AP37	75fr multi	3.25	2.25

Famous inventors: Thomas Alva Edison and Alexander Volta (1745-1827).

POSTAGE DUE STAMPS

Nomad's Milk Jug — D3

Perf. 14x13

1969, Dec. 15 Engr. Unwmk.

J49	D3	1fr red brn, red lil & slate	15	15
J50	D3	2fr red brn, emer & slate	15	15
J51	D3	5fr red brn, bl & slate	28	28
J52	D3	10fr red brn, brn & slate	60	60
		Nos. J49-J52 (4)	1.18	1.18

AFGHANISTAN

LOCATION — Central Asia, bounded by Iran, Russian Turkestan, Pakistan, Baluchistan and China
GOVT. — Republic
AREA — 251,773 sq. mi.
POP. — 17,150,000 (1984 est.)
CAPITAL — Kabul

Afghanistan changed from a constitutional monarchy to a republic in July 1973.

12 Shahi = 6 Sanar = 3 Abasi =
2 Krans = 1 Rupee Kabuli
60 Paisas = 1 Rupee (1921)
100 Pouls = 1 Rupee Afghani (1927)

Catalogue values for unused stamps in this country are for Never Hinged items, beginning with Scott 364 in the regular postage section, Scott B1 in the semi-postal section, Scott C7 in the airpost section, Scott O8 in officials section, and Scott RA6 in the postal tax section.

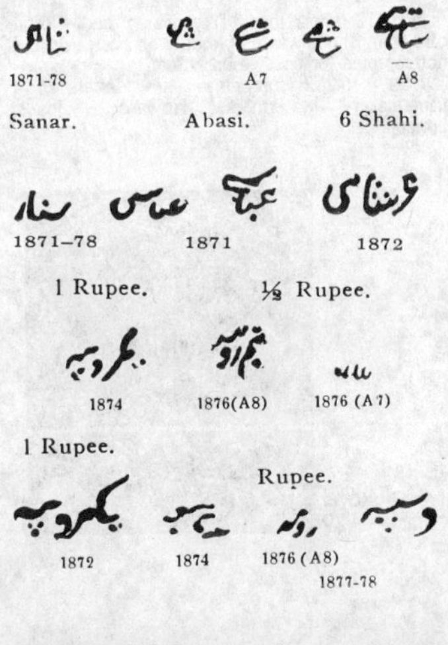

From 1871 to 1892 and 1898 the Moslem year date appears on the stamp. Numerals as follows:

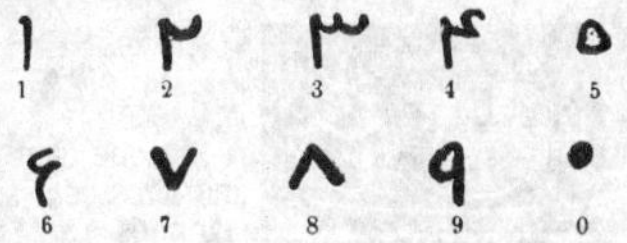

Until 1891 cancellation consisted of cutting or tearing a piece from the stamps. Such copies should not be considered as damaged.

Values are for cut square examples of good color. Cut to shape or faded copies sell for much less, particularly Nos. 2-10.

Nos. 2-108 are on laid paper of varying thickness except where wove is noted.

Until 1907 all stamps were issued ungummed.

The tiger's head on types A2 to A11 symbolizes the name of the contemporary amir, Sher (Tiger) Ali.

Kingdom of Kabul

Tiger's Head A2

(Both circles dotted)

1871 Unwmk. Litho. *Imperf.*
Dated "1288"

2	A2	1sh black	110.00	22.50
3	A2	1sa black	75.00	20.00
4	A2	1ab black	37.50	20.00

Thirty varieties of the shahi, 10 of the sanar and 5 of the abasi.

Similar designs without the tiger's head in the center are revenues.

A3

(Outer circle dotted)

Dated "1288"

5	A3	1sh black	175.00	35.00
6	A3	1sa black	75.00	22.50
7	A3	1ab black	37.50	22.50

Five varieties of each.

A4

1872

Toned Wove Paper
Dated "1289"

8	A4	6sh violet	*850.*	*550.*
9	A4	1rup violet	*1,200.*	*650.*

Two varieties of each. Date varies in location. Printed in sheets of 4 (2x2) containing two of each denomination.

Most used copies are smeared with a greasy ink cancel.

A4a

1873

White Laid Paper
Dated "1290"

10	A4a	1sh black	10.00	4.50
a.		Corner ornament missing	*450.00*	*375.00*
b.		Corner ornament retouched	*60.00*	*25.00*

15 varieties. Nos. 10a, 10b are the sixth stamp on the sheet.

A5

1873

11	A5	1sh black	2.25	2.00
11A	A5	1sh violet	*500.00*	

Sixty varieties of each.

1874

Dated "1291"

12	A5	1ab black	40.00	25.00
13	A5	½rup black	20.00	17.50
14	A5	1rup black	22.50	20.00
		Nos. 12-14 (3)	82.50	62.50

Five varieties of each.

Nos. 12-14 were printed on the same sheet. Se-tenant varieties exist.

A6

A7

1875

Dated "1292"

15	A6	1sa black	*160.00*	*125.00*
a.		Wide outer circle	*600.00*	
16	A6	1ab black	225.00	175.00
17	A6	1sa brown violet	22.50	22.50
a.		Wide outer circle	110.00	
18	A6	1ab brown violet	40.00	25.00

Ten varieties of the sanar, five of the abasi.

Nos. 15-16 and 17-18 were printed in the same sheets. Se-tenant pairs exist.

1876

Dated "1293"

19	A7	1sh black	300.00	150.00
20	A7	1sa black	375.00	200.00
21	A7	1ab black	600.00	325.00
22	A7	½rup black	375.00	200.00
23	A7	1rup black	550.00	200.00
24	A7	1sh violet	375.00	200.00
25	A7	1sa violet	350.00	200.00
26	A7	1ab violet	425.00	200.00
27	A7	½rup violet	90.00	55.00
28	A7	1rup violet	90.00	75.00

12 varieties of the shahi and 3 each of the other values.

A8

1876

Dated "1293"

29	A8	1sh gray	5.00	4.00
30	A8	1sa gray	7.50	4.00
31	A8	1ab gray	15.00	7.50
32	A8	½rup gray	17.50	10.00
33	A8	1rup gray	22.50	10.00
34	A8	1sh olive blk	125.00	
35	A8	1sa olive blk	175.00	
36	A8	1ab olive blk	350.00	
37	A8	½rup olive blk	250.00	
38	A8	1rup olive blk	275.00	
39	A8	1sh green	22.50	3.75
40	A8	1sa green	35.00	15.00
41	A8	1ab green	50.00	37.50
42	A8	½rup green	100.00	40.00
43	A8	1rup green	100.00	80.00
44	A8	1sh ocher	22.50	7.50
45	A8	1sa ocher	35.00	15.00
46	A8	1ab ocher	60.00	27.50
47	A8	½rup ocher	75.00	60.00
48	A8	1rup ocher	125.00	110.00
49	A8	1sh violet	22.50	5.50
50	A8	1sa violet	22.50	7.50
51	A8	1ab violet	35.00	10.00
52	A8	½rup violet	60.00	22.50
53	A8	1rup violet	75.00	35.00

12 varieties of the sanar, 6 of the abasi and 3 each of the ½ rupee and rupee.

24 varieties of the shahi, 4 of which show denomination written:

A9

1877

Dated "1294"

54	A9	1sh gray	3.50	2.25
55	A9	1sa gray	6.00	3.00
56	A9	1ab gray	9.00	6.00
57	A9	½rup gray	12.00	12.00
58	A9	1rup gray	12.00	12.00
59	A9	1sh black	10.00	
60	A9	1sa black	17.50	
61	A9	1ab black	42.50	
62	A9	½rup black	45.00	
63	A9	1rup black	45.00	
64	A9	1sh green	4.50	3.50
a.		Wove paper	12.00	
65	A9	1sa green	7.50	3.50
a.		Wove paper	16.00	12.00
66	A9	1ab green	10.00	10.00
a.		Wove paper	27.50	
67	A9	½rup green	14.00	14.00
a.		Wove paper	30.00	30.00
68	A9	1rup green	14.00	14.00
a.		Wove paper	30.00	30.00
69	A9	1sh ocher	3.50	2.00
70	A9	1sa ocher	10.00	3.50
71	A9	1ab ocher	17.50	16.00
72	A9	½rup ocher	30.00	30.00
73	A9	1rup ocher	30.00	30.00
74	A9	1sh violet	3.75	2.00
75	A9	1sa violet	7.50	2.75
76	A9	1ab violet	11.00	7.50
77	A9	½rup violet	17.50	14.00
78	A9	1rup violet	17.50	14.00

25 varieties of the shahi, 8 of the sanar, 3 of the abasi and 2 each of the ½rupee and rupee.

A10

A11

1878

Dated "1295"

79	A10	1sh gray	1.50	1.50
80	A10	1sa gray	1.75	1.75
81	A10	1ab gray	3.75	3.75
82	A10	½rup gray	10.00	7.50
83	A10	1rup gray	10.00	7.50
84	A10	1sh black	3.00	
85	A10	1sa black	3.00	
86	A10	1ab black	10.00	
87	A10	½rup black	20.00	
88	A10	1rup black	20.00	
89	A10	1sh green	21.00	20.00
90	A10	1sa green	3.00	3.00
91	A10	1ab green	11.00	10.00
92	A10	½rup green	21.00	17.50
93	A10	1rup green	21.00	17.50
94	A10	1sh ocher	10.00	3.00
95	A10	1sa ocher	3.00	2.25
96	A10	1ab ocher	11.00	10.00
97	A10	½rup ocher	21.00	21.00
98	A10	1rup ocher	16.00	16.00
99	A10	1sh violet	1.75	1.75
100	A10	1sa violet	1.75	1.75
101	A10	1ab violet	5.50	5.50
102	A10	½rup violet	21.00	17.50
103	A10	1rup violet	21.00	17.50
104	A11	1sh gray	2.00	1.75
105	A11	1sh black	*90.00*	
106	A11	1sh green	1.75	1.75
107	A11	1sh ocher	1.40	1.40
108	A11	1sh violet	2.00	1.75

40 varieties of the shahi, 30 of the sanar, 6 of the abasi and 2 each of the ½ rupee and 1 rupee.

The 1876, 1877 and 1878 issues were printed in separate colors for each main post office on the Peshawar-Kabul-Khulm (Tashkurghan) postal route. Some specialists consider the black printings to be proofs or trial colors.

There are many shades of these colors.

1ab, Type I (26mm) — A12

1ab, Type II (28mm) — A13

A14

A15

Dated "1298", numerals scattered through design

Handstamped, in watercolor

1881-90

Thin White Laid Batonne Paper

109	A12	1ab violet	1.75	1.10
109A	A13	1ab violet	3.50	2.50
110	A12	1ab black brn	3.50	1.75
111	A12	1ab rose	2.00	2.00
b.		Se-tenant with No. 111A	16.00	
111A	A13	1ab rose	2.50	2.00
112	A14	2ab violet	1.75	1.50
113	A14	2ab black brn	5.00	4.00
114	A14	2ab rose	3.00	3.00
115	A15	1rup violet	2.50	1.50
116	A15	1rup black-brn	6.50	6.50
117	A15	1rup rose	3.00	3.00

Thin White Wove Batonne Paper

118	A12	1ab violet	6.50	4.00
119	A12	1ab vermilion	4.25	
120	A12	1ab rose		
121	A14	2ab violet		
122	A14	2ab vermilion	5.00	
122A	A14	2ab black brn		
123	A15	1rup violet	8.25	
124	A15	1rup vermilion	6.50	
125	A15	1rup black brn	8.25	

Thin White Laid Batonne Paper

126	A12	1ab brown org	2.50	2.50
126A	A13	1ab brn org (II)	3.50	3.50
127	A12	1ab carmine lake	2.50	2.50
a.		Laid paper		
128	A14	2ab brown org	2.50	2.50
129	A14	2ab carmine lake	3.00	3.00
130	A15	1rup brown org	10.00	10.00
131	A15	1rup car lake	4.25	4.25

Yellowish Laid Batonne Paper

132	A12	1ab purple		3.50
133	A12	1ab red	6.50	3.50

1884

Colored Wove Paper

133A	A13	1ab purple, *yel* (II)	17.50	17.50
134	A12	1ab purple, *grn*	20.00	
135	A12	1ab purple, *blue*	32.50	21.00
136	A12	1ab red, *grn*	37.50	
137	A12	1ab red, *yel*	1.75	
139	A12	1ab red, *rose*	6.00	
140	A14	2ab red, *yel*	6.00	
142	A14	2ab red, *rose*	5.50	
143	A15	1rup red, *yel*	6.50	6.50
145	A15	1rup red, *rose*	7.00	7.00

Thin Colored Ribbed Paper

146	A14	2ab red, *yellow*	3.00	
147	A15	1rup red, *yellow*	8.25	
148	A12	1ab lake, *lilac*	4.00	
149	A14	2ab lake, *lilac*	5.00	
150	A15	1rup lake, *lilac*	4.00	
151	A12	1ab lake, *green*	2.00	
152	A14	2ab lake, *green*	4.00	
153	A15	1rup lake, *green*	4.00	

1886-88

Colored Wove Paper

155	A12	1ab black, *magenta*	27.50	
156	A12	1ab claret brn, *org*	20.00	
156A	A12	1ab red, *org*	2.00	
156B	A14	2ab red, *org*	4.75	
156C	A15	1rup red, *org*	3.50	

Laid Batonné Paper

157	A12	1ab black, *lavender*	2.75	
158	A12	1ab cl brn, *grn*	6.50	
159	A12	1ab black, *pink*	17.50	
160	A14	2ab black, *pink*	35.00	
161	A15	1rup black, *pink*	20.00	

Laid Paper

162	A12	1ab black, *pink*	6.50	
163	A14	2ab black, *pink*	6.50	
164	A15	1rup black, *pink*	6.50	
165	A12	1ab brown, *yel*	6.50	
166	A14	2ab brown, *yel*	6.50	
167	A15	1rup brown, *yel*	6.50	
168	A12	1ab blue, *grn*	6.50	
169	A14	2ab blue, *grn*	6.50	
170	A15	1rup blue, *grn*	6.50	

1891

Colored Wove Paper

175	A12	1ab green, *rose*	22.50	
176	A15	1rup pur, *grn batonne*	22.50	

Nos. 109-176 fall into three categories:

1. Those regularly issued and in normal postal use from 1881 on, handstamped on thin white laid or wove paper in strip sheets containing 12 or more impressions of the same denomination arranged in two irregular rows, with the impressions often touching or overlappng.

2. The 1884 postal issues provisionally printed on smooth or ribbed colored wove paper as needed to supplement low stocks of the normal white paper stamps.

3. The "special" printings made in a range of colors on several types of laid or wove colored papers, most of which were never used for normal printings. These were produced periodically from 1886 to 1891 to meet philatelic demands. Although nominally valid for postage, most of the special printings were exported directly to fill dealers' orders, and few were ever postally used. Many of the sheets contained all three denominations with impressions separated by ruled lines. Sometimes different colors were used, so se-tenant multiples of denomination or color exist. Many combinations of stamp and paper colors exist besides those listed.

Various shades of each color exist.

Type A12 is known dated "1297."

Counterfeits, lithographed or typographed, are plentiful.

Kingdom of Afghanistan

A16

A17

A18

Dated "1309"

1891 Pelure Paper Litho.

177	A16	1ab slate blue	85	85
a.		Tete beche pair	14.00	
178	A17	2ab slate blue	6.00	5.00
179	A18	1rup slate blue	12.25	10.00
		Nos. 177-179 (3)	19.10	15.85

Revenue stamps of similar design exist in various colors.

Nos. 177-179 were printed in panes on the same sheet, so se-tenant gutter pairs exist. Examples in black or red are proofs.

A Mosque Gate and Crossed Cannons (National Seal) — A19

Dated "1310" in Upper Right Corner

1892

Flimsy Wove Paper

180	A19	1ab black, *green*	2.00	1.60
181	A19	1ab black, *orange*	2.50	2.50
182	A19	1ab black, *yellow*	2.00	1.60
183	A19	1ab black, *pink*	2.50	1.60
184	A19	1ab black, *lil rose*	2.50	2.50
185	A19	1ab black, *blue*	4.25	3.50
186	A19	1ab black, *salmon*	2.50	2.00
187	A19	1ab black, *magenta*	2.50	2.50
188	A19	1ab black, *violet*	2.50	2.50
188A	A19	1ab black, *scarlet*	2.50	1.75

Many shades exist.

A20

A21

Undated

1894

Flimsy Wove Paper

189	A20	2ab black, *green*	6.50	6.50
190	A21	1rup black, *green*	10.00	10.00

24 varieties of the 2 abasi and 12 varieties of the rupee.

Nos. 189-190 and F3 were printed se-tenant in the same sheet. Pairs exist.

A21a

Dated "1316"

1898

Flimsy Wove Paper

191	A21a	2ab black, *pink*	2.50	
192	A21a	2ab black, *magenta*	2.50	
193	A21a	2ab black, *yellow*	1.10	
193A	A21a	2ab black, *salmon*	3.00	
194	A21a	2ab black, *green*	1.40	
195	A21a	2ab black, *purple*	1.75	
195A	A21a	2ab black, *blue*	17.50	
		Nos. 191-195A (7)	29.75	

Nos. 191-195A were not regularly issued. Genuinely used copies are scarce. No. 195A was found in remainder stocks and probably was never released.

A22

A23

A24

1907 Engr. *Imperf.*

Medium Wove Paper

196	A22	1ab blue green	3.75	2.50
a.		1ab emerald	8.50	5.00
197	A22	1ab brt blue	10.00	10.00
198	A23	2ab deep blue	1.85	1.25
199	A24	1rup green	3.00	2.50
a.		1rup blue green	6.00	6.00

Zigzag Roulette 10

200	A22	1ab green	60.00	
201	A23	2ab blue	80.00	
201A	A24	1rup blue green	*110.00*	

1908 *Perf. 12*

202	A22	1ab green	10.00	6.25
203	A23	2ab deep blue	1.25	1.25
204	A24	1rup blue green	3.00	3.00
		Nos. 202-204 (3)	14.25	10.50

Twelve varieties of the 1 abasi, 6 of the 2 abasi, 4 of the 1 rupee.

Nos. 196-204 were issued in small sheets containing 3 or 4 panes. Gutter pairs, normal and tête bêche, exist.

A25

A26

A27

1909-19 Typo. *Perf. 12*

205	A25	1ab ultra	35	22
a.		Imperf., pair	5.00	
206	A25	1ab red ('16)	22	15
a.		Imperf.		
207	A25	1ab rose ('18)	22	15
208	A26	2ab green	50	25
a.		Imperf., pair	3.00	
b.		Horiz. pair, imperf. btwn.		
208C	A26	2ab yellow ('16)	1.25	1.25
209	A26	2ab bis ('18-'19)	90	90
210	A27	1rup lilac brn	1.50	1.50
a.		1rup red brown	2.50	2.00
211	A27	1rup ol bis ('16)	1.50	1.50
		Nos. 205-211 (8)	6.44	5.92

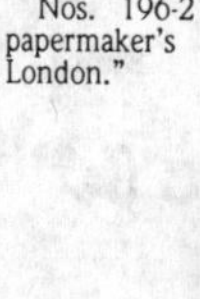

A28

1913

212	A28	2pa drab brown	1.25	1.25
a.		2pa red brown	1.25	1.25

No. 212 is inscribed "Tiket waraq dak" (Postal card stamps). It was usable only on postcards and not accepted for postage on letters.

Nos. 196-212 sometimes show letters of a papermaker's watermark, "Howard & Jones, London."

Royal Star — A29

1920, Aug. 24 *Perf. 12*

Size: 39x47mm

214 A29 10pa rose 20.00 12.00
215 A29 20pa red brown 45.00 18.00
216 A29 30pa green 90.00 60.00
Nos. 214-216 (3) 155.00 90.00

Issued in sheets of two.

1921, Mar.

Size: 22½x28¼mm

217 A29 10pa rose 35 16
a. Perf. 11 ('27) 65 1.00
218 A29 20pa red brown 1.00 50
219 A29 30pa yel green 1.00 50
a. Tete beche pair 6.00 5.50
b. 30pa green 1.50 75
c. As "b," Tete beche pair 6.50 6.50
Nos. 217-219 (3) 2.35 1.16

Two types of the 10pa, three of the 20pa.

Crest of King Amanullah — A32
A30 A32

1924, Feb. 26 *Perf. 12*

220 A30 10pa chocolate 10.00 6.00
a. Tete beche pair 20.00 16.00

6th Independence Day.

Printed in sheets of four consisting of two tete beche pairs, and in sheets of two. Two types exist.

Some authorities believe that Nos. Q15-Q16 were issued as regular postage stamps.

1925, Feb. 26 *Perf. 12*

Size: 29x37mm

222 A32 10pa light brown 10.00 6.00

7th Independence Day.

Printed in sheets of 8 (two panes of 4).

1926, Feb. 28

Wove Paper

Size: 26x33mm

224 A32 10pa dark blue 1.40 1.40
a. Imperf., pair 6.00
b. Horiz. pair, imperf. btwn. 8.00
c. Vert. pair, imperf. btwn. 8.00
d. Laid paper 6.50 5.00

7th anniv. of Independence. Printed in sheets of 4, and in sheets of 8 (two panes of 4). Tete beche gutter pairs exist.

Tughra and Crest of Amanullah — A33

1927, Feb.

225 A33 10pa magenta 10.00 4.25
a. Vertical pair, imperf. between 20.00

Dotted Background

226 A33 10pa magenta 5.50 4.25
a. Horiz. pair, imperf. between 15.00

The surface of No. 226 is covered by a net of fine dots.

8th anniv. of Independence. Printed in sheets of 8 (two panes of 4). Tete beche gutter pairs exist.

National Seal — A34

A35

A35a

A36

1927, Oct. *Imperf.*

227 A34 15p pink 35 35
228 A35 30p Prus green 80 40
229 A36 60p light blue 1.50 1.50
a. Tete beche pair 4.50
Nos. 227-229 (3) 2.65 2.25

1927-30 *Perf. 11, 12*

230 A34 15p pink 22 16
231 A34 15p ultra ('29) 50 30
232 A35 30p Prus green 35 35
233 A35a 30p dp green ('30) 75 70
234 A36 60p bright blue 1.50 1.00
a. Tete beche pair 5.00
235 A36 60p black ('29) 1.40 65
Nos. 230-235 (6) 4.72 3.16

Nos. 230, 232 and 234 are usually imperforate on one or two sides.

No. 233 has been redrawn. A narrow border of pearls has been added and "30", in European and Arabic numerals, inserted in the upper spandrels.

Tughra and Crest of Amanullah A37

1928, Feb. 27

236 A37 15p pink 2.00 2.00
a. Tete beche pair 7.50
b. Horiz. pair, imperf. vert. 6.00
c. As "a," imperf. vert., block of 4 10.00

9th anniv. of Independence. This stamp is always imperforate on one or two sides.

A 15p blue of somewhat similar design was prepared for the 10th anniv., but was not issued due to Amanullah's dethronement. Value, $15.

A38

A39

A40

A41

A42

1928-30 *Perf. 11, 12*

237 A38 2p dull blue 2.50 1.60
a. Vertical pair, imperf. between
238 A38 2p lt rose ('30) 25 25
239 A39 10p gray green 25 15
a. Tete beche pair 5.00 5.00
b. Vert. pair, imperf. horiz. 65
c. Vertical pair, imperf. between 1.00
240 10p choc ('30) 50 50
a. 10p brown purple ('29) 10.00 2.50
241 A40 25p car rose 35 25
242 A40 25p Prus green ('29) 75 60
243 A41 40p ultra 40 35
a. Tete beche pair 5.00
244 A41 40p rose ('29) 1.00 1.00
a. Tete beche pair 7.00
b. Vert. pair, imperf. horiz. 3.50
245 A42 50p red 30 30
246 A42 50p dk blue ('29) 1.50 1.00
Nos. 237-246 (10) 7.80 6.00

The sheets of these stamps are often imperforate at the outer margins.

Nos. 237-238 are newspaper stamps.

This handstamp was used for ten months by the Revolutionary Gov't in Kabul as a control mark on outgoing mail. It occasionally fell on the stamps but there is no evidence that it was officially used as an overprint. Unused copies were privately made.

Independence Monument — A46

Wmk. Large Seal in the Sheet

1931, Aug. **Litho.** *Perf. 12*

Laid Paper

Without Gum

262 A46 20p red 1.00 60

13th Independence Day.

National Assembly Chamber — A47

A48

A50

National Assembly Building A49

National Assembly Chamber A51

National Assembly Building — A52

1932 **Unwmk.** **Typo.** *Perf. 12*

Wove Paper

263 A47 40p olive 1.00 40
264 A48 60p violet 65 50
265 A49 80p dark red 1.00 80
266 A50 1af black 10.00 4.25
267 A51 2af ultra 3.50 2.75
268 A52 3af gray green 4.25 3.50
Nos. 263-268 (6) 20.40 12.20

Formation of the Natl. Council. Imperforate or perforated examples on ungummed chalky paper are proofs.

See Nos. 304-305.

Mosque at Balkh — A53

Kabul Fortress — A54

Parliament House, Darul Funun — A55

Parliament House, Darul Funun — A56

Arch of Qalai Bist — A57

Memorial Pillar of Knowledge and Ignorance — A58

Independence Monument — A59

Minaret at Herat — A60

Arch of Paghman — A61

Ruins at Balkh — A62

Minarets of Herat — A63

Great Buddha at Bamian — A64

1932 **Typo.** *Perf. 12*

269 A53 10p brown 50 15
270 A54 15p dk brown 60 15
271 A55 20p red 28 16
272 A56 25p dk green 75 15
273 A57 30p red 40 28

274 A58 40p orange 65 35
275 A59 50p blue 80 35
a. Tete beche pair 5.50
276 A60 60p blue 1.50 50
277 A61 80p violet 1.75 1.00
278 A62 1af dark blue 2.75 60
279 A63 2af dk red violet 3.75 2.00
280 A64 3af claret 4.25 2.50
Nos. 269-280 (12) 17.98 8.19

Counterfeits of types A53-A65 exist.
See Nos. 290-295, 298-299, 302-303.

Entwined 2's — A65

Two types:
Type I - Numerals shaded. Size about 21x29mm.
Type II - Numerals unshaded. Size about 21¾x30mm.

1931-38 *Perf. 12, 11x12*
281 A65 2p red brn (I) 25 15
282 A65 2p olive blk (I) ('34) 25 15
283 A65 2p grnsh gray (I) ('34) 35 15
283A A65 2p black (II) ('36) 35 15
284 A65 2p salmon (II) ('38) 25 15
284A A65 2p rose (I) ('38) 25 15
b. Imperf., pair 3.00

Imperf
285 A65 2p black (II) ('37) 75 15
286 A65 2p salmon (II) ('38) 25 15
Nos. 281-286 (8) 2.70
Set value 70

The newspaper rate was 2 pouls.

Independence Monument — A66

1932, Aug. *Perf. 12*
287 A66 1af deep rose 2.75 1.50

14th Independence Day.

1929 Liberation Monument, Kabul — A67

1932, Oct. **Typo.**
288 A67 80p red brown 85 50

Arch of Paghman A68

1933, Aug.
289 A68 50p light ultra 1.25 1.25

15th Independence Day.

Types of 1932 and

Royal Palace, Kabul — A69

Darrah- Shikari Pass, Hindu Kush — A70

1934-38 **Typo.** *Perf. 12*
290 A53 10p deep violet 16 15
291 A54 15p turq green 20 15
292 A55 20p magenta 22 15
293 A56 25p deep rose 28 16
294 A57 30p orange 40 20
295 A58 40p blue black 75 28
296 A69 45p dark blue 1.50 1.00
297 A69 45p red ('38) 50 16
298 A59 50p orange 28 16
299 A60 60p purple 85 16
300 A70 75p red 1.00 35
301 A70 75p dk blue ('38) 60 40
302 A61 80p brown vio 1.00 50
303 A62 1af red violet 1.65 1.00
304 A51 2af gray black 3.00 2.00
305 A52 3af ultra 5.00 3.00
Nos. 290-305 (16) 17.39 9.82

Nos. 290, 292, 300, 304, 305 exist imperf.

Independence Monument — A71

1934, Aug. **Litho.**
Without Gum
306 A71 50p pale green 2.50 1.25
a. Tete beche pair 10.00 3.50

16th year of Independence. Each sheet of 40 (4x10) included 4 tete beche pairs as lower half of sheet was inverted.

Independence Monument A74

Fireworks Display A75

1935, Aug. 15
Laid Paper
309 A74 50p dark blue 1.25 1.25

17th year of Independence.

1936, Aug. 15 *Perf. 12*
Wove Paper
310 A75 50p red violet 1.25 1.00

18th year of Independence.

Independence Monument and Nadir Shah — A76

1937
311 A76 50p vio & bis brn 1.00 60
a. Imperf., pair 2.25

19th year of Independence.

Mohammed Nadir Shah
A77 A78

1938 *Perf. 11x12*
Without Gum
315 A77 50p brt blue & sepia 5.00 2.50
a. Imperf. pair 20.00

20th year of Independence.

1939 *Perf. 11, 12x11*
317 A78 50p deep salmon 1.75 1.00

21st year of Independence.

National Arms A79

Parliament House, Darul Funun A80

Royal Palace, Kabul A81

Independence Monument A82

Independence Monument and Nadir Shah — A83

Mohammed Zahir Shah — A84

Mohammed Zahir Shah — A85

Perf. 11, 11x12, 12x11, 12
1939-61 **Typo.**
318 A79 2p intense blk 15 15
318A A79 2p brt pink ('61) 1.50 50
319 A80 10p brt purple 15 15
320 A80 15p brt green 15 15
321 A80 20p red lilac 15 15
322 A81 25p rose red 1.00 25
322A A81 25p green ('41) 50 15
323 A81 30p orange 20 15
324 A81 40p dk gray 20 15
325 A82 45p brt carmine 20 15
326 A82 50p dp orange 30 20
327 A82 60p violet 60 20
328 A83 75p ultra 3.00 75
328A A83 75p red vio ('41) 75 30
328C A83 75p brt red ('44) 3.00 3.00
328D A83 75p chnt brn ('49) 4.00 3.00
329 A83 80p chocolate 50 50
a. 80p dull red violet (error)
330 A84 1af brt red violet 1.50 75
330A A85 1af brt red vio ('44) 3.00 1.50
331 A85 2af copper red 1.75 50
a. 2af dp rose red 2.50 1.35
332 A84 3af deep blue 3.75 1.60
Nos. 318-332 (21) 26.35 14.25

Many shades exist in this issue.
On No. 332 the King faces slightly left.

No. 318A issued with and without gum.
See #795A-795B. For similar design see #907A.

Mohammed Nadir Shah — A86

1940, Aug. 23 *Perf. 11*
333 A86 50p gray green 75 60

22nd year of Independence.

Independence Monument A87

Arch of Paghman A88

1941, Aug. 23 *Perf. 12*
334 A87 15p gray green 8.00 2.75
335 A88 50p red brown 1.25 85

23rd year of Independence.

Sugar Factory, Baghlan — A89

1942, Apr. *Perf. 12*
336 A89 1.25af blue (shades) 2.00 1.00
a. 1.25af ultra 75 50

In 1949, a 1.50af brown, type A89, was sold for 3af by the Philatelic Office, Kabul. It was not valid for postage. Value $3.50.

Independence Monument A90

Mohammed Nadir Shah and Arch of Paghman A91

1942, Aug. 23 *Perf. 12*
337 A90 35p bright green 2.75 2.00
338 A91 125p chalky blue 1.40 1.10

24th year of Independence.

Independence Monument and Nadir Shah — A92

Mohammed Nadir Shah — A93

Perf. 11x12, 12x11
1943, Aug. 25 **Typo.** **Unwmk.**
339 A92 35p carmine 18.00 6.00
340 A93 1.25af dark blue 3.00 1.75

25th year of Independence.

Tomb of Gohar Shad, Herat — A94

Ruins of Qalai Bist — A95

1944, May 1 *Perf. 12, 11x12*

341 A94	35p orange		50	32
342 A95	70p violet		1.00	60
a.	70p rose lilac		3.50	75

A96

A97

1944, Aug. *Perf. 12*

343 A96	35p crimson	80	60
344 A97	1.25af ultra	1.40	1.10

26th year of Independence.

A98

A99

1945, July

345 A98	35p dp red lil	75	65
346 A99	1.25af blue	1.75	1.50

27th year of Independence.

Mohammed Zahir Shah A100

Independence Monument A101

Mohammed Nadir Shah — A102

1946, July

347 A100	15p emerald	45	35
348 A101	20p dp red lilac	70	55
349 A102	125p blue	1.75	1.75
	Nos. 347-349 (3)	2.90	2.65

28th year of Independence.

Zahir Shah and Ruins of Qalai Bist — A103

A104

A105

1947, Aug.

350 A103	15p yellow green	30	15
351 A104	35p plum	38	22
352 A105	125p deep blue	1.40	1.40
	Nos. 350-352 (3)	2.08	1.77

29th year of Independence.

Begging Child — A106

A107

1948, May Unwmk. Typo. *Perf. 12*

353 A106	35p yel green	3.00	2.00
354 A107	125p gray blue	3.00	2.25

Children's Day, May 29, 1948, and valid only on that day. Proceeds were used for Child Welfare.

A108

A109

A110

1948, Aug.

355 A108	15p green	22	15
356 A109	20p magenta	38	18
357 A110	125p dark blue	75	70
	Nos. 355-357 (3)	1.35	1.03

30th year of Independence.

United Nations Emblem A111

1948, Oct. 24

358 A111	125p dk vio bl	6.00	6.00

3rd anniv. of the UN. Valid one day only. Sheets of 9.

Maiwand Victory Column, Kandahar — A112

Zahir Shah and Ruins of Qalai Bist — A113

Independence Monument and Nadir Shah — A114

1949, Aug. Typo. *Perf. 12*

359 A112	25p green	25	16
360 A113	35p magenta	35	25
361 A114	1.25af blue	90	75
	Nos. 359-361 (3)	1.50	1.16

31st year of Independence.

Catalogue values for unused stamps in this section, from this point to the end of the section, are for Never Hinged items.

Nadir Shah — A117

1950, Aug.

364 A117	35p red brown	28	28
365 A117	125p blue	65	65

32nd year of Independence.

Medical School and Nadir Shah A119

1950, Dec. 22 Typo. *Perf. 12*

Size: 38x25mm

367 A119	35p emerald	60	60

Size: 46x30mm

368 A119	1.25af deep blue	1.90	1.90
a.	1.25af black (error)	6.00	

19th anniv. of the founding of Afghanistan's Faculty of Medicine. On sale and valid for use on Dec. 22-28, 1950.

Minaret, Herat — A120

Zahir Shah — A121

Mosque of Khodja Abu Parsar, Balkh — A122

A123

A124

Designs: 20p, Buddha at Bamian. 40p, Ruined arch. 45p, Maiwand Victory Monument. 50p, View of Kandahar. 60p, Ancient tower. 70p, Afghanistan flag. 80p, 1af, Profile of Zahir Shah in uniform.

Photogravure, Engraved, Engraved and Lithographed

Perf. 12, 12½, 13x12½, 13½

1951, Mar. 21 Unwmk.

Imprint: "Waterlow & Sons Limited, London"

369 A120	10p	yel & brn	15	15
370 A120	15p	bl & brn	15	15
371 A120	20p	black	5.00	2.75
372 A121	25p	green	15	15
373 A122	30p	cerise	18	15
374 A121	35p	violet	18	15
375 A122	40p	chnt brn	22	15
376 A120	45p	dp bl	18	15
377 A122	50p	ol blk	45	15
378 A120	60p	black	1.50	75
379 A122	70p	dk grn, blk, red & grn	25	15
380 A123	75p	cerise	75	35
381 A123	80p	car & blk	65	38
382 A123	1af	dp grn & vio	45	38
383 A124	1.25af	rose lil & blk	*5.00*	38
384 A124	2af	ultra	1.10	38
385 A124	3af	ultra & blk	2.50	90
		Nos. 369-385 (17)	18.86	7.62

Nos. 372, 374 and 381 to 385 are engraved, No. 379 is engraved and lithographed.

Imperfs. exist of the photogravure stamps.

See Nos. 445-451, 453, 552A-552D. For surcharges, see Nos. B1-B2.

Arch of Paghman — A125

Nadir Shah and Independence Monument A126

Overprint in Violet

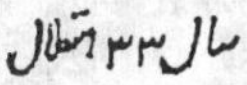

Perf. 13½x13, 13

1951, Aug. 25 Engr.

386 A125	35p dk grn & blk	60	35
387 A126	1.25af deep blue	1.40	85

Overprint reads "Sol 33 Istiqlal" or "33rd Year of Independence." Overprint measures about 11mm wide.

See Nos. 398-399B, 441-442.

Proposed Flag of Pashtunistan — A127

Design: 125p, Flag and Pashtunistan warrior.

1951, Sept. 2 Litho. *Perf. 11½*

388 A127	35p dl choc	80	65
389 A127	125p blue	2.00	1.75

Issued to publicize "Free Pashtunistan" Day.

Imperforates

From 1951 to 1958, quantities of nearly all locally-printed stamps were left imperforate and sold by the government at double face. From 1959 until March, 1964, many of the imperforates were sold for more than face value.

Avicenna — A128

1951, Nov. 4 Typo. *Perf. 11½*

390 A128 35p dp claret 50 35
391 A128 125p blue 1.40 1.10

20th anniv. of the founding of the natl. Graduate School of Medicine.

A129

Dove and UN Symbols — A130

1951, Oct. 24

392 A129 35p magenta 1.40 1.00
393 A130 125p blue 3.50 2.75

7th anniv. of the UN.

Amir Sher Ali Khan and Tiger Head Stamp — A131

Design: Nos. 395 and 397, Zahir Shah and stamp.

1951, Dec. 23 Litho.

394 A131 35p chocolate 35 35
395 A131 35p rose lil 35 35
396 A131 125p ultra 65 60
a. Cliche of 35p in plate of 125p 80.00 80.00
397 A131 125p aqua 65 60
Nos. 394-397 (4) 2.00 1.90

76th anniv. of the UPU.

Stamps of 1951 Without Overprint

Perf. 13½x13, 13

1952, Aug. 24 Engr.

398 A125 35p dk grn & blk 1.25 1.25
399 A126 1.25af deep blue 1.25 1.25

For overprints see #399A-399B, 441-442.

Same Overprinted in Violet

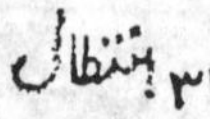

399A A125 35p dk grn & blk 60 40
399B A126 1.25af deep blue 1.60 1.00

#398-399B issued for 34th Independence Day.

Globe — A132

Perf. 11½

1952, Oct. 25 Unwmk. Litho.

400 A132 35p rose 55 45
401 A132 125p aqua 1.10 1.00

Issued to honor the United Nations.

Symbol of Medicine — A134

Tribal Warrior, Natl. Flag — A135

1952, Nov. *Perf. 11½*

403 A134 35p chocolate 40 35
404 A134 125p vio bl 1.10 1.10

21st anniv. of the natl. Graduate School of Medicine.

No. 404 is inscribed in French with white letters on a colored background.

1952, Sept. 1 *Perf. 11*

405 A135 35p red 28 28
406 A135 125p dark blue 60 60

No. 406 is inscribed in French "Pashtunistan Day, 1952."

Flags of Afghanistan & Pashtunistan A139

Badge of Pashtunistan A140

Perf. 10½x11, 11

1953, Sept. 1 Unwmk.

411 A139 35p vermilion 20 16
412 A140 125p blue 60 42

Issued to publicize "Free Pashtunistan" Day.

Nadir Shah and Flag Bearer — A141

A142

1953, Aug. 24 *Perf. 11*

413 A141 35p green 18 15
414 A142 125p violet 75 60

35th anniv. of Independence.

United Nations Emblem — A143

1953, Oct. 24

415 A143 35p lilac 60 60
416 A143 125p vio blue 1.50 1.20

United Nations Day, 1953.

Nadir Shah

A144 A145

1953, Nov. 29

417 A144 35p orange 65 65
418 A145 125p chalky blue 1.50 1.50

22nd anniv. of the founding of the natl. Graduate School of Medicine.

Redrawn

35p. Original- Right character in second line of Persian inscription: ۳

Redrawn- Persian character: ۲

125p: Original- Inscribed "XXIII," "MADECINE" and "ANNIVERAIRE"
Redrawn- Inscribed "XXII," "MEDECINE" and "ANNIVERSAIRE"

1953

419 A144 35p dp orange 3.50
420 A145 125p chalky bl 4.25

Nadir Shah and Symbols of Independence A146

1954, Aug. Typo. *Perf. 11*

421 A146 35p car rose 35 28
422 A146 125p vio bl 1.00 80

36th year of Independence.

Raising Flag of Pashtunistan A147

1954, Sept. *Perf. 11½*

423 A147 35p chocolate 35 28
424 A147 125p blue 1.00 80

Issued to publicize "Free Pashtunistan" Day.

UN Flag and Map — A148

1954, Oct. 24 *Perf. 11*

425 A148 35p car rose 65 65
426 A148 125p dk vio bl 2.00 2.00

9th anniv. of the United Nations.

UN Symbols — A149

Design: 125p, UN emblem & flags.

1955, June 26 Litho. *Perf. 11*

Size: 26½x36mm

427 A149 35p dark green 45 38

Size: 28½x36mm

428 A149 125p aqua 1.10 90

10th anniv. of the UN charter.

Nadir Shah (center) and Brothers — A150

1929 Civil War Scene and Zahir Shah — A151

Tribal Elders' Council and Pashtun Flag — A152

1955, Aug. Unwmk. *Perf. 11*

429 A150 35p brt pink 30 30
430 A150 35p vio blue 30 30
431 A151 125p rose lilac 90 75
432 A151 125p light vio 90 75
Nos. 429-432 (4) 2.40 2.10

37th anniv. of Independence.

1955, Sept. 5

433 A152 35p org brn 22 22
434 A152 125p yel grn 90 65

Issued for "Free Pashtunistan" Day.

UN Flag — A153

A154

1955, Oct. 24 Unwmk. *Perf. 11*

435 A153 35p org brn 75 60
436 A153 125p brt ultra 1.40 1.10

10th anniv. of the United Nations.

1956, Aug. Litho.

437 A154 35p lt grn 25 20
438 A154 140p lt vio bl 90 75

38th year of Independence.

Jesh'n Exhibition Hall — A155

1956, Aug. 25

439 A155 50p chocolate 25 18
440 A155 50p lt vio bl 25 18

International Exposition at Kabul.
Of the 50p face value, only 35p paid postage. The remaining 15p went to the Exposition.

Nos. 398-399 Handstamped in Violet

a

39 em Anv
b

1957, Aug. Engr. *Perf. 13½x13, 13*

441 A125 (a) 35p dk grn & blk 40 20
442 A126 (b) 1.25af deep blue 60 50

Arabic overprint measures 19mm.
39th year of independence.

Pashtunistan Flag — A156

1957, Sept. 1 Litho. *Perf. 11*

443 A156	50p	pale lil rose	60	38
444 A156	155p	lt vio	90	75

Issued for "Free Pashtunistan" Day. French inscription on No. 444. 15p of each stamp went to the Pashtunistan Fund.

Types of 1951 and

Game of Buzkashi A157

Perf. 12, 12½, 12½x13, 13, 13x12, 13x12½, 13½x14

Photo., Engr., Engr.& Litho.

1957, Nov. 23 Unwmk.

Imprint: "Waterlow & Sons Limited, London"

445 A122	30p	brown	15	15
446 A122	40p	rose red	22	15
447 A122	50p	yellow	32	15
448 A120	60p	ultra	40	15
449 A123	75p	brt vio	50	15
450 A123	80p	vio & brn	50	15
451 A123	1af	car & ultra	1.00	15
452 A157	140p	ol & dp cl	2.00	50
453 A124	3af	org & blk	2.50	50
		Nos. 445-453 (9)	7.59	2.05

No. 452 lacks imprint.

Nadir Shah and Flag-bearer A158

1958, Aug. 25 *Perf. 13½x14*

454 A158	35p	dp yel grn	16	15
455 A158	140p	brown	40	35

40th year of Independence.

Exposition Buildings — A159

1958, Aug. 23 Litho. *Perf. 11*

456 A159	35p	brt bl grn	16	15
457 A159	140p	vermilion	50	40

International Exposition at Kabul.

Pres. Celal Bayar of Turkey A160

Flags of UN and Afghanistan A161

1958, Sept. 13 Unwmk.

458 A160	50p	lt bl	20	15
459 A160	100p	brown	35	28

Visit of President Celal Bayar of Turkey.

1958, Oct. 24 Photo. *Perf. 14x13½*

Flags in Original Colors

460 A161	50p	dark gray	60	60
461 A161	100p	green	1.10	90

United Nations Day, Oct. 24.

Atomic Energy Encircling the Hemispheres A162

1958, Oct. 20 *Perf. 13½x14*

462 A162	50p	blue	35	35
463 A162	100p	dp red lil	55	55

Issued to promote Atoms for Peace.

UNESCO Building, Paris — A163

1958, Nov. 3

464 A163	50p	dp yel grn	50	40
465 A163	100p	brn olive	75	60

Opening of UNESCO Headquarters in Paris, Nov. 3.

Globe and Torch — A164

Perf. 13½x14

1958, Dec. 10 Unwmk.

466 A164	50p	lilac rose	35	35
467 A164	100p	maroon	65	65

10th anniv. of the signing of the Universal Declaration of Human Rights.

Nadir Shah and Flags — A165

1959, Aug. Litho. *Perf. 11 Rough*

468 A165	35p	lt ver	20	20
469 A165	165p	lt vio	65	40

41st year of Independence.

Uprooted Oak Emblem — A166

1960, Apr. 7 *Perf. 11*

470 A166	50p	dp org	15	15
471 A166	165p	blue	35	28

Issued to publicize World Refugee Year, July 1, 1959-June 30, 1960.

Two imperf. souvenir sheets exist. Both contain a 50p and a 165p, type A166, with marginal inscriptions and WRY emblem in maroon. On one sheet the stamps are in the colors of Nos. 470-471 (size 108x81mm). On the other, the 50p is blue and the 165p is deep orange (size 107x80mm). Value $4 each.

For surcharges, see Nos. B35-B36.

Buzkashi A167

1960, May 4 *Perf. 11, Imperf.*

472 A167	25p	rose red	22	15
473 A167	50p	bluish green	50	35
a.		Cliche of 25p in plate of 50p	20.00	20.00

See Nos. 549-550A.

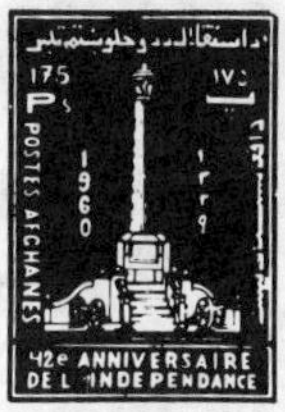

Independence Monument — A168

1960, Aug. *Perf. 11, 12*

474 A168	50p	light blue	15	15
475 A168	175p	bright pink	38	38

42nd Independence Day.

Globe and Flags — A169

1960, Oct. 24 Litho. *Perf. 11, 12*

476 A169	50p	rose lil	22	18
477 A169	175p	ultra	75	65

UN Day.

An imperf. souvenir sheet contains one each of Nos. 476-477 with marginal inscriptions ("La Journée des Nations Unies 1960" in French and Persian) and UN emblem in light blue. Size: 127x85½mm. Value $4.

This sheet was surcharged "+20ps" in 1962. Value $8.50.

Teacher Pointing to Globe — A170

1960, Oct. 23 *Perf. 11*

478 A170	50p	brt pink	18	15
479 A170	100p	brt grn	70	45

Issued to publicize Teacher's Day.

Mohammed Zahir Shah — A171

1960, Oct. 15

480 A171	50p	red brn	30	15
481 A171	150p	dk car rose	90	30

Honoring the King on his 46th birthday.

Buzkashi A172

1960, Nov. 9 *Perf. 11*

482 A172	175p	lt red brn	1.00	40

See Nos. 551-552.

No. 482 Overprinted "1960" and Olympic Rings in Bright Green.

1960, Dec. 24

483 A172	175p	red brn	2.00	1.75
a.		Souv. sheet of 1, imperf.	7.00	

17th Olympic Games, Rome, Aug. 25-Sept. 11.

Mir Wais — A173

1961, Jan. 5 Unwmk. *Perf. 10½*

484 A173	50p	brt rose lil	22	15
485 A173	175p	ultra	60	38
a.		Souv. sheet of 2, #484-485, imperf.	2.00	2.00

Mir Wais (1665-1708), national leader.

No Postal Need

existed for the 1p-15p denominations issued with sets of 1961-63 (between Nos. 486 and 649, B37 and B65).

The lowest denomination actually used for non-philatelic postage in that period was 25p (except for the 2p newspaper rate for which separate stamps were provided).

Horse, Sheep and Camel — A174

Designs: No. 487, 175p, Rock partridge. 10p, 100p, Afghan hound. 15p, 150p, Grain and grasshopper, vert.

1961, Mar. 29 Photo. *Perf. 13½x14*

486 A174	2p	maroon & buff		
487 A174	2p	ultra & org		
488 A174	5p	brn & yel		
489 A174	10p	blk & salmon		
490 A174	15p	bl grn & yel		
491 A174	25p	blk & pink		
492 A174	50p	blk & citron		
493 A174	100p	blk & pink		
494 A174	150p	grn & yel		
495 A174	175p	ultra & pink		
		Nos. 486-495 (10)	2.00	

Two souvenir sheets, perf. and imperf., contain two stamps, one each of Nos. 492-493. Value $2 each.

Afghan Fencing A175

Designs: No. 497, 5p, 25p, 50p, Wrestlers. 10p, 100p, Man with Indian clubs. 15p, 150p, Afghan fencing. 175p, Children skating.

1961, July 6 *Perf. 13½x14*

496 A175	2p	grn & rose lil		
497 A175	2p	brn & citron		
498 A175	5p	gray & rose		
499 A175	10p	bl & bis		

500 A175 15p sl bl & dl lil
501 A175 25p blk & dl bl
502 A175 50p sl grn & bis brn
503 A175 100p brn & bl grn
504 A175 150p brn & org yel
505 A175 175p blk & bl
Nos. 496-505 (10) 1.50

Issued for Children's Day.
A souvenir sheet exists, perf. and imperf., containing one each of Nos. 502-503. Value $3.50 each.
For surcharges, see Nos. B37-B41.

Bande Amir Lakes — A176

1961, Aug. 7 Photo. *Perf. 13½x14*

506 A176 3af brt bl 35 28
507 A176 10af rose claret 1.10 1.00

Nadir Shah — A177

Girl Scout — A178

1961, Aug. 23 *Perf. 14x13½*

508 A177 50p rose red & blk 50 40
509 A177 175p brt grn & org brn 1.00 80

43rd Independence Day.
Two souvenir sheets, perf. and imperf., contain one each of Nos. 508-509. Value, each $2.50.

Perf. 14x13½

1961, July 23 Unwmk.

510 A178 50p dp car & dk gray 28 15
511 A178 175p dp grn & rose brn 60 40

Issued for Women's Day.
Two souvenir sheets exist, perf. and imperf., containing one each of Nos. 510-511. Value $3 each.

Exhibition Hall, Kabul — A179

1961, Aug. 23 *Perf. 13½x14*

512 A179 50p yel brn & yel grn 16 15
513 A179 175p blue & brn 40 28

International Exhibition at Kabul.

Pathan with Pashtunistan Flag — A180

1961, Aug. 31 Photo. *Perf. 14x13½*

514 A180 50p blk, lil & red 15 15
515 A180 175p brn, grnsh bl & red 35 28

Issued for "Free Pashtunistan Day."
Souvenir sheets exist perf. and imperf. containing one each of Nos. 514-515. Value $2 each.

Assembly Building A181

1961, Sept. 10 *Perf. 12*

516 A181 50p dk gray & brt grn 16 15
517 A181 175p ultra & brn 45 30

Anniv. of the founding of the Natl. Assembly.
Souvenir sheets exist, perf. and imperf., containing one each of Nos. 516-517. Value $1 each.

Exterminating Anopheles Mosquito A182

1961, Oct. 5 *Perf. 13½x14*

518 A182 50p blk & brn lil 50 28
519 A182 175p mar & brt grn 1.10 50

Anti-Malaria campaign. Souvenir sheets exist, perf. and imperf., containing one each of Nos. 518-519. Value $4 each.

Zahir Shah — A183

1961, Oct. 15 *Perf. 13½*

520 A183 50p lil & bl 16 15
521 A183 175p emer & red brn 40 35

Issued to honor King Mohammed Zahir Shah on his 47th birthday.
See Nos. 609-612.

Pomegranates A184

Fruit: No. 523, 5p, 25p, 50p, Grapes. 10p, 150p, Apples. 15p, 175p, Pomegranates. 100p, Melons.

1961, Oct. 16 *Perf. 13½x14*

Fruit in Natural Colors

522 A184 2p black
523 A184 2p green
524 A184 5p lil rose
525 A184 10p lilac
526 A184 15p dk bl
527 A184 25p dl red
528 A184 50p purple
529 A184 100p brt bl
530 A184 150p brown
531 A184 175p ol gray
Nos. 522-531 (10) 1.75

For Afghan Red Crescent Society.
Souvenir sheets exist, perf. and imperf., containing one each of Nos. 528-529. Value $1.50 each.
For surcharges, see Nos. B42-B46.

UN Headquarters, NY — A185

1961, Oct. 24 *Perf. 13½x14*

Vertical Borders in Emerald, Red and Black

532 A185 1p rose lil
533 A185 2p slate
534 A185 3p brown
535 A185 4p ultra
536 A185 50p rose red
537 A185 75p gray
538 A185 175p brt grn
Nos. 532-538 (7) 1.25

16th anniv. of the UN. Souvenir sheets exist, perf. and imperf., containing one each of Nos. 536-538. Value $2 each.

Children Giving Flowers to Teacher — A186

People Raising UNESCO Symbol — A187

Designs: No. 540, 5p, 25p, 50p, Tulips. 10p, 100p, Narcissus. 15p, 150p, Children giving flowers to teacher. 175p, Teacher with children in front of school.

1961, Oct. 26 Photo. *Perf. 12*

539 A186 2p multi
540 A186 2p multi
541 A186 5p multi
542 A186 10p multi
543 A186 15p multi
544 A186 25p multi
545 A186 50p multi
546 A186 100p multi
547 A186 150p multi
548 A186 175p multi
Nos. 539-548 (10) 1.75

Issued for Teacher's Day.
Souvenir sheets exist, perf. and imperf. containing one each of Nos. 545-546. Value, 2 sheets, $4.
For surcharges, see Nos. B47-B51.

Buzkashi Types of 1960

1961-72 Litho. *Perf. 10½, 11*

549 A167 25p violet 15 15
b. 25p brt vio, typo. ('72) 15 15
549A A167 25p citron ('63) 18 15
550 A167 50p blue 32 15
550A A167 50p yel org ('69) 15 15
551 A172 100p citron 45 15
551A A172 150p org ('64) 32 15
552 A172 2af lt grn 1.10 45
Nos. 549-552 (7) 2.67
Set value 85

Zahir Shah Types of 1951

Photo., Engr., Engr. & Litho.

1962 *Perf. 13x12, 13*

Imprint: "Thomas De La Rue & Co. Ltd."

552A A123 75p brt pur 1.10 25
552B A123 1af car & ultra 1.40 32
552C A124 2af blue 1.75 75
552D A124 3af org & blk 4.00 1.10
Nos. 552A-552D (4) 8.25 2.42

1962, July 2 Photo. *Perf. 14x13½*

553 A187 2p rose lil & brn
554 A187 2p ol bis & brn
555 A187 5p dp org & dk grn
556 A187 10p gray & mag
557 A187 15p bl & brn
558 A187 25p org yel & pur
559 A187 50p lt grn & pur
560 A187 75p brt cit & brn
561 A187 100p dp org & brn
Nos. 553-561 (9) 1.25

15th anniv. of UNESCO. Souvenir sheets exist, perf. and imperf. One contains Nos. 558-559; the other contains one Value, $3 each.
For surcharges, see Nos. B52-B60.

Ahmad Shah — A188

Afghan Hound — A189

1962, Feb. 24 Photo. *Perf. 13½*

562 A188 50p red brn & gray 15 15
563 A188 75p grn & salmon 25 20
564 A188 100p claret & bis 40 30
Nos. 562-564 (3) 80 65

Ahmad Shah (1724-73), founded the Afghan kingdom in 1747 and ruled until 1773.

1962, Apr. 21 *Perf. 14x13½*

Designs: 5p, 75p, Afghan cock. 10p, 100p, Kondjid plant. 15p, 125p, Astrakhan skins.

565 A189 2p rose & brn
566 A189 2p lt grn & brn
567 A189 5p dp rose & claret
568 A189 10p lt grn & sl grn
569 A189 15p bl grn & blk
570 A189 25p bl & brn
571 A189 50p gray & brn
572 A189 75p rose lil & lil
573 A189 100p gray & dl grn
574 A189 125p rose brn & blk
Nos. 565-574 (10) 2.00

Agriculture Day. Perf. and imperf. souvenir sheets exist. Set of 4 sheets, value $4.

Athletes with Flag and Nadir Shah A190

Woman in National Costume A191

1962, Aug. 23 *Perf. 12*

575 A190 25p multi 15 15
576 A190 50p multi 18 15
577 A190 150p multi 25 15
Nos. 575-577 (3) 58
Set value 19

44th Independence Day.

1962, Aug. 30 *Perf. 11½x12*

578 A191 25p lil & brn 15 15
579 A191 50p grn & brn 25 15
Set value 21

Issued for Women's Day. For souvenir sheet see note after No. C16.

Man and Woman with Flag — A192

Malaria Eradication Emblem and Swamp — A193

1962, Aug. 31 Photo.

580 A192 25p blk, pale bl & red 15 15
581 A192 50p blk, grn & red 18 15
582 A192 150p blk, pink & red 45 15
Nos. 580-582 (3) 78
Set value 29

Issued for "Free Pashtunistan Day."

1962, Sept. 5 *Perf. 14x13½*

583 A193	2p dk grn & ol gray		
584 A193	2p dk grn & sal		
585 A193	5p red brn & ol		
586 A193	10p red brn & brt grn		
587 A193	15p red brn & gray		
588 A193	25p brt bl & bluish grn		
589 A193	50p brt bl & rose lil		
590 A193	75p blk & bl		
591 A193	100p blk & brt pink		
592 A193	150p blk & bis brn		
593 A193	175p blk & org		
	Nos. 583-593 (11)	2.00	

WHO drive to eradicate malaria. Perf. and imperf. souvenir sheets exist. Set of 4 sheets, value $6.50.

For surcharges, see Nos. B61-B71.

National Assembly Building A194

Perf. 10½, 11 (100p)

1962, Sept. 10 **Unwmk.** **Litho.**

594 A194	25p lt grn	35	25
595 A194	50p blue	55	35
596 A194	75p rose	70	55
597 A194	100p violet	1.10	90
598 A194	125p ultra	1.20	1.10
	Nos. 594-598 (5)	3.90	3.15

Establishment of the National Assembly.

Horse Racing — A195

Designs: 2p, Pole vaulting. 3p, Wrestling. 4p, Weight lifting. 5p, Soccer.

1962, Sept. 22 **Photo.** *Perf. 12*

Black Inscriptions

599 A195	1p lt ol & red brn		
600 A195	2p lt grn & red brn		
601 A195	3p yel & dk pur		
602 A195	4p pale bl & grn		
603 A195	5p bluish grn & dk brn		
	Nos. 599-603, C17-C22 (11)	2.50	

4th Asian Games, Djakarta, Indonesia. Two souvenir sheets exist. A perforated one contains a 125p blue, dark blue and brown stamp in horse racing design. An imperf. one contains a 2af buff, purple and black stamp in soccer design. Value, $3.50 each.

Runners A196

Designs: 1p, 2p, Diver, vert. 4p, Peaches. 5p, Iris, vert.

Perf. 11½x12, 12x11½

1962, Oct. 2 **Unwmk.**

604 A196	1p rose lil & brn		
605 A196	2p bl & brn		
606 A196	3p brt bl & lil		
607 A196	4p ol gray & multi		
608 A196	5p gray & multi		
	Nos. 604-608, C23-C25 (8)	2.00	

Issued for Children's Day.

King Type of 1961, Dated "1962"

1962, Oct. 15 *Perf. 13½*

Various Frames

609 A183	25p lil rose & brn	15	15
610 A183	50p org brn & grn	15	15
611 A183	75p bl & lake	15	15
612 A183	100p grn & red brn	20	20
	Set value	50	50

Issued to honor King Mohammed Zahir Shah on his 48th birthday.

Grapes A197

1962, Oct. 16 *Perf. 12*

613 A197	1p shown		
614 A197	2p Grapes		
615 A197	3p Pears		
616 A197	4p Wistaria		
617 A197	5p Blossoms		
	Nos. 613-617, C26-C28 (8)	1.00	

For the Afghan Red Crescent Society.

UN Headquarters, NY and Flags of UN and Afghanistan A198

1962, Oct. 24 **Unwmk.**

618 A198	1p multi		
619 A198	2p multi		
620 A198	3p multi		
621 A198	4p multi		
622 A198	5p multi		
	Nos. 618-622, C29-C31 (8)	1.50	

UN Day. Souvenir sheets exist. One contains a single 4af ultramarine stamp, perforated; the other, a 4af ocher stamp, imperf. Value, 2 sheets, $5.

Boy Scout — A199 Pole Vault — A200

1962, Oct. 18 **Photo.** *Perf. 12*

623 A199	1p yel, dk grn & sal		
624 A199	2p dl yel, sl & sal		
625 A199	3p rose, blk & sal		
626 A199	4p multi		
	Nos. 623-626, C32-C35 (8)	1.50	

Issued to honor the Boy Scouts.

1962, Oct. 25 **Unwmk.** *Perf. 12*

Designs: 3p, High jump. 4p, 5p, Different blossoms.

627 A200	1p lil & dk grn		
628 A200	2p yel grn & brn		
629 A200	3p bis & vio		
630 A200	4p sal pink, grn & ultra		
631 A200	5p yel, grn & bl		
	Nos. 627-631, C36-C37 (7)	1.25	

Issued for Teacher's Day.

Rockets A201

1962, Nov. 29

632 A201	50p pale lil & dk bl	40	
633 A201	100p lt bl & red brn	80	

UN World Meteorological Day. A souvenir sheet contains one 5af pink and green stamp. Value $6.

Ansari Mausoleum, Herat — A202

Perf. 13½

1963, Jan. 3 **Unwmk.** **Photo.**

634 A202	50p pur & grn	15	15
635 A202	75p gray & mag	18	18
636 A202	100p org brn & brn	30	30
	Nos. 634-636 (3)	63	63

Khwaja Abdullah Ansari, Sufi, religious leader and poet, on the 900th anniv. of his death.

Sheep — A203

Silkworm, Cocoons, Moth and Mulberry Branch A204

1963, Mar. 1 *Perf. 12*

637 A203	1p grnsh bl & blk		
638 A203	2p yel grn & blk		
639 A203	3p lil rose & blk		
640 A204	4p gray, grn & brn		
641 A204	5p red lil, grn & brn		
	Nos. 637-641, C42-C44 (8)	1.50	

Issued for the Day of Agriculture.

Rice — A205

Designs: 3p, Corn. 300p, Wheat emblem.

1963, Mar. 27 **Unwmk.** *Perf. 14*

642 A205	2p gray, claret & grn	15	15
643 A205	3p grn, yel & ocher	15	15
644 A205	300p dk bl & yel	30	30
	Set value	44	44

FAO "Freedom from Hunger" campaign.

Meteorological Measuring Instrument A206

Designs: 3p, 10p, Weather station. 4p, 5p, Rockets in space.

1963, May 23 **Photo.** *Perf. 13½x14*

645 A206	1p dp mag & brn		
646 A206	2p brt bl & brn		
647 A206	3p red & brn		
648 A206	4p org & lil		
649 A206	5p grn & dl vio		

Imperf

650 A206	10p red brn & grn		
	Nos. 645-650, C46-C50 (11)	7.50	

3rd UN World Meteorological Day, Mar. 23.

Independence Monument — A207

1963, Aug. 23 **Litho.** *Perf. 10½*

651 A207	25p lt grn	15	15
652 A207	50p orange	15	15
653 A207	150p rose car	35	22
	Set value	56	37

45th Independence Day.

Pathans in Forest — A208

1963, Aug. 31 **Unwmk.** *Perf. 10½*

654 A208	25p pale vio	15	15
655 A208	50p sky blue	15	15
655A A208	150p dl red brn	40	35
	Nos. 654-655A (3)	70	
	Set value		52

Issued for "Free Pashtunistan Day."

4th Asian Games, Djakarta A208a

Designs: 2p, 250p, 300p, Wrestling. 3p, 10p, Tennis. 4p, 500p, Javelin. 5p, 9af, Shot put.

1963, Sept. 3 **Litho.** *Perf. 12*

656 A208a	2p rose vio & brn		
656A A208a	3p olive grn & brn		
656B A208a	4p blue & brn		
656C A208a	5p yel grn & brn		
656D A208a	10p lt bl grn & brn		
656E A208a	300p yellow & vio		
656F A208a	500p lt yel bis & brn		
656G A208a	9af pale grn & vio		

Souvenir Sheets

656H A208a	250p lilac & vio		
656I A208a	300p blue & blk		

Nos. 656-656F are airmail. Nos. 656-656I exist imperf.

National Assembly Building A209

1963, Sept. 10 *Perf. 11*

657 A209	25p gray	15	15
658 A209	50p dull red	15	15
659 A209	75p brown	20	15
660 A209	100p olive	30	15
661 A209	125p lilac	40	20
	Nos. 657-661 (5)	1.20	
	Set value		64

Issued to honor the National Assembly.

Balkh Gate A210

1963, Oct. 8
662 A210 3af choc (screened margins) 40 28
a. White margins 1.00 35

In the original printing a halftone screen extended across the plate, covering the space between the stamps. A retouch removed the screen between the stamps (No. 662a).

Intl. Red Cross, Cent. A210a

Designs: 4p, 5p, 200p, 3af, Nurse holding patient, vert. 10p, 4af, 6af, Crown Prince Ahmed Shah.

1963, Oct. 9 *Perf. 13½*
662B A210a 2p olive, blk & red
662C A210a 3p blue, blk & red
662D A210a 4p lt grn, blk & red
662E A210a 5p lt vio, blk & red
662F A210a 10p gray grn, red & blk
662G A210a 100p dull bl grn, red & blk
662H A210a 200p lt brn, blk & red
662I A210a 4af brt bl grn, red & blk
m. Souv. sheet of 1
662J A210a 6af lt brn, red & blk

Souvenir Sheet

662K A210a 3af dl blue, blk & red

Nos. 662G-662K are airmail. Nos. 662B-662K exist imperf.

Zahir Shah — A211

Kemal Ataturk — A212

1963, Oct. 15 *Perf. 10½*
663 A211 25p green 15 15
663A A211 50p gray 15 15
663B A211 75p car rose 22 15
663C A211 100p dl redsh brn 30 15
Nos. 663-663C (4) 82
Set value 37

King Mohammed Zahir Shah, 49th birthday.

1963, Oct. 10 *Perf. 10½*
664 A212 1af blue 15 15
665 A212 3af rose lilac 40 35

25th anniv. of the death of Kemal Ataturk, president of Turkey.

Protection of Nubian Monuments A213

Designs: 5af, 7.50af, 10af, Ruins, vert.

Perf. 12, Imperf. (150p, 250p, 10af)
1963, Nov. 16 **Photo.**
666 A213 100p lil rose & blk
666A A213 150p rose lil & blk
666B A213 200p brn & blk
666C A213 250p ultra & blk
666D A213 500p grn & blk
666E A213 5af greenish blue & gray bl
666F A213 7.50af red brn & gray bl
666G A213 10af ver & gray bl

Nos. 666E-666G are airmail. No. 666D exists imperf.

Women's Day — A213a

Boy and Girl Scouts — A213c

A213b

1964, Jan. 5 *Perf. 14x13½*
667 A213a 2p multicolored
667A A213a 3p multicolored
667B A213a 4p multicolored
667C A213a 5p multicolored
667D A213a 10p multicolored

Exist imperf.

1964, Jan. 5 *Perf. 13½x14, 14x13½*

Designs: Nos. 668F-668G, 668K-668M, Girl with flag.

668 A213b 2p multi
668A A213b 3p multi
668B A213b 4p multi
668C A213b 5p multi
668D A213b 10p multi
668E A213c 2af multi
668F A213c 2af multi
668G A213c 2.50af multi
668H A213c 3af multi
668I A213c 4af multi
668J A213c 5af multi
668K A213c 12af multi

Souvenir Sheets

668L A213c 5af multi
668M A213c 6af multi
668N A213c 6af multi
668O A213c 10af multi

Nos. 668E-668O are airmail. Nos 668-668K, 668N-668O exist imperf.

Children — A213d

1964, Jan. 22 *Perf. 12*
669 A213d 2p Playing ball
669A A213d 3p like #669
669B A213d 4p Swinging, jumping rope, vert.
669C A213d 5p Skiing, vert.
669D A213d 10p like #669
669E A213d 200p like #669C
669F A213d 300p like #669B

Nos. 669E-669F are airmail. All exist imperf.

Red Crescent Society — A213e

Designs: 100p, 200p, Pierre and Marie Curie, physicists. 2.50af, 7.50af Nurse examining child. 3.50af, 5af, Nurse and patients.

Perf. 14, Imperf. (#670A, 670C-670D)
1964, Feb. 8
670 A213e 100p multi
670A A213e 100p multi
670B A213e 200p multi
670C A213e 2.50af multi
670D A213e 3.50af multi
670E A213e 5af multi
670F A213e 7.50af multi

Nos. 670B-670D are airmail.

Teachers' Day — A213f

Flowers: 2p, 3p, 3af, 4af, Tulips. 4p, 5p, 3.50af, 6af, Flax. 10p, 1.50af, 2af, Iris.

Perf. 12, Imperf. (1.50af, 2af)
1964, Mar. 3
671 A213f 2p multicolored
671A A213f 3p multicolored
671B A213f 4p multicolored
671C A213f 5p multicolored
671D A213f 10p multicolored
671E A213f 1.50af multicolored
671F A213f 2af multicolored
671G A213f 3af multicolored
671H A213f 3.50af multicolored

Souvenir Sheets

671I A213f 4af multicolored
671J A213f 6af multi, imperf

Nos. 671E-671J are airmail. Nos. 671-671D exist imperf.

A213g

UN Day: 5p, 10p, 2af, 3af, 4af, Doctor and nurse, vert.

1964, Mar. 9 *Perf. 14*
672 A213g 2p multicolored
672A A213g 3p multicolored
672B A213g 4p multicolored
672C A213g 5p multicolored
672D A213g 10p multicolored
672E A213g 100p multicolored
672F A213g 2af multicolored
672G A213g 3af multicolored

Souvenir Sheets

672H A213g 4af multi, imperf.
672I A213g 5af multicolored

Nos. 672E-672G are airmail. Nos. 672-672G exist imperf.
For surcharges see Nos. B71A-B71J.

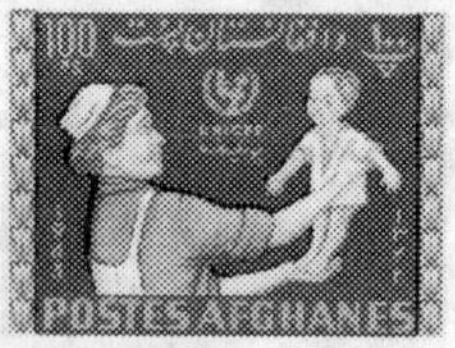

UNICEF A213h

Design: 5af, 7.50af, 10af, Children eating.

Perf. 14x13½, Imperf. (150p, 250p, 10af)
1964, Mar. 15
673 A213h 100p multicolored
673A A213h 150p multicolored
673B A213h 200p multicolored
673C A213h 250p multicolored
673D A213h 5af multicolored
673E A213h 7.50af multicolored
673F A213h 10af multicolored

Nos. 673D-673F are airmail.

Eradication of Malaria A213i

Designs: 4p, 5p, 5af, 10af Spraying mosquitoes.

1964, Mar. 15 *Perf. 13½*
674 A213i 2p lt red brn & yel grn
674A A213i 3p olive grn & buff
674B A213i 4p dk vio & bl grn
674C A213i 5p brn & grn
674D A213i 2af Prus bl & ver
h. Souv. sheet of 1
674E A213i 5af dk grn & lt red brn, imperf.
i. Souv. sheet of 1, imperf.
674F A213i 10af red brn & grnsh bl

X X

10 PS ۱۰ پ

674G A213i 10p on 4p Prus bl & rose

No. 674G not issued without surcharge. Nos. 674-674C, 674G exist imperf. Nos. 674D-674F are airmail.
Exists imperf.

"Tiger's Head" of 1878 — A214

1964, Mar. 22 **Photo.** *Perf. 12*
675 A214 1.25af gold, grn & blk 20 15
676 A214 5af gold, rose car & blk 50 35

Issued to honor philately.

Unisphere and Flags — A215

1964, May 3 *Perf. 13½x14*
677 A215 6af crim, gray & grn 30 22

New York World's Fair, 1964-65.

Hand Holding Torch — A216

1964, May 12 **Photo.** *Perf. 14x13½*
678 A216 3.75af multi 18 18

1st UN Seminar on Human Rights in Kabul, May 1964. The denomination in Persian at right erroneously reads "3.25" but the stamp was sold and used as 3.75af.

Kandahar Airport
A217

1964, Apr. Litho. *Perf. 10½, 11*

679	A217	7.75af	dk red brn	40	20
680	A217	9.25af	lt grn	50	22
681	A217	10.50af	lt grn	50	28
682	A217	13.75af	car rose	70	38
			Nos. 679-682 (4)	2.10	1.08

Inauguration of Kandahar Airport.

Snow Leopard
A218

Designs: 50p, Ibex, vert. 75p, Head of argali. 5af, Yak.

1964, June 25 Photo. *Perf. 12*

683	A218	25p	yel & bl	15	15
684	A218	50p	dl red & grn	15	15
685	A218	75p	Prus bl & lil	15	15
686	A218	5af	brt grn & dk brn	30	30
			Set value	54	54

View of Herat — A219

Flag and Map of Afghanistan
A220

Yourist publicity: 75p, Tomb of Queen Gowhar Shad, vert.

Perf. 13½x14, 14x13½

1964, July 12

687	A219	25p	sepia & bl	15	15
688	A219	75p	dp bl & buff	15	15
689	A220	3af	red, blk & grn	30	15
			Set value	40	20

Wrestling
A221

Designs: 25p, Hurdling, vert. 1af, Diving, vert. 5af, Soccer.

1964, July 26 *Perf. 12*

690	A221	25p	ol bis, blk & car	15	15
691	A221	1af	bl grn, blk & car	15	15
692	A221	3.75af	yel grn, blk & car	22	22
693	A221	5af	brn, blk & car	30	30
a.			Souv. sheet of 4, #690-693, imperf.	90	90
			Nos. 690-693 (4)	82	82

18th Olympic Games, Tokyo, Oct. 10-25, 1964. No. 693a sold for 15af. The additional 5af went to the Afghanistan Olympic Committee.

Flag and Outline of Nadir Shah's Tomb — A222

1964, Aug. 24 Photo.

695	A222	25p	multi	15	15
696	A222	75p	multi	15	15
			Set value	17	17

Independence Day. The stamps were printed with an erroneous inscription in upper left corner: "33rd year of independence." This was locally obliterated with a typographed gold bar.

Pashtunistan Flag — A223

Zahir Shah — A225

1964, Sept. 1 Unwmk.

697	A223	100p	gold, blk, red, bl & grn	15	15

Issued for "Free Pashtunistan Day."

1964, Oct. 17 *Perf. 14x13½*

699	A225	1.25af	gold & yel grn	15	15
700	A225	3.75af	gold & rose	20	15
701	A225	50af	gold & gray	2.00	1.75
			Nos. 699-701 (3)	2.35	2.05

King Mohammed Zahir Shah, 50th birthday.

Coat of Arms of Afghanistan and UN Emblem — A226

1964, Oct. 24 *Perf. 13½x14*

702	A226	5af	gold, blk & dl bl	20	15

Issued for United Nations Day.

Emblem of Afghanistan Women's Association
A227

1964, Nov. 9 Photo. Unwmk.

703	A227	25p	pink, dk bl & emer	50	25
704	A227	75p	aqua, dk bl & emer	75	35
705	A227	1af	sil, dk bl & emer	1.00	50
			Nos. 703-705 (3)	2.25	1.10

Issued for Women's Day.

Poet Mowlana Nooruddin Abdul Rahman Jami (1414-1492) — A228

1964, Nov. 23 Litho. *Perf. 11 Rough*

706	A228	1.50af	blk, emer & yel	85	85

Woodpecker
A229

Birds: 3.75af, Black-throated jay, vert. 5af, Impeyan pheasant, vert.

Perf. 13½x14, 14x13½

1965, Apr. 20 Photo. Unwmk.

707	A229	1.25af	multi	1.00	50
708	A229	3.75af	multi	1.75	75
709	A229	5af	multi	2.50	1.00
			Nos. 707-709 (3)	5.25	2.25

ITU Emblem, Old and New Communication Equipment
A230

1965, May 17 *Perf. 13½x14*

710	A230	5af	lt bl, blk & red	35	35

Cent. of the ITU.

"Red City," Bamian — A231

Designs: 3.75af, Ruins of ancient Bamian city. 5af, Bande Amir, mountain lakes.

1965, May 30 *Perf. 13x13½*

711	A231	1.25af	pink & multi	15	15
712	A231	3.75af	lt bl & multi	18	18
713	A231	5af	yel & multi	30	30
			Nos. 711-713 (3)	63	63

Issued for tourist publicity.

ICY Emblem
A232

1965, June 25 *Perf. 13½x13*

714	A232	5af	multi	25	25

International Cooperation Year, 1965.

ARIANA Air Lines Emblem and DC-3 — A233

Designs: 5af, DC-6 at right. 10af, DC-3 on top.

Perf. 13½x14

1965, July 15 Photo. Unwmk.

715	A233	1.25af	brt bl, gray & blk	15	15
716	A233	5af	red lil, blk & bl	30	30
717	A233	10af	bis, blk, bl gray & grn	75	75
a.			Souv. sheet of 3, #715-717, imperf.	1.00	1.00
			Nos. 715-717 (3)	1.20	1.20

10th anniv. of Afghan Air Lines, ARIANA.

Nadir Shah — A234

1965, Aug. 23 *Perf. 14x13½*

718	A234	1af	dl grn, blk & red brn	25	15

For the 47th Independence Day.

Flag of Pashtunistan
A235

Perf. 13½x14

1965, Aug. 31 Photo. Unwmk.

719	A235	1af	multi	25	15

Issued for "Free Pashtunistan Day."

Zahir Shah Signing Constitution — A236

1965, Sept. 11 *Perf. 13x13½*

720	A236	1.50af	brt grn & blk	25	25

Promulgation of the new Constitution.

Zahir Shah and Oak Leaves — A237

1965, Oct. 14 *Perf. 14x13½*

721	A237	1.25af	blk, ultra & salmon	15	15
722	A237	6af	blk, lt bl & rose lil	40	35

King Mohammed Zahir Shah, 51st birthday.

Flags of UN and Afghanistan
A238

1965, Oct. 24 *Perf. 13½x14*

723	A238	5af	multi	20	20

Issued for United Nations Day.

Dappled Ground Gecko — A239

Designs: 4af, Caucasian agamid (lizard). 8af, Horsfield's tortoise.

Perf. 13½x14

1966, May 10 Photo. Unwmk.

724	A239	3af	tan & multi	75	35
725	A239	4af	brt grn & multi	85	40
726	A239	8af	vio & multi	1.50	75
			Nos. 724-726 (3)	3.10	1.50

Soccer Player and Globe — A240

1966, July 31 Litho. *Perf. 14x13½*

727	A240	2af rose red & blk	60	18
728	A240	6af vio bl & blk	1.10	25
729	A240	12af bis brn & blk	2.25	60
		Nos. 727-729 (3)	3.95	1.03

World Cup Soccer Championship, Wembley, England, July 11-30.

Cotton Flower and Boll — A241

Designs: 5af, Silkworm. 7af, Farmer plowing with oxen.

1966, July 31 *Perf. 13½x14*

730	A241	1af multi	50	15
731	A241	5af multi	1.00	30
732	A241	7af multi	1.40	40
		Nos. 730-732 (3)	2.90	85

Issued for the Day of Agriculture.

Independence Monument A242

1966, Aug. 23 Photo. *Perf. 13½x14*

733	A242	1af multi	25	15
734	A242	3af multi	75	25

Issued to commemorate Independence Day.

Flag of Pashtunistan A243

1966, Aug. 31 Litho. *Perf. 11 Rough*

735	A243	1af bright blue	50	15

"Free Pashtunistan Day."

Bagh-i-Bala Park Casino — A244

Tourist publicity: 2af, Map of Afghanistan. 8af, Tomb of Abd-er-Rahman. The casino on 4af is the former summer palace of Abd-er-Rahman near Kabul.

1966, Oct. 3 Photo. *Perf. 13½x14*

736	A244	2af red & multi	18	15
737	A244	4af multi	40	30
738	A244	8af multi	65	60
a.		Souvenir sheet of 3, #736-738, imperf.	3.50	3.50
		Nos. 736-738 (3)	1.23	1.05

Zahir Shah — A245

UNESCO Emblem — A246

1966, Oct. 14 *Perf. 14x13½*

739	A245	1af dk slate grn	20	15
740	A245	5af red brn	50	25

King Mohammed Zahir Shah, 52nd birthday. See Nos. 760-761.

1967, Mar. 6 Litho. *Perf. 12*

741	A246	2af multi	60	15
742	A246	6af multi	75	15
743	A246	12af multi	1.50	30
		Nos. 741-743 (3)	2.85	60

20th anniv. of UNESCO.

Zahir Shah and UN Emblem A247

1967 Photo.

744	A247	5af multi	38	15
745	A247	10af multi	75	30

UN Intl. Org. for Refugees, 20th anniv..

New Power Station — A248

Designs: 5af, Carpet, vert. 8af, Cement factory.

1967, Jan. 7 Photo. *Perf. 13½x14*

746	A248	2af red lil & ol grn	15	15
747	A248	5af multi	22	18
748	A248	8af blk, dk bl & tan	38	25
		Nos. 746-748 (3)	75	58

Issued to publicize industrial development.

International Tourist Year Emblem — A249

Designs: 6af, International Tourist Year emblem and map of Afghanistan.

1967, May 11 Photo. *Perf. 12*

749	A249	2af yel, blk & lt bl	15	15
750	A249	6af bis brn, blk & lt bl	38	22
a.		Souvenir sheet of 2, #749-750, imperf.	1.00	1.00
		Set value		30

Intl. Tourist Year, 1967. No. 750a sold for 10af.

Power Dam, Dorunta A250

Macaque A251

Designs: 6af, Sirobi Dam, vert. 8af, Reservoir at Jalalabad.

1967, July 2 Photo. *Perf. 12*

751	A250	1af dk grn & lil	15	15
752	A250	6af red brn & grnsh bl	35	35
753	A250	8af plum & dk bl	50	50
		Nos. 751-753 (3)	1.00	1.00

Progress in agriculture through electricity.

1967, July 28 Photo. *Perf. 12*

Designs: 6af, Striped hyena, horiz. 12af, Persian gazelles, horiz.

754	A251	2af dl yel & indigo	25	15
755	A251	6af lt grn & sepia	70	35
756	A251	12af lt bl & red brn	1.50	75
		Nos. 754-756 (3)	2.45	1.25

Pashtun Dancers — A252

1967, Sept. 1 Photo. *Perf. 12*

757	A252	2af magenta & vio	50	15

Issued for "Free Pashtunistan Day."

Retreat of British at Maiwand A253

Fireworks and UN Emblem A254

1967, Aug. 24

758	A253	1af dk brn & org ver	25	15
759	A253	2af dk brn & brt pink	50	15
		Set value		19

Issued to commemorate Independence Day.

King Type of 1966

1967, Oct. 15 Photo. *Perf. 14x13½*

760	A245	2af brown red	15	15
761	A245	8af dark blue	50	25

Issued to honor King Mohammed Zahir Shah on his 53rd birthday.

1967, Oct. 24 Litho. *Perf. 12*

762	A254	10af vio bl & multi	65	35

Issued for United Nations Day.

Greco-Roman Wrestlers A255

Said Jamalluddin Afghan A256

Design: 6af, Wrestlers (free style).

1967, Nov. 20 Photo.

763	A255	4af ol grn & rose lil	50	15
764	A255	6af dp car & brn	80	20
a.		Souvenir sheet of 2, #763-764, imperf.	5.00	5.00

1968 Olympic Games.

1967, Nov. 27

765	A256	1af magenta	15	15
766	A256	5af brown	35	20
		Set value		27

Said Jamalluddin Afghan, politician (1839-97).

Bronze Vase, 11th-12th Centuries A257

WHO Emblem A258

Design: 7af, Bronze vase, Ghasnavide era, 11th-12th centuries.

1967, Dec. 23 Photo. *Perf. 12*

767	A257	3af lt grn & brn	18	15
768	A257	7af yel & slate grn	42	30
a.		Souvenir sheet of 2, #767-768, imperf.	2.50	2.50

1968, Apr. 7 Photo. *Perf. 12*

769	A258	2af citron & brt bl	15	15
770	A258	7af rose & brt bl	28	22
		Set value		30

20th anniv. of the WHO.

Karakul — A259

1968, May 20 Photo. *Perf. 12*

771	A259	1af yel & blk	25	15
772	A259	6af lt bl & blk	70	20
773	A259	12af ultra & dk brn	1.25	40
		Nos. 771-773 (3)	2.20	75

Issued for the Day of Agriculture.

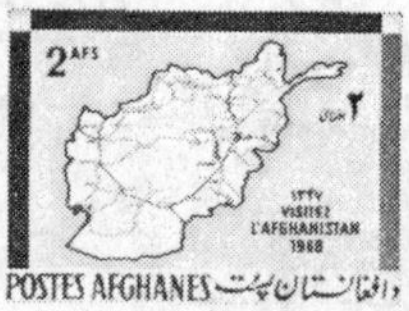

Map of Afghanistan A260

Victory Tower, Ghazni A261

Design: 16af, Mausoleum, Ghazni.

1968, June 3 *Perf. 13½x14, 12*

774	A260	2af red, blk, lt bl & grn	15	15
775	A261	3af yel, dk brn & lt bl	18	15
776	A261	16af pink & multi	95	50
		Nos. 774-776 (3)	1.28	
		Set value		68

Issued for tourist publicity.

Cinereous Vulture — A262

Birds: 6af, Eagle owl. 7af, Greater flamingoes.

1968, July 3 *Perf. 12*

777	A262	1af sky bl & multi	75	15
778	A262	6af yel & multi	1.50	20
779	A262	7af multi	1.75	30
		Nos. 777-779 (3)	4.00	65

Game of "Pegsticking" A263

Designs: 2af, Olympic flame and rings, vert. 12af, Buzkashi.

1968, July 20 Photo. *Perf. 12*

780	A263	2af multi	16	15
781	A263	8af org & multi	65	30
782	A263	12af multi	1.00	45
		Nos. 780-782 (3)	1.81	90

19th Olympic Games, Mexico City, Oct. 12-27.

Flower-decked Armored Car — A264

1968, Aug. 23
783 A264 6af multi 40 20

Issued to commemorate Independence Day.

Flag of Pashtunistan A265

1968 Aug. 31 Photo. *Perf. 12*
784 A265 3af multi 25 15

Issued for "Free Pashtunistan Day."

Zahir Shah — A266

Human Rights Flame — A267

1968, Oct. 14 Photo. *Perf. 12*
785 A266 2af ultra 15 15
786 A266 8af brown 45 28
Set value 34

Issued to honor King Mohammed Zahir Shah on his 54th birthday.

1968, Oct. 24
787 A267 1af multi 15 15
788 A267 2af vio, bis & blk 18 15
789 A267 6af vio blk, bis & vio 38 15
Nos. 787-789 (3) 71
Set value 25

Souvenir Sheet

Imperf

790 A267 10af plum, bis & red org 1.50 1.50

International Human Rights Year.

Maolana Djalalodine Balkhi — A268

Kushan Mural — A269

1968, Nov. 26 Photo. *Perf. 12*
791 A268 4af dk grn & mag 27 15

Balkhi (1207-73), historian.

1969, Jan. 2 *Perf. 12*

Design: 3af, Jug shaped like female torso.

792 A269 1af dk grn, mar & yel 25 15
793 A269 3af vio, gray & mar 75 15
a. Souv. sheet of 2, #792-793, imperf. 1.50 1.50

Archaeological finds at Bagram, 1st cent. B.C. to 2nd cent. A.D.

ILO Emblem A270

1969, Mar. 23 Photo. *Perf. 12*
794 A270 5af lt yel, lemon & blk 30 18
795 A270 8af lt bl, grnsh bl & blk 50 30

50th anniv. of the ILO.

Arms Type of 1939

1969, May (?) Typo.
795A A79 100p dk grn 15 15
795B A79 150p dp brn 25 15
Set value 15

Nos. 795A-795B were normally used as newspaper stamps.

Badakhshan Scene — A271

Tourist Publicity: 2af, Map of Afghanistan. 7af, Three men on mules ascending the Pamir Mountains.

1969, July 6 Photo. *Perf. 13½x14*
796 A271 2af ocher & multi 20 15
797 A271 4af multi 32 15
798 A271 7af multi 75 22
a. Souvenir sheet of 3, #796-798, imperf. 1.75 1.75
Nos. 796-798 (3) 1.27 52

No. 798a sold for 15af.

Bust, from Hadda Treasure, 3rd-5th Centuries — A272

Zahir Shah and Queen Humeira — A273

Designs: 5af, Vase and jug. 10af, Statue of crowned woman. 5af and 10af from Bagram treasure, 1st-2nd centuries.

1969, Aug. 3 Photo. *Perf. 14x13½*
799 A272 1af ol grn & gold 15 15
800 A272 5af purple & gold 20 16
801 A272 10af dp bl & gold 40 32
Nos. 799-801 (3) 75
Set value 52

1969, Aug. 23 *Perf. 12*
802 A273 5af gold, dk bl & red brn 35 20
803 A273 10af gold, dp lil & bl grn 65 35

Issued to commemorate Independence Day.

Map of Pashtunistan and Rising Sun — A274

1969, Aug. 31 Typo. *Perf. 10½*
804 A274 2af lt bl & red 15 15

Issued for "Free Pashtunistan Day."

Zahir Shah — A275

1969, Oct. 14 Photo. *Perf. 12*

Portrait in Natural Colors

805 A275 2af dk brn & gold 15 15
806 A275 6af brn & gold 45 20
Set value 26

Issued to honor King Mohammed Zahir Shah on his 55th birthday.

UN Emblem and Flag of Afghanistan A276

1969, Oct. 24 Litho. *Perf. 13½*
807 A276 5af bl & multi 27 16

Issued for United Nations Day.

ITU Emblem — A277

Wild Boar — A278

1969, Nov. 12
808 A277 6af ultra & multi 30 20
809 A277 12af rose & multi 60 35

Issued for World Telecommunications Day.

1969, Dec. 7 Photo. *Perf. 12*

Designs: 1af, Long-tailed porcupine. 8af, Red deer.

810 A278 1af yel & multi 25 20
811 A278 3af bl & multi 75 50
812 A278 8af pink & multi 2.00 1.00
Nos. 810-812 (3) 3.00 1.70

Man's First Footprints on Moon, and Earth — A279

1969, Dec. 28 *Perf. 13½x14*
813 A279 1af yel grn & multi 15 15
814 A279 3af yel & multi 24 15
815 A279 6af blue & multi 40 20
816 A279 10af rose & multi 65 32
Nos. 813-816 (4) 1.44
Set value 67

Moon landing. See note after Algeria #427.

Anti-cancer Symbol — A280

Mirza Abdul Quader Bedel — A281

1970, Apr. 7 Photo. *Perf. 14*
817 A280 2af dk grn & rose car 15 15
818 A280 6af dk bl & rose claret 40 20
Set value 26

Issued to publicize the fight against cancer.

1970, May 6 *Perf. 14x13½*
819 A281 5af multi 27 15

250th anniv. of the death of Mirza Abdul Quader Bedel (1643-1720), poet.

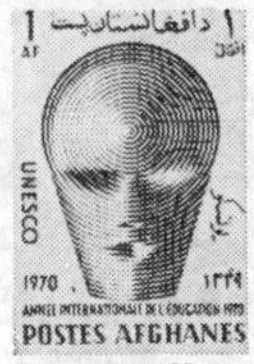

Education Year Emblem A282

Mother and Child A283

1970, June 7 Photo. *Perf. 12*
820 A282 1af black 15 15
821 A282 6af dp rose 35 20
822 A282 12af green 75 35
Nos. 820-822 (3) 1.25
Set value 60

International Education Year 1970.

1970, June 15 *Perf. 13½*
823 A283 6af yel & multi 27 20

Issued for Mother's Day.

UN Emblem, Scales of Justice, Spacecraft A284

1970, June 26
824 A284 4af yel, dk bl & dp bl 20 15
825 A284 6af pink, dk bl & brt bl 35 20

25th anniversary of United Nations.

Mosque of the Amir of the two Swords, Kabul — A285

Designs: 2af, Map of Afghanistan. 7af, Arch of Paghman.

1970, July 6 *Perf. 12*

Size: 30½x30½mm

826 A285 2af lt bl, blk & cit 15 15

Size: 36x26mm

827 A285 3af pink & multi 18 15
828 A285 7af yel & multi 42 22
Nos. 826-828 (3) 75
Set value 38

Issued for tourist publicity.

Zahir Shah Reviewing Troops A286

1970, Aug. 23 Photo. *Perf. 13½*
829 A286 8af multi 60 25

Issued to commemorate Independence Day.

Pathans — A287

1970, Aug. 31 Typo. *Perf. 10½*
830 A287 2af ultra & red 15 15

Issued for "Free Pashtunistan Day."

Quail — A288

Designs: 4af, Golden eagle. 6af, Ringnecked pheasant.

1970, Sept. Photo. *Perf. 12*
831 A288 2af multi 50 25
832 A288 4af multi 1.00 50
833 A288 6af multi 1.50 75
Nos. 831-833 (3) 3.00 1.50

Zahir Shah A289

Red Crescents A290

1970, Oct. 14 Photo. *Perf. 14x13½*
834 A289 3af grn & vio 20 15
835 A289 7af dk bl & vio brn 60 22

Issued to honor King Mohammed Zahir Shah on his 56th birthday.

1970, Oct. 16 Typo. *Perf. 10½*
836 A290 2af blk, gold & red 15 15

Issued for the Red Crescent Society.

UN Emblem and Charter A291

1970, Oct. 24 Photo. *Perf. 14*
837 A291 1af gold & multi 15 15
838 A291 5af gold & multi 20 16
Set value 30 20

United Nations Day.

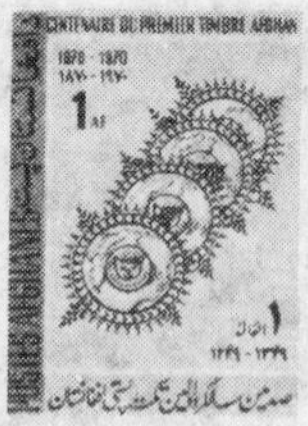

Tiger Heads of 1871 — A292

1970, Nov. 10 *Perf. 12*
839 A292 1af sal, lt grnsh bl & blk 25 15
840 A292 4af lt ultra, yel & blk 50 15
841 A292 12af lil, lt bl & blk 85 35
Nos. 839-841 (3) 1.60
Set value 52

Cent. of the 1st Afghan postage stamps. The postal service was established in 1870, but the 1st stamps were issued in May, 1871.

Globe and Waves A293

1971, May 17 Photo. *Perf. 13½*
842 A293 12af grn, blk & bl 60 35

3rd World Telecommunications Day.

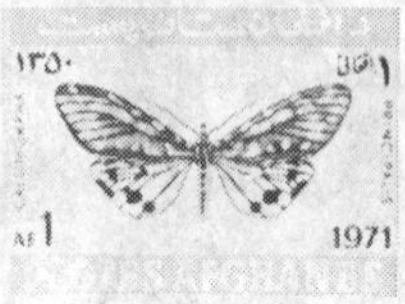

Callimorpha Principalis A294

Designs: 3af, Epizygaenella species. 5af, Parnassius autocrator.

1971, May 30 *Perf. 13½x14*
843 A294 1af ver & multi 1.00 50
844 A294 3af yel & multi 2.25 1.00
845 A294 5af ultra & multi 3.00 1.50
Nos. 843-845 (3) 6.25 3.00

"UNESCO" and Half of Ancient Kushan Statue — A295

1971, June 26 Photo. *Perf. 13½*
846 A295 6af ocher & vio 40 20
847 A295 10af lt bl & mar 65 30

UNESCO-sponsored Intl. Kushani Seminar.

Tughra and Independence Monument — A296

1971, Aug. 23
848 A296 7af rose red & multi 40 22
849 A296 9af red org & multi 65 28

Independence Day.

Pashtunistan Square, Kabul — A297

1971, Aug. 31 Typo. *Perf. 10½*
850 A297 5af deep rose lilac 27 15

"Free Pashtunistan Day."

Zahir Shah — A298

A299

1971, Oct. 14 Photo. *Perf. 12½x12*
851 A298 9af lt grn & multi 40 28
852 A298 17af yel & multi 75 55

57th birthday of King Mohammed Zahir Shah.

1971, Oct. 16 *Perf. 14x13½*

Design: Map of Afghanistan, red crescent, various activities.

853 A299 8af lt bl, red, grn & blk 45 25

For Afghan Red Crescent Society.

Equality Year Emblem A300

1971, Oct. 24 *Perf. 12*
854 A300 24af brt bl 1.25 70

International Year Against Racial Discrimination and United Nations Day.

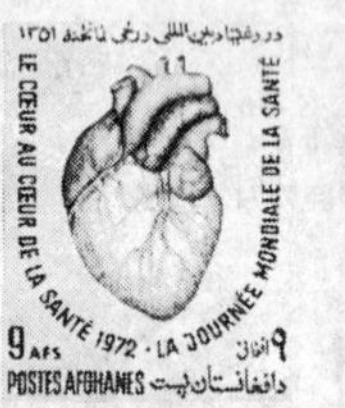

"Your Heart is your Health" — A301

Tulip — A302

1972, Apr. 7 Photo. *Perf. 14*
855 A301 9af pale yel & multi 75 28
856 A301 12af gray & multi 1.50 35

World Health Day.

1972, June 5 Photo. *Perf. 14*

Designs: 10af, Rock partridge, horiz. 12af, Lynx, horiz. 18af, Allium stipitatum (flower).

857 A302 7af grn & multi 50 22
858 A302 10af bl & multi 75 32
859 A302 12af lt grn & multi 1.00 35
860 A302 18af bl grn & multi 1.25 60
Nos. 857-860 (4) 3.50 1.49

Buddhist Shrine, Hadda A302a

Designs: 7af, Greco-Bactrian animal seal, 250 B.C. 9af, Greco-Oriental temple, Ai-Khanoum, 3rd-2nd centuries B.C.

1972, July 16 Photo. *Perf. 12*
861 A302a 3af brn & dl bl 50 15
862 A302a 7af rose claret & dl grn 80 22
863 A302a 9af grn & lilac 1.10 30
Nos. 861-863 (3) 2.40 67

Tourist publicity.

King and Queen Reviewing Parade — A303

1972, Aug. 23 Photo. *Perf. 13½*
864 A303 25af gold & multi 4.00 1.00

Independence Day.

Used as a provisional in 1978 with king and queen portion removed.

Wrestling A304

Designs: 10af, 19af, 21af, Wrestling, different hold.

1972, Aug. 26
865 A304 4af ol bis & multi 28 15
866 A304 8af lt bl & multi 52 25
867 A304 10af yel grn & multi 65 32
868 A304 19af multi 1.20 40
869 A304 21af lil & multi 1.40 45
a. Souv. sheet of 5, #865-869, imperf. 3.00 3.00
Nos. 865-869 (5) 4.05 1.57

20th Olympic Games, Munich, Aug. 26-Sept. 11. No. 869a sold for 60af.

Pathan and View of Tribal Territory — A305

Zahir Shah — A306

1972, Aug. 31 *Perf. 12½x12*
870 A305 5af ultra & multi 27 15

Pashtunistan day.

1972, Oct. 14 Photo. *Perf. 14x13½*
871 A306 7af gold, blk & Prus bl 1.50 30
872 A306 14af gold, blk & lt brn 2.50 50

58th birthday of King Mohammed Zahir Shah.

City Destroyed by Earthquake, Refugees — A307

1972, Oct. 16 *Perf. 13½*
873 A307 7af lt bl, red & blk 40 22

For Afghan Red Crescent Society.

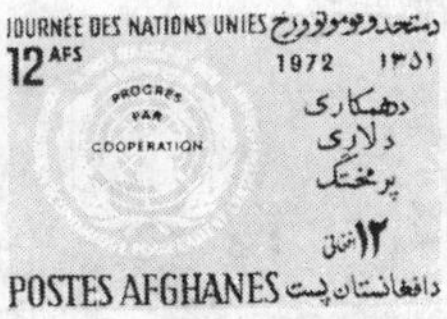
UN Emblem A308

1972, Oct. 24
874 A308 12af lt ultra & blk 65 35

UN Economic Commission for Asia and the Far East (ECAFE), 25th anniv.

Ceramics A309

Designs: 9af, Leather coat, vert. 12af, Metal ware, vert. 16af, Inlaid artifacts.

1972, Dec. 10 Photo. *Perf. 12*

875	A309	7af gold & multi	42	22
876	A309	9af gold & multi	55	28
877	A309	12af gold & multi	70	35
878	A309	16af gold & multi	1.00	50
a.		Souv. sheet of 4, #875-878, imperf.	2.25	2.25
		Nos. 875-878 (4)	2.67	1.35

Handicraft industries. No. 878a sold for 45af.

WMO and National Emblems — A310

1973, Apr. 3 Photo. *Perf. 14*

879	A310	7af lt lil & dk grn	42	22
880	A310	14af lt bl & dp claret	85	45

Cent. of intl. meteorological cooperation.

Abu Rayhan al-Biruni — A311

Family — A312

1973, June 16 Photo. *Perf. 13½*
881 A311 10af multi 55 32

Millennium of birth (973-1048), philosopher and mathematician.

1973, June 30 Photo. *Perf. 13½*
882 A312 9af org & red lil 50 30

Intl. Family Planning Fed., 21st anniv.

Republic

Impeyan Pheasant A313

Birds: 9af, Great crested grebe. 12af, Himalayan snow cock.

1973, July 29 Photo. *Perf. 12x12½*

883	A313	8af yel & multi	1.25	25
884	A313	9af bl & multi	1.75	30
885	A313	12af multi	2.00	35
		Nos. 883-885 (3)	5.00	90

Stylized Buzkashi Horseman A314

1973, Aug. *Perf. 13½*
886 A314 8af black 32 25

Tourist publicity.

Fireworks A315

1973, Aug. 23 Photo. *Perf. 12*
887 A315 12af multi 48 35

55th Independence Day.

Lake Abassine, Pashtunistan Flag — A316

1973, Aug. 31 *Perf. 14x13½*
888 A316 9af multi 50 30

Pashtunistan Day.

Red Crescent — A317

1973, Oct. 16 *Perf. 13½*
889 A317 10af red, blk & gold 60 32

Red Crescent Society.

Kemal Ataturk — A318

1973, Oct. 28 Litho. *Perf. 10½*

890	A318	1af blue	15	15
891	A318	7af reddish brn	42	22
		Set value		27

50th anniversary of the Turkish Republic.

Human Rights Flame, Arms of Afghanistan A319

1973, Dec. 10 Photo. *Perf. 12*
892 A319 12af sil, blk & lt bl 45 35

25th anniversary of the Universal Declaration of Human Rights.

Asiatic Black Bears — A320

1974, Mar. 26 Litho. *Perf. 12*

893	A320	5af shown	35	15
894	A320	7af Afghan hound	50	22
895	A320	10af Persian goat	70	28
896	A320	12af Leopard	90	35
a.		Souv. sheet of 4, #893-896, imperf.	5.00	5.00
		Nos. 893-896 (4)	2.45	1.00

Worker and Farmer A321

1974, May 1 Photo. *Perf. 13½x12½*
897 A321 9af rose red & multi 40 25

International Labor Day, May 1.

Independence Monument and Arch — A322

1974, May 27 Photo. *Perf. 12*

898	A322	4af bl & multi	15	15
899	A322	11af gold & multi	35	30

56th Independence Day.

Arms of Afghanistan and Symbol of Cooperation A323

Pres. Mohammad Daoud Khan — A324

Designs: 5af, Flag of Republic of Afghanistan. 15af, Soldiers and coat of arms of the Republic.

1974, July 25 *Perf. 13½x12½, 14*
Sizes: 4af, 15af, 36x22mm; 5af, 7af, 36x26, 26x36mm

900	A323	4af multi	18	15
901	A323	5af multi	22	15
902	A324	7af grn, brn & blk	32	18
a.		Souv. sheet of 2, #901-902, imperf.	70	70
903	A323	15af multi	65	40
a.		Souv. sheet of 2, #900, 903, imperf.	1.00	1.00
		Nos. 900-903 (4)	1.37	88

1st anniv. of the Republic of Afghanistan.

Lesser Spotted Eagle — A325

Birds: 6af, White-fronted goose, ruddy shelduck and gray-lag goose. 11af, European coots and European crane.

1974, Aug. 6 Photo. *Perf. 13½x13*

904	A325	1af car rose & multi	25	15
905	A325	6af bl & multi	75	18
906	A325	11af yel & multi	1.50	40
a.		Strip of 3, #904-906	1.00	1.00
		Nos. 904-906 (3)	2.50	
		Set value		63

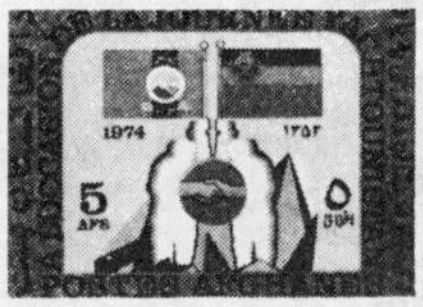
Flags of Pashtunistan and Afghanistan A326

1974, Aug. 31 Photo. *Perf. 14*
907 A326 5af multi 27 15

Pashtunistan Day.

Natl. Arms A326a

1974, Aug. Typo. *Rough Perf. 11*
907A A326a 100p green

Coat of Arms — A327

1974, Oct. 9
908 A327 7af gold, grn & blk 22 18

Centenary of Universal Postal Union.

Buying Sets
It is often less expensive to purchase complete sets than individual stamps that make up the set. Set values are provided for many such sets.

"un" and UN Emblem
A328

1974, Oct. 24 Photo. *Perf. 14*
909 A328 5af lt ultra & dk bl 27 15

United Nations Day.

Minaret of Jam — A329 Buddha, Hadda — A330

Design: 14af, Lady riding griffin, 2nd century, Bagram.

1975, May 5 Photo. *Perf. 13½*
910 A329 7af multi 28 15
911 A330 14af multi 60 30
912 A330 15af multi 65 30
a. Souvenir sheet of 3, #910-912, imperf. 3.50 3.50
Nos. 910-912 (3) 1.53 75

South Asia Tourism Year 1975.

New Flag of Afghanistan
A331

1975, May 27 Photo. *Perf. 12*
913 A331 16af multi 75 35

57th Independence Day.

Celebrating Crowd
A332

1975, July 17 Photo. *Perf. 13½*
914 A332 9af bl & multi 42 20
915 A332 12af car & multi 55 28

Second anniversary of the Republic.

Women's Year Emblems — A333

1975, Aug. 24 Photo. *Perf. 12*
916 A333 9af car, lt bl & blk 28 22

International Women's Year 1975.

Pashtunistan Flag, Sun Rising Over Mountains
A334

Mohammed Akbar Khan
A335

1975, Aug. 31 *Perf. 13½*
917 A334 10af multi 30 25

Pashtunistan Day.

1976, Feb. 4 Photo. *Perf. 14*
918 A335 15af lt brn & multi 45 35

Mohammed Akbar Khan (1816-1846), warrior son of Amir Dost Mohammed Khan.

Pres. Mohammad Daoud Khan
A336 A337

1974-78 Photo. *Perf. 14*
919 A336 10af multi 55 20
920 A336 16af multi ('78) 2.00 *75*
921 A336 19af multi 75 40
922 A336 21af multi 1.10 45
923 A336 22af multi ('78) 3.00 *1.60*
924 A336 30af multi ('78) 4.00 *2.25*
925 A337 50af multi ('75) 2.25 1.10
926 A337 100af multi ('75) 4.50 2.00
Nos. 919-926 (8) 18.15 *8.75*

Arms of Republic, Independence Monument — A338

1976, June 1 Photo. *Perf. 14*
927 A338 22af bl & multi 65 45

58th Independence Day.

Flag Raising — A339

1976, July 17 Photo. *Perf. 14*
928 A339 30af multi 90 75

Republic Day.

Mountain Peaks and Flag of Pashtunistan
A340

1976, Aug. 31 Photo. *Perf. 14*
929 A340 16af multi 48 38

Pashtunistan Day.

Coat of Arms — A340a

1976, Sept. Litho. *Perf. 11 Rough*
930 A340a 25p salmon 25 15
931 A340a 50p lt grn 25 15
932 A340a 1af ultra 25 15
Nos. 930-932 (3) 75 45

Flag and Views on Open Book — A341

1977, May 27 Photo. *Perf. 14*
937 A341 20af grn & multi 60 50

59th Independence Day.

Pres. Daoud and National Assembly — A342

President Taking Oath of Office — A343

Designs: 10af, Inaugural address. 18af, Promulgation of Constitution.

1977, June 22
938 A342 7af multi 65 45
939 A343 8af multi 70 60
940 A343 10af multi 90 75
941 A342 18af multi 1.65 1.25
a. Souvenir sheet of 4 3.00 3.00
Nos. 938-941 (4) 3.90 3.05

Election of 1st Pres. and promulgation of Constitution. No. 941a contains 4 imperf. stamps similar to Nos. 938-941.

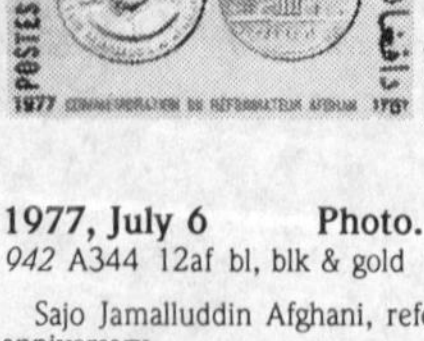

Jamalluddin Medal
A344

1977, July 6 Photo. *Perf. 14*
942 A344 12af bl, blk & gold 35 30

Sajo Jamalluddin Afghani, reformer, 80th death anniversary.

Afghanistan Flag over Crowd — A345

1977, July 17
943 A345 22af multi 65 55

Dancers, Fountain, Pashtunistan Flag — A346

1977, Aug. 31
944 A346 30af multi 90 75

Pashtunistan Day.

Arms and Carrier Pigeon
A346a

1977, Oct. 30 Litho. *Perf. 11*
944A A346a 1af black & blue 15 15

Members of Parliament Congratulating Pres. Daoud — A347

1978, Feb. 5 Litho. *Perf. 14*
945 A347 20af multi 1.75

Election of first president, first anniversary.

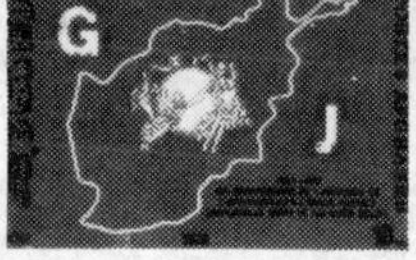

Map of Afghanistan, UPU Emblem
A348

1978, Apr. 1 Photo. *Perf. 14*
946 A348 10af grn, blk & gold 30 25

Afghanistan's UPU membership, 50th anniv.

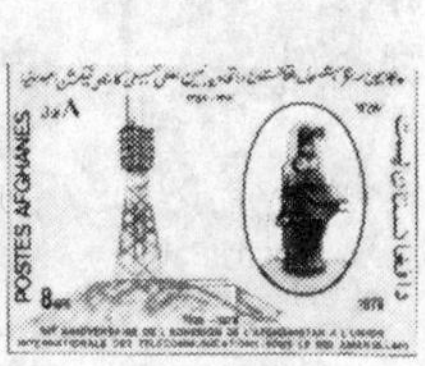

Wall Telephone and Satellite Station
A349

1978, Apr. 12
947 A349 8af multi 24 20

Afghanistan's ITU membership, 50th anniv.

Democratic Republic

Arrows Pointing to Crescent, Cross and Lion — A350

1978, July 6 Litho. *Perf. 11 Rough*
948 A350 3af black 1.00 50

50th anniv. of Afghani Red Crescent Soc.

Khalq Party Emblem A350a

1978, Aug. Litho. *Perf. 11*
948A A350a 1af rose red & gold 1.25 50
948B A350a 4af rose red & gold 1.75 75

Qalai Bist Arch A351

1978, Aug. 19 *Perf. 14*
949 A351 16af Bamian Buddha 1.00 40
949A A351 22af shown 1.25 55
949B A351 30af Hazara Women 1.75 90
Nos. 949-949B (3) 4.00 1.85

Men with Pashtunistan Flag — A352

Coat of Arms and Emblems — A353

1978, Aug. 31 *Perf. 11 Rough*
950 A352 7af ultra & red 22 16

Pashtunistan Day.

1978, Sept. 8 *Perf. 11*
951 A353 20af rose red 60 50

World Literacy Day.

A354

Perf. 11½ Rough
1978, Oct. 25 Litho.
952 A354 18af light green 55 45

Hero of Afghanistan.

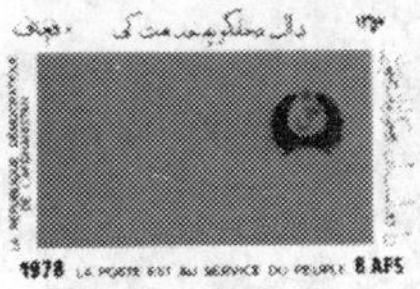

Khalq Party Flag — A355

1978, Oct. 19 Photo. *Perf. 11½*
953 A355 8af blk, red & gold 24 20
954 A355 9af blk, red & gold 30 22

"The mail serving the people."

Nour Mohammad Taraki — A356

1979, Jan. 1 Litho. *Perf. 12*
955 A356 12af multi 35 15

Nour Mohammad Taraki, founder of People's Democratic Party of Afghanistan, installation as president.

Woman Breaking Chain — A357

1979, Mar. 8 Litho. *Perf. 11*
956 A357 14af red & ultra *1.50* 50

Women's Day. Inscribed "POSSTES."

Map of Afghanistan, Census Emblem A358

1979, Mar. 25 Litho. *Perf. 12*
957 A358 3af multi 75 50

First comprehensive population census.

Farmers A359

1979, Mar. 21
958 A359 1af multi 50 25

Agricultural advances.

Pres. Taraki Reading First Issue of Khalq — A360

1979, Apr. 11 *Perf. 12½x12*
959 A360 2af multi 25 15

Khalq, newspaper of People's Democratic Republic of Afghanistan.

Pres. Noor Mohammad Taraki — A361

Plaza with Tank Monument and Fountain — A362

House where Revolution Started — A363

Designs: 50p, Taraki, tank. 12af, House where 1st Khalq Party Congress was held.

Perf. 12, 12½x12 (A362)
1979, Apr. 27 Litho.
959A A363 50p multi 15 15
960 A361 4af multi 16 15
961 A362 5af multi 24 16
962 A363 6af multi 28 24
963 A363 12af multi 52 45
Nos. 959A-963 (5) 1.35 1.15

1st anniversary of revolution.

Carpenter and Blacksmith A364

1979, May 1 *Perf. 12*
964 A364 10af multi 30 25

Int'l Labor Day.

Children, Flag and Map of Afghanistan — A366

1979, June 1 Litho. *Perf. 12½x12*
966 A366 16af multi 1.50 75

International Year of the Child.

Doves Circling Asia in Globe A366a

1979 Litho. *Perf. 11x10½*
966A A366a 2af red & blue 1.00 20

Armed Afghans, Kabul Memorial and Arch — A367

Pashtunistan Citizens, Flag — A368

1979, Aug. 19 Litho. *Perf. 12*
967 A367 30af multi 1.25 75

60th independence day.

1979, Aug. 31
968 A368 9 af multi 28 22

Pashtunistan Day.

UPU Day — A369

1979, Oct. 9 Litho. *Perf. 12*
969 A369 15af multi 45 38

Tombstone — A369a

1979, Oct. 25 Litho. *Perf. 12½x12*
969A A369a 22af multi 2.00 1.00

International Women's Day — A370

1980, Mar. 8 Litho. *Perf. 12*
970 A370 8af multi *3.00 3.00*

Farmers' Day — A371

1980, Mar. 21 Litho. ***Perf. 11½x12***

971 A371 2af multi		50	25

Non-smoker and Smoker — A372

1980, Apr. 7 ***Perf. 11½***

972 A372 5af multi		25	15

Anti-smoking campaign; World Health Day.

Lenin, 110th Birth Anniversary A373

1980, Apr. 22 ***Perf. 12x12½***

973 A373 12af multi		35	30

People and Fist on Map of Afghanistan A374

1980, Apr. 27 Litho. ***Perf. 12½x12***

974 A374 1af multi		25	25

Saur Revolution, 2nd anniversary.

International Workers' Solidarity Day — A375

1980, May 1

975 A375 9af multi		28	22

Wrestling, Moscow '80 Emblem A376

Perf. 12x12½, 12½x12

1980, July 19

976 A376	3af Soccer, vert.	.60	25
977 A376	6af shown	1.00	45
978 A376	9af Buzkashi	1.65	60
979 A376	10af Pegsticking	1.75	75
	Nos. 976-979 (4)	5.00	2.05

22nd Summer Olympic Games, Moscow, July 19-Aug. 3.

61st Anniversary of Independence — A377

1980, Aug. 19 Litho. ***Perf. 12½x12***

980 A377 3af multi		25	15

Pashtunistan Day — A378

1980, Aug. 30

981 A378 25af multi		80	65

Intl. UPU Day — A379

1980, Oct. 9 Litho. ***Perf. 12½x12***

982 A379 20af multi		60	50

International Women's Day — A381

1981, Mar. 9 Litho. ***Perf. 12½x12***

984 A381 15af multi		45	38

Farmers' Day — A382

1981, Mar. 20 Litho. ***Perf. 12½x12***

985 A382 1af multi		25	25

Bighorn Mountain Sheep (Protected Species) — A383

1981, Apr. 4 ***Perf. 12x12½***

986 A383 12af multi		1.00	75

Saur Revolution, 3rd Anniversary A384

Intl. Workers' Solidarity Day A385

1981, Apr. 27 ***Perf. 11***

987 A384 50p brown		15	15

1981, May 1 ***Perf. 12½x12***

988 A385 10af multi		30	25

13th World Telecommunications Day — A387

1981, May 17 Litho. ***Perf. 12½x12***

990 A387 9af multi		28	22

Intl. Children's Day — A388

1981, June 1 ***Perf. 12x12½***

991 A388 15af multi		45	38

People's Independence Monument 62nd Anniv. of Independence A389

1981, Aug. 19

992 A389 4af multi		15	15

Pashtunistan Day — A390

1981, Aug. 31 Litho. ***Perf. 12***

992A A390 2af multi		25	15

Intl. Tourism Day — A391

1981, Sept. 27 ***Perf. 12½x12***

993 A391 5af multi		25	15

World Food Day — A392

1981, Oct. 16

995 A392 7af multi		35	15

Asia-Africa Solidarity Meeting A393

1981, Nov. 18 Litho. ***Perf. 11***

996 A393 8af blue		24	20

Struggle Against Apartheid A394

1300th Anniv. of Bulgaria A395

1981, Dec. 1 ***Perf. 12½x12***

997 A394 4af multi		30	20

1981, Dec. 9 ***Perf. 12x12½***

998 A395 20af multi		1.25	1.00

Buzkashi Game A395a

1980 Photo. ***Perf. 14***

998A A395a	50af multi	3.00	1.00
998B A395a	100af multi	6.00	2.00

Intl. Women's Day — A396

1982, Mar. 8 Litho. ***Perf. 12***

999 A396 6af multi		50	25

Farmers' Day — A397

1982, Mar. 21

1000 A397 4af multi		25	15

Rhubarb Plant — A398

Saur Revolution, 4th Anniv. — A399

Designs: Various local plants.

1982, Apr. 9 Litho. *Perf. 12*
1001 A398 3af Judas trees 25 15
1002 A398 4af Rose of Sharon 35 15
1003 A398 16af shown 1.00 40
Nos. 1001-1003 (3) 1.60
Set value 58

1982, Apr. 27
1004 A399 1af multi 25 15

George Dimitrov (1882-1947), First Prime Minister of Bulgaria — A400

Intl. Workers' Solidarity Day — A401

1982, Apr. 30
1005 A400 30af multi 90 75

1982, May 1
1006 A401 10af multi 30 25

Storks — A402

1982, May 31
1007 A402 6af shown 50 25
1008 A402 11af Nightingales 1.00 45

Hedgehogs A403

1982, July 6 Litho. *Perf. 12*
1009 A403 3af shown 25 15
1010 A403 14af Cobra 75 50

See Nos. 1020-1022.

63rd Anniv. of Independence A404

1982, Aug. 19
1011 A404 20af multi 60 50

Pashtunistan Day — A405

1982, Aug. 31
1012 A405 32af multi 1.00 80

World Tourism Day — A406

1982, Sept. 27 Litho. *Perf. 12*
1013 A406 9af multi 75 50

UPU Day — A407

1982, Oct. 9
1014 A407 4af multi 50 25

World Food Day — A408

1982, Oct. 16
1015 A408 9af multi 30 22

37th Anniv. of UN — A409

1982, Oct. 24
1016 A409 15af multi 45 38

ITU Plenipotentiaries Conference, Nairobi, Sept. — A410

1982, Oct. 26
1017 A410 8af multi 25 20

TB Bacillus Centenary A411

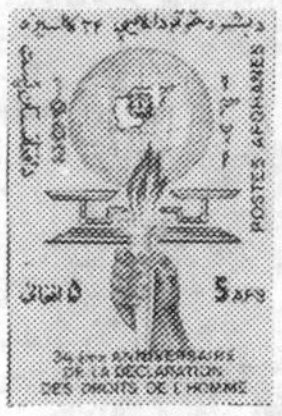

Human Rights Declaration, 34th Anniv. A412

1982, Nov. 24 Litho. *Perf. 12*
1018 A411 7af multi 22 18

1982, Dec. 10
1019 A412 5af multi 25 15

Animal Type of 1982

1982, Dec. 16
1020 A403 2af Lions 25 15
1021 A403 7af Donkeys 75 18
1022 A403 12af Marmots, vert. 1.00 28
Nos. 1020-1022 (3) 2.00
Set value 50

Intl. Women's Day — A413

Mir Alicher Nawai Research Decade — A414

1983, Mar. 8
1023 A413 3af multi 25 15

1983, Mar. 19
1024 A414 22af multi 70 50

Farmers' Day — A415

1983, Mar. 21 Litho. *Perf. 12*
1025 A415 10af multi 30 25

5th Anniv. of Saur Revolution A416

1983, Apr. 27 Litho. *Perf. 12*
1026 A416 15af multi 1.00 50

Intl. Workers' Solidarity Day — A417

1983, May 1
1027 A417 2af multi 60 50

World Communications Year — A418

1983, May 17
1028 A418 4af Modes of communication 25 15
1029 A418 11af Building 75 28

Intl. Children's Day — A419

1983, June 1 Litho. *Perf. 12*
1030 A419 25af multi 1.50 1.50

2nd Anniv. of National Front — A420

1983, June 15
1031 A420 1af multi 15 15

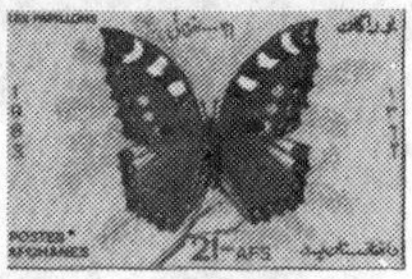

Local Butterflies A421

Various butterflies. 9af, 13af vert.

1983, July 6
1032 A421 9af multi 55 55
1033 A421 13af multi 80 80
1034 A421 21af multi 1.25 1.25
Nos. 1032-1034 (3) 2.60 2.60

Struggle Against Apartheid — A422

1983, Aug. 1 Litho. *Perf. 12*
1035 A422 10af multi 60 60

64th Anniv of Independence A423

1983, Aug. 19
1036 A423 6af multi 35 35

Parliament House A423a

1983, Sept. Litho. *Perf. 12*
1036A A423a 50af shown 3.00 3.00
1036B A423a 100af Afghan Woman, Camel 6.00 6.00

A424

World Tourism Day — A425

1983, Sept. 27 **Litho.** ***Perf. 12***

1037 A424 5af shown 30 30
1038 A425 7af shown 42 42
1039 A424 12af Golden statues 75 75
1040 A425 16af Stone carving 1.00 1.00
Nos. 1037-1040 (4) 2.47 2.47

World Communications Year — A426

1983, Oct. 9 **Litho.** ***Perf. 12***

1041 A426 14af Dish antenna, dove 85 85
1042 A426 15af shown 90 90

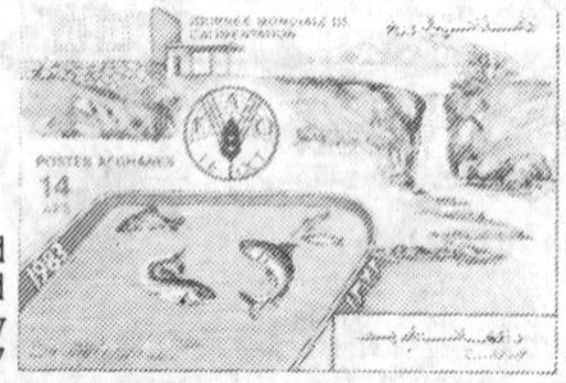

World Food Day A427

1983, Oct. 16 **Litho.** ***Perf. 12***

1043 A427 14af multi 85 85

Boxing A428

1983, Nov. 1 **Litho.** ***Perf. 12***

1044 A428 1af Running 15 15
1045 A428 18af shown 1.10 1.10
1046 A428 21af Wrestling 1.25 1.25
Nos. 1044-1046 (3) 2.50 2.50

Pashtunistan Day — A428a

1983,Nov. **Litho.** ***Perf. 12***

1046A A428a 3af Pathans Waving Flag 18 18

Handicrafts A429

1983, Nov. 22

1047 A429 2af Jewelry 15 15
1048 A429 8af Stone ashtrays, dishes 50 50
1049 A429 19af Furniture 1.10 1.10
1050 A429 30af Leather goods 1.90 1.90
Nos. 1047-1050 (4) 3.65 3.65

UN Declaration of Human Rights, 35th Anniv. A430

1983, Dec. 10 **Litho.** ***Perf. 12***

1051 A430 20af multi 1.25 1.25

Kabul Polytechnical Institute, 20th Anniv. — A431

1983, Dec. 28 ***Perf. 12½x12***

1052 A431 30af multi 1.90 1.90

1984 Winter Olympics A432

1984, Jan. ***Perf. 12***

1053 A432 5af Figure skating 30 30
1054 A432 9af Skiing 55 55
1055 A432 11af Speed skating 65 65
1056 A432 15af Hockey 90 90
1057 A432 18af Biathlon 1.10 1.10
1058 A432 20af Ski jumping 1.25 1.25
1059 A432 22af Bobsledding 1.40 1.40
Nos. 1053-1059 (7) 6.15 6.15

Intl. Women's Day — A433

1984, Mar. 8

1060 A433 4af multi 25 25

Farmers' Day — A434

Various agricultural scenes.

1984, Mar. 21 **Litho.** ***Perf. 12***

1061 A434 2af multi 15 15
1062 A434 4af multi 25 25
1063 A434 7af multi 42 42
1064 A434 9af multi 55 55
1065 A434 15af multi 95 95
1066 A434 18af multi 1.10 1.10
1067 A434 20af multi 1.25 1.25
Nos. 1061-1067 (7) 4.67 4.67

World Aviation Day — A435

1984, Apr. 12

1068 A435 5af Luna 1 30 30
1069 A435 8af Luna 2 50 50
1070 A435 11af Luna 3 70 70
1071 A435 17af Apollo 11 1.00 1.00
1072 A435 22af Soyuz 6 1.40 1.40
1073 A435 28af Soyuz 7 1.75 1.75
1074 A435 34af Soyuz 6, 7, 8 2.00 2.00
Nos. 1068-1074 (7) 7.65 7.65

Souvenir Sheet

Perf. 12x12½

1075 A435 25af S. Koroliov 1.50 1.50

No. 1075 contains one 30x41mm stamp.

Saur Revolution, 6th Anniv. A436

1984, Apr. 27 ***Perf. 12***

1076 A436 3af multi 25 25

65th Anniv. of Independence A437

1984, Aug. 19 **Litho.** ***Perf. 12***

1077 A437 6af multi 38 38

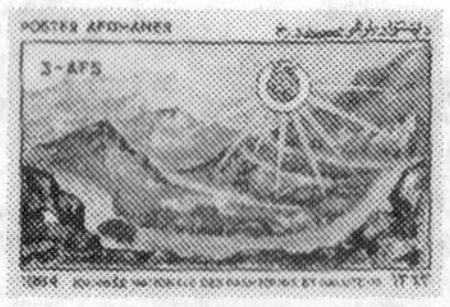

Pashto's and Balutchi's Day — A438

1984, Aug. 31

1078 A438 3af Symbolic sun, tribal terr. 25 25

Wildlife A439

Perf. 12½x12, 12x12½

1984, May 5 **Litho.**

1079 A439 1af Cape hunting dog, vert. 15 15
1080 A439 2af Argali sheep, vert. 15 15
1081 A439 6af Przewalski's horse 38 38
1082 A439 8af Wild boar, vert. 50 50
1083 A439 17af Snow leopard 1.00 1.00
1084 A439 19af Tiger 1.25 1.25
1085 A439 22af Indian elephant, vert. 1.40 1.40
Nos. 1079-1085 (7) 4.83 4.83

19th UPU Congress, Hamburg A440

1984, June 18 ***Perf. 12x12½***

1086 A440 25af German postman, 17th cent. 1.50 1.50
1087 A440 35af Postrider, 16th cent. 2.00 2.00
1088 A440 40af Carrier pigeon, letter 2.50 2.50
Nos. 1086-1088 (3) 6.00 6.00

Souvenir Sheet

1089 A440 50af Hamburg No. 3 in black 4.00 4.00

No. 1089 contains one 30x40mm stamp.

Natl. Aviation, 40th Anniv. A441

Soviet civil aircraft.

1984, June 29

1090 A441 1af Antonov AN-2 15 15
1091 A441 4af Ilyushin IL-12 25 25
1092 A441 9af Tupolev TU-104 55 55
1093 A441 10af Ilyushin IL-18 60 60
1094 A441 13af Tupolev TU-134 80 80
1095 A441 17af Ilyushin IL-62 1.00 1.00
1096 A441 21af Ilyushin IL-28 1.25 1.25
Nos. 1090-1096 (7) 4.60 4.60

Ettore Bugatti (1881-1947), Type 43, Italy — A442

Classic automobiles and their designers: 5af, Henry Ford, 1903 Model A, US. 8af, Rene Panhard (1841-1908), 1899 Landau, France. 11af, Gottlieb Daimler (1834-1900), 1935 Daimler-Benz, Germany. 12af, Carl Benz (1844-1929), 1893 Victoris, Germany. 15af, Armand Peugeot (1848-1915), 1892 Vis-a-Vis, France. 22af, Louis Chevrolet (1879-1941), 1925 Sedan, US.

1984, June 30

1097 A442 2af multi 15 15
1098 A442 5af multi 30 30
1099 A442 8af multi 50 50
1100 A442 11af multi 70 70
1101 A442 12af multi 75 75
1102 A442 15af multi 90 90
1103 A442 22af multi 1.40 1.40
Nos. 1097-1103 (7) 4.70 4.70

Qalai Bist Arch — A443

World Tourism Day: 2af, Ornamental buckled harness. 5af, Victory Monument and Memorial Arch, Kabul. 9af, Standing sculpture of Afghani ruler and attendants. 15af, Buffalo riders in snow. 19af, Camel driver, tent, camel in caparison. 21af, Horsemen playing buzkashi.

1984, Sept. 27

1104 A443 1af multi 15 15
1105 A443 2af multi 15 15
1106 A443 5af multi 30 30
1107 A443 9af multi 55 55
1108 A443 15af multi 60 60
1109 A443 19af multi 1.10 1.10
1110 A443 21af multi 1.25 1.25
Nos. 1104-1110 (7) 4.10 4.10

UN World Food Day — A444

Fruit-bearing trees.

1984, Oct. 16

1111 A444 2af multi 15 15
1112 A444 4af multi 25 25
1113 A444 6af multi 38 38
1114 A444 9af multi 55 55
1115 A444 13af multi 80 80
1116 A444 15af multi 90 90
1117 A444 26af multi 1.65 1.65
Nos. 1111-1117 (7) 4.68 4.68

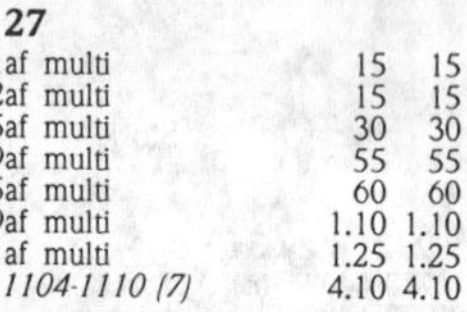

People's Democratic Party, 20th Anniv. A445

1985, Jan. 1

1118 A445 25af multi 1.50 1.50

Farmer's Day — A446

1985, Mar. 2

1119 A446 1af Oxen 15 15
1120 A446 3af Mare, foal 18 18
1121 A446 7af Brown horse 40 40
1122 A446 8af White horse, vert. 50 50
1123 A446 15af Sheep, sheepskins 90 90
1124 A446 16af Shepherd, cattle, sheep 1.00 1.00
1125 A446 25af Family, camels 1.50 1.50
Nos. 1119-1125 (7) 4.63 4.63

Geologist's Day — A447

1985, Apr. 5

1126 A447 4af multi 25 25

Lenin Leading Red Army, 1917 — A448

Lenin and: 10af, Soviet Workers' Party deputies, Smolny. 15af, Revolutionaries, 1917, Leningrad. 50af, Portrait.

1985, Apr. 21 *Perf. 12x12½*

1127 A448 10af multi 60 60
1128 A448 15af multi 90 90
1129 A448 25af multi 1.50 1.50
Nos. 1127-1129 (3) 3.00 3.00

Souvenir Sheet

1130 A448 50af multi 4.00 4.00

Saur Revolution, 7th Anniv. — A449

1985, Apr. 27

1131 A449 21af multi 1.25 1.25

Berlin-Treptow Soviet War Memorial, Red Army at Siege of Berlin, 1945 — A450

Designs: 9af, Victorious Motherland monument, fireworks over Kremlin. 10af, Caecilienhof, site of Potsdam Treaty signing, flags of Great Britain, USSR and US.

1985, May 9 *Perf. 12½x12*

1132 A450 6af multi 38 38
1133 A450 9af multi 55 55
1134 A450 10af multi 65 65
Nos. 1132-1134 (3) 1.58 1.58

End of World War II, defeat of Nazi Germany, 40th anniv.

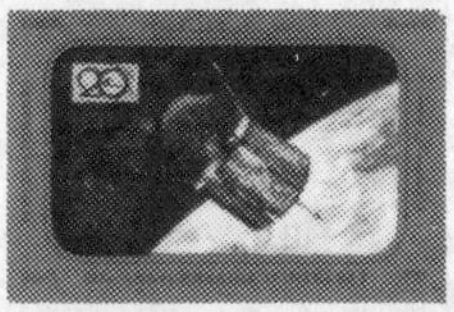

INTELSAT, 20th Anniv. A451

Designs: 6af, INTELSAT satellite orbiting Earth. 9af, INTELSAT III. 10af, Rocket launch, Baikanur Space Center, vert.

Perf. 12x12½, 12½x12

1985, Apr. 6 **Litho.**

1135 A451 6af multi 38 38
1136 A451 9af multi 55 55
1137 A451 10af multi 60 60
Nos. 1135-1137 (3) 1.53 1.53

12th World Youth Festival, Moscow — A452

1985, May 5

1138 A452 7af Olympic stadium, Moscow 50 50
1139 A452 12af Festival emblem 75 75
1140 A452 13af Kremlin 80 80
1141 A452 18af Folk doll, emblem 1.10 1.10
Nos. 1138-1141 (4) 3.15 3.15

Intl. Child Survival Campaign A453

1985, June 1

1142 A453 1af Weighing child 15 15
1143 A453 2af Immunization 15 15
1144 A453 4af Breastfeeding 25 25
1145 A453 5af Mother, child 30 30
Nos. 1142-1145 (4) 85 85

Flowers A454

1985, July 5

1146 A454 2af Oenothera affinis 15 15
1147 A454 4af Erythrina crista-galli 25 25
1148 A454 8af Tillandsia aeranthos 50 50
1149 A454 13af Vinca major 80 80
1150 A454 18af Mirabilis jalapa 1.10 1.10
1151 A454 25af Cypella herbertii 1.50 1.50
1152 A454 30af Clytostoma callistegioides 1.90 1.90
Nos. 1146-1152 (7) 6.20 6.20

Souvenir Sheet

Perf. 12½x11½

1153 A454 75af Sesbania punicea, horiz. 6.00 6.00

ARGENTINA '85.

Independence, 66th Anniv. A455

1985, Aug. 19 *Perf. 12x12½*

1154 A455 33af Mosque 2.00 2.00

Pashto's and Balutchi's Day — A456

1985, Aug. 30

1155 A456 25af multi 1.50 1.50

UN Decade for Women A457

1985, Sept. 22

1156 A457 10af Emblems 60 60

World Tourism Day, 10th Anniv. A457a

1985, Sept. 27 **Litho.** *Perf. 12*

1156A A457a 1af Guldara Stupa 15 15
1156B A457a 2af Mirwais Tomb, vert. 15 15
1156C A457a 10af Statue of Bamyan, vert. 60 60
1156D A457a 13af No Gumbad Mosque, vert. 80 80
1156E A457a 14af Pule Kheshti Mosque 85 85
1156F A457a 15af Bost Citadel 90 90
1156G A457a 20af Ghazni Minaret, vert. 1.25 1.25
Nos. 1156A-1156G (7) 4.70 4.70

Sports A457b

Perf. 12x12½, 12½x12

1985, Oct. 3 **Litho.**

1156H A457b 1af Boxing 15 15
1156I A457b 2af Volleyball 15 15
1156J A457b 3af Soccer, vert. 22 22
1156K A457b 12af Buzkashi 88 88
1156L A457b 14af Weight lifting 1.00 1.00
1156M A457b 18af Wrestling 1.30 1.30
1156N A457b 25af Peg sticking 1.85 1.85
Nos. 1156H-1156N (7) 5.55 5.55

World Food Day — A457c

1985, Oct. 16

1156O A457c 25af multi 1.50 1.50

UN 40th Anniv. — A458

Birds — A459

1985, Oct. 24 *Perf. 12½x12*

1157 A458 22af multi 1.40 1.40

Perf. 12½x12, 12x12½

1985, Oct. 25

1158 A459 2af Jay 15 15
1159 A459 4af Plover, hummingbird 25 25
1160 A459 8af Pheasant 50 50
1161 A459 13af Hoopoe 80 80
1162 A459 18af Falcon 1.10 1.10
1163 A459 25af Partridge 1.50 1.50
1164 A459 30af Pelicans, horiz. 1.90 1.90
Nos. 1158-1164 (7) 6.20 6.20

Souvenir Sheet

Perf. 12x12½

1165 A459 75af Parakeets 6.00 6.00

Mushrooms — A460

1985, June 10 **Litho.** *Perf. 12½x12*

1165A A460 3af Tricholomopsis rutilans 20 20
1166 A460 4af Boletus miniatoporus 25 25
1167 A460 7af Amanita rubescens 45 45
1168 A460 11af Boletus scaber 65 65
1169 A460 12af Coprinus atramentarius 75 75
1170 A460 18af Hypholoma 1.10 1.10
1171 A460 20af Boletus aurantiacus 1.25 1.25
Nos. 1165A-1171 (7) 4.65 4.65

World Wildlife Fund — A461

1985, Nov. 25

1172 A461 2af Leopard, cubs 15 15
1173 A461 9af Adult's head 55 55
1174 A461 11af Adult 70 70
1175 A461 15af Cub 90 90
Nos. 1172-1175 (4) 2.30 2.30

Motorcycle, Cent. — A462

Designs: Different makes and landmarks.

1985, Dec. 16

1176 A462 2af multi 15 15
1177 A462 4af multi 24 24
1178 A462 8af multi 48 48
1179 A462 13af multi 75 75
1180 A462 18af multi 1.00 1.00

1181 A462 25af multi 1.50 1.50
1182 A462 30af multi 1.75 1.75
Nos. 1176-1182 (7) 5.87 5.87

Souvenir Sheet

Perf. 11½x12½

1183 A462 75af multi 6.00 6.00

People's Democratic Party, 21st Anniv. — A463

1986, Jan. 1 ***Perf. 12½x12***
1184 A463 2af multi 25 25

27th Soviet Communist Party Congress — A464

1986, Mar. 31
1185 A464 25af Lenin 1.50 1.50

First Man in Space, 25th Anniv. — A465

Designs: 3af, Spacecraft. 7af, Soviet space achievement medal, vert. 9af, Rocket lift-off, vert. 11af, Yuri Gagarin, military decorations, vert. 13af, Gagarin, cosmonaut. 15af, Gagarin, politician. 17af, Gagarin wearing flight suit, vert.

Perf. 12½x12, 12x12½

1986, Apr. 12 **Litho.**
1186 A465 3af multi
1187 A465 7af multi
1188 A465 9af multi
1189 A465 11af multi
1190 A465 13af multi
1191 A465 15af multi
1192 A465 17af multi
Nos. 1186-1192 (7) 4.50 4.50

Loya Jirgah (Grand Assembly) of the People's Democratic Republic, 1st Anniv. A465a

1986, Apr. 23 **Litho.** ***Perf. 12x12½***
1192A A465a 3af multi 25 25

Intl. Day of Labor Solidarity — A465b

1986, May 1 ***Perf. 12½x12***
1192B A465b 5af multi 30 30

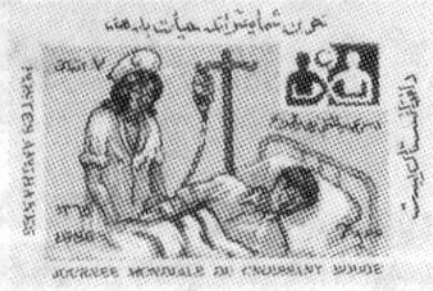

Intl. Red Crescent Day A465c

1986, May 8 ***Perf. 12x12½***
1192C A465c 7af multi 45 45

Intl. Children's Day — A466

1986, June 1 ***Perf. 12***
1193 A466 1af Mother, children, vert. 15 15
1194 A466 3af Mother, child, vert. 25 25
1195 A466 9af Children, map 40 40
Nos. 1193-1195 (3) 80 80

World Youth Day — A466a

1986, July 31 ***Perf. 12x12½***
1195A A466a 15af multi 90 90

Pashtos' and Baluchis' Day — A467

1986, Aug. 31 ***Perf. 12x12½***
1196 A467 4af multi 25 25

Intl. Peace Year — A468

1986, Sept. 30 **Photo.** ***Perf. 12½x12***
1197 A468 12af blk & Prus bl 75 75

A469

1986 World Cup Soccer Championships, Mexico — A470

Various soccer plays.

1986, Apr. 15 **Litho.** ***Perf. 12***
1198 A469 3af multi, vert.
1199 A469 4af multi
1200 A469 7af multi
1201 A469 11af multi, vert.
1202 A469 12af multi
1203 A469 18af multi, vert.
1204 A469 20af multi, vert.
Nos. 1198-1204 (7) 4.50 4.50

Souvenir Sheet

Perf. 12½x12

1205 A470 75af multi 6.00 6.00

A471

A472

1986, Apr. 21 ***Perf. 12½x12***
1206 A471 16af Lenin 1.00 1.00

1986, Apr. 27 **Litho.** ***Perf. 12½x12***
1207 A472 8af multi 50 50

Saur revolution, 8th anniv.

Natl. Independence, 67th Anniv. — A473

1986, Aug. 19 **Litho.** ***Perf. 12½x12***
1208 A473 10af multi 65 65

Literacy Day — A474

1986, Sept. 18 ***Perf. 12x12½***
1209 A474 2af multi 25 25

Dogs — A475

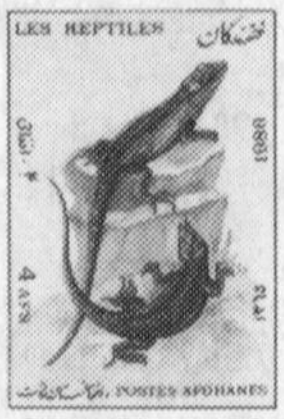

Lizards — A476

1986, May 19 **Litho.** ***Perf. 12x12½***
1210 A475 5af St. Bernard
1211 A475 7af Collie
1212 A475 8af Pointer
1213 A475 9af Golden retriever
1214 A475 11af German shepherd
1215 A475 15af Bulldog
1216 A475 20af Afghan hound
Nos. 1210-1216 (7) 4.50 4.50

1986, July 7 ***Perf. 12x12½, 12½x12***
1217 A476 3af Cobra
1218 A476 4af shown
1219 A476 5af Praying mantis
1220 A476 8af Beetle
1221 A476 9af Tarantula
1222 A476 10af Python
1223 A476 11af Scorpions
Nos. 1217-1223 (7) 3.00 3.00

Nos. 1217, 1219, 1221-1223 horiz.

STOCKHOLMIA '86 — A477

Ships.

1986, Aug. 28 ***Perf. 12½x12***
1224 A477 4af multi
1225 A477 5af multi
1226 A477 6af multi
1227 A477 7af multi
1228 A477 8af multi
1229 A477 9af multi
1230 A477 11af multi
Nos. 1224-1230 (7) 3.00 3.00

Souvenir Sheet

1231 A477 50af Galley 4.00 4.00

A479

A480

1986, Sept. 14 ***Perf. 12***
1232 A479 3af lt blue, blk & olive gray 25 25

Reunion of Afghan tribes under the Supreme Girgah.

1986, Oct. 25 ***Perf. 12½x12***
1233 A480 3af blk & brt ver 25 25

Natl. youth solidarity.

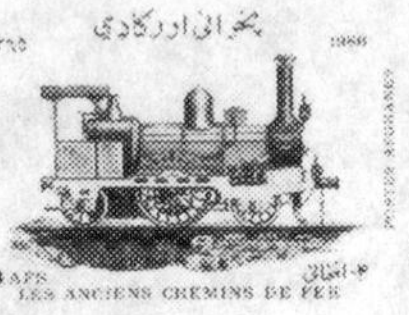

Locomotives — A481

1986, June 21 ***Perf. 12½x12***
1234 A481 4af multi
1235 A481 5af multi
1236 A481 6af multi
1237 A481 7af multi
1238 A481 8af multi
1239 A481 9af multi
1240 A481 11af multi
Nos. 1234-1240 (7) 3.00 3.00

Fish A482

Various fish.

1986, May 25
1241 A482 5af multi
1242 A482 7af multi
1243 A482 8af multi
1244 A482 9af multi
1245 A482 11af multi
1246 A482 15af multi
1247 A482 20af multi
Nos. 1241-1247 (7) 4.50 4.50

Saur Revolution, 9th Anniv. A483

1987, Apr. 27 *Perf. 12*
1248 A483 3af multi 25 25

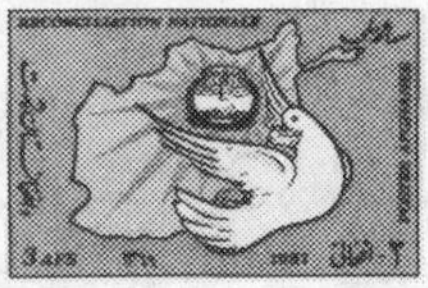
Natl. Reconciliation A484

1987, May 27 *Perf. 12x12½*
1249 A484 3af multi 25 25

A485

A486

UN Child Survival Campaign — A487

1987, June 1 *Perf. 12*
1250 A485 1af multi 15 15
1251 A486 5af multi 30 30
1252 A487 9af multi 55 55
Nos. 1250-1252 (3) 1.00 1.00

Conference of Clergymen and Ulema, 1st Anniv. A488

1987, June 30
1253 A488 5af multi 30 30

Butterflies — A489

A490

1987, July 3
1254 A489 7af multi
1255 A489 9af multi, diff.
1256 A489 10af multi, diff.
1257 A489 12af multi, diff.
1258 A489 15af multi, diff.
1259 A489 22af multi, diff.
1260 A489 25af multi, diff.
Nos. 1254-1260 (7) 6.00 6.00

10af, 15af and 22af horiz.

1987, Aug. 11
1261 A490 1af multi 25 25

1st election of local representatives for State Power and Administration.

Natl. Independence, 68th Anniv. — A490a

1987, Aug. 19
1261A A490a 3af multi 25 25

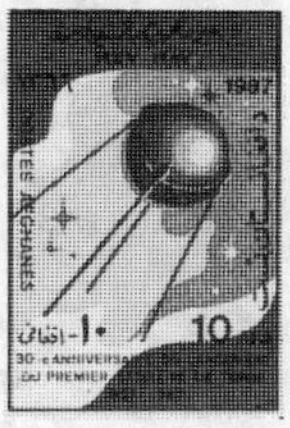
1st Artificial Satellite (Sputnik), 30th Anniv. — A491

1987, Oct. 4 **Litho.** *Perf. 12½x12*
1262 A491 10af Sputnik
1263 A491 15af Rocket launch
1264 A491 25af Soyuz
Nos. 1262-1264 (3) 3.00 3.00

World Post Day — A492

1987, Oct. 9 *Perf. 12x12½*
1265 A492 22af multi 1.40 1.40

Intl. Communications and Transport Day — A493

1987, Oct. 24 *Perf. 12½x12*
1266 A493 42af multi 2.50 2.50

October Revolution in Russia, 70th Anniv. — A494

Mice — A495

1987, Nov. 7
1267 A494 25af Lenin 1.50 1.50

1987, Dec. 6 *Perf. 12½x12, 12x12½*

Various mice. Nos. 1269-1272 horiz.

1268 A495 2af multi
1269 A495 4af multi, diff.
1270 A495 8af multi, diff.
1271 A495 16af multi, diff.
1272 A495 20af multi, diff.
Nos. 1268-1272 (5) 3.00 3.00

Medicinal Plants — A496

Pashto's and Baluchis' Day — A497

1987, Nov. 11 **Litho.** *Perf. 12*
1273 A496 3af Castor bean 18 18
1274 A496 6af Licorice 35 35
1275 A496 9af Chamomile 55 55
1276 A496 14af Datura 80 80
1277 A496 18af Dandelion 1.00 1.00
Nos. 1273-1277 (5) 2.88 2.88

1987, Aug. 30
1278 A497 4af multi 25 25

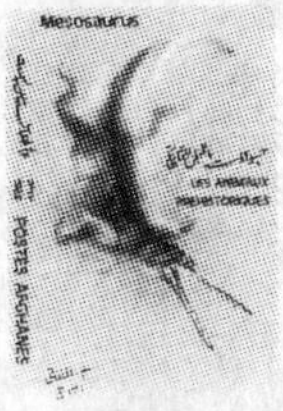
Dinosaurs A498

Pashtos' and Baluchis' Day A499

Perf. 12½x12, 12x12½
1988, June 6 **Litho.**
1279 A498 3af Mesosaurus 18 18
1280 A498 5af Styracosaurus 30 30
1281 A498 10af Uinatherium 60 60
1282 A498 15af Protoceratops 90 90
1283 A498 20af Stegosaurus 1.25 1.25
1284 A498 25af Ceratosaurus 1.50 1.50
1285 A498 30af Dinornis maximus 1.90 1.90
Nos. 1279-1285 (7) 6.63 6.63

Nos. 1280-1283 horiz.

1988, Aug. 30 *Perf. 12½x12*
1286 A499 23af multi 1.40 1.40

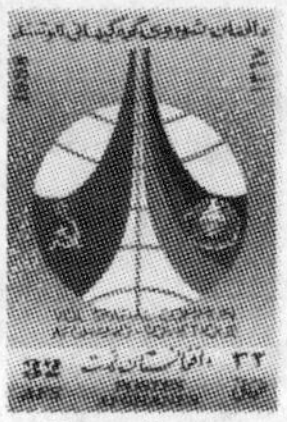
Afghan-Soviet Joint Space Flight — A500

Valentina Tereshkova, 1st Woman in Space, 25th Anniv. — A501

1988, Aug. 30
1287 A500 32af multi 2.00 2.00

Perf. 12x12½, 12½x12
1988, Oct. 16
1288 A501 10af Portrait, rocket, horiz. 60 60
1289 A501 15af Lift-off, dove 90 90
1290 A501 25af Spacecraft, Earth, horiz. 1.50 1.50
Nos. 1288-1290 (3) 3.00 3.00

Traditional Crafts — A502

Precious and Semiprecious Gems — A503

Perf. 12x12½, 12½x12
1988, Nov. 9 **Litho.**
1291 A502 2af Pitcher, bowls 15 15
1292 A502 4af Vases 25 25
1293 A502 5af Dress 30 30
1294 A502 9af Mats, napkins 55 55
1295 A502 15af Pocketbooks 90 90
1296 A502 23af Jewelry 1.40 1.40
1297 A502 50af Furniture 3.00 3.00
Nos. 1291-1297 (7) 6.55 6.55

Nos. 1291-1292, 1294-1297 horiz.

1988, Dec. 5 *Perf. 12½x12*
1298 A503 13af Emeralds 80 80
1299 A503 37af Lapiz lazuli 2.25 2.25
1300 A503 40af Rubies 2.50 2.50
Nos. 1298-1300 (3) 5.55 5.55

1988 Winter Olympics, Calgary — A504

1988, Dec. 25
1301 A504 2af Women's figure skating 15 15
1301A A504 5af Skiing 30 30
1301B A504 9af Bobsledding 55 55
1301C A504 22af Biathlon 1.40 1.40
1301D A504 37af Speed skating 2.25 2.25

Size: 80x60mm
1302 A504 75af Ice hockey 4.50 4.50
Nos. 1301-1302 (6) 9.15 9.15

A510

A511

A512

A513

A513a

Flowers — A514

Various flowering plants.

Perf. 12x12½, 12½x12

1988, Jan. 27 **Litho.**

1303 A510	3af multi	18	18
1304 A511	5af multi	30	30
1305 A511	7af multi, vert.	42	42
1306 A512	9af multi	52	52
1307 A513	12af multi	75	75
1308 A513a	15af multi	90	90
1309 A514	24af multi	1.50	1.50
	Nos. 1303-1309 (7)	4.57	4.57

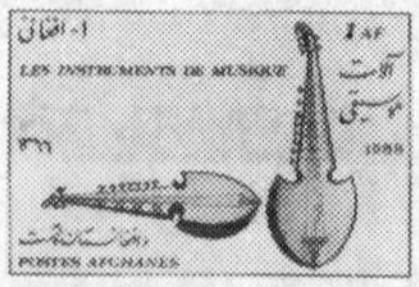
Traditional Musical Instruments A515

String and percussion instruments.

1988, Jan. 15 **Litho.** ***Perf. 12***

1310 A515	1af shown	15	15
1311 A515	3af drums	18	18
1312 A515	5af multi, diff.	30	30
1313 A515	15af multi, diff.	90	90
1314 A515	18af multi, diff.	1.10	1.10
1315 A515	25af multi, diff.	1.50	1.50
1316 A515	33af multi, diff.	2.00	2.00
	Nos. 1310-1316 (7)	6.13	6.13

Admission of Afghanistan to the ITU and UPU, 60th Anniv. — A516

1988, Apr. 13 **Litho.** ***Perf. 12***

1317 A516 20af multi 1.25 1.25

Saur Revolution, 10th Anniv. A517

1988, Apr. 23

1318 A517 10af multi 65 65

Fruit — A518

1988, July 18 **Litho.** ***Perf. 12***

1319 A518	2af Baskets, compote	15	15
1320 A518	4af Four baskets	25	25
1321 A518	7af Basket	42	42
1322 A518	8af Grapes, vert.	50	50
1323 A518	16af Market	1.00	1.00
1324 A518	22af Market, diff.	1.40	1.40
1325 A518	25af Vendor, vert.	1.50	1.50
	Nos. 1319-1325 (7)	5.22	5.22

Jawaharlal Nehru (1889-1964), 1st Prime Minister of Independent India — A519

1988, Nov. 14

1326 A519 40af multi 2.50 2.50

Natl. Independence, 69th Anniv. A520

1988, Aug. 1

1327 A520 24af multi 1.50 1.50

Intl. Red Cross and Red Crescent Organizations, 125th Annivs. — A521

1988, Sept. 26

1328 A521 10af multi 60 60

Natl. Reconciliation Institute, 2nd Anniv. — A522

1989, Jan. 4

1329 A522 4af multi 25 25

Chess A523

Boards, early matches and hand-made chessmen.

1989, Feb. 2 **Litho.** ***Perf. 12x12½***

1330 A523	2af Bishop	15	15
1331 A523	3af Queen	18	18
1332 A523	4af King (bust)	25	25
1333 A523	7af King, diff.	42	42
1334 A523	16af Knight	1.00	1.00
1335 A523	24af Pawn	1.50	1.50
1336 A523	45af Bishop, diff.	2.75	2.75
	Nos. 1330-1336 (7)	6.25	6.25

Paintings by Picasso — A524

Fauna — A525

Designs: 4af, *The Old Jew.* 6af, *The Two Mountebanks.* 8af, *Portrait of Ambrouse Vollar.* 22af, *Woman of Majorca.* 35af, *Acrobat on the Ball.* 75af, *Usine a Horta de Ebro.*

1989, Feb. 13 **Litho.** ***Perf. 12½x12***

1341 A524	4af multi	25	25
1342 A524	6af multi	35	35
1343 A524	8af multi	50	50
1344 A524	22af multi	1.40	1.40
1345 A524	35af multi	2.25	2.25

Size: 71x90mm

Imperf

1346 A524	75af multi	4.50	4.50
	Nos. 1341-1346 (6)	9.25	9.25

1989, Feb. 20 **Litho.** ***Perf. 12½x12***

1347 A525	3af *Allactaga euphratica*	18	18
1348 A525	4af *Equus hemionus*	25	25
1349 A525	14af *Felis lynx*	85	85
1350 A525	35af *Gypaetus barbatus*	2.25	2.25
1351 A525	44af *Capra falconeri*	2.75	2.75

Size: 71x91mm

Imperf

1352 A525	100af *Naja oxiana*	6.00	6.00
	Nos. 1347-1352 (6)	12.28	12.28

Intl. Women's Day — A526

1989, Mar. 8 ***Perf. 12½x12***

1353 A526 8af multi 50 50

Restoration and Development of San'a, Yemen A527

1988, Dec. 27 **Litho.** ***Perf. 12***

1354 A527 32af multi 2.00 2.00

Agriculture Day — A528

1989, Mar. 21

1355 A528	1af Cattle	15	15
1356 A528	2af Old and new plows	15	15
1357 A528	3af Field workers	18	18
	Set value	36	36

World Meteorology Day — A529

1989, Mar. 23

1358 A529	27af shown	1.65	1.65
1359 A529	32af Emblems	2.00	2.00
1360 A529	40af Weather station, balloon, vert.	2.50	2.50
	Nos. 1358-1360 (3)	6.15	6.15

Saur Revolution, 11th Anniv. A530

1989, Apr. 27

1361 A530 20af multi 1.25 1.25

Classic Automobiles — A531

1989 **Litho.** ***Perf. 12½x12***

1362 A531 5af 1910 Duchs, Germany
1363 A531 10af 1911 Ford, US
1364 A531 20af 1911 Renault, France
1365 A531 25af 1911, Russo-Balte, Russia
1366 A531 30af 1926 Fiat, Italy

Asia-Pacific Telecommunity, 10th Anniv. — A532

1989 ***Perf. 12***

1367 A532 3af shown
1368 A532 27af Emblem, satellite dish

Teacher's Day — A533

1989 **Litho.** ***Perf. 12***

1369 A533 42af multicolored 1.30

French Revolution, Bicent. — A534

1989 **Litho.** ***Perf. 12***

1370 A534 25af multicolored 78

Natl. Independence, 70th Anniv. A535

1989 **Litho.** ***Perf. 12***

1371 A535 25af multicolored 78

Pashtos' and Baluchis' Day — A536

1989

1372 A536 3af multicolored 15

Birds — A537

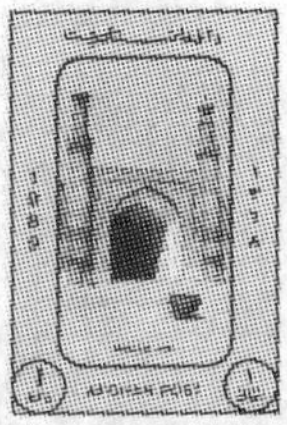

Tourism — A538

1989 **Litho.** ***Perf. 12***

1373 A537 3af Platalea leucorodia 15
1374 A537 5af Porphyrio porhyrio 15
1375 A537 10af Botaurus stellaris, horiz. 30
1376 A537 15af Pelecanus onocrotalus 45
1377 A537 20af Netta rufina 60
1378 A537 25af Cygnus olor 75
1379 A537 30af Phalacrocorax carbo, horiz. 90
Nos. 1373-1379 (7) 3.30

1989

1380 A538 1af Mosque 15
1381 A538 2af Minaret 15
1382 A538 3af Buzkashi, horiz. 15
1383 A538 4af Jet over Hendo Kush, horiz. 15
Set value 28

SEMI-POSTAL STAMPS

Catalogue values for unused stamps in this section are for Never Hinged items.

No. 373 Surcharged in Violet

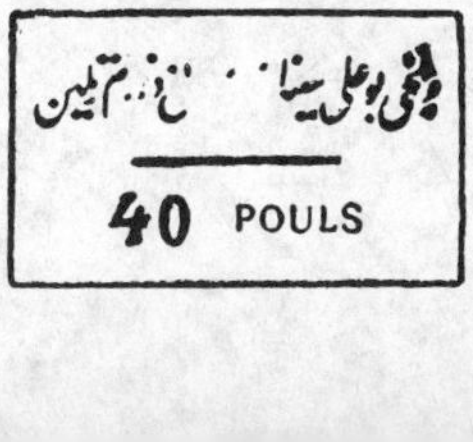

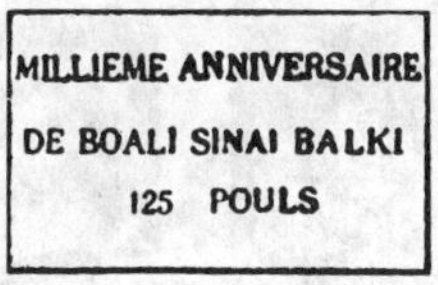

1952, July 12 **Unwmk.** ***Perf. 12½***

B1 A122 40p + 30p cerise 10.00 1.50
B2 A122 125p + 30p cerise 12.50 2.00

1000th anniv. of the birth of Avicenna.

Children at Play — SP1

1955, July 3 **Typo.** ***Perf. 11***

B3 SP1 35p + 15p dk grn 50 35
B4 SP1 125p + 25p purple 1.00 85

The surtax was for child welfare.

Amir Sher Ali Khan, Tiger Head Stamp and Zahir Shah — SP2

Children at Play — SP3

1955, July 2 **Litho.**

B5 SP2 35p + 15p carmine 40 30
B6 SP2 125p + 25p pale vio bl 85 55

85th anniv. of the Afghan post.

1956, June 20 **Typo.**

B7 SP3 35p + 15p brt vio bl 75 25
B8 SP3 140p + 15p dk org brn 1.25 75

Issued for Children's Day. The surtax was for child welfare. No. B8 inscribed in French.

Pashtunistan Monument, Kabul — SP4

1956, Sept. 1 **Litho.**

B9 SP4 35p + 15p dp vio 18 18
B10 SP4 140p + 15p dk brn 60 60

"Free Pashtunistan" Day. The surtax aided the "Free Pashtunistan" movement.

No. B9 measures 30½x19½mm; No. B10, 29x19mm. On sale and valid for use only on Sept. 1-2.

Globe and Sun — SP5

Children on Seesaw — SP6

1956, Oct. 24 ***Perf. 11***

B11 SP5 35p + 15p ultra 65 60
B12 SP5 140p + 15p red brn 1.25 1.00

Afghanistan's UN admission, 10th anniv.

1957, June 20 **Unwmk.**

B13 SP6 35p + 15p brt rose 75 25
B14 SP6 140p + 15p ultra 1.50 90

Children's Day. Surtax for child welfare.

UN Headquarters and Emblems — SP7

1957, Oct. 24 ***Perf. 11 Rough***

B15 SP7 35p + 15p red brn 35 20
B16 SP7 140p + 15p lt ultra 65 55

United Nations Day.

Swimming Pool and Children — SP8

1958, June 22 ***Perf. 11***

B17 SP8 35p + 15p rose 25 20
B18 SP8 140p + 15p dl red brn 75 60

Children's Day. Surtax for child welfare.

Pashtunistan Flag — SP9

1958, Aug. 31

B19 SP9 35p + 15p lt blue 18 18
B20 SP9 140p + 15p red brn 60 60

Issued for "Free Pashtunistan Day."

Children Playing Tug of War — SP10

1959, June 23 **Litho.** ***Perf. 11***

B21 SP10 35p + 15p brn vio 50 20
B22 SP10 165p + 15p brt pink 1.00 60

Children's Day. Surtax for child welfare.

Pathans in Tribal Dance — SP11

1959, Sept. **Unwmk.** ***Perf. 11 Rough***

B23 SP11 35p + 15p green 50 18
B24 SP11 165p + 15p orange 1.00 60

Issued for "Free Pashtunistan Day."

Afghan Cavalryman with UN Flag — SP12

1959, Oct. 24 ***Perf. 11 Rough***

B25 SP12 35p + 15p orange 20 16
B26 SP12 165p + 15p lt bl grn 45 40

Issued for United Nations Day.

Children SP13

1960, Oct. 23 **Litho.**

B27 SP13 75p + 25p lt ultra 75 20
B28 SP13 175p + 25p lt grn 1.50 35

Children's Day. Surtax for child welfare.

Man with Spray Gun — SP14

1960, Sept. 6 ***Perf. 11 Rough***

B29 SP14 50p + 50p orange 80 1.00
B30 SP14 175p + 50p red brn 2.25 2.25

11th anniversary of the WHO malaria control program in Afghanistan.

SP15

1960, Sept. 1 **Unwmk.**

B31 SP15 50p + 50p rose 25 22
B32 SP15 175p + 50p dk bl 55 45

Issued for "Free Pashtunistan Day."

Ambulance — SP16

1960, Oct. 16 ***Perf. 11***

Crescent in Red

B33 SP16 50p + 50p violet 40 30
B34 SP16 175p + 50p blue 90 75

Issued for the Red Crescent Society.

Nos. 470-471 Surcharged in Blue or Orange

1960, Dec. 31 **Litho.** ***Perf. 11***

B35 A166 50p + 25p dp org (Bl) 1.50 1.50
B36 A166 165p + 25p bl (O) 1.50 1.50

The souvenir sheets described after No. 471 were surcharged in carmine "+25 Ps" on each stamp. Value $5 each.

See general note after No. 485.

Nos. 496-500 Surcharged

UNICEF
يونيسف
+25PS

1961 **Unwmk.** **Photo.** ***Perf. 13½x14***

B37 A175 2p + 25p grn & rose lil
B38 A175 2p + 25p brn & cit
B39 A175 5p + 25p gray & rose
B40 A175 10p + 25p bl & bis
B41 A175 15p + 25p sl bl & dl lil
Nos. B37-B41 (5) 1.50

UNICEF. The same surcharge was applied to an imperf. souvenir sheet like that noted after No. 505. Value $4.50.

Nos. 522-526 Surcharged "+25PS" and Crescent in Red

1961, Oct. 16 ***Perf. 13½x14***

B42 A184 2p + 25p blk
B43 A184 2p + 25p grn
B44 A184 5p + 25p lil rose
B45 A184 10p + 25p lilac
B46 A184 15p + 25p dk bl
Nos. B42-B46 (5) 2.00

Issued for the Red Crescent Society.

Nos. 539-543 Surcharged in Red: "UNESCO + 25PS"

1962 ***Perf. 12***

B47 A186 2p + 25p multi
B48 A186 2p + 25p multi
B49 A186 5p + 25p multi

B50 A186 10p + 25p multi
B51 A186 15p + 25p multi
Nos. B47-B51 (5) 1.50

UNESCO. The same surcharge was applied to the souvenir sheets mentioned after No. 548. Value, 2 sheets, $3.50.

Nos. 553-561 Surcharged: "Dag Hammarskjöld +20PS"

1962, Sept. 17 ***Perf. 14x13½***

B52 A187 2p + 20p
B53 A187 2p + 20p
B54 A187 5p + 20p
B55 A187 10p + 20p
B56 A187 15p + 20p
B57 A187 25p + 20p
B58 A187 50p + 20p
B59 A187 75p + 20p
B60 A187 100p + 20p
Nos. B52-B60 (9) 2.00

In memory of Dag Hammarskjold, Sec. Gen. of the UN, 1953-61. Perf. and imperf. souvenir sheets exist. Value, 2 sheets, $3.

Nos. 583-593 Surcharged "+15PS"

1963, Mar. 15 ***Perf. 14x13½***

B61 A193 2p + 15p
B62 A193 2p + 15p
B63 A193 5p + 15p
B64 A193 10p + 15p
B65 A193 15p + 15p
B66 A193 25p + 15p
B67 A193 50p + 15p
B68 A193 75p + 15p
B69 A193 100p + 15p
B70 A193 150p + 15p
B71 A193 175p + 15p
Nos. B61-B71 (11) 7.50

WHO drive to eradicate malaria.
Postally used copies of Nos. B37-B71 are uncommon and command a considerable premium over the values for unused copies.

Nos. 672-672G, 672I Surcharged in Various Positions

15e ANNIVERSAIRE DES DROITS HUMAINS

+
50
POULS

1964, Mar. 9

B71A A213g 2p + 50p
B71B A213g 3p + 50p
B71C A213g 4p + 50p
B71D A213g 5p + 50p
B71E A213g 10p + 50p
B71F A213g 100p + 50p
B71G A213g 2af + 50p
B71H A213g 3af + 50p

Souvenir Sheet

B71J A213g 5af + 50p

Nos. B71E-B71G are airmail semi-postals.

Blood Transfusion Kit — SP17

1964, Oct. 18 **Litho.** ***Perf. 10½***

B72 SP17 1af + 50p blk & rose 50 15

Issued for the Red Crescent Society and Red Crescent Week, Oct. 18-24.

First Aid Station — SP18

1965, Oct. **Photo.** ***Perf. 13½x14***

B73 SP18 1.50af + 50p multi 1.00 50

Issued for the Red Crescent Society.

Children Playing — SP19

1966, Nov. 28 **Photo.** ***Perf. 13½x14***

B74 SP19 1af + 1af yel grn & cl 35 15
B75 SP19 3af + 2af yel & brn 75 20
B76 SP19 7af + 3af rose lil & grn 1.25 40
Nos. B74-B76 (3) 2.35 75

Children's Day.

Nadir Shah Presenting Society Charter — SP20

1967 **Photo.** ***Perf. 13x14***

B77 SP20 2af + 1af red & dk grn 25 15
B78 SP20 5af + 1af lil rose & brn 50 25

Issued for the Red Crescent Society.

Vaccination SP21

Red Crescent SP22

1967, June 6 **Photo.** ***Perf. 12***

B79 SP21 2af + 1af yel & blk 75 15
B80 SP21 5af + 2af pink & brn 1.00 25

The surtax was for anti-tuberculosis work.

1967, Oct. 18 **Photo.** ***Perf. 12***

Crescent in Red

B81 SP22 3af + 1af gray ol & blk 50 15
B82 SP22 5af + 1af dl bl & blk 75 20

Issued for the Red Crescent Society.

Queen Humeira SP23

Red Crescent SP24

1968, June 14 **Photo.** ***Perf. 12***

B83 SP23 2af + 2af red brn 25 20
B84 SP23 7af + 2af dl grn 75 50

Issued for Mother's Day.

1968, Oct. 16 **Photo.** ***Perf. 12***

B85 SP24 4af + 1af yel, blk & red 45 27

Issued for the Red Crescent Society.

Red Cross, Crescent, Lion and Sun Emblems — SP25

Mother and Child — SP26

1969, May 5 **Litho.** ***Perf. 14x13½***

B86 SP25 3af + 1af multi 75 18
B87 SP25 5af + 1af multi 1.25 30

Issued to commemorate the 50th anniversary of the League of Red Cross Societies.

1969, June 14 **Photo.** ***Perf. 12***

B88 SP26 1af + 1af yel org & brn 25 15
B89 SP26 4af + 1af rose lil & pur 40 27
a. Souv. sheet of 2 1.00 1.00

Mother's Day. No. B89a contains 2 imperf. stamps similar to Nos. B88-B89. Sold for 10af.

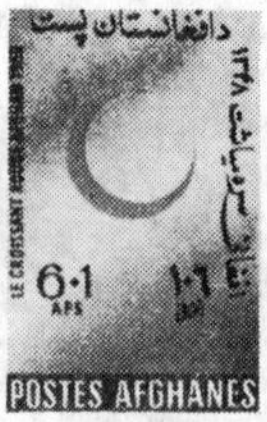

Red Crescent — SP27

1969, Oct. 16 **Photo.** ***Perf. 12***

B90 SP27 6af + 1af multi 75 30

Issued for the Red Crescent Society.

UN and FAO Emblems, Farmer SP28

1973, May 24 **Photo.** ***Perf. 13½***

B91 SP28 14af + 7af grnsh bl & lil 1.10 75

World Food Program, 10th anniversary.

Dome of the Rock, Jerusalem — SP29

1977, Sept. 11 **Photo.** ***Perf. 14***

B92 SP29 12af + 3af multi 1.50 36

Surtax for Palestinian families and soldiers.

15 Cent. (lunar) of Islamic Pilgrimage (Hegira) — SP30

1981, Jan. 17 **Litho.** ***Perf. 12½x12***

B93 SP30 13af + 2af multi 45 38

Red Crescent Aid Programs — SP31

1981, May 8 ***Perf. 12x12½***

B94 SP31 1af + 4af multi 1.00 1.00

Intl. Year of the Disabled — SP32

1981, Oct. 12 ***Perf. 12x12½***

B95 SP32 6af + 1af multi 35 25

AIR POST STAMPS

Plane over Kabul — AP1

Perf. 12, 12x11, 11

1939, Oct. 1 **Typo.** **Unwmk.**

C1 AP1 5af orange 3.75 2.25
a. Imperf., pair ('47) 22.50 22.50
b. Horiz. pair, imperf. vert. 20.00
C2 AP1 10af blue 3.75 1.75
a. 10af lt bl 5.00 5.00
b. Imperf., pair ('47) 22.50
c. Horiz. pair, imperf. vert. 20.00
C3 AP1 20af emerald 7.50 5.00
a. Imperf., pair ('47) 22.50
b. Horiz. pair, imperf. vert. 20.00
c. Vert. pair, imperf. horiz. 22.50
Nos. C1-C3 (3) 15.00 9.00

These stamps come with clean-cut or rough perforations. Counterfeits exist.

1948, June 14 ***Perf. 12x11½***

C4 AP1 5af emerald 15.00 15.00
C5 AP1 10af red orange 15.00 15.00
C6 AP1 20af blue 15.00 15.00
Nos. C4-C6 (3) 45.00 45.00

Imperforates exist.

Catalogue values for unused stamps in this section, from this point to the end of the section, are for Never Hinged items.

Plane over Palace Grounds, Kabul — AP2

1951-54 **Engr.** ***Perf. 13½***

Imprint: "Waterlow & Sons, Limited, London"

C7 AP2 5af henna brn 2.50 55
C8 AP2 5af dp grn ('54) 3.50 50
C9 AP2 10af gray 4.00 1.40
C10 AP2 20af dark blue 6.50 2.25

1957

C11 AP2 5af ultra 90 35
C12 AP2 10af dark vio 1.75 75
Nos. C7-C12 (6) 19.15 5.80

See No. C38.

Ariana Plane over Hindu Kush — AP3

Perf. 11, Imperf.

1960-63 Litho. Unwmk.

C13 AP3 75p light vio 30 30
C14 AP3 125p blue 40 45

Perf. 10½, 11

C14A AP3 5af citron ('63) 1.10 1.10
Nos. C13-C14A (3) 1.80 1.85

Girl Scout — AP4

1962, Aug. 30 Photo. *Perf. 11½x12*

C15 AP4 100p ocher & brn 60 60
C16 AP4 175p brt yel grn & brn 85 85

Women's Day. A souvenir sheet exists containing one each of #578-579, C15-C16. Value $3.

Sports Type of Regular Issue, 1962

Designs: 25p, 50p, Horse racing. 75p, 100p, Wrestling. 150p, Weight lifting. 175p, Soccer.

1962, Sept. 25 Unwmk. *Perf. 12*
Black Inscriptions

C17 A195 25p rose & red brn
C18 A195 50p gray & red brn
C19 A195 75p pale vio & dk grn
C20 A195 100p gray ol & dk pur
C21 A195 150p rose lil & grn
C22 A195 175p sal & brn
Nos. C17-C22 2.25

Children's Day Type of Regular Issue

Perf. 11½x12, 12x11½

1962, Oct. 14 Unwmk.

C23 A196 75p Runners
C24 A196 150p Peaches
C25 A196 200p Iris, vert.

A souvenir sheet contains one each of Nos. C23-C25. Value $2.50.

Red Crescent Type of Regular Issue

1962, Oct. 16 *Perf. 12*
Fruit and Flowers in Natural Colors; Carmine Crescent

C26 A197 25p Grapes
C27 A197 50p Pears
C28 A197 100p Wistaria

Two souvenir sheets exist. One contains a 150p gray brown stamp in blossom design, the other a 200p gray stamp in wistaria design, imperf. Value, each $5.

UN Type of Regular Issue

1962, Oct. 24 Photo.
Flags in Original Colors, Black Inscriptions

C29 A198 75p blue
C30 A198 100p lt brn
C31 A198 125p brt grn

Boy Scout Type of Regular Issue

1962, Oct. 25 Unwmk. *Perf. 12*

C32 A199 25p gray, blk, dl grn & sal
C33 A199 50p grn, brn & sal
C34 A199 75p bl grn, red brn & sal
C35 A199 100p bl, slate & sal

Teacher's Day Type of Regular Issue

1962, Oct. 25

C36 A200 100p Pole vault
C37 A200 150p High jump

A souvenir sheet contains one 250p pink and slate green stamp in design of 150p. Value $2.50.

Type of 1951-54

1962 Engr. *Perf. 13½*
Imprint: "Thomas De La Rue & Co. Ltd."

C38 AP2 5af ultra 6.00 1.00

Agriculture Types of Regular Issue

Unwmk.

1963, Mar. 1 Photo. *Perf. 12*

C42 A204 100p dk car, grn & brn
C43 A203 150p ocher & blk
C44 A204 200p ultra, grn & brn

Hands Holding Wheat Emblem AP5

1963, Mar. 27 Photo. *Perf. 14*

C45 AP5 500p lil, lt brn & brn 1.75 60

FAO "Freedom from Hunger" campaign.
Two souvenir sheets exist. One contains a 1000p blue green, light brown and brown, type AP5, imperf. The other contains a 200p brown and green and 300p ultramarine, yellow and ocher in rice and corn designs, type A205. Values $6 and $2.50.

Meteorological Day Type of Regular Issue

Designs: 100p, 500p, Meteorological measuring instrument. 200p, 400p, Weather station. 300p, Rockets in space.

1963, May 23 *Imperf.*

C46 A206 100p brn & bl

Perf. 13½x14

C47 A206 200p brt grn & lil
C48 A206 300p dk bl & rose
C49 A206 400p bl & dl red brn
C50 A206 500p car rose & gray grn

Nos. C47 and C50 printed se-tenant.
Two souvenir sheets exist. One contains a 125p red and brown stamp in rocket design. The other contains a 100p blue and dull red brown in "rockets in space" design. Values $5 and $7.50.

Kabul International Airport — AP8

Perf. 12x11½

1964, Apr. Unwmk. Photo.

C57 AP8 10af red lil & grn 55 22
C58 AP8 20af dk grn & red lil 80 40
a. Perf. 12 ('68) 5.00 3.00
C59 AP8 50af dk bl & grnsh bl 2.25 1.00
a. Perf. 12 ('68) 8.00 5.00
Nos. C57-C59 (3) 3.60 1.62

Inauguration of Kabul Airport Terminal.
Nos. C58a-C59a are 36mm wide. Nos. C58-C59 are 35½mm wide.

Zahir Shah and Kabul Airport — AP9

Design: 100af, Zahir Shah and Ariana Plane.

1971 Photo. *Perf. 12½x13½*

C60 AP9 50af multi 10.00 8.00
C61 AP9 100af blk, red & grn 5.00 3.00

Remainders of No C60 were used, starting in 1978, with king's portrait removed.

REGISTRATION STAMPS

R1

Dated "1309"

1891 Unwmk. Litho. *Imperf.*
Pelure Paper

F1 R1 1r slate blue 2.00
a. Tete beche pair 12.50

Genuinely used copies of No. F1 are rare. Counterfeit cancellations exist.

R2

Dated "1311"

1893 Thin Wove Paper

F2 R2 1r black, *green* 1.60

Genuinely used copies of No. F2 are rare. Counterfeit cancellations exist.

R3

Undated

1894

F3 R3 2ab black, *green* 8.00 10.00

12 varieties. See note below Nos. 189-190.

R4

Undated

1898-1900

F4 R4 2ab black, *deep rose* 4.00 4.00
F5 R4 2ab black, *lilac rose* 4.00 4.00
F6 R4 2ab black, *magenta* 6.00 4.00
F7 R4 2ab black, *salmon* 2.50 4.00
F8 R4 2ab black, *orange* 6.00 4.00
F9 R4 2ab black, *yellow* 2.50 4.00
F10 R4 2ab black, *green* 6.00 4.00
Nos. F4-F10 (7) 31.00 28.00

Many shades of paper.
Nos. F4-F10 come in two sizes, measured between outer frame lines: 52x36mm, 1st printing; 46x33mm, 2nd printing. The outer frame line (not pictured) is 3-6mm from inner frame line.
Used on P.O. receipts.

OFFICIAL STAMPS

(Used only on interior mail.)

Coat of Arms — O1

1909 Unwmk. Typo. *Perf. 12*
Wove Paper

O1 O1 red 75 1.00
a. Carmine ('19?) 1.25 1.25

Later printings of No. O1 in scarlet, vermilion, claret, etc., on various types of paper, were issued until 1927.

Coat of Arms — O2

1939-68? Typo. *Perf. 11, 12*

O3 O2 15p emerald 35 16
O4 O2 30p ocher ('40) 50 50
O5 O2 45p dark carmine 40 35
O6 O2 50p brt car ('68) 28 28
a. 50p carmine rose ('55) 50 40
O7 O2 1af brt red violet 80 80
Nos. O3-O7 (5) 2.33 2.09

Size of 50p, 24x31mm, others 22½x28mm.

Catalogue values for unused stamps in this section, from this point to the end of the section, are for Never Hinged items.

1964-65 Litho. *Perf. 11*

O8 O2 50p rose 75 75
a. 50p salmon ('65) 1.50 1.50

Stamps of this type are revenues.

PARCEL POST STAMPS

Coat of Arms — PP1

PP2

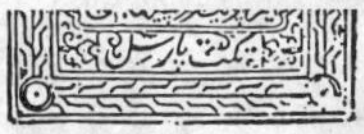

PP3

PP4

1909 Unwmk. Typo. *Perf. 12*

Q1 PP1 3sh bister 85 1.00
a. Imperf., pair 1.00
Q2 PP2 1kr olive gray 1.10 1.25
a. Imperf., pair 1.40
Q3 PP3 1r orange 5.00 3.75
Q4 PP3 1r olive green 2.00 4.00
Q5 PP4 2r red 6.00 4.00
Nos. Q1-Q5 (5) 14.95 14.00

1916-18

Q6 PP1 3sh green 5.00 2.50
Q7 PP2 1kr pale red 2.50 1.25
a. 1kr rose red ('18) 3.25 3.25
Q8 PP3 1r brown org 2.00 1.25
a. 1r deep brown ('18) 2.50 2.50
Q9 PP4 2r blue 5.00 3.00
Nos. Q6-Q9 (4) 14.50 8.00

Nos. Q1-Q9 sometimes show letters of the papermaker's watermark "HOWARD & JONES LONDON."
Ungummed copies are remainders. They sell for one-third the price of mint examples.

Old Habibia College, Near Kabul — PP5

1921

Wove Paper

Q10	PP5	10pa chocolate	3.00	1.75
a.		Tete beche pair	6.25	
Q11	PP5	15pa light brn	4.50	2.50
a.		Tete beche pair	6.25	
Q12	PP5	30pa red violet	5.75	2.75
a.		Tete beche pair	8.75	
b.		Laid paper	*15.00*	*7.50*
Q13	PP5	1r brt blue	7.25	5.50
a.		Tete beche pair	20.00	
		Nos. Q10-Q13 (4)	20.50	12.50

Stamps of this issue are usually perforated on one or two sides only.

The laid paper of No. Q12b has a papermaker's watermark in the sheet.

PP6

1924-26

Wove Paper

Q15	PP6	5kr ultra ('26)	35.00	15.00
Q16	PP6	5r lilac	8.75	8.75

A 15r rose exists, but is not known to have been placed in use.

PP7

PP8

1928-29 *Perf. 11, 11xImperf.*

Q17	PP7	2r yellow orange	10.00	3.00
Q18	PP7	2r green ('29)	3.00	3.00
Q19	PP8	3r deep green	7.50	4.00
Q20	PP8	3r brown ('29)	5.00	5.00
		Nos. Q17-Q20 (4)	25.50	15.00

POSTAL TAX STAMPS

Aliabad Hospital near Kabul — PT1

Pierre and Marie Curie PT2

Perf. 12x11½, 12

1938, Dec. 22 **Typo.** **Unwmk.**

RA1	PT1	10p peacock grn	1.50	2.75
RA2	PT2	15p dull blue	1.50	2.75

Obligatory on all mail Dec. 22-28, 1938. The money was used for the Aliabad Hospital. See note with CD80.

Begging Child

PT3 PT4

1949, May 28 **Typo.** ***Perf. 12***

RA3	PT3	35p red orange	1.60	1.60
RA4	PT4	125p ultra	2.50	2.00

United Nations Children's Day, May 28.

Obligatory on all foreign mail on that date. Proceeds were used for child welfare.

Paghman Arch and UN Emblem PT5

1949, Oct. 24

RA5	PT5	125p dk bl grn	10.00	6.00

4th anniv. of the UN. Valid one day only. Issued in sheets of 9 (3x3).

Catalogue values for unused stamps in this section, from this point to the end of the section, are for Never Hinged items.

Zahir Shah and Map of Afghanistan — PT6

1950, Mar. 30 **Typo.**

RA6	PT6	125p blue green	2.00	1.25

Return of Zahir Shah from a trip to Europe for his health. Valid for two weeks. The tax was used for public health purposes.

Hazara Youth — PT7

1950, May 28 **Typo.** ***Perf. 11½***

RA7	PT7	125p dk bl grn	2.00	1.50

Tax for Child Welfare. Obligatory and valid only on May 28, 1950, on foreign mail.

Ruins of Qalai Bist and Globe PT8

1950, Oct. 24

RA8	PT8	1.25af ultramarine	7.50	4.00

5th anniv. of the UN. Proceeds went to Afghanistan's UN Projects Committee.

Zahir Shah and Medical Center PT9

1950, Dec. 22 **Typo.** ***Perf. 11½***

Size: 38x25mm

RA9	PT9	35p carmine	1.00	1.00
RA10	PT9	1.25af black	4.50	2.25

The tax was for the national Graduate School of Medicine.

Koochi Girl with Lamb — PT10

Kohistani Boy and Sheep — PT11

1951, May 28

RA11	PT10	35p emerald	75	65
RA12	PT11	1.25af ultramarine	75	65

The tax was for Child Welfare.

Distributing Gifts to Children — PT12

Qandahari Boys Dancing the "Attan" — PT13

1952, May 28 **Litho.**

RA13	PT12	35p chocolate	25	25
RA14	PT13	125p violet	75	75

The tax was for Child Welfare.

Soldier Receiving First Aid — PT14

1952, Oct.

RA15	PT14	10p light green	50	35

Stretcher-bearers and Wounded — PT15

Soldier Assisting Wounded PT16

1953, Oct.

RA16	PT15	10p yel grn & org red	50	40
RA17	PT16	10p vio brn & org red	50	40

Prince Mohammed Nadir — PT17

Map and Young Musicians — PT18

1953, May 28

RA18	PT17	35p orange yellow	18	15
RA19	PT17	125p chalky blue	55	55

No. RA19 is inscribed in French "Children's Day." The tax was for child welfare.

1954, May 28 **Unwmk.** ***Perf. 11***

RA20	PT18	35p purple	30	15
RA21	PT18	125p ultra	1.10	1.10

No. RA21 is inscribed in French. The tax was for child welfare.

Red Crescent

PT19 PT20

1954, Oct. 17 ***Perf. 11½***

RA22	PT19	20p blue & red	25	22

1955, Oct. 18 ***Perf. 11***

RA23	PT20	20p dl grn & car	50	25

Zahir Shah and Red Crescent — PT21

1956, Oct. 18

RA24	PT21	20p lt grn & rose car	25	18

Red Crescent Headquarters, Kabul — PT22

1957, Oct. 17

RA25	PT22	20p lt ultra & car	75	50

Map and Crescent — PT23

1958, Oct. Unwmk. *Perf. 11*

RA26	PT23	25p yel grn & red	30	30

PT24

1959, Oct. 17 Litho. *Perf. 11*

RA27	PT24	25p lt vio & red	18	15

The tax on Nos. RA15-RA17, RA22-RA27 was for the Red Crescent Society. Use of these stamps was required for one week.

AGUERA, LA

LOCATION — An administrative district in southern Rio de Oro on the northwest coast of Africa.
GOVT. — Spanish possession
AREA — Because of indefinite political boundaries, figures for area and population are not available.

100 Centimos = 1 Peseta

Type of 1920 Issue of Rio de Oro Overprinted **LA AGÜERA**

1920, June Unwmk. *Perf. 13*

1	A8	1c blue grn	1.40	1.40
2	A8	2c olive brn	1.40	1.40
3	A8	5c deep grn	1.40	1.40
4	A8	10c light red	1.40	1.40
5	A8	15c yellow	1.40	1.40
6	A8	20c lilac	1.40	1.40
7	A8	25c dp blue	1.40	1.40
8	A8	30c dark brn	1.40	1.40
9	A8	40c pink	1.40	1.40
10	A8	50c brt blue	4.00	3.50
11	A8	1p red brn	7.00	5.75
12	A8	4p dark vio	22.50	17.50
13	A8	10p orange	45.00	40.00
		Nos. 1-13 (13)	91.10	79.35

King Alfonso XIII — A2

1922, June Typo.

14	A2	1c turq blue	65	65
15	A2	2c dark green	65	65
16	A2	5c blue green	65	65
17	A2	10c red	65	65
18	A2	15c red brown	65	65
19	A2	20c yellow	65	65
20	A2	25c deep blue	65	65
21	A2	30c dark brn	65	65
22	A2	40c rose red	85	85
23	A2	50c red vio	3.25	2.25
24	A2	1p rose	6.00	4.75
25	A2	4p violet	13.00	10.00
26	A2	10p orange	20.00	15.00
		Nos. 14-26 (13)	48.30	38.05

For later issues see Spanish Sahara.

AJMAN

LOCATION — Oman Peninsula, Arabia, on Persian Gulf
GOVT. — Sheikdom under British Protection
AREA — 100 sq. mi.
POP. — 4,400
CAPITAL — Ajman

Ajman is one of six Persian Gulf sheikdoms to join the United Arab Emirates, which proclaimed its independence Dec. 2, 1971. See United Arab Emirates.

100 Naye Paise = 1 Rupee

Catalogue values for all unused stamps in this country are for Never Hinged items.

Sheik Rashid bin Humaid al Naimi and Arab Stallion — A1

Designs: 2np, 50np, Regal angelfish. 3np, 70np, Camel. 4np, 1r, Angelfish. 5np, 1.50r, Green turtle. 10np, 2r, Jewelfish. 15np, 3r, White storks. 20np, 5r, White-eyed gulls. 30np, 10r, Lanner falcon. 40np as 1np.

Photo. & Litho.
1964 Unwmk. *Perf. 14*
Size: 35x22mm

1	A1	1np gold & multi	15	15
2	A1	2np gold & multi	15	15
3	A1	3np gold & multi	15	15
4	A1	4np gold & multi	15	15
5	A1	5np gold & multi	15	15
6	A1	10np gold & multi	15	15
7	A1	15np gold & multi	15	15
8	A1	20np gold & multi	15	15
9	A1	30np gold & multi	15	15

Size: 42x27mm

10	A1	40np gold & multi	15	15
11	A1	50np gold & multi	15	15
12	A1	70np gold & multi	15	15
13	A1	1r gold & multi	20	15
14	A1	1.50r gold & multi	25	15
15	A1	2r gold & multi	35	15

Size: 53x33 1/2mm

16	A1	3r gold & multi	60	15
17	A1	5r gold & multi	90	25
18	A1	10r gold & multi	2.25	55
		Set value	5.00	1.75

Dates of issue: Nos. 1-9, June 20; Nos. 10-15, Sept. 7; Nos. 16-18, Nov. 4.

Pres. and Mrs. John F. Kennedy with Caroline — A2

Pres. Kennedy: 10np, As a boy in football uniform. 15np, Diving. 50np, As navy lieutenant, receiving Navy and Marine Corps Medal from Capt. Frederic L. Conklin. 1r, Sailing with Jacqueline Kennedy. 2r, With Eleanor Roosevelt. 5r, With Lyndon B. Johnson and Hubert H. Humphrey. 10r, Portrait.

1964, Dec. 15 Photo. *Perf. 13 1/2x14*

19	A2	10np grn & red lil	15	15
20	A2	15np Prus bl & vio	15	15
21	A2	50np org brn & dk bl	15	15
22	A2	1r brn & Prus grn	26	15
23	A2	2r red lil & dp ol	55	15
24	A2	3r grn & red brn	80	20
25	A2	5r vio & brn	1.40	32
26	A2	10r dk bl & red brn	2.75	70
		Nos. 19-26 (8)	6.21	
		Set value		1.50

John F. Kennedy (1917-63). A souvenir sheet contains one each of Nos. 23-26.

Runners at Start — A3

Designs: 10np, 1.50r, Boxing. 25np, 2r, Judo. 50np, 5r, Gymnast on vaulting horse. 1r, 3r, Sailing yacht.

1965, Jan. 12 Photo. *Perf. 13 1/2x14*

27	A3	5np red brn, brt pink & Prus grn	15	15
28	A3	10np dk ol grn, bl gray & red brn	15	15
29	A3	15np dk vio, grn & sep	15	15
30	A3	25np bl sal pink & blk	15	15
31	A3	50np mar, bl & ind	15	15
32	A3	1r dk grn, lil & ultra	26	15
33	A3	1.50r lil, grn & brn	40	16
34	A3	2r red org, bis & dk bl	55	20
35	A3	3r dk brn, grnsh bl & lil	80	26
36	A3	5r grn, yel & red brn	1.40	40
		Nos. 27-36 (10)	4.16	
		Set value		1.35

18th Olympic Games, Tokyo, Oct. 10-25, 1964. A souvenir sheet contains four stamps similar to Nos. 33-36 in changed colors.

Stanley Gibbons Catalogue, 1865, US No. 1X2 — A4

Designs: 10np, Austria, Scarlet Mercury 1856. 15np, British Guiana 1c, 1856. 25np, Canada 12p, 1851. 50np, Hawaii 2c, 1851. 1r, Mauritius 2p, 1847. 3r, Switzerland, Geneva 10c, 1843. 5r, Tuscany 3l, 1860. 5np, 15np, 50np and 3r show first edition of Stanley Gibbons Catalogue; 10np, 25np, 1r and 5r show 1965 Elizabethan Catalogue.

1965, May 6 Unwmk. *Perf. 13*

37	A4	5np multi	15	15
38	A4	10np multi	15	15
39	A4	15np multi	15	15
40	A4	25np multi	15	15
41	A4	50np multi	15	15
42	A4	1r multi	20	15
43	A4	3r multi	60	20
a.		Souv. sheet of 4, #38-39, 42-43	1.00	
44	A4	5r multi	1.00	30
a.		Souv. sheet of 4, #37, 40-41, 44	1.25	
		Set value	2.00	75

Gibbons Catalogue Cent. Exhib., London, Feb. 17-20. Nos. 43a and 44a for 125th anniv. of 1st postage stamp. Sheets exist imperf.

Stamps of Ajman were replaced in 1972 by those of United Arab Emirates.

AIR POST STAMPS

Type of Regular Issue, 1964

Designs: 15np, Arab stallion. 25np, Regal angelfish. 35np, Camel. 50np, Angelfish. 75np, Green turtle. 1r, Jewelfish. 2r, White storks. 3r, White-eyed gulls. 5r, Lanner falcon.

Photo. & Litho.
1965 Unwmk. *Perf. 14*
Size: 42x25 1/2mm

C1	A1	15np silver & multi	15	15
C2	A1	25np silver & multi	15	15
C3	A1	35np silver & multi	15	15
C4	A1	50np silver & multi	15	15
C5	A1	75np silver & multi	16	15
C6	A1	1r silver & multi	24	15

Size: 53x33 1/2mm

C7	A1	2r silver & multi	48	15
C8	A1	3r silver & multi	70	20
C9	A1	5r silver & multi	1.10	32
		Nos. C1-C9 (9)	3.28	
		Set value		95

Issue dates: #C1-C6, Nov. 15, C7-C9, Dec 18.

AIR POST OFFICIAL STAMPS

Type of Regular Issue, 1964

Designs: 75np, Jewelfish. 2r, White storks. 3r, White-eyed gulls. 5r, Lanner falcon.

Photo. & Litho.
1965, Dec. 18 Unwmk. *Perf. 14*
Size: 42x25 1/2mm

CO1	A1	75np gold & multi	18	15

Size: 53x33 1/2mm

CO2	A1	2r gold & multi	50	15
CO3	A1	3r gold & multi	75	20
CO4	A1	5r gold & multi	1.25	32
		Nos. CO1-CO4 (4)	2.68	82

OFFICIAL STAMPS

Type of Regular Issue, 1964

Designs: 25np, Arab stallion. 40np, Regal angelfish. 50np, Camel. 75np, Angelfish. 1r, Green turtle.

Photo. & Litho.
1965, Dec. 1 Unwmk. *Perf. 14*
Size: 42x25 1/2mm

O1	A1	25np gold & multi	15	15
O2	A1	40np gold & multi	15	15
O3	A1	50np gold & multi	15	15
O4	A1	75np gold & multi	20	15
O5	A1	1r gold & multi	26	15
		Set value	77	25

ALAOUITES

LOCATION — A division of Syria, in Western Asia.
GOVT. — Under French Mandate
AREA — 2,500 sq. mi.
POP. — 278,000 (approx. 1930)
CAPITAL — Latakia

This territory became an independent state in 1924, although still administered under the French Mandate. In 1930 it was renamed Latakia and Syrian stamps overprinted "Lattaquie" superseded the stamps of Alaouites. For these and subsequent issues see Latakia and Syria.

100 Centimes = 1 Piaster

Issued under French Mandate

Stamps of France Surcharged:

ALAOUITES 0 P. 25 العلويين ١/٤ الغرش	ALAOUITES 2 PIASTRES العلويين غروش ٢
Nos. 1-6, 16-18	Nos. 7-15, 19-21

1925 Unwmk. *Perf. 14x13 1/2*

1	A16	10c on 2c vio brn	1.00	1.00
2	A22	25c on 5c orange	65	65
3	A20	75c on 15c gray grn	1.25	1.25
4	A22	1p on 20c red brn	80	80
5	A22	1.25p on 25c blue	1.10	1.10
6	A22	1.50p on 30c red	3.50	3.50
7	A22	2p on 35c violet	80	80
8	A18	2p on 40c red & pale bl	1.60	1.60
9	A18	2p on 45c grn & bl	3.50	3.50
10	A18	3p on 60c vio & ultra	2.00	2.00
11	A20	3p on 60c lt vio	3.50	3.50
12	A20	4p on 85c vermilion	60	60
13	A18	5p on 1fr cl & ol grn	2.50	2.50
14	A18	10p on 2fr org & pale bl	3.25	3.25
15	A18	25p on 5fr bl & buff	4.25	4.25
		Nos. 1-15 (15)	30.30	30.30

For overprints, see Nos. C1-C4.

Same Surcharges on Pasteur Stamps of France

16	A23	50c on 10c green	65	65
17	A23	75c on 15c green	65	65
18	A23	1.50p on 30c red	85	85
19	A23	2p on 45c red	1.00	1.00
20	A23	2.50p on 50c blue	1.10	1.10
21	A23	4p on 75c blue	1.60	1.60
		Nos. 16-21 (6)	5.85	5.85

Stamps of Syria, 1925, Overprinted in Red, Black or Blue:

ALAOUITES
العلويين
On A3, A5

ALAOUITES
العلويين
On A4

1925, Mar. 1 *Perf. 12½, 13½*

25 A3 10c dk violet (R) 25 25
a. Double overprint 12.00 12.00
26 A4 25c olive black (R) 50 50
a. Inverted overprint 6.50 6.50
b. Blue overprint 12.00 12.00
27 A4 50c yellow green 40 40
a. Inverted overprint 6.00 6.00
b. Blue overprint 12.00 12.00
c. Red overprint 12.00 12.00
28 A4 75c brown orange 45 45
a. Inverted overprint 6.50 6.50
29 A5 1p magenta 65 65
30 A4 1.25p deep green 50 50
a. Red overprint 10.00 10.00
31 A4 1.50p rose red (Bl) 45 45
a. Inverted overprint 6.50 6.50
b. Black overprint 12.00 12.00
32 A4 2p dk brown (R) 50 50
a. Blue overprint 6.50 6.50
33 A4 2.50p pck blue (R) 60 60
a. Black overprint 6.50 6.50
34 A4 3p orange brown 50 50
a. Inverted overprint 6.50 6.50
b. Blue overprint 14.00 14.00
35 A4 5p violet 55 55
a. Red overprint 14.00 14.00
36 A4 10p violet brown 85 85
37 A4 25p ultra (R) 1.80 1.80
Nos. 25-37 (13) 8.00 8.00

For overprints, see Nos. C5-C19.

Stamps of Syria, 1925, Surcharged in Black or Red:

=4P. غ=
ALAOUITES
العلويين
Nos. 38-42

=4P.50 ٤٫٥٠=
Alaouites
العلويين
Nos. 43-45

1926

38 A4 3.50p on 75c brn org 65 55
a. Surcharged on face and back 4.50 4.50
39 A4 4p on 25c ol blk (R) 65 55
40 A4 6p on 2.50p pck bl (R) 60 55
41 A4 12p on 1.25p dp grn 60 55
a. Inverted surcharge 6.25 6.25
42 A4 20p on 1.25p dp grn 1.00 80
43 A4 4.50p on 75c brn org 2.00 1.10
a. Inverted surcharge 6.50
44 A4 7.50p on 2.50p pck bl 1.50 80
45 A4 15p on 25p ultra 3.00 2.00
Nos. 38-45 (8) 10.00 6.90

For overprint, see No. C21.

Syria #199 Ovptd. like #25 in Red

1928

46 A3 5c on 10c dk violet 28 28
a. Double surcharge 9.00

Syria Nos. 178 and 174 Surcharged like Nos. 43-45 in Red

47 A4 2p on 1.25p dp green 5.75 3.25
48 A4 4p on 25c olive black 3.50 2.25

For overprint, see No. C20.

=4P ٤غ=
ALAOUITES
العلويين

49 A4 4p on 25c olive black 32.50 27.50
a. Double impression
Nos. 46-49 (4) 42.03 33.28

AIR POST STAMPS

Nos. 8, 10, 13 & 14 with Additional Overprint in Black

طيارة Avion

1925, Jan. 1 Unwmk. *Perf. 14x13½*

C1 A18 2p on 40c 3.50 3.50
a. Overprint reversed 42.50
C2 A18 3p on 60c 5.25 5.25
a. Overprint reversed 42.50 42.50
C3 A18 5p on 1fr 3.50 3.50
C4 A18 10p on 2fr 3.50 3.50
Nos. C1-C4 (4) 15.75 15.75

Nos. 32, 34, 35 & 36 With Additional Overprint in Green

AVION طيارة

1925, Mar. 1 *Perf. 13½*

C5 A4 2p dark brown 1.00 1.00
C6 A4 3p orange brown 1.00 1.00
C7 A4 5p violet 1.00 1.00
C8 A4 10p violet brown 1.00 1.00
Nos. C5-C8 (4) 4.00 4.00

Nos. 32, 34, 35 & 36 With Additional Overprint in Red

1926, May 1

C9 A4 2p dark brown 1.40 1.40
C10 A4 3p orange brown 1.40 1.40
C11 A4 5p violet 1.40 1.40
C12 A4 10p violet brown 1.40 1.40
Nos. C9-C12 (4) 5.60 5.60

No. C9 has the original overprint in black.

Double or inverted overprints, original or plane, are known on most of Nos. C9-C12. Value, $8-$10.

The red plane overprint was also applied to Nos. C5-C8. These are believed to have been essays, and were not regularly issued.

Nos. 27, 29, and 37 With Additional Overprint of Airplane in Red or Black

1929, June-July

C17 A4 50c yel grn (R) 75 75
a. Plane overprint double 9.00
b. Plane ovpt. on face and back 9.00
c. Pair with plane overprint tete beche 27.50
C18 A5 1p magenta (Bk) 2.75 2.75
C19 A4 25p ultra (R) 12.00 12.00
a. Plane overprint inverted 42.50 42.50
Nos. C17-C19 (3) 15.50 15.50

Nos. 47 and 45 With Additional Overprint of Airplane in Red

1929-30

C20 A4 2p on 1.25p ('30) 1.20 1.20
a. Surcharge inverted 4.00
b. Double surcharge 3.50
C21 A4 15p on 25p (Bk + R) 17.50 14.00
a. Plane overprint inverted 35.00 35.00

POSTAGE DUE STAMPS

Postage Due Stamps of France, 1893-1920, Surcharged Like No. 1 (Nos. J1-J2) or No. 7 (Nos. J3-J5)

1925 Unwmk. *Perf. 14x13½*

J1 D2 50c on 10c choc 1.50 1.50
J2 D2 1p on 20c ol grn 1.50 1.50
J3 D2 2p on 30c red 1.50 1.50
J4 D2 3p on 50c vio brn 1.50 1.50
J5 D2 5p on 1fr red brn, *straw* 1.50 1.50
Nos. J1-J5 (5) 7.50 7.50

Postage Due Stamps of Syria, 1925, Overprinted Like No. 26 (Type D5) or No. 25 (Type D6) in Black, Blue or Red

1925 *Perf. 13½*

J6 D5 50c brown, *yel* 55 55
J7 D6 1p vio, *rose* (Bl) 55 55
a. Black overprint 9.00 9.00
b. Double overprint (Bk + Bl) 14.00 14.00
J8 D5 2p blk, *blue* (R) 90 90
J9 D5 3p blk, *red org* 1.25 1.25
J10 D5 5p blk, *bl grn* (R) 1.75 1.75
Nos. J6-J10 (5) 5.00 5.00

The stamps of Alaouites were superseded in 1930 by those of Latakia.

ALBANIA

LOCATION — Southeastern Europe
GOVT. — Republic
AREA — 11,101 sq. mi.
POP. — 2,750,000 (1982 est.)
CAPITAL — Tirana

After the outbreak of World War I, the country fell into a state of anarchy when the Prince and all members of the International Commission left Albania. Subsequently General Ferrero in command of Italian troops declared Albania an independent country. A constitution was adopted and a republican form of government was instituted which continued until 1928 when, by constitutional amendment, Albania was declared to be a monarchy. The President of the republic, Ahmed Zogu, became king of the new state. Many unlisted varieties or surcharges and lithographed labels are said to have done postal duty in Albania and Epirus during this unsettled period.

In March 1939, Italy invaded Albania. King Zog fled but did not abdicate. The King of Italy acquired the crown.

Germany occupied Albania from September, 1943, until late 1944 when it became an independent state. The People's Republic began in January, 1946.

40 Paras = 1 Piaster = 1 Grossion
100 Centimes = 1 Franc (1917)
100 Qintar = 1 Franc
100 Qintar (Qindarka) = 1 Lek (1947)

Catalogue values for unused stamps in this country are for Never Hinged items, beginning with Scott 458 in the regular postage section, Scott B34 in the semi-postal section, and Scott C67 in the airpost section.

Watermarks

Wmk. 125- Lozenges

Wmk. 220- Double Headed Eagle

Stamps of Turkey Handstamped

Handstamped on Issue of 1908

Perf. 12, 13½ and Compound

1913, June Unwmk.

1 A19 2½pi violet brown 225.00 190.00

With Additional Overprint in Carmine ب

2 A19 10pa blue green 190.00 175.00

The eagle handstamp was applied to other Turkish stamps of 1908: 25pi green and 50 pi red brown. The 5pa ocher, Albania No. 4, was surcharged "2 paras." These three stamps were retained by officials. Values, $2,250, $5,500, $375.

Handstamped on Issue of 1909

4 A21 5pa ocher 95.00 75.00
5 A21 10pa blue green 75.00 67.50
6 A21 20pa car rose 57.50 45.00
7 A21 1pi ultra 65.00 57.50
8 A21 2pi blue black 110.00 82.50
10 A21 5pi dark violet 350.00 250.00
11 A21 10pi dull red 1,050. 900.00

For surcharge, see No. 19.

With Additional Overprint in Blue or Carmine ب

14 A21 20pa car rose (Bl) 175.00 130.00
15 A21 1pi brt blue (C) 425.00 400.00

Handstamped on Newspaper Stamp of 1911

17 A21 2pa olive green 100.00 90.00

Handstamped on Postage Due Stamp of 1908

18 A19 1pi black, *dp rose* 600.00 450.00

No. 18 was used for regular postage.

No. 6 Surcharged With New Value

19 A21 10pa on 20pa car rose 225.00 210.00

The overprint on #1-19 was handstamped and is found inverted, double, etc.

Nos. 6, 7 and 8 exist with the handstamp in red, blue or violet, but these varieties are not known to have been regularly issued.

Excellent counterfeits exist of Nos. 1 to 19.

A1

1913, July *Imperf.*

Handstamped on White Laid Paper Without Eagle and Value

20 A1 (1pi) black 100.00 *150.00*
Cut to shape 45.00 45.00
a. Sewing machine perf. 150.00 130.00

1913, Aug.

Value Typewritten in Violet With Eagle

21 A1 10pa violet 3.25 2.00
22 A1 20pa red & black 3.25 2.25
23 A1 1gr black 3.25 2.00
24 A1 2gr blue & violet 4.00 3.00
25 A1 5gr violet & blue 5.25 4.25
26 A1 10gr blue 5.50 4.25
Nos. 21-26 (6) 24.50 17.75

Nos. 21-26 exist with the eagle inverted or omitted and with numerous errors in the figures of value and the spelling of the word "grosh."

A2

Skanderberg (George Castriota) — A3

1913, Nov. *Perf. 11½*

Handstamped on White Laid Paper Eagle and Value in Black

27 A2 10pa green 2.75 1.75
b. Eagle and value in green 18.00
c. 10pa red (error) 13.50 13.50
d. 10pa violet (error) 13.50 13.50

29	A2	20pa red	2.75	1.75
b.		20pa green (error)	13.50	13.50
30	A2	30pa violet	3.00	2.25
a.		30pa ultramarine (error)	13.50	13.50
b.		30pa red (error)	13.50	13.50
31	A2	1gr ultramarine	4.50	3.00
a.		1gr green (error)	13.50	13.50
b.		1gr black (error)	13.50	13.50
c.		1gr violet (error)	13.50	13.50
33	A2	2gr black	7.00	6.25
a.		2gr violet (error)	13.50	13.50
b.		2gr blue (error)	13.50	13.50
		Nos. 27-33 (5)	20.00	15.00

The stamps of this issue are known with eagle or value inverted or omitted.

1st anniv. of Albanian independence.

1913, Dec. Typo. *Perf. 14*

35	A3	2q orange brn & buff	60	60
36	A3	5q green & blue grn	60	60
37	A3	10q rose red	60	50
38	A3	25q dark blue	70	80
39	A3	50q violet & red	1.10	1.10
40	A3	1fr deep brown	5.50	*8.00*
		Nos. 35-40 (6)	9.10	*11.60*

For overprints and surcharges, see Nos. 41-52, 105, J1-J9.

Nos. 35-40 Handstamped in Black or Violet

7.Mars

1467. RROFTË MBRETI. 1914

1914, Mar. 7

41	A3	2q orange brn & buff	10.00	*15.00*
42	A3	5q grn & bl grn (V)	10.00	*15.00*
43	A3	10q rose red	10.00	*15.00*
44	A3	25q dark blue (V)	10.00	*15.00*
45	A3	50q violet & red	10.00	*15.00*
46	A3	1fr deep brown	10.00	*15.00*
		Nos. 41-46 (6)	60.00	*90.00*

Issued to celebrate the arrival of Prince Wilhelm zu Wied on Mar. 7, 1914.

Nos. 35-40 Surcharged in Black:

5 • PARA •
a

1 GROSH
b

1914, Apr. 2

47	A3 (a)	5pa on 2q	85	70
48	A3 (a)	10pa on 5q	85	70
49	A3 (a)	20pa on 10q	1.50	1.10
50	A3 (b)	1gr on 25q	1.50	1.10
51	A3 (b)	2gr on 50q	2.25	1.50
52	A3 (b)	5gr on 1fr	12.00	10.00
		Nos. 47-52 (6)	18.95	15.10

For overprints, see Nos. 105, J6-J9.

Inverted Surcharge

47a	A3 (a)	5pa on 2q	4.50	4.50
48a	A3 (a)	10pa on 5q	4.50	4.50
49a	A3 (a)	20pa on 10q	4.50	4.50
50a	A3 (b)	1gr on 25q	5.50	5.50
51a	A3 (b)	2gr on 50q	6.75	6.75
52b	A3 (b)	5gr on 1fr	18.00	18.00
		Nos. 47a-52b (6)	43.75	43.75

Korce (Korytsa) Issues

A4

1914 Handstamped *Imperf.*

52A	A4	10pa violet & red	55.00	45.00
c.		10pa black & red	77.50	62.50
53	A4	25pa violet & red	55.00	45.00
a.		25pa black & red	100.00	90.00

Nos. 52A-53a originally were handstamped directly on the cover, so the paper varies. Later they were also produced in sheets; these are rarely found. Nos. 52A-53a were issued by Albanian military authorities.

A5

A6

1917 Typo. & Litho. *Perf. 11½*

54	A5	1c dk brown & grn	7.50	5.75
55	A5	2c red & green	7.50	5.75
56	A5	3c gray grn & grn	7.50	5.75
57	A5	5c green & black	5.50	3.00
58	A5	10c rose red & black	5.50	3.00
59	A5	25c blue & black	5.50	3.00
60	A5	50c violet & black	5.50	3.00
61	A5	1fr brown & black	7.50	5.75
		Nos. 54-61 (8)	52.00	35.00

1917-18

62	A6	1c dk brown & grn	2.50	1.65
63	A6	2c red brown & grn	2.50	1.65
a.		"CTM" for "CTS"	11.00	11.00
64	A6	3c black & green	2.50	1.65
a.		"CTM" for "CTS"	11.00	11.00
65	A6	5c green & black	2.75	2.25
66	A6	10c dull red & black	2.75	2.25
67	A6	50c violet & black	5.25	4.50
68	A6	1fr red brn & black	9.00	5.00
		Nos. 62-68 (7)	27.25	18.95

Counterfeits abound of Nos. 54-68, 80-81.

No. 65 Surcharged in Red

QARKU
I
KORÇËS
25 CTS

1918

80	A6	25c on 5c green & blk	45.00	37.50

A7

1918

81	A7	25c blue & black	27.50	22.50

General Issue

A8

A9

Handstamped in Rose or Blue

XV I MCMXIX

1919 *Perf. 12½*

84	A8	(2)q on 2h brown	4.00	3.75
85	A8	5q on 16h green	4.00	3.75
86	A8	10q on 8h rose (Bl)	4.00	3.75
87	A8	25q on 64h blue	4.00	3.75
88	A9	25q on 64h blue	165.00	150.00
89	A8	50q on 32h violet	4.00	3.75
90	A8	1fr on 1.28k org, *bl*	4.00	3.75
		Nos. 84-90 (7)	189.00	172.50

See Nos. J10-J13. Compare with types A10-A14. For overprints, see Nos 91-104.

Handstamped in Rose or Blue

1919, Jan. 16

91	A8	(2)q on 2h brown	4.25	4.25
92	A8	5q on 16h green	4.25	4.25
93	A8	10q on 8h rose (Bl)	4.25	4.25
94	A8	25q on 64h blue	25.00	25.00
95	A9	25q on 64h blue	20.00	20.00
96	A8	50q on 32h violet	4.25	4.25
97	A8	1fr on 1.28k org, *bl*	4.25	4.25
		Nos. 91-97 (7)	66.25	66.25

Handstamped in Violet

1919

98	A8	(2)q on 2h brown	5.25	5.25
99	A8	5q on 16h green	5.25	5.25
100	A8	10q on 8h rose	5.25	5.25
101	A8	25q on 64h blue	5.25	5.25
102	A9	25q on 64h blue	22.50	22.50
103	A8	50q on 32h violet	5.25	5.25
104	A8	1fr on 1.28k org, *bl*	5.25	5.25
		Nos. 98-104 (7)	54.00	54.00

No. 50 Overprinted in Violet

SHKODER • 1919

1919 *Perf. 14*

105	A3	1gr on 25q blue	3.00	*3.00*

A10

A11

1919, June 5 *Perf. 11½, 12½*

106	A10	10q on 2h brown	2.75	2.75
107	A11	15q on 8h rose	2.75	2.75
108	A11	20q on 16h green	2.75	2.75
109	A10	25q on 64h blue	2.75	2.75
110	A11	50q on 32h violet	2.75	2.75
111	A11	1fr on 96h orange	2.75	2.75
112	A10	2fr on 1.60k vio, *buff*	5.50	5.50
		Nos. 106-112 (7)	22.00	22.00

Nos. 106-108, 110 exist with inverted surcharge.

A12

A13

Black or Violet Surcharge

1919

113	A12	10q on 8h car	2.75	2.75
114	A12	15q on 8h car (V)	2.75	2.75
115	A13	20q on 16h green	2.75	2.75
116	A13	25q on 35h violet	2.75	2.75
117	A13	50q on 64h blue	5.75	5.75
118	A13	1fr on 96h orange	3.50	3.50
119	A12	2fr on 1.60k vio, *buff*	3.50	3.50
		Nos. 113-119 (7)	23.75	23.75

A14

A15

Overprinted in Blue or Black Without New Value

1920 *Perf. 12½*

120	A14	1q gray (Bl)	20.00	21.00
121	A14	10q rose (Bk)	1.65	2.50
a.		Double overprint	21.00	*24.00*
122	A14	20q brown (Bl)	10.00	10.00
123	A14	25q blue (Bk)	100.00	*100.00*
124	A14	50q brown vio (Bk)	13.00	15.00
		Nos. 120-124 (5)	144.65	*148.50*

Counterfeit overprints exist of Nos. 120-128.

Surcharged with New Value

125	A14	2q on 10q rose (R)	3.75	3.50
126	A14	5q on 10q rose (G)	3.75	3.50
127	A14	25q on 10q rose (Bl)	3.75	3.50
128	A14	50q on 10q rose (Br)	3.75	3.50
		Nos. 125-128 (4)	15.00	14.00

Stamps of type A14 (Portrait of the Prince zu Wied) were not placed in use without overprint or surcharge.

Post Horn Overprinted in Black

1920 *Perf. 14x13*

129	A15	2q orange	1.25	1.25
130	A15	5q deep green	1.65	1.35
131	A15	10q red	4.25	3.25
132	A15	25q light blue	7.50	4.25
133	A15	50q gray green	1.25	1.25
134	A15	1fr claret	1.25	1.25
		Nos. 129-134 (6)	17.15	12.60

Type A15 was never placed in use without post horn or "Besa" overprint.

Stamps of Type A15 (No Post Horn) Overprinted

BESA

1921

135	A15	2q orange	3.00	3.00
136	A15	5q deep green	4.25	4.25
137	A15	10q red	7.25	7.25
138	A15	25q light blue	16.00	12.50
139	A15	50q gray green	5.25	5.25
140	A15	1fr claret	4.25	4.25
		Nos. 135-140 (6)	40.00	36.50

For surcharge, see No. 154. For overprints, see Nos. 156-157.

Stamps of these types, and with "TAKSE" overprint, were unauthorized and never placed in use. They are common.

Gjirokaster
A18

Korcha — A19

Designs: 5q, Kanina. 10q, Berati. 25q, Bridge at Vezirit. 50q, Rozafat. 2fr, Dursit.

1923 Typo. *Perf. 12½, 11½*

147	A18	2q orange	55	55
148	A18	5q yellow green	48	48
149	A18	10q carmine	48	48
150	A18	25q dark blue	48	48
151	A18	50q dark green	48	48
152	A19	1fr dark violet	65	65
153	A19	2fr olive green	1.75	1.75
		Nos. 147-153 (7)	4.87	4.87

For overprints & surcharges see #158-185, B1-B8.

No. 135 Surcharged

Q 1

1922 *Perf. 14x13*

154	A15	1q on 2q orange	3.00	3.00

Stamps of Type A15 (No Post Horn) Overprinted

BESA

1922

156	A15	5q deep green	3.00	2.50
157	A15	10q red	3.00	2.50

Nos. 147-151 Overprinted (top line in Black; diamond in Violet)

Mbledhje Kushtetuese

TIRANE KALLNUER 1924

1924, Jan. *Perf. 12½*

158	A18	2q red orange	3.50	3.00
159	A18	5q yellow green	3.50	3.00
160	A18	10q carmine	3.50	3.00
161	A18	25q dark blue	3.50	3.00
162	A18	50q dark green	3.50	3.00
		Nos. 158-162 (5)	17.50	15.00

The words "Mbledhje Kushtetuese" are in taller letters on the 25q than on the other values. Opening of the Constituent Assembly.

No. 147 Surcharged

= 1 =

1924

163	A18	1q on 2q red orange	2.25	2.25

Nos. 163, 147-152 Overprinted

Triumf' i legalitetit
24 Dhetuer 1924

1924

164	A18	1q on 2q orange	1.40	1.40
165	A18	2q orange	1.40	1.40
166	A18	5q yellow green	1.40	1.40
167	A18	10q carmine	1.40	1.40
168	A18	25q dark blue	1.40	1.40
169	A18	50q dark green	1.40	1.40
170	A19	1fr dark violet	1.40	1.40
		Nos. 164-170 (7)	9.80	9.80

Issued to celebrate the return of the Government to the Capital after a revolution.

Nos. 163, 147-152 Overprinted

Republika Shqiptare
21 Kallnduer 1925

1925

171	A18	1q on 2q orange	1.40	1.40
172	A18	2q orange	1.40	1.40
173	A18	5q yellow green	1.40	1.40
174	A18	10q carmine	1.40	1.40
175	A18	25q dark blue	1.40	1.40
176	A18	50q dark green	1.40	1.40
177	A19	1fr dark violet	1.40	1.40
		Nos. 171-177 (7)	9.80	9.80

Proclamation of the Republic, Jan. 21, 1925. The date "1921" instead of "1925" occurs once in each sheet of 50.

Nos. 163, 147-153 Overprinted

Republika Shqiptare

1925

178	A18	1q on 2q orange	55	55
a.		Inverted overprint	7.00	7.00
179	A18	2q orange	55	55
180	A18	5q yellow green	55	55
a.		Inverted overprint	7.00	7.00
181	A18	10q carmine	55	55
182	A18	25q dark blue	55	55
183	A18	50q dark green	55	55
184	A19	1fr dark violet	65	65
185	A19	2fr olive green	65	65
		Nos. 178-185 (8)	4.60	4.60

President Ahmed Zogu
A25 A26

1925 *Perf. 13½, 13½x13*

186	A25	1q orange	15	15
187	A25	2q red brown	15	15
188	A25	5q green	15	15
189	A25	10q rose red	15	15
190	A25	15q gray brown	1.40	1.40
191	A25	25q dark blue	15	15
192	A25	50q blue green	48	48
193	A26	1fr red & ultra	85	85
194	A26	2fr green & orange	85	85
195	A26	3fr brown & violet	1.40	1.40
196	A26	5fr violet & black	3.50	3.50
		Nos. 186-196 (11)	9.23	9.23

No. 193 in ultramarine and brown, and No. 194 in gray and brown were not regularly issued. Value, both $15.

For overprints and surcharges, see Nos. 197-209, 238-248.

Nos. 186-196 Overprinted in Various Colors

1927

197	A25	1q orange (V)	38	38
198	A25	2q red brn (G)	15	15
199	A25	5q green (R)	75	15
200	A25	10q rose red (Bl)	15	15
201	A25	15q gray brn (G)	7.50	7.50
202	A25	25q dk blue (R)	15	15
203	A25	50q blue grn (Bl)	15	15
204	A26	1fr red & ultra (Bk)	15	15
205	A26	2fr green & org (Bk)	15	15
206	A26	3fr brown & vio (Bk)	55	55
207	A26	5fr violet & blk (Bk)	95	95
		Nos. 197-207 (11)	11.03	10.43

No. 200 exists perf. 11.
For surcharges, see Nos. 208-209, 238-240.

Nos. 200, 202 Surcharged in Black or Red

= 5 =

1928

208	A25	1q on 10q rose red	35	22
a.		Inverted surcharge	3.75	3.75
209	A25	5q on 25q dk blue (R)	35	22
a.		Inverted surcharge	3.75	3.75

King Zog I
A27 A28

Black Overprint

1928 *Perf. 14x13½*

210	A27	1q orange brown	2.00	2.00
211	A27	2q slate	2.00	2.00
212	A27	5q blue green	2.00	2.00
213	A27	10q rose red	2.00	2.00
214	A27	15q bister	11.00	11.00
215	A27	25q deep blue	1.65	1.65
216	A27	50q lilac rose	2.00	2.00

Red Overprint

Perf. 13½x14

217	A28	1fr blue & slate	2.25	2.25
		Nos. 210-217 (8)	24.90	24.90

Compare with types A29-A32.

A29 A30

Black or Red Overprint

1928 *Perf. 14x13½*

218	A29	1q orange brown	6.00	6.00
219	A29	2q slate (R)	6.00	6.00
220	A29	5q blue green	5.00	5.00
221	A29	10q rose red	3.25	3.25
222	A29	15q bister	3.50	3.50
223	A29	25q deep blue (R)	3.50	3.50
224	A29	50q lilac rose	3.75	3.75

Perf. 13½x14

225	A30	1fr blue & slate (R)	5.50	5.50
226	A30	2fr green & slate (R)	6.75	6.75
		Nos. 218-226 (9)	43.25	43.25

Proclamation of Ahmed Zogu as King of Albania.

A31 A32

Black Overprint

1928 *Perf. 14x13½*

227	A31	1q orange brown	35	35
228	A31	2q slate	18	18
229	A31	5q blue green	1.65	18
230	A31	10q rose red	18	15
231	A31	15q bister	11.00	7.25
232	A31	25q deep blue	22	15
233	A31	50q lilac rose	22	15

Perf. 13½x14

234	A32	1fr blue & slate	45	65
235	A32	2fr green & slate	55	65
236	A32	3fr dk red & ol bis	1.10	1.10
237	A32	5fr dull vio & gray	2.25	2.00
		Nos. 227-237 (11)	18.15	12.81

The overprint reads "Kingdom of Albania."

Mbr. Shqiptare

Nos. 203, 202, 200 Surcharged in Black

■ 5 ■

1929 *Perf. 13½x13, 11½*

238	A25	1q on 50q blue green	35	35
239	A25	5q on 25q dark blue	35	35
240	A25	15q on 10q rose red	55	50
		Nos. 238-240 (3)	1.25	1.20

RROFT-MBRETI

Nos. 186-189, 191-194 Overprinted in Black or Red

8 X 1929.

1929 *Perf. 11½, 13½*

241	A25	1q orange	3.00	3.00
242	A25	2q red brown	3.00	3.00
243	A25	5q green	3.00	3.00
244	A25	10q rose red	3.00	3.00
245	A25	25q dark blue	3.00	3.00
246	A25	50q blue green (R)	3.50	3.50
247	A26	1fr red & ultra	5.25	5.25
248	A26	2fr green & orange	6.50	6.50
		Nos. 241-248 (8)	30.25	30.25

34th birthday of King Zog. The overprint reads "Long live the King."

Lake Butrinto — A33

King Zog I — A34

Zog Bridge — A35

Ruin at Zog Manor — A36

Perf. 14, 14½

1930, Sept. 1 **Photo.** **Wmk. 220**

250	A33	1q slate	15	15
251	A33	2q orange red	15	15
252	A34	5q yellow green	15	15
253	A34	10q carmine	15	15
254	A34	15q dark brown	16	16
255	A34	25q dark ultra	20	16
256	A33	50q slate green	30	25
257	A35	1fr violet	75	75
258	A35	2fr indigo	85	85
259	A36	3fr gray green	1.90	1.90
260	A36	5fr orange brown	3.25	3.25
		Nos. 250-260 (11)	8.01	7.92

2nd anniversary of accession of King Zog I.
For overprints, see Nos. 261-270, 299-309, J39.
For surcharges, see Nos. 354-360.

Nos. 250-259 Overprinted in Black

1 1
9 9
2 3
4-24Dhetuer-4

1934, Dec. 24

261	A33	1q slate	1.50	1.50
262	A33	2q orange red	1.50	1.50
263	A34	5q yellow green	1.50	1.50
264	A34	10q carmine	1.50	1.50
265	A34	15q dark brown	1.50	1.50
266	A34	25q dark ultra	1.50	1.50
267	A33	50q slate green	1.50	1.50
268	A35	1fr violet	3.50	3.50
269	A35	2fr indigo	6.75	6.75
270	A36	3fr gray green	9.50	9.50
		Nos. 261-270 (10)	30.25	30.25

Tenth anniversary of the Constitution.

Allegory of Death of Skanderbeg
A37

Albanian Eagle in Turkish Shackles
A38

Designs: 5q, 25q, 40q, 2fr, Eagle with wings spread.

1937 **Unwmk.** *Perf. 14*

271	A37	1q brown violet	15	15
272	A38	2q brown	15	15
273	A38	5q lt green	22	22
274	A37	10q olive brown	30	30
275	A38	15q rose red	38	38
276	A38	25q blue	70	70
277	A37	50q deep green	95	95
278	A38	1fr violet	1.65	1.65
279	A38	2fr orange brown	4.25	4.25
		Nos. 271-279 (9)	8.75	8.75

Souvenir Sheet

280		Sheet of 3	11.50	12.00
a.		A37 20q red violet	2.10	2.50
b.		A38 30q olive brown	2.10	2.50
c.		A38 40q red	2.10	2.50

25th anniv. of independence from Turkey, proclaimed Nov. 26, 1912.

Queen Geraldine and King Zog — A40

1938 *Perf. 14*

281	A40	1q	slate violet	15	15
282	A40	2q	red brown	15	15
283	A40	5q	green	15	15
284	A40	10q	olive brown	20	24
285	A40	15q	rose red	28	40
286	A40	25q	blue	48	60
287	A40	50q	Prus green	1.40	1.65
288	A40	1fr	purple	3.00	3.25
			Nos. 281-288 (8)	5.81	6.59

Souvenir Sheet

289			Sheet of 4	14.00	16.00
a.	A40	20q	dark red violet	1.40	1.40
b.	A40	30q	brown olive	1.40	1.40

Wedding of King Zog and Countess Geraldine Apponyi, Apr. 27, 1938.

No. 289 contains 2 each of Nos. 289a, 289b.

Queen Geraldine — A42

National Emblems — A43

Designs: 10q, 25q, 30q, 1fr, King Zog.

1938

290	A42	1q	dp red violet	15	15
291	A43	2q	red orange	15	15
292	A42	5q	deep green	15	15
293	A42	10q	red brown	15	15
294	A42	15q	deep rose	32	32
295	A42	25q	deep blue	42	52
296	A43	50q	gray black	1.05	1.25
297	A42	1fr	slate green	3.50	3.75
			Nos. 290-297 (8)	5.89	6.44

Souvenir Sheet

298			Sheet of 3	12.50	14.00
b.	A43	20q	Prussian green	1.50	1.50
c.	A42	30q	deep violet	1.50	1.50

10th anniv. of royal rule. They were on sale for 3 days (Aug. 30-31, Sept. 1) only, during which their use was required on all mail.

No. 298 contains Nos. 294, 298b, 298c.

Issued under Italian Dominion

Nos. 250-260 Overprinted in Black

Mbledhja Kushtetuëse 12-IV-1939 XVII

1939 **Wmk. 220** *Perf. 14*

299	A33	1q	slate	15	15
300	A33	2q	orange red	15	15
301	A34	5q	yellow green	15	15
302	A34	10q	carmine	16	16
303	A34	15q	dark brown	16	16
304	A34	25q	dark ultra	22	22
305	A33	50q	slate grn	32	32
306	A35	1fr	violet	60	60
307	A35	2fr	indigo	85	85
308	A36	3fr	gray green	1.75	1.75
309	A36	5fr	orange brown	2.50	2.50
			Nos. 299-309 (11)	7.01	7.01

Resolution adopted by the Natl. Assembly, Apr. 12, 1939, offering the Albanian Crown to Italy.

Native Costumes

A46 A47 A48

King Victor Emmanuel III

A49 A50

Native Costume A51

Monastery A52

Designs: 2fr, Bridge at Vezirit. 3fr, Ancient Columns. 5fr, Amphitheater.

1939 **Unwmk.** **Photo.** *Perf. 14*

310	A46	1q	blue gray	15	15
311	A47	2q	olive green	15	15
312	A48	3q	golden brown	15	15
313	A49	5q	green	15	15
314	A50	10q	brown	15	15
315	A50	15q	crimson	18	15
316	A50	25q	sapphire	25	18
317	A50	30q	brt violet	35	22
318	A51	50q	dull purple	44	22
319	A49	65q	red brown	65	65
320	A52	1fr	myrtle green	85	85
321	A52	2fr	brown lake	1.90	1.90
322	A52	3fr	brown black	3.75	3.75
323	A52	5fr	gray violet	7.50	7.50
			Nos. 310-323 (14)	16.62	16.17

For overprints and surcharges, see Nos. 331-353.

King Victor Emmanuel III — A56

1942 **Photo.**

324	A56	5q	green	15	15
325	A56	10q	brown	15	15
326	A56	15q	rose red	15	15
327	A56	25q	blue	24	24
328	A56	65q	red brown	35	35
329	A56	1fr	myrtle green	70	70
330	A56	2fr	gray violet	1.50	1.50
			Nos. 324-330 (7)	3.24	3.24

Conquest of Albania by Italy, 3rd anniv..

No. 311 Surcharged in Black **1 QIND**

331	A47	1q	on 2q olive green	48	48

Issued under German Administration

Stamps of 1939 Overprinted in Carmine or Brown

14 Shtator 1943

1943

332	A47	2q	olive green	85	1.40
333	A48	3q	golden brown	85	1.40
334	A49	5q	green	85	1.40
335	A50	10q	brown	85	1.40
336	A50	15q	crimson (Br)	85	1.40
337	A50	25q	sapphire	85	1.40
338	A50	30q	brt violet	85	1.40
339	A49	65q	red brown	1.00	2.25
340	A52	1fr	myrtle green	6.00	10.00
341	A52	2fr	brown lake	8.00	*20.00*
342	A52	3fr	brown black	35.00	*52.50*

Surcharged with New Values

343	A48	1q	on 3q gldn brn	85	1.40
344	A49	50q	on 65q red brn	1.00	2.25
			Nos. 332-344 (13)	57.80	*98.20*

Proclamation of Albanian independence.

The overprint "14 Shtator 1943" on Nos. 324 to 328 is private and fraudulent.

Independent State

Nos. 312 to 317 and 319 to 321 Surcharged with New Value and Bars in Black or Carmine, and:

QEVERIJA DEMOKRAT. E SHQIPERISE 22-X-1944

1945

345	A48	30q	on 3q gldn brn	2.25	2.25
346	A49	40q	on 5q green	2.25	2.25
347	A50	50q	on 10q brown	2.25	2.25
348	A50	60q	on 15q crimson	2.25	2.25
349	A50	80q	on 25q saph (C)	2.25	2.25
350	A50	1fr	on 30q brt vio	2.25	2.25
351	A49	2fr	on 65q red brn	2.25	2.25
352	A52	3fr	on 1fr myr grn	2.25	2.25
353	A52	5fr	on 2fr brn lake	2.25	2.25
			Nos. 345-353 (9)	20.25	20.25

"DEMOKRATIKE" is not abbreviated on Nos. 352 and 353.

Nos. 250, 251, 256 and 258 Surcharged in Black or Carmine, and

1943 J.N.Ç.L.SHQ. 1945 10 KORRIK FR.SHQ. 5

1945 **Wmk. 220**

354	A33	30q	on 1q slate	80	80
355	A33	60q	on 1q slate	95	95
356	A33	80q	on 1q slate	1.10	1.10
357	A33	1fr	on 1q slate	1.65	1.65
358	A33	2fr	on 2q org red	2.25	2.25
359	A33	3fr	on 50q sl grn	5.75	5.75
360	A35	5fr	on 2fr indigo	7.50	7.50
			Nos. 354-360 (7)	20.00	20.00

Albanian Natl. Army of Liberation, 2nd anniv.

The surcharge on No. 360 is condensed to fit the size of the stamp.

Country House, Labinot — A57

Designs: 40q, 60q, Bridge at Berat. 1fr, 3fr, Permet.

Unwmk.

1945, Nov. 28 **Typo.** *Perf. 11*

361	A57	20q	bluish green	18	18
362	A57	30q	deep orange	38	38
363	A57	40q	brown	38	38
364	A57	60q	red violet	55	55
365	A57	1fr	rose red	1.10	1.10
366	A57	3fr	dark blue	5.50	5.50
			Nos. 361-366 (6)	8.09	8.09

Counterfeits exist. See note after No. B33.

For overprints and surcharges, see Nos. 367-378, 418-423, B28-B33.

Nos. 361 to 366 Overprinted in Black

ASAMBLEJA KUSHTETUESE 10 KALLHUER 1946

1946

367	A57	20q	bluish green	52	52
368	A57	30q	deep orange	52	52
369	A57	40q	brown	85	85
370	A57	60q	red violet	1.50	1.50
371	A57	1fr	rose red	4.25	4.25
372	A57	3fr	dark blue	6.75	6.75
			Nos. 367-372 (6)	14.39	14.39

Convocation of the Constitutional Assembly, Jan. 10, 1946.

People's Republic

Nos. 361 to 366 Overprinted in Black

REPUBLIKA POPULLORE E SHQIPERISE

1946

373	A57	20q	bluish green	55	55
374	A57	30q	deep orange	95	95
375	A57	40q	brown	1.25	1.25
376	A57	60q	red violet	2.10	2.10
377	A57	1fr	rose red	3.75	3.75
378	A57	3fr	dark blue	6.25	6.25
			Nos. 373-378 (6)	14.85	14.85

Proclamation of the Albanian People's Republic.

For surcharges, see Nos. 418-423.

Globe, Dove and Olive Branch — A60

Perf. 11½, Imperf.

1946, Mar. 8 **Typo.**

Denomination in Black

379	A60	20q	lilac & dull red	15	15
380	A60	40q	dp lilac & dull red	25	25
381	A60	50q	violet & dull red	40	40
382	A60	1fr	lt blue & red	60	60
383	A60	2fr	dk blue & red	1.25	1.25
			Nos. 379-383 (5)	2.65	2.65

International Women's Congress.

Athletes with Shot and Indian Club — A61

Perf. 11½

1946, Oct. 6 **Litho.** **Unwmk.**

384	A61	1q	grnsh black	5.75	5.75
385	A61	2q	green	5.75	5.75
386	A61	5q	brown	5.75	5.75
387	A61	10q	crimson	5.75	5.75
388	A61	20q	ultra	5.75	5.75
389	A61	40q	rose violet	5.75	5.75
390	A61	1fr	deep orange	9.25	9.25
			Nos. 384-390 (7)	43.75	43.75

Balkan Games, Tirana, Oct. 6-13.

Qemal Stafa — A62

1947, May 5 *Perf. 12½x11½*

391	A62	20q	brn & yel brn	1.75	1.75
392	A62	28q	dk blue & blue	1.75	1.75
393	A62	40q	brn blk & gray brn	3.00	3.00
a.			Souvenir sheet, #391-393	6.50	6.50
			Nos. 391-393 (3)	6.50	6.50

5th anniv. of the death of Qemal Stafa.

Young Railway Laborers A64

1947, May 16 *Perf. 11½*

395	A64	1q	brn blk & gray brn	1.00	50
396	A64	4q	dk green & green	1.00	50
397	A64	10q	blk brn & bis brn	1.00	50
398	A64	15q	dk red & red	1.25	50
399	A64	20q	indigo & bl gray	1.75	75
400	A64	28q	dk blue & blue	2.50	75
401	A64	40q	brn vio & rose vio	6.50	3.50
402	A64	68q	dk brn & org brn	10.00	6.50
			Nos. 395-402 (8)	25.00	13.50

Issued to publicize the construction of the Durres Elbasan Railway by Albanian youths.

Citizens Led by Hasim Zeneli — A65

Enver Hoxha and Vasil Shanto — A66

Vojo Kushi — A68

Inauguration of Vithkuq Brigade — A67

1947, July 10			Litho.	
403	A65	16q brn org & red brn	1.65	1.65
404	A66	20q org brn & dk brn	1.65	1.65
405	A67	28q blue & dk blue	1.75	1.75
406	A68	40q lilac & dk brn	2.50	2.50
		Nos. 403-406 (4)	7.55	7.55

4th anniv. of the formation of Albania's army, July 10, 1943.

Conference Building Ruins, Peza — A69

Disabled Soldiers — A70

1947, Sept. 16				
407	A69	2 l red violet	2.00	1.65
408	A69	2.50 l deep blue	2.00	1.65

Peza Conf., Sept. 16, 1942, 5th anniv.

1947, Nov. 17			*Perf. 12½x11½*	
408A	A70	1 l red	2.75	2.75

Disabled War Veterans Cong., Nov. 14-20, 1947.

A71

A73

Designs: 2 l, Banquet. 2.50 l, Peasants rejoicing.

Perf. 11½x12½, 12½x11½

1947, Nov. 17			Unwmk.	
409	A71	1.50 l dull violet	2.25	2.25
410	A71	2 l brown	2.25	2.25
411	A71	2.50 l blue	2.25	2.25
412	A73	3 l rose red	2.25	2.25
		Nos. 409-412 (4)	9.00	9.00

Agrarian reform law of Nov. 17, 1946, 1st anniv.

Burning Farm Buildings A74

Designs: 2.50 l, Trench scene. 5 l, Firing line. 8 l, Winter advance. 12 l, Infantry column.

1947, Nov. 29			*Perf. 11½x12½*	
413	A74	1.50 l red	1.65	1.65
414	A74	2.50 l rose brown	2.00	2.00
415	A74	5 l blue	2.50	2.50
416	A74	8 l purple	4.00	4.00
417	A74	12 l brown	6.00	6.00
		Nos. 413-417 (5)	16.15	16.15

3rd anniv. of Albania's liberation.

Nos. 373 to 378 Surcharged with New Value and Bars in Black

1948, Feb. 22			*Perf. 11*	
418	A57	50q on 30q deep org	24	24
419	A57	1 l on 20q bluish grn	48	48
420	A57	2.50 l on 60q red vio	1.00	1.00
421	A57	3 l on 1fr rose red	1.40	1.40
422	A57	5 l on 3fr dark blue	2.25	2.25
423	A57	12 l on 40q brown	4.75	4.75
		Nos. 418-423 (6)	10.12	10.12

The two bars consist of four type squares each set close together.

Map, Train and Construction Workers A75

1948, June 1		Litho.	*Perf. 11½*	
424	A75	50q dk car rose	1.05	52
425	A75	1 l lt green & blk	1.25	52
426	A75	1.50 l deep rose	1.25	52
427	A75	2.50 l org brn & dk brn	1.25	52
428	A75	5 l dull blue	2.10	1.05
429	A75	8 l salmon & dk brn	4.75	2.10
430	A75	12 l red vio & dk vio	6.50	2.25
431	A75	20 l olive gray	12.50	5.00
		Nos. 424-431 (8)	30.65	12.48

Issued to publicize the construction of the Durres-Tirana Railway.

Marching Soldiers A76

Design: 8 l, Battle scene.

1948, July 10				
432	A76	2.50 l yellow brown	75	75
433	A76	5 l dark blue	1.00	1.00
434	A76	8 l violet gray	2.00	2.00
		Nos. 432-434 (3)	3.75	3.75

5th anniv. of the formation of Albania's army.

Bricklayer, Flag, Globe and "Industry" A77

Map and Soldier A78

1949, May 1		Photo.	*Perf. 12½x12*	
435	A77	2.50 l olive brown	25	25
436	A77	5 l blue	65	65
437	A77	8 l violet brown	1.00	1.00
		Nos. 435-437 (3)	1.90	1.90

Issued to publicize Labor Day, May 1, 1949.

1949, July 10			Unwmk.	
438	A78	2.50 l brown	35	35
439	A78	5 l light ultra	50	50
440	A78	8 l brown orange	1.25	1.25
		Nos. 438-440 (3)	2.10	2.10

6th anniv. of the formation of Albania's army.

Enver Hoxha A79

Albanian Citizen and Spasski Tower, Kremlin A80

1949, Oct. 16		Engr.	*Perf. 12½*	
441	A79	50q purple	15	15
442	A79	1 l dull green	15	15
443	A79	1.50 l car lake	15	15
444	A79	2.50 l brown	25	15
445	A79	5 l violet blue	50	15
446	A79	8 l sepia	85	65
447	A79	12 l rose lilac	1.90	1.05
448	A79	20 l gray blue	3.75	1.75
		Nos. 441-448 (8)	7.70	4.20

1949, Sept. 10		Photo.	*Perf. 12½x12*	
449	A80	2.50 l orange brown	45	45
450	A80	5 l deep ultra	90	90

Albanian-Soviet friendship.

Albanian Soldier and Flag — A81

Battle Scene — A82

1949, Nov. 29		Unwmk.	*Perf. 12*	
451	A81	2.50 l brown	22	22
452	A82	3 l dark red	45	45
453	A81	5 l violet	60	60
454	A82	8 l black	1.65	1.65
		Nos. 451-454 (4)	2.92	2.92

Fifth anniversary of Albania's liberation.

Joseph V. Stalin — A83

Symbols of UPU and Postal Transport — A84

1949, Dec. 21				
455	A83	2.50 l dark brown	44	52
456	A83	5 l violet blue	1.10	1.25
457	A83	8 l rose brown	1.90	2.25
		Nos. 455-457 (3)	3.44	4.02

70th anniv. of the birth of Joseph V. Stalin.

Canceled to Order

Beginning in 1950, Albania sold some issues in sheets canceled to order. Values in second column when much less than unused are for "CTO" copies. Postally used stamps are valued at slightly less than, or the same as, unused.

Catalogue values for unused stamps in this section, from this point to the end of the section, are for Never Hinged items.

1950, July 1		Photo.	*Perf. 12x12½*	
458	A84	5 l blue	1.75	1.25
459	A84	8 l rose brown	2.50	1.75
460	A84	12 l sepia	3.25	2.25
		Nos. 458-460 (3)	7.50	5.25

75th anniv. (in 1949) of the UPU.

Sami Frasheri — A85

Arms and Albanian Flags — A86

Authors: 2.50 l, Andon Zako. 3 l, Naim Frasheri. 5 l, Kostandin Kristoforidhi.

1950, Nov. 5			*Perf. 14*	
461	A85	2 l dark green	48	15
462	A85	2.50 l red brown	65	20
463	A85	3 l brown carmine	95	25
464	A85	5 l deep blue	1.40	60
		Nos. 461-464 (4)	3.48	1.20

"Jubilee of the Writers of the Renaissance."

1951, Jan. 11		Engr.	*Perf. 14x13½*	
465	A86	2.50 l brown carmine	85	25
466	A86	5 l deep blue	1.65	50
467	A86	8 l sepia	2.50	1.00
		Nos. 465-467 (3)	5.00	1.75

5th anniv. of the formation of the Albanian People's Republic.

Skanderbeg A87

Enver Hoxha and Congress of Permet A88

1951, Mar. 1				
468	A87	2.50 l brown	60	25
469	A87	5 l violet	1.25	50
470	A87	8 l olive bister	2.25	1.00
		Nos. 468-470 (3)	4.10	1.75

483rd anniv. of the death of George Castriota (Skanderbeg).

1951, May 24		Photo.	*Perf. 12*	
471	A88	2.50 l dark brown	32	20
472	A88	3 l rose brown	50	30
473	A88	5 l violet blue	85	50
474	A88	8 l rose lilac	1.40	80
		Nos. 471-474 (4)	3.07	1.80

Congress of Permet, 7th anniversary.

Child and Globe — A89

Weighing Baby — A90

1951, July 16				
475	A89	2 l green	52	30
476	A90	2.50 l brown	70	40
477	A90	3 l red	1.00	50
478	A89	5 l blue	1.50	80
		Nos. 475-478 (4)	3.72	2.00

Intl. Children's Day, June 1, 1951.

Enver Hoxha and Birthplace of Albanian Communist Party — A91

1951, Nov. 8 Photo. *Perf. 14*

479	A91	2.50 l	olive brown	30	25
480	A91	3 l	rose brown	42	35
481	A91	5 l	dark slate blue	70	60
482	A91	8 l	black	1.00	85
			Nos. 479-482 (4)	2.42	2.05

10th anniv. of the founding of Albania's Communist Party.

Battle Scene — A92

Designs: 5 l, Schoolgirl, "Agriculture and Industry." 8 l, Four portraits.

1951, Nov. 28 *Perf. 12x12½*

483	A92	2.50 l	brown	32	15
484	A92	5 l	blue	55	40
485	A92	8 l	brown carmine	1.10	75
			Nos. 483-485 (3)	1.97	1.30

Albanian Communist Youth Org., 10th anniv.

Albanian Heroes (Haxhija, Lezhe, Giyebegej, Mezi and Dedej) — A93

Nos. 486-489 each show five "Heroes of the People"; No. 490 shows two (Stafa and Shanto).

1950, Dec. 25 Unwmk. *Perf. 14*

486	A93	2 l	dark green	60	15
487	A93	2.50 l	purple	75	16
488	A93	3 l	scarlet	85	22
489	A93	5 l	brt blue	1.40	35
490	A93	8 l	olive brown	3.50	1.00
			Nos. 486-490 (5)	7.10	1.88

6th anniv. of Albania's liberation.

Tobacco Factory, Shkoder — A94

Composite, Lenin Hydroelectric Plant — A95

Designs: 1 l, Canal. 2.50 l, Textile factory. 3 l, "8 November" Cannery. 5 l, Motion Picture Studio, Tirana. 8 l, Stalin Textile Mill, Tirana. 20 l, Central Hydroelectric Dam.

1953, Aug. 1 *Perf. 12x12½, 12½x12*

491	A94	50q	red brown	15	15
492	A94	1 l	dull green	16	15
493	A94	2.50 l	brown	60	15
494	A94	3 l	rose brown	85	15
495	A94	5 l	blue	1.25	15
496	A94	8 l	brown olive	2.25	16
497	A95	12 l	deep plum	3.50	35
498	A94	20 l	slate blue	6.25	50
			Nos. 491-498 (8)	15.01	
			Set value		1.30

Liberation Scene — A96

1954, Nov. 29 *Perf. 12x12½*

499	A96	50q	brown violet	15	15
500	A96	1 l	olive green	24	15
501	A96	2.50 l	yellow brown	55	15
502	A96	3 l	car rose	70	16
503	A96	5 l	gray blue	90	16
504	A96	8 l	rose brown	1.75	55
			Nos. 499-504 (6)	4.29	
			Set value		1.00

10th anniversary of Albania's liberation.

School — A97

Pandeli Sotiri, Petro Nini Luarasi, Nuci Naci — A98

1956, Feb. 23 Unwmk.

505	A97	2 l	rose violet	25	15
506	A98	2.50 l	lt green	35	15
507	A98	5 l	ultra	80	20
508	A97	10 l	brt grnsh blue	1.65	35
			Nos. 505-508 (4)	3.05	
			Set value		68

70th anniv. of the opening of the 1st Albanian school.

Flags — A99

Designs: 5 l, Labor Party headquarters, Tirana. 8 l, Marx and Lenin.

1957, June 1 Engr. *Perf. 11½x11*

509	A99	2.50 l	brown	32	15
510	A99	5 l	lt violet blue	65	15
511	A99	8 l	rose lilac	1.50	20
			Nos. 509-511 (3)	2.47	
			Set value		40

Albania's Labor Party, 15th anniv.

Congress Emblem A100

1957, Oct. 4 Unwmk. *Perf. 11½*

512	A100	2.50 l	gray brown	28	15
513	A100	3 l	rose red	42	15
514	A100	5 l	dark blue	52	15
515	A100	8 l	green	1.00	30
			Nos. 512-515 (4)	2.22	
			Set value		63

4th Intl. Trade Union Cong., Leipzig, Oct. 4-15.

Lenin and Cruiser "Aurora" — A101

1957, Nov. 7 Litho. *Perf. 10½*

516	A101	2.50 l	violet brown	32	15
517	A101	5 l	violet blue	70	16
518	A101	8 l	gray	95	30
			Nos. 516-518 (3)	1.97	61

40th anniv. of the Russian Revolution.

Albanian Fighter Holding Flag A102

Naum Veqilharxhj A103

1957, Nov. 28 *Perf. 10½*

519	A102	1.50 l	magenta	24	15
520	A102	2.50 l	brown	38	15
521	A102	5 l	blue	70	18
522	A102	8 l	green	1.25	30
			Nos. 519-522 (4)	2.57	
			Set value		60

Proclamation of independence, 45th anniv.

1958, Feb. 1 Unwmk.

523	A103	2.50 l	dark brown	30	15
524	A103	5 l	violet blue	60	15
525	A103	8 l	rose lilac	1.10	30
			Nos. 523-525 (3)	2.00	60

160th anniv. of the birth of Naum Veqilharxhj, patriot and writer.

Luigi Gurakuqi A104

Soldiers A105

1958, Apr. 15 Photo. *Perf. 10½*

526	A104	1.50 l	dark green	18	15
527	A104	2.50 l	brown	25	15
528	A104	5 l	blue	52	15
529	A104	8 l	sepia	1.00	22
			Nos. 526-529 (4)	1.95	
			Set value		50

Transfer of the ashes of Luigi Gurakuqi.

1958, July 10 Litho.

Design: 2.50 l, 11 l, Airman, sailor, soldier and tank.

530	A105	1.50 l	blue green	16	15
531	A105	2.50 l	dark red brown	20	15
532	A105	8 l	rose red	65	16
533	A105	11 l	bright blue	1.00	25
			Nos. 530-533 (4)	2.01	
			Set value		50

15th anniversary of Albanian army.

Cerciz Topulli and Mihal Grameno — A106

Buildings and Tree — A107

1958, July 1

534	A106	2.50 l	dk olive bister	22	15
535	A107	3 l	green	32	15
536	A106	5 l	blue	55	15
537	A107	8 l	red brown	90	22
			Nos. 534-537 (4)	1.99	
			Set value		50

50th anniversary, Battle of Mashkullore.

Ancient Amphitheater and Goddess of Butrinto — A108

1959, Jan. 25 Litho. *Perf. 10½*

538	A108	2.50 l	redsh brown	38	15
539	A108	6.50 l	lt blue green	1.00	18
540	A108	11 l	dark blue	1.65	38
			Nos. 538-540 (3)	3.03	
			Set value		60

Cultural Monuments Week.

Frederic Joliot-Curie and World Peace Congress Emblem A109

Basketball A110

1959, July 1 Unwmk.

541	A109	1.50 l	carmine rose	65	20
542	A109	2.50 l	rose violet	1.10	30
543	A109	11 l	blue	3.25	1.50
			Nos. 541-543 (3)	5.00	2.00

10th anniv. of the World Peace Movement.

1959, Nov. 20 *Perf. 10½*

Sports: 2.50 l, Soccer, 5 l, Runner. 11 l, Man and woman runners with torch and flags.

544	A110	1.50 l	bright violet	25	15
545	A110	2.50 l	emerald	32	15
546	A110	5 l	carmine rose	80	25
547	A110	11 l	ultra	2.25	1.75
			Nos. 544-547 (4)	3.62	2.30

1st Albanian Spartacist Games.

Fighter and Flags A111

Mother and Child, U.N. Emblem A112

Designs: 2.50 l, Miner with drill standing guard. 3 l, Farm woman with sheaf of grain. 6.50 l, Man and woman in laboratory.

1959, Nov. 29

548	A111	1.50 l	brt carmine	25	15
549	A111	2.50 l	red brown	35	15
550	A111	3 l	brt blue green	45	15
551	A111	6.50 l	bright red	90	25
a.			Souvenir sheet	6.00	6.00
			Nos. 548-551 (4)	1.95	
			Set value		42

15th anniversary of Albania's liberation.

No. 551a contains one each of Nos. 548-551, imperf. and all in bright carmine. Inscribed ribbon frame of sheet and frame lines for each stamp are blue green.

1959, Dec. 5 Unwmk.

552	A112	5 l	grnsh blue	2.50	55
a.			Miniature sheet	3.00	3.00

10th anniv. (in 1958) of the signing of the Universal Declaration of Human Rights.

No. 552a contains one imperf. stamp similar to No. 552; ornamental border.

Woman with Olive Branch A113

Alexander Moissi A114

1960, Mar. 8 Litho. *Perf. 10½*

553	A113	2.50 l	chocolate	32	15
554	A113	11 l	rose carmine	1.40	32

50th anniv. of Intl. Women's Day, Mar. 8.

1960, Apr. 20

555 A114	3 l deep brown	22	15
556 A114	11 l Prus green	85	25

80th anniversary of the birth of Alexander Moissi (Moisiu) (1880-1935), German actor.

Lenin
A115

School Building
A116

1960, Apr. 22

557 A115	4 l Prus blue	80	15
558 A115	11 l lake	1.75	18
	Set value		25

90th anniversary of birth of Lenin.

1960, May 30 **Litho.** ***Perf. 10½***

559 A116	5 l green	85	20
560 A116	6.50 l plum	85	20

1st Albanian secondary school, 50th anniv.

Soldier on Guard Duty — A117

Liberation Monument, Tirana, Family and Policeman — A118

1960, May 12 **Unwmk.** ***Perf. 10½***

561 A117	1.50 l carmine rose	20	15
562 A117	11 l Prus blue	1.10	20
	Set value		26

15th anniversary of the Frontier Guards.

1960, May 14

563 A118	1.50 l green	20	15
564 A118	8.50 l brown	1.10	25
	Set value		30

15th anniversary of the People's Police.

Congress Site — A119

Pashko Vasa — A120

1960, Mar. 25

565 A119	2.50 l sepia	18	15
566 A119	7.50 l dull blue	70	25

40th anniversary, Congress of Louchnia.

1960, May 5

Designs: 1.50 l, Jani Vreto. 6.50 l, Sami Frasheri. 11 l, Page of statutes of association.

567 A120	1 l gray olive	18	15
568 A120	1.50 l brown	25	15
569 A120	6.50 l blue	55	15
570 A120	11 l rose red	1.10	18
	Nos. 567-570 (4)	2.08	
	Set value		36

80th anniv. (in 1959) of the Association of Albanian Authors.

Foreign postal stationery (stamped envelopes, postal cards and air letter sheets) is beyond the scope of this catalogue.

Albanian Fighter and Cannon
A121

TU-104 Plane, Clock Tower, Tirana, and Kremlin, Moscow
A122

1960, Aug. 2 **Litho.** ***Perf. 10½***

571 A121	1.50 l olive brown	28	15
572 A121	2.50 l maroon	35	15
573 A121	5 l dark blue	85	20
	Nos. 571-573 (3)	1.48	
	Set value		35

40th anniv. of the Battle of Viona (against Italian troops.)

1960, Aug. 18

574 A122	1 l redsh brown	32	15
575 A122	7.50 l brt grnsh blue	1.25	32
576 A122	11.50 l gray	2.25	60
	Nos. 574-576 (3)	3.82	1.07

TU-104 flights, Moscow-Tirana, 2nd anniv.

Rising Sun and Federation Emblem
A123

Ali Kelmendi
A124

1960, Nov. 10 **Unwmk.** ***Perf. 10½***

577 A123	1.50 l ultra	18	15
578 A123	8.50 l red	70	20
	Set value		26

Intl. Youth Federation, 15th anniv.

1960, Dec. 5 **Litho.** ***Perf. 10½***

579 A124	1.50 l pale gray grn	25	15
580 A124	11 l dull rose lake	65	20
	Set value		26

Ali Kelmendi, communist leader, 60th birthday.

Flags of Russia and Albania and Clasped Hands
A125

Marx and Lenin
A126

1961, Jan. 10 **Unwmk.** ***Perf. 10½***

581 A125	2 l violet	25	15
582 A125	8 l dull red brown	65	20
	Set value		26

15th anniv. of the Albanian-Soviet Friendship Society.

1961, Feb. 13 **Litho.**

583 A126	2 l rose red	20	15
584 A126	8 l violet blue	70	20
	Set value		26

Fourth Communist Party Congress.

Man from Shkoder
A127

Otter
A128

Costumes: 1.50 l, Woman from Shkoder. 6.50 l, Man from Lume. 11 l, Woman from Mirdite.

1961, Apr. 28 ***Perf. 10½***

585 A127	1 l slate	22	15
586 A127	1.50 l dull claret	35	15
587 A127	6.50 l ultra	1.10	18
588 A127	11 l red	1.90	38
	Nos. 585-588 (4)	3.57	
	Set value		66

1961, June 25 **Unwmk.** ***Perf. 10½***

Designs: 6.50 l, Badger. 11 l, Brown bear.

589 A128	2.50 l grayish blue	1.00	22
590 A128	6.50 l blue green	2.25	50
591 A128	11 l dark red brown	4.00	85
	Nos. 589-591 (3)	7.25	1.57

Dalmatian Pelicans
A129

Cyclamen
A130

1961, Sept. 30 ***Perf. 14***

592 A129	1.50 l shown	90	20
593 A129	7.50 l Gray herons	1.75	40
594 A129	11 l Little egret	2.50	60
	Nos. 592-594 (3)	5.15	1.20

1961, Oct. 27 **Litho.**

595 A130	1.50 l shown	85	15
596 A130	8 l Forsythia	1.50	22
597 A130	11 l Lily	2.00	40
	Nos. 595-597 (3)	4.35	77

Milosh G. Nikolla — A131

Flag with Marx and Lenin — A132

1961, Oct. 30 ***Perf. 14***

598 A131	50q violet brown	18	15
599 A131	8.50 l Prus green	70	25
	Set value		31

50th anniv. of the birth of Milosh Gjergi Nikolla, poet.

1961, Nov. 8

600 A132	2.50 l vermilion	30	15
601 A132	7.50 l dull red brn	60	25
	Set value		31

20th anniv. of the founding of Albania's Communist Party.

Worker, Farm Woman and Emblem
A133

Yuri Gagarin and Vostok 1
A134

1961, Nov. 23 **Unwmk.** ***Perf. 14***

602 A133	2.50 l violet blue	38	15
603 A133	7.50 l rose claret	75	30

20th anniv. of the Albanian Workers' Party.

1962, Feb. 15 **Unwmk.** ***Perf. 14***

604 A134	50q blue	30	15
605 A134	4 l red lilac	1.40	15
606 A134	11 l dk slate grn	2.75	65
	Nos. 604-606 (3)	4.45	95

1st manned space flight, made by Yuri A. Gagarin, Soviet astronaut, Apr. 12, 1961.

Nos. 604-606 were overprinted with an over-all yellow tint and with "POSTA AJRORE" (Air Mail) in maroon in 1962. Value, set $50.

Petro Nini Luarasi — A135

Malaria Eradication Emblem — A136

1962, Feb. 28 **Litho.**

607 A135	50q Prus blue	22	15
608 A135	8.50 l olive gray	1.25	25
	Set value		30

50th anniv. (in 1961) of the death of Petro Nini Luarasi, Albanian patriot.

1962, Apr. 30 **Unwmk.** ***Perf. 14***

609 A136	1.50 l brt green	16	15
610 A136	2.50 l brown red	16	15
611 A136	10 l red lilac	55	25
612 A136	11 l blue	85	35
	Nos. 609-612 (4)	1.72	
	Set value		74

WHO drive to eradicate malaria.

Souvenir sheets, perf. and imperf., contain one each of Nos. 609-612. Value $12.50 each. Nos. 609-612 imperf., value, set $12.50.

Camomile
A137

Woman Diver
A138

Medicinal plants.

1962, May 10

613 A137	50q shown	20	15
614 A137	8 l Linden	75	25
615 A137	11.50 l Garden sage	1.75	50
	Nos. 613-615 (3)	2.70	90

Value, imperf. set $10.

1962, May 31 ***Perf. 14***

Designs: 2.50 l, Pole vault. 3 l, Mt. Fuji and torch, horiz. 9 l, Woman javelin thrower. 10 l, Shot putting.

616 A138	50q brt grnsh bl & blk	15	15
617 A138	2.50 l gldn brn & sepia	20	15
618 A138	3 l blue & gray	40	15

619 A138 9 l rose car & dk brn 1.10 25
620 A138 10 l olive & blk 1.25 30
Nos. 616-620 (5) 3.10
Set value 75

1964 Olympic Games, Tokyo. Value, imperf. set $25. A 15 l (like 3 l) exists in souv. sheet, perf. and imperf.

Globe and Orbits — A139

Dog Laika and Sputnik 2 — A140

Designs: 1.50 l, Rocket to the sun. 20 l, Lunik 3 photographing far side of the moon.

1962, June Unwmk. *Perf. 14*

621 A139 50q violet & org 16 15
622 A140 1 l blue grn & brn 28 15
623 A140 1.50 l yellow & ver 40 15
624 A139 20 l magenta & bl 2.75 80
Nos. 621-624 (4) 3.59
Set value 1.05

Russian space explorations.
#621-624 exist imperforate in changed colors.
Two miniature sheets exist, containing one 14-lek picturing Sputnik 1. The perforated 14-lek is yellow and brown; the imperf. red and brown.

Soccer Game, Map of South America — A141

Design: 2.50 l, 15 l, Soccer game and globe as ball.

1962, July Litho.

625 A141 1 l org & dk pur 15 15
626 A141 2.50 l emer & bluish grn 22 15
627 A141 6.50 l lt brn & pink 70 15
628 A141 15 l bluish grn & mar 1.25 35
Nos. 625-628 (4) 2.32
Set value 54

Issued to commemorate the World Soccer Championships, Chile, May 30-June 17.
Exist imperforate in changed colors.
Two miniature sheets exist, each containing a single 20-lek in design similar to A141. The perf. sheet is brown and green; the imperf., brown and orange.

Map of Europe and Albania — A142

Woman of Dardhe — A143

Designs: 1 l, 2.50 l, Map of Adriatic Sea and Albania and Roman statue.

1962, Aug.

630 A142 50q multicolored 32 32
631 A142 1 l ultra & red 80 80
632 A142 2.50 l blue & red 2.50 2.50
633 A142 11 l multicolored 5.00 5.00
Nos. 630-633 (4) 8.62 8.62

Tourist propaganda. Imperforates in changed colors exist.
Miniature sheets containing a 7 l and 8 l stamp, perf. and imperf., exist.

1962, Sept.

Regional Costumes: 1 l, Man from Devoll. 2.50 l, Woman from Lunxheri. 14 l, Man from Gjirokaster.

635 A143 50q car, bl & pur 15 15
636 A143 1 l red brn & ocher 15 15
637 A143 2.50 l vio, yel grn & blk 45 15
638 A143 14 l red brn & pale grn 1.65 50
Nos. 635-638 (4) 2.40
Set value 75

Value, imperf. set $15.

Chamois A144

Ismail Qemali A145

Animals: 1 l, Lynx, horiz. 1.50 l, Wild boar, horiz. 15 l, 20 l, Roe deer.

1962, Oct. 24 Unwmk. *Perf. 14*

639 A144 50q sl grn & dk pur 50 15
640 A144 1 l orange & blk 90 15
641 A144 1.50 l red brn & blk 1.25 15
642 A144 15 l yel ol & red brn 6.25 1.00
Nos. 639-642 (4) 8.90 1.45

Miniature Sheet

643 A144 20 l yel ol & red brn 15.00 15.00

Imperfs. in changed colors, value #639-642 $20, #643 $20.

1962, Dec. 28 Litho.

Designs: 1 l, Albania eagle. 16 l, Eagle over fortress formed by "RPSH."

644 A145 1 l red & red brn 18 15
645 A145 3 l org brn & blk 32 15
646 A145 16 l dk car rose & blk 2.00 52
Nos. 644-646 (3) 2.50
Set value 65

50th anniv. of independence. Imperfs. in changed colors, value, set $12.50.

Monument of October Revolution A146

Henri Dunant, Cross, Globe and Nurse A147

Design: 10 l, Lenin statue.

1963, Jan. 5 Unwmk. *Perf. 14*

647 A146 5 l yel & dull vio 42 15
648 A146 10 l red orange & blk 1.10 22
Set value 30

45th anniv. of the October Revolution (Russia, 1917).

1963, Jan 25 Unwmk. *Perf. 14*

649 A147 1.50 l rose lake, red & blk 18 15
650 A147 2.50 l lt bl, red & blk 25 15
651 A147 6 l emerald, red & blk 60 22
652 A147 10 l dull yel, red & blk 1.10 35
Nos. 649-652 (4) 2.13
Set value 72

Cent. of the Geneva Conf., which led to the establishment of the Intl. Red Cross in 1864.
Imperfs. in changed colors, value, set $15.

Stalin and Battle of Stalingrad A148

Andrian G. Nikolayev A149

1963, Feb. 2

653 A148 8 l dk green & slate 2.50 50

20th anniversary of the Battle of Stalingrad. See No. C67.

1963, Feb. 28 Litho.

Designs: 7.50 l, Vostoks 3 and 4 and globe, horiz. 20 l, Pavel R. Popovich. 25 l, Nikolayev, Popovich and globe with trajectories.

654 A149 2.50 l vio bl & sepia 35 15
655 A149 7.50 l lt blue & blk 70 15
656 A149 20 l violet & sepia 2.00 70
Nos. 654-656 (3) 3.05 1.00

Miniature Sheet

657 A149 25 l vio bl & sepia 12.00 12.00

1st group space flight of Vostoks 3 and 4, Aug. 11-15, 1962. Imperfs. in changed colors, value #654-656 $10, #657 $12.

"Albania" Decorating Police Officer — A150

Polyphylla Fullo — A151

1963, Mar. 20 Unwmk. *Perf. 14*

658 A150 2.50 l crim, mag & blk 38 15
659 A150 7.50 l org ver, dk red & blk 1.40 25

20th anniversary of the security police.

1963, Mar. 20

Beetles: 1.50 l, Lucanus cervus. 8 l, Procerus gigas. 10 l, Cicindela Albanica.

660 A151 50q ol grn & brn 25 15
661 A151 1.50 l blue & brn 55 15
662 A151 8 l dl rose & blk vio 2.75 1.05
663 A151 10 l brt citron & blk 3.00 1.25
Nos. 660-663 (4) 6.55 2.60

1913 Stamp and Postmark — A152

Design: 10 l, Stamps of 1913, 1937 and 1962.

1963, May 5

664 A152 5 l yel, buff, bl & blk 70 25
665 A152 10 l car rose, grn & blk 1.35 45

50th anniversary of Albanian stamps.

Boxer — A153

Crested Grebe — A154

Designs: 3 l, Basketball baskets. 5 l, Volleyball. 6 l, Bicyclists. 9 l, Gymnast. 15 l, Hands holding torch, and map of Japan.

1963, May 25 *Perf. 13½*

666 A153 2 l yel, blk & red brn 22 15
667 A153 3 l ocher, brn & bl 32 15
668 A153 5 l gray bl, red brn & brn 55 15
669 A153 6 l gray, dk gray & grn 75 25
670 A153 9 l rose, red brn & bl 1.50 30
Nos. 666-670 (5) 3.34 1.00

Miniature Sheet

671 A153 15 l lt bl, car, blk & brn 7.50 7.50

1964 Olympic Games in Tokyo. Value, imperfs. #666-670 $7.50, #671 $8.

1963, Apr. 20 Litho. *Perf. 14*

Birds: 3 l, Golden eagle. 6.50 l, Gray partridges. 11 l, Capercaillie.

672 A154 50q multi 15 15
673 A154 3 l multi 60 20
674 A154 6.50 l multi 1.40 45
675 A154 11 l multi 2.25 70
Nos. 672-675 (4) 4.40 1.50

Soldier and Building A155

Designs: 2.50 l, Soldier with pack, ship and plane. 5 l, Soldier in battle. 6 l, Soldier and bulldozer.

1963, July 10 Unwmk. *Perf. 12*

676 A155 1.50 l brick red, yel & blk 20 15
677 A155 2.50 l bl, ocher & brn 28 15
678 A155 5 l bluish grn, gray & blk 65 15
679 A155 6 l red brn, buff & bl 85 25
Nos. 676-679 (4) 1.98
Set value 48

Albanian army, 20th anniversary.

Maj. Yuri A. Gagarin A156

Designs: 5 l, Maj. Gherman Titov. 7 l, Maj. Andrian G. Nikolayev. 11 l, Lt. Col. Pavel R. Popovich. 14 l, Lt. Col. Valeri Bykovski. 20 l, Lt. Valentina Tereshkova.

1963, July 30

Portraits in Yellow and Black

680 A156 3 l brt purple 35 15
681 A156 5 l dull blue 50 15
682 A156 7 l gray 70 15
683 A156 11 l deep claret 1.20 35
684 A156 14 l blue green 1.75 55
685 A156 20 l ultra 2.50 1.00
Nos. 680-685 (6) 7.00 2.35

Man's conquest of space. Value, imperf. set $15.

Volleyball — A157

1963, Aug. 31 *Perf. 12x12½*

686 A157 2 l shown 15 15
687 A157 3 l Weight lifting 25 15
688 A157 5 l Soccer 45 15
689 A157 7 l Boxing 55 25
690 A157 8 l Rowing 1.05 30
Nos. 686-690 (5) 2.45 1.00

European championships. Imperfs. in changed colors, value set $10.

Papilio Podalirius A158

1963, Sept. 29 **Litho.**

Various Butterflies and Moths in Natural Colors

691	A158	1 l red	15	15
692	A158	2 l blue	30	15
693	A158	4 l dull lilac	50	25
694	A158	5 l pale green	90	40
695	A158	8 l bister	1.10	55
696	A158	10 l light blue	1.65	70
		Nos. 691-696 (6)	4.60	2.20

Oil Refinery, Cerrik — A159

Flag and Shield — A160

Designs: 2.50 l, Food processing plant, Tirana, horiz. 30 l, Fruit canning plant. 50 l, Tannery, horiz.

1963, Nov. 15 **Unwmk.** ***Perf. 14***

697	A159	2.50 l rose red, *pnksh*	25	15
698	A159	20 l slate grn, *grnsh*	85	20
699	A159	30 l dull pur, *grysh*	2.00	50
700	A159	50 l ocher, *yel*	2.25	75
		Nos. 697-700 (4)	5.35	1.60

Industrial development in Albania.

1963, Nov. 24 ***Perf. 12½x12***

701	A160	2 l grnsh bl, blk, ocher & red	25	15
702	A160	8 l blue, blk, ocher & red	75	48
		Set value		53

1st Congress of Army Aid Assn.

Chinese, Caucasian and Negro Men — A161

1963, Dec. 10 ***Perf. 12x11½***

703	A161	3 l bister & blk	28	15
704	A161	5 l bister & ultra	52	18
705	A161	7 l bister & vio	85	30
		Nos. 703-705 (3)	1.65	63

15th anniv. of the Universal Declaration of Human Rights.

Slalom Ascent — A162

Lenin — A163

Designs: 50q, Bobsled, horiz. 6.50 l, Ice hockey, horiz. 12.50 l, Women's figure skating. No. 709A, Ski jumper.

1963, Dec. 25 ***Perf. 14***

706	A162	50q grnsh bl & blk	15	15
707	A162	2.50 l red, gray & blk	25	15
708	A162	6.50 l yel, blk & gray	65	20
709	A162	12.50 l red, blk & yel grn	1.50	50
		Nos. 706-709 (4)	2.55	
		Set value		80

Miniature Sheet

709A	A162	12.50 l multi	3.75	3.75

9th Winter Olympic Games, Innsbruck, Jan. 29-Feb. 9, 1964. Imperfs. in changed colors, value #706-709 $20, #709A $25.

1964, Jan. 21 ***Perf. 12½x12***

710	A163	5 l gray & bister	30	15
711	A163	10 l gray & ocher	60	30

40th anniversary, death of Lenin.

Hurdling A164

Fish A165

Designs: 3 l, Track, horiz. 6.50 l, Rifle shooting, horiz. 8 l, Basketball.

Perf. 12½x12, 12x12½

1964, Jan. 30 **Litho.**

712	A164	2.50 l pale vio & ultra	25	15
713	A164	3 l lt grn & red brn	38	15
714	A164	6.50 l blue & claret	75	18
715	A164	8 l lt blue & ocher	1.10	22
		Nos. 712-715 (4)	2.48	
		Set value		60

1st Games of the New Emerging Forces, GANEFO, Jakarta, Indonesia, Nov. 10-22, 1963.

1964, Feb. 26 **Unwmk.** ***Perf. 14***

716	A165	50q Sturgeon	15	15
717	A165	1 l Gilthead	15	15
718	A165	1.50 l Striped mullet	32	15
719	A165	2.50 l Carp	52	15
720	A165	6.50 l Mackerel	1.40	40
721	A165	10 l Lake Ohrid trout	2.50	50
		Nos. 716-721 (6)	5.04	
		Set value		1.25

Wild Animals A166

1964, Mar. 28 ***Perf. 12½x12***

722	A166	1 l Red Squirrel	15	15
723	A166	1.50 l Beech marten	15	15
724	A166	2 l Red fox	40	15
725	A166	2.50 l Hedgehog	45	15
726	A166	3 l Hare	52	15
727	A166	5 l Jackal	90	25
728	A166	7 l Wildcat	1.25	35
729	A166	8 l Wolf	1.65	50
		Nos. 722-729 (8)	5.47	
		Set value		1.50

Lighting Olympic Torch — A167

Designs: 5 l, Torch and globes. 7 l, 15 l, Olympic flag and Mt. Fuji. 10 l, National Stadium, Tokyo.

1964, May 18 ***Perf. 12x12½***

730	A167	3 l lt yel grn, yel & buff	18	15
731	A167	5 l red & vio blue	30	15
732	A167	7 l lt bl, ultra & yel	42	18
733	A167	10 l orange, bl & vio	60	25
		Nos. 730-733 (4)	1.50	
		Set value		55

Miniature Sheet

734	A167	15 l lt bl, ultra & org	8.50	8.50

18th Olympic Games, Tokyo, Oct. 10-25, 1964. No. 734 contains one 49x62mm stamp. Imperfs. in changed colors, value #730-733 $9.50, #734 $12.50.

See No. 745.

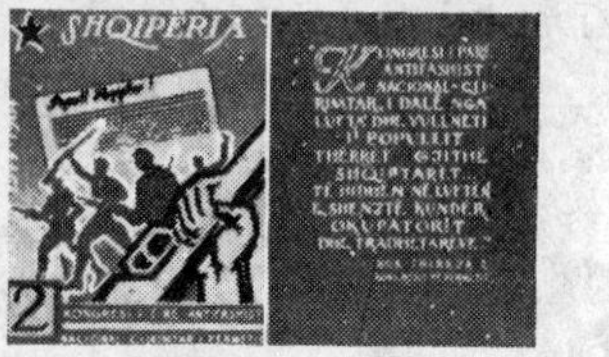
Partisans — A168

Designs: 5 l, Arms of Albania. 8 l, Enver Hoxha.

Perf. 12½x12

1964, May 24 **Litho.** **Unwmk.**

735	A168	2 l orange, red & blk	15	15
736	A168	5 l multicolored	35	15
737	A168	8 l red brn, blk & red	70	20
		Nos. 735-737 (3)	1.20	
		Set value		36

20th anniv. of the Natl. Anti-Fascist Cong. of Liberation, Permet, May 24, 1944. The label attached to each stamp, without perforations between, carries a quotation from the 1944 Congress.

Albanian Flag and Revolutionists A169

Full Moon A170

Perf. 12½x12

1964, June 10 **Litho.** **Unwmk.**

738	A169	2.50 l red & gray	15	15
739	A169	7.50 l lilac rose & gray	35	20

Albanian revolution of 1924, 40th anniv.

1964, June 27 ***Perf. 12x12½***

Designs: 5 l, New moon. 8 l, Half moon. 11 l, Waning moon. 15 l, Far side of moon.

740	A170	1 l purple & yel	18	15
741	A170	5 l violet & yel	45	15
742	A170	8 l blue & yel	80	30
743	A170	11 l green & yel	1.25	45
		Nos. 740-743 (4)	2.68	1.05

Miniature Sheet

Perf. 12 on 2 sides

744	A170	15 l ultra & yel	8.50	8.50

No. 744 contains one stamp, size: 35x36mm, perforated at top and bottom. Imperfs. in changed colors, value #740-743 $9, #744 $9.

No. 733 with Added Inscription: "Rimini 25-VI-64"

1964 ***Perf. 12x12½***

745	A167	10 l orange, bl & vio	3.25	3.00

"Toward Tokyo 1964" Phil. Exhib. at Rimini, Italy, June 25-July 6.

Wren — A171

Birds: 1 l, Penduline titmouse. 2.50 l, Green woodpecker. 3 l, Tree creeper. 4 l, Nuthatch. 5 l, Great titmouse. 6 l, Goldfinch. 18 l, Oriole.

1964, July 31 ***Perf. 12x12½***

746	A171	50q multi	15	15
747	A171	1 l orange & multi	15	15
748	A171	2.50 l multi	20	15
749	A171	3 l blue & multi	30	15
750	A171	4 l yellow & multi	40	15
751	A171	5 l blue & multi	50	15
752	A171	6 l lt vio & multi	70	30
753	A171	18 l pink & multi	2.10	85
		Nos. 746-753 (8)	4.50	
		Set value		1.60

Running and Gymnastics A172

Sport: 2 l, Weight lifting, judo. 3 l, Equestrian, bicycling. 4 l, Soccer, water polo. 5 l, Wrestling, boxing. 6 l, Pentathlon, hockey. 7 l, Swimming, sailing. 8 l, Basketball, volleyball. 9 l, Rowing, canoeing. 10 l, Fencing, pistol shooting. 20 l, Three winners.

Perf. 12x12½

1964, Sept. 25 **Litho.** **Unwmk.**

754	A172	1 l lt bl, rose & emer	15	15
755	A172	2 l bis brn, bluish grn & vio	15	15
756	A172	3 l vio, red org & ol bis	18	15
757	A172	4 l grnsh bl, ol & ultra	18	15
758	A172	5 l grnsh bl, car & pale lil	30	15
759	A172	6 l dk bl, org & lt bl	35	15
760	A172	7 l dk bl, lt ol & org	38	15
761	A172	8 l emerald, gray & yel	52	22
762	A172	9 l bl, yel & lil rose	65	30
763	A172	10 l brt grn, org brn & yel grn	1.65	48
		Nos. 754-763 (10)	4.51	
		Set value		1.60

Miniature Sheet

Perf. 12

764	A172	20 l violet & lemon	8.00	5.00

18th Olympic Games, Tokyo, Oct. 10-25. No. 764 contains one stamp, size: 41x68mm. Imperfs. in changed colors, value #754-763 $12.50, #764 $12.50.

Arms of People's Republic of China — A173

Mao Tse-tung and Flag A174

1964, Oct. 1 ***Perf. 11½x12, 12x11½***

765	A173	7 l black, red & yellow	80	30
766	A174	8 l black, red & yellow	1.25	40

People's Republic of China, 15th anniv.

Karl Marx A175

Jeronim de Rada A176

Designs: 5 l, St. Martin's Hall, London. 8 l, Friedrich Engels.

1964, Nov. 5 ***Perf. 12x11½***

767	A175	2 l red, lt vio & blk	45	15
768	A175	5 l gray blue	1.00	18
769	A175	8 l ocher, blk & red	2.00	30
		Nos. 767-769 (3)	3.45	63

Centenary of First Socialist International.

1964, Nov. 15 *Perf. 12½x11½*

770	A176	7 l slate green	75	30
771	A176	8 l dull violet	1.00	35

Birth of Jeronim de Rada, poet, 150th anniv.

Arms of Albania — A177

Factories A178

Designs: 3 l, Combine harvester. 4 l, Woman chemist. 10 l, Hands holding Constitution, hammer and sickle.

Perf. 11½x12, 12x11½

1964, Nov. 29

772	A177	1 l multicolored	20	15
773	A178	2 l red, yel & vio bl	28	15
774	A178	3 l red, yel & brn	50	15
775	A178	4 l red, yel & gray grn	60	15
776	A177	10 l red, bl & blk	1.00	45
		Nos. 772-776 (5)	2.58	
		Set value		78

20th anniversary of liberation.

Planet Mercury — A179

Planets: 2 l, Venus and rocket. 3 l, Earth, moon and rocket. 4 l, Mars and rocket. 5 l, Jupiter. 6 l, Saturn. 7 l, Uranus. 8 l, Neptune. 9 l, Pluto. 15 l, Solar system and rocket.

1964, Dec. 15 *Perf. 12x12½*

777	A179	1 l yellow & pur	15	15
778	A179	2 l multicolored	15	15
779	A179	3 l multicolored	22	15
780	A179	4 l multicolored	25	15
781	A179	5 l yel, dk pur & brn	42	15
782	A179	6 l lt grn, vio brn & yel	60	15
783	A179	7 l yellow & grn	70	18
784	A179	8 l yellow & vio	85	22
785	A179	9 l lt grn, yel & blk	1.25	38
		Nos. 777-785 (9)	4.59	
		Set value		1.30

Miniature Sheet

Perf. 12 on 2 sides

786	A179	15 l car, bl, yel & grn	7.50	7.50

No. 786 contains one stamp, size: 62x51mm, perforated at top and bottom. Imperfs. in changed colors, value #777-785 $10, #786 $10.

European Chestnut A180

Symbols of Industry A181

1965, Jan. 25 *Perf. 11½x12*

787	A180	1 l shown	15	15
788	A180	2 l Medlars	18	15
789	A180	3 l Persimmon	38	15
790	A180	4 l Pomegranate	42	15
791	A180	5 l Quince	60	20
792	A180	10 l Orange	1.25	35
		Nos. 787-792 (6)	*2.98*	
		Set value		90

1965, Feb. 20

Designs: 5 l, Books, triangle and compass. 8 l, Beach, trees and hotel.

793	A181	2 l blk, car rose & pink	*1.40*	40
794	A181	5 l yel, gray & blk	*2.75*	85
795	A181	8 l blk, vio bl & lt bl	*4.75*	1.60
		Nos. 793-795 (3)	*8.90*	2.85

Professional trade associations, 20th anniv.

Water Buffalo A182

Various designs: Water buffalo.

1965, Mar. *Perf. 12x11½*

796	A182	1 l lt yel grn, yel & brn blk	30	15
797	A182	2 l lt bl, dk gray & blk	70	15
798	A182	3 l yellow, brn & grn	95	15
799	A182	7 l brt grn, yel & brn blk	2.25	35
800	A182	12 l pale lil, dk brn & ind	3.25	65
		Nos. 796-800 (5)	7.45	1.45

Mountain View, Valbona — A183

Views: 1.50 l, Seashore. 3 l, Glacier and peak, vert. 4 l, Gorge, vert. 5 l, Mountain peaks. 9 l, Lake and hills.

1965, Mar. **Litho.** *Perf. 12*

801	A183	1.50 l multi	75	15
802	A183	2.50 l multi	1.00	22
803	A183	3 l multi	1.40	25
804	A183	4 l multi	1.65	38
805	A183	5 l multi	2.50	50
806	A183	9 l multi	4.00	75
		Nos. 801-806 (6)	11.30	2.25

Frontier Guard — A184

Small-bore Rifle Shooting, Prone — A185

1965, Apr. 25 **Unwmk.**

807	A184	2.50 l lt bl & multi	75	15
808	A184	12.50 l lt ultra & multi	3.25	90

20th anniversary of the Frontier Guards.

1965, May 10

Designs: 2 l, Rifle shooting, standing. 3 l, Target over map of Europe, showing Bucharest. 4 l, Pistol shooting. 15 l, Rifle shooting, kneeling.

809	A185	1 l lil, car rose, blk & brn	15	15
810	A185	2 l bl, blk, brn & vio bl	30	15
811	A185	3 l pink & car rose	35	15
812	A185	4 l bis, blk & vio brn	48	15
813	A185	15 l brt grn, brn & vio brn	1.75	50
		Nos. 809-813 (5)	3.03	
		Set value		90

European Shooting Championships, Bucharest.

ITU Emblem, Old and New Communications Equipment — A186

Col. Pavel Belyayev — A187

1965, May 17 *Perf. 12½x12*

814	A186	2.50 l brt grn, blk & lil rose	42	15
815	A186	12.50 l vio, blk & brt bl	2.50	28
		Set value		34

Cent. of the ITU.

1965, June 15 *Perf. 12*

Designs: 2 l, Voskhod II. 6.50 l, Lt. Col. Alexei Leonov. 20 l, Leonov floating in space.

816	A187	1.50 l lt blue & brn	15	15
817	A187	2 l dk bl, lt vio & lt ultra	15	15
818	A187	6.50 l lilac & brn	55	15
819	A187	20 l chlky bl, yel & blk	1.50	35
		Nos. 816-819 (4)	2.35	
		Set value		60

Miniature Sheet

Perf. 12 on 2 sides

820	A187	20 l brt bl, org & blk	5.25	5.25

Space flight of Voskhod II and 1st man walking in space, Lt. Col. Alexei Leonov. No. 820 contains one stamp, size: 51x59½mm, perforated at top and bottom. Imperf., brt grn background, value $5.25.

Marx and Lenin — A188

Mother and Child — A189

1965, June 21 *Perf. 12*

821	A188	2.50 l dk brn, red & yel	70	15
822	A188	7.50 l sl grn, org ver & buff	1.75	25

6th Conf. of Postal Ministers of Communist Countries, Peking, June 21-July 15.

Perf. 12½x12, 12x12½

1965, June 29 **Litho.** **Unwmk.**

Designs: 2 l, Pioneers. 3 l, Boy and girl at play, horiz. 4 l, Child on beach. 15 l, Girl with book.

823	A189	1 l brt bl, rose lil & blk	15	15
824	A189	2 l salmon, vio & blk	22	15
825	A189	3 l green, org & vio	32	15
826	A189	4 l multicolored	45	15
827	A189	15 l lil rose, brn & ocher	1.40	38
		Nos. 823-827 (5)	2.54	
		Set value		70

Issued for International Children's Day.

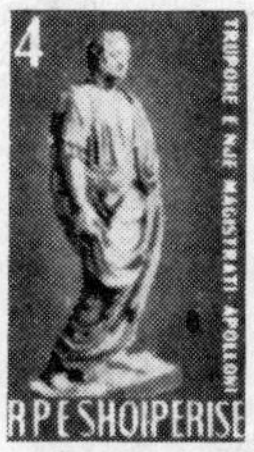

Statue of Magistrate A190

Fuchsia A191

Designs: 1 l, Amphora. 2 l, Illyrian armor. 3 l, Mosaic, horiz. 15 l, Torso, Apollo statue.

1965, July 20 *Perf. 12*

828	A190	1 l lt ol, org & brn	15	15
829	A190	2 l gray grn, grn & brn	20	15
830	A190	3 l tan, brn, car & lil	35	15
831	A190	4 l green, bis & brn	50	20
832	A190	15 l gray & pale cl	1.25	65
		Nos. 828-832 (5)	2.45	
		Set value		1.00

1965, Aug. 11 *Perf. 12½x12*

Flowers: 2 l, Cyclamen. 3 l, Tiger lily. 3.50 l, Iris. 4 l, Dahlia. 4.50 l, Hydrangea. 5 l, Rose. 7 l, Tulips.

833	A191	1 l multi	15	15
834	A191	2 l multi	20	15
835	A191	3 l multi	32	15
836	A191	3.50 l multi	40	15
837	A191	4 l multi	45	15
838	A191	4.50 l multi	52	15
839	A191	5 l multi	65	20
840	A191	7 l multi	1.25	30
		Nos. 833-840 (8)	3.94	
		Set value		1.10

Nos. 698-700 Surcharged New Value and Two Bars

1965, Aug. 16 *Perf. 14*

841	A159	5q on 30 l	15	15
842	A159	15q on 30 l	25	15
843	A159	25q on 50 l	35	15
844	A159	80q on 50 l	70	20
845	A159	1.10 l on 20 l	1.10	30
846	A159	2 l on 20 l	2.00	60
		Nos. 841-846 (6)	4.55	
		Set value		1.32

White Stork — A192

"Homecoming," by Bukurosh Sejdini — A193

Migratory Birds: 20q, Cuckoo. 30q, Hoopoe. 40q, European bee-eater. 50q, European nightjar. 1.50 l, Quail.

1965, Aug. 31 *Perf. 12*

847	A192	10q yellow, blk & gray	15	15
848	A192	20q brt pink, blk & dk bl	18	15
849	A192	30q violet, blk & bis	32	15
850	A192	40q emer, blk yel & org	70	15
851	A192	50q ultra, brn & red brn	85	22
852	A192	1.50 l bis, red brn & dp org	2.25	75
		Nos. 847-852 (6)	4.45	
		Set value		1.35

1965, Sept. 26 **Litho.** *Perf. 12x12½*

853	A193	25q olive black	1.00	16
854	A193	65q blue black	2.50	32
855	A193	1.10 l black	3.75	60
		Nos. 853-855 (3)	7.25	1.08

Second war veterans' meeting.

Hunting — A194

Oleander — A195

1965, Oct. 6 **Litho.** **Unwmk.**

856	A194	10q Capercaillie	15	15
857	A194	20q Deer	22	15
858	A194	30q Pheasant	42	18
859	A194	40q Mallards	65	20
860	A194	50q Boar	75	25
861	A194	1 l Rabbit	2.25	55
		Nos. 856-861 (6)	4.44	1.48

1965, Oct. 26 *Perf. 12½x12*

Flowers: 20q, Forget-me-nots. 30q, Pink. 40q, White water lily. 50q, Bird's foot. 1 l, Corn poppy.

862	A195	10q brt bl, grn & car rose	24	15
863	A195	20q org red, bl, brn & grn	28	15
864	A195	30q vio, car rose & grn	60	15
865	A195	40q emerald, yel & blk	85	18
866	A195	50q org brn, yel & grn	95	20
867	A195	1 l yel grn, blk & rose red	2.15	70
		Nos. 862-867 (6)	5.07	1.53

Hotel Turizmi, Fier — A196

Freighter "Teuta" — A197

Buildings: 10q, Hotel, Peshkopi. 15q, Sanatorium, Tirana. 25q, Rest home, Pogradec. 65q, Partisan Sports Arena, Tirana. 80q, Rest home, Mali Dajt. 1.10 l, Culture House, Tirana. 1.60 l, Hotel Adriatik, Durres. 2 l, Migjeni Theater, Shkoder. 3 l, Alexander Moissi House of Culture, Durres.

1965, Oct. *Perf. 12x12½*

868	A196	5q	blue & blk	15	15
869	A196	10q	ocher & blk	15	15
870	A196	15q	dull grn & blk	15	15
871	A196	25q	violet & blk	15	15
872	A196	65q	lt brn & blk	55	15
873	A196	80q	yel grn & blk	70	15
874	A196	1.10 l	lilac & blk	1.00	20
875	A196	1.60 l	lt vio bl & blk	1.40	35
876	A196	2 l	dull rose & blk	1.90	50
877	A196	3 l	gray & blk	3.00	70
			Nos. 868-877 (10)	9.15	
			Set value		2.15

1965, Nov. 16

Ships: 20q, Raft. 30q, Sailing ship, 19th cent. 40q, Sailing ship, 18th cent. 50q, Freighter "Vlora." 1 l, Illyric galleys.

878	A197	10q	brt grn & dk grn	15	15
879	A197	20q	ol bis & dk grn	20	15
880	A197	30q	lt & dp ultra	35	15
881	A197	40q	vio & dp vio	60	18
882	A197	50q	pink & dk red	75	20
883	A197	1 l	bister & brn	1.50	45
			Nos. 878-883 (6)	3.55	1.28

Brown Bear — A198

Basketball and Players — A199

Designs: Various Albanian bears. 50q, 55q, 60q, horizontal.

1965, Dec. 7 *Perf. 11½x12*

884	A198	10q	bister & dk brn	30	15
885	A198	20q	pale brn & dk brn	42	15
886	A198	30q	bis, dk brn & car	65	15
887	A198	35q	pale brn & dk brn	80	15
888	A198	40q	bister & dk brn	1.25	18
889	A198	50q	bister & dk brn	1.50	20
890	A198	55q	bister & dk brn	1.50	30
891	A198	60q	pale brn, dk brn & car	1.65	45
			Nos. 884-891 (8)	8.07	1.73

1965, Dec. 15 Litho. *Perf. 12½x12*

Designs: 10q, Games' emblem (map of Albania and basket). 30q, 50q, Players with ball (diff. designs). 1.40 l, Basketball medal on ribbon.

892	A199	10q	blue, yel & car	15	15
893	A199	20q	rose lil, lt brn & blk	28	15
894	A199	30q	bis, lt brn, red & blk	35	15
895	A199	50q	lt grn, lt brn & blk	80	15
896	A199	1.40 l	rose, blk, brn & yel	1.50	50
			Nos. 892-896 (5)	3.08	
			Set value		80

7th Balkan Basketball Championships, Tirana, Dec. 15-19.

Arms of Republic and Smokestacks — A200

Designs (Arms and): 10q, Book. 30q, Wheat. 60q, Book, hammer and sickle. 80q, Factories.

1966, Jan. 11 Litho. *Perf. 11½x12*

Coat of Arms in Gold

897	A200	10q	crimson & brn	15	15
898	A200	20q	blue & vio bl	15	15
899	A200	30q	org yel & brn	32	15
900	A200	60q	yel grn & brt grn	50	20
901	A200	80q	crimson & brn	1.10	25
			Nos. 897-901 (5)	2.22	
			Set value		60

Albanian People's Republic, 20th anniv.

Cow — A201

Perf. 12½x12, 12x12½

1966, Feb. 25

902	A201	10q	shown	20	15
903	A201	20q	Pig	32	15
904	A201	30q	Ewe & lamb	45	15
905	A201	35q	Ram	65	15
906	A201	40q	Dog	95	16
907	A201	50q	Cat, vert.	1.00	16
908	A201	55q	Horse, vert.	1.25	25
909	A201	60q	Ass, vert.	1.50	28
			Nos. 902-909 (8)	6.32	
			Set value		1.22

Soccer Player and Map of Uruguay — A202

Andon Zako Cajupi — A203

Designs: 5q, Globe in form of soccer ball. 15q, Player, map of Italy. 20q, Goalkeeper, map of France. 25q, Player, map of Brazil. 30q, Player, map of Switzerland. 35q, Player, map of Sweden. 40q, Player, map of Chile. 50q, Player, map of Great Britain. 70q, World Championship cup and ball.

1966, Mar. 20 Litho. *Perf. 12*

910	A202	5q	gray & dp org	15	15
911	A202	10q	lt brn, bl & vio	15	15
912	A202	15q	cit, dk bl & brt bl	15	15
913	A202	20q	org, vio bl & brt bl	22	15
914	A202	25q	salmon & sepia	25	15
915	A202	30q	lt yel grn & brn	28	15
916	A202	35q	lt ultra & emer	32	15
917	A202	40q	pink & brown	50	15
918	A202	50q	pale grn, mag & rose red	50	15
919	A202	70q	gray, brn, yel & blk	65	24
			Nos. 910-919 (10)	3.17	
			Set value		1.00

World Cup Soccer Championship, Wembley, England, July 11-30.

1966, Mar. 27 **Unwmk.**

920	A203	40q	bluish blk	28	15
921	A203	1.10 l	dark green	80	15
			Set value		22

Centenary of the birth of the poet Andon Zako Cajupi.

Painted Lady — A204

WHO Headquarters, Geneva, and Emblem — A205

Designs: 20q, Blue dragonfly. 30q, Cloudless sulphur butterfly. 35q, 40q, Splendid dragonfly. 50q, Machaon swallow-tail. 55q, Sulphur butterfly. 60q, Whitemarbled butterfly.

1966, Apr. 21 Litho. *Perf. 11½x12*

922	A204	10q	multicolored	15	15
923	A204	20q	yellow & multi	20	15
924	A204	30q	yellow & multi	35	15
925	A204	35q	sky blue & multi	42	15
926	A204	40q	multicolored	45	15
927	A204	50q	rose & multi	60	15
928	A204	55q	multicolored	65	15
929	A204	60q	multicolored	1.10	15
			Nos. 922-929 (8)	3.92	
			Set value		70

Perf. 12x12½, 12½x12

1966, May 3 **Litho.**

Designs (WHO Emblem and): 35q, Ambulance and stretcher bearers, vert. 60q, Albanian mother and nurse weighing infant, vert. 80q, X-ray machine and hospital.

930	A205	25q	lt blue & blk	26	15
931	A205	35q	salmon & ultra	52	15
932	A205	60q	lt grn, bl & red	80	15
933	A205	80q	yel, bl, grn & lt brn	1.10	22
			Nos. 930-933 (4)	2.68	
			Set value		42

Inauguration of the WHO Headquarters, Geneva.

Bird's Foot Starfish — A206

Designs: 25q, Starfish. 35q, Brittle star. 45q, Butthorn starfish. 50q, Starfish. 60q, Sea cucumber. 70q, Sea urchin.

1966, May 10 *Perf. 12x12½*

934	A206	15q	multicolored	20	15
935	A206	25q	multicolored	35	15
936	A206	35q	multicolored	50	15
937	A206	45q	multicolored	70	15
938	A206	50q	multicolored	85	18
939	A206	60q	multicolored	1.00	20
940	A206	70q	multicolored	1.40	35
			Nos. 934-940 (7)	5.00	
			Set value		1.10

Luna 10 — A207

Designs: 30q, 80q, Trajectory of Luna 10, earth and moon.

1966, June 10 *Perf. 12x12½*

941	A207	20q	blue, yel & blk	32	15
942	A207	30q	yel grn, blk & bl	45	15
943	A207	70q	vio, yel & blk	90	20
944	A207	80q	yel, vio, grn & blk	1.25	20
			Nos. 941-944 (4)	2.92	70

Launching of the 1st artificial moon satellite, Luna 10, Apr. 3, 1966.

Jules Rimet Cup and Soccer A208

Designs: Various scenes of soccer play.

1966, July 12 Litho. *Perf. 12x12½*

Black Inscriptions

945	A208	10q	ocher & lilac	15	15
946	A208	20q	lt blue & cit	15	15
947	A208	30q	brick red & Prus bl	20	15
948	A208	35q	lt ultra & rose	25	15
949	A208	40q	yel grn & lt red brn	30	15
950	A208	50q	lt red brn & yel grn	48	15
951	A208	55q	rose lil & yel grn	52	15
952	A208	60q	dp rose & ocher	1.00	22
			Nos. 945-952 (8)	3.05	
			Set value		80

World Cup Soccer Championship, Wembley, England, July 11-30.

Water Level Map of Albania — A209

Designs: 30q, Water measure and fields. 70q, Turbine and pylon. 80q, Hydrological decade emblem.

1966, July *Perf. 12½x12*

953	A209	20q	brick red, blk & org	32	15
954	A209	30q	emer, blk & lt brn	48	15
955	A209	70q	brt violet & blk	1.10	25
956	A209	80q	brt bl, org, yel & blk	52	30
			Nos. 953-956 (4)	2.42	85

Hydrological Decade (UNESCO), 1965-74.

Greek Turtle — A210

Designs: 15q, Grass snake. 25q, European pond turtle. 30q, Wall lizard. 35q, Wall gecko. 45q, Emerald lizard. 50q, Slowworm. 90q, Horned viper (or sand viper).

1966, Aug. 10 Litho. *Perf. 12½x12*

957	A210	10q	gray & multi	15	15
958	A210	15q	yellow & multi	20	15
959	A210	25q	ultra & multi	30	15
960	A210	30q	multicolored	40	18
961	A210	35q	multicolored	55	20
962	A210	45q	multicolored	65	25
963	A210	50q	orange & multi	75	30
964	A210	90q	lilac & multi	1.65	55
			Nos. 957-964 (8)	4.65	1.93

Persian Cat A211

Cats: 10q, Siamese, vert. 15q, European tabby, vert. 25q, Black kitten. 60q, 65q, 80q, Various Persians.

Perf. 12x12½, 12½x12

1966, Sept. 20 **Litho.**

965	A211	10q	multicolored	15	15
966	A211	15q	blk, sep & car	20	15
967	A211	25q	blk, dk & lt brn	28	15
968	A211	45q	blk, org & yel	55	16
969	A211	60q	blk, brn & yel	70	20
970	A211	65q	multicolored	80	20
971	A211	80q	blk, gray & yel	1.40	28
			Nos. 965-971 (7)	4.08	
			Set value		1.00

Pjeter Budi, Writer — A212

1966, Oct. 5 *Perf. 12x12½*

972 A212 25q buff & slate grn 16 15
973 A212 1.75 l gray & dull claret 1.10 45

UNESCO Emblem A213

Designs (UNESCO Emblem and): 15q, Open book, rose and school. 25q, Male folk dancers. 1.55 l, Jug, column and old building.

1966, Oct. 20 Litho. *Perf. 12*

974 A213 5q lt gray & multi 15 15
975 A213 15q dp blue & multi 20 15
976 A213 25q gray & multi 40 15
977 A213 1.55 l multi 1.75 48
Nos. 974-977 (4) 2.50
Set value 75

20th anniv. of UNESCO.

Hand Holding Book with Pictures of Marx, Engels, Lenin and Stalin A214

Hammer and Sickle, Party Emblem in Sunburst A215

Designs: 25q, Map of Albania, hammer and sickle, symbols of agriculture and industry. 65q, Symbolic grain and factories. 95q, Fists holding rifle, spade, axe, sickle and book.

1966, Nov. 1 Litho. *Perf. 11½x12*

978 A214 15q vermilion & gold 22 15
979 A214 25q multicolored 32 15
980 A214 65q brn, brn org & gold 75 15
981 A214 95q yellow & multi 1.10 35
Nos. 978-981 (4) 2.39
Set value 60

Albanian Communist Party, 5th Cong.

1966, Nov. 8

Designs: 25q, Partisan and sunburst. 65q, Steel worker and blast furnace. 95q, Combine harvester, factories, and pylon.

982 A215 15q orange & multi 22 15
983 A215 25q red & multi 30 15
984 A215 65q multicolored 80 15
985 A215 95q blue & multi 1.10 35
Nos. 982-985 (4) 2.42
Set value 60

25th anniv. of the founding of the Albanian Workers Party.

Russian Wolfhound — A216

Dogs: 15q, Sheep dog. 25q, English setter. 45q, English springer spaniel. 60q, Bulldog. 65q, Saint Bernard. 80q, Dachshund.

1966 Litho. *Perf. 12½x12*

986 A216 10q green & multi 18 15
987 A216 15q multicolored 25 15
988 A216 25q lilac & multi 35 15
989 A216 45q rose & multi 70 35
990 A216 60q brown & multi 90 40
991 A216 65q ultra & multi 1.00 45
992 A216 80q blue grn & multi 1.40 52
Nos. 986-992 (7) 4.78 2.17

Ndre Mjeda A217

Proclamation A218

1966 *Perf. 12½x12*

993 A217 25q brt bl & dk brn 52 15
994 A217 1.75 l brt grn & dk brn 2.00 65

Birth Centenary of the priest Ndre Mjeda.

1966 *Perf. 11½x12, 12x11½*

Designs: 10q, Banner, man and woman holding gun and axe, horiz. 1.85 l, man with axe and banner and partisan with gun.

995 A218 5q lt brn, red & blk 15 15
996 A218 10q red, blk, gray & bl 18 15
997 A218 1.85 l red, blk & salmon 1.25 28
Nos. 995-997 (3) 1.58
Set value 38

25th anniv. of the Albanian Communist Party.

Golden Eagle — A219

Birds of Prey: 15q, European sea eagle. 25q, Griffon vulture. 40q, Common sparrowhawk. 50q, Osprey. 70q, Egyptian vulture. 90q, Kestrel.

1966, Dec. 20 Litho. *Perf. 11½x12*

998 A219 10q gray & multi 15 15
999 A219 15q multicolored 20 15
1000 A219 25q citron & multi 35 15
1001 A219 40q multicolored 60 18
1002 A219 50q multicolored 70 22
1003 A219 70q yellow & multi 1.00 35
1004 A219 90q multicolored 1.40 48
Nos. 998-1004 (7) 4.40 1.68

Hake A220

Fish: 15q, Red mullet. 25q, Opah. 40q, Atlantic wolf fish. 65q, Lumpfish. 80q, Swordfish. 1.15 l, Shorthorn sculpin.

1967, Jan. Photo. *Perf. 12x11½*

Fish in Natural Colors

1005 A220 10q blue 15 15
1006 A220 15q lt yellow grn 24 15
1007 A220 25q Prus blue 30 15
1008 A220 40q emerald 75 18
1009 A220 65q brt blue grn 85 25
1010 A220 80q blue 1.25 35
1011 A220 1.15 l brt green 1.65 60
Nos. 1005-1011 (7) 5.19 1.83

White Pelican — A221

Designs: Various groups of pelicans.

1967, Feb. 22 Litho. *Perf. 12*

1012 A221 10q pink & multi 15 15
1013 A221 15q pink & multi 24 15
1014 A221 25q pink & multi 48 15
1015 A221 50q pink & multi 85 15
1016 A221 2 l pink & multi 3.25 75
Nos. 1012-1016 (5) 4.97
Set value 1.05

Camellia — A222

Flowers: 10q, Chrysanthemum. 15q, Hollyhock. 25q, Flowering Maple. 35q, Peony. 65q, Gladiolus. 80q, Freesia. 1.15 l, Carnation.

Unwmk.

1967, Apr. 12 Litho. *Perf. 12*

Flowers in Natural Colors

1017 A222 5q pale brown 15 15
1018 A222 10q lt lilac 15 15
1019 A222 15q gray 18 15
1020 A222 25q ultra 30 15
1021 A222 35q lt blue 55 15
1022 A222 65q lt blue grn 85 15
1023 A222 80q lt bluish gray 1.25 22
1024 A222 1.15 l dull yellow 1.65 40
Nos. 1017-1024 (8) 5.08
Set value 1.00

A223

Rose — A224

Design: Congress emblem and power station.

1967, Apr. 24 Litho. *Perf. 12*

1025 A223 25q multi 22 15
1026 A223 1.75 l multi 1.75 42

Cong. of the Union of Professional Workers, Tirana, Apr. 24.

1967, May 15 *Perf. 12x12½*

Various Roses in Natural Colors.

1027 A224 5q blue gray 15 15
1028 A224 10q brt blue 15 15
1029 A224 15q rose violet 15 15
1030 A224 25q lemon 32 15
1031 A224 35q brt grnsh blue 42 15
1032 A224 65q gray 75 16
1033 A224 80q brown 95 25
1034 A224 1.65 l gray green 2.25 45
Nos. 1027-1034 (8) 5.14
Set value 1.10

Seashore, Bregdet Borsh — A225

Views: 15q, Buthrotum, vert. 25q, Shore, Fshati Piqeras. 45q, Shore, Bregdet. 50q, Shore, Bregdet Himare. 65q, Ship, Sarande (Santi Quaranta). 80q, Shore, Dhermi. 1 l, Sunset, Bregdet, vert.

Perf. 12x12½, 12½x12

1967, June 10

1035 A225 15q multicolored 16 15
1036 A225 20q multicolored 24 15
1037 A225 25q multicolored 25 15
1038 A225 45q multicolored 70 15
1039 A225 50q multicolored 80 16
1040 A225 65q multicolored 1.10 20
1041 A225 80q multicolored 1.25 24
1042 A225 1 l multicolored 1.65 35
Nos. 1035-1042 (8) 6.15
Set value 1.25

Fawn A226

Roe Deer: 20q, Stag, vert. 25q, Doe, vert. 30q, Young stag and doe. 35q, Doe and fawn. 40q, Young stag, vert. 65q, Stag and doe, vert. 70q, Running stag and does.

Perf. 12½x12, 12x12½

1967, July 20 Litho.

1043 A226 15q multicolored 25 15
1044 A226 20q multicolored 25 15
1045 A226 25q multicolored 38 15
1046 A226 30q multicolored 45 15
1047 A226 35q multicolored 55 15
1048 A226 40q multicolored 70 15
1049 A226 65q multicolored 1.10 30
1050 A226 70q multicolored 1.10 35
Nos. 1043-1050 (8) 4.78
Set value 1.15

Man and Woman from Madhe A227

Regional Costumes: 20q, Woman from Zadrimes. 25q, Dancer and drummer, Kukesit. 45q, Woman spinner, Dardhes. 50q, Farm couple, Myseqese. 65q, Dancer with tambourine, Tirana. 80q, Man and woman, Dropullit. 1 l, Piper, Laberise.

1967, Aug. 25 *Perf. 12*

1051 A227 15q tan & multi 15 15
1052 A227 20q lt yellow grn 16 15
1053 A227 25q multicolored 16 15
1054 A227 45q sky blue & multi 32 20
1055 A227 50q lemon & multi 48 24
1056 A227 65q pink & multi 55 35
1057 A227 80q multicolored 70 40
1058 A227 1 l gray & multi 1.00 52
Nos. 1051-1058 (8) 3.52 2.16

Fighters and Newspaper — A228

Designs: 75q, Printing plant, newspapers and microphone. 2 l, People holding newspaper.

1967, Aug. 25 *Perf. 12½x12*

1059 A228 25q multicolored 25 15
1060 A228 75q pink & multi 55 15
1061 A228 2 l multicolored 1.40 32
Nos. 1059-1061 (3) 2.20
Set value 48

Issued for the Day of the Press.

Street Scene, by Kolé Idromeno A229

Hakmarrja Battalion, by Sali Shijaku — A230

Designs: 20q, David, fresco by Onufri, 16th century, vert. 45q, Woman's head, ancient mosaic, vert. 50q, Men on horseback from 16th century icon, vert. 65q, Farm Women, by Zef Shoshi. 80q, Street Scene, by Vangjush Mio. 1 l, Bride, by Kolé Idromeno, vert.

Perf. 12, 12x12½, (A230)

1967, Oct. 25 **Litho.**

1062	A229	15q multicolored	35	15
1063	A229	20q multicolored	40	15
1064	A230	25q multicolored	50	15
1065	A229	45q multicolored	1.00	15
1066	A229	50q multicolored	1.25	15
1067	A230	65q multicolored	1.50	15
1068	A230	80q multicolored	1.75	22
1069	A230	1 l multicolored	2.25	28
		Nos. 1062-1069 (8)	9.00	
		Set value		1.00

Lenin at Storming of Winter Palace — A231

Rabbit — A232

Designs: 15q, Lenin and Stalin, horiz. 50q, Lenin and Stalin addressing meeting. 1.10 l, Storming of the Winter Palace, horiz.

1967, Nov. 7 ***Perf. 12***

1070	A231	15q red & multi	15	15
1071	A231	25q slate grn & blk	20	15
1072	A231	50q brn, blk & brn vio	32	15
1073	A231	1.10 l lilac, gray & blk	1.00	22
		Nos. 1070-1073 (4)	1.67	
		Set value		44

50th anniv. of the Russian October Revolution.

1967, Nov. 25

Designs: Various hares and rabbits. The 15q, 25q, 35q, 40q and 1 l are horizontal.

1074	A232	15q orange & multi	18	15
1075	A232	20q brt yel & multi	18	15
1076	A232	25q lt brn & multi	22	15
1077	A232	35q multicolored	32	15
1078	A232	40q yellow & multi	55	15
1079	A232	50q pink & multi	65	15
1080	A232	65q multicolored	1.10	30
1081	A232	1 l lilac & multi	1.75	45
		Nos. 1074-1081 (8)	4.95	
		Set value		1.20

University, Torch and Book — A233

1967 **Litho.** ***Perf. 12***

1082	A233	25q multi	18	15
1083	A233	1.75 l multi	1.10	28
		Set value		32

10th anniv. of the founding of the State University, Tirana.

Coat of Arms and Soldiers A234

Designs: 65q, Arms, Factory, grain, flag, gun and radio tower. 1.20 l, Arms and hand holding torch.

1967 ***Perf. 12x11½***

1084	A234	15q multi	15	15
1085	A234	65q multi	40	15
1086	A234	1.20 l multi	70	15
		Nos. 1084-1086 (3)	1.25	
		Set value		36

25th anniversary of the Democratic Front.

Turkey — A235

Designs: 20q, Duck. 25q, Hen. 45q, Rooster. 50q, Guinea fowl. 65q, Goose, horiz. 80q, Mallard, horiz. 1 l, Chicks, horiz.

Perf. 12x12½, 12½x12

1967, Nov. 25 **Photo.**

1087	A235	15q gold & multi	18	15
1088	A235	20q gold & multi	18	15
1089	A235	25q gold & multi	22	15
1090	A235	45q gold & multi	35	15
1091	A235	50q gold & multi	52	15
1092	A235	65q gold & multi	70	20
1093	A235	80q gold & multi	1.25	30
1094	A235	1 l gold & multi	1.65	40
		Nos. 1087-1094 (8)	5.05	
		Set value		1.25

Skanderbeg A236

Designs: 10q, Arms of Skanderbeg. 25q, Helmet and sword. 30q, Kruje Castle. 35q, Petreles Castle. 65q, Berati Castle. 80q, Skanderbeg addressing national chiefs. 90q, Battle of Albulenes.

1967, Dec. 10 **Litho.** ***Perf. 12x12½***

Medallion in Bister and Dark Brown

1095	A236	10q gold & violet	15	15
1096	A236	15q gold & rose car	15	15
1097	A236	25q gold & vio bl	15	15
1098	A236	30q gold & dk blue	16	15
1099	A236	35q gold & maroon	22	15
1100	A236	65q gold & green	38	15
1101	A236	80q gold & gray brn	60	15
1102	A236	90q gold & ultra	1.10	18
		Nos. 1095-1102 (8)	2.91	
		Set value		70

500th anniv. of the death of Skanderbeg (George Castriota), national hero.

Ice Hockey — A237

Designs: 15q, 2 l, Winter Olympics emblem. 30q, Women's figure skating. 50q, Slalom. 80q, Downhill skiing. 1 l, Ski jump.

1967-68

1103	A237	15q multicolored	15	15
1104	A237	25q multicolored	15	15
1105	A237	30q multicolored	15	15
1106	A237	50q multicolored	25	15
1107	A237	80q multicolored	52	18
1108	A237	1 l multicolored	75	25
		Nos. 1103-1108 (6)	1.97	
		Set value		65

Miniature Sheet

Imperf

1109	A237	2 l red, gray & brt bl ('68)	5.00	5.00

10th Winter Olympic Games, Grenoble, France, Feb. 6-18.

Nos. 1103-1108 issued Dec. 29, 1967.

Skanderbeg Monument, Kruje — A238

Designs: 10q, Skanderbeg monument, Tirana. 15q, Skanderbeg portrait, Uffizi Galleries, Florence. 25q, engraved portrait of Gen. Tanush Topia. 35q, Portrait of Gen. Gjergj Arianti, horiz. 65q, Portrait bust of Skanderbeg by O. Paskali. 80q, Title page of "The Life of Skanderbeg." 90q, Skanderbeg battling the Turks, painting by S. Rrota, horiz.

Perf. 12x12½, 12½x12

1968, Jan. 17 **Litho.**

1110	A238	10q multicolored	15	15
1111	A238	15q multicolored	22	15
1112	A238	25q blk, yel & lt bl	30	15
1113	A238	30q multicolored	35	15
1114	A238	35q lt vio, pink & blk	52	15
1115	A238	65q multicolored	85	15
1116	A238	80q pink, blk & yel	1.10	18
1117	A238	90q beige & multi	1.50	22
		Nos. 1110-1117 (8)	4.99	
		Set value		82

500th anniv. of the death of Skanderbeg (George Castriota), national hero.

Carnation A239

1968, Feb. 15 ***Perf. 12***

Various Carnations in Natural Colors

1118	A239	15q green	15	15
1119	A239	20q dk brown	15	15
1120	A239	25q brt blue	16	15
1121	A239	50q gray olive	28	15
1122	A239	80q bluish gray	75	16
1123	A239	1.10 l violet gray	1.00	24
		Nos. 1118-1123 (6)	2.49	
		Set value		62

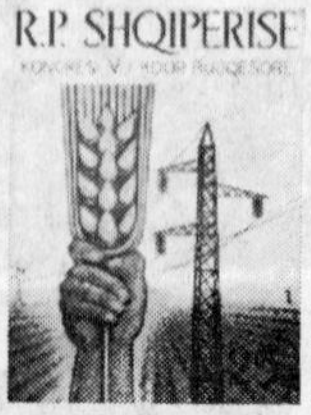

"Electrification" A240

Designs: 65q, Farm tractor, horiz. 1.10 l, Cow and herd.

1968, Mar. 5 **Litho.** ***Perf. 12***

1124	A240	25q multi	16	15
1125	A240	65q multi	48	15
1126	A240	1.10 l multi	70	20
		Nos. 1124-1126 (3)	1.34	
		Set value		32

Fifth Farm Cooperatives Congress.

Goat A241

Designs: Various goats. 15q, 20q and 25q are vertical.

Perf. 12x12½, 12½x12

1968, Mar. 25

1127	A241	15q multi	15	15
1128	A241	20q multi	15	15
1129	A241	25q multi	15	15
1130	A241	30q multi	22	15
1131	A241	40q multi	30	15
1132	A241	50q multi	35	15
1133	A241	80q multi	60	18
1134	A241	1.40 l multi	1.50	35
		Nos. 1127-1134 (8)	3.42	
		Set value		88

Zef N. Jubani — A242

Physician and Hospital — A243

1968, Mar. 30 ***Perf. 12***

1135	A242	25q yellow & choc	18	15
1136	A242	1.75 l lt violet & blk	80	28
		Set value		36

Sesquicentennial of the birth of Zef N. Jubani, writer and scholar.

Perf. 12½x12, 12x12½

1968, Apr. 7 **Litho.**

Designs (World Health Organization Emblem and): 65q, Hospital and microscope, horiz. 1.10 l, Mother feeding child.

1137	A243	25q green & claret	16	15
1138	A243	65q black, yel & bl	48	15
1139	A243	1.10 l black & dp org	70	20
		Nos. 1137-1139 (3)	1.34	
		Set value		36

20th anniv. of WHO.

Scientist A244

Women: 15q, Militia member. 60q, Farm worker. 1 l, Factory worker.

1968, Apr. 14 ***Perf. 12***

1140	A244	15q ver & dk red	15	15
1141	A244	25q blue grn & grn	20	15
1142	A244	60q dull yel & brn	32	15
1143	A244	1 l lt vio & vio	85	28
		Nos. 1140-1143 (4)	1.52	
		Set value		55

Albanian Women's Organization, 25th anniv.

Karl Marx — A245

Designs: 25q, Marx lecturing to students. 65q, "Das Kapital," "Communist Manifesto" and marching crowd. 95q, Full-face portrait.

1968, May 5 Litho. *Perf. 12*

1144	A245	15q gray, dk bl & bis	16	15
1145	A245	25q brn vio, dk brn & dl yel	35	15
1146	A245	65q gray, blk, brn & car	85	18
1147	A245	95q gray, ocher & blk	1.40	35
		Nos. 1144-1147 (4)	2.76	
		Set value		65

Karl Marx, 150th birth anniversary.

Heliopsis — A246

Flowers: 20q, Red flax. 25q, Orchid. 30q, Gloxinia. 40q, Turk's-cap lily. 80q, Amaryllis. 1.40 l, Red magnolia.

1968, May 10 *Perf. 12x12½*

1148	A246	15q gold & multi	15	15
1149	A246	20q gold & multi	15	15
1150	A246	25q gold & multi	15	15
1151	A246	30q gold & multi	15	15
1152	A246	40q gold & multi	40	15
1153	A246	80q gold & multi	50	15
1154	A246	1.40 l gold & multi	75	30
		Nos. 1148-1154 (7)	2.25	
		Set value		70

Proclamation of Prizren A247

Designs: 25q, Abdyl Frasheri. 40q, House in Prizren.

1968, June 10 Litho. *Perf. 12*

1155	A247	25q emerald & blk	20	15
1156	A247	40q multicolored	45	15
1157	A247	85q yellow & multi	85	25
		Nos. 1155-1157 (3)	1.50	
		Set value		40

League of Prizren against the Turks, 90th anniv.

Shepherd, by A. Kushi — A248

Paintings from Tirana Art Gallery: 20q, View of Tirana, by V. Mio, horiz. 25q, Mountaineer, by G. Madhi. 40q, Refugees, by A. Buza. 80q, Guerrillas of Shahin Matrakut, by S. Xega. 1.50 l, Portrait of an Old Man, by S. Papadhimitri. 1.70 l, View of Scutari, by S. Rrota. 2.50 l, Woman in Scutari Costume, by Z. Colombi.

1968, June 20 *Perf. 12x12½*

1158	A248	15q gold & multi	15	15
1159	A248	20q gold & multi	15	15
1160	A248	25q gold & multi	20	15
1161	A248	40q gold & multi	38	15
1162	A248	80q gold & multi	65	15
1163	A248	1.50 l gold & multi	1.10	25
1164	A248	1.70 l gold & multi	1.25	50
		Nos. 1158-1164 (7)	3.88	
		Set value		1.10

Miniature Sheet

Perf. 12½xImperf.

1165	A248	2.50 l multi	2.00	90

No. 1165 contains one stamp, size: 50x71mm.

Soldier and Guns — A249

Designs: 25q, Sailor and warships. 65q, Aviator and planes, vert. 95q, Militiamen and woman.

1968, July 10 Litho. *Perf. 12*

1166	A249	15q multicolored	20	15
1167	A249	25q multicolored	32	15
1168	A249	65q multicolored	85	15
1169	A249	95q multicolored	1.65	20
		Nos. 1166-1169 (4)	3.02	
		Set value		45

25th anniversary of the People's Army.

Squid — A250

Designs: 20q, Crayfish. 25q, Whelk. 50q, Crab. 70q, Spiny lobster. 80q, Shore crab. 90q, Norway lobster.

1968, Aug. 20

1170	A250	15q multicolored	16	15
1171	A250	20q multicolored	16	15
1172	A250	25q multicolored	22	15
1173	A250	50q multicolored	38	15
1174	A250	70q multicolored	60	25
1175	A250	80q multicolored	75	30
1176	A250	90q multicolored	1.10	35
		Nos. 1170-1176 (7)	3.37	
		Set value		1.10

Women's Relay Race — A251

Sport: 20q, Running. 25q, Women's discus. 30q, Equestrian. 40q, High jump. 50q, Women's hurdling. 80q, Soccer. 1.40 l, Woman diver. 2 l, Olympic stadium.

1968, Sept. 23 Photo. *Perf. 12*

1177	A251	15q multicolored	15	15
1178	A251	20q multicolored	15	15
1179	A251	25q multicolored	15	15
1180	A251	30q multicolored	20	15
1181	A251	40q multicolored	22	15
1182	A251	50q multicolored	35	15
1183	A251	80q multicolored	52	15
1184	A251	1.40 l multicolored	95	35
		Nos. 1177-1184 (8)	2.69	
		Set value		85

Souvenir Sheet

Perf. 12½ Horizontally

1185	A251	2 l multicolored	2.25	75

19th Olympic Games, Mexico City, Oct. 12-27. No. 1185 contains one rectangular stamp, size: 64x54mm. Value of imperfs., #1177-1184 $7, #1185 $5.

Enver Hoxha — A252

1968, Oct. 16 Litho. *Perf. 12*

1186	A252	25q blue gray	28	15
1187	A252	35q rose brown	45	18
1188	A252	80q violet	75	35
1189	A252	1.10 l brown	1.00	50
		Nos. 1186-1189 (4)	2.48	1.18

Souvenir Sheet

Imperf

1190	A252	1.50 l rose red, bl vio & gold	*50.00*	*40.00*

60th birthday of Enver Hoxha, First Secretary of the Central Committee of the Communist Party of Albania.

Book and Pupils — A253

1968, Nov. 14 Photo.

1191	A253	15q maroon & slate grn	20	15
1192	A253	85q gray olive & sepia	1.25	18
		Set value		25

60th anniv. of the Congress of Monastir, Nov. 14-22, 1908, which adopted a unified Albanian alphabet.

Waxwing — A254

Birds: 20q, Rose-colored starling. 25q, Kingfishers. 50q, Long-tailed tits. 80q, Wallcreeper. 1.10 l, Bearded tit.

1968, Nov. 15 Litho.

Birds in Natural Colors

1193	A254	15q lt blue & blk	15	15
1194	A254	20q bister & blk	15	15
1195	A254	25q pink & blk	28	15
1196	A254	50q lt yel grn & blk	32	15
1197	A254	80q bis brn & blk	70	22
1198	A254	1.10 l pale green & blk	90	25
		Nos. 1193-1198 (6)	2.50	
		Set value		75

Mao Tse-tung — A255

1968, Dec. 26 Litho. *Perf. 12½x12*

1199	A255	25q gold, red & blk	25	15
1200	A255	1.75 l gold, red & blk	1.25	30

75th birthday of Mao Tse-tung, Chairman of the Communist Party of the People's Republic of China.

Adem Reka and Crane — A256

Portraits: 10q, Pjeter Lleshi and power lines. 15q, Mohammed Shehu and Myrteza Kepi. 25q, Shkurte Vata and women railroad workers. 65q, Agron Elezi, frontier guard. 80q, Ismet Bruçaj and mountain road. 1.30 l, Fuat Cela, blind revolutionary.

1969, Feb. 10 Litho. *Perf. 12x12½*

1201	A256	5q multicolored	15	15
1202	A256	10q multicolored	15	15
1203	A256	15q multicolored	15	15
1204	A256	25q multicolored	15	15
1205	A256	65q multicolored	35	15
1206	A256	80q multicolored	60	15
1207	A256	1.30 l multicolored	95	20
		Set value	2.25	55

Issued to honor a contemporary heroine and heroes.

Meteorological Instruments A257

Designs: 25q, Water gauge. 1.60 l, Radar, balloon and isobars.

1969, Feb. 25 *Perf. 12*

1208	A257	15q multi	20	15
1209	A257	25q ultra, org & blk	35	15
1210	A257	1.60 l rose vio, yel & blk	1.90	25
		Nos. 1208-1210 (3)	2.45	
		Set value		36

20th anniv. of Albanian hydrometeorology.

Partisans, 1944, by F. Haxmiu — A258

Paintings: 5q, Student Revolutionists, by P. Mele, vert. 65q, Steel Mill, by C. Ceka. 80q, Reconstruction, by V. Kilica. 1.10 l, Harvest, by N. Jonuzi. 1.15 l, Terraced Landscape, by S. Kaceli. 2 l, Partisans' Meeting.

Perf. 12x12½, 12½x12

1969, Apr. 25 Litho.

Size: 31½x41½mm

1211	A258	5q buff & multi	15	15

Size: 51½x30½mm

1212	A258	25q buff & multi	15	15

Size: 40½x32mm

1213	A258	65q buff & multi	32	15

Size: 51½x30½mm

1214	A258	80q buff & multi	60	15
1215	A258	1.10 l buff & multi	65	15
1216	A258	1.15 l buff & multi	90	20
		Nos. 1211-1216 (6)	2.77	
		Set value		65

Miniature Sheet

Imperf

Size: 111x90mm

1217	A258	2 l ocher & multi	1.50	1.50

Leonardo da Vinci, Self-portrait A259

Designs (after Leonardo da Vinci): 35q, Lilies. 40q, Design for a flying machine, horiz. 1 l, Portrait of Beatrice. No. 1222, Portrait of a Noblewoman. No. 1223, Mona Lisa.

Perf. 12x12½, 12½x12

1969, May 2 **Litho.**

1218	A259	25q	gold & sepia	18	15
1219	A259	35q	gold & sepia	30	15
1220	A259	40q	gold & sepia	35	15
1221	A259	1 l	gold & multi	95	20
1222	A259	2 l	gold & sepia	1.75	55
			Nos. 1218-1222 (5)	3.53	
			Set value		1.00

Miniature Sheet

Imperf

1223	A259	2 l	gold & multi	3.25	2.25

Leonardo da Vinci (1452-1519), painter, sculptor, architect and engineer.

First Congress Meeting Place — A260

Designs: 1 l, Albanian coat of arms. 2.25 l, Two partisans with guns and flag.

1969, May 24 ***Perf. 12***

1224	A260	25q	lt grn, blk & red	25	15
1225	A260	2.25 l	multi	1.75	85

Souvenir Sheet

1226	A260	1 l	gold, bl, blk & red	*22.50*	*12.50*

25th anniversary of the First Anti-Fascist Congress of Permet, May 24, 1944.

Albanian Violet — A261

Designs: Violets and Pansies.

1969, June 30 **Litho.** ***Perf. 12x12½***

1227	A261	5q	gold & multi	15	15
1228	A261	10q	gold & multi	15	15
1229	A261	15q	gold & multi	15	15
1230	A261	20q	gold & multi	18	15
1231	A261	25q	gold & multi	30	15
1232	A261	80q	gold & multi	48	30
1233	A261	1.95 l	gold & multi	1.25	65
			Nos. 1227-1233 (7)	2.66	
			Set value		1.25

Plum, Fruit and Blossoms — A262

Designs: Blossoms and Fruits.

1969, Aug. 10 **Litho.** ***Perf. 12***

1234	A262	10q	shown	15	15
1235	A262	15q	Lemon	15	15
1236	A262	25q	Pomegranate	18	15
1237	A262	50q	Cherry	38	15
1238	A262	80q	Peach	60	20
1239	A262	1.20 l	Apple	1.10	35
			Nos. 1234-1239 (6)	2.56	
			Set value		75

Basketball — A263

Designs: 10q, 80q, 2.20 l, Various views of basketball game. 25q, Hand aiming ball at basket and map of Europe, horiz.

1969, Sept. 15 **Litho.** ***Perf. 12***

1240	A263	10q	multi	15	15
1241	A263	15q	buff & multi	15	15
1242	A263	25q	blue & multi	28	15
1243	A263	80q	multi	65	16
1244	A263	2.20 l	multi	1.65	50
			Nos. 1240-1244 (5)	2.88	
			Set value		80

16th European Basketball Championships, Naples, Italy, Sept. 27-Oct. 5.

Runner — A264

Designs: 5q, Games' emblem. 10q, Woman gymnast. 20q, Pistol shooting. 25q, Swimmer at start. 80q, Bicyclist. 95q, Soccer.

1969, Sept. 30

1245	A264	5q	multicolored	15	15
1246	A264	10q	multicolored	15	15
1247	A264	15q	multicolored	15	15
1248	A264	20q	multicolored	15	15
1249	A264	25q	multicolored	18	15
1250	A264	80q	multicolored	38	15
1251	A264	95q	multicolored	60	18
			Set value	1.40	50

Second National Spartakiad.

Electronic Technicians, Steel Ladle — A265

Designs: 25q, Mao Tse-tung with microphones, vert. 1.40 l, Children holding Mao's red book, vert.

1969, Oct. 1 **Litho.** ***Perf. 12***

1252	A265	25q	multi	20	15
1253	A265	85q	multi	50	15
1254	A265	1.40 l	multi	80	30
			Nos. 1252-1254 (3)	1.50	60

People's Republic of China, 20th anniv.

Enver Hoxha — A266

Designs: 80q, Pages from Berat resolution. 1.45 l, Partisans with flag.

1969, Oct. 20 **Litho.** ***Perf. 12***

1255	A266	25q	multicolored	20	15
1256	A266	80q	gray & multi	50	15
1257	A266	1.45 l	ocher & multi	80	30
			Nos. 1255-1257 (3)	1.50	60

25th anniv. of the 2nd reunion of the Natl. Antifascist Liberation Council, Berat.

Soldiers — A267

Designs: 30q, Oil refinery. 35q, Combine harvester. 45q, Hydroelectric station and dam. 55q, Militia woman, man and soldier. 1.10 l, Dancers and musicians.

1969, Nov. 29

1258	A267	25q	multi	22	15
1259	A267	30q	multi	22	15
1260	A267	35q	multi	22	15
1261	A267	45q	multi	32	15
1262	A267	55q	multi	80	15
1263	A267	1.10 l	multi	1.65	15
			Nos. 1258-1263 (6)	3.43	
			Set value		38

25th anniv. of the socialist republic.

Joseph V. Stalin, (1879-1953), Russian Political Leader — A268

1969, Dec. 21 **Litho.** ***Perf. 12***

1264	A268	15q	lilac	15	15
1265	A268	25q	slate blue	15	15
1266	A268	1 l	brown	48	15
1267	A268	1.10 l	violet blue	85	20
			Nos. 1264-1267 (4)	1.63	
			Set value		45

Head of Woman — A269

Greco-Roman Mosaics: 25q, Geometrical floor design, horiz. 80q, Bird and tree, horiz. 1.10 l, Floor with birds and grapes, horiz. 1.20 l, Fragment with corn within oval design.

1969, Dec. 25 ***Perf. 12½x12***

1268	A269	15q	gold & multi	15	15
1269	A269	25q	gold & multi	15	15
1270	A269	80q	gold & multi	38	15
1271	A269	1.10 l	gold & multi	55	16
1272	A269	1.20 l	gold & multi	75	28
			Nos. 1268-1272 (5)	1.98	
			Set value		60

Cancellation of 1920 — A270

Design: 25q, Proclamation and congress site.

1970, Jan. 21 **Litho.** ***Perf. 12***

1273	A270	25q	red, gray & blk	15	15
1274	A270	1.25 l	dk grn, yel & blk	85	15
			Set value		17

Congress of Louchnia, 50th anniversary.

Worker, Student and Flag A271

1970, Feb. 11 ***Perf. 12½x12***

1275	A271	25q	red & multi	15	15
1276	A271	1.75 l	red & multi	85	24
			Set value		29

Vocational organizations in Albania, 25th anniv.

Turk's-cap Lily — A272

Lilies: 5q, Cernum, vert. 15q, Madonna, vert. 25q, Royal, vert. 1.10 l, Tiger. 1.15 l, Albanian.

Perf. 11½x12, 12x11½

1970, Mar. 10 **Litho.**

1277	A272	5q	multi	15	15
1278	A272	15q	multi	15	15
1279	A272	25q	multi	20	15
1280	A272	80q	multi	52	15
1281	A272	1.10 l	multi	75	16
1282	A272	1.15 l	multi	95	24
			Nos. 1277-1282 (6)	2.72	
			Set value		65

Lenin A273

Designs (Lenin): 5q, Portrait, vert. 25q, As volunteer construction worker. 95q, Addressing crowd. 1.10 l, Saluting, vert.

1970, Apr. 22 **Litho.** ***Perf. 12***

1283	A273	5q	multi	15	15
1284	A273	15q	multi	15	15
1285	A273	25q	multi	15	15
1286	A273	95q	multi	32	15
1287	A273	1.10 l	multi	52	16
			Set value	1.05	38

Centenary of birth of Lenin (1870-1924).

Frontier Guard A274

1970, Apr. 25

1288	A274	25q multi	15	15
1289	A274	1.25 l multi	75	20
		Set value		25

25th anniversary of Frontier Guards.

Soccer Players — A275

Designs: 5q, Jules Rimet Cup and globes. 10q, Aztec Stadium, Mexico City. 25q, Defending goal. 65q, 80q, No. 1296, Two soccer players in various plays. No. 1297, Mexican horseman and volcano Popocatepetl.

1970, May 15 Litho. *Perf. 12½x12*

1290	A275	5q multicolored	15	15
1291	A275	10q multicolored	15	15
1292	A275	15q multicolored	15	15
1293	A275	25q lt green & multi	15	15
1294	A275	65q pink & multi	28	15
1295	A275	80q lt blue & multi	45	15
1296	A275	2 l yellow & multi	1.25	24
		Set value	2.25	65

Souvenir Sheet

Perf 12 x Imperf

1297	A275	2 l multicolored	2.00	80

World Soccer Championships for the Jules Rimet Cup, Mexico City, May 31-June 21, 1970. No. 1297 contains one large horizontal stamp. Nos. 1290-1297 exist imperf.

UPU Headquarters and Monument, Bern — A276

1970, May 30 Litho. *Perf. 12½x12*

1298	A276	25q ultra, gray & blk	15	15
1299	A276	1.10 l orange, buff & blk	48	20
1300	A276	1.15 l green, gray & blk	65	24
		Nos. 1298-1300 (3)	1.28	59

Inauguration of the new UPU Headquarters in Bern.

Bird and Grapes Mosaic A277

Mosaics, 5th-6th centuries, excavated near Pogradec: 10q, Waterfowl and grapes. 20q, Bird and tree stump. 25q, Bird and leaves. 65q, Fish. 2.25 l, Peacock, vert.

Perf. 12½x12, 12x12½

1970, July 10

1301	A277	5q multi	15	15
1302	A277	10q multi	15	15
1303	A277	20q multi	16	15
1304	A277	25q multi	22	15
1305	A277	65q multi	38	15
1306	A277	2.25 l multi	1.25	32
		Nos. 1301-1306 (6)	2.31	
		Set value		65

Fruit Harvest and Dancers A278

Designs: 25q, Contour-plowed fields and conference table. 80q, Cattle and newspapers. 1.30 l, Wheat harvest.

1970, Aug. 28 Litho. *Perf. 12x11½*

1307	A278	15q brt vio & blk	15	15
1308	A278	25q dp blue & blk	15	15
1309	A278	80q dp brown & blk	40	15
1310	A278	1.30 l org brn & blk	60	16
		Nos. 1307-1310 (4)	1.30	
		Set value		34

25th anniv. of the agrarian reform law.

Attacking Partisans — A279

Designs: 25q, Partisans with horses and flag. 1.60 l, Partisans.

1970, Sept. 3 *Perf. 12*

1311	A279	15q org brn & blk	15	15
1312	A279	25q brn, yel & blk	15	15
1313	A279	1.60 l dp grn & blk	85	28
		Set value	1.00	38

50th anniversary of liberation of Vlona.

Miners, by Nexhmedin Zajmi — A280

Paintings from the National Gallery, Tirana: 5q, Bringing in the Harvest, by Isuf Sulovari, vert. 15q, The Activists, by Dhimitraq Trebicka, vert. 65q, Instruction of Partisans, by Hasan Nallbani. 95q, Architectural Planning, by Vilson Kilica. No. 1319, Woman Machinist, by Zef Shoshi, vert. No. 1320, Partisan Destroying Tank, by Sali Shijaku, vert.

Perf. 12½x12, 12x12½

1970, Sept. 25 Litho.

1314	A280	5q multicolored	15	15
1315	A280	15q multicolored	15	15
1316	A280	25q multicolored	16	15
1317	A280	65q multicolored	20	15
1318	A280	95q multicolored	32	15
1319	A280	2 l multicolored	1.25	30
		Set value	2.00	60

Miniature Sheet

Imperf

1320	A280	2 l multicolored	1.50	95

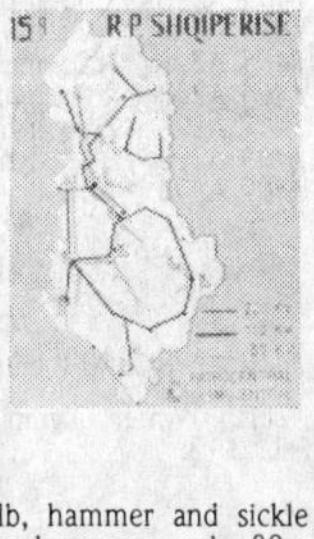

Electrification Map of Albania — A281

Designs: 25q, Light bulb, hammer and sickle emblem, map of Albania and power graph. 80q, Linemen at work. 1.10 l, Use of electricity on the farm, in home and business.

1970, Oct. 25 Litho. *Perf. 12*

1321	A281	15q multi	15	15
1322	A281	25q multi	15	15
1323	A281	80q multi	45	15
1324	A281	1.10 l multi	65	15
		Nos. 1321-1324 (4)	1.40	
		Set value		32

Albanian village electrification completion.

Friedrich Engels — A282

Designs: 1.10 l, Engels as young man. 1.15 l, Engels addressing crowd.

1970, Nov. 28 Litho. *Perf. 12x12½*

1325	A282	25q bister & dk bl	20	15
1326	A282	1.10 l bister & dp claret	60	20
1327	A282	1.15 l bister & dk ol grn	70	25
		Nos. 1325-1327 (3)	1.50	
		Set value		50

150th anniv. of the birth of Friedrich Engels (1820-95), German socialist, collaborator with Karl Marx.

Ludwig van Beethoven — A283

Designs: 5q, Birthplace, Bonn. 25q, 65q, 1.10 l, various portraits. 1.80 l, Scene from Fidelio, horiz.

1970, Dec. 16 Litho. *Perf. 12*

1328	A283	5q dp plum & gold	15	15
1329	A283	15q brt rose lil & sil	15	15
1330	A283	25q green & gold	15	15
1331	A283	65q magenta & sil	30	15
1332	A283	1.10 l dk blue & gold	60	22
1333	A283	1.80 l black & sil	1.25	45
		Nos. 1328-1333 (6)	2.60	
		Set value		90

Bicentenary of the birth of Ludwig van Beethoven (1770-1827), composer.

Coat of Arms A284

Designs: 25q, Proclamation. 80q, Enver Hoxha reading proclamation. 1.30 l, Young people and proclamation.

1971, Jan. 11 Litho. *Perf. 12*

1334	A284	15q lt bl, gold, blk & red	15	15
1335	A284	25q rose lil, blk, gold & gray	15	15
1336	A284	80q emerald, blk & gold	45	15
1337	A284	1.30 l yel org, blk & gold	70	25
		Nos. 1334-1337 (4)	1.45	
		Set value		45

Declaration of the Republic, 25th anniv.

"Liberty" A285

Black Men A286

Designs: 50q, Women's brigade. 65q, Street battle, horiz. 1.10 l, Execution, horiz.

Perf. 12x11½, 11½x12

1971, Mar. 18 Litho.

1338	A285	25q dk bl & bl	15	15
1339	A285	50q slate green	20	15
1340	A285	65q dk brn & chestnut	28	15
1341	A285	1.10 l purple	42	16
		Nos. 1338-1341 (4)	1.05	
		Set value		38

Centenary of the Paris Commune.

1971, Mar. 21 *Perf. 12x12½*

Designs: 1.10 l, Men of 3 races. 1.15 l, Black protest.

1342	A286	25q blk & bis brn	15	15
1343	A286	1.10 l blk & rose car	35	15
1344	A286	1.15 l blk & ver	42	15
		Nos. 1342-1344 (3)	92	
		Set value		32

Intl. year against racial discrimination.

Tulip — A287

Horseman, by Dürer — A288

Designs: Various tulips.

1971, Mar. 25

1345	A287	5q multi	15	15
1346	A287	10q yellow & multi	15	15
1347	A287	15q pink & multi	15	15
1348	A287	20q lt blue & multi	15	15
1349	A287	25q multi	22	15
1350	A287	80q multi	42	15
1351	A287	1 l multi	60	18
1352	A287	1.45 l citron & multi	95	25
		Set value	2.50	75

Perf. 11½x12, 12x11½

1971, May 15 Litho.

Art Works by Dürer: 15q, Three peasants. 25q, Dancing peasant couple. 45q, The bagpiper. 65q, View of Kalkrebut, horiz. 2.40 l, View of Trent, horiz. 2.50 l, Self-portrait.

1353	A288	10q black & pale grn	15	15
1354	A288	15q black & pale lil	15	15
1355	A288	25q black & pale bl	18	15
1356	A288	45q black & pale rose	25	15
1357	A288	65q black & multi	38	15
1358	A288	2.40 l black & multi	1.50	32
		Nos. 1353-1358 (6)	2.61	
		Set value		65

Miniature Sheet

Imperf

1359	A288	2.50 l multi	2.25	80

Albrecht Dürer (1471-1528), German painter and engraver.

Satellite Orbiting Globe — A289

Designs: 1.20 l, Government Building, Tirana, and Red Star emblem. 2.20 l, like 60q. 2.50 l, Flag of People's Republic of China forming trajectory around globe.

1971, June 10 Litho. *Perf. 12x12½*

1360	A289	60q	purple & multi	40	15
1361	A289	1.20 l	ver & multi	1.00	25
1362	A289	2.20 l	grn & multi	1.60	45

Imperf

1363	A289	2.50 l	vio blk & multi	2.50	90
	Nos. 1360-1363 (4)			5.50	1.75

Space developments of People's Republic of China.

Mao Tse-tung — A290

Designs: 1.05 l, House where Communist Party was founded, horiz. 1.20 l, Peking crowd with placards, horiz.

1971, July 1 *Perf. 12x12½, 12½x12*

1364	A290	25q	sil & multi	18	15
1365	A290	1.05 l	sil & multi	55	15
1366	A290	1.20 l	sil & multi	70	25
	Nos. 1364-1366 (3)			1.43	
	Set value				45

50th anniv. of Chinese Communist Party.

Crested Titmouse — A291

1971, Aug. 15 Litho. *Perf. 12½x12*

1367	A291	5q	shown	15	15
1368	A291	10q	European serin	15	15
1369	A291	15q	Linnet	15	15
1370	A291	25q	Firecrest	15	15
1371	A291	45q	Rock thrush	30	15
1372	A291	60q	Blue tit	45	25
1373	A291	2.40 l	Chaffinch	1.50	60
	Nos. 1367-1373 (7)			2.85	
	Set value				1.15

Printed se-tenant in blocks of 8 (2x4) including a label showing bird's nest. The label is se-tenant horizontally with the 5q, and vertically with the 10q.

> ***Set Values***
> *A 15-cent minimum now applies to individual stamps and sets. Where the 15-cent minimum per stamp would increase the value of a set beyond retail, there is a "Set Value" notation giving the retail value of the set.*

Olympic Rings and Running — A292

Designs (Olympic Rings and): 10q, Hurdles. 15q, Canoeing. 25q, Gymnastics. 80q, Fencing. 1.05 l, Soccer. 2 l, Runner at finish line. 3.60 l, Diving, women's.

1971, Sept. 15

1374	A292	5q	green & multi	15	15
1375	A292	10q	multicolored	15	15
1376	A292	15q	blue & multi	15	15
1377	A292	25q	violet & multi	15	15
1378	A292	80q	lilac & multi	28	15
1379	A292	1.05 l	multicolored	38	15
1380	A292	3.60 l	multicolored	1.90	50
	Nos. 1374-1380 (7)			3.16	
	Set value				1.00

Souvenir Sheet

Imperf

1381	A292	2 l	brt blue & multi	1.25	75

20th Olympic Games, Munich, Aug. 26-Sept. 10, 1972.

Workers with Flags — A293

Designs: 1.05 l, Party Headquarters, Tirana, and Red Star. 1.20 l, Rifle, star, flag and "VI," vert.

1971, Nov. 1 *Perf. 12*

1382	A293	25q	gold, sil, red & bl	16	15
1383	A293	1.05 l	gold, sil, red & bl	50	15
1384	A293	1.20 l	gold, sil, red & blk	60	22
	Nos. 1382-1384 (3)			1.26	
	Set value				38

6th Congress of Workers' Party.

Factories and Workers A294

Designs: 80q, "XXX" and flag, vert. 1.55 l, Enver Hoxha and flags.

1971, Nov. 8

1385	A294	15q	gold, sil, lil & yel	18	15
1386	A294	80q	gold, sil & red	70	15
1387	A294	1.55 l	gold, sil, red & brn	1.25	25
	Nos. 1385-1387 (3)			2.13	
	Set value				40

30th anniversary of Workers' Party.

Construction Work, by M. Fushekati — A295

Contemporary Albanian Paintings: 5q, Young Man, by R. Kuci, vert. 25q, Partisan, by D. Jukniu, vert. 80q, Fliers, by S. Kristo. 1.20 l, Girl in Forest, by A. Sadikaj. 1.55 l, Warriors with Spears and Shields, by S. Kamberi. 2 l, Freedom Fighter, by I. Lulani.

Perf. 12x12½, 12½x12

1971, Nov. 20

1388	A295	5q	gold & multi	15	15
1389	A295	15q	gold & multi	15	15
1390	A295	25q	gold & multi	15	15
1391	A295	80q	gold & multi	35	15
1392	A295	1.20 l	gold & multi	80	18
1393	A295	1.55 l	gold & multi	1.00	24
	Nos. 1388-1393 (6)			2.60	
	Set value				65

Miniature Sheet

Imperf

1394	A295	2 l	gold & multi	1.40	70

Young Workers' Emblem — A296

1971, Nov. 23 *Perf. 12x12½*

1395	A296	15q	lt blue & multi	15	15
1396	A296	1.35 l	grnsh gray & multi	75	22
	Set value				27

Albanian Young Workers' Union, 30th anniv.

"Halili and Hajria" Ballet — A297

Scenes from "Halili and Hajria" Ballet: 10q, Brother and sister. 15q, Hajria before Sultan Suleiman. 50q, Hajria and husband. 80q, Execution of Halili. 1.40 l, Hajria killing her husband.

1971, Dec. 27 *Perf. 12½x12*

1397	A297	5q	silver & multi	15	15
1398	A297	10q	silver & multi	15	15
1399	A297	15q	silver & multi	15	15
1400	A297	50q	silver & multi	42	15
1401	A297	80q	silver & multi	70	15
1402	A297	1.40 l	silver & multi	1.10	35
	Nos. 1397-1402 (6)			2.67	
	Set value				72

Albanian ballet Halili and Hajria after drama by Kol Jakova.

Biathlon and Olympic Rings — A298

Designs (Olympic Rings and): 10q, Sledding. 15q, Ice hockey. 20q, Bobsledding. 50q, Speed skating. 1 l, Slalom. 2 l, Ski jump. 2.50 l, Figure skating, pairs.

1972, Feb. 10

1403	A298	5q	lt olive & multi	15	15
1404	A298	10q	lt violet & multi	15	15
1405	A298	15q	multicolored	15	15
1406	A298	20q	pink & multi	15	15
1407	A298	50q	lt blue & multi	20	15
1408	A298	1 l	ocher & multi	50	18
1409	A298	2 l	lilac & multi	1.00	35
	Set value			2.00	75

Souvenir Sheet

Imperf

1410	A298	2.50 l	blue & multi	1.50	50

11th Winter Olympic Games, Sapporo, Japan, Feb. 3-13.

Wild Strawberries A299

Wild Fruits and Nuts: 10q, Blackberries. 15q, Hazelnuts. 20q, Walnuts. 25q, Strawberry-tree fruit. 30q, Dogwood berries. 2.40 l, Rowan berries.

1972, Mar. 20 Litho. *Perf. 12*

1411	A299	5q	lt grn & multi	15	15
1412	A299	10q	yellow & multi	15	15
1413	A299	15q	lt vio & multi	15	15
1414	A299	20q	pink & multi	15	15
1415	A299	25q	multi	20	15
1416	A299	30q	multi	28	15
1417	A299	2.40 l	multi	1.40	42
	Nos. 1411-1417 (7)			2.48	
	Set value				85

"Your Heart is your Health" — A300

Worker and Student — A301

World Health Day: 1.20 l, Cardiac patient and electrocardiogram.

1972, Apr. 7 *Perf. 12x12½*

1418	A300	1.10 l	multi	48	16
1419	A300	1.20 l	rose & multi	60	24

Perf. 11½x12½

1972, Apr. 24 Litho.

7th Trade Union Cong., May 8: 2.05 l, Assembly Hall, dancers and emblem.

1420	A301	25q	multi	15	15
1421	A301	2.05 l	blue & multi	90	40
	Set value				45

Qemal Stafa A302

Designs: 15q, Memorial flame. 25q, Monument "Spirit of Defiance," vert.

1972, May 5 *Perf. 12½x12, 12x12½*

1422	A302	15q	gray & multi	15	15
1423	A302	25q	sal rose, blk & gray	15	15
1424	A302	1.90 l	dull yel & blk	1.10	30
	Nos. 1422-1424 (3)			1.40	
	Set value				42

30th anniversary of the murder of Qemal Stafa and of Martyrs' Day.

Camellia — A303

Designs: Various camellias.

1972, May 10 *Perf. 12x12½*

Flowers in Natural Colors

1425	A303	5q	lt blue & blk	15	15
1426	A303	10q	citron & blk	15	15
1427	A303	15q	grnsh gray & blk	15	15
1428	A303	25q	pale sal & blk	15	15
1429	A303	45q	gray & blk	28	15
1430	A303	50q	sal pink & blk	45	15
1431	A303	2.50 l	bluish gray & blk	1.90	75
			Nos. 1425-1431 (7)	3.23	
			Set value		1.10

High Jump — A304

Designs (Olympic and Motion Emblems and): 10q, Running. 15q, Shot put. 20q, Bicycling. 25q, Pole vault. 50q, Hurdles, women's. 5q, Hockey. 2 l, Swimming. 2.50 l, Diving, women's.

1972, June 30 **Litho.** *Perf. 12½x12*

1432	A304	5q	multicolored	15	15
1433	A304	10q	lt brn & multi	15	15
1434	A304	15q	lt lil & multi	15	15
1435	A304	20q	multicolored	15	15
1436	A304	25q	lt vio & multi	15	15
1437	A304	50q	lt grn & multi	25	15
1438	A304	75q	multicolored	50	15
1439	A304	2 l	multicolored	95	30
			Set value	2.00	75

Miniature Sheet

Imperf

1440	A304	2.50 l	multi	1.50	85

20th Olympic Games, Munich, Aug. 26-Sept. 11. Nos. 1432-1439 each issued in sheets of 8 stamps and one label (3x3) showing Olympic rings in gold.

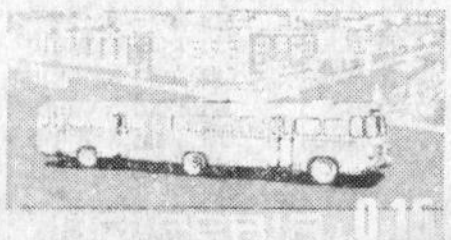

Autobus A305

Designs: 25q, Electric train. 80q, Ocean liner Tirana. 1.05 l, Automobile. 1.20 l, Trailer truck.

1972, July 25 **Litho.** *Perf. 12*

1441	A305	15q	org brn & multi	15	15
1442	A305	25q	gray & multi	15	15
1443	A305	80q	dp grn & multi	32	15
1444	A305	1.05 l	multi	45	15
1445	A305	1.20 l	multi	55	15
			Nos. 1441-1445 (5)	1.62	
			Set value		42

Arm Wrestling A306

Folk Games: 10q, Piggyback ball game. 15q, Women's jumping. 25q, Rope game (srum). 90q, Leapfrog. 2 l, Women throwing pitchers.

1972, Aug. 18

1446	A306	5q	multi	15	15
1447	A306	10q	lt bl & multi	15	15
1448	A306	15q	rose & multi	15	15
1449	A306	25q	lt bl & multi	15	15
1450	A306	90q	ocher & multi	42	15
1451	A306	2 l	lt grn & multi	80	25
			Set value	1.50	55

1st National Festival of People's Games.

Mastheads — A307

30th Press Day: 25q, Printing press. 1.90 l, Workers reading paper.

1972, Aug. 25

1452	A307	15q	lt bl & blk	15	15
1453	A307	25q	red, grn & blk	15	15
1454	A307	1.90 l	lt vio & blk	1.00	35
			Nos. 1452-1454 (3)	1.30	
			Set value		45

Map of Peza Area, Memorial Tablet A308

1972, Sept. 16

1455	A308	15q	shown	15	15
1456	A308	25q	Guerrillas with flag	15	15
1457	A308	1.90 l	Peza Conference memorial	1.00	35
			Nos. 1455-1457 (3)	1.30	
			Set value		45

30th anniversary, Conference of Peza.

Partisans, by Sotir Capo — A309

Paintings: 10q, Woman, by Ismail Lulani, vert. 15q, "Communists," by Lec Shkreli, vert. 20q, View of Nendorit, 1941, by Sali Shijaku, vert. 50q, Woman with Sheaf, by Zef Shoshi, vert. 1 l, Landscape with Children, by Dhimitraq Trebicka. 2 l, Women on Bicycles, by Vilson Kilica. 2.30 l, Folk Dance, by Abdurrahim Buza.

Perf. 12½x12, 12x12½

1972, Sept. 25 **Litho.**

1458	A309	5q	gold & multi	15	15
1459	A309	10q	gold & multi	15	15
1460	A309	15q	gold & multi	15	15
1461	A309	20q	gold & multi	15	15
1462	A309	50q	gold & multi	30	15
1463	A309	1 l	gold & multi	60	15
1464	A309	2 l	gold & multi	1.25	35
			Set value	2.50	75

Miniature Sheet

Imperf

1465	A309	2.30 l	gold & multi	1.25	80

No. 1465 contains one 41x68mm stamp.

Congress Emblem — A310

Design: 2.05 l, Young worker with banner.

1972, Oct. 23 **Litho.** *Perf. 12*

1466	A310	25q	silver, red & gold	15	15
1467	A310	2.05 l	silver & multi	1.00	45
			Set value		50

Union of Working Youth, 6th Congress.

Hammer and Sickle — A311

Ismail Qemali — A312

Design: 1.20 l, Lenin as orator.

1972, Nov. 7 **Litho.** *Perf. 11½x12*

1468	A311	1.10 l	multi	48	20
1469	A311	1.20 l	multi	50	24

55th anniv. of the Russian October Revolution.

Perf. 12x11½, 11½x12

1972, Nov. 29

Designs: 15q, Albanian fighters, horiz. 65q, Rally, horiz. 1.25 l, Coat of arms.

1470	A312	15q	red, brt bl & blk	15	15
1471	A312	25q	yel, blk & red	15	15
1472	A312	65q	red, sal & blk	35	15
1473	A312	1.25 l	dl red & blk	70	25
			Nos. 1470-1473 (4)	1.35	
			Set value		45

60th anniv. of independence.

Cock, Mosaic A313

Mosaics, 2nd-5th centuries, excavated near Buthrotium and Apollonia: 10q, Bird, vert. 15q, Partridges, vert. 25q, Warrior's legs. 45q, Nymph riding dolphin, vert. 50q, Fish, vert. 2.50 l, Warrior with helmet.

Perf. 12½x12, 12x12½

1972, Dec. 10

1474	A313	5q	silver & multi	15	15
1475	A313	10q	silver & multi	15	15
1476	A313	15q	silver & multi	15	15
1477	A313	25q	silver & multi	15	15
1478	A313	45q	silver & multi	20	15
1479	A313	50q	silver & multi	25	15
1480	A313	2.50 l	silver & multi	1.25	38
			Set value	1.95	70

Nicolaus Copernicus — A314

Designs: 10q, 25q, 80q, 1.20 l, Various portraits of Copernicus. 1.60 l, Heliocentric solar system.

1973, Feb. 19 **Litho.** *Perf. 12x12½*

1481	A314	5q	lil rose & multi	15	15
1482	A314	10q	dl ol & multi	15	15
1483	A314	25q	multicolored	15	15
1484	A314	80q	lt vio & multi	45	15
1485	A314	1.20 l	bl & multi	65	24
1486	A314	1.60 l	gray & multi	90	32
			Nos. 1481-1486 (6)	2.45	
			Set value		82

500th anniversary of the birth of Nicolaus Copernicus (1473-1543), Polish astronomer.

Flowering Cactus — A315

Designs: Various flowering cacti.

1973, Mar. 25 **Litho.** *Perf. 12*

1487	A315	10q	multi	15	15
1488	A315	15q	multi	15	15
1489	A315	20q	beige & multi	15	15
1490	A315	25q	gray & multi	20	15
1491	A315	30q	beige & multi	30	15
1492	A315	65q	gray & multi	75	15
1493	A315	80q	multi	95	15
1494	A315	2 l	multi	2.50	28
			Set value		70

Nos. 1487-1494 printed se-tenant.

Guard and Factories A316

Design: 1.80 l, Guard and guards with prisoner.

1973, Mar. 20 **Litho.** *Perf. 12½x12*

1495	A316	25q	ultra & blk	16	15
1496	A316	1.80 l	dk red & multi	75	38
			Set value		44

30th anniv. of the State Security Branch.

Common Tern A317

Sea Birds: 15q, White-winged black terns, vert. 25q, Black-headed gull, vert. 45q, Great black-headed gull. 80q, Slender-billed gull, vert. 2.40 l, Sandwich terns.

Perf. 12½x12, 12x12½

1973, Apr. 30

1497	A317	5q	gold & multi	15	15
1498	A317	15q	gold & multi	15	15
1499	A317	25q	gold & multi	20	15
1500	A317	45q	gold & multi	25	15
1501	A317	80q	gold & multi	55	22
1502	A317	2.40 l	gold & multi	1.75	48
			Nos. 1497-1502 (6)	3.05	
			Set value		90

Letters, 1913 Cancellation and Post Horn A318

Design: 1.80 l, Mailman, 1913 cancel.

1973, May, 5 **Litho.** *Perf. 12x11½*

1503	A318	25q	red & multi	28	15
1504	A318	1.80 l	red & multi	1.65	50

60th anniversary of Albanian stamps.

Farmer, Worker, Soldier A319

Design: 25q, Woman and factory, vert.

1973, June 4 *Perf. 12*

1505	A319	25q car rose	16	15
1506	A319	1.80 l yel, dp org & blk	85	42

7th Congress of Albanian Women's Union.

Creation of General Staff, by G. Madhi — A320

Designs: 40q, "August 1949," sculpture by Sh. Haderi, vert. 60q, "Generation after Generation," sculpture by H. Dule, vert. 80q, "Defend Revolutionary Victories," by M. Fushekati.

1973, July 10 Litho. *Perf. 12½x12*

1507	A320	25q gold & multi	*2.50*	15
1508	A320	40q gold & multi	*4.00*	15
1509	A320	60q gold & multi	*6.00*	22
1510	A320	80q gold & multi	*7.50*	25
		Nos. 1507-1510 (4)	*20.00*	77

30th anniversary of the People's Army.

"Electrification," by S. Hysa — A321

Albanian Paintings: 10q, Woman Textile Worker, by N. Nallbani. 15q, Gymnasts, by M. Fushekati. 50q, Aviator, by F. Stamo. 80q, Fascist Prisoner, by A. Lakuriqi. 1.20 l, Workers with Banner, by P. Mele. 1.30 l, Farm Woman, by Zef Shoshi. 2.05 l, Battle of Tenda, by F. Haxhiu. 10q, 50q, 80q, 1.20 l, 1.30 l, vertical.

Perf. 12½x12, 12x12½

1973, Aug. 10

1511	A321	5q gold & multi	15	15
1512	A321	10q gold & multi	15	15
1513	A321	15q gold & multi	15	15
1514	A321	50q gold & multi	22	15
1515	A321	80q gold & multi	45	15
1516	A321	1.20 l gold & multi	70	15
1517	A321	1.30 l gold & multi	75	18
		Nos. 1511-1517 (7)	2.57	
		Set value		60

Souvenir Sheet

Imperf

1518	A321	2.05 l multi	1.50	65

Mary Magdalene, by Caravaggio A322

Paintings by Michelangelo da Caravaggio: 10q, The Lute Player, horiz. 15q, Self-portrait. 50q, Boy Carrying Fruit and Flowers. 80q, Still Life, horiz. 1.20 l, Narcissus. 1.30 l, Boy Peeling Apple. 2.05 l, Man with Feathered Hat.

Perf. 12x12½, 12½x12

1973, Sept. 28

1519	A322	5q gold & multi	15	15
1520	A322	10q gold & multi	15	15
1521	A322	15q gold, blk & gray	15	15
1522	A322	50q gold & multi	22	15
1523	A322	80q gold & multi	55	15
1524	A322	1.20 l gold & multi	80	25
1525	A322	1.30 l gold & multi	90	25
		Nos. 1519-1525 (7)	2.92	
		Set value		75

Souvenir Sheet

Imperf

1526	A322	2.05 l multi	1.50	60

Michelangelo da Caravaggio (Merisi; 1573?-1609), Italian painter. No. 1526 contains one stamp, size: 63x73mm.

Soccer — A323

Designs: 5q-1.25 l, Various soccer scenes. 2.05 l, Ball in goal and list of cities where championships were held.

1973, Oct. 30 Litho. *Perf. 12½x12*

1527	A323	5q multi	15	15
1528	A323	10q multi	15	15
1529	A323	15q multi	15	15
1530	A323	20q multi	15	15
1531	A323	25q multi	15	15
1532	A323	90q multi	52	15
1533	A323	1.20 l multi	75	15
1534	A323	1.25 l multi	90	18
		Set value	2.50	65

Minature Sheet

Imperf

1535	A323	2.05 l multi	2.00	60

World Soccer Cup, Munich 1974.

Weight Lifter — A324

Designs: Various stages of weight lifting. 1.20 l, 1.60 l, horiz.

1973, Oct. 30 Litho. *Perf. 12*

1536	A324	5q multi	15	15
1537	A324	10q multi	15	15
1538	A324	25q multi	16	15
1539	A324	90q multi	48	18
1540	A324	1.20 l multi	38	15
1541	A324	1.60 l multi	80	15
		Nos. 1536-1541 (6)	2.12	
		Set value		55

Weight Lifting Championships, Havana, Cuba.

Ballet — A325

Harvester Combine — A326

Designs: 5q, Cement factory, Kavaje. 10q, Ali Kelmendi truck factory and tank cars, horiz. 25q, "Communication." 35q, Skiers and hotel, horiz. 60q, Resort, horiz. 80q, Mountain lake. 1 l, Mao Tse-tung textile mill. 1.20 l, Steel workers. 2.40 l, Welder and pipe. 3 l, Skanderbeg Monument, Tirana. 5 l, Roman arches, Durres.

Perf. 12½x12, 12x12½

1973-74 Litho.

1543	A325	5q gold & multi	15	15
1544	A325	10q gold & multi	15	15
1545	A325	15q gold & multi	15	15
1545A	A326	20q gold & multi	15	15
1546	A326	25q gold & multi	18	15
1547	A326	35q gold & multi	18	15
1548	A326	60q gold & multi	28	15
1549	A326	80q gold & multi	40	15
1549A	A326	1 l gold & multi	35	15
1549B	A326	1.20 l gold & multi	60	15
1549C	A326	2.40 l gold & multi	1.25	32
1550	A326	3 l gold & multi	1.40	32
1551	A326	5 l gold & multi	2.25	60
		Nos. 1543-1551 (13)	7.49	
		Set value		1.95

Issue dates: Nos. 1545-1546, 1549-1550, Dec. 5, 1973; others, 1974.

Mao Tse-tung — A327

80th birthday of Mao Tse-tung: 1.20 l, Mao Tse-tung addressing crowd.

1973, Dec. 26 *Perf. 12*

1552	A327	85q gold, red & sepia	60	15
1553	A327	1.20 l gold, red & sepia	90	20

Old Man and Dog, by Gericault — A328

Paintings by Jean Louis André Theodore Gericault: 10q, Horse's Head. 15q, Male Model. 25q, Head of Black Man. 1.20 l, Self-portrait. 2.05 l, Raft of the Medusa, horiz. 2.20 l, Battle of the Giants.

Perf. 12x12½, 12½x12

1974, Jan. 18 Litho.

1554	A328	10q gold & multi	15	15
1555	A328	15q gold & multi	15	15
1556	A328	20q gold & multi	15	15
1557	A328	25q gold & blk	22	15
1558	A328	1.20 l gold & multi	75	15
1559	A328	2.20 l gold & multi	1.50	35
		Nos. 1554-1559 (6)	2.92	
		Set value		65

Souvenir Sheet

Imperf

1560	A328	2.05 l gold & multi	1.25	45

No. 1560 contains one 87x78mm stamp.

Lenin, by Pandi Mele — A329

Designs: 25q, Lenin with Sailors on Cruiser Aurora, by Dhimitraq Trebicka, horiz. 1.20 l, Lenin, by Vilson Kilica.

Perf. 12½x12, 12x12½

1974, Jan. 21

1561	A329	25q gold & multi	15	15
1562	A329	60q gold & multi	35	15
1563	A329	1.20 l gold & multi	75	25
		Nos. 1561-1563 (3)	1.25	
		Set value		40

50th anniv. of the death of Lenin.

Swimming Duck, Mosaic — A330

Designs: Mosaics from the 5th-6th Centuries A.D., excavated near Buthrotium, Pogradec and Apollonia.

1974, Feb. 20 Litho. *Perf. 12½x12*

1564	A330	5q shown	15	15
1565	A330	10q Bird and flower	15	15
1566	A330	15q Vase and grapes	15	15
1567	A330	25q Duck	15	15
1568	A330	40q Donkey and bird	25	15
1569	A330	2.50 l Sea horse	1.25	35
		Nos. 1564-1569 (6)	2.10	
		Set value		60

Soccer — A331

Designs: Various scenes from soccer. 2.05 l, World Soccer Cup and names of participating countries.

1974, Apr. 25 Litho. *Perf. 12½x12*

1570	A331	10q gold & multi	15	15
1571	A331	15q gold & multi	15	15
1572	A331	20q gold & multi	15	15
1573	A331	25q gold & multi	15	15
1574	A331	40q gold & multi	25	15
1575	A331	80q gold & multi	50	15
1576	A331	1 l gold & multi	75	25
1577	A331	1.20 l gold & multi	1.00	35
		Nos. 1570-1577 (8)	3.10	
		Set value		1.00

Souvenir Sheet

Imperf

1578	A331	2.05 l gold & multi	2.25	90

World Cup Soccer Championship, Munich, June 13-July 7. No. 1578 contains one stamp (60x60mm) with simulated perforations. Nos. 1570-1577 exist imperf, No. 1578 with simulated perfs omitted.

Arms of Albania, Soldier — A332

Design: 1.80 l, Soldier and front page of 1944 Congress Book.

1974, May 24 Litho. *Perf. 12*

1579	A332	25q multi	15	15
1580	A332	1.80 l multi	75	25
		Set value		30

30th anniversary of the First Anti-Fascist Liberation Congress of Permet.

Medicinal Plants — A333

40q, 80q, 2.20 l, horiz.

1974, May 5 *Perf. 12x12½*

1581	A333	10q	Bittersweet	15	15
1582	A333	15q	Arbutus	15	15
1583	A333	20q	Lilies of the valley	15	15
1584	A333	25q	Autumn crocus	18	15
1585	A333	40q	Borage	22	15
1586	A333	80q	Soapwort	70	15
1587	A333	2.20 l	Gentian	1.50	40
			Nos. 1581-1587 (7)	3.05	
			Set value		80

Revolutionaries with Albanian Flag — A334

Design: 1.80 l, Portraits of 5 revolutionaries, vert.

Perf. 12½x12, 12x12½

1974, June 10

1588	A334	25q	red, blk & lil	15	15
1589	A334	1.80 l	yel, red & blk	70	25
			Set value		30

50th anniversary Albanian Bourgeois Democratic Revolution.

European Redwing — A335

Designs: Songbirds; Nos. 1597-1600 vert.

Perf. 12½x12, 12x12½

1974, July 15 **Litho.**

1594	A335	10q	shown	15	15
1595	A335	15q	European robin	15	15
1596	A335	20q	Greenfinch	15	15
1597	A335	25q	Bullfinch	15	15
1598	A335	40q	Hawfinch	35	15
1599	A335	80q	Blackcap	85	20
1600	A335	2.20 l	Nightingale	1.90	45
			Nos. 1594-1600 (7)	3.70	
			Set value		90

Globe — A336

Cent. of UPU: 1.20 l, UPU emblem. 2.05 l, Jet over globe.

1974, Aug. 25 **Litho.** *Perf. 12x12½*

1601	A336	85q	green & multi	45	15
1602	A336	1.20 l	vio & ol grn	65	20

Miniature Sheet

Imperf

1603	A336	2.05 l	blue & multi	12.00	12.00

Widows, by Sali Shijaku — A337

Albanian Paintings: 15q, Drillers, by Danish Jukniu, vert. 20q, Workers with Blueprints, by Clirim Ceka. 25q, Call to Action, by Spiro Kristo, vert. 40q, Winter Battle, by Sabaudin Xhaferi. 80q, Comrades, by Clirim Ceka, vert. 1 l, Aiding the Partisans, by Guri Madhi. 1.20 l, Teacher with Pupils, by Kleo Nini Brezat. 2.05 l, Comrades in Arms, by Guri Madhi.

Perf. 12½x12, 12x12½

1974, Sept. 25

1604	A337	10q	silver & multi	15	15
1605	A337	15q	silver & multi	15	15
1606	A337	20q	silver & multi	15	15
1607	A337	25q	silver & multi	15	15
1608	A337	40q	silver & multi	16	15
1609	A337	80q	silver & multi	30	15
1610	A337	1 l	silver & multi	38	15
1611	A337	1.20 l	silver & multi	42	20
			Set value	1.50	65

Miniature Sheet

Imperf

1612	A337	2.05 l	silver & multi	1.05	42

Crowd on Tien An Men Square A338

Design: 1.20 l, Mao Tse-tung, vert.

1974, Oct. 1 *Perf. 12*

1613	A338	85q	gold & multi	32	15
1614	A338	1.20 l	gold & multi	48	15
			Set value		24

25th anniversary of the proclamation of the People's Republic of China.

Women's Volleyball A339

Designs (Spartakiad Medal and): 15q, Women hurdlers. 20q, Women gymnasts. 25q, Mass exercises in Stadium. 40q, Weight lifter. 80q, Wrestlers. 1 l, Military rifle drill. 1.20 l, Soccer.

1974, Oct. 9 *Perf. 12x12½*

1615	A339	10q	multi	15	15
1616	A339	15q	multi	15	15
1617	A339	20q	multi	15	15
1618	A339	25q	gray & multi	15	15
1619	A339	40q	multi	15	15
1620	A339	80q	multi	40	15
1621	A339	1 l	multi	45	15
1622	A339	1.20 l	tan & multi	50	20
			Nos. 1615-1622 (8)	2.10	
			Set value		70

National Spartakiad, Oct. 9-17.

View of Berat — A340

Designs: 80q, Enver Hoxha addressing Congress, bas-relief, horiz. 1 l, Hoxha and leaders leaving Congress Hall.

Perf. 12x12½, 12½x12

1974, Oct. 20 **Litho.**

1623	A340	25q	rose car & blk	16	15
1624	A340	80q	yel, brn & blk	32	15
1625	A340	1 l	dp lilac & blk	50	15
			Nos. 1623-1625 (3)	98	
			Set value		32

30th anniversary of 2nd Congress of Berat.

Anniversary Emblem, Factory Guards A341

Designs (Anniversary Emblem and): 35q, Chemical industry. 50q, Agriculture. 80q, Arts. 1 l, Atomic diagram and computer. 1.20 l, Youth education. 2.05 l, Anniversary emblem: Crowd and History Book.

1974, Nov. 29 **Litho.** *Perf. 12½x12*

1626	A341	25q	green & multi	15	15
1627	A341	35q	ultra & multi	15	15
1628	A341	50q	brown & multi	22	15
1629	A341	80q	multicolored	40	15
1630	A341	1 l	violet & multi	45	15
1631	A341	1.20 l	multicolored	50	20
			Nos. 1626-1631 (6)	1.87	
			Set value		68

Miniature Sheet

Imperf

1632	A341	2.05 l	gold & multi	1.25	50

30th anniv. of liberation from Fascism.

Artemis, from Apolloni — A342

1974, Dec. 25 **Photo.** *Perf. 12x12½*

1633	A342	10q	shown	15	15
1634	A342	15q	Zeus statue	15	15
1635	A342	20q	Poseidon statue	15	15
1636	A342	25q	Illyrian helmet	15	15
1637	A342	40q	Amphora	15	15
1638	A342	80q	Agrippa	40	15
1639	A342	1 l	Demosthenes	45	15
1640	A342	1.20 l	Head of Bilia	55	20
			Nos. 1633-1640 (8)	2.15	
			Set value		65

Miniature Sheet

Imperf

1641	A342	2.05 l	Artemis & amphora	1.75	60

Archaeological discoveries in Albania.

Workers and Factories A343

Design: 25q, Handshake, tools and book, vert.

1975, Feb. 11 **Litho.** *Perf. 12*

1642	A343	25q	brown & multi	15	15
1643	A343	1.80 l	yellow & multi	75	30
			Set value		35

Albanian Trade Unions, 30th anniversary.

Chicory A344

1975, Feb. 15

1644	A344	5q	shown	15	15
1645	A344	10q	Houseleek	15	15
1646	A344	15q	Columbine	15	15
1647	A344	20q	Anemone	15	15
1648	A344	25q	Hibiscus	15	15
1649	A344	30q	Gentian	15	15
1650	A344	35q	Hollyhock	15	15
1651	A344	2.70 l	Iris	1.20	40
			Set value	1.75	75

Protected flowers.

Jesus, from Doni Madonna — A345

Works by Michelangelo: 10q, Slave, sculpture. 15q, Head of Dawn, sculpture. 20q, Awakening Giant, sculpture. 25q, Cumaenian Sybil, Sistine Chapel. 30q, Lorenzo di Medici, sculpture. 1.20 l, David, sculpture. 2.05 l, Self-portrait. 3.90 l, Delphic Sybil, Sistine Chapel.

1975, Mar. 20 **Litho.** *Perf. 12x12½*

1652	A345	5q	gold & multi	15	15
1653	A345	10q	gold & multi	15	15
1654	A345	15q	gold & multi	15	15
1655	A345	20q	gold & multi	15	15
1656	A345	25q	gold & multi	15	15
1657	A345	30q	gold & multi	15	15
1658	A345	1.20 l	gold & multi	35	18
1659	A345	3.90 l	gold & multi	1.50	52
			Set value	2.25	90

Miniature Sheet

Imperf

1660	A345	2.05 l	gold & multi	1.10	52

Michelangelo Buonarroti (1475-1564), Italian sculptor, painter and architect.

Two-wheeled Cart — A346

Albanian Transportation of the Past: 5q, Horseback rider. 15q, Lake ferry. 20q, Coastal three-master. 25q, Phaeton. 3.35 l, Early automobile on bridge.

1975, Apr. 15 **Litho.** *Perf. 12½x12*

1661	A346	5q	bl grn & multi	15	15
1662	A346	10q	ol & multi	15	15
1663	A346	15q	lil & multi	15	15
1664	A346	20q	multi	15	15
1665	A346	25q	multi	15	15
1666	A346	3.35 l	ocher & multi	1.40	50
			Set value	1.75	75

The lack of a value for a listed item does not necessarily indicate rarity.

Guard at Frontier Stone — A347

Guardsman and Militia — A348

1975, Apr. 25 *Perf. 12*

1667	A347	25q multi	15	15
1668	A348	1.80 l multi	85	22
		Set value		26

30th anniversary of Frontier Guards.

Posting Illegal Poster — A349

Designs: 60q, Partisans in battle. 1.20 l, Partisan killing German soldier, and Albanian coat of arms.

1975, May 9 *Perf. 12½x12*

1669	A349	25q multi	15	15
1670	A349	60q multi	22	15
1671	A349	1.20 l red & multi	60	25
		Nos. 1669-1671 (3)	97	
		Set value		40

30th anniversary of victory over Fascism.

European Widgeons — A350

Waterfowl: 10q, Red-crested pochards. 15q, White-fronted goose. 20q, Northern pintails. 25q, Red-breasted merganser. 30q, Eider ducks. 35q, Whooper swan. 2.70 l, Shovelers.

1975, June 15 **Litho.** *Perf. 12*

1672	A350	5q brt bl & multi	15	15
1673	A350	10q yel grn & multi	15	15
1674	A350	15q brt rose lil & multi	15	15
1675	A350	20q bl grn & multi	15	15
1676	A350	25q multi	15	15
1677	A350	30q multi	15	15
1678	A350	35q org & multi	15	15
1679	A350	2.70 l multi	1.10	32
		Set value	1.55	60

Shyqyri Kanapari, by Musa Qarri — A351

Albanian Paintings: 10q, Woman Saving Children in Sea, by Agim Faja. 15q, "November 28, 1912" (revolution), by Petrit Ceno, horiz. 20q, "Workers Unite," by Sali Shijaku. 25q, The Partisan Shota Galica, by Ismail Lulani. 30q, Victorious Resistance Fighters, 1943, by Nestor Jonuzi. 80q, Partisan Couple in Front of Red Flag, by Vilson Halimi. 2.05 l, Dancing Procession, by Abdurahim Buza. 2.25 l, Republic Day Celebration, by Fatmir Haxhiu, horiz.

Perf. 12x12½, 12½x12

1975, July 15 **Litho.**

1680	A351	5q gold & multi	15	15
1681	A351	10q gold & multi	15	15
1682	A351	15q gold & multi	15	15
1683	A351	20q gold & multi	15	15
1684	A351	25q gold & multi	15	15
1685	A351	30q gold & multi	15	15
1686	A351	80q gold & multi	24	15
1687	A351	2.25 l gold & multi	80	28
		Set value	1.50	60

Miniature Sheet

Imperf

1688	A351	2.05 l gold & multi	1.25	48

Nos. 1680-1687 issued in sheets of 8 stamps and gold center label showing palette and easel.

Farmer Holding Reform Law — A352

Design: 2 l, Produce and farm machinery.

1975, Aug. 28 *Perf. 12*

1689	A352	15q multicolored	15	15
1690	A352	2 l multicolored	75	35
		Set value		40

Agrarian reform, 30th anniversary.

Alcynonium Palmatum — A353

Corals: 10q, Paramuricea chamaeleon. 20q, Coralium rubrum. 25q, Eunicella covalini. 3.70 l, Cladocora cespitosa.

1975, Sept. 25 **Litho.** *Perf. 12*

1691	A353	5q blue, ol & blk	15	15
1692	A353	10q blue & multi	15	15
1693	A353	20q blue & multi	15	15
1694	A353	25q blue & blk	15	15
1695	A353	3.70 l blue & blk	1.75	48
		Nos. 1691-1695 (5)	2.35	
		Set value		65

Bicycling — A354

Designs (Montreal Olympic Games Emblem and): 10q, Canoeing. 15q, Fieldball. 20q, Basketball. 25q, Water polo. 30q, Hockey. 1.20 l, Pole vault. 2.05 l, Fencing. 2.15 l, Montreal Olympic Games emblem and various sports.

1975, Oct. 20 **Litho.** *Perf. 12½*

1696	A354	5q multi	15	15
1697	A354	10q multi	15	15
1698	A354	15q multi	15	15
1699	A354	20q multi	15	15
1700	A354	25q multi	15	15
1701	A354	30q multi	15	15
1702	A354	1.20 l multi	35	16
1703	A354	2.05 l multi	75	24
		Set value	1.50	65

Miniature Sheet

Imperf

1704	A354	2.15 l org & multi	2.25	1.75

21st Olympic Games, Montreal, July 18-Aug. 8, 1976. Nos. 1696-1703 exist imperf.

Power Lines Leading to Village — A355

Designs: 25q, Transformers and insulators. 80q, Dam and power station. 85q, Television set, power lines, grain and cogwheel.

1975, Oct. 25 *Perf. 12x12½*

1705	A355	15q ultra & yel	15	15
1706	A355	25q brt vio & pink	15	15
1707	A355	80q lt grn & gray	35	15
1708	A355	85q ocher & brn	35	15
		Nos. 1705-1708 (4)	1.00	
		Set value		35

General electrification, 5th anniversary.

Child, Rabbit and Teddy Bear Planting Tree — A356

Fairy Tales: 10q, Mother fox. 15q, Ducks in school. 20q, Little pigs building house. 25q, Animals watching television. 30q, Rabbit and bear at work. 35q, Working and playing ants. 2.70 l, Wolf in sheep's clothes.

1975, Dec. 25 **Litho.** *Perf. 12½x12*

1709	A356	5q black & multi	15	15
1710	A356	10q black & multi	15	15
1711	A356	15q black & multi	15	15
1712	A356	20q black & multi	15	15
1713	A356	25q black & multi	15	15
1714	A356	30q black & multi	15	15
1715	A356	35q black & multi	16	15
1716	A356	2.70 l black & multi	1.00	28
		Set value	1.50	60

Arms, People, Factories A357

Design: 1.90 l, Arms, government building, celebrating crowd.

1976, Jan. 11 **Litho.** *Perf. 12*

1717	A357	25q gold & multi	15	15
1718	A357	1.90 l gold & multi	55	24
		Set value		29

30th anniversary of proclamation of Albanian People's Republic.

Ice Hockey, Olympic Games' Emblem — A358

Designs: 10q, Speed skating. 15q, Biathlon. 50q, Ski jump. 1.20 l, Slalom. 2.15 l, Figure skating, pairs. 2.30 l, One-man bobsled.

1976, Feb. 4

1719	A358	5q silver & multi	15	15
1720	A358	10q silver & multi	15	15
1721	A358	15q silver & multi	15	15
1722	A358	50q silver & multi	16	15
1723	A358	1.20 l silver & multi	38	15
1724	A358	2.30 l silver & multi	90	35
		Set value	1.60	65

Miniature Sheet

Perf. 12 on 2 sides x Imperf.

1725	A358	2.15 l silver & multi	1.25	80

12th Winter Olympic Games, Innsbruck, Austria, Feb. 4-15.

Meadow Saffron — A359

Medicinal Plants: 10q, Deadly night-shade. 15q, Yellow gentian. 20q, Horse chestnut. 70q, Shield fern. 80q, Marshmallow. 2.30 l, Thorn apple.

1976, Apr. 10 **Litho.** *Perf. 12x12½*

1726	A359	5q black & multi	15	15
1727	A359	10q black & multi	15	15
1728	A359	15q black & multi	15	15
1729	A359	20q black & multi	15	15
1730	A359	70q black & multi	20	15
1731	A359	80q black & multi	40	15
1732	A359	2.30 l black & multi	1.10	35
		Set value	1.90	70

Bowl and Spoon — A360

Designs: 15q, Flask, vert. 20q, Carved handles, vert. 25q, Pistol and dagger. 80q, Wall hanging, vert. 1.20 l, Earrings and belt buckle. 1.40 l, Jugs, vert.

1976 **Litho.** *Perf. 12½x12, 12x12½*

1733	A360	10q lilac & multi	15	15
1734	A360	15q gray & multi	15	15
1735	A360	20q multi	15	15
1736	A360	25q car & multi	15	15
1737	A360	80q yellow & multi	35	15
1738	A360	1.20 l multi	50	15
1739	A360	1.40 l tan & multi	65	25
		Nos. 1733-1739 (7)	2.10	
		Set value		70

Natl. Ethnographic Conf., Tirana, June 28.
For surcharge, see No. 1873.

Founding of Cooperatives, by Zef Shoshi — A361

Paintings: 10q, Going to Work, by Agim Zajmi, vert. 25q, Crowd Listening to Loudspeaker, by Vilson Kilica. 40q, Woman Welder, by Sabaudin Xhaferi, vert. 50q, Factory, by Isuf Sulovari, vert. 1.20 l, 1942 Revolt, by Lec Shkreli, vert. 1.60 l, Coming Home from Work, by Agron Dine. 2.05 l, Honoring a Young Pioneer, by Andon Lakuriqi.

Perf. 12½x12, 12x12½

1976, Aug. 8 **Litho.**

1740	A361	5q	gold & multi	15	15
1741	A361	10q	gold & multi	15	15
1742	A361	25q	gold & multi	15	15
1743	A361	40q	gold & multi	15	15
1744	A361	50q	gold & multi	15	15
1745	A361	1.20 l	gold & multi	48	15
1746	A361	1.60 l	gold & multi	70	28
			Nos. 1740-1746 (7)	1.93	
			Set value		70

Miniature Sheet

Perf. 12 on 2 sides x Imperf.

1747	A361	2.05 l	gold & multi	90	45

Red Flag, Agricultural Symbols — A362

Enver Hoxha, Partisans and Albanian Flag — A363

Design: 1.20 l, Red flag and raised pickax.

1976, Nov. 1

1748	A362	25q	multi	15	15
1749	A362	1.20 l	multi	50	20
			Set value		25

7th Workers Party Congress.

1976, Oct. 28 ***Perf. 12x12½***

Design: 1.90 l, Demonstrators with Albanian flag.

1750	A363	25q	multi	15	15
1751	A363	1.90 l	multi	80	30
			Set value		35

Anti-Fascist demonstrations, 35th anniv.

Attacking Partisans, Meeting House — A364

Designs (Red Flag and): 25q, Partisans, pickax and gun. 80q, Workers, soldiers, pickax and gun. 1.20 l, Agriculture and industry. 1.70 l, Dancers, symbols of science and art.

1976, Nov. 8 **Litho.** ***Perf. 12x12½***

1752	A364	15q	gold & multi	15	15
1753	A364	25q	gold & multi	15	15
1754	A364	80q	gold & multi	22	15
1755	A364	1.20 l	gold & multi	40	15
1756	A364	1.70 l	gold & multi	80	18
			Nos. 1752-1756 (5)	1.72	
			Set value		50

35th anniv. of 1st Workers Party Cong.

Young Workers and Track A365

Design: 1.25 l, Young soldiers and Albanian flag.

1976, Nov. 23 ***Perf. 12***

1757	A365	80q	yellow & multi	28	15
1758	A365	1.25 l	carmine & multi	38	20

Union of Young Communists, 35th anniv.

"Cuca e Maleve" Ballet A366

Designs: Scenes from ballet "Mountain Girl."

1976, Dec. 14 ***Perf. 12***

1759	A366	10q	gold & multi	15	15
1760	A366	15q	gold & multi	15	15
1761	A366	20q	gold & multi	15	15
1762	A366	25q	gold & multi	15	15
1763	A366	80q	gold & multi	40	15
1764	A366	1.20 l	gold & multi	55	18
1765	A366	1.40 l	gold & multi	70	22
			Nos. 1759-1765 (7)	2.25	
			Set value		65

Miniature Sheet

Perf. 12 on 2 sides x Imperf.

1766	A366	2.05 l	gold & multi	1.25	45

Bashtoves Castle A367

Albanian Castles: 15q, Gjirokastres. 20q, Ali Pash Tepelenes. 25q, Petreles. 80q, Beratit. 1.20 l, Durresit. 1.40 l, Krujes.

1976, Dec. 30 **Litho.** ***Perf. 12***

1767	A367	10q	black & dull bl	15	15
1768	A367	15q	black & grn	15	15
1769	A367	20q	black & gray	15	15
1770	A367	25q	black & brn	15	15
1771	A367	80q	black & rose	24	15
1772	A367	1.20 l	black & vio	28	16
1773	A367	1.40 l	black & brn red	55	16
			Set value	1.35	60

Skanderbeg's Shield and Spear — A368

Skanderbeg's Weapons: 80q, Helmet, sword and scabbard. 1 l, Halberd, quiver with arrows, crossbow and spear.

1977, Jan. 28 **Litho.** ***Perf. 12***

1774	A368	15q	silver & multi	25	15
1775	A368	80q	silver & multi	1.00	20
1776	A368	1 l	silver & multi	1.50	25
			Nos. 1774-1776 (3)	2.75	
			Set value		50

Skanderbeg (1403-1468), national hero.

Ilia Oiqi, Messenger in Storm — A369

Modern Heroes: 10q, Ilia Dashi, sailor in battle. 25q, Fran Ndue Ivanaj, fisherman in storm. 80q, Zeliha Allmetaj, woman rescuing child. 1 l, Ylli Zaimi, rescuing goats from flood. 1.90 l, Isuf Plloci, fighting forest fire.

1977, Feb. 28 **Litho.** ***Perf. 12x12½***

1777	A369	5q	brown & multi	15	15
1778	A369	10q	ultra & multi	15	15
1779	A369	25q	blue & multi	15	15
1780	A369	80q	ocher & multi	35	15
1781	A369	1 l	brown & multi	52	15
1782	A369	1.90 l	brown & multi	90	18
			Set value	2.00	50

Polyvinylchloride Plant, Vlore — A370

6th Five-year plan: 25q, Naphtha fractioning plant, Ballsh. 65q, Hydroelectric station and dam, Fjerzes. 1 l, Metailurgical plant and blast furance, Elbasan.

1977, Mar. 29 **Litho.** ***Perf. 12½x12***

1783	A370	15q	silver & multi	15	15
1784	A370	25q	silver & multi	15	15
1785	A370	65q	silver & multi	28	15
1786	A370	1 l	silver & multi	45	16
			Nos. 1783-1786 (4)	1.03	
			Set value		36

Qerime Halil Galica — A371

Victory Monument, Tirana — A372

Design: 1.25 l, Qerime Halil Galica "Shota" and father Azem Galica.

1977, Apr. 20 **Litho.** ***Perf. 12***

1787	A371	80q	dark red	22	15
1788	A371	1.25 l	gray blue	35	15
			Set value		22

"Shota" Galica, communist fighter.

1977, May 5 **Litho.** ***Perf. 12***

Designs (Red Star and): 80q, Clenched fist, Albanian flag. 1.20 l, Bust of Qemal Stafa and poppies.

1789	A372	25q	multi	15	15
1790	A372	80q	multi	35	15
1791	A372	1.20 l	multi	55	20
			Nos. 1789-1791 (3)	1.05	
			Set value		36

35th anniversary of Martyrs' Day.

Physician Visiting Farm, Mobile Clinic — A373

Designs: 10q, Cowherd and cattle ranch. 20q, Militia woman helping with harvest, rifle and combine. 80q, Modern village, highway and power lines. 2.95 l, Tractor and greenhouses.

1977, June 18

1792	A373	5q	multi	15	15
1793	A373	10q	multi	15	15
1794	A373	20q	multi	15	15
1795	A373	80q	multi	22	15
1796	A373	2.95 l	multi	1.40	38
			Nos. 1792-1796 (5)	2.07	
			Set value		60

"Socialist transformation of the villages."

Armed Workers, Flag and Factory — A374

Design: 1.80 l, Workers with proclamation and flags.

1977, June 20

1797	A374	25q	multi	15	15
1798	A374	1.80 l	multi	65	22
			Set value		26

9th Labor Unions Congress.

Kerchief Dance — A375

Designs: Various folk dances.

1977, Aug. 20 **Litho.** ***Perf. 12***

1799	A375	5q	multi	15	15
1800	A375	10q	multi	15	15
1801	A375	15q	multi	15	15
1802	A375	25q	multi	15	15
1803	A375	80q	multi	30	15
1804	A375	1.20 l	multi	60	20
1805	A375	1.55 l	multi	75	25
			Set value	1.90	75

Miniature Sheet

Perf. 12 on 2 sides x Imperf.

1806	A375	2.05 l	multi	85	40

See Nos. 1836-1840, 1884-1888.

Attack A376

Designs: 25q, Enver Hoxha addressing Army. 80q, Volunteers and riflemen. 1 l, Volunteers, hydrofoil patrolboat and MiG planes. 1.90 l, Volunteers and Albanian flag.

1977, July 10 **Litho.** ***Perf. 12***

1807	A376	15q	gold & multi	15	15
1808	A376	25q	gold & multi	15	15
1809	A376	80q	gold & multi	25	15
1810	A376	1 l	gold & multi	38	15
1811	A376	1.90 l	gold & multi	75	22
			Nos. 1807-1811 (5)	1.68	
			Set value		50

"One People-One Army."

Armed Workers, Article 3 of Constitution A377

Design: 1.20 l, Symbols of farming and fertilizer industry, Article 25 of Constitution.

1977, Oct.

1812	A377	25q	red, gold & blk	15	15
1813	A377	1.20 l	red, gold & blk	48	18
			Set value		22

New Constitution.

Picnic — A378

Film Frames: 15q, Telephone lineman in winter. 25q, Two men and a woman. 80q, Workers. 1.20 l, Boys playing in street. 1.60 l, Harvest.

1977, Oct. 25 Litho. *Perf. 12½x12*

1814	A378	10q blue green	15	15
1815	A378	15q multi	15	15
1816	A378	25q black	15	15
1817	A378	80q multi	28	15
1818	A378	1.20 l deep claret	48	15
1819	A378	1.60 l multi	60	20
		Set value	1.50	55

Albanian films.

Farm Workers in Field, by V. Mio — A379

Paintings by V. Mio: 10q, Landscape in Snow. 15q, Grazing Sheep under Walnut Tree in Spring. 25q, Street in Korce. 80q, Horseback Riders on Mountain Pass. 1 l, Boats on Shore. 1.75 l, Tractors Plowing Fields. 2.05 l, Self-portrait.

1977, Dec. 25 Litho. *Perf. 12½x12*

1820	A379	5q gold & multi	15	15
1821	A379	10q gold & multi	15	15
1822	A379	15q gold & multi	15	15
1823	A379	25q gold & multi	15	15
1824	A379	80q gold & multi	28	15
1825	A379	1 l gold & multi	32	15
1826	A379	1.75 l gold & multi	55	16
		Set value	1.35	55

Miniature Sheet

Imperf.; Perf. 12 Horiz. between Vignette and Value Panel

1827	A379	2.05 l gold & multi	70	32

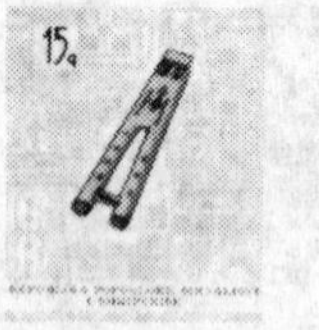

Pan Flute — A380

Albanian Flag, Monument and People — A381

Folk Musical Instruments: 25q, Single-string goat's-head fiddle. 80q, Woodwind. 1.20 l, Drum. 1.70 l, Bagpipe. Background shows various woven folk patterns.

1978, Jan. 20 *Perf. 12x12½*

1828	A380	15q multi	15	15
1829	A380	25q multi	15	15
1830	A380	80q multi	35	15
1831	A380	1.20 l multi	55	15
1832	A380	1.70 l multi	75	20
		Nos. 1828-1832 (5)	1.95	
		Set value		55

1978 *Perf. 12½x12, 12x12½*

Designs: 25q, Ismail Qemali and fighters, horiz. 1.65 l, People dancing around Albanian flag, horiz.

1833	A381	15q multi	15	15
1834	A381	25q multi	15	15
1835	A381	1.65 l multi	60	20
		Nos. 1833-1835 (3)	90	
		Set value		30

65th anniversary of independence.

Folk Dancing Type of 1977

Designs: Various dances.

1978, Feb. 15 Litho. *Perf. 12*

1836	A375	5q multi	15	15
1837	A375	25q multi	15	15
1838	A375	80q multi	32	15
1839	A375	1 l multi	50	15
1840	A375	2.30 l multi	1.00	24
		Nos. 1836-1840 (5)	2.12	
		Set value		55

Nos. 1836-1840 have white background around dancers, Nos. 1799-1805 have pinkish shadows.

Tractor Drivers, by Dhimitraq Trebicka — A382

Working Class Paintings: 80q, Steeplejack, by Spiro Kristo. 85q, "A Point in the Discussion," by Skender Milori. 90q, Oil rig crew, by Anesti Cini, vert. 1.60 l, Metal workers, by Ramadan Karanxha. 2.20 l, Political discussion, by Sotiraq Sholla.

1978, Mar. 25 Litho. *Perf. 12*

1841	A382	25q multi	15	15
1842	A382	80q multi	30	15
1843	A382	85q multi	30	15
1844	A382	90q multi	35	16
1845	A382	1.60 l multi	75	25
		Nos. 1841-1845 (5)	1.85	
		Set value		70

Miniature Sheet

Perf. 12 on 2 sides x Imperf.

1846	A382	2.20 l multi	1.25	40

Woman with Rifle and Pickax — A383

Design: 1.95 l, Farm and Militia women, industrial plant.

1978, June 1 Litho. *Perf. 12*

1847	A383	25q gold & red	15	15
1848	A383	1.95 l gold & red	75	25
		Set value		30

8th Congress of Women's Union.

Children and Flowers — A384

Designs: 10q, Children with rifle, ax, book and flags. 25q, Dancing children in folk costume. 1.80 l, Children in school.

1978, June 1 Litho.

1849	A384	5q multi	15	15
1850	A384	10q multi	15	15
1851	A384	25q multi	15	15
1852	A384	1.80 l multi	60	20
		Set value	80	35

International Children's Day.

Spirit of Skanderbeg as Conqueror — A385

Designs: 10q, Battle at Mostar Bridge. 80q, Marchers and Albanian flag. 1.20 l, Riflemen in winter battle. 1.65 l, Abdyl Frasheri (1839-1892). 2.20 l, Rifles, scroll and pen, League building. 2.60 l, League headquarters, Prizren.

1978, June 10 Litho. *Perf. 12*

1853	A385	10q multi	15	15
1854	A385	25q multi	15	15
1855	A385	80q multi	22	15
1856	A385	1.20 l multi	45	15
1857	A385	1.65 l multi	70	18
1858	A385	2.60 l multi	80	32
		Nos. 1853-1858 (6)	2.47	
		Set value		82

Miniature Sheet

Perf. 12 on 2 sides x Imperf.

1859	A385	2.20 l multi	90	35

Centenary of League of Prizren.

Guerrillas and Flag, 1943 — A386

Designs: 25q, Soldier, sailor, airman, militiaman, horiz. 1.90 l, Members of armed forces, civil guards, and Young Pioneers.

1978, July 10 *Perf. 11½x12½*

1860	A386	5q multi	15	15
1861	A386	25q multi	15	15
1862	A386	1.90 l multi	80	20
		Nos. 1860-1862 (3)	1.10	
		Set value		30

35th anniversary of People's Army.

Woman with Machine Carbine — A387

Kerchief Dance — A388

Designs: 25q, Man with target rifle, horiz. 95q, Man shooting with telescopic sights, horiz. 2.40 l, Woman target shooting with pistol.

Perf. 12½x12, 12x12½

1978, Sept. 20 Litho.

1863	A387	25q blk & yel	15	15
1864	A387	80q org & blk	30	15
1865	A387	95q red & blk	42	15
1866	A387	2.40 l car & blk	1.00	30
		Nos. 1863-1866 (4)	1.87	75

32nd National Rifle-shooting Championships, Sept. 20.

1978, Oct. 6 *Perf. 12*

Designs: 15q, Musicians. 25q, Fiddler with single-stringed instrument. 80q, Dancers, men. 1.20 l, Saber dance. 1.90 l, Singers, women.

1867	A388	10q multi	15	15
1868	A388	15q multi	15	15
1869	A388	25q multi	15	15
1870	A388	80q multi	25	15
1871	A388	1.20 l multi	50	15
1872	A388	1.90 l multi	80	25
		Nos. 1867-1872 (6)	2.00	
		Set value		65

National Folklore Festival.
See Nos. 2082-2085, 2289-2290.

No. 1736 Surcharged with New Value, 2 Bars and "RICCIONE 78"

1978 Litho. *Perf. 12½x12*

1873	A360	3.30 l on 25q multi	5.00	1.10

Riccione 78 Philatelic Exhibition.

Enver Hoxha — A389

1978, Oct. 16 Litho. *Perf. 12x12½*

1874	A389	80q red & multi	30	15
1875	A389	1.20 l red & multi	45	15
1876	A389	2.40 l red & multi	90	25
		Nos. 1874-1876 (3)	1.65	55

Miniature Sheet

Perf. 12½ on 2 sides x Imperf.

1877	A389	2.20 l red & multi	85	40

70th birthday of Enver Hoxha, First Secretary of Central Committee of the Communist Party of Albania.

Woman and Wheat — A390

Designs: 25q, Woman with egg crates. 80q, Shepherd and sheep. 2.60 l, Milkmaid and cows.

1978, Dec. 15 *Perf. 12x12½*

1878	A390	15q multi	15	15
1879	A390	25q multi	15	15
1880	A390	80q multi	40	15
1881	A390	2.60 l multi	1.10	50
		Nos. 1878-1881 (4)	1.80	
		Set value		70

Dora d'Istria — A391

Tower House — A392

Design: 1.10 l, Full portrait of Dora d'Istria, author; birth sesquicentennial.

1979, Jan. 22 Litho. *Perf. 12*

1882	A391	80q lt grn & blk	42	15
1883	A391	1.10 l vio brn & blk	48	15
		Set value		20

Costume Type of 1977

Designs: Various folk dances.

1979, Feb. 25

1884	A375	15q multi	15	15
1885	A375	25q multi	15	15
1886	A375	80q multi	32	15
1887	A375	1.20 l multi	42	15
1888	A375	1.40 l multi	60	22
		Nos. 1884-1888 (5)	1.64	
		Set value		50

Nos. 1884-1888 have white background. Denomination in upper left on No. 1885, in upper right on No. 1802; lower left on No. 1886, upper left on No. 1803.

1979, Mar. 20

Traditional Houses: 15q, Stone gallery house, horiz. 80q, House with wooden galleries, horiz. 1.20 l, Galleried tower house. 1.40 l, 1.90 l, Tower houses, diff.

1889	A392	15q multi	15	15
1890	A392	25q multi	15	15
1891	A392	80q multi	32	15
1892	A392	1.20 l multi	42	15
1893	A392	1.40 l multi	60	22
		Nos. 1889-1893 (5)	1.64	
		Set value		50

Miniature Sheet

Perf. 12 on 2 sides x Imperf.

1894	A392	1.90 l multi	80	40

See Nos. 2015-2018.

Soldier, Factories, Wheat A393

Design: 1.65 l, Soldiers, workers and coat of arms.

1979, May 14 Litho. *Perf. 12*

1895 A393	25q multi		15	15
1896 A393	1.65 l multi		55	18
	Set value			23

Congress of Permet, 35th anniversary.

Albanian Flag — A394

1979, June 4

1897 A394	25q multi		15	15
1898 A394	1.65 l multi		55	18
	Set value			23

5th Congress of Albanian Democratic Front.

Vasil Shanto, (1913-44) A395

Alexander Moissi, (1880-1935), Actor — A396

Design: 25q, 90q, Qemal Stafa (1921-42).

1979

1899 A395	15q multi		15	15
1900 A395	25q multi		15	15
1901 A395	60q multi		35	15
1902 A396	80q multi		45	15
1903 A395	90q multi		45	15
1904 A396	1.10 l multi, diff.		60	18
	Nos. 1899-1904 (6)		2.15	
	Set value			68

Shanto and Stafa, anti-Fascist fighters.
Issued: type A396, Apr. 2, type A395, May 5.
For similar design see A410.

Winter Campaign, by Arben Basha — A397

Paintings of Military Scenes by: 25q, Ismail Lulani. 80q, Myrteza Fushekati. 1.20 l, Muhamet Deliu. 1.40 l, Jorgji Gjikopulli. 1.90 l, Fatmir Haxhiu.

1979, July 15 Litho. *Perf. 12½x12*

1905 A397	15q multi		15	15
1906 A397	25q multi		15	15
1907 A397	80q multi		35	15
1908 A397	1.20 l multi		60	15
1909 A397	1.40 l multi		65	22
	Nos. 1905-1909 (5)		1.90	
	Set value			52

Miniature Sheet

Perf. 12 on 2 sides x Imperf.

1910 A397	1.90 l multi		1.00	40

Athletes Surrounding Flag A398

Literary Society Headquarters A399

1979, Oct. 1 Litho. *Perf. 12*

1911 A398	15q	shown	15	15
1912 A398	25q	Shooting	15	15
1913 A398	80q	Dancing	25	15
1914 A398	1.20 l	Soccer	45	15
1915 A398	1.40 l	High jump	60	22
	Nos. 1911-1915 (5)		1.60	
	Set value			50

Liberation Spartakiad, 35th anniversary.

1979, Oct. 12

Albanian Literary Society Centenary: 25q, Seal and charter. 80q, Founder. 1.55 l, 1879 Headquarters. 1.90 l, Founders.

1916 A399	25q multi		15	15
1917 A399	80q multi		30	15
1918 A399	1.20 l multi		42	15
1919 A399	1.55 l multi		55	18
	Nos. 1916-1919 (4)		1.42	
	Set value			46

Miniature Sheet

Perf. 12½ on 2 sides x Imperf.

1920 A399	1.90 l multi		80	40

Congress Statute, Coat of Arms — A400

1979, Oct. 20 Photo. *Perf. 12x12½*

1921 A400	25q multi		16	15
1922 A400	1.65 l multi		70	25
	Set value			30

2nd Congress of Berat, 35th anniversary.

Children Entering School, Books — A401

1979 Litho. *Perf. 12½x12*

1923	A401	5q	shown	15	15
1924	A401	10q	Communications	15	15
1925	A401	15q	Steel workers	15	15
1926	A401	20q	Dancers, instruments	15	15
1927	A401	25q	Newspapers, radio, television	15	15
1928	A401	60q	Textile worker	22	15
1929	A401	80q	Armed forces	30	15
1930	A401	1.20 l	Industry	42	18
1931	A401	1.60 l	Transportation	55	28
1932	A401	2.40 l	Agriculture	80	35
1932A	A401	3 l	Medicine	1.00	52
			Nos. 1923-1932A (11)	4.04	
			Set value		1.75

Workers and Factory A402

Worker, Red Flag and: 80q, Hand holding sickle and rifle. 1.20 l, Red star and open book. 1.55 l, Open book and cogwheel.

1979, Nov. 29

1933 A402	25q multi		15	15
1934 A402	80q multi		18	15
1935 A402	1.20 l multi		42	15
1936 A402	1.55 l multi		48	15
	Nos. 1933-1936 (4)		1.23	
	Set value			42

35th anniversary of independence.

Joseph Stalin — A403

Design: 1.10 l, Stalin on dais, horiz.

1979, Dec. 21 Litho. *Perf. 12*

1937 A403	80q red & dk bl		35	15
1938 A403	1.10 l red & dk bl		48	18
	Set value			28

Joseph Stalin (1879-1953), birth centenary.

Fireplace and Pottery, Korcar A404

Home Furnishings: 80q, Cupboard bed, dagger, pistol, ammunition pouch, Shkodar. 1.20 l, Stool, pot, chair, Mirdit. 1.35 l, Chimney, dagger, jacket, Gjirokaster.

1980, Feb. 27 Litho. *Perf. 12*

1939 A404	25q multi		15	15
1940 A404	80q multi		35	15
1941 A404	1.20 l multi		55	20
1942 A404	1.35 l multi		60	30
	Nos. 1939-1942 (4)		1.65	
	Set value			66

See Nos. 1985-1988.

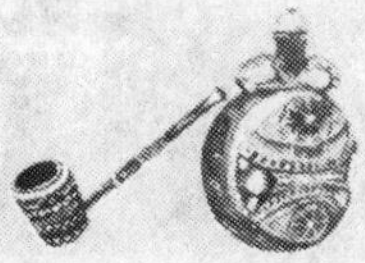

Pipe, Painted Flask — A405

1980, Mar. 4

1943 A405	25q	shown	15	15
1944 A405	80q	Leather handbags	35	15
1945 A405	1.20 l	Carved eagle, embroidered rug	55	20
1946 A405	1.35 l	Lace	60	30
	Nos. 1943-1946 (4)		1.65	
	Set value			66

Prof. Aleksander Xhuvanit Birth Centenary — A406

1980, Mar. 14

1947 A406	80q multi		42	15
1948 A406	1 l multi		52	18

Revolutionaries on Horseback — A407

Insurrection at Kosove, 70th Anniversary: 1 l, Battle scene.

1980, Apr. 4

1949 A407	80q red & black		42	15
1950 A407	1 l red & black		52	18

Soldiers and Workers Laboring to Aid the Stricken Populations, by D. Jukinui and I. Lulani — A408

1980, Apr. 15 Litho. *Perf. 12½*

1951 A408	80q lt blue & multi		42	15
1952 A408	1 l lt blue grn & multi		52	18

Lenin, 110th Birth Anniversary — A409

1980, Apr. 22

1953 A409	80q multi		42	15
1954 A409	1 l multi		52	18

Misto Mame and Ali Demi, War Martyrs A410

War Martyrs: 80q, Sadik Staveleci, Vojo Kusji, Hoxhi Martini. 1.20 l, Bule Naipi, Persefoni Kokedhima. 1.35 l, Ndoc Deda, Hydajet Lezha, Naim Gyylbegu, Ndoc Mazi, Ahmed Haxha.

1980, May 5

1955 A410	25q multi		15	15
1956 A410	80q multi		35	15
1957 A410	1.20 l multi		50	20
1958 A410	1.35 l multi		60	30
	Nos. 1955-1958 (4)		1.60	
	Set value			66

See Nos. 2012A-2012D, 2025-2028, 2064-2067, 2122-2125, 2171-2174, 2207-2209.

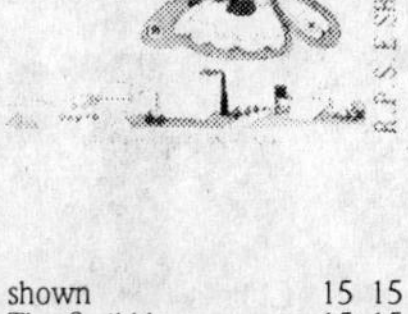

Scene from "Mirela" A411

1980, June 7

1959 A411	15q	shown	15	15
1960 A411	25q	The Scribbler	15	15
1961 A411	80q	Circus Bears	28	15
1962 A411	2.40 l	Waterdrops	80	35
	Nos. 1959-1962 (4)		1.38	
	Set value			55

Carrying Iron Castings in the Enver Hoxha Tractor Combine, by S. Shijaku and M. Fushekati — A412

Paintings (Gallery of Figurative Paintings, Tirana): 80q, The Welder, by Harilla Dhima. 1.20 l, Steel Erectors, by Petro Kokushta. 1.35 l, Pandeli Lena, 1.80 l Communists, by Vilson Kilica.

1980, July 22

1963	A412	25q	multi	15	15
1964	A412	80q	multi	28	15
1965	A412	1.20 l	multi	40	16
1966	A412	1.35 l	multi	52	24
			Nos. 1963-1966 (4)	1.35	
			Set value		55

Souvenir Sheet

1967	A412	1.80 l	multi	70	48

Gate, Parchment Miniature, 11th Cent. — A413

Bas reliefs of the Middle Ages: 80q, Eagle, 13th cent. 1.20 l, Heraldic lion, 14th cent. 1.35 l, Pheasant, 14th cent.

1980, Sept. 27 **Litho.** ***Perf. 12***

1968	A413	25q	gold & blk	15	15
1969	A413	80q	gold & blk	25	15
1970	A413	1.20 l	gold & blk	42	15
1971	A413	1.35 l	gold & blk	52	22
			Nos. 1968-1971 (4)	1.34	
			Set value		54

Divjaka National Park — A414

1980, Nov. 6 **Photo.**

1972	A414	80q	shown	25	15
1973	A414	1.20 l	Lura	42	22
1974	A414	1.60 l	Thethi	55	25
			Nos. 1972-1974 (3)	1.22	62

Souvenir Sheet

Perf. 12½

1975	A414	1.80 l	Llogara Park	75	75

Citizens, Flag and Arms of Albania A415

1981, Jan. 11 **Litho.** ***Perf. 12***

1976	A415	80q	shown	35	15
1977	A415	1 l	People's Party Headquarters, Tirana	50	25

35th anniversary of the Republic.

Child's Bed — A416

1981, Mar. 20 **Litho.** ***Perf. 12***

1978	A416	25q	shown	15	15
1979	A416	80q	Wooden bucket, brass bottle	35	22
1980	A416	1.20 l	Shoes	52	25
1981	A416	1.35 l	Jugs	55	30
			Nos. 1978-1981 (4)	1.57	92

A417

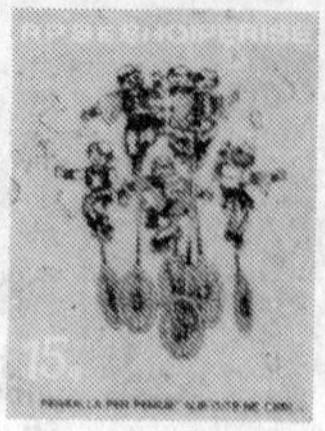

A419

1981, Apr. 20

1982	A417	80q	Soldiers	35	22
1983	A417	1 l	Sword combat	48	25

Souvenir Sheet

Perf. 12½ Vert.

1984	A417	1.80 l	Soldier with pistol	80	80

Battle of Shtimje centenary.

Home Furnishings Type of 1980

1981, Feb. 25 **Litho.** ***Perf. 12***

1985	A404	25q	House interior, Labara	15	15
1986	A404	80q	Labara, diff.	35	22
1987	A404	1.20 l	Mat	52	25
1988	A404	1.35 l	Dibres	55	30
			Nos. 1985-1988 (4)	1.57	92

1981, June ***Perf. 12***

Designs: Children's circus.

1989	A419	15q	multi	15	15
1990	A419	25q	multi	15	15
1991	A419	80q	multi	35	22
1992	A419	2.40 l	multi	1.00	60
			Nos. 1989-1992 (4)	1.65	
			Set value		66

Soccer Players A420

1982 World Cup Soccer Elimination Games: Various soccer players.

1981, Mar. 31 **Litho.** ***Perf. 12***

1993	A420	25q	multi	25	16
1994	A420	80q	multi	1.90	40
1995	A420	1.20 l	multi	2.75	65
1996	A420	1.35 l	multi	3.50	80
			Nos. 1993-1996 (4)	8.40	2.01

Allies, by S. Hysa A421

Paintings: 80q, Warriors, by A. Buza. 1.20 l, Rallying to the Flag, Dec. 1911, by A. Zajmi, vert. 1.35 l, My Flag is My Heart, by L. Cefa, vert. 1.80 l, Circling the Flag in a Common Cause, by N. Vasia.

1981, July 10 ***Perf. 12½x12***

1997	A421	25q	multi	15	15
1998	A421	80q	multi	35	18
1999	A421	1.20 l	multi	50	25
2000	A421	1.35 l	multi	52	28
			Nos. 1997-2000 (4)	1.52	86

Souvenir Sheet

2001	A421	1.80 l	multi	95	85

No. 2001 contains one stamp, size: 55x55mm.

Rifleman A422

1981, Aug. 30 ***Perf. 12***

2002	A422	25q	shown	15	15
2003	A422	80q	Weight lifting	40	20
2004	A422	1.20 l	Volleyball	55	28
2005	A422	1.35 l	Soccer	65	32
			Nos. 2002-2005 (4)	1.75	95

Albanian Workers' Party, 8th Congress A423

1981, Nov. 1

2006	A423	80q	Flag, star	28	18
2007	A423	1 l	Flag, hammer and sickle	38	22

Albanian Workers' Party, 40th Anniv. — A424

Communist Youth Org., 40th Anniv. — A425

1981, Nov. 8

2008	A424	80q	Symbols of industrialization	35	22
2009	A424	2.80 l	Fist, emblem	1.25	70

Souvenir Sheet

2010	A424	1.80 l	Enver Hoxha, Memoirs	85	85

1981, Nov. 23

2011	A425	80q	Star, ax, map	28	18
2012	A425	1 l	Flags, star	38	22

War Martyrs Type of 1980

Portraits: 25q, Perlat Rexhepi (1919-42) and Branko Kadia (1921-42). 80q, Xheladin Beqiri (1908-44) and Hajdar Dushi (1916-44). 1.20 l, Koci Bako (1905-41), Vasil Laci (1923-41) and Mujo Ulqinaku (1898-1939). 1.35 l, Mine Peza (1875-1942) and Zoja Cure (1920-44).

1981, May 5 **Litho.** ***Perf. 12***

2012A	A410	25q	sil & multi	25	15
2012B	A410	80q	gold & multi	80	40
2012C	A410	1.20 l	sil & multi	1.15	55
2012D	A410	1.35 l	gold & multi	1.25	62
			Nos. 2012A-2012D (4)	3.45	1.72

Fan S. Noli, Writer, Birth Centenary A426

Traditional House, Bulqize A427

1982, Jan. 6 **Litho.** ***Perf. 12***

2013	A426	80q	lt ol grn & gold	28	18
2014	A426	1.10 l	lt red brn & gold	38	22

Traditional Houses Type of 1979

1982, Feb. ***Perf. 12½x12***

2015	A392	25q	Bulqize	30	20
2016	A392	80q	Lebush	30	20
2017	A392	1.20 l	Bicaj	50	28
2018	A392	1.55 l	Klos	70	42
			Nos. 2015-2018 (4)	1.80	1.10

TB Bacillus Centenary A428

1982, Mar. 24 ***Perf. 12***

2019	A428	80q	Globe	50	25
2020	A428	1.10 l	Koch	70	35

Albanian League House, Prizren, by K. Buza A429

Kosova Landscapes: 25q, Castle at Prizrenit, by G. Madhi. 1.20 l, Mountain Gorge at Rogove, by K. Buza. 1.55 l, Street of the Hadhji at Zekes, by G. Madhi. 25q, 1.20 l, 1.55 l vert.

Perf. 12x12½, 12½x12

1982, Apr. 15 **Litho.**

2021	A429	25q	multi	15	15
2022	A429	80q	multi	32	15
2023	A429	1.20 l	multi	48	20
2024	A429	1.55 l	multi	65	28
			Nos. 2021-2024 (4)	1.60	
			Set value		66

War Martyr Type of 1980

Designs: 25q, Hibe Palikuqi, Liri Gero. 80q, Mihal Duri, Kajo Karafili. 1.20 l, Fato Dudumi, Margarita Tutulani, Shejnaze Juka. 1.55 l, Memo Meto, Gjok Doci.

1982, May ***Perf. 12***

2025	A410	25q	multi	15	15
2026	A410	80q	multi	32	20
2027	A410	1.20 l	multi	52	28
2028	A410	1.55 l	multi	70	45
			Nos. 2025-2028 (4)	1.69	1.08

Loading Freighter A430

Children's Paintings.

1982, June 15 ***Perf. 12½x12***

2029	A430	15q	shown	15	15
2030	A430	80q	Forest	32	20
2031	A430	1.20 l	City	52	28
2032	A430	1.65 l	Park	75	45
			Nos. 2029-2032 (4)	1.74	1.08

9th Congress of Trade Unions A431

1982, June 6 **Litho.** ***Perf. 12***

2033	A431	80q	Workers, factories	40	18
2034	A431	1.10 l	Emblem, flag	55	22

Alpine Village Festival, by Danish Jukniu A432

Industrial Development Paintings: 80q, Hydroelectric Station Builders, by Ali Miruku. 1.20 l, Steel Workers, by Clirim Ceka. 1.55 l, Oil drillers, by Pandeli Lena. 1.90 l, Trapping the Furnace, by Jorgji Gjikopulli.

1982, July *Perf. 12½*

2035 A432 25q multi 15 15
2036 A432 80q multi 32 15
2037 A432 1.20 l multi 48 20
2038 A432 1.55 l multi 65 28
Nos. 2035-2038 (4) 1.60 78

Souvenir Sheet

Perf. 12

2039 A432 1.90 l multi 1.00 40

No. 2039 contains one 54x48mm stamp.

Communist Party Newspaper "Voice of the People," 40th Anniv. — A432a

1982, Aug. 25 **Litho.** *Perf. 12*

2039A A432a 80q Newspapers
2039B A432a 1.10 l Paper, press

40th Anniv. of Democratic Front — A433

1982, Sept. 16 *Perf. 12*

2040 A433 80q Glory to the Heroes of Peza Monument 40 18
2041 A433 1.10 l Marchers 55 22

8th Youth Congress — A434

Handmade Shoulder Bags — A435

1982, Oct. 4

2042 A434 80q multi 40 18
2043 A434 1.10 l multi 55 22

1982, Nov.

2044 A435 25q Rug, horiz. 15 15
2045 A435 80q shown 32 15
2046 A435 1.20 l Wooden pots, bowls, horiz. 48 20
2047 A435 1.55 l Jug 65 28
Nos. 2044-2047 (4) 1.60
Set value 66

70th Anniv. of Independence A436

1982, Nov. 28

2048 A436 20q Ishamil Qemali 15 15
2049 A436 1.20 l Partisans 48 20
2050 A436 2.40 l Partisans, diff. 95 40
Nos. 2048-2050 (3) 1.58 75

Souvenir Sheet

2051 A436 1.90 l Independence Monument, Tirana 1.00 40

Dhermi Beach A437

1982, Dec. 20

2052 A437 25q shown 15 15
2053 A437 80q Sarande 40 18
2054 A437 1.20 l Ksamil 60 25
2055 A437 1.55 l Lukove 80 35
Nos. 2052-2055 (4) 1.95 93

Handkerchief Dancers A438

Folkdancers.

1983, Feb. 20 **Litho.** *Perf. 12*

2056 A438 25q shown 15 15
2057 A438 80q With kerchief, drum 40 18
2058 A438 1.20 l With guitar, flute, tambourine 60 25
2059 A438 1.55 l Women 80 35
Nos. 2056-2059 (4) 1.95 93

A439

A440

1983, Mar. 14 **Litho.** *Perf. 12*

2060 A439 80q multi 40 18
2061 A439 1.10 l multi 55 22

Karl Marx (1818-83).

1983, Apr. 20

2062 A440 80q Electricity generation 40 18
2063 A440 1.10 l Gas & oil production 55 22

Energy development.

War Martyr Type of 1980

Designs: 25q, Asim Zeneli (1916-43), Nazmi Rushiti (1919-42). 80q, Shyqyri Ishmi (1922-42), Shyqyri Alimerko (1923-43), Myzafer Asqeriu (1918-42). 1.20 l, Qybra Sokoli (1924-44), Qeriba Derri (1905-44), Ylbere Bilibashi (1928-44). 1.55 l, Themo Vasi (1915-43), Abaz Shehu (1905-42).

1983, May 5 **Litho.** *Perf. 12*

2064 A410 25q multi 15 15
2065 A410 80q multi 40 18
2066 A410 1.20 l multi 60 25
2067 A410 1.55 l multi 80 35
Nos. 2064-2067 (4) 1.95 93

Women's Union, 9th Congress — A441

1983, June 1 **Litho.** *Perf. 12x12½*

2068 A441 80q red & gold 40 18
2069 A441 1.10 l bl & gold 55 22

Bicycling A442

1983, June 20 *Perf. 12*

2070 A442 25q shown 15 15
2071 A442 80q Chess 40 18
2072 A442 1.20 l Gymnastics 60 25
2073 A442 1.55 l Wrestling 80 35
Nos. 2070-2073 (4) 1.95 93

40th Anniv. of People's Army — A443

1983, July 10

2074 A443 20q Armed services 15 15
2075 A443 1.20 l Soldier, gun barrels 60 25
2076 A443 2.40 l Factory guard, crowd 1.20 50
Nos. 2074-2076 (3) 1.95 90

Sunny Day, by Myrteza Fushekati A444

Paintings: 80q, Messenger of the Grasp, by Niko Progi. 1.20 l, 29 November 1944, by Harilla Dhimo. 1.55 l, Fireworks, by Pandi Mele. 1.90 l, Partisan Assault, by Sali Shijaku and M. Fushekati.

1983, Aug. 28 **Litho.** *Perf. 12½x12*

2077 A444 25q multi 15 15
2078 A444 80q multi 40 18
2079 A444 1.20 l multi 60 25
2080 A444 1.55 l multi 80 35
Nos. 2077-2080 (4) 1.95 93

Souvenir Sheet

Perf. 12

2081 A444 1.90 l multi 4.00 50

Folklore Festival Type of 1978

Gjirokaster Folklore Festival: folkdances.

1983, Oct. 6 **Litho.** *Perf. 12*

2082 A388 25q Sword dance 15 15
2083 A388 80q Kerchief dance 40 18
2084 A388 1.20 l Shepherd flautists 60 25
2085 A388 1.55 l Garland dance 80 35
Nos. 2082-2085 (4) 1.95 93

World Communications Year — A446

1983, Nov. 10

2086 A446 60q multi 30 15
2087 A446 1.20 l multi 60 25

75th Birthday of Enver Hoxha — A447

1983, Oct. 16 **Litho.** *Perf. 12½*

2088 A447 80q multi 40 18
2089 A447 1.20 l multi 60 25
2090 A447 1.80 l multi 90 38
Nos. 2088-2090 (3) 1.90 81

Souvenir Sheet

Perf. 12

2091 A447 1.90 l multi 1.00 50

The Right to a Joint Triumph, by J. Keraj A448

Era of Skanderbeg in Figurative Art: 80q, The Heroic Center of the Battle of Krujes, by N. Bakalli. 1.20 l, The Rights of the Enemy after our Triumph, by N. Progri. 1.55 l, The Discussion at Lezhes, by B. Ahmeti. 1.90 l, Victory over the Turks, by G. Madhi.

1983, Dec. 10 *Perf. 12½x12*

2092 A448 25q multi 15 15
2093 A448 80q multi 40 18
2094 A448 1.20 l multi 60 25
2095 A448 1.55 l multi 80 35
Nos. 2092-2095 (4) 1.95 93

Souvenir Sheet

Perf. 12

2096 A448 1.90 l multi 1.25 50

Greco-Roman Ruins of Illyria — A449

1983, Dec. 28 *Perf. 12*

2097 A449 80q Amphitheater, Buthroxtum 40 18
2098 A449 1.20 l Colonnade, Apollonium 60 25
2099 A449 1.80 l Vaulted gallery, amphitheater at Epidamnus 90 38
Nos. 2097-2099 (3) 1.90 81

Archeological Discoveries A450

Designs: Apollo, 3rd cent. 25q, Tombstone, Korce, 3rd cent. 80q, Apollo, diff. 1st cent. 1.10 l, Earthenware pot (child's head), Tren, 1st cent. 1.20 l, Man's head, Dyrrah, 2.20 l, Eros with Dolphin, statue Bronze Dyrrah, 3rd cent.

1984, Feb. 25 *Perf. 12x12½*

2100 A450 15q multi 15 15
2101 A450 25q multi 15 15
2102 A450 80q multi 40 18
2103 A450 1.10 l multi 55 22
2104 A450 1.20 l multi 60 25
2105 A450 2.20 l multi 1.10 50
Nos. 2100-2105 (6) 2.95
Set value 1.25

Clock Towers — A451

1984, Mar. 30 Litho. *Perf. 12*

2106	A451	15q	Gjirokaster	15	15
2107	A451	25q	Kavaje	15	15
2108	A451	80q	Elbasan	40	18
2109	A451	1.10 l	Tirana	55	22
2110	A451	1.20 l	Peqin	60	25
2111	A451	2.20 l	Kruje	1.10	50
			Nos. 2106-2111 (6)	2.95	
			Set value		1.25

40th Anniv. of Liberation A452

1984, Apr. 20 Litho. *Perf. 12*

2112	A452	15q	Student & microscope	15	15
2113	A452	25q	Guerrilla with flag	15	15
2114	A452	80q	Children with flag	40	18
2115	A452	1.10 l	Soldier	55	22
2116	A452	1.20 l	Workers with flag	60	25
2117	A452	2.20 l	Militia at dam	1.10	50
			Nos. 2112-2117 (6)	2.95	
			Set value		1.25

Children — A453

1984, May Litho. *Perf. 12*

2118	A453	15q	Children reading	15	15
2119	A453	25q	Young pioneers	15	15
2120	A453	60q	Gardening	30	15
2121	A453	2.80 l	Kite flying	1.40	60
			Nos. 2118-2121 (4)	2.00	
			Set value		84

War Martyr Type of 1980

Designs: 15q, Manush Almani, Mustafa Matohiti, Kastriot Muco. 25q, Zaho Koka, Reshit Collaku, Maliq Muco. 1.20 l, Lefter Talo, Tom Kola, Fuat Babani. 2.20 l, Myslysm Shyri, Dervish Hexali, Skender Caci.

1984, May 5 Litho. *Perf. 12*

2122	A410	15q	multi	15	15
2123	A410	25q	multi	15	15
2124	A410	1.20 l	multi	65	30
2125	A410	2.20 l	multi	1.25	60
			Nos. 2122-2125 (4)	2.20	
			Set value		1.00

A454

A455

1984, May 24 Litho. *Perf. 12*

2126	A454	80q	Enver Hoxha	45	20
2127	A454	1.10 l	Resistance fighter	65	30

40th anniv. of Permet Congress.

1984, June 12 Litho. *Perf. 12*

2128	A455	15q	Goalkeeper	15	15
2129	A455	25q	Referee	20	15
2130	A455	1.20 l	Map of Europe	90	45
2131	A455	2.20 l	Field diagram	1.75	90
			Nos. 2128-2131 (4)	3.00	1.65

European soccer championships.

Freedom Came, by Myrteza Fushekati A456

Paintings, Tirana Gallery of Figurative Art: 25q, Morning, by Zamir Mati, vert. 80q, My Darling, by Agim Zajmi, vert. 2.60 l, For the Partisans, by Arben Basha. 1.90 l, Eagle, by Zamir Mati, vert.

1984, June 12 *Perf. 12½*

2132	A456	15q	multi	15	15
2133	A456	25q	multi	16	15
2134	A456	80q	multi	48	25
2135	A456	2.60 l	multi	1.65	80
			Nos. 2132-2135 (4)	2.44	1.35

Souvenir Sheet

Perf. 12 Horiz.

2136	A456	1.90 l	multi	1.25	60

Flora — A457

1984, Aug. 20 Litho. *Perf. 12*

2137	A457	15q	Moraceae L.	15	15
2138	A457	25q	Plantaginaceae L.	25	15
2139	A457	1.20 l	Hypericaceae L.	1.15	58
2140	A457	2.20 l	Leontopodium alpinum	2.10	1.05
			Nos. 2137-2140 (4)	3.65	1.93

AUSIPEX '84, Melbourne, Sept. 21-30 — A458

1984, Sept. 21 Litho. *Perf. 12 Horiz.*

2141	A458	1.90 l	Sword dancers, emblem	1.50	75

A459

A460

Forestry, logging, UNFAO emblem.

1984, Sept. 25 *Perf. 12*

2142	A459	15q	Beech trees, transport	15	15
2143	A459	25q	Pine forest, logging cable	20	15
2144	A459	1.20 l	Firs, sawmill	90	45
2145	A459	2.20 l	Forester clearing woods	1.75	90
			Nos. 2142-2145 (4)	3.00	1.65

1984, Oct. 13 *Perf. 12½*

2146	A460	1.20 l	View of Gjirokaster	90	45

EURPHILA '84, Rome.

5th National Spartakiad — A461

1984, Oct. 19 *Perf. 12*

2147	A461	15q	Soccer	15	15
2148	A461	25q	Women's track & field	20	15
2149	A461	80q	Weight lifting	60	30
2150	A461	2.20 l	Pistol shooting	1.75	90
			Nos. 2147-2150 (4)	2.70	1.50

Souvenir Sheet

Perf. 12 Horiz.

2151	A461	1.90 l	Opening ceremony, red flags	1.50	75

November 29 Revolution, 40th Anniv. A462

1984, Nov. 29 *Perf. 12*

2152	A462	80q	Industrial reconstruction	60	30
2153	A462	1.10 l	Natl. flag, partisans	80	40

Souvenir Sheet

Perf. 12 Horiz.

2154	A462	1.90 l	Gen. Enver Hoxha reading 1944 declaration	1.50	75

Archaeological Discoveries from Illyria — A463

Designs: 15q, Iron Age water container. 80q, Terra-cotta woman's head, 6th-7th cent. B.C. 1.20 l, Aphrodite, bust, 3rd cent. B.C. 1.70 l, Nike, A.D. 1st-2nd cent. bronze statue.

1985, Feb. 25 *Perf. 12x12½*

2155	A463	15q	multi	16	15
2156	A463	80q	multi	78	40
2157	A463	1.20 l	multi	1.15	55
2158	A463	1.70 l	multi	1.75	85
			Nos. 2155-2158 (4)	3.84	1.95

Hysni Kapo (1915-1980), Natl. Labor Party Leader — A464

1985, Mar. 4 *Perf. 12*

2159	A464	90q	red & blk	85	42
2160	A464	1.10 l	chlky bl & blk	1.10	55

OLYMPHILEX '85, Lausanne A465

1985, Mar. 18

2161	A465	25q	Women's track & field	25	15
2162	A465	60q	Weight lifting	58	30
2163	A465	1.20 l	Soccer	1.15	55
2164	A465	1.50 l	Women's pistol shooting	1.25	65
			Nos. 2161-2164 (4)	3.23	1.65

Johann Sebastian Bach — A466

1985, Mar. 31

2165	A466	80q	Portrait, manuscript	78	40
2166	A466	1.20 l	Eisenach, birthplace	1.15	55

Gen. Enver Hoxha (1908-1985) A467

1985, Apr. 11 *Perf. 12½*

2167	A467	80q	multi	78	40

Souvenir Sheet

Imperf

2168	A467	1.90 l	multi	2.00	1.00

Natl. Frontier Guards, 40th Anniv. A468

1985, Apr. 25 *Perf. 12*

2169	A468	25q	Guardsman, family	25	15
2170	A468	80q	At frontier post	78	40

War Martyrs Type of 1980

Cameo portraits: 25q, Mitro Xhani (1916-44), Nimete Progonati (1929-44), Kozma Nushi (1909-44). 40q, Ajet Xhindoli (1922-43), Mustafa Kacaci (1903-44), Estref Caka Osaja (1919-44). 60q, Celo Sinani (1929-44), Lt. Ambro Andoni (1920-44), Meleq Gosnishti (1913-44). 1.20 l, Thodhori Mastora (1920-44), Fejzi Micoli (1919-45), Hysen Cino (1920-44).

1985, May 5

2171	A410	25q	multi	25	15
2172	A410	40q	multi	40	20
2173	A410	60q	multi	58	30
2174	A410	1.20 l	multi	1.15	55
			Nos. 2171-2174 (4)	2.38	1.20

Victory over Fascism A469

Designs: 25q, Rifle, red flag, inscribed May 9. 80q, Hand holding rifle, globe, broken swastika.

1985, May 9

2175 A469 25q multi 25 15
2176 A469 80q multi 78 40

End of World War II, 40th anniv.

Primary School, by Thoma Malo A470

Paintings, Tirana Gallery of Figurative Art: 80q, The Heroes, by Hysen Devolli, vert. 90q, In Our Days, by Angjelin Dodmasej, vert. 1.20 l, Going Off to Sow, by Ksenofon Dilo. 1.90 l, Foundry Workers, by Mikel Gurashi.

1985, June 25 *Perf. 12½*

2177 A470 25q multi 25 15
2178 A470 80q multi 78 40
2179 A470 90q multi 85 42
2180 A470 1.20 l multi 1.15 55
Nos. 2177-2180 (4) 3.03 1.52

Souvenir Sheet

Perf. 12 Horiz.

2181 A470 1.90 l multi 2.00 1.00

Basketball Championships, Spain — A471

Fruits — A472

Various plays.

1985, July 20 **Litho.** *Perf. 12*

2182 A471 25q dl bl & blk 22 15
2183 A471 80q dl grn & blk 78 40
2184 A471 1.20 l dl vio & blk 1.15 58
2185 A471 1.60 l dl rose & blk 1.50 75
Nos. 2182-2185 (4) 3.65 1.88

1985, Aug. 20

2186 A472 25q Oranges 22 15
2187 A472 80q Plums 78 40
2188 A472 1.20 l Apples 1.15 58
2189 A472 1.60 l Cherries 1.50 75
Nos. 2186-2189 (4) 3.65 1.88

Architecture A473

1985, Sept. 20

2190 A473 25q Kruja 22 15
2191 A473 80q Gjirokastra 78 40
2192 A473 1.20 l Berati 1.15 58
2193 A473 1.60 l Shkodera 1.50 75
Nos. 2190-2193 (4) 3.65 1.88

Natl. Folk Theater Festival — A474

Various scenes from folk plays.

1985, Oct. 6

2194 A474 25q multi 22 15
2195 A474 80q multi 78 40
2196 A474 1.20 l multi 1.15 58
2197 A474 1.60 l multi 1.50 75

Size: 56x82mm

Imperf

2198 A474 1.90 l multi 3.50 1.90
Nos. 2194-2198 (5) 7.15 3.78

Socialist People's Republic, 40th Anniv. A475

1986, Jan. 11 **Litho.** *Perf. 12½*

2199 A475 25q Natl. crest, vert. 25 15
2200 A475 80q Proclamation, 1946 78 40

A476 A477

Designs: 25q, Dam, River Drin, Melgun. 80q, Bust of Enver Hoxha, dam power house.

1986, Feb. 20 *Perf. 12*

2201 A476 25q multi 25 15
2202 A476 80q multi 78 40

Enver Hoxha hydro-electric power station, Koman.

1986, Mar. 20 **Litho.** *Perf. 12*

Flowers.

2203 A477 25q Gymnospermium shqipetarum 22 15
2204 A477 1.20 l Leucojum valentinum 1.15 58

Nos. 2203-2204 printed se-tenant. Sold only in booklets of 2; exist imperf.

A478

Famous Men — A479

Designs: 25q, Maxim Gorky, Russian author. 80q, Andre Marie Ampere, French physicist. 1.20 l, James Watt, English inventor of modern steam engine. 2.40 l, Franz Liszt, Hungarian composer.

1986, Apr. 20

2205 Strip of 4 4.40 2.20
a. A478 25q dull red brown 25 15
b. A478 80q dull violet 78 40
c. A478 1.20 l blue green 1.15 58
d. A478 2.40 l dull lilac rose 2.20 1.10

Size: 88x72mm

Imperf

2206 A479 1.90 l multi 1.75 88

No. 2206 has central area picturing Gorky, Ampere, Watt and Liszt, perf. 12½.

War Martyrs Type of 1980

Portraits: 25q, Ramiz Aranitasi (1923-43), Inajete Dumi (1924-44) and Laze Nuro Ferraj (1897-1944). 80q, Dine Kalenja (1919-44), Kozma Naska (1921-44), Met Hasa (1929-44) and Fahri Ramadani (1920-44). 1.20 l, Hiqmet Buzi (1927-44), Bajram Tusha (1922-42), Mumin Selami (1923-42) and Hajrfdin Bylyshi (1923-42).

1986, May 5 *Perf. 12*

2207 A410 25q multi 25 15
2208 A410 80q multi 78 40
2209 A410 1.20 l multi 1.15 55
Nos. 2207-2209 (3) 2.18 1.10

A480

1986 World Cup Soccer Championships, Mexico — A481

1986, May 31 **Litho.** *Perf. 12*

2210 A480 25q Globe, world cup 22 15
2211 A480 1.20 l Player, soccer ball 1.15 58

Size: 97x64mm

Imperf

2212 A481 1.90 l multi 1.75 88
Nos. 2210-2212 (3) 3.12 1.61

No. 2212 has central label, perf. 12½.

Transportation Workers' Day, 40th Anniv. — A482

1986, Aug. 10 **Litho.** *Perf. 12*

2213 A482 1.20 l multi 1.15 58

Prominent Albanians A483

Designs: 30q, Naim Frasheri (1846-1900), poet. 60q, Ndre Mjeda (1866-1937), poet. 90q, Petro Nini Luarasi (1865-1911), poet, journalist. 1 l, Andon Zako Cajupi (1866-1930), poet. 1.20 l, Millosh Gjergj Nikolla Migjeni (1911-1938), novelist. 2.60 l, Urani Rumbo (1884-1936), educator.

1986, Sept. 20 **Litho.** *Perf. 12*

2214 A483 30q multi 30 15
2215 A483 60q multi 58 30
2216 A483 90q multi 88 45
2217 A483 1 l multi 95 48
2218 A483 1.20 l multi 1.15 58
2219 A483 2.60 l multi 2.50 1.25
Nos. 2214-2219 (6) 6.36 3.21

Albanian Workers' Party, 9th Congress, Tirana A484

1986, Nov. 3 **Litho.** *Perf. 12*

2220 A484 30q multi 30 25

A485 A486

Albanian Workers' Party, 45th Anniv.: 30q, Handstamp, signature of Hoxha. 1.20 l, Marx, Engels, Lenin and Stalin, party building.

1986, Nov. 8

2221 A485 30q multi 30 15
2222 A485 1.20 l multi 1.15 58

1986, Nov. 29 *Perf. 12x12½*

Statue of Mother Albania.

2223 A486 10q peacock blue 15 15
2224 A486 20q henna brn 20 15
2225 A486 30q vermilion 30 15
2226 A486 50q dk olive bis 50 25
2227 A486 60q lt olive grn 58 30
2228 A486 80q rose 78 40
2229 A486 90q ultra 88 45
2230 A486 1.20 l green 1.15 58
2231 A486 1.60 l red vio 1.50 75
2232 A486 2.20 l myrtle grn 2.10 1.05
2233 A486 3 l brn org 2.75 1.40
2234 A486 6 l yel bister 5.50 2.25
Nos. 2223-2234 (12) 16.39 7.88

For surcharges see Nos. 2435-2439.

Artifacts A487

Designs: 30q, Head of Aesoulapius, 5th cent. B.C. Byllis, marble. 80q, Aphrodite, 3rd cent. B.C., Fier, terracotta. 1 l, Pan, 3rd-2nd cent, B.C., Byllis, bronze. 1.20 l, Jupiter, A.D. 2nd cent., Tirana, limestone.

1987, Feb. 20

2235 A487 30q multi 30 15
2236 A487 80q multi 78 40
2237 A487 1 l multi 95 48
2238 A487 1.20 l multi 1.15 58
Nos. 2235-2238 (4) 3.18 1.61

1st Albanian School, Cent. — A488

Famous Men — A489

Gun, quill pen, book of the alphabet and: 30q, Monument, vert. 80q, School, Korca. 1.20 l, Students.

1987, Mar. 7 *Perf. 12*

2239 A488 30q multi	30	15
2240 A488 80q multi	75	38
2241 A488 1.20 l multi	1.15	58
Nos. 2239-2241 (3)	2.20	1.11

1987, Apr. 20

Designs: 30q, Victor Hugo, French author. 80q, Galileo Galilei, Italian mathematician, philosopher. 90q, Charles Darwin, British biologist. 1.30 l, Miguel Cervantes, Spanish novelist.

2242 A489 30q multi	30	15
2243 A489 80q multi	75	38
2244 A489 90q multi	88	45
2245 A489 1.30 l multi	1.25	80
Nos. 2242-2245 (4)	3.18	1.78

World Food Day — A490

10th Trade Unions Cong. — A491

1987, May 20

2246 A490 30q Forsythia europaea	30	15
2247 A490 90q Moltkia doerfleri	88	45
2248 A490 2.10 l Wulfenia baldacii	2.00	1.00
Nos. 2246-2248 (3)	3.18	1.60

1987, June 25

2249 A491 1.20 l multi	1.15	58

Sowing, by Bujar Asllani — A492

Paintings in the Eponymous Museum, Tirana: 30q, The Sustenance of Industry, by Myrteza Fushekati, vert. 80q, The Gifted Partisan, by Skender Kokobobo, vert. 1.20 l, At the Forging Block, by Clirim Ceka.

Perf. 12x12½, 12½x12

1987, July 20 **Litho.**

2250 A492 30q multi	30	15
2251 A492 80q multi	80	40
2252 A492 1 l shown	1.00	50
2253 A492 1.20 l multi	1.20	60
Nos. 2250-2253 (4)	3.30	1.65

A493

OLYMPHILEX '87, Rome, Aug. 29-Sept. 6 — A494

Illustration A494 reduced.

1987, Aug. 29 **Litho.** *Perf. 12½*

2254 A493 30q Hammer throw	30	15
2255 A493 90q Running	90	45
2256 A493 1.10 l Shot put	1.15	58

Size: 85x60mm

2257 A494 1.90 l Runner, globe	2.00	1.00
Nos. 2254-2257 (4)	4.35	2.18

Famous Men — A495

Designs: 30q, Themistokli Germenji (1871-1917), author, politician. 80q, Bajram Curri (1862-1925), founder of the Albanian League. 90q, Aleks Stavre Drenova (1872-1947), poet. 1.30 l, Gjerasim D. Qiriazi (1861-1894), teacher, journalist.

1987, Sept. 30 *Perf. 12*

2258 A495 30q multi	30	15
2259 A495 80q multi	80	40
2260 A495 90q multi	90	45
2261 A495 1.30 l multi	1.30	65
Nos. 2258-2261 (4)	3.30	1.65

Albanian Labor Party Congress, Tirana A496

1987, Oct. 22 **Litho.** *Perf. 12*

2262 A496 1.20 l multi	1.20	60

Natl. Independence, 75th Anniv. — A497

Postal Administration, 75th Anniv. — A498

1987, Nov. 27

2263 A497 1.20 l State flag	1.20	60

1987, Dec. 5

2264 A498 90q P.O. emblem	90	45
2265 A498 1.20 l State seal	1.20	60

Art & Literature — A499

WHO, 40th Anniv. — A500

Portraits: 30q, Lord Byron (1788-1824), English Poet. 1.20 l, Eugene Delacroix (1798-1863), French painter.

1988, Mar. 10

2266 A499 30q org brn & blk	30	15
2267 A499 1.20 l pale vio & blk	1.20	60

1988, Apr. 7

2268 A500 90q multi	90	45
2269 A500 1.20 l multi	1.20	60

Flowers — A501

1988, May 20

2270 A501 30q *Sideritis raeseri*	30	15
2271 A501 90q *Lunaria telekiana*	90	45
2272 A501 2.10 l *Sanguisorba albanica*	2.10	1.05
a. Bklt. pane of 3, plus label	3.50	
Nos. 2270-2272 (3)	3.30	1.65

Nos. 2270-2272 issued in No. 2272a only.

10th Women's Federation Congress A502

1988, June 6

2273 A502 90q blk, red & dark org	90	45

European Soccer Championships — A503

Various athletes. 1.90 l, Goalie designs of Nos. 2274-2276.

1988, June 10

2274 A503 30q multicolored	30	15
2275 A503 80q multicolored	80	40
2276 A503 1.20 l multicolored	1.20	60

Size: 79x68mm

Imperf

2277 A503 1.90 l multicolored	1.90	95
Nos. 2274-2277 (4)	4.20	2.10

Migjeni (1911-1938), Poet — A507

1988, Aug. 26 **Litho.** *Perf. 12*

2285 A507 90q sil & brn	95	48

Ballads — A508

1988, Sept. 5

2286 A508 30q Dede Skurra	32	16
2287 A508 90q Omeri Iri	1.00	50
2288 A508 1.20 l Gjergj Elez Alia	1.30	65
Nos. 2286-2288 (3)	2.62	1.31

Folklore Festival Type of 1978

1988, Oct. 6

2289 A388 30q Kerchief Dance	32	16
2290 A388 1.20 l Dancers with raised arm	1.30	65

Enver Hoxha Museum A510

Perf. 12x12½, 12½x12

1988, Oct. 16 **Litho.**

2291 A510 90q Portrait, vert.	72	36
2292 A510 1.20 l shown	95	48

Enver Hoxha (1908-1985), Communist leader.

Locomotives, Map Showing Rail Network — A512

1989, Feb. 28 **Litho.** *Perf. 12½x12*

2295 A512 30q 1947	22	15
2296 A512 90q 1949	65	32
2297 A512 1.20 l 1978	85	42
2298 A512 1.80 l 1985	1.25	65
2299 A512 2.40 l 1988	1.70	85
Nos. 2295-2299 (5)	4.67	2.39

Archaeological Treasures A513

Designs: 30q, Illyrian grave. 90q, Warrior on horseback.

1989, Mar. 10 **Litho.** *Perf. 12*

2300 A513 30q blk & tan	22	15
2301 A513 90q blk & dl grn	65	34
2302 A513 2.10 l shown	1.50	75
Nos. 2300-2302 (3)	2.37	1.24

Folklore — A514

1989, Apr. 5 **Litho.** *Perf. 12x12½*

2303 A514 30q multicolored	22	15
2304 A514 80q multi, diff.	58	30
2305 A514 1 l multi, diff.	72	36
2306 A514 1.20 l multi, diff.	86	44
Nos. 2303-2306 (4)	2.38	1.25

Flowers — A515

Famous People — A516

Designs: 30q, *Aster albanicus.* 90q, *Orchis x paparisti.* 2.10 l, *Orchis albanica.*

1989, May 10 *Perf. 12*

2307	A515	30q	multicolored	22	15
2308	A515	90q	multicolored	65	32
2309	A515	2.10 l	multicolored	1.50	75
			Nos. 2307-2309 (3)	2.37	1.22

1989, June 3

Designs: 30q, Johann Strauss the Younger (1825-1899), composer. 80q, Marie Curie (1867-1834), chemist. 1 l, Federico Garcia Lorca (1898-1936), poet. 1.20 l, Albert Einstein (1879-1955), physicist.

2310	A516	30q	gold & blk brn	22	15
2311	A516	80q	gold & blk brn	58	30
2312	A516	1 l	gold & blk brn	75	38
2313	A516	1.20 l	gold & blk brn	85	42
			Nos. 2310-2313 (4)	2.40	1.25

6th Congress of Albanian Democratic Front A517

1989, June 26

2314	A517	1.20 l	multicolored	1.30	65

French Revolution, Bicent. — A518

Designs: 90q, Storming of the Bastille. 1.20 l, Statue.

1989, July 7 **Litho.** *Perf. 12½*

2315	A518	90q	multicolored	75	38
2316	A518	1.20 l	shown	1.00	50

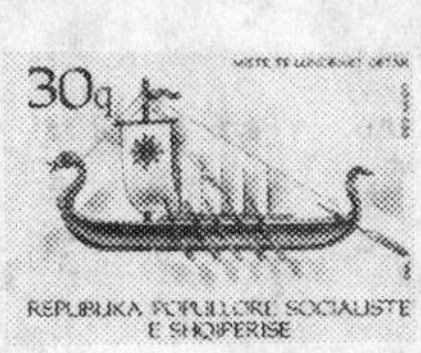

Illyrian Ship — A519

1989, July 25 *Perf. 12*

2317	A519	30q	shown	22	15
2318	A519	80q	Caravel	58	30
2319	A519	90q	3-masted schooner	65	34
2320	A519	1.30 l	Modern cargo ship	95	48
			Nos. 2317-2320 (4)	2.40	1.27

A520

A521

Famous Men: 30q, Pjeter Bogdani (1625-1689), writer. 80q, Gavril Dara (1826-1889), poet. 90q, Thimi Mitko (1820-1890), writer. 1.30 l, Kole Idromeno (1860-1939), painter.

1989, Aug. 30 **Litho.** *Perf. 12*

2321	A520	30q	multicolored	30	15
2322	A520	80q	multicolored	80	40
2323	A520	90q	multicolored	90	45
2324	A520	1.30 l	multicolored	1.30	65
			Nos. 2321-2324 (4)	3.30	1.65

1989, Sept. 29

2325	A521	90q	shown	72	35
2326	A521	1.20 l	Workers	95	48

First Communist International, 125th anniv.

Spartakiad Games — A522

1989, Oct. 27 *Perf. 12x12½*

2327	A522	30q	Gymasnastics	22	15
2328	A522	80q	Soccer	58	30
2329	A522	1 l	Cycling	72	36
2330	A522	1.20 l	Running	86	44
			Nos. 2327-2330 (4)	2.38	1.25

Miniature Sheet

45th Anniv. of Liberation — A523

1989, Nov. 29 *Perf. 12x12½*

2331		Sheet of 4	2.50	1.25
a.	A523	30q Revolutionary	22	15
b.	A523	80q "45"	58	30
c.	A523	1 l Coat of arms	72	36
d.	A523	1.20 l Workers	86	44

Rupicapra Rupicapra — A524

1990, Mar. 15 *Perf. 12*

2332	A524	10q	Two adults	15	15
2333	A524	30q	Adult, kid	32	16
2334	A524	80q	Adult	82	42
2335	A524	90q	Adult head	92	45
a.			Block of 4, #2332-2335	2.16	1.08

World Wildlife Fund.

Tribal Masks — A525

1990, Apr. 4 *Perf. 12x12½*

2336	A525	30q	shown	32	16
2337	A525	90q	multi, diff.	95	48
2338	A525	1.20 l	multi, diff.	1.25	65
2339	A525	1.80 l	multi, diff.	1.90	95
			Nos. 2336-2339 (4)	4.42	2.24

Mushrooms A526

1990, Apr. 28 **Litho.** *Perf. 12*

2340	A526	30q	Amanita caesarea	25	15
2341	A526	90q	Lepiota procera	75	40
2342	A526	1.20 l	Boletus edulis	1.00	50
2343	A526	1.80 l	Clathrus cancelatus	1.50	75
			Nos. 2340-2343 (4)	3.50	1.80

First Postage Stamp, 150th Anniv. A527

1990, May 6 *Perf. 12*

2344	A527	90q	shown	95	48
2345	A527	1.20 l	Post rider	1.25	62
2346	A527	1.80 l	Carriage	1.85	95
a.			Bklt. pane of 3, #2344-2346 + label	4.25	
			Nos. 2344-2346 (3)	4.05	2.05

World Cup Soccer, Italy — A528

1990, June **Litho.** *Perf. 12*

2347	A528	30q	multicolored	48	24
2348	A528	90q	multi, diff.	1.45	75
2349	A528	1.20 l	multi, diff.	1.95	1.00

Size: 80x63mm

Imperf

2350	A528	3.30 l	multi, diff.	5.30	2.65
			Nos. 2347-2350 (4)	9.18	4.64

Vincent Van Gogh, Death Cent. A529

Self portraits and: 30q, Details from various paintings. 90q, Woman in field. 2.10 l, Asylum. 2.40 l, Self-portrait.

1990, July 27

2351	A529	30q	multicolored	48	24
2352	A529	90q	multicolored	1.45	75
2353	A529	2.10 l	multicolored	3.40	1.70

Size: 87x73mm

Imperf

2354	A529	2.40 l	multicolored	1.85	95
			Nos. 2351-2354 (4)	7.18	3.64

Albanian Folklore — A530

Scenes from medieval folktale of "Gjergj Elez Alia": 30q, Alia lying wounded. 90q, Alia being helped onto horse. 1.20 l, Alia fighting Bajloz. 1.80 l, Alia on horseback over severed head of Bajloz.

1990, Aug. 30 *Perf. 12½x12*

2355	A530	30q	multicolored	48	24
2356	A530	90q	multicolored	1.45	72
2357	A530	1.20 l	multicolored	1.95	95
2358	A530	1.80 l	multicolored	2.90	1.45
			Nos. 2355-2358 (4)	6.78	3.36

Founding of Berat, 2400th Anniv. A531

Designs: 30q, Xhamia E Plumbit. 90q, Kisha E Shen Triadhes. 1.20 l, Ura E Beratit. 1.80 l, Onufri-Piktor Mesjetar. 2.40 l, Nikolla-Piktor Mesjetar.

1990, Sept. 20 *Perf. 12½*

2359		Block of 5 + 4 labels	4.20	2.10
a.	A531	30q multi	20	15
b.	A531	90q multi	65	32
c.	A531	1.20 l multi	70	35
d.	A531	1.80 l multi	1.25	65
e.	A531	2.40 l multi	1.40	70

No. 2359 was sold in souvenir folders for 9.90 l.

Illyrian Heroes — A532

1990, Oct. 20 *Perf. 12*

2360	A532	30q	Pirroja	48	24
2361	A532	90q	Teuta	1.45	72
2362	A532	1.20 l	Bato	1.95	95
2363	A532	1.80 l	Bardhyli	2.90	1.45
			Nos. 2360-2363 (4)	6.78	3.36

Intl. Literacy Year — A533

1990, Oct. 30

2364	A533	90q	lt bl & multi	1.45	72
2365	A533	1.20 l	pink & multi	1.95	95

Albanian Horseman by Eugene Delacroix A534

Designs: 1.20 l, Albanian Woman by Camille Corot. 1.80 l, Skanderbeg by unknown artist.

1990, Nov. 30 *Perf. 12x12½*

2366	A534	30q	multicolored	48	24
2367	A534	1.20 l	multicolored	1.95	95
2368	A534	1.80 l	multicolored	2.90	1.45
			Nos. 2366-2368 (3)	5.33	2.64

Isa Boletini (1864-1916), Freedom Fighter — A535

1991, Jan. 23 **Litho.** *Perf. 12x12½*

2369	A535	90q	Portrait	65	32
2370	A535	1.20 l	shown	90	45

Pierre Auguste Renoir (1841-1919), Painter — A537

Paintings: 30q, Girl Reading, 1876, vert. 90q, The Swing, 1876, vert. 1.20 l, Boating Party, 1868-1869. 1.80 l, Flowers and grapes, 1878. 3 l, Self-portrait.

1991, Feb. 25 *Perf. 12½x12*

2373	A537	30q	multicolored	20	15
2374	A537	90q	multicolored	65	32
2375	A537	1.20 l	multicolored	90	45
2376	A537	1.80 l	multicolored	1.30	65

Size: 95x75mm

Imperf

2377	A537	3 l	multicolored	4.80	2.40
			Nos. 2373-2377 (5)	7.85	3.97

Flowers — A538

1991, Mar. 30 *Perf. 12*

2378	A538	30q	Cistus albanicus	48	24
2379	A538	90q	Trifolium pilczii	1.45	72
2380	A538	1.80 l	Lilium albanicum	2.90	1.45
			Nos. 2378-2380 (3)	4.83	2.41

Legend of Rozafa — A539

Various scenes from legend.

1991, Sept. 30 Litho. *Perf. 12x12½*

2381	A539	30q	multicolored	48	24
2382	A539	90q	multicolored	1.45	72
2383	A539	1.20 l	multicolored	1.95	95
2384	A539	1.80 l	multicolored	2.90	1.45
			Nos. 2381-2384 (4)	6.78	3.36

Wolfgang Amadeus Mozart, Death Bicent. — A540

1991, Oct. 5 Litho. *Perf. 12*

2385	A540	90q	Conducting	70	35
2386	A540	1.20 l	Portrait	90	45
2387	A540	1.80 l	Playing piano	1.40	70

Size: 89x70mm

Imperf

2388	A540	3 l	Medal, score	4.00	4.00
			Nos. 2385-2388 (4)	7.00	5.50

Airplanes A541

Designs: 30q, Glider, Otto Lilienthal, 1896. 80q, Avion III, Clement Ader, 1897. 90q, Flyer, Wright Brothers, 1903. 1.20 l, Concorde. 1.80 l, Tupolev 114. 2.40 l, Dornier 31 E.

1992, Jan. 27 Litho. *Perf. 12½x12*

2389	A541	30q	multicolored	48	24
2390	A541	80q	multicolored	1.30	65
2391	A541	90q	multicolored	1.45	72
2392	A541	1.20 l	multicolored	1.95	95
2393	A541	1.80 l	multicolored	2.90	1.45
2394	A541	2.40 l	multicolored	4.00	2.00
			Nos. 2389-2394 (6)	12.08	6.01

No. 2393 misidentifies a Tupolev 144.

Explorers A542

1992, Jan. 10

2395	A542	30q	Bering	48	24
2396	A542	90q	Columbus	1.45	72
2397	A542	1.80 l	Magellan	2.90	1.45
			Nos. 2395-2397 (3)	4.83	2.41

1992 Winter Olympics, Albertville A543

1992, Feb. 15 Litho. *Perf. 12½*

2398	A543	30q	Ski jumping	24	15
2399	A543	90q	Cross country skiing	70	35
2400	A543	1.20 l	Pairs figure skating	95	48
2401	A543	1.80 l	Luge	1.45	70
			Nos. 2398-2401 (4)	3.34	1.68

Participation of Albania in Conference on Security and Cooperation in Europe, Berlin (1991) — A544

1992, Mar. 31 Litho. *Perf. 12½x12*

2402	A544	90q	shown	*95*	*95*
2403	A544	1.20 l	Flags, map	*1.25*	*1.25*
a.			Pair, #2402-2403	*2.25*	*2.25*

Dated 1991. Issued in sheets containing 2 #2403a, 3 each #2402-2403 + 2 labels.

Albanian Admission to CEPT A545

1992, Apr. 25 Litho. *Perf. 12½*

2404	A545	90q	Envelopes, CEPT emblem	90	90
2405	A545	1.20 l	shown	1.20	1.20
a.			Pair, #2404-2405	2.25	2.25

Issued in sheets containing 2 #2405a, 3 each #2404-2405 and 2 labels.

Martyrs' Day — A546

1992, May 5 *Perf. 12x12½*

2406	A546	90q	Freedom flame, vert.	*1.00*	*1.00*

Perf. 12½x12

2407	A546	4.10 l	Flowers	*4.50*	*4.50*

European Soccer Championships, Sweden'92 — A547

Various stylized designs of soccer plays.

1992, June 10 Litho. *Perf. 12*

2408	A547	30q	green & lt grn	15	15
2409	A547	90q	blue & pink	25	25
2410	A547	10.80 l	henna & tan	3.00	3.00

Size: 90x70mm

Imperf

2411	A547	5 l	tan, lt green & pink	1.40	1.40
			Nos. 2408-2411 (4)	4.80	4.80

1992 Summer Olympics, Barcelona A548

1992, June 14 Litho. *Perf. 12*

2412	A548	30q	Tennis	*35*	*35*
2413	A548	90q	Baseball	*1.00*	*1.00*
2414	A548	1.80 l	Table tennis	*2.00*	*2.00*

Size: 90x70mm

Imperf

2415	A548	5 l	Torch bearer	*1.45*	*1.45*
			Nos. 2412-2415 (4)	*4.80*	*4.80*

United Europe A549

1992, July 10 Litho. *Perf. 12*

2416	A549	1.20 l	multicolored	90	45

Horses A550

1992, Aug. 10 Litho. *Perf. 12*

2417	A550	30q	Native	*15*	*15*
2418	A550	90q	Nonius	*24*	*24*
2419	A550	1.20 l	Arabian, vert.	*32*	*32*
2420	A550	10.60 l	Haflinger, vert.	*2.75*	*2.75*
			Nos. 2417-2420 (4)	*3.46*	*3.46*

Discovery of America, 500th Anniv. A551

Map of North and South America and: 60q, Columbus, sailing ships. 3.20 l, Columbus meeting natives.

1992, Aug. 20

2421	A551	60q	blk, bl & gray	*24*	*24*
2422	A551	3.20 l	blk, brn & gray	*1.25*	*1.25*

Size: 90x70mm

Imperf

2423	A551	5 l	Map, Columbus		

A552

A553

Mother Theresa, infant.

1992, Oct. 4 Litho. *Perf. 12x12½*

2424	A552	40q	fawn	*15*	*15*
2425	A552	60q	brown	*15*	*15*
2426	A552	1 l	violet	*15*	*15*
2427	A552	1.80 l	gray	*28*	*28*
2428	A552	2 l	red	*30*	*30*
2429	A552	2.40 l	green	*35*	*35*
2430	A552	3.20 l	blue	*48*	*48*
2431	A552	5.60 l	rose violet	*85*	*85*
2432	A552	7.20 l	olive	*1.05*	*1.05*
2433	A552	10 l	orange brown	*1.50*	*1.50*
			Nos. 2424-2433 (10)	*5.26*	*5.26*

1993, Apr. 25 Litho. *Perf. 12*

2434	A553	16 l	multicolored	*2.50*	*2.50*

Visit of Pope John Paul II.

POSTA SHQIPTARE

Nos. 2223-2226, 2229 Surcharged

3 Lekë

1993, May 2 Litho. *Perf. 12x12½*

2435	A486	3 l	on 10q	*58*	*58*
2436	A486	6.50 l	on 20q	*1.25*	*1.25*
2437	A486	13 l	on 30q	*2.55*	*2.55*
2438	A486	20 l	on 90q	*3.90*	*3.90*
2439	A486	30 l	on 50q	*5.85*	*5.85*
			Nos. 2435-2439 (5)	*14.13*	*14.13*

Lef Nosi (1873-1945), Minister of Posts — A554

1993, May 5 Litho. *Perf. 12*

2440	A554	6.50 l olive brown & bister	*90*	*90*

First Albanian postage stamps, 80th anniv.

Europa A555

Contemporary paintings by: 3 l, A. Zajmi, vert. 7 l, E. Hila. 20 l, B. Ahmeti-Peizazh.

1993, May 28 Litho. *Perf. 12*

2441	A555	3 l multicolored	*55*	*55*
2442	A555	7 l multicolored	*1.25*	*1.25*

Size: 116x122mm

2443	A555	20 l multicolored	*3.75*	*3.75*
		Nos. 2441-2443 (3)	*5.55*	*5.55*

1993 Mediterranean Games, France A556

1993, June 20 Litho. *Perf. 12*

2444	A556	3 l Running	55	55
2445	A556	16 l Kayaking	3.00	3.00
2446	A556	21 l Cycling	3.75	3.75

Size: 111x78mm

Imperf

2447	A556	20 l Mediterranean map	3.50	3.50
		Nos. 2444-2447 (4)	10.80	10.80

Frang Bardhi, Author, 350th Death Anniv. — A557

1993, Aug. 20 Litho. *Perf. 12x12½*

2448	A557	6.50 l shown	1.10	1.10

Size: 89x101mm

Imperf

2449	A557	20 l Writing at desk	3.50	3.50

SEMI-POSTAL STAMPS

Nos. 148-151 Surcharged in Red and Black

+ 5 qind.

1924, Nov. 1

B1	A18	5q + 5q yel grn	2.75	3.50
B2	A18	10q + 5q carmine	2.75	3.50
B3	A18	25q + 5q dark blue	2.75	3.50
B4	A18	50q + 5q dark grn	2.75	3.50
		Nos. B1-B4 (4)	11.00	14.00

Nos. B1 to B4 with Additional Surcharge in Red and Black

+ 5 qind.

1924

B5	A18	5q + 5q + 5q yel grn	2.75	3.50
B6	A18	10q + 5q + 5q car	2.75	3.50
B7	A18	25q + 5q + 5q dk bl	2.75	3.50
B8	A18	50q + 5q + 5q dk grn	2.75	3.50
		Nos. B5-B8 (4)	11.00	14.00

Issued under Italian Dominion

Nurse and Child — SP1

1943, Apr. 1 Unwmk. Photo. *Perf. 14*

B9	SP1	5q + 5q dark grn	15	15
B10	SP1	10q + 10q olive brn	15	15
B11	SP1	15q + 10q rose red	15	15
B12	SP1	25q + 15q saphire	15	18
B13	SP1	30q + 20q violet	18	22
B14	SP1	50q + 25q dk org	22	25
B15	SP1	65q + 30q grnsh blk	32	35
B16	SP1	1fr + 40q chestnut	70	75
		Nos. B9-B16 (8)	2.02	2.20

The surtax was for the control of tuberculosis.
For surcharges, see Nos. B24-B27.

Issued under German Administration

War Victims — SP2

1944, Sept. 22

B17	SP2	5q + 5(q) dp grn	2.10	2.75
B18	SP2	10q + 5(q) dp brn	2.10	2.75
B19	SP2	15q + 5(q) car lake	2.10	2.75
B20	SP2	25q + 10(q) dp blue	2.10	2.75
B21	SP2	1fr + 50q dk olive	2.10	2.75
B22	SP2	2fr + 1(fr) purple	2.10	2.75
B23	SP2	3fr + 1.50(fr) dk org	2.10	2.75
		Nos. B17-B23 (7)	14.70	19.25

Surtax for victims of World War II.

Independent State

Nos. B9 to B12 Surcharged in Carmine

1945, May 4 Unwmk. *Perf. 14*

B24	SP1	30q +15q on 5q+5q	1.40	1.40
B25	SP1	50q +25q on 10q+10q	1.40	1.40
B26	SP1	1fr +50q on 15q+10q	4.00	4.00
B27	SP1	2fr +1fr on 25q+15q	7.00	7.00
		Nos. B24-B27 (4)	13.80	13.80

The surtax was for the Albanian Red Cross.

People's Republic

Nos. 361 to 366 Overprinted in Red (cross) and Surcharged in Black

KONGRESI
K.K.SH.
24-25-11-46
+0.10

1946, July 16 *Perf. 11*

B28	A57	20q + 10q bluish grn	4.50	4.50
B29	A57	30q + 15q dp org	4.50	4.50
B30	A57	40q + 20q brown	4.50	4.50
B31	A57	60q + 30q red vio	4.50	4.50
B32	A57	1fr + 50q rose red	4.50	4.50
B33	A57	3fr + 1.50fr dk bl	4.50	4.50
		Nos. B28-B33 (6)	27.00	27.00

To honor and benefit the Congress of the Albanian Red Cross.

Counterfeits: lithographed, dull gum. Genuine: typographed, shiny gum.

Catalogue values for unused stamps in this section, from this point to the end of the section, are for Never Hinged items.

First Aid and Red Cross — SP3

Designs: 25q+5q, Nurse carrying child on stretcher. 65q+25q, Symbolic blood transfusion. 80q+40q, Mother and child.

1967, Dec. 1 Litho. *Perf. 11½x12*

B34	SP3	15q + 5q blk, red & brn	60	45
B35	SP3	25q + 5q multi	65	60
B36	SP3	65q + 25q multi	2.00	65
B37	SP3	80q + 40q multi	3.25	1.50
		Nos. B34-B37 (4)	6.50	3.20

6th congress of the Albanian Red Cross.

AIR POST STAMPS

Airplane Crossing Mountains AP1

Wmk. 125

1925, May 30 Typo. *Perf. 14*

C1	AP1	5q green	45	45
C2	AP1	10q rose red	45	45
C3	AP1	25q deep blue	48	48
C4	AP1	50q dark green	95	95
C5	AP1	1fr dk vio & blk	1.75	1.75
C6	AP1	2fr ol grn & vio	2.75	2.75
C7	AP1	3fr brn org & dk grn	4.75	4.75
		Nos. C1-C7 (7)	11.58	11.58

Nos. C1-C7 exist imperf.
For overprint, see Nos. C8-C28.

Nos. C1-C7 Overprinted

Rep. Shqiptare

1927, Jan. 18

C8	AP1	5q green	3.00	3.00
a.		Dbl. overprint, one invtd.	30.00	
C9	AP1	10q rose red	3.00	3.00
a.		Inverted overprint	30.00	
b.		Dbl. overprint, one invtd.	30.00	
C10	AP1	25q deep blue	1.60	1.60
C11	AP1	50q dark grn	1.60	1.60
a.		Inverted overprint	30.00	
C12	AP1	1fr dk vio & blk	1.60	1.60
a.		Inverted overprint	30.00	
b.		Double overprint	30.00	
C13	AP1	2fr ol grn & vio	1.60	1.60
C14	AP1	3fr brn org & dk grn	2.75	2.75
		Nos. C8-C14 (7)	15.15	15.15

Nos. C1-C7 Overprinted

REP. SHQYPTARE
Fluturim' i I-ar
Vlonë--Brindisi
21. IV. 1928

1928, Apr. 21

C15	AP1	5q green	90	90
a.		Inverted overprint	18.00	
C16	AP1	10q rose red	90	90
C17	AP1	25q deep blue	90	90
C18	AP1	50q dark grn	90	90
C19	AP1	1fr dk vio & blk	14.00	14.00
C20	AP1	2fr ol grn & vio	14.00	14.00
C21	AP1	3fr brn org & dk grn	14.00	14.00
		Nos. C15-C21 (7)	45.60	45.60

First flight across the Adriatic, Valona to Brindisi, Apr. 21, 1928.

The variety "SHQYRTARE" occurs once in the sheet for each value. Value 3 times normal.

Nos. C1-C7 Overprinted in Red Brown

Mbr. Shqiptare

1929, Dec. 1

C22	AP1	5q green	2.75	2.75
C23	AP1	10q rose red	2.75	2.75
C24	AP1	25q deep blue	2.75	2.75
C25	AP1	50q dk grn	12.00	14.00
C26	AP1	1fr dk vio & blk	150.00	165.00
C27	AP1	2fr ol grn	150.00	165.00
C28	AP1	3fr brn org & dk grn	150.00	165.00
		Nos. C22-C28 (7)	470.25	517.25

Excellent counterfeits exist.

King Zog and Airplane over Tirana — AP2

AP3

1930, Oct. 8 Photo. Unwmk.

C29	AP2	5q yel grn	24	24
C30	AP2	15q rose red	32	32
C31	AP2	20q slate bl	48	48
C32	AP2	50q olive grn	60	60
C33	AP3	1fr dark blue	1.40	1.40
C34	AP3	2fr olive brn	4.75	4.75
C35	AP3	3fr purple	6.00	6.00
		Nos. C29-C35 (7)	13.79	13.79

For overprints and surcharges, see Nos. C36-C45.

Nos. C29-C35 Overprinted

TIRANE-ROME
6 KORRIK 1931

1931, July 6

C36	AP2	5q yel grn	1.25	1.25
a.		Double overprint	*65.00*	
C37	AP2	15q rose red	1.25	1.25
C38	AP2	20q slate blue	1.25	1.25
C39	AP2	50q olive grn	1.25	1.25
C40	AP3	1fr dark blue	10.00	10.00
C41	AP3	2fr olive brn	10.00	10.00
C42	AP3	3fr purple	10.00	10.00
a.		Inverted overprint	*175.00*	
		Nos. C36-C42 (7)	35.00	35.00

1st air post flight from Tirana to Rome.

Only a very small part of this issue was sold to the public. Most of the stamps were given to the Aviation Company to help provide funds for conducting the service.

Issued under Italian Dominion

Nos. C29-C30 Overprinted in Black

Mbledhja Kushtetuëse 12-IV-1939 XVII

1939, Apr. 19 Unwmk. *Perf. 14*

C43	AP2	5q yel green	50	50
C44	AP2	15q rose red	50	50

No. C32 With Additional Surcharge

C45	AP2	20q on 50q ol grn	1.00	1.00
a.		Inverted overprint		
		Nos. C43-C45 (3)	2.00	2.00

See note after No. 309.

King Victor Emmanuel III and Plane over Mountains AP4

1939, Aug. 4 Photo.

C46	AP4	20q brown	5.25	2.75

Shepherds AP5

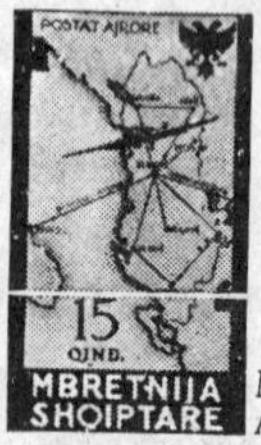

Map of Albania Showing Air Routes — AP6

Designs: 20q, Victor Emmanuel III and harbor view. 50q, Woman and river valley. 1fr, Bridge at Vezirit. 2fr, Ruins. 3fr, Women waving to plane.

1940, Mar. 20 Unwmk.

C47	AP5	5q green	16	16
C48	AP6	15q rose red	16	16
C49	AP5	20q deep blue	16	16
C50	AP6	50q brown	42	42
C51	AP5	1fr myrtle grn	85	90
C52	AP6	2fr brn blk	2.50	3.00
C53	AP6	3fr rose vio	7.50	8.50
		Nos. C47-C53 (7)	11.75	13.30

People's Republic

Vuno-Himare AP12

Albanian Towns: 1 l, 10 l, Rozafat-Shkoder. 2 l, 20 l, Keshtjelle-Butrinto.

1950, Dec. 15 Engr. *Perf. 12½x12*

C54	AP12	50q gray blk	15	15
C55	AP12	1 l red brn	15	15
C56	AP12	2 l ultra	30	15
C57	AP12	5 l dp grn	65	20
C58	AP12	10 l dp bl	1.50	85
C59	AP12	20 l purple	4.25	1.75
		Nos. C54-C59 (6)	7.00	3.25

15-Cent Minimum Value
The minimum value for a single stamp is 15 cents. This value reflects the costs of handling inexpensive stamps.

Nos. C56-C58 Surcharged with New Value and Bars in Red or Black

1952-53

C60	AP12	50q on 2 l (R)	30.00	30.00
C61	AP12	50q on 5 l	5.00	2.75
C62	AP12	2.50 l on 5 l (R)	60.00	60.00
C63	AP12	2.50 l on 10 l	5.00	2.75
		Nos. C60-C63 (4)	100.00	95.50

Issued: #C60, C62, 12/26/52; #C61, C63, 3/14/53.

Catalogue values for unused stamps in this section, from this point to the end of the section, are for Never Hinged items.

Banner with Lenin, Map of Stalingrad and Tanks — AP13

1963, Feb. 2 Litho. *Perf. 14*

C67	AP13	7 l grn & dp car	1.50	60

20th anniversary, Battle of Stalingrad.

Sputnik and Sun — AP14

Designs: 3 l, Lunik 4. 5 l, Lunik 3 photographing far side of the Moon. 8 l, Venus space probe. 12 l, Mars 1.

1963, Oct. 31 Unwmk. *Perf. 12*

C68	AP14	2 l org, yel & blk	22	15
C69	AP14	3 l multi	28	15
C70	AP14	5 l rose lil, yel & blk	65	30
C71	AP14	8 l multi	1.10	42
C72	AP14	12 l blue & org	2.50	95
		Nos. C68-72 (5)	4.75	1.97

Russian interplanetary explorations.

Nos. C68 and C71 Overprinted: "Riccione 23-8-1964"

1964, Aug. 23

C73	AP14	2 l org, yel & blk	7.00	3.50
C74	AP14	8 l multicolored	10.50	5.25

Intl. Space Exhib. in Riccione, Italy.

Plane over Berat AP15

1975, Nov. 25 Litho. *Perf. 12*

C75	AP15	20q multi	15	15
C76	AP15	40q Gjirokaster	15	15
C77	AP15	60q Sarande	15	15
C78	AP15	90q Durres	24	15
C79	AP15	1.20 l Kruje	40	15
C80	AP15	2.40 l Boga	90	32
C81	AP15	4.05 l Tirana	1.40	70
		Nos. C75-C81 (7)	3.39	
		Set value		1.42

SPECIAL DELIVERY STAMPS

Issued under Italian Dominion

King Victor Emmanuel III — SD1

1940 Unwmk. Photo. *Perf. 14*

E1	SD1	25q bright violet	38	38
E2	SD1	50q red orange	1.25	1.50

Issued under German Administration

No. E1 Overprinted in Carmine

14 Shtator 1943

1943

E3	SD1	25q bright violet	12.00	14.00

Proclamation of Albanian independence.

POSTAGE DUE STAMPS

Nos. 35-39 Handstamped in Various Colors

1914, Feb. 23 Unwmk. *Perf. 14*

J1	A3	2q org brn & buff (Bl)	1.00	60
J2	A3	5q green (R)	1.00	75
J3	A3	10q rose red (Bl)	1.40	75
J4	A3	25q dark blue (R)	1.75	1.00
J5	A3	50q vio & red (Bk)	2.00	1.40
		Nos. J1-J5 (5)	7.15	4.50

The two parts of the overprint are handstamped separately. Stamps exist with one or both handstamps inverted, double, omitted or in wrong color.

Nos. 48-51 Overprinted in Black **TAKSË**

1914, Apr. 16

J6	A3 (a)	10pa on 5q green	2.00	2.00
J7	A3 (a)	20pa on 10q rose red	2.00	2.00
J8	A3 (b)	1gr on 25q blue	2.00	2.00
J9	A3 (b)	2gr on 50q vio & red	2.00	2.00
		Nos. J6-J9 (4)	8.00	8.00

Same Design as Regular Issue of 1919, Overprinted

1919, Feb. 10 *Perf. 11½, 12½*

J10	A8	(4)q on 4h rose	3.75	3.75
J11	A8	(10)q on 10k red, *grn*	3.75	3.75
J12	A8	20q on 2k org, *gray*	3.75	3.75
J13	A8	50q on 5k brn, *yel*	3.75	3.75
		Nos. J10-J13 (4)	15.00	15.00

Fortress at Scutari — D3

D5

Post Horn Overprinted in Black

1920, Apr. 1 *Perf. 14x13*

J14	D3	4q olive green	25	32
J15	D3	10q rose red	25	32
J16	D3	20q bister brn	25	32
J17	D3	50q black	45	52
		Nos. J14-J17 (4)	1.20	1.48

1922 *Perf. 12½, 11½*

Background of Red Wavy Lines

J23	D5	4q black, *red*	65	90
J24	D5	10q black, *red*	65	90
J25	D5	20q black, *red*	65	90
J26	D5	50q black, *red*	65	90
		Nos. J23-J26 (4)	2.60	3.60

Same Overprinted in White

Republika Shqiptare

1925

J27	D5	4q black, *red*	60	90
J28	D5	10q black, *red*	60	90
J29	D5	20q black, *red*	60	90
J30	D5	50q black, *red*	60	90
		Nos. J27-J30 (4)	2.40	3.60

The 10q with overprint in gold was a trial printing. It was not put in use.

D7

Coat of Arms — D8

Overprinted "QINDAR" in Red

1926, Dec. 24 *Perf. 13½x13*

J31	D7	10q dark blue	24	20
J32	D7	20q green	48	40
J33	D7	30q red brown	80	60
J34	D7	50q dark brown	1.25	1.00
		Nos. J31-J34 (4)	2.77	2.20

Wmk. Double Headed Eagle (220)

1930, Sept. 1 Photo. *Perf. 14, 14½*

J35	D8	10q dark blue	4.00	4.00
J36	D8	20q rose red	1.00	1.00
J37	D8	30q violet	1.00	1.00
J38	D8	50q dark green	1.25	1.25
		Nos. J35-J38 (4)	7.25	7.25

Nos. J36-J38 exist with overprint "14 Shtator 1943" (see Nos. 332-344) which is private and fraudulent on these stamps.

No. 253 Overprinted **Taksë**

1936 *Perf. 14*

J39	A34	10q carmine	3.50	4.75

Issued under Italian Dominion

Coat of Arms — D9

1940 Unwmk. Photo. *Perf. 14*

J40	D9	4q red orange	5.50	5.50
J41	D9	10q bright violet	1.75	1.75
J42	D9	20q brown	1.75	1.75
J43	D9	30q dark blue	2.00	2.00
J44	D9	50q carmine rose	4.00	4.00
		Nos. J40-J44 (5)	15.00	15.00

ALEXANDRETTA

LOCATION — A political territory in northern Syria, bordering on Turkey
GOVT. — A former French mandate
AREA — 10,000 sq. mi. (approx.)
POP. — 270,000 (approx.)

Included in the Syrian territory mandated to France under the Versailles Treaty, the name was changed to Hatay in 1938. The following year France returned the territory to Turkey in exchange for certain concessions. See Hatay.

100 Centimes = 1 Piaster

Stamps of Syria, 1930-36, Overprinted or Surcharged in Black or Red:

Sandjak d'Alexandrette
a

SANDJAK D'ALEXANDRETTE
b

Sandjak d'Alexandrette
c

Sandjak d'Alexandrette 2P50 ٢٫٥٠ق
d

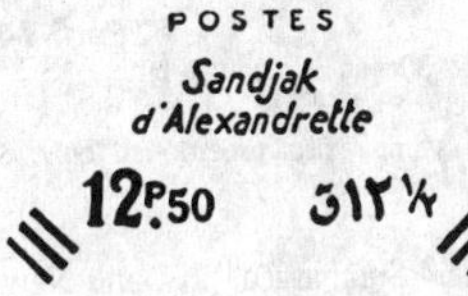

e

1938 Unwmk. *Perf. 12x12½*

1	A6 (a)	10c vio brn	35	35
2	A6 (a)	20c brn org	35	35
		Perf. 13½		
3	A9 (b)	50c vio (R)	35	35
4	A10 (b)	1p bis brn	50	50
5	A9 (b)	2p dk vio (R)	60	60
6	A13 (b)	3p yel grn (R)	1.75	1.75
7	A10 (b)	4p yel org	1.75	1.75
8	A16 (b)	6p grnsh blk (R)	2.00	2.00
9	A18 (b)	25p vio brn	4.75	4.75
10	A15 (c)	75c org red	50	50
11	A10 (d)	2.50p on 4p yel org	90	90
12	AP2 (e)	12.50p on 15p org red	2.50	2.50
		Nos. 1-12 (12)	16.30	16.30

Issue dates: #1-9, Apr. 14, #10-12, Sept. 2.

Nos. 4, 7, 10-12 Overprinted in Black

1938, Nov. 10

13	A15	75c	30.00	30.00
14	A10	1p	20.00	18.00
15	A10	2.50p on 4p	12.50	11.00
16	A10	4p	15.00	13.50
17	AP2	12.50p on 15p	30.00	30.00
		Nos. 13-17 (5)	107.50	102.50

Death of Kemal Ataturk, pres. of Turkey.

AIR POST STAMPS

Air Post Stamps of Syria, 1937, Overprinted Type "b" in Red or Black

1938, Apr. 14 Unwmk. *Perf. 13*

C1	AP14	½p dark vio (R)	75	75
C2	AP15	1p black (R)	35	35
C3	AP14	2p blue grn (R)	1.50	1.50
C4	AP15	3p deep ultra	1.75	1.75
C5	AP14	5p rose lake	4.50	4.50
C6	AP15	10p red brown	5.00	5.00
C7	AP14	15p lake brown	5.75	5.75
C8	AP15	25p dk blue (R)	7.50	7.50
		Nos. C1-C8 (8)	27.10	27.10

POSTAGE DUE STAMPS

Postage Due Stamps of Syria, 1925-31, Ovptd. Type "b" in Black or Red

1938, Apr. 14 Unwmk. *Perf. 13½*

J1	D5	50c brown, *yel*	80	80
J2	D6	1p violet, *rose*	1.10	1.10
J3	D5	2p blk, *blue* (R)	1.60	1.60
J4	D5	3p blk, *red org*	3.25	3.25
J5	D5	5p blk, *bl grn* (R)	5.00	5.00
J6	D7	8p blk, *gray bl* (R)	5.00	5.00
		Nos. J1-J6 (6)	16.75	16.75

On No. J2, the overprint is vertical, reading up, other denominations, horizontal.

Stamps of Alexandretta were discontinued in 1938 and replaced by those of Hatay.

ALGERIA

LOCATION — North Africa
GOVT. — Republic
AREA — 919,595 sq. mi.
POP. — 21,463,000 (1984 est.)
CAPITAL — Algiers

The former French colony of Algeria became an integral part of France on Sept. 1, 1958, when French stamps replaced Algerian stamps. Algeria became an independent country July 3, 1962.

100 Centimes = 1 Franc
100 Centimes = 1 Dinar (1964)

Catalogue values for unused stamps in this country are for Never Hinged items, beginning with Scott 109 in the regular postage section, Scott B27 in the semi-postal section, Scott C1 in the airpost section, Scott CB1 in the airpost semi-postal section, and Scott J25 in the postage due section.

Stamps of France Overprinted in Red, Blue or Black:

ALGÉRIE
a

ALGÉRIE
b

ALGÉRIE
c

ALGÉRIE
d

1924-26 Unwmk. *Perf. 14x13½*

1	A16(a)	1c dk gray (R)	15	15
2	A16(a)	2c violet brn	15	15
3	A16(a)	3c orange	15	15
4	A16(a)	4c yel brn (Bl)	15	15
5	A22(a)	5c orange (Bl)	15	15
6	A16(a)	5c green ('25)	15	15
7	A23(a)	10c green	15	15
b.		Booklet pane of 10	1.50	
8	A22(a)	10c green ('25)	50	15
9	A20(a)	15c slate grn	15	15
10	A23(a)	15c green ('25)	15	15
11	A22(a)	15c red brn (Bl) ('26)	15	15
12	A22(a)	20c red brn (Bl)	15	15
13	A22(a)	25c blue (R)	15	15
a.		Booklet pane of 10	3.00	
14	A23(a)	30c red (Bl)	15	15
15	A22(a)	30c cerise ('25)	50	15
16	A22(a)	30c lt bl (R) ('25)	15	15
a.		Booklet pane of 10	2.00	
17	A22(a)	35c violet	15	15
18	A18(b)	40c red & pale bl	15	15
19	A22(a)	40c ol brn (R) ('25)	75	20
20	A18(b)	45c grn & bl (R)	20	15
21	A23(a)	45c red (Bl) ('25)	30	15
22	A23(a)	50c blue (R)	15	15
23	A20(a)	60c lt violet	15	15
a.		Inverted overprint	250.00	
24	A20(a)	65c rose (Bl)	15	15
25	A23(a)	75c blue (R)	20	15
a.		Double overprint	65.00	
26	A20(a)	80c ver ('26)	40	15
27	A20(a)	85c ver (Bl)	22	15
28	A18(b)	1fr cl & ol grn	1.00	15
29	A22(a)	1.05fr ver ('26)	55	22
30	A18(c)	2fr org & pale bl	40	25
31	A18(b)	3fr vio & bl ('26)	3.00	45
32	A18(d)	5fr bl & buff (R)	6.00	2.75
		Nos. 1-32 (32)	16.87	
		Set value		6.00

No. 15 was issued precanceled only. Values for precanceled stamps in first column are for those which have not been through the post and have original gum. Values in second column are for postally used, gumless stamps.

For surcharges, see Nos. 75, P1.

Street in Kasbah, Algiers
A1

Mosque of Sidi Abd-er-Rahman
A2

La Pêcherie Mosque
A3

Marabout of Sidi Yacoub
A4

1926-39 Typo. *Perf. 14x13½*

33	A1	1c olive	15	15
34	A1	2c red brown	15	15
35	A1	3c orange	16	16
36	A1	5c blue green	15	15
37	A1	10c brt violet	15	15
a.		Booklet pane of 10	3.25	
38	A2	15c orange brn	15	15
39	A2	20c green	15	15
40	A2	20c deep rose	15	15
41	A2	25c blue grn	16	16
42	A2	25c blue ('27)	35	15
43	A2	25c vio bl ('39)	15	15
44	A2	30c blue	22	15
45	A2	30c bl grn ('27)	75	30
46	A2	35c dp violet	85	65
47	A2	40c olive green	15	15
a.		Booklet pane of 10	2.25	
48	A3	45c violet brn	22	20
49	A3	50c blue	22	15
a.		Booklet pane of 10	3.50	
50	A3	50c dk red ('30)	15	15
a.		Booklet pane of 10	4.75	
51	A3	60c yellow grn	15	15
52	A3	65c blk brn ('27)	1.10	85
53	A1	65c ultra ('38)	20	15
a.		Booklet pane of 10	1.75	
54	A3	75c carmine	28	22
55	A3	75c blue ('29)	2.50	18
56	A3	80c orange red	38	25
57	A3	90c red ('27)	3.50	2.75
58	A4	1fr gray grn & red brn	55	18
59	A3	1.05fr lt brown	50	28
60	A3	1.10fr mag ('27)	4.75	1.75
61	A4	1.25fr dk bl & ultra	1.00	80
62	A4	1.50fr dk bl & ultra ('27)	1.75	15
63	A4	2fr Prus bl & blk brn	1.90	18
64	A4	3fr violet & org	2.75	65
65	A4	5fr red & violet	5.00	2.00
66	A4	10fr ol brn & rose ('27)	35.00	20.00
67	A4	20fr vio & grn ('27)	5.75	4.00
		Nos. 33-67 (35)	71.49	37.96

Type A4, 50c blue and rose red, inscribed "CENTENAIRE-ALGERIE" is France No. 255.

For stamps and types surcharged, see Nos. 68-74, 131, 136, 187, B1-B13, J27, P2.

Stamps of 1926 Surcharged with New Values

1927

68	A2	10c on 35c dp violet	15	15
69	A2	25c on 30c blue	15	15
70	A2	30c on 25c blue grn	15	15
71	A3	65c on 60c yel grn	45	35
72	A3	90c on 80c org red	25	20
73	A3	1.10fr on 1.05fr lt brn	25	16
74	A4	1.50fr on 1.25fr dk bl & ultra	90	45
		Set value	2.00	1.35

Bars cancel the old value on #68, 69, 73, 74.

No. 4 Surcharged 5c

1927

75	A16	5c on 4c yellow brown	*75*	*25*

Bay of Algiers — A5

1930, May 4 Engr. *Perf. 11, 12½*

78	A5	10fr red brown	8.00	7.50
a.		Imperf., pair	25.00	

Cent. of Algeria and for Intl. Phil. Exhib. of North Africa, May, 1930.

One copy of No. 78 was sold with each 10fr admission.

Travel across the Sahara — A6

Arch of Triumph, Lambese — A7

Admiralty Building, Algiers — A8

Kings' Tombs near Touggourt — A9

El-Kebir Mosque, Algiers — A10

Oued River at Colomb-Bechar
A11

Sidi Bon Medine Cemetery at Tlemcen
A13

View of Ghardaia
A12

1936-41 Engr. *Perf. 13*

79	A6	1c ultra	15	15
80	A11	2c dk violet	15	15
81	A7	3c dk blue grn	15	15
82	A12	5c red violet	15	15
83	A8	10c emerald	15	15
84	A9	15c red	15	15
85	A13	20c dk blue grn	15	15
86	A10	25c rose vio	32	15
87	A12	30c yellow grn	28	15
88	A9	40c brown vio	15	15
89	A13	45c deep ultra	65	40
90	A8	50c red	40	15
91	A6	65c red brn	2.50	1.75
92	A6	65c rose car ('37)	35	15
93	A6	70c red brn ('39)	15	15
94	A11	75c slate bl	18	15
95	A7	90c henna brn	65	45
96	A10	1fr brown	18	15
97	A8	1.25fr lt violet	35	18
98	A8	1.25fr car rose ('39)	30	15
99	A11	1.50fr turq blue	90	18
99A	A11	1.50fr rose ('40)	35	15
100	A12	1.75fr henna brn	15	15
101	A7	2fr dk brown	15	15
102	A6	2.25fr yellow grn	8.00	6.50
103	A12	2.50fr dk ultra ('41)	28	26
104	A13	3fr magenta	26	15
105	A10	3.50fr pck blue	1.90	1.40
106	A8	5fr slate blue	28	15
107	A11	10fr henna brn	32	20
108	A9	20fr turq blue	60	35
		Nos. 79-108 (31)	20.70	
		Set value		12.90

See Nos. 124-125, 162.

Nos. 82 and 100 with surcharge "E. F. M. 30frs" (Emergency Field Message) were used in 1943 to pay cable tolls for US and Canadian servicemen.

For other surcharges, see Nos. 122, B27.

Catalogue values for unused stamps in this section, from this point to the end of the section, are for Never Hinged items.

Algerian Pavilion — A14

1937 *Perf. 13*

109	A14	40c brt green	40	35
110	A14	50c rose carmine	25	15
111	A14	1.50fr blue	60	25
112	A14	1.75fr brown black	65	50
		Nos. 109-112 (4)	1.90	1.25

Paris International Exposition.

Constantine in 1837 — A15

1937

113	A15	65c deep rose	32	15
114	A15	1fr brown	3.25	50
115	A15	1.75fr blue green	28	20
116	A15	2.15fr red violet	18	15
		Nos. 113-116 (4)	4.03	1.00

Taking of Constantine by the French, cent.

Ruins of a Roman Villa — A16

1938

117	A16	30c green	50	32
118	A16	65c ultra	15	15
119	A16	75c rose violet	55	38
120	A16	3fr carmine rose	1.40	1.40
121	A16	5fr yellow brown	2.25	2.25
		Nos. 117-121 (5)	4.85	4.50

Centenary of Philippeville.

No. 90 Surcharged in Black

0,25

||||| ||||||

1938

122	A8	25c on 50c red	15	15
a.		Double surcharge	27.50	22.50
b.		Inverted surcharge	17.50	15.00

Types of 1936

1939

Numerals of Value on Colorless Background

124	A7	90c henna brown	15	15
125	A10	2.25fr blue green	18	20
		Set value	24	25

For surcharge, see No. B38.

American Export Liner Unloading Cargo — A17

1939

126	A17	20c green	65	65
127	A17	40c red violet	65	50
128	A17	90c brown black	35	22
129	A17	1.25fr rose	2.25	80
130	A17	2.25fr ultra	65	60
		Nos. 126-130 (5)	4.55	2.77

New York World's Fair.

Type of 1926, Surcharged in Black

1F

Two types of surcharge:
I - Bars 6mm
II - Bars 7mm

1939-40 *Perf. 14x13½*

131	A1	1fr on 90c crimson (I)	15	15
a.		Booklet pane of 10		
b.		Double surcharge	35.00	
c.		Inverted surcharge (I)	22.50	
d.		Pair, one without surch. (I)	800.00	
e.		Type II ('40)	1.50	15
f.		Inverted surcharge (II)	27.50	
g.		Pair, one without surch. (II)	800.00	

View of Algiers — A18

1941 **Typo.**

132	A18	30c ultra	15	15
133	A18	70c sepia	15	15
134	A18	1fr carmine rose	15	15
		Nos. 132-134 (3)	45	
		Set value		15

See No. 163.

Marshal Pétain
A19 A20

1941 **Engr.** *Perf. 13*

135	A19	1fr dark blue	30	16

For stamp and type surcharged see #B36-B37.

No. 53 Surcharged in Black with New Value and Bars

1941 *Perf. 14x13½*

136	A1	50c on 65c ultra	28	15
a.		Booklet pane of 10		
b.		Inverted surcharge	21.00	
c.		Pair, one without surch.	52.50	

1942 *Perf. 14x13*

137	A20	1.50fr orange red	15	15

4 other denominations of type A20 exist (4, 5, 10, 20fr), but were not placed in use.

Constantine
A21

Oran
A22

Arms of Algiers — A23

Engraver's Name at Lower Left

1942-43 **Photo.** *Perf. 12*

138	A21	40c dark vio ('43)	15	15
139	A22	60c rose ('43)	15	15
140	A21	1.20fr yel grn ('43)	15	15
141	A23	1.50fr car rose	15	15
142	A22	2fr sapphire	20	15
143	A21	2.40fr rose ('43)	15	15
144	A23	3fr sapphire	20	15
145	A21	4fr blue ('43)	15	15
146	A22	5fr yel grn ('43)	15	15
		Set value	92	58

For type surcharged, see No. 166.

Imperforates

Nearly all of Algeria Nos. 138-285, B39-B96, C1-C12 and CB1-CB3 exist imperforate. See note after France No. 395.

Without Engraver's Name

1942-45 **Typo.** *Perf. 14x13½*

147	A23	10c dull brn vio ('45)	15	15
148	A22	30c dp bl grn ('45)	15	15
149	A21	40c dull brn vio ('45)	15	15
150	A22	60c rose ('45)	15	15
151	A21	70c deep bl ('45)	15	15
152	A23	80c dk bl grn ('43)	22	22
153	A21	1.20fr dp bl grn ('45)	20	15
154	A23	1.50fr brt rose ('43)	15	15
155	A22	2fr dp blue ('45)	20	15
156	A21	2.40fr rose ('45)	30	22
157	A23	3fr dp blue ('45)	15	15
158	A22	4.50fr brown vio	20	15
		Set value	1.50	1.00

For surcharge, see No. 190.

La Pêcherie Mosque — A24

1942 **Typo.**

159	A24	50c dull red	15	15
a.		Booklet pane of 10	2.75	

1942 **Photo.** *Perf. 12*

160	A24	40c gray green	15	15
161	A24	50c red	15	15
		Set value	20	15

Types of 1936-41, Without "RF"

1942 **Engr.** *Perf. 13*

162	A11	1.50fr rose	30	15

Typo. *Perf. 14x13½*

163	A18	30c ultra	15	15

"One Aim Alone - Victory"
A25 A26

1943 **Litho.** *Perf. 12*

164	A25	1.50fr deep rose	15	15
165	A26	1.50fr dark blue	15	15
		Set value	20	15

Type of 1942-3 Surcharged with New Value in Black

1943 **Photo.**

166	A22	2fr on 5fr red orange	15	15
a.		Surcharge omitted	140.00	

Summer Palace, Algiers — A27

1944, Dec. 1 **Litho.**

167	A27	15fr slate	85	65
168	A27	20fr lt blue grn	80	30
169	A27	50fr dk carmine	75	35
170	A27	100fr deep blue	1.10	1.00
171	A27	200fr dull bis brn	1.75	1.10
		Nos. 167-171 (5)	5.25	3.40

Marianne
A28

Gallic Cock
A29

1944-45

172	A28	10c gray	15	15
173	A28	30c red violet	15	15
174	A29	40c rose car ('45)	15	15
175	A28	50c red	15	15
176	A28	80c emerald	15	15
177	A29	1fr green ('45)	15	15
178	A28	1.20fr rose lilac	15	15
179	A28	1.50fr dark blue	15	15
a.		Double impression	20.00	
180	A29	2fr red	15	15
a.		Double impression	22.50	
181	A29	2fr dk brown ('45)	15	15
182	A28	2.40fr rose red	15	15
183	A28	3fr purple	15	15
184	A29	4fr ultra ('45)	15	15
185	A28	4.50fr olive blk	22	22
186	A29	10fr grnsh blk ('45)	38	28
		Set value	1.50	1.20

No. 38 Surcharged in Black **0f.30**

1944 *Perf. 14x13½*

187	A2	30c on 15c orange brn	15	15
a.		Inverted surcharge	10.00	4.00

This stamp exists precanceled only. See note below No. 32.

No. 154 Surcharged "RF" and New Value

1945

190	A23	50c on 1.50fr brt rose	15	15
a.		Inverted surcharge	15.00	

Stamps of France, 1944, Overprinted Type "a" of 1924 in Black

1945-46

191	A99	80c yellow grn	15	15
192	A99	1fr grnsh blue	15	15
193	A99	1.20fr violet	15	15
194	A99	2fr violet brown	22	15
195	A99	2.40fr carmine rose	22	15
196	A99	3fr orange	22	15
		Set value	85	75

Same Overprint on Stamps of France, 1945-47, in Black, Red or Carmine

1945-47

197	A145	40c lilac rose	15	15
198	A145	50c violet bl (R)	15	15
199	A146	60c brt ultra (R)	22	15
200	A146	1fr rose red ('47)	20	15
201	A146	1.50fr rose lilac ('47)	15	15
202	A147	2fr myr grn (R) ('46)	15	15
203	A147	3fr deep rose	15	15
204	A147	4.50fr ultra (C) ('47)	55	15
205	A147	5fr lt green ('46)	15	15
206	A147	10fr ultra	50	25
		Set value	1.75	75

Same Overprint on France No. 383 and New Value Surcharged in Black

1946

207	A99	2fr on 1.50fr henna brn	15	15
a.		Without "2F"	110.00	

Same Overprint on France Nos. 562 and 564, in Carmine or Blue

1947

208	A153	10c dp ultra & blk (C)	15	15
209	A155	50c brown, yel & red (Bl)	22	22
		Set value	27	27

Constantine
A30

Algiers
A31

Arms of Oran — A32

Perf. 14x13½

1947-49 **Unwmk.** **Typo.**

210	A30	10c dk grn & brt red	15	15
211	A31	50c black & orange	15	15
212	A32	1fr ultra & yellow	15	15
213	A30	1.30fr blk & grnsh bl	55	35
214	A31	1.50fr pur & org yel	15	15
215	A32	2fr blk & brt grn	15	15
216	A30	2.50fr blk & brt red	35	28
217	A31	3fr vio brn & grn	15	15
218	A32	3.50fr lt grn & rose lil	15	15
219	A30	4fr dk brn & brt grn	15	15
220	A31	4.50fr ultra & scar	15	15
221	A31	5fr blk & grnsh bl	16	15
222	A32	6fr brown & scarlet	22	15
223	A32	8fr choc & ultra ('48)	18	15
224	A30	10fr car & choc ('48)	32	15
225	A31	15fr black & red ('49)	35	15
		Set value	2.70	1.35

See Nos. 274-280, 285.

Peoples of the World — A33

1949, Oct. 24 Engr. *Perf. 13*

226 A33	5fr green	1.10	90
227 A33	15fr scarlet	1.10	90
228 A33	25fr ultra	2.50	2.50
	Nos. 226-228 (3)	4.70	4.30

75th anniv. of the UPU.

Grapes A34

Apollo of Cherchell A35

Designs: 25fr, Dates. 40fr, Oranges and lemons.

1950, Feb. 25

229 A34	20fr multicolored	1.00	22
230 A34	25fr multicolored	1.25	50
231 A34	40fr multicolored	2.50	65
	Nos. 229-231 (3)	4.75	1.37

1952 Unwmk. *Perf. 13*

Designs: 12fr, 18fr, Isis statue, Cherchell. 15fr, 20fr, Child with eagle.

240 A35	10fr gray black	22	15
241 A35	12fr orange brn	35	15
242 A35	15fr deep blue	22	15
243 A35	18fr rose red	35	22
244 A35	20fr deep green	35	15
245 A35	30fr deep blue	65	35
	Nos. 240-245 (6)	2.14	
	Set value		84

War Memorial, Algiers — A38

Fossilized Nautilus — A39

Phonolite Dike — A40

1952, Apr. 11

246 A38 12fr dark green 48 35

Issued to honor the French Africa Army.

1952, Aug. 11

247 A39	15fr brt crimson	85	60
248 A40	30fr deep ultra	90	65

19th Intl. Geological Cong., Algiers, Sept. 8-15.

French and Algerian Soldiers and Camel — A41

1952, Nov. 30

249 A41 12fr chestnut brown 65 60

50th anniv. of the establishment of the Sahara Companies.

Eugène Millon — A42

François C. Maillot — A43

Oranges — A44

Portrait: 50fr, Alphonse Laveran.

1954, Jan. 4 Unwmk. Engr. *Perf. 13*

250 A42	25fr dk grn & choc	1.10	18
251 A43	40fr org brn & brn car	1.75	60
252 A42	50fr ultra & indigo	1.75	22
	Nos. 250-252 (3)	4.60	1.00

Military Health Service.

1954, May 8

253 A44 15fr indigo & blue 60 40

3rd Intl. Cong. on Agronomy, Algiers, 1954.

Type of France, 1954 Overprinted type "a" in Black

Unwmk.

1954, June 6 Engr. *Perf. 13*

254 A240 15fr rose carmine 45 45

Liberation of France, 10th anniversary.

Darguinah Hydroelectric Works A45

Patio of Bardo Museum A46

1954, June 19

255 A45 15fr lilac rose 55 45

Opening of Darguinah hydroelectric works.

1954 Typo. *Perf. 14x13½*

257 A46	12fr red brn & brn org	50	25
258 A46	15fr dk blue & blue	50	25

See Nos. 267-271.

Type of France, 1954, Overprinted type "a" in Carmine

1954 Engr. *Perf. 13*

260 A247 12fr dark green 50 45

150th anniv. of the 1st Legion of Honor awards at Camp de Boulogne.

St. Augustine — A47

1954, Nov. 11

261 A47 15fr chocolate 75 65

1600th anniv. of the birth of St. Augustine.

Aesculapius Statue and El Kattar Hospital, Algiers — A48

1955, Apr. 3 Unwmk. *Perf. 13*

262 A48 15fr red 50 35

Issued to publicize the 30th French Congress of Medicine, Algiers, April 3-6, 1955.

Chenua Mountain and View of Tipasa — A49

1955, May 31

263 A49 50fr brown carmine 50 18

2000th anniv. of the founding of Tipasa.

Type of France, 1955 Overprinted type "a" in Red

1955, June 13

264 A251 30fr deep ultra 60 45

Rotary Intl., 50th anniv.

Marianne A50

Great Kabylia Mountains A51

Perf. 14x13½

1955, Oct. 3 Typo. Unwmk.

265 A50 15fr carmine 50 25

See No. 284.

1955, Dec. 17 Engr. *Perf. 13*

266 A51 100fr indigo & ultra 2.00 22

Bardo Type of 1954, "Postes" and "Algerie" in White

Perf. 14x13½

1955-57 Unwmk. Typo.

267 A46	10fr dk brown & lt brown	25	15
268 A46	12fr red brn & brn org ('56)	20	15
269 A46	18fr crimson & ver ('57)	45	18
270 A46	20fr grn & yel grn ('57)	35	28
271 A46	25fr purple & brt purple	50	15
	Nos. 267-271 (5)	1.75	
	Set value		60

Marshal Franchet d'Esperey A52

1956, May 25 Engr. *Perf. 13*

272 A52 15fr sapphire & indigo 60 60

Birth cent. of Marshal Franchet d'Esperey.

Marshal Jacques Leclerc — A53

1956, Nov. 29

273 A53 15fr red brown & sepia 48 48

Death of Marshal Leclerc.
For type surcharged, see No. B90.

Type of 1947-49 and

Arms of Bône — A54

Arms: 2fr, Tizi-Ouzou. 3fr, Mostaganem. 5fr, Tlemcen. 10fr, Setif. 12fr, Orleansville.

1956-58 Typo. *Perf. 14x13½*

274 A54	1fr green & ver	15	15
275 A54	2fr ver & ultra ('58)	25	20
276 A54	3fr ultra & emer ('58)	30	15
277 A54	5fr ultra & yellow	15	15
278 A31	6fr red & grn ('57)	35	25
279 A54	10fr dp cl & emer ('58)	35	25
280 A54	12fr ultra & red ('58)	35	25
	Nos. 274-280 (7)	1.90	1.40

Nos. 275 and 279 are inscribed "Republique Francaise." See No. 285.

View of Oran — A55

1956-58 Engr. *Perf. 13*

281 A55	30fr dull purple	45	18
282 A55	35fr car rose ('58)	75	45

Electric Train Crossing Bridge — A56

1957, Mar. 25

283 A56 40fr dk blue grn & emer 60 18

Marianne Type of 1955 Inscribed "Algerie" Vertically

Perf. 14x13½

1957, Dec. 2 Typo. Unwmk.

284 A50 20fr ultra 40 15

Arms Type of 1947-49 Inscribed "Republique Francaise"

1958, July

285 A31 6fr red & green 10.00 10.00

Independent State

France Nos. 939, 968, 945-946 and 1013 Overprinted "EA" and Bars, Handstamped or Typographed, in Black or Red

1962, July 2

286 A336	10c brt green	25	20
a.	Typographed overprint	30	20
287 A349	25c lake & gray	20	15
a.	Handstamped overprint	25	15
288 A339	45c brt vio & ol gray	3.50	3.00
a.	Handstamped overprint	*15.00*	*10.00*
289 A339	50c sl grn & lt cl	5.00	3.00
a.	Handstamped overprint	*15.00*	*12.00*
290 A372	1fr dk bl, sl & bis	2.75	1.00
a.	Handstamped overprint	*4.00*	*1.50*
	Nos. 286-290 (5)	11.70	7.35

Post offices were authorized to overprint their stock of these 5 French stamps. The size of the letters was specified as 3x6mm each, but various sizes were used. The post offices had permission to make their own rubber stamps. Typography, pen or pencil were also used. Many types exist. Colors of handstamped overprints include black, red, blue, violet. "EA" stands for Etat Algérien.

Mosque, Tlemcen — A57

Roman Gates of Lodi, Médéa — A58

Designs: 5c, Kerrata Gorge. 10c, Dam at Foum el Gherza. 95c, Oil field, Hassi Messaoud.

1962, Nov. 1 Engr. *Perf. 13*

291 A57	5c Prus grn, grn & choc	15	15
292 A58	10c ol blk & dk bl	15	15
293 A57	25c sl grn, brn & ver	40	15
294 A57	95c dk bl, blk & bis	1.50	55
295 A58	1fr green & blk	1.50	1.10
	Nos. 291-295 (5)	3.70	
	Set value		1.75

The designs of Nos. 291-295 are similar to French issues of 1959-61 with "Republique Algerienne" replacing "Republique Francaise."

Flag, Rifle, Olive Branch — A59

Design: Nos. 300-303, Broken chain and rifle added to design A59.

1963, Jan. 6 Litho. *Perf. 12½*

Flag in Green and Red

296 A59	5c bister brown	15	15
297 A59	10c blue	15	15
298 A59	25c vermilion	1.00	15
299 A59	95c violet	90	45
300 A59	1fr green	75	15
301 A59	2fr brown	2.00	45
302 A59	5fr lilac	3.00	1.25
303 A59	10fr gray	11.50	7.00
	Nos. 296-303 (8)	19.45	9.75

Nos. 296-299 for the successful revolution and Nos. 300-303 the return of peace.

Men of Various Races, Wheat Emblem and Globe — A60

1963, Mar. 21 Engr. *Perf. 13*

304 A60	25c maroon, dl grn & yel	28	22

FAO "Freedom from Hunger" campaign.

Map of Algeria and Emblems — A61

Physicians from 13th Century Manuscript — A62

1963, July 5 Unwmk. *Perf. 13*

305 A61	25c bl, dk brn, grn & red	40	22

1st anniv. of Algeria's independence.

1963, July 29 Engr.

306 A62	25c brn red, grn & bis	1.00	35

2nd Congress of the Union of Arab physicians.

Orange and Blossom A63

Scales and Scroll A64

1963 *Perf. 14x13*

307 A63	8c gray grn & org	65	65
308 A63	20c slate & org red	75	75
309 A63	40c grnsh bl & org	1.00	1.00
310 A63	55c ol grn & org red	2.00	2.00
	Nos. 307-310 (4)	4.40	4.40

Nos. 307-310 issued precanceled only. See note below No. 32.

1963, Oct. 13 Unwmk. *Perf. 13*

311 A64	25c blk, grn & rose red	42	28

Issued to honor the new constitution.

Guerrillas A65

Centenary Emblem A66

1963, Nov. 1

312 A65	25c dk brn, yel grn & car	55	25

9th anniversary of Algerian revolution.

1963, Dec. 8 Photo. *Perf. 12*

313 A66	25c lt vio bl, yel & dk red	55	28

Centenary of International Red Cross.

UNESCO Emblem, Scales and Globe — A67

Workers — A68

1963, Dec. 16 Unwmk. *Perf. 12*

314 A67	25c lt blue & blk	55	25

15th anniv. of the Universal Declaration of Human Rights.

1964, May 1 Engr. *Perf. 13*

315 A68	50c dull red, red org & bl	90	50

Issued for the Labor Festival.

Map of Africa and Flags — A69

1964, May 25 Unwmk. *Perf. 13*

316 A69	45c blue, orange & car	55	28

Africa Day on the 1st anniv. of the Addis Ababa charter on African unity.

Ramses II Battling the Hittites (from Abu Simbel) — A70

Design: 30c, Two statues of Ramses II.

1964, June 28 Engr. *Perf. 13*

317 A70	20c choc, red & vio bl	55	32
318 A70	30c brn, red & grnsh bl	65	40

UNESCO world campaign to save historic monuments in Nubia.

A71

A72

Designs: 5c, 25c, 85c, Tractors. 10c, 30c, 65c, Men working with lathe. 12c, 15c, 45c, Electronics center and atom symbol. 20c, 50c, 95c, Draftsman and bricklayer.

1964-65 Typo. *Perf. 14x13½*

319 A71	5c red lilac	15	15
320 A71	10c brown	15	15
321 A71	12c emerald ('65)	38	15
322 A71	15c dk blue ('65)	25	15
323 A71	20c yellow	42	15
324 A71	25c red	50	15
325 A71	30c purple ('65)	42	15
326 A71	45c rose car	50	18
327 A71	50c ultra	62	15
328 A71	65c orange	80	18
329 A71	85c green	1.40	22
330 A71	95c car rose	1.75	26
	Nos. 319-330 (12)	7.34	
	Set value		1.40

For surcharges, see Nos. 389, 424.

1964, Aug. 30 Engr. *Perf. 13*

331 A72	85c Communications tower	1.50	75

Inauguration of the Hertzian cable telephone line Algiers-Annaba.

Industrial & Agricultural Symbols — A73

Gas Flames and Pipes — A74

1964, Sept. 26 Typo. *Perf. 13½x14*

332 A73	25c lt ultra, yel & red	60	45

1st Intl. Fair at Algiers, Sept. 26-Oct. 11.

1964, Sept. 27

333 A74	30c violet, blue & yel	45	35

Arzew natural gas liquification plant opening.

Planting Trees A75

Children and UNICEF Emblem A76

1964, Nov. 29 Unwmk.

334 A75	25c slate grn, yel & car	28	20

National reforestation campaign.

1964, Dec. 13 *Perf. 13½x14*

335 A76	15c pink, vio bl & lt grn	25	20

Issued for Children's Day.

Decorated Camel Saddle — A77

1965, May 29 Typo. *Perf. 13½x14*

336 A77	20c blk, red, emer & brn	22	15

Handicrafts of Sahara.

ICY Emblem A78

1965, Aug. 29 Engr. *Perf. 13*

337 A78	30c blk, mar & bl grn	45	32
338 A78	60c blk, brt bl & bl grn	85	38

International Cooperation Year, 1965.

ITU Emblem A79

1965, Sept. 19

339 A79	60c purple, emer & buff	45	30
340 A79	95c dk brn, mar & buff	65	35

Cent. of the ITU.

Musicians A80

Miniatures by Mohammed Racim: 60c, Two female musicians. 5d, Algerian princess and antelope.

1965, Dec. 27 Photo. *Perf. 11½*

341 A80	30c multicolored	70	55
342 A80	60c multicolored	1.10	70
343 A80	5d multicolored	8.00	5.25
	Nos. 341-343 (3)	9.80	6.50

Bulls, Painted in 6000 B.C. A81

Wall Paintings from Tassili-N-Ajjer, c. 6000 B.C.: No. 345, Shepherd, vert. 2d, Fleeing ostriches. 3d, Two girls, vert.

1966, Jan. 29 Photo. *Perf. 11½*

344 A81	1d brn, bis & red brn	2.75	1.90
345 A81	1d gray, blk, ocher & dk brn	2.75	1.90
346 A81	2d brn, ocher & red brn	6.50	3.00
347 A81	3d buff, blk, ocher & brn red	8.00	4.25
	Nos. 344-347 (4)	20.00	11.05

See Nos. 365-368.

Pottery — A82

Handicrafts from Great Kabylia: 50c, Weaving, woman at loom, horiz. 70c, Jewelry.

1966, Feb. 26 Engr. *Perf. 13*

348 A82	40c Prus bl, brn red & blk	28	22
349 A82	50c dk red, ol & ocher	38	28
350 A82	70c vio bl, blk & red	65	40
	Nos. 348-350 (3)	1.31	90

Weather Balloon, Compass Rose and Anemometer A83

1966, Mar. 23 Engr. Unwmk.

351 A83	1d claret, brt bl & grn	85	38

World Meteorological Day.

Book, Grain, Cogwheel and UNESCO Emblem — A84

Design: 60c, Grain, cogwheel, book and UNESCO emblem.

1966, May 2 Typo. *Perf. 13x14*

352 A84	30c yellow bis & blk	22	20
353 A84	60c dk red, gray & blk	40	22

Literacy as basis for development.

WHO Headquarters, Geneva A85

1966, May 30 Engr. *Perf. 13*

354 A85	30c multicolored	35	30
355 A85	60c multicolored	70	40

Inauguration of the WHO Headquarters, Geneva.

Algerian Scout Emblem — A86

Arab Jamboree Emblem — A87

1966, July 23 Photo. *Perf. 12x12½*

356 A86	30c multicolored	65	50
357 A87	1d multicolored	1.75	1.25

No. 356 commemorates the 30th anniv. of the Algerian Mohammedan Boy Scouts. No. 357, the 7th Arab Boy Scout Jamboree, held at Good Daim, Libya, Aug. 12.

Map of Palestine and Victims A88

Abd-el-Kader A89

1966, Sept. 26 Typo. *Perf. 10½*

358 A88	30c red & black	80	40

Deir Yassin Massacre, Apr. 9, 1948.

1966, Nov. 2 Photo. *Perf. 11½*

359 A89	30c multicolored	38	15
360 A89	95c multicolored	1.10	35

Transfer from Damascus to Algiers of the ashes of Abd-el-Kader (1807?-1883), Emir of Mascara. See Nos. 382-387.

UNESCO Emblem — A90

1966, Nov. 19 Typo. *Perf. 10½*

361 A90	1d multicolored	1.00	35

20th anniv. of UNESCO.

Horseman A91

Miniatures by Mohammed Racim: 1.50d, Woman at her toilette. 2d, The pirate Barbarossa in front of the Admiralty.

1966, Dec. 17 Photo. *Perf. 11½*
Granite Paper

362 A91	1d multicolored	3.25	1.40
363 A91	1.50d multicolored	4.25	2.00
364 A91	2d multicolored	7.00	3.50
	Nos. 362-364 (3)	14.50	6.90

Wall Paintings Type of 1966

Wall Paintings from Tassili-N-Ajjer, c. 6000 B.C.: 1d, Cow. No. 366, Antelope. No. 367, Archers. 3d, Warrior, vert.

1967, Jan. 28 Photo. *Perf. 11½*

365 A81	1d brn, bis & dl vio	2.75	1.90
366 A81	2d brn, ocher & red brn	5.00	3.25
367 A81	2d brn, yel & red brn	5.00	3.25
368 A81	3d blk, gray, yel & red brn	7.75	5.00
	Nos. 365-368 (4)	20.50	13.40

Bardo Museum A92

La Kalaa Minaret — A93

Design: 1.30d, Ruins at Sedrata.

1967, Feb. 27 Photo. *Perf. 13*

369 A92	35c multicolored	20	15
370 A93	95c multicolored	45	28
371 A92	1.30d multicolored	75	40
	Nos. 369-371 (3)	1.40	83

Moretti and International Tourist Year Emblem — A94

Design: 70c, Tuareg riding camel, Tassili, and Tourist Year Emblem, vert.

1967, Apr. 29 Litho. *Perf. 14*

372 A94	40c multi	50	22
373 A94	70c multi	1.00	35

International Tourist Year, 1967.

Spiny-tailed Agamid — A95

Designs: 20c, Ostrich, vert. 40c, Slender-horned gazelle, vert. 70c, Fennec.

1967, June 24 Photo. *Perf. 11½*

374 A95	5c bister & blk	60	50
375 A95	20c ocher, blk & pink	1.25	80
376 A95	40c ol bis, blk & red brn	2.00	1.00
377 A95	70c gray, blk & dp org	3.50	2.00
	Nos. 374-377 (4)	7.35	4.30

Dancers — A96

Typographed and Engraved
1967, July 4 *Perf. 10½*

378 A96	50c gray vio, yel & blk	45	32

National Youth Festival.

Map of the Mediterranean and Sport Scenes — A97

1967, Sept. 2 Typo. *Perf. 10½*

379 A97	30c black, red & blue	25	20

Issued to publicize the 5th Mediterranean Games, Tunis, Sept. 8-17.

Skiers — A98

Olympic Emblem and Sports — A99

1967, Oct. 21 Engr. *Perf. 13*

380 A98	30c brt blue & ultra	32	20
381 A99	95c brn org, pur & brt grn	80	52

Issued to publicize the 10th Winter Olympic Games, Grenoble, Feb. 6-18, 1968.

Abd-el-Kader Type of 1966
Lithographed, Photogravure
1967-71 *Perf. 13½, 11½*

382	A89	5c dull pur ('68)	15	15
383	A89	10c green	85	35
383A	A89	10c sl grn (litho., '69)	15	15
383B	A89	25c orange ('71)	18	15
384	A89	30c black ('68)	50	20
385	A89	30c lt violet ('68)	75	30
386	A89	50c rose claret	65	18
387	A89	70c violet blue	85	22
		Nos. 382-387 (8)	4.08	
		Set value		1.40

No. 383, 50c and 70c, issued Nov. 13, 1967, are on granite paper, photo. The 5c, No.383A, 25c and 30c are litho., perf. 13½; others, perf. 11½.

The three 1967 stamps (No. 383, 50c, 70c) have numerals thin, narrow and close together; the Arabic inscription at lower right is 2mm high. The 5 litho. stamps are redrawn, with numerals thicker and spaced more widely; Arabic at lower right 3mm high.

Boy Scouts Holding Jamboree Emblem A100

1967, Dec. 23 Engr. *Perf. 13*

388 A100	1d multicolored	1.00	80

12th Boy Scout World Jamboree, Farragut State Park, Idaho, Aug. 1-9.

No. 324 Surcharged
1967 Typo. *Perf. 14x13½*

389 A71	30c on 25c red	50	20

Mandolin — A101

1968, Feb. 17 Photo. *Perf. 12½x13*

390 A101	30c shown	35	22
391 A101	40c Lute	40	25
392 A101	1.30d Rebec	1.40	65
	Nos. 390-392 (3)	2.15	1.12

Nememcha Rug — A102

Algerian Rugs: 70c, Guergour. 95c, Djebel-Amour. 1.30d, Kalaa.

1968, Apr. 13 Photo. *Perf. 11½*

393 A102	30c multi	75	75
394 A102	70c multi	1.50	1.50
395 A102	95c multi	2.00	2.00
396 A102	1.30d multi	2.50	2.50
	Nos. 393-396 (4)	6.75	6.75

Human Rights Flame A103

1968, May 18 Typo. *Perf. 10½*

397 A103	40c blue, red & yel	40	28

International Human Rights Year, 1968.

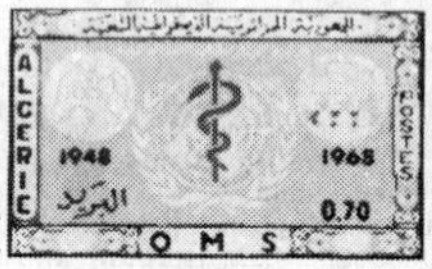

WHO Emblem A104

1968, May 18

398 A104	70c blk, lt bl & yel	55	28

20th anniv. of the WHO.

Welder — A105

Athletes, Olympic Flame and Rings — A106

1968, June 15 Engr. *Perf. 13*

399 A105	30c gray, brn & ultra	25	18

Algerian emigration to Europe.

Perf. 12½x13, 13x12½

1968, July 4 Photo.

Designs: 50c, Soccer player. 1d, Mexican pyramid, emblem, Olympic flame, rings and athletes, horiz.

400 A106	30c green, red & yel	35	28
401 A106	50c rose car & multi	60	32
402 A106	1d dk grn, org, brn & red	1.10	65
	Nos. 400-402 (3)	2.05	1.25

19th Olympic Games, Mexico City, Oct. 12-27.

Scouts and Emblem A107

Barbary Sheep A108

1968, July 4 *Perf. 13*

403 A107	30c multicolored	50	18

8th Arab Boy Scout Jamboree, Algiers, 1968.

1968, Oct. 19 Photo. *Perf. 11½*

404 A108	40c shown	48	25
405 A108	1d Red deer	1.25	60

Hunting Scenes, Djemila A109

"Industry" A110

Design: 95c, Neptune's chariot, Timgad, horiz. Both designs are from Roman mosaics.

Perf. 12½x13, 13x12½

1968, Nov. 23 Photo.

406 A109	40c gray & multi	35	22
407 A109	95c gray & multi	85	50

1968, Dec. 14 *Perf. 11½*

Designs: No. 409, Miner with drill. 95c, "Energy" (circle and rays).

408 A110	30c dp orange & sil	25	18
409 A110	30c brown & multi	25	18
410 A110	95c silver, red & blk	75	35
	Nos. 408-410 (3)	1.25	71

Issued to publicize industrial development.

Opuntia Ficus Indica — A111

Flowers: 40c, Carnations. 70c, Roses. 95c, Bird-of-paradise flower.

1969, Jan. Photo. *Perf. 11½*

Flowers in Natural Colors

411 A111	25c pink & blk	52	25
412 A111	40c yellow & blk	65	32
413 A111	70c gray & blk	1.25	45
414 A111	95c brt blue & blk	2.00	80
	Nos. 411-414 (4)	4.42	1.82

See Nos. 496-499.

Irrigation Dam at Djorf Torba-Oued Guir A112

Design: 1.50d, Truck on Highway No. 51 and camel caravan.

1969, Feb. 22 Photo. *Perf. 11½*

415 A112	30c multi	24	18
416 A112	1.50d multi	1.25	65

Public works in the Sahara.

Mail Coach A113

1969, Mar. 22 Photo. *Perf. 11½*

417 A113	1d multicolored	1.10	60

Issued for Stamp Day, 1969.

Capitol, Timgad — A114

Design: 1d, Septimius Temple, Djemila, horiz.

1969, Apr. 5 Photo. *Perf. 13x12½*

418 A114	30c gray & multi	35	18
419 A114	1d gray & multi	85	35

Second Timgad Festival, Apr. 4-8.

ILO Emblem — A115

Arabian Saddle — A116

1969, May 24 Photo. *Perf. 11½*

420 A115	95c dp car, yel & blk	1.00	38

50th anniv. of the ILO.

1969, June 28 Photo. *Perf. 12x12½*

Algerian Handicrafts: 30c, Bookcase. 60c, Decorated copper plate.

Granite Paper

421 A116	30c multicolored	28	20
422 A116	60c multicolored	55	25
423 A116	1d multicolored	1.00	45
	Nos. 421-423 (3)	1.83	90

No. 321 Surcharged **0,20** ≡

1969 Typo. *Perf. 14x13½*

424 A71	20c on 12c emerald	22	15

Pan-African Culture Festival Emblem — A117

African Development Bank Emblem — A118

1969, July 19 Photo. *Perf. 12½*

425 A117	30c multicolored	32	18

Issued to commemorate the First Pan-African Culture Festival, Algiers, July 21-Aug. 1.

1969, Aug. 23 Typo. *Perf. 10½*

426 A118	30c dull blue, yel & blk	32	20

5th anniversary of the African Development Bank.

Astronauts and Landing Module on Moon — A119

Perf. 12½x11½

1969, Aug. 23 Photo.

427 A119	50c gold & multi	60	35

Man's 1st landing on the moon, July 20, 1969. US astronauts Neil A. Armstrong and Col. Edwin E. Aldrin, Jr., with Lieut. Col. Michael Collins piloting Apollo 11.

Algerian Women, by Dinet — A120

Design: 1.50d, The Watchmen, by Etienne Dinet.

1969, Nov. 29 Photo. *Perf. 14½*

428 A120	1d multi	1.75	90
429 A120	1.50d multi	2.75	1.40

Mother and Child — A121

1969, Dec. 27 Photo. *Perf. 11½*

430 A121	30c multicolored	32	24

Issued to promote mother and child protection.

Agricultural Growth Chart, Tractor and Dam — A122

Designs: 30c, Transportation and development. 50c, Abstract symbols of industrialization.

1970, Jan. 31 Photo. *Perf. 12½*
Size: 37x23mm

431 A122 25c dk brn, yel & org 16 15

Litho. *Perf. 14*
Size: 49x23mm

432 A122 30c blue & multi 24 18

Photo. *Perf. 12½*
Size: 37x23mm

433 A122 50c rose lilac & blk 28 20
Nos. 431-433 (3) 68 53

Four-Year Development Plan.

Old and New Mail Delivery A123

Spiny Lobster A124

1970, Feb. 28 Photo. *Perf. 11½*
Granite Paper

434 A123 30c multicolored 28 18

Issued for Stamp Day.

1970, Mar. 28

Designs: 40c, Mollusks. 75c, Retepora cellulosa. 1d, Red coral.

435 A124 30c ocher & multi 35 18
436 A124 40c multicolored 50 22
437 A124 75c ultra & multi 90 35
438 A124 1d lt blue & multi 1.25 48
Nos. 435-438 (4) 3.00 1.23

Oranges, EXPO '70 Emblem — A125

Designs (EXPO '70 Emblem and): 60c, Algerian pavilion. 70c, Grapes.

1970, Apr. 25 Photo. *Perf. 12½x12*

439 A125 30c lt blue, grn & org 50 15
440 A125 60c multicolored 65 18
441 A125 70c multicolored 1.00 32
Nos. 439-441 (3) 2.15 65

EXPO '70 International Exhibition, Osaka, Japan, Mar. 15-Sept. 13, 1970.

The Scott editorial staff regrettably cannot accept requests to identify, authenticate, or appraise stamps and postal markings.

Olives, Oil Bottle — A126

Saber — A127

1970, May 16 Photo. *Perf. 12½x12*

442 A126 1d yellow & multi 1.00 65

Olive Year, 1969-1970.

UPU Headquarters Issue
Common Design Type

1970, May 30 *Perf. 13*
Size: 36x26mm

443 CD133 75c multicolored 50 40

1970, June 27 Photo. *Perf. 12½*

Designs: 40c, Guns, 18th century, horiz. 1d, Pistol, 18th century, horiz.

444 A127 40c yellow & multi 65 22
445 A127 75c red & multi 80 40
446 A127 1d multicolored 1.25 50
Nos. 444-446 (3) 2.70 1.12

Common Design Types pictured in section at front of book.

Map of Arab Countries and Arab League Flag — A128

Typographed and Engraved
1970, July 25 *Perf. 10½*

447 A128 30c grn, ocher & lt bl 30 20

25th anniversary of the Arab League.

Lenin — A129

1970, Aug. 29 Litho. *Perf. 11½x12*

448 A129 30c brown & buff 25 20

Lenin (1870-1924), Russian communist leader.

Exhibition Hall and Algiers Fair Emblem — A130

1970, Sept. 11 Engr. *Perf. 14x13½*

449 A130 60c lt olive green 40 30

New Exhibition Hall for Algiers International Fair.

Education Year Emblem, Blackboard, Atom Symbol A131

Koran Page — A132

1970, Oct. 24 Photo. *Perf. 14*

450 A131 30c pink, blk, gold & lt bl 22 18
451 A132 3d multicolored 2.50 1.50

Issued for International Education Year.

Great Mosque, Tlemcen — A133

Design: 40c, Ketchaoua Mosque, Algiers, vert. 1d, Mosque, Sidi-Okba, vert.

1970-71 Litho. *Perf. 14*

456 A133 30c multicolored 22 15
457 A133 40c sepia & lemon ('71) 25 15
458 A133 1d multicolored 65 28
Nos. 456-458 (3) 1.12 58

Symbols of the Arts — A134

1970, Dec. 26 Photo. *Perf. 13x12½*

459 A134 1d grn, lt grn & org 80 45

Main Post Office, Algiers A135

1971, Jan. 23 *Perf. 11½*

460 A135 30c multicolored 32 20

Stamp Day, 1971.

Hurdling A136

Designs: 40c, Vaulting, vert. 75c, Basketball, vert.

1971, Mar. 7 Photo. *Perf. 11½*

461 A136 20c lt blue & slate 25 20
462 A136 40c lt ol grn & slate 35 35
463 A136 75c salmon pink & slate 65 50
Nos. 461-463 (3) 1.25 1.05

Mediterranean Games, Izmir, Turkey, Oct. 1971.

Symbolic Head — A137

1971, Mar. 27 *Perf. 12½*

464 A137 60c car rose, blk & sil 32 20

Intl. year against racial discrimination.

Emblem and Technicians A138

1971, Apr. 24 Photo. *Perf. 12½x12*

465 A138 70c claret, org & bluish blk 40 30

Founding of the Institute of Technology.

Woman from Aurès — A139

Regional Costumes: 70c, Man from Oran. 80c, Man from Algiers. 90c, Woman from Amour Mountains.

1971, Oct. 16 *Perf. 11½*

466 A139 50c gold & multi 1.50 65
467 A139 70c gold & multi 1.65 1.00
468 A139 80c gold & multi 2.25 1.10
469 A139 90c gold & multi 2.50 1.25
Nos. 466-469 (4) 7.90 4.00

See Nos. 485-488, 534-537.

UNICEF Emblem, Birds and Plants — A140

1971, Dec. 6 *Perf. 11½*

470 A140 60c multicolored 55 32

25th anniv. of UNICEF.

Lion of St. Mark A141

Design: 1.15d, Bridge of Sighs, Venice, vert.

1972, Jan. 24 Litho. *Perf. 12*

471 A141 80c multi 60 32
472 A141 1.15d multi 90 52

UNESCO campaign to save Venice.

Javelin
A142

Book and Book Year Emblem
A143

Designs: 25c, Bicycling, horiz. 60c, Wrestling. 1d, Gymnast on rings.

1972, Mar. 25 Photo. *Perf. 11½*

473 A142	25c maroon & multi	30	20
474 A142	40c ocher & multi	35	25
475 A142	60c ultra & multi	40	40
476 A142	1d rose & multi	1.00	50
	Nos. 473-476 (4)	2.05	1.35

20th Olympic Games, Munich, Aug. 26-Sept. 11.

1972, Apr. 15

477 A143 1.15d bister, brn & red 65 48

International Book Year 1972.

Mailmen
A144

Flowers
A145

1972, Apr. 22

478 A144 40c gray & multi 25 15

Stamp Day 1972.

1972, May 27

479 A145	50c Jasmine	65	28
480 A145	60c Violets	75	35
481 A145	1.15d Tuberose	1.50	55
	Nos. 479-481 (3)	2.90	1.18

Olympic Stadium, Chéraga — A146

1972, June 10

482 A146 50c gray, choc & grn 60 32

New Day, Algerian Flag — A147

1972, July 5

483 A147 1d green & multi 65 42

10th anniversary of independence.

Festival Emblem — A148

Mailing a Letter — A149

1972, July 5 Litho. *Perf. 10½*

484 A148 40c grn, dk brn & org 22 15

1st Arab Youth Festival, Algiers, July 5-11.

Costume Type of 1971

Regional Costumes: 50c, Woman from Hoggar. 60c, Kabyle woman. 70c, Man from Mzab. 90c, Woman from Tlemcen.

1972, Nov. 18 Photo. *Perf. 11½*

485 A139	50c gold & multi	80	70
486 A139	60c gold & multi	1.10	90
487 A139	70c gold & multi	1.25	1.10
488 A139	90c gold & multi	1.75	1.25
	Nos. 485-488 (4)	4.90	3.95

1973, Jan. 20 Photo. *Perf. 11*

489 A149 40c orange & multi 40 20

Stamp Day.

Ho Chi Minh, Map of Viet Nam — A150

1973, Feb. 17 Photo. *Perf. 11½*

490 A150 40c multicolored 75 50

To honor the people of Viet Nam.

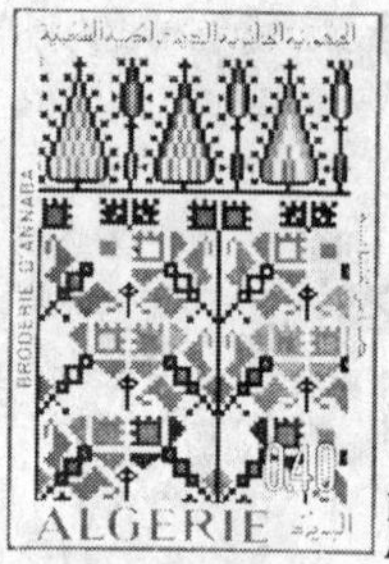
Embroidery from Annaba — A151

Designs: 60c, Tree of Life pattern from Algiers. 80c, Constantine embroidery.

1973, Feb. 24

491 A151	40c gray & multi	75	40
492 A151	60c blue and multi	1.00	60
493 A151	80c dk red, gold & blk	1.50	80
	Nos. 491-493 (3)	3.25	1.80

Stylized Globe and Wheat — A152

1973, Mar. 26 Photo. *Perf. 11½*

494 A152 1.15d brt rose lil, org & grn 75 40

World Food Program, 10th anniversary.

Soldier and Flag
A153

1973, Apr. 23 Photo. *Perf. 14x13½*

495 A153 40c multicolored 25 18

Honoring the National Service.

Flower Type of 1969

Flowers: 30c, Opuntia ficus indica. 40c, Roses. 1d, Carnations. 1.15d, Bird-of-paradise flower.

1973, May 21 Photo. *Perf. 11½*

Flowers in Natural Colors

496 A111	30c pink & blk	40	18
497 A111	40c gray & blk	50	20
498 A111	1d yellow & multi	90	40
499 A111	1.15d multi	1.25	50
	Nos. 496-499 (4)	3.05	1.28

For overprints and surcharges see #518-519, 531.

OAU Emblem — A154

1973, May 28 Photo. *Perf. 12½x13*

500 A154 40c multicolored 40 20

Org. for African Unity, 10th anniv.

Desert and Fruitful Land, Farmer and Family
A155

1973, June 18 *Perf. 11½*

501 A155 40c gold & multi 50 40

Agricultural revolution.

Map of Africa, Scout Emblem — A156

1973, July 16 Litho. *Perf. 10½*

502 A156 80c purple 1.00 50

24th Boy Scout World Conference (1st in Africa), Nairobi, Kenya, July 16-21.

Algerian PTT Emblem — A157

1973, Aug. 6 *Perf. 14*

503 A157 40c blue & orange 22 15

Adoption of new emblem for Post, Telegraph and Telephone System.

Conference Emblem — A158

Perf. 13½x12½

1973, Sept. 5 Photo.

504 A158	40c dp rose & multi	18	15
505 A158	80c blue grn & multi	52	26

4th Summit Conference of Non-aligned Nations, Algiers, Sept. 5-9.

Port of Skikda
A159

1973, Sept. 29 Photo. *Perf. 11½*

506 A159 80c ocher, blk & ultra 48 25

New port of Skikda.

Young Workers — A160

1973, Oct. 22 Photo. *Perf. 13*

507 A160 40c multicolored 22 15

Voluntary work service.

Arms of Algiers
A161

1973, Dec. 22 Photo. *Perf. 13*

508 A161 2d gold & multi 1.60 1.10

Millennium of Algiers.

Infant — A162

1974, Jan. 7 Litho. *Perf. 10½x11*

509 A162 80c orange & multi 60 35

Fight against tuberculosis.

Man and Woman, Industry and Transportation A163

1974, Feb. 18 Photo. *Perf. 11½*
510 A163 80c multicolored 48 20

Four-year plan.

A164

1974, Feb. 25 Photo. *Perf. 11½*
511 A164 1.50d multi 1.10 65

Millennium of the birth of abu-al-Rayhan al-Biruni (973-1048), philosopher and mathematician.

Map and Colors of Algeria, Tunisia, Morocco A165

1974, Mar. 4 Photo. *Perf. 13*
512 A165 40c gold & multi 28 20

Maghreb Committee for Coordination of Posts and Telecommunications.

Hand Holding Rifle A166

Mother and Children A167

1974, Mar. 25 *Perf. 11½*
513 A166 80c red & black 30 20

Solidarity with the struggle of the people of South Africa.

1974, Apr. 8 *Perf. 13½*
514 A167 85c multicolored 35 22

Honoring Algerian mothers.

Village A168

Designs: 80c, Harvest. 90c, Tractor and sun. Designs after children's drawings.

1974, June 15
Size: 45x26mm
515 A168 70c multicolored 40 18

Size: 48x33mm
516 A168 80c multicolored 48 28
517 A168 90c multicolored 60 42
Nos. 515-517 (3) 1.48 88

Nos. 498-499 Overprinted "FLORALIES/1974"

1974, June 22 Photo. *Perf. 11½*
518 A111 1d multi 65 35
519 A111 1.15d multi 70 40

1974 Flower Show.

Stamp Vending Machine — A169

1974, Oct. 7 Photo. *Perf. 13*
520 A169 80c multicolored 42 20

Stamp Day 1974.

UPU Emblem and Globe — A170

1974, Oct. 14 *Perf. 14*
521 A170 80c multicolored 50 28

Centenary of Universal Postal Union.

"Revolution" — A171

Soldiers and Mountains — A172

Raising New Flag — A173

Design: 1d, Algerian struggle for independence (people, sun and fields).

1974, Nov. 4 Photo. *Perf. 14*
522 A171 40c multicolored 28 18
523 A172 70c multicolored 40 22
524 A173 95c multicolored 48 22
525 A171 1d multicolored 60 28
Nos. 522-525 (4) 1.76 90

20th anniv. of the start of the revolution.

"Horizon 1980" — A174

Ewer and Basin — A175

1974, Nov. 23 Photo. *Perf. 13*
526 A174 95c ocher, dk red & blk 55 25

10-year development plan, 1971-1980.

1974, Dec. 21 *Perf. 11½*
527 A175 50c shown 22 15
528 A175 60c Coffee pot 28 20
529 A175 95c Sugar bowl 45 28
530 A175 1d Bath tub 50 35
Nos. 527-530 (4) 1.45 98

17th century Algerian copperware.

No. 497 Surcharged with New Value and Heavy Bar

1975, Jan. 4
531 A111 50c on 40c multi 50 40

Mediterranean Games' Emblem — A176

1975, Jan. 27 *Perf. 13½*
532 A176 50c purple, yel & grn 28 18
533 A176 1d orange, bl & mar 60 22

Mediterranean Games, Algiers, 1975.

Costume Type of 1971

Regional Costumes: No. 534, Woman from Hoggar. No. 535, Woman from Algiers. No. 536, Woman from Oran. No. 537, Man from Tlemcen.

1975, Feb. 22 Photo. *Perf. 11½*
534 A139 1d gold & multi 1.00 80
535 A139 1d gold & multi 1.00 80
536 A139 1d gold & multi 1.00 80
537 A139 1d gold & multi 1.00 80
Nos. 534-537 (4) 4.00 3.20

Map of Arab Countries, ALO Emblem A177

1975, Mar. 10 Litho. *Perf. 10½x11*
538 A177 50c red brown 25 15

Arab Labor Organization, 10th anniversary.

Blood Transfusion A178

1975, Mar. 15 *Perf. 14*
539 A178 50c car rose & multi 32 18

Blood donation and transfusions.

Post Office, Al-Kantara A179

Policeman and Map of Algeria A180

1975, May 10 Photo. *Perf. 11½*
Granite Paper
540 A179 50c multicolored 25 15

Stamp Day 1975.

1975, June 1 Photo. *Perf. 13*
541 A180 50c multicolored 75 40

Natl. Security and 10th Natl. Police Day.

Ground Receiving Station A181

Designs: 1d, Map of Algeria with locations of radar sites, transmission mast and satellite. 1.20d, Main and subsidiary stations.

1975, June 28 Photo. *Perf. 13*
542 A181 50c blue & multi 28 15
543 A181 1d blue & multi 55 20
544 A181 1.20d blue & multi 60 22
Nos. 542-544 (3) 1.43 57

National satellite telecommunications network.

Revolutionary with Flag — A182

1975, Aug. 20 Photo. *Perf. 11½*
545 A182 1d multicolored 50 25

August 20th Revolutionary Movement (Skikda), 20th anniversary.

Swimming and Games' Emblem A183

Perf. 13x13½, 13½x13
1975, Aug. 23 Photo.
546 A183 25c shown 15 15
547 A183 50c Judo, map 25 18
548 A183 70c Soccer, vert. 48 22
549 A183 1d Running, vert. 55 25
550 A183 1.20d Handball, vert. 70 38
a. Souv. sheet of 5, #546-550, perf 13 4.50 4.50
Nos. 546-550 (5) 2.13 1.18

7th Mediterranean Games, Algiers, Aug. 23-Sept. 6.

No. 550a sold for 4.50d. Exists imperf.; same value.

Setif, Guelma, Kherrata — A184

1975 Litho. *Perf. 13½x14*

551 A184 5c orange & blk	15	15
552 A184 10c emerald & brn	15	15
553 A184 25c dl blue & blk	15	15
554 A184 30c lemon & blk	15	15
555 A184 50c brt grn & blk	22	15
556 A184 70c fawn & blk	35	15
557 A184 1d vermilion & blk	50	25
Nos. 551-557 (7)	1.67	
Set value		60

30th anniv. of victory in World War II.
Issue dates: 50c, 1d, Nov. 3; others, Dec. 17.
For surcharge, see No. 611.

Map of Maghreb and APU Emblem A185

1975, Nov. 20 Photo. *Perf. 11½*

558 A185 1d multicolored	55	28

10th Cong. of Arab Postal Union, Algiers.

Mosaic, Bey Constantine's Palace — A186

Dey-Alger Palace — A187

Famous buildings: 2d, Prayer niche, Medersa Sidi-Boumediene, Tlemcen.

1975, Dec. 22

559 A186 1d lt blue & multi	60	22
560 A186 2d buff & multi	1.10	60
561 A187 2.50d buff & blk	1.60	90
Nos. 559-561 (3)	3.30	1.72

Al-Azhar University A188

Perf. 11½x12½
1975, Dec. 29 Litho.

562 A188 2d multicolored	1.10	60

Millennium of Al-Azhar University.

Red-billed Firefinch — A189

Birds: 1.40d, Black-headed bush shrike, horiz. 2d, Blue tit. 2.50d, Blackbellied sandgrouse, horiz.

1976, Jan. 24 Photo. *Perf. 11½*

563 A189 50c multi	35	18
564 A189 1.40d multi	85	55
565 A189 2d multi	1.10	65
566 A189 2.50d multi	1.50	90
Nos. 563-566 (4)	3.80	2.28

See Nos. 595-598.

Telephones 1876 and 1976 — A190

Map of Africa with Angola and its Flag — A191

1976, Feb. 23 Photo. *Perf. 13½x13*

567 A190 1.40d rose, dk & lt bl	65	38

Centenary of first telephone call by Alexander Graham Bell, Mar. 10, 1876.

1976, Feb. 23 *Perf. 11½*

568 A191 50c brown & multi	25	15

Algeria's solidarity with the People's Republic of Angola.

A192

A193

Sahraoui flag and child, map of former Spanish Sahara.

1976, Mar. 15 Photo. *Perf. 11½*

569 A192 50c multicolored	25	15

Algeria's solidarity with Sahraoui Arab Democratic Republic, former Spanish Sahara.

1976, Mar. 22

570 A193 1.40d Mailman	60	32

Stamp Day 1976.

Microscope, Slide with TB Bacilli, Patients A194

1976, Apr. 26 *Perf. 13x13½*

571 A194 50c multicolored	40	20

Fight against tuberculosis.

"Setif, Guelma, Kherrata" — A195

1976, May 24 Photo. *Perf. 13½x13*

572 A195 50c blue & yellow	35	15
a. Booklet pane of 6	4.75	
b. Booklet pane of 10	4.00	

No. 572 was issued in booklets only.

Ram's Head over Landscape — A196

People Holding Torch, Map of Algeria — A197

1976, June 17 Photo. *Perf. 11½*

573 A196 50c multicolored	40	20

Livestock breeding.

1976, June 29 Photo. *Perf. 14x13½*

574 A197 50c multicolored	25	15

National Charter.

Palestine Map and Flag — A198

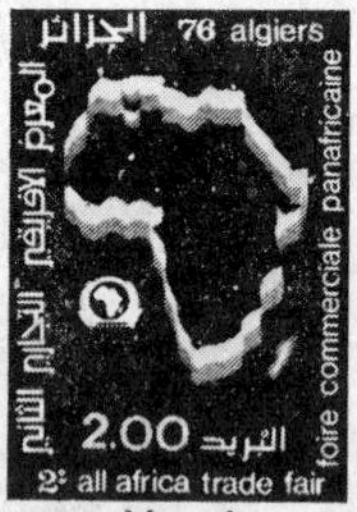

Map of Africa — A199

1976, July 12 *Perf. 11½*
Granite Paper

575 A198 50c multicolored	2.00	1.00

Solidarity with the Palestinians.

1976, Oct. 3 Litho. *Perf. 10½x11*

576 A199 2d dk blue & multi	1.00	50

2nd Pan-African Commercial Fair, Algiers.

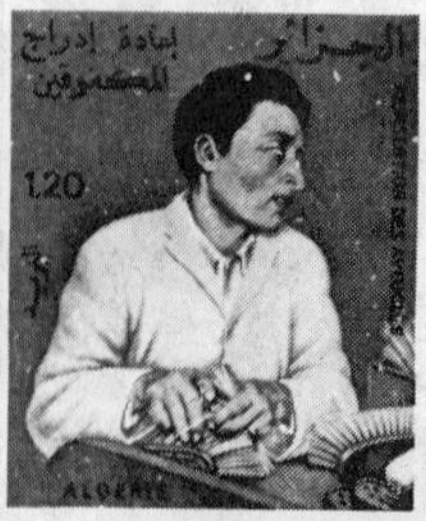

Blind Brushmaker A200

The Blind, by Dinet A201

1976, Oct. 23 Photo. *Perf. 14½*

577 A200 1.20d blue & multi	65	35
578 A201 1.40d gold & multi	1.50	75

Rehabilitation of the blind.

"Constitution 1976" — A202

1976, Nov. 19 Photo. *Perf. 11½*

579 A202 2d multicolored	1.00	55

New Constitution.

Soldiers Planting Seedlings — A203

1976, Nov. 25 Litho. *Perf. 12*

580 A203 1.40d multicolored	75	35

Green barrier against the Sahara.

Ornamental Border and Inscription A204

1976, Dec. 18 Photo. *Perf. 11½*
Granite Paper

581 A204 2d multicolored	1.25	75

Re-election of Pres. Houari Boumediene.
See No. 627.

Map with Charge Zones and Dials A205

People and Buildings A206

1977, Jan. 22 *Perf. 13*

582 A205 40c silver & multi	28	15

Inauguration of automatic national and international telephone service.

1977, Jan. 29 Photo. *Perf. 11½*

583 A206 60c on 50c multi	35	18

2nd General Population and Buildings Census. No. 583 was not issued without the typographed red brown surcharge, date, and bars.

Sahara Museum, Uargla — A207

1977, Feb. 12 Litho. *Perf. 14*

584 A207 60c multicolored 35 20

El-Kantara Gorge — A208

Perf. 12½x13½

1977, Feb. 19 Photo.

585 A208 20c green & yellow		15	15
a. Bklt. pane, 3 #585, 4 #586 + label		8.00	
b. Bklt. pane, 5 #585, 2 #587 + label		6.50	
586 A208 60c brt lilac & yel		18	15
587 A208 1d brown & yellow		40	15
Set value		63	30

National Assembly — A209

1977, Feb. 27 *Perf. 11½*

588 A209 2d multicolored 1.00 60

People and Flag — A210

Soldier and Flag — A211

Perf. 13½, 11½ (3d)

1977, Mar. 12 Photo.

589 A210 2d multicolored	1.25	40
590 A211 3d multicolored	1.75	65

Solidarity with the peoples of Zimbabwe (Rhodesia), 2d; Namibia, 3d.

Winter, Roman Mosaic — A212

The Seasons from Roman Villa, 2nd century A.D.: 1.40d, Fall. 2d, Summer. 3d, Spring.

1977, Apr. 21 Photo. *Perf. 11½*

Granite Paper

591 A212 1.20d multi	95	52
592 A212 1.40d multi	1.25	52
593 A212 2d multi	1.65	95
594 A212 3d multi	2.50	1.65
a. Souv. sheet of 4, #591-594, perf., imperf.	10.00	10.00
Nos. 591-594 (4)	6.35	3.64

No. 594a sold for 8d.

Bird Type of 1976

Birds: 60c, Tristram's warbler. 1.40d, Moussier's redstart, horiz. 2d, Temminck's horned lark, horiz. 3d, Eurasian hoopoe.

1977, May 21 Photo. *Perf. 11½*

595 A189 60c multi	75	22
596 A189 1.40d multi	1.25	40
597 A189 2d multi	1.75	65
598 A189 3d multi	2.50	1.10
Nos. 595-598 (4)	6.25	2.37

Horseman — A213

Design: 5d, Attacking horsemen, horiz.

1977, June 25 Photo. *Perf. 11½*

599 A213 2d multicolored	1.65	75
600 A213 5d multicolored	3.50	2.00

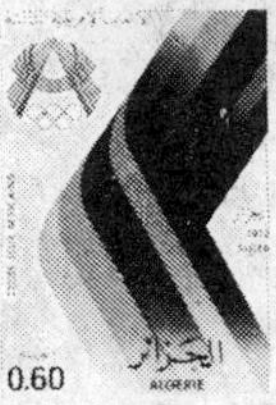
Flag Colors, Games Emblem — A214

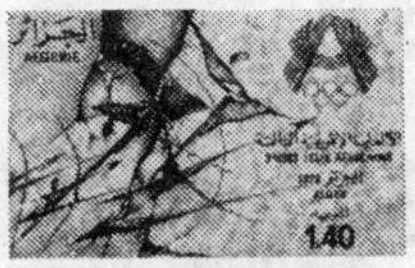
Wall Painting, Games Emblem A215

1977, Sept. 24 Photo. *Perf. 11½*

601 A214 60c multi	35	22
602 A215 1.40d multi	80	45

3rd African Games, Algiers 1978.

Village and Tractor A216

1977, Nov. 12 *Perf. 14x13*

603 A216 1.40d multi 90 65

Socialist agricultural village.

Almohades Dirham, 12th Century — A217

Ancient Coins: 1.40d, Almohades coin, 12th century. 2d, Almoravides dinar, 11th century.

1977, Dec. 17 Photo. *Perf. 11½*

604 A217 60c ultra, sil & blk	50	35
605 A217 1.40d green, gold & brn	1.10	50
606 A217 2d red brn, gold & brn	1.50	90
Nos. 604-606 (3)	3.10	1.75

Flowering Trees — A218

1978, Feb. 11 Photo. *Perf. 11½*

607 A218 60c Cherry	35	24
608 A218 1.20d Peach	85	50
609 A218 1.30d Almond	85	50
610 A218 1.40d Apple	90	55
Nos. 607-610 (4)	2.95	1.79

No. 555 Surcharged with New Value and Bar

1978, Feb. 11 Litho. *Perf. 13½x14*

611 A184 60c on 50c 50 16

Children with Traffic Signs and Car — A219

1978, Apr. 29 Photo. *Perf. 11½*

612 A219 60c multicolored 28 15

Road safety and protection of children.

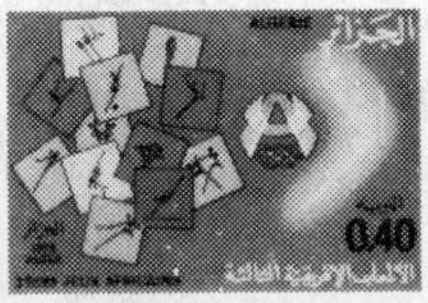
Sports and Games Emblems A220

Designs (Games Emblem and): 60c, Rower, vert. 1.20d, Flag colors. 1.30d, Fireworks, vert. 1.40d, Map of Africa and dancers, vert.

1978, July 13 Photo. *Perf. 11½*

613 A220 40c multi	18	15
614 A220 60c multi	28	18
615 A220 1.20d multi	60	28
616 A220 1.30d multi	60	35
617 A220 1.40d multi	65	35
Nos. 613-617 (5)	2.31	1.31

3rd African Games, Algiers, July 13-28.

TB Patient Returning to Family A221

1978, Oct. 5 Photo. *Perf. 13½x14*

618 A221 60c multicolored 35 16

Anti-tuberculosis campaign.

Holy Kaaba — A222

1978, Oct. 28 Photo. *Perf. 11½*

619 A222 60c multicolored 28 15

Pilgrimage to Mecca.

National Servicemen Building Road — A223

1978, Nov. 4

620 A223 60c multicolored 28 15

African Unity Road from El Goleah to In Salah, inauguration.

Fibula A224

Pres. Boumediene A225

Jewelry: 1.35d, Pendant. 1.40d, Ankle ring.

1978, Dec. 21 Photo. *Perf. 12x11½*

621 A224 1.20d multi	65	28
622 A224 1.35d multi	70	28
623 A224 1.40d multi	1.10	1.10
Nos. 621-623 (3)	2.45	1.66

1979, Jan. 7 Photo. *Perf. 12x11½*

624 A225 60c green, red & brown 28 15

Houari Boumediene, president of Algeria 1965-1978.

Torch and Books A226

1979, Jan. 27 Photo. *Perf. 11½*

625 A226 60c multicolored 28 18

Natl. Front of Liberation Party Cong.

Pres. Boumediene A227

1979, Feb. 4 Photo. *Perf. 11½*

626 A227 1.40d multi 65 28

Forty days after death of Pres. Houari Boumediène.

Ornamental Type of 1976

Proclamation of new President.

1979, Feb. 10
627 A204 2d multicolored 1.00 35

Election of Pres. Chadli Bendjedid.

A229

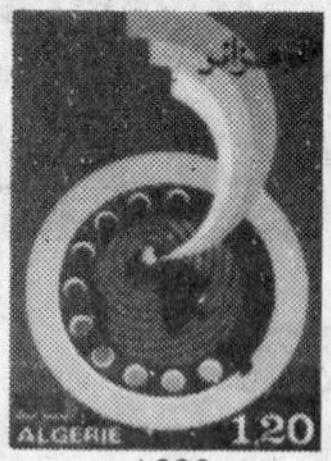

A230

1979, Apr. 18 Photo. *Perf. 11½*
628 A229 60c multicolored 28 15

Sheik Abdul-Hamid Ben Badis (1889-1940).

1979, May 19 Photo. *Perf. 13½x14*

Designs: 1.20d, Telephone dial, map of Africa. 1.40d, Symbolic Morse key and waves.

629 A230 1.20d multi 55 22
630 A230 1.40d multi 60 22

Telecom '79 Exhib., Geneva, Sept. 20-26.

Harvest, IYC Emblem — A231

Design: 1.40d, Dancers and IYC emblem, vert.

Perf. 11½x11, 11x11½

1979, June 21
631 A231 60c multi 40 20
632 A231 1.40d multi 60 45

International Year of the Child.

A232

A233

1979, Oct. 20 Photo. *Perf. 11½*
633 A232 1.40d Nuthatch 90 40

1979, Nov. 1 Photo. *Perf. 12½*

Designs: 1.40d, Flag, soldiers and workers. 3d, Revolutionaries and emblem.

634 A233 1.40d multi 90 22

Size: 37x48mm
Perf. 11½

635 A233 3d multi 2.25 65

November 1 revolution, 25th anniversary.

Hegira, 1500 Anniv. A234

1979, Dec. 2 Photo. *Perf. 11½*
636 A234 3d multicolored 1.25 65

Camels, Lion, Men and Slave — A235

Dionysian Procession (Setif Mosaic): 1.35d, Elephants, tigers and women. Men in tiger-drawn cart. No. 639a has continuous design.

1980, Feb. 16 Photo. *Perf. 11½*
Granite Paper

637 A235 1.20d multi 55 22
638 A235 1.35d multi 60 35
639 A235 1.40d multi 65 55
a. Strip of 3, #637-639 1.80 1.25
Nos. 637-639 (3) 1.80 1.12

Science Day — A236

1980, Apr. 19 Photo. *Perf. 12*
640 A236 60c multicolored 28 20

Dam and Workers — A237

1980, June 17 Photo. *Perf. 11½*
641 A237 60c multicolored 28 15

Extraordinary Congress of the National Liberation Front Party.

Olympic Sports, Moscow '80 Emblem A238

1980, June 28
642 A238 50c Flame, rings, vert. 22 15
643 A238 1.40d shown 65 35

22nd Summer Olympic Games, Moscow, July 19-Aug. 3.

20th Anniversary of OPEC — A239

Perf. 11x10½, 10½x11

1980, Sept. 15 Engr.
644 A239 60c Men holding OPEC emblem, vert. 28 15
645 A239 1.40d shown 65 35

Aures Valley A240

1980, Sept. 25 Litho. *Perf. 13½x14*
646 A240 50c shown 22 15
647 A240 1d El Oued Oasis 40 18
648 A240 1.40d Tassili Rocks 60 22
649 A240 2d View of Algiers 90 40
Nos. 646-649 (4) 2.12 95

World Tourism Conf., Manila, Sept. 27.

Avicenna (980-1037), Philosopher and Physician A241

1980, Oct. 25 Photo. *Perf. 12*
650 A241 2d multicolored 1.50 75

Ruins of El Asnam A242

1980, Nov. 13 Photo. *Perf. 12*
651 A242 3d multicolored 1.25 45

Earthquake relief.

Crown A243

1980, Dec. 20 Photo. *Perf. 12*
Granite Paper

652 A243 60c Necklace, vert. 28 18
653 A243 1.40d Earrings, bracelet, vert. 60 28
654 A243 2d shown 80 45
Nos. 652-654 (3) 1.68 91

See Nos. 705-707.

1980-1984 Five-Year Plan — A244

1981, Jan. 29 Litho. *Perf. 14*
655 A244 60c multicolored 25 15

Basket Weaving — A245

1981, Feb. 19 Photo. *Perf. 12½*
Granite Paper

656 A245 40c shown 20 15
657 A245 60c Rug weaving 28 15
658 A245 1d Coppersmith 40 18
659 A245 1.40d Jeweler 60 32
Nos. 656-659 (4) 1.48 80

Cedar Tree — A246

Arbor Day: 1.40d, Cypress tree, vert.

1981, Mar. 19 Photo. *Perf. 12*
Granite Paper

660 A246 60c multi 30 15
661 A246 1.40d multi 60 32

Mohamed Bachir el Ibrahimi (1869-1965) A247

Children Going to School — A248

1981, Apr. 16
Granite Paper

662 A247 60c multicolored 25 15
663 A248 60c multicolored 25 15
Set value 17

Science Day.

12th International Hydatidological Congress, Algiers — A249

1981, Apr. 23 *Perf. 14x13½*

664 A249	2d multicolored		80	32

13th World Telecommunications Day — A250

1981, May 14 Photo. *Perf. 14x13½*

665 A250	1.40d multi	60	20

Disabled People and Hand Offering Flower A251

Perf. 12½x13, 13x12½

1981, June 20 Litho.

666 A251	1.20d Symbolic globe, vert.	55	18
667 A251	1.40d shown	60	18

Intl. Year of the Disabled.

Papilio Machaon A252

1981, Aug. 20 Photo. *Perf. 11½*

Granite Paper

668 A252	60c shown	25	15
669 A252	1.20d Rhodocera rhamni	55	20
670 A252	1.40d Charaxes jasius	60	25
671 A252	2d Papilio podalirius	80	38
	Nos. 668-671 (4)	2.20	98

Monk Seal — A253

1981, Sept. 17 *Perf. 14x13½*

672 A253	60c shown	25	15
673 A253	1.40d Macaque	60	35

World Food Day — A254

Cave Drawings of Tassili — A255

1981, Oct. 16 Photo. *Perf. 14x14½*

674 A254	2d multicolored	65	35

1981, Nov. 21 *Perf. 11½*

Designs: Various cave drawings. 1.60d, 2d horiz.

675 A255	60c multi	30	15
676 A255	1d multi	50	18
677 A255	1.60d multi	75	32
678 A255	2d multi	90	40
	Nos. 675-678 (4)	2.45	1.05

Galley, 17-18th Cent. A256

1981, Dec. 17 Photo. *Perf. 11½*

679 A256	60c shown	40	18
680 A256	1.60d Ship, diff.	90	35

1982 World Cup Soccer A257

Designs: Various soccer players.

Perf. 13x12½x 12½x13

1982, Feb. 25 Litho.

681 A257	80c multi, vert.	35	15
682 A257	2.80d multi	1.10	50

TB Bacillus Centenary — A258

1982, Mar. 20 Photo. *Perf. 14½x14*

683 A258	80c multi	35	15

Painted Stand A259

1982, Apr. 24 Photo. *Perf. 11½*

Granite Paper

684 A259	80c Mirror, vert.	35	18
685 A259	2d shown	80	40

Size: 48x33mm

686 A259	2.40d Chest	1.00	55
	Nos. 684-686 (3)	2.15	1.13

Djamaael Djadid Mosque, Algiers — A260

1982, May 15 Litho. *Perf. 14*

687 A260	80c shown	35	15
688 A260	2.40d Sidi Boumediene Mosque, Tlemcen	1.00	50
689 A260	3d Garden of Dey, Algiers	1.25	55
	Nos. 687-689 (3)	2.60	1.20

See Nos. 731-734, 745-747, 774, 778-783.

Callitris Articulata A261

Independence, 20th Anniv. A262

Designs: Medicinal plants.

1982, May 27 Photo. *Perf. 11½*

Granite Paper

690 A261	50c shown	20	15
691 A261	80c Artemisia herba-alba	25	15
692 A261	1d Ricinus communis	50	20
693 A261	2.40d Thymus fontanesii	90	45
	Nos. 690-693 (4)	1.85	95

1982, July 5

Granite Paper

694 A262	50c Riflemen	20	15
695 A262	80c Soldiers, horiz.	32	18
696 A262	2d Symbols, citizens, horiz.	80	45
	Nos. 694-696 (3)	1.32	78

Souvenir Sheet

697 A262	5d Emblem	2.00	2.00

No. 697 contains one 32x39mm stamp.

Soummam Congress A263

1982, Aug. 20 Litho.

698 A263	80c Congress building	35	15

Scouting Year — A264

1982, Oct. 21 Photo.

Granite Paper

699 A264	2.80d multi	1.10	45

Palestinian Child — A265

Chlamydotis Undulata — A266

1982, Nov. 25 Litho. *Perf. 10½*

700 A265	1.60d multi	2.00	75

Perf. 15x14, 14x15

1982, Dec. 23 Photo.

Protected birds. 50c, 2d horiz.

701 A266	50c Geronticus eremita	40	15
702 A266	80c shown	65	18
703 A266	2d Aguila rapax	1.25	40
704 A266	2.40d Gypaetus barbatus	1.75	45
	Nos. 701-704 (4)	4.05	1.18

Jewelry Type of 1980

1983, Feb. 10 *Perf. 11½*

Granite Paper

705 A243	50c Picture frame	18	15
706 A243	1d Flaska	38	28
707 A243	2d Brooch, horiz.	75	45
	Nos. 705-707 (3)	1.31	88

A267

A268

1983, Mar. 17 Photo.

Granite Paper

708 A267	80c Abies numidica, vert.	32	15
709 A267	2.80d Acacia raddiana	1.10	60

Intl. Arbor Day.

Perf. 12x12½, 12½x12

1983, Apr. 21 Photo.

Various minerals. 1.20d, 2.40d horiz.

Granite Paper

710 A268	70c multi	28	15
711 A268	80c multi	32	18
712 A268	1.20d multi	50	28
713 A268	2.40d multi	1.00	60
	Nos. 710-713 (4)	2.10	1.21

30th Anniv. of Intl. Customs Cooperation Council A269

1983, May 14 Photo. *Perf. 11½*

Granite Paper

714 A269	80c multi	35	18

Emir Abdelkader Death Centenary — A270

1983, May 22 Photo. *Perf. 12*

Granite Paper

715 A270	4d multi	1.60	75

A271

A272

Local mushrooms.

1983, July 21 *Perf. 14x15*
716 A271 50c Amanita muscaria 20 15
717 A271 80c Amanita phalloides 32 18
718 A271 1.40d Pleurotus eryngii 55 35
719 A271 2.80d Tefezia leonis 1.00 60
Nos. 716-719 (4) 2.07 1.28

1983, Sept. 1 **Photo.** *Perf. 11½*
720 A272 80c multi 35 15

ibn-Khaldun, historian, philosopher.

World Communications Year — A273

Perf. 11½x12½
1983, Sept. 22 **Litho.**
721 A273 80c Post Office, Algiers 35 15
722 A273 2.40d Telephone, circuit box 1.00 38

Goat and Tassili Mountains A274

1983, Oct. 20 **Litho.** *Perf. 12½x13*
723 A274 50c shown 20 15
724 A274 80c Tuaregs in native costume 32 18
725 A274 2.40d Animals, rock painting 1.00 40
726 A274 2.80d Rock formation 1.00 60
Nos. 723-726 (4) 2.52 1.33

Sloughi Dog — A275

Perf. 14x14½, 14½x14
1983, Nov. 24 **Photo.**
727 A275 80c shown 60 40
728 A275 2.40d Sloughi, horiz. 1.50 75

Natl. Liberation Party, 5th Congress — A276

1983, Dec. 19 **Photo.** *Perf. 11½*
729 A276 80c Symbols of development 35 22

Souvenir Sheet

730 A276 5d Emblem 3.00 2.50

No. 730 contains one 32x38mm stamp.

View Type of 1982

1984, Jan. 26 **Litho.** *Perf. 14*
731 A260 10c View of Oran, 1830 15 15
732 A260 1d Sidi Abderahman and Taalibi Mosques 40 18
733 A260 2d Bejaia, 1830 80 35
734 A260 4d Constantine, 1830 1.75 60
Nos. 731-734 (4) 3.10 1.28

See Nos. 745-747, 781, 783.

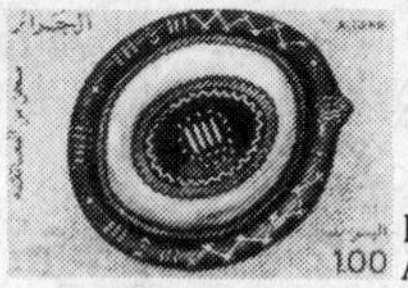

Pottery A278

Perf. 11½x12, 12x11½
1984, Feb. 23 **Photo.**

Granite Paper

735 A278 80c Jug, vert. 35 22
736 A278 1d Platter 40 22
737 A278 2d Oil lamp, vert. 80 45
738 A278 2.40d Pitcher 1.00 60
Nos. 735-738 (4) 2.55 1.49

Fountains of Old Algiers — A279

1984 Summer Olympics — A280

Various fountains.

1984, Mar. 22 **Photo.** *Perf. 11½*

Granite Paper

739 A279 50c multi 20 15
740 A279 80c multi 38 20
741 A279 2.40d multi 1.00 60
Nos. 739-741 (3) 1.58 95

1984, May 19 **Photo.** *Perf. 11½*

Granite Paper

742 A280 1d multi 45 28

Brown Stallion — A281

1984, June 14 **Photo.** *Perf. 11½*

Granite Paper

743 A281 80c shown 35 18
744 A281 2.40d White mare 1.00 60

View Type of 1982

1984 **Litho.** *Perf. 14*
745 A260 5c Mustapha Pacha 15 15
746 A260 20c Bab Azzoun 15 15
746A A260 30c Algiers 15 15
746B A260 40c Kolea 15 15
746C A260 50c Algiers 15 15
747 A260 70c Mostaganem 32 15
Set value 84 40

Issue dates: Nos. 745, 746, 747, July 19. Nos. 746A-746C, Oct. 20.

Lute — A282

Native musical instruments.

1984, Sept. 22 **Litho.** *Perf. 15x14*
748 A282 80c shown 22 15
749 A282 1d Drum 28 15
750 A282 2.40d Fiddle 65 35
751 A282 2.80d Bagpipe 70 40
Nos. 748-751 (4) 1.85 1.05

30th Anniv. of Algerian Revolution — A284

1984, Nov. 3 **Photo.** *Perf. 11½x12*
757 A284 80c Partisans 22 15

Souvenir Sheet

758 A284 5d Algerian flags, vert. 2.00 1.00

M'Zab Valley A285

1984, Dec. 15 *Perf. 15x14, 14x15*
759 A285 80c Map of valley 22 15
760 A285 2.40d Town of M'Zab, vert. 65 32

18th and 19th Century Metalware — A286

1985, Jan. 26 **Photo.** *Perf. 11½*
761 A286 80c Coffee pot 22 15
762 A286 2d Bowl, horiz. 50 25
763 A286 2.40d Covered bowl 65 32
Nos. 761-763 (3) 1.37 72

Fish — A287

1985, Feb. 23 **Photo.** *Perf. 15x14*
764 A287 50c Thunnus thynnus 15 15
765 A287 80c Sparus aurata 20 15
766 A287 2.40d Epinephelus guaza 60 30
767 A287 2.80d Mustelus mustelus 65 35
Nos. 764-767 (4) 1.60
Set value 82

National Games — A288

1985, Mar. 28 *Perf. 11½x12*

Granite Paper

768 A288 80c Doves, emblem 20 15

Environmental Conservation A289

1985, Apr. 25 *Perf. 13½*
769 A289 80c Stylized trees 20 15
770 A289 1.40d Stylized waves 38 20

View Type of 1982 and

The Casbah — A290

View of Constantine — A290a

Street Scene in Algiers — A290b

Designs: 2.50d, Djamaael Djadid Mosque, Algiers. 2.90d, like #746. 5d, like #746A. 1.50d, like #746B. 4.20d, like #764.

Perf. 13½x12½, 13 (#778B, 4.20d),
Perf. 13½x14 (#778C)
Perf. 14½x14 (2d)

Photo., Litho. (2d, 6,20d, 7.50d, #778C)

1985-94
771 A290 20c dk blue & buff 15 15
772 A290 80c sage grn & buff 20 15
773 A290a 1d dk olive grn 50 25
a. Bklt. pane of 5 + label 2.50
774 A260 1.50d dull red 55 30
775 A290b 1.50d red brown & brn 25 15
a. Booklet pane of 6 1.50
776 A290b 2d dk blue & lt blue 15 15
a. Booklet pane of 5 + label 95
777 A290 2.40d chestnut & buff 60 30
a. Bklt. pane of 5 (20c, 3 80c, 2.40d) + label 1.40
778 A260 2.50d bluish green 98 50
779 A260 2.90d slate 1.15 58
780 A260 4.20d gray green 1.60 85
781 A260 5d deep bister & black 1.95 98

Perf. 14

782 A260 6.20d like #731 1.05 52
783 A260 7.50d like #745 1.30 65
Nos. 771-783 (13) 10.43 5.53

Nos. 771-772, 777 issued only in booklet panes.

Issue dates: 20c, 80c, 2.40d, June 1, 1985. 1d, Jan. 26, 1989. 2.50d, 2.90d, 5d, Feb. 23, 1989. No. 774, 4.20d, Mar. 21, 1991. No. 775, May 20, 1992. 6.20d, 7.50d, Apr. 22, 1992. 2d, Oct. 21, 1993. No. 776a, Oct. 21, 1994.

See No. 1010.

UN, 40th Anniv. — A291

Natl. Youth Festival — A292

1985, June 26 **Photo.** *Perf. 14*
784 A291 1d Dove, emblem, 40 25 15

1985, July 5 **Litho.** *Perf. 13½*
785 A292 80c multicolored 20 15

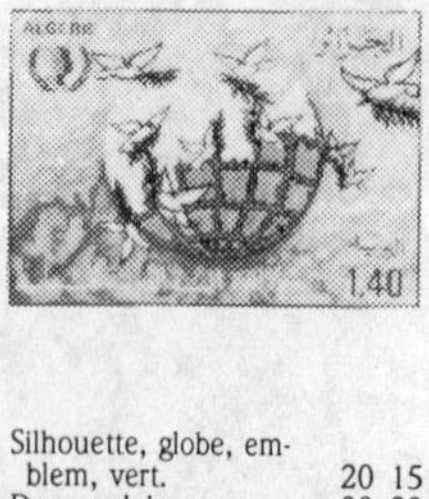

Intl. Youth Year — A293

1985, July 5
786 A293 80c Silhouette, globe, emblem, vert. 20 15
787 A293 1.40d Doves, globe 38 20

World Map, OPEC — A294

1985, Sept. 14 Photo. *Perf. 12½x13*

788	A294	80c	multicolored	20	15

Organization of Petroleum Exporting Countries, 25th anniv.

Family Planning A295

El-Meniaa Township A296

1985, Oct. 3 Litho. *Perf. 14*

789	A295	80c	Mother and sons	20	15
790	A295	1.40d	Weighing infant	38	18
791	A295	1.70d	Breast-feeding	45	22
			Nos. 789-791 (3)	1.03	55

1985, Oct. 24 Engr. *Perf. 13*

792	A296	80c	Chetaibi Bay, horiz.	20	15
793	A296	2d	shown	50	25
794	A296	2.40d	Bou Noura Town, horiz.	65	32
			Nos. 792-794 (3)	1.35	72

The Palm Grove, by N. Dinet — A297

1985, Nov. 21 Photo. *Perf. 11½x12*

Granite Paper

795	A297	2d	multi	50	25
796	A297	3d	multi, diff.	70	40

Tapestries A298

Various designs.

1985, Dec. 19

Granite Paper

797	A298	80c	multi	20	15
798	A298	1.40d	multi	38	20
799	A298	2.40d	multi	60	32
800	A298	2.80d	multi	70	40
			Nos. 797-800 (4)	1.88	1.07

Wildcats A299

Perf. 12x11½, 11½x12

1986, Jan. 23

Granite Paper

801	A299	80c	Felis margarita	60	15
802	A299	1d	Felis caracal	80	15
803	A299	2d	Felis sylvestris	1.50	80
804	A299	2.40d	Felis serval, vert.	2.00	95
			Nos. 801-804 (4)	4.90	2.05

UN Child Survival Campaign — A300

Algerian General Worker's Union, 30th Anniv. — A301

1986, Feb. 13 Litho. *Perf. 13½*

805	A300	80c	Oral vaccine	20	15
806	A300	1.40d	Mother, child, sun	40	18
807	A300	1.70d	Three children	45	22
			Nos. 805-807 (3)	1.05	55

1986, Feb. 24 *Perf. 12½*

Granite Paper

808	A301	2d	multi	50	25

National Charter — A302

Natl. Day of the Disabled — A303

1986, Mar. 6 Photo. *Perf. 11½*

Granite Paper

809	A302	4d	multi	1.50	55

1986, Mar. 15 *Perf. 12½x13*

810	A303	80c	multi	20	15

A304

A305

1986, Apr. 17 Litho. *Perf. 14x15*

811	A304	80c	multi	20	15

Anti-Tuberculosis campaign.

1986, Apr. 24 *Perf. 14*

812	A305	2d	Soccer ball, sombrero	50	25
813	A305	2.40d	Soccer players	65	32

1986 World Cup Soccer Championships, Mexico.

Inner Courtyards — A306

Blood Donation Campaign — A307

1986, May 15 Photo. *Perf. 11½*

Granite Paper

814	A306	80c	multi	20	15
815	A306	2.40d	multi, diff.	65	32
816	A306	3d	multi, diff.	80	40
			Nos. 814-816 (3)	1.65	87

1986, June 26 Litho. *Perf. 13½*

817	A307	80c	multi	22	15

Southern District Radio Communication Inauguration — A308

1986, July *Perf. 13*

818	A308	60c	multi	16	15

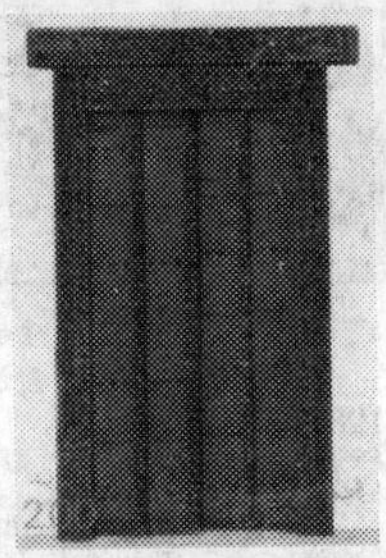

Mosque Gateways A309

1986, Sept. 27 Photo. *Perf. 12x11½*

Granite Paper

819	A309	2d	Door	50	25
820	A309	2.40d	Ornamental arch	65	32

Intl. Peace Year — A310

Perf. 13½x14½

1986, Oct. 16 Photo.

821	A310	2.40d	multi	65	32

Folk Dancing A311

1986, Nov. 22 Litho. *Perf. 14x13½*

822	A311	80c	Woman, scarf	22	15
823	A311	2.40d	Woman, diff.	65	32
824	A311	2.80d	Man, sword	70	40
			Nos. 822-824 (3)	1.57	87

Flowers — A312

1986, Dec. 18 Photo. *Perf. 14*

825	A312	80c	Narcissus tazetta	22	15
826	A312	1.40d	Iris unguicularis	40	20
827	A312	2.40d	Capparis spinosa	65	32
828	A312	2.80d	Gladiolus segetum	70	40
			Nos. 825-828 (4)	1.97	1.07

See Nos. 936-938.

Abstract Paintings by Mohammed Issia Khem A313

Perf. 11½x12, 12x11½

1987, Jan. 29 Litho.

829	A313	2d	Man and woman, vert.	65	35
830	A313	5d	Man and books	1.60	80

Jewelry from Aures A314

1987, Feb. 27 Photo. *Perf. 12*

Granite Paper

831	A314	1d	Earrings	35	16
832	A314	1.80d	Bracelets	60	30
833	A314	2.90d	Nose rings	1.00	50
834	A314	3.30d	Necklace	1.10	55
			Nos. 831-834 (4)	3.05	1.51

Nos. 831-833 vert.

Petroglyphs, Atlas A315

1987, Mar. 26 Litho. *Perf. 12x11½*

Granite Paper

835	A315	1d	Man and woman	35	16
836	A315	2.90d	Goat	1.00	50
837	A315	3.30d	Horse, bull	1.10	60
			Nos. 835-837 (3)	2.45	1.26

Syringe as an Umbrella — A316

1987, Apr. 7 *Perf. 11½*

Granite Paper

838	A316	1d	multi	35	16

Child Immunization Campaign, World Health Day.

Volunteers — A317

Third General Census — A318

1987, Apr. 23 *Perf. 10½*
839 A317 1d multi 35 16

1987, May 21 *Perf. 13½*
840 A318 1d multi 35 16

Algerian Postage, 25th Anniv. — A319

Design: War Orphans' Fund label (1fr + 9fr) of 1962.

1987, July 5 Photo. *Perf. 11½x12*
Granite Paper
841 A319 1.80d multi 60 32

A320

A321

1987, July 5
Granite Paper
842 A320 1d multi 35 16
Souvenir Sheet
843 A321 5d multi 1.60 1.60

Natl. independence, 25th anniv.

Amateur Theater Festival, Mostaganem A322

1987, July 20 *Perf. 12x11½*
Granite Paper
844 A322 1d Actors on stage 35 16
845 A322 1.80d Theater 60 32
a. Pair, #844-845 1.00 50

No. 845a has continuous design.

Mediterranean Games, Latakia A323

1987, Aug. 6 *Perf. 13x12½, 12½x13*
846 A323 1d Discus 35 16
847 A323 2.90d Tennis, vert. 1.00 50
848 A323 3.30d Team handball 1.10 55
Nos. 846-848 (3) 2.45 1.21

Birds — A324

1987 Litho. *Perf. 13½*
849 A324 1d Phoenicopterus ruber roseus 55 24
850 A324 1.80d Porphyrio porphyrio 1.00 50
851 A324 2.50d Elanus caeruleus 1.40 65
852 A324 2.90d Milvus milvus 1.65 75
Nos. 849-852 (4) 4.60 2.14

Agriculture A325

Perf. 10½x11, 11x10½
1987, Nov. 26 Litho.
853 A325 1d Planting 35 16
854 A325 1d Reservoir 35 16
855 A325 1d Harvesting crop, vert. 35 16
856 A325 1d Produce, vert. 35 16
Nos. 853-856 (4) 1.40 64

African Telecommunications Day — A326

1987, Dec. 7 *Perf. 10½*
857 A326 1d multi 35 16

Transportation A327

1987, Dec. 18 Litho. *Perf. 10½x11*
858 A327 2.90d shown 1.00 50
859 A327 3.30d Diesel train 1.10 55

Algerian Universities A328

Various campuses.

Perf. 10½x11, 11x10½
1987, Dec. 26
860 A328 1d shown 35 16
861 A328 2.50d multi, diff. 80 40
862 A328 2.90d multi, diff. 1.00 50
863 A328 3.30d multi, diff., vert. 1.10 55
Nos. 860-863 (4) 3.25 1.61

Intl. Rural Development Fund, 10th Anniv. A329

1988, Jan. 27 *Perf. 10½x11*
864 A329 1d multi 50 25

Autonomy of State-owned Utilities — A330

1988, Feb. 27 Litho. *Perf. 11x10½*
865 A330 1d multi 50 25

Intl. Women's Day — A331

Arab Scouts, 75th Anniv. — A332

1988, Mar. 10 Litho. *Perf. 11x10½*
866 A331 1d multi 50 25

1988, Apr. 7 Litho. *Perf. 10½*
867 A332 2d multi 95 48

1988 Summer Olympics, Seoul — A333

Hot Springs — A334

1988, July 23 Litho. *Perf. 10½*
868 A333 2.90d multi 1.40 70

1988, July 16
869 A334 1d shown 50 25
870 A334 2.90d Caverns, horiz. 1.40 70
871 A334 3.30d Gazebo, fountain, horiz. 1.60 80
Nos. 869-871 (3) 3.50 1.75

World Wildlife Fund — A335

Barbary apes, *Macaca sylvanus.*

1988, Sept. 17 Litho. *Perf. 10½*
872 A335 50c Adult 25 15
873 A335 90c Family 45 22
874 A335 1d Close-up, vert. 50 25
875 A335 1.80d Seated on branch, vert. 90 45
Nos. 872-875 (4) 2.10 1.07

Intl. Literacy Day — A336

WHO, 40th Anniv. — A337

1988, Sept. 10 Photo. *Perf. 10½*
876 A336 2.90d multi 1.40 70

1988, Oct. 15
877 A337 2.90d multi 1.40 70

Fight Apartheid A338

1988, Nov. 19 Litho. *Perf. 10½x11*
878 A338 2.50d multi 1.20 60

Natl. Front Congress — A339

1988, Nov. 29 *Perf. 11x10½*
879 A339 1d multi 50 25

Agriculture A340

1988, Dec. 24 *Perf. 10½*
880 A340 1d Irrigation 50 25
881 A340 1d Orchard, fields, livestock 50 25

Natl. Goals — A342

Airports — A343

1989, Mar. 9 Litho. *Perf. 11½*
Granite Paper
886 A342 1d shown 50 25
887 A342 1d Ancient fort 50 25
888 A342 1d Telecommunications 50 25
889 A342 1d Modern buildings 50 25
Nos. 886-889 (4) 2.00 1.00

Nos. 887-889 horiz.

Perf. 10½x11, 11x10½
1989, Mar. 23
890 A343 2.90d Oran Es Senia, horiz. 1.45 72
891 A343 3.30d Tebessa, horiz. 1.65 82
892 A343 5d shown 2.50 1.25
Nos. 890-892 (3) 5.60 2.79

Development of the South A344

1989, Apr. 24 Litho. *Perf. 13½*

893 A344	1d	Irrigation	48	25
894 A344	1.80d	Building	88	45
895 A344	2.50d	Fossil fuel extraction, vert.	1.20	60
		Nos. 893-895 (3)	2.56	1.30

Eradicate Locusts A345

1989, May 25 *Perf. 10½*

896 A345	1d	multi	50	25

National Service — A346

1989, May 11 Litho. *Perf. 13½*

897 A346	2d	multicolored	78	40

1st Moon Landing, 20th Anniv. A347

Designs: 4d, Astronaut, lunar module, Moon's surface, vert.

1989, July 23 Litho. *Perf. 13½*

898 A347	2.90d	shown	1.10	55
899 A347	4d	multi	1.50	75

Interparliamentary Union, Cent. — A348

1989, Sept. 4 *Perf. 10½*

900 A348	2.90d	gold, brt rose lil & blk	1.10	55

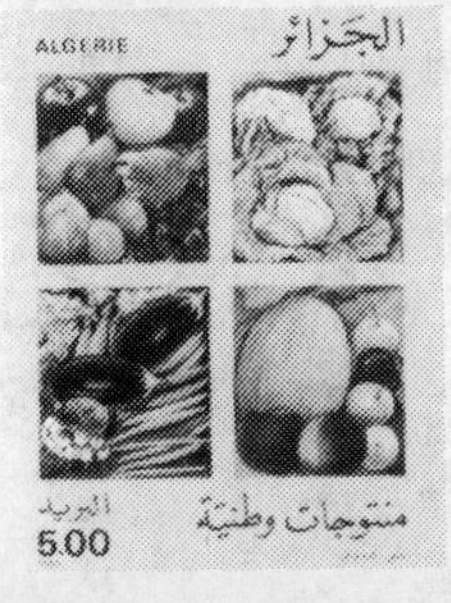
Produce A349

1989, Sept. 23 Litho. *Perf. 11½*
Granite Paper

901	Strip of 3	4.00	
a.	A349 2d multi, diff.	78	40
b.	A349 3d multi, diff.	1.15	58
c.	A349 5d shown	1.95	98

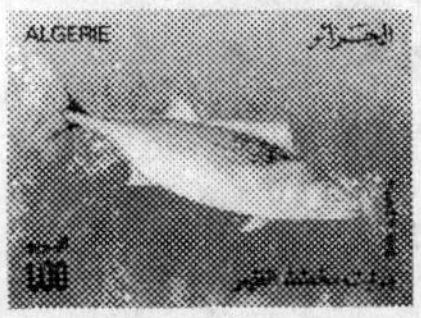
Fish — A350

1989, Oct. 27 Litho. *Perf. 13½*

902 A350	1d	*Sarda sarda*	40	20
903 A350	1.80d	*Zeus faber*	70	35
904 A350	2.90d	*Pagellus bogaraveo*	1.15	58
905 A350	3.30d	*Xiphias gladius*	1.30	65
		Nos. 902-905 (4)	3.55	1.78

Algerian Revolution, 35th Anniv. — A351

1989, Nov. 4 Litho. *Perf. 13½*

906 A351	1d	multicolored	40	20

African Development Bank, 25th Anniv. A352

Mushrooms A353

1989, Nov. 18 *Perf. 10½*

907 A352	1d	multicolored	40	20

1989, Dec. 16 *Perf. 13½*

908 A353	1d	*Boletus satanas*	40	20
909 A353	1.80d	*Psalliota xanthoderma*	70	35
910 A353	2.90d	*Lepiota procera*	1.15	58
911 A353	3.30d	*Lactarius deliciosus*	1.30	65
		Nos. 908-911 (4)	3.55	1.78

A354

A355

1990, Jan. 18 Litho. *Perf. 10½*

912 A354	1d	multicolored	40	20

Pan-African Postal Union, 10th anniv.

1990, Feb. 22 Litho. *Perf. 14*

913 A355	1d	Energy conservation	25	15

A356

A357

1990, Mar. 2 Photo. *Perf. 11½*

914 A356	3d	multicolored	65	32

African Soccer Championships.

1990, May 17 Litho. *Perf. 13½*

917 A357	2.90d	shown	75	38
918 A357	5d	Trophy	1.25	65

World Cup Soccer Championships, Italy.

Rural Electrification A358

1990, June 21

919 A358	2d	multicolored	50	25

Youth A359

Youth Holding Rainbow — A360

1990, July 6 *Perf. 13½*

920 A359	2d	multicolored	50	25
921 A360	3d	multicolored	75	36

Maghreb Arab Union — A361

1990 *Perf. 14x13½*

922 A361	1d	multicolored	38	20

Vocations — A362

1990, Apr. 26 Litho. *Perf. 12½*

923 A362	2d	Craftsmen	75	40
924 A362	2.90d	Auto mechanics	1.15	60
925 A362	3.30d	Deep sea fishing	1.25	65
		Nos. 923-925 (3)	3.15	1.65

Organization of Petroleum Exporting Countries (OPEC), 30th Anniv. A363

1990 *Perf. 13½*

926 A363	2d	multicolored	75	40

Savings Promotion — A364

1990, Oct. 31 Litho. *Perf. 14*

927 A364	1d	multicolored	38	20

Namibian Independence A365

1990, Nov. 8

928 A365	3d	multicolored	1.15	60

A366

A367

Farm animals.

1990, Nov. 29 *Perf. 13½*

929 A366	1d	Duck	38	20
930 A366	2d	Rabbit, horiz.	75	40
931 A366	2.90d	Turkey	1.10	60
932 A366	3d	Rooster, horiz.	1.15	60
		Nos. 929-932 (4)	3.38	1.80

1990, Dec. 11

933 A367	1d	multicolored	38	20

Anti-French Riots, 30th anniv.

A368

A369

1990, Dec. 20 *Perf. 14*

934 A368	1d	multicolored	38	20

Fight against respiratory diseases.

1991, Feb. 24 Litho. *Perf. 13½*

935 A369	1d	multicolored	36	18

Constitution, 2nd anniv.

Flower Type of 1986

1991, May 23 Litho. *Perf. 13½*

Size: 26x36mm

936 A312 2d Jasminum fruticans 65 32
937 A312 4d Dianthus crinitus 1.30 65
938 A312 5d Cyclamen africanum 1.65 85
Nos. 936-938 (3) 3.60 1.82

Children's Drawings A370

1991, June 3 Litho. *Perf. 13½*

939 A370 3d shown 1.00 50
940 A370 4d Children playing 1.30 65

Maghreb Arab Union Summit — A371

1991, June 10

941 A371 1d multicolored 32 16

Geneva Convention on Refugees, 40th Anniv. A372

Perf. 14½x13½

1991, July 28 Litho.

942 A372 3d multicolored 1.05 52

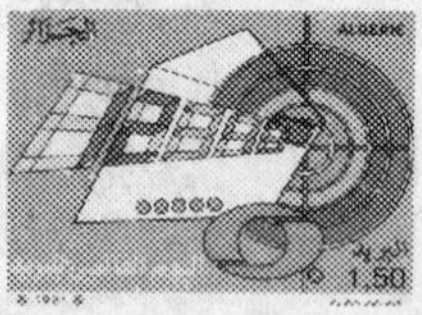

Postal Service A373

1991, Oct. 12 *Perf. 14*

943 A373 1.50d shown 55 28
944 A373 4.20d Expo emblem, vert. 1.50 75

Telecom '91, 6th World Forum and Exposition on Telecommunications, Geneva, Switzerland (No. 944).

Butterflies A374

1991, Nov. 21 Litho. *Perf. 11½*

Granite Paper

945 A374 2d Zerynthia rumina 32 16
946 A374 4d Melitaea didyma 65 32
947 A374 6d Vanessa atalanta 1.00 50
948 A374 7d Nymphalis polychloros 1.15 58
Nos. 945-948 (4) 3.12 1.56

A375

A376

1991, Dec. 21 *Perf. 12*

Granite Paper

949 A375 3d Necklace 50 25
950 A375 4d Jewelry of Southern Tuaregs 65 32
951 A375 5d Brooch 85 42
952 A375 7d Rings, horiz. 1.15 58
Nos. 949-952 (4) 3.15 1.57

1992, Mar. 8 Litho. *Perf. 14*

953 A376 1.50d Algerian Women 22 15

Gazelles A377

Designs: 1.50d, Gazella dorcas. 6.20d, Gazella cuvieri. 8.60d, Gazella dama.

1992, May 13 *Perf. 14½x13*

954 A377 1.50d multicolored 25 15
955 A377 6.20d multicolored 1.05 52
956 A377 8.60d multicolored 1.45 75
Nos. 954-956 (3) 2.75 1.42

1992 Summer Olympics, Barcelona A379

1992, June 24 Litho. *Perf. 14*

958 A379 6.20d Runners 1.10 55

A381

A382

1992, July 7 Litho. *Perf. 14*

960 A381 5d multicolored 90 45

Independence, 30th anniv.

1992, Sept. 23 Litho. *Perf. 14*

Designs: Medicinal plants.

961 A382 1.50d Ajuga iva 20 15
962 A382 5.10d Rhamnus alaternus 70 35
963 A382 6.20d Silybum marianum 85 42
964 A382 8.60d Lavandula stoechas 1.15 58
Nos. 961-964 (4) 2.90 1.50

Post Office Modernization A383

1992, Oct. 10 Litho. *Perf. 14*

965 A383 1.50d multicolored 22 15

Marine Life — A384

Designs: 1.50d, Hippocampus hippocampus. 2.70d, Caretta caretta. 6.20d, Muraena helena. 7.50d, Palinurus elephas.

1992, Dec. 23

966 A384 1.50d multicolored 20 15
967 A384 2.70d multicolored 35 18
968 A384 6.20d multicolored 85 42
969 A384 7.50d multicolored 1.00 50
Nos. 966-969 (4) 2.40 1.25

Pres. Mohammad Boudiaf (1919-92) A385

1992, Nov. 3 Litho. *Perf. 11½*

Granite Paper

970 A385 2d green & multi 28 15
971 A385 8.60d blue & multi 1.15 58

Coins A386

1992, Dec. 16 Litho. *Perf. 11½*

Granite Paper

972 A386 1.50d Numidia, 2nd cent. BC 20 15
973 A386 2d Dinar, 14th cent. 28 15
974 A386 5.10d Dinar, 11th cent. 68 35
975 A386 6.20d Abdelkader, 19th cent. 85 40
Nos. 972-975 (4) 2.01 1.05

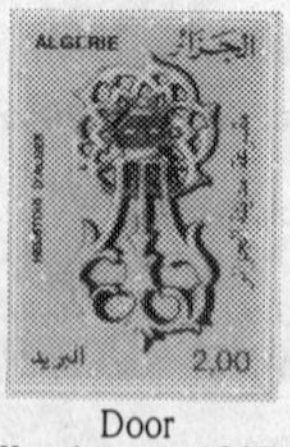

Door Knockers — A387

Flowering Trees — A388

1993, Feb. 17 Litho. *Perf. 14*

976 A387 2d Algiers 28 15
977 A387 5.60d Constantine 75 38
978 A387 8.60d Tlemcen 1.15 58
Nos. 976-978 (3) 2.18 1.11

Perf. 12x11½, 11½x12

1993, Mar. 17

Granite Paper

979 A388 4.50d Neflier (medlar), horiz. 60 30
980 A388 8.60d Cognassier (quince) 1.20 60
981 A388 11d Abricotier (apricot) 1.50 75
Nos. 979-981 (3) 3.30 1.65

Natl. Coast Guard Service, 20th Anniv. A389

1993, Apr. 3 Litho. *Perf. 14*

982 A389 2d multicolored 28 15

Traditional Grain Processing — A390

1993, May 19 Litho. *Perf. 14*

983 A390 2d Container 26 15
984 A390 5.60d Millstone 75 38
985 A390 8.60d Press 1.15 58
Nos. 983-985 (3) 2.16 1.11

Royal Mausoleums A391

1993, June 16 Litho. *Perf. 14*

986 A391 8.60d Mauretania 1.15 58
987 A391 12d El Khroub 1.60 80

Ports — A392

1993, Oct. 20 Litho. *Perf. 14x13½*

988 A392 2d Annaba 25 15
989 A392 8.60d Arzew 1.10 55

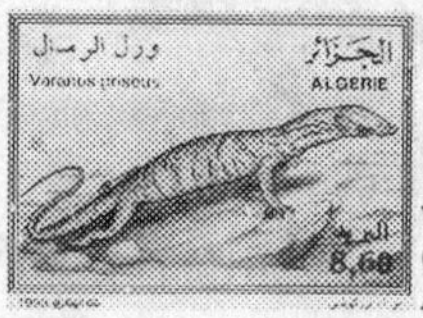

Varanus Griseus A393

Design: 2d, Chamaeleo vulgaris, vert.

Perf. 13½x14, 14x13½

1993, Nov. 20

990 A393 2d multicolored 25 15
991 A393 8.60d multicolored 1.10 55

Tourism A394

1993, Dec. 18 Litho. *Perf. 14x13½*

992	A394	2d Tipaza	22	15
993	A394	8.60d Kerzaz	80	40

A395

Chahid Day — A396

1994, Jan. 2 *Perf. 13½x14*

994	A395	2d multicolored	22	15

SONATRACH (Natl. Society for Research, Transformation, and Commercialization of Hydrocarbons), 30th anniv.

1994, Feb. 18 Litho. *Perf. 13½x14*

995	A396	2d multicolored	22	15

1994 World Cup Soccer Championships, US — A397

1994, Mar. 16 *Perf. 14x13½*

996	A397	8.60d multicolored	80	40

A398

Ancient Petroglyphs — A399

Orchids: 5.60d, Orchis simia lam. 8.60d, Ophrys lutea cavan. 11d, Ophrys apifera huds.

1994, Apr. 20 Litho. *Perf. 11½*
Granite Paper

997	A398	5.60d multicolored	55	28
998	A398	8.60d multicolored	85	42
999	A398	11d multicolored	1.10	55
		Nos. 997-999 (3)	2.50	1.25

1994, May 21 Litho. *Perf. 13x14*

1000	A399	3d Inscriptions	35	18
1001	A399	10d Man on horse	1.25	60

A400

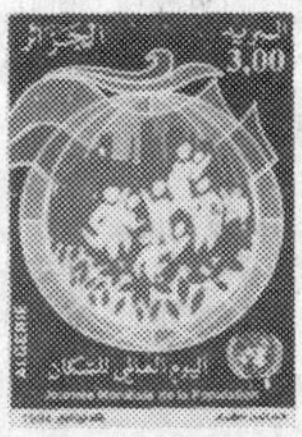
A401

1994, June 25

1002	A400	12d multicolored	1.25	65

Intl. Olympic Committee, cent.

1994, July 13

1003	A401	3d multicolored	35	18

World Population Day.

SEMI-POSTAL STAMPS

Regular Issue of 1926 Surcharged in Black or Red

+10c

1927 Unwmk. *Perf. 14x13½*

B1	A1	5c +5c bl grn	35	35
B2	A1	10c +10c lilac	35	35
B3	A2	15c +15c org brn	35	35
B4	A2	20c +20c car rose	35	35
B5	A2	25c +25c bl grn	35	35
B6	A2	30c +30c lt bl	35	35
B7	A2	35c +35c dp vio	35	35
B8	A2	40c +40c ol grn	35	35
B9	A3	50c +50c dp bl (R)	35	35
a.		Double surcharge	110.00	110.00
B10	A3	80c +80c red org	35	35
B11	A4	1fr +1fr gray grn & red brn	35	35
B12	A4	2fr +2fr Prus bl & blk brn	11.50	11.50
B13	A4	5fr +5fr red & vio	16.00	16.00
		Nos. B1-B13 (13)	31.35	31.35

The surtax was for the benefit of wounded soldiers. Government officials speculated in this issue.

Railroad Terminal, Oran — SP1

Ruins at Djemila SP2

Mosque of Sidi Abd-er-Rahman SP3

Designs: 10c+10c, Rummel Gorge, Constantine. 15c+15c, Admiralty Buildings, Algiers. 25c+25c, View of Algiers. 30c+30c, Trajan's Arch, Timgad. 40c+40c, Temple of the North, Djemila. 75c+75c Mansourah Minaret, Tlemcen. 1f+1f, View of Ghardaia. 1.50f+1.50f, View of Tolga. 2f+2f, Tuareg warriors. 3f+3f, Kasbah, Algiers.

1930 Engr. *Perf. 12½*

B14	SP1	5c +5c orange	4.45	4.50
B15	SP1	10c +10c ol grn	4.50	4.50
B16	SP1	15c +15c dk brn	4.50	4.50
B17	SP1	25c +25c black	4.50	4.50
B18	SP1	30c +30c dk red	4.50	4.50
B19	SP1	40c +40c ap grn	4.50	4.50
B20	SP2	50c +50c ultra	4.50	4.50
B21	SP2	75c +75c red pur	4.50	4.50
B22	SP2	1fr +1fr org red	4.50	4.50
B23	SP2	1.50fr +1.50fr deep ultra	4.50	4.50
B24	SP2	2fr +2fr dk car	4.50	4.50
B25	SP2	3fr +3fr dk grn	4.50	4.50
B26	SP3	5fr +5fr grn & car	9.00	9.00
a.		Center inverted	325.00	
		Nos. B14-B26 (13)	62.95	63.00

Centenary of the French occupation of Algeria. The surtax on the stamps was given to the funds for the celebration.

Nos. B14-B26 exist imperf. Value, set in pairs, $350.

Catalogue values for unused stamps in this section, from this point to the end of the section, are for Never Hinged items.

No. 102 Surcharged in Red

1918-11 Nov.-1938
0.65 + 0.35

1938 *Perf. 13*

B27	A6	65c +35c on 2.25fr yel grn	40	40

20th anniversary of Armistice.

René Caillié, Charles Lavigerie and Henri Duveyrier SP14

1939 Engr.

B28	SP14	30c +20c dk bl grn	90	60
B29	SP14	90c +60c car rose	1.00	60
B30	SP14	2.25fr +75c ultra	6.50	6.00
B31	SP14	5fr +5fr brn blk	12.00	12.00
		Nos. B28-B31 (4)	20.40	19.20

Pioneers of the Sahara.

French and Algerian Soldiers SP15

1940 Photo. *Perf. 12*

B32	SP15	1fr +1fr bl & car	40	40
B33	SP15	1fr +2fr brn rose & blk	40	40
B34	SP15	1fr +4fr dp grn & red	60	60
B35	SP15	1fr +9fr brn & car	1.00	1.00
		Nos. B32-B35 (4)	2.40	2.40

The surtax was used to assist the families of mobilized men.

Type of Regular Issue, 1941 Surcharged in Carmine

+ 4f

1941 Engr. *Perf. 13*

B36	A19	1fr +4fr black	20	20

No. 135 Surcharged in Carmine

SECOURS NATIONAL
+ 4f

B37	A19	1fr +4fr dark blue	20	20

The surtax was for National Relief.

No. 124 Surcharged in Black "+60c"

1942

B38	A7	90c +60c henna brn	15	15
a.		Double surcharge	55.00	

The surtax was used for National Relief. The stamp could also be used as 1.50 francs for postage.

Mother and Child — SP16

1943, Dec. 1 Litho. *Perf. 12*

B39	SP16	50c +4.50fr brt pink	30	25
B40	SP16	1.50fr +8.50fr lt grn	30	25
B41	SP16	3fr +12fr dp bl	30	25
B42	SP16	5fr +15fr vio brn	30	25
		Nos. B39-B42 (4)	1.20	1.00

The surtax was for the benefit of soldiers and prisoners of war.

Planes over Fields — SP17

1945, July 2 Unwmk. Engr. *Perf. 13*

B43	SP17	1.50fr +3.50fr lt ultra, red org & blk	20	20

The surtax was for the benefit of Algerian airmen and their families.

France No. B192 Overprinted Type "a" of 1924 in Black

1945

B44	SP146	4fr +6fr dk vio brn	20	20

The surtax was for war victims of the P.T.T.

Overprinted in Blue on Type of France, 1945

1945, Oct. 15

B45	SP150	2fr +3fr dk brn	35	35

For Stamp Day.

Overprinted in Blue on Type of France, 1946

1946, June 29

B46	SP160	3fr +2fr red	45	45

For Stamp Day.

Children Playing by Stream SP18

Girl — SP19

Athlete — SP20

Repatriated Prisoner and Bay of Algiers SP21

1946, Oct. 2 Engr. *Perf. 13*

B47	SP18	3fr +17fr dark grn	65	65
B48	SP19	4fr +21fr red	65	65
B49	SP20	8fr +27fr rose lilac	2.75	2.75
B50	SP21	10fr +35fr dark blue	70	70
		Nos. B47-B50 (4)	4.75	4.75

Type of France, 1947, Overprinted type "a" of 1924 in Carmine

1947, Mar. 15

B51	SP172	4.50fr +5.50fr dp ultra	35	35

For Stamp Day.

Same on Type of France, 1947, Surcharged Like No. B36 in Carmine

1947, Nov. 13

B52	A173	5fr +10fr dk Prus grn	50	40

Type of France, 1948, Overprinted in Dark Green — f

ALGÉRIE

1948, Mar. 6

B53	SP176	6fr +4fr dk grn	40	40

For Stamp Day.

Type of France, 1948, Overprinted type "a" of 1924 in Blue and New Value

1948, May

B54	A176	6fr +4fr red	30	30

Battleship Richelieu and the Admiralty, Algiers SP22

Aircraft Carrier Arromanches SP23

Unwmk.

1949, Jan. 15 Engr. *Perf. 13*

B55 SP22 10fr +15fr dp blue		4.00	4.00
B56 SP23 18fr +22fr red		4.00	4.00

The surtax was for naval charities.

Type of France, 1949, Overprinted in Blue — g

ALGÉRIE

1949, Mar. 26

B57 SP180 15fr +5fr lilac rose	80	80

For Stamp Day, Mar. 26-27.

Type of France, 1950, Overprinted type "f" in Green

1950, Mar. 11

B58 SP183 12fr +3fr blk brn	1.00	1.00

For Stamp Day, Mar. 11-12.

Foreign Legionary — SP24

1950, Apr. 30

B59 SP24 15fr +5fr dk grn	1.25	1.25

Charles de Foucauld and Gen. J. F. H. Laperrine SP25

1950, Aug. 21 Unwmk. *Perf. 13*

B60 SP25 25fr +5fr brn ol & brn blk	3.00	3.00

50th anniversary of the presence of the French in the Sahara.

Emir Abd-el-Kader and Marshal T. R. Bugeaud SP26

1950, Aug. 21

B61 SP26 40fr +10fr dk brn & blk brn	2.50	2.50

Unveiling of a monument to Emir Abd-el-Kader at Cacheron.

Col. Colonna d'Ornano and Fine Arts Museum, Algiers SP27

1951, Jan. 11

B62 SP27 15fr +5fr blk brn, vio brn & red brn	60	60

Death of Col. Colonna d'Ornano, 10th anniv.

Type of France, 1951, Overprinted type "a" of 1924 in Black

1951, Mar. 10

B63 SP186 12fr +3fr brown	80	80

For Stamp Day.

Type of France, 1952, Overprinted type "g" in Dark Blue

1952, Mar. 8 Unwmk. *Perf. 13*

B64 SP190 12fr +3fr dk bl	1.25	1.25

For Stamp Day.

French Military Medal — SP28

1952, July 5 Unwmk. Engr. *Perf. 13*

B65 SP28 15fr +5fr grn, yel & brn	1.25	1.25

Centenary of the creation of the French Military Medal.

Type of France 1952, Surcharged type "g" and Surtax in Black

1952, Sept. 15

B66 A222 30fr +5fr dp ultra	1.10	1.10

10th anniv. of the defense of Bir-Hakeim.

View of El Oued — SP29

Design: 12fr+3fr, View of Bou-Noura.

1952, Nov. 15 Engr.

B67 SP29 8fr +2fr ultra & red	90	90
B68 SP29 12fr +3fr red	1.25	1.25

The surtax was for the Red Cross.

Type of France, 1953, Overprinted type "a" of 1924 in Black

1953, Mar. 14 Engr.

B69 SP193 12fr +3fr purple	1.00	90

For Stamp Day. Surtax for Red Cross.

Victory of Cythera — SP30

Unwmk.

1953, Dec. 18 Engr. *Perf. 13*

B70 SP30 15fr +5fr blk brn & brn	60	60

The surtax was for army welfare work.

Type of France, 1954, Overprinted type "a" of 1924 in Black

1954, Mar. 20 Unwmk. *Perf. 13*

B71 SP196 12fr +3fr scarlet	65	65

For Stamp Day.

Soldiers and Flags SP31

Foreign Legionary SP32

1954, Mar. 27

B72 SP31 15fr +5fr dk brn	50	50

The surtax was for old soldiers.

1954, Apr. 30

B73 SP32 15fr +5fr dk grn	1.00	1.00

The surtax was for the welfare fund of the Foreign Legion.

Nurses and Verdun Hospital, Algiers — SP33

Design: 15fr+5fr, J. H. Dunant & ruins at Djemila.

1954, Oct. 30

B74 SP33 12fr +3fr indigo & red	1.50	1.50
B75 SP33 15fr +5fr pur & red	1.75	1.75

The surtax was for the Red Cross.

Earthquake Victims and Ruins — SP34

First Aid — SP35

Design: #B80-B81, Removing wounded.

1954, Dec. 5

B76 SP34 12fr +4fr dk vio brn	1.00	1.00
B77 SP34 15fr +5fr dp bl	1.00	1.00
B78 SP35 18fr +6fr lil rose	1.25	1.25
B79 SP35 20fr +7fr vio	1.25	1.25
B80 SP35 25fr +8fr rose brn	1.50	1.50
B81 SP35 30fr +10fr brt bl grn	1.50	1.50
Nos. B76-B81 (6)	7.50	7.50

The surtax was for victims of the Orleansville earthquake disaster of September 1954.

Type of France, 1955, Overprinted type "a" of 1924 in Black

1955, Mar. 19

B82 SP199 12fr +3fr dp ultra	80	80

For Stamp Day, Mar. 19-20.

Women and Children SP36

Cancer Victim SP37

1955, Nov. 5

B83 SP36 15fr +5fr bl & ind	60	60

The tax was for war victims.

1956, Mar. 3 Unwmk. *Perf. 13*

B84 SP37 15fr +5fr dk brn	45	45

The surtax was for the Algerian Cancer Society. The male figure in the design is Rodin's "Age of Bronze."

Type of France, 1956, Overprinted type "a" of 1924 in Black

1956, Mar.

B85 SP202 12fr +3fr red	45	45

For Stamp Day, Mar. 17-18.

Foreign Legion Rest Home — SP38

1956, Apr. 29

B86 SP38 15fr +5fr dk bl grn	1.00	1.00

Honoring the French Foreign Legion.

Type of France, 1957, Overprinted type "f" in Black

1957, Mar. 16 Engr. *Perf. 13*

B87 SP204 12fr +3fr dull purple	65	65

For Stamp Day and to honor the Maritime Postal Service.

Fennec SP39

Design: 15fr+5fr, Stork flying over roofs.

1957, Apr. 6

B88 SP39 12fr +3fr red brn & red	3.00	3.00
B89 SP39 15fr +5fr sepia & red	3.00	3.00

The surtax was for the Red Cross.

Type of Regular Issue, 1956 Surcharged in Dark Blue

18 JUIN 1940
+ 5F

1957, June 18

B90 A53 15fr +5fr scar & rose red	75	75

17th anniv. of General de Gaulle's appeal for a Free France.

The Giaour, by Delacroix — SP40

On the Banks of the Oued, by Fromentin SP41

Design: 35fr+10fr, Dancer, by Chasseriau.

Unwmk.

1957, Nov. 30 **Engr.** ***Perf. 13***

B91	SP40 15fr +5fr dk car	3.75	3.75
B92	SP41 20fr +5fr grn	3.75	3.75
B93	SP40 35fr +10fr dk bl	3.75	3.75
	Nos. B91-B93 (3)	11.25	11.25

Surtax for army welfare organizations.

Type of France Overprinted type "f" in Blue

1958, Mar. 15 **Unwmk.** ***Perf. 13***

B94 SP206 15fr +5fr org brn 65 65

For Stamp Day.

Bird-of-Paradise Flower — SP42

Arms & Marshal's Baton — SP43

1958, June 14 **Engr.** ***Perf. 13***

B95 SP42 20fr +5fr grn, org & vio 2.00 2.00

The surtax was for Child Welfare.

1958, Juiy 20

B96 SP43 20fr +5fr ultra, car & grn 1.00 1.00

Marshal de Lattre Foundation.

Independent State

Clasped Hands, Wheat, Olive Branch — SP44

Burning Books — SP45

1963, May 27 **Unwmk.** ***Perf. 13***

B97 SP44 50c +20c sl grn, brt grn & car 80 60

Surtax for the Natl. Solidarity Fund.

1965, June 7 **Engr.** ***Perf. 13***

B98 SP45 20c +5c ol grn, red & blk 50 40

Issued to commemorate the burning of the Library of Algiers, June 7, 1962.

Soldiers and Woman Comforting Wounded Soldier — SP46

1966, Aug. 20 **Photo.** ***Perf. 11½***

B99	SP46 30c +10c multi	1.25	70
B100	SP46 95c +10c multi	1.75	1.10

Day of the Moudjahid (Moslem volunteers).

Red Crescent, Boy and Girl — SP47

1967, May 27 **Litho.** ***Perf. 14***

B101 SP47 30c +10c brt grn, brn & car 45 35

Algerian Red Crescent Society.

Flood Victims — SP48

Design: 95c+25c, Rescuing flood victims.

1969, Nov. 15 **Typo.** ***Perf. 10½***

B102 SP48 30c +10c dl bl, sal & blk 45 35

Litho.

B103 SP48 95c +25c multi 1.00 65

Red Crescent Flag — SP49

1971, May 17 **Engr.** ***Perf. 10½***

B104 SP49 30c +10c sl grn & car 35 28

Algerian Red Crescent Society.

Intl. Children's Day — SP50

1989, June 1 **Litho.** ***Perf. 10½x11***

B105 SP50 1d +30c multi 65 48

Surtax for child welfare.

Solidarity with Palestinians SP51

1990, Dec. 9 **Litho.** ***Perf. 10½x11***

B106 SP51 1d +30c multi 50 30

AIR POST STAMPS

Catalogue values for unused stamps in this section are for Never Hinged items.

Plane over Algiers Harbor — AP1

Two types of 20fr:

Type I - Monogram "F" without serifs. "POSTE" indented 3mm.

Type II - Monogram "F" with serifs. "POSTE" indented 4½mm.

Unwmk.

1946, June 20 **Engr.** ***Perf. 13***

C1	AP1	5fr red	15	15
C2	AP1	10fr deep blue	15	15
C3	AP1	15fr deep green	35	15
C4	AP1	20fr brown (II)	18	15
C4A	AP1	20fr brown (I)	72.50	45.00
C5	AP1	25fr violet	40	15
C6	AP1	40fr gray black	45	15
		Set value, #C1-C4, C5-C6	1.45	40

For surcharges, see Nos, C7, CB1-CB2.

No. C1 Surcharged in Black **— 10 %**

1947, Jan. 18

C7 AP1 (4.50fr) on 5fr red 15 15

Storks over Mosque — AP2

Plane over Village — AP3

1949-53

C8	AP2	50fr green	2.00	25
C9	AP3	100fr brown	1.75	25
C10	AP2	200fr bright red	4.00	3.00
C11	AP3	500fr ultra ('53)	14.00	10.00
		Nos. C8-C11 (4)	21.75	13.50

Beni Bahdel Dam — AP4

1957, July 1 **Unwmk.** ***Perf. 13***

C12 AP4 200fr dark red 3.25 75

Caravelle over Ghardaia — AP5

Designs: 2d, Caravelle over El Oued. 5d, Caravelle over Tipasa.

1967-68 **Engr.** ***Perf. 13***

C13	AP5 1d lil, org brn & emer	1.00	50
C14	AP5 2d brt bl, org brn & emer	2.50	1.25
C15	AP5 5d brt bl, grn & org brn ('68)	6.00	2.75
	Nos. C13-C15 (3)	9.50	4.50

Plane over Casbah, Algiers — AP6

Designs: 3d, Plane over Oran. 4d, Plane over Rhumel Gorge.

1971-72 **Photo.** ***Perf. 12½***

C16	AP6 2d grysh blk & multi	1.65	80
C17	AP6 3d vio & blk	2.50	1.40
C18	AP6 4d blk & multi	3.25	1.75
	Nos. C16-C18 (3)	7.40	3.95

Issued: 2d, 6/12/71; 3d, 4d, 2/28/72.

Storks and Plane — AP7

1979, Mar. 24 **Photo.** ***Perf. 11½***

C19 AP7 10d multi 4.00 1.60

Plane Approaching Coastal City — AP8

1991, Apr. 26 **Litho.** ***Perf. 13½***

C20	AP8 10d shown	3.60	1.80
C21	AP8 20d Plane over city	7.20	3.60

Plane Over Djidjelli Corniche — AP9

1993, Sept. 25 **Engr.** ***Perf. 13½x14***

C22 AP9 50d blue, green & brown 6.25 3.25

AIR POST SEMI-POSTAL STAMPS

Catalogue values for unused stamps in this section are for Never Hinged items.

No. C2 Surcharged in Carmine

‡
18 Juin 1940
+10Fr.

1947, June 18 ***Perf. 13***

CB1 AP1 10fr +10fr deep blue 60 60

7th anniv. of Gen. Charles de Gaulle's speech in London, June 18, 1940.

No. C1 Surcharged in Blue

‡
18 JUIN 1940
+10 Fr.

1948, June 18
CB2 AP1 5fr +10fr red 60 60

8th anniv. of Gen. Charles de Gaulle's speech in London, June 18, 1940.

Monument, Clock Tower and Plane — SPAP1

1949, Nov. 10 Engr. Unwmk.
CB3 SPAP1 15fr +20fr dk brn 3.75 3.75

25th anniv. of Algeria's 1st postage stamps.

POSTAGE DUE STAMPS

D1

D2

Perf. 14x13½
1926-27 Typo. Unwmk.
J1 D1 5c light blue 15 15
J2 D1 10c dk brn 15 15
J3 D1 20c olive grn 15 15
J4 D1 25c car rose 28 28
J5 D1 30c rose red 15 15
J6 D1 45c blue grn 40 40
J7 D1 50c brn vio 15 15
J8 D1 60c green ('27) 1.00 30
J9 D1 1fr red brn, *straw* 15 15
J10 D1 2fr lil rose ('27) 15 15
J11 D1 3fr deep blue ('27) 15 15
Set value 2.50 1.74

See Nos. J25-J26, J28-J32. For surcharges, see Nos. J18-J20.

1926-27
J12 D2 1c olive grn 15 15
J13 D2 10c violet 40 18
J14 D2 30c bister 28 20
J15 D2 60c dull red 22 20
J16 D2 1fr brt vio ('27) 10.00 1.75
J17 D2 2fr lt bl ('27) 6.50 65
Nos. J12-J17 (6) 17.55 3.13

See note below France No. J51.
For surcharges, see Nos. J21-J24.

Stamps of 1926 Surcharged

1927
J18 D1 60c on 20c olive grn 80 28
J19 D1 2fr on 45c blue grn 1.00 65
J20 D1 3fr on 25c car rose 45 28
Nos. J18-J20 (3) 2.25 1.21

Recouvrement Stamps of 1926 Surcharged

=
10c

1927-32
J21 D2 10c on 30c bis ('32) 2.25 1.50
J22 D2 1fr on 1c olive grn 65 60
J23 D2 1fr on 60c dl red ('32) 11.00 22
J24 D2 2fr on 10c violet 6.25 6.25
Nos. J21-J24 (4) 20.15 8.57

Catalogue values for unused stamps in this section, from this point to the end of the section, are for Never Hinged items.

Type of 1926, Without "R F"
1942 Typo. *Perf. 14x13½*
J25 D1 30c dark red 15 15
J26 D1 2fr magenta 18 18
Set value 23 23

Type of 1926 Surcharged in Red

T
0.50

1944 *Perf. 14x13½*
J27 A2 50c on 20c yel grn 15 15
a. Inverted surcharge 3.50
b. Double surcharge 9.50

No. J27 was issued precanceled only. See note after No. 32.

Type of 1926
1944 Litho. *Perf. 12*
J28 D1 1.50fr brt rose lilac 28 22
J29 D1 2fr greenish blue 28 22
J30 D1 5fr rose carmine 28 22
Nos. J28-J30 (3) 84 66

Type of 1926
1947 Typo. *Perf. 14x13½*
J32 D1 5fr green 60 45

France Nos. J80-J81 Overprinted Type "a" of 1925 in Carmine or Black
1947
J33 D5 10c sepia (C) 15 15
J34 D5 30c bright red violet 15 15
Set value 24 20

D3

1947-55 Unwmk. Engr. *Perf. 14x13*
J35 D3 20c red 15 15
J36 D3 60c ultra 22 20
J37 D3 1fr dk org brn 15 15
J38 D3 1.50fr dull green 40 38
J39 D3 2fr red 15 15
J40 D3 3fr violet 15 15
J41 D3 5fr ultra ('49) 15 15
J42 D3 6fr black 20 18
J43 D3 10fr lil rose 20 15
J44 D3 15fr ol grn ('55) 45 45
J45 D3 20fr brt grn 22 15
J46 D3 30fr red org ('55) 40 38
J47 D3 50fr indigo ('51) 95 95
J48 D3 100fr brt bl ('53) 4.00 3.50
Nos. J35-J48 (14) 7.79 7.09

Independent State

France Nos. J93-J97 Overprinted "EA" in Black like Nos. 286-290

Perf. 14x13½
1962, July 2 Typo. Unwmk.
Handstamped Overprint
J49 D6 5c bright pink 2.25 1.60
J50 D6 10c red orange 2.25 1.40
J51 D6 20c olive bister 2.25 1.40
J52 D6 50c dark green 3.00 2.75
J53 D6 1fr deep green 4.25 4.00
Nos. J49-J53 (5) 14.00 11.15

Typographed Overprint
J49a D6 5c bright pink 6.00 6.00
J50a D6 10c red orange 6.00 6.00
J51a D6 20c olive bister 5.50 5.50
J52a D6 50c dark green 14.00 14.00
J53a D6 1fr deep green 25.00 25.00
Nos. J49a-J53a (5) 56.50 56.50

See note after No. 290.

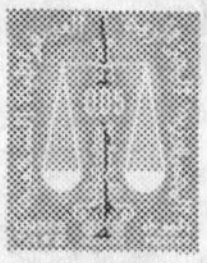
Scales — D4

Grain — D5

1963, June 25 *Perf. 14x13½*
J54 D4 5c car rose & blk 15 15
J55 D4 10c olive & car 15 15
J56 D4 20c ultra & blk 18 15
J57 D4 50c bister brn & grn 50 28
J58 D4 1fr lilac & org 85 50
Nos. J54-J58 (5) 1.83
Set value 95

#J58 Surcharged with New Value & 3 Bars
1968, Mar. 28 Typo. *Perf. 14x13½*
J59 D4 60c on 1fr lilac & org 40 28

1972-93 Litho. *Perf. 13½x14*
J60 D5 10c bister 15 15
J61 D5 20c deep brown 15 15
J62 D5 40c orange 20 15
J63 D5 50c dk vio blue 22 15
J64 D5 80c dk olive gray 38 15
J65 D5 1d green 42 25
J66 D5 2d blue 95 42
J67 D5 3d violet 45 22
J68 D5 4d lilac rose 58 28
Nos. J60-J68 (9) 3.50
Set value 1.50

Issued: 3d, 4d, 1/21/93; others, 10/21/72.

NEWSPAPER STAMPS

Nos. 1 and 33 Surcharged in Red

½
centime

1924-26 Unwmk. *Perf. 14x13½*
P1 A16 ½c on 1c dk gray 15 15
a. Triple surcharge 87.50
P2 A1 ½c on 1c olive ('26) 15 15
Set value 19 19

ALLENSTEIN

LOCATION — In East Prussia
AREA — 4,457 sq. mi.
POP. — 540,000 (estimated 1920)
CAPITAL — Allenstein

Allenstein, a district of East Prussia, held a plebiscite in 1920 under the Versailles Treaty, voting to join Germany rather than Poland. Later that year, Allenstein became part of the German Republic.

100 Pfennig = 1 Mark

Stamps of Germany, 1906-20, Overprinted

PLÉBISCITE
OLSZTYN
ALLENSTEIN

Perf. 14, 14½, 14x14½, 14½x14
1920 Wmk. 125
1 A16 5pf green 15 15
2 A16 10pf carmine 15 15
3 A22 15pf dk vio 15 15
4 A22 15pf vio brn 5.25 4.50
5 A16 20pf bl vio 15 15
6 A16 30pf org & blk, *buff* 24 24
7 A16 40pf lake & blk 18 18
8 A16 50pf pur & blk, *buff* 20 20
9 A16 75pf grn & blk 20 18
10 A17 1m car rose 65 65
a. Double overprint 375.00 600.00
11 A17 1.25m green 55 55
a. Double overprint 475.00 1,000.
12 A17 1.50m yel brn 55 55
13 A21 2.50m lilac rose 65 1.40
14 A19 3m blk vio 1.25 1.25
a. Double overprint 350.00 925.00
b. Inverted overprint 375.00 600.00
Nos. 1-14 (14) 10.32 10.30

Overprinted

15 A16 5pf green 15 24
16 A16 10pf carmine 15 24
17 A22 15pf dark vio 15 15
18 A22 15pf vio brn 25.00 25.00
19 A16 20pf blue vio 15 24
20 A16 30pf org & blk, *buff* 24 24
21 A16 40pf lake & blk 24 24
22 A16 50pf pur & blk, *buff* 15 15
23 A16 75pf grn & blk 15 15
24 A17 1m car rose 55 55
a. Inverted overprint 550.00 750.00
25 A17 1.25m green 55 55
26 A17 1.50m yel brn 55 55
27 A21 2.50m lilac rose 85 1.50
28 A19 3m blk vio 1.00 1.00
a. Inverted overprint 350.00 550.00
b. Double overprint 275.00 450.00
Nos. 15-28 (14) 29.88 30.71

The 40pf carmine rose (Germany No. 124) exists with this oval overprint, but it is doubtful whether it was regularly issued. Value $250.

ANDORRA

LOCATION — On the southern slope of the Pyrenees Mountains between France and Spain.
GOVT. — Co-principality
AREA — 179 sq. mi.
POP. — 26,500 (1976)
CAPITAL — Andorre-la-Vieille

Andorra is subject to the joint control of France and the Spanish Bishop of Urgel and pays annual tribute to both. The country has no monetary unit of its own, the peseta and franc both being in general use.

100 Centimos = 1 Peseta
100 Centimes = 1 Franc

Catalogue values for unused stamps in the Spanish Administration for this country are for Never Hinged items, beginning with Scott 50 in the regular postage section and Scott C2 in the airpost section; for the French Administration of this country, Never Hinged items begin at Scott 78 for regular postage, Scott B1 for the semi-postal section, Scott C1 for the airpost section, and Scott J21 for the postage due section.

SPANISH ADMINISTRATION

Stamps of Spain, 1922-26, Overprinted in Red or Black

:-: CORREOS :-:
ANDORRA

Perf. 14, 13½x12½, 12½x11½
1928 Unwmk.
1 A49 2c olive green 30 20

Control Numbers on Back
2 A49 5c car rose (Bk) 40 30
3 A49 10c green 40 30
4 A49 15c slate blue 2.00 2.00
5 A49 20c violet 2.00 2.00
6 A49 25c rose red (Bk) 2.00 2.00
7 A49 30c black brown 10.00 7.00
8 A49 40c deep blue 10.00 5.00
9 A49 50c orange (Bk) 10.00 7.25
10 A49a 1p blue blk 12.00 10.00
11 A49a 4p lake (Bk) 85.00 70.00
12 A49a 10p brown (Bk) 140.00 100.00
Nos. 1-12 (12) 274.10 206.05

Counterfeit overprints exist.

La Vall
A1

St. Juan de Caselles
A2

St. Julia de Loria — A3

St. Coloma — A4

General Council — A5

1929, Nov. 25 Engr. *Perf. 14*
13 A1 2c olive green 50 15

Control Numbers on Back

14 A2 5c carmine lake 1.10 20
15 A3 10c yellow green 1.10 75
16 A4 15c slate green 1.10 75
17 A3 20c violet 1.10 75
18 A4 25c carmine rose 2.75 1.10
19 A1 30c olive brown 50.00 32.50
20 A2 40c dark blue 2.25 50
21 A3 50c deep orange 2.25 75
22 A5 1p slate 4.75 2.50
23 A5 4p deep rose 32.50 17.50
24 A5 10p bister brown 35.00 25.00
Nos. 13-24 (12) 134.40 82.45

Nos. 13-24, 26, 28, 32 exist imperforate.

1931-38
Perf. 11½
13a A1 2c 3.00 30

Control Numbers on Back

14a A2 5c 4.00 90
15a A3 10c 6.00 1.10
16a A4 15c 20.00 14.00
17a A3 20c 6.00 3.50
18a A4 25c 6.00 3.50
19a A1 30c ('33) 50.00 37.50
20a A2 40c ('35) 10.00 7.50
22a A5 1p ('38) 25.00 14.00
b. Control number omitted 1,400.

Without Control Numbers

1936-43 *Perf. 11½x11*
25 A1 2c red brown ('37) 2.00 90
26 A2 5c dark brown 2.00 90
27 A3 10c blue green 10.00 2.00
a. 10c yellow green 80.00 30.00
28 A4 15c green ('37) 6.25 2.00
29 A3 20c violet 6.25 2.00
30 A4 25c deep rose ('37) 2.25 2.00
31 A1 30c carmine 4.50 2.00
31A A2 40c dark blue *600.00* 37.50
32 A1 45c rose red ('37) 2.00 90
33 A3 50c deep orange 8.75 3.50
34 A1 60c deep blue ('37) 5.00 2.00
35 A5 4p deep rose ('43) 32.50 30.00
36 A5 10p bister brn ('43) 45.00 30.00
Nos. 25-36 (13) *726.50* 115.70

Edelweiss — A6

Provost — A7

Coat of Arms — A8

Plaza of Ordino — A9

Chapel of Meritxell A10

Map A11

1948-53 Unwmk. Photo. *Perf. 12½*
37 A6 2c dark olive grn ('51) 35 20
38 A6 5c deep orange ('53) 35 20
39 A6 10c deep blue ('53) 35 20

Engr. *Perf. 9½x10*
40 A7 20c brown vio 6.25 65
41 A7 25c org, perf. 12½ ('53) 4.50 45
42 A8 30c dk slate grn 8.50 1.25
43 A9 50c deep green 10.00 1.50
44 A10 75c dark blue 14.00 1.50
45 A9 90c dp car rose 6.50 1.50
46 A10 1p brt orange ver 10.00 1.50
47 A8 1.35p dk blue vio 6.50 1.75

Perf. 10
48 A11 4p ultra ('53) 10.00 3.50
49 A11 10p dk violet brn ('51) 20.00 7.50
Nos. 37-49 (13) 97.30 21.70

Catalogue values for unused stamps in this section, from this point to the end of the section, are for Never Hinged items.

Bridge of St. Anthony — A12

Madonna of Meritxell, 8th Century — A13

Designs: 70c, Aynos pasture. 1p, View of Canillo. 2p, St. Coloma. 2.50p, Arms of Andorra. 3p, Old Andorra, horiz. 5p, View of Ordino, horiz.

1963-64 Unwmk. Engr. *Perf. 13*
50 A12 25c dk gray & sepia 25 15
51 A12 70c dk sl grn & brn blk 25 15
52 A12 1p slate & dull pur 38 15
53 A12 2p violet & dull pur 38 15
54 A12 2.50p rose claret 1.00 60
55 A12 3p blk & grnsh gray 1.75 60
56 A12 5p dk brn & choc 2.00 1.10
57 A13 6p sepia & car 3.00 1.10
Nos. 50-57 (8) 9.01 4.00

Issue dates: 25c-2p, July 20, 1963. 2.50p-6p, Feb. 29, 1964.

Narcissus — A14

Encamp Valley — A15

1966, June 10 Engr. *Perf. 13*
58 A14 50c shown 15 15
59 A14 1p Pinks 22 15
60 A14 5p Jonquils 1.40 55
61 A14 10p Hellebore 2.75 65
Nos. 58-61 (4) 4.52 1.50

Europa Issue 1972
Common Design Type

1972, May 2 Photo. *Perf. 13*
Size: 25½x38mm
62 CD15 8p multicolored 125.00 80.00

1972, July 4 Photo. *Perf. 13*

Tourist publicity: 1.50p, Massana (village). 2p, Skiing on De La Casa Pass. 5p, Pessons Lake, horiz.

63 A15 1p multicolored 30 15
64 A15 1.50p multicolored 90 55
65 A15 2p multicolored 2.25 55
66 A15 5p multicolored 3.00 90
Nos. 63-66 (4) 6.45 2.15

Butterfly Stroke — A16

Design: 2p, Volleyball, vert.

1972, Oct. Photo. *Perf. 13*
67 A16 2p lt blue & multi 28 15
68 A16 5p multicolored 32 20

20th Olympic Games, Munich, Aug. 26-Sept. 11.

St. Anthony Singers A17

1972, Dec. 5 Photo. *Perf. 13*
69 A17 1p shown 15 15
70 A17 1.50p Les Caramelles (boys' choir) 15 15
71 A17 2p Nativity scene 15 15
72 A17 5p Man holding giant cigar, vert 70 15
73 A17 8p Hermit of Meritxell, vert 85 35
74 A17 15p Marratxa dancers 2.00 50
Nos. 69-74 (6) 4.00
Set value 1.10

Andorran customs. No. 71 is for Christmas.

Common Design Types pictured in section at front of book.

Europa Issue 1973
Common Design Type and

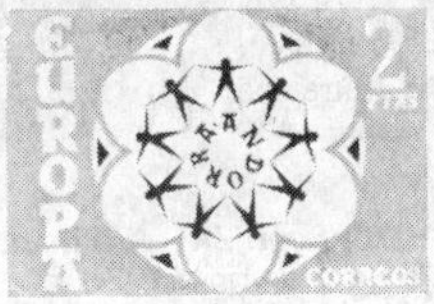
Symbol of Unity — A18

1973, Apr. 30 Photo. *Perf. 13*
75 A18 2p ultra, red & blk 20 15
Size: 37x25mm
76 CD16 8p tan, red & blk 85 30

Nativity — A19

Virgin of Ordino — A20

Christmas: 5p, Adoration of the Kings. Designs are from altar panels of Meritxell Parish Church.

1973, Dec. 14 Photo. *Perf. 13*
77 A19 2p multicolored 22 15
78 A19 5p multicolored 90 38

1974, Apr. 29 Photo. *Perf. 13*

Europa: 8p, Les Banyes Cross.

79 A20 2p multicolored 1.50 38
80 A20 8p slate & brt blue 4.50 1.25

Cupboard — A21

Crowns of Virgin and Child of Roser — A22

1974, July 30 Photo. *Perf. 13*
81 A21 10p multicolored 2.25 85
82 A22 25p dark red & multi 5.00 1.90

UPU Monument, Bern — A23

1974, Oct. 9 Photo. *Perf. 13*
83 A23 15p multicolored 1.40 55

Centenary of Universal Postal Union.

Nativity A24

Christmas: 5p, Adoration of the Kings.

1974, Dec. 4 Photo. *Perf. 13*
84 A24 2p multicolored 60 20
85 A24 5p multicolored 2.25 45

Mail Delivery, Andorra, 19th Century — A25

12th Century Painting, Ordino Church — A26

1975, Apr. 4 Photo. *Perf. 13*
86 A25 3p multicolored 30 15

Espana 75 International Philatelic Exhibition, Madrid, Apr. 4-13.

1975, Apr. 28 Photo. *Perf. 13*

Design: 12p, Christ in Glory, 12th century Romanesque painting, Ordino church.

87 A26 3p multicolored 1.65 35
88 A26 12p multicolored 3.00 60

Urgel Cathedral and Document — A27

1975, Oct. 4 Photo. *Perf. 13*
89 A27 7p multicolored 1.00 50

Millennium of consecration of Urgel Cathedral, and Literary Festival 1975.

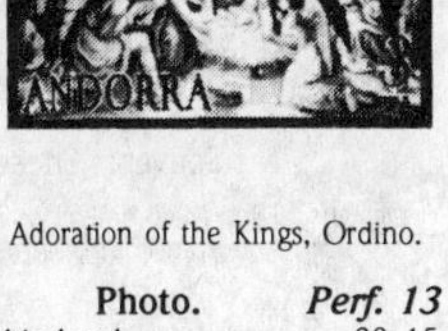
Nativity, Ordino A28

Christmas: 7p, Adoration of the Kings, Ordino.

1975, Dec. 3 Photo. *Perf. 13*
90 A28 3p multicolored 30 15
91 A28 7p multicolored 40 22

Caldron and CEPT Emblem — A29

Slalom and Montreal Olympic Emblem — A30

Europa: 12p, Chest and CEPT emblem, horiz.

1976, May 3 Photo. *Perf. 13*

92	A29 3p bister & multi	20	15
93	A29 12p yellow & multi	60	16

1976, July 9 Photo. *Perf. 13*

Design: 15p, One-man canoe and Montreal Olympic emblem, horiz.

94	A30 7p multicolored	18	15
95	A30 15p multicolored	42	25

21st Olympic Games, Montreal, Canada, July 17-Aug. 1.

Nativity A31

Christmas: 25p, Adoration of the Kings. Wall paintings in La Massana Church.

1976, Dec. 7 Photo. *Perf. 13*

96	A31 3p multicolored	15	15
97	A31 25p multicolored	55	25

View of Ansalonge A32

Europa: 12p, Xuclar, valley, mountains.

1977, May 2 Litho. *Perf. 13*

98	A32 3p multicolored	16	15
99	A32 12p multicolored	55	22

Cross of Terme — A33

Map of Post Offices — A34

Christmas: 12p, Church of St. Miguel d'Engolasters.

1977, Dec. 2 Photo. *Perf. 13x12½*

100	A33 5p multicolored	35	22
101	A33 12p multicolored	90	50

Souvenir Sheet

Designs: 10p, Mail delivery. 20p, Post Office, 1928. 25p, Andorran coat of arms.

1978, Mar. 31 Photo. *Perf. 13x13½*

102	Sheet of 4	1.00	1.00
a.	A34 5p multicolored	15	15
b.	A34 10p multicolored	20	15
c.	A34 20p multicolored	30	30
d.	A34 25p multicolored	35	35

Spanish postal service in Andorra, 50th anniversary.

La Vall — A35

Europa: 12p, St. Juan de Caselles.

1978, May 2 *Perf. 13*

103	A35 5p multicolored	15	15
104	A35 12p multicolored	30	15
	Set value		21

Crown, Bishop's Mitre and Staff — A36

1978, Sept. 24 Photo. *Perf. 13*

105	A36 5p brown, car & yel	45	15

700th anniversary of the signing of treaty establishing Co-Principality of Andorra.

Holy Family — A37

Young Woman — A38

Christmas: 25p, Adoration of the Kings. Both designs after frescoes in the Church of St. Mary d'Encamp.

1978, Dec. 5 Photo. *Perf. 13*

106	A37 5p multicolored	15	15
107	A37 25p multicolored	42	20
	Set value		26

1979, Feb. 14 Photo. *Perf. 13*

Designs: 5p, Young man. 12p, Bridegroom and bride riding mule.

108	A38 3p multicolored	15	15
109	A38 5p multicolored	15	15
110	A38 12p multicolored	25	15
	Set value	45	24

Old Mail Truck A39

Europa: 12p, Stampless covers of 1846 and 1854.

1979, Apr. 30 Engr. *Perf. 13*

111	A39 5p yel grn & dk blue	15	15
112	A39 12p dk red & violet	35	15
	Set value		21

Children Holding Hands A40

1979, Oct. 18 Photo. *Perf. 13*

113	A40 19p multicolored	40	20

International Year of the Child.

St. Coloma's Church — A41

Christmas: 25p, Agnus Dei roundel, St. Coloma's Church.

1979, Nov. 28 Photo. *Perf. 13½*

114	A41 8p multicolored	16	15
115	A41 25p multicolored	45	24
	Set value		29

Bishop Pere d'Arg A42

Bishops of Urgel: 5p, Josep Caixal. 13p, Joan Benlloch.

1979, Dec. 27 Engr.

116	A42 1p dk blue & brown	15	15
117	A42 5p rose lake & purple	15	15
118	A42 13p brown & dk green	25	15
	Set value	40	26

See Nos. 132-133, 159, 175, C4.

Antoni Fiter, Magistrate — A43

Europa: 19p, Francesc Cairat, magistrate.

1980, Apr. 28 Photo. *Perf. 13x13½*

119	A43 8p bister, blk & brn	15	15
120	A43 19p lt green & blk	40	18

Boxing, Moscow '80 Emblem A44

1980, July 23 Photo. *Perf. 13½x13*

121	A44 5p Downhill skiing	15	15
122	A44 8p shown	15	15
123	A44 50p Target shooting	85	50
	Nos. 121-123 (3)	1.15	
	Set value		69

12th Winter Olympic Games, Lake Placid, NY, Feb. 12-24 (5p); 22nd Summer Olympic Games, Moscow, July 19-Aug. 3.

Nativity A45

1980, Dec. 12 Litho. *Perf. 13*

124	A45 10p Nativity, vert.	15	15
125	A45 22p shown	40	20

Christmas 1980.

Children Dancing at Santa Anna Feast — A46

Europa: 30p, Going to church on Aplec de la Verge de Canolich Day.

1981, May 7 Photo. *Perf. 13*

126	A46 12p multicolored	20	15
127	A46 30p multicolored	45	25

50th Anniv. of Police Force — A47

1981, July 2 Photo. *Perf. 13½x13*

128	A47 30p multicolored	45	20

Intl. Year of the Disabled A48

1981, Oct. 8 Photo. *Perf. 13½*

129	A48 50p multicolored	75	30

Christmas 1981 — A49

Designs: Encamp Church retable.

1981, Dec. 3 Photo. *Perf. 13½*

130	A49 12p Nativity	20	15
131	A49 30p Adoration	50	20

Bishops of Urgel Type of 1979

1981, Dec. 12 Engr. *Perf. 13½*

132	A42 7p Salvador Casanas	15	15
133	A42 20p Josep de Boltas	38	15
	Set value		22

Natl. Arms — A51

1982, Feb. 17 Photo. *Perf. 13x13½*

134	A51 1p bright pink	15	15
135	A51 3p bister brown	15	15
136	A51 7p red orange	15	15
137	A51 12p lake	15	15
138	A51 15p ultra	18	15
139	A51 20p blue green	22	15
140	A51 30p crimson rose	35	15

Perf. 13½x12½

1982, Sept. 30 **Engr.**

Size: 25½x30½mm

141 A51	50p	dark green		80	18
142 A51	100p	dark blue		1.65	52
		Set value, #134-142		1.85	70

For type A51 without "PTA" see #192-198.

Europa 1982 — A52

1982, May 12 **Photo.** ***Perf. 13***

143 A52	14p	New Reforms, 1866, vert.	18	15
144 A52	33p	Reform of Institutions, 1981	48	25

1982 World Cup — A53

Designs: Various soccer players.

1982, June 13 **Photo.** ***Perf. 13x13½***

145 A53	14p	multicolored	60	60
146 A53	33p	multicolored	1.25	1.25
a.		Pair, #145-146 + label	1.85	1.85

A54

A55

Anniversaries: 9p, Permanent Spanish and French delegations, cent. 14p, 50th anniv. of Andorran stamps. 23p, St. Francis of Assisi (1182-1226). 33p, Anyos Pro-Vicarial District membership centenary (Relacio sobre la Vall de Andorra titlepage).

1982, Sept. 7 **Engr.** ***Perf. 13***

147 A54	9p	dk blue & brown	15	15
148 A54	14p	black & green	48	20
149 A54	23p	dk blue & brown	30	15
150 A54	33p	black & olive grn	90	45
		Nos. 147-150 (4)	1.83	
		Set value		80

Perf. 13x13½, 13½x13

1982, Dec. 9 **Photo.**

Christmas: 14p, Madonna and Child, Andorra la Vieille Church, vert. 33p, El Tio de Nadal (children in traditional costumes striking hollow tree).

151 A55	14p	multicolored	20	15
152 A55	33p	multicolored	50	25

Europa 1983 A56

1983, June 7 **Photo.** ***Perf. 13***

153 A56	16p	La Cortinada Church, architect, 12th cent.	30	15
154 A56	38p	Water mill, 16th cent.	75	40

Local Mushrooms — A57

1983, July 20 **Photo.** ***Perf. 13x12½***

155 A57	16p	Lactarius sanguifluus	1.65	50

See Nos. 165, 169, 172.

Universal Suffrage, 50th Anniv. A58

Photogravure and Engraved

1983, Sept. 6 ***Perf. 13***

156 A58	10p	multicolored	25	15

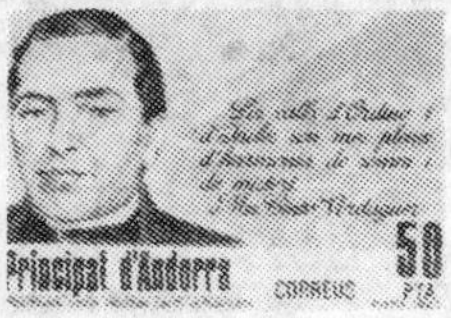

Visit of Monsignor Jacinto Verdaguer Bishop and Co-Prince A59

1983, Sept. 6

157 A59	50p	multicolored	95	45

Christmas 1983 — A60

Saint Cerni de Nagol, Romanesque fresco, Church of San Cerni de Nagol.

1983, Nov. 24 **Photo.** ***Perf. 13½***

158 A60	16p	multicolored	30	15

Bishops of Urgel Type of 1979

1983, Dec. 7 **Engr.** ***Perf. 13***

159 A42	26p	Joan J. Laguarda Fenollera	40	18

1984 Winter Olympics A62

1984, Feb. 17 **Litho.** ***Perf. 13½x14***

160 A62	16p	Ski jumping	40	15

ESPANA '84 — A63

1984, Apr. 27 **Photo.** ***Perf. 13***

161 A63	26p	Emblems	40	15

Europa (1959-84) A64

1984, May 5 **Engr.**

162 A64	16p	brown	30	15
163 A64	38p	blue	75	38

1984 Summer Olympics A65

1984, Aug. 9 **Litho.** ***Perf. 13½x14***

164 A65	40p	Running	70	38

Mushroom Type of 1983

1984, Sept. 27 **Photo.** ***Perf. 13x12½***

165 A57	11p	Morchella esculenta	*13.00*	1.50

Christmas 1984 — A66

1984, Dec. 6 **Photo.** ***Perf. 13½***

166 A66	17p	Nativity carving	35	15

Europa 1985 A67

Designs: 18p, Mossen Enric Arfany, composer, natl. hymn score. 45p, Musician Playing Viol, Romanesque fresco detail, La Cortinada Church, vert.

1985, May 3 **Engr.** ***Perf. 13½***

167 A67	18p	dk vio, grn & choc	38	15
168 A67	45p	green & choc	90	25

Mushroom Type of 1983

Perf. 13½x12½

1985, Sept. 19 **Photo.**

169 A57	30p	Gyromitra esculenta	65	25

Pal Village — A68

1985, Nov. 7 **Engr.** ***Perf. 13½***

170 A68	17p	brt ultra & dk blue	35	15

Christmas 1985 — A69

Fresco: Angels Playing Trumpet and Psaltery, St. Bartholomew Chapel.

1985, Dec. 11 **Photo.** ***Perf. 13½x13***

171 A69	17p	multicolored	35	15

Mushroom Type of 1983

Perf. 13½x12½

1986, Apr. 10 **Photo.**

172 A57	30p	Marasmius oreades	60	25

Europa 1986 — A70

1986, May 5 **Engr.** ***Perf. 13***

173 A70	17p	Water	30	15
174 A70	45p	Soil and air	85	25

Bishops of Urgel Type of 1979

1986, Sept. 11 **Engr.** ***Perf. 13½***

175 A42	35p	Justi Guitart	60	20

A72

A73

Santa Roma de Les Bons Church bell.

1986, Dec. 11 **Litho.** ***Perf. 14***

176 A72	19p	multicolored	30	15

Christmas.

1987, Mar. 27 **Photo.** ***Perf. 14***

Contemporary Natl. Coat of Arms.

177 A73	48p	multicolored	78	40

Visit of the co-princes: the Bishop of Urgel and president of France, September 26, 1986.

Europa 1987 A74

Modern architecture: 19p, Meritxell Sanctuary interior. 48p, Sanctuary exterior, vert.

1987, May 15 **Engr.** ***Perf. 14x13½***

178 A74	19p	dark blue & brown	30	15
179 A74	48p	dark blue & brown	78	28

Souvenir Sheet

1992 Summer Olympics, Barcelona A75

Designs: 20p, House of the Valleys. 50p, Bell tower, Chapel of the Archangel Michael, and torch-bearer.

1987, July 20 **Photo.** ***Perf. 14***

180		Sheet of 2	5.00	5.00
a.		A75 20p multicolored	1.40	1.40
b.		A75 50p multicolored	3.50	3.50

Local Mushrooms — A76

1987, Sept. 11 *Perf. 13½x12½*
181 A76 100p Boletus edulis 1.65 60

Christmas A77

Design: Detail from a Catalan manuscript, De Nativitat, by R. Llull.

1987, Nov. 18 Litho. *Perf. 14*
182 A77 20p multicolored 38 15

Lance and Arrowhead (Bronze Age) — A78

1988, Mar. 25 Photo. *Perf. 14*
183 A78 50p multicolored 90 30

Europa 1988 — A79

Pyrenean Mastiff — A80

Transport and communications: 20p, Les Bons, a medieval road. 45p, Trader and pack mules, early 20th cent.

1988, May 5 Engr. *Perf. 14x13½*
184 A79 20p dark blue & dark red 32 15
185 A79 45p dark blue & dark red 70 25

1988, July 26 Litho. *Perf. 14x13½*
186 A80 20p multicolored 35 15

Bishop of Urgel and Seigneur of Caboet Confirming Co-Principality, 700th Anniv. — A81

1988, Oct. 24 Litho. *Perf. 14x13½*
187 A81 20p gold, blk & int blue 35 15

Andorra, Spanish Administration, stamps can be mounted in the Scott annual Spain and Spanish Andorra supplement.

Christmas 1988 A82

1988, Nov. 30 Litho. *Perf. 14x13½*
188 A82 20p multicolored 35 15

Arms Type of 1982 Without "PTA"

1988, Dec. 2 Photo. *Perf. 13x13½*
192 A51 20p brt blue green 35 15

Size: 25x30½mm

Perf. 13½x12½

Engr.

194 A51 50p grnsh black 90 30
196 A51 100p dark blue 1.80 60
198 A51 500p dark brown 9.00 3.00
Nos. 192-198 (4) 12.05 4.05

This is an expanding set. Numbers will change if necessary.

Europa 1989 A83

Perf. 14x13½, 13½x14

1989, May 8 Litho. & Engr.
200 A83 20p Leapfrog, vert. 32 15
201 A83 45p Tug of war 72 24

Santa Roma Church, Les Bons — A84

Perf. 13½x14

1989, June 20 Litho. & Engr.
202 A84 50p blk, dp blue & grn blue 90 28

Anniv. Emblem — A85

Christmas — A86

1989, Oct. 26 Litho. *Perf. 14x13½*
203 A85 20p multicolored 35 15

Intl. Red Cross and Red Crescent societies, 125th annivs.; Year for the Protection of Human Life.

1989, Dec. 1
204 A86 20p *The Immaculate Conception* 35 15

Europa 1990 A87

Post offices.

Perf. 13½x14, 14x13½

1990, May 17 Photo.
205 A87 20p shown 38 15
206 A87 50p Post office, vert. 95 32

Gomphidius Rutilus — A88

1990, June 21 Litho. *Perf. 13x13½*
207 A88 45p multicolored 95 35

Plandolit House — A89

Christmas — A90

Perf. 13x12½

1990, Oct. 17 Litho. & Engr.
208 A89 20p brown & org yel 45 16

1990, Nov. 26 Litho. *Perf. 14x13½*
209 A90 25p lake, brn & bister 55 20

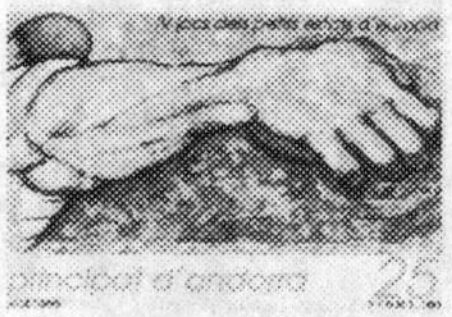

4th Games of the Small European States A91

1991, Apr. 29 Photo. *Perf. 13½x14*
210 A91 25p Discus 55 20
211 A91 45p High jump, runner 95 35

Europa — A92

Perf. 14x13½, 13½x14

1991, May 10 Litho.
212 A92 25p Olympus-1 satellite 55 20
213 A92 55p Olympus-1, horiz. 1.25 45

A93

Christmas — A94

1991, Sept. 20 Litho. *Perf. 13x12½*
214 A93 45p Macrolepiota Procera 95 35

1991, Nov. 29 Photo. *Perf. 14x13½*
215 A94 25p multicolored 55 20

Woman Carrying Water Pails — A95

1992, Feb. 14 Photo. *Perf. 13½x14*
216 A95 25p multicolored 55 20

Discovery of America, 500th Anniv. A96

Perf. 14x13½, 13½x14

1992, May 8 Photo.
217 A96 27p Santa Maria, vert. 65 22
218 A96 45p King Ferdinand 1.00 38

Europa.

1992 Summer Olympics, Barcelona A97

1992, July 22 Photo. *Perf. 13½x14*
219 A97 27p Kayak 85 30

Nativity Scene, by Fra Angelico — A98

1992, Nov. 18 Photo. *Perf. 14*
220 A98 27p multicolored 65 22

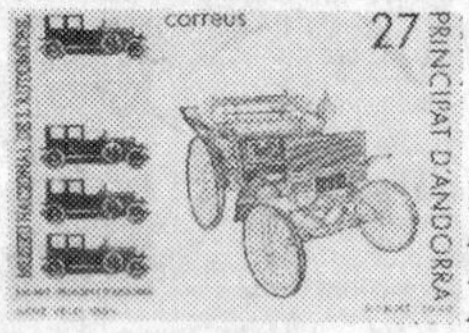

Natl. Automobile Museum A99

Perf. 13½x14

1992, Sept. 10 Litho. & Engr.
221 A99 27p 1894 Benz 85 30

Cantharellus Cibarius A100

1993, Mar. 25 Photo. *Perf. 13½x14*
222 A100 28p multicolored 90 32

Contemporary Paintings — A101

Europa: 28p, Upatream, by John Alan Morrison. 45p, Rhythm, by Angel Calvente, vert.

Perf. 13½x14, 14x13½

1993, May 20 **Litho.**

223	A101	28p multicolored	90	32
224	A101	45p multicolored	1.40	50

A102

A103

1993, Sept. 23 **Litho.** *Perf. 14*

225	A102	28p multicolored	90	32

Art and Literature Society, 25th anniv.

Perf. 14x13½

1993, Nov. 25 **Litho. & Engr.**

226	A103	28p Christmas	90	32

Souvenir Sheet

Constitution, 1st Anniv. — A104

1994, Mar. 14 **Photo.** *Perf. 14*

227	A104	29p multicolored	95	95

Sir Alexander Fleming (1881-1955), Co-discoverer of Penicillin A105

1994, May 6 **Photo.** *Perf. 13½x14*

228	A105	29p Portrait	95	95
229	A105	55p AIDS virus	1.75	1.75

Europa.

Hygrophorus Gliocyclus A106

1994, Sept. 27 **Photo.** *Perf. 14*

230	A106	29p multicolored	95	95

Christmas — A107

1994, Nov. 29 **Photo.** *Perf. 14x13½*

231	A107	29p multicolored	95	95

SPANISH ADMINISTRATIONAIR POST STAMPS

AP1

Unwmk.

1951, June 27 **Engr.** *Perf. 11*

C1	AP1	1p dk violet brn	25.00	2.25

Catalogue values for unused stamps in this section, from this point to the end of the section, are for Never Hinged items.

AP2

AP3

Litho. & Engr.

1983, Oct. 20 *Perf. 13*

C2	AP2	20p brown & bis brn	30	20

Jaime Sansa Nequi, Episcopal Church official.

1984, Oct. 25 **Photo.** *Perf. 13*

C3	AP3	20p multicolored	40	25

Pyrenees Art Center.

Bishops of Urgel Type of 1979

1985, June 13 **Engr.** *Perf. 13½*

C4	A42	20p Ramon Iglesias	35	18

SPECIAL DELIVERY STAMPS

Special Delivery Stamp of Spain, 1905 Overprinted

CORREOS

ANDORRA

1928 **Unwmk.** *Perf. 14*

Without Control Number on Back

E1	SD1	20c red	62.50	42.50

With Control Number on Back

E2	SD1	20c pale red	32.50	17.50

Eagle over Mountain Pass — SD2

Arms and Squirrel — SD3

1929 *Perf. 14*

With Control Number on Back

E3	SD2	20c scarlet	13.50	5.00
a.		Perf. 11½	300.00	

1937 *Perf. 11½x11*

Without Control Number on Back

E4	SD2	20c red	7.50	4.00

1949 **Unwmk.** **Engr.** *Perf. 10x9½*

E5	SD3	25c red	4.00	2.50

FRENCH ADMINISTRATION

Stamps and Types of France, 1900-1929, Overprinted **ANDORRE**

Perf. 14x13½

1931, June 16 **Unwmk.**

1	A16	1c gray	50	50
a.		Double overprint	950.00	950.00
2	A16	2c red brn	55	55
3	A16	3c orange	55	55
4	A16	5c green	95	95
5	A16	10c lilac	1.40	1.40
6	A22	15c red brn	2.75	2.75
7	A22	20c red vio	3.75	3.75
8	A22	25c yel brn	3.75	3.75
9	A22	30c green	3.75	3.75
10	A22	40c ultra	6.75	6.75
11	A20	45c lt vio	7.25	7.25
12	A20	50c vermilion	6.25	6.25
13	A20	65c gray green	9.00	9.00
14	A20	75c rose lilac	12.50	12.50
15	A22	90c red	16.00	16.00
16	A20	1fr dull blue	17.00	17.00
17	A22	1.50fr light blue	22.50	22.50

Overprinted **ANDORRE**

18	A18	2fr org & pale bl	16.00	16.00
19	A18	3fr brt vio & rose	57.50	57.50
20	A18	5fr dk bl & buff	90.00	90.00
21	A18	10fr grn & red	175.00	175.00
22	A18	20fr mag & grn	225.00	225.00
		Nos. 1-22 (22)	678.70	678.70

See No. P1 for ½c on 1c gray.

Nos. 9, 15 and 17 were not issued in France without overprint.

Chapel of Meritxell A50

Bridge of St. Anthony A51

St. Miguel d'Engolasters A52

Gorge of St. Julia A53

Old Andorra — A54

1932-43 **Engr.** *Perf. 13*

23	A50	1c gray blk	30	25
24	A50	2c violet	42	42
25	A50	3c brown	30	22
26	A50	5c bl grn	42	35
27	A51	10c dull lilac	65	55
28	A50	15c dp red	1.00	1.00
29	A51	20c lt rose	6.25	4.50
30	A52	25c brown	2.25	2.25
31	A51	25c brn car ('37)	4.50	6.50
32	A51	30c emerald	1.75	1.50
33	A51	40c ultra	5.00	4.25
34	A51	40c brn blk ('39)	65	60
35	A51	45c lt red	6.00	4.75
36	A51	45c bl grn ('39)	3.00	2.50
37	A52	50c lil rose	6.50	4.75
38	A51	50c lt vio ('39)	3.00	2.50
38A	A51	50c grn ('40)	1.40	1.40
39	A51	55c lt vio ('38)	9.50	6.00
40	A51	60c yel brn ('38)	60	50
41	A52	65c yel grn	25.00	25.00
42	A51	65c blue ('38)	6.50	5.50
43	A51	70c red ('39)	1.40	1.00
44	A52	75c violet	3.25	2.50
45	A51	75c ultra ('39)	2.50	2.25
46	A51	80c green ('38)	13.00	9.50
46A	A53	80c bl grn ('40)	28	30
47	A53	90c dp rose	3.25	2.00
48	A53	90c dk grn ('39)	2.25	2.25
49	A53	1fr blue grn	9.50	5.75
50	A53	1fr scar ('38)	12.50	9.50
51	A53	1fr dp ultra ('39)	25	25
51A	A53	1.20fr brt vio ('42)	25	22
52	A50	1.25fr rose car ('33)	22.50	14.00
52A	A50	1.25fr rose ('38)	3.00	1.40
52B	A53	1.30fr sep ('40)	25	22
53	A54	1.50fr ultra	8.25	7.50
53A	A53	1.50fr crim ('40)	25	22
54	A53	1.75fr vio ('33)	65.00	50.00
55	A53	1.75fr dk bl ('38)	22.50	16.00
56	A53	2fr red vio	3.75	3.50
56A	A50	2fr rose red ('40)	1.00	65
56B	A50	2fr dk bl grn ('42)	25	20
57	A50	2.15fr dk vio ('38)	27.50	20.00
58	A50	2.25fr ultra ('39)	4.00	3.00
58A	A50	2.40fr red ('42)	25	20
59	A50	2.50fr gray blk ('39)	4.00	3.00
59A	A50	2.50fr dp ultra ('40)	1.40	1.25
60	A53	3fr org brn	3.75	3.50
60A	A50	3fr red brn ('40)	30	25
60B	A50	4fr sl bl ('42)	30	25
60C	A50	4.50fr dp vio ('42)	80	80
61	A54	5fr brown	40	30
62	A54	10fr violet	45	40
62B	A54	15fr dp ultra ('42)	50	38
63	A54	20fr rose lake	50	40
63A	A51	50fr turq bl ('43)	1.00	50
		Nos. 23-63A (56)	305.32	238.73

A 20c ultra exists. Value $12,500.

No. 37 Surcharged with Bars and New Value in Black

1935, Sept. 25

64	A52	20c on 50c lil rose	10.00	8.00
a.		Double surcharge	650.00	

Coat of Arms
A55 A56

1936-42 *Perf. 14x13*

65	A55	1c black ('37)	15	15
66	A55	2c blue	15	15
67	A55	3c brown	15	15
68	A55	5c rose lil	15	15
69	A55	10c ultra ('37)	15	15
70	A55	15c red vio	55	55
71	A55	20c emer ('37)	15	15
72	A55	30c cop red ('38)	25	25
72A	A55	30c blk brn ('42)	15	15
73	A55	35c Prus grn ('38)	25.00	25.00
74	A55	40c cop red ('42)	15	15
75	A55	50c Prus grn ('42)	15	15
76	A55	60c turq bl ('42)	15	15
77	A55	70c vio ('42)	15	15
		Nos. 65-77 (14)	27.45	27.45

Catalogue values for unused stamps in this section, from this point to the end of the section, are for Never Hinged items.

1944

78	A56	10c violet	15	15
79	A56	30c dp magenta	15	15
80	A56	40c dull blue	15	15
81	A56	50c orange red	15	15
82	A56	60c black	15	15
83	A56	70c brt red vio	15	15
84	A56	80c blue green	15	15
		Set value	58	58

See No. 114.

St. Jean de Caselles A57

La Maison des Vallees — A58

Old Andorra A59

Provost A60

1944-47 *Perf. 13*

85	A57	1fr brn vio	18	15
86	A57	1.20fr blue	15	15
87	A57	1.50fr red	18	15
88	A57	2fr dk bl grn	15	15
89	A58	2.40fr rose red	22	18
90	A58	2.50fr rose red ('46)	1.25	50
91	A58	3fr sepia	15	15
92	A58	4fr ultra	18	15
93	A59	4.50fr brn blk	18	15
94	A58	4.50fr dk bl grn ('47)	4.00	3.50
95	A59	5fr ultra	22	18
96	A59	5fr Prus grn ('46)	40	30
97	A59	6fr rose car ('45)	30	15
98	A59	10fr Prus grn	15	15
99	A59	10fr ultra ('46)	18	15
100	A60	15fr rose lilac	38	25
101	A60	20fr deep blue	55	45
102	A60	25fr lt rose red ('46)	1.40	1.10
103	A60	40fr dk grn ('46)	1.40	1.10
104	A60	50fr sepia	1.40	1.10
		Nos. 85-104 (20)	13.02	10.16

1948-49

105	A58	4fr lt bl grn	70	70
106	A59	6fr vio brn	35	35
107	A59	8fr indigo	1.00	1.00
108	A59	12fr brt red	75	75
109	A59	12fr bl grn ('49)	90	75
110	A59	15fr crimson ('49)	45	45
111	A60	18fr deep blue	2.50	1.50
112	A60	20fr dark vio	2.00	1.65
113	A60	25fr ultra ('49)	1.40	1.10
		Nos. 105-113 (9)	10.05	8.25

1949-51 *Perf. 14x13, 13*

114	A56	1fr deep blue	60	55
115	A57	3fr red ('51)	4.50	3.25
116	A57	4fr sepia	2.00	2.00
117	A58	5fr emerald	2.25	1.65
118	A58	5fr pur ('51)	2.25	1.40
119	A58	6fr blue grn ('51)	2.00	1.65
120	A58	8fr brown	60	60
121	A59	15fr blk brn ('51)	2.00	1.65
122	A59	18fr rose red ('51)	11.00	7.25
123	A60	30fr ultra ('51)	17.50	7.50
		Nos. 114-123 (10)	44.70	27.50

Les Escaldres Spa — A61

St. Coloma Belfry — A62

Designs: 15fr, 18fr, 20fr, 25fr, Gothic cross. 30fr, 35fr, 40fr, 50fr, 65fr, 70fr, 75fr, Village of Les Bons.

1955-58 Unwmk. Engr. *Perf. 13*

124	A61	1fr dk gray bl	18	15
125	A61	2fr dp grn	18	15
126	A61	3fr red	18	15
127	A61	5fr chocolate	18	15
128	A62	6fr dk bl grn	45	38
129	A62	8fr rose brn	45	45
130	A62	10fr brt vio	70	55
131	A62	12fr indigo	75	60
132	A61	15fr red	1.00	85
133	A61	18fr bl grn	1.00	85
134	A61	20fr dp pur	1.65	1.50
135	A61	25fr sepia	2.00	1.50
136	A62	30fr deep blue	24.00	16.00
137	A62	35fr Prus bl ('57)	9.00	6.75
138	A62	40fr dk grn	25.00	18.00
139	A62	50fr cerise	3.00	2.25
140	A62	65fr pur ('58)	8.50	5.75
141	A62	70fr chnt ('57)	6.00	5.75
142	A62	75fr vio bl	40.00	32.50
		Nos. 124-142 (19)	124.22	94.28

Issue dates: 35fr, 70fr, Aug. 19, 65fr, Feb. 10, others, Feb. 15.

Coat of Arms — A63

Gothic Cross, Meritxell — A64

Designs: 65c, 85c, 1fr, Pond of Engolasters.

1961, June 19 Typo. *Perf. 14x13*

143	A63	5c brt grn & blk	15	15
144	A63	10c red, pink & blk	15	15
145	A63	15c bl & blk	15	15
146	A63	20c yel & brn	15	15

Engr. *Perf. 13*

147	A64	25c vio, bl & grn	22	22
148	A64	30c mar, ol grn & brn	38	38
149	A64	45c indigo, bl & grn	13.00	8.00
150	A64	50c pur, lt brn & ol grn	1.40	1.40
151	A64	65c bl, ol & brn	16.00	12.00
152	A64	85c rose lil, vio bl & brn	16.00	12.00
153	A64	1fr grnsh bl, ind & brn	1.25	90
		Nos. 143-153 (11)	48.85	35.50

See Nos. 161-166A.

Imperforates

Most stamps of Andorra, French Administration, from 1961 onward exist imperforate in issued and trial colors, and also in small presentation sheets in issued colors.

Telstar and Globe Showing Andover and Pleumeur-Bodou — A65

1962, Sept. 29 **Engr.**

154	A65	50c ultra & purple	1.35	1.35

1st television connection of the US and Europe through the Telstar satellite, July 11-12.

"La Sardane" A66

Charlemagne Crossing Andorra — A67

Design: 1fr, Louis le Debonnaire giving founding charter.

1963, June 22 Unwmk. *Perf. 13*

155	A66	20c lil rose, cl & ol grn	3.50	3.50
156	A67	50c sl grn & dk car rose	6.00	6.00
157	A67	1fr red brn, ultra & dk grn	9.50	9.50
		Nos. 155-157 (3)	19.00	19.00

Old Andorra Church and Champs-Elysées Palace — A68

1964, Jan. 20 **Engr.**

158	A68	25c blk, grn & vio brn	1.20	75

"PHILATEC," Intl. Philatelic and Postal Techniques Exhib., Paris, June 5-21, 1964.

Bishop of Urgel and Seigneur of Caboet Confirming Co-Principality, 1288 — A69

Design: 60c, Napoleon re-establishing Co-principality, 1806.

1964, Apr. 25 Engr. *Perf. 13*

159	A69	60c dk brn, red brn & sl grn	11.50	11.50
160	A69	1fr brt bl, org brn & blk	11.50	11.50

Arms Type of 1961

1964, May 16 Typo. *Perf. 14x13*

161	A63	1c dk bl & gray	15	15
162	A63	2c blk & org	15	15
163	A63	12c pur, emer & yel	30	30
164	A63	18c blk, lil & pink	30	30
		Set value	75	75

Scenic Type of 1961

Designs: 40c, 45c, Gothic Cross, Meritxell. 60c, 90c, Pond of Engolasters.

1965-71 Engr. *Perf. 13*

165	A64	40c dk brn, org brn & sl grn	50	50
165A	A64	45c vio bl, ol bis & slate	1.00	75
166	A64	60c org brn & dk brn	60	60
166A	A64	90c ultra, bl grn & bister	50	50
		Nos. 165-166A (4)	2.60	2.35

Issued: 40c, 60c, Apr. 24, 1965. 45c, June 13, 1970. 90c, Aug. 28, 1971.

Syncom Satellite over Pleumeur-Bodou Station — A70

Andorra House, Paris — A71

1965, May 17 **Unwmk.**

167	A70	60c dp car, lil & bl	4.00	3.25

Cent. of the ITU.

1965, June 5

168	A71	25c dk bl, org brn & ol gray	90	75

Ski Lift — A72

Design: 25c, Chair lift, vert.

1966, Apr. 2 Engr. *Perf. 13*

169	A72	25c brt bl, grn & dk brn	1.00	80
170	A72	40c mag, brt ultra & sep	1.40	1.25

Winter sports in Andorra.

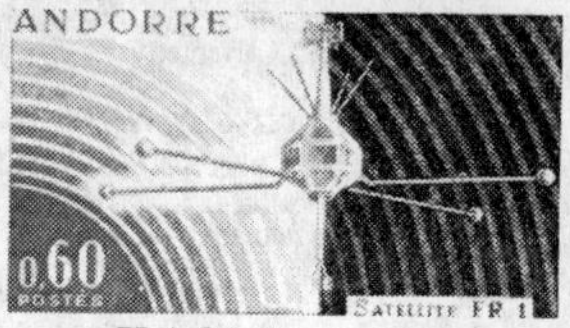

FR-1 Satellite — A73

1966, May 7 *Perf. 13*

171	A73	60c brt bl, grn & dk grn	1.50	1.50

Issued to commemorate the launching of the scientific satellite FR-1, Dec. 6, 1965.

Europa Issue, 1966

Common Design Type

1966, Sept. 24 Engr. *Perf. 13*

Size: 21½x35½mm

172	CD9	60c brown	3.00	2.25

Folk Dancers, Sculpture by Josep Viladomat A74

Telephone Encircling the Globe A75

1967, Apr. 29 Engr. *Perf. 13*

173	A74	30c ol grn, dp grn & slate	60	45

Cent. (in 1966) of the New Reform, which reaffirmed and strengthened political freedom in Andorra.

Europa Issue, 1967

Common Design Type

1967, Apr. 29

Size: 22x36mm

174	CD10	30c bluish blk & lt bl	1.75	1.50
175	CD10	60c dk red & brt pink	2.75	2.00

1967, Apr. 29

176	A75	60c dk car, vio & blk	1.25	1.00

Automatic telephone service.

Injured Father at Home — A76

1967, Sept. 23 Engr. *Perf. 13*

177	A76	2.30fr ocher, dk red brn & brn red	6.50	4.25

Introduction of Social Security System.

Jesus in Garden of Gethsemane A77

Designs (from 16th century frescoes in La Maison des Vallees): 30c, The Kiss of Judas. 60c, The Descent from the Cross (Pieta).

1967, Sept. 23

178 A77 25c blk & red brn	50	40
179 A77 30c pur & red lilac	75	50
180 A77 60c indigo & Prus bl	1.40	90
Nos. 178-180 (3)	2.65	1.80

See Nos. 185-187.

Downhill Skier — A78

1968, Jan. 27 **Engr.** ***Perf. 13***

181 A78 40c org, ver & red lil	75	60

10th Winter Olympic Games, Grenoble, France, Feb. 6-18.

Europa Issue, 1968

Common Design Type

1968, Apr. 27 **Engr.** ***Perf. 13***

Size: 36x22mm

182 CD11 30c gray & brt bl	4.00	3.00
183 CD11 60c brn & lilac	5.00	3.75

High Jump — A79

1968, Oct. 12 **Engr.** ***Perf. 13***

184 A79 40c brt bl & brn	1.20	1.00

19th Olympic Games, Mexico City, Oct. 12-27.

Fresco Type of 1967

Designs (from 16th century frescoes in La Maison des Vallees): 25c, The Scourging of Christ. 30c, Christ Carrying the Cross. 60c, The Crucifixion. (All horiz.)

1968, Oct. 12

185 A77 25c dk grn & gray grn	60	60
186 A77 30c dk brn & lil	1.00	1.00
187 A77 60c dk car & vio brn	1.40	1.40
Nos. 185-187 (3)	3.00	3.00

Europa Issue, 1969

Common Design Type

1969, Apr. 26 **Engr.** ***Perf. 13***

188 CD12 40c rose car, gray & dl bl	3.75	3.00
189 CD12 70c indigo, dl red & ol	5.75	4.25

10th anniv. of the Conf. of European Postal and Telecommunications Administrations.

Kayak on Isère River A80

Drops of Water and Diamond A80a

1969, Aug. 2 **Engr.** ***Perf. 13***

190 A80 70c dk sl grn, ultra & ind	1.75	1.75

Intl. Canoe & Kayak Championships, Bourg-Saint-Maurice, Savoy, July 31-Aug. 6.

1969, Sept. 27 **Engr.** ***Perf. 13***

191 A80a 70c blk, dp ultra & grnsh bl	3.25	3.25

European Water Charter.

St. John, the Woman and the Dragon — A81

The Revelation (From the Altar of St. John, Caselles): 40c, St. John Hearing Voice from Heaven on Patmos. 70c, St. John and the Seven Candlesticks.

1969, Oct. 18

192 A81 30c brn, dp pur & brn red	65	65
193 A81 40c gray, dk brn & brn ol	1.00	1.00
194 A81 70c dk red, maroon & brt rose lilac	1.75	1.75
Nos. 192-194 (3)	3.40	3.40

See Nos. 199-201, 207-209, 214-216.

Field Ball — A82

Shot Put — A83

1970, Feb. 21 **Engr.** ***Perf. 13***

195 A82 80c multi	1.75	1.25

Issued to publicize the 7th International Field Ball Games, France, Feb. 26-Mar. 8.

Europa Issue, 1970

Common Design Type

1970, May 2 **Engr.** ***Perf. 13***

Size: 36x22mm

196 CD13 40c orange	2.50	1.90
197 CD13 80c vio bl	3.50	2.75

1970, Sept. 11 **Engr.** ***Perf. 13***

198 A83 80c bl & dk brn	1.25	1.00

1st European Junior Athletic Championships, Colombes, France, Sept. 11-13.

Altar Type of 1969

The Revelation (from the Altar of St. John, Caselles): 30c, St. John recording angel's message. 40c, Angel erecting column symbolizing faithful in heaven. 80c, St. John's trial in kettle of boiling oil.

1970, Oct. 24

199 A81 30c dp car, dk brn & brt pur	75	75
200 A81 40c vio & sl grn	90	90
201 A81 80c ol, dk bl & car rose	1.75	1.75
Nos. 199-201 (3)	3.40	3.40

Ice Skating A84

1971, Feb. 20 **Engr.** ***Perf. 13***

202 A84 80c dk red, red lil & pur	2.25	1.50

World Figure Skating Championships, Lyons, France, Feb. 23-28.

Andorra, French Administration stamps can be mounted in the Scott annual Monaco and French Andorra supplement.

Capercaillie — A85

Nature protection: No. 204, Brown bear.

1971, Apr. 24 **Photo.** ***Perf. 13***

203 A85 80c multi	2.25	1.40

Engr.

204 A85 80c bl, grn & brn	2.25	1.40

Europa Issue, 1971

Common Design Type

1971, May 8 **Engr.** ***Perf. 13***

Size: 35 1/2x22mm

205 CD14 50c rose red	3.00	2.25
206 CD14 80c lt bl grn	4.25	3.00

Altar Type of 1969

The Revelation (from the Altar of St. John, Caselles): 30c, St. John preaching, Rev. 1:3. 50c, "The Sign of the Beast . . ." Rev. 16:1-2. 90c, The Woman, Rev. 17:1.

1971, Sept. 18

207 A81 30c dl grn, ol & brt grn	75	75
208 A81 50c rose car, org & ol brn	1.00	1.00
209 A81 90c blk, dk pur & bl	1.60	1.60
Nos. 207-209 (3)	3.35	3.35

Europa Issue 1972

Common Design Type

1972, Apr. 29 **Photo.** ***Perf. 13***

Size: 21 1/2x37mm

210 CD15 50c brt mag & multi	3.00	2.75
211 CD15 90c multi	4.00	3.25

Golden Eagle — A86

1972, May 27 **Engr.**

212 A86 60c dk grn, ol & plum	2.00	1.65

Nature protection.

Shooting A87

1972, July 8

213 A87 1fr dk pur	1.75	1.40

20th Olympic Games, Munich, Aug. 26-Sept. 11.

Altar Type of 1969

The Revelation (from the Altar of St. John, Caselles): 30c, St. John, bishop and servant. 50c, Resurrection of Lazarus. 90c, Angel with lance and nails.

1972, Sept. 16 **Engr.** ***Perf. 13***

214 A81 30c dk ol, gray & red lil	75	75
215 A81 50c vio bl & sl	1.10	1.10
216 A81 90c dk Prus bl & sl grn	1.75	1.75
Nos. 214-216 (3)	3.60	3.60

De Gaulle as Coprince of Andorra — A88

Design: 90c, De Gaulle in front of Maison des Vallées.

1972, Oct. 23 **Engr.** ***Perf. 13***

217 A88 50c vio bl	1.25	1.25
218 A88 90c dk car	1.75	1.75
a. Pair, #217-218 + label	3.00	3.00

Visit of Charles de Gaulle to Andorra, 5th anniv.

See Nos. 399-400.

Europa Issue 1973

Common Design Type

1973, Apr. 28 **Photo.** ***Perf. 13***

Size: 36x22mm

219 CD16 50c vio & multi	3.00	2.75
220 CD16 90c dk red & multi	4.00	3.00

Virgin of Canolich A89

1973, June 16 **Engr.** ***Perf. 13***

221 A89 1fr ol, Prus bl & vio	1.65	1.65

Lily — A90

Blue Titmouse — A91

Designs: 45c, Iris. 50c, Columbine. 65c, Tobacco. No. 226, Pinks. No. 227, Narcissuses.

1973-74 **Photo.** ***Perf. 13***

222 A90 30c car rose & multi	35	35
223 A90 45c yel grn & multi	20	20
224 A90 50c buff & multi	1.10	1.10
225 A90 65c gray & multi	30	30
226 A90 90c ultra & multi	70	70
227 A90 90c grnsh bl & multi	60	60
Nos. 222-227 (6)	3.25	3.25

See Nos. 238-240.

1973-74 **Photo.** ***Perf. 13***

Nature protection: 60c, Citril finch and mistletoe. 80c, Eurasian bullfinch. 1fr, Lesser spotted woodpecker.

228 A91 60c buff & multi	1.40	1.10
229 A91 80c gray & multi	1.40	1.10
230 A91 90c gray & multi	1.10	90
231 A91 1fr yel grn & multi	1.65	1.20
Nos. 228-231 (4)	5.55	4.30

Europa Issue 1974

Virgin of Pal — A92

Design: 90c, Virgin of Santa Coloma. Statues are polychrome 12th century carvings by rural artists.

1974, Apr. 27 **Engr.** ***Perf. 13***

232 A92 50c multi	5.00	3.75
233 A92 90c multi	7.00	5.00

Arms of Andorra and Cahors Bridge — A93

Mail Box, Chutes and Globe — A94

1974, Aug. 24 **Engr.** ***Perf. 13***
234 A93 1fr bl, vio & org 1.00 60

First anniversary of meeting of the co-princes of Andorra: Pres. Georges Pompidou of France and Msgr. Juan Marti Alanis, Bishop of Urgel.

1974, Oct. 5 **Engr.** ***Perf. 13***
235 A94 1.20fr multi 1.25 1.10

Centenary of Universal Postal Union.

Coronation of St. Marti, 16th Century — A95

Europa: 80c, Crucifixion, 16th cent., vert.

Perf. 11½x13, 13x11½

1975, Apr. 26 **Photo.**
236 A95 80c gold & multi 5.00 4.00
237 A95 1.20fr gold & multi 5.75 4.00

Flower Type of 1973

Designs: 60c, Gentian. 80c, Anemone. 1.20fr, Autumn crocus.

1975, May 10 **Photo.** ***Perf. 13***
238 A90 60c ol & multi 32 32
239 A90 80c brt rose & multi 75 75
240 A90 1.20fr grn & multi 80 80
Nos. 238-240 (3) 1.87 1.87

Abstract Design — A96

1975, June 7 **Engr.** ***Perf. 13***
241 A96 2fr bl, magenta & emer 2.00 2.00

ARPHILA 75 International Philatelic Exhibition, Paris, June 6-16.

Pres. Georges Pompidou — A97

1975, Aug. 23 **Engr.** ***Perf. 13***
242 A97 80c vio bl & blk 80 80

Georges Pompidou (1911-74), pres. of France and co-prince of Andorra (1969-74).

Costume and IWY Emblem — A98

1975, Nov. 8 **Engr.** ***Perf. 13***
243 A98 1.20fr multi 1.20 1.00

International Women's Year.

Skier and Snowflake A99

1976, Jan. 31 **Engr.** ***Perf. 13***
244 A99 1.20fr multi 1.20 1.00

12th Winter Olympic Games, Innsbruck, Austria, Feb. 4-15.

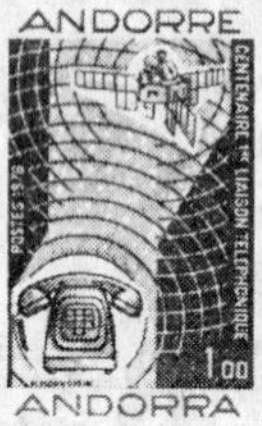

Telephone and Satellite — A100

1976, Mar. 20 **Engr.** ***Perf. 13***
245 A100 1fr multi 80 80

Centenary of first telephone call by Alexander Graham Bell, Mar. 10, 1976.

Catalan Forge — A101

Europa: 1.20fr, Lacemaker.

1976, May 8 **Engr.** ***Perf. 13***
246 A101 80c multi 1.25 1.10
247 A101 1.20fr multi 1.75 1.65

Thomas Jefferson A102

Trapshooting A103

1976, July 3 **Engr.** ***Perf. 13***
248 A102 1.20fr multi 1.10 90

American Bicentennial.

1976, July 17 **Engr.** ***Perf. 13***
249 A103 2fr multi 1.40 1.00

21st Olympic Games, Montreal, Canada, July 17-Aug. 1.

Meritxell Sanctuary and Old Chapel — A104

1976, Sept. 4 **Engr.** ***Perf. 13***
250 A104 1fr multi 1.00 80

Dedication of rebuilt Meritxell Church, Sept. 8, 1976.

Apollo — A105

Ermine — A106

Design: 1.40fr, Morio butterfly.

1976, Oct. 16 **Photo.** ***Perf. 13***
251 A105 80c blk & multi 1.00 90
252 A105 1.40fr salmon & multi 1.50 1.25

Nature protection.

1977, Apr. 2 **Photo.** ***Perf. 13***
253 A106 1fr vio bl, gray & blk 1.40 1.10

Nature protection.

St. Jean de Caselles A107

Manual Digest, 1748, Arms of Andorra A108

Europa: 1.40fr, Sant Vicens Castle.

1977, Apr. 30 **Engr.** ***Perf. 13***
254 A107 1fr multi 1.25 90
255 A107 1.40fr multi 1.65 1.40

1977, June 11 **Engr.** ***Perf. 13***
256 A108 80c grn, bl & brn 80 70

Establishment of Institute of Andorran Studies.

St. Romanus of Caesarea A109

1977, July 23 **Engr.** ***Perf. 12½x13***
257 A109 2fr multi 1.25 1.00

Design from altarpiece in Church of St. Roma de les Bons.

General Council Chamber A110

Guillem d'Arény Plandolit — A111

1977, Sept. 24 **Engr.** ***Perf. 13***
258 A110 1.10fr multi 1.10 90
259 A111 2fr car & dk brn 1.25 90

Andorran heritage. Guillem d'Arény Plandolit started Andorran reform movement in 1866.

Squirrel A112

Flag and Valira River Bridge A113

1978, Mar. 18 **Engr.** ***Perf. 13***
260 A112 1fr multi 75 55

1978, Apr. 8
261 A113 80c multi 60 55

Signing of the treaty establishing the Co-Principality of Andorra, 700th anniv.

Pal Church A114

Europa: 1.40fr, Charlemagne's Castle, Charlemagne on horseback, vert.

1978, Apr. 29 **Engr.** ***Perf. 13***
262 A114 1fr multi 1.25 1.00
263 A114 1.40fr multi 1.75 1.50

Virgin of Sispony A115

1978, May 20 **Engr.** ***Perf. 12x13***
264 A115 2fr multi 1.25 1.00

Visura Tribunal A116

1978, June 24 **Engr.** ***Perf. 13***
265 A116 1.20fr multi 75 50

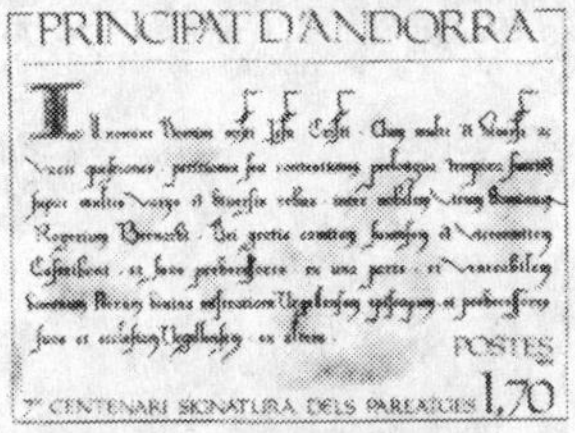

Preamble of 1278 Treaty — A117

1978, Sept. 2 **Engr.** ***Perf. 13x12½***
266 A117 1.70fr multi 75 50

700th anniversary of the signing of treaty establishing Co-Principality of Andorra.

Pyrenean Chamois A118

White Partridges A119

1979, Mar. 26 **Engr.** ***Perf. 13***
267 A118 1fr multi 50 35

1979, Apr. 9 **Photo.** ***Perf. 13***
268 A119 1.20fr multi 75 60

Nature protection. See Nos. 288-289.

French Mailman, 1900 — A120

Europa: 1.70fr, 1st French p.o. in Andorra.

1979, Apr. 28 **Engr.** ***Perf. 13***
269 A120 1.20fr multi 1.10 90
270 A120 1.70fr multi 1.50 1.10

Falcon, Pre-Roman Painting A121

1979, June 2 **Engr.** ***Perf. 12½x13***
271 A121 2fr multi 1.00 75

A122

A123

Child with Lambs, Church, IYC emblem.

1979, July 7 **Photo.** ***Perf. 13***
272 A122 1.70fr multi 75 50

International Year of the Child.

1979, Sept. 29 **Engr.** ***Perf. 13***

Bas-relief, Trobada monument.

273 A123 2fr multi 1.00 75

700th anniversary of Co-Principality of Andorra

Judo Hold — A124

Farm House, Cortinada — A125

1979, Nov. 24 **Engr.** ***Perf. 13***
274 A124 1.30fr multi 65 45

World Judo Championships, Paris, Dec. 1979.

1980, Jan. 26 **Engr.** ***Perf. 13***
275 A125 1.10fr multi 50 45

Cross-Country Skiing — A126

1980, Feb. 9
276 A126 1.80fr ultra & lil rose 1.50 90

13th Winter Olympic Games, Lake Placid, NY, Feb. 12-24.

A128

A129

1980, Aug. 30 **Engr.** ***Perf. 13***
278 A128 1.20fr multi 45 38

World Bicycling championships.

1980, Apr. 26 **Engr.** ***Perf. 13***

Europa: 1.30fr, Charlemagne (742-814). 1.80fr, Napoleon I (1769-1821).

279 A129 1.30fr multi 45 35
280 A129 1.80fr gray grn & brn 75 55

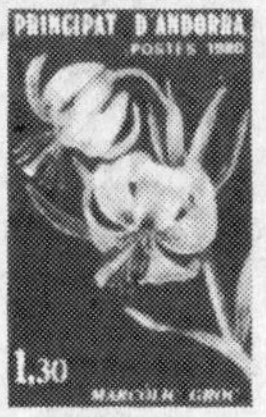

Pyrenees Lily — A130

1980 **Photo.**
281 A130 1.10fr Dog-toothed violet 45 28
282 A130 1.30fr shown 50 35

Nature protection. Issue dates: 1.10fr, June 21, 1.30fr, May 17.

De La Vall House, 400th Anniversary of Restoration A131

1980, Sept. 6 **Engr.**
283 A131 1.40fr multi 50 38

Angel, Church of St. Cerni de Nagol, Pre-Romanesque Fresco — A132

1980, Oct. 27 ***Perf. 13x12½***
284 A132 2fr multi 1.00 70

Bordes de Mereig Mountain Village A133

1981, Mar. 21 **Engr.** ***Perf. 13***
285 A133 1.40fr bl gray & dk brn 50 40

Europa Issue 1981

Ball de l'Ossa, Winter Game A134

1981, May 16 **Engr.**
286 A134 1.40fr shown 65 45
287 A134 2fr El Contrapas dance 80 60

Bird Type of 1979

1981, June 20 **Photo.**
288 A119 1.20fr Phylloscopus bonelli 45 30
289 A119 1.40fr Tichodroma muraria 55 38

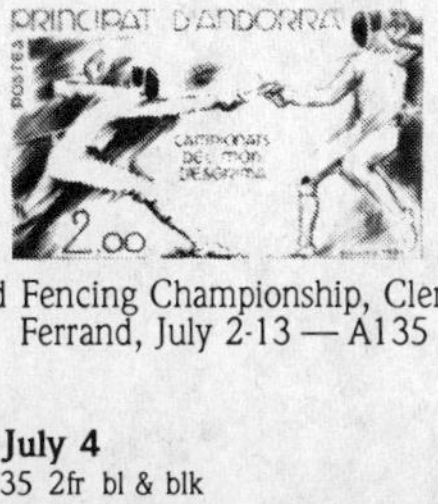

World Fencing Championship, Clermont-Ferrand, July 2-13 — A135

1981, July 4 **Engr.**
290 A135 2fr bl & blk 60 40

St. Martin, 12th Cent. Tapestry — A136

1981, Sept. 5 **Engr.** ***Perf. 12x13***
291 A136 3fr multi 1.10 80

Intl. Drinking Water Decade A137

Intl. Year of the Disabled A138

1981, Oct. 17 ***Perf. 13***
292 A137 1.60fr multi 55 40

1981, Nov. 7
293 A138 2.30fr multi 80 70

Europa 1982 — A139

1982, May 8 **Engr.** ***Perf. 13***
294 A139 1.60fr Creation of Andorran govt., 1982 55 40
295 A139 2.30fr Land Council, 1419 80 55

1982 World Cup — A140

Designs: Various soccer players. Nos. 296-297 se-tenant with label showing natl. arms.

1982, June 12 **Engr.** ***Perf. 13***
296 A140 1.60fr red & dk brn 60 45
297 A140 2.60fr red & dk brn 90 65

Souvenir Sheet

No. 52 — A141

1982, Aug. 21 **Engr.**
298 A141 5fr blk & rose car 1.60 1.60

1st Andorran Stamp Exhib., Aug. 21-Sept. 19.

Horse, Roman Wall Painting — A142

1982, Sept. 4 Photo. *Perf. 13x12½*
299 A142 3fr multi 1.10 90

Wild Cat — A143

1982, Oct. 9 Engr. *Perf. 13*
300 A143 1.80fr shown 75 50
301 A143 2.60fr Pine trees 1.10 65

TB Bacillus Centenary A144

St. Thomas Aquinas (1225-74) A145

1982, Nov. 13
302 A144 2.10fr Koch, lungs 75 60

1982, Dec. 4
303 A145 2fr multi 75 60

Manned Flight Bicentenary A146

1983, Feb. 26 Engr.
304 A146 2fr multi 75 60

Nature Protection A147

1983, Apr. 16 Engr. *Perf. 13*
305 A147 1fr Birch trees 40 22
306 A147 1.50fr Trout 55 38

See Nos. 325-326.

Europa 1983 — A148

Catalane Gold Works.

1983, May 7 Engr. *Perf. 13*
307 A148 1.80fr Exterior 60 45
308 A148 2.60fr Interior 80 60

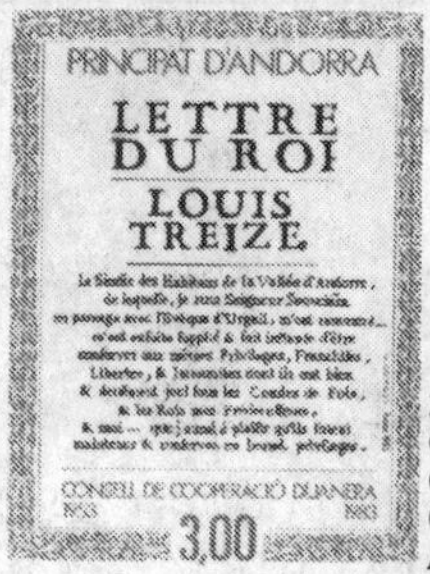

30th Anniv. of Customs Cooperation Council A149

1983, May 14
309 A149 3fr Letter of King Louis XIII 1.10 80

First Arms of Valleys of Andorra A150

1983, Sept. 3 Engr. *Perf. 13*
310 A150 5c olive grn & red 15 15
311 A150 10c grn & olive grn 15 15
312 A150 20c brt pur & red 15 15
313 A150 30c brn vio & red 15 15
314 A150 40c dk bl & ultra 15 15
315 A150 50c gray & red 15 15
316 A150 1fr deep magenta 30 18
317 A150 2fr org red & red brn 55 35
318 A150 5fr dk brn & red 1.40 85
Set value 2.65 1.65

See Nos. 329-335, 380-383.

Painting, Cortinada Church A151

1983, Sept. 24 *Perf. 12x13*
319 A151 4fr multi 1.40 1.00

Plandolit House — A152

1983, Oct. 15 Photo. *Perf. 13*
320 A152 1.60fr dp ultra & brn 50 38

1984 Winter Olympics A153

1984, Feb. 18 Engr.
321 A153 2.80fr multi 90 70

Pyrenees Region Work Community (Labor Org.) — A154

1984, Apr. 28 Engr. *Perf. 13*
322 A154 3fr brt bl & sepia 90 65

Europa (1959-84) A155

1984, May 5 Engr.
323 A155 2fr brt grn 70 50
324 A155 2.80fr rose car 1.00 75

Nature Protection Type of 1983

1984, July 7 Engr. *Perf. 13*
325 A147 1.70fr Chestnut tree 65 40
326 A147 2.10fr Walnut tree 80 50

Pyrenees Art Center A155a

1984, Sept. 7 Engr.
327 A155a 3fr multi 1.10 80

Romanesque Fresco, Church of St. Cerni de Nagol A156

1984, Nov. 17 *Perf. 12x13*
328 A156 5fr multi 1.75 1.25

First Arms Type of 1983

1984-87 Engr. *Perf. 13*
329 A150 1.90fr emerald 65 15
330 A150 2.20fr red orange 75 15
a. Bklt. pane, 2 #329, 6 #330 6.25
331 A150 3fr bl grn & red brn 75 45
332 A150 4fr brt org & brn 1.15 85
333 A150 10fr brn org & blk 2.50 1.50
334 A150 15fr grn & dk grn 4.25 3.25
335 A150 20fr brt bl & red brn 5.25 3.00
Nos. 329-335 (7) 15.30 9.35

Nos. 329-330 issued in booklets only.
Issue dates: 3fr, 20fr, Dec. 1, 1984. 10fr, Feb. 9, 1985. 4fr, 15fr, Apr. 19, 1986. 1.90fr, 2.20fr, Mar. 28, 1987.

Saint Julia Valley A157

1985, Apr. 13 Engr.
336 A157 2fr multi 55 45

The index in each volume of the Scott Catalogue contains many listings that help identify stamps.

Europa 1985 — A158

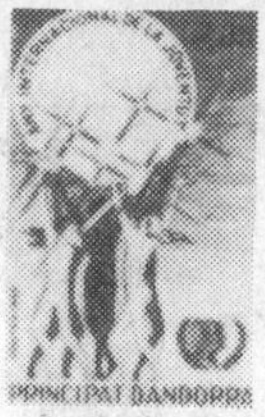

Intl. Youth Year — A159

1985, May 4 Engr.
337 A158 2.10fr Le Val D'Andorre 70 52
338 A158 3fr Instruments 90 75

1985, June 8 Engr.
339 A159 3fr multi 80 60

Wildlife Conservation A160

1985, Aug. 3 Photo.
340 A160 1.80fr Anas platyrhynchos 50 38
341 A160 2.20fr Carduelis carduelis 60 45

Two Saints, Medieval Fresco in St. Cerni de Nagol Church A161

1985, Sept. 14 Engr. *Perf. 12½x13*
342 A161 5fr multi 1.40 1.10

Postal Museum Inauguration — A162

1986, Mar. 22 Engr. *Perf. 13*
343 A162 2.20fr like No. 269 62 15

Europa 1986 A163

1986, May 3 Engr. *Perf. 13*
344 A163 2.20fr Ansalonga 62 15
345 A163 3.20fr Isard 80 16

1986 World Cup Soccer Championships, Mexico — A164

1986, June 14
346 A164 3fr multi 75 15

Angonella Lake — A165

1986, June 28
347 A165 2.20fr multi 62 15

Manual Digest Frontispiece, 1748 A166

1986, Sept. 6 **Engr.**
348 A166 5fr chnt brn, gray ol & blk 1.55 30

Intl. Peace Year — A167

1986, Sept. 29
349 A167 1.90fr bl gray & grnsh bl 58 15

A168 A169

1986, Oct. 18 **Engr.** ***Perf. 13¹/₂x13***
350 A168 1.90fr St. Vicenc D'Enclar 60 15

1987, Mar. 27 **Litho.** ***Perf. 12¹/₂x13***
351 A169 2.20fr Contemporary natl. coat of arms 75 15

Visit of the French co-prince.

Europa 1987 — A170

1987, May 2 **Engr.** ***Perf. 13***
352 A170 2.20fr Meritxell Sanctu- ary 75 15
353 A170 3.40fr Pleta D'Ordino 1.15 24

Ransol Village — A171

1987, June 13 **Photo.**
354 A171 1.90fr multi 62 15

Nature A172

1987, July 4
355 A172 1.90fr Cavall rogenc 62 15
356 A172 2.20fr Graellsia isabellae 72 15

Aryalsu, Romanesque Painting, La Cortinada Church A173

Perf. 12¹/₂x13
1987, Sept. 5 **Litho. & Engr.**
357 A173 5fr multi 1.70 35

Hiker Looking at Map — A174

1987, Sept. 19 **Engr.** ***Perf. 13***
358 A174 2fr olive, grn & dark brn vio 68 15

Medieval Iron Key, La Cortinada A175

1987, Oct. 17 **Litho.**
359 A175 3fr multi 1.00 20

Andorran Coat of Arms — A176

Booklet Stamp
1988, Feb. 6 **Engr.** ***Perf. 13***
360 A176 2.20fr red 80 16
a. Bklt. pane of 10 8.00

See Nos. 388-389B.

Shoemaker's Last from Roc de l'Oral — A177

1988, Feb. 13 **Photo.**
361 A177 3fr multi 1.10 22

Rugby — A178

1988, Mar. 19 **Engr.** ***Perf. 13¹/₂x13***
362 A178 2.20fr emer grn, Prus grn & brn 80 16

Europa 1988 — A179 Hot Springs, Escaldes — A180

Transport and communication: 2.20fr, Broadcast tower. 3.60fr, Computer graphics.

1988, May 2 **Engr.** ***Perf. 13***
363 A179 2.20fr multicolored 78 16
364 A179 3.60fr multicolored 1.30 25

1988, May 14 **Engr.**
365 A180 2.20fr Prus bl, org brn & emer 80 16

Tor D'Ansalonga Farmhouse, Ansalonga Pass — A181

1988, June 13 **Engr.**
366 A181 2fr multi 70 15

Sheepdog — A182

1988, July 2 **Photo.**
367 A182 2fr shown 70 15
368 A182 2.20fr Hare 78 16

Roman Fresco, 8th Cent., St. Steven's Church, Andorre-La-Vieille — A183

1988, Sept. 3 **Engr.** ***Perf. 13x12¹/₂***
369 A183 5fr multicolored 1.60 32

French Revolution, Bicent. — A184

1989, Jan. 1 **Litho.** ***Perf. 13***
370 A184 2.20fr red & vio bl 75 15

Poble de Pal Village A185

1989, Mar. 4 **Engr.** ***Perf. 13***
371 A185 2.20fr 70 15

Europa 1989 — A186

Children's games.

1989, June 9 **Engr.** ***Perf. 13***
372 A186 2.20fr Human tower 72 15
373 A186 3.60fr The handkerchief 1.20 24

Red Cross — A187

1989, May 6
374 A187 3.60fr multi 1.20 24

Visigothic- Merovingian Age Cincture from a Column, St. Vicenc D'Anclar — A188

1989, June 3 **Photo.**
375 A188 3fr multi 1.00 20

Wildlife A189

1989, Sept. 18 Engr. *Perf. 13*
376 A189 2.20fr Wild boar 68 15
377 A189 3.60fr Newt 1.10 22

Scene of Salome from the Retable of St. Michael of Mosquera, Encamp — A190

1989, Oct. 16 *Perf. 13x13½*
378 A190 5fr multi 1.50 30

La Margineda Bridge A191

1990, Feb. 26 Engr. *Perf. 13*
379 A191 2.30fr multi 82 16

Tourism.

Arms Types of 1983 and 1988

1990-93 Engr. *Perf. 13*
380 A150 2.10fr green 78 16
381 A150 2.20fr green 1.50 50
382 A150 2.30fr vermilion 85 18
383 A150 2.40fr green 90 30
384 A150 2.50fr vermilion 1.70 55
385 A150 2.80fr vermilion 1.00 32
Nos. 380-385 (6) 6.73 2.01

Booklet Stamps

Perf. 13

386 A176 2.30fr red 85 18
a. Booklet pane of 5 4.25
387 A176 2.50fr vermilion 1.70 55
a. Booklet pane of 5 8.50
388 A176 2.80fr red 1.00 32
c. Booklet pane of 5 5.00
Nos. 386-388 (3) 3.55 1.05

Issued: 2.20fr, #384, 10/28/91; #387, 10/21/91; 2.40fr, 2.80fr, 8/9/93; 2.10fr, 2.30fr, 1990.

Llorts Mines A193

1990, Apr. 21 Engr. *Perf. 12½x13*
390 A193 3.20fr multicolored 1.20 25

Europa A194

Designs: 2.30fr, Early post office. 3.20fr, Modern post office.

1990, May 5 *Perf. 13*
391 A194 2.30fr blk & scar 85 18
392 A194 3.20fr scar & vio 1.20 25

Otter A195

1990, May 25 *Perf. 12x13*
393 A195 2.30fr Roses, vert. 85 18
394 A195 3.20fr shown 1.20 25

Censer of St. Roma of Les Bons A196

1990, June 25 *Perf. 12½x13*
395 A196 3fr multicolored 1.15 30

Tobacco Drying Sheds, Les Bons A197

1990, Sept. 15 Engr. *Perf. 12½x13*
396 A197 2.30fr multi 85 18

St. Coloma (Detail) A198

1990, Oct. 8 *Perf. 12½x13*
397 A198 5fr multi 2.00 72

Coin from Church of St. Eulalia d'Encamp A199

1990, Oct. 27 Litho. *Perf. 13*
398 A199 3.20fr multi 1.15 38

De Gaulle Type of 1972 Dated 1990

1990, Oct. 23 Engr. *Perf. 13*
399 A88 2.30fr vio bl 1.00 35
400 A88 3.20fr dk car 1.40 55
a. Pair, #399-400 + label 2.40 85

Birth centenary of De Gaulle.

4th Games of the Small European States — A200

1991, Apr. 8 Photo. *Perf. 13*
401 A200 2.50fr multicolored 90 30

Chapel of St. Roma Dels Vilars — A201

1991, Mar. 9 Engr. *Perf. 13*
402 A201 2.50fr multicolored 90 30

Europa — A202

Perf. 13x12½, 12½x13

1991, Apr. 27
403 A202 2.50fr TV satellite 90 30
404 A202 3.50fr Telescope, horiz. 1.30 45

Bottles from Tombs of St. Vincenc d'Enclar A203

1991, May 11 Photo. *Perf. 13*
405 A203 3.20fr multicolored 1.20 40

Farm Animals A204

1991, June 22 Engr. *Perf. 13*
406 A204 2.50fr Sheep 90 30
407 A204 3.50fr Cow 1.25 42

Petanque World Championships — A205

1991, Sept. 14 Engr. *Perf. 13*
408 A205 2.50fr multicolored 90 30

Wolfgang Amadeus Mozart, Death Bicent. A206

1991, Oct. 5
409 A206 3.40fr multicolored 1.35 45

Virgin and Child of St. Julia and St. Germa A207

1991, Nov. 16 Engr. *Perf. 12½x13*
410 A207 5fr multicolored 2.00 65

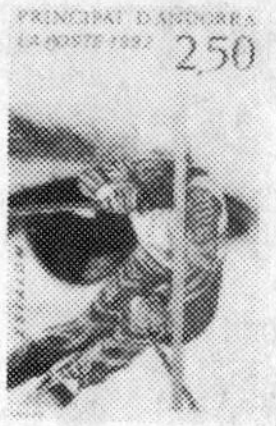

1992 Winter Olympics, Albertville — A208

1992, Feb. 10 Litho. *Perf. 13*
411 A208 2.50fr Slalom skiing 90 30
412 A208 3.40fr Figure skating 1.20 40
a. Pair, #411-412 + label 2.10 70

Church of St. Andrew of Arinsal A209

1992, Mar. 21 Engr. *Perf. 12x13*
413 A209 2.50fr black & tan 90 30

Discovery of America, 500th Anniv. A210

1992, Apr. 25 *Perf. 13*
414 A210 2.50fr Columbus' fleet 90 30
415 A210 3.40fr Landing in New World 1.25 40

Europa.

1992 Summer Olympics, Barcelona A211

European Globeflower A212

1992, June 8 Litho. *Perf. 13*
416 A211 2.50fr Kayaking 1.00 35
417 A211 3.40fr Shooting 1.40 45
a. Pair, #416-417 + label 2.40 80

1992, July 6

Design: 3.40fr, Vulture, horiz.

418 A212 2.50fr multicolored 1.00 35
419 A212 3.40fr multicolored 1.40 45

Martyrdom of St. Eulalia A213

1992, Sept. 14 Photo. *Perf. 13*
420 A213 4fr multicolored 1.65 55

Sculpture by Mauro Staccioli A214

1992, Oct. 5 Engr. *Perf. 12½x13*

421	A214	5fr	multicolored	2.05	68

Ordino Arcalis '91.

Tempest in a Tea Cup, by Dennis Oppenheim — A215

1992, Nov. 14 Engr. *Perf. 13x12½*

422	A215	5fr	multicolored	2.00	68

Skiing in Andorra — A216

Ski resorts: No. 423a, 2.50fr, Soldeu El Tarter. b, 3.40fr, Arinsal.

No. 424a, 2.50fr, Pas de la Casa-Grau Roig. b, 2.50fr, Ordino Arcalis. c, 3.40fr, Pal.

1993, Mar. 13 Litho. *Perf. 13*

423	A216	Pair, #a.-b. + label		2.20	75
424	A216	Strip of 3, #a.-c.		3.25	1.05

Sculptures — A217

Europa: 2.50fr, "Estructures Autogeneradores," by Jorge du Bon, vert. 3.40fr, Sculpture, "Fisicromia per Andorra," by Carlos Cruz-Diez.

1993, May 15 Engr. *Perf. 12½x13*

425	A217	2.50fr	multicolored	1.00	35

Litho.

Perf. 14x13½

426	A217	3.40fr	multicolored	1.35	45

Butterflies A218

1993, June 28 Litho. *Perf. 13*

427	A218	2.50fr	Polymmatus icarus	95	32
428	A218	4.20fr	Nymphalidae	1.55	52

Tour de France Bicycle Race — A219

1993, July 20 Litho. *Perf. 13*

429	A219	2.50fr	multicolored	90	30

Andorra School, 10th Anniv. A220

1993, Sept. 20 Litho. *Perf. 13*

430	A220	2.80fr	multicolored	1.00	35

Un Lloc Paga, by Michael Warren A221

1993, Oct. 18 Engr. *Perf. 12½x13*

431	A221	5fr	blue & black	1.75	60

Sculpture, by Erik Dietman A222

1993, Nov. 8 Engr. *Perf. 12½x13*

432	A222	5fr	multicolored	1.75	60

1994 Winter Olympics, Lillehammer A223

1994, Feb. 21 Litho. *Perf. 13*

433	A223	3.70fr	multicolored	1.25	45

1st Anniversary of the Constitution — A224

Designs: 2.80fr, Monument, by Emili Armengol. 3.70fr, Stone tablet with inscription.

1994, Mar. 15 Litho. *Perf. 13*

434	A224	2.80fr	multicolored	1.00	35
435	A224	3.70fr	multicolored	1.40	48
a.		Pair, #434-435 + label		2.40	85

European Discoveries A225

Europa: 2.80fr, Discovery of AIDS virus. 3.70fr, Radio diffusion.

1994, May 9 Litho. *Perf. 13*

436	A225	2.80fr	multicolored	1.10	35
437	A225	3.70fr	multicolored	1.50	50

1994 World Cup Soccer Championships, US — A226

1994, June 20

438	A226	3.70fr	multicolored	1.50	50

Tourist Sports — A227

Designs: No. 439, Mountain climbing. No. 440, Fishing. No. 441, Horseback riding. No. 442, Mountain biking.

1994, July 11

439	A227	2.80fr	multicolored	1.10	35
440	A227	2.80fr	multicolored	1.10	35
a.		Pair, #439-440 + label		2.20	70
441	A227	2.80fr	multicolored	1.10	35
442	A227	2.80fr	multicolored	1.10	35
a.		Pair, #441-442 + label		2.20	70
		Nos. 439-442 (4)		4.40	1.40

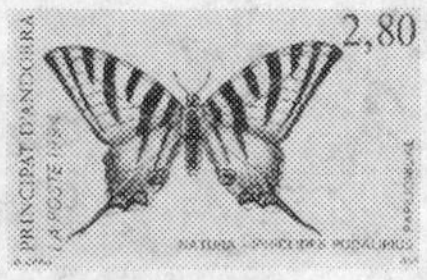

Butterflies A228

1994, Sept. 5 Litho. *Perf. 13*

443	A228	2.80fr	Iphiclides podalirus	1.10	35
444	A228	4.40fr	Aglais urticae	1.75	60

Meeting of the Co-Princes, 1st Anniv. — A229

1994, Oct. 22 Litho. *Perf. 13*

445	A229	2.80fr	multicolored	1.25	42

SEMI-POSTAL STAMP

Catalogue values for unused stamps in this section are for Never Hinged items.

Virgin of St. Coloma — SP1

Unwmk.

1964, July 25 Engr. *Perf. 13*

B1	SP1	25c + 10c	multi	21.00	21.00

The surtax was for the Red Cross.

AIR POST STAMPS

Catalogue values for unused stamps in this section are for Never Hinged items.

Chamois AP1

Unwmk.

1950, Feb. 20 Engr. *Perf. 13*

C1	AP1	100fr	indigo	60.00	45.00

East Branch of Valira River — AP2

1955-57

C2	AP2	100fr	dark green	8.50	6.50
C3	AP2	200fr	cerise	17.50	14.00
C4	AP2	500fr	deep blue ('57)	90.00	65.00
		Nos. C2-C4 (3)		116.00	85.50

D'Inclès Valley — AP3

1961-64 Unwmk. *Perf. 13*

C5	AP3	2fr	red, ol gray & claret	75	60
C6	AP3	3fr	bl, mar & slate grn	1.10	1.10
C7	AP3	5fr	rose lil & red org	1.75	1.60
C8	AP3	10fr	bl grn & slate grn	3.50	3.25
		Nos. C5-C8 (4)		7.10	6.55

Issued: 10fr, 4/25/64; others, 6/19/61.

POSTAGE DUE STAMPS

Postage Due Stamps of France, 1893-1931, Overprinted

ANDORRE

On Stamps of 1893-1926

1931-33 Unwmk. *Perf. 14x13½*

J1	D2	5c blue	1.00	1.00
J2	D2	10c brown	1.00	1.00
J3	D2	30c rose red	30	30
J4	D2	50c vio brn	1.00	1.00
J5	D2	60c green	10.00	10.00
J6	D2	1fr red brn, *straw*	50	50
J7	D2	2fr brt vio	6.00	6.00
J8	D2	3fr magenta	1.10	1.10
		Nos. J1-J8 (8)	20.90	20.90

On Stamps of 1927-31

J9	D4	1c olive grn	1.25	1.25
J10	D4	10c rose	2.50	2.50
J11	D4	60c red	16.00	16.00
J12	D4	1fr Prus grn ('32)	65.00	65.00
J13	D4	1.20fr on 2fr bl	47.50	47.50
J14	D4	2fr ol brn ('33)	110.00	110.00
J15	D4	5fr on 1fr vio	60.00	60.00
		Nos. J9-J15 (7)	302.25	302.25

D5

D6

1935-41 Typo.

J16	D5	1c gray grn	1.65	1.25
J17	D6	5c lt bl ('37)	4.75	4.50
J18	D6	10c brn ('41)	3.75	4.50
J19	D6	2fr vio ('41)	5.50	3.25
J20	D6	5fr red org ('41)	7.00	3.25
		Nos. J16-J20 (5)	22.65	16.75

Catalogue values for unused stamps in this section, from this point to the end of the section, are for Never Hinged items.

Wheat Sheaves — D7

1943-46 *Perf. 14x13½*

J21	D7	10c sepia	1.00	1.00
J22	D7	30c brt red vio	1.50	1.50
J23	D7	50c blue grn	1.75	1.75
J24	D7	1fr brt ultra	80	80
J25	D7	1.50fr rose red	5.75	5.75
J26	D7	2fr turq blue	1.50	1.50
J27	D7	3fr brown org	2.75	2.75
J28	D7	4fr dp vio ('45)	4.50	4.50
J29	D7	5fr brt pink	4.50	4.50
J30	D7	10fr red org ('45)	5.75	5.75
J31	D7	20fr olive brn ('46)	6.00	6.00
		Nos. J21-J31 (11)	35.80	35.80

Inscribed: "Timbre Taxe"

1946-53

J32	D7	10c sepia ('46)	1.10	1.10
J33	D7	1fr ultra	75	75
J34	D7	2fr turq blue	1.00	1.00
J35	D7	3fr orange brn	2.00	2.00
J36	D7	4fr violet	2.75	2.75
J37	D7	5fr brt pink	1.75	1.75
J38	D7	10fr red orange	2.75	2.75
J39	D7	20fr olive brn	6.25	6.25
J40	D7	50fr dk green ('50)	16.50	16.50
J41	D7	100fr dp green ('53)	87.50	87.50
		Nos. J32-J41 (10)	122.35	122.35

Inscribed: "Timbre Taxe"

1961, June 19 *Perf. 14x13½*

J42	D7	5c rose pink	2.75	2.75
J43	D7	10c red orange	5.50	5.50
J44	D7	20c olive	8.25	8.25
J45	D7	50c dark slate green	13.00	13.00
		Nos. J42-J45 (4)	29.50	29.50

D8

D9

1964-71 Typo. *Perf. 14x13½*

J46	D8	5c Centaury ('65)	15	15
J47	D8	10c Gentian ('65)	15	15
J48	D8	15c Corn poppy	15	15
J49	D8	20c Violets ('71)	15	15
J50	D8	30c Forget-me-not	15	15
J51	D8	40c Columbine ('71)	15	15
J52	D8	50c Clover ('65)	22	22
		Set value	74	74

1985, Oct. 21 Engr. *Perf. 13*

J53	D9	10c Holly	15	15
J54	D9	20c Blueberries	15	15
J55	D9	30c Raspberries	15	15
J56	D9	40c Bilberries	15	15
J57	D9	50c Blackberries	15	15
J58	D9	1fr Broom	30	30
J59	D9	2fr Rosehips	60	38
J60	D9	3fr Nightshade	90	58
J61	D9	4fr Nabiu	1.25	75
J62	D9	5fr Strawberries	1.50	95
		Nos. J53-J62 (10)	5.30	3.71

NEWSPAPER STAMP

France No. P7 Overprinted **ANDORRE**

1931 Unwmk. *Perf. 14x13½*

P1	A16	½c on 1c gray	75	75

ANGOLA

LOCATION — Southwestern Africa between Zaire and Namibia.
GOVT. — Republic
AREA — 481,351 sq. mi.
POP. — 7,108,000 (1983 est.)
CAPITAL — Luanda

Angola was a Portuguese overseas territory until it became independent November 11, 1975, as the People's Republic of Angola.

1000 Reis = 1 Milreis
100 Centavos = 1 Escudo (1913, 1954)
100 Centavos = 1 Angolar (1932)
10 Lweys = 1 Kwanza (1977)

Catalogue values for unused stamps in this country are for Never Hinged items, beginning with Scott 328 in the regular postage section, Scott C26 in the airpost section, Scott J31 in the postage due section, Scott RA7 in the postal tax section, and Scott RAJ4 in the postal tax postage due section.

Watermark

Wmk. 232- Maltese Cross

Portuguese Crown — A1

Perf. 12½, 13½

1870-77 Typo. Unwmk.

1	A1	5r black	1.25	1.10
a.		Perf. 13½	6.50	3.25
2	A1	10r yellow	14.00	6.50
3	A1	20r bister	1.75	1.25
a.		Perf. 13½	65.00	50.00
4	A1	25r red	6.00	2.00
a.		25r rose	6.00	2.00
c.		25r rose, perf. 14	110.00	65.00
d.		Perf. 13½	16.00	8.00
5	A1	40r blue ('77)	100.00	60.00
6	A1	50r green	32.50	8.50
a.		Perf. 13½	165.00	65.00
7	A1	100r lilac	1.50	1.25
a.		Perf. 12½	6.50	4.00
8	A1	200r orange ('77)	2.00	1.25
a.		Perf. 12½	3.00	1.65
9	A1	300r choc ('77)	2.50	2.00
a.		Perf. 12½	8.00	4.75

1881-85

10	A1	10r green ('83)	3.00	1.50
a.		Perf. 12½	11.50	2.25
11	A1	20r carmine rose ('85)	6.00	5.00
12	A1	25r violet ('85)	2.50	2.00
a.		Perf. 13½	4.50	2.75
13	A1	40r buff ('82)	3.50	2.00
a.		Perf. 12½	4.00	2.00
15	A1	50r blue	12.50	1.65
a.		Perf. 13½	17.00	1.65
		Nos. 10-15 (5)	27.50	12.15

Two types of numerals are found on #2, 11, 13, 15.

The cliche of 40r in plate of 20r error, was discovered before the stamps were issued. All copies were defaced by a blue pencil mark.

In perf. 12½, Nos. 1-4, 4a and 6, as well as 7a, were printed in 1870 on thicker paper and 1875 on normal paper. Stamps of the earlier printing sell for 2 to 5 times more than those of the 1875 printing.

Some reprints of the 1870-85 issues are on a smooth white chalky paper, ungummed and perf. 13½.

Other reprints of these issues are on thin ivory paper with shiny white gum and clear-cut perf. 13½.

King Luiz — A2

King Carlos — A3

1886 Embossed *Perf. 12½*

16	A2	5r black	3.50	3.25
a.		Perf. 13½	11.50	8.50
17	A2	10r green	3.50	3.00
a.		Perf. 13½	13.00	7.25
18	A2	20r rose	10.00	6.25
a.		Perf. 13½	12.50	6.50
19	A2	25r red violet	7.25	1.25
20	A2	40r chocolate	8.00	5.00
21	A2	50r blue	10.50	2.00
22	A2	100r yellow brn	14.00	6.00
23	A2	200r gray violet	18.00	9.00
24	A2	300r orange	20.00	11.00
		Nos. 16-24 (9)	94.75	46.75

For surcharges see #61-69, 172-174, 208-210.

Reprints of 5r, 20r & 100r have cleancut perf. 13½.

Perf. 11½, 12½, 13½

1893-94 Typo.

25	A3	5r yellow	90	75
26	A3	10r redsh violet	2.00	85
27	A3	15r chocolate	2.75	1.25
28	A3	20r lavender	2.75	1.25
29	A3	25r green	1.10	75
a.		Perf. 12½	4.00	2.00
30	A3	50r light blue	3.25	1.25
a.		Perf. 13½	5.00	2.75
31	A3	75r carmine	6.00	3.50
a.		Perf. 11½	8.00	6.25
32	A3	80r lt green	6.75	3.50
33	A3	100r brown, *buff*	6.75	3.50
a.		Perf. 11½	50.00	32.50
34	A3	150r car, *rose*	12.00	9.00
35	A3	200r dk blue, *lt bl*	14.00	11.00
36	A3	300r dk blue, *sal*	14.00	11.00
		Nos. 25-36 (12)	72.25	47.60

For surcharges see Nos. 70-81, 175-179, 213-216, 234.

No. P1 Surcharged in Blue

1894, Aug.

37	N1	25r on 2½r brown	62.50	22.50

King Carlos — A5

1898-1903 *Perf. 11½*

Name and Value in Black except 500r

38	A5	2½r gray	15	15
39	A5	5r orange	15	15
40	A5	10r yellow grn	15	15
41	A5	15r violet brn	1.50	70
42	A5	15r gray green ('03)	65	50
43	A5	20r gray violet	25	20
44	A5	25r sea green	1.00	40
45	A5	25r car ('03)	50	15
46	A5	50r blue	1.65	35
47	A5	50r brown ('03)	3.00	2.00
48	A5	65r dull blue ('03)	5.25	5.00
49	A5	75r rose	4.50	1.65
50	A5	75r red violet ('03)	1.25	90
51	A5	80r violet	5.25	1.75
52	A5	100r dk blue, *blue*	90	65
53	A5	115r org brn, *pink* ('03)	5.75	4.00
54	A5	130r brn, *straw* ('03)	5.75	4.00
55	A5	150r brn, *straw*	5.75	3.75
56	A5	200r red vio, *pink*	2.25	1.00
57	A5	300r dk blue, *rose*	3.25	3.25
58	A5	400r dull bl, *straw* ('03)	2.50	2.25
59	A5	500r blk & red, *bl* ('01)	2.75	2.75
60	A5	700r vio, *yelsh* ('01)	14.00	10.00
		Nos. 38-60 (23)	68.15	45.70

For surcharges and overprints see Nos. 83-102, 113-117, 159-171, 181-183, 217-218, 221-225.

Stamps of 1886-94 Surcharged in Black or Red **65 RÉIS**

Two types of surcharge:
I - 3mm between numeral and REIS.
II - 4½mm spacing.

1902 *Perf. 12½*

61	A2	65r on 40r choc	4.50	3.50
62	A2	65r on 300r org, I	4.50	3.50
a.		Type II	32.50	25.00
63	A2	115r on 10r green	3.75	3.25
a.		Inverted surcharge		
b.		Perf. 13½	18.00	17.00
64	A2	115r on 200r gray vio	3.50	2.75
65	A2	130r on 50r blue	5.75	4.75
66	A2	130r on 100r brown	4.00	3.00
67	A2	400r on 20r rose	35.00	22.50
a.		Perf. 13½	45.00	35.00
68	A2	400r on 25r violet	8.50	6.00
69	A2	400r on 5r black (R)	6.75	6.25
a.		Double surcharge		
		Nos. 61-69 (9)	76.25	55.50

For surcharges see Nos. 172-174, 208-210.

Perf. 11½, 12½, 13½

70	A3	65r on 5r yel, I	4.00	2.75
a.		Type II	10.00	10.00
71	A3	65r on 10r red vio, I	3.25	2.25
a.		Type II	13.00	5.25
b.		Perf. 11½, type I	8.75	5.25
c.		Perf. 11½, type II	3.50	2.50
72	A3	65r on 20r lav	4.00	2.75
a.		Type II	6.50	6.00
73		65r on 25r green	3.00	2.25
a.		Perf. 11½	9.25	7.25
74	A3	115r on 80r lt grn	5.25	4.00
75	A3	115r on 100r brn, *buff*	5.25	3.25
a.		Perf. 13½	9.25	6.50
76	A3	115r on 150r car, *rose*	8.00	5.25
a.		Perf. 13½	10.00	6.00
77	A3	130r on 15r choc	2.75	2.00
78	A3	130r on 75r carmine	3.00	2.25
a.		Perf. 13½	14.00	11.50
79	A3	130r on 300r dk bl, *sal*	8.25	6.00
80	A3	400r on 50r lt bl	3.25	2.75
81	A3	400r on 200r bl, *bl*	3.25	3.25
a.		Perf. 13½	21.00	8.75
82	N1	400r on 2½r brn	1.10	1.10
a.		Type II	2.50	2.25
		Nos. 70-82 (13)	54.35	39.85

For surcharges see #175-180, 211-216, 234-235.

Reprints of Nos. 65, 67, 68 and 69 have clean-cut perforation 13½.

Stamps of 1898 Overprinted — a **PROVISORIO**

1902 *Perf. 11½*
83 A5 15r brown 1.00 60
84 A5 25r sea green 85 35
85 A5 50r blue 1.50 85
86 A5 75r rose 2.75 2.00
Nos. 83-86 (4) 6.10 3.80

For surcharge see No. 116.

No. 48 Surcharged in Black

50 RÉIS

1905
87 A5 50r on 65r dull blue 2.75 1.25

For surcharge see No. 183.

Stamps of 1898-1903 Overprinted in Carmine or Green — b

REPUBLICA

1911
88 A5 2½r gray 15 15
89 A5 5r orange yel 15 15
90 A5 10r light green 22 20
91 A5 15r gray green 25 20
92 A5 20r gray violet 25 20
93 A5 25r car (G) 25 15
94 A5 50r brown 1.50 90
95 A5 75r lilac 2.50 2.50
96 A5 100r dk blue, *bl* 2.50 2.50
97 A5 115r org brn, *pink* 90 60
98 A5 130r brn, *straw* 90 60
99 A5 200r red lil, *pnksh* 90 60
100 A5 400r dull bl, *straw* 1.25 65
101 A5 500r blk & red, *bl* 1.10 65
102 A5 700r violet, *yelsh* 1.25 70
Nos. 88-102 (15) 14.07 10.75

Inverted and double overprints of Nos. 88-102 were made intentionally.

For surcharges see Nos. 217-218, 221-222, 224.

King Manuel II — A6

Ceres — A7

Overprinted in Carmine or Green

1912 *Perf. 11½x12*
103 A6 2½r violet 22 32
104 A6 5r black 25 40
105 A6 10r gray green 35 30
106 A6 20r carmine (G) 35 30
107 A6 25r violet brown 35 30
108 A6 50r dk blue 60 50
109 A6 75r bister brown 65 65
110 A6 100r brown, *lt green* 1.65 70
111 A6 200r dk green, *salmon* 1.10 70
112 A6 300r black, *azure* 1.10 70
Nos. 103-112 (10) 6.62 4.87

For surcharges see Nos. 219-220, 226-227.

No. 91 Surcharged with New Values as 5 ■

1912, June *Perf. 11½*
113 A5 2½r on 15r gray green 2.25 2.25
114 A5 5r on 15r gray green 1.75 1.50
115 A5 10r on 15r gray green 1.75 1.50
Nos. 113-115 (3) 5.75 5.25

Inverted and double surcharges of Nos. 113-115 were made intentionally.

Nos. 86 and 50 Surcharged "25" in Black and Overprinted in Violet — c

REPUBLICA

1912
116 A5 25r on 75r rose 52.50 40.00
117 A5 25r on 75r red violet 2.75 1.50
a. "REUPBLICA" 27.50 25.00
b. "25" omitted 27.50 25.00
c. "REPUBLICA" omitted 27.50 25.00

1914-26 Typo. *Perf. 12x11½, 15x14*
Name and Value in Black
118 A7 ¼c olive brown 15 *15*
a. Inscriptions inverted 6.00
119 A7 ½c black 15 *15*
120 A7 1c blue green 15 *15*
121 A7 1c yel grn ('22) 15 15
122 A7 1½c lilac brown 15 15
123 A7 2c carmine 15 15
124 A7 2c gray ('25) 30 *1.00*
125 A7 2½c lt violet 15 15
126 A7 3c orange ('21) 15 *60*
127 A7 4c dull rose ('21) 15 15
128 A7 4½c gray ('21) 15 *80*
130 A7 5c blue 15 15
131 A7 6c lilac ('21) 15 15
132 A7 7c ultra ('21) 15 15
133 A7 7½c yellow brn 15 15
134 A7 8c slate 15 15
135 A7 10c orange brn 20 15
136 A7 12c olive brn ('21) 35 22
137 A7 12c dp green ('25) 20 15
138 A7 15c plum 40 15
139 A7 15c brown rose ('21) 15 15
140 A7 20c yel green 25 15
141 A7 24c ultra ('25) 1.10 75
142 A7 25c choc ('25) 1.10 75
143 A7 30c brown, *green* 1.25 *2.00*
144 A7 30c gray grn ('21) 65 15
145 A7 40c brown, *pink* 3.00 2.00
146 A7 40c turq blue ('21) 60 15
147 A7 50c orange, *sal* 6.00 4.25
148 A7 50c lt violet ('25) 1.00 15
149 A7 60c dk blue ('22) 55 15
150 A7 60c dp rose ('26) 40.00 40.00
151 A7 80c pink ('22) 1.25 15
152 A7 1e green, *blue* 3.00 2.25
153 A7 1e rose ('22) 1.50 15
154 A7 1e dp blue ('25) 3.00 3.00
155 A7 2e dk violet ('22) 1.25 50
156 A7 5e buff ('25) 5.00 2.25
157 A7 10e pink ('25) 14.00 10.00
158 A7 20e pale turq ('25) 50.00 35.00
Nos. 118-158 (40) 138.35 108.97

Two kinds of paper, chalky-surfaced paper and ordinary, were used for Nos. 118-120, 122-123, 125, 130, 133-135, 138 and 140. Those on coated paper sell unused for 10 to 40 times the values listed; used for about 5 to 20 times.

All but #143, 145, 147 come perf 12x11½. All but #124, 137, 141-142, 146, 148, 151, 153-154, 156-158 come perf 15x14.

For surcharges see Nos. 228-229, 236-239.

Stamps of 1898-1903 Overprinted type "c" in Red or Green
On Stamps of 1898-1903

1914 *Perf. 11½, 12*
159 A5 10r yel green (R) 3.25 2.50
160 A5 15r gray green (R) 3.25 2.50
161 A5 20r gray violet (G) 80 80
163 A5 75r red violet (G) 80 80
164 A5 100r blue, *blue* (R) 1.25 1.25
165 A5 115r org brn, *pink* (R) *35.00*
167 A5 200r red vio, *pnksh* (G) 90 50
169 A5 400r dl bl, *straw* (R) 24.00 20.00
170 A5 500r blk & red, *bl* (R) 2.50 2.00
171 A5 700r vio, *yelsh* (G) 10.00 8.00

Inverted and double overprints were made intentionally. No. 165 was not regularly issued. Red overprints on the 20r, 75r, 200r were not regularly issued. The 130r was not regularly issued without surcharge (No. 225).

On Nos. 63-65, 74-76, 78-79, 82
Perf. 11½, 12½, 13½
172 A2 115r on 10r (R) 10.00 9.25
a. Perf. 13½ 11.00 10.00
173 A2 115r on 200r (R) 14.00 11.00
174 A2 130r on 50r (R) 14.00 11.00
175 A3 115r on 80r (R) 125.00 92.50
176 A3 115r on 100r (R) 175.00 125.00
177 A3 115r on 150r (G) 140.00 125.00
178 A3 130r on 75r (G) 1.75 1.65
179 A3 130r on 300r (R) 4.00 3.25
a. Perf. 12½ 7.00 4.50
180 N1 400r on 2½r (R) 40 40
a. Perf. 11½ 1.65 1.25
Nos. 172-180 (9) 484.15 379.05

Overprinted PROVISORIO

On Stamps of 1902
Perf. 11½, 12
181 A5 50r blue (R) 90 60
182 A5 75r rose (G) 2.75 2.00

On No. 87
183 A5 50r on 65r dull blue (R) 2.50 2.50
Nos. 181-183 (3) 6.15 5.10

Inverted and double surcharges of Nos. 181-183 were made intentionally.

Vasco da Gama Issue of Various Portuguese Colonies

Common Design Types CD20-CD27 Surcharged

REPUBLICA
ANGOLA
¼ C.

On Stamps of Macao

1913 *Perf. 12½ to 16*
184 ¼c on ½a blue grn 2.00 2.00
185 ½c on 1a red 1.75 1.75
186 1c on 2a red violet 1.75 1.75
187 2½c on 4a yel green 1.25 1.25
188 5c on 8a dk blue 1.25 1.25
189 7½c on 12a vio brn 3.00 3.00
190 10c on 16a bister brn 2.00 2.00
191 15c on 24a bister 2.00 2.00
Nos. 184-191 (8) 15.00 15.00

On Stamps of Portuguese Africa
Perf. 14 to 15
192 ¼c on 2½r blue grn 75 75
193 ½c on 5r red 75 75
194 1c on 10r red violet 75 75
195 2½c on 25r yel grn 75 75
196 5c on 50r dk blue 75 75
197 7½c on 75r vio brn 2.50 2.50
198 10c on 100r bister brn 1.25 1.25
199 15c on 150r bister 1.75 1.75
Nos. 192-199 (8) 9.25 9.25

On Stamps of Timor
200 ¼c on ½a blue grn 2.00 2.00
201 ½c on 1a red 2.00 2.00
202 1c on 2a red vio 2.00 2.00
203 2½c on 4a yel grn 2.00 2.00
204 5c on 8a dk blue 2.00 2.00
205 7½c on 12a vio brn 3.00 3.00
206 10c on 16a bis brn 2.00 2.00
207 15c on 24a bister 2.00 2.00
Nos. 200-207 (8) 17.00 17.00
Nos. 184-207 (24) 41.25 41.25

Provisional Issue of 1902 Overprinted in Carmine

REPUBLICA

1915 *Perf. 11½, 12½, 13½*
208 A2 115r on 10r green 1.00 *2.00*
209 A2 115r on 200r gray vio 90 *2.00*
210 A2 130r on 100r brown 70 *2.00*
211 A3 115r on 80r lt green 1.10 *2.00*
212 A3 115r on 100r brn, *buff* 90 *2.00*
a. Perf. 11½ 17.00 *17.00*
213 A3 115r on 150r car, *rose* 1.75 *2.00*
214 A3 130r on 15r choc 65 *2.00*
a. Perf. 12½ 7.00 7.00
215 A3 130r on 75r carmine 1.50 *1.75*
216 A3 130r on 300r dk bl, *sal* 1.10 *1.75*
Nos. 208-216 (9) 9.60 *17.50*

Stamps of 1911-14 Surcharged in Black:

½ C.

½ C. ═ ═ ═
d e

On Stamps of 1911

1919 *Perf. 11½*
217 A5 (d) ½c on 75r red lilac 1.50 *2.00*
218 A5 (d) 2½c on 100r blue, *grysh* 1.75 *2.00*

On Stamps of 1912
Perf. 11½x12
219 A6 (e) ½c on 75r bis brn 65 *65*
220 A6 (e) 2½c on 100r brn, *lt grn* 85 40

On Stamps of 1914
221 A5 (d) ½c on 75r red lil 65 40
222 A5 (d) 2½c on 100r bl, *grysh* 70 60
Nos. 217-222 (6) 6.10 *6.05*

Inverted and double surcharges were made for sale to collectors.

Nos. 163, 98 and Type of 1914 Surcharged with New Values and Bars in Black

1921
223 A5 (c) 00.5c on 75r *200.00 200.00*
224 A5 (b) 4c on 130r (#98) 70 *70*
225 A5 (c) 4c on 130r brn, *straw* 2.75 2.50

Nos. 109 and 108 Surcharged with New Values and Bars in Black
226 A6 00.5c on 75c 85 85
227 A6 1c on 50r 75 65

Nos. 133 and 138 Surcharged with New Values and Bars in Black
228 A7 00.5c on 7½c 70 60
229 A7 04c on 15c 1.10 1.10

The 04c surcharge exists on the 15c brown rose, perf 12x11½, No. 139.

Nos. 81-82 Surcharged

República
═
40 C.

1925 *Perf. 12½*
234 A3 40c on 400r on 200r bl, *bl* 80 65
a. Perf. 13½ 3.25 2.25
235 N1 40c on 400c on 2½r brn 60 60
a. Perf. 13½ 60 60

Nos. 150-151, 154-155 Surcharged

═ ═
70 C.

1931 *Perf. 11½*
236 A7 50c on 60c deep rose 1.10 80
237 A7 70c on 80c pink 2.25 1.00
238 A7 70c on 1e deep blue 2.00 1.10
239 A7 1.40e on 2e dark violet 2.00 1.10
Nos. 236-239 (4) 7.35 4.00

Ceres — A14

Perf. 12x11½
1932-46 Typo. Wmk. 232
243 A14 1c bister brn 15 15
244 A14 5c dk brown 15 15
245 A14 10c dp violet 15 15
246 A14 15c black 15 15
247 A14 20c gray 25 15
248 A14 30c myrtle grn 25 15
249 A14 35c yel grn ('46) 4.50 2.00
250 A14 40c dp orange 25 15
251 A14 45c lt blue 85 65
252 A14 50c lt brown 15 15
253 A14 60c olive grn 30 15
254 A14 70c orange brn 65 15
255 A14 80c emerald 25 15
256 A14 85c rose 2.00 2.00
257 A14 1a claret 65 18
258 A14 1.40a dk blue 4.50 1.10
258A A14 1.75a dk blue ('46) 6.00 1.10
259 A14 2a dull vio 2.25 35
260 A14 5a pale yel grn 3.00 50
261 A14 10a olive bis 10.00 90
262 A14 20a orange 17.50 2.00
Nos. 243-262 (21) 53.95 12.43

For surcharges see Nos. 263-267, 271-273, 294A-300, J31-J36.

Surcharged with New Value and Bars

5½mm between bars and new value.

1934
263 A14 10c on 45c lt bl 1.25 70
264 A14 20c on 85c rose 1.10 70
265 A14 30c on 1.40a dk bl 1.10 70
266 A14 70c on 2a dl vio 1.50 1.10
267 A14 80c on 5a pale yel grn 2.25 1.00
Nos. 263-267 (5) 7.20 4.20

See Nos. 294A-300.

Nos. J26, J30 Surcharged in Black

CORREIOS
═ 5
CENTAVOS
═

1935 Unwmk. *Perf. 11½*

268	D2	5c on 6c lt brown	90	60
269	D2	30c on 50c gray	90	60
270	D2	40c on 50c gray	90	60
		Nos. 268-270 (3)	2.70	1.80

No. 255 Surcharged in Black

0,15 Cent.

1938 Wmk. 232 *Perf. 12x11½*

271	A14	5c on 80c emerald	40	*1.00*
272	A14	10c on 80c emerald	50	*1.75*
273	A14	15c on 80c emerald	65	*2.50*
		Nos. 271-273 (3)	1.55	*5.25*

Vasco da Gama Issue

Common Design Types

Engr.; Name & Value Typo. in Black

Perf. 13½x13

1938, July 26 Unwmk.

274	CD34	1c gray green	15	15
275	CD34	5c orange brn	15	15
276	CD34	10c dk carmine	15	15
277	CD34	15c dk violet brn	15	15
278	CD34	20c slate	20	15
279	CD35	30c rose violet	25	15
280	CD35	35c brt green	35	20
281	CD35	40c brown	25	15
282	CD35	50c brt red vio	25	15
283	CD36	60c gray black	35	15
284	CD36	70c brown vio	30	15
285	CD36	80c orange	30	15
286	CD36	1a red	30	15
287	CD37	1.75a blue	85	30
288	CD37	2a brown car	1.50	30
289	CD37	5a olive grn	3.00	30
290	CD38	10a blue vio	6.50	60
291	CD38	20a red brown	15.00	1.10
		Nos. 274-291 (18)	30.00	4.60

For surcharges see Nos. 301-304.

Marble Column and Portuguese Arms with Cross — A20

1938, July 29 *Perf. 12½*

292	A20	80c blue green	1.00	95
293	A20	1.75a deep blue	5.00	1.00
294	A20	20a dk red brown	14.00	11.00
		Nos. 292-294 (3)	20.00	12.95

Visit of the President of Portugal to this colony in 1938.

Common Design Types pictured in section at front of book.

Stamps of 1932 Surcharged with New Value and Bars

8mm between bars and new value.

1941-45 Wmk. 232 *Perf. 12x11½*

294A	A14	5c on 80c emer ('45)	22	20
295	A14	10c on 45c lt blue	65	55
296	A14	15c on 45c lt blue	1.00	70
297	A14	20c on 85c rose	65	55
298	A14	35c on 85c rose	65	55
299	A14	50c on 1.40a dk blue	65	55
300	A14	60c on 1a claret	5.75	4.00
		Nos. 294A-300 (7)	9.57	7.10

Nos. 285 to 287 Surcharged with New Values and Bars in Black or Red

1945 Unwmk. *Perf. 13½x13*

301	CD36	5c on 80c org	28	20
302	CD36	50c on 1a red	60	20
303	CD37	50c on 1.75a bl (R)	42	20
304	CD37	50c on 1.75a bl	60	20
		Nos. 301-304 (4)	1.90	80

Sao Miguel Fort, Luanda — A21

John IV — A22

Designs: 10c, Our Lady of Nazareth Church, Luanda. 50c, Salvador Correia de Sa e Bene vides. 1a, Surrender of Luanda. 1.75a, Diogo Cao. 2a, Manuel Cerveira Pereira. 5a, Stone Cliffs, Yelala. 10a, Paulo Dias de Novais. 20a, Massangano Fort.

Perf. 14½

1948, May Unwmk. Litho.

305	A21	5c dk violet	15	15
306	A21	10c dk brown	25	20
307	A22	30c blue grn	15	15
308	A22	50c vio brown	15	15
309	A21	1a carmine	32	15
310	A22	1.75a slate blue	65	20
311	A22	2a green	65	20
312	A21	5a gray black	1.00	32
313	A22	10a rose lilac	2.00	35
314	A21	20a gray blue	5.00	1.10
a.		Sheet of 10, #305-314	40.00	40.00
		Nos. 305-314 (10)	10.32	2.97

300th anniv. of the restoration of Angola to Portugal. No. 314a sold for 42.50a.

Lady of Fatima Issue

Common Design Type

1948, Dec.

315	CD40	50c carmine	65	50
316	CD40	3a ultra	2.00	1.00
317	CD40	6a red orange	7.00	2.50
318	CD40	9a dp claret	17.00	3.00
		Nos. 315-318 (4)	26.65	7.00

Our Lady of the Rosary at Fatima, Portugal.

Chiumbe River — A24

Black Rocks — A25

Designs: 50c, View of Luanda. 2.50a, Sa da Bandeira. 3.50a, Mocamedes. 15a, Cubal River. 50a, Duke of Bragança Falls.

1949 Unwmk. *Perf. 13½*

319	A24	20c dk slate blue	15	15
320	A25	40c black brown	15	15
321	A24	50c rose brown	15	15
322	A24	2.50a blue violet	1.10	25
323	A24	3.50a slate gray	1.10	25
323A	A24	15a dk green	8.25	1.50
324	A24	50a dp green	22.50	3.75
		Nos. 319-324 (7)	33.40	6.20

Sailing Vessel — A26

UPU Symbols — A27

1949, Aug. *Perf. 14*

325	A26	1a chocolate	4.00	32
326	A26	4a dk Prus green	10.00	85

Centenary of founding of Mocamedes.

1949, Oct.

327	A27	4a dk grn & lt grn	3.50	1.50

75th anniv. of the UPU.

Catalogue values for unused stamps in this section, from this point to the end of the section, are for Never Hinged items.

Stamp of 1870 — A28

1950, Apr. 2 *Perf. 11½x12*

328	A28	50c yellow green	65	22
329	A28	1a fawn	65	25
330	A28	4a black	2.75	70
a.		Sheet of 3, #328-330	5.00	5.00
		Nos. 328-330 (3)	4.05	1.17

Angola's first philatelic exhibition, marking the 80th anniversary of Angola's first stamps.

No. 330a contains Nos. 328, 329 (inverted), 330, perf. 11½ and sold for 6.50a. Size: 119x80mm. All copies carry an oval exhibition cancellation in the margin but the stamps were valid for postage.

Holy Year Issue

Common Design Types

1950, May *Perf. 13x13½*

331	CD41	1a dull rose vio	32	15
332	CD42	4a black	3.00	32

Dark Chanting Goshawk A31

European Bee Eater A32

Designs: 10c, Racquet-tailed roller. 15c, Bataleur eagle. 50c, Giant kingfisher. 1a, Yellow-fronted barbet. 1.50a, Openbill (stork). 2a, Southern ground hornbill. 2.50a, African skimmer. 3a, Shikra. 3.50a, Denham's bustard. 4a, African golden oriole. 4.50a, Long-tailed shrike. 5a, Red-shouldered glossy starling. 6a, Sharp-tailed glossy starling. 7a, Red-shouldered widow bird. 10a, Half-colored kingfisher. 12.50a, White-crowned shrike. 15a, White-winged babbling starling. 20a, Yellow-billed hornbill. 25a, Amethyst starling. 30a, Orange-breasted shrike. 40a, Secretary bird. 50a, Rosy-faced lovebird.

Photogravure and Lithographed

1951 Unwmk. *Perf. 11½*

Birds in Natural Colors

333	A31	5c lt blue	15	*50*
334	A32	10c aqua	15	15
335	A32	15c salmon pink	22	*1.00*
336	A32	20c pale yellow	38	22
337	A31	50c gray blue	22	15
338	A31	1a lilac	22	15
339	A31	1.50a gray buff	32	15
340	A31	2a cream	32	15
341	A32	2.50a gray	32	15
342	A32	3a lemon yel	28	18
343	A31	3.50a lt gray	28	18
344	A31	4a rose buff	48	18
345	A32	4.50a rose lilac	48	20
346	A31	5a green	3.25	20
347	A31	6a blue	3.25	55
348	A31	7a orange	3.25	75
349	A31	10a lilac rose	27.50	1.10
350	A32	12.50a slate gray	3.75	1.75
351	A31	15a pale olive	3.75	1.75
352	A31	20a pale bis brn	37.50	4.50
353	A31	25a lilac rose	13.00	2.50
354	A32	30a pale salmon	13.00	3.00
355	A31	40a yellow	26.00	3.75
356	A31	50a turquoise	62.50	14.00
		Nos. 333-356 (24)	200.57	37.21

Holy Year Extension Issue

Common Design Type

1951, Oct. Litho. *Perf. 14*

357	CD43	4a orange	1.25	50

Sheets contain alternate vertical rows of stamps and labels bearing quotations from Pope Pius XII or the Patriarch Cardinal of Lisbon.

Medical Congress Issue

Common Design Type

Design: Medical examination

1952, June *Perf. 13½*

358	CD44	1a vio blue & brn blk	40	20

Head of Christ — A35

1952, Oct. Unwmk. *Perf. 13*

359	A35	10c dk blue & buff	15	15
360	A35	50c dk ol grn & ol gray	20	15
361	A35	2a rose vio & cream	1.25	15
		Nos. 359-361 (3)	1.60	
		Set value		26

Issued to commemorate the Exhibition of Sacred Missionary Art held at Lisbon in 1951.

Leopard A36

Sable Antelope A37

Animals: 20c, Elephant. 30c, Eland. 40c, African crocodile. 50c, Impala. 1a, Mountain zebra. 1.50a, Sitatunga. 2a, Black rhinoceros. 2.30a, Gemsbok. 2.50a, Lion. 3a, Buffalo. 3.50a, Springbok. 4a, Brindled gnu. 5a, Hartebeest. 7a, Wart hog. 10a, Defassa waterbuck. 12.50a, Hippopotamus. 15a, Greater kudu. 20a, Giraffe.

1953, Aug. 15 *Perf. 12½*

362	A36	5c multicolored	15	15
363	A37	10c multicolored	15	15
364	A37	20c multicolored	15	15
365	A37	30c multicolored	15	15
366	A36	40c multicolored	15	15
367	A37	50c multicolored	15	15
368	A37	1a multicolored	20	15
369	A37	1.50a multicolored	15	15
370	A36	2a multicolored	18	15
371	A37	2.30a multicolored	24	15
372	A37	2.50a multicolored	30	15
373	A36	3a multicolored	30	15
374	A37	3.50a multicolored	18	15
375	A37	4a multicolored	6.00	24
376	A37	5a multicolored	32	15
377	A37	7a multicolored	75	24
378	A37	10a multicolored	1.25	20
379	A37	12.50a multicolored	4.00	1.65
380	A37	15a multicolored	4.00	1.25
381	A37	20a multicolored	5.00	35
		Nos. 362-381 (20)	23.77	6.03

Stamp of Portugal and Arms of Colonies — A38

1953, Nov. Photo. *Perf. 13*

Stamp and Arms Multicolored

382	A38	50c gray & dark gray	55	32

Cent. of Portugal's 1st postage stamps.

Map and Plane — A39

Typographed and Lithographed

1954, May 27 *Perf. 13½*

383	A39	35c multicolored	15	15
384	A39	4.50e multicolored	70	30

Visit of Pres. Francisco H C. Lopes.

Sao Paulo Issue

Common Design Type

1954 Litho.

385	CD46	1e bister & gray	32	20

Map of Angola — A41

Artur de Paiva — A42

1955, Aug. Unwmk. *Perf. 13½*

386	A41	5c	multicolored	15	15
387	A41	20c	multicolored	15	15
388	A41	50c	multicolored	15	15
389	A41	1e	multicolored	15	15
390	A41	2.30e	multicolored	28	15
391	A41	4e	multicolored	50	15
392	A41	10e	multicolored	50	15
393	A41	20e	multicolored	1.00	20
			Nos. 386-393 (8)	2.88	
			Set value		78

For overprints see Nos. 593, 598, 604.

1956, Oct. 9 *Perf. 13½x12½*

394	A42	1e	blk, dk bl & ocher	20	15

Cent. of the birth of Col. Artur de Paiva.

Man of Malange — A43

Jose M. Antunes — A44

Various Costumes in Multicolor; Inscriptions in Black Brown

1957, Jan. 1 Photo. *Perf. 11½*

Granite Paper

395	A43	5c	gray	15	15
396	A43	10c	orange yel	15	15
397	A43	15c	lt blue grn	15	15
398	A43	20c	pale rose vio	15	15
399	A43	30c	brt rose	15	15
400	A43	40c	blue gray	15	15
401	A43	50c	pale olive	15	15
402	A43	80c	lt violet	15	15
403	A43	1.50e	buff	1.00	15
404	A43	2.50e	lt yel grn	1.00	15
405	A43	4e	salmon	50	15
406	A43	10e	salmon pink	1.00	25
			Nos. 395-406 (12)	4.70	
			Set value		1.25

1957, Apr. *Perf. 13½*

407	A44	1e	aqua & brown	65	20

Birth cent. of Father Jose Maria Antunes.

Fair Emblem, Globe and Arms — A45

1958, July Litho. *Perf. 12x11½*

408	A45	1.50e	multicolored	25	15

World's Fair, Brussels, Apr. 17-Oct. 19.

Tropical Medicine Congress Issue

Common Design Type

Design: Securidaca longipedunculata.

1958, Dec. 15 *Perf. 13½*

409	CD47	2.50e	multicolored	1.10	70

Medicine Man — A47

Welwitschia Mirabilis — A48

Designs: 1.50e, Early government doctor. 2.50e, Modern medical team.

1958, Dec. 18 *Perf. 11½x12*

410	A47	1e	blue blk & brown	20	15
411	A47	1.50e	gray, blk & brown	50	20
412	A47	2.50e	multicolored	75	40
			Nos. 410-412 (3)	1.45	75

75th anniversary of the Maria Pia Hospital, Luanda.

1959, Oct. 1 Litho. *Perf. 14½*

Various Views of Plant and Various Frames

413	A48	1.50e	lt brown, grn & blk	55	45
414	A48	2.50e	multicolored	85	50
415	A48	5e	multicolored	1.10	75
416	A48	10e	multicolored	2.75	1.00
			Nos. 413-416 (4)	5.25	2.70

Centenary of discovery of Welwitschia mirabilis, desert plant.

Map of West Africa, c. 1540, by Jorge Reinel — A49

1960, June 25 *Perf. 13½*

417	A49	2.50e	multicolored	20	15

500th anniv. of the death of Prince Henry the Navigator.

Distributing Medicines — A50

Girl of Angola — A51

1960, Oct. Litho. *Perf. 14½*

418	A50	2.50e	multicolored	30	15

10th anniv. of the Commission for Technical Co-operation in Africa South of the Sahara (C.C.T.A.).

1961, Nov. 30 Unwmk. *Perf. 13*

419	A51	10c	multicolored	15	15
420	A51	15c	multicolored	15	15
421	A51	30c	multicolored	15	15
422	A51	40c	multicolored	15	15
423	A51	60c	multicolored	15	15
424	A51	1.50e	multicolored	15	15
425	A51	2e	multicolored	60	15
426	A51	2.50e	multicolored	85	15
427	A51	3e	multicolored	2.00	20
428	A51	4e	multicolored	90	20
429	A51	5e	multicolored	70	20
430	A51	7.50e	multicolored	90	45
431	A51	10e	multicolored	70	25
432	A51	15e	multicolored	65	40
432A	A51	25e	multicolored	1.90	65
432B	A51	50e	multicolored	3.25	1.00
			Nos. 419-432B (16)	13.35	4.55

Sports Issue

Common Design Type

Sports: 50c, Flying. 1e, Rowing. 1.50e, Water polo. 2.50e, Hammer throwing. 4.50e, High jump. 15e, Weight lifting.

1962, Jan. 18 *Perf. 13½*

Multicolored Design

433	CD48	50c	lt blue	15	15
434	CD48	1e	olive bister	70	15
435	CD48	1.50e	salmon	32	15
436	CD48	2.50e	lt green	40	15
437	CD48	4.50e	pale blue	32	25
438	CD48	15e	yellow	1.50	65
			Nos. 433-438 (6)	3.39	1.50

For overprint see No. 608.

Anti-Malaria Issue

Common Design Type

Design: Anopheles funestus.

1962, April Litho. *Perf. 13½*

439	CD49	2.50e	multicolored	60	32

Gen. Norton de Matos — A54

Locusts — A56

1962, Aug. 8 Unwmk. *Perf. 14½*

440	A54	2.50e	multicolored	30	15

50th anniv. of the founding of Nova Lisboa.

1963, June 2 Litho. *Perf. 14*

447	A56	2.50e	multicolored	40	20

15th anniv. of the Intl. Anti-Locust Organ.

Arms of Luanda A57

Vila de Santo Antonio do Zaire — A58

Coats of Arms (Provinces and Cities): 10c, Massangano. 15c, Sanza-Pombo. 25c, Ambriz. 30c, Muxima. 40c, Ambrizete. 50c, Carmona. 60c, Catete. 70c, Quibaxe. No. 458, Maquelo do Zombo. 1e, Salazar. 1.20e, Bembe. No. 461, Caxito. 1.50e, Malanje. 1.80e, Dondo. 2e, Henrique de Carvalho. No. 465, Moçamedes. No. 466, Damba. 3e, Novo Redondo. 3.50e, S. Salvador do Congo. 4e, Cuimba. 5e, Luso. 6.50e, Negage. 7e, Quitexe. 7.50e, S. Filipe de Benguela. 8e, Mucaba. 9e, 31 de Janeiro. 10e, Lobito. 11e, Nova Caipemba. 12.50e, Gabela. 14e, Songo. 15e Sa da Bandeira. 17e, Quimbele. 17.50e, Silva Porto. 20e, Nova Lisboa. 22.50e, Cabinda. 25e, Noqui. 30e, Serpa Pinto. 35e, Santa Cruz. 50e, General Freire.

1963 *Perf. 13½*

Arms in Original Colors; Red and Violet Blue Inscriptions

448	A57	5c	tan	15	15
449	A57	10c	lt blue	15	15
450	A58	15c	salmon	15	15
451	A58	20c	olive	15	15
452	A58	25c	lt blue	15	15
453	A57	30c	buff	15	15
454	A58	40c	gray	15	15
455	A57	50c	lt green	15	15
456	A58	60c	brt yellow	15	15
457	A58	70c	dull rose	15	15
458	A57	1e	pale lilac	30	15
459	A58	1e	dull yellow	20	15
460	A58	1.20e	rose	15	15
461	A57	1.50e	pale salmon	60	15
462	A58	1.50e	lt green	40	15
463	A58	1.80e	yel olive	22	15
464	A57	2e	lt yel green	30	15
465	A57	2.50e	lt gray	1.50	15
466	A58	2.50e	dull blue	1.25	15
467	A57	3e	yel olive	42	15
468	A57	3.50e	gray	50	15
469	A58	4e	citron	35	15
470	A57	5e	citron	40	22
471	A58	6.50e	tan	40	25
472	A58	7e	rose lilac	42	25
473	A57	7.50e	pale lilac	55	30
474	A58	8e	lt aqua	45	30
475	A58	9e	yellow	60	30
476	A57	10e	dp salmon	70	35
477	A58	11e	dull yel grn	70	55
478	A57	12.50e	pale blue	90	45
479	A58	14e	lt gray	90	45
480	A57	15e	lt blue	1.00	45
481	A58	17e	pale blue	1.10	70
482	A57	17.50e	dull yellow	1.50	1.00
483	A57	20e	lt aqua	1.50	70
484	A57	22.50e	gray	1.50	1.00
485	A58	25e	citron	1.50	70
486	A57	30e	yellow	2.00	1.25
487	A58	35e	grysh blue	2.00	1.50
488	A58	50e	dp yellow	3.00	1.25
			Nos. 448-488 (41)	28.81	15.27

Pres. Américo Rodrigues Thomaz — A59

1963, Sept. 16 Litho.

489	A59	2.50e	multicolored	50	30

Visit of the President of Portugal.

Airline Anniversary Issue

Common Design Type

1963, Oct. 5 Unwmk. *Perf. 14½*

490	CD50	1e	lt blue & multi	25	15

Cathedral of Sá da Bandeira A61

Malange Cathedral A62

Churches: 20c, Landana. 30c, Luanda Cathedral. 40c, Gabela. 50c, St. Martin's Chapel, Baia dos Tigres. 1.50e, St. Peter, Chibia. 2e, Church of Our Lady, Benguela. 2.50e, Church of Jesus, Luanda. 3e, Camabatela. 3.50e, Mission, Cabinda. 4e, Vila Folgares. 4.50e, Church of Our Lady, Lobito. 5e, Church of Cabinda. 7.50e, Cacuso Church, Malange. 10e, Lubango Mission. 12.50e, Huila Mission. 15e, Church of Our Lady, Luanda Island.

1963, Nov. 1 Litho.

Multicolored Design and Inscription

491	A61	10c	gray blue	15	15
492	A61	20c	pink	15	15
493	A61	30c	lt blue	15	15
494	A61	40c	tan	15	15
495	A61	50c	lt green	15	15
496	A62	1e	buff	15	15
497	A61	1.50e	lt vio blue	15	15
498	A62	2e	pale rose	15	15
499	A61	2.50e	gray	15	15
500	A62	3e	buff	18	15
501	A61	3.50e	olive	22	15
502	A62	4e	buff	22	20
503	A62	4.50e	pale blue	25	22
504	A61	5e	tan	30	22
505	A62	7.50e	gray	45	32
506	A61	10e	dull yellow	60	40
507	A62	12.50e	bister	80	80
508	A62	15e	pale gray vio	1.25	70
			Nos. 491-508 (18)	5.62	
			Set value		3.65

National Overseas Bank Issue

Common Design Type

Design: Antonio Teixeira de Sousa.

1964, May 16 *Perf. 13½*

509	CD51	2.50e	multicolored	40	22

Angola stamps can be mounted in the Scott annual Portugal supplement.

Commerce Building and Arms of Chamber of Commerce A64

1964, Nov. Litho. *Perf. 12*

510 A64 1e multicolored 15 15

Luanda Chamber of Commerce centenary.

ITU Issue
Common Design Type

1965, May 17 Unwmk. *Perf. 14½*

511 CD52 2.50e gray & multi 70 25

Plane over Luanda Airport — A65

Harquebusier, 1539 — A66

1965, Dec. 3 Litho. *Perf. 13*

512 A65 2.50e multicolored 22 15

25th anniv. of DTA, Direccao dos Transportes Aereos.

1966, Feb. 25 Litho. *Perf. 14½*

Designs: 50c, Harquebusier, 1539. 1e, Harquebusier, 1640. 1.50e, Infantry officer, 1777. 2e, Standard bearer, infantry, 1777. 2.50e, Infantry soldier, 1777. 3e, Cavalry officer, 1783. 4e, Cavalry soldier, 1783. 4.50e, Infantry officer, 1807. 5e, Infantry soldier, 1807. 6e, Cavalry officer, 1807. 8e, Cavalry soldier, 1807. 9e, Infantry soldier, 1873.

513	A66	50c	multicolored	15	15
514	A66	1e	multicolored	15	15
515	A66	1.50e	multicolored	15	15
516	A66	2e	multicolored	15	15
517	A66	2.50e	multicolored	20	15
518	A66	3e	multicolored	20	15
519	A66	4e	multicolored	40	25
520	A66	4.50e	multicolored	40	25
521	A66	5e	multicolored	60	18
522	A66	6e	multicolored	75	50
523	A66	8e	multicolored	1.25	85
524	A66	9e	multicolored	1.50	1.00
			Nos. 513-524 (12)	5.90	3.93

National Revolution Issue
Common Design Type

Design: St. Paul's Hospital and Commercial and Industrial School.

1966, May 28 Litho. *Perf. 12*

525 CD53 1e multicolored 20 15

Emblem of Holy Ghost Society — A68

1966 Litho. *Perf. 13*

526 A68 1e blue & multi 15 15

Centenary of the Holy Ghost Society.

Navy Club Issue
Common Design Type

Designs: 1e, Mendes Barata and cruiser Dom Carlos I. 2.50e, Capt. Augusto de Castilho and corvette Mindelo.

1967, Jan. 31 Litho. *Perf. 13*

527	CD54	1e	multicolored	38	15
528	CD54	2.50e	multicolored	65	18

Fatima Basilica — A70

Angola Map, Manuel Cerveira Pereira — A71

1967, May 13 Litho. *Perf. 12½x13*

529 A70 50c multicolored 15 15

50th anniv. of the apparition of the Virgin Mary to 3 shepherd children at Fatima.

1967, Aug. 15 Litho. *Perf. 12½x13*

530 A71 50c multicolored 15 15

350th anniv. of the founding of Benguela.

Administration Building, Carmona — A72

1967 Litho. *Perf. 12*

531 A72 1e multicolored 15 15

50th anniv. of the founding of Carmona.

Military Order of Valor — A73

Our Lady of Hope — A74

Designs: 50c, Ribbon of the Three Orders. 1.50e, Military Order of Avis. 2e, Military Order of Christ. 2.50e, Military Order of St. John of Espada. 3e, Order of the Empire. 4e, Order of Prince Henry. 5e, Order of Benemerencia. 10e, Order of Public Instruction. 20e, Order for Industrial and Agricultural Merit.

1967, Oct. 31 *Perf. 14*

532	A73	50c	lt gray & multi	15	15
533	A73	1e	lt green & multi	15	15
534	A73	1.50e	yellow & multi	15	15
535	A73	2e	multicolored	15	15
536	A73	2.50e	multicolored	15	15
537	A73	3e	lt olive & multi	18	15
538	A73	4e	gray & multi	20	15
539	A73	5e	multicolored	25	15
540	A73	10e	lilac & multi	40	25
541	A73	20e	lt blue & multi	1.00	52
			Nos. 532-541 (10)	2.78	
			Set value		1.28

1968, Apr. 22 Litho. *Perf. 14*

Designs: 1e, Belmonte Castle, horiz. 1.50e, St. Jerome's Convent. 2.50e, Cabral's Armada.

542	A74	50c	yellow & multi	15	15
543	A74	1e	gray & multi	25	15
544	A74	1.50e	lt blue & multi	40	15
545	A74	2.50e	buff & multi	60	15
			Nos. 542-545 (4)	1.40	
			Set value		32

500th anniv. of the birth of Pedro Alvares Cabral, navigator who took possession of Brazil for Portugal.

Francisco Inocencio de Souza Coutinho — A75

1969, Jan. 7 Litho. *Perf. 14*

546 A75 2e multicolored 25 20

200th anniversary of the founding of Novo Redondo.

Admiral Coutinho Issue
Common Design Type

Design: Adm. Gago Coutinho and his first ship.

1969, Feb. 17 Litho. *Perf. 14*

547 CD55 2.50e multicolored 30 15

Compass Rose A77

Portal of St. Jeronimo's Monastery A79

1969, Aug. 29 Litho. *Perf. 14*

548 A77 1e multicolored 15 15

500th anniv. of the birth of Vasco da Gama (1469-1524), navigator.

Administration Reform Issue
Common Design Type

1969, Sept. 25 Litho. *Perf. 14*

549 CD56 1.50e multicolored 15 15

1969, Dec. 1 Litho. *Perf. 14*

550 A79 3e multicolored 20 15

500th anniv. of the birth of King Manuel I.

Angolasaurus Bocagei — A80

Fossils and Minerals: 1e, Ferrometeorite. 1.50e, Dioptase crystals. 2e, Gondwanidium. 2.50e, Diamonds. 3e, Estromatolite. 3.50e, Procarcharodon megalodon. 4e, Microceratodus angolensis. 4.50e, Moscovite. 5e, Barite. 6e, Nostoceras. 10e, Rotula orbiculus angolensis.

1970, Oct. 31 Litho. *Perf. 13*

551	A80	50c	tan & multi	15	15
552	A80	1e	multicolored	15	15
553	A80	1.50e	multicolored	15	15
554	A80	2e	multicolored	20	15
555	A80	2.50e	lt gray & multi	20	15
556	A80	3e	multicolored	20	15
557	A80	3.50e	blue & multi	30	15
558	A80	4e	lt gray & multi	30	15
559	A80	4.50e	gray & multi	30	15
560	A80	5e	gray & multi	30	15
561	A80	6e	pink & multi	60	20
562	A80	10e	lt blue & multi	75	32
			Nos. 551-562 (12)	3.60	
			Set value		1.40

Marshal Carmona Issue
Common Design Type

1970, Nov. 15 *Perf. 14*

563 CD57 2.50e multicolored 22 15

Arms of Malanje, Cotton Boll and Field — A82

1970, Nov. 20 *Perf. 13*

564 A82 2.50e multicolored 22 15

Centenary of the municipality of Malanje.

Mail Ships and Angola No. 1 — A83

Designs: 4.50e, Steam locomotive and Angola No. 4.

1970, Dec. 1 *Perf. 13½*

565	A83	1.50e	multicolored	30	15
566	A83	4.50e	multicolored	65	22

Cent. of stamps of Angola. See No. C36. For overprint see No. 616B.

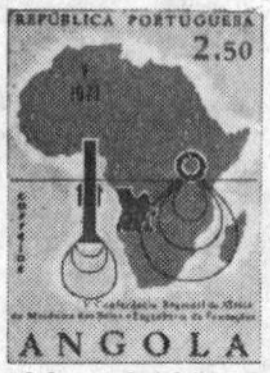

Map of Africa, Diagram of Seismic Tests — A84

Galleon on Congo River — A85

1971, Aug. 22 Litho. *Perf. 13*

567 A84 2.50e multicolored 15 15

5th Regional Conference of Soil and Foundation Engineers, Luanda, Aug. 22-Sept. 5.

1972, May 25 Litho. *Perf. 13*

568 A85 1e emerald & multi 15 15

4th centenary of the publication of The Lusiads by Luiz Camoens.

Olympic Games Issue
Common Design Type

1972, June 20 *Perf. 14x13½*

569 CD59 50c multicolored 15 15

Lisbon-Rio de Janeiro Flight Issue
Common Design Type

1972, Sept. 20 Litho. *Perf. 13½*

570 CD60 1e multicolored 15 15

WMO Centenary Issue
Common Design Type

1973, Dec. 15 Litho. *Perf. 13*

571 CD61 1e dk gray & multi 15 15

Radar Station A89

1974, June 25 Litho. *Perf. 13*

572 A89 2e multicolored 22 15

Establishment of satellite communications network via Intelsat among Portugal, Angola and Mozambique.

For overprint see No. 616A

Harpa Doris — A90

Designs: Sea shells.

1974, Oct. 25 Litho. *Perf. 12x12½*

573	A90	25c	shown	15	15
574	A90	30c	Murex melanamathos	15	15
575	A90	50c	Venus foliaceo lamellosa	15	15
576	A90	70c	Lathyrus filosus	15	15
577	A90	1e	Cymbium cisium	18	15
578	A90	1.50e	Cassis tesselata	18	15
579	A90	2e	Cypraea stercoraria	18	15
580	A90	2.50e	Conus prometheus	18	18
581	A90	3e	Strombus latus	18	18
582	A90	3.50e	Tympanotonus fuscatus	18	18
583	A90	4e	Cardium costatum	25	20
584	A90	5e	Natica fulminea	25	20
585	A90	6e	Lyropecten nodosus	30	20
586	A90	7e	Tonna galea	75	25
587	A90	10e	Donax rugosus	90	30
588	A90	25e	Cymatium trigonum	1.50	40
589	A90	30e	Olivancilaria acuminata	2.50	75
590	A90	35e	Semifusus morio	2.50	75
591	A90	40e	Clavatula lineata	3.00	1.00
592	A90	50e	Solarium granulatum	4.00	1.50
			Nos. 573-592 (20)	17.63	
			Set value		4.00

For overprints see Nos. 605-607, 617-630.

No. 386 Overprinted in Blue: "1974 / FILATELIA / JUVENIL"

1974, Dec. 21 Litho. *Perf. 13½*

593 A41 5c multicolored 15 15

Youth philately.

Republic

Star and Hand Holding Rifle — A91

1975, Nov. 11 Litho. *Perf. 13x13½*

594 A91 1.50e red & multi 15 15

Independence in 1975.

Diquiche Mask — A92

Design: 3e, Bui ou Congolo mask.

1976, Feb. 6 *Perf. 13½*

595	A92	50c	lt blue & multi	15	15
596	A92	3e	multicolored	20	15
			Set value	27	15

Workers — A93

President Agostinho Neto — A94

1976, May 1 Litho. *Perf. 12*

597 A93 1e red & multi 15 15

International Workers' Day.

No. 392 Overprinted Bar and: "DIA DO SELO / 15 Junho 1976 / REP. POPULAR / DE"

1976, June 15 Litho. *Perf. 13½*

598 A41 10e multicolored 40 25

Stamp Day.

1976, Nov. 11 Litho. *Perf. 13*

599	A94	50c	yel & dk brown	15	15
600	A94	2e	lt gray & plum	15	15
601	A94	3e	gray & indigo	15	15
602	A94	5e	buff & brown	20	15
603	A94	10e	tan & sepia	40	15
a.			Souv. sheet of 1, imperf.	2.00	1.25
			Nos. 599-603 (5)	1.05	
			Set value		40

First anniversary of independence.

Nos. 393, 588-589, 592 Overprinted with Bar over Republica Portuguesa and: "REPUBLICA POPULAR DE"

1977, Feb. 9 *Perf. 13½, 12x12½*

604	A41	20e	multicolored	85	24
605	A90	25e	multicolored	1.00	32
606	A90	30e	multicolored	1.25	40
607	A90	50e	multicolored	2.00	65
			Nos. 604-607 (4)	5.10	1.61

Overprint in 3 lines on No. 604, in 2 lines on others.

No. 438 Overprinted with Bar over Republica Portuguesa and: "S. Silvestre / 1976 / Rep. Popular / de"

1976, Dec. 31 *Perf. 13½*

608 CD48 15e multicolored 60 25

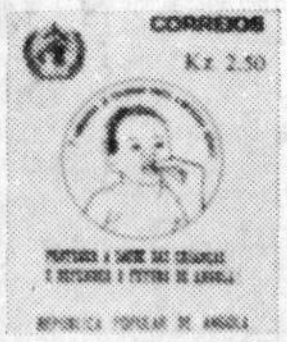
Child and WHO Emblem — A95

Map of Africa, Flag of Angola — A96

1977 Litho. *Perf. 10½*

609 A95 2.50k blk & lt blue 15 15

Campaign for vaccination against poliomyelitis.

1977 Photo.

610 A96 6k blk, red & bl 20 15

First congress of Popular Movement for the Liberation of Angola.

Anti-Apartheid Emblem — A97

1979, June 20 Litho. *Perf. 13½*

611 A97 1k multicolored 15 15

Anti-Apartheid Year.

Human Rights Emblem — A98

Child Flowers, Globe, IYC Emblem — A99

1979, June 15 Litho. *Perf. 13½*

612 A98 2.50k multicolored 15 15

Declaration of Human Rights, 30th anniv. (in 1975).

1980, May 1 Litho. *Perf. 14x14½*

613 A99 3.50k multicolored 15 15

International Year of the Child (1979).

Running, Moscow '80 Emblem A100

5th Anniv. of Independence A101

1980, Dec. 15 Litho. *Perf. 13½*

614	A100	9k	shown	32	15
615	A100	12k	Swimming, horiz.	40	20

22nd Summer Olympic Games, Moscow, July 19-Aug. 3.

1980, Nov. 11

616 A101 5.50k multicolored 15 15

Nos. 572, 566 Overprinted with Bar and: "REPUBLICA POPULAR / DE"

1980-81 Litho. *Perf. 13½x13*

616A	A89	2e	multi (bar only)	50	
616B	A83	4.50e	multicolored	1.00	

Issue dates: 2e, May 17, 1981, 4.50e, June 15. See No. C37.

Nos. 577-580, 582-591 Overprinted with Black Bar over "Republica Portuguesa"

1981, June 15 Litho. *Perf. 12x12½*

617	A90	1e	multicolored		
618	A90	1.50e	multicolored		
619	A90	2e	multicolored		
620	A90	2.50e	multicolored		
621	A90	3.50e	multicolored		
622	A90	4e	multicolored		
623	A90	5e	multicolored		
624	A90	6e	multicolored		
625	A90	7e	multicolored		
626	A90	10e	multicolored		
627	A90	25e	multicolored		
628	A90	30e	multicolored		
629	A90	35e	multicolored		
630	A90	40e	multicolored		
			Nos. 617-630 (14)	10.00	5.50

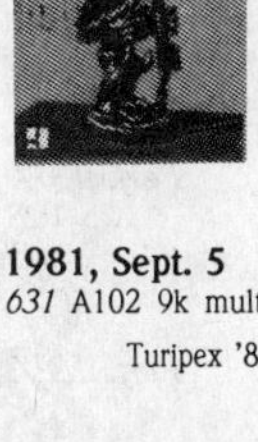
Man Walking with Canes, Tchibinda Ilunga Statue — A102

1981, Sept. 5 Litho. *Perf. 13½*

631 A102 9k multicolored 32 20

Turipex '81 tourism exhibition.

M.P.L.A. Workers' Party Congress — A103

1980, Dec. 23 Litho. *Perf. 14*

632	A103	50 l	Millet	15	15
633	A103	5k	Coffee	20	15
634	A103	7.50k	Sunflowers	25	15
635	A103	13.50k	Cotton	40	20
636	A103	14k	Oil	45	25
637	A103	16k	Diamonds	45	25
			Nos. 632-637 (6)	1.90	1.15

People's Power — A104

Natl. Heroes' Day — A105

1980, Nov. 11

638 A104 40k lt blue & blk 1.25 40

1980, Sept. 17 *Perf. 14x13½*

639	A105	4.50k	Former Pres. Neto	15	15
640	A105	50k	Neto, diff.	1.50	65

Soweto Uprising, 5th Anniv. A106

1981

641 A106 4.50k multicolored 20 15

2nd Central African Games A107

1981, Sept. 3 Litho. *Perf. 13½*

642	A107	50 l	Bicycling, tennis	15	15
643	A107	5k	Judo, boxing	20	15
644	A107	6k	Basketball, volleyball	22	15
645	A107	10k	Handball, soccer	40	25
			Nos. 642-645 (4)	97	
			Set value		52

Souvenir Sheet

Imperf

646 A107 15k multicolored *2.00*

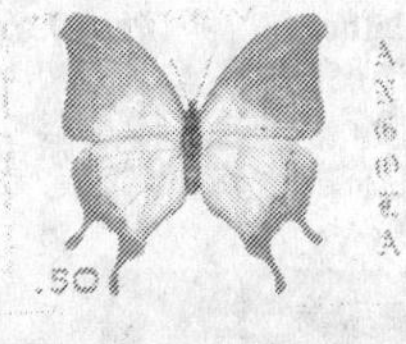
Charaxes Kahldeni A108

1982, Feb. 26 Litho. *Perf. 13½*

647	A108	50 l	shown	15	15
648	A108	1k	Abantis zambesiaca	15	15
649	A108	5k	Catacroptera cloanthe	20	15
650	A108	9k	Myrina ficedula, vert.	40	15
651	A108	10k	Colotis danae	40	15
652	A108	15k	Acraea acrita	52	25

653 A108 100k Precis hierta 2.75 1.25
a. Souvenir sheet 2.00 1.00
Nos. 647-653 (7) 4.57 2.25

No. 653a contains Nos. 647-653, imperf., and sold for 30k (stamps probably not valid individually).

5th Anniv. of UN Membership A109

Designs: 5.50k, The Silence of the Night, by Musseque Catambor. 7.50k, Cotton picking, Catete.

1982, Sept. 22 **Litho.**
654 A109 5.50k multicolored 20 15
655 A109 7.50k multicolored 25 15

20th Anniv. of Engineering Laboratory A110

1982, Dec. 21 **Litho.** ***Perf. 14***
656 A110 9k Lab 25 15
657 A110 13k Worker, vert. 40 20
658 A110 100k Equipment, vert. 3.25 1.25
Nos. 656-658 (3) 3.90 1.60

Local Flowers A111

1983, Feb. 18 ***Perf. 13½***
659 A111 5k Dichrostachys glomerata 15 15
660 A111 12k Amblygonocarpus obtusangulus 40 15
661 A111 50k Albizzia versicolor 2.00 65
Nos. 659-661 (3) 2.55 95

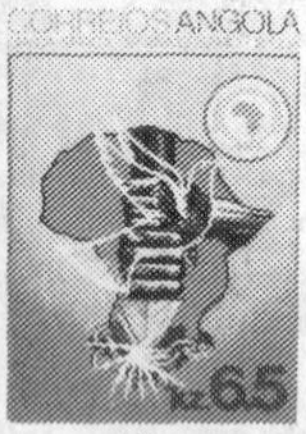

Women's Org., First Congress — A112

Africa Day — A113

1983 **Litho.** ***Perf. 13½***
662 A112 20k multicolored 80 80

1983, June 30 ***Perf. 13***
663 A113 6.5k multi 25 25

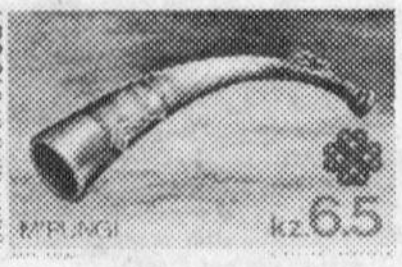

World Communications Year — A114

1983, June 30 **Litho.** ***Perf. 13½***
664 A114 6.5k M'pungi 25 25
665 A114 12k Mondu 40 40

BRASILIANA '83 Stamp Exhibition, Rio de Janeiro, July 29-Aug. 7 — A115

Crop-eating insects.

1983, July 29 **Litho.** ***Perf. 13***
666 A115 4.5k Antestiopsis lineaticollis 18 18
667 A115 6.5k Stephanoderes hampei ferr. 25 25
668 A115 10k Zonocerus variegatus 40 40
Nos. 666-668 (3) 83 83

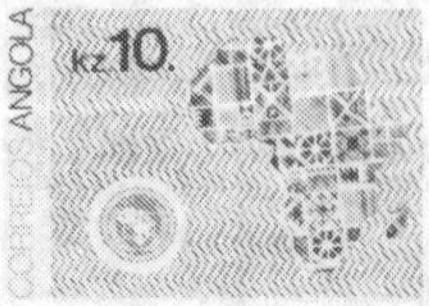

25th Anniv. of Economic Commission for Africa A116

1983, Aug. 2
669 A116 10k Map, emblem 40 40

185th Anniv. of Post Office A117

1983, Dec. 7 **Litho.** ***Perf. 13½***
670 A117 50 l Mail collection, vert. 15 15
671 A117 3.5k Unloading mail plane 15 15
672 A117 5k Sorting mail 20 20
673 A117 15k Mailing letter, vert. 60 60
674 A117 30k Post office box delivery 1.25 1.25
a. Min. sheet of 3, #671-672, 674 4.00 4.00
Nos. 670-674 (5) 2.35 2.35

No. 674a sold for 100k.

Local Butterflies A118

1984, Jan. 20 **Litho.** ***Perf. 13½***
675 A118 50 l Parasa karschi 15 15
676 A118 1k Diaphone angolensis 15 15
677 A118 3.5k Choeropasis jucunda 15 15
678 A118 6.5k Hespagarista rendalli 25 25
679 A118 15k Euchromia guineensis 60 60
680 A118 17.5k Mazuca roseistriga 70 70
681 A118 20k Utetheisa callima 85 85
Nos. 675-681 (7) 2.85 2.85

A119 A120

1984, Apr. 11 **Litho.** ***Perf. 13½***
682 A119 30k multicolored 1.25 1.25

First Natl. Worker's Union Congress, Apr. 11-16.

1984, Oct. 24 **Litho.** ***Perf. 13½***

Local birds.

683 A120 10.50k Bucorvos leadbeateri 45 40
684 A120 14k Gypohicax angolensis 55 50
685 A120 16k Ardea goliath 60 50
686 A120 19.50k Pelicanus onocrotalus 80 75
687 A120 22k Platelea alba 90 90
688 A120 26k Balearica pavonnia 1.00 1.00
Nos. 683-688 (6) 4.30 4.05

Local Animals A121

1984, Nov. 12
689 A121 1k Tragelephus strepsicerus 15 15
690 A121 4k Antidorcos marsupialis angolerusis 15 15
691 A121 5k Pan troglodytes 20 20
692 A121 10k Sycerus caffer 40 40
693 A121 15k Hippotragus niger variani 60 60
694 A121 20k Orycteropus afer 80 80
695 A121 25k Crocuta crocuta 1.00 1.00
Nos. 689-695 (7) 3.30 3.30

Angolese Monuments A122

1985, Feb. 21 **Litho.** ***Perf. 13½***
696 A122 5k San Pedro da Barra 22 22
697 A122 12.5k Nova Oeiras 55 55
698 A122 18k M'Banza Kongo 80 80
699 A122 26k Massangano 1.10 1.10
700 A122 39k Escravatura Museum 1.65 1.65
Nos. 696-700 (5) 4.32 4.32

United Workers' Party, 25th Anniv. A123

1985, May **Litho.** ***Perf. 12***
701 A123 77k XXV, red flags 1.50 1.50

Printed in sheets of 5.

A124 A125

1985, May
702 A124 1k Flags 15 15
703 A124 11k Oil drilling platform, Cabinda 22 22
704 A124 57k Conference 1.10 1.10
a. Strip of 3, #702-704 1.40 1.40

Southern African Development Council, 5th anniv.

Lithographed and Typographed

1985, July 5 ***Perf. 11***

Medicinal plants.

705 A125 1k Lonchocarpus sericeus 15 15
706 A125 4k Gossypium 15 15
707 A125 11k Cassia occidentalis 22 22
708 A125 25.50k Gloriosa superba 50 50
709 A125 55k Cochlospermum angolensis 1.10 1.10
Nos. 705-709 (5) 2.12 2.12

ARGENTINA '85 exhibition.

5th Natl. Heroes Day — A126

Natl. flag and: 10.50k, Portrait of Agostinho Neto, party leader. 36.50k, Neto working.

1985 **Litho.** ***Perf. 13½***
710 A126 10.50k multicolored 20 20
711 A126 36.50k multicolored 70 70

Ministerial Conference of Non-Aligned Countries, Luanda A127

1985, Sept. 4 **Photo.** ***Perf. 11***
712 A127 35k multicolored 1.50 1.50

UN, 40th Anniv. A128

1985, Oct. 29 **Litho.** ***Perf. 11***
713 A128 12.50k multicolored 55 55

Industry and Natural Resources A129

1985, Nov. 11
714 A129 50 l Cement Factory 15 15
715 A129 5k Logging 22 22
716 A129 7k Quartz 30 30
717 A129 10k Iron mine 42 42
a. Souvenir sheet of 4, #714-717, imperf. 1.00 1.00
Nos. 714-717 (4) 1.09 1.09

Natl. independence, 10th anniv.

2nd Natl. Workers' Party Congress (MPLA) A130

1985, Nov. 28 ***Perf. 13½***
718 A130 20k multicolored 85 85

Demostenes de Almeida Clington Races, 30th Anniv. — A131

Various runners.

1985, Dec. 13

719 A131	50 l	multicolored	15	15
720 A131	5k	multicolored	22	22
721 A131	6.50k	multicolored	28	28
722 A131	10k	multicolored	42	42
		Nos. 719-722 (4)	1.07	1.07

1986 World Cup Soccer Championships, Mexico — A132

Map, soccer field and various plays.

1986, May 6 Litho. *Perf. 11½x11*

723 A132	50 l	multi	15	15
724 A132	3.50k	multi	15	15
725 A132	5k	multi	22	22
726 A132	7k	multi	30	30
727 A132	10k	multi	42	42
728 A132	18k	multi	85	85
		Nos. 723-728 (6)	2.09	2.09

Struggle Against Portugal, 25th Anniv. A133

1986, May 6 *Perf. 11x11½*

729 A133	15k	multicolored	65	65

First Man in Space, 25th Anniv. A134

1986, Aug. 21 Litho. *Perf. 11x11½*

730 A134	50 l	Skylab, US	15	15
731 A134	1k	Spacecraft	15	15
732 A134	5k	A. Leonov space-walking	22	22
733 A134	10k	Lunokhod on Moon	42	42
734 A134	13k	Apollo-Soyuz link-up	60	60
		Nos. 730-734 (5)	1.54	1.54

Admission of Angola to UN, 10th Anniv. — A135

1986, Dec. 1 Litho. *Perf. 11x11½*

735 A135	22k	multi	90	90

Liberation Movement, 30th Anniv. — A136

Angolese at work, fighting and: No. 736a, "1956." No. 736b, Congress emblem, "1980." No. 736c, Labor Party emblem, "1985."

1986, Dec. 3 *Perf. 11½x11*

736 A136		Strip of 3	65	65
a.-c.		5k any single	20	20

Agostinho Neto University, 10th Anniv. A137

1986, Dec. 30 Litho. *Perf. 11x11½*

737 A137	50 l	Mathematics	15	15
738 A137	1k	Law	15	15
739 A137	10k	Medicine	45	45
		Nos. 737-739 (3)	75	75

Tribal Hairstyles — A138

1987, Apr. 15 Litho. *Perf. 11½x11*

740 A138	1k	Ouioca	15	15
741 A138	1.50k	Luanda	15	15
742 A138	5k	Humbe	15	15
743 A138	7k	Muila	15	15
744 A138	20k	Muila, diff.	45	45
745 A138	30k	Dilolo	70	70
		Nos. 740-745 (6)	1.75	1.75

Landscapes — A139

Lenin — A140

Perf. 11½x12, 12x11½

1987, July 7 Litho.

746 A139	50 l	Pambala Shore	15	15
747 A139	1.50k	Dala Waterfalls	15	15
748 A139	3.50k	Black Stones	15	15
749 A139	5k	Cuango River	15	15
750 A139	10k	Launda coast	22	22
751 A139	20k	Hills of Leba	50	50
		Set value	1.00	1.00

Nos. 746-747, 749 and 751 horiz.

1987, Nov. 25 *Perf. 12x12½*

752 A140	15k	multi	58	58

October Revolution, Russia, 70th anniv.

2nd Congress of the Organization of Angolan Women (OMA) — A141

1988, May 30 Litho. *Perf. 13x13½*

753 A141	2k	shown	15	15
754 A141	10k	Soldier, nurse, technician, student	35	35

Victory Carnival, 10th Anniv. — A142

Various carnival scenes.

1988, June 15 Litho. *Perf. 13½x13*

755 A142	5k	shown	16	16
756 A142	10k	multi, diff.	32	32

Augusto N'Gangula (1956-1968), Youth Pioneer Killed by Portuguese Colonial Army — A143

Agostinho Neto Pioneers' Organization (OPA), 25th Anniv. — A144

1989, Oct. 2 Litho. *Perf. 12x11½*

757 A143	12k	multicolored	40	40
758 A144	15k	multicolored	48	48

Pioneer Day.

10th Natl. Soccer Championships, Benguela, May 1 — A145

1989, Oct. 16

759 A145	5k	shown	16	16
760 A145	5k	Luanda, 3 years	16	16
761 A145	5k	Luanda, 5 years	16	16
		Nos. 759-761 (3)	48	48

Intl. Fund for Agricultural Development, 10th Anniv. — A146

1990, Feb. 15 Litho. *Perf. 11½x12*

762 A146	10k	multicolored	70	70

Ingombotas' Houses A147

Architecture: 2k, Alta Train Station. 5k, National Museum of Anthropology. 15k, Ana Joaquina Palace. 23k, Iron Palace. 36k, Meteorological observatory, vert. 50k, People's Palace.

Perf. 12x11½, 11½x12

1990, Feb. 20

763 A147	1k	shown	15	15
764 A147	2k	multicolored	15	15
765 A147	5k	multicolored	32	32
766 A147	15k	multicolored	98	98
767 A147	23k	multicolored	1.50	1.50
768 A147	36k	multicolored	2.30	2.30
769 A147	50k	multicolored	3.25	3.25
		Nos. 763-769 (7)	8.65	8.65

Luanda and Benguela Railways A148

Various maps and locomotives.

1990, Mar. 1 *Perf. 12x11½*

770 A148	5k	shown	35	35
771 A148	12k	Garrat T (left)	80	80
772 A148	12k	Garrat T (right)	80	80
a.		Pair, #771-772	1.60	1.60
773 A148	14k	Mikado	95	95
		Nos. 770-773 (4)	2.90	2.90

Souvenir Sheet

774 A148	25k	Diesel electric	2.35	2.35

No. 772a has a continuous design.

Southern Africa Development Coordinating Conf. (SADCC), 10th Anniv. A149

1990, Apr. 1 Litho. *Perf. 14*

775 A149	5k	shown	*35*	*35*
776 A149	9k	Floating oil rig	*65*	*65*

Pan-African Postal Union (PAPU), 10th Anniv. A150

1990, Apr. 6

777 A150	4k	shown	28	28
778 A150	10k	Simulated stamp, map	70	70

Paintings by Raul Indipwo A151

1990, Apr. 24

779 A151	6k	*Tres Gracas*	42	42
780 A151	9k	*Muxima*, vert.	65	65

Stamp World London 90.

Hippotragus Niger Variani, Adult Male and Female — A152

1990, May 9 *Perf. 14x13½*

781 A152	5k	Adult male	35	35
782 A152	5k	shown	35	35
783 A152	5k	Adult female	35	35
784 A152	5k	Female, calf	35	35
		Nos. 781-784 (4)	1.40	1.40

World Wildlife Fund. Various combinations available in blocks or strips of four.

Rosa de Porcelana — A153

1990, June 2 Litho. *Perf. 14*

785	A153	5k shown	35	35
786	A153	8k Cravo burro	56	56
787	A153	10k Alamandra	70	70
		Nos. 785-787 (3)	1.61	1.61

Souvenir Sheet

788	A153	40k Hibiscus	2.70	2.70

Belgica '90.

Miniature Sheet

Intl. Literacy Year — A154

Various animals and forest scenes.

1990, July 26 Litho. *Perf. 14*

789		Sheet of 30	2.25	2.25
a.		A154 1k any single	15	15
790	A154	5k Zebra	35	35
791	A154	5k Butterfly	35	35
792	A154	5k Horse	35	35
a.		Block of 3, #790-792 + label	1.05	1.05

People's Assembly, 10th Anniv. A155

1990, Nov. 11 *Perf. 14*

793	A155	10k multicolored	70	70

3rd Natl. Labor Congress — A156

1990 Litho. *Perf. 13½*

794	A156	14k multicolored	1.35	1.35

War of Independence, 30th Anniv. A157

Uniforms.

1991, Feb. 28 Litho. *Perf. 14*

795	A157	6k Machete, 1961	42	42
a.		Perf. 13½ vert.	42	42
796	A157	6k Rifle, 1962-63	42	42
a.		Perf. 13½ vert.	42	42
797	A157	6k Rifle, 1968	42	42
a.		Perf. 13½ vert.	42	42
798	A157	6k Automatic rifle, 1972	42	42
a.		Perf. 13½ vert.	42	42
b.		Bklt. pane of 4, #795a-798a	1.70	
		Nos. 795-798 (4)	1.68	1.68

Musical Instruments A158

Designs: a, Marimba. b, Mucupela. c, Ngoma la Txina. d, Kissange.

1991, Apr. 5 Litho. *Perf. 14*

799	A158	6k Block or strip of 4, #799a-799d	1.70	1.70

Tourism A159

Designs: 3k, Iona National Park. 7k, Kalandula Waterfalls. 35k, Lobito Bay. 60k, Weltwitschia Mirabilis plant.

1991, June 25 Litho. *Perf. 14*

800	A159	3k multi	15	15
801	A159	7k multi	24	24
802	A159	35k multi	1.15	1.15
803	A159	60k multi	2.00	2.00
		Nos. 800-803 (4)	3.54	3.54

Dogs — A160

1991, July 5 Litho. *Perf. 14*

804	A160	5k Kabir of dembos	16	16
805	A160	7k Ombua	24	24
806	A160	11k Kabir massongo	38	38
807	A160	12k Kawa tchowe	40	40
		Nos. 804-807 (4)	1.18	1.18

1992 Summer Olympics, Barcelona A161

1991, July 26 *Perf. 13*

808	A161	4k Judo	15	15
809	A161	6k Sailing	20	20
810	A161	10k Running	35	35
811	A161	100k Swimming	3.35	3.35
		Nos. 808-811 (4)	4.05	4.05

Navigation Aids — A162

1991, Nov. 8 Litho. *Perf. 12*

812	A162	5k Quadrant	16	16
813	A162	15k Astrolabe	52	52
814	A162	20k Cross-staff	70	70
815	A162	50k Portolano	1.75	1.75
		Nos. 812-815 (4)	3.13	3.13

Iberex '91.

Rays — A163

1992, Mar. 30 Litho. *Perf. 14*

816	A163	40k Myliobatis aquila	15	15
817	A163	50k Aetobatus narinari	18	18
818	A163	66k Manta birostris	24	24
819	A163	80k Raja miraletus	30	30
		Nos. 816-819 (4)	87	87

Souvenir Sheet

Perf. 13½

820	A163	25k Manta birostris, diff.	15	15

Quioca Masks — A164

1992, Apr. 30 Litho. *Perf. 13½*

821	A164	60k Kalelwa	22	22
822	A164	100k Mukixe Wa Kino	38	38
823	A164	150k Cikunza	55	55
824	A164	250k Mukixi Wa Mbwesu	92	92
		Nos. 821-824 (4)	2.07	2.07

See Nos. 854-857, 868-871, 883-886, 895-898.

Medicinal Plants — A165

Designs: 200k, Ptaeroxylon obliquum. 300k, Spondias mombin. 500k, Parinari curatellifolia. 600k, Cochlospermum angolense.

1992, May 8 *Perf. 14*

825	A165	200k brown & pale yel	75	75
826	A165	300k brown & pale yel	1.10	1.10
827	A165	500k brown & pale yel	1.85	1.85
828	A165	600k brown & pale yel	2.20	2.20
a.		Block or strip of 4, #825-828	5.90	5.90

Evangelization of Angola, 500th Anniv. — A166

1992, May 10 *Perf. 13½*

829	A166	150k King, missionaries	55	55
830	A166	420k Ruins of M'banza Congo	1.55	1.55
831	A166	470k Maxima Church	1.75	1.75
832	A166	500k Faces of people	1.90	1.90
		Nos. 829-832 (4)	5.75	5.75

Traditional Houses — A167

Perf. 14, 13½ Vert. (#832A)

1992, May 22

832A	A167	150k Dimbas	45	45
b.		Bklt. pane of 4, #832A, 833a-835a	4.60	
833	A167	330k Cokwe	1.25	1.25
a.		Perf. 13½ vert.	1.25	1.25
834	A167	360k Mbali	1.35	1.35
a.		Perf. 13½ vert.	1.35	1.35
835	A167	420k Ambwelas	1.55	1.55
a.		Perf. 13½ vert.	1.55	1.55
836	A167	500k Upper Zambezi	1.90	1.90
		Nos. 832A-836 (5)	6.50	6.50

Expo '92, Seville.

Agapornis Roseicollis A168

1992, June 2 *Perf. 12x11½*

837	A168	150k Two birds on branch	55	55
838	A168	200k Birds feeding	75	75
839	A168	250k Hand holding bird	92	92
840	A168	300k Bird on perch	1.10	1.10
a.		Strip of 4, #837-840	3.35	3.35

Expo '92, Seville.

Souvenir Sheet

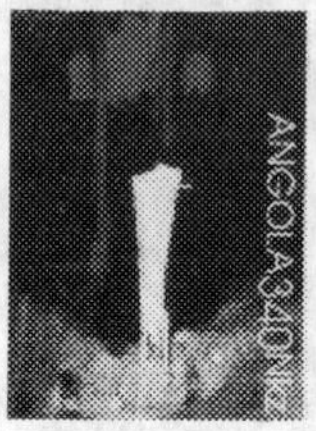

Visit of Pope John Paul II to Angola — A169

Abstract paintings: a, 340k, The Crucifixion. b, 370k, The Resurrection.

1992, June 4 Litho. *Perf. 13½*

841	A169	Sheet of 2, #a.-b. + 2 labels	1.80	1.80

1992 Summer Olympics, Barcelona A170

1992, July 30 *Perf. 14*

842	A170	120k Hurdles	32	32
843	A170	180k Cycling	50	50
844	A170	240k Roller hockey	65	65
845	A170	360k Basketball	1.00	1.00
		Nos. 842-845 (4)	2.47	2.47

Native Fishing — A171

1992, Aug. 5 *Perf. 11½x12*

846	A171	65k Building traps	18	18
847	A171	90k Using nets	25	25
848	A171	100k Laying traps	28	28
849	A171	120k Fisherman in boats	32	32
		Nos. 846-849 (4)	1.03	1.03

Souvenir Sheet

Discovery of America, 500th Anniv. — A172

1992, Sept. 18 Litho. *Perf. 12*

850 A172 500k multicolored 1.35 1.35

Genoa '92.

First Free Elections in Angola — A173

Designs: 120k, People voting. 150k, Map, ballot box, peace doves. 200k, People, dove, hand dropping ballot into ballot box.

1992, Oct. 27 Litho. *Perf. 11½x12*

851 A173 120k multicolored 32 32
852 A173 150k multicolored 42 42
853 A173 200k multicolored 55 55
Nos. 851-853 (3) 1.29 1.29

Quioca Mask Type of 1992

1992, Nov. 6 *Perf. 13½*

854 A164 72k Cihongo 28 28
855 A164 80k Mbwasu 30 30
856 A164 120k Cinhanga 45 45
857 A164 210k Kalewa 80 80
Nos. 854-857 (4) 1.83 1.83

Inauguration of Express Mail Service A174

1992, Dec. 14 Litho. *Perf. 12x11½*

858 A174 450k Truck 1.05 1.05
859 A174 550k Airplane 1.25 1.25

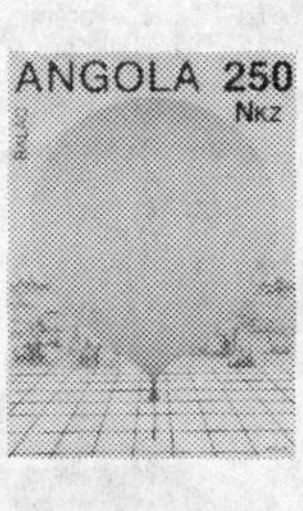

Meteorological Instruments — A175

1993, Mar. 23 Litho. *Perf. 11½x12*

860 A175 250k Weather balloon 58 58
861 A175 470k Actinometer 1.10 1.10
862 A175 500k Rain gauge 1.15 1.15
Nos. 860-862 (3) 2.83 2.83

Seashells A176

1993, Apr. 6 *Perf. 12x11½*

863 A176 210k Trochita trochiformis 48 48
864 A176 330k Strombus latus 75 75
865 A176 400k Aporrhais pesgallinae 95 95
866 A176 500k Fusos aff. albinus 1.15 1.15
Nos. 863-866 (4) 3.33 3.33

Souvenir Sheet

867 A176 1000k Pusionella nifat 2.30 2.30

Quioca Art Type of 1992

1993, June 7 Litho. *Perf. 12*

868 A164 72k Men with vehicles 15 15
869 A164 210k Cavalier 45 45
870 A164 420k Airplane 90 90
871 A164 600k Men carrying stretcher 1.25 1.25
Nos. 868-871 (4) 2.75 2.75

Flowering Plants — A177

1993, June 28 *Perf. 11½x12*

872 A177 360k Sansevieria cylindrica 75 75
873 A177 400k Euphorbia tirucalli 85 85
874 A177 500k Opuntia ficus-indica 1.05 1.05
875 A177 600k Dracaena aubryana 1.25 1.25
Nos. 872-875 (4) 3.90 3.90

Souvenir Sheet

Africa Day — A178

1993, May 31 *Perf. 12*

876 A178 1500k Leopard 3.15 3.15

Tribal Pipes — A179

1993, Aug. 16 Litho. *Perf. 11½x12*

877 A179 72k Vimbundi 15 15
878 A179 200k Vimbundi, diff. 42 42
879 A179 420k Mutopa 88 88
880 A179 600k Pexi 1.25 1.25
Nos. 877-880 (4) 2.70 2.70

Souvenir Sheet

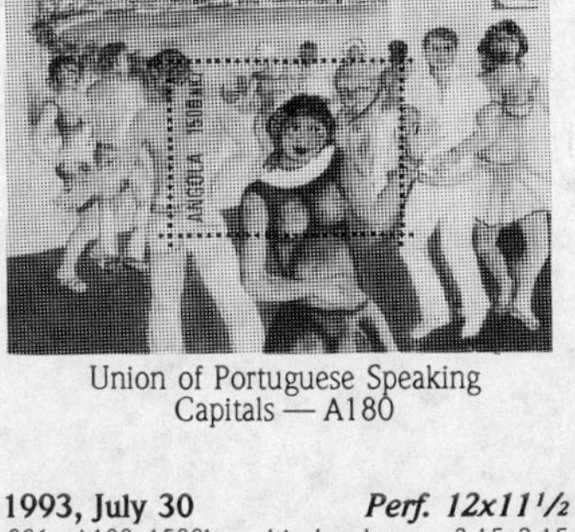

Union of Portuguese Speaking Capitals — A180

1993, July 30 *Perf. 12x11½*

881 A180 1500k multicolored 3.15 3.15

Turtles — A181

Designs: a, 180k, Chelonia mydas (b). b, 450k, Eretmochelys imbricata. c, 550k, Dermochelys coriacea. d, 630k, Caretta caretta.

1993, July 9 Litho. *Perf. 12½x12*

882 A181 Block of 4, #a.-d. 3.50 3.50

Quioca Art Type of 1992

1993, Sept. 1 Litho. *Perf. 12*

883 A164 300k Leopard 65 65
884 A164 600k Malhado 1.25 1.25
885 A164 800k Birds 1.65 1.65
886 A164 1000k Chickens 2.00 2.00
Nos. 883-886 (4) 5.55 5.55

Mushrooms — A182

A183

1993 Litho. *Perf. 12*

887 A182 300k Tricholoma georgii 55 55
 a. Perf. 11½ vert. 55 55
888 A182 500k Amanita phalloides 95 95
 a. Perf. 11½ vert. 95 95
889 A182 600k Amanita vaginata 1.10 1.10
 a. Perf. 11½ vert. 1.10 1.10
890 A182 1000k Macrolepiota procera 1.90 1.90
 a. Perf. 11½ vert. 1.90 1.90
 b. Booklet pane of 4, #887a-890a 4.50
Nos. 887-890 (4) 4.50 4.50

1994, Jan. 10 Litho. *Perf. 12*

Natl. Culture Day: 500k, Cinganji, wood carving of dancer. 1000k, Ohunya yo soma, staff with woman's face. 1200k, Ongende, sculpture of man on donkey. 2200k, Upi, corn pestle.

891 A183 500k multicolored 45 45
892 A183 1000k multicolored 90 90
893 A183 1200k multicolored 1.10 1.10
894 A183 2200k multicolored 2.00 2.00
Nos. 891-894 (4) 4.45 4.45

Hong Kong '94.

Quioca Art Type of 1992

1994, Feb. 21 Litho. *Perf. 12*

895 A164 500k Bird on flower 32 32
896 A164 2000k Plant with roots 1.30 1.30
897 A164 2500k Feto 1.65 1.65
898 A164 3000k Plant 2.00 2.00
Nos. 895-898 (4) 5.27 5.27

Social Responsibilities of AIDS — A184

Designs: 500k, Mass of people. 1000k, Witchdoctor receiving AIDS through needle, people being educated. 3000k, Stylized man, woman.

1994, May 5 Litho. *Perf. 12*

899 A184 500k multicolored 32 32
900 A184 1000k multicolored 65 65
901 A184 3000k multicolored 2.00 2.00
Nos. 899-901 (3) 2.97 2.97

1994 World Cup Soccer Championships, US — A185

1994, June 17 *Perf. 14*

902 A185 500k Large arrows, small ball 32 32
903 A185 700k Small arrows, large ball 45 45
904 A185 2200k Ball in goal 1.50 1.50
905 A185 2500k Ball, foot 1.65 1.65
Nos. 902-905 (4) 3.92 3.92

Dinosaurs A186

1994, Aug. 16 Litho. *Perf. 12*

906 A186 1000k Brachiosaurus 15 15
907 A186 3000k Spinosaurus 55 55
908 A186 5000k Ouranosaurus 90 90
909 A186 10,000k Lesothosaurus 1.90 1.90
Nos. 906-909 (4) 3.50 3.50

Souvenir Sheet

910 A186 19,000k Lesothosaurus, map of Africa 3.50 3.50

PHILAKOREA '94, SINGPEX '94. No. 910 contains one 44x34mm stamp.

Tourism A187

1994 Litho. *Perf. 12x11½*

911 A187 2000k Birds 18 18
912 A187 4000k Wild animals 35 35
913 A187 8000k Native women 75 75
914 A187 10,000k Native men 90 90
Nos. 911-914 (4) 2.18 2.18

Post Boxes — A188

Designs: 5000k, Letters, bundled mail wall box. 7500k, Wall box for letters. 10,000k, Pillar box. 21,000k, Multi-function units.

1994 *Perf. 14½*

915 A188 5000k multicolored 45 45
916 A188 7500k multicolored 70 70
917 A188 10,000k multicolored 90 90
918 A188 21,000k multicolored 1.90 1.90
Nos. 915-918 (4) 3.95 3.95

Cotton Pests — A189

Insects: 5000k, Heliothis armigera. 6000k, Bemisia tabasi. 10,000k, Dysdercus. 27,000k, Spodoptera exigua.

1994 Litho. *Perf. 14*

919	A189	5000k	multicolored	45	45
920	A189	6000k	multicolored	55	55
921	A189	10,000k	multicolored	95	95
922	A189	27,000k	multicolored	2.50	2.50
			Nos. 919-922 (4)	4.45	4.45

Intl. Olympic Committee, Cent. — A190

1994

923	A190	27,000k	multicolored	2.75	2.75

SEMI-POSTAL STAMPS

Angolan Red Cross — SP1

1991, Sept. 19 Litho. *Perf. 14*

B1	SP1	20k +5k	Mother and child	85	85
B2	SP1	40k +5k	Zebra and foal	1.50	1.50

AIR POST STAMPS

Common Design Type

Perf. 13½x13

1938, July 26 Engr. Unwmk.

Name and Value in Black

C1	CD39	10c	scarlet	15	15
C2	CD39	20c	purple	25	15
C3	CD39	50c	orange	15	15
C4	CD39	1a	ultra	38	15
C5	CD39	2a	lilac brn	85	15
C6	CD39	3a	dk green	2.25	25
C7	CD39	5a	red brown	3.25	35
C8	CD39	9a	rose carmine	4.25	1.10
C9	CD39	10a	magenta	5.50	1.10
			Nos. C1-C9 (9)	17.03	3.55

No. C7 exists with overprint "Exposicao Internacional de Nova York, 1939-1940" and Trylon and Perisphere.

AP2

Planes Circling Globe — AP3

1947, Aug. Litho. *Perf. 10½*

C10	AP2	1a	red brown	6.25	1.65
C11	AP2	2a	yellow grn	6.25	1.65
C12	AP2	3a	orange	8.00	1.65
C13	AP2	3.50a	orange	10.00	4.00
C14	AP2	5a	olive grn	90.00	10.00
C15	AP2	6a	rose	90.00	12.00
C16	AP2	9a	red	275.00	140.00
C17	AP2	10a	green	175.00	40.00
C18	AP2	20a	blue	175.00	40.00
C19	AP2	50a	black	300.00	150.00
C20	AP2	100a	yellow	575.00	450.00
			Nos. C10-C20 (11)	1,710.	850.95

1949, May 1 Photo. *Perf. 11½*

C21	AP3	1a	henna brown	15	15
C22	AP3	2a	red brown	40	15
C23	AP3	3a	plum	65	15
C24	AP3	6a	dull green	2.00	40
C25	AP3	9a	violet brown	3.00	1.00
			Nos. C21-C25 (5)	6.20	1.85

Catalogue values for unused stamps in this section, from this point to the end of the section, are for Never Hinged items.

Cambambe Dam — AP4

Designs: 1.50e, Oil refinery, vert. 3e, Salazar Dam. 4e, Capt. Teófilo Duarte Dam. 4.50e, Craveiro Lopes Dam. 5e, Cuango Dam. 6e, Quanza River Bridge. 7e, Capt. Teófilo Duarte Bridge. 8.50e, Oliveira Salazar Bridge. 12.50e, Capt. Silva Carvalho Bridge.

Perf. 11½x12, 12x11½

1965, July 12 Litho. Unwmk.

C26	AP4	1.50e	multicolored	1.00	15
C27	AP4	2.50e	multicolored	60	15
C28	AP4	3e	multicolored	1.00	15
C29	AP4	4e	multicolored	40	15
C30	AP4	4.50e	multicolored	40	15
C31	AP4	5e	multicolored	65	20
C32	AP4	6e	multicolored	65	20
C33	AP4	7e	multicolored	1.00	20
C34	AP4	8.50e	multicolored	1.25	55
C35	AP4	12.50e	multicolored	1.50	65
			Nos. C26-C35 (10)	8.45	2.55

Stamp Centenary Type

Design: 2.50e, Boeing 707 jet & Angola #2.

1970, Dec. 1 Litho. *Perf. 13½*

C36	A83	2.50e	multicolored	45	15
a.			Souv. sheet of 3, #565-566, C36	2.50	2.50

No. C36a sold for 15e.

No. C36 Overprinted with Bar and: "REPUBLICA POPULAR / DE"

1980, June 15 Litho. *Perf. 13½*

C37	A83	2.50e	multicolored	15	

POSTAGE DUE STAMPS

D1

D2

1904 Unwmk. Typo. *Perf. 11½x12*

J1	D1	5r	yellow grn	25	15
J2	D1	10r	slate	25	15
J3	D1	20r	yellow brn	35	32
J4	D1	30r	orange	60	60
J5	D1	50r	gray brown	60	60
J6	D1	60r	red brown	4.00	2.50
J7	D1	100r	lilac	1.75	1.65
J8	D1	130r	dull blue	1.75	1.65
J9	D1	200r	carmine	4.00	3.00
J10	D1	500r	gray violet	4.00	3.00
			Nos. J1-J10 (10)	17.55	13.62

Postage Due Stamps of 1904 Overprinted in Carmine or Green

REPUBLICA

1911

J11	D1	5r	yellow grn	20	20
J12	D1	10r	slate	20	20
J13	D1	20r	yellow brn	20	20
J14	D1	30r	orange	30	30
J15	D1	50r	gray brown	30	30
J16	D1	60r	red brown	60	60
J17	D1	100r	lilac	60	60
J18	D1	130r	dull blue	60	60
J19	D1	200r	carmine (G)	60	60
J20	D1	500r	gray violet	70	70
			Nos. J11-J20 (10)	4.30	4.30

1921 *Perf. 11½*

J21	D2	½c	yellow green	15	15
J22	D2	1c	slate	15	15
J23	D2	2c	orange brown	15	15
J24	D2	3c	orange	15	15
J25	D2	5c	gray brown	15	15
J26	D2	6c	lt brown	15	15
J27	D2	10c	red violet	15	15
J28	D2	13c	dull blue	20	20
J29	D2	20c	carmine	20	20
J30	D2	50c	gray	20	20
			Set value	1.15	1.15

For surcharges see Nos. 268-270.

Catalogue values for unused stamps in this section, from this point to the end of the section, are for Never Hinged items.

Stamps of 1932 Surcharged in Black

= =
PORTEADO
10
Centavos

1948 Wmk. 232 *Perf. 12x11½*

J31	A14	10c	on 20c gray	20	20
J32	A14	20c	on 30c myrtle grn	20	20
J33	A14	30c	on 50c lt brown	45	45
J34	A14	40c	on 1a claret	45	45
J35	A14	50c	on 2a dull vio	90	45
J36	A14	1a	on 5a pale yel grn	1.25	1.00
			Nos. J31-J36 (6)	3.45	2.75

Common Design Type

Photogravure and Typographed

1952 Unwmk. *Perf. 14*

Numeral in Red, Frame Multicolored

J37	CD45	10c	red brown	15	15
J38	CD45	30c	olive green	15	15
J39	CD45	50c	chocolate	15	15
J40	CD45	1a	dk vio blue	15	15
J41	CD45	2a	red brown	20	20
J42	CD45	5a	black brown	32	32
			Set value	92	92

NEWSPAPER STAMP

N1

Perf. 11½, 12½, 13½

1893 Typo. Unwmk.

P1	N1	2½r	brown	1.00	70

No. P1 was also used for ordinary postage. For surcharges see Nos. 37, 82, 180, 235.

POSTAL TAX STAMPS

Pombal Issue

Common Design Types

1925, May 8 Unwmk. *Perf. 12½*

RA1	CD28	15c	lilac & black	32	25
RA2	CD29	15c	lilac & black	32	25
RA3	CD30	15c	lilac & black	32	25
			Nos. RA1-RA3 (3)	96	75

"Charity" PT1

Coat of Arms PT2

1929 Litho. *Perf. 11*

Without Gum

RA4	PT1	50c	dark blue	2.00	70

1939 Without Gum *Perf. 10½*

RA5	PT2	50c	turq green	1.75	15
RA6	PT2	1a	red	3.25	1.50

A 1.50a, type PT2, was issued for fiscal use.

Catalogue values for unused stamps in this section, from this point to the end of the section, are for Never Hinged items.

Old Man — PT3

Mother and Child — PT4

Designs: 1e, Boy. 1.50e, Girl.

Imprint: "Foto-Lito-E.G.A.-Luanda"

1955 Unwmk. *Perf. 13*

Heads in dark brown

RA7	PT3	50c	dk ocher	15	15
RA8	PT3	1e	orange ver	75	40
RA9	PT3	1.50e	brt yel grn	50	25
			Nos. RA7-RA9 (3)	1.40	80

A 2.50e, type PT3 showing an old woman, was issued for revenue use.

See Nos. RA16, RA19-RA21, RA25-RA27.

No. RA7 Surcharged with New Values and two Bars in Red or Black

1957-58

Head in dark brown

RA11	PT3	10c	on 50c dk ocher (R)	25	25
RA12	PT3	10c	on 50c dk ocher ('58)	20	20
RA13	PT3	30c	on 50c dk ocher	22	22
			Nos. RA11-RA13 (3)	67	67

1959 Litho. *Perf. 13*

Design: 30c, Boy and girl.

RA14	PT4	10c	orange & blk	15	15
RA15	PT4	30c	slate & blk	15	15
			Set value	24	24

Type of 1955 Redrawn

Design: 1e, Boy.

1961, Nov. *Perf. 13*

RA16	PT3	1e	sal pink & dk brn	20	20

Denomination in italics.

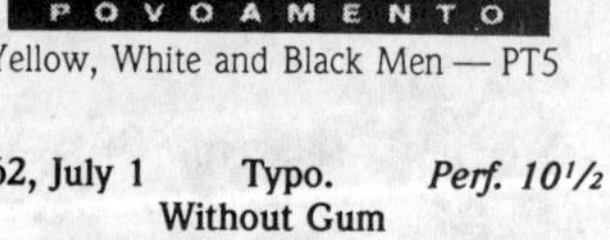

Yellow, White and Black Men — PT5

1962, July 1 Typo. *Perf. 10½*

Without Gum

RA17	PT5	50c	multicolored	65	65
RA18	PT5	1e	multicolored	32	32

Issued for the Provincial Settlement Committee (Junta Provincial do Povoamento). The tax was used to promote Portuguese settlement in Angola, and to raise educational and living standards of recent immigrants.

Denominations higher than 1e were used for revenue purposes.

Head Type of 1955
Without Imprint

Designs: 50c, Old man. 1e, Boy. 1.50e, Girl.

1964-65 Litho. *Perf. 11½*

Heads in dark brown

RA19	PT3	50c orange	15	15
RA20	PT3	1e dull red org ('65)	20	20
RA21	PT3	1.50e yel grn ('65)	25	25
		Nos. RA19-RA21 (3)	60	60

No. RA20 is second redrawing of 1e, with bolder lettering and denomination in gothic. Space between "Assistencia" and denomination on RA19-RA21 is ½mm; on 1955 issue space is 2mm.

Map of Angola, Industrial and Farm Workers — PT6

1965, Sept. 1 Litho. *Perf. 13*

RA22	PT6	50c multicolored	35	15
RA23	PT6	1e multicolored	35	25

The 2e was used for revenue purposes.

Head Type of 1955
Imprint: "I.N.A." or "INA" (1e)

Designs: 50c, Old man. 1e, Boy. 1.50e, Girl.

1966

Heads in dark brown

RA25	PT3	50c dull orange	15	15
RA26	PT3	1e dull brick red	15	15
RA27	PT3	1.50e lt yel grn	32	15
		Nos. RA25-RA27 (3)	62	
		Set value		32

Woman Planting Tree — PT7

1972 Litho. *Perf. 13*

RA28	PT7	50c shown	15	15
RA29	PT7	1e Workers	15	15
RA30	PT7	2e Produce	20	20
		Set value	39	39

POSTAL TAX DUE STAMPS

Pombal Issue
Common Design Types

1925, May 8 Unwmk. *Perf. 12½*

RAJ1	CD31	30c lilac & black	50	*1.25*
RAJ2	CD32	30c lilac & black	50	*1.25*
RAJ3	CD33	30c lilac & black	50	*1.25*
		Nos. RAJ1-RAJ3 (3)	1.50	

See note after Portugal No. RAJ4.

ANGRA

LOCATION — An administrative district of the Azores, consisting of the islands of Terceira, Sao Jorge and Graciosa.
GOVT. — A district of Portugal
AREA — 275 sq. mi.
POP. — 70,000 (approx.)
CAPITAL — Angra do Heroismo

1000 Reis = 1 Milreis

King Carlos
A1 A2

Perf. 11½, 12½, 13½

1892-93 Typo. Unwmk.

1	A1	5r yellow	1.25	85
a.		Perf. 11½	4.00	2.00
2	A1	10r redsh vio	1.75	1.10
3	A1	15r chocolate	2.50	1.50
4	A1	20r lavender	3.50	1.50
a.		Perf. 13½	5.50	1.65
5	A1	25r green	2.25	15
a.		Perf. 12½	7.00	50
7	A1	50r blue	7.00	1.50
a.		Perf. 13½	7.00	3.25
8	A1	75r carmine	9.00	2.75
9	A1	80r yel grn	7.00	4.00
10	A1	100r brn, *yel*, perf. 13½ ('93)	22.50	10.00
a.		Perf. 12½	82.50	65.00
11	A1	150r car, *rose* ('93)	25.00	15.00
12	A1	200r dk bl, *bl* ('93)	27.50	22.50
13	A1	300r dk bl, *sal* ('93)	27.50	22.50

Reprints of 50r, 150r, 200r and 300r, made in 1900, are perf. 11½ and ungummed. Value, each $7.50. Reprints of all values, made in 1905, have shiny white gum and clean-cut perf. 13½.

1897-1905 *Perf. 11½*

Name and Value in Black except Nos. 26 and 35

14	A2	2½r gray	20	15
15	A2	5r orange	20	15
a.		Diagonal half used as 2½r on cover		*12.50*
16	A2	10r yel green	20	15
17	A2	15r brown	5.50	1.75
18	A2	15r gray grn ('99)	85	45
19	A2	20r gray vio	1.40	30
20	A2	25r sea green	1.00	25
21	A2	25r car rose ('99)	60	15
22	A2	50r dark blue	3.50	60
23	A2	50r ultra ('05)	12.50	8.00
24	A2	65r slate bl ('98)	30	20
25	A2	75r rose	1.25	50
26	A2	75r gray brn & car, *straw* ('05)	14.00	17.50
27	A2	80r violet	42	30
28	A2	100r dk bl, *bl*	1.50	40
29	A2	115r org brn, *pink* ('98)	1.00	60
30	A2	130r gray brn, *straw* ('98)	1.00	60
31	A2	150r lt brn, *straw*	1.00	55
32	A2	180r sl, *pnksh* ('98)	1.50	85
33	A2	200r red vio, *pnksh*	3.00	1.50
34	A2	300r blue, *rose*	5.50	2.75
35	A2	500r blk & red, *bl*	11.00	5.25
a.		Perf. 12½	14.00	9.25
		Nos. 14-35 (22)	67.42	42.95

Azores stamps were used in Angra from 1906 to 1931, when they were superseded by those of Portugal.

ANJOUAN

LOCATION — One of the Comoro Islands in the Mozambique Channel between Madagascar and Mozambique.
GOVT. — Former French colony.
AREA — 89 sq. mi.
POP. — 20,000 (approx. 1912)
CAPITAL — Mossamondu
See Comoro Islands.

100 Centimes = 1 Franc

Navigation and Commerce — A1

Perf. 14x13½

1892-1907 Typo. Unwmk.

Name of Colony in Blue or Carmine

1	A1	1c black, *blue*	75	75
2	A1	2c brown, *buff*	1.10	1.00
3	A1	4c claret, *lav*	1.25	1.10
4	A1	5c green, *grnsh*	3.00	2.00
5	A1	10c blk, *lavender*	3.00	2.25
6	A1	10c red ('00)	7.50	6.00
7	A1	15c blue, quadrille paper	3.75	2.75
8	A1	15c gray, *lt gray* ('00)	5.75	4.50
9	A1	20c red, *green*	3.75	2.75
10	A1	25c black, *rose*	4.25	3.50
11	A1	25c blue ('00)	6.25	6.25
12	A1	30c brn, *bister*	8.50	6.75
13	A1	35c blk, *yel* ('06)	4.50	3.50
14	A1	40c red, *straw*	13.50	11.00
15	A1	45c blk, *gray grn* ('07)	62.50	52.50
16	A1	50c car, *rose*	16.00	11.00
17	A1	50c brn, *az* ('00)	11.00	7.50
18	A1	75c vio, *orange*	15.00	11.00
19	A1	1fr brnz grn, *straw*	32.50	32.50
		Nos. 1-19 (19)	203.85	168.60

Perf. 13½x14 stamps are counterfeits.

Issues of 1892-1907 Surcharged in Black or Carmine **05 10**

1912

20	A1	5c on 2c brn, *buff*	38	38
21	A1	5c on 4c cl, *lav* (C)	38	38
22	A1	5c on 15c blue (C)	38	38
23	A1	5c on 20c red, *green*	38	38
24	A1	5c on 25c blk, *rose* (C)	38	38
25	A1	5c on 30c brn, *bis* (C)	38	38
26	A1	10c on 40c red, *straw*	55	55
27	A1	10c on 45c black, *gray green* (C)	75	75
28	A1	10c on 50c car, *rose*	1.40	1.40
29	A1	10c on 75c vio, *org*	95	95
30	A1	10c on 1fr brnz grn, *straw*	1.10	1.10
		Nos. 20-30 (11)	7.03	7.03

Nos. 21-23, 30 exist in pairs, one without surcharge. Value, $225 each.

Two spacings between the surcharged numerals are found on Nos. 20-30.

Nos. 20-30 were available for use in Madagascar and the Comoro archipelago.

The stamps of Anjouan were superseded by those of Madagascar, and in 1950 by those of Comoro Islands.

ANNAM AND TONKIN

LOCATION — In French Indo-China bordering on the China Sea on the east and Siam on the west.
GOVT. — French Protectorate
AREA — 97,503 sq. mi.
POP. — 14,124,000 (approx. 1890)
CAPITAL — Annam: Hue; Tonkin: Hanoi

For administrative purposes, the Protectorates of Annam, Tonkin, Cambodia, Laos and the Colony of Cochin-China were grouped together and were known as French Indo-China.

100 Centimes = 1 Franc

Stamps of French Colonies, 1881-86 Surcharged in Black:

A & T 1 **A & T 5**

1888 Unwmk. *Perf. 14x13½*

1	A9	1c on 2c brn, *buff*	15.00	13.00
a.		Inverted surcharge	55.00	55.00
2	A9	1c on 4c claret, *lav*	11.00	10.00
a.		Inverted surcharge	55.00	55.00
3	A9	5c on 10c blk, *lav*	12.00	11.00
a.		Inverted surcharge	55.00	55.00

Hyphen between "A" and "T"

7	A9	1c on 2c brn, *buff*	135.00	135.00
8	A9	1c on 4c claret, *lav*	210.00	200.00
9	A9	5c on 10c blk, *lav*	110.00	110.00

A 5c on 2c was prepared but not issued.

In these surcharges there are different types of numerals and letters.

These stamps were superseded in 1892 by those of Indo-China.

ARGENTINA

LOCATION — In South America
GOVT. — Republic
AREA — 1,084,120 sq. mi.
POP. — 27,949,480 (1980)
CAPITAL — Buenos Aires

100 Centavos = 1 Peso

Watermarks

Wmk. 84- Italic RA

Wmk. 85- Small Sun, 4½mm

Wmk. 86- Large Sun, 6mm

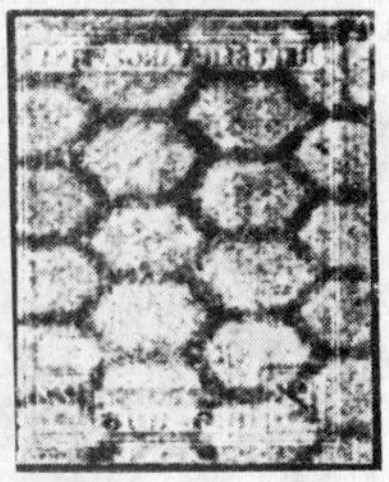

Wmk. 87- Honeycomb

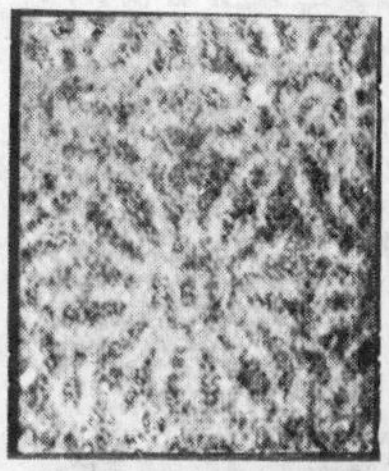

Wmk. 88- Multiple Suns

Wmk. 89- Large Sun

In this watermark the face of the sun is 7mm in diameter, the rays are heavier than in the large sun watermark of 1896-1911 and the watermarks are placed close together, so that parts of several frequently appear on one stamp. This paper was intended to be used for fiscal stamps and is usually referred to as "fiscal sun paper."

Wmk. 90- RA in Sun

In 1928 watermark 90 was slightly modified, making the diameter of the Sun 9mm instead of 10mm. Several types of this watermark exist.

Wmk. 205- AP in Oval

The letters "AP" are the initials of "AHORRO POSTAL." This paper was formerly used exclusively for Postal Savings stamps.

Wmk. 287- Double Circle and Letters in Sheet

Wmk. 288- RA in Sun with Straight Rays

Wmk. 365- Argentine Arms, "Casa de Moneda de la Nacion" & "RA" Multiple

Argentine Confederation

Symbolical of the Argentine Confederation
A1 A2

1858, May 1 Unwmk. Litho. *Imperf.*

1	A1	5c red	1.40	*8.50*
a.		Colon after "5"	1.10	*11.00*
b.		Colon after "V"	1.10	*11.00*
2	A1	10c green	2.25	*47.50*
a.		Half used as 5c on cover		*190.00*
3	A1	15c blue	14.00	*125.00*
a.		One-third used as 5c on cover		*3,500.*
		Nos. 1-3 (3)	17.65	

1860, Jan.

4	A2	5c red	3.00	*62.50*
4A	A2	10c green	6.50	
4B	A2	15c blue	25.00	
		Nos. 4-4B (3)	34.50	

Nos. 4A and 4B were never placed in use. There are nine varieties of Nos. 1, 2 and 3, sixteen of No. 4 and eight of Nos. 4A and 4B. Counterfeits and forged cancellations of Nos. 1-4B are plentiful.

> Values for Unused
> Unused values for Nos. 5-15, 17-67 are for copies without gum. Copies with original gum command higher prices. From No. 68 onward, unused values are for stamps with original gum.

Argentine Republic

Seal of the Republic — A3

Broad "C" in "CENTAVOS," Accent on "U" of "REPUBLICA"

1862, Jan. 11

5	A3	5c rose	40.00	37.50
a.		5c rose lilac	87.50	35.00
6	A3	10c green	140.00	65.00
b.		Diagonal half used as 5c on cover		*4,250.*
7	A3	15c blue	275.00	225.00
a.		Without accent on "U"	*5,500.*	*2,400.*
b.		Tete beche pair	*45,000.*	*27,500.*
i.		15c ultramarine	425.00	325.00

Broad "C" in "CENTAVOS," No Accent on "U"

1863

7C	A3	5c rose	18.00	21.00
d.		5c rose lilac	100.00	110.00
e.		Worn plate	200.00	52.50
7F	A3	10c yellow green	350.00	140.00
g.		10c olive green	*500.00*	250.00

Narrow "C" in "CENTAVOS," No Accent on "U"

1864

7H	A3	5c rose red	160.00	32.50

The so-called reprints of 10c and 15c are counterfeits. They have narrow "C" and straight lines in shield. Nos. 7C and 7H have been extensively counterfeited.

Rivadavia Issue

Bernardino Rivadavia
A4 A5

Rivadavia — A6

1864-67 Engr. Wmk. 84 *Imperf.*
Clear Impressions

8	A4	5c brown rose	*1,300.*	*160.*
a.		5c orange red ('67)	*1,500.*	*110.*
9	A5	10c green	*1,500.*	*900.*
10	A6	15c blue	*7,250.*	*3,000.*

Perf. 11½
Dull to Worn Impressions

11	A4	5c brown rose ('65)	30.00	12.00
11B	A4	5c lake	77.50	17.50
12	A5	10c green	70.00	30.00
a.		Diagonal half used as 5c on cover		*750.00*
13	A6	15c blue	140.00	60.00

1867-72 Unwmk. *Imperf.*

14	A4	5c carmine ('72)	225.	55.
15	A4	5c rose	200.	100.
15A	A5	10c green	*4,000.*	*4,000.*
16	A6	15c blue	*1,750.*	*1,750.*

Nos. 15A-16 issued without gum.

1867 *Perf. 11½*

17	A4	5c carmine	350.00	150.00

Nos. 14, 15 and 17 exist with part of papermaker's wmk. "LACROIX FRERES."

Rivadavia
A7

Manuel Belgrano
A8

Jose de San Martin — A9

Groundwork of Horizontal Lines

1867-68 *Perf. 12*

18	A7	5c vermilion	200.00	9.00
18A	A8	10c green	30.00	4.50
b.		Diag. half used as 5c on cover		*525.00*
19	A9	15c blue	45.00	13.00

Groundwork of Crossed Lines

20	A7	5c vermilion	10.50	65
21	A9	15c blue	92.50	10.50

See Nos. 27, 33-34, 39 and types A19, A33, A34, A37. For surcharges and overprints see Nos. 30-32, 41-42, 47-51, O6-O7, O26.

Gen. Antonio G. Balcarce
A10

Mariano Moreno
A11

Carlos Maria de Alvear — A12

Gervasio Antonio Posadas — A13

Cornelio Saavedra — A14

1873

22	A10	1c purple	3.50	2.00
a.		1c gray violet	6.25	2.00
23	A11	4c brown	4.75	38
a.		4c red brown	17.00	2.00
24	A12	30c orange	100.00	15.00
25	A13	60c black	100.00	4.75
26	A14	90c blue	25.00	2.25

For overprints see Nos. O5, O12-O14, O19-O21, O25, O29.

1873

Laid Paper

27	A8	10c green	150.00	16.00

Nos.18, 18A Surcharged in Black

Nos. 30-31

No. 32

1877, Feb.

Wove Paper

30	A7	1c on 5c vermilion	47.50	15.00
a.		Inverted surcharge	350.00	200.00
31	A7	2c on 5c vermilion	92.50	60.00
a.		Inverted surcharge	700.00	500.00
32	A8	8c on 10c green	125.00	30.00
b.		Inverted surcharge	500.00	425.00

Forgeries of these surcharges include the inverted and double varieties.

1876-77 *Rouletted*

33	A7	5c vermilion	150.00	60.00
34	A7	8c lake ('77)	25.00	32

Belgrano
A17

Dalmacio Vélez Sarsfield
A18

San Martín — A19

1878 *Rouletted*

35	A17	16c green	8.00	1.10
36	A18	20c blue	8.50	3.00
37	A19	24c blue	17.00	3.00
		Nos. 35-37 (3)	33.50	7.10

See No. 56. For overprints see Nos. O9-O10, O15-O17, O22, O28.

Vicente Lopez — A20

Alvear — A21

1877-80 *Perf. 12*

38	A20	2c yellow green	4.25	90
39	A7	8c lake ('80)	4.25	32
a.		8c brown lake	*27.50*	32
40	A21	25c lake ('78)	22.50	6.00
		Nos. 38-40 (3)	31.00	7.22

For overprints see Nos. O4, O11, O18, O24.

No. 18 Surcharged in Black

½

(PROVISORIO

1882

41	A7	½c on 5c ver	90	80
a.		Double surcharge	25.00	14.00
b.		Inverted surcharge	17.50	14.00
c.		"PROVISORIO" omitted	35.00	35.00
d.		Fraction omitted	25.00	
e.		"PROVISORIO"	8.75	8.75
f.		Pair, one without surcharge	87.50	

Perforated across Middle of Stamp

42	A7	½c on 5c ver	2.00	2.00
a.		"PROVISORIO"	12.00	12.00

The "½ (PROVISORIO)" surcharge on Nos. 41-42 is found in two types: I - Small "P" and narrow "V." II - Large "P" and wider "V."

A23

1882 Typo. *Perf. 12*

43	A23	½c brown	1.40	80
a.		Imperf., pair	25.00	25.00
44	A23	1c red, perf. 14	3.50	1.00
a.		Perf. 12	9.00	4.25
45	A23	12c ultra	55.00	8.75
a.		Perf. 14	45.00	8.75
46	A23	12c grnsh blue, perf. 14	125.00	11.00

See type A29. For overprints see Nos. O2, O8, O23, O27.

No. 21 Surcharged in Red:

1884 ½ — a

1 C 1884 — b

CUATRO Centavos 1884 — c

1884 Engr. *Perf. 12*

47	A9 (a)	½c on 15c blue	1.90	1.50
a.		Groundwork of horiz. lines	62.50	50.00
b.		Inverted surcharge	15.00	10.50
48	A9 (b)	1c on 15c blue	9.50	8.50
a.		Groundwork of horiz. lines	6.25	5.00
b.		Inverted surcharge	42.50	35.00
c.		Double surcharge	16.00	14.00
d.		Triple surcharge	325.00	

Nos. 20-21 Surcharged in Black

49	A7 (a)	½c on 5c ver	2.50	2.25
a.		Inverted surcharge	87.50	70.00
b.		Date omitted	32.50	
c.		Pair, one without surch.	110.00	
50	A9 (a)	½c on 15c blue	7.00	6.50
a.		Groundwork of horiz. lines	22.50	17.50
b.		Inverted surcharge	22.50	21.00
51	A7 (c)	4c on 5c ver	8.75	5.00
a.		Inverted surcharge	14.00	10.50
b.		Double surcharge	250.00	150.00
c.		Pair, one without surcharge but with "4" in manuscript	190.00	100.00
		Nos. 47-51 (5)	29.65	23.75

A29

1884-85 Engr. *Perf. 12*

52	A29	½c red brown	90	42
a.		Imperf., pair	45.00	
53	A29	1c rose red	5.25	42
a.		Imperf., pair	45.00	
54	A29	12c grnsh blue ('85)	25.00	1.25
a.		12c deep blue	25.00	1.25
b.		Imperf., pair	45.00	
		Nos. 52-54 (3)	31.15	2.09

For overprints see Nos. O1, O3, O9.

San Martin Type of 1878

1887 Engr.

56	A19	24c blue	17.50	1.40

Justo Jose de Urquiza A30

Lopez A31

Miguel Juarez Celman — A32

Rivadavia (Large head) — A33

Rivadavia (Small head) A34

Domingo F. Sarmiento A35

Nicolas Avellaneda A36

San Martin A37

Julio A. Roca A37a

Belgrano A37b

Manuel Dorrego — A38

Moreno — A39

Bartolome Mitre — A40

CINCO CENTAVOS.
A33 - Shows collar on left side only.
A34 - Shows collar on both sides. Lozenges in background larger and clearer than in A33.

1888-90 Litho. *Perf. 11½*

57	A30	½c blue	50	45
58	A31	2c yellow green	9.25	6.00
59	A32	3c blue green	1.75	60
b.		Horiz. pair, imperf. vert.	25.00	
c.		Horiz. pair, imperf. btwn.	27.50	
d.		Vert. pair, imperf. btwn.	10.50	
60	A33	5c carmine	10.50	1.90
61	A34	5c carmine	8.00	60
b.		Vert. pair, imperf. btwn.	*35.00*	
62	A35	6c red	21.00	15.00
b.		Vert. pair, imperf. btwn.	*35.00*	
c.		Perf. 12	52.50	42.50
63	A36	10c brown	15.00	1.10
64	A37	15c orange	15.00	1.65
64A	A37a	20c green	12.00	1.25
64B	A37b	25c purple	15.00	1.65
65	A38	30c chocolate	21.00	2.50
66	A39	40c slate, perf. 12	21.00	3.00
a.		Perf. 11½	60.00	16.00
67	A40	50c blue	80.00	8.25
		Nos. 57-67 (13)	230.00	43.95

In this issue there are several varieties of each value, the difference between them being in the relative position of the head to the frame.

Imperf., Pairs

57a	A30	½c	35.00	25.00
58a	A31	2c	27.50	
59a	A32	3c	17.50	12.50
61a	A34	5c		*52.50*
62a	A35	6c	*27.50*	
63a	A36	10c	*27.50*	
64c	A37	15c		*110.00*
65a	A38	30c	*140.00*	*110.00*

Urquiza A41

Velez Sarsfield A42

Miguel Juarez Celman A43

Rivadavia (Large head) A44

Sarmiento A45

Juan Bautista Alberdi A46

1888-89 Engr. *Perf. 11½, 11½x12*

68	A41	½c ultra	28	15
a.		Vert. pair, imperf. horiz.	16.00	10.00
b.		Imperf., pair	16.00	10.00
69	A42	1c brown	85	16
a.		Vert. pair, imperf. horiz.	16.00	
b.		Vert. pair, imperf. btwn.	16.00	
c.		Imperf., pair	16.00	
70	A43	3c blue green	2.00	42
71	A44	5c rose	2.75	15
a.		Imperf., pair	22.50	16.00
72	A45	6c blue black	1.40	55
b.		Perf. 11½x12	10.00	2.50
73	A46	12c blue	4.25	1.10
a.		Imperf., pair	13.00	
b.		bluish paper	2.75	80
c.		Perf. 11½	8.25	3.25
		Nos. 68-73 (6)	11.53	2.53

#69-70 exist with papermakers' watermarks.
See No. 77, types A50, A61. For surcharges see Nos. 83-84.

Jose Maria Paz A48

Santiago Derqui A49

Rivadavia (Small head) A50

Avellaneda A51

Moreno A53

Mitre A54

Posadas — A55

1890 Engr. *Perf. 11½*

75	A48	¼c green	15	15
76	A49	2c violet	85	16
a.		2c purple	85	16
b.		2c slate	1.25	28
c.		Horiz. pair, imperf. btwn.	15.00	
d.		Imperf., pair	18.00	
e.		Perf. 11½x12	3.50	28
77	A50	5c carmine	1.90	15
a.		Imperf., pair	40.00	20.00
b.		Perf. 11½x12	1.90	32
78	A51	10c brown	1.65	26
b.		Imperf., pair		100.00
80	A53	40c olive green	4.00	80
a.		Imperf., pair	20.00	
81	A54	50c orange	4.00	80
a.		Imperf., pair	30.00	
b.		Perf. 11½x12	4.25	1.10
82	A55	60c black	15.00	2.75
a.		Imperf., pair	35.00	35.00
		Nos. 75-82 (7)	27.55	5.07

Type A50 differs from type A44 in having the head smaller, the letters of "Cinco Centavos" not as tall, and the curved ornaments at sides close to the first and last letters of "Republica Argentina."

Lithographed Surcharge on No. 73 in Black or Red

1/4

1890 *Perf. 11½x12*

83	A46	¼c on 12c blue	38	32
a.		Perf. 11½	35.00	21.00
84	A46	¼c on 12c blue (R)	38	32
a.		Double surcharge	52.50	52.50
b.		Perf. 11½	7.00	2.00

Surcharge is different on #83 and 84.

Rivadavia A57

Jose de San Martin A58

Gregorio Araoz de Lamadrid — A59

Admiral Guillermo Brown — A60

1891 Engr. *Perf. 11½*

85	A57	8c carmine rose	1.25	22
a.		Imperf., pair	52.50	

86	A58	1p deep blue	40.00	5.50
87	A59	5p ultra	200.00	21.00
88	A60	20p green	275.00	60.00

A 10p brown and a 50p red were prepared but not issued. Values $1,500 and $1,000.

Velez Sarsfield — A61

"Santa Maria," "Nina" and "Pinta" — A62

1890 *Perf. 11½*

89	A61	1c brown	80	24

Type A61 is a re-engraving of A42. The figure "1" in each upper corner has a short horizontal serif instead of a long one pointing downward. In type A61 the first and last letters of "Correos y Telegrafos" are closer to the curved ornaments below than in type A42. Background is of horizontal lines (crosshatching on No. 69).

1892, Oct. 12 Wmk. 85 *Perf. 11½*

90	A62	2c light blue	6.00	3.00
a.		Double impression	190.00	
91	A62	5c dark blue	8.50	5.00

Discovery of America, 400th anniv. Counterfeits of Nos. 90-91 are litho.

Rivadavia A63

Belgrano A64

San Martin — A65

Perf. 11½, 12 and Compound

1892-95 Wmk. 85

92	A63	½c dull blue	18	15
a.		½c bright ultra	25.00	7.00
93	A63	1c brown	35	15
94	A63	2c green	35	15
95	A63	3c orange ('95)	1.00	15
96	A63	5c carmine	1.50	15
b.		5c green (error)	190.00	140.00
98	A64	10c carmine rose	5.50	15
99	A64	12c deep blue ('93)	5.50	22
100	A64	16c gray	10.00	55
101	A64	24c gray brown	10.00	55
b.		Perf. 12	25.00	7.00
102	A64	50c blue green	15.00	55
b.		Perf. 12	25.00	2.75
103	A65	1p lake ('93)	9.00	70
a.		1p red brown	17.50	5.00
104	A65	2p dark green	21.00	2.25
a.		Perf. 12	77.50	27.50
105	A65	5p dark blue	38.00	2.75
		Nos. 92-105 (13)	117.38	8.47

Part-perforate varieties of Nos. 92-98 include vert. or horiz. pairs imperf. between and pairs imperf. vert. or horiz. Value $6-$35.

The high values of this and succeeding issues are frequently punched with the word "INUTILIZADO," parts of the letters showing on each stamp. These punched stamps sell for only a small fraction of the catalogue values.

Reprints of No. 96b have white gum. The original stamp has yellowish gum. Value $125.

Imperf., Pairs

92b	A63	½c	27.50	
93a	A63	1c	27.50	
94a	A63	2c	12.50	
96a	A63	5c	12.50	12.50
98a	A64	10c	32.50	
99a	A64	12c	32.50	
100a	A64	16c	32.50	
101a	A64	24c	32.50	
102a	A64	50c	25.00	
103b	A65	1p	35.00	
105a	A65	5p	70.00	

1896-97 Wmk. 86

106	A63	½c slate	35	15
a.		½c gray blue	35	15
b.		½c indigo	35	15
107	A63	1c brown	35	15
108	A63	2c yellow green	60	15
109	A63	3c orange	60	15
110	A63	5c carmine	60	15
a.		Imperf., pair	18.00	
111	A64	10c carmine rose	5.00	15
112	A64	12c deep blue	2.50	15
a.		Imperf., pair	*27.50*	
113	A64	16c gray	6.00	52
114	A64	24c gray brown	10.50	1.25
a.		Imperf., pair	15.00	
115	A64	30c orange ('97)	7.50	45
116	A64	50c blue green	9.50	45
117	A64	80c dull violet	11.00	60
118	A65	1p lake	16.00	75
119	A65	1p20c black ('97)	8.50	3.50
120	A65	2p dark green	15.00	7.00
121	A65	5p dark blue	75.00	7.00
a.		Perf. 12	165.00	42.50
		Nos. 106-121 (16)	169.00	22.57

Allegory, Liberty Seated

A66 A67

Perf. 11½, 12 and Compound

1899-1903

122	A66	½c yellow brown	15	15
123	A66	1c green	20	15
124	A66	2c slate	20	15
125	A66	3c orange ('01)	85	15
126	A66	4c yellow ('03)	1.50	16
127	A66	5c carmine rose	20	15
128	A66	6c black ('03)	1.00	18
129	A66	10c dark green	1.50	15
130	A66	12c dull blue	1.00	28
131	A66	12c olive grn ('01)	1.00	24
132	A66	15c sea green ('01)	2.75	15
132B	A66	15c dull blue ('01)	3.00	25
133	A66	16c orange	7.50	3.75
134	A66	20c claret	2.00	15
135	A66	24c violet	3.50	70
136	A66	30c rose	7.50	40
137	A66	30c vermilion ('01)	3.75	15
a.		30c scarlet	50.00	2.50
138	A66	50c brt blue	4.75	16
139	A67	1p bl & blk, perf. 11½	14.00	70
a.		Center inverted	*1,500.*	*475.00*
b.		Perf. 12	190.00	47.50
140	A67	5p orange & blk	57.50	9.25
		Punch cancellation		75
a.		Center inverted	*1,700.*	
141	A67	10p green & blk	50.00	9.25
		Punch cancellation		75
a.		Center inverted	*2,400.*	
		Punch cancellation		675.00
142	A67	20p red & black	200.00	27.50
		Punch cancellation		35
a.		Center invtd.(punch cancel)		*2,000.*
		Nos. 122-142 (22)	363.85	54.17

Part-perforate varieties of Nos. 122-129 include vert. or horiz. pairs imperf. between and pairs imperf. vert. or horiz. Value 35 cents to $7.

Imperf., Pairs

122a	A66	½c	17.00	
123a	A66	1c	24.00	
124a	A66	2c	6.00	3.00
125a	A66	3c	95.00	50.00
127a	A66	5c	5.00	3.50
128a	A66	6c	30.00	
129a	A66	10c	30.00	
132a	A66	15c	30.00	

River Port of Rosario A68

1902, Oct. 26 *Perf. 11½, 11½x12*

143	A68	5c deep blue	4.50	2.50
a.		Imperf., pair	95.00	

Completion of port facilities at Rosario.

San Martin

A69 A70

Perf. 13½, 13½x12½

1908-09 Typo.

144	A69	½c violet	15	15
145	A69	1c brnsh buff	18	15
146	A69	2c chocolate	55	15
147	A69	3c green	70	32
148	A69	4c redsh violet	1.40	32
149	A69	5c carmine	32	15
150	A69	6c olive bister	80	25
151	A69	10c gray green	1.50	15
152	A69	12c yellow buff	40	38
153	A69	12c dk blue ('09)	1.25	15
154	A69	15c apple green	1.75	85
155	A69	20c ultra	1.25	15
156	A69	24c red brown	3.25	60
157	A69	30c dull rose	5.00	60
158	A69	50c black	4.75	42
159	A70	1p sl bl & pink	11.00	1.75
		Nos. 144-159 (16)	34.25	6.54

The 1c blue was not issued. Value $250.

Wmk. 86 appears on ½, 1, 6, 20, 24 and 50c. Other values have similar wmk. with wavy rays.

Stamps lacking wmk. are from outer rows printed on sheet margin.

Pyramid of May — A71

Nicolas Rodriguez Pena and Hipolito Vieytes — A72

Meeting at Pena's Home — A73

Designs: 3c, Miguel de Azcuenaga (1754-1833) and Father Manuel M. Alberti (1763-1811). 4c, Viceroy's house and Fort Buenos Aires. 5c, Cornelio Saavedra (1759-1829). 10c, Antonio Luis Beruti (1772-1842) and French distributing badges. 12c, Congress building. 20c, Juan Jose Castelli (1764-1812) and Domingo Matheu (1765-1831). 24c, First council. 30c, Manuel Belgrano (1770-1820) and Juan Larrea (1782-1847). 50c, First meeting of republican government, May 25, 1810. 1p, Mariano Moreno (1778-1811) and Juan Jose Paso (1758-1833). 5p, Oath of the Junta. 10p, Centenary Monument. 20p, Jose Francisco de San Martin (1778-1850).

Inscribed "1810 1910"

Various Frames

1910, May 1 Engr. *Perf. 11½*

160	A71	½c bl & gray bl	32	15
161	A72	1c blue grn & blk	32	15
b.		Horiz. pair, imperf. btwn.	*65.00*	
162	A73	2c olive & gray	22	15
163	A72	3c green	70	15
164	A73	4c dk blue & grn	70	24
165	A71	5c carmine	45	15
166	A73	10c yel brn & blk	1.75	22
167	A73	12c brt blue	1.40	24
168	A72	20c gray brn & blk	3.25	35
169	A73	24c org brn & bl	1.75	90
170	A72	30c lilac & blk	1.75	65
171	A71	50c carmine & blk	4.50	90
172	A72	1p brt blue	10.00	3.50
173	A73	5p orange & vio	70.00	30.00
		Punch cancel		2.50
174	A71	10p orange & blk	90.00	65.00
		Punch cancel		3.00
175	A71	20p dp blue & ind	150.00	90.00
		Punch cancel		4.50
		Nos. 160-175 (16)	337.11	192.75

Centenary of the republic.

Center Inverted

160a	A71	½c	*650.00*	
161a	A72	1c	*650.00*	
162a	A73	2c	*800.00*	
164a	A73	4c	*375.00*	
167a	A73	12c	*650.00*	
171a	A71	50c	*650.00*	
173a	A73	5p	*650.00*	

Domingo F. Sarmiento A87

Agriculture A88

1911, May 15 Typo. *Perf. 13½*

176	A87	5c gray brn & blk	75	50

Domingo Faustino Sarmiento (1811-88), pres. of Argentina, 1868-74.

Wmk. 86, without Face

1911 Engr. *Perf. 12*

Size: 19x25mm

177	A88	5c vermilion	30	15
178	A88	12c deep blue	4.00	18
		Set value		24

Wmk. 86, with Face

1911 Typo. *Perf. 13½x12½*

Size: 18x23mm

179	A88	½c violet	15	15
180	A88	1c brown ocher	15	15
181	A88	2c chocolate	18	15
a.		Perf. 13½	4.25	1.75
b.		Imperf., pair	*26.00*	
182	A88	3c green	42	15
183	A88	4c brown violet	35	25
184	A88	10c gray green	52	15
185	A88	20c ultra	4.25	1.00
186	A88	24c red brown	5.25	3.50
187	A88	30c claret	1.75	48
188	A88	50c black	8.00	85
		Nos. 179-188 (10)	21.02	6.83

The 5c dull red is a proof. In this issue Wmk. 86 comes: straight rays (4c, 20c, 24c) and wavy rays (2c). All other values exist with both forms.

Wmk. 87 (Horiz. or Vert.)

1912-14 *Perf. 13½x12½*

189	A88	½c violet	16	15
190	A88	1c ocher	16	15
191	A88	2c chocolate	32	15
192	A88	3c green	60	16
193	A88	4c brown violet	60	16
194	A88	5c red	16	15
195	A88	10c deep green	1.40	15
196	A88	12c deep blue	1.40	15
197	A88	20c ultra	8.00	70
198	A88	24c red brown	3.25	1.65
199	A88	30c claret	8.00	60
200	A88	50c black	5.00	60
		Nos. 189-200 (12)	29.05	4.77

See Nos. 208-212. For overprints see Nos. OD1-OD8, OD47-OD54, OD102-OD108, OD146-OD152, OD183-OD190, OD235-OD241, OD281-OD284, OD318-OD323.

Perf. 13½

189a	A88	½c	80	28
190a	A88	1c	80	28
191a	A88	2c	80	16
192a	A88	3c	35.00	16.00
193a	A88	4c	1.65	70
194a	A88	5c	32	15
196a	A88	12c	3.25	80
197a	A88	20c	5.00	70
		Nos. 189a-197a (8)	47.62	19.07

A89

1912-13 *Perf. 13½*

201	A89	1p dull bl & rose	6.00	1.00
		Punch cancel		28
202	A89	5p slate & ol grn	19.00	6.00
		Punch cancel		60
203	A89	10p violet & blue	75.00	9.00
		Punch cancel		1.40
204	A89	20p blue & claret	175.00	60.00
		Punch cancel		2.00
		Nos. 201-204 (4)	275.00	76.00

1915 Unwmk. *Perf. 13½x12½*

208	A88	1c ocher	50	15
209	A88	2c chocolate	50	15
212	A88	5c red	50	15
		Nos. 208-212 (3)	1.50	
		Set value		20

Only these denominations were printed on paper without watermark.

Other stamps of the series are known unwatermarked but they are from the outer rows of sheets the other parts of which are watermarked.

Francisco Narciso de Laprida A90

Declaration of Independence A91

Jose de San Martin
A92 A92a

Perf. 13½, 13½x12½

1916, July 9 Litho. Wmk. 87

215	A90	½c violet	18	15
216	A90	1c buff	24	15

Perf. 13½x12½

217	A90	2c chocolate	18	15
218	A90	3c green	45	15
219	A90	4c red violet	68	15

Perf. 13½

220	A91	5c red	30	15
a.		Imperf., pair	40.00	
221	A91	10c gray green	1.50	15
222	A92	12c blue	65	15
223	A92	20c ultra	1.00	25
224	A92	24c red brown	1.65	75
225	A92	30c claret	1.65	32
226	A92	50c gray black	3.25	42
227	A92a	1p sl bl & red	9.25	4.00
		Punch cancel		50
a.		Imperf., pair	325.00	
228	A92a	5p blk & gray grn	110.00	40.00
		Punch cancel		3.25
229	A92a	10p violet & blue	110.00	75.00
		Punch cancel		2.50
230	A92a	20p dull blue & cl	165.00	67.50
		Punch cancel		1.00
a.		Imperf., pair	650.00	
		Nos. 215-230 (16)	405.98	189.44

Cent. of Argentina's declaration of independence of Spain, July 9, 1816.

The watermark is either vert. or horiz. on Nos. 215-220, 222; only vert. on No. 221, and only horiz. on Nos. 223-230.

For overprints see #OD9, OD55-OD56, OD109, OD153, OD191-OD192, OD285, OD324.

A93

A94

A94a

Juan Gregorio Pujol — A95

1917 *Perf. 13½, 13½x12½*

231	A93	½c violet	20	15
232	A93	1c buff	25	15
233	A93	2c brown	25	15
234	A93	3c lt green	75	15
235	A93	4c red violet	75	40
236	A93	5c red	25	15
a.		Imperf., pair	14.00	
237	A93	10c gray green	1.50	15

Perf. 13½

238	A94	12c blue	1.00	15
239	A94	20c ultra	1.50	18
240	A94	24c red brown	4.50	2.00
241	A94	30c claret	4.50	60
242	A94	50c gray black	4.00	60
243	A94a	1p slate bl & red	4.00	35
244	A94a	5p black & gray grn	17.00	3.00
		Punch cancel		1.50
245	A94a	10p violet & blue	40.00	9.25
		Punch cancel		1.00
246	A94a	20p dull blue & cl	77.50	15.00
		Punch cancel		80
a.		Center inverted	1,200.	875.00
		Nos. 231-246 (16)	157.95	32.43

The watermark is either vert. or horiz. on Nos. 231-236, 238; only vert. on No. 237, and only horiz. on Nos. 239-246.

1918, June 15 Litho. *Perf. 13½*

247	A95	5c bister & gray	70	25

Cent. of the birth of Juan G. Pujol (1817-61), lawyer and legislator.

Perf. 13½, 13½x12½

1918-19 Unwmk.

248	A93	½c violet	15	15
249	A93	1c buff	15	15
a.		Imperf., pair	14.00	
250	A93	2c brown	15	15
251	A93	3c lt green	25	15
252	A93	4c red violet	25	15
253	A93	5c red	15	15
254	A93	10c gray green	1.10	15

Perf. 13½

255	A94	12c blue	1.25	15
256	A94	20c ultra	1.65	15
257	A94	24c red brown	2.00	50
258	A94	30c claret	2.50	30
259	A94	50c gray black	5.50	26
		Nos. 248-259 (12)	15.10	
		Set value		1.50

The stamps of this issue sometimes show letters of papermakers' watermarks.

There were two printings, in 1918 and 1923, using different ink and paper.

Perf. 13½, 13½x12½

1920 Wmk. 88

264	A93	½c violet	20	15
265	A93	1c buff	26	15
266	A93	2c brown	26	15
267	A93	3c green	1.50	32
268	A93	4c red violet	2.00	1.25
269	A93	5c red	40	15
270	A93	10c gray green	3.25	15

Perf. 13½

271	A94	12c blue	1.75	15
272	A94	20c ultra	2.50	15
274	A94	30c claret	8.25	70
275	A94	50c gray black	5.00	90
		Nos. 264-275 (11)	25.37	
		Set value		3.50

See #292-300, 304-307A, 310-314, 318, 322.

For overprints see Nos. OD10-OD20, OD57-OD71, OD74, OD110-OD121, OD154-OD159, OD161-OD162, OD193-OD207, OD209-OD211, OD242-OD252, OD254-OD255, OD286-OD290, OD325-OD328, OD330.

Belgrano's Mausoleum
A96

Creation of Argentine Flag
A97

Gen. Manuel Belgrano — A98

1920, June 18 *Perf. 13½*

280	A96	2c red	38	20
a.		Perf. 13½x12½	38	20
281	A97	5c rose & blue	38	15
282	A98	12c green & blue	75	75
		Nos. 280-282 (3)	1.51	1.10

Belgrano (1770-1820), Argentine general, patriot and diplomat.

Gen. Justo Jose de Urquiza — A99

Bartolome Mitre — A100

1920, Nov. 11

283	A99	5c gray blue	24	15

Gen. Justo Jose de Urquiza (1801-70), pres. of Argentina, 1854-60. See No. 303.

1921, June 26 Unwmk.

284	A100	2c violet brown	26	20
285	A100	5c light blue	26	15
		Set value		29

Bartolome Mitre (1821-1906), pres. of Argentina, 1862-65.

Allegory, Pan-America — A101

1921, Aug. 25 *Perf. 13½*

286	A101	3c violet	55	30
287	A101	5c blue	80	15
288	A101	10c vio brown	1.40	35
289	A101	12c rose	2.00	75
		Nos. 286-289 (4)	4.75	1.55

Inscribed "Buenos Aires-Agosto de 1921"
A102

Inscribed "Republica Argentina"
A103

1921, Oct. *Perf. 13½x12½*

290	A102	5c rose	28	15
a.		Perf. 13½	1.25	15
291	A103	5c rose	1.50	15
a.		Perf. 13½	2.50	15
		Set value		15

1st Pan-American Postal Cong., Buenos Aires, Aug., 1921.

See Nos. 308-309, 319. For overprints see Nos. OD72, OD160, OD208, OD253, OD329.

Perf. 13½, 13½x12½

1920 Wmk. 89

292	A93	½c violet	2.00	75
293	A93	1c buff	5.00	75
294	A93	2c brown	3.00	75
297	A93	5c red	4.00	50
298	A93	10c gray green	4.00	38

Perf. 13½

299	A94	12c blue	*3,000.*	125.00
300	A94	20c ultra	12.00	75
		Nos. 292-298,300 (6)	30.00	3.88

1920

303	A99	5c gray blue	275.00	190.00

Perf. 13½, 13½x12½

1922-23 Wmk. 90

304	A93	½c violet	15	15
305	A93	1c buff	15	15
306	A93	2c brown	15	15
307	A93	3c green	45	28
307A	A93	4c red violet	3.75	1.00
308	A102	5c rose	2.25	15
309	A103	5c red	1.50	15
310	A93	10c gray green	4.75	28

Perf. 13½

311	A94	12c blue	85	15
312	A94	20c ultra	1.25	15
313	A94	24c red brown	9.25	4.50
314	A94	30c claret	5.50	50
		Nos. 304-314 (12)	30.00	7.61

Paper with Gray Overprint RA in Sun

Perf. 13½, 13½x12½

1922-23 Unwmk.

318	A93	2c brown	3.00	1.00
319	A103	5c red	2.00	30

Perf. 13½

322	A94	20c ultra	15.00	1.50
		Nos. 318-322 (3)	20.00	2.80

San Martín
A104 A105

With Period after Value

1923, May Litho. Wmk. 90

323	A104	½c red violet	20	18
324	A104	1c buff	32	15
325	A104	2c dark brown	32	15
326	A104	3c lt green	32	22
327	A104	4c red brown	32	18
328	A104	5c red	32	15
329	A104	10c dull green	2.50	15
330	A104	12c deep blue	40	15
331	A104	20c ultra	1.00	15
332	A104	24c lt brown	2.50	1.50
333	A104	30c claret	7.75	60
334	A104	50c black	4.00	35

Without Period after Value

Wmk. 87 *Perf. 13½*

335	A105	1p blue & red	4.00	15
336	A105	5p gray lilac & grn	16.00	1.75
		Punch cancel		60
337	A105	10p claret & blue	55.00	10.50
		Punch cancel		1.00
338	A105	20p slate & brn lake	90.00	30.00
		Punch cancel		60
a.		Center inverted		
		Nos. 323-338 (16)	184.95	46.33

Nos. 335-338 and 353-356 canceled with round or oval killers in purple (revenue cancellations) sell for one-fifth to one-half as much as postally used copies.

For overprints see Nos. 399-404.

Design of 1923
Without Period after Value

Perf. 13½, 13½x12½

1923-24 Litho. Wmk. 90

340	A104	½c red violet	15	15
341	A104	1c buff	15	15
342	A104	2c dk brown	15	15
343	A104	3c green	15	15
a.		Imperf., pair	8.00	
344	A104	4c red brown	40	15
345	A104	5c red	15	15
346	A104	10c dull green	28	15
347	A104	12c deep blue	48	15
348	A104	20c ultra	65	15
349	A104	24c lt brown	1.65	70
350	A104	25c purple	80	15
351	A104	30c claret	1.65	15
352	A104	50c black	1.65	15
353	A105	1p blue & red	2.00	15
354	A105	5p dk violet & grn	15.00	75
		Punch cancel		20
355	A105	10p claret & blue	32.50	3.25
		Punch cancel		22
356	A105	20p slate & lake	47.50	7.50
		Punch cancel		22
		Nos. 340-356 (17)	105.31	14.15

1931-33

Typographed

343b	A104	3c	1.40	26
345a	A104	5c	2.50	15
346a	A104	10c	4.00	20
347a	A104	12c	8.50	1.50
348a	A104	20c	32.50	1.65
350a	A104	25c	20.00	75
351a	A104	30c	15.00	40
		Nos. 343b-351a (7)	83.90	4.91

The typographed stamps were issued only in coils and have a rough impression with heavy shading about the eyes and nose. Nos. 343 and 346 are known without watermark.

Nos. 341-345, 347-349, 351a may be found in pairs, one with period.

See note after No. 338. See Nos. 362-368. For overprints see Nos. OD21-OD33, OD75-OD87, OD122-OD133, OD163-OD175, OD212-OD226, OD256-OD268, OD291-OD304, OD331-OD345.

Rivadavia — A106

1926, Feb. 8 *Perf. 13½*

357	A106	5c rose	42	15

Centenary of the Presidency of Bernardino Rivadavia.

Rivadavia
A108

San Martin
A109

General Post Office, 1926 — A110

General Post Office, 1826 — A111

1926, July 1 *Perf. 13½x12½*

358	A108	3c gray green	15	15
359	A109	5c red	15	15

Perf. 13½

360	A110	12c deep blue	90	18
361	A111	25c chocolate	1.65	15
a.		"1326" for "1826"	6.00	75
		Nos. 358-361 (4)	2.85	
		Set value		38

Centenary of the Post Office.

For overprints see Nos. OD34, OD88, OD134, OD227-OD228, OD269, OD305, OD346.

Type of 1923-31 Issue Without Period after Value

1927 Wmk. 205 *Perf. 13½x12½*

362	A104	½c red violet	24	24
a.		Pelure paper	1.75	1.50
363	A104	1c buff	24	24
364	A104	2c dark brown	24	15
a.		Pelure paper	35	18
365	A104	5c red	30	15
a.		Period after value	3.50	1.90
b.		Pelure paper	45	22
366	A104	10c dull green	4.50	2.25
367	A104	20c ultra	18.00	2.25

Perf. 13½

368	A105	1p blue & red	35.00	7.00
		Nos. 362-368 (7)	58.52	12.28

Arms of Argentina and Brazil — A112

Wmk. RA in Sun (90)

1928, Aug. 27 *Perf. 12½x13*

369	A112	5c rose red	1.00	25
370	A112	12c deep blue	1.50	50

Cent. of peace between the Empire of Brazil and the United Provinces of the Rio de la Plata.

Allegory, Discovery of the New World A113

"Spain" and "Argentina" A114

"America" Offering Laurels to Columbus — A115

1929, Oct. 12 Litho. *Perf. 13½*

371	A113	2c lilac brown	85	25
372	A114	5c light red	85	15
373	A115	12c dull blue	2.00	75
		Nos. 371-373 (3)	3.70	1.15

437th anniversary of the discovery of America by Columbus.

Spirit of Victory Attending Insurgents A116

March of the Victorious Insurgents A117

Perf. 13½x12½ (A116), 12½x13 (A117)

1930

374	A116	½c violet gray	15	15
375	A116	1c myrtle green	18	18
376	A117	2c dull violet	24	15
377	A116	3c green	32	25
378	A116	4c violet	25	25
379	A116	5c rose red	15	15
380	A116	10c gray black	75	35
381	A117	12c dull blue	55	25
382	A117	20c ocher	55	25
383	A117	24c red brown	2.25	1.50
384	A117	25c green	2.50	1.50
385	A117	30c deep violet	4.50	2.00
386	A117	50c black	6.25	2.50
387	A117	1p sl bl & red	11.00	10.00
388	A117	2p black & org	22.50	10.00
389	A117	5p dull grn & blk	65.00	40.00
390	A117	10p dp red brn & dull blue	90.00	42.50
391	A117	20p yel grn & dl bl	225.00	100.00
392	A117	50p dk grn & vio	600.00	450.00
		Nos. 374-390 (17)	207.14	111.98

Revolution of 1930.

Nos. 387-392 with oval (parcel post) cancellation sell for less.

For overprint see No. 405.

1931 *Perf. 12½x13*

393	A117	½c red violet	15	15
394	A117	1c gray black	1.25	50
395	A117	3c green	60	30
396	A117	4c red brown	35	25
397	A117	5c red	18	15
a.		Plane omitted, top left corner	3.00	1.65
398	A117	10c dl grn	1.25	28
		Nos. 393-398 (6)	3.78	1.63

Revolution of 1930.

Stamps of 1924-25 Overprinted in Red or Green

-6-
Septiembre
1930 - 1931

1931, Sept. 6 *Perf. 13½, 13½x12½*

399	A104	3c green	20	20
400	A104	10c dull green	60	60
401	A104	30c claret (G)	3.25	3.25
402	A104	50c black	3.25	3.25

Overprinted in Blue

1930
Septiembre
6
1931

403	A105	1p blue & red	3.75	3.25
404	A105	5p dk violet & grn	70.00	20.00

No. 388 Overprinted in Blue

6 Septiembre 1931

Perf. 12½x13

405	A117	2p black & orange	13.00	9.00
		Nos. 399-405 (7)	94.05	39.55

1st anniv. of the Revolution of 1930.

See Nos. C30-C34.

Refrigeration Compressor — A118

Perf. 13½x12½

1932, Aug. 29 Litho.

406	A118	3c green	40	24
407	A118	10c scarlet	1.25	15
408	A118	12c gray blue	3.25	1.25
		Nos. 406-408 (3)	4.90	1.64

6th Intl. Refrigeration Congress.

Port of La Plata — A119

Pres. Julio A. Roca — A120

Municipal Palace — A121

Cathedral of La Plata — A122

Dardo Rocha — A123

Perf. 13½x13, 13x13½ (10c)

1933, Jan.

409	A119	3c green & dk brn	32	30
410	A120	10c orange & dk vio	50	20
411	A121	15c dk blue & dp blue	3.50	1.75
412	A122	20c violet & yel brn	1.65	1.00
413	A123	30c dk grn & vio brn	14.00	5.50
		Nos. 409-413 (5)	19.97	8.75

50th anniv. of the founding of the city of La Plata, Nov. 19th, 1882.

Christ of the Andes — A124

Buenos Aires Cathedral A125

1934, Oct. 1 *Perf. 13x13½, 13½x13*

414	A124	10c rose & brown	70	18
415	A125	15c dark blue	1.40	45

32nd Intl. Eucharistic Cong., Oct. 10-14.

"Liberty" with Arms of Brazil and Argentina A126

Symbolical of "Peace" and "Friendship" A127

1935, May 15 *Perf. 13x13½*

416	A126	10c red	85	24
417	A127	15c blue	1.65	48

Visit of Pres. Getulio Vargas of Brazil.

Belgrano A128

Sarmiento A129

Urquiza A130

Louis Braille A131

San Martin A132

Brown A133

Moreno A134

Alberdi A135

Nicolas Avellaneda A136

Rivadavia A137

Mitre A138

Bull (Cattle Breeding) A139

Martin Güemes A140

Agriculture A141

Merino Sheep (Wool) — A142

Sugar Cane
A143

Oil Well
(Petroleum)
A144

Map of South America
A145 A146

Fruit
A147

Iguacu Falls
(Scenic
Wonders)
A148

Grapes
(Vineyards)
A149

Cotton
A150

Two types of A140:
Type I - Inscribed Juan Martin Guemes.
Type II - Inscribed Martin Güemes.

Perf. 13, 13½x13, 13x13½

1935-51 Litho. Wmk. 90

418	A128	½c red violet	15	15
419	A129	1c buff	15	15
a.		Typo.	15	15
420	A130	2c dark brown	15	15
421	A131	2½c black ('39)	15	15
422	A132	3c green	15	15
423	A132	3c lt gray ('39)	15	15
424	A134	3c lt gray ('46)	15	15
425	A133	4c lt gray	15	15
426	A133	4c sage green ('39)	15	15
427	A134	5c yel brn, typo.	15	15
a.		Tete beche pair, typo.	4.50	2.25
b.		Booklet pane of 8, typo.		
c.		Booklet pane of 4, typo.		
d.		Litho.	1.40	15
428	A135	6c olive green	22	15
429	A136	8c orange ('39)	15	15
430	A137	10c car, typo.	28	15
431	A137	10c brown ('42)	15	15
a.		Typo.	42	15
432	A138	12c brown	20	15
433	A138	12c red ('39)	15	15
434	A139	15c slate bl ('36)	85	15
435	A139	15c pale ultra ('39)	52	15
436	A140	15c lt gray bl (II) ('42)	37.50	1.75
437	A140	20c lt ultra (I)	60	15
438	A140	20c lt ultra (II) ('36)	35	15
439	A140	20c bl gray (II) ('39)	35	15
439A	A139	20c dk bl & pale bl, ('42) 22x33mm	85	15
440	A139	20c blue ('51)	15	15
a.		Typo.	15	15
441	A141	25c carmine ('36)	22	15
442	A142	30c org brn ('36)	52	15
443	A143	40c dk violet ('36)	42	15
444	A144	50c red & org ('36)	35	15
445	A145	1p brn blk & lt bl ('36)	17.00	70
446	A146	1p brn blk & lt bl ('37)	7.00	16
a.		Chalky paper	42.50	85
447	A147	2p brn lake & dk ultra ('36)	85	15
448	A148	5p ind & ol grn ('36)	6.00	28
449	A149	10p brn lake & blk	35.00	1.95
450	A150	20p bl grn & brn ('36)	47.50	7.50
		Nos. 418-450 (34)	158.68	
		Set value		12.00

See Nos. 485-500, 523-540, 659, 668. For overprints see Nos. O37-O41, O43-O51, O53-O56, O58-O78, O108, O112, OD35-OD46, OD89-OD101, OD135-OD145, OD176-OD182C, OD229-OD234F, OD270-OD280, OD306-OD317, OD347-OD357.

No. 439A exists with attached label showing medallion. Value $42.50 unused, $22.50 used.

Souvenir Sheet

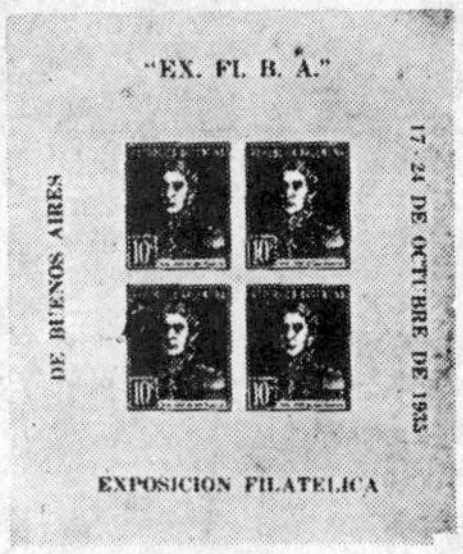

A151

Without Period after Value

1935, Oct. 17 Litho. *Imperf.*

452	A151	Sheet of 4	52.50	30.00
a.		10c dull green	7.00	4.00

Phil. Exhib. at Buenos Aires, Oct. 17-24, 1935. The stamps were on sale during the 8 days of the exhibition only. Sheets measure 83x101mm.

Plaque — A152

1936, Dec. 1 *Perf. 13x13½*

453	A152	10c rose	52	25

Inter-American Conference for Peace.

Domingo
Faustino
Sarmiento
A153

"Presidente
Sarmiento"
A154

1938, Sept. 5

454	A153	3c sage green	18	15
455	A153	5c red	18	15
456	A153	15c deep blue	60	15
457	A153	50c orange	1.75	1.00
		Nos. 454-457 (4)	2.71	
		Set value		1.20

50th anniv. of the death of Domingo Faustino Sarmiento, pres., educator and author.

1939, Mar. 16

458	A154	5c greenish blue	35	15

Final voyage of the training ship "Presidente Sarmiento."

Allegory of the
UPU — A155

Coat of
Arms — A157

Post Office,
Buenos
Aires — A156

Iguacu
Falls — A158

Bonete Hill,
Nahuel Huapi
Park — A159

Allegory of Modern
Communications
A160

Argentina, Land
of Promise
A161

Lake Frias,
Nahuel Huapi
Park — A162

Perf. 13x13½, 13½x13

1939, Apr. 1 Photo.

459	A155	5c rose carmine	16	15
460	A156	15c grnsh black	42	26
461	A157	20c brt blue	42	15
462	A158	25c dp blue grn	85	40
463	A159	50c brown	1.65	65
464	A160	1p brown violet	1.90	80
465	A161	2p magenta	8.75	5.25
466	A162	5p purple	35.00	16.00
		Nos. 459-466 (8)	49.15	23.66

Universal Postal Union, 11th Congress.

Souvenir Sheets

A163

A164

1939, May 12 Wmk. 90 *Imperf.*

467	A163	Sheet of 4	6.00	4.25
a.		5c rose carmine (A155)	1.25	75
b.		20c bright blue (A157)	1.25	75
c.		25c deep blue green (A158)	1.25	75
d.		50c brown (A159)	1.25	75
468	A164	Sheet of 4	6.00	4.28

Issued in four forms:

a.	Unsevered horizontal pair of sheets, type A163 at left, A164 at right	15.00	15.00
b.	Unsevered vertical pair of sheets, type A163 at top, A164 at bottom	15.00	15.00
c.	Unsevered block of 4 sheets, type A163 at left, A164 at right	52.50	52.50
d.	Unsevered block of 4 sheets, type A163 at top, A164 at bottom	52.50	52.50

11th Cong. of the UPU and the Argentina Intl. Phil. Exposition (C.Y.T.R.A.).

No. 468 contains Nos. 467a-467d.

Family and New
House — A165

Perf. 13½x13

1939, Oct. 2 Litho. Wmk. 90

469	A165	5c bluish green	25	15

1st Pan-American Housing Congress.

Bird Carrying
Record — A166

Head of Liberty and
Arms of
Argentina — A167

Record and
Winged
Letter — A168

1939, Dec. 11 Photo. *Perf. 13*

470	A166	1.18p indigo	15.00	7.00
471	A167	1.32p brt blue	15.00	7.00
472	A168	1.50p dark brown	50.00	27.50
		Nos. 470-472 (3)	80.00	41.50

These stamps were issued for the recording and mailing of flexible phonograph records.

Map of the
Americas — A169

1940, Apr. 14 *Perf. 13x13½*

473	A169	15c ultra	42	15

50th anniv. of the Pan American Union.

Souvenir Sheet

Reproductions of Early Argentine
Stamps — A170

Wmk. RA in Sun (90)

1940, May 25 Litho. *Imperf.*

474 A170 Sheet of 5 9.50 5.50
a. 5c dark blue (Corrientes A2) 1.10 70
b. 5c red (Argentina A1) 1.10 70
c. 5c dark blue (Cordoba #1) 1.10 70
d. 5c red (Argentina A3) 1.10 70
e. 10c dark blue (Buenos Aires A1) 1.10 70

100th anniv. of the first postage stamp.

General Domingo French and Colonel Antonio Beruti — A171

1941, Feb. 20 *Perf. 13½x13*

475 A171 5c dk gray blue & lt blue 32 15

Issued in honor of General French and Colonel Beruti, patriots.

Marco M. de Avellaneda A172

Statue of Gen. Julio Roca A173

1941, Oct. 3 *Perf. 13x13½*

476 A172 5c dull slate blue 32 15

Marco M. de Avellaneda, (1814-41), Army leader and martyr.

1941, Oct. 19 Photo. Wmk. 90

477 A173 5c dark olive green 32 15

Dedication of a monument to Lt. Gen. Julio Argentino Roca (1843-1914).

Carlos Pellegrini and Bank of the Nation — A174

1941, Oct. 26 *Perf. 13½x13*

478 A174 5c brown carmine 32 15

Founding of the Bank of the Nation, 50th anniv.

Gen. Juan Lavalle — A175

1941, Dec. 5 *Perf. 13x13½*

479 A175 5c bright blue 32 15

Gen. Juan Galo de Lavalle (1797-1841).

National Postal Savings Bank — A176

1942, Apr. 5 Litho. *Perf. 13½x13*

480 A176 1c pale olive 20 15

Jose Manuel Estrada — A177

1942, July 13 *Perf. 13x13½*

481 A177 5c brown violet 32 15

Jose Estrada (1842-1894), writer and diplomat.
No. 481 exists with label, showing medallion, attached. Value, pair $10.

Types of 1935-51

Perf. 13, 13x13½, 13½x13

1942-50 Litho. Wmk. 288

485 A128 ½c brown violet 4.75 1.00
486 A129 1c buff ('50) 15 15
487 A130 2c dk brown ('50) 15 15
488 A132 3c lt gray 16.00 1.25
489 A134 3c lt gray ('49) 16 15
490 A137 10c red brown ('49) 20 15
491 A138 12c red 20 15
492 A140 15c lt gray blue (II) 28 15
493 A139 20c dk sl bl & pale bl 1.25 15
494 A141 25c dull rose ('49) 60 15
495 A142 30c orange brn ('49) 1.25 15
496 A143 40c violet ('49) 8.00 15
497 A144 50c red & org ('49) 8.00 18
498 A146 1p brn blk & lt bl 6.50 18
499 A147 2p brn lake & bl ('49) 13.00 75
500 A148 5p ind & ol grn ('49) 50.00 4.50
Nos. 485-500 (16) 110.49 9.36

No. 493 measures 22x33mm.

Post Office, Buenos Aires — A178

Proposed Columbus Lighthouse — A179

Inscribed: "Correos y Telegrafos."

1942, Oct. 5 Litho. *Perf. 13*

503 A178 35c lt ultra 2.75 15

See Nos. 541-543.

1942, Oct. 12 Wmk. 288

504 A179 15c dull blue 3.00 15

Wmk. 90

505 A179 15c dull blue 60.00 5.00

450th anniv. of the discovery of America by Columbus.

Jose C. Paz — A180

Books and Argentine Flag — A181

1942, Dec. 15 Wmk. 288

506 A180 5c dark gray 35 15

Cent. of the birth of Jose C. Paz, stateman and founder of the newspaper La Prensa.

1943, Apr. 1 Litho. *Perf. 13*

507 A181 5c dull blue 18 15

1st Book Fair of Argentina.

Arms of Argentina Inscribed "Honesty, Justice, Duty" — A182

1943-50 Wmk. 288 *Perf. 13*

Size: 20x26mm

508 A182 5c red ('50) 2.50 15

Wmk. 90

509 A182 5c red 22 15
a. 5c dull red, unsurfaced paper 3.00 15
510 A182 15c green 70 15

Perf. 13x13½

Size: 22x33mm

511 A182 20c dark blue 1.10 15
Nos. 508-511 (4) 4.52
Set value 30

Change of political organization, June 4, 1943.

Independence House, Tucuman A183

Liberty Head and Savings Bank A184

1943-51 Wmk. 90 *Perf. 13*

512 A183 5c blue green 90 15

Wmk. 288

513 A183 5c blue green ('51) 35 15
Set value 15

Restoration of Independence House.

1943, Oct. 25 Wmk. 90

514 A184 5c violet brown 15 15

Wmk. 288

515 A184 5c violet brown 37.50 3.00

1st conference of National Postal Savings.

Port of Buenos Aires in 1800 — A185

1943, Dec. 11 Wmk. 90

516 A185 5c gray black 15 15

Day of Exports.

Warship, Merchant Ship and Sailboat A186

Arms of Argentine Republic A187

1944, Jan. 31 *Perf. 13*

517 A186 5c blue 18 15

Issued to commemorate Sea Week.

1944, June 4

518 A187 5c dull blue 15 15

1st anniv. of the change of political organization in Argentina.

St. Gabriel A188

Cross at Palermo A189

1944, Oct. 11

519 A188 3c yellow green 15 15
520 A189 5c deep rose 15 15
Set value 15

Fourth national Eucharistic Congress.

Allegory of Savings A190

Reservists A191

1944, Oct. 24

521 A190 5c gray 15 15

20th anniv. of the National Savings Bank.

1944, Dec. 1

522 A191 5c blue 15 15

Day of the Reservists.

Types of 1935-51

Perf. 13x13½, 13½x13

1945-47 Litho. Unwmk.

523 A128 ½c brown vio ('46) 15 15
524 A129 1c yellow brown 15 15
525 A130 2c sepia 15 15
526 A132 3c lt gray (San Martin) 42 15
527 A134 3c lt gray (Moreno) ('46) 15 15
528 A135 6c olive grn ('47) 18 15
529 A137 10c brown ('46) 1.25 15
530 A140 15c lt gray bl (II) 75 15
531 A139 20c dk sl bl & pale bl 1.25 15
532 A141 25c dull rose 45 15
533 A142 30c orange brown 35 15
534 A143 40c violet 1.25 15
535 A144 50c red & orange 1.25 15
536 A146 1p brown blk & lt bl 1.65 15
537 A147 2p brown lake & bl 8.00 22
538 A148 5p ind & ol grn ('46) 45.00 2.50
539 A149 10p dp cl & int blk 5.50 90
540 A150 20p bl grn & brn ('46) 5.75 90
Nos. 523-540 (18) 73.65
Set value 5.25

No. 531 measures 22x33mm.

Post Office Type Inscribed: "Correos y Telecommunicaciones"

1945 Unwmk. *Perf. 13x13½*

541 A178 35c lt ultra 1.25 15

Wmk. 90

542 A178 35c lt ultra 1.25 15

Wmk. 288

543 A178 35c lt ultra 35 15
Nos. 541-543 (3) 2.85
Set value 15

Bernardino Rivadavia A192 A193

Mausoleum of Rivadavia A194

Perf. 13½x13

1945, Sept. 1 Litho. Unwmk.

544 A192 3c blue green 15 15
545 A193 5c rose 15 15
546 A194 20c blue 28 15
Nos. 544-546 (3) 58
Set value 15

Cent. of the death of Bernardino Rivadavia, Argentina's first president.
No. 546 exists with mute label attached. The pair sells for four times the price of the single stamp.

San Martin
A195

Monument to Army of the Andes, Mendoza
A196

1945-46 Wmk. 90 Typo. or Litho.

547 A195	5c carmine		15	15
a.	Litho. ('46)		15	15

Wmk. 288

548 A195	5c carmine, litho.	120.00	20.00

Unwmk.

549 A195	5c carmine ('46)	52	15
a.	Litho. ('46)	20	15

For overprints see Nos. O42, O57.

1946, Jan. 14 Litho. *Perf. 13½x13*

550 A196 5c violet brown 15 15

Issued to honor the Unknown Soldier of the War for Independence.

Franklin D. Roosevelt — A197

1946, Apr. 12

551 A197 5c slate black 15 15

Liberty Administering Presidential Oath — A198

1946, June 4 *Perf. 13x13½*

552 A198 5c blue 15 15

Issued to commemorate the inauguration of President Juan D. Perón, June 4, 1946.

Argentina Receiving Popular Acclaim
A199

1946, Oct. 17 *Perf. 13½x13*

553 A199	5c rose violet	16	15
554 A199	10c blue green	24	15
555 A199	15c dark blue	48	18
556 A199	50c red brown	70	30
557 A199	1p carmine rose	1.40	70
	Nos. 553-557 (5)	2.98	
	Set value		1.25

First anniversary of the political organization change of Oct. 17, 1945.

Coin Bank and World Map — A200

1946, Oct. 31 Unwmk.

558 A200 30c dk rose car & pink 60 15

Universal Day of Savings, October 31, 1946.

Argentine Industry
A201

International Bridge Connecting Argentina and Brazil
A202

1946, Dec. 6 *Perf. 13x13½*

559 A201 5c violet brown 15 15

Day of Argentine Industry, Dec. 6.

1947, May 21 Litho. *Perf. 13½x13*

560 A202 5c green 15 15

Opening of the Argentina-Brazil International Bridge, May 21, 1947.

Map of Argentine Antarctic Claims — A203

Justice — A204

1947-49 Unwmk. *Perf. 13x13½*

561 A203	5c violet & lilac	35	15
562 A203	20c dk car rose & rose	70	15

Wmk. 90

563 A203	20c dk car rose & rose	2.00	20

Wmk. 288

564 A203	20c dk car rose & rose ('49)	2.00	15
	Nos. 561-564 (4)	5.05	
	Set value		35

1st Argentine Antarctic mail, 43rd anniv.

1947, June 4 Unwmk.

565 A204 5c brn vio & pale yel 15 15

1st anniversary of the Peron government.

Icarus Falling — A205

1947, Sept. 25 *Perf. 13½x13*

566 A205 15c red violet 15 15

Aviation Week.

Training Ship Presidente Sarmiento — A206

1947, Oct. 5 *Perf. 13x13½*

567 A206 5c blue 18 15

50th anniv. of the launching of the Argentine training frigate "Presidente Sarmiento."

Cervantes and Characters from Don Quixote — A207

Perf. 13½x13

1947, Oct. 12 Photo. Wmk. 90

568 A207 5c olive green 15 15

400th anniv. of the birth of Miguel de Cervantes Saavedra, playwright and poet.

Gen. Jose de San Martin — A208

Perf. 13½x13

1947-49 Unwmk. Litho.

569 A208 5c dull green 15 15

Wmk. 288

570 A208	5c dull green ('49)	15	15
	Set value		15

Transfer of the remains of Gen. Jose de San Martin's parents.

School Children — A209

Statue of Araucanian Indian — A210

1947-49 Unwmk. *Perf. 13x13½*

571 A209 5c green 15 15

Wmk. 90

574 A209 20c brown 35 15

Wmk. 288

575 A209	5c green ('49)	35	15
	Nos. 571-575 (3)	85	
	Set value		22

Argentine School Crusade for World Peace.

1948, May 21 Wmk. 90

576 A210 25c yellow brown 30 15

American Indian Day, Apr. 19.

Cap of Liberty — A211

Manual Stop Signal — A212

1948, July 16

577 A211 5c ultra 15 15

Revolution of June 4, 1943, 5th anniv.

1948, July 22

578 A212 5c chocolate & yellow 15 15

Traffic Safety Day, June 10.

Post Horn and Oak Leaves — A213

Argentine Farmers — A214

1948, July 22 Unwmk.

579 A213 5c lilac rose 15 15

200th anniversary of the establishment of regular postal service on the Plata River.

Perf. 13x13½

1948, Sept. 20 Wmk. 288

580 A214 10c red brown 15 15

Agriculture Day, Sept. 8, 1948.

Liberty and Symbols of Progress — A215

Perf. 13x13½

1948, Nov. 23 Photo. Wmk. 287

581 A215 25c red brown 18 15

3rd anniversary of President Juan D. Peron's return to power, October 17, 1945.

Souvenir Sheets

A216

Designs: 15c, Mail coach. 45c, Buenos Aires in 18th century. 55c, First train, 1857. 85c, Sailing ship, 1767.

1948, Dec. 21 Unwmk. *Imperf.*

582 A216	Sheet of 4	3.00	3.00
a.	15c dark green	45	45
b.	45c orange brown	45	45
c.	55c lilac brown	45	45
d.	85c ultramarine	45	45

A217

Designs: 85c, Domingo de Basavilibaso (1709-75). 1.05p, Postrider. 1.20p, Sailing ship, 1798. 1.90p, Courier in the Andes, 1772.

583 A217	Sheet of 4	14.00	11.00
a.	85c brown	3.00	2.50
b.	1.05p dark green	3.00	2.50
c.	1.20p dark blue	3.00	2.50
d.	1.90p red brown	3.00	2.50

200th anniversary of the establishment of regular postal service on the Plata River.

Winged Wheel — A218

Perf. 13½x13

1949, Mar. 1 Wmk. 288

584 A218 10c blue	22	15

Railroad nationalization, 1st anniv.

Liberty A219

1949, June 20 Engr. Wmk. 90

585 A219 1p red & red violet	42	15

Ratification of the Constitution of 1949.

Allegory of the UPU A220

1949, Nov. 19

586 A220 25c dk grn & yel grn	22	15

75th anniv. of the UPU.

Catalogue values for unused stamps in this section, from this point to the end of the section, are for Never Hinged items.

Gen. Jose de San Martin — A221

San Martin at Boulogne sur Mer A222

Mausoleum of San Martin — A223

Designs: 20c, 50c, 75c, Different Portraits of San Martin. 1p, House where San Martin died.

Engr., Photo. (25c, 1p, 2p)

1950, Aug. 17 Wmk. 90 ***Perf. 13½***

587 A221	10c indigo & dk pur	15	15
588 A221	20c red brn & dk brn	15	15
589 A222	25c brown	15	15
590 A221	50c dk green & ind	42	15
591 A221	75c choc & dk grn	42	15
a.	Souv. sheet of 4, #587, 588, 590, 591, imperf.	1.25	80
592 A222	1p dark green	85	25
593 A223	2p dp red lilac	70	35
	Nos. 587-593 (7)	2.84	
	Set value		90

Death cent. of General Jose de San Martin.

Map Showing Antarctic Claims — A224

1951, May 21 Litho. ***Perf. 13x13½***

594 A224 1p choc & lt blue	70	15

For overprint see No. O52.

Pegasus and Train A225

Communications Symbols — A226

Design: 25c, Ship and dolphin.

1951, Oct. 17 Photo. ***Perf. 13½***

595 A225	5c dark brown	15	15
596 A225	25c Prus green	24	15
597 A226	40c rose brown	28	15
	Nos. 595-597 (3)	67	
	Set value		32

Close of Argentine Five Year Plan.

Woman Voter and "Argentina" A227

1951, Dec. 14 ***Perf. 13½x13***

598 A227 10c brown violet	15	15

Granting of women's suffrage.

Eva Peron
A228 A229

Litho. or Engraved (#605)

1952, Aug. 26 Wmk. 90 ***Perf. 13***

599 A228	1c orange brown	15	15
600 A228	5c gray	15	15
601 A228	10c rose lilac	15	15
602 A228	20c rose pink	15	15
603 A228	25c dull green	15	15
604 A228	40c dull violet	15	15
605 A228	45c deep blue	15	15
606 A228	50c dull brown	15	15

Photo.

607 A229	1p dark brown	26	15
608 A229	1.50p deep green	1.50	15
609 A229	2p brt carmine	45	15
610 A229	3p indigo	75	15
	Nos. 599-610 (12)	4.16	
	Set value		75

For overprints see Nos. O79-O85.

Inscribed: "Eva Peron"

1952-53 ***Perf. 13x13½***

611 A229	1p dark brown	50	15
612 A229	1.50p deep green	50	15
613 A229	2p brt car ('53)	1.10	15
614 A229	3p indigo	1.50	15

Engr.

Perf. 13½x13

Size: 30x40mm

615 A229	5p red brown	1.50	35
616 A228	10p red	4.25	1.40
617 A229	20p green	11.00	4.00
618 A228	50p ultra	17.00	10.00
	Nos. 611-618 (8)	37.35	16.35

For overprints see Nos. O86-O93.

Indian Funeral Urn — A230

1953, Aug. 28 Photo. ***Perf. 13x13½***

619 A230 50c blue green	18	15

Founding of Santiago del Estero, 400th anniv.

Rescue Ship "Uruguay" A231

1953, Oct. 8 ***Perf. 13½***

620 A231 50c ultra	85	15

50th anniv. of the rescue of the Antarctic expedition of Otto C. Nordenskjold.

Planting Argentine Flag in the Antarctic — A232

1954, Jan. 20 Engr. ***Perf. 13½x13***

621 A232 1.45p blue	1.25	15

50th anniv. of Argentina's 1st antarctic p.o. and the establishing of the La Hoy radio p.o. in the South Orkneys.

Wired Communications A233

Television A234

Perf. 13x13½, 13½x13

1954, Apr. Photo. Wmk. 90

622 A233	1.50p shown	35	25
623 A233	3p Radio	1.10	28
624 A234	5p shown	1.40	55
	Nos. 622-624 (3)	2.85	1.08

Intl. Plenipotentiary Conf. of Telecommunications, Buenos Aires, 1952.

Pediment, Buenos Aires Stock Exchange A235

1954, July 13 ***Perf. 13½x13***

625 A235 1p dark green	28	15

Cent. of the establishment of the Buenos Aires Stock Exchange.

Eva Peron — A236

1954 Wmk. 90

626 A236 3p dp car rose	1.25	25

Wmk. 288

627 A236 3p dp car rose	175.00	32.50

2nd anniv. of the death of Eva Peron.

Jose de San Martin A237

Wheat A238

Industry A238a

Eva Peron Foundation Building A239

Cliffs of Humahuaca
A240

Gen. Jose de San Martin — A241

Designs: 50c, Buenos Aires harbor. 1p, Cattle ranch (Ganaderia). 3p, Nihuil Dam. 5p, Iguacu Falls, vert. 20p, Mt. Fitz Roy, vert.

Perf. 13½, 13x13½ (80c), 13½x13 (#639, 641-642)
Engraved (#632, 638-642), Photogravure (#634-637)

1954-59 Wmk. 90

628	A237	20c brt red, typo.	15	15
629	A237	20c red, litho. ('55)	60	15
630	A237	40c red, litho. ('56)	16	15
631	A237	40c brt red, typo. ('55)	25	15
632	A239	50c blue ('56)	15	15
633	A239	50c bl, litho. ('59)	16	15
634	A238	80c brown	22	15
635	A239	1p brown ('58)	26	15
636	A238a	1.50p ultra ('58)	20	15
637	A239	2p dk rose lake	32	15
638	A239	3p violet brn ('56)	32	15
639	A240	5p gray grn ('55)	5.25	15
a.		Perf. 13½	6.50	15
640	A240	10p yel grn ('55)	3.75	15
641	A240	20p dull vio ('55)	7.75	15
a.		Perf. 13½	9.50	15
642	A241	50p ultra & ind ('55)	7.75	15
a.		Perf. 13½	7.75	15
		Nos. 628-642 (15)	27.29	
		Set value		80

See Nos. 699-700. For similar designs inscribed "Republica Argentina" see Nos. 823-827, 890, 935, 937, 940, 990, 995, 1039, 1044, 1048.
For overprints see Nos. O94-O106, O142, O153-O157.

Allegory — A242

1954, Aug. 26 Typo. *Perf. 13½*

643	A242	1.50p slate black	65	15

Cent. of the establishment of the Buenos Aires Grain Exchange.

Clasped Hands and Congress Medal — A243

1955, Mar. 21 Photo. *Perf. 13½x13*

644	A243	3p red brown	80	15

Issued to publicize the National Productivity and Social Welfare Congress.

Allegory of Aviation — A244

Argentina Breaking Chains — A245

1955, June 18 Wmk. 90 *Perf. 13½*

645	A244	1.50p olive gray	65	15

Commercial aviation in Argentina, 25th anniv.

1955, Oct. 16 Litho.

647	A245	1.50p olive green	32	15

Liberation Revolution of Sept. 16, 1955.

Army Navy and Air Force Emblems
A246

Perf. 13½x13
1955, Dec. 31 Photo. Wmk. 90

648	A246	3p blue	42	15

"Brotherhood of the Armed Forces."

A247

A248

1956, Feb. 3 *Perf. 13½*

649	A247	1.50p Justo Jose de Urquiza	28	15

Battle of Caseros, 104th anniversary.

1956, July 28 Engr. *Perf. 13½x13*

650	A248	2p Coin and die	28	15

75th anniversary of the Argentine Mint.

1856 Stamp of Corrientes
A249

Juan G. Pujol — A250

Design: 2.40p, Stamp of 1860-78.

1956, Aug. 21

651	A249	40c dk grn & blue	15	15
652	A249	2.40p brn & lil rose	30	15

Photo.

653	A250	4.40p brt blue	65	18
a.		Souv. sheet of 3, #651-653, imperf.	2.25	2.00
		Nos. 651-653 (3)	1.10	48

Centenary of Argentine postage stamps.
No. 653a for the Argentine stamp cent. and Philatelic Exhib. for the Cent. of Corrientes Stamps, Oct. 12-21. The 4.40p is photo., the other two stamps and border litho. Colors of 40c and 2.40p differ slightly from engraved stamps.

Felling Trees, La Pampa
A251

Maté Herb and Gourd, Misiones
A252

Design: 1p, Cotton plant and harvest, Chaco.

1956, Sept. 1 *Perf. 13½*

654	A251	50c ultra	15	15
655	A251	1p magenta	18	15
656	A252	1.50p green	22	15
		Nos. 654-656 (3)	55	
		Set value		15

Elevation of the territories of La Pampa, Chaco and Misiones to provinces.

"Liberty"
A253

Florentino Ameghino
A254

Perf. 13½
1956, Sept. 15 Wmk. 90 Photo.

657	A253	2.40p lilac rose	30	15

1st anniv. of the Revolution of Liberation.

1956, Nov. 30

658	A254	2.40p brown	30	15

Issued to honor Florentino Ameghino (1854-1911), anthropologist.
For overprint see No. O110.

Adm. Brown Type of 1935-51

1956 Litho. *Perf. 13*

Two types:
I. Bust touches upper frame line of name panel at bottom.
II. White line separates bust from frame line.

Size: 19½-20½x26-27mm

659	A133	20c dull purple (I)	18	15
a.		Type II	18	15
b.		Size 19½x25¾mm (I)	15	15

For overprint see No. O108.

Benjamin Franklin
A255

1956, Dec. 22 Photo. *Perf. 13½*

660	A255	40c intense blue	30	15

250th anniv. of the birth of Benjamin Franklin.

Frigate "Hercules"
A256

Guillermo Brown
A257

1957, Mar. 2

661	A256	40c brt blue	15	15
662	A257	2.40p gray black	35	15
		Nos. 661-662,C63-C65 (5)	1.02	
		Set value		42

Admiral Guillermo (William) Brown (1777-1857), founder of the Argentine navy.

Roque Saenz Pena (1851-1914)
A258

Church of Santo Domingo, 1807
A259

1957, Apr. 1

663	A258	4.40p grnsh gray	45	15

Roque Saenz Pena, pres. 1910-14.
For overprint see No. O111.

1957, July 6 Wmk. 90

664	A259	40c brt blue green	15	15

150th anniv. of the defense of Buenos Aires.

"La Portena" — A260

1957, Aug. 31 Wmk. 90 *Perf. 13½*

665	A260	40c pale brown	18	15

Centenary of Argentine railroads.

Esteban Echeverria
A261

"Liberty"
A262

1957, Sept. 2 *Perf. 13x13½*

666	A261	2p claret	22	15

Esteban Echeverria (1805-1851), poet.
For overprint see No. O109.

1957, Sept. 28 *Perf. 13½*

667	A262	40c carmine rose	15	15

Constitutional reform convention.

Portrait Type of 1935-51

1957, Oct. 28 Litho. *Perf. 13½*
Size: 16½x22mm

668	A128	5c Jose Hernandez	15	15

For overprint see No. O112.

Oil Derrick and Hands Holding Oil — A263

Perf. 13½

1957, Dec. 21 Wmk. 90 Photo.

669 A263 40c bright blue		18	15

50th anniv. of the national oil industry.

Museum, La Plata — A264

1958, Jan. 11

670 A264 40c dark gray		15	15

City of La Plata, 75th anniversary.

A265

A266

Designs: 40c, Locomotive and arms of Argentina and Bolivia. 1p, Map of Argentine-Bolivian boundary and plane.

1958, Apr. 19 Wmk. 90 *Perf. 13½*

671 A265 40c slate & dp car		28	15
672 A266 1p dark brown		28	15
Set value			25

Argentine-Bolivian friendship. No. 671 for the opening of the Jacuiba-Santa Cruz railroad; No. 672, the exchange of presidential visits.

Symbols of the Republic A267

Flag Monument A268

1958, Apr. 30 Photo. & Engr.

673 A267 40c multicolored		15	15
674 A267 1p multicolored		16	15
675 A267 2p multicolored		25	15
Nos. 673-675 (3)		56	
Set value			25

Transmission of Presidential power.

1958, June 21 Litho. Wmk. 90

676 A268 40c blue & violet bl		15	15

1st anniv. of the Flag Monument of Rosario.

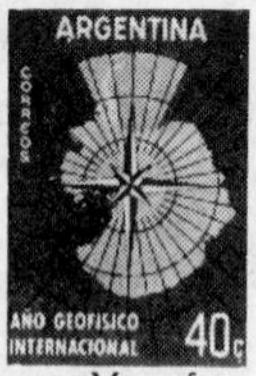

Map of Antarctica A269

Stamp of Cordoba and Mail Coach A270

1958, July 12 *Perf. 13½*

677 A269 40c car rose & blk		48	18

International Geophysical Year, 1957-58.

1958, Oct. 18

678 A270 40c pale blue & slate		15	15
Nos. 678,C72-C73 (3)		59	
Set value			25

Centenary of Cordoba postage stamps.

"Slave" by Michelangelo and UN Emblem — A271

Engraved and Lithographed

1959, Mar. 14 Wmk. 90 *Perf. 13½*

679 A271 40c violet brn & gray		15	15

10th anniv. (in 1958) of the signing of the Universal Declaration of Human Rights.

Orchids and Globe — A272

1959, May 23 Photo. *Perf. 13½*

680 A272 1p dull claret		22	15

1st International Horticulture Exposition.

Pope Pius XII — A273

William Harvey — A274

1959, June 20 Engr. *Perf. 13½*

681 A273 1p yellow & black		18	15

Pope Pius XII, 1876-1958.

1959, Aug. 8 Litho. Wmk. 90

Portraits: 1p, Claude Bernard. 1.50p, Ivan P. Pavlov.

682 A274 50c green		15	15
683 A274 1p dark red		15	15
684 A274 1.50p brown		22	15
Nos. 682-684 (3)		52	
Set value			18

21st International Congress of Physiological Sciences, Buenos Aires.

Type of 1958 and

Domestic Horse A275

Jose de San Martin A276

Tierra del Fuego — A277

Inca Bridge, Mendoza A278

Ski Jumper A279

Mar del Plata A280

Designs: 10c, Cayman. 20c, Llama. 50c, Puma. No. 690, Sunflower. 3p, Zapata Slope, Catamarca. 12p, 23p, 25p, Red Quebracho tree. 20p, Nahuel Huapi Lake. 22p, "Industry" (cogwheel and factory).

Two overall paper sizes for 1p, 5p:

I - 27x37½mm or 37½x27mm.

II - 27x39mm or 39x27mm.

Perf. 13x13½

1959-70 Litho. Wmk. 90

685	A275	10c	slate green	15	15
686	A275	20c	dl red brn ('61)	15	15
687	A275	50c	bister ('60)	15	15
688	A275	50c	bis, typo. ('60)	18	15
689	A275	1p	rose red	15	15

Perf. 13½

690	A278	1p	brn, photo., I ('61)	15	15
a.			Paper II ('69)	18	15
690B	A278	1p	brown, I	65	15
691	A276	2p	rose red ('61)	25	15
692	A276	2p	red, typo. (19½ x 26mm) ('61)	32	15
a.			Redrawn (19½ x 25mm)	4.75	15
693	A277	3p	dk bl, photo. ('60)	16	15
694	A276	4p	red, typo ('62)	18	15
694A	A276	4p	red ('62)	38	15
695	A277	5p	gray brn, photo., I	38	15
e.			5p dk brn, paper II ('70)	6.25	15
695A	A276	8p	ver ('65)	1.25	15
695B	A276	8p	red, typo. ('65)	32	15
695C	A276	10p	ver ('66)	65	15
695D	A276	10p	red, typo. ('66)	48	15

Photo.

696	A278	10p	lt red brn ('60)	48	15
697	A278	12p	dk brn vio ('62)	80	15
697A	A278	12p	dk brn, litho. ('64)	8.00	15
698	A278	20p	Prus grn ('60)	2.75	15
698A	A276	20p	red, typo. ('67)	25	15
699	A238a	22p	ultra ('62)	1.50	15
700	A238a	22p	ultra, litho. ('62)	24.00	15
701	A278	23p	green ('65)	4.75	15
702	A278	25p	dp vio ('66)	1.25	15
703	A278	25p	pur, litho. ('66)	6.25	15
704	A279	100p	blue ('61)	5.00	15
705	A280	300p	dp vio ('62)	2.75	15
			Nos. 685-705 (29)	63.73	
			Set value		1.50

See Nos. 882-887, 889, 892, 923-925, 928-930, 938, 987-989, 991.

For overprints and surcharges see Nos. 1076, C82-C83, O113-O118, O122-O124, O126-O141, O143-O145, O163.

The 300p remained on sale as a 3p stamp after the 1970 currency exchange.

Symbolic Sailboat — A281

Child Playing with Doll — A282

1959, Oct. 3 Litho. *Perf. 13½*

706 A281 1p blk, red & bl		15	15

Red Cross sanitary education campaign.

1959, Oct. 17

707 A282 1p red & blk		15	15

Issued for Mother's Day, 1959.

Buenos Aires 1p Stamp of 1859 — A283

1959, Nov. 21 Wmk. 90 *Perf. 13½*

708 A283 1p gray & dk bl		15	15

Issued for the Day of Philately.

Bartolomé Mitre and Justo José de Urquiza A284

1959, Dec. 12 Photo. *Perf. 13½*

709 A284 1p purple		15	15

Treaty of San Jose de Flores, centenary.

WRY Emblem A285

Abraham Lincoln A286

1960, Apr. 7 Litho. Wmk. 90

710 A285 1p bister & car		15	15
711 A285 4.20p apple grn & dp claret		32	20
Set value			27

World Refugee Year, July 1, 1959-June 30, 1960. See No. B25.

1960, Apr. 14 Photo. *Perf. 13½*

712 A286 5p ultra		42	18

Sesquicentennial (in 1959) of the birth of Abraham Lincoln.

Cornelio Saavedra and Cabildo, Buenos Aires — A287

"Cabildo" and: 2p, Juan José Paso. 4.20p, Manuel Alberti and Miguel Azcuénaga. 10.70p, Juan Larrea and Domingo Matheu.

Perf. 13½

1960, May 28 Wmk. 90 Photo.

713 A287	1p rose lilac	15	15
714 A287	2p bluish grn	15	15
715 A287	4.20p gray & grn	24	15
716 A287	10.70p gray & ultra	45	20
Nos. 713-716,C75-C76 (6)		1.46	
Set value			55

150th anniversary of the May Revolution. Souvenir sheets are Nos. C75a and C76a.

Luis Maria Drago — A288

Juan Bautista Alberdi — A289

1960, July 8

717 A288 4.20p brown 22 15

Ccentenary of the birth of Dr. Luis Maria Drago, statesman and jurist.

1960, Sept. 10 Wmk. 90 *Perf. 13½*

718 A289 1p green 15 15

150th anniversary of the birth of Juan Bautista Alberdi, statesman and philosopher.

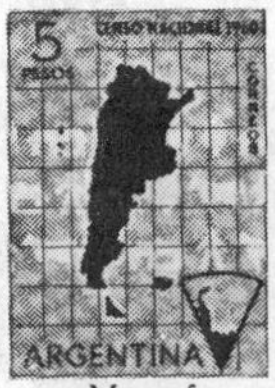

Map of Argentina and Antarctic Sector — A290

Caravel and Emblem — A291

1960, Sept. 24 Litho. *Perf. 13½*

719 A290 5p violet 85 22

National census of 1960.

1960, Oct. 1 Photo.

720 A291 1p dk olive grn	15	15
721 A291 5p brown	45	15
Nos. 720-721,C78-C79 (4)	1.13	
Set value		15

8th Congress of the Postal Union of the Americas and Spain.

Virgin of Luján, Patroness of Argentina A292

Argentine Boy Scout Emblem A293

1960, Nov. 12 Wmk. 90 *Perf. 13½*

722 A292 1p dark blue 15 15

First Inter-American Marian Congress.

1961, Jan. 17 Litho.

723 A293 1p car rose & blk 28 15

International Patrol Encampment of the Boy Scouts, Buenos Aires.

"Shipment of Cereals," by Quinquela Martin A294

1961, Feb. 11 Photo. *Perf. 13½*

724 A294 1p red brown 28 15

Export drive: "To export is to advance."

Naval Battle of San Nicolás — A295

Mariano Moreno by Juan de Dios Rivera — A296

1961, Mar. 2 *Perf. 13½*

725 A295 2p gray 28 15

Naval battle of San Nicolas, 150th anniv.

1961, Mar. 25 *Perf. 13½*

726 A296 2p blue 15 15

Mariano Moreno (1778-1811), writer, politician, member of the 1810 Junta.

Emperor Trajan Statue — A297

Rabindranath Tagore — A298

1961, Apr. 11

727 A297 2p slate green 15 15

Visit of Pres. Giovanni Gronchi of Italy to Argentina, April 1961.

1961, May 13 Photo. *Perf. 13½*

728 A298 2p purple, *grysh* 15 15

Centenary of the birth of Rabindranath Tagore, Indian poet.

San Martin Statue, Madrid — A299

1961, May 24 Wmk. 90

729 A299 1p olive gray 15 15

Unveiling of a statue of General José de San Martin in Madrid.

Manuel Belgrano — A300

1961, June 17 *Perf. 13½*

730 A300 2p violet blue 15 15

Erection of a monument by Hector Rocha, to General Manuel Belgrano in Buenos Aires.

Explorers, Sledge and Dog Team — A301

1961, Aug. 19 Photo. Wmk. 90

731 A301 2p black 70 22

10th anniversary of the General San Martin Base, Argentine Antarctic.

Spanish Conquistador and Sword — A302

Sarmiento Statue by Rodin, Buenos Aires — A303

1961, Aug. 19 Litho.

732 A302 2p red & blk 15 15

First city of Jujuy, 400th anniversary.

1961, Sept. 9 Photo.

733 A303 2p violet 15 15

Domingo Faustino Sarmiento (1811-88), political leader and writer.

Symbol of World Town Planning A304

1961, Nov. 25 Litho. *Perf. 13½*

734 A304 2p ultra & yel 15 15

World Town Planning Day, Nov. 8.

Manuel Belgrano Statue, Buenos Aires A305

Grenadier, Flag and Regimental Emblem A306

1962, Feb. 24 Photo.

735 A305 2p Prus blue 15 15

150th anniversary of the Argentine flag.

1962, Mar. 31 Wmk. 90 *Perf. 13½*

736 A306 2p carmine rose 15 15

150th anniversary of the San Martin Grenadier Guards regiment.

Mosquito and Malaria Eradication Emblem — A307

1962, Apr. 7 Litho.

737 A307 2p vermilion & blk 15 15

WHO drive to eradicate malaria.

Church of the Virgin of Lujàn — A308

Bust of Juan Jufrè — A309

1962, May 12 *Perf. 13½*

738 A308 2p org brn & blk 15 15

75th anniversary of the pontifical coronation of the Virgin of Lujan.

1962, June 23 Photo.

739 A309 2p Prus blue 15 15

Founding of San Juan, 4th cent.

"Soaring into Space" A310

Juan Vucetich A311

1962, Aug. 18 Litho. *Perf. 13½*

740 A310 2p maroon, blk & bl 15 15

Argentine Air Force, 50th anniversary.

1962, Oct. 6 Photo. Wmk. 90

741 A311 2p green 15 15

Juan Vucetich (1864-1925), inventor of the Argentine system of fingerprinting.

Domingo F. Sarmiento A312

February 20th Monument, Salta A313

Design: 4p, Jose Hernandez.

1962-66 Photo. *Perf. 13½*

742	A312 2p deep green	65	15
	Litho.		
742A	A312 2p lt green ('64)	55	15
	Photo.		
742B	A312 4p dull red ('65)	45	15
	Litho.		
742C	A312 4p rose red ('66)	60	15
	Nos. 742-742C (4)	2.25	
	Set value		20

See No. 817-819. For overprints see Nos. O119-O121, O125, O149.

1963, Feb. 23 Photo. Wmk. 90

743 A313 2p dark green 15 15

150th anniversary of the Battle of Salta, War of Independence.

Gear Wheels — A314

1963, Mar. 16 **Litho.** ***Perf. 13½***
744 A314 4p gray, blk & brt rose 15 15

Argentine Industrial Union, 75th anniv.

National College, Buenos Aires — A315

Child Draining Cup — A316

1963, Mar. 16 **Wmk. 90**
745 A315 4p dull org & blk 18 15

National College of Buenos Aires, cent.

1963, Apr. 6
746 A316 4p multicolored 15 15

FAO "Freedom from Hunger" campaign.

Frigate "La Argentina," 1817, by Emilio Biggeri — A317

1963, May 18 **Photo.**
747 A317 4p bluish green 28 15

Issued for Navy Day, May 17.

Seat of 1813 Assembly and Official Seal — A318

1963, July 13 **Litho.** ***Perf. 13½***
748 A318 4p lt blue & blk 15 15

150th anniversary of the 1813 Assembly.

Battle of San Lorenzo, 1813 A319

1963, Aug. 24
749 A319 4p grn & blk, *grnsh* 20 15

Sesquicentennial of the Battle of San Lorenzo.

Queen Nefertari Offering Papyrus Flowers, Abu Simbel — A320

1963, Sept. 14 ***Perf. 13½***
750 A320 4p ocher, blk & bl grn 28 15

Campaign to save the historic monuments in Nubia.

Government House, Buenos Aires A321

1963, Oct. 12 **Wmk. 90** ***Perf. 13½***
751 A321 5p rose & brown 16 15

Inauguration of President Arturo Illia.

"Science" A322

Francisco de las Carreras, Supreme Court Justice A323

1963, Oct. 16 **Litho.**
752 A322 4p org brn, bl & blk 15 15

10th Latin-American Neurosurgery Congress.

1963, Nov. 23 **Photo.** ***Perf. 13½***
753 A323 5p bluish green 15 15

Centenary of judicial power.

Blackboards A324

1963, Nov. 23 **Litho.**
754 A324 5p red, blk & bl 15 15

Issued to publicize "Teachers for America" through the Alliance for Progress program.

Kemal Atatürk A325

"Payador" by Juan Carlos Castagnino A326

1963, Dec. 28 **Photo.** ***Perf. 13½***
755 A325 12p dark gray 28 15

25th anniversary of the death of Kemal Atatürk, president of Turkey.

1964, Jan. 25 **Litho.**
756 A326 4p ultra, blk & lt bl 32 15

Fourth National Folklore Festival.

Maps of South Georgia, South Orkney and South Sandwich Islands — A327

Design: 4p, Map of Argentina and Antarctic claims, vert.

1964, Feb. 22 **Wmk. 90** ***Perf. 13½***
Size: 33x22mm
757 A327 2p lt & dk bl & bister 1.25 24

Size: 30x40mm
758 A327 4p lt & dk bl & ol grn 1.75 30
Nos. 757-758,C92 (3) 4.75 1.24

60th anniversary of Argentina's claim to Antarctic territories.

Jorge Newbery in Cockpit — A328

1964, Feb. 23 **Photo.**
759 A328 4p deep green 16 15

Newbery, aviator, 50th death anniv.

John F. Kennedy — A329

José Brochero by José Cuello — A330

1964, Apr. 14 **Engr.** **Wmk. 90**
760 A329 4p claret & dk bl 35 15

President John F. Kennedy (1917-63).

1964, May 9 **Photo.** ***Perf. 13½***
761 A330 4p light sepia 16 15

50th anniversary of the death of Father Jose Gabriel Brochero.

Soldier of Patricios Regiment — A331

1964, May 29 **Litho.** **Wmk. 90**
762 A331 4p blk, ultra & red 38 20

Issued for Army Day. Later Army Day stamps, inscribed "Republica Argentina," are of type A340a.

Pope John XXIII — A332

1964, June 27 **Engr.**
763 A332 4p orange & blk 22 15

Issued in memory of Pope John XXIII.

University of Cordoba Arms — A333

Pigeons and UN Building, NYC — A334

1964, Aug. 22 **Litho.** **Wmk. 90**
764 A333 4p blk, ultra & yel 15 15

350th anniv. of the University of Cordoba.

1964, Oct. 24 ***Perf. 13½***
765 A334 4p dk blue & lt blue 15 15

Issued for United Nations Day.

Joaquin V. Gonzalez — A335

Julio Argentino Roca — A336

1964, Nov. 14 **Photo.**
766 A335 4p dk rose carmine 15 15

Centenary (in 1963) of the birth of Joaquin V. Gonzalez, writer.

1964, Dec. 12 ***Perf. 13½***
767 A336 4p violet blue 15 15

General Julio A. Roca, (1843-1914), president of Argentina, (1880-86, 1898-1904).

Market at Montserrat Square, by Carlos Morel — A337

1964, Dec. 19 **Photo.**
768 A337 4p sepia 30 18

19th century Argentine painter Carlos Morel.

Icebreaker General San Martin — A338

Girl with Piggy Bank — A339

Design: 2p, General Belgrano Base, Antarctica.

1965 ***Perf. 13½***
769 A338 2p dull purple 42 15
770 A338 4p ultra 48 15

Issued to publicize the national territory of Tierra del Fuego, Antarctic and South Atlantic Isles.
Issue dates: 4p, Feb. 27; 2p, June 5.

1965, Apr. 3 **Litho.**
771 A339 4p red org & blk 15 15

National Postal Savings Bank, 50th anniv.

Sun and Globe — A340

1965, May 29
772 A340 4p blk, org & dl bl 24 15
Nos. 772,C98-C99 (3) 1.66 85

International Quiet Sun Year, 1964-65.

Hussar of Pueyrredon Regiment A340a

Ricardo Rojas (1882-1957) A341

1965, June 5 Wmk. 90 *Perf. 13½*
773 A340a 8p dp ultra, blk & red 48 18

Issued for Army Day. See Nos. 796, 838, 857, 893, 944, 958, 974, 1145.

1965, June 26 Photo.

Portraits: No. 775, Ricardo Guiraldes (1886-1927). No. 776, Enrique Larreta (1873-1961). No. 777, Leopoldo Lugones (1874-1938). No. 778, Roberto J. Payro (1867-1928).

774 A341 8p brown 35 16
775 A341 8p brown 35 16
776 A341 8p brown 35 16
777 A341 8p brown 35 16
778 A341 8p brown 35 16
Nos. 774-778 (5) 1.75 80

Issued to honor Argentine writers. Printed se-tenant in sheets of 100 (10x10); 2 horizontal rows of each design with Guiraldes in top rows and Rojas in bottom rows.

Hipolito Yrigoyen — A342

1965, July 3 Litho.
779 A342 8p pink & black 20 15

Hipolito Yrigoyen (1852-1933), president of Argentina 1916-22, 1928-30.

Children Looking Through Window A343

1965, July 24 Photo.
780 A343 8p salmon & blk 24 15

International Seminar on Mental Health.

Child's Funerary Urn and 16th Century Map A344

1965, Aug. 7 Litho.
781 A344 8p lt grn, dk red, brn & ocher 32 15

City of San Miguel de Tucuman, 400th anniv.

Cardinal Cagliero A345

Dante Alighieri A346

1965, Aug. 21 Photo.
782 A345 8p violet 20 15

Juan Cardinal Cagliero (1839-1926), missionary to Argentina and Bishop of Magida.

1965, Sept. 16 Wmk. 90 *Perf. 13½*
783 A346 8p light ultra 28 15

Dante Alighieri (1265-1321), Italian poet.

Clipper "Mimosa" and Map of Patagonia A347

1965, Sept. 25 Litho.
784 A347 8p red & black 28 15

Centenary of Welsh colonization of Chubut, and the founding of the city of Rawson.

Map of Buenos Aires, Cock and Compass Emblem of Federal Police — A348

1965, Oct. 30 Photo. *Perf. 13½*
785 A348 8p carmine rose 32 15

Issued for Federal Police Day.

Child's Drawing of Children — A349

1965, Nov. 6 Litho. Wmk. 90
786 A349 8p lt yel grn & blk 28 15

Public education law, 81st anniversary.

Church of St. Francis, Catamarca A350

Ruben Dario A351

1965, Dec. 8
787 A350 8p org yel & red brn 20 15

Brother Mamerto de la Asuncion Esquiu, preacher, teacher and official of 1885 Provincial Constitutional Convention.

Litho. and Photo.

1965, Dec. 22 *Perf. 13½*
788 A351 15p bl vio, *gray* 20 15

Ruben Dario (pen name of Felix Ruben Garcia Sarmiento, 1867-1916), Nicaraguan poet, newspaper correspondent and diplomat.

"The Orange Seller" A352

Pueyrredon Paintings: No. 790, "Stop at the Grocery Store." No. 791, "Landscape at San Fernando" (sailboats). No. 792, "Bathing Horses at River Plata."

1966, Jan. 29 Photo. *Perf. 13½*
789 A352 8p bluish green 70 40
790 A352 8p bluish green 70 40
791 A352 8p bluish green 70 40
792 A352 8p bluish green 70 40
Nos. 789-792 (4) 2.80 1.60

Prilidiano Pueyrredon (1823-1870), painter. Nos. 789-792 are printed in one sheet of 40 stamps and 20 labels.

Sun Yat-sen, Flags of Argentina and China — A353

1966, Mar. 12 Wmk. 90 *Perf. 13½*
793 A353 8p dk red brown 70 22

Dr. Sun Yat-sen (1866-1925), founder of the Republic of China.

Souvenir Sheet

Rivadavia Issue of 1864 — A354

Wmk. 90

1966, Apr. 20 Litho. *Imperf.*
794 A354 Sheet of 3 95 95
a. 4p gray & red brown 15 15
b. 5p gray & green 15 15
c. 8p gray & dark blue 16 16

2nd Rio de la Plata Stamp Show, Buenos Aires, Mar. 16-24.

People of Various Races and WHO Emblem A355

1966, Apr. 23 *Perf. 13½*
795 A355 8p brown & blk 28 15

Opening of the WHO Headquarters, Geneva.

Soldier Type of 1965

Army Day: 8p, Cavalryman, Guemes Infernal Regiment.

1966, May 28 Litho.
796 A340a 8p multicolored 55 30

Coat of Arms — A356

Arms: a, Buenos Aires. b, Federal Capital. c, Catamarca. d, Cordoba. e, Corrientes. f, Chaco. g, Chubut. h, Entre Rios. i, Formosa. j, Jujuy. k, La Pampa. l, La Rioja. m, Mendoza. n, Misiones. o, Neuquen. p, Salta. q, San Juan. r, San Luis. s, Santa Cruz. t, Santa Fe. u, Santiago del Estero. v, Tucuman. w, map of Rio Negro. x, map of Tierra del Fuego, Antarctica. y, South Atlantic Islands.

1966, July 30 Wmk. 90 *Perf. 13½*
797 Sheet of 25 40.00
a.-y. A356 10p black & multi 1.00 65

150th anniv. of Argentina's Declaration of Independence.

Three Crosses, Caritas Emblem — A357

1966, Sept. 10 Litho. *Perf. 13½*
798 A357 10p ol grn, blk & lt bl 22 15

Caritas, charity organization.

Hilario Ascasubi (1807-75) — A358

Portraits: #800, Estanislao del Campo (1834-80). #801, Miguel Cane (1851-1905). #802, Lucio V. Lopez (1848-94). #803, Rafael Obligado (1851-1920). #804, Luis Agote (1868-1954), M.D. #805, Juan B. Ambrosetti (1865-1917), naturalist and archaeologist. #806, Miguel Lillo (1862-1931), botanist and chemist. #807, Francisco P. Moreno (1852-1919), naturalist and paleontologist. #808, Francisco J. Muñiz (1795-1871), physician.

1966 Photo. Wmk. 90
799 A358 10p dk blue green 42 35
800 A358 10p dk blue green 42 35
801 A358 10p dk blue green 42 35
802 A358 10p dk blue green 42 35
803 A358 10p dk blue green 42 35
804 A358 10p deep violet 42 35
805 A358 10p deep violet 42 35
806 A358 10p deep violet 42 35
807 A358 10p deep violet 42 35
808 A358 10p deep violet 42 35
Nos. 799-808 (10) 4.20 3.50

Nos. 799-803 issued Sept. 17 to honor Argentine writers. Printed se-tenant in sheets of 100 (10x10); 2 horizontal rows of each portrait with Ascasubi in top two rows and Obligado in bottom rows. Nos. 804-808 issued Oct. 22 to honor Argentine scientists; 2 horizontal rows of each portrait with Agote in top two rows and Muniz in bottom rows. Scientists set has value at upper left, frame line with rounded corners.

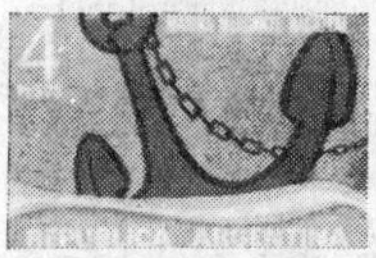

Anchor — A359

1966, Oct. 8 Litho.
809 A359 4p multicolored 22 15

Argentine merchant marine.

Flags and Map of the Americas — A360

Argentine National Bank — A361

1966, Oct. 29 *Perf. 13½*

810 A360 10p gray & multi 24 15

7th Conference of American Armies.

1966, Nov. 5 **Photo.**

811 A361 10p brt blue green 20 15

75th anniv. of the Argentine National Bank.

La Salle Monument and College, Buenos Aires — A362

1966, Nov. 26 **Litho.** *Perf. 13½*

812 A362 10p brown org & blk 20 15

75th anniv. of the Colegio de la Salle, Buenos Aires, and to honor Saint Jean Baptiste de la Salle (1651-1719), educator.

Map of Argentine Antarctica and Expedition Route — A363

1966, Dec. 10 **Wmk. 90**

813 A363 10p multicolored 70 45

1965 Argentine Antarctic expedition, which planted the Argentine flag on the South Pole. See No. 851.

Juan Martin de Pueyrredon A364

Gen. Juan de Las Heras A365

1966, Dec. 17 **Photo.** *Perf. 13½*

814 A364 10p dull red brn 18 15

Issued to honor Juan Martin de Pueyrredon (1777-1850), Governor of Cordoba and of the United Provinces of the River Plata.

1966, Dec. 17 **Engr.**

815 A365 10p black 18 15

Issued to honor Gen. Juan Gregorio de Las Heras (1780-1866), Peruvian field marshal and aide-de-camp to San Martin.

Inscribed "Republica Argentina"
Types of 1955-61 and

Guillermo Brown — A366

Trout Leaping in National Park — A366a

Designs: 6p, Jose Hernandez. 50p, Gen. Jose de San Martin. 500p, Red deer in forest.

Two overall paper sizes for 6p, 50p (No. 827) and 90p:
I - 27x37½mm
II - 27x39mm

1965-68 Wmk. 90 Photo. *Perf. 13½*

817	A366	6p rose red, litho, I ('67)	1.25	15
818	A366	6p rose red ('67)	2.25	15
819	A366	6p brn, 15x22mm ('68)	15	15
823	A238a	43p dk car rose	6.25	15
824	A238a	45p brn ('66)	4.25	15
825	A238a	45p brn, litho ('67)	7.00	15
826	A241	50p dk bl, 29x40mm	7.00	15
827	A241	50p dk bl, 22x31½mm, I ('67)	4.75	15
a.		Paper II	2.75	15
828	A366	90p ol bis, I ('67)	3.00	15
a.		Paper II	12.00	15

Engr.

829	A495	500p yel grn ('66)	1.40	28
829A	A366a	1,000p vio bl ('68)	5.50	1.25
		Nos. 817-829A (11)	42.80	
		Set value		2.25

The 500p and 1,000p remained on sale as 5p and 10p stamps after the 1970 currency exchange.

See Nos. 888, 891, 939, 941, 992, 1031, 1040, 1045-1047. For surcharge and overprints see Nos. 1077, O153-O158, O162.

Pre-Columbian Pottery — A367

1967, Feb. 18 **Litho.** *Perf. 13½*

830 A367 10p multi 28 15

20th anniv. of UNESCO.

"The Meal" by Fernando Fader A368

1967, Feb. 25 **Photo.** **Wmk. 90**

831 A368 10p red brn 28 15

Issued in memory of the Argentine painter Fernando Fader (1882-1935).

Col. Juana Azurduy de Padilla (1781-1862), Soldier — A369

Schooner "Invencible," 1811 — A370

Famous Argentine Women: #833, Juana Manuela Gorriti, writer. #834, Cecilia Grierson (1858-1934), physician. #835, Juana Paula Manso (1819-75), writer and educator. #836, Alfonsina Storni (1892-1938), writer and educator.

1967, May 13 **Photo.** *Perf. 13½*

832	A369	6p dark brown	32	20
833	A369	6p dark brown	32	20
834	A369	6p dark brown	32	20
835	A369	6p dark brown	32	20
836	A369	6p dark brown	32	20
		Nos. 832-836 (5)	1.60	1.00

Printed se-tenant in sheets of 100 (10x10); 2 horizontal rows of each portrait with Azurduy in two top rows and Storni in bottom rows.

1967, May 20 **Litho.**

837 A370 20p multi 85 35

Issued for Navy Day.

Soldier Type of 1965

Army Day: 20p, Highlander (Arribeños Corps).

1967, May 27

838 A340a 20p multi 70 28

Souvenir Sheet

Manuel Belgrano and José Artigas — A371

1967, June 22 ***Imperf.***

839	A371	Sheet of 2	40	40
a.		6p gray & brown	15	15
b.		22p brown & gray	24	24

Third Rio de la Plata Stamp Show, Montevideo, Uruguay, June 18-25.

Peace Dove and Valise A372

PADELAI Emblem A373

1967, Aug. 5 **Litho.** *Perf. 13½*

840 A372 20p multi 22 15

Issued for International Tourist Year 1967.

1967, Aug. 12 **Litho.**

841 A373 20p multi 22 15

75th anniv. of the Children's Welfare Association (Patronato de la Infancia-PADELAI).

Stagecoach and Modern City — A374

1967, Sept. 23 **Wmk. 90** *Perf. 13½*

842 A374 20p rose, yel & blk 26 15

Centenary of Villa Maria, Cordoba.

San Martin by Ibarra — A375

"Battle of Chacabuco" by P. Subercaseaux — A376

1967, Sept. 30 **Litho.**

843 A375 20p blk brn & pale yel 55 15

Engr.

844 A376 40p bl blk 85 20

Set value 27

Battle of Chacabuco, 150th anniversary.

Exhibition Rooms — A377

1967, Oct. 11 **Photo.**

845 A377 20p bl gray 20 15

Government House Museum, 10th anniv.

Pedro L. Zanni, Fokker and 1924 Flight Route — A378

1967, Oct. 21 **Litho.** *Perf. 13½*

846 A378 20p multi 28 15

Issued for Aviation Week and to commemorate the 1924 flight of the Fokker seaplane "Province of Buenos Aires" from Amsterdam, Netherlands, to Osaka, Japan.

Training Ship General Brown, by Emilio Biggeri A379

1967, Oct. 28 **Wmk. 90**
847 A379 20p multi 85 35

Issued to honor the Military Naval School.

Ovidio Lagos and Front Page — A380

St. Barbara — A381

1967, Nov. 11 **Photo.**
848 A380 20p sepia 15 15

Centenary of La Capital, Rosario newspaper.

1967, Dec. 2 ***Perf. 13½***
849 A381 20p rose red 28 15

St. Barbara, patron saint of artillerymen.

Portrait of his Wife, by Eduardo Sivori — A382

1968, Jan. 27 **Photo.** ***Perf. 13½***
850 A382 20p bl grn 28 15

Eduardo Sivori (1847-1918), painter.

Antarctic Type of 1966 and

Admiral Brown Scientific Station A383

Planes over Map of Antarctica A384

Design: 6p, Map showing radio-postal stations 1966-67.

1968, Feb. 17 **Litho.** **Wmk. 90**
851 A363 6p multi 45 18
852 A383 20p multi 60 24
853 A384 40p multi 1.00 30
Nos. 851-853 (3) 2.05 72

Issued to publicize Argentine research projects in Argentine Antarctica.

The Annunciation, by Leonardo da Vinci — A385

Man in Wheelchair and Factory — A386

1968, Mar. 23 **Photo.** ***Perf. 13½***
854 A385 20p lil rose 20 15

Issued for the Day of the Army Communications System and its patron saint, Gabriel.

1968, Mar. 23 **Litho.**
855 A386 20p green & black 20 15

Day of Rehabilitation of the Handicapped.

Children and WHO Emblem — A387

1968, May 11 **Wmk. 90** ***Perf. 13½***
856 A387 20p dk vio bl & ver 20 15

20th anniv. of WHO.

Soldier Type of 1965

Army Day: 20p, Uniform of First Artillery Regiment "General Iriarte."

1968, June 8 **Litho.**
857 A340a 20p multi 75 24

Frigate "Libertad," Painting by Emilio Biggeri A388

1968, June 15 **Wmk. 90**
858 A388 20p multi 75 24

Issued for Navy Day.

Guillermo Rawson and Old Hospital — A389

1968, July 20 **Photo.** ***Perf. 13½***
859 A389 6p olive bister 16 15

Cent. of Rawson Hospital, Buenos Aires.

Student Directing Traffic for Schoolmates A390

1968, Aug. 10 **Litho.** ***Perf. 13½***
860 A390 20p lt bl, blk, buff & car 15 15

Traffic safety and education.

O'Higgins Joining San Martin at Battle of Maipu, by P. Subercaseaux — A391

1968, Aug. 15 **Engr.**
861 A391 40p bluish blk 65 30

Sesquicentennial of the Battle of Maipu.

Osvaldo Magnasco (1864-1920), Lawyer, Professor of Law and Minister of Justice — A392

1968, Sept. 7 **Photo.** ***Perf. 13½***
862 A392 20p brown 22 15

Grandmother's Birthday, by Patricia Lynch — A393

The Sea, by Edgardo Gomez — A394

1968, Sept. 21 **Litho.**
863 A393 20p multicolored 24 15
864 A394 20p multicolored 24 15
Set value 16

The designs were chosen in a competition among kindergarten and elementary school children.

Mar del Plata at Night — A395

1968, Oct. 19 **Litho.** ***Perf. 13½***
865 A395 20p blk, ocher & bl 22 15
Nos. 865,C113-C114 (3) 1.27 61

4th Plenary Assembly of the Intl. Telegraph and Telephone Consultative Committee, Mar del Plata, Sept. 23-Oct. 25.

Frontier Gendarme A396

Patrol Boat A397

1968, Oct. 26
866 A396 20p multi 30 15
867 A397 20p bl, vio bl & blk 30 15

No. 866 honors the Gendarmery; No. 867 the Coast Guard.

Aaron de Anchorena and Pampero Balloon — A398

1968, Nov. 2 **Photo.**
868 A398 20p bl & multi 32 15

22nd Aeronautics and Space Week.

St. Martin of Tours, by Alfredo Guido — A399

1968, Nov. 9 **Litho.**
869 A399 20p lil & dk brn 20 15

St. Martin of Tours, patron saint of Buenos Aires.

Municipal Bank Emblem — A400

1968, Nov. 16
870 A400 20p multi 20 15

90th anniv. of the Buenos Aires Municipal Bank.

Anniversary Emblem A401

1968, Dec. 14 **Wmk. 90** ***Perf. 13½***
871 A401 20p car rose & dk grn 20 15

25th anniversary of ALPI (Fight Against Polio Association).

Shovel and State Coal Fields Emblem A402

Pouring Ladle and Army Manufacturing Emblem A403

1968, Dec. 21 **Litho.**
872 A402 20p org, bl & blk 26 15
873 A403 20p dl vio, dl yel & blk 26 15
Set value 18

Issued to publicize the National Coal and Steel industry at the Rio Turbio coal fields and the Zapla blast furnaces.

Woman Potter, by Ramon Gomez Cornet — A404

1968, Dec. 21 Photo. *Perf. 13½*

874 A404 20p car rose 48 40

Centenary of the Witcomb Gallery.

View of Buenos Aires and Rio de la Plata by Ulrico Schmidl A405

1969, Feb. 8 Litho. Wmk. 90

875 A405 20p yel, blk & ver 48 35

Ulrico Schmidl (c. 1462-1554) who wrote "Journey to the Rio de la Plata and Paraguay."

Types of 1955-67

Designs: 50c, Puma. 1p, Sunflower. 3p, Zapata Slope, Catamarca. 5p, Tierra del Fuego. 6p, José Hernandez. 10p, Inca Bridge, Mendoza. 50p, José de San Martin. 90p, Guillermo Brown. 100p, Ski jumper.

Photo.; Litho. (50c, 3p, 10p)

1969-70 Wmk. 365 *Perf. 13½*

882 A275 50c bister ('70) 70 15
883 A277 5p brown 1.25 15
884 A279 100p blue 26.00 70

Unwmk.

885 A278 1p brown ('70) 65 15
886 A277 3p dk blue ('70) 65 15
a. Wmk. 90 5.25 35
887 A277 5p brown ('70) 75 15
888 A366 6p red brn, 15x22mm ('70) 1.25 15
889 A278 10p dl red ('70) 52 15
a. Wmk. 90 425.00 32.50
890 A241 50p dk bl, 22x31½mm ('70) 1.75 15
891 A366 90p ol brn, 22x32mm ('70) 3.50 18
892 A279 100p blue ('70) 9.00 30
Nos. 882-892 (11) 46.02
Set value 1.78

For surcharges see Nos. 1076-1077.

Soldier Type of 1965

Army Day: 20p, Sapper (gastador) of Buenos Aires Province, 1856.

Perf. 13½

1969, May 31 Wmk. 365 Litho.

893 A340a 20p multicolored 85 35

Frigate Hercules, by Emilio Biggeri — A406

1969, May 31

894 A406 20p multicolored 1.00 28

Issued for Navy Day.

"All Men are Equal" A407

ILO Emblem A408

1969, June 28 Wmk. 90

895 A407 20p black & ocher 20 15

International Human Rights Year.

1969, June 28 Litho. Wmk. 365

896 A408 20p lt green & multi 20 15

50th anniv. of the ILO.

Pedro N. Arata (1849-1922), Chemist — A409

Radar Antenna, Balcarce Station and Satellite — A410

Portraits: No. 898, Miguel Fernandez (1883-1950), zoologist. No. 899, Angel P. Gallardo (1867-1934), biologist. No. 900, Cristobal M. Hicken (1875-1933), botanist. No. 901, Eduardo Ladislao Holmberg, M.D. (1852-1937), natural scientist.

1969, Aug. 9 Wmk. 365 *Perf. 13½*

897 A409 6p Arata 42 15
898 A409 6p Fernandez 42 15
899 A409 6p Gallardo 42 15
900 A409 6p Hicken 42 15
901 A409 6p Holmberg 42 15
Nos. 897-901 (5) 2.10
Set value 50

Argentine scientists. See No. 778 note.

1969, Aug. 23 Wmk. 99

902 A410 20p yellow & blk 28 15

Communications by satellite through Intl. Telecommunications Satellite Consortium (INTELSAT). See No. C115.

Nieuport 28, Flight Route and Map of Buenos Aires Province A411

1969, Sept. 13 Litho. Wmk. 90

903 A411 20p multicolored 28 15

50th anniv. of the first Argentine airmail service from El Palomar to Mar del Plata, flown Feb. 23-24, 1919, by Capt. Pedro L. Zanni.

Military College Gate and Emblem A412

1969, Oct. 4 Wmk. 365 *Perf. 13½*

904 A412 20p multicolored 28 15

Cent. of the National Military College, El Palomar (Greater Buenos Aires).

Gen. Angel Pacheco A413

La Farola, Logotype of La Prensa A414

1969, Nov. 8 Photo. Wmk. 365

905 A413 20p deep green 22 15

Gen. Angel Pacheco (1795-1869).

1969, Nov. 8 Litho. *Perf. 13½*

Design: No. 907, Bartolomé Mitre and La Nacion logotype.

906 A414 20p org, yel & blk 70 22
907 A414 20p brt green & blk 70 22

Cent. of newspapers La Prensa and La Nacion.

Julian Aguirre — A415

Musicians: No. 909, Felipe Boero. No. 910, Constantino Gaito. No. 911, Carlos Lopez Buchardo. No. 912, Alberto Williams.

Perf. 13½

1969, Dec. 6 Wmk. 365 Photo.

908 A415 6p Aguirre 55 30
909 A415 6p Boero 55 30
910 A415 6p Gaito 55 30
911 A415 6p Buchardo 55 30
912 A415 6p Williams 55 30
Nos. 908-912 (5) 2.75 1.50

Argentine musicians. See No. 778 note.

Lt. Benjamin Matienzo and Nieuport Plane A416

1969, Dec. 13 Litho.

913 A416 20p multicolored 55 35

23rd Aeronautics and Space Week.

High Power Lines and Map A417

Design: 20p, Map of Santa Fe Province and schematic view of tunnel.

1969, Dec. 13

914 A417 6p multicolored 50 15
915 A417 20p multicolored 1.00 15
Set value 18

Completion of development projects: 6p for the hydroelectric dams on the Limay and Neuquen Rivers, the 20p the tunnel under Rio Grance from Sante Fe to Parana.

Lions Emblem A418

1969, Dec. 20 Wmk. 365 *Perf. 13½*

916 A418 20p blk, emer & org 60 24

Argentine Lions Intl. Club, 50th anniv.

Madonna and Child, by Raul Soldi — A419

1969, Dec. 27 Litho.

917 A419 20p multicolored 70 28

Christmas 1969.

Manuel Belgrano, by Jean Gericault — A420

The Creation of the Flag, Bas-relief by Jose Fioravanti — A421

Perf. 13½

1970, July 4 Unwmk. Photo.

918 A420 20c deep brown 35 15

Litho. *Perf. 12½*

919 A421 50c bis, blk & bl 85 50

Gen. Manuel Belgrano (1770-1820), Argentine patriot.

San Jose Palace A422

1970, Aug. 9 Litho. *Perf. 13½*

920 A422 20c yel grn & multi 22 15

Cent. of the death of Gen. Justo Jose de Urquiza (1801-70), pres. of Argentina, 1854-60.

Schooner "Juliet" A423

1970, Aug. 8 Unwmk.

921 A423 20c multi 1.00 40

Issued for Navy Day.

Receiver of 1920 and Waves A424

1970, Aug. 29

922 A424 20c lt bl & multi 30 15

50th anniv. of Argentine broadcasting.

Types of 1955-67 Inscribed "Republica Argentina" and Types A425, A426

Belgrano A425

Lujan Basilica A426

Designs: 1c, Sunflower. 3c, Zapata Slope, Catamarca. 5c, Tierra del Fuego. 8c, No. 931, Belgrano. 10c, Inca Bridge, Mendoza. 25c, 50c, 70c, Jose de San Martin. 65c, 90c, 1.20p, San Martin. 1p, Ski jumper. 1.15p, 1.80p, Adm. Brown.

1970-73 Photo. Unwmk. *Perf. 13½*

923	A278	1c	dk grn ('71)	15	15
924	A277	3c	car rose ('71)	15	15
925	A277	5c	blue ('71)	15	15
926	A425	6c	dp bl	15	15
927	A425	8c	grn ('72)	15	15
928	A278	10c	dl red ('71)	38	15
929	A278	10c	brn, litho. ('71)	52	15
930	A278	10c	org brn ('72)	45	15
931	A425	10c	brown ('73)	20	15
932	A426	18c	yel & dk brn, litho ('73)	20	15
933	A425	25c	brown ('71)	32	15
934	A425	50c	scar ('72)	1.25	15
935	A241	65c	brn, 22x31½mm, paper II ('71)	65	15
936	A425	70c	dk bl ('73)	32	15
937	A241	90c	emer, 22x31½ mm ('72)	3.25	15
938	A279	1p	brn, 22½x29½ mm ('71)	1.90	15
939	A366	1.15p	dk bl, 22½x32 mm ('71)	1.10	15
940	A241	1.20p	org, 22x31½ mm ('73)	1.10	15
941	A366	1.80p	brn ('73)	1.10	15
			Nos. 923-941 (19)	13.49	
			Set value		1.00

The imprint "Casa de Moneda de la Nacion" (in capitals) appears on 3c, 5c, Nos. 928-929; 65c, 90c, 1p, 1.20p.

On type A425 only the 6c is inscribed "Ley 18.188" below denomination.

Fluorescent paper was used in printing the 25c, 50c, and 70c. The 3c, 5c, 8c, No. 931 and 65c were issued on both ordinary and fluorescent paper.

See Nos. 987-996, 1032-1038, 1042-1043, 1089-1107. For overprint and surcharge see Nos. 1010, 1078.

Soldier Type of 1965

Design: 20c, Galloping messenger of Field Army, 1879.

1970, Oct. 17 Litho. *Perf. 13½*

944 A340a 20c multi 80 26

Dome of Cathedral of Cordoba — A430

1970, Nov. 7 Unwmk.

945 A430 50c gray & blk 80 15

Bishopric of Tucuman, 400th anniversary. See No. C131.

People Around UN Emblem — A431

1970, Nov. 7

946 A431 20c tan & multi 20 15

25th anniversary of the United Nations.

State Mint and Medal A432

1970, Nov. 28 Unwmk. *Perf. 13½*

947 A432 20c gold, grn & blk 20 15

Inauguration of the State Mint Building, 25th anniversary.

St. John Bosco and Dean Funes College A433

1970, Dec. 19 Litho.

948 A433 20c olive & blk 20 15

Honoring the work of the Salesian Order in Patagonia.

Nativity, by Horacio Gramajo Gutierrez — A434

1970, Dec. 19

949 A434 20c multi 55 35

Christmas 1970.

Argentine Flag, Map of Argentine Antarctica — A435

1971, Feb. 20 Litho. *Perf. 13½*

950 A435 20c multi 1.25 50

Argentine South Pole Expedition, 5th anniv.

Phosphorescent Sorting Code and Albert Einstein — A436

1971, Apr. 30 Unwmk. *Perf. 13½*

951 A436 25c multi 48 30

Electronics in postal development.

Symbolic Road Crossing A437

1971, May 29 Litho.

952 A437 25c bl & blk 25 18

Inter-American Regional Meeting of the Intl. Federation of Roads, Buenos Aires, Mar. 28-31.

Elias Alippi — A438

Actors: No. 954, Juan Aurelio Casacuberta. No. 955, Angelina Pagano. No. 956, Roberto Casaux. No. 957, Florencio Parravicini. See No. 778 note.

1971, May 29 Litho.

953	A438	15c	Alippi	35	20
954	A438	15c	Casacuberta	35	20
955	A438	15c	Pagano	35	20
956	A438	15c	Casaux	35	20
957	A438	15c	Parravicini	35	20
			Nos. 953-957 (5)	1.75	1.00

Soldier Type of 1965

Army Day, May 29: Artilleryman, 1826.

1971, July 3 Unwmk. *Perf. 13½*

958 A340a 25c multi 1.25 50

Bilander "Carmen," by Emilio Biggeri A439

1971, July 3

959 A439 25c multi 1.25 25

Navy Day

Peruvian Order of the Sun A440

1971, Aug. 28

960 A440 31c multi 32 15

Sesquicentennial of Peru's independence.

Güemes in Battle, by Lorenzo Gigli A441

Design: No. 962, Death of Güemes, by Antonio Alice.

1971, Aug. 28

Size: 39x29mm

961 A441 25c multi 48 30

Size: 84x29mm

962 A441 25c multi 48 30

Sesquicentennial of the death of Martin Miguel de Güemes, leader in Gaucho War, Governor and Captain General of Salta Province.

Stylized Tulip — A442

1971, Sept. 18

963 A442 25c tan & multi 26 15

3rd Intl. and 8th Natl. Horticultural Exhib.

Father Antonio Saenz, by Juan Gut — A443

1971, Sept. 18

964 A433 25c gray & multi 26 15

Sesquicentennial of University of Buenos Aires, and to honor Father Antonio Saenz, first Chancellor and Rector.

Fabricaciones Militares Emblem — A444

1971, Oct. 16 Unwmk. *Perf. 13½*

965 A444 25c brn, gold, bl & blk 26 15

30th anniv. of military armament works.

Cars and Trucks A445

Design: 65c, Tree converted into paper.

1971, Oct. 16

966	A445	25c	dl bl & multi	52	20
967	A445	65c	grn & multi	1.25	50
			Nos. 966-967,C134 (3)	2.37	94

Nationalized industries.

Luis C. Candelaria and his Plane, 1918
A446

1971, Nov. 27
968 A446 25c multi 25 18

25th Aeronautics and Space Week.

Observatory and Nebula of Magellan
A447

1971, Nov. 27
969 A447 25c multi 25 15

Cordoba Astronomical Observatory, cent.

Christ in Majesty — A448

1971, Dec. 18 **Litho.**
970 A448 25c blk & multi 25 15

Christmas 1971. Design is from a tapestry by Horacio Butler in Basilica of St. Francis, Buenos Aires.

Mother and Child, by J. C. Castagnino — A449

1972, May 6 **Unwmk.** ***Perf. 13½***
971 A449 25c fawn & black 25 18

25th anniv. (in 1971) of UNICEF.

Mailman's Bag
A450

1972, Sept. 2 **Litho.** ***Perf. 13½***
972 A450 25c lemon & multi 16 15

Bicentenary of appointment of first Argentine mailman.

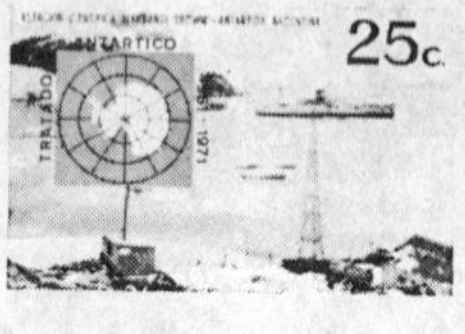

Adm. Brown Station, Map of Antarctica
A451

1972, Sept. 2
973 A451 25c blue & multi 70 35

10th anniv. (in 1971) of Antarctic Treaty.

Soldier Type of 1965

Army Day: 25c, Sergeant, Negro and Mulatto Corps, 1806-1807.

1972, Sept. 23
974 A340a 25c multi 75 35

Brigantine "Santisima Trinidad"
A452

1972, Sept. 23
975 A452 25c multi 75 35

Navy Day. See No. 1006.

A453 A454

1972, Sept. 30 **Litho.** ***Perf. 13½***
976 A453 45c Oil pump 90 20

50th anniv. of the organ. of the state oil fields (Yacimientos Petroliferos Fiscales).

1972, Sept. 30
977 A454 25c Sounding balloon 25 15

Cent. of Natl. Meteorological Service.

Trees and Globe — A455

1972, Oct. 14 ***Perf. 13x13½***
978 A455 25c bl, blk & lt bl 70 20

7th World Forestry Congress, Buenos Aires, Oct. 4-18.

Arms of Naval School, Frigate "Presidente Sarmiento" — A456

1972, Oct. 14
979 A456 25c gold & multi 65 35

Centenary of Military Naval School.

Early Balloon and Plane, Antonio de Marchi — A457

Bartolomé Mitre — A458

1972, Nov. 4 ***Perf. 13½***
980 A457 25c multi 26 20

Aeronautics and Space Week, and in honor of Baron Antonio de Marchi (1875-1934), aviation pioneer.

1972, Nov. 4 **Engr.**
981 A458 25c dark blue 16 15

Pres. Bartolome Mitre (1821-1906), writer, historian, soldier.

Flower and Heart — A459

1972, Dec. 2 **Litho.** ***Perf. 13½***
982 A459 90c lt bl, ultra & blk 60 35

"Your heart is your health," World Health Day.

"Martin Fierro," by Juan C. Castignano — A460

"Spirit of the Gaucho," by Vicente Forte — A461

1972, Dec. 2 **Litho.** ***Perf. 13½***
983 A460 50c multi 32 20
984 A461 90c multi 65 35

Intl. Book Year 1972, and cent. of publication of the poem, Martin Fierro, by Jose Hernandez (1834-86).

Iguacu Falls and Tourist Year Emblem — A462

1972, Dec. 16 ***Perf. 13x13½***
985 A462 45c multi 28 15

Tourism Year of the Americas.

Market value for a particular scarce stamp may remain relatively low if few collectors want it.

King, Wood Carving, 18th Century — A463

1972, Dec. 16 ***Perf. 13½***
986 A463 50c multi 50 25

Christmas 1972.

Types of 1955-73 Inscribed "Republica Argentina" and

Moon Valley, San Juan Province — A463a

Designs: 1c, Sunflower. 5c, Tierra del Fuego. 10c, Inca Bridge, Mendoza. 50c, Lujan Basilica. 65c, 22.50p, San Martin. 1p, Ski jumper. 1.15p, 4.50p, Guillermo Brown. 1.80p, Manuel Belgrano.

Litho.; Photo. (1c, 65c, 1p)
Perf. 13½, 12½ (1.80p)

1972-75 **Wmk. 365**

987	A278	1c	dk grn	16	15
988	A277	5c	dark blue	16	15
989	A278	10c	bis brn	16	15
989A	A426	50c	dl pur ('75)	16	15
990	A241	65c	gray brn	3.25	15
991	A279	1p	brown	1.40	15
992	A366	1.15p	dk gray bl	1.40	15
993	A425	1.80p	bl ('75)	16	15
994	A366	4.50p	grn ('75)	65	15
995	A241	22.50p	vio bl ('75)	1.40	15
996	A463a	50p	multi ('75)	2.75	32
	Nos. 987-996 (11)			11.65	
			Set value		1.05

Paper size of 1c is 27½x39mm; others of 1972, 37x27, 27x37mm.
Size of 22.50p, 50p: 26½x38½mm.
See Nos. 1050, 1108.

Cock (Symbolic of Police) — A464

First Coin of Bank of Buenos Aires — A465

1973, Feb. 3 **Litho.** **Unwmk.**
997 A464 50c lt grn & multi 30 15

Sesqui. of Federal Police of Argentina.

1973, Feb. 3 ***Perf. 13½***
998 A465 50c pur, yel & brn 15 15

Sesquicentennial of the Bank of Buenos Aires Province.

DC-3 Planes Over Antarctica A466

1973, Apr. 28 **Litho.** ***Perf.* 13½**
999 A466 50c lt bl & multi 1.50 60

10th anniversary of Argentina's first flight to the South Pole.

Rivadavia's Chair, Argentine Arms and Colors — A467

1973, May 19 **Litho.** ***Perf.* 13½**
1000 A467 50c multi 25 15

Inauguration of Pres. Hector J. Campora, May 25, 1973.

San Martin, by Gil de Castro — A468

San Martin and Bolivar A469

1973, July 7 **Litho.** ***Perf.* 13½**
1001 A468 50c lt grn & multi 35 15
1002 A469 50c yel & multi 35 15

Gen. San Martin's farewell to the people of Peru and his meeting with Simon Bolivar at Guayaquil July 26-27, 1822.

Eva Peron A470

1973, July 26 **Litho.** ***Perf.* 13½**
1003 A470 70c blk, org & bl 20 15

Maria Eva Duarte de Peron (1919-1952), political leader.

House of Viceroy Sobremonte, by Hortensia de Virgilion — A471

1973, July 28 ***Perf.* 13x13½**
1004 A471 50c bl & multi 20 15

400th anniversary of the city of Cordoba.

Woman, by Lino Spilimbergo A472

New and Old Telephones A473

1973, Aug. 28 **Litho.** ***Perf.* 13½**
1005 A472 70c multi 70 15

Philatelists' Day. See Nos. B60-B61.

Ship Type of 1972

Navy Day: 70c, Frigate "La Argentina."

1973, Oct. 27 **Litho.** ***Perf.* 13½**
1006 A452 70c multi 60 35

1973, Oct. 27
1007 A473 70c brt bl & multi 40 20

25th anniv. of natl. telecommunications system.

Plume Made of Flags of Participants A474

1973, Nov. 3 ***Perf.* 13½**
1008 A474 70c yel bis & multi 25 15

12th Cong. of Latin Notaries, Buenos Aires.

No. 940 Overprinted

TRANSMISION DEL MANDO PRESIDENCIAL
12 OCTUBRE 1973

1973, Nov. 30 **Photo.**
1010 A241 1.20p orange 85 20

Assumption of presidency by Juan Peron, Oct. 12.

Virgin and Child, Window, La Plata Cathedral — A476

Christmas: 1.20p, Nativity, by Bruno Venier, b. 1914.

1973, Dec. 15 **Litho.** ***Perf.* 13½**
1011 A476 70c gray & multi 35 18
1012 A476 1.20p black & multi 70 35

The Lama, by Juan Batlle Planas — A477

Paintings: 50c, Houses in Boca District, by Eugenio Daneri, horiz. 90c, The Blue Grotto, by Emilio Pettoruti, horiz.

1974, Feb. 9 **Litho.** ***Perf.* 13½**
1013 A477 50c multicolored 28 15
1014 A477 70c multicolored 35 20
1015 A477 90c multicolored 60 28
Nos. 1013-1015,B64 (4) 1.51 85

Argentine painters.

Mar del Plata A478

1974, Feb. 9
1016 A478 70c multicolored 28 15

Centenary of Mar del Plata.

Weather Symbols A479

Justo Santa Maria de Oro A480

1974, Mar. 23 **Litho.** ***Perf.* 13½**
1017 A479 1.20p multi 35 20

Cent. of intl. meteorological cooperation.

1974, Mar. 23
1018 A480 70c multi 20 15

Bicentenary of the birth of Brother Justo Santa Maria de Oro (1772-1836), theologian, patriot, first Argentine bishop.

Belisario Roldan (1873-1922), Writer — A481

1974, June 29 **Photo.** **Unwmk.**
1019 A481 70c bl & brn 20 15

Poster with Names of OAS Members A482

1974, June 29 **Litho.**
1020 A482 1.38p multi 18 15

Organization of American States, 25th anniv.

ENCOTEL Emblem — A483

1974, Aug. 10 **Litho.** ***Perf.* 13**
1021 A483 1.20p bl, gold & blk 42 15

ENCOTEL, Natl. Post and Telegraph Press.

Flags of Argentina, Bolivia, Brazil, Paraguay, Uruguay — A484

1974, Aug. 16 ***Perf.* 13½**
1022 A484 1.38p multi 22 15

6th Meeting of Foreign Ministers of Rio de la Plata Basin Countries.

El Chocon Hydroelectric Complex, Limay River — A485

Somisa Steel Mill, San Nicolas — A486

Gen. Belgrano Bridge, Chaco-Corrientes — A487

***Perf.* 13½, 13x13½ (4.50p)**
1974, Sept. 14
1023 A485 70c multi 40 18
1024 A486 1.20p multi 60 35
1025 A487 4.50p multi 2.00 52
Nos. 1023-1025 (3) 3.00 1.05

Development projects.

Brigantine Belgrano, by Emilio Biggeri A488

1974, Oct. 26 **Litho.** ***Perf.* 13½**
1026 A488 1.20p multi 60 30

Departure into exile in Chile of General San Martin, Sept. 22, 1822.

Alberto R. Mascias and Bleriot Plane — A489

1974, Oct. 26 **Unwmk.**
1027 A489 1.20p multi 50 25

Air Force Day, Aug. 10, and to honor Alberto Roque Garcias (1878-1951), aviation pioneer.
Exists with wmk. 365.

Hussar, 1812, by Eleodoro Marenco — A490

1974, Oct. 26
1028 A490 1.20p multi 50 25

Army Day.

Post Horn and Flags A491

1974, Nov. 23 **Unwmk.** ***Perf. 13½***
1029 A491 2.65p multi 85 20

Centenary of Universal Postal Union.
Exists with wmk. 365.

Franciscan Monastery A492

1974, Nov. 23 **Litho.**
1030 A492 1.20p multi 40 15

400th anniversary, city of Santa Fe.

Trout Type of 1968

1974 **Engr.** **Unwmk.**
1031 A366a 1000p vio bl 3.25 80

Due to a shortage of 10p stamps a quantity of this 1,000p was released for use as 10p.

Types of 1954-73 Inscribed "Republica Argentina" and

Red Deer in Forest — A495

Congress Building A497

Designs: 30c, 60c, 1.80p, Manuel Belgrano. 50c, Lujan Basilica. No. 1036, 2p, 6p, San Martin (16x22½mm). 2.70p, 7.50p, 22.50p, San Martin (22x31½mm). 4.50p, 13.50p, Guillermo Brown. 10p, Leaping trout.

1974-76 **Unwmk.** **Photo.** ***Perf. 13½***

1032	A425	30c	brn vio	15	15
1033	A426	50c	blk & brn red	15	15
1034	A426	50c	bis & bl	15	15
1035	A425	60c	ocher	15	15
1036	A425	1.20p	red	30	15
1037	A425	1.80p	dp bl	15	15
1038	A425	2p	dk pur	20	15
1039	A241	2.70p	dk bl, 22 x 31½mm	24	15
1040	A366	4.50p	green	85	15
1041	A495	5p	yel grn	40	15
1042	A425	6p	red org	20	15
1043	A425	6p	emer	20	15
1044	A241	7.50p	grn, 22 x 31½mm	85	15
1045	A366a	10p	vio bl	1.00	15
1046	A366	13.50p	scar, 16 x 22½mm	85	15
1047	A366	13.50p	scar, 22 x 31½mm	85	15
1048	A241	22.50p	dp bl, 22 x 31½mm	75	15
1049	A497	30p	yel & dk red brn	1.10	15
1050	A463a	50p	multi	1.50	15
			Nos. 1032-1050 (19)	10.04	
			Set value		1.50

Nos. 1033-1035, 1037-1038, 1042-1044, 1046-1048 issued in 1976, No. 1050 in 1976.

Fluorescent paper was used in printing No. 1036, 2p, Nos. 1044 and 1047. The 30p was issued on both ordinary and fluorescent paper.

See No. 829. For type of A495 overprinted see No. 1144.

Miniature Sheet

A498

1974, Dec. 7 **Litho.** ***Perf. 13½***
1052 A498 Sheet of 6 3.50 2.75

a.	1p Mariano Necochea	25
b.	1.20p Jose de San Martin	25
c.	1.70p Manuel Isidoro Suarez	35
d.	1.90p Juan Pascual Pringles	42
e.	2.70p Latin American flags	65
f.	4.50p Jose Felix Bogado	1.10

Sesqui. of Battles of Junin and Ayacucho.

Dove, by Vito Campanella A499

St. Anne, by Raul Soldi — A500

1974, Dec. 21 **Litho.** ***Perf. 13½***
1053 A499 1.20p multi 48 18
1054 A500 2.65p multi 75 30

Christmas 1974.

Boy Looking at Stamp — A501

1974, Dec. 21
1055 A501 1.70p blk & yel 38 15

World Youth Philately Year.

Space Monsters, by Raquel Forner A502

Argentine modern art: 4.50p, Dream, by Emilio Centurion.

1975, Feb. 22 **Litho.** ***Perf. 13½***
1056 A502 2.70p multi 90 26
1057 A502 4.50p multi 1.75 40

Indian Woman and Cathedral, Catamarca — A503

Tourist Publicity: #1059, Carved chancel and street scene. #1060, Grazing cattleand monastery yard. #1061, Painted pottery and power station. #1062, Farm cart and colonial mansion. #1063, Perito Moreno glacier and spinning mill. #1064, Lake Lapataia and scientific surveyor. #1065, Los Alerces National Park and oil derrick.

1975 **Litho.** **Unwmk.** ***Perf. 13½***

1058	A503	1.20p	shown	22	16
1059	A503	1.20p	Jujuy	22	16
1060	A503	1.20p	Salta	22	16
1061	A503	1.20p	Santiago del Estero	22	16
1062	A503	1.20p	Tucuman	22	16
1063	A503	6p	Santa Cruz	48	16
1064	A503	6p	Tierra del Fuego	48	16
1065	A503	6p	Chubut	48	16
			Nos. 1058-1065 (8)	2.54	1.28

Issue dates: 1.20p, Mar. 8; 6p, Dec. 20.

"We Have Been Inoculated" A504

1975, Apr. 26 **Unwmk.** ***Perf. 13½***
1066 A504 2p multi 45 22

Children's inoculation campaign (child's painting).

Hugo A. Acuña and South Orkney Station — A505

Designs: No. 1068, Francisco P. Moreno and Lake Nahuel Huapi. No. 1069, Lt. Col. Luis Piedra Buena and cutter, Luisito. No. 1070, Ensign José M. Sobral and Snow Hill House. No. 1071, Capt. Carlos M. Moyano and Cerro del Toro (mountain).

1975, June 28 **Litho.** ***Perf. 13***

1067	A505	2p	grnsh bl & multi	26	15
1068	A505	2p	yel grn & multi	26	15
1069	A505	2p	lt vio & multi	26	15
1070	A505	2p	gray bl & multi	26	15
1071	A505	2p	pale grn & multi	26	15
			Nos. 1067-1071 (5)	1.30	75

Pioneers of Antarctica.

Frigate "25 de Mayo" A506

1975, Sept. 27 **Unwmk.** ***Perf. 13½***
1072 A506 6p multi 42 22

Navy Day 1975.

Eduardo Bradley and Balloon — A507

1975, Sept. 27 **Wmk. 365**
1073 A507 6p multi 42 22

Air Force Day.

Declaration of Independence, by Juan M. Blanes — A508

1975, Oct. 25
1074 A508 6p multi 32 15

Sesquicentennial of Uruguay's declaration of independence.

Flame A509

1975, Oct. 17 **Unwmk.**
1075 A509 6p gray & multi 32 15

Loyalty Day, 30th anniversary of Pres. Peron's accession to power.

Nos. 886, 891 and 932 Surcharged

REVALORIZADO
6 c.

REVALORIZADO 30 c

REVALORIZADO
5 pesos

1975 Lithographed, Photogravure

1076	A277	6c on 3p		15	15
1077	A366	30c on 90p		15	15
1078	A426	5p on 18c		35	18
		Nos. 1076-1078 (3)		65	
		Set value			38

Issue dates: 6c, Oct. 30; 30c, Nov. 20; 5p, Oct. 24. The 6c also exists on No. 886a.

International Bridge, Flags of Argentina and Uruguay A510

1975, Oct. 25 Litho. Wmk. 365

1081 A510 6p multi 35 18

Opening of bridge connecting Colon, Argentina, and Paysandu, Uruguay.

Post Horn, Surcharged A511

1975, Nov. 8

1082 A511 10p on 20c multi 45 15

Introduction of postal code. Not issued without surcharge.

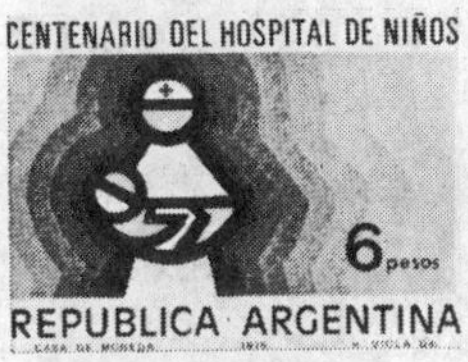

Nurse Holding Infant A512

1975, Dec. 13 Litho. *Perf. 13½*

1083 A512 6p multi 45 15

Children's Hospital, centenary.

Nativity, Nueva Pompeya Church — A513

1975, Dec. 13 Litho. Unwmk.

1084 A513 6p multi 30 18

Christmas 1975.

Types of 1970-75 and

Church of St. Francis, Salta — A515

Designs: 3p, No. 1099, 60p, 90p, Manuel Belgrano. 12p, 15p, 20p, 30p, No. 1100, 100p, 110p, 120p, 130p, San Martin. 15p, 70p, Guillermo Brown. 300p, Moon Valley (lower inscriptions italic). 500p, Adm. Brown Station, Antarctica.

1976-78 Photo. Unwmk. *Perf. 13½*

1089	A425	3p slate	15	15
1090	A425	12p rose red	25	15

Perf. 12½x13

Litho. Wmk. 365

1091	A425	12p rose red	20	15
1092	A425	12p emerald	20	15

Perf. 13½

Photo. Unwmk.

1093	A425	12p emer ('77)	20	15
1094	A425	15p rose red	20	15
1095	A425	15p vio bl ('77)	20	15
1097	A425	20p rose red ('77)	35	15
1098	A425	30p rose red ('77)	35	15
1099	A425	40p dp grn	52	15
1100	A425	40p rose red ('77)	35	15
1101	A425	60p dk bl ('77)	70	20
1102	A425	70p dk bl ('77)	85	20
1103	A425	90p emer ('77)	1.00	28
1104	A425	100p red	75	24
1105	A425	110p rose red ('78)	52	18
1106	A425	120p rose red ('78)	60	20
1107	A425	130p rose red ('78)	70	24

Litho.

1108	A463a	300p multi	3.50	1.50
1109	A515	500p multi ('77)	8.25	1.40
1110	A515	1000p multi ('77)	10.00	2.00
		Nos. 1089-1110 (21)	29.84	8.09

Fluorescent paper was used in printing both 12p rose red, 15p rose red, 20p, 30p, 40p rose red, 100p, 110p, 120p, 130p. No. 1099 and the 300p were issued on both ordinary and fluorescent paper.
300p and 500p exist with wmk. 365.
See Nos. B73-B74.

A516

1976 Photo. Unwmk. *Perf. 13½*

1112	A516	12c gray & blk	15	15
1113	A516	50c gray & grn	15	15
1114	A516	1p red & blk	15	15
1115	A516	4p bl & blk	15	15
1116	A516	5p org & blk	15	15
1117	A516	6p dp brn & blk	15	15
1118	A516	10p gray & vio bl	22	15
1119	A516	27p lt grn & blk	52	15
1120	A516	30p lt bl & blk	90	15
1121	A516	45p yel & blk	90	15
1122	A516	50p dl grn & blk	1.25	15
1123	A516	100p brt grn & red	1.65	25

Perf. 13x12½

1976 Litho. Wmk. 365

1124	A516	5p org & blk	20	15
1125	A516	27p lt grn & blk	52	15
1126	A516	45p yel & blk	1.25	15
		Nos. 1112-1126 (15)	8.31	
		Set value		1.35

The 1p, 6p, 10p, 50p and No. 1116 were issued on both ordinary and fluorescent paper.

Jet and Airlines Emblem — A517

Perf. 13x13½

1976, Apr. 24 Litho. Unwmk.

1130 A517 30p bl, lt bl & dk bl 1.00 20

Argentine Airlines, 25th anniversary.

Frigate Heroina and Map of Falkland Islands — A518

1976, Apr. 26

1131 A518 6p multi 1.00 40

Argentina's claim to Falkland Islands.

Louis Braille — A519

Perf. 13½

1976, May 22 Engr. Wmk. 365

1132 A519 19.70 dp bl 28 15

Sesquicentennial of the invention of the Braille system of writing for the blind by Louis Braille (1809-1852).

Private, 7th Infantry Regiment — A520

1976, May 29 Litho. Unwmk.

1133 A520 12p multi 38 18

Army Day.

Schooner Rio de la Plata, by Emilio Biggeri A521

1976, June 19

1134 A521 12p multi 38 18

Navy Day.

Dr. Bernardo Houssay A522

Argentine Nobel Prize Winners: 15p, Luis F. Leloir, chemistry, 1970. 20p, Carlos Saavedra Lamas, peace, 1936. Bernardo Houssay, medicine and physiology, 1947.

1976, Aug. 14 Litho. *Perf. 13½*

1135	A522	10p org & blk	22	15
1136	A522	15p yel & blk	32	16
1137	A522	20p ocher & blk	45	22
		Nos. 1135-1137 (3)	99	53

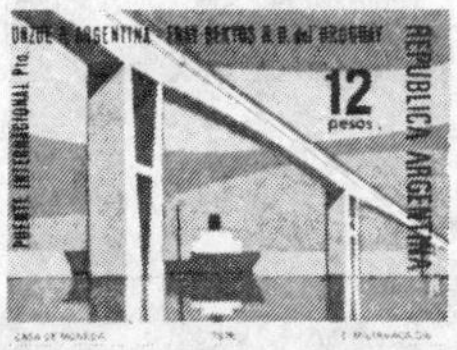

Rio de la Plata International Bridge A523

1976, Sept. 18 Litho. *Perf. 13½*

1138 A523 12p multi 28 15

Inauguration of International Bridge connecting Puerte Unzue, Argentina, and Fray Bentos, Uruguay.

Pipelines and Cooling Tower, Gen. Mosconi Plant A524

1976, Nov. 20 Litho. *Perf. 13½*

1139 A524 28p multi 42 20

Pablo Teodoro Fels and Bleriot Monoplane, 1910 A525

1976, Nov. 20

1140 A525 15p multi 32 15

Air Force Day.

Nativity A526

1976, Dec. 18 Litho. *Perf. 13½*

1141 A526 20p multi 65 28

Christmas. Painting by Edith Chiapetto.

Water Conference Emblem — A527

1977, Mar. 19 Litho. *Perf. 13½*

1142 A527 70p multi 70 25

UN Water Conf., Mar del Plata, Mar. 14-25.

15-Cent Minimum Value
The minimum catalogue value is 15 cents. Separating se-tenant pieces into individual stamps does not increase the value of the stamps since demand for the separated stamps may be small.

Dalmacio Velez Sarsfield A528

1977, Mar. 19 **Engr.**
1143 A528 50p blk & red brn 70 28

Dalmacio Velez Sarsfield (1800-1875), author of Argentine civil code.

Red Deer Type of 1974 Surcharged

1977, July 30 **Photo.** ***Perf. 13½***
1144 A495 100p on 5p brn 1.40 35

Sesquicentennial of Uruguayan postal service. Not issued without surcharge.

Soldier, 16th Lancers — A529

1977, July 30
1145 A529 30p multi 40 20

Army Day.

Schooner Sarandi, by Emilio Biggeri A530

1977, July 30
1146 A530 30p multi 42 22

Navy Day.

Soccer Games' Emblem — A531

Design: 70p, Argentina '78 emblem, flags and soccer field.

1977, May 14
1147 A531 30p multi 40 18
1148 A531 70p multi 85 42

11th World Cup Soccer Championship, Argentina, June 1-25, 1978.

The Visit, by Horacio Butler A532

Consecration, by Miguel P. Caride — A533

1977, Mar. 26 **Litho.**
1149 A532 50p multi 52 25
1150 A533 70p multi 65 38

Argentine artists.

Sierra de la Ventana — A534

Views: No. 1152, Civic Center, Santa Rosa. No. 1153, Skiers, San Martin de los Andes. No. 1154, Boat on Lake Fonck, Rio Negro.

1977, Oct. 8 **Litho.** ***Perf. 13x13½***
1151 A534 30p multi 32 16
1152 A534 30p multi 32 16
1153 A534 30p multi 32 16
1154 A534 30p multi 32 16
Nos. 1151-1154 (4) 1.28 64

Guillermo Brown, by R. del Villar — A535

1977, Oct. 8 ***Perf. 13½***
1155 A535 30p multi 38 22

Adm. Guillermo Brown (1777-1857), leader in fight for independence, bicentenary of birth.

Jet — A536

Double-decker, 1926 — A537

1977 **Litho.** ***Perf. 13½***
1156 A536 30p multi 24 15
1157 A537 40p multi 32 20

50th anniversary of military plane production (30p); Air Force Day (40p).
Issue dates: 30p, Dec. 3; 40p, Nov. 26.

Adoration of the Kings — A538

1977, Dec. 17
1158 A538 100p multi 1.00 28

Christmas 1977.

Historic City Hall, Buenos Aires — A539

Chapel of Rio Grande Museum, Tierra del Fuego — A540

Designs: 5p, 20p, La Plata Museum. 10p, Independence Hall, Tucuman. 40p, City Hall, Salta, vert. No. 1165, City Hall, Buenos Aires. 100p, Columbus Theater, Buenos Aires. 200p, flag Monument, Rosario. 280p, 300p, Chapel of Rio Grande Museum, Tierra del Fuego. 480p, 520p, 800, Ruins of Jesuit Mission Church of San Ignacio, Misiones. 500p, Candonga Chapel, Cordoba. 1000p, G.P.O., Buenos Aires. 2000p, Civic Center, Bariloche, Rio Negro.

Three types of 10p: I. Nine vertical window bars; small imprint "E. MILIAVACA Dib." II. Nine bars; large imprint "E. MILIAVACA DIB." III. Redrawn; 5 bars; large imprint.

1977-81 Photo. Unwmk. *Perf. 13½*
Size: 32x21mm, 21x32mm

1159 A540 5p gray & blk 15 15
1160 A540 10p lt ultra & blk, I 15 15
a. Type II 15 15
1161 A540 10p lt bl & blk, III 15 15
1162 A540 20p cit & blk, litho. 15 15
1163 A540 40p gray bl & blk 24 15
1164 A539 50p yel & blk 28 15
1165 A540 50p cit & blk 16 15
1166 A540 100p org & blk, litho. 35 15
a. Wmk. 365 92.50 24.00
1167 A540 100p red org & blk 15 15
1168 A540 100p turq & blk 15 15
1169 A539 200p lt bl & blk 48 24
1170 A540 280p rose & blk 14.00 20
1171 A540 300p lem & blk 95 15
1172 A540 480p org & blk 1.75 24
1173 A540 500p yel grn & blk 1.75 20
1174 A540 520p org & blk 1.75 30
1175 A540 800p rose lil & blk 2.25 32
1176 A540 1000p lem bis & blk 2.50 38
1177 A540 1000p gold & blk, 40x29mm 3.75 38
1178 A540 2000p multi 2.25 38
Nos. 1159-1178 (20) 33.36
Set value 3.35

Nos. 1161, 1163, 1165, 1167, 1169, 1171, 1173, 1176 and 1177 were issued on both ordinary and fluorescent paper. No. 1174 was issued only on fluorescent paper. All others were issued only on ordinary paper.

Issue dates: No. 1164, May 30, 1977. 280p, Dec. 15, 1977. No. 1160, Mar. 14, 1978. 480p, May 22, 1978. 5p, July 25, 1978. 20p, 500p, Sept. 8, 1978. No. 1166, Sept. 20, 1978. No. 1177, Sept. 28, 1978. 520p, Sept. 30, 1978. 300p, Oct. 5, 1978. 40p, Dec. 1, 1978. No. 1161, 1979. No. 1165, Jan. 8, 1979. 800p, Mar. 20, 1979. No. 1167, Apr. 25, 1979. 200p, June 23, 1979. No. 1176, Dec. 15, 1979. 2000p, June 25, 1980. No. 1168, May 26, 1981.

For overprints see Nos. 1253, 1315.

Soccer Games' Emblem A544

1978, Feb. 10 **Photo.** ***Perf. 13½***
1179 A544 200p yel grn & bl 85 28

11th World Cup Soccer Championship, Argentina, June 1-25. Exists with wmk. 365.

View of El Rio, Rosario — A545

Designs (Argentina '78 Emblem and): 100p, Rio Tercero Dam, Cordoba. 150p, Cordillera Mountains, Mendoza. 200p, City Center, Mar del Plata. 300p, View of Buenos Aires.

1978, May 6 **Litho.** ***Perf. 13***
1180 A545 50p multi 16 15
1181 A545 100p multi 32 15
1182 A545 150p multi 50 16
1183 A545 200p multi 50 24
1184 A545 300p multi 1.10 32
Nos. 1180-1184 (5) 2.58 1.02

Sites of 11th World Cup Soccer Championship, June 1-25.

Children — A546

1978, May 20
1185 A546 100p multi 35 15

50th anniversary of Children's Institute.

Labor Day, by B. Quinquela Martin — A547

Design: No. 1187, Woman's torso, sculpture by Orlando Pierri.

1978, May 20 ***Perf. 13½***
1186 A547 100p multi 35 15
1187 A547 100p multi 35 15

Argentina, Hungary, France, Italy and Emblem — A548

Stadium A549

Teams and Argentina '78 Emblem: 200p, Poland, Fed. Rep. of Germany, Tunisia, Mexico. 300p, Austria, Spain, Sweden, Brazil. 400p, Netherlands, Iran, Peru, Scotland.

1978 Litho. *Perf. 13*
1188 A548 100p multi 32 15
1189 A548 200p multi 65 15
1190 A548 300p multi 95 25
1191 A548 400p multi 1.25 30
Nos. 1188-1191 (4) 3.17 85

Souvenir Sheet
Lithographed and Engraved
Perf. 13½

1192 A549 700p buff & blk 2.50 1.40

11th World Cup Soccer Championship, Argentina, June 1-25. Issued: Nos. 1188-1191, June 6, No. 1192, June 3.

Stadium Type of 1978 Inscribed in Red: "ARGENTINA / CAMPEON"

Lithographed and Engraved

1978, Sept. 2 *Perf. 13½*
1193 A549 1000p bulf, blk & red 3.25 1.40

Argentina's victory in 1978 Soccer Championship. No. 1193 has margin similar to No. 1192 with Rimet Cup emblem added in red.

Young Tree Nourished by Old Trunk, UN Emblem A550

1978 Sept. 2 Litho.
1194 A550 100p multi 35 22

Technical Cooperation among Developing Countries Conf., Buenos Aires, Sept. 1978.

Emblems of Buenos Aires and Bank A551

1978, Sept. 16
1195 A551 100p multi 35 22

Bank of City of Buenos Aires, centenary.

General Savio and Steel Production A552

1978, Sept. 16
1196 A552 100p multi 35 22

Gen. Manuel N. Savio (1892-1948), general manager of military heavy industry.

San Martin — A553

1978, Oct. Engr.
1197 A553 2000p grnsh blk 6.25 1.10

1979 Wmk. 365
1198 A553 2000p grnsh blk 4.75 35

Gen Jose de San Martin (1778-1850), soldier and statesman. See No. 1292.

Globe and Argentine Flag — A554

1978, Oct. 7 Litho. *Perf. 13½*
1199 A554 200p multi 70 28

12th International Cancer Congress, Buenos Aires, Oct. 5-11.

Chessboard, Queen and Pawn — A555

1978, Oct. 7
1200 A555 200p multi 2.00 65

23rd National Chess Olympics, Buenos Aires, Oct. 25-Nov. 12.

Correct Positioning of Stamps — A557

Design: 50p, Use correct postal code number.

1978 Photo. *Perf. 13½*
1201 A557 20p ultra 15 15
1203 A557 50p carmine 22 15
Set value 15

No. 1201 issued on both ordinary and fluorescent paper.

A558

A559

1978-82 Photo. *Perf. 13½*
1204 A558 150p bl & ultra 35 15
1205 A558 180p bl & ultra 45 15
1206 A558 200p bl & ultra 32 15
1207 A559 240p ol bis & bl ('79) 38 15
1208 A559 260p blk & lt bl ('79) 42 15
1209 A559 290p blk & lt bl ('79) 45 15
1210 A559 310p mag & bl ('79) 50 18
1211 A559 350p ver & bl ('79) 65 20
1212 A559 450p ultra & bl 52 18
1213 A559 600p grn & bl ('80) 70 24
1214 A559 700p blk & bl ('80) 70 24
1215 A559 800p red & bl ('81) 65 15
1216 A559 1100p gray & bl ('81) 90 15
1217 A559 1500p blk & bl ('81) 35 15
1218 A559 1700p grn & bl ('82) 45 15
Nos. 1204-1218 (15) 7.79
Set value 2.00

No. 1204 issued on fluorescent and ordinary paper. No. 1206 issued only on fluorescent paper.

For overprint see No. 1338.

Balsa "24" A561

Ships: 200p, Tug Legador. 300p, River Parana tug No. 34. 400p, Passenger ship Ciudad de Parana.

1978, Nov. 4 Litho. *Perf. 13½*
1220 A561 100p multi 24 15
1221 A561 200p multi 48 20
1222 A561 300p multi 70 30
a. Pair, #1221-1222 1.20
1223 A561 400p multi 95 40
a. Pair, #1220, 1223 1.20
Nos. 1220-1223 (4) 2.37 1.05

20th anniversary of national river fleet. Issued on fluorescent paper.

View and Arms of Bahia Blanca A562

1978, Nov. 25 Litho. *Perf. 13½*
1224 A562 20p multi 48 15

Sesquicentennial of Bahia Blanca.

"Spain," (Queen Isabella and Columbus) by Arturo Dresco A563

1978, Nov. 25
1225 A563 300p multi 2.75 30

Visit of King Juan Carlos and Queen Sofia of Spain to Argentina, Nov. 26.

Virgin and Child, San Isidro Cathedral — A564

1978, Dec. 16
1226 A564 200p gold & multi 55 28

Christmas 1978.

Slope at Chacabuco, by Pedro Subercaseaux — A565

Painting: 1000p, The Embrace of Maipu (San Martin and O'Higgins), by Pedro Subercaseaux, vert.

1978, Dec. 16 Litho. *Perf. 13½*
1227 A565 500p multi 1.00 26
1228 A565 1000p multi 2.00 40

José de San Martin, 200th birth anniversary.

Adolfo Alsina A566

Design: No. 1230, Mariano Moreno.

1979, Jan. 20
1229 A566 200p lt bl & blk 30 15
1230 A566 200p yel red & blk 30 15
Set value 16

Adolfo Alsina (1828-1877), political leader, vice-president; Mariano Moreno (1778-1811), lawyer, educator, political leader.

Argentina No. 37 and UPU Emblem A567

1979, Jan. 20
1231 A567 200p multi 22 15

Centenary of Argentina's UPU membership.

Still-life, by Carcova A568

Painting: 300p, The Laundresses, by Faustino Brughetti.

1979, Mar. 3
1232 A568 200p multi 45 15
1233 A568 300p multi 60 20

Ernesto de la Carcova (1866-1927) and Faustino Brughetti (1877-1956), Argentine painters.

A569

A570

1979, Mar. 3
1234 A569 200p Balcarce Earth station 55 25

Third Inter-American Telecommunications Conference, Buenos Aires, March 5-9.

1979
1235 A570 30p Stamp collecting 15 15

Printed on ordinary and fluorescent paper.

European Olive — A571

Laurel and Regimental Emblem — A572

1979, June 2 Litho. *Perf. 13½*

1236 A571 100p shown	26	15
1237 A571 200p Tea	55	26
1238 A571 300p Sorghum	85	40
1239 A571 400p Common flax	1.10	55
Nos. 1236-1239 (4)	2.76	1.36

1979, June 9
1240 A572 200p gold & multi 42 22

Founding of Subteniente Berdina Village in memory of Sub-lieutenant Rodolfo Hernan Berdina, killed by terrorists in 1975.

"75" and Automobile Club Emblem A573

1979, June 9
1241 A573 200p gold & multi 40 20

Argentine Automobile Club, 75th anniv.

Exchange Building and Emblem A574

1979, June 9
1242 A574 200p bl, blk & gold 40 20

Grain Exchange, 125th anniversary.

Cavalry Officer, 1817 — A575

1979, July 7 Litho. *Perf. 13½*
1243 A575 200p multi 1.00 30

Army Day.

Corvette Uruguay and Navy Emblem — A576

Design: No. 1245, Hydrographic service ship and emblem.

1979 *Perf. 13*
1244 A576 250p multi 85 35
1245 A576 250p multi 85 35

Navy Day; Cent. of Naval Hydrographic Service. Issued: #1244, July 28; #1245, July 7.

Tree and Man — A577

1979, July 28 *Perf. 13½*
1246 A577 250p multi 60 22

Protection of the Environment Day, June 5.

"Spad" Flying over Andes, and Vicente Almandos Almonacid A578

1979, Aug. 4
1247 A578 250p multi 70 22

Air Force Day.

Gen. Julio A. Roca Occupying Rio Negro, by Juan M. Blanes A579

1979, Aug. 4
1248 A579 250p multi 70 22

Conquest of Rio Negro Desert, centenary.

Rowland Hill — A580

1979, Sept. 29 Litho. *Perf. 13½*
1249 A580 300p gray red & blk 55 22

Sir Rowland Hill (1795-1879), originator of penny postage.

Viedma Navarez Monument A581

1979, Sept. 29
1250 A581 300p multi 60 22

Viedma and Carmen de Patagones towns, bicentenary.

Pope Paul VI — A582

Design: No. 1252, Pope John Paul I.

1979, Oct. 27 Engr. *Perf. 13½*
1251 A582 500p black 1.00 28
1252 A582 500p sepia 1.00 28

No. 1169 Overprinted in Red: "75 ANIV. / SOCIEDAD/ FILATELICA / DE ROSARIO"

1979, Nov. 10 Photo. *Perf. 13½*
1253 A539 200p lt bl & blk 60 20

Rosario Philatelic Society, 75th anniversary.

Frontier Resettlement A583

1979, Nov. 10 Litho.
1254 A583 300p multi 70 28

Military Geographic Institute Centenary — A584

1979, Dec. 1 Litho. *Perf. 13½*
1255 A584 300p multi 70 28

Christmas 1979 A585

1979, Dec. 1
1256 A585 300p multi 55 22

General Mosconi Birth Centenary — A586

1979, Dec. 15 Engr. *Perf. 13½*
1257 A586 1000p blk & bl 1.50 24

Rotary Emblem and Globe A587

1979, Dec. 29 Litho.
1258 A587 300p multi 1.75 35

Rotary International, 75th anniversary.

Child and IYC Emblem — A588

Family, by Pablo Menicucci A589

1979, Dec. 29
1259 A588 500p lt bl & sep 75 15
1260 A589 1000p multi 1.50 22

International Year of the Child.

Microphone, Waves, ITU Emblem — A590

1980, Mar. 22 Litho. *Perf. 13x13½*

1261 A590 500p multi 95 26

Regional Administrative Conference on Broadcasting by Hectometric Waves for Area 2, Buenos Aires, Mar. 10-29.

Guillermo Brown — A591

1980 Engr. *Perf. 13½*

1262 A591 5000p black 4.50 15

See No. 1372.

Argentine Red Cross Centenary A592

1980, Apr. 19 Litho. *Perf. 13½*

1263 A592 500p multi 52 20

OAS Emblem — A593

1980, Apr. 19

1264 A593 500p multi 55 22

Day of the Americas, Apr. 14.

Dish Antennae, Balcarce A594

1980, Apr. 26 Litho. & Engr.

1265 A594 300p shown 38 20

1266 A594 300p Hydroelectric Station, Salto Grande 38 20

1267 A594 300p Bridge, Zarate-Brazo Largo 38 20

Nos. 1265-1267 (3) 1.14 60

Capt. Hipolito Bouchard, Frigate "Argentina" — A595

1980, May 31 Litho. *Perf. 13x13½*

1268 A595 500p multi 70 28

Navy Day.

"Villarino," San Martin, by Theodore Gericault — A596

1980, May 31

1269 A596 500p multi 70 28

Return of the remains of Gen. Jose de San Martin to Argentina, centenary.

Buenos Aires Gazette, 1810, Signature A597

1980, June 7 *Perf. 13½*

1270 A597 500p multi 55 22

Journalism Day.

Coaches in Victoria Square — A598

1980 June 14

1271 Block of 14 9.00 3.25

a. A598 500p any single 60 22

Buenos Aires, 400th anniv. No. 1271 shows ceramic mural of Victoria Square by Rodolfo Franco in continuous design. See No. 1285.

Gen. Pedro Aramburu — A599

1980, July 12 Litho. *Perf. 13½*

1272 A599 500p yel & blk 55 22

Gen. Pedro Eugenio Aramburu (1903-1970), provisional president, 1955.

Army Day A600

1980, July 12

1273 A600 500p multicolored 85 28

Gen. Juan Gregorio de Las Heras (1780-1866), Hero of 1817 War of Independence — A601

Grandees of Argentina Bicentenary: No. 1275, Rivadavia. No. 1276, Brig. Gen Jose Matias Zapiola (1780-1874), naval commander and statesman.

1980, Aug. 2 Litho. *Perf. 13½*

1274 A601 500p tan & blk 55 22

1275 A601 500p multicolored 55 22

1276 A601 500p lt lilac & blk 55 22

Nos. 1274-1276 (3) 1.65 66

Avro "Gosport" Biplane, Maj. Francisco de Artega — A602

1980, Aug. 16 *Perf. 13*

1277 A602 500p multicolored 70 22

Air Force Day. Artega (1882-1930) was first director of Military Aircraft Factory where Avro "Gosport" was built (1927).

University of La Plata, 75th Anniversary A603

1980, Aug. 16 *Perf. 13½*

1278 A603 500p multi 55 22

Souvenir Sheets

Emperor Penguin — A604

South Orkneys Argentine Base

A605 A606

No. 1279 (A604): a, shown. b, Bearded penguin. c, Adelie penguins. d, Papua penguins. e, Sea elephants. f, A605 shown. g, A606 shown. h, Fur seals. i, Giant petrels. j, Blue-eyed cororants. k, Stormy petrels. m, Anarctic doves.

1980, Sept. 27 Litho. *Perf. 13½*

1279 Sheet of 12 11.00 11.00

a.-m. A604 500p, any single 75 60

1280 Sheet of 12 11.00 11.00

a. A605 500p Puerto Soledad 75 60

b. A606 500p Different view 75 60

75th anniv. of Argentina's presence in the South Orkneys and 150th anniv. of political and military command in the Falkland Islands. Nos. 1279-1280 each contain 12 stamps (4x3) with landscape designs in center of sheets. Silhouettes of Argentine exploration ships in margins. #1280 contains #1279a-1279e, 1279h-1279m, 1280a-1280b.

Anti-smoking Campaign — A608

1980, Oct. 11

1282 A608 700p multi 90 22

National Census — A609

1980, Sept.

1283 A609 500p blk & bl 1.00 20

Madonna and Child (Congress Emblem) A610

1980, Oct. 1 Litho.

1284 A610 700p multi 85 15

National Marian Cong., Mendoza, Oct. 8-12

Mural Type of 1980

1980, Oct. 25

1285 Block of 14 7.75 7.75

a. A598 500p, any single 52 40

Buenos Aires, 400th anniv./Buenos Aires '80 Stamp Exhib., Oct. 24-Nov. 2. No. 1285 shows ceramic mural Arte bajo la Ciudad by Alfredo Guido in continuous design.

Technical Military Academy, 50th Anniversary A611

Amateur Radio Operation A612

1980, Nov. 1

1286 A611 700p multi 75 15

1980, Nov. 1

1287 A612 700p multi 75 15

Medal — A613

Lujan Cathedral Floor Plan — A614

1980, Nov. 29 **Litho.** ***Perf. 13½***
1288 A613 700p multi 75 25
1289 A614 700p olive & brn 75 25

Christmas 1980. 150th anniv. of apparition of Holy Virgin to St. Catherine Laboure, Paris (No. 1288), 350th anniv. of apparition at Lujan.

150th Death Anniversary of Simon Bolivar — A615

1980, Dec. 13
1290 A615 700p multi 75 25

Soccer Gold Cup Championship, Montevideo, 1980 — A616

1981, Jan. 3 **Litho.**
1291 A616 1000p multi 1.10 25

San Martin Type of 1978

1981, Jan. 20 **Engr.** ***Perf. 13½***
1292 A553 10,000p dark blue 7.25 16

Landscape in Lujan, by Marcos Tiglio A617

Paintings: No. 1304, Expansion of Light along a Straight Line, by Miguel Angel Vidal, vert.

1981, Apr. 11 **Litho.**
1303 A617 1000p multi 85 30
1304 A617 1000p multi 85 30

Intl. Sports Medicine Congress, June 7-12 — A618

1981, June 6 **Litho.** ***Perf. 13½***
1305 A618 1000p bl & dk brn 75 20

Esperanza Base, Antarctica A619

Cargo Plane, Map of Vice-Commodore Marambio Island — A620

Perf. 13½, 13x13½ (No. 1308)
1981, June 13
1306 A619 1000p shown 1.40 42
1307 A619 2000p Almirante Irizar 2.50 55
1308 A620 2000p shown 2.50 85
Nos. 1306-1308 (3) 6.40 1.82

Antarctic Treaty 20th anniv.

Antique Pistols (Military Club Centenary) A621

1981, June 27 ***Perf. 13½***
1309 A621 1000p Club building 80 15
1310 A621 2000p shown 80 15

Gen. Juan A. Alvarez de Arenales (1770-1831) A622

Famous Men: No. 1312, Felix G. Frias (1816-1881), writer. No. 1313, Jose E. Uriburu (1831-1914), statesman.

1981, Aug. 8 **Litho.** ***Perf. 13½***
1311 A622 1000p multi 70 15
1312 A622 1000p multi 70 15
1313 A622 1000p multi 70 15
Nos. 1311-1313 (3) 2.10 45

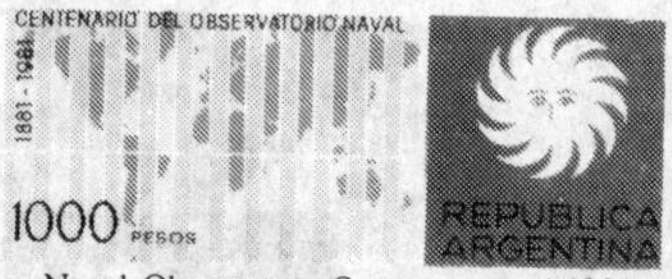

Naval Observatory Centenary — A623

1981, Aug. 15 **Litho.** ***Perf. 13x13½***
1314 A623 1000p multi 75 24

No. 1176 Overprinted in Red: "50 ANIV. DE LA ASOCIACION / FILATELICA Y NUMISMATICA / DE BAHIA BLANCA"

1981, Aug. 15 **Photo.** ***Perf. 13½***
1315 A540 1000p lem & blk 1.90 25

50th anniv. of Bahia Blanca Philatelic and Numismatic Society.

St. Cayetano, Stained-glass Window, Buenos Aires — A624

1981, Sept. 5 **Litho.** ***Perf. 13½***
1316 A624 1000p multi 70 15

St. Cayetano, founder of Teatino Order, 500th birth anniv.

Pablo Castaibert (1883-1909) and his Monoplane (Air Force Day) — A625

1981, Sept. 5 ***Perf. 13x13½***
1317 A625 1000p multi 65 15

Intl. Year of the Disabled A626

1981, Sept. 10 ***Perf. 13½***
1318 A626 1000p multi 65 15

22nd Latin-American Steelmakers' Congress, Buenos Aires, Sept. 21-23 — A627

1981, Sept. 19
1319 A627 1000p multi 65 15

Army Regiment No. 1 (Patricios), 175th Anniv. — A628

1981, Oct. 10 **Litho.** ***Perf. 13½***
1320 A628 1500p Natl. arms 45 15
1321 A628 1500p shown 45 15
a. Pair, #1320-1321 90 30

A629

A630

San Martin as artillery Captain in Battle of Bailen, 1808.

1981, Oct. 5
1322 Sheet of 8 + 4 labels 4.75 1.75
a. A629 1000p multi 35 18
b. A629 1500p multi 52 18

Espamer '81 Intl. Stamp Exhib. (Americas, Spain, Portugal), Buenos Aires, Nov. 13-22.
No. 1322 contains 4 se-tenant pairs.

1981, Oct. 5
1323 A630 1000p multi 2.25 32

Anti-indiscriminate whaling.

Espamer '81 Emblem and Ship — A631

1981
1324 A631 1300p multi 55 16

No. 1324 Overprinted in Blue: "CURSO SUPERIOR DE ORGANIZACIONES DE FILATELICOS-UPAE-BUENOS AIRES-1981"

1981, Nov. 7 **Photo.** ***Perf. 13½***
1325 A631 1300p multi 1.25 18

Postal Administration philatelic training course.

Soccer Players — A632

Designs: Soccer players.

1981, Nov. 13 **Litho.**
1326 Sheet of 4 + 2 labels 7.25 4.50
a. A632 1000p multi 22 15
b. A632 3000p multi 65 22
c. A632 5000p multi 1.10 38
d. A632 15,000p multi 3.25 1.10

Espamer '81.

"Peso" Coin Centenary A633

1981, Nov. 21
1327 A633 2000p Patacon, 1881 38 15
1328 A633 3000p Argentine Oro, 1881 60 15
Set value 20

Christmas 1981 — A634

1981, Dec. 12
1329 A634 1500p multi 85 24

Traffic Safety A635

1981, Dec. 19 **Litho.**

1330 A635 1000p Observe traffic lights, vert. 75 38
1331 A635 2000p Drive carefully, vert. 75 38
1332 A635 3000p Cross at white lines 75 38
1333 A635 4000p Don't shine headlights 1.50 38
Nos. 1330-1333 (4) 3.75 1.52

Francisco Luis Bernardez, Ciuda Laura — A636

Writers and title pages from their works: 2000p, Lucio V. Mansilla, Excursion a los indios ranqueles. 3000p, Conrado Nale Roxlo, El Grillo. 4000p, Victoria Ocampo, Sur.

1982, Mar. 20 **Litho.**

1334 A636 1000p shown 60 20
1335 A636 2000p multi 85 20
1336 A636 3000p multi 1.25 28
1337 A636 4000p multi 1.75 28
Nos. 1334-1337 (4) 4.45 96

No. 1218 Overprinted: "LAS / MALVINAS / SON/ ARGENTINAS"

1982, Apr. 17 **Photo.** ***Perf. 13½***

1338 A559 1700p grn & bl 48 20

Argentina's claim on Falkland Islds.

Robert Koch — A637

American Airforces Commanders' 22nd Conf. — A638

1982, Apr. 17 **Litho.** **Wmk. 365**

1339 A637 2000p multi 48 25

TB bacillus centenary and 25th Intl. Tuberculosis Conference.

1982, Apr. 17

1340 A638 2000p multi 70 28

Stone Carving, City Founder's Signature (Don Hernando de Lerma) A639

1982, Apr. 17

1341 A639 2000p multi 70 28

Souvenir Sheet

1342 A639 5000p multi 2.00 2.00

City of Salta, 400th anniv. No. 1342 contains one 43x30mm stamp.

Naval Center Centenary — A640

1982, Apr. 24 ***Perf. 13x13½***

1343 A640 2000p multi 70 28

Chorisia Speciosa — A641

1982 **Unwmk.** **Photo.** ***Perf. 13½***

1344 A641 200p Zinnia peruviana 15 15
1345 A641 300p Ipomoea purpurea 15 15
1346 A641 400p Tillandsia aeranthos 15 15
1347 A641 500p shown 15 15
1348 A641 800p Oncidium bifolium 15 15
1349 A641 1000p Erythrina crista-galli 15 15
1350 A641 2000p Jacaranda mimosi-folia 22 15
1351 A641 3000p Bauhinia candicans 32 15
1352 A641 5000p Tecoma stans 52 15
1353 A641 10,000p Tabebuia ipe 1.10 22
1354 A641 20,000p Passiflora coerulea 2.25 35
1355 A641 30,000p Aristolochia littoralis 3.25 52
1356 A641 50,000p Oxalis enneaphylla 5.25 70
Nos. 1344-1356 (13) 13.81
Set value 2.35

Nos. 1344-1346, 1348-1350 issued on fluorescent paper. Nos. 1353-1356 issued on ordinary paper. Others issued on both fluorescent and ordinary paper.

Issue dates: 500p, 2000p, 5000p, 10,000p, May 22. 200p, 300p, 1000p, 20,000p, Sept. 25. 400p, 800p, 30,000p, 50,000p, Dec. 4. 3000p, Dec. 18.

See Nos. 1429-1443A, 1515-1527, 1683-1691. For overprint see No. 1382.

10th Death Anniv. of Gen. Juan C. Sanchez A641a

1982, May 29 **Litho.** **Wmk. 365**

1364 A641a 5000p grn & blk 90 28

Luis Venet, First Commander — A641b

1982, June 12

1365 A641b 5000p org & blk 1.10 45

Size: 83x28mm

1366 A641b 5000p Map 75 30

153rd Anniv. of Malvinas Political and Military Command District.

Visit of Pope John Paul II — A641c

1982, June 12

1367 A641c 5000p multi 1.75 55

Organ Grinder, by Aldo Severi (b. 1928) — A641d

Design: 3000p, Still Life, by Santiago Cogorno (b. 1915).

1982, July 3 **Wmk. 365**

1368 A641d 2000p shown 26 20
1369 A641d 3000p multi 40 20

Guillermo Brown Type of 1980 and:

Jose de San Martin — A641e

Litho. and Engr.

1982 **Unwmk.** ***Perf. 13½***

1372 A591 30,000p blk & bl 3.25 65
1376 A641e 50,000p sepia & car 6.50 85

Issue dates: 30,000p, June; 50,000p, July.

Scouting Year A641f

Perf. 13½

1982, Aug. 7 **Litho.** **Wmk. 365**

1380 A641f 5000p multi 1.25 15

Alconafta Fuel Campaign A641g

1982, Aug. 7 **Wmk. 365**

1381 A641g 2000p multi 32 15

No. 1352 Overprinted: "50 ANIVERSARIO SOCIEDAD FILATELICA DE TUCUMAN"

1982, Aug. 7 **Photo.** **Unwmk.**

1382 A641 5000p multi 1.25 95

Rio III Central Nuclear Power Plant, Cordoba A642

Perf. 13½

1982, Sept. 4 **Litho.** **Wmk. 365**

1383 A642 2000p shown 30 15
1384 A642 2000p Control room 30 15
Set value 15

Namibia Day — A643

1982, Sept. 4

1385 A643 5000p Map 75 15

Formosa Cathedral A644

Churches and Cathedrals of the Northeast: 2000p, Our Lady of Itati, Corrientes, vert. 3000p, Resistencia Cathedral, Chaco, vert. 10,000p, St. Ignatius Church ruins, Misiones.

1982, Sept. 18 **Litho. & Engr.**

1386 A644 2000p dk grn & blk 24 15
1387 A644 3000p dk brn & brn 35 15
1388 A644 5000p dk bl & brn 60 20
1389 A644 10,000p dp org & blk 1.10 35
Nos. 1386-1389 (4) 2.29 85

Tension Sideral, by Mario Alberto Agatiello — A645

Sculpture (Espamer '81 and Juvenex '82 Exhibitions): 3000p, Sugerencia II, by Eduardo Mac Entyre. 5000p, Storm, by Carlos Silva.

1982, Oct. 2 **Litho.** ***Perf. 13½***

1390 A645 2000p multi 24 15
1391 A645 3000p multi 45 15
1392 A645 5000p multi 60 18
Nos. 1390-1392 (3) 1.29
Set value 39

Sante Fe Bridge A646

1982, Oct. 16 **Litho. & Engr.**
1393 A646 2000p bl & blk 38 15

2nd Southern Cross Games, Santa Fe and Rosario, Nov. 26-Dec. 5.

10th World Men's Volleyball Championship — A647

1982, Oct. 16 **Litho.** **Wmk. 365**
1394 A647 2000p multi 24 15
1395 A647 5000p multi 48 18

Los Andes Newspaper Centenary A648

Design: Army of the Andes Monument, Hill of Glory, Mendoza.

1982, Oct. 30
1396 A648 5000p multi 50 18

A649

A650

1982, Oct. 30 **Wmk. 365**
1397 A649 5000p Signs 55 22

50th Anniv. of Natl. Roads, Administration.

1982, Nov. 20 **Litho.**

La Plata City Cent.: No. 1400: a, Cathedral, diff. b, Head, top. c, Observatory. d, City Hall, diff. e, Head, bottom. f, University.

1398 A650 5000p Cathedral 75 15
1399 A650 5000p City Hall 75 15
1400 Sheet of 6 2.25 1.00
a.-f. A650 2500p any single 28 15

Well, Natl. Hydrocarbon Congress Emblem — A651

1982, Nov. 20
1401 A651 5000p multi 50 20

75th Anniv. of Oil Discovery, Comodoro Rivadavia.

Jockey Club of Buenos Aires Centenary — A652

Christmas 1982 — A653

Design: No. 1403, Carlos Pellegrini, first president.

1982, Dec. 4 **Litho.**
1402 A652 5000p Emblem 52 15
1403 A652 5000p multi 52 15
Set value 20

1982, Dec. 18 ***Perf. 13½***
1404 A653 3000p St. Vincent de Paul 1.50 15

Size: 29x38mm

1405 A653 5000p St. Francis of Assisi 1.25 15
Set value 15

Pedro B. Palacios (1854-1917), Writer — A654

Writers: 2000p, Leopoldo Marechal (1900-1970). 3000p, Delfina Bunge de Galvez (1881-1952). 4000p, Manuel Galvez (1882-1962). 5000p, Evaristo Carriego (1883-1912).

1983, Mar. 26 **Litho.** ***Perf. 13½***
1406 A654 1000p multi 15 15
1407 A654 2000p multi 22 15
1408 A654 3000p multi 32 15
1409 A654 4000p multi 42 15
1410 A654 5000p multi 55 18
a. Strip of 5, #1406-1410 1.75 1.00
Nos. 1406-1410 (5) 1.66
Set value 57

Recovery of the Malvinas (Falkland Islands) — A655

1983, Apr. 9 **Litho.** ***Perf. 13½***
1411 A655 20,000p Map, flag 60 30

Telecommunications Systems — A656

1983, Apr. 16 **Wmk. 365**
1412 A656 5000p SITRAM 75 15
1413 A656 5000p RED ARPAC 75 15
Set value 15

Naval League Emblem — A657

1983, May 14 **Litho.** ***Perf. 13½***
1414 A657 5000p multi 35 15

Navy Day and 50th anniv. of Naval League.

Allegory, by Victor Rebuffo — A658

1983, May 14
1415 A658 5000p multi 35 15

Natl. Arts Fund, 25th Anniv.

75th Anniv. of Colon Opera House, Buenos Aires — A659

1983, May 28 **Wmk. 365**
1416 A659 5000p Main hall 70 15
1417 A659 10000p Stage 1.00 15
Set value 17

Protected Species A660

1983, July 2 **Litho.** ***Perf. 13½***
1418 A660 1p Chrysocyon brachyurus 32 15
1419 A660 1.50p Ozotocerus bezoarticus 48 15
1420 A660 2p Myrmecophaga tridactyla 55 15
1421 A660 2.50p Leo onca 65 16
Nos. 1418-1421 (4) 2.00
Set value 42

City of Catamarca, 300th Anniv. — A661

Foundation of the City of Catamarca, by Luis Varela Lezana (1900-1982).

1983, July 16 **Litho.** ***Perf. 13½***
1422 A661 1p multi 32 15

Mamerto Esquiu (1826-1883) A662

1983, July 16
1423 A662 1p multi 32 15

Bolivar, by Herrera Toro — A663

Bolivar, Engraving by Kepper — A664

Perf. 13 (A663), 13½ (A664)

1983 **Unwmk.**
1424 A663 1p multi 30 15
1425 A664 2p black 60 15
1426 A664 10p San Martin 3.00 1.50
Nos. 1424-1426 (3) 3.90 1.80

Issue dates: 1p, 2p, July 23. 10p, Aug. 20.
See Nos. 1457-1462B.

Gen. Toribio de Luzuriaga (1782-1842) A665

1983, Aug. 20 **Litho.** ***Perf. 13½***
1427 A665 1p multi 30 15

50th Anniv. of San Martin National Institute A666

1983, Aug. 20 **Engr.** **Unwmk.**
1428 A666 2p sepia 60 16

Flower Type of 1982 in New Currency

1983-85 **Photo.** ***Perf. 13½***
1429 A641 5c like #1347 15 15
1430 A641 10c like #1349 15 15
1431 A641 20c like #1350 15 15
1432 A641 30c like #1351 15 15
1433 A641 40c Eichhornia crassipes 15 15
1434 A641 50c like #1352 15 15
1435 A641 1p like #1353 15 15
1435A A641 1.80p Mutisia retusa 15 15
1436 A641 2p like #1354 22 15
1437 A641 3p like #1355 32 15
1438 A641 5p like #1356 55 20
1439 A641 10p Alstroemeria aurantiaca 1.10 80

1440	A641	20p like #1345	55	16
1441	A641	30p Embothrium coccineum	3.50	2.50
1442	A641	50p like #1346	1.10	40
1443	A641	100p like #1348	1.65	48
1443A	A641	300p Cassia carnaval	80	24
		Nos. 1429-1443A (17)	10.99	
		Set value		5.25

Issue Dates: 20p, Aug. 27, 1984. 50p, Oct. 19, 1984. 100p, Dec. 1984. 300p, June 15, 1985.

Nos. 1429, 1433, 1435A issued on fluorescent paper. Nos. 1443, 1443A issued on ordinary paper. Others issued on both ordinary and fluorescent paper.

For overprint and surcharge see #1489, 1530.

Intl. Rotary South American Regional Conference, Buenos Aires, Sept. 25-28 — A667

1983, Sept. 24 **Litho.**

1444 A667 1p multi 55 24

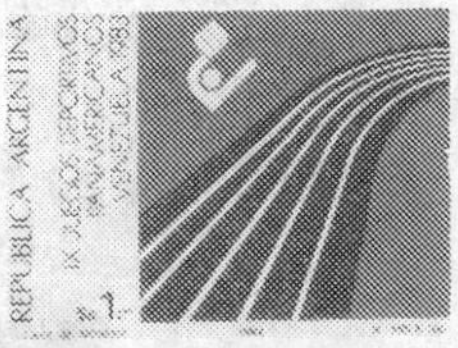

9th Pan American Games, Caracas, Aug. 13-28 A668

1983, Sept. 24

1445 A668 1p Track 32 15
1446 A668 2p Emblem 65 28

World Communications Year — A669

1983, Oct. 8 ***Perf. 13½***

1447 A669 2p multi 60 24

Squash Peddler by Antonio Berni (1905-1981) A670

Designs: 2p, Figure in Yellow by Luis Seoane (1910-1979).

1983, Oct. 15 ***Perf. 13½***

1448 A670 1p multi 32 15
1449 A670 2p multi 52 22

World Communications Year — A671

Designs: 1p, Wagon, 18th cent. 2p, Post chaise, 19th cent. 4p, Steam locomotive, 1857. 5p, Tramway, 1910.

1983, Nov. 19 **Litho.** ***Perf. 13½***

1450 A671 1p multi 15 15
1451 A671 2p multi 24 15
1452 A671 4p multi 50 20
1453 A671 5p multi 65 26
Nos. 1450-1453 (4) 1.54 76

A672 A673

1983, Nov. 26 **Litho.** ***Perf. 12½x12***

1454 A672 2p General Post Office 42 18

World Communications Year.

1983, Dec. 10 **Photo.** ***Perf. 13½***

1455 A673 2p Coin, 1813 30 18

Return to elected government.

Eudyptes Crestatus A674

Designs: b, Diomedea exulans. c, Diomedea melanophris. d, Eudyptes chrysolophus. e, Luis Piedra Buena. f, Carlos Maria Moyano. g, Luis Py. h, Augusto Lasserre. i, Phoebetria palpebrata. j, Hydrurga leptonyx. k, Lobodon carcinophagus. l, Leptonychotes weddelli.

1983, Dec. 10 **Litho.**

1456 Sheet of 12 4.50 2.25
a.-l. A674 2p any single 35 15

Southern pioneers and fauna. Margin depicts various airplanes and emblems.

Bolivar Type of 1983

Famous men: 10p, Angel J. Carranza (1834-99), historian. No. 1458, 500p, Guillermo Brown. No. 1459, Estanislao del Campo (1834-80), poet. 30p, Jose Hernandez (1834-86), author. 40p, Vicente Lopez y Planes (1784-1856), poet and patriot. 50p, San Martin. 200p, Belgrano.

1983-85 **Litho. & Engr.** ***Perf. 13½***

1457	A664	10p pale bl & dk bl	15	15
1458	A664	20p dk bl & blk	2.75	1.40
1459	A664	20p dl brn ol & ol blk	15	15
1460	A664	30p pale bl & bluish blk	15	15
1461	A664	40p lt bl grn & blk	18	15
1462	A664	50p Prus & choc	1.10	24
1462A	A664	200p int bl & blk	3.00	95
1462B	A664	500p brn & int bl	1.50	32
		Nos. 1457-1462B (8)	8.98	3.51

Issue dates: #1458, Oct. 6, 1983. 10p, #1459, 30p, 40p, Mar. 23, 1985. 50p, Apr. 23, 1985. 200p, Nov. 2, 1985. 500p, May 2, 1985.

Christmas 1983 A675

Nativity Scenes: 2p, Tapestry, by Silke. 3p, Stained-glass window, San Carlos de Bariloche's Wayn Church, vert.

1983, Dec. 17 **Litho.** ***Perf. 13½***

1463 A675 2p multi 30 15
1464 A675 3p multi 55 28

Centenary of El Dia Newspaper — A676

1984, Mar. 24 **Litho.**

1465 A676 4p Masthead, printing roll 38 20

Alejandro Carbo Teachers' College Centenary A677

1984, June 2 **Litho.** ***Perf. 13½***

1466 A677 10p Building 42 22

1984 Olympics A678

Designs: #1468, Weightlifting, discus, shot put. #1469, Javelin, fencing. #1470, Bicycling, swimming.

1984, July 28 **Litho.** ***Perf. 13½***

1467	A678	5p shown	22	15
1468	A678	5p multicolored	22	15
1469	A678	10p multicolored	45	22
1470	A678	10p multicolored	45	22
		Nos. 1467-1470 (4)	1.34	74

Rosario Stock Exchange Centenary A679

1984, Aug. 11

1471 A679 10p multicolored 45 22

Wheat A680

1984, Aug. 11

1472	A680	10p shown	48	24
1473	A680	10p Corn	48	24
1474	A680	10p Sunflower	48	24
		Nos. 1472-1474 (3)	1.44	72

18th FAO Regional Conference for Latin America and Caribbean (No. 1472); 3rd Natl. Corn Congress (No. 1473); World Food Day (No. 1474).

Wildlife Protection A681

1984, Sept. 22 **Litho.** ***Perf. 13½***

1475	A681	20p Hippocamelus bisulcus	40	15
1476	A681	20p Vicugna vicugna	40	15
1477	A681	20p Aburria jacutinga	40	15
1478	A681	20p Mergus octosetaceus	40	15
1479	A681	20p Podiceps gallardoi	40	15
		Nos. 1475-1479 (5)	2.00	75

First Latin American Theater Festival, Cordoba, Oct. — A682

1984, Oct. 13 **Litho.** ***Perf. 13½***

1480 A682 20p Mask 25 15

Intl. Eucharistic Congress, 50th Anniv. A683

Design: Apostles' Communion, by Fra Angelico.

1984, Oct. 13

1481 A683 20p multicolored 30 15

Glaciares Natl. Park (UNESCO World Heritage List) A684

1984, Nov. 17 **Litho.**

1482 A684 20p Sea 25 15
1483 A684 30p Glacier 42 15
Set value 25

City of Puerto Deseado Centenary A685

1984, Nov. 17 ***Perf. 13½***

1484 A685 20p shown 30 15
1485 A685 20p Ushuaia centenary 30 15
Set value 15

Childrens' Paintings, Christmas 1984 A686

1984, Dec. 1 Litho. *Perf. 13½*

1486 A686 20p Diego Aguero 32 15
1487 A686 30p Leandro Ruiz 60 15
1488 A686 50p Maria Castillo, vert. 60 15
Nos. 1486-1488 (3) 1.52 45

No. 1439 Overprinted

1984, Dec. 1 Photo. *Perf. 13½*

1489 A641 10p multicolored 26 22

50th anniversary of the Buenos Aires Philatelic Center.

Vista Del Jardin Zoologico, by Fermin Eguia — A687

Paintings: No. 1491, El Congreso Iluminado, by Francisco Travieso. No. 1492, Galpones (La Boca), by Marcos Borio.

1984, Dec. 15 *Perf. 13½*

1490 A687 20p multi 28 15
1491 A687 20p multi, vert. 28 15
1492 A687 20p multi, vert. 28 15
Nos. 1490-1492 (3) 84 45

Gen. Martin Miguel de Guemes (1785-1821) — A688

1985, Mar. 23 Litho. *Perf. 13½*

1493 A688 30p multicolored 26 15

ARGENTINA '85 Exhibition — A689

First airmail service from: 20p, Buenos Aires to Montevideo, 1917. 40p, Cordoba to Villa Dolores, 1925. 60p, Bahia Blanca to Comodoro Rivadavia, 1929. 80p, Argentina to Germany, 1934. 100p, naval service to the Antarctic, 1952.

1985, Apr. 27

1494 A689 20p Bleriot Gnome 16 15
1495 A689 40p Junker F-13L 32 15
1496 A689 60p Latte 25 50 20
1497 A689 80p L.Z. 127 Graf Zeppelin 65 30
1498 A689 100p Consolidated PBY Catalina 85 40
Nos. 1494-1498 (5) 2.48 1.20

Central Bank, 50th Anniv. A690

1985, June 1

1499 A690 80p Bank Bldg., Buenos Aires 55 18

Jose A. Ferreyra (1889-1943), Director of Munequitas Portenas A691

Famous directors and their films: No. 1501, Leopoldo Torre Nilsson (1924-1978), scene from Martin Fierro.

1985, June 1

1500 A691 100p shown 60 18
1501 A691 100p multi 60 18

Carlos Gardel (1890-1935), Entertainer — A692

Paintings: No. 1502, Gardel playing the guitar on stage, by Carlos Alonso (b. 1929). No. 1503, Gardel in a wide-brimmed hat, by Hermegildo Sabat (b. 1933). No. 1504, Portrait of Gardel in an ornamental frame, by Aldo Severi (b. 1928) and Martiniano Arce (b. 1939).

1985, June 15

1502 A692 200p multi 95 45
1503 A692 200p multi 95 45
1504 A692 200p multi 95 45
Nos. 1502-1504 (3) 2.85 1.35

The Arrival, by Pedro Figari A693

A Halt on the Plains, by Prilidiano Pueyrredon — A693a

Oil paintings (details): 30c, The Wagon Square, by C. B. de Quiros. Illustration A693a is reduced.

1985, July 6 Litho. *Perf. 13½*

1505 A693 20c multi 1.00 24
1506 A693 30c multi 1.25 24

Souvenir Sheet

Perf. 12

1507 A693a Sheet of 2 2.50
a. 20c Pilgrims, vert. 26
b. 30c Wagon 40

ARGENTINA '85. No. 1507 contains 2 30x40mm stamps. See No. 1542.

Buenos Aires to Montevideo, 1917 Teodoro Fels Flight A694

Historic flight covers: No. 1508, Shown. No. 1509, Villa Dolores to Cordoba, 1925. No. 1510, Buenos Aires to France, 1929 St. Exupery flight. No. 1511, Buenos Aires to Bremerhaven, 1934 Graf Zeppelin flight. No. 1512, First Antarctic flight, 1952.

1985, July 13 *Perf. 12x12½*

1508 A694 10c emer & multi 40 15
1509 A694 10c ultra & multi 40 15
1510 A694 10c lt choc & multi 40 15
1511 A694 10c chnt & multi 40 15
1512 A694 10c ap grn & multi 40 15
Nos. 1508-1512 (5) 2.00
Set value 60

ARGENTINA '85.

Illuminated Fruit, by Fortunato Lacamera (1887-1951) — A695

Paintings: 20c, Woman with Bird, by Juan del Prete, vert.

1985, Sept. 7 *Perf. 13½*

1513 A695 20c multi 85 30
1514 A695 30c multi 1.00 30

Flower Types of 1982-85

Designs: 1a, Begonia micranthera var. hieronymi. 5a, Gymnocalycium bruchii.

1985-88 Photo. *Perf. 13½*

1515 A641 ½c like #1356 15 15
1516 A641 1c like #1439 15 15
1517 A641 2c like #1345 15 15
1518 A641 3c like #1441 15 15
1519 A641 5c like #1346 22 15
1520 A641 10c like #1348 35 15
1521 A641 20c like #1347 70 16
1522 A641 30c like #1443A 1.10 25
1523 A641 50c like #1344 1.75 35
1524 A641 1a multi 3.50 65
1525 A641 2a like #1351 38 15
1526 A641 5a multi 6.75 3.00

Size: 15x23mm

1527 A641 8½c like #1349 32 15
Nos. 1515-1527 (13) 15.67 5.61

Issue dates: ½c, 1c, Dec. 16. 2c, 8½c, 30c, Sept. 18. 3c, 5c, 10c, 50c, 1a, Sept. 7. 20c, Oct. 17. 5a, Mar. 21, 1987. 2a, Dec. 5, 1988.

No. 1435 Surcharged

1986, Nov. 4 Photo. *Perf. 13½*

1530 A641 10c on 1p No. 1435 15 15

Folk Musical Instruments A699

1985, Sept. 14 Litho. *Perf. 13½*

1531 A699 20c Frame drum 55 22
1532 A699 20c Long flute 55 22
1533 A699 20c Jew's harp 55 22
1534 A699 20c Pan flutes 55 22
1535 A699 20c Musical bow 55 22
Nos. 1531-1535 (5) 2.75 1.10

Juan Bautista Alberdi (1810-1884), Historian, Politician A700

Famous men: Nicolas Avellaneda (1836-1885), President in 1874. 30c, Fr. Luis Beltran (1784-1827), military and naval engineer. 40c, Ricardo Levene (1885-1959), historian, author.

1985, Oct. 5

1536 A700 10c multi 22 15
1537 A700 20c multi 45 22
1538 A700 30c multi 65 32
1539 A700 40c multi 1.10 45
Nos. 1536-1539 (4) 2.42 1.14

Type of 1985 and

Skaters A701

Deception, by J. H. Rivoira A702

1985, Oct. 19 Litho. *Perf. 13½*

1540 A701 20c multi 35 32
1541 A702 30c multi 50 48

Size: 147x75mm

Imperf

1542 A693a 1a multi 1.90

IYY. No. 1542 is inscribed in silver with the UN 40th anniversary and IYY emblems.

Provincial Views — A703

Designs: No. 1543, Rock Window, Buenos Aires. No. 1544, Forclaz Windmill, Entre Rios. No. 1545, Lake Potrero de los Funes, San Luis. No. 1546, Mission church, north-east province. No. 1547, Penguin colony, Punta Tombo, Chubut. No. 1548, Water Mirrors, Cordoba.

1985, Nov. 23 *Perf. 13½*

1543 A703 10c multi 26 25
1544 A703 10c multi 26 25
1545 A703 10c multi 26 25
1546 A703 10c multi 26 25
1547 A703 10c multi 26 25
1548 A703 10c multi 26 25
Nos. 1543-1548 (6) 1.56 1.50

Christmas 1985 — A704

Designs: 10c, Birth of Our Lord, by Carlos Cortes. 20c, Christmas, by Hector Viola.

1985, Dec. 7

1549 A704 10c multi 24 18
1550 A704 20c multi 48 45

Natl. Campaign for the Prevention of Blindness A705

1985, Dec. 7
1551 A705 10c multi 24 18

Rio Gallegos City, Cent. — A716

1985, Dec. 21 Litho. ***Perf. 13½***
1552 A716 10c Church 24 18

Natl. Grape Harvest Festival, 50th Anniv. A717

1986, Mar. 15
1553 A717 10c multi 24 18

Historical Architecture in Buenos Aires — A718

Designs: No. 1554, Valentin Alsina House, Italian Period, 1860-70. No. 1555, House on Cerrito Street, French influence, 1880-1900. No. 1556, House on the Avenida de Mayo y Santiago del Estero, Art Nouveau, 1900-10. No. 1557, Customs Building, academic architecture, 1900-15. No. 1558, Isaac Fernandez Blanco Museum, house of architect Martin Noel, natl. restoration, 1910-30. Nos. 1554-1556 vert.

1986, Apr. 19
1554 A718 20c multi 40 30
1555 A718 20c multi 40 30
1556 A718 20c multi 40 30
1557 A718 20c multi 40 30
1558 A718 20c multi 40 30
Nos. 1554-1558 (5) 2.00 1.50

Antarctic Bases, Pioneers and Fauna — A719

Designs: a, Base, Jubany. b, Arctocephalus gazella. c, Otaria byronia. d, Gen. Belgrano Base. e, Daption capensis. f, Diomedia melanophris. g, Apterodytes patagonica. h, Macronectes giganteus. i, Hugo Alberto Acuna (1885-1953). j, Spheniscus magellanicus. k, Gallinago gallinage. l, Capt. Agustin del Castillo (1855-89).

1986, May 31
1559 Sheet of 12 2.50 3.50
a.-l. A719 10c any single 20 25

Famous People — A720

Statuary, Buenos Aires — A721

Designs: No. 1560, Dr. Alicia Moreau de Justo, human rights activist. No. 1561, Dr. Emilio Ravignani (1886-1954), historian. No. 1562, Indira Gandhi.

1986, July 5 Litho. ***Perf. 13½***
1560 A720 10c multi 26 22
1561 A720 10c multi 26 22
1562 A720 30c multi 80 65
Nos. 1560-1562 (3) 1.32 1.09

1986, July 5

Designs: 20c, Fountain of the Nereids, by Dolores Lola Mora (1866-1936). 30c, Lamenting at Work, by Rogelio Yrurtia (1879-1950), horiz.

1563 A721 20c multi 52 45
1564 A721 30c multi 80 65

Famous Men — A722

Designs: No. 1565, Francisco N. Laprida (1786-1829), politician. No. 1566, Estanislao Lopez (1786-1838), brigadier general. No. 1567, Francisco Ramirez (1786-1821), general.

1986, Aug. 9 Litho. ***Perf. 13***
1565 A722 20c dl yel, brn & blk 42 38
1566 A722 20c dl yel, brn & blk 42 38
1567 A722 20c dl yel, brn & blk 42 38
Nos. 1565-1567 (3) 1.26 1.14

Fr. Ceferino Namuncura (1886-1905) A723

1986, Aug. 30 ***Perf. 13½***
1568 A723 20c multi 42 38

Miniature Sheets

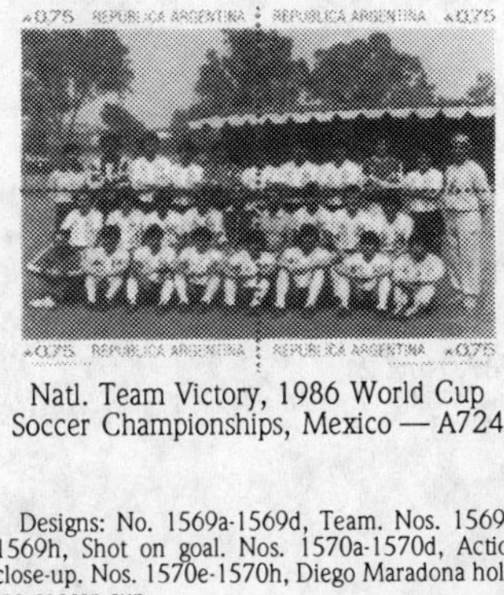

Natl. Team Victory, 1986 World Cup Soccer Championships, Mexico — A724

Designs: No. 1569a-1569d, Team. Nos. 1569e-1569h, Shot on goal. Nos. 1570a-1570d, Action close-up. Nos. 1570e-1570h, Diego Maradona holding soccer cup.

1986, Nov. 8 Litho. ***Perf. 13½***
1569 A724 Sheet of 8 9.25 12.00
a.-h. 75c any single 1.15 1.50
1570 A724 Sheet of 8 9.25 12.00
a.-h. 75c any single 1.15 1.50

San Francisco (Cordoba), Cent. A725

1986, Nov. 8
1571 A725 20c Municipal Building 45 42

Trelew City (Chubut), Cent. A726

1986, Nov. 22 Litho. ***Perf. 13½***
1572 A726 20c Old railroad station, 1865 42 42

Mutualism Day A727

1986, Nov. 22
1573 A727 20c multi 42 42

Christmas A728

Designs: 20c, Naif retable, by Aniko Szabo (b. 1945). 30c, Everyone's Tree, by Franca Delacqua (b. 1947).

1986, Dec. 13 Litho. ***Perf. 13½***
1574 A728 20c multicolored 35
1575 A728 30c multicolored 50

Santa Rosa de Lima, 400th Birth Anniv. — A729

Rio Cuarto Municipal Building — A730

1986, Dec. 13
1576 A729 50c multicolored 80

1986, Dec. 20
1577 A730 20c shown 35
1578 A730 20c Court Building, Cordoba 35

Rio Cuarto City, bicent. Court Building, Cordoba, 50th anniv.

Antarctic Treaty, 25th Anniv. — A731

1987, Mar. 7 Litho. ***Perf. 13½***
1579 A731 20c Marine biologist 35
1580 A731 30c Ornithologist 52

Souvenir Sheet

Perf. 12

1581 Sheet of 2 90
a. A731 20c like No. 1579 35
b. A731 30c like No. 1580 52

No. 1581 contains 2 stamps, size: 40x50mm.

Natl. Mortgage Bank, Cent. A732

1987, Mar. 21 ***Perf. 13½***
1582 A732 20c multi 35

Natl. Cooperative Associations Movement — A733

1987, Mar. 21
1583 A733 20c multi 35

Second State Visit of Pope John Paul II — A734

Engr., Litho. (No. 1585)
1987, Apr. 4 ***Perf. 13½***
1584 A734 20c shown 35
1585 A734 80c Papal blessing 1.40

Souvenir Sheet

Perf. 12

1586 A734 1a like 20c 1.75

No. 1586 contains one 40x50mm stamp.

Intl. Peace Year A735

Designs: 30c, Pigeon, abstract sculpture by Victor Kaniuka.

1987, Apr. 11 **Litho.**
1587 A735 20c multi 35
1588 A735 30c multi 52

Low Handicap World Polo Championships A736

Design: Polo Players, painting by Alejandro Moy.

1987, Apr. 11
1589 A736 20c multi 35

Miniature Sheet

ICOM '86 — A737

Designs: a, Emblem. b, Family crest, National History Museum, Buenos Aires. c, St. Bartholomew, Enrique Larreta Museum of Spanish Art, Buenos Aires. d, Zoomorphic club, Patagonian Museum, San Carlos de Bariloche. e, Supplication, anthropomorphic sculpture, Natural Sciences Museum, La Plata. f, Wrought iron lattice from the house of J. Urquiza, president of the Confederation of Argentina, Entre Rios History Museum, Parana. g, St. Joseph, 18th cent. wood figurine, Northern History Museum, Salta. h, Funerary urn, Provincial Archaeological Museum, Santiago del Estero.

1987, May 30
1590 Sheet of 8 3.05
a.-h. A737 25c any single 38

14th General Conference of the Intl. Council of Museums.

Natl. College of Monserrat, Cordoba, 300th Anniv. — A738

1987, July 4 ***Imperf.***
1591 A738 1a multi 1.10

Monserrat '87 Philatelic Exposition.

Fight Drug Abuse A739

Design: The Proportions of Man, by da Vinci.

1987, Aug. 15 ***Perf. 13½***
1592 A739 30c multi 35

Famous Men A740

Portraits and quotations: 20c, Jorge Luis Borges (1899-1986), writer. 30c, Armando Discepolo (1887-1971), playwright. 50c, Carlos A. Pueyrredon (1887-1962), professor, Legion of Honor laureate.

1987, Aug. 15
1593 A740 20c multi 22
1594 A740 30c multi 35
1595 A740 50c multi 55
Nos. 1593-1595 (3) 1.12

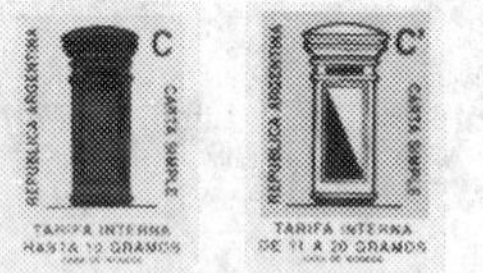

Pillar Boxes
A741 A742

1987 **Photo.** ***Perf. 13½***
1596 A741 (30c) yel, blk & dark red 35
1597 A742 (33c) lt blue grn, blk & yel 38

Issue dates: (30c), June 8; (33c), July 13.

The Sower, by Julio Vanzo A743

1987, Sept. 12
1598 A743 30c multi 35

Argentine Agrarian Federation, 75th anniv.

10th Pan American Games, Indianapolis, Aug. 7-25 — A744

1987, Sept. 26
1599 A744 20c Basketball 22
1600 A744 30c Rowing 35
1601 A744 50c Yachting 55
Nos. 1599-1601 (3) 1.12

Children Playing Doctor, WHO Emblem A745

1987, Oct. 7
1602 A745 30c multi 35

Vaccinate every child campaign.

Heroes of the Revolution A746

Signing of the San Nicolas Accord, 1852, by Rafael del Villar A747

Independence anniversaries and historic events: No. 1603, Maj.-Col. Ignacio Alvarez Thomas (1787-1857). No. 1604, Col. Manuel Crispulo Bernabe Dorrego (1787-1829). No. 1606, 18th cent. Spanish map of the Falkland Isls., administered by Jacinto de Altolaguirre.

1987, Oct. 17
1603 A746 25c shown 28
1604 A746 25c multi 28
1605 A747 50c shown 55
1606 A747 50c multi 55
Nos. 1603-1606 (4) 1.66

Museum established in the House of the San Nicholas Accord, 50th anniv. (#1605); Jacinto de Altolaguirre (1754-1787), governor the Malvinas Isls. for the King of Spain (#1606).

Celedonio Galvan Moreno, 1st Director A748

1987, Nov. 21
1607 A748 50c multi 55

Postas Argentinas magazine, 50th anniv.

LRA National Radio, Buenos Aires, 50th Anniv. — A749

1987, Nov. 21
1608 A749 50c multi 55

Natl. Philatelic Society, Cent. A750

1987, Nov. 21
1609 A750 1a Jose Marco del Pont 1.10

Christmas A751

Tapestries: 50c, *Navidad,* by Alisia Frega. 1a, *Vitral,* by Silvina Trigos.

1987, Dec. 5
1610 A751 50c multi 55
1611 A751 1a multi 1.10

Natl. Parks — A752

1987, Dec. 19 ***Perf. 13x13½***
1612 A752 50c Baritu 55
1613 A752 50c Nahuel Huapi 55
1614 A752 50c Rio Pilcomayo 55
1615 A752 50c Tierra del Fuego 55
1616 A752 50c Iguacu 55
Nos. 1612-1616 (5) 2.75

See Nos. 1647-1651, 1715-1719, 1742-1746.

Landscapes in Buenos Aires Painted by Jose Cannella A753

1988-89 **Litho.** ***Perf. 13½***
1617 A753 5a Caminito 2.00
1618 A753 10a Viejo Almacen 4.00
1618A A753 10a like No. 1618 1.05
1618B A753 50a like No. 1617 1.05
Nos. 1617-1618B (4) 8.10

No. 1618 inscribed "Viejo Almacen"; No. 1618A inscribed "El Viejo Almacen."
Issue dates: 5a, #1618, Mar. 15; 50a, 1989.
For overprint see No. 1635.

Minstrel in a Tavern, by Carlos Morel A754

Paintings: No. 1620, Interior of Curuzu, by Candido Lopez.

1988, Mar. 19 **Litho.** ***Perf. 13½***
1619 A754 1a shown 45
1620 A754 1a multi 45

See Nos. 1640-1641.

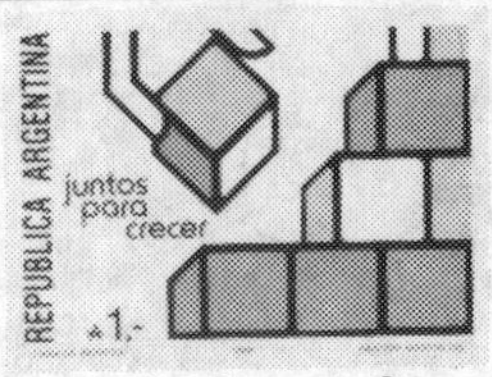

Argentine-Brazilian Economic Cooperation and Integration Program for Mutual Growth — A755

1988, Mar. 19

1621 A755 1a multi 42

Cities of Alta Gracia and Corrientes, 400th Annivs. A756

1988, Apr. 9 Litho. *Perf. 13½*

1622 A756 1a Alta Gracia Church 40
1623 A756 1a Chapel of St. Anne, Corrientes 40

Labor Day — A757

Grain Carriers, a tile mosaic by Alfredo Guido, Line D of Nueve de Julio station, Buenos Aires subway: a, (UL). b, (UR). c, (LL). d, (LR).

1988, May 21

1624 A757 Block of 4 80
a.-d. 50c any single 20

1988 Summer Olympics, Seoul — A758

1988, July 16 Litho. *Perf. 13½*

1625 A758 1a Running 18
1626 A758 2a Soccer 35
1627 A758 3a Field hockey 55
1628 A758 4a Tennis 68
Nos. 1625-1628 (4) 1.76

Mendoza Bank, Cent. A759

Natl. Gendarmerie, Cent. — A760

1988, Aug. 13

1629 A759 2a multi 35
1630 A760 2a multi 35

Sarmiento and Cathedral School to the North, Buenos Aires A761

1988, Sept. 10 Litho. *Perf. 13½*

1631 A761 3a multi 50

Domingo Faustino Sarmiento (1811-1888), educator, politician.

St. Cayetano, Patron of Workers — A762

El Amor, by Antonio Berni, Pacific Gallery, Buenos Aires — A763

1988, Sept. 10 Litho.

1632 A762 2a multi 35
1633 A762 3a Our Lady of Carmen, Cuyo 50

Souvenir Sheet

Perf. 12

1634 A763 5a multi 85

Liniers Philatelic Circle and the Argentine Western Philatelic Institution (IFADO), 50th annivs.

No. 1634 contains one stamp, size: 40x30mm.

No. 1617 Ovptd. with Congress Emblem and:
"XXI CONGRESO
DE LA SOCIEDAD
INTERNACIONAL
DE UROLOGIA"

1988, Oct. 29 Litho. *Perf. 13½*

1635 A753 5a multi 85

21st Congress of the Intl. Urology Soc.

Tourism A763a

1988, Nov. 1 Litho. *Perf. 13½*

1635A A763a 3a Purmamarca, Jujuy 50

Size: 28½x38mm

1635B A763a 20a Ushuaia 3.35

Buenos Aires Subway, 75th Anniv. A764

1988, Dec. 17 Litho. *Perf. 13½*

1636 A764 5a Train, c. 1913 85

Christmas A765

Frescoes in Ucrania Cathedral, Buenos Aires: No. 1637, *Virgin Patron.* No. 1638, *Virgin of Tenderness.*

1988, Dec. 17

1637 A765 5a multi 85
1638 A765 5a multi 85

St. John Bosco (1815-1888), Educator, and Church in Ushuaia — A766

1989, Apr. 8 Litho. *Perf. 13½*

1639 A766 5a multi 30

Dated 1988.

Art Type of 1988

Paintings: No. 1640, *Blancos,* by Fernando Fader (1882-1935). No. 1641, *Rincon de los Areneros,* by Justo Lynch (1870-1953).

1989, Apr. 8

1640 A754 5a multi 30
1641 A754 5a multi 30

Holy Week A767

Sculpture and churches: No. 1642, *The Crown of Thorns,* Calvary of Tandil, and Church of Our Lady Carmelite, Tandil. No. 1643, *Jesus the Nazarene* and Metropolitan Cathedral, Buenos Aires. No. 1644, *Jesus Encounters His Mother* (scene of the crucifixion), La Quebrada Village, San Luis. No. 1645, *Our Lady of Sorrow* and Church of Humahuaca, Jujuy.

1989, Apr. 22 Litho. *Perf. 13½*

1642 A767 2a multi 15
1643 A767 2a multi 15
1644 A767 3a multi 15
1645 A767 3a multi 15
Set value 40

Printed in sheets of 16+4 labels containing blocks of 4 of each design. Labels picture Jesus's arrival in Jerusalem (Palm Sunday).

Prevent Alcoholism A768

1989, Apr. 22

1646 A768 5a multi 22

Natl. Park Type of 1987

1989, May 6 *Perf. 13x13½*

1647 A752 5a Lihue Calel 16
1648 A752 5a El Palmar 16
1649 A752 5a Calilegua 16
1650 A752 5a Chaco 16
1651 A752 5a Los Glaciares 16
Nos. 1647-1651 (5) 80

Admission of Argentina to the ITU, Cent. A769

1989, May 6 *Perf. 13½*

1652 A769 10a multi 32

World Model Aircraft Championships — A770

1989, May 27 Litho. *Perf. 13½*

1653 A770 5a F1A glider 15
1654 A770 5a F1B rubber band motor 15
1655 A770 10a F1C gas motor 28
Nos. 1653-1655 (3) 58

French Revolution, Bicent. — A771

Designs: 10a, "All men are born free and equal." 15a, French flag and *La Marianne,* by Gandon. 25a, *Liberty Guiding the People,* by Delacroix.

1989, July 1 Litho. *Perf. 13½*

1656 A771 10a shown 15
1657 A771 15a multi 15
Set value 21

Souvenir Sheet

Perf. 12

1658 A771 25a multi 22

No. 1658 contains one 40x30mm stamp.

The Republic, a Bronze Bust in the Congreso de la Nacion, Buenos Aires — A772

1989, Aug. 12 Litho. *Perf. 13½*
1659 A772 300a on 50a multi

Peaceful transition of power (presidential office). Not issued without surcharge.

Immigration to Argentina — A773

1989, Aug. 19 *Perf. 13½*
1660 A773 150a S.S. *Weser,* 1889
1661 A773 200a Immigrant hotel, 1889

Souvenir Sheet
Perf. 12

1662 Sheet of 2
a. A773 150a like No. 1660
b. A773 200a like No. 1661

No. 1662 contains 40c30mm stamps.

Famous Men A774

Designs: No. 1663, Fr. Guillermo Furlong (1889-1974), historian, and title page of *The Jesuits.* No. 1664, Dr. Gregorio Alvarez (1889-1986), physician, and title page of *Canto a Chos Malal.* 200a, Brig.-Gen. Enrique Martinez (1789-1870) and lithograph *La Batalla de Maipu,* by Teodoro Gericault.

1989, Oct. 7 Litho. *Perf. 13½*
1663 A774 150a multi
1664 A774 150a multi
1665 A774 200a multi

America Issue — A775

Emblem of the Postal Union of the Americas and Spain (PUAS) and pre-Columbian art from Catamarca Province: 200a, Wooden mask from Atajo, Loma Morada. 300a, Urn of the Santa Maria Culture (Phase 3) from Punta de Balastro, Santa Maria Department.

1989, Oct. 14
1666 A775 200a multi
1667 A775 300a multi

Federal Police Week — A776

Children's drawings: No. 1668, Diego Molinari, age 13. No. 1669, Carlos Alberto Sarago, age 8. No. 1670, Roxana Andrea Osuna, age 7. No. 1671, Pablo Javier Quaglia, age 9.

1989, Oct. 28 Litho. *Perf. 13½*
1668 A776 100a multi
1669 A776 100a multi
1670 A776 150a multi
1671 A776 150a multi

Battle of Vuelta de Obligado, 1845 — A777

(Illustration reduced.)

1989, Dec. 2 Litho. *Perf. 13x13½*
1672 A777 300a multicolored

Paintings A778

Cristo de los Cerros, Sculpture by Chipo Cespedes — A779

1989, Dec. 2 *Perf. 13½*
1673 A778 200a Gato Frias
1674 A778 200a Maria Carballido
1675 A779 300a shown

Christmas.

Buenos Aires Port, Cent. — A780

(Illustration reduced.)

1990, Mar. 3 Litho. *Perf. 13½*
1676 A780 Strip of 4
a.-d. 200a any single

Aconcagua Intl. Fair, Mendoza — A781

Design: Aconcagua mountain, Los Horcones Lagoon and fair emblem.
(Illustration reduced.)

1990, Mar. 3
1677 A781 Pair
a.-b. 500a any single

Natl. Savings and Insurance Fund, 75th Anniv. A782

1990, May 5 Litho. *Perf. 13½*
1678 A782 1000a multicolored

Miniature Sheet

1990 World Cup Soccer Championships, Italy — A783

Designs: a, Athlete's torso (striped jersey). b, Athlete's torso (solid jersey). c, Players' feet, soccer ball. d, Player (knee to waist).

1990, May 5
1679 Sheet of 4
a.-d. A783 2500a multicolored

Carlos Pellegrini, Commercial High School Founder, Cent. — A784

1990, June 2 Litho. *Perf. 13½*
1680 A784 2000a multicolored

Youth Against Drugs A785

1990, June 2
1681 A785 2000a multicolored

Intl. Literacy Year A786

1990, July 14 Litho. *Perf. 13½*
1682 A786 2000a multicolored

Flower Type of 1982 in New Currency

1989-90 Photo. *Perf. 13½*
1683 A641 10a like #1433
1684 A641 20a like #1435A
1685 A641 50a like #1354
1686 A641 100a like #1439
1687 A641 300a like #1345
1688 A641 500a like #1441
1689 A641 1000a like #1355
1690 A641 5000a like #1349
1691 A641 10,000a like #1350

Issue dates: 20a, 100a, 300a, 500a, Aug. 1, 1989. 10a, Aug. 24, 1989. 50a, Aug. 30, 1989. 1000, Mar. 8, 1990. 5000a, Apr. 6, 1990. 10,000a, July 2, 1990.

World Basketball Championships A787

1990, Aug. 11 Litho. *Perf. 13½*
1703 A787 2000a multicolored .95

Souvenir Sheet
Perf. 12

1704 A787 5000a Jump ball 2.40

Postal Union of the Americas and Spain, 14th Congress A788

1990, Sept. 15 Litho. *Perf. 13½*
1705 A788 3000a Arms, seal 1.50
1706 A788 3000a Sailing ships 1.50
1707 A788 3000a Modern freighter 1.50
1708 A788 3000a Van, cargo plane 1.50
Nos. 1705-1708 (4) 6.00

America Issue A789

1990, Oct. 13
1709 A789 3000a Iguacu Falls, hamelia erecta 1.50
1710 A789 3000a Puerto Deseado, elephant seal 1.50

Natl. Parks Type of 1987

1990, Oct. 27 *Perf. 13x13½*
1715 A752 3000a Lanin 1.50
1716 A752 3000a Laguna Blanca 1.50
1717 A752 3000a Perito Moreno 1.50
1718 A752 3000a Puelo 1.50
1719 A752 3000a El Rey 1.50
Nos. 1715-1719 (5) 7.50

Stamp Day A790

1990, Oct. 27 *Perf. 13½*
1720 A790 3000a multicolored 1.50

Salvation Army, Cent. A793

Designs: No. 1722, Natl. University of the Littoral, Santa Fe, cent.

1990, Dec. 1 **Litho.** *Perf. 13½*
1721 A793 3000a multicolored
1722 A793 3000a multicolored
a. Pair, #1721-1722 + label

Miniature Sheets

Christmas — A794

Stained glass windows: No. 1723, The Immaculate Conception. No. 1724, The Nativity. No. 1725, Presentation of Jesus at the Temple.

1990, Dec. 1 *Perf. 13½x13*
Sheets of 4
1723 A794 3000a #a.-d.
1724 A794 3000a #a.-d.
1725 A794 3000a #a.-d.

Landscapes A795

Paintings: No. 1726, Los Sauces, by Atilio Malinverno. No. 1727, Paisaje, by Pio Collivadino, vert.

1991, May 4 **Litho.** *Perf. 13½*
1726 A795 4000a multicolored 1.00
1727 A795 4000a multicolored 1.00

Return of Remains of Juan Manuel de Rosas (1793-1877) A796

1991, June 1 **Litho.** *Perf. 13½*
1728 A796 4000a multicolored 1.00

Swiss Confederation, 700th Anniv. — A797

1991, Aug. 3 **Litho.** *Perf. 13½*
1729 A797 4000a multicolored 95

Miniature Sheet

Cartoons — A798

Designs: a, Hernan, the Corsair by Jose Luis Salinas. b, Don Fulgencio by Lino Palacio. c, Medical Rules of Salerno by Oscar Esteban Conti. d, Buenos Aires Undershirt by Alejandro del Prado. e, Girls! by Jose A.G. Divito. f, Langostino by Eduardo Carlos Ferro. g, Mafalda by Joaquin Salvador Lavoro. h, Mort Cinder by Alberto Breccia.

1991, Aug. 3
1730 A798 4000a Sheet of 8, #a.-h. 7.75

City of La Rioja, 400th Anniv. — A799

1991, Sept. 14 **Litho.** *Perf. 13½*
1731 A799 4000a multicolored 1.00

First Balloon Flight over the Andes, 75th Anniv. — A800

Illustration reduced.

1991, Sept. 14
1732 A800 4000a multicolored 1.00

America Issue A801

Designs: No. 1733, Magellan's caravel, Our Lady of Victory. No. 1734, Ships of Juan Diaz de Solis.

1991, Nov. 9 **Litho.** *Perf. 13½*
1733 A801 4000a multicolored 1.00
1734 A801 4000a multicolored 1.00

Anniversaries — A802

Designs: a, J. Enrique Pestalozzi, founder of newspaper, Daily Argentinian. b, Leandro N. Alem, founder of Radical People's Party. c, Man with rifle, emblem of Argentine Federal Shooting Club. d, Dr. Nicasio Etchepareborda, emblem of College of Odontology. e, Dalmiro Huergo, emblem of Graduate School of Economics.

1991, Nov. 30
1735 A802 4000a Strip of 5, #a.-e. 5.00

Christmas — A803

Stained glass windows from Our Lady of Lourdes Basilica, Buenos Aires: Nos. 1736a-1736b, Top and bottom portions of Virgin of the Valley, Catamarca. Nos. 1736c-1736d, Top and bottom portions of Virgin of the Rosary of the Miracle, Cordoba.

1991, Nov. 30
1736 A803 4000a Block of 4, #a.-d. 4.00

Famous Men A804

Designs: a, Gen. Juan de Lavalle (1797-1841), Peruvian medal of honor. b, Brig. Gen. Jose Maria del Rosario Siriaco Paz (1791-1854), medal. c, Marco Manuel de Avellaneda (1813-1841), lawyer. d, Guillermo Enrique Hudson (1841-1922), author.

1991, Dec. 14 **Litho.** *Perf. 13½*
1737 A804 4000a Block of 4, #a.-d. 4.00

Birds — A805

1991, Dec. 28
1738 A805 4000a Pterocnemia pennata 1.00
1739 A805 4000a Morphnu guianensis 1.00
1740 A805 4000a Ara chloroptera 1.00
Nos. 1738-1740 (3) 3.00

Miniature Sheet

Arbrafex '92, Argentina-Brazil Philatelic Exhibition — A806

Traditional costumes: a, Gaucho, woman. b, Gaucho, horse. c, Gaucho in store. d, Gaucho holding lariat.

1992 **Litho.** *Perf. 13½*
1741 A806 38c Sheet of 4, #a.-d. 4.10

Natl. Parks Type of 1987

1992, Apr. 4 **Litho.** *Perf. 13x13½*
1742 A752 38c Alerces 90
1743 A752 38c Formosa Nature Reserve 90
1744 A752 38c Petrified Forest 90
1745 A752 38c Arrayanes 90
1746 A752 38c Laguna de los Pozuelos 90
Nos. 1742-1746 (5) 4.50

Mushrooms — A807

1992-94 **Photo.** *Perf. 13½*
1748 A807 10c Psilocybe cubensis 25 15
1749 A807 25c Coprinus atramentarius 60
1750 A807 38c Psilocybe cubensis 90
1752 A807 48c Coprinus atramentarius 1.20
1753 A807 50c Suillus granulatus 1.25
1754 A807 51c Morchella esculenta 1.30
1756 A807 61c Amanita muscaria 1.55
1760 A807 1p like #1756 2.50
1763 A807 1.77p Stropharia oeruginosa 4.25
1764 A807 2p like #1754 5.00
Nos. 1748-1764 (10) 18.80

No. 1763 not issued without overprint "Centro Filatelico de Neuquen y Rio Negro 50th Aniversario."

Issued: 38c, 4/4/92; 48c, 51c, 61c, 8/1/92; 1.77p, 11/7/92; 25c, 50c, 8/17/93; 1p, 2p, 8/26/93; 10c, 1/11/94. This is an expanding set. Numbers will change if necessary.

Falkland Islands War, 10th Anniv. A808

1992, May 2 **Litho.** *Perf. 13½*
1767 A808 38c Pucara 1A-58 95
1768 A808 38c Cruiser Gen. Belgrano 95
1769 A808 38c Soldier and truck 95
Nos. 1767-1769 (3) 2.85

Miniature Sheet

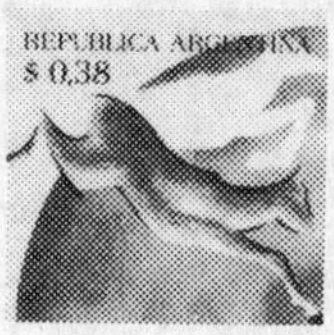

Preserve the Environment
A809

Designs: a, Deer. b, Geese. c, Butterflies. d, Whale.

1992, June 6 Litho. *Perf. 12*
1770 A809 38c Sheet of 4, #a.-d. 3.70

Paintings by Florencio Molina Campos
A810

1992, June 6 *Perf. 13½*
1771 A810 38c A La Sombra 95
1772 A810 38c Tileforo Areco, vert. 95

Famous Men
A811

Designs: No. 1773, Gen. Lucio N. Mansilla (1792-1871). No. 1774, Jose Manuel Estrada (1842-1894), writer. No. 1775, Brig. Gen. Jose I. Garmendia (1842-1915).

1992, July 4 Litho. *Perf. 13½*
1773 A811 38c multicolored 95
1774 A811 38c multicolored 95
1775 A811 38c multicolored 95
Nos. 1773-1775 (3) 2.85

Fight Against Drugs — A812

1992, Aug. 1 *Perf. 13½x13*
1776 A812 38c multicolored 95

Col. Jose M. Calaza, 140th Birth Anniv.
A813

1992, Sept. 5 Litho. *Perf. 13½*
1777 A813 38c multicolored 95

Discovery of America, 500th Anniv. — A814

Designs: a, Columbus, castle, ship. b, Native drawings, Columbus.

1992, Oct. 10 Litho. *Perf. 13½*
1778 A814 38c Pair, #a.-b. 1.90

Argentine Film Posters — A815

1992, Nov. 7 Litho. *Perf. 13½*
1779 A815 38c Dios Se Lo Pague, 1948 90
1780 A815 38c Las Aguas Bajan Turbias, 1952 90
1781 A815 38c Un Guapo Del 900, 1960 90
1782 A815 38c La Tregua, 1974 90
1783 A815 38c La Historia Oficial, 1984 90
Nos. 1779-1783 (5) 4.50

Christmas — A816

1992, Nov. 28
1784 A816 38c multicolored 90

Miniature Sheet

Iberoprenfil '92 — A817

Lighthouses: a, Punta Mogotes. b, Rio Negro. c, San Antonio. d, Cabo Blanco.

1992, Dec. 5
1785 A817 38c Sheet of 4, #a.-d. 3.60

Fight Against AIDS
A818 A819

1992, Dec. 12 Litho. *Perf. 13½*
1786 A818 10c multicolored 22
1787 A819 26c multicolored 65

Intl. Space Year
A820

1992, Dec. 19
1788 A820 38c multicolored 90

Souvenir Sheet

Miraculous Lord Crucifix, 400th Anniv. of Arrival in America — A821

1992, Dec. 26 *Perf. 12*
1789 A821 76c multicolored 2.00

Jujuy City, 400th Anniv. — A822

1993, Apr. 24 Litho. *Perf. 13½*
1790 A822 38c multicolored 90

Argentina Soccer Assoc., Cent.
A823

1993, Mar. 27
1791 A823 38c multicolored 1.00

Souvenir Sheet

Intl. Philatelic Exhibitions — A824

Designs: a, 38c, City Hall, Poznan, Poland. b, 48c, Statue of Christ the Redeemer, Rio de Janeiro, Brazil. c, 76c, Royal Palace, Bangkok, Thailand.

1993, May 8 Litho. *Perf. 12*
1792 A824 Sheet of 3, #a.-c. 3.85

Polska '93 (#1792a), Brasiliana '93 (#1792b), Bangkok '92 (#1792c).

Luis C. Candelaria's Flight Over Andes Mountains, 75th Anniv. — A825

1993, June 26 Litho. *Perf. 13x13½*
1793 A825 38c multicolored 95

Illustration reduced.

Order of San Martin, 50th Anniv. — A826

National History Academy, Cent. — A827

1993, May 29 *Perf. 13½*
1794 A826 38c multicolored 95
1795 A827 38c multicolored 95

Armed Forces Memorial Day — A828

1993, June 12
1796 A828 38c National Gendarmerie 95
1797 A828 38c Coast Guard 95

Paintings
A829

Designs: No. 1798, Old House, by Norberto Russo. No. 1799, Pa'las Casas, by Adriana Zaefferer.

1993, Aug. 14 Litho. *Perf. 13½*
1798 A829 38c multicolored 90
1799 A829 38c multicolored 90

Pato — A830

1993, Aug. 28 Litho. *Perf. 12*

1800 A830 1p multicolored	2.50	

Nut-Bearing Trees — A831

Designs: No. 1801, Enterolobium contortisiliquum. No. 1802, Prosopis alba. No. 1803, Magnolia grandiflora. No. 1804, Erythrina falcata. Illustration reduced.

1993, Sept. 25 Litho. *Perf. 13x13½*

1801 A831 75c multicolored	1.75	
1802 A831 75c multicolored	1.75	
1803 A831 1.50p multicolored	3.50	
1804 A831 1.50p multicolored	3.50	
Nos. 1801-1804 (4)	10.50	

America Issue A832

Whales: 50c, Eubalaena australis. 75c, Cephalorhynchus commersonii.

1993, Oct. 9 *Perf. 13½*

1805 A832 50c multicolored	1.10	
1806 A832 75c multicolored	1.75	

Miniature Sheet

Christmas, New Year — A833

Denomination at: a, UL. b, UR. c, LL. d, LR.

1993, Dec. 4 Litho. *Perf. 13½*

1807 A833 75c Sheet of 4, #a.-d.	6.00	

Cave of the Hands, Santa Cruz — A834

1993, Dec. 18

1808 A834 1p multicolored	2.00	

New Emblem, Argentine Postal Service — A835

Illustration reduced.

1994, Jan. 8 *Perf. 11½*

1809 A835 75c multicolored	1.75	

A836

1994 World Cup Soccer Championships, US — A837

Players from: 25c, Germany, 1990. 50c, Brazil, 1970. 75c, 1.50p, Argentina, 1986. 1p, Italy, 1982.

1994, June 11 Litho. *Perf. 13½*

1810 A836 25c multicolored	50	
1811 A836 50c multicolored	1.00	
1812 A836 75c multicolored	1.50	
1813 A836 1p multicolored	2.00	
Nos. 1810-1813 (4)	5.00	

Souvenir Sheet

Perf. 12

1814 A836 1.50p multicolored	3.00	

No. 1814 contains one 40x50mm stamp with continuous design.

1994, July 23 *Perf. 13½*

Drawings of championships by: No. 1815, Julian Lisenberg. No. 1816, Matias Taylor, vert. No. 1817, Torcuato S. Gonzalez Agote, vert. No. 1818, Maria Paula Palma.

1815 A837 75c multicolored	1.50	
1816 A837 75c multicolored	1.50	
1817 A837 75c multicolored	1.50	
1818 A837 75c multicolored	1.50	
Nos. 1815-1818 (4)	6.00	

A838

1994 Litho. *Perf. 13½*

1819 A838 10c like #1748	20	
1820 A838 25c like #1749	50	
1823 A838 50c like #1753	1.00	
1828 A838 1p like #1760	2.00	
1832 A838 2p like #1764	4.00	
Nos. 1819-1832 (5)	7.70	

Issued: 10c, 25c, 50c, 1p, 2p, 6/14/94. This is expanding set. Numbers may change.

Wildlife of Falkland Islands A839

Designs: 25c, Melanodera melanodera. 50c, Pygoscelis papua. 75c, Tachyeres brachypterus. 1p, Mirounga leonina.

1994, Aug 6

1839 A839 25c multicolored	50	
1840 A839 50c multicolored	1.00	
1841 A839 75c multicolored	1.50	
1842 A839 1p multicolored	2.00	
Nos. 1839-1842 (4)	5.00	

City of San Luis, 400th Anniv. — A840

1994, Aug. 20

1843 A840 75c multicolored	1.50	

Province of Tierra del Fuego, Antarctica and South Atlantic Islands — A841

1994, Aug. 20

1844 A841 75c multicolored	3.00	

Argentine Inventors — A842

Designs: No. 1845, Ladislao Jose Biro (1899-1985), ball point pen. No. 1846, Raul Pateras de Pescara (1890-1966), helicopter. No. 1847, Quirino Cristiani (1896-1984), animated drawings. No. 1848, Enrique Finochietto (1881-1948), surgical instruments.

1994, Oct. 1

1845 A842 75c multicolored	1.50	
1846 A842 75c multicolored	1.50	
1847 A842 75c multicolored	1.50	
1848 A842 75c multicolored	1.50	
Nos. 1845-1848 (4)	6.00	

SEMI-POSTAL STAMPS

Samuel F. B. Morse — SP1

Globe — SP2

Landing of Columbus — SP5

Map of Argentina — SP6

Designs: 10c+5c, Alexander Graham Bell. 25c+15c, Rowland Hill.

Wmk. RA in Sun (90)

1944, Jan. 5 Litho. *Perf. 13*

B1 SP1 3c +2c lt vio & sl bl	32	26
B2 SP2 5c +5c dl red & sl bl	65	16
B3 SP1 10c +5c org & slate bl	1.25	70
B4 SP1 25c +15c red brn & sl bl	1.75	1.10
B5 SP5 1p +50c lt grn & sl bl	8.00	7.25
Nos. B1-B5 (5)	11.97	9.47

The surtax was for the Postal Employees Benefit Association.

1944, Feb. 17 Wmk. 90 *Perf. 13*

B6 SP6 5c +10c ol yel & slate	75	50
B7 SP6 5c +50c vio brn & slate	3.25	2.00
B8 SP6 5c +1p dl org & slate	9.00	6.50
B9 SP6 5c +20p dp bl & slate	22.50	15.00
Nos. B6-B9 (4)	35.50	24.00

The surtax was for the victims of the San Juan earthquake.

Souvenir Sheets

National Anthem and Flag — SP7

Illustration reduced.

1944, July 17 *Imperf.*

B10 SP7 5c +1p vio brn & lt bl 1.90 1.90
B11 SP7 5c +50p bl blk & lt bl 250.00 225.00

Surtax for the needy in the provinces of La Rioja and Catamarca.

Catalogue values for unused stamps in this section, from this point to the end of the section, are for Never Hinged items.

Stamp Designing — SP8

1950, Aug. 26 **Photo.** *Perf. 13½*

B12 SP8 10c +10c violet 24 24
Nos. B12,CB1-CB5 (6) 20.42 15.61

Argentine Intl. Philatelic Exhibition, 1950.

Poliomyelitis Victim — SP9

1956, Apr. 14 *Perf. 13½x13*

B13 SP9 20c +30c slate 30 15

The surtax was for the poliomyelitis fund. Head in design is from Correggio's "Antiope," Louvre.

Stamp of 1858 and Mail Coach on Raft — SP10

Designs: 2.40p+1.20p, Album, magnifying glass and stamp of 1858. 4.40p+2.20p, Government seat of Confederation, Parana.

1958, Mar. 29 **Litho.** *Perf. 13½*

B14 SP10 40c +20c brt grn & dl pur 32 24
B15 SP10 2.40p +1.20p ol gray & bl 40 26
B16 SP10 4.40p +2.20p lt bl & dp claret 60 40
Nos. B14-B16,CB8-CB12 (8) 5.84 4.66

Surtax for Intl. Centennial Philatelic Exhibition, Paraná, Entre Rios, Apr. 19-27.

View of Flooded Land — SP11

1958, Oct. 4 **Photo.** *Perf. 13½*

B17 SP11 40c +20c brown 15 15
Nos. B17,CB13-CB14 (3) 1.20 1.10

The surtax was for flood victims in the Buenos Aires district.

Child Receiving Blood — SP12

Runner — SP13

1958, Dec. 20 **Litho.** **Wmk. 90**

B18 SP12 1p +50c blk & rose red 16 15

The surtax went to the Anti-Leukemia Foundation.

1959, Sept. 5 *Perf. 13½*

Designs: 50c+20c, Basketball players, vert. 1p+50c, Boxers, vert.

B19 SP13 20c +10c emer & blk 20 16
B20 SP13 50c +20c yel & blk 15 15
B21 SP13 1p +50c mar & blk 16 16
Nos. B19-B21,CB15-CB16 (5) 1.51 1.21

3rd Pan American Games, Chicago, Aug. 27-Sept. 7, 1959.

Condor — SP14

Birds: 50c+20c, Fork-tailed flycatchers. 1p+50c, Magellanic woodpecker.

1960, Feb. 6

B22 SP14 20c +10c dk bl 15 15
B23 SP14 50c +20c dp vio bl 15 15
B24 SP14 1p +50c brn & buff 20 15
Nos. B22-B24,CB17-CB18 (5) 1.25
Set value 72

The surtax was for child welfare work. See Nos. B30, CB29.

Souvenir Sheet

Uprooted Oak Emblem — SP15

1960, Apr. 7 **Wmk. 90** *Imperf.*

B25 SP15 Sheet of 2 1.25 1.25
a. 1p + 50c bister & carmine 55 55
b. 4.20p + 2.10p apple grn & dp claret 55 55

WRY, July 1, 1959-June 30, 1960.
The surtax was for aid to refugees.

Jacaranda — SP16

Flowers: 1p+1p, Passionflower. 3p+3p, Orchid. 5p+5p, Tabebuia.

1960, Dec. 3 **Photo.** *Perf. 13½*

B26 SP16 50c +50c deep blue 15 15
B27 SP16 1p +1p bluish grn 15 15
B28 SP16 3p +3p henna brn 32 22
B29 SP16 5p +5p dark brn 52 35
Nos. B26-B29 (4) 1.14
Set value 70

"TEMEX 61" (Intl. Thematic Exposition).
For overprints see Nos. B31-B34.

Type of 1960

Bird: 4.20p+2.10p, Blue-eyed shag.

1961, Feb. 25 **Wmk. 90** *Perf. 13½*

B30 SP14 4.20p +2.10p chestnut brn 48 32

Surtax for child welfare work. See #CB29.

Nos. B26-B29 Overprinted in Black, Brown, Blue or Red: "14 DE ABRIL DIA DE LAS AMERICAS"

1961, Apr. 15

B31 SP16 50c +50c deep blue 15 15
B32 SP16 1p +1p bluish grn (Brn) 15 15
B33 SP16 3p +3p henna brn (Bl) 32 25
B34 SP16 5p +5p dk brn (R) 52 42
Nos. B31-B34 (4) 1.14 97

Day of the Americas, Apr. 14.

Cathedral, Cordoba — SP17

Stamp of 1862 — SP18

Flight into Egypt, by Ana Maria Moncalvo — SP19

Design: 10p+10p, Cathedral, Buenos Aires.

Perf. 13½

1961, Oct. 21 **Wmk. 90** **Photo.**

B35 SP17 2p +2p rose claret 22 15
B36 SP18 3p +3p green 32 18
B37 SP17 10p +10p brt blue 90 52
a. Souvenir sheet of 3 1.75 1.10
Nos. B35-B37 (3) 1.44 85

1962 International Stamp Exhibition.
No. B37a contains three imperf. stamps similar to Nos. B35-B37 in dark blue.

1961, Dec. 16 **Litho.**

B38 SP19 2p +1p lilac & blk brn 15 15
B39 SP19 10p +5p light & deep claret 52 15
Set value 22

The surtax was for child welfare.

Chalk-browed Mockingbird — SP20

Soccer — SP21

Design: 12p+6p, Rufous-collared sparrow.

1962, Dec. 29 *Perf. 13½*

B40 SP20 4p +2p bis, brn & bl grn 90 60
B41 SP20 12p +6p gray, yel, grn & brn 1.50 1.10

The surtax was for child welfare. See Nos. B44, B47, B48-B50, CB32, CB35-CB36.

1963, May 18 *Perf. 13½*

B42 SP21 4p +2p multi 22 15
B43 SP21 12p +6p Horsemanship 45 35
a. Dark carmine (jacket) omitted
Nos. B42-B43,CB31 (3) 1.22 1.00

4th Pan American Games, Sao Paulo.

Bird Type of 1962

Design: Vermilion flycatcher.

1963, Dec. 21 **Litho.**

B44 SP20 4p +2p blk, red, org & grn 60 28

The surtax was for child welfare. See No. CB32.

Fencers — SP22

Design: 4p+2p, National Stadium, Tokyo, horiz.

1964, July 18 **Wmk. 90** *Perf. 13½*

B45 SP22 4p +2p red, ocher & brn 16 15
B46 SP22 12p +6p bl grn & blk 40 32
Nos. B45-B46,CB33 (3) 1.06 97

18th Olympic Games, Tokyo, Oct. 10-25, 1964. See No. CB33.

Bird Type of 1962

Design: Red-crested cardinal.

1964, Dec. 23 **Litho.**

B47 SP20 4p +2p dk bl, red & grn 60 30

The surtax was for child welfare. See #CB35.

Bird Type of 1962
Inscribed "R. ARGENTINA"

Designs: 8p+4p, Lapwing. 10p+5p, Scarlet-headed marshbird, horiz. 20p+10p, Amazon kingfisher.

1966-67 *Perf. 13½*

B48 SP20 8p +4p blk, ol, brt grn & red 80 35
B49 SP20 10p +5p blk, bl, org & grn 80 55
B50 SP20 20p +10p blk, yel, bl & pink 40 35
Nos. B48-B50,CB36,CB38-CB39 (6) 4.30 3.25

The surtax was for child welfare.
Issue dates: 8p+4p, Mar. 26, 1966. 10p+5p, Jan. 14, 1967. 20p+10p, Dec. 23, 1967.

Grandmother's Birthday, by Patricia Lynch; Lions Emblem — SP23

Perf. 12½x13½

1968, Dec. 14 Litho. Wmk. 90

B51	SP23 40p + 20p multi	45	38

1st Lions Intl. Benevolent Phil. Exhib. Surtax for the Children's Hospital Benevolent Fund.

White-faced Tree Duck — SP24

1969, Sept. 20 Wmk. 365 *Perf. 13½*

B52	SP24 20p + 10p multi	48	35

Surtax for child welfare. See No. CB40.

Slender-tailed Woodstar (Hummingbird) SP25

1970, May 9 Wmk. 365 *Perf. 13½*

B53	SP25 20c + 10c multi	45	40

The surtax was for child welfare. See Nos. CB41, B56-B59, B62-B63.

Dolphinfish — SP26

1971, Feb. 20 Unwmk. *Perf. 12½*
Size: 75x15mm

B54	SP26 20c + 10c multi	52	45

Surtax for child welfare. See No. CB42.

Children with Stamps, by Mariette Lydis — SP27

1971, Dec. 18 Litho. *Perf. 13½*

B55	SP27 1p + 50p multi	48	32

2nd Lions Intl. Solidarity Stamp Exhib.

Bird Type of 1970

Birds: 25c+10c, Saffron finch. 65c+30c, Rufous-bellied thrush, horiz.

1972, May 6 Unwmk. *Perf. 13½*

B56	SP25 25c + 10c multi	32	20
B57	SP25 65c + 30c multi	45	32

Surtax was for child welfare.

Bird Type of 1970

Birds: 50c+25c, Southern screamer (chaja). 90c+45c, Saffron-cowled blackbird, horiz.

1973, Apr. 28

B58	SP25 50c + 25c multi	48	32
B59	SP25 90c + 45c multi	70	48

Surtax was for child welfare.

Painting Type of Regular Issue

Designs: 15c+15c, Still Life, by Alfredo Guttero, horiz. 90c+90c, Nude, by Miguel C. Victorica, horiz.

1973, Aug. 28 Litho. *Perf. 13½*

B60	A472 15c + 15c multi	28	18
B61	A472 90c + 90c multi	1.00	70

Bird Type of 1970

Birds: 70c+30c, Blue seed-eater. 1.20p+60c, Hooded siskin.

1974, May 11 Litho. *Perf. 13½*

B62	SP25 70c + 30c multi	50	35
B63	SP25 1.20p + 60c multi	75	42

Surtax was for child welfare.

Painting Type of 1974

Design: 70c+30c, The Lama, by Juan Batlle Planas.

1974, May 11 Litho. *Perf. 13½*

B64	A477 70c + 30c multi	28	22

PRENFIL-74 UPU, Intl. Exhib. of Phil. Periodicals, Buenos Aires, Oct. 1-12.

Plushcrested Jay — SP28

Designs: 13p+6.50p, Golden-collared macaw. 20p+10p, Begonia. 40p+20p, Teasel.

1976, June 12 Litho. *Perf. 13½*

B65	SP28 7p + 3.50p multi	20	15
B66	SP28 13p + 6.50p multi	32	20
B67	SP28 20p + 10p multi	48	32
B68	SP28 40p + 20p multi	95	48
	Nos. B65-B68 (4)	1.95	1.15

Argentine philately.

Telegraph, Communications Satellite — SP29

Designs: 20p+10p, Old and new mail trucks. 60p+30p, Old, new packet boats. 70p+35p, Biplane and jet.

1977, July 16 Litho. *Perf. 13½*

B69	SP29 10p + 5p multi	30	20
B70	SP29 20p + 10p multi	50	60
B71	SP29 60p + 30p multi	1.00	85
B72	SP29 70p + 35p multi	1.25	85
	Nos. B69-B72 (4)	3.05	2.50

Surtax was for Argentine philately.
No. B70 exists with wmk. 365.

Church of St. Francis Type, 1977, Inscribed: "EXPOSICION ARGENTINA '77"

1977, Aug. 27

B73	A515 160p + 80p multi	2.50	2.00

Surtax was for Argentina '77 Philatelic Exhibition. Issued in sheets of 4.

No. B73 Overprinted with Soccer Cup Emblem

1978, Feb. 4 Litho. *Perf. 13½*

B74	A515 160p + 80p multi	4.50	4.25
a.	Souvenir sheet of 4	20.00	19.00

11th World Cup Soccer Championship, Argentina, June 1-25.

Spinus Magellanicus SP30

Birds: 100p+100p, Variable seedeater. 150p+150p, Yellow thrush. 200p+200p, Pyrocephalus rubineus. 500p+500p, Great kiskadee.

1978, Aug. 5 Litho. *Perf. 13½*

B75	SP30 50p + 50p multi	90	60
B76	SP30 100p + 100p multi	1.10	90
B77	SP30 150p + 150p multi	1.40	1.25
B78	SP30 200p + 200p multi	1.75	1.75
B79	SP30 500p + 500p multi	8.50	7.25
	Nos. B75-B79 (5)	13.65	11.75

ARGENTINA '78, Inter-American Philatelic Exhibition, Buenos Aires, Oct. 27-Nov. 5. Nos. B75-B79 issued in sheets of 4 with marginal inscriptions commemorating Exhibition and 1978 Soccer Championship.

Caravel "Magdalena," 16th Century — SP31

Sailing Ships: 500+500p, 3 master "Rio de la Plata," 17th cent. 600+600p, Corvette "Descubierta," 18th cent. 1500+1500p, Naval Academy yacht "A.R.A. Fortuna," 1979.

1979, Sept. 8 Litho. *Perf. 13½*

B80	SP31 400p +400p multi	3.25	2.25
B81	SP31 500p +500p multi	3.75	2.50
B82	SP31 600p +600p multi	4.75	3.25
B83	SP31 1500p +1500p multi	12.00	8.00
	Nos. B80-B83 (4)	23.75	16.00

Buenos Aires '80, International Philatelic Exhibition, Buenos Aires, Oct. 24-Nov. 2, 1980. Issued in sheets of 4.

Purmamarca Church — SP32

Churches: 200p + 100p, Molinos. 300p + 150p, Animana. 400p + 200p, San Jose de Lules.

1979, Nov. 3 Litho. *Perf. 13½*

B84	SP32 100p + 50p multi	24	15
B85	SP32 200p + 100p multi	45	15
B86	SP32 300p + 150p multi	60	18
B87	SP32 400p + 200p multi	90	24
	Nos. B84-B87 (4)	2.19	
	Set value		62

Buenos Aires No. 3, Exhibition and Society Emblems — SP33

Argentine Stamps: 750p+750p, type A580. 1000p+1000p, No. 91. 2000p+2000p, type A588.

1979, Dec. 15 Litho. *Perf. 13½*

B88	SP33 250p + 250p multi	90	70
B89	SP33 750p + 750p multi	2.25	1.75
B90	SP33 1000p + 1000p multi	3.00	2.50
B91	SP33 2000p + 2000p multi	6.00	5.00
	Nos. B88-B91 (4)	12.15	9.95

PRENFIL '80, Intl. Philatelic Literature and Publications Exhib., Buenos Aires, Nov. 7-16, 1980.

Minuet, by Carlos E. Pellegrini SP34

Paintings: 700p+350p, Media Cana, by Carlos Morel. 800p+400p, Cielito, by Pellegrini. 1000p+500p, El Gato, by Juan Leon Palliere.

1981, July 11 Litho. *Perf. 13½*

B92	SP34 500p + 250p multi	70	35
B93	SP34 700p + 350p multi	1.00	70
B94	SP34 800p + 400p multi	1.10	90
B95	SP34 1000p + 500p multi	1.40	1.25
	Nos. B92-B95 (4)	4.20	3.20

Espamer '81 Intl. Stamp Exhib. (Americas, Spain, Portugal), Buenos Aires, Nov. 13-22.

Canal, by Beatrix Bongliani (b. 1933) SP35

Tapestries: 1000p+500p, Shadows, by Silvia Sieburger, vert. 2000p+1000p, Interpretation of a Rectangle, by Silke R. de Haupt, vert. 4000p+2000p, Tilcara, by Tana Sachs.

1982, July 31 Litho. *Perf. 13½*

B96	SP35 1000p + 500p multi	20	20
B97	SP35 2000p + 1000p multi	40	40
B98	SP35 3000p + 1500p multi	60	60
B99	SP35 4000p + 2000p multi	80	80
	Nos. B96-B99 (4)	2.00	2.00

Boy Playing Marbles — SP36

1983, July 2 Litho. *Perf. 13½*

B100	SP36 20c + 10c shown	15	15
B101	SP36 30c + 15c Jumping rope	32	16
B102	SP36 50c + 25c Hopscotch	32	20
B103	SP36 1p + 50c Flying kites	60	48
B104	SP36 2p + 1p Spinning top	65	65
	Nos. B100-B104 (5)	2.04	1.64

Surtax was for natl. philatelic associations.
See Nos. B106-B110.

Compass, 15th Cent. SP37

ARGENTINA '85 Intl. Stamp Show: b, Arms of Spain, Argentina. c, Columbus' arms. d-f, Columbus' arrival at San Salvador Island. Nos. B105d-B105f in continuous design; ships shown on singles range in size, left to right, from small to large. Surtax was for exhibition.

1984, Apr. 28 Litho. *Perf. 13½*

B105 Block of 6 3.75 3.75
a.-f. SP37 5p + 2.50p, any single 52 26

Children's Game Type of 1983

1984, July 7 Litho. *Perf. 13½*

B106 SP36 2p + 1p Blind Man's Buff 15 15
B107 SP36 3p + 1.50p The Loop 30 24
B108 SP36 4p + 2p Leap Frog 35 30
B109 SP36 5p + 2.50p Rolling the loop 45 35
B110 SP36 6p + 3p Ball Mold 55 45
Nos. B106-B110 (5) 1.80 1.49

Butterflies SP38

1985, Nov. 9 Litho. *Perf. 13½*

B111 SP38 5c + 2c Rothschildia jacobaeae 15 15
B112 SP38 10c + 5c Heliconius erato phyllis 30 30
B113 SP38 20c + 10c Precis evarete hilaris 60 60
B114 SP38 25c + 13c Cyanopepla pretiosa 75 75
B115 SP38 40c + 20c Papilio androgeus 1.10 1.10
Nos. B111-B115 (5) 2.90 2.90

Children's Drawings SP39

1986, Aug. 30 Litho.

B116 SP39 5c + 2c N. Pastor 15 15
B117 SP39 10c + 5c T. Valleistein 30 30
B118 SP39 20c + 10c J.M. Flores 60 60
B119 SP39 25c + 13c M.E. Pezzuto 75 75
B120 SP39 40c + 20c E. Diehl 1.10 1.10
Nos. B116-B120 (5) 2.90 2.90

Surtax for natl. philatelic associations.

Miniature Sheets

Fresh-water Fish — SP40

No. B121: a, Metynnis maculatus. b, Cynolebias nigripinnis. c, Leporinus solarii. d, Aphyocharax rathbuni. e, Corydoras aeneus. f, Thoracocharax securis. g, Cynolebias melanotaenia. h, Cichlasoma facetum.

No. B122: a, Tetragonopterus argenteus. b, Hemigrammus caudovittatus. c, Astyanax bimaculatus. d, Gymnocorymbus ternetzi. e, Hoplias malabaricus. f, Aphyocharax rubripinnis. g, Apistogramma agassizi. h, Pyrrhulina rachoviana.

1987, June 27

B121 Sheet of 8 2.00
a.-h. SP40 10c +5c, any single 25
B122 Sheet of 8 4.00
a.-h. SP40 20c +10c, any single 50

PRENFIL '88, Intl. Philatelic Literature and Media Exhibition, Buenos Aires, Nov. 25-Dec. 2 — SP41

Locomotives and railroad car: No. B123, Yatay locomotive, 1888. No. B124, FCCA electric passenger car, 1914. No. B125, B-15 locomotive, 1942. No. B126, GT-22 No. 200 locomotive, 1988.

1988, June 4 Litho. *Perf. 13½*

B123 SP41 1a +50c multi 40
B124 SP41 1a +50c multi 40
B125 SP41 1a +50c multi 40
B126 SP41 1a +50c multi 40
Nos. B123-B126 (4) 1.60

Nos. B123-B125 each issued in sheets of 4.

Horses SP42

Paintings: No. B127, *The Waiting*, by Gustavo Solari. No. B128, *Mare and Foal*, by E. Castro. No. B129, *Saint Isidor*, by Castro. No. B130, *At Lagoon's Edge*, by F. Romero Carranza. No. B131, *Under the Tail*, by Castro.

1988, Oct. 29 Litho. *Perf. 13½*

B127 SP42 2a +1a multi 50
B128 SP42 2a +1a multi 50
B129 SP42 2a +1a multi 50
B130 SP42 2a +1a multi 50
B131 SP42 2a +1a multi 50
Nos. B127-B131 (5) 2.50

PRENFIL '88 — SP43

Covers of philatelic magazines.

1988, Nov. 26 Litho. *Perf. 13½*

B132 SP43 1a +1a *Cronaca Filatelica*, Italy 32
B133 SP43 1a +1a *CO-FI*, Brazil 32
B134 SP43 1a +1a *References de la Poste*, France 32
B135 SP43 2a +2a *Postas Argentinas* 65
Nos. B132-B135 (4) 1.61

Souvenir Sheet

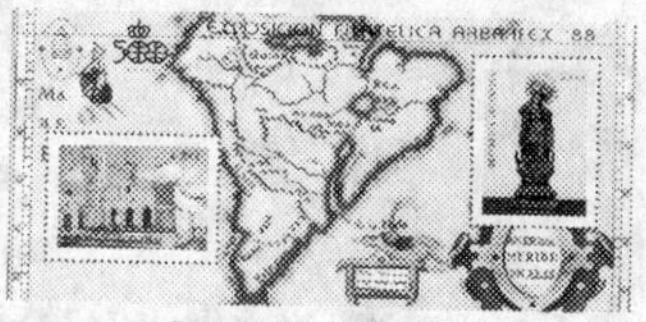

ARBRAPEX '88 — SP44

Designs: No. B136a, *Candel Delivery at San Ignacio*, by Leonie Matthis, Cornelio Saavedra Museum, Buenos Aires. No. B136b, *Immaculate Conception*, a statue in the Isaac Fernandez Blanco Museum, Buenos Aires.

1988, Nov. 26 *Perf. 12*

B136 SP44 Sheet of 2 1.60
a. 2a +2a multi 65
b. 3a +3a multi 95

Fish SP45

Designs: No. B137, *Diplomystes viedmensis*. No. B138, *Haplochiton taeniatus*. No. B139, *Percichthys trucha*. No. B140, *Galaxias platei*. No. B141, *Salmo fario*.

1989, June 24 Litho. *Perf. 13½*

B137 SP45 10a +5a multi 15
B138 SP45 10a +5a multi 15
B139 SP45 10a +5a multi 15
B140 SP45 10a +5a multi 15
B141 SP45 10a +5a multi 15
Set value 50

Printed in sheets of 4.

Discovery of America 500th Anniv. (in 1992) and ESPAMER '90 — SP46

Documents and chronicles: No. B142, Columbus's coat of arms, *Book of Privileges* title page. No. B143, Illustration from *New Chronicle and Good Government*, by Guaman Poma de Ayala. No. B144, Illustration from *Discovery and Conquest of Peru*, by Pedro de Cieza de Leon. No. B145, Illustration from *Travel to the River Plate*, by Ulrico Schmidl.

1989, Sept. 16 Litho. *Perf. 13½*
Yellow, Rose Violet & Black

B142 SP46 100a +50a
B143 SP46 150a +50a
B144 SP46 200a +100a
B145 SP46 250a +100a

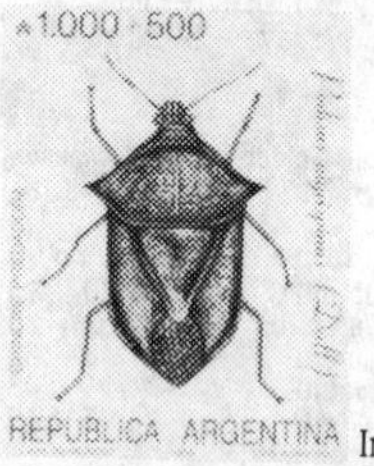

Insects — SP47

Designs: No. B146, *Podisus nigrispinus*. No. B147, *Adalia bipunctata*. No. B148, *Nabis punctipennis*. No. B149, *Hippodamia convergens*. No. B150, *Calleida suturalis*.

1990, June 30 Litho. *Perf. 13½*

B146 SP47 1000a +500a multi
B147 SP47 1000a +500a multi
B148 SP47 1000a +500a multi
B149 SP47 1000a +500a multi
B150 SP47 1000a +500a multi

Souvenir Sheet

First Natl. Exposition of Aerophilately — SP48

Designs: a, Lieut. Marcos A. Zar, Macchi seaplane. b, Capt. Antonio Parodi, Ansaldo SVA biplane. (Illustration reduced).

1990, July 14 Litho. *Perf. 12*

B151 Sheet of 2
a. SP48 2000a +2000a multi
b. SP48 3000a +3000a multi

Souvenir Sheet

1992 Summer Olympics, Barcelona SP49

Designs: a, Shot put. b, High jump. c, Hurdles. d, Pole vault.

1990, Dec. 15 Litho. *Perf. 13½*

B152 Sheet of 4
a.-d. SP49 2000a +2000a multi

Espamer '91 Philatelic Exhibition. See No. B155.

Souvenir Sheet

Discovery of America, 500th Anniv. (in 1992) — SP50

Voyage of Alesandro Malaspina, 1789-1794: a, Sailing ship. b, Malaspina. c, Indian, hut. d, Indian, horse, artist drawing.

1990, Oct. 13 Litho. *Perf. 13½*

B153 Sheet of 4 6.00
a.-d. SP50 2000a +1000a, any single 1.50

Espamer '91, Buenos Aires.

Souvenir Sheet

Race Cars and Drivers — SP51

Designs: a, Juan Manuel Fangio. b, Juan Manuel Bordeu. c, Carlos Alberto Reutemann. d, Oscar and Juan Galvez.

1991 Litho. *Perf. 13½*

B154 SP51 Sheet of 4 4.80
a.-d. 2500a +2500a, any single 1.20

Espamer '91.

Souvenir Sheet
1992 Summer Olympics Type of 1990

Women's gymnastics routines: a, Floor exercise. b, Uneven parallel bars. c, Balance beam. d, Rhythmic gymnastics.

1991, June 29 Litho. *Perf. 13½*

B155 Sheet of 4 4.80
a.-d. SP49 2500a +2500a, any single 1.20

Espamer '91.

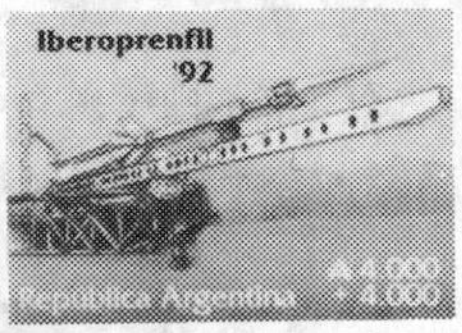

Iberoprenfil '92 SP52

Designs: No. B156, Castor missile. No. B157, Satellite LUSAT 1.

1991, Dec. 28 Litho. *Perf. 13½*

B156 SP52	4000a +4000a multi	2.00
B157 SP52	4000a +4000a multi	2.00

Dinosaurs — SP53

1992, May 2 Litho. *Perf. 13½*

B158 SP53	38c +38c Carnotaurus	1.90
B159 SP53	38c +38c Amargasaurus	1.90

Iberoprenfil '92, Buenos Aires SP54

Paintings by Raul Soldi (b. 1905): No. B160, The Fiesta. No. B161, Church of St. Anne of Glew.

1992, Sept. 5 Litho. *Perf. 13½*

B160 SP54	76c +76c multi	3.75
B161 SP54	76c +76c multi	3.75

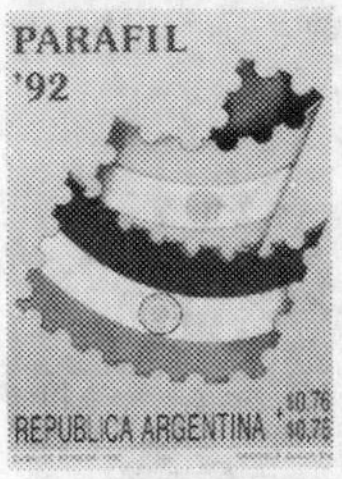

Parafil '92 — SP55

1992, Nov. 21 Litho. *Perf. 13½*

B162 SP55	76c +76c multi	3.60

2nd Argentine-Paraguayan Philatelic Exhibition, Buenos Aires.

Souvenir Sheet

Birds — SP56

Designs: a, Egretta thula. b, Amblyramphus holosericeus. c, Paroaria coronata. d, Chloroceryle amazona.

1993, July 17 Litho. *Perf. 13½*

B163 SP56	38c +38c Sheet of 4	7.25

AIR POST STAMPS

Airplane Circles the Globe — AP1

Eagle — AP2

Wings Cross the Sea — AP3

Condor on Mountain Crag — AP4

Perforations of Nos. C1-C37 vary from clean-cut to rough and uneven, with many skipped perfs.

Perf. 13x13½, 13½x13

1928, Mar. 1 Litho. Wmk. 90

C1	AP1	5c lt red	1.00	45
C2	AP1	10c Prus blue	2.00	1.00
C3	AP2	15c lt brown	2.00	75
C4	AP1	18c lilac gray	2.75	2.50
a.		18c brown lilac	3.00	2.50
b.		Double impression	*375.00*	
C5	AP2	20c ultra	2.00	75
C6	AP2	24c deep blue	3.25	2.50
C7	AP3	25c brt violet	3.25	1.50
C8	AP3	30c rose red	4.75	90
C9	AP4	35c rose	3.25	90
C10	AP1	36c bister brn	2.25	1.50
C11	AP4	50c gray black	3.75	45
C12	AP2	54c chocolate	3.25	1.90
C13	AP2	72c yellow grn	4.25	1.90
a.		Double impression	*300.00*	
C14	AP3	90c dk brown	7.25	1.65
C15	AP3	1p slate bl & red	9.25	60
C16	AP3	1.08p rose & dk bl	14.00	4.25
C17	AP4	1.26p dull vio & grn	18.00	7.25
C18	AP4	1.80p blue & lil rose	18.00	7.25
C19	AP4	3.60p gray & blue	37.50	18.00
		Nos. C1-C19 (19)	141.75	56.00

The watermark on No. C4a is larger than on the other stamps of this set, measuring 10mm across Sun.

Zeppelin First Flight

Air Post Stamps of 1928 Overprinted in Blue

"ZEPPELIN" 1er VUELO 1930

1930, May

C20	AP2	20c ultra	9.50	4.75
C21	AP4	50c gray black	20.00	9.50
a.		Inverted overprint	*475.00*	
C22	AP3	1p slate bl & red	21.00	9.50
a.		Inverted overprint	*550.00*	
C23	AP4	1.80p blue & lil rose	55.00	24.00
C24	AP4	3.60p gray & blue	150.00	70.00
		Nos. C20-C24 (5)	255.50	117.75

Overprinted in Green

C25	AP2	20c ultra	8.50	5.50
C26	AP4	50c gray black	11.00	7.00
C27	AP3	90c dark brown	8.50	5.50
C28	AP3	1p slate bl & red	18.00	11.00
C29	AP4	1.80p blue & lil rose	475.00	350.00
a.		Thick paper	*725.00*	
		Nos. C25-C29 (5)	521.00	379.00

Air Post Stamps of 1928 Overprinted in Red or Blue

1930
6
Septiembre
-1931-

On AP1-AP2

6 de Septiembre
1930 — 1931

On AP3-AP4

1931

C30	AP1	18c lilac gray	2.00	1.50
C31	AP2	72c yellow green	14.00	10.50
C32	AP3	90c dark brown	14.00	10.50
C33	AP4	1.80p bl & lil rose (Bl)	30.00	22.50
C34	AP4	3.60p gray & blue	57.50	40.00
		Nos. C30-C34 (5)	117.50	85.00

1st anniv. of the Revolution of 1930.

Zeppelin Issue

Nos. C1, C4, C4a, C14 Overprinted in Blue or Red

GRAF ZEPPELIN 1932

On AP1

GRAF ZEPPELIN 1932

On AP3

1932, Aug. 4

C35	AP1	5c lt red (Bl)	2.40	2.00
C36	AP1	18c lilac gray (R)	8.50	9.00
a.		18c brown lilac (R)	100.00	60.00
C37	AP3	90c dark brown (R)	27.50	26.00
		Nos. C35-C37 (3)	38.40	37.00

Plane and Letter — AP5

Mercury — AP6

Plane in Flight — AP7

Perf. 13½x13, 13x13½

1940, Oct. 23 Photo. Wmk. 90

C38	AP5	30c deep orange	5.00	15
C39	AP6	50c dark brown	7.50	18
C40	AP5	1p carmine	1.75	15
C41	AP7	1.25p deep green	45	15
C42	AP5	2.50p bright blue	1.25	18
		Nos. C38-C42 (5)	15.95	
		Set value		67

Plane and Letter — AP8

Mercury and Plane — AP9

Perf. 13½x13, 13x13½

1942, Oct. 6 Litho. Wmk. 90

C43	AP8	30c orange	15	15
C44	AP9	50c dull brn & buff	38	15
		Set value		15

See Nos. C49-C52, C57, C61.

Plane over Iguaçu Falls — AP10

Plane over the Andes — AP11

Perf. 13½x13

1946, June 10 Unwmk.

C45	AP10	15c dull red brn	22	15
C46	AP11	25c gray green	15	15
		Set value		15

See Nos. C53-C54.

Allegory of Flight — AP12

Astrolabe — AP13

Perf. 13½x13, 13x13½

1946, Sept. 25 Litho. Unwmk.

Surface-Tinted Paper

C47	AP12	15c sl grn, *pale grn*	55	15
C48	AP13	60c vio brn, *ocher*	55	35

Types of 1942

1946-48 Unwmk. *Perf. 13½x13*

C49	AP8	30c orange	1.40	15
C50	AP9	50c dull brn & buff	2.50	15
C51	AP8	1p carmine ('47)	1.25	15
C52	AP8	2.50p brt blue ('48)	5.50	75
		Nos. C49-C52 (4)	10.65	1.20

Types of 1946

1948 Wmk. 90

C53	AP10	15c dull red brn	15	15
C54	AP11	25c gray green	24	15
		Set value		15

Atlas (National Museum, Naples) — AP14

Map of Argentine Republic, Globe and Caliper AP15

Perf. 13½x13, 13x13½

1948-49 Photo. Wmk. 288

C55	AP14	45c dk brown ('49)	32	16
C56	AP15	70c dark green	50	22

4th Pan-American Reunion of Cartographers, Buenos Aires, Oct.-Nov., 1948.

Mercury Type of 1942

1949 Litho. *Perf. 13x13½*

C57	AP9	50c dull brn & buff	40	15

Marksmanship Trophy — AP16

1949, Nov. 4 Photo.

C58	AP16	75c brown	75	20

World Rifle Championship, 1949.

Catalogue values for unused stamps in this section, from this point to the end of the section, are for Never Hinged items.

Douglas DC-3 and Condor AP17

Perf. 13x13½

1951, June 20 **Wmk. 90**

C59 AP17 20c dk olive grn 16 15

10th anniversary of the State air lines.

Douglas DC-6 and Condor — AP18

1951, Oct. 17 *Perf. 13½*

C60 AP18 20c blue 16 15

End of Argentine 5-year Plan.

Plane-Letter Type of 1942

1951 **Litho.** *Perf. 13½x13*

C61 AP8 1p carmine 40 15

Jesus by Leonardo da Vinci (detail, "Virgin of the Rocks") — AP19

Perf. 13½x13

1956, Sept. 29 **Photo.** **Wmk. 90**

C62 AP19 1p dull purple 35 15

Issued to express the gratitude of the children of Argentina to the people of the world for their help against poliomyelitis.

Battle of Montevideo AP20

Leonardo Rosales and Tomas Espora — AP21

Guillermo Brown — AP22

AP23

1957, Mar. 2 *Perf. 13½*

C63 AP20 60c blue gray	15	15
C64 AP21 1p brt pink	15	15
C65 AP22 2p brown	22	15
Set value	45	22

Cent. of the death of Admiral Guillermo Brown, founder of the Argentine navy.

1957, Aug. 16

Map of Americas and Arms of Buenos Aires.

C66 AP23 2p rose violet 42 18

Issued to publicize the Inter-American Economic Conference in Buenos Aires.

AP24

AP25

1957, Aug. 31 **Wmk. 90** *Perf. 13½*

C67 AP24 60c Modern locomotive 15 15

Centenary of Argentine railroads.

1957, Sept. 14

C68 AP25 1p Globe, Flag,Compass Rose	18	15
C69 AP25 2p Key	28	15
Set value		15

1957 International Congress for Tourism.

Birds Carrying Letters — AP26

1957, Nov. 6

C70 AP26 1p bright blue 15 15

Issued for Letter Writing Week, Oct. 6-12.

Early Plane — AP27

1958, May 31 *Perf. 13½*

C71 AP27 2p maroon 16 15

50th anniversary of the Argentine Aviation Club.

Stamp Anniv. Type

Designs: 80c, Stamp of Buenos Aires and view of the Plaza de la Aduana. 1p, Stamp of 1858 and "The Post of Santa Fe."

1958 **Litho.** *Perf. 13½*

C72 A270 80c pale bis & sl bl	20	15
C73 A270 1p red org & dk bl	24	15

Centenary of the first postage stamps of Buenos Aires and the Argentine Confederation.
Issue dates: 80c, Oct. 18; 1p, Aug. 23.

Comet Jet over World Map AP29

1959, May 16 *Perf. 13½*

C74 AP29 5p black & olive 35 15

Inauguration of jet flights by Argentine Airlines.

Type of Regular Issue, 1960.

"Cabildo" and: 1.80p, Mariano Moreno. 5p, Manuel Belgrano and Juan Jose Castelli.

Perf. 13½

1960, May 28 **Wmk. 90** **Photo.**

C75 A287 1.80p red brown	15	15
a. Souvenir sheet of 3	65	38
C76 A287 5p buff & purple	32	15
a. Souvenir sheet of 3	1.25	80
Set value		16

Souvenir sheets are imperf. No. C75a contains one No. C75 and 1p and 2p resembling Nos. 713-714; stamps in reddish brown. No. C76a contains one No. C76 and 4.20p and 10.70p resembling Nos. 715-716; stamps are in green.

Symbolic of New Provinces — AP30

1960, July 8 **Litho.**

C77 AP30 1.80p dp car & blue 15 15

Elevation of the territories of Chubut, Formosa, Neuquen, Rio Negro and Santa Cruz to provinces.

Type of Regular Issue, 1960

1960, Oct. 1 **Photo.** *Perf. 13½*

C78 A291 1.80p rose lilac	15	15
C79 A291 10.70p brt grnsh blue	38	15

UNESCO Emblem AP31

1962, July 14 **Litho.**

C80 AP31 13p ocher & brown 38 24

15th anniv. of UNESCO.

Mail Coach — AP32

1962, Oct. 6 **Wmk. 90** *Perf. 13½*

C81 AP32 5.60p gray brn & blk 18 15

Mailman's Day, Sept. 14, 1962.

No. 695 and Type of 1959 Surcharged in Green

AEREO
5 60
PESOS

1962, Oct. 31 **Photo.**

C82 A277 5.60p on 5p brown	28	15
C83 A277 18p on 5p brn, *grnsh*	1.00	20

UPAE Emblem AP33

Skylark AP34

1962, Nov. 24 **Photo.** *Perf. 13½*

C84 AP33 5.60p dark blue 18 15

50th anniv. of the founding of the Postal Union of the Americas and Spain, UPAE.

1963, Feb. 9 **Litho.**

Design: 11p, Super Albatros.

C85 AP34 5.60p blue & black	18	15
C86 AP34 11p blue, blk & red	30	15

9th World Gliding Championships.

Symbolic Plane — AP35

1963-65 **Wmk. 90** *Perf. 13½*

C87 AP35 5.60p dk pur, car & brt grn	35	15
C88 AP35 7p black & bis ('64)	52	15
C88A AP35 7p black & bis ('65)	4.00	52
C89 AP35 11p blk, dk pur & grn	52	24
C90 AP35 18p dk pur, red & vio bl	1.00	35
C91 AP35 21p brown, red & gray	1.40	52
Nos. C87-C91 (6)	7.79	1.93

"Argentina" reads down on No. C88, up on No. C88A. See Nos. C101-C104, C108-C111, C123-C126, C135-C141. For overprint and surcharges see Nos. C96, C146-C150.

Type of Regular Issue, 1964

Design: 18p, Map of Falkland Islands (Islas Malvinas).

1964, Feb. 22 *Perf. 13½*

Size: 33x22mm

C92 A327 18p lt & dk bl & ol grn 1.75 70

UPU Monument, Bern, and UN Emblem — AP36

1964, May 23 **Engr.** *Perf. 13½*

C93 AP36 18p red & dk brown 52 25

15th UPU Cong., Vienna, Austria, May-June 1964.

Discovery of America, Florentine Woodcut — AP37

1964, Oct. 10 **Litho.**

C94 AP37 13p tan & black 35 30

Day of the Race, Columbus Day.

Lt. Matienzo Base, Antarctica AP38

1965, Feb. 27 **Photo.** *Perf. 13½*

C95 AP38 11p salmon pink 52 15

Issued to publicize the national territory of Tierra del Fuego, Antarctic and South Atlantic Isles.

No. C88A Overprinted in Silver: "PRIMERS / JORNADAS FILATELICAS / RIOPLATENSES"

1965, Mar. 17 **Litho.**
C96 AP35 7p black & bister 24 15

1st Rio de la Plata Stamp Show, sponsored jointly by the Argentine and Uruguayan Philatelic Associations, Montevideo, Mar. 19-28.

ITU Emblem — AP39

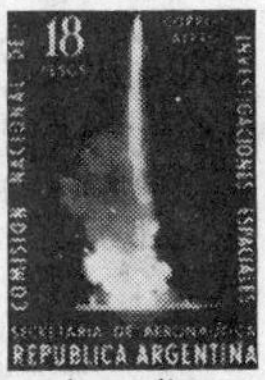

Ascending Rocket — AP40

1965, May 11 **Wmk. 90** ***Perf. 13½***
C97 AP39 18p slate, blk & red 42 22

Centenary of the ITU.

1965, May 29 **Photo.** ***Perf. 13½***

Design: 50p, Earth with trajectories and magnetic field, horiz.

C98 AP40 18p vermilion 42 20
C99 AP40 50p dp violet blue 1.00 50

6th Symposium on Space Research, held in Buenos Aires, and to honor the Natl. Commission of Space Research.

Type of 1963-65 Inscribed "Republica Argentina" Reading Down

1965, Oct. 13 **Litho.** **Wmk. 90**
C101 AP35 12p dk car rose & brn 1.40 20
C102 AP35 15p vio blue & dk red 85 26
C103 AP35 27.50p dk bl grn & gray 1.40 40
C104 AP35 30.50p dk brown & dk bl 2.00 60
Nos. C101-C104 (4) 5.65 1.46

Argentine Antarctica Map and Centaur Rocket — AP41

1966, Feb. 19 ***Perf. 13½***
C105 AP41 27.50p blue, blk & dp org 1.00 75

Launchings of sounding balloons and of a Gamma Centaur rocket in Antarctica during February, 1965.

Sea Gull and Southern Cross AP42

1966, May 14 ***Perf. 13½***
C106 AP42 12p Prus blue, blk & red 32 15

50th anniv. of the Naval Aviation School.

Blériot Plane Flown by Fels, 1917 — AP43

1967, Sept. 2 **Litho.** ***Perf. 13½***
C107 AP43 26p olive, bl & blk 26 15

Flight by Theodore Fels from Buenos Aires to Montevideo, Sept. 2, 1917, allegedly the 1st intl. airmail flight.

Type of 1963-65 Inscribed "Republica Argentina" Reading Down

1967, Dec. 20 ***Perf. 13½***
C108 AP35 26p brown 60 22
C109 AP35 40p violet 4.50 30
C110 AP35 68p blue green 3.00 45
C111 AP35 78p ultra 1.25 60
Nos. C108-C111 (4) 9.35 1.57

Vito Dumas and Ketch "Legh II" AP44

1968, July 27 **Litho.** **Wmk. 90**
C112 AP44 68p bl, blk, red & vio bl 65 40

Issued to commemorate Vito Dumas's one-man voyage around the world in 1943.

Type of Regular Issue and

Assembly Emblem AP45

Design: 40p, Globe and map of South America.

1968, Oct. 19 **Litho.** ***Perf. 13½***
C113 A395 40p brt pink, lt bl & blk 40 16
C114 AP45 68p bl, lt bl, gold & blk 65 30

4th Plenary Assembly of the Intl. Telegraph and Telephone Consultative Committee, Mar del Plata, Sept. 23-Oct. 25.

Radar Antenna, Balcarce Station — AP46

Perf. 13½
1969, Aug. 23 **Wmk. 90** **Photo.**
C115 AP46 40p blue gray 70 22

Communications by satellite through Intl. Telecommunications Consortium (INTELSAT).

Atucha Nuclear Center AP47

1969, Dec. 13 **Litho.** **Wmk. 365**
C116 AP47 26p blue & multi 1.40 80

Completion of Atucha Nuclear Center.

Type of 1963-65 Inscribed "Republica Argentina" Reading Down

1969-71 ***Perf. 13½***
C123 AP35 40p violet 5.00 32
C124 AP35 68p dk blue grn ('70) 2.00 60

Unwmk.
C125 AP35 26p yellow brn ('71) 32 20
C126 AP35 40p violet ('71) 2.75 40
Nos. C123-C126 (4) 10.07 1.52

Old Fire Engine and Fire Brigade Emblem AP48

1970, Aug. 8 **Litho.** **Unwmk.**
C128 AP48 40c green & multi 55 28

Centenary of the Fire Brigade.

Education Year Emblem — AP49

1970, Aug. 29 ***Perf. 13½***
C129 AP49 68c blue & blk 42 25

Issued for International Education Year.

Fleet Leaving Valparaiso, by Antonio Abel AP50

1970, Oct. 17 **Litho.** ***Perf. 13½***
C130 AP50 26c multicolored 1.00 35

150th anniv. of the departure for Peru of the liberation fleet from Valparaiso, Chile.

Sumampa Chapel AP51

1970, Nov. 7 **Photo.**
C131 AP51 40c multicolored 95 35

Bishopric of Tucuman, 400th anniversary.

Buenos Aires Planetarium AP52

1970, Nov. 28 **Litho.** ***Perf. 13½***
C132 AP52 40c multicolored 60 26

Jorge Newbery and Morane Saulnier Plane AP53

1970, Dec. 19
C133 AP53 26c bl, blk, yel & grn 38 25

24th Aeronautics and Space Week.

Industries Type of Regular Issue

Design: 31c, Refinery.

1971, Oct. 16 **Litho.** ***Perf. 13½***
C134 A445 31c red, blk & yel 60 24

Type of 1963-65 Inscribed "Republica Argentina" Reading Down

1971-74 **Unwmk.**
C135 AP35 45c brown 3.25 15
C136 AP35 68c red 48 15
C137 AP35 70c vio blue ('73) 80 15
C138 AP35 90c emerald ('73) 1.90 15
C139 AP35 1.70p blue ('74) 48 25
C140 AP35 1.95p emerald ('74) 48 30
C141 AP35 2.65p dp claret ('74) 48 40
Nos. C135-C141 (7) 7.87
Set value 1.30

Fluorescent paper was used for Nos. C135-C136, C138-C141. The 70c was issued on both papers.

Don Quixote, Drawing by Ignacio Zuloaga — AP54

1975, Apr. 26 **Photo.** ***Perf. 13½***
C145 AP54 2.75p yellow, blk & red 60 35

Day of the Race and for Espana 75 Intl. Philatelic Exhibition, Madrid, Apr. 4-13.

No. C87 Surcharged

100 PESOS

1975, Sept. 15 **Litho.** **Wmk. 90**
C146 AP35 9.20p on 5.60p 90 18
C147 AP35 19.70p on 5.60p 1.25 45
C148 AP35 100p on 5.60p 5.50 2.25
Nos. C146-C148 (3) 7.65 2.88

No. C87 Surcharged

REVALORIZADO
920 PESOS

1975, Oct. 15
C149 AP35 9.20p on 5.60p 70 30
C150 AP35 19.70p on 5.60p 1.25 60

Argentine State Airline, 50th Anniv. AP55

1990, Sept. 15 Litho. *Perf. 13½*

C151	AP55 2500a Junkers JU52-3M	1.25	
C152	AP55 2500a Grumman SA-16	1.25	
C153	AP55 2500a Fokker F-27	1.25	
C154	AP55 2500a Fokker F-28	1.25	
	Nos. C151-C154 (4)	5.00	

AIR POST SEMI-POSTAL STAMPS

Catalogue values for unused stamps in this section are for Never Hinged items.

Philatelic Exhibition Type

Designs: 45c+45c, Stamp engraving. 70c+70c, Proofing stamp die. 1p+1p, Sheet of stamps. 2.50p+2.50p, The letter. 5p+5p, Gen. San Martin.

Perf. 13½

1950, Aug. 26 Wmk. 90 Photo.

CB1	SP8 45c + 45c violet bl	38	24
CB2	SP8 70c + 70c dark brown	55	38
a.	Souv. sheet of 3, #B12, CB1, CB2, imperf.	3.00	3.00
CB3	SP8 1p + 1p cerise	1.50	1.50
CB4	SP8 2.50p + 2.50p ol gray	8.50	6.00
CB5	SP8 5p + 5p dull green	9.25	7.25
	Nos. CB1-CB5 (5)	20.18	15.37

Argentine Intl. Philatelic Exhib., 1950.

Pieta by Michelangelo SPAP2

1951, Dec. 22 *Perf. 13½x13*

CB6	SPAP2 2.45p +7.55p grnsh blk	21.00	14.00

Surtax as for the Eva Peron Foundation.

Flower and Child's Head — SPAP3

Stamp of 1858 — SPAP4

1958, Mar. 15 *Perf. 13½*

CB7	SPAP3 1p +50c deep claret	28	28

Surtax for National Council for Children.

1958, Mar. 29 Litho. Wmk. 90

CB8	SPAP4 1p + 50c gray ol & bl	40	32
CB9	SPAP4 2p + 1p rose lilac & vio	52	42
CB10	SPAP4 3p + 1.50p green & brown	60	52
CB11	SPAP4 5p + 2.50p gray ol & car rose	1.00	85
CB12	SPAP4 10p + 5p gray ol & brn	2.00	1.65
	Nos. CB8-CB12 (5)	4.52	3.76

The surtax was for the Intl. Centennial Philatelic Exhibition, Buenos Aires, Apr. 19-27.

Type of Semi-Postal Issue, 1958

Designs: 1p+50c, Flooded area. 5p+2.50p, House and truck under water.

1958, Oct. 4 Photo. *Perf. 13½*

CB13	SP11 1p + 50c dull purple	25	20
CB14	SP11 5p + 2.50p grnsh blue	80	75

The surtax was for victims of a flood in the Buenos Aires district.

Type of Semi-Postal Issue, 1959

1959, Sept. 5 Litho. *Perf. 13½*

CB15	SP13 2p + 1p Rowing	40	26
CB16	SP13 3p + 1.50p Woman diver	60	48

Type of Semi-Postal Issue, 1960

Birds: 2p+1p, Rufous tinamou. 3p+1.50p, Rhea.

1960, Feb. 6 *Perf. 13½*

CB17	SP14 2p + 1p rose car & sal	30	20
CB18	SP14 3p + 1.50p slate green	45	35

The surtax was for child welfare work.
See No. CB29.

Buenos Aires Market Place, 1810 — SPAP5

Seibo, National Flower — SPAP6

Designs: 6p+3p, Oxcart water carrier. 10.70p+5.30p, Settlers landing. 20p+10p, The Fort.

1960, Aug. 20 Photo. Wmk. 90

CB19	SPAP5 2 + 1p rose brown	16	15
CB20	SPAP5 6 + 3p gray	35	24
CB21	SPAP5 10.70 + 5.30p blue	60	35
CB22	SPAP5 20 + 10p bluish grn	1.00	85
	Nos. CB19-CB22 (4)	2.11	1.59

Inter-American Philatelic Exhibition EFIMAYO 1960, Buenos Aires, Oct. 12-24, held to for the sesquicentennial of the May Revolution of 1910.
For overprints see Nos. CB25-CB28.

1960, Sept. 10 *Perf. 13½*

Design: 10.70p+5.30p, Copihue, Chile's national flower.

CB23	SPAP6 6 + 3p lilac rose	35	28
CB24	SPAP6 10.70 + 5.30p vermilion	52	42

The surtax was for earthquake victims in Chile.

Nos. CB19-CB22 Overprinted: "DIA DE LAS NACIONES UNIDAS 24 DE OCTUBRE"

1960, Oct. 8

CB25	SPAP5 2 + 1p rose brown	20	15
CB26	SPAP5 6 + 3p gray	32	28
CB27	SPAP5 10.70 + 5.30p blue	48	42
CB28	SPAP5 20 + 10p bluish green	85	75
	Nos. CB25-CB28 (4)	1.85	1.60

United Nations Day, Oct. 24, 1960.

Type of Semi-Postal Issue, 1960

Design: Emperor penguins.

1961, Feb. 25 Photo. Wmk. 90

CB29	SP14 1.80p + 90c gray	32	20

The surtax was for child welfare work.

Stamp of 1862 — SPAP7

Crutch, Olympic Torch and Rings — SPAP8

1962, May 19 Litho.

CB30	SPAP7 6.50p + 6.50p Prus bl & grnsh bl	70	65

Opening of the "Argentina 62" Philatelic Exhibition, Buenos Aires, May 19-29.

Type of Semi-Postal Issue, 1963

1963, May 18 Wmk. 90 *Perf. 13½*

CB31	SP21 11p + 5p Bicycling	55	50

Type of Semi-Postal Issue, 1962

1963, Dec. 21 *Perf. 13½*

CB32	SP20 11p + 5p Great kiskadee	70	60

The surtax was for child welfare.

Type of Semi-Postal Issue, 1964

1964, July 18 Litho.

CB33	SP22 11p + 5p Sailboat	50	50

1964, Sept. 19 Litho. *Perf. 13½*

CB34	SPAP8 18p + 9p bluish grn, blk, red & yel	60	60

13th "Olympic" games for the handicapped, Tokyo, 1964.

Bird Type of Semi-Postal Issue, 1962

1964, Dec. 23 Litho. Wmk. 90

CB35	SP20 18p + 9p Chilean swallow	90	75

The surtax was for child welfare.

Bird Type of Semi-Postal Issue, 1962, Inscribed "R. ARGENTINA"

Design: Rufous ovenbird.

1966, Mar. 26 *Perf. 13½*

CB36	SP20 27.50p + 12.50p bl, ocher, yel & grn	80	70

The surtax was for child welfare.

Coat of Arms — SPAP9

1966, June 25 Litho. *Perf. 13½*

CB37	SPAP9 10p + 10p yellow & multi	1.75	1.40

ARGENTINA '66 Philatelic Exhibition held in connection with the sesquicentennial celebration of the Declaration of Independence, Buenos Aires, July 16-23. The surtax was for the Exhibition. Issued in sheets of 4.

Bird Type of Semi-Postal Issue, 1962, Inscribed "R. ARGENTINA"

Designs: 15p+7p, Blue and yellow tanager. 26p+13p, Toco toucan.

1967 Litho. Wmk. 90

CB38	SP20 15p + 7p blk, bl, grn & yel	1.00	90
CB39	SP20 26p + 13p blk, org, yel & bl	50	40

The surtax was for child welfare.
Issue dates: 15p+7p, Jan. 14. 26p+13p, Dec. 23.

Bird Type of Semi-Postal Issue, 1969

Design: 26p+13p, Lineated woodpecker.

1969, Sept. 20 Wmk. 365 *Perf. 13½*

CB40	SP24 26p + 13p multi	48	40

The surtax was for child welfare.

Bird Type of Semi-Postal Issue, 1970

Design: 40c+20c, Chilean flamingo.

1970, May 9 Litho. Wmk. 365

CB41	SP25 40c + 20c multi	45	40

The surtax was for child welfare.

Fish Type of Semi-Postal Issue, 1971

Design: Pejerrey (atherinidae family).

1971, Feb. 20 Unwmk. *Perf. 12½*
Size: 75x15mm

CB42	SP26 40c + 20c lt blue & multi	40	40

The surtax was for child welfare.

OFFICIAL STAMPS

Regular Issues Overprinted in Black

OFICIAL

1884-87 Unwmk. *Perf. 12, 14*

O1	A29 ½c brown	7.00	5.00
O2	A23 1c red	4.50	3.25
b.	Perf. 12	37.50	27.50
O3	A29 1c red	40	26
b.	Double overprint	20.00	20.00
O4	A20 2c green	40	26
b.	Double overprint	20.00	20.00
O5	A11 4c brown	38	26
O6	A7 8c lake	38	26
O7	A8 10c green	37.50	19.00
O8	A23 12c ultra (#45)	3.50	2.50
a.	Perf. 14	37.50	37.50
O9	A29 12c grnsh bl	60	50
O10	A19 24c blue	1.00	60
O11	A21 25c lake	8.50	5.50
O12	A12 30c orange	15.00	10.00
O13	A13 60c black	10.00	6.50
O14	A14 90c blue	7.50	5.50
b.	Double overprint	30.00	
	Nos. O1-O14 (14)	96.66	59.39

Inverted Overprint

O1a	A29 ½c	10.00	10.00
O2a	A23 1c perf. 14	32.50	25.00
c.	perf. 12	24.00	24.00
O3a	A29 1c	85	55
O4a	A20 2c	37.50	18.00
O5a	A11 4c	27.50	18.00
O6a	A7 8c	37.50	37.50
O9a	A29 12c	72.50	67.50
O10a	A19 24c	2.75	1.65
O13a	A13 60c	37.50	24.00
O14a	A14 90c	30.00	24.00

1884 *Rouletted*

O15	A17 16c green	1.75	65
a.	Double overprint	10.00	10.00
b.	Inverted overprint	72.50	
O16	A18 20c blue	7.00	5.00
a.	Inverted overprint	37.50	25.00
O17	A19 24c blue	1.25	75
a.	Inverted overprint	3.00	2.25
b.	Double ovpt., one inverted	18.00	
	Nos. O15-O17 (3)	10.00	6.40

Overprinted Diagonally in Red

1885 *Perf. 12*

O18	A20 2c green	1.75	1.00
a.	Inverted overprint	30.00	18.00
O19	A11 4c brown	1.75	85
a.	Inverted overprint	30.00	18.00
b.	Double overprint	30.00	30.00
O20	A13 60c black	17.00	10.00
O21	A14 90c blue	185.00	125.00

1885 *Rouletted*

O22	A19 24c blue	13.00	7.50

On all of these stamps, the overprint is found reading both upwards and downwards.
Counterfeits exist of No. O21 overprint and others.

Regular Issues Handstamped Horizontally in Black

OFICIAL

1884 *Perf. 12, 14*

O23	A23 1c red	47.50	17.00
a.	Perf. 12	150.00	85.00
O24	A20 2c green, diagonal overprint	24.00	14.00
a.	Horizontal overprint	150.00	125.00
O25	A11 4c brown	10.00	7.50
O26	A7 8c lake	10.00	7.50
O27	A23 12c ultra	27.50	17.00

Overprinted Diagonally

O28	A19 24c bl, rouletted	20.00	14.00
O29	A13 60c black	14.00	6.75

Counterfeit overprints exist.

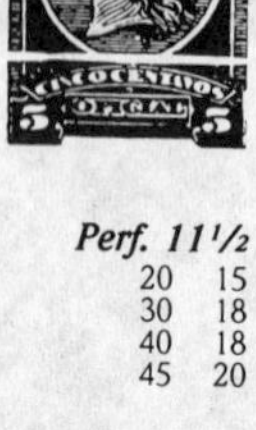

Liberty Head — O1

1901, Dec. 1 Engr. *Perf. 11½*

O31	O1 1c gray	20	15
O32	O1 2c org brn	30	18
O33	O1 5c red	40	18
O34	O1 10c dk grn	45	20

O35	O1	30c dk bl	3.00	75
O36	O1	50c orange	1.65	52
		Nos. O31-O36 (6)	6.00	1.98

Regular Stamps of 1935-51 Overprinted in Black

SERVICIO OFICIAL
c

Perf. 13x13½, 13½x13, 13

1938-54 Wmk. RA in Sun (90)

O37	A129	1c buff ('40)	15	15
O38	A130	2c dk brn ('40)	15	15
O39	A132	3c grn ('39)	15	15
O40	A132	3c lt gray ('39)	15	15
O41	A134	5c yel brn	15	15
O42	A195	5c car ('53)	15	15
O43	A137	10c carmine	15	15
O44	A137	10c brn ('39)	15	15
O45	A140	15c lt gray bl, type II ('47)	15	15
O46	A139	15c slate blue	50	15
O47	A139	15c pale ultra ('39)	15	15
O48	A139	20c blue ('53)	28	15
O49	A141	25c carmine	15	15
a.		Overprint 11mm	18	15
O49B	A143	40c dk vio	90	15
O50	A144	50c red & org	15	15
a.		Overprint 11mm	24	15
O51	A146	1p brn blk & lt bl ('40)	18	15
a.		Overprint 11mm		
O52	A224	1p choc & lt bl ('51)	18	15
a.		Overprint 11mm	18	15
O53	A147	2p brn lake & dk ultra (ovpt. 11mm) ('54)	70	15
		Nos. O37-O53 (18)	4.54	
		Set value		1.05

Overprinted in Black on Stamps and Types of 1945-47

Perf. 13x13½, 13½x13

1945-46 Unwmk.

O54	A130	2c sepia	1.50	40
O55	A134	3c lt gray	1.25	30
O56	A134	5c yel brn	35	15
O57	A195	5c dp car	15	15
O58	A137	10c brown	15	15
a.		Double overprint		
O59	A140	15c lt gray bl, type II	15	15
O61	A141	25c dl rose	16	15
O62	A144	50c red & org	28	15
O63	A146	1p brn blk & lt bl	15	15
O64	A147	2p brn lake & bl	20	15
O65	A148	5p ind & ol grn	15	15
O66	A149	10p dp cl & int blk	24	15
O67	A150	20p bl grn & brn	48	30
		Nos. O54-O67 (13)	5.21	
		Set value		1.50

Overprinted in Black on Stamps and Types of 1942-50

Perf. 13, 13x13½

1944-51 Wmk. 288

O73	A134	3c lt gray	1.10	50
O74	A134	5c yel brn	25	15
O75	A137	10c red brn	15	15
O76	A140	15c lt gray bl, type II	25	15
O77	A144	50c red & org (overprint 11 mm)	1.50	50
O78	A146	1p brn blk & lt bl (overprint 11mm)	1.75	35
		Nos. O73-O78 (6)	5.00	
		Set value		1.50

Catalogue values for unused stamps in this section, from this point to the end of the section, are for Never Hinged items.

Nos. 600-606 Overprinted in Black

SERVICIO OFICIAL
d

1953 Wmk. 90 *Perf. 13*

O79	A228	5c gray	15	15
O80	A228	10c rose lil	15	15
O81	A228	20c rose pink	15	15
O82	A228	25c dl grn	15	15
O83	A228	40c dl vio	15	15
O84	A228	45c dp bl	18	15
O85	A228	50c dl brn	15	15

SERVICIO OFICIAL
e

SERVICIO OFICIAL
f

Nos. 611-617 Overprinted Type "e" in Blue

Perf. 13x13½, 13½x13

O86	A229	1p dk brn	15	15
O87	A229	1.50p dp grn	28	15
O88	A229	2p brt car	18	15
O89	A229	3p indigo	55	25

Size: 30x40mm

O90	A229	5p red brn	55	45
O91	A228	10p red	2.75	1.75
O92	A229	20p green	30.00	20.00
		Nos. O79-O92 (14)	35.54	23.95

No. 612 Overprinted Type "f" in Blue

O93	A229	1.50p dp grn	1.00	30

Regular Issues of 1954-59 Variously Overprinted in Black or Blue

S. OFICIAL
g

SERVICIO OFICIAL
h

Perf. 13½, 13x13½, 13½x13

1955-61 Litho. Wmk. 90

O94	A237(c)	20c red (#629)	15	15
O95	A237(d)	20c red (#629)	15	15
O96	A237(d)	40c red, ovpt. 15mm (#630)	15	15

Engr.

O97	A239(g)	50c bl (#632)	15	15

Photo.

O98	A239(h)	1p brn (#635)	15	15
O99	A239(e)	1p brn (Bl, #635)	15	15
O100	A239(e)	1p brn (Bk, #635)	15	15

Engr.

O101	A239(h)	3p vio brn (#638)	15	15
O102	A240(h)	5p gray grn (#639)	28	15
O103	A240(e)	10p yel grn (#640)	42	15
O104	A240(f)	20p dl vio (#641)	75	30
O105	A240(h)	20p dl vio (#641)	75	25
O106	A241(e)	50p ultra & ind (#642)	1.10	20
		Nos. O94-O106 (13)	4.50	
		Set value		1.30

The overprints on Nos. O99-O100 and O103-O104 are horizontal; that on No. O109 is vertical. On No. O106 overprint measures 23mm.

Issue dates: Nos. O102, 1957. Nos. O97, O101, O103, O105, 1958. Nos. O98-O99, O104, 1959. No. O100, 1960. No. O106, 1961.

No. 659 Overprinted Type "d"

1957 Wmk. 90 Litho. *Perf. 13*

O108	A133	20c dl pur (ovpt. 15mm)	15	15

Nos. 666, 658 and 663 Variously Overprinted

1957 Photo. *Perf. 13x13½, 13½*

O109	A261(g)	2p claret	22	15
O110	A254(e)	2.40p brown	22	15
O111	A258(c)	4.40p grnsh gray	26	15
		Nos. O109-O111 (3)	70	
		Set value		18

Nos. 668, 685-687, 690-691, 693-705, 742, 742C and Types of 1959-65 Overprinted in black, Blue or Red Types "e," "g," or

S. OFICIAL
i

S. OFICIAL
j

S. OFICIAL
k

S. OFICIAL
m

S. OFICIAL
n

Lithographed; Photogravure

1960-68 *Perf. 13x13½, 13½*

O112	A128(g)	5c buff (vert. ovpt.)	15	15
O113	A275(j)	10c sl grn	15	15
O114	A275(j)	20c dl red brn	15	15
O115	A275(i)	50c bister	15	15
O116	A278(k)	1p brn	15	15
O117	A278(j)	1p brn, photo. (vert. ovpt.)	18	15
O117A	A278(j)	1p brn, litho., (down)	18	15
O118	A276(j)	2p rose red	15	15
O119	A312(m)	2p dp grn (down)	22	15
O120	A312(j)	2p brt grn (up)	15	15
O121	A312(j)	2p grn litho. (down)	22	15
O122	A277(e)	3p dk bl (horiz.)	18	15
O123	A277(j)	3p dk bl	18	15
O124	A276(j)	4p red, litho.	18	15
O125	A312(j)	4p rose red, litho. (down)	18	15
O126	A277(e)	5p brn (Bl) (horiz.)	22	15
O127	A277(e)	5p brn (Bk) (horiz.)	22	15
O128	A277(j)	5p sep	15	15
O129	A277(e)	5p sep (horiz. ovpt.)	15	15
O130	A276(j)	8p red	18	15
O131	A278(i)	10p lt red brn	45	15
O132	A276(j)	10p ver	18	15
O133	A278(j)	10p brn car (up)	18	15
O134	A278(m)	12p dk brn vio	35	15
O135	A278(k)	20p Prus grn	52	15
O136	A278(j)	20p Prus grn (up)	40	15
O137	A276(j)	20p red, litho.	35	15
O138	A276(m)	20p red, litho.	22	15
O139	A278(j)	23p grn (vert. ovpt.)	52	15
O140	A278(j)	25p dp vio, photo. (R) (up)	52	15
O141	A278(j)	25p pur, litho. (R) (down)	52	15
O142	A241(n)	50p dk bl	1.10	15
O143	A279(m)	100p bl (horiz. ovpt.)	1.10	35
O144	A279(m)	100p bl (up)	1.10	35
O145	A280(m)	300p dp vio	2.25	60
		Nos. O112-O145 (35)	13.25	
		Set value		3.20

The "m" overprint measures 15½mm on 2p; 14½mm on 12p, 100p and 300p; 13mm on 20p.

Issue dates: Nos. O122, O127, O135, 1961. Nos. O122-O114, O116, O118, 1962. No. O124, 1963. Nos. O119, O134, O143, 1964. Nos. O117, O125, O130, O139, O144, 1965. Nos. O120, O128, O132-O133, O136, O140, O142, O145, 1966. Nos. O121, O129, O137-O138, O141, 1967. No. O117A, 1968.

Nos. 699, 823-825, 827-829, and Type of 1962 Overprinted in Black or Red Types "j," "m," or "o"

SERVICIO OFICIAL
o

Inscribed: "Republica Argentina"

Litho., Photo., Engr.

1964-67 Wmk. 90 *Perf. 13½*

O149	A312(j)	6p rose red (down)	26	15
O153	A238a(m)	22p ultra	52	15
O154	A238a(j)	43p dk car rose (down)	75	15
O155	A238a(j)	45p brn, photo. (up)	75	15
O156	A238a(j)	45p brn, litho. (up)	1.10	20
O157	A241(j)	50p dk bl (up) (R)	2.25	15
O158	A366(j)	90p ol bis (up)	2.75	20
O162	A495(o)	500p yel grn	3.50	80
		Nos. O149-O162 (8)	11.88	
		Set value		1.50

Issued: No. O153, 1964; No. O155, 1966; Nos. O149, O156-O162, 1967.

Type of 1959-67 Ovptd. Type "j"

1969 Litho. Wmk. 365 *Perf. 13½*

O163	A276	20p vermilion	22	15

OFFICIAL DEPARTMENT STAMPS

Regular Issues of 1911-37 Overprinted in Black

M. A.
Type I

M. A.
Type II

Ministry of Agriculture (M. A.)

Type I

1913-37

On Stamp of 1911

OD1	A88	2c #181	15	15

On Stamps of 1912-14

OD2	A88	1c #190	15	15
OD3	A88	2c #191	15	15
OD4	A88	5c #194	30	15
OD5	A88	12c #196	15	15
		Set value	65	25

On Stamps of 1915-16

OD6	A88	1c #208	15	15
OD7	A88	2c #209	15	15
OD8	A88	5c #212	15	15
OD9	A91	5c #220	15	15
		Set value	45	32

On Stamp of 1917

OD10	A94	12c #238	30	15

On Stamps of 1918-19

OD11	A93	1c #249	15	15
OD12	A93	2c #250	15	15
OD13	A93	5c #253	15	15
OD14	A94	12c #255	15	15
OD15	A94	20c #256	15	15
		Set value	55	35

On Stamps of 1920

OD16	A93	1c #265	30	25
OD17	A93	2c #266	50	25
OD18	A93	5c #269	20	15
		Nos. OD16-OD18 (3)	1.00	
		Set value		55

On Stamps of 1922-23

OD19	A94	12c #311	1.00	40
OD20	A94	20c #312	25.00	

On Stamps of 1923

OD21	A104	1c #324	15	15
OD22	A104	2c #325	25	15
OD23	A104	5c #328	15	15
OD24	A104	12c #330	15	15
OD25	A104	20c #331	15	15
		Set value	45	30

On Stamps of 1923-31

OD26	A104	1c #341	15	15
OD27	A104	2c #342, I	15	15
a.		Type II	1.50	75
OD28	A104	3c #343	15	15
OD29	A104	5c #345, II	15	15
a.		Type I	15	15
OD30	A104	10c #346, II	15	15
a.		Type I	15	15
OD31	A104	12c #347	15	15
OD32	A104	20c #348, I	15	15
a.		Type II	15	15
OD33	A104	30c #351	15	15
		Set value	70	40

On Stamp of 1926

OD34	A110	12c #360	15	15

Type II

On Stamps of 1935-37

OD35	A129	1c #419	15	15
OD36	A130	2c #420	15	15
OD37	A132	3c #422	15	15
OD38	A134	5c #427	15	15
OD39	A137	10c #430	15	15
OD40	A139	15c #434	50	15
OD41	A140	20c #437	30	15
OD42	A140	20c #438	20	15
OD43	A141	25c #441	25	15
OD44	A142	30c #442	15	15
OD45	A145	1p #445	2.50	1.50
OD46	A146	1p #446	50	25
		Nos. OD35-OD46 (12)	5.15	
		Set value		2.00

Ministry of War (M. G.)

Type I

On Stamp of 1911

OD47	A88	2c #181	15	15

On Stamps of 1912-14

OD48	A88	1c #190	15	15
OD49	A88	2c #191	75	15
OD50	A88	5c #194	15	15
OD51	A88	12c #196	15	15
		Set value	1.05	20

On Stamps of 1915-16

OD52	A88	1c #208	6.00	75
OD53	A88	2c #209	60	15
OD54	A88	5c #212	75	15
OD55	A91	5c #220	1.00	25
OD56	A92	12c #222	1.00	35
		Nos. OD52-OD56 (5)	9.35	1.65

On Stamps of 1917

OD57	A93	1c #232	30	15
OD58	A93	2c #233	40	15
OD59	A93	5c #236	30	15
OD60	A94	12c #238	60	15
		Nos. OD57-OD60 (4)	1.60	
		Set value		20

On Stamps of 1918-19

OD61	A93	1c #249	15	15
OD62	A93	2c #250	15	15
OD63	A93	5c #253	15	15
OD64	A94	12c #255	40	15
OD65	A94	20c #256	1.25	15
		Nos. OD61-OD65 (5)	2.10	
		Set value		25

On Stamps of 1920

OD66	A93	2c #266	40	15
OD67	A93	5c #269	40	15
OD68	A94	12c #271	35	15
		Nos. OD66-OD68 (3)	1.15	
		Set value		15

On Stamp of 1920

OD69	A94	12c #299	2.00	25

On Stamps of 1922-23

OD70	A93	1c #305	75	15
OD71	A93	2c #306	1.50	45
OD72	A103	5c #309	75	15
OD73	A94	20c #312	30	15
		Nos. OD70-OD73 (4)	3.30	
		Set value		70

On Stamp of 1922-23

OD74	A93	2c #318	5.00	50

On Stamps of 1923

OD75	A104	1c #324	15	15
OD76	A104	2c #325	15	15
OD77	A104	5c #328	15	15
OD78	A104	12c #330	15	15
OD79	A104	20c #331	1.00	15
		Nos. OD75-OD79 (5)	1.60	
		Set value		25

On Stamps of 1923-31

OD80	A104	1c #341	1.25	45
OD81	A104	2c #342	20	15
OD82	A104	3c #343, I	15	15
a.	Type II		40	15
OD83	A104	5c #345, I	15	15
a.	Type II		20	15
OD84	A104	10c #346, II	15	15
a.	Type I		60	15
OD85	A104	20c #348, I	15	15
a.	Type II		40	15
OD86	A104	30c #351, II	20	15
a.	Type I		1.00	15
OD87	A105	1p #353	2.00	30
		Nos. OD80-OD87 (8)	4.25	
		Set value		75

On Stamp of 1926

OD88	A109	5c #359	60	15

Type II

On Stamps of 1935-37

OD89	A129	1c #419	15	15
OD90	A130	2c #420	15	15
OD91	A132	3c #422	15	15
OD92	A134	5c #427	15	15
OD93	A137	10c #430	15	15
OD94	A139	15c #434	25	15
OD95	A140	20c #437	1.00	15
OD96	A140	20c #438	25	15
OD97	A141	25c #441	15	15
OD98	A142	30c #442	15	15
OD99	A144	50c #444	25	15
OD100	A145	1p #445	1.25	50
OD101	A146	1p #446	50	25
		Set value	4.00	1.30

Ministry of Finance (M. H.)

Type I

On Stamp of 1911

OD102	A88	2c #181	15	15

On Stamps of 1912-14

OD103	A88	1c #190	15	15
OD104	A88	2c #191	15	15
OD105	A88	5c #194	20	15
OD106	A88	12c #196	15	15
		Set value	40	20

On Stamps of 1915-16

OD107	A88	2c #209	15	15
OD108	A88	5c #212	15	15
OD109	A91	5c #220	15	15
		Set value	30	16

On Stamps of 1917

OD110	A93	2c #233	15	15
OD111	A93	5c #236	1.25	15
OD112	A94	12c #238	15	15
		Nos. OD110-OD112 (3)	1.55	
		Set value		25

On Stamps of 1918-19

OD113	A93	2c #250		25.00
OD114	A93	5c #253	20	15
OD115	A94	12c #255	45	15
OD116	A94	20c #256	45	15

On Stamps of 1920

OD117	A93	1c #265	75	45
OD118	A93	2c #266	1.25	45
OD119	A93	5c #269	30	15
OD120	A94	12c #271	60	20
		Nos. OD117-OD120 (4)	2.90	1.25

On Stamp of 1922-23

OD121	A94	20c #312	12.50	2.50

On Stamps of 1923

OD122	A104	1c #324	75	40
OD123	A104	2c #325	15	15
OD124	A104	5c #328	15	15
OD125	A104	12c #330	15	15
OD126	A104	20c #331	15	15
		Set value	90	60

On Stamps of 1923-31

OD127	A104	3c #343	7.00	1.50
OD128	A104	5c #345	15	15
OD129	A104	10c #346	15	15
OD130	A104	12c #347	7.00	3.75
OD131	A104	20c #348, I	15	15
a.	Type II		35	15
OD132	A104	30c #351	25	15
OD133	A105	1p #353	40	15
		Nos. OD127-OD133 (7)	15.10	6.00

On Stamp of 1926

OD134	A110	12c #360	12.50	12.50

Type II

On Stamps of 1935-37

OD135	A129	1c #419	15	15
OD136	A130	2c #420	15	15
OD137	A132	3c #422	15	15
OD138	A134	5c #427	15	15
OD139	A137	10c #430	15	15
OD140	A139	15c #434	45	15
OD141	A140	20c #437	15	15
OD142	A140	20c #438	15	15
OD143	A142	30c #442	15	15
OD144	A145	1p #445	2.00	1.00
OD145	A146	1p #446	50	25
		Set value	3.50	1.70

Ministry of the Interior (M. I.)

Type I

On Stamp of 1911

OD146	A88	2c #181	25	15

On Stamps of 1912-14

OD147	A88	1c #190	15	15
OD148	A88	2c #191	15	15
OD149	A88	5c #194	15	15
OD150	A88	12c #196	15	15
		Set value	40	30

On Stamps of 1915-17

OD151	A88	2c #209	80	30
OD152	A88	5c #212	75	15
OD153	A91	5c #220	60	15
OD154	A93	5c #236	1.50	15
		Nos. OD151-OD154 (4)	3.65	
		Set value		65

On Stamps of 1918-19

OD155	A93	2c #250	15	15
OD156	A93	5c #253	15	15
		Set value	20	15

On Stamps of 1920

OD157	A93	1c #265	3.75	1.25
OD158	A93	5c #269	75	35

On Stamps of 1922-23

OD159	A93	2c #306	12.50	12.50
OD160	A103	5c #309	3.50	1.25
OD161	A94	12c #311	1.25	40
OD162	A94	20c #312	1.25	40
		Nos. OD159-OD162 (4)	18.50	14.55

On Stamps of 1923

OD163	A104	1c #324	15	15
OD164	A104	2c #325	15	15
OD165	A104	5c #328	15	15
OD166	A104	12c #330	2.00	2.00
OD167	A104	20c #331	75	15
		Nos. OD163-OD167 (5)	3.20	
		Set value		2.10

On Stamps of 1923-31

OD168	A104	1c #341	15	15
OD169	A104	2c #342	15	15
OD170	A104	3c #343, II	15	15
a.	Type I		1.25	30
OD171	A104	5c #345, I	15	15
a.	Type II		15	15
OD172	A104	10c #346, II	15	15
OD173	A104	12c #347	30	15
OD174	A104	20c #348, II	15	15
a.	Type I		75	15
OD175	A104	30c #351	15	15
		Set value	60	45

Type II

On Stamps of 1935-37

OD176	A129	1c #419	15	15
OD177	A130	2c #420	15	15
OD178	A132	3c #422	15	15
OD178A	A134	5c #427	15	15
OD179	A137	10c #430	15	15
OD180	A139	15c #434	30	15
OD181	A140	20c #437	75	15
OD182	A140	20c #438	20	15
OD182A	A142	30c #442	15	15
OD182B	A145	1p #445	2.00	1.00
OD182C	A146	1p #446	50	25
		Set value	4.00	1.65

Ministry of Justice and Instruction (M. J. I.)

Type I

On Stamp of 1911

OD183	A88	2c #181	1.25	15

On Stamps of 1912-14

OD184	A88	1c #190	1.50	15
OD185	A88	2c #191	1.00	15
OD186	A88	5c #194	45	15
OD187	A88	12c #196	45	15
		Nos. OD184-OD187 (4)	3.40	
		Set value		30

On Stamps of 1915-17

OD188	A88	1c #208	30	15
OD189	A88	2c #209	30	15
OD190	A88	5c #212	1.00	15
OD191	A91	5c #220	25	15
OD192	A92	12c #222	75	15
		Nos. OD188-OD192 (5)	2.60	
		Set value		45

On Stamps of 1917

OD193	A93	1c #232	25	15
OD194	A93	2c #233	75	15
OD195	A93	5c #236	25	15
OD196	A94	12c #238	17.50	5.00
		Nos. OD193-OD196 (4)	18.75	5.45

On Stamps of 1918-19

OD197	A93	1c #249	15	15
OD198	A93	2c #250	15	15
OD199	A93	5c #253	15	15
OD200	A94	12c #255	20	15
OD201	A94	20c #256	50	15
		Set value	1.00	35

On Stamps of 1920

OD202	A93	1c #265	25	15
OD203	A93	2c #266	20	15
OD204	A93	5c #269	20	15
OD205	A94	12c #271	40	15
		Nos. OD202-OD205 (4)	1.05	
		Set value		30

On Stamps of 1922-23

OD206	A93	1c #305	25	15
OD207	A93	2c #306	1.50	50
OD208	A103	5c #309	25	15
OD209	A94	12c #311	10.00	1.75
OD210	A94	20c #312	1.50	30
		Nos. OD206-OD210 (5)	13.50	2.85

On Stamp of 1922-23

OD211	A93	2c #318	2.50	2.50

On Stamps of 1923

OD212	A104	1c #324	15	15
OD213	A104	2c #325	15	15
OD214	A104	5c #328	15	15
OD215	A104	12c #330	15	15
OD216	A104	20c #331	50	15
		Set value	1.00	30

On Stamps of 1923-31

OD217	A104	½c #340	2.00	75
OD218	A104	1c #341, I	15	15
a.	Type II		15	15
OD219	A104	2c #342	15	15
OD220	A104	3c #343, I	15	15
a.	Type II		15	15
OD221	A104	5c #345, I	15	15
a.	Type II		15	15
OD222	A104	10c #346, II	15	15
a.	Type I		30	15
OD223	A104	12c #347, I	15	15
a.	Type II		30	15
OD224	A104	20c #348, I	15	15
a.	Type II		15	15
OD225	A104	30c #351	15	15
OD226	A105	1p #353	40	50
		Set value	2.10	1.30

On Stamps of 1926

OD227	A109	5c #359	15	15
OD228	A110	12c #360	20	15
		Set value	30	15

Type II

On Stamps of 1935-37

OD229	A129	1c #419	15	15
OD230	A130	2c #420	15	15
OD231	A132	3c #422	15	15
OD232	A134	5c #427	15	15
OD233	A137	10c #430	15	15
OD234	A139	15c #434	45	15
OD234A	A140	20c #437	15	15
OD234B	A140	20c #438	20	15
OD234C	A141	25c #441	15	15
OD234D	A142	30c #442	15	15
OD234E	A145	1p #445	1.00	60
OD234F	A146	1p #446	30	20
		Set value	2.60	1.20

Ministry of Marine (M. M.)

Type I

On Stamp of 1911

OD235	A88	2c #181	20	15

On Stamps of 1912-14

OD236	A88	1c #190	15	15
OD237	A88	2c #191	15	15
OD238	A88	5c #194	2.00	15
OD239	A88	12c #196	15	15
		Nos. OD236-OD239 (4)	2.45	
		Set value		25

On Stamps of 1915-16

OD240	A88	2c #209	60	15
OD241	A88	5c #212	40	15
		Set value		15

On Stamps of 1917

OD242	A93	1c #232	15	15
OD243	A93	2c #233	15	15
OD244	A93	5c #236	15	15
		Nos. OD242-OD244 (3)	45	
		Set value		15

On Stamps of 1918-19

OD245	A93	1c #249	15	15
OD246	A93	2c #250	15	15
OD247	A93	5c #253	25	15
OD248	A94	12c #255	25	15
OD249	A94	20c #256	3.00	35
		Nos. OD245-OD249 (5)	3.80	
		Set value		60

On Stamps of 1920

OD250	A93	1c #265	15	15
OD251	A93	2c #266	20	15
OD252	A93	5c #269	25	15
		Nos. OD250-OD252 (3)	60	
		Set value		20

On Stamps of 1922-23

OD253	A103	5c #309	1.00	15
OD254	A94	12c #311	7.00	7.00
OD255	A94	20c #312	7.00	1.50
		Nos. OD253-OD254 (2)	8.00	7.15

On Stamps of 1923

OD256	A104	1c #324	15	15
OD257	A104	2c #325	15	15
OD258	A104	5c #328	35	15
OD259	A104	12c #330	65	15
OD260	A104	20c #331	65	15
		Nos. OD256-OD260 (5)	1.95	
		Set value		35

On Stamps of 1923-31

OD261	A104	1c #341	75	25
OD262	A104	2c #342	15	15
OD263	A104	3c #343	60	20
OD264	A104	5c #345, I	15	15
a.	Type II		60	15
OD265	A104	10c #346	60	15
OD266	A104	20c #348, II	60	15
a.	Type I		75	15
OD267	A104	30c #351	1.00	15
OD268	A105	1p #353	11.00	3.00
		Nos. OD261-OD268 (8)	14.85	
		Set value		3.60

On Stamp of 1926

OD269	A109	5c #359	50	15

Type II

On Stamps of 1935-37

OD270	A129	1c #419	15	15
OD271	A130	2c #420	15	15
OD272	A132	3c #422	15	15
OD273	A134	5c #427	15	15
OD274	A137	10c #430	25	15
OD275	A139	15c #434	30	15
OD276	A140	20c #437	40	15
OD277	A140	20c #438	30	15
OD278	A142	30c #442	25	15
OD279	A145	1p #445	3.25	1.00
OD280	A146	1p #446	75	25
		Nos. OD270-OD280 (11)	6.10	
		Set value		1.65

Ministry of Public Works (M. O. P.)

Type I

On Stamp of 1911

OD281	A88	2c #181	30	15

On Stamps of 1912-14

OD282	A88	1c #190	30	15
OD283	A88	5c #194	15	15
OD284	A88	12c #196	1.50	35
		Nos. OD282-OD284 (3)	1.95	
		Set value		45

On Stamps of 1916-19

OD285	A91	5c #220	10.00	1.00
OD286	A94	12c #238	25.00	
OD287	A94	20c #256	25.00	

On Stamps of 1920

OD288	A93	2c #266	6.00	2.50
OD289	A93	5c #269	2.00	15
OD290	A94	12c #271	20.00	6.00
		Nos. OD288-OD290 (3)	28.00	8.65

On Stamps of 1923

OD291	A104	1c #324	40	15
OD292	A104	2c #325	30	15
OD293	A104	5c #328	40	15
OD294	A104	12c #330	60	15
OD295	A104	20c #331	1.00	15
		Nos. OD291-OD295 (5)	2.70	
		Set value		50

On Stamps of 1923-31

OD296	A104	1c #341	15	15
OD297	A104	2c #342	15	15
OD298	A104	3c #343	15	15
OD299	A104	5c #345, I	15	15
a.	Type II		15	15
OD300	A104	10c #346	15	15
OD301	A104	12c #347	9.00	1.25
OD302	A104	20c #348, I	15	15
a.	Type II		2.50	50
OD303	A104	30c #351	40	15
OD304	A105	1p #353	20.00	6.00
		Nos. OD296-OD304 (9)	30.30	8.30

On Stamp of 1926

OD305	A109	5c #359	60	15

Type II

On Stamps of 1935-37

OD306	A129	1c #419	15	15
OD307	A130	2c #420	15	15
OD308	A132	3c #422	15	15
OD309	A134	5c #427	15	15
OD310	A137	10c #430	30	15
OD311	A139	15c #434	60	15
OD312	A140	20c #437	75	15
OD313	A140	20c #438	15	15
OD314	A142	30c #442	15	15
OD315	A144	50c #444	15	15
OD316	A145	1p #445	2.00	1.00
OD317	A146	1p #446	50	25
		Set value	4.75	1.70

Ministry of Foreign Affairs and Religion (M. R. C.)
Type I
On Stamp of 1911

OD318 A88 2c #181 5.00 1.25

On Stamps of 1912-14

OD319 A88 1c #190 15 15
OD320 A88 2c #191 15 15
OD321 A88 5c #194 40 15
OD322 A88 12c #196 1.50 25
Nos. OD319-OD322 (4) 2.20
Set value 40

On Stamps of 1915-19

OD323 A88 5c #212 40 15
OD324 A91 5c #220 15 15
OD325 A94 20c #256 2.00 75
Nos. OD323-OD325 (3) 2.55
Set value 90

On Stamps of 1920

OD326 A93 1c #265 40 15
OD327 A93 5c #269 15 15
Set value 15

On Stamps of 1922-23

OD328 A93 2c #306 9.00 3.50
OD329 A103 5c #309 27.50
OD330 A93 10c #311 22.50
Nos. OD328-OD330 (3) 59.00

On Stamps of 1923

OD331 A104 1c #324 15 15
OD332 A104 2c #325 15 15
OD333 A104 5c #328 15 15
OD334 A104 12c #330 15 15
OD335 A104 20c #331 15 15
Set value 40 30

On Stamps of 1923-31

OD336 A104 ½c #340 1.00 50
OD337 A104 1c #341 15 15
OD338 A104 2c #342 15 15
OD339 A104 3c #343 15 15
OD340 A104 5c #345 15 15
OD341 A104 10c #346, II 15 15
a. Type I 1.50 15
OD342 A104 12c #347 15 15
OD343 A104 20c #348, I 15 15
a. Type II 15 15
OD344 A104 30c #351, I 15 15
a. Type II 15 15
OD345 A105 1p #353 40 20
Set value 2.00 1.10

On Stamp of 1926

OD346 A110 12c #360 15 15

Type II
On Stamps of 1935-37

OD347 A129 1c #419 15 15
OD348 A130 2c #420 15 15
OD349 A132 3c #422 15 15
OD350 A134 5c #427 15 15
OD351 A137 10c #430 15 15
OD352 A139 15c #434 15 15
OD353 A140 20c #437 15 15
OD354 A140 20c #438 15 15
OD355 A142 30c #442 15 15
OD356 A145 1p #445 2.50 1.25
OD357 A146 1p #446 1.00 50
Set value 4.25 2.25

BUENOS AIRES

The central point of the Argentine struggle for independence. At intervals Buenos Aires maintained an independent government but after 1862 became a province of the Argentine Republic.

8 Reales = 1 Peso

> Values of Buenos Aires Nos. 1-8 vary according to condition. Quotations are for fine copies. Very fine to superb specimens sell at much higher prices, and inferior or poor copies sell at reduced values, depending on the condition of the individual specimen.

Steamship — A1

1858 Unwmk. Typo. *Imperf.*

1 A1 1 (in) pesos lt brn *350.* *250.*
2 A1 2 (dos) pesos blue 175. 140.
3 A1 3 (tres) pesos grn 1,400. *750.*
a. 3p dark green 1,700. *825.*
4 A1 4 (cuatro) pesos ver 4,750. *1,500.*
5 A1 5 (cinco) pesos org 4,250. *1,400.*
a. 5p ocher 4,250. *1,400.*
b. 5p olive yellow 4,250. *1,400.*

Issued: #2-5, Apr. 29; #1, Oct. 26.

1858, Oct. 26

6 A1 4 (cuatro) reales brown 250. 200.
a. 4r gray brown 250. 200.
b. 4r yellow brown 250. 200.

1859, Jan. 1

7 A1 1 (in) pesos blue 165. 225.
a. 1p indigo 200. 250.
b. Impression on reverse of stamp in blue *2,100.*
c. Double impression 200. 165.
d. Tete beche pair *45,000.*
8 A1 1 (to) pesos blue 350. 225.

Nos. 1, 2, 3 and 7 have been reprinted on very thick, hand-made paper. The same four stamps and No. 8 have been reprinted on thin, hard, white wove paper.

Counterfeits of Nos. 1-8 are plentiful.

Liberty Head — A2

1859, Sept. 3

9 A2 4r green, *bluish* 190.00 90.00
10 A2 1p blue 35.00 17.50
11 A2 2p vermilion 350.00 150.00
a. 2p red 350.00 150.00

Both clear and rough impressions of these stamps may be found. They have generally been called Paris and Local prints, respectively, but the opinion now obtains that the differences are due to the impression and that they do not represent separate issues.

Many shades exist of Nos. 1-11.

1862, Oct. 4

12 A2 1p rose 125.00 60.00
13 A2 2p blue 350.00 75.00

All three values have been reprinted in black, brownish black, blue and red brown on thin hard white paper. The 4r has also been reprinted in green on bluish paper.

CORDOBA

A province in the central part of the Argentine Republic.

100 Centavos = 1 Peso

Arms of Cordoba — A1

Unwmk.
1858, Oct. 28 Litho. *Imperf.*
Laid Paper

1 A1 5c blue 125.
2 A1 10c black *2,500.*

Cordoba stamps were printed on laid paper, but stamps from edges of the sheets sometimes do not show any laid lines and appear to be on wove paper. Counterfeits are plentiful.

CORRIENTES

The northeast province of the Argentine Republic.

1 Real M(oneda) C(orriente) =
12½ Centavos M.C. = 50 Centavos
100 Centavos Fuertes = 1 Peso Fuerte

Ceres
A1 A2

1856, Aug. 21 Unwmk. *Imperf.*

1 A1 1r black, *blue* 85.00 *275.00*

Pen Stroke Through "Un Real"

1860, Feb. 8

2 A1 (3c) black, *blue* 350.00 *525.00*

1860-78

3 A2 (3c) black, *blue* 9.50 *30.00*
4 A2 (2c) blk, *yel grn* ('64) 37.50 37.50
a. (2c) black, *blue green* 92.50 110.00
5 A2 (2c) blk, *yel* ('67) 7.50 *19.00*
6 A2 (3c) blk, *dk bl* ('71) 3.00 *19.00*
7 A2 (3c) blk, *lil rose* ('75)
a. (3c) black, *rose red* ('76)
8 A2 (3c) blk, *red vio* ('78) 60.00 35.00

Pen canceled copies sell for much less.

Printed from settings of 8 varieties, 3 or 4 impressions constituting a sheet. Some impressions were printed inverted and tete beche pairs may be cut from adjacent impressions.

From Jan. 1 to Feb. 24, 1864, No. 4 was used as a 5 centavos stamp but copies so used can only be distinguished when they bear dated cancellations.

The reprints show numerous spots and small defects which are not found on the originals. They are printed on gray blue, dull blue, gray green, dull orange and light magenta papers.

ARMENIA

LOCATION — South of Russia bounded by Georgia, Azerbaijan, Iran and Turkey
GOVT. — Republic
AREA — 11,306 sq. mi.
POP. — 3,300,000 (1989)
CAPITAL — Yerevan

With Azerbaijan and Georgia, Armenia made up the Transcaucasian Federation of Soviet Republics.

Stamps of Armenia were replaced in 1923 by those of Transcaucasian Federated Republics.

With the breakup of the Soviet Union on Dec. 26, 1991, Armenia and ten former Soviet republics established the Commonwealth of Independent States.

100 Kopecks = 1 Ruble
100 Luma = 1 Dram (1993)

> **Catalogue values for unused stamps in this country are for Never Hinged items, beginning with Scott 430 in the regular postage section.**

Counterfeits abound of all overprinted and surcharged stamps.

Watermark

Diamonds — Wmk. 171

> Perforations
> Perforations are the same as the basic Russian stamps.

National Republic

Russian Stamps of 1902-19 Handstamped

Thirteen types exist of both framed and unframed overprints. The device is the Armenian "H," initial of Hayasdan (Armenia). Inverted and double overprints are found.

Surcharged **K 60 K**

Type I - Without periods.
Type II - Periods after 1st "K" and "60."

Black Surcharge

1919 Unwmk. *Perf. 14x14½*

1 A14 60k on 1k orange (II) 2.00 40
a. Imperf. (I) 1.00 24
b. Imperf. (II) 1.00 24

Violet Surcharge

2 A14 60k on 1k orange (II) 45 50

Handstamped in Violet — a 

Perf.

6 A15 4k carmine 2.00 2.00
7 A14 5k claret, imperf. 7.50 7.50
a. Perf. 5.00 5.00
9 A14 10k on 7k lt blue 1.10 1.25
10 A11 15k red brn & bl 25 25
11 A8 20k blue & car 85 1.00
13 A11 35k red brn & grn 3.50 3.50
14 A8 50k violet & green 3.50 3.50
15 A14 60k on 1k orange (II) 2.00 2.00
a. Imperf. (I) 1.90 2.00
b. Imperf. (II) 8.50 9.00
18 A13 5r dk bl, grn & pale bl 3.50 4.25
a. Imperf. 1.00 1.00
19 A12 7r dk green & pink 1.75 2.00
20 A13 10r scarlet, yel & gray 1.75 2.00

Handstamped in Black

31 A14 2k green, imperf. 15 15
a. Perf. 3.25 4.25
32 A14 3k red, imperf. 22 22
a. Perf. 2.00 2.00
33 A15 4k carmine 15 20
34 A14 5k claret 50 20
a. Imperf. 5.00 5.00
36 A15 10k dark blue 2.00 65
37 A14 10k on 7k lt blue 50 15
38 A11 15k red brn & bl 50 15
a. Imperf. 3.00 3.00
39 A8 20k blue & car 50 20
40 A11 25k green & gray vio 50 20
41 A11 35k red brn & grn 50 15
42 A8 50k violet & green 1.00 15
43 A14 60k on 1k orange (II) 2.50 2.50
43A A11 70k brown & org 50 32
b. Imperf. 50 30
44 A9 1r pale brn, dk brn & org 1.50 32
a. Imperf. 50 50
45 A12 3½r mar & lt grn, imperf. 60 65
a. Perf. 1.00 85
46 A13 5r dk bl, grn & pale bl 60 65
a. Imperf. 1.00 1.00
47 A12 7r dk green & pink 5.00 1.10
48 A13 10r scar, yel & gray 5.00 1.00

Wmk. Wavy Lines (168)
1920 *Imperf.*
Vertically Laid Paper

60 A13 5r dk bl, grn & pale bl 20.00

Handstamped in Violet — c 

Unwmk. *Perf.*
Wove Paper

62 A14 2k green, imperf. 40 40
a. Perf. 4.50 4.50
63 A14 3k red, imperf. 25 25
a. Perf. 3.00 2.75
64 A15 4k carmine 50 50
65 A14 5k claret 40 40
a. Imperf. 60 60
67 A15 10k dark blue 1.00 85
68 A14 10k on 7k lt bl 1.00 65
69 A11 15k red brn & bl 2.50 2.50
70 A8 20k blue & car 40 40
71 A11 25k grn & gray vio 1.00 1.00
72 A11 35k red brn & grn 1.50 1.50
73 A8 50k violet & grn 50 50
74 A14 60k on 1k org (II) 2.50 2.00
a. Imperf. (I) 1.65 1.65
b. Imperf. (II) 2.00 2.00
75 A9 1r pale brn, dk brn & org 60 60
a. Imperf. 1.50 1.50
76 A12 3½r mar & lt grn, imperf. 75 75
a. Perf. 1.00 1.00

77 A13 5r dk bl, grn & pale bl, imperf. 5.00 5.00
a. Perf. 4.00 4.00
78 A12 7r dk green & pink 7.50 7.50
79 A13 10r scar, yel & gray 2.25 1.90

Imperf

85 A11 70k brown & org 2.00 2.00

Handstamped in Black

Perf.

90 A14 1k orange 5.00 4.50
a. Imperf. 6.00 6.00
91 A14 2k green, imperf. 15 15
a. Perf. 3.00 2.50
92 A14 3k red, imperf. 22 22
a. Perf. 3.25 2.75
93 A15 4k carmine 50 50
94 A14 5k claret 15 15
a. Imperf. 60 60
95 A14 7k light blue 15.00 15.00
96 A15 10k dark blue 12.00 12.00
97 A14 10k on 7k lt bl 15 15
98 A11 15k red brn & bl 18 15
99 A8 20k blue & car 15 15
100 A11 25k grn & gray vio 50 20
101 A11 35k red brn & grn 18 15
102 A8 50k violet & grn 18 15
102A A14 60k on 1k org, imperf. (I) 30 30
b. Imperf. (II) 50 50
c. Perf. (II) 2.50 1.25
103 A9 1r pale brn, dk brn & org 1.00 1.00
a. Imperf. 75 75
104 A12 3½r maroon & lt grn 50 50
a. Imperf. 32 32
105 A13 5r dk bl, grn & pale bl 2.50 2.50
a. Imperf. 2.50 2.50
106 A12 7r dk green & pink 2.50 2.50
107 A13 10r scar, yel & gray 3.50 3.50

Imperf

113 A11 70k brown & org 25 25

Handstamped in Violet or Black:

f

g

Violet Surcharge, Type f

1920 ***Perf.***

120 A14 3r on 3k red, imperf. 85 85
a. Perf. 2.50 2.50
121 A14 5r on 3k red 3.75 3.25
122 A15 5r on 4k car 10.00 8.00
123 A14 5r on 5k claret, imperf. 10.00 10.00
a. Perf. 10.00 8.00
124 A15 5r on 10k dk blue 10.00 8.00
125 A14 5r on 10k on 7k lt bl 10.00 8.00
126 A8 5r on 20k bl & car

Imperf

127 A14 5r on 2k green 7.00 7.00
128 A11 5r on 35k red brn & grn 7.00 7.00

Black Surcharge, Type f or Type g (#130)

Perf.

130 A14 1r on 1k orange 50 50
a. Imperf. 75 75
131 A14 3r on 3k red 15 15
a. Imperf. 15 15
132 A15 3r on 4k carmine 3.00 3.00
133 A14 5r on 2k green, imperf. 15 15
a. Perf. 2.00 2.00
134 A14 5r on 3k red 5.00 5.00
a. Imperf. 2.50 2.50
135 A15 5r on 4k carmine 40 40
a. Imperf. 4.75 4.75
136 A14 5r on 5k claret 50 50
a. Imperf. 50 50
137 A14 5r on 7k lt blue 2.00 2.00
138 A15 5r on 10k dk blue 50 50
139 A14 5r on 10k on 7k lt bl 50 50
140 A11 5r on 14k bl & rose 2.00 2.00
141 A11 5r on 15k red brn & blue 50 50
a. Imperf. 2.00 2.00
142 A8 5r on 20k bl & car 50 50
a. Imperf. 10.00 10.00
143 A11 5r on 20k on 14k bl & rose 12.00 12.00
144 A11 5r on 25k grn & gray vio 12.00 12.00

Black Surcharge, Type g or Type f (#148A, 151)

145 A14 10r on 1k org, imperf. 90 90
a. Perf. 250.00 250.00
146 A14 10r on 3k red 200.00 200.00
147 A14 10r on 5k claret 15.00 15.00
a. Imperf. 6.00
148 A8 10r on 20k bl & car 15.00 15.00
148A A11 10r on 25k grn & gray vio 8.00 8.00
149 A11 10r on 25k grn & gray vio 5.00 5.00
a. Imperf. 8.00 8.00
150 A11 10r on 35k red brn & grn 50 50
151 A8 10r on 50k brn vio & grn 1.75 1.75
152 A8 10r on 50k brn vio & grn 45 45
152A A11 10r on 70k brn & org, imperf. 3.00 3.00
b. Perf. 200.00 200.00
152C A8 25r on 20k bl & car 4.00 4.00
153 A11 25r on 25k grn & gray vio 2.00 2.00
154 A11 25r on 35k red brn & grn 2.00 2.00
a. Imperf. 3.50 3.50
155 A8 25r on 50k vio & grn 4.00 4.00
a. Imperf. 5.00 5.00
156 A11 25r on 70k brn & org 8.00 8.00
a. Imperf. 5.00 5.00
157 A9 50r on 1r pale brn, dk brn & org, imperf. 1.00 1.00
a. Perf. 5.00 5.00
158 A13 50r on 5r dk bl, grn & lt bl 10.00 10.00
a. Imperf. 10.00 10.00
159 A12 100r on 3½r mar & lt grn 7.00 7.00
a. Imperf. 7.00 7.00
160 A13 100r on 5r dk bl, grn & pale bl 10.00 10.00
a. Imperf. 7.00 7.00
161 A12 100r on 7r dk grn & pink 10.00 10.00
a. Imperf. 35.00 35.00
162 A13 100r on 10r scar, yel & gray 10.00 10.00

Wmk. Wavy Lines (168)

Perf. 11½

Vertically Laid Paper

163 A12 100r on 3½r blk & gray 50.00 50.00
164 A12 100r on 7r blk & yel 35.00 35.00

1920 Unwmk. *Imperf.*

Wove Paper

166 A14 (g) 1r on 60k on 1k org (I) 12.00 12.00
168 A14 (f) 5r on 1k orange 9.00 9.00
173 A11 (f) 5r on 35k red brn & grn 2.50 2.50
177 A11 (g) 50r on 70k brn & org 5.00 5.00
179 A12 (g) 50r on 3½r mar & lt grn 2.00 2.00
181 A9 (g) 100r on 1r pale brn, dk brn & org 4.00 4.00

Romanov Issues Surcharged Type g or Type f (#185-187, 190)
On Stamps of 1913

1920 ***Perf. 13½***

184 A16 1r on 1k brn org 10.00 10.00
185 A18 3r on 3k rose red 15.00 15.00
186 A19 5r on 4k dull red 10.00 10.00
187 A22 5r on 14k blue grn 60.00 60.00
187A A19 10r on 4k dull red 30.00
187B A26 10r on 35k gray vio & dk grn
187C A19 25r on 4k dull red 10.00 10.00
188 A26 25r on 35k gray vio & dk grn 2.75 2.75
189 A28 25r on 70k yel grn & brn 2.75 2.75
190 A31 50r on 3r dk violet 2.00 2.00
190A A16 100r on 1k brn org 55.00 55.00
190B A17 100r on 2k green 55.00 55.00
191 A30 100r on 2r brown 10.50 10.50
192 A31 100r on 3r dk vio 10.50 10.50

On Stamps of 1915, Type g

Thin Cardboard

Inscriptions on Back

Perf. 12

193 A21 100r on 10k blue 3.00
194 A23 100r on 15k brown 3.00
195 A24 100r on 20k ol grn 3.00

On Stamps of 1916, Type f

Perf. 13½

196 A20 5r on 10k on 7k brown 5.00 5.00
197 A22 5r on 20k on 14k bl grn 8.00 8.00

Surch. Type f or Type g (#204-205A, 207-207C, 210-211) over Type c

Type c in Violet

Perf.

200 A15 5r on 4k carmine 1.00 1.00
201 A15 5r on 10k dk blue 1.00 1.00
202 A11 5r on 15k red brn & bl 2.00 2.00
203 A8 5r on 20k blue & car 1.75 1.75
204 A11 10r on 25k grn & gray vio 1.50 1.50
205 A11 10r on 35k red brn & grn 3.00 3.00
205A A8 10r on 50k brn vio & grn 3.50 3.50
206 A8 25r on 50k brn vio & grn 150.00 150.00
207 A9 50r on 1r pale brn, dk brn & org, imperf. 3.50 3.50
a. Perf. 25.00 25.00
207B A12 100r on 3½r mar & lt grn 30.00
207C A12 100r on 7r dk grn & pink 9.00

Imperf

208 A14 5r on 2k green 25.00 25.00
209 A14 5r on 5k claret 25.00 25.00
210 A11 25r on 70k brn & org 5.50 5.50
211 A13 100r on 5r dk bl, grn & pale bl 1.00 1.00

Surcharged Type g or Type f (212-213, 215, 219-219A, 221-222) over Type c

Type c in Black

Perf.

212 A14 5r on 7k lt bl 150.00 150.00
213 A14 5r on 10k on 7k lt bl 5.00 5.00
214 A11 5r on 15k red brn & bl 50 50
215 A8 5r on 20k blue & car 3.00 3.00
215A A11 10r on 5r on 25k grn & gray vio 5.00 5.00
216 A11 10r on 35k red brn & grn 50 50
217 A8 10r on 50k brn vio & grn 1.00 1.00
217A A9 50r on 1r pale brn, dk brn & org 1.00 1.00
b. Imperf. 1.10 1.10
217C A12 100r on 3½r mar & lt grn 1.50 1.50
218 A13 100r on 5r dk bl, grn & pale bl 10.00 10.00
a. Imperf. 1.75 1.75
219 A12 100r on 7r dk grn & pink 15.00 15.00
219A A13 100r on 10r scar, yel & gray 10.00 10.00

Imperf

220 A14 1r on 60k on 1k org (I) 20.00 20.00
221 A14 5r on 2k green 80 80
222 A14 5r on 5k claret 3.00 3.00
223 A11 10r on 70k brn & org 2.00 2.00
224 A11 25r on 70k brn & org 2.00 2.00

Surcharged Type g or Type f (#233) over Type a

Type a in Violet

Imperf

231 A9 50r on 1r pale brn, dk brn & org 140.00 140.00
232 A13 100r on 5r dk bl, grn & pale bl 10.50

Type a in Black

Perf.

233 A8 5r on 20k blue & car 80 80
233A A11 10r on 25k grn & gray vio 55.00 55.00
234 A11 10r on 35k red brn & grn 90 90
235 A12 100r on 3½r mar & lt grn 1.25 1.25
a. Imperf. 1.50 1.50

Imperf

237 A14 5r on 2k green 125.00 125.00
237A A11 10r on 70k brn & org

Surcharged Type a and New Value

Type a in Violet

Perf.

238 A11 10r on 15k red brn & blue 80 80

Type a in Black

239 A8 5r on 20k blue & car 3.00 3.00
239A A8 10r on 20k blue & car 3.00 3.00
239B A8 10r on 50k brn red & grn 7.50

Imperf

240 A12 100r on 3½r mar & lt grn 1.90 1.90

Surcharged Type c and New Value
Type c in Black

1920 ***Perf.***

241 A15 5r on 4k red 1.75 1.75
242 A11 5r on 15k red brn & bl 1.00 1.00
243 A8 10r on 20k blue & car 1.75 1.75
243A A11 10r on 25k grn & gray vio 1.00 1.00
244 A11 10r on 35k red brn & grn 1.00 1.00
a. With additional surch. "5r" 1.50 1.50
245 A12 100r on 3½r mar & lt grn 1.50 1.50

Imperf

247 A14 3r on 3k red 4.75 4.75
248 A14 5r on 2k green 30 30
249 A9 50r on 1r pale brn, dk brn & org 90 90

Type c in Violet

249A A14 5r on 2k green 6.50

Postal Savings Stamps Surcharged

A1

A2

A3

Perf. 14½x15

Wmk. 171

250 A1 60k on 1k red & buff 50.00 50.00
251 A2 1r on 1k red & buff 5.00 5.00
252 A3 5r on 5k green & buff 7.25 7.25
253 A3 5r on 10k brown & buff 30.00 3.00

Russian Semi-Postal Stamps of 1914-18 Surcharged with Armenian Monogram and New Values like Regular Issues
On Stamps of 1914

Unwmk. ***Perf.***

255 SP5 25r on 1k red brn & dk grn, *straw* 60.00 60.00
256 SP6 25r on 3k mar & gray grn, *pink* 60.00 60.00
257 SP7 50r on 7 dk brn & dk grn, *buff* 20.00 20.00
258 SP5 100r on 1k red brn & dk grn, *straw* 3.25 3.50
259 SP6 100r on 3k mar & gray grn, *pink* 3.25 3.50
260 SP7 100r on 7k dk brn & dk grn, *buff* 3.25 3.50

On Stamps of 1915-19

261 SP5 25r on 1k org brn & gray 75.00 75.00
262 SP6 25r on 3k car & gray 30.00 30.00
263 SP8 50r on 10k dk bl & brn 25.00 25.00
264 SP5 100r on 1k org brn & gray 3.25 3.50
265 SP8 100r on 10k dk bl & brn 3.25 3.50

These surcharged semi-postal stamps were used for ordinary postage.

A set of 10 stamps in the above designs, and in a third design showing a woman quilling, was prepared in 1920, but not issued. Value of set, $4. Exist with "SPECIMEN" overprint and imperf. Reprints exist.

Soviet Socialist Republic

Hammer and Sickle — A7

Mythological Monster — A8

Symbols of Soviet Republics on Designs from old Armenian Manuscripts — A9

Ruined City of Ani — A10

Mythological Monster — A11

Armenian Soldier — A12

Soviet Symbols, Armenian Designs — A14

Mythological Monster — A13

Mt. Alagöz and Plain of Shirak A15

Fisherman on River Aras — A16

Post Office in Erevan and Mt. Ararat A17

Ruin in City of Ani — A18

Street in Erevan — A19

Lake Gökcha and Sevan Monastery A20

Mythological Subject from old Armenian Monument — A21

Mt. Ararat A22

1921 Unwmk. *Perf. 11½, Imperf.*

278	A7	1r	gray green	28	
279	A8	2r	slate gray	28	
280	A9	3r	carmine	28	
281	A10	5r	dark brown	28	
282	A11	25r	gray	28	18
283	A12	50r	red	15	
284	A13	100r	orange	15	
285	A14	250r	dark blue	15	
286	A15	500r	brown vio	15	
287	A16	1000r	sea green	28	
288	A17	2000r	bister	30	
289	A18	5000r	dark brown	30	
290	A19	10,000r	dull red	30	
291	A20	15,000r	slate blue	30	
292	A21	20,000r	lake	30	
293	A22	25,000r	gray blue	65	
294	A22	25,000r	brown olive	5.50	
			Nos. 278-294 (17)	9.93	

Except the 25r, Nos. 278-294 were not regularly issued and used. Counterfeits exist.

For surcharges see Nos. 347-390.

Russian Stamps of 1909-17 Surcharged

Wove Paper
Lozenges of Varnish on Face

1921, Aug. ***Perf. 13½***

295	A9	5000r on 1r	2.00	
296	A12	5000r on 3½r	2.00	
297	A13	5000r on 5r	2.00	
298	A12	5000r on 7r	2.00	
299	A13	5000r on 10r	2.00	
		Nos. 295-299 (5)	10.00	

Nos. 295-299 were not officially issued. Counterfeits abound.

Mt. Ararat and Soviet Star
A23 A24

Soviet Symbols — A25

Crane — A26

Peasant — A27

Harpy — A28

Peasant Sowing — A29

Soviet Symbols — A30

Forging — A31

Plowing A32

1922 ***Perf. 11½***

300	A23	50r	green & red	35	
301	A24	300r	slate bl & buff	40	
302	A25	400r	blue & pink	40	
303	A26	500r	vio & pale lil	40	
304	A27	1000r	dull bl & pale bl	40	
305	A28	2000r	black & gray	65	
306	A29	3000r	black & grn	65	
307	A30	4000r	black & lt brn	65	
308	A31	5000r	black & dull red	50	
309	A32	10,000r	black & pale rose	50	
a.			Tête bêche pair	11.00	
			Nos. 300-309 (10)	4.90	

Nos. 300 to 309 were not placed in use without surcharge.

Stamps of types A23 to A32, printed in other colors than Nos. 300 to 309, are essays.

Nos. 300-309 with Handstamped Surcharge of New Values in Rose, Violet or Black

1922

310	10,000 on 50r (R)	4.75	4.75
311	10,000 on 50r (V)	5.00	5.00
312	10,000 on 50r	2.00	2.00
313	15,000 on 300r (R)	25.00	25.00
314	15,000 on 300r (V)	5.00	5.00
315	15,000 on 300r	3.00	3.00
316	25,000 on 400r (V)	5.00	5.00
317	25,000 on 400r	2.00	2.00
318	30,000 on 500r (R)	9.00	9.00
319	30,000 on 500r (V)	75	75
320	30,000 on 500r	2.00	2.00
321	50,000 on 1000r (R)	7.25	7.25
322	50,000 on 1000r (V)	10.00	10.00
323	50,000 on 1000r	3.00	3.00
324	75,000 on 3000r	4.00	4.00
325	100,000 on 2000r (R)	50.00	50.00
326	100,000 on 2000r (V)	20.00	20.00
327	100,000 on 2000r	3.00	3.00
328	200,000 on 4000r (V)	5.00	5.00
329	200,000 on 4000r	15.00	15.00
330	300,000 on 5000r (V)	20.00	20.00
331	300,000 on 5000r	2.00	2.00
332	500,000 on 10,000r (V)	10.00	10.00
333	500,000 on 10,000r	5.00	5.00
	Nos. 310-333 (24)	217.75	217.75

Goose — A33

Armenian Woman at Well — A35

Armenian Village Scene — A34

Mt. Ararat — A36

Mt. Ararat A37

New Values in Gold Kopecks, Handstamped Surcharge in Black

1922 ***Imperf.***

334	A33	1(k) on 250r rose	7.00	7.00
335	A33	1(k) on 250r gray	13.00	13.00
336	A34	2(k) on 500r rose	5.00	5.00
337	A34	3(k) on 500r gray	5.00	5.00
338	A35	4(k) on 1000r rose	5.00	5.00
339	A35	4(k) on 1000r gray	9.25	9.25
340	A36	5(k) on 2000r gray	5.00	5.00
341	A36	10(k) on 2000r rose	5.00	5.00
342	A37	15(k) on 5000r rose	30.00	30.00
343	A37	20(k) on 5000r gray	5.00	5.00
		Nos. 334-343 (10)	89.25	89.25

Nos. 334-343 were issued for postal tax purposes.

Nos. 334-343 exist without surcharge but are not known to have been issued in that condition. Counterfeits exist of both sets.

Regular Issue of 1921 Handstamped with New Values in Black or Red
Short, Thick Numerals

1922 ***Imperf.***

347	A8	2(k) on 2r (R)	25.00	25.00
350	A11	4(k) on 25r (R)	10.00	10.00
353	A13	10(k) on 100r (R)	7.50	7.50
354	A14	15(k) on 250r	3.00	3.00
355	A15	20(k) on 500r	10.00	10.00
a.		With "k" written in red	10.00	10.00
357	A22	50(k) on 25,000r bl (R)	12.00	12.00
358	A22	50(k) on 25,000r brn ol (R)	9.00	9.00
359	A22	50(k) on 25,000r brn ol	76.50	76.50
		Nos. 347-358 (7)		

Perf. 11½

360	A7	1(k) on 1r, imperf.	1.75	1.75
a.		Perf.	6.00	6.00
361	A7	1(k) on 1r (R)	15.00	15.00
a.		Imperf.	20.00	20.00
362	A8	2(k) on 2r, imperf.	15.00	15.00
a.		Perf.	25.00	25.00
363	A15	2(k) on 500r	2.00	2.00
a.		Imperf.	1.75	1.75
364	A15	2(k) on 500r (R)	9.00	9.00
365	A11	4(k) on 25r, imperf.	3.50	3.50
a.		Perf.	25.00	25.00
366	A12	5(k) on 50r, imperf.	1.75	1.75
a.		Perf.	2.50	2.50
367	A13	10(k) on 100r	8.00	8.00
a.		Imperf.	8.00	8.00
368	A21	35(k) on 20,000r, imperf.	3.50	3.50
a.		With "k" written in violet	3.50	3.50
b.		Perf.	15.00	15.00
c.		As "a," perf.	15.00	15.00
d.		With "kop" written in violet, imperf.		
		Nos. 360-368 (9)	59.50	59.50

Manuscript Surcharge in Red

Perf. 11½

371	A14	1k on 250r dk bl	2.50	2.50

Handstamped in Black or Red
Tall, Thin Numerals

Imperf

377	A11	4(k) on 25r (R)	4.25	4.25
379	A13	10(k) on 100r	10.00	10.00
380	A15	20(k) on 500r	6.00	6.00
381	A22	50k on 25,000r bl	1.00	1.00
a.		Surcharged "50" only	15.00	15.00
382	A22	50k on 25,000r bl (R)	12.00	12.00
382A	A22	50k on 25,000r brn ol	24.00	24.00
		Nos. 377-382A (6)	57.25	57.25

On Nos. 381, 382 and 382A the letter "k" forms part of the surcharge.

Perf. 11½

383	A7	1(k) on 1r (R)	3.00	3.00
a.		Imperf.		
384	A14	1(k) on 250r	1.75	1.75
385	A15	2(k) on 500r	8.00	8.00
a.		Imperf.	12.00	12.00
386	A15	2(k) on 500r (R)	4.75	4.75
387	A9	3(k) on 3r	20.00	20.00
a.		Imperf.	20.00	20.00
388	A21	3(k) on 20,000r, imperf.	10.00	10.00
a.		Perf.	50.00	50.00
389	A11	4(k) on 25r	2.50	2.50
a.		Imperf.	4.25	4.25

390	A12	5(k) on 50r, imperf.		4.00	5.00
a.		Perf.		6.00	7.00
		Nos. 383-390 (8)		54.00	54.00

Catalogue values for unused stamps in this section, from this point to the end of the section, are for Never Hinged items.

Mt. Ararat — A45

Designs: a, 20k. b, 2r. c, 5r. 7r, Eagle and Mt. Ararat.

1992, Apr. 28 Litho. *Perf. 14*

430	A45	Strip of 3, #a.-c.	*3.75*

Souvenir Sheet

431	A45	7r multicolored	*35.00*

AT & T Communications System in Armenia — A45a

1992 Litho. *Perf. 13x13½*

431A	A45a	50k multicolored	*5.00*

A46

A47

1992 Summer Olympics, Barcelona: a, 40k, Ancient Greek wrestlers. b, 3.60r, Boxing. c, 5r, Weight lifting. d, 12r, Gymnastics.

1992 Litho. *Perf. 14*

432	A46	Strip of 4, #a.-d.	*7.50*

Perf. 14½, 15x14½

1992, Aug. 25 Litho.

Designs: 20k, Natl. flag. 2r, Yerevan Airport. 1r, Goddess Waroubini, Orgov radio telescope. No. 435, Goddess Anahit. No. 435A, Runic message, 7th cent B.C. 5r, UPU emblem. 20r, Silver cup.

433	A47	20k	multicolored	*15*
434	A47	1r	black	*15*
435	A47	2r	blue	*1.10*
436	A47	3r	brown	*1.65*
437	A47	3r	brown	*15*
438	A47	5r	brown black	*2.75*
439	A47	20r	gray	*15*
			Nos. 433-439 (7)	*6.10*

No. 435 is airmail. See Nos. 464-471.

Armenia stamps can be mounted in the Scott annually supplemented Russia album part 1.

David of Sassoun, by Hakop Kojoian — A50a

Religious Artifacts — A50

Yerevan '93 — A52

Scenic Views — A51

1993, May 23 Litho. *Perf. 14*

448	A50	40k	Marker	*15*
449	A50	80k	Gospel page	*30*
450	A50	3.60r	Bas-relief, 13th cent.	*1.25*
451	A50	5r	Icon of the Madonna	*1.90*
			Nos. 448-451 (4)	*3.60*

Souvenir Sheet

Perf. 14x13½

451A	A50a	12r multicolored	*4.50*

1993, May 24 *Perf. 14*

Designs (illustration reduced): 40k, Garni Canyon, vert. 80k, Shaki Waterfall, Zangezur, vert. 3.60r, Arpa River Canyon, vert. 5r, Lake Sevan. 12r, Mount Aragats.

452	A51	40k	multicolored	*15*
453	A51	80k	multicolored	*15*
454	A51	3.60r	multicolored	*60*
455	A51	5r	multicolored	*80*
456	A51	12r	multicolored	*2.00*
			Nos. 452-456 (5)	*3.70*

1993, May 25 *Perf. 14½*

457	A52	10r multicolored	*70*
a.		Min. sheet of 6 + 2 labels	*7.50*

Souvenir Sheet

Noah's Descent from Mt. Ararat, by Hovhannes Aivazovsky — A52

1993, May 24 Litho. *Perf. 14½*

458	A52	7r multicolored	*1.10*

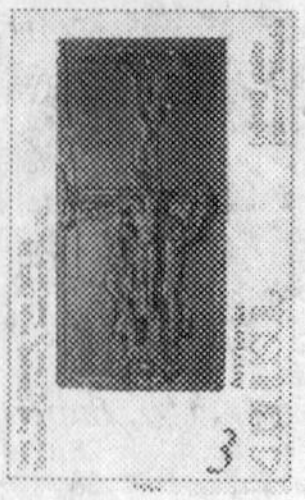

Religious Relics, Echmiadzin — A53

Designs: 3r, Wooden panel, descent from cross, 9th cent. 5r, Gilded silver reliquary for Holy Cross of Khotakerats. 12r, Cross depicting right hand of St. Karapet, 14th cent. 30r, Reliquary for arm of St. Thaddeus the Apostle, 17th cent. 50r, Gilded silver vessel for consecrated ointment, 1815.

1994, Aug. 4 Litho. *Perf. 14x14½*

459	A53	3d	multicolored	*15*
460	A53	5d	multicolored	*20*
461	A53	12d	multicolored	*48*
462	A53	30d	multicolored	*1.25*
463	A53	50d	multicolored	*2.00*
			Nos. 459-463 (5)	*4.08*

Artifacts and Landmarks Type of 1993

Gods of Van (Urartu): 10 l, Shivini, god of the sun. 50 l, Tayshaba, god of elements. 10d, Khaldi, supreme god.
25d, Natl. arms.

1994 *Perf. 14½*

464	A47	10 l	black & brown	*15*
465	A47	50 l	black & red brown	*15*
469	A47	10d	black & gray	*55*
471	A47	25d	red & bister	*1.40*
			Nos. 464-471 (4)	*2.25*

Issued: 10 l, 50 l, 10d, 25d, 8/4/94.
This is an expanding set. Numbers may change.

ARUBA

LOCATION — West Indies, north of Venezuela
AREA — 78 sq. mi.
POP. — 67,014

On Jan. 1, 1986 Aruba, formerly part of Netherlands Antilles, achieved a separate status within the Kingdom.

100 Cents = 1 Gulden

Catalogue values for all unused stamps in this country are for Never Hinged items.

Traditional House — A1

1986-87 Litho. *Perf. 14x13*

1	A1	5c	shown	15	15
2	A1	15c	King William III Tower	15	15
3	A1	20c	Loading crane	18	18
4	A1	25c	Lighthouse	22	22
5	A1	30c	Snake	26	26
6	A1	35c	Owl	32	32
7	A1	45c	Shell	40	40
8	A1	55c	Frog	50	50
9	A1	60c	Water skier	55	55
10	A1	65c	Net fishing	60	60
11	A1	75c	Music box	70	70
12	A1	85c	Pre-Columbian bisque pot	75	75
13	A1	90c	Bulb cactus	80	80
14	A1	100c	Grain	90	90
15	A1	150c	Watapana tree	1.40	1.40
16	A1	250c	Aloe plant	2.25	2.25
			Nos. 1-16 (16)	10.13	10.13

Issue dates: 5c, 30c, 60c, 150c, Jan. 1. 15c, 35c, 65c, 250c, Feb. 5. 20c, 45c, 75c, 100c, Apr. 7, 1987. 25c, 55c, 85c, 90c, July 17, 1987.

Independence A2

1986, Jan. 1 *Perf. 14x13, 13x14*

18	A2	25c	Map	20	20
19	A2	45c	Coat of arms, vert.	35	35
20	A2	55c	Natl. anthem, vert.	42	42
21	A2	100c	Flag	75	75
			Nos. 18-21 (4)	1.72	1.72

Intl. Peace Year — A3

1986, Aug. 29 Litho. *Perf. 14x13*

22	A3	60c	shown	45	45
23	A3	100c	Barbed wire	75	75

Princess Juliana and Prince Bernhard, 50th Wedding Anniv. — A4

1987, Jan. 7 Photo. *Perf. 13x14*

24	A4	135c	multicolored	1.25	1.25

State Visit of Queen Beatrix and Prince Claus of the Netherlands A5

1987, Feb. 16 Litho. *Perf. 14x13*

25	A5	55c	shown	48	48
26	A5	60c	Prince William-Alexander	50	50

Tourism — A6

1987, June 5 Litho.

27	A6	60c	Beach and sea	90	90
28	A6	100c	Rock and cacti	1.50	1.50

Aloe Vera Plant — A7

Coins — A8

1988, Jan. 27 Litho. *Perf. 13x14*

29	A7	45c	Field	50	50
30	A7	60c	Plant	65	65
31	A7	100c	Harvest	1.10	1.10
			Nos. 29-31 (3)	2.25	2.25

1988, Mar. 16 Litho. *Perf. 13x14*

32	A8	25c	25-cent	35	35
33	A8	55c	50-cent	70	70
34	A8	65c	5 and 10-cent	85	85
35	A8	150c	1-florin	2.00	2.00
			Nos. 32-35 (4)	3.90	3.90

Love Issue — A9 A10

1988, May 4

36 A9 70c shown 75 75
37 A9 135c Seashells, coastal scenery 1.45 1.45

1988, Aug. 24

38 A10 35c shown 38 38
39 A10 100c Emblems 1.10 1.10

Aruba, the 162nd member of the Intl. Olympic Committee (35c), 1988 Summer Olympics, Seoul (100c).

Carnival — A11

1989, Jan. 5 *Perf. 14x13*

40 A11 45c Two children 45 45
41 A11 60c Girl 60 60
42 A11 100c Entertainer 1.00 1.00
Nos. 40-42 (3) 2.05 2.05

Maripampun, *Omphalophalmum zumbrum* — A12

1989, Mar. 16 Litho. *Perf. 14x13*

43 A12 35c Leaves 35 35
44 A12 55c Pods 55 55
45 A12 200c Blossom 1.95 1.95
Nos. 43-45 (3) 2.85 2.85

New Year 1990 — A13 UPU — A14

Dande band members playing instruments or singing: 25c, Violin, tambor, cuatro, marimba. 70c, Lead singer, guitar. 150c, Accordion, urri, guitar.

1989, Nov. 16 Litho. *Perf. 13x14*

46 A13 25c multicolored 25 25
47 A13 70c multicolored 70 70
48 A13 150c multicolored 1.50 1.50
Nos. 46-48 (3) 2.45 2.45

1989, June 8 Litho. *Perf. 13x14*

49 A14 250c multicolored 2.50 2.50

Crotalus durissus unicolor — A15

1989, Aug. 24 *Perf. 14x13*

50 A15 45c shown 52 52
51 A15 55c multi, diff. 62 62
52 A15 60c multi, diff. 68 68
Nos. 50-52 (3) 1.82 1.82

Species in danger of extinction.

Man Living in Harmony with Nature — A16

1990, Feb. 7 *Perf. 13x14, 14x13*

53 A16 45c The land 52 52
54 A16 55c shown 62 62
55 A16 100c The sea 1.15 1.15
Nos. 53-55 (3) 2.29 2.29

Environmental protection. #53, 55 horiz.

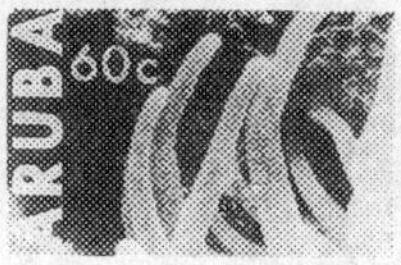

Marine Life — A17

Designs: 60c, Giant caribbean anemone, Pederson's cleaning shrimp. 70c, Queen angelfish, red and orange coral. 100c, Banded coral shrimp, fire sponge, yellow boring sponge.

1990, Apr. 4 Litho. *Perf. 14x13*

56 A17 60c multicolored 70 70
57 A17 70c multicolored 80 80
58 A17 100c multicolored 1.15 1.15
Nos. 56-58 (3) 2.65 2.65

A18 A19

1990, May 30 Litho. *Perf. 13x14*

59 A18 35c multicolored 28 28
60 A18 200c Character trademark 1.75 1.75

World Cup Soccer Championships, Italy.

1990, Sept. 12

61 A19 45c Tools 48 48
62 A19 60c Stone figure 65 65
63 A19 100c Jar 1.05 1.05
Nos. 61-63 (3) 2.18 2.18

Archeological discoveries.

Landscapes A20

1991, Jan. 31 Litho. *Perf. 14x13*

64 A20 55c Seashore 60 60
65 A20 65c Desert 72 72
66 A20 100c Cactus, ocean view 1.10 1.10
Nos. 64-66 (3) 2.42 2.42

Working Women — A21 Medicinal Plants — A22

Designs: 35c, Taking care of others. 70c, Housewife. 100c, Women in society.

1991, Mar. 28 Litho. *Perf. 13x14*

67 A21 35c multicolored 40 40
68 A21 70c multicolored 85 85
69 A21 100c multicolored 1.25 1.25
Nos. 67-69 (3) 2.50 2.50

Style of inscriptions varies.

1991, May 29

70 A22 65c Ocimum sanctum 72 72
71 A22 75c Jatropha gossypifolia 82 82
72 A22 95c Croton flavens 1.05 1.05
Nos. 70-72 (3) 2.59 2.59

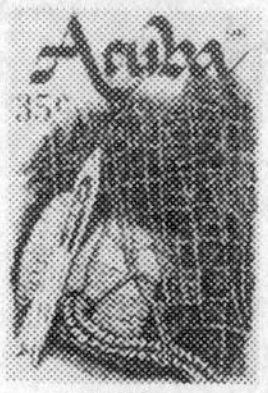

A23 A24

Aruban Handicrafts: 35c, Fish net, wood float, wooden needle. 250c, Straw hat, hat block.

1991, July 31 Litho. *Perf. 13x14*

73 A23 35c lt bl, dk bl & blk 42 42
74 A23 250c pink, lil rose & blk 2.75 2.75

1991, Nov. 28 Litho. *Perf. 13x14*

75 A24 35c Toucan 38 38
76 A24 70c People shaking hands 75 75
77 A24 100c Windmill 1.10 1.10
Nos. 75-77 (3) 2.23 2.23

Welcome to Aruba.

Aruba Postal Service, Cent. — A25

Designs: 60c, Government decree, 1892, vert. 75c, First post office. 80c, Current post office.

Perf. 13x14, 14x13

1992, Jan. 31 Litho.

78 A25 60c multicolored 65 65
79 A25 75c multicolored 85 85
80 A25 80c multicolored 90 90
Nos. 78-80 (3) 2.40 2.40

Equality Day — A26

1992, Mar. 25 Litho. *Perf. 14x13*

81 A26 100c People of five races 1.00 1.00
82 A26 100c Woman, man, scales 1.00 1.00

Aruba stamps can be mounted in the Scott annual Netherlands supplement.

Discovery of America, 500th Anniv. — A27

1992, July 30 Litho. *Perf. 13x14*

83 A27 30c Columbus 32 32
84 A27 40c Sailing ship 42 42
85 A27 50c Natives, map 55 55
Nos. 83-85 (3) 1.29 1.29

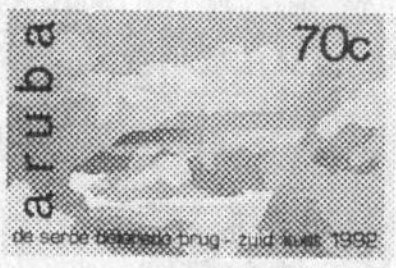

Natural Bridges in Aruba — A28

Designs: 70c, Seroe Colorado Bridge, south coast. 80c, Natural Bridge, north coast.

1992, Nov. 30 Litho. *Perf. 14x13*

86 A28 70c multicolored 85 85
87 A28 80c multicolored 90 90

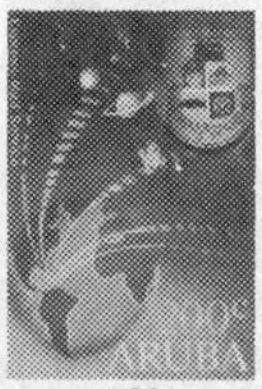

A29 A30

1993, Jan. 29 Litho. *Perf. 13x14*

88 A29 200c multicolored 2.50 2.50

Express mail service.

1993, Mar. 31 Litho. *Perf. 13x14*

Various rock formations found in Districts of Ayo and Casibari.

89 A30 50c multicolored 65 65
90 A30 60c multicolored 75 75
91 A30 100c multicolored 1.25 1.25
Nos. 89-91 (3) 2.65 2.65

Folklore — A31 Sailing Sports — A32

Designs: 40c, String instruments, drum. 70c, Traditional music and games. 80c, Dera Gai song lyrics.

1993, May 28 Litho. *Perf. 13x14*

92 A31 40c multicolored 50 50
93 A31 70c multicolored 85 85
94 A31 80c multicolored 1.00 1.00
Nos. 92-94 (3) 2.35 2.35

1993, July 30 Litho. *Perf. 13x14*

95 A32 50c Sailboating 60 60
96 A32 65c Land sailing 80 80
97 A32 75c Wind surfing 95 95
Nos. 95-97 (3) 2.35 2.35

Iguana Iguana — A33

Perf. 14x13, 13x14

1993, Sept. 1 **Litho.**

98	A33	35c Young	45	45
99	A33	60c Almost grown	75	75
100	A33	100c Mature, vert.	1.25	1.25
		Nos. 98-100 (3)	2.45	2.45

Burrowing Owl — A34

Perf. 14x13, 13x14

1994, Jan. 28 **Litho.**

101	A34	5c Two adults	15	15
102	A34	10c Two adults, young	15	15
103	A34	35c Adult with prey, vert.	45	45
104	A34	40c Adult, vert.	50	50
		Nos. 101-104 (4)	1.25	1.25

World Wildlife Fund.

A35

A36

Intl. Olympic Committee, Cent.: 90c, Baron Pierre de Coubertin (1863-1937), founder of modern Olympics.

1994, Mar. 29 **Litho.** ***Perf. 13x14***

105	A35	50c multicolored	65	65
106	A35	90c multicolored	1.10	1.10

1994, July 7 **Litho.** ***Perf. 13x14***

107	A36	65c shown	80	80
108	A36	150c Mascot, soccer ball	1.90	1.90

1994 World Cup Soccer Championships, US.

Wild Fruit — A37

Designs: 40c, Malpighia punicifolia. 70c, Cordia sebestena. 85c, Pithecellobium unguis-cati. 150c, Coccoloba uvifera.

1994, Sept. 28 **Litho.** ***Perf. 13x14***

109	A37	40c multicolored	50	50
110	A37	70c multicolored	90	90
111	A37	85c multicolored	1.10	1.10
112	A37	150c multicolored	1.90	1.90
		Nos. 109-112 (4)	4.40	4.40

SEMI-POSTAL STAMPS

Solidarity SP1

1986, May 7 **Litho.** ***Perf. 14x13***

B1	SP1	30c + 10c shown	28	28
B2	SP1	35c + 15c Three ropes	38	38
B3	SP1	60c + 25c One rope	60	60
		Nos. B1-B3 (3)	1.26	1.26

Surtax for social and cultural projects.

Child Welfare — SP2

1986, Oct. 29 **Litho.** ***Perf. 14x13***

B4	SP2	45c + 20c Boy, caterpillar	70	70
B5	SP2	70c + 25c Boy, cocoon	1.00	1.00
B6	SP2	100c + 40c Girl, butterfly	1.50	1.50
		Nos. B4-B6 (3)	3.20	3.20

Surtax for child welfare organizations.

Christmas SP3

1987, Oct. 27 **Litho.** ***Perf. 14x13***

B7	SP3	25c +10c Boy on beach	35	35
B8	SP3	45c +20c Drawing Christmas tree	70	70
B9	SP3	70c +30c Child, creche figures	1.10	1.10
		Nos. B7-B9 (3)	2.15	2.15

Surtax for child welfare organizations.

Solidarity SP4

YMCA emblem in various geometric designs.

1988, Aug. 3 **Litho.** ***Perf. 14x13***

B10	SP4	45c +20c shown	70	70
B11	SP4	60c +25c multi, diff.	90	90
B12	SP4	100c +50c multi, diff.	1.60	1.60
		Nos. B10-B12 (3)	3.20	3.20

11th YMCA world council.
Surtax for social and cultural projects.

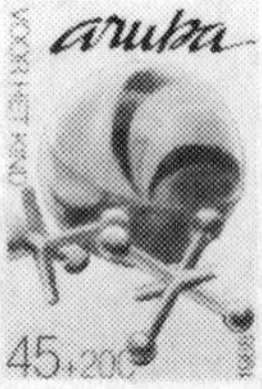
Children's Toys — SP5

1988, Oct. 26 ***Perf. 13x14***

B13	SP5	45c +20c Jacks	70	70
B14	SP5	70c +30c Top	1.10	1.10
B15	SP5	100c +50c Kite	1.60	1.60
		Nos. B13-B15 (3)	3.40	3.40

Surtax for child welfare organizations.

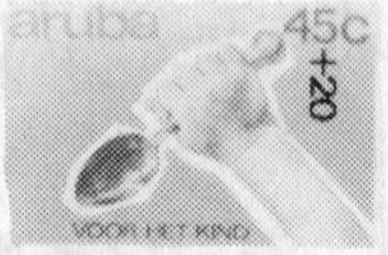
Children — SP6

1989, Oct. 26 ***Perf. 14x13***

B16	SP6	45c +20c Baby spoon	65	65
B17	SP6	60c +30c Chasing a ball	85	85
B18	SP6	100c +50c Adult & child holding hands	1.50	1.50
		Nos. B16-B18 (3)	3.00	3.00

Surtax for child welfare organizations.

Solidarity — SP7

1990, July 25

B19	SP7	55c +25c shown	1.10	1.10
B20	SP7	100c +50c Family, house	2.00	2.00

Surtax for social and cultural projects.

SP8

SP9

1990, Oct. 24 **Litho.** ***Perf. 13x14***

B21	SP8	45c +20c Wind surfboards	75	75
B22	SP8	60c +30c shown	1.05	1.05
B23	SP8	100c +50c Kites, lizard	1.70	1.70
		Nos. B21-B23 (3)	3.50	3.50

Surtax for child welfare organizations.

1991, Oct. 25 **Litho.** ***Perf. 13x14***

Designs: 45c+25c, Discovery of reading. 60c+35c, Pointing to letter. 100c+50c, Child reading.

B24	SP9	45c +25c multi	75	75
B25	SP9	60c +35c multi	1.00	1.00
B26	SP9	100c +50c multi	1.65	1.65
		Nos. B24-B26 (3)	3.40	3.40

Surtax for child welfare organizations.

Solidarity SP10

Designs: 55c+30c, Girl scouts, flag and emblem. 100c+50c, Hand holding cancer fund emblem, people.

1992, May 27 **Litho.** ***Perf. 14x13***

B27	SP10	55c +30c multi	90	90
B28	SP10	100c +50c multi	1.65	1.65

Surtax for social and cultural projects.

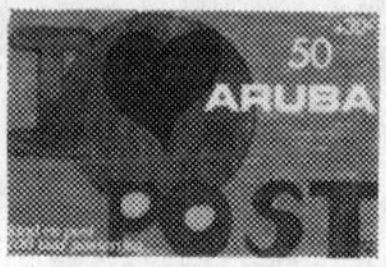
Postal Services of Aruba, Cent. — SP11

Designs: 50c+30c, Heart. 70c+35c, Airplane, letters. 100c+55c, Pigeon with letter in beak, vert.

1992, Oct. 30 **Litho.** ***Perf. 14x13***

B29	SP11	50c +30c multi	1.00	1.00
B30	SP11	70c +35c multi	1.40	1.40

Perf. 13x14

B31	SP11	100c +50c multi	2.00	2.00
		Nos. B29-B31 (3)	4.40	4.40

Surtax for child welfare organizations.

Youth Foreign Study Programs SP12

Abstract designs of: 50c+30c, Landscapes. 75c+40c, Young man, scenes of other countries, vert. 100c+50c, Integrating cultures.

Perf. 14x13, 13x14

1993, Oct. 27 **Litho.**

B32	SP12	50c +30c multi	1.00	1.00
B33	SP12	75c +40c multi	1.40	1.40
B34	SP12	100c +50c multi	1.90	1.90
		Nos. B32-B34 (3)	4.30	4.30

Surtax for child welfare organizations.

Intl. Year of the Family — SP13

Designs: 50c+35c, Family seated, reading, studying. 100c+50c, Family playing in front of house.

1994, May 30 **Litho.** ***Perf. 14x13***

B35	SP13	50c +35c multi	1.10	1.10
B36	SP13	100c +50c multi	1.90	1.90

Surtax for social and cultural projects.

Child Welfare — SP14

Designs: 50c+30c, Children on anchor with umbrella. 80c+35c, Children inside Sun. 100c+50c, Child riding owl.

1994, Oct. 27 **Litho.** ***Perf. 14x13***

B37	SP14	50c +30c multi	1.00	1.00
B38	SP14	80c +35c multi	1.40	1.40
B39	SP14	100c +50c multi	1.90	1.90
		Nos. B37-B39 (3)	4.30	4.30

Surtax for child welfare organizations.

AUSTRIA

LOCATION — Central Europe
GOVT. — Republic
AREA — 32,376 sq. mi.
POP. — 7,555,338 (1981)
CAPITAL — Vienna

Before 1867 Austria was an absolute monarchy, which included Hungary and Lombardy-Venetia. In 1867 the Austro-Hungarian Monarchy was established, with Austria and Hungary as equal partners. After World War I, in 1918, the different nationalities established their own states and only the German-speaking parts remained, forming a republic under the name "Deutschosterreich" (German Austria), which name was shortly again changed to "Austria." In 1938 German forces occupied Austria, which became part of the German Reich. After the liberation by Allied troops in 1945, an independent republic was re-established.

60 Kreuzer = 1 Gulden
100 Neu-Kreuzer = 1 Gulden (1858)
100 Heller = 1 Krone (1899)
100 Groschen = 1 Schilling (1925)

Catalogue values for unused stamps in this country are for Never Hinged items, beginning with Scott 432 in the regular postage section, Scott B165 in the semi-postal section, Scott C47 in the airpost section, Scott J175 in the postage due section, and Scott 4N1 in the AMG section.

Values of early Austrian stamps vary according to condition. Quotations for Nos. 1-5, P1-P7 and PR1-PR4 are for fine copies. Very fine to superb specimens sell at much higher prices, and inferior or poor copies sell at reduced prices, depending on the condition of the individual specimen.

Values for unused stamps of 1850-80 issues are for copies in fine condition with original gum. Specimens without gum sell for about one-third of the figures quoted.

Watermark

Wmk. 91 - "BRIEF-MARKEN" In Double-lined Capitals Across the Middle of the Sheet

Wmk. 140- Crown

Issues of the Austrian Monarchy (including Hungary)

Coat of Arms — A1

NINE KREUZER

Type I. One heavy line around coat of arms center. On the 9kr the top of "9" is about on a level with "Kreuzer" and not near the top of the label. Each cliche has the "9" in a different position.

Type IA. As type I, but with 1¼mm between "9" and "K."

Type II. One heavy line around coat of arms center. On the 9kr the top of "9" is much higher than the top of the word "Kreuzer" and nearly touches the top of the label.

Type III. As type II, but with two, thinner, lines around the center.

Wmk. K.K.H.M. in Sheet or Unwmk.

1850 Typo. *Imperf.*

The stamps of this issue were at first printed on a rough hand-made paper, varying in thickness and having a watermark in script letters K.K.H.M., the initials of Kaiserlich Königliches Handels-Ministerium (Imperial and Royal Ministry of Commerce), vertically in the gutter between the panes. Parts of these letters show on margin stamps in the sheet. From 1854 a thick, smooth machine-made paper without watermark was used.

Thin to Thick Paper

1	A1	1kr yellow	650.00	55.00
a.		Printed on both sides	*1,450.*	130.00
b.		1kr orange	1,050.	60.00
c.		1kr brown orange	1,900.	300.00
2	A1	2kr black	525.00	45.00
a.		Ribbed paper		*1,350.*
b.		2kr gray black	1,000.	50.00
3	A1	3kr red	275.00	2.00
a.		Ribbed paper	*1,500.*	45.00
b.		Laid paper		*7,500.*
c.		Printed on both sides		*7,500.*
4	A1	6kr brown	300.00	2.75
a.		Ribbed paper		*1,150.*
5	A1	9kr blue, type II	650.00	2.25
a.		9kr blue, type I	*1,150.*	7.00
b.		9kr blue, type IA		*1,000.*
c.		Laid paper, type III		*6,250.*
d.		Printed on both sides, type II		*7,500.*

1854 Machine-made Paper, Type III

1d	A1	1kr yellow	*800.00*	40.00
2c	A1	2kr black	*675.00*	37.50
3e	A1	3kr red	*250.00*	2.00
f.		3kr red, type I	*1,750.*	10.00
4b	A1	6kr brown	*325.00*	2.25
5e	A1	9kr blue	*500.00*	2.25

In 1852-54, Nos. 1 to 5, rouletted 14, were used in Tokay and Homonna. A 12kr blue exists, but was not issued.

The reprints are type III in brighter colors, some on paper watermarked "Briefmarken" in the sheet.

For similar design see Lombardy-Venetia A1.

Emperor Franz Josef

A2 A3 A4

A5

A6

1858-59 Embossed *Perf. 14½*

Two Types of Each Value.

Type I. Loops of the bow at the back of the head broken, except the 2kr. In the 2kr, the "2" has a flat foot, thinning to the right. The frame line in the UR corner is thicker than the line below. In the 5kr the top frame line is unbroken.

Type II. Loops complete. Wreath projects further at top of head. In the 2kr, the "2" has a more curved foot of uniform thickness, with a shading line in the upper and lower curves. The frame line UR is thicker than the line below. In the 5kr the top frame line is broken.

6	A2	2kr yellow, type II	450.00	16.00
a.		2kr yellow, type I	900.00	350.00
b.		2kr orange, type II	900.00	200.00
7	A3	3kr black, type II	*1,350.*	100.00
a.		3kr black, type I	450.00	140.00
8	A3	3kr green, type II ('59)	375.00	62.50
9	A4	5kr red, type II	125.00	50
a.		5kr red, type I	150.00	5.75
b.		5kr red, type II with type I frame	200.00	12.50
10	A5	10kr brown, type II	300.00	1.40
a.		10kr brown, type I	300.00	12.50
11	A6	15kr blue, type II	250.00	1.00
a.		Type I	550.00	7.50

The reprints are of type II and are perforated 10½, 11, 12, 12½ and 13. There are also imperforate reprints of Nos. 6 to 8.

For similar designs see Lombardy-Venetia A2-A6.

Franz Josef — A7

Coat of Arms — A8

1860-61 Embossed *Perf. 14*

12	A7	2kr yellow	225.00	16.00
13	A7	3kr green	200.00	12.00
14	A7	5kr red	150.00	52
15	A7	10kr brown	175.00	1.10
16	A7	15kr blue	145.00	65

The reprints are perforated 9, 9½, 10, 10½, 11, 11½, 12, 12½, 13 and 13½. There are also imperforate reprints of the 2 and 3kr.

For similar design see Lombardy-Venetia A7.

1863

17	A8	2kr yellow	325.00	55.00
18	A8	3kr green	225.00	50.00
19	A8	5kr rose	140.00	3.75
20	A8	10kr blue	475.00	4.50
21	A8	15kr yellow brown	550.00	5.50

For similar design see Lombardy-Venetia A1.

Wmk. 91, or, before July 1864, Unwmkd.

1863-64 *Perf. 9½*

22	A8	2kr yellow ('64)	75.00	6.00
23	A8	3kr green ('64)	75.00	5.50
24	A8	5kr rose	30.00	15
25	A8	10kr blue	70.00	1.40
26	A8	15kr yellow brown	75.00	85
		Nos. 22-26 (5)	325.00	13.90

The reprints are perforated 10½, 11½, 13 and 13½. There are also imperforate reprints of the 2 and 3kr.

Issues of Austro-Hungarian Monarchy

From 1867 to 1871 the independent postal administrations of Austria and Hungary used the same stamps.

A9

A10

5 kr:

Type I. In arabesques in lower left corner, the small ornament at left of the curve nearest the figure "5" is short and has three points at bottom.

Type II. The ornament is prolonged within the curve and has two points at bottom. The corresponding ornament at top of the lower left corner does not touch the curve (1872).

Type III. Similar to type II but the top ornament is joined to the curve (1881). Two different printing methods were used for the 1867-74 issues. The first produced stamps on which the hair and whiskers were coarse and thick, from the second they were fine and clear.

1867-72 Wmk. 91 Typo. *Perf. 9½*

Coarse Print

27	A9	2kr yellow	85.00	1.25
28	A9	3kr green	80.00	1.10
29	A9	5kr rose, type I	47.50	15
a.		5kr rose, type II	45.00	15
b.		Perf. 10½, type II	85.00	
c.		Cliché of 3kr in plate of 5kr		*25,000.*
30	A9	10kr blue	90.00	1.00
31	A9	15kr brown	95.00	2.75
32	A9	25kr lilac	14.00	9.25
a.		25kr gray lilac	14.00	9.25
b.		25kr brown violet	65.00	21.00

Perf. 12

33	A10	50kr light brown	20.00	*42.50*
a.		50kr pale red brown	85.00	52.50
b.		50kr brownish rose	275.00	95.00
c.		Pair, imperf. btwn., vert. or horizontal	350.00	*825.00*

Issues for Austria only

1874-80 *Perf. 9½*

Fine Print

34	A9	2kr yellow ('76)	7.00	50
35	A9	3kr green ('76)	22.50	50
36	A9	5kr rose, type III	2.50	15
37	A9	10kr blue ('75)	50.00	15
38	A9	15kr brown ('77)	4.75	2.00
39	A9	25kr gray lil ('78)	1.25	*40.00*

Perf. 9

34a	A9	2kr	100.00	11.00
35a	A9	3kr	95.00	10.00
36a	A9	5kr	45.00	1.75
37a	A9	10kr	180.00	11.00
38a	A9	15kr	225.00	35.00

Perf. 10½

34b	A9	2kr	27.50	2.00
35b	A9	3kr	27.50	1.25
36b	A9	5kr	6.50	38
37b	A9	10kr	47.50	1.25
38b	A9	15kr	115.00	10.00

Perf. 12

34c	A9	2kr	150.00	42.50
35c	A9	3kr	115.00	4.50
36c	A9	5kr	35.00	1.25
37c	A9	10kr	225.00	50.00
38c	A9	15kr	350.00	55.00
40	A10	50kr brown ('80)	8.00	*32.50*
b.		perf. 10½x12	210.00	

Perf. 13

34d	A9	2kr	115.00	75.00
35d	A9	3kr	90.00	11.00
36d	A9	5kr	55.00	5.00
37d	A9	10kr	115.00	40.00
38d	A9	15kr	210.00	100.00
40a	A10	50kr	9.00	*37.50*

Various compound perforations exist.

For similar designs see Offices in the Turkish Empire A1-A2.

A11

Perf. 9, 9½, 10, 10½, 11½, 12, 12½

1883

Inscriptions in Black

41	A11	2kr brown	3.50	25
42	A11	3kr green	3.75	18
43	A11	5kr rose	6.50	15
a.		Vert. pair, imperf. btwn.	200.00	275.00
44	A11	10kr blue	4.00	20
45	A11	20kr gray	40.00	3.00
46	A11	50kr red lilac	200.00	35.00

The last printings of Nos. 41 to 46 are watermarked "ZEITUNGS-MARKEN" instead of "BRIEF-MARKEN."

The 5kr has been reprinted in a dull red rose, perforated 10½.

For similar design see Offices in the Turkish Empire A3.

For surcharges see Offices in the Turkish Empire Nos. 15-19.

A12

A13

Perf. 9 to 13½, also Compound

1890-96 **Unwmk.**

Granite Paper

Numerals in black, Nos. 51 to 61

51	A12	1kr dark gray	1.25	15
a.		Pair, imperf. between	180.00	300.00
52	A12	2kr light brown	22	15
53	A12	3kr gray green	28	15
a.		Pair, imperf. between	195.00	300.00
54	A12	5kr rose	22	15
a.		Pair, imperf. between	180.00	240.00
55	A12	10kr ultramarine	40	15
a.		Pair, imperf. between	225.00	325.00
56	A12	12kr claret	1.50	15
57	A12	15kr lilac	1.00	15
a.		Pair, imperf. between	225.00	325.00
58	A12	20kr olive green	20.00	1.25
59	A12	24kr gray blue	2.00	42
a.		Pair, imperf. between	240.00	325.00
60	A12	30kr dark brown	1.75	20
61	A12	50kr violet	7.25	3.75

Engr.

62	A13	1gld dark blue	1.25	1.40
63	A13	1gld pale lilac ('96)	32.50	1.90
64	A13	2gld carmine	3.00	5.00
65	A13	2gld gray green ('96)	17.50	15.00
		Nos. 51-65 (15)	90.12	29.97

Nearly all values of the 1890-1907 issues are found with numerals missing in one or more corners, some with numerals printed on the back.

For surcharges see Offices in the Turkish Empire Nos. 20-25, 28-31.

A14

Perf. 9 to 13½, also Compound

1891 **Typo.**

Numerals in black

66	A14	20kr olive green	1.25	15
67	A14	24kr gray blue	2.25	30
68	A14	30kr brown	1.25	15
a.		Pair, imperf. between	250.00	350.00
b.		Perf. 9	100.00	20.00
69	A14	50kr violet	1.75	18
		Nos. 66-69 (4)	6.50	
		Set value		60

For surcharges see Offices in the Turkish Empire Nos. 26-27.

A15

A16

A17

A18

Perf. 10½ to 13½ and Compound

1899

Without Varnish Bars

Numerals in black, Nos. 70-82

70	A15	1h lilac	60	15
b.		Imperf.	55.00	75.00
c.		Perf. 10½	12.00	3.25
d.		Numerals inverted	375.00	500.00
71	A15	2h dark gray	2.00	25
72	A15	3h bister brown	2.75	15
b.		"3" in lower right corner sideways		*825.00*
73	A15	5h blue green	7.00	15
c.		Perf. 10½	10.50	3.00
74	A15	6h orange	32	15
75	A16	10h rose	4.50	15
b.		Perf. 10½	240.00	65.00
76	A16	20h brown	55	15
77	A16	25h ultramarine	47.50	15
78	A16	30h red violet	16.00	1.65
b.		Horiz. pair, imperf. btwn.	275.00	
80	A17	40h green	26.00	1.65
81	A17	50h gray blue	17.50	2.25
b.		All four "50's" parallel		*1,150.*
82	A17	60h brown	32.50	65
b.		Horiz. pair, imperf. btwn.	275.00	
c.		Perf. 10½	40.00	75

Engr.

83	A18	1k carmine rose	1.65	15
a.		1k carmine	4.50	15
b.		Vert. pair, imperf. btwn.	275.00	300.00
84	A18	2k gray lilac	40.00	25
a.		Vert. pair, imperf. btwn.	300.00	400.00
85	A18	4k gray green	4.00	3.50
		Nos. 70-85 (15)	202.87	11.40

For surcharges see Offices in Crete Nos. 1-7, Offices in the Turkish Empire Nos. 32-45.

1901 **With Varnish Bars**

70a	A15	1h lilac	1.10	18
71a	A15	2h dark gray	1.10	15
72a	A15	3h bister brown	35	15
73a	A15	5h blue green	20	15
74a	A15	6h orange	20	15
75a	A16	10h rose	24	15
76a	A16	20h brown	75	15
77a	A16	25h ultra	85	15
78a	A16	30h red violet	85	55
79	A17	35h green	85	15
80a	A17	40h green	1.65	2.75
81a	A17	50h gray blue	4.00	4.00
82a	A17	60h brown	2.00	32
		Nos. 70a-78a,79,80a-82a (13)	14.14	9.00

The diagonal yellow bars of varnish were printed across the face to prevent cleaning.

A19

A20

A21

Perf. 12½ to 13½ and Compound

1905-07 **Typo.**

Colored Numerals

Without Varnish Bars

86	A19	1h lilac	15	15
87	A19	2h dark gray	15	15
88	A19	3h bister brown	15	15
89	A19	5h dk blue green	7.50	15
90	A19	5h yellow grn ('06)	28	15
91	A19	6h deep orange	28	15
92	A20	10h carmine ('06)	40	15
93	A20	12h violet ('07)	80	28
94	A20	20h brown ('06)	1.65	15
95	A20	25h ultra ('06)	2.50	18
96	A20	30h red violet ('06)	4.50	15

Black Numerals

97	A20	10h carmine	5.50	15
98	A20	20h brown	30.00	70
99	A20	25h ultra	30.00	1.65
100	A20	30h red violet	30.00	1.65

White Numerals

101	A21	35h green	1.75	18
102	A21	40h deep violet	1.75	55
103	A21	50h dull blue	2.25	2.50
104	A21	60h yellow brown	2.25	28
105	A21	72h rose	2.25	95
		Nos. 86-105 (20)	124.11	10.42

For surcharges see Offices in Crete #8-14.

1904

With Varnish Bars

86a	A19	1h lilac	40	30
87a	A19	2h dark gray	1.50	30
88a	A19	3h bister brown	1.50	15
89a	A19	5h dk blue green	3.50	15
91a	A19	6h deep orange	5.50	22
97a	A20	10h carmine	2.00	15
98a	A20	20h brown	27.50	40
99a	A20	25h ultra	32.50	40
100a	A20	30h red violet	35.00	75
101a	A21	35h green	30.00	32
102a	A21	40h deep violet	27.50	2.75
103a	A21	50h dull blue	27.50	4.00
104a	A21	60h yellow brown	27.50	70
105a	A21	72h rose	80	50
		Nos. 86a-105a (14)	222.70	11.09

Stamps of the 1901, 1904 and 1905 issues perf. 9 or 10½, also compound with 12½, were not sold at any post office, but were supplied only to some high-ranking officials. This applies also to the contemporary issues of Austrian Offices Abroad.

Karl VI — A22

Franz Josef — A23

Schönbrunn Castle — A24

Franz Josef — A25

Designs: 2h, Maria Theresa. 3h, Joseph II. 5h, 10h, 25h, Franz Josef. 6h, Leopold II. 12h, Franz I. 20h, Ferdinand I. 30h, Franz Josef as youth. 35h, Franz Josef in middle age. 60h, Franz Josef on horseback. 1k, Franz Josef in royal robes. 5k, Hofburg, Vienna.

1908-13 **Typo.** ***Perf. 12½***

110	A22	1h gray black	30	15
111	A22	2h blue violet ('13)	22	15
a.		2h violet	28	15
112	A22	3h magenta	15	15
113	A22	5h yellow green	15	15
a.		Booklet pane of 6	20.00	
114	A22	6h buff	55	35
b.		6h orange brown ('13)	95	90
115	A22	10h rose	15	15
a.		Booklet pane of 6	70.00	
116	A22	12h scarlet	1.10	25
117	A22	20h chocolate	1.65	15
118	A22	25h ultra ('13)	1.00	15
a.		25h deep blue	1.65	20
119	A22	30h olive green	3.25	20
120	A22	35h slate	2.50	20

Engr.

121	A23	50h dark green	55	20
a.		Pair, imperf. btwn., vert. or horiz.	210.00	225.00
122	A23	60h deep carmine	30	15
a.		Pair, imperf. btwn., vert. or horiz.	300.00	325.00
123	A23	72h dk brown ('13)	1.40	20
124	A23	1k purple	10.00	20
a.		Pair, imperf. btwn., vert. or horiz.	210.00	225.00
125	A24	2k lake & olive grn	14.00	30
126	A24	5k bister & dk vio	25.00	3.00
127	A25	10k blue, bis & dp brn	140.00	42.50
		Nos. 110-127 (18)	202.27	48.60

Definitive set issued for the 60th year of the reign of Emperor Franz Josef.

The 1h-35h exist on both ordinary (1913) and chalk-surfaced (1908) paper.

All values exist imperforate. They were not sold at any post office, but presented to a number of high government officials. This applies also to all imperforate stamps of later issues, including semi-postals, etc., and those of the Austrian Offices Abroad.

Litho. forgeries of No. 127 exist.

For overprint and surcharge see #J47-J48. For similar designs see Offices in Crete A5-A6, Offices in the Turkish Empire A16-A17.

Birthday Jubilee Issue

Similar to 1908 Issue, but designs enlarged by labels at top and bottom bearing dates "1830" and "1910"

1910 **Typo.**

128	A22	1h gray black	3.25	3.50
129	A22	2h violet	4.25	5.25
130	A22	3h magenta	4.25	5.25
131	A22	5h yellow green	15	15
132	A22	6h buff	1.75	1.75
133	A22	10h rose	15	15
134	A22	12h scarlet	2.50	2.75
135	A22	20h chocolate	3.25	4.25
136	A22	25h deep blue	70	85
137	A22	30h olive green	3.25	4.25
138	A22	35h slate	3.25	4.25

Engr.

139	A23	50h dark green	3.75	5.25
140	A23	60h deep carmine	3.75	5.25
141	A23	1k purple	3.75	7.00
142	A24	2k lake & ol grn	100.00	125.00
143	A24	5k bister & dk vio	77.50	140.00
144	A25	10k blue, bis & dp brn	150.00	200.00
		Nos. 128-144 (17)	365.50	514.90

80th birthday of Emperor Franz Josef.
All values exist imperforate.
Litho. forgeries of Nos. 142 to 144 exist.

Austrian Crown — A37

Franz Josef — A38

Coat of Arms
A39 A40

1916-18 **Typo.**

145	A37	3h brt violet	15	15
146	A37	5h lt green	15	15
a.		Booklet pane of 6	14.00	
b.		Booklet pane of 4 + 2 labels	25.00	
147	A37	6h deep orange	20	35
148	A37	10h magenta	15	15
a.		Booklet pane of 6	25.00	
149	A37	12h light blue	28	85
150	A38	15h rose red	35	15
a.		Booklet pane of 6	14.00	
151	A38	20h chocolate	3.50	15
152	A38	25h blue	5.00	38
153	A38	30h slate	4.50	55
154	A39	40h olive green	15	15
155	A39	50h blue green	24	15
156	A39	60h deep blue	15	15
157	A39	80h orange brown	15	15
158	A39	90h red violet	15	15
159	A39	1k car, *yel* ('18)	28	15

Engr.

160	A40	2k dark blue	38	15
161	A40	3k claret	4.50	70
162	A40	4k deep green	85	1.40
163	A40	10k deep violet	15.00	27.50
		Nos. 145-163 (19)	36.13	33.53

Stamps of type A38 have two varieties of the frame. Stamps of type A40 have various decorations about the shield.

Nos. 145-163 exist imperf. Value, set $400.

1917 **Ordinary Paper**

164	A40	2k light blue	60	35
165	A40	3k carmine rose	7.50	60
166	A40	4k yellow green	95	95
167	A40	10k violet	85.00	42.50
		Nos. 164-167 (4)	94.05	44.40

Nos. 164-167 exist imperf. Value, set $250.

See Nos. 172-175 (granite paper). For overprints and surcharges see Nos. 181-199, C1-C3, J60-J63, N1-N5, N10-N19, N33-N37, N42-N51. Western Ukraine 2-7, 11-15, 19-28, 57-58, 85-89, 94-103, N3-N14, NJ13.

Emperor Karl I — A42

1917-18 **Typo.**

168	A42	15h dull red	15	15
a.		Booklet pane of 6	14.00	
169	A42	20h dk green ('18)	15	15
a.		20h green ('17)	40	15
170	A42	25h blue	15	15
171	A42	30h dull violet	15	15
		Set value	34	20

Nos. 168-171 exist imperf. Value, set $40.

For overprints and surcharges see Nos. N6-N9, N20, N38-N41, N52, N64. Western Ukraine 1, 8, 16-18, 90-93, N15-N18.

1918-19 **Engr.**

Granite Paper

172	A40	2k light blue	15	38
a.		Perf. 11½	425.00	350.00
173	A40	3k carmine rose	18	90
174	A40	4k yellow green ('19)	3.00	8.25
175	A40	10k lt violet ('19)	3.50	7.00
		Nos. 172-175 (4)	6.83	16.53

Issues of the Republic

Austrian Stamps of 1916-18 Overprinted

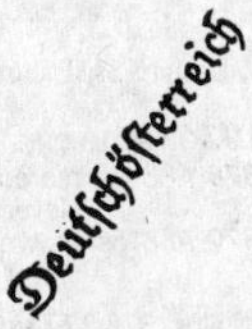

1918-19 **Unwmk.** ***Perf. 12½***

181	A37	3h bright violet	15	15
182	A37	5h light green	15	15
183	A37	6h deep orange	15	18
184	A37	10h magenta	15	15
185	A37	12h light blue	15	32
186	A42	15h dull red	15	32
187	A42	20h deep green	15	15
188	A42	25h blue	15	15
189	A42	30h dull violet	15	15
190	A39	40h olive green	15	15
191	A39	50h deep green	28	32
192	A39	60h deep blue	20	32
193	A39	80h orange brown	15	15
a.		Inverted overprint	175.00	175.00
194	A39	90h red violet	15	15
195	A39	1k carmine, *yel*	15	15

Granite Paper

196	A40	2k light blue	15	15
a.		Pair, imperf. between	175.00	175.00
b.		Perf. 11½	10.00	5.00
197	A40	3k carmine rose	15	30
198	A40	4k yellow green	85	1.10
a.		Perf. 11½	14.00	9.50
199	A40	10k deep violet	6.25	7.50
		Nos. 181-199 (19)	9.83	12.01
		Set, never hinged	20.00	

Nos. 181, 182, 184, 187-191, 194, 197 and 199 exist imperforate.

Post Horn — A43

Coat of Arms — A44

Allegory of New Republic — A45

1919-20 **Typo.** ***Perf. 12½***

Ordinary Paper

200	A43	3h gray	15	15
201	A44	5h yellow green	15	15
202	A44	5h gray ('20)	15	15
203	A43	6h orange	15	32
204	A44	10h deep rose	15	15
205	A44	10h red ('20)	15	15
a.		Thick grayish paper ('20)	15	15
206	A43	12h grnsh blue	15	40
207	A43	15h bister ('20)	22	65
a.		Thick grayish paper ('20)	15	15
208	A45	20h dark green	15	15
a.		20h yellow green	15	15
b.		As "a," thick grysh paper ('20)	45	1.25
209	A44	25h blue	15	15
210	A43	25h violet ('20)	15	15
211	A45	30h dark brown	15	15
212	A45	40h violet	15	15
213	A45	40h lake ('20)	15	15
214	A44	45h olive green	18	45
215	A45	50h dark blue	15	15
a.		Thick grayish paper ('20)	15	15
216	A43	60h olive green ('20)	15	15
217	A44	1k carmine, *yel*	15	15
218	A44	1k light blue ('20)	15	15
		Set value	1.30	2.75
		Set, never hinged	2.40	

All values exist imperf. (For regularly issued imperfs, see Nos. 227-235).

For overprints and surcharge see Nos. B11-B19, B30-B38, J102, N21, N27, N53, N58, N65, N71.

Parliament Building — A46

1919-20 **Engr.** ***Perf. 12½, 11½***

Granite Paper

219	A46	2k vermilion & blk	25	45
a.		Center inverted	*3,250.*	
220	A46	2½k olive bis ('20)	15	20
221	A46	3k blue & blk brn	15	15
222	A46	4k carmine & blk	15	15
a.		Center inverted	*1,600.*	*1,200.*
223	A46	5k black ('20)	15	15
a.		Perf. 11½x12½	45.00	60.00
224	A46	7½k plum	15	32
a.		Perf. 11½	75.00	100.00
b.		Perf. 11½x12½	75.00	125.00
225	A46	10k olive grn & blk brn	20	45
a.		Perf. 11½x12½	100.00	110.00
b.		Perf. 11½	16.00	20.00
226	A46	20k lilac & red ('20)	15	55
a.		Center inverted	*6,500.*	*5,750.*
b.		Perf. 11½	40.00	70.00
		Set value	87	
		Set, never hinged	2.50	

A number of values exist imperforate between. Values, $300 to $400 a pair.

See No. 248. For overprints and surcharge see Nos. B43-B49, N30, N60, N74.

1920 **Typo.** ***Imperf.***

Ordinary Paper

227	A44	5h yellow green	15	30
228	A44	5h gray	15	15
229	A44	10h deep rose	15	15
230	A44	10h red	15	15
231	A43	15h bister	15	15
232	A43	25h violet	15	15
233	A45	30h dark brown	15	15
234	A45	40h violet	15	15
235	A43	60h olive green	15	15
		Set value	48	88
		Set, never hinged	80	

Arms
A47 A48

1920-21 **Typo.** ***Perf. 12½***

Ordinary Paper

238	A47	80h rose	15	15
239	A47	1k black brown	15	15
241	A47	1½k green ('21)	15	15
242	A47	2k blue	15	15
243	A48	3k yel grn & dk grn ('21)	15	15
244	A48	4k red & claret ('21)	15	15
245	A48	5k vio & claret ('21)	15	15
246	A48	7½k yellow & brown ('21)	15	15
247	A48	10k ultra & blue ('21)	15	15
		Set value	48	55
		Set, never hinged	1.65	

Nos. 238-245, 247 exist on white paper of good quality and on thick grayish paper of inferior quality; No. 246 only on white paper.

For overprints and surcharges see Nos. N22-N23, N31, N54-N55, N61-N62, N66-N67.

1921 **Engr.**

248	A46	50k dk violet, *yel*	30	80
a.		Perf. 11½	30.00	47.50
		Never hinged	50	

Symbols of Agriculture
A49

Symbols of Labor and Industry
A50

1922-24 **Typo.** ***Perf. 12½***

250	A49	½k olive bister	15	*32*
251	A50	1k brown	15	15
252	A50	2k cobalt blue	15	15
253	A49	2½k orange brown	15	15
254	A50	4k dull violet	15	*40*
255	A50	5k gray green	15	15
256	A49	7½k gray violet	15	15
257	A50	10k claret	15	15
258	A49	12½k gray green	15	15
259	A49	15k bluish green	15	15
260	A49	20k dark blue	15	15
261	A49	25k claret	15	15
262	A50	30k pale gray	15	15
263	A50	45k pale red	15	15
264	A50	50k orange brown	15	15
265	A50	60k yellow green	15	15
266	A50	75k ultramarine	15	15
267	A50	80k yellow	15	15
268	A49	100k gray	15	15
269	A49	120k brown	15	15
270	A49	150k orange	15	15
271	A49	160k light green	15	15
272	A49	180k red	15	15
273	A49	200k pink	15	15
274	A49	240k dark violet	15	15
275	A49	300k light blue	15	15
276	A49	400k deep green	70	15
a.		400k gray green	70	15
277	A49	500k yellow	15	15
278	A49	600k slate	15	15
279	A49	700k brown ('24)	35	15
280	A49	800k violet ('24)	70	*1.75*
281	A50	1000k violet ('23)	35	15
282	A50	1200k car rose ('23)	15	28
283	A50	1500k orange ('24)	1.00	15
284	A50	1600k slate ('23)	1.50	1.50
285	A50	2000k deep blue ('23)	3.00	28
286	A50	3000k lt blue ('23)	9.75	55
287	A50	4000k dk bl, *bl* ('24)	4.25	1.40
		Nos. 250-287 (38)	25.95	
		Set value		8.90
		Set, never hinged	57.50	

Nos. 250-287 exist imperf. Value, set $500.

For overprints and surcharges see Nos. N24-N26, N28-N29, N32, N56, N59, N63, N68-N70, N72-N73.

Symbols of Art and Science — A51

1922-24 Engr. *Perf. 12½*

288	A51	20k	dark brown	15	15
a.			Perf. 11½	1.10	1.25
a.			Never hinged	1.65	
289	A51	25k	blue	15	15
a.			Perf. 11½	1.10	1.25
a.			Never hinged	1.65	
290	A51	50k	brown red	15	15
a.			Perf. 11½	2.50	3.50
a.			Never hinged	4.25	
291	A51	100k	deep green	15	15
a.			Perf. 11½	6.00	7.00
a.			Never hinged	9.00	
292	A51	200k	dark violet	15	15
a.			Perf. 11½	9.00	15.00
a.			Never hinged	12.00	
293	A51	500k	dp orange	15	1.00
294	A51	1000k	blk vio, *yel*	15	15
a.			Perf. 11½	125.00	190.00
a.			Never hinged	325.00	
295	A51	2000k	olive grn, *yel*	15	15
296	A51	3000k	claret brn ('23)	7.00	35
297	A51	5000k	gray black ('23)	1.75	95

Granite Paper

298	A51	10,000k	red brown ('24)	2.50	2.50
			Nos. 288-298 (11)	12.45	5.85
			Set, never hinged	27.50	

On Nos. 281-287, 291-298 "kronen" is abbreviated to "k" and transposed with the numerals.
Nos. 288-298 exist imperf. Value, set $300.

Numeral A52

Fields Crossed by Telegraph Wires A53

White-Shouldered Eagle — A54

Church of Minorite Friars — A55

1925-27 Typo. *Perf. 12*

303	A52	1g	dark gray	15	15
304	A52	2g	claret	18	15
305	A52	3g	scarlet	28	15
306	A52	4g	grnsh blue ('27)	70	15
307	A52	5g	brown orange	1.40	15
308	A52	6g	ultramarine	85	15
309	A52	7g	chocolate	1.50	15
310	A52	8g	yellow green	6.25	15
311	A53	10g	orange	15	15
313	A53	15g	red lilac	15	15
314	A53	16g	dark blue	15	15
315	A53	18g	olive green	90	18
316	A54	20g	dark violet	28	15
317	A54	24g	carmine	40	18
318	A54	30g	dark brown	35	15
319	A54	40g	ultramarine	50	15
320	A54	45g	yellow brown	70	15
321	A54	50g	gray	85	15
322	A54	80g	turquoise blue	3.00	2.00

Perf. 12½

Engr.

323	A55	1s	deep green	14.00	18
a.			1s light green	125.00	1.25
324	A55	2s	brown rose	6.25	5.00
			Nos. 303-324 (21)	38.99	
			Set value		8.35
			Set, never hinged	120.00	

Nos. 303-305 and 307-324 exist imperf. Value, set $275.
For type A52 surcharged see Nos. B118.

Güssing — A56

National Library, Vienna — A57

Designs: 15g, Hochosterwitz. 16g, 20g, Durnstein. 18g, Traunsee. 24g, Salzburg. 30g, Seewiesen. 40g, Innsbruck. 50g, Worthersee. 60g, Hohenems. 2s, St. Stephen's Cathedral, Vienna.

1929-30 Typo. *Perf. 12½*

Size: 25½x21½mm

326	A56	10g	brown orange	65	15
327	A56	10g	bister ('30)	65	15
328	A56	15g	violet brown	45	*75*
329	A56	16g	dark gray	15	15
330	A56	18g	blue green	32	28
331	A56	20g	dark gray ('30)	32	15
332	A56	24g	maroon	3.25	3.75
333	A56	24g	lake ('30)	5.75	28
334	A56	30g	dark violet	3.25	15
335	A56	40g	dark blue	6.25	15
336	A56	50g	gray violet ('30)	24.00	15
337	A56	60g	olive green	18.00	16

Engr.

Size: 21x26mm

338	A57	1s	black brown	4.00	15
339	A57	2s	dark green	7.25	4.00
			Nos. 326-339 (14)	74.29	10.42
			Set, never hinged	275.00	

Type of 1929-30 Issue

Designs: 12g, Traunsee. 64g, Hohenems.

1932 *Perf. 12*

Size: 21x16½mm

340	A56	10g	olive brown	65	15
341	A56	12g	blue green	1.10	15
342	A56	18g	blue green	52	*1.75*
343	A56	20g	dark gray	85	15
344	A56	24g	carmine rose	4.00	15
345	A56	24g	dull violet	3.25	15
346	A56	30g	dark violet	13.00	15
347	A56	30g	carmine rose	3.00	15
348	A56	40g	dark blue	15.00	55
349	A56	40g	dark violet	4.50	18
350	A56	50g	gray violet	17.50	18
351	A56	50g	dull blue	5.00	18
352	A56	60g	gray green	37.50	1.40
353	A56	64g	gray green	6.00	15
			Nos. 340-353 (14)	111.87	
			Set value		*4.75*
			Set, never hinged	440.00	

For overprints and surcharges see Nos. B87-B92, B119-B121.

Burgenland A67

Tyrol A68

Designs (costumes of various districts): 3g, Burgenland. 4g, 5g, Carinthia. 6g, 8g, Lower Austria. 12g, 20g, Upper Austria. 24g, 25g, Salzburg. 30g, 35g, Styria. 45g, Tyrol. 60g, Vorarlberg bridal couple. 64g, Vorarlberg. 1s, Viennese family. 2s, Military.

1934-35 Typo. *Perf. 12*

354	A67	1g	dark violet	15	15
355	A67	3g	scarlet	15	15
356	A67	4g	olive green	15	15
357	A67	5g	red violet	15	15
358	A67	6g	ultramarine	16	15
359	A67	8g	green	15	15
360	A67	12g	dark brown	15	15
361	A67	20g	yellow brown	15	15
362	A67	24g	grnsh blue	15	15
363	A67	25g	violet	16	15
364	A67	30g	maroon	15	15
365	A67	35g	rose carmine	30	24

Perf. 12½

366	A68	40g	slate gray	35	15
367	A68	45g	brown red	30	15
368	A68	60g	ultramarine	55	15
369	A68	64g	brown	65	15
370	A68	1s	deep violet	60	25
371	A68	2s	dull green	32.50	42.50

Designs Redrawn

Perf. 12 (6g), 12½ (2s)

372	A67	6g	ultra ('35)	15	15
373	A68	2s	emerald ('35)	2.25	3.75
			Nos. 354-373 (20)	39.32	49.14
			Set, never hinged	75.00	

The design of No. 358 looks as though the man's ears were on backwards, while No. 372 appears correctly.
On No. 373 there are seven feathers on each side of the eagle instead of five.
Nos. 354-373 exist imperf. Value, set $375.
For surcharges see Nos. B128-B131.

Dollfuss Mourning Issue

Engelbert Dollfuss — A85

1934-35 Engr. *Perf. 12½*

374	A85	24g	greenish black	40	20
			Never hinged	70	
375	A85	24g	indigo ('35)	70	55
			Never hinged	1.25	

"Mother and Child," by Joseph Danhauser — A86

"Madonna and Child," after Painting by Dürer — A87

1935, May 1

376	A86	24g	dark blue	40	16
			Never hinged	70	

Mother's Day. Nos. 376-377 exist imperf. Value, each $165.

1936, May 5 Photo.

377	A87	24g	violet blue	15	20
			Never hinged	30	

Mother's Day.

Farm Workers — A88

Design: 5s, Factory workers.

1936, June Engr. *Perf. 12½*

378	A88	3s	red orange	11.00	14.00
			Never hinged	20.00	
379	A88	5s	brown black	22.50	37.50
			Never hinged	35.00	

Nos. 378-379 exist imperf. Value, set $250.

Engelbert Dollfuss — A90

Mother and Child — A91

1936, July 25

380	A90	10s	dark blue	575.00	675.00
			Never hinged	775.00	

Second anniv. of death of Engelbert Dollfuss, chancellor. Exists imperf. Value, $1,750.

1937, May 5 Photo. *Perf. 12*

381	A91	24g	henna brown	20	15
			Never hinged	40	

Mother's Day. Exists imperf. Value, $175.

S.S. Maria Anna — A92

Steamships: 24g, Uranus, 64g, Oesterreich.

1937, June 9

382	A92	12g	red brown	45	18
383	A92	24g	deep blue	45	18
384	A92	64g	dark green	45	60
			Nos. 382-384 (3)	1.35	96
			Set, never hinged	3.00	

Cent. of steamship service on Danube River. Exist imperf. Value, set $135.

First Locomotive, "Austria" — A95

Designs: 25g, Modern steam locomotive. 35g, Modern electric train.

1937, Nov. 22

385	A95	12g	black brown	15	15
386	A95	25g	dark violet	30	60
387	A95	35g	brown red	75	90
			Nos. 385-387 (3)	1.20	1.65
			Set, never hinged	3.25	

Centenary of Austrian railways. Exist imperf. Value, set $135.

Rose and Zodiac Signs — A98

1937 Engr. *Perf. 13x12½*

388	A98	12g	dark green	15	15
389	A98	24g	dark carmine	15	15
			Set value	20	24
			Set, never hinged	30	

For Use in Vienna, Lower Austria and Burgenland

Germany Nos. 509-511 and 511B Overprinted in Black

a

b

1945 Unwmk. *Perf. 14*

390	A115(a)	5pf	dp yellow green	15	15
391	A115(b)	6pf	purple	15	15
392	A115(a)	8pf	red	15	15
393	A115(b)	12pf	carmine	15	15
			Set value	22	42
			Set, never hinged	30	

Nos. 390-393 exist with overprint inverted or double.
Germany No. 507, the 3pf, with overprint "a" was prepared, not issued, but sold to collectors after the definitive Republic issue had been placed in use. Value $30, hinged, $60, never hinged.

German Semi-Postal Stamps, #B207, B209, B210, B283 Surcharged in Black

c

d 

1945 *Perf. 14, 14x13½, 13½x14*

394	SP181(c)	5pf on 12pf + 88pf	40	90
395	SP184(d)	6pf on 6pf + 14pf	2.25	5.50
396	SP242(d)	8pf on 42pf + 108pf	40	90
397	SP183(d)	12pf on 3pf + 7pf	40	90
		Nos. 394-397 (4)	3.45	8.20
		Set, never hinged	8.00	

The surcharges are spaced to fit the stamps.

Stamps of Germany, Nos. 509 to 511, 511B, 519 and 529 Overprinted

e

f

1945 **Typo.** *Perf. 14*

Size: 18½x22½mm

398	A115(e)	5pf dp yellow green	22	*42*
399	A115(f)	5pf dp yellow green	4.00	*7.75*
400	A115(e)	6pf purple	15	*28*
401	A115(e)	8pf red	15	*28*
402	A115(e)	12pf carmine	20	*35*

Engr.

Size: 21½x26mm

403	A115(e)	30pf olive green	3.25	*6.50*
a.		Thin bar at bottom	12.00	*15.00*
a.		Never hinged	19.00	
404	A118(e)	42pf brt green	12.00	*24.00*
a.		Thin bar at bottom	12.00	16.00
a.		Never hinged	19.00	
		Nos. 398-404 (7)	19.97	*39.58*
		Set, never hinged	52.50	

On Nos. 403a and 404a, the bottom bar of the overprint is 2½mm wide, and, as the overprint was applied in two operations, "Osterreich" is usually not exactly centered in its diagonal slot. On Nos. 403 and 404, the bottom bar is 3mm wide, and "Osterreich" is always well centered.

Germany Nos. 524-527 (the 1m, 2m, 3m and 5m), overprinted with vertical bars and "Osterreich" similar to "e" and "f," were prepared, not issued, but sold to collectors after the definitive Republic issue had been placed in use. Value for set, $70 hinged, $150 ever hinged.

Counterfeits exist of Nos. 403-404, 403a-404a and 1m-5m overprints.

For Use in Styria

Stamps of Germany Nos. 506 to 511, 511A, 511B, 514 to 523 and 529 Overprinted in Black

1945 **Unwmk.** **Typo.** *Perf. 14*

Size: 18½x22½mm

405	A115	1pf gray black	1.40	3.00
406	A115	3pf lt brown	1.40	3.00
407	A115	4pf slate	4.75	10.00
408	A115	5pf dp yellow grn	1.00	2.00
409	A115	6pf purple	15	30
410	A115	8pf red	75	1.65
411	A115	10pf dark brown	1.40	3.25
412	A115	12pf carmine	15	30

Engr.

413	A115	15pf brown lake	75	1.75
414	A115	16pf pck green	8.75	18.00
415	A115	20pf blue	2.25	5.25
416	A115	24pf orange brown	8.75	18.00

Size: 22½x26mm

417	A115	25pf brt ultra	1.00	2.75
418	A115	30pf olive green	1.00	2.00
419	A115	40pf brt red violet	1.25	2.25
420	A118	42pf brt green	1.40	3.50
421	A115	50pf myrtle green	1.40	3.50
422	A115	60pf dk red brown	2.25	4.75
423	A115	80pf indigo	1.75	3.75
		Nos. 405-423 (19)	41.55	89.00
		Set, never hinged	82.50	

Overprinted on Nos. 524-527

Perf. 12½, 14

424	A116	1m dk slate grn	7.25	*20.00*
a.		Perf. 12½	100.00	
425	A116	2m violet	6.25	*20.00*
a.		Perf. 14	12.00	*45.00*
426	A116	3m copper red	15.00	*47.50*
a.		Perf. 14	125.00	
427	A116	5m dark blue	160.00	*500.00*
a.		Perf. 14	*575.00*	
		Nos. 424-427 (4)	188.50	
		Set, never hinged	400.00	

On the preceding four stamps the innermost vertical lines are 10½mm apart; on the pfennig values 6½mm apart.

Counterfeits exist of Nos. 405-427 overprints.

Germany Nos. 524 to 527 Overprinted in Black

Perf. 14

428	A116	1m dk slate grn	8.25	*18.00*
429	A116	2m violet	8.25	*20.00*

Perf. 12½

430	A116	3m copper red	17.00	*37.50*
431	A116	5m dark blue	115.00	*265.00*
a.		Perf. 14	*600.00*	
		Nos. 428-431 (4)	148.50	
		Set, never hinged	300.00	

On the preceding four stamps, "Osterreich" is thinner, measuring 16mm. On the previous set of 23 values it measures 18mm.

Counterfeits exist of Nos. 428-431 overprints.

Catalogue values for unused stamps in this section, from this point to the end of the section, are for Never Hinged items.

For Use in Vienna, Lower Austria and Burgenland

Coat of Arms
A99 A100

Typographed or Lithographed

1945, July 3 **Unwmk.** *Perf. 14x13½*

Size: 21x25mm

432	A99	3pf brown	15	15
433	A99	4pf slate	15	15
434	A99	5pf dark green	15	15
435	A99	6pf deep violet	15	15
436	A99	8pf orange brown	15	15
437	A99	10pf deep brown	15	15
438	A99	12pf rose carmine	15	15
439	A99	15pf orange red	15	15
440	A99	16pf dull blue green	15	32

Perf. 14

Size: 24x28½mm

441	A99	20pf light blue	15	15
442	A99	24pf orange	15	18
443	A99	25pf dark blue	15	15
444	A99	30pf deep gray grn	15	15
445	A99	38pf ultramarine	15	15
446	A99	40pf brt red vio	15	15
447	A99	42pf sage green	15	15
448	A99	50pf blue green	15	*45*
449	A99	60pf maroon	15	15
450	A99	80pf dull lilac	15	15

Engr. *Perf. 14x13½*

451	A100	1m dark green	15	*45*
452	A100	2m dark purple	15	*45*
453	A100	3m dark violet	15	*45*
454	A100	5m brown red	15	*45*
		Set value	1.30	*4.00*

Nos. 432, 433, 437, 439, 440, 443, 446, 448 and 449 are typographed. Nos. 434, 435, 441 and 442 are lithographed; the other values exist both ways.

For overprint see No. 604.

For General Use

Lermoos, Winter Scene — A101

The Prater Woods, Vienna — A105

Hochosterwitz, Carinthia A106

Lake Constance A110

Dürnstein, Lower Austria A124

Designs: 4g, Eisenerz surface mine. 5g, Leopoldsberg, near Vienna. 6g, Hohensalzburg, Salzburg Province. 12g, Wolfgang See, near Salzburg. 15g, Forchtenstein Castle, Burgenland. 16g, Gesäuse Valley. 24g, Höldrichs Mill, Lower Austria. 25g, Oetz Valley Outlet, Tyrol. 30g, Neusiedler Lake, Burgenland. 35g, Belvedere Palace, Vienna. 38g, Langbath Lake. 40g, Mariazell, Styria. 42g, Traunkirchen. 45g, Hartenstein Castle. 50g, Silvretta Mountains, Vorarlberg. 60g, Railroad viaducts near Semmering. 70g, Waterfall of Bad-Gastein, Salzburg. 80g, Kaiser Mountains, Tyrol. 90g, Wayside Shrine, Tragöss, Styria. 2s, St. Christof am Arlberg, Tyrol. 3s, Heiligenblut, Carinthia. 5s, Schönbrunn, Vienna.

Perf. 14x13½

1945-46 **Photo.** **Unwmk.**

455	A101	3g sapphire	15	15
456	A101	4g dp orange ('46)	15	15
457	A101	5g dk carmine rose	15	15
458	A101	6g dk slate green	15	15
459	A105	8g golden brown	15	15
460	A106	10g dark green	15	15
461	A106	12g dark brown	15	15
462	A106	15g dk slate bl ('46)	15	15
463	A106	16g chnt brn ('46)	15	15

Perf. 13½x14

464	A110	20g dp ultra ('46)	15	15
465	A110	24g dp yellow grn ('46)	15	15
466	A110	25g gray black ('46)	15	15
467	A110	30g dark red	15	15
468	A110	35g brown red ('46)	15	15
469	A110	38g brown olive ('46)	15	15
470	A110	40g gray	15	15
471	A110	42g brown orange ('46)	15	15
472	A110	45g dark blue ('46)	15	22
473	A110	50g dark blue	15	15
474	A110	60g dark violet	15	15
a.		Imperf., pair	50.00	60.00
475	A110	70g Prus blue ('46)	15	22
476	A110	80g brown	15	32
477	A110	90g Prussian green	80	85
478	A124	1s dk red brn ('46)	55	55
479	A124	2s blue gray ('46)	2.00	2.00
480	A124	3s dk slate grn ('46)	60	65
481	A124	5s dark red ('46)	1.10	1.25
		Set value	6.25	7.00

See Nos. 486-488, 496-515. For overprints and surcharges see Nos. 492-493, B166, B280, B287.

No. 461 Overprinted in Carmine

1946, Sept. 26

482	A106	12g dark brown	15	20

Meeting of the Soc. for Cultural and Economic Relations with the USSR, Vienna, Sept. 26-29.

City Hall Park, Vienna A128

Hochosterwitz, Carinthia A129

Perf. 14x13½

1946-47 **Photo.** **Unwmk.**

483	A128	8g deep plum	15	15
484	A128	8g olive brown	15	15
a.		8g dark olive green	15	15
485	A129	10g dk brn vio ('47)	15	15

Perf. 13½x14

486	A110	30g blue gray ('47)	15	15
487	A110	50g brown violet ('47)	25	25
488	A110	60g violet blue ('47)	2.00	1.10
		Set value	2.45	1.60

See No. 502.

Franz Grillparzer — A130

Franz Schubert — A131

1947 **Engr.** *Perf. 14x13½*

489	A130	18g chocolate	15	15

Photo.

490	A130	18g dk violet brn	15	15
		Set value	15	18

Death of Franz Grillparzer, dramatic poet, 75th anniv.

A second printing of No. 490 on thicker paper has a darker frame and clearer delineation of the portrait.

Issue dates: #489, Feb. 10; #490, Mar. 31.

1947, Mar. 31 **Engr.**

491	A131	12g dark green	15	15

150th birth anniv. of Franz Schubert, musician and composer.

Nos. 469 and 463 Surcharged in Brown

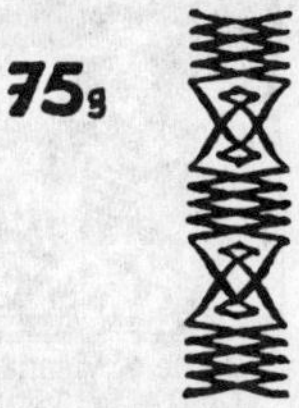

1947, Sept. 1 **Photo.** *Perf. 14*

492	A110	75g on 38g brown ol	20	80
493	A106	1.40s on 16g chnt brn	15	15

The surcharge on No. 493 varies from brown to black brown.

Symbols of Global Telegraphic Communication A132

1947, Nov. 5 Engr. *Perf. 14x13½*
495 A132 40g dark violet 15 15

Centenary of the telegraph in Austria.

Scenic Type of 1946

1946, Aug. Photo. *Perf. 13½x14*
496 A124 1s dark brown 1.25 38
497 A124 2s dark blue 6.50 2.50
498 A124 3s dark slate green 2.00 65
499 A124 5s dark red 32.00 7.75
Nos. 496-499 (4) 41.75 11.28

On Nos. 478 to 481 the upper and lower panels show a screen effect. On Nos. 496 to 499 the panels appear to be solid color.

Scenic Types of 1945-46

1947-48 Photo. *Perf. 14x13½*
500 A101 3g bright red 15 15
501 A101 5g bright red 15 15
502 A129 10g bright red 15 15
503 A106 15g brt red ('48) 1.40 50

Perf. 13½x14
504 A110 20g bright red 45 15
505 A110 30g bright red 70 15
506 A110 40g bright red 70 15
507 A110 50g bright red 95 15
508 A110 60g brt red ('48) 6.00 1.10
509 A110 70g brt red ('48) 3.25 15
510 A110 80g brt red ('48) 3.25 15
511 A110 90g brt red ('48) 3.50 24
512 A124 1s dark violet 70 15
513 A124 2s dark violet 95 15
514 A124 3s dk violet ('48) 8.25 80
515 A124 5s dk violet ('48) 10.00 1.10
Nos. 500-515 (16) 40.55
Set value 4.50

Carl Michael Ziehrer (1843-1922), Composer — A133

Designs: No. 517, Adalbert Stifter (1805-68), novelist. No. 518, Anton Bruckner (1824-96), composer. 60g, Friedrich von Amerling (1803-87), painter.

1948-49 Engr.
516 A133 20g dull green 32 15
517 A133 40g chocolate 5.00 2.50
518 A133 40g dark green 5.00 4.00
519 A133 60g rose brown 65 28
Nos. 516-519 (4) 10.97 6.93

Issue dates: 20g, Jan. 21, No. 517, Sept. 6, No. 518, Sept. 3, 1949, 60g, Jan. 26.

Vorarlberg, Montafon Valley — A134

Costume of Vienna, 1850 — A135

Designs (Austrian Costumes): 3g, Tyrol, Inn Valley. 5g, Salzburg, Pinzgau. 10g, Styria, Salzkammergut. 15g, Burgenland, Lutzmannsburg. 25g, Vienna, 1850. 30g, Salzburg, Pongau. 40g, Vienna, 1840. 45g, Carinthia, Lesach Valley. 50g, Vorarlberg, Bregenzer Forest. 60g, Carinthia, Lavant Valley. 70g, Lower Austria, Wachau. 75g, Styria, Salzkammergut. 80g, Styria, Enns Valley. 90g, Central Styria. 1s, Tyrol, Puster Valley. 1.20s, Lower Austria, Vienna Woods. 1.40s, Upper Austria, Inn District. 1.45s, Wilten. 1.50s, Vienna, 1853. 1.60s, Vienna, 1830. 1.70s, East Tyrol, Kals. 2s, Upper Austria. 2.20s, Ischl, 1820. 2.40s, Kitzbuhel. 2.50s, Upper Steiermark, 1850. 2.70s, Little Walser Valley. 3s, Burgenland. 3.50s, Lower Austria, 1850. 4.50s, Gail Valley. 5s, Ziller Valley. 7s, Steiermark, Sulm Valley.

Perf. 14x13½
1948-52 Unwmk. Photo.
520 A134 3g gray ('50) 60 42
521 A134 5g dark green ('49) 15 15
522 A134 10g deep blue 15 15
523 A134 15g brown 60 15
524 A134 20g yellow green 15 15
525 A134 25g brown ('49) 15 15
526 A134 30g dk car rose 2.50 15
527 A134 30g dk violet ('50) 60 15
528 A134 40g violet 2.50 15
529 A134 40g green ('49) 18 15
530 A134 45g violet blue 2.25 28
531 A134 50g orange brn ('49) 60 15
532 A134 60g scarlet 18 15
533 A134 70g brt blue grn ('49) 18 15
534 A134 75g blue 3.75 28
535 A134 80g carmine rose ('49) 38 15
536 A134 90g brown vio ('49) 22.50 20
537 A134 1s ultramarine 4.00 15
538 A134 1s rose red ('50) 62.50 15
539 A134 1s dk green ('51) 18 15
540 A134 1.20s violet ('49) 38 15
541 A134 1.40s brown 2.50 15
542 A134 1.45s dk carmine ('51) 1.10 15
543 A134 1.50s ultra ('51) 60 15
544 A134 1.60s orange red ('49) 18 15
545 A134 1.70s violet blue ('50) 2.50 55
546 A134 2s blue green 38 15
547 A134 2.20s slate ('52) 4.75 15
548 A134 2.40s blue ('51) 1.00 15
549 A134 2.50s brown ('52) 4.50 15
550 A134 2.70s dk brown ('51) 45 35
551 A134 3s brown car ('49) 1.90 15
552 A134 3.50s dull grn ('51) 9.75 15
553 A134 4.50s brown vio ('51) 60 35
554 A134 5s dark red vio 1.00 15
555 A134 7s olive ('52) 1.50 15

Engr.
556 A135 10s gray ('50) 26.00 3.00
Nos. 520-556 (37) 163.19
Set value 6.25

In 1958-59, 21 denominations of this set were printed on white paper, differing from the previous grayish paper with yellowish gum.

Pres. Karl Renner — A136

1948, Nov. 12 *Perf. 14x13½*
557 A136 1s deep blue 1.90 1.10

Founding of the Austrian Republic, 30th anniv. See Nos. 573, 636.

Franz Gruber and Josef Mohr — A137

1948, Dec. 18 *Perf. 13½x14*
558 A137 60g red brown 4.25 4.00

130th anniv. of the hymn "Silent Night, Holy Night".

Symbolical of Child Welfare — A138

Johann Strauss, the Younger — A139

1949, May 14 Photo. *Perf. 14x13½*
559 A138 1s bright blue 11.50 1.25

1st year of activity of UNICEF in Austria.

1949 Engr.

Designs: 30g, Johann Strauss, the elder. No. 561, Johann Strauss, the younger. No. 562, Karl Millöcker.

560 A139 30g violet brown 2.25 1.65
561 A139 1s dark blue 3.00 1.10
562 A139 1s dark blue 12.00 6.25
Nos. 560-562 (3) 17.25 9.00

Johann Strauss, the elder (1804-49), Johann Strauss, the younger (1825-99), and Karl Millöcker (1842-1899), composers. See #574.

Esperanto Star, Olive Branches — A140

St. Gebhard — A141

1949, June 25 Photo.
563 A140 20g blue green 1.00 50

Austrian Esperanto Congress at Graz.

1949, Aug. 6 Engr.
564 A141 30g dark violet 1.50 1.25

St. Gebhard (949-995), Bishop of Vorarlberg.

Letter, Roses and Post Horn — A142

UPU, 75th Anniv.: 60g, Plaque. 1s, "Austria," wings and monogram.

1949, Oct. 8 *Perf. 13½x14*
565 A142 40g dark green 3.75 1.65
566 A142 60g dk carmine 3.75 1.65
567 A142 1s dk violet blue 6.50 4.75
Nos. 565-567 (3) 14.00 8.05

Moritz Michael Daffinger — A143

Andreas Hofer — A144

Designs: 30g, Alexander Girardi. No. 569, Daffinger. No. 570, Hofer. No. 571, Josef Madersperger.

1950 Unwmk. *Perf. 14x13½*
568 A144 30g dark blue 1.50 85
569 A143 60g red brown 6.00 3.25
570 A144 60g dark violet 10.50 6.50
571 A144 60g purple 4.50 2.25
Nos. 568-571 (4) 22.50 12.85

Alexander Girardi (1850-1918), actor; Moritz Michael Daffinger (1790-1849), painter; Andreas Hofer (1767-1810), patriot; Josef Madersperger (1768-1850), inventor.

Issue dates: 30g, Dec. 5; No. 569, Jan. 25; No. 570, Feb. 20; No. 571, Oct. 2.

Austrian Stamp of 1850 — A146

1950, May 20 *Perf. 14½*
572 A146 1s black, *straw* 1.50 90

Centenary of Austrian postage stamps.

Renner Type of 1948, Frame and Inscriptions Altered

1951, Mar. 3
573 A136 1s black, *straw* 1.40 18

In memory of Pres. Karl Renner, 1870-1950.

Strauss Type of 1949

Portrait: 60g, Joseph Lanner.

1951, Apr. 12
574 A139 60g dk blue green 3.50 1.10

150th birth anniv. of Joseph Lanner, composer.

Martin Johann Schmidt — A147

Boy Scout Emblem — A148

1951, June 28 Engr. *Perf. 14x13½*
575 A147 1sh brown red 4.50 2.00

150th death anniv. of Martin Johann Schmidt, painter.

1951, Aug. 3 Engr. and Litho.
576 A148 1sh dk grn, ocher & pink 3.50 2.75

7th World Scout Jamboree, Bad Ischl-St. Wolfgang, Aug. 3-13, 1951.

Wilhelm Kienzl A149

Josef Schrammel A150

Design: 1s, Karl von Ghega.

1951-52 Engr. Unwmk.
577 A149 1s deep green ('52) 6.50 1.10
578 A149 1.50s indigo 3.00 90
579 A150 1.50s violet blue ('52) 6.50 1.10
Nos. 577-579 (3) 16.00 3.10

Ghega (1802-60), civil engineer; Kienzl (1857-1941), composer; Schrammel (1852-95), composer. See #582.

Issued: 1s, Mar. 2; #578, Oct. 3; #579, Mar. 3.

Breakfast Pavilion, Schönbrunn A151

1952, May 24 *Perf. 13½x14*
580 A151 1.50s dark green 5.75 1.00

Vienna Zoological Gardens, 200th anniv.

Globe as Dot Over "i" — A152

School Girl — A153

1952, July 1 *Perf. 14x13½*
581 A152 1.50s dark blue 6.00 65

Formation of the Intl. Union of Socialist Youth Camp, Vienna, July 1-10, 1952.

Type Similar to A150

Portrait: 1s, Nikolaus Lenau.

1952, Aug. 13
582 A150 1s deep green 6.50 1.10

Nikolaus Lenau, pseudonym of Nikolaus Franz Niembsch von Strehlenau (1802-50), poet.

1952, Sept. 6
583 A153 2.40s dp violet blue 10.00 1.75

Issued to stimulate letter-writing between Austrian and foreign school children.

Hugo Wolf — A154

Pres. Theodor Körner — A155

1953, Feb. 21 **Engr.** *Perf. 14x13½*
587 A154 1.50s dark blue 6.75 70

Hugo Wolf, composer, 50th death anniv.

1953, Apr. 24
588 A155 1.50s dk violet blue 6.75 70

80th birthday of Pres. Theodor Körner. See Nos. 591, 614.

State Theater, Linz, and Masks — A156

1953, Oct. 17 *Perf. 13½x14*
589 A156 1.50s dark gray 15.00 1.50

State Theater at Linz, 150th anniv.

Child and Christmas Tree — A157

Karl von Rokitansky — A158

1953, Nov. 30 *Perf. 14x13½*
590 A157 1s dark green 1.40 16

See No. 597.

Type Similar to A155

Portrait: 1.50s, Moritz von Schwind.

1954, Jan. 21 *Perf. 14x13½*
591 A155 1.50s purple 12.00 1.10

Moritz von Schwind, painter, 150th birth anniv.

1954, Feb. 19
592 A158 1.50s purple 14.00 1.40

Karl von Rokitansky, physician, 150th birth anniv. See No. 595.

Esperanto Star and Wreath A159

Engr. and Photo.

1954, June 5 *Perf. 13½x14*
593 A159 1s dk brown & emer 4.25 16

Esperanto movement in Austria, 50th anniv.

A160

A161

1954, Aug. 4 **Engr.** *Perf. 14x13½*
594 A160 1s dark blue green 11.00 1.65

300th birth anniv. of Johann Michael Rottmayr von Rosenbrunn, painter.

Type Similar to A158

Portrait: 1.50s, Carl Auer von Welsbach.

1954, Aug. 4
595 A158 1.50s violet blue 30.00 1.50

25th death anniv. of Carl Auer von Welsbach (1858-1929), chemist.

1954, Oct. 2 **Unwmk.**

Organ, St. Florian Monastery and Cherub.

596 A161 1s brown 2.25 18

2nd Intl. Congress for Catholic Church Music, Vienna, Oct. 4-10, 1954.

Christmas Type of 1953

1954, Nov. 30
597 A157 1s dark blue 2.75 25

Arms of Austria and Official Publication A162

1954, Dec. 18 **Engr.**
598 A162 1s salmon & black 2.25 16

Austria's State Printing Plant, 150th anniv., and Wiener Zeitung, government newspaper, 250th year of publication.

Parliament Building A163

Designs: 1s, Western railroad station, Vienna. 1.45s, Letters forming flag. 1.50s, Public housing, Vienna. 2.40s, Limberg dam.

1955, Apr. 27 *Perf. 13½x14*

599 A163	70g	rose violet	1.40	16
600 A163	1s	deep ultra	5.00	16
601 A163	1.45s	scarlet	7.75	1.50
602 A163	1.50s	brown	17.00	16
603 A163	2.40s	dk blue green	7.75	3.00
	Nos. 599-603 (5)		38.90	4.98

10th anniv. of Austria's liberation.

Type of 1945 Overprinted in Blue **STAATSVERTRAG 1955**

1955, May 15 *Perf. 14x13½*
604 A100 2s blue gray 1.90 20

Signing of the state treaty with the US, France, Great Britain and Russia, May 15, 1955.

Workers of Three Races Climbing Globe — A164

1955, May 20 *Perf. 13½x14*
605 A164 1s indigo 2.00 1.35

4th congress of the Intl. Confederation of Free Trade Unions, Vienna, May.

Burgtheater, Vienna — A165

Design: 2.40s, Opera House, Vienna.

1955, July 25
606 A165 1.50s light sepia 3.00 16
607 A165 2.40s dark blue 4.00 1.25

Re-opening of the Burgtheater and Opera House in Vienna.

Symbolic of Austria's Desire to Join the UN — A166

1955, Oct. 24 **Unwmk.**
608 A166 2.40s green 14.00 1.40

Tenth anniversary of UN.

Wolfgang Amadeus Mozart — A167

Symbolic of Austria's Joining the UN — A168

1956, Jan. 21 *Perf. 14x13½*
609 A167 2.40s slate blue 3.75 50

200th birth anniv. of Wolfgang Amadeus Mozart, composer.

1956, Feb. 20
610 A168 2.40s chocolate 11.00 1.10

Austria's admission to the UN.

Globe Showing Energy of the Earth — A169

1956, May 8 *Perf. 13½x14*
611 A169 2.40s deep blue 10.00 1.40

Fifth Intl. Power Conf., Vienna, June 17-23.

Map of Europe and City Maps — A170

J.B. Fischer von Erlach — A171

Photo. and Typo.

1956, June 8 *Perf. 14x13½*
612 A170 1.45s lt grn blk & red 2.50 50

23rd Intl. Housing and Town Planning Congress, Vienna, July 22-28.

1956, July 20 **Engr.**
613 A171 1.50s brown 1.25 1.10

300th birth anniv. of Johann Bernhard Fischer von Erlach, architect.

Körner Type of 1953

1957, Jan. 11
614 A155 1.50s gray black 1.50 1.25

Death of Pres. Theodor Körner.

Dr. Julius Wagner-Jauregg A172

Anton Wildgans A173

1957, Mar. 7 *Perf. 14x13½*
615 A172 2.40s brn violet 3.50 1.25

Birth cent. of Dr. Julius Wagner-Jauregg, psychiatrist.

1957, May 3 **Unwmk.**
616 A173 1s violet blue 35 15

Anton Wildgans, poet, 25th death anniv.

Old and New Postal Motor Coach — A174

1957, June 14 *Perf. 13½x14*
617 A174 1s black, *yellow* 35 15

Austrian Postal Motor Coach Service, 50th anniv.

Gasherbrum II and Glacier A175

1957, July 27
618 A175 1.50s gray blue 42 15

Austrian Karakorum Expedition, which climbed Mount Gasherbrum II on July 7, 1956.

A176

A177

Designs: 20g, Farmhouse at Mörbisch. 50g, Heiligenstadt, Vienna. 1s, Mariazell. 1.40s, County seat, Klagenfurt. 1.50s, Rabenhof Building, Erdberg, Vienna. 1.80s, The Mint, Hall, Tyrol. 2s, Christkindl Church. 3.40s, Steiner Gate, Krems. 4s, Vienna Gate, Hainburg. 4.50s, Schwechat Airport, Vienna. 5.50s, Chur Gate, Feldkirch. 6s, County seat, Graz. 6.40s, "Golden Roof," Innsbruck. 10s, Heidenreichstein Castle.

1957-61 Litho. *Perf. 14x13½*
Size: 20x25mm

618A A176 20g vio blk ('61) 15 15
619 A176 50g bluish black ('59) 15 15

Engr.

620 A176 1s chocolate 1.25 15

Typo.

621 A176 1s chocolate 1.75 15

Litho.

622 A176 1s choc ('59) 90 15
622A A176 1.40s brt greenish bl ('60) 30 15
623 A176 1.50s rose lake ('58) 50 15
624 A176 1.80s brt ultra ('60) 30 15
625 A176 2s dull blue ('58) 6.00 15
626 A176 3.40s yel grn ('60) 90 80
627 A176 4s brt red lil ('60) 75 15
627A A176 4.50s dl green ('60) 1.00 50
628 A176 5.50s grnsh gray ('60) 55 20
629 A176 6s brt vio ('60) 1.00 15
629A A176 6.40s brt blue ('60) 95 90

Engr.
Size: 22x28mm

630 A177 10s dk bl grn 3.00 45
Nos. 618A-630 (16) 19.45
Set value 3.50

Of the three 1s stamps above, Nos. 620 and 621 have two names in imprint (designer H. Strohofer, engraver G. Wimmer). No. 622 has only Strohofer's name.

Values for Nos. 618A-624, 626-630 are for stamps on white paper. Most denominations also come on grayish paper with yellowish gum.

See Nos. 688-702.

1960-65 Photo. *Perf. 14½x14*
Size: 17x21mm

630A A176 50g slate ('64) 15 15

Size: 18x21½mm

630B A176 1s chocolate 15 15

Size: 17x21mm

630C A176 1.50s dk car ('65) 18 15
Set value 36 25

Nos. 630A-630C issued in sheets and coils.

Graukogel, Badgastein — A180

1958, Feb. 1 Engr. *Perf. 14x13½*
631 A180 1.50s dark blue 22 15

Intl. Ski Federation Alpine championships, Badgastein, Feb. 2-7.

Plane over Map of Austria — A181

1958, Mar. 27 *Perf. 13½x14*
632 A181 4s red 45 15

Re-opening of Austrian Airlines.

Mother and Daughter A182

Walther von der Vogelweide A183

1958, May 8 Unwmk. *Perf. 14x13½*
633 A182 1.50s dark blue 25 15

Issued for Mother's Day.

1958, July 17 Litho. and Engr.
634 A183 1.50s multicolored 25 15

3rd Austrian Song Festival, Vienna, July 17-20.

Oswald Redlich — A184

Giant "E" on Map — A185

1958, Sept. 17 Engr.
635 A184 2.40s ultramarine 55 15

Prof. Oswald Redlich (1858-1944), historian, birth cent.

Renner Type of 1948

1958, Nov. 12
636 A136 1.50s deep green 45 22

Austrian Republic, 40th anniv.

1959, Mar. 9
637 A185 2.40s emerald 35 20

Idea of a United Europe.

Cigarette Machine and Trademark of Tobacco Monopoly — A186

Archduke Johann — A187

1959, May 8 Unwmk. *Perf. 13½*
638 A186 2.40s dark olive bister 25 15

Austrian tobacco monopoly, 175th anniv.

1959, May 11 *Perf. 14x13½*
639 A187 1.50s deep green 25 18

Archduke Johann of Austria, military leader and humanitarian, death cent.

Capercaillie A188

Joseph Haydn A189

Animals: 1.50s, Roe buck. 2.40s, Wild boar. 3.50s, Red deer, doe and fawn.

1959, May 20 Engr.
640 A188 1s rose violet 22 15
641 A188 1.50s blue violet 55 15
642 A188 2.40s dk bl green 40 35
643 A188 3.50s dark brown 28 18
Nos. 640-643 (4) 1.45 83

Congress of the Intl. Hunting Council, Vienna, May 20-24.

1959, May 30 Unwmk.
644 A189 1.50s violet brown 45 18

Joseph Haydn, composer, 150th death anniv.

Coat of Arms, Tyrol A190

Antenna, Zugspitze A191

1959, June 13 *Perf. 14x13½*
645 A190 1.50s rose red 25 15

Fight for liberation of Tyrol, 150th anniv.

1959, June 19 *Perf. 13½*
646 A191 2.40s dk bl grn 30 15

Inauguration of Austria's relay system.

Field Ball Player A192

Orchestral Instruments A193

Designs: 1s, Runner. 1.80s, Gymnast on vaulting horse. 2s, Woman hurdler. 2.20s, Hammer thrower.

1959-70 Engr. *Perf. 14x13½*
647 A192 1s lilac 18 16
648 A192 1.50s blue green 50 20
648A A192 1.80s carmine ('62) 45 32
648B A192 2s rose lake ('70) 25 15
648C A192 2.20s bluish blk ('67) 25 15
Nos. 647-648C (5) 1.63 98

Litho. and Engr.

1959, Aug. 19 *Perf. 14x13½*
649 A193 2.40s dull bl & blk 30 15

World tour of the Vienna Philharmonic Orchestra.

Family Fleeing over Mountains A194

1960, Apr. 7 Engr. *Perf. 13½x14*
650 A194 3s Prussian green 65 25

WRY, July 1, 1959-June 30, 1960.

President Adolf Schärf — A195

1960, Apr. 20 *Perf. 14x13½*
651 A195 1.50s gray olive 65 15

Pres. Adolf Scharf, 70th birthday.

Young Hikers and Hostel — A196

1960, May 20 *Perf. 13½x14*
652 A196 1s carmine rose 20 15

Youth hiking; youth hostel movement.

Anton Eiselsberg — A197

Gustav Mahler — A198

Litho. and Engr.

1960, June 20 *Perf. 14x13½*
653 A197 1.50s buff & dk brn 70 15

Dr. Anton Eiselsberg, surgeon, birth cent.

1960, July 7 Engr.
654 A198 1.50s chocolate 70 15

Gustav Mahler, composer, birth cent.

Jakob Prandtauer, Melk Abbey — A199

Gross Glockner Mountain Road — A200

1960, July 16 Unwmk.
655 A199 1.50s red brown 70 15

Jakob Prandtauer, architect, 300th birth anniv.

1960, Aug. 3
656 A200 1.80s dark blue 75 48

Gross Glockner Mountain Road, 25th anniv.

Ionic Capital — A201

1960, Aug. 29 *Perf. 14x13½*

657 A201 3s black 1.40 75

Europa: Idea of a United Europe.

Griffen, Carinthia A202

1960, Oct. 10 Engr. *Perf. 13½x14*

658 A202 1.50s slate green 30 15

40th anniv. of the plebiscite which kept Carinthia with Austria.

Flame and Broken Chain — A203

1961, May 8 Unwmk. *Perf. 14x13½*

659 A203 1.50s scarlet 30 15

Victims in Austria's fight for freedom.

First Austrian Mail Plane, 1918 — A204

1961, May 15 *Perf. 13½x14*

660 A204 5s violet blue 70 30

Airmail Phil. Exhib., LUPOSTA 1961, Vienna, May.

Transportation by Road, Rail and Waterway — A205

Mountain Mower, by Albin Egger-Lienz — A206

Engraved and Typographed

1961, May 29 *Perf. 13½*

661 A205 3s rose red & olive 45 30

13th European Conference of Transportation ministers, Vienna, May 29-31.

1961, June 12 Engr. *Perf. 13½x14*

Designs: 1.50s, The Kiss, by August von Pettenkofen. 3s, Girl, by Anton Romako. 5s, Ariadne's Triumph, by Hans Makart.

Inscriptions in Red Brown

662 A206 1s rose lake 15 15
663 A206 1.50s dull violet 22 22
664 A206 3s olive green 75 70
665 A206 5s blue violet 45 40
Nos. 662-665 (4) 1.57 1.47

Society of Creative Artists, Künstlerhaus, Vienna, cent.

Sonnblick Mountain and Observatory A207

Mercury and Globe A208

1961, Sept. 1 *Perf. 14x13½*

666 A207 1.80s violet blue 38 28

Sonnblick meteorological observatory, 75th anniv.

1961, Sept. 18

667 A208 3s black 65 40

Intl. Banking Congress, Vienna, Sept. 1961. English inscription listing UN financial groups.

Coal Mine Shaft — A209

Designs: 1.50s, Generator. 1.80s, Iron blast furnace. 3s, Pouring steel. 5s, Oil refinery.

1961, Sept. 15 Engr. *Perf. 14x13½*

668 A209 1s black 16 15
669 A209 1.50s green 25 18
670 A209 1.80s dark car rose 52 40
671 A209 3s bright lilac 70 52
672 A209 5s blue 90 70
Nos. 668-672 (5) 2.53 1.95

15th anniversary of nationalized industry.

Arms of Burgenland A210

Franz Liszt A211

1961, Oct. 9 Engr. and Litho.

673 A210 1.50s blk, yel & dk red 35 15

Burgenland as part of the Austrian Republic, 40th anniv.

1961, Oct. 20 Engr.

674 A211 3s dark brown 55 38

Franz Liszt, composer, 150th birth anniv.

Parliament A212

1961, Dec. 18 *Perf. 13½x14*

675 A212 1s brown 20 15

Austrian Bureau of Budget, 200th anniv.

Kaprun-Mooserboden Reservoir — A213

Hydroelectric Power Plants: 1.50s, Ybbs-Persenbeug dam and locks. 1.80s, Lünersee dam and reservoir. 3s, Grossraming dam. 4s, Bisamberg transformer plant. 6.40s, St. Andrä power plant.

1962, Mar. 26 Unwmk.

676 A213 1s violet blue 15 15
677 A213 1.50s red lilac 24 20
678 A213 1.80s green 38 32
679 A213 3s brown 38 32
680 A213 4s rose red 38 32
681 A213 6.40s gray 1.25 1.10
Nos. 676-681 (6) 2.78 2.41

Nationalization of the electric power industry, 15th anniv.

Johann Nestroy A214

Friedrich Gauermann A215

1962, May 25 *Perf. 14x13½*

682 A214 1s violet 20 15

Johann Nepomuk Nestroy, Viennese playwright, author and actor, death cent.

1962, July 6 Engr.

683 A215 1.50s intense blue 20 15

Friedrich Gauermann (1807-1862), landscape painter, death cent.

Scout Emblem and Handshake — A216

1962, Oct. 5

684 A216 1.50s dark green 35 18

Austria's Boy Scouts, 50th anniv.

Lowlands Forest A217

Designs: 1.50s, Deciduous forest. 3s, Fir and larch forest.

1962, Oct. 12 *Perf. 13½x14*

685 A217 1s greenish gray 16 15
686 A217 1.50s reddish brown 25 22
687 A217 3s dk sl green 90 70
Nos. 685-687 (3) 1.31 1.07

Buildings Types of 1957-61

Designs: 30g, City Hall, Vienna. 40g, Porcia Castle, Spittal on the Drau. 60g, Tanners' Tower, Wels. 70g, Residenz Fountain, Salzburg. 80g, Old farmhouse, Pinzgau. 1s, Romanesque columns, Millstatt Abbey. 1.20s, Kornmesser House, Bruck on the Mur. 1.30s, Schatten Castle, Feldkirch, Vorarlberg. 2s, Dragon Fountain, Klagenfurt. 2.20s, Beethoven House, Vienna. 2.50s, Danube Bridge, Linz. 3s, Swiss Gate, Vienna. 3.50s, Esterhazy Palace, Eisenstadt. 8s, City Hall, Steyr. 20s, Melk Abbey

1962-70 Litho. *Perf. 14x13½*

Size: 20x25mm

688 A176 30g greenish gray 50 15
689 A176 40g rose red 15 15
690 A176 60g violet brown 32 15
691 A176 70g dark blue 25 15
692 A176 80g yellow brown 32 15
693 A176 1s brown ('70) 20 15
694 A176 1.20s red lilac 40 15
695 A176 1.30s green ('67) 15 15
696 A176 2s dk blue ('68) 25 15
697 A176 2.20s green 1.40 15
698 A176 2.50s violet 80 15
699 A176 3s bright blue 70 15
700 A176 3.50s rose carmine 80 15
701 A176 8s claret ('65) 1.00 15

Perf. 13½

Engr.

Size: 28x36½mm

702 A177 20s rose claret ('63) 2.40 35
Nos. 688-702 (15) 9.64
Set value 1.15

Values for Nos. 688-702 are for stamps on white paper. Some denominations also come on grayish paper with yellowish gum.

Electric Locomotive and Train of 1837 A218

Lithographed and Engraved

1962, Nov. 9 *Perf. 13½x14*

703 A218 3s buff & black 1.00 40

125th anniversary of Austrian railroads.

Postilions and Postal Clerk, 1863 — A219

Hermann Bahr — A220

1963, May 7 Photo. *Perf. 14x13½*

704 A219 3s dk brn & citron 70 40

First Intl. Postal Conference, Paris, cent.

Lithographed and Envraved

1963, July 19 *Perf. 14x13½*

705 A220 1.50s blue & black 24 15

Centenary of birth of Hermann Bahr, poet.

The Scott Catalogue value is a retail value; that is, what you could expect to pay for the stamp in a grade of Fine-Very Fine. The value listed reflects recent actual dealer selling prices.

St. Florian Statue, Kefermarkt, Contemporary and Old Fire Engines — A221

1963, Aug. 30 **Unwmk.**
706 A221 1.50s brt rose & blk 24 15

Austrian volunteer fire brigades, cent.

Factory, Flag and "ÖGB" on Map of Austria A222

1963, Sept. 23 **Litho.** ***Perf. 13½x14***
707 A222 1.50s gray, red & dk brn 24 15

5th Congress of the Austrian Trade Union Federation (ÖGB), Sept. 23-28.

Arms of Austria and Tyrol — A223

1963, Sept. 27 **Unwmk.**
708 A223 1.50s tan, blk, red & yel 24 15

Tyrol's union with Austria, 600th anniv.

Prince Eugene of Savoy — A224

Centenary Emblem — A225

1963, Oct. 18 **Engr.** ***Perf. 14x13½***
709 A224 1.50s violet 24 15

Prince Eugene of Savoy (1663-1736), Austrian general, 300th birth anniv.

1963, Oct. 25 **Engr. and Photo.**
710 A225 3s blk, sil & red 48 20

Intl. Red Cross, cent.

Slalom A226

Sports: 1.20s, Biathlon (skier with rifle). 1.50s, Ski jump. 1.80s, Women's figure skating. 2.20s, Ice hockey. 3s, Tobogganing. 4s, Bobsledding.

Photo. and Engr.

1963, Nov. 11 ***Perf. 13½x14***
711 A226 1s multi 15 15
712 A226 1.20s multi 16 15
713 A226 1.50s multi 20 15
714 A226 1.80s multi 25 15
715 A226 2.20s multi 40 25
716 A226 3s multi 32 20
717 A226 4s multi 60 40
Nos. 711-717 (7) 2.08 1.45

9th Winter Olympic Games, Innsbruck, Jan. 29-Feb. 9, 1964.

Baroque Creche by Josef Thaddäus Stammel — A227

1963, Nov. 29 **Engr.** ***Perf. 14x13½***
718 A227 2s dk Prussian grn 22 15

Flowers A228

1964, Apr. 17 **Litho.** ***Perf. 14***
719 A228 1s Nasturtium 15 15
720 A228 1.50s Peony 20 15
721 A228 1.80s Clematis 25 15
722 A228 2.20s Dahlia 32 20
723 A228 3s Morning glary 38 24
724 A228 4s Hollyhock 50 32
Nos. 719-724 (6) 1.80 1.21

Vienna Intl. Garden Show, Apr. 16-Oct. 11.

St. Mary Magdalene and Apostle — A229

Pallas Athena and National Council Chamber — A230

1964, May 21 **Engr.** ***Perf. 13½***
725 A229 1.50s bluish black 22 15

Romanesque art in Austria. The 12th century stained-glass window is from the Weitensfeld Church, the bust of the Apostle from the portal of St. Stephen's Cathedral, Vienna.

Engr. and Litho.

1964, May 25 ***Perf. 14x13½***
726 A230 1.80s black & emer 28 15

2nd Parliamentary and Scientific Conf., Vienna.

The Kiss, by Gustav Klimt A231

1964, June 5 **Litho.** ***Perf. 13½***
727 A231 3s multicolored 35 25

Re-opening of the Vienna Secession, a museum devoted to early 20th century art (art nouveau).

Brother of Mercy and Patient — A232

1964, June 11 **Engr.** ***Perf. 14x13½***
728 A232 1.50s dark blue 22 15

Brothers of Mercy in Austria, 350th anniv.

"Bringing the News of Victory at Kunersdorf" by Bernardo Bellotto A233

"The Post in Art": 1.20s, Changing Horses at Relay Station, by Julius Hörmann. 1.50s, The Honeymoon Trip, by Moritz von Schwind. 1.80s, After the Rain, by Ignaz Raffalt. 2.20s, Mailcoach in the Mountains, by Adam Klein. 3s, Changing Horses at Bavarian Border, by Friedrich Gauermann. 4s, Postal Sleigh (Truck) in the Mountains, by Adalbert Pilch. 6.40s, Saalbach Post Office, by Adalbert Pilch.

1964, June 15 ***Perf. 13½x14***
729 A233 1s rose claret 15 15
730 A233 1.20s sepia 15 15
731 A233 1.50s violet blue 15 15
732 A233 1.80s brt violet 15 15
733 A233 2.20s black 18 15
734 A233 3s dl car rose 30 16
735 A233 4s slate green 38 20
736 A233 6.40s dull claret 80 45
Nos. 729-736 (8) 2.26
Set value 1.22

15th UPU Cong., Vienna, May-June 1964.

Workers — A234

1964, Sept. 4 ***Perf. 14x13½***
737 A234 1s black 15 15

Centenary of Austrian Labor Movement.

Europa Issue, 1964

Common Design Type

1964, Sept. 14 **Litho.** ***Perf. 12***

Size: 21x36mm

738 CD7 3s dark blue 50 15

Emblem of Radio Austria and Transistor Radio Panel A235

1964, Oct. 1 **Photo.** ***Perf. 13½***
739 A235 1s black brn & red 15 15

Forty years of Radio Austria.

A236

A237

Litho. and Engr.

1964, Oct. 12 ***Perf. 14x13½***
740 A236 1.50s Old printing press 15 15

6th Congress of the Intl. Graphic Federation, Vienna, Oct. 12-17.

Typo. and Engr.

1965, Apr. 20 ***Perf. 12***

Pres. Adolf Schärf and Scharf Student Center.

741 A237 1.50s bluish black 20 15

Dr. Adolf Schärf (1890-1965), Pres. of Austria (1957-65).

Ruins and New Buildings — A238

1965, Apr. 27 **Engr.** ***Perf. 14x13½***
742 A238 1.80s carmine lake 20 15

Twenty years of reconstruction.

Oldest Seal of Vienna University — A239

St. George, 16th Century Wood Sculpture — A240

Photo. and Engr.

1965, May 10 ***Perf. 14x13½***
743 A239 3s gold & red 35 18

University of Vienna, 600th anniv.

1965, May 17 **Engr.**
744 A240 1.80s bluish black 25 15

Art of the Danube Art School, 1490-1540, exhibition, May-Oct. 1965. The stamp background shows an engraving by Albrecht Altdorfer.

ITU Emblem, Telegraph Key and TV Antenna — A241

Ferdinand Raimund — A242

1965, May 17 **Unwmk.**
745 A241 3s violet blue 32 18

ITU, cent.

1965 **Engr.** ***Perf. 14x13½***

Portraits: No. 746, Dr. Ignaz Philipp Semmelweis. No. 747, Bertha von Suttner. No. 749, Ferdinand Georg Waldmüller.

746 A242 1.50s violet 30 15
747 A242 1.50s bluish black 30 15
748 A242 3s dark brown 55 15
749 A242 3s greenish blk 55 20
Nos. 746-749 (4) 1.70
Set value 53

Semmelweis (1818-65), who discovered the cause of puerperal fever and introduced antisepsis into obstetrics (#746). 60th anniv. of the awarding of the Nobel Prize for Peace to von Suttner (1843-1914), pacifist and author (#747). Raimund (1790-1836), actor and playwright (#748). Waldmüller (1793-1865), painter (#749).

Issue dates: No. 746, Aug. 13; No. 747, Dec. 1; No. 748, June 1; No. 749, Aug. 23.

Dancers with Tambourines A243

Red Cross and Strip of Gauze A244

Design: 1.50s, Male gymnasts with practice bars.

1965, July 20 Photo. and Engr.

750 A243 1.50s gray & black	16	15
751 A243 3s bister & blk	35	22

4th Gymnaestrada, intl. athletic meet, Vienna, July 20-24.

1965, Oct. 1 Litho. *Perf. 14x13½*

752 A244 3s black & red	32	15

20th Intl. Red Cross Conference, Vienna.

Austrian Flag and Eagle with Mural Crown — A245

Austrian Flag, UN Headquarters and Emblem — A246

1965, Oct. 7 Photo. and Engr.

753 A245 1.50s gold, red & blk	15	15

50th anniv. of the Union of Austrian Towns.

Lithographed and Engraved

1965, Oct. 25 Unwmk. *Perf. 12*

754 A246 3s blk, brt bl & red	45	15

Austria's admission to the UN, 10th anniv.

University of Technology, Vienna — A247

1965, Nov. 8 Engr. *Perf. 13½x14*

755 A247 1.50s violet	15	15

Vienna University of Technology, 150th anniv.

Map of Austria with Postal Zone Numbers — A248

1966, Jan. 14 Photo. *Perf. 12*

756 A248 1.50s yel, red & blk	15	15

Introduction of postal zone numbers, Jan. 1, 1966.

PTT Building, Emblem and Churches of Sts. Maria Rotunda and Barbara A249

Maria von Ebner Eschenbach A250

Lithographed and Engraved

1966, Mar. 4 *Perf. 14x13½*

757 A249 1.50s blk, *dull yellow*	15	15

Headquarters of the Post and Telegraph Administration, cent.

1966, Mar. 11 Engr.

758 A250 3s plum	35	15

50th death anniv. of Maria von Ebner Eschenbach (1830-1916), novelist and poet.

Ferris Wheel, Prater — A251

1966, Apr. 19 Engr. *Perf. 14x13½*

759 A251 1.50s slate green	15	15

Opening of the Prater (park), Vienna, to the public by Emperor Joseph II, 200th anniv.

A252

A253

1966, May 6 Unwmk. *Perf. 12*

760 A252 3s dark brown	35	15

Josef Hoffmann (1870-1956), architect, 10th death anniv.

Photo. and Engr.

1966, May 27 *Perf. 14*

761 A253 1.50s Wiener Neustadt Arms	15	15

Wiener Neustadt Art Exhib., centered around the time and person of Frederick III (1440-93).

Austrian Eagle and Emblem of National Bank A254

1966, May 27 *Perf. 14*

762 A254 3s gray grn, dk brn & dk green	35	15

Austrian National Bank, 150th anniv.

Puppy — A255

A256

Litho. and Engr.

1966, June 16 *Perf. 12*

763 A255 1.80s yellow & blk	25	15

120th anniv. of the Vienna Humane Society.

1966, Aug. 17 Litho. *Perf. 13½*

Alpine Flowers: 1.50s, Columbine. 1.80s, Turk's cap. 2.20s, Wulfenia carinthiaca. 3s, Globeflowers. 4s, Fire lily. 5s, Pasqueflower.

Flowers in Natural Colors

764 A256 1.50s dark blue	15	15
765 A256 1.80s dark blue	16	15
766 A256 2.20s dark blue	28	20
767 A256 3s dark blue	42	30
768 A256 4s dark blue	45	32
769 A256 5s dark blue	45	32
Nos. 764-769 (6)	1.91	1.44

Fair Building A257

1966, Aug. 26 Engr. *Perf. 13½x13*

770 A257 3s violet blue	35	15

First International Fair at Wels.

Peter Anich, Map, Globe and Books — A258

Sick Worker and Health Emblem — A259

1966, Sept. 1 *Perf. 14x13½*

771 A258 1.80s black	20	15

Peter Anich (1723-1766), Tirolean cartographer and farmer, 200th death anniv.

1966, Sept. 19 Engr. and Litho.

772 A259 3s black & ver	35	15

15th Occupational Medicine Congress, Vienna, Sept. 19-24.

Theater Collection: "Eunuchus" by Terence from a 1496 Edition A260

Designs: 1.80s, Map Collection: Title page of Geographia Blavania (Cronus, Hercules and celestial sphere). 2.20s, Picture Archive and Portrait Collection: View of Old Vienna after a watercolor by Anton Stutzinger. 3s, Manuscript Collection: Illustration from the 15th century "Livre du Cuer d'Amours Espris" of the Duke René d'Anjou.

Photogravure and Engraved

1966, Sept. 28 *Perf. 13½x14*

773 A260 1.50s multicolored	15	15
774 A260 1.80s multicolored	20	15
775 A260 2.20s multicolored	25	16
776 A260 3s multicolored	28	18
Nos. 773-776 (4)	88	64

Austrian National Library.

Young Girl A261

Strawberries A262

Litho. and Engr.

1966, Oct. 3 *Perf. 14x13½*

777 A261 3s light bl & blk	35	15

"Save the Child" society, 10th anniv.

1966, Nov. 25 Photo. *Perf. 13½x13*

778 A262 50g shown	20	15
779 A262 1s Grapes	18	15
780 A262 1.50s Apple	18	15
781 A262 1.80s Blackberries	28	18
782 A262 2.20s Apricots	28	18
783 A262 3s Cherries	35	22
Nos. 778-783 (6)	1.47	1.03

Coat of Arms of University of Linz — A263

Ice Skater, 1866 — A264

Photo. and Engr.

1966, Dec. 9 *Perf. 14x13½*

784 A263 3s multi	35	15

Inauguration of the Universary of Linz, Oct. 8, 1966.

Photo. and Engr.

1967, Feb. 3 *Perf. 14x13½*

785 A264 3s pale bl & dk bl	35	15

Centenary of Vienna Ice Skating Club.

Ballet Dancer — A265

Karl Schönherr — A266

1967, Feb. 15 Engr. *Perf. 11½x12*

786 A265 3s deep claret	35	15
a. Perf. 12	1.25	1.10

"Blue Danube" waltz by Johann Strauss, cent.

1967, Feb. 24 Engr. *Perf. 14x13½*

787 A266 3s gray brown	35	15

Dr. Karl Schönherr (1867-1943), poet, playwright and physician.

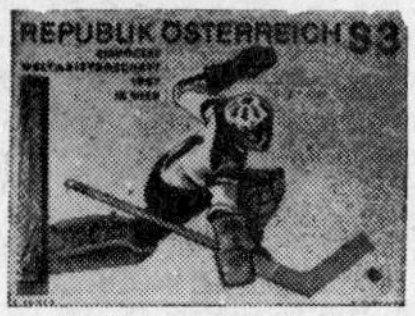

Ice Hockey Goalkeeper A267

Photogravure and Engraved

1967, Mar. 17 *Perf. 13½x14*
788 A267 3s pale grn & dk bl 35 15

Ice Hockey Championships, Vienna, Mar. 18-29.

Violin, Organ and Laurel — A268

1967, Mar. 28 **Engr.** *Perf. 13½*
789 A268 3.50s indigo 40 15

Vienna Philharmonic Orchestra, 125th anniv.

Motherhood, Watercolor by Peter Fendi A269

1967, Apr. 28 **Litho.** *Perf. 14*
790 A269 2s multicolored 25 15

Mother's Day.

Gothic Mantle Madonna — A270

1967, May 19 **Engr.** *Perf. 13½x14*
791 A270 3s slate 35 15

"Austrian Gothic," art exhibition, Krems, 1967. The Gothic wood carving is from Frauenstein in Upper Austria.

Medieval Gold Cross — A271

Swan, Tapestry by Oscar Kokoschka — A272

Litho. and Engr.

1967, June 9 *Perf. 13½*
792 A271 3.50s Prus grn & multi 40 15

Salzburg Treasure Chamber; exhibition at Salzburg Cathedral, June 12-Sept. 15.

1967, June 9 **Photo.**
793 A272 2s multicolored 25 15

Nibelungen District Art Exhibition, Pöchlarn, celebrating the 700th anniversary of Pöchlarn as a city. The design is from the border of the Amor and Psyche tapestry at the Salzburg Festival Theater.

View and Arms of Vienna A273

Engraved and Photogravure

1967, June 12 *Perf. 13x13½*
794 A273 3s black & red 35 15

10th Europa Talks, "Science and Society in Europe," Vienna, June 13-17.

Prize Bull "Mucki" A274

1967, Aug. 28 **Engr.** *Perf. 13½*
795 A274 2s deep claret 35 15

Centenary of the Ried Festival and the Agricultural Fair.

Potato Beetle — A275

Engraved and Photogravure

1967, Aug. 29 *Perf. 13½x14*
796 A275 3s black & multi 35 15

6th Intl. Congress for Plant Protection, Vienna.

First Locomotive Used on Brenner Pass — A276

1967, Sept. 23 **Photo.** *Perf. 12*
797 A276 3.50s tan & slate grn 40 15

Centenary of railroad over Brenner Pass.

Christ in Glory — A277

1967, Oct. 9 *Perf. 13½*
798 A277 2s multicolored 25 15

Restoration of the Romanesque (11th century) frescoes in the Lambach monastery church.

Main Gate to Fair, Prater, Vienna — A278

1967, Oct. 24 **Photo.** *Perf. 13½x14*
799 A278 2s choc & buff 25 15

Congress of Intl. Trade Fairs, Vienna, Oct., 1967.

Medal Showing Minerva and Art Symbols A279

Frankfurt Medal for Reformation, 1717 A280

Litho. & Engr.

1967, Oct. 25 *Perf. 13½*
800 A279 2s dk brn, dk bl & yel 25 15

Vienna Academy of Fine Arts, 275th anniv. The medal was designed by Georg Raphael Donner (1693-1741) and is awarded as an artist's prize.

1967, Oct. 31 **Engr.** *Perf. 14x13½*
801 A280 3.50s blue black 40 15

450th anniversary of the Reformation.

Mountain Range and Stone Pines A281

1967, Nov. 7 *Perf. 13½*
802 A281 3.50s green 40 15

Centenary of academic study of forestry.

Land Survey Monument, 1770 — A282

St. Leopold, Window, Heiligenkreuz Abbey — A283

1967, Nov. 7 **Photo.**
803 A282 2s olive black 25 15

150th anniversary of official land records.

1967, Nov. 15 **Engr. & Photo.**
804 A283 1.80s multicolored 25 15

Margrave Leopold III (1075-1136), patron saint of Austria.

Tragic Mask and Violin — A284

Nativity from 15th Century Altar — A285

1967, Nov. 17 *Perf. 13½*
805 A284 3.50s bluish lil & blk 40 15

Academy of Music and Dramatic Art, 150th anniv.

1967, Nov. 27 **Engr.** *Perf. 14x13½*
806 A285 2s green 25 15

Christmas.

The design shows the late Gothic carved center panel of the altar in St. John's Chapel in Nonnberg Convent, Salzburg.

Innsbruck Stadium, Alps and FISU Emblem — A286

Camillo Sitte — A287

1968, Jan. 22 **Engr.** *Perf. 13½*
807 A286 2s dark blue 25 15

Winter University Games under the auspices of FISU (Fédération Internationale du Sport Universitaire), Innsbruck, Jan. 21-28.

1968, Apr. 17 *Perf. 13½*
808 A287 2s black brown 25 15

125th birth anniv. of Camillo Sitte (1843-1903), architect and city planner.

Mother and Child — A288

1968, May 7
809 A288 2s slate green 25 15

Mother's Day.

Cup and Serpent Emblem — A289

1968, May 7 **Photo.**
810 A289 3.50s dp plum, gray & gold 40 15

Bicentenary of the Veterinary College.

Bride with Lace Veil — A290

1968, May 24 Engr. *Perf. 12*

811 A290 3.50s blue black 40 15

Embroidery industry of Vorarlberg, cent.

Horse Race A291

1968, June 4 *Perf. 13½*

812 A291 3.50s sepia 40 18

Centenary of horse racing at Freudenau, Vienna.

Dr. Karl Landsteiner A292

Peter Rosegger A293

1968, June 14 *Perf. 14x13½*

813 A292 3.50s dark blue 40 18

Birth cent. of Dr. Karl Landsteiner (1868-1943), pathologist, discoverer of the four main human blood types.

1968, June 26

814 A293 2s slate green 25 15

50th death anniv. of Peter Rosegger (1843-1918), poet and writer.

Angelica Kauffmann, Self-portrait A294

Bronze Statue of Young Man, 1st Century B.C. A295

1968, July 15 Engr. *Perf. 14x13½*

815 A294 2s intense black 25 15

"Angelica Kauffmann and her Contemporaries," art exhibitions, Bregenz, July 28-Oct. 13, and Vienna, Oct. 22, 1968-Jan. 6, 1969.

1968, July 15 Litho. & Engr.

816 A295 2s grnsh gray & blk 25 15

20 years of excavations on Magdalene Mountain, Carinthia.

Bishop, Romanesque Bas-relief — A296

1968, Sept. 20 Engr. *Perf. 14x13½*

817 A296 2s blue gray 25 15

Graz-Seckau Bishopric, 750th anniv.

Koloman Moser — A297

Human Rights Flame — A298

Engr. & Photo.

1968, Oct. 18 *Perf. 12*

818 A297 2s black brn & ver 25 15

50th death anniv. of Koloman Moser (1868-1918), stamp designer and painter.

1968, Oct. 18 Photo. *Perf. 14x13½*

819 A298 1.50s gray, dp car & dk green 28 15

International Human Rights Year.

A299

A300

Designs: No. 820, Pres. Karl Renner and States' arms. No. 821, Coats of arms of Austria and Austrian states. No. 822, Article I of Austrian Constitution and States' coats of arms.

Engr. & Photo.

1968, Nov. 11 *Perf. 13½*

820	A299	2s black & multi	35	30
821	A299	2s black & multi	35	30
822	A299	2s black & multi	35	30
		Nos. 820-822 (3)	1.05	90

50th anniversary of Republic of Austria.

1968, Nov. 29 Engr. *Perf. 14x13½*

Crèche, Memorial Chapel, Oberndorf-Salzburg.

823 A300 2s slate green 25 15

Christmas; 150th anniv. of "Silent Night, Holy Night" hymn.

Angels, from Last Judgment by Troger (Röhrenbach-Greillenstein Chapel) — A301

Baroque Frescoes: No. 825, Vanquished Demons, by Paul Troger, Altenburg Abbey. No. 826, Sts. Peter and Paul, by Troger, Melk Abbey. No. 827, The Glorification of Mary, by Franz Anton Maulpertsch, Maria Treu Church, Vienna. No. 828, St. Leopold Carried into Heaven, by Maulpertsch, Ebenfurth Castle Chapel. No. 829, Symbolic figures from The Triumph of Apollo, by Maulpertsch, Halbthurn Castle.

Engr. & Photo.

1968, Dec. 11 *Perf. 13½x14*

824	A301	2s multicolored	28	28
825	A301	2s multicolored	28	28
826	A301	2s multicolored	28	28
827	A301	2s multicolored	28	28
828	A301	2s multicolored	28	28
829	A301	2s multicolored	28	28
		Nos. 824-829 (6)	1.68	1.68

St. Stephen — A302

Statues in St. Stephen's Cathedral, Vienna: No. 831, St. Paul. No. 832, Mantle Madonna. No. 833, St. Christopher. No. 834, St. George and the Dragon. No. 835, St. Sebastian.

1969, Jan. 28 Engr. *Perf. 13½*

830	A302	2s black	28	28
831	A302	2s rose claret	28	28
832	A302	2s gray violet	28	28
833	A302	2s slate blue	28	28
834	A302	2s slate green	28	28
835	A302	2s dk red brn	28	28
		Nos. 830-835 (6)	1.68	1.68

500th anniversary of Diocese of Vienna.

Parliament and Pallas Athena Fountain, Vienna A303

1969, Apr. 8 Engr. *Perf. 13½*

836 A303 2s greenish blk 25 15

Interparliamentary Union Conf., Vienna, Apr. 7-13.

Europa Issue, 1969

Common Design Type

1969, Apr. 28 Photo. *Perf. 12*

837 CD12 2s gray grn, brick red & blue 25 15

Council of Europe Emblem — A304

1969, May 5

838 A304 3.50s gray, ultra, blk & yel 42 25

20th anniversary of Council of Europe.

Frontier Guards — A305

Engr. & Photo.

1969, May 14 *Perf. 12*

839 A305 2s sepia & red 25 15

Austrian Federal Army.

Don Giovanni, by Mozart — A306

Cent. of Vienna Opera House: a, Don Giovanni, Mozart. b, Magic Flute, Mozart. c, Fidelio, Beethoven. d, Lohengrin, Wagner. e, Don Carlos, Verdi. f, Carmen, Bizet. g, Rosencavalier, Richard Strauss. h, Swan Lake, Ballet by Tchaikovsky.

1969, May 23 *Perf. 13½*

840 A306 Sheet of 8 4.00 4.00

a.-h. 2s, any single 32 32

Centenary of Vienna Opera House.

No. 840 contains 8 stamps arranged around gold and red center label showing Opera House. Printed in sheets containing 4 Nos. 840 with wide gutters between.

A307

A308

Gothic armor of Maximilian I.

1969, June 4 Engr.

841 A307 2s bluish black 25 15

Emperor Maximilian I Exhibition, Innsbruck, May 30-Oct. 5.

1969, June 16 Photo. *Perf. 13½*

Oldest Municipal Seal of Vienna.

842 A308 2s tan, red & black 25 15

19th Cong. of the Intl. Org. of Municipalities, Vienna, June 1969.

A309

A310

Girl's head and village house.

Engraved and Photogravure

1969, June 16 *Perf. 13½x14*

843 A309 2s yel grn & sepia 25 15

20th anniv. of the Children's Village Movement in Austria (SOS Villages).

1969, Aug. 22 Photo. *Perf. 13x13½*

Hands holding wrench, and UN emblem.

844 A310 2s deep green 25 15

ILO, 50th anniv.

Austria stamps can be mounted in the Scott annually supplemented Austria album.

A311

A312

Austria's flag and shield circling the world.

Engraved and Lithographed

1969, Aug. 22 *Perf. 14x13½*

845 A311 3.50s slate & red	40	16

Year of Austrians Living Abroad, 1969.

Engraved and Photogravure

1969, Sept. 26 *Perf. 13½*

Etchings: No. 846, Young Hare, by Dürer. No. 847, El Cid Killing a Bull, by Francisco de Goya. No. 848, Madonna with the Pomegranate, by Raphael. No. 849, The Painter, by Peter Brueghel. No. 850, Rubens' Son Nicolas, by Rubens. No. 851, Self-portrait, by Rembrandt. No. 852, Lady Reading, by Francois Guerin. No. 853, Wife of the Artist, by Egon Schiele.

Gray Frame, Buff Background

846 A312 2s black & brn	24	24
847 A312 2s black	24	24
848 A312 2s black	24	24
849 A312 2s black	24	24
850 A312 2s blk & salmon	24	24
851 A312 2s black	24	24
852 A312 2s blk & salmon	24	24
853 A312 2s black	24	24
Nos. 846-853 (8)	1.92	1.92

Etching collection in the Albertina, Vienna, 200th anniv.

President Franz Jonas — A313

1969, Oct. 3

854 A313 2s gray & vio blue	25	15

70th birthday of Franz Jonas, Austrian Pres.

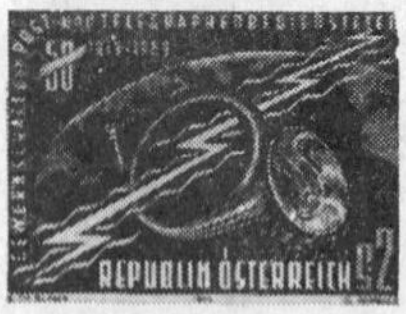

Post Horn, Globe and Lightning A314

1969, Oct. 17 *Perf. 13½x14*

855 A314 2s multicolored	25	15

Union of Postal and Telegraph employees, 50th anniv.

Savings Box, about 1450 A315

Madonna, by Albin Egger-Lienz A316

1969, Oct. 31 Photo. *Perf. 13x13½*

856 A315 2s silver & slate green	25	15

The importance of savings.

Engr. & Photo.

1969, Nov. 24 *Perf. 12*

857 A316 2s dp cl & pale yel	25	15

Christmas.

Josef Schöffel — A317

St. Klemens M. Hofbauer — A318

1970, Feb. 6 Engr. *Perf. 14x13½*

858 A317 2s dull purple	25	15

60th death anniv. of Josef Schöffel, (1832-1910), who saved the Vienna Woods.

Engraved and Photogravure

1970, Mar. 13 *Perf. 14x13½*

859 A318 2s dk brn & lt tan	25	15

150th death anniv. St. Klemens Maria Hofbauer (1751-1820); Redemptorist preacher in Poland and Austria, canonized in 1909.

Chancellor Leopold Figl A319

Belvedere Palace, Vienna A320

1970, Apr. 27 Engr. *Perf. 13½*

860 A319 2s dark ol gray	25	15
861 A320 2s dark rose brn	25	15
Set value		20

25th anniversary of Second Republic.

A321

A322

1970, May 19 Engr. *Perf. 13½*

862 A321 2s Krimml waterfalls	25	15

European Nature Conservation Year, 1970.

Litho. & Engr.

1970, June 5 *Perf. 13½*

St. Leopold on oldest seal of Innsbruck University.

863 A322 2s red & black	25	15

Leopold Franzens University, Innsbruck, 300th anniv.

Organ, Great Hall, Music Academy — A323

Photo. & Engr.

1970, June 5 *Perf. 14*

864 A323 2s gold & deep claret	25	15

Vienna Music Academy Building, cent.

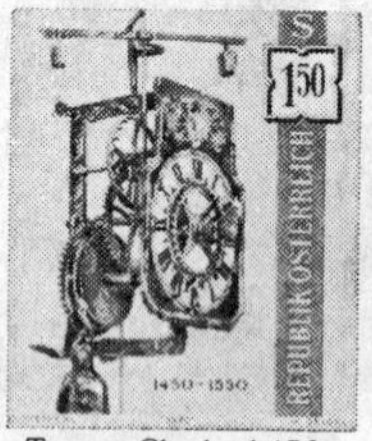

Tower Clock, 1450-1550 A324

The Beggar Student, by Carl Millöcker A325

Old Clocks from Vienna Horological Museum: #866, Lyre clock, 1790-1815. #867, Pendant clock 1600-50. #868, Pendant watch, 1800-30. #869, Bracket clock, 1720-60. #870, French column clock, 1820-50.

1970

865 A324 1.50s buff & sepia	22	22
866 A324 1.50s greenish & grn	22	22
867 A324 2s pale bl & dk bl	28	28
868 A324 2s pale rose & lake	28	28
869 A324 3.50s buff & brown	50	50
870 A324 3.50s pale lil & brn vio	50	50
Nos. 865-870 (6)	2.00	2.00

Issue dates: Nos. 865, 867, 869, June 22. Others, Oct. 23.

1970 Photo & Engr. *Perf. 13½*

Operettas: No. 872, Fledermaus, by Johann Strauss. No. 873, The Dream Waltz, by Oscar Strauss. No. 874, The Bird Seller, by Carl Zeller. No. 875, The Merry Widow, by Franz Lehar. No. 876, Two Hearts in Three-quarter Time, by Robert Stolz.

871 A325 1.50s pale grn & grn	22	22
872 A325 1.50s yel & vio blue	22	22
873 A325 2s pale rose & vio brn	28	28
874 A325 2s pale grn & sep	28	28
875 A325 3.50s pale bl & ind	50	50
876 A325 3.50s beige & slate	50	50
Nos. 871-876 (6)	2.00	2.00

Issue dates: Nos. 871, 873, 875, July 3. Others Sept. 11.

Bregenz Festival Stage — A326

1970, July 23 **Photo.**

877 A326 3.50s dark bl & buff	40	20

25th anniversary of Bregenz Festival.

Salzburg Festival Emblem — A327

1970, July 27 *Perf. 14*

878 A327 3.50s blk, red, gold & gray	40	20

50th anniversary of Salzburg Festival.

A328

A329

1970, Aug. 31 **Engr.**

879 A328 3.50s dark gray	40	20

13th General Assembly of the World Veterans Federation, Aug. 28-Sept. 4. The head of St. John is from a sculpture showing the Agony in the Garden in the chapel of the Parish Church in Ried. It is attributed to Thomas Schwanthaler (1634-1702).

1970, Sept. 16 *Perf. 14x13½*

880 A329 2s chocolate	25	15

Thomas Koschat (1845-1914), Carinthian composer of songs.

Mountain Scene A330

1970, Sept. 16 Photo. *Perf. 14x13½*

881 A330 2s vio bl & pink	25	15

Hiking and mountaineering in Austria.

Alfred Cossmann
A331

Arms of Carinthia
A332

1970, Oct. 2 Engr. *Perf. 14x13½*
882 A331 2s dark brown 25 15

Birth cent. of Alfred Cossmann (1870-1951), engraver.

1970, Oct. 2 Photo. & Engr. *Perf. 14*
883 A332 2s ol, red, gold, blk & sil 25 15

Carinthian plebiscite, 50th anniversary.

UN Emblem — A333

1970, Oct. 23 Litho. *Perf. 14x13½*
884 A333 3.50s light bl & blk 50 20

25th anniversary of the United Nations.

Adoration of the Shepherds, Carving from Garsten Vicarage
A334

1970, Nov. 27 Engr. *Perf. 13½x14*
885 A334 2s dark vio bl 25 15

Christmas.

Karl Renner — A335

Beethoven, by Georg Waldmüller — A336

1970, Dec. 14 Engr. *Perf. 14x13½*
886 A335 2s deep claret 25 15

Karl Renner (1870-1950), Austrian Pres., birth cent.

Photo. & Engr.
1970, Dec. 16 *Perf. 13½*
887 A336 3.50s black & buff 40 20

Ludwig van Beethoven (1770-1827), composer, birth bicentenary.

Enrica Handel-Mazzetti
A337

1971, Jan. 11 Engr. *Perf. 14x13½*
888 A337 2s sepia 25 15

Birth cent. of Enrica von Handel-Mazzetti (1871-1955), novelist and poet.

"Watch Out for Children!"
A338

1971, Feb. 18 Photo. *Perf. 13½*
889 A338 2s blk, red brn & brt grn 25 15

Traffic safety.

Saltcellar, by Benvenuto Cellini
A339

Art Treasures: 1.50s, Covered vessel, made of prase, gold and precious stones, Florentine, 1580. 2s, Emperor Joseph I, ivory statue by Matthias Steinle, 1693.

Photo. & Engr.
1971, Mar. 22 *Perf. 14*

890	A339	1.50s gray & slate grn	20	15
891	A339	2s gray & deep plum	25	20
892	A339	3.50s gray, blk & bister	48	35
		Nos. 890-892 (3)	93	70

Emblem of Austrian Wholesalers' Organization
A340

1971, Apr. 16 Photo. *Perf. 13½*
893 A340 3.50s multicolored 40 20

Intl. Chamber of Commerce, 23rd Congress, Vienna, Apr. 17-23.

Jacopo de Strada, by Titian — A341

Paintings in Vienna Museum: 2s, Village Feast, by Peter Brueghel, the Elder. 3.50s, Young Venetian Woman, by Albrecht Dürer.

1971, May 6 Engr. *Perf. 13½*

894	A341	1.50s rose lake	20	15
895	A341	2s greenish black	25	20
896	A341	3.50s deep brown	48	35
		Nos. 894-896 (3)	93	70

Seal of Paulus of Franchenfordia, 1380 — A342

Photo. & Engr.
1971, May 6 *Perf. 13½x14*
897 A342 3.50s dk brn & bister 40 20

Congress commemorating the centenary of the Austrian Notaries' Statute, May 5-8.

St. Matthew
A343

August Neilreich
A344

1971, May 27 *Perf. 12½x13½*
898 A343 2s brt rose lil & brn 25 15

Exhibition of "1000 Years of Art in Krems." The statue of St. Matthew is from the Lentl Altar, created about 1520 by the Master of the Pulkau Altar.

1971, June 1 Engr. *Perf. 14x13½*
899 A344 2s brown 25 15

August Neilreich (1803-71), botanist.

Singer with Lyre — A345

Photo. & Engr.
1971, July 1 *Perf. 13½x14*
900 A345 4s lt bl, vio bl & gold 48 28

Intl. Choir Festival, Vienna, July 1-4.

Coat of Arms of Kitzbuhel — A346

1971, Aug. 23 *Perf. 14*
901 A346 2.50s gold & multi 28 15

700th anniversary of the town of Kitzbuhel.

Vienna Stock Exchange — A347

1971, Sept. 1 Engr. *Perf. 13½x14*
902 A347 4s reddish brown 45 18

Bicentenary of the Vienna Stock Exchange.

First and Latest Exhibition Halls — A348

1971, Sept. 6 Photo. *Perf. 13½x13*
903 A348 2.50s dp rose lilac 32 15

Vienna Intl. Fair, 50th anniv.

Trade Union Emblem
A349

Arms of Burgenland
A350

1971, Sept. 20 *Perf. 14x13½*
904 A349 2s gray, buff & red 25 15

Austrian Trade Union Assoc., 25th anniv.

1971, Oct. 1
905 A350 2s dk bl, gold, red & blk 25 15

50th anniv. of Burgenland joining Austria.

Marcus Car — A351

1971, Oct. 1 Photo. & Engr. *Perf. 14*
906 A351 4s pale green & blk 50 22

Austrian Automobile, Motorcycle and Touring Club, 75th anniv.

Europa Bridge — A352

1971, Oct. 8 Engr. *Perf. 14x13½*
907 A352 4s violet blue 50 22

Opening of highway over Brenner Pass.

Styria's Iron Mountain
A353

Designs: 2s, Austrian Nitrogen Products, Ltd., Linz. 4s, United Austrian Iron and Steel Works, Ltd. (VÖEST), Linz Harbor.

1971, Oct. 15 *Perf. 13½*

908	A353	1.50s reddish brown	18	15
909	A353	2s bluish black	25	20
910	A353	4s dk slate grn	40	32
		Nos. 908-910 (3)	83	67

25 years of nationalized industry.

High-speed Train on Semmering A354

Trout Fisherman A355

1971, Oct. 21 *Perf. 14*
911 A354 2s claret 25 15

Inter-city rapid train service.

1971, Nov. 15 *Perf. 13½*
912 A355 2s dark red brn 25 15

Erich Tschermak-Seysenegg A356

Infant Jesus as Savior, by Dürer A357

Photo. & Engr.

1971, Nov. 15 *Perf. 14x13½*
913 A356 2s pale ol & dk pur 25 15

Birth cent. of Dr. Erich Tschermak-Seysenegg (1871-1962), botanist.

1971, Nov. 26 *Perf. 13½*
914 A357 2s gold & multi 25 15

Christmas.

Franz Grillparzer, by Moritz Daffinger — A358

Fountain, Main Square, Friesach — A359

Perf. 14x13½

1972, Jan. 21 **Litho. & Engr.**
915 A358 2s buff, gold & blk 25 15

Death cent. of Franz Grillparzer (1791-1872), dramatic poet.

1972, Feb. 23 **Engr.** *Perf. 14x13½*

Designs: 2s, Fountain, Heiligenkreuz Abbey. 2.50s, Leopold Fountain, Innsbruck.

916 A359 1.50s rose lilac 22 15
917 A359 2s brown 28 16
918 A359 2.50s olive 35 24
Nos. 916-918 (3) 85 55

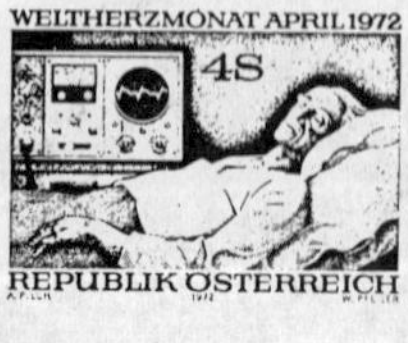

Cardiac Patient and Monitor A360

1972, Apr. 11 *Perf. 13½x14*
919 A360 4s violet brown 45 25

World Health Day.

A361

A362

Design: St. Michael's Gate, Royal Palace, Vienna.

1972, Apr. 11 *Perf. 14x13½*
920 A361 4s violet blue 45 25

Conference of European Post and Telecommunications Ministers, Vienna, Apr. 11-14.

1972, May 5 **Photo. & Engr.** *Perf. 14*
921 A362 2s Sculpture, Gurk Cathedral 25 15

900th anniv. of Gurk (Carinthia) Diocese. The design is after the central column supporting the sarcophagus of St. Hemma in Gurk Cathedral.

City Hall, Congress Emblem — A363

1972, May 23 **Litho. & Engr.**
922 A363 4s red, blk & yel 45 22

9th Intl. Congress of Public and Cooperative Economy, Vienna, May 23-25.

Power Line in Carnic Alps — A364

Designs: 2.50s, Power Station, Simmering. 4s, Zemm Power Station (lake in Zillertaler Alps).

1972, June 28 *Perf. 13½x14*
923 A364 70g gray & violet 15 15
924 A364 2.50s gray & red brn 32 32
925 A364 4s gray & slate 45 45
Nos. 923-925 (3) 92 92

Nationalization of the power industry, 25th anniv.

Runner with Olympic Torch — A365

St. Hermes, by Conrad Laib — A366

Engr. & Photo.

1972, Aug. 21 *Perf. 14x13½*
926 A365 2s sepia & red 25 15

Olympic torch relay from Olympia, Greece, to Munich, Germany, passing through Austria.

1972, Aug. 21 **Engr.**
927 A366 2s violet brown 25 15

Exhibition of Late Gothic Art, Salzburg.

Pears — A367

1972, Sept. *Perf. 14*
928 A367 2.50s dk bl & multi 28 15

World Congress of small plot Gardeners, Vienna, Sept. 7-10.

Souvenir Sheet

Spanish Walk — A368

1972, Sept. 12 *Perf. 13½*
929 A368 Sheet of 6 2.75 2.75
a. 2s Spanish walk 25 25
b. 2s Piaffe 25 25
c. 2.50s Levade 32 32
d. 2.50s On long rein 32 32
e. 4s Capriole 52 52
f. 4s Courbette 52 52

400th anniv. of the Spanish Riding School in Vienna.

Arms of University of Agriculture A369

Church and Old University A370

Photo. & Engr.

1972, Oct. 17 *Perf. 14x13½*
930 A369 2s black & multi 25 15

University of Agriculture, Vienna, cent.

1972, Nov. 7 **Engr.**
931 A370 4s red brown 45 20

Paris Lodron University, Salzburg, 350th anniv.

Carl Michael Ziehrer — A371

1972, Nov. 14
932 A371 2s rose claret 25 15

50th death anniv. of Carl Michael Ziehrer (1843-1922), composer.

Virgin and Child, Wood, 1420-30 A372

Photo. & Engr.

1972, Dec. 1 *Perf. 13½*
933 A372 2s olive & choc 25 15

Christmas.

Racing Sleigh, 1750 A373

Designs: 2s, Coronation landau, 1824. 2.50s, Imperial state coach, 1763.

1972, Dec. 12
934 A373 1.50s pale gray & brn 22 15
935 A373 2s pale gray & sl grn 28 16
936 A373 2.50s pale gray & plum 35 24
Nos. 934-936 (3) 85 55

Collection of historic state coaches and carriages in Schönbrunn Palace.

Map of Austrian Telephone System — A374

1972, Dec. 14 **Photo.** *Perf. 14*
937 A374 2s yellow & blk 25 15

Completion of automation of Austrian telephone system.

"Drugs are Death" — A375

1973, Jan. 26 **Photo.** *Perf. 13½x14*
938 A375 2s scar & multi 1.50 45

Fight against drug abuse.

Alfons Petzold — A376

Theodor Körner — A377

1973, Jan. 26 **Engr.** *Perf. 14x13½*
939 A376 2s reddish brn 25 15

50th death anniv. of Alfons Petzold (1882-1923), poet.

Photo. & Engr.

1973, Apr. 24 *Perf. 14x13½*
940 A377 2s gray & dp cl 25 15

Theodor Korner (1873-1957), Austrian Pres., birth cent.

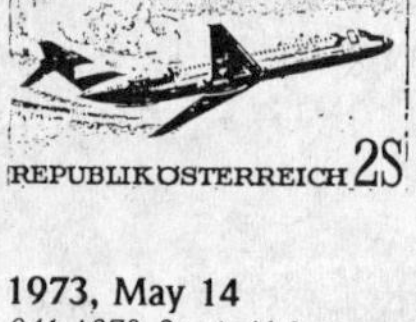

Douglas DC-9 — A378

1973, May 14 *Perf. 13½x14*
941 A378 2s vio bl & rose red 25 15

First intl. airmail service, Vienna to Kiev, Mar. 31, 1918, 55th anniv.; Austrian Aviation Corporation, 50th anniv.; Austrian Airlines, 15th anniv.

Otto Loewi — A379

"Support" — A380

1973, June 4 Engr. *Perf. 14x13½*

942 A379 4s deep violet 50 20

Birth cent. of Otto Loewi (1873-1961), pharmacologist, winner of 1936 Nobel prize.

1973, June 25

943 A380 2s dark blue 25 15

Federation of Austrian Social Insurance Institutes, 25th anniv.

Europa Issue 1973

Post Horn and Telephone — A381

1973, July 9 Photo. *Perf. 14*

944 A381 2.50s ocher, blk & yel 28 15

Dornbirn Fair Emblem A382

1973, July 27 *Perf. 13½x14*

945 A382 2s multicolored 25 15

Dornbirn Trade Fair, 25th anniversary.

Hurdles — A383

Leo Slezak — A384

1973, Aug. 13 Engr. *Perf. 14x13½*

946 A383 4s gray olive 50 22

23rd Intl. Military Pentathlon Championships, Wiener Neustadt, Aug. 13-18.

1973, Aug. 17 *Perf. 14*

947 A384 4s dark brown 50 22

Birth cent. of Leo Slezak (1873-1946), operatic tenor.

Gate, Vienna Hofburg, and ISI Emblem — A385

Photogravure and Engraved

1973, Aug. 20 *Perf. 14x13½*

948 A385 2s gray, dk brn & ver 25 15

39th Congress of Intl. Statistical Institute, Vienna, Aug. 20-30.

Tegetthoff off Franz Josef Land, by Julius Prayer — A386

1973, Aug. 30 Engr. *Perf. 13½x14*

949 A386 2.50s Prussian grn 28 15

Discovery of Franz Josef Land by an Austrian North Pole expedition, cent.

Academy of Science, by Canaletto A387

1973, Sept. 4

950 A387 2.50s violet 28 15

Intl. meteorological cooperation, cent.

Arms of Viennese Tanners A388

Max Reinhardt A389

Photo. & Engr.

1973, Sept. 4 *Perf. 14*

951 A388 4s red & multi 38 22

13th Congress of the Intl. Union of Leather Chemists' Societies, Vienna, Sept. 1-7.

1973, Sept. 7 Engr. *Perf. 13x13½*

952 A389 2s rose magenta 25 15

Max Reinhardt (1873-1943), theatrical director and stage manager, birth cent.

Trotter A390

1973, Sept. 28 *Perf. 13½*

953 A390 2s green 30 15

Centenary of Vienna Trotting Association.

Ferdinand Hanusch — A391

1973, Sept. 28 *Perf. 14x13½*

954 A391 2s rose brown 25 15

50th death anniv. of Ferdinand Hanusch (1866-1923), secretary of state.

Police Radio Operator A392

1973, Oct. 2 *Perf. 13½x14*

955 A392 4s violet blue 50 22

50th anniv. of Intl. Criminal Police Org. (INTERPOL).

Josef Petzval's Photographic Lens — A393

1973, Oct. 8 Litho. & Engr. *Perf. 14*

956 A393 2.50s blue & multi 28 15

EUROPHOT Photographic Cong., Vienna.

Emperor's Spring, Hell Valley — A394

Photo. & Engr.

1973, Oct. 23 *Perf. 13½x14*

957 A394 2s sepia, bl & red 25 15

Vienna's first mountain spring water supply system, cent.

Almsee, Upper Austria — A395

Hofburg and Prince Eugene Statue, Vienna — A395a

Designs: 50g, Farmhouses, Zillertal, Tirol. 1s, Kahlenbergerdorf. 1.50s, Bludenz, Vorarlberg. 2s, Inn Bridge, Alt Finstermunz. 2.50s, Murau, Styria. 3s, Bischofsmütze, Salzburg. 3.50s, Easter Church, Oberwart. 4.50s, Windmill, Retz. 5s, Aggstein Castle, Lower Austria. 6s, Lindauer Hut, Vorarlberg. 6.50s, Holy Cross Church, Villach, Carinthia. 7s, Falkenstein Castle, Carinthia. 7.50s, Hohensalzburg. 8s, Votive column, Reiteregg, Styria. 10s, Lake Neusiedl, Burgenland. 11s, Old Town, Enns. 16s, Openair Museum, Bad Tatzmannsdorf. 20s. Myra waterfalls.

Photo. & Engr.

1973-78 *Perf. 13½x14*

Size: 23x29mm

Type A395

958	50g	gray & sl green	15	15
959	1s	brn & dk brown	15	15
960	1.50s	rose & brown	22	15
961	2s	gray bl & dk blue	30	15
962	2.50s	vio & dp violet	35	15
963	3s	lt ultra & vio blue	45	15
963A	3.50s	dl org & brown	50	15
964	4s	brt lil & pur	55	15
965	4.50s	brt grn & bl green	60	15
966	5s	lilac & vio	65	15
967	6s	dp rose & dk violet	80	15
968	6.50s	bl grn & indigo	90	15
969	7s	sage grn & sl green	95	15
970	7.50s	lil rose & claret	1.00	24
971	8s	dl red & dp brown	1.10	18
972	10s	gray grn & dk green	1.40	18
973	11s	ver & dk carmine	1.65	15
974	16s	ocher & black	2.25	60
975	20s	ol bis & ol grn	2.75	1.25

Type A395a

976	50s gray vio & vio bl	6.75	2.50
	Nos. 958-976 (20)	23.47	
	Set value		5.75

Issue dates: 1974, Nos. 960-963. 1975, Nos. 958-959, 967, 976. 1976, Nos. 965, 971, 973. 1977, Nos. 968, 970, 974-975. 1978, No. 963A. See Nos. 1100-1109.

Nativity — A396

Pregl — A397

1973, Nov. 30 *Perf. 14*

977 A396 2s multicolored 25 15

Christmas. Design from 14th century stained-glass window.

1973, Dec. 12 Engr. *Perf. 14x13½*

978 A397 4s deep blue 50 22

50th anniv. of the awarding of the Nobel prize for chemistry to Fritz Pregl (1869-1930).

Telex Machine A398

Hofmannsthal A399

1974, Jan. 14 Photo. *Perf. 14x13½*

979 A398 2.50s ultramarine 28 15

50th anniversary of Radio Austria.

1974, Feb. 1 Engr. *Perf. 14*

980 A399 4s violet blue 50 22

Birth cent. of Hugo Hofmannsthal (1874-1929), poet and playwright.

Anton Bruckner and Bruckner House A400

1974, Mar. 22 Engr. *Perf. 14*

981 A400 4s brown 50 22

Founding of Anton Bruckner House (concert hall), Linz, and birth of Anton Bruckner (1824-1896), composer, 150th anniv.

Vegetables A401

Photo. & Engr.

1974, Apr. 18 *Perf. 14*

982 A401	2s	shown	28	20
983 A401	2.50s	Fruits	35	30
984 A401	4s	Flowers	50	50
		Nos. 982-984 (3)	1.13	1.00

Intl. Garden Show, Vienna, Apr. 18-Oct. 14.

Seal of Judenburg
A402

Karl Kraus
A403

1974, Apr. 24 Photo. ***Perf. 14x13½***

985 A402 2s plum & multi 25 15

750th anniversary of Judenburg.

1974, Apr. 6 **Engr.**

986 A403 4s dark red 50 22

Karl Kraus (1874-1936), poet and satirist, birth cent.

St. Michael, by Thomas Schwanthaler — A404

1974, May 3

987 A404 2.50s slate green 28 15

Exhibition of the works by the Schwanthaler Family of sculptors, (1633-1848), Reichersberg am Inn, May 3-Oct. 13.

A405

A406

Europa: King Arthur, from tomb of Maximilian I

1974, May 8 ***Perf. 13½***

988 A405 2.50s ocher & slate blue 28 15

Photo. & Engr.

1974, May 17 ***Perf. 14x13½***

De Dion Bouton motor tricycle.

989 A406 2s gray & vio brn 25 15

Austrian Automobile Assoc., 75th anniv.

Satyr's Head, Terracotta
A407

1974, May 22 ***Perf. 13½x14***

990 A407 2s org brn, gold & blk 25 15

Exhibition, "Renaissance in Austria," Schallaburg Castle, May 22-Nov. 14.

Road Transport Union Emblem
A408

Maulbertsch, Self-portrait
A409

1974, May 24 Photo. ***Perf. 14x13½***

991 A408 4s deep org & blk 50 22

14th Congress of the Intl. Road Transport Union, Innsbruck.

1974, June 7 Engr. ***Perf. 14x13½***

992 A409 2s violet brown 25 15

Franz Anton Maulbertsch (1724-96), painter, 250th birth anniv.

Gendarmes, 1824 and 1974 — A410

1974, June 7 Photo. ***Perf. 13½x14***

993 A410 2s red & multi 25 15

125th anniversary of Austrian gendarmery.

Fencing
A411

Photo. & Engr.

1974, June 14 ***Perf. 13½***

994 A411 2.50s red org & blk 28 15

Transportation Symbols — A412

St. Virgil, Sculpture from Nonntal Church — A413

1974, June 18 Photo. ***Perf. 14x13½***

995 A412 4s lt ultra & multi 50 22

European Conference of Transportation Ministers, Vienna, June 18-21.

1974, June 28 Engr. ***Perf. 13½x14***

996 A413 2s violet blue 25 15

Consecration of the Cathedral of Salzburg by Scotch-Irish Bishop Feirgil (St. Virgil), 1200th anniv. Salzburg was a center of Christianization in the 8th century.

Franz Jonas and Austrian Eagle — A414

1974, June 28

997 A414 2s black 25 15

Franz Jonas (1899-1974), Austrian Pres., 1965-1974.

Franz Stelzhamer — A415

Diver — A416

1974, July 12 Engr. ***Perf. 14x13½***

998 A415 2s indigo 25 15

Franz Stelzhamer (1802-1874), poet who wrote in Upper Austrian vernacular, death cent.

Photo. & Engr.

1974, Aug. 16 ***Perf. 13x13½***

999 A416 4s blue & sepia 50 22

13th European Swimming, Diving and Water Polo Championships, Vienna, Aug. 18-25.

Ferdinand Ritter von Hebra — A417

1974, Sept. 10 Engr. ***Perf. 14x13½***

1000 A417 4s brown 50 22

30th Meeting of the Assoc. of German-speaking Dermatologists, Graz, Sept. 10-14. Dr. von Hebra (1816-1880) was a founder of modern dermatology.

Arnold Schonberg
A418

1974, Sept. 13 ***Perf. 13½x14***

1001 A418 2.50s purple 28 15

Arnold Schönberg (1874-1951), composer, birth cent.

Radio Station, Salzburg
A419

1974, Oct. 1 Photo. ***Perf. 13½x14***

1002 A419 2s multicolored 25 15

50th anniversary of Austrian broadcasting.

Edmund Eysler (1874-1949), Composer — A420

1974, Oct. 4 Engr. ***Perf. 14x13½***

1003 A420 2s dark olive 25 15

Mailman, Mail Coach and Train, UPU Emblem
A421

Design: 4s, Mailman, jet, truck, 1974, and UPU emblem.

1974, Oct. 9 Photo. ***Perf. 13½***

1004 A421 2s deep claret & lil 25 15

1005 A421 4s dark blue & gray 50 22

Centenary of Universal Postal Union.

Gauntlet Protecting Rose — A422

1974, Oct. 23 Photo. ***Perf. 13½x14***

1006 A422 2s multicolored 25 15

Environment protection.

Austrian Sports Pool Emblem
A423

1974, Oct. 23 Photo. ***Perf. 13½x14***

1007 A423 70g multicolored 15 15

Austrian Sports Pool (lottery), 25th anniv.

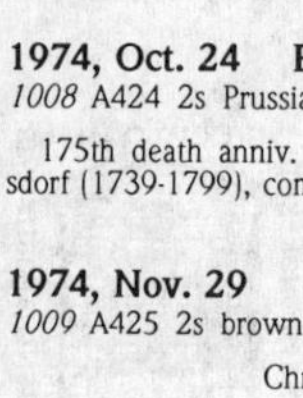

Carl Ditters von Dittersdorf
A424

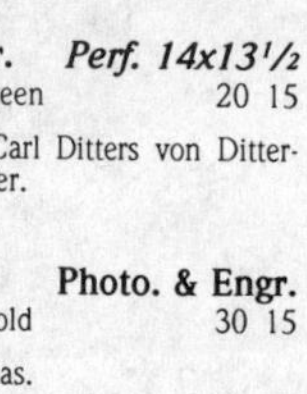

Virgin and Child, Wood, c. 1600
A425

1974, Oct. 24 Engr. ***Perf. 14x13½***

1008 A424 2s Prussian green 20 15

175th death anniv. of Carl Ditters von Dittersdorf (1739-1799), composer.

1974, Nov. 29 **Photo. & Engr.**

1009 A425 2s brown & gold 30 15

Christmas.

Values quoted in this catalogue are for stamps graded Fine-Very Fine and with no faults. An illustrated guide to grade is provided in the "Catalogue Information" section of the Introduction.

A426

A427

1974, Dec. 18
1010 A426 4s gray & black 50 22

Franz Schmidt (1874-1939), composer.

Photo. & Engr.

1975, Jan. 24 *Perf. 13½*
1011 A427 2.50s St. Christopher 38 15

European Architectural Heritage Year. The design shows part of a wooden figure from central panel of the retable in the Kefermarkt Church, 1490-1497.

Safety Belt and Skeleton Arms — A428

Stained Glass Window, Vienna City Hall — A429

1975, Apr. 1 Photo. *Perf. 14x13½*
1012 A428 70g violet & multi 15 15

Introduction of obligatory use of automobile safety belts.

1975, Apr. 2 *Perf. 14*
1013 A429 2.50s multicolored 32 15

11th meeting of the Council of European Municipalities, Vienna, Apr. 2-5.

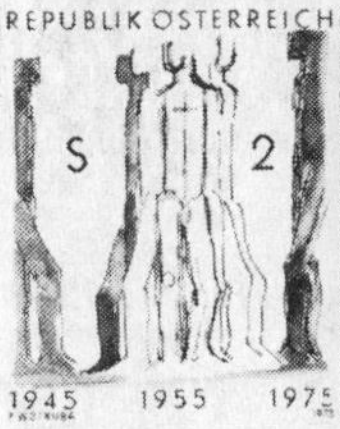
Austria as Mediator — A430

Forest — A431

1975, May 2 Litho. *Perf. 14*
1014 A430 2s blk & bister 25 15

2nd Republic of Austria, 30th anniv.

1975, May 6 **Engr.**
1015 A431 2s green 25 15

National forests, 50th anniversary.

High Priest, by Michael Pacher — A432

Gosaukamm Funicular — A433

Europa Issue 1975
Photo. & Engr.

1975, May 27 *Perf. 14x13½*
1016 A432 2.50s black & multi 38 15

Design is detail from painting "The Marriage of Joseph and Mary," by Michael Pacher (c. 1450-1500).

1975, June 23 *Perf. 14x13½*
1017 A433 2s slate & red 30 15

4th Intl. Funicular Cong., Vienna, June 23-27.

Josef Misson and Mühlbach am Manhartsberg A434

1975, June 27 *Perf. 13½x14*
1018 A434 2s choc & redsh brn 25 15

Josef Misson (1803-1875), poet who wrote in Lower Austrian vernacular, death cent.

Setting Sun and "P" — A435

1975, Aug. 27 Litho. *Perf. 14x13½*
1019 A435 1.50s org, blk & bl 20 15

Austrian Assoc. of Pensioners 25th anniv. meeting, Vienna, Aug. 1975.

Ferdinand Porsche A436

Photo. & Engr.

1975, Sept. 3 *Perf. 13½x14*
1020 A436 1.50s gray & purple 20 15

Ferdinand Porsche (1875-1951), engineer, developer of Porsche and Volkswagen cars, birth cent.

Leo Fall (1873-1925), Composer — A437

1975, Sept. 16 Engr. *Perf. 14x13½*
1021 A437 2s violet 25 15

Judo Throw — A438

Heinrich Angeli — A439

1975, Oct. 20 Photo. *Perf. 14x13½*
1022 A438 2.50s gold & multi 28 15

10th World Judo Championships, Vienna, Oct. 20-26.

1975, Oct. 21 Engr. *Perf. 14x13½*
1023 A439 2s rose lake 25 15

Heinrich Angeli (1840-1925), painter, 50th death anniv.

Johann Strauss and Dancers A440

Photo. & Engr.

1975, Oct. 24 *Perf. 13½x14*
1024 A440 4s ocher & sepia 50 22

Johann Strauss (1825-1899), composer, 150th birth anniv.

Stylized Musician Playing a Viol — A441

Symbolic House — A442

1975, Oct. 30 *Perf. 14x13½*
1025 A441 2.50s sil & vio bl 28 15

Vienna Symphony Orchestra, 75th anniv.

1975, Oct. 31 **Photo.**
1026 A442 2s multicolored 25 15

Austrian building savings societies, 50th anniv.

Fan with "Hanswurst" Scene, 18th Century A443

1975, Nov. 14 Photo. *Perf. 13½x14*
1027 A443 1.50s green & multi 20 15

Salzburg Theater bicentenary.

Virgin and Child, from 15th Century Altar A444

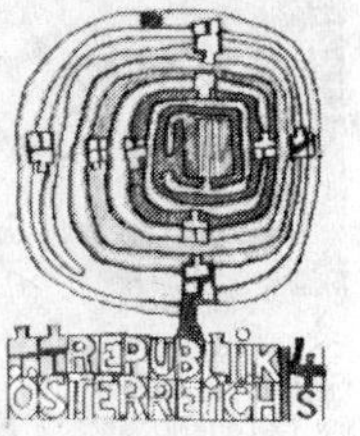
"The Spiral Tree," by Hundertwasser A445

Photo. & Engr.

1975, Nov. 28 *Perf. 13x13½*
1028 A444 2s gold & dull pur 25 15

Christmas.

Photo., Engr. & Typo.

1975, Dec. 11 *Perf. 13½x14*
1029 A445 4s multicolored 60 25

Austrian modern art. Friedenstreich Hundertwasser is the pseudonym of Friedrich Stowasser (b. 1928).

Old Burgtheater A446

Design: No. 1030b, Grand staircase, new Burgtheater.

Perf. 14 (pane), 13½x14 (stamps)

1976, Apr. 8 **Engr.**
1030 Pane of 2 + label 85 85
a. A446 3s violet blue 28 28
b. A446 3s deep brown 28 28

Bicentenary of Vienna Burgtheater. Printed in sheets of 5 panes. Label (head of Pan) and commemorative inscription in vermilion.

Dr. Robert Barany (1876-1936), Winner of Nobel Prize for Medicine, 1914 — A447

Photo. & Engr.

1976, Apr. 22 *Perf. 14x13½*
1031 A447 3s blue & brown 35 15

Ammonite A448

1976, Apr. 30 Photo. *Perf. 13½x14*
1032 A448 3s red & multi 35 15

Vienna Museum of Natural History, Centenary Exhibition.

Carinthian Dukes' Coronation Chair — A449

Siege of Linz, 17th Century Etching — A450

Photo. & Engr.

1976, May 6 *Perf. 14x13½*
1033 A449 3s grnsh blk & org 35 15

Millennium of Carinthia.

1976, May 14
1034 A450 4s blk & gray grn 50 22

Upper Austrian Peasants' War, 350th anniv.

Skittles — A451

1976, May 14 *Perf. 13½x14*
1035 A451 4s black & org 50 22

11th World Skittles Championships, Vienna.

Duke Heinrich II, Stained-glass Window — A452

1976, May 14 *Perf. 14*
1036 A452 3s multicolored 35 15

Babenberg Exhibition, Lilienfeld.

St. Wolfgang, from Pacher Altar — A453

1976, May 26 Engr. *Perf. 13½*
1037 A453 6s bright vio 77 40

Intl. Art Exhibition at St. Wolfgang.

Europa Issue 1976

Tassilo Cup, Kremsmunster, 777 — A454

Photo. & Engr.

1976, Aug. 13 *Perf. 14x13½*
1038 A454 4s ultra & multi 60 22

Timber Fair Emblem — A455

Constantin Economo, M.D. — A456

1976, Aug. 13 **Photo.**
1039 A455 3s green & multi 35 15

Austrian Timber Fair, Klagenfurt, 25th anniv.

1976, Aug. 23 **Engr.**
1040 A456 3s dark red brn 35 15

Dr. Economo (1876-1931), neurologist.

Administrative Court, by Salomon Klein — A457

1976, Oct. 25 Engr. *Perf. 13½x14*
1041 A457 6s deep brown 75 32

Austrian Central Administrative Court, cent.

Souvenir Sheet

Coats of Arms of Austrian Provinces — A458

Millennium of Austria: a, Lower Austria. b, Upper Austria. c, Styria. d, Carinthia. e, Tyrol. f, Voralberg. g, Salzburg. h, Burgenland. i, Vienna.

Photo. & Engr.

1976, Oct. 25 *Perf. 14*
1042 Sheet of 9 2.75 2.75
a.-i. A458 2s any single 28 28

"Cancer" A459

1976, Nov. 17 Photo. *Perf. 14x13½*
1043 A459 2.50s multicolored 35 15

Fight against cancer.

UN Emblem and Bridge — A460

1976, Nov. 17
1044 A460 3s blue & gold 40 15

UN Industrial Development Org. (UNIDO), 10th anniv.

Punched Tape, Map of Europe — A461

1976, Nov. 17 *Perf. 14*
1045 A461 1.50s multicolored 15 15

Austrian Press Agency (APA), 30th anniv.

Viktor Kaplan, Kaplan Turbine — A462

Photo. & Engr.

1976, Nov. 26 *Perf. 13½x14*
1046 A462 2.50s multicolored 30 15

Viktor Kaplan (1876-1934), inventor of Kaplan turbine, birth centenary.

Nativity, by Konrad von Friesach, c. 1450 A463

1976, Nov. 26 *Perf. 13½*
1047 A463 3s multicolored 32 15

Christmas.

Augustin, the Piper — A464

Photo. & Engr.

1976, Dec. 29 *Perf. 13½*
1048 A464 6s multicolored 75 25

Modern Austrian art.

Rainer Maria Rilke (1875-1926), Poet A465

Vienna City Synagogue A466

1976, Dec. 29 Engr. *Perf. 14x13½*
1049 A465 3s deep violet 30 15

1976, Dec. 29 Photo. *Perf. 13½*
1050 A466 1.50s multicolored 15 15

Sesquicentennial of Vienna City Synagogue.

Nikolaus Joseph von Jacquin (1727-1817), Botanist — A467

1977, Feb. 16 Engr. *Perf. 14x13½*
1051 A467 4s chocolate 45 22

Oswald von Wolkenstein (1377-1445), Poet — A468

Photo. & Engr.

1977, Feb. 16 *Perf. 14*
1052 A468 3s multicolored 35 15

Handball A469

1977, Feb. 25 Photo. *Perf. 13½x14*
1053 A469 1.50s multicolored 15 15

World Indoor Handball Championships, Austria, Feb. 5-Mar. 6.

A470

A471

1977, Apr. 12 Engr. *Perf. 14x13½*
1054 A470 6s dk violet bl 70 25

Alfred Kubin (1877-1959), illustrator and writer.

1977, Apr. 22 Engr. *Perf. 13½*

Designs: 2.50s, Great Spire, St. Stephen's Cathedral. 3s, Heathen Tower and Frederick's Gable. 4s, Interior view with Albertinian Choir.

1055	A471	2.50s dark brown	35	15
1056	A471	3s dark blue	38	28
1057	A471	4s rose lake	52	32
		Nos. 1055-1057 (3)	1.25	75

Restoration and re-opening of St. Stephen's Cathedral, Vienna, 25th anniversary.

Fritz Hermanovsky-Orlando (1877-1954), Poet and Artist — A472

Photo. & Engr.

1977, Apr. 29 *Perf. 13½x14*
1058 A472 6s Prus green & gold 70 25

IAEA Emblem A473

Arms of Schwanenstadt A474

1977, May 2 **Photo.** ***Perf. 14***
1059 A473 3s brt bl, lt bl & gold 35 15

Intl. Atomic Energy Agency (IAEA), 20th anniv.

1977, June 10 **Photo.** ***Perf. 14x13½***
1060 A474 3s dk brown & multi 35 15

Town of Schwanenstadt, 350th anniv.

Europa Issue 1977

Attersee, Upper Austria — A475

1977, June 10 **Engr.** ***Perf. 14***
1061 A475 6s olive green 90 30

Globe, by Vincenzo Coronelli, 1688 — A476

Photo. & Engr.

1977, June 29 ***Perf. 14***
1062 A476 3s black & buff 35 15

5th Intl. Symposium of the Coronelli World Federation of Friends of the Globe, Austria, June 29-July 3.

Kayak Race — A477

1977, July 15 **Photo.** ***Perf. 13½x14***
1063 A477 4s multicolored 48 18

3rd Kayak Slalom White Water Race on Lieser River, Spittal.

The Good Samaritan, by Francesco Bassano — A478

1977, Sept. 16 **Photo. & Engr.**
1064 A478 1.50s brown & red 20 15

Workers' Good Samaritan Org., 50th anniv.

Papermakers' Coat of Arms — A479

Man with Austrian Flag Lifting Barbed Wire — A480

1977, Oct. 10 ***Perf. 14x13½***
1065 A479 3s multicolored 35 15

17th Conf. of the European Committee of Pulp and Paper Technology (EUCEPA), Vienna.

1977, Nov. 3 ***Perf. 14***
1066 A480 2.50s slate & red 30 15

Honoring the martyrs for Austria's freedom.

"Austria," First Steam Locomotive in Austria — A481

Designs: 2.50s, Steam locomotive 214. 3s, Electric locomotive 1044.

Photo. & Engr.

1977, Nov. 17 ***Perf. 13½***

1067 A481 1.50s multicolored		20	15
1068 A481 2.50s multicolored		38	15
1069 A481 3s multicolored		45	22
Nos. 1067-1069 (3)		1.03	
Set value			40

140th anniversary of Austrian railroads.

A482

A483

Virgin and Child, wood statue, Mariastein, Tyrol.

1977, Nov. 25 ***Perf. 14x13½***
1070 A482 3s multicolored 32 15

Christmas.

1977, Dec. 2 ***Perf. 13½x14***

The Danube Maiden, by Wolfgang Hutter.

1071 A483 6s multicolored 75 18

Modern Austrian art.

Egon Friedell (1878-1938), Writer and Historian A484

1978, Jan. 23 **Photo. & Engr.**
1072 A484 3s light bl & blk 35 15

Subway Train — A485

1978, Feb. 24 **Photo.** ***Perf. 13½x14***
1073 A485 3s multicolored 50 15

New Vienna subway system.

Biathlon Competition A486

1978, Feb. 28 **Photo. & Engr.**
1074 A486 4s multicolored 45 22

Biathlon World Championships, Hochfilzen, Tyrol, Feb. 28-Mar. 5.

Leopold Kunschak (1871-1953), Political Leader — A487

1978, Mar. 13 **Engr.** ***Perf. 14x13½***
1075 A487 3s violet blue 32 15

Coyote, Aztec Feather Shield — A488

1978, Mar. 13 **Photo.** ***Perf. 13½x14***
1076 A488 3s multicolored 32 15

Ethnographical Museum, 50th anniv. exhibition.

Alpine Farm, Woodcut by Suitbert Lobisser — A489

1978, Mar. 23 **Engr.** ***Perf. 13½***
1077 A489 3s dark brown, *buff* 32 15

Lobisser (1878-1943), graphic artist.

Capercaillie, Hunting Bag, 1730, and Rifle, 1655 — A490

Photo. & Engr.

1978, Apr. 28 ***Perf. 13½***
1078 A490 6s multicolored 75 35

Intl. Hunting Exhibition, Marchegg.

Europa Issue 1978

Riegersburg, Styria — A491

1978, May 3 **Engr.**
1079 A491 6s deep rose lilac 75 35

Parliament, Vienna, and Map of Europe — A492

Admont Pietà, c. 1410 — A493

1978, May 3 **Photo.** ***Perf. 14x13½***
1080 A492 4s multicolored 45 20

3rd Interparliamentary Conference for European Cooperation and Security, Vienna.

1978, May 26 **Photo. & Engr.**
1081 A493 2.50s ocher & black 25 15

Gothic Art in Styria Exhibition, St. Lambrecht, 1978.

Ort Castle, Gmunden — A494

1978, June 9
1082 A494 3s multicolored 32 15

700th anniversary of Gmunden City.

Child with Flowers and Fruit — A495

Lehar and his Home, Bad Ischl — A496

Photo. & Engr.

1978, June 30 ***Perf. 14x13½***
1083 A495 6s gold & multi 75 35

25 years of Social Tourism.

1978, July 14 **Engr.** ***Perf. 14x13½***
1084 A496 6s slate 75 30

International Lehar Congress, Bad Ischl. Franz Lehar (1870-1948), operetta composer.

Congress Emblem A497

1978, Aug. 21 Photo. ***Perf. 13½x14***
1085 A497 1.50s black, red & yel 20 15

Cong. of Intl. Fed. of Building Construction and Wood Workers, Vienna, Aug. 20-24.

Ottokar of Bohemia and Rudolf of Hapsburg A498

1978, Aug. 25 Photo. & Engr.
1086 A498 3s multicolored 35 15

Battle of Durnkrut and Jedenspeigen (Marchfeld), which established Hapsburg rule in Austria, 700th anniversary.

First Documentary Reference to Villach, "ad pontem uillah" A499

1978, Sept. 8 Litho. ***Perf. 13½x14***
1087 A499 3s multicolored 35 15

1100th anniversary of Villach, Carinthia.

Seal of Graz, 1440 — A500

Emperor Maximilian Fishing — A501

Photo. & Engr.
1978, Sept. 13 ***Perf. 14x13½***
1088 A500 4s multicolored 50 25

850th anniversary of Graz.

1978, Sept. 15 ***Perf. 14x13½***
1089 A501 4s multicolored 50 22

World Fishing Championships, Vienna, Sept. 1978.

"Aid to the Handicapped" A502

1978, Oct. 2 Photo. ***Perf. 13½x14***
1090 A502 6s orange brn & blk 75 30

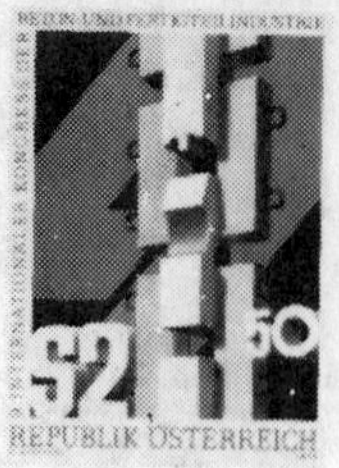

Symbolic Column — A503

1978, Oct. 9 Photo. ***Perf. 13½***
1091 A503 2.50s orange, blk & gray 30 15

9th Intl. Congress of Concrete and Prefabrication Industries, Vienna, Oct. 8-13.

Grace, by Albin Egger-Lienz A504

1978, Oct. 27 ***Perf. 13½x14***
1092 A504 6s multicolored 75 30

European Family Congress, Vienna, Oct. 26-29.

Lise Meitner (1878-1968), Physicist, and Atom Symbol — A505

1978, Nov. 7 Engr. ***Perf. 14x13½***
1093 A505 6s dark violet 75 30

Viktor Adler, by Anton Hanak A506

Photo. & Engr.
1978, Nov. 10 ***Perf. 13½x14***
1094 A506 3s vermilion & black 35 15

Viktor Adler (1852-1918), leader of Social Democratic Party, 60th death anniversary.

Franz Schubert, by Josef Kriehuber — A507

Virgin and Child, Wilhering Church — A508

1978, Nov. 17 Engr. ***Perf. 14***
1095 A507 6s reddish brown 75 35

Franz Schubert (1797-1828), composer.

Perf. 12½x13½
1978, Dec. 1 Photo. & Engr.
1096 A508 3s multicolored 35 15

Christmas.

Archduke Johann Shelter, Grossglockner A509

1978, Dec. 6 ***Perf. 13½x14***
1097 A509 1.50s gold & dk vio bl 20 15

Austrian Alpine Club, centenary.

A510

A511

Adam, by Rudolf Hausner.

1978, Dec. 6 Photo. ***Perf. 13½x14***
1098 A510 6s multicolored 75 35

Modern Austrian art.

1978, Dec. 6 ***Perf. 14x13½***
1099 A511 6s Bound Hands 75 30

Universal Declaration of Human Rights, 30th anniv.

Type of 1973

Designs: 20g, Freistadt, Upper Austria. 3s, Bishofsmutze, Salzburg. 4.20s, Hirschegg, Kleinwalsertal. 5.50s, Peace Chapel, Stoderzinken. 5.60s, Riezlern, Kleinwalsertal. 9s, Asten Carinthia. 12s, Kufstein Fortress. 14s, Weiszsee, Salzburg.

Photo. & Engr.
1978-83 ***Perf. 13½x14***

Size: 23x29mm

1100 A395 20g vio bl & dk bl 15 15

Size: 17x21mm

1102 A395 3s lt ultra & vio bl 45 15

Size: 23x29mm

1104 A395 4.20s blk & grysh bl 55 15
1105 A395 5.50s lilac & pur 75 18
1106 A395 5.60s yel grn & ol grn 75 20
1107 A395 9s red 1.25 45
1108 A395 12s ocher & vio brn 1.75 15
1109 A395 14s lt green & green 2.00 22
Nos. 1100-1109 (8) 7.65 1.65

Issue dates: 3s, Dec. 7. 4.20s, June 22, 1979. 20g, June 27, 1980. 12s, Oct. 3, 1980. 14s, Jan. 27, 1982. 5.50s, 5.60s, July 1, 1982. 9s, Feb. 9, 1983.

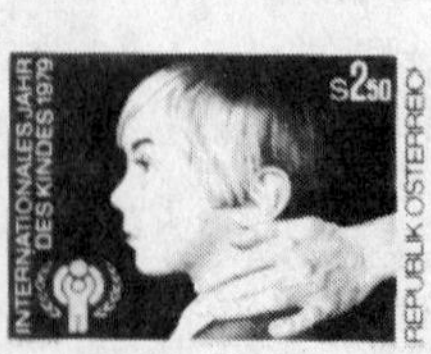

Child and IYC Emblem A512

Photo. & Engr.
1979, Jan. 16 ***Perf. 14***
1110 A512 2.50s dk blue, blk & brn 25 15

International Year of the Child.

CCIR Emblem A513

1979, Jan. 16 Photo. ***Perf. 13½x14***
1111 A513 6s multicolored 75 30

Intl. Radio Consultative Committee (CCIR) of the ITU, 50th anniv.

Air Rifle, Air Pistol and Club Emblem A514

Photo. & Engr.
1979, Mar. 7 ***Perf. 13½***
1112 A514 6s multicolored 75 30

Austrian Shooting Club, cent., and European Air Rifle and Air Pistol Championships, Graz.

Figure Skater — A515

1979, Mar. 7 Photo. ***Perf. 14x13½***
1113 A515 4s multicolored 45 25

World Ice Skating Championships, Vienna.

Steamer Franz I A516

Designs: 2.50s, Tugboat Linz. 3s, Passenger ship Theodor Körner.

1979, Mar. 13 Engr. ***Perf. 13½***
1114 A516 1.50s violet blue 22 15
1115 A516 2.50s sepia 30 15
1116 A516 3s magenta 35 18
Nos. 1114-1116 (3) 87
Set value 40

1st Danube Steamship Company, 150th anniv.

Fashion Design, by Theo Zasche, 1900 — A517

Photo. & Engr.
1979, Mar. 26 ***Perf. 13x13½***
1117 A517 2.50s multicolored 30 15

50th Intl. Fashion Week, Vienna.

Wiener Neustadt Cathedral A518

1979, Mar. 27 Engr. *Perf. 13½*

1118 A518 4s violet blue 50 25

Cathedral of Wiener Neustadt, 700th anniv.

Teacher and Pupils, by Franz A. Zauner — A519

Population Chart and Barock Angel — A520

Photo. & Engr.

1979, Mar. 30 *Perf. 14x13½*

1119 A519 2.50s multicolored 30 15

Education of the deaf in Austria, 200th anniv.

1979, Apr. 6

1120 A520 2.50s multicolored 30 15

Austrian Central Statistical Bureau, 150th anniv.

Laurenz Koschier — A521

Diesel Motor — A522

Europa Issue, 1979

1979, May 4

1121 A521 6s ocher & purple 80 30

1979, May 4 Photo.

1122 A522 4s multicolored 45 22

13th CIMAC Congress (Intl. Org. for Internal Combustion Machines).

Arms of Ried, Schärding and Braunau — A523

Photo. & Engr.

1979, June 1 *Perf. 14x13½*

1123 A523 3s multicolored 32 15

200th anniversary of Innviertel District.

Flood and City — A524

1979, June 1 *Perf. 13½x14*

1124 A524 2.50s multicolored 30 15

Control and eliminate water polution.

Arms of Rottenmann A525

Jodok Fink A526

Photo. & Engr.

1979, June 22 *Perf. 14x13½*

1125 A525 3s multicolored 32 15

700th anniversary of Rottenmann.

1979, June 29 Engr. *Perf. 14*

1126 A526 3s brown carmine 32 15

Jodok Fink (1853-1929), governor of Vorarlberg.

Arms of Wels, Returnees' Emblem, "Europa Sail" — A527

1979, July 6 Photo. *Perf. 14x13½*

1127 A527 4s yellow grn & blk 45 22

5th European Meeting of the Intl. Confederation of Former Prisoners of War, Wels, July 6-8.

Symbolic Flower, Conference Emblem — A528

1979, Aug. 20 Litho. *Perf. 14x13½*

1128 A528 4s turq blue 45 22

UN Conf. for Science and Technology, Vienna, Aug. 20-31.

Donaupark, UNIDO and IAEA Emblems A529

1979, Aug. 24 Engr. *Perf. 13½x14*

1129 A529 6s grayish blue 75 30

Opening of the Donaupark Intl. Center in Vienna, seat of the UN Industrial Development Org. (UNIDO) and the Intl. Atomic Energy Agency (IAEA).

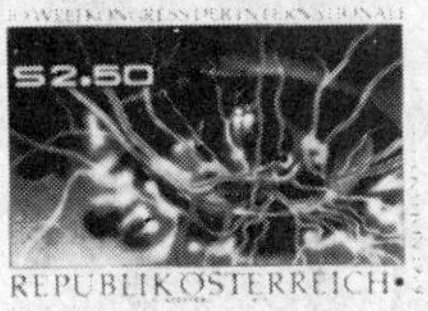

Diseased Eye and Blood Vessels A530

1979, Sept. 10 Photo. *Perf. 14*

1130 A530 2.50s multicolored 35 15

10th World Congress of Intl. Diabetes Federation, Vienna, Sept. 9-14.

View of Stanz Valley through East Portal of Arlberg Tunnel A531

1979, Sept. 14 Photo. & Engr.

1131 A531 4s multicolored 45 20

16th World Road Cong., Vienna, Sept. 16-21.

Steam Printing Press A532

Photo. & Engr.

1979, Sept. 18 *Perf. 13½x14*

1132 A532 3s multicolored 32 15

Austrian Government Printing Office, 175th anniv.

Richard Zsigmondy (1865-1929), Chemist — A533

1979, Sept. 21 Engr. *Perf. 14x13½*

1133 A533 6s multicolored 75 30

"Save Energy" A534

1979, Oct. 1 Photo. *Perf. 14x13½*

1134 A534 2.50s multicolored 30 15

Festival and Convention Center, Bregenz (Model) A535

1979, Oct. 1 Engr. *Perf. 14*

1135 A535 2.50s purple 30 15

Lions International Emblem — A536

1979, Oct. 11 Photo. & Engr.

1136 A536 4s multicolored 45 22

25th Lions Europa Forum, Vienna, Oct. 11-13.

A537

A538

Photo. & Engr.

1979, Oct. 19 *Perf. 13½x14*

1137 A537 2.50s Wilhelm Exner 30 15

Centenary of Technological Handicraft Museum, founded by Wilhelm Exner.

1979, Oct. 23 Litho. *Perf. 13½x14*

The Compassionate Christ, by Hans Fronius.

1138 A538 4s olive & ol blk 50 22

Modern Austrian art.

Locomotive and Arms A539

1979, Oct. 24 Photo. *Perf. 13½x14*

1139 A539 2.50s multicolored 30 15

Raab-Odenburg-Ebenfurt railroad, cent.

August Musger — A540

Photo. & Engr.

1979, Oct. 30 *Perf. 14x13½*

1140 A540 2.50s bl gray & blk 30 15

August Musger (1868-1929), developer of slow-motion film technique.

Nativity, St. Barbara's Church A541

1979, Nov. 30 *Perf. 13½x14*

1141 A541 4s multicolored 45 22

Christmas.

Arms of Baden — A542

1980, Jan. 25 ***Perf. 14***
1142 A542 4s multicolored 45 22

Baden, 500th anniversary.

A543

A544

1980, Feb. 21 ***Perf. 13½***
1143 A543 2.50s red & aqua 30 15

Fight rheumatism.

1980, Feb. 21 Photo. ***Perf. 14x13½***
1144 A544 4s dark blue & red 45 22

Austrian exports.

Austrian Red Cross Centenary A545

1980, Mar. 14 Photo. ***Perf. 13½x14***
1145 A545 2.50s multicolored 30 15

Rudolph Kirchschlager — A546

Photo. & Engr.

1980, Mar. 20 ***Perf. 14x13½***
1146 A546 4s sepia & red 45 22

Robert Hamerling (1830-1889), Poet — A547

1980, Mar. 24 Engr. ***Perf. 13½x14***
1147 A547 2.50s olive green 30 15

Seal of Hallein — A548

Maria Theresa, by Andreas Moller — A549

Photo. & Engr.

1980, Apr. 30 ***Perf. 14x13½***
1148 A548 4s red & black 45 22

Hallein, 750th anniversary.

1980, May 13 Engr. ***Perf. 13½***

Empress Maria Theresa (1717-1780) Paintings by: 4s, Martin van Meytens. 6s, Josef Ducreux.

1149 A549 2.50s violet brown		28	20
1150 A549 4s dark blue		45	35
1151 A549 6s rose lake		65	50
	Nos. 1149-1151 (3)	1.38	1.05

Flags of Austria and Four Powers — A550

1980, May 14 Photo. ***Perf. 13½x14***
1152 A550 4s multicolored 45 22

State Treaty, 25th anniversary.

St. Benedict, by Meinrad Guggenbichler A551

1980, May 16 Engr. ***Perf. 14½***
1153 A551 2.50s olive green 30 15

Congress of Benedictine Order of Austria.

Hygeia by Gustav Klimt — A552

1980, May 20 Photo. ***Perf. 14***
1154 A552 4s multicolored 45 22

Academic teaching of hygiene, 175th anniv.

Aflenz Ground Satellite Receiving Station Inauguration — A553

1980, May 30 Photo. ***Perf. 14***
1155 A553 6s multicolored 75 30

Steyr, Etching, 1693 A554

Photo. & Engr.

1980, June 4 ***Perf. 13½***
1156 A554 4s multicolored 45 22

Millennium of Steyr.

Worker, Oil Drill Head — A555

1980, June 12
1157 A555 2.50s multicolored 30 15

Austrian oil production, 25th anniversary.

Seal of Innsbruck, 1267 — A556

1980, June 23 ***Perf. 13½x14½***
1158 A556 2.50s multicolored 30 15

Innsbruck, 800th anniversary.

Duke's Hat — A557

Bible Illustration, Book of Genesis — A559

Leo Ascher (1880-1942), Composer A558

Perf. 14½x13½

1980, June 23 Photo.
1159 A557 4s multicolored 45 22

800th anniversary of Styria as a Duchy.

1980, Aug. 18 Engr. ***Perf. 14***
1160 A558 3s dark purple 38 18

1980, Aug. 25 ***Perf. 13½***
1161 A559 4s multicolored 45 25

10th Intl. Cong. of the Org. for Old Testament Studies.

Europa Issue 1980

Robert Stolz (1880-1975), Composer — A560

1980, Aug. 25 Engr. ***Perf. 14x13½***
1162 A560 6s red brown 85 30

Old and Modern Bridges A561

1980, Sept. 1 Photo. ***Perf. 13½***
1163 A561 4s multicolored 45 25

11th Congress of the Intl. Assoc. for Bridge and Structural Engineering, Vienna.

Moon Figure, by Karl Brandstätter A562

Customs Service, Sesquicentennial A563

Photo. & Engr.

1980, Oct. 10 ***Perf. 14x13½***
1164 A562 4s multicolored 45 25

1980, Oct. 13 **Photo.**
1165 A563 2.50s multicolored 30 15

Gazette Masthead, 1810 A564

1980, Oct. 23 Photo. ***Perf. 13½***
1166 A564 2.50s multicolored 30 15

Official Gazette of Linz, 350th anniversary.

Waidhofen Town Book Title Page, 14th Century — A565

Photo. & Engr.

1980, Oct. 24 ***Perf. 14***
1167 A565 2.50s multicolored 30 15

Waidhofen on Thaya, 750th anniversary.

Federal Austrian Army, 25th Anniversary A566

1980, Oct. 24 Photo. *Perf. 13½x14*
1168 A566 2.50s grnsh black & red 30 15

Alfred Wegener A567

1980, Oct. 31 Engr.
1169 A567 4s violet blue 45 25

Alfred Wegener (1880-1930), scientist, formulated theory of continental drift.

A568

A569

1980, Nov. 6 *Perf. 14x13½*
1170 A568 4s dark red brown 45 25

Robert Musil (1880-1942), poet.

Photo. & Engr.
1980, Nov. 28 *Perf. 13½*

Nativity, stained glass window, Klagenfurt.

1171 A569 4s multicolored 45 25

Christmas.

25th Anniversary of Social Security A570

1981, Jan. 19 Litho. *Perf. 13½x14*
1172 A570 2.50s multicolored 30 15

Niebelungen Saga, 1926, by Dachauer A571

Machinist in Wheelchair A572

1981, Apr. 6 Engr. *Perf. 14x13½*
1173 A571 3s sepia 40 15

Wilhelm Dachauer (1881-1951), artist and engraver.

1981, Apr. 6 Photo. & Engr.
1174 A572 6s multicolored 75 35

Rehabilitation International, 3rd European Regional Conference.

Sigmund Freud — A573

Congress, Vienna — A574

1981, May 6 Engr.
1175 A573 3s rose violet 35 15

Sigmund Freud (1856-1939), psychoanalyst.

1981, May 11 Photo.
1176 A574 4s multicolored 45 25

A575

Europa — A576

Azzo (founder of House of Kuenringer) and his followers, bear-skin manuscript.

1981, May 15 Photo. & Engr.
1177 A575 3s multicolored 35 15

Kuenringer Exhibition, Zwettl Monastery.

1981, May 22 Photo.
1178 A576 6s Maypole 80 35

Telephone Service Centenary A577

Photo. and Engr.
1981 May 29 *Perf. 13½x14*
1179 A577 4s multicolored 45 25

Seibersdorf Research Center, 25th Anniv. A578

1981, June 29 Photo. *Perf. 13½*
1180 A578 4s multicolored 45 25

The Frog King (Child's Drawing) A579

1981, June 29 *Perf. 13½x14*
1181 A579 3s multicolored 35 15

Town Hall and Town Seal of 1250 — A580

Photo. & Engr.
1981, July 17 *Perf. 13½x14*
1182 A580 4s multicolored 45 25

St. Veit an der Glan, 800th anniv.

Johann Florian Heller (1813-1871), Pioneer of Urinalysis — A581

1981, Aug. 31 *Perf. 14x13½*
1183 A581 6s red brown 75 35

11th Intl. Clinical Chemistry Congress.

Ludwig Boltzmann (1844-1906), Physicist — A582

Scale — A583

1981, Sept. 4 Engr. *Perf. 14x13½*
1184 A582 3s dark green 35 15

Photo. & Engr.
1981, Sept. 7 *Perf. 14*
1185 A583 6s multicolored 75 35

Intl. Pharmaceutical Federation World Congress, Vienna, Sept. 6-11.

Otto Bauer, Politician, Birth Centenary A584

Escher's Impossible Cube A585

1981, Sept. 7 Photo. *Perf. 14x13½*
1186 A584 4s multicolored 45 25

1981, Sept. 14
1187 A585 4s dk blue & brt blue 45 25

10th Intl. Mathematicians' Cong., Innsbruck.

Kneeling Virgin, Detail of Coronation of Mary Altarpiece, St. Wolfgang, 500th Anniv. — A586

1981, Sept. 25 Engr. *Perf. 14x13½*
1188 A586 3s dark blue 35 15

South-East Fair, Graz, 75th Anniv. — A587

1981, Sept. 25 Photo. *Perf. 13½x14*
1189 A587 4s multicolored 45 25

Holy Trinity, 12th Cent. Byzantine Miniature A588

1981, Oct. 5
1190 A588 6s multicolored 75 35

16th Intl. Byzantine Congress.

Hans Kelsen (1881-1973), Co-author of Federal Constitution A589

1981, Oct. 9 Engr.
1191 A589 3s dark carmine 35 15

Edict of Tolerance Bicen. — A590

1981, Oct. 9 Photo. & Engr. *Perf. 14*
1192 A590 4s Joseph II 45 25

World Food Day — A591

1981, Oct. 16 Photo. *Perf. 13½*
1193 A591 6s multicolored 75 35

Between the Times, by Oscar Asboth A592

1981, Oct. 22 Litho. *Perf. 13½x14*
1194 A592 4s multicolored 45 25

Intl. Catholic Workers' Day — A593

Photo. & Engr.

1981, Oct. 23 *Perf. 14x13½*

1195 A593 3s multicolored 35 15

Baron Josef Hammer-Purgstall, Founder of Oriental Studies, 125th Death Anniv. — A594

Photo. & Engr.

1981, Nov. 23 *Perf. 14*

1196 A594 3s multicolored 35 15

Julius Raab (1891-1964), Politician — A595

1981, Nov. 27 **Engr.** *Perf. 13½*

1197 A595 6s rose lake 75 35

Nativity, Corn Straw Figures A596

1981, Nov. 27 **Photo. & Engr.**

1198 A596 4s multicolored 52 22

Christmas.

Stefan Zweig (1881-1942), Poet — A597

1981, Nov. 27 **Engr.** *Perf. 14x13½*

1199 A597 4s dull violet 52 22

800th Anniv. of St. Nikola on the Danube — A598

1981, Dec. 4 **Photo. & Engr.**

1200 A598 4s multicolored 45 22

Vienna Emergency Medical Service Centenary A599

1981, Dec. 9 **Photo.** *Perf. 13½x14*

1201 A599 3s multicolored 35 15

Schladming-Haus Alpine World Skiing Championship A600

1982, Jan. 27 *Perf. 14*

1202 A600 4s multicolored 45 22

Dorotheum (State Auction Gallery), 275th Anniv. — A601

Photo. & Engr.

1982, Mar. 12 *Perf. 14*

1203 A601 4s multicolored 45 22

A602

A603

1982, Mar. 19 **Photo.** *Perf. 14x13½*

1204 A602 5s multicolored 60 30

Water Rescue Service, 25th anniv.

Photo. & Engr.

1982, Apr. 23 *Perf. 14x13½*

1205 A603 3s St. Severin 35 15

St. Severin and the End of the Roman Era exhibition.

A604

A605

1982, May 4 *Perf. 14*

1206 A604 4s multicolored 45 22

Intl. Kneipp Hydropathy Congress, Vienna.

1982, May 7

1207 A605 4s Printers' guild arms 45 22

Printing in Austria, 500th anniv.

A606

A607

Design: Urine analysis, Canone di Avicenna manuscript.

1982, May 12 **Photo.**

1208 A606 6s multicolored 75 35

5th European Urology Soc. Cong., Vienna.

1982, May 14 **Photo. & Engr.**

1209 A607 3s multicolored 35 15

800th birth anniv. of St. Francis of Assisi.

A608

A609

1982, May 19 **Engr.** *Perf. 13½*

1210 A608 3s olive green 35 15

Haydn and His Time Exhibition, Rohrau.

1982, May 25 **Photo.** *Perf. 14x13½*

1211 A609 7s multicolored 85 40

25th World Milk Day.

800th Anniv of Gfohl (Market Town) — A610

Photo. & Engr.

1982, May 28 *Perf. 14*

1212 A610 4s multicolored 45 22

Tennis Player and Austrian Tennis Federation Emblem — A611

1982, June 11

1213 A611 3s multicolored 35 15

900th Anniv. of City of Langenlois A612

Photo. & Engr.

1982, June 11 *Perf. 13½x14*

1214 A612 4s multicolored 45 22

800th Anniv. of City of Weiz — A613

Ignaz Seipel (1876-1932), Statesman — A614

1982, June 18 **Photo.** *Perf. 14x13½*

1215 A613 4s Arms 45 22

1982, July 30 **Engr.** *Perf. 14x13½*

1216 A614 3s brown violet 35 15

Europa Issue 1982

Sesquicentennial of Linz-Freistadt-Budweis Horse-drawn Railroad — A615

1982, July 30 *Perf. 13½*

1217 A615 6s brown 90 35

Mail Bus Service, 75th Anniv. — A616

Rocket Lift-off — A617

1982, Aug. 6 **Photo.** *Perf. 14x13½*

1218 A616 4s multicolored 45 22

1982, Aug. 9 *Perf. 14*

1219 A617 4s multicolored 45 22

2nd UN Conference on Peaceful Uses of Outer Space, Vienna, Aug. 9-21.

Geodesists' Day — A618

Photo. & Engr.

1982, Sept. 1 *Perf. 13½x14*

1220 A618 3s Tower, Office of Standards 35 15

Protection of Endangered Species — A619

1982, Sept. 9 *Perf. 14*

1221 A619 3s Bustard	45	25
1222 A619 4s Beaver	60	30
1223 A619 6s Capercaillie	90	45
Nos. 1221-1223 (3)	1.95	1.00

10th Anniv. of Intl. Institute for Applied Systems Anaysis, Vienna A620

1982, Oct. 4 **Photo.**
1224 A620 3s Laxenburg Castle 35 15

St. Apollonia (Patron Saint of Dentists) A621

1982, Oct. 11 **Photo. & Engr.**
1225 A621 4s multicolored 45 22

70th Annual World Congress of Dentists.

Emmerich Kalman (1882-1953), Composer A622

1982, Oct. 22 **Engr.** ***Perf. 13½***
1226 A622 3s dark blue 35 15

Max Mell (1882-1971), Poet — A623

Christmas — A624

1982, Nov. 10 **Photo.** ***Perf. 14x13½***
1227 A623 3s multicolored 35 15

Photo. & Engr.

1982, Nov. 25 ***Perf. 13½***

Design: Christmas crib, Damuls Church, Vorarlberg, 1630.

1228 A624 4s multicolored 45 22

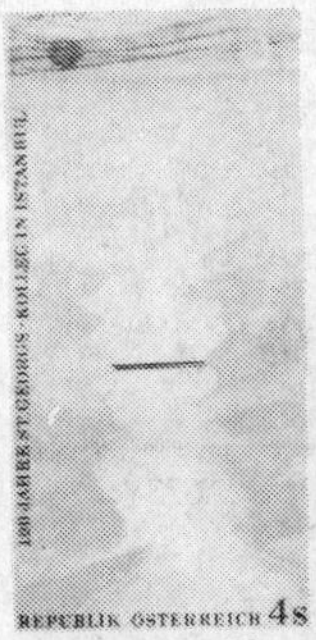

Centenary of St. George's College, Istanbul — A625

Portrait of a Girl, by Ernst Fuchs — A626

1982, Nov. 26 **Litho.** ***Perf. 14***
1229 A625 4s Bosporus 45 22

1982, Dec. 10 **Photo. & Engr.**
1230 A626 4s multicolored 45 22

Postal Savings Bank Centenary A627

Photo. & Engr.

1983, Jan. 12 ***Perf. 14***
1231 A627 4s Bank 55 22

Hildegard Burjan (1883-1933), Founder of Caritas Socialis — A628

1983, Jan. 28 **Engr.**
1232 A628 4s rose lake 55 22

World Communications Year — A629

1983, Feb. 18 **Photo.** ***Perf. 13½x14***
1233 A629 7s multicolored 95 40

75th Anniv. Children's Friends Org. — A630

Photo. & Engr.

1983, Feb. 23 ***Perf. 14x13½***
1234 A630 4s multicolored 55 22

Josef Matthias Hauer (1883-1959), Composer A631

1983, Mar. 18 **Engr.** ***Perf. 14***
1235 A631 3s deep lilac rose 42 15

25th Anniv. of Austrian Airlines A632

1983, Mar. 31 **Photo.** ***Perf. 13½x14***
1236 A632 6s multicolored 85 35

Work Inspection Centenary A633

1983, Apr. 8 **Photo.** ***Perf. 13½***
1237 A633 4s multicolored 55 22

Upper Austria Millennium Provincial Exhibition A634

1983, Apr. 28 **Photo.** ***Perf. 13½***
1238 A634 3s Wels Castle, by Matthaus Merian 42 15

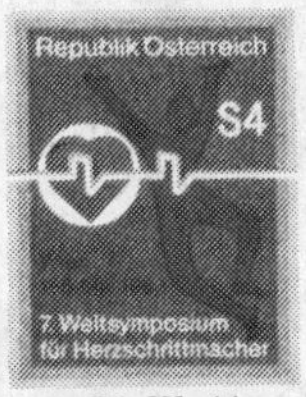

Gottweig Monastery, 900th Anniv. A635

7th World Pacemakers Symposium A636

Photo. & Engr.

1983, Apr. 29 ***Perf. 13½***
1239 A635 3s multicolored 42 15

1983, Apr. 29 **Photo.** ***Perf. 14x13½***
1240 A636 4s multicolored 55 22

Catholic Students' Org. — A637

1983, May 20 **Photo.** ***Perf. 14***
1241 A637 4s multicolored 55 22

Weitra, 800th Anniv. A638

Photo. & Engr.

1983, May 20 ***Perf. 13½***
1242 A638 4s multicolored 55 22

Granting of Town Rights to Hohenems, 650th Anniv. — A639

1983, May 27 **Photo.** ***Perf. 14***
1243 A639 4s multicolored 55 22

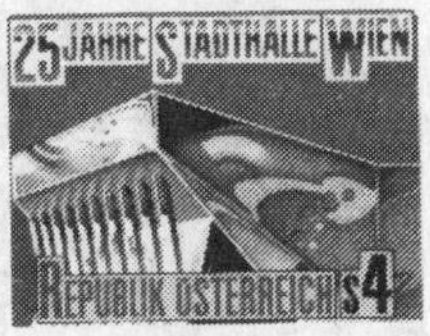

25th Anniv. of Stadthall, Vienna A640

1983, June 24 **Photo.** ***Perf. 14***
1244 A640 4s multicolored 55 22

Europa Issue 1983

A641 A642

1983, June 24 **Engr.** ***Perf. 14x13½***
1245 A641 6s dark green 95 35

Europa: Viktor Franz Hess (1883-1964), 1936 Nobel Prize winner in physics.

1983, July 1 **Photo.** ***Perf. 13½***
1246 A642 5s multicolored 70 30

Kiwanis Intl. Convention, Vienna, July 3-6.

7th World Congress of Psychiatry, Vienna — A643

1983, July 11 **Photo.** ***Perf. 14***
1247 A643 4s Emblem, St. Stephen's Cathedral 55 22

Baron Carl von Hasenauer (1833-1894), Architect A644

1983, July 20 **Engr.** ***Perf. 13½x14***
1248 A644 3s Natural History Museum, Vienna 42 15

27th Intl. Chamber of Commerce Professional Competition, Linz — A645

1983, Aug. 16 **Photo.**
1249 A645 4s Chamber building 55 22

13th Intl. Chemotherapy Congress, Vienna, Aug. 28-Sept. 2 — A646

1983, Aug. 26
1250 A646 5s Penicillin test on cancer 70 30

Catholics' Day — A647

Visit of Pope John Paul II — A648

1983, Sept. 9 Photo. *Perf. 14x13½*
1251 A647 3s multicolored 42 15

Photo. & Engr.

1983, Sept. 9 *Perf. 13½*
1252 A648 6s multicolored 90 35

Souvenir Sheet

Battle of 1683 to Relieve Vienna, by Frans Geffel A649

1983, Sept. 9 *Perf. 14*
1253 A649 6s multicolored 95 50

300th anniv. of Vienna's rescue from Turkey.

Vienna Rathaus Centenary — A650

1983, Sept. 23 *Perf. 13½x14*
1254 A650 4s multicolored 55 22

Karl von Terzaghi (1883-1963), Founder of Scientific Subterranean Engineering A651

1983, Oct. 3 Engr.
1255 A651 3s dark blue 42 15

10th Trade Unions Federal Congress, Oct. 3-8 — A652

1983, Oct. 3 Photo. *Perf. 13½*
1256 A652 3s black & red 42 15

Evening Sun in Burgenland, by Gottfried Kumpf — A653

Photo. & Engr.

1983, Oct. 7 *Perf. 13½x14*
1257 A653 4s multicolored 55 22

Modling-Hinterbruhl Electric Railroad Centenary — A654

1983, Oct. 21 Photo.
1258 A654 3s multicolored 42 15

Provincial Museum of Upper Austria Sesquicentennial — A655

1983, Nov. 4 Photo. & Engr.
1259 A655 4s Francisco-Carolinum Museum 55 22

Creche, St. Andreas Parish Church, Kitzbuhel A656

1983, Nov. 25 *Perf. 14*
1260 A656 4s multicolored 55 22

Christmas.

Parliament Bldg. Vienna, 100th Anniv. — A657

1983, Dec. 2 Engr.
1261 A657 4s slate blue 55 22

A658

A659

Altar picture, St. Nikola/Pram Church.

1983, Dec. 6 Photo. *Perf. 14x13½*
1262 A658 3s multicolored 42 15

Perf. 14½x13½

1983, Dec. 15 Engr.
1263 A659 6s dark red brn 90 35

Wolfgang Pauli (1900-58), physicist, Nobel Prize winner.

Gregor Mendel (1822-1884), Genetics Founder — A660

Photo. & Engr.

1984, Jan. 5 *Perf. 13½*
1264 A660 4s multicolored 55 22

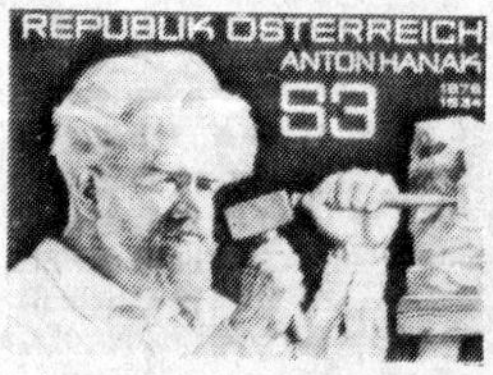

Anton Hanak (1875-1934), Sculptor — A661

1984, Jan. 5
1265 A661 3s red brown & blk 42 15

50th Anniv. of 1934 Uprising — A662

1984, Feb. 10 Photo. *Perf. 14*
1266 A662 4.50s Memorial, Woellersdorf 65 28

Wernher von Reichersberg Family, Bas-relief, 15th Cent. — A663

Photo. & Engr.

1984, Apr. 25 *Perf. 14x13½*
1267 A663 3.50s brown & blue 48 25

900th anniv. of Reichersberg Monastery.

Tobacco Monopoly Bicentenary A665

1984, May 4 *Perf. 13½*
1269 A665 4.50s Cigar wrapper, tobacco plant 65 28

1200th Anniv. of Kostendorf Municipality — A666

1984, May 4
1270 A666 4.50s View, arms 65 28

Automobile Engineers World Congress A667

1984, May 4 Photo. *Perf. 13½x14*
1271 A667 5s Wheel bearing cross-section 70 30

Europa (1959-1984) A668

1984, May 4 *Perf. 13½*
1272 A668 6s multicolored 90 35

A669

Aragonite — A670

Archduke Johann (1782-1859) by S. von Carolsfeld.

Photo. & Engr.

1984, May 11 *Perf. 14*
1273 A669 4.50s multicolored 65 28

1984, May 11 *Perf. 13½*
1274 A670 3.50s multicolored 48 18

Ore and Iron Provincial Exhibition.

Era of Emperor Francis Joseph Exhibition — A671

Design: Cover of Viribus Unitis, publ. by Max Herzig, 1898.

1984, May 18
1275 A671 3.50s red & gold 48 18

A672

A673

Photo. & Engr.

1984, May 30 *Perf. 14x13½*
1276 A672 4.50s Tower, arms 65 28

City of Vocklabruck, 850th anniv.

1984, June 1 *Perf. 13½*

Dionysius, Virinum mosaic.

1277 A673 3.50s multicolored 48 18

Museum of Carinthia, centenary.

Erosion Prevention Systems Centenary A674

1984, June 5 **Engr.** ***Perf. 14***
1278 A674 4.50s Stone reinforcement wall 65 28

Tyrol Provincial Celebration, 1809-1984 — A675

Art Exhibition: Meeting of Imperial Troops with South Tyrolean Reserves under Andreas Hofer near Sterzing in April 1809, by Ludwig Schnorr von Carolsfeld, 1830.

Photo. & Engr.
1984, June 5 ***Perf. 14x13 1/2***
1279 A675 3.50s multicolored 48 18

A676 A677

1984, June 5 **Engr.**
1280 A676 4s violet brown 55 22

Ralph Benatzky (1884-1957), composer.

1984, June 22 **Photo.** ***Perf. 14***
1281 A677 3.50s multicolored 48 18

Christian von Ehrenfels (1859-1932), philosopher.

25th Anniv. of Minimundus (Model City) — A678

1984, June 22 ***Perf. 13 1/2x14***
1282 A678 4s Eiffel Tower, Tower of Pisa, ferris wheel 55 22

Blockheide Eibenstein Nature Park — A679

1984 **Photo. & Engr.**
1283 A679 4s shown 55 22
1284 A679 4s Lake Neusiedl 55 22

Issued: #1283, June 29; #1284, Aug. 13.
See Nos. 1349-1354, 1492-1496.

Monasteries and Abbeys — A679a

Designs: 3.50s, Geras Monastery, Lower Austria. 4s, Stams. 4.50s, Schlagl. 5s, Benedictine Abbey of St. Paul Levanttal. 6s, Rein-Hohenfurth.

1984-85 ***Perf. 14***
1285 A679a 3.50s multicolored 48 18
1286 A679a 4s multicolored 48 20
1287 A679a 4.50s multicolored 65 28
1288 A679a 5s multicolored 65 28
1288A A679a 6s multicolored 90 32
Nos. 1285-1288A (5) 3.16 1.26

Issue dates: 3.50s. Apr. 27; 4s, Sept. 28; 4.50s, May 18; 5s, Sept. 27, 1985; 6s, Oct. 4. See Nos. 1361-1365, 1464A-1468.

Schanatobel Railroad Bridge A680

Railroad Anniversaries: 3.50s, Arlberg centenary. 4.50s, Tauern, 75th.

1984, July 6 ***Perf. 14***
1289 A680 3.50s shown 48 18
1290 A680 4.50s Falkenstein Bridge 65 18

A681 A682

1984, July 6 **Photo.**
1291 A681 6s Johan Stuwer's balloon 90 35

Balloon flight in Austria bicentenary.

1984, Aug. 31 **Photo. & Engr.**
1292 A682 7s Vienna Palace of Justice, emblem 95 45

Intl. Lawyers' Congress, Vienna.

A683 A684

1984, Sept. 3 **Photo.**
1293 A683 6s Josef Hyrtl, anatomist 90 35

7th European Anatomy Congress, Innsbruck, Sept. 3-7.

1984, Oct. 12
1294 A684 4s Window, by Karl Korab 55 22

A685 A686

1984, Oct. 18
1295 A685 3.50s Clock (Immset Uhr), 1555 48 18

Johannes of Gmunden, mathematician, 600th birth anniv.

1984, Nov. 9 **Photo.** ***Perf. 13 1/2***
1296 A686 4.50s Quill 65 28

Concordia Press Club, 125th anniv.

Fanny Eissler, Dancer, Birth Centenary — A687

1984, Nov. 23 **Photo. & Engr.**
1297 A687 4s multicolored 55 28

Christmas A688

Design: Christ is Born, Aggsbacher Altar, Herzogenburg Monastery.

1984, Nov. 30 ***Perf. 14***
1298 A688 4.50s multicolored 65 20

A689 A690

1985, Jan. 4 ***Perf. 14x13 1/2***
1299 A689 3.50s Seal 48 15

Karl Franzens University, Graz, 400th anniv.

1985, Jan. 15 **Engr.**
1300 A690 4.50s dk rose lake 60 18

Dr. Lorenz Bohler, Surgeon, birth cent.

Nordic Events, Ski Championships, Seefeld — A691

1985, Jan. 17 **Photo.** ***Perf. 13 1/2***
1301 A691 4s Ski jumper, cross country racer 55 15

Linz Diocese Bicentenary A692

1985, Jan. 25
1302 A692 4.50s Linz Cathedral interior 60 18

Alban Berg (1885-1935), Composer — A693

1985, Feb. 8 **Engr.**
1303 A693 6s bluish black 80 25

Vocational Training Inst., 25th Anniv. — A694

1985, Feb. 15 **Photo.** ***Perf. 13 1/2x14***
1304 A694 4.50s multicolored 60 18

City of Bregenz, Bimillennium — A695

1985, Feb. 22 ***Perf. 14x13 1/2***
1305 A695 4s multicolored 55 15

Austrian Registration Labels Cent. — A696

1985, Mar. 15 ***Perf. 13 1/2x14***
1306 A696 4.50s Label, 1885 60 18

Josef Stefan (1835-1893), Physicist — A697

Photo. & Engr.
1985, Mar. 22 ***Perf. 14x13 1/2***
1307 A697 6s buff, dl red brn & dk brn 80 25

A698

A699

St. Leopold 16th-17th cent. embroidery.

1985, Mar. 29
1308 A698 3.50s multicolored 48 15

St. Leopold Exhibition, Klosterneuberg.

1985, Apr. 26 **Photo.**
1309 A699 4.50s multicolored 60 18

Liberation from German occupation forces, 40th anniv.

Painter Franz von Defregger (1835-1921) A700

1985, Apr. 26
1310 A700 3.50s Fairy tale teller 48 15

Europa Issue 1985

Johann Joseph Fux (1660-1741), Composer, Violin and Trombone A701

Photo. & Engr.
1985, May 3 ***Perf. 13½***
1311 A701 6s lil gray & dk brn 90 25

Boheimkirchen (Market Town) Millennium — A702

1985, May 10 ***Perf. 14***
1312 A702 4.50s View, coat of arms 60 18

A703

A704

Mercury staff, flags of member and affiliate nations.

1985, May 10 **Photo.** ***Perf. 13½***
1313 A703 4s multicolored 55 15

European Free Trade Assoc., 25th anniv.

1985, May 15 **Photo. & Engr.**

Episcopal residence gate, St. Polten diocese arms.

1314 A704 4.50s multicolored 60 18

St. Polten Diocese, bicentenary.

The Gumpp Family of Builders, Innsbruck — A705

Perf. 14½x13½
1985, May 17 **Photo.**
1315 A705 3.50s multicolored 48 15

Garsten Market Town Millennium A706

Design: 17th century engraving by George Mathaus Fischer (1628-1696).

Photo. & Engr.
1985, June 7 ***Perf. 13½x14***
1316 A706 4.50s multicolored 60 22

UN, 40th Anniv. A707

Perf. 13½x14½
1985, June 26 **Photo.**
1317 A707 4s multicolored 55 20

Austrian membership, 30th anniv.

Intl. Assoc. for the Prevention of Suicide, 13th Congress — A708

Photo. & Engr.
1985, June 28 ***Perf. 14***
1318 A708 5s brn, lt ap grn & yel 70 28

Souvenir Sheet

Year of the Forest A709

1985, June 28 ***Perf. 13½***
1319 A709 6s Healthy and damaged woodland 1.00 35

Kurhaus, Bad Ischl Operetta Activities Emblem A710

1985, July 5 ***Perf. 14***
1320 A710 3.50s multicolored 48 15

Bad Ischl Festival, 25th anniv.

Intl. Competition of Fire Brigades, Vocklabruck — A711

1985, July 18 **Photo.** ***Perf. 14x13½***
1321 A711 4.50s Fireman, emblem 60 22

Grossglockner Alpine Motorway, 50th Anniv. — A712

Photo. & Engr.
1985, Aug. 2 ***Perf. 13½***
1322 A712 4s View of Fuschertorl 55 20

World Chess Federation Congress, Graz — A713

1985, Aug. 28 **Photo.** ***Perf. 13½***
1323 A713 4s Checkered globe, emblem 55 20

The Legendary Foundation of Konigstetten by Charlemagne, by Auguste Stephan, c. 1870 — A714

Photo. & Engr.
1985, Aug. 30 ***Perf. 14***
1324 A714 4.50s multicolored 60 22

Konigstetten millennium.

Hofkirchen-Taufkirchen-Weibern Municipalities, 1200th Anniv. — A715

1985, Aug. 30 ***Perf. 13½x14***
1325 A715 4.50s View of Weiburn, municipal arms 60 22

Dr. Adam Politzer (1835-1923), Physician — A716

1985, Sept. 12 **Engr.** ***Perf. 14***
1326 A716 3.50s blue violet 48 15

Politzer pioneered aural therapy for auditory disorders.

Intl. Assoc. of Forwarding Agents, World Congress, Vienna — A717

1985, Oct. 7 **Photo.** ***Perf. 13½***
1327 A717 6s multicolored 85 35

Carnival Figures Riding High Bicycles, By Paul Flora A718

Photo. & Engr.
1985, Oct. 25 ***Perf. 14***
1328 A718 4s multicolored 55 22

St. Martin on Horseback A719

1985, Nov. 8 **Photo.**
1329 A719 4.50s multicolored 60 28

Eisenstadt Diocese, 25th anniv.

Creche, Marble Bas-relief, Salzburg — A720

Photo. & Engr.
1985, Nov. 29 ***Perf. 13½***
1330 A720 4.50s gold, dl vio & buff 60 28

Christmas.

Hanns Horbiger (1860-1931), Inventor — A721

1985, Nov. 29 *Perf. 14*
1331 A721 3.50s gold & sepia 48 20

Aqueduct, Hundsau Brook, Near Gostling A722

1985, Nov. 29 *Perf. 13½x14½*
1332 A722 3.50s red, bluish blk & brt ultra 48 20

Vienna Aqueduct, 75th anniv.

Chateau de la Muette, Paris Headquarters A723

1985, Dec. 13
1333 A723 4s sep, rose lil & gold 55 25

Org. for Economic Cooperation and Development, 25th anniv.

Johann Bohm (1886-1959), Pres. Austrian Trade Fed. — A724

1986, Jan. 24 **Photo.** *Perf. 14*
1334 A724 4.50s blk, ver & grayish black 65 28

Intl. Peace Year — A725

Perf. 13½x14½
1986, Jan. 24 **Photo.**
1335 A725 6s multicolored 85 35

Digital Telephone Service Introduction A726

1986, Jan. 29 **Photo.**
1336 A726 5s Push-button keyboard 75 30

Johann Georg Albrechtsberger (b. 1736), Composer — A727

Perf. 13½x14½
1986, Jan. 31 **Photo. & Engr.**
1337 A727 3.50s Klosterneuberg organ 52 22

Korneuberg, 850th Anniv. A728

1986, Feb. 7 **Photo.** *Perf. 14*
1338 A728 5s multicolored 75 30

A729 A730

Self-portrait, by Oskar Kokoschka (b.1886).

Perf. 14½x13½
1986, Feb. 28 **Photo.**
1339 A729 4s multicolored 60 28

1986, Feb. 28 **Photo.** *Perf. 13x13½*
1340 A730 6s multicolored 85 35

Admission to Council of Europe, 30th anniv.

Clemens Holzmeister (b. 1886), Architect, Salzburg Festival Theater, 1926 — A731

Photo. & Engr.
1986, Mar. 27 *Perf. 13½*
1341 A731 4s sep & redsh brn 60 28

3rd Intl. Geotextile Congress, Vienna A732

Perf. 13½x14½
1986, Apr. 7 **Photo.**
1342 A732 5s multicolored 75 30

Prince Eugen and Schlosshof Castle — A733

Photo. & Engr.
1986, Apr. 21 *Perf. 14*
1343 A733 4s multicolored 60 28

Prince Eugen Exhibition, Schlosshof and Niederweiden.

St. Florian Monastery, Upper Austria A734

1986, Apr. 24
1344 A734 4s multicolored 60 28

The World of Baroque provincial exhibition, St. Florian.

Herberstein Castle, Arms of Styria — A735

1986, May 2 *Perf. 13½x14½*
1345 A735 4s multicolored 60 28

Europa 1986 — A736

1986, May 2 *Perf. 13½*
1346 A736 6s Pasque flower 85 45

Wagner, Scene from Opera Lohengrin A737

1986, May 21
1347 A737 4s multicolored 60 28

Intl. Richard Wagner Congress, Vienna.

Antimonite A738

1986, May 23 *Perf. 13½x14½*
1348 A738 4s multicolored 60 28

Burgenland Provincial Minerals Exhibition.

Scenery Type of 1984

1986-89 **Photo. & Engr.** *Perf. 14*

1349	A679	5s	Martinswall, Tyrol	65	35
1350	A679	5s	Tschauko Falls, Carinthia	65	35
1351	A679	5s	Dachstein Ice Caves	82	45
1352	A679	5s	Gauertal, Montafon	80	45
1353	A679	5s	Krimmler Waterfalls	78	60
1354	A679	5s	Lusthauswasser	78	58
			Nos. 1349-1354 (6)	4.48	2.78

Issue dates: No. 1351, June 11, 1987. No. 1352, Aug. 21, 1987. No. 1353, Aug. 19, 1988. No. 1354, Sept. 1, 1989.

Waidhofen on Ybbs Township, 800th Anniv. A739

1986, June 20 **Photo.** *Perf. 13½*
1355 A739 4s multicolored 52 28

Salzburg Local Railway, Cent. A740

1986, Aug. 8 **Photo.** *Perf. 14*
1356 A740 4s multicolored 55 28

Seals of Dukes Leopold Of Austria, Otakar of Styria, and Georgenberg Church A741

1986, Aug. 14 **Photo. & Engr.**
1357 A741 5s multicolored 68 30

Georgenberg Treaty, 800th anniv.

Julius Tandler (1869-1936), Social Reformer — A742

1986, Aug. 22
1358 A742 4s multicolored 60 28

Sonnblick Observatory, Cent. — A743

Perf. 13½x14½
1986, Aug. 27 **Photo. & Engr.**
1359 A743 4s Observatory, 1886 60 28

Discovery of Mandrake Root — A744

1986, Aug. 27 *Perf. 14½x13½*

1360 A744 5s multicolored 75 30

European Assoc. for Anesthesiology, 7th cong.

Monasteries and Abbeys Type of 1984

Designs: 5.50s, St. Gerold's Provostry, Vorarlberg. 7s, Loretto Monastery, Burgenland. 7.50s, Dominican Convent, Vienna. 8s, Zwettl Monastery. 10s, Wilten Monastery.

1986-88 **Photo. & Engr.** *Perf. 14*

1361	A679a	5.50s	multicolored	78	60
1362	A679a	7s	multicolored	1.15	88
1363	A679a	7.50s	multicolored	1.10	85
1364	A679a	8s	multicolored	1.35	1.05
1365	A679a	10s	multicolored	1.75	1.30
	Nos. 1361-1365 (5)			6.13	4.68

Issue dates: 5.50s, Sept. 12. 7.50s, Oct. 3. 7s, Aug. 14, 1987. 8s, May 27, 1988. 10s, Mar. 18, 1988

A745

A746

Photo. & Engr.

1986, Sept. 3 *Perf. 14*

1366 A745 4s multicolored 60 28

Otto Stoessl (d. 1936), writer.

1986, Sept. 3 **Photo.**

1367 A746 4s Fireman, 1686 60 28

Vienna fire brigade, 300th anniv.

Silk Viennese Hunting Tapestry — A747

Photo. & Engr.

1986, Sept. 3 *Perf. 14*

1368 A747 5s multicolored 75 40

Intl. conf. on Oriental Carpets, Vienna, Budapest.

A748

A749

Photo. & Engr.

1986, Oct. 10 *Perf. 14*

1369 A748 5s Minister at pulpit 72 40

Protestant Act, 25th anniv., and Protestant Patent of Franz Josef I ensuring religious equality, 125th anniv.

1986, Oct. 17 *Perf. 13½x14*

Disintegration, by Walter Schmogner.

1370 A749 4s multicolored 58 28

Franz Liszt, Composer, and Birthplace, Burgenland A750

1986, Oct. 17 *Perf. 13½*

1371 A750 5s green & sepia 72 40

Souvenir Sheet

European Security Conference, Vienna — A751

Illustration reduced.

1986, Nov. 4 *Perf. 13½x14*

1372 A751 6s Vienna 95 65

Strettweg Cart, 7th Cent. B.C. — A752

Photo. & Engr.

1986, Nov. 26 *Perf. 14*

1373 A752 4s multicolored 65 28

Joanneum Styrian Land Museum, 175th anniv.

Christmas A753

Design: The Little Crib, bas-relief by Schwanthaler (1740-1810), Schlierbach Monastery.

1986, Nov. 28

1374 A753 5s gold & rose lake 80 40

Federal Chamber of Commerce, 40th Anniv. — A754

1986, Dec. 2 **Photo.**

1375 A754 5s multicolored 80 40

Industry A755

1986-91 *Perf. 14x13½*

1376	A755	4s	Steel workers	80	28
1377	A755	4s	Office worker, computer	80	35
1378	A755	4s	Lab assistant	80	30
1378A	A755	4.50s	Textile worker	75	60
1379	A755	5s	Bricklayer	78	58
	Nos. 1376-1379 (5)			3.93	2.11

Issue dates: No. 1376, Dec. 4. No. 1377, Oct. 5, 1987. No. 1378, Oct. 21, 1988. No. 1379, Oct. 10, 1989. 4.50s, Oct. 11, 1991.

This is an expanding set. Numbers will change if necessary.

The Educated Eye, by Arnulf Rainer — A756

1987, Jan. 13 **Photo.** *Perf. 13½x14*

1386 A756 5s multicolored 80 40

Adult education in Vienna, cent.

The Large Blue Madonna, by Anton Faistauer (1887-1970) A757

Paintings: 6s, Self-portrait, 1922, by A. Paris Gutersloh (1887-1973).

1987, Jan. 29 *Perf. 14*

1387 A757 4s multicolored 55 20

1388 A757 6s multicolored 90 40

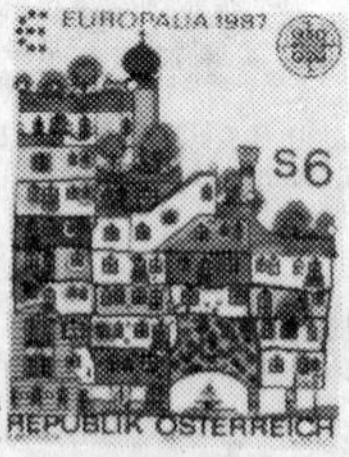

Europa 1987 — A758

Photo. & Engr.

1987, Apr. 6 *Perf. 13½x14*

1389 A758 6s Hundertwasser House 95 55

World Ice Hockey Championships, Vienna — A759

Perf. 13½x14½

1987, Apr. 17 **Photo.**

1390 A759 5s multicolored 80 60

Opening of the Austria Center, Vienna A760

1987, Apr. 22

1391 A760 5s multicolored 80 60

Salzburg City Charter, 700th Anniv. A761

1987, Apr. 24

1392 A761 5s multicolored 80 60

A762

A763

Photo. & Engr.

1987, Apr. 29 *Perf. 14*

1393 A762 4s Factory, 1920 65 48

Work-Men-Machines, provincial exhibition, Upper Austria.

1987, Apr. 29 **Photo.** *Perf. 13½*

1394 A763 5s multicolored 80 60

Equal rights for men and women.

Adele Block-Bauer I, Abstract by Gustav Klimt — A764

Photo. & Engr.

1987, May 8 *Perf. 13½*

1395 A764 4s multicolored 65 48

The Era of Emperor Franz Joseph, provincial exhibition, Lower Austria.

Arthur Schnitzler (1862-1931), Poet — A765

1987, May 15 *Perf. 14½x13½*

1396 A765 6s multicolored 1.00 75

Von Raitenau, View of Salzburg
A766

1987, May 15 *Perf. 14*
1397 A766 4s multicolored 65 48

Prince Archbishop Wolf Dietrich von Raitenau, patron of baroque architecture in Salzburg, provincial exhibition.

Lace, Lustenau Municipal Arms — A767

1987, May 22
1398 A767 5s multicolored 82 62

Lustenau, 1100th anniv.

Souvenir Sheet

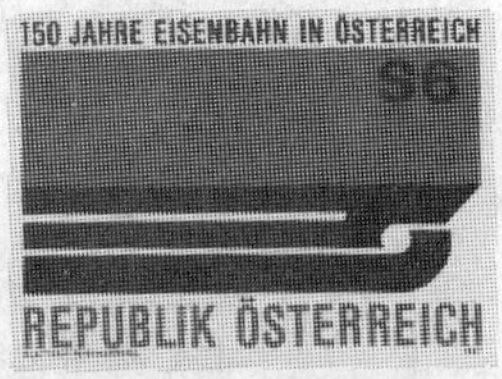

Austrian Railways Sesquicentenary — A768

1987, June 5 **Photo.** *Perf. 13½*
1399 A768 6s multicolored 1.00 75

8th Intl. Congress of Engravers, Vienna
A769

Photo. & Engr.

1987, June 17 *Perf. 14*
1400 A769 5s gray, gray brn & dull rose 82 62

Dr. Karl Josef Bayer (1847-1904), Chemist — A770

Shipping on Achensee, Cent. — A771

1987, June 22 *Perf. 14x13½*
1401 A770 5s multicolored 80 60

Eighth Intl. Light Metals Congress, June 22-26, Leoben and Vienna; Bayer Technique for producing aluminum oxide from bauxite, cent.

1987, June 26 **Photo.**
1402 A771 4s multicolored 65 50

A772 A773

1987, July 1
1403 A772 5s Palais Rottal, Vienna 80 60

Ombudsmen's office, 10th anniv.

1987, Aug. 11 **Photo. & Engr.**
1404 A773 5s dull olive bister, choc & buff 80 60

Dr. Erwin Schrodinger (1887-1961), 1933 Nobel laureate in physics.

Freistadt Exhibitions, 125th Anniv.
A774

1987, Aug. 11 *Perf. 14x14½*
1405 A774 5s multicolored 80 60

Arbing, 850th Anniv. — A775

1987, Aug. 21 *Perf. 13½*
1406 A775 5s multicolored 80 60

1987 World Cycling Championships, Villach to Vienna — A776

1987, Aug. 25 *Perf. 14*
1407 A776 5s multicolored 80 60

World Congress of Savings Banks, Vienna
A777

Perf. 13½x14½

1987, Sept. 9 **Photo.**
1408 A777 5s multicolored 80 60

Johann Michael Haydn (1737-1806), Composer
A778

Perf. 13½x14½

1987, Sept. 14 **Engr.**
1409 A778 4s dull violet 65 50

Paul Hofhaymer (1459-1537), Composer
A779

Photo. & Engr.

1987, Sept. 11 *Perf. 14*
1410 A779 4s gold, blk & ultra 65 50

Bearded Vulture — A780

1987, Sept. 25
1411 A780 4s multicolored 65 50

Innsbruck Zoo, 25th anniv.

Baumgottinnen, by Arnulf Neuwirth — A781

1987, Oct. 9 *Perf. 14x13½*
1412 A781 5s multicolored 80 60

Modern Art.

Gambling Monopoly, 200th Anniv. — A782

Perf. 14½x13½

1987, Oct. 30 **Photo.**
1413 A782 5s Lottery drum 80 60

Christoph Willibald Gluck (1714-1787), Composer
A784

Photo. & Engr.

1987, Nov. 13 *Perf. 14*
1415 A784 5s cream & blk 88 65

Oskar Helmer (b. 1887), Politician — A785

1987, Nov. 13
1416 A785 4s multicolored 70 52

Joseph Mohr (1792-1848) and Franz Gruber (1787-1863), Opening Bars of "Silent Night, Holy Night" — A786

1987, Nov. 27
1417 A786 5s multicolored 88 65

Christmas.

A787 A788

Photo. & Engr.

1988, Jan. 12 *Perf. 13½*
1418 A787 5s St. John Bosco, children 88 65

Intl. Education Congress of Salesian Fathers.

Perf. 14½x13½

1988, Feb. 19 **Photo. & Engr.**
1419 A788 6s multicolored 1.05 78

Ernst Mach (1838-1916), physicist.

Village with Bridge (1904), by Franz von Zulow (1883-1963), Painter — A789

1988, Feb. 25 **Photo.** *Perf. 14½x14*
1420 A789 4s multicolored 70 52

Biedermeier Provincial Exhibition, Vormarz in Vienna
A790

Painting: Confiscation, by Ferdinand Georg Waldmuller (1793-1865).

Photo. & Engr.

1988, Mar. 11 *Perf. 14*
1421 A790 4s multicolored 70 52

Anschluss of March 11, 1938 A791

1988, Mar. 11 **Photo.** ***Perf. 13½***

1422 A791 5s gray olive, brn blk & ver 85 65

No. 2 Aigen Steam Locomotive, 1887 — A792

1988, Mar. 22 ***Perf. 13½x14½***

1423 A792 4s shown 70 52
1424 A792 5s Electric train, Josepsplatz 85 65

Muhlkreis Railway, cent. (4s); Vienna Local Railway, cent. (5s).

World Wildlife Fund — A793

Photo. & Engr.

1988, Apr. 15 ***Perf. 13½x14***

1425 A793 5s Bee eater 88 65

Styrian Provincial Exhibition on Glass and Coal, Barnbach A794

1988, Apr. 29 ***Perf. 13½***

1426 A794 4s Frosted glass 70 52

Intl. Red Cross, 125th Anniv. — A795

1988, May 6 **Photo.** ***Perf. 14***

1427 A795 12s grn, brt red & blk 2.10 1.60

Gothic Silver Censer — A796

1988, May 6 **Photo. & Engr.**

1428 A796 4s multicolored 70 52

Art and Monasticism at the Birth of Austria, lower Austrian provincial exhibition, Seitenstetten.

Europa 1988 A797

Communication and transportation.

1988, May 13 **Photo.**

1429 A797 6s multicolored 1.05 78

Mattsee Monastery and Lion of Alz — A798

1988, May 18 **Photo. & Engr.**

1430 A798 4s multicolored 68 50

Provincial exhibition at Mattsee Monastery: Bavarian Tribes in Salzburg.

Weinberg Castle — A799

Perf. 13½x14½

1988, May 20 **Photo.**

1431 A799 4s multicolored 68 50

Upper Austrian provincial exhibition: Weinberg Castle.

Odon von Horwath (1901-1938), Dramatist — A800

Perf. 14½x13½

1988, June 1 **Photo. & Engr.**

1432 A800 6s olive bis & slate grn 1.05 78

Stockerau Festival, 25th Anniv. — A801

1988, June 17 ***Perf. 14***

1433 A801 5s Stockerau Town Hall 80 60

Tauern Motorway Opening — A802

1988, June 24 **Photo.** ***Perf. 13½x14***

1434 A802 4s multicolored 65 48

Brixlegg, 1200th Anniv. A803

Perf. 13½x14½

1988, July 1 **Photo. & Engr.**

1435 A803 5s multicolored 80 60

View of Klagenfurt, Engraving by Matthaus Merian (1593-1650) A804

Photo. & Engr.

1988, Aug. 12 ***Perf. 14***

1436 A804 5s multicolored 78 60

Carinthian Postal Service, 400th Anniv.

Brixen-im-Thale, 1200th Anniv. — A805

1988, Aug. 12

1437 A805 5s multicolored 78 60

Feldkirchen, 1100th Anniv. — A806

1988, Sept. 2 ***Perf. 13½***

1438 A806 5s multicolored 78 60

Feldbach, 800th Anniv. A807

1988, Sept. 15 **Photo. & Engr.**

1439 A807 5s multicolored 78 60

Ansfelden, 1200th Anniv. — A808

1988, Sept. 23 ***Perf. 14***

1440 A808 5s multicolored 78 60

Exports — A809

1988, Oct. 18 **Photo.** ***Perf. 14x13½***

1441 A809 8s multicolored 1.50 1.25

No. 1441 has a holographic image. Soaking in water may affect the hologram.

Vienna Concert Hall, 75th Anniv. A810

Photo. & Engr.

1988, Oct. 19 ***Perf. 13½***

1442 A810 5s multicolored 78 58

The Watchmen, by Giselbert Hoke — A811

1988, Oct. 21 ***Perf. 14***

1443 A811 5s multicolored 78 58

Social Democrats Unification Party Congress, Cent. — A812

1988, Nov. 11 **Photo.** ***Perf. 14½x14***

1444 A812 4s multicolored 65 48

Leopold Schonbauer (1888-1963), Physician — A813

Perf. 14½x13½

1988, Nov. 11 **Photo. & Engr.**
1445 A813 4s multicolored 65 48

Christmas
A814

Design: Nativity painting from St. Barbara's Church.

1988, Nov. 25 *Perf. 14*
1446 A814 5s multicolored 82 62

Benedictine Monastery, Melk, 900th Anniv.
A815

Design: Fresco by Paul Troger.

1989, Mar. 17 **Photo. & Engr.**
1447 A815 5s multicolored 80 60

Madonna and Child, by Lucas Cranach (1472-1553)
A816

Marianne Hainisch (1839-1936), Women's Rights Activist
A817

1989, Mar. 17 *Perf. 14½x13½*
1448 A816 4s multicolored 62 48

Diocese of Innsbruck, 25th anniv.

1989, Mar. 24 *Perf. 14x13½*
1449 A817 6s multicolored 95 72

Glider Plane and Parachutist
A818

1989, Mar. 31 **Photo.** *Perf. 14*
1450 A818 6s multicolored 1.00 75

World Gliding Championships, Wiener Neustadt, and World Parachuting Championships, Damuls.

Bruck an der Leitha Commune, 750th Anniv.
A819

Painting by Georg Matthaus Vischer (1628-1696).

1989, Apr. 21
1451 A819 5s multicolored 85 62

A820

A821

Die Malerei, 1904, by Rudolf Jettmar (1869-1939).

Perf. 14½x13½

1989, Apr. 21 **Photo.**
1452 A820 5s multicolored 85 62

1989, Apr. 26 **Photo. & Engr.**

Holy Trinity Church, Stadl-Paura.

1453 A821 5s multicolored 85 62

Michael Prunner (1669-1739), baroque architect.

A822

A823

Eduard Suess (1831-1914, structural geologist) portrait by J. Krieher (1800-1876) and map.

1989, Apr. 26
1454 A822 6s multicolored 1.00 75

1989, Apr. 26
1455 A823 5s multicolored 85 62

Ludwig Wittgenstein (1889-1951), philosopher.

Styrian Provincial Exhibition, Judenburg
A824

Design: Judenberg, 17th cent., an engraving by Georg Matthaus Vischer.

1989, Apr. 28 *Perf. 14x13½*
1456 A824 4s multicolored 70 52

Industrial Technology Exhibition, Pottenstein — A825

1989, Apr. 28 **Photo.** *Perf. 13½*
1457 A825 4s Steam engine 70 52

Radstadt Township, 700th Anniv.
A826

1989, May 3 **Photo.** *Perf. 13½x14½*
1458 A826 5s multicolored 85 62

Europa 1989 — A827

1989, May 5
1459 A827 6s Toy boat 1.00 75

Monastery Church at Lambach, 900th Anniv. — A828

Photo. & Engr.

1989, May 19 *Perf. 14*
1460 A828 4s multicolored 70 52

Paddle Steamer *Gisela* — A829

1989, May 19 **Photo.** *Perf. 13½*
1461 A829 5s multicolored 85 62

Shipping on the Traunsee, 150th anniv.

St. Andra im Lavanttal, 650th Anniv.
A830

Period cityscape by Matthaus Merian.

1989, May 26 **Photo. & Engr.**
1462 A830 5s multicolored 85 62

Richard Strauss (1864-1949), Composer — A831

Perf. 14½x13½

1989, June 1 **Photo. & Engr.**
1463 A831 6s dark brn, gold & red brn 1.00 75

Achensee Railway, Cent. — A832

1989, June 8 **Photo.** *Perf. 13½*
1464 A832 5s multicolored 85 62

Monastery Type of 1984

Design: 50g, Vorau Abbey, Styria. 1s, Monastery of Mehrerau, Vorarlberg. 1.50s, Monastery of the German Order in Vienna. 2s, Bendictine Monastery, Michaelbeuern. 11s, Engelszell Abbey. 12s, Monastery of the Hospitalers, Eisenstadt. 17s, St. Peter, Salzburg. 20s, Wernberg Monastery.

1989-92 **Photo. & Engr.** *Perf. 14*

1464A	A679a	50g multicolored	15	15
1465	A679a	1s multicolored	16	15
1465A	A679a	1.50s multicolored	30	24
1466	A679a	2s multicolored	32	25
1467	A679a	11s multicolored	1.85	1.40
1467A	A679a	12s multicolored	2.25	1.80
1468	A679a	17s multicolored	2.65	2.00
1469	A679a	20s multicolored	2.65	2.00
		Nos. 1464A-1469 (8)	10.33	7.99

Issue dates: 1s, Sept. 1. 17s, June 29. 11s, Mar. 9, 1990. 50g, Oct. 12, 1990. 20s, May 3, 1991. 2s, Sept. 27, 1991. 1.50s, Oct. 23, 1992. 12s, June 17, 1992.

This is an expanding set. Numbers will change if necessary.

Interparliamentary Union, Cent. — A833

Photo. & Engr.

1989, June 30 *Perf. 14*
1475 A833 6s Parliament, Vienna 1.00 75

Social Security in Austria, Cent. — A834

1989, Aug. 1 **Photo.**
1476 A834 5s multicolored 70 52

UN Offices in Vienna, 10th Anniv.
A835

1989, Aug. 23
1477 A835 8s multicolored 1.15 85

Wildalpen, 850th Anniv.
A836

Photo. & Engr.

1989, Sept. 15 *Perf. 13½x14*
1478 A836 5s Foundry, coat of arms 78 58

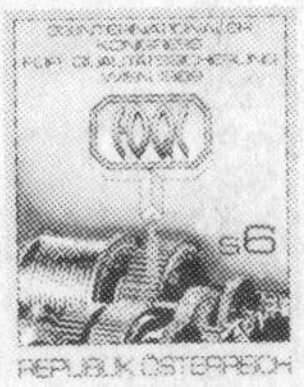

33rd Congress of the Association for Quality Assurance (EOQC) — A837

1989, Sept. 18 **Photo.** *Perf. 14x13½*
1479 A837 6s multicolored 92 70

14th World Congress of the Soc. for Criminal Law (AIDP) A838

Photo. & Engr.

1989, Oct. 2 *Perf. 13½*

1480 A838 6s Justice Palace, Vienna 92 70

Lebensbaum, by Ernst Steiner — A839

1989, Oct. 10 *Perf. 13½x14*

1481 A839 5s multicolored 78 58

A840 A841

Perf. 14½x13½

1989, Nov. 6 **Photo.**

1482 A840 4s Trakl 60 45
1483 A840 4s Anzengruber 60 45

Georg Trakl (1887-1914), expressionist poet; Ludwig Anzengruber (1839-1889), playwright and novelist.

1989, Nov. 10 **Photo. & Engr.**

1484 A841 6s multicolored 90 68

Alfred Fried (1864-1921), pacifist and publisher awarded the Nobel peace prize for 1911 with Tobias Asser.

Parish Church Christ Child, by Johann Carl Reslfeld A842

1989, Dec. 1 *Perf. 13½x14½*

1485 A842 5s multicolored 75 58

Christmas.

A843 A844

The Young Post Rider, an Engraving by Albrecht Durer

1990, Jan. 12 Photo. & Engr. *Perf. 14*

1486 A843 5s multicolored 78 58

Postal communications in Europe, 500th anniv.

See Belgium No. 1332, Germany No. 1592, Berlin No. 9N584 and German Democratic Republic No. 2791.

Perf. 13½x14½

1990, Jan. 12 **Photo.**

1487 A844 5s multicolored 78 58

Hahnenkamm alpine competition, Kitzbuhel, 50th anniv.

A845 A846

Perf. 14½x13½

1990, Jan. 17 **Photo.**

1488 A845 4.50s multicolored 72 54

Salomon Sulzer (1804-90), cantor and composer.

1990, Jan. 22 **Photo. & Engr.**

1489 A846 6s claret & pale green 95 70

Friedrich Emich (1860-1940), chemist.

Miniature from the *Market Book of Grein,* by Ulrich Schreier, c. 1490 A847

1990, Mar. 9 *Perf. 14*

1490 A847 5s sepia, buff & gray 80 60

City of Linz, 500th anniv.

University Seals — A848

1990, Apr. 6

1491 A848 5s multicolored 85 65

625th Anniv. of Vienna University and 175th anniv. of Vienna Technical University.

Scenery Type of 1984

1990-94 *Perf. 14*

1492 A679 5s Styrian Vineyards 85 65
1493 A679 5s Obir Caverns 95 72
1494 A679 5s Natural Bridge, Vorarlberg 90 75
1495 A679 6s Wilder Kaiser Mountain, Tyrol 1.20 95
1496 A679 6s Peggau Cave, Styria 1.00 80
Nos. 1492-1496 (5) 4.90 3.87

Issued: #1492, 4/27/90; #1493, 3/26/91; #1494, 2/5/92; #1495, 2/19/93; #1496, 4/29/94.

This is an expanding set. Numbers will change if necessary.

A849 A850

Church and municipal arms.

1990, Apr. 27 Photo. *Perf. 14x13½*

1500 A849 7s multicolored 1.20 25

1200th anniv. of Anthering.

1990, Apr. 30 Photo. *Perf. 13½*

1501 A850 4.50s multicolored 82 62

Labor Day, cent.

Seckau Abbey, 850th Anniv. — A851

Ebene Reichenau Post Office — A852

1990, May 4 Engr. *Perf. 14x13½*

1502 A851 4.50s bluish black 82 62

1990, May 4 Photo. *Perf. 13½x14*

1503 A852 7s multicolored 1.20 25

A853 A854

Self Portraits: 4.50s, Hans Makart (1840-84). 5s, Egon Schiele (1890-1918).

Photo. & Engr.

1990, May 29 *Perf. 14*

1504 A853 4.50s multicolored 82 62
1505 A853 5s multicolored 85 65

1990, June 1 Photo. *Perf. 14x13½*

1506 A854 4.50s multicolored 82 62

Ferdinand Raimund (1790-1836), actor.

Christ Healing the Sick by Rembrandt A855

1990, June 5 Photo. & Engr. *Perf. 14*

1507 A855 7s multicolored 1.30 1.00

Second Intl. Christus Medicus Congress, Bad Ischl.

Hardegg, 700th Anniv. — A856

Photo. & Engr.

1990, June 8 *Perf. 13½x14*

1508 A856 4.50s multicolored 82 62

Oberdrauburg, 750th Anniv. A857

1990, June 8 **Photo.**

1509 A857 5s multicolored 85 65

Gumpoldskirchen, 850th Anniv. — A858

Photo. & Engr.

1990, June 15 *Perf. 13½*

1510 A858 5s multicolored 85 65

Mathias Zdarsky (1856-1940), Alpine Skier — A859

1990, June 20 *Perf. 14x13½*

1511 A859 5s multicolored 85 65

Telegraph, 1880, Anton Tschechow, 1978 — A860

1990, June 28 Photo. *Perf. 14*

1512 A860 9s multicolored 1.50 1.10

Modern shipbuilding in Austria, 150th anniv.

A861 A862

Photo. & Engr.

1990, Aug. 3 *Perf. 14x13½*
1513 A861 5s gold & brown 85 65

Joseph Friedrich Perkonig (1890-1959), poet.

Photo. & Engr.

1990, Aug. 30 *Perf. 13½x14*

Herr des Regenbogens, by Robert Zeppel-Sperl.

1514 A862 5s gold & brown 85 65

European Dialysis and Transplantation Society, 27th Congress — A863

1990, Sept. 4 **Photo.** *Perf. 14*
1515 A863 7s multicolored 1.30 1.00

Franz Werfel (1890-1945), Writer — A864

Photo. & Engr.

1990, Sept. 11 *Perf. 14x13½*
1516 A864 5s multicolored 95 70

Austrian Forces in UN Peace Keeping Forces, 30th Anniv. A865

1990, Sept. 20 **Photo.** *Perf. 13½*
1517 A865 7s multicolored 1.30 1.00

Federal and State Arms A866

1990, Sept. 24 **Photo. & Engr.**
1518 A866 5s multicolored 95 70

Federalism in Austria.

A867 A868

1990, Oct. 22 **Photo & Engr.** *Perf. 14*
1519 A867 4.50s blk, bl grn & red 85 65

Mining Univ., Leoben, 150th anniv.

Photo. & Engr.

1990, Nov. 8 *Perf. 14x13½*
1520 A868 4.50s multicolored 85 65

Karl Freiherr von Vogelsang (1818-90), politician.

Metalworkers and Miners Trade Union, Cent. — A869

1990, Nov. 16 *Perf. 14*
1521 A869 5s multicolored 95 72

3rd World Curling Championships A870

1990, Nov. 23 **Photo.** *Perf. 14x13½*
1522 A870 7s multicolored 1.35 1.00

Palmhouse at Schonbrunn A871

1990, Nov. 30 *Perf. 14*
1523 A871 5s multicolored 95 72

A872 A873

Christmas: Altar in Klosterneuburg Abbey by the Master from Verdun.

Photo. & Engr.

1990, Nov. 23 *Perf. 13½*
1524 A872 5s multicolored 95 72

Photo. & Engr.

1991, Jan. 15 *Perf. 14x13½*
1525 A873 4.50s multicolored 85 65

Franz Grillparzer (1791-1872), dramatic poet.

A874 A875

1991, Jan. 21 *Perf. 13½*
1526 A874 5s multicolored 95 72

Alpine Skiing World Championship, Saalbach-Hinterglemm.

1991, Jan. 21 **Photo.** *Perf. 14x13½*
1527 A875 5s multicolored 95 72

Bruno Kreisky (1911-90), chancellor.

Friedrich Freiherr von Schmidt (1825-1891), Architect A876

1991, Jan. 21 *Perf. 14*
1528 A876 7s multicolored 1.35 1.00

Visual Arts — A877

Designs: 4.50s, Donner Fountain, Vienna, by Raphael Donner (1693-1741), sculptor. 5s, Kitzbuhel in Winter, by Alfons Walde (1891-1958), painter. 7s, Vienna Stock Exchange, Theophil Hansen (1813-1891), architect.

1991, Feb. 8

1529	A877	4.50s multicolored	85	65
1530	A877	5s multicolored	95	72
1531	A877	7s multicolored	1.35	1.00
		Nos. 1529-1531 (3)	3.15	2.37

See No. 1543.

Marie von Ebner Eschenbach (1830-1916), Poet — A878

Perf. 13½x14½

1991, Mar. 12 **Engr.**
1532 A878 4.50s rose violet 85 65

Miniature Sheet

Wolfgang Amadeus Mozart (1756-1791), Composer — A879

Design: b, Magic Flute Fountain, Vienna.

1991, Mar. 22 *Perf. 13½*
1533 Sheet of 2 + label 1.65 1.25
a.-b. A879 5s any single 80 60

Spittal an der Drau, 800th Anniv. A880

1991, Apr. 11 *Perf. 14*
1534 A880 4.50s multicolored 75 60

Europa A881

1991, May 3 **Photo.** *Perf. 14*
1535 A881 7s ERS-1 satellite 1.10 82

Garden Banquet by Anthony Bays A882

1991, May 10 **Photo.** *Perf. 13½*
1536 A882 5s multicolored 75 60

Vorarlberg Provincial Exhibition, Hohenems.

Museum of Military History, Cent. A883

Design: 7s, Interior of Museum of Art History.

Photo. & Engr.

1991, May 24 *Perf. 13½*
1537 A883 5s multicolored 95 78
1538 A883 7s multicolored 1.30 1.05

Museum of Art History, Cent. (#1538).

Grein, 500th Anniv. A884

1991, May 24 **Photo.** *Perf. 14*
1539 A884 4.50s multicolored 90 45

Tulln, 1200th Anniv. A885

1991, May 24 *Perf. 13½x14*
1540 A885 5s multicolored 95 78

Completion of Karawanken Tunnels — A886

1991, May 31 *Perf. 14x13½*
1541 A886 7s multicolored 1.30 1.05

5th Anniv. of St. Polten as Provincial Capital of Lower Austria A887

1991, July 5 Photo. *Perf. 14*
1542 A887 5s multicolored 80 65

Visual Arts Type of 1991

Design: 4.50s, Karlsplatz Station of Vienna Subway by Otto Wagner (1841-1918), Architect.

1991, July 12 Photo. & Engr.
1543 A877 4.50s multicolored 75 60

Rowing and Junior Canoeing World Championships, Vienna — A888

1991, Aug. 20 Photo. *Perf. 13½x14*
1544 A888 5s multicolored 85 70

European Congress of Radiologists A889

1991, Sept. 13 *Perf. 14*
1545 A889 7s multicolored 1.15 95

Paracelsus (1493-1541), Physician — A890

1991, Sept. 27 *Perf. 14x13½*
1546 A890 4.50s multicolored 75 60

Joint Austrian-Soviet Space Mission — A891

1991, Oct. 2 *Perf. 14*
1547 A891 9s multicolored 1.50 1.20

Austrian Folk Festivals — A892

Designs: 4.50s, Almabtrieb, Tyrol. 5s, Winzerkrone, Vienna. 7s, Ernte-Monstranz, Styria.

1991, Oct. 4 Photo. & Engr.
1548 A892 4.50s multicolored 75 60
1549 A892 5s multicolored 85 70
1550 A892 7s multicolored 1.15 95
Nos. 1548-1550 (3) 2.75 2.25

See Nos. 1577-1579, 1619-1621.

The General by Rudolph Pointner — A893

Photo. & Engr.
1991, Oct. 11 *Perf. 13½x14*
1551 A893 5s multicolored 85 70

Birth of Christ, Baumgartenberg Church — A894

1991, Nov. 29
1552 A894 5s multicolored 85 70

Christmas.

Julius Raab, Politician, Birth Cent. — A895

1991, Nov. 29 *Perf. 14x13½*
1553 A895 4.50s red brn & brn 75 60

1992 Winter and Summer Olympic Games A897

1992, Jan. 14 Photo. *Perf. 14*
1555 A897 7s multicolored 1.25 1.00

Trade Union of Clerks in Private Enterprises, Cent. — A898

1992, Jan. 14
1556 A898 5.50s multicolored 95 78

A899

A900

1992, Jan. 29 *Perf. 14x13½*
1557 A899 5s multicolored 90 75

8th Natural Run Toboggan World Championships.

1992, Feb. 5 Engr. *Perf. 14x13½*
1558 A900 5.50s brown 95 78

George Saiko, Poet, nirth cent.

Worker's Sports, Cent. — A901

1992, Feb. 5 Photo. *Perf. 14*
1559 A901 5.50s multicolored 95 78

Souvenir Sheet

Vienna Philharmonic Orchestra, 150th Anniv. — A902

Photo. & Engr.
1992, Mar. 27 *Perf. 14*
1560 A902 5.50s multicolored 95 78

Scientists — A903

Designs: 5s, Franz Joseph Muller von Reichenstein (1742-1825), discoverer of tellurium. 5.50s, Dr. Paul Kitaibel (1757-1817), botanist. 6s, Christian Johann Doppler (1803-1853), physicist. 7s, Richard Kuhn (1900-1967), chemist.

1992, Mar. 27 **Photo.**
1561 A903 5s multicolored 85 68
1562 A903 5.50s multicolored 95 78
1563 A903 6s multicolored 1.05 85
1564 A903 7s multicolored 1.20 95
Nos. 1561-1564 (4) 4.05 3.26

Railway Workers Union, Cent. A904

1992, Apr. 2 *Perf. 14x13½*
1565 A904 5.50s black & red 95 78

Norbert Hanrieder (1842-1913), Poet — A905

Photo. & Engr.
1992, Apr. 30 *Perf. 14x13½*
1566 A905 5.50s purple & buff 95 78

Carl Zeller (1842-1898) and Karl Millocker (1842-1899), Operetta Composers A906

Photo. & Engr.
1992, Apr. 30 *Perf. 14*
1567 A906 6s multicolored 1.05 85

LD Steel Mill, 40th Anniv. A907

1992, May 8 Photo. *Perf. 14x13½*
1568 A907 5s multicolored 85 68

Discovery of America, 500th Anniv. A908

1992, May 8 Photo. & Engr. *Perf. 14*
1569 A908 7s multicolored 1.20 95

Europa.

Austro-Swiss Treaty on Regulation of Rhine River, Cent. — A909

1992, May 8 Photo. *Perf. 13½x14*

1570 A909 7s multicolored 1.20 95

Protection of the Alps — A910

1992, May 22 *Perf. 14x13½*

1571 A910 5.50s multicolored 95 78

Dr. Anna Dengel (1892-1980), Physician — A911

Sebastian Rieger (1867-1953), Poet — A912

1992, May 22 Photo. & Engr.

1572 A911 5.50s multicolored 95 78

1992, May 22 Engr.

1573 A912 5s red brown 85 68

Lienz, 750th Anniv. A913

1992, June 17 Photo. *Perf. 14x13½*

1574 A913 5s Town Hall 90 72

Intl. Congress of Austrian Society of Surgeons — A914

Photo. & Engr.

1992, June 17 *Perf. 14*

1575 A914 6s multicolored 1.15 90

Dr. Kurt Waldheim, President of Austria, 1986-92 — A915

1992, June 22 *Perf. 14x13½*

1576 A915 5.50s multicolored 95 75

Folk Festivals Type of 1991

Designs: 5s, Marksman's target, Lower Austria. 5.50s, Peasant's chest, Carinthia. 7s, Votive icon, Vorarlberg.

Photo. & Engr.

1992, Sept. 18 *Perf. 14*

1577 A892 5s multicolored 90 72
1578 A892 5.50s multicolored 95 75
1579 A892 7s multicolored 1.25 1.00
Nos. 1577-1579 (3) 3.10 2.47

Marchfeld Canal — A917

1992, Oct. 9 Photo. *Perf. 13½x14*

1580 A917 5s multicolored 90 72

5th Intl. Ombudsman Conference, Vienna A918

1992, Oct. 9 Photo & Engr. *Perf. 14*

1581 A918 5.50s multicolored 95 75

The Clearance of Seawater, by Peter Pongratz A919

1992, Oct. 9

1582 A919 5.50s multicolored 95 75

Academy of Fine Arts, 300th Anniv. — A920

Photo. & Engr.

1992, Oct. 23 *Perf. 14*

1583 A920 5s red & blue 1.05 85

Birth of Christ, by Johann Georg Schmidt A921

1992, Nov. 27 *Perf. 14x13½*

1584 A921 5.50s multicolored 1.15 92

Christmas.

Veit Koniger, Sculptor, Death Bicent. — A922

Photo. & Engr.

1992, Nov. 27 *Perf. 14*

1585 A922 5s multicolored 1.00 80

Herman Potocnik, Theoretician of Geosynchronous Satellite Orbit, Birth Cent. — A923

1992, Nov. 27 Photo.

1586 A923 10s multicolored 2.00 1.60

Famous Buildings A924

Designs: 5s, Statues and dome of Imperial Palace, Vienna, designed by Joseph Emanuel Fischer von Erlach. 5.50s, Kinsky Palace, designed by Lukas von Hildebrandt. 7s, Vienna State Opera, designed by Eduard van der Null and August Siccard von Siccardsburg.

1993, Jan. 22 Photo. & Engr.

1587 A924 5s multicolored 1.00 80
1588 A924 5.50s multicolored 1.10 90
1589 A924 7s multicolored 1.40 1.15
Nos. 1587-1589 (3) 3.50 2.85

Joseph Emanuel Fischer von Erlach, 300th birth anniv. (#1587). Johann Lukas von Hildebrandt, 325th birth anniv. (#1588). Eduard van der Null, August Siccard von Siccardsburg, 125th death anniv. (#1589).

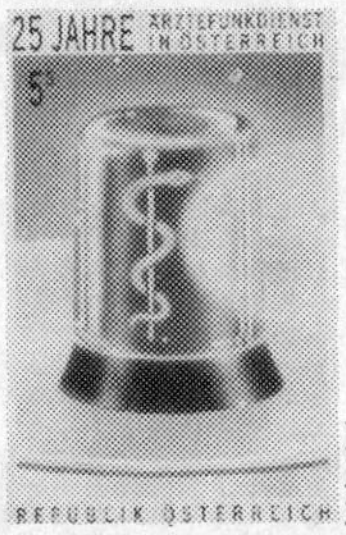

Radio Dispatched Medical Service, 25th Anniv. — A925

1993, Feb. 19 Photo.

1590 A925 5s multicolored 1.00 80

Typewriter Made by Peter Mitterhofer (1822-1893) A926

1993, Feb. 19 *Perf. 13½x14*

1591 A926 17s multicolored 3.50 2.75

Popular Entertainers — A927

Design: 5.50s, Strada del Sole, by Rainhard Fendrich.

1993, Mar. 19 Photo. *Perf. 14*

1592 A927 5.50s multicolored 1.00 80

See Nos. 1626, 1639.

Charles Sealsfield (1793-1864), Writer A928

Photo. & Engr.

1993, Mar. 19 *Perf. 13½x14*

1593 A928 10s multicolored 1.75 1.40

Rights of the Child — A930

1993, Apr. 16 Photo. *Perf. 13½x14*

1595 A930 7s multicolored 1.25 1.00

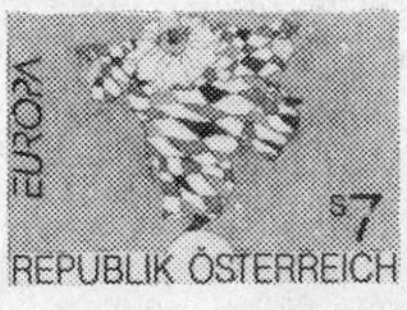

Flying Harlequin, by Paul Flora — A931

1993, Apr. 16 Photo. & Engr.

1596 A931 7s multicolored 1.25 1.00

Europa.

Monastery of Admont — A932

Designs: 5.50s, Death, wooden statue by Josef Stammel (1695-1765). 6s, Stained glass, Mariastern-Gwiggen Monastery. 7s, Marble lion, Franciscan Monastery, Salzburg. 7.50s, Cupola fresco, by Paul Troger, Monastery of Altenburg. 10s, Altarpiece, St. Peregrinus praying, Maria Luggau Monastery. 20s, Crosier, Fiecht Monastery.

Photo. & Engr.

1993-94 *Perf. 14x13½*

1603 A932 5.50s green, black & yel 1.00 80

Perf. 14

1606 A932 6s multicolored 1.10 85
1606A A932 7s gray, blk & yel 1.25 1.00
1607 A932 7.50s brown, blk & bl 1.25 1.00
1609 A932 10s multicolored 1.75 1.40
1613 A932 20s multicolored 3.50 1.75
Nos. 1606-1613 (5) 8.85 6.00

Issued: 5.50s, 4/16/93; 6s, 9/17/93; 20s, 10/8/93; 7.50s, 4/4/94; 10s, 8/26/94; 7s, 11/18/94.

This is an expanding set. Numbers may change.

Peter Rosegger (1843-1918), Writer — A933

1993, May 5 **Photo.** *Perf. 14x13½*
1617 A933 5.50s green & black 1.00 80

Lake Constance Steamer Hohentwiel A934

1993, May 5 **Photo.** *Perf. 14*
1618 A934 6s multicolored 1.05 85

See Germany No. 1786, Switzerland No. 931.

Folk Festivals Type of 1991

Designs: 5s, Corpus Christi Day Procession, Upper Austria. 5.50s, Blockdrawing, Burgenland. 7s, Cracking whip when snow is melting, Salzburg.

Photo. & Engr.

1993, June 11 *Perf. 14*
1619 A892 5s multicolored 90 70
1620 A892 5.50s multicolored 1.00 80
1621 A892 7s multicolored 1.25 1.00
Nos. 1619-1621 (3) 3.15 2.50

UN Conference on Human Rights, Vienna — A935

1993, June 11 **Photo.**
1622 A935 10s multicolored 1.75 1.40

Franz Jagerstatter (1907-1943), Resistance Fighter — A936

1993, Aug. 6 **Photo.** *Perf. 14x13½*
1623 A936 5.50s multicolored 1.00 80

Schafberg Railway, Cent. — A937

1993, Aug. 6 *Perf. 13½x14*
1624 A937 6s multicolored 1.10 90

Self-portrait with Puppet, by Rudolf Wacker (1893-1939) A938

1993, Aug. 6 **Photo. & Engr.** *Perf. 14*
1625 A938 6s multicolored 1.10 90

Popular Entertainers Type of 1993

Design: 5.50s, Granny, by Ludwig Hirsch.

1993, Sept. 3 **Photo.** *Perf. 14*
1626 A927 5.50s multicolored 1.00 80

Vienna Mens' Choral Society, 150th Anniv. A940

1993, Sept. 17 **Photo.** *Perf. 14*
1627 A940 5s multicolored 90 75

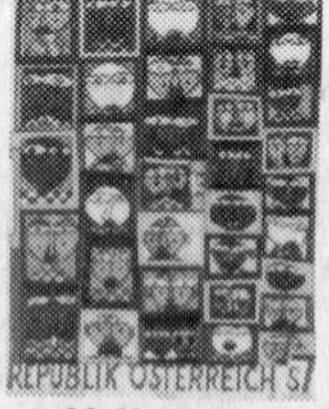

Easter, by Max Weiler A941

99 Heads, by Hundertwasser A942

Photo. & Engr.

1993, Oct. 8 *Perf. 13½x14*
1628 A941 5.50s multicolored 1.00 80

1993, Oct. 8
1629 A942 7s multicolored 1.25 1.00

Council of Europe Conference, Vienna.

Austrian Republic, 75th Anniv. — A943

Design: 5.50s, Statue of Pallas Athena.

Photo. & Engr.

1993, Nov. 12 *Perf. 13½x14*
1630 A943 5.50s multicolored 1.00 80

Trade Unions in Austria, Cent. A944

1993, Nov. 12 **Photo.** *Perf. 14*
1631 A944 5.50s multicolored 1.00 80

Birth of Christ, by Master of the Krainburger Altar — A945

Photo. & Engr.

1993, Nov. 26 *Perf. 13½x14*
1632 A945 5.50s multicolored 1.00 80

Christmas.

Folklore and Customs Type of 1991

Antiques: 5.50s, Dolls, cradle, Vorarlberg. 6s, Sled, Steiermark. 7s, Godparent's bowl, Upper Austria.

1994, Jan. 28 **Photo. & Engr.** *Perf. 14*
1633 A892 5.50s multicolored 1.00 80
1634 A892 6s multicolored 1.10 90
1635 A892 7s multicolored 1.25 1.00
Nos. 1633-1635 (3) 3.35 2.70

1994 Winter Olympics, Lillehammer, Norway — A946

1994, Feb. 9
1636 A946 7s multicolored 1.25 1.00

Vienna Mint, 800th Anniv. A947

1994, Feb. 18
1637 A947 6s multicolored 1.10 90

Lying Lady, by Herbert Boeckl (1894-1966) A948

1994, Mar. 18 **Photo.** *Perf. 14x13½*
1638 A948 5.50s multicolored 95 70

Popular Entertainers Type of 1993

Design: 6s, Rock Me Amadeus, by Falco.

1994, Mar. 18 *Perf. 14*
1639 A927 6s multicolored 1.00 80

Wiener Neustadt, 800th Anniv. — A949

1994, Mar. 18
1640 A949 6s multicolored 1.00 80

Lake Rudolph, Teleki-Hohnel Expedition — A950

Photo. & Engr.

1994, May 27 *Perf. 14x13½*
1641 A950 7s multicolored 1.25 1.00

Europa.

Daniel Gran, 300th Birth Anniv. A951

Fresco: 20s, Allegory of Theology, Jurisprudence and Medicine.

1994, May 27
1642 A951 20s multicolored 3.50 2.75

Carinthian Summer Festival, 25th Anniv. — A952

Design: 5.50s, Scene from The Prodigal Son.

Photo. & Engr.

1994, June 17 *Perf. 14*
1643 A952 5.50s lake & gold 95 75

Railway Centennials — A953

1994 **Photo. & Engr.** *Perf. 14*

1647	A953	5.50s Gailtal	95	75
1648	A953	6s Murtal	1.00	80

Issued: 5.50s, 6s, 6/17/94.

Hermann Gmeiner, 75th Birth Anniv. — A954

1994, June 17 *Perf. 14x13½*

1656	A954	7s multicolored	1.25	1.00

Karl Seitz (1869-1950) Politician — A955

Karl Bohm (1894-1981), Conductor — A956

1994, Aug. 12 **Photo.** *Perf. 14*

1657	A955	5.50s multicolored	1.00	80

Photo. & Engr.

1994, Aug. 26 *Perf. 14x13½*

1658	A956	7s gold & dk blue	1.25	1.00

Ethnic Minorities in Austria A957

1994, Sept. 9 **Photo.** *Perf. 13½*

1659	A957	5.50s multicolored	1.00	80

Franz Theodor Csokor (1885-1969), Writer — A958

Design: 7s, Joseph Roth (1894-1939), writer.

1994, Sept. 9 *Perf. 14x13½*

1660	A958	6s multicolored	1.00	80
1661	A958	7s multicolored	1.25	1.00

Austrian Working Environment — A961

1994, Nov. 18 **Photo.** *Perf. 14*

1664	A961	6s Stewardess, child	1.10	90

Richard Coudenhove Kalergi, Founder of PanEuropean Union, Birth Cent. — A962

Photo. & Engr.

1994, Nov. 18 *Perf. 13½*

1665	A962	10s multicolored	1.90	1.50

Birth of Christ, by Anton Wollenek A963

1994, Nov. 25 *Perf. 14*

1666	A963	6s multicolored	1.10	90

Christmas.

SEMI-POSTAL STAMPS

Issues of the Monarchy

Emperor Franz Josef — SP1

The Firing Step — SP2

Perf. 12½

1914, Oct. 4 **Typo.** **Unwmk.**

B1	SP1	5h green	15	15
B2	SP1	10h rose	15	15
		Set value	17	15
		Set, never hinged	40	

Nos. B1-B2 were sold at an advance of 2h each over face value. Exist imperf.; value, set $60.

1915, May 1

Designs: 5h+2h, Cavalry. 10h+2h, Siege gun. 20h+3h, Battleship. 35h+3h, Airplane.

B3	SP2	3h + 1h violet brn	15	30
B4	SP2	5h + 2h green	15	15
B5	SP2	10h + 2h deep rose	15	15
B6	SP2	20h + 3h Prus blue	15	70
B7	SP2	35h + 3h ultra	1.65	1.10
		Nos. B3-B7 (5)	2.25	2.40
		Set, never hinged	4.75	

Exist imperf. Value, set $110.

Issues of the Republic

Types of Austria, 1919-20, Overprinted in Black

Kärnten

Abstimmung

1920, Sept. 16 *Perf. 12½*

B11	A44	5h gray, *yellow*	20	52
B12	A44	10h red, *pink*	42	85
B13	A43	15h bister, *yel*	20	52
B14	A45	20h dark grn, *bl*	20	52
B15	A43	25h violet, *pink*	20	52
B16	A45	30h brown, *buff*	52	1.65
B17	A45	40h carmine, *yel*	32	70
B18	A45	50h dark bl, *blue*	32	70
B19	A43	60h ol grn, *azure*	85	1.75
B20	A47	80h red	20	52
B21	A47	1k orange brown	28	55
B22	A47	2k pale blue	20	52

Granite Paper

Imperf

B23	A46	2½k brown red	28	65
B24	A46	3k dk blue & green	28	65
B25	A46	4k carmine & violet	42	1.00
B26	A46	5k blue	55	1.10
B27	A46	7½k yellow green	55	1.10
B28	A46	10k gray grn & red	55	1.10
B29	A46	20k lilac & orange	55	1.10
		Nos. B11-B29 (19)	7.09	16.02
		Set, never hinged	18.00	

Carinthia Plebiscite. Sold at three times face value for the benefit of the Plebiscite Propaganda Fund.

Nos. B11-B19 exist imperf. Value, set $125.

Types of Regular Issues of 1919-21 Overprinted

Hochwasser

1920

1921, Mar. 1 *Perf. 12½*

B30	A44	5h gray, *yellow*	18	32
B31	A44	10h orange brown	18	32
B32	A43	15h gray	18	32
B33	A45	20h green, *yellow*	18	32
B34	A43	25h blue, *yellow*	18	32
B35	A45	30h violet, *bl*	18	32
B36	A45	40h org brn, *pink*	22	52
B37	A45	50h green, *blue*	70	1.90
B38	A43	60h lilac, *yellow*	18	32
B39	A47	80h pale blue	18	32
B40	A47	1k red org, *blue*	45	1.25
B41	A47	1½k green, *yellow*	22	32
B42	A47	2k lilac brown	22	32

Overprinted

Hochwasser

1920

B43	A46	2½k light blue	22	32
B44	A46	3k ol grn & brn red	22	32
B45	A46	4k lilac & orange	52	1.40
B46	A46	5k olive green	30	70
B47	A46	7½k brown red	30	70
B48	A46	10k blue & olive grn	42	1.10
B49	A46	20k car rose & vio	50	1.25
		Nos. B30-B49 (20)	5.73	12.66
		Set, never hinged	15.00	

Nos. B30-B49 were sold at three times face value, the excess going to help flood victims. Exists imperf. Value, set $175.

Franz Joseph Haydn — SP9

View of Bregenz — SP16

Musicians: 5k, Mozart. 7½k, Beethoven. 10k, Schubert. 25k, Anton Bruckner. 50k, Johann Strauss (son). 100k, Hugo Wolf.

1922, Apr. 24 **Engr.** *Perf. 12½*

B50	SP9	2½k brown	4.25	4.50
a.		Perf. 11½	4.25	4.50
B51	SP9	5k dark blue	90	1.25
B52	SP9	7½k black	1.00	1.90
a.		Perf. 11½	65.00	110.00
B53	SP9	10k dark violet	1.65	2.00
a.		Perf. 11½	2.00	2.50
B54	SP9	25k dark green	2.00	2.75
a.		Perf. 11½	3.25	4.00
B55	SP9	50k claret	1.40	2.50
B56	SP9	100k brown olive	4.50	6.00
a.		Perf. 11½	6.00	8.75
		Nos. B50-B56 (7)	15.70	20.90
		Set, never hinged	47.50	

These stamps were sold at 10 times face value, the excess being given to needy musicians.

All values exist imperf. on both regular and hand-made papers. Value, set $425.

A 1969 souvenir sheet without postal validity contains reprints of the 5k in black, 7½k in claret and 50k in dark blue, each overprinted "NEUDRUCK" in black at top. It was issued for the Vienna State Opera Centenary Exhibition.

1923, May 22 *Perf. 12½*

Designs: 120k, Mirabelle Gardens, Salzburg. 160k, Church at Eisenstadt. 180k, Assembly House, Klagenfurt. 200k, "Golden Roof," Innsbruck. 240k, Main Square, Linz. 400k, Castle Hill, Graz. 600k, Abbey at Melk. 1000k, Upper Belvedere, Vienna.

Various Frames

B57	SP16	100k dk green	2.00	3.00
B58	SP16	120k deep blue	2.00	3.00
B59	SP16	160k dk violet	2.00	3.00
B60	SP16	180k red violet	2.00	3.00
B61	SP16	200k lake	2.00	3.00
B62	SP16	240k red brown	2.00	3.00
B63	SP16	400k dark brown	2.00	3.00
B64	SP16	600k olive brn	2.00	3.00
B65	SP16	1000k black	2.00	3.00
		Nos. B57-B65 (9)	18.00	27.00
		Set, never hinged	52.50	

Nos. B57-B65 were sold at five times face value, the excess going to needy artists.

All values exist imperf. on both regular and hand-made papers. Value, set $350.

Feebleness SP25

Siegfried Slays the Dragon SP30

Designs: 300k+900k, Aid to industry. 500k+1500k, Orphans and widow. 600k+1800k, Indigent old man. 1000k+3000k, Alleviation of hunger.

1924, Sept. 6 **Photo.**

B66	SP25	100k + 300k yel green	2.50	2.50
B67	SP25	300k + 900k red brn	3.75	6.00
B68	SP25	500k + 1500k brn vio	3.75	6.00
B69	SP25	600k + 1800k pck bl	3.75	6.00
B70	SP25	1000k + 3000k brn org	6.25	9.25
		Nos. B66-B70 (5)	20.00	29.75
		Set, never hinged	50.00	

The surtax was for child welfare and anti-tuberculosis work. Set exists imperf. Value, $300.

1926, Mar. 8 **Engr.**

Designs: 8g+2g, Gunther's voyage to Iceland. 15g+5g, Brunhild accusing Kriemhild. 20g+5g, Nymphs telling Hagen the future. 24g+6g, Rudiger von Bechelaren welcomes the Nibelungen. 40g+10g, Dietrich von Bern vanquishes Hagen.

B71	SP30	3g + 2g olive blk	70	28
B72	SP30	8g + 2g indigo	16	28
B73	SP30	15g + 5g dk claret	16	28
B74	SP30	20g + 5g olive grn	32	50
B75	SP30	24g + 6g dk violet	32	50
B76	SP30	40g + 10g red brn	2.25	2.75
		Nos. B71-B76 (6)	3.91	4.59
		Set, never hinged	10.00	

Nibelungen issue.

The surtax was for child welfare. Set exists imperf. Value, $225.

Pres. Michael Hainisch — SP36

Pres. Wilhelm Miklas — SP37

1928, Nov. 5

B77	SP36	10g dark brown	3.50	6.00
B78	SP36	15g red brown	3.50	6.00
B79	SP36	30g black	3.50	6.00
B80	SP36	40g indigo	3.50	6.00
		Nos. B77-B80 (4)	14.00	24.00
		Set, never hinged	29.00	

Tenth anniversary of Austrian Republic. Sold at double face value, the premium aiding war orphans and children of war invalids.

Set exists imperf. Value $300.

1930, Oct. 4

B81 SP37	10g light brown	5.50	8.50
B82 SP37	20g red	5.50	8.50
B83 SP37	30g brown violet	5.50	8.50
B84 SP37	40g indigo	5.50	8.50
B85 SP37	50g dark green	5.50	8.50
B86 SP37	1s black brown	5.50	8.50
	Nos. B81-B86 (6)	33.00	51.00
	Set, never hinged	78.00	

Nos. B81-B86 were sold at double face value. The excess aided the anti-tuberculosis campaign and the building of sanatoria in Carinthia.
Set exists imperf. Value, $325.

Regular Issue of 1929-30 Overprinted in Various Colors

1931, June 20

B87 A56	10g bister (Bl)	25.00	32.50
B88 A56	20g dk gray (R)	25.00	32.50
B89 A56	30g dk violet (Gl)	25.00	32.50
B90 A56	40g dk blue (Gl)	25.00	32.50
B91 A56	50g gray vio (O)	25.00	32.50
B92 A57	1s black brn (Bk)	25.00	32.50
	Nos. B87-B92 (6)	150.00	195.00
	Set, never hinged	340.00	

Rotary convention, Vienna.
Nos. B87 to B92 were sold at double their face values. The excess was added to the beneficent funds of Rotary International.
Exists imperf.

Ferdinand Raimund — SP38

Poets: 20g, Franz Grillparzer. 30g, Johann Nestroy. 40g, Adalbert Stifter. 50g, Ludwig Anzengruber. 1s, Peter Rosegger.

1931, Sept. 12

B93 SP38	10g dark violet	9.00	14.00
B94 SP38	20g gray black	9.00	14.00
B95 SP38	30g orange red	9.00	14.00
B96 SP38	40g dull blue	9.00	14.00
B97 SP38	50g gray green	9.00	14.00
B98 SP38	1s yellow brown	9.00	14.00
	Nos. B93-B98 (6)	54.00	84.00
	Set, never hinged	130.00	

Nos. B93-B98 were sold at double face value. The surtax aided unemployed young people.
Set exists imperf. Value, $500.

Chancellor Ignaz Seipel SP44

Ferdinand Georg Waldmüller SP45

1932, Oct. 12 *Perf. 13*

B99 SP44	50g ultra	9.50	11.50
	Never hinged	17.50	

Msgr. Ignaz Seipel, Chancellor of Austria, 1922-29. Sold at double face value, the excess aiding wounded veterans of World War I.
Exists imperf. Value, $150.

1932, Nov. 21

Artists: 24g, Moritz von Schwind. 30g, Rudolf von Alt. 40g, Hans Makart. 64g, Gustav Klimt. 1s, Albin Egger-Lienz.

B100 SP45	12g slate green	13.00	25.00
B101 SP45	24g dp violet	13.00	25.00
B102 SP45	30g dark red	13.00	25.00
B103 SP45	40g dark gray	13.00	25.00
B104 SP45	64g dark brown	13.00	25.00
B105 SP45	1s claret	13.00	25.00
	Nos. B100-B105 (6)	78.00	150.00
	Set, never hinged	170.00	

Nos. B100 to B105 were sold at double their face values. The surtax was for the assistance of charitable institutions.
Set exists imperf. Value, $600.

Mountain Climbing SP51

Designs: 24g, Ski gliding. 30g, Walking on skis. 50g, Ski jumping.

1933, Jan. 9 **Photo.** *Perf. 12½*

B106 SP51	12g dark green	5.50	8.25
B107 SP51	24g dark violet	47.50	75.00
B108 SP51	30g brown red	10.50	14.00
B109 SP51	50g dark blue	47.50	75.00
	Nos. B106-B109 (4)	111.00	172.25
	Set, never hinged	315.00	

Meeting of the Intl. Ski Federation, Innsbruck, Feb. 8-13.
These stamps were sold at double their face value. The surtax was for the benefit of "Youth in Distress."
#B106-B109 exist imperf. Value $1,500.

Stagecoach, after Painting by Moritz von Schwind SP55

1933, June 23 **Engr.** *Perf. 12½*
Ordinary Paper

B110 SP55	50g deep ultra	125.00	140.00
	Never hinged	200.00	
a.	Granite paper	265.00	300.00
a.	Never hinged	375.00	

Sheets of 25.
Nos. B110 and B110a exist imperf. Values $750 and $1,500.

Souvenir Sheet
Perf. 12
Granite Paper

B111	Sheet of 4	1,800.	2,500.
a.	SP55 50g deep ultra	300.00	450.00
a.	Never hinged	450.00	

Intl. Phil. Exhib., Vienna, 1933. In addition to the postal value of 50g the stamp was sold at a premium of 50g for charity and of 1.60s for the admission fee to the exhibition.
Size of No. B111: 126x103mm.
A 50g dark red in souvenir sheet, with dark blue overprint ("NEUDRUCK WIPA 1965"), had no postal validity.

St. Stephen's Cathedral in 1683 — SP56

Marco d'Aviano, Papal Legate — SP57

Designs: 30g, Count Ernst Rudiger von Starhemberg. 40g, John III Sobieski, King of Poland. 50g, Karl V, Duke of Lorraine. 64g, Burgomaster Johann Andreas von Liebenberg.

1933, Sept. 6 **Photo.** *Perf. 12½*

B112 SP56	12g dark green	16.00	21.00
B113 SP57	24g dark violet	15.00	19.00
B114 SP57	30g brown red	15.00	19.00
B115 SP57	40g blue black	21.00	32.50
B116 SP57	50g dark blue	15.00	19.00
B117 SP57	64g olive brown	21.00	30.00
	Nos. B112-B117 (6)	103.00	140.50
	Set, never hinged	240.00	

Deliverance of Vienna from the Turks, 250th anniv., and Pan-German Catholic Congress, Sept. 6, 1933.
The stamps were sold at double their face value, the excess being for the aid of Catholic works of charity.
Set exists imperf. Value, $750.

Types of Regular Issue of 1925-30 Surcharged:

+2g
Winterhilfe
a

WINTERHILFE
+6g
b

+50g

WINTERHILFE
c

1933, Dec. 15

B118 A52(a)	5g + 2g olive grn	25	55
B119 A56(b)	12g + 3g lt blue	25	55
B120 A56(b)	24g + 6g brn orange	25	55
B121 A57(c)	1s + 50g orange red	25.00	35.00
	Nos. B118-B121 (4)	25.75	36.65
	Set, never hinged	45.00	

Winterhelp. Exists imperf. Value, set $175.

Anton Pilgram — SP62

Architects: 24g, J. B. Fischer von Erlach. 30g, Jakob Prandtauer. 40g, A. von Siccardsburg & E. van der Null. 60g, Heinrich von Ferstel. 64g, Otto Wagner.

1934, Dec. 2 **Engr.** *Perf. 12½*
Thick Yellowish Paper

B122 SP62	12g black	7.00	10.00
B123 SP62	24g dull violet	7.00	10.00
B124 SP62	30g carmine	7.00	10.00
B125 SP62	40g brown	7.00	10.00
B126 SP62	60g blue	7.00	10.00
B127 SP62	64g dull green	7.00	10.00
	Nos. B122-B127 (6)	42.00	60.00
	Set, never hinged	85.00	

Exist imperf. Value, set $500.
Nos. B124-B127 exist in horiz. pairs imperf. between. Value, $175 to $225.
These stamps were sold at double their face value. The surtax on this and the following issues was devoted to general charity.

Types of Regular Issue of 1934 Surcharged in Black:

+50g
Winterhilfe
+2g
a

WINTERHILFE
b

1935, Nov. 11 *Perf. 12, 12½*

B128 A67(a)	5g + 2g emerald	45	75
B129 A67(a)	12g + 3g blue	45	75
B130 A67(a)	24g + 6g lt brown	45	75
B131 A68(b)	1s + 50g ver	17.00	30.00
	Nos. B128-B131 (4)	18.35	32.25
	Set, never hinged	45.00	

Winterhelp. Set exists imperf. Value, $140.

Prince Eugene of Savoy — SP68

Slalom Turn — SP74

Military Leaders: 24g, Field Marshal Laudon. 30g, Archduke Karl. 40g, Field Marshal Josef Radetzky. 60g, Admiral Wilhelm Tegetthoff. 64g, Field Marshal Franz Conrad Hotzendorff.

1935, Dec. 1 *Perf. 12½*

B132 SP68	12g brown	8.50	11.00
B133 SP68	24g dark green	8.50	11.00
B134 SP68	30g claret	8.50	11.00
B135 SP68	40g slate	8.50	11.00
B136 SP68	60g deep ultra	8.50	11.00
B137 SP68	64g dark violet	8.50	11.00
	Nos. B132-B137 (6)	51.00	66.00
	Set, never hinged	100.00	

These stamps were sold at double their face value. Set exists imperf. Value, $500.

1936, Feb. 20 **Photo.**

Designs: 24g, Jumper taking off. 35g, Slalom turn. 60g, Innsbruck view.

B138 SP74	12g Prus green	2.00	2.50
B139 SP74	24g dp violet	3.75	4.00
B140 SP74	35g rose car	17.50	27.50
B141 SP74	60g sapphire	17.50	30.00
	Nos. B138-B141 (4)	40.75	64.00
	Set, never hinged	95.00	

Ski concourse issue. These stamps were sold at double their face value. Set exists imperf. Value, $475.

St. Martin of Tours — SP78

Designs: 12g+3g, Medical clinic. 24g+6g, St. Elizabeth of Hungary. 1s+1s, "Flame of Charity."

1936, Nov. 2 **Unwmk.**

B142 SP78	5g + 2g dp green	25	32
B143 SP78	12g + 3g dp violet	25	32
B144 SP78	24g + 6g dp blue	25	32
B145 SP78	1s + 1s dk carmine	5.00	8.75
	Nos. B142-B145 (4)	5.75	9.71
	Set, never hinged	11.00	

Winterhelp. Set exists imperf. Value, $175.

Josef Ressel — SP82

Nurse and Infant — SP88

Inventors: 24g, Karl von Ghega. 30g, Josef Werndl. 40g, Carl Auer von Welsbach. 60g, Robert von Lieben. 64g, Viktor Kaplan.

1936, Dec. 6 **Engr.**

B146 SP82	12g dk brown	1.50	3.00
B147 SP82	24g dk violet	1.50	3.00
B148 SP82	30g dp claret	1.50	3.00
B149 SP82	40g gray violet	1.50	3.00
B150 SP82	60g vio blue	1.50	3.00
B151 SP82	64g dk slate green	1.50	3.00
	Nos. B146-B151 (6)	9.00	18.00
	Set, never hinged	24.00	

These stamps were sold at double their face value. Exists imperf. Value, set $325.

1937, Oct. 18 **Photo.**

Designs: 12g+3g, Mother and child. 24g+6g, Nursing the aged. 1s+1s, Sister of Mercy with patient.

B152	SP88	5g + 2g dk green	15	24
B153	SP88	12g + 3g dk brown	15	24
B154	SP88	24g + 6g dk blue	15	24
B155	SP88	1s + 1s dk carmine	2.75	5.00
		Nos. B152-B155 (4)	3.20	5.72
		Set, never hinged	6.50	

Winterhelp. Set exists imperf. Value, $85.

Gerhard van Swieten — SP92

The Dawn of Peace — SP101

Physicians: 8g, Leopold Auenbrugger von Auenbrugg. 12g, Karl von Rokitansky. 20g, Joseph Skoda. 24g, Ferdinand von Hebra. 30g, Ferdinand von Arlt. 40g, Joseph Hyrtl. 60g, Theodor Billroth. 64g, Theodor Meynert.

1937, Dec. 5 **Engr.** ***Perf. 12½***

B156	SP92	5g choc	1.50	2.75
B157	SP92	8g dk red	1.50	2.75
B158	SP92	12g brown blk	1.50	2.75
B159	SP92	20g dk green	1.50	2.75
B160	SP92	24g dk violet	1.50	2.75
B161	SP92	30g brown car	1.50	2.75
B162	SP92	40g dp olive grn	1.50	2.75
B163	SP92	60g indigo	1.50	2.75
B164	SP92	64g brown vio	1.50	2.75
		Nos. B156-B164 (9)	13.50	24.75
		Set, never hinged	30.00	

These stamps were sold at double their face value. Set exists imperf. Value, $450.

Catalogue values for unused stamps in this section, from this point to the end of the section, are for Never Hinged items.

1945, Sept. 10 **Photo.** ***Perf. 14***

B165	SP101	1s + 10s dk green	60	1.40

No. 467 Surcharged in Black

1946, June 25

B166	A110	30g + 20g dk red	3.00	3.00

First anniversary of United Nations.

Pres. Karl Renner SP102

1946 **Engr.** ***Perf. 13½x14***

B167	SP102	1s + 1s dk slate grn	2.00	3.00
B168	SP102	2s + 2s dk blue vio	2.00	3.00
B169	SP102	3s + 3s dk purple	2.00	3.00
B170	SP102	5s + 5s dk violet brn	2.00	3.00
		Nos. B167-B170 (4)	8.00	12.00

See Nos. B185-B188.

Nazi Sword Piercing Austria — SP103

Sweeping Away Fascist Symbols — SP104

Designs: 8g+6g, St. Stephen's Cathedral in Flames. 12g+12g, Pleading hand in concentration camp. 30g+30g, Hand choking Nazi serpent. 42g+42g, Hammer breaking Nazi pillar. 1s+1s, Oath of allegiance. 2s+2s, Austrian eagle and burning swastika.

Unwmk.

1946, Sept. 16 **Photo.** ***Perf. 14***

B171	SP103	5g + (3g) dk brown	42	55
B172	SP104	6g + (4g) dk slate grn	32	45
B173	SP104	8g + (6g) orange red	32	45
B174	SP104	12g + (12g) slate blk	32	45
B175	SP104	30g + (30g) violet	32	45
B176	SP104	42g + (42g) dull brn	32	45
B177	SP104	1s + 1s dk red	42	55
B178	SP104	2s + 2s dk car rose	60	55
		Nos. B171-B178 (8)	3.04	3.90

Anti-fascist propaganda.

Race Horse with Foal — SP111

Various Race Horses.

1946, Oct. 20 **Engr.** ***Perf. 13½x14***

B179	SP111	16g + 16g rose brown	1.90	2.25
B180	SP111	24g + 24g dk purple	1.90	2.25
B181	SP111	60g + 60g dk green	1.90	2.25
B182	SP111	1s + 1s dk blue gray	1.90	2.25
B183	SP111	2s + 2s yel brown	1.90	2.25
		Nos. B179-B183 (5)	9.50	11.25

Austria Prize race, Vienna.

St. Ruprecht's Church, Vienna — SP116

1946, Oct. 30 ***Perf. 14x13½***

B184	SP116	30g + 70g dark red	32	60

Founding of Austria, 950th anniv. The surtax aided the Stamp Day celebration.

Renner Type of 1946
Souvenir Sheets

1946, Sept. 5 ***Imperf.***

B185	Sheet of 8	450.00	*900.00*
a.	SP102 1s+1s dk slate grn	47.50	*75.00*
B186	Sheet of 8	450.00	*900.00*
a.	SP102 2s+2s dk blue vio	47.50	*75.00*
B187	Sheet of 8	450.00	*900.00*
a.	SP102 3s+3s dark purple	47.50	*75.00*
B188	Sheet of 8	450.00	*900.00*
a.	SP102 5s+5s dk vio brown	47.50	*75.00*

1st anniv. of Austria's liberation. Sheets of 8 plus center label showing arms.

Statue of Rudolf IV the Founder — SP118

Reaping Wheat — SP128

Designs: 5g+20g, Tomb of Frederick III. 6g+24g, Main pulpit. 8g+32g, Statue of St. Stephen. 10g+40g, Madonna of the Domestics statue. 12g+48g, High altar. 30g+1.20s, Organ, destroyed in 1945. 50g+1.80s, Anton Pilgram statue. 1s+5s, Cathedral from northeast. 2s+10s, Southwest corner of cathedral.

1946, Dec. 12 **Engr.** ***Perf. 14x13½***

B189	SP118	3g + 12g brown	20	30
B190	SP118	5g + 20g dk vio brown	20	30
B191	SP118	6g + 24g dk blue	20	30
B192	SP118	8g + 32g dk green	20	30
B193	SP118	10g + 40g dp blue	34	38
B194	SP118	12g + 48g dk vio	40	48
B195	SP118	30g + 1.20s car	1.00	1.10
B196	SP118	50g + 1.80s dk bl	1.10	1.25
B197	SP118	1s + 5s brn vio	1.50	1.75
B198	SP118	2s + 10s vio brn	3.00	3.50
		Nos. B189-B198 (10)	8.14	9.66

The surtax aided reconstruction of St. Stephen's Cathedral, Vienna.

1947, Mar. 23 ***Perf. 14x13½***

Designs: 8g+2g, Log raft. 10g+5g, Cement factory. 12g+8g, Coal mine. 18g+12g, Oil derricks. 30g+10g, Textile machinery. 35g+15g, Iron furnace. 60g+20g, Electric power lines.

B199	SP128	3g + 2g yel brown	30	32
B200	SP128	8g + 2g dk bl grn	30	32
B201	SP128	10g + 5g slate blk	30	32
B202	SP128	12g + 8g dark pur	30	32
B203	SP128	18g + 12g ol green	30	32
B204	SP128	30g + 10g deep cl	30	32
B205	SP128	35g + 15g crimson	30	32
B206	SP128	60g + 20g dk blue	30	32
		Nos. B199-B206 (8)	2.40	2.56

Vienna International Sample Fair, 1947.

Race Horse and Jockey SP136

1947, June 29 ***Perf. 13½x14***

B207	SP136	60g + 20g deep blue, *pale pink*	15	20

Cup of Corvinus — SP137

Prisoner of War — SP147

Designs: 8g+2g, Statue of Providence, Vienna. 10g+5g, Abbey at Melk. 12g+8g, Picture of a Woman, by Kriehuber. 18g+12g, Children at the Window, by Waldmuller. 20g+10g, Entrance, Upper Belvedere Palace. 30g+10g, Nymph Egeria, Schönbrunn Castle. 35g+15g, National Library, Vienna. 48g+12g, "Workshop of a Printer of Engravings," by Schmutzer. 60g+20g, Girl with Straw Hat, by Amerling.

1947, June 20 ***Perf. 14x13½***

B208	SP137	3g + 2g brown	25	28
B209	SP137	8g + 2g dk blue grn	25	28
B210	SP137	10g + 5g dp claret	25	28
B211	SP137	12g + 8g dk purple	25	28
B212	SP137	18g + 12g golden brn	25	28
B213	SP137	20g + 10g sepia	25	28
B214	SP137	30g + 10g dk yel grn	25	28
B215	SP137	35g + 15g deep car	25	28
B216	SP137	48g + 12g dk brn vio	25	28
B217	SP137	60g + 20g dp blue	25	28
		Nos. B208-B217 (10)	2.50	2.80

1947, Aug. 30

Designs: 12g+8g, Prisoners' Mail. 18g+12g, Prison camp visitor. 35g+15g, Family reunion. 60g+20g, "Industry" beckoning. 1s+40g, Sower.

B218	SP147	8g + 2g dk green	15	15
B219	SP147	12g + 8g dk vio brn	15	15
B220	SP147	18g + 12g black brn	15	15
B221	SP147	35g + 15g rose brn	15	15
B222	SP147	60g + 20g dp blue	15	15
B223	SP147	1s + 40g redsh brn	15	15
		Nos. B218-B223 (6)	90	90

Olympic Flame and Emblem SP153

Laabenbach Bridge Neulengbach SP154

1948, Jan. 16 **Engr.**

B224	SP153	1s + 50g dark blue	28	35

The surtax was used to help defray expenses of Austria's 1948 Olympics team.

1948, Feb. 18 ***Perf. 14x13½***

Designs: 20g+10g, Dam, Vermunt Lake. 30g+10g, Danube Port, Vienna. 40g+20g, Mining, Erzberg. 45g+20g, Tracks, Southern Railway Station, Vienna. 60g+30g, Communal housing project, Vienna. 75g+35g, Gas Works, Vienna. 80g+40g, Oil refinery. 1s+50g, Gesäuse Highway, Styria. 1.40s+70g, Parliament Building, Vienna.

B225	SP154	10g + 5g slate blk	16	16
B226	SP154	20g + 10g lilac	16	16
B227	SP154	30g + 10g dull grn	50	35
B228	SP154	40g + 20g ol brn	15	15
B229	SP154	45g + 20g dk blue	15	15
B230	SP154	60g + 30g dk red	15	15
B231	SP154	75g + 35g dk vio brn	15	15
B232	SP154	80g + 40g vio brn	15	15
B233	SP154	1s + 50g dp blue	15	15
B234	SP154	1.40s + 70g dp car	38	35
		Set value	1.60	1.55

The surtax was for the Reconstruction Fund.

Violet — SP155

Designs: 20g+10g, Anemone. 30g+10g, Crocus. 40g+20g, Yellow primrose. 45g+20g, Pasqueflower. 60g+30g, Rhododendron. 75g+35g, Dogrose. 80g+40g, Cyclamen. 1s+50g, Alpine Gentian. 1.40s+70g, Edelweiss.

1948, May 14 **Engr. & Typo.**

B235	SP155	10g + 5g multi	34	15
B236	SP155	20g + 10g multi	15	15
B237	SP155	30g + 10g multi	2.50	1.65
B238	SP155	40g + 20g multi	52	20
B239	SP155	45g + 20g multi	15	15
B240	SP155	60g + 30g multi	15	15
B241	SP155	75g + 35g multi	15	15
B242	SP155	80g + 40g multi	30	15
B243	SP155	1s + 50g multi	38	25
B244	SP155	1.40s + 70g multi	65	45
		Nos. B235-B244 (10)	5.29	3.45

Hans Makart — SP156

St. Rupert — SP157

Designs: 20g+10g, Künstlerhaus, Vienna. 40g+20g, Carl Kundmann. 50g+25g, A. S. von Siccardsburg. 60g+30g, Hans Cannon. 1s+50g, William Unger. 1.40s+70g, Friedrich von Schmidt.

1948, June 15 **Unwmk.** **Engr.**

B245	SP156	20g + 10g dp yel green	6.25	4.25
B246	SP156	30g + 15g dark brown	3.00	1.65
B247	SP156	40g + 20g indigo	3.00	1.65
B248	SP156	50g + 25g dk vio	3.50	2.50
B249	SP156	60g + 30g dk red	3.50	2.50
B250	SP156	1s + 50g dk blue	6.25	4.25

B251 SP156 1.40s + 70g red brown 8.50 6.00
Nos. B245-B251 (7) 34.00 22.80

Kunstlerhaus, home of the leading Austrian Artists Association, 80th anniv.

1948, Aug. 6 ***Perf. 14x13½***

Designs: 30g+15g, Cathedral and Fountain. 40g+20g, Facade of Cathedral. 50g+25g, Cathedral from South. 60g+30g, Abbey of St. Peter. 80g+40g, Inside Cathedral. 1s+50g, Salzburg Cathedral and Castle. 1.40s+70g, Madonna by Michael Pacher.

B252	SP157	20g + 10g dp grn	5.50	5.00
B253	SP157	30g + 15g red brn	2.25	2.25
B254	SP157	40g + 20g sl blk	1.75	1.65
B255	SP157	50g + 25g choc	35	35
B256	SP157	60g + 30g dk red	35	35
B257	SP157	80g + 40g dk brn vio	35	35
B258	SP157	1s + 50g dp blue	65	45
B259	SP157	1.40s + 70g dk grn	1.25	95
		Nos. B252-B259 (8)	12.45	11.35

The surtax was to aid in the reconstruction of Salzburg Cathedral.

Easter — SP158

Arms of Austria, 1230 — SP159

Designs: 60g+20g, St. Nicholas Day. 1s+25g, Birthday. 1.40s+35g, Christmas.

1949, Apr. 13 **Unwmk.**
Inscribed: "Gluckliche Kindheit"

B260	SP158	40g + 10g brn vio	17.00	11.00
B261	SP158	60g + 20g brn red	17.00	11.00
B262	SP158	1s + 25g dp ultra	17.00	11.00
B263	SP158	1.40s + 35g dk grn	17.00	11.00
		Nos. B260-B263 (4)	68.00	44.00

The surtax was for Child Welfare.

1949, Aug. 17 **Engr. & Photo.**

B264 SP159 40g + 10g 1230 6.50 5.25

Engraved and Typographed

B265	SP159	60g + 15g 1450	6.50	5.25
B266	SP159	1s + 25g 1600	6.50	5.25
B267	SP159	1.60s + 40g 1945	6.50	5.25
		Nos. B264-B267 (4)	26.00	21.00

Surtax was for returned prisoners of war.

Laurel Branch, Stamps and Magnifier — SP160

1949, Dec. 3 **Engr.**

B268 SP160 60g + 15g dk red 2.25 1.50

Stamp Day, Dec. 3-4.

Arms of Austria and Carinthia — SP161

Carinthian with Austrian Flag — SP162

Design: 1.70s+40g, Casting ballot.

1950, Oct. 10 **Photo.** ***Perf. 14x13½***

B269	SP161	60g + 15g	21.00	16.00
B270	SP162	1s + 25g	27.50	18.00
B271	SP162	1.70s + 40g	32.50	25.00
		Nos. B269-B271 (3)	81.00	59.00

Plebiscite in Carinthia, 30th anniv.

Collector Examining Cover — SP163

Miner and Mine — SP164

1950, Dec. 2 **Engr.**

B272 SP163 60g + 15g blue grn 8.00 4.00

Stamp Day.

1951, Mar. 10 **Unwmk.**

Designs: 60g+15g, Mason holding brick and trowel. 1s+25g, Bridge builder with hook and chain. 1.70s+40g, Electrician, pole and insulators.

B273	SP164	40g + 10g dark brown	12.50	10.50
B274	SP164	60g + 15g dk grn	12.50	10.50
B275	SP164	1s + 25g red brown	12.50	10.50
B276	SP164	1.70s + 40g vio bl	12.50	10.50
		Nos. B273-B276 (4)	50.00	42.00

Issued to publicize Austrian reconstruction.

Laurel Branch and Olympic Circles SP165

1952, Jan. 26 ***Perf. 13½x14***

B277 SP165 2.40s + 60g grnsh black 15.00 12.00

The surtax was used to help defray expenses of Austria's athletes in the 1952 Olympic Games.

Cupid as Postman — SP166

1952, Mar. 10 ***Perf. 14x13½***

B278 SP166 1.50s + 35g dark brn car 16.00 15.00

Stamp Day.

Sculpture, "Christ, The Almighty" SP167

1952, Sept. 6 ***Perf. 13½x14***

B279 SP167 1s + 25g grnsh gray 10.00 8.50

Austrian Catholic Conv., Vienna, Sept. 11-14.

Type of 1945-46 Overprinted in Gold

GEWERKSCHAFTS BEWEGUNG
60 JAHRE
1s+25g

1953, Aug. 29 **Unwmk.**

B280 A124 1s + 25g on 5s dl bl 2.50 2.00

60th anniv. of labor unions in Austria.

Bummerlhaus Steyr SP168

Globe and Philatelic Accessories SP169

Designs: 1s+25g, Johannes Kepler. 1.50s+40g, Lutheran Bible, 1st edition. 2.40s+60g, Theophil von Hansen. 3s+75g, Reconstructed Lutheran School, Vienna.

1953, Nov. 5 **Engr.** ***Perf. 14x13½***

B281	SP168	70g + 15g vio brn	25	20
B282	SP168	1s + 25g dk gray blue	25	20
B283	SP168	1.50s + 40g choc	80	60
B284	SP168	2.40s + 60g dk grn	2.75	2.00
B285	SP168	3s + 75g dk pur	6.25	5.50
		Nos. B281-B285 (5)	10.30	8.50

The surtax was used toward reconstruction of the Lutheran School, Vienna.

1953, Dec. 5

B286 SP169 1s + 25g choc 5.00 3.75

Stamp Day.

Type of 1945-46 with Denomination Replaced by Asterisks

Overprinted in Brown

LAWINENOPFER
1954
1s + 20g

1954, Feb. 19 ***Perf. 13½x14***

B287 A124 1s + 20g blue gray 15 15

Surtax for aid to avalanche victims.

Patient Under Sun Lamp — SP170

Designs: 70g+15g, Physician using microscope. 1s+25g, Mother and children. 1.45s+35g, Operating room. 1.50s+35g, Baby on scale. 2.40s+60g, Nurse.

1954 **Engr.** ***Perf. 14x13½***

B288	SP170	30g + 10g purple	1.25	95
B289	SP170	70g + 15g dk brn	20	15
B290	SP170	1s + 25g dk bl	25	18
B291	SP170	1.45s + 35g dk bl green	38	25
B292	SP170	1.50s + 35g dk red	4.75	3.50
B293	SP170	2.40s + 60g dk red brown	5.75	4.75
		Nos. B288-B293 (6)	12.58	9.78

The surtax was for social welfare.

Early Vienna-Ulm Ferryboat SP171

1954, Dec. 4 ***Perf. 13½x14***

B294 SP171 1s + 25g dk gray grn 4.25 4.00

Stamp Day.

"Industry" Welcoming Returned Prisoner of War — SP172

1955, June 29

B295 SP172 1s + 25g red brn 2.00 1.50

Surtax for returned prisoners of war and relatives of prisoners not yet released.

Collector Looking at Album — SP173

Ornamental Shield and Letter — SP174

1955, Dec. 3 ***Perf. 14x13½***

B296 SP173 1s + 25g vio brn 3.00 2.75

Stamp Day. The surtax was for the promotion of Austrian philately.

1956, Dec. 1 **Engr.**

B297 SP174 1s + 25g scarlet 2.75 2.50

Stamp Day. See note after No. B296.

Arms of Austria, 1945 — SP175

Perf. 14x13½

1956, Dec. 21 **Engr. & Typo.**

B298 SP175 1.50s + 50g on 1.60s + 40g gray & red 25 22

The surtax was for Hungarian refugees.

New Post Office, Linz 2 — SP176

Design: 2.40s+60g, Post office, Kitzbuhel.

1957-58 **Engr.** ***Perf. 13½x14***

B299	SP176	1s + 25g dk sl grn	2.75	2.50
B300	SP176	2.40s + 60g blue	65	60

Stamp Day. See note after B296. Issue dates: 1s, Nov. 30, 1957. 2.40s, Dec. 6, 1957. See No. B303.

Roman Carriage from Tomb at Maria Saal — SP177

Perf. 13½x14

1959, Dec. 5 **Litho. & Engr.**

B301 SP177 2.40s + 60g pale lil & blk 52 50

Stamp Day.

Progressive Die Proof under Magnifying Glass — SP178

1960, Dec. 2 **Engr.** *Perf. 13½x14*

B302 SP178 3s + 70g vio brn 85 70

Stamp Day.

Post Office Type of 1957

Design: 3s+70g, Post Office, Rust.

1961, Dec. 1 **Unwmk.** *Perf. 13½*

B303 SP176 3s + 70g dk bl grn 90 70

Stamp Day. See note after No. B296.

Hands of Stamp Engraver at Work — SP179

1962, Nov. 30 *Perf. 13½x14*

B304 SP179 3s + 70g dull pur 1.25 90

Stamp Day.

Railroad Exit, Post Office Vienna 101 — SP180

1963, Nov. 29 **Litho. & Engr.**

B305 SP180 3s + 70g tan & blk 80 80

Stamp Day.

View of Vienna, North SP181

Designs: Various view of Vienna with compass indicating direction.

1964, July 20 **Litho.** *Perf. 13½x14*

B306 SP181 1.50s + 30g ("N") 18 15
B307 SP181 1.50s + 30g ("NO") 18 15
B308 SP181 1.50s + 30g ("O") 18 15
B309 SP181 1.50s + 30g ("SO") 18 15
B310 SP181 1.50s + 30g ("S") 18 15
B311 SP181 1.50s + 30g ("SW") 18 15
B312 SP181 1.50s + 30g ("W") 18 15
B313 SP181 1.50s + 30g ("NW") 18 15
Nos. B306-B313 (8) 1.44 1.20

Vienna Intl. Phil. Exhib. (WIPA 1965).

Post Bus Terminal, St. Gilgen, Wolfgangsee SP182

1964, Dec. 4 **Unwmk.** *Perf. 13½*

B314 SP182 3s + 70g multi 45 45

Stamp Day.

Wall Painting, Tomb at Thebes — SP183

Development of Writing: 1.80s+50g, Cuneiform writing on stone tablet and man's head from Assyrian palace. 2.20s+60g, Wax tablet with Latin writing, Corinthian column. 3s+80g, Gothic writing on sealed letter, Gothic window from Munster Cathedral. 4s+1s, Letter with seal and postmark and upright desk. 5s+1.20s, Typewriter.

Perf. 14x13½

1965, June 4 **Litho. & Engr.**

B315 SP183 1.50s + 40g dp rose & black 15 15
B316 SP183 1.80s + 50g yel & black 16 16
B317 SP183 2.20s + 60g pale vio & black 32 32
B318 SP183 3s + 80g ap grn & black 20 20
B319 SP183 4s + 1s lt bl & black 45 45
B320 SP183 5s + 1.20s brt grn & black 60 60
Nos. B315-B320 (6) 1.88 1.88

Vienna Intl. Phil. Exhib., WIPA, June 4-13.

Mailman Distributing Mail — SP184

1965, Dec. 3 **Engr.** *Perf. 13½x14*

B321 SP184 3s + 70g blue grn 38 32

Stamp Day.

Letter Carrier, 16th Century SP185

Letter Carrier, 16th Century Playing Card SP186

Litho. & Engr.

1966, Dec. 2 *Perf. 13½*

B322 SP185 3s + 70g multi 38 32

Stamp Day. Design is from Ambras Heroes' Book, Austrian National Library.

Engr. & Photo.

1967, Dec. 1 *Perf. 13x13½*

B323 SP186 3.50s + 80g multi 40 32

Stamp Day.

Mercury, Bas-relief from Purkersdorf SP187

Unken Post Station Sign, 1710 SP188

1968, Nov. 29 **Engr.** *Perf. 13½*

B324 SP187 3.50s + 80g sl green 40 32

Stamp Day.

Engr. & Photo.

1969, Dec. 5 *Perf. 12*

B325 SP188 3.50s + 80g tan, red & blk 40 35

Stamp Day. Design is from a watercolor by Friedrich Zeller.

Saddle, Bag, Harness and Post Horn — SP189

Perf. 13½x14

1970, Dec. 4 **Engr. & Litho.**

B326 SP189 3.50s + 80g gray blk & yel 40 35

Stamp Day.

"50 Years" SP190

Engr. & Photo.

1971, Dec. 3 *Perf. 13½*

B327 SP190 4s + 1.50s gold & red brn 60 42

50th anniversary of the Federation of Austrian Philatelic Societies.

Local Post Carrier — SP191

Gabriel, by Lorenz Luchsperger, 15th Century — SP192

1972, Dec. 1 **Engr.** *Perf. 14x13½*

B328 SP191 4s + 1s olive green 60 42

Stamp Day.

1973, Nov. 30

B329 SP192 4s + 1s maroon 60 42

Stamp Day.

Mail Coach Leaving Old PTT Building — SP193

1974, Nov. 29 **Engr.** *Perf. 14x13½*

B330 SP193 4s + 2s violet blue 70 70

Stamp Day.

Alpine Skiing, Women's SP194

Designs: 1.50s+70g, Ice hockey. 2s+90g, Ski jump. 4s+1.90s, Bobsledding.

1975, Mar. 14 **Photo.** *Perf. 13½x14*

B331 SP194 1s + 50g multi 20 20
B332 SP194 1.50s + 70g multi 25 25
B333 SP194 2s + 90g multi 32 32
B334 SP194 4s + 1.90s multi 65 65
Nos. B331-B334 (4) 1.42 1.42

1975, Nov. 14

Designs: 70g+30g, Figure skating, pair. 2s+1s, Cross-country skiing. 2.50s+1s, Luge. 4s+2s, Biathlon.

B335 SP194 70g + 30g multi 15 15
B336 SP194 2s + 1s multi 28 28
B337 SP194 2.50s + 1s multi 32 32
B338 SP194 4s + 2s multi 60 60
Nos. B335-B338 (4) 1.35 1.35

12th Winter Olympic Games, Innsbruck, Feb. 4-15, 1976.

Austria Nos. 5, 250, 455 — SP195

Photo. & Engr.

1975, Nov. 28 *Perf. 14*

B339 SP195 4s + 2s multi 65 65

Stamp Day; 125th anniv. of Austrian stamps.

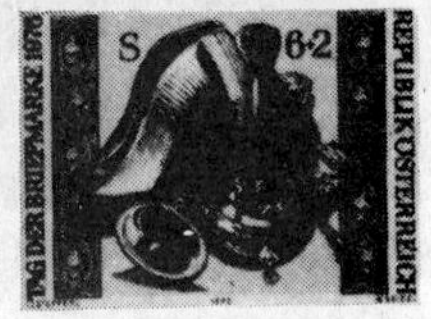

Postilion's Gala Hat and Horn — SP196

1976, Dec. 3 *Perf. 13½x14*

B340 SP196 6s + 2s blk & lt vio 80 80

Stamp Day.

Emanuel Herrmann — SP197

1977, Dec. 2 **Perf. 14x13½**

B341 SP197 6s + 2s multi 80 80

Stamp Day. Emanuel Herrmann (1839-1902), economist, invented postal card. Austria issued first postal card in 1869.

Post Bus, 1913 — SP198

1978, Dec. 1 **Photo.** **Perf. 13½x14**

B342 SP198 10s + 5s multi 1.40 1.40

Stamp Day.

Heroes' Square, Vienna SP199

Photo. & Engr.

1979, Nov. 30 **Perf. 13½**

B343 SP199 16s + 8s multi 3.00 2.50

No. B343 Inscribed "2. Phase"

1980, Nov. 21

B344 SP199 16s + 8s multi 2.90 2.50

Souvenir Sheet

1981, Feb. 20

B345 SP199 16s + 8s multi 3.00 2.50

WIPA 1981 Phil. Exhib., Vienna, May 22-31. No. B345 contains one stamp without inscription.

Mainz-Weber Mailbox, 1870 — SP200

1982, Nov. 26 **Photo. & Engr.**

B346 SP200 6s + 3s multi 1.00 1.00

Stamp Day.

Boy Examining Cover — SP201

Photo. & Engr.

1983, Oct. 21 **Perf. 14**

B347 SP201 6s + 3s multi 1.25 1.25

Stamp Day. See Nos. B349-B352, B354-B355.

World Winter Games for the Handicapped SP202

1984, Jan. 5 **Photo.** **Perf. 13½x13**

B348 SP202 4s + 2s Downhill skier 75 75

Stamp Day Type of 1983

Designs: No. B349, Seschemnofer III burial chamber detail, pyramid of Cheops, Gizeh. No. B350, Roman messenger on horseback. No. B351, Nuremberg messenger, 16th cent. No. B352, *The Postmaster* (detail), 1841, lithograph by Carl Schuster.

1984-87 **Photo. & Engr.** **Perf. 14**

B349 SP201 6s + 3s multi		1.25	1.25
B350 SP201 6s + 3s multi		1.25	1.25
B351 SP201 6s + 3s multi		1.30	1.30
B352 SP201 6s + 3s multi		1.55	1.55
	Nos. B349-B352 (4)	5.35	5.35

Issue dates: No. B349, Nov. 30, 1984. No. B350, Nov. 28, 1985. No. B351, Nov. 28. 1986. No. B352, Nov. 19, 1987.

4th World Winter Sports Championships for the Disabled, Innsbruck — SP203

1988, Jan. 15 **Photo.** **Perf. 13½**

B353 SP203 5s + 2.50s multi 1.30 1.30

Stamp Day Type of 1983

Designs: No. B354, Railway mail car. No. B355, Hansa-Brandenburg CI mail plane.

1988-89 **Photo. & Engr.** **Perf. 14**

B354 SP201 6s +3s multi 1.45 1.45

B355 SP201 6s +3s multi 1.50 1.15

Issued: #B354, Nov. 17; #B355, May 24, 1989.

Stamp Day — SP204

1990, May 25 **Photo.** **Perf. 13½**

B356 SP204 7s +3s multi 1.70 1.25

Stamp Day — SP205

1991, May 29 **Photo. & Engr.**

B357 SP205 7s +3s "B" and "P" 1.85 1.30

1992, May 22

B358 SP205 7s +3s "R" and "H" 1.70 1.35

1993, May 5

B359 SP205 7s +3s "I" and "I" 1.80 1.45

1994, May 27

B360 SP205 7s +3s "E" and "L" 1.75 1.40

Nos. B357-B360 (4) 7.10 5.50

The first letters will spell "Briefmarke," the second "Philatelie."

Special Olympics Winter Games SP206

1993, Mar. 19 **Photo.** **Perf. 13½x14**

B367 SP206 6s +3s multi 1.60 1.30

AIR POST STAMPS

Issues of the Monarchy

FLUGPOST

Types of Regular Issue of 1916 Surcharged

2·50 K 2·50

1918, Mar. 30 **Unwmk.** **Perf. 12½**

C1	A40 1.50k on 2k lilac	1.75	2.25
C2	A40 2.50k on 3k ocher	7.25	16.00
a.	Inverted surcharge	*1,250.*	
b.	Perf. 11½	325.00	225.00
c.	Perf. 12½x11½	27.50	37.50

Overprinted **FLUGPOST**

C3 A40 4k gray 4.00 8.00
Set, never hinged 30.00

Set exists imperf. Value, $325.

Nos. C1-C3 also exist without surcharge or overprint. Value, set perf., $625; imperf., $625.

Nos. C1-C3 were printed on grayish and on white paper.

A 7k on 10k red brown was prepared but not regularly issued. Value, perf. or imperf., $400.

Issues of the Republic

Hawk — AP1

Wilhelm Kress — AP2

1922-24 **Typo.** **Perf. 12½**

C4	AP1 300k claret	25	1.10
C5	AP1 400k green ('24)	4.25	9.00
C6	AP1 600k bister	15	52
C7	AP1 900k brn orange	15	52
	Engr.		
C8	AP2 1200k brn violet	15	52
C9	AP2 2400k slate	15	52
C10	AP2 3000k dp brn ('23)	1.65	2.50
C11	AP2 4800k dark bl ('23)	2.00	2.75
	Nos. C4-C11 (8)	8.75	17.43
	Set, never hinged	16.00	

Set exists imperf. Value, $300.

Plane and Pilot's Head — AP3

Airplane Passing Crane — AP4

1925-30 **Typo.** **Perf. 12½**

C12	AP3 2g gray brown	38	85
C13	AP3 5g red	22	20
a.	Horiz. pair, imperf. btwn.	205.00	
C14	AP3 6g dark blue	80	1.25
C15	AP3 8g yel green	90	1.40
C16	AP3 10g dp org ('26)	90	1.40
a.	Horiz. pair, imperf. btwn.	225.00	
C17	AP3 15g red vio ('26)	42	75
a.	Horiz. pair, imperf. btwn.	275.00	
C18	AP3 20g org brn ('30)	9.25	3.50
C19	AP3 25g blk vio ('30)	2.00	5.25
C20	AP3 30g bister ('26)	5.75	5.25
C21	AP3 50g bl gray ('26)	10.50	8.75
C22	AP3 80g dk grn ('30)	1.10	3.50
	Photo.		
C23	AP4 10g orange red	80	2.25
a.	Horiz. pair, imperf. btwn.	225.00	
C24	AP4 15g claret	55	1.10
C25	AP4 30g brn violet	70	2.25
C26	AP4 50g gray black	65	2.25
C27	AP4 1s deep blue	1.65	3.00
C28	AP4 2s dark green	1.25	3.00
a.	Vertical pair, imperf. btwn.	225.00	
C29	AP4 3s red brn ('26)	32.50	32.50
C30	AP4 5s indigo ('26)	9.50	19.00
	Size: 25½x32mm		
C31	AP4 10s blk brown, *gray* ('26)	8.75	15.00
	Nos. C12-C31 (20)	88.57	112.45
	Set, never hinged	200.00	

Exists imperf. Value, set $900.

Airplane over Güssing Castle — AP5

Airplane over the Danube — AP6

Designs (each includes plane): 10g, Maria-Worth. 15g, Durnstein. 20g, Hallstatt. 25g, Salzburg. 30g, Upper Dachstein and Schladminger Glacier. 40g, Lake Wetter. 50g, Arlberg. 60g, St. Stephen's Cathedral. 80g, Church of the Minorites. 2s, Railroad viaduct, Carinthia. 3s, Gross Glockner mountain. 5s, Aerial railway. 10s, Seaplane and yachts.

1935, Aug. 16 **Engr.** **Perf. 12½**

C32	AP5 5g rose violet	15	15
C33	AP5 10g red orange	15	15
C34	AP5 15g yel green	55	32
C35	AP5 20g gray blue	15	18
C36	AP5 25g violet brn	15	18
C37	AP5 30g brn orange	15	22
C38	AP5 40g gray green	15	22
C39	AP5 50g light sl bl	15	22
C40	AP5 60g black brn	30	40
C41	AP5 80g light brown	30	40
C42	AP6 1s rose red	30	55
C43	AP6 2s olive green	1.40	*3.50*
C44	AP6 3s yellow brn	6.50	*10.00*
C45	AP6 5s dark green	4.00	*10.00*
C46	AP6 10s slate blue	27.50	*55.00*
	Nos. C32-C46 (15)	41.90	*81.49*
	Set, never hinged	90.00	

Set exists imperf. Value, $275.

Catalogue values for unused stamps in this section, from this point to the end of the section, are for Never Hinged items.

Windmill, Neusiedler Lake Shore — AP20

Designs: 1s, Roman arch, Carnuntum. 2s, Town Hall, Gmund. 3s, Schieder Lake, Hinterstoder. 4s, Praegraten, Eastern Tyrol. 5s, Torsäule, Salzburg. 10s, St. Charles Church, Vienna.

1947 **Unwmk.** **Perf. 14x13½**

C47	AP20 50g black brown	15	18
C48	AP20 1s dark brn vio	28	24
C49	AP20 2s dark green	32	30
C50	AP20 3s chocolate	1.90	2.00
C51	AP20 4s dark green	1.25	1.40

C52	AP20	5s dark blue	1.25	1.40
C53	AP20	10s dark blue	65	90
		Nos. C47-C53 (7)	5.80	6.42

Rooks — AP27

Birds: 1s, Barn swallows. 2s, Blackheaded gulls. 3s, Great cormorants. 5s, Buzzard. 10s, Gray heron. 20s, Golden eagle.

1950-53 *Perf. 13½x14*

C54	AP27	60g dark bl vio	2.50	1.10
C55	AP27	1s dark vio blue ('53)	16.00	12.50
C56	AP27	2s dark blue	11.00	3.75
C57	AP27	3s dk slate green ('53)	90.00	52.50
C58	AP27	5s red brn ('53)	90.00	52.50
C59	AP27	10s gray vio ('53)	40.00	20.00
C60	AP27	20s brn blk ('52)	7.50	3.00
		Nos. C54-C60 (7)	257.00	145.35
		Set, hinged	165.00	

Value at lower left on Nos. C59 and C60.
No. C60 exists imperf.

Etrich "Dove" AP28

Designs: 3.50s, Twin-engine jet airliner. 5s, Four-engine jet airliner.

1968, May 31 Engr. *Perf. 13½x14*

C61	AP28	2s olive bister	30	25
C62	AP28	3.50s slate green	48	42
C63	AP28	5s dark blue	75	60
		Nos. C61-C63 (3)	1.53	1.27

IFA WIEN 1968 (International Air Post Exhibition), Vienna, May 30-June 4.

POSTAGE DUE STAMPS

Issues of the Monarchy

D1

D2

Perf. 10 to 13½

1894-95 Typo. Wmk. 91

J1	D1	1kr brown	1.65	1.40
a.		Perf. 13½	17.00	5.75
J2	D1	2kr brown ('95)	3.50	1.40
a.		Pair, imperf. btwn.	150.00	200.00
J3	D1	3kr brown	3.00	15
J4	D1	5kr brown	2.25	35
a.		Perf. 13½	12.75	6.50
b.		Pair, imperf. btwn.	125.00	175.00
J5	D1	6kr brown ('95)	2.25	2.50
J6	D1	7kr brown ('95)	70	1.40
a.		Pair, imperf. btwn.	200.00	250.00
J7	D1	10kr brown	4.00	35
J8	D1	20kr brown	60	1.90
J9	D1	50kr brown	30.00	32.50
		Nos. J1-J9 (9)	47.95	41.95

See Nos. J204-J231.

1899-1900 *Imperf.*

J10	D2	1h brown	15	26
J11	D2	2h brown	15	26
J12	D2	3h brown ('00)	15	20
J13	D2	4h brown	3.25	70
J14	D2	5h brown ('00)	2.75	20
J15	D2	6h brown	28	95
J16	D2	10h brown	15	20
J17	D2	12h brown	38	1.75
J18	D2	15h brown	38	95
J19	D2	20h brown	17.50	50
J20	D2	40h brown	80	1.75
J21	D2	100h brown	4.00	1.50
		Nos. J10-J21 (12)	29.94	9.22

Perf. 10½, 12½, 13½ and Compound

J22	D2	1h brown	55	15
J23	D2	2h brown	42	15
J24	D2	3h brown ('00)	38	15
J25	D2	4h brown	38	15
J26	D2	5h brown ('00)	28	15
J27	D2	6h brown	28	15
J28	D2	10h brown	38	15
J29	D2	12h brown	42	28
J30	D2	15h brown	75	28
J31	D2	20h brown	45	22
J32	D2	40h brown	80	60
J33	D2	100h brown	20.00	1.00
		Nos. J22-J33 (12)	25.09	
		Set value		3.00

Nos. J10-J33 exist on unwmkd. paper.
For surcharges see Offices in the Turkish Empire Nos. J1-J5.

D3

1908-13 Unwmk. *Perf. 12½*

J34	D3	1h carmine	1.10	60
J35	D3	2h carmine	42	24
J36	D3	4h carmine	42	15
J37	D3	6h carmine	42	15
J38	D3	10h carmine	42	15
J39	D3	14h carmine ('13)	3.25	70
J40	D3	20h carmine	4.25	15
J41	D3	25h carmine ('10)	8.25	1.25
J42	D3	30h carmine	4.75	15
J43	D3	50h carmine	6.00	16
J44	D3	100h carmine	13.00	20
		Nos. J34-J44 (11)	42.28	3.90

All values exist on ordinary paper, Nos. J34-J38, J40, J42-J44 on chalky paper and Nos. J34-J38, J40, J44 on thin ordinary paper. Thin paper copies sell for 5 to 10 times the listed values. All values exist imperf.
See Offices in the Turkish Empire type D2.

1911, July 16

J45	D3	5k violet	30.00	6.00
J46	D3	10k violet	175.00	3.00

Regular Issue of 1908 Overprinted or Surcharged in Carmine or Black:

PORTO

a

PORTO
15 15

b

1916, Oct. 21

J47	A22	1h gray (C)	15	15
a.		Pair, one without overprint	125.00	
J48	A22	15h on 2h vio (Bk)	20	25
		Set value	28	33
		Set, never hinged	90	

D4

D5

1916, Oct. 1

J49	D4	5h rose red	15	15
J50	D4	10h rose red	15	15
J51	D4	15h rose red	15	15
J52	D4	20h rose red	15	15
J53	D4	25h rose red	35	30
J54	D4	30h rose red	15	15
J55	D4	40h rose red	18	15
J56	D4	50h rose red	90	90
J57	D5	1k ultramarine	30	15
a.		Horiz. pair, imperf. btwn.	350.00	350.00
J58	D5	5k ultramarine	1.25	1.40
J59	D5	10k ultramarine	1.25	90
		Nos. J49-J59 (11)	4.98	4.55
		Set, never hinged	16.00	

Exists imperf. Value, set $80.
For overprints see Western Ukraine Nos. 54-55, NJ1-NJ6.

Type of Regular Issue of 1916 Surcharged

PORTO
15 * 15

1917

J60	A38	10h on 24h blue	1.25	20
J61	A38	15h on 36h violet	20	15
J62	A38	20h on 54h orange	20	20
J63	A38	50h on 42h chocolate	20	15
		Nos. J60-J63 (4)	1.85	70
		Set, never hinged	5.00	

All values of this issue are known imperforate, also without surcharge, perforated and imperforate.
For overprints see Western Ukraine Nos. 57-58.

Issues of the Republic

Postage Due Stamps of 1916 Overprinted

Deutschösterreich

1919

J64	D4	5h rose red	15	16
a.		Inverted overprint	200.00	225.00
J65	D4	10h rose red	15	16
J66	D4	15h rose red	15	30
J67	D4	20h rose red	25	24
J68	D4	25h rose red	4.75	12.00
J69	D4	30h rose red	15	16
J70	D4	40h rose red	15	24
J71	D4	50h rose red	30	80
J72	D5	1k ultramarine	4.50	4.25
J73	D5	5k ultramarine	6.00	4.25
J74	D5	10k ultramarine	6.50	3.00
		Nos. J64-J74 (11)	23.05	25.56
		Set, never hinged	70.00	

Nos. J64, J65, J67 and J70 exist imperforate.

D6

D7

1920-21 *Perf. 12½*

J75	D6	5h bright red	15	15
J76	D6	10h bright red	15	15
J77	D6	15h bright red	15	28
J78	D6	20h bright red	15	15
J79	D6	25h bright red	15	28
J80	D6	30h bright red	15	15
J81	D6	40h bright red	15	15
J82	D6	50h bright red	15	15
J83	D6	80h bright red	15	15
J84	D7	1k ultramarine	15	15
J85	D7	1½k ultra ('21)	15	15
J86	D7	2k ultra ('21)	15	15
J87	D7	3k ultra ('21)	15	15
J88	D7	4k ultra ('21)	15	15
J89	D7	5k ultramarine	15	15
J90	D7	8k ultra ('21)	15	15
J91	D7	10k ultramarine	15	15
J92	D7	20k ultra ('21)	15	35
		Set value	95	2.18
		Set, never hinged	3.00	

Nos. J84 to J92 exist on white paper and on grayish white paper. They also exist imperf.; value, set $65.

Imperf

J93	D6	5h bright red	15	18
J94	D6	10h bright red	15	15
J95	D6	15h bright red	15	22
J96	D6	20h bright red	15	15
J97	D6	25h bright red	15	28
J98	D6	30h bright red	15	15
J99	D6	40h bright red	15	15
J100	D6	50h bright red	15	20
J101	D6	80h bright red	15	15
		Set value	48	1.30
		Set, never hinged	1.25	

No. 207a Surcharged in Dark Blue

Nachmarke
7½ K

1921, Dec. *Perf. 12½*

J102	A43	7½k on 15h bister	15	18
		Never hinged	15	
a.		Inverted surcharge	185.00	185.00

D8

D9

D10

1922

J103	D8	1k reddish buff	15	*15*
J104	D8	2k reddish buff	15	*15*
J105	D8	4k reddish buff	15	*15*
J106	D8	5k reddish buff	15	*15*
J107	D8	7½k reddish buff	15	*15*
J108	D8	10k blue green	15	*15*
J109	D8	15k blue green	15	*15*
J110	D8	20k blue green	15	*15*
J111	D8	25k blue green	15	*15*
J112	D8	40k blue green	15	*15*
J113	D8	50k blue green	15	*25*
		Set value	60	*1.44*
		Set, never hinged	1.00	

Issue date: Nos. J108-J113, June 2.

1922-24

J114	D9	10k cobalt blue	15	*15*
J115	D9	15k cobalt blue	15	*15*
J116	D9	20k cobalt blue	15	*15*
J117	D9	50k cobalt blue	15	*18*
J118	D10	100k plum	15	15
J119	D10	150k plum	15	*15*
J120	D10	200k plum	15	15
J121	D10	400k plum	15	15
J122	D10	600k plum ('23)	15	*15*
J123	D10	800k plum	15	15
J124	D10	1,000k plum ('23)	15	15
J125	D10	1,200k plum ('23)	38	*1.25*
J126	D10	1,500k plum ('24)	15	15
J127	D10	1,800k plum ('24)	1.25	*3.75*
J128	D10	2,000k plum ('23)	16	35
J129	D10	3,000k plum ('24)	5.00	6.50
J130	D10	4,000k plum ('24)	3.25	*8.50*
J131	D10	6,000k plum ('24)	3.25	*13.00*
		Nos. J114-J131 (18)	15.09	*35.18*
		Set, never hinged	40.00	

Value, Nos. J103-J131 imperf, $200.

D11

D12

1925-34 *Perf. 12½*

J132	D11	1g red	15	15
J133	D11	2g red	15	15
J134	D11	3g red	15	15
J135	D11	4g red	15	15
J136	D11	5g red ('27)	15	15
J137	D11	6g red	15	32
J138	D11	8g red	15	16
J139	D11	10g dark blue	15	15
J140	D11	12g dark blue	15	15
J141	D11	14g dark blue ('27)	15	15
J142	D11	15g dark blue	15	15
J143	D11	16g dark blue ('29)	25	15
J144	D11	18g dark blue ('34)	95	3.00
J145	D11	20g dark blue	15	15
J146	D11	23g dark blue	52	15
J147	D11	24g dark blue ('32)	85	15
J148	D11	28g dark blue ('27)	35	22
J149	D11	30g dark blue	15	15
J150	D11	31g dark blue ('29)	68	15
J151	D11	35g dark blue ('30)	42	15
J152	D11	39g dark blue ('32)	75	15
J153	D11	40g dark blue	75	1.50
J154	D11	60g dark blue	52	85
J155	D12	1s dark green	2.75	85
J156	D12	2s dark green	22.50	3.00

J157	D12	5s	dark green	67.50	24.00
J158	D12	10s	dark green	35.00	3.50
			Nos. J132-J158 (27)	135.74	39.95
			Set, never hinged	275.00	

Issues of 1925-27 (21 values) imperf, value, set $400.

Issue dates: 3g, 2s-10s, Dec. 5g, 28g, Jan. 1. 14g, June. 31g, Feb. 1. 35g, Jan. 24g, 39g, Sept. 16g, May. 18g, June 25. Others, June 1.

Coat of Arms
D13 D14

1935, June 1

J159	D13	1g	red	15	15
J160	D13	2g	red	15	15
J161	D13	3g	red	15	15
J162	D13	5g	red	15	15
J163	D13	10g	blue	15	15
J164	D13	12g	blue	15	15
J165	D13	15g	blue	15	38
J166	D13	20g	blue	15	15
J167	D13	24g	blue	15	15
J168	D13	30g	blue	15	15
J169	D13	39g	blue	20	15
J170	D13	60g	blue	35	1.10
J171	D14	1s	green	60	38
J172	D14	2s	green	90	52
J173	D14	5s	green	2.50	1.10
J174	D14	10s	green	3.50	60
			Nos. J159-J174 (16)	9.55	
			Set value		5.00
			Set, never hinged	50.00	

On Nos. J163-J170, background lines are horizontal.

Nos. J159-J174 exist imperf. Value, set $125.

Catalogue values for unused stamps in this section, from this point to the end of the section, are for Never Hinged items.

D15

1945 Unwmk. Typo. *Perf. 10½*

J175	D15	1g	vermilion	15	*15*
J176	D15	2g	vermilion	15	*15*
J177	D15	3g	vermilion	15	*15*
J178	D15	5g	vermilion	15	15
J179	D15	10g	vermilion	15	15
J180	D15	12g	vermilion	15	15
J181	D15	20g	vermilion	15	*15*
J182	D15	24g	vermilion	15	15
J183	D15	30g	vermilion	15	*15*
J184	D15	60g	vermilion	15	*18*
J185	D15	1s	violet	15	*35*
J186	D15	2s	violet	15	*45*
J187	D15	5s	violet	15	*20*
J188	D15	10s	violet	15	*20*
			Set value	1.00	*2.15*

Issue dates: 1g-60g, Sept. 10, 1s-10s, Sept. 24.

Occupation Stamps of the Allied Military Government Overprinted in Black

PORTO

1946 ***Perf. 11***

J189	OS1	3g	deep orange	15	15
J190	OS1	5g	bright green	15	15
J191	OS1	6g	red violet	15	15
J192	OS1	8g	rose pink	15	15
J193	OS1	10g	light gray	15	20
J194	OS1	12g	pale buff brown	15	15
J195	OS1	15g	rose red	15	20
J196	OS1	20g	copper brown	15	15
J197	OS1	25g	deep blue	15	15
J198	OS1	30g	bright violet	15	15
J199	OS1	40g	light ultra	15	15
J200	OS1	60g	light olive grn	15	15
J201	OS1	1s	dark violet	15	18
J202	OS1	2s	yellow	25	28
J203	OS1	5s	deep ultra	25	28
			Set value	1.42	1.88

Nos. J189-J203 were issued by the Renner Government. Inverted overprints exist on about half of the denominations.

Issue dates: 3g-60g, Apr. 23, 1s-5s, May 20.

Type of 1894-95
Inscribed "Republik Osterreich"

1947 Typo. *Perf. 14*

J204	D1	1g	chocolate	15	15
J205	D1	2g	chocolate	15	15
J206	D1	3g	chocolate	15	15
J207	D1	5g	chocolate	15	15
J208	D1	8g	chocolate	15	15
J209	D1	10g	chocolate	15	15
J210	D1	12g	chocolate	15	15
J211	D1	15g	chocolate	15	15
J212	D1	16g	chocolate	22	40
J213	D1	17g	chocolate	22	40
J214	D1	18g	chocolate	22	40
J215	D1	20g	chocolate	48	15
J216	D1	24g	chocolate	30	30
J217	D1	30g	chocolate	18	25
J218	D1	36g	chocolate	48	60
J219	D1	40g	chocolate	15	15
J220	D1	42g	chocolate	50	60
J221	D1	48g	chocolate	52	60
J222	D1	50g	chocolate	60	15
J223	D1	60g	chocolate	18	15
J224	D1	70g	chocolate	15	15
J225	D1	80g	chocolate	3.75	1.65
J226	D1	1s	blue	18	15
J227	D1	1.15s	blue	2.50	28
J228	D1	1.20s	blue	3.00	1.00
J229	D1	2s	blue	38	40
J230	D1	5s	blue	38	40
J231	D1	10s	blue	45	40
			Nos. J204-J231 (28)	16.04	9.78

Issue dates: 1g, 20g, 50g, 80g, 1.15s, 1.20s, Sept. 25, others, Aug. 14.

D16

D17

1949-57

J232	D16	1g	carmine	18	15
J233	D16	2g	carmine	18	15
J234	D16	4g	carmine ('51)	75	15
J235	D16	5g	carmine	1.75	25
J236	D16	8g	carmine ('51)	2.25	1.20
J237	D16	10g	carmine	15	15
J238	D16	20g	carmine	15	15
J239	D16	30g	carmine	15	15
J240	D16	40g	carmine	15	15
J241	D16	50g	carmine	15	15
J242	D16	60g	carmine ('50)	6.25	15
J243	D16	63g	carmine ('57)	3.75	3.25
J244	D16	70g	carmine	15	15
J245	D16	80g	carmine	15	15
J246	D16	90g	carmine ('50)	18	15
J247	D16	1s	purple	18	15
J248	D16	1.20s	purple	28	15
J249	D16	1.35s	purple	22	15
J250	D16	1.40s	purple ('51)	38	20
J251	D16	1.50s	purple ('53)	18	15
J252	D16	1.65s	purple ('50)	30	15
J253	D16	1.70s	purple	30	15
J254	D16	2s	purple	28	15
J255	D16	2.50s	purple ('51)	38	15
J256	D16	3s	purple ('51)	75	15
J257	D16	4s	purple ('51)	75	40
J258	D16	5s	purple	1.40	20
J259	D16	10s	purple	2.25	20
			Nos. J232-J259 (28)	23.99	
			Set value		7.20

Issue dates: 60g, 90g, 1.65s, Aug. 7. 4g, 8g, 1.40s, 2.50s-4s, Dec. 4. 1.50s, Feb. 18. 63g, Apr. 30. Others, Nov. 17.

1985-89 Photo. *Perf. 14*
Background Color

J260	D17	10g	brt yel ('86)	15	15
J261	D17	20g	pink ('86)	15	15
J262	D17	50g	orange ('86)	15	15
J263	D17	1s	lt blue ('86)	15	15
J264	D17	2s	pale brn ('86)	28	20
J265	D17	3s	violet ('86)	40	30
J266	D17	5s	ocher	58	42
J267	D17	10s	pale grn ('89)	1.55	1.15
			Nos. J260-J267 (8)	3.41	2.67

Issue dates: 5s, Dec. 12. 20g, 1s, 3s, Mar. 19. 10g, 50g, 2s, Oct. 3. 10s, June 30.

This is an expanding set. Numbers will change if necessary.

MILITARY STAMPS

Issues of the Austro-Hungarian Military Authorities for the Occupied Territories in World War I

See Bosnia and Herzegovina for similar designs inscribed "MILITARPOST" instead of "FELDPOST."

Stamps of Bosnia of 1912-14 Overprinted

K.U.K.
FELDPOST

1915 Unwmk. *Perf. 12½*

M1	A23	1h	olive green	15	22
M2	A23	2h	bright blue	15	22
M3	A23	3h	claret	15	22
M4	A23	5h	green	15	15
M5	A23	6h	dark gray	15	22
M6	A23	10h	rose carmine	15	15
M7	A23	12h	deep ol grn	22	35
M8	A23	20h	orange brn	32	40
M9	A23	25h	ultramarine	32	35
M10	A23	30h	orange red	2.75	*5.00*
M11	A24	35h	myrtle grn	2.50	*4.00*
M12	A24	40h	dark violet	2.50	*4.00*
M13	A24	45h	olive brown	2.75	*4.50*
M14	A24	50h	slate blue	2.50	*4.00*
M15	A24	60h	brn violet	35	50
M16	A24	72h	dark blue	2.50	*4.00*
M17	A25	1k	brn vio, *straw*	2.75	*5.00*
M18	A25	2k	dk gray, *blue*	2.75	*4.00*
M19	A26	3k	car, *green*	18.00	24.00
M20	A26	5k	dk vio, *gray*	18.00	24.00
M21	A25	10k	dk ultra, *gray*	125.00	135.00
			Nos. M1-M21 (21)	184.11	*220.28*

Exists imperf. Value, set $300.

Nos. M1-M21 also exist with overprint double, inverted and in red. These varieties were made by order of an official but were not regularly issued.

Emperor Franz Josef
M1 M2

Perf. 11½, 12½ and Compound

1915-17 Engr.

M22	M1	1h	olive green	15	15
M23	M1	2h	dull blue	15	15
M24	M1	3h	claret	15	15
M25	M1	5h	green	15	15
a.			Perf. 11½	35.00	*40.00*
b.			Perf. 11½x12½	47.50	*70.00*
c.			Perf. 12½x11½	75.00	*100.00*
M26	M1	6h	dark gray	15	15
M27	M1	10h	rose carmine	15	15
M28	M1	10h	gray bl ('17)	15	15
M29	M1	12h	dp olive grn	15	15
M30	M1	15h	car rose ('17)	15	15
a.			Perf. 11½	7.50	7.50
M31	M1	20h	orange brn	28	15
M32	M1	20h	ol green ('17)	28	15
M33	M1	25h	ultramarine	15	15
M34	M1	30h	vermilion	15	15
M35	M1	35h	dark green	24	28
M36	M1	40h	dark violet	24	28
M37	M1	45h	olive brown	22	28
M38	M1	50h	myrtle green	22	16
M39	M1	60h	brown violet	22	28
M40	M1	72h	dark blue	22	28
M41	M1	80h	org brn ('17)	15	15
M42	M1	90h	magenta ('17)	65	60
M43	M2	1k	brn vio, *straw*	1.10	1.40
M44	M2	2k	dk gray, *blue*	1.00	55
M45	M2	3k	car, *green*	70	75
M46	M2	4k	dark violet, *gray* ('17)	70	75
M47	M2	5k	dk vio, *gray*	16.00	17.00
M48	M2	10k	dk ultra, *gray*	2.25	4.25
			Nos. M22-M48 (27)	26.12	28.96

Nos. M22-M48 exist imperf. Value, set $75.

Emperor Karl I
M3 M4

1917-18 *Perf. 12½*

M49	M3	1h	grnsh blue ('18)	15	15
a.			Perf. 11½	3.50	4.00
M50	M3	2h	red org ('18)	15	15
M51	M3	3h	olive gray	15	15
a.			Perf. 11½	12.00	15.00
b.			Perf. 11½x12½	18.00	27.00
M52	M3	5h	olive green	15	15
M53	M3	6h	violet	15	15
M54	M3	10h	orange brn	15	15
M55	M3	12h	blue	15	15
a.			Perf. 11½	2.75	3.50
M56	M3	15h	bright rose	15	15
M57	M3	20h	red brown	15	15
M58	M3	25h	ultramarine	35	35
M59	M3	30h	slate	15	15
M60	M3	40h	olive bister	15	15
a.			Perf. 11½	1.40	1.50
M61	M3	50h	deep green	15	15
a.			Perf. 11½	4.25	6.00
M62	M3	60h	car rose	15	15
M63	M3	80h	dull blue	15	15
M64	M3	90h	dk violet	38	45
M65	M4	2k	rose, *straw*	15	15
a.			Perf. 11½	2.25	3.50
M66	M4	3k	green, *blue*	95	95
M67	M4	4k	rose, *green*	15.00	12.00
a.			Perf. 11½	27.50	35.00
M68	M4	10k	dl vio, *gray*	2.25	3.50
a.			Perf. 11½	11.00	17.50
			Nos. M49-M68 (20)	21.18	19.50

Nos. M49-M68 exist imperf. Value, set $36.

See No. M82. For overprints see Western Ukraine Nos. 34-53, 75-81.

Emperor Karl I — M5

1918 Typo. *Perf. 12½*

M69	M5	1h	grnsh blue	19.00	
M70	M5	2h	orange	9.50	
M71	M5	3h	olive gray	7.50	
M72	M5	5h	yellow green	30	
M73	M5	10h	dark brown	30	
M74	M5	20h	red	70	
M75	M5	25h	blue	70	
M76	M5	30h	bister	72.50	
M77	M5	45h	dark slate	72.50	
M78	M5	50h	deep green	47.50	
M79	M5	60h	violet	90.00	
M80	M5	80h	rose	47.50	
M81	M5	90h	brown violet	1.75	
			Engr.		
M82	M4	1k	ol bister, *blue*	30	
			Nos. M69-M82 (14)	370.05	

Nos. M69-M82 were on sale at the Vienna post office for a few days before the Armistice signing. They were never issued at the Army Post Offices. They exist imperf.; value, set $400.

MILITARY SEMI-POSTAL STAMPS

Emperor Karl I — MSP7

Empress Zita — MSP8

Perf. 12½x13

1918, July 20 Unwmk. Typo.

MB1	MSP7	10h	gray green	18	20
MB2	MSP8	20h	magenta	18	20
MB3	MSP7	45h	blue	18	20
			Nos. MB1-MB3 (3)	54	60
			Set, never hinged	1.25	

These stamps were sold at a premium of 10h each over face value. The surtax was for "Karl's Fund."

For overprints see Western Ukraine Nos. 31-33.

Exist imperf. Value, set $8.

MILITARY NEWSPAPER STAMPS

Mercury — MN1

1916 Unwmk. Typo. *Perf. 12½*

MP1	MN1	2h blue	15	15
a.		Perf. 11½	1.50	1.00
b.		Perf. 12½x11½	125.00	*125.00*
MP2	MN1	6h orange	55	50
MP3	MN1	10h carmine	70	50
MP4	MN1	20h brown	38	45
a.		Perf. 11½	1.90	1.25
		Nos. MP1-MP4 (4)	1.78	1.60
		Set, never hinged	4.50	

Exist imperf. Values, Nos. MP2-MP3, $1 each, Nos. MP1, MP4, $18 each.

NEWSPAPER STAMPS

From 1851 to 1866, the Austrian Newspaper Stamps were also used in Lombardy-Venetia.

> Values for unused stamps 1851-67 are for fine copies with original gum. Specimens without gum sell for about a third of the figures quoted.

Issues of the Monarchy

Mercury — N1

Three Types

Type I - The "G" has no crossbar.

Type II - The "G" has a crossbar.

Type IIa - as type II but the rosette is deformed. Two spots of color in the "G."

1851-56 Unwmk. Typo. *Imperf.*

Machine-made Paper

P1	N1	(0.6kr) bl, type IIa	130.00	52.50
a.		Blue, type I	175.00	85.00
b.		Ribbed paper	400.00	125.00
c.		Blue, type II	375.00	150.00
P2	N1	(6kr) yel, type I	*12,500.*	*7,500.*
P3	N1	(30kr) rose, type I	*17,500.*	*10,000.*
P4	N1	(6kr) scar, type II ('56)	*37,500.*	*40,000.*

From 1852 No. P3 and from 1856 No. P2 were used as 0.6 kreuzer values.

Pale shades of Nos. P2 and P3 sell at considerably lower values.

Originals of Nos. P2 and P3 are usually in pale colors and poorly printed. Values are for stamps clearly printed and in bright colors. Numerous reprints of Nos. P1 to P4 were made between 1866 and 1904. Those of Nos. P2 and P3 are always well printed and in much deeper colors. All reprints are in type I, but occasionally show faint traces of a crossbar on "G" of "ZEITUNGS."

N2

N3

Two Types of the 1858-59 Issue

Type I - Loops of the bow at the back of the head broken.

Type II - Loops complete. Wreath projects further at top of head.

1858-59 Embossed

P5	N2	(1kr) blue, type I	325.00	425.00
P6	N2	(1kr) lilac, type II ('59)	450.00	165.00

1861

P7	N3	(1kr) gray	100.00	75.00
a.		(1kr) gray lilac	250.00	100.00
b.		(1kr) deep lilac	1,200.	325.00

The embossing on the reprints of the 1858-59 and 1861 issues is not as sharp as on the originals.

N4

Wmk. 91, or, before July 1864, Unwmkd.

1863

P8	N4	(1.05kr) gray	22.50	6.75
a.		Tete beche pair	*20,000.*	
b.		(1.05kr) gray lilac	45.00	12.00

The embossing of the reprints is not as sharp as on the originals.

Mercury

N5 N6

Three Types

Type I - Helmet not defined at back, more or less blurred. Two thick short lines in front of wing of helmet. Shadow on front of face not separated from hair.

Type II - Helmet distinctly defined. Four thin short lines in front of wing. Shadow on front of face clearly defined from hair.

Type III - Outer white circle around head is open at top (closed on types I and II). Greek border at top and bottom is wider than on types I and II.

1867-73 Typo. Wmk. 91

Coarse Print

P9	N5	(1kr) vio, type I	37.50	1.25
a.		(1kr) violet, type II ('73)	150.00	10.00

1874-76

Fine Print

P9B	N5	(1kr) violet, type III ('76)	30	15
c.		(1kr) gray lilac, type I ('76)	100.00	15.00
d.		(1kr) violet, type II	30.00	2.25
e.		Double impression, type III		125.00

Stamps of this issue, except No. P9c, exist in many shades, from gray to lilac brown and deep violet. Stamps in type III exist also privately perforated or rouletted.

1880

P10	N6	½kr green	5.00	45

Nos. P9B and P10 also exist on thicker paper without sheet watermark and No. P10 exists with unofficial perforation.

N7

1899 Unwmk. *Imperf.*

Without Varnish Bars

P11	N7	2h dark blue	16	15
P12	N7	6h orange	2.00	75
P13	N7	10h brown	90	75
P14	N7	20h rose	1.25	1.10
		Nos. P11-P14 (4)	4.31	2.75

1901

With Varnish Bars

P11a	N7	2h dark blue	65	18
P12a	N7	6h orange	9.50	10.00
P13a	N7	10h brown	8.25	7.50
P14a	N7	20h rose	17.00	18.00
		Nos. P11a-P14a (4)	35.40	35.68

Nos. P11 to P14 were re-issued in 1905.

Mercury

N8 N9

1908 *Imperf.*

P15	N8	2h dark blue	1.40	15
a.		Tete beche pair	190.00	275.00
P16	N8	6h orange	2.25	30
P17	N8	10h carmine	2.25	30
P18	N8	20h brown	2.25	22
		Nos. P15-P18 (4)	8.15	97

All values are found on chalky, regular and thin ordinary paper. They exist privately perforated.

1916 *Imperf.*

P19	N9	2h brown	15	15
P20	N9	4h green	15	30
P21	N9	6h dark blue	18	60
P22	N9	10h orange	18	30
P23	N9	30h claret	22	30
		Nos. P19-P23 (5)	88	1.65
		Set, never hinged	2.00	

Issues of the Republic

Newspaper Stamps of 1916 Overprinted

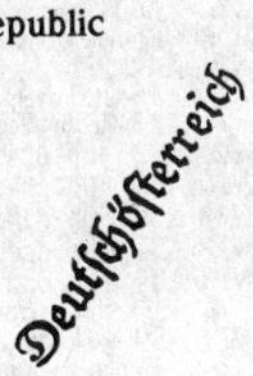

1919

P24	N9	2h brown	15	15
P25	N9	4h green	15	*45*
P26	N9	6h dark blue	15	*70*
P27	N9	10h orange	25	*45*
P28	N9	30h claret	15	*70*
		Set value	58	
		Set, never hinged	1.65	

Mercury

N10 N11

1920-21 *Imperf.*

P29	N10	2h violet	15	15
P30	N10	4h brown	15	15
P31	N10	5h slate	15	15
P32	N10	6h turq blue	15	15
P33	N10	8h green	15	15
P34	N10	9h yellow ('21)	15	15
P35	N10	10h red	15	15
P36	N10	12h blue	15	15
P37	N10	15h lilac ('21)	15	15
P38	N10	18h blue grn ('21)	15	15
P39	N10	20h orange	15	15
P40	N10	30h yellow brn ('21)	15	15
P41	N10	45h green ('21)	15	15
P42	N10	60h claret	15	22
P43	N10	72h chocolate ('21)	15	35
P44	N10	90h violet ('21)	15	35
P45	N10	1.20k red ('21)	15	35
P46	N10	2.40k yellow grn ('21)	15	35
P47	N10	3k gray ('21)	15	35
		Set value	1.10	2.92
		Set, never hinged	1.75	

Nos. P37-P40, P42, P44 and P47 exist also on thick gray paper.

1921-22

P48	N11	45h gray	15	18
P49	N11	75h brown org ('22)	15	15
P50	N11	1.50k ol bister ('22)	15	18
P51	N11	1.80k gray blue ('22)	15	18
P52	N11	2.25k light brown	15	18
P53	N11	3k dull green ('22)	15	35
P54	N11	6k claret ('22)	15	35
P55	N11	7.50k bister	18	35
		Set value	60	
		Set, never hinged	1.25	

Nos. P24-P55 exist privately perforated.

NEWSPAPER TAX STAMPS

> Values for unused stamps 1853-59 are for copies in fine condition with gum. Specimens without gum sell for about one-third of the figures quoted.

Issues of the Monarchy

NT1

NT2

Unwmk.

1853, Mar. 1 Typo. *Imperf.*

PR1	NT1	2kr green	1,500.	45.00

The reprints are in finer print than the more coarsely printed originals, and on a smooth toned paper.

Wmk. 91, or, before July 1864, Unwmkd.

1858-59

Two Types.

Type I - The banderol on the Crown of the left eagle touches the beak of the eagle.

Type II - The banderol does not touch the beak.

PR2	NT2	1kr blue, type II ('59)	27.50	5.00
a.		1kr blue, type I	700.00	150.00
b.		Printed on both sides, type II		
PR3	NT2	2kr brown, type II ('59)	17.50	5.00
a.		2kr red brown, type II	400.00	150.00
PR4	NT2	4kr brn, type I	400.00	*1,000.*

Nos. PR2a, PR3a, and PR4 were printed only on unwatermarked paper. Nos. PR2 and PR3 exist on unwatermarked and watermarked paper.

Nos. PR2 and PR3 exist in coarse and (after 1874) in fine print, like the contemporary postage stamps.

The reprints of the 4kr brown are of type II and on a smooth toned paper.

Issue date: 4kr, Nov. 1.

See Lombardy-Venetia for the 1kr in black and the 2kr, 4fk in red.

NT3

NT4

1877 Redrawn

PR5	NT3	1kr blue	12.50	70
a.		1kr pale ultramarine		*1,200.*
PR6	NT3	2kr brown	10.50	80

In the redrawn stamps the shield is larger and the vertical bar has eight lines above the white square and nine below, instead of five.

Nos. PR5 and PR6 exist also watermarked "WECHSEL" instead of "ZEITUNGS-MARKEN."

1890, June 1

PR7	NT4	1kr brown	6.75	45
PR8	NT4	2kr green	7.75	80

#PR5-PR8 exist with private perforation.

NT5

Perf. 13, 12½

1890, June 1 Wmk. 91

PR9	NT5	25kr carmine	85.00	110.00

Nos. PR1-PR9 did not pay postage, but were a fiscal tax, collected by the postal authorities on newspapers.

SPECIAL HANDLING STAMPS

(For Printed Matter Only)
Issues of the Monarchy

Mercury — SH1

1916 Unwmk. *Perf. 12½*
QE1 SH1 2h claret, *yel* 28 40
QE2 SH1 5h dp green, *yel* 28 40
Set, never hinged 1.75

SH2

1917 *Perf. 12½*
QE3 SH2 2h claret, *yel* 15 15
a. Pair, imperf. between 200.00 200.00
b. Perf. 11½x12½ 45.00 60.00
c. Perf. 12½x11½ 60.00 90.00
d. Perf. 11½ 95 1.40
QE4 SH2 5h dp green, *yel* 15 15
a. Pair, imperf. between 175.00 175.00
b. Perf. 11½x12½ 45.00 60.00
c. Perf. 12½x11½ 60.00 90.00
d. Perf. 11½ 95 1.40
Set value 18 20
Set, never hinged 35

Nos. QE1-QE4 exist imperforate.

Issues of the Republic

Nos. QE3 and QE4 Overprinted

Deutschösterreich

1919
QE5 SH2 2h claret, *yel* 15 15
a. Inverted overprint 175.00
b. Perf. 11½x12½ 5.00 8.00
c. Perf. 12½x11½ 65.00 85.00
d. Perf. 11½ 22 70
QE6 SH2 5h deep green, *yel* 15 20
a. Perf. 11½x12½ 2.25 3.75
b. Perf. 12½x11½ 25.00 35.00
c. Perf. 11½ 18 48
Set value 15
Set, never hinged 20

Nos. QE5 and QE6 exist imperforate.

SH3

Dark Blue Surcharge

1921
QE7 SH3 50h on 2h claret, *yel* 15 15
Never hinged 15

SH4

1922 *Perf. 12½*
QE8 SH4 50h lilac, *yel* 15 18
Never hinged 15

#QE5-QE8 exist in vertical pairs, imperf between. No. QE8 exists imperf.

OCCUPATION STAMPS

Issued under Italian Occupation

Issued in Trieste

Austrian Stamps of 1916-18 Overprinted

Regno d'Italia
Venezia Giulia
3. XI. 18.

1918 Unwmk. *Perf. 12½*
N1 A37 3h bright vio 20 22
a. Double overprint 7.00 9.00
b. Inverted overprint 7.00 9.00
N2 A37 5h light grn 20 22
a. Inverted overprint 7.00 9.00
b. "3.XI." omitted 7.00 7.00
c. Double overprint 9.00
N3 A37 6h dp orange 22 28
N4 A37 10h magenta 18 22
a. Inverted overprint 5.00 6.00
N5 A37 12h light bl 52 70
a. Double overprint 7.00 9.00
N6 A42 15h dull red 18 22
a. Inverted overprint 6.00 8.25
b. Double overprint 7.00 9.00
c. "3.XI." omitted 7.00 7.00
N7 A42 20h dark green 18 22
a. Inverted overprint 5.00 6.00
b. "3.XI." omitted 7.00 8.25
c. Double overprint 14.00
N8 A42 25h deep blue 1.40 1.75
a. Inverted overprint 20.00 25.00
b. "3.XI." omitted 40.00 40.00
N9 A42 30h dl violet 40 55
N10 A39 40h olive grn 14.00 17.50
N11 A39 50h dark green 60 80
N12 A39 60h deep blue 1.00 1.40
N13 A39 80h orange brn 70 80
a. Inverted overprint
N14 A39 1k car, *yel* 60 80
a. Double overprint 14.00 14.00
N15 A40 2k light bl 25.00 27.50
N16 A40 4k yellow grn 55.00 72.50

Handstamped
N17 A40 10k dp violet *8,000. 10,000.*

Granite Paper
N18 A40 2k light blue
N19 A40 3k car rose 40.00 72.50
Nos. N1-N16,N19 (17) 140.38 198.18

Some authorities question the authenticity of No. N18. Counterfeits of Nos. N10, N15-N19 are plentiful.

Italian Stamps of 1901-18 Overprinted

Venezia
Giulia

Wmk. 140 *Perf. 14*
N20 A42 1c brown 18 40
a. Inverted overprint 3.25 5.00
N21 A43 2c orange brn 18 40
a. Inverted overprint 2.50 *3.75*
N22 A48 5c green 15 30
a. Inverted overprint 5.00 *7.00*
b. Double overprint 14.00
N23 A48 10c claret 15 30
a. Inverted overprint 7.00 *10.00*
b. Double overprint 14.00
N24 A50 20c brn orange 15 30
a. Inverted overprint 10.00 *15.00*
b. Double overprint 14.00 *20.00*
N25 A49 25c blue 15 30
a. Double overprint *40.00*
b. Inverted overprint 14.00 *20.00*
N26 A49 40c brown 80 *2.00*
a. Inverted overprint *35.00*
N27 A45 45c olive grn 22 50
a. Inverted overprint 14.00 *20.00*
N28 A49 50c violet 30 *75*
N29 A49 60c brown car 3.25 *8.25*
N30 A46 1 l brn & green 1.40 *3.50*
Nos. N20-N30 (11) 6.93 *17.00*

Italian Stamps of 1901-18 Surcharged

Venezia
Giulia
5 Heller

N31 A48 5h on 5c green 15 30
a. "5" omitted 10.00 *15.00*
b. Inverted surcharge 12.50 *17.50*
N32 A50 20h on 20c brn org 15 28
a. Double surcharge 12.50 *17.50*

Issued in the Trentino

Austrian Stamps of 1916-18 Overprinted

Regno d Italia.
Trentino
3 nov 1918

1918 Unwmk. *Perf. 12½*
N33 A37 3h bright vio 50 70
a. Double overprint 14.00 *20.00*
b. Inverted overprint 12.50 *16.00*
N34 A37 5h light grn 30 45
a. "8 nov. 1918" *750.00*
b. Inverted overprint 12.50 *16.00*
N35 A37 6h dp orange 13.00 17.50
N36 A37 10h magenta 40 60
a. "8 nov. 1918" 16.00 22.50
N37 A37 12h light blue 40.00 60.00
N38 A42 15h dull red 1.10 1.65
N39 A42 20h dark green 18 28
a. "8 nov. 1918" 20.00 *32.50*
b. Double overprint 14.00 20.00
c. Inverted overprint 5.00 6.00
N40 A42 25h deep blue 9.00 13.00
N41 A42 30h dl violet 2.00 3.00
N42 A39 40h olive grn 13.00 17.50
N43 A39 50h dark green 5.00 7.25
a. Inverted overprint 20.00 26.00
N44 A39 60h deep blue 9.00 13.00
a. Double overprint 25.00 *32.50*
N45 A39 80h orange brn 14.00 20.00
N46 A39 90h red violet 200.00 300.00
N47 A39 1k car, *yel* 14.00 20.00
N48 A40 2k light blue 62.50 92.50
N49 A40 4k yel green *375.00 700.00*
N50 A40 10k dp violet *25,000.*

Granite Paper
N51 A40 2k light blue *100.00*

Counterfeits of Nos. N33-N51 are plentiful.

Italian Stamps of 1901-18 Overprinted

Venezia
Tridentina

Wmk. 140 *Perf. 14*
N52 A42 1c brown 22 50
a. Inverted overprint 6.00 9.00
N53 A43 2c orange brn 22 50
a. Inverted overprint 6.00 9.00
N54 A48 5c green 22 50
a. Inverted overprint 6.00 9.00
b. Double overprint 8.25 12.50
N55 A48 10c claret 22 50
a. Inverted overprint 8.25 12.50
b. Double overprint 8.25 12.50
N56 A50 20c brn orange 22 50
a. Inverted overprint 8.25 12.50
N57 A49 40c brown 4.00 10.50
N58 A45 45c olive grn 2.50 6.00
a. Double overprint 26.00 *40.00*
N59 A49 50c violet 2.50 6.00
N60 A46 1 l brn & green 2.50 6.00
a. Double overprint 26.00 *40.00*
Nos. N52-N60 (9) 12.60 31.00

Italian Stamps of 1906-18 Surcharged

Venezia
Tridentina
5 Heller

N61 A48 5h on 5c green 15 25
N62 A48 10h on 10c claret 15 25
a. Inverted surcharge 9.50 *13.00*
N63 A50 20h on 20c brn org 15 25
a. Double surcharge 9.50 *13.00*
Set value 27

General Issue

Italian Stamps of 1901-18 Surcharged

5
centesimi
di corona

1919
N64 A42 1c on 1c brown 15 18
a. Inverted surcharge 1.80 2.75
N65 A43 2c on 2c org brn 15 18
a. Double surcharge 32.50
b. Inverted surcharge 95 1.50
N66 A48 5c on 5c green 15 18
a. Inverted surcharge 4.50 6.50
b. Double surcharge 9.00 9.00
N67 A48 10c on 10c claret 15 18
a. Inverted surcharge 4.50 6.50
b. Double surcharge 9.00 *13.00*
N68 A50 20c on 20c brn org 15 18
a. Double surcharge 13.00 *19.00*
N69 A49 25c on 25c blue 15 18
a. Double surcharge 13.00 13.00
N70 A49 40c on 40c brown 15 18
a. "ccrona" 15.00 *22.50*
N71 A45 45c on 45c ol grn 15 18
a. Inverted surcharge 13.00 19.00
N72 A49 50c on 50c violet 15 18
N73 A49 60c on 60c brn car 15 18
a. "00" for "60" 15.00 *22.50*

Surcharged

1
corona

N74 A46 1cor on 1 l brn & grn 15 18
Set value, N64-N74 88

Surcharges similar to these but differing in style or arrangement of type were used in Dalmatia.

OCCUPATION SPECIAL DELIVERY STAMPS

Issued in Trieste

Special Delivery Stamp of Italy of 1903 Overprinted

Venezia Giulia

1918 Wmk. 140 *Perf. 14*
NE1 SD1 25c rose red 2.50 6.00
a. Inverted overprint 16.00 25.00

General Issue

Special Delivery Stamps of Italy of 1903-09 Surcharged

25 centesimi
di corona

1919
NE2 SD1 25c on 25c rose 15 22
a. Double surcharge 8.25 *12.50*
NE3 SD2 30c on 30c bl & rose 15 40
Set value 25

OCCUPATION POSTAGE DUE STAMPS

Issued in Trieste

Postage Due Stamps of Italy, 1870-94, Overprinted

Venezia
Giulia

1918 Wmk. 140 *Perf. 14*
NJ1 D3 5c buff & mag 15 30
a. Inverted overprint 3.75 3.00
b. Double overprint 25.00
NJ2 D3 10c buff & mag 15 30
a. Inverted overprint 7.25 *10.50*
NJ3 D3 20c buff & mag 15 30
a. Double overprint 25.00
b. Inverted overprint 7.25 *10.50*
NJ4 D3 30c buff & mag 22 50
NJ5 D3 40c buff & mag 2.00 5.00
a. Inverted overprint 37.50 *55.00*
NJ6 D3 50c buff & mag 5.00 12.50
a. Inverted overprint 37.50 *55.00*
NJ7 D3 1 l bl & mag 13.00 32.50
Nos. NJ1-NJ7 (7) 20.67 51.40

General Issue

Postage Due Stamps of Italy, 1870-1903 Surcharged

5
centesimi
di corona

1919

Buff & Magenta
NJ8 D3 5c on 5c 15 30
a. Inverted overprint 2.00 3.00
NJ9 D3 10c on 10c 15 30
a. Center and surcharge invtd. 10.00 *15.00*
NJ10 D3 20c on 20c 15 30
a. Double overprint 20.00 *30.00*
NJ11 D3 30c on 30c 15 30
NJ12 D3 40c on 40c 15 30
NJ13 D3 50c on 50c 15 30

Surcharged **una corona**

NJ14	D3	1cor on 1 l bl & mag	15	30
NJ15	D3	2cor on 2 l bl & mag	4.50	11.00
NJ16	D3	5cor on 5 l bl & mag	4.50	11.00
		Nos. NJ8-NJ16 (9)	10.05	24.10

A. M. G. ISSUE FOR AUSTRIA

Catalogue values for unused stamps in this section are for Never Hinged items.

Issued jointly by the Allied Military Government of the US and Great Britain, for civilian use in areas under American, British and French occupation. (Upper Austria, Salzburg, Tyrol, Vorarlberg, Styria and Carinthia).

OS1

1945 Unwmk. Litho. *Perf. 11*

4N1	OS1	1g aquamarine	15	15
4N2	OS1	3g deep orange	15	15
4N3	OS1	4g buff	15	15
4N4	OS1	5g bright green	15	15
4N5	OS1	6g red violet	15	15
4N6	OS1	8g rose pink	15	15
4N7	OS1	10g light gray	15	15
4N8	OS1	12g pale buff brown	15	15
4N9	OS1	15g rose red	15	15
4N10	OS1	20g copper brown	15	15
4N11	OS1	25g deep blue	15	15
4N12	OS1	30g bright violet	15	15
4N13	OS1	40g light ultra	15	15
4N14	OS1	60g light olive grn	15	18
4N15	OS1	1s dark violet	15	28
4N16	OS1	2s yellow	20	30
4N17	OS1	5s deep ultra	42	45
		Set value	1.40	1.90

For Nos. 4N2, 4N4-4N17 overprinted "PORTO" see Nos. J189-J203.

AUSTRIAN OFFICES ABROAD

These stamps were on sale and usable at all Austrian post-offices in Crete and in the Turkish Empire.

100 Centimes = 1 Franc

OFFICES IN CRETE

Used values are italicized for stamps often found with false cancellations.

Stamps of Austria of 1899-1901 Issue, Surcharged in Black:

CENTIMES a

CENTIMES b

CENTIMES c

FRANC d

1903-04 Unwmk. *Perf. 12½, 13½*
On Nos. 73a, 75a, 77a, 81a
Granite Paper
With Varnish Bars

1	A15(a)	5c on 5h blue green	1.50	2.00
2	A16(b)	10c on 10h rose	70	*2.25*
3	A16(b)	25c on 25h ultra	30.00	20.00
4	A17(c)	50c on 50h gray blue	6.00	*37.50*

On Nos. 83, 83a, 84, 85
Without Varnish Bars

5	A18(d)	1fr on 1k car rose	2.25	*40.00*
a.		1fr on 1k carmine	4.00	
b.		Horiz. or vert. pair, imperf. between	175.00	
6	A18(d)	2fr on 2k ('04)	9.50	*145.00*
7	A18(d)	4fr on 4k ('04)	10.50	*200.00*
		Nos. 1-7 (7)	60.45	

Surcharged on Austrian Stamps of 1904-05

1905
On Nos. 89, 97
Without Varnish Bars

8	A19(a)	5c on 5h bl grn	40.00	16.00
9	A20(b)	10c on 10h car	80	*5.00*

On Nos. 89a, 97a, 99a, 103a
With Varnish Bars

8a	A19(a)	5c on 5h blue green	3.75	4.00
9a	A20(b)	10c on 10h carmine	20.00	14.00
10	A20(b)	25c on 25h ultra	65	*35.00*
11	A21(b)	50c on 50h dl bl	1.00	*150.00*

Surcharged on Austrian Stamps and Type of 1906-07

1907 *Perf. 12½, 13½*
Without Varnish Bars

12	A19(a)	5c on 5h yel green (#90)	80	*3.25*
13	A20(b)	10c on 10h car (#92)	1.10	*12.00*
14	A20(b)	15c on 15h vio	1.25	*14.00*
		Nos. 12-14 (3)	3.15	

A5

A6

1908 Typo. *Perf. 12½*

15	A5	5c green, *yellow*	35	18
16	A5	10c scarlet, *rose*	40	30
17	A5	15c brown, *buff*	45	*2.75*
18	A5	25c dp blue, *blue*	11.50	2.75

Engr.

19	A6	50c lake, *yellow*	1.75	*18.00*
20	A6	1fr brown, *gray*	2.50	*25.00*
a.		Vert pair, imperf. btwn.	175.00	
		Nos. 15-20 (6)	16.95	*48.98*

Nos. 15 to 18 are on paper colored on the surface only. All values exist imperforate.

60th year of the reign of Emperor Franz Josef, for permanent use.

Paper Colored Through

1914 Typo.

21	A5	10c rose, *rose*	1.65	*575.00*
22	A5	25c ultra, *blue*	65	*65.00*

Nos. 21 and 22 exist imperforate.

OFFICES IN THE TURKISH EMPIRE

From 1863 to 1867 the stamps of Lombardy-Venetia (Nos. 15 to 24) were used at the Austrian Offices in the Turkish Empire.

100 Soldi = 1 Florin
40 Paras = 1 Piaster

Values for unused stamps are for copies with gum. Specimens without gum sell for about one-third the figures quoted.

Used values are italicized for stamps often found with false cancellations.

For similar designs in Kreuzers, see early Austria.

A1

A2

Two different printing methods were used, as in the 1867-74 issues of Austria. They may be distinguished by the coarse or fine lines of the hair and whiskers and by the paper, which is more transparent on the later issue.

1867 Typo. Wmk. 91 *Perf. 9½*
Coarse Print

1	A1	2sld orange	1.25	*12.50*
a.		2sld yellow	45.00	20.00
2	A1	3sld green	80.00	22.50
a.		3sld dark green	85.00	25.00
3	A1	5sld red	80.00	9.00
a.		5sld carmine	90.00	12.50
4	A1	10sld blue	80.00	1.25
a.		10sld light blue	85.00	1.65
b.		10sld dark blue	85.00	1.90
5	A1	15sld brown	12.50	4.00
a.		15sld dark brown	40.00	12.50
b.		15sld reddish brown	14.00	8.00
6	A1	25sld gray lilac	9.00	*22.50*
a.		25sld brown violet	11.00	*25.00*
7	A2	50sld brn, perf. 10½	85	*32.50*
a.		Perf. 12	67.50	*47.50*
b.		Perf. 13	225.00	
k.		Perf. 9	20.00	*40.00*
l.		50sld pale red brn, perf. 12	32.50	35.00
m.		Vert. pair, imperf. btwn.	325.00	*600.00*
n.		Horiz. pair, imperf. btwn.	300.00	*675.00*
o.		Perf. 10½x9	45.00	50.00

Perf. 9, 9½, 10½ and Compound

1876-83
Fine Print

7C	A1	2sld yellow ('83)	15	*1,200.*
7D	A1	3sld green ('78)	80	*15.00*
7E	A1	5sld red ('78)	30	*14.00*
7F	A1	10sld blue	55.00	65
7I	A1	15sld org brn ('81)	6.00	*80.00*
7J	A1	25sld gray lil ('83)	42	*175.00*
		Nos. 7C-7J (6)	62.67	

The 10 soldi has been reprinted in deep dull blue, perforated 10½.

A3

1883 *Perf. 9½, 10, 10½*

8	A3	2sld brown	15	*65.00*
9	A3	3sld green	75	*12.50*
10	A3	5sld rose	15	*6.50*
11	A3	10sld blue	60	28
12	A3	20sld gray	1.50	*3.50*
13	A3	50sld red lilac	1.50	*9.00*
		Nos. 8-13 (6)	4.65	

A4

A5

10 PARAS ON 3 SOLDI:

Type I - Surcharge 16½mm across. "PARA" about ½mm above bottom of "10." 2mm space between "10" and "P"; 1½mm between "A" and "10." Perf. 9½ only.

Type II - Surcharge 15¼ to 16mm across. "PARA" on same line with figures or slightly higher or lower. 1½mm space between "10" and "P"; 1mm between "A" and "10." Perf. 9½ and 10.

1886 *Perf. 9½ and 10*

14	A4	10pa on 3sld green, type II	18	*3.50*
a.		10pa on 3sld green, type I	185.00	250.00
b.		Inverted surcharge, type I		*1,750.*

1888

15	A5	10pa on 3kr grn	3.00	4.50
a.		"01 PARA 10"		*375.00*
16	A5	20pa on 5kr rose	60	*4.50*
17	A5	1pi on 10kr blue	45.00	85
a.		Perf. 13½		150.00
b.		Double surcharge		140.00
18	A5	2pi on 20kr gray	1.50	2.25
19	A5	5pi on 50kr vio	2.25	*11.50*
		Nos. 15-19 (5)	52.35	

A6

1890-92 Unwmk. *Perf. 9 to 13½*
Granite Paper

20	A6	8pa on 2kr brn ('92)	15	15
a.		Perf. 9½	2.75	1.65
21	A6	10pa on 3kr green	65	15
a.		Pair, imperf. between		
22	A6	20pa on 5kr rose	15	15
23	A6	1pi on 10kr ultra	35	15
24	A6	2pi on 20kr ol grn	10.00	*16.00*
25	A6	5pi on 50kr violet	12.50	*35.00*
		Nos. 20-25 (6)	23.80	

See note after Austria No. 65 on missing numerals, etc.

Austria Nos. 66, 69 Surcharged **2 PIASTER 2**

1891 *Perf. 9 to 13½*

26	A14	2pi on 20kr	4.75	40
a.		Perf. 9½	80.00	20.00
27	A14	5pi on 50kr	2.75	1.75

Two types of the surcharge on No. 26 exist.

A8

1892 *Perf. 10½, 11½*

28	A8	10pi on 1gld blue	11.00	16.00
29	A8	20pi on 2gld car	13.00	20.00
a.		Double surcharge		

1896 *Perf. 10½, 11½, 12½*

30	A8	10pi on 1gld pale lilac	13.00	16.00
31	A8	20pi on 2gld gray grn	42.50	40.00

A9

A10

A11

A12

Perf. 10½, 12½, 13½ and Compound

1900
Without Varnish Bars

32	A9	10pa on 5h bl grn	3.50	75
33	A10	20pa on 10h rose	3.50	75
b.		Perf. 12½x10½	225.00	30.00
34	A10	1pi on 25h ultra	3.50	15
35	A11	2pi on 50h gray bl	7.25	1.10
36	A12	5pi on 1k car rose	1.10	15
a.		5pi on 1k carmine	1.25	65
b.		Horiz. or vert. pair, imperf. btwn.	115.00	
37	A12	10pi on 2k gray lil	2.75	1.65
a.		Horiz. pair, imperf. btwn.		
38	A12	20pi on 4k gray grn	2.00	*3.75*
		Nos. 32-38 (7)	23.60	*8.30*

In the surcharge on Nos. 37 and 38 "piaster" is printed "PIAST."

1901
With Varnish Bars

32a	A9	10pa on 5h blue green	2.00	1.10
33a	A10	20pa on 10h rose	2.00	*65.00*
34a	A10	1pi on 25h ultra	1.65	24
35a	A11	2pi on 50h gray blue	3.75	1.00
		Nos. 32a-35a (4)	9.40	

A13

A14

A15

1906 *Perf. 12½ to 13½*

Without Varnish Bars

39	A13	10pa dark green	12.00	1.00
40	A14	20pa rose	80	35
41	A14	1pi ultra	35	15
42	A15	2pi gray blue	90	38
		Nos. 39-42 (4)	14.05	1.88

1903 **With Varnish Bars**

39a	A13	10pa dark green	4.75	75
40a	A14	20pa rose	2.25	35
41a	A14	1pi ultra	1.75	20
42a	A15	2pi gray blue	105.00	1.10

1907

Without Varnish Bars

43	A13	10pa yellow green	35	*1.25*
45	A14	30pa violet	52	*2.25*

A16

A17

1908 **Typo.** *Perf. 12½*

46	A16	10pa green, *yellow*	15	15
47	A16	20pa scarlet, *rose*	20	15
48	A16	30pa brown, *buff*	30	40
49	A16	1pi deep bl, *blue*	12.00	15
50	A16	60pa vio, *bluish*	55	2.25

Engr.

51	A17	2pi lake, *yellow*	35	15
52	A17	5pi brown, *gray*	48	40
53	A17	10pi green, *yellow*	80	1.10
54	A17	20pi blue, *gray*	1.50	2.25
		Nos. 46-54 (9)	16.33	7.00

Nos. 46 to 50 are on paper colored on the surface only. 60th year of the reign of Emperor Franz Josef I, for permanent use. All values exist imperforate.

1913-14 **Typo.**

Paper Colored Through

57	A16	20pa rose, *rose* ('14)	80	*175.00*
58	A16	1pi ultra, *blue*	35	30

Nos. 57 and 58 exist imperforate.

POSTAGE DUE STAMPS

D1

D2

Black Surcharge

1902 **Unwmk.** *Perf. 12½, 13½*

J1	D1	10pa on 5h green	1.25	2.75
J2	D1	20pa on 10h green	1.25	2.50
J3	D1	1pi on 20h green	2.00	3.50
J4	D1	2pi on 40h green	2.00	2.75
J5	D1	5pi on 100h green	3.00	1.65
		Nos. J1-J5 (5)	9.50	13.15

Shades of Nos. J1 to J5 exist, varying from yellowish green to dark green.

1908 **Typo.** *Perf. 12½*

J6	D2	¼pi green	3.00	5.00
J7	D2	½pi green	1.50	*3.50*
J8	D2	1pi green	2.00	*5.00*
J9	D2	1½pi green	65	*6.25*
J10	D2	2pi green	2.25	*8.00*
J11	D2	5pi green	2.25	*5.00*
J12	D2	10pi green	18.00	*85.00*
J13	D2	20pi green	16.00	*110.00*
J14	D2	30pi green	12.00	7.00
		Nos. J6-J14 (9)	57.65	*234.75*

Nos. J6 to J14 exist in distinct shades of green and on thick chalky, regular and thin ordinary paper. Values are for the least expensive variety. No. J6-J14 exist imperforate.

Forgeries exist.

LOMBARDY-VENETIA

Formerly a kingdom in the north of Italy forming part of the Austrian Empire. Milan and Venice were the two principal cities. Lombardy was annexed to Sardinia in 1859, and Venetia to the kingdom of Italy in 1866.

100 Centesimi = 1 Lira
100 Soldi = 1 Florin (1858)

Values of the earliest Lombardy-Venetia stamps vary according to condition. Quotations for Nos. 1-6, PR1-PR3 are for fine copies. Very fine to superb specimens sell at much higher prices, and inferior or poor copies sell at reduced prices, depending on the condition of the individual specimen.

Values for unused stamps are for fine copies with gum. Specimens without gum sell for about one-quarter of the values quoted.

For similar designs in Kreuzers, see early Austria.

Coat of Arms — A1

15 CENTESIMI:

Type I- "5" is on a level with the "1." One heavy line around coat of arms center.

Type II- As type I, but "5" is a trifle sideways and is higher than the "1."

Type III- As type II, but two, thinner, lines around center.

45 CENTESIMI:

Type I- Lower part of "45" is lower than "Centes." One heavy line around coat of arms center. "45" varies in height and distance from "Centes."

Type II- One heavy line around coat of arms center. Lower part of "45" is on a level with lower part of "Centes."

Type III- As type II, but two, thinner, lines around center.

Wmk. K.K.H.M. in Sheet or Unwmkd.
1850 **Typo.** *Imperf.*

Thick to Thin Paper

1	A1	5c buff	675.00	42.50
a.		Printed on both sides	*4,000.*	110.00
b.		5c yellow	*3,500.*	325.00
c.		5c orange	650.00	72.50
d.		5c lemon yellow		*400.00*
3	A1	10c black	950.00	37.50
a.		10c gray black	1,050.	45.00
4	A1	15c red, type III	300.00	1.00
b.		15c red, type I	*1,050.*	9.00
c.		Ribbed paper, type II	*10,000.*	150.00
d.		Ribbed paper, type I	*5,500.*	47.50
f.		15c red, type II	*600.00*	6.00
5	A1	30c brown	825.00	2.00
a.		Ribbed paper	2,250.	24.00
6	A1	45c blue, type III	*2,500.*	5.50
a.		45c blue, type I	*4,000.*	11.00
b.		Ribbed paper, type I	*10,000.*	100.00
c.		45c blue, type II	*7,500.*	15.00

1854 **Machine-made Paper, Type III**

3c	A1	10c black	*2,000.*	100.00
4g	A1	15c pale red	*150.00*	60
5b	A1	30c brown	*600.00*	1.50
6d	A1	45c blue	*4,000.*	5.50

See note about the paper of the 1850 issue of Austria. *The reprints are type III, in brighter colors.*

A2

A3

A4

A5

A6

Two Types of Each Value.

Type I- Loops of the bow at the back of the head broken.

Type II- Loops complete. Wreath projects further at top of head.

1858-62 **Embossed** *Perf. 14½*

7	A2	2s yel, type II	250.00	40.00
a.		2s yellow, type I	675.00	225.00
8	A3	3s black, type II	1,000.	62.50
a.		3s black, type I	500.00	130.00
b.		Perf. 16, type I		300.00
c.		Perf. 15x16 or 16x15, type I	*900.00*	265.00
9	A3	3s grn, type II ('62)	150.00	30.00
10	A4	5s red, type II	100.00	1.65
a.		5s red, type I	110.00	6.50
b.		Printed on both sides, type II		*1,750.*
11	A5	10s brown, type II	465.00	4.50
a.		10s brown, type I	135.00	17.50
12	A6	15s blue, type II	485.00	6.00
a.		15s blue, type I	675.00	37.50

The reprints are of type II and are perforated 10½, 11, 11½, 12, 12½ and 13. There are also imperforate reprints of Nos. 7-9.

A7

A8

1861-62 *Perf. 14*

13	A7	5s red	550.00	1.15
14	A7	10s brown ('62)	500.00	9.50

The reprints are perforated 9, 9½, 10½, 11, 12, 12½ and 13. There are also imperforate reprints of the 2 and 3s.

The 2, 3 and 15s of this type exist only as reprints.

1863

15	A8	2s yellow	57.50	72.50
16	A8	3s green	425.00	45.00
17	A8	5s rose	425.00	5.00
18	A8	10s blue	1,000.	37.50
19	A8	15s yellow brown	800.00	62.50

1864-65 **Wmk. 91** *Perf. 9½*

20	A8	2s yellow ('65)	55.00	*150.00*
21	A8	3s green	9.00	6.25
22	A8	5s rose	1.00	75
23	A8	10s blue	8.25	2.75
24	A8	15s yellow brown	12.00	12.00

Nos. 15-24 reprints are perforated 10½ and 13. There are also imperforate reprints of the 2s and 3s.

NEWSPAPER TAX STAMPS

From 1853 to 1858 the Austrian Newspaper Tax Stamp 2kr green (No. PR1) was also used in Lombardy-Venetia, at the value of 10 centesimi.

NT1

Type I- The banderol of the left eagle touches the beak of the eagle.

Type II- The banderol does not touch the beak.

1858-59 **Unwmk.** **Typo.** *Imperf.*

PR1	NT1	1kr black, type I ('59)	775.00	*2,750.*
PR2	NT1	2kr red, type II ('59)	100.00	35.00
PR3	NT1	4kr red, type I	*32,500.*	*1,750.*

No. PR2 exists with watermark 91.

The reprints are on a smooth toned paper and are all of type II.

AZERBAIJAN

(Azerbaidjan)

LOCATION — Southernmost part of Russia in Eastern Europe, bounded by Georgia, Dagestan, Caspian Sea, Persia and Armenia

GOVT. — A Soviet Socialist Republic

AREA — 32,686 sq. mi.

POP. — 2,096,973 (1923)

CAPITAL — Baku

100 Kopecks = 1 Ruble

Catalogue values for unused stamps in this country are for Never Hinged items, beginning with Scott 350 in the regular postage section.

National Republic

Standard Bearer — A1

Farmer at Sunset — A2

Baku — A3

Temple of Eternal Fires — A4

1919 **Unwmk.** **Litho.** *Imperf.*

1	A1	10k multicolored	15	28
2	A1	20k multicolored	15	28
3	A2	40k green, yellow & blk	15	28
4	A2	60k red, yellow & blk	20	28
5	A2	1r blue, yellow & blk	30	50
6	A3	2r red, bister & blk	30	50
7	A3	5r blue, bister & blk	42	85
8	A3	10r olive grn, bis & blk	60	95
9	A4	25r blue, red & black	1.00	1.50
10	A4	50r ol grn, red & black	1.25	1.75
		Nos. 1-10 (10)	4.52	7.17

The two printings of Nos. 1-10 are distinguished by the grayish or thin white paper. Both have yellowish gum. White paper copies are worth five times the above values.

For surcharges see Nos. 57-64, 75-80.

Soviet Socialist Republic

Symbols of Labor — A5

Oil Well — A6

Bibi Eibatt Oil Field — A7

Khan's Palace, Baku — A8

Globe and Workers — A9

Maiden's Tower, Baku — A10

Goukasoff House A11

Blacksmiths A12

Hall of Judgment, Baku — A13

1922

15	A5	1r gray green	20	35
16	A6	2r olive black	50	50
17	A7	5r gray brown	20	35
18	A8	10r gray	50	65
19	A9	25r orange brown	20	40
20	A10	50r violet	20	40
21	A11	100r dull red	35	50
22	A12	150r blue	35	50
23	A9	250r violet & buff	35	50
24	A13	400r dark blue	35	50
25	A12	500r gray vio & blk	35	50
26	A13	1000r dk blue & rose	35	60
27	A8	2000r blue & black	35	50
28	A7	3000r brown & blue	35	50
a.		Tete beche pair	13.00	14.00
29	A11	5000r black, *ol grn*	60	75
		Nos. 15-29 (15)	5.20	7.50

Counterfeits exist of Nos. 1-29. They generally sell for more than genuine copies.

For overprints and surcharges see Nos. 32-41, 43, 45-55, 65-72, 300-304, 307-333.

Nos. 15, 17, 23, 28, 27 Handstamped from Metal Dies in a Numbering Machine

15000

1922

32	A5	10,000r on 1r	8.00	8.00
33	A7	15,000r on 5r	9.50	10.00
34	A9	33,000r on 250r	5.00	5.00
35	A7	50,000r on 3000r	5.00	5.00
36	A8	66,000r on 2000r	11.00	10.00
		Nos. 32-36 (5)	38.50	38.00

Same Surcharges on Regular Issue and Semi-Postal Stamps of 1922

1922-23

36A	A7	500r on 5r	60.00	67.50
37	A6	1000r on 2r	15.00	15.00
38	A8	2000r on 10r	5.00	4.00
39	A8	5000r on 2000r	5.00	3.00
40	A11	15,000r on 5000r	12.00	10.00
41	A5	20,000r on 1r	10.00	9.00
42	SP1	25,000r on 500r	35.00	
43	A7	50,000r on 5r	12.50	12.50
44	SP2	50,000r on 1000r	26.00	
45	A11	50,000r on 5000r	5.00	4.50
45A	A8	60,000r on 2000r	12.50	14.00
46	A11	70,000r on 5000r	20.00	20.00
47	A6	100,000r on 2r	15.00	15.00
48	A8	200,000r on 10r	10.00	10.00
49	A9	200,000r on 25r	15.00	15.00
50	A7	300,000r on 3000r	5.00	5.00
51	A8	500,000r on 2000r	15.00	10.00

Revalued

52	A7	500r on #33	30.00	*52.50*
53	A11	15,000r on #46	30.00	*52.50*
54	A7	300,000r on #35	45.00	*55.00*
55	A8	500,000r on #36	50.00	*75.00*

The surcharged semi-postal stamps were used for regular postage.

Same Surcharges on Stamps of 1919

57	A1	25,000r on 10k	70	1.00
58	A1	50,000r on 20k	70	1.00
59	A2	75,000r on 40k	1.75	2.50
60	A2	100,000r on 60k	70	95
61	A2	200,000r on 1r	70	95
62	A3	300,000r on 2r	88	1.10
63	A3	500,000r on 5r	1.00	1.10
64	A2	750,000r on 40k	3.50	2.75
		Nos. 57-64 (8)	9.93	11.35

Handstamped from Settings of Rubber Type in Black or Violet

100000 **200.000**

Nos. 65-66, 71-80 Nos. 67-70

On Stamps of 1922

65	A6	100,000r on 2r	12.00	12.00
66	A8	200,000r on 10r	13.00	14.00
67	A8	200,000r on 10r (V)	17.50	15.00
68	A9	200,000r on 25r (V)	15.00	11.00
a.		Black surcharge	26.00	27.50
69	A7	300,000r on 3000r (V)	25.00	25.00
70	A8	500,000r on 2000r (V)	20.00	20.00
a.		Black surcharge	27.50	29.00
72	A11	1,500,000r on 5000r (V)	16.00	15.00
a.		Black surcharge	16.00	15.00

On Stamps of 1919

75	A1	50,000r on 20k	1.00	
76	A2	75,000r on 40k	65	
77	A2	100,000r on 60k	1.25	
78	A2	200,000r on 1r	15	15
79	A3	300,000r on 2r	1.00	
80	A3	500,000r on 5r	1.25	

Inverted and double surcharges of Nos. 32-80 sell for twice the normal price.

Counterfeits exist of Nos. 32-80.

Baku Province

Regular and Semi-Postal Stamps of 1922 Handstamped in Violet or Black

БАКИНСКОИ П. К.

The overprint reads "Bakinskoi P(ochtovoy) K(ontory)," meaning Baku Post Office.

1922		**Unwmk.**	***Imperf.***
300	A5	1r gray green	*13.00*
301	A7	5r gray brown	*13.00*
302	A12	150r blue	*4.00*
303	A9	250r violet & buff	*6.00*
304	A13	400r dark blue	*5.25*
305	SP1	500r blue & pale blue	*6.00*
306	SP2	1000r brown & bister	*8.00*
307	A8	2000r blue & black	*8.00*
308	A7	3000r brown & blue	*13.00*
309	A11	5000r black, *ol grn*	*13.00*
		Nos. 300-309 (10)	*89.25*

Stamps of 1922 Handstamped in Violet

Бакинскаго Г-П-Т.О.№1

Ovpt. reads: Baku Post, Telegraph Office No. 1.

1924

Overprint 24x2mm

312	A12	150r blue	*6.00*
313	A9	250r violet & buff	*6.00*
314	A13	400r dark blue	*6.00*
317	A8	2000r blue & black	*6.50*
318	A7	3000r brown & blue	*6.50*
319	A11	5000r black, *ol grn*	*6.50*

Overprint 30x3½mm

323	A12	150r blue	*6.00*
324	A9	250r violet & buff	*6.00*
325	A13	400r dark blue	*6.00*
328	A8	2000r blue & black	*6.00*
329	A7	3000r brown & blue	*6.00*
330	A11	5000r black, *ol grn*	*6.00*

Overprinted on Nos. 32-33, 35

331	A5	10,000r on 1r	*22.50*
332	A7	15,000r on 5r	*22.50*
333	A7	50,000r on 3000r	*27.50*
		Nos. 312-333 (15)	*146.50*

The overprinted semipostal stamps were used for regular postage.

This handstamp on Nos. 17, B1-B2 in size 24x2mm, and on Nos. 15, 17, B1-B2 in size 30x3½mm, was of private origin and not officially issued.

With the breakup of the Soviet Union on Dec. 26, 1991, Azerbaijan and ten former Soviet republics established the Commonwealth of Independent States.

100 Kopecks = 1 Ruble

100 Giapiks = 1 Manat (1992)

Catalogue values for unused stamps in this section, from this point to the end of the section, are for Never Hinged items.

Flag, Map — A20

Unwmk.

1992, Mar. 26	**Litho.**	***Perf. 14***
350 A20 35k multicolored		3.00

Park — A21

1992, May 7		***Perf. 12***
351 A21	25g on 15k multicolored	*35*
352 A21	35g on 15k multicolored	*50*
353 A21	50g on 15k multicolored	*70*
354 A21	1.50m on 15k multicolored	*2.10*
355 A21	2.50m on 15k multicolored	*3.50*
	Nos. 351-355 (5)	*7.15*

Nos. 351-355 are overprints on a National Park series prepared for the former republics of Soviet Union. Not issued without surcharges.

For surcharge see No. 435.

Iran-Azerbaijan Telecommunications — A21a

1992	**Photo.**	***Perf. 13x13½***
355A A21a 15g multicolored		*5.00*

See Iran No. 2544.

For surcharges see Nos. 403-406.

Horses — A22

1993, Feb. 1		**Litho.**	***Perf. 13***
356	A22	20g shown	*28*
357	A22	30g Kabarda	*42*
358	A22	50g Qarabair	*70*
359	A22	1m Don	*1.40*
360	A22	2.50m Yakut	*3.50*
361	A22	5m Orlov	*7.00*
362	A22	10m Diliboz	*14.00*
		Nos. 356-362 (7)	*27.30*

Perf. 12½

Souvenir Sheet

362A	A22	8m Qarabag	*5.25*

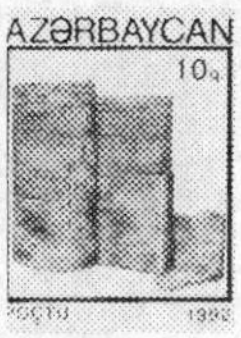

Ruins — A23

Government Building — A24

1992-93		**Litho.**	***Perf. 12½x12***
363	A23	10g blk & blue grn	*15*
365	A23	20g black & red	*20*
367	A23	50g black & green	*15*
368	A23	50g black & yellow	*48*
370	A23	1m black & rose lilac	*20*
372	A23	1.50m black & blue	*1.50*
373	A23	2.50m black & yellow	*48*
374	A23	5m black & green	*95*
		Nos. 363-374 (8)	*4.11*

Issued: 10g, 20g, 1.50m, #367, Dec. 20; #368, 1m, 2.50m, 5m, June 20, 1993.

This is an expanding set. Numbers may change.

1993	**Litho.**	***Perf. 12½***
375 A24	25g yellow & black	*15*
376 A24	30g green & black	*18*
377 A24	50g blue & black	*28*
378 A24	1m red & black	*55*
	Nos. 375-378 (4)	*1.16*

For surcharges see No. 407-414.

Flowers — A25

1993		**Litho.**	***Perf. 12½***
379	A25	25g Tulipa eichleri	*15*
380	A25	50g Puschkinia scilloides	*15*
381	A25	1m Iris elegantissima	*28*
382	A25	1.50m Iris acutiloba	*40*
383	A25	5m Tulipa florenskyii	*1.40*
384	A25	10m Iris reticulata	*2.75*
		Nos. 379-384 (6)	*5.13*

Souvenir Sheet

Perf. 13

385	A25	10m Muscari elecostomum	*2.75*

No. 385 contains one 32x40mm stamp.

Fish A26

Designs: 25g, Acipenser guldenstadti. 50g, Acipenser stellatus. 1m, Rutilus frisii kutum. 1.50m, Rutilus rutilus caspicus. 5m, Salmo trutta caspius. No. 391, Alosa kessleri. No. 392, Huso huso.

1993			***Perf. 12½***
386	A26	25g multicolored	*15*
387	A26	50g multicolored	*15*
388	A26	1m multicolored	*28*
389	A26	1.50m multicolored	*40*
390	A26	5m multicolored	*1.40*
391	A26	10m multicolored	*2.75*
		Nos. 386-391 (6)	*5.13*

Souvenir Sheet

Perf. 13

392	A26	10m multicolored	*2.75*

No. 392 contains one 40x32mm stamp.

Pres. Geidar A. Aliyev — A27

Design: No. 394, Map of Nakhichevan.

1993 **Litho.** ***Perf. 12½x13***

393	A27	25m multicolored	*1.90*
394	A27	25m multicolored	*1.90*
a.		Souvenir sheet, #393-394, perf. 12	*3.80*

Historic Buildings, Baku — A28

Style of tombs: 2m, Fortress, 13th-14th cent. 4m, Moorish gate, 15th cent. 8m, Oriental-style columns, 15th cent.

1993 **Litho.** ***Perf. 11***

395	A28	2m red, silver & black	*18*
396	A28	4m green, silver & black	*35*
397	A28	8m blue, silver & black	*75*
		Nos. 395-397 (3)	*1.28*

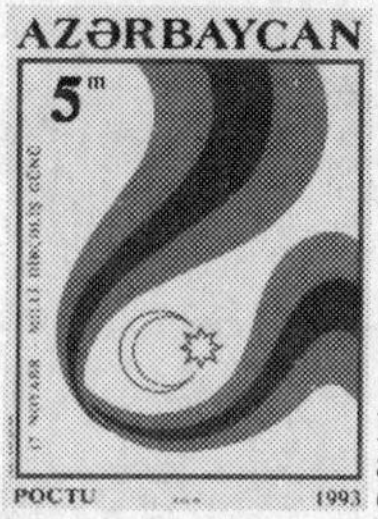

Natl. Colors, Star and Crescent — A29

1993 ***Perf. 12½***

398	A29	5m shown	*60*
399	A29	8m Natl. coat of arms	*1.00*

Mohammed Fizuli (1494-1556), Poet — A30

1993 ***Perf. 12½***

400	A30	10m multicolored	*1.40*

No. 400 printed se-tenant with label.

Mammed Amin Rasulzade (1884-1955), Politician A31

Jalil Mamedkulizade, Politician, 125th Birth Anniv. — A32

1994 ***Perf. 12½, 13 (#402)***

401	A31	15m black, yellow & brown	*1.65*
402	A32	20m black, blue & gold	*1.90*

No. 402 printed se-tenant with label.

No. 355A Surchaged

2 m.

1994 **Photo.** ***Perf. 13x13½***

403	A21a	2m on 15g	*15*
404	A21a	20m on 15g	*80*
405	A21a	25m on 15g	*1.00*
406	A21a	50m on 15g	*2.00*
		Nos. 403-406 (4)	*3.95*

Nos. 375-378 Surcharged

5 m.

1994 **Litho.** ***Perf. 12½***

407	A24	5m on 1m #375	*15*
408	A24	10m on 30g #377	*15*
409	A24	15m on 30g #377	*20*
a.		Pair, #408-409	*35*
410	A24	20m on 50g #378	*28*
411	A24	25m on 1m #375	*35*
a.		Pair, #407, 411	*50*
412	A24	40m on 50g #378	*55*
a.		Pair, #410, 412	*85*
413	A24	50m on 25g #376	*65*
414	A24	100m on 25g #376	*1.40*
a.		Pair, #413-414	*2.05*
		Nos. 407-414 (8)	*3.73*

Baku Oil Fields — A33

Designs: 15m, Temple of Eternal Fires. 20m, Oil derricks. 25m, Early tanker. 50m, Ludwig Nobel, Robert Nobel, Petr Bilderling, Alfred Nobel.

1994, June 10 **Photo.** ***Perf. 13***

415	A33	15m multicolored	*70*
416	A33	20m multicolored	*90*
417	A33	25m multicolored	*1.10*
418	A33	50m multicolored	*2.25*
a.		Souvenir sheet of 1	*2.25*
		Nos. 415-418 (4)	*4.95*

See Turkmenistan Nos. 39-43.

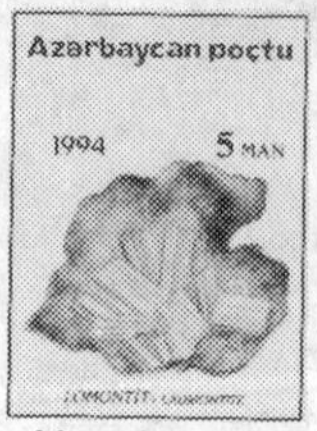

Minerals — A34

Posthorn — A35

1994, June 15 **Litho.** ***Perf. 13***

419	A34	5m Laumontite	*42*
420	A34	10m Epidot calcite	*85*
421	A34	15m Andradite	*1.25*
422	A34	20m Amethyst	*1.65*
a.		Souvenir sheet, #420-423 + 2 labels, perf. 12	*4.75*
		Nos. 419-422 (4)	*4.17*

1994 **Litho.** ***Perf. 12½***

426	A35	5m black & red	*15*
427	A35	10m black & green	*15*
428	A35	20m black & blue	*22*
429	A35	25m black & yellow	*28*
431	A35	40m black & brown	*45*
		Nos. 426-431 (5)	*1.25*

400 м.

No. 351 Surcharged

25q.

1994 **Litho.** **Unwmk.** ***Perf. 12***

435	A21	400m on 25g multi	*85*

SEMI-POSTAL STAMPS

Carrying Food to Sufferers — SP1

1922 **Unwmk.** ***Imperf.***

B1	SP1	500r blue & pale blue	40	75

For overprint and surcharge see Nos. 42, 305.

Widow and Orphans — SP2

1922

B2	SP2	1000r brown & bister	50	1.25

Counterfeits exist.
For overprint and surcharge see Nos. 44, 306.

OCCUPATION AZIRBAYEDJAN

Russian stamps of 1909-18 were privately overprinted as above in red, blue or black by a group of Entente officers working with Russian soldiers returning from Persia. Azerbaijan was not occupied by the Allies. There is evidence that existing covers (some seemingly postmarked at Baku, dated Oct. 19, 1917, and at Tabriz, Russian Consulate, Apr. 25, 1917) are fakes.

AZORES

LOCATION — Group of islands in the North Atlantic Ocean, due west of Portugal
GOVT. — Integral part of Portugal, former colony
AREA — 922 sq. mi.
POP. — 253,935 (1930)
CAPITAL — Ponta Delgada

Azores stamps were supplanted by those of Portugal in 1931.

1000 Reis = 1 Milreis
100 Centavos = 1 Escudo (1912)

Values of early Azores stamps vary according to condition. Quotations for Nos. 1-37 are for fine copies. Very fine to superb specimens sell at much higher prices, and inferior or poor copies sell at reduced prices, depending on the condition of the individual specimen.

See Portugal for other recent issues.

Stamps of Portugal Overprinted in Black or Carmine

AÇORES
a

A second type of this overprint has a broad "O" and open "S."

1868 **Unwmk.** ***Imperf.***

1	A14	5r black	*1,800.*	*900.00*
2	A14	10r yellow	*4,250.*	*1,800.*
3	A14	20r bister	100.00	40.00
4	A14	50r green	100.00	40.00
5	A14	80r orange	100.00	40.00
6	A14	100r lilac	100.00	40.00

The reprints are on thick chalky white wove paper, ungummed, and on thin ivory paper with shiny white gum. Value $20 each.

1868-70 ***Perf. 12½***

5 REIS:
Type I- The "5" at the right is 1mm from end of label.
Type II- The "5" is 1½mm from end of label.

7	A14	5r blk (C)	20.00	17.50
8	A14	10r yellow	42.50	35.00
a.		Inverted overprint	*110.00*	*110.00*
9	A14	20r bister	35.00	27.50
10	A14	25r rose	32.50	4.25
a.		Inverted overprint	*80.00*	*80.00*
11	A14	50r green	110.00	55.00
12	A14	80r orange	110.00	55.00
13	A14	100r lilac	110.00	55.00
14	A14	120r blue	62.50	42.50
15	A14	240r violet	275.00	150.00

The reprints are on thick chalky white paper ungummed, perf 13½, and on thin ivory paper with shiny white gum, perf 13½. Value $10 each.

1871-75 ***Perf. 12½, 13½***

21	A15	5r blk (C)	6.75	4.75
a.		Inverted overprint	*60.00*	*60.00*
23	A15	10r yellow	11.00	8.00
a.		Inverted overprint	*60.00*	*60.00*
24	A15	20r bister	10.00	8.00
25	A15	25r rose	8.00	1.75
a.		Inverted overprint	*60.00*	*60.00*
b.		Double overprint	*60.00*	
c.		Perf. 14	*125.00*	*37.50*
d.		Dbl. impression of stamp		
26	A15	50r green	35.00	12.00
27	A15	80r orange	50.00	30.00
28	A15	100r lilac	37.50	18.00
a.		Perf. 14	*125.00*	*72.50*
29	A15	120r blue	82.50	47.50
a.		Inverted overprint	*165.00*	*165.00*
30	A15	240r violet	525.00	225.00

Nos. 21-29 exist with overprint "b."

The reprints are of type "b." They are on thick chalky white paper ungummed, perf 13½, and also on thin white paper with shiny white gum and perforated 13½.

Overprinted in Black

AÇORES
b

1875-80

15 REIS:
Type I - The figures of value, 1 and 5, at the right in upper label are close together.
Type II - The figures of value at the right in upper label are spaced.

31	A15	10r bl grn	85.00	60.00
32	A15	10r yel grn	42.50	30.00
33	A15	15r lil brn	7.25	6.25
a.		Inverted overprint	*60.00*	*60.00*

34	A15	50r blue	65.00	30.00
35	A15	150r blue	90.00	65.00
36	A15	150r yellow	110.00	80.00
37	A15	300r violet	30.00	24.00

The reprints have the same papers, gum and perforations as those of the preceding issue.

Black Overprint

1880 ***Perf. 11½, 12½ and 13½***

38	A17	25r gray	50.00	10.00
39	A18	25r red lilac	12.00	4.00
a.		25r gray	12.00	4.00
b.		Double overprint		

Overprinted in Carmine or Black

1881-82

40	A16	5r black (C)	8.00	3.50
41	A23	25r brown ('82)	10.50	2.25
a.		Double overprint		
42	A19	50r blue	65.00	12.00
		Nos. 40-42 (3)	83.50	17.75

Reprints of Nos. 38, 39, 39a, 40 and 42 have the same papers, gum and perforations as those of preceding issues.

Overprinted in Red or Black

AÇORES
c

1882-85

15, 20 REIS

Type I - The figures of value are some distance apart and close to the end of the label.

Type II - The figures are closer together and farther from the end of the label. On the 15 reis this is particularly apparent in the upper right figures.

43	A16	5r blk (R)	7.50	4.50
44	A21	5r slate	3.50	1.00
a.		Double overprint		
c.		Inverted overprint		
45	A15	10r green	30.00	24.00
a.		Inverted overprint		
46	A22	10r green	7.25	3.25
a.		Double overprint		
47	A15	15r lil brn	18.00	10.50
b.		Inverted overprint		
48	A15	20r bister	37.50	27.50
a.		Inverted overprint		
49	A15	20r carmine	50.00	35.00
a.		Double overprint		
50	A23	25r brown	10.00	1.75
51	A15	50r blue	*650.00*	*550.00*
52	A24	50r blue	10.50	1.75
a.		Double overprint		
53	A15	80r yellow	20.00	10.00
a.		80r orange	30.00	24.00
b.		Double overprint		
54	A15	100r lilac	18.00	12.00
55	A15	150r blue	*500.00*	*350.00*
56	A15	150r yellow	20.00	12.00
57	A15	300r violet	30.00	24.00

Reprints of the 1882-85 issues have the same papers, gum and perforations as those of preceding issues.

Red Overprint

58	A21	5r slate	7.50	1.75
59	A24a	500r black	90.00	72.50
60	A15	1000r black	45.00	35.00

1887 **Black Overprint**

61	A25	20r pink	9.50	4.75
a.		Inverted overprint		
b.		Double overprint		
62	A26	25r lilac rose	9.50	1.00
a.		Inverted overprint		
b.		Double ovpt., one invtd.		
63	A26	25r red violet	9.50	1.00
a.		Double overprint		
64	A24a	500r red violet	67.50	35.00
a.		Perf. 13½	100.00	72.50
		Nos. 61-64 (4)	96.00	41.75

Nos. 58-64 inclusive have been reprinted on thin white paper with shiny white gum and perforated 13½.

Prince Henry the Navigator Issue

Portugal Nos. 97-109 Overprinted AÇORES

1894, Mar. 4 ***Perf. 14***

65	A46	5r org yel	1.75	1.25
a.		Inverted overprint	20.00	13.00
66	A46	10r vio rose	1.75	1.25
a.		Double overprint	25.00	
b.		Inverted overprint	20.00	13.00
67	A46	15r brown	2.25	1.25
68	A46	20r violet	2.25	1.25
a.		Double overprint		20.00
69	A47	25r green	2.25	1.25
a.		Double overprint	20.00	20.00
b.		Inverted overprint	20.00	20.00
70	A47	50r blue	4.75	2.50
71	A47	75r dp car	10.00	4.75
72	A47	80r yel grn	12.00	4.75
73	A47	100r lt brn, *pale buff*	10.00	3.50
a.		Double overprint	35.00	
74	A48	150r lt car, *pale rose*	18.00	8.75
75	A48	300r dk bl, *sal buff*	24.00	10.50
76	A48	500r brn vio, *pale lil*	40.00	16.00
77	A48	1000r gray blk, *yelsh*	70.00	30.00
a.		Double overprint		
		Nos. 65-77 (13)	199.00	87.00

St. Anthony of Padua Issue

Portugal Nos. 132-146 Overprinted in Red or Black AÇORES

1895, June 13 ***Perf. 12***

78	A50	2½r black (R)	1.75	1.50
79	A51	5r brown yel	3.50	1.50
80	A51	10r red lilac	3.50	2.50
81	A51	15r red brown	4.25	2.50
82	A51	20r gray lilac	4.25	2.50
83	A51	25r green & vio	3.50	2.75
84	A52	50r blue & brn	14.00	7.00
85	A52	75r rose & brn	21.00	18.00
86	A52	80r lt green & brn	32.50	22.50
87	A52	100r choc & blk	40.00	18.00
88	A53	150r vio rose & bis	60.00	50.00
89	A53	200r blue & bis	75.00	42.50
90	A53	300r slate & bis	100.00	52.50
91	A53	500r vio brn & grn	150.00	85.00
92	A53	1000r violet & grn	250.00	150.00
		Nos. 78-92 (15)	763.25	458.75

7th cent. of the birth of Saint Anthony of Padua.

Vasco da Gama Issue
Common Design Types

1898, Apr. 1 ***Perf. 14, 15***

93	CD20	2½r blue grn	1.00	60
94	CD21	5r red	1.10	70
95	CD22	10r gray lilac	2.00	1.25
96	CD23	25r yel green	1.75	70
97	CD24	50r dk blue	3.50	2.75
98	CD25	75r violet brn	8.00	4.75
99	CD26	100r bister brn	8.00	4.50
100	CD27	150r bister	12.00	6.25
		Nos. 93-100 (8)	37.35	21.50

For overprints and surcharges see Nos. 141-148.

King Carlos — A28

King Manuel II — A29

1906 **Typo.** ***Perf. 11½x12***

101	A28	2½r gray	18	15
a.		Inverted overprint	15.00	15.00
102	A28	5r orange yel	18	15
a.		Inverted overprint	15.00	15.00
103	A28	10r yellow grn	18	15
104	A28	20r gray vio	40	20
105	A28	25r carmine	20	15
106	A28	50r ultra	3.00	2.00
107	A28	75r brown, *straw*	65	*60*
108	A28	100r dk blue, *bl*	65	*80*
109	A28	200r red lilac, *pnksh*	1.25	*1.00*
110	A28	300r dk blue, *rose*	2.00	*1.65*
111	A28	500r black, *blue*	2.75	1.25
		Nos. 101-111 (11)	11.44	8.10

"Acores" and letters and figures in the corners are in red on the 2½, 10, 20, 75 and 500r and in black on the other values.

1910, Apr. 1 ***Perf. 14x15***

112	A29	2½r violet	20	15
113	A29	5r black	20	18
114	A29	10r dk green	28	24
115	A29	15r lilac brn	48	45
116	A29	20r carmine	45	40
117	A29	25r violet brn	20	15
a.		Perf. 11½	1.25	80
118	A29	50r blue	1.00	60
119	A29	75r bister brn	1.75	1.25
120	A29	80r slate	1.75	1.25
121	A29	100r brown, *lt grn*	2.25	1.75
122	A29	200r green, *sal*	2.25	1.75
123	A29	300r black, *blue*	3.50	2.50
124	A29	500r olive & brown	7.00	7.00
125	A29	1000r blue & black	12.00	12.00
		Nos. 112-125 (14)	33.31	29.67

The errors of color 10r black, 15r dark green, 25r black and 50r carmine are considered to be proofs.

Stamps of 1910 Overprinted in Carmine or Green REPUBLICA

1910

126	A29	2½r violet	15	15
a.		Inverted overprint	9.00	9.00
127	A29	5r black	20	15
a.		Inverted overprint	9.00	9.00
128	A29	10r dk green	20	16
a.		Inverted overprint	9.00	9.00
129	A29	15r lilac brn	80	65
a.		Inverted overprint	9.00	9.00
130	A29	20r carmine (G)	1.00	80
a.		Inverted overprint	16.00	16.00
b.		Double overprint	16.00	16.00
131	A29	25r violet brn	22	15
a.		Perf. 11½	40.00	30.00
132	A29	50r blue	60	52
133	A29	75r bister brn	35	20
a.		Double overprint	9.00	9.00
134	A29	80r slate	45	32
135	A29	100r brown, *grn*	40	24
136	A29	200r green, *sal*	60	*60*
137	A29	300r black, *blue*	1.10	1.10
138	A29	500r olive & brn	1.25	*1.75*
139	A29	1000r blue & blk	3.50	*4.00*
		Nos. 126-139 (14)	10.82	*10.79*

Vasco da Gama Issue Overprinted or Surcharged in Black:

REPUBLICA
d

REPUBLICA **REIS 15 REIS**
e

REPUBLICA **1$000**
f

1911 ***Perf. 14, 15***

141	CD20(d)	2½r blue green	35	28
142	CD21(e)	15r on 5r red	20	20
143	CD23(d)	25r yellow grn	40	25
144	CD24(d)	50r dk blue	1.00	70
145	CD25(d)	75r violet brn	60	60
146	CD27(e)	80r on 150r bister	60	60
147	CD26(d)	100r yellow brn	60	60
a.		Double surcharge	35.00	35.00
148	CD22(f)	1000r on 10r lilac	8.50	6.50
		Nos. 141-148 (8)	12.25	9.73

Postage Due Stamps of Portugal Overprinted or Surcharged in Black "ACORES" and

REPUBLICA

REPUBLICA **Rs 300 Rs**

1911 ***Perf. 12***

149	D1	5r black	75	35
150	D1	10r magenta	1.75	1.25
a.		"Açores" double	20.00	20.00
151	D1	20r orange	2.00	2.00
152	D1	200r brn, *buff*	7.25	6.00
a.		"Açores" inverted		
153	D1	300r on 50r slate	7.25	6.00
154	D1	500r on 100r car, *pink*	7.25	6.00
		Nos. 149-154 (6)	26.25	21.60

Ceres — A30

Ceres Issue of Portugal Overprinted "ACORES" in Black or Carmine
With Imprint

1912-31 ***Perf. 12x11½, 15x14***

155	A30	¼c olive brown	15	15
a.		Inverted overprint	9.00	
156	A30	½c black (C)	15	15
157	A30	1c deep green	55	32
a.		Inverted overprint	9.00	
158	A30	1c deep brown ('18)	15	15
a.		Inverted overprint		
159	A30	1½c choc ('13)	48	40
a.		Inverted overprint	9.00	
160	A30	1½c deep green ('18)	35	15
a.		Inverted overprint		
161	A30	2c carmine	28	20
a.		Inverted overprint	14.00	
162	A30	2c orange ('18)	16	15
a.		Inverted overprint	18.00	
163	A30	2½c violet	24	15
164	A30	3c rose ('18)	18	15
165	A30	3c dull ultra ('25)	18	15
166	A30	3½c lt green ('18)	30	15
167	A30	4c lt green ('19)	15	15
168	A30	4c orange ('30)	26	20
169	A30	5c dp blue	26	15
170	A30	5c yellow brn ('18)	26	18
171	A30	5c olive brn ('23)	15	15
172	A30	5c black brn ('30)	2.75	2.50
173	A30	6c dull rose ('20)	20	15
174	A30	6c choc ('25)	20	15
175	A30	6c red brn ('31)	35	*80*
176	A30	7½c yel brn	4.75	1.25
177	A30	7½c deep blue ('18)	60	40
178	A30	8c slate ('13)	55	20
179	A30	8c blue grn ('22)	24	20
180	A30	8c orange ('25)	48	24
181	A30	10c orange brown	28	15
182	A30	12c blue gray ('20)	1.00	70
183	A30	12c deep green ('22)	45	32
184	A30	13½c chlky bl ('20)	1.00	*3.25*
185	A30	14c dk bl, *yel* ('20)	3.25	*6.00*
186	A30	15c plum ('13)	60	60
187	A30	15c blk (R) ('23)	40	40
188	A30	16c brt ultra ('24)	80	40
189	A30	16c dp bl ('30)	1.25	*1.50*
190	A30	20c vio brn, *grn* ('13)	8.00	3.25
191	A30	20c choc ('20)	60	20
192	A30	20c deep green ('23)	80	80
a.		Double overprint		
193	A30	20c gray ('24)	55	20
194	A30	24c grnsh bl ('21)	55	40
195	A30	25c salmon ('23)	28	18
196	A30	30c brn, *pink* ('13)	40.00	22.50
197	A30	30c brn, *yel* ('19)	2.25	2.25
198	A30	30c gray brn ('21)	80	65
199	A30	32c dp green ('25)	1.40	1.00
200	A30	36c red ('21)	40	20
201	A30	40c dp blue ('23)	40	40
202	A30	40c black brn ('24)	20	15
203	A30	40c brt green ('30)	1.40	40
204	A30	48c brt rose ('24)	1.40	1.00
205	A30	48c dull pink ('31)	3.00	3.00
206	A30	50c org, *sal* ('13)	5.00	1.00
207	A30	50c yellow ('23)	1.25	1.00
208	A30	50c bister ('30)	2.50	1.75
209	A30	50c red brn ('31)	2.00	1.40
210	A30	60c blue ('21)	90	70
211	A30	64c pale ultra ('24)	1.40	1.00
212	A30	64c brown rose ('31)	22.50	16.00
213	A30	75c dull rose ('23)	4.00	4.00
214	A30	75c car rose ('30)	1.50	1.25
215	A30	80c dull rose ('21)	1.25	60
216	A30	80c violet ('24)	1.25	80
217	A30	80c dk green ('31)	1.50	1.25
218	A30	90c chlky bl ('21)	1.25	65
219	A30	96c dp rose ('26)	8.00	4.50
220	A30	1e dp grn, *bl*	4.50	1.50
221	A30	1e violet ('21)	1.25	65
222	A30	1e gray vio ('24)	1.50	1.00
223	A30	1e brn lake ('30)	12.00	10.00
224	A30	1.10e yel brn ('21)	1.25	1.25
225	A30	1.20e yel grn ('21)	1.40	1.00
226	A30	1.20e buff ('24)	3.50	1.75
227	A30	1.25e dk blue ('30)	1.40	65
228	A30	1.50e blk vio ('23)	2.75	1.75
229	A30	1.50e lilac ('25)	2.75	1.75
230	A30	1.60e dp bl ('25)	2.75	1.75
231	A30	2e slate grn ('21)	4.00	2.00
232	A30	2.40e apple grn ('26)	30.00	17.00
233	A30	3e lilac pink ('26)	30.00	17.00
234	A30	3.20e gray grn ('25)	10.00	4.50
235	A30	5e emerald ('24)	11.00	5.50
236	A30	10e pink ('24)	22.50	10.00
237	A30	20e pale turq ('25)	75.00	45.00
		Nos. 155-237 (83)	357.28	218.84

For same overprint on surcharged stamps see Nos. 300-306. For same design without imprint see Nos. 307-313.

Castello-Branco Issue

Stamps of Portugal, 1925, Overprinted in Black or Red AÇORES

1925, Mar. 29 ***Perf. 12½***

238	A73	2c orange	18	*50*
239	A73	3c green	18	*50*
240	A73	4c ultra (R)	18	*50*
241	A73	5c scarlet	18	*50*
242	A74	10c pale blue	16	*50*
243	A74	16c red orange	24	*75*
244	A75	25c car rose	24	*75*
245	A74	32c green	55	*85*
246	A75	40c grn & blk (R)	24	*75*
247	A74	48c red brn	1.10	*2.25*
248	A76	50c blue green	80	*2.25*
249	A76	64c orange brn	1.40	*2.25*
250	A76	75c gray blk (R)	1.00	*3.00*
251	A75	80c brown	1.00	*3.00*
252	A76	96c car rose	1.25	*3.00*
253	A77	1.50e dk bl, *bl* (R)	1.25	*2.25*
254	A75	1.60e indigo (R)	1.25	*2.25*
255	A77	2e dk grn, *grn* (R)	1.50	*3.00*
256	A77	2.40e red, *org*	2.00	*3.25*
257	A77	3.20e blk, *grn* (R)	3.00	*5.00*
		Nos. 238-257 (20)	17.70	*37.10*

First Independence Issue

Stamps of Portugal, 1926, Overprinted in Red **AÇÔRES**

1926, Aug. 13 *Perf. 14, 14½*

Center in Black

258	A79	2c orange	24	*70*
259	A80	3c ultra	24	*70*
260	A79	4c yellow grn	24	*70*
261	A80	5c black brn	24	*70*
262	A79	6c ocher	24	*70*
263	A80	15c dk green	48	*90*
264	A81	20c dull violet	48	*90*
265	A82	25c scarlet	48	*90*
266	A81	32c deep green	48	*90*
267	A82	40c yellow brn	48	*90*
268	A82	50c olive bis	1.25	*1.90*
269	A82	75c red brown	1.25	*1.90*
270	A83	1e black violet	1.75	*3.25*
271	A84	4.50e olive green	2.00	*6.75*
		Nos. 258-271 (14)	9.85	*21.80*

The use of these stamps instead of those of the regular issue was obligatory on Aug. 13th and 14th, Nov. 30th and Dec. 1st, 1926.

Second Independence Issue

Same Overprint on Stamps of Portugal, 1927, in Red

1927, Nov. 29

Center in Black

272	A86	2c lt brown	26	*70*
273	A87	3c ultra	26	*70*
274	A86	4c orange	26	*70*
275	A88	5c dk brown	26	*70*
276	A89	6c orange brn	26	*70*
277	A87	15c black brn	26	*70*
278	A86	25c gray	1.00	*3.00*
279	A89	32c blue grn	1.00	*3.00*
280	A90	40c yellow grn	1.00	*3.00*
281	A90	96c red	2.50	*5.75*
282	A88	1.60e myrtle grn	2.50	*5.75*
283	A91	4.50e bister	4.50	*8.00*
		Nos. 272-283 (12)	14.06	*32.70*

Third Independence Issue

Same Overprint on Stamps of Portugal, 1928, in Red

1928, Nov. 27

Center in Black

284	A93	2c lt blue	26	*70*
285	A94	3c lt green	26	*70*
286	A95	4c lake	26	*70*
287	A96	5c olive grn	26	*70*
288	A97	6c orange brn	26	*70*
289	A94	15c slate	40	*1.25*
290	A95	16c dk violet	65	*2.25*
291	A93	25c ultra	65	*2.00*
292	A97	32c dk green	65	*2.00*
293	A96	40c olive brn	65	*2.00*
294	A95	50c red orange	1.25	*3.00*
295	A94	80c lt gray	1.25	*3.00*
296	A97	96c carmine	1.75	*6.00*
297	A96	1e claret	1.75	*6.00*
298	A93	1.60e dk blue	1.75	*6.00*
299	A98	4.50e yellow	4.00	*8.50*
		Nos. 284-299 (16)	16.05	*45.50*

A31

A32

1929-30 *Perf. 12x11½, 15x14*

300	A31	4c on 25c pink ('30)	32	32
301	A31	4c on 60c dp blue	32	32
302	A31	10c on 25c pink	80	40
303	A31	12c on 25c pink	80	40
304	A31	15c on 25c pink	60	60
305	A31	20c on 25c pink	80	65
306	A31	40c on 1.10e yel brn	2.75	2.25
		Nos. 300-306 (7)	6.39	4.94

Black or Red Overprint

1930 *Perf. 14*

Without Imprint at Foot

307	A32	4c orange	40	40
308	A32	5c dp brown	1.50	1.00
309	A32	10c vermilion	80	55
310	A32	15c black (R)	80	55
311	A32	40c brt green	80	55
312	A32	80c violet	11.00	8.75
313	A32	1.60e dk blue	1.75	1.00
		Nos. 307-313 (7)	17.05	12.80

POSTAGE DUE STAMPS

D2

D3

Portugal Nos. J7-J13 Overprinted in Black

1904 **Unwmk.** *Perf. 12*

J1	D2	5r brown	40	60
J2	D2	10r orange	40	60
J3	D2	20r lilac	80	1.10
J4	D2	30r gray green	85	1.10
	a.	Double overprint		
J5	D2	40r gray violet	1.75	1.75
J6	D2	50r carmine	2.75	3.00
J7	D2	100r dull blue	4.25	4.50
		Nos. J1-J7 (7)	11.20	12.65

Same Overprinted in Carmine or Green (Portugal Nos. J14-J20) **REPUBLICA**

1911

J8	D2	5r brown	20	20
J9	D2	10r orange	20	20
J10	D2	20r lilac	20	20
J11	D2	30r gray green	20	20
J12	D2	40r gray violet	40	40
J13	D2	50r carmine (G)	2.00	2.00
J14	D2	100r dull blue	1.25	1.25
		Nos. J8-J14 (7)	4.45	4.45

Portugal Nos. J21-J27 Overprinted in Black

1918

J15	D3	½c brown	15	15
	a.	Inverted overprint	4.00	4.00
	b.	Double overprint	4.00	4.00
J16	D3	1c orange	15	15
	a.	Inverted overprint	4.00	4.00
	b.	Double overprint	4.00	4.00
J17	D3	2c red lilac	15	15
	a.	Inverted overprint	4.00	4.00
	b.	Double overprint	4.00	4.00
J18	D3	3c green	15	15
	a.	Inverted overprint	4.00	4.00
	b.	Double overprint	4.00	4.00
J19	D3	4c gray	15	15
	a.	Inverted overprint	4.00	4.00
	b.	Double overprint	4.00	4.00
J20	D3	5c rose	15	15
	b.	Double overprint	4.00	4.00
J21	D3	10c dark blue	20	20
		Nos. J15-J21 (7)	1.10	1.10

Stamps and Type of Portugal Postage Dues, 1921-27, Overprinted in Black

1922-24 *Perf. 11½x12*

J30	D3	½c gray green ('23)	15	15
J31	D3	1c gray green ('23)	15	15
J32	D3	2c gray green ('23)	15	15
J33	D3	3c gray green ('24)	32	32
J34	D3	8c gray green ('24)	20	20
J35	D3	10c gray green ('24)	20	20
J36	D3	12c gray green ('24)	20	20
J37	D3	16c gray green ('24)	20	20
J38	D3	20c gray green	60	48
J39	D3	24c gray green	20	20
J40	D3	32c gray green ('24)	20	20
J41	D3	36c gray green	20	20
J42	D3	40c gray green ('24)	48	48
J43	D3	48c gray green ('24)	28	28
J44	D3	50c gray green	60	48
J45	D3	60c gray green	60	32
J46	D3	72c gray green	60	32
J47	D3	80c gray green ('24)	1.75	1.40
J48	D3	1.20e gray green	1.75	1.40
		Nos. J30-J48 (19)	8.83	7.33

NEWSPAPER STAMPS

Newspaper Stamps of Portugal, Nos. P1, P1a, Overprinted Types b & c in Black or Red and:

N3

Perf. 11½, 12½ and 13½

1876-88 **Unwmk.**

P1	N1	2½r (a) olive	4.50	1.75
	a.	Inverted overprint		
P2	N1	2½r (b) olive ('82)	3.25	1.00
	a.	Inverted overprint		
	b.	Double overprint		
P3	N3	2r black ('85)	1.50	1.00
	a.	Inverted overprint		
	b.	Double overprint, one inverted		
P4	N1	2½r (b) bister ('82)	3.25	80
	a.	Double overprint		
P5	N3	2r black (R) ('88)	5.25	3.50
		Nos. P1-P5 (5)	17.75	8.05

Reprints of the newspaper stamps have the same papers, gum and perforations as reprints of the regular issues. Value $2 each.

PARCEL POST STAMPS

Portugal Nos. Q1-Q17 Overprinted Like Nos. 155-237 in Black or Red

1921-22 **Unwmk.** *Perf. 12*

Q1	PP1	1c lilac brown	15	15
	a.	Inverted overprint	4.00	4.00
Q2	PP1	2c orange	15	15
	a.	Inverted overprint	4.00	4.00
Q3	PP1	5c light brown	15	15
	a.	Inverted overprint	5.00	5.00
	b.	Double overprint	5.00	5.00
Q4	PP1	10c red brown	15	24
	a.	Inverted overprint	5.00	5.00
	b.	Double overprint	5.00	5.00
Q5	PP1	20c gray blue	28	24
	a.	Inverted overprint	5.00	5.00
	b.	Double overprint	5.00	5.00
Q6	PP1	40c carmine	28	28
	a.	Double overprint	6.50	6.50
Q7	PP1	50c black (R)	55	55
Q8	PP1	60c dark blue (R)	55	55
Q9	PP1	70c gray brown	1.40	1.25
	a.	Double overprint		
Q10	PP1	80c ultra	1.40	1.25
Q11	PP1	90c light violet	1.40	1.25
Q12	PP1	1e light green	1.75	1.25
Q13	PP1	2e pale lilac	2.50	2.50
Q14	PP1	3e olive	3.00	3.25
Q15	PP1	4e ultra	3.50	5.00
Q16	PP1	5e gray	3.50	5.00
Q17	PP1	10e chocolate	15.00	13.00
		Nos. Q1-Q17 (17)	35.71	36.06

POSTAL TAX STAMPS

These stamps represent a special fee for the delivery of postal matter on certain days in the year. The money derived from their sale is applied to works of public charity.

Nos. 114 and 157 Overprinted in Carmine **ASSISTENCIA**

1911-13 **Unwmk.** *Perf. 14x15*

RA1	A29	10r dark green	55	40

The 20r of this type was for use on telegrams.

Perf. 15x14

RA2	A30	1c deep green	1.25	1.25

The 2c of this type was for use on telegrams.

Postal Tax Stamp of Portugal, No. RA4, Overprinted Like Nos. 155-237 in Black

1915 *Perf. 12*

RA3	PT2	1c carmine	15	15

The 2c of this type was for use on telegrams.

Postal Tax Stamp of 1915 Surcharged **15 ctvs.**

1924

RA4	PT1	15c on 1c rose	75	*1.25*

Comrades of the Great War Issue

Postal Tax Stamps of Portugal, 1925, Overprinted **AÇORES**

1925, Apr. 8 *Perf. 11*

RA5	PT3	10c brown	38	28
RA6	PT3	10c green	38	28
RA7	PT3	10c rose	38	28
RA8	PT3	10c ultra	38	28
		Nos. RA5-RA8 (4)	1.52	1.12

The use of Nos. RA5-RA11 in addition to the regular postage was compulsory on certain days. If the tax represented by these stamps was not prepaid, it was collected by means of Postal Tax Due Stamps.

In 1934-45, #RA5-RA11, RAJ1-RAJ4 were used for regular postage in Portugal.

Pombal Issue

Common Design Types

1925 *Perf. 12½*

RA9	CD28	20c dp green & black	35	28
RA10	CD29	20c dp green & black	35	28
RA11	CD30	20c dp green & black	35	28
		Nos. RA9-RA11 (3)	1.05	84

POSTAL TAX DUE STAMPS

Postal Tax Due Stamp of Portugal Overprinted like Nos. RA5-RA8

1925, Apr. 8 **Unwmk.** *Perf. 11x11½*

RAJ1	PTD1	20c brown orange	40	40

See note after No. RA8.

Pombal Issue

Common Design Types

1925, May 8 *Perf. 12½*

RAJ2	CD31	40c dp green & black	60	*4.00*
RAJ3	CD32	40c dp green & black	60	*4.00*
RAJ4	CD33	40c dp green & black	60	*4.00*
		Nos. RAJ2-RAJ4 (3)	1.80	

See note after No. RA8.

See Portugal for later issues.

BELARUS

(Byelorussia)

(White Russia)

LOCATION — Eastern Europe, bounded by Russia, Latvia, Lithuania and Poland

GOVT. — Independent republic, member of the Commonwealth of Independent States

AREA — 80,200 sq. mi.

POP. — 10,200,000 (1989)

CAPITAL — Minsk

With the breakup of the Soviet Union on Dec. 26, 1991, Belarus and ten former Soviet republics established the Commonwealth of Independent States.

100 Kopecks = 1 Ruble

Catalogue values for all unused stamps in this country are for Never Hinged items.

Five denominations, perf and imperf, of this design produced in 1920 were not put in use and were probably propaganda labels. They are common.

Cross of Ephrosinia of Polotsk — A1

1992, Mar. 20 **Litho.** *Perf. 12x12½*

1	A1	1r multicolored		*40*

R.R. Schurma (1892-1978), Composer — A2

1992, Apr. 10 Photo. *Perf. 12x11½*

2	A2	20k blue & black	*60*

Arms of Polotsk — A3

Designs: No. 13, Stag jumping fence. No. 14, Man's head, sword.

1992-94 Photo. *Perf. 12x11½*

11	A3	2r shown	*60*

Perf. 12x12½

12	A3	25r Minsk	*15*
13	A3	700r Grodno	*22*
14	A3	700r Vitebsk	*22*
		Nos. 11-14 (4)	*1.19*

Issued: 2r, 6/9/92; 25r, 11/11/93; #13, 14, 10/17/94.

This is an expanding set. Numbers will change if necessary.

National Symbols — A4

Designs: No. 15, Natl. arms. No. 16, Map, flag.

1992, Aug. 31 Litho. *Perf. 12x12½*

15	A4	5r black, red & yellow	*38*
16	A4	5r multicolored	*38*

For surcharges see Nos. 55-58, 61-64.

1000—ГОДДЗЕ БЕЛАРУСКАЙ ПРАВАСЛАЎНАЙ ЦАРКВЫ

No. 1 Overprinted

Cross of Ephrosinia of Polotsk — A5

A5 illustration reduced.

1992, Sept. 25 Litho. *Perf. 12x12½*

17	A1	1r on #1 multi	*24*

Souvenir Sheet

Perf. 12

18	A5	5r multicolored	*38*

Orthodox Church in Belarus, 1000th anniv.

No. 18, imperf, was issued Feb. 15, 1993.

Orthodox Church in Belarus, 1000th anniv. For surcharges see Nos. 59-60, 65-66.

Buildings A6

Designs: No. 19, Church of Boris Gleb, Grodno, 12th cent. No. 20, World Castle, 16th cent. No. 21, Nyasvizh Castle, 16th-19th cent. No. 22, Kamyanets Tower, 12th-13th cent, vert. No. 23, Church of Ephrosinia of Polotsk, 12th cent., vert. No. 24, Calvinist Church, Zaslaw, 16th cent., vert.

1992, Oct. 15 Litho. *Perf. 12*

19	A6	2r multicolored	*15*
20	A6	2r multicolored	*15*
21	A6	2r multicolored	*15*
22	A6	2r multicolored	*15*
23	A6	2r multicolored	*15*
24	A6	2r multicolored	*15*
		Set value	*70*

Centuries of construction are in Roman numerals.

Natl. Arms — A7

1992 Litho. *Perf. 12x12½*

27	A7	30k light blue	*15*
29	A7	45k olive green	*15*
30	A7	50k green	*15*
32	A7	1r brown	*15*
33	A7	2r green	*16*
34	A7	3r green	*24*
35	A7	5r blue	*15*
36	A7	10r green	*80*
37	A7	15r violet	*25*
39	A7	25r yellow green	*42*
40	A7	50r bright pink	*28*
40A	A7	100r henna brown	*55*
40B	A7	150r plum	*85*
		Nos. 27-40B (13)	*4.30*

Issued: 30k, 45k, 50k, Nov. 10; 50r, 100r, 150r, June 16, 1993; others, 1992.

This is an expanding set. Numbers may change.

Ceramics — A8

Designs: No. 41, Pitcher and bowl. No. 42, Four pieces on tree branches. No. 43, Two large pitchers. No. 44, One large pitcher.

1992 Litho. *Perf. 11½*

41	A8	1r multicolored	*15*
42	A8	1r multicolored	*15*
43	A8	1r multicolored	*15*
44	A8	1r multicolored	*15*
		Set value	*50*

M. I. Garetzky (1893-1938), Writer — A9

1993, June 22 Photo. *Perf. 12x11½*

45	A9	50r magenta	*30*

Straw Figures — A10

Designs: 5r, Chickens. 10r, Child, mother, vert. 15r, Woman, vert. 25r, Man with scythe, woman with rake, vert.

Perf. 12x11½, 11½x12

1993, Apr. 22 Litho.

47	A10	5r multicolored	*18*
48	A10	10r multicolored	*35*
49	A10	15r multicolored	*55*
50	A10	25r multicolored	*90*
		Nos. 47-50 (4)	*1.98*

First World Congress of White Russians — A11

1993, July 8 Litho. *Perf. 12*

51	A11	50r multicolored	*3.50*

Europa — A12

Paintings by Chagall: No. 52, Promenade, vert. No. 53, Man Over Vitebsk. 2500r, Allegory.

1993, Oct. 12 Litho. *Perf. 14*

52	A12	1500r multicolored	*3.00*
53	A12	1500r multicolored	*3.00*
a.		Pair, #52-53	*6.00*

Souvenir Sheet

54	A12	2500r multicolored	*17.50*

Nos. 15-16, 18 Surcharged

XVII ЗІМОВЫЯ
АЛІМПІЙСКІЯ
ГУЛЬНІ
ЛІЛЕХАМЕР,
НАРВЕГІЯ, 1994

1500
a

WINTER
PRE-OLYMPICS
GAMES
LILLEHAMMER,
NORWAY

1500
b

Size and location of surcharge varies.

1993, Oct. 15 Litho. *Perf. 12x12½*

55	A4(a)	1500r on 5r #15	*3.50*
56	A4(b)	1500r on 5r #15	*3.50*
a.		Pair, #55-56	*7.00*
57	A4(a)	1500r on 5r #16	*3.50*
58	A4(b)	1500r on 5r #16	*3.50*
a.		Pair, #57-58	*7.00*
		Nos. 55-58 (4)	*14.00*

Souvenir Sheets

Perf. 12

59	A5(a)	1500r on 5r #18	*3.50*
60	A5(b)	1500r on 5r #18	*3.50*

No. 59 exists imperf.

Nos. 15-16, 18 Surcharged

ЧЭМПІЯНАТ СВЕТУ
ПА ФУТБОЛУ,
ЗША. 1994

1500
c

WORLD CUP
USA **94**

1500
d

Size and location of surcharge varies.

1993, Oct. 15 Litho. *Perf. 12x12½*

61	A4(c)	1500r on 5r #15	*3.50*
62	A4(d)	1500r on 5r #15	*3.50*
a.		Pair, #61-62	*7.00*
63	A4(c)	1500r on 5r #16	*3.50*
64	A4(d)	1500r on 5r #16	*3.50*
a.		Pair, #63-64	*7.00*
		Nos. 61-64 (4)	*14.00*

Souvenir Sheets

Perf. 12

65	A5(c)	1500r on 5r #18	*3.50*
66	A5(d)	1500r on 5r #18	*3.50*

Stansilavski Church A13

1993, Nov. 24 Litho. *Perf. 12*

67	A13	150r multicolored	*50*

Famous People — A14

Designs: 50r, Kastus Kalinovsky, led 1863 independence movement. No. 69, Prince Rogvold of Polotsk, map of Polotsk. No. 70, Princess Rogneda, daughter of Rogvold, fortress. 100r, Statue of Simon Budny (1530-93), writer and printer, vert.

1993 *Perf. 12x12½, 12½x12*

68	A14	50r multicolored	*16*
69	A14	75r multicolored	*25*
70	A14	75r multicolored	*25*
71	A14	100r multicolored	*35*
		Nos. 68-71 (4)	*1.01*

Issued: 50r, Dec. 29. 75r, Dec. 30. 100r, Dec. 31.

Nos. 27, 29, 30 Surcharged

15.00

1994, Feb. 1 Photo. *Perf. 12x12½*

72	A7	15r on 30k light green	15	
73	A7	25r on 45k olive green	15	
74	A7	50r on 50k green	15	
		Set value	18	

Birds A15

1994, Jan. 19 Litho. *Perf. 11½*

75	A15	20r Aguila chrysaetos	15	
76	A15	40r Cygnus olor	15	
77	A15	40r Alcedo atthis	15	
a.		Block of 3, #75-77 + label	38	

See Nos. 87-89.

Liberation of Russian Areas, 50th Anniv. A16

Battle maps and: a, Katyusha rockets, liberation of Russia. b, Russian fighter planes, liberation of Ukraine. c, Combined offensive, liberation of Belarus.

1994, July 3 Litho. *Perf. 12*

78	A16	500r Block of 3 + label	45	30

See Russia No. 6213, Ukraine No. 195.

1994 Winter Olympics, Lillehammer — A17

1994, Aug. 30 Litho. *Perf. 12x12½*

79	A17	1000r Speed skating	15	
80	A17	1000r Women's figure skating	15	
81	A17	1000r Hockey	15	
82	A17	1000r Cross-country skiing	15	
83	A17	1000r Biathlon	15	
		Set value	65	

Painters — A18

Designs: No. 84, Farmer, oxen in field, by Ferdinand Rushchyts. No. 85, Knight on horseback, by Jasev Drazdovich. No. 86, Couple walking up path, by Petra Sergievich. Illustration reduced

1994, July 18 Litho. *Perf. 12*

84	A18	300r multicolored	15	
85	A18	300r multicolored	15	
86	A18	300r multicolored	15	
		Set value	28	

Bird Type of 1994

1994, Sept. 30 *Perf. 11½*

87	A15	300r like #75	15	
88	A15	400r like #76	15	
89	A15	400r like #77	15	
		Set value	22	

BELGIAN CONGO

LOCATION — Central Africa
GOVT. — Belgian colony
AREA — 902,082 sq. mi. (estimated)
POP. — 12,660,000 (1956)
CAPITAL — Léopoldville

Congo was an independent state, founded by Leopold II of Belgium, until 1908 when it was annexed to Belgium as a colony. In 1960 it became the independent Republic of the Congo. See Congo Democratic Republic and Zaire.

100 Centimes = 1 Franc

Catalogue values for unused stamps in this country are for Never Hinged items, beginning with Scott 187 in the regular postage section, Scott B32 in the semi-postal section, Scott C17 in the airpost section, and Scott J8 in the postage due section.

Independent State

King Leopold II

A1 A2 A3

1886 Unwmk. Typo. *Perf. 15*

1	A1	5c green	5.50	12.00
2	A1	10c rose	2.25	3.00
3	A2	25c blue	27.50	24.00
4	A3	50c olive grn	3.75	3.75
5	A1	5fr lilac	225.00	135.00
a.		Perf. 14	500.00	

Counterfeits exist.

For surcharge see No. Q1.

King Leopold II — A4

1887-94

6	A4	5c grn ('89)	40	40
7	A4	10c rose ('89)	65	60
8	A4	25c blue ('89)	50	50
9	A4	50c brown	30.00	10.50
10	A4	50c gray ('94)	1.25	*9.00*
11	A4	5fr violet	325.00	190.00
12	A4	5fr gray ('92)	65.00	55.00
13	A4	10fr buff ('91)	150.00	125.00

The 25fr and 50fr in gray were not issued. Values, each $15.

Counterfeits exist of Nos. 10-13, 25fr and 50fr, unused, used, genuine stamps with faked cancels and counterfeit stamps with genuine cancels.

For surcharges see Nos. Q3-Q6.

Port Matadi — A5

River Scene on the Congo, Stanley Falls — A6

Inkissi Falls — A7

Railroad Bridge on M'pozo River — A8

Hunting Elephants A9

Bangala Chief and Wife — A10

1894-1901 Engr. *Perf. 12½ to 15*

14	A5	5c pale bl & blk	9.00	7.00
15	A5	5c red brn & blk ('95)	2.00	75
16	A5	5c grn & blk ('00)	1.40	25
17	A6	10c red brn & blk	9.00	7.00
18	A6	10c grnsh bl & blk ('95)	75	65
a.		Center inverted	*1,750.*	*1,900.*
19	A6	10c car & blk ('00)	1.75	25
20	A7	25c yel org & blk	2.25	1.10
21	A7	25c lt bl & blk ('00)	1.90	65
22	A8	50c grn & blk	85	65
23	A8	50c ol & blk ('00)	1.90	32
24	A9	1fr lil & blk	14.00	5.50
a.		1fr rose lilac & black	125.00	8.50
25	A9	1fr car & blk ('01)	125.00	1.00
26	A10	5fr lake & blk	22.50	7.00
		Nos. 14-26 (13)	192.30	32.12

For overprints see Nos. 31-32, 34, 36-37, 39.

Climbing Oil Palms — A11

Congo Canoe — A12

1896

27	A11	15c ocher & blk	2.25	30
28	A12	40c bluish grn & blk	2.50	1.65

For overprints see Nos. 33, 35.

Congo Village — A13

River Steamer on the Congo — A14

1898

29	A13	3.50fr red & blk	85.00	30.00
30	A14	10fr yel grn & blk	55.00	8.50
a.		Center inverted	*25,000.*	
b.		Perf. 12	300.00	10.50
c.		Perf. 12x14	225.00	85.00

For overprints see Nos. 38, 40.

Belgian Congo

Overprinted **CONGO BELGE**

1908

31	A5	5c grn & blk	5.00	4.50
a.		Handstamped	1.65	1.10
32	A6	10c car & blk	8.25	7.50
a.		Handstamped	1.65	1.10
33	A11	15c ocher & blk	4.00	2.00
a.		Handstamped	3.25	1.75
34	A7	25c lt bl & blk	3.25	2.00
a.		Handstamped	5.00	2.00
35	A12	40c bluish grn & blk	1.50	1.40
a.		Handstamped	5.00	3.50
36	A8	50c ol & blk	2.75	1.50
a.		Handstamped	2.50	1.65
37	A9	1fr car & blk	14.00	1.50
a.		Handstamped	16.00	1.25
38	A13	3.50fr red & blk	13.00	7.50
a.		Handstamped	100.00	55.00
39	A10	5fr car & blk	25.00	12.00
a.		Handstamped	40.00	15.00
40	A14	10fr yel grn & blk	57.50	10.50
a.		Perf. 14	110.00	55.00
b.		Handstamped	70.00	17.50
c.		Handstamped, perf. 14	150.00	100.00
		Nos. 31-40 (10)	134.25	50.40

Most of the above handstamps are also found inverted and double.

Values for handstamped overprints are for those applied locally.

Counterfeits of the handstamped overprints exist.

Port Matadi — A15

River Scene on the Congo, Stanley Falls — A16

Climbing Oil Palms — A17

Railroad Bridge on M'pozo River — A18

1909 *Perf. 14*

41	A15	5c grn & blk	45	45
42	A16	10c car & blk	40	30
43	A17	15c ocher & blk	12.50	7.25
44	A18	50c olive & blk	1.90	1.50
		Nos. 41-44 (4)	15.25	9.50

Port Matadi — A19

River Scene on the Congo, Stanley Falls — A20

Climbing Oil Palms — A21

Inkissi Falls — A22

Congo Canoe — A23

Railroad Bridge on M'pozo River — A24

Hunting Elephants A25

Congo Village — A26

Bangala Chief and Wife — A27

River Steamer on the Congo — A28

1910-15 Engr. *Perf. 14, 15*

45	A19	5c grn & blk	75	15
46	A20	10c car & blk	42	15
47	A21	15c ocher & blk	42	15
48	A21	15c grn & blk ('15)	22	15
a.		Booklet pane of 10	10.00	
49	A22	25c bl & blk	1.10	22
50	A23	40c bluish grn & blk	1.40	1.25
51	A23	40c brn red & blk ('15)	2.75	1.25
52	A24	50c ol & blk	2.25	1.10
53	A24	50c brn lake & blk ('15)	4.25	1.25
54	A25	1fr car & blk	2.00	1.50
55	A25	1fr ol bis & blk ('15)	1.40	50
56	A26	3fr red & blk	10.50	7.25
57	A27	5fr car & blk	12.00	9.75
58	A27	5fr ocher & blk ('15)	1.10	50
59	A28	10fr grn & blk	11.50	8.75
		Nos. 45-59 (15)	52.06	33.92

Nos. 48, 51, 53, 55 and 58 exist imperforate.

For overprints and surcharges see Nos. 64-76, 81-86, B5-B9.

Port Matadi — A29

Stanley Falls, Congo River — A30

Inkissi Falls — A31

TEN CENTIMES.

Type I - Large white space at top of picture and two small white spots at lower edge. Vignette does not fill frame.

Type II - Vignette completely fills frame.

1915

60	A29	5c green & blk	15	15
a.		Booklet pane of 10	7.00	
61	A30	10c car & blk (II)	18	15
a.		10c carmine & black (I)	18	15
d.		Booklet pane of 10 (II)	10.00	
62	A31	25c blue & blk	75	22
a.		Booklet pane of 10	40.00	
		Nos. 60-62 (3)	1.08	52

Nos. 60 to 62 exist imperforate.

For surcharges see Nos. 77-80, 87, B1-B4.

Stamps of 1910 Issue Surcharged in Red or Black

10c 10c

1921

64	A23	5c on 40c bluish grn & blk (R)	18	18
65	A19	10c on 5c grn & blk (R)	18	18
66	A24	15c on 50c ol & blk (R)	18	18
67	A21	25c on 15c ocher & blk (R)	1.00	75
68	A20	30c on 10c car & blk	18	18
69	A22	50c on 25c bl & blk (R)	95	70
		Nos. 64-69 (6)	2.67	2.17

The position of the new value and the bars varies on Nos. 64 to 69.

Overprinted **1921**

1921

70	A25	1fr car & blk	55	55
a.		Double overprint	11.50	
71	A26	3fr red & blk	1.65	1.65
72	A27	5fr car & blk	3.00	3.00
73	A28	10fr grn & blk (R)	2.50	1.40
		Nos. 70-73 (4)	7.70	6.60

Belgian Surcharges

Nos. 51, 53, 60-62 Surcharged in Black or Red **·10c**

1922

74	A24	5c on 50c	28	25
75	A29	10c on 5c (R)	28	22
76	A23	25c on 40c (R)	1.40	25
77	A30	30c on 10c (II)	15	15
a.		30c on 10c (I)	15	15
b.		Double surcharge	3.25	3.25
78	A31	50c on 25c (R)	32	22
		Nos. 74-78 (5)	2.43	1.09

No. 74 has the surcharge at each side.

Congo Surcharges

Nos. 60, 51 Surcharged in Red or Black:

10 c.

a

25 c.

b

1922

80	A29	10c on 5c (R)	40	40
a.		Inverted surcharge	13.00	13.00
b.		Double surcharge	3.25	
c.		Double surch., one invtd.	27.50	
d.		Pair, one without surcharge	30.00	
e.		On No. 45	100.00	100.00
81	A23	25c on 40c	55	28
a.		Inverted surcharge	13.00	13.00
b.		Double surcharge	3.75	
c.		"25c" double		
d.		25c on 5c, No. 60	70.00	70.00

Nos. 55, 58 Surcharged with vertical bars over original values **10 c.**

1922

84	A25	10c on 1fr (R)	40	40
a.		Double surcharge	10.00	
b.		Inverted surcharge	13.00	13.00
85	A27	25c on 5fr	1.10	1.10

Nos. 68, 77 Handstamped **0,25**

86	A20	25c on 30c on 10c	5.00	6.25
87	A30	25c on 30c on 10c (II)	5.00	6.25

Nos. 86-87 exist with handstamp surcharge inverted.

Counterfeit handstamped surcharges exist.

Ubangi Woman — A32

Watusi Cattle — A44

Designs: 10c, Baluba woman. 15c, Babuende woman. No. 90, 40c, 1.25fr, 1.50fr, 1.75fr. Ubangi man. 25c, Basketmaking. 30c, 35c, Nos. 101, 102, Carving wood. 50c, Archer. Nos. 92, 100, Weaving. 1fr, Making pottery. 3fr, Working rubber. 5fr, Making palm oil. 10fr, African elephant.

1923-27 Engr. *Perf. 12*

88	A32	5c yellow	15	15
89	A32	10c green	15	15
90	A32	15c olive brn	15	15
91	A32	20c ol grn ('24)	15	15
92	A44	20c grn ('26)	15	15
93	A44	25c red brn	18	15
94	A44	30c rose red ('24)	40	60
95	A44	30c ol grn ('25)	15	15
96	A44	35c green ('27)	28	32
97	A32	40c violet ('25)	15	15
98	A44	50c gray blue	18	15
99	A44	50c buff ('25)	20	15
100	A44	75c red org	25	28
101	A44	75c gray bl ('25)	28	18
102	A44	75c sal red ('26)	15	15
103	A44	1fr bister brn	30	15
104	A44	1fr dl bl ('25)	28	15
105	A44	1fr rose red ('27)	40	15
106	A32	1.25fr dl bl ('26)	20	18
107	A32	1.50fr dl bl ('26)	20	15
108	A32	1.75fr dl bl ('27)	2.00	1.90
109	A44	3fr gray brn ('24)	2.50	90
110	A44	5fr gray ('24)	5.00	2.50
111	A44	10fr gray blk ('24)	11.50	4.00

1925-26

112	A44	45c dk vio ('26)	25	24
113	A44	60c carmine rose	25	15
		Nos. 88-113 (26)	25.85	13.50

For surcharges see Nos. 114, 136-138, 157.

No. 107 Surcharged **1.75**

1927, June 14

114	A32	1.75fr on 1.50fr dl bl	28	24

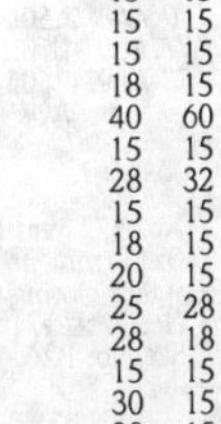
Sir Henry Morton Stanley — A45

1928, June 30 *Perf. 14*

115	A45	5c gray blk	15	15
116	A45	10c dp vio	15	15
117	A45	20c org red	15	15
118	A45	35c green	40	65
119	A45	40c red brn	16	15
120	A45	60c blk brn	16	15
121	A45	1fr carmine	16	15
122	A45	1.60fr dk gray	1.75	1.75
123	A45	1.75fr dp bl	70	55
124	A45	2fr dk brn	50	22
125	A45	2.75fr red vio	2.00	28
126	A45	3.50fr rose lake	65	45
127	A45	5fr slate grn	50	18
128	A45	10fr vio bl	70	45
129	A45	20fr claret	2.50	1.65
		Nos. 115-129 (15)	10.63	7.08

Sir Henry M. Stanley (1841-1904), explorer.

Nos. 118, 121-123, 125-126 Surcharged in Red, Blue or Black

1F25

1931, Jan. 15

130	A45	40c on 35c	42	32
131	A45	1.25fr on 1fr (Bl)	32	15
132	A45	2fr on 1.60fr	65	22
133	A45	2fr on 1.75fr	60	20
134	A45	3.25fr on 2.75fr (Bk)	1.75	1.40
135	A45	3.25fr on 3.25fr (Bk)	2.25	1.50

Nos. 96, 108, 112 Surcharged in Red

50c

136	A44	40c on 35c grn	2.50	2.25
137	A44	50c on 45c dk vio	1.50	85

Surcharged **2**

138	A32	2(fr) on 1.75fr dl bl	6.00	5.50
		Nos. 130-138 (9)	15.99	12.39

View of Sankuru River — A46

Flute Players — A50

Designs: 15c, Kivu Kraal. 20c, Sankuru River rapids. 25c, Uele hut. 50c, Musicians of Lake Leopold II. 60c, Batetelas drummers. 75c, Mangbetu woman. 1fr, Domesticated elephant of Api. 1.25fr, Mangbetu chief. 1.50fr, 2fr, Village of Mondimbi. 2.50fr, 3.25fr, Okapi. 4fr, Canoes at Stanleyville. 5fr, Woman preparing cassava. 10fr, Baluba chief. 20fr, Young woman of Irumu.

1931-37 Engr. *Perf. 11½*

139	A46	10c gray brn ('32)	15	15
140	A46	15c gray ('32)	15	15
141	A46	20c brn lil ('32)	15	15
142	A46	25c dp bl ('32)	15	15
143	A50	40c dp grn ('32)	15	15
144	A46	50c vio ('32)	15	15
b.		Booklet pane of 8	5.25	
145	A50	60c vio brn ('32)	15	15
146	A50	75c rose ('32)	15	15
b.		Booklet pane of 8	1.00	
147	A50	1fr rose red ('32)	15	15
148	A50	1.25fr red brn	15	15
b.		Booklet pane of 8	1.00	
149	A46	1.50fr dk ol gray ('37)	15	15
b.		Booklet pane of 8	5.00	
150	A46	2fr ultra ('32)	15	15
151	A46	2.50fr dp bl ('37)	28	15
b.		Booklet pane of 8	7.00	
152	A46	3.25fr gray blk ('32)	42	24
153	A46	4fr dl vio ('32)	18	15
154	A50	5fr dp vio ('32)	42	18
155	A50	10fr red ('32)	45	30
156	A50	20fr blk brn ('32)	1.10	90
		Set value	4.00	2.85

No. 109 Surcharged in Red

3F25

═ ═

1932, Mar. 15		Perf. 12	
157 A44 3.25fr on 3fr gray brn		2.00	1.50

King Albert Memorial Issue

King Albert — A62

1934, May 7 Photo.		Perf. 11½	
158 A62 1.50fr	black	50	15

Leopold I, Leopold II, Albert I, Leopold III A63

1935, Aug. 15 Engr.		Perf. 12½x12	
159 A63 50c	green	45	32
160 A63 1.25fr	dk car	45	15
161 A63 1.50fr	brn vio	45	15
162 A63 2.40fr	brn org	1.50	1.25
163 A63 2.50fr	lt bl	1.25	50
164 A63 4fr	brt vio	1.50	75
165 A63 5fr	blk brn	1.50	85
Nos. 159-165 (7)		7.10	3.97

Founding of Congo Free State, 50th anniv.
For surcharges see Nos. B21-B22.

Molindi River — A64

Bamboos — A65

Suza River — A66

Rutshuru River — A67

Karisimbi — A68

Mitumba Forest — A69

1937-38 Photo.		Perf. 11½	
166 A64 5c	pur & blk	15	15
167 A65 90c	car & brn	35	28
168 A66 1.50fr	dp red brn & blk	15	15
169 A67 2.40fr	ol blk & brn	15	15
170 A68 2.50fr	dp ultra & blk	22	15
171 A69 4.50fr	dk grn & brn	22	15
172 A69 4.50fr	car & sep	18	18
Nos. 166-172 (7)		1.42	
Set value			94

National Parks.
No. 172 was issued in sheets of four measuring 140x111mm. It was sold by subscription, the subscription closing Oct. 20, 1937. Value, $1.60.
Nos. 166-171 were issued Mar. 1, 1938.
See No. B26. For surcharges see Nos. 184, 186.

King Albert Memorial, Leopoldville — A70

1941, Feb. 7 Litho.		Perf. 11	
173 A70 10c	lt gray	15	15
174 A70 15c	brown vio	15	15
175 A70 25c	lt blue	18	15
176 A70 50c	lt violet	15	15
177 A70 75c	rose pink	65	25
178 A70 1.25fr	gray	15	15
179 A70 1.75fr	orange	50	40
180 A70 2.50fr	carmine	30	15
181 A70 2.75fr	vio blue	65	50
182 A70 5fr	lt olive grn	1.25	1.25
183 A70 10fr	rose red	1.40	1.40
Nos. 173-183 (11)		5.53	4.70

Exist imperforate.
For surcharge see No. 185.

Nos. 168, 179, 169 Surcharged in Blue or Black

5 c.

75 c.

Nos. 184, 186 — No. 185

1941-42		Perf. 11½, 11	
184 A66	5c on 1.50fr (Bl)	15	15
a.	Inverted surcharge	12.00	12.00
185 A70	75c on 1.75fr ('42)	28	28
a.	Inverted surcharge	12.00	12.00
186 A67	2.50(fr) on 2.40fr ('42)	70	55
a.	Double surcharge	24.00	24.00
b.	Inverted surcharge	12.00	12.00
Nos. 184-186 (3)		1.13	98

Catalogue values for unused stamps in this section, from this point to the end of the section, are for Never Hinged items.

Oil Palms
A71 A72

Congo Woman — A73

Askari — A75

Leopard A74

Okapi — A76

Inscribed "Congo Belge Belgisch Congo"

1942, May 23 Engr.		Perf. 12½	
187 A71 5c	red	15	15
188 A72 10c	olive grn	15	15
189 A72 15c	brn car	15	15
190 A72 20c	dp ultra	15	15
191 A72 25c	brn vio	15	15
192 A72 30c	blue	15	15
193 A72 50c	dp grn	15	15
194 A72 60c	chestnut	15	15
195 A73 75c	dl lil & blk	15	15
196 A73 1fr	dk brn & blk	18	15
197 A73 1.25fr	rose red & blk	18	15
198 A74 1.75fr	dk gray brn	85	35
199 A74 2fr	ocher	85	15
200 A74 2.50fr	carmine	85	15
201 A75 3.50fr	dk ol grn	32	15
202 A75 5fr	orange	60	15
203 A75 6fr	brt ultra	55	15
204 A75 7fr	black	55	15
205 A75 10fr	dp brn	70	15
206 A76 20fr	plum & blk	4.50	65
Nos. 187-206 (20)		11.48	
Set value			2.40

Same Inscribed "Belgisch Congo Congo Belge"

207 A72 10c	olive grn	15	15
208 A72 15c	brn car	15	15
209 A72 20c	dp ultra	15	15
210 A72 25c	brn vio	15	15
211 A72 30c	blue	15	15
212 A72 50c	dp grn	15	15
213 A72 60c	chestnut	15	15
214 A73 75c	dl lil & blk	15	15
215 A73 1fr	dk brn & blk	18	15
216 A73 1.25fr	rose red & blk	18	15
217 A74 1.75fr	dk gray brn	85	35
218 A74 2fr	ocher	85	15
219 A74 2.50fr	carmine	85	15
220 A75 3.50fr	dk ol grn	32	15
221 A75 5fr	orange	60	15
222 A75 6fr	brt ultra	55	15
223 A75 7fr	black	55	15
224 A75 10fr	dp brn	70	15
225 A76 20fr	plum & blk	4.50	65
Nos. 207-225 (19)		11.33	
Set value			2.35

Miniature sheets of Nos. 193, 194, 197, 200, 211, 214, 217 and 219 were printed in 1944 by the Belgian Government in London and given to the Belgian political review, Message, which distributed them to its subscribers, one a month. Value per sheet, about $12.50.

Remainders of these eight miniature sheets received marginal overprints in various colors in 1950, specifying a surtax of 100fr per sheet and paying tribute to the UPU. These sheets, together with four of Ruanda-Urundi, were sold by the Committee of Cultural Works (and not at post offices) in sets of 12 for 1,217.15 francs. Set value, about $150.

Nos. 187-227 imperforate had no franking value.
For surcharges see Nos. B34-B37.

Congo Woman — A77

Askari — A78

1943, Jan. 1			
226 A77 50fr	ultra & blk	5.00	40
227 A78 100fr	car & blk	6.50	60

Slaves and Arab Guards A79

Auguste Lambermont A80

Design: 10fr, Leopold II.

Perf. 13x11½, 12½x12

1947 Engr.		Unwmk.	
228 A79 1.25fr	black brown	25	15
229 A80 3.50fr	dark blue	38	15
230 A80 10fr	red orange	75	15
Nos. 228-230 (3)		1.38	
Set value			29

50th anniv. of the abolition of slavery in Belgian Congo. See Nos. 261-262.

Baluba Carving of Former King — A82

Carved Figures and Masks of Baluba Tribe: 10c, 50c, 2fr, "Ndoha," figure of tribal king. 15c, 70c, 1.20fr, 2.50fr, "Tshimanyi," an idol. 20c, 75c, 1.60fr, 3.50fr, "Buangakokoma," statue of kneeling beggar. 25c, 1fr, 2.40fr, 5fr, "Mbuta," sacred double cup, carved with two faces, Man and Woman. 40c, 1.25fr, 6fr, 8fr, "Ngadimuashi," female mask. 1.50fr, 3fr, 10fr, 50fr, "Buadi-Muadi," mask with squared features. 6.50fr, 20fr, 100fr, "Mbowa," executioner's mask with buffalo horns.

1947-50 *Perf. 12½*

231	A82	10c	dp org ('48)	15	15
232	A82	15c	ultra ('48)	15	15
233	A82	20c	brt bl ('48)	15	15
234	A82	25c	rose car ('48)	25	15
235	A82	40c	vio ('48)	15	15
236	A82	50c	olive brn	15	15
237	A82	70c	yel grn ('48)	15	15
238	A82	75c	mag ('48)	15	15
239	A82	1fr	yel org & dk vio	1.25	15
240	A82	1.20fr	gray & brn ('50)	15	15
241	A82	1.25fr	lt bl grn & mag ('48)	25	15
242	A82	1.50fr	ol & mag ('50)	8.00	1.10
243	A82	1.60fr	bl gray & brt bl ('50)	20	15
244	A82	2fr	org & mag ('48)	18	15
245	A82	2.40fr	bl grn & dk grn ('50)	25	15
246	A82	2.50fr	brn red & bl grn	15	15
247	A82	3fr	lt ultra & ind ('49)	3.75	15
248	A82	3.50fr	lt bl & blk ('48)	2.75	15
249	A82	5fr	bis & mag ('48)	50	15
250	A82	6fr	brn org & ind ('48)	65	15
251	A82	6.50fr	red org & red brn ('49)	1.25	15
252	A82	8fr	gray bl & dk grn ('50)	65	15
253	A82	10fr	pale vio & red brn ('48)	2.00	15
254	A82	20fr	red org & vio brn ('48)	1.00	15
255	A82	50fr	dp org & blk ('48)	2.50	15
256	A82	100fr	crim & blk brn ('48)	3.75	30
			Nos. 231-256 (26)	30.53	
			Set value		3.75

Railroad Train and Map — A83

1948, July 1 **Unwmk.** *Perf. 13½*

257	A83	2.50fr	dp bl & grn	1.00	15

50th anniv. of railway service in the Congo.

Globe and Ship — A84

1949, Nov. 21 *Perf. 11½*

Granite Paper

258	A84	4fr	violet blue	85	15

75th anniv. of the UPU.

Allegorical Figure and Map — A85

1950, Aug. 12 *Perf. 12x12½*

259	A85	3fr	blue & indigo	1.75	15
260	A85	6.50fr	car rose & blk brn	2.00	25

Establishment of Katanga Province, 50th anniv.

Portrait Type of 1947

Designs: 1.50fr, Cardinal Lavigerie. 3fr, Baron Dhanis.

Perf. 12½x12

1951, June 25 **Unwmk.**

261	A80	1.50fr	purple	2.00	25
262	A80	3fr	black brown	2.00	15

Littonia — A86

St. Francis Xavier — A86a

Flowers: 10c, Dissotis. 15c, Protea. 20c, Vellozia. 40c, Ipomoea. 50c, Angraecum. 60c, Euphorbia. 75c, Ochna. 1fr, Hibiscus. 1.25fr, Protea. 1.50fr, Schizoglossum. 2fr, Ansellia. 3fr, Costus. 4fr, Nymphaea. 5fr, Thunbergia. 6.50fr, Thonningia. 7fr, Gerbera. 8fr, Gloriosa. 10fr, Silene. 20fr, Aristolochia. 50fr, Eulophia. 100fr, Crytosepalum.

1952-53 **Photo.** *Perf. 11½*

Granite Paper

Flowers in Natural Colors

Size: 21x25½mm

263	A86	10c	dp plum & ocher	15	15
264	A86	15c	red & yel grn	15	15
265	A86	20c	grn & gray	15	15
266	A86	25c	dk grn & dl org	15	15
267	A86	40c	grn & sal	18	15
268	A86	50c	dk car & aqua	15	15
269	A86	60c	bl grn & pink	15	15
270	A86	75c	dp plum & gray	15	15
271	A86	1fr	car & yel	15	15
272	A86	1.25fr	dk grn & bl ('53)	65	45
273	A86	1.50fr	vio & ap grn	15	15
274	A86	2fr	ol grn & buff	25	15
275	A86	3fr	ol grn & pink	25	15
276	A86	4fr	choc & lil	30	15
277	A86	5fr	dp plum & lt bl grn	45	15
278	A86	6.50fr	dk car & lil	55	15
279	A86	7fr	dk grn & fawn	55	15
280	A86	8fr	grn & lt yel ('53)	90	15
281	A86	10fr	dp plum & pale ol ('53)	1.65	15
282	A86	20fr	vio bl & dl salmon	1.40	15

Size: 22x32mm

283	A86	50fr	dp plum & gray bl ('53)	7.00	45
284	A86	100fr	grn & buff ('53)	11.00	1.00
			Nos. 263-284 (22)	26.48	
			Set value		2.90

Nos. 264, 269 and 270 with additional surcharges are varieties of Congo Democratic Republic Nos. 324, 327 and 328.

1953, Jan. 5 **Engr.** *Perf. 12½x13*

285	A86a	1.50fr	ultra & gray blk	75	30

400th death anniv. of St. Francis Xavier.

Canoe on Lake Kivu — A87

1953, Jan. 5 *Perf. 14*

286	A87	3fr	car & blk	1.25	18
287	A87	7fr	dp bl & brn org	1.25	28

Issued to publicize the Kivu Festival, 1953.

Royal Colonial Institute Jubilee Medal A88

Design: 6.50fr, Same with altered background and transposed inscriptions.

1954, Dec. 27 **Photo.** *Perf. 13½*

288	A88	4.50fr	indigo & gray	1.10	28
289	A88	6.50fr	dk grn & brn	90	15

25th anniv. of the founding of the Belgian Royal Colonial Institute.

King Baudouin and Tropical Scene — A89

Designs: King and various views.

Inscribed "Congo Belge-Belgisch Congo"

Engr.; Portrait Photo.

1955, Feb. 15 **Unwmk.** *Perf. 11½*

Portrait in Black

290	A89	1.50fr	rose car	70	25
291	A89	3fr	green	25	15
292	A89	4.50fr	ultra	32	15
293	A89	6.50fr	dp claret	52	15

Inscribed "Belgisch Congo-Congo Belge"

294	A89	1.50fr	rose car	32	16
295	A89	3fr	green	25	15
296	A89	4.50fr	ultra	32	15
297	A89	6.50fr	deep claret	52	15
			Nos. 290-297 (8)	3.20	
			Set value		90

Map of Africa and Emblem of Royal Touring Club — A90

1955, July 26 **Engr.** *Perf. 11½*

Inscription in French

298	A90	6.50fr	vio blue	3.25	25

Inscription in Flemish

299	A90	6.50fr	vio blue	3.25	25

5th International Congress of African Tourism, Elisabethville, July 26-Aug. 4. Nos. 298-299 printed in alternate rows.

Kings of Belgium A91

1958, July 1 **Unwmk.** *Perf. 12½*

300	A91	1fr	rose vio	22	15
301	A91	1.50fr	ultra	22	15
302	A91	3fr	rose car	22	15
303	A91	5fr	green	70	32
304	A91	6.50fr	brn red	45	15
305	A91	10fr	dl vio	65	15
			Nos. 300-305 (6)	2.46	
			Set value		73

Belgium's annexation of Congo, 50th anniv.

Roan Antelope — A92

Black Buffaloes — A93

Animals: 20c, White rhinoceros. 40c, Giraffe. 50c, Thick-tailed bushbaby. 1fr, Gorilla. 2fr, Black-and-white colobus (monkey). 3fr, Elephants. 5fr, Okapis. 6.50fr, Impala. 8fr, Giant pangolin. 10fr, Eland and zebras.

1959, Oct. 15 **Photo.** *Perf. 11½*

Granite Paper

306	A92	10c	bl & brn	15	15
307	A93	20c	red org & slate	15	15
308	A92	40c	brn & bl	15	15
309	A93	50c	brt ultra, red & sep	15	15
310	A92	1fr	brn, grn & blk	15	15
311	A93	1.50fr	blk & org yel	15	15
312	A92	2fr	crim, blk & brn	15	15
313	A93	3fr	blk, gray & lil rose	25	15
314	A92	5fr	brn, dk brn & brt grn	40	18
315	A93	6.50fr	bl, brn & org yel	45	15
316	A92	8fr	org brn, ol bis & lil	50	30
317	A93	10fr	multi	60	15
			Set value	2.80	1.30

Madonna and Child — A94

1959, Dec. 1 **Unwmk.** *Perf. 11½*

318	A94	50c	golden brn, ocher & red brn	15	15
319	A94	1fr	dk bl, pur & red brn	15	15
320	A94	2fr	gray, brt bl & red brn	18	15
			Set value	38	26

Map of Africa and Symbolic Honeycomb A95

1960, Feb. 19 **Unwmk.** *Perf. 11½*

Inscription in French

321	A95	3fr	gray & red	25	15

Inscription in Flemish

322	A95	3fr	gray & red	25	15

10th anniv. of the Commission for Technical Co-operation in Africa South of the Sahara (C. C. T. A.).

Succeeding issues are listed under Congo Democratic Republic.

SEMI-POSTAL STAMPS

Types of 1910-15 Issues Surcharged in Red **+ 10c**

1918, May 15 **Unwmk.** *Perf. 14, 15*

B1	A29	5c	+ 10c grn & bl	18	22
B2	A30	10c	+ 15c car & bl (I)	18	22
B3	A21	15c	+ 20c bl grn & bl	18	22
B4	A31	25c	+ 25c dp bl & pale bl	22	22
B5	A23	40c	+ 40c brn red & bl	30	40
B6	A24	50c	+ 50c brn lake & bl	30	40
B7	A25	1fr	+ 1fr ol bis & bl	1.10	1.40
B8	A27	5fr	+ 5fr ocher & bl	7.00	7.25
B9	A28	10fr	+ 10fr grn & bl	55.00	55.00
			Nos. B1-B9 (9)	64.46	65.33

The position of the cross and the added value varies on the different stamps.

Nos. B1-B9 exist imperforate.

SP1

Design: #B11 inscribed "Belgisch Congo."

1925, July 8 *Perf. 12½*

B10	SP1	25c	+ 25c carmine & blk	16	16
B11	SP1	25c	+ 25c carmine & blk	16	16

Colonial campaigns in 1914-1918.

The stamps with French and Flemish inscriptions alternate in the sheet.

The surtax helped erect at Kinshasa a monument to those who died in World War I.

Nurse Weighing Child — SP3

First Aid Station — SP5

Designs: 20c+10c, Missionary and Child. 60c+30c, Congo hospital. 1fr+50c, Dispensary service. 1.75fr+75c, Convalescent area. 3.50fr+1.50fr, Instruction on bathing infant. 5fr+2.50fr, Operating room. 10fr+5fr, Students.

1930, Jan. 16 Engr. *Perf. 11½*

B12	SP3	10c + 5c ver	28	32
B13	SP3	20c + 10c dp brn	35	42
B14	SP5	35c + 15c dp grn	65	75
B15	SP5	60c + 30c dl vio	75	90
B16	SP3	1fr + 50c dk car	1.10	1.40
B17	SP5	1.75fr + 75c dp bl	1.65	1.90
B18	SP5	3.50fr + 1.50fr rose lake	3.00	3.75
B19	SP5	5fr + 2.50fr red brn	3.00	3.50
B20	SP5	10fr + 5fr gray blk	3.00	3.75
		Nos. B12-B20 (9)	13.78	16.69

The surtax on these stamps was intended to aid welfare work among the natives, especially the children.

Nos. 161, 163 Surcharged "+50c" in Blue or Red

1936, May 15 *Perf. 12½x12*

B21	A63	1.50fr + 50c (Bl)	1.50	2.00
B22	A63	2.50fr + 50c (R)	1.50	2.00

The surtax was for the benefit of the King Albert Memorial Fund.

Queen Astrid with Congolese Children — SP12

1936, Aug. 29 Photo. *Perf. 12½*

B23	SP12	1.25fr + 5c dark brown	40	35
B24	SP12	1.50fr + 10c dull rose	40	35
B25	SP12	2.50fr + 25c dark blue	50	50
		Nos. B23-B25 (3)	1.30	1.20

Issued in memory of Queen Astrid. The surtax was for the aid of the National League for Protection of Native Children.

Souvenir Sheet

SP13

1938, Oct. 3 *Perf. 11½*

B26	SP13	Sheet of 9	6.00	6.00
a.		A64 5c ultra & light brown	1.00	1.00
b.		A65 90c ultra & light brown	1.00	1.00
c.		A66 1.50fr ultra & light brown	1.00	1.00
d.		A67 2.40fr ultra & light brown	1.00	1.00
e.		A68 2.50fr ultra & light brown	1.00	1.00
f.		A69 4.50fr ultra & light brown	1.00	1.00

Intl. Tourist Cong. The star is printed in yellow. A surtax of 3.15fr was for the benefit of the Congo Tourist Service.

Marabou Storks and Vultures — SP14

Buffon's Kob — SP15

Designs: 1.50fr+1.50fr, Pygmy chimpanzees. 4.50fr+4.50fr, Dwarf crocodiles. 5fr+5fr, Lioness.

1939 Photo. *Perf. 14*

B27	SP14	1fr + 1fr dp claret	2.75	2.75
B28	SP15	1.25fr + 1.25fr car	2.75	2.75
B29	SP15	1.50fr + 1.50fr brt pur	4.00	4.00
B30	SP14	4.50fr + 4.50fr sl grn	2.75	2.75
B31	SP15	5fr + 5fr brown	3.00	3.00
		Nos. B27-B31 (5)	15.25	15.25

The surtax was for the Leopoldville Zoological Gardens.

Nos. B27-B31 were sold in full sets by subscription.

Catalogue values for unused stamps in this section, from this point to the end of the section, are for Never Hinged items.

Lion of Belgium and Inscription "Belgium Shall Rise Again" — SP19

1942, Feb. 17 Engr. *Perf. 12½*

B32	SP19	10fr + 40fr brt grn	1.10	75
B33	SP19	10fr + 40fr vio bl	1.10	75

Nos. 193, 216, 198 and 220 Surcharged in Red

Au profit de la Croix Rouge + 50 Fr. Ten voordeele van het Roode Kruis
a

Ten voordeele van het Roode Kruis + 100 Fr. Au profit de la Croix Rouge
b

c
Au profit de la Croix Rouge + 100 Fr. Ten voordeele van het Roode Kruis

1945

B34	A72	(a)	50c + 50fr	2.00	1.75
B35	A73	(b)	1.25fr + 100fr	2.00	1.75
B36	A74	(c)	1.75fr + 100fr	2.00	1.90
B37	A75	(b)	3.50fr + 100fr	2.00	1.90
			Nos. B34-B37 (4)	8.00	7.30

The surtax was for the Red Cross.

Nos. B34-B37 were sold in full sets by subscription.

Mozart at Age 7 — SP20

Queen Elisabeth and Sonata by Mozart — SP21

Perf. 11½

1956, Oct. 10 Unwmk. Engr.

B38	SP20	4.50fr + 1.50fr brt lil	2.00	1.50
B39	SP21	6.50fr + 2.50fr ultra	3.00	2.50

200th anniv. of the birth of Wolfgang Amadeus Mozart.

The surtax was for the Pro-Mozart Committee.

Nurse and Children — SP22

Designs: 4.50fr+50c, Patient receiving injection. 6.50fr+40c, Patient being bandaged.

1957, Dec. 10 Photo. *Perf. 13x10½*
Cross in Carmine

B40	SP22	3fr + 50c dk bl	90	65
B41	SP22	4.50fr + 50c dk grn	80	60
B42	SP22	6.50fr + 50c red brn	1.00	75
		Nos. B40-B42 (3)	2.70	2.00

The surtax was for the Red Cross.

High Jump — SP23

1960, May 2 Unwmk. *Perf. 13½*

B43	SP23	50c + 25c shown	15	15
B44	SP23	1.50fr + 50c Hurdles	18	15
B45	SP23	2fr + 1fr Soccer	18	15
B46	SP23	3fr + 1.25fr Javelin	75	55
B47	SP23	6.50fr + 3.50fr Discus	1.00	75
		Nos. B43-B47 (5)	2.26	1.75

17th Olympic Games, Rome, Aug. 25-Sept. 11. The surtax was for the youth of Congo.

AIR POST STAMPS

Wharf on Congo River AP1

Congo "Country Store" AP2

View of Congo River AP3

Stronghold in the Interior — AP4

1920, July 1 Unwmk. Engr. *Perf. 12*

C1	AP1	50c orange & blk	15	15
C2	AP2	1fr dull vio & blk	15	15
C3	AP3	2fr blue & blk	48	18
C4	AP4	5fr green & blk	90	42
		Nos. C1-C4 (4)	1.68	90

Kraal — AP5

Porters on Safari AP6

1930, Apr. 2

C5	AP5	15fr dk brn & blk	1.90	75
C6	AP6	30fr brn vio & blk	2.25	75

Fokker F VII over Congo — AP7

1934, Jan. 22 *Perf. 13½x14*

C7	AP7	50c gray black	15	15
C8	AP7	1fr dk carmine	18	15
a.		Booklet pane of 8	5.25	
C9	AP7	1.50fr green	15	15
C10	AP7	3fr brown	18	15
C11	AP7	4.50fr brt ultra	25	15
a.		Booklet pane of 8	10.00	
C12	AP7	5fr red brown	20	15
C13	AP7	15fr brown vio	38	25
C14	AP7	30fr red orange	70	60
C15	AP7	50fr violet	2.00	95
		Nos. C7-C15 (9)	4.19	2.70

The 1, 3, 4.50, 5 and 15fr exist imperf.

No. C10 Surcharged in Blue with New Value and Bars

1936, Mar. 25

C16	AP7	3.50fr on 3fr brown	20	15

Catalogue values for unused stamps in this section, from this point to the end of the section, are for Never Hinged items.

No. C9 Surcharged in Black

50 c.

1942, Apr. 27

C17	AP7	50c on 1.50fr green	35	15
a.		Inverted surcharge	6.50	6.50

POSTAGE DUE STAMPS

In 1908-23 regular postage stamps handstamped "TAXES" or "TAXE," usually boxed, were used in lieu of postage due stamps.

D1

D2

1923-29(?) Typo. Unwmk. *Perf. 14*

J1	D1	5c black brown	15	15
J2	D1	10c rose red	15	15
J3	D1	15c violet	15	15
J4	D1	30c green	24	20
J5	D1	50c ultramarine	32	28
J6	D1	50c blue ('29)	32	28
J7	D1	1fr gray	45	25
		Nos. J1-J7 (7)	1.78	1.46

Catalogue values for unused stamps in this section, from this point to the end of the section, are for Never Hinged items.

1943 *Perf. 14x14½*

J8	D2	10c olive green	15	15
J9	D2	20c dark ultra	15	15
J10	D2	50c green	15	15
J11	D2	1fr dark brown	18	18
J12	D2	2fr yellow orange	22	22
		Set value	67	67

1943 *Perf. 12½*

J8a	D2	10c olive green	28	28
J9a	D2	20c dark ultramarine	28	28
J10a	D2	50c green	28	28
J11a	D2	1fr dark brown	42	42
J12a	D2	2fr yellow orange	42	42
		Nos. J8a-J12a (5)	1.68	1.68

D3

1957 Engr. *Perf. 11½*

J13	D3	10c olive brown	15	15
J14	D3	20c claret	15	15
J15	D3	50c green	15	15
J16	D3	1fr light blue	28	20
J17	D3	2fr vermilion	40	25
J18	D3	4fr purple	55	35
J19	D3	6fr violet blue	75	45
		Nos. J13-J19 (7)	2.43	1.70

PARCEL POST STAMPS

PP1

PP2

PP3

Handstamped Surcharges on Nos. 5, 11-12

1887-93 Unwmk. *Perf. 15*

Blue-Black Surcharge

Q1	PP1	3.50fr on 5fr lil	400.00	400.00

Black Surcharge

Q3	PP2	3.50fr on 5fr vio	450.00	300.00
Q4	PP3	3.50fr on 5fr vio ('88)	325.00	225.00
a.		Blue surcharge	350.00	240.00
Q6	PP3	3.50fr on 5fr gray ('93)	62.50	42.50

Nos. Q1, Q3-Q4, Q4a and Q6 are known with inverted surcharge, No. Q1 with double surcharge and No. Q6 in pair with unsurcharged stamp. Most of these handstamp varieties sell for more than the normal surcharges.

Genuine stamps with counterfeit surcharges, counterfeit stamps with counterfeit surcharges, and both with counterfeit cancels exist.

BELGIUM

LOCATION — Western Europe, bordering the North Sea
GOVT. — Constitutional Monarchy
AREA — 11,778 sq. mi.
POP. — 9,853,000 (est. 1983)
CAPITAL — Brussels

100 Centimes = 1 Franc

Catalogue values for unused stamps in this country are for Never Hinged items, beginning with Scott 322 in the regular postage section, Scott B370 in the semi-postal section, Scott C8 in the airpost section, Scott CB1 in the airpost semi-postal section, Scott J40 in the postage due section, Scott M1 in the military stamp section, Scott O36 in the officials section, and Scott Q267 in the parcel post section.

Values of early Belgian stamps vary according to condition. Quotations for Nos. 1-12 are for fine copies. Very fine to superb specimens sell at much higher prices, and inferior or poor copies sell at much reduced prices, depending on the condition of the individual specimen.

Values for unused stamps of 1849-1863 issues are for copies with original gum. Copies without gum generally sell for one third off the figures quoted.

Watermark

Wmk. 96 (No Frame)

King Leopold I
A1 A2

Wmk. Two "L's" Framed (96)

1849 Engr. *Imperf.*

1	A1	10c brown	*1,250.*	65.00
a.		10c red brown	*1,800.*	200.00
2	A1	20c blue	*1,750.*	52.50
a.		20c milky blue	*1,900.*	125.00

The reprints are on thick and thin wove and thick laid paper unwatermarked.

A souvenir sheet containing reproductions of the 10c, 20c and 40c of 1849-51 with black burelage on back was issued Oct. 17, 1949, for the cent. of the 1st Belgian stamps. It was sold at BEPITEC 1949, an intl. stamp exhib. at Brussels, and was not valid.

1849-50

3	A2	10c brown ('50)	*1,000.*	55.00
4	A2	20c blue ('50)	*1,250.*	47.50
5	A2	40c carmine rose	*1,000.*	200.00

Nos. 3-5 on thin paper are as valued. Copies on thick paper sell for 5 to 12 percent more.

Wmk. Two "L's" Without Frame (96)

1851-54

6	A2	10c brown	425.00	7.00
a.		Ribbed paper ('54)	650.00	32.50
7	A2	20c blue	425.00	7.00
a.		Ribbed paper ('54)	650.00	32.50
8	A2	40c car rose	*850.00*	72.50
a.		Ribbed paper ('54)	*1,300.*	135.00

Nos. 6-8 were printed on thin and thick paper. Nos. 6-7 on thick paper, unused, sell for 7 to 10 percent more.

1858-61 Unwmk.

9	A2	1c green ('61)	*225.00*	110.00
10	A2	10c brown	275.00	6.00
11	A2	20c blue	325.00	6.00
12	A2	40c car rose	*1,700.*	60.00

Nos. 9 and 13 were valid for postage on newspapers and printed matter only.

Reprints of Nos. 9 to 12 are on thin wove paper. The colors are brighter than those of the originals. They were made from the dies and show lines outside the stamps.

Perf. 12½, 12½x13, 12½x13½, 14½

1863

13	A2	1c green	52.50	45.00
14	A2	10c brown	75.00	2.25
15	A2	20c blue	80.00	2.25
16	A2	40c carmine rose	400.00	35.00

Values for Nos. 13-16 are for copies with perfs cutting into design.

King Leopold I
A3 A3a

A4

A4a

A5

London Print

1865 Typo. *Perf. 14*

17	A5	1fr pale violet	700.00	100.00

Brussels Print
Thick or Thin Paper

1865-66 *Perf. 15, 14½x14*

18	A3	10c slate ('66)	85.00	1.25
a.		Pair, imperf. between		115.00
19	A3a	20c blue ('66)	100.00	1.25
a.		20c lilac blue	100.00	1.40
20	A4	30c brown	200.00	10.00
a.		Pair, imperf. between	675.00	
21	A4a	40c rose ('66)	300.00	18.00
22	A5	1fr violet	750.00	90.00

Nos. 18 to 22 on thin paper are perf. 14½x14; on thick paper, perf. 15.

The reprints are on thin paper, imperforate and ungummed.

Coat of Arms — A6

1866-67 *Imperf.*

23	A6	1c gray	250.00	150.00

Perf. 15, 14½x14

24	A6	1c gray	37.50	16.00
25	A6	2c blue ('67)	135.00	90.00
a.		2c ultramarine	150.00	110.00
26	A6	5c brown	135.00	90.00

Nos. 23-26 were valid for postage on newspapers and printed matter only.

Nos. 24 to 26 on thin paper are perf. 14½ x 14; on thick paper, perf. 15.

Counterfeits exist.

Reprints of Nos. 24 to 26 are on thin paper, imperforate and ungummed.

Imperf. varieties of 1869-1912 (between Nos. 28-105) are without gum.

A7 A8 A9

A10 A11 A12

King Leopold II
A13 A14 A15

1869-70 *Perf. 15*

28	A7	1c green	6.00	28
29	A7	2c ultra ('70)	9.50	28
30	A7	5c buff ('70)	37.50	50
31	A7	8c lilac ('70)	75.00	50.00
32	A8	10c green	17.50	38
33	A9	20c lt ultra ('70)	70.00	70
34	A10	30c buff ('70)	70.00	4.00
35	A11	40c brt rose ('70)	70.00	5.00
36	A12	1fr dull lilac ('70)	200.00	17.00
a.		1fr rose lilac	215.00	19.00

The frames and inscriptions of Nos. 30, 31 and 42 differ slightly from the illustration.

Minor "broken letter" varieties exist on several values.

Nos. 28-36, 40 also were printed in aniline colors. These are not valued separately.

See Nos. 40-43, 49-51, 55.

1875-78

37	A13	25c olive bister	55.00	1.25
a.		25c ocher	55.00	1.25
38	A14	50c gray	200.00	7.50
a.		50c gray black	325.00	55.00
39	A15	5fr dp red brown	*1,000.*	500.00
		Roller cancel		250.00
a.		5fr pale brown ('78)	*1,700.*	250.00

Dangerous counterfeits of No. 39 exist.

Printed in Aniline Colors

1881 *Perf. 14*

40	A7	1c gray green	8.00	45
41	A7	2c lt ultra	9.00	85
42	A7	5c orange buff	40.00	65
a.		5c red orange	40.00	65
43	A8	10c gray green	30.00	45
44	A13	25c olive bister	55.00	1.40
		Nos. 40-44 (5)	142.00	3.80

See note following No. 36.

A16

A17

A18

A19

1883

45	A16	10c carmine	27.50	1.75
46	A17	20c gray	115.00	4.50
47	A18	25c blue	225.00	27.50
		Roller cancel		12.50
48	A19	50c violet	200.00	35.00
		Roller cancel		12.50

A20

A21

A22

1884-85 *Perf. 14*

49	A7	1c olive green	6.50	55
50	A7	1c gray	2.75	15
51	A7	5c green	14.00	15
52	A20	10c rose, *bluish*	4.50	15
a.		Grayish paper	5.00	35
c.		Yellowish paper	50.00	20.00
53	A21	25c blue, *pink* ('85)	8.00	38
54	A22	1fr brown, *grnsh*	*500.00*	13.00

The frame and inscription of No. 51 differ slightly from the illustration.

See note after No. 36.

A23

A24

A25

A26

1886-91

55	A7	2c purple brn ('88)	7.75	45
56	A23	20c olive, *grnsh*	95.00	55
57	A24	35c vio brn, *brnsh* ('91)	18.00	2.50
58	A25	50c bister, *yelsh*	9.50	1.50
59	A26	2fr violet, *pale lil*	90.00	30.00
		Roller cancel		6.00

Coat of Arms
A27

King Leopold
A28

1893-1900

60	A27	1c gray	1.10	15
61	A27	2c yellow	1.25	1.10
a.		Wmkd. coat of arms in sheet ('95)		
62	A27	2c violet brn ('94)	1.65	18
63	A27	2c red brown ('98)	3.25	18
64	A27	5c yellow grn	5.00	15
65	A28	10c orange brn	5.00	15
66	A28	10c brt rose ('00)	3.50	15
67	A28	20c olive green	22.50	38
68	A28	25c ultra	20.00	38
a.		No ball to "5" in upper left corner	32.50	12.00
69	A28	35c violet brn	37.50	95
a.		35c brown	42.50	1.25
70	A28	50c bister	62.50	8.25
71	A28	50c gray ('97)	57.50	1.90
72	A28	1fr car, *lt grn*	75.00	11.00
73	A28	1fr orange ('00)	105.00	5.00
74	A28	2fr lilac, *rose*	110.00	82.50
75	A28	2fr lilac ('00)	150.00	13.50

Values quoted for Nos. 60-107 are for stamps with label attached. Stamps without label sell for about one tenth.

Antwerp Exhibition Issue

Arms of Antwerp — A29

1894

76	A29	5c green, *rose*	4.75	3.25
77	A29	10c carmine, *bluish*	3.75	1.25
78	A29	25c blue, *rose*	80	90
		Nos. 76-78 (3)	9.30	5.40

Brussels Exhibition Issue

St. Michael and Satan
A30 A31

1896-97 *Perf. 14x14½*

79	A30	5c dp violet	90	45
80	A31	10c orange brown	8.50	3.00
81	A31	10c lilac brown	65	35
		Nos. 79-81 (3)	10.05	3.80

A32

A33

A34

A35

A36

A37

A38

A39

Two types of 1c:

I - Periods after "Dimanche" and "Zondag" in label.

II - No period after "Dimanche." Period often missing after "Zondag."

1905-07 *Perf. 14*

82	A32	1c gray (I) ('07)	65	22
a.		Type II ('08)	65	25
83	A32	2c red brown ('07)	4.50	2.25
84	A32	5c green ('07)	4.50	22
85	A33	10c dull rose	1.65	20
86	A34	20c olive grn	12.00	90
87	A35	25c ultra	9.75	75
a.		25c dull blue	9.75	75
88	A36	35c purple brn	18.00	1.90
89	A37	50c bluish gray	47.50	2.50
90	A38	1fr yellow	62.50	8.00
91	A39	2fr violet	62.50	22.50
		Bar cancellation		4.00
		Nos. 82-91 (10)	223.55	39.44

A40

A41

Lion of Belgium — A42

A43

King Albert I — A44

1912

92	A40	1c orange	22	15
93	A41	2c orange brn	45	55
94	A42	5c green	35	15
95	A43	10c red	1.10	42
96	A43	20c olive grn	8.50	1.75
97	A43	35c bister brn	1.25	80
98	A43	40c green	13.00	8.75
99	A43	50c gray	1.25	1.10
100	A43	1fr orange	6.00	5.50
101	A43	2fr violet	14.00	15.00
102	A44	5fr plum	90.00	24.00
		Nos. 92-102 (11)	136.12	58.17

Counterfeits exist of Nos. 97-102. Those of No. 102 are common.

For overprints see Nos. Q49-Q50, Q52, Q55-Q55A, Q57-Q60.

A45

1912-13

Larger Head

103	A45	10c red	35	22
a.		Without engraver's name	25	15
104	A45	20c olive grn ('13)	50	50
a.		Without engraver's name	1.10	1.10
105	A45	25c ultra	35	45
a.		With engraver's name	2.75	1.90
107	A45	40c green ('13)	60	75
		Nos. 103-107 (4)	1.80	1.92

For overprints see #Q51, Q53-Q54, Q56.

Albert I
A46

Cloth Hall of Ypres
A47

Bridge of Dinant — A48

Library of Louvain — A49

Scheldt River at Antwerp A50

Anti-slavery Campaign in the Congo — A51

King Albert I at Furnes — A52

Kings of Belgium Leopold I, Albert I, Leopold II A53

1915-20 Typo. *Perf. 14, 14½*

108	A46	1c orange	15	15
109	A46	2c chocolate	15	15
110	A46	3c gray blk ('20)	18	15
111	A46	5c green	35	15
112	A46	10c carmine	65	15
113	A46	15c purple	80	15
114	A46	20c red vio	80	15
115	A46	25c blue	95	16

Engr.

116	A47	35c brown org & blk	65	16
117	A48	40c green & black	1.10	16
a.		Vert. pair, imperf. btwn.		
118	A49	50c car rose & blk	3.50	16
119	A50	1fr violet	13.00	30
120	A51	2fr slate	16.00	1.25
121	A52	5fr dp blue	150.00	62.50
		Telegraph or railroad cancel		47.50
122	A53	10fr brown	16.00	15.00
		Nos. 108-122 (15)	204.28	80.74

Two types each of the 1c, 10c and 20c; three of the 2c and 15c; four of the 5c, differing in the top left corner.

Nos. 108-120, 122 exist imperforate. See No. 138. For surcharges see Nos. B34-B47.

Perron of Liege (Fountain) A54

King Albert in Trench Helmet A55

1919 *Perf. 11½*

123	A54	25c deep blue	1.50	20
a.		Sheet of 10	*5,500.*	*5,500.*

Perf. 11, 11½, 11½x11, 11x11½

1919

Size: 18½x22mm

124	A55	1c lilac brn	15	15
125	A55	2c olive	15	15

Size: 23x26mm

126	A55	5c green	18	15
127	A55	10c carmine	15	15
128	A55	15c gray vio	15	15
129	A55	20c olive blk	45	55
130	A55	25c deep blue	55	60
131	A55	35c bister brn	85	70
132	A55	40c red	1.25	1.25
133	A55	50c red brn	3.25	3.25
134	A55	1fr lt orange	18.00	18.00
135	A55	2fr violet	195.00	180.00

Size: 28x33½mm

136	A55	5fr car lake	65.00	65.00
137	A55	10fr claret	72.50	72.50
		Nos. 124-137 (14)	357.63	342.60

Type of 1915 Inscribed: "FRANK" instead of "FRANKEN"

1919, Dec. *Perf. 14, 15*

138	A52	5fr deep blue	1.50	85

Town Hall at Termonde
A56 A57

1920 *Perf. 11½*

139	A56	65c claret & black	1.10	20
a.		Center inverted		*25,000.*

For surcharge see No. 143.

Semi-Postal Stamps of 1920 Surcharged in Red or Black

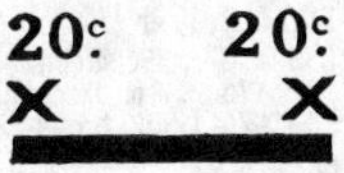

1921 *Perf. 12*

140	SP6	20c on 5c (R)	60	22
a.		Inverted surcharge	185.00	185.00
141	SP7	20c on 10c	42	22
b.		Inverted surcharge	185.00	185.00
142	SP8	20c on 15c (R)	45	22
a.		Inverted surcharge	185.00	185.00

Red Surcharge

143	A57	55c on 65c claret & blk	1.10	35
a.		Pair, one without surcharge	1.75	85
		Nos. 140-143 (4)	2.57	1.01

A58

A59

1922-27 Typo. *Perf. 14*

144	A58	1c orange	15	15
145	A58	2c olive ('26)	15	15
146	A58	3c fawn	15	15
147	A58	5c gray	15	15
148	A58	10c blue grn	15	15
149	A58	15c plum ('23)	15	15
150	A58	20c black brn	20	15
151	A58	25c dull violet	15	15
152	A58	30c vermilion	50	15
153	A58	30c rose ('25)	38	15
154	A58	35c red brown	30	15
155	A58	35c blue grn ('27)	55	30
156	A58	40c rose	50	15
157	A58	50c bister ('25)	50	15
158	A58	60c olive brn ('27)	2.00	15
159	A58	1.25fr dp blue ('26)	60	60
160	A58	1.50fr brt blue ('26)	1.50	22
161	A58	1.75fr ultra ('27)	1.00	15
a.		Tete beche pair	7.50	4.50
c.		Bklt. pane of 4 + 2 labels	37.50	
		Nos. 144-161 (18)	9.08	
		Set value		2.30

See Nos. 185-190. For overprints and surcharges see Nos. 191-195, 197, B56, O1-O6.

Perf. 11½, 11½x11, 11½x12, 11½x12½

1921-25 Engr.

162	A59	50c dull blue	30	15
163	A59	75c scarlet ('22)	15	15
164	A59	75c ultra ('24)	38	15
165	A59	1fr black brn ('22)	75	15
166	A59	1fr dk blue ('25)	52	15
167	A59	2fr dk green ('22)	60	20
168	A59	5fr brown vio ('23)	10.50	13.00
169	A59	10fr magenta ('22)	7.00	1.75
		Nos. 162-169 (8)	20.20	15.70

No. 162 measures 18x20¾mm and was printed in sheets of 100.

Philatelic Exhibition Issues

1921, May 26 *Perf. 11½*

170	A59	50c dark blue	3.50	3.50
a.		Sheet of 25	225.00	175.00

No. 170 measures 17½x21¼mm, was printed in sheets of 25 and sold at the Philatelic Exhibition at Brussels.

The sheet normally has pin holes and a cancellation-like marking in the margin. These are considered unused and the condition valued here.

Souvenir Sheet

1924, May 24 *Perf. 11½*

171		Sheet of 4	125.00	110.00
a.		A59 5fr red brown	15.00	15.00

Sold only at the Intl. Phil. Exhib., Brussels. Sheet size: 130x145mm.

The sheet normally has pin holes and a cancellation-like marking in the margin. These are considered unused and the condition valued here.

Kings Leopold I and Albert I — A60

1925 *Perf. 14*

172	A60	10c dp green	5.75	6.00
173	A60	15c dull vio	3.75	4.50
174	A60	20c red brown	3.75	4.50
175	A60	25c grnsh black	3.75	4.50
176	A60	30c vermilion	3.75	4.50
177	A60	35c lt blue	3.75	4.50
178	A60	40c brnsh blk	3.75	4.50
179	A60	50c yellow brn	3.75	4.50
180	A60	75c dk blue	3.75	4.50
181	A60	1fr dk violet	5.75	6.50
182	A60	2fr ultra	3.75	4.50
183	A60	5fr blue blk	3.75	4.50
184	A60	10fr dp rose	5.75	7.75
		Nos. 172-184 (13)	54.75	65.25

75th anniv. of Belgian postage stamps.

Nos. 172-184 were sold only in sets and only by The Administration of Posts, not at post offices.

A61

1926-27 Typo.

185	A61	75c dk violet	65	65
186	A61	1fr pale yellow	52	22
187	A61	1fr rose red ('27)	75	15
a.		Tete beche pair	7.50	4.50
c.		Bklt. pane 4 + 2 labels	22.50	
188	A61	2fr Prus blue	2.00	15
189	A61	5fr emerald ('27)	14.00	90
190	A61	10fr dk brown ('27)	25.00	4.00
		Nos. 185-190 (6)	42.92	6.07

For overprints and surcharge see Nos. 196, Q174-Q175.

Stamps of 1921-27 Surcharged in Carmine, Red or Blue

1927

191	A58	3c on 2c olive (C)	15	15
192	A58	10c on 15c plum (R)	15	15
193	A58	35c on 40c rose (Bl)	50	15
194	A58	1.75fr on 1.50fr brt bl (C)	2.50	80
		Nos. 191-194 (4)	3.30	1.25

Nos. 153, 185 and 159 Surcharged in Black

1929, Jan. 1

195	A58	5c on 30c rose	15	15
196	A61	5c on 75c dk violet	30	30
197	A58	5c on 1.25fr dp blue	15	15
		Nos. 195-197 (3)	60	60

The surcharge on Nos. 195 to 197 is a precancelation which alters the value of the stamp to which it is applied.

Values for precanceled stamps in unused column are for those which have not been through the post and have original gum. Values in second column are for postally used, gumless stamps.

A63

A64

1929-32 Typo. *Perf. 14*

198	A63	1c orange	15	15
199	A63	2c emerald ('31)	20	35
200	A63	3c red brown	15	15
201	A63	5c slate	15	15
c.		Bklt. pane of 4 + 2 labels	8.25	
202	A63	10c olive grn	15	15
c.		Bklt. pane of 4 + 2 labels	4.50	
203	A63	20c brt violet	1.00	15
204	A63	25c rose red	45	15
c.		Bklt. pane of 4 + 2 labels	8.25	
205	A63	35c green	65	15
c.		Bklt. pane of 4 + 2 labels	9.75	
206	A63	40c red vio ('30)	30	15
c.		Bklt. pane of 4 + 2 labels	9.75	
207	A63	50c dp blue	52	15
c.		Bklt. pane of 4 + 2 labels	8.25	
208	A63	60c rose ('30)	1.10	20
c.		Bklt. pane of 4 + 2 labels	30.00	
209	A63	70c org brn ('30)	70	15
c.		Bklt. pane of 4 + 2 labels	22.50	
210	A63	75c dk blue ('30)	1.75	15
211	A63	75c dp brown ('32)	6.00	15
b.		Bklt. pane of 4 + 2 labels	100.00	
		Nos. 198-211 (14)	13.27	
		Set value		1.35

For overprints and surcharges see Nos. 225-226, 240-241, 254-256, 309, O7-O15.

Tete Beche Pairs

201a	A63	5c	1.00	90
202a	A63	10c	65	60
204a	A63	25c	2.00	2.00
205a	A63	35c	3.00	3.00
206a	A63	40c	3.00	3.00
207a	A63	50c	2.50	2.50
208a	A63	60c	9.00	8.50
209a	A63	70c	6.50	5.50
210a	A63	75c	10.00	9.50
211a	A63	75c	32.50	27.50
		Nos. 201a-211a (10)	70.15	63.00

1929, Jan. 25 Engr. *Perf. 14½, 14*

212	A64	10fr dk brown	9.25	4.00
213	A64	20fr dk green	60.00	5.50
214	A64	50fr red violet	5.75	5.50
a.		Perf. 14½	18.00	18.00
215	A64	100fr rose lake	7.50	10.00
a.		Perf. 14½	24.00	24.00
		Nos. 212-215 (4)	82.50	25.00

Peter Paul Rubens — A65

Zenobe Gramme — A66

1930, Apr. 26 Photo. *Perf. 12½x12*

216	A65	35c blue green	45	25
217	A66	35c blue green	45	25

No. 216 issued for the Antwerp Exhibition, No. 217 the Liege Exhibition.

Leopold I, by Jacques de Winne — A67

Leopold II, by Joseph Lempoels — A68

Design: 1.75fr, Albert I.

1930, July 1 **Engr.** ***Perf. 11½***

218 A67 60c brown vio 24 15
219 A68 1fr carmine 1.25 1.25
220 A68 1.75fr dk blue 3.00 95
Nos. 218-220 (3) 4.49 2.35

Centenary of Belgian independence.
For overprints see Nos. 222-224.

Antwerp Exhibition Issue
Souvenir Sheet

Arms of Antwerp — A70

1930, Aug. 9 ***Perf. 11½***

221 A70 4fr Sheet of 1 140.00 160.00

Size: 142x141mm. Inscription in lower margin "ATELIER DU TIMBRE-1930-ZEGELFABRIEK." Each purchaser of a ticket to the Antwerp Phil. Exhib., Aug. 9-15, was allowed to purchase one stamps. The ticket cost 6 francs.

The sheet normally has pin holes and a cancellation-like marking in the margin. These are considered unused and the condition valued here.

Nos. 218-220 Overprinted in Blue or Red

B.I.T.
OCT. 1930

1930, Oct.

222 A67 60c brown vio (Bl) 1.75 1.50
223 A68 1fr carmine (Bl) 8.25 7.50
224 A68 1.75fr dk blue (R) 14.00 14.00
Nos. 222-224 (3) 24.00 23.00

50th meeting of the administrative council of the Intl. Labor Bureau at Brussels.

The names of the painters and the initials of the engraver have been added at the foot of these stamps.

Stamps of 1929-30 Surcharged in Blue or Black:

BELGIQUE
1931
BELGIË
10c

2c

1931, Feb. 20 ***Perf. 14***

225 A63 2c on 3c red brown (Bl) 15 15
226 A63 10c on 60c rose (Bk) 50 22

The surcharge on No. 226 is a precancelation which alters the denomination. See note after No. 197.

King Albert
A71 A71a

1931, June 15 **Photo.**

227 A71 1fr brown carmine 85 15

1932, June 1

228 A71a 75c bister brown 45 15
a. Tete beche pair 11.00 11.00
c. Bklt. pane 4 + 2 labels 27.50

See No. 257. For overprint see No. O18.

A72

1931-32 **Engr.**

229 A72 1.25fr gray black 85 35
230 A72 1.50fr brown vio 1.10 30
231 A72 1.75fr dp blue 85 15
232 A72 2fr red brown 1.10 15
233 A72 2.45fr dp violet 1.50 30
234 A72 2.50fr black brn ('32) 11.50 35
235 A72 5fr dp green 12.50 90
236 A72 10fr claret 30.00 11.00
Nos. 229-236 (8) 59.40 13.50

Nos. 206 and 209 Surcharged as No. 226, but dated "1932"

1932, Jan. 1

240 A63 10c on 40c red vio 2.75 32
241 A63 10c on 70c org brn 2.25 16

See note after No. 197.

Gleaner
A73

Mercury
A74

1932, June 1 **Typo.** ***Perf. 13½x14***

245 A73 2c pale green 15 45
246 A74 5c dp orange 15 15
247 A73 10c olive grn 22 15
a. Tete beche pair 4.50 4.50
c. Bklt. pane 4 + 2 labels 15.00
248 A74 20c brt violet 45 15
249 A73 25c deep red 45 15
a. Tete beche pair 4.00 4.00
c. Bklt. pane 4 + 2 labels 15.00
250 A74 35c dp green 1.65 15
Nos. 245-250 (6) 3.07
Set value 85

For overprints see Nos. O16-O17.

Auguste Piccard's Balloon — A75

1932, Nov. 26 **Engr.** ***Perf. 11½***

251 A75 75c red brown 3.25 30
252 A75 1.75fr dk blue 7.75 1.75
253 A75 2.50fr dk violet 9.50 8.50
Nos. 251-253 (3) 20.50 10.55

Issued in commemoration of Prof. Auguste Piccard's two ascents to the stratosphere.

Nos. 206 and 209 Surcharged as No. 226, but dated "1933"

1933, Nov. ***Perf. 14***

254 A63 10c on 40c red vio 14.00 4.00
255 A63 10c on 70c org brn 11.00 1.50

No. 206 Surcharged as No. 226, but dated "1934"

1934, Feb.

256 A63 10c on 40c red vio 11.00 1.50

For Nos. 254 to 256 see note after No. 197. Regummed copies of Nos. 254-256 abound.

King Albert Memorial Issue
Type of 1932 with Black Margins

1934, Mar. 10 **Photo.**

257 A71a 75c black 30 15

Congo Pavilion — A76

Designs: 1fr, Brussels pavilion. 1.50fr, "Old Brussels." 1.75fr, Belgian pavilion.

1934, July 1 ***Perf. 14x13½***

258 A76 35c green 50 15
259 A76 1fr dk carmine 65 18
260 A76 1.50fr brown 1.75 75
261 A76 1.75fr blue 4.00 15
Nos. 258-261 (4) 6.90 1.23

Brussels Intl. Exhib. of 1935.

King Leopold III
A80 A81

1934-35 ***Perf. 13½x14***

262 A80 70c ol blk ('35) 35 15
a. Tete beche pair 1.75 1.00
c. Bklt. pane 4 + 2 labels 6.25
263 A80 75c brown 70 15

Perf. 14x13½

264 A81 1fr rose car ('35) 3.50 35
Nos. 262-264 (3) 4.55
Set value 52

For overprint see No. O19.

Coat of Arms — A82

1935-48 **Typo.** ***Perf. 14***

265 A82 2c green ('37) 15 15
266 A82 5c orange 15 15
267 A82 10c ol bister 15 15
a. Tete beche pair 35 30
b. Bklt. pane 4 + 2 labels 4.50
268 A82 15c dk violet 15 15
269 A82 20c lilac 15 15
270 A82 25c car rose 15 15
a. Tete beche pair 59 45
c. Bklt. pane 4 + 2 labels 4.50
271 A82 25c yel org ('46) 15 15
272 A82 30c brown 15 15
273 A82 35c green 15 15
a. Tete beche pair 30 20
c. Bklt. pane 4 + 2 labels 3.00
274 A82 40c red vio ('38) 20 15
275 A82 50c blue 25 15
276 A82 60c slate ('41) 15 15
277 A82 65c red lilac ('46) 30 15
278 A82 70c lt blue grn ('45) 15 15
279 A82 75c lilac rose ('45) 25 15
280 A82 80c green ('48) 3.50 45
281 A82 90c dull vio ('46) 20 15
282 A82 1fr red brown ('45) 15 15
Nos. 265-282 (18) 6.50
Set value 1.25

Several stamps of type A82 exist in various shades.

Nos. 265, 361 were privately overprinted and surcharged "+10FR." by the Association Belgo-Americaine for the dedication of the Bastogne Memorial, July 16, 1950. The overprint is in six types.

See design O1. For overprints and surcharges see Nos. 312-313, 361-364, 390-394, O20-O22, O24, O26-O28, O33.

A83

A83a

Perf. 14, 14x13½, 11½

1936-51 **Photo.**

Size: 17½x21¾mm

283 A83 70c brown 35 15
a. Tete beche pair 75 65
c. Bklt. pane 4 + 2 labels 7.50

Size: 20¾x24mm

284 A83a 1fr rose car 30 15
285 A83a 1.20fr dk brown ('51) 90 15
286 A83a 1.50fr brt red vio ('43) 25 15
287 A83a 1.75fr dp ultra ('43) 15 18
288 A83a 1.75fr dk car ('50) 15 15
289 A83a 2fr dk pur ('43) 90 85
290 A83a 2.25fr grnsh blk ('43) 25 15
291 A83a 2.50fr org red ('51) 1.90 15
292 A83a 3.25fr chestnut ('43) 15 15
293 A83a 5fr dp green ('43) 90 40
Nos. 283-293 (11) 6.20
Set value 2.00

Nos. 287-288, 290-291, 293 inscribed "Belgie-Belgique."

See designs A85, A91. For overprints and surcharges see Nos. 314, O23, O25, O29, O31, O34.

A84

A85

1936-51 **Engr.** ***Perf. 14x13½***

294 A84 1.50fr rose lilac 30 15
295 A84 1.75fr dull blue 20 15
296 A84 2fr dull vio 30 15
297 A84 2.25fr gray vio ('41) 25 15
298 A84 2.45fr black 22.50 45
299 A84 2.50fr ol blk ('40) 2.00 25
300 A84 3.25fr org brn ('41) 30 15
301 A84 5fr dull green 1.50 35
302 A84 10fr dk vio brn 60 15
a. 10fr light brown 22.50 35
303 A84 20fr vermilion 1.00 15

Perf. 11½

304 A84 3fr yel brn ('51) 60 15
305 A84 4fr bl, *bluish* ('50) 1.50 15
a. White paper 5.50 15
306 A84 6fr brt rose car ('51) 3.00 15
307 A84 10fr brn vio ('51) 60 15
308 A84 20fr red ('51) 1.25 15
Nos. 294-308 (15) 35.90
Set value 2.00

See No. 1159. For overprint and surcharges see Nos. 316-317, O32.

No. 206 Surcharged as No. 226, but dated "1937"

1937 **Unwmk.** ***Perf. 14***

309 A63 10c on 40c red vio 15 20

See note after No. 197.

1938-41 **Photo.** ***Perf. 13½x14***

310 A85 75c olive gray 30 15
a. Tete beche pair 1.50 1.25
c. Bklt. pane 4 + 2 labels 6.75
311 A85 1fr rose pink ('41) 15 15
a. Tete beche pair 35 22
b. Booklet pane of 6 2.25
c. Bklt. pane 4 + 2 labels 2.25
Set value 15

For overprints and surcharges see Nos. 315, O25, O30, O35.

Nos. 272, 274, 283, 310, 299, 298 Surcharged in Blue, Black, Carmine or Red

10
c
a

10c.
b

≡ 2F25
c

1938-42

312	A82 (a)	10c on 30c (Bl)	15	15
313	A82 (a)	10c on 40c (Bl)	15	15
314	A83 (b)	10c on 70c (Bk)	15	15
315	A85 (b)	50c on 75c (C)	16	15
316	A84 (c)	2.25fr on 2.50fr (C)	50	60
317	A84 (c)	2.50fr on 2.45fr (R)	12.00	15
		Nos. 312-317 (6)	13.11	1.35

Issue date: No. 317, Oct. 31, 1938.

Basilica and Bell Tower — A86

Water Exhibition Buildings — A87

Designs: 1.50fr, Albert Canal and Park. 1.75fr, Eygenbilsen Cut in Albert Canal.

Perf. 14x13½, 13½x14

1938, Oct. 31

318	A86	35c dk blue grn	15	15
319	A87	1fr rose red	50	18
320	A87	1.50fr vio brn	1.25	70
321	A87	1.75fr ultra	1.40	22
		Nos. 318-321 (4)	3.30	1.25

Intl. Water Exhibition, Liège, 1939.

Catalogue values for unused stamps in this section, from this point to the end of the section, are for Never Hinged items.

Lion Rampant A90

Leopold III, Crown and V A91

1944 Unwmk. Photo. *Perf. 12½*

Inscribed: "Belgique-Belgie"

322	A90	5c chocolate	15	15
323	A90	10c green	15	15
324	A90	25c lt blue	15	15
325	A90	35c brown	15	15
326	A90	50c lt bl grn	15	15
327	A90	75c purple	15	15
328	A90	1fr vermilion	15	15
329	A90	1.25fr chestnut	18	16
330	A90	1.50fr orange	45	38
331	A90	1.75fr brt ultra	15	15
332	A90	2fr aqua	3.75	1.90
333	A90	2.75fr dp mag	20	15
334	A90	3fr claret	75	60
335	A90	3.50fr sl blk	75	60
336	A90	5fr dk olive	6.75	4.75
337	A90	10fr black	1.25	1.10
		Nos. 322-337 (16)	15.28	10.84

Inscribed: "Belgie-Belgique"

338	A90	5c chocolate	15	15
339	A90	10c green	15	15
340	A90	25c lt bl	15	15
341	A90	35c brown	15	15
342	A90	50c lt bl grn	15	15
343	A90	75c purple	15	15
344	A90	1fr vermilion	15	15
345	A90	1.25fr chestnut	15	20
346	A90	1.50fr orange	32	45
347	A90	1.75fr brt ultra	15	15
348	A90	2fr aqua	2.00	2.00
349	A90	2.75fr dp magenta	18	15
350	A90	3fr claret	65	75
351	A90	3.50fr slate blk	65	75
352	A90	5fr dark olive	5.75	5.00
353	A90	10fr black	1.00	1.25
		Nos. 338-353 (16)	11.90	11.75

1944-57 *Perf. 14x13½*

354	A91	1fr brt rose red	35	15
355	A91	1.50fr magenta	50	15
356	A91	1.75fr dp ultra	50	55
357	A91	2fr dp vio	1.50	15
358	A91	2.25fr grnsh blk	55	65
359	A91	3.25fr chnt brn	75	15
360	A91	5fr dk bl grn	3.00	15
a.		Perf. 11½ ('57)	45.00	15
		Nos. 354-360 (7)	7.15	
		Set value		1.50

Nos. 355, 357, 359 inscribed "Belgique-Belgie."

For surcharges see Nos. 365-367 and footnote following No. 367.

Stamps of 1935-41 Overprinted in Red

V

1944 *Perf. 14*

361	A82	2c pale grn	15	15
362	A82	15c indigo	15	15
363	A82	20c brt vio	15	15
364	A82	60c slate	24	15
		Set value	48	32

See note following No. 282.

Nos. 355, 357, and 360 Surcharged Typographically in Black or Carmine

−10%

1946 *Perf. 14x13½*

365	A91	On 1.50fr magenta	52	15
366	A91	On 2fr dp vio (C)	1.90	45
367	A91	On 5fr dk bl grn (C)	2.50	28
		Nos. 365-367 (3)	4.92	88

To provide denominations created by a reduction in postal rates, the Government produced Nos. 365-367 by surcharging typographically. Also, each post office was authorized on May 20, 1946, to surcharge its stock of 1.50fr, 2fr and 5fr stamps "-10 percent." Hundreds of types and sizes of this surcharge exist, both hand-stamped and typographed. These include the "1,35," "1,80" and "4,50" applied at Ghislenghien.

M. S. Prince Baudouin — A92

Designs: 2.25fr, S.S. Marie Henriette. 3.15fr, S.S. Diamant.

Perf. 14x13½, 13½x14

1946, June 15 Photo. Unwmk.

368	A92	1.35fr brt bluish grn	15	15
369	A92	2.25fr slate green	30	15
370	A92	3.15fr slate black	30	15
		Nos. 368-370 (3)	75	
		Set value		31

Centenary of the steamship line between Ostend and Dover.

#368 exists in two sizes: 21¼x18¼mm and 21x17mm. #369-370 are 24½x20mm.

Capt. Adrien de Gerlache A95

Belgica and Explorers A96

1947, June *Perf. 14x13½, 11½*

371	A95	1.35fr crimson rose	38	15
372	A96	2.25fr gray black	2.25	2.00

50th anniv. of Capt. Adrien de Gerlache's Antarctic Expedition.

Joseph A. F. Plateau — A97

1947, June *Perf. 14x13½*

373	A97	3.15fr deep blue	80	15

Issued to mark the World Film and Fine Arts Festival, Brussels, June, 1947.

Chemical Industry — A98

Industrial Arts — A99

Agriculture — A100

Textile Industry — A102

Communications Center — A101

Iron Manufacture A103

Photogravure (#374-376, 378), Typographed (#377, 380), Engraved

1948 Unwmk. *Perf. 11½*

374	A98	60c bl grn	80	22
375	A98	1.20fr brown	2.00	16
376	A99	1.35fr red brown	80	15
377	A100	1.75fr brt red	1.40	15
378	A99	1.75fr dk gray grn	1.00	15
379	A101	2.25fr gray blue	1.75	1.75
380	A100	2.50fr dk car rose	6.25	18
381	A101	3fr brt red vio	8.50	28
382	A102	3.15fr deep blue	1.75	22
383	A102	4fr brt ultra	7.50	18
384	A103	6fr bl grn	12.50	18
385	A103	6.30fr brt red vio	3.50	3.75
		Nos. 374-385 (12)	47.75	7.37

See Nos. O42-O46.

Leopold I — A104

1949, July 1 Engr. *Perf. 14x13½*

386	A104	90c dk green	1.10	65
387	A104	1.75fr brown	90	15
388	A104	3fr red	3.50	3.25
389	A104	4fr deep blue	5.00	1.40
		Nos. 386-389 (4)	10.50	5.45

Cent. of Belgium's 1st postage stamps. See note on souvenir sheet below No. 2.

Stamps of 1935-45 Precanceled and Surcharged in Black

= 20c =

1949 *Perf. 14*

390	A82	5c on 15c dk vio	15	15
391	A82	5c on 30c brown	15	15
392	A82	5c on 40c red vio	15	15
393	A82	20c on 70c lt bl grn	35	45
394	A82	20c on 75c lil rose	20	18

Similar Surcharge and Precancellation in Black on Nos. B455-B458

Perf. 14x13½

395	SP251	10c on #B455	4.00	4.00
396	SP251	40c on #B456	1.25	1.10
397	SP251	80c on #B457	70	65
398	SP251	1.20fr on #B458	2.50	2.00
		Nos. 390-398 (9)	9.45	8.83

See note after No. 197.

St. Mary Magdalene, from Painting by Gerard David — A105

1949, July 15 Photo. *Perf. 11*

399	A105	1.75fr dk brown	65	35

Gerard David Exhibition at Bruges, 1949.

Allegory of UPU — A106

1949, Oct. 1 Engr. *Perf. 11½*

400	A106	4fr deep blue	4.50	2.50

75th anniv. of the UPU.

Symbolical of Pension Fund A107

Lion Rampant A108

Perf. 11½

1950, May 1 Unwmk. Photo.

401	A107	1.75fr dark brown	50	25

General Pension Fund founding, cent.

1951, Feb. 15 Engr. *Perf. 11½*

402	A108	20c blue	25	15

1951-75 Typo. *Perf. 13½x14*

Size: 17½x21mm

403	A108	2c org brn ('60)	15	15
404	A108	3c brt lil ('60)	15	15
405	A108	5c pale violet	15	15
406	A108	5c brt pink ('74)	15	15
407	A108	10c red orange	15	15
408	A108	15c brt pink ('59)	15	15
409	A108	20c claret	15	15
410	A108	25c green	1.50	22
411	A108	25c lt bl grn ('66)	15	15
412	A108	30c gray grn ('57)	15	15
413	A108	40c brown olive	15	15
414	A108	50c ultra	15	15
a.		50c light blue	15	15
415	A108	60c lilac rose	15	15
416	A108	65c violet brn	12.50	55
417	A108	75c bluish lilac	30	15
418	A108	80c emerald	1.00	15
419	A108	90c deep blue	1.25	15
420	A108	1fr rose	15	15
421	A108	2fr emerald ('73)	30	15
422	A108	2.50fr brown ('70)	30	15
423	A108	3fr brt pink ('70)	30	15
424	A108	4fr brt rose lil ('74)	30	15
425	A108	4.50fr blue ('74)	45	15
426	A108	5fr brt lilac ('75)	30	15

Size: 17x20½mm

427	A108	1.50fr dk sl grn ('69)	15	15

Perf. 13½x13

428	A108	2fr emerald ('68)	25	15

Photo. *Perf. 11½*
Size: 20½x24mm

429	A108	50c lt blue ('61)	1.00	15
430	A108	60c lil rose ('66)	2.25	2.00
431	A108	1fr car rose ('59)	15	15

Perf. 13½x12½
Size: 17½x22mm

432	A108	50c lt blue ('75)	15	15
a.		Booklet pane of 4 (#432, 784 and 2 #785) + labels	1.00	
b.		Booklet pane of 4 (#432 and 3 #787) + labels	1.35	
433	A108	1fr rose ('69)	4.00	1.00
434	A108	2fr emerald ('72)	60	30
e.		Booklet pane of 6 (4 #434 + 2 #475)	5.50	
f.		Booklet pane of 5 (#434, 4 #476 + label)	8.00	
		Nos. 403-434 (32)	29.00	
		Set value		6.00

Counterfeits exist of No. 416. Nos. 429, 431 also issued in coils with black control number on back of every fifth stamp. Nos. 432-434 issued in booklet panes only. No. 432 has one straightedge, and stamps in the pane are tete-beche. Each pane has 2 labels showing Belgian postal emblem and a large selvage with postal code instructions.

Nos. 433-434 have 1 or 2 straight-edges. Panes have a large selvage with inscription or map of Belgium showing postal zones.

See designs A386, O5. For surcharges see Nos. 477-478, 563-567.

Francois de Tassis (Franz von Taxis) — A109

Portraits: 1.75fr, Jean-Baptiste of Thurn & Taxis. 2fr, Baron Leonard I. 2.50fr, Count Lamoral I. 3fr, Count Leonard II. 4fr, Count Lamoral II. 5fr, Prince Eugene Alexander. 5.75fr, Prince Anselme Francois. 8fr, Prince Alexander Ferdinand. 10fr, Prince Charles Anselme. 20fr, Prince Charles Alexander.

1952, May 14 **Engr.** *Perf. 11½*
Laid Paper

435	A109	80c olive grn	85	1.00
436	A109	1.75fr red org	85	32
437	A109	2fr violet brn	1.65	55
438	A109	2.50fr carmine	2.25	1.65
439	A109	3fr olive bis	2.00	1.00
440	A109	4fr ultra	3.00	85
441	A109	5fr red brn	4.00	1.75
442	A109	5.75fr blue vio	6.75	2.25
443	A109	8fr gray	11.00	2.75
444	A109	10fr rose vio	19.00	4.50
445	A109	20fr brown	47.50	22.00
		Nos. 435-445,B514 (12)	208.85	178.62

13th UPU Cong., Brussels, 1952.

King Baudouin
A110 A111

1952-58 **Engr.** *Perf. 11½*
Size: 21x24mm

446	A110	1.50fr gray	55	15
447	A110	2fr crimson	42	15
448	A110	4fr ultra	3.50	20

Size: 24½x35mm

449	A110	50fr gray brn	1.75	20
a.		50fr violet brown	20.00	60
450	A110	100fr rose red ('58)	5.00	24

1953-72 **Photo.** *Perf. 11½*

451	A111	1.50fr gray	25	15
452	A111	2fr rose carmine	6.75	15
453	A111	2fr green	25	15
454	A111	2.50fr red brn ('57)	60	15
a.		2.50fr orange brown ('70)	45	15
455	A111	3fr rose lilac ('58)	38	15
456	A111	3.50fr brt yel grn ('58)	75	15
457	A111	4fr brt ultra	50	15
458	A111	4.50fr dk red brn ('62)	3.00	15
459	A111	5fr violet ('57)	1.25	15
460	A111	6fr dp pink ('58)	75	15
461	A111	6.50fr gray ('60)	60.00	12.00
462	A111	7fr blue ('60)	90	15
463	A111	7.50fr grysh brn ('58)	42.50	14.00
464	A111	8fr bluish gray ('58)	1.25	15
465	A111	8.50fr claret ('58)	15.00	30
466	A111	9fr gray ('58)	45.00	75
467	A111	12fr lt bl grn ('66)	90	15
468	A111	30fr red org ('58)	5.50	15

Redrawn

469	A111	2.50fr orange brn ('71)	35	15
470	A111	4.50fr brown ('72)	2.25	60
471	A111	7fr blue ('71)	60	15

Perf. 13½x12½
Size: 17½x22mm

472	A111	1.50fr gray ('70)	60	30
b.		Bklt. pane of 10	6.50	
c.		Bklt. pane, 3 #472, 3 #475	15.00	
473	A111	2.50fr org brn ('70)	9.00	6.25
h.		Bklt. pane, 1 #473, 5 #475	16.00	
474	A111	3fr lilac rose ('69)	60	15
a.		Bklt. pane of 5 + label	25.00	
b.		Bklt. pane, 2 #433, 6 #474	18.00	
475	A111	3.50fr brt yel grn ('70)	60	24
476	A111	4.50fr dull red brn ('72)	75	45
		Nos. 446-476 (31)	211.50	38.38

Nos. 451, 453, 454a, 455, 456, 458 also issued in coils with black control number on back of every fifth stamp. These coils, except for No. 451, are on luminescent paper.

On Nos. 469-471, the 2, 4 and 7 are 3mm high. The background around the head is white. On Nos. 454, 458, 462 the 2, 4 and 7 are 2½mm high and the background is tinted.

Nos. 472-476 issued in booklets only and have 1 or 2 straight-edges. All panes have a large selvage with inscription or map.

See designs M1, O3.

Luminescent Paper

Stamps issued on both ordinary and luminescent paper include: Nos. 307-308, 430-431, 449-451, 453-460, 462, 464, 467-468, 472, 643-644, 650-651, 837, Q385, Q410.

Stamps issued only on luminescent paper include: Nos. 433, 454a, 472b, 473-474, 649, 652-658, 664-670, 679-682, 688-690, 694-696, 698-703, 705-711, 713-726, 729-747, 751-754, 756-757, 759, 761-762, 764, 766, 769, 772, 774, 778, 789, 791-793, 795, 797-799, 801-807, 809-811, 814-818, 820-834, 836, 838-848.

See note after No. 857.

Nos. 396 and 398 Surcharged and Precanceled in Black

20c
I-I-54
31-XII-54

1954, Jan. 1 **Unwmk.** *Perf. 13½x14*

477	A108	20c on 65c vio brn	1.75	65
478	A108	20c on 90c dp blue	1.75	45

See note after No. 197.

Map and Rotary Emblem A112

Designs: 80c, Mermaid and Mercury holding emblem. 4fr, Rotary emblem and two globes.

1954, Sept. 10 **Engr.** *Perf. 11½*

479	A112	20c red	25	25
480	A112	80c dark green	65	50
481	A112	4fr ultra	1.40	75
		Nos. 479-481 (3)	2.30	1.50

5th regional conf. of Rotary Intl. at Ostend. No. 481 for Rotary 50th Anniv. (in 1955).

A souv. sheet containing one each, imperf., was sold for 500 francs. It was not valid for postage.

The Rabot and Begonia — A113

Designs: 2.50fr, The Oudeburg and azalea. 4fr, "Three Towers" and orchid.

1955, Feb. 15 **Photo.**

482	A113	80c brt carmine	70	38
483	A113	2.50fr black brn	4.25	3.75
484	A113	4fr dk rose brn	4.00	1.25
		Nos. 482-484 (3)	8.95	5.38

Ghent Intl. Flower Exhibition, 1955.

Homage to Charles V as a Child, by Albrecht de Vriendt — A114

Charles V, by Titian — A115

Design: 4fr, Abdication of Charles V, by Louis Gallait.

1955, Mar. 25 **Unwmk.** *Perf. 11½*

485	A114	20c rose red	20	18
486	A115	2fr dk gray green	1.50	15
487	A114	4fr blue	4.00	1.25
		Nos. 485-487 (3)	5.70	1.58

Charles V Exhibition, Ghent, 1955.

Emile Verhaeren, by Montald Constant — A116

1955, May 11 **Engr.**

488	A116	20c dark gray	15	15

Birth cent. of Verhaeren, poet.

Allegory of Textile Manufacture A117

1955, May 11

489	A117	2fr violet brown	1.00	18

2nd Intl. Textile Exhibition, Brussels, June 1955.

"The Foolish Virgin" by Rik Wouters — A118

"Departure of Volunteers from Liege, 1830" by Charles Soubre — A119

1955, June 10

490	A118	1.20fr olive green	1.00	1.10
491	A118	2fr violet	1.50	15

3rd biennial exhibition of sculpture, Antwerp, June 11-Sept. 10, 1955.

1955, Sept. 10 **Photo.**

492	A119	20c grnsh slate	18	18
493	A119	2fr chocolate	90	22

Exhibition "The Romantic Movement in Liege Province," Sept. 10-Oct. 31, 1955; and 125th anniv. of Belgium's independence from the Netherlands.

Pelican Giving Blood to Young — A120

Buildings of Tournai, Ghent and Antwerp — A121

1956, Jan. 14 **Engr.**

494	A120	2fr brt carmine	42	18

Blood donor service of the Belgian Red Cross.

1956, July 14 **Photo.**

495	A121	2fr brt ultra	28	18

The Scheldt exhibition (Scaldis) at Tournai, Ghent and Antwerp, July-Sept. 1956.

Europa Issue

"Rebuilding Europe" — A122

1956, Sept. 15 **Engr.**

496	A122	2fr lt green	1.40	15
497	A122	4fr purple	6.50	70

Issued to symbolize the cooperation among the six countries comprising the Coal and Steel Community.

Train on Map of Belgium and Luxembourg A123

1956, Sept. 29

498	A123	2fr dark blue	55	18

Issued to mark the electrification of the Brussels-Luxembourg railroad.

Edouard Anseele — A124

"The Atom" and Exposition Emblem — A125

1956, Oct. 27

499	A124	20c violet brown	15	15

Cent. of the birth of Edouard Anseele, statesman, and in connection with an exhibition held in his honor at Ghent.

1957-58 **Unwmk.**

500	A125	2fr car rose	22	15
501	A125	2.50fr green ('58)	30	15
502	A125	4fr brt vio bl	75	18
503	A125	5fr claret ('58)	65	50
		Nos. 500-503 (4)	1.92	98

1958 World's Fair at Brussels.

Emperor Maximilian I Receiving Letter — A126

1957, May 19

504	A126	2fr claret	40	15

Day of the Stamp, May 19, 1957.

Sikorsky S-58 Helicopter A127

1957, June 15

505	A127	4fr gray grn & brt bl	90	80

100,000th passenger carried by Sabena helicopter service, June 15, 1957.

Zeebrugge Harbor A128

1957, July 6

506	A128	2fr dark blue	38	15

50th anniv. of the completion of the port of Zeebrugge-Bruges.

Leopold I Entering Brussels, 1831 — A129

Leopold I Arriving at Belgian Border — A130

1957, July 17 **Photo.**

507	A129	20c dk gray grn	15	15
508	A130	2fr lilac	52	20

126th anniv. of the arrival in Belgium of King Leopold I.

Boy Scout and Girl Scout Emblems A131

Design: 4fr, Robert Lord Baden-Powell, painted by David Jaggers, vert.

Perf. 11½

1957, July 29 **Unwmk.** **Engr.**

509	A131	80c gray	24	15
510	A131	4fr light green	1.00	45

Cent. of the birth of Lord Baden-Powell, founder of the Boy Scout movement.

"Kneeling Woman" by Lehmbruck A132

"United Europe" A133

1957, Aug. 20 **Photo.**

511	A132	2.50fr dk blue grn	1.10	1.50

4th Biennial Exposition of Sculpture, Antwerp, May 25-Sept. 15.

1957, Sept. 16 **Engr.** ***Perf. 11½***

512	A133	2fr dk violet brn	85	15
513	A133	4fr dark blue	1.65	45

Europa: United Europe for peace and prosperity.

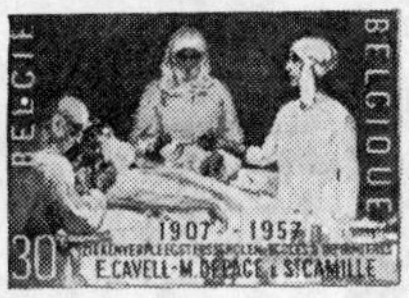

Queen Elisabeth Assisting at Operation, by Allard L'Olivier A134

Perf. 11½

1957, Nov. 23 **Unwmk.** **Engr.**

514	A134	30c rose lilac	15	15

50th anniv. of the founding of the Edith Cavell-Marie Depage and St. Camille schools of nursing.

Post Horn and Historic Postal Insignia A135

1958, Mar. 16 **Photo.** ***Perf. 11½***

515	A135	2.50fr gray	24	15

Postal Museum Day.

United Nations Issue

International Labor Organization A136

Allegory of UN — A137

Designs: 1fr, FAO. 2fr, World Bank. 2.50fr, UNESCO. 3fr, UN Pavilion. 5fr, ITU. 8fr, Intl. Monetary Fund. 11fr, WHO. 20fr, UPU.

Perf. 11½

1958, Apr. 17 **Unwmk.** **Engr.**

516	A136	50c gray	90	1.40
517	A136	1fr claret	28	45
518	A137	1.50fr dp ultra	28	45
519	A137	2fr gray brown	85	1.25
520	A136	2.50fr olive grn	28	45
521	A136	3fr grnsh blue	85	1.25
522	A137	5fr rose lilac	55	90
523	A136	8fr red brown	1.00	1.65
524	A136	11fr dull lilac	1.25	2.00
525	A136	20fr car rose	1.65	2.50
		Nos. 516-525,C15-C20 (16)	11.49	18.00

World's Fair, Brussels, Apr. 17-Oct. 19.

Postally valid only from the UN pavilion at the Brussels Fair. Proceeds went toward financing the UN exhibits.

Eugène Ysaye — A138

1958, Sept. 1

526	A138	30c dk blue & plum	15	15

Ysaye (1858-1931), violinist, composer.

Europa Issue, 1958

Common Design Type

1958, Sept. 13 **Photo.**

Size: 24½x35mm

527	CD1	2.50fr brt red & blue	22	15
528	CD1	5fr brt blue & red	38	45

Issued to show the European Postal Union at the service of European integration.

Infant and UN Emblem — A140

Charles V and Jean-Baptiste of Thurn and Taxis — A141

1958, Dec. 10 **Engr.**

529	A140	2.50fr blue gray	28	15

10th anniv. of the signing of the Universal Declaration of Human Rights.

1959, Mar. 15 **Unwmk.**

530	A141	2.50fr green	35	15

Issued for the Day of the Stamp. Design from painting by J.-E. van den Bussche.

NATO Emblem A142

City Hall, Audenarde A143

1959, Apr. 3 **Photo.** ***Perf. 11½***

531	A142	2.50fr dp red & dk bl	45	15
532	A142	5fr emerald & dk bl	1.25	1.40

10th anniv. of NATO. See No. 720.

1959, Aug. 17 **Engr.**

533	A143	2.50fr deep claret	28	15

Pope Adrian VI, by Jan van Scorel — A144

1959, Aug. 31 ***Perf. 11½***

534	A144	2.50fr dark red	20	15
535	A144	5fr Prus blue	55	55

500th anniv. of the birth of Pope Adrian VI.

Europa Issue, 1959

Common Design Type

1959, Sept. 19 **Photo.**

Size: 24x35½mm

536	CD2	2.50fr dark red	18	15
537	CD2	5fr brt grnsh blue	40	50

Boeing 707 A146

Engraved and Photogravure

1959, Dec. 1 ***Perf. 11½***

538	A146	6fr dk bl gray & car	1.40	1.00

Inauguration of jet flights by Sabena Airlines.

Countess of Taxis — A147

Indian Azalea — A148

1960, Mar. 21 **Engr.** ***Perf. 11½***

539	A147	3fr dark blue	85	15

Alexandrine de Rye, Countess of Taxis, Grand Mistress of the Netherlands Posts, 1628-1645, and day of the stamp, Mar. 21, 1960. The painting of the Countess is by Nicholas van der Eggermans.

1960, Mar. 28 **Unwmk.**

540	A148	40c shown	22	15
541	A148	3fr Begonia	90	15
542	A148	6fr Anthurium, bromelia	1.00	90
		Nos. 540-542 (3)	2.12	1.20

24th Ghent Intl. Flower Exhibition, Apr. 23-May 2, 1960.

Steel Workers, by Constantin Meunier — A149

Design: 3fr, The sower, field and dock workers, from "Monument to Labor," Brussels, by Constantin Meunier, horiz.

Engraved and Photogravure

1960, Apr. 30 ***Perf. 11½***

543	A149	40c claret & brt red	15	15
544	A149	3fr brown & brt red	85	28

Socialist Party of Belgium, 75th anniv.

Congo River Boat Pilot — A150

Designs: 40c, Medical team. 1fr, Planting tree. 2fr, Sculptors. 2.50fr, Shot put. 3fr, Congolese officials. 6fr, Congolese and Belgian girls playing with doll. 8fr, Boy pointing on globe to independent Congo.

1960, June 30 **Photo.** ***Perf. 11½***

Size: 35x24mm

545	A150	10c bright red	30	15
546	A150	40c rose claret	45	15
547	A150	1fr brt lilac	85	55
548	A150	2fr gray green	95	65
549	A150	2.50fr blue	85	55
550	A150	3fr dk bl gray	1.00	35

Size: 51x35mm

551	A150	6fr violet bl	3.00	1.40
552	A150	8fr dk brown	5.00	3.00
		Nos. 545-552 (8)	12.40	6.80

Independence of Congo.

Europa Issue, 1960

Common Design Type

1960, Sept. 17

Size: 35x24½mm

553	CD3	3fr claret	60	15
554	CD3	6fr gray	1.25	40

Children Examining Stamp and Globe A152

H. J. W. Frère-Orban A153

1960, Oct. 1 **Photo.** ***Perf. 11½***

555	A152	40c bister & blk + label	15	15

Promoting stamp collecting among children.

Common Design Types pictured in section at front of book.

Engraved and Photogravure

1960, Oct. 17 **Unwmk.**

Portrait in Brown

556	A153	10c orange yel	15	15
557	A153	40c blue grn	15	15
558	A153	1.50fr bright violet	70	70
559	A153	3fr red	1.10	15
		Nos. 556-559 (4)	2.10	1.15

Centenary of Communal Credit Society.

King Baudouin and Queen Fabiola A154

1960, Dec. 13 **Photo.** ***Perf. 11½***

Portraits in Dark Brown

560	A154	40c green	15	15
561	A154	3fr red lilac	28	15
562	A154	6fr dull blue	1.25	60
		Nos. 560-562 (3)	1.68	90

Wedding of King Baudouin and Dona Fabiola de Mora y Aragon, Dec. 15, 1960.

Nos. 412, 414 Surcharged

1961-68 **Typo.** ***Perf. 13½x14***

563	A108	15c on 30c gray grn	24	15
564	A108	15c on 50c blue ('68)	15	15
565	A108	20c on 30c gray grn	24	15
		Nos. 563-565 (3)	63	
		Set value		28

No. 412 Surcharged and Precanceled

1961

566	A108	15c on 30c gray grn	90	15
567	A108	20c on 30c gray grn	1.90	1.40

See note after No. 197.

Nicolaus Rockox, by Anthony Van Dyck — A155

Seal of Jan Bode, Alderman of Antwerp, 1264 — A156

Engraved and Photogravure

1961, Mar. 18 ***Perf. 11½***

568	A155	3fr bister, blk & brn	32	15

400th anniv. of the birth of Nicolaus Rockox, mayor of Antwerp.

1961, Apr. 16 **Photo.**

569	A156	3fr buff & brown	32	15

Issued for Stamp Day, April 16.

Senate Building, Brussels, Laurel and Sword — A157

Engraved and Photogravure

1961, Sept. 14 **Unwmk.** ***Perf. 11½***

570	A157	3fr brn & Prus grn	20	15
571	A157	6fr dk brn & dk car	1.50	1.25

50th Conference of the Interparliamentary Union, Brussels, Sept. 14-22.

Europa Issue, 1961

Common Design Type

1961, Sept. 16 **Photo.**

Size: 35x25½mm

572	CD4	3fr yel grn & dk grn	20	15
573	CD4	6fr org brn & blk	30	25

Atomic Reactor Plant, BR2, Mol — A159

Designs: 3fr, Atomic Reactor BR3, vert. 6fr, Atomic Reactor plant BR3.

1961, Nov. 8 **Unwmk.** ***Perf. 11½***

574	A159	40c dk bl grn	15	15
575	A159	3fr red lilac	15	15
576	A159	6fr bright blue	30	22
		Nos. 574-576 (3)	60	
		Set value		36

Aatomic nuclear research center at Mol.

Horta Museum — A160

1962, Feb. 15 **Engr.**

577	A160	3fr red brown	25	15

Baron Victor Horta (1861-1947), architect.

Postrider, 16th Century A161

Engraved and Photogravure

1962, Mar. 25 ***Perf. 11½***

Chalky Paper

578	A161	3fr brn & slate grn	30	15

Stamp Day. See No. 677.

Gerard Mercator — A162

Bro. Alexis-Marie Gochet — A163

Engraved and Photogravure

1962, Apr. 14 **Unwmk.**

579	A162	3fr sepia & gray	30	15

Mercator (Gerhard Kremer, 1512-1594), geographer and map maker.

1962, May 19 **Engr.** ***Perf. 11½***

Portrait: 3fr, Canon Pierre-Joseph Triest.

580	A163	2fr dark blue	30	18
581	A163	3fr golden brown	30	15

Brother Alexis-Marie Gochet (1835-1910), geographer and educator, and Canon Pierre-Joseph Triest (1760-1836), educator and founder of hospitals and orphanages.

Europa Issue, 1962

Common Design Type

1962, Sept. 15 **Photo.**

Size: 35x24mm

582	CD5	3fr dp car, citron & blk	24	15
583	CD5	6fr olive, citron & blk	35	35

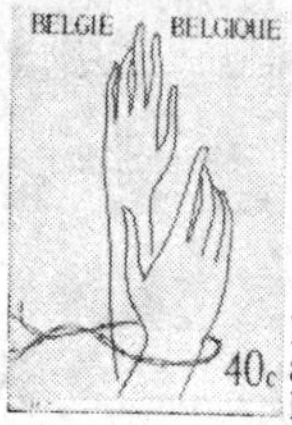

Hand with Barbed Wire and Freed Hand — A165

1962, Sept. 16 **Engr. & Photo.**

584	A165	40c lt bl & blk	15	15

Issued in memory of concentration camp victims.

Adam, by Michelangelo, Broken Chain and UN Emblem A166

1962, Nov. 24 ***Perf. 11½***

585	A166	3fr gray & blk	20	15
586	A166	6fr lt redsh brn & dk brn	35	30

UN Declaration of Human Rights.

Henri Pirenne (1862-1935), Historian — A167

1963, Jan. 15 **Engr.**

587	A167	3fr ultra	30	15

Swordsmen and Ghent Belfry — A168

Designs: 3fr, Modern fencers. 6fr, Arms of the Royal and Knightly Guild of St. Michael, vert.

Engraved and Photogravure

1963, Mar. 23 **Unwmk.** ***Perf. 11½***

588	A168	1fr brn red & pale bl	15	15
589	A168	3fr dk vio & yel grn	15	15
590	A168	6fr gray, blk, red, bl & gold	28	28
		Nos. 588-590 (3)	58	
		Set value		43

350th anniv. of the granting of a charter to the Ghent guild of fencers.

Stagecoach A169

1963, Apr. 7

591	A169	3fr gray & ocher	25	15

Stamp Day. See No. 678.

Hotel des Postes, Paris, Stagecoach and Stamp, 1863
A170

Perf. 11½

1963, May 7 Unwmk. Engr.

592 A170 6fr dk brn, gray & yel grn	38	38

Cent. of the 1st Intl. Postal Conf., Paris, 1863.

"Peace," Child in Rye Field — A171

1963, May 8 Engr. & Photo.

593 A171 3fr grn, blk, yel & brn	16	15
594 A171 6fr buff, blk, brn & org	32	28

May 8th Movement for Peace. (On May 8, 1945, World War II ended in Europe).

Allegory and Shields of 17 Member Nations
A172

1963, June 13 Unwmk. *Perf. 11½*

595 A172 6fr bl & blk	38	30

10th anniversary of the Conference of European Transport Ministers.

Seal of Union of Belgian Towns — A173

1963, June 17

596 A173 6fr grn, red, blk & gold	38	38

Intl. Union of Municipalities, 50th anniv.

Caravelle over Brussels National Airport
A174

Photogravure and Engraved

1963, Sept. 1 Unwmk. *Perf. 11½*

597 A174 3fr green & gray	22	15

40th anniversary of SABENA airline.

Europa Issue, 1963

Common Design Type

1963, Sept. 14 Photo.

Size: 35x24mm

598 CD6 3fr blk, dl red & lt brn	60	15
599 CD6 6fr blk, lt bl & lt brn	1.65	32

Jules Destrée
A176

Design: No. 601, Henry Van de Velde.

Perf. 11½

1963, Nov. 16 Unwmk. Engr.

600 A176 1fr rose lilac	15	15
601 A176 1fr green	15	15
Set value	18	16

Jules Destrée (1863-1936), statesman and founder of the Royal Academy of French Language and Literature, and of Henry Van de Velde (1863-1957), architect.

No. 600 incorrectly inscribed "1864."

Development of the Mail, Bas-relief
A177

1963, Nov. 23 Engr. & Photo.

602 A177 50c dl red, slate & blk	15	15

50th anniversary of the establishment of postal checking service.

Dr. Armauer G. Hansen
A178

Fight Against Leprosy: 2fr, Leprosarium. 5fr, Father Joseph Damien.

1964, Jan. 25 Unwmk. *Perf. 11½*

603 A178 1fr brn org & blk	15	15
604 A178 2fr brn org & blk	18	15
605 A178 5fr brn org & blk	25	20
a. Souvenir sheet of 3, #603-605	1.50	1.50
Nos. 603-605 (3)	58	
Set value		36

No. 605a sold for 12fr.

Andreas Vesalius (1514-64), Anatomist — A179

Jules Boulvin (1855-1920), Mechanical Engineer
A180

Design: 2fr, Henri Jaspar (1870-1939), statesman and lawyer.

Engraved and Photogravure

1964, Mar. 2 Unwmk. *Perf. 11½*

606 A179 50c pale grn & blk	15	15
607 A180 1fr pale grn & blk	15	15
608 A180 2fr pale grn & blk	16	15
Set value	36	27

Postilion of Liege, 1830-40 — A181

1964, Apr. 5 Engr. *Perf. 11½*

609 A181 3fr black	22	15

Issued for Stamp Day 1964.

Arms of Ostend
A182

1964, May 16 Photo.

610 A182 3fr ultra, ver, gold & blk	22	15

Millennium of Ostend.

Flame, Hammer and Globe — A183

Designs: 1fr, "SI" and globe. 2fr, Flame over wavy lines.

1964, July 18 Unwmk. *Perf. 11½*

611 A183 50c dark blue & red	15	15
612 A183 1fr dark blue & red	15	15
613 A183 2fr dark blue & red	15	15
Set value	27	23

Centenary of the First Socialist International, founded in London, Sept. 28, 1864.

Europa Issue, 1964

Common Design Type

1964, Sept. 12 Photo. *Perf. 11½*

Size: 24x35½mm

614 CD7 3fr yel grn, dk car & gray	25	15
615 CD7 6fr car rose, yel grn & bl	38	38

Benelux Issue

King Baudouin, Queen Juliana and Grand Duchess Charlotte — A185

1964, Oct. 12

616 A185 3fr ol, lt grn & mar	15	15

20th anniv. of the customs union of Belgium, Netherlands and Luxembourg.

Hand, Round & Pear-shaped Diamonds
A186

Symbols of Textile Industry
A187

1965, Jan. 23 Unwmk. *Perf. 11½*

617 A186 2fr ultra, dp car & blk	15	15

Diamond Exhibition "Diamantexpo," Antwerp, July 10-28, 1965.

1965, Jan. 25 Photo.

618 A187 1fr bl, red & blk	15	15

Eighth textile industry exhibition "Textirama," Ghent, Jan. 29-Feb. 2, 1965.

Vriesia — A188

Paul Hymans — A189

Designs: 2fr, Echinocactus. 3fr, Stapelia.

1965, Feb. 13 Engr. & Photo.

619 A188 1fr multi	15	15
620 A188 2fr multi	15	15
621 A188 3fr multi	15	15
a. Souvenir sheet of 3, #619-621	1.50	1.50
Set value	30	30

25th Ghent International Flower Exhibition, Apr. 24-May 3, 1965.

No. 621a was issued Apr. 26 and sold for 20fr.

1965, Feb. 24 Engr. *Perf. 11½*

622 A189 1fr dl pur	15	15

Paul Hymans (1865-1941), Belgian Foreign Minister and first president of the League of Nations.

Peter Paul Rubens
A190

Sir Rowland Hill as Philatelist
A191

Portraits: 2fr, Frans Snyders. 3fr, Adam van Noort. 6fr, Anthony Van Dyck. 8fr, Jacob Jordaens.

1965, Mar. 15 Photo. & Engr.

Portraits in Sepia

623 A190 1fr car rose	15	15
624 A190 2fr bl grn	15	15
625 A190 3fr plum	15	15
626 A190 6fr dp car	24	15
627 A190 8fr dk bl	35	35
Nos. 623-627 (5)	1.04	95

Issued to commemorate the founding of the General Savings and Pensions Bank.

1965, Mar. 27 Engr. *Perf. 11½*

628 A191 50c blue green	15	15

Issued to publicize youth philately. The design is from a mural by J. E. Van den Bussche in the General Post Office, Brussels.

Postmaster, c. 1833 — A192

Staircase, Affligem Abbey — A194

Set Values

A 15-cent minimum now applies to individual stamps and sets. Where the 15-cent minimum per stamp would increase the value of a set beyond retail, there is a "Set Value" notation giving the retail value of the set.

Telephone, Globe and Teletype Paper — A193

1965, Apr. 26 Unwmk. *Perf. 11½*

629 A192 3fr emerald 15 15

Issued for Stamp Day.

1965, May 8 Photo.

630 A193 2fr dl pur & blk 15 15

Cent. of the ITU.

1965, May 27 Engr.

631 A194 1fr gray blue 15 15

St. Jean Berchmans and his Birthplace A195

1965, May 27 Engr. & Photo.

632 A195 2fr dk brn & red brn 15 15

Issued to honor St. Jean Berchmans (1599-1621), Jesuit "Saint of the Daily Life."

TOC H Lamp and Arms of Poperinge A196

Farmer with Tractor A197

1965, June 19 Photo. *Perf. 11½*

633 A196 3fr ol bis, blk & car 15 15

50th anniv. of the founding of Talbot House in Poperinge, which served British soldiers in World War I, and where the TOC H Movement began (Christian Social Service; TOC H is army code for Poperinge Center).

Engraved and Photogravure

1965, July 17 Unwmk. *Perf. 11½*

Design: 3fr, Farmer with horse-drawn roller.

634 A197 50c bl, ol, bis brn & blk 15 15
635 A197 3fr bl, ol grn, ol & blk 15 15
Set value 20 15

75th anniv. of the Belgian Farmers' Association (Boerenbond).

Europa Issue, 1965

Common Design Type

1965, Sept. 25 *Perf. 11½*

Size: 35½x24mm

636 CD8 1fr dl rose & blk 15 15
637 CD8 3fr grnsh gray & blk 15 15
Set value 22 16

Leopold I A199

Joseph Lebeau A200

1965, Nov. 13 Engr.

638 A199 3fr sepia 18 15
639 A199 6fr bright violet 25 25
Set value 31

King Leopold I (1790-1865). The designs of the vignettes are similar to A4 and A5.

1965, Nov. 13 Photo.

640 A200 1fr multi 15 15

Joseph Lebeau (1794-1865), Foreign Minister.

Tourist Issue

Grapes and Houses, Hoeilaart A201

Bridge and Castle, Huy A202

Designs: No. 643, British War Memorial, Ypres. No. 644, Castle Spontin. No. 645, City Hall, Louvain. No. 646, Ourthe Valley. No. 647, Romanesque Cathedral, gothic fountain, Nivalles. No. 648, Water mill, Kasterlee. No. 649, City Hall, Cloth Guild and Statue of Margarethe of Austria, Malines. No. 650, Town Hall, Lier. No. 651, Castle Bouillon. No. 652, Fountain and Kursaal Spa. No. 653, Windmill, Bokrijk. No. 654, Mountain road, Vielsalm. No. 655, View of Furnes. No. 656, City Hall and Belfry, Mons. No. 657, St. Martin's Church, Aalst. No. 658, Abbey and fountain, St. Hubert.

1965-71 Engr. *Perf. 11½*

641 A201 50c vio bl, lt bl & yel grn 15 15
642 A202 50c sl grn, lt bl & red brn 15 15
643 A202 1fr grn, lt bl, sal & brn 15 15
644 A202 1fr ind, lt bl & ol 15 15
645 A201 1fr brt rose lil, lt bl & blk 15 15
646 A202 1fr blk, grnsh bl & ol 15 15
647 A201 1.50fr sl, sky bl & bis 15 15
648 A202 1.50fr blk, bl & ol 15 15
649 A202 1.50fr dk bl & buff 18 15
650 A201 2fr brn, lt bl & ind 18 15
651 A202 2fr dk brn, grn & ocher 18 15
652 A202 2fr bl, brt grn & blk 15 15
653 A202 2fr blk, lt bl & yel 15 15
654 A202 2fr blk, lt bl & yel grn 15 15
655 A202 2fr car, lt bl & dk brn 15 15
656 A201 2.50fr vio, buff & blk 18 15
657 A201 2.50fr vio, lt bl, blk & ol 25 15
658 A201 2.50fr vio bl & yel 25 15
Nos. 641-658 (18) 3.02
Set value 1.50

Issue dates: Nos. 641-642, Nov. 13, 1965; Nos. 643-644, July 15, 1967; Nos. 645-646, Dec. 16, 1968; Nos. 647-648, July 6, 1970; Nos. 649, 656, Dec. 11, 1971; Nos. 650-651, Nov. 11, 1966; Nos. 652-653, June 24, 1968; Nos. 654-655, Sept. 6, 1969; Nos. 657-658, Sept. 11, 1971.

Queen Elisabeth Type of Semi-Postal Issue, 1956

1965, Dec. 23 Photo. *Perf. 11½*

659 SP305 3fr dark gray 22 15

Queen Elisabeth (1876-1965).

A dark frame has been added in design of No. 659; 1956 date has been changed to 1965; inscription in bottom panel is Koningin Elisabeth Reine Elisabeth 3F.

"Peace on Earth" — A203

Arms of Pope Paul VI — A204

Rural Mailman, 19th Century — A205

Design: 1fr, "Looking toward a Better Future" (family, new buildings, sun and landscape).

1966, Feb. 12 Photo. *Perf. 11½*

660 A203 50c multi 15 15
661 A203 1fr ocher, blk & bl 15 15
662 A204 3fr gray, gold, car & blk 15 15
Set value 25 19

75th anniv. of the encyclical by Pope Leo XIII "Rerum Novarum," which proclaimed the general principles for the organization of modern industrial society.

1966, Apr. 17 Photo. Unwmk.

663 A205 3fr blk, dl yel & pale lil 18 15

Stamp Day. For overprint see No. 673.

Iguanodon, Natural Science Institute A206

Arend-Roland Comet, Observatory — A207

Designs: No. 665, Ancestral head and spiral pattern, Kasai; Central Africa Museum. No. 666, Snowflakes, Meteorological Institute. No. 667, Seal of Charles V, Royal Archives. No. 668, Medieval scholar, Royal Library. 8fr, Satellite and rocket, Space Aeronautics Institute.

1966, May 28 Engr. & Photo.

664 A206 1fr grn & blk 15 15
665 A206 2fr gray, blk & brn org 15 15
666 A206 2fr bl, blk & yel 15 15
667 A207 3fr dp rose, blk & gold 15 15
668 A207 3fr multi 15 15
669 A207 6fr ultra, yel & blk 22 15
670 A207 8fr multi 30 30
Set value 1.00 78

National scientific heritage.

Atom Symbol and Retort — A208

August Kekulé, Benzene Ring — A209

Engraved and Photogravure

1966, July 9 Unwmk. *Perf. 11½*

671 A208 6fr gray, blk & red 30 18

Issued to publicize the European chemical plant, EUROCHEMIC, at Mol.

1966, July 9

672 A209 3fr brt bl & blk 18 15

August Friedrich Kekule (1829-96), chemistry professor at University of Ghent (1858-67).

No. 663 Overprinted with Red and Blue Emblem

1966, July 11 Photo.

673 A205 3fr multi 18 15

19th Intl. P.T.T. Cong., Brussels, July 11-15.

Rik Wouters (1882-1916), Self-portrait — A210

1966, Sept. 6 Photo. *Perf. 11½*

674 A210 60c multi 15 15

Europa Issue, 1966

Common Design Type

1966, Sept. 24 Engr. *Perf. 11½*

Size: 24x34mm

675 CD9 3fr brt grn 15 15
676 CD9 6fr brt rose lil 32 28

Types of 1962-1963 Overprinted in Black and Red

1966, Nov. 11 Engr. & Photo.

677 A161 60c sepia & grnsh gray 15 15
678 A169 3fr sepia & pale bister 15 15
Set value 19 16

75th anniv., Royal Fed. of Phil. Circles of Belgium. Overprint shows emblem of F.I.P.

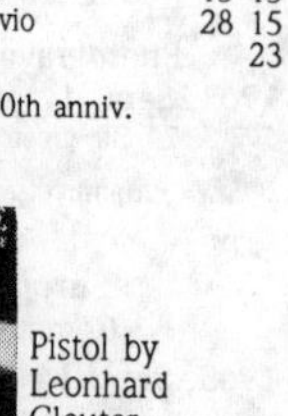

Lions Emblem — A214

1967, Jan. 14 *Perf. 11½*

679 A214 3fr gray, blk & bl 15 15
680 A214 6fr lt grn, blk & vio 28 15
Set value 23

Lions Club Intl., 50th anniv.

Pistol by Leonhard Cleuter A215

1967, Feb. 11 Photo.

681 A215 2fr dp car, blk & cream 15 15

Fire Arms Museum in Liege.

International Tourist Year Emblem A216

1967, Feb. 11
682 A216 6fr ver, ultra & blk 28 15

International Tourist Year, 1967.

Birches and Trientalis A217

Design: No. 684, Dunes, beach grass, privet and blue thistles.

1967, Mar. 11 Photo. *Perf. 11½*
683 A217 1fr multi 15 15
684 A217 1fr multi 15 15
Set value 16 16

Issued to publicize the nature preserves at Hautes Fagnes and Westhoek.

Paul E. Janson — A218

1967, Apr. 15 Engr. *Perf. 11½*
685 A218 10fr blue 35 18

Issued in memory of Paul Emile Janson (1872-1944), lawyer and statesman.

Postilion A219

1967, Apr. 16 Photo. & Engr.
686 A219 3fr rose red & claret 18 15

Issued for Stamp Day, 1967.

Inscribed: "FITCE"

1967, June 24 *Perf. 11½*
687 A219 10fr ultra, sep & emer 42 30

Issued to commemorate the meeting of the Federation of Common Market Telecommunications Engineers, Brussels, July 3-8.

Europa Issue, 1967
Common Design Type

1967, May 2 Photo.
Size: 24x35mm
688 CD10 3fr blk, lt bl & red 18 15
689 CD10 6fr blk, grnsh gray & yel 30 28

Flax, Shuttle and Mills — A221

1967, June 3 Photo. *Perf. 11½*
690 A221 6fr tan & multi 28 20

Belgian linen industry.

Old Kursaal, Ostend — A222

1967, June 3 Engr. & Photo.
691 A222 2fr dk brn, lt bl & yel 15 15

700th anniversary of Ostend as a city.

A223

A224

Designs: #692, Caesar Crossing Rubicon, 15th Century Tapestry. #693, Emperor Maximilian Killing a Boar, 16th cent. tapestry.

1967, Sept. 2 Photo. *Perf. 11½*
692 A223 1fr multi 15 15
693 A223 1fr multi 15 15
Set value 20 16

Issued for the Charles Plisnier and Lodewijk de Raet Foundations.

Arms of Universities: #694, Ghent. #695, Liege.

Engraved and Photogravure

1967, Sept. 30 *Perf. 11½*
694 A224 3fr gray & multi 15 15
695 A224 3fr gray & multi 15 15
Set value 20

Universities of Ghent and Liège, 150th anniv.

Princess Margaret of York — A225

"Virga Jesse," Hasselt — A226

1967, Sept. 30 Photo.
696 A225 6fr multi 28 24

British Week, Sept. 28-Oct. 2.

1967, Nov. 11 Engr. *Perf. 11½*
697 A226 1fr slate blue 15 15

Christmas, 1967.

Hand Guarding Worker — A227

Military Mailman, 1916, by James Thiriar — A228

1968, Feb. 3 Photo. *Perf. 11½*
698 A227 3fr multi 18 15

Issued to publicize industrial safety.

Engraved and Photogravure

1968, Mar. 17 *Perf. 11½*
699 A228 3fr sepia, lt bl & brn 18 15

Issued for Stamp Day, 1968.

View of Grammont and Seal of Baudouin VI — A229

Stamp of 1866, No. 23 — A230

Historic Sites: 3fr, Theux-Franchimont fortress, sword and seal. 6fr, Neolithic cave and artifacts, Spiennes. 10fr, Roman oil lamp and St. Medard's Church, Wervik.

1968, Apr. 13 Photo. *Perf. 11½*
700 A229 2fr bl, blk, lil & rose 15 15
701 A229 3fr org, blk & car 15 15
702 A229 6fr ultra, ind & bis 25 15
703 A229 10fr tan, blk, yel & gray 40 28
Nos. 700-703 (4) 95 73

1968, Apr. 13 Engr. *Perf. 13*
704 A230 1fr black 15 15

Centenary of the Malines Stamp Printery.

Europa Issue, 1968
Common Design Type

1968, Apr. 27 Photo. *Perf. 11½*
Size: 35x24mm
705 CD11 3fr dl grn, gold & blk 15 15
706 CD11 6fr car, sil & blk 35 25

St. Laurent Abbey, Liège A232

Designs: 3fr, Gothic Church, Lisseweghe. No. 709. Barges in Zandvliet locks. No. 710, Ship in Neuzen lock, Ghent Canal. 10fr, Ronquieres canal ship lift.

Engraved and Photogravure

1968, Sept. 7 *Perf. 11½*
707 A232 2fr ultra, gray ol & sep 15 15
708 A232 3fr ol bis, gray & sep 15 15
709 A232 6fr ind, brt bl & sep 30 15
710 A232 6fr blk, grnsh bl & ol 22 15
711 A232 10fr bis, brt bl & sep 50 32
Nos. 707-711 (5) 1.32 92

No. 710 issued Dec. 14 for opening of lock at Neuzen, Netherlands.

Christmas Candle — A233

1968, Dec. 7 *Perf. 11½*
712 A233 1fr multi 15 15

Christmas, 1968.

St. Albertus Magnus — A234

1969, Feb. 15 Engr. *Perf. 11½*
713 A234 2fr sepia 15 15

The Church of St. Paul in Antwerp (16th century) was destroyed by fire in Apr. 1968.

Ruins of Aulne Abbey, Gozee A235

1969, Feb. 15 Engr. & Photo.
714 A235 3fr brt pink & blk 15 15

Aulne Abbey was destroyed in 1794 during the French Revolution.

The Travelers, Roman Sculpture — A236

Broodjes Chapel, Antwerp — A237

1969, Mar. 15 Engr. *Perf. 11½*
715 A236 2fr vio brn 15 15

2,000th anniversary of city of Arlon.

1969, Mar. 15 Engr. & Photo.
716 A237 3fr gray & blk 15 15

150th anniv. of public education in Antwerp.

Post Office Train — A238

1969, Apr. 13 Photo. *Perf. 11½*
717 A238 3fr multi 15 15

Issued for Stamp Day.

Europa Issue, 1969
Common Design Type

1969, Apr. 26
Size: 35x24mm

718 CD12 3fr lt grn, brn & blk	20	15
719 CD12 6fr sal, rose car & blk	30	30

NATO Type of 1959 Redrawn and Dated "1949-1969"

1969, May 31 Photo. *Perf. 11½*
720 A142 6fr org brn & ultra 28 28

20th anniv. of NATO. No. 720 inscribed Belgique-Belgie and OTAN-NAVO.

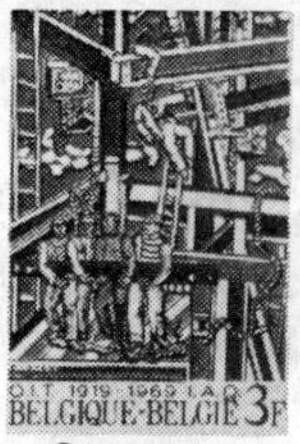

Construction Workers, by F. Leger A240

Bicyclist A241

1969, May 31
721 A240 3fr multi 15 15

50th anniversary of the ILO.

1969, July 5 Photo. *Perf. 11½*
722 A241 6fr rose & multi 28 24

World Bicycling Road Championships, Terlaemen to Zolder, Aug. 10.

Ribbon in Benelux Colors — A242

1969, Sept. 6 Photo. *Perf. 11½*
723 A242 3fr blk, red, ultra & yel 20 15

25th anniv. of the signing of the customs union of Belgium, Netherlands and Luxembourg.

Annevoie Garden and Pascali Rose — A243

Design: No. 725, Lochristi Garden and begonia.

1969, Sept. 6

724 A243 2fr multi	15	15
725 A243 2fr multi	15	15
Set value	20	16

Armstrong, Collins, Aldrin and Map Showing Tranquillity Base — A245

1969, Sept. 20 Photo.
726 A245 6fr black 28 24

See note after Algeria #427. See #B846.

Wounded Veteran — A246

Mailman — A247

1969, Oct. 11 Engr. *Perf. 11½*
727 A246 1fr blue gray 15 15

Natl. war veterans' aid organization (O.N.I.G.). The design is similar to type SP10.

1969, Oct. 18 Photo.
728 A247 1fr deep rose & multi 15 15

Issued to publicize youth philately. Design by Danielle Saintenoy, 14.

Kennedy Tunnel Under the Schelde, Antwerp A248

Design: 6fr, Three highways crossing near Loncin.

1969, Nov. 8 Engr. *Perf. 11½*

729 A248 3fr multi	22	15
730 A248 6fr multi	28	28

Issued to publicize the John F. Kennedy Tunnel under the Schelde and the Walloon auto route and interchange near Loncin.

Henry Carton de Wiart, by Gaston Geleyn — A249

1969, Nov. 8
731 A249 6fr sepia 28 20

Count de Wiart (1869-1951), statesman.

The Census at Bethlehem (detail), by Peter Brueghel A250

1969, Dec. 13 Photo.
732 A250 1.50fr multi 15 15

Christmas, 1969.

Symbols of Bank's Activity, 100fr Coin — A251

1969, Dec. 13 Engr. & Photo.
733 A251 3.50fr lt ultra, blk & sil 15 15

50th anniv. of the Industrial Credit Bank (Societe nationale de credit a l'industrie).

Camellia — A252

Beeches in Botanical Garden — A253

1970, Jan. 31 Photo. *Perf. 11½*

734 A252 1.50fr shown	15	15
735 A252 2.50fr Water lily	15	15
736 A252 3.50fr Azalea	15	15
a. Souvenir sheet of 3, #734-736	2.00	2.00
Nos. 734-736 (3)	45	
Set value		26

Ghent Int'l Flower Exhibition. No. 736a was issued Apr. 25 and sold for 25fr.

1970, Mar. 7 Engr. & Photo.

737 A253 3.50fr shown	20	15
738 A253 7fr Birches	30	30

European Nature Conservation Year.

Mailman A254

1970, Apr. 4 Photo.
739 A254 1.50fr multi 15 15

Issued for Youth Stamp Day.

New UPU Headquarters and Monument, Bern — A255

1970, Apr. 12 Engr. & Photo.
740 A255 3.50fr grn & lt grn 30 15

Opening of the new UPU Headquarters, Bern.

Europa Issue, 1970
Common Design Type

1970, May 1 Photo. *Perf. 11½*
Size: 35x24mm

741 CD13 3.50fr rose cl, yel & blk	20	15
742 CD13 7fr ultra, pink & blk	40	30

Cooperative Alliance Emblem — A257

1970, June 27 Photo. *Perf. 11½*
743 A257 7fr blk & org 30 15

Intl. Cooperative Alliance, 75th anniv.

Ship in Ghent Terneuzen Lock, Zelzate A258

Design: No. 745, Clock Tower, Virton, vert.

1970, June 27 Engr. & Photo.

744 A258 2.50fr ind & lt bl	15	15
745 A258 2.50fr dk pur & ocher	15	15

King Baudouin — A259

1970-80 Engr. *Perf. 11½*

746 A259	1.75fr green ('71)	24	15
747 A259	2.25fr gray grn ('72)	35	15
748 A259	2.50fr gray grn ('74)	16	15
749 A259	3fr emer ('73)	3.00	2.00
750 A259	3.25fr vio brn ('75)	20	15
751 A259	3.50fr org brn	24	15
752 A259	3.50fr brown ('71)	24	15
753 A259	4fr blue ('72)	35	15
754 A259	4.50fr brown ('72)	24	15
755 A259	4.50fr grnsh bl ('74)	24	15
756 A259	5fr lilac ('72)	24	15
757 A259	6fr rose car ('72)	28	15
758 A259	6.50fr vio blk ('74)	35	15
759 A259	7fr ver ('71)	35	15
760 A259	7.50fr brt pink ('75)	35	15
761 A259	8fr black ('72)	35	15
762 A259	9fr ol bis ('71)	60	15
763 A259	9fr red brn ('80)	45	15
764 A259	10fr rose car ('71)	48	15
765 A259	11fr gray ('76)	52	15
766 A259	12fr Prus bl ('72)	60	15
767 A259	13fr slate ('75)	70	15
768 A259	14fr gray grn ('76)	65	15
769 A259	15fr lt vio ('71)	70	15
770 A259	16fr green ('77)	70	15
771 A259	17fr dl mag ('75)	80	15
772 A259	18fr steel bl ('71)	1.00	20
773 A259	18fr grnsh bl ('80)	90	15
774 A259	20fr vio bl ('71)	1.00	15
775 A259	22fr black ('74)	1.40	1.25
776 A259	22fr lt grn ('79)	1.10	15
777 A259	25fr lilac ('75)	1.25	15
778 A259	30fr ocher ('72)	1.50	15
779 A259	35fr emer ('80)	1.50	20
780 A259	40fr dk bl ('77)	2.00	15
781 A259	45fr brown ('80)	2.25	20

Perf. 12½x13½
Photo.
Size: 22x17mm

782 A259	3fr emer ('73)	3.00	2.50
a.	Booklet pane of 4 (#782 and 3 #783) + labels	10.00	
783 A259	4fr blue ('73)	70	60
784 A259	4.50fr grnsh bl ('75)	40	30
785 A259	5fr lilac ('73)	24	15
a.	Booklet pane of 4 + labels	2.75	
786 A259	6fr car ('78)	28	16
787 A259	6.50fr dl pur ('75)	45	20
788 A259	8fr gray ('78)	35	15
	Nos. 746-788 (43)	32.70	
	Set value		10.75

No. 751 issued Sept. 7, 1970, King Baudouin's 40th birthday, and is inscribed "1930-1970." Dates are omitted on other stamps of type A259.

Nos. 754, 756 also issued in coils in 1973 and Nos. 757, 761 in 1978, with black control number on back of every fifth stamp.

Nos. 782-788 issued in booklets only. Nos. 782, 784 have one straight-edge, Nos. 786, 788 have two. The rest have one or two. Stamps in the panes are tete-beche. Each pane has two labels showing Belgian Postal emblem with a large selvage with postal code instructions. Nos. 786, 788 not luminescent.

See designs M2, O4. See Nos. 432a, 432b, 977a, 977b.

UN Headquarters, NY — A260

Fair Emblem — A261

1970, Sept. 12 Engr. & Photo.
789 A260 7fr dk brn & Prus bl 30 15

25th anniversary of the United Nations.

1970, Sept. 19
790 A261 1.50fr bis, org & brn 15 15

Issued to publicize the 25th International Fair at Ghent, Sept. 12-27.

Queen Fabiola — A262

The Mason, by Georges Minne — A263

1970, Sept. 19
791 A262 3.50fr lt bl & blk 15 15

Issued to publicize the Queen Fabiola Foundation for Mental Health.

1970, Oct. 17 ***Perf. 11½***
792 A263 3.50fr dl yel & sep 15 15

50th anniv. of the National Housing Society.

Man, Woman and City — A264

1970, Oct. 17 **Photo.**
793 A264 2.50fr blk & multi 15 15

Social Security System, 25th anniv.

Madonna with the Grapes, by Jean Gossaert — A265

1970, Nov. 14 **Engr.** ***Perf. 11½***
794 A265 1.50fr dk brn 15 15

Christmas 1970.

Arms of Eupen, Malmédy and Saint-Vith A266

Engraved and Photogravure
1970, Dec. 12 ***Perf. 11½***
795 A266 7fr sepia & dk brn 30 15

The 50th anniversary of the return of the districts of Eupen, Malmédy and Saint-Vith.

Automatic Telephone — A267

Touring Club Emblem — A269

"Auto" A268

1971, Jan. 16 **Photo.** ***Perf. 11½***
796 A267 1.50fr multi 15 15

Automatization of Belgian telephone system.

1971, Jan. 16
797 A268 2.50fr car & blk 15 15

50th Automobile Show, Brussels, Jan. 19-31.

1971, Feb. 13
798 A269 3.50fr ultra & multi 18 15

Belgian Touring Club, 75th anniversary.

Tournai Cathedral A270

1971, Feb. 13 **Engr.**
799 A270 7fr brt bl 30 20

Cathedral of Tournai, 8th centenary.

"The Letter Box," by T. Lobrichon — A271

1971, Mar. 13 **Engr.** ***Perf. 11½***
800 A271 1.50fr dk brn 15 15

Youth philately.

Albert I, Jules Destrée and Academy — A272

Engraved and Photogravure
1971, Apr. 17 ***Perf. 11½***
801 A272 7fr gray & blk 30 20

50th anniversary of the founding of the Royal Academy of Language and French Literature.

Stamp Day — A273

1971, Apr. 25
802 A273 3.50fr Mailman 15 15

Europa Issue, 1971
Common Design Type

1971, May 1 **Photo.**
Size: 35x24mm
803 CD14 3.50fr olive & blk 24 15
804 CD14 7fr dk ol grn & blk 35 15
Set value 20

Radar Ground Station A275

1971, May 15 **Photo.** ***Perf. 11½***
805 A275 7fr multi 30 15

3rd World Telecommunications Day.

Antarctic Explorer, Ship and Penguins — A276

1971, June 19 **Photo.** ***Perf. 11½***
806 A276 10fr multi 50 50

Tenth anniversary of the Antarctic Treaty pledging peaceful uses of and scientific cooperation in Antarctica.

A277

A278

1971, June 26 **Engr.** ***Perf. 11½***
807 A277 2.50fr Orval Abbey 15 15

9th cent. of the Abbey of Notre Dame, Orval.

1971, June 26 **Engr. & Photo.**
808 A278 1.50fr vio bl & blk 15 15

Georges Hubin (1863-1947), socialist leader and Minister of State.

Mr. and Mrs. Goliath, the Giants of Ath — A279

View of Ghent A280

1971, Aug. 7 **Photo.**
809 A279 2.50fr multi 15 15

Engr.
810 A280 2.50fr gray brn 15 15

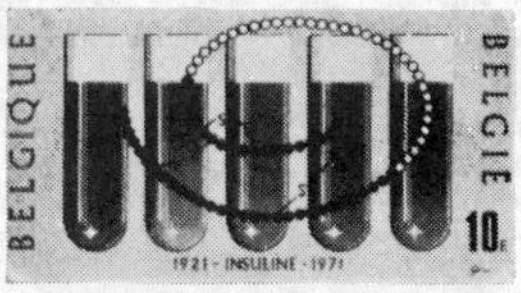

Test Tubes and Insulin Molecular Diagram — A281

1971, Aug. 7 **Photo.**
811 A281 10fr lt gray & multi 40 30

50th anniversary of the discovery of insulin.

Family and "50" — A283

1971, Sept. 11 **Photo.**
812 A283 1.50fr grn & multi 15 15

Belgian Large Families League, 50th anniv.

Achaemenidaen Tomb, Buzpar, and Persian Coat of Arms — A284

Engraved and Photogravure
1971, Oct. 2 ***Perf. 11½***
813 A284 7fr multi 30 15

2500th anniversary of the founding of the Persian empire by Cyrus the Great.

Dr. Jules Bordet A285

Flight into Egypt, Anonymous A286

Portrait: No. 815, Stijn Streuvels.

1971, Oct. 2 **Engr.**
814 A285 3.50fr slate green 15 15
815 A285 3.50fr dark brown 15 15
Set value 16

No. 814 honors Dr. Jules Bordet (1870-1945), serologist and immunologist; No. 815, Stijn

Streuvels (1871-1945), novelist whose pen name was Frank Lateur.

1971, Nov. 13 **Photo.**
816 A286 1.50fr multi 15 15

Christmas 1971.

Federation Emblem — A287

Book Year Emblem — A288

1971, Nov. 13
817 A287 3.50fr blk, ultra & gold 18 15

25th anniversary of the Federation of Belgian Industries (FIB).

1972, Feb. 19
818 A288 7fr bis, blk & bl 30 20

International Book Year 1972.

Coins of Belgium and Luxembourg — A289

Traffic Signal and Road Signs — A290

1972, Feb. 19 **Engr. & Photo.**
819 A289 1.50fr org blk & sil 15 15

Economic Union of Belgium and Luxembourg, 50th anniversary.

1972, Feb. 19 **Photo.**
820 A290 3.50fr bl & multi 15 15

Via Secura (road safety), 25th anniversary.

Belgica '72 Emblem A291

1972, Mar. 27
821 A291 3.50fr choc, bl & lil 15 15

International Philatelic Exhibition, Brussels, June 24-July 9.

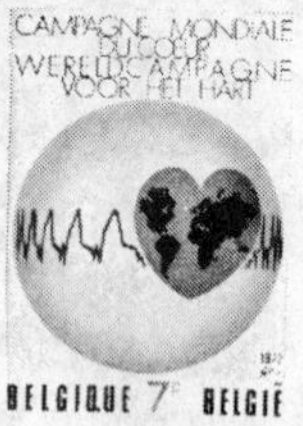

"Your Heart is your Health" A292

Auguste Vermeylen A293

1972, Mar. 27
822 A292 7fr blk, gray, red & bl 25 18

World Health Day.

1972, Mar. 27
823 A293 2.50fr multi 15 15

Centenary of the birth of Auguste Vermeylen (1872-1945), Flemish writer and educator. Portrait by Isidore Opsomer.

A294

A296

1972, Apr. 23
824 A294 3.50fr Astronaut on Moon 15 15

Stamp Day 1972.

Europa Issue 1972
Common Design Type

1972, Apr. 29
Size: 24x35mm
825 CD15 3.50fr light blue & multi 20 15
826 CD15 7fr rose & multi 40 30

1972, May 13 **Photo.** ***Perf. 11½***
827 A296 2.50fr "Freedom of the Press" 15 15

50th anniv. of the BELGA news information agency and 25th Congress of the Intl. Federation of Newspaper Editors (F.I.E.J.), Brussels, May 15-19.

Freight Cars with Automatic Coupling A297

1972, June 3
828 A297 7fr bl & multi 30 20

Intl. Railroad Union, 50th anniv.

View of Couvin — A298

Design: No. 830, Aldeneik Church, Maaseik, vert.

1972, June 24 **Engr.** ***Perf. 13½x14***
829 A298 2.50fr bl, vio brn & sl grn 20 20
830 A298 2.50fr dk brn & bl 20 20

Beatrice, by Gustave de Smet — A299

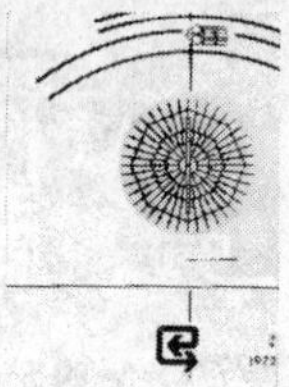

Radar Station, Intelsat 4 — A300

1972, Sept. 9 **Photo.** ***Perf. 11½***
831 A299 3fr multi 18 15

Youth philately.

1972, Sept. 16
832 A300 3.50fr lt bl, sil & blk 18 15

Opening of the Lessive satellite earth station.

Frans Masereel, Self-portrait A301

Adoration of the Kings, by Felix Timmermans A302

1972, Oct. 21
833 A301 4.50fr lt ol & blk 18 15

Frans Masereel (1889-1972), wood engraver.

1972, Nov. 11 **Photo.** ***Perf. 11½***
834 A302 3.50fr blk & multi 18 15

Christmas 1972.

Maria Theresa, Anonymous A303

1972, Dec. 16 **Photo.** ***Perf. 11½***
835 A303 2fr multi 15 15

200th anniversary of the Belgian Academy of Science, Literature and Art, founded by Empress Maria Theresa.

WMO Emblem, Meteorological Institute, Ukkel — A304

1973, Mar. 24 **Photo.** ***Perf. 11½***
836 A304 9fr bl & multi 38 18

Cent. of intl. meteorological cooperation.

"Fire" — A305

Man and WHO Emblem — A306

1973, Mar. 24
837 A305 2fr multi 15 15

Natl. industrial fire prevention campaign.

1973, Apr. 7
838 A306 8fr dk red, ocher & blk 32 24

25th anniv. of WHO.

Europa Issue 1973
Common Design Type

1973, Apr. 28
Size: 35x24mm
839 CD16 4.50fr org brn, vio bl & yel 22 15
840 CD16 8fr ol, dk bl & yel 55 45

Thurn and Taxis Courier — A308

Arrows Circling Globe — A309

Engraved and Photogravure

1973, Apr. 28 ***Perf. 11½***
841 A308 4.50fr blk & red brn 20 15

Stamp Day.

1973, May 12 **Photo.**
842 A309 3.50fr dp ocher & multi 16 15

5th International Telecommunications Day.

Workers' Sports Exhibition Poster, Ghent, 1913 — A310

1973, May 12
843 A310 4.50fr multi 20 15

60th anniversary of the International Workers' Sports Movement.

Fair Emblem A311

1973, May 12 **Photo.** ***Perf. 11½***
844 A311 4.50fr multi 18 15

25th International Fair, Liege, May 12-27.

DC-10 and 1923 Biplane over Brussels Airport
A312

Design: 10fr, Tips biplane, 1908.

1973, May 19 **Engr. & Photo.**

845 A312 8fr gray bl, blk & ultra 28 20
846 A312 10fr grn, lt bl & blk 45 35

50th anniv. of SABENA, Belgian airline (8fr) and 25th anniv. of the "Vieilles Tiges" Belgian flying pioneers' society (10fr).

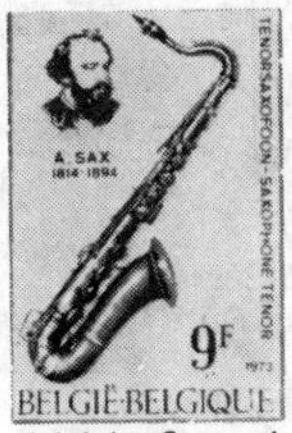

Adolphe Sax and Tenor Saxophone
A313

Fresco from Bathhouse, Ostend
A314

1973, Sept. 15 **Photo.**

847 A313 9fr grn, blk & bl 40 20

Adolphe Sax (1814-1894), inventor of saxophone.

1973, Sept. 15

848 A314 4.50fr multi 22 15

Year of the Spa.

St. Nicholas Church, Eupen
A315

Charley, by Henri Evenepoel
A316

Designs: No. 850, Town Hall, Leau. No. 851, Aarshot Church. No. 852, Chiman Castle. No. 853, Gemmenich Border: Belgium, Germany, Netherlands. No. 854, St. Monan and church, Nassogne. No. 855, Church tower, Dottignes. No. 856, Grand-Place, Sint-Truiden.

1973-75 **Engr.** ***Perf. 13***

849 A315 2fr plum, sep & lt vio 20 15
850 A315 3fr blk, lt bl & mar 50 15
851 A315 3fr brn blk & yel 32 15
852 A315 4fr grnsh blk & grnsh bl 35 15
853 A315 4fr grnsh blk & bl 40 18
854 A315 4fr grnsh blk & bl 40 18
855 A315 4.50fr multi 50 20
856 A315 5fr multi 50 18
Nos. 849-856 (8) 3.17 1.34

Nos. 851, 855 not luminescent. Nos. 850, 852-854, 856 horiz.

1973, Oct. 13 **Photo.** ***Perf. 11½***

857 A316 3fr multi 18 15

Youth philately.

Luminescent Paper
Starting with No. 858, all stamps are on luminescent paper unless otherwise noted.

Jean-Baptiste Moens
A317

1973, Oct. 13 **Engr. & Photo.**

858 A317 10fr gray & multi 42 20

50th anniversary of the Belgian Stamp Dealers' Association. Printed in sheets of 12 stamps and 12 labels showing association emblem.

Adoration of the Shepherds, by Hugo van der Goes
A318

Louis Pierard, by M. I. Ianchelevici
A319

1973, Nov. 17 **Engr.** ***Perf. 11½***

859 A318 4fr blue 18 15

Christmas 1973.

1973, Nov. 17 **Engr. & Photo.**

860 A319 4fr ver & buff 25 15

Louis Pierard (1886-1952), journalist, member of Parliament.

Highway, Automobile Club Emblem
A320

1973, Nov. 17 **Photo.**

861 A320 5fr yellow & multi 25 15

Flemish Automobile Club, 50th anniv.

Early Microphone, Emblem of Radio Belgium — A321

1973, Nov. 24 **Engr. & Photo.**

862 A321 4fr blue & black 18 15

50th anniversary of Radio Belgium.

Felicien Rops, Self-portrait
A323

Engraved and Photogravure

1973, Dec. 8 ***Perf. 11½***

863 A323 7fr tan & black 32 15

Felicien Rops (1833-1898), painter and engraver.

King Albert, (1875-1934) — A324

Sun, Bird, Flowers and Girl — A325

1974, Feb. 16 **Photo.** ***Perf. 11½***

864 A324 4fr Prus grn & blk 22 15

1974, Mar. 25 **Photo.** ***Perf. 11½***

865 A325 3fr vio & multi 15 15

Protection of the environment.

NATO Emblem
A326

1974, Apr. 20 **Photo.** ***Perf. 11½***

866 A326 10fr dp to lt bl 45 25

25th anniversary of the signing of the North Atlantic Treaty.

Hubert Krains — A327

"Destroyed City," by Ossip Zadkine — A328

1974, Apr. 27 **Engr. & Photo.**

867 A327 5fr blk & gray 20 15

Stamp Day.

Europa Issue 1974

1974, May 4

Design: 10fr, Solidarity, by Georges Minne.

868 A328 5fr blk & red 24 15
869 A328 10fr blk & ultra 60 30

Children
A329

1974, May 18 **Photo.** ***Perf. 11½***

870 A329 4fr lt bl & multi 20 15

10th Lay Youth Festival.

Planetarium, Brussels
A330

Soleilmont Abbey Ruins — A331

Designs: 4fr, Pillory, Braine-le-Chateau. 7fr, Fountain, Ghent (procession symbolic of Chamber of Rhetoric). 10fr, Belfry, Bruges, vert.

Engr. and Photo.

1974, June 22 ***Perf. 11½***

871 A330 3fr sky bl & blk 15 15
872 A330 4fr lil rose & blk 18 15
873 A331 5fr lt grn & blk 28 15
874 A331 7fr dl yel & blk 35 20
875 A330 10fr blk, bl & brn 45 15
Nos. 871-875 (5) 1.41
Set value 55

Historic buildings and monuments.

"BENELUX"
A332

1974, Sept. 7 **Photo.** ***Perf. 11½***

876 A332 5fr bl grn, dk grn & lt bl 25 15

30th anniversary of the signing of the customs union of Belgium, Netherlands and Luxembourg.

Jan Vekemans, by Cornelis de Vos — A333

1974, Sept. 14

877 A333 3fr multi 18 15

Youth philately.

Leon Tresignies, Willebroek Canal Bridge
A334

1974, Sept. 28 **Engr. & Photo.**

878 A334 4fr brn & ol grn 18 15

60th death anniversary of Corporal Leon Tresignies (1886-1914), hero of World War I.

Montgomery Blair, UPU Emblem
A335

Design: 10fr, Heinrich von Stephan and UPU emblem.

1974, Oct. 5 ***Perf. 11½***

879 A335 5fr grn & blk 20 15
880 A335 10fr brick red & blk 40 28

Centenary of Universal Postal Union.

Symbolic Chart — A336

1974, Oct. 12 **Photo.** ***Perf. 11½***

881 A336 7fr multi 30 20

Central Economic Council, 25th anniv.

Rotary Emblem A337

1974, Oct. 19

882 A337 10fr multi 42 20

Rotary International of Belgium.

A338

A341

Wild boar (regiment's emblem).

1974, Oct. 26

883 A338 3fr multi 18 15

Granting of the colors to the Ardennes Chasseurs Regiment, 40th anniversary.

1974, Nov. 16 *Perf. 11½*

Angel, by Van Eyck brothers.

884 A341 4fr rose lilac 20 15

Christmas 1974. The Angel shown is from the triptyque "The Mystical Lamb" in the Saint-Bavon Cathedral, Ghent.

A342

A343

Adolphe Quetelet, by J. Odevaere.

1974, Dec. 14 **Engr. & Photo.**

885 A342 10fr blk & buff 42 20

Death centenary of Adolphe Quetelet (1796-1874), statistician, astronomer and Secretary of Royal Academy of Brussels.

1975, Feb. 15 **Photo.** *Perf. 11½*

912 A343 6.50fr Themabelga emblem 30 15

Themabelga, International Thematic Stamp Exhibition, Brussels, Dec. 13-21, 1975.

A344

A345

1975, Feb. 22

913 A344 4.50fr Neoregelia carolinae 22 15

Photogravure and Engraved

914 A344 5fr Coltsfoot 25 16
915 A344 6.50fr Azalea 30 15
Nos. 913-915 (3) 77 46

Ghent Intl. Flower Exhib., Apr. 26-May 5.

1975, Mar. 15 *Perf. 11½*

School emblem, man Leading boy.

916 A345 4.50fr blk & multi 20 15

Centenary of the founding of the Charles Buls Normal School for Boys, Brussels.

Davids Foundation Emblem A346

1975, Mar. 22 **Photo.**

917 A346 5fr yel & multi 25 15

Centenary of the Davids Foundation, a Catholic organization for the promotion of Flemish through education and books.

King Albert (1875-1934) A347

Mailman, 1840, by James Thiriar A348

1975, Apr. 5 **Engr. & Photo.**

918 A347 10fr blk & mar 45 25

1975, Apr. 19 **Engr.** *Perf. 11½*

919 A348 6.50fr dl mag 30 15

Stamp Day 1975.

St. John, from Last Supper, by Bouts — A349

Concentration Camp Symbols — A350

Europa: 10fr, Woman's Head, detail from "Trial by Fire," by Dirk Bouts.

1975, Apr. 26 **Engr. & Photo.**

920 A349 6.50fr blk, grn & bl 35 15
921 A349 10fr blk, ocher & red 60 32

1975, May 3 **Photo.**

Design: "B" denoted political prisoners, "KG" prisoners of war.

922 A350 4.50fr multi 20 15

Liberation of concentration camps, 30th anniversary.

Hospice of St. John, Bruges A351

Church of St. Loup, Namur — A352

Design: 10fr, Martyrs' Square, Brussels.

1975, May 12 **Engr.** *Perf. 11½*

926 A351 4.50fr deep rose lilac 22 20
927 A352 5fr slate grn 22 15
928 A351 10fr brt blue 45 32
Nos. 926-928 (3) 89 67

European Architectural Heritage Year.

Library, Louvain University, Ryckmans and Cerfaux A355

1975, June 7 **Photo.** *Perf. 11½*

931 A355 10fr dl bl & sepia 40 20

25th anniversary of Louvain Bible Colloquium, founded by Professors Gonzague Ryckmans (1887-1969) and Lucien Cerfaux (1883-1968).

"Metamorphose" by Pol Mara — A356

Marie Popelin, Palace of Justice, Brussels — A357

1975, June 14

932 A356 7fr multi 30 20

Queen Fabiola Mental Health Foundation.

1975, June 21 **Engr. & Photo.**

933 A357 6.50fr grn & claret 30 15

International Women's Year 1975. Marie Popelin (1846-1913), first Belgian woman doctor of law.

Assia, by Charles Despiau — A358

Cornelia Vekemans, by Cornelis de Vos — A359

1975, Sept. 6 *Perf. 11½*

934 A358 5fr yel grn & blk 24 15

Middelheim Outdoor Museum, 25th anniv.

1975, Sept. 20 **Photo.**

935 A359 4.50fr multi 20 15

Youth philately.

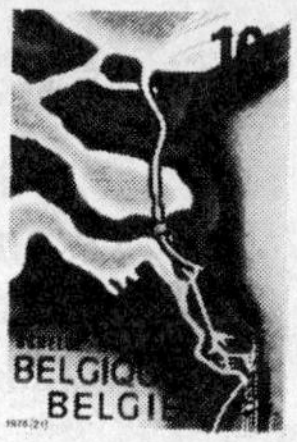
Map of Schelde-Rhine Canal — A360

1975, Sept. 20

936 A360 10fr multi 45 22

Opening of connection between the Schelde and Rhine, Sept. 23, 1975.

National Bank, W. F. Orban, Founder A361

Photogravure and Engraved

1975, Oct. 11 *Perf. 12½x13*

937 A361 25fr multi 1.00 30

Natl. Bank of Belgium, 125th anniv.

Edmond Thieffry and Plane, 1925 — A362

1975, Oct. 18 *Perf. 11½*

938 A362 7fr blk & lil 30 20

First flight Brussels to Kinshasa, Congo, 50th anniversary.

"Seat of Wisdom" St. Peter's, Louvain — A363

1975, Nov. 8 *Perf. 11½*

939 A363 6.50fr bl, blk & grn 28 15

University of Louvain, 550th anniversary.

Angels, by Rogier van der Weyden A364

1975, Nov. 15

940 A364 5fr multi 24 15

Christmas 1975.

Willemsfonds Emblem — A365

American Bicentennial Emblem — A366

1976, Feb. 21 **Photo.** ***Perf. 11½***
941 A365 5fr multi 24 15

125th anniversary of the Willems Foundation, which supports Flemish language and literature.

1976, Mar. 13 **Photo.** ***Perf. 11½***
942 A366 14fr gold, red, bl & blk 60 30

American Bicentennial. No. 942 printed checkerwise in sheets of 30 stamps and 30 gold and black labels which show medal with 1626 seal of New York. Black engraved inscription on labels commemorates arrival of first Walloon settlers in Nieu Nederland.

Cardinal Mercier — A367

Symbolic of V.E.V. — A368

1976, Mar. 20 **Engr.**
943 A367 4.50fr brt rose lil 20 15

Desire Joseph Cardinal Mercier (1851-1926), professor at Louvain University, spiritual and patriotic leader during World War I, 50th death anniversary.

1976, Apr. 3 **Photo.** ***Perf. 11½***
944 A368 6.50fr multi 28 15

Flemish Economic Organization (Vlaams Ekonomisch Verbond), 50th anniversary.

General Post Office, Brussels A369

1976, Apr. 24 **Engr.** ***Perf. 11½***
945 A369 6.50fr sepia 28 15

Stamp Day.

Potter's Hands — A370

Europa: 6.50fr, Basket maker, vert.

1976, May 8 **Photo.**
946 A370 6.50fr multi 45 15
947 A370 14fr multi 65 38

Truck on Road — A371

1976, May 8
948 A371 14fr blk, yel & red 65 35

15th International Road Union Congress, Brussels, May 9-13.

Queen Elisabeth (1876-1965) — A372

1976, May 24 ***Perf. 11½***
949 A372 14fr green 60 30

Ardennes Draft Horses — A373

1976, June 19
950 A373 5fr multicolored 22 15

Ardennes Draft Horses Association, 50th anniversary.

Souvenir Sheets

King Baudouin — A374

1976, June 26
951 A374 Sheet of 3 2.25 2.25
a. 4.50fr gray 70 70
b. 6.50fr ocher 70 70
c. 10fr brick red 70 70
952 A374 Sheet of 2 3.25 3.25
a. 20fr yellow green 85 85
b. 30fr Prussian blue 85 85

25th anniv. of the reign of King Baudouin. No. 951 sold for 30fr, No. 952 for 70fr. The surtax went to a new foundation for the improvement of living conditions in honor of the King.

Electric Train and Society Emblem A375

1976, Sept. 11 **Photo.** ***Perf. 11½***
953 A375 6.50fr multi 30 15

Natl. Belgian Railroad Soc., 50th anniv.

William of Nassau, Prince of Orange — A376

1976, Sept. 11 **Engr.**
954 A376 10fr slate green 42 20

400th anniv. of the pacification of Ghent.

New Subway Train — A377

1976, Sept. 18 **Photo.**
955 A377 6.50fr multi 30 15

Opening of first line of Brussels subway.

Young Musician, by W. C. Duyster — A378

1976, Oct. 2 **Photo.** ***Perf. 11½***
956 A378 4.50fr multi 20 15

Young musicians and youth philately.

Charles Bernard — A379

St. Jerome in the Mountains, by Le Patinier — A380

Blind Leading the Blind, by Breughel the Elder — A381

Design: No. 958, Fernand Victor Toussaint van Boelaere.

1976, Oct. 16 **Engr.**
957 A379 5fr violet 16 16
958 A379 5fr red brn & sepia 16 16
959 A380 6.50fr dark brown 28 15
960 A381 6.50fr slate green 28 15
Nos. 957-960 (4) 88
Set value 48

Charles Bernard (1875-1961), Frenchspeaking journalist; Toussaint van Boelaere (1875-1947), Flemish journalist; No. 959, Charles Plisnier Belgian-French Cultural Society. No. 960, Assoc. for Language Promotion.

Remouchamps Caves — A382

Hunnegem Priory, Gramont, and Madonna A383

Designs: No. 963, River Lys and St. Martin's Church. No. 964, Ham-sur-Heure Castle.

1976, Oct. 23 **Engr.** ***Perf. 13***
961 A382 4.50fr multi 15 15
962 A383 4.50fr multi 15 15
963 A383 5fr multi 22 15
964 A383 5fr multi 22 15
Nos. 961-964 (4) 74
Set value 48

Tourism. #961-962 are not luminescent.

Nativity, by Master of Flemalle — A384

1976, Nov. 20 ***Perf. 11½***
965 A384 5fr violet 22 18

Christmas 1976.

Rubens' Monogram — A385

1977, Feb. 12 **Photo. & Engr.**
966 A385 6.50fr lilac & blk 30 15

Peter Paul Rubens (1577-1640), painter.

Heraldic Lion — A386

1977-85 **Typo.** ***Perf. 13½x14***
Size: 17x20mm
967 A386 50c brn ('80) 15 15
a. 50c orange brown ('85) 15 15
968 A386 1fr brt lil 15 15
a. 1fr bright rose lilac ('84) 15 15
969 A386 1.50fr gray ('78) 15 15
970 A386 2fr yel ('78) 15 15
970A A386 2.50fr yel brn ('81) 15 15
971 A386 2.75fr Prus bl ('80) 30 15
972 A386 3fr vio ('78) 30 15
a. 3fr dull violet ('84) 18 15
973 A386 4fr red brn ('80) 25 15
a. 4fr rose brown ('85) 25 15
974 A386 4.50fr lt ultra 30 15
975 A386 5fr grn ('80) 30 15
a. 5fr emerald green ('84) 20 15
976 A386 6fr dl red brn 35 15
a. 6fr light red brown ('85) 35 15
Nos. 967-976 (11) 2.55
Set value 60

Perf. 13½x12½, 12½x13½

1978, Aug. **Photo.**

Size: 17x22mm, 22x17mm

Booklet Stamps

977 A386 1fr brt lilac	15	15
a. Bklt. pane, #977-978, 2 #786	1.50	
b. Bklt. pane, #977, 979, 2 #788	2.00	
978 A386 2fr yellow	30	30
979 A386 3fr violet	45	45
Nos. 977-979 (3)	90	90

See Nos. 1084-1088. Each pane has 2 labels showing Belgian Postal emblem, also a large selvage with zip code instructions. No. 977-979 not luminescent.

See design O5.

Anniversary Emblem A387

1977, Mar. 14 **Photo.** ***Perf. 11½***

982 A387 6.50fr sil & multi	30	15

Royal Belgian Association of Civil and Agricultural Engineers, 50th anniversary.

Birds and Lions Emblem A388

1977, Mar. 28

983 A388 14fr multi	60	30

Belgian District No. 112 of Lions International, 25th anniversary.

BELGIË-BELGIQUE Pillar Box, 1852 — A389

1977, Apr. 23 **Engr.**

984 A389 6.50fr slate green	45	15

Stamp Day 1977.

Gileppe Dam, Jalhay — A390

Europa: 14fr, War Memorial, Yser at Nieuport.

1977, May 7 **Photo.** ***Perf. 11½***

985 A390 6.50fr multi	40	15
986 A390 14fr multi	90	15
Set value		20

Buying Sets

It is often less expensive to purchase complete sets than individual stamps that make up the set. Set values are provided for many such sets.

Mars and Mercury Association Emblem — A391

1977, May 14

987 A391 5fr multi	22	15

Mars and Mercury Association of Reserve and Retired Officers, 50th anniversary.

Prince de Hornes Coat of Arms — A392

Conversion of St. Hubertus — A394

Battle of the Golden Spur, from Oxford Chest A393

Design: 6.50fr, Froissart writing book.

1977, June 11 **Engr.** ***Perf. 11½***

988 A392 4.50fr violet	22	15
989 A393 5fr red	25	16
990 A394 6.50fr dark brown	28	15
991 A394 14fr slate green	55	35
Nos. 988-991 (4)	1.30	
Set value		66

300th anniv. of the Principality of Overijse (4.50fr); 675th anniv. of the Battle of the Golden Spur (5f); 600th anniv. of publication of 1st volume of the Chronicles of Jehan Froissart (6.50fr); 1250th anniv. of the death of St. Hubertus (14fr).

Rubens, Self-portrait — A395

1977, June 25 **Photo.**

992 A395 5fr multi	25	15
a. Souvenir sheet of 3	1.00	90

Peter Paul Rubens (1577-1640), painter. No. 992a sold for 20fr.

Open Book, from The Lamb of God, by Van Eyck Brothers A396

1977, Sept. 3 **Photo.** ***Perf. 11½***

993 A396 10fr multi	45	25

Intl. Federation of Library Associations (IFLA), 50th Anniv. Congress, Brussels, Sept. 5-10.

Gymnast and Soccer Player — A397

Designs: 6.50fr, Fencers in wheelchairs, horiz. 10fr, Basketball players. 14fr, Hockey players.

1977, Sept. 10

994 A397 4.50fr multi	20	15
995 A397 6.50fr multi	30	15
996 A397 10fr multi	45	20
997 A397 14fr multi	60	30
Nos. 994-997 (4)	1.55	
Set value		65

Workers' Gymnastics and Sports Center, 50th anniversary (4.50fr); sport for the Handicapped (6.50fr); 20th European Basketball Championships (10fr); First World Hockey Cup (14fr).

Europalia 77 Emblem — A398

1977, Sept. 17

998 A398 5fr gray & multi	22	15

5th Europalia Arts Festival, featuring German Federal Republic, Belgium, Oct.-Nov. 1977.

The Egg Farmer, by Gustave De Smet — A399

1977, Oct. 8 **Engr. & Photo.**

999 A399 4.50fr bister & blk	22	15

Publicity for Belgian eggs.

Mother and Daughter with Album, by Constant Cap — A400

1977, Oct. 15 **Engr.**

1000 A400 4.50fr dark brown	22	15

Youth Philately.

Bailiff's House, Gembloux — A401

Market Square, St. Nicholas A402

Designs: No. 1002, St. Aldegonde Church and Cultural Center. No. 1004, Statue and bridge, Liège.

1977, Oct. 22

1001 A401 4.50fr multi	22	15
1002 A401 4.50fr multi	22	15
1003 A402 5fr multi	22	18
1004 A402 5fr multi	22	18
Nos. 1001-1004 (4)	88	
Set value		56

Tourism. Nos. 1001-1004 not luminescent. See Nos. 1017-1018, 1037-1040.

Nativity, by Rogier van der Weyden — A403

1977, Nov. 11 **Engr.**

1005 A403 5fr rose red	30	15

Christmas 1977.

Symbols of Transportation and Map — A404

Parliament of Europe, Strasbourg, and Emblem — A405

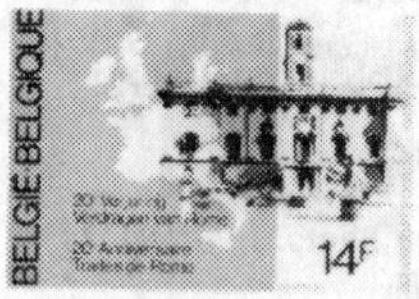

Campidoglio Palace, Rome, and Map — A406

Design: No. 1009, Paul-Henri Spaak and map of 19 European member countries.

1978, Mar. 18 **Photo.** ***Perf. 11½***

1006 A404 10fr blue & multi	45	18
1007 A405 10fr blue & multi	90	18
1008 A406 14fr blue & multi	52	52
1009 A406 14fr blue & multi	52	52
Nos. 1006-1009 (4)	2.39	1.40

European Action: 25th anniversary of the European Transport Ministers' Conference; 1st general elections for European Parliament; 20th anniversary of the signing of the Treaty of Rome; Paul Henri Spaak (1899-1972), Belgian statesman who worked for the establishment of European Community.

Grimbergen Abbey — A407

1978, Apr. 1 **Engr.**

1010 A407 4.50fr red brown	22	15

850th anniversary of the Premonstratensian Abbey at Grimbergen.

Emblem — A408

No. 39 with First Day Cancel — A409

1978, Apr. 8 **Photo.**
1011 A408 8fr multicolored 50 15

Ostend Chamber of Commerce and Industry, 175th anniversary.

1978, Apr. 15
1012 A409 8fr multicolored 35 15

Stamp Day.

Europa Issue

Pont des Trous, Tournai A410

Design: 8fr, Antwerp Cathedral, by Vaclav Hollar, vert.

Photogravure and Engraved

1978, May 6 ***Perf. 11½***
1013 A410 8fr multicolored 50 15
1014 A410 14fr multicolored 75 30

Virgin of Ghent, Porcelain Plaque — A411

Paul Pastur Workers' University, Charleroi — A412

1978, Sept. 16 **Photo.** ***Perf. 11½***
1015 A411 6fr multicolored 42 15
1016 A412 8fr multicolored 55 15
Set value 21

Municipal education in Ghent, 150th anniversary; Paul Pastur Workers' University, Charleroi, 75th anniv. #1015-1016 are not luminescent.

Types of 1977 and

Tourist Guide, Brussels A413

Designs: No. 1017, Jonathas House, Enghien. No. 1018, View of Wetteren and couple in local costume. No. 1020, Prince Carnival, Eupen-St. Vith.

1978, Sept. 25 **Photo. & Engr.**
1017 A401 4.50fr multi 16 15
1018 A402 4.50fr multi 16 15
1019 A413 6fr multi 25 15
1020 A413 6fr multi 25 15
Nos. 1017-1020 (4) 82
Set value 48

Tourism. #1017-1020 are not luminescent.

Emblem A414

1978, Oct. 7 **Photo.**
1021 A414 8fr red & blk 35 15

Royal Flemish Engineer's Organization, 50th anniversary.

Young Philatelist A415

1978, Oct. 14 **Engr.** ***Perf. 11½***
1022 A415 4.50fr dk violet 22 15

Youth philately.

Nativity, Notre Dame, Huy — A416

1978, Nov. 18 **Engr.** ***Perf. 11½***
1023 A416 6fr black 28 15

Christmas 1978.

Tyll Eulenspiegel, Lay Action Emblem — A417

European Parliament Emblem — A418

1979, Mar. 3 **Photo.** ***Perf. 11½***
1024 A417 4.50fr multi 28 15

10th anniversary of Lay Action Centers.

1979, Mar. 3
1025 A418 8fr multicolored 50 15

European Parliament, first direct elections, June 7-10.

St. Michael Banishing Lucifer — A419

1979, Mar. 17 **Photo. & Engr.**
1026 A419 4.50fr rose red & blk 20 15
1027 A419 8fr brt green & blk 30 15
Set value 19

Millennium of Brussels.

NATO Emblem and Monument A420

1979, Mar. 31 **Photo.**
1028 A420 3fr multicolored 1.10 45

NATO, 30th anniv.

Prisoner's Head — A421

1979, Apr. 7 **Photo. & Engr.**
1029 A421 6fr orange & blk 25 15

25th anniversary of the National Political Prisoners' Monument at Breendonk.

Belgium No. O2 — A422

1979, Apr. 21 **Photo.** ***Perf. 11½***
1030 A422 8fr multicolored 50 15

Stamp Day 1979.

Mail Coach and Truck A423

Europa: 14fr, Chappe's heliograph, Intelsat satellite and dish antenna.

1979, Apr. 28 **Photo. & Engr.**
1031 A423 8fr multicolored 45 15
1032 A423 14fr multicolored 90 40

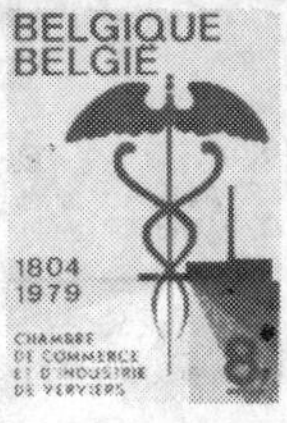
Chamber of Commerce Emblem — A424

1979, May 19 **Photo.** ***Perf. 11½***
1033 A424 8fr multicolored 35 15

Verviers Chamber of Commerce and Industry, 175th anniversary.

"50" Emblem A425

1979, June 9 **Photo.** ***Perf. 11½***
1034 A425 4.50fr gold & ultra 28 15

Natl. Fund for Professional Credit, 50th anniv.

Merchants, Roman Bas-relief A426

1979, June 9
1035 A426 10fr multicolored 45 16

Belgian Chamber of Trade and Commerce, 50th anniversary.

"Tintin" as Philatelist A427

1979, Sept. 29 **Photo.** ***Perf. 11½***
1036 A427 8fr multicolored 32 15

Youth philately.

Tourism Types of 1977

Designs: No. 1037, Belfry, Thuin. No. 1038, Royal Museum of Central Africa, Tervuren. No. 1039, St. Nicholas Church and cattle, Ciney. No. 1040, St. John's Church and statue of Our Lady, Poperinge.

Perf. 11½ (A401), 13 (A402)
1979, Oct. 22 **Photo. & Engr.**
1037 A401 5fr multicolored 18 15
1038 A402 5fr multicolored 18 15
1039 A401 6fr multicolored 28 15
1040 A402 6fr multicolored 28 15
Nos. 1037-1040 (4) 92
Set value 44

Francois Auguste Gevaert A429

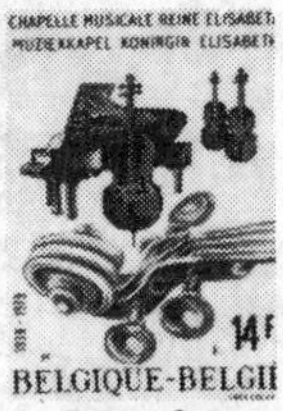
Piano, String Instruments A430

Design: 6fr, Emmanuel Durlet.

1979, Nov. 3 ***Perf. 11½***
1041 A429 5fr brown 35 15
1042 A429 6fr brown 42 15
1043 A430 14fr brown 90 35
Nos. 1041-1043 (3) 1.67
Set value 53

Francois Auguste Gevaert (1828-1908), musicologist and composer; Emmanuel Durlet (1893-1977), pianist; Queen Elisabeth Musical Chapel Foundation, 40th anniv.

Virgin and Child, Notre Dame, Foy — A431

1979, Nov. 24 **Photo. & Engr.**
1044 A431 6fr lt grnsh blue 30 15

Christmas 1979.

Independence, 150th Anniversary A432

1980, Jan. 26 **Photo.** ***Perf. 11½***
1045 A432 9fr purple 40 15

Frans van Cauwelaert A433

Spring Flowers A434

1980, Feb. 25 **Engr.**
1046 A433 5fr gray 22 15

Frans van Cauwelaert (1880-1961), Minister of State.

1980, Mar. 10 **Photo.**
1047 A434 5fr shown 24 15
1048 A434 6.50fr Summer flowers 32 15
1049 A434 9fr Autumn flowers 45 15
Nos. 1047-1049 (3) 1.01
Set value 28

Ghent Flower Show, Apr. 19-27.

P.T.T., 50th Anniv. A435

1980, Apr. 14 **Photo.** ***Perf. 11½***
1050 A435 10fr multicolored 45 22

Belgium No. C4 — A436

1980, Apr. 21
1051 A436 9fr multicolored 50 15

Stamp Day.

A437

A438

Europa: 9fr, St. Benedict, by Hans Memling. 14fr, Margaret of Austria (1480-1530).

1980, Apr. 28
1052 A437 9fr multicolored 45 15
1053 A437 14fr multicolored 70 24

1980, May 10 **Photo.** ***Perf. 11½***
1054 A438 5fr Palais des Nations, Brussels 25 15

4th Interparliamentary Conference for European Cooperation and Security, Brussels, May 12-18.

Golden Carriage, 1780, Mons — A439

Tourism: #1056, Canal landscape, Damme.

1980, May 17
1055 A439 6.50fr multi 32 20
1056 A439 6.50fr multi 32 20

Souvenir Sheet

Royal Mint Theater, Brussels — A440

Photo. & Engr.

1980, May 31 ***Perf. 11½***
1057 A440 50fr black 3.25 3.25

150th anniv. of independence. Sold for 75fr.

King Baudouin, 50th Birthday — A441

1980, Sept. 6 **Photo.** ***Perf. 11½***
1058 A441 9fr rose claret 42 15

View of Chiny A442

Portal and Court, Diest — A443

1980 **Engr.** ***Perf. 13***
1059 A442 5fr multicolored 25 15
1060 A443 5fr multicolored 25 15
Set value 20

Tourism. Nos. 1059-1060 are not luminescent. Issue dates: No. 1059, Sept. 27; No. 1060, Dec. 13. See Nos. 1072-1075, 1120-1125.

Emblem of Belgian Heart League A444

1980, Oct. 4 **Photo.** ***Perf. 11½***
1061 A444 14fr blue & magenta 55 25

Heart Week, Oct. 20-25.

Rodenbach Statue, Roulers — A445

1980, Oct. 11
1062 A445 9fr multicolored 40 15

Albrecht Rodenbach (1856-1880), poet.

Youth Philately — A446

1980, Oct. 27 **Photo.** ***Perf. 11½***
1063 A446 5fr multicolored 22 15

National Broadcasting Service, 50th Anniversary — A447

1980, Nov. 10
1064 A447 10fr gray & blk 45 22

Garland and Nativity, by Daniel Seghers, 17th Century A448

1980, Nov. 17
1065 A448 6.50fr multicolored 40 15

Christmas 1980.

Baron de Gerlache, by F.J. Navez — A449

Leopold I, By Geefs — A450

Design: 9fr, Baron de Stassart, by F.J. Navez.

1981, Mar. 16 **Photo.** ***Perf. 11½***
1066 A449 6fr multicolored 25 15
1067 A449 9fr multicolored 40 15

Photogravure and Engraved
1068 A450 50fr multicolored 2.25 55

Sesquicentennial of Chamber of Deputies, Senate and Dynasty.

Europa Issue 1981

Tchantchès and Op-Signoorke, Puppets — A451

Photogravure and Engraved

1981, May 4 ***Perf. 11½***
1069 A451 9fr shown 40 15
1070 A451 14fr d'Artagnan and Woltje 65 35

Impression of M.A. de Cock (Founder of Post Museum) — A452

1981, May 18 **Photo.**
1071 A452 9fr multicolored 40 15

Stamp Day.

Tourism Types of 1980

Designs: No. 1072, Virgin and Child statue, Our Lady's Church, Tongre-Notre Dame. No. 1073, Egmont Castle, Zottegem. No. 1074, Eau d'Heure River. No. 1075, Tongerlo Abbey, Antwerp.

1981, June 15 **Engr.** ***Perf. 11½***
1072 A442 6fr multi 35 15
1073 A442 6fr multi 35 20
1074 A443 6.50fr multi 35 20
1075 A443 6.50fr multi 35 20
Nos. 1072-1075 (4) 1.40 75

Soccer Player — A453

E. Remouchamps, Founder — A454

1981, Sept. 5 **Photo.** ***Perf. 11½***
1076 A453 6fr multicolored 28 15

Soccer in Belgium centenary; Royal Antwerp Soccer Club.

1981, Sept. 5 **Photo. & Engr.**
1077 A454 6.50fr multi 32 15

Walloon Language and Literature Club 125th anniv.

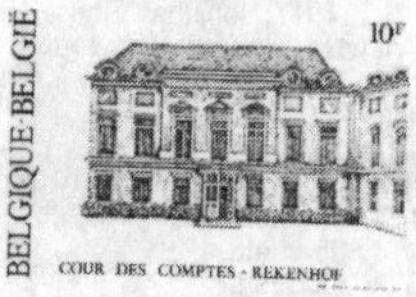

Audit Office Sesquicentennial — A455

1981, Sept. 12 **Engr.**
1078 A455 10fr tan & dk brn 48 24

French Horn — A456

1981, Sept. 12 **Photo.**

1079 A456 6.50fr multi 32 15

Vredekring (Peace Circle) Band of Antwerp centenary.

Souvenir Sheet

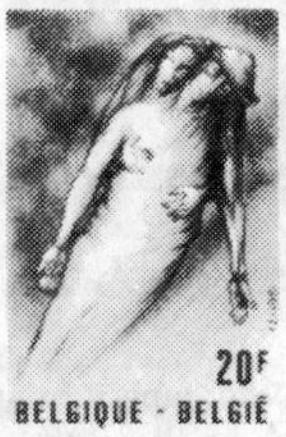
Pieta, by Ben Genaux — A457

1981, Sept. 19 **Photo.** ***Perf. 11½***

1080 A457 20fr multicolored 1.40 1.40

Mining disaster at Marcinelle, 25th anniv. Sold for 30fr.

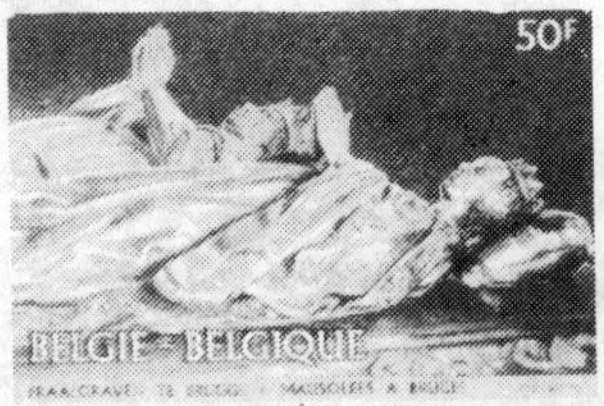
Mausoleum of Marie of Burgundy and Charles the Bold, Bruges — A458

1981, Oct. 10 **Photo. & Engr.**

1081 A458 50fr multi 2.25 60

Youth Philately — A459

1981, Oct. 24 **Photo.**

1082 A459 6fr multi 28 15

Type of 1977 and

A459a

A460

King Baudouin A460a

Photo. and Engr.; Photo.

1980-86 ***Perf. 13½x14, 11½***

1084	A386	65c brt rose	15	15
1085	A386	1fr on 5fr grn ('82)	15	15
1086	A386	7fr brt rose ('82)	32	15
1087	A386	8fr grnsh bl ('83)	35	15
1088	A386	9fr dl org ('85)	30	15
1089	A459a	10fr blue ('82)	48	15
1090	A459a	11fr dl red ('83)	52	15
1091	A459a	12fr grn ('84)	55	15
1092	A459a	13fr scar ('86)	48	15
1093	A459a	15fr red org ('84)	70	20
1094	A459a	20fr dk bl ('84)	90	28
1095	A459a	22fr lil ('84)	1.00	30
1096	A459a	23fr gray grn ('85)	60	55
1097	A459a	30fr brn ('84)	1.25	40
1098	A459a	40fr red org ('84)	1.50	55
1099	A460	50fr lt grnsh bl & bl	2.00	30
1100	A460a	50fr tan & dk brn ('84)	2.00	60
1101	A460	65fr pale lil & blk ('81)	2.75	90
1102	A460	100fr lt bis brn & dk bl ('81)	4.00	1.25
1103	A460a	100fr lt bl & dk bl ('84)	4.00	1.25
		Nos. 1084-1103 (20)	24.00	7.93

See Nos. 1231-1234.

Max Waller, Movement Founder A461

The Spirit Drinkers, by Gustave van de Woestyne A462

Fernand Severin, Poet, 50th Death Anniv. — A463

Jan van Ruusbroec, Flemish Mystic, 500th Birth Anniv. — A464

Thought and Man TV Series, 25th Anniv. A465

Nativity, 16th Cent. Engraving A466

1981, Nov. 7

1104	A461	6fr multi	25	15
1105	A462	6.50fr multi	30	18
1106	A463	9fr multi	40	15
1107	A464	10fr multi	65	22
1108	A465	14fr multi	60	35
		Nos. 1104-1108 (5)	2.20	1.05

La Jeune Belgique cultural movement cent. (6fr).

1981, Nov. 21

1109 A466 6.50fr multi 30 15

Christmas 1981.

Royal Conservatory of Music Sesquicentennial — A467

Design: 9fr, Judiciary sesquicentennial.

1982, Jan. 25 **Photo.** ***Perf. 11½***

1110	A467	6.50fr multi	30	15
1111	A467	9fr multi	40	15
		Set value		22

A468

A469

1982, Mar. 1

1112	A468	6fr Cyclotron	25	15
1113	A468	14fr Galaxy, telescope	60	35
1114	A468	50fr Koch	2.25	65
		Nos. 1112-1114 (3)	3.10	1.15

Radio-isotope production, Natl. Radio-elements Institute, Fleurus (6fr); Royal Belgian Observatory (14fr); centenary of TB bacillus discovery (50fr).

1982, Apr. 17 **Photo.** ***Perf. 11½***

1115 A469 6.50fr multi 32 15

Joseph Lemaire (1882-1966), Minister of State.

Europa 1982 — A470

1982, May 1

1116	A470	10fr Universal suffrage	48	15
1117	A470	17fr Edict of Tolerance, 1781	80	40

Stamp Day — A471

1982, May 22 **Photo. & Engr.**

1118 A471 10fr multi 50 15

67th World Esperanto Congress, Anvers A472

1982, June 7 **Photo.** ***Perf. 11½***

1119 A472 12fr Tower of Babel 60 30

Tourism Type of 1980

Designs: No. 1120, Tower of Gosselies. No. 1121, Zwijveke Abbey, Dendermonde. No. 1122, Stavelot Abbey. No. 1123, Villers-la-Ville Abbey ruins. No. 1124, Geraardsbergen Abbey entrance. No. 1125, Beveren Pillory.

1982, June 21 **Photo. & Engr.**

1120	A443	7fr lt bl & blk	35	15
1121	A443	7fr lt grn & blk	35	15
1122	A442	7.50fr tan & dk brn	38	25
1123	A442	7.50fr lt vio & pur	38	25
1124	A443	7.50fr slate & blk	38	25
1125	A443	7.50fr beige & blk	38	25
		Nos. 1120-1125 (6)	2.22	1.30

Self Portrait, by L.P. Boon (b. 1912) A473

Abraham Hans, Writer (1882-1932) A474

Designs: 10fr, Adoration of the Shepherds, by Hugo van der Goes (1440-1482). 12fr, The King on His Throne, carving by M. de Ghelderode (1898-1962). 17fr, Madonna and Child, by Pieter Paulus (1881-1959).

1982, Sept. 13 **Photo.** ***Perf. 11½***

1126	A473	7fr multi	35	15
1127	A473	10fr multi	45	15
1128	A473	12fr multi	55	35
1129	A473	17fr multi	75	35
		Nos. 1126-1129 (4)	2.10	
		Set value		82

1982, Sept. 27

1130 A474 17fr multi 75 35

Youth Philately and Scouting A475

1982, Oct. 2 **Photo.** ***Perf. 11½***

1131 A475 7fr multi 35 15

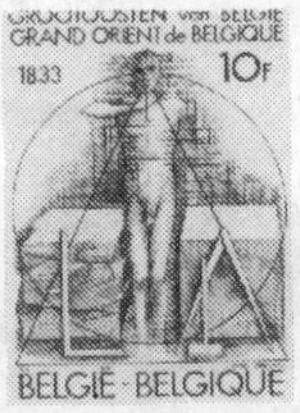
Grand Orient Lodge of Belgium Sesquicentennial A476

1982, Oct. 16 **Photo. & Engr.**

1132 A476 10fr Man taking oath 48 15

Cardinal Joseph Cardijn (1882-1967) A477

1982, Nov. 13 **Photo.**

1133 A477 10fr multi 48 15

St. Francis of Assisi (1182-1226) — A478

1982, Nov. 27

1134 A478 20fr multi 90 30

Horse-drawn Trolley A479

1983, Feb. 12 Photo. *Perf. 11½*

1135 A479	7.50fr shown		38	22
1136 A479	10fr Electric trolley		50	15
1137 A479	50fr Trolley, diff.		2.50	50
	Nos. 1135-1137 (3)		3.38	87

Intl. Fed. for Periodical Press, 24th World Congress, Brussels, May 11-13 — A480

1983, Mar. 19 Photo. *Perf. 11½*

1138 A480 20fr multi 1.00 25

Homage to Women A481

1983, Apr. 16

1139 A481	8fr Operator	45	15
1140 A481	11fr Homemaker	55	15
1141 A481	20fr Executive	95	25
	Nos. 1139-1141 (3)	1.95	
	Set value		38

Stamp Day — A482

1983, Apr. 23

1142 A482 11fr multi 60 15

Procession of the Precious Blood, Bruges A483

1983, Apr. 30 Photo. *Perf. 11½*

1143 A483 8fr multi 60 15

Europa 1983 A484

Paintings by P. Delvaux. 11fr vert.

1983, May 14

1144 A484	11fr Common Man	65	15
1145 A484	20fr Night Train	1.25	45

Manned Flight Bicentenary A485

1983, June 11 Photo. *Perf. 11½*

1146 A485	11fr Balloon over city	65	15
1147 A485	22fr Country	1.40	45

Our Lady's Church, Hastiere A486

1983, June 25

1148 A486	8fr shown	40	18
1149 A486	8fr Landen	40	18
1150 A486	8fr Park, Mouscron	40	18
1151 A486	8fr Wijnendale Castle, Torhout	40	18
	Nos. 1148-1151 (4)	1.60	72

Tineke Festival, Heule — A487

1983, Sept. 10 Photo.

1152 A487 8fr multi 40 15

Enterprise Year Emblem A488

1983, Sept. 24

1153 A488 11fr multicolored 55 15

European year for small and medium-sized enterprises and craft industry.

Youth Philately — A489

1983, Oct. 10 Photo. *Perf. 11½*

1154 A489 8fr multicolored 40 15

Belgian Exports — A490

1983, Oct. 24 *Perf. 11½*

1155 A490	10fr Diamond industry	55	15
1156 A490	10fr Metallurgy	55	15
1157 A490	10fr Textile industry	55	15
	Nos. 1155-1157 (3)	1.65	
	Set value		30

See Nos. 1161-1164.

A491

A492

1983, Nov. 7

1158 A491 20fr multi 1.00 25

Hendrik Conscience, novelist (1812-1883).

Leopold III Type of 1936

1983, Dec. 12 Engr. *Perf. 12x11½*

1159 A84 11fr black 55 15

Leopold III memorial (1901-1983), King 1934-1951.

Photogravure and Engraved

1984, Jan. 14 *Perf. 11½*

1160 A492 11fr multi 55 15

Free University of Brussels, sesquicentennial.

Exports Type of 1983

1984, Jan. 28 Photo.

1161 A490	11fr Chemicals	55	15
1162 A490	11fr Food	55	15
1163 A490	11fr Transportation equipment	55	15
1164 A490	11fr Technology	55	15
	Nos. 1161-1164 (4)	2.20	
	Set value		48

A494

A495

1984, Feb. 11 Photo. & Engr.

1165 A494 8fr tan & dk brn 40 15

50th death anniv. of King Albert I.

1984, Mar. 3 Photo.

Souvenir Sheet

1166	Sheet of 2	2.00	2.00
a.	A495 10fr Archery	55	55
b.	A495 24fr Dressage	1.40	1.40

1984 Olympics. See Nos. B1029-B1030.

Family, Globe, Birds A496

St. John Bosco Canonization A497

1984, Mar. 24 Photo. *Perf. 11½*

1167 A496 12fr multicolored 60 15

"Movement without a Name" peace org.

1984, Apr. 7

1168 A497 8fr multicolored 40 15

Europa (1959-84) A498

1984, May 5 Photo. *Perf. 11½*

1169 A498	12fr black & red	75	15
1170 A498	22fr black & ultra	1.40	30

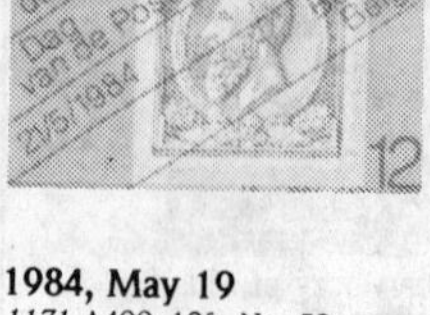

Stamp Day — A499

1984, May 19

1171 A499 12fr No. 52 60 15

2nd European Parliament Elections A500

1984, May 26

1172 A500 12fr multicolored 60 15

Royal Military School, 150th Anniv. — A501

1984, June 9 Photo. *Perf. 11½*

1173 A501 22fr Hat 1.10 25

Notre-Dame de la Chappelle, Brussels A502

Churches: No. 1175, St. Martin's, Montignyle-Tilleul. No. 1176, Tielt, vert.

Perf. 11½x12, 12x11½

1984, June 23 Photo. & Engr.

1174 A502	10fr multicolored	55	15
1175 A502	10fr multicolored	55	15
1176 A502	10fr multicolored	55	15
	Nos. 1174-1176 (3)	1.65	45

50th Anniv. of Chirojeugd (Christian Youth Movement) A503

1984, Sept. 15 Photo. *Perf. 11½*

1177 A503 10fr Emblem 50 15

Affligem Abbey A504

1984, Oct. 6 Photo. & Engr.

1178 A504	8fr Averbode, vert.	40	25
1179 A504	22fr Chimay, vert.	1.25	25
1180 A504	24fr Rochefort, vert.	1.25	38
1181 A504	50fr shown	2.50	50
	Nos. 1178-1181 (4)	5.40	1.38

Youth Philately A505

1984, Oct. 20 Photo.

1182 A505 8fr Postman smurf 45 15

Arthur Meulemans (1884-1966), Composer — A506

1984, Nov. 17 **Photo. & Engr.**
1183 A506 12fr multi 60 15

St. Norbert, 850th Death Anniv. — A507

Europalia '85 — A508

1985, Jan. 14 **Photo. & Engr.**
1184 A507 22fr sepia & beige 1.10 30

1985, Jan. 21 **Photo.**
1185 A508 12fr Virgin with Lion 65 15

Belgian Assoc. of Professional Journalists, Cent. — A509

1985, Feb. 11 **Photo.**
1186 A509 9fr multicolored 42 15

Ghent Flower Festival, Orchids A510

Visit of Pope John Paul II A511

Photogravure and Engraved

1985, Mar. 18 ***Perf. 11½***
1187 A510 12fr Vanda coerules 70 15
1188 A510 12fr Phalaenopsis 70 15
1189 A510 12fr Suphrolaelio cattlea riffe 70 15
Nos. 1187-1189 (3) 2.10 45

1985, Apr. 1 **Photo.**
1190 A511 12fr multicolored 60 15

Belgian Worker's Party Cent. — A512

1985, Apr. 15 **Photo.**
1191 A512 9fr Chained factory gate 42 15
1192 A512 12fr Broken wall, red flag 60 15
Set value 24

Jean de Bast (1883-1975), Engraver A513

1985, Apr. 22 **Engr.**
1193 A513 12fr blue black 60 15

Stamp Day.

Public Transportation Year — A514

Design: 9fr, Steam tram locomotive Type 18, 1896. 12fr, Locomotive Elephant and tender, 1835. 23fr, Type 23 tank engine, 1904. 24fr, Type 1 Pacific locomotive, 1935. 50fr, Type 27 electric locomotive, 1975.

1985, May 6 **Photo.**
1194 A514 9fr multicolored 45 15
1195 A514 12fr multicolored 60 15
1196 A514 23fr multicolored 1.00 25
1197 A514 24fr multicolored 1.25 28
Nos. 1194-1197 (4) 3.30 83

Souvenir Sheet

1198 A514 50fr multicolored 3.00 1.00

Europa 1985 — A515

1985, May 13 **Photo.**
1199 A515 12fr Cesar Franck at organ, 1887 80 15
1200 A515 23fr Folk figures 1.50 25

26th Navigation Congress, Brussels A516

1985, June 10 **Photo.** ***Perf. 11½***
1201 A516 23fr Zeebruge Harbor 1.25 25
1202 A516 23fr Projected lock at Strepy-Thieu 1.25 25

St. Martin's Church, Marcinelle A517

Tourism: No. 1203, Church of the Assumption of Our Lady, Avernas-le-Baudouin, vert. No. 1204, Church of the Old Beguinage, Tongres, vert. No. 1206, Private residence, Puyenbroeck.

1985, June 24 ***Perf. 11½***
1203 A517 12fr multicolored 60 15
1204 A517 12fr multicolored 60 15
1205 A517 12fr multicolored 60 15
1206 A517 12fr multicolored 60 15
Nos. 1203-1206 (4) 2.40
Set value 48

Queen Astrid (1905-1935) A518

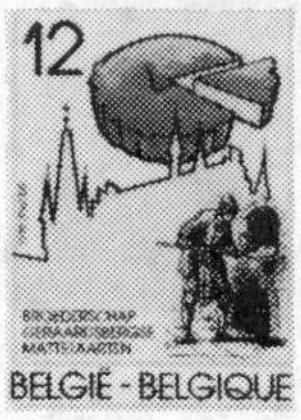

Baking Pies for the Mattetart of Geraardsbergen A519

1985, Sept. 2 ***Perf. 11½***
1207 A518 12fr brown 60 15

1985, Sept. 16

Folk events: 24fr, Children dancing, centenary of the St. Lambert de Hermalle-Argenteau Le Rouges youth organization.

1208 A519 12fr multicolored 60 15
1209 A519 24fr multicolored 95 28

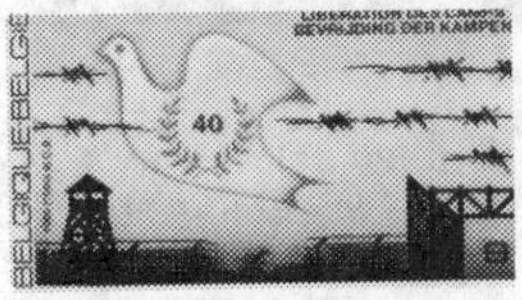

Liberation from German Occupation, 40th Anniv. — A520

Allegories: 9fr, Dove, liberation of concentration camps. 23fr, Battle of Ardennes. 24fr, Destroyer, liberation of the River Scheldt estuary.

1985, Sept. 30 **Photo.** ***Perf. 11½***
1210 A520 9fr multicolored 50 25
1211 A520 23fr multicolored 1.25 65
1212 A520 24fr multicolored 1.25 68
Nos. 1210-1212 (3) 3.00 1.58

Ernest Claes (1885-1968), Author A521

1985, Oct. 7
1213 A521 9fr Portrait, book character 48 25

Intl. Youth Year — A522

1985, Oct. 21
1214 A522 9fr Nude in repose, angel 50 25

King Baudouin & Queen Fabiola, 25th Wedding Anniv. — A523

1985, Dec. 9
1215 A523 12fr multicolored 52 38

Birds — A524

Photo. (50c-2fr, No. 1220, 4.50fr-6fr, No. 1229, 10fr), Typo. (Others)

1985-91 ***Perf. 11½***
1216 A524 50c Crested wren 15 15
1217 A524 1fr Lesser spotted woodpecker 15 15
1218 A524 2fr Tree sparrow 15 15
1219 A524 3fr Hawkfinch 15 15
1220 A524 3fr Reed bunting (Rietgors) 20 15
1221 A524 3.50fr Robin 18 15
1222 A524 4fr Blue throat 20 15
1223 A524 4.50fr Stone chat 30 15
1224 A524 5fr Nuthatch 28 15
1225 A524 6fr Bullfinch 35 15
1226 A524 7fr Blue tit 40 15
1227 A524 8fr Kingfisher 40 15
1228 A524 9fr Goldfinch 30 15
1229 A524 9fr Song thrush (Zanglijster) 58 15
1230 A524 10fr Chaffinch 58 15
Nos. 1216-1230 (15) 4.37
Set value 1.00

Issue dates: 7fr, Sept. 7, 1987. 5fr, 6fr, Sept. 12, 1988. 4fr, Apr. 17, 1989. 2fr, Dec. 4, 1989. 1fr, Jan. 8, 1990. 10fr, Jan. 15, 1990. 50c, Nos. 1220, 1229, Sept. 30, 1991. Others, Sept. 30, 1985.

See Nos. 1432-1447.

King Type of 1981

1986-90 **Photo.** ***Perf. 11½***
1231 A459a 14fr black 80 20
1232 A459a 24fr dk grysh green 1.10 85
1233 A459a 25fr blue black 1.45 38
1234 A460a 200fr sage grn & dl gray grn 9.50 2.00
Nos. 1231-1234 (4) 12.85 3.43

Issue dates: 14fr, Jan. 15, 1990. 25fr, Feb. 19, 1990.

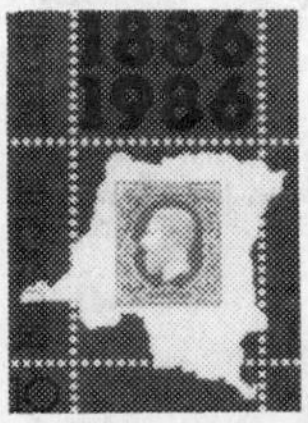

Congo Stamp Cent. — A525

1986, Jan. 27 **Photo.** ***Perf. 11½***
1236 A525 10fr Belgian Congo #3 42 15

See Zaire No. 1230.

Carnival Cities of Aalst and Binche A526

Folklore: masks, giants.

1986, Feb. 3
1237 A526 9fr Aalst Belfry 48 15
1238 A526 12fr Binche Gilles 60 18

Intl. Peace Year — A527

1986, Mar. 10
1239 A527 23fr Emblem, dove 1.25 35

Stamp Day — A528

1986, Apr. 21 Photo. *Perf. 11½*
1240 A528 13fr Artifacts 65 42

Europa 1986 — A529

1986, May 5
1241 A529 13fr Fish 65 42
1242 A529 24fr Flora 1.40 85

Dogs — A530

St. Ludger's Church, Zele — A531

1986, May 26 Photo. *Perf. 11½*
1243 A530 9fr Malines sheepdog 50 30
1244 A530 13fr Tervueren sheepdog 70 45
1245 A530 24fr Groenendael sheepdog 1.40 82
1246 A530 26fr Flemish cattle dog 1.40 85
Nos. 1243-1246 (4) 4.00 2.42

1986, June 30 Photo. & Engr.

Designs: No. 1248, Waver Town Hall. No. 1249, Nederzwalm Canal, horiz. No. 1250, Chapel of Our Lady of the Dunes, Bredene. No. 1251, Licot Castle, Viroinval, horiz. No. 1252, Eynenbourg Castle, La Calamine, horiz.

1247 A531 9fr multi 50 30
1248 A531 9fr multi 50 30
1249 A531 13fr multi 70 45
1250 A531 13fr multi 70 45
1251 A531 13fr multi 70 45
1252 A531 13fr multi 70 45
Nos. 1247-1252 (6) 3.80 2.40

Youth Philately A532

1986, Sept. 1 Photo. *Perf. 11½*
1253 A532 9fr dl ol grn, blk & dk red 50 32

Cartoon Exhibition, Knokke.

Famous Men — A533

Designs: 9fr, Constant Permeke, painter, sculptor. 13fr, Baron Michel-Edmond de Selys Longchamps, scientist. 24fr, Felix Timmermans, writer. 26fr, Maurice Careme, poet.

1986, Sept. 29
1254 A533 9fr multi 52 32
1255 A533 13fr multi 75 45
1256 A533 24fr multi 1.40 82
1257 A533 26fr multi 1.50 90
Nos. 1254-1257 (4) 4.17 2.49

Royal Academy for Dutch Language and Literature, Cent. — A534

1986, Oct. 6 Engr.
1258 A534 9fr dark blue 52 32

Natl. Beer Industry A535

Perf. 12½x11½
1986, Oct. 13 Photo.
1259 A535 13fr Glass, barley, hops 70 50

Provincial Law and Councils, 150th Anniv. A536

1986, Oct. 27 *Perf. 11½*
1260 A536 13fr Stylized map 70 50

Christian Trade Union, Cent. — A537

1986, Dec. 13 Photo. *Perf. 11½*
1261 A537 9fr shown 45 35
1262 A537 13fr design reversed 65 50

Flanders Technology Intl. — A538

1987, Mar. 2 Photo.
1263 A538 13fr multi 70 50

EUROPALIA '87, Austrian Cultural Events — A539

Design: Woman, detail of a fresco by Gustav Klimt, Palais Stoclet, Brussels.

1987, Apr. 4 Photo. *Perf. 11½*
1264 A539 13fr multi 70 50

Stamp Day 1987 — A540

Portrait: Jakob Wiener (1815-1899), 1st engraver of Belgian stamps.

1987, Apr. 11 Photo. & Engr.
1265 A540 13fr lt greenish blue & sage grn 70 50

Folklore A541

1987, Apr. 25 Photo.
1266 A541 9fr Penitents procession, Veurne 45 35
1267 A541 13fr Play of John and Alice, Wavre 65 50

Europa 1987 — A542

Modern architecture: 13fr, Louvain-la-Neuve Church. 24fr, Regional Housing Assoc. Tower, St. Maartensdal at Louvain.

1987, May 9 Photo.
1268 A542 13fr multi 75 55
1269 A542 24fr multi 1.35 1.00

Statue of Andre-Ernest Gretry (1741-1813), French Composer A543

1987, May 23
1270 A543 24fr multi 1.35 1.00

Wallonie Royal Opera, Liege, 20th anniv.

Tourism — A544

Designs: No. 1271, Statues of Jan Breydel and Pieter de Conin, Bruges. No. 1272, Boondael Chapel, Brussels. No. 1273, Windmill, Keerbergen. No. 1274, St. Christopher's Church, Racour. No. 1275, Virelles Lake, Chimay.

1987, June 13
1271 A544 13fr multi 75 55
1272 A544 13fr multi 75 55
1273 A544 13fr multi 75 55
1274 A544 13fr multi 75 55
1275 A544 13fr multi 75 55
Nos. 1271-1275 (5) 3.75 2.75

Royal Belgian Rowing Assoc., Cent. — A545

European Volleyball Championships A546

1987, Sept. 5
1276 A545 9fr multi 50 38
1277 A546 13fr multi 75 55

Foreign Trade Year — A547

1987, Sept. 12
1278 A547 13fr multi 75 55

Belgian Social Reform, Cent. — A548

1987, Sept. 19
1279 A548 26fr Leisure, by P. Paulus 1.45 1.10

Youth Philately A549

1987, Oct. 3
1280 A549 9fr multi 50 38

Newspaper Centennials A550

1987, Dec. 12
1281 A550 9fr Le Soir 55 42
1282 A550 9fr Hett Lattste Nieuws, vert. 55 42

The Sea — A551

Designs: a, Lighthouse, trawler, rider and mount. b, Trawler, youths playing volleyball on beach. c, Cruise ship, sailboat, beach and cabana. d, Shore, birds.

1988, Feb. 6 **Photo.** ***Perf. 11½***
1283 Strip of 4 + label 2.50 1.80
a.-d. A551 10fr any single 62 45

No. 1283 has a continuous design.

Dynamism of the Regions A552

1988, Mar. 5 **Photo.** ***Perf. 11½***
1284 A552 13fr Operation Athena 80 58
1285 A552 13fr Flanders Alive Campaign 80 58

Stamp Day — A553

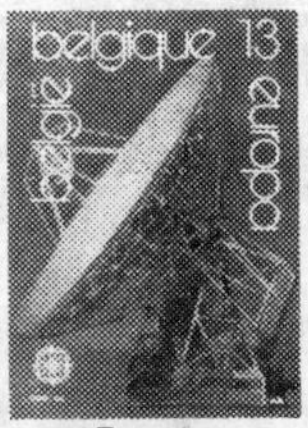
Europa 1988 — A554

Painting: 19th Cent. Postman, by James Thiriar.

1988, Apr. 16 **Photo. & Engr.**
1286 A553 13fr buff & sepia 80 58

1988, May 9 **Photo.** ***Perf. 11½***

Transport and communication.

1287 A554 13fr Satellite dish 80 58
1288 A554 24fr Non-polluting combustion engine 1.45 1.10

Tourism A555

Designs: No. 1289, Romanesque watchtower, ca. 12th-13th cent., Amay, vert. No. 1290, Our Lady of Hanswijk Basilica, 988, Mechelen, vert. No. 1291, St. Sernin's Church, 16th cent., Waimes. No. 1292, Old Town Hall, 1637, and village water pump, 1761, Peer, vert. No. 1293, Our Lady of Bon-Secours Basilica, 1892, Peruwelz.

Photo. & Engr.
1988, June 20 ***Perf. 11½***
1289 A555 9fr beige & blk 50 38
1290 A555 9fr lt blue & blk 50 38
1291 A555 9fr pale blue grn & blk 50 38
1292 A555 13fr pale pink & blk 75 55
1293 A555 13fr pale gray & blk 75 55
Nos. 1289-1293 (5) 3.00 2.24

Our Lady of Hanswijk Basilica millennium (No. 1290); Waimes village, 1100th anniv. (No. 1291).

Jean Monnet (1888-1979), French Economist — A556

Tapestry in the Hall of the Royal Academy of Medicine — A557

1988, Sept. 12 ***Perf. 11½***
1294 A556 13fr black 70 52

1988, Sept. 17 **Photo.**

Academies building and: No. 1296, Lyre, quill pen, open book and atomic symbols.

1295 A557 9fr shown 50 38
1296 A557 9fr multi 50 38

Royal Academy of Medicine (#1295); Royal Academy of Science, Literature and Fine Arts (#1296).

Cultural Heritage A558

Artifacts: 9fr, Statue and mask in the Antwerp Ethnographical Museum. 13fr, Sarcophagus, St. Martin's Church, Trazegnies. 24fr, Church organ, Geraardsbergen. 26fr, Shrine, St. Hadelin's Church, Vise.

1988, Sept. 24
1297 A558 9fr multi 50 38
1298 A558 13fr multi 70 52
1299 A558 24fr multi 1.30 1.00
1300 A558 26fr multi 1.40 1.05
Nos. 1297-1300 (4) 3.90 2.95

Youth Philately A559

1988, Oct. 10
1301 A559 9fr multi 50 38

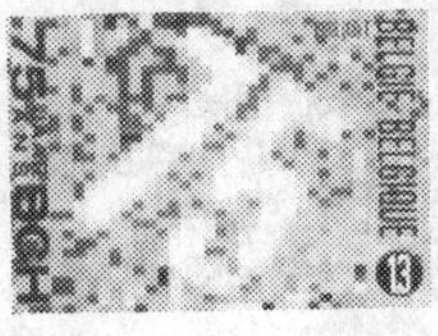
Natl. Postal Savings Bank, 75th Anniv. A560

1988, Nov. 7
1302 A560 13fr multi 70 52

Christmas 1988 and New Year 1989 — A561

1988, Nov. 21
1303 A561 9fr Winter landscape 50 38

Royal Mounted Guard, 50th Anniv. A562

1988, Dec. 12
1304 A562 13fr multi 75 55

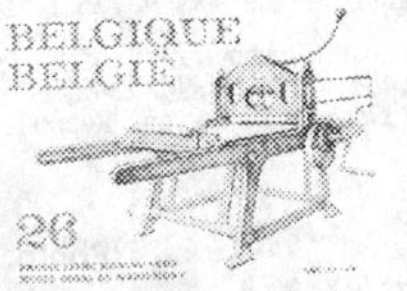
Printing Presses A563

Designs: 9fr, J. Moretus I, Antwerp Museum, vert. 24fr, Stanhope, Printing Museum, Brussels, vert. 26fr, Litho Krause, Royal Museum, Mariemont.

1988, Dec. 19 **Engr.**
1305 A563 9fr bl blk & blk 52 40
1306 A563 24fr dark red brn 1.40 1.05
1307 A563 26fr grn & slate grn 1.50 1.15
Nos. 1305-1307 (3) 3.42 2.60

Lace — A564

1989, Mar. 20 **Photo.**
1308 A564 9fr Marche-en-Famenne 50 38
1309 A564 13fr Brussels 70 52
1310 A564 13fr Brugge 70 52
Nos. 1308-1310 (3) 1.90 1.42

Stamp Day — A565

1989, Apr. 24 **Photo. & Engr.**
1311 A565 13fr Mail coach, post chaise 75 55

Europa 1989 — A566

Royal Academy of Fine Arts, Antwerp, 325th Anniv. — A567

Children's toys.

1989, May 8 **Photo.**
1312 A566 13fr Marbles, horiz. 75 52
1313 A566 24fr Jumping-jack 1.35 1.00

1989, May 22 ***Perf. 11½***
1314 A567 13fr multi 75 52

European Parliament 3rd Elections — A568

Illustration reduced.

1989, June 5 **Photo.**
1315 A568 13fr Brussels 75 52

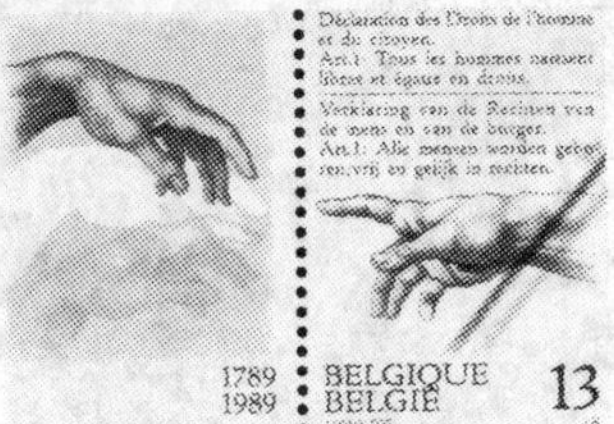
Declaration of Rights of Man and the Citizen, Bicent. — A569

1989, June 12 ***Perf. 11½***
1316 A569 13fr multi + label 75 52

Tourism A570

Designs: No. 1317, St. Tillo's Church, Izegem. No. 1318, Logne Castle, Ferrieres. No. 1319, St. Laurentius's Church, Lokeren. No. 1320, Antoing Castle, Antoing. Nos. 1318-1320 vert.

1989, June 26 **Photo. & Engr.**
1317 A570 9fr shown 50 38
1318 A570 9fr multi 50 38
1319 A570 13fr multi 75 52
1320 A570 13fr multi 75 52
Nos. 1317-1320 (4) 2.50 1.80

Ducks — A571

1989, Sept. 4 **Photo.** ***Perf. 12***
Booklet Stamps
1321 A571 13fr Mallard (8a) 68 52
1322 A571 13fr Winter teal (8b) 68 52
1323 A571 13fr Shoveller (8c) 68 52
1324 A571 13fr Pintail (8d) 68 52
a. Bklt. pane of 4, #1321-1324 2.75

Shigefusa Uesugi, a Seated Japanese Warrior, 13th Cent. A572

1989, Sept. 18 ***Perf. 11½***
1325 A572 24fr multi 1.25 92

Europalia.

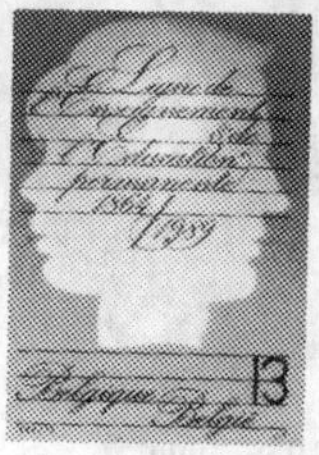

Education League, 125th Anniv. — A573

1989, Sept. 25

1326 A573 13fr multi 68 52

Treaty of London, 150th Anniv. — A574

Mr. Nibbs — A575

1989, Oct. 2 **Photo.**

1327 A574 13fr Map of Limburg Provinces 65 50

See Netherlands No. 750.

1989, Oct. 9 ***Perf. 11½***

1328 A575 9fr multi 45 32

Youth philately promotion.

Christmas, New Year 1990 A576

1989, Nov. 20 **Photo.**

1329 A576 9fr Salvation Army band 45 32

Fr. Damien (1840-89), Missionary, Molokai Is. Leper Colony, Hawaii A577

1989, Nov. 27 **Photo.**

1330 A577 24fr multicolored 1.25 95

Father Adolf Daens — A578

1989, Dec. 11 **Photo. & Engr.**

1331 A578 9fr pale & dk grn 48 35

The Young Post Rider, an Engraving by Albrecht Durer A579

Ghent Flower Festival A580

1990, Jan. 12 **Photo. & Engr.**

1332 A579 14fr buff & red blk 75 55

Postal communications in Europe, 500th anniv.

See Austria No. 1486, Germany No. 1592, Berlin No. 9N584 and German Democratic Republic No. 2791.

1990, Mar. 3 **Photo.**

1333 A580 10fr *Iris florentina* 55 40

1334 A580 14fr *Cattleya harrisoniana* 75 55

1335 A580 14fr *Lilium bulbiferum* 75 55

Nos. 1333-1335 (3) 2.05 1.50

Intl. Women's Day — A581

1990, Mar. 12 **Photo.** ***Perf. 11½***

1336 A581 25fr Emilienne Brunfaut 1.45 1.05

Wheelchair Basketball — A582

Sports.

1990, Mar. 19

1337 A582 10fr multicolored 58 42

1338 A582 14fr multicolored 80 60

1339 A582 25fr shown 1.45 1.05

Nos. 1337-1339 (3) 2.83 2.07

Special Olympics (10fr); and 1990 World Cup Soccer Championships, Italy (14fr).

Natl. Water Supply Soc., 75th Anniv. A583

1990, Apr. 2

1340 A583 14fr Water means life 80 60

Postman Roulin, by Van Gogh — A584

1990, Apr. 9

1341 A584 14fr multicolored 80 60

Stamp Day.

Labor Day, Cent. A585

1990, Apr. 30

1342 A585 25fr multicolored 1.45 1.05

Europa 1990 A586

Post offices.

1990, May 7 **Photo. & Engr.**

1343 A586 14fr Ostend 1 80 60

1344 A586 25fr Liege 1, vert. 1.45 1.05

18-Day Campaign, 1940 — A587

1990, May 14 **Photo.** ***Perf. 11½***

1345 A587 14fr Lys Monument, Courtrai 80 60

Resistance of German occupation.

Stamp Collecting Promotion Type of 1988 Souvenir Sheet

Various flowers from *Sixty Roses for a Queen,* by P.J. Redoute (1759-1840): a, *Rose tricolore.* b, Belle Rubaree. c, *Mycrophylla.* d, Amelie rose. e, Adelaide rose. f, Helene rose.

1990, June 2 **Photo. & Engr.**

1346 Sheet of 6 13.50 13.50

a.-c. SP487 14fr any single 80 60

d.-f. SP487 25fr any single 1.45 1.05

BELGICA '90, Brussels, June 2-10. sold for 220fr.

Battle of Waterloo, 1815 — A588

Design: Marshal Ney leading the French cavalry. (Illustration reduced).

1990, June 18 **Photo.**

1352 A588 25fr multi + label 1.60 1.15

Tourism A589

1990, July 9

1353 A589 10fr Antwerp 58 45

1354 A589 10fr Dendermonde 58 45

1355 A589 14fr Gerpinnes, vert. 80 60

1356 A589 14fr Lommel 80 60

1357 A589 14fr Watermael 80 60

Nos. 1353-1357 (5) 3.56 2.70

A590

A590a

King Baudouin A590b

1990-92 **Photo.** ***Perf. 11½***

1364 A590 14fr multicolored 80 60

1365 A590a 15fr rose car 85 65

1366 A590a 28fr blue green 1.75 1.30

1367 A590b 100fr slate green 6.00 1.50

Nos. 1364-1367 (4) 9.40 4.05

Issue dates: 14fr, Sept. 7; 15fr, Apr. 1; 28fr, Aug. 3, 1992; 100fr, Sept. 14, 1992.

Fish — A591

Designs: No. 1383, Perch (Perche). No. 1384, Minnow (Vairon). No. 1385, Bitterling (Bouviere). No. 1386, Stickleback (Epinoche).

1990, Sept. 8 ***Perf. 12***

1383 A591 14fr multicolored 80 60

1384 A591 14fr multicolored 80 60

1385 A591 14fr multicolored 80 60

1386 A591 14fr multicolored 80 60

a. Bklt. pane of 4, #1383-1386 3.20

Youth Philately A592

1990, Oct. 13 ***Perf. 11½***

1387 A592 10fr multicolored 58 45

St. Bernard, 900th Birth Anniv. — A593

1990, Nov. 5 **Photo & Engr.**

1388 A593 25fr black & buff 1.45 1.10

Winter Scene by Jozef Lucas A594

1990, Nov. 12 **Photo.**
1389 A594 10fr 58 42

Christmas.

Self-Portrait A595

Paintings by David Teniers (1610-1690).

1990, Dec. 3

1390	A595 10fr shown		58	42
1391	A595 14fr Dancers		82	62
1392	A595 25fr Bowlers		1.45	1.10
	Nos. 1390-1392 (3)		2.85	2.14

A596

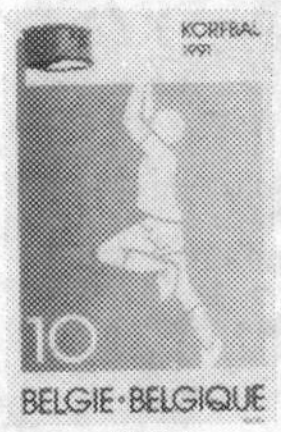

A597

Designs: 14fr, The Sower by Constantin Meunier (1831-1905). 25fr, Brabo Fountain by Jef Lambeaux (1852-1908).

Photo. & Engr.

1991, Mar. 18 ***Perf. 11½***

1393	A596 14fr buff & blk	82	62
1394	A596 25fr lt bl & dk bl	1.45	1.10

1991, Apr. 8 **Photo.** ***Perf. 11½***

1395	A597 10fr Rhythmic gymnastics	65	50
1396	A597 10fr Korfball	65	50

No. 1395, European Youth Olympics. No. 1396, Korfball World Championships.

Stamp Printing Office, Mechlin — A598

1991, Apr. 22
1397 A598 14fr multicolored 90 65

Stamp Day.

Liberal Trade Union, Cent. A599

1991, Apr. 29
1398 A599 25fr blue & lt blue 1.50 1.15

Europa A600

1991, May 6

1399	A600 14fr Olympus-1 satellite	90	65
1400	A600 25fr Hermes space shuttle	1.50	1.15

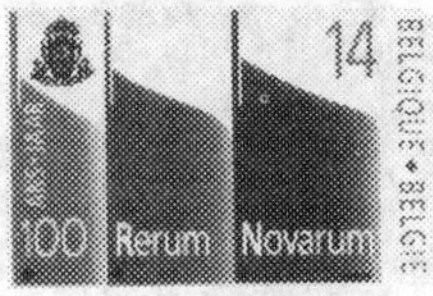

Rerum Novarum Encyclical, Cent. A601

1991, May 13 **Photo.** ***Perf. 11½***
1401 A601 14fr multicolored 85 65

Princess Isabel & Philip le Bon — A602

1991, May 27 **Photo.** ***Perf. 11½***
1402 A602 14fr multicolored 85 65

Europalia '91. See Portugal No. 1861.

Tourism A603

Designs: No. 1403, Neptune's Grotto, Couvin. No. 1404, Dieleghem Abbey, Jette. No. 1405, Town Hall, Niel, vert. No. 1406, Nature Reserve, Hautes Fagnes. No. 1407, Legend of giant Rolarius, Roeselare, vert.

1991, June 17 **Photo. & Engr.**

1403	A603 14fr multicolored	85	65
1404	A603 14fr multicolored	85	65
1405	A603 14fr multicolored	85	65
1406	A603 14fr multicolored	85	65
1407	A603 14fr multicolored	85	65
	Nos. 1403-1407 (5)	4.25	3.25

King Baudouin, Coronation, 40th Anniv. and 60th Birthday A604

1991, June 24 **Photo.**
1408 A604 14fr multicolored 85 65

Royal Academy of Medicine, 150th Anniv. — A605

Photo. & Engr.

1991, Sept. 2 ***Perf. 11½***
1409 A605 10fr multicolored 65 50

The English Coast at Dover by Alfred W. Finch (1854-1930) — A606

1991, Sept. 9 **Photo.**
1410 A606 25fr multicolored 1.50 1.15

See Finland Nos. 868-869.

Mushrooms — A607

1991, Sept. 16 **Photo.** ***Perf. 12***

Booklet Stamps

1411	A607 14fr Amanita phalloides (13A)	85	65
1412	A607 14fr Amanita rubescens (13B)	85	65
1413	A607 14fr Boletus erythropus (13C)	85	65
1414	A607 14fr Hygrocybe persistens (13D)	85	65
a.	Bklt. pane of 4, #1411-1414	3.40	

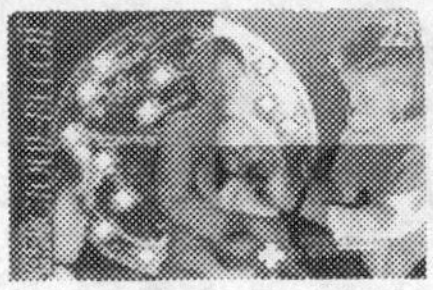

Doctors Without Borders A608

Design: No. 1415, Amnesty Intl.

1991, Sept. 23 ***Perf. 11½***

1415	A608 25fr multicolored	1.50	1.15
1416	A608 25fr multicolored	1.50	1.15

Telecom '91 — A609

1991, Oct. 7 **Photo.** ***Perf. 11½***
1417 A609 14fr multicolored 90 70

6th World Forum and Exposition on Telecommunications, Geneva, Switzerland.

Youth Philately — A610

Cartoon characters: No. 1418, Blake and Mortimer, by Edgar P. Jacobs (16a). No. 1419, Cori the ship boy, by Bob De Moor (16b). No. 1420, Cities of the Fantastic, by Francois Schuiten (16c). No. 1421, Boule and Bill, by Jean Roba (16d).

1991, Oct. 14 ***Perf. 12***

Booklet Stamps

1418	A610 14fr multicolored	90	70
1419	A610 14fr multicolored	90	70
1420	A610 14fr multicolored	90	70
1421	A610 14fr multicolored	90	70
a.	Bklt. pane of 4, #1418-1421	3.60	

Belgian Newspapers, Cent. A611

1991, Nov. 4 **Photo.** ***Perf. 11½***

1422	A611 10fr Gazet Van Antwerpen	65	50
1423	A611 10fr Het Volk	65	50

Icon of Madonna and Child, Chevetogne Abbey — A612

1991, Nov. 25 **Photo.** ***Perf. 11½***
1424 A612 10fr multicolored 65 50

Christmas.

Wolfgang Amadeus Mozart, Death Bicent. — A613

1991, Dec. 2 **Photo.** ***Perf. 11½***
1425 A613 25fr multicolored 1.70 1.30

A614

A615

1992, Feb. 10 Photo. *Perf. 11½*

1426 A614 14fr Fire fighting	80	60

1992, Feb. 24

1427 A615 14fr multicolored	80	60

Belgian resistance in WWII.

Belgian Carpet Industry — A616

Antwerp Diamond Club, Cent. A617

Design: 14fr, Chef's hat, cutlery.

1992, Mar. 9

1428 A616 10fr multicolored	55	42
1429 A616 14fr multicolored	80	60
1430 A617 27fr multicolored	1.50	1.15
Nos. 1428-1430 (3)	2.85	2.17

Belgian Association of Master Chefs.

Expo '92, Seville A618

1992, Mar. 23

1431 A618 14fr multicolored	80	60

Bird Type of 1985

1992-94 Photo. *Perf. 11½*

1432	A524	1fr Sizerin flamme	15	15
1433	A524	2fr Merle noir	15	15
1435	A524	4fr Bergeronette grise	25	15
1436	A524	5fr Hirondelle de cheminee	32	15
1436A	A524	5.50fr Geai des chenes	30	22
1437	A524	6fr Cincle flongeur	35	15
1437A	A524	6.50fr Phragmite des jongs	45	30
1438	A524	7fr Loriot	45	15
1439	A524	8fr Mesange charbonniere	45	15
1442	A524	10fr Verdier	58	15
1444	A524	11fr Troglodyte mignon	65	15
1446	A524	13fr Moineau domestique	70	18
1447	A524	16fr Jaseur boreal	90	22
		Nos. 1432-1447 (13)	5.70	
		Set value		70

Issued: 11fr, 4/1/92; 1fr, 2fr, 6fr, 8fr, 10fr, 6/92; 4fr, 5fr, 7fr, 9/7/92; 5.50fr, 9/27/93; 13fr, 16fr, 1/3/94; 6.50fr, 10/3/94.

This is an expanding set. Numbers may change.

Jean Van Noten (1903-1982), Stamp Designer — A619

Photo. & Engr.

1992, Apr. 13 *Perf. 11½*

1448 A619 15fr ver & black	90	70

Stamp Day.

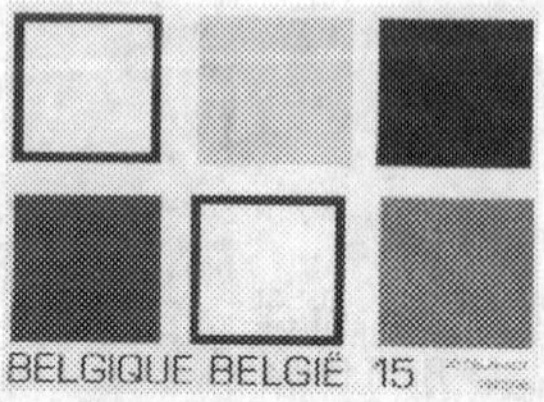
Abstract Painting by Jo Delahaut — A620

Design: No. 1449, Witte Magie No. 6, by Roger Raveel, vert.

1992, Apr. 27 Photo. *Perf. 11½*

1449 A620 15fr multicolored	85	65
1450 A620 15fr multicolored	85	65

Discovery of America, 500th Anniv. — A621

1992, May 4

1451 A621 15fr shown	85	65
1452 A621 28fr 500, globe, astrolabe	1.60	1.20

Europa.

Fight Racism — A622

1992, May 18 Photo. *Perf. 11½*

1453 A622 15fr black, gray & pink	90	70

Paintings from Orsay Museum, Paris — A623

Paintings by Belgian artists: 11fr, The Hamlet, by Jacob Smits. 15fr, The Bath, by Alfred Stevens. 30fr, The Man at the Helm, by Theo Van Rysselberghe.

1992, June 15 Photo. *Perf. 11½*

1454 A623 11fr multicolored	65	48
1455 A623 15fr multicolored	90	70
1456 A623 30fr multicolored	1.75	1.35
Nos. 1454-1456 (3)	3.30	2.53

Tourism — A624

Designs: No. 1457, Manneken Pis Fountain, Brussels. No. 1458, Landcommander Castle Alden Biesen, Bilzen, horiz. No. 1459, Building facade, Andenne. No. 1460, Fools' Monday Carnival, Renaix, horiz. No. 1461, Great Procession, Tournai, horiz.

Photo. & Engr.

1992, July 6 *Perf. 11½*

1457 A624 15fr multicolored	90	70
1458 A624 15fr multicolored	90	70
1459 A624 15fr multicolored	90	70
1460 A624 15fr multicolored	90	70
1461 A624 15fr multicolored	90	70
Nos. 1457-1461 (5)	4.50	3.50

Village of Andenne, 1300th anniv. (#1459). Grand Procession of Tournai, 900th anniv. (#1461).

Animals — A625

1992, Sept. 7 Photo. *Perf. 12*

Booklet Stamps

1462 A625 15fr Polecat (13a)	1.05	80
1463 A625 15fr Squirrel (13b)	1.05	80
1464 A625 15fr Hedgehog (13c)	1.05	80
1465 A625 15fr Dormouse (13d)	1.05	80
a. Bklt. pane of 4, #1462-1465	4.20	

Brabant Revolution — A626

Design: 15fr, Troops fighting and Henri Van der Noot, Jean Andre Van der Meersch, and Jean Francois Vonck, rebel leaders.

Photo. & Engr.

1992, Sept. 21 *Perf. 11½*

1466 A626 15fr multicolored	90	70

Arms of Thurn and Taxis — A627

1992, Oct. 5 Photo. *Perf. 11½*

1467 A627 15fr multicolored	90	70

Gaston Lagaffe, by Andre Franquin A628

1992, Oct. 12

1468 A628 15fr multicolored	90	70

Youth philately.

Single European Market — A629

1992, Oct. 26

1469 A629 15fr multicolored	90	70

Antwerp Zoo, 150th Anniv. — A630

1992, Nov. 16

1470 A630 15fr Okapi	90	70
1471 A630 30fr Tamarin	1.80	1.40

The Brussels Place Royale in Winter, by Luc De Decker A631

1992, Nov. 23

1472 A631 11fr multicolored	70	52

Christmas.

History A632

Designs: 11fr, Council of Leptines, 1250th anniv.. 15fr, 28fr, Missale Romanum of Matthias Corvinus (Matyas Hunyadi, King of Hungary) (diff. details). 30fr, Battles of Neerwinden (1693, 1793).

1993, Mar. 15 Photo. *Perf. 11½*

1473 A632 11fr multicolored	65	48
1474 A632 15fr multicolored	90	70
1475 A632 30fr multicolored	1.80	1.35
Nos. 1473-1475 (3)	3.35	2.53

Souvenir Sheet

1476 A632 28fr multicolored	1.75	1.30

Size of No. 1474, 80x28mm. No. 1476 contains one 55x40mm stamp.

See Hungary No. 3385-3386.

A633

A634

Antwerp, Cultural City of Europe
A635

Designs: No. 1477, Panoramic view of Antwerp (illustration reduced). No. 1478, Antwerp Town Hall, designed by Cornelis Floris. No. 1479, Woman's Head and Warrior's Torso, by Jacob Jordaens. No. 1480, St. Job's Altar (detail), Schoonbroek. No. 1481, Angels on stained glass window, Mater Dei Chapel of Institut Marie-Josee, by Eugeen Yoors, vert.

1993, Mar. 22

1477	A633	15fr	multicolored	90	70
1478	A634	15fr	multicolored	90	70
1479	A635	15fr	gray & multi	90	70
1480	A635	15fr	green & multi	90	70
1481	A635	15fr	blue & multi	90	70
			Nos. 1477-1481 (5)	4.50	3.50

Antwerp '93.

Stamp Day — A636

1993, Apr. 5

1482	A636	15fr	No. 74	90	70

Contemporary Paintings — A637

Europa: 15fr, Florence 1960, by Gaston Bertrand. 28fr, De Sjees, by Constant Permeke.

1993, Apr. 26 Photo. *Perf. 11½*

1483	A637	15fr	multicolored	90	70
1484	A637	28fr	multicolored	1.70	1.35

Butterflies — A638

1993, May 10

1485	A638	15fr	Vanessa atalanta	90	70
1486	A638	15fr	Apatura iris	90	70
1487	A638	15fr	Inachis io	90	70
1488	A638	15fr	Aglais urticae	90	70
			Nos. 1485-1488 (4)	3.60	2.80

Alumni Assoc. (UAE), Free University of Brussels, 150th Anniv.
A639

1993, May 17

1489	A639	15fr	blue & black	90	70

Europalia '93 — A640

1993, May 24

1490	A640	15fr	Mayan statuette	90	70

Folklore
A641

Designs: 11fr, Ommegang Procession, Brussels. 15fr, Royal Moncrabeau Folk Group, Namur. 28fr, Stilt walkers of Merchtem, vert.

1993, June 7 Photo. *Perf. 11½*

1491	A641	11fr	multicolored	65	48
1492	A641	15fr	multicolored	90	70
1493	A641	28fr	multicolored	1.65	1.30
			Nos. 1491-1493 (3)	3.20	2.48

Tourism
A642

Castles: No. 1494, La Hulpe. No. 1495, Cortewalle (Beveren). No. 1496, Jehay. No. 1497, Arenberg (Heverlee), vert. No. 1498, Raeren.

Photo. & Engr.

1993, June 21 *Perf. 11½*

1494	A642	15fr	pale green & black	90	70
1495	A642	15fr	pale lilac & black	90	70
1496	A642	15fr	pale blue & black	90	70
1497	A642	15fr	pale brown & black	90	70
1498	A642	15fr	pale olive & black	90	70
			Nos. 1494-1498 (5)	4.50	3.50

Intl. Triennial Exhibition of Tournai
A643

1993, July 5 Photo. *Perf. 11½*

1499	A643	15fr	black, blue & red	90	70

Belgian Presidency of European Community Council
A644

1993, Aug. 9 Photo. *Perf. 11½*

1500	A644	15fr	multicolored	90	70

Rene Magritte (1898-1967), Artist
A645

1993, Aug. 9

1501	A645	30fr	multicolored	1.75	1.40

King Baudouin (1930-1993) — A646

1993, Aug. 17 Photo. *Perf. 11½*

1502	A646	15fr	black & gray	90	70

European House Cats — A647

1993, Sept. 6 Photo. *Perf. 12*

Booklet Stamps

1503	A647	15fr	Brown & white (10a)	90	70
1504	A647	15fr	Black & white (10b)	90	70
1505	A647	15fr	Gray tabby (10c)	90	70
1506	A647	15fr	Calico (10d)	90	70
a.			Booklet pane of 4, #1503-1506	3.75	

Publication of De Humani Corporis Fabrica, by Andreas Vesalius, 1543 — A648

1993, Oct. 4 Photo. *Perf. 11½*

1507	A648	15fr	multicolored	90	70

Air Hostess Natacha, by Francois Walthery — A649

1993, Oct. 18

1508	A649	15fr	multicolored	85	65

Youth philately.

Publication of "Faux Soir," 50th Anniv. — A650

1993, Nov. 8 Photo. *Perf. 11½*

1509 A650 11fr multicolored 60 45

Notre-Dame de la Chapelle, Brussels A651

1993, Nov. 22 Photo. *Perf. 11½*

1510 A651 11fr multicolored 65 48

Christmas, New Year.

Children, Future Decisionmakers — A652

1993, Dec. 13 Photo. *Perf. 11½*

1511 A652 15fr multicolored 90 70

King Albert II

A653 A654

1993-94 Photo. *Perf. 11½*

1519 A653	16fr	multicolored	95	25
1522 A653	20fr	cream & brown	1.25	32
1526 A653	30fr	red lilac	1.65	40
1527 A653	32fr	cream & org brn	1.90	48
1528 A653	40fr	pink & carmine	2.50	60
1529 A653	50fr	green	3.00	75
1533 A654	100fr	multicolored	6.25	4.75
		Nos. 1519-1533 (7)	17.50	7.55

Issued: 16fr, 12/15/93; 30fr, 2/4/94; 32fr, 3/7/94; 50fr, 4/18/94; 20fr, 6/6/94; 40fr, 6/20/94; 100fr, 10/3/94.

This is part of an expanding set. Numbers may change.

Paintings A656

Designs: No. 1537, The Malleable Darkness, by Octave Landuyt. No. 1538, Ma Toute Belle, by Serge Vandercam, vert.

1994, Jan. 31 Photo. *Perf. 11½*

1537 A656 16fr multicolored 90 70
1538 A656 16fr multicolored 90 70

Airplanes A657

Designs: 13fr, Hanriot-Dupont HD-1. 15fr, Spad XIII. 30fr, Schreck FBA-H. 32fr, Stampe-Vertongen SV-4B.

1994, Feb. 28

1539 A657 13fr multicolored		70	52
1540 A657 15fr multicolored		85	65
1541 A657 30fr multicolored		1.65	1.25
1542 A657 32fr multicolored		1.75	1.40
	Nos. 1539-1542 (4)	4.95	3.82

Daily Newspapers A658

Designs: No. 1543, "Le Jour-Le Courier," cent., vert. No. 1544, "La Wallonie," 75th anniv.

1994, Mar. 21 Photo. *Perf. 11½*

1543 A658 16fr multicolored 95 70
1544 A658 16fr multicolored 95 70

Fall of the Golden Calf (Detail), by Fernand Allard l'Olivier — A659

1994, Mar. 28

1545 A659 16fr multicolored 95 70

Charter of Quaregnon, cent.

Stamp Day — A660

1994, Apr. 11 Photo. *Perf. 11½*

1546 A660 16fr No. 102 95 70

History A661

Scenes from Brabantse Yeesten, 15th cent. illuminated manuscript: 13fr, Reconciliation between John I and Arnold, squire of Wezemaal. 16fr, Tournament at wedding of John II and Margaret of York. 30fr, Battle of Woeringen.

1994, Apr. 25

1547 A661 13fr multicolored		75	55
1548 A661 16fr multicolored		95	70
1549 A661 30fr multicolored		1.75	1.25
	Nos. 1547-1549 (3)	3.45	2.50

No. 1549 is 81x28mm.

Europa — A662

Designs: 16fr, Abbe Georges Lemaitre (1894-1966), proposed "big-bang" theory of origins of universe. 30fr, Gerardus Mercator (1512-94), cartographer, astronomer.

1994, May 9 Photo. *Perf. 11½*

1550 A662 16fr multicolored 95 70
1551 A662 30fr multicolored 1.75 1.25

Papal Visit A663

Designs: No. 1552, Father Damien (1840-89). No. 1553, St. Mutien-Marie (1841-1917), Christian educator.

1994, May 16 *Perf. 11½x12*

1552 A663 16fr multicolored 95 70
1553 A663 16fr multicolored 95 70

Tourism A664

Churches: No. 1554, St. Peter's, Bertem. No. 1555, St. Bavo's, Kanegem, vert. No. 1556, Royal St. Mary's, Schaarbeek. No. 1557, St. Gery's, Aubechies. No. 1558, Sts. Peter and Paul, Saint-Severin, Condroz, vert.

1994, June 13 Photo. *Perf. 11½*

1554 A664 16fr multicolored		95	70
1555 A664 16fr multicolored		95	70
1556 A664 16fr multicolored		95	70
1557 A664 16fr multicolored		95	70
1558 A664 16fr multicolored		95	70
	Nos. 1554-1558 (5)	4.75	3.50

Guillaume Lekeu (1870-94), Composer A665

Design: No. 1560, Detail of painting by Hans Memling (c.1430-94).

1994, Aug. 16 Photo. *Perf. 11½*

1559 A665 16fr multicolored 1.10 75
1560 A665 16fr multicolored 1.10 75

Liberation of Belgium, 50th Anniv. — A666

Design: 16fr, General Crerar, Field Marshal Montgomery, Gen. Bradley, Belgium landscape. Illustration reduced.

1994, Sept. 5 Photo. *Perf. 11x11½*

1561 A666 16fr multicolored 95 70

Wildflowers — A667

Designs: No. 1562, Caltha palustris. No. 1563, Cephalanthera damasonium. No. 1564, Calystegia soldanella. No. 1565, Epipactis helleborine.

1994, Sept. 26 Photo. *Perf. 12*

Booklet Stamps

1562 A667 16fr multi (14a)	1.10	75
1563 A667 16fr multi (14b)	1.10	75
1564 A667 16fr multi (14c)	1.10	75
1565 A667 16fr multi (14d)	1.10	75
a. Booklet pane of 4, #1562-1565	4.50	

Cubitus the Dog, by Luc Dupanloup — A668

1994, Oct. 10 *Perf. 11½*

1566 A668 16fr multicolored	1.10	75

Youth philately.

Georges Simenon (1903-89), Writer A669

Photo. & Engr.

1994, Oct. 17 *Perf. 11½*

1567 A669 16fr multicolored	1.10	75

See France No. 2443, Switzerland No. 948.

Christmas A670

1994, Dec. 5 Photo. *Perf. 11½*

1568 A670 13fr multicolored	85	65

SEMI-POSTAL STAMPS

Values quoted for Nos. B1-B24 are for stamps with label attached. Copies without label sell for one-tenth or less.

St. Martin of Tours Dividing His Cloak with a Beggar
SP1 SP2

Unwmk.

1910, June 1 Typo. *Perf. 14*

B1 SP1 1c gray	85	1.25
B2 SP1 2c purple brn	6.25	9.25
B3 SP1 5c peacock blue	1.75	2.50
B4 SP1 10c brown red	1.75	2.50
B5 SP2 1c gray green	1.75	2.50
B6 SP2 2c violet brn	5.00	7.25
B7 SP2 5c peacock blue	1.75	2.50
B8 SP2 10c carmine	1.75	2.50
Nos. B1-B8 (8)	20.85	30.25

Overprinted "1911" in Black

1911, Apr. 1

B9 SP1 1c gray	11.00	12.00
a. Inverted overprint		
B10 SP1 2c purple brn	26.00	40.00
B11 SP1 5c peacock blue	3.00	3.50
B12 SP1 10c brown red	3.00	3.50
B13 SP2 1c gray green	21.00	32.50
B14 SP2 2c violet brn	19.00	24.00
B15 SP2 5c peacock blue	3.00	3.50
B16 SP2 10c carmine	3.00	3.50
Nos. B9-B16 (8)	89.00	122.50

Overprinted "CHARLEROI-1911"

1911, June

B17 SP1 1c gray	2.50	4.00
B18 SP1 2c purple brn	8.50	13.00
B19 SP1 5c peacock blue	4.00	6.00
B20 SP1 10c brown red	3.50	5.25
B21 SP2 1c gray green	2.50	4.00
B22 SP2 2c violet brn	7.75	12.00
B23 SP2 5c peacock blue	3.25	4.75
B24 SP2 10c carmine	2.50	4.00
Nos. B17-B24 (8)	34.50	53.00

Nos. B1-B24 were sold at double face value, except the 10c denominations which were sold for 15c. The surtax benefited the national anti-tuberculosis organization.

SP3

Merode Monument — SP4

King Albert I — SP5

1914, Oct. 3 Litho.

B25 SP3 5c green & red	*1.65*	*2.00*
B26 SP3 10c red	*45*	*52*
B27 SP3 20c violet & red	*10.50*	*13.00*
Nos. B25-B27 (3)	*12.60*	*15.52*

Counterfeits of Nos. B25-B27 abound. Probably as many as 90% of the stamps on the market are counterfeits. Competently certified copies sell for much more.

1914, Oct. 3

B28 SP4 5c green & red	3.50	5.00
B29 SP4 10c red	3.50	5.00
B30 SP4 20c violet & red	32.50	47.50
Nos. B28-B30 (3)	39.50	57.50

Counterfeits of Nos. B28-B30 abound. Probably as many as 90% of the stamps on the market are counterfeits. Competently certified copies sell for much more.

1915, Jan. 1 *Perf. 12, 14*

B31 SP5 5c green & red	3.50	2.25
a. Perf. 12x14	11.00	8.50
B32 SP5 10c rose & red	6.75	4.50
B33 SP5 20c violet & red	18.00	11.00
a. Perf. 14x12	325.00	325.00
b. Perf. 12	60.00	35.00
Nos. B31-B33 (3)	28.25	17.75

Nos. B25-B33 were sold at double face value. The surtax benefited the Red Cross.

Types of Regular Issue of 1915 Surcharged in Red:

+ 1/c Nos. B34-B40 **+ 35c** Nos. B41-B43

+ 1F Nos. B44-B47

1918, Jan. 15 Typo. *Perf. 14*

B34 A46 1c + 1c dp orange	22	22
B35 A46 2c + 2c brown	28	28
B36 A46 5c + 5c blue grn	60	60
B37 A46 10c + 10c red	1.10	1.10
B38 A46 15c + 15c brt violet	1.65	1.65
B39 A46 20c + 20c plum	3.50	3.50
B40 A46 25c + 25c ultra	3.50	3.50
Engr.		
B41 A47 35c + 35c lt vio & blk	5.00	5.00
B42 A48 40c + 40c dull red & blk	5.00	5.00
B43 A49 50c + 50c turq blue & blk	6.00	6.00
B44 A50 1fr + 1fr bluish slate	17.50	17.50
B45 A51 2fr + 2fr dp gray grn	47.50	47.50
B46 A52 5fr + 5fr brown	125.00	125.00
B47 A53 10fr + 10fr dp blue	250.00	250.00
Nos. B34-B47 (14)	466.85	466.85

Discus Thrower — SP6

Racing Chariot — SP7

Runner — SP8

1920, May 20 Engr. *Perf. 12*

B48 SP6 5c + 5c dp green	2.25	2.50
B49 SP7 10c + 5c carmine	2.25	2.50
B50 SP8 15c + 15c dk brown	4.50	1.25
Nos. B48-B50 (3)	9.00	6.25

7th Olympic Games, 1920. Surtax benefited wounded soldiers. Exists imperf.

For surcharges see Nos. 140-142.

Allegory: Asking Alms from the Crown — SP9

Wounded Veteran — SP10

1922, May 20

B51 SP9 20c + 20c brown	1.25	1.00

1923, July 5

B52 SP10 20c + 20c slate gray	1.65	1.65

Surtax on #B51-B52 was to aid wounded veterans.

SP11

SP12

St. Martin, by Van Dyck
SP13 SP14

1925, Dec. 15 Typo. *Perf. 14*

B53 SP11 15c + 15c dull vio & red	30	15
B54 SP11 30c + 5c gray & red	16	15
B55 SP11 1fr + 10c chalky blue & red	85	1.00
Nos. B53-B55 (3)	1.31	1.30

Surtax for the Natl. Anti-Tuberculosis League.

1926, Feb. 10

B56 SP12 30c + 30c bluish grn (red surch.)	50	55
B57 SP13 1fr + 1fr lt blue	7.25	7.25
B58 SP14 1fr + 1fr lt blue	1.10	1.25
Nos. B56-B58 (3)	8.85	9.05

The surtax aided victims of the Meuse flood.

Lion and Cross of Lorraine SP15

Queen Elisabeth and King Albert SP16

1926, Dec. 6 Typo. *Perf. 14*

B59 SP15 5c + 5c dk brown	22	16
B60 SP15 20c + 5c red brown	42	35
B61 SP15 50c + 5c dull violet	28	16
Engr. *Perf. 11½*		
B62 SP16 1.50fr + 25c dk blue	65	60
B63 SP16 5fr + 1fr rose red	6.00	5.50
Nos. B59-B63 (5)	7.57	6.77

Surtax was used to benefit tubercular war veterans.

Boat Adrift — SP17

1927, Dec. 15 Engr. *Perf. 11½, 14*

B64 SP17 25c + 10c dk brown	70	70
B65 SP17 35c + 10c yel grn	70	70
B66 SP17 60c + 10c dp violet	55	38
B67 SP17 1.75fr + 25c dk blue	1.50	2.00
B68 SP17 5fr + 1fr plum	4.50	4.75
Nos. B64-B68 (5)	7.95	8.53

The surtax on these stamps was divided among several charitable associations.

Ogives of Orval Abbey — SP18

Monk Carving Capital of Column — SP19

Ruins of Orval Abbey — SP20

Design: 60c+15c, 1.75fr+25c, 3fr+1fr, Countess Matilda recovering her ring.

1928, Sept. 15 Photo. *Perf. 11½*

B69 SP18 5c + 5c red & gold	20	35
B70 SP18 25c + 5c dk vio & gold	42	75
Engr.		
B71 SP19 35c + 10c dp green	1.00	1.25
B72 SP19 60c + 15c red brown	1.40	55
B73 SP19 1.75fr + 25c dk blue	3.25	2.75
B74 SP19 2fr + 40c dp violet	12.00	8.00
B75 SP19 3fr + 1fr red	14.00	9.75
Perf. 14		
B76 SP20 5fr + 5fr rose lake	14.00	12.50
B77 SP20 10fr + 10fr ol green	14.00	14.00
Nos. B69-B77 (9)	60.27	49.90

Surtax for the restoration of the ruined Orval Abbey.

For overprints see Nos. B84-B92.

St. Waudru, Mons — SP22

St. Rombaut, Malines — SP23

Designs: 25c + 15c, Cathedral of Tournai. 60c + 15c, St. Bavon, Ghent. 1.75fr + 25c, St. Gudule, Brussels. 5fr + 5fr, Louvain Library.

1928, Dec. 1 Photo. *Perf. 14, 11½*

B78 SP22	5c + 5c carmine		16	20
B79 SP22	25c + 15c ol brn		30	38

Engr.

B80 SP23	35c + 10c dp green	1.10	1.25
B81 SP23	60c + 15c red brn	42	25
B82 SP23	1.75fr + 25c vio blue	7.25	7.00
B83 SP23	5fr + 5fr red vio	14.00	15.00
	Nos. B78-B83 (6)	23.23	24.08

The surtax was for anti-tuberculosis work.

Nos. B69-B77 with this overprint in blue or red was privately produced. They are for the laying of the 1st stone toward the restoration of the ruined Abbey of Orval. Forgeries of the overprint exist. Value, set, $575.

Waterfall at Coo — SP28

Bayard Rock, Dinant — SP29

Designs: 35c+10c, Menin Gate, Ypres. 60c+15c, Promenade d'Orleans, Spa. 1.75fr+25c, Antwerp Harbor. 5fr+5fr, Quai Vert, Bruges.

1929, Dec. 2 Engr. *Perf. 11½*

B93 SP28	5c + 5c red brown	18	20
B94 SP29	25c + 15c gray blk	60	55
B95 SP28	35c + 10c green	70	85
B96 SP28	60c + 15c rose lake	48	42
B97 SP28	1.75fr + 25c dp blue	4.00	4.25

Perf. 14

B98 SP29	5fr + 5fr dl vio	25.00	25.00
	Nos. B93-B98 (6)	30.96	31.27

Bornhem — SP34

Beloeil — SP35

Gaesbeek SP36

Designs: 25c + 15c, Wynendaele. 70c + 15c, Oydonck. 1fr + 25c, Ghent. 1.75fr + 25c, Bouillon.

1930, Dec. 1 Photo. *Perf. 14*

B99 SP34	10c + 5c violet	20	28
B100 SP34	25c + 15c olive brn	55	55

Engr.

B101 SP35	40c + 10c brown vio	70	90
B102 SP35	70c + 15c gray blk	50	50
B103 SP35	1fr + 25c rose lake	3.25	3.25
B104 SP35	1.75fr + 25c dp blue	4.00	2.50
B105 SP36	5fr + 5fr gray grn	22.50	30.00
	Nos. B99-B105 (7)	31.70	37.98

Prince Leopold SP41

Queen Elisabeth SP42

Philatelic Exhibition Issue

Souvenir Sheet

1931, July 18 Photo. *Perf. 14*

B106 SP41	2.45fr + 55c car brown	80.00	80.00

Sold exclusively at the Brussels Phil. Exhib., July 18-21, 1931. Size: 122x159mm. Surtax for the Veterans' Relief Fund.

The sheet normally has pin holes and a cancellation-like marking in the margin. These are considered unused and the condition valued here.

1931, Dec. 1 Engr.

B107 SP42	10c + 5c red brown	30	52
B108 SP42	25c + 15c dk violet	1.10	1.25
B109 SP42	50c + 10c dk green	95	1.00
B110 SP42	75c + 15c black brn	90	65
B111 SP42	1fr + 25c rose lake	6.75	6.00
B112 SP42	1.75fr + 25c ultra	4.75	4.00
B113 SP42	5fr + 5fr brown vio	55.00	55.00
	Nos. B107-B113 (7)	69.75	68.42

The surtax was for the National Anti-Tuberculosis League.

Désiré Cardinal Mercier SP43

Mercier Protecting Children and Aged at Malines SP44

Mercier as Professor at Louvain University — SP45

Mercier in Full Canonicals, Giving His Blessing SP46

1932, June 10 Photo. *Perf. 14½x14*

B114 SP43	10c + 10c dk violet	35	35
B115 SP43	50c + 30c brt violet	1.25	1.40
B116 SP43	75c + 25c olive brn	1.25	1.10
B117 SP43	1fr + 2fr brown red	3.50	3.25

Engr. *Perf. 11½*

B118 SP44	1.75fr + 75c dp blue	40.00	47.50
B119 SP45	2.50fr + 2.50fr dk brn	40.00	40.00
B120 SP44	3fr + 4.50fr dull grn	40.00	40.00
B121 SP45	5fr + 20fr vio brn	47.50	47.50
B122 SP46	10fr + 40fr brn lake	110.00	125.00
	Nos. B114-B122 (9)	283.85	306.10

Issued in commemoration of Cardinal Mercier and to obtain funds to erect a monument to his memory.

Belgian Infantryman SP47

Sanatorium at Waterloo SP48

1932, Aug. 4 *Perf. 14½x14*

B123 SP47	75c + 3.25fr red brn	27.50	27.50
B124 SP47	1.75fr + 4.25fr dk blue	27.50	27.50

Honoring Belgian soldiers who fought in WWI and to obtain funds to erect a natl. monument to their glory.

1932, Dec. 1 Photo. *Perf. 13½x14*

B125 SP48	10c + 5c dk vio	22	80
B126 SP48	25c + 15c red vio	80	1.10
B127 SP48	50c + 10c red brn	80	1.10
B128 SP48	75c + 15c ol brn	80	70
B129 SP48	1fr + 25c dp red	10.50	9.50
B130 SP48	1.75fr + 25c dp blue	8.25	8.25
B131 SP48	5fr + 5fr gray grn	67.50	80.00
	Nos. B125-B131 (7)	88.87	101.45

Surtax for the assistance of the Natl. Anti-Tuberculosis Society at Waterloo.

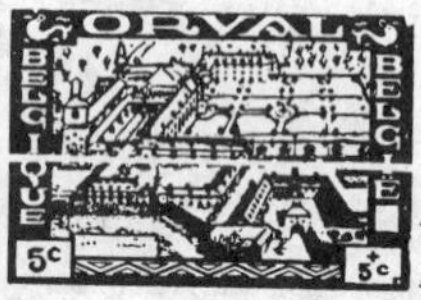

View of Old Abbey — SP49

Ruins of Old Abbey — SP50

Count de Chiny Presenting First Abbey to Countess Matilda SP56

Restoration of Abbey in XVI and XVII Centuries SP57

Abbey in XVIII Century, Maria Theresa and Charles V — SP58

Madonna and Arms of Seven Abbeys — SP60

Designs: 25c+15c, Guests, courtyard. 50c+25c, Transept. 75c+50c, Bell Tower. 1fr+1.25fr, Fountain. 1.25fr+1.75fr, Cloisters. 5fr+20fr, Duke of Brabant placing 1st stone of new abbey.

1933, Oct. 15 *Perf. 14*

B132 SP49	5c + 5c dull grn	25.00	27.50
B133 SP50	10c + 15c ol grn	22.50	25.00
B134 SP49	25c + 15c dk brn	22.50	25.00
B135 SP50	50c + 25c red brn	22.50	25.00
B136 SP50	75c + 50c dp grn	22.50	25.00
B137 SP50	1fr + 1.25fr cop red	22.50	25.00
B138 SP49	1.25fr + 1.75fr gray blk	22.50	25.00
B139 SP56	1.75fr + 2.75fr blue	27.50	27.50
B140 SP57	2fr + 3fr mag	27.50	27.50
B141 SP58	2.50fr + 5fr dull brn	27.50	27.50
B142 SP56	5fr + 20fr vio	27.50	27.50

Perf. 11½

B143 SP60	10fr + 40fr blue	180.00	150.00
	Nos. B132-B143 (12)	450.00	437.50

The surtax was for a fund to aid in the restoration of Orval Abbey. Counterfeits exist.

"Tuberculosis Society" SP61

Peter Benoit SP62

1933, Dec. 1 Engr. *Perf. 14x13½*

B144 SP61	10c + 5c black	50	65
B145 SP61	25c + 15c violet	1.65	1.75
B146 SP61	50c + 10c red brn	1.40	1.65
B147 SP61	75c + 15c blk brn	5.25	50
B148 SP61	1fr + 25c claret	6.00	7.25
B149 SP61	1.75fr + 25c vio bl	7.25	6.25
B150 SP61	5fr + 5fr lilac	65.00	72.50
	Nos. B144-B150 (7)	87.05	90.55

The surtax was for anti-tuberculosis work.

1934, June 1 Photo.

B151 SP62	75c + 25c ol brn	5.50	5.50

The surtax was to raise funds for the Peter Benoit Memorial.

King Leopold III SP63 SP64

1934, Sept. 15

B152 SP63	75c + 25c ol blk	18.00	17.00
a.	Sheet of 20	750.00	750.00
B153 SP64	1fr + 25c red vio	17.00	16.00
a.	Sheet of 20	750.00	750.00

The surtax aided the National War Veterans' Fund. Sold for 4.50fr a set at the Exhibition of War Postmarks 1914-18, held at Brussels by the Royal Philatelic Club of Veterans. The price included an exhibition ticket. Sold at Brussels post office Sept. 18-22. No. B152 printed in sheets of 20 (4x5) and 100 (10x10). No. B153 printed in sheets of 20 (4x5) and 150 (10x15).

1934, Sept. 24

B154	SP63	75c + 25c violet	1.25	1.25
B155	SP64	1fr + 25c red brn	7.00	7.00

The surtax aided the National War Veterans' Fund. No. B154 printed in sheets of 100 (10x10); No. B155 in sheets of 150 (10x15). These stamps remained in use one year.

Crusader — SP65

1934, Nov. 17 Engr. *Perf. 13½x14*

Cross in Red

B156	SP65	10c + 5c black	60	28
B157	SP65	25c + 15c brown	1.00	90
B158	SP65	50c + 10c dull grn	1.00	90
B159	SP65	75c + 15c vio brn	48	28
B160	SP65	1fr + 25c rose	5.00	5.50
B161	SP65	1.75fr + 25c ultra	4.25	4.50
B162	SP65	5fr + 5fr brn vio	60.00	60.00
		Nos. B156-B162 (7)	72.33	72.36

The surtax was for anti-tuberculosis work.

Prince Baudouin, Princess Josephine and Prince Albert SP66

1935, Apr. 10 Photo.

B163	SP66	35c + 15c dk green	85	75
B164	SP66	70c + 30c red brn	85	60
B165	SP66	1.75fr + 50c dk blue	3.00	3.50
		Nos. B163-B165 (3)	4.70	4.85

Surtax was for Child Welfare Society.

Stagecoach SP67

Franz von Taxis — SP68

Queen Astrid — SP69

1935, Apr. 27

B166	SP67	10c + 10c ol blk	48	60
B167	SP67	25c + 25c bis brn	1.65	1.50
B168	SP67	35c + 25c dk green	2.25	2.00
		Nos. B166-B168 (3)	4.38	4.10

Printed in sheets of 10. Value, set of 3, $175.

Souvenir Sheet

1935, May 25 Engr. *Perf. 14*

B169	SP68	5fr + 5fr grnsh blk	80.00	80.00

Sheets measure 91½x117mm.

Nos. B166-B169 were issued for the Brussels Philatelic Exhibition (SITEB).

The sheet normally has pin holes and a cancellation-like marking in the margin. These are considered unused and the condition valued here.

1935, Dec. 1 Photo. *Perf. 11½*

Borders in Black

B170	SP69	10c + 5c ol blk	15	15
B171	SP69	25c + 15c brown	15	28
B172	SP69	35c + 5c dk green	18	24
B173	SP69	50c + 10c rose lil	65	52
B174	SP69	70c + 5c gray blk	15	15
B175	SP69	1fr + 25c red	90	70
B176	SP69	1.75fr + 25c blue	2.00	1.50
B177	SP69	2.45fr + 55c dk vio	2.50	2.75
		Nos. B170-B177 (8)	6.68	6.29

Queen Astrid Memorial issue. The surtax was divided among several charitable organizations.

Borgerhout Philatelic Exhibition Issue

Souvenir Sheet

Town Hall, Borgerhout — SP70

1936, Oct. 3

B178	SP70	70c + 30c pur brn	35.00	35.00

Sheet measures 115x126mm.

The sheet normally has pin holes and a cancellation-like marking in the margin. These are considered unused and the condition valued here.

Town Hall and Belfry of Charleroi SP71

Prince Baudouin SP72

Charleroi Youth Exhibition

Souvenir Sheet

1936, Oct. 18 Engr.

B179	SP71	2.45fr + 55c gray blue	32.50	30.00

Sheet measures 95x120mm.

The sheet normally has pin holes and a cancellation-like marking in the margin. These are considered unused and the condition valued here.

1936, Dec. 1 Photo. *Perf. 14x13½*

B180	SP72	10c + 5c dk brown	15	16
B181	SP72	25c + 5c violet	20	25
B182	SP72	35c + 5c dk green	20	25
B183	SP72	50c + 5c vio brn	30	35
B184	SP72	70c + 5c ol grn	20	16
B185	SP72	1fr + 25c cerise	65	45
B186	SP72	1.75fr + 25c ultra	1.10	65
B187	SP72	2.45fr + 2.55fr vio rose	3.00	4.00
		Nos. B180-B187 (8)	5.80	6.27

The surtax was for the assistance of the National Anti-Tuberculosis Society.

1937, Jan. 10

B188	SP72	2.45fr + 2.55fr slate	1.50	1.50

Intl. Stamp Day. Surtax for the benefit of the Brussels Postal Museum, the Royal Belgian Phil. Fed. and the Anti-Tuberculosis Soc.

Queen Astrid and Prince Baudouin SP73

Queen Mother Elisabeth SP74

1937, Apr. 15 *Perf. 11½*

B189	SP73	10c + 5c magenta	15	15
B190	SP73	25c + 5c ol blk	20	25
B191	SP73	35c + 5c dk grn	20	25
B192	SP73	50c + 5c violet	52	55
B193	SP73	70c + 5c slate	20	30
B194	SP73	1fr + 25c dk car	65	65
B195	SP73	1.75fr + 25c dp ultra	1.10	1.10
B196	SP73	2.45fr + 1.55fr dk brn	2.75	2.75
		Nos. B189-B196 (8)	5.77	6.00

The surtax was to raise funds for Public Utility Works.

1937, Sept. 15 *Perf. 14x13½*

B197	SP74	70c + 5c int black	30	30
B198	SP74	1.75fr + 25c brt ultra	70	70

Souvenir Sheet

Perf. 11½

B199	Sheet of 4	21.00	15.00
a.	SP74 1.50fr+2.50fr red brn	3.75	3.25
b.	SP74 2.45fr+3.55fr red vio	3.25	2.00

Issued for the benefit of the Queen Elisabeth Music Foundation in connection with the Eugene Ysaye intl. competition.

No. B199 contains two se-tenant pairs of Nos. B199a and B199b. Size: 111x145mm. On sale one day, Sept. 15, at Brussels.

The sheet normally has pin holes and a cancellation-like marking in the margin. These are considered unused and the condition valued here.

Princess Josephine-Charlotte SP75

1937, Dec. 1 *Perf. 14x13½*

B200	SP75	10c + 5c sl grn	15	16
B201	SP75	25c + 5c lt brn	20	18
B202	SP75	35c + 5c yel grn	20	18
B203	SP75	50c + 5c ol gray	40	35
B204	SP75	70c + 5c brn red	15	18
B205	SP75	1fr + 25c red	70	55
B206	SP75	1.75fr + 25c vio bl	80	70
B207	SP75	2.45fr + 2.55fr mag	3.25	3.50
		Nos. B200-B207 (8)	5.85	5.80

King Albert Memorial Issue

Souvenir Sheet

King Albert Memorial — SP76

1938, Feb. 17 *Perf. 11½*

B208	SP76	2.45fr + 7.55fr brn vio	8.75	8.75

Dedication of the monument to King Albert.

The sheet normally has pin holes and a cancellation-like marking in the margin. These are considered unused and the condition valued here.

King Leopold III in Military Plane — SP77

1938, Mar. 15

B209	SP77	10c + 5c car brn	18	32
B210	SP77	35c + 5c dp grn	35	90
B211	SP77	70c + 5c gray blk	65	48
B212	SP77	1.75fr + 25c ultra	1.50	1.40
B213	SP77	2.45fr + 2.55fr pur	3.50	3.00
		Nos. B209-B213 (5)	6.18	6.10

The surtax was for the benefit of the National Fund for Aeronautical Propaganda.

Basilica of Koekelberg SP78

Interior View of the Basilica of Koekelberg — SP79

1938, June 1 Photo.

B214	SP78	10c + 5c lt brn	15	18
B215	SP78	35c + 5c grn	18	18
B216	SP78	70c + 5c gray grn	18	18
B217	SP78	1fr + 25c car	65	55
B218	SP78	1.75fr + 25c ultra	65	65
B219	SP78	2.45fr + 2.55fr brn vio	2.75	3.50

Engr.

B220	SP79	5fr + 5fr dl grn	11.00	10.50
		Nos. B214-B220 (7)	15.56	15.74

Souvenir Sheet

1938, July 21 Engr. *Perf. 14*

B221	SP79	5fr + 5fr lt vio	12.00	10.50

The surtax was for a fund to aid in completing the National Basilica of the Sacred Heart at Koekelberg.

Nos. B214, B216 and B218 are different views of the exterior of the Basilica.

The sheet normally has pin holes and a cancellation-like marking in the margin. These are considered unused and the condition valued here.

Stamps of 1938 Surcharged in Black:

40c

Nos. B222-B223

2 Fr 50   2 F 50

No. B224

1938, Nov. 10 *Perf. 11½*

B222	SP78	40c on 35c+5c grn	30	35
B223	SP78	75c on 70c+5c gray grn	40	52
B224	SP78	2.50 +2.50fr on 2.45+2.55fr	4.25	4.75
		Nos. B222-B224 (3)	4.95	5.62

Prince Albert of Liege — SP81

1938, Dec. 10 Photo. *Perf. 14x13½*

B225	SP81	10c + 5c brn	15	18
B226	SP81	30c + 5c mag	22	30
B227	SP81	40c + 5c ol gray	22	30
B228	SP81	75c + 5c sl grn	16	18
B229	SP81	1fr + 25c dk car	55	75
B230	SP81	1.75fr + 25c ultra	55	75
B231	SP81	2.50fr + 2.50fr dp grn	3.50	5.50
B232	SP81	5fr + 5fr brn lake	11.00	8.50
		Nos. B225-B232 (8)	16.35	16.46

Henri Dunant SP82

Florence Nightingale SP83

Queen Mother Elisabeth and Royal Children — SP84

Queen Astrid — SP86

King Leopold and Royal Children SP85

Queen Mother Elisabeth and Wounded Soldier — SP87

1939, Apr. 1 Photo. *Perf. 11½*
Cross in Carmine

B233	SP82	10c + 5c brn	15	18
B234	SP83	30c + 5c brn car	30	30
B235	SP84	40c + 5c ol gray	22	30
B236	SP85	75c + 5c sl blk	42	18
B237	SP84	1fr + 25c brt rose	1.90	1.10
B238	SP85	1.75fr + 25c brt ultra	60	85
B239	SP86	2.50fr + 2.50fr dl vio	1.25	1.65
B240	SP87	5fr + 5fr gray grn	4.25	5.50
		Nos. B233-B240 (8)	9.09	10.06

75th anniversary of the founding of the International Red Cross Society.

Rubens' House, Antwerp SP88

"Albert and Nicolas Rubens" — SP89

Arcade, Rubens' House SP90

"Helena Fourment and Her Children" — SP91

Rubens and Isabelle Brandt — SP92

Peter Paul Rubens — SP93

"The Velvet Hat" — SP94

"Descent from the Cross" SP95

1939, July 1

B241	SP88	10c + 5c brn	15	18
B242	SP89	40c + 5c brn car	30	30
B243	SP90	75c + 5c ol blk	60	50
B244	SP91	1fr + 25c rose	1.65	1.50
B245	SP92	1.50fr + 25c sep	1.65	1.50
B246	SP93	1.75fr + 25c dp ultra	2.25	1.65
B247	SP94	2.50fr + 2.50fr brt red vio	9.25	10.50
B248	SP95	5fr + 5fr sl gray	14.00	14.00
		Nos. B241-B248 (8)	29.85	30.13

Issued to honor Peter Paul Rubens. The surtax was used to restore Rubens' home in Antwerp.

"Martin van Nieuwenhove" by Hans Memling (1430?-1495), Flemish Painter — SP96

1939, July 1

B249	SP96	75c + 75c olive blk	2.75	2.75

Twelfth Century Monks at Work — SP97

Reconstructed Tower Seen through Cloister — SP98

Monks Laboring in the Fields — SP99

Orval Abbey, Aerial View — SP100

Bishop Heylen of Namur, Madonna and Abbot General Smets of the Trappists — SP101

King Albert I and King Leopold III and Shrine — SP102

1939, July 20

B250	SP97	75c + 75c ol blk	2.50	2.75
B251	SP98	1fr + 1fr rose red	1.65	1.65
B252	SP99	1.50fr + 1.50fr dl brn	1.65	1.65
B253	SP100	1.75fr + 1.75fr saph	1.65	1.65
B254	SP101	2.50fr + 2.50fr brt red vio	7.25	6.50
B255	SP102	5fr + 5fr brn car	7.25	7.25
		Nos. B250-B255 (6)	21.95	21.45

The surtax was used for the restoration of the Abbey of Orval.

Bruges SP103

Furnes SP104

Belfries: 30c+5c, Thuin. 40c+5c, Lierre. 75c+5c, Mons. 1.75fr+25c, Namur. 2.50fr+2.50fr, Alost. 5fr+5fr, Tournai.

1939, Dec. 1 Photo. *Perf. 14x13½*

B256	SP103	10c + 5c ol gray	15	18
B257	SP103	30c + 5c brn org	18	28
B258	SP103	40c + 5c brt red vio	30	35
B259	SP103	75c + 5c olive blk	15	18

Engr.

B260	SP104	1fr + 25c rose car	75	90
B261	SP104	1.75fr + 25c dk blue	75	90
B262	SP104	2.50fr + 2.50fr dp red brn	5.75	6.25
B263	SP104	5fr + 5fr purple	7.50	8.50
		Nos. B256-B263 (8)	15.53	17.54

Mons SP111

Ghent SP112

Coats of Arms: 40c+10c, Arel. 50c+10c, Bruges. 75c+15c, Namur. 1fr+25c, Hasselt. 1.75fr+50c, Brussels. 2.50fr+2.50fr, Antwerp. 5fr+5fr, Liege.

1940-41 Typo. *Perf. 14x13½*

B264	SP111	10c + 5c multi	15	15
B265	SP112	30c + 5c multi	18	15
B266	SP111	40c + 10c multi	18	15
B267	SP112	50c + 10c multi	18	15
B268	SP111	75c + 15c multi	15	15
B269	SP112	1fr + 25c multi	28	30
B270	SP111	1.75fr + 50c multi	45	38
B271	SP112	2.50fr + 2.50fr multi	1.25	1.25
B272	SP111	5fr + 5fr multi	1.50	1.50
		Nos. B264-B272 (9)	4.32	4.18

Nos. B264, B269-B272 issued in 1941. Surtax for winter relief. See No. B279.

Queen Elisabeth Music Chapel SP120

Bust of Prince Albert of Liege — SP121

1940, Nov. Photo. *Perf. 11½*

B273	SP120	75c + 75c slate	1.75	1.75
B274	SP120	1fr + 1fr rose red	1.10	1.10
B275	SP121	1.50fr + 1.50fr Prus grn	1.25	1.25
B276	SP121	1.75fr + 1.75fr ultra	1.25	1.25
B277	SP120	2.50fr + 2.50fr brn org	2.50	2.50
B278	SP121	5fr + 5fr red vio	3.00	3.00
		Nos. B273-B278 (6)	10.85	10.85

The surtax was for the Queen Elisabeth Music Foundation. Nos. B273-B278 were not authorized for postal use, but were sold to advance subscribers either mint or canceled to order. See Nos. B317-B318.

Arms Types of 1940-41
Souvenir Sheets
Perf. 14x13½, Imperf.

1941, May Typo.
Cross and City Name in Carmine
Arms in Color of Stamp

B279		Sheet of 9	10.00	11.00
a.	SP111	10c + 5c slate	85	90
b.	SP112	30c + 5c emerald	85	90
c.	SP111	40c + 10c chocolate	85	90
d.	SP112	50c + 10c light violet	85	90
e.	SP111	75c + 15c dull purple	85	90
f.	SP112	1fr + 25c carmine	85	90
g.	SP111	1.75fr + 50c dull blue	85	90
h.	SP112	2.50fr + 2.50fr olive gray	85	90
i.	SP111	5fr + 5fr dull violet	3.00	3.25

The sheets measure 106x148mm. The surtax was used for relief work.

Painting SP123

Sculpture SP124

Monks Studying Plans of Orval Abbey — SP128

Designs: 40c+60c, 2fr+3.50fr, Monk carrying candle. 50c+65c, 1.75fr+2.50fr, Monk praying. 75c+1fr, 3fr+5fr, Two monks singing.

1941, June Photo. *Perf. 11½*

B281	SP123	10c + 15c brn org	35	40
B282	SP124	30c + 30c ol gray	35	40
B283	SP124	40c + 60c dp brn	35	40
B284	SP124	50c + 65c vio	35	40
B285	SP124	75c + 1fr brt red vio	35	40
B286	SP124	1fr + 1.50fr rose red	35	40

B287	SP123	1.25fr + 1.75fr dp yel grn	35	40
B288	SP123	1.75fr + 2.50fr dp ultra	35	40
B289	SP123	2fr + 3.50fr red vio	35	40
B290	SP124	2.50fr + 4.50fr dl red brn	35	40
B291	SP124	3fr + 5fr dk ol grn	35	40
B292	SP128	5fr + 10fr grnsh blk	1.25	1.25
		Nos. B281-B292 (12)	5.10	5.65

The surtax was used for the restoration of the Abbey of Orval.

Maria Theresa — SP129

Charles the Bold — SP130

Portraits (in various frames): 35c+5c, Charles of Lorraine. 50c+10c, Margaret of Parma. 60c+10c, Charles V. 1fr+15c, Johanna of Castile. 1.50fr+1fr, Philip the Good. 1.75fr+1.75fr, Margaret of Austria. 3.25fr+3.25fr, Archduke Albert. 5fr+5fr, Archduchess Isabella.

1941-42 **Photo.**

B293	SP129	10c + 5c ol blk	15	15
B294	SP129	35c + 5c dl grn	15	15
B295	SP129	50c + 10c brn	15	15
B296	SP129	60c + 10c pur	15	15
B297	SP129	1fr + 15c brt car rose	15	15
B298	SP129	1.50fr + 1fr red vio	20	20
B299	SP129	1.75fr + 1.75fr ryl bl	20	20
B300	SP130	2.25fr + 2.25fr dl red brn	28	30
B301	SP129	3.25fr + 3.25fr lt brn	35	45
B302	SP129	5fr + 5fr sl grn	40	45
		Nos. B293-B302 (10)	2.18	2.35

Souvenir Sheet

Archduke Albert and Archduchess Isabella — SP139

B302A	SP139	Sheet of 2 ('42)	3.25	3.25
b.		3.25fr+6.75fr turquoise blue	1.40	1.40
c.		5fr+10fr dark carmine	1.40	1.40

The surtax was for the benefit of National Social Service Work among soldiers' families.

Souvenir Sheets

Monks Studying Plans of Orval Abbey SP140

1941, Oct. **Photo.** ***Perf. 11½***

Inscribed "Belgie-Belgique"

B303	SP140	5fr + 15fr ultra	4.50	6.25

Inscribed "Belgique-Belgie"

B304	SP140	5fr + 15fr ultra	4.50	6.25

Surtax for the restoration of Orval Abbey.
No. B304 exists perforated.
In 1942 these sheets were privately trimmed and overprinted "1142 1942" and ornament.

St. Martin Statue, Church of Dinant SP141

Lennik, Saint-Quentin SP142

St. Martin's Church, Saint-Trond SP146

Designs (Statues of St. Martin): 50c+10c, 3.25fr+3.25fr, Beck, Limburg. 60c+10c, 2.25fr+2.25fr, Dave on the Meuse. 1.75fr+50c, Hal, Brabant.

1941-42 **Photo.** ***Perf. 11½***

B305	SP141	10c + 5c chnt	15	16
B306	SP142	35c + 5c dk bl grn	15	16
B307	SP142	50c + 10c vio	15	16
B308	SP142	60c + 10c dp brn	15	16
B309	SP142	1fr + 15c car	15	16
B310	SP141	1.50fr + 25c sl grn	22	25
B311	SP142	1.75fr + 50c dk ultra	25	32
B312	SP142	2.25fr + 2.25fr red vio	25	32
B313	SP142	3.25fr + 3.25fr brn vio	25	32
B314	SP146	5fr + 5fr dk ol grn	40	45
		Nos. B305-B314 (10)	2.12	2.46

Souvenir Sheets

Inscribed "Belgie-Belgique"

B315	SP146	5fr + 20fr vio brn ('42)	8.25	8.25

Inscribed "Belgique-Belgie"

B316	SP146	5fr + 20fr vio brn ('42)	6.75	6.75

In 1956, the Bureau Europeen de la Jeunesse et de l'Enfance privately overprinted Nos. B315-B316: "Congres Europeen de l'education 7-12 Mai 1956," in dark red and dark green respectively. A black bar obliterates "Winterhulp-Secours d'Hiver."

Souvenir Sheets

Queen Elisabeth Music Chapel — SP147

1941, Dec. 1 **Photo.** ***Perf. 11½***

Inscribed "Belgique-Belgie"

B317	SP147	10fr + 15fr ol blk	1.40	2.50

Inscribed "Belgie-Belique"

B318	SP147	10fr + 15fr ol blk	1.40	2.50

The surtax was for the Queen Elisabeth Music Foundation. These sheets were perforated with the monogram of Queen Elisabeth in 1942.
In 1954 Nos. B317-B318 were overprinted to for the birth cent. of Edgar Tinel, composer. These overprinted sheets were not postally valid.

Jean Bollandus SP148

Christophe Plantin SP156

Designs: 35c+5c, Andreas Vesalius. 50c+10c, Simon Stevinus. 60c+10c, Jean Van Helmont. 1fr+15c, Rembert Dodoens. 1.75fr+50c, Gerardus Mercator. 3.25fr+3.25fr, Abraham Ortelius. 5fr+5fr, Justus Lipsius.

1942, May 15 **Photo.** ***Perf. 14x13½***

B319	SP148	10c + 5c dl brn	15	15
B320	SP148	35c + 5c gray grn	15	15
B321	SP148	50c + 10c fawn	15	15
B322	SP148	60c + 10c grnsh blk	15	15

Engr.

B323	SP148	1fr + 15c brt rose	15	18
B324	SP148	1.75fr + 50c dl bl	22	18
B325	SP148	3.25fr + 3.25fr lil rose	22	18
B326	SP148	5fr + 5fr vio	25	25

Perf. 13½x14

B327	SP156	10fr + 30fr red org	95	1.00
		Nos. B319-B327 (9)	2.39	2.39

The surtax was used to help fight tuberculosis.
No. B327 was sold by subscription at the Brussels Post Office, July 1-10, 1942.

Belgian Prisoner — SP158

1942, Oct. 1 ***Perf. 11½***

B331	SP158	5fr + 45fr olive gray	5.50	5.50

The surtax was for prisoners of war. Value includes a brown label, inscribed "1942 POUR NOS PRISONNIERS/VOOR ONZE GEVANGENEN," which alternates with the stamps in the sheet.

SP159

SP164

SP162

SP168

Various Statues of St. Martin

1942-43

B332	SP159	10c + 5c org	15	15
B333	SP159	35c + 5c dk bl grn	15	15
B334	SP159	50c + 10c dp brn	15	15
B335	SP162	60c + 10c blk	15	15
B336	SP159	1fr + 15c brt rose	15	15
B337	SP164	1.50fr + 25c grnsh blk	18	18
B338	SP164	1.75fr + 50c dk bl	20	20
B339	SP162	2.25fr + 2.25fr brn	30	25
B340	SP162	3.25fr + 3.25fr brt red vio	35	30
B341	SP168	5fr + 10fr hn brn	50	45
B342	SP168	10fr + 20fr rose brn & vio brn ('43)	65	65

Inscribed "Belgique-Belgie"

B343	SP168	10fr + 20fr gldn brn & vio brn ('43)	65	65
		Nos. B332-B343 (12)	3.58	3.43

The surtax was for winter relief.
Issue dates: Nos. B332-B341, Nov. 12, 1942. Nos. B342-B343, Apr. 3, 1943.

Prisoners of War — SP170

Design: No. B345, Two prisoners with package from home.

1943, May **Photo.** ***Perf. 11½***

B344	SP170	1fr + 30fr ver	2.25	2.50
B345	SP170	1fr + 30fr brn rose	2.25	2.50

The surtax was used for prisoners of war.

Roof Tiler SP172

Coppersmith SP173

Statues in Petit Sablon Park, Brussels: 35c+5c, Blacksmith. 60c+10c, Gunsmith. 1fr+15c, Armsmith. 1.75fr+75c, Goldsmith. 3.25fr+3.25fr, Fishdealer. 5fr+25fr, Watchmaker.

1943, June 1

B346	SP172	10c + 5c chnt brn	15	15
B347	SP172	35c + 5c grn	15	15
B348	SP173	50c + 10c dk brn	15	15
B349	SP173	60c + 10c slate	15	15
B350	SP173	1fr + 15c dl rose brn	15	18
B351	SP173	1.75fr + 75c ultra	18	24
B352	SP173	3.25fr + 3.25fr brt red vio	30	40
B353	SP173	5fr + 25fr dk pur	50	55
		Set value	1.45	1.75

Surtax for the control of tuberculosis.

"O" — SP180

"ORVAL" — SP185

1943, Oct. 9

B354	SP180	50c + 1fr "O"	52	60
B355	SP180	60c + 1.90fr "R"	30	25
B356	SP180	1fr + 3fr "V"	30	25
B357	SP180	1.75fr + 5.25fr "A"	30	25
B358	SP180	3.25fr + 16.75fr "L"	40	45
B359	SP185	5fr + 30fr dp brn	75	75
		Nos. B354-B359 (6)	2.57	2.55

Surtax aided restoration of Orval Abbey.

St. Leonard Church, Leau — SP186

St. Martin Church, Courtrai SP190

Basilica of St. Martin, Angre SP191

Notre Dame, Hal — SP193

St. Martin SP194

Designs: 35c+5c, St. Martin Church, Dion-le-Val. 50c+15c, St. Martin Church, Alost. 60c+20c, St. Martin Church, Liege. 3.25fr+11.75fr, St. Martin Church, Loppem. No. B369, St. Martin, beggar and Meuse landscape.

1943-44

B360	SP186	10c	+ 5c dp brn	15	15
B361	SP186	35c	+ 5c dk bl grn	22	28
B362	SP186	50c	+ 15c ol blk	28	32
B363	SP186	60c	+ 20c brt red vio	32	40
B364	SP190	1fr	+ 1fr rose brn	40	40
B365	SP191	1.75fr	+ 4.25fr dp ultra	90	60
B366	SP186	3.25fr	+ 11.75fr red lil	90	65
B367	SP193	5fr	+ 25fr dk bl	1.25	1.25
B368	SP194	10fr	+ 30fr gray grn ('44)	90	90
B369	SP194	10fr	+ 30fr blk brn ('44)	90	90
			Nos. B360-B369 (10)	6.22	5.85

Surtax for winter relief.

Catalogue values for unused stamps in this section, from this point to the end of the section, are for Never Hinged items.

"Daedalus and Icarus" SP196

Sir Anthony Van Dyck, Self-portrait SP200

Paintings by Van Dyck: 50c+2.50fr. "The Good Samaritan." 60c+3.40fr, Detail of "Christ Healing the Paralytic." 1fr+5fr, "Madonna and Child." 5fr+30fr, "St. Sebastian."

1944, Apr. 16 Photo. *Perf. 11½*
Crosses in Carmine

B370	SP196	35c	+ 1.65fr dk sl grn	42	30
B371	SP196	50c	+ 2.50fr grnsh blk	42	30
B372	SP196	60c	+ 3.40fr blk brn	42	30
B373	SP196	1fr	+ 5fr dk car	60	45
B374	SP200	1.75fr	+ 8.25fr int bl	75	60
B375	SP196	5fr	+ 30fr cop brn	75	60
			Nos. B370-B375 (6)	3.36	2.55

The surtax was for the Belgian Red Cross.

Jan van Eyck SP202

Godfrey of Bouillon SP203

Designs: 50c+25c, Jacob van Maerlant. 60c+40c, Jean Joses de Dinant. 1fr+50c, Jacob van Artevelde. 1.75fr+4.25fr, Charles Joseph de Ligne. 2.25fr+8.25fr, Andre Gretry. 3.25fr+11.25fr, Jan Moretus-Plantin. 5fr+35fr, Jan van Ruysbroeck.

1944, May 31

B376	SP202	10c	+ 15c dk pur	32	30
B377	SP203	35c	+ 15c grn	32	30
B378	SP203	50c	+ 25c chnt brn	32	30
B379	SP203	60c	+ 40c ol blk	32	30
B380	SP203	1fr	+ 50c rose brn	32	30
B381	SP203	1.75fr	+ 4.25fr ultra	32	30
B382	SP203	2.25fr	+ 8.25fr grnsh blk	85	75
B383	SP203	3.25fr	+ 11.25fr dk brn	32	30
B384	SP203	5fr	+ 35fr sl bl	65	90
			Nos. B376-B384 (9)	3.74	3.75

The surtax was for prisoners of war.

Sons of Aymon Astride Bayard SP211

Brabo Slaying the Giant Antigoon SP212

Till Eulenspiegel Singing to Nele SP214

Designs: 50c+10c, St. Hubert converted by stag with crucifix. 1fr+15fr, St. George slaying the dragon. 1.75fr+5.25fr, Genevieve of Brabant with son and roe-deer. 3.25fr+11.75fr, Tchantches wrestling with the Saracen. 5fr+25fr, St. Gertrude rescuing the knight with the cards.

1944, June 25

B385	SP211	10c	+ 5c choc	15	20
B386	SP212	35c	+ 5c dk bl grn	15	20
B387	SP211	50c	+ 10c dl vio	15	20
B388	SP214	60c	+ 10c blk brn	15	20
B389	SP214	1fr	+ 15c rose brn	15	20
B390	SP214	1.75fr	+ 5.25fr ultra	22	40
B391	SP211	3.25fr	+ 11.75fr grnsh blk	32	60
B392	SP211	5fr	+ 25fr dk bl	45	80
			Nos. B385-B392 (8)	1.74	2.80

The surtax was for the control of tuberculosis.

Nos. B385-B389 were overprinted "Breendonk+10fr." in 1946 by the Union Royale Philatelique for an exhibition at Brussels. They had no postal validity.

Union of the Flemish and Walloon Peoples in their Sorrow — SP219

Union in Reconstruction — SP220

Perf. 11½

1945, May 1 Unwmk. Photo.

B395	SP219	1fr	+ 30fr car	1.10	1.25
B396	SP220	1¾fr	+ 30fr brt ultra	1.10	1.25

1945, July 21
Size: 34½x23½mm

B397	SP219	1fr	+ 9fr scarlet	30	22
B398	SP220	1fr	+ 9fr car rose	30	22
			Nos. B395-B398 (4)	2.80	2.94

The surtax was for the postal employees' relief fund.

Prisoner of War — SP221

Reunion SP222

Awaiting Execution SP223

Symbolical Figures "Recovery of Freedom" SP225

Design: 70c+30c, 3.50fr+3.50fr, Member of Resistance Movement.

1945, Sept. 10

B399	SP221	10c	+ 15c org	15	15
B400	SP222	20c	+ 20c dp pur	15	15
B401	SP223	60c	+ 25c sepia	15	15
B402	SP221	70c	+ 30c dp yel grn	15	15
B403	SP221	75c	+ 50c org brn	15	18
B404	SP222	1fr	+ 75c brt bl grn	22	22
B405	SP223	1.50fr	+ 1fr brt red	22	22
B406	SP221	3.50fr	+ 3.50fr brt bl	1.00	1.10
B407	SP225	5fr	+ 40fr brown	85	1.00
			Nos. B399-B407 (9)	3.04	3.32

The surtax was for the benefit of prisoners of war, displaced persons, families of executed victims and members of the Resistance Movement.

Arms of West Flanders — SP226

Arms of Provinces: 20c+20c, Luxembourg. 60c+25c, East Flanders. 70c+30c, Namur. 75c+50c, Limburg. 1fr+75c, Hainaut. 1.50fr+1fr, Antwerp. 3.50fr+1.50fr, Liege. 5fr+45fr, Brabant.

1945, Dec. 1

B408	SP226	10c	+ 15c sl blk & sl gray	15	15
B409	SP226	20c	+ 20c rose car & rose	15	15
B410	SP226	60c	+ 25c dk brn & pale brn	15	15
B411	SP226	70c	+ 30c dk grn & lt grn	15	15
B412	SP226	75c	+ 50c org brn & pale org brn	20	20
B413	SP226	1fr	+ 75c pur & lt pur	15	15
B414	SP226	1.50fr	+ 1fr car & rose	15	15
B415	SP226	3.50fr	+ 1.50fr dp bl & gray bl	24	24
B416	SP226	5fr	+ 45fr dp mag & cer	1.75	1.90
			Nos. B408-B416 (9)	3.09	3.24

The surtax was for tuberculosis prevention.

Father Joseph Damien — SP227

Father Damien Comforting Leper — SP229

Leper Colony, Molokai Island, Hawaii SP228

Symbols of Wisdom and Patriotism SP230

"In Memoriam" SP232

François Bovesse SP231

Emile Vandervelde SP233

Sower SP235

Vandervelde, Laborer and Family
SP234

Perf. 11½

1946, July 15 Unwmk. Photo.

B417	SP227	65c + 75c dk bl	85	60
B418	SP228	1.35fr + 2fr brn	85	60
B419	SP229	1.75fr + 18fr rose brn	1.25	1.00

The surtax was for the erection of a museum in Louvain.

1946, July 15

B420	SP230	65c + 75c vio	85	60
B421	SP231	1.35fr + 2fr dk org brn	1.00	75
B422	SP232	1.75fr + 18fr car rose	1.50	1.00

The surtax was for the erection of a "House of the Fine Arts" at Namur.

1946, July 15

B423	SP233	65c + 75c dk sl grn	90	60
B424	SP234	1.35fr + 2fr dk vio bl	1.00	75
B425	SP235	1.75fr + 18fr dp car	1.50	1.00
		Nos. B417-B425 (9)	9.70	6.90

The surtax was for the Emile Vanderveide Institute, to promote social, economic and cultural activities.
For surcharges see Nos. CB4-CB12.

Pepin of Herstal — SP236

Malines — SP241

Designs: 1fr+50c, Charlemagne. 1.50fr+1fr, Godfrey of Bouillon. 3.50fr+1.50fr, Robert of Jerusalem. Nos. B430-B431, Baldwin of Constantinople.

1946, Sept. 15 Engr. *Perf. 11½x11*

B426	SP236	75c + 25c grn	45	35
B427	SP236	1fr + 50c vio	70	50
B428	SP236	1.50fr + 1fr plum	80	60
B429	SP236	3.50fr + 1.50fr brt bl	1.00	75
B430	SP236	5fr + 45fr red vio	8.25	7.00
B431	SP236	5fr + 45fr red org	10.50	7.75
		Nos. B426-B431 (6)	21.70	16.95

The surtax on Nos. B426-B429 was for the benefit of former prisoners of war, displaced persons, the families of executed patriots, and former members of the Resistance Movement.
The surtax on Nos. B430-B431 was divided among several welfare, national celebration and educational organizations.
Issue dates: Nos. B426-B429, Apr. 15; No. B430, Sept. 15; No. B431, Nov. 15.
See Nos. B437-B441, B465-B466, B472-B476.

1946, Dec. 2 *Perf. 11½*

Coats of Arms: 90c+60c, Dinant. 1.35fr+1.15fr, Ostend. 3.15fr+1.85fr, Verviers. 4.50fr+45.50fr, Louvain.

B432	SP241	65c + 35c rose car	55	35
B433	SP241	90c + 60c lemon	55	35
B434	SP241	1.35fr + 1.15fr dp grn	55	35
B435	SP241	3.15fr + 1.85fr blue	1.40	52
B436	SP241	4.50fr + 45.50fr dk vio brn	13.00	8.75
		Nos. B432-B436 (5)	16.05	10.32

The surtax was for anti-tuberculosis work. See Nos. B442-B446.

Type of 1946

Designs: 65c+35c, John II, Duke of Brabant. 90c+60c, Count Philip of Alsace. 1.35fr+1.15fr, William the Good. 3.15fr+1.85fr, Bishop Notger of Liege. 20fr+20fr, Philip the Noble.

1947, Sept. 25 Engr. *Perf. 11½x11*

B437	SP236	65c + 35c Prus grn	45	55
B438	SP236	90c + 60c yel grn	75	75
B439	SP236	1.35fr + 1.15fr car	1.00	1.00
B440	SP236	3.15fr + 1.85fr ultra	1.50	2.00
B441	SP236	20fr + 20fr red vio	40.00	25.00
		Nos. B437-B441 (5)	43.70	29.30

The surtax was for victims of World War II.

Arms Type of 1946 Dated "1947"

Coats of Arms: 65c+35c, Nivelles. 90c+60c, St. Trond. 1.35fr+1.15fr, Charleroi. 3.15fr+1.85fr, St. Nicolas. 20fr+20fr, Bouillon.

1947, Dec. 15 *Perf. 11½*

B442	SP241	65c + 35c org	75	45
B443	SP241	90c + 60c dp cl	60	45
B444	SP241	1.35fr + 1.15fr dk brn	90	50
B445	SP241	3.15fr + 1.85fr dp bl	2.00	1.25
B446	SP241	20fr + 20fr dk grn	17.00	9.00
		Nos. B442-B446 (5)	21.25	11.65

The surtax was for anti-tuberculosis work.

St. Benedict and King Totila — SP247

Achel Abbey
SP248

Designs: 3.15fr+2.85fr, St. Benedict, legislator and builder. 10fr+10fr, Death of St. Benedict.

1948, Apr. 5 Photo.

B447	SP247	65c + 65c red brn	1.00	45
B448	SP248	1.35fr + 1.35fr gray	1.40	45
B449	SP247	3.15fr + 2.85fr dp ultra	2.00	1.50
B450	SP247	10fr + 10fr brt red vio	10.00	8.00
		Nos. B447-B450 (4)	14.40	10.40

The surtax was to aid the Abbey of the Trappist Fathers at Achel.

St. Begga and Chevremont Castle — SP249

Chevremont Basilica and Convent
SP250

Designs: 3.15fr+2.85fr, Madonna of Chevremont and Chapel. 10fr+10fr, Madonna of Mt. Carmel.

1948, Apr. 5 Unwmk.

B451	SP249	65c + 65c bl grn	1.00	45
B452	SP250	1.35fr + 1.35fr dk car rose	1.40	45
B453	SP249	3.15fr + 2.85fr dp bl	2.00	1.50
B454	SP249	10fr + 10fr dp brn	10.00	8.00
		Nos. B451-B454 (4)	14.40	10.40

The surtax was to aid the Basilica of the Carmelite Fathers of Chèvremont.

Anseele Monument Showing French Inscription — SP251

Designs: 90c+60c, View of Ghent. 1.35fr+1.15fr, Van Artevelde monument, Ghent. 3.15fr+1.85fr. Anseele Monument, Flemish inscription.

1948, June 21 *Perf. 14x13½*

B455	SP251	65c + 35c rose red	2.50	1.40
B456	SP251	90c + 60c gray	3.25	2.25
B457	SP251	1.35fr + 1.15fr hn brn	2.00	1.75
B458	SP251	3.15fr + 1.85fr brt bl	7.50	4.00
a.		Souv. sheet of 4, #B455-B458	65.00	30.00
		Nos. B455-B458 (4)	15.25	9.40

Issued to honor Edouard Anseele, statesman, founder of the Belgian Socialist Party.
No. B458a sold for 50fr.
For surcharges see Nos. 395-398.

Statue "The Unloader"
SP252

Underground Fighter
SP253

1948, Sept. 4 *Perf. 11½x11*

B460	SP252	10fr + 10fr gray grn	32.50	21.00
B461	SP253	10fr + 10fr red brn	19.00	13.00

The surtax was used toward erection of monuments at Antwerp and Liege.

Portrait Type of 1946 and

Double Barred Cross — SP254

Designs: 4fr+3.25fr, Isabella of Austria. 20fr+20fr, Archduke Albert of Austria.

1948, Dec. 15 Photo. *Perf. 13½x14*

B462	SP254	20c + 5c dk sl grn	40	22
B463	SP254	1.20fr + 30c mag	1.00	1.00
B464	SP254	1.75fr + 25c red	1.40	90

Engr. *Perf. 11½x11*

B465	SP236	4fr + 3.25fr ultra	8.00	9.50
B466	SP236	20fr + 20fr Prus grn	35.00	45.00
		Nos. B462-B466 (5)	45.80	56.62

The surtax was divided among several charities.

Souvenir Sheets

Rogier van der Weyden Paintings — SP255

Paintings by van der Weyden (No. B466A): 90c, Virgin and Child. 1.75fr, Christ on the Cross. 4fr, Mary Magdalene.
Paintings by Jordaens (No. B466B): 90c, Woman Reading. 1.75fr, The Flutist. 4fr, Old Woman Reading Letter.

1949, Apr. 1 Photo. *Perf. 11½*

B466A	SP255	Sheet of 3	90.00	85.00
c.		90c deep brown	27.50	25.00
d.		1.75fr deep rose lilac	27.50	25.00
e.		4fr dark violet blue	27.50	25.00
B466B	SP255	Sheet of 3	90.00	85.00
f.		90c dark violet	27.50	25.00
g.		1.75fr red	27.50	25.00
h.		4fr blue	27.50	25.00

The surtax went to various cultural and philanthropic organizations. Sheets sold for 50fr each.
Gum on Nos. B466A-B466B is irregularly applied.

Guido Gezelle — SP256

1949, Nov. 15 Photo. *Perf. 14x13½*

B467	SP256	1.75fr + 75c dk Prus grn	2.25	1.75

50th anniversary of the death of Guido Gezelle, poet. The surtax was for the Guido Gezelle Museum, Bruges.

Portrait Type of 1946 and

Arnica — SP257

Designs: 65c+10c, Sand grass. 90c+10c, Wood myrtle. 1.20fr+30c, Field poppy. 1.75fr+25c, Philip the Good. 3fr+1.50fr, Charles V. 4fr+2fr, Maria-Christina. 6fr+3fr, Charles of Lorraine. 8fr+4fr, Maria-Theresa.

1949, Dec. 20 Typo. *Perf. 13½x14*

B468	SP257	20c + 5c multi	35	42
B469	SP257	65c + 10c multi	90	85
B470	SP257	90c + 10c multi	1.40	1.10
B471	SP257	1.20fr + 30c multi	1.75	1.25

Engr. *Perf. 11½x11*

B472	SP236	1.75fr + 25c red org	1.00	60
B473	SP236	3fr + 1.50fr dp claret	5.50	5.00
B474	SP236	4fr + 2fr ultra	7.00	5.75
B475	SP236	6fr + 3fr choc	11.50	8.00
B476	SP236	8fr + 4fr dl grn	11.50	6.50
		Nos. B468-B476 (9)	40.90	29.47

The surtax was apportioned among several welfare organizations.

Arms of Belgium and Great Britain
SP258

British Memorial
SP260

Design: 2.50fr+50c, British tanks at Hertain.

Perf. 13½x14, 11½

1950, Mar. 15 Engr.

B477	SP258	80c + 20c green	1.50	1.10
B478	SP258	2.50fr + 50c red	5.00	4.50
B479	SP260	4fr + 2fr dp bl	9.25	7.50
		Nos. B477-B479 (3)	15.75	13.10

6th anniv. of the liberation of Belgian territory by the British army.

Hurdling SP261

Relay Race SP262

Designs: 90c+10c, Javelin throwing. 4fr+2fr, Pole vault. 8fr+4fr, Foot race.

Perf. 14x13½, 13½x14

1950, July 1 Engr. Unwmk.

B480	SP261	20c + 5c brt grn	65	60
B481	SP261	90c + 10c vio brn	2.75	1.50
B482	SP262	1.75fr + 25c car	3.25	1.50
a.		Souvenir sheet of 1	35.00	22.50
B483	SP261	4fr + 2fr lt bl	26.00	15.00
B484	SP261	8fr + 4fr dp grn	30.00	19.00
		Nos. B480-B484 (5)	62.65	37.60

Issued to publicize the European Athletic Games, Brussels, August 1950.

The margins of No. B482a were trimmed in April, 1951, and an overprint ("25 Francs pour le Fonds Sportif-25e Fofre Internationale Bruxelles") was added in red in French and in black in Flemish by a private committee. These pairs of altered sheets were sold at the Brussels Fair.

Gentian SP263

Sijsele Sanatorium SP264

Tombeek Sanatorium — SP265

Designs: 65c+10c, Cotton Grass. 90c+10c, Foxglove. 1.20fr+30c, Limonia. 4fr+2fr, Jauche Sanatorium.

1950, Dec. 20 Typo. *Perf. 14x13½*

B485	SP263	20c + 5c multi	70	35
B486	SP263	65c + 10c multi	1.40	70
B487	SP263	90c + 10c multi	1.50	90
B488	SP263	1.20fr + 30c multi	2.50	1.75

Perf. 11½

Engr.

Cross in Red

B489	SP264	1.75fr + 25c car	2.25	1.10
B490	SP264	4fr + 2fr blue	12.00	5.25
B491	SP265	8fr + 4fr bl grn	19.00	13.00
		Nos. B485-B491 (7)	39.35	23.05

The surtax was for tuberculosis prevention and other charitable purposes.

Chemist — SP266

Allegory of Peace — SP268

Colonial Instructor and Class — SP267

1951, Mar. 27 Unwmk.

B492	SP266	80c + 20c grn	1.10	1.00
B493	SP267	2.50fr + 50c vio brn	7.50	5.00
B494	SP268	4fr + 2fr dp bl	8.00	6.00
		Nos. B492-B494 (3)	16.60	12.00

Surtax for the reconstruction fund of the UNESCO.

Monument to Political Prisoners SP269

Fort of Breendonk SP270

Design: 8fr+4fr, Monument: profile of figure on pedestal.

1951, Aug. 20 Photo. *Perf. 11½*

B495	SP269	1.75fr + 25c blk brn	2.00	1.25
B496	SP270	4fr + 2fr bl & sl gray	16.00	9.25
B497	SP269	8fr + 4fr dk bl grn	20.00	11.50
		Nos. B495-B497 (3)	38.00	22.00

The surtax was for the erection of a national monument.

Queen Elisabeth — SP271

1951, Sept. 22

B498	SP271	90c + 10c grnsh gray	1.10	60
B499	SP271	1.75fr + 25c plum	1.40	1.00
B500	SP271	3fr + 1fr grn	13.00	6.50
B501	SP271	4fr + 2fr gray bl	14.00	8.50
B502	SP271	8fr + 4fr sep	18.00	10.00
		Nos. B498-B502 (5)	47.50	26.60

The surtax was for the Queen Elisabeth Medical Foundation.

Cross, Sun Rays and Dragon SP272

Beersel Castle SP273

Horst Castle — SP274

Castles: 4fr+2fr, Lavaux St. Anne. 8fr+4fr, Veves.

1951, Dec. 17 Engr. Unwmk.

B503	SP272	20c + 5c red	18	16
B504	SP272	65c + 10c dp ultra	70	45
B505	SP272	90c + 10c sepia	75	60
B506	SP272	1.20fr + 30c rose vio	95	65
B507	SP273	1.75fr + 75c red brn	1.45	1.10
B508	SP274	3fr + 1fr yel grn	10.00	5.50
B509	SP273	4fr + 2fr bl	12.50	6.50
B510	SP274	8fr + 4fr gray	17.00	8.50
		Nos. B503-B510 (8)	43.53	23.46

The surtax was for anti-tuberculosis work.

See Nos. B523-B526, B547-B550.

Main Altar SP275

Basilica of the Sacred Heart Koekelberg SP276

Procession Bearing Relics of St. Albert of Louvain — SP277

1952, Mar. 1 Photo. *Perf. 11½*

B511	SP275	1.75fr + 25c blk brn	1.25	90
B512	SP276	4fr + 2fr indigo	9.50	6.50

Engr.

B513	SP277	8fr + 4fr vio brn	12.00	8.50
a.		Souv. sheet, #B511-B513	125.00	72.50
		Nos. B511-B513 (3)	22.75	15.90

25th anniv. of the Cardinalate of J. E. Van Roey, Primate of Belgium. The surtax was for the Basilica. No. B513a sold for 30fr.

Beaulieu Castle, Malines SP278

August Vermeylen SP279

1952, May 14 Engr.

Laid Paper

B514	SP278	40fr + 10fr lt grnsh bl	110.00	140.00

Issued on the occasion of the 13th Universal Postal Union Congress, Brussels, 1952.

Perf. 11½

1952, Oct. 24 Unwmk. Photo.

Portraits: 80c+40c, Karel Van de Woestijne. 90c+45c, Charles de Coster. 1.75fr+75c, M. Maeterlinck. 4fr+2fr, Emile Verhaeren. 8fr+4fr, Hendrik Conscience.

B515	SP279	65c + 30c pur	1.65	80
B516	SP279	80c + 40c dk grn	3.25	1.00
B517	SP279	90c + 45c sep	2.50	1.25
B518	SP279	1.75fr + 75c cer	3.25	1.40
B519	SP279	4fr + 2fr bl vio	26.00	15.00
B520	SP279	8fr + 4fr dk brn	26.00	17.00
		Nos. B515-B520 (6)	62.65	36.45

1952, Nov. 15

Portraits: 4fr, Emile Verhaeren. 8fr, Hendrik Conscience.

B521	SP279	4fr (+ 9fr) blue	70.00	85.00
B522	SP279	8fr (+ 9fr) dk car rose	70.00	85.00

On Nos. B521-B522, the denomination is repeated at either side of the stamp. The surtax is expressed on se-tenant labels bearing quotations of Verhaeren (in French) and Conscience (in Flemish). Value is for stamp with label.

A 9-line black overprint was privately applied to these labels: "Conference Internationale de la Musique Bruxelles UNESCO International Music Conference Brussels 1953*"

Type of 1951 Dated "1952," and

Arms of Malmédy — SP281

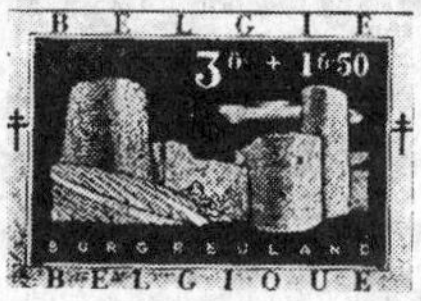

Castle Ruins, Burgreuland SP282

Designs: 4fr+2fr, Vesdre Dam, Eupen. 8fr+4fr, St. Vitus, patron saint of Saint-Vith.

1952, Dec. 15 Engr.

B523	SP272	20c + 5c red brn	38	30
B524	SP272	80c + 20c grn	75	45
B525	SP272	1.20fr + 30c lil rose	1.50	70
B526	SP272	1.50fr + 50c ol brn	1.50	70
B527	SP281	2fr + 75c car	2.50	1.65
B528	SP282	3fr + 1.50fr choc	11.50	6.50
B529	SP281	4fr + 2fr bl	9.75	5.75
B530	SP281	8fr + 4fr vio brn	17.00	8.50
		Nos. B523-B530 (8)	44.88	24.55

The surtax on Nos. B523-B530 was for anti-tuberculosis and other charitable works.

Walthère Dewé SP283

Princess Josephine-Charlotte SP284

1953, Feb. 16 Photo.

B531	SP283	2fr + 1fr brn car	2.50	2.00

The surtax was for the construction of a memorial to Walthère Dewé, Underground leader in World War II.

1953, Mar. 14 Cross in Red

B532	SP284	80c + 20c ol grn	90	65
B533	SP284	1.20fr + 30c brn	1.25	80
B534	SP284	2fr + 50c rose lake	90	1.10
a.		Booklet pane of 8	90.00	90.00
B535	SP284	2.50fr + 50c crim	10.50	6.00
B536	SP284	4fr + 1fr brt bi	7.00	4.75
B537	SP284	5fr + 2fr sl grn	8.50	6.00
		Nos. B532-B537 (6)	29.05	19.30

The surtax was for the Belgian Red Cross.

The selvage of No. B534a is inscribed in French or Dutch. The value is for the French.

Boats at Dock — SP285

Bridge and Citadel, Namur — SP286

Allegory — SP287

Designs: 1.20fr+30c, Bridge at Bouillon. 2fr+50c, Antwerp waterfront. 4fr+2fr, Wharf at Ghent. 8fr+4fr, Meuse River at Freyr.

1953, June 22 Unwmk. *Perf. 11½*

B538 SP285	80c + 20c green	70	65
B539 SP285	1.20fr + 30c redsh brn	1.40	1.10
B540 SP285	2fr + 50c sepia	1.75	1.50
B541 SP286	2.50fr + 50c dp mag	8.75	6.50
B542 SP286	4fr + 2fr vio bl	13.00	6.50
B543 SP286	8fr + 4fr gray blk	16.00	6.50
	Nos. B538-B543 (6)	41.60	22.75

The surtax was used to promote tourism in the Ardenne-Meuse region and for various cultural works.

1953, Oct. 26 Engr.

B544 SP287	80c + 20c green	3.25	2.75
B545 SP287	2.50fr + 1fr rose car	30.00	27.50
B546 SP287	4fr + 1.50fr blue	35.00	35.00
	Nos. B544-B546 (3)	68.25	65.25

The surtax was for the European Bureau of Childhood and Youth.

Type of 1951 Dated "1953," and

Ernest Malvoz — SP288

Robert Koch — SP289

Portraits: 3fr+1.50fr, Carlo Forlanini. 4fr+2fr, Leon Charles Albert Calmette.

1953, Dec. 15

B547 SP272	20c + 5c blue	32	35
B548 SP272	80c + 20c rose vio	85	45
B549 SP272	1.20fr + 30c choc	90	65
B550 SP272	1.50fr + 50c dk gray	1.40	80
B551 SP288	2fr + 75c dk grn	2.25	1.25
B552 SP288	3fr + 1.50fr dk red	10.00	6.50
B553 SP288	4fr + 2fr ultra	8.50	5.50
B554 SP289	8fr + 4fr choc	13.00	7.75
	Nos. B547-B554 (8)	37.22	23.25

The surtax was for anti-tuberculosis and other charitable works.

King Albert I Statue — SP290

Albert I Monument, Namur SP291

Design: 9fr+4.50fr, Cliffs of Marche-les-Dames.

1954, Feb. 17 Photo.

B555 SP290	2fr + 50c chnt brn	1.90	1.25
B556 SP291	4fr + 2fr blue	11.00	7.75
B557 SP290	9fr + 4.50fr ol blk	15.00	8.25
	Nos. B555-B557 (3)	27.90	17.25

20th anniv. of the death of King Albert I. The surtax aided in the erection of the monument pictured on #B556.

Political Prisoners' Monument — SP292

Camp and Fort, Breendonk SP293

Design: 9fr+4.50fr, Political prisoners' monument (profile).

1954, Apr. 1 Unwmk. *Perf. 11½*

B558 SP292	2fr + 1fr red	9.00	5.50
B559 SP293	4fr + 2fr dk brn	20.00	13.00
B560 SP292	9fr + 4.50fr ol grn	22.50	13.00
	Nos. B558-B560 (3)	51.50	31.50

The surtax was used toward the creation of a monument to political prisoners.

Gatehouse and Gateway SP294

Nuns in Courtyard — SP295

Our Lady of the Vine — SP296

Designs: 2fr+1fr, Swans in stream. 7fr+3.50fr Nuns at well. 8fr+4fr, Statue above door.

1954, May 15

B561 SP294	80c + 20c dk bl grn	90	85
B562 SP294	2fr + 1fr crim	9.25	1.50
B563 SP295	4fr + 2fr vio	13.00	9.25
B564 SP295	7fr + 3.50fr lil rose	27.50	22.50
B565 SP295	8fr + 4fr brn	26.00	19.00
B566 SP296	9fr + 4.50fr gray bl	45.00	30.00
	Nos. B561-B566 (6)	121.65	83.10

The surtax was for the Friends of the Beguinage of Bruges.

Child's Head SP297

"The Blind Man and the Paralytic," by Antoine Carte SP298

1954, Dec. 1 Engr.

B567 SP297	20c + 5c dk grn	45	38
B568 SP297	80c + 20c dk gray	80	60
B569 SP297	1.20fr + 30c org brn	1.25	75
B570 SP297	1.50fr + 50c pur	1.50	1.25
B571 SP298	2fr + 75c rose car	6.00	2.75
B572 SP298	4fr + 1fr brt bl	13.00	7.00
	Nos. B567-B572 (6)	23.00	12.73

The surtax was for anti-tuberculosis work.

Ernest Solvay SP299

Jean-Jacques Dony — SP300

Portraits: 1.20fr+30c, Egide Walschaerts. 25fr+50c, Leo H. Baekeland. 3fr+1fr, Jean-Etienne Lenoir. 4fr+2fr, Emile Fourcault and Emile Gobbe.

Perf. 11½

1955, Oct. 22 Unwmk. Photo.

B573 SP299	20c + 5c brn & dk brn	35	30
B574 SP300	80c + 20c vio	90	45
B575 SP299	1.20fr + 30c ind	1.00	60
B576 SP300	2fr + 50c dp car	3.50	2.00
B577 SP300	3fr + 1fr dk grn	10.50	5.00
B578 SP299	4fr + 2fr brn	10.50	5.00
	Nos. B573-B578 (6)	26.75	13.35

Issued in honor of Belgian scientists.
The surtax was for the benefit of various cultural organizations.

"The Joys of Spring" by E. Canneel — SP301

Einar Holböll — SP302

Portraits: 4fr+2fr, John D. Rockefeller. 8fr+4fr, Sir Robert W. Philip.

1955, Dec. 5 Unwmk. *Perf. 11½*

B579 SP301	20c + 5c red lil	50	20
B580 SP301	80c + 20c grn	70	45
B581 SP301	1.20fr + 30c redsh brn	95	60
B582 SP301	1.50fr + 50c vio bl	1.00	75
B583 SP302	2fr + 50c car	6.50	3.25
B584 SP302	4fr + 2fr ultra	13.00	7.75
B585 SP302	8fr + 4fr ol gray	16.00	9.00
	Nos. B579-B585 (7)	38.65	22.00

The surtax was for anti-tuberculosis work.

Palace of Charles of Lorraine — SP303

Queen Elisabeth and Sonata by Mozart — SP304

Design: 2fr+1fr, Mozart at age 7.

1956, Mar. 5 Engr.

B586 SP303	80c + 20c steel bl	75	1.00
B587 SP303	2fr + 1fr rose lake	3.00	3.00
B588 SP304	4fr + 2fr dull pur	5.00	3.75
	Nos. B586-B588 (3)	8.75	7.75

200th anniversary of the birth of Wolfgang Amadeus Mozart, composer.
The surtax was for the benefit of the Pro-Mozart Committee in Belgium.

Queen Elisabeth — SP305

1956, Aug. 16 Photo.

B589 SP305	80c + 20c slate grn	90	1.00
B590 SP305	2fr + 1fr deep plum	2.50	1.50
B591 SP305	4fr + 2fr brown	3.50	2.50
	Nos. B589-B591 (3)	6.90	5.00

Issued in honor of the 80th birthday of Queen Elisabeth. The surtax went to the Queen Elisabeth Foundation. See No. 659.

Ship with Cross SP306

Infant on Scales SP307

Rehabilitation — SP308

Design: 4fr+2fr, X-Ray examination.

1956, Dec. 17 Engr.

B592 SP306	20c + 5c redsh brn	32	28
B593 SP306	80c + 20c grn	65	55
B594 SP306	1.20fr + 30c dl lil	80	52
B595 SP306	1.5fr + 50c lt sl bl	85	80
B596 SP307	2fr + 50c ol grn	2.00	1.40
B597 SP307	4fr + 2fr dl pur	10.00	5.75
B598 SP308	8fr + 4fr dp car	10.00	6.50
	Nos. B592-B598 (7)	24.62	15.80

The surtax was for anti-tuberculosis work.

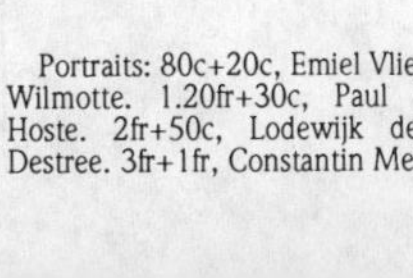

Charles Plisnier and Albrecht Rodenbach SP309

Portraits: 80c+20c, Emiel Vliebergh and Maurice Wilmotte. 1.20fr+30c, Paul Pastur and Julius Hoste. 2fr+50c, Lodewijk de Raet and Jules Destree. 3fr+1fr, Constantin Meunier and Constant

Permeke. 4fr+2fr, Lieven Gevaert and Edouard Empain.

Perf. 11½

1957, June 8 Unwmk. Photo.

B599	SP309	20c + 5c brt vio	35	28
B600	SP309	80c + 20c lt red brn	55	32
B601	SP309	1.20f + 30c blk brn	65	50
B602	SP309	2fr + 50c claret	1.65	85
B603	SP309	3fr + 1fr dk ol grn	2.25	1.65
B604	SP309	4fr + 2fr vio bl	3.25	2.50
		Nos. B599-B604 (6)	8.70	6.10

The surtax was for the benefit of various cultural organizations.

Dogs and Antarctic Camp SP310

1957, Oct. 18 Engr. *Perf. 11½*

B605	SP310	5fr + 2.50fr gray, org & vio brn	2.50	3.75
a.		Sheet of 4, #B605b	120.00	130.00
b.		Blue, slate & red brown	25.00	40.00

Surtax for Belgian Antarctic Expedition, 1957-58.

Gen. Patton's Grave and Flag — SP311

Gen. George S. Patton, Jr. — SP312

Designs: 2.50fr+50c, Memorial, Bastogne. 3fr+1fr, Gen. Patton decorating Brig. Gen. Anthony C. McAuliffe. 6fr+3fr, Tanks of 1918 and 1944.

1957, Oct. 28 Photo.

Size: 36x25mm, 25x36mm

B606	SP311	1fr + 50c dk gray	1.10	75
B607	SP311	2.50fr + 50c ol grn	1.50	1.40
B608	SP311	3fr + 1fr red brn	2.25	1.50
B609	SP312	5fr + 2.50fr grysh bl	5.25	4.25

Size: 53x35mm

B610	SP311	6fr + 3fr pale brn car	8.00	5.50
		Nos. B606-B610 (5)	18.10	13.40

The surtax was for the General Patton Memorial Committee and Patriotic Societies.

Adolphe Max — SP313

1957, Nov. 10 Engr.

B611	SP313	2.50fr + 1fr ultra	1.40	3.25

18th anniversary of the death of Adolphe Max, mayor of Brussels. The surtax was for the national "Adolphe Max" fund.

"Chinels," Fosses SP314

"Op Signoorken," Malines SP315

Infanta Isabella Shooting Crossbow SP316

Legends: 1.50fr+50c, St. Remacle and the wolf. 2fr+1fr, Longman and the pea soup. 5fr+2fr, The Virgin with Inkwell, vert. 6fr+2.50fr, "Gilles" (clowns), Binche.

1957, Dec. 14 Engr. & Photo.

B612	SP314	30c + 20c pur & org yel	22	30
B613	SP315	1fr + 50c brn & lt bl	40	30
B614	SP314	1.50fr + 50c gray & red	85	50
B615	SP315	2fr + 1fr gray & brt grn	1.00	1.00
B616	SP316	2.50fr + 1fr bl grn & lil	1.10	90
B617	SP316	5fr + 2fr bl & dk gray	3.00	2.25
B618	SP316	6fr + 2.50fr vio brn & red org	4.00	3.25
		Nos. B612-B618 (7)	10.57	8.50

The surtax was for anti-tuberculosis work. See Nos. B631-B637.

Benelux Gate — SP317

Designs: 1fr+50c, Civil Engineering Pavilion. 1.50fr+50c, Ruanda-Urundi Pavilion. 2.50fr+1fr, Belgium 1900. 3fr+1.50fr, Atomium. 5fr+3fr, Telexpo Pavilion.

Perf. 11½

1958, Apr. 15 Unwmk. Engr.

Size: 35½x24½mm

B619	SP317	30c + 20c multi	15	15
B620	SP317	1fr + 50c multi	15	15
B621	SP317	1.50fr + 50c multi	25	24
B622	SP317	2.50fr + 1fr multi	38	45
B623	SP317	3fr + 1.50fr multi	85	50

Size: 49x33mm

B624	SP317	5fr + 3fr multi	1.00	50
		Nos. B619-B624 (6)	2.78	1.99

World's Fair, Brussels, Apr. 17-Oct. 19.

Marguerite van Eyck by Jan van Eyck — SP318

Christ Carrying Cross, by Hieronymus Bosch — SP319

Paintings: 1.50fr+50c, St. Donatien, Jan Gossart. 2.50fr+1fr, Self-portrait, Lambert Lombard. 3fr+1.50fr, The Rower, James Ensor. 5fr+3fr, Henriette, Henri Evenepoel.

1958, Oct. 30 Photo. *Perf. 11½*

Various Frames in Ocher and Brown

B625	SP318	30c + 20c dk ol grn	24	30
B626	SP319	1fr + 50c mar	75	70
B627	SP318	1.50fr + 50c vio bl	1.00	75
B628	SP318	2.50fr + 1fr dk brn	2.00	1.40
B629	SP319	3fr + 1.50fr dl red	2.50	2.00
B630	SP318	5fr + 3fr brt bl	4.75	5.00
		Nos. B625-B630 (6)	11.24	10.15

The surtax was for the benefit of various cultural organizations.

Type of 1957

Legends: 40c+10c, Elizabeth, Countess of Hoogstraten. 1fr+50c, Jean de Nivelles. 1.50fr+50c, St. Evermare play, Russon. 2fr+1fr, The Penitents of Furnes. 2.50fr+1fr, Manger and "Pax." 5fr+2fr, Sambre-Meuse procession. 6fr+2.50fr, Our Lady of Peace and "Pax," vert.

Engraved and Photogravure

1958, Dec. 6 Unwmk. *Perf. 11½*

B631	SP314	40c + 10 ultra & brt grn	30	20
B632	SP315	1fr + 50 gray brn & org	42	28
B633	SP315	1.50fr + 50c cl & brt grn	60	35
B634	SP314	2fr + 1fr brn & red	75	50
B635	SP316	2.50fr + 1fr vio brn & bl grn	2.50	1.90
B636	SP316	5fr + 2fr cl & bl	3.75	3.00
B637	SP316	6fr + 2.50fr bl & rose red	4.75	4.50
		Nos. B631-B637 (7)	13.07	10.73

The surtax was for anti-tuberculosis work.

"Europe of the Heart" SP320

1959, Feb. 25 Photo. Unwmk.

B638	SP320	1fr + 50c red lil	90	45
B639	SP320	2.50fr + 1fr dk grn	1.50	1.25
B640	SP320	5fr + 2.50fr dp brn	2.00	1.50
		Nos. B638-B640 (3)	4.40	3.20

The surtax was for aid for displaced persons.

Allegory of Blood Transfusion — SP321

Henri Dunant and Battlefield at Solferino — SP322

Design: 2.50fr+1fr, 3fr+1.50fr, Red Cross, broken sword and drop of blood, horiz.

1959, June 10 Photo. *Perf. 11½*

B641	SP321	40c + 10c bl gray & car	50	30
B642	SP321	1fr + 50c brn & car	85	45
B643	SP321	1.50fr + 50c dl vio & car	1.00	60
B644	SP321	2.50fr + 1fr sl grn & car	1.40	1.10
B645	SP321	3fr + 1.50fr vio bl & car	3.50	2.50
B646	SP322	5fr + 3fr dk brn & car	5.50	3.25
		Nos. B641-B646 (6)	12.75	8.20

Cent. of the Intl. Red Cross idea. Surtax for the Red Cross and patriotic organizations.

Philip the Good — SP323

Arms of Philip the Good SP324

Designs: 1fr+50c, Charles the Bold. 1.50fr+50c, Emperor Maximilian of Austria. 2.50fr+1fr, Philip the Fair. 3fr+1.50fr, Charles V. Portraits from miniatures by Simon Bening (c. 1483-1561).

1959, July 4 Engr.

B647	SP323	40c + 10c multi	45	30
B648	SP323	1fr + 50c multi	75	45
B649	SP323	1.50fr + 50c multi	90	60
B650	SP323	2.50fr + 1fr multi	1.25	1.10
B651	SP323	3fr + 1.50fr multi	3.00	2.50
B652	SP324	5fr + 3fr multi	5.00	3.25
		Nos. B647-B652 (6)	11.35	8.20

The surtax was for the Royal Library, Brussels. Portraits show Grand Masters of the Order of the Golden Fleece.

Whale, Antwerp SP325

Carnival, Stavelot SP326

Designs: 1fr+50c, Dragon, Mons. 2fr+50c, Prince Carnival, Eupen. 3fr+1fr, Jester and cats, Ypres. 6fr+2fr, Holy Family, horiz. 7fr+3fr, Madonna, Liége, horiz.

Engraved and Photogravure

1959, Dec. 5 *Perf. 11½*

B653	SP325	40c + 10c cit, Prus bl & red	45	30
B654	SP325	1fr + 50c ol & grn	70	45
B655	SP325	2fr + 50c lt brn, org & cl	52	30
B656	SP326	2.50fr + 1fr gray, pur & ultra	75	45
B657	SP326	3fr + 1fr gray, mar & yel	1.75	90
B658	SP326	6fr + 2fr ol, brt bl & hn brn	3.25	2.00
B659	SP326	7fr + 3fr chlky bl & org yel	4.75	3.00
		Nos. B653-B659 (7)	12.17	7.40

The surtax was for anti-tuberculosis work.

Child Refugee — SP327

Designs: 3fr+1.50fr, Man. 6fr+3fr, Woman.

1960, Apr. 7 — **Engr.**

B660 SP327	40c + 10c rose claret	18	15
B661 SP327	3fr + 1.50fr gray brn	70	45
B662 SP327	6fr + 3fr dk bl	1.90	1.00
a.	Souvenir sheet of 3	45.00	45.00
	Nos. B660-B662 (3)	2.78	1.60

Issued to publicize World Refugee Year, July 1, 1959-June 30, 1960.

No. B662a contains Nos. B660-B662 with colors changed: 40c+10c, dull purple; 3fr+1.50fr, red brown; 6fr+3fr, henna brown.

Parachutists and Plane SP328

Designs: 2fr+50c, 2.50fr+1fr, Parachutists coming in for landing, vert 3fr+1fr, 6fr+2fr, Parachutist walking with parachute.

Photogravure and Engraved

1960, June 13 — *Perf. 11½*

B663 SP328	40c + 10c lt ultra & blk	15	15
B664 SP328	1fr + 50c bl & blk	60	60
B665 SP328	2fr + 50c bl, blk & ol	1.65	1.25
B666 SP328	2.50fr + 1fr grnsh bl, blk & gray ol	2.00	2.00
B667 SP328	3fr + 1fr bl, blk & sl grn	2.00	2.00
B668 SP328	6fr + 2fr lt vio bl, blk & ol	4.00	3.75
	Nos. B663-B668 (6)	10.40	9.75

The surtax was for various patriotic and cultural organizations.

Mother and Child, Planes and Rainbow SP329

Designs: 40c+10c, Brussels Airport, planes and rainbow. 6fr+3fr, Rainbow connecting Congo and Belgium, and planes, vert

Perf. 11½

1960, Aug. 3 — **Unwmk.** — **Photo.**

Size: 35x24mm

B669 SP329	40c + 10c grnsh blue	16	15
B670 SP329	3fr + 1.50fr brt red	2.75	1.90

Size: 35x52mm

B671 SP329	6fr + 3fr violet	4.25	2.50
	Nos. B669-B671 (3)	7.16	4.55

The surtax was for refugees from Congo.

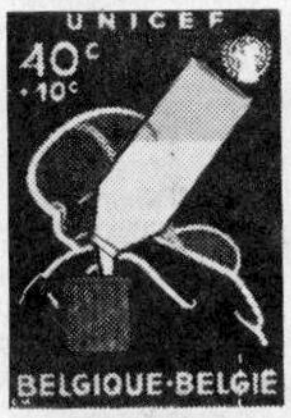

Infant, Milk Bottle and Mug — SP330

UNICEF: 1fr+50c, Nurse and children of 3 races. 2fr+50c, Refugee woman carrying gift clothes. 2.50fr+1fr, Negro nurse weighing infant. 3fr+1fr, Children of various races dancing. 6fr+2fr, Refugee boys.

Photogravure and Engraved

1960, Oct. 8 — *Perf. 11½*

B672 SP330	40c + 10c gldn brn, yel & bl grn	15	15
B673 SP330	1fr + 50c ol gray, mar & slate	1.10	70
B674 SP330	2fr + 50c vio, pale brn & brt grn	1.25	95
B675 SP330	2.50fr + 1fr dk red, sep & lt bl	1.50	1.25
B676 SP330	3fr + 1fr bl grn, red org & dl vio	80	80
B677 SP330	6fr + 2fr ultra, emer & brn	3.00	2.75
	Nos. B672-B677 (6)	7.80	6.60

Tapestry SP331

Belgian handicrafts: 1fr+50c, Cut crystal vases, vert. 2fr+50c, Lace, vert. 2.50fr+1fr, Metal plate & jug. 3fr+1fr, Diamonds. 6fr+2fr, Ceramics.

1960, Dec. 5 — *Perf. 11½*

B678 SP331	40c + 10c bl, bis & brn	15	15
B679 SP331	1fr + 50c ind & org brn	1.10	1.10
B680 SP331	2fr + 50c dk red brn, blk & cit	2.00	1.65
B681 SP331	2.50fr + 1fr choc & yel	2.50	2.50
B682 SP331	3fr + 1fr org brn, blk & ultra	1.25	1.25
B683 SP331	6fr + 2fr dp blk & yel	5.00	4.00
	Nos. B678-B683 (6)	12.00	10.65

The surtax was for anti-tuberculosis work.

Jacob Kats and Abbe Nicolas Pietkin SP332

Portraits: 1fr+50c, Albert Mockel and J. F. Willems. 2fr+50c, Jan van Rijswijck and Xavier M. Neujean. 2.50fr+1fr, Joseph Demarteau and A. Van de Perre. 3fr+1fr, Canon Jan-Baptist David and Albert du Bois. 6fr+2fr, Henri Vieuxtemps and Willem de Mol.

1961, Apr. 22 — **Unwmk.** — *Perf. 11½*

Portraits in Gray Brown

B684 SP332	40c + 10c ver & mar	15	15
B685 SP332	1fr + 50c bis brn & mar	1.10	1.00
B686 SP332	2fr + 50c yel & crim	1.50	1.40
B687 SP332	2.50fr + 1fr pale cit & dk grn	2.25	1.50
B688 SP332	3fr + 1fr lt & dk bl	2.25	2.25
B689 SP332	6fr + 2fr lil & ultra	4.00	4.00
	Nos. B684-B689 (6)	11.25	10.30

The surtax was for the benefit of various cultural organizations.

White Rhinoceros SP333

Antonius Cardinal Perrenot de Granvelle SP334

Animals: 1fr+50c, Przewalski horses. 2fr+50c, Okapi. 2.50fr+1fr, Giraffe, horiz. 3fr+1fr, Lesser panda, horiz. 6fr+2fr, European elk, horiz.

Perf. 11½

1961, June 5 — **Unwmk.** — **Photo.**

B690 SP333	40c + 10c bis brn & dk brn	15	15
B691 SP333	1fr + 50c gray & brn	90	90
B692 SP333	2fr + 50c dp rose & blk	1.25	1.10
B693 SP333	2.50fr + 1fr red org & brn	1.00	90
B694 SP333	3fr + 1fr org & brn	90	90
B695 SP333	6fr + 2fr bl & bis brn	2.25	1.40
	Nos. B690-B695 (6)	6.45	5.35

The surtax was for various philanthropic organizations.

1961, July 29 — **Engr.**

Designs: 3fr+1.50fr, Arms of Cardinal de Granvelle. 6fr+3fr, Tower and crosier, symbolic of collaboration between Malines and the Archbishopric.

B696 SP334	40c + 10c magenta, car & brn	15	15
B697 SP334	3fr + 1.50fr multi	90	60
B698 SP334	6fr + 3fr mag pur & bis	1.75	1.50
	Nos. B696-B698 (3)	2.80	2.25

400th anniv. of Malines as an Archbishopric.

Mother and Child by Pierre Paulus — SP335

Castle of the Counts of Male — SP336

Plaintings: 1fr+50c, Mother Love, Francois-Joseph Navez. 2fr+50c, Motherhood, Constant Permeke. 2.50fr+1fr, Madonna and Child, Rogier van der Weyden. 3fr+1fr, Madonna with Apple, Hans Memling. 6fr+2fr, Madonna of the Forget-me-not, Peter Paul Rubens.

1961, Dec. 2 — **Photo.** — *Perf. 11½*

Gold Frame

B699 SP335	40c + 10c dp brn	15	15
B700 SP335	1fr + 50c brt bl	40	30
B701 SP335	2fr + 50c rose red	60	45
B702 SP335	2.50fr + 1fr mag	90	70
B703 SP335	3fr + 1fr vio bl	1.00	85
B704 SP335	6fr + 2fr dk sl grn	1.75	1.50
	Nos. B699-B704 (6)	4.80	3.95

The surtax was for anti-tuberculosis work.

1962, Mar. 12 — **Engr.** — *Perf. 11½*

Designs: 90c+10c, Royal library, horiz. 1fr+50c, Church of Our Lady, Tongres. 2fr+50c, Collegiate Church, Soignies (horiz.). 2.50fr+1fr, Church of Our Lady, Malines. 3fr+1fr, St. Denis Abbey, Broqueroi. 6fr+2fr, Cloth Hall, Ypres, horiz.

B705 SP336	40c + 10c brt grn	15	15
B706 SP336	90c + 10c lil rose	22	22
B707 SP336	1fr + 50c dl vio	45	45
B708 SP336	2fr + 50c vio	65	65
B709 SP336	2.50fr + 1fr red brn	95	95
B710 SP336	3fr + 1fr bl grn	95	95
B711 SP336	6fr + 2fr car rose	1.50	1.40
	Nos. B705-B711 (7)	4.87	4.77

The surtax was for various cultural and philanthropic organizations.

Andean Cock of the Rock — SP337

Handicapped Child — SP338

Birds: 1fr+50c, Red lory. 2fr+50c, Guinea touraco. 2.50fr+1fr, Keel-billed toucan. 3fr+1fr, Great bird of paradise. 6fr+2fr, Congolese peacock.

Engraved and Photogravure

1962, June 23 — **Unwmk.** — *Perf. 11½*

B712 SP337	40c + 10c multi	15	15
B713 SP337	1fr + 50c multi	45	38
B714 SP337	2fr + 50c multi	52	45
B715 SP337	2.50fr + 1fr multi	60	52
B716 SP337	3fr + 1fr multi	1.25	1.10
B717 SP337	6fr + 2fr multi	2.25	2.00
	Nos. B712-B717 (6)	5.22	4.60

The surtax was for various philanthropic organizations.

1962, Sept. 22 — **Photo.**

Handicapped Children: 40c+10c, Reading Braille. 2fr+50c, Deaf-mute girl with earphones and electronic equipment, horiz. 2.50fr+1fr, Child with ball (cerebral palsy). 3fr+1fr, Girl with crutches (polio). 6fr+2fr, Sitting boys playing ball, horiz.

B718 SP338	40c + 10c choc	15	15
B719 SP338	1fr + 50c rose red	32	30
B720 SP338	2fr + 50c brt lil	65	55
B721 SP338	2.50fr + 1fr dl grn	70	65
B722 SP338	3fr + 1fr dk bl	90	85
B723 SP338	6fr + 2fr dk brn	1.65	1.25
	Nos. B718-B723 (6)	4.37	3.75

The surtax was for various institutions for handicapped children.

Queen Louise-Marie — SP339

Belgian Queens: No. B725, like No. B724 with "ML" initials. 1fr+50c, Marie-Henriette. 2fr+1fr, Elisabeth. 3fr+1.50fr, Astrid. 8fr+2.50fr, Fabiola.

1962, Dec. 8 — **Photo. & Engr.**

Gray, Black & Gold

B724 SP339	40c + 10c ("L")	15	15
B725 SP339	40c + 10c ("ML")	15	15
B726 SP339	1fr + 50c	52	52
B727 SP339	2fr + 1fr	90	90
B728 SP339	3fr + 1.50fr	1.00	90
B729 SP339	8fr + 2.50fr	1.50	1.10
	Nos. B724-B729 (6)	4.22	3.72

The surtax was for anti-tuberculosis work.

British War Memorial (Porte de Menin), Ypres — SP340

1962, Dec. 26 — **Engr.** — *Perf. 11½*

B730 SP340	1fr + 50c multi	65	65

Millennium of the city of Ypres. Issued in sheets of eight.

Peace Bell Ringing over Globe SP341

The Sower by Brueghel SP342

Engraved and Photogravure

1963, Feb. 18 — **Unwmk.** — *Perf. 11½*

B731 SP341	3fr + 1.50fr blk, bl, org & grn	1.75	1.75
a.	Sheet of 4	8.00	8.00
B732 SP341	6fr + 3fr blk, brn & org	1.10	1.10

The surtax was for the installation of the Peace Bell (Bourdon de la Paix) at Koekelberg Basilica and for the benefit of various cultural organizations.

No. B731 was issued in sheets of 4. No. B732 was issued in sheets of 30.

1963, Mar. 21 — *Perf. 11½*

Designs: 3fr+1fr, The Harvest, by Brueghel, horiz. 6fr+2fr, "Bread," by Anton Carte, horiz.

B733 SP342	2fr + 1fr grn, ocher & blk	20	20
B734 SP342	3fr + 1fr red lil, ocher & blk	52	45
B735 SP342	6fr + 2fr red brn, cit & blk	75	60
	Nos. B733-B735 (3)	1.47	1.25

FAO "Freedom from Hunger" campaign.

Speed Racing — SP343

Designs: 2fr+1fr, Bicyclists at check point, horiz. 3fr+1.50fr, Team racing, horiz. 6fr+3fr, Pace setters.

Perf. 11½

1963, July 13 Unwmk. Engr.

B736	SP343 1fr + 50c multi	15	15
B737	SP343 2fr + 1fr bl, car, blk & ol gray	25	25
B738	SP343 3fr + 1.50fr multi	42	42
B739	SP343 6fr + 3fr multi	60	60
	Nos. B736-B739 (4)	1.42	1.42

80th anniversary of the founding of the Belgian Bicycle League. The surtax was for athletes at the 1964 Olympic Games.

Princess Paola with Princess Astrid — SP344

Prince Albert and Family SP345

Designs: 40c+10c, Prince Philippe. 2fr+50c, Princess Astrid. 2.50fr+1fr, Princess Paola. 6fr+2fr, Prince Albert.

1963, Sept. 28 Photo.

B740	SP344 40c + 10c	15	15
B741	SP344 1fr + 50c	30	30
B742	SP344 2fr + 50c	38	38
B743	SP344 2.50fr + 1fr	45	45
B744	SP345 3fr + 1fr	45	45
B745	SP345 3fr + 1fr	1.40	1.40
a.	Booklet pane of 8	17.00	17.00
B746	SP344 6fr + 2fr	80	80
	Nos. B740-B746 (7)	3.93	3.93

Cent. of the Intl. Red Cross. No. B745 issued in booklet panes of 8, which are in two forms: French and Flemish inscriptions in top and bottom margins transposed.

Daughter of Balthazar Gerbier, Painted by Rubens — SP346

Jesus, St. John and Cherubs by Rubens — SP347

Portraits (Rubens' sons): 1fr+40c, Nicolas, 2 yrs. old. 2fr+50c, Franz. 2.50fr+1fr, Nicolas, 6 yrs. old. 3fr+1fr, Albert.

Photogravure and Engraved

1963, Dec. 7 Unwmk. *Perf. 11½*

B747	SP346 50c + 10c	15	15
B748	SP346 1fr + 40c	15	15
B749	SP346 2fr + 50c	28	28
B750	SP346 2.50fr + 1fr	55	55
B751	SP346 3fr + 1fr	45	45
B752	SP347 6fr + 2fr	60	60
	Nos. B747-B752 (6)	2.18	2.18

The surtax was for anti-tuberculosis work. See No. B771.

John Quincy Adams and Lord Gambier Signing Treaty of Ghent, by Amédée Forestier — SP348

1964, May 16 Photo. *Perf. 11½*

B753	SP348 6fr + 3fr dk blue	75	75

150th anniv. of the signing of the Treaty of Ghent between the US and Great Britain, Dec. 24, 1814.

Philip van Marnix — SP349

Portraits: 3fr+1.50fr, Ida de Bure Calvin. 6fr+3fr, Jacob Jordaens.

1964, May 30 Engr.

B754	SP349 1fr + 50c blue gray	15	15
B755	SP349 3fr + 1.50fr rose pink	25	25
B756	SP349 6fr + 3fr redsh brn	45	45
	Nos. B754-B756 (3)	85	85

Issued to honor Protestantism in Belgium. The surtax was for the erection of a Protestant church.

Foot Soldier, 1918 — SP350

Battle of Bastogne — SP351

Designs: 2fr+1fr, Flag bearer, Guides Regiment, 1914. 3fr+1.50fr, Trumpeter of the Grenadiers and drummers, 1914.

1964, Aug. 1 Photo. *Perf. 11½*

B757	SP350 1fr + 50c multi	15	15
B758	SP350 2fr + 1fr multi	24	24
B759	SP350 3fr + 1.50fr multi	24	24
	Nos. B757-B759 (3)	63	63

50th anniversary of the German aggression against Belgium in 1914. The surtax aided patriotic undertakings.

1964, Aug. 1 Unwmk.

Design: 6fr+3fr, Liberation of the estuary of the Escaut.

B760	SP351 3fr + 1fr multi	18	18
B761	SP351 6fr + 3fr multi	28	28

Belgium's Resistance and liberation of World War II. The surtax was to help found an International Student Center at Antwerp and to aid cultural undertakings.

Souvenir Sheets

Rogier van der Weyden Paintings — SP352

Descent From the Cross — SP353

1964, Sept. 19 Photo. *Perf. 11½*

B762	SP352 Sheet of 3	2.25	2.25
a.	1fr Philip the Good	52	52
b.	2fr Portrait of a Lady	52	52
c.	3fr Man with Arrow	52	52

Engr.

B763	SP353 8fr red brown	2.25	2.25

Rogier van der Weyden (Roger de La Pasture, 1400-64). The surtax went to various cultural organizations. No. B762 sold for 14fr, No. B763 for 16fr.

Ancient View of the Pand SP354

Design: 3fr+1fr, Present view of the Pand from Lys River.

1964, Oct. 10 Photo.

B764	SP354 2fr + 1fr blk, grnsh bl & ultra	40	40
B765	SP354 3fr + 1fr lil rose, bl & dk brn	40	40

The surtax was for the restoration of the Pand Dominican Abbey in Ghent.

Type of 1963 and

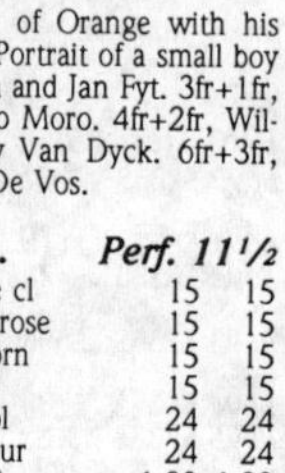

Child of Charles I, Painted by Van Dyck — SP355

Designs: 1fr+40c, William of Orange with his bride, by Van Dyck. 2fr+1fr, Portrait of a small boy with dogs by Erasmus Quellin and Jan Fyt. 3fr+1fr, Alexander Farnese by Antonio Moro. 4fr+2fr, William II, Prince of Orange by Van Dyck. 6fr+3fr, Artist's children by Cornelis De Vos.

1964, Dec. 5 Engr. *Perf. 11½*

B766	SP355 50c + 10c rose cl	15	15
B767	SP355 1fr + 40c car rose	15	15
B768	SP355 2fr + 1fr vio brn	15	15
B769	SP355 3fr + 1fr gray	15	15
B770	SP355 4fr + 2fr vio bl	24	24
B771	SP347 6fr + 3fr brt pur	24	24
	Nos. B766-B771 (6)	1.08	1.08

The surtax was for anti-tuberculosis work.

Liberator, Shaking Prisoner's Hand, Concentration Camp — SP356

Designs: 1fr+50c, Prisoner's hand reaching for the sun. 3fr+1.50fr, Searchlights and tank breaking down barbed wire, horiz. 8fr+5fr, Rose growing amid the ruins, horiz.

Engraved and Photogravure

1965, May 8 Unwmk. *Perf. 11½*

B772	SP356 50c + 50c tan, blk & buff	15	15
B773	SP356 1fr + 50c multi	15	15
B774	SP356 3fr + 1.50fr dl lil & blk	18	18
B775	SP356 8fr + 5fr multi	35	35
	Nos. B772-B775 (4)	83	83

20th anniv. of the liberation of the concentration camps for political prisoners and prisoners of war.

Stoclet House, Brussels SP357

Stoclet House: 6fr+3fr, Hall with marble foundation, vert. 8fr+4fr, View of house from garden.

1965, June 21

B776	SP357 3fr + 1fr slate & tan	22	22
B777	SP357 6fr + 3fr sepia	32	32
B778	SP357 8fr + 4fr vio brn & tan	42	42
	Nos. B776-B778 (3)	96	96

Austrian architect Josef Hoffmann (1870-1956), builder of the art nouveau residence of Adolphe Stoclet, engineer and financier.

Jackson's Chameleon SP358

Animals from Antwerp Zoo: 2fr+1fr, Common iguanas. 3fr+1.50fr, African monitor. 6fr+3fr, Komodo monitor. 8fr+4fr, Nile softshell turtle.

1965, Oct. 16 Photo. *Perf. 11½*

B779	SP358 1fr + 50c multi	15	15
B780	SP358 2fr + 1fr multi	16	16
B781	SP358 3fr + 1.50fr multi	22	22
B782	SP358 6fr + 3fr multi	45	45
	Nos. B779-B782 (4)	98	98

Miniature Sheet

B783	SP358 8fr + 4fr multi	1.75	1.75

The surtax was for various cultural and philanthropic organizations. No. B783 contains one stamp, size: 52x35mm.

Boatmen's and Archers' Guild Halls — SP359

Buildings on Grand-Place, Brussels: 1fr+40c, Brewers' Hall. 2fr+1fr, "King of Spain." 3fr+1.50fr, "Dukes of Brabant." 10fr+4.50fr, Tower of City Hall and St. Michael.

1965, Dec. 4 Engr. *Perf. 11½*

Size: 35x24mm

B784	SP359 50c + 10c ultra	15	15
B785	SP359 1fr + 40c bl grn	15	15
B786	SP359 2fr + 1fr rose claret	18	18
B787	SP359 3fr + 1.50fr vio	20	20

Size: 24x44mm

B788	SP359 10fr + 4.50fr sep & gray	32	32
	Nos. B784-B788 (5)	1.00	1.00

The surtax was for anti-tuberculosis work.

Souvenir Sheets

Queen Elisabeth — SP360

Design: No. B790, Types of 1931 and 1956.

1966, Apr. 16 Photo. *Perf. 11½*

B789 SP360 Sheet of 2 + label 1.50 1.50
a. SP74 3fr dk brn & gray grn 60 60
b. SP87 3fr dk brn, yel grn & gold 60 60
B790 SP360 Sheet of 2 + label 1.50 1.50
a. SP42 3fr dk brn & dl bl 60 60
b. SP304 3fr dk brn & gray 60 60

The surtax went to various cultural organizations. Each sheet sold for 20fr.

Luminescent Paper was used in printing Nos. B789-B790, B801-B806, B808-B809, B811-B823, B825-B831, B833-B835, B837-B840, B842-B846, B848-B850, B852-B854, B856-B863, and from B865 onward unless otherwise noted.

Diver — SP361

Design: 10fr+4fr, Swimmer at start.

1966, May 9 Engr.

B791 SP361 60c + 40c Prus grn, ol & org brn 15 15
B792 SP361 10fr + 4fr ol grn, org brn & mag 38 38

Issued to publicize the importance of swimming instruction.

Minorites' Convent, Liège — SP362

Designs: 1fr+50c, Val-Dieu Abbey, Aubel. 2fr+1fr, View and seal of Huy. 10fr+4.50fr, Statue of Ambiorix by Jules Bertin, and tower, Tongeren.

1966, Aug. 27 Engr. *Perf. 11½*

B793 SP362 60c + 40c multi 15 15
B794 SP362 1fr + 50c multi 15 15
B795 SP362 2fr + 1fr multi 15 15
B796 SP362 10fr + 4.50fr multi 42 42
Set value 69 69

The surtax was for various patriotic and cultural organizations.

Surveyor and Dog Team — SP363

Designs: 3fr+1.50fr, Adrien de Gerlache and "Belgica." 6fr+3fr, Surveyor, weather balloon and ship. 10fr+5fr, Penguins and "Magga Dan" (ship used for 1964, 1965 and 1966 expeditions).

1966, Oct. 8 Engr. *Perf. 11½*

B797 SP363 1fr + 50c bl grn 15 15
B798 SP363 3fr + 1.50fr pale vio 20 20
B799 SP363 6fr + 3fr dk car 35 35
Nos. B797-B799 (3) 70 70

Souvenir Sheet

Engraved and Photogravure

B800 SP363 10fr + 5fr dk gray, sky bl & dk red 70 70

Belgian Antarctic expeditions. #B800 contains one 52x35mm stamp.

Boy with Ball and Dog — SP364

Designs: 2fr+1fr, Girl skipping rope. 3fr+1.50fr, Girl and boy blowing soap bubbles. 6fr+3fr, Girl and boy rolling hoops, horiz. 8fr+3.50fr, Four children at play and cat, horiz.

1966, Dec. 3 *Perf. 11½*

B801 SP364 1fr + 1fr pink & blk 15 15
B802 SP364 2fr + 1fr lt bluish grn & blk 15 15
B803 SP364 3fr + 1.50fr lt vio & blk 15 15
B804 SP364 6fr + 3fr pale sal & dk brn 24 24
B805 SP364 8fr + 3.50fr lt yel grn & dk brn 28 28
Nos. B801-B805 (5) 97 97

The surtax was for anti-tuberculosis work.

Souvenir Sheet

Refugees — SP365

Designs: 1fr, Boy receiving clothes. 2fr, Tibetan children. 3fr, African mother and children.

1967, Mar. 11 Photo. *Perf. 11½*

B806 SP365 Sheet of 3 1.25 1.25
a. 1fr black & yellow 28 28
b. 2fr black & blue 28 28
c. 3fr black & orange 40 40

Issued to help refugees around the world. Sheet has black border with Belgian P.T.T. and UN Refugee emblems. Sold for 20fr.

Robert Schuman — SP366

Colonial Brotherhood Emblem — SP368

Kongolo Memorial, Gentinnes SP367

1967, June 24 Engr. *Perf. 11½*

B807 SP366 2fr + 1fr gray blue 24 24

Engraved and Photogravure

B808 SP367 5fr + 2fr brn & olive 28 28
B809 SP368 10fr + 5fr multi 45 35

Robert Schuman (1886-1963), French statesman, one of the founders of European Steel and Coal Community, 1st pres. of European Parliament (2fr+1fr); Kongolo Memorial, erected in memory of missionary and civilian victims in the Congo (5fr+2fr); a memorial for African Troops, Brussels (10fr+5fr).

Preaching Fool from "Praise of Folly" by Erasmus — SP369

Erasmus, by Quentin Massys — SP370

Designs: 2fr+1fr, Exhorting Fool from Praise of Folly. 5fr+2fr, Thomas More's Family, by Hans Holbein, horiz. 6fr+3fr, Pierre Gilles (Aegidius), by Quentin Massys.

Photogravure and Engraved (SP369); Photogravure (SP370)

1967, Sept. 2 Unwmk. *Perf. 11*

B810 SP369 1fr + 50c tan, blk, bl & car 15 15
B811 SP369 2fr + 1fr tan, blk & car 15 15
B812 SP370 3fr + 1.50fr multi 15 15
B813 SP369 5fr + 2fr tan, blk & car 18 18
B814 SP370 6fr + 3fr multi 24 24
Nos. B810-B814 (5) 87 87

Issued to commemorate Erasmus (1466(?)-1536), Dutch scholar and his era.

Souvenir Sheet

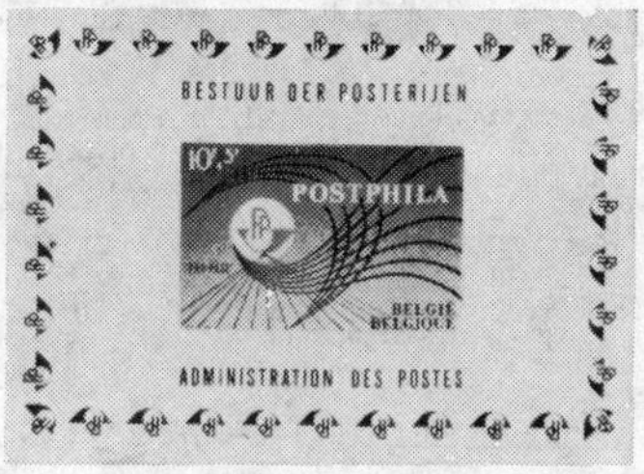

Pro-Post Association Emblem — SP371

Engraved and Photogravure

1967, Oct. 21 *Perf. 11½*

B815 SP371 10fr + 5fr multi 75 75

Issued to publicize the POSTPHILA Philatelic Exhibition, Brussels, Oct. 21-29.

Detail from Brueghel's "Children's Games" — SP372

Designs: Various Children's Games. Singles of Nos. B816-B821 arranged in 2 rows of 3 show complete painting by Pieter Brueghel.

1967, Dec. 9 Photo. *Perf. 11½*

B816 SP372 1fr + 50c multi 15 15
B817 SP372 2fr + 50c multi 18 18
B818 SP372 3fr + 1fr multi 18 18
B819 SP372 6fr + 3fr multi 30 30
B820 SP372 10fr + 4fr multi 40 40
B821 SP372 13fr + 6fr multi 60 60
Nos. B816-B821 (6) 1.81 1.81

Queen Fabiola Holding Refugee Child from Congo — SP373

Design: 6fr+3fr, Queen Elisabeth and Dr. Depage.

1968, Apr. 27 Photo. *Perf. 11½*

Cross in Red

B822 SP373 6fr + 3fr sepia & gray 25 25
B823 SP373 10fr + 5fr sepia & gray 45 45

The surtax was for the Red Cross.

Woman Gymnast and Calendar Stone SP374

Yachting and "The Swimmer" by Andrien SP375

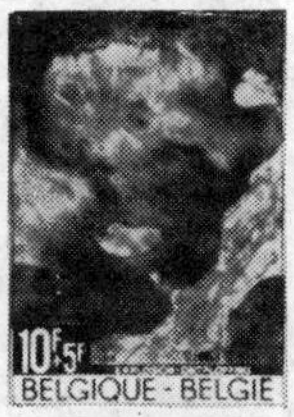

"Explosion" SP376

Designs: 2fr+1fr, Weight lifter and Mayan motif. 3fr+1.50fr, Hurdler, colossus of Tula and animal head from Kukulkan. 6fr+2fr, Bicyclists and Chichen Itza Temple.

Engraved and Photogravure

1968, May 27 *Perf. 11½*

B824 SP374 1fr + 50c multi 15 15
B825 SP374 2fr + 1fr multi 15 15
B826 SP374 3fr + 1.50fr multi 15 15
B827 SP374 6fr + 2fr multi 24 24

Photo.

B828 SP375 13fr + 5fr multi 52 52
Nos. B824-B828 (5) 1.21 1.21

Issued to publicize the 19th Olympic Games, Mexico City, Oct. 12-27.

1968, June 22 Photo.

Designs (Paintings by Pol Mara): 12fr+5fr, "Fire." 13fr+5fr, "Tornado."

B829 SP376 10fr + 5fr multi 40 40
B830 SP376 12fr + 5fr multi 65 65
B831 SP376 13fr + 5fr multi 70 70
Nos. B829-B831 (3) 1.75 1.75

The surtax was for disaster victims.

Undulate Triggerfish
SP377

Tropical Fish: 3fr+1.50fr, Angelfish. 6fr+3fr, Turkeyfish (Pterois volitans). 10fr+5fr, Orange butterflyfish.

1968, Oct. 19 **Engr. & Photo.**

B832	SP377	1fr + 50c multi	15	15
B833	SP377	3fr + 1.50fr multi	15	15
B834	SP377	6fr + 3fr multi	30	30
B835	SP377	10fr + 5fr multi	42	42
		Nos. B832-B835 (4)	1.02	1.02

King Albert and Queen Elisabeth Entering Brussels
SP378

Tomb of the Unknown Soldier and Eternal Flame, Brussels — SP379

Designs: 1fr+50c, King Albert, Queen Elisabeth and Crown Prince Leopold on balcony, Bruges, vert. 6fr+3fr, King and Queen entering Liège.

1968, Nov. 9 **Photo.** ***Perf. 11½***

B836	SP378	1fr + 50c multi	15	15
B837	SP378	3fr + 1.50fr multi	15	15
B838	SP378	6fr + 3fr multi	30	30

Engraved and Photogravure

B839	SP379	10fr + 5fr multi	40	40
		Nos. B836-B839 (4)	1.00	1.00

50th anniv. of the victory in World War I.

Souvenir Sheet

The Painter and the Amateur, by Peter Brueghel — SP380

1969, May 10 **Engr.** ***Perf. 11½***

B840	SP380	10fr + 5fr sepia	1.10	1.10

Issued to publicize the POSTPHILA 1969 Philatelic Exhibition, Brussels, May 10-18.

Huts, by Ivanka D. Pancheva, Bulgaria
SP381

Msgr. Victor Scheppers
SP382

Children's Drawings and UNICEF Emblem: 3fr+1.50fr, "My Art" (Santa Claus), by Claes Patric, Belgium. 6fr+3fr, "In the Sun" (young boy), by Helena Rejchlova, Czechoslovakia. 10fr+5fr, "Out for a Walk" by Phillis Sporn, US, horiz.

1969, May 31 **Photo.** ***Perf. 11½***

B841	SP381	1fr + 50c multi	15	15
B842	SP381	3fr + 1.50fr multi	16	16
B843	SP381	6fr + 3fr multi	35	35
B844	SP381	10fr + 5fr multi	52	52
		Nos. B841-B844 (4)	1.18	1.18

The surtax was for philanthropic purposes.

1969, July 5 **Engr.**

B845	SP382	6fr + 3fr rose claret	45	45

Msgr. Victor Scheppers (1802-77), prison reformer and founder of the Brothers of Mechlin (Scheppers).

Moon Landing Type of 1969
Souvenir Sheet

Design: 20fr+10fr, Armstrong, Collins and Aldrin and moon with Tranquillity Base, vert.

1969, Sept. 20 **Photo.** ***Perf. 11½***

B846	A245	20fr + 10fr indigo	3.00	3.00

See note after No. 726.

Heads from Alexander the Great Tapestry, 15th Century — SP383

Designs from Tapestries: 3fr+1.50fr, Fiddler from "The Feast," c. 1700. 10fr+4fr, Head of beggar from "The Healing of the Paralytic," 16th century.

1969, Sept. 20

B847	SP383	1fr + 50c multi	15	15
B848	SP383	3fr + 1.50fr multi	18	18
B849	SP383	10fr + 4fr multi	45	45
		Nos. B847-B849 (3)	78	78

The surtax was for philanthropic purposes.

Bearded Antwerp Bantam
SP384

1969, Nov. 8 **Engr. & Photo.**

B850	SP384	10fr + 5fr multi	70	70

Angel Playing Lute — SP385

Designs from Stained Glass Windows: 1.50fr+50c, Angel with trumpet, St. Waudru's, Mons. 7fr+3fr, Angel with viol, St. Jacques', Liege. 9fr+4fr, King with bagpipes, Royal Art Museum, Brussels.

1969, Dec. 13 **Photo.**

Size: 24x35mm

B851	SP385	1.50fr + 50c multi	15	15
B852	SP385	3.50fr + 1.50fr multi	18	18
B853	SP385	7fr + 3fr multi	35	35

Size: 35x52mm

B854	SP386	9fr + 4fr multi	52	52
		Nos. B851-B854 (4)	1.20	1.20

The surtax was for philanthropic purposes.

Farm and Windmill, Open-air Museum, Bokrijk
SP386

Belgian Museums: 3.50fr+1.50fr, Stage Coach Inn, Courcelles. 7fr+3fr, "The Thresher of Trevires," Gallo-Roman sculpture, Gaumais Museum, Virton. 9fr+4fr, "The Sovereigns," by Henry Moore, Middelheim Museum, Antwerp.

Engraved and Photogravure

1970, May 30 ***Perf. 11½***

B855	SP386	1.50fr + 50c multi	15	15
B856	SP386	3.50fr + 1.50fr multi	25	25
B857	SP386	7fr + 3fr multi	35	35
B858	SP386	9fr + 4fr multi	40	40
		Nos. B855-B858 (4)	1.15	1.15

The surtax went to various culture organizations.

"Resistance" — SP387

Design: 7fr+3fr, "Liberation of Camps." The designs were originally used as book covers.

1970, July 4 **Photo.** ***Perf. 11½***

B859	SP387	3.50fr + 1.50fr blk, gray grn & dp car	20	20
B860	SP387	7fr + 3fr blk, lil & dp car	40	40

Honoring the Resistance Movement and 25th anniv. of the liberation of concentration camps.

Fishing Rod and Reel — SP388

Design: 9fr+4fr, Hockey stick and puck, vert.

1970, Sept. 19 **Engr. & Photo.**

B861	SP388	3.50fr + 1.50fr multi	28	28
B862	SP388	9fr + 4fr brt grn & multi	48	48

Souvenir Sheet

Belgium Nos. 31, 36, 39 — SP389

1970, Oct. 10 ***Perf. 11½***

B863	SP389	Sheet of 3	4.75	4.75
a.		1.50fr + 50c black & dull lilac	1.40	1.40
b.		3.50fr + 1.50fr black & lilac	1.40	1.40
c.		9fr + 4fr black & red brown	1.40	1.40

BELGICA 72 International Philatelic Exhibition, Brussels, June 24-July 9.

Camille Huysmans (1871-1968)
SP390

"Anxious City" (Detail) by Paul Delvaux
SP391

Portraits: 3.50fr+1.50fr, Joseph Cardinal Cardijn (1882-1967). 7fr+3fr, Maria Baers (1883-1959). 9fr+4fr, Paul Pastur (1866-1938).

1970, Nov. 14 ***Perf. 11½***

Portraits in Sepia

B864	SP390	1.50fr + 50c car rose	15	15
B865	SP390	3.50fr + 1.50fr lilac	20	20
B866	SP390	7fr + 3fr green	40	40
B867	SP390	9fr + 4fr blue	48	48
		Nos. B864-B867 (4)	1.23	1.23

1970, Dec. 12 **Photo.**

Design: 7fr+3fr, "The Memory," by Rene Magritte.

B868	SP391	3.50fr + 1.50fr multi	18	18
B869	SP391	7fr + 3fr multi	38	38

Notre Dame du Vivier, Marche-les-Dames — SP392

Design: 7fr+3fr, Turnhout Beguinage and Beguine.

1971, Mar. 13 ***Perf. 11½***

B870	SP392	3.50fr + 1.50fr multi	20	20
B871	SP392	7fr + 3fr multi	40	40

The surtax was for philanthropic purposes.

Red Cross — SP393

1971, May 22 **Photo.** ***Perf. 11½***

B872	SP393	10fr + 5fr crim & blk	75	75

Belgian Red Cross.

Discobolus and Munich Cathedral SP394

Festival of Flanders SP395

1971, June 19 **Engr. & Photo.**

B873 SP394	7fr + 3fr bl & blk	42	42

Publicity for the 20th Summer Olympic Games, Munich 1972.

1971, Sept. 11 **Photo.** ***Perf. 11½***

Design: 7fr+3fr, Wallonia Festival.

B874 SP395	3.50fr + 1.50fr multi	18	18
B875 SP395	7fr + 3fr multi	38	38

Attre Palace — SP396

Steen Palace, Elewijt — SP397

Design: 10fr+5fr, Royal Palace, Brussels.

1971, Oct. 23 **Engr.**

B876 SP396	3.50fr + 1.50fr sl grn	30	30
B877 SP397	7fr + 3fr red brn	50	50
B878 SP396	10fr + 5fr vio bl	70	70
	Nos. B876-B878 (3)	1.50	1.50

Surtax was for BELGICA 72, International Philatelic Exposition.

Ox Fly — SP398

Insects: 1.50fr+50c, Luna moth, vert. 7fr+3fr, Wasp, polistes gallicus. 9fr+4fr, Tiger beetle, vert.

1971, Dec. 11 **Photo.** ***Perf. 11½***

B879 SP398	1.50fr + 50c multi	20	20
B880 SP398	3.50fr + 1.50fr multi	20	20
B881 SP398	7fr + 3fr multi	40	40
B882 SP398	9fr + 4fr multi	60	60
	Nos. B879-B882 (4)	1.40	1.40

Surtax was for philanthropic purposes.

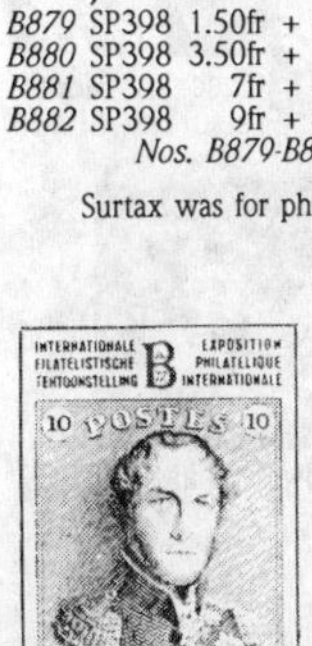

Leopold I on #1 — SP399

Epilepsy Emblem — SP400

Designs: 2fr+1fr, Leopold I on No. 5. 2.50fr+1fr, Leopold II on No. 45. 3.50fr+1.50fr, Leopold II on No. 48. 6fr+3fr, Albert I on No. 135. 7fr+3fr, Albert I on No. 214. 10fr+5fr, Albert I on No. 231. 15fr+7.50fr, Leopold III on No. 290. 20fr+10fr, King Baudouin on No. 718.

Engraved and Photogravure

1972, June 24 ***Perf. 11½***

B883 SP399	1.50fr + 50c	16	16
B884 SP399	2fr + 1fr	16	16
B885 SP399	2.50 + 1fr	20	20
B886 SP399	3.50fr + 1.50fr	32	32
B887 SP399	6fr + 3fr	52	52
B888 SP399	7fr + 3fr	70	70
B889 SP399	10fr + 5fr	90	90
B890 SP399	15fr + 7fr	1.10	1.10
B891 SP399	20fr + 10fr	2.00	2.00
	Nos. B883-B891 (9)	6.06	6.06

Belgica 72, Intl. Philatelic Exhibition, Brussels, June 24-July 9. Nos. B883-B891 issued in sheets of 10 and of 20 (2 tete beche sheets with gutter between). Sold in complete sets.

1972, Sept. 9 **Photo.** ***Perf. 11½***

B892 SP400	10fr + 5fr multi	55	55

The surtax was for the William Lennox Center for epilepsy research and treatment.

Gray Lag Goose — SP401

Designs: 4.50fr+2fr, Lapwing. 8fr+4fr, Stork. 9fr+4.50fr, Kestrel, horiz.

1972, Dec. 16 **Photo.** ***Perf. 11½***

B893 SP401	2fr + 1fr multi	22	22
B894 SP401	4.50fr + 2fr multi	32	32
B895 SP401	8fr + 4fr multi	60	60
B896 SP401	9fr + 4.50fr multi	60	60
	Nos. B893-B896 (4)	1.74	1.74

Bijloke Abbey, Ghent — SP402

Designs: 4.50fr+2fr, St. Ursmer Collegiate Church, Lobbes. 8fr+4fr, Park Abbey, Heverle. 9fr+4.50fr, Abbey, Floreffe.

1973, Mar. 24 **Engr.** ***Perf. 11½***

B897 SP402	2fr + 1fr slate grn	16	16
B898 SP402	4.50fr + 2fr brown	24	24
B899 SP402	8fr + 4fr rose lil	48	48
B900 SP402	9fr + 4.50fr brt bl	60	60
	Nos. B897-B900 (4)	1.48	1.48

Basketball SP403

1973, Apr. 7 **Photo. & Engr.**

B901 SP403	10fr + 5fr multi	60	60

First World Basketball Championships of the Handicapped, Bruges, Apr. 16-21.

Dirk Martens' Printing Press — SP404

Lady Talbot, by Petrus Christus — SP405

Hadrian and Marcus Aurelius Coins — SP406

Council of Malines, by Coussaert — SP407

Designs: 3.50fr+1.50fr, Head of Amon and Tutankhamen's cartouche. 10fr+5fr, Three-master of Ostend Merchant Company.

Photogravure and Engraved; Photogravure (#B906)

1973, June 23 ***Perf. 11½***

B902 SP404	2fr + 1fr multi	15	15
B903 SP404	3.50fr + 1.50fr multi	15	15
B904 SP405	4.50fr + 2fr multi	20	20
B905 SP406	8fr + 4fr multi	60	60
B906 SP407	9fr + 4.50fr multi	85	85
B907 SP407	10fr + 5fr multi	1.50	1.50
	Nos. B902-B907 (6)	3.45	3.45

500th anniv. of 1st book printed in Belgium (#B902); 50th anniv. of Queen Elisabeth Egyptological Foundation (#B903); 500th anniv. of death of painter Petrus Christus (#B904); Discovery of Roman treasure at Luttre-Liberchies (#B905); 500th anniv. of Great Council of Malines (#B906); 250th anniv. of the Ostend Merchant Company (#B907).

No. B902 is not luminescent.

Queen of Hearts SP408

Symbol of Blood Donations SP409

Old Playing Cards: #B909, King of Clubs. #B910, Jack of Diamonds. #B911, King of Spades.

1973, Dec. 8 **Photo.** ***Perf. 11½***

B908 SP408	5fr + 2.50fr multi	38	38
B909 SP408	5fr + 2.50fr multi	38	38
B910 SP408	5fr + 2.50fr multi	38	38
B911 SP408	5fr + 2.50fr multi	38	38
a.	Block of 4, #B908-B911	1.60	1.60

Surtax was for philanthropic purposes.

1974, Feb. 23 **Photo.** ***Perf. 11½***

Design: 10fr+5fr, Traffic lights, Red Cross (symbolic of road accidents).

B912 SP409	4fr + 2fr multi	24	24
B913 SP409	10fr + 5fr multi	55	55

The Red Cross as blood collector and aid to accident victims.

Armand Jamar, Self-portrait SP410

Van Gogh, Self-portrait and House at Cuesmes SP411

Designs: 5fr+2.50fr, Anton Bergmann and view of Lierre. 7fr+3.50fr, Henri Vieuxtemps and view of Verviers. 10fr+5fr, James Ensor, self-portrait, and masks.

1974, Apr. 6 **Photo.** ***Perf. 11½***

Size: 24x35mm

B914 SP410	4fr + 2fr multi	24	24
B915 SP410	5fr + 2.50fr multi	32	32
B916 SP410	7fr + 3.50fr multi	40	40

Size: 35x52mm

B917 SP410	10fr + 5fr multi	65	65
	Nos. B914-B917 (4)	1.61	1.61

1974, Sept. 21 **Photo.** ***Perf. 11½***

B918 SP411	10fr + 5fr multi	55	55

Opening of Vincent van Gogh House at Cuesmes, where he worked as teacher.

Gentian — SP412

Spotted Cat's Ear — SP414

Badger SP413

Design: 7fr+3.50fr, Beetle.

1974, Dec. 8 **Photo.** ***Perf. 11½***

B919 SP412	4fr + 2fr multi	25	25
B920 SP413	5fr + 2.50fr multi	30	30
B921 SP413	7fr + 3.50fr multi	40	40
B922 SP414	10fr + 5fr multi	60	60
	Nos. B919-B922 (4)	1.55	1.55

Pesaro Palace, Venice SP415

St. Bavon Abbey, Ghent SP416

Virgin and Child, by Michelangelo — SP417

1975, Apr. 12 Engr. *Perf. 11½*

B923 SP415	6.50fr + 2.50fr brn	35	35
B924 SP416	10fr + 4.50 vio brn	60	60
B925 SP417	15fr + 6.50fr brt bl	80	80
	Nos. B923-B925 (3)	1.75	1.75

Surtax was for various cultural organizations.

Frans Hemerijckx and Leprosarium, Kasai — SP418

1975, Sept. 13 Photo. *Perf. 11½*

B926 SP418	20fr + 10fr multi	1.40	1.40

Dr. Frans Hemerijckx (1902-1969), tropical medicine and leprosy expert.

Emile Moyson — SP419

Beheading of St. Dympna — SP420a

Hand Reading Braille SP420

Design: 6.50fr+3fr, Dr. Ferdinand Augustin Snellaert.

1975, Nov. 22 Engr. *Perf. 11½*

B927 SP419	4.50fr + 2fr lilac	24	24
B928 SP419	6.50fr + 3fr green	35	35

Engraved and Photogravure

B929 SP420	10fr + 5fr multi	50	50

Photo.

B930 SP420a	13fr + 6fr multi	70	70
	Nos. B927-B930 (4)	1.79	1.79

Emile Moyson (1838-1868), freedom fighter for the rights of Flemings and Walloons; Dr. Snellaert (1809-1872), physician and Flemish patriot; Louis Braille (1809-1852), sesquicentennial of invention of Braille system of writing for the blind; St. Dympna, patron saint of Geel, famous for treatment of mentally ill.

The Cheese Vendor — SP421

Designs (THEMABELGA Emblem and): No. B932, Potato vendor. No. B933, Basket carrier. No. B934, Shrimp fisherman with horse, horiz. No. B935, Knife grinder, horiz. No. B936, Milk vendor with dog cart, horiz.

1975, Dec. 13 Engr. & Photo.

B931 SP421	4.50fr + 1.50fr multi	15	15
B932 SP421	6.50fr + 3fr multi	32	32
B933 SP421	6.50fr + 3fr multi	32	32
B934 SP421	10fr + 5fr multi	45	45
B935 SP421	10fr + 5fr multi	45	45
B936 SP421	30fr + 15fr multi	1.50	1.50
	Nos. B931-B936 (6)	3.19	3.19

THEMABELGA International Topical Philatelic Exhibition, Brussels, Dec. 13-21. Issued in sheets of 10 (5x2).

Blackface Fund Collector — SP422

1976, Feb. 14 Photo. *Perf. 11½*

B937 SP422	10fr + 5fr multi	55	55

Centenary of the "Conservatoire Africain" philanthropic society, and to publicize the Princess Paola creches.

Swimming and Olympic Emblem SP423

Designs (Montreal Olympic Games Emblem and): 5fr+2fr, Running, vert. 6.50fr+2.50fr, Equestrian.

1976, Apr. 10 Photo. *Perf. 11½*

B938 SP423	4.50fr + 1.50fr multi	18	18
B939 SP423	5fr + 2fr multi	25	25
B940 SP423	6.50fr + 2.50fr multi	45	45
	Nos. B938-B940 (3)	88	88

21st Olympic Games, Montreal, Canada, July 17-Aug. 1.

Queen Elisabeth Playing Violin SP424

Perf. 11½

1976, May 1 Engr. Photo.

B941 SP424	14fr + 6fr blk & claret	95	95

Queen Elisabeth International Music Competition, 25th anniversary.

Souvenir Sheet

Jan Olieslagers, Bleriot Monoplane, Aero Club Emblem SP425

Engraved and Photogravure

1976, June 12 *Perf. 11½*

B942 SP425	25fr + 10fr multi	2.25	2.25

Royal Belgian Aero Club, 75th anniversary, and Jan Olieslagers (1883-1942), aviation pioneer.

Adoration of the Shepherds (detail), by Rubens SP426

Dwarf, by Velazquez SP427

Rubens Paintings (Details): 4.50fr, Descent from the Cross. No. B945, The Virgin with the Parrot. No. B946, Adoration of the Kings. No. B947, Last Communion of St. Francis. 30fr+15fr, Virgin and Child.

1976, Sept. 4 Photo. *Perf. 11½*

Size: 35x52mm

B943 SP426	4.50fr + 1.50fr multi	35	35

Size: 24x35mm

B944 SP426	6.50fr + 3fr multi	55	55
B945 SP426	6.50fr + 3fr multi	55	55
B946 SP426	10fr + 5fr multi	85	85
B947 SP426	10fr + 5fr multi	85	85

Size: 35x52mm

B948 SP426	30fr + 15fr multi	1.75	1.75
	Nos. B943-B948 (6)	4.90	4.90

Peter Paul Rubens (1577-1640), Flemish painter, 400th birth anniversary.

1976, Nov. 6 Photo. *Perf. 11½*

B949 SP427	14fr + 6fr multi	80	80

Surtax was for the National Association for the Mentally Handicapped.

Dr. Albert Hustin — SP428

Red Cross and Rheumatism Year Emblem — SP429

1977, Feb. 19 Photo. *Perf. 11½*

B950 SP428	6.50fr + 2.50 multi	38	38
B951 SP429	14fr + 7fr multi	75	75

Belgian Red Cross.

Bordet Atheneum, Empress Maria Theresa — SP430

Conductor and Orchestra, by E. Tytgat — SP431

Lucien Van Obbergh, Stage — SP432

Humanistic Society Emblem SP433

Camille Lemonnier SP434

Design: No. B953, Marie-Therese College, Herve, and coat of arms.

1977, Mar. 21 Photo. *Perf. 11½*

B952 SP430	4.50fr + 1fr multi	20	20
B953 SP430	4.50fr + 1fr multi	20	20
B954 SP431	5fr + 2fr multi	24	24
B955 SP432	6.50fr + 2fr multi	32	32
B956 SP433	6.50fr + 2fr blk & red	32	32

Engr.

B957 SP434	10fr + 5fr slate bl	48	48
	Nos. B952-B957 (6)	1.76	1.76

Bicentenaries of the Jules Bordet Atheneum, Brussels, and the Marie-Therese College, Herve (#B952-B953); 50th anniv. of the Brussels Philharmonic Soc., and Artists' Union (#B954-B955); 25th anniv. of the Flemish Humanistic Organization (#B956); 75th anniv. of the French-speaking Belgian writers' organization (#957).

Young Soccer Players — SP435

Albert-Edouard Janssen, Financier — SP436

1977, Apr. 18 Photo.

B958 SP435	10fr + 5fr multi	55	55

30th Intl. Junior Soccer Tournament.

1977, Dec. 3 Engr. *Perf. 11½*

Famous Men: No. B960, Joseph Wauters (1875-1929), editor of Le Peuple, and newspaper. No. B961, Jean Capart (1877-1947), Egyptologist, and hieroglyph. No. B962, August de Boeck (1865-1937), composer, and score.

B959 SP436	5fr + 2.50fr brown	28	28
B960 SP436	5fr + 2.50fr red	28	28
B961 SP436	10fr + 5fr magenta	55	55
B962 SP436	10fr + 5fr blue gray	55	55
	Nos. B959-B962 (4)	1.66	1.66

Abandoned Child — SP437

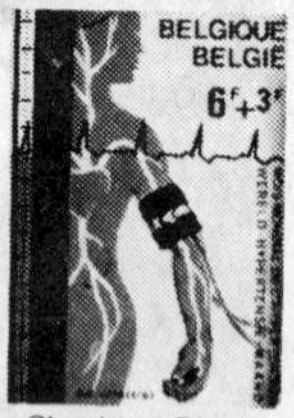

Checking Blood Pressure — SP438

De Mick Sanatorium, Brasschaat — SP439

1978, Feb. 18 Photo. *Perf. 11½*

B963	SP437	4.50fr + 1.50fr multi	15	15
B964	SP438	6fr + 3fr multi	38	38
B965	SP439	10fr + 5fr multi	60	60
		Nos. B963-B965 (3)	1.13	1.13

Help for abandoned children (No. B963); fight against hypertension (No. B964); fight against tuberculosis (No. B965).

Actors and Theater SP440

Karel van de Woestijne SP441

Designs: No. B967, Harquebusier, Harquebusier Palace and coat of arms. 10fr+5fr, John of Austria and his signature.

Engraved and Photogravure

1978, June 17 *Perf. 11½*

B966	SP440	6fr + 3fr multi	38	38
B967	SP440	6fr + 3fr multi	38	38

Engr.

B968	SP441	8fr + 4fr black	45	45
B969	SP441	10fr + 5fr black	55	55
		Nos. B966-B969 (4)	1.76	1.76

Cent. of Royal Flemish Theater, Brussels (#B966); 400th anniv. of Harquebusiers' Guild of Vise, Liege (#967); Karel van de Woestijne (1878-1929), poet (#B968); 400th anniv. of signing of Perpetual Edict by John of Austria (#969).

Lake Placid '80 and Belgian Olympic Emblems — SP442

Designs (Moscow '80 Emblem and): 8fr+3.50fr, Kremlin Towers and Belgian Olympic Committee emblem. 7fr+3fr, Runners from Greek vase, Lake Placid '80 emblem and Olympic rings. 14fr+6fr, Olympic flame, Lake Placid '80 and Belgian emblems, Olympic rings.

1978, Nov. 4 Photo. *Perf. 11½*

B970	SP442	6fr + 2.50fr multi	30	30
B971	SP442	8fr + 3.50fr multi	45	45

Souvenir Sheet

B972		Sheet of 2	1.40	1.40
a.		SP442 7fr + 3fr multi	55	55
b.		SP442 14fr + 6fr multi	90	90

Surtax was for 1980 Olympic Games.

Great Synagogue, Brussels — SP443

Dancers SP444

Father Pire, African Village SP445

1978, Dec. 2 Engr. *Perf. 11½*

B973	SP443	6fr + 2fr sepia	45	45

Photo.

B974	SP444	8fr + 3fr multi	35	35
B975	SP445	14fr + 7fr multi	65	65
		Nos. B973-B975 (3)	1.45	1.45

Centenary of Great Synagogue of Brussels; Flemish Catholic Youth Action Organization, 50th anniversary; Nobel Peace Prize awarded to Father Dominique Pire for his "Heart Open to the World" movement, 20th anniversary.

Young People Giving First Aid — SP446

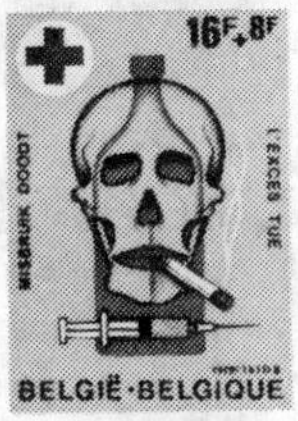

Skull with Bottle, Cigarette, Syringe — SP447

1979, Feb. 10 Photo. *Perf. 11½*

B976	SP446	8fr + 3fr multi	35	35
B977	SP447	16fr + 8fr multi	85	85

Belgian Red Cross.

Beatrice Soetkens with Statue of Virgin Mary — SP448

Details from Tapestries, 1516-1518, Showing Legend of Our Lady of Sand: 8fr+3fr, Francois de Tassis accepting letter from Emperor Frederick III (beginning of postal service). 14fr+7fr, Arrival of statue, Francois de Tassis and Philip the Fair. No. B981, Statue carried in procession by future Emperor Charles V and his brother Ferdinand. No. B982, Ship carrying Beatrice Soetkens with statue to Brussels, horiz.

1979, May 5 Photo. *Perf. 11½*

B978	SP448	6fr + 2fr multi	25	25
B979	SP448	8fr + 3fr multi	40	40
B980	SP448	14fr + 7fr multi	65	65
B981	SP448	20fr + 10fr multi	1.10	1.10
		Nos. B978-B981 (4)	2.40	2.40

Souvenir Sheet

B982	SP448	20fr + 10fr multi	90	90

The surtax was for festivities in connection with the millennium of Brussels.

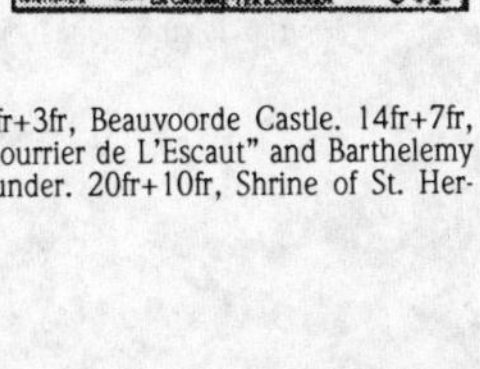

Notre Dame Abbey, Brussels SP449

Designs: 8fr+3fr, Beauvoorde Castle. 14fr+7fr, 1st issue of "Courrier de L'Escaut" and Barthelemy Dumortier, founder. 20fr+10fr, Shrine of St. Hermes, Renaix.

Engraved and Photogravure

1979, Sept. 15 *Perf. 11½*

B983	SP449	6fr + 2fr multi	35	35
B984	SP449	8fr + 3fr multi	50	50
B985	SP449	14fr + 7fr multi	60	60
B986	SP449	20fr + 10fr multi	1.10	1.10
		Nos. B983-B986 (4)	2.55	2.55

50th anniv. of restoration of Notre Dame de la Cambre Abbey; historic Beauvoorde Castle, 15th cent. sesquicentennial of the regional newspaper "Le Courrier de L'Escaut"; 850th anniv. of the consecration of the Collegiate Church of St. Hermes, Renaix.

Grand-Hornu Coal Mine — SP450

1979, Oct. 22 Engr. *Perf. 11½*

B987	SP450	10fr + 5fr blk	55	55

Henry Heyman — SP451

Veterans Organization Medal — SP452

Boy and IYC Emblem SP453

1979, Dec. 8 Photo. *Perf. 11½*

B988	SP451	8fr + 3fr multi	45	45
B989	SP452	10fr + 5fr multi	55	55
B990	SP453	16fr + 8fr multi	75	75
		Nos. B988-B990 (3)	1.75	1.75

Henri Heyman (1879-1958), Minister of State; Disabled Veterans' Organization, 50th anniv.; Intl. Year of the Child.

Ivo Van Damme, Olympic Rings — SP454

1980, May 3 Photo. *Perf. 11½*

B991	SP454	20fr + 10fr multi	1.10	1.10

Ivo Van Damme (1954-1976), silver medalist, 800-meter race, Montreal Olympics, 1976. Surtax was for Van Damme Memorial Foundation.

Queen Louis, King Leopold I SP455

150th Anniversary of Independence (Queens and Kings): 9fr+3fr, Marie Henriette. Leopold II. 14fr+6fr, Elisabeth, Albert I. 17fr+8fr, Astrid, Leopold III. 25fr+10fr, Fabiola, Baudouin.

Photogravure and Engraved

1980, May 31 *Perf. 11½*

B992	SP455	6.50 + 1.50fr multi	28	28
B993	SP455	9 + 3fr multi	50	50
B994	SP455	14 + 6fr multi	70	70
B995	SP455	17 + 8fr multi	1.00	1.00
B996	SP455	25 + 10fr multi	1.25	1.25
		Nos. B992-B996 (5)	3.73	3.73

Miner, by Constantine Meunier SP456

Seal of Bishop Notger, First Prince-Bishop — SP457

Designs: 9fr+3fr, Brewer, 16th century, from St. Lambert's reliquary, vert. 25fr+10fr, Virgin and Child, 13th century, St. John's Collegiate Church, Liege.

1980, Sept. 13 Photo. *Perf. 11½*

B997	SP456	9 + 3fr multi	35	35
B998	SP456	17 + 6fr multi	70	70
B999	SP456	25 + 10fr multi	1.10	1.10
		Nos. B997-B999 (3)	2.15	2.15

Souvenir Sheet

B1000	SP457	20 + 10fr multi	1.25	1.25

Millennium of the Principality of Liege.

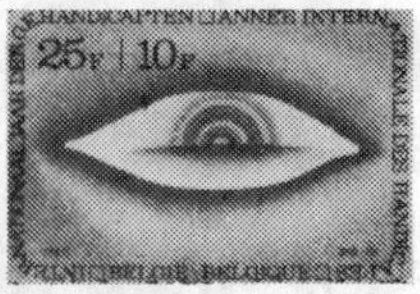

Visual and Oral Handicaps SP458

Intl. Year of the Disabled: 10fr+5fr, Cerebral handicap, vert.

1981, Feb. 9 Photo. *Perf. 11½*

B1001	SP458	10 + 5fr multi	70	70
B1002	SP458	25 + 10fr multi	1.65	1.65

Dove with Red Cross Carrying Globe SP459

Design: 10fr+5fr, Atomic model, vert.

1981, Apr. 6 Photo. *Perf. 11½*

B1003	SP459	10 + 5fr multi	70	70
B1004	SP459	25 + 10fr multi	1.65	1.65

Red Cross and: 15th Intl. Radiology Congress, Brussels, June 24-July 1 (#B1003); intl. disaster relief (#B1004).

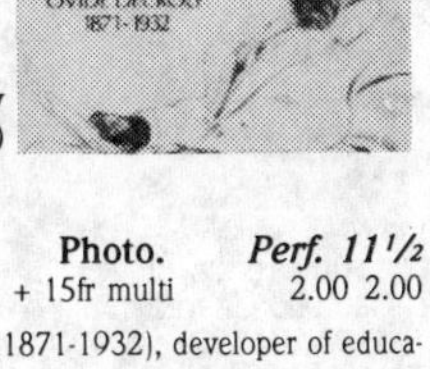

Ovide Decroly SP460

1981, June 1 Photo. *Perf. 11½*

B1005	SP460	35 + 15fr multi	2.00	2.00

Ovide Decroly (1871-1932), developer of educational psychology.

Mounted Police Officer — SP461

Billiards — SP462

Anniversaries: 9fr+4fr, Gendarmerie (State Police Force), 150th. 20fr+7fr, Carabineers Regiment, 150th. 40fr+20fr, Guides Regiment.

1981, Dec. 7 Photo. *Perf. 11½*

B1006 SP461 9 + 4fr multi 60 60
B1007 SP461 20 + 7fr multi 1.25 1.25
B1008 SP461 40 + 20fr multi 2.75 2.75
Nos. B1006-B1008 (3) 4.60 4.60

1982, Mar. 29 Photo. *Perf. 11½*

B1009 SP462 6 + 2fr shown 38 38
B1010 SP462 9 + 4fr Cycling 60 60
B1011 SP462 10 + 5fr Soccer 70 70
B1012 SP462 50 + 14fr Yachting 3.00 3.00
Nos. B1009-B1012 (4) 4.68 4.68

Souvenir Sheet

B1013 Sheet of 4 5.00 5.00
a. SP462 25fr like #B1009 1.40 1.40
b. SP462 25fr like #B1010 1.40 1.40
c. SP462 25fr like #B1011 1.40 1.40
d. SP462 25fr like #B1012 1.40 1.40

#B1013 shows designs in changed colors.

Christmas SP463

1982, Nov. 6

B1014 SP463 10 + 1fr multi 60 45

Surtax was for tuberculosis research.

Belgica '82 Intl. Stamp Exhibition, Brussels, Dec. 11-19 SP464

Messengers (Prints). Nos. B1016-B1018 vert.

Photogravure and Engraved

1982, Dec. 11 *Perf. 11½*

B1015 SP464 7 + 2fr multi 38 38
B1016 SP464 7.50 + 2.50fr multi 45 45
B1017 SP464 10 + 3fr multi 55 55
B1018 SP464 17 + 7fr multi 1.10 1.10
B1019 SP464 20 + 9fr multi 1.25 1.25
B1020 SP464 25 + 10fr multi 1.50 1.50
Nos. B1015-B1020 (6) 5.23 5.23

Souvenir Sheet

B1021 SP464 50 + 25fr multi 6.00 6.00

No. B1021 contains one 48x37mm stamp.

50th Anniv. of Catholic Charities SP465

Mountain Climbing SP466

1983, Jan. 22 Photo. *Perf. 11½*

B1022 SP465 10 + 2fr multi 65 65

1983, Mar. 7 Photo.

B1023 SP466 12 + 3fr shown 80 80
B1024 SP466 20 + 5fr Hiking 1.25 1.25

Surtax was for Red Cross.

Madonna by Jef Wauters — SP467

Rifles Uniform — SP468

1983, Nov. 21 Photo. *Perf. 11½*

B1025 SP467 11 + 1fr multi 60 60

1983, Dec. 5 Photo. *Perf. 11½*

B1026 SP468 8 + 2fr shown 50 50
B1027 SP468 11 + 2fr Lancers uniform 75 75
B1028 SP468 50 + 12fr Grenadiers uniform 3.50 3.50
Nos. B1026-B1028 (3) 4.75 4.75

Type of 1984

1984, Mar. 3 Photo. *Perf. 11½*

B1029 A495 8 + 2fr Judo, horiz. 55 55
B1030 A495 12 + 3fr Wind surfing 85 85

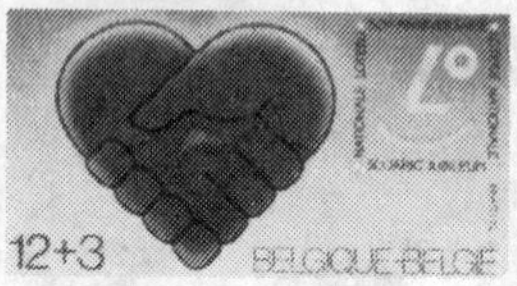

50th Anniv. of Natl. Lottery SP469

1984, Mar. 31 Photo. *Perf. 11½*

B1031 SP469 12 + 3fr multi 75 75

Brussels Modern Art Museum Opening SP470

Paintings: 8fr+2fr, Les Masques Singuliers, by James Ensor. 12fr+3fr, Empire des Lumieres, by Rene Magritte. 22fr+5fr, The End, by Jan Cox. 50fr+13fr, Rhythm No. 6, by Jo Delahaut.

1984, Sept. 1 Photo.

B1032 SP470 8 + 2fr multi 60 60
B1033 SP470 12 + 3fr multi 90 90
B1034 SP470 22 + 5fr multi 1.65 1.65
B1035 SP470 50 + 13fr multi 3.75 3.75
Nos. B1032-B1035 (4) 6.90 6.90

Child with Parents — SP471

1984, Nov. 3 Photo.

B1036 SP471 10 + 2fr shown 60 60
B1037 SP471 12 + 3fr Siblings 75 75
B1038 SP471 15 + 3fr Merry-go-round 85 85
Nos. B1036-B1038 (3) 2.20 2.20

Surtax was for children's programs.

Christmas 1984 SP472

1984, Dec. 1

B1039 SP472 12 + 1fr Three Kings 75 75

Belgian Red Cross Blood Transfusion Service, 50th Anniv. — SP473

1985, Mar. 4 Photo. *Perf. 11½*

B1040 SP473 9 + 2fr Tree 60 60
B1041 SP473 23 + 5fr Hearts 1.40 1.40

Surtax was for the Belgian Red Cross.

Solidarity SP474

Castles.

1985, Nov. 4 Photo. & Engr.

B1042 SP474 9 + 2fr Trazegnies 60 60
B1043 SP474 12 + 3fr Laarne 80 80
B1044 SP474 23 + 5fr Turnhout 1.40 1.40
B1045 SP474 50 + 12fr Colonster 3.50 3.50
Nos. B1042-B1045 (4) 6.30 6.30

Christmas 1985, New Year 1986 — SP475

Painting: Miniature from the Book of Hours, by Jean duc de Berry.

1985, Nov. 25 Photo.

B1046 SP475 12 + 1fr multi 70 70

King Baudouin Foundation SP476

1986, Mar. 24 Photo.

B1047 SP476 12 + 3fr Emblem 80 80

Surtax for the foundation.

Madonna SP477

Adoration of the Mystic Lamb, St. Bavon Cathedral Altarpiece, Ghent — SP478

Paintings by Hubert van Eyck (c. 1370-1426).

1986, Apr. 5 Photo. *Perf. 11½*

B1048 SP477 9 + 2fr shown 65 65
B1049 SP477 13 + 3fr Christ in Majesty 95 95
B1050 SP477 24 + 6fr St. John the Baptist 1.75 1.75
Nos. B1048-B1050 (3) 3.35 3.35

Souvenir Sheet

B1051 SP478 50 + 12fr multi 5.25 5.25

Surtax for cultural organizations.

Antique Automobiles SP479

1986, Nov. 3 Photo.

B1052 SP479 9 + 2fr Lenoir, 1863 65 65
B1053 SP479 13 + 3fr Pipe de Tourisme, 1911 90 90
B1054 SP479 24 + 6fr Minerva 22 HP, 1930 1.75 1.75
B1055 SP479 26 + 6fr FN 8 Cylinder, 1931 1.90 1.90
Nos. B1052-B1055 (4) 5.20 5.20

Christmas 1986, New Year 1987 — SP480

1986, Nov. 24 Photo.

B1056 SP480 13 + 1fr Village in winter 75 75

Natl. Red Cross — SP482

European Conservation Year — SP483

Nobel Prize winners for physiology (1938) and medicine (1974): No. B1058, Corneille Heymans (1892-1968). No. B1059, A. Claude (1899-1983).

Photogravure and Engraved

1987, Feb. 16 *Perf. 11½*

B1058 SP482 13 + 3fr dk brn & red 90 90
B1059 SP482 24 + 6fr dk brn & red 1.65 1.65

1987, Mar. 16 Photo.

B1060 SP483 9 + 2fr Bee orchid 60 60
B1061 SP483 24 + 6fr Horseshoe bat 1.65 1.65
B1062 SP483 26 + 6fr Peregrine falcon 1.75 1.75
Nos. B1060-B1062 (3) 4.00 4.00

Castles — SP484

1987, Oct. 17 Photo. & Engr.

B1063 SP484 9 + 2fr Rixensart 60 60
B1064 SP484 13 + 3fr Westerlo 90 90
B1065 SP484 26 + 5fr Fallais 1.75 1.75
B1066 SP484 50 + 12fr Gaasbeek 3.50 3.50
Nos. B1063-B1066 (4) 6.75 6.75

Christmas 1987 — SP485

White and Yellow Cross of Belgium, 50th Anniv. — SP486

Painting: Holy Family, by Rev. Father Lens.

1987, Nov. 14 Photo.

B1067 SP485 13 + 1fr multi 85 85

1987, Dec. 5

B1068 SP486 9 + 2fr multi 70 70

Promote Philately — SP487

Various flowers from Sixty Roses for a Queen, by P. J. Redoute (1759-1840).

1988, Apr. 25 Photo. *Perf. 11½*

B1069 SP487 13 + 3fr shown 98 98
B1070 SP487 24 + 6fr multi, diff. 1.80 1.80

Souvenir Sheet

B1071 SP487 50 + 12fr multi, diff. 3.75 3.75

See Nos. B1081-B1083, B1089-B1091, 1346.

1988 Summer Olympics, Seoul — SP488

1988, June 6 Photo. *Perf. 11½*

B1072 SP488 9fr + 2fr Table tennis 65 65
B1073 SP488 13fr + 3fr Cycling 95 95

Souvenir Sheet

B1074 SP488 50fr + 12fr Marathon runners 3.70 3.70

Solidarity — SP489

1988, Oct. 24 Photo. *Perf. 12x11½*

B1075 SP489 9fr + 2fr Jacques Brel 60 60
B1076 SP489 13fr + 3fr Jef Denyn 88 88
B1077 SP489 26fr + 6fr Fr. Ferdinand Verbiest 1.75 1.75
Nos. B1075-B1077 (3) 3.23 3.23

Belgian Red Cross SP490

Paintings: No. B1078, *Crucifixion of Christ,* by Rogier van der Weyden (c. 1399-1464). No. B1079, *Virgin and Child,* by David (c. 1460-1523). B1089, *The Good Samaritan,* by Denis van Alsloot.

1989, Feb. 20 Photo. *Perf. 11½*

B1078 SP490 9fr + 2fr multi 60 60
B1079 SP490 13fr + 3fr multi 88 88
B1080 SP490 24fr + 6fr multi 1.65 1.65
Nos. B1078-B1080 (3) 3.13 3.13

Stamp Collecting Promotion Type of 1988

Various flowers from *Sixty Roses for a Queen,* by P.J. Redoute (1759-1840) and inscriptions: No. B1081, "Centfeuille unique melee de rouge." No. B1082, "Bengale a grandes feuilles." No. B1083, Aeme vibere (tea roses).

1989, Apr. 17

B1081 SP487 13fr + 5fr multi 1.00 1.00
B1082 SP487 24fr + 6fr multi 1.65 1.65

Souvenir Sheet

B1083 SP487 50fr + 17fr multi 3.75 3.75

Solidarity SP491

Royal Greenhouses of Laeken.

1989, Oct. 23

B1084 SP491 9fr + 3fr Exterior 60 60
B1085 SP491 13fr + 4fr Interior, vert. 82 82
B1086 SP491 24fr + 5fr Dome exterior, vert. 1.40 1.40
B1087 SP491 26fr + 6fr Dome interior, vert. 1.55 1.55
Nos. B1084-B1087 (4) 4.37 4.37

Queen Elisabeth Chapelle Musicale, 50th Anniv. — SP492

1989, Nov. 6

B1088 SP492 24fr + 6fr G clef 1.45 1.45

Stamp Collecting Promotion Type of 1988

Various flowers from *Sixty Roses for a Queen,* by P.J. Redoute (1759-1840): No. B1089, *Bengale desprez.* No. B1090, *Bengale philippe.* No. B1091, *Maria leonida.*

1990, Feb. 5

B1089 SP487 14fr + 7fr multi 1.15 1.15
B1090 SP487 25fr + 12fr multi 2.00 2.00

Souvenir Sheet

B1091 SP487 50fr + 20fr multi 3.75 3.75

Youth and Music — SP493

Designs: 14fr+3fr, Beethoven and Lamoraal, Count of Egmont (1522-1568). 25fr+6fr, Joseph Cantre (1890-1957), drawing and sculpture.

1990, Oct. 6

B1092 SP493 10fr + 2fr multi 70 70
B1093 SP493 14fr + 3fr multi 1.00 1.00
B1094 SP493 25fr + 6fr multi 1.80 1.80
Nos. B1092-B1094 (3) 3.50 3.50

King Baudouin & Queen Fabiola, 30th Wedding Anniv. — SP494

1990, Dec. 10

B1095 SP494 50fr +15fr multi 4.25 4.25

Belgian Red Cross SP495

Details from paintings: No. B1096, The Temptation of St. Anthony by Hieronymus Bosch. No. B1097, The Annunciation by Dirk Bouts.

1991, Feb. 25, Photo. *Perf. 11½*

B1096 SP495 14fr +3fr multi 1.10 1.10
B1097 SP495 25fr +6fr multi 2.00 2.00

Belgian Film Personalities — SP496

Designs: 10fr+2fr, Charles Dekeukeleire (1905-1971), producer. 14fr+3fr, Jacques Ledoux (1921-1988), film conservationist. 25fr+6fr, Jacques Feyder (1899-1948), director.

1991, Oct. 28 Photo. *Perf. 11½*

B1098 SP496 10fr +2fr multi 75 75
B1099 SP496 14fr +3fr multi 1.05 1.05
B1100 SP496 25fr +6fr multi 1.90 1.90
Nos. B1098-B1100 (3) 3.70 3.70

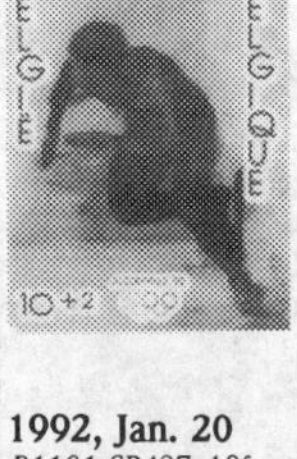

1992 Winter and Summer Olympics, Albertville and Barcelona — SP497

1992, Jan. 20 Photo. *Perf. 11½*

B1101 SP497 10fr +2fr Speed skating 75 75
B1102 SP497 10fr +2fr Baseball 75 75
B1103 SP497 14fr +3fr Women's tennis, horiz. 1.05 1.05
B1104 SP497 25fr +6fr Skeet shooting 1.90 1.90
Nos. B1101-B1104 (4) 4.45 4.45

Folk Legends SP498

Designs: 11fr + 2fr, Proud Margaret. 15fr + 3fr, Gustine Maca and the Witches. 28fr + 6fr, Reynard the Fox.

1992, June 22 Photo. *Perf. 11½*

B1105 SP498 11fr +2fr multi 78 78
B1106 SP498 15fr +3fr multi 1.10 1.10
B1107 SP498 28fr +6fr multi 2.00 2.00
Nos. B1105-B1107 (3) 3.88 3.88

Belgian Red Cross SP499

Paintings: 15fr + 3fr, Man with the Pointed Hat, by Adriaen Brouwer (1605-1638). 28fr + 7fr, Nereid and Triton, by Peter Paul Rubens, horiz.

1993, Feb. 15 Photo. *Perf. 11½*

B1108 SP499 15fr +3fr multi 1.10 1.10
B1109 SP499 28fr +7fr multi 2.10 2.10

Fight Against Cancer SP500

1993, Sept. 20 Photo. *Perf. 11½*

B1110 SP500 15fr +3fr multicolored 1.10 1.10

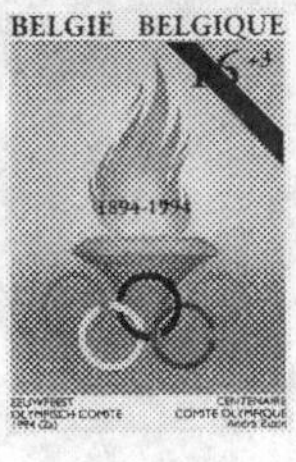

Intl. Olympic Committee, Cent. — SP501

Designs: No. B1112, Soccer players. No. B1113, Figure skater.

1994, Feb. 14 Photo. *Perf. 11½*

B1111 SP501 16fr +3fr multi 1.00 1.00
B1112 SP501 16fr +3fr multi 1.00 1.00
B1113 SP501 16fr +3fr multi 1.00 1.00
Nos. B1111-B1113 (3) 3.00 3.00

1994 World Cup Soccer Championships, Los Angeles (#B1112). 1994 Winter Olympics, Lillehammer, Norway (#B1113).

Porcelain — SP502

Designs: No. B1114, Tournai plate, Museum of Mariemont-Morlanweiz. No. B1115, Etterbeek cup, saucer, Municipal Museum, Louvain. 50fr+11fr, Delft earthenware jars, Pharmacy Museum of Maaseik.

1994, June 27 Photo. *Perf. 11½*

B1114	SP502	16fr +3fr multi	1.10	1.10
B1115	SP502	16fr +3fr multi	1.10	1.10

Souvenir Sheet

B1116	SP502	50fr +11fr multi	3.50	3.50

No. B1116 contains one 49x38mm stamp.

Solidarity SP503

Design: 16fr+3fr, Hearing-impaired person.

1994, Nov. 14 Photo. *Perf. 11½*

B1117	SP503	16fr +3fr multi	1.25	1.25

AIR POST STAMPS

Fokker FVII/3m over Ostend — AP1

Designs: 1.50fr, Plane over St. Hubert. 2fr, over Namur. 5fr, over Brussels.

Perf. 11½

1930, Apr. 30 Unwmk. Photo.

C1	AP1	50c blue	40	40
C2	AP1	1.50fr black brn	2.25	2.50
C3	AP1	2fr deep green	2.00	55
C4	AP1	5fr brown lake	1.75	95
		Nos. C1-C4 (4)	6.40	4.40

Exist imperf.

1930, Dec. 5

C5	AP1	5fr dark violet	27.50	27.50

Issued for use on a mail carrying flight from Brussels to Leopoldville, Belgian Congo, starting Dec. 7. Exists imperf.

Nos. C2 and C4 Surcharged in Carmine or Blue

1Fr ✕ 1Fr ✕

1935, May 23

C6	AP1	1fr on 1.50fr (C)	55	55
C7	AP1	4fr on 5fr (Bl)	7.50	4.75

Catalogue values for unused stamps in this section, from this point to the end of the section, are for Never Hinged items.

DC-4 Skymaster, Sabena Airline AP5

1946, Apr. 20 Engr. *Perf. 11½*

C8	AP5	6fr blue	70	24
C9	AP5	8.50fr vio brn	90	35
C10	AP5	50fr yel grn	4.50	55
a.		Perf. 12x11½ ('54)	225.00	80
C11	AP5	100fr gray	7.25	75
a.		Perf. 12x11½ ('54)	125.00	1.10
		Nos. C8-C11 (4)	13.35	1.89

Evolution of Postal Transportation — AP6

1949, July 1

C12	AP6	50fr dark brown	20.00	12.00

Centenary of Belgian postage stamps.

Glider — AP7

Design: 7fr, "Tipsy" plane.

1951, June 18 Photo. *Perf. 13½*

C12A	Strip of 2 + label	55.00	60.00
b.	AP7 6fr dark blue	20.00	25.00
c.	AP7 7fr carmine rose	20.00	25.00

For the 50th anniv. of the Aero Club of Belgium. The strip sold for 50fr.

1951, July 25 *Perf. 13½*

C13	AP7	6fr sepia	4.50	15
C14	AP7	7fr Prus grn	3.50	95

UN Types of Regular Issue, 1958

Designs: 5fr, ICAO. 6fr, World Meteorological Organization. 7.50fr, Protection of Refugees. 8fr, General Agreement on Tariffs and Trade. 9fr, UNICEF. 10fr, Atomic Energy Agency.

Perf. 11½

1958, Apr. 17 Unwmk. Engr.

C15	A137	5fr dl bl	35	55
C16	A136	6fr yel grn	60	1.00
C17	A137	7.50fr lilac	35	55
C18	A136	8fr sepia	35	55
C19	A137	9fr carmine	85	1.40
C20	A136	10fr redsh brn	1.10	1.65
		Nos. C15-C20 (6)	3.60	5.70

World's Fair, Brussels, Apr. 17-Oct. 19. See note after No. 476.

AIR POST SEMI-POSTAL STAMPS

Catalogue values for unused stamps in this section are for Never Hinged items.

American Soldier in Combat — SPAP1

Perf. 11x11½

1946, June 15 Unwmk. Engr.

CB1	SPAP1	17.50fr + 62.50fr dl brn	90	1.40
CB2	SPAP1	17.50fr + 62.50fr dl gray grn	90	1.40

Surtax for an American memorial at Bastogne.

An overprint, "Hommage a Roosevelt," was privately applied to Nos. CB1-CB2 in 1947 by the Association Belgo-Americaine.

In 1950 another private overprint was applied, in red, to Nos. CB1-CB2. It consists of "16-12-1944, 25-1-1945, Dedication July 16, 1950" and outlines of the American eagle emblem and the Bastogne Memorial. Similar overprints were applied to Nos. 265 and 345.

Flight Allegory SPAP2

1946, Sept. 7 *Perf. 11½*

CB3	SPAP2	2fr + 8fr brt vio	60	1.00

The surtax was for the benefit of aviation.

Nos. B417-B425 Surcharged in Various Arrangements in Red or Dark Blue

POSTE AERIENNE
LUCHTPOST
1F + 2F

LUCHTPOST
POSTE AERIENNE
1F +2F

Type I- Top line "POSTE AERIENNE"
Type II- Top line "LUCHTPOST"

1947, May 18 Photo. *Perf. 11½*

Type I

CB4	1fr + 2fr on #B417 (R)	60	90
CB5	1.50fr + 2.50fr on #B418	60	90
CB6	2fr + 45fr on #B419	60	90
CB7	1fr + 2fr on #B420 (R)	60	90
CB8	1.50fr + 2.50fr on #B421	60	90
CB9	2fr + 45fr on #B422	60	90
CB10	1fr + 2fr on #B423 (R)	60	90
CB11	1.50fr + 2.50fr on #B424 (R)	60	90
CB12	2fr + 45fr on #B425	60	90

Type II

CB4a	1fr + 2fr on #B417 (R)	60	90
CB5a	1.50fr + 2.50fr on #B418	60	90
CB6a	2fr + 45fr on #B419	60	90
CB7a	1fr + 2fr on #B420 (R)	60	90
CB8a	1.50fr + 2.50fr on #B421	60	90
CB9a	2fr + 45fr on #B422	60	90
CB10a	1fr + 2fr on #B423 (R)	60	90
CB11a	1.50fr + 2.50fr on #B424 (R)	60	90
CB12a	2fr + 45fr on #B425	60	90
	Nos. CB4-CB12 (9)	5.40	8.10
	Nos. CB4a-CB12a (9)	5.40	8.10

In 1948 Nos. CB4-CB12 and CB4a-CB12a were punched with the letters "IMABA," and the inscription "Imaba du 21 au 29 aout 1948" was applied to the backs. Value $20.

Helicopter Leaving Airport SPAP3

1950, Aug. 7

CB13	SPAP3	7fr + 3fr blue	8.00	5.25

Surtax for the Natl. Aeronautical Committee.

SPECIAL DELIVERY STAMPS

From 1874 to 1903 certain hexagonal telegraph stamps were used as special delivery stamps.

Town Hall, Brussels — SD1

Eupen — SD2

Designs: 2.35fr, Street in Ghent. 3.50fr, Bishop's Palace, Liege. 5.25fr, Notre Dame Cathedral, Antwerp.

1929 Unwmk. Photo. *Perf. 11½*

E1	SD1	1.75fr dark blue	80	32
E2	SD1	2.35fr carmine	1.50	45
E3	SD1	3.50fr dark vio	4.00	6.50
E4	SD1	5.25fr olive grn	4.00	4.75

1931

E5	SD2	2.45fr dark green	11.00	1.75
		Nos. E1-E5 (5)	21.30	13.77

No. E5 Surcharged in Red

2 Fr 50 ✕

1932

E6	SD2	2.50fr on 2.45fr dk grn	8.00	1.25

POSTAGE DUE STAMPS

D1

D2

1870 Unwmk. Typo. *Perf. 15*

J1	D1	10c green	3.50	1.50
a.		Half used as 5c on piece		3.50
J2	D1	20c ultra	25.00	2.25

1895-09 *Perf. 14*

J3	D2	5c yel grn	15	15
J4	D2	10c org brn	4.50	1.10
J5	D2	10c carmine ('00)	15	15
J6	D2	20c olive green	15	15
J7	D2	30c pale bl ('09)	30	22
J8	D2	50c yel brn	10.00	3.50
J9	D2	50c gray ('00)	60	42
J10	D2	1fr carmine	21.00	11.50
J11	D2	1fr ocher ('00)	7.25	4.75
		Nos. J3-J11 (9)	44.10	21.94

1916 Redrawn

J12	D2	5c blue grn	6.00	3.00
J13	D2	10c carmine	6.00	2.25
J14	D2	20c dp gray grn	14.00	7.50
J15	D2	30c brt blue	2.25	1.75
J16	D2	50c gray	30.00	25.00
		Nos. J12-J16 (5)	58.25	39.50

In the redrawn stamps the lions have a heavy, colored outline. There is a thick vertical line at the outer edge of the design on each side.

D3

D4

1919 *Perf. 14*

J17	D3	5c green	35	25
J18	D3	10c carmine	85	22
J19	D3	20c gray green	6.50	65
J20	D3	30c bright blue	1.25	20
J21	D3	50c gray	2.50	25
		Nos. J17-J21 (5)	11.45	1.57

1922-32

J22	D4	5c dk gray	15	15
J23	D4	10c green	15	15
J24	D4	20c deep brn	15	15
J25	D4	30c ver ('24)	22	15
a.		30c rose red	75	45
J26	D4	40c red brn ('25)	22	15
J27	D4	50c ultra	1.90	15
J28	D4	70c red brn ('29)	28	15
J29	D4	1fr vio ('25)	45	15
J30	D4	1fr rose lil ('32)	38	15
J31	D4	1.20fr ol grn ('29)	65	45
J32	D4	1.50fr ol grn ('32)	65	45
J33	D4	2fr vio ('29)	75	18
J34	D4	3.50fr dp bl ('29)	1.00	22
		Nos. J22-J34 (13)	6.95	
		Set value		2.25

1934-46 *Perf. 14x13½*

J35	D4	35c green ('35)	38	45
J36	D4	50c slate	22	15
J37	D4	60c carmine ('38)	38	28
J38	D4	80c slate ('38)	30	18
J39	D4	1.40fr gray ('35)	65	45

J39A	D4	3fr org brn ('46)	1.10	60
J39B	D4	7fr brt red vio ('46)	2.25	3.25
		Nos. J35-J39B (7)	5.28	5.36

See Nos. J54-J61.

Catalogue values for unused stamps in this section, from this point to the end of the section, are for Never Hinged items.

D5

D6

1945 Typo. *Perf. 12½*

Inscribed "TE BETALEN" at Top

J40	D5	10c gray olive	15	15
J41	D5	20c ultramarine	15	15
J42	D5	30c carmine	15	15
J43	D5	40c black violet	15	15
J44	D5	50c dl bl grn	15	15
J45	D5	1fr sepia	15	15
J46	D5	2fr red orange	18	15

Inscribed "A PAYER" at Top

J47	D5	10c gray olive	15	15
J48	D5	20c ultramarine	15	15
J49	D5	30c carmine	15	15
J50	D5	40c black vio	15	15
J51	D5	50c dl bl grn	15	15
J52	D5	1fr sepia	15	15
J53	D5	2fr red orange	18	15
		Set value	1.58	1.70

Type of 1922-32

1949-53 Typo. *Perf. 14x13½*

J54	D4	65c emerald	6.25	8.00
J55	D4	1.60fr lilac rose ('53)	7.50	11.00
J56	D4	1.80fr red	11.00	11.00
J57	D4	2.40fr gray lilac ('53)	6.50	3.00
J58	D4	4fr deep blue ('53)	7.50	1.75
J59	D4	5fr red brn	3.00	65
J60	D4	8fr lilac rose	7.50	10.00
J61	D4	10fr dark violet	6.25	8.00
		Nos. J54-J61 (8)	55.50	53.40

Numerals 6½mm or More High

1966-70 Photo.

J62	D6	1fr brt pink	15	15
J63	D6	2fr blue green	15	15
J64	D6	3fr blue	15	15
J65	D6	5fr purple	28	25
J66	D6	6fr bis brn	32	32
J67	D6	7fr red org ('70)	38	38
J68	D6	20fr slate grn	1.40	1.40
		Nos. J62-J68 (7)	2.83	2.80

Printed on various papers.

Numerals 4½-5½mm High

1985-87 Photo. *Perf. 14x13½*

J69	D6	1fr lilac rose	15	15
J70	D6	2fr dull blue grn	15	15
J71	D6	3fr greenish blue	15	15
J72	D6	4fr green	20	15
J73	D6	5fr light vio	25	18
J74	D6	7fr brt orange	35	28
J75	D6	8fr pale gray	40	30
J76	D6	9fr rose lake	45	35
J77	D6	10fr lt red brn	50	38
J78	D6	20fr lt olive grn	1.10	1.10
		Nos. J69-J78 (10)	3.70	3.19

Printed on various papers.

Issue dates: 3fr, 4fr, 8fr-10fr, Mar. 25, 1985. 2fr, 20fr, 1986. 1fr, 5fr, 7fr, 1987.

This is an expanding set. Numbers will change again if necessary.

MILITARY STAMPS

Catalogue values for unused stamps in this section are for Never Hinged items.

King Baudouin

M1 M2

Unwmk.

1967, July 17 Photo. *Perf. 11*

M1	M1	1.50fr greenish gray	55	45

1971-75 Engr. *Perf. 11½*

M2	M2	1.75fr green	1.10	55
M3	M2	2.25fr gray green ('72)	1.00	38
M4	M2	2.50fr gray green ('74)	38	32
M5	M2	3.25fr vio brown ('75)	30	16
		Nos. M2-M5 (4)	2.78	1.41

#M1-M3 are luminescent, #M4-M5 are not.

MILITARY PARCEL POST STAMP

Type of Parcel Post Stamp of 1938 Surcharged with New Value and "M" in Blue.

1939 Unwmk. *Perf. 13½*

MQ1	PP19	3fr on 5.50fr copper red	30	20

OFFICIAL STAMPS

For franking the official correspondence of the Administration of the Belgian National Railways.

Counterfeits exist of Nos. O1-O25.

Regular Issue of 1921-27 Overprinted in Black

1929-30 Unwmk. *Perf. 14*

O1	A58	5c gray	15	20
O2	A58	10c bl grn	22	38
O3	A58	35c bl grn	30	30
O4	A58	60c ol grn	35	28
O5	A58	1.50fr brt bl	6.25	6.25
O6	A58	1.75fr ultra ('30)	1.40	2.00
		Nos. O1-O6 (6)	8.67	9.41

Same Overprint, in Red or Black, on Regular Issues of 1929-30

1929-31

O7	A63	5c slate (R)	15	28
O8	A63	10c olive grn (R)	30	35
O9	A63	25c rose red (Bk)	90	75
O10	A63	35c dp green (R)	1.10	45
O11	A63	40c red vio (Bk)	75	38
O12	A63	50c dp blue (R) ('31)	50	28
O13	A63	60c rose (Bk)	4.25	5.25
O14	A63	70c orange brn (Bk)	2.75	1.00
O15	A63	75c black vio (R) ('31)	2.50	75
		Nos. O7-O15 (9)	13.20	9.49

Overprinted on Regular Issue of 1932

1932

O16	A73	10c olive grn (R)	52	60
O17	A74	35c dp green	9.00	75
O18	A71a	75c bister brn (R)	1.50	28
		Nos. O16-O18 (3)	11.02	1.63

Overprinted on No. 262 in Red

1935 *Perf. 13½x14*

O19	A80	70c olive black	1.90	28

Regular Stamps of 1935-36 Overprinted in Red

1936-38 *Perf. 13½, 13½x14, 14*

O20	A82	10c olive bister	15	24
O21	A82	35c green	18	28
O22	A82	50c dark blue	38	24
O23	A83	70c brown	1.25	52

Overprinted in Black or Red on Regular Issue of 1938

Perf. 13½x14

O24	A82	40c red violet (Bk)	24	24
O25	A85	75c olive gray (R)	55	20
		Nos. O20-O25 (6)	2.75	1.72

Regular Issues of 1935-41 Overprinted in Red or Dark Blue

1941-44 *Perf. 14, 14x13½, 13½x14*

O26	A82	10c olive bister	15	15
a.		Inverted overprint		*40.00*
O27	A82	40c red violet	55	75
O28	A82	50c dark blue	15	15
a.		Inverted overprint		
O29	A83a	1fr rose car (Bl)	45	35
O30	A85	1fr rose pink (Bl)	15	15
O31	A83a	2.25fr grnsh blk ('44)	28	50
O32	A84	2.25fr gray violet	45	70
		Nos. O26-O32 (7)	2.18	2.75

Nos. O21, O23 and O25 Surcharged with New Values in Black or Red

1942

O33	A82	10c on 35c green	18	32
O34	A83	50c on 70c brown	15	18
O35	A85	50c on 75c ol gray (R)	15	18
		Nos. O33-O35 (3)	48	68

Catalogue values for unused stamps in this section, from this point to the end of the section, are for Never Hinged items.

O1

O2

1946-48 Unwmk. *Perf. 14*

O36	O1	10c olive bister	20	20
O37	O1	20c brt violet	1.75	75
O38	O1	50c dk blue	25	22
O39	O1	65c red lilac ('48)	2.75	1.10
O40	O1	75c lilac rose	20	30
O41	O1	90c brown violet	3.50	50
		Nos. O36-O41 (6)	8.65	3.07

Types A99, A101 and A102 with "B" Emblem Added to Design

1948 *Perf. 11½*

O42	A99	1.35fr red brown	3.25	80
O43	A99	1.75fr dk gray green	4.00	30
O44	A101	3fr brt red violet	21.00	4.00
O45	A102	3.15fr deep blue	9.00	8.00
O46	A102	4fr brt ultra	16.00	15.00
		Nos. O42-O46 (5)	53.25	28.10

1953-66 Typo. *Perf. 13½x14*

O47	O2	10c orange	65	85
O48	O2	20c red lilac	75	60
O49	O2	30c gray green ('58)	75	1.00
O50	O2	40c olive gray	50	40
O51	O2	50c light blue	70	50
O51A	O2	60c lilac rose ('66)	1.10	90
O52	O2	65c red lilac	27.50	42.50
O53	O2	80c emerald	1.50	85
O54	O2	90c deep blue	3.00	1.25
O55	O2	1fr rose	38	40
		Nos. O47-O55 (10)	36.83	49.25

See Nos. O66, O68.

King Baudouin

O3 O4

1954-70 Photo. *Perf. 11½*

O56	O3	1.50fr gray	65	38
O57	O3	2fr rose red	25.00	75
O58	O3	2fr blue grn ('59)	50	30
O59	O3	2.50fr red brown ('58)	16.00	75
O60	O3	3fr red lilac ('58)	1.25	60
O61	O3	3.50fr yel green ('70)	70	60
O62	O3	4fr brt blue	1.50	1.00
O63	O3	6fr car rose ('58)	3.25	1.65
		Nos. O56-O63 (8)	48.85	6.03

Type of 1953-66 Redrawn

1970-75 Typo. *Perf. 13½x14*

O66	O2	1.50fr grnsh gray ('75)	18	15
O68	O2	2.50fr brown	18	15
		Set value		20

1971-73 Engr. *Perf. 11½*

O71	O4	3.50fr org brn ('73)	1.75	1.25
O72	O4	4.50fr brown ('73)	1.10	90
O73	O4	7fr red	45	40
O74	O4	15fr violet	90	90
		Nos. O71-O74 (4)	4.20	3.45

Nos. O71-O74 are on luminescent paper.

1974-80

O75	O4	3fr yel grn	4.00	1.25
O76	O4	4fr blue	1.50	75
O77	O4	4.50fr grnsh bl ('75)	45	25
O78	O4	5fr lilac	20	20
O79	O4	6fr carmine ('78)	28	28
O80	O4	6.50fr black ('76)	45	45
O81	O4	8fr bluish blk ('78)	35	30
O82	O4	9fr lt red brn ('80)	35	30
O83	O4	10fr rose car	38	35
O84	O4	25fr lilac ('76)	1.00	1.00
O85	O4	30fr org brn ('78)	1.40	1.25
		Nos. O75-O85 (11)	10.36	6.38

Heraldic Lion — O5

1977-82 Typo. *Perf. 13½x14*

O87	O5	50c brown ('82)	15	15
O92	O5	1fr lilac ('82)	15	15
O94	O5	2fr orange ('82)	15	15
O95	O5	4fr red brown	30	25
O96	O5	5fr green ('80)	35	28
		Set value	90	74

NEWSPAPER STAMPS

Counterfeits exist of Nos. P1-P40.

Parcel Post Stamps of 1923-27 Overprinted

JOURNAUX
DAGBLADEN
1928

Perf. 14½x14, 14x14½

1928 Unwmk.

P1	PP12	10c vermilion	15	20
P2	PP12	20c turq blue	15	20
P3	PP12	40c olive grn	15	20
P4	PP12	60c orange	30	45
P5	PP12	70c dk brown	18	20
P6	PP12	80c violet	25	35
P7	PP12	90c slate	1.00	1.00
P8	PP13	1fr brt blue	38	28
a.		1fr ultramarine	5.50	2.50
P10	PP13	2fr olive grn	70	30
P11	PP13	3fr orange red	75	45
P12	PP13	4fr rose	1.00	55
P13	PP13	5fr violet	1.00	52
P14	PP13	6fr bister brn	1.90	90
P15	PP13	7fr orange	2.25	1.10
P16	PP13	8fr dk brown	2.50	1.40
P17	PP13	9fr red violet	4.75	1.50
P18	PP13	10fr blue green	4.00	1.40
P19	PP13	20fr magenta	7.00	3.50
		Nos. P1-P8,P10-P19 (18)	28.41	14.50

Parcel Post Stamps of 1923-28 Overprinted

JOURNAUX
DAGBLADEN

1929-31

P20	PP12	10c vermilion	18	16
P21	PP12	20c turq blue	18	16
P22	PP12	40c olive green	22	20
a.		Inverted overprint		
P23	PP12	60c orange	30	35
P24	PP12	70c dk brown	38	20
P25	PP12	80c violet	45	22
P26	PP12	90c gray	1.25	1.00
P27	PP13	1fr ultra	42	25
a.		1fr bright blue	2.00	50
P28	PP13	1.10fr org brn ('31)	6.25	1.40
P29	PP13	1.50fr gray vio ('31)	6.25	1.90
P30	PP13	2fr olive green	1.25	25
P31	PP13	2.10fr sl gray ('31)	22.50	9.00
P32	PP13	3fr orange red	1.40	42
P33	PP13	4fr rose	1.40	70
P34	PP13	5fr violet	2.00	55
P35	PP13	6fr bister brn	2.50	1.00
P36	PP13	7fr orange	2.50	1.00
P37	PP13	8fr dk brown	2.50	1.10
P38	PP13	9fr red violet	3.50	1.50
P39	PP13	10fr blue green	2.50	1.10
P40	PP13	20fr magenta	8.75	4.50
		Nos. P20-P40 (21)	66.68	26.96

PARCEL POST AND RAILWAY STAMPS

Values for used Railway Stamps (Chemins de Fer) stamps are for copies with railway cancellations. Railway Stamps with postal cancellations sell for twice as much.

Coat of Arms — PP1

1879-82 Unwmk. Typo. *Perf. 14*

Q1	PP1	10c violet brown	27.50	1.90
Q2	PP1	20c blue	92.50	8.25
Q3	PP1	25c green ('81)	115.00	4.50
Q4	PP1	50c carmine	900.00	3.75
Q5	PP1	80c yellow	925.00	25.00
Q6	PP1	1fr gray ('82)	82.50	6.25

Used copies of Nos. Q1-Q6 with pinholes, a normal state, sell for half price.

Most of the stamps of 1882-1902 (Nos. Q7 to Q28) are without watermark. Twice in each sheet of 100 stamps they have one of three watermarks: (1) A winged wheel and "Chemins de Fer de l'Etat Belge," (2) Coat of Arms of Belgium and "Royaume de Belgique," (3) Larger Coat of Arms, without inscription.

PP2

1882-94 *Perf. 15½x14½*

Q7	PP2	10c brown ('86)	9.25	60
Q8	PP2	15c gray ('94)	8.00	6.00
Q9	PP2	20c blue ('86)	40.00	2.00
a.		20c ultra ('90)	35.00	2.00
Q10	PP2	25c yel grn ('91)	35.00	2.25
a.		25c blue green ('87)	40.00	2.25
Q11	PP2	50c carmine	40.00	30
Q12	PP2	80c brnsh buff	35.00	42
Q13	PP2	80c lemon	42.50	1.75
Q14	PP2	1fr lavender	215.00	1.75
Q15	PP2	2fr yel buff ('94)	140.00	32.50

Counterfeits exist.

PP3

Name of engraver below frame

1895-97

Numerals in Black, except 1fr, 2fr

Q16	PP3	10c red brown ('96)	6.50	28
Q17	PP3	15c gray	6.25	4.75
Q18	PP3	20c blue	13.00	60
Q19	PP3	25c green	13.00	85
Q20	PP3	50c carmine	14.00	28
Q21	PP3	60c violet ('96)	25.00	35
Q22	PP3	80c ol yel ('96)	21.00	35
Q23	PP3	1fr lilac brown	92.50	60
Q24	PP3	2fr yel buff ('97)	100.00	3.00

Counterfeits exist.

1902

Numerals in Black

Q25	PP3	30c orange	14.00	90
Q26	PP3	40c green	15.00	90
Q27	PP3	70c blue	27.50	45
a.		Numerals omitted	*750.00*	
Q28	PP3	90c red	30.00	60
		Nos. Q25-CQ28 (4)	86.50	2.85

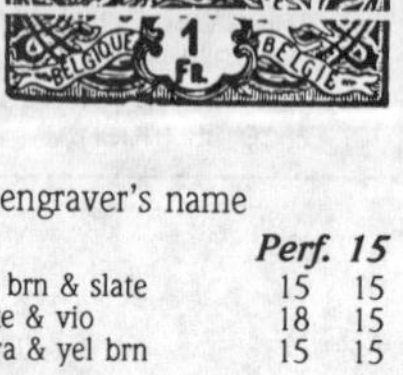

Winged Wheel — PP4

Without engraver's name

1902-14 *Perf. 15*

Q29	PP3	10c yel brn & slate	15	15
Q30	PP3	15c slate & vio	18	15
Q31	PP3	20c ultra & yel brn	15	15
Q32	PP3	25c yel grn & red	18	15
Q33	PP3	30c orange & bl grn	18	15
Q34	PP3	35c bister & bl grn ('12)	32	20
Q35	PP3	40c blue grn & vio	18	15
Q36	PP3	50c pale rose & vio	15	15
Q37	PP3	55c lilac brn & ultra ('14)	32	20
Q38	PP3	60c violet & red	18	15
Q39	PP3	70c blue & red	15	15
Q40	PP3	80c lemon & vio brn	15	15
Q41	PP3	90c red & yel grn	18	15
Q42	PP4	1fr vio brn & org	18	15
Q43	PP4	1.10fr rose & blk ('06)	20	15
Q44	PP4	2fr ocher & bl grn	20	15
Q45	PP4	3fr black & ultra	32	20
Q46	PP4	4fr yel grn & red ('13)	1.25	70
Q47	PP4	5fr org & bl grn ('13)	52	52
Q48	PP4	10fr ol yel & brn vio ('13)	90	55
		Nos. Q29-Q48 (20)	6.04	
		Set value		3.70

Exist imperforate.

Regular Issues of 1912-13 Handstamped in Violet

1915 *Perf. 14*

Q49	A42	5c green	130.00	130.00
Q50	A43	10c red	465.00	465.00
Q51	A45	10c red	82.50	82.50
a.		With engraver's name	300.00	300.00
Q52	A43	20c olive grn	*725.00*	*725.00*
Q53	A45	20c olive grn	90.00	90.00
a.		With engraver's name	300.00	300.00
Q54	A45	25c ultra	90.00	90.00
a.		With engraver's name	300.00	300.00
Q55	A43	35c bister brn	130.00	130.00
Q55A	A45	40c green	*1,050.*	*1,050.*
Q56	A45	40c green	90.00	90.00
Q57	A43	50c gray	110.00	110.00
Q58	A43	1fr orange	140.00	140.00
Q59	A43	2fr violet	*800.00*	*800.00*
Q60	A44	5fr plum	*1,800.*	*1,800.*

Excellent forgeries of this overprint exist.

PP5

PP6

1916 Litho. *Perf. 13½*

Q61	PP5	10c pale blue	75	18
Q62	PP5	15c olive grn	85	35
Q63	PP5	20c red	1.40	35
Q64	PP5	25c lt brown	1.40	35
Q65	PP5	30c lilac	85	30
Q66	PP5	35c gray	85	30
Q67	PP5	40c orange yel	1.90	90
Q68	PP5	50c bister	1.50	30
Q69	PP5	55c brown	1.90	1.25
Q70	PP5	60c gray vio	1.40	30
Q71	PP5	70c green	1.40	30
Q72	PP5	80c red brown	1.40	30
Q73	PP5	90c blue	1.40	30
Q74	PP6	1fr gray	1.40	30
Q75	PP6	1.10fr ultra *(Franken)*	19.00	15.00
Q76	PP6	2fr red	15.00	30
Q77	PP6	3fr violet	15.00	30
Q78	PP6	4fr emerald	25.00	60
Q79	PP6	5fr brown	25.00	90
Q80	PP6	10fr orange	25.00	60
		Nos. Q61-Q80 (20)	142.40	23.48

Type of 1916 Inscribed "FRANK" instead of "FRANKEN"

1920

Q81	PP6	1.10fr ultra	1.25	30

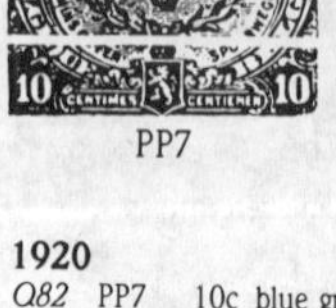

PP7

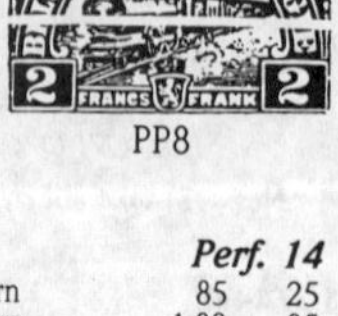

PP8

1920 *Perf. 14*

Q82	PP7	10c blue grn	85	25
Q83	PP7	15c olive grn	1.00	85
Q84	PP7	20c red	1.00	25
Q85	PP7	25c gray brn	1.25	65
Q86	PP7	30c red vio	8.25	6.50
Q87	PP7	40c pale org	5.75	52
Q88	PP7	50c bister	4.00	40
Q89	PP7	55c pale brown	3.00	1.25
Q90	PP7	60c dk violet	5.00	65
Q91	PP7	70c green	7.25	1.10
Q92	PP7	80c red brown	21.00	90
Q93	PP7	90c dull blue	4.00	40
Q94	PP8	1fr gray	37.50	65
Q95	PP8	1.10fr ultra	10.50	2.00
Q96	PP8	1.20fr dk green	8.25	32
Q97	PP8	1.40fr black brn	4.75	32
Q98	PP8	2fr vermilion	40.00	52
Q99	PP8	3fr red vio	50.00	85
Q100	PP8	4fr yel grn	50.00	50
Q101	PP8	5fr bister brn	50.00	50
Q102	PP8	10fr brown org	50.00	50
		Nos. Q82-Q102 (21)	363.35	19.88

PP9

PP10

Types PP7 and PP9 differ in the position of the wheel and the tablet above it.

Types PP8 and PP10 differ in the bars below "FR".

There are many other variations in the designs.

1920-21 Typo.

Q103	PP9	10c carmine	30	15
Q104	PP9	15c yel grn	28	15
Q105	PP9	20c blue grn	70	22
Q106	PP9	25c ultra	65	22
Q107	PP9	30c chocolate	85	22
Q108	PP9	35c orange brn	90	30
Q109	PP9	40c orange	1.10	15
Q110	PP9	50c rose	1.10	15
Q111	PP9	55c yel ('21)	2.25	1.10
Q112	PP9	60c dull rose	1.10	15
Q113	PP9	70c emerald	2.00	20
Q114	PP9	80c violet	2.00	15
Q115	PP9	90c lemon	9.25	10.00
Q116	PP9	90c claret	4.50	40
Q117	PP10	1fr buff	4.50	32
Q118	PP10	1fr red brown	4.00	25
Q119	PP10	1.10fr ultra	1.50	45
Q120	PP10	1.20fr orange	2.00	15
Q121	PP10	1.40fr yellow	8.25	1.00
Q122	PP10	1.60fr turq blue	14.00	32
Q123	PP10	1.60fr emerald	32.50	32
Q124	PP10	2fr pale rose	15.00	20
Q125	PP10	3fr dp rose	14.00	20
Q126	PP10	4fr emerald	14.00	25
Q127	PP10	5fr lt violet	12.00	22
Q128	PP10	10fr lemon	75.00	2.50
Q129	PP10	10fr dk brown	12.50	18
Q130	PP10	15fr dp rose ('21)	12.50	22
Q131	PP10	20fr dk blue ('21)	180.00	1.65
		Nos. Q103-Q131 (29)	428.73	21.79

PP11

1922 Engr. *Perf. 11½*

Q132	PP11	2fr black	2.75	15
Q133	PP11	3fr brown	27.50	18
Q134	PP11	4fr green	6.50	15
Q135	PP11	5r claret	6.50	15
Q136	PP11	10fr yel brown	7.50	15
Q137	PP11	15fr rose red	7.50	22
Q138	PP11	20fr blue	47.50	24
		Nos. Q132-Q138 (7)	105.75	1.24

PP12

PP13

Perf. 14x13½, 13½x14

1923-40 Typo.

Q139	PP12	5c red brown	18	24
Q140	PP12	10c vermilion	15	15
Q141	PP12	15c ultra	22	30
Q142	PP12	20c turq blue	15	15
Q143	PP12	30c brn vio ('27)	22	15
Q144	PP12	40c olive grn	18	15
Q145	PP12	50c magenta ('27)	18	15
Q146	PP12	60c orange	22	15
Q147	PP12	70c dk brown ('24)	15	15
Q148	PP12	80c violet	18	15
Q149	PP12	90c slate ('27)	1.00	15
Q150	PP13	1fr ultra	28	15
Q151	PP13	1fr brt blue ('28)	55	15
Q152	PP13	1.10fr orange	3.00	15
Q153	PP13	1.50fr turq blue	3.25	24
Q154	PP13	1.70fr dp brown ('31)	75	16
Q155	PP13	1.80fr claret	5.50	16
Q156	PP13	2fr olive grn ('24)	28	16
Q157	PP13	2.10fr gray grn	6.00	25
Q158	PP13	2.40fr dp violet	6.00	38
Q159	PP13	2.70fr gray ('24)	12.00	16
Q160	PP13	3fr orange red	45	15
Q161	PP13	3.30fr brown ('24)	12.50	25
Q162	PP13	4fr rose ('24)	55	15
Q163	PP13	5fr violet ('24)	90	15
Q163A	PP13	5fr brn vio ('40)	45	38
Q164	PP13	6fr bis brn ('27)	52	15
Q165	PP13	7fr orange ('27)	90	15
Q166	PP13	8fr dp brown ('27)	75	15
Q167	PP13	9fr red vio ('27)	2.00	15
Q168	PP13	10fr blue grn ('27)	90	15
Q168A	PP13	10fr black ('40)	2.50	2.75
Q169	PP13	20fr magenta ('27)	1.90	15
Q170	PP13	30fr turq green ('31)	6.00	16
Q171	PP13	40fr gray ('31)	42.50	30
Q172	PP13	50fr bister ('27)	9.00	20
		Nos. Q139-Q172 (36)	122.26	
		Set value		7.75

See Nos. Q239-Q262. For overprints see Nos. Q216-Q238. Stamps overprinted "Bagages Reisgoed" are revenues.

PP14

1924

Green Surcharge

Q173	PP14	2.30fr on 2.40fr violet	4.50	25
a.		Inverted surcharge	57.50	

Type of Regular Issue of 1926-27 Overprinted

1928 *Perf. 14*

Q174	A61	4fr buff	6.50	90
Q175	A61	5fr bister	6.50	1.10

Central P.O., Brussels PP15

1929-30 Engr. *Perf. 11½*

Q176	PP15	3fr black brn	1.10	15
Q177	PP15	4fr gray	1.10	15
Q178	PP15	5fr carmine	1.10	15
Q179	PP15	6fr vio brn ('30)	18.00	20.00
		Nos. Q176-Q179 (4)	21.30	20.45

No. Q179 Surcharged in Blue

×4 4×

1933

Q180	PP15	4(fr) on 6fr vio brn	18.00	18

Modern Locomotive PP16

1934 **Photo.** ***Perf. 13½x14***

Q181	PP16	3fr dk green	3.00	1.50
Q182	PP16	4fr red violet	90	15
Q183	PP16	5fr dp rose	3.25	15
		Nos. Q181-Q183 (3)	7.15	1.80

Modern Railroad Train — PP17

Old Railroad Train — PP18

1935 **Engr.** ***Perf. 14x13½, 13½x14***

Q184	PP17	10c rose car	26	15
Q185	PP17	20c violet	32	15
Q186	PP17	30c black brn	42	32
Q187	PP17	40c dk blue	52	15
Q188	PP17	50c orange red	55	15
Q189	PP17	60c green	65	15
Q190	PP17	70c ultra	70	15
Q191	PP17	80c olive blk	65	15
Q192	PP17	90c rose lake	85	45
Q193	PP18	1fr brown vio	85	15
Q194	PP18	2fr gray blk	1.65	15
Q195	PP18	3fr red org	2.00	15
Q196	PP18	4fr violet brn	2.25	15
Q197	PP18	5fr plum	2.75	15
Q198	PP18	6fr dp green	3.00	15
Q199	PP18	7fr dp violet	3.50	15
Q200	PP18	8fr olive blk	4.50	20
Q201	PP18	9fr dk blue	5.25	15
Q202	PP18	10fr car lake	5.25	15
Q203	PP18	20fr green	24.00	20
Q204	PP18	30fr violet	75.00	1.00
Q205	PP18	40fr black brn	75.00	1.50
Q206	PP18	50fr rose car	85.00	1.10
Q207	PP18	100fr ultra	190.00	20.00
		Nos. Q184-Q207 (24)	484.92	27.17

Centenary of Belgian State Railway.

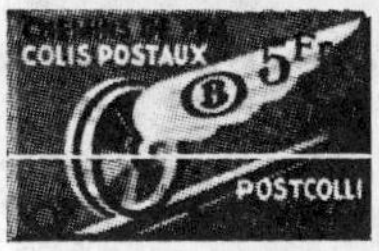

Winged Wheel — PP19

Surcharge in Red or Blue

1938 **Photo.** ***Perf. 13½***

Q208	PP19	5fr on 3.50fr dk grn	6.50	42
Q209	PP19	5fr on 4.50fr rose vio (Bl)	15	15
Q210	PP19	6fr on 5.50fr cop red (Bl)	32	15
a.		Half used as 3fr on piece		1.50
		Nos. Q208-Q210 (3)	6.97	
		Set value		59

See Nos. MQ1, Q297-Q299.

Symbolizing Unity Achieved Through Railroads PP20

1939 **Engr.** ***Perf. 13½x14***

Q211	PP20	20c redsh brn	2.00	2.25
Q212	PP20	50c vio bl	2.00	2.25
Q213	PP20	2fr rose red	2.00	2.25
Q214	PP20	9fr sl grn	2.00	2.25
Q215	PP20	10fr dk vio	2.00	2.25
		Nos. Q211-Q215 (5)	10.00	11.25

Issued in commemoration of the Railroad Exposition and Congress held at Brussels.

Parcel Post Stamps of 1925-27 Overprinted in Blue or Carmine

Perf. 14½x14, 14x14½

1940 **Unwmk.**

Q216	PP12	10c vermilion	15	15
Q217	PP12	20c turq bl (C)	15	15
Q218	PP12	30c brn vio	15	15
Q219	PP12	40c ol grn (C)	15	15
Q220	PP12	50c magenta	15	15
Q221	PP12	60c orange	15	20
Q222	PP12	70c dk brn	15	15
Q223	PP12	80c vio (C)	15	15
Q224	PP12	90c slate (C)	18	20
Q225	PP13	1fr ultra (C)	18	15
Q226	PP13	2fr ol grn (C)	18	15
Q227	PP13	3fr org red	18	15
Q228	PP13	4fr rose	18	15
Q229	PP13	5fr vio (C)	18	15
Q230	PP13	6fr bis brn	25	22
Q231	PP13	7fr orange	25	15
Q232	PP13	8fr dp brn	25	15
Q233	PP13	9fr red vio	25	15
Q234	PP13	10fr bl grn (C)	25	20
Q235	PP13	20fr magenta	45	20
Q236	PP13	30fr turq grn (C)	85	65
Q237	PP13	40fr gray (C)	1.10	1.65
Q238	PP13	50fr bister	1.25	85
		Nos. Q216-Q238 (23)	7.18	6.42

Types of 1923-40

1941

Q239	PP12	10c dl olive	15	15
Q240	PP12	20c lt vio	15	15
Q241	PP12	30c fawn	15	15
Q242	PP12	40c dull blue	15	15
Q243	PP12	50c lt grn	15	15
Q244	PP12	60c gray	15	15
Q245	PP12	70c chalky grn	15	15
Q246	PP12	80c orange	15	15
Q247	PP12	90c rose lilac	15	15
Q248	PP13	1fr lt yel grn	15	15
Q249	PP13	2fr vio brn	20	15
Q250	PP13	3fr slate	22	15
Q251	PP13	4fr dl olive	28	15
Q252	PP13	5fr rose lilac	35	15
Q253	PP13	5fr black	52	22
Q254	PP13	6fr org ver	50	20
Q255	PP13	7fr lilac	50	15
Q256	PP13	8fr chalky grn	50	15
Q257	PP13	9fr blue	60	15
Q258	PP13	10fr rose lilac	60	15
Q259	PP13	20fr milky blue	1.25	15
Q260	PP13	30fr orange	3.00	22
Q261	PP13	40fr rose	3.50	25
Q262	PP13	50fr brt red vio	4.50	15
		Nos. Q239-Q262 (24)	18.02	
		Set value		3.00

Adjusting Tie Plates — PP21

Engineer at Throttle — PP22

Freight Station Interior — PP23

Signal and Electric Train — PP24

1942 **Engr.** ***Perf. 14x13½***

Q263	PP21	9.20fr red org	60	80
Q264	PP22	12.30fr dp grn	60	85
Q265	PP23	14.30fr dk car	85	1.25

Perf. 11½

Q266	PP24	100fr ultra	16.00	24.00
		Nos. Q263-Q266 (4)	18.05	26.90

Catalogue values for unused stamps in this section, from this point to the end of the section, are for Never Hinged items.

PP25

PP26

PP27

1945-46 **Photo.** **Unwmk.**

Q267	PP25	10c ol blk ('46)	20	15
Q268	PP25	20c dp vio	20	15
Q269	PP25	30c chnt brn ('46)	20	15
Q270	PP25	40c dp bl ('46)	20	15
Q271	PP25	50c peacock grn	20	15
Q272	PP25	60c blk ('46)	22	15
Q273	PP25	70c emer ('46)	30	25
Q274	PP25	80c orange	50	20
Q275	PP25	90c brn vio ('46)	30	25
Q276	PP26	1fr bl grn ('46)	20	15
Q277	PP26	2fr blk brn	22	15
Q278	PP26	3fr grnsh blk ('46)	1.25	20
Q279	PP26	4fr dark blue	30	20
Q280	PP26	5fr sepia	30	15
Q281	PP26	6fr dk ol grn ('46)	1.50	15
Q282	PP26	7fr dk vio ('46)	50	18
Q283	PP26	8fr red org	50	15
Q284	PP26	9fr dp bl ('46)	65	15
Q285	PP27	10fr dk red ('46)	2.25	15
Q286	PP27	10fr sepia ('46)	1.10	25
Q287	PP27	20fr dk yel grn ('46)	50	15
Q288	PP27	30fr dp vio	75	15
Q289	PP27	40fr rose pink	65	15
Q290	PP27	50fr brt bl ('46)	8.00	15
		Nos. Q267-Q290 (24)	20.99	
		Set value		3.00

Mercury — PP28

1945-46 ***Perf. 13½x13***

Q291	PP28	3fr emer ('46)	35	25
Q292	PP28	5fr ultra	15	18
Q293	PP28	6fr red	18	15

Inscribed "Belgique-Belgie"

Q294	PP28	3fr emer ('46)	35	25
Q295	PP28	5fr ultra	15	18
Q296	PP28	6fr red	18	15
		Nos. Q291-Q296 (6)	1.36	1.16

Winged Wheel Type of 1938 Carmine Surcharge

1946 ***Perf. 13½x14***

Q297	PP19	8fr on 5.50fr brn	65	15
Q298	PP19	10fr on 5.50fr dk bl	75	25
Q299	PP19	12fr on 5.50fr vio	1.10	25
		Nos. Q297-Q299 (3)	2.50	65

Railway Crossing PP29

1947 **Engr.** ***Perf. 12½***

Q300	PP29	100fr dark green	6.25	25

Crossbowman with Train — PP30

1947 **Photo.** ***Perf. 11½***

Q301	PP30	8fr dk ol brn	1.00	25
Q302	PP30	10fr gray & bl	1.10	30
Q303	PP30	12fr dk vio	1.75	50
		Nos. Q301-Q303 (3)	3.85	1.05

Surcharged with New Value and Bars in Carmine

1948

Q304	PP30	9fr on 8fr	1.00	25
Q305	PP30	11fr on 10fr	1.10	40
Q306	PP30	13.50fr on 12fr	1.75	40
		Nos. Q304-Q306 (3)	3.85	1.05

Delivery of Parcel — PP31

1948

Q307	PP31	9fr chocolate	5.25	15
Q308	PP31	11fr brn car	5.50	15
Q309	PP31	13.50fr gray	8.00	35
		Nos. Q307-Q309 (3)	18.75	65

Locomotive of 1835 — PP32

Various Locomotives.

Lathe Work in Frame Differs

1949 **Engr.** ***Perf. 12½***

Q310	PP32	½fr dk brn	40	15
Q311	PP32	1fr car rose	52	15
Q312	PP32	2fr dp ultra	60	15
Q313	PP32	3fr dp mag	1.25	15
Q314	PP32	4fr bl grn	1.50	15
Q315	PP32	5fr org red	1.50	15
Q316	PP32	6fr brn vio	1.90	18
Q317	PP32	7fr yel grn	2.25	15
Q318	PP32	8fr grnsh bl	2.75	15
Q319	PP32	9fr yel brn	3.75	18
Q320	PP32	10fr citron	4.75	15
Q321	PP32	20fr orange	7.50	15
Q322	PP32	30fr blue	10.50	15
Q323	PP32	40fr lil rose	14.00	18
Q324	PP32	50fr violet	15.00	25
Q325	PP32	100fr red	42.50	18

Engraved; Center Typographed

Q326	PP32	10fr car rose & blk	6.00	70
		Nos. Q310-Q326 (17)	116.67	3.32

See No. Q337.

1949 **Engr.**

Design: Electric locomotive.

Q327	PP32	60fr blk brn	20.00	25

Opening of Charleroi-Brussels electric railway line, Oct. 15, 1949.

Mailing Parcel Post — PP33

Sorting PP34

Loading PP35

1950-52 ***Perf. 12, 12½***

Q328	PP33	11fr red org	5.25	40
Q329	PP33	12fr red vio ('51)	13.00	1.10
Q330	PP34	13fr dk bl grn	4.75	20
Q331	PP34	15fr ultra ('51)	12.50	30
Q332	PP35	16fr gray	5.00	20
Q333	PP33	17fr brn ('52)	6.75	40

Q334	PP35	18fr brt car ('51)	11.50	40
Q335	PP35	20fr brn org ('52)	6.75	45
		Nos. Q328-Q335 (8)	65.50	3.45

For surcharges see Nos. Q338-Q340.

Mercury and Winged Wheel — PP36

1951

Q336	PP36	25fr dark blue	9.00	8.00

25th anniv. of the founding of the Natl. Soc. of Belgian Railroads.

Type of 1949

Design: Electric locomotive.

1952 Unwmk. ***Perf. 11½***

Q337	PP32	300fr red violet	100.00	65

Nos. Q331, Q328 and Q334 Surcharged with New Value and "X" in Red, Blue or Green

1953 ***Perf. 12***

Q338	PP34	13fr on 15fr (R)	50.00	1.65
Q339	PP33	17fr on 11fr (Bl)	30.00	1.40
Q340	PP35	20fr on 18fr (G)	26.00	1.75
		Nos. Q338-Q340 (3)	106.00	4.80

Electric Train, 1952 — PP37

1953 **Engr.**

Q341	PP37	200fr dk yel grn & vio brn	175.00	4.00
Q342	PP37	200fr dk green	140.00	1.00

No. Q341 was issued to commemorate the opening of the railway link connecting Brussels North and South Stations, Oct. 4, 1952.

New North Station, Brussels — PP38

Chapelle Station, Brussels PP39

Designs: No. Q348, 15fr, Congress Station. 10fr, 20fr, 30fr, 40fr, 50fr, South Station. 100fr, 200fr, 300fr, Central Station.

1953-57 Unwmk. ***Perf. 11½***

Q343	PP38	1fr bister	50	15
Q344	PP38	2fr slate	65	15
Q345	PP38	3fr blue grn	85	15
Q346	PP38	4fr orange	1.40	15
Q347	PP38	5fr red brn	1.40	15
Q348	PP38	5fr dk red brn	9.25	25
Q349	PP38	6fr rose vio	1.65	15
Q350	PP38	7fr brt green	1.65	15
Q351	PP38	8fr rose red	1.65	15
Q352	PP38	9fr brt grnsh bl	2.75	15
Q353	PP38	10fr lt grn	2.75	15
Q354	PP38	15fr dl red	11.50	15
Q355	PP38	20fr blue	4.25	15
Q356	PP38	30fr purple	6.75	15
Q357	PP38	40fr brt purple	8.25	15
Q358	PP38	50fr lilac rose	10.00	15
Q359	PP39	60fr brt purple	20.00	15
Q360	PP39	80fr brown vio	24.00	15
Q361	PP39	100fr emerald	23.50	15
Q361A	PP39	200fr brt vio bl	52.50	1.65
Q361B	PP39	300fr lilac rose	82.50	2.25
		Nos. Q343-Q361B (21)	267.75	
		Set value		5.25

Issue dates: No. Q347, 20fr and 30fr, 1953; 80fr, 1955; 200fr, 1956; 300fr, 1957. Rest of set, 1954.

See Nos. Q407, Q431-Q432.

Electric Train — PP40

Mercury and Winged Wheel — PP41

1954

Q362	PP40	13fr chocolate	8.75	15
Q363	PP40	18fr dark blue	10.00	15
Q364	PP40	21fr lilac rose	11.00	50
		Nos. Q362-Q364 (3)	29.75	80

Nos. Q362-Q364 Surcharged with New Value and "X" in Blue, Red or Green

1956

Q365	PP40	14fr on 13fr (B)	6.25	15
Q366	PP40	19fr on 18fr (R)	6.75	25
Q367	PP40	22fr on 21fr (G)	7.25	45
		Nos. Q365-Q367 (3)	20.25	85

1957 Engr. ***Perf. 11½***

Q368	PP41	14fr brt green	6.00	25
Q369	PP41	19fr olive gray	7.00	35
Q370	PP41	22fr carmine rose	7.25	60
		Nos. Q368-Q370 (3)	20.25	1.20

Nos. Q369-Q370 Surcharged with New Value and "X" in Pink or Green

1959

Q371	PP41	20fr on 19fr (P)	20.00	38
Q372	PP41	20fr on 22fr (G)	22.50	60

Old North Station, Brussels PP42

1959 Engr. ***Perf. 11½***

Q373	PP42	20fr olive green	11.00	38

See Nos. Q381, Q383. For surcharges see Nos. Q378, Q382, Q384.

Diesel and Electric Locomotives and Association Emblem PP43

1960 Unwmk. ***Perf. 11½***

Q374	PP43	20fr red	40.00	30.00
Q375	PP43	50fr dark blue	40.00	27.50
Q376	PP43	60fr red lilac	40.00	27.50
Q377	PP43	70fr emerald	40.00	27.50
		Nos. Q374-Q377 (4)	160.00	112.50

75th anniv. of the Intl. Assoc. of Railway Congresses.

No. Q373 Surcharged with New Value and "X" in Red

1961

Q378	PP42	24fr on 20fr ol grn	60.00	38

South Station, Brussels — PP44

1962 Unwmk. ***Perf. 11½***

Q379	PP44	24fr dull red	6.00	38

No. Q379 Surcharged with New Value and "X" in Light Green

1963

Q380	PP44	26fr on 24fr dl red	5.00	38

Type of 1959

Design: 26fr, Central Station, Antwerp.

1963 Engr. ***Perf. 11½***

Q381	PP42	26fr blue	5.25	75

No. Q381 Surcharged in Red

1964, Apr. 20

Q382	PP42	28fr on 26fr blue	5.50	50

Type of 1959

Design: 28fr, St. Peter's Station, Ghent.

1965 Engr. ***Perf. 11½***

Q383	PP42	28fr red lilac	5.25	1.25

Nos. Q383 Surcharged with New Value and "X" in Green

1966

Q384	PP42	35fr on 28fr red lil	5.25	1.00

Arlon Railroad Station — PP45

Perf. 11½

1967, Aug. Unwmk. Engr.

Q385	PP45	25fr bister	6.50	30
Q386	PP45	30fr blue green	3.50	38
Q387	PP45	35fr deep blue	4.75	65
		Nos. Q385-Q387 (3)	14.75	1.33

See #Q408. For surcharges see #Q410-Q412.

Electric Train — PP46

Designs: 2fr, 3fr, 4fr, 5fr, 6fr, 7fr, 8fr, 9fr, like 1fr. 10fr, 20fr, 30fr, 40fr, Train going right. 50fr, 60fr, 70fr, 80fr, 90fr, Train going left. 100fr, 200fr, 300fr, Diesel train.

1968-73 Engr. ***Perf. 11½***

Q388	PP46	1fr olive bis	15	15
Q389	PP46	2fr slate	15	15
Q390	PP46	3fr bl grn	15	15
Q391	PP46	4fr orange	16	15
Q392	PP46	5fr brown	20	15
Q393	PP46	6fr plum	28	15
Q394	PP46	7fr brt grn	30	15
Q395	PP46	8fr carmine	35	15
Q396	PP46	9fr blue	38	15
Q397	PP46	10fr green	45	15
Q398	PP46	20fr dk bl	75	15
Q399	PP46	30fr dk pur	1.10	15
Q400	PP46	40fr brt lil	1.40	15
Q401	PP46	50fr brt pink	1.75	15
Q402	PP46	60fr brt vio	2.00	15
Q402A	PP46	70fr dp bis ('73)	2.75	1.00
Q403	PP46	80fr dk brn	2.75	25
Q403A	PP46	90fr yel grn ('73)	3.75	1.25
Q404	PP46	100fr emerald	4.00	45
Q405	PP46	200fr vio bl	8.75	80
Q406	PP46	300fr lil rose	19.00	1.25
		Nos. Q388-Q406 (21)	50.57	
		Set value		5.90

See No. Q409.

Types of 1953-68

Designs: 10fr, Congress Station, Brussels. 40fr, Arlon Station. 500fr, Electric train going left.

1968, June Engr. ***Perf. 11½***

Q407	PP38	10fr gray	50	15
Q408	PP45	40fr vermilion	18.00	40
Q409	PP46	500fr yellow	20.00	2.25
		Nos. Q407-Q409 (3)	38.50	2.80

Nos. Q385, Q387 and Q408 Surcharged with New Value and "X"

1970, Dec.

Q410	PP45	37fr on 25fr bister	35.00	3.50
Q411	PP45	48fr on 35fr dp bl	10.50	5.50
Q412	PP45	53fr on 40fr ver	12.00	6.75
		Nos. Q410-Q412 (3)	57.50	15.75

Ostend Station PP47

1971, Mar. Engr. ***Perf. 11½***

Q413	PP47	32fr bis & blk	1.50	60
Q414	PP47	37fr gray & blk	1.75	85
Q415	PP47	42fr bl & blk	2.00	90
Q416	PP47	44fr brt rose & blk	2.25	1.00
Q417	PP47	46fr vio & blk	2.25	1.00
Q418	PP47	50fr brick red & blk	2.75	1.10
Q419	PP47	52fr sep & blk	2.75	1.10
Q420	PP47	54fr yel grn & blk	3.00	1.10
Q421	PP47	61fr grnsh bl & blk	3.00	1.25
		Nos. Q413-Q421 (9)	21.25	8.90

Nos. Q413-Q416, Q419-Q421 Surcharged with New Value and "X"

1971, Dec. 15

Denomination in Black

Q422	PP47	34fr on 32fr bister	1.25	48
Q423	PP47	40fr on 37fr gray	1.50	60
Q424	PP47	47fr on 44fr brt rose	1.65	65
Q425	PP47	53fr on 42fr blue	1.90	75
Q426	PP47	56fr on 52fr sepia	2.00	85
Q427	PP47	59fr on 54fr yel grn	2.50	85
Q428	PP47	66fr on 61fr grnsh blue	3.00	1.00
		Nos. Q422-Q428 (7)	13.80	5.18

Track, Underpinning of Railroad Car and Emblems PP48

1972, Mar. Photo.

Q429	PP48	100fr emer, red & blk	10.00	1.75

Centenary of International Railroad Union.

Congress Emblem — PP49

1974, Apr. Photo. ***Perf. 11½***

Q430	PP49	100fr yel, blk & red	8.50	1.25

4th International Symposium on Railroad Cybernetics, Washington, DC, Apr. 1974.

Type of 1953-1957

1975, June 1 Engr. ***Perf. 11½***

Q431	PP38	20fr emerald	90	52
Q432	PP38	50fr blue	2.00	1.25

Railroad Tracks — PP50

1976, June 10 Photo. *Perf. 11½*

Q433	PP50	20fr	ultra & multi	3.00	60
Q434	PP50	50fr	brt grn & multi	1.75	1.40
Q435	PP50	100fr	dp org & multi	4.00	2.75
Q436	PP50	150fr	brt lil & multi	6.00	4.75
			Nos. Q433-Q436 (4)	14.75	9.50

Railroad Station — PP51

1977 Photo. *Perf. 11½*

Q437	PP51	1000fr	multi	35.00	*30.00*

Freight Car — PP52

Designs: 1fr-9fr, Freight car. 10fr-40fr, Hopper car. 50fr-90fr, Maintenance car. 100fr-500fr, Liquid fuel car.

1980, Dec. 16 Engr. *Perf. 11½*

Q438	PP52	1fr	bis brn & blk	15	15
Q439	PP52	2fr	cl & blk	15	15
Q440	PP52	3fr	brt bl & blk	15	15
Q441	PP52	4fr	grnsh blk & blk	15	15
Q442	PP52	5fr	sep & blk	18	15
Q443	PP52	6fr	dp org & blk	20	15
Q444	PP52	7fr	pur & blk	25	15
Q445	PP52	8fr	black	28	15
Q446	PP52	9fr	grn & blk	30	15
Q447	PP52	10fr	yel bis & blk	35	15
Q448	PP52	20fr	grnsh bl & blk	75	28
Q449	PP52	30fr	bis & blk	1.10	45
Q450	PP52	40fr	lt lil & blk	1.40	55
Q451	PP52	50fr	dk brn & blk	1.90	70
Q452	PP52	60fr	ol & blk	2.00	90
Q453	PP52	70fr	vio bl & blk	2.50	1.00
Q454	PP52	80fr	vio brn & blk	3.00	1.10
Q455	PP52	90fr	lil rose & blk	3.25	1.25
Q456	PP52	100fr	crim rose & blk	3.75	1.40
Q457	PP52	200fr	brn & blk	7.00	2.75
Q458	PP52	300fr	ol gray & blk	10.50	4.25
Q459	PP52	500fr	dl pur & blk	18.00	7.00
			Nos. Q438-Q459 (22)	57.31	23.13

Train in Station PP53

Electric Locomotives PP54

1982 Engr. *Perf. 11½*

Q460	PP53	10fr	red & blk	45	20
Q461	PP53	20fr	green & blk	90	40
Q462	PP53	50fr	sepia & blk	2.50	1.00
Q463	PP53	100fr	blue & blk	5.00	2.00
			Nos. Q460-Q463 (4)	8.85	3.60

1985, May 3 Photo. *Perf. 11½*

Q464	PP54	250fr	BB-150	8.00	6.00
Q465	PP54	500fr	BB-120	16.00	12.00

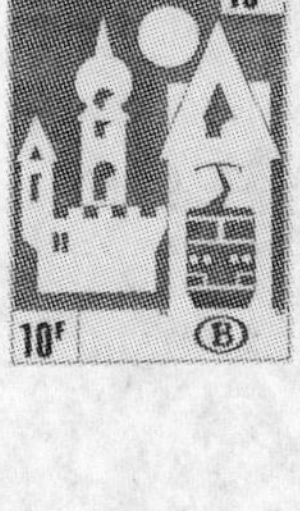

Stylized Castle, Gabled Station and Electric Rail Car — PP55

1987, Oct. 12 Engr. *Perf. 11½*

Q466	PP55	10fr	dk red & blk	50	38
Q467	PP55	20fr	dk grn & blk	1.00	75
Q468	PP55	50fr	dk brn & blk	2.50	1.90
Q469	PP55	100fr	dk lil & blk	5.00	3.75
Q470	PP55	150fr	dark olive bister & blk	7.50	5.65
			Nos. Q466-Q470 (5)	16.50	12.43

ISSUED UNDER GERMAN OCCUPATION

German Stamps of 1906-11 Surcharged

Belgien
3 Centimes
Nos. N1-N6

✻ 1Fr.25C. ✻

Belgien
Nos. N7-N9

Wmk. Lozenges (125)

1914-15 *Perf. 14, 14½*

N1	A16	3c	on 3pf brown	20	15
N2	A16	5c	on 5pf green	18	15
N3	A16	10c	on 10pf car	25	15
N4	A16	25c	on 20pf ultra	30	22
N5	A16	50c	on 40pf lake & blk	1.25	95
N6	A16	75c	on 60pf mag	50	70
N7	A16	1fr	on 80pf lake & blk, *rose*	1.40	1.10
N8	A17	1fr25c	on 1m car	12.50	9.75
N9	A21	2fr50c	on 2m gray bl	11.00	12.50
			Nos. N1-N9 (9)	27.58	25.67

German Stamps of 1906-18 Surcharged

Belgien **Belgien**
3 Cent. **1F.**
Nos. N10-N21 No. N22

✻ 1F.25Cent. ✻

Belgien
Nos. N23-N25

1916-18

N10	A22	2c	on 2pf drab	15	15
N11	A16	3c	on 3pf brn	16	15
N12	A16	5c	on 5pf grn	16	15
N13	A22	8c	on 7½pf org	28	28
N14	A16	10c	on 10pf car	15	15
N15	A22	15c	on 15pf yel brn	30	15
N16	A22	15c	on 15pf dk vio	30	28
N17	A16	20c	on 25pf org & blk, *yel*	16	16
N18	A16	25c	on 20pf ultra	16	15
a.			25c on 20pf blue	20	15
N19	A16	40c	on 30pf org & blk, *buff*	18	16
N20	A16	50c	on 40pf lake & blk	16	16
N21	A16	75c	on 60pf mag	30	*8.50*
N22	A16	1fr	on 80pf lake & blk, *rose*	1.00	*2.50*
N23	A17	1fr25c	on 1m car	1.65	1.65
N24	A21	2fr50c	on 2m gray bl	15.00	15.00
a.			2fr50c on 1m car (error)		*3,500.*
N25	A20	6fr25c	on 5m sl & car	20.00	24.00
			Nos. N10-N25 (16)	40.11	53.59

A similar series of stamps without "Belgien" was used in parts of Belgium and France while occupied by German forces. See France Nos. N15-N26.

BENIN

French Colony

LOCATION — West Coast of Africa
GOVT. — French Possession
AREA — 8,627 sq. mi.
POP. — 493,000 (approx.)
CAPITAL — Benin

In 1895 the French possessions known as Benin were incorporated into the colony of Dahomey and postage stamps of Dahomey superseded those of Benin. Dahomey took the name Benin when it became a republic in 1975.

100 Centimes = 1 Franc

Catalogue values for unused stamps in this country are for Never Hinged items, beginning with Scott 342 in the regular postage section, Scott C240 in the airpost section, Scott J44 in the postage due section, and Scott Q8 in the parcel post section.

Handstamped on Stamps of French Colonies **BÉNIN**

1892 Unwmk. *Perf. 14x13½*

Black Overprint

1	A9	1c	blk, *bluish*	85.00	65.00
2	A9	2c	brn, *buff*	65.00	60.00
3	A9	4c	claret, *lav*	25.00	20.00
4	A9	5c	grn, *grnsh*	7.50	6.25
5	A9	10c	blk, *lavender*	40.00	32.50
6	A9	15c	blue	16.00	6.50
7	A9	20c	red, *grn*	90.00	110.00
8	A9	25c	blk, *rose*	47.50	25.00
9	A9	30c	brn, *yelsh*	90.00	75.00
10	A9	35c	blk, *orange*	90.00	75.00
11	A9	40c	red, *straw*	75.00	67.50
12	A9	75c	car, *rose*	160.00	140.00
13	A9	1fr	brnz grn, *straw*	175.00	150.00

Red Overprint

14	A9	15c	blue	47.50	40.00

Blue Overprint

15	A9	5c	grn, *grnsh*	1,400.	350.00
15A	A9	15c	blue	1,400.	350.00

Nos. 1-13 all exist with overprint inverted, and several with it double. These sell for slightly more than normal stamps. The overprints of Nos. 1-15A are of four types, three without accent mark on "E." They exist diagonal.

Counterfeits exist of Nos. 1-19.

Additional Surcharge in Red or Black **40**

1892

16	A9	01c	on 5c grn, *grnsh*	150.	110.
17	A9	40c	on 15c blue	110.	35.
18	A9	75c	on 15c blue	625.	425.
19	A9	75c	on 15c bl (Bk)	2,500.	1,900.

Counterfeits exist.

Navigation and Commerce
A3 A4

1893 Typo. *Perf. 14x13½*

Name of Colony in Blue or Carmine

20	A3	1c	blk, *bluish*	1.40	1.10
21	A3	2c	brn, *buff*	1.75	1.40
22	A3	4c	claret, *lav*	1.90	1.40
23	A3	5c	grn, *grnsh*	2.50	1.60
24	A3	10c	blk, *lavender*	2.50	1.75
25	A3	15c	blue, quadrille paper	12.50	7.50
26	A3	20c	red, *grn*	7.50	3.75
27	A3	25c	blk, *rose*	17.50	7.50
28	A3	30c	brn, *bis*	8.25	6.00
29	A3	40c	red, *straw*	2.25	1.40
30	A3	50c	car, *rose*	1.65	1.40
31	A3	75c	vio, *org*	5.00	3.25
32	A3	1fr	brnz grn, *straw*	30.00	22.50
			Nos. 20-32 (13)	94.70	60.55

Perf. 13½x14 stamps are counterfeits.

1894 *Perf. 14x13½*

33	A4	1c	blk, *bluish*	1.25	90
34	A4	2c	brn, *buff*	1.25	90
35	A4	4c	claret, *lav*	1.25	90
36	A4	5c	grn, *grnsh*	1.50	90
37	A4	10c	blk, *lavender*	2.25	1.60
38	A4	15c	bl, quadrille paper	3.00	1.50
39	A4	20c	red, *grn*	3.25	2.50
40	A4	25c	blk, *rose*	3.75	1.75
41	A4	30c	brn, *bis*	2.50	1.75
42	A4	40c	red, *straw*	7.50	4.50
43	A4	50c	car, *rose*	9.00	5.00
44	A4	75c	vio, *org*	6.00	4.50
45	A4	1fr	brnz grn, *straw*	1.40	1.40
			Nos. 33-45 (13)	43.90	28.10

Perf. 13½x14 stamps are counterfeits.

PEOPLE'S REPUBLIC OF BENIN

LOCATION — West Coast of Africa
GOVT. — Republic.
AREA — 43,483 sq. mi.
POP. — 3,832,000 (est. 1984)
CAPITAL — Porto Novo

The Republic of Dahomey proclaimed itself the People's Republic of Benin on Nov. 30, 1975. See Dahomey for stamps issued before then.

Catalogue values for unused stamps in this section are for Never Hinged items.

Allamanda Cathartica — A83

Flag Bearers, Arms of Benin — A84

Flowers: 35fr, Ixora coccinea. 45fr, Hibiscus, 60fr, Phaemeria magnifica.

Unwmk.

1975, Dec. 8 Photo. *Perf. 13*

342	A83	10fr	lilac & multi	15	15
343	A83	35fr	gray & multi	22	15
344	A83	45fr	multi	35	22
345	A83	60fr	blue & multi	40	30
			Nos. 342-345 (4)	1.12	82

1976, Apr. 30 Litho. *Perf. 12*

Design: 60fr, Speaker, wall with "PRPB," flag and arms of Benin. 100fr, Flag and arms of Benin.

346	A84	50fr	ocher & multi	28	20
347	A84	60fr	ocher & multi	30	20
348	A84	100fr	multi	55	40
			Nos. 346-348 (3)	1.13	80

Proclamation of the People's Republic of Benin. Nov. 30, 1975.

A.G. Bell, Satellite and 1876 Telephone — A85

1976, July 9 Litho. *Perf. 13*

349	A985	200fr	lilac, red & brn	1.10	45

Centenary of first telephone call by Alexander Graham Bell, Mar. 10, 1876.

Dahomey Nos. 277-278 Surcharged

1976, July 19 Photo. *Perf. 12½x13*

350	A57	50fr	on 1fr multi	32	15
351	A57	60fr	on 2fr multi	42	15

African Jamboree, Nigeria 1976 — A86

1976, Aug. 16 Litho. *Perf. 12½x13*
352 A86 50fr Scouts Cooking 28 20
353 A86 70fr Three scouts 38 28

Blood Bank, Cotonou — A87

Designs: 50fr, Accident and first aid station. 60fr, Blood donation.

1976, Sept. 24 Litho. *Perf. 13*
354 A87 5fr multicolored 15 15
355 A87 50fr multicolored 28 20
356 A87 60fr multicolored 35 22
Nos. 354-356 (3) 78
Set value 47

National Blood Donors Day.

A88

A89

1976, Oct. 4 Litho. *Perf. 13x12½*
357 A88 20fr Manioc 15 15
358 A88 50fr Corn 28 20
359 A88 60fr Cacao 30 20
360 A88 150fr Cotton 80 60
Nos. 357-360 (4) 1.53 1.15

Natl. agricultural production campaign. For surcharge see No. 565.

1976, Oct. 25
361 A89 50fr Classroom 28 20

Third anniversary of KPARO newspaper, used in local language studies.

Roan Antelope — A90

Flags, Wall, Broken Chains — A91

Penhari National Park: 30fr, Buffalo. 50fr, Hippopotamus, horiz. 70fr, Lion.

1976, Nov. 8 Photo.
362 A90 10fr multicolored 15 15
363 A90 30fr multicolored 16 15
364 A90 50fr multicolored 28 20
365 A90 70fr multicolored 38 22
Nos. 362-365 (4) 97
Set value 59

1976, Nov. 30 Litho. *Perf. 12½*

Design: 150fr, Corn, raised hands with weapons.

366 A91 40fr multicolored 20 15
367 A91 150fr multicolored 80 60

First anniversary of proclamation of the People's Republic of Benin.

Table Tennis, Map of Africa (Games' Emblem) — A92

Design: 50fr, Stadium, Cotonou.

1976, Dec. 26 Litho. *Perf. 13*
368 A92 10fr multi 15 15
369 A92 50fr multi 28 20
Set value 35 25

West African University Games, Cotonou, Dec. 26-31.

Europafrica Issue

Planes over Africa and Europe — A93

1977, May 13 Litho. *Perf. 13*
370 A93 200fr multi 70 55

For surcharge see No. 590.

Snake — A94

1977, June 13 Litho. *Perf. 13x13½*
371 A94 2fr shown 15 15
372 A94 3fr Tortoise 15 15
373 A94 5fr Zebus 15 15
374 A94 10fr Cats 16 15
Set value 37 20

Patients at Clinic — A95

1977, Aug. 2 Litho. *Perf. 12½*
375 A95 100fr multi 60 40

World Rheumatism Year.

Karate, Map of Africa — A96

Designs: 100fr, Javelin, map of Africa, Benin Flag, horiz. 150fr, Hurdles.

1977, Aug. 30 Litho. *Perf. 12½*
376 A96 90fr multi 35 25
377 A96 100fr multi 45 35
378 A96 150fr multi 60 45
a. Souvenir sheet of 3, #376-378 2.00 2.00
Nos. 376-378 (3) 1.40 1.05

2nd West African Games, Lagos, Nigeria.

Chairman Mao — A97

Lister and Vaporizer — A98

1977, Sept. 9 Litho. *Perf. 13x12½*
379 A97 100fr multicolored 50 40

Mao Tse-tung (1893-1976), Chinese communist leader.

1977, Sept. 20 Engr. *Perf. 13*

Designs: 150fr, Scalpels and flames, symbols of antisepsis, and Red Cross.

380 A98 150fr multi 80 60
381 A98 210fr multi 1.20 80

Joseph Lister (1827-1912), surgeon, founder of antiseptic surgery.
For surcharges see Nos. 560, 566.

Guelege Mask, Ethnographic Museum, Porto Novo — A99

Designs: 50fr, Jar, symbol of unity, emblem of King Ghezo, Historical Museum, Abomey, vert. 210fr, Abomey Museum.

1977, Oct. 17 *Perf. 13*
382 A99 50fr red & multi 28 20
383 A99 60fr blk, bl & bister 35 22
384 A99 210fr multi 1.20 80
Nos. 382-384 (3) 1.83 1.22

For surcharge see No. 562.

Atacora Falls — A100

Mother and Child, Owl of Wisdom — A101

Tourist Publicity: 60fr, Pile houses, Ganvie, horiz. 150fr, Round huts, Savalou.

1977, Oct. 24 Litho. *Perf. 12½*
385 A100 50fr multi 32 24
386 A100 60fr multi 42 25
387 A100 150fr multi 1.00 70
a. Souvenir sheet of 3, #385-387 2.00 2.00
Nos. 385-387 (3) 1.74 1.19

Perf. 12½x13, 13x12½
1977, Dec. 3 Photo.

Designs: 150fr, Chopping down magical tree, horiz.

388 A101 60fr multi 35 22
389 A101 150fr multi 80 60

Campaign against witchcraft.
For surcharge see No. 576.

Battle Scene A102

1978, Jan. 16 Litho. *Perf. 12½*
390 A102 50fr multi 35 20

Victory of people of Benin over imperialist forces.

Map, People and Houses of Benin — A103

1978, Feb. 1
391 A103 50fr multi 35 20

General population and dwelling census.

Alexander Fleming, Microscope and Penicillin — A104

1978, Mar. 12 Litho. *Perf. 13*
392 A104 300fr multi 2.00 1.10

Alexander Fleming (1881-1955), 50th anniversary of discovery of penicillin.

Abdoulaye Issa, Weapons and Fighters A105

1978, Apr. 1 *Perf. 12½x13*
393 A105 100fr red, blk & gold 65 38

First anniversary of death of Abdoulaye Issa and National Day of Benin's Youth.

Ed Hadj Omar and Horseback Rider — A106

Design: 90fr, L'Almamy Samory Toure (1830-1900) and horseback riders.

1976, Apr. 10 *Perf. 13x12½*

394 A106	90fr red & multi	60	35
395 A106	100fr multi	65	38

African heroes of resistance against colonialism.

ITU Emblem, Satellite, Landscape — A107

1978, May 17 **Litho.** *Perf. 13*

396 A107	100fr multi	65	38

10th World Telecommunications Day.

Soccer Player, Stadium, Argentina '78 Emblem — A108

Designs (Argentina '78 Emblem and): 300fr, Soccer players and ball, vert. 500fr, Soccer player, globe with ball on map.

1978, June 1 **Litho.** *Perf. 12½*

397 A108	200fr multi	1.40	70
398 A108	300fr multi	2.00	1.10
399 A108	500fr multi	3.50	1.75
a.	Souvenir sheet of 3	7.00	7.00
	Nos. 397-399 (3)	6.90	3.55

11th World Cup Soccer Championship, Argentina, June 1-25. No. 399a contains 3 stamps similar to Nos. 397-399 in changed colors.

For surcharges see Nos. 591, 593, 595-596.

Nos. 397-399a Overprinted in Red Brown:
a. FINALE / ARGENTINE: 3 / HOLLANDE: 1
b. CHAMPION / 1978 / ARGENTINE
c. 3e BRESIL / 4e ITALIE

1978, June 25 **Litho.** *Perf. 12½*

400 A108 (a)	200fr multi	1.40	75
401 A108 (b)	300fr multi	2.00	1.10
402 A108 (c)	500fr multi	3.50	1.75
a.	Souvenir sheet of 3	7.00	7.00
	Nos. 400-402 (3)	6.90	3.60

Argentina's victory in 1978 Soccer Championship.

Games' Flag over Africa, Basketball Players — A109

Designs: 60fr, Map of Africa, volleyball players. 80fr, Map of Benin, bicyclists.

1978, July 13 *Perf. 13x12½*

403 A109	50fr lt bl & multi	35	20
404 A109	60fr ultra & multi	40	22
405 A109	80fr multi	55	35
a.	Souvenir sheet of 3	1.40	1.40
	Nos. 403-405 (3)	1.30	77

3rd African Games, Algiers, July 13-28. No. 405a contains 3 stamps in changed colors similar to Nos. 403-405.

Martin Luther King, Jr. — A110

1978, July 30 *Perf. 12½*

406 A110	300fr multi	2.00	1.10

Martin Luther King, Jr. (1929-1968), American civil rights leader.

For surcharge see No. 592.

Kanna Taxi, Oueme A111

Designs: 60fr Leatherworker and goods. 70fr, Drummer and tom-toms. 100fr, Metalworker and calabashes.

1978, Aug. 26

407 A111	50fr multi	35	20
408 A111	60fr multi	40	22
409 A111	70fr multi	45	28
410 A111	100fr multi	65	40
	Nos. 407-410 (4)	1.85	1.10

Getting to know Benin through its provinces.

Map of Italy and Exhibition Poster — A112

1978, Aug. 26 **Litho.** *Perf. 13*

411 A112	200fr multi	1.40	70

Riccione 1978 Philatelic Exhibition.

For overprint see No. 537.

Poultry Breeding — A113

1978 Oct. 5 **Photo.** *Perf. 12½x13*

412 A113	10fr Turkeys	15	15
413 A113	20fr Ducks	15	15
414 A113	50fr Chicken	35	35
415 A113	60fr Guinea fowl	40	40
	Nos. 412-415 (4)	1.05	1.05

Royal Messenger, UPU Emblem A114

Designs (UPU Emblem and): 60fr, Boatsman, ship and car, vert. 90fr, Special messenger and plane, vert.

Perf. 13x12½, 12½x13

1978, Oct. 16

416 A114	50fr multi	35	35
417 A114	60fr multi	40	40
418 A114	90fr multi	60	60
	Nos. 416-418 (3)	1.35	1.35

Centenary of change of "General Postal Union" to "Universal Postal Union."

Raoul Follereau A115

1978, Dec. 17 **Litho.** *Perf. 12½*

419 A115	200fr multi	1.75	1.75

Raoul Follereau (1903-1977), apostle to the lepers and educator of the blind.

IYC Emblem A116

Intl. Year of the Child: 20fr, Glove as balloon carrying childern. 50fr, Children of various races surrounding globe.

1979, Feb. 20 **Litho.** *Perf. 12x13*

420 A116	10fr multi	15	15
421 A116	20fr multi	15	15
422 A116	50fr multi	35	35
	Nos. 420-422 (3)	65	65

Hydrangea — A117

Flowers: 25fr, Assangokan. 30fr, Geranium. 40fr, Water lilies, horiz.

Perf. 13x12½, 12½x13

1979, Feb. 28 **Litho.**

423 A117	20fr multi	15	15
424 A117	25fr multi	16	16
425 A117	30fr multi	20	20
426 A117	40fr mutli	25	25
	Nos. 423-426 (4)	76	76

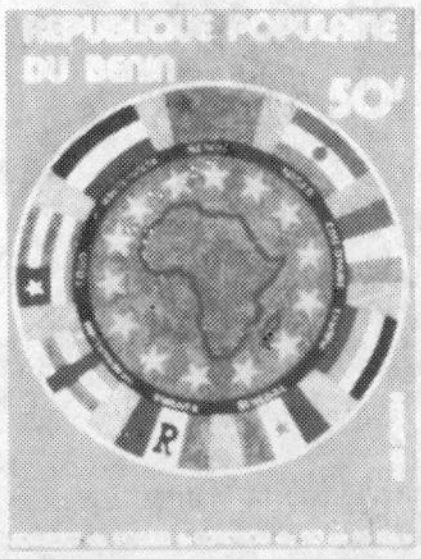

Emblem: Map of Africa and Members' Flags — A118

Designs: 60fr, Map of Benin and flags. 80fr, OCAM flag and map of Africa showing member states.

1979, Mar. 20 **Litho.** *Perf. 12x13*

427 A118	50fr multi	40	40
428 A118	60fr multi	45	45
429 A118	80fr multi	65	65
	Nos. 427-429 (3)	1.50	1.50

OCAM Summit Conf., Cotonou, Mar. 20-28.

For overprints see Nos. 434-436.

Tower, Waves, Satellite, ITU Emblem A119

1979, May 17 **Litho.** *Perf. 12½*

430 A119	50fr multi	40	40

World Telecommunications Day.

Bank Building and Sculpture — A120

1979, May 26 **Litho.**

431 A120	50fr multi	35	35

Opening of Headquarters of West African Savings Bank in Dakar.

Guelede Mask, Abomey Tapestry, Malaconotus Bird — A121

Design: 50fr, Jet, canoe, satellite, UPU and exhibition emblems.

1979, June 8 **Litho.** *Perf. 13*

432 A121	15fr multi	15	15

Engr.

433 A121	50fr multi	35	35

Philexafrique II, Libreville, Gabon, June 8-17. Nos. 432, 433 each printed in sheets of 10 with 5 labels showing exhibition emblem.

Nos. 427-429 Overprinted: "26 au 28 juin 1979" and Dots

1979, June 26

434 A118	50fr multi	35	35
435 A118	60fr multi	40	40
436 A118	80fr multi	55	55
	Nos. 434-436 (3)	1.30	1.30

2nd OCAM Summit Conf., June 26-28.

Olympic Flame, and Emblems
A122

Pre-Olympic Year: 50fr, High jump.

1979, July 1 **Litho.**

437 A122	10fr multi	15	15
438 A122	50fr multi	35	35

Antelope
A123

Animals: 10fr, Giraffes, map of Benin, vert 20fr, Chimpanzee. 50fr, Elephants, map of Benin, vert.

1979, Oct. 1 **Litho.** ***Perf. 13***

439 A123	5fr multi	15	15
440 A123	10fr multi	15	15
441 A123	20fr multi	15	15
442 A123	50fr multi	35	35
	Set value	60	60

Map of Africa, Emblem and Jet — A124

1979, Dec. 12 **Litho.** ***Perf. 12½***

443 A124	50fr multi	35	35
444 A124	60fr multi	40	40

ASECNA (Air Safety Board), 20th anniv.

Mail Services — A125

Design: 50fr, Post Office and headquarters, vert.

1979, Dec. 19 **Litho.** ***Perf. 13***

445 A125	50fr multi	35	35
446 A125	60fr multi	40	40

Office of Posts and Telecommunications, 20th anniversary.

Lenin and Globe
A126

1980, Apr. 22 **Litho.** ***Perf. 12½***

447 A126	50fr shown	25	25
448 A126	150fr Lenin in library	80	80

Lenin, 110th birth anniversary.

Monument to King Behanzin
A126a

Litho. & Embossed

1980, May 31 ***Perf. 12½***

448A	A126a 1000fr gold & multi	5.50	5.50

For overprint see No. Q10A.

Cotonou Club Emlem — A127

Galileo, Astrolabe — A128

1980, Feb. 23 **Litho.** ***Perf. 12½***

449 A127	90fr shown	60	60
450 A127	200fr Rotary emblem on globe, horiz.	1.40	1.40

Rotary International, 75th anniversary.

1980, Apr. 2

451 A128	100fr shown	45	45
452 A128	100fr Copernicus, solar system	65	65

Discovery of Pluto, 50th anniversary.

Abu Simbel, UNESCO Emblem — A129

1980, Apr. 15 ***Perf. 13***

453 A129	50fr Column, vert.	35	35
454 A129	60fr Ramses II, vert.	40	40
455 A129	150fr shown	1.00	1.00
	Nos. 453-455 (3)	1.75	1.75

UNESCO campaign to save Nubian monuments, 20h anniversary.

Monument, Martyrs' Square, Cotonou
A130

Designs: Various monuments in Martyrs' Square. Cotonou. 60fr, 70fr, 100fr, horiz.

1980, May 2 ***Perf. 12½x13, 13x12½***

456 A130	50fr multi	35	35
457 A130	60fr multi	40	40
458 A130	70fr multi	45	45
459 A130	100fr multi	65	65
	Nos. 456-459 (4)	1.85	1.85

For surcharge see No. 539.

Musical Instruments
A131

1980, May 20 ***Perf. 12½***

460 A131	5fr Assan, vert.	15	15
461 A131	10fr Tinbo	15	15
462 A131	15fr Tam-tam sato, vert.	15	15
463 A131	20fr Kora	15	15
464 A131	30fr Gangan	20	20
465 A131	50fr Sinhoun	35	35
	Set value	90	90

First Non-stop Flight, Paris-New York — A132

1980, June 2 **Litho.** ***Perf. 12½***

466 A132	90fr shown	60	60
467 A132	100fr Dieudonne Coste, Maurice Bellonte	65	65

For surcharge see No. 564.

Lunokhod I on the Moon — A133

1980, June 15 **Engr.** ***Perf. 13***

468 A133	90fr multi	60	60

Lunokhod I Soviet unmanned moon mission, 10th anniv. See #C290. For surcharge see #C305.

Olympic Flame and Mischa, Moscow '80 Emblem — A134

1980, July 16 **Litho.** ***Perf. 12½***

469 A134	50fr shown	35	35
470 A134	60fr Equestrian, vert.	40	40
471 A134	70fr Judo	50	50
472 A134	200fr Flag, sports, globe, vert.	1.40	1.40
473 A134	300fr Weight lifting, vert.	2.25	2.25
	Nos. 469-473 (5)	4.90	4.90

22nd Summer Olympic Games, Moscow, July 19-Aug. 3.

For surcharges see Nos. 559, 561.

Telephone and Rising Sun — A135

World Telecommunications Day: 50fr, Farmer on telephone, vert.

1980, May 17 **Litho.** ***Perf. 12½***

474 A135	50fr multi	35	35
475 A135	60fr multi	40	40

Cotonou West African Community Village
A136

Designs: View of Cotonou.

1980, July 26 ***Perf. 13x13½***

476 A136	50fr multi	35	35
477 A136	60fr multi	40	40
478 A136	70fr multi	45	45
	Nos. 476-478 (3)	1.20	1.20

For surcharge see No. 540.

Agbadja Dancers — A137

Designs: Dancers and muscians.

1980, Aug. 1 ***Perf. 12½***

479 A137	30fr multi	20	20
480 A137	50fr multi	35	35
481 A137	60fr multi	40	40
	Nos. 479-481 (3)	95	95

Fisherman
A138

Philippines under Magnifier
A139

Designs: 5fr, Throwing net. 15fr, Canoe and shore fishing. 20fr, Basket traps. 50fr, Hauling net. 60fr, River fishing. All horiz.

1980, Sept. 1

482 A138	5fr multi	15	15
483 A138	10fr multi	15	15
484 A138	15fr multi	15	15
485 A138	20fr multi	15	15
486 A138	50fr multi	35	35
487 A138	60fr multi	40	40
	Set value	1.10	1.10

For surcharge see No. 535.

Perf. 13x13½, 13x½x13

1980, Sept. 27

World Tourism Conference, Manila, Sept. 27: 60fr, Emblem on flag, hand pointing to Manila on globe, horiz.

488 A139	50fr multi	35	35
489 A139	60fr multi	40	40

For surcharge see No. 557.

A140

A141

1980, Oct. 1 *Perf. 12½*

490 A140 40fr Othreis materna 25 25
491 A140 50fr Othreis fullonia 35 35
492 A140 200fr Oryctes sp. 1.40 1.40
Nos. 490-492 (3) 2.00 2.00

1980, Oct. 24 **Photo.** *Perf. 13½*

493 A141 75fr multi 50 50

African Postal Union, 5th Anniv.

A142

A143

1980, Nov. 4 *Perf. 12½x13*

494 A142 30fr shown 20 20
495 A142 50fr Freed prisoner 35 35
496 A142 60fr Man holding torch 40 40
Nos. 494-496 (3) 95 95

Declaration of human rights, 30th anniv.

1980, Dec. 1 **Litho.** *Perf. 13*

Self-portrait, by Vincent van Gogh, 1888.

497 A143 100fr shown 75 75
498 A143 300fr Facteur Roulin 2.25 2.25

Vincent van Gogh (1853-1890), artist.
For surcharge see No. 579.

Offenbach and Scene from Orpheus in the Underworld — A144

1980, Dec. 15 **Engr.**

499 A144 50fr shown 40 40
500 A144 60fr Paris Life 45 45

Jacques Offenbach (1819-1880), composer.

Kepler and Satellites — A145

1980, Dec. 20

501 A145 50fr Kepler, diagram, vert. 35 35
502 A145 60fr shown 40 40

Johannes Kepler (1571-1630), astronomer.

Intl. Year of the Disabled — A146

1981, Apr. 10 **Litho.** *Perf. 12½*

503 A146 115fr multi 75 75

For surcharge see No. 582.

20th Anniv. of Manned Space Flight — A147

1981, May 30 *Perf. 13*

504 A147 500fr multi 3.50 3.50

For surcharge see No. 580.

13th World Telecommunications Day — A148

1981, May 30 **Litho.** *Perf. 12½*

505 A148 115fr multi 75 75

For surcharge see No. 583.

Amaryllis A149

1981, June 20 *Perf. 12½*

506 A149 10fr shown 15 15
507 A149 20fr Eischornia crassipes, vert. 15 15
508 A149 80fr Parkia biglobosa, vert. 55 55
Nos. 506-508 (3) 85 85

For surcharge see No. 542.

Benin Sheraton Hotel — A150

1981, July

509 A150 100fr multi 65 65

For surcharge see No. 541.

Guinea Pig — A151

1981, July 31 *Perf. 13x13½*

510 A151 5fr shown 15 15
511 A151 60fr Cat 40 40
512 A151 80fr Dogs 55 55
Nos. 510-512 (3) 1.10 1.10

For surcharges see Nos. 536, 543, 563.

World UPU Day — A152

1981, Oct. 9 **Engr.** *Perf. 13*

513 A152 100fr red brn & blk 65 65

25th Intl. Letter Writing Week, Oct. 6-12 — A153

1981, Oct. 15

514 A153 100fr dk bl & pur 65 65

For surcharge see No. 558.

West African Economic Community A154

1981, Nov. 20 **Litho.** *Perf. 12½*

515 A154 60fr multi 40 40

West African Rice Development Assoc. 10th Anniv. A155

1981, Dec. 10 *Perf. 13x13½*

516 A155 60fr multi 40 40

TB Bacillus Centenary A156

1982, Mar. 1 **Litho.** *Perf. 13*

517 A156 115fr multi 1.20 1.20

For surcharge see No. 584.

West African Economic Community, 5th Summit Conference — A157

1982, May 27 *Perf. 12½*

518 A157 60fr multi 40 40

1982 World Cup A158

1982, June 1 *Perf. 13*

519 A158 90fr Players 65 65
520 A158 300fr Flags on leg 2.25 2.25

For overprints and surcharge see #523-524, 594.

France No. B349 Magnified, Map of France — A159

1982, June 11

521 A159 90fr multi 60 60

PHILEXFRANCE '82 Stamp Exhibition, Paris, June 11-21.

George Washington A160

1982, Mar. 10 **Litho.** *Perf. 14*

522 A160 200fr Washington, flag, map 1.00 1.00

For surcharge see No. 577.

Nos. 519-520 Overprinted with Finalists Names

1982, Aug. 16 *Perf. 12½*

523 A158 90fr multi 60 60
524 A158 300fr multi 2.00 2.00

Italy's victory in 1982 World Cup.

Bluethroat A161

Perf. 14x14½, 14½x14

1982, Sept. 1

525 A161 5fr Daoelo gigas, vert. 15 15
526 A161 10fr shown 15 15
527 A161 15fr Swallow, vert. 15 15
528 A161 20fr Kingfisher, weaver bird, vert. 16 16
529 A161 30fr Great sedge warbler 25 25
530 A161 60fr Common warbler 50 50

531 A161 80fr Owl, vert. 65 65
532 A161 100fr Cockatoo, vert. 80 80
Nos. 525-532 (8) 2.81 2.81

ITU Plenipotentiaries Conference, Nairobi, Sept. — A162

1982, Sept. 26 *Perf. 13*
533 A162 200fr Map 1.00 1.00

For surcharge see No. 585.

13th World UPU Day A163

1982, Oct. 9 **Engr.** *Perf. 13*
534 A163 100fr Monument 65 65

Nos. 482, 510, 411 Overprinted in Red or Blue:
#535 "Croix Rouge / 8 Mai 1982"
#536 "UAPT 1982"
#537 "RICCONE 1982"

Perf. 13, 12½, 13x13½

1982, Nov. **Litho.**
535 A138 60fr on 5fr multi 40 40
536 A151 60fr on 5fr multi 40 40
537 A112 200fr multi (Bl) 1.40 1.40
Nos. 535-537 (3) 2.20 2.20

Visit of French Pres. Francois Mitterand A164

1983, Jan. 15 **Litho.** *Perf. 12½x13*
538 A164 90fr multi 60 60

Nos. 458, 476, 508-509, 512 Surcharged
Perf. 13x12½, 13x13½, 12½

1983 **Litho.**
539 A130 60fr on 70fr multi 40 40
540 A136 60fr on 50fr multi 40 40
541 A150 60fr on 100fr multi 40 40
542 A149 75fr on 80fr multi 50 50
543 A151 75fr on 80fr multi 50 50
Nos. 539-543 (5) 2.20 2.20

Seme Oil Rig — A165

1983, Apr. 28 **Litho.** *Perf. 13x12½*
544 A165 125fr multi 80 80

World Communications Year — A166

1983, May 17 **Litho.** *Perf. 13*
545 A166 185fr multi 1.00 1.00

Riccione '83, Stamp Show — A167

1983, Aug. 27 **Litho.** *Perf. 13*
546 A167 500fr multi 3.25 3.25

Benin Red Cross, 20th Anniv. A168

1983, Sept. 5 **Photo.** *Perf. 13*
547 A168 105fr multi 70 70

For surcharge see No. 581.

Handicrafts A169

Designs: 75fr, Handcarved lion chairs and table. 90fr, Natural tree table and stools. 200fr, Monkeys holding jar.

1983, Sept. 18 **Litho.** *Perf. 13*
548 A169 75fr multi 40 40
549 A169 90fr multi 50 50
550 A169 200fr multi 1.10 1.10
Nos. 548-550 (3) 2.00 2.00

For surcharge see No. 578.

14th UPU Day — A170

1983, Oct. 9 **Engr.** *Perf. 13*
551 A170 125fr multi 80 80

For surcharge see No. 575.

Religious Movements A171

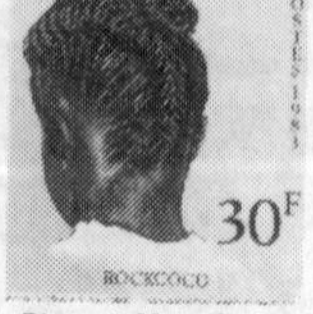

Plaited Hair Styles A172

1983, Oct. 31 **Litho.** *Perf. 14x15*
552 A171 75fr Zangbeto 35 35
553 A171 75fr Egoun 35 35

1983, Nov. 14
554 A172 30fr Rockcoco 15 15
555 A172 75fr Serpent 35 35
556 A172 90fr Songas 40 40
Nos. 554-556 (3) 90 90

Stamps of 1976-81 Surcharged

1983, Nov.
557 A139 5fr on 50fr #488 15 15
558 A153 10fr on 100fr #514 15 15
559 A134 15fr on 200fr #472 15 15
560 A98 15fr on 210fr #381 15 15
561 A134 25fr on 70fr #471 15 15
562 A99 25fr on 210fr #384 15 15
563 A151 75fr on 5fr #510 35 35
564 A132 75fr on 100fr #467 35 35
565 A88 75fr on 150fr #360 35 35
566 A98 75fr on 150fr #380 35 35
Set value 1.85 1.85

Alfred Nobel (1833-96) A173

1983, Dec. 19 **Litho.** *Perf. 15x14*
567 A173 300fr multi 1.40 1.40

Council of Unity — A174

1984, May 29 **Litho.** *Perf. 12*
568 A174 75fr multi 35 35
569 A174 90fr multi 40 40

1984 UPU Congress A175

1984, June 18 **Litho.** *Perf. 13*
570 A175 90fr multi 40 40

Abomey Calavi Earth Station A176

1984, June 29 **Litho.** *Perf. 12½x13*
571 A176 75fr Satellite dish 35 35

Traditional Costumes — A177

1984, July 2 **Litho.** *Perf. 13½x13*
572 A177 5fr Koumboro 15 15
573 A177 10fr Taka 15 15
574 A177 20fr Toko 15 15
Set value 17 17

Nos. 389, 498, 503-505, 517, 522, 533, 547, 550 and 551 Surcharged

1984, Sept.
575 A170 5fr on 125fr #551 15 15
576 A101 5fr on 150fr #389 15 15
577 A160 10fr on 200fr #522 15 15
578 A169 10fr on 200fr #550 15 15
579 A143 15fr on 300fr #498 15 15
580 A147 40fr on 500fr #504 15 15
581 A168 75fr on 105fr #547 35 35
582 A146 75fr on 115fr #503 35 35
583 A148 75fr on 115fr #505 35 35
584 A156 75fr on 115fr #517 35 35
585 A162 75fr on 200fr #533 35 35
Set value 2.15 2.15

World Food Day — A178

Dinosaurs — A179

1984, Oct. 16 **Litho.** *Perf. 12½*
586 A178 100fr Malnourished child 30 30

1984, Dec. 14 **Litho.** *Perf. 13½*
587 A179 75fr Anatosaurus 22 22
588 A179 90fr Brontosaurus 25 25

Cultural & Technical Cooperation Agency, 15th Anniv. A180

1985, Mar 20 **Litho.** *Perf. 13*
589 A180 300fr Emblem, globe, hands, book 90 90

Stamps of 1977-82 Surcharged

1985, Mar.
590 A93 75fr on 200fr No. 370 20 20
591 A108 75fr on 200fr No. 397 20 20
592 A110 75fr on 300fr No. 406 20 20
593 A108 75fr on 300fr No. 398 20 20
594 A158 90fr on 300fr No. 520 25 25
595 A108 90fr on 500fr No. 399 25 25
596 A108 90fr on 500fr No. 402 25 25
Nos. 590-596 (7) 1.55 1.55

Traditional Dances A181

1985, June 1 **Litho.** *Perf. 15x14½*
597 A181 75fr Teke, Borgou Tribe 20 20
598 A181 100fr Tipen'ti, L'Atacora Tribe 28 28

Intl. Youth Year — A182

1985, July 16 *Perf. 13½*

599 A182 150fr multi 45 45

1986 World Cup Soccer Championships, Mexico — A183

1985, July 22 *Perf. 13x12½*

600 A183 200fr multi 60 60

Dahomey No. 336 Ovptd. "REPUBLIQUE POPULAIRE DU BENIN" and Surcharged with Black Bars and New Value

1985, Aug. *Perf. 12½*

601 A78 15fr on 40fr multi 18 18

ASECNA Airlines, 25th Anniv. — A184

1985, Sept. 16 *Perf. 13*

602 A184 150fr multi 45 45

UN 40th Anniv. A185

1985, Oct. 24 *Perf. 12½*

603 A185 250fr multi 90 90

Benin UN membership, 25th anniv.

ITALIA'85, Rome — A186

1985, Oct. 25 *Perf. 13½*

604 A186 200fr multi 75 75

PHILEXAFRICA '85, Lome — A187

1985, Nov. 16 *Perf. 13*

605 A187 250fr #569, labor emblem 90 90
606 A187 250fr #C252, Gabon #365, magnified stamp 90 90

Nos. 605-606 printed se-tenant with center label picturing map of Africa or UAPT emblem.

Audubon Birth Bicent. — A188

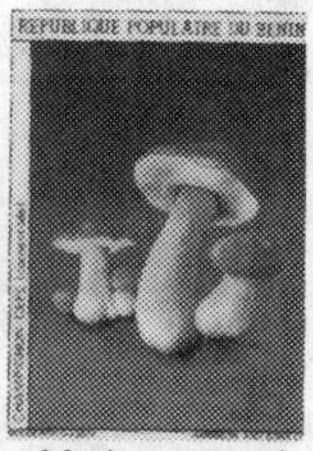

Mushrooms and Toadstools — A189

1985, Oct. 17 **Litho.** *Perf. 14x15*

607 A188 150fr Skua gull 55 55
608 A188 300fr Oyster catcher 1.10 1.10

1985, Oct. 17

609 A189 35fr Boletus edible 15 15
610 A189 40fr Amanite phalloide 15 15
611 A189 100fr Brown chanterelle 38 38
Nos. 609-611 (3) 68 68

Dahomey Nos. 282, 292, 343 Surcharged and Ovptd. with 2 Black Bars and "Populaire Republique du Benin" in 3 lines

1986, Mar. **Photo.**

612 A83 75fr on 35fr #343 25 25
613 A57 90fr on 75fr #282 35 35
614 A60 90fr on 140fr #292 35 35
Nos. 612-614 (3) 95 95

African Parliamentary Union, 10th Anniv. — A190

1986, May 8 **Litho.** *Perf. 13x12½*

615 A190 100fr multi 38 38

9th Conference, Cotonou, May 8-10.

Halley's Comet — A191

1986, May 30 *Perf. 12½x12*

616 A191 250fr multi 75 75

Dahomey Nos. 283, 344 Surcharged with Bar, "Republique/Populaire/du Benin" and New Value

Engraved, Photogravure

1986, June *Perf. 13*

617 A58 100fr on 40fr #283 38 38
618 A83 150fr on 45fr #344 55 55

1986 World Cup Soccer Championships, Mexico — A192

1986, June 29 **Litho.**

619 A192 500fr multi 1.75 1.75

Fight against Desert Encroachment A193

1986, July 16 *Perf. 13½*

620 A193 150fr multi 55 55

King Behanzin A194

Amazon A194a

1986-88 **Engr.** *Perf. 13*

621 A194 40fr black 20 20
622 A194a 100fr brt blue 40 40
623 A194 125fr maroon 60 60
624 A194a 150fr violet 60 60
625 A194 190fr dark ultra 90 90
627 A194 220fr dark grn 1.00 1.00
Nos. 621-627 (6) 3.70 3.70

Issued: 100fr, 150fr, Aug. 1; others, Oct. 1, 1988.

See No. 636.

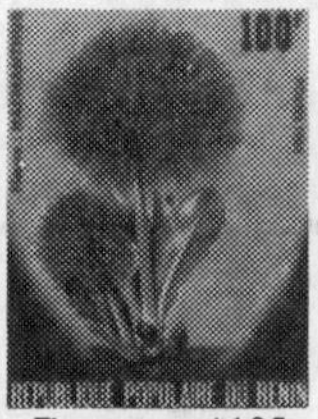

Flowers — A195

Butterflies — A196

Perf. 13x12½, 12½x13

1986, Sept. 1 **Litho.**

631 A195 100fr Haemanthus 42 42
632 A195 205fr Hemerocalle, horiz. 90 90

1986, Sept. 15

Designs: No. 633, Day peacock, little tortoise-shell, morio. No. 634, Aurora, machaon and fair lady.

633 A196 150fr multi 60 60
634 A196 150fr multi 60 60

Statue of Liberty, Cent. — A197

King Behanzin — A198

1986, Oct. 28 **Litho.** *Perf. 12½*

635 A197 250fr multi 90 90

1986, Oct. 30 *Perf. 13½*

636 A198 440fr multi 1.60 1.60

Behanzin, leader of resistance movement against French occupation (1886-1894).

Brazilian Cultural Week, Cotonou — A200

1987, Jan. 17 *Perf. 12½*

638 A200 150fr multi 88 88

Rotary Intl. District 910 Conference, Cotonou, Apr. 23-25 — A201

1987, Apr. 23 **Litho.** *Perf. 13½*

639 A201 300fr Center for the Blind, Cotonou 1.75 1.75

Automobile Cent. — A202

Modern car and: 150fr, Steam tricycle, by De Dion-Bouton and Trepardoux, 1887. 300fr, Gas-driven Victoria, by Daimler, 1886.

1987, July 1 *Perf. 12½*

640 A202 150fr multi 88 88
641 A202 300fr multi 1.75 1.75

Snake Temple Baptism — A203

1987, July 20 *Perf. 13½*

642 A203 100fr multi 55 55

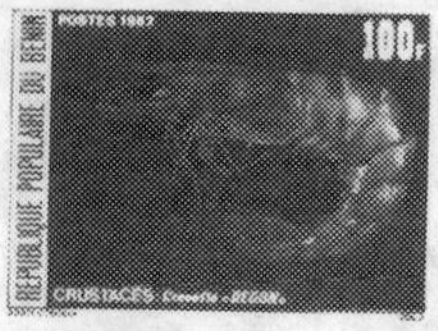

Shellfish
A204

1987, July 24 *Perf. 12½*
643 A204 100fr crayfish 55 55
644 A204 150fr crab 90 90

Cure
Leprosy — A205

1987, Sept. 4 *Perf. 13*
645 A205 200fr G. Hansen, R. Follereau 1.10 1.10

Locust Control
A206

1987, Dec. 7 Litho. *Perf. 12½x13*
646 A206 100fr multi 72 72

Christmas
1987 — A207

1987, Dec. 21 *Perf. 13*
647 A207 150fr multi 1.10 1.10

Dahomey No. 268 Ovptd.

[redacted]

Republique
Populaire
du Bénin

1987 Engr. *Perf. 13*
647B A53 40fr ultra, brn & sl grn

See Nos. C362, C369. Eleven other stamps exist in this set. The editors need to see these stamps before listings can be created.

Intl. Red Cross and Red Crescent Organizations, 125th Anniv. — A208

1988, May 25 Litho. *Perf. 13½*
648 A208 200fr multi 1.30 1.30

A209

A210

1988, July 11 *Perf. 12½*
649 A209 200fr multi 1.30 1.30

Martin Luther King, Jr. (1929-68), American civil rights leader.

1988, May 25 Litho. *Perf. 13½*
650 A210 125fr multi 88 88

Organization of African Unity, 25th anniv.

WHO, 40th Anniv. — A211

1988, Sept. 1 Litho. *Perf. 13x12½*
651 A211 175fr multi 1.15 1.15

Alma Ata Declaration, 10th anniv.; Health Care for All on Earth by the Year 2000.

Ganvie Lake Village A212

1988, Sept. 4 *Perf. 13½*
652 A212 125fr shown 85 85
653 A212 190fr Boatman, village, diff. 1.25 1.25

A213

A214

1988, Aug. 14 *Perf. 12½*
654 A213 125fr multi 88 88

1st Benin Scout Jamboree, Aug. 12-19.

1988, Dec. 30 Litho. *Perf. 13*

Ritual Offering to Hebiesso, God of Thunder and Lightning.

655 A214 125fr multi 82 82

Dahomey No. 247 Surcharged

50 f
République
Populaire
du Lénin

1988 Photo. *Perf. 12½x13*
655E A45 50fr on 45fr #247

This is one stamp from a set of 13 known to exist. Another set of 19 surcharges also is known to exist. The editors need to see these stamps before listings can be created.

World Wildlife Fund — A216

Roseate terns, *Sterna dougalli.*

1989, Jan. 30 Litho. *Perf. 13*
657 A216 10fr Three terns 15 15
658 A216 15fr Feeding on fish 15 15
659 A216 50fr Perched 32 32
660 A216 125fr In flight 82 82
Nos. 657-660 (4) 1.44 1.44

Eiffel Tower
Cent. — A217

1989, Apr. 24 Litho. *Perf. 13x12½*
661 A217 190fr multi 1.10 1.10

PHILEXFRANCE '89, French Revolution Bicent. — A218

Design: Bastille, emblems, Declaration of Human Rights and Citizenship, France No. B252-B253.

1989, July 7 *Perf. 13*
662 A218 190fr multicolored 1.10 1.10

Electric Corp. of Benin, 20th Anniv.
A219

1989, Oct. Litho. *Perf. 12½x13*
663 A219 125fr multicolored 80 80

Fish — A220

1989, Sept. 22 *Perf. 13½*
664 A220 125fr Lote 80 80
665 A220 190fr Pike, salmon 1.20 1.20

Death of King Glele, Cent. — A221

1989, Dec. 16 Litho. *Perf. 13½*
666 A221 190fr multicolored 1.25 1.25

Christmas
A222

1989, Dec. 25 *Perf. 13*
667 A222 200fr Holy family 1.30 1.30

Benin Posts & Telecommunications, Cent. — A223

1990, Jan. 1 *Perf. 13½*
668 A223 125fr multicolored 82 82

Fruits and Flora
A224

1990, Jan. 23 Litho. *Perf. 11½*

669 A224 60fr Oranges 42 42
670 A224 190fr Kaufmann Tulips, vert. 1.40 1.40
671 A224 250fr Cashews, vert. 1.75 1.75
Nos. 669-671 (3) 3.57 3.57

Dated 1989.

Moon Landing, 20th Anniv. A225

1990, Jan. 23

672 A225 190fr multicolored 1.40 1.40

Dated 1989.

World Cup Soccer Championships, Italy — A226

1990, June 8 Litho. *Perf. 12½*

673 A226 125fr shown 1.00 1.00
674 A226 190fr Character trademark, vert. 1.50 1.50

For overprint see No. 676.

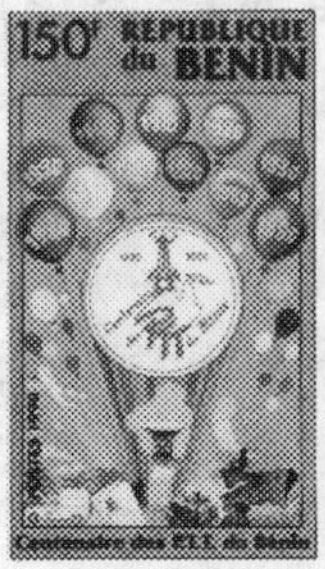

Post, Telephone & Telegraph Administration in Benin, Cent. — A227

1990, July 1 *Perf. 13*

675 A227 150fr multicolored 1.25 1.25

No. 673 Ovptd. **FINALE R.F.A. - ARGENTINE 1 - 0**

1990 Litho. *Perf. 12½*

676 A226 125fr multicolored 1.00 1.00

Charles de Gaulle (1890-1970) A228

1990, Nov. 22 Litho. *Perf. 13*

677 A228 190fr multicolored 1.50 1.50

See No. 689.

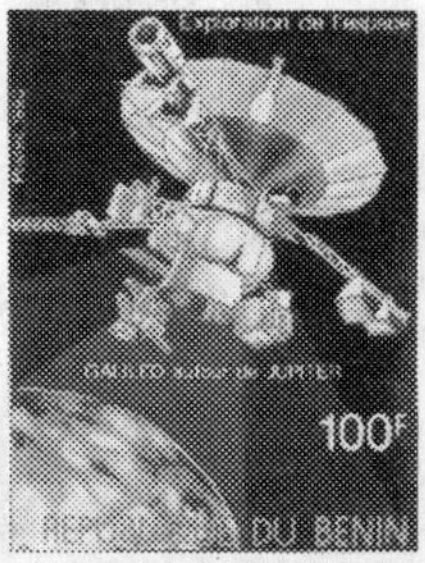

Galileo Probe and Jupiter A229

1990, Dec. 1

678 A229 100fr multicolored 75 75

For overprint see No. 681.

A230

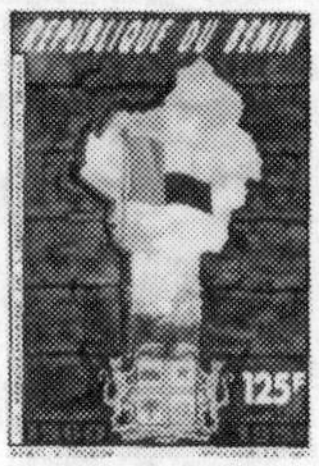

A231

1990, Dec. 25 Litho. *Perf. 12½x13*

679 A230 200fr multicolored 1.75 1.75

Christmas.

1991, Sept. 3 Litho. *Perf. 13½*

680 A231 125fr multicolored 1.05 1.05

Independence, 31st anniv.

No. 678 Ovptd. in Red **"Riccione 91"**

1991 *Perf. 13*

681 A229 100fr multicolored 85 85

French Open Tennis Championships, Cent. — A232

1991 *Perf. 13½*

682 A232 125fr multicolored 1.05 1.05

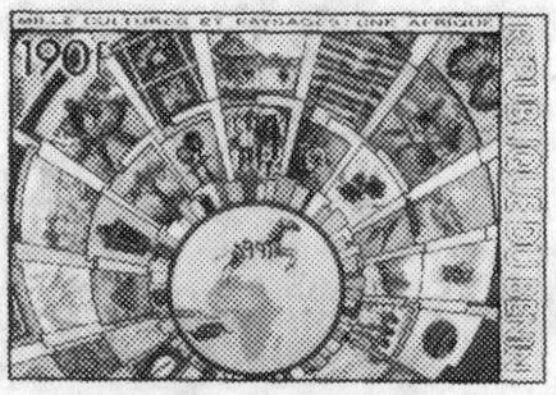

African Tourism Year — A233

1991

683 A233 190fr multicolored 1.65 1.65

Christmas A234

1991, Dec. 2 Litho. *Perf. 13½*

684 A234 125fr multicolored 1.05 1.05

Dancer of Guelede — A235

Wolfgang Amadeus Mozart, Death Bicent. — A236

1991, Dec. 2

685 A235 190fr multicolored 1.65 1.65

1991, Dec. 2

686 A236 1000fr multicolored 8.50 8.50

Discovery of America, 500th Anniv. A237

Design: 1000fr, Columbus coming ashore, horiz.

1992, Apr. 24 Litho. *Perf. 13*

687 A237 500fr blk, blue & brn 3.75 3.75
688 A237 1000fr multicolored 7.50 7.50
a. Souvenir sheet of 2, #687-688 11.25 11.25

De Gaulle Type of 1990

1992 Litho. *Perf. 13*

689 A228 300fr like #677 2.25 2.25

Intl. Conference on Nutrition, Rome — A238

1992, Dec. 5 Litho. *Perf. 13*

690 A238 190fr multicolored 1.60 1.60

Visit of Pope John Paul II, Feb. 3-5 — A239

Ouidah 92, First Festival of Voodoo Culture — A240

1993, Feb. 3 Litho. *Perf. 13x12½*

691 A239 190fr multicolored 1.50 1.50

1993, Feb. 8 *Perf. 13½*

692 A240 125fr multicolored 1.00 1.00

Well of Possotome, Eurystome A241

1993, May 25 Litho. *Perf. 12½*

693 A241 125fr multicolored 1.00 1.00

OAU, 30th Anniv. A242

1993, June 7 Litho. *Perf. 13½*

694 A242 125fr multicolored 1.00 1.00

John F. Kennedy — A243

1993, June 24 *Perf. 13*

695 A243 190fr shown 1.50 1.50
696 A243 190fr Martin Luther King, vert. 1.50 1.50

Assassinations of Kennedy, 30th anniv. (#695), and King, 25th anniv. (#696).

AIR POST STAMPS

PEOPLE'S REPUBLIC

Catalogue values for unused stamps in this section are for Never Hinged items.

Nativity, by Aert van Leyden — AP84

Christmas: 85fr, Adoration of the Kings, by Rubens, vert. 140fr, Adoration of the Shepherds, by Charles Lebrun. 300fr, The Virgin with the Blue Diadem, by Raphael, vert.

1975, Dec. 19 Litho. *Perf. 13*

C240 AP84	40fr gold & multi	20	15
C241 AP84	85fr gold & multi	42	15
C242 AP84	140fr gold & multi	60	25
C243 AP84	300fr gold & multi	1.40	65
	Nos. C240-C243 (4)	2.62	1.20

For surcharge see No. C362.

Slalom, Innsbruck Olympic Emblem — AP85

Designs (Innsbruck Olympic Games Emblem and): 150fr, Bobsledding, vert. 300fr, Figure skating, pairs.

1976, June 28 Litho. *Perf. 12½*

C244 AP85	60fr multi	25	15
C245 AP85	150fr multi	65	25
C246 AP85	300fr multi	1.25	55
	Nos. C244-C246 (3)	2.15	95

12th Winter Olympic Games, Innsbruck, Austria, Feb. 4-15.

Dahomey Nos. C235-C237 Overprinted or Surcharged: "POPULAIRE / DU BENIN" and Bars

1976, July 4 Engr. *Perf. 13*

C247 AP82	135fr multi	55	25
C248 AP82	210fr on 300fr multi	90	35
C249 AP82	380fr on 500fr multi	1.50	65
	Nos. C247-C249 (3)	2.95	1.25

The overprint includes a bar covering "DU DAHOMEY" in shades of brown; "POPULAIRE DU BENIN" is blue on Nos. C247-C248, red on No. C249. The surcharge and bars over old value are blue on No. C248, red, brown on No. C249.

Long Jump AP86

Designs (Olympic Rings and): 150fr, Basketball, vert. 200fr, Hurdles.

1976, July 16 Photo. *Perf. 13*

C250 AP86	60fr multi	32	15
C251 AP86	150fr multi	85	30
C252 AP86	200fr multi	1.25	45
a.	Souv. sheet of 3, #C250-C252	3.00	3.00
	Nos. C250-C252 (3)	2.42	90

21st Olympic Games, Montreal, Canada, July 17-Aug 1.

Konrad Adenauer and Cologne Cathedral — AP87

Design: 90fr, Konrad Adenauer, vert.

1976, Aug. 27 Engr. *Perf. 13*

C253 AP87	90fr multi	60	25
C254 AP87	250fr multi	1.75	70

Konrad Adenauer (1876-1967), German Chancellor, birth centenary.

Children's Heads and Flying Fish (Dahomey Type A32) — AP88

Design: 210fr, Lion cub's head and Benin type A3, vert.

1976, Sept. 13

C255 AP88	60fr Prus bl & vio bl	35	15
C256 AP88	210fr multi	1.10	45

JUVAROUEN 76, Intl. Youth Phil. Exhib., Rouen, France, Apr. 25-May 2.
For surcharge see No. C300.

Apollo 14 Emblem and Blast-off — AP89

Design: 270fr, Landing craft and man on moon.

1976, Oct. 18 Engr. *Perf. 13*

C257 AP89	130fr multi	45	30
C258 AP89	270fr multi	1.00	65

Apollo 14 Moon Mission, 5th anniversary.
For surcharge see No. C312.

Annunciation, by Master of Jativa — AP90

Christmas: 60fr, Nativity, by Gerard David. 270fr, Adoration of the Kings, Dutch School. 300fr, Flight into Egypt, by Gentile Fabriano, horiz.

1976, Dec. 20 Litho. *Perf. 12½*

C259 AP90	50fr gold & multi	25	16
C260 AP90	60fr gold & multi	35	22
C261 AP90	270fr gold & multi	1.50	60
C262 AP90	300fr gold & multi	1.60	1.00
	Nos. C259-C262 (4)	3.70	1.98

For surcharges see Nos. C310, C321.

Gamblers and Lottery Emblem — AP91

1977, Mar. 13 Litho. *Perf. 13*

C263 AP91	50fr multi	25	20

National lottery, 10th anniversary.

Sassenage Castle, Grenoble — AP92

1977, May 16 *Perf. 12½*

C264 AP92	200fr multi	80	60

10th anniv. of Intl. French Language Council.
For surcharge see No. C334.

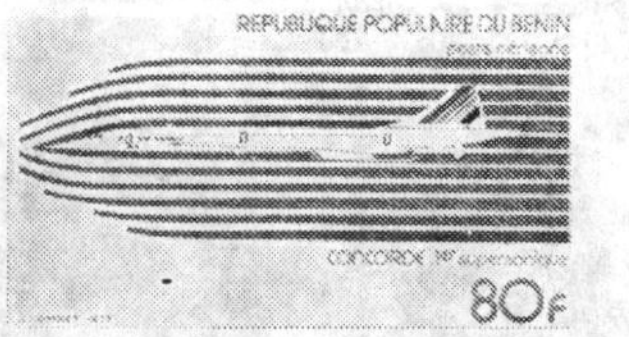

Concorde, Supersonic Plane — AP93

Designs: 150fr, Zeppelin. 300fr, Charles A. Lindbergh and Spirit of St. Louis. 500fr, Charles Nungesser and François Coli, French aviators lost over Atlantic, 1927.

1977, July 25 Engr. *Perf. 13*

C265 AP93	80fr ultra & red	40	35
C266 AP93	150fr multi	80	60
C267 AP93	300fr multi	1.60	1.20
C268 AP93	500fr multi	2.50	2.00
	Nos. C265-C268 (4)	5.30	4.15

Aviation history.
For overprint and surcharges see Nos. C274, C316, C336.

Soccer Player — AP94

Design: 200fr, Soccer players and Games' emblem.

1977, July 28 Litho. *Perf. 12½x12*

C269 AP94	60fr multi	35	20
C270 AP94	200fr multi	1.10	80

World Soccer Cup elimination games.
For surcharge see No. C308.

Miss Haverfield, by Gainsborough AP95

Designs: 150fr, Self-portrait, by Rubens. 200fr, Anguish, man's head by Da Vinci.

1977, Oct. 3 Engr. *Perf. 13*

C271 AP95	100fr sl grn & mar	55	40
C272 AP95	150fr red brn & dk brn	80	60
C273 AP95	200fr brn & red	1.10	80
	Nos. C271-C273 (3)	2.45	1.80

For surcharges see Nos. C309, C317.

No. C265 Overprinted: "1er VOL COMMERCIAL / 22.11.77 PARIS NEW-YORK"

1977, Nov. 22 Engr. *Perf. 13*

C274 AP93	80fr ultra & red	42	35

Concorde, 1st commercial flight, Paris to NY.

Viking on Mars AP96

Designs: 150fr, Isaac Newton, apple globe, stars. 200fr, Vladimir M. Komarov, spacecraft and earth. 500fr, Dog Laika, rocket and space.

1977, Nov. 28 Engr. *Perf. 13*

C275 AP96	100fr multi	55	40
C276 AP96	150fr multi	80	60
C277 AP96	200fr multi	1.10	80
C278 AP96	500fr multi	2.75	2.00
	Nos. C275-C278 (4)	5.20	3.80

Operation Viking on Mars; Isaac Newton (1642-1727); 10th death anniv. of Russian cosmonaut Vladimir M. Komarov; 20th anniv. of 1st living creature in space.
For surcharges see Nos. C301, C314.

Monument, Red Star Place, Cotonou AP97

Lithographed; Gold Embossed

1977 Nov. 30 *Perf. 12½*

C279 AP97	500fr multi	1.75	1.10

Suzanne Fourment, by Rubens — AP98

Design: 380fr, Nicholas Rubens, By Rubens.

1977, Dec. 12 Engr. *Perf. 13*

C280 AP98	200fr multi	1.10	80
C281 AP98	380fr claret & ocher	2.00	1.40

For surcharges see Nos. C311, C313.

Parthenon and UNESCO Emblem — AP99

Designs: 70fr, Acropolis and frieze showing Pan-Athenaic procession, vert. 250fr, Parthenon and frieze showing horsemen, vert.

1978, Sept. 22 Litho. *Perf. 12½x12*

C282 AP99 70fr multi 35 20
C283 AP99 250fr multi 1.25 80
C284 AP99 500fr multi 2.75 1.50
Nos. C282-C284 (3) 4.35 2.50

Save the Parthenon in Athens campaign.
For surcharge see No. C338.

Philexafrique II—Essen Issue
Common Design Types

Designs: No. C285, Buffalo and Dahomey #C33. No. C286, Wild ducks and Baden #1.

1978, Nov. 1 Litho. *Perf. 12½*

C285 CD138 100fr multi 65 40
C286 CD139 100fr multi 65 40
a. Pair, #C285-C286 1.30 1.00

Wilbur and Orville Wright and Flyer — AP100

1978, Dec. 28 Engr. *Perf. 13*

C287 AP100 500fr multi 3.50 2.00

75th anniversary of 1st powered flight.
For surcharge see No. C339.

Cook's Ships, Hawaii, World Map — AP101

Design: 50fr, Battle at Kowrowa.

1979, June 1 Engr. *Perf. 13*

C288 AP101 20fr multi 20 20
C289 AP101 50fr multi 45 45

Capt. James Cook (1728-1779), explorer.

Lunokhod Type of 1980

1980, June 15 Engr. *Perf. 13*
Size: 27x48mm

C290 A133 210fr multi 1.40 1.40

For surcharge see No. C305.

Soccer Players — AP102

1981, Mar. 31 Litho. *Perf. 13*

C291 AP102 200fr Ball, globe 90 90
C292 AP102 500fr shown 2.50 2.50

ESPANA '82 World Soccer Cup eliminations.
For surcharges see Nos. C335, Q10B.

Prince Charles and Lady Diana, London Bridge — AP103

1981, July 29 Litho. *Perf. 12½*

C293 AP103 500fr multi 3.00 3.00

Royal wedding.
For surcharge see No. C323.

Three Musicians, by Pablo Picasso (1881-1973) — AP104

Perf. 12½x13, 13x12½
1981, Nov. 2 Litho.

C294 AP104 300fr Dance, vert. 2.00 2.00
C295 AP104 500fr shown 3.50 3.50

For surcharges see Nos. C320, C340.

1300th Anniv. of Bulgaria — AP105

1981, Dec. 2 Litho. *Perf. 13*

C296 AP105 100fr multi 60 60

Visit of Pope John Paul II — AP106

1982, Feb. 17 Litho. *Perf. 13*

C297 AP106 80fr multi 55 55

20th Anniv. of John Glenn's Flight — AP107

1982, Feb. 21 Litho. *Perf. 13*

C298 AP107 500fr multi 3.00 3.00

For surcharge see No. C315.

Scouting Year AP108

1982, June 1 *Perf. 12½*

C299 AP108 105fr multi 70 70

For surcharge see No. C324.

Nos. C256, C275 Surcharged

1982, Nov. Engr. *Perf. 13*

C300 AP88 50fr on 210fr multi 35 35
C301 AP96 50fr on 100fr multi 35 35

Monet in Boat, by Claude Monet (1832-1883) — AP109

1982, Dec. 6 Litho. *Perf. 13x12½*

C302 AP109 300fr multi 2.00 2.00

For surcharge see No. C326.

Christmas 1982 AP110

Virgin and Child Paintings.

1982, Dec. 20 *Perf. 12½x13*

C303 AP110 200fr Matthias Grunewald 1.25 1.25
C304 AP110 300fr Correggio 1.75 1.75

For surcharges see Nos. C325, C337.

No. C290 Surcharged

1983 Engr. *Perf. 13*

C305 A133 75fr on 210fr multi 50 50

Bangkok '83 Stamp Exhibition AP111

1983, Aug. 4 Photo. *Perf. 13*

C306 AP111 300fr multi 1.50 1.50

For surcharge see No. C322.

Christmas 1983 AP112

1983, Dec. 26 Litho. *Perf. 12½x13*

C307 AP112 200fr Loretto Madonna, by Raphael 65 65

For surcharge see No. C319.

Types of 1976-82 Surcharged

1983, Nov.

C308 AP94 10fr on 200fr C270 15 15
C309 AP95 15fr on 200fr C273 15 15
C310 AP90 15fr on 270fr C261 15 15
C311 AP98 20fr on 200fr C280 15 15
C312 AP89 25fr on 270fr C258 15 15
C313 AP98 25fr on 380fr C281 15 15
C314 AP96 30fr on 200fr C277 15 15
C315 AP107 40fr on 500fr C298 20 20
C316 AP93 75fr on 150fr C266 38 38
C317 AP95 75fr on 150fr C272 38 38
Set value 1.60 1.60

Summer Olympics — AP113

1984, July 16 Litho. *Perf. 13x13½*

C318 AP113 300fr Sam the Eagle, mascot 1.00 1.00

Nos. C262, C293-C294, C299, C302-C303, C306-C307 Surcharged

1984, Sept.

C319 AP112 15fr on 200fr multi 15 15
C320 AP104 15fr on 300fr multi 15 15
C321 AP90 25fr on 300fr multi 15 15
C322 AP111 25fr on 300fr multi 15 15
C323 AP103 40fr on 500fr multi 15 15
C324 AP108 75fr on 105fr multi 25 25
C325 AP110 90fr on 200fr multi 30 30
C326 AP109 90fr on 300fr multi 30 30
Set value 1.25 1.25

Christmas 1984 AP114

1984, Dec. 17 Litho. *Perf. 12½x13*

C327 AP114 500fr Virgin and Child, by Murillo 1.50 1.50

Ships — AP115

1984, Dec. 28 Litho. *Perf. 13*

C328 AP115 90fr Sidon merchant ship 30 30
C329 AP115 125fr Wavertree, vert. 38 38

Benin-S.O.M. Postal Convention AP116

1985, Apr. 15 Litho. *Perf. 13½*

C330	AP116	75fr Benin arms	22	22
C331	AP116	75fr Sovereign Order of Malta	22	22
a.		Pair, #C330-C331	45	45

PHILEXAFRICA III, Lome — AP117

1985, June 24 *Perf. 13*

C332	AP117	200fr Oil platform	60	60
C333	AP117	200fr Soccer players	60	60
a.		Pair, #C332-C333 + label	1.25	1.25

Stamps of 1977-82 Surcharged

1985, Mar.

C334	AP92	75fr on 200fr #C264	20	20
C335	AP102	75fr on 200fr #C291	20	20
C336	AP93	75fr on 300fr #C267	20	20
C337	AP110	75fr on 300fr #C304	20	20
C338	AP99	90fr on 500fr #C284	25	25
C339	AP100	90fr on 500fr #C287	25	25
C340	AP104	90fr on 500fr #C295	25	25
		Nos. C334-C340 (7)	1.55	1.55

Dahomey Stamps of 1971-75 Ovptd. "REPUBLIQUE POPULAIRE DU BENIN" or "POPULAIRE DU BENIN" and Surcharged with Black Bar and New Value

1985, Aug.

C341	AP83	25fr on 40fr #C238	15	15
C342	AP49	40fr #C142	15	15
C343	AP56	75fr on 85fr #C164	20	20
C344	AP60	75fr on 100fr #C173	20	20
C345	AP64	75fr on 125fr #C186	20	20
C346	AP56	90fr on 20fr #C163	25	25
C347	A61	90fr on 150fr #C153	25	25
C348	AP49	90fr on 200fr #C143	25	25
C349	AP76	90fr on 200fr #C221	25	25
C350	AP76	150fr #C220	45	45
		Nos. C341-C350 (10)	2.35	2.35

Christmas — AP118

1985, Dec. 20 Litho. *Perf. 13x12½*

C351	AP118	500fr multi	1.75	1.75

Dahomey Nos. C34-C37, C84, C131 Surcharged and Overprinted with 1 or 2 Black Bars and "Republique Populaire du Benin" in 3 lines

1986 Photo. Perfs. as before

C352	AP33	75fr on 70fr #C84	25	25
C353	AP14	75fr on 100fr #C34	25	25
C354	AP15	75fr on 200fr #C35	25	25
C355	AP15	90fr on 250fr #C36	35	35
C356	AP45	100fr #C131	38	38
C357	AP14	150fr on 500fr #C37	55	55
		Nos. C352-C357 (6)	2.03	2.03

Issued: 75fr, 90fr, Mar; 100fr, 150fr, June.

Christmas — AP119

1986, Dec. 24 Litho. *Perf. 13x12½*

C358	AP119	300fr multi	1.20	1.20

Air Africa, 25th Anniv. AP120

1986, Dec. 30 *Perf. 12½*

C359	AP120	100fr multi	40	40

Intl. Agricultural Development Fund (FIDA), 10th Anniv. AP121

1987, Dec. 14 Litho. *Perf. 13½*

C360	AP121	500fr multi	3.50	3.50

Christmas — AP122

1988, Dec. 23 Litho. *Perf. 13x12½*

C361	AP122	500fr Adoration of the Magi, storyteller	3.25	3.25

No. C241 Surcharged

République
Populaire
du Bénin

15 f

1989, Apr. 24 Litho. *Perf. 13*

C362	AP84	15fr on 85fr multi	15	15

Dahomey No. C53 Overprinted

République
Populaire
du Bénin

1987 Photo. *Perf. 13*

C369	AP22	80fr multicolored		

POSTAGE DUE STAMPS

French Colony

Handstamped in Black on Postage Due Stamps of French Colonies

BENIN

1894 Unwmk. *Imperf.*

J1	D1	5c black	65.00	30.00
J2	D1	10c black	65.00	30.00
J3	D1	20c black	65.00	30.00
J4	D1	30c black	65.00	30.00
		Nos. J1-J4 (4)	260.00	120.00

Nos. J1-J4 exist with overprint in various positions.

Catalogue values for unused stamps in this section are for Never Hinged items.

People's Republic

Pineapples D6

Mail Delivery — D7

Designs: 20fr, Cashew, vert. 40fr, Oranges. 50fr, Akee. 80fr, Mail delivery by boat.

1978, Sept. 5 Photo. *Perf. 13*

J44	D6	10fr multi	15	15
J45	D6	20fr multi	15	15
J46	D6	40fr multi	28	16
J47	D6	50fr multi	45	25

Engr.

J48	D7	60fr multi	32	22
J49	D7	80fr multi	45	28
		Nos. J44-J49 (6)	1.80	1.21

PARCEL POST STAMPS

Catalogue values for unused stamps in this section are for Never Hinged items.

Nos. 448-448A, 459, 473, C292 Overprinted or Surcharged "Colis Postaux"

Perfs. and Printing Methods as Before

1982, Nov.

Q8	A126	100fr on 150fr	40	20
Q9	A130	100fr multi	40	20
Q10	A134	300fr multi	1.20	60
Q10A	A126a	1000fr multi	5.50	5.50
Q10B	AP102	5000fr on 500fr	27.50	27.50
		Nos. Q8-Q10B (5)	35.00	34.00

Dahomey No. C205 Surcharged

500 f

République
Populaire
du Bénin

colis postaux

1989 Photo. *Perf. 12½x13*

Q11	AP71	500fr on 200fr multi	3.25	3.25

BHUTAN

LOCATION — Eastern Himalayas
GOVT. — Kingdom
AREA — 18,000 sq. mi.
POP. — 1,250,000 (est. 1983)
CAPITAL — Thimphu

100 Chetrum = 1 Ngultrum or Rupee

Catalogue values for all unused stamps in this country are for Never Hinged items.

Postal Runner — A1

Designs: 3ch, 70ch, Archer. 5ch, 1.30nu, Yak. 15ch, Map of Bhutan, portrait of Druk Gyalpo (Dragon King) Ugyen Wangchuk (1867-1902) and Paro Dzong (fortress-monastery). 33ch, Postal runner. All horiz. except 2ch and 33ch.

Perf. 14x14½, 14½x14

1962 Litho. Unwmk.

1	A1	2ch red & gray	15	15
2	A1	3ch red & ultra	15	15
3	A1	5ch green & brown	40	40
4	A1	15ch red, blk & org yel	15	15
5	A1	33ch blue grn & lil	15	15
6	A1	70ch dp ultra & lt blue	30	30
7	A1	1.30nu blue & black	80	80
		Set value	1.80	1.80

Nos. 1-7 were issued for inland use in April, 1962, and became valid for international mail on Oct. 10, 1962.

For overprint and surcharges see #42, 72-73.

Refugee Year Emblem and Arms of Bhutan — A2

1962, Oct. 10 *Perf. 14½x14*

8	A2	1nu dk blue & dk car rose	40	40
9	A2	2nu yel grn & red lilac	1.00	1.00

World Refugee Year. For surcharges see #68-69.

Equipment of Ancient Warrior — A3

Boy Filling Grain Box and Wheat Emblem — A4

1963 Unwmk. *Perf. 14x14½*

10	A3	33ch multicolored	15	15
11	A3	70ch multicolored	28	28
12	A3	1.30nu multicolored	60	60
		Nos. 10-12 (3)	1.03	1.03

Bhutan's membership in Colombo Plan.

1963, July 15 *Perf. 13½x14*

13	A4	20ch lt blue, yel & red brn	16	16
14	A4	1.50nu rose lil, bl & red brn	65	65

FAO "Freedom from Hunger" campaign. For surcharge see No. 117M.

Masked Dancer A5

Various Bhutanese Dancers (Five Designs; 2ch, 5ch, 20ch, 1nu, 1.30nu vert.)

Perf. 14½x14, 14x14½

1964, Apr. 16

15	A5	2ch	multicolored	15	15
16	A5	3ch	multicolored	15	15
17	A5	5ch	multicolored	15	15
18	A5	20ch	multicolored	15	15
19	A5	33ch	multicolored	15	15
20	A5	70ch	multicolored	22	22
21	A5	1nu	multicolored	40	40
22	A5	1.30nu	multicolored	45	45
23	A5	2nu	multicolored	75	75
			Set value	2.10	2.10

For surcharges see Nos. 70-71, 74-75, 129A, 129G. For overprints see Nos. C1-C3, C11-C13.

Stone Throwing — A6

Sport: 5ch, 33ch, Boxing. 1nu, 3nu, Archery. 2nu, Soccer.

1964, Oct. 10 Litho. *Perf. 14½*

24	A6	2ch	emerald & multi	15	15
25	A6	5ch	orange & multi	15	15
26	A6	15ch	brt cit & multi	15	15
27	A6	33ch	rose lil & multi	15	15
28	A6	1nu	multicolored	35	35
29	A6	2nu	rose lilac & multi	55	55
30	A6	3nu	lt blue & multi	80	80
			Set value	1.95	1.95

18th Olympic Games, Tokyo, Oct. 10-25. See No. B4.
Nos. 24-30 exist imperf. Value $4.

Flags of the World at Half-mast — A7

1964, Nov. 22 Unwmk. *Perf. 14½*
Flags in Original Colors

31	A7	33ch	steel gray	15	15
32	A7	1nu	silver	50	50
33	A7	3nu	gold	1.20	1.20
a.			Souv. sheet, perf. 13½ or imperf.	2.75	2.75
			Nos. 31-33 (3)	1.85	1.85

Issued in memory of those who died in the service of their country. Nos. 31-33 exist imperf.
No. 33a contains 2 stamps similar to Nos. 32-33.
For overprints see Nos. 44, 46.

Flowers — A8

1965, Jan. 6 Litho. *Perf. 13*

34	A8	2ch	Primrose	15	15
35	A8	5ch	Gentian	15	15
36	A8	15ch	Primrose	15	15
37	A8	33ch	Gentian	15	15
38	A8	50ch	Rhododendron	15	15
39	A8	75ch	Peony	20	20
40	A8	1nu	Rhododendron	22	22
41	A8	2nu	Peony	45	45
			Set value	1.20	1.20

For overprints see Nos. 43, 45, C4-C5, C14-C15.

Nos. 5, 40, 32, 41 and 33 Overprinted: "WINSTON CHURCHILL 1874-1965"

1965, Feb. 27

42	A1	33ch	bl grn & lilac	16	16
43	A8	1nu	pink, grn & dk gray	42	42
44	A7	1nu	silver & multi	42	42
45	A8	2nu	sepia, yel & grn	75	75
46	A7	3nu	gold & multi	1.00	1.00
			Nos. 42-46 (5)	2.75	2.75

Issued in memory of Sir Winston Churchill (1874-1965), British statesman. The overprint is in three lines on Nos. 42-43 and 45; in two lines on Nos. 43 and 46.
Nos. 44 and 46 exist imperf. Value, both, $4.50.

Skyscraper, Pagoda and World's Fair Emblem — A9

Designs: 10ch, 2nu, Pieta by Michelangelo and statue of Khmer Buddha. 20ch, Skyline of NYC and Bhutanese village. 33ch, George Washington Bridge, NY, and foot bridge, Bhutan.

1965, Apr. 21 Litho. *Perf. 14½*

47	A9	1ch	blue & multi	15	15
48	A9	10ch	green & multi	15	15
49	A9	20ch	rose lilac & multi	15	15
50	A9	33ch	bister & multi	15	15
51	A9	1.50nu	bister & multi	50	50
52	A9	2nu	multicolored	65	65
a.			Souv. sheet, perf. 13½ or imperf.	2.00	2.00
			Set value	1.45	1.45

Nos. 47-52 exist imperf.; value $3.50.
No. 52a contains two stamps similar to Nos. 51-52.
For overprints see #87-87B, C6-C10, C16-C20.

Telstar, Short-wave Radio and ITU Emblem — A10

Designs (ITU Emblem and): 2nu, Telstar and Morse key. 3nu, Syncom and ear phones.

1966, Mar. 2 Litho. *Perf. 14½*

53	A10	35ch	multicolored	15	15
54	A10	2nu	multicolored	60	60
55	A10	3nu	multicolored	85	85
			Nos. 53-55 (3)	1.60	1.60

Cent. (in 1965) of the ITU. Souvenir sheets exist containing two stamps similar to Nos. 54-55, perf. 13½ and imperf. Value, 2 sheets, $5.

BHUTAN Leopard — A11

Animals: 1ch, 4nu, Asiatic black bear. 4ch, 2nu, Pigmy hog. 8ch, 75ch, Tiger. 10ch, 1.50nu, Dhole (Asiatic hunting dog). 1nu, 5nu, Takin (goat).

1966, Mar. 24 Litho. *Perf. 13*

56	A11	1ch	yellow & blk	15	15
57	A11	2ch	pale grn & blk	15	15
58	A11	4ch	lt citron & blk	15	15
59	A11	8ch	lt blue & blk	15	15
60	A11	10ch	lt lilac & blk	15	15
61	A11	75ch	lt yel grn & blk	20	20
62	A11	1nu	lt green & blk	50	50
63	A11	1.50nu	lt bl grn & blk	40	40
64	A11	2nu	dull org & blk	50	50
65	A11	3nu	bluish lil & blk	75	75
66	A11	4nu	lt green & blk	1.00	1.00
67	A11	5nu	pink & black	1.40	1.40
			Nos. 56-67 (12)	5.50	5.50

For surcharges see Nos. 115C, 115E, 115I, 117N, 117P, 129B, 129J.

Nos. 6-9, 20-23 Surcharged

1965(?) *Perf. 14½x14, 14x14½*

68	A2	5ch	on 1nu	*26.00*	*26.00*
69	A2	5ch	on 2nu	*26.00*	*26.00*
70	A5	10ch	on 70ch	*4.25*	*4.25*
71	A5	10ch	on 2nu	*4.25*	*4.25*
72	A1	15ch	on 70ch	*6.25*	*6.25*
73	A1	15ch	on 1.30nu	*6.25*	*6.25*
74	A5	20ch	on 1nu	*8.25*	*8.25*
75	A5	20ch	on 1.30nu	*8.25*	*8.25*
			Nos. 68-75 (8)	*89.50*	*89.50*

The surcharges on Nos. 68-69 contain two bars at left and right obliterating the denomination on both sides of the design. Four bars on Nos. 72-73.

Simtokha Dzong A12

Tashichho Dzong — A13

Daga Dzong — A14

Designs: 5ch, Rinpung Dzong. 50ch, Tongsa Dzong. 1nu, Lhuntsi Dzong.

Perf. 14½x14 (A12), 13½ (A13, A14)
1966-70 Photo.

76	A12	5ch	orange brn ('67)	15	15
77	A13	10ch	dk grn & rose vio ('68)	15	15
78	A12	15ch	brown	15	15
79	A12	20ch	green	15	15
80	A13	50ch	blue grn ('68)	20	15
81	A14	75ch	dk bl & ol gray ('70)	20	20
82	A14	1nu	dk vio & vio bl ('70)	28	28
			Set value	1.05	90

Sizes: 5ch, 15ch, 20ch, 37x20½mm. 10ch, 53½x28½mm. 50ch, 35½x25½mm.

King Jigme Wangchuk A14a

Coins: 1.30nu, 3nu, 5nu, reverse.

Litho. & Embossed on Gold Foil
1966, July 8 Die Cut *Imperf.*

83	A14a	10ch	green	15	15
83A	A14a	25ch	green	22	22
83B	A14a	50ch	green	45	45
83C	A14a	1nu	red	90	90
83D	A14a	1.30nu	red	1.10	1.10
83E	A14a	2nu	red	1.75	1.75
83F	A14a	3nu	red	2.50	2.50
83G	A14a	4nu	red	3.50	3.50
83H	A14a	5nu	red	4.25	4.25
			Nos. 83-83H (9)	14.82	14.82

See Nos. 98-98B.

Abominable Snowman — A14b

1966 Photo. *Perf. 13½*

84	A14b	1ch	multicolored	15	15
84A	A14b	2ch	multi, diff.	15	15
84B	A14b	3ch	multi, diff.	15	15
84C	A14b	4ch	multi, diff.	15	15
84D	A14b	5ch	multi, diff.	15	15
84E	A14b	15ch	like #84	15	15
84F	A14b	30ch	like #84A	15	15
84G	A14b	40ch	like #84B	15	15
84H	A14b	50ch	like #84C	15	15
84I	A14b	1.25nu	like #84D	30	30
84J	A14b	2.50nu	like #84	65	65
84K	A14b	3nu	like #84A	75	75
84L	A14b	5nu	like #84B	1.25	1.25
84M	A14b	6nu	like #84C	1.50	1.50
84N	A14b	7nu	like #84D	1.75	1.75
			Set value	6.50	6.50

Issue dates: 1ch, 2ch, 3ch, 4ch, 5ch, 15ch, 30ch, 40ch, 50ch, Oct. 12. Others, Nov. 15. Exist imperf.
For overprints see Nos. 93-93G. For surcharges see Nos. 115D, 115K, 115O, 115P, 117I, 117S.

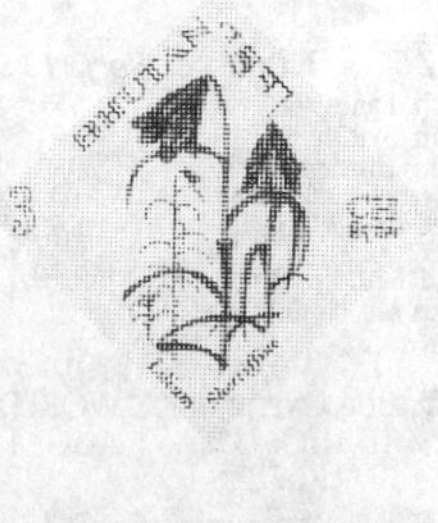
Flowers A14c

Designs: 3ch, 50ch, Lilium sherriffiae. 5ch, 1nu, Meconopsis dhwoju. 7ch, 2.50nu, Rhododendron chaetomallum. 10ch, 4nu, Pleione hookeriana. 5nu, Rhododendron giganteum.

1967, Feb. 9 Litho. *Perf. 13*

85	A14c	3ch	multicolored	15	15
85A	A14c	5ch	multicolored	15	15
85B	A14c	7ch	multicolored	15	15
85C	A14c	10ch	multicolored	15	15

Gray Background

85D	A14c	50ch	multicolored	15	15
85E	A14c	1nu	multicolored	30	30
85F	A14c	2.50nu	multicolored	75	75
85G	A14c	4nu	multicolored	1.20	1.20
85H	A14c	5nu	multicolored	1.50	1.50
			Nos. 85-85H (9)	4.50	4.50

For surcharges see Nos. 115F, 115L.

Boy Scouts — A14d

1967, Mar. 28 Photo. *Perf. 13½*
86 A14d 5ch Planting tree 15 15
86A A14d 10ch Cooking 15 15
86B A14d 15ch Mountain climbing 15 15

Emblem, Border in Gold
86C A14d 50ch like #86 16 16
86D A14d 1.25nu like #86A 40 40
86E A14d 4nu like #86B 1.25 1.25
f. Souv. sheet of 2, #86D, 86E 1.75 1.75
Nos. 86-86E (6) 2.26 2.26

Exist imperf.
See Nos. 89-89E for overprints. For surcharges see Nos. 115G, 117J, 129K.

Nos. 50-52, 52a Ovptd.

expo67

1967, May 25 Litho. *Perfs. as Before*
87 A9 33ch on #50 15 15
87A A9 1.50nu on #51 40 40
87B A9 2nu on #52 50 50
c. Souv. sheet of 2, on #52a 1.50 1.50
Nos. 87-87B (3) 1.05 1.05

Nos. 87-87B exist imperf.

Airplanes — A14f

1967, June 26 Litho. *Perf. 13½*
88 A14f 45ch Lancaster 15 15
88A A14f 2nu Spitfire 45 45
88B A14f 4nu Hurricane 95 95
c. Souv. sheet of 2, #88A, 88B 2.00 2.00
Nos. 88-88B (3) 1.55 1.55

Churchill and Battle of Britain. Exist imperf.
For surcharges see Nos. 117Q, 117T.

Nos. 86-86D, 86e Overprinted "WORLD JAMBOREE / IDAHO, U.S.A. / AUG. 1-9,/67"

1967, Aug. 8 Photo. *Perf. 13½*
89 A14d 5ch Planting tree 15 15
89A A14d 10ch Cookout 15 15
89B A14d 15ch Mountain climbing 15 15
89C A14d 50ch like #89 16 16
89D A14d 1.25nu like #89A 45 45
89E A14d 4nu like #89B 1.50 1.50
f. Souv. sheet of 2, #89D, 89E 2.00 2.00
Nos. 89-89E (6) 2.56 2.56

No. 89f sold for 6.25nu. Exist imperf.

Girl Scouts — A14g

1967, Sept. 28 Photo. *Perf. 13½*
90 A14g 5ch Painting 15 15
90A A14g 10ch Making music 15 15
90B A14g 15ch Picking fruit 15 15

Emblem, Border in Gold
90C A14g 1.50nu like #90 25 25
90D A14g 2.50nu like #90A 40 40
90E A14g 5nu like #90B 80 80
f. Souv. sheet of 2, #90A, 90B 1.75 1.75
Set value 1.50 1.50

Exist imperf.
For surcharge see No. 266.

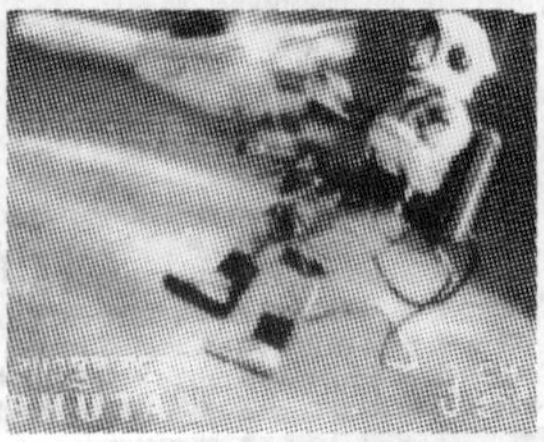

Astronaut, Space Capsule — A14h

Astronaut walking in space and: 5ch, 30ch, 4nu, Orbiter, Lunar modules docked. 7ch, 50ch, 5nu, Lunar module. 10ch, 1.25nu, 9nu, Other astronauts.

1967, Oct. 30 Litho. *Imperf.*
91 A14h 3ch multi 15 15
91A A14h 5ch multi 15 15
91B A14h 7ch multi 18 18
91C A14h 10ch multi 25 25
m. Souv. sheet of 4, #91-91C 75 75
91D A14h 15ch multi 35 35
91E A14h 30ch multi 75 75
91F A14h 50ch multi 1.25 1.25
91G A14h 1.25nu multi 3.00 3.00
n. Souv. sheet of 4, #91D-91G 6.75 6.75
91H A14h 2.50nu multi 1.75 1.75
91I A14h 4nu multi 3.00 3.00
91J A14h 5nu multi 3.75 3.75
91K A14h 9nu multi 6.50 6.50
o. Souv. sheet of 4, #91H-91K 20.00 20.00
Nos. 91-91K (12) 21.08 21.08

Nos. 91H-91K are airmail. Simulated 3-dimensions using a plastic overlay.
For other space issues see types A15a, A15e.

Pheasants — A14i

Designs: 1ch, 2nu, Tragopan satyra. 2ch, 4nu, Lophophorus sclareti. 4ch, 5nu, Lophophorus impeyanus. 8ch, 7nu, Lophura leucomelana. 15ch, 9nu, Crossoptilon crossoptilon.

1968 Photo. *Perf. 13½*
92 A14i 1ch multicolored 15 15
92A A14i 2ch multicolored 15 15
92B A14i 4ch multicolored 15 15
92C A14i 8ch multicolored 15 15
92D A14i 15ch multicolored 15 15

Border in Gold
92E A14i 2nu multicolored 35 35
92F A14i 4nu multicolored 70 70
92G A14i 5nu multicolored 90 90
92H A14i 7nu multicolored 1.25 1.25
92I A14i 9nu multicolored 1.65 1.65
Set value 5.00 5.00

Issue dates: 1ch, 2ch, 4ch, 8ch, 15ch, 2nu, 4nu, 7nu, Jan 20. 5nu, 9nu, Apr. 23.
Unauthorized imperfs. exist.
For surcharges see Nos. 115H, 117R, 117V, 129D, 129L.

Nos. 84G, 84I, 84K, 84M Ovptd. in Black on Silver

a

b

1968, Feb. 16 Photo. *Perfs. as Before*

Overprint Type "a"
93 A14b 40ch on #84G 15 15
93A A14b 1.25nu on #84I 20 20
93B A14b 3nu on #84K 50 50
93C A14b 6nu on #84M 1.00 1.00

Overprint Type "b"
93D A14b 40ch on #84G 15 15
93E A14b 1.25nu on #84I 20 20
93F A14b 3nu on #84K 50 50
93G A14b 6nu on #84M 1.00 1.00
Nos. 93-93G (8) 3.70 3.70

Exist imperf.

Snow Lion — A14j

1968, Mar. 14 Photo. *Perf. 12½*
94 A14j 2ch Elephant 15 15
94A A14j 3ch Garuda 15 15
94B A14j 4ch Monastery Tiger 15 15
94C A14j 5ch Wind Horse 15 15
94D A14j 15ch Snow Lion 15 15
94E A14j 20ch like #94 15 15
94F A14j 30ch like #94A 15 15
94G A14j 50ch like #94B 15 15
94H A14j 1.25nu like #94C 20 20
94I A14j 1.50nu like #94 25 25
94J A14j 2nu like #94D 32 32
94K A14j 2.50nu like #94A 40 40
94L A14j 4nu like #94B 65 65
94M A14j 5nu like #94C 80 80
94N A14j 10nu like #94D 1.65 1.65
Set value 4.50 4.50

Nos. 94I, 94K-94N are airmail. All exist imperf.
For surcharges see Nos. 115, 115M, 115Q, 117-117E, 129C, C35-C36.

Butterflies A14k

Designs: 15ch, Catagramma sorana. 50ch, Delias hyparete. 1.25nu, Anteos maerula. 2nu, Ornithoptera priamus urvilleanus. 3nu, Euploea mulciber. 4nu, Morpho rhetenor. 5nu, Papilio androgeous. 6nu, Troides magellanus.

1968, May 20 Litho. *Imperf.*
95 A14k 15ch multi 15 15
95A A14k 50ch multi 45 45
95B A14k 1.25nu multi 1.10 1.10
95C A14k 2nu multi 1.75 1.75
h. Souv. sheet of 4, #95-95C 3.50 3.50
95D A14k 3nu multi 1.25 1.25
95E A14k 4nu multi 1.65 1.65
95F A14k 5nu multi 2.00 2.00
95G A14k 6nu multi 2.50 2.50
i. Souv. sheet of 4, #95D-95G 7.50 7.50
Nos. 95-95G (8) 10.85 10.85

Souv. sheets issued Oct. 23. Nos. 95D-95G, 95i are airmail. Simulated 3-dimensions using a plastic overlay.

Paintings — A14m

1968 Litho. & Embossed *Imperf.*
96 A14m 2ch Van Gogh 15 15
96A A14m 4ch Millet 15 15
96B A14m 5ch Monet 15 15
96C A14m 10ch Corot 15 15
p. Souv. sheet of 4, #96-96C 15 15
96D A14m 45ch like #96 20 20
96E A14m 80ch like #96A 35 35
96F A14m 1.05nu like #96B 45 45
96G A14m 1.40nu like #96C 60 60
q. Souv. sheet of 4, #96D-96G 1.65 1.65
96H A14m 1.50nu like #96 65 65
96I A14m 2nu like #96 85 85
96J A14m 2.50nu like #96A 1.10 1.10
96K A14m 3nu like #96A 1.25 1.25
96L A14m 4nu like #96B 1.10 1.10
96M A14m 5nu like #96C 1.40 1.40
r. Souv. sheet of 4, #96I, 96K-96M 4.75 4.75
96N A14m 6nu like #96B 1.75 1.75
96O A14m 8nu like #96C 2.25 2.25
s. Souv. sheet of 4, #96H, 96J, 96N-96O 6.00 6.00
Nos. 96-96O (16) 12.55 12.55

Issue dates: Nos. 96-96G, 96I, 96K-96M, July 8. Nos. 96p, 96q, 96r, Aug. 5. Others, Aug. 28. Nos. 96H, 96J, 96N-96O are airmail.
See Nos. 114-114O, 144-144G.

Summer Olympics, Mexico, 1968 A14n

1968, Oct. 1 Photo. *Perf. 13½*
97 A14n 5ch Discus 15 15
97A A14n 45ch Basketball 15 15
97B A14n 60ch Javelin 15 15
97C A14n 80ch Shooting 15 15
97D A14n 1.05nu like #97 15 15
97E A14n 2nu like #97B 24 24
97F A14n 3nu like #97C 35 35
97G A14n 5nu Soccer 60 60
h. Souv. sheet of 2, #97D, 97G 2.25 2.25
Set value 1.50 1.50

Exist imperf.
For surcharges see Nos. 129E, B5-B7.

Coin Type of 1966 Overprinted

Embossed on Gold Foil

1968, Nov. 12 Die Cut *Imperf.*
98 A14a 15ch green 15 15
98A A14a 33ch green 16 16
98B A14a 9nu green 4.25 4.25
Nos. 98-98B (3) 4.56 4.56

Human Rights Year.

Birds — A14p

Designs: 2ch, 20ch, 1.50nu, Crimson-winged laughing thrush. 3ch, 30ch, 2.50nu, Ward's trogon, vert. 4ch, 50ch, 4nu, Grey peacock-pheasant. 5ch, 1.25nu, 5nu, Rufous necked hornbill, vert. 15ch, 2nu, 10nu, Myzornis.

1968-69 Photo. *Perf. 12½*

99	A14p	2ch multicolored	15	15
99A	A14p	3ch multicolored	15	15
99B	A14p	4ch multicolored	15	15
99C	A14p	5ch multicolored	15	15
99D	A14p	15ch multicolored	15	15
99E	A14p	20ch multicolored	15	15
99F	A14p	30ch multicolored	15	15
99G	A14p	50ch multicolored	15	15
99H	A14p	1.25nu multicolored	30	30
99I	A14p	1.50nu multicolored	38	38
99J	A14p	2nu multicolored	42	42
99K	A14p	2.50nu multicolored	52	52
99L	A14p	4nu multicolored	85	85
99M	A14p	5nu multicolored	1.10	1.10
99N	A14p	10nu multicolored	2.00	2.00
		Nos. 99-99N (15)	6.77	6.77

Issue dates: 2ch, 3ch, 4ch, 5ch, 15ch, 30ch, 50ch, Dec. 7, 1968. 20ch, 1.25nu, 2nu, Dec. 28, 1968. Others, Jan. 29, 1969.

1.50nu, 2.50nu, 4nu, 5nu, 10nu are airmail.

Exist imperf.

For surcharges see Nos. 115A-115B, 115I, 115M, 115R, 117F-117G, 117K, 117O, 129H.

Fish A14q

1969, Feb. 27 Litho. *Imperf.*

100	A14q	15ch multicolored	80	80
100A	A14q	20ch multi, diff.	1.00	1.00
100B	A14q	30ch multi, diff.	1.50	1.50
100C	A14q	5nu multi, diff.	2.00	2.00
100D	A14q	6nu multi, diff.	2.50	2.50
100E	A14q	7nu multi, diff.	3.00	3.00
f.		Souv. sheet of 4, #100B-100E	9.00	9.00
		Nos. 100-100E (6)	10.80	10.80

Nos. 100C-100E are airmail. Simulated 3-dimensions using a plastic overlay.

Insects — A14r

1969, Apr. 10 Litho. *Imperf.*

101	A14r	10ch multicolored	15	15
101A	A14r	75ch multi, diff.	35	35
101B	A14r	1.25nu multi, diff.	60	60
101C	A14r	2nu multi, diff.	1.00	1.00
h.		Souv. sheet of 4, #101-101C	3.75	3.75
101D	A14r	3nu multi, diff.	1.10	1.10
101E	A14r	4nu multi, diff.	1.50	1.50
101F	A14r	5nu multi, diff.	1.90	1.90
101G	A14r	6nu multi, diff.	2.25	2.25
i.		Souv. sheet of 4, #101D-101G	8.00	8.00
		Nos. 101-101G (8)	8.85	8.85

Nos. 101D-101G, 101i are airmail. Stamps from souvenir sheets have inscription at lower right. Simulated 3-dimensions using a plastic overlay.

Admission to UPU — A14s

Illustration reduced.

1969, May 2 Photo. *Perf. 13*

102	A14s	5ch multicolored	15	15
102A	A14s	10ch multicolored	15	15
102B	A14s	15ch multicolored	15	15
102C	A14s	45ch multicolored	15	15
102D	A14s	60ch multicolored	16	16
102E	A14s	1.05nu multicolored	25	25
102F	A14s	1.40nu multicolored	35	35
102G	A14s	4nu multicolored	1.00	1.00
		Set value	2.00	2.00

Exist imperf.

For surcharges see #117H, 117L, 117U, 129.

History of Steel Making — A14t

Designs: 2ch, Pre-biblical. 5ch, Damascus sword. 15ch, 3nu, Saugus Mill. 45ch, Beehive coke ovens. 75ch, 4nu, Bessemer converter. 1.50nu, 5nu, Rolling mill. 1.75nu, Steel mill. 2nu, 6nu, Future applications.

Litho. on Steel Foil

1969, June 2 *Imperf.*

Without Gum

103	A14t	2ch multicolored	15	15
103A	A14t	5ch multicolored	15	15
103B	A14t	15ch multicolored	15	15
m.		Souv. sheet of 2, #103A-103B	15	15
103C	A14t	45ch multicolored	15	15
n.		Souv. sheet of 2, #103, 103C	30	30
103D	A14t	75ch multicolored	22	22
103E	A14t	1.50nu multicolored	45	45
103F	A14t	1.75nu multicolored	52	52
o.		Souv. sheet of 2, #103E-103F	2.25	2.25
103G	A14t	2nu multicolored	60	60
p.		Souv. sheet of 2, #103D, 103G	1.90	1.90
103H	A14t	3nu multicolored	85	85
103I	A14t	4nu multicolored	1.10	1.10
103J	A14t	5nu multicolored	1.40	1.40
q.		Souv. sheet of 2, #103I-103J	3.75	3.75
103K	A14t	6nu multicolored	1.65	1.65
r.		Souv. sheet of 2, #103H,103K	3.75	3.75
		Nos. 103-103K (12)	7.39	7.39

Nos. 103H-103K, 103q, 103r are airmail. Souv. sheets issued June 30.

Birds A14u

1969, Aug. 5 Litho. *Imperf.*

104	A14u	15ch Owl	15	15
104A	A14u	50ch Red birds	38	38
104B	A14u	1.25nu Hawk	95	95
104C	A14u	2nu Penguin	1.50	1.50
h.		Souv. sheet of 4, #104-104C	3.25	3.25
104D	A14u	3nu Macaws	1.10	1.10
104E	A14u	4nu Bird of paradise	1.40	1.40
104F	A14u	5nu Duck	1.75	1.75
104G	A14u	6nu Pheasant	2.00	2.00
i.		Souv. sheet of 4, #104D-104G	6.75	6.75
		Nos. 104-104G (8)	9.23	9.23

Nos. 104D-104G, 104i are airmail. Simulated 3-dimensions using a plastic overlay. Souv. sheets issued Aug. 28.

Buddhist Prayer Banners — A14v

Litho. on Cloth

1969, Sep. 30 *Imperf.*

Self-adhesive

Sizes: 15ch, 75ch, 2nu, 57x57mm, 5nu, 6nu, 70x37mm

105	A14v	15ch multicolored	15	15
105A	A14v	75ch multi, diff.	26	26
105B	A14v	2nu multi, diff.	70	70
105C	A14v	5nu multi, diff.	1.75	1.75
105D	A14v	6nu multi, diff.	2.25	2.25
		Nos. 105-105D (5)	5.11	5.11

Souvenir Sheet

105E		Sheet of 3	5.00	5.00

No. 105E shows denominations of 75ch, 5nu, 6nu with design elements of Nos. 105A, 105C, 105D with gray frame. Exists perf. 13½.

Mahatma Gandhi — A15

1969, Oct. 2 Litho. *Perf. 13x13½*

106	A15	20ch light blue & brn	15	15
107	A15	2nu lemon & brn ol	75	75

Mohandas K. Gandhi (1869-1948), leader in India's struggle for independence.

Apollo 11 Moon Landing — A15a

Designs: 3ch, Separation from third stage. 5ch, Entering lunar orbit. 15ch, Lunar module separating from orbiter. 20ch, 3nu, Astronaut standing on lunar module's foot pad. 25ch, Astronaut, lunar module on moon. 45ch, Astronaut, flag. 50ch, 4nu, Setting up experiments. 1.75nu, Lunar module docking with orbiter. 5nu, Lift-off from Cape Canaveral. 6nu, Recovery at sea.

1969 Litho. *Imperf.*

108	A15a	3ch multi	15	15
108A	A15a	5ch multi	15	15
108B	A15a	15ch multi	16	16
108C	A15a	20ch multi	20	20
m.		Souv. sheet of 4, #108-108C	55	55
108D	A15a	25ch multi	25	25
108E	A15a	45ch multi	48	48
108F	A15a	50ch multi	52	52
108G	A15a	1.75nu multi	1.75	1.75
n.		Souv. sheet of 4, #108D-108G	4.00	4.00
108H	A15a	3nu multi	1.50	1.50
108I	A15a	4nu multi	2.00	2.00
108J	A15a	5nu multi	2.50	2.50
108K	A15a	6nu multi	3.00	3.00
o.		Souv. sheet of 4, #108H-108K	21.00	21.00
		Nos. 108-108K (12)	12.66	12.66

Issue dates: Nos. 108-108G, Nov. 3. Nos. 108H-108K, Nov. 20. Souv. sheets, Dec. 20.

Nos. 108H-108K, 108o are airmail. Simulated 3-dimensions using a plastic overlay.

"Aldrin" misspelled on No. 108o.

Paintings A15b

1970, Jan. 19 Litho. *Imperf.*

109	A15b	5ch Clouet	15	15
109A	A15b	10ch van Eyck	15	15
109B	A15b	15ch David	15	15
109C	A15b	2.75nu Rubens	1.75	1.75
h.		Souv. sheet of 4, #109-109C	2.50	2.50
109D	A15b	3nu Homer	1.10	1.10
109E	A15b	4nu Gentileschi	1.40	1.40
109F	A15b	5nu Raphael	1.75	1.75
109G	A15b	6nu Ghirlandaio	2.25	2.25
i.		Souv. sheet of 4, #109D-109G	7.50	7.50
		Nos. 109-109G (8)	8.70	8.70

Nos. 109D-109G, 109i are airmail. Simulated 3-dimensions using a plastic overlay. Souv. sheets issued Feb. 25.

Various Forms of Mail Transport, UPU Headquarters, Bern — A15c

1970, Feb. 27 Photo. *Perf. 13½*

110	A15c	3ch ol grn & gold	15	15
111	A15c	10ch red brn & gold	15	15
112	A15c	20ch Prus bl & gold	15	15
113	A15c	2.50nu dp mag & gold	65	65
		Set value	75	75

New Headquarters of Universal Postal Union, Bern, Switzerland.

Exist imperf. Value $5.

For surcharge see No. 129I.

Painting Type of 1968

Paintings of flowers.

Litho. & Embossed

1970, May 6 *Imperf.*

114	A14m	2ch Van Gogh	15	15
114A	A14m	3ch Redon	15	15
114B	A14m	5ch Kuroda	15	15
114C	A14m	10ch Renoir	15	15
p.		Souv. sheet of 4, #114-114C	15	15
114D	A14m	15ch Renoir, diff.	15	15
114E	A14m	75ch Monet	32	32
114F	A14m	80ch like #114	20	20
114G	A14m	90ch like #114A	22	22
114H	A14m	1nu La Tour	42	42
114I	A14m	1.10nu like #114B	28	28
114J	A14m	1.40nu Oudot	60	60
q.		Souv. sheet of 4, #114D, 114E, 114H, 114J	1.90	1.90
114K	A14m	1.40nu like #114C	35	35
r.		Souv. sheet of 4, #114F, 114G, 114I, 114K	1.25	1.25
114L	A14m	1.60nu like #114D	40	40
114M	A14m	1.70nu like #114E	42	42
114N	A14m	3nu like #114H	75	75
114O	A14m	3.50nu like #114J	85	85
s.		Souv. sheet of 4, #114L-114O	2.75	2.75
		Nos. 114-114O (16)	5.56	5.56

#114F-114G, 114I, 114K-114O are airmail.

Stamps of 1966-69 Surcharged

1970, June 19

115	A14j	20ch on 2nu, #94J	*2.50*	*2.50*
115A	A14p	20ch on 2nu, #99J	*2.50*	*2.50*
115B	A14p	20ch on 2.50nu, #99K	*2.50*	*2.50*
115C	A11	20ch on 3nu, #65	*2.50*	*2.50*
115D	A14b	20ch on 3nu, #84K	*2.50*	*2.50*
115E	A11	20ch on 4nu, #66	*2.50*	*2.50*
115F	A14c	20ch on 4nu, #85G	*2.50*	*2.50*
115G	A14d	20ch on 4nu, #86E	*2.50*	*2.50*
115H	A14i	20ch on 4nu, #92F	*2.50*	*2.50*
115I	A14p	20ch on 4nu, #99L	*2.50*	*2.50*
115J	A11	20ch on 5nu, #67	*2.50*	*2.50*
115K	A14b	20ch on 5nu, #84L	*2.50*	*2.50*
115L	A14c	20ch on 5nu, #85H	*2.50*	*2.50*
115M	A14j	20ch on 5nu, #94M	*2.50*	*2.50*
115N	A14p	20ch on 5nu, #99M	*2.50*	*2.50*
115O	A14b	20ch on 6nu, #84M	*2.50*	*2.50*
115P	A14b	20ch on 7nu, #84N	*2.50*	*2.50*

115Q	A14j	20ch on 10nu, #94N	*2.50*	*2.50*
115R	A14p	20ch on 10nu, #99N	*2.50*	*2.50*
		Nos. 115-115R (19)	*47.50*	*47.50*

Nos. 115B, 115I, 115M-115N, 115Q-115R are airmail.

Animals — A15d

1970, Oct. 15 Litho. *Imperf.*

116	A15d	5ch African elephant	15	15
116A	A15d	10ch Leopard	15	15
116B	A15d	20ch Ibex	15	15
116C	A15d	25ch Tiger	15	15
116D	A15d	30ch Abominable snow-man	16	16
116E	A15d	40ch Water buffalo	22	22
116F	A15d	65ch Rhinoceros	35	35
116G	A15d	75ch Giant pandas	42	42
116H	A15d	85ch Snow leopard	48	48
116I	A15d	2nu Young deer	65	65
116J	A15d	3nu Wild boar, vert.	95	95
116K	A15d	4nu Collared bear, vert.	1.25	1.25
116L	A15d	5nu Takin	1.65	1.65
		Nos. 116-116L (13)	6.73	6.73

Nos. 116I-116L are airmail. Simulated 3-dimensions using a plastic overlay.

Stamps of 1963-69 Surcharged

1970, Nov. 2

117	A14j	5ch on 30ch, #94F	*60*	*60*
117A	A14j	5ch on 50ch, #94G	*60*	*60*
117B	A14j	5ch on 1.25nu, #94H	*60*	*60*
117C	A14j	5ch on 1.50nu, #94I	*60*	*60*
117D	A14j	5ch on 2nu, #94J	*60*	*60*
117E	A14j	5ch on 2.50nu, #94K	*60*	*60*
117F	A14p	20ch on 30ch, #99F	*2.50*	*2.50*
117G	A14p	20ch on 50ch, #99G	*2.50*	*2.50*
117H	A14s	20ch on 1.05nu, #102E	*2.50*	*2.50*
117I	A14b	20ch on 1.25nu, #84I	*2.50*	*2.50*
117J	A14d	20ch on 1.25nu, #86D	*2.50*	*2.50*
117K	A14p	20ch on 1.25nu, #99H	*2.50*	*2.50*
117L	A14s	20ch on 1.40nu, #102F	*2.50*	*2.50*
117M	A4	20ch on 1.50nu, #14	*2.50*	*2.50*
117N	A11	20ch on 1.50nu, #63	*2.50*	*2.50*
117O	A14p	20ch on 1.50nu, #99I	*2.50*	*2.50*
117P	A11	20ch on 2nu, #64	*2.50*	*2.50*
117Q	A14f	20ch on 2nu, #88A	*2.50*	*2.50*
117R	A14i	20ch on 2nu, #92E	*2.50*	*2.50*
117S	A14b	20ch on 2.50nu, #84J	*2.50*	*2.50*
117T	A14f	20ch on 4nu, #88B	*2.50*	*2.50*
117U	A14s	20ch on 4nu, #102G	*2.50*	*2.50*
117V	A14i	20ch on 7nu, #92H	*2.50*	*2.50*
		Nos. 117-117V (23)	*46.10*	*46.10*

Nos. 117C, 117E, 117O are airmail.

Conquest of Space — A15e

Designs: 2ch, Jules Verne's "From the Earth to the Moon." 5ch, V-2 rocket. 15ch, Vostok. 25ch, Mariner 2. 30ch, Gemini 7. 50ch, Lift-off. 75ch, Edward White during space walk. 1.50nu, Apollo 13. 2nu, View of Earth from moon. 3nu, Another galaxy. 6nu, Moon, Earth, Sun, Mars, Jupiter. 7nu, Future space station.

1970 Litho. *Imperf.*

118	A15e	2ch multicolored	15	15
118A	A15e	5ch multicolored	15	15
118B	A15e	15ch multicolored	15	15
118C	A15e	25ch multicolored	18	18
m.		Souv. sheet of 4, #118-118C	40	40
118D	A15e	30ch multicolored	22	22
118E	A15e	50ch multicolored	35	35
118F	A15e	75ch multicolored	55	55
118G	A15e	1.50nu multicolored	1.10	1.10
n.		Souv. sheet of 4, #118D-118G	2.50	2.50
118H	A15e	2nu multicolored	65	65
118I	A15e	3nu multicolored	1.00	1.00
118J	A15e	6nu multicolored	2.00	2.00
118K	A15e	7nu multicolored	2.25	2.25
o.		Souv. sheet of 4, #118H-118K	6.50	6.50
		Nos. 118-118K (12)	8.75	8.75

Issue dates: Nos. 118-118G, Nov. 9. Nos. 118H-118K, Nov. 30. Souv. sheets, Dec. 18. Nos. 118H-118K are airmail. Simulated 3-dimensions using a plastic overlay.

See Nos. 127-127C. For surcharge see No. 129F.

Wangdiphodrang Dzong and Bridge — A15f

1971-72 Photo. *Perf. 13½*

119	A15f	2ch gray	15	15
120	A15f	3ch deep red lilac	15	15
121	A15f	4ch violet	15	15
122	A15f	5ch dark green	15	15
123	A15f	10ch orange brown	15	15
124	A15f	15ch deep blue	15	15
125	A15f	20ch deep plum	15	15
		Set value	55	55

Issued: 5ch-20ch, Feb. 22. 2ch-4ch, Apr. 1972.

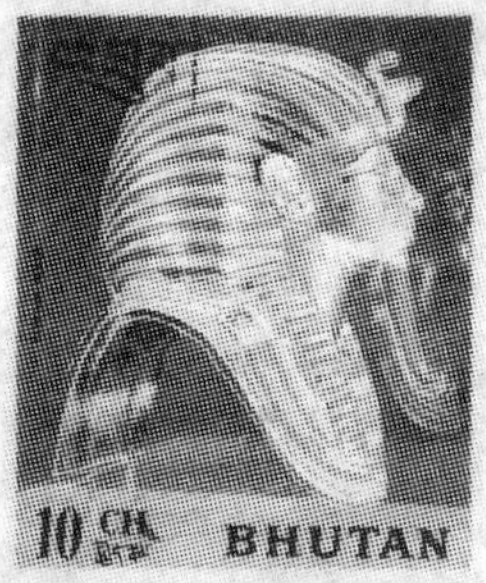

Funeral Mask of King Tutankhamen — A15g

History of Sculpture: 75ch, Winged Bull. 1.25nu, Head of Zeus. 2nu, She-wolf Suckling Romulus and Remus, horiz. 3nu, Head of Cicero. 4nu, Head of David, by Michaelangelo. 5nu, Age of Bronze, by Rodin. 6nu, Head of Woman, by Modigliani.

1971, Feb. 27 Litho. *Imperf.*
Self-adhesive

126	A15g	10ch multicolored	15	15
126A	A15g	75ch multicolored	35	35
126B	A15g	1.25nu multicolored	60	60
126C	A15g	2nu multicolored	1.00	1.00
h.		Souv. sheet of 4, #126-126C	2.50	2.50
126D	A15g	3nu multicolored	80	80
126E	A15g	4nu multicolored	1.10	1.10
126F	A15g	5nu multicolored	1.40	1.40
126G	A15g	6nu multicolored	1.65	1.65
i.		Souv. sheet of 4, #126D-126G	5.50	5.50
		Nos. 126-126G (8)	7.05	7.05

Stamps are plastic heat molded into three dimensions. Nos. 126D-126G are airmail.

Conquest of Space Type of 1970

Designs: 10ch, 2.50nu, Lunokhod 1. 1.70nu, 4nu, Apollo 15.

1971, Mar. 20 Litho. *Imperf.*

127	A15e	10ch multicolored	15	15
127A	A15e	1.70nu multicolored	1.00	1.00
127B	A15e	2.50nu multicolored	1.50	1.50
127C	A15e	4nu multicolored	2.25	2.25
d.		Souv. sheet of 4, #127-127C	5.00	5.00
		Nos. 127-127C (4)	4.90	4.90

Nos. 127B-127C are airmail. Simulated 3-dimensions using a plastic overlay.

Antique Automobiles — A15h

1971 Litho. *Imperf.*

128	A15h	2ch Mercedes Benz, Germany	15	15
128A	A15h	5ch Ford, US	15	15
128B	A15h	10ch Alfa Romeo, Italy	15	15
128C	A15h	15ch Cord, US	15	15
128D	A15h	20ch Hispano Suiza, Spain	15	15
128E	A15h	30ch Invicta, Britain	15	15
128F	A15h	60ch Renault, France	20	20
128G	A15h	75ch Talbot, Britain	25	25
128H	A15h	85ch Mercer, US	30	30
128I	A15h	1nu Sunbeam, Britain	35	35
128J	A15h	1.20nu Austrian Daimler	42	42
128K	A15h	1.55nu Bugatti, Italy	55	55
128L	A15h	1.80nu Simplex, US	60	60
128M	A15h	2nu Amilcar, France	65	65
128N	A15h	2.50nu Bentley, Britain	85	85
128O	A15h	4nu Morris Garage, Britain	85	85
128P	A15h	6nu Duesenberg, US	1.10	1.10
128Q	A15h	7nu Aston Martin, Britain	1.25	1.25
128R	A15h	9nu Packard, US	1.65	1.65
128S	A15h	10nu Rolls Royce, Britain	1.75	1.75
		Nos. 128-128S (20)	11.67	11.67

Issue dates: Nos. 128-128F, May 20. Nos. 128G-128N, June 10. Nos. 128O-128S, July 5. Nos. 128O-128S are airmail. Simulated 3-dimensions using a plastic overlay.

"Romeo" misspelled.

Stamps of 1964-71 Surcharged

1971, July 1

129	A14s	55ch on 60ch, #102D	75	75
129A	A5	55ch on 1.30nu, #22	38	38
129B	A11	55ch on 3nu, #65	38	38
129C	A14j	55ch on 4nu, #94L	38	38
129D	A14i	55ch on 5nu, #92G	38	38
129E	A14n	90ch on 1.05nu, #97D	1.90	1.90
129F	A15e	90ch on 1.70nu, #127A	4.25	4.25
129G	A5	90ch on 2nu, #23	38	38
129H	A14p	90ch on 2nu, #99J	75	75
129I	A15c	90ch on 2.50nu, #88	1.10	1.10
129J	A11	90ch on 4nu, #66	75	75
129K	A14d	90ch on 4nu, #86E	1.90	1.90
129L	A14i	90ch on 7nu, #92I	75	75
		Nos. 129-129L (13)	14.05	14.05

No. 129C is airmail. No. 129F comes with lines 8mm or 18mm long.

UN Emblem and Bhutan Flag A16

Designs (Bhutan Flag and): 10ch, UN Headquarters, NY. 20ch, Security Council Chamber and mural by Per Krohg. 3nu, General Assembly Hall.

1971, Sept. 21 Photo. *Perf. 13½*

130	A16	5ch gold, bl & multi	15	15
131	A16	10ch gold & multi	15	15
132	A16	20ch gold & multi	15	15
133	A16	3nu gold & multi	45	45
		Set value, Nos. 130-133, C21-C23	2.50	2.50

Bhutan's admission to the United Nations. Exist imperf.

For overprints see Nos. 140-143. For surcharge see No. 252.

Boy Scout Crossing Stream in Rope Sling — A17

Designs (Emblem and Boy Scouts): 20ch, 2nu, mountaineering. 50ch, 6nu, reading map. 75ch, as 10ch.

1971, Nov. 30 Litho. *Perf. 13½*

134	A17	10ch gold & multi	15	15
135	A17	20ch gold & multi	15	15
136	A17	50ch gold & multi	15	15
137	A17	75ch silver & multi	16	16
138	A17	2nu silver & multi	40	40
139	A17	6nu silver & multi	1.00	1.00
a.		Souv. sheet of 2, #138-139 + 2 labels	2.00	2.00
		Nos. 134-139 (6)	2.01	2.01

60th anniv. of the Boy Scouts. Exist imperf.

For overprint and surcharge see #253, 383.

Nos. 130-133 Overprinted in Gold

UNHCR
UNRWA
1971

1971, Dec. 23

140	A16	5ch gold & multi	15	15
141	A16	10ch gold & multi	15	15
142	A16	20ch gold & multi	15	15
143	A16	3nu gold & multi	65	65
		Nos. 140-143,C24-C26 (7)	4.15	4.15

World Refugee Year. Exist imperf.

The Bathing Girl by Renoir A17a

Designs: 20ch, A Bar at the Follies, by Monet, horiz. 90ch, Mona Lisa, by da Vinci. 1.70nu, Cart of Father Junier, by Rousseau, horiz. 2.50nu, The Gleaners, by Millet, horiz. 4.60nu, White Horse, by Gaugin. 5.40nu, The Dancing Lesson, by Degas. 6nu, After the Rain, by Gaillauman, horiz.

1972 Litho. & Embossed *Imperf.*

144	A17a	15ch multicolored	15	15
144A	A17a	20ch multicolored	15	15
144B	A17a	90ch multicolored	35	35
144C	A17a	1.70nu multicolored	52	52
144D	A17a	2.50nu multicolored	1.00	1.00
h.		Souv. sheet of 4, #144-144B, 144D	3.50	3.50
144E	A17a	4.60nu multicolored	1.40	1.40
144F	A17a	5.40nu multicolored	1.65	1.65
144G	A17a	6nu multicolored	1.90	1.90
i.		Souv. sheet of 4, #144C, 144E-144G	6.00	6.00
		Nos. 144-144G (8)	7.12	7.12

Issue dates: Nos. 144-144B, 144D, Jan. 29. Others, Feb. 28. Nos. 144C, 144E-144G are airmail.

Famous Men A17b

1972, Apr. 17 Litho. *Imperf.*

Self-adhesive

145	A17b	10ch	John F. Kennedy	15	15
145A	A17b	15ch	Gandhi	15	15
145B	A17b	55ch	Churchill	45	45
145C	A17b	2nu	De Gaulle	50	50
145D	A17b	6nu	Pope John XVIII	1.50	1.50
145E	A17b	8nu	Eisenhower	2.00	2.00
f.			Souv. sheet of 4, #145B-145E	5.00	5.00
			Nos. 145-145E (6)	4.75	4.75

Nos. 145C-145E are airmail. Stamps are plastic heat molded into three dimensions.

Book Year Emblem A17c

1972, May 15 Photo. *Perf. 13½x13*

146	A17c	2ch	multicolored	15	15
146A	A17c	3ch	multicolored	15	15
146B	A17c	5ch	multicolored	15	15
146C	A17c	20ch	multicolored	15	15
			Set value	26	26

International Book Year.

1972 Summer Olympics, Munich A17d

1972, June 6 Photo. *Perf. 13½*

147	A17d	10ch	Handball	15	15
147A	A17d	15ch	Archery	15	15
147B	A17d	20ch	Boxing	15	15
147C	A17d	30ch	Discus	15	15
147D	A17d	35ch	Javelin	15	15
147E	A17d	45ch	Shooting	15	15
147F	A17d	1.35nu	like #147A	38	38
147G	A17d	7nu	like #147	1.90	1.90
h.			Souv. sheet of 3, #147D, 147F-147G	3.00	3.00
			Set value	2.75	2.75

Nos. 147D, 147F-147G are airmail and have a gold border.
Exist imperf.
For overprint see No. 384.

Apollo 11 Type of 1969

Apollo 16: 15ch, Lift-off, vert. 20ch, Achieving lunar orbit. 90ch, Astronauts Young, Mattingly, Duke, vert. 1.70nu, Lunar module. 2.50nu, Walking on moon. 4.60nu, Gathering rock samples. 5.40nu, Apollo 16 on launch pad, vert. 6nu, Looking at earth, vert.

1972, Sept. 1 Litho. *Imperf.*

148	A15a	15ch	multicolored	15	15
148A	A15a	20ch	multicolored	15	15
148B	A15a	90ch	multicolored	18	18
148C	A15a	1.70nu	multicolored	35	35
148D	A15a	2.50nu	multicolored	50	50
h.			Souv. sheet of 4, #148-148B, 148D	3.00	3.00
148E	A15a	4.60nu	multicolored	90	90
148F	A15a	5.40nu	multicolored	1.10	1.10
148G	A15a	6nu	multicolored	1.20	1.20
i.			Souv. sheet of 4, #148C, 148E-148G	5.00	5.00
			Nos. 148-148G (8)	4.53	4.53

Nos. 148C, 148E-148G are airmail. Simulated 3-dimensions using a plastic overlay.

Dogs A17f

1972-73 Photo. *Perf. 13½*

149	A17f	2ch	Pointer	15	15
149A	A17f	3ch	Irish Setter	15	15
149B	A17f	5ch	Lhasa Apso, vert	15	15
149C	A17f	10ch	Dochi	15	15
149D	A17f	15ch	Damci	15	15
149E	A17f	15ch	Collie	15	15
149F	A17f	20ch	Basset hound	15	15
149G	A17f	25ch	Damci, diff	15	15
149H	A17f	30ch	Fox terrier	15	15
149I	A17f	55ch	Lhasa Apso, diff.	15	15
149J	A17f	99ch	Boxer	22	22
149K	A17f	2.50nu	St. Bernard	55	55
149L	A17f	4nu	Cocker Spaniel	90	90
o.			Souv. sheet of 3, #149J-149L, perf. 14	3.00	3.00
149M	A17f	8nu	Damci, diff.	1.90	1.90
p.			Souv. sheet of 2, #149I, 149M, perf. 14	3.25	3.25
			Set value	4.00	4.00

Souvenir Sheet

Perf. 14

149N	A17f	18nu	Poodle	5.00	5.00

Issue dates: Nos. 149B-149D, 149G, 149I, 149M, 149p, Oct. 5. Nos. 149-149A, 149E-149F, 149H, 149J-149L, 149o, Jan. 1, 1973. No. 149N, Jan. 15, 1973. No. 149N is airmail. All exist imperf.
For surcharges and overprints see Nos. 268-269, 385.

Roses — A17g

1973, Jan. 30 Photo. *Perf. 13½*

Scented Paper

150	A17g	15ch	Wendy Cussons	15	15
150A	A17g	25ch	Iceberg	15	15
150B	A17g	30ch	Marchioness of Urquio	15	15
150C	A17g	3nu	Pink parfait	70	70
150D	A17g	6nu	Roslyn	1.40	1.40
150E	A17g	7nu	Blue moon	1.65	1.65
f.			Souv. sheet of 2, #150D-150E	2.50	2.50
			Nos. 150-150E (6)	4.20	4.20

#150D-150E are airmail. Exist imperf.

Apollo 11 Type of 1969

Apollo 17: 10ch, Taking photographs on moon. 15ch, Setting up experiments. 55ch, Earth. 2nu, Driving lunar rover. 7nu, Satellite. 9nu, Astronauts Cernan, Evans, Schmitt.

1973, Feb. 28 Litho. *Imperf.*

Size: 50x49mm

151	A15a	10ch	multicolored	15	15
151A	A15a	15ch	multicolored	15	15
151B	A15a	55ch	multicolored	20	20
151C	A15a	2nu	multicolored	70	70
f.			Souv. sheet of 4, #151-151C	2.50	2.50
151D	A15a	7nu	multicolored	2.25	2.25
151E	A15a	9nu	multicolored	3.25	3.25
g.			Souv. sheet of 2, #151D-151E	10.00	10.00
			Nos. 151-151E (6)	6.70	6.70

Simulated 3-dimensions using a plastic overlay. Nos. 151D-151E are airmail. No. 151g is circular, 160mm in diameter.

Phonograph Records

A17h

Recordings: 10ch, Bhutanese History. 25ch, Royal Bhutan Anthem. 1.25nu, Bhutanese History (English). 3nu, Bhutanese History (Bhutanese), Folk Song #1. 7nu, Folk Song #1. 8nu, Folk Song #2. 9nu, History in English, Folk Songs #1 & 2.

1973, Apr. 15

Self-adhesive

Diameter: #152-152B, 152D-152E, 69mm, #152C, 152F, 100mm

152	A17h	10ch	yel on red	*45*	*45*
152A	A17h	25ch	gold on grn	*65*	*65*
152B	A17h	1.25nu	sil on bl	*3.25*	*3.25*
152C	A17h	3nu	sil on pur	*7.50*	*7.50*
152D	A17h	7nu	sil on blk	*18.00*	*18.00*
152E	A17h	8nu	red on white	*21.00*	*21.00*
152F	A17h	9nu	blk on yel	*24.00*	*24.00*
			Nos. 152-152F (7)	*74.85*	*74.85*

Nos. 152C, 152F are airmail.

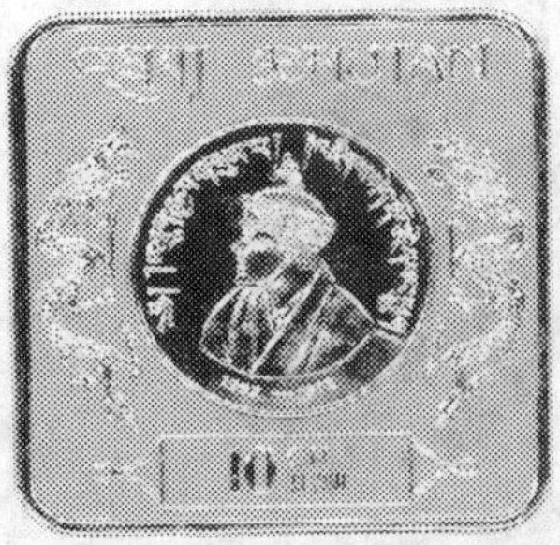

King Jigme Dorji Wangchuk (d. 1972) — A17i

Embossed on Gold Foil

1973, May 2 Die Cut *Imperf.*

153	A17i	10ch	orange	15	15
153A	A17i	25ch	red	15	15
153B	A17i	3nu	green	70	70
153C	A17i	6nu	blue	1.40	1.40
153D	A17i	8nu	purple	1.90	1.90
e.			Souv. sheet of 2, #153C-153D	2.75	2.75
			Nos. 153-153D (5)	4.30	4.30

Nos. 153C-153D are airmail.

Mushrooms — A17j

Different mushrooms.

1973, Sept. 25 Litho. *Imperf.*

154	A17j	15ch	multicolored	*15*	*15*
154A	A17j	25ch	multicolored	*20*	*20*
154B	A17j	30ch	multicolored	*24*	*24*
154C	A17j	3nu	multicolored	*2.50*	*2.50*
f.			Souvenir sheet of 4, #154-154C	*15.00*	*15.00*
154D	A17j	6nu	multicolored	*5.75*	*5.75*
154E	A17j	7nu	multicolored	*6.75*	*6.75*
g.			Souvenir sheet of 2, #154D-154E	*35.00*	*35.00*
			Nos. 154-154E (6)	15.59	15.59

Simulated 3-dimensions using a plastic overlay. Nos. 154D-154E are airmail.

Bhutanese Mail Service — A17k

Designs: 5ch, 6nu, Letter carrier at mail box. 10ch, 5nu, Postmaster, letter carrier. 15ch, Sacking mail. 25ch, Mailtruck. 1.25nu, Sorting mail. 3nu, Hand-delivered mail.

1973, Nov. 14 Photo. *Perf. 13½*

155	A17k	5ch	multicolored	15	15
155A	A17k	10ch	multicolored	15	15
155B	A17k	15ch	multicolored	15	15
155C	A17k	25ch	multicolored	15	15
155D	A17k	1.25nu	multicolored	28	28
155E	A17k	3nu	multicolored	65	65
155F	A17k	5nu	multicolored	1.10	1.10
155G	A17k	6nu	multicolored	1.25	1.25
h.			Souv. sheet of 2, #155F-155G	6.00	6.00
			Nos. 155-155G (8)	3.88	3.88

Indipex '73. Nos. 155F-155G are airmail. All exist imperf.
For surcharges and overprint see Nos. 267, 382, C37-C38.

A set of 15 stamps plus souvenir sheet of 3 showing paintings with reading and writing themes was not authorized.

King Jigme Singye Wangchuk and Royal Crest — A18

Designs (King and): 25ch, 90ch, Flag of Bhutan. 1.25nu, Wheel with 8 good luck signs. 2nu, 4nu, Punakha Dzong, former winter capital. 3nu, 5nu, Crown. 5ch, same as 10ch.

1974, June 2 Litho. *Perf. 13½*

157	A18	10ch	maroon & multi	15	15
158	A18	25ch	gold & multi	15	15
159	A18	1.25nu	multi	35	35
160	A18	2nu	gold & multi	55	55
161	A18	3nu	multi	75	75
			Nos. 157-161 (5)	1.95	1.95

Souvenir Sheets

Perf. 13½, Imperf.

162	Sheet of 2	2.75	2.75
a.	A18 5ch maroon & multi	15	
b.	A18 5nu red orange & multi	2.50	
163	Sheet of 2	2.75	2.75
a.	A18 90ch gold & multi	75	
b.	A18 4nu gold & multi	2.00	

Coronation of King Jigme Singye Wangchuk, June 2, 1974.

Mailman on Horseback
A19

Old and New Locomotives
A20

Designs (UPU Emblem, Carrier Pigeon and): 3ch, Sailing and steam ships. 4ch, Old biplane and jet. 25ch, Mail runner and jeep.

1974, Oct. 9 Litho. *Perf. 14½*

164	A19	1ch	grn & multi	15	15
165	A20	2ch	lilac & multi	15	15
166	A20	3ch	ocher & multi	15	15
167	A20	4ch	yel grn & multi	15	15
168	A20	25ch	salmon & multi	15	15
			Set value, #164-168, C27-C29	1.25	1.25

Centenary of Universal Postal Union. Issued in sheets of 50 and sheets of 5 plus label with multicolored margin. Exist imperf.

Family and WPY Emblem — A21

1974, Dec. 17 *Perf. 13½*

169	A21	25ch	bl & multi	15	15
170	A21	50ch	org & multi	15	15
171	A21	90ch	ver & multi	28	28
172	A21	2.50nu	brn & multi	75	75
a.			Souvenir sheet, 10nu	2.25	2.25
			Nos. 169-172 (4)	1.33	1.33

For surcharge see No. 254.

Sephisa Chandra
A22

Designs: Indigenous butterflies.

1975, Sept. 15 Litho. *Perf. 14½*

173	A22	1ch	*shown*	15	15
174	A22	2ch	*Lethe kansa*	15	15
175	A22	3ch	*Neope bhadra*	15	15
176	A22	4ch	*Euthalia duda*	15	15
177	A22	5ch	*Vindula erota*	15	15
178	A22	10ch	*Bhutanitis Lidderdale*	15	15
179	A22	3nu	*Limenitis zayla*	60	60
180	A22	5nu	*Delis thysbe*	1.40	1.40
			Set value	2.25	2.25

Souvenir Sheet

Perf. 13

181	A22	10nu	*Dabasa gyas*	2.50	2.50

For surcharges see Nos. 255-256.

Apollo and Apollo-Soyuz Emblem — A23

Design: No. 183, Soyuz and emblem.

1975, Dec. 1 Litho. *Perf. 14x13½*

182	A23	10nu	multicolored	2.25	2.25
183	A23	10nu	multicolored	2.25	2.25
a.			Souvenir sheet of 2, 15nu	7.00	7.00

Apollo Soyuz link-up in space, July 17. Nos. 182-183 printed se-tenant in sheets of 10. No. 183a contains two 15nu stamps similar to Nos 182-183. Exist imperf.

For surcharges see Nos. 257-258.

Jewelry
A24

Designs: 2ch, Coffee pot, bell and sugar cup. 3ch, Container and drinking horn. 4ch, Pendants and box cover. 5ch, Painter. 15ch, Silversmith. 20ch, Wood carver with tools. 1.50nu, Mat maker. 5nu, 10nu, Printer.

1975, Dec. 17 *Perf. 14½*

184	A24	1ch	multicolored	15	15
185	A24	2ch	multicolored	15	15
186	A24	3ch	multicolored	15	15
187	A24	4ch	multicolored	15	15
188	A24	5ch	multicolored	15	15
189	A24	15ch	multicolored	15	15
190	A24	20ch	multicolored	15	15
191	A24	1.50nu	multicolored	40	40
192	A24	10nu	multicolored	2.50	2.50
			Set value	3.20	3.20

Souvenir Sheet

Perf. 13

193	A24	5nu	multicolored	1.40	1.40

Handicrafts and craftsmen.

For surcharges see No. 259, 381.

King Jigme Singye Wangchuk
A25

Designs: 25ch, 90ch, 1nu, 2nu, 4nu, like 15ch. 1.30nu, 3nu, 5nu, Coat of arms. Sizes (Diameter): 15ch, 1nu, 1.30nu, 38mm. 25ch, 2nu, 3nu, 49mm. 90ch, 4nu, 5nu, 63mm.

Lithographed, Embossed on Gold Foil

1975, Nov. 11 *Imperf.*

194	A25	15ch	emerald	15	15
195	A25	25ch	emerald	15	15
196	A25	90ch	emerald	35	35
197	A25	1nu	bright carmine	40	40
198	A25	1.30nu	bright carmine	45	45
199	A25	2nu	bright carmine	65	65
200	A25	3nu	bright carmine	1.00	1.00
201	A25	4nu	bright carmine	1.65	1.65
202	A25	5nu	bright carmine	2.00	2.00
			Nos. 194-202 (9)	6.80	6.80

King Jigme Singye Wangchuk's 20th birthday.

Rhododendron Cinnabarinum — A28

Designs (Rhododendron): 2ch, Campanulatum. 3ch, Fortunei. 4ch, Red arboreum. 5ch, Pink arboreum. 1nu, Falconeri. 3nu, Hodgsonii. 5nu, Keysii. 10nu, Cinnabarinum.

1976, Feb. 15 Litho. *Perf. 15*

203	A28	1ch	rose & multi	15	15
204	A28	2ch	lt grn & multi	15	15
205	A28	3ch	gray & multi	15	15
206	A28	4ch	lil & multi	15	15
207	A28	5ch	ol gray & multi	15	15
208	A28	1nu	brn org & multi	25	20
209	A28	3nu	ultra & multi	75	60
210	A28	5nu	gray & multi	1.25	90
			Set value	2.40	1.85

Souvenir Sheet

Perf. 13½

211	A28	10nu	multicolored	2.50	2.50

For surcharge see No. 260.

Slalom and Olympic Games Emblem — A29

Designs (Olympic Games Emblem and): 2ch, 4-men bobsled. 3ch, Ice hockey. 4ch, Cross-country skiing. 5ch, Figure skating, women's. 2nu, Downhill skiing. 4nu, Speed skating. 6nu, Ski jump. 10nu, Figure skating, pairs.

1976, Mar. 29 Litho. *Perf. 13½*

212	A29	1ch	multicolored	15	15
213	A29	2ch	multicolored	15	15
214	A29	3ch	multicolored	15	15
215	A29	4ch	multicolored	15	15
216	A29	5ch	multicolored	15	15
217	A29	2nu	multicolored	40	35
218	A29	4nu	multicolored	90	75
219	A29	10nu	multicolored	2.50	1.75
			Nos. 212-219 (8)	4.55	
			Set value		3.00

Souvenir Sheet

220	A29	6nu	multicolored	1.50	1.50

12th Winter Olympic Games, Innsbruck, Austria, Feb. 4-15.

For surcharges see Nos. 261-262.

Ceremonial Masks
A29a

Various masks.

1976, Apr. 23 Litho. *Imperf.*

220A	A29a	5ch	multicolored	15	15
220B	A29a	10ch	multicolored	15	15
220C	A29a	15ch	multicolored	15	15
220D	A29a	20ch	multicolored	15	15
220E	A29a	25ch	multi, horiz.	15	15
220F	A29a	30ch	multi, horiz.	15	15
220G	A29a	35ch	multi, horiz.	16	16
220H	A29a	1nu	multi, horiz.	45	45
220I	A29a	2nu	multi, horiz.	90	90
220J	A29a	2.50nu	multi, horiz.	1.10	1.10
220K	A29a	3nu	multi, horiz.	1.40	1.40
			Nos. 220A-220K (11)	4.91	4.91

Souvenir Sheets

220L	A29a	5nu	like #220C	1.65	1.65
220M	A29a	10nu	like #220F	3.25	3.25

Simulated 3-dimensions using a plastic overlay. Nos. 220H-220M are airmail.

Sizes of stamps: No. 220L, 59x70mm, No. 220M, 69x57mm.

Orchid
A30

Designs: Various flowers.

1976, May 29 Litho. *Perf. 14½*

221	A30	1ch	multicolored	15	15
222	A30	2ch	multicolored	15	15
223	A30	3ch	multicolored	15	15
224	A30	4ch	multicolored	15	15
225	A30	5ch	multicolored	15	15
226	A30	2nu	multicolored	40	30
227	A30	4nu	multicolored	80	60
228	A30	6nu	multicolored	1.25	1.00
			Set value	2.60	2.00

Souvenir Sheet

Perf. 13½

229	A30	10nu	multicolored	2.75	2.50

For surcharges see Nos. 263-264.

Double Carp Design
A31

Designs: Various symbolic designs and Colombo Plan emblem.

1976, July 1 Litho. *Perf. 14½*

230	A31	3ch	red & multi	15	15
231	A31	4ch	ver & multi	15	15
232	A31	5ch	multicolored	15	15
233	A31	25ch	bl & multi	20	15
234	A31	1.25nu	multicolored	38	30
335	A31	2nu	yel & multi	60	48
236	A31	2.50nu	vio & multi	75	60
237	A31	3nu	multicolored	90	72
			Nos. 230-237 (8)	3.28	2.70

Colombo Plan, 25th anniversary.

For surcharge see No. 265.

Bandaranaike Conference Hall — A32

1976, Aug. 16 Litho. *Perf. 13½*

238	A32	1.25nu	multicolored	35	22
239	A32	2.50nu	multicolored	65	45

5th Summit Conference of Non-aligned Countries, Colombo, Sri Lanka, Aug. 9-19.

Elizabeth II — A33

Liberty Bell — A34

Spirit of St. Louis — A35

Bhutanese Archer, Olympic Rings — A36

Designs: No. 242, Alexander Graham Bell. No. 245, LZ 3 Zeppelin docking, 1907. No. 246, Alfred B. Nobel.

626 A77 25nu multicolored 4.00 3.00
627 A77 25nu multicolored 4.00 3.00
628 A77 25nu multicolored 4.00 3.00
629 A77 25nu multicolored 4.00 3.00
630 A77 25nu multicolored 4.00 3.00
Nos. 607-630 (24) 60.81 45.72

1988 Winter Olympics, Calgary — A78

Emblem and Disney animated characters as competitors in Olympic events.

1988, Feb. 15 Litho. *Perf. 14*
631 A78 50ch Slalom 15 15
632 A78 1nu Downhill skiing 16 15
633 A78 2nu Ice hockey 32 24
634 A78 4nu Biathlon 65 48
635 A78 7nu Speed skating 1.15 85
636 A78 8nu Figure skating 1.30 95
637 A78 9nu Figure skating, diff. 1.45 1.10
638 A78 20nu Bobsled 3.20 2.40
Nos. 631-638 (8) 8.38 6.32

Souvenir Sheets
639 A78 25nu Ski jumping 4.00 4.00
640 A78 25nu Ice dancing 4.00 4.00

Transportation Innovations — A79

1988, Mar. 31
41 A79 50ch Pullman Pioneer, 1865 15 15
A79 1nu Stephenson's Rocket, 1829 16 15
A79 2nu Pierre L'Allement's Velocipede, 1866 32 25
9 3nu Benz Velocipede, 1886 48 35
4nu Volkswagen Beetle, c. 1960 65 48
5nu Natchez Vs. Robert E. Lee, 1870 80 60
nu American La France, 1910 1.00 75
USS Constitution, 1787, vert. 1.15 85
Bell Rocket Belt, 1961, vert. 1.45 1.10
revithick Locomo- ve, 1804 1.60 1.20
650 (10) 7.76 5.88

enir Sheets
rde jet 4.00 4.00
, 1938, vert. 4.00 4.00
sen 4.00 4.00
81 4.00 4.00

Litho.
5 15
6 15
24
48
85
95
10
0

BHUTAN 50CH

Paintings by Titian — A81

Designs: 50ch, *Gentleman with a Book.* 1nu, *Venus and Cupid, with a Lute Player.* 2nu, *Diana and Actaeon.* 3nu, *Cardinal Ippolito dei Medici.* 4nu, *Sleeping Venus.* 5nu, *Venus Risen from the Waves.* 6nu, *Worship of Venus.* 7nu, *Fete Champetre.* 10nu, *Perseus and Andromeda.* 15nu, *Danae.* 20nu, *Venus at the Mirror.* 25nu, *Venus and the Organ Player.* No. 677, *The Pardo Venus,* horiz. No. 678, *Venus and Cupid, with an Organist.* No. 679, *Miracle of the Irascible Son.* No. 680, *Diana and Callisto.* No. 681, *Saint John the Almsgiver.* No. 682, *Danae with the Shower of Gold,* horiz. No. 683, *Bacchus and Ariadne.* No. 684, *Venus Blindfolding Cupid.* No. 685, *Portrait of Laura Dianti.* No. 686, *Venus of Urbino.* No. 687, *Portrait of Johann Friedrich.* No. 688, *Mater Dolorosa with Raised Hands.*

Perf. 13½x14, 14x13½
1989, Feb. 15 Litho.
665 A81 50ch multicolored 15 15
666 A81 1nu multicolored 16 15
667 A81 2nu multicolored 32 24
668 A81 3nu multicolored 48 35
669 A81 4nu multicolored 65 48
670 A81 5nu multicolored 80 60
671 A81 6nu multicolored 95 72
672 A81 7nu multicolored 1.15 85
673 A81 10nu multicolored 1.60 1.20
674 A81 15nu multicolored 2.40 1.80
675 A81 20nu multicolored 3.20 2.40
676 A81 25nu multicolored 4.00 3.00
Nos. 665-676 (12) 15.86 11.94

Souvenir Sheets
677-688 A81 25nu each 4.00 4.00

Mickey Mouse, 60th Anniv. (in 1988) — A82

Movie posters.

1989, June 20 Litho. *Perf. 13½x14*
689 A82 1ch Mickey Mouse, 1930s 15 15
690 A82 2ch *Barnyard Olympics,* 1932 15 15
691 A82 3ch *Society Dog Show,* 1939 15 15
692 A82 4ch *Fantasia,* 1980s re-release 15 15
693 A82 5ch *The Mad Dog,* 1932 15 15
694 A82 10ch *A Gentleman's Gentleman,* 1941 15 15
695 A82 50ch *Symphony hour,* 1942 15 15
696 A82 10nu *The Moose Hunt,* 1931 1.50 1.20
697 A82 15nu *Wild Waves,* 1929 2.25 1.80
698 A82 20nu *Mickey in Arabia,* 1932 3.00 2.40
699 A82 25nu *Tugboat Mickey,* 1940 3.75 3.00
700 A82 30nu *Building a Building,* 1933 4.25 3.50
Nos. 689-700 (12) 15.80 12.95

Souvenir Sheets
701 A82 25nu *The Mad Doctor,* 1933 4.00 4.00
702 A82 25nu *The Meller Drammer,* 1933 4.00 4.00
703 A82 25nu *Ye Olden Days,* 1933 4.00 4.00
704 A82 25nu *Mickey's Good Deed,* 1932 4.00 4.00
705 A82 25nu *Mickey's Pal Pluto,* 1933 4.00 4.00
706 A82 25nu *Trader Mickey,* 1932 4.00 4.00
707 A82 25nu *Touchdown Mickey,* 1932 4.00 4.00
708 A82 25nu *Steamboat Willie,* 1928 4.00 4.00
709 A82 25nu *The Whoopee Party,* 1932 4.00 4.00
710 A82 25nu *Mickey's Nightmare,* 1932 4.00 4.00
711 A82 25nu *The Klondike Kid,* 1932 4.00 4.00
712 A82 25nu *The Wayward Canary,* 1932 4.00 4.00

Mushrooms — A83

1989, Aug. 22 Litho. *Perf. 14*
713 A83 50ch *Tricholoma pardalotum* 15 15
714 A83 1nu *Suillus placidus* 16 15
715 A83 2nu *Boletus regius* 32 24
716 A83 3nu *Gomphidius glutinosus* 48 35
717 A83 4nu *Boletus calopus* 65 48
718 A83 5nu *Suillus grevillei* 80 60
719 A83 6nu *Boletus appendiculatus* 95 70
720 A83 7nu *Lactarius torminosus* 1.10 82
721 A83 10nu *Macrolepiota rhacodes* 1.60 1.20
722 A83 15nu *Amanita rubescens* 2.40 1.80
723 A83 20nu *Amanita phalloides* 3.20 2.40
724 A83 25nu *Amanita citrina* 4.00 3.00
Nos. 713-724 (12) 15.81 11.89

Souvenir Sheets
725 A83 25nu *Russula aurata* 4.00 4.00
726 A83 25nu *Gyroporus castaneus* 4.00 4.00
727 A83 25nu *Cantharellus cibarius* 4.00 4.00
728 A83 25nu *Boletus rhodoxanthus* 4.00 4.00
729 A83 25nu *Paxillus involutus* 4.00 4.00
730 A83 25nu *Gyroporus cyanescens* 4.00 4.00
731 A83 25nu *Lepista nuda* 4.00 4.00
732 A83 25nu *Dentinum repandum* 4.00 4.00
733 A83 25nu *Lepista saeva* 4.00 4.00
734 A83 25nu *Hydnum imbricatum* 4.00 4.00
735 A83 25nu *Xerocomus subtomentosus* 4.00 4.00
736 A83 25nu *Russula olivacea* 4.00 4.00

Intl. Maritime Organization, 30th Anniv. — A84

Ships: 50ch, Spanish galleon *La Reale,* 1680. 1nu, Submersible *Turtle,* 1776. 2nu, *Charlotte Dundas,* 1802. 3nu, *Great Eastern,* c. 1858. 4nu, HMS *Warrior,* 1862. 5nu, Mississippi steamer, 1884. 6nu, *Preussen,* 1902. 7nu, USS *Arizona,* 1915. 10nu, *Bluenose,* 1921. 15nu, Steam trawler, 1925. 20nu, American liberty ship, 1943. No. 748, S.S. *United States,* 1952. No. 749, Moran tug, c. 1950. No. 750, Sinking of the *Titanic,* 1912. No. 751, U-boat, c. 1942. No. 752, Japanese warship *Yamato,* 1944. No. 753, HMS *Dreadnought.* No. 754, S.S. *Normandie,* c. 1933, and a Chinese junk. No. 755, HMS *Victory,* 1805. No. 756, USS *Monitor,* 1862. No. 757, *Cutty Sark,* 1869. No. 758, USS *Constitution.* No. 759, HMS *Resolution.* No. 760, Chinese junk.

1989, Aug. 24 Litho. *Perf. 14*
737 A84 50ch multicolored 15 15
738 A84 1nu multicolored 16 15
739 A84 2nu multicolored 32 24
740 A84 3nu multicolored 48 35
741 A84 4nu multicolored 65 48
742 A84 5nu multicolored 80 60
743 A84 6nu multicolored 95 70
744 A84 7nu multicolored 1.10 82
745 A84 10nu multicolored 1.60 1.20
746 A84 15nu multicolored 2.40 1.80
747 A84 20nu multicolored 3.20 2.40
748 A84 25nu multicolored 4.00 3.00
Nos. 737-748 (12) 15.81 11.89

Souvenir Sheets
749-760 A84 25nu each 4.00 4.00

Nos. 289-291 Overprinted: WORLD / AIDS DAY

1988, Dec. 1 Litho. *Perf. 14x13½*
761 A37 2nu multicolored 45 35
762 A37 5nu multicolored 1.15 88
763 A37 10nu multicolored 2.25 1.70
Nos. 761-763 (3) 3.85 2.93

Nos. 486-494 Ovptd. in Silver: ASIA-PACIFIC EXPOSITION FUKUOKA '89

1989, Mar. 17 *Perf. 13½*
764 A61 5ch multicolored 15 15
765 A61 35ch multicolored 15 15
766 A61 50ch multicolored 15 15
767 A61 2.50nu multicolored 40 30
768 A61 3nu multicolored 48 35
769 A61 4nu multicolored 65 50
770 A61 5nu multicolored 80 60
771 A61 5.50nu multicolored 88 65
772 A61 6nu multicolored 1.05 80
Nos. 764-772 (9) 4.71 3.65

This set exists overprinted in Japanese.

Chhukha Hydroelectric Project — A85

1988, Oct. 21 Litho. *Perf. 13½*
773 A85 50ch multicolored 15 15

Jawaharlal Nehru (1889-1964), Indian Prime Minister — A85a

1989, Nov. 14 Photo. *Perf. 14*
773A A85a 100ch olive brown 16 16

Denomination is shown as 1.00ch in error.

Birds A86

Designs: 50ch, Larger goldenbacked woodpecker. 1nu, Black-naped monarch. 2nu, White-crested laughing thrush. 3nu, Blood-pheasant. 4nu, Blossom-headed parakeet. 5nu, Rosy minivet. 6nu, Chestnut-headed tit babbler. 7nu, Blue pitta. 10nu, Black-naped oriole. 15nu, Green magpie. 20nu, Indian three-toed kingfisher. No. 785, Ibisbill. No. 786, Great pied hornbill. No. 787, Himalayan red-breasted falconet. No. 788, Lammergeier. No. 789, Large racket-tailed drongo. No. 790, Fire-tailed sunbird. No. 791, Indian crested swift. No. 792, White-eared pheasant. No. 793, Satyr tragopan. No. 794, Wallcreeper. No. 795, Fairy bluebird. No. 796, Little spiderhunter. No. 797, Spotted forktail. Nos. 774-779 vert.

1989, Nov. 22 Litho. *Perf. 14*
774 A86 50ch multicolored 15 15
775 A86 1nu multicolored 16 15
776 A86 2nu multicolored 32 24
777 A86 3nu multicolored 48 35
778 A86 4nu multicolored 65 48
779 A86 5nu multicolored 80 60
780 A86 6nu multicolored 95 70
781 A86 7nu multicolored 1.10 82
782 A86 10nu multicolored 1.60 1.20
783 A86 15nu multicolored 2.40 1.80
784 A86 20nu multicolored 3.20 2.40
785 A86 25nu multicolored 4.00 3.00
Nos. 774-785 (12) 15.81 11.89

Souvenir Sheets
786-797 A86 25nu each 4.00 4.00

1978, Nov. 15 Litho. *Perf. 14½*
240 A33 20nu multicolored 5.00 5.00
241 A34 20nu multicolored 5.00 5.00
242 A33 20nu multicolored 5.00 5.00
243 A35 20nu multicolored 5.00 5.00
244 A36 20nu multicolored 5.00 5.00
245 A35 20nu multicolored 5.00 5.00
246 A33 20nu multicolored 5.00 5.00
Nos. 240-246 (7) 35.00 35.00

25th anniv. of coronation of Elizabeth II; American Bicentennial; cent. of 1st telephone call by Alexander Graham Bell; Charles A. Lindbergh crossing the Atlantic, 50th anniv.; Olympic Games; 75th anniv. of the Zeppelin; 75th anniv. of Nobel Prize. Seven souvenir sheets exist, each 25nu, commemorating same events with different designs. Size: 103x80mm.

Issues of 1967-1976 Surcharged with New Value and Bars

Perforations and Printing as Before

1978
252 A16 25ch on 3nu (#133)
253 A17 25ch on 6nu (#139)
254 A21 25ch on 2.50nu (#172)
255 A22 25ch on 3nu (#179)
256 A22 25ch on 5nu (#180)
257 A23 25ch on 10nu (#182)
258 A23 25ch on 10nu (#183)
259 A24 25ch on 10nu (#192)
260 A28 25ch on 5nu (#210)
261 A29 25ch on 4nu (#218)
262 A29 25ch on 10nu (#219)
263 A30 25ch on 4nu (#227)
264 A30 25ch on 6nu (#228)
265 A31 25ch on 2.50nu (#236)
266 A14g 25ch on 5nu (#90E)
267 A17k 25ch on 3nu (#155E)
268 A17f 25ch on 4nu (#149L)
269 A17f 25ch on 8nu (#149M)
Nos. 252-269, C31-C38 (26) *37.50 37.50*

Mother and Child, IYC Emblem — A37

IYC Emblem and: 5nu, Mother and two children. 10nu, Boys with blackboards and stylus.

1979, June Litho. *Perf. 14x13½*
289 A37 2nu multicolored 52 40
290 A37 5nu multicolored 1.40 1.00
291 A37 10nu multicolored 2.50 2.00
a. Souv. sheet of 3, #289-291 + label, perf. 15x13½ 4.25 3.25
Nos. 289-291 (3) 4.42 3.40

International Year of the Child.
For overprints see Nos. 761-763.

Conference Emblem and Dove — A38

Design: 10nu, Emblem and Bhutanese symbols.

1979, Sept. 3 Litho. *Perf. 14x13½*
292 A38 25ch multicolored 15 15
293 A38 10nu multicolored 3.25 2.50

6th Non-Aligned Summit Conference, Havana, August 1979.

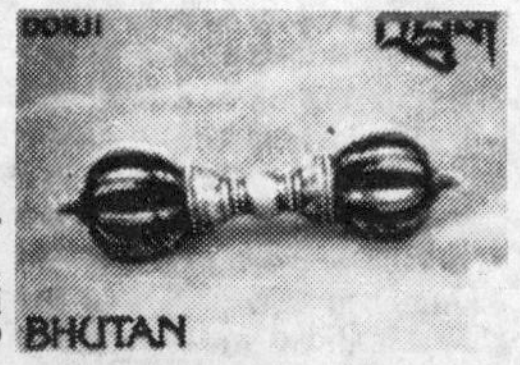

Silver Rattle, Dorji A39

Antiques: 10ch, Silver handell, Dilbu, vert. 15ch, Cylindrical jar, Jadum, vert. 25ch, Ornamental teapot, Jamjee. 1nu, Leather container, Kem, vert. 1.25nu, Brass teapot, Jamjee. 1.70nu, Vessel with elephant-head legs, Sangphor, vert. 2nu, Teapot with ornamental spout, Jamjee, vert. 3nu, Metal pot on claw-shaped feet, Yangtho, vert. 4nu, Dish inlaid with precious stones, Battha. 5nu, Metal circular flask, Chhap, vert.

1979, Dec. 17 Photo. *Perf. 14*
294 A39 5ch multicolored 15 15
295 A39 10ch multicolored 15 15
296 A39 15ch multicolored 15 15
297 A39 25ch multicolored 15 15
298 A39 1nu multicolored 45 38
299 A39 1.25nu multicolored 52 52
300 A39 1.70nu multicolored 70 70
301 A39 2nu multicolored 90 75
302 A39 3nu multicolored 1.25 1.10
303 A39 4nu multicolored 1.65 1.50
304 A39 5nu multicolored 2.25 1.90
Nos. 294-304 (11) 8.32 7.45

Hill, Rinpiang Dzong — A40

Hill Statue, Stamps of Bhutan and: 2nu, Dzong. 5nu, Ounsti Dzong. 10nu, Lingzi Dzong, Gt. Britain Type 81. 20nu, Rope bridge, Penny Black.

1980, May 6 Litho. *Perf. 14x13½*
305 A40 1nu multicolored 30 25
306 A40 2nu multicolored 60 50
307 A40 5nu multicolored 1.60 1.25
308 A40 10nu multicolored 3.00 2.50
Nos. 305-308 (4) 5.50 4.50

Souvenir Sheet
309 A40 20nu multicolored 5.75 4.25

Sir Rowland Hill (1795-1879), originator of penny postage.

Kichu Lhakhang Monastery, Phari — A41

Guru Padma Sambhava's Birthday: Monasteries.

1981, July 11 Litho. *Perf. 14*
310 A41 1nu Dungtse, Phari, vert 32 25
311 A41 2nu shown 65 50
312 A41 2.25nu Kurjey 75 55
313 A41 3nu Tangu, Thimphu 1.00 75
314 A41 4nu Cheri, Thimphu 1.30 1.00
315 A41 5nu Chorten, Kora 1.65 1.25
316 A41 7nu Tak-Tsang, Phari, vert 2.30 1.75
Nos. 310-316 (7) 7.97 6.05

Prince Charles and Lady Diana — A42

Orange- bellied Chloropsis — A43

1981, Sept. 10 Litho. *Perf. 14½*
317 A42 1nu St. Paul's Cathedral 20 15
318 A42 5nu like #317 1.00 65
319 A42 20nu shown 4.00 2.50
320 A42 25nu like #319 4.50 3.50
Nos. 317-320 (4) 9.70 6.80

Souvenir Sheet
321 A42 20nu Wedding procession 5.00 4.00

Royal wedding. Nos. 318-319 issued in sheets of 5 plus label.
For surcharges see Nos. 471-475.

1982, Apr. 19 Litho. *Perf. 14*
322 A43 2nu shown 52 40
323 A43 3nu Monal pheasant 80 60
324 A43 5nu Ward's trogon 1.40 1.00
325 A43 10nu Mrs. Gould's sunbird 2.50 2.00
Nos. 322-325 (4) 5.22 4.00

Souvenir Sheet
326 A43 25nu Maroon oriole 7.00 5.00

1982 World Cup — A44

Designs: Various soccer players.

1982, June 25 Litho. *Perf. 14½x14*
327 A44 1nu multicolored 25 20
328 A44 2nu multicolored 52 40
329 A44 3nu multicolored 80 60
330 A44 20nu multicolored 5.25 4.00
Nos. 327-330 (4) 6.82 5.20

Souvenir Sheet
331 A44 25nu multicolored 12.00 7.50

Nos. 331 have margins continuing design and listing finalists (Algeria, etc. or Hungary, etc.).
For surcharges see Nos. 481-485.

21st Birthday of Princess Diana — A45

1982, Aug.
332 A45 1nu St. James' Palace 25 22
332A A45 10nu Diana, Charles 2.50 1.75
332B A45 15nu Windsor Castle 4.00 4.50
333 A45 25nu Wedding 6.50 4.50
Nos. 332-333 (4) 13.25 10.97

Souvenir Sheet
334 A45 20nu Diana 5.50 4.00

10nu-15nu issued only in sheets of 5 + label.
For overprints and surcharges see Nos. 361-363, 455-459, 476-480.

Scouting Year — A46

1982, Aug. 23 Litho. *Perf. 14*
335 A46 3nu Baden-Powell, vert. 65 50
336 A46 5nu Eating around fire 1.10 85
337 A46 15nu Reading map 3.50 2.50
338 A46 20nu Pitching tents 4.50 3.50
Nos. 335-338 (4) 9.75 7.45

Souvenir Sheet
339 A46 25nu Mountain climbing 6.00 4.50

For surcharges see Nos. 450-454.

Rama and Cubs with Mowgli — A47

Designs: Scenes from Walt Disney's The Jungle Book.

1982, Sept. 1 *Perf. 11*
340 A47 1ch multicolored 15 15
341 A47 2ch multicolored 15 15
342 A47 3ch multicolored 15 15
343 A47 4ch multicolored 15 15
344 A47 5ch multicolored 15 15
345 A47 10ch multicolored 15 15
346 A47 30ch multicolored 15 15
347 A47 2nu multicolored 50 40
348 A47 20nu multicolored 5.50 4.25
Nos. 340-348 (9) 7.05
Set value 5.00

Souvenir Sheets
Perf. 13½
349 A47 20nu Baloo and Mowgli in forest 5.25 4.00
350 A47 20nu Baloo and Mowgli floating 5.25 4.00

George Washington Surveying A48

1982, Nov. 15 Litho. *Perf. 15*
351 A48 50ch shown 15 15
352 A48 1nu FDR, Harvard 16 15
353 A48 2nu Washington at Valley Forge 32 25
354 A48 3nu FDR, family 50 38
355 A48 4nu Washington, Battle of Monmouth 65 50
356 A48 5nu FDR, White House 85 65
357 A48 15nu Washington, Mt. Vernon 2.50 2.00
358 A48 20nu FDR, Churchill, Stalin 3.25 2.50
Nos. 351-358 (8) 8.38 6.58

Souvenir Sheets
359 A48 25nu Washington, vert. 4.25 3.25
360 A48 25nu FDR, vert. 4.25 3.25

Washington and Franklin D. Roosevelt.

Nos. 332-334 Overprinted: "ROYAL BABY / 21.6.82"

1982, Nov. 19 *Perf. 14½x14*
361 A45 1nu multicolored 25 25
361A A45 10nu multicolored 2.50 1.75
361B A45 15nu multicolored 3.75 3.00
362 A45 25nu multicolored 6.25 4.75
Nos. 361-362 (4) 12.75 9.75

Souvenir Sheet
363 A45 20nu multicolored 5.25 4.25

Birth of Prince William of Wales, June 21.

500th Birth Anniv. of Raphael — A51

Portraits.

1983, Mar. 23 *Perf. 13½*
375 A51 1nu Angelo Doni 25 18
376 A51 4nu Maddalena Doni 1.00 75
377 A51 5nu Baldassare Castiglione 1.25 90
378 A51 20nu La Donna Velata 5.00 3.75
Nos. 375-378 (4) 7.50 5.58

Souvenir Sheets

379 A51 25nu Expulsion of Heliodorus 6.25 4.75
380 A51 25nu Mass of Bolsena 6.25 4.75

Nos. 184, 155F, 139, 184, 147G, 149M Surchd. or Ovptd.: "Druk Air"

1983, Feb. 11

381 A24 30ch on 1ch multi 15 15
382 A17k 5nu multicolored 1.25 85
383 A17 6nu multicolored 1.50 1.00
384 A17d 7nu multicolored 1.75 1.10
385 A17f 8nu multicolored 1.75 1.40
Nos. 381-385 (5) 6.40 4.50

Druk Air Service inauguration. Overprint of 8nu all caps. Nos. 382, 384 air mail.

Manned Flight Bicentenary A52

1983, Aug. 15 Litho. *Perf. 15*

386 A52 50ch Dornier Wal 15 15
387 A52 3nu Savoia-Marchetti S-66 75 55
388 A52 10nu Hawker Osprey 2.50 1.75
389 A52 20nu Ville de Paris 5.00 3.75
Nos. 386-389 (4) 8.40 6.20

Souvenir Sheet

390 A52 25nu Balloon Captif 5.00 3.75

Buddhist Symbols — A53

1983, Aug. 11 Litho. *Perf. 13½*

391 A53 25ch Sacred vase 15 15
392 A53 50ch Five Sensory Symbols 15 15
393 A53 2nu Seven Treasures 38 30
394 A53 3nu Five Sensory Organs 60 45
395 A53 8nu Five Fleshes 1.50 1.10
396 A53 9nu Sacrificial cake 1.75 1.25
a. Souv. sheet of 6, #391-396 6.00 4.50
Nos. 391-396 (6) 4.53 3.40

Size of Nos. 393, 396: 45x40mm.

World Communications Year (1983) — A54

Various Disney characters and history of communications.

1984, Apr. 10 Litho. *Perf. 14½x14*

397 A54 4ch multicolored 15 15
398 A54 5ch multicolored 15 15
399 A54 10ch multicolored 15 15
400 A54 20ch multicolored 15 15
401 A54 25ch multicolored 15 15
402 A54 50ch multicolored 16 15
403 A54 1nu multicolored 32 25
404 A54 5nu multicolored 1.10 95
405 A54 20nu multicolored 4.25 3.75
Nos. 397-405 (9) 6.58 5.85

Souvenir Sheets
Perf. 14x14½

406 A54 20nu Donald Duck on phone, horiz. 4.75 4.00
407 A54 20nu Mickey Mouse on TV 4.75 4.00

1984 Winter Olympics — A55

1984, June 16 *Perf. 14*

408 A55 50ch Skiing 15 15
409 A55 1nu Cross-country skiing 25 20
410 A55 3nu Speed skating 60 45
411 A55 20nu Bobsledding 3.75 3.00
Nos. 408-411 (4) 4.75 3.80

Souvenir Sheet

412 A55 25nu Hockey 5.00 3.25

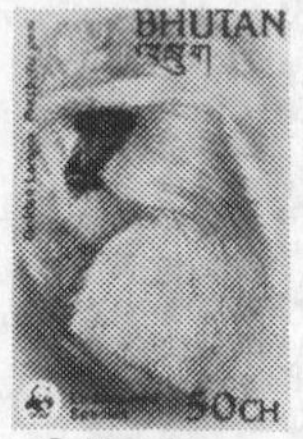

Golden Langur A56

Locomotives A57

1984, June 10 Litho. *Perf. 14½*

413 A56 50ch shown 15 15
414 A56 1nu Group in tree, horiz. 20 15
415 A56 2nu Family, horiz. 40 30
416 A56 4nu Group walking 80 60
Nos. 413-416 (4) 1.55 1.20

Souvenir Sheets

417 A56 20nu Snow leopard 3.00 2.00
418 A56 25nu Yak 3.00 2.00
419 A56 25nu Blue sheep, horiz. 3.00 2.00

1984, July 16

420 A57 50ch Sans Pareil, 1829 15 15
421 A57 1nu Planet, 1830 20 15
422 A57 3nu Experiment, 1832 60 45
423 A57 4nu Black Hawk, 1835 80 60
424 A57 5.50nu Jenny Lind, 1847 1.10 85
425 A57 8nu Semmering-Bavaria, 1851 1.60 1.25
426 A57 10nu Great Northern #1, 1870 2.00 1.50
427 A57 25nu German Natl. Tinder, 1880 5.00 3.75
Nos. 420-427 (8) 11.45 8.70

Souvenir Sheets

428 A57 20nu Darjeeling Himalayan Railway, 1984 4.00 3.00
429 A57 20nu Sondermann Freight, 1896 4.00 3.00
430 A57 20nu Crampton's locomotive, 1846 4.00 3.00
431 A57 20nu Erzsebet, 1870 4.00 3.00

Nos. 424-427 horiz.

Classic Cars A58

1984, Aug. 29 Litho. *Perf. 14*

432 A58 50ch Riley Sprite, 1936 15 15
433 A58 1nu Lanchester, 1919 20 15
434 A58 3nu Itala, 1907 65 45
435 A58 4nu Morris Oxford Bullnose, 1913 90 60
436 A58 5.50nu Lagonda LG6, 1939 1.25 85
437 A58 6nu Wolseley, 1903 1.40 90
438 A58 8nu Buick Super, 1952 1.75 1.20
439 A58 20nu Maybach Zeppelin, 1933 4.50 3.00
Nos. 432-439 (8) 10.80 7.30

Souvenir Sheets

440 A58 25nu Simplex, 1912 2.50 1.50
441 A58 25nu Renault, 1901 2.50 1.50

For surcharges see Nos. 537-544.

Summer Olympic Games — A59

1984, Oct. 27 Litho.

442 A59 15ch Women's archery 15 15
443 A59 25ch Men's archery 15 15
444 A59 2nu Table tennis 40 30
445 A59 2.25nu Basketball 45 35
446 A59 5.50nu Boxing 1.10 85
447 A59 6nu Running 1.20 90
448 A59 8nu Tennis 1.60 1.20
Nos. 442-448 (7) 5.05 3.90

Souvenir Sheet

449 A59 25nu Archery 5.00 3.50

For overprints see Nos. 537-544.

Nos. 335-339 Surcharged with New Values and Bars in Black or Silver

1985 Litho. *Perf. 14*

450 A46 10nu on 3nu multi 2.00 1.50
451 A46 10nu on 5nu multi 2.00 1.50
452 A46 10nu on 15nu multi 2.00 1.50
453 A46 10nu on 20nu multi 2.00 1.50
Nos. 450-453 (4) 8.00 6.00

Souvenir Sheet

454 A46 20nu on 25nu multi 4.00 3.00

Nos. 332, 332A, 332B, 333-334 Surcharged with New Values and Bars

1985, Feb. 28

455 A45 5nu on 1nu multi 1.00 68
456 A45 5nu on 10nu multi 1.00 68
457 A45 5nu on 15nu multi 1.00 68
458 A45 40nu on 25nu multi 8.00 5.25
Nos. 455-458 (4) 11.00 7.29

Souvenir Sheet

459 A45 25nu on 20nu multi 5.00 4.00

50th Anniv. of Donald Duck — A60

1984, Dec. 10 Litho. *Perf. 13½x14*

460 A60 4ch Magician Mickey 15 15
461 A60 5ch Slide, Donald, Slide 15 15
462 A60 10ch Donald's Golf Game 15 15
463 A60 20ch Mr. Duck Steps Out 15 15
464 A60 25ch Lion Around 15 15
465 A60 50ch Alpine Climbers 15 15
466 A60 1nu Flying Jalopy 25 15
467 A60 5nu Frank Duck 1.10 75
468 A60 20nu Good Scouts 4.50 3.25
Nos. 460-468 (9) 6.75 5.05

Souvenir Sheets

469 A60 20nu Three Caballeros 4.50 3.25
470 A60 20nu Sea Scouts 4.50 3.25

Nos. 317-321 Surcharged with New Values and Bars

1985, Feb. 28 *Perf. 14½*

471 A42 10nu on 1nu multi 2.00 1.50
472 A42 10nu on 5nu multi 2.00 1.50
473 A42 10nu on 20nu multi 2.00 1.50
474 A42 10nu on 25nu multi 2.00 1.50
Nos. 471-474 (4) 8.00 6.00

Souvenir Sheet

475 A42 30nu on 20nu multi 6.00 5.00

Nos. 361, 361A, 361B, 362-363 Surcharged with New Values and Bars

1985, Feb. 28 *Perf. 14½x14*

476 A45 5nu on 1nu multi 75 75
477 A45 5nu on 10nu multi 75 55
478 A45 5nu on 15nu multi 75 55
479 A45 40nu on 25nu multi 7.50 5.50
Nos. 476-479 (4) 9.75 7.35

Souvenir Sheet

480 A45 25nu on 20nu multi 5.00 3.75

Nos. 327-331 Surcharged with New Values and Bars in Black or Silver

1985, June

481 A44 5nu on 1nu multi 1.50 1.10
482 A44 5nu on 2nu multi 1.50 1.10
483 A44 5nu on 3nu multi 1.50 1.10
484 A44 5nu on 20nu multi 1.50 1.10
Nos. 481-484 (4) 6.00 4.40

Souvenir Sheets

485 A44 20nu on 25nu multi 7.50 5.50

Mask Dance of the Judgement of Death — A61

1985, Apr. 27 *Perf. 13½*

486 A61 5ch Shinje Choegyel 15 15
487 A61 35ch Raksh Lango 15 15
488 A61 50ch Druelgo 15 15
489 A61 2.50nu Pago 45 35
490 A61 3nu Telgo 55 42
491 A61 4nu Due Nakcung 75 58
492 A61 5nu Lha Karpo 90 68
a. Souvenir sheet of 4, #486-487, 491-492 1.90 1.50
493 A61 5.50nu Nyalbum 1.00 75
494 A61 6nu Khimda Pelkyi 1.10 85
Nos. 486-494 (9) 5.20 4.08

For overprints see Nos. 764-772.

Monasteries A62

1984, Dec. 1 Litho. *Perf. 12*

495 A62 10ch Domkhar 15 15
496 A62 25ch Shemgang 15 15
497 A62 50ch Chapcha 15 15
498 A62 1nu Tashigang 15 15
499 A62 2nu Pungthang Chhug 28 28
500 A62 5nu Dechhenphoda 70 70
Set value 1.25 1.25

Veteran's War Memorial Building, San Francisco A63

1985, Oct. 24 Litho. *Perf. 14*

502 A63 50ch Flags of Bhutan, UN, vert. 15 15
503 A63 15nu Headquarters, NY, vert. 2.75 2.00
504 A63 20nu shown 3.75 2.75
Nos. 502-504 (3) 6.65 4.90

Souvenir Sheet

505 A63 25nu UN Human Rights Declaration 4.25 3.00

UN, 40th anniv.

Audubon Birth Bicentenary A64

Illustrations of North American bird species by Audubon.

1985

506 A64 50ch Anas breweri 15 15
507 A64 1nu Lagopus lagopus 18 15
508 A64 2nu Charadrius montanus 35 25
509 A64 3nu Cavia stellata 52 40
510 A64 4nu Canachites canadensis 70 52
511 A64 5nu Mergus cucullatus 85 62
512 A64 15nu Olor buccinator 2.50 1.75
513 A64 20nu Bucephala clangula 3.50 2.50
Nos. 506-513 (8) 8.75 6.34

Souvenir Sheets

514 A64 25nu Accipiter striatus 3.75 2.25
515 A64 25nu Parus bicolor 3.75 2.25

Issue dates: Nos. 507, 510-511, 514 Nov. 15. Nos. 506, 508-509, 513, 515 Dec. 6.

A Tramp Abroad, by Mark Twain (1835-1910) A65

Walt Disney animated characters.

1985, Nov. 15

516 A65 50ch multicolored 15 15
517 A65 2nu multicolored 35 25
518 A65 5nu multicolored 85 62
519 A65 9nu multicolored 1.50 1.15
520 A65 20nu multicolored 3.50 2.50
Nos. 516-520 (5) 6.35 4.67

Souvenir Sheet

521 A65 25nu Goofy, Mickey Mouse 5.00 3.50

Intl. Youth Year.
For overprints see Nos. 554, 556-557.

Rapunzel, by Jacob and Wilhelm Grimm — A66

Walt Disney animated characters.

1985, Nov. 15

522 A66 1nu multicolored 18 15
523 A66 4nu multicolored 70 52
524 A66 7nu multicolored 1.25 95
525 A66 8nu multicolored 1.40 1.05
526 A66 15nu multicolored 2.50 1.75
Nos. 522-526 (5) 6.03 4.42

Souvenir Sheet

527 A66 25nu multicolored 5.00 4.00

No. 525 printed in sheets of 8.
For overprints see Nos. 553, 555, 558.

First South Asian Regional Cooperation Summit, Dec. 7-8, Dacca, Bangladesh A67

1985, Dec. 8 *Perf. 14*

528 A67 50ch multicolored 15 15
529 A67 5nu multicolored 85 62

Seven Precious Attributes of the Universal King — A68

1986, Feb. 12 Litho. *Perf. 13x12½*

530 A68 30ch Wheel 15 15
531 A68 50ch Gem 15 15
532 A68 1.25nu Queen 18 18
533 A68 2nu Minister 28 28
534 A68 4nu Elephant 55 55
535 A68 6nu Horse 85 85
536 A68 8nu General 1.15 1.15
Nos. 530-536 (7) 3.31 3.31

Nos. 442-443, 445-449 Ovptd. with Medal, Winners' Names and Countries. No. 449 Ovptd. for Men's and Women's Events

1986, May 5 Litho. *Perf. 14*

537 A59 15ch Hyang Soon Seo, So. Korea 15 15
538 A59 25ch Darrell Pace, US 15 15
539 A59 2.25nu US 32 32
540 A59 5.50nu Mark Breland, US 78 78
541 A59 6nu Daley Thompson, Britain 85 85
542 A59 8nu Stefan Edberg, Sweden 1.15 1.15
Nos. 537-542 (6) 3.40 3.40

Souvenir Sheets

543 A59 25nu Hyang Soon Seo 3.50 3.50
544 A59 25nu Darrel Pace 3.50 3.50

Kilkhor Mandalas, Deities — A69

Religious art: 10ch, 1nu, Phurpa, ritual dagger. 25ch, 3nu, Amitayus in wrath. 50ch, 5nu, Overpowering Deities. 75ch, 7nu, Great Wrathful One, Guru Rinpoche.

1986, June 17 *Perf. 13½*

545 A69 10ch multicolored 15 15
546 A69 25ch multicolored 15 15
547 A69 50ch multicolored 15 15
548 A69 75ch multicolored 15 15
549 A69 1nu multicolored 15 15
550 A69 3nu multicolored 42 42
551 A69 5nu multicolored 70 70
552 A69 7nu multicolored 1.00 1.00
Nos. 545-552 (8) 2.87 2.87

Nos. 525, 519, 526, 520, 521 and 527 Ovptd. with AMERIPEX '86 Emblem

1986, June 16 Litho. *Perf. 14*

553 A66 8nu multi 1.40 1.05
554 A65 9nu multi 1.50 1.15
555 A66 15nu multi 2.50 1.75
556 A65 20nu multi 3.50 2.50
Nos. 553-556 (4) 8.90 6.45

Souvenir Sheets

557 A65 25nu #521 4.25 3.00
558 A66 25nu #527 4.25 3.00

A70

A71

Halley's Comet A72

Designs: 50ch, Babylonian tablet fragments, 2349 B.C. sighting. 1nu, 17th cent. print, A.D. 66 sighting. 2nu, French silhouette art, 1835 sighting. 3nu, Bayeux Tapestry, 1066 sighting. 4nu, Woodblock, 684 sighting. 5nu, Illustration from Bybel Printen, 1650. 15nu, 1456 Sighting, Cancer constellation. 20nu, Delft plate, 1910 sighting. No. 572, Comet over Himalayas. No. 573, Comet over domed temple Dug-gye Jong.

1986, Nov. 4 Litho. *Perf. 15*

564 A70 50ch multicolored 18 15
565 A70 1nu multicolored 18 15
566 A71 2nu multicolored 35 28
567 A70 3nu multicolored 50 35
568 A70 4nu multicolored 68 52
569 A71 5nu multicolored 85 65
570 A70 15nu multicolored 2.50 2.00
571 A70 20nu multicolored 3.50 2.50
Nos. 564-571 (8) 8.71 6.60

Souvenir Sheets

572 A72 25nu multicolored 4.25 3.00
573 A72 25nu multicolored 4.25 3.00

A73

Statue of Liberty, Cent. — A74

Statue and ships: 50ch, Mircea, Romania. 1nu, Shalom, Israel. 2nu, Leonardo da Vinci, Italy. 3nu, Libertad, Argentina. 4nu, France, France. 5nu, SS United States, US. 15nu, Queen Elizabeth II, England. 20nu, Europa, West Germany. No. 5[illegible] Statue. No. 583, Statue, World Trade Center

1986, Nov. 4

574 A73 50ch multicolored
575 A73 1nu multicolored
576 A73 2nu multicolored
577 A73 3nu multicolored
578 A73 4nu multicolored
579 A73 5nu multicolo[illegible]
580 A73 15nu multicolo[illegible]
581 A73 20nu multi[illegible]
Nos. 5[illegible]

582 A74 25[illegible]
583 A74 [illegible]

1987, May 25

584 A75 20ch Santa Ma[illegible]
585 A75 25ch Queen Isabe[illegible]
586 A75 50ch Ship, flying fish
587 A75 1nu Columbus's coat o[illegible] arms
588 A75 2nu Christopher Columbus
589 A75 3nu Landing in the New World 75 55
a. Miniature sheet of 6, #584-589 1.75 1.75
Nos. 584-589 (6) 1.95
Set value 1.30

Souvenir Sheets

590 A75 20ch Pineapple
591 A75 25ch Indian hammock
592 A75 50ch Tobacco plant
593 A75 1nu Flamingo
594 A75 2nu Navigator, astrolabe, 15th cent.
595 A75 3nu Lizard
596 A75 5nu Iguana 1.25 95

All stamps are vertical except those contained in Nos. 591, 595 and 596. Stamps from No. 589a have white background.

CAPEX '87 — A76

Locomotives.

1987, June 15

597 A76 50ch Canadian Natl. U1-f 15 15
598 A76 1nu Via Rail L.R.C. 18 15
599 A76 2nu Canadian Natl. GM GF-30t 35 28
600 A76 3nu Canadian Natl. 4-8-4 50 35
601 A76 8nu Canadian Pacific 4-6-2 1.35 1.00
602 A76 10nu Via Express passenger train 1.75 1.30
603 A76 15nu Canadian Nat. Turbotrain 2.50 1.90
604 A76 20nu Canadian Pacific Diesel-Electric Express 3.25 2.50
Nos. 597-604 (8) 10.03 7.63

Souvenir Sheets

605 A76 25nu Royal Hudson 4-6-4 4.25
606 A76 25nu Canadian Natl. 4-8-4, diff.

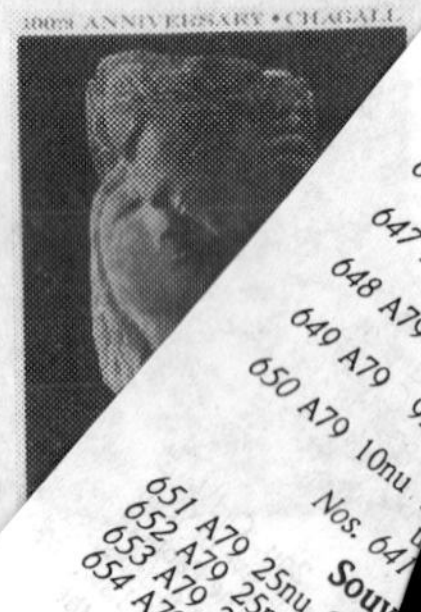

1988 Summer Olympics, Seoul A80

7nu-20nu vert.

1989, Feb. 15

655 A80 50ch Women's gymnastics
656 A80 1nu Tae kwon do
657 A80 2nu Shot put
658 A80 4nu Women's volleyball
659 A80 7nu Basketball
660 A80 8nu Soccer
661 A80 9nu Women's high jump
662 A80 20nu Running
Nos. 655-662 (8)

Souvenir Sheets

663 A80 25nu Archery, vert. 4.00 4.00
664 A80 25nu Fencing 4.00 4.00

Steam Locomotives A87

Designs: 50ch, *Best Friend of Charleston,* 1830, US 1nu, Class U, 1949, France. 2nu, *Consolidation,* 1866, US. 3nu, *Luggage Engine,* 1843, Great Britain. 4nu, Class 60-3 Shay, 1913, US. 5nu, *John Bull,* 1831, US. 6nu, *Hercules,* 1837, US. 7nu, Eight-wheel tank engine, 1874, Great Britain. 10nu, *The Illinois,* 1852, US. 15nu, German State 4-6-4, 1935. 20nu, American Standard, 1865. No. 809, Class Ps-4, 1926, US. No. 810, *Puffing Billy,* 1814, Great Britain. No. 811, Stephenson's *Rocket,* 1829, Great Britain. No. 812, *Cumberland,* 1845, US, vert. No. 813, *John Stevens,* 1849, US, vert. No. 814, No. 22 Baldwin Locomotive Works, 1873, US, No. 815, *Ariel,* 1877, US. No. 816, 1899 *No. 1301* Webb Compound Engine, Great Britain. No. 817, 1893 *No. 999* Empire State Express, US. No. 818, 1923 Class K-36, US. No. 819, 1935 Class A4, Great Britain. No. 820, 1935 Class A, US. No. 821, 1943 Class P-1, US.

1990, Jan. 30

798	A87	50ch	multi	15	15
799	A87	1nu	multi	16	15
800	A87	2nu	multi	32	24
801	A87	3nu	multi	48	35
802	A87	4nu	multi	65	48
803	A87	5nu	multi	80	60
804	A87	6nu	multi	95	70
805	A87	7nu	multi	1.10	82
806	A87	10nu	multi	1.60	1.20
807	A87	15nu	multi	2.40	1.80
808	A87	20nu	multi	3.20	2.40
809	A87	25nu	multi	4.00	3.00
			Nos. 798-809 (12)	15.81	11.89

Souvenir Sheets

810-821	A87	25nu each	4.00	4.00

Butterflies A88 3 NU

1990, Jan. 30 Litho. *Perf. 14*

822	A88	50ch	*Charaxes harmodius*	15	15
823	A88	1nu	*Prioneris thestylis*	16	15
824	A88	2nu	*Sephisa chandra*	32	24
825	A88	3nu	*Penthema usarda*	48	35
826	A88	4nu	*Troides aecus*	65	48
827	A88	5nu	*Polyura eudamippus*	80	60
828	A88	6nu	*Polyura dolon*	95	70
829	A88	7nu	*Neope bhadra*	1.10	82
830	A88	10nu	*Delias descombesi*	1.60	1.20
831	A88	15nu	*Childreni childrena*	2.40	1.80
832	A88	20nu	*Kallima inachus*	3.20	2.40
833	A88	25nu	*Elymnias malelas*	4.00	3.00
			Nos. 822-833 (12)	15.81	11.89

Souvenir Sheets

834	A88	25nu	Red lacewing	4.00	4.00
835	A88	25nu	Bhutan glory	4.00	4.00
836	A88	25nu	Great eggfly	4.00	4.00
837	A88	25nu	Kaiser-I-Hind	4.00	4.00
838	A88	25nu	Chestnut tiger	4.00	4.00
839	A88	25nu	Common map	4.00	4.00
840	A88	25nu	Swallowtail	4.00	4.00
841	A88	25nu	Jungle glory	4.00	4.00
842	A88	25nu	Checkered swallowtail	4.00	4.00
843	A88	25nu	Common birdwing	4.00	4.00
844	A88	25nu	Blue banded peacock	4.00	4.00
845	A88	25nu	Camberwell beauty	4.00	4.00

Nos. 822-824, 826-827, 830-831, 834-835, 844-845 are vert.

Paintings by Hiroshige A89

BHUTAN 10CH

Designs: 10ch, Plum Estate, Kameido. 20ch, Yatsumi Bridge. 50ch, Ayase River and Kanegafuchi. 75ch, View of Shiba Coast. 1nu, Grandpa's Teahouse, Meguro. 2nu, Kameido Tenjin Shrine. 6nu, Yoroi Ferry, Koami-cho. 7nu, Sakasai Ferry. 10nu, Fukagawa Lumberyards. 15nu, Suido Bridge and Surugadai. 20nu, Meguro Drum Bridge and Sunset Hill. No. 857, Atagoshita and Yabu Lane. No. 858, Towboats Along the Yotsugi-dori Canal. No. 859, Minowa, Kanasugi, Mikawashima. No. 860, Horikiri Iris Garden. No. 861, Fukagawa Susaki and Jumantsubo. No. 862, Suijin Shrine and Massaki on the Sumida River. No. 863, New Year's Eve Foxfires at the Changing Tree, Oji. No. 864, Nihonbashi, Clearing After Snow. No. 865, View to the North from Asukayama. No. 866, Komakata Hall and Azuma Bridge. No. 867, The City Flourishing, Tanabata Festival. No. 868, Suruga-cho. No. 869, Sudden Shower over Shin-Ohashi Bridge and Atake.

1990, May 21 Litho. *Perf. 13½*

846	A89	10ch	multicolored	15	15
847	A89	20ch	multicolored	15	15
848	A89	50ch	multicolored	15	15
849	A89	75ch	multicolored	15	15
850	A89	1nu	multicolored	16	15
851	A89	2nu	multicolored	32	25
852	A89	6nu	multicolored	95	70
853	A89	7nu	multicolored	1.10	85
854	A89	10nu	multicolored	1.60	1.20
855	A89	15nu	multicolored	2.40	1.80
856	A89	20nu	multicolored	3.20	2.40
857	A89	25nu	multicolored	4.00	3.00
			Nos. 846-857 (12)	14.33	10.95

Souvenir Sheets

858-869	A89	25nu each	4.00	3.00

Hirohito (1901-1989) and enthronement of Akihito as emperor of Japan.

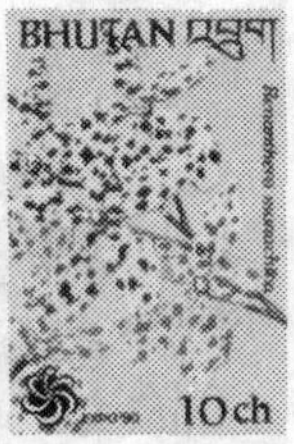

Orchids — A90

1990, Apr. 6 Litho. *Perf. 14*

870	A90	10ch	*Renanthera monachica*	15	15
871	A90	50ch	*Vanda coerulea*	15	15
872	A90	1nu	*Phalaenopsis violacea*	16	15
873	A90	2nu	*Dendrobium nobile*	32	24
874	A90	5nu	*Vandopsis lissochiloides*	80	60
875	A90	6nu	*Paphiopedilum rothschildianum*	95	70
876	A90	7nu	*Phalaenopsis schilleriana*	1.10	82
877	A90	9nu	*Paphiopedilum insigne*	1.45	1.10
878	A90	10nu	*Paphiopedilum bellatulum*	1.60	1.20
879	A90	20nu	*Doritis pulcherrima*	3.20	2.40
880	A90	25nu	*Cymbidium giganteum*	4.00	3.00
881	A90	35nu	*Phalaenopsis mariae*	5.50	4.15
			Nos. 870-881 (12)	19.38	14.66

Souvenir Sheets

882	A90	30nu	*Vanda coerulescens*	4.75	4.75
883	A90	30nu	*Vandopsis parishi*	4.75	4.75
884	A90	30nu	*Dendrobium aphyllum*	4.75	4.75
885	A90	30nu	*Phalaenopsis amabilis*	4.75	4.75
886	A90	30nu	*Paphiopedilum haynaldianum*	4.75	4.75
887	A90	30nu	*Dendrobium lodigesii*	4.75	4.75
888	A90	30nu	*Vanda alpina*	4.75	4.75
889	A90	30nu	*Phalaenopsis equestris*	4.75	4.75
890	A90	30nu	*Vanda cristata*	4.75	4.75
891	A90	30nu	*Phalaenopsis cornu cervi*	4.75	4.75
892	A90	30nu	*Paphiopedilum niveum*	4.75	4.75
893	A90	30nu	*Dendrobium margaritaceum*	4.75	4.75

EXPO '90 Intl. Garden and Greenery Exposition, Osaka, Apr. 1-Dec. 31.

G.P.O., Thimphu — A90a

1990, May 29 Photo. *Perf. 14*

893A	A90a	1nu	multicolored	16	16

Penny Black, 150th Anniv. A90b

Penny Black and: 50ch, Bhutan #1. 1nu, Oldenburg #1. 2nu, Bergedorf #3. 4nu, German Democratic Republic #48. 5nu, Brunswick #1. 6nu, Basel #3L1. 8nu, Geneva #2L1. 10nu, Zurich #1L1. No. 902, France #3. 20nu, Vatican City #1. 25nu, Israel #1. No. 905, Japan #1.

Penny Black and: No. 906a, Mecklenburg-Schwerin #1. b, Mecklenburg-Strelitz #1. No. 907a, Germany #5, #9. b, Prussia #2. No. 908a, Hamburg #1. b, North German Confederation #1, #7. No. 909a, Baden #1. b, Wurttemberg #1. No. 910a, Heligoland #1. b, Hanover #1. No. 911a, Thurn & Taxis #3. b, Thurn & Taxis #42. No. 912a, Schleswig-Holstein #1. b, Lubeck #5. No. 913, Saxony #1. No. 914, Berlin #9N1. No. 915, No other stamp. No. 916, US #1. No. 917, Bavaria #1.

1990, Oct. 9 *Perf. 14*

894	A90b	50ch	multicolored	15	15
895	A90b	1nu	multicolored	16	15
896	A90b	2nu	multicolored	32	24
897	A90b	4nu	multicolored	65	50
898	A90b	5nu	multicolored	80	60
899	A90b	6nu	multicolored	1.00	75
900	A90b	8nu	multicolored	1.30	1.00
901	A90b	10nu	multicolored	1.60	1.20
902	A90b	15nu	multicolored	2.40	1.80
903	A90b	20nu	multicolored	3.20	2.40
904	A90b	25nu	multicolored	4.00	3.00
905	A90b	30nu	multicolored	4.80	3.60
			Nos. 894-905 (12)	20.38	15.39

Souvenir Sheets

Sheets of 2 (#906-912) or 1

906-912	A90b	15nu each	4.75	4.75
913-917	A90b	30nu each	4.75	4.75

Stamp World London '90.

Giant Pandas A91

Tiger A92

Endangered wildlife of Asia.

1990 *Perf. 14*

918	A91	50ch	multi, diff.	15	15
919	A91	1nu	multi, diff.	16	15
920	A91	2nu	multi, diff.	32	24
921	A91	3nu	shown	48	35
922	A91	4nu	multi, diff.	65	48
923	A92	5nu	shown	80	60
924	A91	6nu	multi, diff.	95	70
925	A91	7nu	multi, diff.	1.10	82
926	A92	10nu	Elephant	1.60	1.20
927	A91	15nu	multi, diff.	2.40	1.80
928	A92	20nu	Barking deer	3.20	2.40
929	A92	25nu	Snow leopard	4.00	3.00
			Nos. 918-929 (12)	15.81	11.89

Souvenir Sheets

930	A92	25nu	Rhinoceros	4.00	4.00
931	A92	25nu	Clouded leopard	4.00	4.00
932	A92	25nu	Asiatic wild dog	4.00	4.00
933	A92	25nu	Himalayan shou	4.00	4.00
934	A92	25nu	Golden cat	4.00	4.00
935	A92	25nu	Himalayan musk deer	4.00	4.00
936	A91	25nu	multi, diff.	4.00	4.00
937	A92	25nu	Asiatic black bear	4.00	4.00
938	A92	25nu	Gaur	4.00	4.00
939	A92	25nu	Pygmy hog	4.00	4.00
940	A92	25nu	Wolf	4.00	4.00
941	A92	25nu	Sloth bear	4.00	4.00

Nos. 919-920 and 927 vert.

Buddhist Musical Instruments — A93

1990, Sept. 29 Litho. *Perf. 13½x13*

942	A93	10ch	Dungchen	15	15
943	A93	20ch	Dungkar	15	15
944	A93	30ch	Roim	15	15
945	A93	50ch	Tinchag	15	15
946	A93	1nu	Dradu & drilbu	16	15
947	A93	2nu	Gya-ling	32	24
948	A93	2.50nu	Nga	40	30
a.			Souv. sheet of 4, #943, 945, 947-948	85	65
949	A93	3.50nu	Kang-dung	56	42
a.			Souv. sheet of 4, #942, 944, 946, 949	85	65
			Set value	1.65	1.25

Year of the Girl Child — A94 BHUTAN 50CH

1990, Dec. 8

950	A94	50ch	shown	15	15
951	A94	20nu	Young girl	3.20	2.40

Wonders of the World A95

Walt Disney characters viewing: 1ch, Temple of Artemis, Ephesus. 2ch, Statue of Zeus, Olympia. 3ch, Egyptian pyramids. 4ch, Lighthouse, Alexandria. 5ch, Mausoleum at Halicarnassus. 10ch, Colossus of Rhodes. 50ch, Hanging gardens of Babylon. 5nu, Mauna Loa volcano, Hawaii. 6nu, Carlsbad Caverns, New Mexico. 10nu, Rainbow Bridge, Utah. 15nu, Grand Canyon of the Colorado, Arizona. 20nu, Old Faithful geyser, Wyoming. 25nu, Giant sequoias, California. 30nu, Crater Lake and Wizard Island, Oregon. 5nu, 6nu, 10nu, 15nu, 20nu, 25nu, 30nu are horiz.

Walt Disney characters viewing: No. 966, Great Wall of China, horiz. No. 967, Mosque of St. Sophia, Istanbul, Turkey. No. 968, The Leaning Tower of Pisa, Italy. No. 969, Colosseum, Rome. No. 970, Stonehenge, England. No. 971, Catacombs of Alexandria, Egypt. No. 972, Porcelain Tower, Nanking, China, horiz. No. 973, The Panama Canal, horiz. No. 974, Golden Gate Bridge, San Francisco, horiz. No. 975, Sears Tower, Chicago, horiz. No. 976, Gateway Arch, St. Louis. No. 977, Alcan Highway, Alaska and Canada, horiz. No. 978, Hoover Dam, Nevada. No. 979, Empire State Building, New York.

1991, Feb. 2 Litho. *Perf. 14*

952	A95	1ch	multicolored	15	15
953	A95	2ch	multicolored	15	15
954	A95	3ch	multicolored	15	15
955	A95	4ch	multicolored	15	15
956	A95	5ch	multicolored	15	15
957	A95	10ch	multicolored	15	15

958 A95	50ch multicolored	15	15
959 A95	5nu multicolored	80	60
960 A95	6nu multicolored	95	70
961 A95	10nu multicolored	1.60	1.20
962 A95	15nu multicolored	2.40	1.80
963 A95	20nu multicolored	3.20	2.40
964 A95	25nu multicolored	4.00	3.00
965 A95	30nu multicolored	4.80	3.60
	Nos. 952-965 (14)	18.80	14.35

Souvenir Sheets

Perf. 14x13½, 13½x14

966-979 A95	25nu each	4.00	4.00

Peter Paul Rubens (1577-1640), Painter — A96

Entire paintings or different details from: 10ch, 5nu, 6nu, 10nu, No. 992, Atalanta and Meleager. 50ch, Fall of Phaethon. 1nu, No. 993, Feast of Venus Verticordia. 2nu, Achilles Slaying Hector. 3nu, No. 994, Arachne Punished by Minerva. 4nu, No. 995, Jupiter Receives Psyche on Olympus. 7nu, Venus in Vulcan's Furnace. 20nu, No. 996, Briseis Returned to Achilles. 30nu, No. 997, Mars and Rhea Sylvia. No. 998, Venus Shivering. No. 999, Ganymede and the Eagle. No. 1000, Origin of the Milky Way. No. 1001, Adonis and Venus. No. 1002, Hero and Leander. No. 1003, Fall of the Titans.

Nos. 994, 996-997, 1000-1003 are horiz.

1991, Feb. 2

980 A96	10ch multicolored	15	15
981 A96	50ch multicolored	15	15
982 A96	1nu multicolored	16	15
983 A96	2nu multicolored	32	15
984 A96	3nu multicolored	48	15
985 A96	4nu multicolored	64	15
986 A96	5nu multicolored	80	60
987 A96	6nu multicolored	95	70
988 A96	7nu multicolored	1.15	85
989 A96	10nu multicolored	1.60	1.20
990 A96	20nu multicolored	3.20	2.40
991 A96	30nu multicolored	4.80	3.60
	Nos. 980-991 (12)	14.40	10.25

Souvenir Sheets

992-1003 A96	25nu each	4.00	4.00

Vincent Van Gogh (1853-1890), Painter — A97

Paintings: 10ch, Cottages, Reminiscence of the North. 50ch, Head of a Peasant Woman with Dark Cap. 1nu, Portrait of a Woman in Blue. 2nu, The Midwife. 8nu, Vase with Hollyhocks. 10nu, Portrait of a Man with a Skull Cap. 12nu, Agostina Segatori Sitting in the Cafe du Tambourin. 15nu, Vase with Daisies and Anemones. 18nu, Fritillaries in a Copper Vase. 20nu, Woman Sitting in the Grass. 25nu, On the Outskirts of Paris, horiz. 30nu, Chrysanthemums and Wild Flowers in a Vase.

No. 1016, Le Moulin de la Galette. No. 1017, Bowl with Sunflowers, Roses and Other Flowers, horiz. No. 1018, Poppies and Butterflies. No. 1019, Trees in the Garden of Saint-Paul Hospital. No. 1020, Le Moulin de Blute Fin. No. 1021, Le Moulin de la Galette, diff. No. 1022, Vase with Peonies. No. 1023, Vase with Zinnias. No. 1024, Fishing in the Spring, Pont de Clichy, horiz. No. 1025, Village Street in Auvers, horiz. No. 1026, Vase with Zinnias and Other Flowers, horiz. No. 2027, Vase with Red Poppies.

1991, July 22 Litho. *Perf. 13½*

1004 A97	10ch multicolored	15	15
1005 A97	50ch multicolored	15	15
1006 A97	1nu multicolored	16	15
1007 A97	2nu multicolored	32	15
1008 A97	8nu multicolored	1.30	1.00
1009 A97	10nu multicolored	1.60	1.20
1010 A97	12nu multicolored	2.00	1.50
1011 A97	15nu multicolored	2.40	1.80
1012 A97	18nu multicolored	2.90	2.15
1013 A97	20nu multicolored	3.20	2.40
1014 A97	25nu multicolored	4.00	3.00
1015 A97	30nu multicolored	4.80	3.60
	Nos. 1004-1015 (12)	22.98	17.25

Size: 76x102mm, 102x76mm

Imperf

1016-1027 A97	30nu each	4.80	4.80

History of World Cup Soccer — A98

Winning team pictures, plays or possible future site: 50ch, Uruguay, 1930. 1nu, Italy, 1934. 2nu, Italy, 1938. 3nu, Uruguay, 1950. 5nu, West Germany, 1954. 10nu, Brazil, 1958. 20nu, Brazil, 1962. 25nu, England, 1966. 29nu, Brazil, 1970. 30nu, West Germany, 1974. 31nu, Argentina, 1978. 32nu, Italy, 1982. 33nu, Argentina, 1986. 34nu, West Germany, 1990. 35nu, Los Angeles Coliseum, 1994.

Players: No. 1043, Claudio Caniggia, Argentina, vert. No. 1044, Salvatore Schillaci, Italy, vert. No. 1045, Roberto Baggio, Italy, vert. No. 1046, Peter Shilton, England, vert. No. 1047, Lothar Matthaus, West Germany, vert. No. 1048, Paul Gascoigne, England, vert.

1991, Aug. 1 Litho. *Perf. 13½*

1028 A98	50ch multicolored	15	15
1029 A98	1nu multicolored	16	15
1030 A98	2nu multicolored	32	15
1031 A98	3nu multicolored	48	15
1032 A98	5nu multicolored	80	60
1033 A98	10nu multicolored	1.60	1.20
1034 A98	20nu multicolored	3.20	2.40
1035 A98	25nu multicolored	4.00	3.00
1036 A98	29nu multicolored	4.75	3.55
1037 A98	30nu multicolored	4.80	3.60
1038 A98	31nu multicolored	5.10	3.80
1039 A98	32nu multicolored	5.25	3.95
1040 A98	33nu multicolored	5.40	4.05
1041 A98	34nu multicolored	5.60	4.20
1042 A98	35nu multicolored	5.75	4.30
	Nos. 1028-1042 (15)	47.36	35.25

Souvenir Sheets

1043-1048 A98	30nu each	4.80	4.00

Phila Nippon '91 — A99

1991, Nov. 16 *Perf. 13*

1049 A99	15nu multicolored	2.40	1.80

Education in Bhutan A100

1992, Mar. 5 Photo. *Perf. 13½*

1050 A100	1nu multicolored	18	15

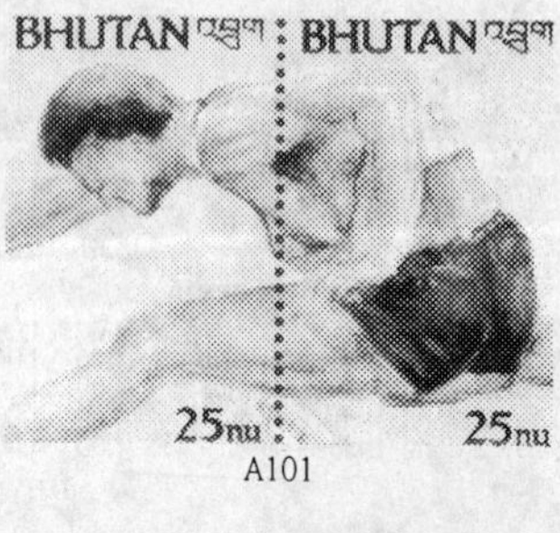

A101

1992 Summer Olympics, Barcelona — A102

1992, July 24 Litho. *Perf. 12*

1051 A101	25nu Pair, #a.-b.	8.25	8.25

Souvenir Sheet

1052 A102	25nu Archer	4.10	4.10

German Reunification — A103

1992, Oct. 3 Litho. *Perf. 12*

1053 A103	25nu multicolored	2.00	2.00

Souvenir Sheet

1054 A103	25nu multicolored	2.00	2.00

Stamp from No. 1054 does not have white inscription or border.

Bhutan Postal Service, 30th Anniv. A104

Designs: 1nu, Mail truck, plane. 3nu, Letter carrier approaching village. 5nu, Letter carrier emptying mail box.

1992, Oct. 9

1055 A104	1nu multicolored	15	15
1056 A104	3nu multicolored	24	24
1057 A104	5nu multicolored	40	40
	Nos. 1055-1057 (3)	79	79

This miniature sheet of four was never officially issued.

Discovery of America, 500th Anniv. — A106

1992, Sept. 18 *Perf. 12*

1059 A106	15nu Ship	1.20	1.20
1060 A106	20nu Portrait	1.60	1.60

Souvenir Sheet

1061 A106	25nu like #1060	2.00	2.00

Stamp from No. 1061 does not have silver inscription or white border.

Reign of King Jigme Singye Wangchuk, 20th Anniv. — A107

Designs: a, 1nu, Man tilling field, factory. b, 5nu, Airplane. c, 10nu, House, well. d, 15nu, King. 20nu, People, flag, King, horiz.

1992, Nov. 11 Litho. *Perf. 12*

1062 A107	Block of 4, #a.-d.	2.50	2.50

Souvenir Sheet

1063 A107	20nu multicolored	1.70	1.70

Intl. Volunteer Day A108

Designs: a, 1.50nu, White inscription. b, 9nu, Green inscription. c, 15nu, Red inscription.

1992, Dec. 5 Litho. *Perf. 14*

1067 A108	Block of 4, #a.-c. + label	2.05	2.05

Medicinal Plants — A109

1993, Jan. 1 Litho. *Perf. 12*

1068 A109	1.50nu Meconopsis grandis prain	15	15
1069 A109	7nu Meconopsis sp.	58	58
1070 A109	10nu Meconopsis wallichii	40	40
1071 A109	12nu Meconopsis horridula	1.00	1.00
1072 A109	20nu Meconopsis discigera	1.70	1.70
	Nos. 1068-1072 (5)	3.83	3.83

Souvenir Sheet

1073 A109	25nu Meconopsis horridula, diff.	2.00	2.00

Miniature Sheet

Lunar New Year — A110

1993, Feb. 22 Litho. *Perf. 14*

1074 A110 25nu multicolored 2.05 2.05

No. 1074 Surcharged "TAIPEI '93" in Silver and Black

1993, Aug. 14 Litho. *Perf. 14*

1075 A110 30nu on 25nu 2.50 2.50

Door Gods — A112

Flowers — A113

1993, Dec. 17 Litho. *Perf. 12*

1091 A112 1.50nu Namtheo-Say 15 15
1092 A112 5nu Pha-Ke-Po 50 50
1093 A112 10nu Chen-Mi-Jang 1.00 1.00
1094 A112 15nu Yul-Khor-Sung 1.50 1.50
Nos. 1091-1094 (4) 3.15 3.15

1993, Jan. 1 *Perf. 13*

Designs: No. 1095a, 1nu, Rhododendron mucronatum. b, 1.5nu. Anemone rupicola. c, 2nu, Polemonium coeruleum. d, 2.5nu, Rosa marophylla. e, 4nu, Paraquilegia microphylla. f, 5nu, Aquilegia nivalis. g, 6nu, Geranium wallichianum. h, 7nu, Rhodendron campanulatum. i, 9nu, Viola suavis. j, 10nu, Cyananthus lobatus.
13nu, Red flower, horiz.

1095 A113 Strip of 10, #a.-j. 4.75 4.75

Souvenir Sheet

1096 A113 13nu multicolored 1.40 1.40

New Year 1994 (Year of the Dog) — A114

1994, Feb. 11 Litho. *Perf. 14*

1097 A114 11.50nu multicolored 80 80

Souvenir Sheet

1098 A114 20nu like #1097 1.40 1.40

Hong Kong '94.

Stamp Cards — A115

Designs: 16nu, Tagtshang Monastery. 20nu, Map of Bhutan. Illustration reduced.

Rouletted 26 on 2 or 3 Sides

1994, Aug. 15 Litho.

Self-Adhesive

Cards of 6 + 6 labels

1099 A115 16nu #a.-f. 6.25 6.25
1100 A115 20nu #a.-f. 7.75 7.75

Individual stamps measure 70x9mm and have a card backing. Se-tenant labels inscribed "AIR MAIL."

Souvenir Sheet

First Manned Moon Landing, 25th Anniv. — A116

Designs: a, 30nu, Astronaut on moon. b, 36nu, Space shuttle, earth, moon. Illustration reduced.

1994 Litho. *Perf. 14x14½*

1101 A116 Sheet of 2, #a.-b. 4.25 4.25

Nos. 1101a, 1101b have holographic images. Soaking in water may affect the holograms.

SEMI-POSTAL STAMPS

Nos. 10-12 Surcharged

+ 50 ch

Perf. 14x14½

1964, Mar. Litho. Unwmk.

B1 A3 33ch + 50ch multi 2.00 2.00
B2 A3 70ch + 50ch multi 2.00 2.00
B3 A3 1.30nu + 50ch multi 2.00 2.00
Nos. B1-B3 (3) 6.00 6.00

9th Winter Olympic Games, Innsbruck, Jan. 29-Feb. 9, 1964.

Olympic Games Type of Regular Issue, 1964

Souvenir Sheet

1964, Oct. 10 *Perf. 13½, Imperf.*

B4 A6 Sheet of 2 7.50 7.50
a. 1nu + 50ch Archery 90 90
b. 2nu + 50ch Soccer 2.00 2.00

18th Olympic Games, Tokyo, Oct. 10-25.

Nos. 97, 97C, 97E Surcharged

FLOOD RELIEF

+ 5Ch

1968, Dec. 7 Photo. *Perf. 13½*

B5 A14n 5ch +5ch 15 15
B6 A14n 80ch +25ch 35 35
B7 A14n 2nu +50ch 85 85
Nos. B5-B7 (3) 1.35 1.35

AIR POST STAMPS

Nos. 19-21, 38-39, 63-67 Ovptd.

a

b

1967, Jan. 10 Litho. *Perfs. as Before*

Overprint "a"

C1 A5 33ch on #19 15 15
C2 A5 70ch on #20 30 30
C3 A5 1nu on #21 42 42
C4 A8 50ch on #38 22 22
C5 A8 75ch on #39 32 32
C6 A11 1.50nu on #63 65 65
C7 A11 2nu on #64 85 85
C8 A11 3nu on #65 1.25 1.25
C9 A11 4nu on #66 1.75 1.75
C10 A11 5nu on #67 2.25 2.25

Overprint "b"

C11 A5 33ch on #19 15 15
C12 A5 70ch on #20 30 30
C13 A5 1nu on #21 42 42
C14 A8 50ch on #38 22 22
C15 A8 75ch on #39 32 32
C16 A11 1.50nu on #63 65 65
C17 A11 2nu on #64 85 85
C18 A11 3nu on #65 1.25 1.25
C19 A11 4nu on #66 1.75 1.75
C20 A11 5nu on #67 2.25 2.25
Nos. C1-C20 (20) 16.32 16.32

UN Type of Regular Issue

Bhutan Flag and: 2.50nu, UN Headquarters, NYC. 5nu, Security Council Chamber and mural by Per Krohg. 6nu, General Assembly Hall.

1971, Sept. 21 Photo. *Perf. 13½*

C21 A16 2.50nu silver & multi 38 38
C22 A16 5nu silver & multi 75 75
C23 A16 6nu silver & multi 90 90
Nos. C21-C23 (3) 2.03 2.03

Bhutan's admission to the United Nations. Exist imperf.

Nos. C21-C23 Overprinted in Gold: "UNHCR / UNRWA / 1971" like Nos. 145-145C

1971, Dec. 23 Litho. *Perf. 13½*

C24 A16 2.50nu silver & multi 55 55
C25 A16 5nu silver & multi 1.10 1.10
C26 A16 6nu silver & multi 1.40 1.40
Nos. C24-C26 (3) 3.05 3.05

World Refugee Year. Exist imperf.

UPU Types of 1974

UPU Emblem, Carrier Pigeon and: 1nu, Mail runner and jeep. 1.40nu, 10nu, Old and new locomotives. 2nu, Old biplane and jet.

1974, Oct. 9 Litho. *Perf. 14½*

C27 A19 1nu salmon & multi 25 25
C28 A20 1.40nu lilac & multi 38 38
C29 A20 2nu multicolored 48 48
Nos. C27-C29 (3) 1.11 1.11

Souvenir Sheet

Perf. 13

C30 A20 10nu lilac & multi 2.75 2.75

Cent. of the UPU. Nos. C27-C29 were issued in sheets of 50 and sheets of 5 plus label with multicolored margin. Exist imperf.

Issues of 1968-1974 Surcharged 25ch and Bars

1978 Perf. & Printing as Before

C31 A16 25ch on 5nu, #C22
C32 A16 25ch on 6nu, #C23
C33 A20 25ch on 1.40nu, #C28
C34 A20 25ch on 2nu, #C29
C35 A14j 25ch on 4nu, #94L
C36 A14j 25ch on 10nu, #94N
C37 A17k 25ch on 5nu, #154F
C38 A17k 25ch on 6nu, #154G

BOLIVIA

LOCATION — Central South America, separated from the Pacific Ocean by Chile and Peru.
GOVT. — Republic
AREA — 424,165 sq. mi.
POP. — 6,252,250 (est. 1984)
CAPITAL — Sucre (La Paz is the actual seat of government).

100 Centavos = 1 Boliviano
100 Centavos = 1 Peso Boliviano (1963)
100 Centavos = 1 Boliviano (1987)

Catalogue values for unused stamps in this country are for Never Hinged items, beginning with Scott 308 in the regular postage section, Scott C112 in the airpost section, Scott RA5 in the postal tax section, and Scott RAC1 in airpost postal tax section.

On Feb. 21, 1863, the Bolivian Government decreed contracts for carrying the mails should be let to the highest bidder, the service to commence on the day the bid was accepted, and stamps used for the payment of postage. On Mar. 18, the contract was awarded to Sr. Justiniano Garcia and was in effect until Apr. 29, 1863, when it was rescinded. Stamps in the form illustrated above were prepared in denominations of ½, 1, 2 and 4 reales. All values exist in black and in blue. The blue are twice as scarce as the black. Value, black, $75 each.

It is said that used copies exist on covers, but the authenticity of these covers remains to be established.

Condor — A1

A2

A3

72 varieties of each of the 5c, 78 varieties of the 10c, 30 varieties of each of the 50c and 100c.

The plate of the 5c stamps was entirely reengraved 4 times and retouched at least 6 times. Various states of the plate have distinguishing characteristics, each of which is typical of most, though not all the stamps in a sheet. These characteristics (usually termed types) are found in the shading lines at the right side of the globe. a, vertical and diagonal lines. b, diagonal lines only. c, diagonal and horizontal with traces of vertical lines. d, diagonal and horizontal lines. e, horizontal lines only. f, no lines except the curved ones forming the outlines of the globe.

1867-68 Unwmk. Engr. *Imperf.*

1 A1 5c yel grn, thin paper (a, b) 3.50 *4.50*
a. 5c blue green (a) 4.50 *14.00*
b. 5c deep green (a) 4.50 *14.00*
c. 5c ol grn, thick paper (a) 35.00 25.00
d. 5c yel grn, thick paper (a) 80.00 80.00
e. 5c yel grn, thick paper (b) 80.00 80.00
f. 5c blue green (b) 4.50 14.00
2 A1 5c green (d) 4.00 7.00
a. 5c green (c) 4.00 7.00
b. 5c green (e) 4.00 7.00
c. 5c green (f) 4.00 7.00
3 A1 5c vio ('68) 185.00 140.00
a. 5c rose lilac ('68) 185.00 140.00
Revenue cancel 28.00
4 A3 10c brown 225.00 140.00
5 A2 50c orange 20.00
6 A2 50c blue ('68) *325.00*
a. 50c dark blue ('68) *325.00*
Revenue cancel 28.00
7 A3 100c blue 60.00
Revenue cancel 15.00
8 A3 100c green ('68) 140.00
a. 100c pale blue grn ('68) 140.00
Revenue cancel 28.00

Used values are for postally canceled copies. Pen cancellations usually indicate that the stamps have been used fiscally and such stamps sell for about one-fifth as much as those with postal cancellations.

The 500c is an essay.

Reprints of Nos. 3,4, 6 and 8 are common. Value, $10 each. Reprints of Nos. 2 and 5 are scarcer. Value, $25 each.

Coat of Arms
A4 A5

1868-69 *Perf. 12*

Nine Stars

10	A4	5c green	16.00	8.00
11	A4	10c vermilion	22.50	8.00
12	A4	50c blue	40.00	22.50
13	A4	100c orange	40.00	25.00
14	A4	500c black	350.00	300.00

Eleven Stars

15	A5	5c green	8.00	5.00
16	A5	10c vermilion	11.00	8.00
a.		Half used as 5c as cover		400.00
17	A5	50c blue	30.00	14.00
18	A5	100c dp org	27.50	14.00
19	A5	500c black	*1,400.*	*1,400.*

See Nos. 26-27, 31-34.

Arms and "The Law" — A6

1878 Various Frames *Perf. 12*

20	A6	5c ultra	8.00	3.50
21	A6	10c orange	6.50	2.75
a.		Half used as 5c on cover		50.00
22	A6	20c green	20.00	3.50
a.		Half used as 10c on cover		160.00
23	A6	50c dull carmine	100.00	10.00
		Nos. 20-23 (4)	134.50	19.75

Numerals Upright
(11 Stars)-A7 (9 Stars)-A8

1887 *Rouletted*

24	A7	1c rose	2.00	1.75
25	A7	2c violet	2.00	1.75
26	A5	5c blue	6.50	3.00
27	A5	10c orange	6.50	3.00
		Nos. 24-27 (4)	17.00	9.50

See No. 37.

1890 *Perf. 12*

28	A8	1c rose	1.50	75
29	A8	2c violet	4.00	2.00
30	A4	5c blue	2.75	75
31	A4	10c orange	6.00	90
32	A4	20c dk grn	12.00	1.50
33	A4	50c red	6.00	1.50
34	A4	100c yellow	12.00	3.00
		Nos. 28-34 (7)	44.25	10.40

See Nos. 35-36, 38-39.

1893 Litho. *Perf. 11*

35	A8	1c rose	3.00	2.00
a.		Imperf. pair	35.00	
b.		Horiz. pair, imperf. vert.	20.00	
c.		Horiz. pair, imperf. btwn.	35.00	
36	A8	2c violet	3.00	2.00
a.		Block of 4 imperf. vert. and horiz. through center	50.00	
b.		Horiz. pair, imperf. btwn.	27.50	
37	A7	5c blue	5.00	2.00
a.		Vert. pair, imperf. horiz.	27.50	
b.		Horiz. pair, imperf. btwn.	35.00	
38	A8	10c orange	14.00	3.00
a.		Horiz. pair, imperf. btwn.	50.00	
39	A8	20c dark green	32.50	14.00
a.		Imperf. pair, vert. or horiz.	140.00	
b.		Pair, imperf. btwn., vert. or horiz.	140.00	
		Nos. 35-39 (5)	57.50	23.00

Coat of Arms — A9

1894 Unwmk. Engr. *Perf. 14, 14½*

Thin Paper

40	A9	1c bister	1.00	60
41	A9	2c red orange	1.00	60
42	A9	5c green	1.00	60
43	A9	10c yellow brn	1.00	60
44	A9	20c dark blue	3.00	1.25
45	A9	50c claret	7.50	1.75
46	A9	100c brown rose	17.50	6.25
		Nos. 40-46 (7)	32.00	11.65

Stamps of type A9 on thick paper were surreptitiously printed in Paris on the order of an official and without government authorization. Some of these stamps were substituted for part of a shipment of stamps on thin paper, which had been printed in London on government order. When the thick paper stamps reached Bolivia they were at first repudiated but afterwards were allowed to do postal duty. A large quantity of the thick paper stamps were fraudulently canceled in Paris with a cancellation of heavy bars forming an oval.

To be legitimate, copies of the thick paper stamps must have genuine cancellations of Bolivia. Value, on cover, each $125.

The 10c blue on thick paper is not known to have been issued.

Some copies of Nos. 40-46 show part of a papermakers' watermark "1011."

For overprints see Nos. 55-59.

President Tomas Frias — A10

President Jose M. Linares — A11

Pedro Domingo Murillo A12

Bernardo Monteagudo A13

Gen. Jose Ballivian — A14

Gen. Antonio Jose de Sucre — A15

Simon Bolivar — A16

Coat of Arms — A17

1897 Litho. *Perf. 12*

47	A10	1c pale yellow grn	1.00	65
a.		Vert. pair, imperf. horiz.	50.00	
b.		Vert. pair, imperf. btwn.	50.00	
48	A11	2c red	1.50	1.10
49	A12	5c dk green	2.00	65
a.		Horiz. pair, imperf. btwn.	50.00	
50	A13	10c brown vio	2.00	65
a.		Vert. pair, imperf. btwn.	50.00	
51	A14	20c lake & blk	4.00	75
a.		Imperf., pair		150.00
52	A15	50c orange	4.00	2.00
53	A16	1b Prus blue	4.00	4.50
54	A17	2b red, yel, grn & blk	30.00	40.00
		Nos. 47-54 (8)	48.50	50.30

Excellent forgeries of No. 54, perf and imperf, exist, some postally used.

Reprint of No. 53 has dot in numeral. Same value.

Nos. 40-44 Handstamped in Violet or Blue

E.F.
1899

1899 *Perf. 14½*

55	A9	1c yellow bis	12.50	12.50
56	A9	2c red orange	15.00	15.00
57	A9	5c green	10.00	10.00
58	A9	10c yellow brn	12.50	10.00
59	A9	20c dark blue	20.00	20.00
		Nos. 55-59 (5)	70.00	67.50

The handstamp is found inverted, double, etc. Values twice the listed amounts. Forgeries of this handstamp are plentiful. "E.F." stands for Estado Federal.

The 50c and 100c (Nos. 45-46) were overprinted at a later date in Brazil.

Antonio José de Sucre — A18

Perf. 11½, 12

1899 Engr. Thin Paper

62	A18	1c gray blue	2.00	65
63	A18	2c brnsh red	1.50	65
64	A18	5c dk green	5.00	1.25
65	A18	10c yellow org	2.00	1.00
66	A18	20c rose pink	2.50	65
67	A18	50c bister brn	5.00	2.00
68	A18	1b gray violet	1.50	1.50
		Nos. 62-68 (7)	19.50	7.70

1901

69	A18	5c dark red	1.60	50

Col. Adolfo Ballivian A19

Eliodoro Camacho A20

President Narciso Campero A21

Jose Ballivian A22

Gen. Andres Santa Cruz — A23

Coat of Arms — A24

1901-02 Engr.

70	A19	1c claret	50	15
71	A20	2c green	50	18
73	A21	5c scarlet	50	20
74	A22	10c blue	1.25	15
75	A23	20c violet & blk	75	15
76	A24	2b brown	3.50	2.50
		Nos. 70-71,73-76 (6)	7.00	3.33

Nos. 73, 74 exist imperf. Value, pairs, each $50.

For surcharges see #95-96, 193.

1904 Litho.

77	A19	1c claret	2.00	50

In No. 70 the panel above "CENTAVO" is shaded with continuous lines. In No. 77 the shading is of dots.

See Nos. 103-105, 107, 110.

Coat of Arms of Dept. of La Paz — A25

Murillo — A26

Jose Miguel Lanza — A27

Ismael Montes — A28

1909 Litho. *Perf. 11*

78	A25	5c blue & blk	7.50	4.00
79	A26	10c green & blk	7.50	4.00
80	A27	20c orange & blk	7.50	4.00
81	A28	2b red & black	7.50	4.00
		Nos. 78-81 (4)	30.00	16.00

Centenary of Revolution of July, 1809.

Nos. 78-81 exist imperf. and tête bêche. Nos. 79-81 exist with center inverted.

Miguel Betanzos A29

Col. Ignacio Warnes A30

Murillo A31

Monteagudo A32

Esteban Arce — A33

Antonio Jose de Sucre — A34

Simon Bolivar A35

Manuel Belgrano A36

1909 Dated 1809-1825 *Perf. 11½*

82	A29	1c lt brn & blk	50	30
83	A30	2c green & blk	50	38
84	A31	5c red & blk	50	25

85	A32	10c dull bl & blk	50	25
86	A33	20c violet & blk	60	38
87	A34	50c olive bister & blk	90	50
88	A35	1b gray brn & blk	90	75
89	A36	2b chocolate & blk	1.50	1.00
		Nos. 82-89 (8)	5.90	3.81

War of Independence, 1809-1825.
Exist imperf. For surcharge see #97.

Warnes
A37

Betanzos
A38

Arce — A39

Dated 1910-1825

1910 ***Perf. 13x13½***

92	A37	5c green & black	35	15
a.		Imperf., pair	5.00	
93	A38	10c claret & indigo	35	15
a.		Imperf., pair	5.00	
94	A39	20c dull blue & indigo	60	35
a.		Imperf., pair	5.00	
		Nos. 92-94 (3)	1.30	65

War of Independence.
Nos. 92-94 may be found with parts of a papermaker's watermark: "A I & Co/EXTRA STRONG/9303."
Exist with inverted centers.

Nos. 71 and 75 Surcharged in Black

5 Centavos 1911

1911 ***Perf. 11½, 12***

95	A20	5c on 2c green	40	20
a.		Inverted surcharge	5.00	5.00
b.		Double surcharge	15.00	
c.		Period after "1911"	3.50	80
d.		Blue surcharge	75.00	60.00
e.		Double dsurch., one invtd.	15.00	
96	A23	5c on 20c vio & blk	15.00	15.00
a.		Inverted surcharge	30.00	30.00
b.		Double surch., one invtd.	60.00	

No. 83 Handstamp Surcharged in Green

20 CENTS 1911

97	A30	20c on 2c grn & blk		*1,100.*

This provisional was issued by local authorities at Villa Bella, a town on the Brazilian border. The 20c surcharge was applied after the stamp had been affixed to the cover. Excellent forgeries of No. 96-97 exist.

"Justice"
A40 A41

1912

Black or Dark Blue Overprint On Revenue Stamps

98	A40	2c green (Bk)	30	20
a.		Inverted overprint	5.00	
99	A41	10c ver (Bl)	1.00	35
a.		Inverted overprint	5.00	

A42

A43

Red or Black Overprint

Engr.

100	A42	5c orange (R)	50	35
a.		Inverted overprint	5.00	
b.		Pair, one without overprint	12.50	
c.		Black overprint	50.00	

Red or Black Surcharge

101	A43	10c on 1c bl (R)	50	16
a.		Inverted surcharge	6.00	
b.		Double surcharge	6.00	
c.		Dbl. surcharge, one invtd.	7.50	
d.		Black surcharge	100.00	100.00
e.		As "d," inverted		
f.		As "d," double surcharge		
g.		Pair, one without black surch.	200.00	

Revenue Stamp Surcharged "CORREOS / 10 Cts. / - 1917 -" in Red

1917 **Litho.**

102		10c on 1c blue	*6,000.*	*1,750.*

Design similar to type A43.
Excellent forgeries exist.

Types of 1901 and

Frias-A45 Sucre-A46 Bolivar-A47

1913 **Engr.** ***Perf. 12***

103	A19	1c car rose	35	20
104	A20	2c vermilion	35	15
105	A21	5c green	40	15
106	A45	8c yellow	75	45
107	A22	10c gray	75	20
108	A46	50c dull violet	1.40	50
109	A47	1b slate blue	2.00	1.25
110	A24	2b black	4.00	2.50
		Nos. 103-110 (8)	10.00	5.40

No. 107, litho., was not regularly issued.

Nine values commemorating the Guiqui-La Paz railroad were printed in 1915 but never issued. Typographed forgeries exist.

Monolith of Tiahuanacu
A48

Mt. Potosí
A49

Lake Titicaca — A50

Mt. Illimani — A51

Legislature Building — A53

FIVE CENTAVOS.
Type I - Numerals have background of vertical lines. Clouds formed of dots.

Type II - Numerals on white background. Clouds near the mountain formed of wavy lines.

1916-17 **Litho.** ***Perf. 11½***

111	A48	½c brown	15	15
a.		Horiz. pair, imperf. vert.	5.00	
112	A49	1c gray green	15	15
a.		Imperf., pair	2.00	
113	A50	2c car & blk	25	15
a.		Imperf., pair	2.00	
b.		Vert. pair, imperf. horiz.		
c.		Center inverted	12.50	11.25
d.		Imperf., center inverted	17.50	
114	A51	5c dk blue (I)	50	18
a.		Imperf., pair	2.00	
b.		Vert. pair, imperf. horiz.	3.50	
c.		Horiz. pair, imperf. vert.	3.50	
115	A51	5c dk blue (II)	50	15
a.		Imperf., pair	2.50	
116	A53	10c org & bl	1.00	15
a.		Imperf., pair	3.50	
b.		No period after "Legislativo"	1.00	15
c.		Center inverted	40.00	40.00
d.		Vertical pair, imperf. between	5.00	
		Nos. 111-116 (6)	2.55	
		Set value		69

For surcharges see Nos. 194-196.

Coat of Arms
A54 A55

Printed by the American Bank Note Co.

1919-20 **Engr.** ***Perf. 12***

118	A54	1c carmine	20	18
119	A54	2c dk violet	4.00	2.50
120	A54	5c dk green	40	15
121	A54	10c vermilion	40	15
122	A54	20c dk blue	1.25	25
123	A54	22c lt blue	75	65
124	A54	24c purple	50	40
125	A54	50c orange	4.00	50
126	A55	1b red brown	5.00	1.50
127	A55	2b black brn	7.50	3.75
		Nos. 118-127 (10)	24.00	10.03

Printed by Perkins, Bacon & Co., Ltd.

1923-27 **Re-engraved** ***Perf. 13½***

128	A54	1c carmine ('27)	15	15
129	A54	2c dk violet	20	15
130	A54	5c dp green	65	15
131	A54	10c vermilion	12.00	10.00
132	A54	20c slate blue	1.50	18
135	A54	50c orange	2.25	50
136	A55	1b red brown	60	25
137	A55	2b black brown	40	25
		Nos. 128-137 (8)	17.75	11.63

There are many differences in the designs of the two issues but they are too minute to be illustrated or described.
Nos. 128-137 exist imperf.
See Nos. 144-146, 173-177. For surcharges see Nos. 138-143, 160, 162, 181-186, 236-237.

Stamps of 1919-20 Surcharged in Blue, Black or Red

Habilitada 15 cts.

1924 ***Perf. 12***

138	A54	5c on 1c car (Bl)	35	18
a.		Inverted surcharge	5.00	5.00
b.		Double surcharge	5.00	5.00
139	A54	15c on 10c ver (Bk)	60	40
a.		Inverted surcharge	6.00	6.00
140	A54	15c on 22c lt bl (Bk)	60	25
a.		Inverted surcharge	5.25	5.25
b.		Double surcharge, one inverted		

No. 140 surcharged in red or blue probably are trial impressions. They appear jointly, and with black in blocks.

Same Surcharge on No. 131
Perf. 13½

142	A54	15c on 10c ver (Bk)	60	20
a.		Inverted surcharge	6.00	6.00

No. 121 Surcharged

Habilitada 15 cts.

Perf. 12

143	A54	15c on 10c ver (Bk)	75	25
a.		Inverted surcharge	6.00	6.00
b.		Double surcharge	5.00	5.00
		Nos. 138-143 (5)	2.90	1.28

Type of 1919-20 Issue
Printed by Waterlow & Sons
Second Re-engraving

1925 **Unwmk.** ***Perf. 12½***

144	A54	5c deep green	75	22
145	A54	15c ultra	75	15
146	A54	20c dark blue	30	15
		Nos. 144-146 (3)	1.80	52

These stamps may be identified by the perforation.

Miner — A56

Condor Looking Toward the Sea — A57

Designs: 2c, Sower. 5c, Torch of Eternal Freedom. 10c, National flower (kantuta). 15c, Pres. Bautista Saavedra. 50c, Liberty head. 1b, Archer on horse. 2b, Mercury. 5b, Gen. A. J. de Sucre.

1925 **Engr.** ***Perf. 14***

150	A56	1c dark green	75	
151	A56	2c rose	75	
152	A56	5c red, *grn*	75	35
153	A56	10c car, *yel*	1.25	75
154	A56	15c red brown	50	25
155	A57	25c ultra	50	50
156	A56	50c dp violet	50	50
157	A56	1b red	1.25	1.25
158	A57	2b orange	1.75	1.75
159	A56	5b black brn	2.00	2.00
		Nos. 150-159 (10)	10.00	

Cent. of the Republic. The 1c and 2c were not released for general use.
Nos. 150-159 exist imperf. Value, $60 each pair.
For surcharges see Nos. C59-C62.

Stamps of 1919-27 Surcharged in Blue, Black or Red

1927 5 CENTAVOS

1927

160	A54	5c on 1c car (Bl)	2.00	75
a.		Inverted surcharge	6.00	6.00
b.		Black surcharge	22.50	22.50

Perf. 12

162	A54	10c on 24c pur (Bk)	2.00	1.25
a.		Inverted surcharge	30.00	30.00
b.		Red surcharge	22.50	22.50

Coat of Arms — A66

Printed by Waterlow & Sons

1927 **Litho.** ***Perf. 13½***

165	A66	2c yellow	40	20
166	A66	3c pink	50	50
167	A66	4c red brown	40	40
168	A66	20c lt ol grn	65	20
169	A66	25c deep blue	65	30
170	A66	30c violet	80	80
171	A66	40c orange	1.50	1.25
172	A66	50c dp brown	1.50	50
173	A55	1b red	1.75	1.25
174	A55	2b plum	2.50	2.50
175	A55	3b olive grn	2.50	2.50
176	A55	4b claret	4.00	3.50
177	A55	5b bister brn	4.75	4.00
		Nos. 165-177 (13)	21.90	17.90

For overprints and surcharges see Nos. 178-180, 208, 211-212.

Type of 1927 Issue Overprinted

Octubre / 1927

1927

178 A66	5c dark green	20	15
179 A66	10c slate	40	15
180 A66	15c carmine	60	25
	Nos. 178-180 (3)	1.20	55

Exist with inverted overprint. Value $20 each.

Stamps of 1919-27 Surcharged

15 cts. 1928

1928 *Perf. 12, 12½, 13½*

Red Surcharge

181 A54	15c on 20c #122	7.50	7.50
182 A54	15c on 20c #132	7.50	7.50
a.	Black surcharge	25.00	
183 A54	15c on 20c #146	140.00	140.00

Black Surcharge

184 A54	15c on 24c #124	1.40	75
a.	Inverted surcharge	4.25	4.25
b.	Blue surcharge	42.50	
185 A54	15c on 50c #125	42.50	35.00
186 A54	15c on 50c #135	1.00	60
	Nos. 181-186 (6)	199.90	191.35

Condor — A67

Hernando Siles — A68

Map of Bolivia — A69

Printed by Perkins, Bacon & Co., Ltd.

1928 **Engr.** *Perf. 13½*

189 A67	5c green	1.25	15
190 A68	10c slate	25	15
191 A69	15c carmine lake	50	15
	Nos. 189-191 (3)	2.00	
	Set value		15

Nos. 104, 111, 113, Surcharged in Various Colors

0.03 Centavos R.S. 21-4 1930

1930 *Perf. 12, 11½*

193 A20	1c on 2c (Bl)	75	75
a.	"0.10" for "0.01"	12.50	12.50
194 A50	3c on 2c (Br)	75	75
195 A48	25c on ½c (Bk)	75	75
196 A50	25c on 2c (V)	75	75
	Nos. 193-196 (4)	3.00	3.00

The lines of the surcharges were spaced to fit the various shapes of the stamps. The surcharges exist inverted, double, etc.

Trial printings were made of the surcharges on Nos. 193 and 194 in black and on No. 196 in brown.

Mt. Potosi — A70

Mt. Illimani — A71

Eduardo Abaroa — A72

Map of Bolivia — A73

Sucre — A74

Bolivar — A75

1931 **Engr.** *Perf. 14*

197 A70	2c green	1.25	45
198 A71	5c light blue	1.25	16
199 A72	10c red orange	1.25	16
200 A73	15c violet	1.25	16
201 A73	35c carmine	1.75	75
202 A73	45c orange	1.75	65
203 A74	50c gray	50	50
204 A75	1b brown	50	50
	Nos. 197-204 (8)	9.50	3.33

No. 198 exists imperf.
See #207, 241. For surcharges see #209-210.

Symbols of 1930 Revolution — A76

1931 **Litho.** *Perf. 11*

205 A76	15c scarlet	2.00	35
a.	Pair, imperf. between		
206 A76	50c brt violet	65	65
a.	Pair, imperf. between	7.50	

Revolution of June 25, 1930.
For surcharges see Nos. 239-240.

Map Type of 1931 Without Imprint

1932 **Litho.**

207 A73	15c violet	1.25	30

Stamps of 1927-31 Surcharged

Habilitada A 15 Cts. D. S. 13-7.1933

1933 *Perf. 13½, 14*

208 A66	5c on 1b red	50	30
a.	Without period after "Cts"	1.25	1.25
209 A73	15c on 35c car	30	30
a.	Inverted surcharge	20.00	
210 A73	15c on 45c orange	30	30
a.	Inverted surcharge	3.00	3.00
211 A66	15c on 50c dp brn	1.25	25
212 A66	25c on 40c orange	50	20
	Nos. 208-212 (5)	2.85	1.35

The hyphens in "13-7-33" occur in three positions.

Coat of Arms — A77

1933 **Engr.** *Perf. 12*

213 A77	2c blue green	20	15
214 A77	5c blue	20	15
215 A77	10c red	40	25
216 A77	15c deep violet	30	15
217 A77	25c dark blue	60	50
	Nos. 213-217 (5)	1.70	1.20

For surcharges see Nos. 233-235, 238.

Mariano Baptista — A78

Map of Bolivia — A79

1935

218 A78	15c dull violet	40	18

1935

219 A79	2c dark blue	15	15
220 A79	3c yellow	15	15
221 A79	5c vermilion	15	15
222 A79	5c blue grn	30	15
223 A79	10c black brn	30	15
224 A79	15c deep rose	30	15
225 A79	15c ultra	30	15
226 A79	20c yellow grn	35	15
227 A79	25c lt blue	35	15
228 A79	30c deep rose	75	50
229 A79	40c orange	75	50
230 A79	50c gray violet	75	20
231 A79	1b yellow	50	32
232 A79	2b olive brown	75	60
	Nos. 219-232 (14)	5.85	3.47

Regular Stamps of 1925-33 Surcharged in Black

Comuni- caciones D. S. 25-2-37 0.05

1937 *Perf. 11, 12, 13½*

233 A77	5c on 2c bl grn	20	20
234 A77	15c on 25c dk bl	25	25
235 A77	30c on 25c dk bl	40	40
236 A55	45c on 1b red brn	50	50
237 A55	1b on 2b plum	60	60
a.	"1" missing	6.00	6.00
238 A77	2b on 25c dk bl	60	60

"Comunicaciones" on one line

239 A76	3b on 50c brt vio	1.00	1.00
a.	"3" of value missing	5.00	5.00
240 A76	5b on 50c brt vio	1.00	1.00
	Nos. 233-240 (8)	4.55	4.55

Exist inverted, double, etc.

President Siles — A80

1937 **Unwmk.** *Perf. 14*

241 A80	1c yellow brown	30	30

Native School — A81

Oil Wells — A82

Modern Factories A83

Torch of Knowledge A84

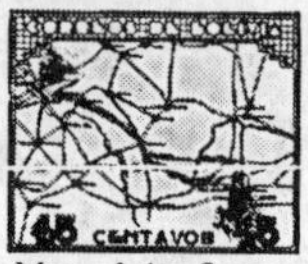
Map of the Sucre-Camiri R. R. — A85

Allegory of Free Education — A86

Allegorical Figure of Learning A87

Symbols of Industry A88

Modern Agriculture — A89

1938 **Litho.** *Perf. 10½, 11*

242 A81	2c dull red	25	25
243 A82	10c pink	30	18
244 A83	15c yellow grn	40	20
245 A84	30c yellow	50	25
246 A85	45c rose red	90	50
247 A86	60c dk violet	75	25
248 A87	75c dull blue	1.00	25
249 A88	1b lt brown	1.50	25
250 A89	2b bister	1.40	50
	Nos. 242-250 (9)	7.00	2.63

For surcharge see No. 314.

Llamas — A90

Vicuna — A91

Coat of Arms — A92

Cocoi Herons — A93

Chinchilla — A94

Toco Toucan — A95

Condor — A96

Jaguar — A97

1939, Jan. 21 *Perf. 10½, 11½x10½*

251 A90	2c green	25	25
252 A90	4c fawn	25	25
253 A90	5c red violet	25	20
254 A91	10c black	40	25
255 A91	15c emerald	40	30
256 A91	20c dk slate grn	40	20
257 A92	25c lemon	40	20
258 A92	30c dark blue	40	25
259 A93	40c vermilion	1.00	25
260 A93	45c gray	1.00	25
261 A94	60c rose red	1.00	50
262 A94	75c slate blue	2.00	50
263 A95	90c orange	1.50	50
264 A95	1b blue	1.50	50
265 A96	2b rose lake	2.00	50
266 A96	3b dark violet	2.50	75

267 A97 4b brown org 3.00 1.00
268 A97 5b gray brown 3.75 1.25
Nos. 251-268 (18) 22.00 7.90

All but 20c exist imperf.
Imperf. counterfeits with altered designs exist of some values.
For surcharges see Nos. 315-317.

Flags of 21 American Republics
A98

1940, Apr. Litho. *Perf. 10½*
269 A98 9b multicolored 1.00 1.00

Pan American Union, 150th anniversary.

Statue of Murillo — A99

Urns of Murillo and Sagarnaga — A100

Dream of Murillo
A101

Murillo
A102

1941, Apr. 15
270 A99 10c dl vio brn 15 15
271 A100 15c lt grn 16 15
a. Imperf., pair 3.50
b. Double impression 6.00
272 A101 45c car rose 16 15
a. Double impression 6.00
273 A102 1.05b dk ultra 35 15
Nos. 270-273 (4) 82
Set value 43

130th anniv. of the execution of Pedro Domingo Murillo (1759-1810), patriot.
For surcharge see No. 333.

First Stamp of Bolivia and 1941 Airmail Stamp — A103

1942, Oct. Litho. *Perf. 13½*
274 A103 5c pink 50 45
275 A103 10c orange 50 35
276 A103 20c yel grn 1.00 60
277 A103 40c car rose 1.25 75
278 A103 90c ultra 2.50 90
279 A103 1b violet 3.00 1.50
280 A103 10b ol bis 10.00 7.50
Nos. 274-280 (7) 18.75 12.05

1st School Phil. Exposition held in La Paz, Oct., 1941.

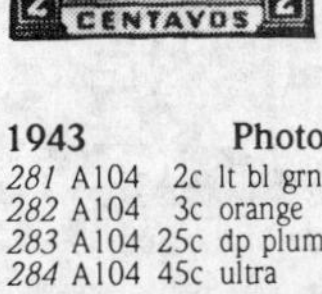
Gen. Ballivian Leading Cavalry Charge, Battle of Ingavi — A104

1943 Photo. *Perf. 12½*
281 A104 2c lt bl grn 15 15
282 A104 3c orange 15 15
283 A104 25c dp plum 15 15
284 A104 45c ultra 18 15
285 A104 3b scarlet 38 28
286 A104 4b brt rose lil 55 40
287 A104 5b black brn 80 50
Nos. 281-287 (7) 2.36 1.78

Souvenir Sheets
Perf. 13, Imperf.
288 A104 Sheet of 4 1.50 1.50
289 A104 Sheet of 3 4.50 4.50

Centenary of the Battle of Ingavi, 1841. No. 288 contains 4 stamps similar to Nos. 281-284, No. 289 three stamps similar to Nos. 285-287.

Potosi
A107

Quechisla
A108

Miner — A109

Dam
A110

Mine Interior
A111

Chaquiri Dam
A112

Entrance to Pulacayo Mine
A113

1943 Engr. *Perf. 12½*
290 A107 15c red brown 20 15
291 A108 45c vio blue 20 15
292 A109 1.25b brt rose vio 25 25
293 A110 1.50b emerald 25 25
294 A111 2b brown blk 30 30
295 A112 2.10b lt blue 40 40
296 A113 3b red orange 50 50
Nos. 290-296 (7) 2.10 2.00

General José Ballivián and Cathedral at Trinidad
A114

1943, Nov. 18
297 A114 5c dk green & brn 15 15
298 A114 10c dull pur & brn 15 15
299 A114 30c rose red & brn 15 15
300 A114 45c brt ultra & brn 20 20
301 A114 2.10b dp org & brn 28 28
Nos. 297-301,C91-C95 (10) 2.03 1.86

Department of Beni centenary.

"Honor, Work, Law"
A115

"United for the Country"
A116

1944 Litho. *Perf. 13½*
302 A115 20c orange 15 15
303 A115 90c ultra 15 15
304 A116 1b brt red vio 15 15
305 A116 2.40b dull brown 20 15

1945
306 A115 20c green 15 15
307 A115 90c dp rose 15 15
Set value, #302-307, C96-C99 1.48 92

Nos. 302-307 were issued to commemorate the Revolution of Dec. 20, 1943.

Catalogue values for unused stamps in this section, from this point to the end of the section, are for Never Hinged items.

Leopold Benedetto Vincenti, Joseph Ignacio de Sanjines and Bars of Anthem
A117

1946, Aug. 21 Litho. *Perf. 10½*
308 A117 5c rose vio & blk 15 15
309 A117 10c ultra & blk 15 15
310 A117 15c blue grn & blk 15 15
311 A117 30c vermilion & brn 15 15
a. Souv. sheet of 1, imperf. 65 65
312 A117 90c dk blue & brn 15 15
313 A117 2b black & brn 30 15
a. Souv. sheet of 1, imperf. 1.25 1.25
Set value 84 56

Cent. of the adoption of Bolivia's natl. anthem.
Nos. 311a and 313a sold for 4b over face.

Nos. 248 and 262 Surcharged in Carmine, Black or Orange

1947
Habilitada
Bs. 1.40

1947, Mar. 12 *Perf. 10½, 11*
314 A87 1.40b on 75c (C) 15 15
315 A94 1.40b on 75c (Bk) 15 15
316 A94 1.40b on 75c (C) 15 15
317 A94 1.40b on 75c (O) 15 15
Set value, #314-317, C112 66 62

People Attacking Presidential Palace — A118

Arms of Bolivia and Argentina — A119

1947, Sept. Litho. *Perf. 13½*
318 A118 20c blue grn 15 15
319 A118 50c lilac rose 15 15
320 A118 1.40b grnsh bl 15 15
321 A118 3.70b dull org 15 15
322 A118 4b violet 18 15
323 A118 10b olive 40 22
Set value, #318-323, C113-C117 1.52 1.00

1st anniv. of the Revolution of July 21, 1946. Exist imperf.

1947, Oct. 23
324 A119 1.40b deep orange 18 15

Meeting of Presidents Enrique Hertzog of Bolivia and Juan D. Peron of Argentina at Yacuiba on Oct. 23, 1947. Exist imperf.

See No. C118.

Statue of Christ above La Paz — A120

Designs: 2b, Child kneeling before cross of Golgotha. 3b, St. John Bosco. No. 328, Virgin of Copacabana. No. 329, Pope Pius XII blessing University of La Paz.

1948, Sept. 26 Unwmk. *Perf. 11½*
325 A120 1.40b blue & yel 30 15
326 A120 2b yel grn & sal 40 15
327 A120 3b green & gray 65 16
328 A120 5b violet & sal 80 20
329 A120 5b red brn & lt grn 1.10 20
Nos. 325-329,C119-C123 (10) 6.05 2.37

3rd Inter-American Cong. of Catholic Education.

Map and Emblem of Bolivia Auto Club — A125

Pres. Gregorio Pacheco, Map and Post Horn — A126

1948, Oct. 20
330 A125 5b indigo & salmon 1.50 15

Intl. Automobile Races of South America, Sept.-Oct. 1948. See No. C124.

1950, Jan. 2 Litho. *Perf. 11½*
331 A126 1.40b violet blue 15 15
332 A126 4.20b red 15 15
Set value, #331-332, C125-C127 60 54

75th anniv. of the UPU.

No. 273 Surcharged in Black

Bs.2.-
Habilitada
D.S.6·VII·50

1950 *Perf. 10½*
333 A102 2b on 1.05b dk ultra 16 15

Crucifix and View of Potosi — A127

Symbols of United Nations — A128

Perf. 11½
1950, Sept. 14 Litho. Unwmk.
334 A127 20c violet 15 15
335 A127 30c dp orange 15 15
336 A127 50c lilac rose 15 15
337 A127 1b carmine 15 15
338 A127 2b blue 30 15
339 A127 6b chocolate 22 15
Set value 83 35

400th anniv. of the appearance of a crucifix at Potosi. Exist imperf.

1950, Oct. 24

340 A128 60c ultra 1.00 15
341 A128 2b green 1.40 22

5th anniv. of the UN, Oct. 24, 1945. See Nos. C138-C139.

Gate of the Sun and Llama
A129

Church of San Francisco
A130

Designs: 40c, Avenue Camacho. 50c, Consistorial Palace. 1b, Legislative Palace. 1.40b, Communications Bldg. 2b, Arms. 3b, La Gasca ordering Mendoza to found La Paz. 5b, Capt. Alonso de Mendoza founding La Paz. 10b, Arms; portrait of Mendoza.

1951, Mar. Engr. *Perf. 12½*
Center in Black

342 A129 20c green 15 15
343 A130 30c dp orange 15 15
344 A129 40c bister brn 15 15
345 A129 50c dk red 15 15
346 A129 1b dp purple 15 15
347 A129 1.40b dk vio blue 15 15
348 A129 2b dp purple 15 15
349 A129 3b red lilac 20 15
a. Sheet, Nos. 345, 346, 348, 349 1.10 1.10
b. As "a," imperf. 1.10 1.10
350 A129 5b dk red 22 16
a. Sheet, Nos. 344, 347, 350 1.10 1.10
b. As "a," imperf. 1.10 1.10
351 A129 10b sepia 50 22
a. Sheet, Nos. 342, 343, 351 1.10 1.10
b. As "a," imperf. 1.10 1.10
Nos. 342-351,C140-C149 (20) 4.97 4.58

400th anniv. of the founding of La Paz.
For surcharges see Nos. 393-402.

Boxing — A131

Perf. 12½

1951, July 1 Unwmk. Engr.

352 A131 20c shown 16 15
353 A131 50c Tennis 16 15
354 A131 1b Diving 20 15
355 A131 1.40b Soccer 20 15
356 A131 2b Skiing 38 30
357 A131 3b Handball 80 80
a. Sheet, Nos. 352, 353, 356, 357 2.25 1.75
b. As "a," imperf. 2.25 1.75
358 A131 4b Cycling 1.00 1.00
a. Sheet, Nos. 354, 355, 358 2.00 1.50
b. As "a," imperf. 2.00 1.50
Nos. 352-358,C150-C156 (14) 8.15 5.85

The stamps were intended to commemorate the 5th athletic championship matches held at La Paz, October 1948.

Eagle and Flag of Bolivia — A132

1951, Nov. 5 Litho. *Perf. 11½*
Flag in Red, Yellow and Green.

359 A132 2b aqua 15 15
360 A132 3.50b ultra 15 15
361 A132 5b purple 15 15
362 A132 7.50b gray 20 15
363 A132 15b dp car 25 22
364 A132 30b sepia 50 50
Nos. 359-364 (6) 1.40 1.32

Cent. of the adoption of Bolivia's natl. flag.

Eduardo Abaroa
A133

Queen Isabella I
A134

1952, Mar. *Perf. 11*

365 A133 80c dk carmine 15 15
366 A133 1b red orange 15 15
367 A133 2b emerald 20 15
368 A133 5b ultra 25 15
369 A133 10b lilac rose 50 16
370 A133 20b dk brown 75 65
Nos. 365-370,C157-C162 (12) 5.00 4.11

73rd anniversary of the death of Eduardo Abaroa.

1952, July 16 Unwmk. *Perf. 13½*

371 A134 2b vio bl 15 15
372 A134 6.30b carmine 20 20
Set value 30 30

500th anniv. of the birth of Isabella I of Spain. See Nos. C163-C164.

Columbus Lighthouse
A135

1952, July 16 Litho.

373 A135 2b vio bl, *bl* 15 15
374 A135 5b car, *sal* 50 40
375 A135 9b emer, *grn* 85 60
Nos. 373-375,C165-C168 (7) 2.50 1.90

Miner — A136

1953, Apr. 9

376 A136 2.50b vermilion 15 15
377 A136 8b violet 15 15
Set value 25 20

Nationalization of the mines.

Gualberto Villarroel, Victor Paz Estenssoro and Hernan Siles Zuazo — A137

1953, Apr. 9 *Perf. 11½*

378 A137 50c rose lil 15 15
379 A137 1b brt rose 15 15
380 A137 2b vio bl 15 15
381 A137 3b lt grn 15 15
382 A137 4b yel org 15 15
383 A137 5b dl vio 16 15
Set value, #378-383, C169-C175 1.90 1.50

Revolution of Apr. 9, 1952, 1st anniv.

Map of Bolivia and Cow's Head — A138

Designs: 17b, Same as 5b. 25b, 85b, Map and ear of wheat.

1954, Aug. 2 *Perf. 12x11½*

384 A138 5b car rose 15 15
385 A138 17b aqua 15 15
386 A138 25b chalky blue 15 15
387 A138 85b blk brn 25 20
Set value, #384-387, C176-C181 2.35 1.15

Nos. 384-385 for the agrarian reform laws of 1953-54. Nos. 386-387 for the 1st National Congress of Agronomy. Exist imperf.

Oil Refinery
A139

1955, Oct. 9 Unwmk. *Perf. 12x11½*

388 A139 10b ultra & lt ultra 15 15
389 A139 35b rose car & rose 15 15
390 A139 40b dk & lt yel grn 15 15
391 A139 50b red vio & lil rose 15 15
392 A139 80b brn & bis brn 18 15
Nos. 388-392,C182-C186 (10) 3.28
Set value 2.25

Exist imperf.

Nos. 342-351, Surcharged with New Values and Bars in Ultramarine

1957, Feb. 14 Engr. *Perf. 12½*
Center in Black

393 A129 50b on 3b red lilac 15 15
394 A129 100b on 2b dp pur 15 15
395 A129 200b on 1b dp pur 15 15
396 A129 300b on 1.40b dk vio bl 16 15
397 A129 350b on 20c green 22 15
398 A129 400b on 40c bis brn 22 15
399 A130 600b on 30c dp org 35 15
400 A129 800b on 50c dk red 40 15
401 A129 1000b on 10b sepia 40 15
402 A129 2000b on 5b dk red 65 20
Nos. 393-402 (10) 2.85
Set value 75

See Nos. C187-C196.

CEPAL Building, Santiago de Chile, and Meeting Hall in La Paz — A140

1957, May 15 Litho. *Perf. 13*

403 A140 150b gray & ultra 15 15
404 A140 350b bis brn & gray 18 18
405 A140 550b chlky bl & brn 20 20
406 A140 750b dp rose & grn 30 20
407 A140 900b grn & brn blk 40 15
Nos. 403-407,C197-C201 (10) 5.03 3.48

7th session of the C. E. P. A. L. (Comision Economica para la America Latina de las Naciones Unidas), La Paz. Exist imperf.
For surcharges see Nos. 482-484,

Presidents Siles Zuazo and Aramburu
A141

1957, Dec. 15 Unwmk. *Perf. 11½*

408 A141 50b red org 15 15
409 A141 350b blue 25 15
410 A141 1000b redsh brn 50 15
Nos. 408-410,C202-C204 (6) 1.97
Set value 48

Opening of the Santa Cruz-Yacuiba Railroad and the meeting of the Presidents of Bolivia and Argentina. Exist imperf.
For surcharge see No. 699.

Flags of Bolivia and Mexico and Presidents Hernan Siles Zuazo and Adolfo Lopez Mateos
A142

1960, Jan. 30 Litho. *Perf. 11½*

411 A142 350b olive 16 16
412 A142 600b red brn 22 22
413 A142 1500b blk brn 50 50
Nos. 411-413,C205-C207 (6) 3.03 2.18

Issued for an expected visit of Mexico's President Adolfo Lopez Mateos. On sale Jan. 30-Feb. 1, 1960.

Indians and Mt. Illimani
A143

Refugee Children
A144

1960, Mar. 26 Unwmk.

414 A143 500b ol bis 50 15
415 A143 1000b blue 90 30
416 A143 2000b brown 2.00 50
417 A143 4000b green 3.75 2.50
Nos. 414-417,C208-C211 (8) 22.15 12.90

1960, Apr. 7 *Perf. 11½*

418 A144 50b brown 15 15
419 A144 350b claret 15 15
420 A144 400b steel blue 16 16
421 A144 1000b gray brn 50 50
422 A144 3000b slate grn 1.00 1.00
Nos. 418-422,C212-C216 (10) 4.26 4.21

Issued to publicize World Refugee Year, July 1, 1959-June 30, 1960.
For surcharges see Nos. 454-458, 529.

Jaime Laredo
A145

Rotary Emblem and Nurse with Children
A146

1960, Aug. 15 Litho. *Perf. 11½*

423 A145 100b olive 20 15
424 A145 350b dp rose 30 25
425 A145 500b Prus grn 38 20
426 A145 1000b brown 50 50
427 A145 1500b vio bl 90 90
428 A145 5000b gray 3.00 3.00
Nos. 423-428,C217-C222 (12) 13.03 8.70

Issued to honor violinist Jaime Laredo.
For surcharge see No. 485.

1960, Nov. 19 *Perf. 11½*

429 A146 350b multi 16 15
430 A146 500b multi 22 15
431 A146 600b multi 35 35
432 A146 1000b multi 40 20
Nos. 429-432,C223-C226 (8) 6.13 3.49

Issued for the Children's Hospital, sponsored by the Rotary Club of La Paz.
For surcharges see Nos. 486-487.

Designs from Gate of the Sun
A147 A148

Designs: Various prehistoric gods and ornaments from Tiahuanacu excavations.

1960, Dec. 16 *Perf. 13x12, 12x13*

Gold Background

Surcharge in Black or Dark Red

Sizes: 21x23mm, 23x21mm

433	A147	50b on ½c red	45	30
434	A147	100b on 1c red	35	15
435	A147	200b on 2c blk	75	35
436	A147	300b on 5c grn (DR)	25	20
437	A147	350b on 10c grn	25	75
438	A148	400b on 15c ind	35	15
439	A148	500b on 20c red	35	30
440	A148	500b on 50c red	40	15
441	A148	600b on 22½c grn	45	45
442	A148	600b on 60c vio	60	50
443	A148	700b on 25c vio	75	15
444	A148	700b on 1b grn	1.00	1.00
445	A148	800b on 30c red	60	15
446	A148	900b on 40c grn	45	20
447	A148	1000b on 2b bl	60	50
448	A148	1800b on 3b gray	5.00	3.50

Perf. 11

Size: 49½x23mm

449	A148	4000b on 4b gray	30.00	25.00

Perf. 11x13½

Size: 49x53mm

450	A147	5000b on 5b gray	7.50	7.00
		Nos. 433-450 (18)	50.10	40.80

Nos. 433-450 were not regularly issued without surcharge. Value, set $20.

The decree for Nos. 433-450 stipulated that 7 were for air mail (500b on 50c, 600b on 60c, 700b on 1b, 1000b, 1800b, 4000b and 5000b), but the overprinting failed to include "Aereo."

The 800b surcharge also exists on the 1c red and gold. This was not listed in the decree.

For surcharges see Nos. 528, 614.

Miguel de Cervantes A149

Nuflo de Chaves A150

1961, Nov. **Photo.** *Perf. 13x12½*

451	A149	600b ocher & dl vio	38	15

Cervantes' appointment as Chief Magistrate of La Paz. See No. C230.

1961, Nov. **Unwmk.**

452	A150	1500b dk bl, *buff*	75	30

400th anniv. of the founding of Santa Cruz de la Sierra. See Nos. 468, C246. For surcharge see No. 533.

People below Eucharist Symbol — A151

Flowers — A152

1962, Mar. 19 **Litho.** *Perf. 10½*

453	A151	1000b gray grn, red & yel	65	35

4th Natl. Eucharistic Congress, Santa Cruz, 1961. See No. C231.

Nos. 418-422 Surcharged Horizontally with New Value and Bars or Greek Key Border Segment

1962, June *Perf. 11½*

454	A144	600b on 50b brown	18	18
455	A144	900b on 350b claret	22	15
456	A144	1000b on 400b steel blue	32	15
457	A144	2000b on 1000b gray brn	38	22
458	A144	3500b on 3000b slate grn	65	65
		Nos. 454-458,C232-C236 (10)	5.15	4.45

Old value obliterated with two short bars on No. 454; four short bars on Nos. 455-456 and Greek key border on Nos. 457-458. The Greek key obliteration comes in two positions: two full "keys" on top, and one full and two half keys on top.

1962, June 28 **Litho.** *Perf. 10½*

459	A152	200b Hibiscus	30	15
460	A152	400b Bicolored vanda	45	15
461	A152	600b Lily	75	15
462	A152	1000b Orchid	1.00	18
		Nos. 459-462,C237-C240 (8)	7.50	3.18

Bolivia's Armed Forces A153

Anti-Malaria Emblem A154

1962, Sept. 5 *Perf. 11½*

463	A153	400b Infantry	15	15
464	A153	500b Cavalry	15	15
465	A153	600b Artillery	16	15
466	A153	2000b Engineers	50	35
		Nos. 463-466,C241-C244 (8)	3.96	2.15

1962, Oct. 4

467	A154	600b dk & lt vio & yel	25	25

WHO drive to eradicate malaria. See #C245.

Portrait Type of 1961

Design: 600b, Alonso de Mendoza.

1962 **Photo.** *Perf. 13x12½*

468	A150	600b rose vio, *bluish*	25	15

Soccer and Flags — A155

Design: 1b, Goalkeeper catching ball, vert.

1963, Mar. 21 **Litho.** *Perf. 11½*

Flags in National Colors

469	A155	60c gray	40	40
470	A155	1b gray	60	20

21st South American Soccer Championships. See Nos. C247-C248.

Globe and Wheat Emblem — A156

1963, Aug. 1 **Unwmk.** *Perf. 11½*

471	A156	60c dk bl, bl & yel	25	25

"Freedom from Hunger" campaign of the FAO. See No. C249.

Oil Derrick and Chart — A157

Designs: 60c, Map of Bolivia. 1b, Students.

1963, Dec. 21 **Litho.** *Perf. 11½*

472	A157	10c grn & dk brn	15	15
473	A157	60c ocher & dk brn	22	15
474	A157	1b dk bl, grn & yel	28	15
		Nos. 472-474,C251-C253 (6)	2.55	1.80

Revolution of Apr. 9, 1952, 10th anniv.

Flags of Bolivia and Peru — A158

1966, Aug. 10 **Wmk. 90** *Perf. 13½*

Flags in National Colors

475	A158	10c blk & tan	15	15
476	A158	60c blk & lt grn	20	20
477	A158	1b blk & gray	35	35
478	A158	2b blk & rose	50	50
		Nos. 475-478,C254-C257 (8)	2.85	2.85

Marshal Andrés Santa Cruz (1792-1865), president of Bolivia and of Peru-Bolivian Confederation.

Children — A159

Perf. 13½

1966, Dec. 16 **Unwmk.** **Litho.**

479	A159	30c ocher & sepia	15	15

Issued to help poor children. See No. C258.

Map and Flag of Bolivia and Generals Ovando and Barrientos A160

1966, Dec. 16 **Litho.** *Perf. 13½*

Flag in Red, Yellow and Green

480	A160	60c vio brn & tan	30	20
481	A160	1b dl grn & tan	45	15

Issued to honor Generals Rene Barrientos Ortuno and Alfredo Ovando C., co-Presidents, 1965-66. See Nos. C259-C260.

Various Issues 1957-60 and Type A161 Surcharged with New Values and Bars

A161

1966, Dec. 21

On No. 403: "Centenario de la / Cruz Roja / Internacional"

482	A140	20c on 150b gray & ultra	20	15

On Nos. 405-406: "Homenaje a la / Generala / J. Azurduy de / Padilla"

483	A140	30c on 550b chlky bl & brn	30	15
484	A140	2.80b on 750b dp rose & grn	75	50

On No. 424: "CL Aniversario / Heroinas Coronilla"

485	A145	60c on 350b dp rose	50	15

Nos. 429-430 Surcharged

486	A146	1.60b on 350b multi	75	50
487	A146	2.40b on 500b multi	1.00	75

Revenue Stamps of 1946 surcharged with New Value, "X" and: "XXV Aniversario / Gobierno Busch"

488	A161	20c on 5b red	20	15

Overprinted: "XX Aniversario / Gob. Villaroel"

489	A161	60c on 2b grn	30	15

Overprinted: "Centenario do / Rurrenabaque"

490	A161	1b on 10b brn	50	15

Overprinted: "XXV Aniversario / Dpto. Pando"

491	A161	1.60b on 50c vio	50	16
		Nos. 482-491,C261-C272 (22)	14.50	8.86

For surcharge see No. C272.

Sower A162

"Macheteros" A163

1967, Sept. 20 **Litho.** *Perf. 13½x13*

492	A162	70c multi	35	15

50th anniv. of Lions Intl. See #C273-C273a.

1968, June 24 *Perf. 13½x13*

Designs (Folklore characters): 60c, Chunchos. 1p, Wiphala. 2p, Diablada.

493	A163	30c gray & multi	15	15
494	A163	60c sky bl & multi	25	25
495	A163	1b gray & multi	40	15
496	A163	2b gray ol & multi	60	20
		Nos. 493-496,C274-C277 (8)	3.90	1.65

Issued to publicize the 9th Congress of the Postal Union of the Americas and Spain.

A souvenir sheet exists containing 4 imperf. stamps similar to #493-496. Size: 131x81½mm.

Arms of Tarija — A164

Pres. Gualberto Villaroel — A165

1968, Oct. 29 **Litho.** *Perf. 13½x13*

497	A164	20c pale sal & multi	15	15
498	A164	30c gray & multi	15	15
499	A164	40c dl yel & multi	15	15
500	A164	60c lt yel grn & multi	20	20
		Nos. 497-500,C278-C281 (8)	3.15	2.40

Battle of Tablada sesquicentennial.

1968, Nov. 6 **Unwmk.**

501	A165	20c sep & org	30	15
502	A165	30c sep & dl bl grn	30	15
503	A165	40c sep & dl rose	30	20
504	A165	50c sep & yel grn	30	15
505	A165	1b sep & ol bis	30	15
		Nos. 501-505 (5)	1.50	
		Set value		45

4th centenary of the founding of Cochabamba. See Nos. C282-C286.

ITU Emblem — A166

1968, Dec. 3 **Litho.** *Perf. 13x13½*

506	A166	10c gray, blk & yel	20	20
507	A166	60c org, blk & ol	40	40

Cent. (in 1965) of the ITU. See Nos. C287-C288.

Polychrome Painted Clay Cup, Inca Period — A167

1968, Nov. 14 *Perf. 13½x13*
508 A167 20c dk bl grn & multi 15 15
509 A167 60c vio bl & multi 35 35

20th anniv. (in 1966) of UNESCO. See Nos. C289-C290.

John F. Kennedy — A168

Tennis Player — A169

1968, Nov. 22 *Perf. 13x13½*
510 A168 10c yel grn & blk 15 15
511 A168 4b vio & blk 1.40 1.40

A souvenir sheet contains one imperf. stamp similar to No. 511. Green marginal inscription. Size: 131x81½mm.
See Nos. C291-C292.

1968, Dec. 10 *Perf. 13x13½*
512 A169 10c gray, blk & lt brn 25 25
513 A169 20c yel, blk & lt brn 25 25
514 A169 30c ultra, blk & lt brn 25 25
Nos. 512-514 (3) 75 75

32nd South American Tennis Championships, La Paz, 1965. See Nos. C293-C294.
A souvenir sheet exists containing 3 imperf. stamps similar to Nos. 512-514. Size: 131x81½mm.

Issue of 1863 — A170

1968, Dec. 23 **Litho.** *Perf. 13x13½*
515 A170 10c yel grn, brn & blk 35 20
516 A170 30c lt bl, brn & blk 35 35
517 A170 2b gray, brn & blk 35 35
Nos. 515-517,C295-C297 (6) 3.55 3.40

Cent. of Bolivian postage stamps. See Nos. C295-C297.
A souvenir sheet exists containing 3 imperf. stamps similar to Nos. 515-517. Yellow green marginal inscription. Size: 131x81½mm.

Rifle Shooting — A171

Sports: 50c, Equestrian. 60c, Canoeing.

1969, Oct. 29 **Litho.** *Perf. 13x13½*
518 A171 40c red brn, org & blk 40 40
519 A171 50c emer, red & blk 40 40
520 A171 60c bl, emer & blk 40 40
Nos. 518-520,C299-C301 (6) 4.20 3.85

Issued to commemorate the 19th Olympic Games, Mexico City, Oct. 12-27, 1968.
A souvenir sheet exists containing 3 imperf. stamps similar to Nos. 518-520. Size: 130½x81mm.

Temenis Laothoe Violetta A172

Butterflies: 10c, Papilio crassus. 20c, Catagramma cynosura. 30c, Eunica eurota flora. 80c, Ituna phenarete.

1970, Apr. 24 **Litho.** *Perf. 13x13½*
521 A172 5c pale lil & multi 50 50
522 A172 10c pink & multi 1.00 1.00
523 A172 20c gray & multi 1.00 1.00
524 A172 30c yel & multi 1.00 1.00
525 A172 80c multicolored 1.00 1.00
Nos. 521-525,C302-C306 (10) 15.00 15.00

A souvenir sheet exists containing 3 imperf. stamps similar to Nos. 521-523. Black marginal inscription. Size: 129½x80mm.

Boy Scout — A173

Design: 10c, Girl Scout planting rose bush.

1970, June 17 *Perf. 13½x13*
526 A173 5c multicolored 20 15
527 A173 10c multicolored 20 15

Issued to honor the Bolivian Scout movement. See Nos. C307-C308.

No. 437 Surcharged "EXFILCA 70 / $b. 0.30" and Two Bars in Red

1970, Dec. 6 **Litho.** *Perf. 13x12*
528 A147 30c on 350b on 10c 25 25

EXFILCA 70, 2nd Interamerican Philatelic Exhib., Caracas, Venezuela, Nov. 27-Dec. 6.

Nos. 455 and 452 Surcharged in Black or Red

1970, Dec. **Photo.** *Perf. 11½*
529 A144 60c on 900b on 350b 25 20
533 A150 1.20b on 1500b (R) 50 15

Amaryllis Yungacensis A174

Sica Sica Church, EXFILIMA Emblem A175

Bolivian Flowers: 30c, Amaryllis escobar uriae, horiz. 40c, Amaryllis evansae, horiz. 2b, Gymnocalycium chiquitanum.

Perf. 13x13½, 13½x13
1971, Aug. 9 **Litho.** **Unwmk.**
534 A174 30c gray & multi 30 30
535 A174 40c multi 30 30
536 A174 50c multi 35 35
537 A174 2b multi 1.00 60
Nos. 534-537,C310-C313 (8) 6.95 4.45

1971, Nov. 6 *Perf. 14x13½*
538 A175 20c red & multi 20 15

EXFILIMA '71, 3rd Inter-American Philatelic Exhibition, Lima, Peru, Nov. 6-14.

A176

A177

Design: Pres. Hugo Banzer Suarez.

1972, Jan. 24 **Litho.** *Perf. 13½*
539 A176 1.20b blk & multi 50 15

Bolivia's development, Aug. 19, 1971, to Jan. 24, 1972.

1972, Mar. 23 **Litho.** *Perf. 13½x13*

Folk Dances: 20c, Chiriwano de Achocalla. 40c, Rueda Chapaca. 60c, Kena-kena. 1b, Waca Thokori.

540 A177 20c red & multi 15 15
541 A177 40c rose lil & multi 30 25
542 A177 60c cream & multi 45 20
543 A177 1b citron & multi 55 22
Nos. 540-543,C314-C315 (6) 2.60 1.14

Madonna and Child by B. Bitti — A178

Tarija Cathedral, EXFILBRA Emblem — A179

Bolivian paintings: 10c, Nativity, by Melchor Perez de Holguin. 50c, Coronation of the Virgin, by G. M. Berrio. 70c, Harquebusier, anonymous. 80c, St. Peter of Alcantara, by Holguin.

1972 **Litho.** *Perf. 14x13½*
544 A178 10c gray & multi 15 15
545 A178 50c sal & multi 25 15
546 A178 70c lt grn & multi 35 15
547 A178 80c buff & multi 40 15
548 A178 1b multi 50 15
Nos. 544-548,C316-C319 (9) 3.40
Set value 1.10

Issue dates: 1b, Aug. 17; others, Dec. 4.

1972, Aug. 26
549 A179 30c multi 16 15

4th Inter-American Philatelic Exhibition, EXFILBRA, Rio de Janeiro, Brazil, Aug. 26-Sept. 2.

Echinocactus Notocactus — A180

Designs: Various cacti.

1973, Aug. 6 **Litho.** *Perf. 13½*
550 A180 20c crim & multi 30 25
551 A180 40c multi 30 25
552 A180 50c multi 30 15
553 A180 70c multi 30 20
Nos. 550-553,C321-C323 (7) 2.70 1.45

Power Station, Santa Isabel A181

Designs: 20c, Tin industry. 90c, Bismuth industry. 1b, Natural gas plant.

1973, Nov. 26 **Litho.** *Perf. 13½*
554 A181 10c gray & multi 15 15
555 A181 20c tan & multi 15 15
556 A181 90c lt grn & multi 25 20
557 A181 1b yel & multi 25 15
Nos. 554-557,C324-C325 (6) 1.80
Set value 75

Bolivia's development.

Cattleya Nobilior — A182

Orchids: 50c, Zygopetalum bolivianum. 1b, Huntleya melagris.

1974, May 15 *Perf. 13½*
558 A182 20c gray & multi 40 15
559 A182 50c lt bl & multi 40 15
560 A182 1b cit & multi 40 15
Nos. 558-560,C327-C330 (7) 7.70 1.97

For surcharge see No. 704.

UPU and Philatelic Exposition Emblems A183

1974, Oct. 9
561 A183 3.50b grn, blk & bl 1.00 40

Centenary of Universal Postal Union: PRENFIL-UPU Philatelic Exhibition, Buenos Aires, Oct. 1-12; EXPO-UPU Philatelic Exhibition, Montevideo, Oct. 20-27.

Gen. Sucre, by I. Wallpher — A184

1974, Dec. 9 **Litho.** *Perf. 13½*
562 A184 5b multicolored 1.10 50

Sesquicentennial of the Battle of Ayacucho.

Lions Emblem and Steles A185

1975, Mar. **Litho.** *Perf. 13½*
563 A185 30c red & multi 35 35

Lions Intl. in Bolivia, 25th anniv.

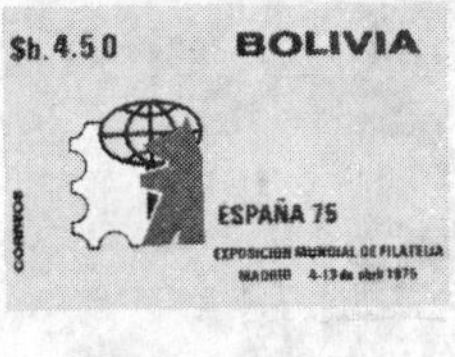
España 75 Emblem A186

1975, Mar.

564 A186 4.50b yel, red & blk		80	35

Espana 75 International Philatelic Exhibition, Madrid, Apr. 4-13.

Emblem A187

1975 **Litho.** ***Perf. 13½***

565 A187 2.50b lil, blk & sil		65	25

First meeting of Postal Ministers, Quito, Ecuador, March 1974, and for the Cartagena Agreement.

Pando Coat of Arms — A188

Designs: Departmental coats of arms.

1975, July 16 **Litho.** ***Perf. 13½***

566 A188	20c shown	15	15
567 A188	2b Chuquisaca	40	40
568 A188	3b Cochabamba	50	50
	Nos. 566-568,C336-C341 (9)	4.10	4.10

Sesquicentennial of Republic of Bolivia.

Simón Bolívar — A189

Presidents and Statesmen of Bolivia: 30c, Victor Paz Estenssoro. 60c, Tomas Frias. 1b, Ismael Montes. 2.50b, Aniceto Arce. 7b, Bautista Saavedra. 10b, Jose Manuel Pando. 15b, Jose Maria Linares. 50b, Simon Bolivar.

1975 **Litho.** ***Perf. 13½***

Size: 24x32mm

569	A189	30c multi	15	15
569A	A189	60c multi	20	20
570	A189	1b multi	30	30
571	A189	2.50b multi	50	50
572	A189	7b multi	1.40	50
573	A189	10b multi	2.00	75
574	A189	15b multi	2.50	2.50

Size: 28x39mm

575	A189	50b multi	10.00	10.00
		Nos. 569-575,C346-C353 (16)	36.05	31.15

Sesquicentennial of Republic of Bolivia.

"EXFIVIA 75" A190

1975, Dec. 1 **Litho.** ***Perf. 13½***

576 A190 3b multicolored		75	60
a. Souvenir sheet		1.50	1.50

EXFIVIA 75, first Bolivian Philatelic Exposition. No. 576a contains one stamp similar to No. 576 with simulated perforations. Sold for 5b.

A191

A192

Chiang Kai-shek, flags of Bolivia and China.

1976, Apr. 4 **Litho.** ***Perf. 13½***

577 A191	2.50b multi, red circle	1.00	1.00
578 A191	2.50b multi, bl circle	1.00	1.00

Pres. Chiang Kai-shek of China (1887-1975).

Erroneous red of sun's circle on Chinese flag of No. 577 was corrected on No. 578 with a dark blue overlay.

1976, Apr. **Litho.** ***Perf. 13½***

579 A192 50c Naval insignia		40	35

Navy anniversary.

Geological Map, Pickax and Lamp A193

1976, May

580 A193 4b multicolored		80	60

Bolivian Geological Institute.

Lufthansa Jet, Bolivian and German Colors A194

1976, May

581 A194 3b multicolored		80	35

Lufthansa, 50th anniversary.

Boy Scout and Scout Emblem — A195

1976, May **Litho.** ***Perf. 13½***

582 A195 1b multicolored		50	50

Bolivian Boy Scouts, 60th anniversary.

Battle Scene, US Bicentennial Emblem A196

1976, May 25

583 A196 4.50b bis & multi		1.40	65

American Bicentennial.

A souvenir sheet contains one stamp similar to No. 583 with simulated perforations. Size: 130x80mm.

Family, Map of Bolivia — A197

Vicente Bernedo — A198

1976 ***Perf. 13½***

584 A197 2.50b multicolored		50	40

National Census 1976.

1976, Oct.

585 A198 1.50b multicolored		35	30

Brother Vicente Bernedo de Potosi (1544-1619), missionary to the Indians.

Policeman with Dog, Rainbow over La Paz — A199

1976, Oct.

586 A199 2.50b multicolored		60	60

Bolivian Police, 150 years of service.

Emblem, Bolivar and Sucre A200

1976, Nov. 18 **Litho.** ***Perf. 13½***

587 A200 1.50b multicolored		60	60

Intl. Congress of Bolivarian Societies.

Pedro Poveda, View of La Paz — A201

1976, Dec.

588 A201 1.50b multicolored		35	25

Pedro Poveda (1874-1936), educator.

A202

Boy and Girl — A203

1976, Dec. 17 ***Perf. 10½***

594 A202	20c brown	30	15
595 A202	1b ultra	45	15
596 A202	1.50b green	75	50
	Nos. 594-596 (3)	1.50	
	Set value		62

1977, Feb. 4 **Litho.** ***Perf. 13½***

599 A203 50c multicolored		15	15

Christmas 1976, and for 50th anniversary of the Inter-American Children's Institute.

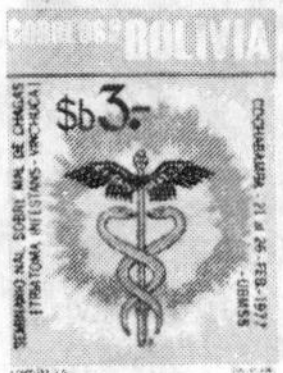
Staff of Aesculapius A204

Supreme Court, La Paz A205

1977, Mar. 18 **Litho.** ***Perf. 13½x13***

600 A204 3b multicolored		75	30

National Seminar on Chagas' disease, Cochabamba, Feb. 21-26.

1977, May 3

Designs: 4b, Manuel Maria Urcullu, first President of Supreme Court. 4.50b, Pantaleon Dalence, President 1883-1889.

601 A205	2.50b multi	30	30
602 A205	4b multi	42	15
603 A205	4.50b multi	50	20
	Nos. 601-603 (3)	1.22	65

Sesquicentennial of Bolivian Supreme Court.

Newspaper Mastheads A206

Map of Bolivia, Tower and Flag A207

Designs: 2.50b, Alfredo Alexander and Hoy, horiz. 3b, Jose Carrasco and El Diario, horiz. 4b, Demetrio Canelas and Los Tiempos. 5.50b, Frontpage of Presencia.

1977, June **Litho.** ***Perf. 13½***

604 A206	1.50b multi	22	15
605 A206	2.50b multi	35	30
606 A206	3b multi	42	25
607 A206	4b multi	50	35
608 A206	5.50b multi	65	20
	Nos. 604-608 (5)	2.14	1.25

Bolivian newspapers and their founders.

1977, June

609 A207 3b multi		50	16

90th anniversary of Oruro Club.

Games' Poster — A208

Tin Miner and Emblem — A209

1977, Oct. 20 Litho. *Perf. 13½*
610 A208 5b blue & multi 75 20

8th Bolivian Games, La Paz, Oct. 1977.

1977, Oct. 31 Litho. *Perf. 13*
611 A209 3b multicolored 60 40

Bolivian Mining Corp., 25th anniv.

Miners, Globe, Tin Symbol — A210

Map of Bolivia, Radio Masts — A211

1977, Nov. 3
612 A210 6b silver & multi 80 25

Intl. Tin Symposium, La Paz, Nov. 14-21.

1977, Nov. 11
613 A211 2.50b blue & multi 50 35

Radio Bolivia, ASBORA, 50th anniversary.

No. 450 Surcharged with New Value, 3 Bars and "EXFIVIA-77"

1977, Nov. 25 Litho. *Perf. 11x13½*
614 A147 5b on 5000b on 5b 1.00 1.25

EXFIVIA '77 Philatelic Exhibition, Cochabamba.

Eye, Compass, Book of Law — A212

1978, May 3 Litho. *Perf. 13½x13*
615 A212 5b multi 65 16

Audit Department, 50th anniversary.

Mt. Illimani — A213

Pre-Columbian Monolith — A214

Design: 1.50b, Mt. Cerro de Potosi.

Perf. 11x10½, 10½x11

1978, June 1 Litho.
616 A213 50c bl & Prus bl 15 15
617 A214 1b brn & lemon 20 15
618 A213 1.50b red & bl gray 35 25
Nos. 616-618 (3) 70
Set value 35

Andean Countries, Staff of Aesculapius — A215

Map of Americas with Bolivia — A216

1978, June 1 *Perf. 10½x11*
626 A215 2b org & blk 35 15

Health Ministers of Andean Countries, 5th meeting.

1978, June 1
627 A216 2.50b dp ultra & red 35 15

World Rheumatism Year.
For surcharge see No. 697.

Central Bank Building — A217

Jesus and Children — A218

1978, July 26 Litho. *Perf. 13½*
628 A217 7b multi 1.00 25

50th anniversary of Bank of Bolivia.

1979, Feb. 20 Litho. *Perf. 13½*
629 A218 8b multicolored 90 16

International Year of the Child.

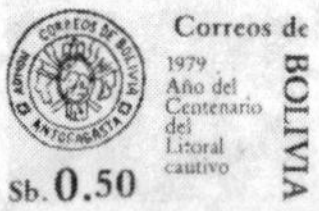

Antofagasta Cancel — A219

Eduardo Abaroa, Chain — A220

Designs: 1b, La Chimba cancel. 1.50b, Mejillones cancel. 5.50b, View of Antofagasta (horiz.). 6.50b, Woman in chains, symbolizing captive province. 8b, Map of Antofagasta Province, 1876. 10b, Arms of province.

1979, Mar. 23 Litho. *Perf. 10½*
630 A219 50c buff & blk 30 20
631 A219 1b pink & blk 50 25
632 A219 1.50b pale grn & blk 50 25

Perf. 13½
633 A220 5.50b multi 60 25
634 A220 6.50b multi 80 30
635 A220 7b multi 80 30
636 A220 8b multi 90 35
637 A220 10b multi 1.10 35
Nos. 630-637 (8) 5.50 2.25

Centenary of loss of Antofagasta coastal area to Chile.
For surcharge see No. 696.

Emblem and Map of Bolivia A221

Gymnast A222

1979, Mar. 26 *Perf. 13½x13*
638 A221 3b multicolored 75 50

Radio Club of Bolivia.

Perf. 13x13½, 13½x13
1979, Mar. 27

Design: 6.50b, Runner and Games emblem, horiz.

639 A222 6.50b multi 80 50
640 A222 10b multi 1.10 25

Southern Cross Sports Games, Bolivia, Nov. 3-12, 1978.
A souvenir sheet contains 1 stamp similar to No. 640 with simulated perforations. Sold for 20b. Size: 80x130mm.

Bulgaria No. 1 — A223

EXFILMAR Emblem — A224

1979, Mar. 30 *Perf. 10½*
641 A223 2.50b multi 35 25

PHILASERDICA '79 International Philatelic Exhibition, Sofia, Bulgaria, May 18-27.
For surcharge see No. 694.

1979, Apr. 2
642 A224 2b multi 20 20

Bolivian Maritime Philatelic Exhibition, La Paz, Nov. 18-28.
For surcharge see No. 698.

OAS Emblem, Map of Bolivia — A226

1979, Oct. 22 Litho. *Perf. 14x13½*
644 A226 6b multi 75 25

Organization of American States, 9th Congress, La Paz, Oct.-Nov.

Franz Tamayo — A227

Bolivian and Japanese Flags, Hospital — A228

UN Emblem and Meeting — A229

Radio Tower and Waves — A230

1979, Dec.
645 A227 2.80b blk & gray 35 25
646 A228 5b multi 50 35
648 A229 5b multi 50 35
649 A230 6b multi 65 25
Nos. 645-649 (4) 2.00 1.20

Franz Tamayo, lawyer, birth centenary; Japanese-Bolivian health care cooperation; CEPAL, 18th Congress, La Paz, Sept. 18-26; Bolivian National Radio, 50th anniversary.
For surcharge see No. 695.

Puerto Suarez Iron Ore Deposits A231

1979 Litho. *Perf. 13½x14*
650 A231 9.50b multi 1.10 50

Bolivia No. 19, EXFILMAR Emblem, Bolivian Flag — A232

1980 Litho. *Perf. 13½*
651 A232 4b multi 55 30

EXFILMAR, Bolivian Maritime Philatelic Exhibition, La Paz, Nov. 18-28, 1979.

Juana Azurduy on Horseback — A233

1980 Litho. *Perf. 14x13½*
652 A233 4b multi 55 30

Juana Azurduy de Padilla, independence fighter, birth bicentenary.

La Salle and World Map A234

1980 *Perf. 13½x14*
653 A234 9b multi 1.10 60

St. Jean Baptiste de la Salle (1651-1719), educator.

"Victory" in Chariot, Madrid, Exhibition Emblem, Flags of Bolivia and Spain
A235

1980, Oct. Litho. *Perf. 13½x14*
654 A235 14b multi 1.60 75

ESPAMER '80 Stamp Exhibition, Madrid.

Map of South America, Flags of Argentina, Bolivia and Peru — A236

1980, Oct. *Perf. 14x13½*
655 A236 2b multi 25 20

Ministers of Public Works and Transport of Argentina, Bolivia and Peru meeting.

Santa Cruz-Trinidad Railroad, Inauguration of Third Section — A237

1980, Oct.
656 A237 3b multi 35 20

Flag on Provincial Map — A238

Parrots — A239

Perf. 14x13½, 13½x14
1981, May 11 Litho.

657	A238	1b Soldier, flag, map	15	15
658	A238	3b Flag, map	35	15
659	A238	40b shown	5.00	1.25
660	A238	50b Soldier, civilians, horiz.	6.00	1.25
		Nos. 657-660 (4)	11.50	2.80

July 17 Revolution memorial.

1981, May 11 *Perf. 14x13½*

661	A239	4b Ara macao	50	30
662	A239	7b Ara chloroptera	80	50
663	A239	8b Ara ararauna	1.00	60
664	A239	9b Ara rubrogenys	1.10	65
665	A239	10b Ara auricollis	1.10	65
666	A239	12b Anodorynchus hyacinthinus	1.50	75
667	A239	15b Ara militaris	1.75	1.00
668	A239	20b Ara severa	2.25	1.25
		Nos. 661-668 (8)	10.00	5.70

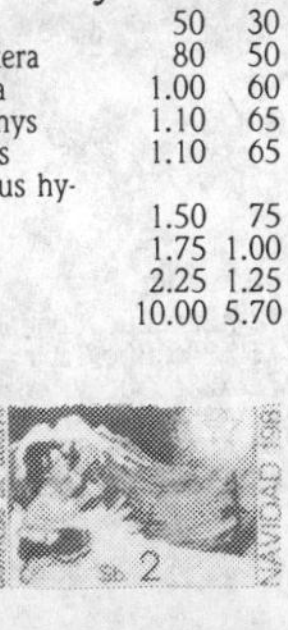

Christmas 1981 — A240

1981, Dec. 7 Litho. *Perf. 10½*

669	A240	1b Virgin and Child, vert.	15	15
670	A240	2b Child, star	25	15

American Airforces Commanders' 22nd Conference, Buenos Aires — A241

1982, Apr. 12 Litho. *Perf. 13½*
671 A241 14b multi 1.60 50

75th Anniv. of Cobija — A242

Simon Bolivar Birth Bicentenary (1983) — A243

1982, July 8 Litho. *Perf. 13½*
672 A242 28b multi 40 25

1982, July 12
673 A243 18b multi 25 20

1983 World Telecommunications Day — A244

1982 World Cup — A245

1982, July 15
674 A244 26b Receiving station 40 25

1982, July 21 *Perf. 11*

675	A245	4b shown	15	15
676	A245	100b Final Act, by Picasso	1.75	95

For surcharge see No. 701.

Girl Playing Piano — A246

1982, July 25 *Perf. 13½*

677	A246	16b Boy playing soccer, vert.	25	15
678	A246	20b shown	35	20

Bolivian-Chinese Agricultural Cooperation, 1972-1982 — A247

1982, Aug. 12
679 A247 30b multi 50 25

First Bolivian-Japanese Gastroenterology Conference, La Paz, Jan. — A248

1982, Aug. 26
680 A248 22b multi 35 25

A249

A250

1982, Aug. 31 Litho. *Perf. 14x13½*
681 A249 19b Stamps 35 20

10th Anniv. of Bolivian Philatelic Federation.

1982, Sept. 1
682 A250 20b tan & dk brown 30 20

Pres. Hernando Siles, birth centenary.

Scouting Year — A251

Cochabamba Philatelic Center, 25th Anniv. — A252

1982, Sept. 3 *Perf. 11*
683 A251 5b Baden-Powell 15 15

For surcharge see No. 703.

1982, Sept. 14
684 A252 3b multicolored 15 15

For surcharge see No. 700.

Cochabamba Superior Court of Justice Sesquicentennial
A253

1982 Litho. *Perf. 13½*
685 A253 10b multicolored 20 15

Enthronement of Virgin of Copacabana, 400th Anniv. — A254

Navy Day — A255

1982, Nov. 15 Litho. *Perf. 13½*
686 A254 13b multicolored 25 15

1982, Nov. 17
687 A255 14b Port Busch Naval Base 25 15

A256

A257

1982, Nov. 19 *Perf. 11*
688 A256 10b grn & gray 20 15

Christmas. For surcharge see No. 702.

1983, Feb. 13 Litho. *Perf. 13½*
689 A257 50b multicolored 80 40

10th Youth Soccer Championship, Jan. 22-Feb. 13.

EXFIVIA '83 Philatelic Exhibition
A258

1983, Nov. 5 Litho. *Perf. 13½*
690 A258 150b brn car 1.00 50

Visit of Brazilian Pres. Joao Figueiredo, Feb.
A259

1984, Feb. 7 Litho. *Perf. 13½x14*
691 A259 150b multicolored 40 20

Simon Bolivar Entering La Paz, by Carmen Baptista
A260

Paintings of Bolivar: 50b, Riding Horse, by Mulato Gil de Quesada, vert.

Perf. 14x13½, 13½x14
1984, Mar. 30

692	A260	50b multi	15	15
693	A260	200b multi	55	22
		Set value		28

Types of 1957-79 Surcharged

1984, Mar.

694	A223	40b on 2.50b #641	15	15
695	A227	40b on 2.80b #645	15	15
696	A219	60b on 1.50b #632	18	15
697	A216	60b on 2.50b #627	18	15

698 A224 100b on 2b #642 30 15
699 A141 200b on 350b #409 60 25
Nos. 694-699 (6) 1.56
Set value 80

Nos. 675, 683-684, 688, C328 Surcharged

1984, June 27 Litho. *Perf. 11*

700 A252 500b on 3b #684 75 35
701 A245 1000b on 4b #675 1.50 75
702 A256 2000b on 10b #688 3.00 1.25
703 A251 5000b on 5b #683 7.50 3.00

Perf. 13½

704 A182 10,000b on 3.80b #C328 10.00 6.00
Nos. 700-704 (5) 22.75 11.35

Road Safety Education A261

Jose Eustaquio Mendez, 200th Birth Anniv. A262

Cartoons.

1984, Sept. 7 Litho. *Perf. 11*

705 A261 80b Jaywalker 15 15
706 A261 120b Motorcycle policeman, ambulance 15 15
Set value 15 15

Perf. 14x13½, 13½x14

1984, Sept. 19

Paintings: 300b, Birthplace, by Jorge Campos. 500b, Mendez Leading the Battle of La Tablada, by M. Villegas, horiz.

707 A262 300b multi 15 15
708 A262 500b multi 15 15
Set value 15

1983 World Cup Soccer Championships, Mexico — A263

Chasqui, Postal Runner — A264

Sponsoring shoe-manufacturers' trademarks and: 100b, 200b, Outline map of Bolivia, national colors. 600b, World map and soccer ball, horiz.

1984, Oct. 26 *Perf. 11*

709 A263 100b multi 15 15
710 A263 200b multi 15 15
711 A263 600b multi 15 15
Set value 25 16

1985

712 A264 11000b vio bl 25 15

Intl. Year of Professional Education A265

Intl. Anti-Polio Campaign A266

1985, Apr. 25

713 A265 2000b Natl. Manual Crafts emblem 15 15

For surcharges see Nos. 721-722.

1985, May 22

714 A266 20000b lt bl & vio 25 15

Endangered Wildlife — A267

1985, May 22

715 A267 23000b Altiplano boliviano 20 15
716 A267 25000b Sarcorhamphus gryphus 22 15
717 A267 30000b Blastocaros dichotomus 30 15
Nos. 715-717 (3) 72
Set value 30

Nos. 716-717 vert.

Dona Vicenta Juaristi Eguino (b. 1785), Independence Heroine — A268

UN, 40th Anniv. — A269

1985, Oct. Litho. *Perf. 13½*

718 A268 300000b multi 20 15

1985, Oct. 24 *Perf. 11*

719 A269 1000000b bl & gold 65 30

A270

A271

1985, Nov.

720 A270 200000b multi 15 15

Natl. Soccer Team, 75th anniv.

No. 713 Surcharged

1986 Litho. *Perf. 11*

721 A265 200000b on 2000b 22 15
722 A265 5000000b on 2000b 5.25 2.50

1986

723 A271 300000 Emblems, vert. 32 15
724 A271 550000 Pique trademark, vert. 58 24
725 A271 1000000 Azteca Stadium 1.05 50
726 A271 2500000 World cup, vert. 2.65 1.25
Nos. 723-726 (4) 4.60 2.14

1986 World Cup Soccer Championships.

Intl. Youth Year A272 A273

1986

727 A272 150000 brt car rose 16 15
728 A272 500000 bl grn 55 35
729 A273 3000000 multi 3.15 1.50
Nos. 727-729 (3) 3.86 2.00

Inscribed 1985.

Alfonso Sobieta Viaduct, Carretera Quillacollo, Confital — A274

1986 *Perf. 13½*

730 A274 400000 int bl & gray 42 20

Inter-American Development Bank, 25th anniv.

Admission of Bolivia to the UPU, Cent. — A275

Postal Workers Soc., 50th Anniv. — A276

1986, Apr. 3 *Perf. 11*

731 A275 800000 multi 85 40

1986, Sept. 5

732 A276 2000000 brn & pale brn 2.10 1.00

Founding of Trinidad, 300th Anniv. A277

1986, May 25 *Perf. 13½x14*

733 A277 1400000 Bull and Rider, by Vaca 1.50 75

Bolivian Philatelic Federation, 15th Anniv. A278

1986, Nov. 28

734 A278 600000b No. 19 62 30

Death of a Priest, by Jose Antonio Zampa — A279

Intl. Peace Year — A280

1986, Nov. 21 *Perf. 14x13½*

735 A279 400000b multi 42 20

1986, Sept. 16 *Perf. 11*

736 A280 200000 yel grn & pale grn 22 15

Natl. Oil Corp. (YPBF), 50th Anniv. — A281

1986, Dec. 22 Litho. *Perf. 11*

737 A281 1000000b multi 1.50 50

A282 A283

Photograph of a Devil-mask Dancer, by Jimenez Cordero.

1987, Feb. 13 Litho. *Perf. 14x13½*

738 A282 20c multi 30 15

February 10th Society, cent. (in 1985).

1987, Mar. 20 Litho. *Perf. 14x13½*

739 A283 30c Crossed flags 45 25

State Visit of Richard von Weizsacker, Pres. of Germany, Mar. 20.

State Visit of King Juan Carlos of Spain, May 20 — A284

1987, May 20 *Perf. 13½x14*

740 A284 60c Natl. arms 90 40

EXFIVIA '87 — A285

Mount Potosi, 18th cent. engraving.

1987, Oct. Litho. *Perf. 13½*

741 A285 50c multi 72 35

See No. 750.

Wildlife Conservation A286

1987, Oct.

742 A286 20c Condor 30 15
743 A286 20c Tapir 30 15
744 A286 30c Vicuna 45 25
745 A286 30c Armadillo 45 25
746 A286 40c Spectacled bears 58 30
747 A286 60c Toucans 88 40
Nos. 742-747 (6) 2.96 1.50

Wildlife in danger of extinction.

ESPAMER '87, La Coruna A287

1987, Oct. Litho. *Perf. 14x13½*

748 A287 20c Nina, stern of Santa Maria 30 15
749 A287 20c Bow of Santa Maria, Pinta 30 15
a. Pair, #748-749 60 25

No. 749a has a continuous design.

EXFIVIA Type of 1987

Design: Photograph of Mt. Potosi by Jimenez Cordero.

1987, Aug. 5 Litho. *Perf. 13½*

750 A285 40c multi 58 30

Musical Instruments A288

1987, Dec. 3 *Perf. 13½x14, 14x13½*

751 A288 50c Zampona and quena (wind instruments) 72 35
752 A288 1b Charango, vert. 1.45 70

A289

State Visit of Pope John Paul II A290

Pontiff, religious architecture and art: No. 753, Cathedral of Kings, Beni. No. 754, Carabuco Church. No. 755, Tihuanacu Church. No. 756, St. Francis's Church, Sucre. No. 757, St. Joseph's of Chiquitos Church. 40c, Cobija Chapel, vert. No. 759, Jayu Kcota Church. No. 760, Cochabamba Cathedral, vert. 60c, St. Francis's Basilica, La Paz, vert. No. 762, Christ of Machaca Church. No. 763, St. Lawrence's Church, Potosi, vert. No. 764, *The Holy Family*, by Rubens, vert. No. 765, *The Virgin of Copacabana*, statue, vert. No. 766, Vallegrande Church. No. 767, Tarija Cathedral, vert. No. 768, Concepcion Church.

1988 Litho. *Perf. 13½x14, 14x13½*

753 A289 20c multi 25 15
754 A289 20c multi 25 15
755 A289 20c multi 25 15
756 A289 30c multi 38 20
757 A289 30c multi 38 20
758 A289 40c multi 50 25
759 A289 50c multi 65 30
760 A289 50c multi 65 30
761 A289 60c multi 75 35
762 A289 70c multi 90 35
763 A289 70c multi 90 35
764 A289 80c multi 1.00 45
765 A289 80c multi 1.00 45
766 A289 80c multi 1.00 45
767 A289 1.30b multi 1.65 75
768 A289 1.30b multi 1.65 75
769 A290 1.50b shown 1.90 90
Nos. 753-769 (17) 14.06 6.50

Issue dates; 1.50b, May 9. Others, Mar. 3.

Visit of Pres. Jose Sarney of Brazil A291

1988, Aug. 2 Litho. *Perf. 13½x14*

770 A291 50c multi 60 30

St. John Bosco (1815-1888) — A292

1988, Aug. 16 *Perf. 13½*

771 A292 30c multi 42 20

Bolivian Railways, Cent. — A293

Design: 1b, Steam locomotive from the La Paz-Beni line, made by Marca Shy Ohio, Natl. Railway Museum, Sucre.

1988, Aug. 29

772 A293 1b multi 1.20 60

Nataniel Aguirre (b. 1888), Author — A294

Department of Pando, 50th Anniv. — A295

1988, Sept. 14 Litho. *Perf. 13½*

773 A294 1b blk & beige 1.20 60

1988, Sept. 26 *Perf. 13½*

Designs: 40c, *Columna Porvenir*, memorial to the Battle of Bahio. 60c, Siringuero rubber production (worker sapping latex from *Hevea brasiliensis*).

774 A295 40c multi 48 25
775 A295 60c multi 72 35

A296

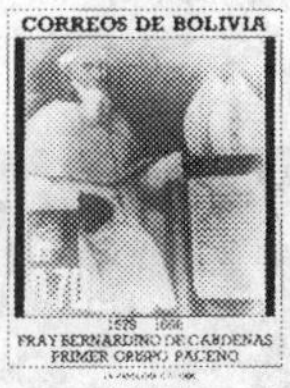

A297

1988, Sept. 27

776 A296 1.50b multi 1.85 90

1988 Summer Olympics, Seoul.

1988

Designs: 70c, Archbishop Bernardino de Cardenas (1579-1668). 80c, Mother Rosa Gattorno (1831-1900), founder of the Sisters of Santa Ana.

777 A297 70c multi 90 45
778 A297 80c multi 1.05 50

Issue dates: 70c, Oct. 20, 80c, Oct. 14.

Ministry of Transportation & Communications A298

1988, Oct. 24 Litho. *Perf. 14x13½*

779 A298 2b deep car, blk & pale olive grn 2.35 1.00

Army Communications, 50th Anniv. (in 1987) — A299

1988, Nov. 29 Litho. *Perf. 13½*

780 A299 70c multi 95 45

Bolivian Automobile Club, 50th Anniv. — A300

1988, Dec. 29 Litho. *Perf. 13½*

781 A300 1.50b multi 1.45 70

Flowering Plants and Emblems A301

Designs: 50c, Orchid, BULGARIA '89 emblem, vert. 60c, Kantuta blossoms, ITALIA '90 emblem. 70c, *Heliconia humilis*, Albertville '86 emblem, vert. 1b, Hoffmanseggia, Barcelona '92 Games emblem, vert. 2b, Puya raymondi, Seoul '88 Games and five-ring emblems, vert.

1989, Feb. 17 Litho. *Perf. 13½*

782 A301 50c multi 58 24
783 A301 60c multi 70 28
784 A301 70c multi 80 32
785 A301 1b multi 1.15 45
786 A301 2b multi 2.30 92
Nos. 782-786 (5) 5.53 2.21

Radio FIDES, 50th Anniv. — A302

1989, Feb. 2

787 A302 80c multi 92 38

Gold Quarto of 1852 A303

1989, Feb. 9 *Perf. 13½x14*

788 A303 1b multi 1.20 48

French Revolution, Bicent. — A304

1989, June 23 Litho. *Perf. 14x13½*

789 A304 70c red, blk & blue 90 35

Uyuni Township, Cent. — A305

1989, July 9 Litho. *Perf. 14x13½*

790 A305 30c blue, black & gray 38 15

Noel Kempff Mercado Natl. Park, Santa Cruz — A306

Designs: 1.50b, Federico Ahlfeld Falls, Pauserna River. 3b, *Ozotoceros bezcarticus* (deer).

1989, Sept. 24 Litho. *Perf. 13½x14*

791 A306 1.50b multicolored 1.70 68
792 A306 3b multicolored 3.40 1.35

UPAEP — A306a

1989, Oct. 12 Litho. *Perf. 13½*

792A A306a 50c Metalworking 52 20
792B A306a 1b Temple of Kalasasaya 1.05 42

See Nos. 808-809

State Visit by Dr. Carlos Andres Perez, Pres. of Venezuela A306b

1989, Oct. 14

792C A306b 2b multi 2.05 82

See Nos. 825-826, 832.

City of Potosi — A306c

1989, Nov. 10 Litho. *Perf. 13½*

792D	A306c 60c Cobija Arch	75	30
792E	A306c 80c Mint	85	40
f.	Pair, #792D-792E	1.60	70

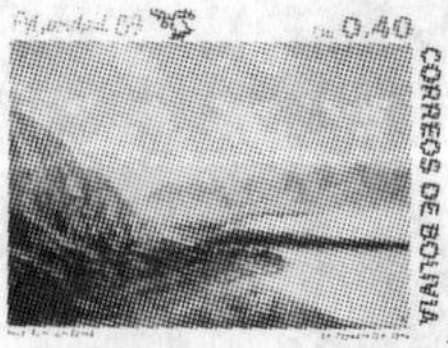

Christmas A307

Paintings: 40c, *Andean Stillwaters*, by Arturo Borda. 60c, *The Virgin of the Roses*, anonymous. 80c, *The Conquistador*, by Jorge de la Reza. 1b, *Native Harmony*, by Juan Rimsa. 1.50b, *Woman with Jug*, by Cecilio Guzman de Rojas. 2b, *Bloom of Tenderness*, by Gil Imana. Nos. 794-798 vert.

Perf. 13½x14, 14x13½

1989, Dec. 18

793	A307 40c multicolored	42	17
794	A307 60c multicolored	62	25
795	A307 80c multicolored	82	32
796	A307 1b multicolored	1.05	42
797	A307 1.50b multicolored	1.55	62
798	A307 2b multicolored	2.05	82
	Nos. 793-798 (6)	6.51	2.60

A308 A309

1990, Jan. 23 Litho. *Perf. 13½*

799	A308 80c multicolored	85	35

Fight against drug abuse.

1990, May 13 *Perf. 14x13½*

Design: Great Britain No. 1, Sir Rowland Hill and Bolivia No. 1

800	A309 4b multicolored	4.10	1.70

Penny Black, 150th anniv.

World Cup Soccer Championships, Italy — A310

1990, June 16 *Perf. 13½*

801	A310 2b Stadium, Milan	2.00	80
802	A310 6b Game	6.00	2.40

Organization of American States, Cent. — A311

1990, Apr. 14

803	A311 80c dark bl & brt bl	82	32

A312 A313

1990, Apr. 16

804	A312 1.20b multi	1.22	62

1990 Litho. *Perf. 14x13½*

805	A313 70c Telecommunications	72	55

National Chamber of Commerce, Cent. — A314

1990, June

806	A314 50c gold, blk & bl	58	42

Cochabamba Social Club, Cent. — A315

1990, Sept. 14 Litho. *Perf. 13½*

807	A315 40c multicolored	42	32

UPAEP Type of 1989

Perf. 13½x14, 14x13½

1990, Oct. 12 Litho.

808	A306a 80c Huts	75	30
809	A306a 1b Mountains, lake, vert.	95	38

A317 A318

1990, Oct. 19 *Perf. 14x13½*

810	A317 1.20b multicolored	1.05	42

Magistrate's District of Larecaja, 400th Anniv.

1990, Oct. 12 *Perf. 14x13½*

811	A318 2b multicolored	1.75	70

Discovery of America, 500th anniv. (in 1992).

German Reunification A319

1990, Nov. 19 Litho. *Perf. 14x13½*

812	A319 2b multicolored	1.70	70

Visit of Carlos Salinas de Gortari, Pres. of Mexico — A320

Design: 80c, Visit of Rodrigo Borja Cevallos, Pres. of Ecuador.

1990, Dec. 13 Litho. *Perf. 13½*

813	A320 60c multicolored	75	30
814	A320 80c multicolored	85	40

4th Congress of the Andean Presidents A321

1990, Nov. 29 *Perf. 13½x14*

815	A321 1.50b multicolored	1.35	55

Exfivia '90 A322

Christmas A323

1990, Dec. 9 *Perf. 13½*

816	A322 40c dk blue	40	15

1990, Nov. 20 *Perf. 11*

817	A323 50c multicolored	45	18

Express Mail Service A324

1990, Dec. 14 *Perf. 13½x14*

818	A324 1b multicolored	90	35

Bolivian Radio Club, 50th Anniv. — A325

1991, Mar. 1 Litho. *Perf. 14x13½*

819	A325 2.40b multicolored	2.00	80

End of Chaco War, 56th Anniv. — A326

National Museums — A327

Map of Heroes of Chaco Highway.

1991, June 14 Litho. *Perf. 14x13½*

820	A326 60c multicolored	55	22

1991, June 13 *Perf. 13½*

821	A327 50c Archaeology	42	18
822	A327 50c Art	42	18
823	A327 1b Ethnology, Folklore	85	35
a.	Strip of 3, #821-823	1.70	70

Espamer '91.

A328 A329

Our Lady of Peace, Metropolitan Cathedral.

1991, July 15 Litho. *Perf. 14x13½*

824	A328 1.20b multicolored	1.15	45

Presidential State Visit Type of 1989

Jaime Paz Zamora, Pres. of Bolivia and: No. 825, Dr. Carlos Saul Menem, Pres. of Argentina. No. 826, Dr. Luis Alberto Lacalle, Pres. of Uruguay.

1991 *Perf. 13½x14*

825	A306b 1b multicolored	85	35
826	A306b 1b multicolored	85	35

Issue dates: #825, Aug. 5; #826, Aug. 12.

1991, May 31 *Perf. 13½*

Tremarctos ornatus.

827	A329 30c Adult, 2 cubs	28	15
828	A329 30c Adult's head	28	15
829	A329 30c Adult on tree limb	28	15
830	A329 30c Adult, cubs on tree limb	28	15
	Nos. 827-830 (4)	1.12	60

World Wildlife Fund.

A330 A331

1991, Aug. 21 Litho. *Perf. 14x13½*

831	A330 70c multicolored	68	28

Bolivian Philatelic Federation, 20th anniv.

Presidential State Visit Type of 1989

Design: 50c, Jaime Paz Zamora, Pres. of Bolivia and Alberto Fujimori, Pres. of Peru.

1991, Aug. 29 *Perf. 13½x14*

832 A306b 50c multicolored 45 18

1991, Nov. 19 Litho. *Perf. 14x13½*

833 A331 50c multicolored 45 18

National census.

America Issue — A332

UPAEP emblem and: 60c, First Discovery of Chuquiago, 1535, by Arturo Reque M. 1.20c, Founding of the City of La Paz, 1548, by J. Rimsa, vert.

Perf. 13½x14, 14x13½

1991, Oct. 12

834 A332 60c multicolored 58 25
835 A332 1.20b multicolored 1.15 45

First National Grand Prix Auto and Motorcycle Race — A332a

1991, Sept. 5 Litho. *Perf. 14x13½*

835A A332a 50c multicolored 45 18

ECOBOL, Postal Security System A333

1991, Sept. 9 *Perf. 13½x14*

836 A333 1.40b multicolored 1.35 52

Simon Bolivar — A334

1992, Feb. 15 Litho. *Perf. 13½*

837 A334 1.20b buff, brn & org brn 1.15 45

Exfilbo '92.

Scouting in Bolivia, 75th Anniv. (in 1990) and 1992 Andes Jamboree A335

1992, Jan. 13 *Perf. 13½x14*

838 A335 1.20b multicolored 1.15 45

Dated 1991.

Christmas A336

Paintings: 2b, Landscape, by Daniel Pena y Sarmiento. 5b, Woman with Fruit, by Cecilio Guzman de Rojas. 15b, Native Mother, by Crespo Gastelu.

1991, Dec.19 Litho. *Perf. 13½*

839 A336 2b multicolored 1.50 60
840 A336 5b multicolored 3.75 1.50
841 A336 15b multicolored 11.20 4.50
Nos. 839-841 (3) 16.45 6.60

Pacific Ocean Access Pact Between Bolivia and Peru A337

Designs: 1.20b, Pres. Zamora raising flag, vert. 1.50b, Pres. Jaime Paz Zamora of Bolivia and Pres. Alberto Fujimori, Peru. 1.80b, Shoreline of access zone near Ilo, Peru.

Perf. 14x13½, 13½x14

1992, Mar. 23

842 A337 1.20b multicolored 95 40
843 A337 1.50b multicolored 1.15 48
844 A337 1.80b multicolored 1.40 55
Nos. 842-844 (3) 3.50 1.43

Expo '92, Seville A338

1992, Apr. 15 *Perf. 13½x14*

845 A338 30c multicolored 28 15
846 A338 50c Columbus' ships 45 18

Miraflores Rotary Club, District 4690, Mt. Illimani — A339

1992, Apr. 30 Litho. *Perf. 13½*

847 A339 90c multicolored 70 45

Prof. Elizardo Perez, Founder of Ayllu of Warisata School, Birth Cent. — A340

1992, June 6 Litho. *Perf. 13½*

848 A340 60c multicolored 52 22

Government Palace, Sucre A341

1992, July 10 Litho. *Perf. 13½x14*

849 A341 50c multicolored 42 16

A342

A343

1992, Sept. 11 *Perf. 14x13½*

850 A342 50c multicolored 42 16

Los Tiempos Newpaper, 25th anniv.

1992, Aug. 9 *Perf. 13½*

Design: 1.50b, Mario Martinez Guzman, tennis player.

851 A343 1.50b multicolored 1.15 48

1992 Summer Olympics, Barcelona.

First Intl. Whitewater Canoe Regatta, Bermejo River — A343a

1992, Sept. 17 Litho. *Perf. 13½*

851A A343a 1.20b multicolored 1.10 48

1994 World Cup Soccer Championships, US — A344

1992, Oct. 2 Litho. *Perf. 13½*

852 A344 1.20b multicolored 1.85 75

Oruro Technical University, Cent. — A345

1992, Oct. 15 *Perf. 13½x14*

853 A345 50c multicolored 38 15

Interamerican Institute for Agricultural Cooperation, 50th Anniv. — A346

1992, Oct. 7 *Perf. 13½*

854 A346 1.20b Chenopodium quinoa 1.15 48

Discovery of America, 500th Anniv. A347

Paintings: 60c, Columbus departing from Palos, vert. 2b, Columbus with Caribbean natives.

1992, Oct. 1 *Perf. 14x13½, 13½x14*

855 A347 60c multicolored 42 18
856 A347 2b multicolored 1.40 58

Battle of Ingavi, 150th Anniv. (in 1991) A348

1992, Nov. 18 Litho. *Perf. 13½x14*

857 A348 1.20b sepia & black 95 38

12th Bolivian Games, Cochabamba and Santa Cruz — A349

1992, Nov. 13

858 A349 2b multicolored 1.50 60

Fauna, Events — A350

Event emblem and fauna: 20c, Beni Dept., sesquicentennial, caiman. 50c, Polska '93, paca. 1b, Bangkok '93, chinchilla. 2b, 1994 Winter Olympics, Lillehammer, Norway, anteater. 3b, Brandenburg Gate, jaguar. 4b, Brasiliana '93, hummingbird, vert. 5b, 1994 World Cup Soccer Championships, US, piranhas.

1992, Nov. 18 Litho. *Perf. 13½*

859 A350 20c multicolored 15 15
860 A350 50c multicolored 35 15
861 A350 1b multicolored 75 30
862 A350 2b multicolored 1.50 60
863 A350 3b multicolored 2.25 90
864 A350 4b multicolored 3.00 1.25
865 A350 5b multicolored 3.75 1.50
Nos. 859-865 (7) 11.75 4.85

Christmas A350a

Designs: 1.20b, Man in canoe, star. 2.50b, Star over churches. 6b, Flowers, church, infant on hay.

1992, Dec. 1 Litho. *Perf. 13½*

865A A350a 1.20b multicolored 90 35
865B A350a 2.50b multicolored 1.90 75
865C A350a 6b multicolored 4.50 1.75
Nos. 865A-865C (3) 7.30 2.85

A351

A352

Nicolaus Copernicus (1473-1543), Polish Astronomer: 50c, Santa Ana Intl. astrometrical observatory, Tarija, horiz.

Perf. 13x13½, 13½x13

1993, Feb. 18 **Litho.**

866 A351 50c multicolored	38	15
867 A351 2b black	1.50	60

1993, Apr. 14 **Litho.** *Perf. 13½*

868 A352 60c multicolored	58	24

Beatification of Mother Nazaria.

12th Bolivar Games A353

1993, Apr. 24 *Perf. 13½x14*

869 A353 2.30b multicolored	1.65	65

Bolivia #C240, Brazil #3 — A354

1993, May 31

870 A354 2.30b multicolored	1.65	65

First Brazilian Stamp, 150th anniv.

A355 A356

Eternal Father, by Gaspar de la Cueva.

1993, June 9 **Litho.** *Perf. 13½*

871 A355 1.80b multicolored	1.30	52

1993, July 31 **Litho.** *Perf. 14x13½*

872 A356 50c Virgin of Urkupina	35	15

City of Quillacollo, 400th anniv.

Pedro Domingo Murillo Industrial School — A357

1993 *Perf. 13½*

873 A357 60c multicolored	42	16

Butterflies A358

1993, June 4 *Perf. 13½x14*

874 A358 60c Archaeoprepona demophon	40	16
875 A358 60c Morpho sp.	40	16
876 A358 80c Papilio sp.	55	22
877 A358 80c Historis odius	55	22
878 A358 80c Euptoieta hegesia	55	22
879 A358 1.80b Morpho deidamia	1.25	48
880 A358 1.80b Papilio thoas	1.25	48
881 A358 1.80b Danaus plexippus	1.25	48
882 A358 2.30b Caligo sp.	1.50	60
883 A358 2.30b Anaea marthesia	1.50	60
884 A358 2.30b Rothschildia sp.	1.50	60
885 A358 2.70b Heliconius sp.	1.75	75
886 A358 2.70b Marpesia corinna	1.75	75
887 A358 2.70b Prepona chromus	1.75	75
888 A358 3.50b Heliconius sp., diff.	2.25	95
889 A358 3.50b Siproeta epaphus	2.25	95
a. Sheet of 16, #874-889	20.50	20.50
Nos. 874-889 (16)	20.45	8.37

Pan-American Health Organization, 90th Anniv. — A359

1993, Oct. 13 **Litho.** *Perf. 13½*

890 A359 80c multicolored	52	20

Archaeological Finds — A360

Location of cave paintings: No. 891, Oruro. No. 892, Santa Cruz, vert. No. 893, Beni, vert. No. 894, Chuquisaca, vert. No. 895, Chuquisaca. No. 896, Potosi. No. 897, La Paz, vert. No. 898, Tarija, vert. No. 899, Cochabamba.

1993, Sept. 28

891 A360 80c multicolored	52	20
892 A360 80c multicolored	52	20
893 A360 80c multicolored	52	20
894 A360 80c multicolored	52	20
895 A360 80c multicolored	52	20
896 A360 80c multicolored	52	20
897 A360 80c multicolored	52	20
898 A360 80c multicolored	52	20
899 A360 80c multicolored	52	20
Nos. 891-899 (9)	4.68	1.80

America Issue — A361

1993, Oct. 9 **Litho.** *Perf. 13½*

900 A361 80c Saimiri sciereus	52	20
901 A361 2.30b Felis pordalis	1.50	60

Famous People — A361a

Christmas — A361b

Designs: 50c, Yolanda Bedregal, poet. 70c, Simon Martinic, President of Cochabamba Philatelic Center. 90c, Eugenio von Boeck, politician, President of Bolivian Philatelic Federation. 1b, Marina Nunez del Prado, sculptor.

1993, Nov. 17 **Litho.** *Perf. 11*

901A A361a 50c sepia	32	15
901B A361a 70c sepia	45	18
901C A361a 90c sepia	55	22
901D A361a 1b sepia	60	25
Nos. 901A-901D (4)	1.92	80

1993, Dec. 8 *Perf. 14x13½*

Paintings: 2.30b, Adoration of the Shepherds, by Leonardo Flores. 3.50b, Virgin with Child and Saints, by unknown artist. 6b, Virgin of the Milk, by Melchor Perez de Holguin.

901E A361b 2.30b multicolored	1.40	55
901F A361b 3.50b multicolored	2.25	85
901G A361b 6b multicolored	3.75	1.50
Nos. 901E-901G (3)	7.40	2.90

Town of Riberalta, Cent. — A362

1994, Feb. 3 **Litho.** *Perf. 13½*

902 A362 2b multicolored	1.25	60

World Population Day A363

1994, Feb. 17 **Litho.** *Perf. 13½*

903 A363 2.30b multicolored	1.50	60

A364 A365

1994, Feb. 21 *Perf. 13½*

904 A364 2b buff & multi	1.25	60
905 A364 2.30b multi	1.50	60

Inauguration of Pres. Gonzalo Sanchez de Lozada.

1994, Mar. 22

1994 World Cup Soccer Championships, US: 80c, Mascot. 1.80b, Bolivia, Uruguay. 2.30b, Bolivia, Venezuela. No. 909, Part of Bolivian team, goalies in black. No. 910, Part of Bolivian team, diff. 2.70b, Bolivia, Ecuador. 3.50b, Bolivia, Brazil.

906 A365 80c multicolored	48	20
907 A365 1.80b multicolored	1.10	45
908 A365 2.30b multicolored	1.40	55
909 A365 2.50b multicolored	1.50	60
910 A365 2.50b multicolored	1.50	60
a. Pair, #909-910	3.00	1.25
911 A365 2.70b multicolored	1.65	65
912 A365 3.50b multicolored	2.25	85
Nos. 906-912 (7)	9.88	3.90

SOS Children's Village, Bolivia — A366

1994, Apr. 12 **Litho.** *Perf. 13½*

913 A366 2.70b multicolored	1.65	65

Catholic Archdiocese La Paz, 50th Anniv. — A367

Churches, priests: 1.80b, Church of San Pedro, Msgr. Jorge Manrique Hurtado. 2b, Archbishop Abel I. Antezana y Rojas, Church of the Sacred Heart of Mary, vert. 3.50b, Msgr. Luis Sainz Hinojosa, Church of Santo Domingo, vert.

1994, July 12 **Litho.** *Perf. 13½*

914 A367 1.80b multicolored	1.10	45
915 A367 2b multicolored	1.25	60
916 A367 3.50b multicolored	2.25	85
Nos. 914-916 (3)	4.60	1.90

A368 A369

1994 **Litho.** *Perf. 13½*

Design: 2b, Pres. Victor Paz Estenssoro.

917 A368 2b multicolored	1.25	50

1994, Oct. 9

918 A369 1.80b No. 46	1.10	45

Battle of Ft. Boqueron A370

Design: 80c, Col. Manuel Marzana Oroza, battle scene.

1994, Oct. 6

919 A370 80c multicolored	50	20

San Borja, 300th Anniv. — A371

1994

920 A371 1.60b Erythrina fusca	1.00	40

America Issue — A372

Old, new methods of postal transport: 1b, Streetcar, van. 5b, Airplane, ox cart.

1994, Oct. 12

921 A372 1b multicolored	65	25
922 A372 5b multicolored	3.25	1.25

1994 Solar Eclipse — A373

Environmental Protection — A374

1994

923	A373	3.50b multicolored	2.25	85

1994

Trees: 60c, Buddleja coriacea. 1.80b, Bertholletia exelsa. 2b, Schinus molle, horiz. 2.70b, Polylepis racemosa. 3, Tabebuia chrysantha. 3.50b, Erythrina falcata, horiz.

924	A374	60c multicolored	38	15
925	A374	1.80b multicolored	1.10	45
926	A374	2b multicolored	1.25	50
927	A374	2.70b multicolored	1.65	65
928	A374	3b multicolored	1.90	75
929	A374	3.50b multicolored	2.25	85
		Nos. 924-929 (6)	8.53	3.35

AIR POST STAMPS

Aviation School
AP1 AP2

1924, Dec. Unwmk. Engr. *Perf. 14*

C1	AP1	10c ver & blk	20	25
a.		Inverted center	800.00	
C2	AP1	15c carmine & blk	1.25	40
C3	AP1	25c dk bl & blk	50	50
C4	AP1	50c orange & blk	1.25	1.00
C5	AP2	1b red brn & blk	80	80
C6	AP2	2b blk brn & blk	1.50	1.50
C7	AP2	5b dk vio & blk	4.50	4.50
		Nos. C1-C7 (7)	10.00	8.95

Natl. Aviation School establishment.

These stamps were available for ordinary postage.

Nos. C1, C3, C5 and C6 exist imperforate. Proofs of the 2b with inverted center exist imperforate and privately perforated.

For overprints and surcharges see Nos. C11-C23, C56-C58.

Emblem of Lloyd Aéreo Boliviano — AP3

1928 Litho. *Perf. 11*

C8	AP3	15c green	80	80
a.		Imperf., pair	50.00	
C9	AP3	20c dark blue	20	20
C10	AP3	35c red brown	50	50
		Nos. C8-C10 (3)	1.50	1.50

No. C8 exists imperf. between.

For surcharges see #C24-C26, C53-C55.

Graf Zeppelin Issues

Nos. C1-C5 Surcharged or Overprinted in Various Colors:

CORREO AEREO

R. S. 6-V-1930

5 Cts.

Nos. C11, C19

CORREO AEREO

R. S.

6-V- 1930

Nos. C12-C18, C20-C23

1930, May 6 *Perf. 14*

C11	AP1	5c on 10c ver & blk (G)	8.00	8.00
C12	AP1	10c ver & blk (Bl)	8.00	8.00
C13	AP1	10c ver & blk (Br)	500.00	700.00
C14	AP1	15c car & blk (V)	8.00	8.00
C15	AP1	25c dk bl & blk (R)	8.00	8.00
C16	AP1	50c org & blk (Br)	8.00	8.00
C17	AP1	50c org & blk (R)	400.00	550.00
C18	AP2	1b red brn & blk (gold)	110.00	100.00

Experts consider the 50c with gold or silver overprint and 5c with black to be a trial color proofs.

Nos. C11-C18 exist with the surcharges inverted, double, or double with one inverted, but the regularity of these varieties is questioned.

See notes following No. C23.

Surcharged or Overprinted in Bronze Inks of Various Colors

C19	AP1	5c on 10c ver & blk (G)	65.00	65.00
C20	AP1	10c ver & blk (Bl)	55.00	55.00
C21	AP1	15c car & blk (V)	65.00	65.00
C22	AP1	25c dk bl & blk (cop)	65.00	65.00
C23	AP2	1b red brn & blk (gold)	140.00	140.00
		Nos. C19-C23 (5)	390.00	390.00

Flight of the airship Graf Zeppelin from Europe to Brazil and return via Lakehurst, NJ.

Nos. C19 to C23 were intended for use on postal matter forwarded by the Graf Zeppelin.

No. C18 was overprinted with light gold or gilt bronze ink. No. C23 was overprinted with deep gold bronze ink. Nos. C13 and C17 were overprinted with trial colors but were sold with the regular printings. The 5c on 10c is known surcharged in black and in blue.

No. C8-C10 Surcharged

Z 1930

Bs. 3.—

1930, May 6 *Perf. 11*

C24	AP3	1.50b on 15c	20.00	20.00
a.		Inverted surcharge	45.00	45.00
b.		Comma instead of period after "1"	27.50	27.50
C25	AP3	3b on 20c	20.00	20.00
a.		Inverted surcharge	50.00	50.00
b.		Comma instead of period after "3"	32.50	32.50
C26	AP3	6b on 35c	30.00	32.50
a.		Inverted surcharge	90.00	90.00
b.		Comma instead of period after "6"	50.00	50.00
		Nos. C24-C26 (3)	70.00	72.50

Airplane and Bullock Cart — AP6

Airplane and River Boat — AP7

1930, July 24 Litho. *Perf. 14*

C27	AP6	5c dp violet	1.25	1.00
C28	AP7	15c red	1.25	1.00
C29	AP7	20c yellow	50	50
C30	AP6	35c yellow grn	40	25
C31	AP7	50c deep blue	40	25
C32	AP6	1b lt brown	40	25
C33	AP7	2b deep rose	40	40
C34	AP6	3b slate	1.40	1.40
		Nos. C27-C34 (8)	6.00	5.05

Nos. C27 to C34 exist imperforate.

For surcharge see No. C52.

Air Service Emblem AP8

1932, Sept. 16 *Perf. 11*

C35	AP8	5c ultra	65	50
C36	AP8	10c gray	40	30
C37	AP8	15c dark rose	65	50
C38	AP8	25c orange	65	50
C39	AP8	30c green	55	25
C40	AP8	50c violet	55	30
C41	AP8	1b dk brown	55	30
		Nos. C35-C41 (7)	4.00	2.65

Map of Bolivia — AP9

1935, Feb. 1 Engr. *Perf. 12*

C42	AP9	5c brown red	15	15
C43	AP9	10c dk green	15	15
C44	AP9	20c dk violet	15	15
C45	AP9	30c ultra	20	15
C46	AP9	50c orange	25	15
C47	AP9	1b bister brn	25	20
C48	AP9	1½b yellow	55	15
C49	AP9	2b carmine	55	25
C50	AP9	5b green	1.00	35
C51	AP9	10b dk brown	1.60	65
		Nos. C42-C51 (10)	4.85	2.35

Nos. C1, C4, C10, C30 Surcharged in Red (#C52-C56) or Green (#C57-C58) — c

Correo Aéreo
D. S. 25-2-37
0.05

1937, Oct. 6 *Perf. 11, 14*

C52	AP6	5c on 35c yel grn	30	25
a.		"Carreo"	12.50	
b.		Inverted surcharge		
C53	AP3	20c on 35c red brn	40	30
a.		Inverted surcharge		
C54	AP3	50c on 35c red brn	1.10	90
a.		Inverted surcharge	17.50	
C55	AP3	1b on 35c red brn	90	50
a.		Inverted surcharge		
C56	AP1	2b on 50c org & blk	1.25	75
a.		Inverted surcharge		
C57	AP1	12b on 10c ver & blk	4.50	3.50
a.		Inverted surcharge	22.50	
C58	AP1	15b on 10c ver & blk	4.50	2.00
a.		Inverted surcharge		

Regular Postage Stamps of 1925 Surcharged in Green or Red — d

Correo
Aéreo
D. S.
25-2-37
Bs. 4.—

C59	A56 (d)	3b on 50c dp vio (G)	90	75
C60	A56 (d)	4b on 1b red (G)	1.10	1.00
C61	A57 (c)	5b on 2b org (G)	1.40	1.25
a.		Double surcharge	90.00	
C62	A56 (d)	10b on 5b blk brn	3.50	2.50
a.		Double surcharge	35.00	
		Nos. C52-C62 (11)	19.85	13.70

No. C59-C62 exist with inverted surcharge, No. C62 with black and black and red surcharges.

Courtyard of Potosi Mint — AP10

Miner — AP11

Emancipated Woman — AP12

Pincers, Torch and Good Will Principles — AP15

Airplane over Field — AP13

Airplanes and Liberty Monument AP14

Airplane over River — AP16

Emblem of New Government AP17

Transport Planes over Map of Bolivia AP18

1938, May Litho. *Perf. 10½*

C63	AP10	20c deep rose	20	20
C64	AP11	30c gray	20	20
C65	AP12	40c yellow	20	20
C66	AP13	50c yellow grn	40	20
C67	AP14	60c dull blue	40	20
C68	AP15	1b dull red	60	20
C69	AP16	2b bister	1.00	20
C70	AP17	3b lt brown	1.00	20
C71	AP18	5b dk violet	1.50	20
		Nos. C63-C71 (9)	5.50	1.80

40c, 1b, 2b exist imperf.

Chalice — AP19

Virgin of Copacabana AP20

Jesus Christ AP21

Church of San Francisco, La Paz — AP22

St. Anthony of Padua — AP23

Perf. 13½, 10½

1939, July 19 **Litho.**

C72 AP19	5c dull violet	35	35
a.	Pair, imperf. between	30.00	
C73 AP20	30c lt bl grn	30	20
C74 AP21	45c violet bl	60	20
a.	Vertical pair, imperf. between	42.50	
C75 AP22	60c carmine	40	35
C76 AP23	75c vermilion	65	60
C77 AP23	90c deep blue	45	25
C78 AP22	2b dull brown	75	25
C79 AP21	4b deep plum	1.00	40
C80 AP20	5b lt blue	2.50	25
C81 AP19	10b yellow	5.00	25
	Nos. C72-C81 (10)	12.00	3.10

2nd National Eucharistic Congress.
For surcharge see No. C112.

Plane over Lake Titicaca — AP24

Mt. Illimani and Condor — AP25

1941, Aug. 21 *Perf. 13½*

C82 AP24	10b dull green	3.25	38
C83 AP24	20b light ultra	3.75	65
C84 AP25	50b rose lilac	6.50	1.00
C85 AP25	100b olive bister	16.00	6.00
	Nos. C82-C85 (4)	29.50	8.03

Counterfeits exist.

Liberty and Clasped Hands — AP26

1942, Nov. 12

C86 AP26	40c rose lake	25	25
C87 AP26	50c ultra	25	25
C88 AP26	1b orange brn	1.25	75
C89 AP26	5b magenta	75	25
a.	Double impression		
C90 AP26	10b dull brn vio	2.50	1.25
	Nos. C86-C90 (5)	5.00	2.75

Conference of Chancellors, Jan. 15, 1942.

General José Ballivián; Old and Modern Transportation — AP27

1943, Nov. 18 **Engr.** *Perf. 12½*

C91 AP27	10c rose vio & brn	15	15
C92 AP27	20c emerald & brn	15	15
C93 AP27	30c rose car & brn	18	15
C94 AP27	3b blue & brn	22	18
C95 AP27	5b black & brn	40	30
	Nos. C91-C95 (5)	1.10	93

Department of Beni centenary.

Condor and Sun Rising — AP28

Plane — AP29

1944, Sept. 19 **Litho.** *Perf. 13½*

C96 AP28	40c red violet	15	15
C97 AP28	1b blue violet	15	15
C98 AP29	1.50b yellow green	18	15
C99 AP29	2.50b dk gray blue	38	18
	Nos. C96-C99 (4)	86	
	Set value		42

Revolution of Dec. 20, 1943.

Map of Natl. Airways — AP30

Map of Bolivian Air Lines — AP31

1945, May 31 *Perf. 11*

C100 AP30	10c red	15	15
a.	Imperf., pair	9.00	
C101 AP30	50c yellow	15	15
a.	Imperf., pair	27.50	
C102 AP30	90c lt green	20	15
a.	Imperf., pair	30.00	
C103 AP30	5b lt ultra	35	15
C104 AP30	20b deep brown	1.00	45
	Nos. C100-C104 (5)	1.85	
	Set value		84

10th anniversary of first flight, La Paz to Tacha, Peru, by Panagra Airways.
For surcharges see Nos. C128-C129.

1945, Sept. 15 *Perf. 13½*

Centers in Red and Blue

C105 AP31	20c violet	15	15
C106 AP31	30c orange brn	15	15
C107 AP31	50c brt blue grn	15	15
C108 AP31	90c brt violet	15	15
C109 AP31	2b blue	15	15
C110 AP31	3b magenta	20	15
C111 AP31	4b olive bister	35	16
	Set value	1.00	68

20th anniv. of the founding of Lloyd Aéreo Boliviano.

Catalogue values for unused stamps in this section, from this point to the end of the section, are for Never Hinged items.

No. C76 Surcharged in Blue

1947, Mar. 23

C112 AP23	1.40b on 75c ver	18	18

Mt. Illimani — AP32

Arms of Bolivia and Argentina — AP33

1947, Sept. 15 **Litho.** *Perf. 11½*

C113 AP32	1b rose car	15	15
C114 AP32	1.40b emerald	15	15
C115 AP32	2.50b blue	15	15
C116 AP32	3b dp orange	18	15
C117 AP32	4b rose lilac	20	15
	Set value	64	46

1st anniv. of the Revolution of July 21, 1946. 1.40b, 2.50b exist imperf.
For surcharge see No. C137.

1947, Oct. 23 *Perf. 13½*

C118 AP33	2.90b ultra	25	25
a.	Imperf., pair	20.00	
b.	Perf. 10½	5.00	4.00

Meeting of Presidents Enrique Hertzog of Bolivia and Juan D. Perón of Argentina at Yacuiba, Oct. 23, 1947.

Types of Regular Issue of 1948

Designs: 2.50b, Statue of Christ above La Paz. 3.70b, Child kneeling before cross. No. C121, St. John Bosco. No. C122, Virgin of Copacabana. 13.60b, Pope Pius XII blessing University of La Paz.

1948, Sept. 26 *Perf. 11½*

C119 A120	2.50b ver & yel	45	35
C120 A120	3.70b rose & cream	55	35
C121 A120	4b rose lil & gray	55	25
C122 A120	4b lt ultra & sal	55	16
C123 A120	13.60b ultra & lt grn	70	40
	Nos. C119-C123 (5)	2.80	1.51

Type of Regular Issue of 1948

1948, Oct.

C124 A125	10b emerald & salmon	1.60	18

Pres. Gregorio Pacheco, Map and Post Horn — AP34

L. A. B. Plane — AP35

1950, Jan. 2 **Unwmk.**

C125 AP34	1.40b orange brown	15	15
C126 AP34	2.50b orange	15	15
C127 AP34	3.30b rose violet	15	15
	Nos. C125-C127 (3)	45	45

75th anniv. of the UPU.

Nos. C100 and C104 Surcharged in Black

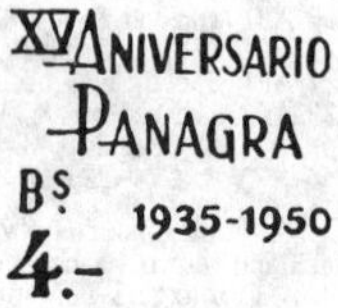

1950, May 31 *Perf. 11*

C128 AP30	4b on 10c red	15	15
a.	Inverted surcharge	17.50	17.50
C129 AP30	10b on 20b dp brn	30	22
a.	Inverted surcharge	17.50	17.50

Panagra air services in Bolivia, 15th anniv.

1950, Sept. 15 **Litho.** *Perf. 13½*

C130 AP35	20c red orange	15	15
C131 AP35	30c purple	15	15
C132 AP35	50c green	15	15
C133 AP35	1b orange	15	15
C134 AP35	3b ultra	25	15
C135 AP35	15b carmine	50	15
C136 AP35	50b chocolate	1.00	35
	Nos. C130-C136 (7)	2.35	
	Set value		1.00

25th anniv. of the founding of Lloyd Aero Boliviano. 30c, 50c, 15b exist imperforate.
No. C132 exists without imprint at bottom of stamp.

No. C116 Surcharged in Black

1950, Sept. 24 *Perf. 11½*

C137 AP32	1.40b on 3b dp orange	25	25

1st anniv. of the ending of the Civil War of Aug. 24-Sept. 24, 1949.
Exists with inverted and double surcharge.

Symbols of United Nations — AP36

1950, Oct. 24 **Unwmk.**

C138 AP36	3.60b crimson rose	50	16
C139 AP36	4.70b black brown	65	16

5th anniv. of the UN.

Gate of the Sun and Llama AP37

Church of San Francisco AP38

Designs: 40c, Avenue Camacho. 50c, Consistorial Palace. 1b, Legislative Palace. 2b, Communications Bldg. 3b, Arms. 4b, La Gasca ordering Mendoza to found La Paz. 5b, Capt. Alonso de Mendoza founding La Paz. 10b, Arms; portrait of Mendoza.

1951, Mar. 1 **Engr.** *Perf. 12½*

Center in Black

C140 AP37	20c carmine	15	15
C141 AP38	30c dk vio bl	15	15
C142 AP37	40c dark blue	15	15
C143 AP37	50c blue green	15	15
C144 AP37	1b red	20	20
C145 AP37	2b red orange	35	35
C146 AP37	3b deep blue	35	35
C147 AP37	4b vermilion	45	45
a.	Souvenir sheet of 4	1.00	1.00
C148 AP37	5b dark green	40	40
a.	Souvenir sheet of 3	1.00	1.00
C149 AP37	10b red brown	65	65
a.	Souvenir sheet of 3	1.00	1.00
	Nos. C140-C149 (10)	3.00	3.00

400th anniv. of the founding of La Paz.
No. C147a contains C143-C145, C147; No. C148a contains C142, C146, C148; No. C149a contains C140, C141, C149. Perf. and imperf., size: 150x100mm.
For surcharges see Nos. C187-C196.

Horsemanship AP39

Designs: 30c, Basketball. 50c, Fencing. 1b, Hurdling. 2.50b, Javelin throwing. 3b, Relay race. 5b, La Paz stadium.

1951, Aug. 23 **Unwmk.**

Center in Black

C150 AP39	20c purple	20	15
C151 AP39	30c rose vio	30	15
C152 AP39	50c dp red org	50	15
C153 AP39	1b chocolate	50	15
C154 AP39	2.50b orange	75	30
C155 AP39	3b black brn	1.00	75
a.	Souvenir sheet of 3	4.00	3.50
C156 AP39	5b red	2.00	1.50
a.	Souvenir sheet of 4	4.50	4.00
	Nos. C150-C156 (7)	5.25	3.15

The stamps were intended to commemorate the 5th South American Games and the 2nd National Sports Congress held at La Paz, October 1948.
No. C155a contains C153-C155; No. C156a contains C150-C152, C156. Perf. and imperf., size: 150x100mm.

Eduardo Abaroa — AP40

Queen Isabella I — AP41

1952, Mar. 24 **Litho.** *Perf. 11*

C157 AP40	70c rose red	15	15
C158 AP40	2b orange yel	25	25
C159 AP40	3b yellow green	25	15
C160 AP40	5b blue	25	15
C161 AP40	50b rose lilac	1.00	90
C162 AP40	100b gray black	1.10	1.10
a.	Perf. 14	10.00	
	Nos. C157-C162 (6)	3.00	2.70

73rd anniv. of the death of Abaroa.

1952, July 16 *Perf. 13½*
C163 AP41 50b emerald 35 25
C164 AP41 100b brown 65 35

500th anniversary of the birth of Queen Isabella I of Spain. Exist imperforate.

Columbus Lighthouse AP42

1952, July 16
C165 AP42 2b rose lilac, *salmon* 20 20
C166 AP42 3.70b blue grn, *bl* 20 20
C167 AP42 4.40b orange, *salmon* 20 20
C168 AP42 20b dk brn, *cream* 40 15
Nos. C165-C168 (4) 1.00 75

No. C168 exists imperforate.

Soldiers — AP43

Gualberto Villarroel, Victor Paz Estenssoro and Hernan Siles Zuazo — AP44

Perf. 13½ (AP43), 11½ (AP44)
1953, Apr. 9 **Litho.**
C169 AP44 3.70b chocolate 15 15
C170 AP43 6b red violet 15 15
C171 AP44 9b brown rose 15 15
C172 AP44 10b aqua 15 15
C173 AP44 16b vermilion 15 15
C174 AP43 22.50b dk brown 25 20
C175 AP44 40b gray 40 15
Nos. C169-C175 (7) 1.40 1.10

1st anniv. of the Revolution of Apr. 9, 1952. Nos. C169-C170 and C174 exist imperf.

Pres. Victor Paz Estenssoro Embracing Indian — AP45

Map and Peasant — AP46

1954, Aug. 2 *Perf. 12x11½*
C176 AP45 20b orange brn 15 15
C177 AP46 27b brt pink 15 16
C178 AP46 30b red org 15 15
C179 AP46 45b violet brn 20 15
C180 AP45 100b blue grn 38 15
C181 AP46 300b yellow grn 1.00 28
Nos. C176-C181 (6) 2.03
Set value 77

Nos. C176, C180 for 3rd Inter-American Indian Congress. Nos. C177-C179, C181 agrarian reform laws of 1953-1954.
Nos. C176-C180 exist imperf.
For surcharge see No. C261.

Oil Derricks — AP47

Map of South America and La Paz Arms — AP48

1955, Oct. 9 *Perf. 10½*
C182 AP47 55b dk & lt grnsh bl 20 15
C183 AP47 70b dk gray & gray 20 15
C184 AP47 90b dk & lt grn 20 15

Perf. 13
C185 AP47 500b red lilac 65 40
C186 AP47 1000b blk brn & fawn 1.25 1.25
Nos. C182-C186 (5) 2.50 2.10

For surcharge see No. C262.

Nos. C140-C149 Surcharged with New Values and Bars in Black or Carmine

1957 **Engr.** *Perf. 12½*
Center in Black
C187 AP37 100b on 3b (C) 15 15
C188 AP37 200b on 2b 15 15
C189 AP37 500b on 4b 16 15
C190 AP37 600b on 1b 16 15
C191 AP37 700b on 20c 25 15
C192 AP37 800b on 40c (C) 35 15
C193 AP38 900b on 30c (C) 40 15
C194 AP37 1800b on 50c (C) 65 25
C195 AP37 3000b on 5b (C) 1.00 45
C196 AP37 5000b on 10b (C) 1.60 75
Nos. C187-C196 (10) 4.87
Set value 2.15

Unwmk.
1957, May 25 **Litho.** *Perf. 12*
C197 AP48 700b lilac & vio 35 35
C198 AP48 1200b pale brn 40 35
C199 AP48 1350b rose car 55 50
C200 AP48 2700b blue grn 1.10 65
C201 AP48 4000b violet bl 1.40 75
Nos. C197-C201 (5) 3.80 2.60

7th session of the C. E. P. A. L. (Comision Economica para la America Latina de las Naciones Unidas), La Paz.
Exist imperf.
For surcharges see Nos. C263-C265.

Type of Regular Issue, 1957

1957, Dec. 19 *Perf. 11½*
C202 A141 600b magenta 22 15
C203 A141 700b violet bl 35 15
C204 A141 900b pale grn 50 15
Nos. C202-C204 (3) 1.07
Set value 27

Type of Regular Issue, 1960

1960, Jan. 30
C205 A142 400b rose claret 50 30
C206 A142 800b slate blue 65 40
C207 A142 2000b slate 1.00 60
Nos. C205-C207 (3) 2.15 1.30

Gate of the Sun, Tiahuanacu AP49

Uprooted Oak Emblem AP50

1960, Mar. 26 **Litho.** *Perf. 11½*
C208 AP49 3000b gray 1.75 1.10
C209 AP49 5000b orange 2.75 1.10
C210 AP49 10,000b rose claret 4.25 2.75
C211 AP49 15,000b blue violet 6.25 4.50
Nos. C208-C211 (4) 15.00 9.45

1960, Apr. 7 *Perf. 11½*
C212 AP50 600b ultra 35 35
C213 AP50 700b lt red brn 35 35
C214 AP50 900b dk bl grn 35 35
C215 AP50 1800b violet 60 60
C216 AP50 2000b gray 65 60
Nos. C212-C216 (5) 2.30 2.25

WRY, July 1, 1959-June 30, 1960.

No. C215 exists with "1961" overprint in dark carmine, but was not regularly issued in this form.

Jaime Laredo — AP51

Perf. 11½
1960, Aug. 15 **Unwmk.** **Litho.**
C217 AP51 600b rose vio 75 45
C218 AP51 700b ol gray 75 25
C219 AP51 800b vio brn 75 25
C220 AP51 900b dk bl 1.00 25
C221 AP51 1800b green 1.50 1.50
C222 AP51 4000b dk gray 3.00 1.00
Nos. C217-C222 (6) 7.75 3.70

Issued to honor the violinist Jaime Laredo.
For surcharges see Nos. C266-C267.

Children's Hospital Type of 1960

1960, Nov. 21 *Perf. 11½*
C223 A146 600b multi 40 22
C224 A146 1000b multi 60 22
C225 A146 1800b multi 1.00 1.00
C226 A146 5000b multi 3.00 1.20
Nos. C223-C226 (4) 5.00 2.64

For surcharges see No. C268-C269.

Pres. Paz Estenssoro and Pres. Getulio Vargas of Brazil AP52

1960, Dec. 14 **Litho.** *Perf. 11½*
C227 AP52 1200b on 10b org & blk 70 70

Exists with surcharge inverted.
No. C227 without surcharge was not regularly issued, although a decree authorizing its circulation was published. Value, 50-cents.
Postally-used counterfeits of surcharge exist.

Pres. Paz Estenssoro and Pres. Frondizi of Argentina AP53

Design: 4000b, Flags of Bolivia and Argentina.

1961, May 23 *Perf. 10½*
C228 AP53 4000b brn, red, yel, grn & bl 75 75
C229 AP53 6000b dk grn & blk 1.50 1.50

Visit of the President of Argentina, Dr. Arturo Frondizi, to Bolivia.
For surcharge see No. C309.

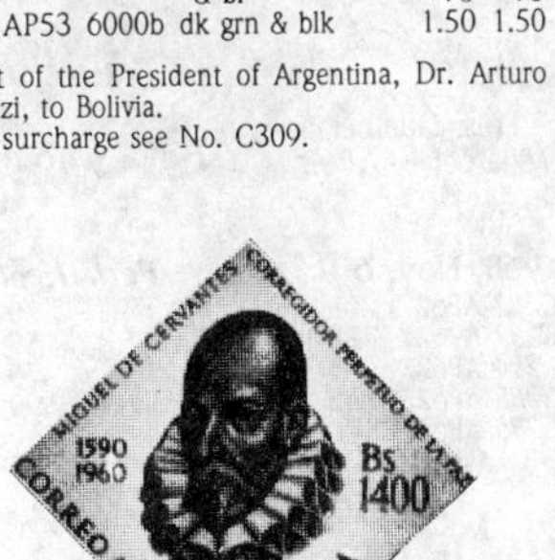

Miguel de Cervantes — AP54

1961, Oct. **Photo.** *Perf. 13*
C230 AP54 1400b pale grn & dk ol grn 58 22

Cervantes' appointment as Chief Magistrate of La Paz.

Virgin of Cotoca and Symbol of Eucharist AP55

Planes and Parachutes AP56

1962, Mar. 19 **Litho.** *Perf. 10½*
C231 AP55 1400b brn, pink & yel 65 35

4th Natl. Eucharistic Cong., Santa Cruz, 1961.

Nos. C212-C216 Surcharged Vertically with New Value and Greek Key Border

1962, June **Unwmk.** *Perf. 11½*
C232 AP50 1200b on 600b 55 55
C233 AP50 1300b on 700b 50 50
C234 AP50 1400b on 900b 55 55
C235 AP50 2800b on 1,800b 90 75
C236 AP50 3000b on 2,000b 90 75
Nos. C232-C236 (5) 3.40 3.10

The overprinted segment of Greek key border on Nos. C232-C236 comes in two positions: two full "keys" on top, and one full and two half keys on top.

Flower Type of 1962

Flowers: 100b, 1800b, Cantua buxifolia. 800b, 10,000b, Cantua bicolor.

1962, June 28 **Litho.** *Perf. 10½*
Flowers in Natural Colors
C237 A152 100b dk bl 25 15
C238 A152 800b green 50 15
C239 A152 1800b violet 1.00 50
a. Souvenir sheet of 3 3.50 3.50
C240 A152 10,000b dk bl 3.25 1.75
Nos. C237-C240 (4) 5.00 2.55

No. C239a contains 3 imperf. stamps similar to Nos. C237-C239, but with the 1,800b background color changed to dark violet blue.
For surcharges see Nos. C270-C271.

1962, Sept. 5 **Litho.** *Perf. 11½*

Designs: 1200b, 5000b, Plane and oxcart. 2000b, Aerial photography (plane over South America).

Emblem in Red, Yellow & Green
C241 AP56 600b blk & bl 25 15
C242 AP56 1200b multi 50 20
C243 AP56 2000b multi 75 35
C244 AP56 5000b multi 1.50 65
Nos. C241-C244 (4) 3.00 1.35

Armed Forces of Bolivia.

Malaria Type of 1962

Design: Inscription around mosquito, laurel around globe.

1962, Oct. 4
C245 A154 2000b ind, grn & yel 80 50

Type of Regular Issue, 1961

Design: Pedro de la Gasca (1485-1567).

1962 **Unwmk.** **Photo.** *Perf. 13x12½*
C246 A150 1200b brn, *yel* 35 20

Condor, Soccer Ball and Flags AP57

Alliance for Progress Emblem AP58

Design: 1.80b, Map of Bolivia, soccer ball, goal and flags.

1963, Mar. 21 Litho. *Perf. 11½*
C247 AP57 1.40b multi 1.00 65
C248 AP57 1.80b multi 1.00 1.00

Issued to publicize the 21st South American Soccer Championships.

Freedom from Hunger Type

Design: Wheat, globe and wheat emblem.

1963, Aug. 1 Unwmk. *Perf. 11½*
C249 A156 1.20b dk grn, bl & yel 75 75

1963, Nov. 15 *Perf. 11½*
C250 AP58 1.20b dl yel, ultra & grn 80 75

2nd anniv. of the Alliance for Progress, which aims to stimulate economic growth and raise living standards in Latin America.

Type of Regular Issue, 1963

Designs: 1.20b, Ballot box and voters. 1.40b, Map and farmer breaking chain. 2.80b, Miners.

1963, Dec. 21 *Perf. 11½*
C251 A157 1.20b gray, dk brn & rose 40 20
C252 A157 1.40b bis & grn 50 25
C253 A157 2.80b sl & buff 1.00 90
Nos. C251-C253 (3) 1.90 1.35

Andrés Santa Cruz — AP59

Perf. 13½
1966, Aug. 10 Wmk. 90 Litho.
C254 AP59 20c dp bl 15 15
C255 AP59 60c dp grn 20 20
C256 AP59 1.20b red brn 50 50
C257 AP59 2.80b black 80 80
Nos. C254-C257 (4) 1.65 1.65

Cent. (in 1965) of the death of Marshal Andrés Santa Cruz (1792-1865), pres. of Bolivia and of Peru-Bolivia Confederation.

Children Type of 1966

Design: 1.40b, Mother and children.

1966, Dec. 16 Unwmk. *Perf. 13½*
C258 A159 1.40b gray bl & blk 1.00 42

Co-Presidents Type of Regular Issue

1966, Dec. 16 Litho. *Perf. 12½*
Flag in Red, Yellow and Green
C259 A160 2.80b gray & tan 1.40 1.00
C260 A160 10b sep & tan 1.60 50
a. Souvenir sheet of 4 6.50 6.50

No. C260a contains 4 imperf. stamps similar to Nos. 480-481 and C259-C260. Dark green marginal inscription. Size: 135x82mm.

Various Issues 1954-62 Surcharged with New Values and Bars

1966, Dec. 21
On No. C177: "XII Aniversario / Reforma / Agraria"
C261 AP46 10c on 27b 20 15
a. Agraria/Agraria 10.00
On No. C182: "XXV / Aniversario Paz / del Chaco"
C262 AP47 10c on 55b 20 15
On No. C199: "Centenario de / Tupiza"
C263 AP48 60c on 1350b 50 20
On No. C200: "XXV / Aniversario / Automovil Club / Boliviano"
C264 AP48 2.80b on 2700b 2.00 1.60
On No. C201: "Centenario de la / Cruz Roja / Internacional"
C265 AP48 4b on 4000b 1.40 1.00
On No. C219: "CL Aniversario / Heroinas Coronilla"
C266 AP51 1.20b on 800b 75 50
On No. C222: "Centenario Himno / Paceño"
C267 AP51 1.40b on 4,000b 75 50

Nos. C224-C225 Surcharged
C268 A146 1.40b on 1,000b 60 60
C269 A146 1.40b on 1,800b 60 60

On Nos. C238-C239: "Aniversario / Centro Filatelico / Cochabamba"
C270 A152 1.20b on 800b 1.00 25
C271 A152 1.20b on 1,800b 1.00 25

Revenue Stamp of 1946 Surcharged with New Value "X" and: "XXV Aniversario / Dpto. Pando / Aéreo"
C272 A161 1.20b on 1b dk bl 50 25
Nos. C261-C272 (12) 9.50 6.05

Lions Emblem and Pre-historic Sculptures AP60

1967, Sept. 20 Litho. *Perf. 13x13½*
C273 AP60 2b red & multi 80 65
a. Souvenir sheet of 2 3.75 3.75

50th anniv. of Lions Intl. No. C273a contains 2 imperf. stamps similar to Nos. 492 and C273.

Folklore Type of Regular Issue

Designs (Folklore characters): 1.20p, Pujllay. 1.40p, Ujusiris. 2p, Morenada. 3p, Auki-aukis.

1968, June 24 *Perf. 13½x13*
C274 A163 1.20b lt yel grn & multi 35 20
C275 A163 1.40b gray & multi 40 20
C276 A163 2b dk ol bis & multi 75 25
C277 A163 3b sky bl & multi 1.00 25
Nos. C274-C277 (4) 2.50 90

A souvenir sheet exists containing 4 imperf. stamps similar to Nos. C274-C277. Size: 131x81½mm.

Moto Mendez — AP61

1968, Oct. 29 Litho. *Perf. 13½x13*
C278 AP61 1b multi 35 15
C279 AP61 1.20b multi 40 35
C280 AP61 2b multi 75 50
C281 AP61 4b multi 1.00 75
Nos. C278-C281 (4) 2.50 1.75

Battle of Tablada sesquicentennial.

Pres. Gualberto Villaroel — AP62

1968, Nov. 6 *Perf. 13x13½*
C282 AP62 1.40b org & blk 30 22
C283 AP62 3b lt bl & blk 55 32
C284 AP62 4b rose & blk 70 40
C285 AP62 5b gray grn & blk 90 55
C286 AP62 10b pale pur & blk 1.60 1.10
Nos. C282-C286 (5) 4.05 2.59

4th centenary of Cochabamba.

ITU Type of Regular Issue

1968, Dec. 3 Litho. *Perf. 13x13½*
C287 A166 1.20b gray, blk & yel 60 30
C288 A166 1.40b bl, blk & gray ol 60 20

UNESCO Emblem — AP63

1968, Nov. 14 *Perf. 13½x13*
C289 AP63 1.20b pale vio & blk 35 35
C290 AP63 2.80b yel grn & blk 65 65

20th anniv. (in 1966) of UNESCO.

Kennedy Type of Regular Issue

1968, Nov. 22 Unwmk.
C291 A168 1b grn & blk 25 15
C292 A168 10b scar & blk 2.75 2.75

A souvenir sheet contains one imperf. stamp similar to No. C291. Dark violet marginal inscription. Size: 131x81½mm.

Tennis Type of Regular Issue

1968, Dec. 10 *Perf. 13x13½*
C293 A169 1.40b org, blk & lt brn 35 35
C294 A169 2.80b sky bl, blk & lt brn 65 65

A souvenir sheet exists containing one imperf. stamp similar to No. C293. Size: 131x81½mm.

Stamp Centenary Type of Regular Issue

Design: 1.40b, 2.80b, 3b, Bolivia No. 1.

1968, Dec. 23 Litho. *Perf. 13x13½*
C295 A170 1.40b org, grn & blk 50 50
C296 A170 2.80b pale rose, grn & blk 1.00 1.00
C297 A170 3b lt vio, grn & blk 1.00 1.00
Nos. C295-C297 (3) 2.50 2.50

A souvenir sheet exists containing 3 imperf. stamps similar to Nos. C295-C297. Size: 131x81½mm.

Franklin D. Roosevelt — AP64

1969, Oct. 29 Litho. *Perf. 13½x13*
C298 AP64 5b brn, blk & buff 1.75 1.10

Olympic Type of Regular Issue

Sports: 1.20b, Woman runner, vert. 2.80b, Discus thrower, vert. 5b, Hurdler.

Perf. 13½x13, 13x13½
1969, Oct. 29 Litho.
C299 A171 1.20b yel grn, bis & blk 50 40
C300 A171 2.80b red, org & blk 1.00 75
C301 A171 5b bl, lt bl, red & blk 1.50 1.50
Nos. C299-C301 (3) 3.00 2.65

A souvenir sheet exists containing 3 imperf. stamps similar to Nos. C299-C301. Size: 130½x81mm.

Butterfly Type of Regular Issue

Butterflies: 1b, Metamorpha dido wernichei. 1.80b, Heliconius felix. 2.80b, Morpho casica. 3b, Papilio yuracares. 4b, Heliconius melitus.

1970, Apr. 24 Litho. *Perf. 13x13½*
C302 A172 1b sal & multi 1.00 1.00
C303 A172 1.80b lt bl & multi 1.50 1.50
C304 A172 2.80b multi 2.50 2.50
C305 A172 3b multi 2.50 2.50
C306 A172 4b multi 3.00 3.00
Nos. C302-C306 (5) 10.50 10.50

A souvenir sheet exists containing 3 imperf. stamps similar to Nos. C302-C304. Black marginal inscription. Size: 129½x80mm.

Scout Type of Regular Issue

Designs: 50c, Boy Scout building brick wall. 1.20b, Bolivian Boy Scout emblem.

1970, June 17 Litho. *Perf. 13½x13*
C307 A173 50c yel & multi 15 15
C308 A173 1.20b multi 40 40

No. C228 Surcharged

1970, Dec. Litho. *Perf. 10½*
C309 AP53 1.20b on 4000b multi 25 15

Flower Type of Regular Issue

Bolivian Flowers: 1.20b, Amaryllis pseudopardina, horiz. 1.40b, Rebutia kruegeri. 2.80b, Lobivia pentlandii, horiz. 4b, Rebutia tunariensis.

Perf. 13x13½, 13½x13
1971, Aug. 9 Litho. Unwmk.
C310 A174 1.20b multi 70 40
C311 A174 1.40b multi 80 50
C312 A174 2.80b multi 1.50 75
C313 A174 4b multi 2.00 1.25
Nos. C310-C313 (4) 5.00 2.90

Two souvenir sheets of 4 exist. One contains imperf. stamps similar to Nos. 534-535 and C310, C312. The other contains imperf. stamps similar to Nos. 536-537, C311, C313. Size: 130x80mm.

Folk Dance Type of Regular Issue

1972, Mar. 23 Litho. *Perf. 13½x13*
C314 A177 1.20b Kusillo 50 16
C315 A177 1.40b Taquirari 65 16

Two souvenir sheets of 3 exist. One contains imperf. stamps similar to Nos. 542-543, C314. The other contains imperf. stamps similar to Nos. 540-541, C315. Size: 80x129mm.

Painting Type of Regular Issue

Bolivian Paintings: 1.40b, Portrait of Chola Paceña, by Cecilio Guzman de Rojas. 1.50b, Adoration of the Kings, by G. Gamarra. 1.60b, Adoration of Pachamama (mountain), by A. Borda. 2b, The Kiss of the Idol, by Guzman de Rojas.

1972 Litho. *Perf. 13½*
C316 A178 1.40b multi 40 15
C317 A178 1.50b multi 40 15
C318 A178 1.60b multi 40 20
C319 A178 2b multi 55 20
Nos. C316-C319 (4) 1.75 70

Two souvenir sheets of 2 exist. One contains imperf. stamps similar to Nos. 548 and C318. The other contains imperf. stamps similar to Nos. C317 and C319. Size: 129x80mm.
Issue dates: 1.40b, Dec. 4. Others, Aug. 17.

Bolivian Coat of Arms AP65

1972, Dec. 4 *Perf. 13½x14*
C320 AP65 4b lt bl & multi 1.40 50

Cactus Type of Regular Issue

Designs: Various cacti.

1973, Aug. 6 Litho. *Perf. 13½*
C321 A180 1.20b tan & multi 35 15
C322 A180 1.90b org & multi 50 20
C323 A180 2b multi 65 25
Nos. C321-C323 (3) 1.50 60

Development Type of Regular Issue

Designs: 1.40b, Highway 1Y4. 2b, Rail car on bridge.

1973, Nov. 26 Litho. *Perf. 13½*
C324 A181 1.40b sal & multi 40 15
C325 A181 2b multi 60 20

Santos-Dumont and 14-Bis Plane — AP66

1973, July 20
C326 AP66 1.40b yel & blk 65 35

Centenary of the birth of Alberto Santos-Dumont (1873-1932), Brazilian aviation pioneer.

Orchid Type of 1974

Orchids: 2.50b, Cattleya luteola, horiz. 3.80b, Stanhopaea. 4b, Catasetum, horiz. 5b, Maxillaria.

1974 Litho. Perf. 13½

C327	A182	2.50b multi	1.00	22
C328	A182	3.80b rose & multi	1.50	45
C329	A182	4b multi	1.50	40
C330	A182	5b sal & multi	2.50	45
		Nos. C327-C330 (4)	6.50	1.52

Air Force Emblem, Plane over Map of Bolivia — AP67

Designs: 3.80b, Plane over Andes. 4.50b, Triple decker and jet. 8b, Rafael Pabon and double decker. 15b, Jet and "50."

1974 Litho. Perf. 13x13½

C331	AP67	3b multi	65	25
C332	AP67	3.80b multi	1.00	25
C333	AP67	4.50b multi	1.00	25
C334	AP67	8b multi	1.60	40
C335	AP67	15b multi	3.50	50
		Nos. C331-C335 (5)	7.75	1.65

Bolivian Air Force, 50th anniv. Exist imperf.

Coat of Arms Type of 1975

Designs: Departmental coats of arms.

1975, July 16 Litho. Perf. 13½

C336	A188	20c Beni	15	15
C337	A188	30c Tarija	15	15
C338	A188	50c Potosi	25	25
C339	A188	1b Oruro	50	50
C340	A188	2.50b Santa Cruz	1.00	1.00
C341	A188	3b La Paz	1.00	1.00
		Nos. C336-C341 (6)	3.05	3.05

LAB Emblem — AP68

Bolivia on Map of Americas — AP69

Map of Bolivia, Plane and Kyllmann AP70

1975 Litho. Perf. 13½

C342	AP68	1b gold, bl & blk	40	40
C343	AP69	1.50b multi	60	60
C344	AP70	2b multi	75	75
		Nos. C342-C344 (3)	1.75	1.75

Lloyd Aereo Boliviano, 50th anniversary, founded by Guillermo Kyllmann.

Bolivar, Presidents Perez and Banzer, and Flags AP71

1975, Aug. 4 Litho. Perf. 13½

C345	AP71	3b gold & multi	75	65

Visit of Pres. Carlos A. Perez of Venezuela.

Bolivar Type of 1975

Presidents and Statesmen of Bolivia: 50c, Rene Barrientos O. 2b, Francisco B. O'Connor. 3.80b, Gualberto Villarroel. 4.20b, German Busch. 4.50b, Hugo Banzer Suarez. 20b, José Ballivian. 30b, Andres de Santa Cruz. 40b, Antonio Jose de Sucre.

1975 Litho. Perf. 13½

Size: 24x33mm

C346	A189	50c multi	25	25
C347	A189	2b multi	50	50
C348	A189	3.80b multi	75	75
C349	A189	4.20b multi	1.00	75

Size: 28x39mm

C350	A189	4.50b multi	1.00	50

Size: 24x33mm

C351	A189	20b multi	4.00	2.00
C352	A189	30b multi	5.00	5.00
C353	A189	40b multi	6.50	6.50
		Nos. C346-C353 (8)	19.00	16.25

UPU Emblem AP72

1975, Dec. 7 Litho. Perf. 13½

C358	AP72	25b bl & multi	3.00	3.00

Cent. of UPU (in 1974).

POSTAGE DUE STAMPS

D1

1931 Unwmk. Engr. Perf. 14, 14½

J1	D1	5c ultra	1.00	1.00
J2	D1	10c red	1.00	1.00
J3	D1	15c yellow	1.50	1.50
J4	D1	30c deep green	1.50	1.50
J5	D1	40c deep violet	2.50	2.50
J6	D1	50c black brown	3.50	3.50
		Nos. J1-J6 (6)	11.00	11.00

Symbol of Youth — D2

Torch of Knowledge — D3

Symbol of the Revolution of May 17, 1936 — D4

1938 Litho. Perf. 11

J7	D2	5c deep rose	50	40
a.		Pair, imperf. between		
J8	D3	10c green	50	40
J9	D4	30c gray blue	50	40
		Nos. J7-J9 (3)	1.50	1.20

POSTAL TAX STAMPS

Worker PT1

Symbols of Communications PT2

Imprint: "LITO. UNIDAS LA PAZ."

Perf. 13½x10½, 10½, 13½

1939 Litho. Unwmk.

RA1	PT1	5c dl vio	50	15
a.		Double impression		

Redrawn

Imprint: "TALL. OFFSET LA PAZ."

1940 Perf. 12x11, 11

RA2	PT1	5c violet	42	15
a.		Horizontal pair, imperf. between	2.00	
b.		Imperf. horiz., pair		

Tax of Nos. RA1-RA2 was for the Workers' Home Building Fund.

1944-45 Litho. Perf. 10½

RA3	PT2	10c salmon	35	15
RA4	PT2	10c blue ('45)	35	15

A 30c orange inscribed "Centenario de la Creacion del Departmento del Beni" was issued in 1946 and required to be affixed to all air and surface mail to and from the Department of Beni in addition to regular postage. Five higher denominations in the same scenic design were used for local revenue purposes.

Catalogue values for unused stamps in this section, from this point to the end of the section, are for Never Hinged items.

Type of 1944 Redrawn

1947-48 Unwmk. Perf. 10½

RA5	PT2	10c carmine	35	15
RA6	PT2	10c org yel ('48)	30	15
RA7	PT2	10c yel brn ('48)	30	15
RA8	PT2	10c emer ('48)	30	15
		Nos. RA5-RA8 (4)	1.25	
		Set value		24

Post horn and envelope reduced in size.

Condor, Envelope and Post Horn — PT3

Communication Symbols — PT4

1951-52

RA9	PT3	20c dp org	35	16
a.		Imperf., pair	20.00	
RA10	PT3	20c green ('52)	45	16
a.		Imperf., pair	20.00	
RA11	PT3	20c blue ('52)	45	16
a.		Imperf., pair	20.00	
		Nos. RA9-RA11 (3)	1.25	48

For surcharges see Nos. RA17-RA18.

1952-54 Perf. 13½, 10½, 10½x12

RA12	PT4	50c green	50	15
RA13	PT4	50c carmine	50	15
RA14	PT4	3b green	50	15
RA15	PT4	3b olive bister	50	50
RA16	PT4	5b vio ('54)	50	50
		Nos. RA12-RA16 (5)	2.50	1.45

For surcharges see Nos. RA21-RA22.

No. RA10 and Type of 1951-52 Surcharged with New Value in Black

1953 Perf. 10½

RA17	PT3	50c on 20c green	25	15
RA18	PT3	50c on 20c red vio	25	15

Postman Blowing Horn — PT5

1954-55 Unwmk. Perf. 10½

RA19	PT5	1b brown	20	15
RA20	PT5	1b car rose ('55)	20	15
		Set value		20

Exist imperf.

Nos. RA15 and RA14 Surcharged in Black "Bs. 5.-/D. S./21-IV-55"

1955 Perf. 10½, 10½x12

RA21	PT4	5b on 3b olive bister	25	15
RA22	PT4	5b on 3b green	25	15
		Set value		16

Tax of Nos. RA3-RA22 was for the Communications Employees Fund.

No. RA21 is known with surcharge in thin type of different font and with comma added after "55."

Plane over Airport — PT6

Planes — PT7

Perf. 10½, 12, 13½

1955 Unwmk. Litho.

RA23	PT6	5b dp ultra	25	15
a.		Vertical pair imperf. between		

Perf. 11½

RA24	PT7	10b light green	20	15

PT8

PT9

1955 Litho. Perf. 10½

RA25	PT8	5b red	7.50	7.50

Perf. 12

RA26	PT9	20b dark brown	25	15

Tax of Nos. RA23-RA26 was for the building of new airports.

General Alfredo Ovando and Three Men — PT10

1970, Sept. 26 Litho. Perf. 13x13½

RA27	PT10	20c black & red	50	15

See No. RAC1.

Pres. German Busch — PT11

1971, May 13 Litho. Perf. 13x13½

RA28	PT11	20c lilac & black	50	15

AIR POST POSTAL TAX STAMPS

Catalogue values for unused stamps in this section are for Never Hinged items.

Type of Postal Tax Issue

Design: 30c, General Ovando and oil well.

1970, Sept. 26 Litho. Perf. 13x13½

RAC1	PT10	30c blk & grn	50	15

Pres. Gualberto Villarroel, Refinery
PTAP1

1971, May 25 Litho. ***Perf. 13x13½***

RAC2	PTAP1	30c lt bl & blk	50	15

Type of 1971 Inscribed: "XXV ANIVERSARIO DE SU GOBIERNO"

1975 Litho. ***Perf. 13x13½***

RAC3	PTAP1	30c lt bl & blk	3.00	3.00

BOSNIA AND HERZEGOVINA

LOCATION — Dalmatia and Serbia
GOVT. — Provinces of Turkey under Austro-Hungarian occupation, 1879-1908; provinces of Austria-Hungary 1908-1918
AREA — 19,768 sq. mi.
POP. — 2,000,000 (approx. 1918)
CAPITAL — Sarajevo

Following World War I Bosnia and Herzegovina united with the kingdoms of Montenegro and Serbia, and Croatia, Dalmatia and Slovenia, to form the Kingdom of Yugoslavia (See Yugoslavia.)

100 Novcica (Neukreuzer) = 1 Florin (Gulden)
100 Heller = 1 Krone (1900)

Watermark

Wmk. 91- BRIEF-MARKEN or (from 1890) ZEITUNGS-MARKEN in Double-lined Capitals, Across the Sheet

Coat of Arms — A1

Type I - The heraldic eaglets on the right side of the escutcheon are entirely blank. The eye of the lion is indicated by a very small dot, which sometimes fails to print.

Type II - There is a colored line across the lowest eaglet. A similar line sometimes appears on the middle eaglet. The eye of the lion is formed by a large dot which touches the outline of the head above it.

Type III - The eaglets and eye of the lion are similar to type I. Each tail feather of the large eagle has two lines of shading and the lowest feather does not touch the curved line below it. In types I and II there are several shading lines in these feathers, and the lowest feather touches the curved line.

Varieties of the Numerals

2 NOVCICA:
A - The "2" has curved tail. All are type I.
B - The "2" has straight tail. All are type II.

15 NOVCICA:
C - The serif of the "1" is short and forms a wide angle with the vertical stroke.
D - The serif of the "1" forms an acute angle with the vertical stroke.

The numerals of the 5n were retouched several times and show minor differences, especially in the flag.

Other Varieties

½ NOVCICA:
There is a black dot between the curved ends of the ornaments near the lower spandrels.
G - This dot touches the curve at its right. Stamps of this (1st) printing are litho.
H - This dot stands clear of the curved lines. Stamps of this (2nd) printing are typo.

10 NOVCICA:
Ten stamps in each sheet of type II show a small cross in the upper section of the right side of the escutcheon.

Perf. 9 to 13½ and Compound

1879-94 Litho. Wmk. 91

Type I

1	A1	½n blk (type II) ('94)	6.00	*12.50*
2	A1	1n gray	4.00	1.25
c.		1n gray lilac		1.50
4	A1	2n yellow	7.00	75
5	A1	3n green	5.00	1.50
6	A1	5n rose red	7.50	35
7	A1	10n blue	25.00	65
8	A1	15n brown	27.50	3.75
9	A1	20n gray green ('93)	125.00	5.50
10	A1	25n violet	22.50	5.50

No. 2c was never issued. It is usually canceled by blue pencil marks and "mint" copies generally have been cleaned.

Perf. 10½ to 13 and Compound

1894-98 Typo.

Type II

1a	A1	½n black	8.00	*12.00*
2a	A1	1n gray	3.25	85
4a	A1	2n yellow	2.50	45
5a	A1	3n green	3.25	1.10
6a	A1	5n rose red	45.00	30
7a	A1	10n blue	4.50	60
8a	A1	15n brown	4.00	2.75
9a	A1	20n gray green	5.50	3.00
10a	A1	25n violet	6.00	4.75

Type III

6b	A1	5n rose red ('98)	1.25	30

All the preceding stamps exist in various shades.

Nos. 1a to 10a were reprinted in 1911 in lighter colors, on very white paper and perf. 12½. Value, set $25.

A2

A3

Perf. 10½, 12½ and Compound

1900 Typo.

11	A2	1h gray black	24	15
12	A2	2h gray	24	15
13	A2	3h yellow	25	15
14	A2	5h green	24	15
15	A2	6h brown	50	15
16	A2	10h red	22	15
17	A2	20h rose	85.00	3.25
18	A2	25h blue	70	15
19	A2	30h bister brown	95.00	4.00
20	A2	40h orange	125.00	6.50
21	A2	50h red lilac	85	30
22	A3	1k dark rose	1.00	42
23	A3	2k ultra	1.25	1.10
24	A3	5k dull blue grn	3.00	3.00
		Nos. 11-24 (14)	313.49	19.62

All values of this issue except the 3h exist on ribbed paper.

Nos. 17, 19 and 20 were reprinted in 1911. The reprints are in lighter colors and on whiter paper than the originals. Reprints of Nos. 17 and 19 are perf. 10½ and those of No. 20 are perf. 12½. Value each $1.50.

Numerals in Black

1901-04 ***Perf. 12½***

25	A2	20h pink ('02)	55	30
26	A2	30h bister brn ('03)	55	30
27	A2	35h blue	75	30
a.		35h ultramarine	*80.00*	4.75
28	A2	40h orange ('03)	1.00	60
29	A2	45h grnsh blue ('04)	65	35
		Nos. 25-29 (5)	3.50	1.85

Nos. 11-16, 18, 21-29 exist imperf. Most of Nos. 11-29 exist perf. 6½; compound with 12½; part perf.; in pairs imperf. between. These were supplied only to some high-ranking officials and never sold at any P.O.

View of Deboj — A4

The Carsija at Sarajevo — A5

Designs: 2h, View of Mostar. 3h, Pliva Gate, Jajce. 5h, Narenta Pass and Prenj River. 6h, Rama Valley. 10h, Vrbas Valley. 20h, Old Bridge, Mostar. 25h, Bey's Mosque, Sarajevo. 30h, Donkey post. 35h, Jezero and tourists' pavilion. 40h, Mail wagon. 45h, Bazaar at Sarajevo. 50h, Postal car. 2k, St. Luke's Campanile, Jajce. 5k, Emperor Franz Josef.

Perf. 6½, 9½, 10½ and 12½, also Compounds

1906 Engr. Unwmk.

30	A4	1h black	15	15
31	A4	2h violet	15	15
32	A4	3h olive	15	15
33	A4	5h dark green	15	15
34	A4	6h brown	15	15
a.		Perf. 13½	15.00	18.00
35	A4	10h carmine	15	15
36	A4	20h dark brown	35	18
a.		Perf. 13½	37.50	37.50
37	A4	25h deep blue	1.00	75
38	A4	30h green	1.10	30
39	A4	35h myrtle green	1.25	30
40	A4	40h orange red	1.25	30
41	A4	45h brown red	1.25	90
42	A4	50h dull violet	1.40	60
43	A5	1k maroon	3.25	1.25
44	A5	2k gray green	4.25	6.00
45	A5	5k dull blue	3.50	4.50
		Nos. 30-45 (16)	19.50	15.98

Nos. 30-45 exist imperf. Value, set $50 unused, $37.50 canceled.

For overprint and surcharges see Nos. 126, B1-B4.

Birthday Jubilee Issue

Designs of 1906 Issue, with "1830-1910" in Label at Bottom

1910 ***Perf. 12½***

46	A4	1h black	30	15
47	A4	2h violet	35	15
48	A4	3h olive	35	18
49	A4	5h dark green	42	15
50	A4	6h orange brn	45	18
51	A4	10h carmine	42	15
52	A4	20h dark brown	90	1.10
53	A4	25h deep blue	2.00	2.25
54	A4	30h green	1.50	1.90
55	A4	35h myrtle grn	2.00	1.90
56	A4	40h orange red	2.00	2.50
57	A4	45h brown red	3.50	4.25
58	A4	50h dull violet	3.50	4.50
59	A5	1k maroon	3.50	4.50
60	A5	2k gray green	13.00	13.00
61	A5	5k dull blue	2.50	3.00
		Nos. 46-61 (16)	36.69	39.86

80th birthday of Emperor Franz Josef.

Scenic Type of 1906

Designs (Views): 12h, Jaice. 60h, Konjica. 72h, Vishegrad.

1912

62	A4	12h ultra	3.25	4.00
63	A4	60h dull blue	2.00	3.50
64	A4	72h carmine	10.00	13.00
		Nos. 62-64 (3)	15.25	20.50

Value, imperf. set, $75.

See Austria for similar designs inscribed "FELDPOST" instead of "MILITARPOST."

Emperor Franz Josef
A23 A24

Bosnia and Herzegovina stamps can be mounted in the Scott Austria album.

A25

A26

1912-14

Various Frames

65	A23	1h olive green	35	15
66	A23	2h brt blue	35	15
67	A23	3h claret	35	15
68	A23	5h green	35	15
69	A23	6h dark gray	35	15
70	A23	10h rose car	35	15
71	A23	12h dp olive grn	1.10	20
72	A23	20h orange brn	4.50	15
73	A23	25h ultra	2.25	15
74	A23	30h orange red	2.25	15
75	A24	35h myrtle grn	2.25	15
76	A24	40h dk violet	6.75	15
77	A24	45h olive brn	3.00	15
78	A24	50h slate blue	3.00	15
79	A24	60h brown vio	2.75	15
80	A24	72h dark blue	3.25	2.75
81	A25	1k brn vio, *straw*	12.50	32
82	A25	2k dk gray, *bl*	7.25	22
83	A26	3k carmine, *grn*	11.00	8.25
84	A26	5k dk vio, *gray*	22.50	20.00
85	A25	10k dk ultra, *gray* ('14)	82.50	70.00
		Nos. 65-85 (21)	168.95	103.84

Value, imperf. set, $450.

For overprint and surcharges see #127, B5-B8.

A27

A28

1916-17 ***Perf. 12½***

86	A27	3h dark gray	15	18
87	A27	5h olive green	24	32
88	A27	6h violet	28	32
89	A27	10h bister	1.25	1.65
90	A27	12h blue gray	32	45
91	A27	15h car rose	15	15
92	A27	20h brown	30	40
93	A27	25h blue	22	32
94	A27	30h dark green	22	32
95	A27	40h vermilion	22	32
96	A27	50h green	22	32
97	A27	60h lake	24	35
98	A27	80h orange brn	1.00	37
a.		Perf. 11½	3.25	3.00
99	A27	90h dark violet	60	50
a.		Perf. 11½	450.00	*675.00*
101	A28	2k claret, *straw*	60	75
102	A28	3k green, *bl*	1.75	3.25
103	A28	4k carmine, *grn*	5.25	7.25
104	A28	10k dp vio, *gray*	14.00	20.00
		Nos. 86-104 (18)	27.01	37.22

Value, imperf. set, $175.

For overprints see Nos. B11-B12.

Emperor Karl I
A29 A30

1917 ***Perf. 12½***

105	A29	3h olive gray	15	20
a.		Perf. 11½	75.00	75.00
b.		Perf. 12½x11½	13.00	21.00
106	A29	5h olive green	15	15
107	A29	6h violet	32	55
108	A29	10h orange brn	15	15
a.		Perf. 11½x12½	62.50	95.00
b.		Perf. 11½		
109	A29	12h blue	50	70
110	A29	15h brt rose	15	15
111	A29	20h red brown	15	15
112	A29	25h ultra	1.00	45
113	A29	30h gray green	22	16
114	A29	40h olive bis	24	15
115	A29	50h dp green	85	45
116	A29	60h car rose	85	38
a.		Perf. 11½	15.00	21.00
117	A29	80h steel blue	22	20
118	A29	90h dull violet	1.00	1.40
119	A30	2k carmine, *straw*	52	42
120	A30	3k green, *bl*	13.00	16.00

121 A30	4k carmine, *grn*	5.25	7.25
122 A30	10k dp violet, *gray*	3.25	5.75
	Nos. 105-122 (18)	27.97	34.66

Value, imperf. set, $85.

Nos. 47 and 66 Overprinted in Red **1918**

1918

126 A4 2h violet		42	50
b.	Inverted overprint	15.00	
d.	Double overprint	35.00	
f.	Double overprint, one inverted		
127 A23 2h bright blue		50	60
a.	Pair, one without overprint		
b.	Inverted overprint	15.00	
c.	Double overprint	13.00	
d.	Double overprint, one inverted		

Emperor Karl I — A31

1918 Typo. *Perf. 12½, Imperf.*

128 A31	2h orange	9.00
129 A31	3h dark green	9.00
130 A31	5h lt green	9.00
131 A31	6h blue green	9.00
132 A31	10h brown	9.00
133 A31	20h brick red	9.00
134 A31	25h ultra	9.00
135 A31	45h dk slate	9.00
136 A31	50h lt bluish grn	9.00
137 A31	60h blue violet	9.00
138 A31	70h ocher	9.00
139 A31	80h rose	9.00
140 A31	90h violet brn	9.00

Engr.

141 A30	1k ol grn, *grnsh*	*1,900.*
	Nos. 128-140 (13)	117.00

Nos. 128-141 were prepared for use in Bosnia and Herzegovina, but were not issued there. They were sold after the Armistice at the Vienna post office for a few days.

SEMI-POSTAL STAMPS

Nos. 33 and 35 Surcharged in Red **1914. 7 Heller**

1914 Unwmk. *Perf. 12½*

B1 A4	7h on 5h dk grn	40	40
B2 A4	12h on 10h car	40	40

Various minor varieties of the surcharge include "4" with open top, narrow "4" and wide "4."

Nos. B1-B2 exist with double and inverted surcharges. Value about $20 each.

Nos. 33 and 35 Surcharged in Red or Blue **❖ 1915. ❖ 7 Heller**

1915 *Perf. 12½*

B3 A4	7h on 5h (R)	8.75	8.75
a.	Perf. 9½	140.00	140.00
B4 A4	12h on 10h (Bl)	28	28

Nos. B3-B4 exist with double and inverted surcharges. Value about $18.50 each.

❖ 1915 ❖

Nos. 68 and 70 Surcharged in Red or Blue

7 Heller.

1915

B5 A23	7h on 5h (R)	75	75
a.	"1915" at top and bottom	35.00	37.50
B6 A23	12h on 10h (Bl)	1.25	1.50
a.	Surcharged "7 Heller."	35.00	37.50

Nos. B5-B6 are found in three types differing in length of surcharge lines:

I- date 18mm, denomination 14mm.
II- date 16mm, denomination 14mm.
III- date 18mm, denomination 16mm.

Nos. B5-B6 exist with double and inverted surcharges. Value $25 each.

Nos. B5a and B6a exist double and inverted.

❖ 1916. ❖

Nos. 68 and 70 Surcharged in Red or Blue

7 Heller.

1916

B7 A23	7h on 5h (R)	50	65
B8 A23	12h on 10h (Bl)	50	65

Nos. B7-B8 exist with double and inverted surcharges. Value $12.50 each.

Wounded Soldier — SP1

Blind Soldier — SP2

1916 Engr.

B9 SP1	5h (+ 2h) green	60	60
B10 SP2	10h (+ 2h) magenta	90	90

Nos. B9-B10 exist imperf. Value, set $27.50.

Nos. 89, 91 Overprinted **WITWEN- UND WAISENWOCHE 1917**

1917

B11 A27	10h bister	15	15
B12 A27	15h carmine rose	15	15
	Set value	20	20

Nos. B11-B12 exist imperf. Value set, $16.

Nos. B11-B12 exist with double and inverted overprint. Value $9 each.

Design for Memorial Church at Sarajevo SP3

Archduke Francis Ferdinand — SP4

Duchess Sophia and Archduke Francis Ferdinand SP5

1917 Typo. *Perf. 11½, 12½*

B13 SP3	10h violet black	15	25
B14 SP4	15h claret	15	25
B15 SP5	40h deep blue	15	25
	Set value	36	

Assassination of Archduke Ferdinand and Archduchess Sophia. Sold at a premium of 2h each which helped build a memorial church at Sarajevo.

Exist imperf. Value, set $2.50.

Blind Soldier — SP6

Emperor Karl I — SP8

Design: 15h, Wounded soldier.

1918 Engr. *Perf. 12½*

B16 SP6	10h (+ 10h) grnsh bl	45	52
B17 SP6	15h (+ 10h) red brn	45	52

#B16-B17 exist imperf. Value, set $18.50.

1918 Typo. *Perf. 12½x13*

Design: 15h, Empress Zita.

B18 SP8	10h gray green	30	45
B19 SP8	15h brown red	30	45
B20 SP8	40h violet	30	45
	Nos. B18-B20 (3)	90	1.35

Sold at a premium of 10h each which went to the "Karl's Fund."

#B18-B20 exist imperf. Value, set $22.50.

POSTAGE DUE STAMPS

D1

D2

Perf. 9½, 10½, 12½ and Compound

1904 Unwmk.

J1	D1	1h black, red & yel	38	15
J2	D1	2h black, red & yel	38	16
J3	D1	3h black, red & yel	38	15
J4	D1	4h black, red & yel	38	15
J5	D1	5h black, red & yel	38	15
J6	D1	6h black, red & yel	18	15
J7	D1	7h black, red & yel	2.25	2.50
J8	D1	8h black, red & yel	2.25	50
J9	D1	10h black, red & yel	55	15
J10	D1	15h black, red & yel	50	15
J11	D1	20h black, red & yel	2.75	16
J12	D1	50h black, red & yel	1.90	15
J13	D1	200h black, red & grn	7.75	70
		Nos. J1-J13 (13)	20.03	5.22

Value, imperf. set, $150.

For overprints see Western Ukraine Nos. 61-72.

1916-18 *Perf. 12½*

J14	D2	2h red ('18)	38	38
J15	D2	4h red ('18)	28	28
J16	D2	5h red	38	38
J17	D2	6h red ('18)	28	28
J18	D2	10h red	35	35
J19	D2	15h red	3.00	3.00
J20	D2	20h red	35	35
J21	D2	25h red	1.10	1.10
J22	D2	30h red	95	95
J23	D2	40h red	7.50	7.50
J24	D2	50h red	24.00	24.00
J25	D2	1k dark blue	3.00	3.00
J26	D2	3k dark blue	13.00	13.00
		Nos. J14-J26 (13)	54.57	54.57

Nos. J25-J26 have colored numerals on a white tablet.

Value, imperf. set, $110.

NEWSPAPER STAMPS

Bosnian Girl — N1

1913 Unwmk. *Imperf.*

P1	N1	2h ultra	38	38
P2	N1	6h violet	1.50	1.50
P3	N1	10h rose	1.50	1.50
P4	N1	20h green	1.90	1.90
		Nos. P1-P4 (4)	5.28	5.28

After Bosnia and Herzegovina became part of Yugoslavia stamps of type N1 perf., and imperf. copies surcharged with new values, were used as regular postage stamps. See Yugoslavia Nos. 1L21-1L22, 1L43-1L45.

SPECIAL HANDLING STAMPS

"Lightning" — SH1

1916 Unwmk. Engr. *Perf. 12½*

QE1 SH1	2h vermilion	20	20
a.	Perf. 11½x12½	250.00	250.00
QE2 SH1	5h deep green	32	32
a.	Perf. 11½	13.00	13.00

BRAZIL

Brasil (after 1918)

LOCATION — On the north and east coasts of South America, bordering on the Atlantic Ocean.
GOVT. — Republic
AREA — 3,286,000 sq. mi.
POP. — 132,580,000 (est. 1984)
CAPITAL — Brasilia

Brazil was an independent empire from 1822 to 1889, when a constitution was adopted and the country became officially known as The United States of Brazil.

1000 Reis = 1 Milreis
100 Centavos = 1 Cruzeiro (1942)
100 Centavos = 1 Cruzado (1986)
100 Centavos = 1 Cruzeiro (1990)
100 Centavos = 1 Cruzeiro Real (Aug. 2, 1993)

Catalogue values for unused stamps in this country are for Never Hinged items, beginning with Scott 680 in the regular postage section, Scott C66 in the airpost section, Scott RA2 in the postal tax section, and Scott RAB1 in the postal tax semi-postal section.

Values of Brazil Nos. 1-13 vary according to condition. Quotations are for fine-very fine copies. Very fine to superb specimens sell at much higher prices, and inferior or poor copies sell at reduced prices, depending on the condition of the individual specimen.

Watermarks

Wmk. 97- "CORREIO FEDERAL REPUBLICA DOS ESTADOS UNIDOS DO BRAZIL" in Sheet

Wmk. 98- "IMPOSTO DE CONSUMO REPUBLICA DOS ESTADOS UNIDOS DO BRAZIL" in Sheet

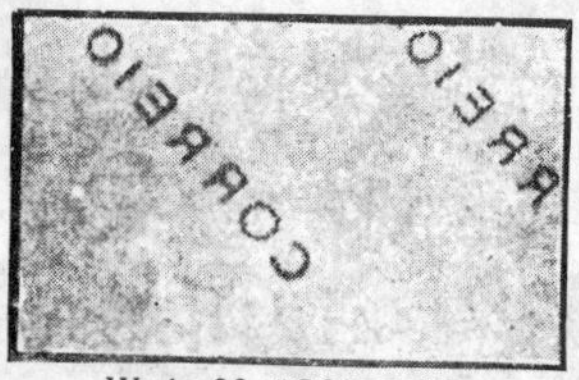
Wmk. 99- "CORREIO"

Wmk. 100- "CASA DA MOEDA" in Sheet

Because of the spacing of this watermark, a few stamps in each sheet may show no watermark.

Wmk. 101- Stars and CASA DA MOEDA

Wmk. 193- ESTADOS UNIDOS DO BRASIL

Wmk. 206- Star-framed CM, Multiple

Wmk. 218- E U BRASIL Multiple, Letters 8mm High

Wmk. 221- ESTADOS UNIDOS DO BRASIL, Multiple, Letters 6mm High

Wmk. 222- CORREIO BRASIL and 5 Stars in Squared Circle

Wmk. 236- Coat of Arms in Sheet

Watermark (reduced illustration) covers 22 stamps in sheet.

Wmk. 245- Multiple "CASA DA MOEDA DO BRASIL" and Small Formee Cross

Wmk. 249- "CORREIO BRASIL" multiple

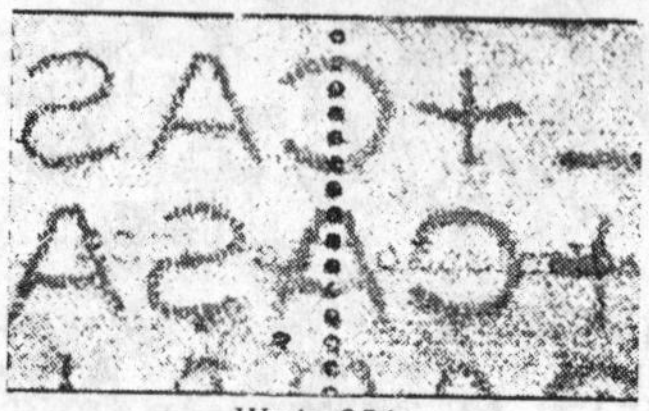
Wmk. 256- "CASA+DA+MOEDA+DO+BRAZIL" in 8mm Letters

Wmk. 264- "*CORREIO*BRASIL*" Multiple, Letters 7mm High

Wmk. 267- "*CORREIO*BRASIL*" Multiple in Small Letters 5mm High

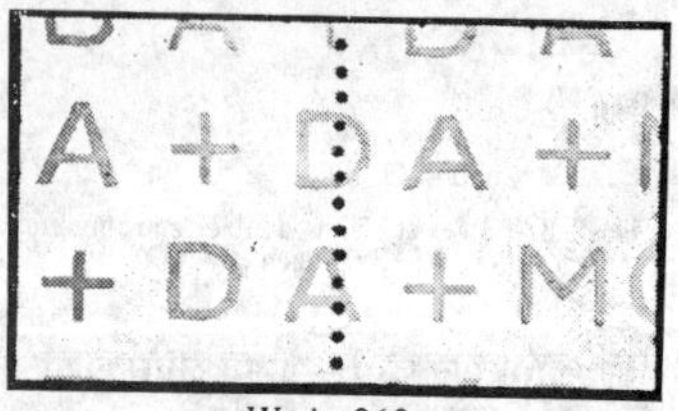
Wmk. 268- "CASA+DA+MOEDA+DO+BRASIL" in 6mm Letters

Wmk. 270- Wavy Lines and Seal

Wmk. 271- Wavy Lines

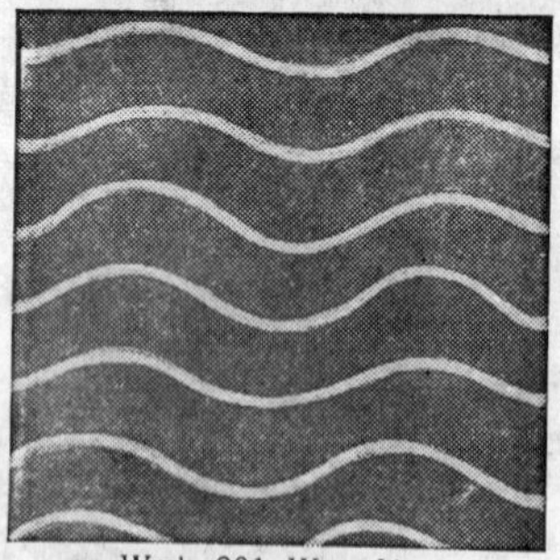
Wmk. 281- Wavy Lines

Issues of the Empire

A1

Grayish or Yellowish Paper

1843, Aug. 1 Unwmk. Engr. ***Imperf.***

1	A1 30r black		1,650.	400.
a.	In pair with No. 2			*200,000.*
2	A1 60r black		450.	175.
3	A1 90r black		2,750.	950.

Values are for early or fine impressions. Intermediate or worn impressions sell for less.

A2

A3

Grayish or Yellowish Paper

1844-46

7	A2	10r black	60.00	15.00
8	A2	30r black	75.00	30.00
9	A2	60r black	65.00	22.50
10	A2	90r black	500.00	100.00
11	A2	180r black	3,500.	1,300.
12	A2	300r black	5,250.	1,800.
13	A2	600r black	5,000.	2,000.

Nos. 8, 9 and 10 exist on thick paper and are considerably scarcer.

Grayish or Yellowish Paper

1850, Jan. 1

21	A3	10r black	22.50	15.00
22	A3	20r black	55.00	95.00
23	A3	30r black	8.50	3.00
24	A3	60r black	8.50	2.25
25	A3	90r black	80.00	11.50
26	A3	180r black	80.00	52.50
27	A3	300r black	325.00	60.00
28	A3	600r black	275.00	90.00

All values except the 90r were reprinted in 1910 on very thick paper.

1854

37	A3	10r blue	12.00	11.50
38	A3	30r blue	32.50	45.00

A4

1861

39	A4	280r red	140.00	95.00
40	A4	430r yellow	175.00	90.00

Nos. 39 and 40 have been reprinted on thick white paper with white gum. They are printed in aniline inks and the colors are brighter than those of the originals.

1866 ***Perf. 13½***

42	A3	10r blue	60.00	*95.00*
43	A3	20r black	375.00	260.00
44	A3	30r black	165.00	82.50
45	A3	30r blue	*500.00*	*575.00*
46	A3	60r black	60.00	17.50
47	A3	90r black	300.00	165.00
48	A3	180r black	300.00	165.00
49	A4	280r red	350.00	500.00
50	A3	300r black	575.00	260.00
51	A4	430r yellow	350.00	325.00
52	A3	600r black	350.00	165.00

Fraudulent perforations abound.
A 10r black is questioned.

A5

A6

A7

A8

A8a

A9

Emperor Dom Pedro — A9a

Thick or Thin White Wove Paper

1866, July 1 *Perf. 12*

No.	Type	Description	Unused	Used
53	A5	10r vermilion	5.25	3.50
54	A6	20r red lilac	6.25	2.00
a.		20r dull violet	52.50	25.00
56	A7	50r blue	11.00	1.40
57	A8	80r slate violet	30.00	4.25
58	A8a	100r blue green	11.00	35
a.		100r yellow green	62.50	3.50
59	A9	200r black	47.50	4.25
60	A9a	500r orange	100.00	16.00
		Nos. 53-60 (7)	211.00	31.75

The 10r and 20r exist imperf. on both white and bluish paper. Some authorities consider them proofs.

Nos. 58 and 65 are found in two types.

Bluish Paper

No.	Type	Description	Unused	Used
53a	A5	10r	300.00	375.00
54b	A6	20r	125.00	22.50
56a	A7	50r	125.00	11.00
57a	A8	80r	165.00	25.00
58b	A8a	100r	550.00	105.00

1876-77 ***Rouletted***

No.	Type	Description	Unused	Used
61	A5	10r vermilion ('77)	27.50	20.00
62	A6	20r red lilac ('77)	40.00	20.00
63	A7	50r blue ('77)	37.50	5.00
64	A8	80r violet ('77)	85.00	12.50
65	A8a	100r green	11.00	70
66	A9	200r black ('77)	32.50	4.25
67	A9a	500r orange	110.00	20.00
		Nos. 61-67 (7)	343.50	82.45

A10

A11

A12

A13

A14

A15

A16

A17

A18

A19

A20

1878-79 ***Rouletted***

No.	Type	Description	Unused	Used
68	A10	10r vermilion	4.50	2.00
69	A11	20r violet	6.25	1.75
70	A12	50r blue	9.25	1.00
71	A13	80r lake	10.50	6.25
72	A14	100r green	10.50	35
73	A15	200r black	67.50	10.00
74	A16	260r dk brown	42.50	17.00
75	A18	300r bister	42.50	4.25
76	A19	700r red brown	92.50	80.00
77	A20	1000r gray lilac	125.00	32.50
		Nos. 68-77 (10)	411.00	155.10

1878, Aug. 21 ***Perf. 12***

No.	Type	Description	Unused	Used
78	A17	300r orange & grn	50.00	15.00

Nos. 68-78 exist imperforate.

A21

A22

A23

Small Heads

Laid Paper

Perf. 13, 13¹/₂ and Compound

1881, July 15

No.	Type	Description	Unused	Used
79	A21	50r blue	62.50	14.00
80	A22	100r olive green	250.00	27.50
81	A23	200r pale red brn	425.00	87.50

On Nos. 79 and 80 the hair above the ear curves forward. On Nos. 83 and 88 it is drawn backward. On the stamps of the 1881 issue the beard is smaller than in the 1882-85 issues and fills less of the space between the neck and the frame at the left.

See No. 88.

A24

A25

A26

A27

Two types each of the 100 and 200 reis.

100 REIS:

Type I - Groundwork formed of diagonal crossed lines and horizontal lines.

Type II - Groundwork formed of diagonal crossed lines and vertical lines.

200 REIS:

Type I - Groundwork formed of diagonal and horizontal lines.

Type II - Groundwork formed of diagonal crossed lines.

Larger Heads

Laid Paper

Perf. 12¹/₂ to 14 and Compound

1882-84

No.	Type	Description	Unused	Used
82	A24	10r black	5.00	11.00
83	A25	100r ol grn, type I	21.00	2.50
a.		100r dark green, type I	19.00	2.50
b.		100r dark green, type II	110.00	7.50
84	A26	200r pale red brn, type I	42.50	20.00
85	A27	200r pale rose, type II	21.00	3.50
a.		Diagonal half used as 100r on cover		14.00
		Nos. 82-85 (4)	89.50	37.00

See No. 86.

A28

A29

A30

Three types of A29

Type I - Groundwork of horizontal lines.

Type II - Groundwork of diagonal crossed lines.

Type III - Groundwork solid.

Perf. 13, 13¹/₂, 14 and Compound

1884-85

No.	Type	Description	Unused	Used
86	A24	10r orange	1.40	1.40
87	A28	20r slate green	5.50	2.00
a.		20r olive green	5.00	1.40
88	A21	50r bl, head larger	14.00	2.50
89	A29	100r lil, type II,III	165.00	42.50
90	A29	100r lil, type I	42.50	1.75
91	A30	100r lilac	92.50	2.75

A31

A32

Southern Cross

A33

Crown

A34

Perf. 13, 13¹/₂, 14 and Compound

1885

No.	Type	Description	Unused	Used
92	A31	100r lilac	22.50	1.00

Compare design A31 with A35.

1887

No.	Type	Description	Unused	Used
93	A32	50r chalky blue	12.50	2.75
94	A33	300r gray blue	77.50	16.00
95	A34	500r olive	52.50	10.00

A35

A36

Entrance to Bay of Rio de Janeiro — A37

1888

No.	Type	Description	Unused	Used
96	A35	100r lilac	17.00	70
a.		Imperf., pair	62.50	87.50
97	A36	700r violet	37.50	62.50
98	A37	1000r dull blue	125.00	62.50

Issues of the Republic

Southern Cross — A38

Wove Paper, Thin to Thick

Perf. 12¹/₂ to 14, 11 to 11¹/₂, and 12¹/₂ to 14x11 to 11¹/₂, Rough or Clean-Cut

Engraved; Typographed (#102)

1890-91

No.	Type	Description	Unused	Used
99	A38	20r gray green	1.10	90
a.		20r blue green	1.25	90
b.		20r emerald	9.00	4.25
100	A38	50r gray green	1.75	70
a.		50r olive green	7.00	70
b.		50r yellow green	7.00	3.50
c.		50r dark slate green	7.00	3.50
d.		Horiz. pair, imperf. btwn.		
101	A38	100r lilac rose	190.00	2.75
102	A38	100r red lil, redrawn	17.50	45
a.		Tete beche pair	9,500.	14,500.
103	A38	200r purple	5.00	70
a.		200r violet	10.00	1.65
b.		200r violet blue	21.00	2.10
104	A38	300r slate vio	32.50	1.75
a.		300r gray	35.00	5.25
b.		300r gray blue	50.00	7.00
c.		300r dark violet	25.00	4.25
105	A38	500r olive bister	11.00	5.25
a.		500r olive gray	11.00	7.00
106	A38	500r slate	11.00	5.50
107	A38	700r chocolate	14.00	14.00
a.		700r fawn	16.00	16.00
108	A38	1000r bister	8.50	1.75
a.		1000r yellow buff	17.00	3.50
		Nos. 99-108 (10)	292.35	33.75

The redrawn 100r may be distinguished by the absence of the curved lines of shading in the left side of the central oval. The pearls in the oval are not well aligned and there is less shading at right and left of "CORREIO" and "100 REIS."

A 100 reis stamp of type A38 but inscribed "BRAZIL" instead of "E. U. DO BRAZIL" was not placed in issue but postmarked copies are known. A reprint on thick paper was made in 1910.

No. 101 exists imperf., not regularly issued.

For surcharges see Nos. 151-158.

Liberty Head

A39 A40

Perf. 12¹/₂ to 14, 11 to 11¹/₂ and 12¹/₂ to 14x11 to 11¹/₂

1891, May 1 **Typo.**

No.	Type	Description	Unused	Used
109	A39	100r blue & red	17.50	35
a.		Head inverted	77.50	62.50
b.		Tete beche pair	400.00	400.00
c.		100r ultra & red	19.00	42

Perf. 11, 11¹/₂, 13, 13¹/₂, 14 and Compound

1893, Jan. 18 **Litho.**

No.	Type	Description	Unused	Used
111	A40	100r rose	25.00	35

Sugarloaf Mountain
A41 A41a

Liberty Head
A42 A42a

Hermes — A43

Perf. 11 to 11½, 12½ to 14 and 12½ to 14x11 to 11½

1894-97 **Unwmk.**

112	A41	10r rose & blue	1.40	35
113	A41a	10r rose & blue	1.00	25
114	A41a	20r orange & bl	90	20
115	A41a	50r dk blue & blue	3.50	1.00
116	A42	100r carmine & blk	1.75	18
a.		Vert. pair, imperf. btwn.	70.00	
118	A42a	200r orange & blk	1.00	18
a.		Imperf. horiz., pair	52.50	
b.		Vert. pair, imperf. btwn.	52.50	
119	A42a	300r green & blk	10.00	35
120	A42a	500r blue & blk	17.50	90
121	A42a	700r lilac & blk	12.50	1.25
122	A43	1000r green & vio	42.50	1.00
124	A43	2000r blk & gray lil	42.50	10.50
		Nos. 112-124 (11)	134.55	16.16

The head of No. 116 exists in five types. See Nos. 140-150A, 159-161, 166-171d.

Newspaper Stamps Surcharged:

100 1898 100
a

200 1898 200
b

100 1898 100
c

Surcharged on 1889 Issue of type N1

1898 ***Rouletted***

Green Surcharge

125	(b)	700r on 500r yel	5.00	7.00
126	(c)	1000r on 700r yel	21.00	21.00
a.		Surcharged "700r"	325.00	375.00
127	(c)	2000r on 1000r yel	14.00	8.75
128	(c)	2000r on 1000r brn	12.50	4.25

Violet Surcharge

129	(a)	100r on 50r brn yel	1.40	*17.50*
130	(c)	100r on 50r brn yel	32.50	35.00
131	(c)	300r on 200r blk	2.50	90
a.		Double surcharge	105.00	87.50

The surcharge on No. 130 is handstamped. The impression is blurred and lighter in color than on No. 129. The two surcharges differ most in the shapes and serifs of the figures "1."

Counterfeits exist of No. 126a.

Black Surcharge

132	(b)	200r on 100r violet	2.10	90
a.		Double surcharge	60.00	*105.00*
b.		Inverted surcharge	60.00	*105.00*
132C	(b)	500r on 300r car	3.25	1.75
133	(b)	700r on 500r green	5.00	1.65

Blue Surcharge

134	(b)	500r on 300r car	5.25	3.50

Red Surcharge

135	(c)	1000r on 700r ultra	14.00	8.75
a.		Inverted surcharge	125.00	125.00

Surcharged on 1890-94 Issues:

200 1898
d

1898 50 RÉIS 50
e

Black Surcharge

136	N3(e)	20r on 10r blue	90	1.75
137	N2(d)	200r on 100r red lilac	6.25	4.50
a.		Double surcharge	77.50	77.50

Surcharge on No. 137 comes blue to deep black.

Blue Surcharge

138	N3(e)	50r on 20r green	2.10	4.25

Red Surcharge

139	N3(e)	100r on 50r green	6.25	7.00
a.		Blue surcharge	12.50	

The surcharge on Nos. 139 and 139a exists double, inverted, one missing, etc.

Types of 1894-97

Perf. 5½-7 and 11-11½x5½-7

140	A41a	10r rose & bl	2.75	5.50
141	A41a	20r orange & bl	5.50	5.50
142	A41a	50r dk bl & lt bl	6.25	12.50
143	A42	100r carmine & blk	10.50	2.75
144	A42a	200r orange & blk	6.25	2.75
145	A42a	300r green & blk	37.50	6.25

Perf. 8½-9½, 8½-9½x11-11½

146	A41a	10r rose & bl	3.50	1.75
147	A41a	20r orange & bl	10.50	1.75
147A	A41a	50r dk bl & bl	87.50	25.00
148	A42	100r carmine & blk	17.50	1.00
149	A42a	200r orange & blk	7.00	90
150	A42a	300r green & blk	42.50	4.25
150A	A43	1000r green & vio	85.00	8.50

Issue of 1890-93 Surcharged in Violet or Magenta

1899
50 RÉIS

Perf. 11 to 11½, 12½ to 14 and Compound

1899, June 25

151	A38	50r on 20r gray grn	70	1.00
a.		Double surcharge		
152	A38	100r on 50r gray grn	1.00	1.00
b.		Double surcharge	42.50	42.50
153	A38	300r on 200r pur	4.25	*6.25*
a.		Double surcharge	42.50	42.50
154	A38	500r on 300r sl vio	12.50	5.50
a.		500r on 300r gray lilac	11.00	4.25
b.		Pair, one without surcharge	210.00	
155	A38	700r on 500r ol bis	14.00	3.50
a.		Pair, one without surcharge	250.00	
156	A38	1000r on 700r choc	8.50	3.50
157	A38	1000r on 700r fawn	10.50	3.50
a.		Pair, one without surcharge	250.00	
158	A38	2000r on 1000r yel buff	32.50	2.50
a.		2000r on 1000r bister	12.50	2.50
b.		Pair, one without surcharge	250.00	
		Nos. 151-158 (8)	83.95	26.75

Types of 1894-97

Perf. 11, 11½, 13 and Compound

1900

159	A41a	50r green	6.00	35
160	A42	100r rose	12.50	18
a.		Frame around inner oval	70.00	3.50
161	A42a	200r blue	8.50	18
		Nos. 159-161 (3)	27.00	71

Three types exist of No. 161, all of which have the frame around inner oval.

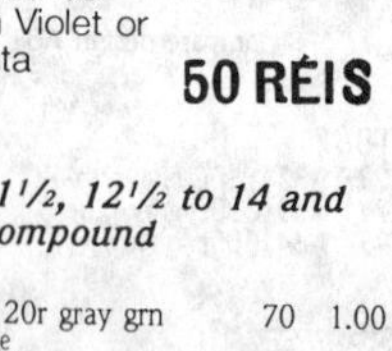

Cabral Arrives at Brazil — A44

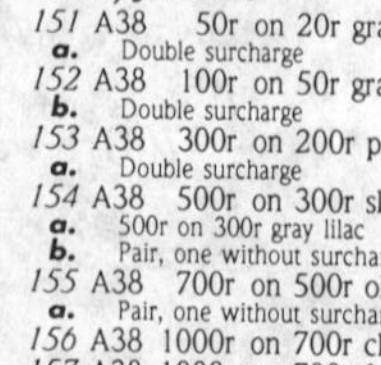

Independence Proclaimed
A45

"Emancipation of Slaves" — A46

Allegory, Republic of Brazil — A47

1900, Jan. 1 **Litho.** ***Perf. 12½***

162	A44	100r red	4.25	3.75
a.		Imperf., pair	250.00	250.00
163	A45	200r green & yel	4.25	3.75
164	A46	500r blue	4.25	3.75
165	A47	700r emerald	4.25	3.75
		Nos. 162-165 (4)	17.00	15.00

Discovery of Brazil, 400th anniversary.

Types of 1894-97

Wmk. (97? or 98?)

1905 ***Perf. 11, 11½***

166	A41a	10r rose & bl	2.75	1.40
167	A41a	20r orange & bl	5.00	52
168	A41a	50r green	8.75	42
169	A42	100r rose	12.50	20
170	A42a	200r dark blue	12.50	15
171	A42a	300r green & blk	25.00	1.00
		Nos. 166-171 (6)	66.50	3.69

Positive identification of Wmk. 97 or 98 places stamp in specific watermark groups below.

Wmk. 97

166b	A41a	10r rose & blue	21.00	9.00
167b	A41a	20r orange & blue	21.00	5.25
168b	A41a	50r green	32.50	5.25
169b	A42	100r rose	165.00	17.50
170b	A42a	200r dark blue	62.50	1.40
171b	A42a	300r green & blk	190.00	12.50
171A	A43	1000r green & vio	165.00	16.00
		Nos. 166b-171A (7)	657.00	66.90

Wmk. 98

166c	A41a	10r rose & blue	22.50	19.00
167c	A41a	20r orange & blue	42.50	8.75
168c	A41a	50r green	77.50	16.00
169c	A42	100r rose	45.00	1.50
170c	A42a	200r dark blue	62.50	70
171d	A42a	300r green & blk	140.00	16.00
		Nos. 166c-171d (6)	390.00	61.95

Allegory, Pan-American Congress
A48

1906, July 23 **Litho.** **Unwmk.**

172	A48	100r carmine rose	15.00	15.00
173	A48	200r blue	30.00	4.00

Third Pan-American Congress.

Aristides Lobo — A48a

Benjamin Constant — A49

Pedro Alvares Cabral — A50

Eduardo Wandenkolk — A51

Manuel Deodoro da Fonseca — A52

Floriano Peixoto — A53

Prudente de Moraes — A54

Manuel Ferraz de Campos Salles — A55

Francisco de Paula Rodrigues Alves — A56

Liberty Head — A57

A58

A59

1906-16 **Engr.** ***Perf. 12***

174	A48a	10r bluish slate	24	15
175	A49	20r aniline vio	15	15
176	A50	50r green	30	15
a.		Booklet pane of 6 ('08)	25.00	*47.50*
177	A51	100r anil rose	65	15
a.		Imperf. vert., coil ('16)	2.50	30
b.		Booklet pane of 6 ('08)	35.00	*47.50*
178	A52	200r blue	65	15
a.		Booklet pane of 6 ('08)	27.50	*47.50*
179	A52	200r ultra ('15)	90	15
a.		Imperf. vert., coil ('16)	1.25	30
180	A53	300r gray blk	2.00	15
181	A54	400r olive grn	13.00	90
182	A55	500r dk violet	2.75	15
183	A54	600r olive grn ('10)	90	30
184	A56	700r red brown	2.75	1.25
185	A57	1000r vermilion	20.00	35
186	A58	2000r yellow grn	9.00	24
187	A58	2000r Prus blue ('15)	5.50	30
188	A59	5000r carmine rose	3.50	75
		Nos. 174-188 (15)	62.29	5.29

Allegorical Emblems: Liberty, Peace, Industry, etc. — A60

1908, July 14

189	A60	100r carmine	10.00	50

National Exhibition, Rio de Janeiro.

Emblems of Peace Between Brazil and Portugal
A61

1908, July 14

190	A61	100r red	4.00	40

Opening of Brazilian ports to foreign commerce, cent. Medallions picture King Carlos I of Portugal and Pres. Affonso Penna of Brazil.

Bonifacio, Bolivar, Hidalgo, O'Higgins, San Martin, Washington — A62

1909

191	A62	200r deep blue	2.00	30

For surcharge see No. E1.

Nilo Peçanha — A63

Baron of Rio Branco — A64

1910, Nov. 15

192	A63	10,000r brown	5.00	75

1913-16

193	A64	1000r deep green	90	15
194	A64	1000r slate ('16)	9.00	18

Cabo Frio — A65

Perf. 11½

1915, Nov. 13 Litho. Wmk. 99

195	A65	100r dk grn, *yelsh*	2.00	2.00

Founding of the town of Cabo Frio, 300th anniversary.

Bay of Guajara — A66

1916, Jan. 5

196	A66	100r carmine	4.00	2.25

City of Belem, 300th anniversary.

Revolutionary Flag — A67

1917, Mar. 6

197	A67	100r deep blue	10.00	3.50

Revolution of Pernambuco, Mar. 6, 1817.

Rodrigues Alves — A68

Unwmk.

1917, Aug. 31 Engr. *Perf. 12*

198	A68	5000r red brown	35.00	4.00

Liberty Head

A69 A70

Perf. 12½, 13, 13x13½.

1918-20 Typo. Unwmk.

200	A69	10r orange brn	20	15
201	A69	20r slate	20	15
202	A69	25r ol gray ('20)	20	15
203	A69	50r green	20.00	1.40
204	A70	100r rose	55	15
a.		Imperf., pair		
205	A70	300r red orange	9.75	1.10
206	A70	500r dull violet	9.75	60
		Nos. 200-206 (7)	40.65	3.70

1918-20 Wmk. 100

207	A69	10r red brown	2.50	75
a.		Imperf., pair		
207B	A69	20r slate	60	48
c.		Imperf., pair		
208	A69	25r ol gray ('20)	30	18
209	A69	50r green	30	15
210	A70	100r rose	22.50	15
a.		Imperf., pair		
211	A70	200r dull blue	3.25	18
212	A70	300r orange	22.50	1.75
213	A70	500r dull violet	22.50	4.25
214	A70	600r orange	90	4.25
		Nos. 207-214 (9)	75.35	12.14

Because of the spacing of this watermark, a few stamps in each sheet may show no watermark.

"Education" — A72

1918 Engr. *Perf. 11½*

215	A72	1000r blue	2.50	15
216	A72	2000r red brown	17.00	3.25
217	A72	5000r dark violet	5.25	3.75
		Nos. 215-217 (3)	24.75	7.15

Watermark note below No. 257 also applies to Nos. 215-217.

See Nos. 233-234, 283-285, 404, 406, 458, 460. For surcharge see No. C30.

Railroad A73

"Industry" A74

"Aviation" A75

Mercury A76

"Navigation" — A77

Perf. 13½x13, 13x13½

1920-22 Typo. Unwmk.

218	A73	10r red violet	40	20
219	A73	20r olive green	40	20
220	A74	25r brown violet	30	20
221	A74	50r blue green	50	20
222	A74	50r orange brn ('22)	80	20
223	A75	100r rose red	1.50	20
224	A75	100r orange ('22)	3.00	20
225	A75	150r violet ('21)	80	20
226	A75	200r blue	1.50	20
227	A75	200r rose red ('22)	5.00	20
228	A76	300r olive gray	5.00	30
229	A76	400r dull blue ('22)	15.00	1.75
230	A76	500r red brown	10.00	40
		Nos. 218-230 (13)	44.20	4.45

See Nos. 236-257, 265-266, 268-271, 273-274, 276-281, 302-311, 316-322, 326-340, 357-358, 431-434, 436-441, 461-463B, 467-470, 472-474, 488-490, 492-494. For surcharges see Nos. 356-358, 376-377.

Perf. 11, 11½

Engr. Wmk. 100

231	A77	600r red orange	1.25	20
232	A77	1000r claret	3.00	15
a.		Perf. 8½	22.50	4.00
233	A72	2000r dull violet	12.00	40
234	A72	5000r brown	10.00	5.00
		Nos. 231-234 (4)	26.25	5.75

Nos. 233 and 234 are inscribed "BRASIL CORREIO." Watermark note below No. 257 also applies to Nos. 231-234.

See No. 282.

King Albert of Belgium and President Epitacio Pessoa A78

1920, Sept. 19 Engr. *Perf. 11½x11*

235	A78	100r dull red	50	50

Visit of the King and Queen of Belgium.

Types of 1920-22 Issue

Perf. 13x13½, 13x12½

1922-29 Typo. Wmk. 100

236	A73	10r red violet	20	15
237	A73	20r olive green	20	15
238	A75	20r gray violet ('29)	20	15
239	A74	25r brown violet	25	15
240	A74	50r blue grn	2.50	30.00
241	A74	50r org brn ('23)	35	25
a.		Booklet pane of 6		
242	A75	100r rose red	18.00	30
243	A75	100r orange ('26)	40	15
a.		Booklet pane of 6		
244	A75	100r turq grn ('28)	25	15
245	A75	150r violet	2.00	15
246	A75	200r blue	300.00	10.00
247	A75	200r rose red	30	15
a.		Booklet pane of 6		
248	A75	200r ol grn ('28)	2.00	2.50
249	A76	300r olive gray	1.50	20
a.		Booklet pane of 6		
250	A76	300r rose red ('29)	25	20
251	A76	400r blue	1.50	15
252	A76	400r orange ('29)	60	50
253	A76	500r red brown	6.00	40
a.		Booklet pane of 6		
254	A76	500r ultra ('29)	7.00	15
255	A76	600r brn org ('29)	6.00	2.50
256	A76	700r dull vio ('29)	6.00	1.40
257	A76	1000r turq bl ('29)	8.00	60
		Nos. 236-257 (22)	363.50	50.35

Because of the spacing of the watermark, a few stamps in each sheet show no watermark.

"Agriculture" — A79

1922 Unwmk. *Perf. 13x13½*

258	A79	40r orange brown	40	15
259	A79	80r grnsh blue	32	1.50

See Nos. 263, 267, 275.

Declaration of Ypiranga — A80

Dom Pedro I and Jose Bonifacio — A81

National Exposition and President Pessoa — A82

Unwmk.

1922, Sept. 7 Engr. *Perf. 14*

260	A80	100r ultra	3.00	20
261	A81	200r red	1.25	15
262	A82	300r green	2.25	15
		Nos. 260-262 (3)	6.50	50

Cent. of independence and Natl. Exposition of 1922.

Agriculture Type of 1922

Perf. 13½x12

1923 Wmk. 100 Typo.

263	A79	40r orange brown	50	50

Brazilian Army Entering Bahia — A83

Unwmk.

1923, July 12 Litho. *Perf. 13*

264	A83	200r rose	5.00	2.50

Centenary of the taking of Bahia from the Portuguese.

Types of 1920-22 Issues

Perf. 13x13½

1924 Typo. Wmk. 193

265	A73	10r red violet	4.50	3.00
266	A73	20r olive green	5.00	3.00
267	A79	40r orange brown	3.50	50
268	A74	50r orange brown	3.00	15.00
269	A75	100r orange	3.50	25
270	A75	200r rose	5.00	20
271	A76	400r blue	3.00	3.00
		Nos. 265-271 (7)	27.50	24.95

Arms of Equatorial Confederation, 1824 — A84

Unwmk.

1924, July 2 Litho. *Perf. 11*

272	A84	200r bl, blk, yel, & red	2.00	1.25
a.		Red omitted	275.00	275.00

Centenary of the Equatorial Confederation.

Types of 1920-22 Issues

Perf. 9½ to 13½ and Compound

1924-28 Typo. Wmk. 101

273	A73	10r red violet	15	15
274	A73	20r olive gray	15	15
275	A79	40r orange brn	30	15
276	A74	50r orange brn	30	15
277	A75	100r red orange	60	15
278	A75	200r rose	40	15
279	A76	300r ol gray ('25)	7.00	80
280	A76	400r blue	2.00	25
281	A76	500r red brown	9.00	35
		Engr.		
282	A77	600r red orange ('26)	75	15
283	A72	2000r dull vio ('26)	2.00	15
284	A72	5000r brown ('26)	10.00	60
285	A72	10,000r rose ('28)	12.00	75
		Nos. 273-285 (13)	44.65	3.95

Nos. 283-285 are inscribed "BRASIL CORREIO."

Ruy Barbosa — A85

1925 Wmk. 100 *Perf. 11½*

286	A85	1000r claret	3.50	1.25

1926 Wmk. 101

287	A85	1000r claret	1.50	25

"Justice" — A86

Scales of Justice and Map of Brazil — A87

Perf. 13½x13

1927, Aug. 11 Typo. Wmk. 206

288	A86	100r deep blue	65	30
289	A87	200r rose	65	30

Founding of the law courses, cent.

Liberty Holding Coffee Leaves — A88

1928, Mar. 5

290	A88	100r blue green	75	30
291	A88	200r carmine	50	25
292	A88	300r olive black	4.25	20
		Nos. 290-292 (3)	5.50	75

Introduction of the coffee tree in Brazil, bicent.

Official Stamps of 1919 Surcharged in Red or Black **700 Réis**

Perf. 11, 11½

1928 Wmk. 100 Engr.

293	O3	700r on 500r orange	2.10	1.40
a.		Inverted surcharge	175.00	175.00
294	O3	1000r on 100r rose red (Bk)	1.40	25
295	O3	2000r on 200r dull bl	2.00	38
296	O3	5000r on 50r green	2.00	48
297	O3	10,000r on 10r ol grn	10.00	80
		Nos. 293-297 (5)	17.50	3.31

#293-297 were used for ordinary postage.

Stamps in the outer rows of the sheets are often without watermark.

Ruy Barbosa — A89

Perf. 9, 9½x11, 11, and Compound

1929 Wmk. 101

300	A89	5000r blue violet	8.00	50

See #405, 459. For surcharge see #C29.

Types of 1920-21 Issue

Perf. 13½x12½

1929 Typo. Wmk. 218

302	A75	20r gray violet	15	15
303	A75	50r red brown	15	15
304	A75	100r turq green	20	15
305	A75	200r olive green	10.50	2.00
306	A76	300r rose red	48	15
307	A76	400r orange	60	20
308	A76	500r ultra	6.00	40
309	A76	600r brown org	7.25	48
310	A76	700r dp violet	2.00	15
311	A76	1000r turq blue	3.25	15
		Nos. 302-311 (10)	30.58	3.98

Wmk. 218 exists both in vertical alignment and in echelon.

Wmk. in echelon

302a	A75	20r	16	28
303a	A75	50r	72.50	25.00
306a	A76	300r	60	24
308a	A76	500r	100.00	14.00
311a	A76	1000r	6.00	6.00

Architectural Fantasies
A90 A91

Architectural Fantasy — A92

Perf. 13x13½

1930, June 20 Wmk. 206

312	A90	100r turq blue	90	50
313	A91	200r olive gray	1.50	40
314	A92	300r rose red	2.50	50
		Nos. 312-314 (3)	4.90	1.40

Fourth Pan-American Congress of Architects and Exposition of Architecture.

Types of 1920-21 Issues

1930 Wmk. 221 ***Perf. 13x12½***

316	A75	20r gray violet	15	15
317	A75	50r red brown	15	15
318	A75	100r turq blue	20	15
319	A75	200r olive green	2.50	20
320	A76	300r rose red	50	20
321	A76	500r ultra	1.25	20
322	A76	1000r turq blue	17.50	60
		Nos. 316-322 (7)	22.25	1.65

Imperforates

Since 1930, imperforate or partly perforated sheets of nearly all commemorative and some definitive issues have become obtainable.

Types of 1920-29 Issue

Perf. 11, 13½x13, 13x12½

1931-34 Typo. Wmk. 222

326	A75	10r deep brown	15	15
327	A75	20r gray violet	15	15
328	A74	25r brn vio ('34)	15	50
330	A75	50r blue green	15	15
331	A75	50r red brown	15	15
332	A75	100r orange	25	15
334	A75	200r dp carmine	35	15
335	A76	300r olive green	50	15
336	A76	400r ultra	70	15
337	A76	500r red brown	3.00	15
338	A76	600r brown org	3.00	15
339	A76	700r deep violet	3.00	15
340	A76	1000r turq blue	10.00	15
		Nos. 326-340 (13)	21.55	
		Set value		1.65

Getulio Vargas and Joao Pessoa — A93

Vargas and Pessoa — A94

Oswaldo Aranha
A95 A96

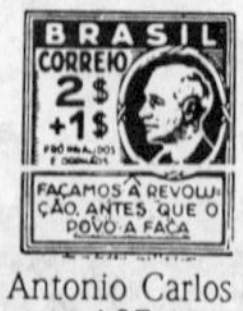

Antonio Carlos A97

Pessoa A98

Vargas — A99

Unwmk.

1931, Apr. 29 Litho. ***Perf. 14***

342	A93	10r + 10r lt bl	15	*4.50*
343	A93	20r + 20r yel brn	15	*3.25*
344	A95	50r + 50r bl grn, red & yel	15	15
a.		Red missing at left	70	70
345	A93	100r + 50r orange	22	22
346	A93	200r + 100r green	22	22
347	A94	300r + 150r multi	22	22
348	A93	400r + 200r dp rose	85	50
349	A93	500r + 250r dk blue	55	45
350	A93	600r + 300r brn vio	38	*5.50*
351	A94	700r + 350r multi	70	42
352	A96	1000r + 500r brt grn, red & yel	1.65	16
353	A97	2000r + 1000r gray blk & red	3.25	42
354	A98	5000r + 2500r blk & red	14.00	3.75
355	A99	10000r + 5000r brt grn & yel	32.50	8.25
		Nos. 342-355 (14)	54.99	28.01

Revolution of Oct. 3, 1930. Prepared as semi-postal stamps, Nos. 342-355 were sold as ordinary postage stamps with stated surtax ignored.

Nos. 306, 320 and 250 Surcharged **1931 200 Réis**

Wmk. E U BRASIL Multiple (218)

1931, July 20 ***Perf. 13½x12½***

356	A76	200r on 300r rose red	75	75
a.		Wmk. in echelon	15.00	15.00
b.		Inverted surcharge	35.00	

Perf. 13x12½

Wmk. 221

357	A76	200r on 300r rose red	25	18
a.		Inverted surcharge	40.00	40.00

Perf. 13½x12½

Wmk. 100

358	A76	200r on 300r rose red	50.00	50.00

Map of South America Showing Meridian of Tordesillas
A100

Joao Ramalho and Tibiriça A101

Martim Affonso de Souza A102

King John III of Portugal A103

Disembarkation of M. A. de Souza at Sao Vicente — A104

Wmk. 222

1932, June 3 Typo. ***Perf. 13***

359	A100	20r dk violet	15	15
360	A101	100r black	16	28
361	A102	200r purple	85	15
362	A103	600r red brown	1.65	65

Engr.

Wmk. 101

Perf. 9½, 11, 9½x11

363	A104	700r ultra	2.00	1.00
		Nos. 359-363 (5)	4.81	2.23

1st colonization of Brazil at Sao Vicente, in 1532, under the hereditary captaincy of Martim Affonso de Souza.

Revolutionary Issue

Map of Brazil — A105

Soldier and Flag — A106

Allegory: Freedom, Justice, Equality — A107

Soldier's Head — A108

"LEX" and Sword A109

Symbolical of Law and Order A110

Symbolical of Justice A111

Perf. 11½

1932, Sept. 13 Litho. Unwmk.

364	A105	100r brown org	35	1.75
365	A106	200r dk carmine	30	60
366	A107	300r gray green	1.75	3.00
367	A108	400r dark blue	6.00	6.00
368	A105	500r black brown	6.00	6.00
369	A107	600r red	6.00	6.00
370	A106	700r violet	2.75	*6.00*
371	A108	1000r orange	1.50	*6.00*
372	A109	2000r dark brown	12.00	17.00
373	A110	5000r yellow grn	15.00	27.50
374	A111	10000r plum	17.00	32.50
		Nos. 364-374 (11)	68.65	112.35

Issued by the revolutionary forces in the state of Sao Paulo during the revolt of September, 1932. Subsequenty the stamps were recognized by the Federal Government and placed in general use.

Excellent counterfeits of Nos. 373 and 374 exist. Counterfeit cancellations abound.

City of Vassouras and Illuminated Memorial — A112

Wmk. 222

1933, Jan. 15 Typo. ***Perf. 12***

375	A112	200r rose red	80	50

City of Vassouras founding, cent.

Nos. 306, 320 Surcharged **200 RÉIS**

Perf. 13½x12½

1933, July 28 Wmk. 218

376	A76	200r on 300r rose red	50	50
a.		Wmk. 218 in echelon (No. 306a)	11.50	11.50
b.		Wmk. 100 (No. 250)	82.50	82.50

Perf. 13x12½

Wmk. 221

377	A76	200r on 300r rose red	38	38
a.		Inverted surcharge	30.00	
b.		Double surcharge	30.00	

Religious Symbols and Inscriptions — A113

Wmk. 222

1933, Sept. 3 Typo. *Perf. 13*

378	A113	200r dark red	70	40

1st Natl. Eucharistic Congress in Brazil.

"Flag of the Race" A114

1933, Aug. 18

379	A114	200r deep red	70	40

The raising of the "Flag of the Race" and the 441st anniv. of the sailing of Columbus from Palos, Spain, Aug. 3, 1492.

Republic Figure, Flags of Brazil and Argentina — A115

Perf. 11½

1933, Oct. 7 Wmk. 101 Engr.

380	A115	200r blue	25	18

Thick Laid Paper

Perf. 11, 11½

Wmk. 236

381	A115	400r green	45	35
382	A115	600r brt rose	1.75	1.75
383	A115	1000r lt violet	2.75	1.50
		Nos. 380-383 (4)	5.20	3.78

Visit of President Justo of the Argentina to Brazil, Oct. 2-7, 1933.

Allegory: "Faith and Energy" — A116

Allegory of Flight — A117

1933 Typo. Wmk. 222

384	A116	200r dark red	18	15
385	A116	200r dark violet	22	15
		Set value		17

See Nos. 435, 471 and 491.

Wmk. 236

1934, Apr. 15 Engr. *Perf. 12*

386	A117	200r blue	50	50

1st Natl. Aviation Congress at Sao Paulo.

A118

Wmk. 222

1934, May 12 Typo. *Perf. 11*

387	A118	200r dark olive	25	25
388	A118	400r carmine	1.25	1.25
389	A118	700r ultra	1.25	75
390	A118	1000r orange	3.00	50
		Nos. 387-390 (4)	5.75	2.75

7th Intl. Fair at Rio de Janeiro.

Christ of Corcovado — A119

1934, Oct. 20

392	A119	300r dark red	1.65	1.65
a.		Tete beche pair	5.00	6.00
393	A119	700r ultra	6.50	4.25
a.		Tete beche pair	19.00	22.50

Visit of Eugenio Cardinal Pacelli, later Pope Pius XII, to Brazil.

The three printings of Nos. 392-393, distinguishable by shades, sell for different prices.

José de Anchieta A120

Thick Laid Paper

1934, Nov. 8 Wmk. 236 *Perf. 11, 12*

394	A120	200r yellow brown	50	15
395	A120	300r violet	38	20
396	A120	700r blue	1.50	1.25
397	A120	1000r lt green	3.00	50
		Nos. 394-397 (4)	5.38	2.10

Jose de Anchieta, S.J. (1534-1597), Portuguese missionary and "father of Brazilian literature."

"Brazil" and "Uruguay"
A121 A122

Wmk. 222

1935, Jan. 8 Typo. *Perf. 11*

398	A121	200r orange	60	35
399	A122	300r yellow	75	45
400	A122	700r ultra	3.00	3.00
401	A121	1000r dk violet	7.25	3.50
		Nos. 398-401 (4)	11.60	7.30

Visit of President Terra of Uruguay.

View of Town of Igarassu A123

1935, July 1

402	A123	200r maroon & brn	75	38
403	A123	300r vio & olive brn	75	30

Captaincy of Pernambuco founding, 400th anniv.

Types of 1918-29

Thick Laid Paper

Perf. 9½, 11, 12, 12x11

1934-36 Engr. Wmk. 236

404	A72	2000r violet	3.50	32
405	A89	5000r blue vio ('36)	10.00	40
406	A72	10000r claret ('36)	8.00	65
		Nos. 404-406 (3)	21.50	1.37

No. 404 is inscribed "BRASIL CORREIO."

Revolutionist — A124

Bento Gonçalves da Silva — A125

Duke of Caxias A126

1935, Sept. 20 *Perf. 11, 12*

407	A124	200r black	50	38
408	A124	300r rose lake	50	30
409	A125	700r dull blue	2.00	2.00
410	A126	1000r light violet	2.25	1.25
		Nos. 407-410 (4)	5.25	3.93

Centenary of the "Ragged" Revolution.

Federal District Coat of Arms A127

Wmk. 222

1935, Oct. 19 Typo. *Perf. 11*

411	A127	200r blue	2.00	2.00

8th Intl. Sample Fair held at Rio de Janeiro.

Coutinho's Ship A128

Arms of Fernandes Coutinho — A129

1935, Oct. 25

412	A128	300r maroon	2.00	60
413	A129	700r turq blue	2.75	1.50

400th anniversary of the establishment of the first Portuguese colony at Espirito Santo by Vasco Fernandes Coutinho.

Gavea, Rock near Rio de Janeiro A130

1935, Oct. 12 Wmk. 245 *Perf. 11*

414	A130	300r brown & vio	1.25	90
415	A130	300r blk & turq bl	1.25	90
416	A130	300r Prus bl & ultra	1.25	90
417	A130	300r crimson & blk	1.25	90
		Nos. 414-417 (4)	5.00	3.60

"Child's Day," Oct. 12.

Viscount of Cairu — A131

Perf. 11, 12x11

1936, Jan. 20 Engr. Wmk. 236

418	A131	1200r violet	5.00	2.50

Jose da Silva Lisboa, Viscount of Cairu (1756-1835).

View of Cametá A132

1936, Feb. 26 *Perf. 11, 12*

419	A132	200r brown orange	1.25	85
420	A132	300r green	1.25	50

300th anniversary of the founding of the city of Cameta, Dec. 24, 1635.

Coining Press A133

Thick Laid Paper

1936, Mar. 24 *Perf. 11*

421	A133	300r pur brn, *cr*	75	45

1st Numismatic Cong. at Sao Paulo, Mar., 1936.

Carlos Gomes A134

"Il Guarany" A135

Thick Laid Paper

1936, July 11 *Perf. 11, 11x12*

422	A134	300r dull rose	32	25
423	A134	300r black brown	32	25
424	A135	700r ocher	2.00	75
425	A135	700r blue	1.50	90
		Nos. 422-425 (4)	4.14	2.15

100th anniversary of the birth of Antonio Carlos Gomes, who composed the opera "Il Guarany."

Scales of Justice — A136

Wmk. 222

1936, July 4 Typo. *Perf. 11*

426 A136 300r rose		1.25	45

First National Judicial Congress.

Federal District Coat of Arms A137

1936, Nov. 13 Typo. Wmk. 249

427 A137 200r rose red		75	45

Ninth International Sample Fair held at Rio de Janeiro.

Eucharistic Congress Seal — A138

1936, Dec. 17 Wmk. 245 *Perf. 11½*

428 A138 300r grn, yel, bl & blk		70	45

2nd Natl. Eucharistic Congress in Brazil.

Botafogo Bay — A139

Thick Laid Paper

Wmk. 236

1937, Jan. 2 Engr. *Perf. 11*

429 A139 700r blue		75	45
430 A139 700r black		75	45

Birth cent. of Francisco Pereira Passos, engineer who planned the modern city of Rio de Janeiro.

Types of 1920-21, 1933

Perf. 11, 11½ and Compound

1936-37 Typo. Wmk. 249

431	A75	10r deep brown	15	15
432	A75	20r dull violet	15	15
433	A75	50r blue green	15	15
434	A75	100r orange	20	15
435	A116	200r dk violet	40	15
436	A76	300r olive green	20	15
437	A76	400r ultra	40	15
438	A76	500r lt brown	60	15
439	A76	600r brn org ('37)	1.40	15
440	A76	700r deep violet	2.50	15
441	A76	1000r turq blue	2.75	15
		Nos. 431-441 (11)	8.90	
		Set value		88

Massed Flags and Star of Esperanto A140

1937, Jan. 19

442 A140 300r green		1.00	50

Ninth Brazilian Esperanto Congress.

Bay of Rio de Janeiro A141

1937, June 9 Unwmk. *Perf. 12½*

443 A141 300r orange red & blk		42	42
444 A141 700r blue & dk brn		1.10	42

2nd South American Radio Communication Conf. held in Rio, June 7-19.

Globe — A142

1937, Sept. 4 Wmk. 249 *Perf. 11, 12*

445 A142 300r green		75	40

50th anniversary of Esperanto.

Monroe Palace, Rio de Janeiro — A143

Botanical Garden, Rio de Janeiro — A144

1937, Sept. 30 Unwmk. *Perf. 12½*

446 A143	200r lt brn & bl	42	28
447 A144	300r org & ol grn	42	28
448 A143	2000r grn & cerise	3.50	5.00
449 A144	10000r lake & indigo	30.00	25.00
	Nos. 446-449 (4)	34.34	30.56

Brig. Gen. Jose da Silva Paes — A145

Eagle and Shield — A146

1937, Oct. 11 Wmk. 249 *Perf. 11½*

450 A145 300r blue		75	30

Bicentenary of Rio Grande do Sul.

1937, Dec. 2 Typo. *Perf. 11*

451 A146 400r dark blue		75	30

150th anniversary of the US Constitution

Bags of Brazilian Coffee — A147

Frame Engraved, Center Typographed

1938, Jan. 17 Unwmk. *Perf. 12½*

452 A147 1200r multi		3.00	40

Arms of Olinda A148

Perf. 11, 11x11½

1938, Jan. 24 Engr. Wmk. 249

453 A148 400r violet		50	25

4th cent. of the founding of the city of Olinda.

Independence Memorial, Ypiranga — A149

1938, Jan. 24 Typo. *Perf. 11*

454 A149 400r brown olive		60	25

Proclamation of Brazil's independence by Dom Pedro, Sept. 7, 1822.

Iguaçu Falls — A150

Perf. 12½

1938, Jan. 10 Unwmk. Engr.

455 A150 1000r sepia & yel brn		1.50	75
456 A150 5000r ol blk & grn		17.00	7.50

Couto de Magalhaes — A151

Perf. 11, 11x11½

1938, Mar. 17 Wmk. 249

457 A151 400r dull green		50	25

General Couto de Magalhaes (1837-1898), statesman, soldier, explorer, writer, developer.

Types of 1918-38

Perf. 11, 12x11, 12x11½, 12

1938 Engr. Wmk. 249

458 A72	2000r blue violet	6.50	15
459 A89	5000r violet blue	24.00	48
a.	5000r deep blue	20.00	48
460 A72	10000r rose lake	27.50	95
	Nos. 458-460 (3)	58.00	1.58

No. 458 is inscribed "BRASIL CORREIO."

Types of 1920-22

1938 Wmk. 245 Typo. *Perf. 11*

461	A75	50r blue green	50	75
462	A75	100r orange	50	75
463	A76	300r olive green	50	15
463A	A76	400r ultra	100.00	35.00
463B	A76	500r red brown	50	*10.00*
		Nos. 461-463B (5)	102.00	46.65

National Archives Building A152

1938, May 20 Wmk. 249

464 A152 400r brown		40	25

Centenary of National Archives.

Souvenir Sheets

Sir Rowland Hill A153

1938, Oct. 22 *Imperf.*

465 A153	Sheet of 10	12.50	12.50
a.	400r dull green, single stamp	75	75

Brazilian Intl. Philatelic Exposition (Brapex). Issued in sheets measuring 106x118mm. A few perforated sheets exist.

President Vargas A154

1938, Nov. 10 *Perf. 11*

Without Gum

466 A154	Sheet of 10	5.00	8.50
a.	400r slate blue, single stamp	40	40

Constitution of Brazil, set up by President Vargas, Nov. 10, 1937. Size: 113x135½mm.

Types of 1920-33

1939 Typo. Wmk. 256 *Perf. 11*

467	A75	10r red brown	28	22
468	A75	20r dull violet	28	15
469	A75	50r blue green	28	15
470	A75	100r yellow org	42	15
471	A116	200r dk violet	50	15
472	A76	400r ultra	90	15
473	A76	600r dull orange	90	15
474	A76	1000r turq blue	6.25	15
		Nos. 467-474 (8)	9.81	
		Set value		74

View of Rio de Janeiro — A155

View of Santos — A156

1939, June 14 Engr. Wmk. 249

475 A155 1200r dull violet		1.25	25

1939, Aug. 23

476 A156 400r dull blue		40	20

Centenary of founding of Santos.

Chalice Vine and Blossoms — A157

Eucharistic Congress Seal — A158

1939, Aug. 23

477	A157	400r green	1.00	25

1st South American Botanical Congress held in January, 1938.

1939, Sept. 3

478	A158	400r rose red	40	20

Third National Eucharistic Congress.

Duke of Caxias, Army Patron — A159

1939, Sept. 12 Photo. *Rouletted*

479	A159	400r deep ultra	40	25

Issued for Soldiers' Day.

A159a

A159b

A159d

A159c

Designs: 400r, George Washington. 800r, Emperor Pedro II. 1200r, Grover Cleveland. 1600r, Statue of Friendship, given by US.

1939, Oct. 7 Unwmk. Engr. *Perf. 12*

480	A159a	400r yellow orange	38	22
481	A159b	800r dark green	22	15
482	A159c	1200r rose car	50	15
483	A159d	1600r dark blue	50	22
		Nos. 480-483 (4)	1.60	74

New York World's Fair.

Benjamin Constant A160

Fonseca on Horseback A161

Manuel Deodoro da Fonseca and President Vargas — A162

Wmk. 249

1939, Nov. 15 Photo. *Rouletted*

484	A160	400r deep green	30	20
485	A162	1200r chocolate	75	28

Engr. *Perf. 11*

486	A161	800r gray black	45	30
		Nos. 484-486 (3)	1.50	78

50th anniv. of the Proclamation of the Republic.

President Roosevelt, President Vargas and Map of the Americas A163

1940, Apr. 14

487	A163	400r slate blue	70	40

Pan American Union, 50th anniversary.

Types of 1920-33

1940-41 Typo. Wmk. 264 *Perf. 11*

488	A75	10r red brown	15	22
489	A75	20r dull violet	22	22
489A	A75	50r blue grn ('41)	70	*1.25*
490	A75	100r yellow org	85	15
491	A116	200r violet	65	15
492	A76	400r ultra	4.25	15
493	A76	600r dull orange	4.25	15
494	A76	1000r turq blue	10.50	15
		Nos. 488-494 (8)	21.57	
		Set value		2.00

Map of Brazil — A164

1940, Sept. 7 Engr.

495	A164	400r carmine	40	20
a.		Unwmkd.	50.00	30.00

9th Brazilian Congress of Geography held at Florianopolis.

Victoria Regia Water Lily — A165

President Vargas — A166

Relief Map of Brazil — A167

1940, Oct. 30 Wmk. 249 *Perf. 11*

Without Gum

496	A165	1000r dull violet	85	85
a.		Sheet of 10	8.50	*25.00*
497	A166	5000r red	6.75	5.00
a.		Sheet of 10	72.50	*110.00*
498	A167	10,000r slate blue	7.50	2.50
a.		Sheet of 10	100.00	110.00
		Nos. 496-498 (3)	15.10	8.35

New York World's Fair.

All three sheets exist unwatermarked and also with papermaker's watermark of large globe and "AMERICA BANK" in sheet. A few imperforate sheets also exist.

Joaquim Machado de Assis — A168

Pioneers and Buildings of Porto Alegre — A169

1940, Nov. 1

499	A168	400r black	50	20

Birth centenary of Joaquim Maria Machado de Assis, poet and novelist.

1940, Nov. 2 Wmk. 264

500	A169	400r green	40	15

Colonization of Porto Alegre, bicent.

Proclamation of King John IV of Portugal A173

1940, Dec. 1 Wmk. 249

501	A173	1200r blue black	1.00	25

800th anniv. of Portuguese independence and 300th anniv. of the restoration of the monarchy.

No. 501 was also printed on paper with papermaker's watermark of large globe and "AMERICA BANK." Unwatermarked copies are from these sheets.

Brazilian Flags and Head of Liberty — A175

Wmk. 256

1940, Dec. 18 Engr. *Perf. 11*

502	A175	400r dull violet	50	20
b.		Unwmkd.	40.00	40.00

Wmk. 245

502A	A175	400r dull violet	40.00	40.00

10th anniv. of the inauguration of President Vargas.

Calendar Sheet and Inscription "Day of the Fifth General Census of Brazil" — A176

Wmk. 256

1941, Jan. 14 Typo. *Perf. 11*

503	A176	400r bl & red	40	20

Wmk. 245

504	A176	400r bl & red	3.00	80

Fifth general census of Brazil.

King Alfonso Henriques A177

Father Antonio Vieira A178

Salvador Corrêia de Sa e Benevides — A179

President Carmona of Portugal and President Vargas A180

Wmk. 264

1940-41 Photo. *Rouletted*

504A	A177	200r pink	15	15
505	A178	400r ultra	22	15
506	A179	800r brt vio	25	15
506A	A180	5400r sl grn	1.65	70

Wmk. 249

507	A177	200r pink	5.25	3.25
507A	A178	400r ultra	25.00	8.50
508	A180	5400r sl grn	2.50	1.25
		Nos. 504A-508 (7)	35.02	14.15

Portuguese Independence, 800th anniv.

For surcharge and overprint see Nos. C45, C47.

Jose de Anchieta A181

Amador Bueno A182

Wmk. 264

1941, Aug. 1 Engr. *Perf. 11*

509	A181	1000r gray vio	1.00	50

Society of Jesus, 400th anniversary.

1941, Oct. 20 *Perf. 11½*

510	A182	400r black	50	30

300th anniv. of the acclamation of Amador Bueno (1572-1648) as king of Sao Paulo.

Air Force Emblem A183

1941, Oct. 20 *Perf. 11*

511	A183	5400r slate grn	3.00	2.00

Issued in connection with Aviation Week, as propaganda for the Brazilian Air Force.

Petroleum — A184

Agriculture — A185

Steel Industry — A186

Commerce — A187

Marshal Peixoto — A188

Count of Porto Alegre — A189

Admiral J. A. C. Maurity — A190

"Armed Forces" — A191

Vargas — A192

1941-42 Wmk. 264 Typo. *Perf. 11*

512	A184	10r yel brn	18	18
513	A184	20r ol grn	15	15
514	A184	50r ol bis	15	15
515	A184	100r bl grn	18	15
516	A185	200r brn org	42	15
517	A185	300r lil rose	22	15
518	A185	400r grnsh bl	65	15
519	A185	500r salmon	30	15
520	A186	600r violet	65	15
521	A186	700r brt rose	30	15
522	A186	1000r gray	1.75	15
523	A186	1200r dl bl	3.00	15
524	A187	2000r gray vio	2.50	15
		Engr.		
525	A188	5000r blue	5.25	15
526	A189	10,000r rose red	6.50	18
527	A190	20,000r dp brn	6.50	35
528	A191	50,000r red ('42)	26.00	20.00
529	A192	100,000r bl ('42)	52	*8.50*
		Nos. 512-529 (18)	55.22	31.16

Nos. 512 to 527 and later issues come on thick or thin paper. The stamps on both papers also exist with three vertical green lines printed on the back, a control mark.

See Nos. 541-587, 592-593, 656-670.

Bernardino de Campos A193

Prudente de Morais A194

1942, May 25

533	A193	1000r red	1.25	40
534	A194	1200r blue	3.00	25

100th anniversary of the birth of Bernardino de Campos and Prudente de Morais, lawyers and statesmen of Brazil.

Head of Indo-Brazilian Bull — A195

1942, May 1 Wmk. 264 *Perf. 11½*

535	A195	200r blue	42	22
536	A195	400r org brn	42	22
a.		Wmk. 267	45.00	45.00

2nd Agriculture and Livestock Show of Central Brazil held at Uberaba.

Outline of Brazil and Torch of Knowledge A196

Map of Brazil Showing Goiania A197

Wmk. 264

1942, July 5 Typo. *Perf. 11*

537	A196	400r org brn	30	25

8th Brazilian Congress of Education.

1942, July 5

538	A197	400r lt vio	40	30

Founding of Goiania city.

Seal of Congress — A198

1942, Sept. 20 Wmk. 264

539	A198	400r olive bister	25	20
a.		Wmk. 267	25.00	12.50

4th Natl. Eucharistic Cong. at Sao Paulo.

Types of 1941-42

1942-47 Wmk. 245 *Perf. 11*

541	A184	20r olive green	15	40
542	A184	50r olive bister	15	15
543	A184	100r bl grn	40	40
544	A185	200r brn org	65	50
545	A185	400r grnsh bl	40	15
546	A186	600r lt vio	3.00	15
547	A186	700r brt rose	35	80
548	A186	1200r dl bl	1.25	15
549	A187	2000r gray vio ('47)	9.00	9.00
		Engr.		
550	A188	5000r blue	10.00	40
551	A189	10,000r rose red	6.00	1.50
552	A190	20,000r dp brn ('47)	4.50	45
553	A192	100,000r blue	3.50	8.00
		Nos. 541-553 (13)	39.35	22.05

Types of 1941-42

1941-47 Typo. Wmk. 268 *Perf. 11*

554	A184	20r ol grn	18	15
555	A184	50r ol bis ('47)	52	52
556	A184	100r bl grn ('43)	18	15
557	A185	200r brn org ('43)	18	15
558	A185	300r lil rose ('43)	15	15
559	A185	400r grnsh bl ('42)	30	15
560	A185	500r sal ('43)	18	15
561	A186	600r violet	60	15
562	A186	700r brt rose ('45)	35	*1.75*
563	A186	1000r gray	65	15
564	A186	1200r dp bl ('44)	85	15
565	A187	2000r gray vio ('43)	3.00	15
		Engr.		
566	A188	5000r bl ('43)	4.25	15
567	A189	10,000r rose red ('43)	8.50	38
568	A190	20,000r dp brn ('42)	19.00	42
569	A191	50,000r red ('42)	21.00	3.00
a.		50,000r dk brn red ('47)	15.00	8.50
570	A192	100,000r blue	55	55
		Nos. 554-570 (17)	60.44	8.27

Types of 1941-42

1942-47 Typo. Wmk. 267

573	A184	20r ol grn ('43)	15	15
574	A184	50r ol bis ('43)	15	15
575	A184	100r bl grn ('43)	18	15
576	A185	200r brn org ('43)	22	25
577	A185	400r grnsh bl	22	15
578	A185	500r sal ('43)	70.00	10.00
579	A186	600r vio ('43)	42	28
580	A186	700r brt rose ('47)	35	*3.50*
581	A186	1000r gray ('44)	2.10	15
582	A186	1200r dl bl	2.50	15
583	A187	2000r gray vio	2.50	15
		Engr.		
584	A188	5000r blue	4.25	15
585	A189	10,000r rose red ('44)	7.00	60
586	A190	20,000r dp brn ('45)	8.50	42
587	A191	50,000r red ('43)	25.00	5.25
		Nos. 573-587 (15)	123.54	21.50

1942 Typo. Wmk. 249

592	A184	100r bl grn	4.00	2.50
593	A186	600r violet	4.00	80

Map Showing Amazon River — A199

1943, Mar. 19 Wmk. 267 *Perf. 11*

607	A199	40c orange brown	32	32

Discovery of the Amazon River, 400th anniv.

Reproduction of Brazil Stamp of 1866 — A200

1943, Mar. 28 Wmk. 267

608	A200	40c violet	48	25
a.		Wmk. 268	*650.00*	

Centenary of city of Petropolis.

Adaptation of 1843 "Bull's-eye" A201

1943, Aug. 1 Engr. *Imperf.*

609	A201	30c black	45	25
610	A201	60c black	55	25
611	A201	90c black	45	25
		Nos. 609-611 (3)	1.45	75

Cent. of the 1st postage stamp of Brazil. The 30c and 90c exist unwatermarked; values $25 and $65.

Souvenir Sheet

A202

Wmk. 281 Horizontally or Vertically

1943 Engr. *Imperf.*

Without Gum

612	A202	Sheet of 3	7.50	6.75
a.		30c black	1.90	1.90
b.		60c black	1.90	1.90
c.		90c black	1.90	1.90

Ubaldino do Amaral A203

"Justice" A204

Perf. 11, 12

1943, Aug. 27 Typo. Wmk. 264

613	A203	40c dull slate grn	40	20
a.		Wmk. 267	20.00	15.00

Birth centenary of Ubaldino do Amaral, banker and statesman.

1943, Aug. 30 Wmk. 267

614	A204	2cr bright rose	70	40

Centenary of Institute of Brazilian Lawyers.

Indo-Brazilian Bull — A205

1943, Aug. 30 Engr.

615	A205	40c dk red brn	70	40

9th Livestock Show at Bahia.

José Barbosa Rodrigues A206

1943, Nov. 13 Typo.

616	A206	40c bluish grn	40	20

Birth cent. of Jose Barbosa Rodrigues, botanist.

Charity Hospital, Santos A207

1943, Nov. 7 Engr.

617	A207	1cr blue	40	30

400th anniv. of Charity Hospital, Santos.

Pedro Americo de Figueirido e Melo (1843-1905), Artist-hero and Statesman — A208

Wmk. 267

1943, Dec. 16 Typo. *Perf. 11*

618	A208	40c brn org	20	16

Gen. A. E. Gomes Carneiro A209

1944, Feb. 9 Engr.

619	A209	1.20cr rose	50	35

50th anniversary of the Lapa siege.

Statue of Baron of Rio Branco — A210

1944, May 13 **Typo.**

620 A210 1cr blue		40	25

Statue of the Baron of Rio Branco unveiling.

Duke of Caxias A211

1944, May 13 **Unwmk.** ***Perf. 12***
Granite Paper

621 A211 1.20cr bl grn & pale org		50	30

Centenary of pacification of Sao Paulo and Minas Gerais in an independence movement in 1842.

YMCA Seal — A212

1944, June 7 **Litho.** ***Perf. 11***
Granite Paper

622 A212 40c dp bl, car & yel		30	20

Centenary of Young Men's Christian Assn.

Chamber of Commerce Rio Grande — A213

Wmk. 268
1944, Sept. 25 **Engr.** ***Perf. 12***

623 A213 40c lt yel brn		30	25

Issued to commemorate the centenary of the Chamber of Commerce of Rio Grande.

Martim F. R. de Andrada A214

1945, Jan. 30 ***Perf. 11***

624 A214 40c blue		30	25

Ccentenary of the death of Martim F. R. de Andrada, statesman.

Meeting of Duke of Caxias and David Canabarro A215

1945, Mar. 19 **Photo.**

625 A215 40c ultra		30	20

Pacification of Rio Grande do Sul, cent.

Globe and "Esperanto" A216

1945, Apr. 16

626 A216 40c lt bl grn		50	25

10th Esperanto Congress, Rio, Apr. 14-22.

Baron of Rio Branco's Bookplate — A217

1945, Apr. 20 **Wmk. 268** ***Perf. 11***

627 A217 40c violet		50	25

Cent. of the birth of Jose Maria da Silva Paranhos, Baron of Rio Branco.

Tranquility — A218

Glory — A219

Victory A220

Peace A221

Cooperation A222

Rouletted 7
1945, May 8 **Engr.** **Wmk. 268**

628 A218 20c dk rose vio		15	15
629 A219 40c dk car		15	15
630 A220 1cr dl org		32	28
631 A221 2cr stl bl		85	42
632 A222 5cr green		1.65	55
	Nos. 628-632 (5)	3.12	1.55

Victory of the Allied Nations in Europe.

Nos. 628-632 exist on thin card, imperf. and unwatermarked.

Francisco Manoel da Silva (1795-1865), Composer (in 1831) of the National Anthem — A223

Wmk. 245
1945, May 30 **Typo.** ***Perf. 12***

633 A223 40c brt rose		45	30
a.	Wmk. 268	6.75	6.75

Bahia Institute of Geography and History A224

1945, May 30 **Wmk. 268** ***Perf. 11***

634 A224 40c lt ultra		25	20

50th anniv. of the founding of the Institute of Geography and History at Bahia.

Emblems of 5th Army and B.E.F.
A225 A226

US Flag and Shoulder Patches A227

Brazilian Flag and Shoulder Patches A228

Victory Symbol and Shoulder Patches — A229

1945, July 18 **Litho.**

635 A225 20c multi		15	15
636 A226 40c multi		15	15
637 A227 1cr multi		65	40
638 A228 2cr multi		95	55
639 A229 5cr multi		2.75	55
	Nos. 635-639 (5)	4.65	1.80

Honoring the Brazilian Expeditionary Force and the US 5th Army Battle against the Axis in Italy.

Radio Tower and Map — A230

1945, Sept. 3 **Engr.**

640 A230 1.20cr gray		45	25

Third Inter-American Conference on Radio Communications.

No. 640 was reproduced on a souvenir card with blue background and inscriptions. Size: 145x161mm.

A 40c lilac stamp, picturing the International Bridge between Argentina and Brazil and portraits of Presidents Justo and Vargas, was prepared late in 1945. It was not issued, but later was sold, without postal value, to collectors. Value, 15 cents.

Admiral Luiz Felipe Saldanha da Gama (1846-1895) A231

1946, Apr. 7

641 A231 40c gray blk		16	16

Princess Isabel d'Orleans-Braganca Birth Cent. — A232

1946, July 29 **Unwmk.**

642 A232 40c black		25	25

Post Horn, V and Envelope — A233

Post Office, Rio de Janeiro — A234

Bay of Rio de Janeiro and Plane A235

Wmk. 268
1946, Sept. 2 **Litho.** ***Perf. 11***

643 A233 40c blk & pale org		15	15

Perf. 12½
Engr. **Unwmk.**
Center in Ultramarine

644 A234	2cr slate	32	15
645 A234	5cr org brn	2.00	85
646 A234	10cr dk vio	2.25	42

Center in Brown Orange

647 A235	1.30cr dk grn		22	28
648 A235	1.70cr car rose		22	28
649 A235	2.20cr dp ultra		32	42
	Nos. 643-649 (7)		5.48	2.55

5th Postal Union Congress of the Americas and Spain.

No. 643 was reproduced on a souvenir card. Size: 188x239mm. Sold for 10cr.

Liberty — A236

Perf. 11x11½

1946, Sept. 18 **Wmk. 268**

650 A236 40c blk & gray 16 15
a. Unwmkd. 150.00

Adoption of the Constitution of 1946.

Columbus Lighthouse, Dominican Republic A237

1946, Sept. 14 **Litho.** ***Perf. 11***

651 A237 5cr Prus grn 4.00 1.50

Orchid — A238

Gen. A. E. Gomes Carneiro — A239

1946, Nov. 8 **Wmk. 268**

652 A238 40c ultra, red & yel 40 22
a. Unwmkd. 55.00

4th National Exhibition of Orchids, Rio de Janeiro, November, 1946.

Perf. 10½x12

1946, Dec. 6 **Engr.** **Unwmk.**

653 A239 40c dp grn 20 20

Centenary of the birth of Gen. Antonio Ernesto Gomes Carneiro.

Brazilian Academy of Letters A240

1946, Dec. 14 ***Perf. 11***

654 A240 40c blue 25 20

50th anniv. of the foundation of the Brazilian Academy of Letters, Rio de Janeiro.

15-Cent Minimum Value
The minimum catalogue value is 15 cents. Separating se-tenant pieces into individual stamps does not increase the value of the stamps since demand for the separated stamps may be small.

Antonio de Castro Alves (1847-1871), Poet — A241

1947, Mar. 14 **Litho.** **Wmk. 267**

655 A241 40c bluish grn 20 20

Types of 1941-42, Values in Centavos or Cruzeiros

1947-54 **Wmk. 267** **Typo.** ***Perf. 11***

656	A184	2c olive	15	15
657	A184	5c yel brn	15	15
658	A184	10c green	15	15
659	A185	20c brn org	15	15
660	A185	30c dk lil rose	50	15
661	A185	40c blue	25	15
b.		Wmk. 268	800.00	60.00
661A	A185	50c salmon	50	15
662	A186	60c lt vio	90	15
663	A186	70c brt rose ('54)	30	15
664	A186	1cr gray	90	15
665	A186	1.20cr dl bl	2.25	15
a.		Wmk. 268	10.00	9.00
666	A187	2cr gray vio	3.50	15
		Engr.		
667	A188	5cr blue	7.00	15
668	A189	10cr rose red	7.00	15
		Perf. 11, 13		
669	A190	20cr dp brn	14.00	75
670	A191	50cr red	27.50	50
		Nos. 656-670 (16)	65.20	
		Set value		2.45

The 5, 20, 50cr also exist with perf. 12-13.

Pres. Gonzalez Videla of Chile — A242

1947, June 26 **Unwmk.** ***Perf. 12x11***

671 A242 40c dk brn org 20 15

Visit of President Gabriel Gonzalez Videla of Chile, June 1947.

A souvenir folder contains four impressions of No. 671, and measures 6½x8¼ inches.

"Peace" and Western Hemisphere — A243

1947, Aug. 15 ***Perf. 11x12***

672 A243 1.20cr blue 20 15

Inter-American Defense Conference at Rio de Janeiro, August-September, 1947.

Pres. Harry S Truman, Map and Statue of Liberty A244

1947, Sept. 1 **Typo.** ***Perf. 12x11***

673 A244 40c ultra 20 15

Visit of US President Harry S Truman to Brazil, Sept. 1947.

Pres. Eurico Gaspar Dutra — A245

Mother and Child — A246

Wmk. 268

1947, Sept. 7 **Engr.** ***Perf. 11***

674 A245	20c green		15	15
675 A245	40c rose car		15	15
676 A245	1.20cr dp bl		25	15
	Nos. 674-676 (3)		55	
	Set value			30

The souvenir sheet containing Nos. 674-676 is listed as No. C73A. See No. 679.

1947, Oct. 10 **Typo.** **Unwmk.**

677 A246 40c brt ultra 20 15

Issued to mark Child Care Week, 1947.

Arms of Belo Horizonte A247

Globe A248

1947, Dec. 12 **Engr.** **Wmk. 267**

678 A247 1.20cr rose car 30 15

50th anniversary of the founding of the city of Belo Horizonte.

Dutra Type of 1947

1948 **Engr.** **Wmk. 267**

679 A245 20c green 1.50 1.50

Catalogue values for unused stamps in this section, from this point to the end of the section, are for Never Hinged items.

1948, July 10 **Litho.**

680 A248 40c dl grn & pale lil 35 15

International Exposition of Industry and Commerce, Petropolis, 1948.

Arms of Paranagua A249

Child Reading Book A250

1948, July 29

681 A249 5cr bister brown 1.75 50

300th anniversary of the founding of the city of Paranagua, July 29, 1648.

1948, Aug. 1

682 A250 40c green 25 20

National Education Campaign.

No. 682 was reproduced on a souvenir card. Size: 124x157mm.

Tiradentes A251

Symbolical of Cancer Eradication A252

1948, Nov. 12

683 A251 40c brn org 25 20

200th anniversary of the birth of Joaquim José da Silva Xavier (Tiradentes).

1948, Dec. 14

684 A252 40c claret 25 25

Anti-cancer publicity.

Adult Student A253

1949, Jan. 3 **Wmk. 267** ***Perf. 12x11***

685 A253 60c red vio & pink 25 15

Campaign for adult education.

"Battle of Guararapes," by Vitor Meireles — A254

1949, Feb. 15 ***Perf. 11½x12***

686 A254 60c lt bl 95 60

2nd Battle of Guararapes, 300th anniv.

Church of Sao Francisco de Paula — A255

Manuel de Nobrega — A256

Perf. 11x12

1949, Mar. 8 **Unwmk.** **Engr.**

687 A255 60c dark brown 20 16
a. Souvenir sheet 27.50 27.50

Bicentenary of city of Ouro Fino, state of Minas Gerais.

No. 687a contains one imperf. stamp similar to No. 687, with dates in lower margin. Size: 70x89mm.

1949, Mar. 29 ***Imperf.***

688 A256 60c violet 25 25

Founding of the City of Salvador, 400th anniv.

Emblem of Brazilian Air Force and Plane — A257

1949, June 18
689 A257 60c blue violet 25 25

Issued to honor the Brazilian Air Force.

Star and Angel — A258

1949 Wmk. 267 Litho. *Perf. 11x12*
690 A258 60c pink 20 16

1st Ecclesiastical Cong., Salvador, Bahia.

Globe — A259

1949, Oct. 31 Typo. *Perf. 12x11*
691 A259 1.50cr blue 25 16

75th anniv. of the UPU.

Ruy Barbosa A260

Unwmk.
1949, Dec. 14 Engr. *Perf. 12*
692 A260 1.20cr rose carmine 65 32

Centenary of birth of Ruy Barbosa.

Joaquim Cardinal Arcoverde A. Cavalcanti, Birth Centenary — A261

Perf. 11x12
1950, Feb. 27 Litho. Wmk. 267
693 A261 60c rose 25 20

Grapes and Factory A262

1950, Mar. 15 *Perf. 12x11*
694 A262 60c rose lake 25 20

75th anniversary of Italian immigration to the state of Rio Grande do Sul.

Virgin of the Globe — A263

Globe and Soccer Players — A264

1950, May 31 *Perf. 11x12*
695 A263 60c blk & lt bl 25 20

Establishment in Brazil of the Daughters of Charity of St. Vincent de Paul, cent.

1950, June 24
696 A264 60c ultra, bl & gray 85 50

4th World Soccer Championship.

Symbolical of Brazilian Population Growth A265

1950, July 10 Typo. *Perf. 12x11*
697 A265 60c rose lake 25 20

Issued to publicize the 6th Brazilian census.

Dr. Oswaldo Cruz — A266

1950, Aug. 23 Litho. *Perf. 11x12*
698 A266 60c orange brown 25 20

5th International Congress of Microbiology.

View of Blumenau and Itajai River — A267

1950, Sept. 9 Wmk. 267 *Perf. 12x11*
699 A267 60c bright pink 25 20

Centenary of the founding of Blumenau.

Amazonas Theater, Manaus A268

1950, Sept. 27
700 A268 60c light brn red 20 16

Centenary of Amazonas Province.

Arms of Juiz de Fora — A269

1950, Oct. 24 *Perf. 11x12*
701 A269 60c carmine 25 25

Centenary of the founding of Juiz de Fora.

Post Office at Recife — A270

1951, Jan. 10 Typo. *Perf. 12x11*
702 A270 60c carmine 20 20
703 A270 1.20cr carmine 30 20

Opening of the new building of the Pernambuco Post Office.

Arms of Joinville — A271

Jean-Baptiste de La Salle — A272

1951, Mar. 9 *Perf. 11x12*
704 A271 60c orange brown 25 20

Centenary of the founding of Joinville.

1951, Apr. 30 Litho.
705 A272 60c blue 25 20

300th anniversary of the birth of Jean-Baptiste de La Salle.

Heart and Flowers — A273

Sylvio Romero — A274

1951, May 13 Engr.
706 A273 60c deep plum 25 20

Mother's Day, May 14, 1951.

1951, Apr. 21 Litho.
707 A274 60c dl vio brn 20 20

Romero (1851-1914), poet and author.

Joao Caetano, Stage and Masks — A275

1951, July 9 *Perf. 12x11*
708 A275 60c lt gray bl 25 20

Issued to publicize the first Brazilian Theater Congress, Rio de Janeiro, July 9-13, 1951.

Orville A. Derby — A276

First Mass Celebrated in Brazil — A277

1951, July 23 *Perf. 11x12*
709 A276 2cr slate 35 35

Centenary of the birth (in New York State) of Orville A. Derby, geologist.

1951, July 25
710 A277 60c dl brn & buff 20 16

4th Inter-American Congress on Catholic Education, Rio de Janeiro, 1951.

Euclides Pinto Martins A278

1951, Aug. 16 *Perf. 12x11*
711 A278 3.80cr brn & citron 1.50 35

1st flight from NYC to Rio, 29th anniv.

Monastery of the Rock — A279

1951, Sept. 8
712 A279 60c dl brn & cream 20 20

Founding of Vitoria, 4th centenary.

Santos-Dumont and Model Plane Contest — A280

Dirigible and Eiffel Tower — A281

Perf. 11x12
1951, Oct. 19 Wmk. 267 Litho.
713 A280 60c sal & dk brn 42 35

Unwmk. Engr.
714 A281 3.80cr dk pur 1.25 40

Week of the Wing and 50th anniv. of Santos-Dumont's flight around the Eiffel Tower.

In December 1951, Nos. 713 and 714 were privately overprinted: "Exposicao Filatelica Regional Distrito Federal 15-XII-1951 23-XII-1951." These were attached to souvenir sheets bearing engraved facsimiles of Nos. 38, 49 and 51, which were sold by Clube Filatelico do Brasil to mark its 20th anniversary. The overprinted stamps on the sheets were canceled, but 530 "unused" sets were sold by the club.

Farmers and Ear of Wheat — A282

1951, Nov. 10 Litho. Wmk. 267

715 A282 60c dp grn & gray 25 25

Festival of Grain at Bage, 1951.

Map and Open Bible — A283

1951, Dec. 9 *Perf. 12x11*

716 A283 1.20cr brn org 50 35

Issued to publicize the Day of the Bible.

Queen Isabella — A284

Henrique Oswald — A285

1952, Mar. 10 *Perf. 11x12*

717 A284 3.80cr lt bl 60 30

500th anniversary of the birth of Queen Isabella I of Spain.

1952, Apr. 22

718 A285 60c brown 25 20

Oswald (1852-1931), composer.

Vicente Licinio Cardoso A286

Map and Symbol of Labor A287

1952, May 2

719 A286 60c gray bl 25 20

4th Brazilian Homeopathic Congress.

1952, Apr. 30

720 A287 1.50cr brnsh pink 25 20

5th International Labor Organization Conference for American Countries.

Gen. Polidoro da Fonseca — A288

Luiz de Albuquerque M. P. Caceres — A289

Portraits: 5cr, Baron de Capanema. 10cr, Minister Eusebio de Queiros.

Unwmk.

1952, May 11 Engr. *Perf. 11*

721 A288	2.40cr lt car	35	20
722 A288	5cr blue	2.25	28
723 A288	10cr dk bl grn	2.25	28
	Nos. 721-723 (3)	4.85	76

Centenary of telegraph in Brazil.

Perf. 11x12

1952, June 8 Litho. Wmk. 267

724 A289 1.20cr vio bl 25 20

200th anniversary of the founding of the city of Mato Grosso.

Symbolizing the Glory of Sports — A290

1952, July 21 *Perf. 12x11*

725 A290 1.20cr dp bl & bl 60 40

Fluminense Soccer Club, 50th anniversary.

José Antonio Saraiva — A291

Emperor Dom Pedro — A292

1952, Aug. 16 *Perf. 11x12*

726 A291 60c lil rose 25 20

Centenary of the founding of Terezina, capital of Piaui State.

1952, Sept. 3 Wmk. 267

727 A292 60c lt bl & blk 25 20

Issued for Stamp Day and the 2nd Philatelic Exhibition of Sao Paulo.

Flag-encircled Globe — A293

1952, Oct. 24 *Perf. 13½*

728 A293 3.80cr blue 85 50

Issued to publicize United Nations Day.

View of Sao Paulo, Sun and Compasses A294

1952, Nov. 8 Litho. *Perf. 12x11*

729 A294 60c dl bl, yel & gray grn 25 20

City Planning Day.

Father Diogo Antonio Feijo — A295

1952, Nov. 9 *Perf. 11x12*

730 A295 60c fawn 25 20

Rodolpho Bernardelli and His "Christ and the Adultress" A297

1952, Dec. 18 *Perf. 12x11*

732 A297 60c gray bl 25 20

Bernardelli, sculptor and painter, birth cent.

Map of Western Hemisphere and View of Rio de Janeiro A298

1952, Sept. 20

733 A298 3.80cr vio brn & lt grn 80 30

2nd Congress of American Industrial Medicine, Rio de Janeiro, 1952.

Arms and Head of Pioneer A299

Coffee, Cotton and Sugar Cane — A300

Designs: 2.80cr, Jesuit monk planting tree. 3.80cr and 5.80cr, Spiral, symbolizing progress.

1953, Jan. 25 Litho. *Perf. 11*

734 A299	1.20cr ol brn & blk brn	52	35
735 A300	2cr olive grn & yel	1.75	35
736 A300	2.80cr red brn & dp org	1.20	20
737 A300	3.80cr dk brn & yel grn	1.00	20
738 A300	5.80cr int bl & yel grn	70	20
	Nos. 734-738 (5)	5.17	1.30

400th anniversary of Sao Paulo.

Used copies of No. 734 exist with design inverted.

Ledger and Winged Cap — A301

1953, Feb. 22 *Perf. 12x11*

739 A301 1.20cr dl brn & fawn 25 20

6th Brazilian Accounting Congress.

Joao Ramalho — A302

Perf. 11½

1953, Apr. 8 Wmk. 264 Engr.

740 A302 60c blue 25 20

Founding of the city of Santo Andre, 4th cent.

Aarao Reis and Plan of Belo Horizonte A303

1953, May 6 Photo.

741 A303 1.20cr red brn 25 20

Aarao Leal de Carvalho Reis (1853-1936), civil engineer.

A304

A305

1953, May 16

742 A304 1.50cr Almirante Saldanha 40 25

4th globe-circling voyage of the training ship Almirante Saldanha.

1953, July 5 Photo.

Joaquim Jose Rodrigues Torres, Viscount of Itaborai.

743 A305 1.20cr violet 20 16

Centenary of the Bank of Brazil.

Lamp and Rio-Petropolis Highway A306

1953, July 14

744 A306 1.20cr gray 25 20

Issued to publicize the tenth International Congress of Nursing, Petropolis, 1953.

Bay of Rio de Janeiro
A307

1953, July 15

745 A307 3.80cr dk bl grn 40 20

Issued to publicize the fourth World Congress of Baptist Youth, July 1953.

Arms of Jau and Map — A308

1953, Aug. 15 **Engr.**

746 A308 1.20cr purple 25 20

Centenary of the city of Jau.

Ministry of Health and Education Building, Rio — A309

Maria Quiteria de Jesus Medeiros — A310

1953, Aug. 1

747 A309 1.20cr dp grn 25 20

Day of the Stamp and the first Philatelic Exhibition of National Education.

1953, Aug. 21 **Photo.**

748 A310 60c vio bl 25 20

Centenary of the death of Maria Quiteria de Jesus Medeiros (1792-1848), independence heroine.

Pres. Odria of Peru — A311

Duke of Caxias Leading his Troops — A312

1953, Aug. 25

749 A311 1.40cr rose brn 25 20

Issued to publicize the visit of Gen. Manuel A. Odria, President of Peru, Aug. 25, 1953.

Engr. (60c, 5.80cr); Photo.
1953, Aug. 25

Designs: 1.20cr, Caxias' tomb. 1.70cr, 5.80cr, Portrait of Caxias. 3.80cr, Arms of Caxias.

750	A312	60c dp grn	32	16
751	A312	1.20cr dp cl	40	16
752	A312	1.70cr sl grn	40	16
753	A312	3.80cr rose brn	65	16
754	A312	5.80cr gray vio	65	16
		Nos. 750-754 (5)	2.42	80

150th anniversary of the birth of Luis Alves de Lima e Silva, Duke of Caxias.

Quill Pen, Map and Tree — A313

Horacio Hora — A314

1953, Sept. 12 **Photo.**

755 A313 60c ultra 25 20

5th National Congress of Journalism.

1953, Sept. 17 **Litho.** **Wmk. 267**

756 A314 60c org & dp plum 25 20

Horacio Pinto de Hora (1853-1890), painter.

Pres. Somoza of Nicaragua A315

Auguste de Saint-Hilaire A316

1953, Sept. 24 **Photo.** **Wmk. 264**

757 A315 1.40cr dk vio brn 25 20

Issued to publicize the visit of Gen. Anastasio Somoza, president of Nicaragua.

1953, Sept. 30

758 A316 1.20cr dk brn car 25 25

Centenary of the death of Auguste de Saint-Hilaire, explorer and botanist.

Jose Carlos do Patrocinio A317

Clock Tower, Crato A318

1953, Oct. 9 **Photo.**

759 A317 60c dk slate gray 25 20

Jose Carlos do Patrocinio, (1853-1905), journalist and abolitionist.

1953, Oct. 17

760 A318 60c blue green 25 20

Centenary of the city of Crato.

Joao Capistrano de Abreu — A319

Allegory: "Justice" — A320

1953, Oct. 23

761 A319 60c dull blue 20 20
762 A319 5cr purple 85 85

Joao Capistrano de Abreu (1853-1927), historian.

1953, Nov. 17

763 A320 60c indigo 25 20
764 A320 1.20cr dp magenta 25 20

50th anniv. of the Treaty of Petropolis.

Farm Worker in Wheat Field — A321

Teacher and Pupils — A322

1953, Nov. 29 **Photo.** ***Perf. 11½***

766 A321 60c dk green 25 20

3rd Natl. Wheat Festival, Erechim, 1953.

1953, Dec. 14

767 A322 60c red 25 25

First National Conference of Primary School Teachers, Salvador, 1953.

Zacarias de Gois e Vasconsellos A323

Alexandre de Gusmao A324

Design: 5cr, Porters with Trays of Coffee Beans.

1953-54 **Photo.**

768 A323 2cr org brn & blk, *buff* ('54) 65 40
a. White paper 1.75 40
769 A323 5cr dp org & blk 1.25 40

Centenary of the state of Parana.

1954, Jan. 13

770 A324 1.20cr brn vio 25 20

Gusmao (1695-1753), statesman, diplomat and writer.

Symbolical of Sao Paulo's Growth — A325

Arms and View of Sao Paulo A326

Designs: 2cr, Priest, settler and Indian. 2.80cr, José de Anchieta.

1954, Jan. 25 ***Perf. 11½x11***

771 A325 1.20cr dk vio brn 75 50
a. Buff paper 1.75 1.00

Engr.

772 A325 2cr lilac rose 1.05 60
773 A325 2.80cr pur gray 1.05 1.00

Perf. 11x11½

774 A326 3.80cr dl grn 1.25 50
a. Buff paper 2.25 2.00
775 A326 5.80cr dl red 1.25 60
a. Buff paper 5.00 75
Nos. 771-775 (5) 5.35 3.20

400th anniversary of Sao Paulo.

J. Fernandes Vieira, A. Vidal de Negreiros, A. F. Camarao and H. Dias — A327

Perf. 11x11½

1954, Feb. 18 **Photo.** **Unwmk.**

776 A327 1.20cr ultra 25 25

300th anniversary of the recovery of Pernambuco from the Dutch.

Sao Paulo and Minerva A328

1954, Feb. 24

777 A328 1.50cr dp plum 25 25

10th International Congress of Scientific Organizations, Sao Paulo, 1954.

Stylized Grapes, Jug and Map A329

Monument of the Immigrants A330

1954, Feb. 27 **Photo.** ***Perf. 11½x11***

778 A329 40c dp claret 25 20

Grape Festival, Rio Grande do Sul.

1954, Feb. 28

779 A330 60c dp vio bl 25 20

Unveiling of the Monument to the Immigrants of Caxias do Sul.

First Brazilian Locomotive A331

Perf. 11x11½

1954, Apr. 30 **Unwmk.**

781 A331 40c carmine 25 20

Centenary of the first railroad engine built in Brazil.

The Scott Catalogue value is a retail value; that is, what you could expect to pay for the stamp in a grade of Fine-Very Fine. The value listed reflects recent actual dealer selling prices.

Pres. Chamoun of Lebanon — A332

1954, May 12 Photo. *Perf. 11½x11*

782	A332	1.50cr maroon	25	25

Issued to commemorate the visit of Pres. Camille Chamoun of Lebanon, 1954.

Sao Jose College, Rio de Janeiro A333

J. B. Champagnat Marcelin A334

Apolonia Pinto A335

1954, June 6 *Perf. 11x11½, 11½x11*

783	A333	60c purple	18	15
784	A334	120cr vio blue	22	20

50th anniversary of the founding of the Marist Brothers in Brazil.

1954, June 21 **Photo.**

785	A335	1.20cr bright green	15	15

Apolonia Pinto (1854-1937), actress.

Adm. Margues Tamandare — A336

Portraits: 2c, 5c, 10c, Admiral Margues Tamandare. 20c, 30c, 40c, Oswaldo Cruz. 50c, 60c, 90c, Joaquim Murtinho. 1cr, 1.50cr, 2cr, Duke of Caxias. 5cr, 10cr, Ruy Barbosa. 20cr, 50cr, Jose Bonifacio.

1954-60 Wmk. 267 *Perf. 11x11½*

786	A336	2c vio blue	15	15
787	A336	5c org red	15	15
788	A336	10c brt green	15	15
789	A336	20c magenta	15	15
790	A336	30c dk gray grn	15	15
791	A336	40c rose red	26	15
792	A336	50c violet	16	15
793	A336	60c gray grn	15	15
794	A336	90c orange ('55)	26	15
795	A336	1cr brown	15	15
796	A336	1.50cr blue	15	15
a.		Wmk. 264	16.00	8.00
797	A336	2cr dk bl grn ('56)	32	15
798	A336	5cr rose lil ('56)	26	15
799	A336	10cr lt grn ('60)	65	15
800	A336	20cr crim rose ('59)	65	15
801	A336	50cr ultra ('59)	4.00	20
		Nos. 786-801 (16)	7.76	
		Set value		1.25

See Nos. 890, 930-933.

Boy Scout Waving Flag (Statue) A337

Baltasar Fernandes, Explorer A338

1954, Aug. 2 Unwmk. *Perf. 11½x11*

802	A337	1.20cr vio bl	40	24

Issued to publicize the International Boy Scout Encampment, Sao Paulo, 1954.

1954, Aug. 15

803	A338	60c dk red	25	25

300th anniversary of city of Sorocaba.

Adeodato Giovanni Cardinal Piazza — A339

Our Lady of Aparecida, Map of Brazil — A340

1954, Sept. 2

804	A339	4.20cr red org	50	35

Visit of Adeodato Cardinal Piazza, papal legate to Brazil.

1954

Design: 1.20cr, Virgin standing on globe.

805	A340	60c claret	32	32
806	A340	1.20cr vio bl	42	28

No. 805 was issued to commemorate the 1st Congress of Brazil's Patron Saint (Our Lady of Aparecida); No. 806, the centenary of the proclamation of the dogma of the Immaculate Conception. Both stamps also commemorate the Marian Year.

Issue dates: 60c, Sept. 6; 1.20cr, Sept. 8.

Benjamin Constant and Hand Reading Braille A341

1954, Sept. 27 Photo. Unwmk.

807	A341	60c dk grn	25	20

Centenary of the founding of the Benjamin Constant Institute.

River Battle of Riachuelo A342

Admiral F. M. Barroso A343

Dr. Christian F. S. Hahnemann A344

1954, Oct. 6 *Perf. 11x11½, 11½x11*

808	A342	40c redsh brown	30	20
809	A343	60c purple	20	20

Admiral Francisco Manoel Barroso da Silva (1804-82).

1954, Oct. 8 *Perf. 11½x11*

810	A344	2.70cr dk green	30	25

1st World Cong. of Homeopathic Medicine.

Nizia Floresta A345

Ears of Wheat A346

1954, Oct. 12

811	A345	60c lilac rose	25	20

Reburial of the remains of Nizia Floresta (Dio Nizia Pinto Lisboa), writer and educator.

1954, Oct. 22

812	A346	60c olive green	20	16

4th National Wheat Festival, Carazinho.

Basketball Player and Ball-Globe A347

Allegory of the Spring Games A348

1954, Oct. 23 **Photo.**

813	A347	1.40cr orange red	30	30

Issued to publicize the second World Basketball Championship Matches, 1954.

Perf. 11½x11

1954, Nov. 6 Wmk. 267

814	A348	60c red brown	25	20

Issued to publicize the 6th Spring Games.

San Francisco Hydroelectric Plant — A349

1955, Jan. 15 *Perf. 11x11½*

815	A349	60c brown org	20	15

Issued to publicize the inauguration of the San Francisco Hydroelectric Plant.

Itutinga Hydroelectric Plant — A350

1955, Feb. 3

816	A350	40c blue	20	15

Issued to publicize the inauguration of the Itutinga Hydroelectric Plant at Lavras.

Rotary Emblem and Bay of Rio de Janeiro — A351

1955, Feb. 23 *Perf. 12x11½*

817	A351	2.70cr slate gray & blk	85	25

Rotary International, 50th anniversary.

Fausto Cardoso Palace A352

1955, Mar. 17 *Perf. 11x11½*

818	A352	40c henna brown	25	25

Centenary of Aracaju.

Aviation Symbols A353

1955, Mar. 13 Photo. *Perf. 11½*

819	A353	60c dark gray green	16	15

Issued to publicize the third National Aviation Congress at Sao Paulo, Mar. 6-13.

Arms of Botucatu A354

1955, Apr. 14

820	A354	60c orange brn	15	15
821	A354	1.20cr brt green	25	15

Centenary of Botucatu.

Young Racers at Starting Line — A355

Perf. 11½

1955, Apr. 30 Photo. Unwmk.

823	A355	60c orange brn	25	20

5th Children's Games.

Marshal Hermes da Fonseca — A356

Congress Altar, Sail and Sugarloaf Mountain — A357

1955, May 12 **Wmk. 267**

824 A356 60c purple 20 16

Centenary of the birth of Marshal Hermes da Fonseca.

Engraved; Photogravure (2.70cr)

1955, July 17 **Unwmk.** ***Perf. 11½***

Designs: 2.70cr, St. Pascoal. 4.20cr, Aloisi Benedetto Cardinal Masella.

825 A357 1.40cr green 15 15
826 A357 2.70cr deep claret 25 20
827 A357 4.20cr blue 30 15
Nos. 825-827 (3) 70 50

36th World Eucharistic Cong. in Rio de Janeiro.

Girl Gymnasts A358

1955, Nov. 12 **Engr.**

Granite Paper

828 A358 60c rose lilac 20 20

Issued to publicize the 7th Spring Games.

José B. Monteiro Lobato, Author A359

1955, Dec. 8

Granite Paper

829 A359 40c dark green 20 15

Adolfo Lutz — A360

Lt. Col. Vilagran Cabrita — A361

1955, Dec. 18

Granite Paper

830 A360 60c dk green 20 15

Centenary of the birth of Adolfo Lutz, public health pioneer.

1955, Dec. 22 **Photo.** **Wmk. 267**

831 A361 60c vio bl 20 15

First Battalion of Engineers, cent.

Salto Grande Hydroelectric Dam — A362

1956, Jan. 15 **Unwmk.** ***Perf. 11½***

Granite Paper

832 A362 60c brick red 20 15

Arms of Mococa — A363

"G" and Globe — A364

Perf. 11½

1956, Apr. 17 **Wmk. 256** **Photo.**

833 A363 60c brick red 16 15

Centenary of Mococa, Sao Paulo.

1956, Apr. 14 **Unwmk.**

Granite Paper

834 A364 1.20cr violet blue 16 20

18th Intl. Geographic Cong., Rio, Aug. 1956.

Girls' Foot Race — A365

1956, Apr. 28 **Photo.**

Granite Paper

835 A365 2.50cr brt blue 30 20

6th Children's Games.

Plane over Map of Brazil — A366

1956, June 12 **Wmk. 267** ***Perf. 11½***

836 A366 3.30cr brt vio bl 40 20

National Airmail Service, 25th anniv.

Fireman Rescuing Child — A367

1956, July 2 **Wmk. 264**

837 A367 2.50cr crimson 40 25
a. Buff paper 2.25 2.00

Centenary of the Fire Brigade.

Map of Brazil and Open Book — A368

1956, Sept. 8 **Wmk. 267**

838 A368 2.50cr brt vio bl 30 20

50th anniversary of the arrival of the Marist Brothers in Northern Brazil.

Church and Monument, Franca — A369

1956, Sept. 7 **Engr.**

839 A369 2.50cr dk blue 30 20

Centenary of city of Franca, Sao Paulo.

Woman Hurdler A370

1956, Sept. 22 **Photo.** **Unwmk.**

Granite Paper

840 A370 2.50cr dk car 40 20

Issued to publicize the 8th Spring Games.

Forest and Map of Brazil — A371

1956, Sept. 30 **Wmk. 267** ***Perf. 11½***

841 A371 2.50cr dk green 25 20

Issued to publicize education in forestry.

Baron da Bocaina A372

1956, Oct. 8 **Engr.** **Wmk. 268**

842 A372 2.50cr reddish brown 25 20

Centenary of the birth of Baron da Bocaina, who introduced the special delivery mail system to Brazil.

Marbleized Paper

Paper with a distinct wavy-line or marbleized watermark (which Brazilians call *marmorizado* paper) has been found on many stamps of Brazil, 1956-68, including Nos. 843-845, 847, 851-854, 858-858A, 864, 878, 880, 882, 884, 886-887, 896, 909, 918, 920-921, 925-928, 936-939, 949, 955-958, 960, 962-964, 978-979, 983, 985-987, 997-998, 1002-1003, 1005, 1009-1012, 1017, 1024, 1026, 1055, 1075, 1078, 1082, C82, C82a, C83-C87, C96, C99, C109.

Quantities are much less than those of stamps on regular paper.

Panama Stamp Showing Pres. Juscelino Kubitschek — A373

1956, Oct. 12 **Photo.** **Wmk. 267**

843 A373 3.30cr green & blk 40 20

Issued on America Day, Oct. 12, to commemorate the meeting of the Presidents and the Pan-American Conference at Panama City, July 21-22.

Symbolical of Steel Production A374

Perf. 11½

1957, Jan. 31 **Wmk. 267** **Photo.**

844 A374 2.50cr chocolate 25 15

2nd expansion of the National Steel Company at Volta Redonda.

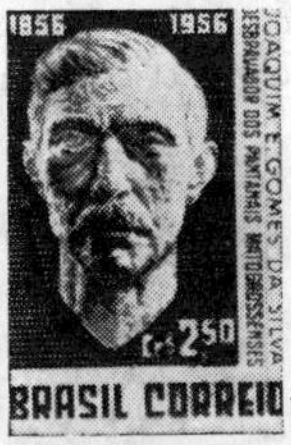

Joaquim E. Gomes da Silva — A375

1957, Mar. 1 **Photo.** **Unwmk.**

Granite Paper

845 A375 2.50cr dk bl grn 25 15

Centenary of the birth (in 1856) of Joaquim E. Gomes da Silva.

Allan Kardec A376

Perf. 11½

1957, Apr. 18 **Wmk. 268** **Engr.**

846 A376 2.50cr dk brown 25 15

Issued in honor of Allan Kardec, pen name of Leon Hippolyto Denizard Rivail, and for the centenary of the publication of his "Codification of Spiritism."

Boy Gymnast A377

1957, Apr. 27 **Photo.** **Unwmk.**

Granite Paper

847 A377 2.50cr lake 48 25

7th Children's Games.

Pres. Craveiro Lopes — A378

Stamp of 1932 — A379

1957, June 7 **Engr.** **Wmk. 267**
848 A378 6.50cr blue 40 20

Visit of Gen. Francisco Higino Craveiro Lopes, President of Portugal.

1957, July 9 **Photo.**
849 A379 2.50cr rose 25 15

25th anniv. of the movement for a constitution.

St. Antonio Monastery, Pernambuco A380

1957, Aug. 24 **Engr.** **Wmk. 267**
850 A380 2.50cr dp magenta 25 15

300th anniv. of the emancipation of the Franciscan province of St. Antonio in Pernambuco State.

Volleyball A381

Basketball A382

1957, Sept. 28 **Photo.** ***Perf. 11½***
851 A381 2.50cr dull org red 45 25

Issued for the 9th Spring Games.

1957, Oct. 12
852 A382 3.30cr org & brt grn 45 25

2nd Women's International Basketball Championship, Rio de Janeiro.

Count of Pinhal and Sao Carlos A383

1957, Nov. 4 **Wmk. 267** ***Perf. 11½***
853 A383 2.50cr rose 28 25

Centenary of the city of Sao Carlos and honoring the Count of Pinhal, its founder.

Auguste Comte — A384

1957, Nov. 15
854 A384 2.50cr dk red brn 25 20

Centenary of the death of Auguste Comte, French mathematician and philosopher.

Radio Station A385

1957, Dec. 10 **Wmk. 268**
855 A385 2.50cr dk green 20 15

Opening of Sarapui Central Radio Station.

Admiral Tamandare and Warship A386

Design: 3.30cr, Aircraft carrier.

1957-58 **Photo.**
856 A386 2.50cr light blue 25 20

Engr.

857 A386 3.30cr green ('58) 28 20

150th anniversary of the birth of Admiral Joaquin Marques de Tamandare, founder of the Brazilian navy.

Coffee Plant and Symbolic "R" — A387

Perf. 11½

1957-58 **Wmk. 267** **Photo.**
858 A387 2.50cr magenta 52 35

Unwmk.

Granite Paper

858A A387 2.50cr magenta ('58) 45 35

Centenary (in 1956) of the city of Ribeirao Preto in Sao Paulo state.

Dom John VI — A388

1958, Jan. 28 **Engr.** **Wmk. 268**
859 A388 2.50cr magenta 35 25

150th anniversary of the opening of the ports of Brazil to foreign trade.

Bugler A389

1958, Mar. 18 **Wmk. 267**
860 A389 2.50cr red 35 25

Brazilian Marine Corps, 150th anniv.

Station at Rio and Locomotive of 1858 — A390

Court House — A391

Perf. 11½

1958, Mar. 29 **Wmk. 267** **Photo.**
861 A390 2.50cr red brn 35 25

Central Railroad of Brazil, cent.

1958, Apr. 1 **Engr.** **Wmk. 256**
862 A391 2.50cr green 25 15

150th anniv. of the Military Superior Court.

Emblem and Brazilian Pavilion A392

1958, Apr. 17 **Wmk. 267**
863 A392 2.50cr dk blue 25 25

World's Fair, Brussels, Apr. 17-Oct. 19.

High Jump — A393

1958, Apr. 20 **Photo.** **Unwmk.**

Granite Paper

864 A393 2.50cr crimson rose 25 15

8th Children's Games.

Marshal Mariano da Silva Rondon A394

1958, Apr. 19 **Engr.** **Wmk. 267**
865 A394 2.50cr magenta 25 15

Issued to honor Marshal Mariano da Silva Rondon and the "Day of the Indian."

Hydroelectric Station A395

1958, Apr. 28 **Wmk. 267** ***Perf. 11½***
866 A395 2.50cr magenta 25 15

Opening of Sao Paulo State power plant.

National Printing Plant — A396

1958, May 22 **Photo.**
867 A396 2.50cr redsh brn 20 15

150th anniversary of the founding of the National Printing Plant.

Marshal Osorio — A397

1958, May 24
868 A397 2.50cr brt violet 20 15

150th anniversary of the birth of Marshal Manoel Luiz Osorio.

Pres. Ramon Villeda Morales — A398

Fountain — A399

1958, June 7 **Engr.** ***Perf. 11½***
869 A398 6.50cr dk green 1.25 75
a. Wmk. 268 5.00 2.00

Visit of Pres. Ramon Villeda Morales of Honduras.

1958, June 13
870 A399 2.50cr dk green 25 15

Botanical Garden, Rio de Janeiro, 150th anniv.

Symbols of Agriculture A400

Prophet Joel A401

1958, June 18 **Photo.**
871 A400 2.50cr rose carmine 25 15

50th anniv. of Japanese immigration to Brazil.

1958, June 21 **Engr.**
872 A401 2.50cr dk blue 25 15

Bicentenary of the Cathedral of Bom Jesus at Matosinhos.

Stylized Globe — A402

1958, July 10 **Photo.**
873 A402 2.50cr dk brown 20 15

Issued to publicize the International Investment Conference, Belo Horizonte.

Julio Bueno Brandao — A403

1958, Aug. 1 **Wmk. 268** ***Perf. 11½***
874 A403 2.50cr red brown 25 15

Centenary of the birth of Julio Bueno Brandao, President of Minas Gerais.

Palacio Tiradentes (House of Congress) A404

1958, July 24 **Engr.**
875 A404 2.50cr sepia 25 15

47th Interparliamentary Conference, Rio de Janeiro, July 24-Aug. 1.

Presidential Palace, Brasilia A405

1958, Aug. 8 **Photo.** **Wmk. 267**
876 A405 2.50cr ultra 20 15

Issued to publicize the construction of Brazil's new capital, Brasilia.

Freighters A406

1958, Aug. 22
877 A406 2.50cr blue 25 15

Brazilian merchant marine.

Joaquim Caetano da Silva — A407

1958, Sept. 2 **Unwmk.**
Granite Paper
878 A407 2.50cr redsh brn 25 15

Issued in honor of Joaquim Caetano da Silva, scientist and historian.

Giovanni Gronchi — A408

Archers — A409

1958, Sept. 4 **Engr.** **Wmk. 268**
879 A408 7cr dk blue 50 15

Visit of Italy's President Giovanni Gronchi to Brazil.

Perf. 11½
1958, Sept. 21 **Photo.** **Unwmk.**
Granite Paper
880 A409 2.50cr red org 35 20

Issued to publicize the 10th Spring Games.

Elderly Couple — A410

Machado de Assis — A411

1958, Sept. 27 **Wmk. 267**
881 A410 2.50cr magenta 25 15

Day of the Old People, Sept. 27.

1958, Sept. 28 **Unwmk.**
882 A411 2.50cr red brn 25 15

50th anniversary of the death of Joaquim Maria Machado de Assis, writer.

Pres. Vargas and Oil Derrick A412

1958, Oct. 6 **Wmk. 268**
883 A412 2.50cr blue 25 15

5th anniv. of Pres. Getulio D. Vargas' oil law.

Globe — A413

Gen. Lauro Sodré — A414

Perf. 11½
1958, Nov. 14 **Photo.** **Wmk. 267**
884 A413 2.50cr blue 30 15

7th Inter-American Congress of Municipalities.

1958, Nov. 15 **Engr.**
885 A414 3.30cr green 25 15

Cent. of the birth of Gen. Lauro Sodré.

UN Emblem — A415

Soccer Player — A416

1958, Dec. 26 **Photo.** ***Perf. 11½***
886 A415 2.50cr brt blue 20 15

10th anniv. of the signing of the Universal Declaration of Human Rights.

1959, Jan. 20
887 A416 3.30cr emer & red brn 40 20

World Soccer Championships of 1958.

Railroad Track and Map A417

Pres. Sukarno of Indonesia A418

1959, Apr. **Wmk. 267** ***Perf. 11½***
888 A417 2.50cr dp orange 25 20

Centenary of the linking of Patos and Campina Grande by railroad.

1959, May 20
889 A418 2.50cr blue 25 15

Visit of President Sukarno of Indonesia.

Dom John VI — A419

Boy Polo Players — A420

Perf. 10½x11½
1959, June 12 **Wmk. 267**
890 A419 2.50cr crimson 25 15

1959, June 13 ***Perf. 11½***
891 A420 2.50cr orange brn 25 15

9th Children's Games.

Loading Freighter A421

Organ and Emblem A422

1959, July 10
892 A421 2.50cr dk green 25 15

Issued to honor the merchant marine.

1959, July 16 **Photo.**
893 A422 3.30cr magenta 25 15

Bicentenary of the Carmelite Order in Brazil.

Joachim Silverio de Souza — A423

Symbolic Road — A424

1959, July 20 ***Perf. 11½***
894 A423 2.50cr red brown 25 15

Birth centenary of Joachim Silverio de Souza, first bishop of Diamantina, Minas Gerais.

1959, Sept. 27 **Wmk. 267**
895 A424 3.30cr bl grn & ultra 25 15

11th International Roadbuilding Congress.

Woman Athlete — A425

1959, Oct. 4
896 A425 2.50cr lilac rose 25 15

11th Spring Games.

Map of Parana A426

1959, Sept. 27
897 A426 2.50cr dk green 25 15

Founding of Londrina, Parana, 25th anniv.

Globe and Snipes
A427

Cross of Lusitania
A428

1959, Oct. 22 *Perf. 11½*
898 A427 6.50cr dull grn 20 15

World Championship of Snipe Class Sailboats, Porto Alegre, won by Brazilian yachtsmen.

1959, Oct. 24 **Engr.**
899 A428 6.50cr dull blue 20 15

4th Intl. Conf. on Brazilian-Portuguese Studies, University of Bahia, Aug. 10-20.

Factory Entrance and Order of Southern Cross — A429

Corcovado Christ, Globe and Southern Cross — A430

1959, Nov. 19 **Photo.**
900 A429 3.30cr orange red 20 15

Pres. Vargas Gunpowder Factory, 50th anniv.

1959, Nov. 26 *Perf. 11½*
901 A430 2.50cr blue 20 15

Universal Thanksgiving Day.

Burning Bush — A431

1959, Dec. 24 **Wmk. 267**
902 A431 3.30cr lt grn 20 15

Centenary of Presbyterian work in Brazil.

Piraja da Silva and Schistosoma Mansoni A432

1959, Dec. 28
903 A432 2.50cr rose violet 20 15

25th anniv. of the discovery and identification of schistosoma mansoni, a parasite of the fluke family, by Dr. Piraja da Silva.

Luiz de Matos — A433

1960, Jan. 3 **Photo.**
904 A433 3.30cr red brown 16 15

Birth centenary of Luiz de Matos.

Zamenhof
A434

Adél Pinto
A435

1960, Mar. 10 **Wmk. 267** *Perf. 11½*
905 A434 6.50cr emerald 20 15

Lazarus Ludwig Zamenhof (1859-1917), Polish oculist who invented Esperanto in 1887.

1960, Mar. 19 **Engr.** **Wmk. 268**
906 A435 11.50cr rose red 20 15

Centenary of the birth of Adél Pinto, civil engineer and railroad expert.

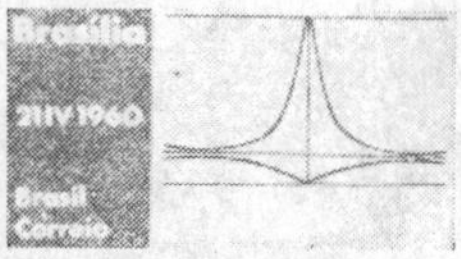

Presidential Palace, Colonnade A436

Design: 27cr, Plan of Brasilia (like #C98).

Perf. 11x11½

1960 **Photo.** **Wmk. 267**
907 A436 2.50cr brt green 22 15
908 A436 27cr salmon 60 60
Nos. 907-908,C95-C98 (6) 2.02 1.35

No. 907 issued Apr. 21 to commemorate the inauguration of Brazil's new capital, Brasilia, Apr. 21, 1960.

No. 908 issued Sept. 12 to commemorate the birthday of Pres. Juscelino Kubitschek. It measures 105x46½mm, carrying at center a 27cr in design of No. C98, flanked by the chief design features of Nos. 907, C95-C97, with Kubitschek signature below. Issued in sheets of 4 with wide horizontal gutter.

Grain, Coffee, Cotton and Cacao — A437

Paulo de Frontin — A438

Perf. 11½x11

1960, July 28 **Wmk. 267**
909 A437 2.50cr brown 20 15

Centenary of Ministry of Agriculture.

1960, Oct. 12 **Wmk. 268**
910 A438 2.50cr orange red 20 15

Cent. of the birth of Paulo de Frontin, engineer.

Woman Athlete Holding Torch — A439

1960, Oct. 18 *Perf. 11½x11*
911 A439 2.50cr blue grn 20 15

12th Spring Games.

Volleyball and Net
A440

Locomotive Wheels
A441

Perf. 11½x11

1960, Nov. 12 **Wmk. 268**
912 A440 11cr blue 20 15

International Volleyball Championships.

1960, Oct. 15 *Perf. 11½x11*
913 A441 2.50cr ultra 20 15

10th Pan-American Railroad Congress.

Symbols of Flight
A442

1960, Dec. 16 **Photo.** *Perf. 11½*
914 A442 2.50cr brn & yel 16 15

Intl. Fair of Industry and Commerce, Rio.

Emperor Haile Selassie — A443

1961, Jan. 31 *Perf. 11½x11*
915 A443 2.50cr dk brown 16 15

Visit of Emperor Haile Selassie of Ethiopia to Brazil, Dec. 1960.

Map of Brazil, Open Book and Sacred Heart Emblem
A444

Perf. 11x11½

1961, Mar. 13 **Wmk. 268**
916 A444 2.50cr blue 20 15

50th anniv. of the operation in Brazil of the Order of the Blessed Heart of Mary.

Map of Guanabara
A445

1961, Mar. 27 **Wmk. 267**
917 A445 7.50cr org brn 20 15

Promulgation of the constitution of the state of Guanabara.

Arms of Agulhas Negras
A446

Brazil and Senegal Linked on Map
A447

Design: 3.30cr, Dress helmet and sword.

Perf. 11½x11

1961, Apr. 23 **Wmk. 267**
918 A446 2.50cr green 20 15
919 A446 3.30cr rose car 15 15

Sesquicentennial of the Agulhas Negras Military Academy.

1961, Apr. 28 **Photo.**
920 A447 27cr ultra 25 20

Issued to commemorate the visit of Afonso Arinos, Brazilian foreign minister, to Senegal to attend its independence ceremonies.

View of Ouro Preto, 1711
A448

1961, June 6 *Perf. 11x11½*
921 A448 1cr orange 20 20

250th anniversary of Ouro Preto.

War Arsenal
A449

1961, June 20 **Wmk. 256**
924 A449 5cr dk red brn 25 15

150th anniv. of the War Arsenal, Rio de Janeiro.

Coffee Bean and Branch
A450

Rabindranath Tagore
A451

Perf. 11½x11

1961, June 26 **Wmk. 267**
925 A450 20cr redsh brn 80 25

8th Directorial Committee meeting of the Intl. Coffee Convention, Rio, June 26.

1961, July 28 **Photo.** **Wmk. 267**
926 A451 10cr rose car 20 15

Rabindranath Tagore, Indian poet, birth cent.

Stamp of 1861 and Map of English Channel
A452

Design: 20cr, 430r stamp of 1861 and map of Netherlands.

1961, Aug. 1 *Perf. 11x11½*

927 A452 10cr rose 75 20
928 A452 20cr salmon pink 2.00 30

Centenary of 1861 stamp issue.

Portrait Type of 1954-60
Designs as Before

1961 Wmk. 268 *Perf. 11x11½*

930 A336 1cr brown 80 50
931 A336 2cr dk bl grn 1.25 50
932 A336 5cr red lilac 3.75 30
933 A336 10cr emerald 7.25 30
Nos. 930-933 (4) 13.05 1.60

1cr, 5cr and 10cr have patterned background.

Sun, Clouds, Rain and Weather Symbols — A453

Dedo de Deus Peak — A454

1962, Mar. 23 *Perf. 11½x11*

936 A453 10cr red brown 75 30

World Meteorological Day, Mar. 23.

1962, Apr. 14 Photo. Wmk. 267

937 A454 8cr emerald 20 25

50th anniversary of the climbing of Dedo de Deus (Finger of God) peak.

Dr. Gaspar Vianna and Leishmania Protozoa A455

1962, Apr. 24 *Perf. 11x11½*

938 A455 8cr blue 25 15

Discovery by Gaspar Oliveiro Vianna (1885-1914) of a cure for leishmaniasis, 50th anniv.

Henrique Dias A456

1962, June 18 Wmk. 267

939 A456 10cr dk vio brn 32 15

300th anniversary of the death of Henrique Dias, Negro military leader who fought against the Dutch and Spaniards.

Millimeter Gauge — A457

Sailboats, Snipe Class — A458

1962, June 26 *Perf. 11½x11*

940 A457 100cr car rose 35 20

Centenary of the introduction of the metric system in Brazil.

1962, July 21 Photo. Wmk. 267

941 A458 8cr Prus grn 20 15

Issued to commemorate the 13th Brazilian championships for Snipe Class sailing.

Julio Mesquita A459

1962, Aug. 18 *Perf. 11x11½*

942 A459 8cr dull brown 20 15

Centenary of the birth of Julio Mesquita, journalist and founder of Sao Paulo.

Empress Leopoldina — A460

1962, Sept. 7 *Perf. 11½x11*

943 A460 8cr rose claret 20 15

140th anniversary of independence.

Buildings, Brasilia A461

Perf. 11x11½

1962, Oct. 24 Wmk. 267

944 A461 10cr orange 30 15

51st Interparliamentary Conf., Brasilia.

Pouring Ladle — A462

1962, Oct. 26 *Perf. 11½x11*

945 A462 8cr orange 20 15

Issued to mark the inauguration of the Usiminas State Iron and Steel Foundry at Belo Horizonte, Minas Gerais.

UPAE Emblem A463

1962, Nov. 19 *Perf. 11x11½*

946 A463 8cr bright magenta 20 15

Founding of the Postal Union of the Americas and Spain, UPAE, 50th anniv.

Chimney and Cogwheel Forming "10" — A464

1962, Nov. 26 *Perf. 11½x11*

947 A464 10cr lt blue grn 20 15

Natl. Economic and Development Bank, 10th anniv.

Quintino Bocaiuva A465

Soccer Player and Globe A466

Perf. 11½x11

1962, Dec. 27 Photo. Wmk. 267

948 A465 8cr brown org 20 15

50th anniversary of the death of Quintino Bocaiuva, journalist.

1963, Jan. 14

949 A466 10cr blue grn 40 15

World Soccer Championship of 1962.

Carrier Pigeon A467

1963, Jan. Unwmk. Litho. *Perf. 14*

950 A467 8cr yel, dk bl, red & grn 20 15

Souvenir Sheet

Imperf

951 A467 100cr yel, dk bl, red & grn 1.25 *3.00*

300 years of Brazilian postal service.
Issue dates: 8cr, Jan. 25; 100cr, Jan. 31.

Severino Neiva — A468

Perf. 10½x11½

1963, Jan. 31 Photo. Wmk. 267

952 A468 8cr brt vio 20 15

Radar Tracking Station and Rockets — A469

"Cross of Unity" — A470

Perf. 11½x11

1963, Mar. 15 Wmk. 268

953 A469 21cr lt ultra 20 15

Issued to publicize the International Aeronautics and Space Exhibition, Sao Paulo.

1963 Wmk. 267 *Perf. 11½x11*

954 A470 8cr red lilac 20 15

Vatican II, the 21st Ecumenical Council of the Roman Catholic Church.

"ABC" in Geometric Form — A471

Basketball Player — A472

1963, Apr. 22 Photo. Wmk. 267

955 A471 8cr brt bl & lt bl 16 15

Education Week, Apr. 22-27, 3-year alphabetization program.

1963, May 15

956 A472 8cr dp lilac rose 20 15

4th International Basketball Championships, Rio de Janeiro, May 10-25, 1963.

Games Emblem A473

"OEA" and Map of the Americas A474

1963, May 22 *Perf. 11½x11*

957 A473 10cr car rose 30 15

4th Pan American Games, Sao Paulo.

1963, June 6

958 A474 10cr org & dp org 30 15

15th anniversary of the charter of the Organization of American States.

The first value column gives the catalogue value of an unused stamp, the second that of a used stamp.

José Bonifacio de Andrada — A475

1963, June 13

959 A475 8cr dk brown		15	15

Bicentenary of the birth of José Bonifacio de Andrada de Silva, statesman.

Wheat A476

Perf. 11x11½

1963, June 19 **Photo.** **Wmk. 267**

960 A476 10cr blue		30	15

FAO "Freedom from Hunger" campaign.

Centenary Emblem A477

Joao Caetano A478

1963, Aug. 19 *Perf. 11½x11*

961 A477 8cr yel org & red		25	15

Centenary of International Red Cross.

1963, Aug. 24 *Perf. 11½x11*

962 A478 8cr slate		20	15

Death centenary of Joao Caetano, actor.

Symbols of Agriculture, Industry and Atomic Energy A479

Hammer Thrower A480

1963, Aug. 28

963 A479 10cr car rose		25	15

Atomic Development Law, 1st anniv.

1963, Sept. 13

964 A480 10cr gray		42	15

Intl. College Students' Games, Porto Alegre.

Marshal Tito — A481

Compass Rose, Map of Brazil and View of Rio — A482

1963, Sept. 19

965 A481 80cr sepia		35	30

Visit of Marshal Tito of Yugoslavia.

1963, Sept. 20

966 A482 8cr lt blue grn		16	15

8th International Leprology Congress.

Oil Derrick and Storage Tank A483

1963, Oct. 3 *Perf. 11x11½*

967 A483 8cr dk slate grn		16	15

10th anniv. of Petrobras, the natl. oil company.

"Spring Games" A484

1963, Nov. 5 **Photo.** **Wmk. 267**

968 A484 8cr yel & org		20	20

1963 Spring Games.

Dr. Borges de Medeiros (1863-1962), Governor of Rio Grande do Sul — A485

1963, Nov. 29 *Perf. 11½x11*

969 A485 8cr red brown		16	15

Sao Joao del Rei — A486

1963, Dec. 8 *Perf. 11x11½*

970 A486 8cr violet blue		16	15

250th anniversary of Sao Joao del Rei.

Dr. Alvaro Alvim A487

1963, Dec. 19

971 A487 8cr dk gray		16	15

Alvaro Alvim (1863-1928), X-ray specialist and martyr of science.

Viscount de Mauá A488

Mandacaru Cactus and Emblem A489

1963, Dec. 28 *Perf. 11½x11*

972 A488 8cr rose car		16	15

Sesquicentennial of the birth of Viscount de Mauá, founder of first Brazilian railroad.

1964, Jan. 23 **Photo.** **Wmk. 267**

973 A489 8cr dull green		16	15

Bank of Northeast Brazil, 10th anniv.

Coelho Netto — A490

Lauro Müller — A491

1964, Feb. 21 *Perf. 11½x11*

974 A490 8cr brt violet		16	15

Birth centenary of Coelho Netto, writer.

1964, Mar. 8 **Wmk. 267**

975 A491 8cr dp orange		16	15

Lauro Siverino Müller, politician and member of the Brazilian Academy of Letters, birth cent.

Child Holding Spoon A492

1964, Mar. 25 *Perf. 11x11½*

976 A492 8cr yel brn & yel		16	15

Issued for "School Meals Week."

Chalice Rock — A493

Allan Kardec — A494

1964, Apr. 9 **Engr.** *Perf. 11½x11*

977 A493 80cr red orange		20	15

Issued for tourist publicity.

1964, Apr. 18 **Photo.**

978 A494 30cr slate green		45	15

Cent. of "O Evangelho" (Gospel) of the codification of Spiritism.

Heinrich Lübke — A495

Pope John XXIII — A496

Perf. 11½x11

1964, May 8 **Photo.** **Wmk. 267**

979 A495 100cr red brown		60	18

Visit of President Heinrich Lübke of Germany.

1964, June 29 **Wmk. 267**

980 A496 20cr dk car rose		20	18
a. Unwmkd.		20	18

Issued in memory of Pope John XXIII.

Pres. Senghor of Senegal — A497

1964, Sept. 19 **Wmk. 267**

981 A497 20cr dk brown		25	15

Visit of Leopold Sedar Senghor, President of Senegal.

Botafogo Bay and Sugarloaf Mountain A498

Designs: 100cr, Church of Our Lady of the Rock, vert. 200cr, Copacabana beach.

Perf. 11x11½, 11½x11

1964-65 **Photo.**

983 A498 15cr org & bl		30	22
984 A498 100cr brt grn & red brn, *yel*		18	16
985 A498 200cr black & red		1.75	30
a. Souvenir sheet of 3 ('65)		4.75	4.00
Nos. 983-985 (3)		2.23	68

4th cent. of Rio de Janeiro.

No. 985a contains three imperf. stamps similar to Nos. 983-985, but printed in brown. Sold for 320cr. Issued Dec. 30, 1965.

A souvenir card containing one lithographed facsimile of No. 984, imperf., exists, but has no franking value. Size: 100x125mm. Sold by P.O. for 250cr.

Buying Sets

It is often less expensive to purchase complete sets than individual stamps that make up the set. Set values are provided for many such sets.

Pres. Charles de Gaulle
A499

Pres. John F. Kennedy
A500

1964, Oct. 13 ***Perf. 11½x11***

986 A499 100cr orange brn 35 15

Visit of Charles de Gaulle, President of France, Oct. 13-15.

1964, Oct. 24 **Photo.** **Wmk. 267**

987 A500 100cr slate 20 15

"Prophet" by A. F. Lisbao — A501

1964, Nov. 18 ***Perf. 11½x11***

988 A501 10cr slate 16 15

150th death anniv. of the sculptor Antonio Francisco Lisbao, "O Aleijadinho" (The Cripple).

Antonio Goncalves Dias — A502

Designs: 30cr, Euclides da Cunha. 50cr, Prof. Angelo Moreira da Costa Lima. 200cr, Tiradentes. 500cr, Dom Pedro I. 1000cr, Dom Pedro II.

1965-66 **Wmk. 267** ***Perf. 11x11½***

989	A502	30cr brt bluish grn ('66)	2.00	25
989A	A502	50cr dull brn ('66)	1.50	15
990	A502	100cr blue	60	15
991	A502	200cr brown org	2.00	15
992	A502	500cr red brown	6.00	50
992A	A502	1000cr sl bl ('66)	10.00	50
		Nos. 989-992A (6)	22.10	1.70

Statue of St. Sebastian, Guanataro Bay — A503

The Arches
A504

Design: 35cr, Estacio de Sa (1520-67), founder of Rio de Janeiro.

1965 **Photo.** ***Perf. 11½***
Size: 24x37mm

993 A503 30cr bl & rose red 30 15

Lithographed and Engraved
Perf. 11x11½

994 A504 30cr lt bl & blk 30 15

Photo. ***Perf. 11½***
Size: 21x39mm

995 A503 35cr blk & org		18	25
a.	Souvenir sheet of 3	3.25	4.00
	Nos. 993-995 (3)	78	55

4th cent. of Rio de Janeiro. Issue dates: No. 993, Mar. 5. No. 994, Nov. 30. No. 995, July 28. No. 995a, Dec. 30.

No. 995a contains three imperf. stamps similar to Nos. 993-995, but printed in deep orange. Size: 130x79mm. Sold for 100cr.

Sword and Cross — A505

1965, Apr. 15 **Wmk. 267** ***Perf. 11½***

996 A505 120cr gray 30 15

1st anniv, of the democratic revolution.

Vital Brazil — A506

Shah of Iran — A507

1965, Apr. 28 **Wmk. 267** ***Perf. 11½***

997 A506 120cr dp orange 30 15

Centenary of birth of Vital Brazil, M.D.

A souvenir card containing one impression similar to No. 997, imperf., exists, printed in dull plum. Sold by P.O. for 250cr. Size: 114x180mm.

1965, May 5 **Photo.**

998 A507 120cr rose claret 25 15

Issued to commemorate the visit of Shah Mohammed Riza Pahlavi of Iran.

Marshal Mariano da Silva Rondon
A508

Lions' Emblem
A509

1965, May 7 **Engr.**

999 A508 30cr claret 25 15

Marshal Mariano da Silva Rondon (1865-1958), explorer and expert on Indians.

1965, May 14 **Photo.**

1000 A509 35cr pale vio & blk 20 15

12th convention of the Lions Clubs of Brazil, Rio de Janeiro, May 11-16.

ITU Emblem, Old and New Communication Equipment — A510

1965, May 21 ***Perf. 11½***

1001 A510 120cr yellow & grn 30 20

Centenary of the ITU.

Epitácio Pessoa — A511

Statue of Admiral Barroso — A512

1965, May 23 **Photo.**

1002 A511 35cr blue gray 20 15

Epitácio da Silva Pessoa (1865-1942), jurist, president of Brazil, 1919-22.

1965, June 11

1003 A512 30cr blue 25 15

Cent. of the naval battle of Riachuelo.

A souvenir card containing one lithographed facsimile of No. 1003, imperf., exists. Size: 100x139½mm.

José de Alencar and Indian Princess — A513

1965, June 24 ***Perf. 11½x11***

1004 A513 30cr deep plum 25 15

Centenary of the publication of "Iracema" by Joséde Alencar.

A souvenir card containing one lithographed facsimile of No. 1004, printed in rose red and imperf., exists. Size: 100x141½mm.

Winston Churchill
A514

1965, June 25 ***Perf. 11x11½***

1005 A514 200cr slate 50 25

Scout Jamboree Emblem — A515

1965, July 17 **Photo.**

1006 A515 30cr dull bl grn 30 15

1st Pan-American Boy Scout Jamboree, Fundao Island, Rio de Janeiro, July 15-25.

ICY Emblem
A516

1965, Aug. 25 **Wmk. 267** ***Perf. 11½***

1007 A516 120cr dl bl & blk 25 15

International Cooperation Year, 1965.

Leoncio Correias
A517

Emblem
A518

1965, Sept. 1 ***Perf. 11½x11***

1008 A517 35cr slate grn 25 15

Leoncio Correias, poet, birth cent.

1965, Sept. 4

1009 A518 30cr brt rose 20 15

Issued to publicize the Eighth Biennial Fine Arts Exhibition, Sao Paulo, Nov.-Dec., 1965.

Pres. Saragat of Italy — A519

1965, Sept. 11 **Photo.** **Wmk. 267**

1010 A519 100cr slate grn, *pink* 25 15

Visit of Pres. Giuseppe Saragat of Italy.

Grand Duke and Duchess of Luxembourg — A520

1965, Sept. 17 ***Perf. 11x11½***

1011 A520 100cr brn olive 25 15

Visit of Grand Duke Jean and Grand Duchess Josephine Charlotte of Luxembourg.

Biplane — A521

1965, Oct. 8 **Photo.** ***Perf. 11½x11***

1012 A521 35cr ultra 20 15

Issued to publicize the 3rd Aviation Week Philatelic Exhibition, Rio de Janeiro.

A souvenir card carries one impression of this 35cr, imperf. Size: 102x140mm. Sold for 100cr.

Flags of OAS Members
A522

1965, Nov. 17 *Perf. 11x11½*

1013 A522 100cr brt bl & blk 25 20

2nd meeting of Foreign Ministers of the OAS, Rio.

King Baudouin and Queen Fabiola of Belgium
A523

1965, Nov. 18

1014 A523 100cr gray 25 20

Visit of King and Queen of Belgium.

"Coffee Beans" — A524

Perf. 11½x11

1965, Dec. 21 Photo. Wmk. 267

1015 A524 30cr brown 30 15

Brazilian coffee publicity.

Conveyor and Loading Crane
A525

1966, Apr. 1 *Perf. 11x11½*

1016 A525 110cr tan & dk sl grn 25 20

Opening of the new terminal of the Rio Doce Iron Ore Company at Tubarao.

Pouring Ladle and Steel Beam — A526

Prof. de Rocha Dissecting Cadaver — A527

Perf. 11½x11

1966, Apr. 16 Photo. Wmk. 267

1017 A526 30cr blk, *dp org* 25 15

25th anniv. of the National Steel Company (nationalization of the steel industry).

1966, Apr. 26

1018 A527 30cr brt bluish grn 40 15

50th anniv. of the discovery and description of Rickettsia prowazeki, the cause of typhus fever, by Prof. Henrique de Rocha Lima.

Battle of Tuiuti
A528

Perf. 11x11½

1966, May 24 Photo. Wmk. 267

1019 A528 30cr gray grn 30 15

Centenary of the Battle of Tuiuti.

Symbolic Water Cycle — A529

Pres. Shazar of Israel — A530

1966, July 1 *Perf. 11½x11*

1020 A529 100cr lt brn & bl 25 20

Hydrological Decade (UNESCO), 1965-74.

1966, July 18 Photo. Wmk. 267

1021 A530 100cr ultra 30 20

Visit of Pres. Zalman Shazar of Israel.

Imperial Academy of Fine Arts
A531

Perf. 11x11½

1966, Aug. 12 Engr. Wmk. 267

1022 A531 100cr red brown 60 20

150th anniversary of French art mission.

Military Service Emblem
A532

1966, Sept. 6 Photo. *Perf. 11x11½*

1023 A532 30cr yel, ultra & grn 25 15

a. With commemorative border 3.50 3.00

New Military Service Law.

No. 1023a issued in sheets of 4. It carries at left a 30cr, type A532, in deeper tones of yellow and ultramarine, Wmk. 264. Without gum. Sold for 100cr.

Ruben Dario — A533

Perf. 11½x11

1966, Sept. 20 Photo. Wmk. 267

1024 A533 100cr brt rose lilac 25 15

Ruben Dario (pen name of Felix Ruben Garcia Sarmiento (1867-1916), Nicaraguan poet, newspaper correspondent and diplomat.

Ceramic Candlestick from Santarém
A534

1966, Oct. 6 *Perf. 11x11½*

1025 A534 30cr dk brn, *sal* 25 15

Centenary of Goeldi Museum at Belem.

Arms of Santa Cruz — A535

Perf. 11½x11

1966, Oct. 15 Photo. Wmk. 267

1026 A535 30cr slate grn 25 15

1st Natl. Tobacco Exposition, Santa Cruz.

UNESCO Emblem — A536

1966, Oct. 24 Engr. *Perf. 11½*

1027 A536 120cr black 75 25

a. With commemorative border 6.00 6.00

20th anniv. of UNESCO. No. 1027a issued in sheets of 4. It carries at right a design similar to No. 1027. Unwatermarked granite paper, without gum. Sold for 150cr.

Captain Antonio Correia Pinto and Map of Lages — A537

Cross of Lusitania and Southern Cross — A538

Perf. 11½x11

1966, Nov. 22 Photo. Wmk. 267

1028 A537 30cr salmon pink 25 15

Arrival of Capt. Antonio Correia Pinto, cent.

1966, Dec. 4 *Perf. 11½*

1029 A538 100cr blue green 30 15

LUBRAPEX 1966 philatelic exhibition at the National Museum of Fine Arts, Rio.

Madonna and Child — A539

A540

Perf. 11½x11

1966, Dec. Photo. Wmk. 267

1030 A539 30cr blue green 25 15

Perf. 11½

1031 A540 35cr salmon & ultra 20 20

a. 150cr salmon & ultra 2.50 3.00

Christmas 1966.

No. 1031a measures 46x103mm and is printed in sheets of 4. It is inscribed "Pax Hominibus" (but not "Brasil Correio") and carries the Madonna shown on No. 1031. Issued without gum.

Issue dates: 30cr, Dec. 8; 35cr, Dec. 22; 150cr, Dec. 28.

Arms of Laguna
A541

1967, Jan. 4 Engr. *Perf. 11x11½*

1032 A541 60cr sepia 20 15

Centenary of the Post and Telegraph Agency of Laguna, Santa Catarina.

Railroad Bridge
A542

1967, Feb. 16 Photo. Wmk. 267

1033 A542 50cr deep orange 45 20

Centenary of the Santos-Jundiai railroad.

Black Madonna of Czestochowa, Polish Eagle and Cross — A543

1967, Mar. 12 *Perf. 11x11½*

1034 A543 50cr yel, bl & rose red 35 20

Adoption of Christianity in Poland, 1,000th anniv.

Research Rocket
A544

Anita Garibaldi
A545

1967, Mar. 23 *Perf. 11½x11*

1035 A544 50cr blk & brt bl 60 30

World Meteorological Day, March 23.

Perf. 11x11½

1967-69 Photo. Wmk. 267

Portraits: 1c, Mother Joana Angelica. 2c, Marilia de Dirceu. 3c, Dr. Rita Lobato. 6c, Ana Neri. 10c, Darcy Vargas.

1036 A545	1c dp ultra	15	15
1037 A545	2c red brn	15	15
1038 A545	3c brt grn	18	15
1039 A545	5c black	35	15
1040 A545	6c brown	35	15
1041 A545	10c dk slate grn ('69)	1.10	30
	Nos. 1036-1041 (6)	2.28	
	Set value		64

Issue dates: 1c, May 3; 2c, Aug. 14; 3c, June 7; 5c, Apr. 14; 6c, May 14, 1967; 10c, June 18, 1969.

VARIG Airlines
A546

Madonna and Child, by Robert Feruzzi
A548

Lions Emblem and Globes
A547

1967, May 8 *Perf. 11½x11*

1046 A546 6c brt bl & blk 30 25

40th anniversary of VARIG Airlines.

1967, May 9 Engr. *Perf. 11x11½*

1047 A547 6c green 30 25
a. Souvenir sheet 2.50 *3.00*

50th anniv. of Lions Intl. No. 1047a contains one imperf. stamp similar to No. 1047. Sold for 15c.

1967, May 14 Photo. *Perf. 11½x11*

1048 A548 5c violet 25 20
a. 15c Souvenir sheet 2.25 *2.25*

Mother's Day. No. 1048a contains one 15c imperf. stamp in design of No. 1048.

Prince Akihito and Princess Michiko
A549

1967, May 25 *Perf. 11x11½*

1049 A549 10c black & pink 30 20

Visit to Brazil of Crown Prince Akihito and Princess Michiko of Japan.

Carrier Pigeon and Radar Screen
A550

Brother Vicente do Salvador
A551

Perf. 11½x11

1967, June 20 Photo. Wmk. 267

1050 A550 10c sl & brt pink 25 20

Issued to commemorate the opening of the Communications Ministry in Brasilia.

1967, June 28 Engr.

1051 A551 5c brown 25 20

400th birth anniv. of Brother Vicente do Salvador (1564-1636), founder of Franciscan convent in Rio de Janeiro, and historian.

Boy, Girl and 4-S Emblem
A552

1967, July 12 Photo. *Perf. 11½*

1052 A552 5c green & blk 25 20

National 4-S (4-H) Day.

Möbius Strip
A553

1967, July 21 *Perf. 11x11½*

1053 A553 5c brt bl & blk 25 20

6th Brazilian Mathematical Congress.

Fish — A554

1967, Aug. 1 *Perf. 11½*

1054 A554 5c slate 30 20

Bicentenary of city of Piracicaba.

Golden Rose and Papal Arms — A555

1967, Aug. 15

1055 A555 20c mag & yel 1.00 40

Offering of a golden rose by Pope Paul VI to the Virgin Mary of Fatima (Our Lady of Peace), Patroness of Brazil.

General Sampaio
A556

King Olaf of Norway
A557

1967, Aug. 25 Engr. *Perf. 11½x11*

1056 A556 5c blue 25 20

Issued to honor General Antonio de Sampaio, hero of the Battle of Tutui.

1967, Sept. 8 Photo.

1057 A557 10c brown org 25 20

Visit of King Olaf of Norway.

Sun over Sugar Loaf, Botafogo Bay
A558

Nilo Peçanha
A559

Photogravure and Embossed

1967, Sept. 25 Wmk. 267 *Perf. 11½*

1058 A558 10c blk & dp org 25 20

22nd meeting of the Intl. Monetary Fund, Intl. Bank for Reconstruction and Development, Intl. Financial Corporation and Intl. Development Assoc.

Perf. 11½x11

1967, Oct. 1 Photo. Wmk. 267

1059 A559 5c brown violet 25 20

Peçanha (1867-1924), Pres. of Brazil 1909-10.

Virgin of the Apparition and Basilica of Aparecida
A560

Cockerel, Festival Emblem
A561

1967, Oct. 11 *Perf. 11½*

1060 A560 5c ultra & dl yel 30 20
a. Souvenir sheet of 2 3.25 *3.25*

250th anniv. of the discovery of the statue of Our Lady of the Apparition, now in the National Basilica of the Apparition at Aparecida do Norte.

No. 1060a contains imperf. 5c and 10c stamps similar to No. 1060. Issued Dec. 27, 1967, for Christmas.

Engraved and Photogravure

1967, Oct. 16 *Perf. 11½x11*

1061 A561 20c black & multi 50 40

Second International Folksong Festival.

Balloon, Plane and Rocket
A562

Perf. 11x11½

1967, Oct. 18 Photo. Unwmk.

1062 A562 10c blue 50 30
a. 15c souvenir sheet 4.50 *4.50*

Week of the Wing, Oct. 18-23. No. 1062a contains one imperf. 15c stamp similar to No. 1062 and was issued Oct. 23.

Pres. Arthur Bernardes — A563

Portraits of Brazilian Presidents: 20c, Campos Salles. 50c, Wenceslau Pereira Gomes Braz. 1cr, Washington Pereira de Souza Luiz. 2cr, Castello Branco.

Perf. 11x11½

1967-68 Photo. Wmk. 267

1063 A563 10c blue 24 20
1064 A563 20c dk red brn 75 20

Engr.

1065 A563 50c black ('68) 3.75 30
1066 A563 1cr lil rose ('68) 6.00 30
1067 A563 2cr emerald ('68) 1.10 30
Nos. 1063-1067 (5) 11.84 1.30

Carnival of Rio — A564

Ships, Anchor and Sailor — A565

1967, Nov. 22 *Perf. 11½x11*

1070 A564 10c lem, ultra & pink 30 20
a. 15c souvenir sheet 3.50 *4.50*

Issued for International Tourist Year, 1967. No. 1070a contains a 15c imperf. stamp in design of No. 1070. Issued Nov. 24.

1967, Dec. 6

1071 A565 10c ultra 30 25

Issued for Navy Week.

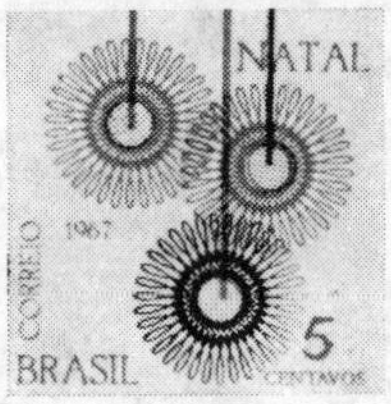

Christmas Decorations
A566

1967, Dec. 8 *Perf. 11½*

1072 A566 5c car, yel & bl 25 20

Christmas 1967.

Olavo Bilac, Planes, Tank and Aircraft Carrier
A567

Perf. 11x11½

1967, Dec. 16 Photo. Wmk. 267

1073 A567 5c brt blue & yel 30 20

Issued for Reservists' Day and to honor Olavo Bilac, sponsor of compulsory military service.

Rodrigues de Carvalho — A568

1967, Dec. 18 Engr. *Perf. 11½x11*

1074 A568 10c green 25 20

Cent. of the birth of Rodrigues de Carvalho, poet and lawyer.

Orlando Rangel A569

1968, Feb. 29 Photo. *Perf. 11x11½*

1075 A569 5c lt grnsh bl & blk 35 25

Orlando de Fonseca Rangel, pioneer of pharmaceutical industry in Brazil, birth cent.

Virgin of Paranagua and Diver A570

Map of Brazil Showing Manaus A571

1968, Mar. 9 *Perf. 11½x11*

1076 A570 10c dk sl grn & brt yel grn 35 25

250th anniversary of the first underwater explorations at Paranagua.

1968, Mar. 13 Photo. Wmk. 267

1077 A571 10c yel, grn & red 35 25

Free port of Manaus on the Amazon River.

Human Rights Flame A572

Paul Harris and Rotary Emblem A573

1968, Mar. 21 *Perf. 11½x11*

1078 A572 10c blue & salmon 35 25

International Human Rights Year.

1968, Apr. 19 Litho. Unwmk.

Without Gum

1079 A573 20c grn & org brn 1.25 70

Paul Percy Harris (1868-1947), founder of Rotary International.

Pedro Alvares Cabral and his Fleet — A574

Design: 20c, First Mass celebrated in Brazil.

1968 Without Gum *Perf. 11½*

1080 A574 10c multicolored 55 45

1081 A574 20c multicolored 80 60

500th anniversary of the birth of Pedro Alvares Cabral, navigator, who took possession of Brazil for Portugal.

Issue dates: 10c, Apr. 22; 20c, July 11.

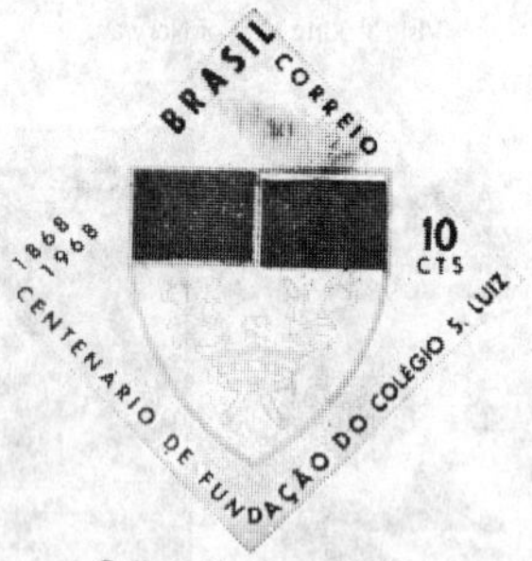

College Arms — A575

1968, Apr. 22 Photo. Wmk. 267

1082 A575 10c vio bl, red & gold 55 35

Centenary of St. Luiz College, Sao Paulo.

Motherhood, by Henrique Bernardeli A576

1968, May 12 Litho. Unwmk.

Without Gum

1083 A576 5c multicolored 35 25

Issued for Mother's Day.

Harpy Eagle — A577

Photogravure and Engraved

1968, May 28 Wmk. 267

1084 A577 20c brt bl & blk 1.50 50

Sesquicentennial of National Museum.

Brazilian and Japanese Women — A578

1968, June 28 Litho. Unwmk.

Without Gum

1085 A578 10c yellow & multi 60 40

Issued to commemorate the inauguration of Varig's direct Brazil-Japan airline.

Horse Race A579

Perf. 11x11½

1968, July 16 Litho. Unwmk.

Without Gum

1086 A579 10c multicolored 35 25

Centenary of the Jockey Club of Brazil.

Musician Wren A580

Designs: 10c, Red-crested cardinal, vert. 50c, Royal flycatcher, vert.

Perf. 11½x11, 11x11½

1968-69 Engr. Wmk. in Sheet

Without Gum

1087 A580 10c multi ('69)	45	28
1088 A580 20c multicolored	75	28
1089 A580 50c multicolored	1.00	55
Nos. 1087-1089 (3)	2.20	1.11

Some stamps in each sheet of Nos. 1087-1089 show parts of a two-line papermaker's watermark: "WESTERPOST / INDUSTRIA BRASILEIRA" with diamond-shaped emblem between last two words. Entire watermark appears in one sheet margin.

Issue dates: 10c, Aug. 20, 1969. 20c, July 19, 1968. 50c, Aug. 2, 1968.

Mailbox and Envelope A581

Photogravure and Engraved

1968, Aug. 1 Wmk. 267 *Perf. 11*

1091 A581 5c citron, blk & grn 20 20

Stamp Day, 1968 and for 125th anniv. of the 1st Brazilian postage stamps.

Emilio Luiz Mallet A582

Map of South America A583

Perf. 11½x11

1968, Aug. 25 Engr. Wmk. 267

1092 A582 10c pale purple 20 20

Issued to honor Marshal Emilio Luiz Mallet, Baron of Itapevi, patron of the marines.

1968, Sept. 5 Photo.

1093 A583 10c deep orange 20 20

Visit of President Eduardo Frei of Chile.

Seal of Portuguese Literary School — A584

Photogravure and Engraved

1968, Sept. 10 *Perf. 11½*

1094 A584 5c pink & grn 20 20

Centenary of Portuguese Literary School.

Map of Brazil and Telex Tape A585

1968, Sept. Photo. *Perf. 11x11½*

1095 A585 20c citron & brt grn 50 25

Linking of 25 Brazilian cities by teletype.

Soldiers' Heads on Medal — A586

Perf. 11½x11

1968, Sept. 24 Litho. Unwmk.

Without Gum

1096 A586 5c blue & gray 20 25

8th American Armed Forces Conference.

Clef, Notes and Sugarloaf Mountain A587

1968, Sept. 30 *Perf. 11½*

Without Gum

1097 A587 6c blk, yel & red 50 30

Third International Folksong Festival.

Catalytic Cracking Plant — A588

1968, Oct. 4
Without Gum

1098 A588 6c blue & multi 50 40

Petrobras, the natl. oil company, 15th anniv.

Child Protection A589

Whimsical Girl — A590

Design: 5c, School boy walking toward the sun.

Perf. 11½x11, 11x11½
1968, Oct. 16 Litho. Unwmk.
Without Gum

1099 A590	5c gray & lt bl	32	30
1100 A589	10c brt bl, dk red & blk	40	25
1101 A590	20c multicolored	48	25
	Nos. 1099-1101 (3)	1.20	80

22nd anniv. of UNICEF.

Children with Books A591

1968, Oct. 23 *Perf. 11x11½*
Without Gum

1102 A591 5c multicolored 25 25

Issued to publicize Book Week.

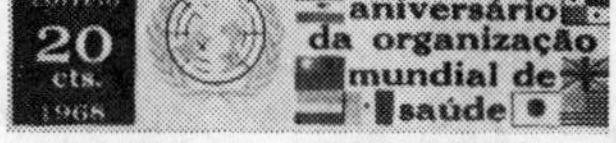

UN Emblem and Flags — A592

1968, Oct. 24 *Perf. 11½x11*
Without Gum

1103 A592 20c black & multi 45 24

20th anniv. of WHO.

Jean Baptiste Debret, Self-portrait — A593

Perf. 11x11½
1968, Oct. 30 Litho. Unwmk.
Without Gum

1104 A593 10c dk gray & pale yel 35 25

Jean Baptiste Debret, (1768-1848), French painter who worked in Brazil (1816-31). Design includes his "Burden Bearer."

Queen Elizabeth II A594

1968, Nov. 4 *Perf. 11½*
Without Gum

1105 A594 70c lt bl & multi 1.75 1.00

Visit of Queen Elizabeth II of Great Britain.

Francisco Braga — A595

Perf. 11½x11
1968, Nov. 19 Wmk. 267

1106 A595 5c dull red brn 40 25

Cent. of the birth of Antonio Francisco Braga, composer of the Hymn of the Flag.

Brazilian Flag — A596

1968, Nov. 19 Unwmk. *Perf. 11½*
Without Gum

1107 A596 10c multicolored 40 30

Issued for Flag Day.

Clasped Hands and Globe A597

Perf. 11x11½
1968, Nov. 25 Typo. Unwmk.
Without Gum

1108 A597 5c multicolored 25 25

Issued for Voluntary Blood Donor's Day.

Old Locomotive — A598

1968, Nov. 28 Litho. *Perf. 11½*
Without Gum

1109 A598 5c multicolored 1.00 50

Centenary of the Sao Paulo Railroad.

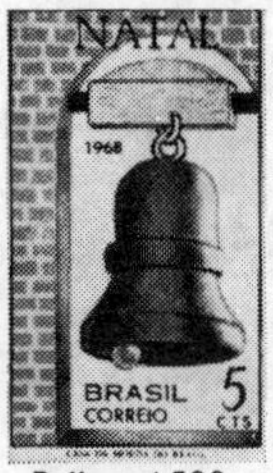

Bell — A599

Francisco Caldas, Jr. — A600

Design: 6c, Santa Claus and boy.

1968 Without Gum *Perf. 11½x11*

1110 A599 5c multicolored 30 25
1111 A599 6c multicolored 30 25

Christmas 1968.
Issue dates: 5c, Dec. 12; 6c, Dec. 20.

1968, Dec. 13
Without Gum

1112 A600 10c crimson & blk 20 18

Cent. of the birth of Francisco Caldas, Jr., journalist and founder of Correio de Povo, newspaper.

Map of Brazil, War Memorial and Reservists' Emblem A601

Perf. 11x11½
1968, Dec. 16 Photo. Wmk. 267

1113 A601 5c bl grn & org brn 30 22

Issued for Reservists' Day.

Radar Antenna A602

Viscount of Rio Branco A603

Perf. 11½x11
1969, Feb. 28 Litho. Unwmk.
Without Gum

1114 A602 30c ultra, lt bl & blk 70 55

Inauguration of EMBRATEL, satellite communications ground station bringing US television to Brazil via Telstar.

1969, Mar. 16
Without Gum

1115 A603 5c black & buff 25 25

José Maria da Silva Paranhos, Viscount of Rio Branco (1819-1880), statesman.

St. Gabriel — A604

1969, Mar. 24
Without Gum

1116 A604 5c multicolored 40 25

Issued to honor St. Gabriel as patron saint of telecommunications.

Shoemaker's Last and Globe — A605

Perf. 11x11½
1969, Mar. 29 Litho. Unwmk.
Without Gum

1117 A605 5c multicolored 25 25

4th Intl. Shoe Fair, Novo Hamburgo.

Allan Kardec A606

1969, Mar. 31 Photo. Wmk. 267

1118 A606 5c brt grn & org brn 25 25

Allan Kardec (pen name of Leon Hippolyto Denizard Rivail, 1803-1869), French physician and spiritist.

Men of 3 Races and Arms of Cuiabá A607

1969, Apr. 8 Litho. Unwmk.
Without Gum

1119 A607 5c black & multi 25 25

250th anniversary of the founding of Cuiabá, capital of Matto Grosso.

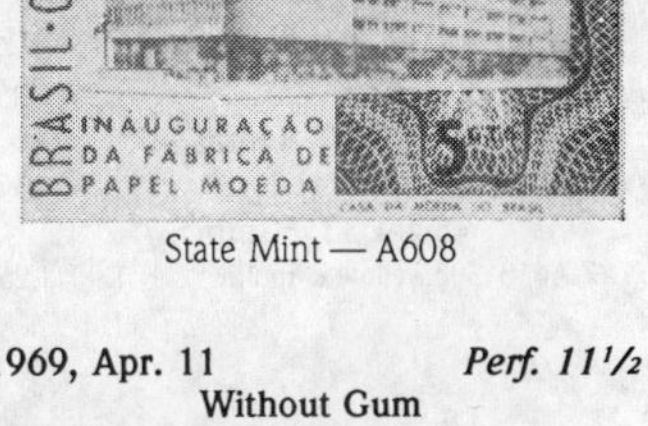

State Mint — A608

1969, Apr. 11 *Perf. 11½*
Without Gum

1120 A608 5c ol bis & org 45 35

Opening of the state money printing plant.

Brazilian Stamps and Emblem A609

Perf. 11x11½

1969, Apr. 30 Litho. Unwmk.

Without Gum

1121 A609 5c multicolored 25 25

Sao Paulo Philatelic Society, 50th anniv.

St. Anne, Baroque Statue — A610

1969, May 8 *Perf. 11½*

Without Gum

1122 A610 5c lemon & multi 50 40

Issued for Mother's Day.

ILO Emblem A611

Perf. 11x11½

1969, May 13 Photo. Wmk. 267

1123 A611 5c dp rose red & gold 25 20

50th anniv. of the ILO.

Diving Platform and Swimming Pool — A612

Mother and Child at Window — A613

Lithographed and Photogravure

Perf. 11½x11

1969, June 13 Unwmk.

Without Gum

1124 A612 20c bis brn, blk & bl grn 55 42

40th anniversary of the Cearense Water Sports Club, Fortaleza.

1969 Litho. *Perf. 11½*

Designs: 20c, Modern sculpture by Felicia Leirner. 50c, "The Sun Sets in Brasilia," by Danilo di Prete. 1cr, Angelfish, painting by Aldemir Martins.

Size: 24x36mm

1125 A613 10c orange & multi 55 25

Size: 33x34mm

1126 A613 20c red & multi 55 50

Size: 33x53mm

1127 A613 50c yellow & multi 1.90 1.25

Without Gum

1128 A613 1cr gray & multi 2.50 1.25

Nos. 1125-1128 (4) 5.50 3.25

Issued to publicize the 10th Biennial Art Exhibition, Sao Paulo, Sept.-Dec. 1969.

Angelfish A614

Fish — A615

Fish: 10c, Tetra. 15c, Piranha. No. 1130c, Megalamphodus megalopterus. 30c, Black tetra.

Perf. 11½

1969, July 21 Litho. Wmk. 267

1129 A614 20c multicolored 70 40

Souvenir Sheet

1969, July 24 Unwmk. ***Imperf.***

1130 A615 Sheet of 4 4.50 *5.00*

a.	10c yellow & multi	90	90
b.	15c bright blue & multi	90	90
c.	20c green & multi	90	90
d.	30c orange & multi	90	90

Issued to publicize the work of ACAPI, an organization devoted to the preservation and development of fish in Brazil.

No. 1130 contains 4 stamps, size: 38½x21mm.

L. O. Teles de Menezes A616

Mailman A617

Perf. 11½x11

1969, July 26 Photo. Wmk. 267

1131 A616 50c dp org & bl grn 1.25 1.00

Centenary of Spiritism press in Brazil.

1969, Aug. 1

1132 A617 30c blue 1.10 90

Issued for Stamp Day.

Map of Brazil A618

Gen. Tasso Fragoso A620

Railroad Bridge A619

Perf. 11½

1969, Aug. 25 Unwmk. Litho.

Without Gum

1133 A618 10c lt ultra, grn & yel 24 22

Perf. 11x11½

1134 A619 20c multicolored 80 40

Perf. 11½x11

Engr. Wmk. 267

With Gum

1135 A620 20c green 80 50

Nos. 1133-1135 (3) 1.84 1.12

No. 1133 honors the Army as guardian of security; No. 1134, as promoter of development. No. 1135 commemorates the birth centenary of Gen. Tasso Fragoso.

Jupia Dam, Parana River — A621

Perf. 11½

1969, Sept. 10 Litho. Unwmk.

Without Gum

1136 A621 20c lt blue & multi 35 35

Inauguration of the Jupia Dam, part of the Urubupunga hydroelectric system serving Sao Paulo.

Gandhi and Spinning Wheel A622

1969, Oct. 2 *Perf. 11x11½*

1137 A622 20c yellow & blk 40 30

Mohandas K. Gandhi (1869-1948), leader in India's fight for independence.

Santos Dumont, Eiffel Tower and Module Landing on Moon — A623

1969, Oct. 17 *Perf. 11½*

Without Gum

1138 A623 50c dk bl & multi 1.75 1.25

Man's first landing on the moon, July 20, 1969. See note after U.S. No. C76.

Smelting Plant — A624

1969, Oct. 26 Unwmk. *Perf. 11½*

Without Gum

1139 A624 20c multicolored 45 40

Expansion of Brazil's steel industry.

Steel Furnace A625

1969, Oct. 31 Litho.

Without Gum

1140 A625 10c yellow & multi 45 40

25th anniversary of Acesita Steel Works.

Water Vendor, by J. B. Debret — A626

Design: 30c, Street Scene, by Debret.

1969-70

Without Gum

1141 A626 20c multicolored 1.25 50

1141A A626 30c multicolored 1.25 1.00

Jean Baptiste Debret (1768-1848), painter.

Issue dates: 20c, Nov. 5, 1969; 30c, May 19, 1970.

Exhibition Emblem — A627

1969, Nov. 15 *Perf. 11½x11*

Without Gum

1142 A627 10c multicolored 35 22

Issued to publicize the ABUEXPO 69 Philatelic Exposition, Sao Paulo, Nov. 15-23.

Plane — A628

1969, Nov. 23

Without Gum

1143 A628 50c multicolored 2.75 1.40

Issued to publicize the year of the expansion of the national aviation industry.

Pelé Scoring — A629

1969-70

Without Gum

1144 A629 10c multicolored 38 30

Souvenir Sheet

Imperf

1145 A629 75c multi ('70) 4.50 3.50

Issued to commemorate the 1,000th goal scored by Pele, Brazilian soccer player.

No. 1145 contains one imperf. stamp with simulated perforations.

Issued dates: 10c, Nov. 28, 1969. 75c, Jan. 23, 1970.

Madonna and Child from Villa Velha Monastery A630

Perf. 11½

1969, Dec. Unwmk. Litho.

Without Gum

1146 A630 10c gold & multi 35 20

Souvenir Sheet

Imperf

1147 A630 75c gold & multi 12.00 *15.00*

Christmas 1969.

No. 1147 has simulated perforations.

Issue dates: 10c, Dec. 8; 75c, Dec. 18.

Destroyer and Submarine A631

Perf. 11x11½

1969, Dec. 9 Engr. Wmk. 267

1148 A631 5c bluish gray 40 25

Issued for Navy Day.

Dr. Herman Blumenau A632

1969, Dec. 26 *Perf. 11½*

1149 A632 20c gray grn 85 40

Dr. Herman Blumenau (1819-1899), founder of Blumenau, Santa Catarina State.

Carnival Scene — A633

Sugarloaf Mountain, Mask, Confetti and Streamers A634

Designs: 5c, Jumping boy and 2 women, vert. 20c, Clowns. 50c, Drummer.

1969-70 Litho. Unwmk.

Without Gum

1150 A633 5c multicolored 40 30

1151 A633 10c multicolored 40 30

1152 A633 20c multicolored 52 40

1153 A634 30c multicolored 3.00 3.00

1154 A634 50c multicolored 2.75 2.50

Nos. 1150-1154 (5) 7.07 6.50

Carico Carnival, Rio de Janeiro.

Issue dates: Nos. 1150-1152, Dec. 29, 1969. Nos. 1153-1154, Feb. 5, 1970.

Opening Bars of "Il Guarani" with Antonio Carlos Gomes Conducting A635

1970, Mar. 19 Litho. *Perf. 11½*

Without Gum

1155 A635 20c blk, yel, gray & brn 60 40

Centenary of the opera Il Guarani, by Antonio Carlos Gomes.

Church of Penha — A636

1970, Apr. 6 Unwmk. *Perf. 11½*

Without Gum

1156 A636 20c black & multi 30 20

400th anniversary of the Church of Penha, State of Esperito Santo.

Assembly Building A637

10th anniv. of Brasilia: 50c, Reflecting Pool. 1cr, Presidential Palace.

1970, Apr. 21

Without Gum

1157 A637 20c multicolored 90 70

1158 A637 50c multicolored 2.25 1.75

1159 A637 1cr multicolored 2.25 1.75

Nos. 1157-1159 (3) 5.40 4.20

Symbolic Water Design — A638

1970, May 5 Unwmk. *Perf. 11½*

Without Gum

1161 A638 50c multicolored 2.50 3.00

Issued to publicize the Rondon Project for the development of the Amazon River basin.

Marshal Manoel Luiz Osorio and Osorio Arms — A639

1970, May 8

Without Gum

1162 A639 20c multicolored 1.50 1.00

Issued to commemorate the inauguration of the Marshal Osorio Historical Park.

Madonna, from San Antonio Monastery, Rio de Janeiro A640

Detail from Brasilia Cathedral A641

1970, May 10

Without Gum

1163 A640 20c multicolored 40 40

Issued for Mother's Day.

1970, May 27 Engr. Wmk. 267

1164 A641 20c lt yellow grn 25 25

8th National Eucharistic Congress, Brasilia.

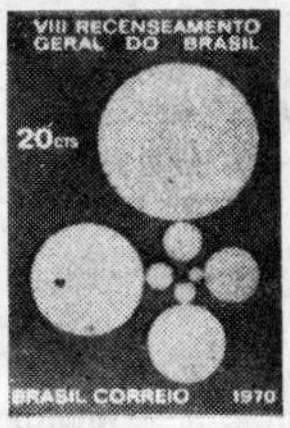

Census Symbol — A642

Perf. 11½

1970, June 22 Unwmk. Litho.

Without Gum

1165 A642 20c green & yel 60 60

Issued to publicize the 8th general census.

Soccer Cup, Maps of Brazil and Mexico A643

Swedish Flag and Player Holding Rimet Cup — A644

Designs: 2cr, Chilean flag and soccer. 3cr, Mexican flag and soccer.

1970

Without Gum

1166 A643 50c blk, lt bl & gold 90 90

1167 A644 1cr pink & multi 2.75 1.50

1168 A644 2cr gray & multi 5.25 1.50

1169 A644 3cr multicolored 4.50 1.00

Nos. 1166-1169 (4) 13.40 4.90

9th World Soccer Championships for the Jules Rimet Cup, Mexico City, May 30-June 21. No. 1166 honors Brazil's victory.

Issued: #1166, June 24; #1167-1169, Aug. 4.

Corcovado Christ and Map of South America A645

1970, July 18

Without Gum

1170 A645 50c brn, dk red & bl 2.50 2.50

6th World Cong. of Marist Brothers' Alumni.

Pandia Calogeras, Minister of War — A646

Perf. 11½x11

1970, Aug. 25 Photo. Unwmk.

1171 A646 20c blue green 50 50

Brazilian Military Emblems and Map
A647

Perf. 11x11½

1970, Sept. 8 Litho. Unwmk.

Without Gum

1172 A647 20c gray & multi 50 50

25th anniv. of victory in World War II.

Annunciation (Brazilian Primitive Painting)
A648

1970, Sept. 29 *Perf. 11½*

Without Gum

1173 A648 20c multicolored 1.25 1.00

Issued for St. Gabriel's (patron saint of communications) Day.

Boy in Library — A649

UN Emblem — A650

1970, Oct. 23

Without Gum

1174 A649 20c multicolored 1.25 1.00

Issued to publicize Book Week.

1970, Oct. 24

Without Gum

1175 A650 50c dk bl, lt bl & sil 1.25 1.25

25th anniversary of the United Nations.

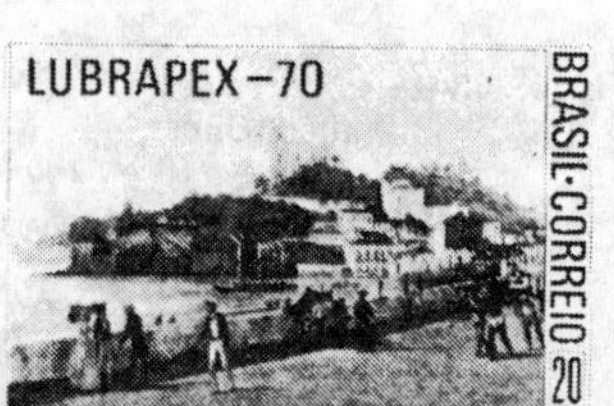

Rio de Janeiro, 1820 — A651

Designs: 50c, LUBRAPEX 70 emblem. 1cr, Rio de Janeiro with Sugar Loaf Mountain, 1970. No. 1179, like 20c.

1970, Oct.

Without Gum

1176 A651 20c multicolored		1.75	1.00
1177 A651 50c yel brn & blk		3.50	2.00
1178 A651 1cr multicolored		3.50	3.75
	Nos. 1176-1178 (3)	8.75	6.75

Souvenir Sheet

Imperf

1179 A651 1cr multicolored 11.00 *17.00*

LUBRAPEX 70, 3rd Portuguese-Brazilian Phil. Exhib., Rio de Janeiro, Oct. 24-31.

Issued: #1176-1178, Oct. 27; #1179, Oct. 31.

Holy Family by Candido Portinari
A652

1970, Dec. Litho. *Perf. 11½*

Without Gum

1180 A652 50c multicolored 1.25 1.50

Souvenir Sheet

Imperf

1181 A652 1cr multicolored 15.00 *24.00*

Christmas 1970. No. 1181 contains one stamp with simulated perforations.

Issue dates: 50c, Dec. 1; 1cr, Dec. 8.

Battleship
A653

CIH Emblem
A654

1970, Dec. 11 Litho. *Perf. 11½*

Without Gum

1182 A653 20c multicolored 1.25 75

Navy Day.

1971, Mar. 28 Litho. *Perf. 11½*

Without Gum

1183 A654 50c black & red 1.50 1.75

3rd Inter-American Housing Congress, Mar. 27-Apr. 3.

Links Around Globe — A655

1971, Mar. 31 Litho. *Perf. 12½x11*

Without Gum

1184 A655 20c grn, yel, blk & red 65 50

Intl. year against racial discrimination.

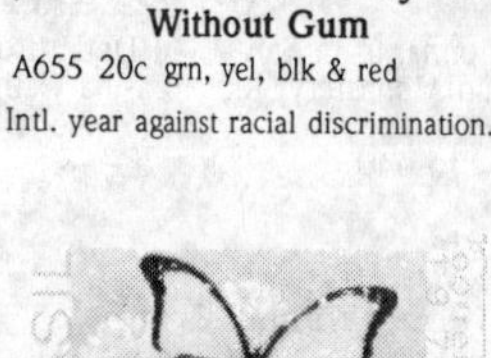

Morpho Melacheilus — A656

Design: 1cr, Papilio thoas brasiliensis.

Perf. 11x11½

1971, Apr. 28 Litho. Unwmk.

Without Gum

1185 A656 20c multicolored	1.25	60
1186 A656 1cr multicolored	5.50	3.25

Madonna and Child — A657

1971, May 9 Litho. *Perf. 11½*

Without Gum

1187 A657 20c multicolored 85 40

Mother's Day, 1971.

Basketball
A658

1971, May 19

Without Gum

1188 A658 70c multicolored 1.50 1.00

6th World Women's Basketball Championship.

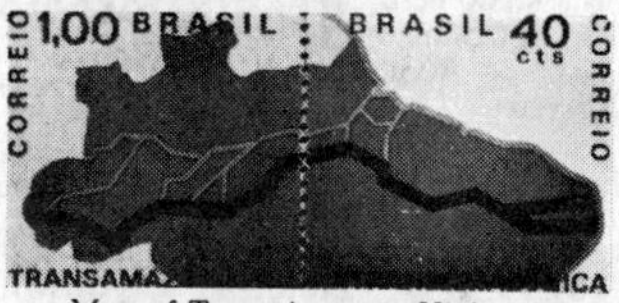

Map of Trans-Amazon Highway
A660 A659

Perf. 11½

1971, July 1 Unwmk. Litho.

Without Gum

1189 A659 40c multicolored	5.50	2.75
1190 A660 1cr multicolored	5.50	5.50
a. Pair, #1189-1190	11.00	11.00

Trans-Amazon Highway. No. 1190a printed in sheets of 28 (4x7). Horizontal rows contain 2 No. 1190a with a label between. Each label carries different inscription.

Man's Head, by Victor Mairelles de Lima — A661

Stamp Day: 1cr, Arab Violinist, by Pedro Américo.

1971, Aug. 1

Without Gum

1191 A661 40c pink & multi	1.25	80
1192 A661 1cr gray & multi	3.25	1.65

Duke of Caxias and Map of Brazil — A662

1971, Aug. 23 Photo.

1193 A662 20c yel grn & red brn 50 60

Army Day.

Anita Garibaldi — A663

1971, Aug. 30 Litho.

Without Gum

1194 A663 20c multicolored 42 42

Anita Garibaldi (1821-1849), heroine in liberation of Brazil.

Xavante Jet and Santos Dumont's Plane, 1910 — A664

1971, Sept. 6

Without Gum

1195 A664 40c yellow & multi 1.40 75

First flight of Xavante jet plane.

Flags and Map of Central American Nations — A665

"71" in French Flag Colors — A666

1971, Sept. 15

Without Gum

1196 A665 40c ocher & multi 1.25 60

Sesquicentennial of the independence of Central American nations.

1971, Sept. 16

Without Gum

1197 A666 1.30cr ultra & multi 1.25 1.10

French Exhibition.

Black Mother, by Lucilio de Albuquerque
A667

Archangel Gabriel
A668

1971, Sept. 28

Without Gum

1198 A667 40c multicolored 60 50

Centenary of law guaranteeing personal freedom starting at birth.

1971, Sept. 29 *Perf. 11½x11*

Without Gum

1199 A668 40c multicolored 75 65

St. Gabriel's Day.

Bridge over River — A669

Children's Drawings: 35c, People crossing bridge. 60c, Woman with hat.

1971, Oct. 25 *Perf. 11½*

Without Gum

1200 A669 35c pink, bl & blk 55 45
1201 A669 45c black & multi 1.40 45
1202 A669 60c olive & multi 55 45
Nos. 1200-1202 (3) 2.50 1.35

Children's Day.

Werkhäuserii Superba
A670

1971, Nov. 16

Without Gum

1203 A670 40c blue & multi 2.00 1.00

In memory of Carlos Werkhauser, botanist.

Greek Key Pattern "25" — A671

Design: 40c, like 20c but inscribed "sesc / servicio social / do comercio."

1971, Dec. 3

Without Gum

1204 A671 20c black & blue 1.25 1.00
1205 A671 40c black & org 1.25 1.00
a. Pair, #1204-1205 2.50 2.50

25th anniversary of SENAC (national apprenticeship system) and SESC (commercial social service).

Gunboat
A672

1971, Dec. 8 *Perf. 11*

Without Gum

1206 A672 20c blue & multi 85 50

Navy Day.

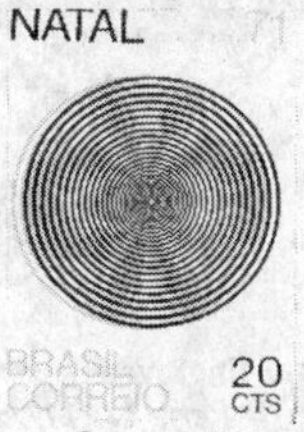

Cross and Circles — A673

Washing of Bonfim Church, Salvador, Bahia — A674

1971, Dec. 11

1207 A673 20c car & blue 40 40
1208 A673 75c silver & gray 80 *3.00*
1209 A673 1.30cr blk, yel, grn & bl 4.75 2.50
Nos. 1207-1209 (3) 5.95 *5.90*

Christmas 1971.

1972, Feb. 18 **Litho.** *Perf. 11½x11*

Designs: 40c, Grape Festival, Rio Grande do Sul. 75c, Festival of the Virgin of Nazareth, Belém. 1.30cr, Winter Arts Festival, Ouro Preto.

Without Gum

1210 A674 20c silver & multi 1.50 75
1211 A674 40c silver & multi 2.75 75
1212 A674 75c silver & multi 2.75 3.00
1213 A674 1.30cr silver & multi 6.00 3.00
Nos. 1210-1213 (4) 13.00 7.50

Pres. Lanusse and Flag of Argentina
A675

1972, Mar. 13 *Perf. 11x11½*

Without Gum

1214 A675 40c blue & multi 2.00 2.50

Visit of Lt. Gen. Alejandro Agustin Lanusse, president of Argentina.

Presidents Castello Branco, Costa e Silva and Garrastazu Medici
A676

1972, Mar. 29

Without Gum

1215 A676 20c emerald & multi 1.25 60

Anniversary of 1964 revolution.

Post Office Emblem — A677

Perf. 11½x11

1972, Apr. 10 **Photo.** **Unwmk.**

1216 A677 20c red brown 2.00 20

No. 1216 is luminescent.

Pres. Thomas and Portuguese Flag
A678

1972, Apr. 22 **Litho.** *Perf. 11*

Without Gum

1217 A678 75c ol brn & multi 1.75 1.75

Visit of Pres. Americo Thomas of Portugal to Brazil, Apr. 22-27.

Soil Research (CPRM)
A679

1972, May 3 *Perf. 11½*

Without Gum

1218 A679 20c shown 1.50 50
1219 A679 40c Offshore oil rig 3.50 85
1220 A679 75c Hydroelectric dam 1.50 1.75
1221 A679 1.30cr Iron ore production 3.50 1.40
Nos. 1218-1221 (4) 10.00 4.50

Industrial development. Stamps are inscribed with names of industrial firms.
See Nos. 1228-1229.

Souvenir Sheet

Poster for Modern Art Week 1922 — A680

1972, May 5

1222 A680 1cr black & car 26.00 26.00

50th anniversary of Modern Art Week.

Mailman, Map of Brazil and Letters
A681

Designs: 45c, "Telecommunications", vert. 60c, Tropospheric scatter system. 70c, Road map of Brazil and worker.

1972, May 26

Without Gum

1223 A681 35c blue & multi 1.25 40
1224 A681 45c silver & multi 1.50 1.50
1225 A681 60c black & multi 1.50 1.25
1226 A681 70c multicolored 1.75 1.25
Nos. 1223-1226 (4) 6.00 4.40

Unification of communications in Brazil.

Development Type and

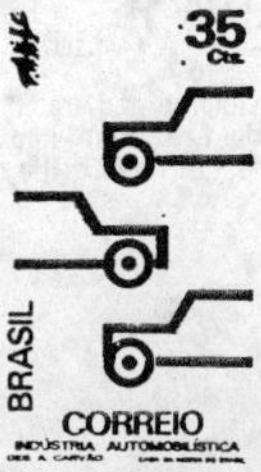

Automobiles — A682

Perf. 11x11½, 11½x11

1972, June 21 **Photo.**

1227 A682 35c shown 1.00 50

Litho.

1228 A679 45c Ships 1.00 60
1229 A679 70c Ingots 1.00 40
Nos. 1227-1229 (3) 3.00 1.50

Industrial development. The 35c is luminescent.

Soccer — A683

Designs: 75c, Folk music. 1.30cr, Plastic arts.

Perf. 11½x11

1972, July 7 **Photo.** **Unwmk.**

1230 A683 20c black & yel 1.00 50
1231 A683 75c black & ver 2.00 3.50
1232 A683 1.30cr black & ultra 4.00 3.50
Nos. 1230-1232 (3) 7.00 7.50

150th anniversary of independence. No. 1230 publicizes the 1972 sports tournament, a part of independence celebrations. Luminescent.

Souvenir Sheet

Shout of Independence, by Pedro Americo de Figueiredo e Melo — A684

1972, July 19 **Litho.** *Perf. 11½*

Without Gum

1233 A684 1cr multicolored 4.00 *9.00*

4th Interamerican Philatelic Exhibition, EXFILBRA, Rio de Janeiro, Aug 26-Sept. 2.

Figurehead
A685

Brazilian folklore: 60c, Gauchos dancing fandango. 75c, Acrobats (capoeira). 1.15cr, Karajá (ceramic) doll. 1.30cr, Mock bullfight (bumba meu boi).

1972, Aug. 6

Without Gum

1234 A685 45c multicolored 85 35
1235 A685 60c orange & multi 1.65 1.50
1236 A685 75c gray & multi 30 30
1237 A685 1.15cr multicolored 55 55
1238 A685 1.30cr yellow & multi 5.00 2.00
Nos. 1234-1238 (5) 8.35 4.70

15-Cent Minimum Value
The minimum value for a single stamp is 15 cents. This value reflects the costs of handling inexpensive stamps.

Map of Brazil, by Diego Homem, 1568 — A686

Designs: 1cr, Map of Americas, by Nicholas Visscher, 1652. 2cr, Map of Americas, by Lopo Homem, 1519.

1972, Aug. 26 Litho. *Perf. 11½*

Without Gum

1239	A686	70c multicolored	50	50
1240	A686	1cr multicolored	9.00	1.00
1241	A686	2cr multicolored	4.50	1.50
		Nos. 1239-1241 (3)	14.00	3.00

4th Inter-American Philatelic Exhibition, EXFILBRA, Rio de Janeiro, Aug. 26-Sept. 2.

Dom Pedro Proclaimed Emperor, by Jean Baptiste Debret A687

Designs: 30c, Founding of Brazil (people with imperial flag; vert.). 1cr, Coronation of Emperor Dom Pedro, vert. 2cr, Dom Pedro commemorative medal. 3.50cr, Independence Monument, Ipiranga.

1972, Sept. 4 Litho. *Perf. 11½x11*

1242	A687	30c yellow & grn	1.25	1.25
1243	A687	70c pink & rose lil	1.25	80
1244	A687	1cr buff & red brn	8.00	1.25
1245	A687	2cr pale yel & blk	4.00	1.25
1246	A687	3.50cr gray & blk	7.25	4.00
		Nos. 1242-1246 (5)	21.75	8.55

Sesquicentennial of independence.

Souvenir Sheet

"Automobile Race" — A688

1972, Nov. 14 *Perf. 11½*

1247	A688	2cr multicolored	10.00	15.00

Emerson Fittipaldi, Brazilian world racing champion.

Numeral and Post Office Emblem — A689

Mö — A689a

Perf. 11½x11

1972-75 Unwmk. Photo.

1248	A689	5c orange	35	15
a.		Wmk. 267	20	15
1249	A689	10c brown ('73)	20	15
a.		Wmk. 267	4.00	15
1250	A689	15c brt blue ('75)	15	15
1251	A689	20c ultra	35	15
1252	A689	25c sepia ('75)	25	15
1253	A689	30c dp carmine	40	15
1254	A689	40c dk grn ('73)	20	15
1255	A689	50c olive	30	15
1256	A689	70c red lilac ('75)	30	15

Engr. *Perf. 11½*

1257	A689a	1cr lilac ('74)	45	15
1258	A689a	2cr grnsh bl ('74)	65	15
1259	A689a	4cr org & vio ('75)	1.40	20
1260	A689a	5cr brn, car & buff ('74)	2.00	20
1261	A689a	10cr grn, blk & buff ('74)	4.50	30
		Nos. 1248-1261 (14)	11.50	
		Set value		1.55

The 5cr and 10cr have beige lithographed multiple Post Office emblem underprint.

Nos. 1248-1261 are luminescent. Nos. 1248a and 1249a are not.

Hand Writing "Mobral" A690

Designs: 20c, Multiracial group and population growth curve. 1cr, People and hands holding house. 2cr, People, industrial scene and upward arrow.

1972, Nov. 28 Litho. *Perf. 11½*

Without Gum

1262	A690	10c black & multi	20	*50*
1263	A690	20c black & multi	1.00	75
1264	A690	1cr black & multi	8.75	30
1265	A690	2cr black & multi	2.00	75
		Nos. 1262-1265 (4)	11.95	2.30

Publicity for: "Mobral" literacy campaign (10c); Centenary of census (20c); Housing and retirement fund (1cr); Growth of gross national product (2cr).

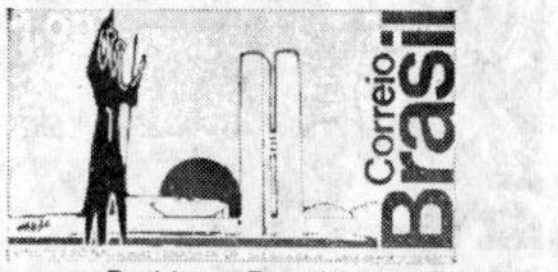

Congress Building, Brasilia, by Oscar Niemeyer, and "Os Guerreiros," by Bruno Giorgi A691

1972, Dec. 4

Without Gum

1266	A691	1cr blue, blk & org	10.00	6.00

Meeting of Natl. Cong., Brasilia, Dec. 4-8.

Holy Family (Clay Figurines) A692

Retirement Plan A693

1972, Dec. 13 Photo. *Perf. 11½x11*

1267	A692	20c ocher & blk	85	50

Christmas 1972. Luminescent.

Perf. 11½x11, 11x11½

1972, Dec. 20 Litho.

Designs: No. 1269, School children and traffic lights, horiz. 70c, Dr. Oswaldo Cruz with Red Cross, caricature. 2cr, Produce, fish and cattle, horiz.

Without Gum

1268	A693	10c blk, bl & dl org	50	50
1269	A693	10c orange & multi	1.00	1.00
1270	A693	70c blk, red & brn	9.00	3.75
1271	A693	2cr green & multi	15.00	6.50
		Nos. 1268-1271 (4)	25.50	11.75

Publicity for: Agricultural workers' assistance program (No. 1268); highway and transportation development (No. 1269); centenary of the birth of Dr. Oswaldo Cruz (1872-1917), Director of Public Health Institute (70c); agricultural and cattle export (2cr). Nos. 1268-1271 are luminescent.

Sailing Ship, Navy A694

Designs: 10c, Monument, Brazilian Expeditionary Force. No. 1274, Plumed helmet, Army. No. 1275, Rocket, Air Force.

Lithographed and Engraved

1972, Dec. 28 *Perf. 11x11½*

Without Gum

1272	A694	10c brn, dk brn & blk	1.50	1.10
1273	A694	30c lt ultra, grn & blk	1.50	1.10
1274	A694	30c yel grn, bl grn & blk	1.50	1.10
1275	A694	30c lilac, mar & blk	1.50	1.10
a.		Block of 4, #1272-1275	6.00	5.00

Armed Forces Day.

Rotary Emblem and Cogwheels A695

Perf. 11½

1973, Mar. 21 Litho. Unwmk.

1276	A695	1cr ultra, grnsh bl & yel	1.75	1.50

Rotary International serving Brazil 50 years.

Swimming A696

Designs: No. 1278, Gymnastics. No. 1279, Volleyball, vert.

1973 Photo. *Perf. 11x11½, 11½x11*

1277	A696	40c brt bl & red brn	35	35
1278	A696	40c green & org brn	2.75	70
1279	A696	40c violet & org brn	70	70
		Nos. 1277-1279 (3)	3.80	1.75

Issue dates: No. 1277, Apr. 19; No. 1278, May 22; No. 1279, Oct. 15.

Flag of Paraguay A697

Perf. 11½

1973, Apr. 27 Litho. Unwmk.

1280	A697	70c multicolored	1.75	1.25

Visit of Pres. Alfredo Stroessner of Paraguay, Apr. 25-27.

"Communications" — A698

Design: 1cr, Neptune, map of South America and Africa.

1973, May 5 *Perf. 11x11½*

1281	A698	70c multicolored	80	70
1282	A698	1cr multicolored	4.25	3.00

Inauguration of the Ministry of Communications Building, Brasilia (70c); and of the first underwater telephone cable between South America and Europe, Bracan 1 (1cr).

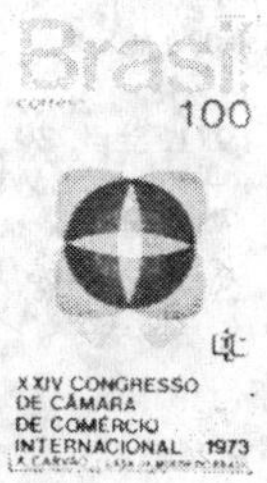

Congress Emblem — A699

1973, May 19 *Perf. 11½x11*

1283	A699	1cr orange & pur	4.00	3.00

24th Congress of the International Chamber of Commerce, Rio de Janeiro, May 19-26.

Swallowtailed Manakin — A700

Birds: No. 1285, Orange-backed oriole. No. 1286, Brazilian ruby (hummingbird).

1973 Litho. *Perf. 11x11½*

1284	A700	20c multicolored	50	20
1285	A700	20c multicolored	50	20
1286	A700	20c multicolored	50	20
		Nos. 1284-1286 (3)	1.50	60

Issue dates: No. 1284, May 26; No. 1285, June 6; No. 1286, June 19.

Tourists A701

1973, June 28 Litho. *Perf. 11x11½*

1287	A701	70c multicolored	90	85

National Tourism Year.

Conference at Itu — A702

Satellite and Multispectral Image — A703

1973 *Perf. 11½x11*

1288 A702 20c shown 52 35
1289 A702 20c Decorated wagon 52 35
1290 A702 20c Indian 52 35
1291 A702 20c Graciosa Road 52 35
Nos. 1288-1291 (4) 2.08 1.40

Centenary of the Itu Convention (1288); sesquicentennial of the July 2 episode (1289); 400th anniversary of the founding of Niteroi (1290); centenary of Graciosa Road (1291).
Issue dates: #1291, July 29; others July 2.

1973, July 11 *Perf. 11½*

Designs: 70c, Official opening of Engineering School, 1913. 1cr, Möbius strips and "IMPA."

1292 A703 20c black & multi 25 40
1293 A703 70c dk blue & multi 2.25 1.00
1294 A703 1cr lilac & multi 3.00 1.00
Nos. 1292-1294 (3) 5.50 2.40

Institute for Space Research (20c); School of Engineering, Itajubá, 60th anniversary (70c); Institute for Pure and Applied Mathematics (1cr).

Santos-Dumont and 14-Bis Plane — A704

Designs (Santos-Dumont and): 70c, No. 6 Balloon and Eiffel Tower. 2cr Demoiselle plane.

Lithographed and Engraved

1973, July 20 *Perf. 11x11½*

1295 A704 20c lt grn, brt grn & brn 75 25
1296 A704 70c yel, rose red & brn 1.75 1.25
1297 A704 2cr bl, vio bl & brn 1.75 1.25
Nos. 1295-1297 (3) 4.25 2.75

Centenary of the birth of Alberto Santos-Dumont (1873-1932), aviation pioneer.

Mercator Map A705

Design: No. 1299, Same, red border on top and at left.

Photogravure and Engraved

1973, Aug. 1 **Wmk. 267**

1298 A705 40c red & black 2.50 1.50
1299 A705 40c red & black 2.10 2.10
a. Block of 4 21.00 15.00

Stamp Day. Nos. 1298-1299 are printed se-tenant horizontally and tête bêche vertically in sheets of 55. Blocks of 4 have red border all around.

Gonçalves Dias (1823-1864), Poet — A706

Perf. 11½x11

1973, Aug. 10 **Wmk. 267**

1300 A706 40c violet & blk 70 42

Souvenir Sheet

Copernicus and Sun — A707

Perf. 11x11½

1973, Aug. 15 **Litho.** **Unwmk.**

1301 A707 1cr multicolored 4.00 5.00

500th anniversary of the birth of Nicolaus Copernicus (1473-1543), Polish astronomer.

Folklore Festival Banner — A708

1973, Aug. 22 *Perf. 11½*

1302 A708 40c ultra & multi 75 52

Folklore Day, Aug. 22.

Masonic Emblem A709

1973, Aug. 24 **Photo.** *Perf. 11x11½*

1303 A709 1cr Prus blue 3.00 2.00

Free Masons of Brazil, 1822-1973.

Nature Protection A710

Designs: No. 1305, Fire protection. No. 1306, Aviation safety. No. 1307, Safeguarding cultural heritage.

1973, Sept. 20 **Litho.** *Perf. 11x11½*

1304 A710 40c brt grn & multi 75 40
1305 A710 40c dk blue & multi 75 40
1306 A710 40c lt blue & multi 75 40
1307 A710 40c pink & multi 75 40
Nos. 1304-1307 (4) 3.00 1.60

Souvenir Sheet

St. Gabriel and Proclamation of Pope Paul VI — A711

Lithographed and Engraved

1973, Sept. 29 **Unwmk.** *Perf. 11½*

1308 A711 1cr bister & blk 7.50 10.00

1st National Exhibition of Religious Philately, Rio de Janeiro, Sept. 29-Oct. 6.

St. Teresa — A712

Photogravure and Engraved

Perf. 11½x11

1973, Sept. 30 **Wmk. 267**

1309 A712 2cr dk org & brn 3.50 2.50

St. Teresa of Lisieux, the Little Flower (1873-1897), Carmelite nun.

Monteiro Lobato and Emily A713

Perf. 11½

1973, Oct. 12 **Litho.** **Unwmk.**

1310 A713 40c shown 80 50
1311 A713 40c Aunt Nastacia 80 50
1312 A713 40c Snubnose, Peter and Rhino 80 50
1313 A713 40c Viscount de Sabugosa 80 50
1314 A713 40c Dona Benta 80 50
a. Block of 5 + label 4.00 4.00

Monteiro Lobato, author of children's books.

Soapstone Sculpture of Isaiah (detail) — A714

Baroque Art in Brazil: No. 1316, Arabesque, gilded wood carving, horiz. 70c, Father José Maurício Nuñes Garcia and music score. 1cr, Church door, Salvador, Bahia. 2cr, Angels, church ceiling painting by Manoel da Costa Athayde, horiz.

1973, Nov. 5

1315 A714 40c multicolored 30 30
1316 A714 40c multicolored 30 30
1317 A714 70c multicolored 1.50 1.40
1318 A714 1cr multicolored 9.00 3.00
1319 A714 2cr multicolored 4.00 3.00
Nos. 1315-1319 (5) 15.10 8.00

Old and New Telephones A715

1973, Nov. 28 *Perf. 11x11½*

1320 A715 40c multicolored 35 30

50th anniv. of Brazilian Telephone Co.

Symbolic Angel — A716

1973, Nov. 30 *Perf. 11½*

1321 A716 40c ver & multi 35 30

Christmas 1973.

River Boats A717

1973, Nov. 30 **Litho.** *Perf. 11x11½*

1322 A717 40c "Gaiola" 35 35
1323 A717 70c "Regatao" 1.05 1.05
1324 A717 1cr "Jangada" 4.50 3.00
1325 A717 2cr "Saveiro" 4.25 3.00
Nos. 1322-1325 (4) 10.15 7.40

Nos. 1322-1325 are luminescent.

Scales of Justice — A718

1973, Dec. 5 *Perf. 11½*

1326 A718 40c magenta & vio 50 32

To honor the High Federal Court, created in 1891. Luminescent.

José Placido de Castro — A719

Scarlet Ibis and Victoria Regia — A720

Lithographed and Engraved

Perf. 11½x11

1973, Dec. 12 **Wmk. 267**

1327 A719 40c lilac rose & blk 60 35

Centenary of the birth of Jose Placido de Castro, liberator of the State of Acre.

Perf. 11½x11

1973, Dec. 28 **Litho.** **Unwmk.**

Designs: 70c, Jaguar and spathodea campanulata. 1cr, Scarlet macaw and carnauba palm. 2cr, Rhea and coral tree.

1328 A720 40c brown & multi 80 50
1329 A720 70c brown & multi 2.25 1.50
1330 A720 1cr bister & multi 3.50 40
1331 A720 2cr bister & multi 6.25 3.50
Nos. 1328-1331 (4) 12.80 5.90

Nos. 1328-1331 are luminescent.

Saci Perere, Mocking Goblin — A721

Characters from Brazilian Legends: 80c, Zumbi, last chief of rebellious slaves. 1cr, Chico Rei, African king. 1.30cr, Little Black Boy of the Pasture. 2.50cr, Iara, Queen of the Waters.

Perf. 11½x11

1974, Feb. 28 **Litho.** **Unwmk.**

Size: 21x39mm

1332 A721 40c multicolored 32 22
1333 A721 80c multicolored 65 60
1334 A721 1cr multicolored 1.40 42

Perf. 11½

Size: 32½x33mm

1335	A721	1.30cr multicolored	2.25	85
1336	A721	2.50cr multicolored	9.25	2.50
		Nos. 1332-1336 (5)	13.87	4.59

Nos. 1332-1336 are luminescent.

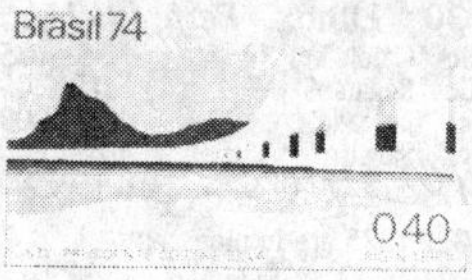

Pres. Costa e Silva Bridge A722

1974, Mar. 11

1337 A722 40c multicolored 60 30

Inauguration of the Pres. Costa e Silva Bridge, Rio Niteroi, connecting Rio de Janeiro and Guanabara State.

"The Press" — A723

1974, Mar. 25 *Perf. 11½*

1338	A723	40c shown	48	32
1339	A723	40c "Radio"	24	24
1340	A723	40c "Television"	40	32
		Nos. 1338-1340 (3)	1.12	88

Communications Commemorations: No. 1338, bicentenary of first Brazilian newspaper, published in London by Hipolito da Costa; No. 1339, founding of the Radio Sociedade do Rio de Janeiro by Roquette Pinto; No. 1340, installation of first Brazilian television station by Assis Chateaubriand. Luminescent.

"Reconstruction" A724

1974, Mar. 31

1341 A724 40c multicolored 70 45

10 years of progress. Luminescent.

Corcovado Christ, Marconi, Colors of Brazil and Italy — A725

1974, Apr. 25 Litho. *Perf. 11½*

1342 A725 2.50cr multi 6.00 3.00

Guglielmo Marconi (1874-1937), Italian physicist and inventor. Luminescent.

Values quoted in this catalogue are for stamps graded Fine-Very Fine and with no faults. An illustrated guide to grade is provided in the "Catalogue Information" section of the Introduction.

Stamp Printing Press, Stamp Designing A726

1974, May 6

1343 A726 80c multicolored 1.00 50

Brazilian mint.

World Map, Indian, Caucasian and Black Men — A727

Designs (World Map and): No. 1345, Brazilians. No. 1346, Cabin and German horseback rider. No. 1347, Italian farm wagon. No. 1348, Japanese woman and torii.

1974, May 3 **Unwmk.**

1344	A727	40c multicolored	28	28
1345	A727	40c multicolored	18	18
1346	A727	2.50cr multicolored	3.00	1.50
1347	A727	2.50cr multicolored	4.25	1.50
1348	A727	2.50cr multicolored	1.10	85
		Nos. 1344-1348 (5)	8.81	4.31

Ethnic and migration influences in Brazil.

Sandstone Cliffs, Sete Cidades National Park A728

Tourist publicity: 80c, Ruins of Cathedral of Sao Miguel das Missões.

Lithographed and Engraved

1974, June 8 *Perf. 11x11½*

1349	A728	40c multicolored	75	50
1350	A728	80c multicolored	75	50

Souvenir Sheet

Soccer — A729

1974, June 20 Litho. *Perf. 11½*

1351 A729 2.50cr multi 3.50 *6.00*

World Cup Soccer Championship, Munich, June 13-July 7.

Church and College, Caraça A730

1974, July 6 Litho. *Perf. 11x11½*

1352 A730 40c multicolored 45 30

College (Seminary) of Caraça, bicent.

Wave on Television Screen A731

1974, July 15 *Perf. 11½*

1353 A731 40c black & blue 30 40

TELEBRAS, Third Brazilian Congress of Telecommunications, Brasilia, July 15-20.

Fernao Dias Paes — A732

1974, July 21 *Perf. 11½*

1354 A732 20c green & multi 30 30

3rd centenary of the expedition led by Fernao Dias Paes exploring Minas Gerais and the passage from South to North in Brazil.

Mexican Flag — A733

1974, July 24 Litho. *Perf. 11½*

1355 A733 80c multicolored 2.25 1.10

Visit of Pres. Luis Echeverria Alvares of Mexico, July 24-29.

Flags of Brazil and Germany A734

1974, Aug. 5 *Perf. 11x11½*

1356 A734 40c multicolored 50 50

World Cup Soccer Championship, 1974, victory of German Federal Republic.

Souvenir Sheet

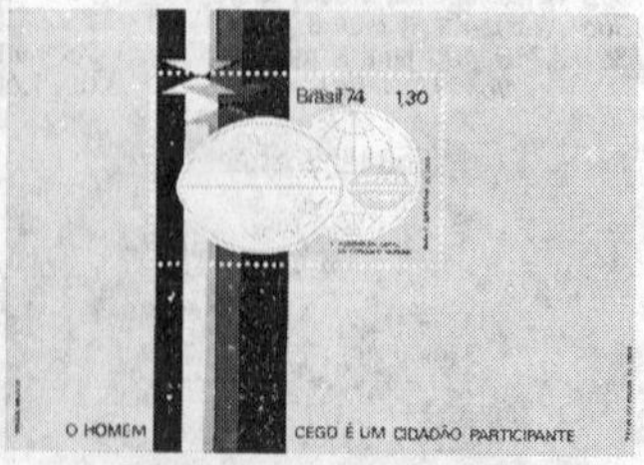

Congress Emblem — A735

1974, Aug. 7 *Perf. 11½*

1357 A735 1.30cr multi 85 *1.75*

5th World Assembly of the World Council for the Welfare of the Blind, Sao Paulo, Aug. 7-16. Stamp and margin inscribed in Braille with name of Assembly.

Raul Pederneiras (1874-1953, Journalist, Professor of Law and Fine Arts), Caricature by J. Carlos — A736

Lithographed and Engraved

1974, Aug. 15 *Perf. 11½x11*

1358 A736 40c buff, blk & ocher 30 40

Society Emblem and Landscape A737

1974, Aug. 19 Litho. *Perf. 11x11½*

1359 A737 1.30cr multi 1.25 90

13th Congress of the International Union of Building and Savings Societies.

Souvenir Sheet

Five Women, by Di Cavalcanti — A738

1974, Aug. 26 Litho. *Perf. 11½*

1360 A738 2cr multicolored 2.50 *6.00*

LUBRAPEX 74, 5th Portuguese-Brazilian Phil. Exhib., Sao Paulo, Nov. 26-Dec. 4.

"UPU" and World Map — A739

1974, Oct. 9 Litho. *Perf. 11½*

1361 A739 2.50cr blk & brt bl 4.50 1.75

Centenary of Universal Postal Union.

Hammock (Antillean Arawak Culture) — A740

Bilro Lace — A741

Singer of "Cord" Verses — A742

Ceramic Figure by Master Vitalino — A743

1974, Oct. 16 Litho. *Perf. 11½*

1362 A740 50c deep rose lilac	2.00	40
1363 A741 50c lt & dk blue	2.50	40
1364 A742 50c yel & red brn	60	40
1365 A743 50c brt yel & dk brn	75	40
Nos. 1362-1365 (4)	5.85	1.60

Popular Brazilian crafts.

Branch of Coffee A744

1974, Oct. 27 Unwmk. *Perf. 11*

1366 A744 50c multicolored 1.00 60

Centenary of city of Campinas.

Hornless Tabapua A745

Animals of Brazil: 1.30cr, Creole horse. 2.50cr, Brazilian mastiff.

1974, Nov. 10 *Perf. 11½*

1367 A745 80c multi	1.10	75
1368 A745 1.30cr multi	1.10	75
1369 A745 2.50cr multi	7.75	2.50
Nos. 1367-1369 (3)	9.95	4.00

Christmas — A746

1974, Nov. 18 *Perf. 11½x11*

1370 A746 50c Angel 70 30

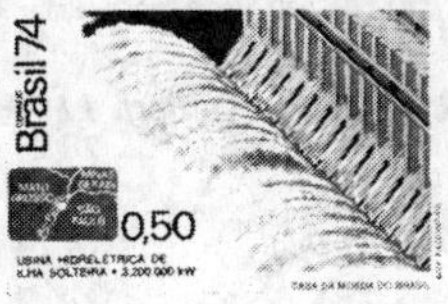

Solteira Island Hydroelectric Dam A747

1974, Nov. 11 *Perf. 11½*

1371 A747 50c black & yel 1.40 50

Inauguration of the Solteira Island Hydroelectric Dam over Parana River.

The Girls, by Carlos Reis — A748

1974, Nov. 26

1372 A748 1.30cr multi 70 50

LUBRAPEX 74, 5th Portuguese-Brazilian Phil. Exhib., Sao Paulo, Nov. 26-Dec. 4.

Youths, Judge, Scales A749

1974, Dec. 20 Litho. *Perf. 11½*

1373 A749 90c yel, red & bl 30 35

Juvenile Court of Brazil, 50th anniversary.

Long Distance Runner — A750

1974, Dec. 23

1374 A750 3.30cr multi 75 75

Sao Silvestre long distance running, 50th anniversary.

News Vendor, 1875, Masthead, 1975 — A751

1975, Jan. 4

1375 A751 50c multicolored 1.25 75

Newspaper "O Estado de S. Paulo," cent.

Sao Paulo Industrial Park A752

Designs: 1.40cr, Natural rubber industry, Acre. 4.50cr, Manganese mining, Amapá.

1975, Jan. 24 Litho. *Perf. 11x11½*

1376 A752 50c vio bl & yel	1.25	40
1377 A752 1.40cr yellow & brn	60	40
1378 A752 4.50cr yellow & blk	6.00	40
Nos. 1376-1378 (3)	7.85	1.20

Economic development.

Fort of the Holy Cross A753

Colonial forts: No. 1380, Fort of the Three Kings. No. 1381, Fort of Monteserrat. 90c, Fort of Our Lady of Help.

Litho. & Engr.

1975, Mar. 14 *Perf. 11½*

1379 A753 50c yel & red brn	24	16
1380 A753 50c yel & red brn	40	16
1381 A753 50c yel & red brn	80	16
1382 A753 90c yel & red brn	24	16
Nos. 1379-1382 (4)	1.68	64

House on Stilts, Amazon Region A754

Designs: 50c, Modern houses and plan of Brasilia. 1.40cr, Indian hut, Rondonia. 3.30cr, German-style cottage (Enxaimel), Santa Catarina.

1975, Apr. 18 Litho. *Perf. 11½*

1383 A754 50c yel & multi	1.25	2.25
1384 A754 50c yel & multi	8.50	6.25
a. Pair, #1383-1384	10.00	8.50
1385 A754 1cr yel & multi	85	22
1386 A754 1.40cr yel & multi	1.75	2.50
1387 A754 1.40cr yel & multi	50	85
a. Pair, #1386-1387	2.25	3.50
1388 A754 3.30cr yel & multi	75	1.25
1389 A754 3.30cr yel & multi	3.50	4.00
a. Pair, #1388-1380	4.25	5.25
Nos. 1383-1389 (7)	17.10	17.32

Brazilian architecture. Nos. 1383, 1386, 1388 have yellow strip at right side, others at left.

Astronotus Ocellatus A755

Designs: Brazilian fresh-water fish.

1975, May 2 Litho. *Perf. 11½*

1390 A755 50c *shown*	1.40	40
1391 A755 50c *Colomesus psitacus*	25	25
1392 A755 50c *Phallocerus caudimaculatus*	25	40
1393 A755 50c *Symphysodon discus*	48	50
Nos. 1390-1393 (4)	2.38	1.55

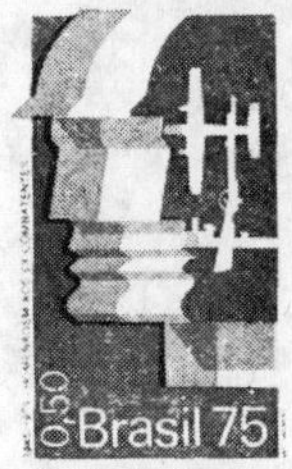

Soldier's Head in Brazil's Colors, Plane, Rifle and Ship — A756

Brazilian Otter — A757

1975, May 8 *Perf. 11½x11*

1394 A756 50c vio bl & multi 35 30

In honor of the veterans of World War II, on the 30th anniversary of victory.

1975, June 17 Litho. *Perf. 11½*

Nature protection: 70c, Brazilian pines, horiz. 3.30cr, Marsh cayman, horiz.

1395 A757 70c bl, grn & blk	1.05	50
1396 A757 1cr multi	1.05	1.00
1397 A757 3.30cr multi	90	75
Nos. 1395-1397 (3)	3.00	2.25

Petroglyphs, Stone of Ingá — A758

Marjoara Vase, Pará — A759

Vinctifer Comptoni, Petrified Fish — A760

1975, July 8 Litho. *Perf. 11½*

1398 A758 70c multicolored	55	40
1399 A759 1cr multicolored	35	40
1400 A760 1cr multicolored	35	40
Nos. 1398-1400 (3)	1.25	1.20

Archaeological discoveries.

Immaculate Conception, Franciscan Monastery, Vitoria — A761

Post and Telegraph Ministry — A762

1975, July 15

1401 A761 3.30cr blue & multi 95 95

Holy Year 1975 and 300th anniv. of establishment of the Franciscan Province in Southern Brazil.

1975, Aug. 8 Engr. *Perf. 11½*

1402 A762 70c dk carmine 70 30

Stamp Day 1975.

Sword Dance, Minas Gerais — A763

Folk Dances: No. 1404, Umbrella Dance, Pernambuco. No. 1405, Warrior's Dance, Alagoas.

1975, Aug. 22 Litho. *Perf. 11½*

1403 A763 70c gray & multi	35	35
1404 A763 70c pink & multi	35	35
1405 A763 70c yellow & multi	35	35
Nos. 1403-1405 (3)	1.05	1.05

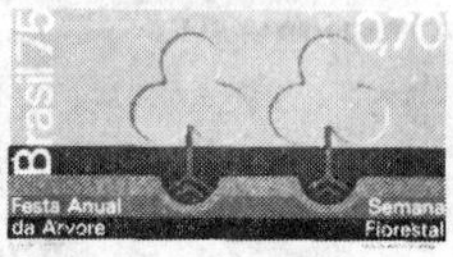

Trees A764

1975, Sept. 15 *Perf. 11x11½*

1406 A764 70c multicolored 30 25

Annual Tree Festival.

Globe, Radar and Satellite — A765

1975, Sept. 16 *Perf. 11½*

1407 A765 3.30cr multi 70 75

Inauguration of 2nd antenna of Tangua Earth Station, Rio de Janeiro State.

Woman Holding Flowers and Globe A766

1975, Sept. 23

1408 A766 3.30cr multi 1.00 1.00

International Women's Year 1975.

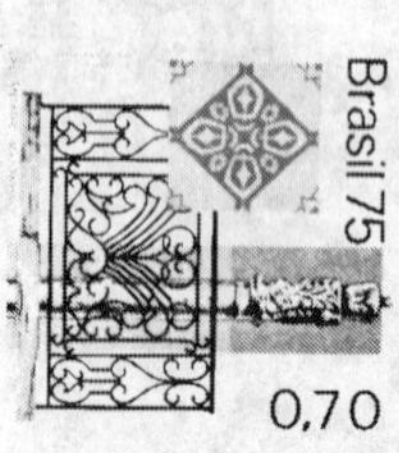

Tile, Railing and Column, Alcantara A767

Cross and Monastery, Sao Cristovao — A768

Historic cities: No. 1411, Jug and Clock Tower, Goiás, vert.

1975, Sept. 27 Litho. *Perf. 11½*

1409 A767 70c multicolored	32	45
1410 A768 70c multicolored	60	45
1411 A768 70c multicolored	60	45
Nos. 1409-1411 (3)	1.52	1.35

"Books teach how to live" — A769

1975, Oct. 23 Litho. *Perf. 11½*

1412 A769 70c multicolored 25 30

Day of the Book.

ASTA Congress Emblem A770

1975, Oct. 27 *Perf. 11x11½*

1413 A770 70c multicolored 25 30

American Society of Travel Agents, 45th World Congress, Rio, Oct. 27-Nov. 1.

Angels — A771

1975, Nov. 11

1414 A771 70c red & brown 25 20

Christmas 1975.

Map of Americas, Waves — A772

Dom Pedro II — A773

1975, Nov. 19 *Perf. 11½x12*

1415 A772 5.20cr gray & multi 2.75 2.00

2nd Interamerican Conference of Telecommunications (CITEL), Rio, Nov. 19-27.

1975, Dec. 2 Engr. *Perf. 12*

1416 A773 70c violet brown 75 45

Dom Pedro II (1825-1891), emperor of Brazil, birth sesquicentennial.

People and Cross A774

1975, Nov. 27 Litho. *Perf. 11x11½*

1417 A774 70c lt bl & dp bl 50 65

National Day of Thanksgiving.

Guarapari Beach, Espirito Santo A775

Tourist Publicity: #1419, Salt Stone beach, Piaui. #1420, Cliffs, Rio Grande Do Sul.

1975, Dec. 19 Litho. *Perf. 11½*

1418 A775 70c multicolored	28	28
1419 A775 70c multicolored	28	28
1420 A775 70c multicolored	28	28
Nos. 1418-1420 (3)	84	84

Triple Jump, Games Emblem A776

1975, Dec. 22 *Perf. 11x11½*

1421 A776 1.60cr bl grn & blk 25 35

Triple jump world record by Joao Carlos de Oliveira in 7th Pan-American Games, Mexico City, Oct. 12-26.

UN Emblem and Headquarters A777

1975, Dec. 29 *Perf. 11½*

1422 A777 1.30cr dp bl & vio bl 25 30

United Nations, 30th anniversary.

Light Bulbs, House and Sun A778

Energy conservation: No. 1424, Gasoline drops, car and sun.

1976, Jan. 16

1423 A778 70c multicolored	30	20
1424 A778 70c multicolored	30	15

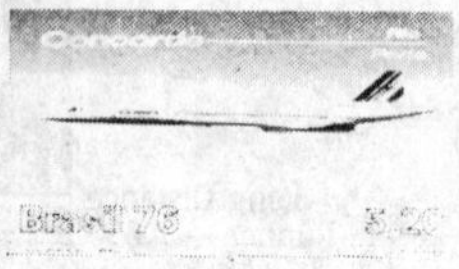

Concorde A779

1976, Jan. 21 Litho. *Perf. 11x11½*

1425 A779 5.20cr bluish blk 50 35

First commercial flight of supersonic jet Concorde from Paris to Rio, Jan. 21.

Souvenir Sheet

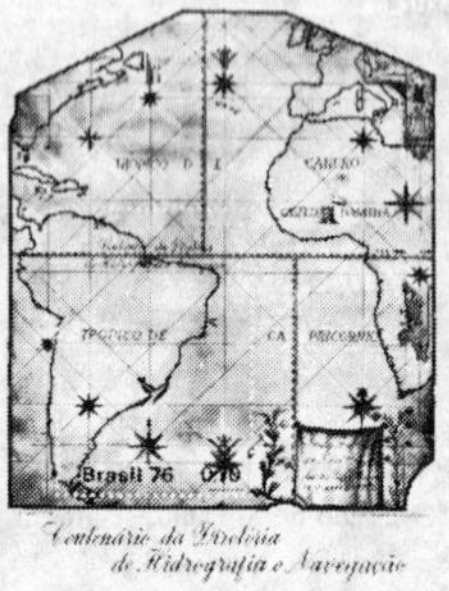

Nautical Map of South Atlantic, 1776 A780

1976, Feb. 2 *Perf. 11½*

1426 A780 70c salmon & multi 85 1.50

Centenary of the Naval Hydrographic and Navigation Institute.

Telephone Lines, 1876 Telephone A781

1976, Mar. 10 Litho. *Perf. 11x11½*

1427 A781 5.20cr orange & bl 65 48

Centenary of first telephone call by Alexander Graham Bell, March 10, 1876.

Eye and Exclamation Point — A782

Kaiapo Body Painting — A783

1976, Apr. 7 Litho. *Perf. 11½x11*

1428 A782 1cr vio red brn & brn 50 75

World Health Day: "Foresight prevents blindness."

1976, Apr. 19 Litho. *Perf. 11½*

Designs: No. 1430, Bakairi ceremonial mask. No. 1431, Karajá feather headdress.

1429 A783 1cr lt violet & multi	16	16
1430 A783 1cr lt violet & multi	16	16
1431 A783 1cr lt violet & multi	16	16
Nos. 1429-1431 (3)	48	48

Preservation of indigenous culture.

Itamaraty Palace, Brasilia A784

1976, Apr. 20

1432 A784 1cr multicolored 60 60

Diplomats' Day. Itamaraty Palace, designed by Oscar Niemeyer, houses the Ministry of Foreign Affairs.

Watering Can over Stones, by José Tarcisio A785

Fingers and Ribbons, by Pietrina Checcacci A786

1976, May 14 Litho. *Perf. 11½*

1433 A785 1cr multi	22	20
1434 A786 1.60cr multi	28	20

Modern Brazilian art.

Basketball — A787

Orchid — A788

Designs (Olympic Rings and): 1.40cr, Yachting. 5.20cr, Judo.

1976, May 21 Litho. *Perf. 11½*

1435	A787	1cr emerald & blk	16	15
1436	A787	1.40cr dk blue & blk	20	15
1437	A787	5.20cr orange & blk	65	50
		Nos. 1435-1437 (3)	1.01	80

21st Olympic Games, Montreal, Canada, July 17-Aug. 1.

1976, June 4 *Perf. 11½x11*

Nature protection: No. 1439, Golden-faced lion monkey.

1438	A788	1cr multicolored	22	20
1439	A788	1cr multicolored	22	20

Film Camera, Brazilian Colors — A789

1976, June 19

1440	A789	1cr vio bl, brt grn & yel	20	25

Brazilian film industry.

Bahia Woman — A790

Designs: 10c, Oxcart driver, horiz. 20c, Raft fishermen, horiz. 30c, Rubber plantation worker. 40c, Cowboy, horiz. 50c, Gaucho. 80c, Gold panner. 1cr, Banana plantation worker. 1.10cr, Grape harvester. 1.30cr, Coffee picker. 1.80cr, Farmer gathering wax palms. 2cr, Potter. 5cr, Sugar cane cutter. 7cr, Salt mine worker. 10cr, Fisherman. 15cr, Coconut seller. 20cr, Lacemaker.

Perf. 11½x11, 11x11½

1976-78 Photo.

1441	A790	10c red brn ('77)	15	15
1442	A790	15c brown	24	32
1443	A790	20c vio blue	15	15
1444	A790	30c lilac rose	15	15
1445	A790	40c org ('77)	15	15
1446	A790	50c citron	15	15
1447	A790	80c slate grn	38	15
1448	A790	1cr black	16	15
1449	A790	1.10cr mag ('77)	16	15
1450	A790	1.30cr red ('77)	16	15
1451	A790	1.80cr dk vio bl ('78)	18	15

Engr.

1452	A790	2cr brown ('77)	22	15
1453	A790	5cr dk pur ('77)	50	15
1454	A790	7cr violet	1.50	15
1455	A790	10cr yel grn ('77)	55	15
1456	A790	15cr gray grn ('78)	1.40	15
1457	A790	20cr blue	1.40	15
		Nos. 1441-1457 (17)	7.60	
		Set value		1.10

See Nos. 1653-1657.

Hyphessobrycon Innesi — A791

Designs: Brazilian fresh-water fish.

1976, July 12 Litho. *Perf. 11x11½*

1460	A791	1cr *shown*	42	40
1461	A791	1cr *Copeina arnoldi*	42	40
1462	A791	1cr *Prochilodus insignis*	42	40
1463	A791	1cr *Crenicichla lepidota*	42	40
1464	A791	1cr *Ageneiosus*	42	40
1465	A791	1cr *Corydoras reticulatus*	42	40
a.		Block of 6, #1460-1465	2.50	2.50
		Nos. 1460-1465 (6)	2.52	2.40

Santa Marta Lighthouse — A792

1976, July 29 Engr. *Perf. 12x11½*

1466	A792	1cr blue	20	30

300th anniversary of the city of Laguna.

Children on Magic Carpet A793

1976, Aug. 1 Litho. *Perf. 11½x12*

1467	A793	1cr multicolored	20	20

Stamp Day.

Nurse's Lamp and Head A794

1976, Aug. 12 Litho. *Perf. 11½*

1468	A794	1cr multicolored	20	20

Brazilian Nurses' Assoc., 50th anniv.

Puppet, Soldier — A795

Winner's Medal — A796

Designs: 1.30cr, Girl's head. 1.60cr, Hand with puppet head on each finger, horiz.

1976, Aug. 20

1469	A795	1cr multi	20	20
1470	A795	1.30cr multi	20	20
1471	A795	1.60cr multi	20	20
		Nos. 1469-1471 (3)	60	60

Mamulengo puppet show.

1976, Aug. 21

1472	A796	5.20cr multi	70	50

27th International Military Athletic Championships, Rio de Janeiro, Aug. 21-28.

Family Protection — A797

1976, Sept. 12

1473	A797	1cr lt & dk blue	20	20

National organizations SENAC and SESC helping commercial employees to improve their living standard, both commercially and socially.

Dying Tree — A798

1976, Sept. 20 Litho. *Perf. 11½*

1474	A798	1cr gray & multi	20	20

Protection of the environment.

Atom Symbol, Electron Orbits A799

1976, Sept. 21

1475	A799	5.20cr multi	70	50

20th General Conference of the International Atomic Energy Agency, Rio de Janeiro, Sept. 21-29.

Train in Tunnel — A800

1976, Sept. 26

1476	A800	1.60cr multi	25	25

Sao Paulo subway, 1st in Brazil.

St. Francis and Birds A801

1976, Oct. 4

1477	A801	5.20cr multi	60	42

St. Francis of Assisi, 750th death anniv.

Ouro Preto School of Mining — A802

1976, Oct. 12 Engr. *Perf. 12x11½*

1478	A802	1cr dk vio	40	50

Ouro Preto School of Mining, centenary.

Three Kings — A803

Designs: Children's drawings.

1976, Nov. 4 Litho. *Perf. 11½*

1479	A803	80c shown	28	28
1480	A803	80c Santa Claus on donkey	28	28
1481	A803	80c Virgin and Child and Angels	28	28
1482	A803	80c Angels with candle	28	28
1483	A803	80c Nativity	28	28
a.		Strip of 5, #1479-1483	1.40	1.40
		Nos. 1479-1483 (5)	1.40	1.40

Christmas 1976.

Souvenir Sheet

30,000 Reis Banknote — A804

1976, Nov. 5 Litho. *Perf. 11½*

1484	A804	80c multicolored	40	*1.50*

Opening of 1000th branch of Bank of Brazil, Barra do Bugres, Mato Grosso.

Virgin of Monte Serrat, by Friar Agostinho A805

St. Joseph, 18th Century Wood Sculpture — A806

Designs: 5.60cr, The Dance, by Rodolfo Bernadelli, 19th century. 6.50cr, The Caravel, by Bruno Giorgi, 20th century abstract sculpture.

1976, Nov. 5

1485 A805 80c multi 15 15
1486 A806 5cr multi 65 40
1487 A805 5.60cr multi 65 40
1488 A806 6.50cr multi 65 40
Nos. 1485-1488 (4) 2.10 1.35

Development of Brazilian sculpture.

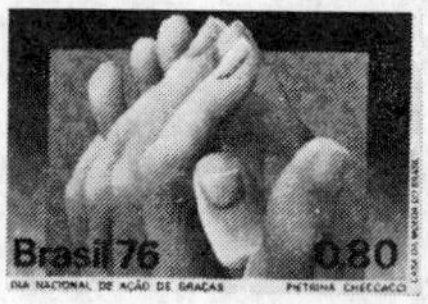

Praying Hands A807

1976, Nov. 25

1489 A807 80c multicolored 25 25

National Day of Thanksgiving.

Sailor, 1840 — A808

Design: 2cr, Marine's uniform, 1808.

1976, Dec. 13 Litho. *Perf. 11½x11*

1490 A808 80c multicolored 22 22
1491 A808 2cr multicolored 32 22

Brazilian Navy.

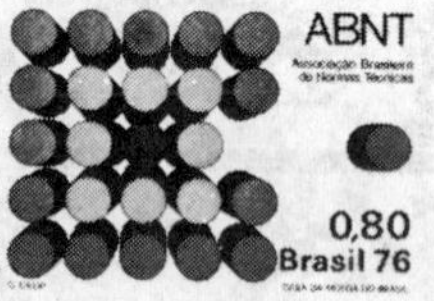

"Natural Resources and Development" — A809

1976, Dec. 17 *Perf. 11½*

1492 A809 80c multicolored 20 16

Brazilian Bureau of Standards, founded 1940.

Wheel of Life — A810

Designs: 5.60cr, Beggar, sculpture by Agnaldo dos Santos. 6.50cr, Benin mask.

1977, Jan. 14

1493 A810 5cr multi 55 35
1494 A810 5.60cr multi 55 35
1495 A810 6.50cr multi 1.10 35
Nos. 1493-1495 (3) 2.20 1.05

FESTAC '77, 2nd World Black and African Festival, Lagos, Nigeria, Jan. 15-Feb. 12.

A811

1977, Jan. 20 Litho. *Perf. 11½*

1496 A811 6.50cr bl & yel grn 85 65

Rio de Janeiro International Airport.

Seminar Emblem with Map of Americas A812

Salicylate, Microphoto A813

1977, Feb. 6

1497 A812 1.10cr gray, vio bl & bl 35 18

6th Inter-American Budget Seminar.

1977, Apr. 10 Litho. *Perf. 11½*

1498 A813 1.10cr multi 20 15

International Rheumatism Year.

Lions International Emblem A814

1977, Apr. 16

1499 A814 1.10cr multi 20 20

25th anniv. of Brazilian Lions Intl.

Heitor Villa Lobos A815

1977, Apr. 26 *Perf. 11x11½*

1500 A815 1.10cr shown 15 20
1501 A815 1.10cr Chiquinha Gonzaga 15 20
1502 A815 1.10cr Noel Rosa 15 20
Nos. 1500-1502 (3) 45 60

Brazilian composers.

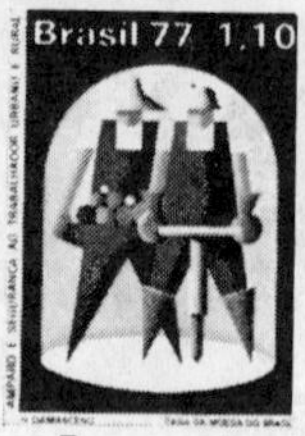

Farmer and Worker — A816

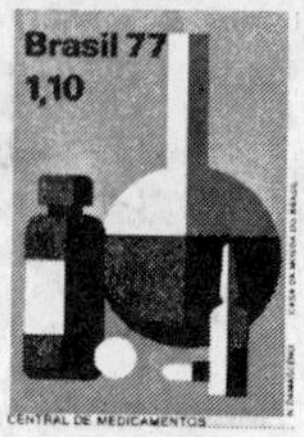

Medicine Bottles and Flask — A817

1977, May 8 Litho. *Perf. 11½*

1503 A816 1.10cr grn & multi 15 20
1504 A817 1.10cr lt & dk grn 15 20

Support and security for rural and urban workers (No. 1503) and establishment in 1971 of Medicine Distribution Center (CEME) for low-cost medicines (No. 1504).

Churchyard Cross, Porto Seguro A818

Views, Porto Seguro: 5cr, Beach and boats. 5.60cr, Our Lady of Pena Chapel. 6.50cr, Town Hall.

1977, May 25 Litho. *Perf. 11½*

1505 A818 1.10cr multi 15 15
1506 A818 5cr multi 1.40 35
1507 A818 5.60cr multi 55 45
1508 A818 6.50cr multi 80 55
Nos. 1505-1508 (4) 2.90 1.50

Cent. of Brazil's membership in UPU.

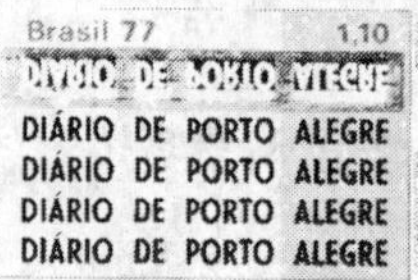

Diario de Porto Alegre A819

1977, June 1

1509 A819 1.10cr multi 20 20

Diario de Porto Alegre, newspaper, 150th anniv.

Blue Whale A820

1977, June 3

1510 A820 1.30cr multi 20 20

Protection of marine life.

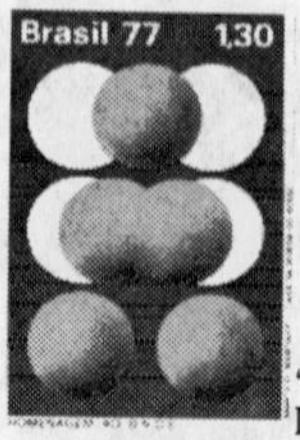

"Life and Development" — A821

1977, June 20

1511 A821 1.30cr multi 20 20

National Development Bank, 25th anniversary.

Train Leaving Tunnel — A822

1977, July 8 Engr. *Perf. 11½*

1512 A822 1.30cr black 20 20

Centenary of Sao Paulo-Rio de Janeiro railroad.

Vasum Cassiforme A823

Caduceus, Formulas for Water and Fluoride A824

Sea Shells: No. 1514, Strombus goliath. No. 1515, Murex tenuivaricosus.

1977, July 14 Litho.

1513 A823 1.30cr blue & multi 20 20
1514 A823 1.30cr brown & multi 20 20
1515 A823 1.30cr green & multi 20 20
Nos. 1513-1515 (3) 60 60

1977, July 15 *Perf. 11½x11*

1516 A824 1.30cr multi 20 20

3rd Intl. Odontology Congress, Rio, July 15-21.

Masonic Emblem, Map of Brazil — A825

"Stamps Don't Sink or Lose their Way" — A826

1977, July 18 *Perf. 11½*

1517 A825 1.30cr bl, lt bl & blk 20 20

50th anniversary of the founding of the Brazilian Grand Masonic Lodge.

1977, Aug. 1

1518 A826 1.30cr multi 20 20

Stamp Day 1977.

Dom Pedro's Proclamation — A827

Horses and Bulls — A828

1977, Aug. 11 Litho. *Perf. 11½*

1519 A827 1.30cr multi 20 20

150th anniversary of Brazilian Law School.

Perf. 11½x11, 11x11½

1977, Aug. 20 **Litho.**

Brazilian folklore: No. 1521, King on horseback. No. 1522, Joust, horiz.

1520 A828 1.30cr ocher & multi	20	20
1521 A828 1.30cr blue & multi	20	20
1522 A828 1.30cr yel & multi	20	20
Nos. 1520-1522 (3)	60	60

2000-reis Doubloon A829

Brazilian Colonial Coins: No. 1524, 640r pataca. No. 1525, 20r copper "vintem."

1977, Aug. 31 *Perf. 11½*

1523 A829 1.30cr vio bl & multi	20	15
1524 A829 1.30cr dk red & multi	20	15
1525 A829 1.30cr yel & multi	20	15
Nos. 1523-1525 (3)	60	45

Pinwheel A830

Neoregelia Carolinae A831

1977, Sept. 1

1526 A830 1.30cr multi	20	15

National Week.

1977, Sept. 21 **Litho.** *Perf. 11½*

1527 A831 1.30cr multi	20	15

Nature preservation.

Pen, Pencil, Letters — A832

1977, Oct. 15 **Litho.** *Perf. 11½*

1528 A832 1.30cr multi	20	15

Primary education, sesquicentennial.

Dome and Telescope A833

1977, Oct. 15

1529 A833 1.30cr multi	20	15

National Astrophysics Observatory, Brasópolis, sesquicentennial.

"Jahu" Hydroplane (Savoia Marchetti S-55) — A834

Design: No. 1531, PAX, dirigible.

1977, Oct. 17

1530 A834 1.30cr multi	25	25
1531 A834 1.30cr multi	25	25

50th anniv. of crossing of South Atlantic by Joao Ribeiro de Barros, Genoa-Sao Paulo (#1530) and 75th anniv. of the PAX airship (#1531).

A835

A836

1977, Oct. 24

1532 A835 1.30cr Il'Guarani	20	15

Book Day and to honor Jose Martiniano de Alencar, writer, jurist.

1977, Nov. 5 **Litho.** *Perf. 11½*

1533 A836 1.30cr Waves	20	15

Amateur Radio Operators' Day.

Nativity — A837

Christmas (folk art): 2cr, Annunciation. 5cr, Nativity.

1977, Nov. 10

1534 A837 1.30cr bister & multi	22	15
1535 A837 2cr bister & multi	32	15
1536 A837 5cr bister & multi	65	25
Nos. 1534-1536 (3)	1.19	55

A838

A839

1977, Nov. 19

1537 A838 1.30cr Emerald	20	20
1538 A838 1.30cr Topaz	20	20
1539 A838 1.30cr Aquamarine	20	20
Nos. 1537-1539 (3)	60	60

PORTUCALE 77, 2nd International Topical Exhibition, Porto, Nov. 19-20.

1977, Nov. 24 **Litho.** *Perf. 11½*

1540 A839 1.30cr Angel, cornucopia	20	20

National Thanksgiving Day.

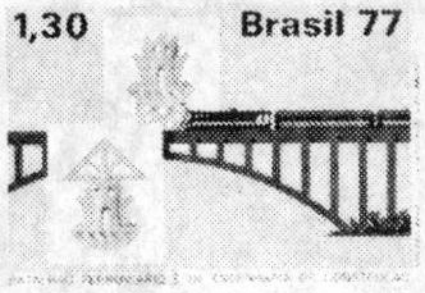

Army's Railroad Construction Battalion A840

Civilian services of armed forces: No. 1542, Navy's Amazon flotilla. No. 1543, Air Force's postal service (plane).

1977, Dec. 5

1541 A840 1.30cr multi	20	20
1542 A840 1.30cr multi	20	20
1543 A840 1.30cr multi	20	20
Nos. 1541-1543 (3)	60	60

Varig Emblem, Jet A841

1977, Dec. *Perf. 11x11½*

1544 A841 1.30cr bl & blk	20	20

50th anniversary of Varig Airline.

Sts. Cosme and Damiao Church, Igaracu — A842

Woman Holding Sheaf — A843

Brazilian Architecture: 7.50cr, St. Bento Monastery Church, Rio de Janeiro. 8.50cr, Church of St. Francis of Assisi, Ouro Preto. 9.50cr, St. Anthony Convent Church, Joao Pessoa.

1977, Dec. 8

1545 A842 2.70cr multi	30	15
1546 A842 7.50cr multi	90	35
1547 A842 8.50cr multi	90	40
1548 A842 9.50cr multi	1.25	45
Nos. 1545-1548 (4)	3.35	1.35

1977, Dec. 19 *Perf. 11½*

1549 A843 1.30cr multi	20	20

Brazilian diplomacy.

Soccer Ball and Foot — A844

Designs: No. 1551, Soccer ball in net. No. 1552, Symbolic soccer player.

1978, Mar. 1 **Litho.** *Perf. 11½*

1550 A844 1.80cr multi	28	20
1551 A844 1.80cr multi	28	20
1552 A844 1.80cr multi	28	20
Nos. 1550-1552 (3)	84	60

11th World Cup Soccer Championship, Argentina, June 1-25.

"La Fosca" on La Scala Stage and Carlos Gomes A845

1978, Feb. 9

1553 A845 1.80cr multi	20	20

Bicentenary of La Scala in Milan, and to honor Carlos Gomes (1836-1893), Brazilian composer.

Symbols of Postal Mechanization — A846

1978, Mar. 15 **Litho.** *Perf. 11½*

1554 A846 1.80cr multi	20	20

Opening of Postal Staff College.

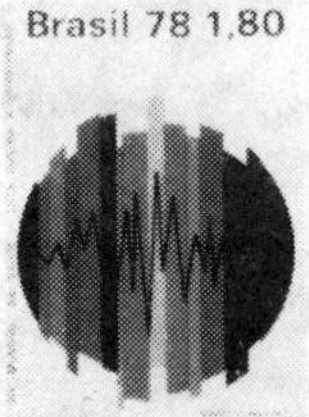

Hypertension Chart — A847

Waves from Antenna Uniting World — A848

1978, Apr. 4

1555 A847 1.80cr multi	20	20

World Health Day, fight against hypertension.

1978, May 17 **Litho.** *Perf. 12x11½*

1556 A848 1.80cr multi	20	20

10th World Telecommunications Day.

Brazilian Canary A849

Birds: 8.50cr, Cotinga. 9.50cr, Tanager fastuosa.

1978, June 5 *Perf. 11½x12*

1557 A849 7.50cr multi	1.00	75
1558 A849 8.50cr multi	1.00	80
1559 A849 9.50cr multi	1.00	1.00
Nos. 1557-1559 (3)	3.00	2.55

Inocencio Serzedelo Correa and Manuel Francisco Correa, 1893 A850

1978, June 20 **Litho.** *Perf. 11x11½*

1560 A850 1.80cr multi	20	20

85th anniversary of Union Court of Audit.

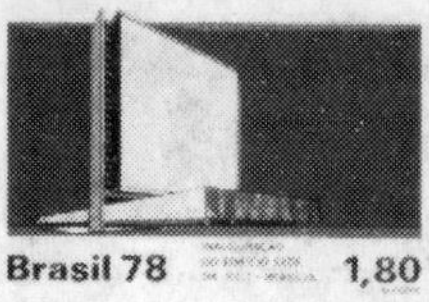

Post and Telegraph Building A851

1978, June 22 *Perf. 11½*
1561 A851 1.80cr multi 20 25

Souvenir Sheet

Imperf

1562 A851 7.50cr multi 75 1.50

Inauguration of Post and Telegraph Building (ECT), Brasilia, and for BRAPEX, 3rd Brazilian Philatelic Exhibition, Brasilia, June 23-28 (No. 1562).

Ernesto Geisel, President of Brazil — A852

1978, June 22 **Engr.** *Perf. 11½*
1563 A852 1.80cr dl grn 20 15

Savoia-Marchetti S-64, Map of South Atlantic A853

1978, July 3 **Litho.**
1564 A853 1.80cr multi 20 20

50th anniv. of 1st crossing of South Atlantic by Carlos del Prete and Arturo Ferrarin.

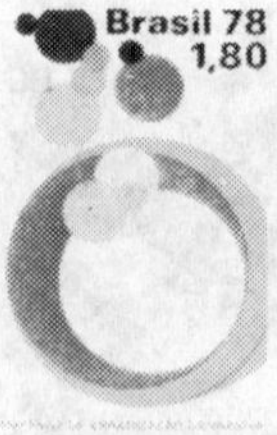

Symbolic of Smallpox Eradication A854

Brazil No. 68 A855

1978, July 25
1565 A854 1.80cr multi 20 20

Eradication of smallpox.

1978, Aug. 1
1566 A855 1.80cr multi 20 20

Stamp Day, centenary of the "Barba Branca" (white beard) issue.

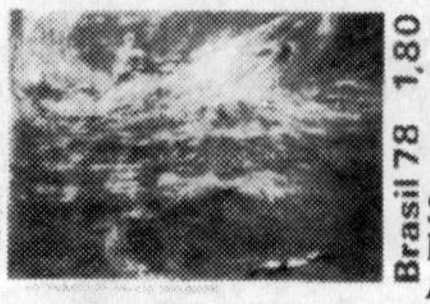

Stormy Sea, by Seelinger A856

1978, Aug. 4
1567 A856 1.80cr multi 20 20

Helios Seelinger, painter, birth centenary.

Guitar Players — A857

Musicians and Instruments: No. 1569, Flutes. No. 1570, Percussion instruments.

1978, Aug. 22 **Litho.** *Perf. 11½*
1568 A857 1.80cr multi 20 15
1569 A857 1.80cr multi 20 15
1570 A857 1.80cr multi 20 20
Nos. 1568-1570 (3) 60 50

Children at Play A858

1978, Sept. 1 **Litho.** *Perf. 11½*
1571 A858 1.80cr multi 20 20

National Week.

Collegiate Church A859

1978, Sept. 6 **Engr.**
1572 A859 1.80cr red brn 20 20

Restoration of patio of Collegiate Church, Sao Paulo.

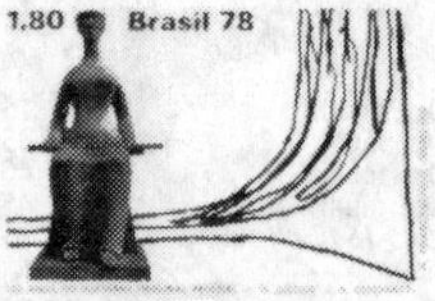

Justice by A. Geschiatti A860

1978, Sept. 18 **Litho.**
1573 A860 1.80cr blk & olive 20 20

Federal Supreme Court, sesquicentennial.

Iguacu Falls — A861

Design: No. 1575, Yellow ipecac.

1978, Sept. 21
1574 A861 1.80cr multi 20 20
1575 A861 1.80cr multi 20 20

Iguacu National Park.

Stages of Intelsat Satellite — A862

1978, Oct. 9 **Litho.** *Perf. 11½*
1576 A862 1.80cr multi 20 20

Flag of Order of Christ A863

Brazilian Flags: No. 1578, Principality of Brazil. No. 1579, United Kingdom. No. 1580, Imperial Brazil. No. 1581, National flag (current).

1978, Oct. 13
1577 A863 1.80cr multi 65 55
1578 A863 1.80cr multi 65 55
1579 A863 1.80cr multi 65 55
1580 A863 8.50cr multi 65 55
1581 A863 8.50cr multi 65 55
a. Block of 5, #1577-1581 + label 3.25 6.50
Nos. 1577-1581 (5) 3.25 2.75

7th LUBRAPEX Philatelic Exhibition, Porto Alegre.

Mail Street Car A864

Mail Transportation: No. 1583, Overland mail truck. No. 1584, Mail delivery truck. 7.50cr. Railroad mail car. 8.50cr, Mail coach. 9.50cr, Post riders.

1978, Oct. 21 *Perf. 11x11½*
1582 A864 1.80cr multi 50 40
1583 A864 1.80cr multi 50 40
1584 A864 1.80cr multi 50 40
1585 A864 7.50cr multi 50 40
1586 A864 8.50cr multi 50 40
1587 A864 9.50cr multi 50 50
a. Block of 6, #1582-1587 3.00 3.00
Nos. 1582-1587 (6) 3.00 2.50

18th UPU Congress, Rio de Janeiro, 1979.

Gaucho Herding Cattle, and Cactus — A865

1978, Oct. 23 *Perf. 11½x11*
1588 A865 1.80cr multi 20 20

Joao Guimaraes Rosa, poet and diplomat, 70th birthday.

St. Anthony's Hill, by Nicholas A. Taunay A866

Landscape Paintings: No. 1590, Castle Hill, by Victor Meirelles. No. 1591, View of Sabara, by Alberto da Veiga Guignard. No. 1592, View of Pernambuco, by Frans Post.

1978, Nov. 6 **Litho.** *Perf. 11½*
1589 A866 1.80cr multi 20 20
1590 A866 1.80cr multi 20 20
1591 A866 1.80cr multi 20 20
1592 A866 1.80cr multi 20 20
Nos. 1589-1592 (4) 80 80

Angel with Harp — A867

Christmas: No. 1594, Angel with lute. No. 1595, Angel with oboe.

1978, Nov. 10
1593 A867 1.80cr multi 20 20
1594 A867 1.80cr multi 20 20
1595 A867 1.80cr multi 20 20
Nos. 1593-1595 (3) 60 60

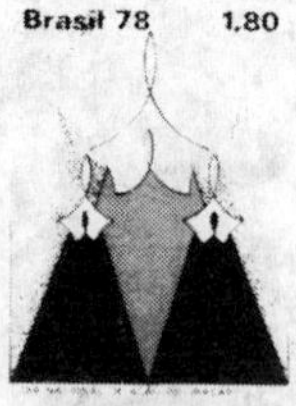

Symbolic Candles — A868

1978, Nov. 23
1596 A868 1.80cr blk, gold & car 20 20

National Thanksgiving Day.

Red Crosses and Activities A869

1978, Dec. 5 **Litho.** *Perf. 11x11½*
1597 A869 1.80cr blk & red 20 20

70th anniversary of Brazilian Red Cross.

Paz Theater, Belem — A870

Designs: 12cr, José de Alencar Theater, Portaleza. 12.50cr, Municipal Theater, Rio de Janeiro.

1978, Dec. 6 *Perf. 11½*
1598 A870 10.50cr multi 70 25
1599 A870 12cr multi 70 25
1600 A870 12.50cr multi 70 25
Nos. 1598-1600 (3) 2.10 75

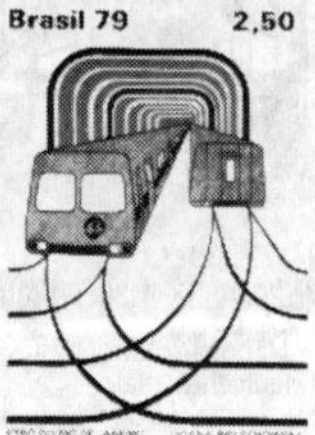

Subway Trains — A871

1979, Mar. 5 **Litho.** *Perf. 11½*
1601 A871 2.50cr multi 20 18

Inauguration of Rio subway system.

Old and New Post Offices A872

Designs: No. 1603, Old and new mail boxes. No. 1604, Manual and automatic mail sorting. No. 1605, Old and new planes. No. 1606, Telegraph and telex machine. No. 1607, Mailmen's uniforms.

1979, Mar. 20 Litho. *Perf. 11x11½*

1602 A872 2.50cr multi		25	20
1603 A872 2.50cr multi		25	20
1604 A872 2.50cr multi		25	20
1605 A872 2.50cr multi		25	20
1606 A872 2.50cr multi		25	20
1607 A872 2.50cr multi		25	20
	Nos. 1602-1607 (6)	1.50	1.20

10th anniv. of the new Post and Telegraph Dept., and 18th Universal Postal Union Cong., Rio de Janeiro, Sept.-Oct., 1979.

O'Day 23 Class Yacht A873

Yachts and Stamp Outlines: 10.50cr, Penguin Class. 12cr, Hobie Cat Class. 12.50cr, Snipe Class.

1979, Apr. 18 Litho. *Perf. 11x11½*

1608 A873 2.50cr multi		28	26
1609 A873 10.50cr multi		55	45
1610 A873 12cr multi		55	35
1611 A873 12.50cr multi		75	35
	Nos. 1608-1611 (4)	2.13	1.41

Brasiliana '79, 3rd World Thematic Stamp Exhibition, Sao Conrado, Sept. 15-23.

Children, IYC Emblem — A874

1979, May 30 Litho. *Perf. 11½*

1612 A874 2.50cr multi	25	20

Intl. Year of the Child & Children's Book Day.

Giant Water Lily — A875

Designs: 12cr, Amazon manatee. 12.50cr, Arrau (turtle).

1979, June 5 Litho. *Perf. 11½*

1613 A875 10.50cr multi		70	50
1614 A875 12cr multi		90	60
1615 A875 12.50cr multi		90	60
	Nos. 1613-1615 (3)	2.50	1.70

Amazon National Park, nature conservation.

Bank Emblem — A876

1979, June 7

1616 A876 2.50cr multi	20	15

Northwest Bank of Brazil, 25th anniversary.

Physician Tending Patient 15th Cent. Woodcut A877

1979, June 30

1617 A877 2.50cr multi	20	15

Natl. Academy of Medicine, 50th anniv.

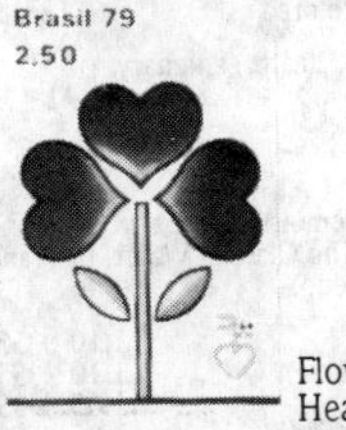

Flower made of Hearts — A878

1979, July 8 Litho. *Perf. 11½*

1618 A878 2.50cr multi	20	15

35th Brazilian Cardiology Congress.

Souvenir Sheet

Hotel Nacional, Rio de Janeiro A879

1979, July 16

1619 A879 12.50cr multi	75	1.50

Brasiliana '79 comprising 1st Inter-American Exhibition of Classical Philately and 3rd World Topical Exhibition, Rio de Janeiro, Sept. 15-23.

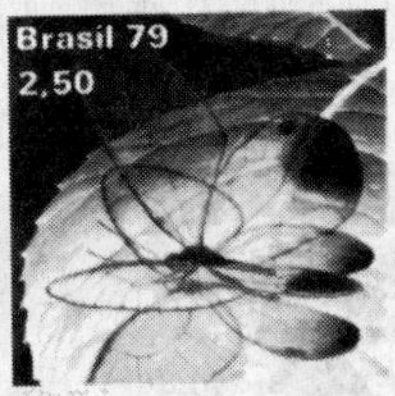

Cithaerias Aurora — A880

Moths: 10.50cr, Evenus regalis. 12cr, Caligo eurilochus. 12.50cr, Diaethria clymena janeira.

1979, Aug. 1

1620 A880 2.50cr multi		18	15
1621 A880 10.50cr multi		60	40
1622 A880 12cr multi		70	52
1623 A880 12.50cr multi		70	52
	Nos. 1620-1623 (4)	2.18	1.59

Stamp Day 1979.

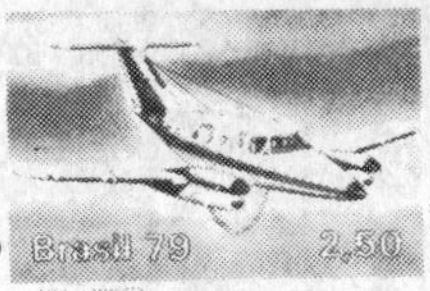

EMB-121 Xingo A881

1979, Aug. 19 Litho. *Perf. 11½*

1624 A881 2.50cr vio blue	20	20

Embraer, Brazilian aircraft company, 10th anniversary.

A882 A883

Natl. emblem over landscape.

1979, Sept. 12

1625 A882 3.20cr multi	20	20

National Week.

1979, Sept. 8 Litho. *Perf. 11½*

1626 A883 2.50cr multi	20	20

Statue of Our Lady of the Apparition, 75th anniversary of coronation.

"UPU," Envelope and Mail Transport A884

"UPU" and: No. 1628, Post Office emblems. 10.50cr, Globe. 12cr, Flags of Brazil and UN. 12.50cr, UPU emblem.

1979, Sept. 12 *Perf. 11x11½*

1627 A884 2.50cr multi		16	16
1628 A884 2.50cr multi		16	16
1629 A884 10.50cr multi		52	52
1630 A884 12cr multi		70	70
1631 A884 12.50cr multi		70	70
	Nos. 1627-1631 (5)	2.24	2.24

18th UPU Cong., Rio, Sept.-Oct. 1979.

Pyramid Fountain, Rio de Janeiro — A885

Fountains: 10.50cr, Facade, Marilia, Ouro Preto, horiz. 12cr, Boa Vista, Recife.

Perf. 12x11½, 11½x12

1979, Sept. 15

1632 A885 2.50cr multi		16	16
1633 A885 10.50cr multi		50	50
1634 A885 12cr multi		60	60
	Nos. 1632-1634 (3)	1.26	1.26

Brasiliana '79, 1st Interamerican Exhibition of Classical Philately.

Church of the Glory — A886

Landscapes by Leandro Joaquim: 12cr, Fishing on Guanabara Bay. 12.50cr, Boqueirao Lake and Carioca Arches.

1979, Sept. 15 *Perf. 11½*

1635 A886 2.50cr multi		16	16
1636 A886 12cr multi		60	60
1637 A886 12.50cr multi		60	60
	Nos. 1635-1637 (3)	1.36	1.36

Brasiliana '79, 3rd World Topical Exhibition, Sao Conrado, Sept. 15-23.

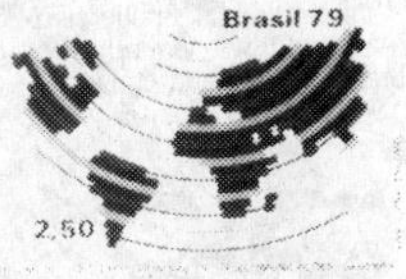

World Map — A887

1979, Sept. 20

1638 A887 2.50cr multi	20	20

3rd World Telecommunications Exhibition, Geneva, Sept. 20-26.

"UPU" and UPU Emblem — A888

1979, Oct. 9 Litho. *Perf. 11½x11*

1639 A888 2.50cr multi		18	18
1640 A888 10.50cr multi		55	55
1641 A888 12cr multi		65	65
1642 A888 12.50cr multi		65	65
	Nos. 1639-1642 (4)	2.03	2.03

Universal Postal Union Day.

IYC Emblem, Feather Toy A889

IYC Emblem and Toys: No. 1644, Bumble bee, ragdoll. No. 1645, Flower, top. No. 1646, Wooden acrobat.

1979, Oct. 12 *Perf. 11½*

1643 A889 2.50cr multi		25	20
1644 A889 3.20cr multi		25	25
1645 A889 3.20cr multi		25	25
1646 A889 3.20cr multi		25	25
	Nos. 1643-1646 (4)	1.00	95

International Year of the Child.

Adoration of the Kings — A890

Christmas 1979: No. 1648, Nativity. No. 1649 Jesus and the Elders in the Temple.

1979, Nov. 12 Litho. *Perf. 11½*

1647	A890	3.20cr multi	20	18
1648	A890	3.20cr multi	20	18
1649	A890	3.20cr multi	20	18
		Nos. 1647-1649 (3)	60	54

Souvenir Sheet

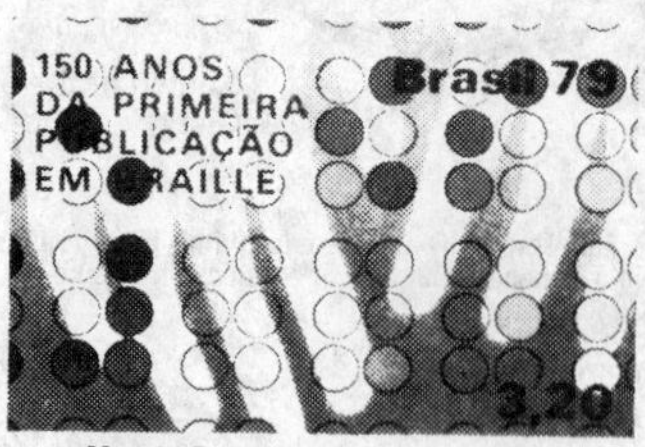

Hands Reading Braille — A891

Lithographed and Embossed

1979, Nov. 20. *Perf. 11½*

1650	A891	3.20cr multi	50	1.25

Publication of Braille script, 150th anniversary. Margin shows extension of stamp design with Braille printed and embossed.

Wheat Harvester — A892

Steel Mill — A893

1979, Nov. 22

1651	A892	3.20cr multi	20	15

Thanksgiving 1979.

1979, Nov. 23

1652	A893	3.20cr multi	20	15

COSIPA Steelworks, Sao Paulo, 25th anniversary.

Type of 1976

Designs: 70c, Women grinding coconuts. 2.50cr, Basket weaver. 3.20cr, River boatman. 21cr, Harvesting ramie (China grass). 27cr, Man leading pack mule. 3.20cr, 27cr, horiz.

Photogravure, Engraved (21cr)

1979 *Perf. 11x11½, 11½x11*

1653	A790	70c gray grn	15	15
1654	A790	2.50cr sepia	15	15
1655	A790	3.20cr blue	15	15
1656	A790	21cr purple	38	15
1657	A790	27cr sepia	45	15
		Nos. 1653-1657 (5)	1.28	
		Set value		40

A894

Designs: 2cr, Coconuts. 3cr, Mangoes. 4cr, Corn. 5cr, Onions. 7cr, Oranges. 10cr, Maracuja. 12cr, Pineapple. 15cr, Bananas. 17cr, Guarana. 20cr, Sugar cane. 24cr, Beekeeping. 30cr, Silkworm. 34cr, Cacao. 38cr, Coffee. 42cr, Soybeans. 45cr, Mandioca. 50cr, Wheat. 57cr, Peanuts. 66cr, Grapes. 100cr, Cashews. 140cr, Tomatoes. 200cr, Mamona. 500cr, Cotton.

1980-83 Photo. *Perf. 11½x11*

1658	A894	2cr yel brn ('82)	15	15
1659	A894	3cr red ('82)	15	15
1660	A894	4cr orange	15	15
1661	A894	5cr dk pur ('82)	15	15
1662	A894	7cr org ('81)	15	15
1663	A894	10cr bl grn ('82)	15	15
1664	A894	12cr dk grn ('81)	22	15
1665	A894	15cr gldn brn ('83)	15	15
1666	A894	17cr brn org ('82)	24	15
1667	A894	20cr olive ('82)	22	15
1668	A894	24cr bis ('82)	15	15
1669	A894	30cr blk ('82)	15	15
1670	A894	34cr brown	35	15
1671	A894	38cr red ('83)	15	15
1672	A894	42cr green	5.75	50
1673	A894	45cr sepia ('83)	55	15
1674	A894	50cr yel org ('82)	16	15
1675	A894	57cr brn ('83)	16	15
1676	A894	66cr pur ('81)	3.75	15
1677	A894	100cr dk red brn ('81)	2.25	15
1678	A894	140cr red ('82)	2.75	15

Engr.

1678A	A894	200cr grn ('82)	2.75	15
1679	A894	500cr brn ('82)	5.75	15
		Nos. 1658-1679 (23)	26.40	
		Set value		2.25

See Nos. 1934-1941.

Plant Inside Raindrop — A896

Light Bulb Containing: 17cr+7cr, Sun. 20cr+8cr, Windmill. 21cr+9cr, Dam.

1980, Jan. 2 Litho. *Perf. 12*

1680	A896	3.20cr multi	15	15
1681	A896	24cr (17 + 7)	1.25	65
1682	A896	28cr (20 + 8)	1.50	75
1683	A896	30cr (21 + 9)	2.25	85
		Nos. 1680-1683 (4)	5.15	2.40

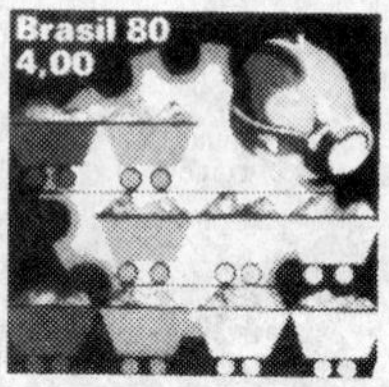

Anthracite Industry — A897

1980, Mar. 19 Litho. *Perf. 11½*

1684	A897	4cr multi	20	15

Map of Americas, Symbols of Development — A898

1980, Apr. 14 Litho. *Perf. 11x11½*

1685	A898	4cr multi	20	15

21st Assembly of Inter-American Development Bank Governors, Rio, Apr. 14-16.

Tapirape Mask, Mato Grosso A899

1980, Apr. 18 *Perf. 11½*

1686	A899	4cr shown	20	15
1687	A899	4cr Tukuna mask, Amazonas, vert.	20	15
1688	A899	4cr Kanela mask, Maranhao, vert.	20	15
		Nos. 1686-1688 (3)	60	45

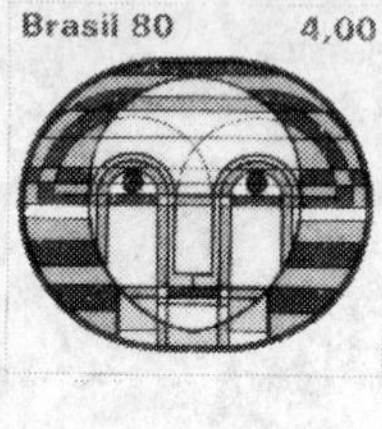

Brazilian Television, 30th Anniversary A900

1980, May 5 Litho. *Perf. 11½*

1689	A900	4cr multicolored	18	15

Duke of Caixas, by Miranda — A901

The Worker, by Candido Partinari — A902

1980, May 7

1690	A901	4cr multicolored	18	15

Duke of Caixas, death centenary.

1980, May 18

Paintings: 28cr, Mademoiselle Pogany, by Constantin Brancusi. 30cr, The Glass of Water, by Francisco Aurelio de Figueiredo.

1691	A902	24cr multi	1.10	55
1692	A902	28cr multi	1.10	55
1693	A902	30cr multi	1.65	55
		Nos. 1691-1693 (3)	3.85	1.65

Graf Zeppelin, 50th Anniversary of Atlantic Crossing A903

1980, June Litho. *Perf. 11x11½*

1694	A903	4cr multicolored	20	15

Pope John Paul II, St. Peter's, Rome, Congress Emblem A904

Pope, Emblem and Brazilian Churches: No. 1696, Fortaleza, vert. 24cr, Apericida 28cr, Rio de Janeiro. 30cr, Brasilia.

1980, June 24 *Perf. 12*

1695	A904	4cr multi	18	15
1696	A904	4cr multi	18	15
1697	A904	24cr multi	90	40
1698	A904	28cr multi	90	40
1699	A904	30cr multi	1.75	40
		Nos. 1695-1699 (5)	3.91	1.50

Visit of Pope John Paul II to Brazil, June 30-July 12; 10th National Eucharistic Congress, Fortaleza, July 9-16.

First Transatlantic Flight, 50th Anniversary — A905

1980, June Litho. *Perf. 11x11½*

1700	A905	4cr multicolored	20	15

Souvenir Sheet

Yacht Sail, Exhibition Emblem — A906

1980, June *Perf. 11½*

1701	A906	30cr multi	1.00	1.50

Brapex IV Stamp Exhib., Fortaleza, June 13-21.

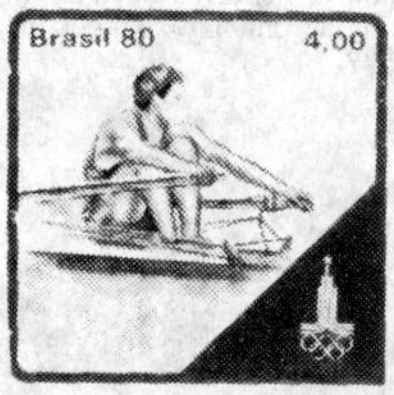

Rowing, Moscow '80 Emblem A907

1980, June 30

1702	A907	4cr shown	20	15
1703	A907	4cr Target shooting	20	15
1704	A907	4cr Bicycling	20	15
		Nos. 1702-1704 (3)	60	45

22nd Summer Olympic Games, Moscow, July 19-Aug. 3.

Rondon Community Works Project A908

1980, July 11

1705	A908	4cr multicolored	20	15

Helen Keller and Anne Sullivan A909

1980, July 28

1706	A909	4cr multicolored	20	15

Helen Keller (1880-1968), blind deaf writer and lecturer taught by Anne Sullivan (1867-1936).

Souvenir Sheet

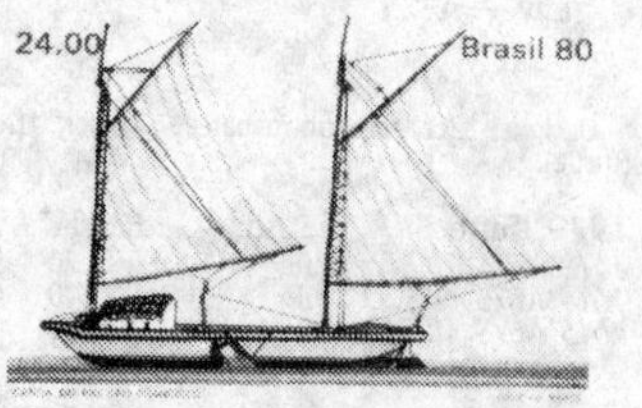

São Francisco River Canoe — A910

1980, Aug. 1 Litho. *Perf. 11½*

1707	A910	24cr multi	1.00	1.50

Stamp Day.

Microscope, Red Cross, Insects, Brick and Tile Houses — A911

1980, Aug. 5 *Perf. 11½x11*
1708 A911 4cr multi 25 15

National Health Day.

Brazilian Postal Administration, 15th Anniversary — A912

1980, Sept. 16 **Litho.** *Perf. 12*
1709 A912 5cr multi 25 20

Souvenir Sheet

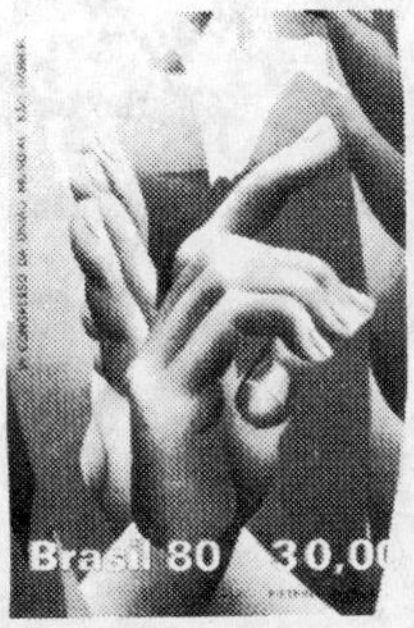

St. Gabriel World Union, 6th Congress A913

1980, Sept. 29 *Perf. 11½x12*
1710 A913 30cr multi 1.00 1.50

Cattleya Amethystoglossa A914

1980, Oct. 3 *Perf. 11½*
1711 A914 5cr *shown* 18 15
1712 A914 5cr *Laelia cinnabarina* 18 15
1713 A914 24cr *Zygopetalum crinitum* 1.10 60
1714 A914 28cr *Laelia tenebrosa* 1.10 60
Nos. 1711-1714 (4) 2.56 1.50

Espamer 80, American-European Philatelic Exhibition, Madrid, Oct. 3-12.

Red-tailed Amazon Parrot — A915

Capitao Rodrigo, Hero of Erico Verissimo's "O Continento" — A916

Parrots: No. 1716, Vinaceous Amazon. No. 1717, Brown-backed. No. 1718, Red-spectacled.

1980, Oct. 18 **Litho.** *Perf. 12*
1715 A915 5cr multi 18 15
1716 A915 5cr multi 18 15
1717 A915 28cr multi 1.10 60
1718 A915 28cr multi 1.10 60
Nos. 1715-1718 (4) 2.56 1.50

Lubrapex '80 Stamp Exhib., Lisbon, Oct. 18-26.

1980, Oct. 23
1719 A916 5cr multi 25 20

Book Day.

Flight into Egypt — A917

1980, Nov. 5
1720 A917 5cr multi 25 20

Christmas 1980.

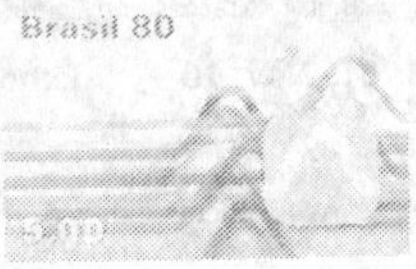

Sound Waves and Oscillator Screen A918

1980, Nov. 7
1721 A918 5cr multi 25 20

Telebras Research Center inauguration.

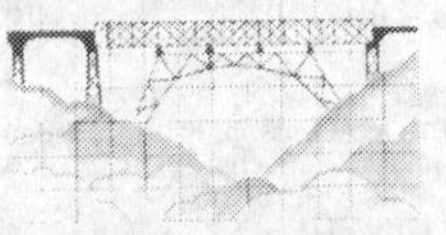

Carvalho Viaduct, Paranagua-Curitiba Railroad — A919

1980, Nov. 10
1722 A919 5cr multi 25 20

Engineering Club centenary.

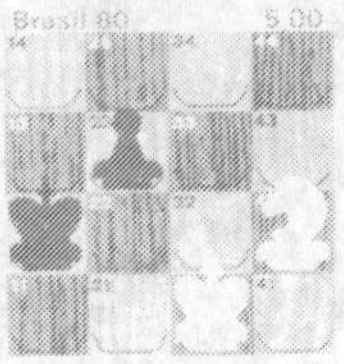

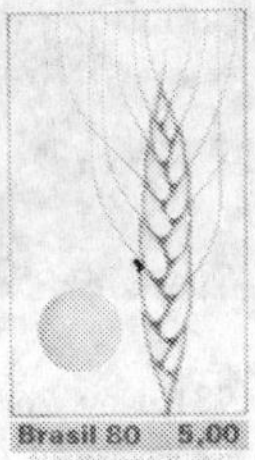

A920 A921

1980, Nov. 18 **Litho.** *Perf. 11½*
1723 A920 5cr Portable chess board 25 50

Postal chess contest.

1980, Nov. 27 *Perf. 11½x11*
1724 A921 5cr Sun, wheat 25 40

Thanksgiving 1980

Footnotes near stamp listings often refer to other stamps of the same design.

Father Anchieta Writing "Virgin Mary, Mother of God" on Sand of Iperoig Beach — A922

1980, Dec. 8 *Perf. 12*
1725 A922 5cr multi 25 20

Christ Carrying Cross, By O Aleijadinho A923

Antonio Francisco Lisboa (O Aleijadinho), 250th Birth Anniv.: Paintings of the life of Christ: a, Mount of Olives. b, Arrest in the Garden. c, Flagellation. d, Crown of Thorns. f, Crucifixion.

1980, Dec. 29
1726 Block of 6 1.65 1.65
a.-f. A923 5cr any single 24 16

Agricultural Productivity A924

1981, Jan. 2 **Litho.** *Perf. 11x11½*
1727 A924 30cr shown 1.25 35
1728 A924 35cr Domestic markets 1.10 35
1729 A924 40cr Exports 1.10 35
Nos. 1727-1729 (3) 3.45 1.05

Boy Scout and Campfire A925

1981, Jan. 22 **Litho.** *Perf. 11x11½*
1730 A925 5cr shown 25 20
1731 A925 5cr Scouts cooking 25 20
1732 A925 5cr Scout, tents 25 20
Nos. 1730-1732 (3) 75 60

4th Pan-American Scout Jamboree.

Souvenir Sheet

Mailman, 1930 — A926

1981, Mar. 11 **Litho.** *Perf. 11*
1733 Sheet of 3 4.00 4.00
a. A926 30cr shown 1.00 1.00
b. A926 35cr Mailman, 1981 1.00 1.00
c. A926 40cr Telegram messenger, 1930 1.00 1.00

Dept. of Posts & Telegraphs, 50th anniv.

Souvenir Sheet

The Hunter and the Jaguar, by Felix Taunay (1795-1881) A927

1981, Apr. 10 **Litho.** *Perf. 11*
1734 A927 30cr multi 1.00 *2.00*

Lima Barreto and Rio de Janeiro, 1900 A928

1981, May 13 **Litho.** *Perf. 11½*
1735 A928 7cr multi 25 20

Lima Barreto, writer, birth centenary.

Maraca Indian Funerary Urn — A929

1981, May 18
1736 A929 7cr shown 25 20
1737 A929 7cr Marajoara triangular jug 25 20
1738 A929 7cr Tupi-Guarani bowl 25 20
Nos. 1736-1738 (3) 75 60

Lophornis Magnifica A930

Designs: Hummingbirds.

1981, May 22 *Perf. 11½*
1739 A930 7cr shown 30 20
1740 A930 7cr Phaethornis pretrei 30 20
1741 A930 7cr Chrysolampis mosquitus 30 20
1742 A930 7cr Heliactin cornuta 30 20
Nos. 1739-1742 (4) 1.20 80

Rotary Emblem and Faces — A931

1981, May 31
1743 A931 7cr Emblem, hands 20 15
1744 A931 35cr shown 1.00 80

72nd Convention of Rotary Intl., Sao Paulo.

Environmental Protection A932

1981, June 5 *Perf. 12*

1745 A932 7cr shown 25 20
1746 A932 7cr Forest 25 20
1747 A932 7cr Clouds (air) 25 20
1748 A932 7cr Village (soil) 25 20
a. Block of 4, #1745-1748 1.00 1.00

Biplane, 1931 (Airmail Service, 50th Anniv.) A933

1981, June 10 *Perf. 11½*

1749 A933 7cr multi 25 20

Madeira-Mamore Railroad, 50th Anniv. of Nationalization — A934

1981, July 10 **Litho.** *Perf. 11x11½*

1750 A934 7cr multi 25 20

66th Intl. Esperanto Congress, Brasilia A935

1981, July 26 *Perf. 12*

1751 A935 7cr green & blk 25 20

No. 79 A936

1981, Aug. 1

1752 A936 50cr shown 1.40 30
1753 A936 55cr No. 80 1.40 30
1754 A936 60cr No. 81 1.40 30
Nos. 1752-1754 (3) 4.20 90

Stamp Day; cent. of "small head" stamps.

Institute of Military Engineering, 50th Anniv. — A937

1981, Aug. 11 **Litho.** *Perf. 11½*

1755 A937 12cr multi 25 20

Reisado Dancers — A938

1981, Aug. 22

1756 A938 50cr Dancers, diff. 80 22
1757 A938 55cr Sailors 80 25
1758 A938 60cr shown 80 20
Nos. 1756-1758 (3) 2.40 67

Intl. Year of the Disabled A939

1981, Sept. 17 **Litho.** *Perf. 11½*

1759 A939 12cr multi 25 20

Flowers of the Central Plateau A940

1981, Sept. 21 **Litho.** *Perf. 12*

1760 A940 12cr Palicourea rigida 25 20
1761 A940 12cr Dalechampia caperonioides 25 20
1762 A940 12cr Cassia clausseni, vert. 25 20
1763 A940 12cr Eremanthus sphaerocephalus, vert. 25 20
Nos. 1760-1763 (4) 1.00 80

Virgin of Nazareth Statue — A941

Christ the Redeemer Statue, Rio de Janeiro, 50th Anniv. — A942

1981, Oct. 10 **Litho.** *Perf. 12*

1764 A941 12cr multi 25 20

Candle Festival of Nazareth, Belem.

1981, Oct. 12

1765 A942 12cr multi 25 20

World Food Day — A943

1981, Oct. 16

1766 A943 12c multi 25 20

75th Anniv. of Santos-Dumont's First Flight — A944

1981, Oct. 23 **Litho.** *Perf. 12*

1767 A944 60cr multi 1.00 35

Father José de Santa Rita Durao, Titlepage of his Epic Poem Caramuru, Diego Alvares Correia (Character) A945

1981, Oct. 29

1768 A945 12cr multi 25 20

Caramuru publication centenary; World Book Day.

Christmas 1981 — A946

Designs: Creches and figurines.

1981, Nov. 10 **Litho.** *Perf. 12*

1769 A946 12cr multi 15 15
1770 A946 50cr multi 1.25 25
1771 A946 55cr multi, vert. 1.25 28
1772 A946 60cr multi, vert. 1.25 30
Nos. 1769-1772 (4) 3.90 98

State Flags — A947

Designs: a, Alagoas. b, Bahia. c, Federal District. d, Pernambuco. e, Sergipe.

1981, Nov. 19

1773 Block of 5 + label 1.25 1.25
a.-e. A947 12cr, any single 20 20

Label shows arms of Brazil.

Thanksgiving 1981 — A948

1981, Nov. 26 **Litho.** *Perf. 11½*

1776 A948 12cr multi 25 15

Ministry of Labor, 50th Anniv. A949

1981, Nov. 26

1777 A949 12cr multi 20 15

School of Engineering, Itajuba A950

1981, Nov. 30 *Perf. 11x11½*

1778 A950 15cr lt grn & pur 35 15

Theodomiro C. Santiago, founder, birth centenary.

Sao Paulo State Police Sesquicentennial A951

1981, Dec. 15 **Litho.** *Perf. 12*

1779 A951 12cr Policeman with saxophone 20 15
1780 A951 12cr Mounted policemen 20 15

Army Library Centenary A952

1981, Dec. 17

1781 A952 12cr multi 20 15

Souvenir Sheet

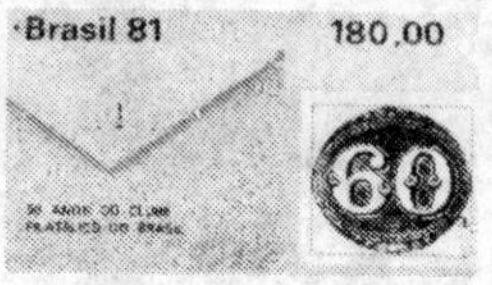

Philatelic Club of Brazil, 50th Anniv. A953

1981, Dec. 18 *Perf. 11*

1782 A953 180cr multi 4.50 *4.50*

Brigadier Eduardo Gomes A954

1982, Jan. 20 **Litho.** *Perf. 11x11½*

1783 A954 12cr blue & blk 30 15

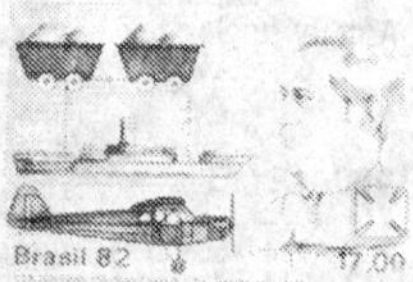

Birth Centenary of Henrique Lage, Industrialist A956

1982, Mar. 14 **Litho.** *Perf. 11½*

1785 A956 17cr multi 50 16

1982 World Cup Soccer — A957

TB Bacillus Cent. — A958

Designs: Various soccer players.

1982, Mar. 19

1786 A957 75cr multi 75 25
1787 A957 80cr multi 75 28
1788 A957 85cr multi 75 28
Nos. 1786-1788 (3) 2.25 81

Souvenir Sheet
Imperf

1789	Sheet of 3	3.00	*6.00*
a.	A957 100cr like #1786	1.00	
b.	A957 100cr like #1787	1.00	
c.	A957 100cr like #1788	1.00	

1982, Mar. 24 ***Perf. 12***

1790	A958 90cr Microscope, lung	1.25	80
1791	A958 100cr Lung, pills	1.25	90
a.	Pair, #1790-1791	2.50	2.00

Souvenir Sheet

A959

1982, Apr. 17 **Litho.** ***Perf. 11***

1792	Sheet of 3	3.50	3.25
a.	A959 75cr Laelia Purpurata	1.00	50
b.	A959 80cr Oncidium flexuosum	1.00	50
c.	A959 85cr Cleistes revoluta	1.25	55

BRAPEX V Stamp Exhibition, Blumenau.

Oil Drilling Centenary A960

1982, Apr. 18 ***Perf. 11½***

1793 A960 17cr multi 25 15

400th Birth Anniv. of St. Vincent de Paul — A961

1982, Apr. 24 **Litho.** ***Perf. 11½***

1794 A961 17cr multi 25 15

Seven Steps of Guaira (Waterfalls) A962

1982, Apr. 29

1795	A962 17cr Fifth Fall	20	15
1796	A962 21cr Seventh Fall	30	20

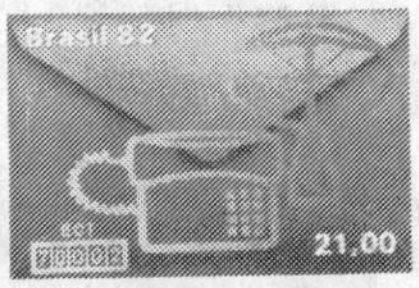

Ministry of Communications, 15th Anniv. — A963

1982, May 15

1797 A963 21cr multi 25 20

Museology Course, Natl. Historical Museum, 50th Anniv. A964

1982, May 18

1798 A964 17cr blk & sal pink 20 15

Vale de Rio Doce Mining Co. — A965

1982, June 1

1799 A965 17cr Gears 25 15

Martin Afonso de Souza Reading Charter to Settlers A966

1982, June 3 **Litho.** ***Perf. 11½***

1800 A966 17cr multi 25 15

Town of Sao Vincente, 450th anniv.

Armadillo A967

1982, June 4

1801	A967 17cr shown	55	15
1802	A967 21cr Wolves	55	18
1803	A967 30cr Deer	1.65	22
	Nos. 1801-1803 (3)	2.75	55

Film Strip and Award A968

1982, June 19

1804 A968 17cr multi 25 15

20th anniv. of Golden Palm award for The Promise Keeper, Cannes Film Festival.

Souvenir Sheet

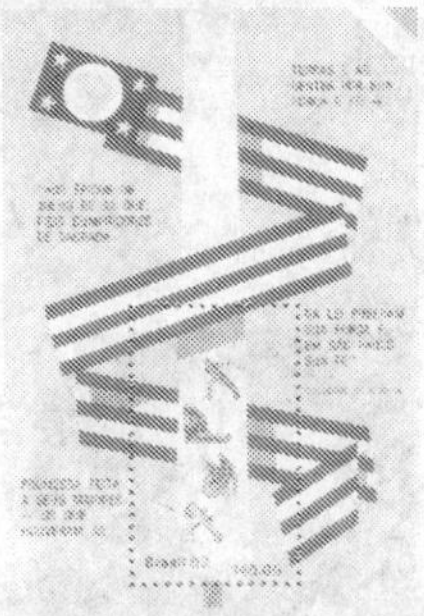
50th Anniv. of Constitutionalist Revolution — A969

1982, July 9 **Litho.** ***Perf. 11***

1805 A969 140cr multi 1.75 1.75

Church of Our Lady of O'Sabara — A970

St. Francis of Assisi, 800th Birth Anniv. — A971

Baroque Architecture, Minas Gerais State: No. 1807, Church of Our Lady of the Rosary, Diamantina, horiz. No. 1808, Town Square, Mariana, horiz.

1982, July 16 ***Perf. 11½***

1806	A970 17cr multi	25	15
1807	A970 17cr multi	25	15
1808	A970 17cr multi	25	15
	Nos. 1806-1808 (3)	75	45

1982, July 24

1809 A971 21cr multi 20 16

Stamp Day and Centenary of Pedro II "Large Head" Stamps A972

1982, Aug. 1

1810 A972 21cr No. 82 25 20

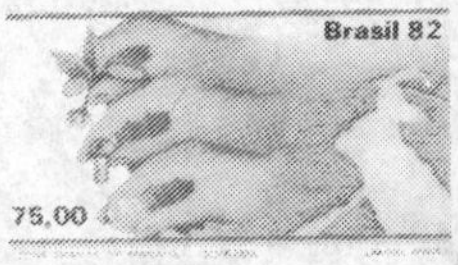

Port of Manaus Free Trade Zone A973

1982, Aug. 15 ***Perf. 11x11½***

1811 A973 75cr multi 65 35

Scouting Year — A974

1982, Aug. 21 **Litho.** ***Perf. 11***

1812	Sheet of 2	2.75	*3.75*
a.	A974 85cr Baden-Powell	1.00	*1.10*
b.	A974 185cr Scout	1.65	*2.00*

Orixas Folk Costumes of African Origin — A975

1982, Aug. 21 ***Perf. 11½***

1813	A975 20cr Iemanja	20	16
1814	A975 20cr Xango	20	16
1815	A975 20cr Oxumare	20	16
	Nos. 1813-1815 (3)	60	48

10th Anniv. of Central Bank of Brazil Currency Museum A976

1982, Aug. 31

1816	A976 25cr 12-florin coin, 1645, obverse and reverse	25	20
1817	A976 25cr Emperor Pedro's 6.40-reis coronation coin, 1822	25	20

National Week — A977

1982, Sept. 1

1818 A977 25cr Don Pedro proclaiming independence 38 25

A978

A979

1982, Oct. 4

1819 A978 85cr Portrait 1.00 60

St. Theresa of Avila (1515-1582).

1982, Oct. 15 **Litho.** ***Perf. 11½x11***

1820	A979 75cr Instruments	65	38
1821	A979 80cr Dancers	65	38
1822	A979 85cr Musicians	70	40
a.	Souvenir sheet of 3, #1820-1822, perf. 11	2.75	*2.75*
	Nos. 1820-1822 (3)	2.00	1.16

Lubrapex '82, 4th Portuguese-Brazilian Stamp Exhibition. Stamps in No. 1822a are without "LUBRAPEX 82."

Aviation Industry Day — A980

1982, Oct. 17 ***Perf. 12***

1823 A980 24cr Embraer EMB-312 trainer plane 25 20

Bastos Tigre, Poet, Birth Centenary, and "Saudade" Text — A981

1982, Oct. 29

1824 A981 24cr multi 25 20

Book Day.

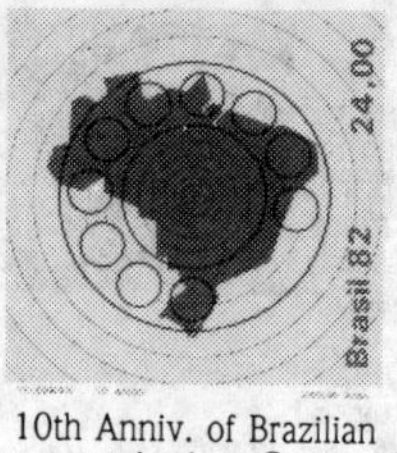

10th Anniv. of Brazilian Telecommunications Co. — A982

1982, Nov. 9 Litho. *Perf. 11½*
1825 A982 24cr multi 25 20

Christmas 1982 — A983

Children's Drawings.

1982, Nov. 10
1826 A983 24cr Nativity 25 20
1827 A983 24cr Angels 25 20
1828 A983 30cr Nativity, diff. 32 45
1829 A983 30cr Flight into Egypt 32 45
Nos. 1826-1829 (4) 1.14 1.30

State Flags — A984

Designs: a, Ceara. b, Espirito Santo. c, Paraiba. d, Grande de Norte. e, Rondonia.

1982, Nov. 19
1830 Block of 5 + label 5.25 5.25
a.-e. A984 24cr any single 1.00 20

Thanksgiving 1982 — A985

1982, Nov. 25
1835 A985 24cr multi 25 20

Homage to the Deaf — A986

1982, Dec. 1
1836 A986 24cr multi 25 20

Naval Academy Bicentenary A987

Training Ships.

1982, Dec. 14
1837 A987 24cr Brazil 35 20
1838 A987 24cr Benjamin Constant 35 20
1839 A987 24cr Almirante Saldanha 35 20
Nos. 1837-1839 (3) 1.05 60

Souvenir Sheet

No. 12 — A988

1982, Dec. 18 Litho. *Perf. 11*
1840 A988 200cr multi 4.00 *5.00*

BRASILIANA '83 Intl. Stamp Exhibition, Rio de Janeiro, July 29-Aug. 7.

Brasiliana '83 Carnival A989

1983, Feb. 9 Litho. *Perf. 11½*
1841 A989 24cr Samba drummers 20 15
1842 A989 130cr Street parade 1.40 50
1843 A989 140cr Dancer 1.40 52
1844 A989 150cr Male dancer 1.40 55
Nos. 1841-1844 (4) 4.40 1.72

Antarctic Expedition A990

1983, Feb. 20 Litho. *Perf. 11½*
1845 A990 150cr Support ship Barano de Teffe 2.00 55

50th Anniv. of Women's Rights — A991

1983, Mar. 8
1846 A991 130cr multi 1.25 50

Itaipu Hydroelectric Power Station Opening A992

1983, Mar. Litho. *Perf. 12*
1847 A992 140cr multi 1.90 42

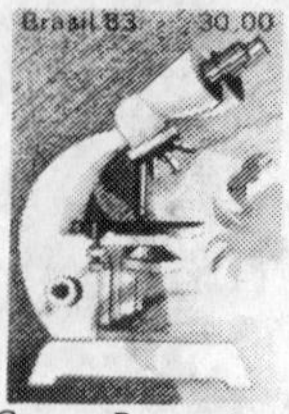

Cancer Prevention A993

Martin Luther (1483-1546) A994

Designs: 30cr, Microscope. 38cr, Antonio Prudente, Paulista Cancer Assoc. founder, Camargo Hospital.

1983, Apr. 18
1848 A993 30cr multi 30 15
1849 A993 38cr multi 32 15
a. Pair, #1848-1849 65 35
Set value 22

1983, Apr. 18
1850 A994 150cr pale grn & blk 1.25 50

Agricultural Research A995

1983, Apr. 26 Litho. *Perf. 11½*
1851 A995 30cr Chestnut tree 20 15
1852 A995 30cr Genetic research 20 15
1853 A995 38cr Tropical soy beans 25 15
Nos. 1851-1853 (3) 65
Set value 20

Father Rogerio Neuhaus (1863-1934), Centenary of Ordination — A996

1983, May 3 *Perf. 11½x11*
1854 A996 30cr multi 25 15

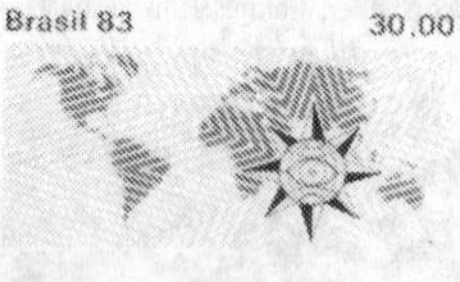

30th Anniv. of Customs Cooperation Council A997

1983, May 5 *Perf. 11x11½*
1855 A997 30cr multi 25 15

World Communications Year — A998

1983, May 17 Litho. *Perf. 11½*
1856 A998 250cr multi 1.50 45

Toucans A999

1983, May 21
1857 A999 30cr Tucanucu 15 15
1858 A999 185cr White-breasted 1.25 38
1859 A999 205cr Green-beaked 1.25 40
1860 A999 215cr Black-beaked 1.25 45
Nos. 1857-1860 (4) 3.90 1.38

Souvenir Sheet

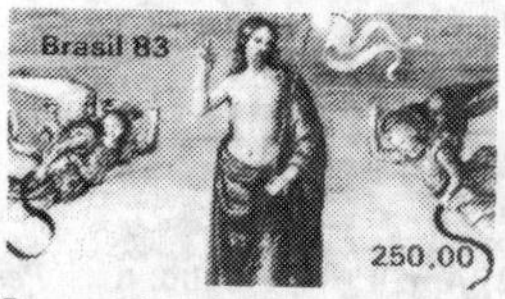

Resurrection, by Raphael (1483-1517) — A1000

1983, May 25 *Perf. 11*
1861 A1000 250cr multi 2.50 *3.00*

Hohenzollern 980 Locomotive, 1875 A1001

Various locomotives.

1983, June 12 Litho. *Perf. 11½*
1862 A1001 30cr shown 25 15
1863 A1001 30cr Baldwin #1, 1881 25 15
1864 A1001 38cr Fowler #1, 1872 30 15
Nos. 1862-1864 (3) 80
Set value 20

9th Women's Basketball World Championship — A1002

1983, July 24 Litho. *Perf. 11½x11*
1865 A1002 30cr Players, front view 20 15
1866 A1002 30cr Players, rear view 20 15
Set value 15

Simon Bolivar (1783-1830) A1003

1983, July 24 *Perf. 12*
1867 A1003 30cr multi 20 15

Children's Polio and Measles Vaccination Campaign A1004

1983, July 25
1868 A1004 30cr Girl, measles 20 15
1869 A1004 30cr Boy, polio 20 15
Set value 15

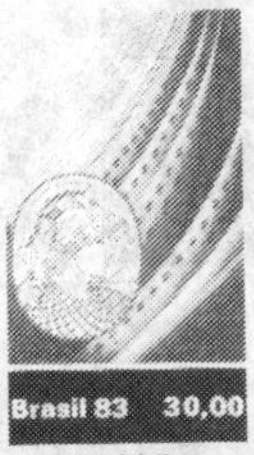

A1005

A1006

1983, July 28 *Perf. 11½x11*

1870 A1005 30cr Minerva (goddess of wisdom), computer tape	20	15

20th Anniv. of Master's program in engineering.

1983, July 29 **Engr.**

Guanabara Bay.

1871 A1006 185cr No. 1	1.50	38
1872 A1006 205cr No. 2	1.50	40
1873 A1006 215cr No. 3	1.50	45
Nos. 1871-1873 (3)	4.50	1.23

Souvenir Sheet

Perf. 11

1874 Sheet of 3	8.00	*10.00*
a. A1006 185cr No. 1	2.00	*3.00*
b. A1006 205cr No. 2	2.00	*3.00*
c. A1006 215cr No. 3	2.00	*3.00*

BRASILIANA '83 Intl. Stamp Show, Rio de Janeiro, July 29-Aug. 7.

Souvenir Sheet

The First Mass in Brazil, by Vitor Meireles (1833-1903) — A1007

1983, Aug. 18 *Perf. 11*

1875 A1007 250cr multi 3.00 1.50

EMB-120 Brasilia Passenger Plane A1008

1983, Aug. 19 *Perf. 12*

1876 A1008 30cr multi 25 15

Vision of Don Bosco Centenary A1009

1983, Aug. 30

1877 A1009 130cr multi 75 25

Independence Week A1010

1983, Sept. 1 **Litho.** *Perf. 11½*

1878 A1010 50cr multi 25 15

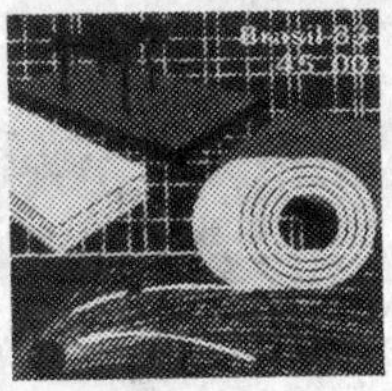

National Steel Corp., 10th Anniv. — A1011

1983, Sept. 17 **Litho.** *Perf. 11½*

1879 A1011 45cr multi 25 15

Cactus — A1012

1983, Sept. 12 **Litho.** *Perf. 11½*

1880 A1012 45cr Pilosocereus gounellei	32	15
1881 A1012 45cr Melocactus bahiensis	32	15
1882 A1012 57cr Cereus jamacaru	40	15
Nos. 1880-1882 (3)	1.04	
Set value		32

1st National Eucharistic Congress — A1013

1983, Oct. 12 **Litho.** *Perf. 11½*

1883 A1013 45cr multi 25 15

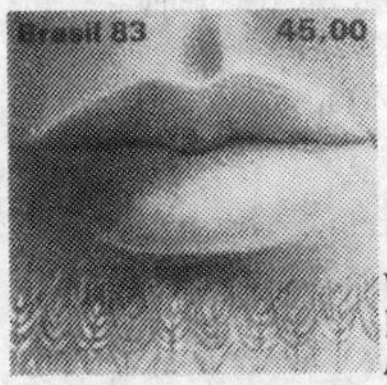

World Food Program A1014

1983, Oct. 14 **Litho.** *Perf. 11½*

1884 A1014 45cr Mouth, grain	30	15
1885 A1014 57cr Fish, sailboat	40	15
Set value		22

Souvenir Sheet

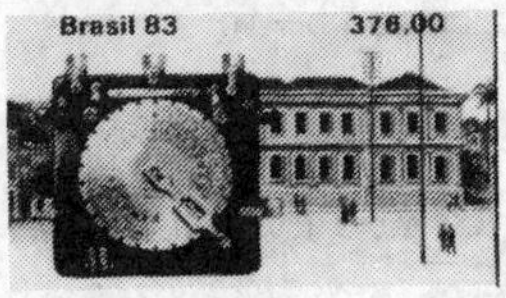

Louis Breguet, Death Centenary A1015

1983, Oct. 27 **Litho.** *Perf. 11*

1886 A1015 376cr Telegraph transmitter 4.25 1.50

Christmas 1983 — A1016

17th-18th Cent. Statues: 45cr, Our Lady of the Angels. 315cr, Our Lady of the Parturition. 335cr, Our Lady of Joy. 345cr, Our Lady of the Presentation.

1983, Nov. 10 **Litho.** *Perf. 11½*

1887 A1016 45cr multi	25	15
1888 A1016 315cr multi	1.65	60
1889 A1016 335cr multi	1.65	65
1890 A1016 345cr multi	1.65	70
Nos. 1887-1890 (4)	5.20	2.10

Marshal Mascarenhas Birth Centenary A1017

1983, Nov. 13 **Litho.** *Perf. 11½*

1891 A1017 45cr Battle sites 20 15

Commander of Brazilian Expeditionary Force in Italy.

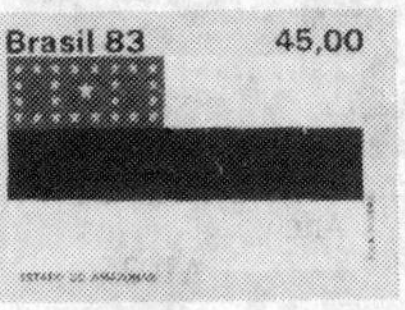

State Flags A1018

Designs: a, Amazonas. b, Goias. c, Rio. d, Mato Grosso Do Sol. e, Parana.

1983, Nov. 17 **Litho.** *Perf. 11½*

1892 Block of 5 + label	3.00	3.00
a.-e. A1018 45cr any single	50	20

Thanksgiving A1018a

1983, Nov. 24 **Litho.** *Perf. 12*

1896 A1018a 45cr Madonna, wheat 35 15

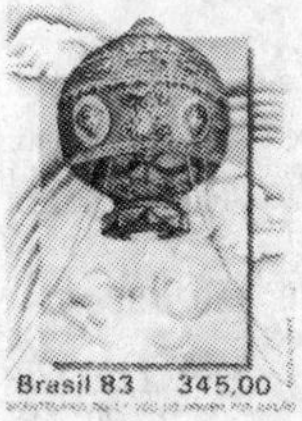

Manned Flight Bicentenary — A1019

1983, Dec. 15 **Litho.** *Perf. 12*

1897 A1019 345cr Montgolfiere balloon, 1783 5.00 50

Ethnic Groups A1020

1984, Jan. 20 **Litho.** *Perf. 12*

1898 A1020 45cr multi 20 15

50th anniv. of publication of Masters and Slaves, sociological study by Gilberto Freyre.

Centenary of Crystal Palace, Petropolis A1021

1984, Feb. 2

1899 A1021 45cr multi 18 15

Souvenir Sheet

Flags (Sculpture with 40 Figures), by Victor Brecheret (b. 1894) A1022

1984, Feb. 22 **Litho.** *Perf. 11*

1900 A1022 805cr multi 1.50 1.00

Naval Museum Centenary A1023

1984, Mar. 23 **Litho.** *Perf. 11½*

1901 A1023 620cr Figurehead, frigate, 1847 85 52

Slavery Abolition Centenary A1024

1984, Mar. 25

1902 A1024 585cr Broken chain, raft	85	55
1903 A1024 610cr Freed slave	90	60

Souvenir Sheet

Visit of King Carl XVI Gustaf of Sweden A1025

1984, Apr. 2 *Perf. 11*

1904 A1025 2105cr multi 3.50 2.50

1984 Summer Olympics A1026

1984, Apr. 13 *Perf. 11½*

1905 A1026 65cr Long jump	15	15
1906 A1026 65cr 100-meter race	15	15
1907 A1026 65cr Relay race	15	15
1908 A1026 585cr Pole vault	80	65
1909 A1026 610cr High jump	85	70
1910 A1026 620cr Hurdles	90	80
a. Block of 6, #1905-1910	3.00	3.00
Nos. 1905-1910 (6)	3.00	2.60

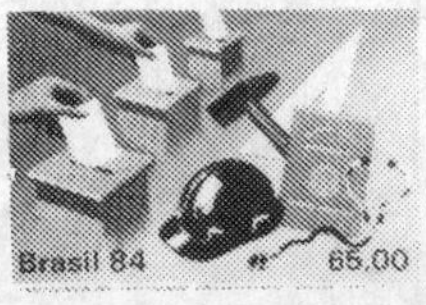

Voters Casting Ballots, Symbols of Labor A1027

Pres. Getulio Vargas Birth Centenary: Symbols of Development.

1984, Apr. 19 Litho. *Perf. 11½*

1911 A1027 65cr shown 15 15
1912 A1027 65cr Oil rig, blast furnace 15 15
1913 A1027 65cr High-tension towers 15 15
Nos. 1911-1913 (3) 45
Set value 24

Columbus, Espana '84 Emblem — A1028

1984, Apr. 27

1914 A1028 65cr Pedro Cabral 15 15
1915 A1028 610cr shown 1.25 70

Map of Americas, Heads — A1029

Lubrapex '84 — A1030

1984, May 7 Litho. *Perf. 11½*

1916 A1029 65cr multi 15 15

Pan-American Association of Finance and Guarantees, 8th Assembly.

1984, May 8 *Perf. 11½x11*

18th Century Paintings, Mariana Cathedral.

1917 A1030 65cr Hunting scene 15 15
1918 A1030 585cr Pastoral scene 75 42
1919 A1030 610cr People under umbrellas 80 50
1920 A1030 620cr Elephants 85 50
Nos. 1917-1920 (4) 2.55 1.57

Souvenir Sheet

Intl. Fedn. of Soccer Associations, 80th Anniv. — A1031

1984, May 21 *Perf. 11*

1921 A1031 2115cr Globe 3.50 1.75

Matto Grosso Lowland Fauna A1032

1984, June 5 Litho. *Perf. 11½*

1922 Strip of 3 60 30
a. A1032 65cr Deer 20 15
b. A1032 65cr Jaguar 20 15
c. A1032 80cr Alligator 20 15

First Letter Mailed in Brazil, by Guido Mondin — A1033

1984, June 8 *Perf. 12x11½*

1923 A1033 65cr multi 15 15

Postal Union of Americas and Spain, first anniv. of new headquarters.

Brazil-Germany Air Service, 50th Anniv.
A1034 A1035

1984, June 19

1924 A1034 610cr Dornier-Wal seaplane 1.00 70
1925 A1035 620cr Steamer Westfalen 1.05 72
a. Pair, #1924-1925 2.05 1.50

Woolly Spider Monkey, World Wildlife Fund Emblem — A1036

1984, July 6 *Perf. 11½*

1926 A1036 65cr Mother, baby 48 15
1927 A1036 80cr Monkey 32 15
Set value 18

Agriculture Type of 1980

Designs: 65cr, Rubber tree. 80cr, Brazil nuts. 120cr, Rice. 150cr, Eucalyptus. 300cr, Pinha da Parana. 800cr, Carnauba. 1000cr, Babacu. 2000cr, Sunflower.

Photogravure (65, 80, 120, 150cr), Engraved

1984-85 *Perf. 11x11½*

1934 A894 65cr lilac 20 15
1935 A894 80cr brn red 25 15
1936 A894 120cr dk sl bl 35 15
1937 A894 150cr green 15 15
1938 A894 300cr rose mag 50 15
1939 A894 800cr grnsh bl 1.40 15
1940 A894 1000cr lemon 1.40 15
1941 A894 2000cr yel org ('85) 70 25
Nos. 1934-1941 (8) 4.95
Set value 1.00

Marajo Isld. Buffalo A1037

1984, July 9 Litho. *Perf. 12*

1942 Strip of 3 50 28
a. A1037 65cr Approaching stream 15 15
b. A1037 65cr Standing on bank 15 15
c. A1037 80cr Drinking 18 15

Continuous design.

Banco Economico Sesquicentenary — A1038

1984, July 13 *Perf. 11½*

1943 A1038 65cr Bank, coins 15 15

Historic Railway Stations A1039

1984, July 23 Litho. *Perf. 11½*

1944 A1039 65cr Japeri 15 15
1945 A1039 65cr Luz, vert. 15 15
1946 A1039 80cr Sao Joao del Rei 16 15
Nos. 1944-1946 (3) 46
Set value 26

A1040

A1041

1984, Aug. 13 *Perf. 11*

Souvenir Sheet

1947 A1040 585cr Girl scout 1.40 1.00

Girl Scouts in Brazil, 65th anniv.

1984, Aug. 21 Litho. *Perf. 11½*

1948 A1041 65cr Couple sheltered from rain 15 15

Housing project bank, 20th anniv.

Independence Week A1042

Children's Drawings.

1984, Sept. 3

1949 A1042 100cr Explorer & ship 15 15
1950 A1042 100cr Sailing ships 15 15
1951 A1042 100cr "BRASIL" mural 15 15
1952 A1042 100cr Children under rainbow 15 15
Nos. 1949-1952 (4) 60
Set value 48

Rio de Janeiro Chamber of Commerce Sesquicentenary — A1043

1984, Sept. 10

1953 A1043 100cr Monument, worker silhouette 15 15

Death Sesquicentenary of Don Pedro I (IV of Portugal) — A1044

1984, Sept. 23 *Perf. 12x11½*

1954 A1044 1000cr Portrait 1.50 1.10

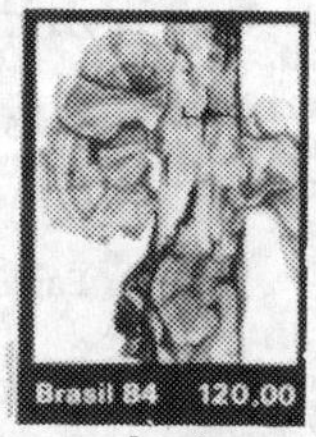

Local Mushrooms — A1045

Book Day — A1046

1984, Oct. 22 *Perf. 11½*

1955 A1045 120cr Pycnoporus sanguineus 15 15
1956 A1045 1050cr Calvatia sp 1.10 1.25
1957 A1045 1080cr Pleurotus sp, horiz. 1.20 1.30
Nos. 1955-1957 (3) 2.45 2.70

1984, Oct. 23 *Perf. 11½*

1958 A1046 120cr Girl in open book 15 15

New State Mint Opening — A1047

1984, Nov. 1

1959 A1047 120cr multi 15 15

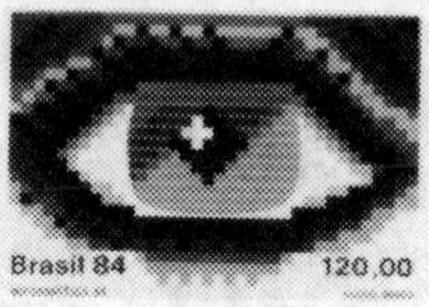

Informatics Fair & Congress A1048

1984, Nov. 5 Litho. *Perf. 12*

1960 A1048 120cr Eye, computer terminal 15 15

Org. of American States, 14th Assembly — A1049

1984, Nov. 14

1961 A1049 120cr Emblem, flags 15 15

State Flags A1050

Designs: a, Maranhaio. b, Mato Grosso. c, Minas Gerais. d, Piaui. e, Santa Catarina.

1984, Nov. 19 *Perf. 11½*
1962 Block of 5 + label 1.00 1.00
a.-e. A1050 120cr, any single 20 15

See Nos. 2037, 2249.

Thanksgiving 1984 — A1051

1984, Nov. 22
1963 A1051 120cr Bell tower, Brasilia 15 15

Christmas 1984 A1052

Paintings: No. 1964, Nativity, by Djanira. No. 1965, Virgin and Child, by Glauco Rodrigues. No. 1966, Flight into Egypt, by Paul Garfunkel. No. 1967, Nativity, by Di Cavalcanti.

1984, Dec. 3 Litho. *Perf. 12*
1964 A1052 120cr multi 15 15
1965 A1052 120cr multi 15 15
1966 A1052 1050cr multi 85 40
1967 A1052 1080cr multi 85 40
Nos. 1964-1967 (4) 2.00
Set value 90

40th Anniv., International Civil Aviation Organization A1053

1984, Dec. 7 Litho. *Perf. 12*
1968 A1053 120cr Aircraft, Earth globe 15 15

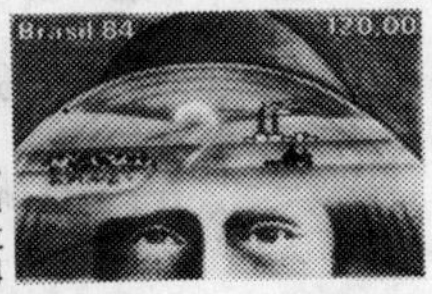

25th Anniv., North-Eastern Development A1054

1984, Dec. 14 Litho. *Perf. 12*
1969 A1054 120cr Farmer, field 15 15

Emilio Rouede A1055

Painting: Church of the Virgin of Safe Travels, by Rouede.

1985, Jan. 22 Litho. *Perf. 12*
1970 A1055 120cr multi 15 15

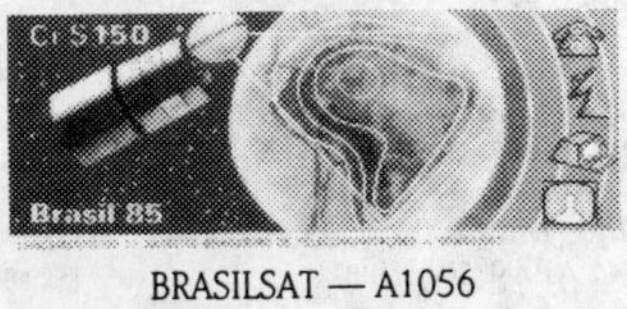

BRASILSAT — A1056

1985, Feb. 8 Litho. *Perf. 11½x12*
1971 A1056 150cr Satellite, Brazil 15 15

Metropolitan Railways — A1057

1985, Mar. 2 Litho. *Perf. 11x11½*
1972 A1057 200cr Passenger trains 15 15

Brasilia Botanical Gardens A1058

1985, Mar. 8 Litho. *Perf. 11½x12*
1973 A1058 200cr Caryocar brasiliense 15 15

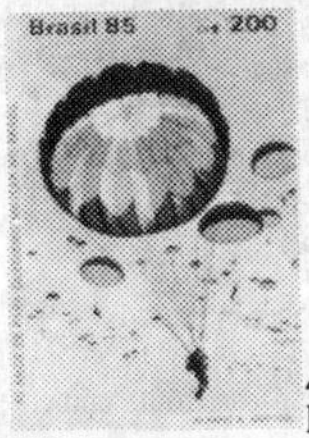

40th Anniv., Brazilian Paratroops — A1059

1985, Mar. 8 Litho. *Perf. 11½x12*
1974 A1059 200cr Parachute drop 15 15

Natl. Climate Awareness Program — A1060

1985, Mar. 18 Litho. *Perf. 11½x12*
1975 A1060 500cr multi 20 15

Thoroughbred Horses A1061

1985, Mar. 19 Litho. *Perf. 12*
1976 A1061 1000cr Campolina 38 22
1977 A1061 1500cr Marajoara 70 35
1978 A1061 1500cr Mangalarga marchador 70 35
Nos. 1976-1978 (3) 1.78 92

Ouro Preto — A1062

1985, Apr. 18 Litho. *Perf. 11½x12*
1979 A1062 220cr shown 15 15
1980 A1062 220cr St. Miguel des Missoes 15 15
1981 A1062 220cr Olinda 15 15
Set value 30 18

Polivolume, by Mary Vieira — A1063

1985, Apr. 20 **Litho.**
1982 A1063 220cr multi 15 15

Rio Branco Inst., 40th anniv.

Natl. Capital, Brasilia, 25th Anniv. — A1064

1985, Apr. 22 **Litho.**
1983 A1064 220cr Natl. Theater, acoustic shell 15 15
1984 A1064 220cr Catetinho Palace, JK Memorial 15 15
Set value 20 15

A1065

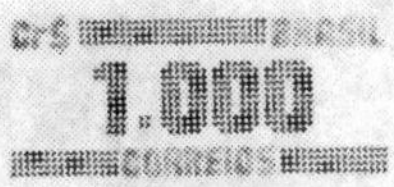

A1065a

1985-86 Photo. *Perf. 11½*
1985 A1065 50cr lake 15 15
1986 A1065 100cr dp vio 15 15
1987 A1065 150cr violet 15 15
1988 A1065 200cr ultra 15 15
1989 A1065 220cr green 15 15
1990 A1065 300cr royal bl 18 15
1991 A1065 500cr olive blk 30 22
1992 A1065a 1000cr brn ol ('86) 18 15
1993 A1065a 2000cr brt grn ('86) 35 22
1994 A1065a 3000cr dl vio 42 32
1995 A1065a 5000cr brn 58 42
Set value 2.35 1.65

Marshal Rondon, 120th Birth Anniv. A1066

1985, May 5 *Perf. 11x11½*
1996 A1066 220cr multi 15 15

Educator, protector of the Indians, building superintendent of telegraph lines.

Candido Fontoura (1885-1974) A1067

Brapex VI A1068

1985, May 14 *Perf. 12x11½*
1997 A1067 220cr multi 15 15

Pioneer of the Brazilian pharmaceutical industry.

1985, May 18 *Perf. 11½x11*

Cave paintings: No. 1998, Deer, Cerca Grande. No. 1999, Lizards, Lapa do Caboclo. No. 2000, Running deer, Grande Abrigo de Santana do Riacho.

1998 A1068 300cr multi 15 15
1999 A1068 300cr multi 15 15
2000 A1068 2000cr multi 75 50
a. Souvenir sheet of 3, #1998-2000, perf. 10½x11 1.00 1.00
Nos. 1998-2000 (3) 1.05
Set value 66

Wildlife Conservation A1069

Birds in Marinho dos Abrolhos National Park.

1985, June 5 *Perf. 11½x12*
2001 A1069 220cr Fregata magnificens 15 15
2002 A1069 220cr Sula dactylatra 15 15
2003 A1069 220cr Anous stolidus 15 15
2004 A1069 2000cr Pluvialis squatarola 60 25
Nos. 2001-2004 (4) 1.05
Set value 40

A1070

A1071

1985, June 11 *Perf. 12x11½*
2005 A1070 220cr Mother breastfeeding infant 15 15
2006 A1070 220cr Hand, eyedropper, children 15 15
a. Pair, #2005-2006 25 15

UN infant survival campaign.

1985, June 22 Litho. *Perf. 11½x11*

Helicopter rescue, search ship, diver.

2007 A1071 220cr multi 15 15

Sea Search & Rescue.

Souvenir Sheet

World Cup Soccer, Mexico, 1986 A1072

1985, June 23 *Perf. 11*
2008 A1072 2000cr Player dribbling, World Cup 4.00 85

Intl. Youth Year — A1073

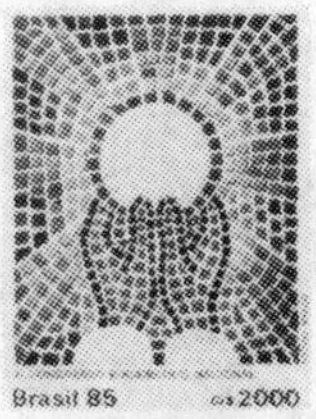

11th Natl. Eucharistic Congress — A1074

1985, June 28 *Perf. 12*
2009 A1073 220cr Circle of children 15 15

1985, July 16 *Perf. 12x11½*
2010 A1074 2000cr Mosaic, Priest raising host 55 38

Director Humberto Mauro, Scene from Sangue Mineiro, 1929
A1075

1985, July 27
2011 A1075 300cr multi 15 15

Cataguases Studios, 60th anniv.

Escola e Sacro Museum, Convent St. Anthony, Joao Pessoa, Paraiba
A1076

1985, Aug. 5 *Perf. 11½x12*
2012 A1076 330cr multi 15 15

Paraiba State 400th anniv.

Inconfidencia Museum — A1077

Cabanagem Insurrection, 150th Anniv. — A1078

1985, Aug. 11 *Perf. 12x11½*
2013 A1077 300cr shown 15 15
2014 A1077 300cr Museum of History & Diplomacy 15 15
Set value 20 16

1985, Aug. 14

Design: Revolutionary, detail from an oil painting by Guido Mondin.

2015 A1078 330cr multi 15 15

AMX Subsonic Air Force Fighter Plane
A1079

1985, Aug. 19 *Perf. 11½x12*
2016 A1079 330cr multi 15 15

AMX Project, joint program with Italy.

16th-17th Century Military Uniforms — A1080

1985, Aug. 26 *Perf. 12x11½*
2017 A1080 300cr Captain, crossbowman 16 15
2018 A1080 300cr Harquebusier, sergeant 16 15
2019 A1080 300cr Musketeer, pikeman 16 15
2020 A1080 300cr Fusilier, pikeman 16 15
Nos. 2017-2020 (4) 64
Set value 48

Farrouphilha Insurrection, 150th Anniv.
A1081

Design: Bento Goncalves and insurrectionist cavalry on Southern battlefields, detail of an oil painting by Guido Mondin.

1985, Sept. 20 *Perf. 11½x12*
2021 A1081 330cr multi 15 15

Aparados da Serra National Park
A1082

1985, Sept. 23
2022 A1082 3100cr Ravine 65 52
2023 A1082 3320cr Mountains 70 55
2024 A1082 3480cr Forest, waterfall 75 60
Nos. 2022-2024 (3) 2.10 1.67

President-elect Tancredo Neves — A1083

Design: Portrait, Natl. Congress, Alvorada Palace, Federal Supreme Court.

1985, Oct. 10 **Litho.** *Perf. 11x11½*
2025 A1083 330cr multi 15 15

FEB, Postmark
A1084

1985, Oct. 10 *Perf. 11½x12*
2026 A1084 500cr multi 15 15

Brazilian Expeditionary Force Postal Service, 41st anniv.

Rio de Janeiro-Niteroi Ferry Service, 150th Anniv. — A1085

1985, Oct. 14 *Perf. 11½x12*
2027 A1085 500cr Segunda 20 15
2028 A1085 500cr Terceira 20 15
2029 A1085 500cr Especuladora 20 15
2030 A1085 500cr Urca 20 15
Nos. 2027-2030 (4) 80 60

Muniz M-7 Inaugural Flight, 50th Anniv. — A1086

1985, Oct. 22
2031 A1086 500cr multi 15 15

UN 40th Anniv. — A1087

Natl. Press System — A1088

1985, Oct. 24 *Perf. 11½x11*
2032 A1087 500cr multi 15 15

1985, Nov. 7
2033 A1088 500cr Newspaper masthead, reader 15 15

Diario de Pernambuco, newspaper, 160th anniv.

Christmas 1985
A1089

1985, Nov. 11 *Perf. 11½x12*
2034 A1089 500cr Christ in Manger 20 15
2035 A1089 500cr Adoration of the Magi 20 15
2036 A1089 500cr Flight to Egypt 20 15
Nos. 2034-2036 (3) 60 45

State Flag Type

State Flags: a, Para. b, Rio Grande do Sul. c, Acre. d, Sao Paulo.

1985, Nov. 19 *Perf. 12*
2037 Block of 4 80 60
a.-d. A1050 500cr, any single 20 15

Thanksgiving Day — A1091

1985, Nov. 28 *Perf. 12x11½*
2038 A1091 500cr Child gathering wheat 20 15

Economic Development of Serra dos Carajas Region
A1092

1985, Dec. 11 **Litho.** *Perf. 11½x12*
2039 A1092 500cr multi 15 15

Fr. Bartholomeu Lourenco de Gusmao (1685-1724), Inventor, the Aerostat
A1093

1985, Dec. 19 **Litho.** *Perf. 11x11½*
2040 A1093 500cr multi 15 15

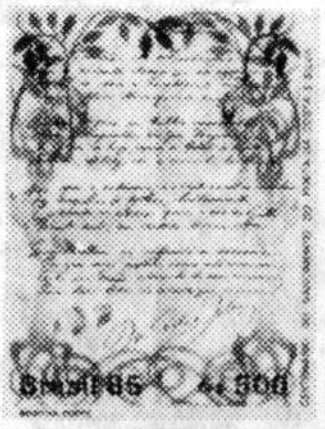
A1094

A1095

The Trees, by Da Costa E Silva (b. 1885), poet.

1985, Dec. 20 **Litho.** *Perf. 12x11½*
2041 A1094 500cr multi 15 15

1986, Mar. 3 **Litho.** *Perf. 11*
Souvenir Sheet
2042 A1095 10000cr multi 2.25 2.00

1986 World Cup Soccer Championships, Mexico. LUBRAPEX '86, philatelic exhibition.

Halley's Comet — A1096

1986, Apr. 11 **Litho.** *Perf. 11½x12*
2043 A1096 50c multi 15 15

Commander Ferraz Antarctic Station, 2nd Anniv.
A1097

1986, Apr. 25
2044 A1097 50c multi 15 15

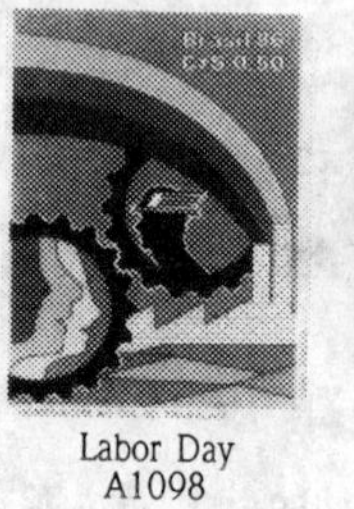
Labor Day
A1098

Maternity, by Henrique Bernardelli (1858-1936)
A1099

1986, May 1 **Litho.** *Perf. 12x11½*
2045 A1098 50c multi 15 15

1986, May 8
2046 A1099 50c multi 15 15

Amnesty Intl., 25th Anniv. A1100

1986, May 28 Litho. *Perf. 11½x12*

2047 A1100 50c multi	15	15

Butterflies — A1101

1985, June 5 *Perf. 12x11½*

2048 A1101 50c Pyrrhopyge ruficauda	15	15
2049 A1101 50c Prepona eugenes diluta	15	15
2050 A1101 50c Pierriballia mandel molione	15	15
Nos. 2048-2050 (3)	45	
Set value		15

Score from Opera "Il Guarani" and Antonio Carlos Gomes (1836-1896), Composer A1102

1986, July 11 *Perf. 11½x12*

2051 A1102 50c multi	18	15

Natl. Accident Prevention Campaign — A1103

Stamp Day — A1104

1986, July 30 Litho. *Perf. 11½x11*

2052 A1103 50c Lineman	15	15

Souvenir Sheet

1986, Aug. 1 *Perf. 11*

2053 A1104 5cz No. 53	85	35

Brazilian Phil. Soc., 75th anniv., and Dom Pedro II issue, Nos. 53-60, 120th anniv.

Architecture A1105

Famous Men A1106

Designs: 10c, House of Garcia D'Avila, Nazare de Mata, Bahia. 20c, Church of Our Lady of the Assumption, Anchieta Village. 50c, Fort Reis Magos, Natal. 1cz, Pilgrim's Column, Alcantara Village, 1648. 2cz, Cloisters, St. Francis Convent, Olinda. 5cz, St. Anthony's Chapel, Sao Roque. 10cz, St. Lawrence of the Indians Church, Niteroi. 20cz, Principe da Beiro Fort, Mato Dentro. 50cz, Jesus of Matozinhos Church, vert. 100cz, Church of our Lady of Sorrow, Campanha. 200cz, Casa dos Contos, Ouro Preto. 500cz, Antiga Alfandega, Belem, Para.

Perf. 11½x11, 11x11½

1986-88 **Photo.**

2055 A1105	10c sage grn	15	15
2057 A1105	20c brt blue	15	15
2059 A1105	50c orange	15	15
2064 A1105	1cz golden brn	15	15
2065 A1105	2cz dull rose	25	18
a.	Litho. ('88)	15	15
2067 A1105	5cz lt olive grn	60	45
a.	Litho. ('88)	15	15
2068 A1105	10cz slate blue	50	35
2069 A1105	20cz lt red brn	75	58
2070 A1105	50cz brn org	2.25	1.75
2071 A1105	100cz dull grn	2.70	2.00
2072 A1105	200cz deep blue	2.50	1.85
2073 A1105	500cz dull red brn	1.30	1.00
Nos. 2055-2073 (12)		11.45	8.76

Issue dates: 10c, Aug. 11. 20c, Dec. 8; 50c, Aug. 19. 1cz, Nov. 19; 2cz, Nov. 9; 5cz, Dec. 30; 10cz, June 2, 1987; 20cz, 50cz, Sept. 18, 1987. 100cz, Dec. 21, 1987. 200cz, May 9, 1988. 500cz, Nov. 22, 1988.

This is an expanding set. Numbers will change if necessary.

1986 *Perf. 12x11½, 11½x12*

Designs: No. 2074, Juscelino Kubitschek de Oliveira, president 1956-61, and Alvorado Palace, Brasilia. No. 2075, Octavio Mangabeira, statesman, and Itamaraty Palace, Rio de Janeiro, horiz.

2074 A1106	50c multi	15	15
2075 A1106	50c multi	15	15
	Set value	15	15

Issue dates: #2074, Aug. 21. #2075, Aug. 27.

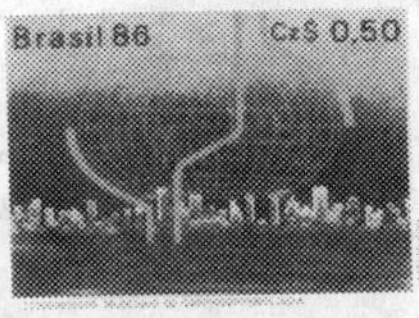

World Gastroenterology Congress, Sao Paulo — A1107

1986, Sept. 7 *Perf. 11½x12*

2076 A1107	50c multi	15	15

Federal Broadcasting System, 50th Anniv. — A1108

Intl. Peace Year — A1109

1986, Sept. 15 *Perf. 12x11½*

2077 A1108	50c multi	15	15

1986, Sept. 16

Painting (detail): War and Peace, by Candido Portinari.

2078 A1109	50c multi	15	15

Ernesto Simoes Filho (b. 1886), Publisher of La Tarde A1110

1986, Oct. 4 Litho. *Perf. 11½x12*

2079 A1110	50c multi	15	15

Famous Men — A1111

Federal Savings Bank, 125th Anniv. — A1112

Designs: No. 2080, Title page from manuscript, c. 1683-94, by Gregorio Mattose e Guerra (b. 1636), author. No. 2081, Manuel Bandeira (1886-1968), poet, text from I'll Go Back to Pasargada.

1986, Oct. 29 *Perf. 11½x11*

2080 A1111	50c lake & beige	15	15
2081 A1111	50c lake & dl grn	15	15
	Set value	20	15

1986, Nov. 4 *Perf. 12x11½*

2082 A1112	50c multi	15	15

Flowering Plants A1113

Glauber Rocha, Film Industry Pioneer A1114

Perf. 12x11½, 11½x12

1986, Sept. 23

2083 A1113	50c Urera mitis	15	15
2084 A1113	6.50cz Couroupita guyanensis	52	40
2085 A1113	6.90cz Bauhinia variegata, horiz.	55	42
Nos. 2083-2085 (3)		1.22	97

1986, Nov. 20 *Perf. 12x11½*

2086 A1114	50c multi	15	15

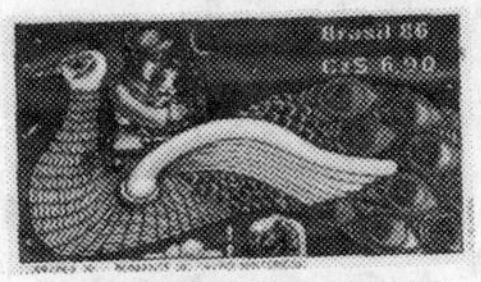

LUBRAPEX '86 — A1115

Cordel Folk Tales: No. 2087, Romance of the Mysterious Peacock. No. 2088, History of the Empress Porcina.

1986, Nov. 21 *Perf. 11x12*

2087 A1115	6.90cz multi	45	35
2088 A1115	6.90cz multi	45	35
a.	Souvenir sheet of 2, #2087-2088, perf. 11	1.10	85

Christmas A1116

Birds: 50c, And Christ child. 6.50cz, And tree. 7.30cz, Eating fruit.

1986, Nov. 10 *Perf. 11½x12*

2089 A1116	50c multi	15	15
2090 A1116	6.50cz multi	65	48
2091 A1116	7.30cz multi	75	58
Nos. 2089-2091 (3)		1.55	1.21

Military Uniforms, c. 1930 — A1117

Bartolomeu de Gusmao Airport, 50th Anniv. — A1118

Designs: No. 2092, Navy lieutenant commander, dreadnought Minas Gerais. No. 2093, Army flight lieutenant, WACO S.C.O. biplane, Fortaleza Airport.

1986, Dec. 15 *Perf. 12x11½*

2092 A1117	50c multi	15	15
2093 A1117	50c multi	15	15
	Set value	15	15

Fortaleza Air Base, 50th anniv. (No. 2093).

1986, Dec. 26

2094 A1118	1cz multi	15	15

Heitor Villa Lobos (1887-1959), Conductor — A1119

1987, Mar. 5 Litho. *Perf. 12x11½*

2095 A1119	1.50cz multi	15	15

Natl. Air Force C-130 Transport Plane, Flag, the Antarctic A1120

1987, Mar. 9 *Perf. 11x11½*

2096 A1120	1cz multi	15	15

Antarctic Project.

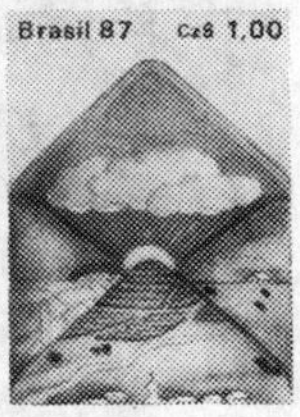

Special Mail Services — A1121

1987, Mar. 20 *Perf. 12x11½*

2097 A1121	1cz Rural delivery	15	15
2098 A1121	1cz Intl. express	15	15
	Set value	20	16

TELECOM '87, Geneva A1122

1987, May 5 *Perf. 11½x12*

2099 A1122 2cz Brazilsat, wave, globe 20 15

10th Pan American Games, Indianapolis, Aug. 7-25 — A1123

1987, May 20 *Perf. 12x11½*

2100 A1123 18cz multi 1.00 75

Natl. Fine Arts Museum, 150th Anniv A1124

1987, Jan. 13 *Perf. 11½x12*

2101 A1124 1cz multi 15 15

Marine Conservation — A1125

1987, June 5

2102 A1125	2cz	Eubalaena australis	15	15
2103 A1125	2cz	Eretmochelys imbricata	15	15
		Set value		20

Federal Court of Appeal, 40th Anniv. A1126

1987, June 15

2104 A1126 2cz multi 15 15

Military Club, Cent. — A1127

1987, June 26 *Perf. 12x11½*

2105 A1127 3cz multi 18 15

> ***Set Values***
> *A 15-cent minimum now applies to individual stamps and sets. Where the 15-cent minimum per stamp would increase the value of a set beyond retail, there is a "Set Value" notation giving the retail value of the set.*

Agriculture Institute of Campinas, Cent. A1128

1987, June 27 *Perf. 11½x12*

2106 A1128 2cz multi 15 15

Entomological Society, 50th Anniv. A1129

1987, July 17

2107 A1129	3cz	Zoolea lopiceps	15	15
2108 A1129	3cz	Fulgora servillei	15	15
		Set value		20

Natl. Tourism Year A1130

Designs: No. 2109, Monuments and Sugarloaf Mountain, Rio de Janeiro. No. 2110, Colonial church, sailboats, parrot, cashews.

1987, Aug. 4

2109 A1130	3cz	multi	15	15
2110 A1130	3cz	multi	15	15

Royal Portuguese Cabinet of Literature, 150th Anniv. — A1131

1987, Aug. 27 *Perf. 12x11½*

2111 A1131 30cz ver & brt grn 1.10 85

Sport Club Intl. — A1132

Championship soccer clubs, Brazil's Gold Cup: b, Sao Paulo. c, Guarani. d, Regatas do Flamengo.

1987, Aug. 29 *Perf. 11½x12*

2112	Block of 4	60	40
a.-d.	A1132 3cz any single	15	15

St. Francis Convent, 400th Anniv. A1133

1987, Oct. 4

2113 A1133 4cz multi 20 15

Jose Americo de Almeida, Author A1134

Design: Characters from romance novel, "A Bagaceira," 1928, and portrait of author.

1987, Oct. 23 **Litho.** *Perf. 11x11½*

2114 A1134 4cz multi 18 15

Spanish Galleons Anchored in Recife Port, 1537 A1135

1987, Nov. 12 **Litho.** *Perf. 11½x12*

2115 A1135 5cz Harbor entrance 18 15

Recife City, 450th anniv.

Thanksgiving A1136

1987, Nov. 26 *Perf. 12x11½*

2116 A1136 5cz multi 18 15

Christmas 1987 A1137

1987, Nov. 30 *Perf. 11½x12*

2117 A1137	6cz	Shepherd and flock	20	15
2118 A1137	6cz	Christmas pageant	20	15
2119 A1137	6cz	Six angels	20	15
		Nos. 2117-2119 (3)	60	45

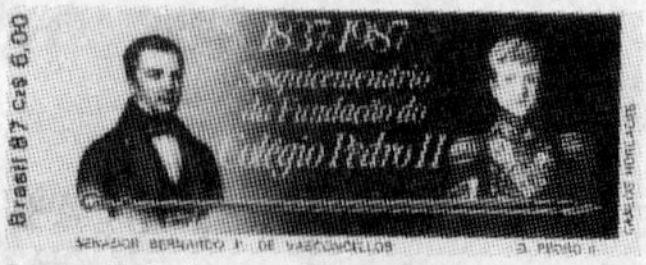

Pedro II College, 150th Anniv. — A1138

Gold pen Emperor Pedro II used to sign edict establishing the school, and Senator Bernardo Pereira de Vasconcellos, founder.

1987, Dec. 2

2120 A1138 6cz multi 18 15

Natl. Orchid Growers' Soc., 50th Anniv. A1139

1987, Dec. 3

2121 A1139	6cz	Laelia lobata veitch	20	15
2122 A1139	6cz	Cattleya guttata lindley	20	15

Marian Year — A1140

Statue of Our Lady and Basilica at Fatima, Portugal.

1987, Dec. 20 *Perf. 12x11½*

2123 A1140 50cz multi 1.10 85

Exhibit of the Statue of Our Lady of Fatima in Brazil.

Descriptive Treatise of Brazil, by Gabriel S. de Sousa, 400th Anniv. A1141

1987, Dec. 21 **Litho.** *Perf. 11x11½*

2124 A1141 7cz multi 20 16

Natl. Archives, 150th Anniv. A1142

Design: Text from illuminated Gregorian canticle and computer terminal.

1988, Jan. 5 *Perf. 11½x12*

2125 A1142 7cz multi 20 16

Opening of Brazilian Ports to Ships of Friendly Nations, 180th Anniv. A1143

1988, Jan. 28 *Perf. 11x11½*

2126 A1143 7cz multi 24 18

Souvenir Sheet

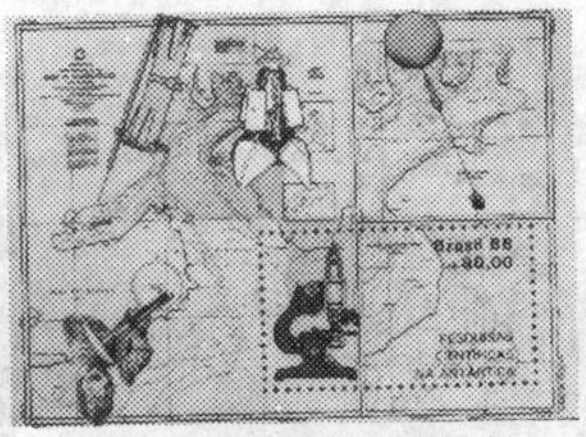

Antarctic Research — A1144

1988, Feb. 9 Litho. *Perf. 11*
2127 A1144 80cz multi 2.00 2.00

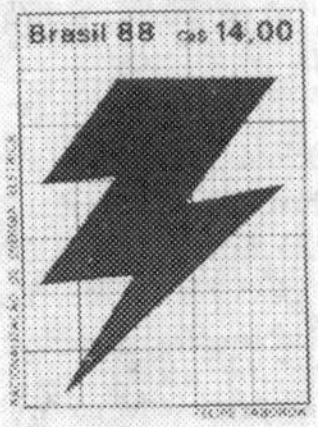

Energy Resources — A1145

1988, Mar. 15 Litho. *Perf. 12x11½*
2128 A1145 14cz Electricity 22 16
2129 A1145 14cz Fossil fuels 22 16

Souvenir Sheet

Brazilians as Formula 1 World Champions in 1981, 1983, 1987 — A1146

1988, Mar. 30 *Perf. 11*
2130 A1146 300cz multi 4.50 4.50

Jose Bonifacio, Armorial and Masonic Emblems — A1147

1988, Apr. 6 *Perf. 12x11½*
2131 A1147 20cz multi 30 24

Jose Bonifacio de Andrada e Silva (c. 1763-1838), geologist and prime minister under Pedro I who supported the movement for independence from Portugal and was exiled for opposing the emperor's advisors.

Abolition of Slavery, Cent. — A1148

Telecom '88 — A1149

Designs: 20cz, Declaration and quill pen. 50cz, Slave ship and maps of African coastline and slave trade route between Africa and South America.

1988, May 12 Litho. *Perf. 12x11½*
2132 A1148 20cz multi 25 18
2133 A1148 50cz multi 65 50

1988, May 16 *Perf. 11½x11*
2134 A1149 50cz multi 60 45

Jesus of Matosinhos Sanctuary A1150

1988, May 16 *Perf. 11½x12*
2135 A1150 20cz shown 22 16
2136 A1150 50cz Pilot plan of Brazilia 58 45
2137 A1150 100cz Salvador historic district 1.20 90
Nos. 2135-2137 (3) 2.00 1.51

LUBRAPEX '88. World heritage list.

Japanese Immigrants in Brazil, 80th Anniv. — A1151

1988, June 18 Litho. *Perf. 11½x11*
2138 A1151 100cz multi 75 55

A1152

A1153

1988, July 1 Photo. *Perf. 13*
2139 A1152 (A) brt blue 22 16

No. 2139 met the first class inland letter postage rate (28cz).
See Nos. 2201, 2218.

1988, July 14 Litho. *Perf. 12x11½*
2140 A1153 20cz Judo 22 16

1988 Summer Olympics, Seoul.

Wildlife Conservation A1154

1988, July 24 *Perf. 11½x12*
2141 A1154 20cz Myrmecophaga tridactyla 15 15
2142 A1154 50cz Chaetomys subspinosus 32 24
2143 A1154 100cz Speothos venaticus 65 48
Nos. 2141-2143 (3) 1.12 87

Souvenir Sheet

The Motherland, 1919 by Pedro Bruno — A1155

1988, Aug. 1 Litho. *Perf. 11*
2144 A1155 250cz multi 1.50 1.50

Stamp Day, BRASILIANA '89.

Natl. Confederation of Industries, 50th Anniv. — A1156

1988, Aug. 12 *Perf. 11½x12*
2145 A1156 50cz multi 26 20

Soccer Clubs A1157

No. 2146, Recife, Pernambuco. No. 2147, Coritiba, Parana. 100cz, Gremio, Porto Alegre, Rio Grando do Sul. 200cz, Fluminense, Rio de Janeiro.

1988, Sept. 29 *Perf. 11½x12*
2146 A1157 50cz multi 16 15
2147 A1157 50cz multi 16 15
2148 A1157 100cz multi 32 22
2149 A1157 200cz multi 60 48
a. Block of 4, #2146-2149 1.25 95

Poems, 1888 A1158

Portraits and text: 50cz, *O Ateneu*, by Raul Pompeia. 100cz, *Poesias*, by Olavo Bilac.

1988, Oct. 28 *Perf. 11x11½*
2150 A1158 50cz multi 15 15
2151 A1158 100cz multi 26 20

Souvenir Sheet

1988 Democratic Constitution for the Union of the People and the State — A1159

1988, Oct. 5 Litho. *Perf. 11*
2152 A1159 550cz Government building 2.40 2.40

Origami Art — A1160

1988, Nov. 11 Litho. *Perf. 11½x12*
2153 A1160 50cz Abbey, nuns 15 15
2154 A1160 100cz Nativity 25 20
2155 A1160 200cz Santa Claus, presents 52 38
Nos. 2153-2155 (3) 92 73

Christmas.

ARBRAFEX Philatelic Exhibition of Argentina and Brazil A1161

1988, Nov. 26
2156 A1161 400cz multi 85 65

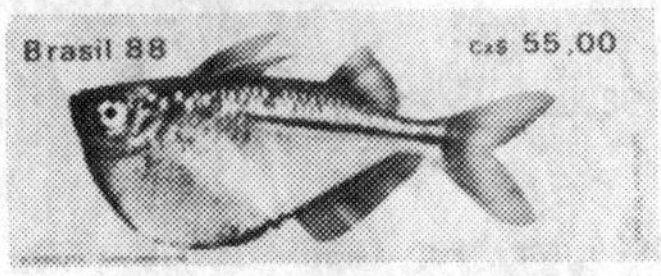

Fresh-water Fish — A1162

Designs: a, *Gasteropelecus*. b, *Osteoglossum ferreirai*. c, *Moenkhausia*. d, *Xavantei*. e, *Ancistrus hoplogenys*. f, *Brochis splendens*. Se-tenant in a continuous design.
Illustration reduced.

1988, Nov. 29 Litho. *Perf. 11½x12*
2157 Block of 6 90 72
a.-f. A1162 55cz any single 15 15

Souvenir Sheet

BRAPEX '88, Ecological Preservation — A1163

1988, Dec. 10 *Perf. 11*
2158 Sheet of 3 1.80 1.80
a. A1163 100cz Parrot 25 25
b. A1163 250cz Plant 60 60
c. A1163 400cz Pelican 95 95

Satellite Dishes
A1164

Performing Arts
A1165

1988, Dec. 20 ***Perf. 12x11½***
2159 A1164 70cz multi 18 15

Ansat 10-Earth satellite station communication.

1988, Dec. 21
2160 A1165 70cz multi 18 15

Court of Justice, Bahia, 380th Anniv. A1166

1989, Mar. 10 Litho. ***Perf. 11½x12***
2161 A1166 25c multi 42 32

Public Library Year — A1167

1989, Mar. 13 ***Perf. 11½***
2162 A1167 25c Library, Bahia, 1811 42 32

Brazilian Post & Telegraph Enterprise, 20th Anniv. A1168

Intl. and domestic postal services: a, Facsimile transmission (Post-Grama). b, Express mail (EMS). c, Parcel post (Sedex). d, Postal savings (CEFPostal).

1989, Mar. 20 ***Perf. 11½x12***
2163 Block of 4 1.65 1.25
a.-d. A1168 25c any single 40 30

Souvenir Sheet

Ayrton Senna, 1988 Formula 1 World Champion — A1169

1989, Mar. 23
2164 A1169 2cz multi 4.00 4.00

Environmental Conservation A1170

1989, Apr. 6 Litho. ***Perf. 12x11½***
2165 A1170 25c multi 35 25

Mineira Inconfidencia Independence Movement, Bicent. — A1171

Designs: a, Pyramid, hand. b, Figure of a man, houses. c, Destruction of houses.

1989, Apr. 21 ***Perf. 11½x12***
2166 Strip of 3 1.30 95
a.-b. A1171 30c any single 38 28
c. A1171 40c multi 52 38

First rebellion against Portuguese dominion.

Military School, Rio de Janeiro, Cent. A1172

1989, May 6 Litho. ***Perf. 11½x12***
2167 A1172 50c multi 50 38

Flowering Plants A1173

1989, June 5 ***Perf. 11½x12, 12x11½***
2168 A1173 50c *Pavonia alnifolia* 60 45
2169 A1173 1cz *Worsleya rayneri* 1.25 90
2170 A1173 1.50cz *Heliconia farinosa* 1.75 1.40
Nos. 2168-2170 (3) 3.60 2.75

Nos. 2169-2170 vert.

Barreto and Recife Law School, Pedro II Square A1174

1989, June 7 ***Perf. 11x11½***
2171 A1174 50c multi 65 48

Tobias Barreto (b. 1839), advocate of Germanization of Brazil.

Cultura Broadcasting System, 20th Anniv. — A1175

1989, June 27 Litho. ***Perf. 11½x12***
2172 A1175 50c multi 60 45

Aviation A1176

1989, July 7
2173 A1176 50c Ultra-light aircraft 52 40
2174 A1176 1.50cz Eiffel Tower, *Demoiselle* 1.65 1.10

Flight of Santos-Dumont's *Demoiselle,* 80th anniv (1.50cz).

Indigenous Flora — A1177

1989 Photo. ***Perf. 11x11½, 11½x11***
2176 A1177 10c *Dichorisandra,* vert. 15 15
2177 A1177 20c *Quiabentia zehnteri* 22 16
2178 A1177 50c *Bougainvillea glabra* 52 42
2179 A1177 1cz *Impatiens specie* 1.00 80
2180 A1177 2cz *Chorisia crispiflora* 25 18
2181 A1177 5cz *Hibiscus trilineatus* 60 45
Nos. 2176-2181 (6) 2.74 2.16

Issue dates: 10c, July 4; 20c, June 21; 50c, June 26; 1cz, June 19. 2cz, 5cz, Dec. 4.
No. 2181 vert.
See Nos. 2259-2273.

Souvenir Sheet

Largo da Carioca, by Nicolas Antoine Taunay — A1179

1989, July 7 Litho. ***Perf. 11***
2197 A1179 3cz multi 3.00 3.00

PHILEXFRANCE '89, French revolution bicent.

Cut and Uncut Gemstones — A1180

1989, July 12 Litho. ***Perf. 12x11½***
2198 A1180 50c Tourmaline 40 30
2199 A1180 1.50cz Amethyst 1.20 90

Souvenir Sheet

Paco Imperial, Rio de Janeiro, and Map — A1181

1989, July 28 ***Perf. 11***
2200 A1181 5cz multi 3.75 3.75

BRASILANA '89.

Type of 1988 Redrawn

1989, July 26 Photo. ***Perf. 13***

Size: 17x21mm

2201 A1152 (A) org & brt blue 18 15

Size of type and postal emblem are smaller on No. 2201; "le PORTE" is at lower left.

No. 2201 met the first class inland letter postage rate (cz).

Pernambuco Commercial Assoc., 150th Anniv. A1182

1989, Aug. 1 Litho. ***Perf. 11½x12***
2202 A1182 50c multi 40 30

Photography, 150th Anniv. — A1183

1989, Aug. 14
2203 A1183 1.50cz multi 1.10 85

1st Hydroelecric Power Station in South America, Marmelos-o, Cent. A1184

1989, Sept. 5 Litho. ***Perf. 11½x12***
2204 A1184 50c multi 35 25

Conchs Endemic to the Brazilian Coast A1185

1989, Sept. 8
2205 A1185 50c *Voluta ebraea* 32 22
2206 A1185 1cz *Morum matthewsi* 60 45
2207 A1185 1.50cz *Agaronia travassosi* 90 65
Nos. 2205-2207 (3) 1.82 1.32

Wildlife conservation.

America Issue
A1186

UPAE emblem and pre-Columbian stone carvings: 1cz, Muiraquita ritual statue, vert. 4cz, Ceramic brazier under three-footed votive urn.

Perf. 12x11½, 11½x12

1989, Oct. 12 — Litho.

2208 A1186	1cz multicolored	48	35
2209 A1186	4cz shown	1.85	1.40

Discovery of America 500th anniv. (in 1992).

A1187

A1188

Hologram and: a. *Lemons*, by Danilo di Prete. b. *O Indio E A Suacuapara*, by sculptor Victor Brecheret. c. Francisco Matarazzo.

1989, Oct. 14 — *Perf. 11*

Souvenir Sheet

2210	Sheet of 3	3.75	3.75
a.	A1187 2cz multicolored	.72	.72
b.	A1187 3cz multicolored	1.10	1.10
c.	A1187 5cz multicolored	1.75	1.75

Sao Paulo 20th intl. art biennial.

1989, Oct. 26 — *Perf. 11½x11*

Writers, residences and quotes: No. 2211, Casimiro de Abreu (b. 1839). No. 2212, Cora Coralina (b. 1889). No. 2213, Joaquim Machado de Assis (b. 1839).

2211 A1188	1cz shown	57	42
2212 A1188	1cz multicolored	57	42
2213 A1188	1cz multicolored	57	42
	Nos. 2211-2213 (3)	1.71	1.26

Federal Police Department, 25th Anniv. A1189

1989, Nov. 9 — *Perf. 11½x12*

2214 A1189	1cz multicolored	27	20

Christmas — A1190

Thanksgiving Day — A1191

1989, Nov. 10 — *Perf. 12x11½*

2215 A1190	70c Heralding angel	18	15
2216 A1190	1cz Holy family	24	18

1989, Nov. 23

2217 A1191	1cz multicolored	24	18

Type of 1988 Redrawn

1989, Nov. 6 — Photo. — *Perf. 13x13½*

Size: 22x26mm

2218 A1152	(B) org & dark red	2.00	1.50

Size of type and postal emblem are smaller on No. 2218; "1e PORTE" is at lower left.

No. 2218 met the first class intl. letter postage rate, initially at 9cz.

Souvenir Sheet

Proclamation of the Republic, Cent. — A1192

1989, Nov. 19 — Litho. — *Perf. 11*

2225 A1192	15cz multicolored	4.50	4.50

Bahia Sports Club, 58th Anniv. A1193

1989, Nov. 30 — *Perf. 11½x12*

2226 A1193	50c Soccer	15	15

Yellow Man, by Anita Malfatti (b. 1889) — A1194

1989, Dec. 2 — *Perf. 12x11½*

2227 A1194	1cz multicolored	26	20

Bahia State Public Archives, Cent. — A1195

1990, Jan. 16 — Litho. — *Perf. 11½x12*

2228 A1195	2cz multicolored	28	20

Brazilian Botanical Soc., 40th Anniv. A1196

1990, Jan. 21

2229 A1196	2cz Sabia, Caatinga	22	16
2230 A1196	13cz Pau, Brazil	1.40	1.10

Churches
A1197

Designs: 2cz, St. John the Baptist Cathedral, Santa Cruz do Sul, vert. 3cz, Our Lady of Victory Church, Oeiras. 5cz, Our Lady of the Rosary Church, Ouro Preto, vert.

1990, Feb. 5 — *Perf. 12x11½, 11½x12*

2231 A1197	2cz multicolored	16	15
2232 A1197	3cz multicolored	25	20
2233 A1197	5cz multicolored	42	32
	Nos. 2231-2233 (3)	83	67

Lloyd's of London in Brazil, Cent. A1198

1990, Feb. 19 — Litho. — *Perf. 11½x12*

2234 A1198	3cz multicolored	15	15

Souvenir Sheet

Antarctic Research Program — A1199

1990, Feb. 22 — Litho. — *Perf. 11*

2235 A1199	20cz Fauna, map	1.55	1.55

Vasco da Gama Soccer Club A1200

1990, Mar. 5

2236 A1200	10cz multicolored	48	38

Lindolfo Collor (b. 1890), Syndicated Columnist, and Labor Monument A1201

1990, Mar. 7

2237 A1201	20cz multicolored	95	70

A1202

A1203

Pres. Jose Sarney.

1990, Mar. 8 — *Perf. 12x11½*

2238 A1202	20cz chalky blue	95	70

1990, Apr. 6 — *Perf. 12x11½*

2239 A1203	20cz multicolored	70	52

AIDS prevention.

Souvenir Sheet

Penny Black, 150th Anniv. — A1204

Designs: 20cz, Dom Pedro, Brazil No. 1. 100cz, Queen Victoria, Great Britain No. 1.

1990, May 3 — Litho. — *Perf. 11*

2240 A1204	Sheet of 2	2.35	1.75
a.	20cr multicolored		
b.	100cr multicolored		

Central Bank, 25th Anniv. A1205

1990, Mar. 30 — Litho. — *Perf. 11½x12*

2241 A1205	20cr multicolored	70	52

Amazon River Postal Network, 21st Anniv. A1207

1990, Apr. 20 — *Perf. 11x11½*

2243 A1207	20cr multicolored	70	52

Souvenir Sheet

World Cup Soccer Championships, Italy — A1208

1990, May 12 — Litho. — *Perf. 12x11½*

2244 A1208	120cr multicolored	3.00	3.00

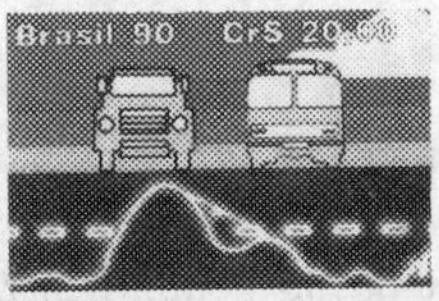

22nd Congress of the Intl. Union of Highway Transportation — A1209

1990, May 14 *Perf. 11½x12*
2245 A1209 20cr multicolored 65 48
2246 A1209 80cr multicolored 3.00 2.25
a. Pair, #2245-2246 3.75 2.75

No. 2246a has a continuous design.

Imperial Crown, 18th Cent. — A1210

Designs: No. 2248, Our Lady of Immaculate Conception, 18th cent.

1990, May 18 *Perf. 12x11½*
2247 A1210 20cr shown 68 52
2248 A1210 20cr multicolored 68 52

Imperial Museum, 50th anniv.(No. 2247). Mission Museum, 50th anniv. (No. 2248).

State Flags Type

1990, May 20 *Perf. 11½x12*
2249 A1050 20cr Tocantins 68 52

Army Geographical Service, Cent. — A1212

1990, May 30 *Perf. 11x11½*
2250 A1212 20cr multicolored 68 52

Film Personalities A1213

1990, June 19 *Perf. 11½x12*
2251 A1213 25cr Adhemar Gonzaga 80 60
2252 A1213 25cr Carmen Miranda 80 60
2253 A1213 25cr Carmen Santos 80 60
2254 A1213 25cr Oscarito 80 60
a. Block of 4, #2251-2254 3.20 2.40

France-Brazil House, Rio de Janeiro A1214

1990, July 14 Litho. *Perf. 11½x11*
2255 A1214 50cr multicolored 1.50 1.10

See France No. 2226.

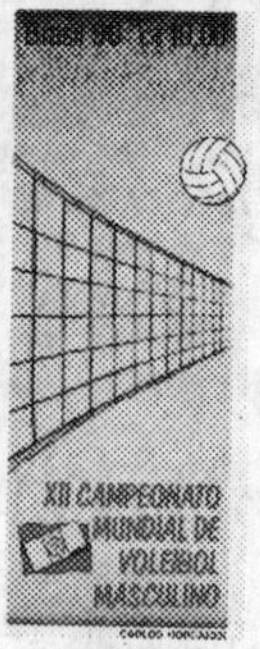

World Men's Volleyball Chmpships. A1215

Intl. Literacy Year A1217

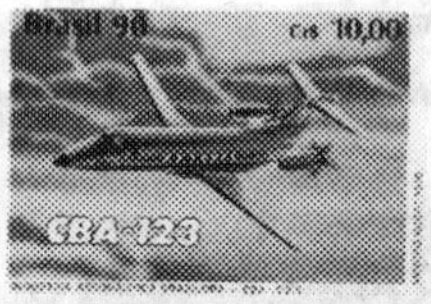

CBA 123 — A1216

1990, July 28 Litho. *Perf. 12x11½*
2256 A1215 10cr multicolored 30 24

1990, July 30 *Perf. 11½x12*
2257 A1216 10cr multicolored 30 24

1990, Aug. 22 *Perf. 12x11½*
2258 A1217 10cr multicolored 30 24

Flora Type of 1989
Perf. 11x11½, 11½x11

1989-93 **Photo.**

Design A1177

2259	1cr	like #2179	15	15
2260	2cr	like #2180	15	15
2261	5cr	like #2181	15	15
2262	10cr	Tibouchina granulosa	15	15
2263	20cr	Cassia macranthera	15	15
2264	50cr	Clitoria fairchildiana	28	15
2265	50cr	Tibouchina mutabilis	35	35
2266	100cr	Erythrina crista-galli, perf. 13	55	28
2267	200cr	Jacaranda mimosifolia	1.10	55
2268	500cr	Caesalpinia peltophoroides	2.75	1.40
2269	1000cr	Pachira aquatica	15	15
2270	2000cr	Hibiscus pernambucensis	15	15
2271	5000cr	Triplaris surinamensis	85	85
2272	10,000cr	Tabebuia heptaphylla	1.65	1.65
2273	20,000cr	Erythrina speciosa	2.25	2.25
		Nos. 2259-2273 (15)	10.83	8.53

Issued: 1cr, 11/8/90; 2cr, 11/12/90; 5cr, 11/16/90; #2264, 6/1/89; 10cr, 4/18/90; 20cr, 5/4/90; 100cr, 8/24/90; 200cr, 6/16/91; 500cr, 5/14/91; 1000cr, 9/2/92; 2000cr, 9/8/92; 5000cr, 10/16/92; 10,000cr, 11/16/92; 20,000cr, 4/25/93; #2265, 10/20/93.

Granbery Instutute, Cent. A1218

1990, Sept. 8 Litho. *Perf. 11½x12*
2279 A1218 13cr multicolored 40 28

18th Panamerican Railroad Congress A1219

1990, Sept. 9
2280 A1219 95cr multicolored 2.00 1.50

Embratel, 25th Anniv. — A1220

1990, Sept. 21
2281 A1220 13cr multicolored 40 30

LUBRAPEX '90 — A1221

Statues by Ceschiatti and Giorgi (No. 2283).

1990, Sept. 22
2282 A1221 25cr As Banhistas 62 45
2283 A1221 25cr Os Candangos 62 45
2284 A1221 100cr Evangelista Sao Joao 1.25 90
2285 A1221 100cr A Justica 1.25 90
a. Block of 4, #2282-2285 4.00 3.00
b. Souv. sheet of 4, #2282-2285 6.00 6.00

Praia Do Sul Wildlife Reserve A1222

1990, Oct. 12
2286 A1222 15cr Flowers 45 32
2287 A1222 105cr Shoreline 2.60 1.80
a. Pair, #2286-2287 3.05 2.12

Discovery of America, 500th anniv. (in 1992).

Natl. Library, 180th Anniv. A1223

Writers: No. 2289, Guilherme de Almeida (1890-1969). No. 2290, Oswald de Andrade (1890-1954).

1990, Oct. 29 Litho. *Perf. 11x11½*
2288 A1223 15cr multicolored 40 30
2289 A1223 15cr multicolored 40 30
2290 A1223 15cr multicolored 40 30
Nos. 2288-2290 (3) 1.20 90

Natl. Tax Court, Cent. A1224

1990, Nov. 7 Litho. *Perf. 11½x12*
2291 A1224 15cr multicolored 40 30

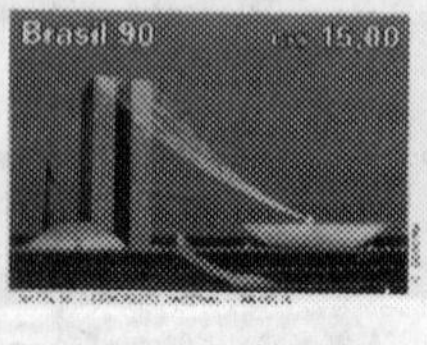

Christmas A1225

Architecture of Brasilia: No. 2292, National Congress. No. 2293, Television tower.

1990, Nov. 20
2292 A1225 15cr multicolored 40 30
2293 A1225 15cr multicolored 40 30

A1226

A1227

1990, Dec. 13 Litho. *Perf. 12x11½*
2294 A1226 15cr multicolored 18 15

Organization of American States, cent.

1990, Dec. 14
2295 A1227 15cr multicolored 18 15

First Flight of Nike Apache Missile, 25th anniv.

Colonization of Sergipe, Founding of Sao Cristovao, 400th Anniv. A1228

1990, Dec. 18 Litho. *Perf. 11½x12*
2296 A1228 15cr multicolored 18 15

World Congress of Physical Education A1229

1991, Jan. 7 *Perf. 11½x12*
2297 A1229 17cr multicolored 18 15

Rock in Rio II — A1230

1991, Jan. 9 *Perf. 12x11½*
2298 A1230 25cr Cazuza 20 15
2299 A1230 185cr Raul Seixas 1.65 1.00
a. Pair, #2298-2299 2.00 1.10

Printed in sheets of 12.

Ministry of Aviation, 50th Anniv. A1231

1991, Jan. 20 *Perf. 11x11½*
2300 A1231 17cr multicolored 20 15

A1232

A1233

Carnivals.

1991, Feb. 8 Litho. *Perf. 12x11½*

2301 A1232	25cr	Olinda	24	16
2302 A1232	30cr	Salvador	28	20
2303 A1232	280cr	Rio de Janeiro	2.50	2.00
		Nos. 2301-2303 (3)	3.02	2.36

1991, Feb. 20

2304 A1233 300cr multicolored 3.00 2.25

Visit by Pres. Collor to Antarctica.

Hang Gliding World Championships — A1234

1991, Feb. 24 *Perf. 11½x12*

2305 A1234 36cr multicolored 36 28

11th Pan American Games, 25th Summer Olympics A1235

1991, Mar. 30 Litho. *Perf. 11½x12*

2306 A1235	36cr	Sailing	32	24
2307 A1235	36cr	Rowing	32	24
2308 A1235	300cr	Swimming	2.50	1.90
a.		Block of 3, #2306-2308 + label	3.25	2.50

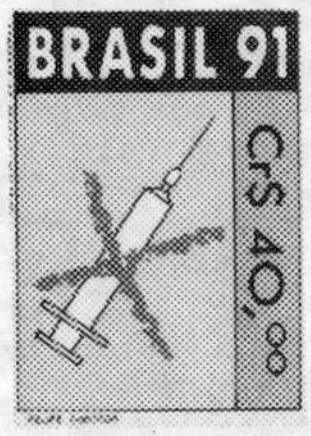

Fight Against Drugs A1236

Yanomami Indian Culture A1237

1991, Apr. 7 Litho. *Perf. 12x11½*

2309 A1236	40cr	Drugs	35	30
2310 A1236	40cr	Alcohol	35	30
2311 A1236	40cr	Smoking	35	30
		Nos. 2309-2311 (3)	1.05	90

Perf. 11½x11, 11x11½

1991, Apr. 19

2312 A1237	40cr	shown	35	28
2313 A1237	400cr	Indian, horiz.	3.50	2.75

Journal of Brazil, Cent. A1238

1991, Apr. 8 Litho. *Perf. 11x11½*

2314 A1238 40cr multicolored 35 28

Neochen Jubata (Orinoco Goose) — A1239

1991, June 5 Litho. *Perf. 12x11½*

2315 A1239 45cr multi 30 22

UN Conference on Development.

Snakes & Dinosaurs A1240

1991, June 6 *Perf. 11½x12*

2316 A1240	45cr	Bothrops jararaca	30	22
2317 A1240	45cr	Corallus caninus	30	22
a.		Pair, #2316-2317	60	45
2318 A1240	45cr	Teropods	30	22
2319 A1240	350cr	Sauropods	2.10	1.60
a.		Pair, #2318-2319	2.40	1.85
		Nos. 2316-2319 (4)	3.00	2.26

Flag of Brazil — A1241

1991, June 10 Photo. *Perf. 13x13½*

2320 A1241 A multicolored 25 20

Valued at inland letter rate (cr) on day of issue.

Fire Pumper A1242

1991, July 2 Litho. *Perf. 11½x12*

2321 A1242 45cr multicolored 30 22

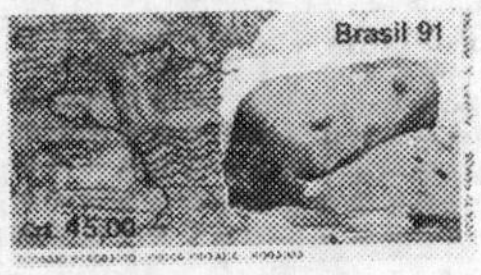

Tourism A1243

Map location and: 45cr, Painted stones, Roraima. 350cr, Dedo de Deus Mountain, Rio De Janeiro.

1991, July 6 *Perf. 11x11½*

2322 A1243	45cr	multicolored	28	20
2323 A1243	350cr	multicolored	2.00	1.50

Labor Laws, 50th Anniv. A1244

1991, Aug. 11 *Perf. 11½x12*

2324 A1244 45cr multicolored 30 22

Leonardo Mota, Birth Cent. A1245

1991, Aug. 22

2325 A1245 45cr buff, blk & red 30 22

Folklore Festival.

Jose Basilio da Gama (1741-1795), Poet A1246

Designs: No. 2327, Fagundes Varela (b. 1841), poet. No. 2328, Jackson de Figueiredo (b. 1891), writer.

1991, Aug. 29

2326 A1246	45cr	multicolored	26	18
2327 A1246	50cr	multicolored	30	22
2328 A1246	50cr	multicolored	30	22
		Nos. 2326-2328 (3)	86	62

12th Natl. Eucharistic Congress — A1247

1991, Oct. 6 Litho. *Perf. 12x11½*

2329 A1247	50cr	Pope John Paul II	18	15
2330 A1247	400cr	Map, crosses	1.40	1.05
a.		Pair, #2329-2330	1.60	1.20

Visit by Pope John Paul II.

First Brazilian Constitution, Cent. A1248

1991, Oct. 7 *Perf. 11½x12*

2331 A1248 50cr multicolored 18 15

Telecom '91 — A1249

1991, Oct. 8 *Perf. 12x11½*

2332 A1249 50cr multicolored 18 15

Sixth World Forum and Exposition on Telecommunications, Geneva, Switzerland.

America Issue A1250

UPAEP emblem and explorers: 50cr, Ferdinand Magellan (c. 1480-1521). 400cr, Francisco de Orellana (c. 1490-c. 1546).

1991, Oct. 12 *Perf. 11½x12*

2333 A1250	50cr	multicolored	18	15
2334 A1250	400cr	multicolored	1.40	1.05

Discovery of America, 500th anniv. (in 1992).

A1251

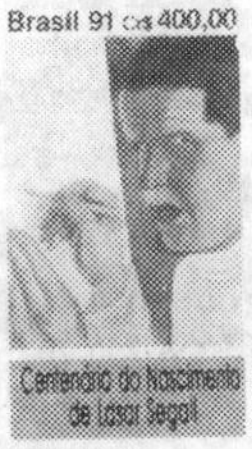

A1252

BRAPEX VIII (Orchids and Hummingbirds): 50cr, Colibri serrirostris, cattleya warneri. No. 2336, Chlorostilbon aureoventris, rodriguezia venusta. No. 2337, Clytolaema rubricauda, zygopetalum intermedium. No. 2338a, 50cr, Colibri serrirostris. b, 50cr, Chlorostilbon aureoventris. c, 500cr, Clytolaema rubricauda.

1991, Oct. 29 Litho. *Perf. 12x11½*

2335 A1251	50cr	multicolored	15	15
2336 A1251	65cr	multicolored	18	15
2337 A1251	65cr	multicolored	18	15
		Nos. 2335-2337 (3)	51	45

Souvenir Sheet

2338 A1251 Sheet of 3, #a.-c. 2.20 1.65

1991, Oct. 29 Litho. *Perf. 11½x11*

2339 A1252 400cr multicolored 90 65

Lasar Segall, artist, birth cent.

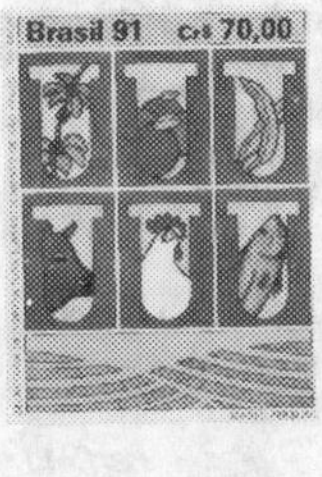

Bureau of Agriculture and Provision of Sao Paulo, Cent. — A1253

1991, Nov. 11 *Perf. 12x11½*

2340 A1253 70cr multicolored 20 15

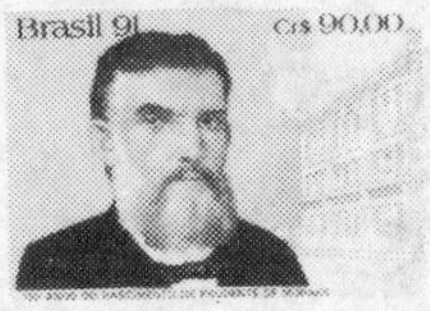

First Civilian Presidents, Birth Sesquicentennials — A1254

1991, Nov. 14 *Perf. 11½x12*

2341 A1254	70cr	Manuel de Campos Salles	20	15
2342 A1254	90cr	Prudente de Moraes Barros	25	18
a.		Pair, #2341-2342	45	35

Christmas
A1255

Thanksgiving
A1256

1991, Nov. 20 *Perf. 12x11½*
2343 A1255 70cr multicolored 20 15

1991, Nov. 28
2344 A1256 70cr multicolored 20 15

Military Police
A1257

1991, Dec. 1 *Perf. 11½x12*
2345 A1257 80cr multicolored 22 16

Souvenir Sheet

Emperor Dom Pedro (1825-1891) — A1258

Designs: No. 2346a, 80cr, Older age. b, 800cr, Wearing crown.

Litho. & Engr.
1991, Nov. 29 *Perf. 11*
2346 A1258 Sheet of 2, #a.-b. 2.50 2.50

BRASILIANA 93.

Churches — A1259

Designs: No. 2347, Presbyterian Church, Rio de Janeiro. No. 2348, First Baptist Church, Niteroi.

1992, Jan. 12 Litho. *Perf. 12x11½*
2347 A1259 250cr multicolored 30 22
2348 A1259 250cr multicolored 30 22

1992 Summer Olympics, Barcelona
A1260

Medalists in shooting, Antwerp, 1920: 300cr, Afranio Costa, silver. 2500cr, Guihlherme Paraense, gold.

1992, Jan. 28 *Perf. 11½x12*
2349 A1260 300cr multicolored 32 24
2350 A1260 2500cr multicolored 2.75 2.00

Port of Santos, Cent. — A1261

1992, Feb. 3 Litho. *Perf. 11½*
2351 A1261 300cr multicolored 45 35

Fauna of Fernando de Noronha Island
A1262

1992, Feb. 25 Litho. *Perf. 11½x12*
2352 A1262 400cr White-tailed tropicbirds 40 30
2353 A1262 2500cr Dolphins 2.50 1.75

Earth Summit, Rio de Janeiro.

Yellow Amaryllis — A1263

1992, Feb. 27 Photo. *Perf. 13½*
2354 A1263 (A) multicolored 25 20

No. 2354 met the second class domestic letter postage rate of 265cr on date of issue.

ARBRAFEX '92, Argentina-Brazil Philatelic Exhibition — A1264

Designs: No. 2355, Gaucho throwing bola at rhea. No. 2356, Man playing accordion, couple dancing. No. 2357, Couple in horse-drawn cart, woman. 1000cr, Gaucho throwing lasso at steer.
No. 2358c, 250cr, like #2356. d, 500cr, like #2355. e, 1500cr, like #2358.

1992, Mar. 20 Litho. *Perf. 11½x12*
2355 A1264 250cr multicolored 15 15
2356 A1264 250cr multicolored 15 15
2357 A1264 250cr multicolored 15 15
2358 A1264 1000cr multicolored 60 60
a. Block of 4, Nos. 2355-2358 1.05 1.05

Souvenir Sheet

2358B A1264 Sheet of 4, #2357, 2358c-2358e 1.05 1.05

1992 Summer Olympics, Barcelona — A1265

1992, Apr. 3 *Perf. 12x11½*
2359 A1265 300cr multicolored 18 18

Discovery of America, 500th Anniv.
A1266

1992, Apr. 24 *Perf. 11½x12*
2360 A1266 500cr Columbus' fleet 30 30
2361 A1266 3500cr Columbus, map 2.10 2.10
a. Pair, #2360-2361 2.40 2.40

Telebras Telecommunications System — A1267

1992, May 5 *Perf. 11x11½*
2362 A1267 350cr multicolored 20 20

Installation of 10 million telephones.

Langsdorff Expedition to Brazil, 170th Anniv.
A1268

Designs: No. 2363, Aime-Adrien Taunay, natives. No. 2364, Johann Moritz Rugendas, monkey . No. 2365, Hercule Florence, flowering plant. 3000cr, Gregory Ivanovitch Langsdorff, map.

1992, June 2 *Perf. 11½x12*
2363 A1268 500cr multicolored 25 25
2364 A1268 500cr multicolored 25 25
2365 A1268 500cr multicolored 25 25
2366 A1268 3000cr multicolored 1.50 1.50
Nos. 2363-2366 (4) 2.25 2.25

UN Conf. on Environmental Development, Rio.

UN Conference on Environmental Development, Rio de Janeiro — A1269

Globe and: No. 2367, Flags of Sweden and Brazil. No. 2368, City, grain, mountain and tree. 3000cr, Map of Brazil, parrot, orchid.

1992, June 3 Litho. *Perf. 11x11½*
2367 A1269 450cr multicolored 20 20
2368 A1269 450cr multicolored 20 20
2369 A1269 3000cr multicolored 1.50 1.50
Nos. 2367-2369 (3) 1.90 1.90

Ecology
A1270

Designs: No. 2370, Flowers, waterfall, and butterflies. No. 2371, Butterflies, canoe, and hummingbirds. No. 2372, Boy taking pictures of tropical birds. No. 2373, Armadillo, girl picking fruit.

1992, June 4 *Perf. 11½x12*
2370 A1270 500cr multicolored 25 25
2371 A1270 500cr multicolored 25 25
2372 A1270 500cr multicolored 25 25
2373 A1270 500cr multicolored 25 25
a. Strip of 4, #2370-2373 1.00 1.00

UN Conf. on Environmental Development, Rio.

Floral Paintings by Margaret Mee — A1271

1992, June 5 *Perf. 12x11½*
2374 A1271 600cr Nidularium innocentii 35 35
2375 A1271 600cr Canistrum exiguum 35 35
2376 A1271 700cr Canistrum cyathiforme 42 42
2377 A1271 700cr Nidularium rubens 42 42
Nos. 2374-2377 (4) 1.54 1.54

UN Conf. on Environmental Development, Rio.

Souvenir Sheet

Joaquim Jose da Silva Xavier (1748-1792), Patriot — A1272

1992, Apr. 21 Litho. & Engr. *Perf. 11*
2378 A1272 3500cr multicolored 2.10 2.10

Souvenir Sheet

Expedition of Alexandre Rodrigues Ferreira, Bicent.
A1273

Designs: a, 500cr, Sailing ships, gray and green hulls. b, 1000cr, Sailing ships, red hulls. c, 2500cr, Sailing ship at shore.

1992, May 9 Litho. *Perf. 11½x12*
2379 A1273 Sheet of 3, #a.-c. 2.40 2.40

Lubrapex '92.

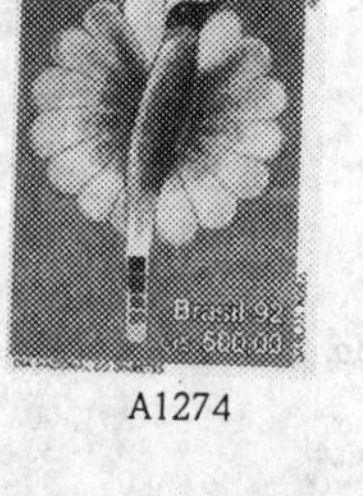

A1274

A1275

1992, June 5 Litho. *Perf. 12x11½*
2380 A1274 600cr Hummingbird 25 25

Diabetes Day.

1992, July 13 Litho. *Perf. 11½x11*
2381 A1275 550cr multicolored 25 25

Volunteer firemen of Joinville.

A1276 A1277

Serra da Capivara National Park: No. 2382, Leopard, animals, map of park. No. 2383, Canyon, map of Brazil.

1992, July 17 *Perf. 12x11½*

2382 A1276 550cr multicolored		22	22
2383 A1276 550cr multicolored		22	22
a. Pair, #2382-2383		45	45

1992, July 24

2384 A1277 550cr multicolored	25	25

Financing for studies and projects.

Natl. Service for Industrial Training, 50th Anniv. — A1278

1992, Aug. 5 *Perf. 11½x12*

2385 A1278 650cr multicolored	35	35

Fortresses A1279

1992, Aug. 19 Litho. *Perf. 11½x12*

2386 A1279 650cr Santa Cruz	28	28
2387 A1279 3000cr Santo Antonio	1.25	1.25

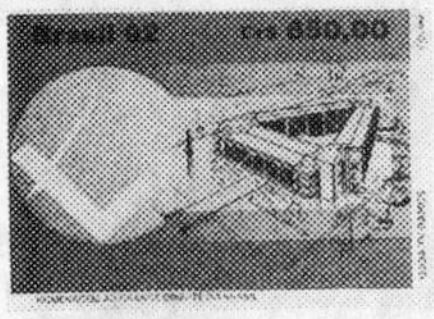

Masonic Square, Compass and Lodge A1280

1992, Aug. 20

2388 A1280 650cr multicolored	28	28

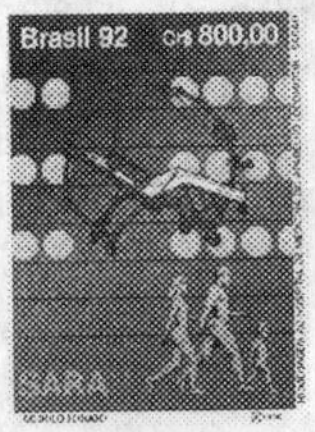

Brazilian Assistance Legion, 50th Anniv. A1281

Hospital of Medicine and Orthopedics A1282

1992, Aug. 28 *Perf. 12x11½*

2389 A1281 650cr multicolored	28	28

1992, Sept. 11

2390 A1282 800cr multicolored	30	30

Merry Christmas A1283

1992, Nov. 20 *Perf. 11½*

2391 A1283 (1) multicolored	25	25

No. 2391 met the first class domestic letter postage rate of 1090cr on day of issue.

Writers A1284

Designs: No. 2392, Graciliano Ramos (1892-1953), vert. No. 2393, Menotti del Picchia (1892-1988), vert. 1000cr, Assis Chateaubriand (1892-1968).

Perf. 12x11½, 11½x12

1992, Oct. 29 **Litho.**

2392 A1284 900cr multicolored	22	22
2393 A1284 900cr multicolored	22	22
2394 A1284 1000cr multicolored	28	28
Nos. 2392-2394 (3)	72	72

Expedition of Luis Cruls, Cent. A1285

1992, Nov. 11 *Perf. 11½x12*

2395 A1285 900cr multicolored	22	22

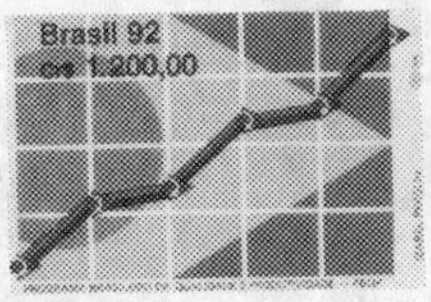

Brazillian Program for Quality and Productivity A1286

1992, Nov. 12

2396 A1286 1200cr multicolored	28	28

Souvenir Sheet

Tourism Year in the Americas — A1287

Designs: a, 1200cr, Mountains, coastline. b, 9000cr, Sugarloaf Mt., aerial tram, Rio de Janeiro.

1992, Nov. 18 Litho. *Perf. 11½x12*

2397 A1287 Sheet of 2, #a.-b.	2.00	2.00

Brasiliana '93.

Sister Irma Dulce A1288

1993, Mar. 13 Litho. *Perf. 11½x12*

2398 A1288 3500cr multicolored	35	35

Souvenir Sheet

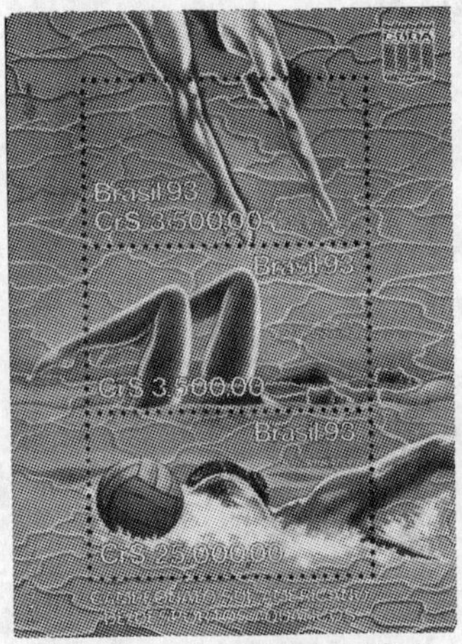

Water Sports Championships of South America — A1289

Designs: a, 3500cr, Diver. b, 3500cr, Synchronized swimmers. c, 25,000cr, Water polo.

1993, Mar. 21 Litho. *Perf. 11*

2399 A1289 Sheet of 3, #a.-c.	2.75	2.75

Curitiba, 300th Anniv. A1290

1993, Mar. 29

2400 A1290 4500cr multicolored	40	40

Health and Preservation of Life — A1291

Pedro Americo, 150th Birth Anniv. — A1292

Red Cross emblem and: No. 2401, Bleeding heart, flowers. No. 2402, Cancer symbol, breast. No. 2403, Brain waves, rainbow emerging from head.

1993, Apr. 7 Litho. *Perf. 12x11½*

2401 A1291 4500cr multicolored	30	30
2402 A1291 4500cr multicolored	30	30
2403 A1291 4500cr multicolored	30	30
a. Strip of 3, #2401-2403	90	90

Perf. 12x11½, 11½x12

1993, Apr. 29

Paintings: 5500cr, A Study of Love, 1883. No. 2405, David and Abizag, 1879, horiz. No. 2406, Seated Nude, 1882.

2404 A1292 5500cr multi	25	25
2405 A1292 36,000cr multi	1.65	1.65
2406 A1292 36,000cr multi	1.65	1.65
Nos. 2404-2406 (3)	3.55	3.55

Natl. Flag — A1292a

1993, May 26 Litho. *Die Cut*

Self-adhesive

2407 A1292a A multicolored	35	35

No. 2407 valued at first class domestic letter rate of 9570cr on day of issue.

Beetles A1293

1993, June 5 Litho. *Perf. 11½x12*

2408 A1293 8000cr Dynastes hercules	35	35
2409 A1293 55,000cr Batus barbicornis	2.25	2.25

3rd Iberian-American Conference of Chiefs of State and Heads of Government, Salvador — A1294

1993, July 15 Litho. *Perf. 11x11½*

2410 A1294 12,000cr multi	15	15

1st Brazilian Postage Stamps, 150th Anniv. — A1295

Perf. 12x11½

1993, July 30 **Litho. & Engr.**

2411 A1295 30,000cr No. 1	30	30
2412 A1295 60,000cr No. 2	60	60
2413 A1295 90,000cr No. 3	90	90
a. Souvenir sheet of 3, #2411-2413, wmk. 268	2.00	2.00
Nos. 2411-2413 (3)	1.80	1.80

No. 2413a sold for 200,000cr.

Union of Portuguese Speaking Capitals A1296

Designs: a, 15,000cr, Brasilia. b, 71,000cr, Rio de Janiero.

1993, July 30 Litho. ***Perf. 11½x12***

2414 A1296 Pair, #a.-b. 90 90

No. 2414 printed in continuous design.

Monica & Friends, by Mauricio de Sousa A1297

Monica, Cebolinha, Cascao, Magali, and Bidu: a, Engraving die. b, Reading proclamation, king, No. 1. c, Writing and sending letter, No. 2. d, Receiving letter, No. 3.

1993, Aug. 1

2415 A1297 (1) Strip of 4, #a.-d. 85 85

First Brazilian postage stamps, 150th anniv. Nos. 2415a-2415d paid the first class rate in the new currency on day of issue.

Brazilian Post, 330th Anniv. A1298

Postal buildings: a, Imperial Post Office, Rio de Janeiro. b, Petropolis. c, Central office, Rio de Janeiro. d, Niteroi.

1993, Aug. 3 Litho. ***Perf. 11½x12***

2416 A1298 20,000cr Block of 4, #a.-d. 45 45

Brazilian Engineering Schools A1299

Designs: No. 2417, School of Engineering, Federal University, Rio de Janeiro. No. 2418, Polytechnical School, University of Sao Paulo.

1993, Aug. 24 Litho. ***Perf. 11x11½***

2417 A1299 17cr multicolored 30 30
2418 A1299 17cr multicolored 30 30

Preservation of Sambaquis Archaelogical Sites — A1300

1993, Sept. 19 ***Perf. 12x11½***

2419 A1300 17cr Two artifacts 22 22
2420 A1300 17cr Six artifacts 22 22

Ulysses Guimaraes, Natl. Congress — A1301

1993, Oct. 6 Litho. ***Perf. 11x11½***

2421 A1301 22cr multicolored 28 28

A1302

A1303

1993, Oct. 8 Litho. ***Perf. 12x11½***

2422 A1302 22cr multicolored 28 28

Virgin of Nazare Religious Festival, bicent.

1993, Oct. 13 Litho. ***Perf. 11½x11***

Endangered birds (America Issue): 22cr, Anodorhynchus hyacinthinus, anodorhynchus glaucus, anodorhynchus leari. 130cr, Cyanopsitta spixii.

2423 A1303 22cr multicolored 25 25
2424 A1303 130cr multicolored 1.40 1.40

Composers — A1304

A1307

1993, Oct. 19 Litho. ***Perf. 12x11½***

2425 A1304 22cr Vinicius de Moraes 18 18
2426 A1304 22cr Pixinguinha 18 18

1993, Oct. 29 Litho. ***Perf. 12x11½***

Poets: No. 2427, Mario de Andrade (1893-1945). No. 2428, Alceu Amoroso Lima (Tristao de Athayde) (1893-1983). No. 2429, Gilka Machado (1893-1980).

2427 A1307 30cr multicolored 28 28
2428 A1307 30cr multicolored 28 28
2429 A1307 30cr multicolored 28 28
Nos. 2427-2429 (3) 84 84

Natl. Book Day.

Brazil-Portugal Treaty of Consultation and Friendship, 40th Anniv. — A1308

1993, Nov. 3 Litho. ***Perf. 11½x12***

2430 A1308 30cr multicolored 28 28

See Portugal No. 1980.

Image of the Republic — A1309

1993, Nov. 3 Photo. & Engr. ***Perf. 13***

2431 A1309 (B) multicolored 2.50 2.50

Valued at first class international letter rate (cr) on day of issue.

2nd Intl. Biennial of Comic Strips A1310

Cartoon drawings: No. 2432, Nho-Quim. No. 2433, Benjamin. No. 2434, Lamparina. No. 2435, Reco-Reco, Bolao, Azeitona.

1993, Nov. 11 Litho. ***Perf. 11½x12***

2432 A1310 (1) multicolored 42 42
2433 A1310 (1) multicolored 42 42
2434 A1310 (1) multicolored 42 42
2435 A1310 (1) multicolored 42 42
a. Block of 4, #2432-2435 1.75 1.75

Valued at first class domestic letter rate (cr) on day of issue.

Launching of First Brazilian-Built Submarine — A1311

1993, Nov. 18 ***Perf. 11½***

2436 A1311 240cr multicolored 1.75 1.75

Christmas A1312

1993, Nov. 20

2437 A1312 (1) multicolored 45 45

Valued at first class domestic letter rate (cr) on day of issue.

First Fighter Group, 50th Anniv. A1313

1993, Dec. 18 Litho. ***Perf. 11½***

2438 A1313 42cr multicolored 35 35

Convent of Merces, 340th Anniv. A1314

1994, Jan. 31 Litho. ***Perf. 11½x12***

2439 A1314 58cr multicolored 32 32

Mae Menininha of Gantois, Birth Cent. A1315

1994, Feb. 10 Litho. ***Perf. 11x11½***

2440 A1315 80cr multicolored 40 40

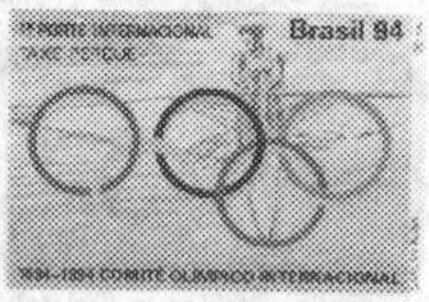

Intl. Olympic Committee, Cent. A1316

1994, Feb. 17 ***Perf. 11½x12***

2441 A1316 (1) multicolored 2.25 2.25

No. 2441 valued at first class international letter rate (cr) on day of issue.

Natl. Flag — A1317

1994, Jan. 31 Litho. ***Die Cut***

Self-Adhesive

2442 A1317 (1) multicolored 40 40

No. 2442 valued at first class domestic letter rate (cr) on day of issue.

Birds — A1318

1994 Photo. ***Perf. 11x11½***

2443 A1318 10cr Notiochelidon cyanoleuca 15 15
2444 A1318 20cr Buteo magnirostris 15 15
2445 A1318 50cr Turdus rufiventris 15 15
2446 A1318 100cr Columbina talpacoti 15 15
2447 A1318 200cr Vanellus chilensis 20 20
2448 A1318 500cr Zonotrichia capensis 50 50
Set value 90 90

Issued: 10cr, 3/17/94. 20cr, 3/9/94. 50cr, 3/1/94. 100cr, 200cr, 4/4/94. 500cr, 4/13/94.

See Nos. 2484-2494.

Image of the Republic — A1318a

1994, May 10 Litho. ***Perf. 12x11½***

Size: 25x35mm

2449 A1318a (5) henna brown 20 20
2450 A1318a (4) green 60 60

Self-Adhesive
Die Cut

2451 A1318a (3) claret 80 80
2452 A1318a (1) blue 1.00 1.00
Nos. 2449-2452 (4) 2.60 2.60

Nos. 2449, 2450, 2451 valued at 5th, 4th and 3rd class domestic letter rate (cr) on day of issue. No. 2452 valued at 1st class printed matter category II rate (cr) on day of issue.

Prince Henry the Navigator (1394-1460) — A1319

1994, Mar. 4 Litho. ***Perf. 11½x12***
2463 A1319 635cr multicolored 2.25 2.25

See Macao No. 719, Portugal No. 1987.

America Issue A1320

Postal vehicles: 110cr, Bicycle, country scene. 635cr, Motorcycle, city scene.

1994, Mar. 18
2464 A1320 110cr multicolored 20 20
2465 A1320 635cr multicolored 1.10 1.10

Father Cicero Romao Batista, 150th Birth Anniv. A1321

1994, Mar. 24 ***Perf. 11x11½***
2466 A1321 (1) multicolored 35 35

No. 2466 valued at first class domestic letter rate (cr) on day of issue.

Albert Sabin, Campaign Against Polio A1322

1994, Apr. 7 ***Perf. 11½x12***
2467 A1322 160cr multicolored 30 30

Carlos Castello Branco, Journalist A1323

1994, Apr. 14
2468 A1323 160cr multicolored 30 30

Karl Friedrich Phillip von Martius, Naturalist — A1324

Flowers: No. 2469, Euterpe oleracea. No. 2470, Jacaranda paucifoliolata. No. 2471, Barbacernia tomentosa.

1994, Apr. 24 ***Perf. 12x11½***
2469 A1324 (1) multicolored 35 35
2470 A1324 (1) multicolored 35 35
2471 A1324 (1) multicolored 2.00 2.00
Nos. 2469-2471 (3) 2.70 2.70

Nos. 2469-2470 were valued at first class domestic letter rate (cr) on day of issue. No. 2471 valued at first class intl. letter rate (cr) on day of issue.

Monkeys — A1326

Designs: No. 2474, Leontopithecus rosalia. No. 2475, Saguinus imperator. No. 2476, Saguinus bicolor.

1994, May 24
2474 A1326 (1) multicolored 35 35
2475 A1326 (1) multicolored 35 35
2476 A1326 (1) multicolored 35 35
Nos. 2474-2476 (3) 1.05 1.05

Nos. 2474-2476 were valued at first class domestic letter rate (cr) on day of issue.

1994 World Cup Soccer Championships, US — A1327

1994, May 19 ***Perf. 11½x12***
2477 A1327 (1) multicolored 2.00 2.00

No. 2477 was valued at first class intl. rate (cr) on day of issue.
Soccer in Brazil, cent.

Souvenir Sheet

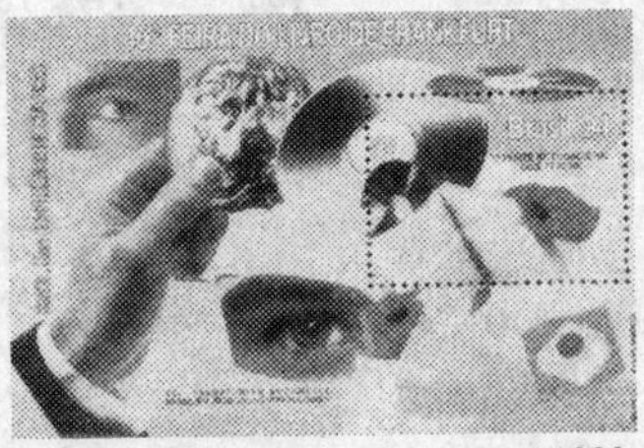

46th Frankfurt Intl. Book Fair — A1328

Illustration reduced.

1994, May 27
2478 A1328 (1) multicolored 2.00 2.00

No. 2478 was valued at first class intl. rate (cr) on day of issue.

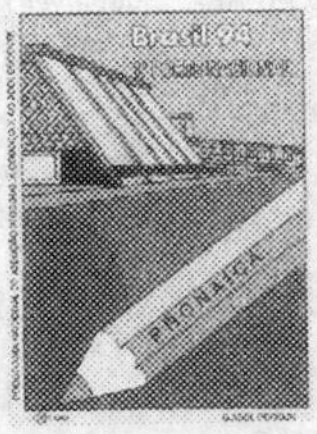

Natl. Literacy Program — A1329

Designs: No. 2479, Pencil, buildings. No. 2480, Pencil, people on television, people watching. No. 2481, Classroom, pencil. No. 2482, Pencils crossed over fingerprint, map of Brazil.

1994, June 3 Litho. ***Perf. 12x11½***
2479 A1329 (1) multicolored 32 32
2480 A1329 (1) multicolored 32 32
2481 A1329 (1) multicolored 32 32
2482 A1329 (1) multicolored 32 32
Nos. 2479-2482 (4) 1.28 1.28

Nos. 2479-2482 were valued at first class domestic letter rate (cr) on day of issue.

Souvenir Sheet

Treaty of Tordesillas, 500th Anniv. — A1330

1994, June 7
2483 A1330 (1) multicolored 2.25 2.25

No. 2483 was valued at first class intl. letter rate (cr) on day of issue.

Bird Type of 1994

1994 Photo. ***Perf. 11x11½***
2484 A1318 1c like No. 2443 15 15
2485 A1318 2c like No. 2444 15 15
2486 A1318 5c like No. 2445 15 15
2487 A1318 10c like No. 2446 20 20
2489 A1318 20c like No. 2447 42 42
2491 A1318 50c like No. 2448 1.00 1.00
2494 A1318 1r Furnarius rufus 2.25 2.25
Nos. 2484-2494 (7) 4.32 4.32

Issued: 1c, 2c, 5c, 20c, 20c, 50c, 1r, 7/1/94.
This is an expanding set. Numbers may change.

Prominent Brazilians A1331

Designs: No. 2504, Edgard Santos (1894-1962), surgeon, educator. No. 2505, Oswaldo Aranha (1894-1960), politician. No. 2507, Otto Lara Resende (1922-92), writer, educator.

1994, July 5 Litho. ***Perf. 11½x12***
2504 A1331 (1) multicolored 28 28
2505 A1331 (1) multicolored 28 28
2506 A1331 (1) multicolored 28 28
Nos. 2504-2506 (3) 84 84

Nos. 2504-2506 were valued at first class domestic letter rate (12c) on day of issue.

A1332

A1333

1994, July 15 ***Perf. 12x11½***
2507 A1332 12c multicolored 28 28

Petrobras, 40th anniv.

Litho. & Engr.
1994, July 26 ***Perf. 11½***
2508 A1333 12c multicolored 28 28

Brazilian State Mint, 300th anniv.

Campaign Against Famine & Misery A1334

1994, July 27 Litho. ***Perf. 11½x12***
2509 A1334 (1) Fish 28 28
2510 A1334 (1) Bread 28 28

Nos. 2509-2510 were valued at first class domestic letter rate (12c) on day of issue.

Institute of Brazilian Lawyers, 150th Anniv. A1335

1994, Aug. 11
2511 A1335 12c multicolored 28 28

Intl. Year of the Family A1336

1994, Aug. 16 ***Perf. 11½***
2512 A1336 84c multicolored 2.00 2.00

Maternity Hospital of Sao Paulo, Cent. A1337

1994, Aug. 26 ***Perf. 11½x12***
2513 A1337 12c multicolored 28 28

Vincente Celestino (1894-1968), Singer A1338

1994, Sept. 12
2514 A1338 12c multicolored 28 28

SEMI-POSTAL STAMPS

National Philatelic Exhibition Issue

SP1

Wmk. Coat of Arms in Sheet (236)
1934, Sept. 16 Engr. *Imperf.*
Thick Paper

B1	SP1	200r + 100r dp cl	52	75
B2	SP1	300r + 100r ver	52	75
B3	SP1	700r + 100r brt bl	5.50	7.50
B4	SP1	1000r + 100r blk	5.50	7.50
		Nos. B1-B4 (4)	12.04	16.50

The surtax was to help defray the expenses of the exhibition. Issued in sheets of 60, inscribed "EXPOSICAO FILATELICA NACIONAL."

Red Cross Nurse and Soldier SP2

Wmk. 222
1935, Sept. 19 Typo. *Perf. 11*

B5	SP2	200r + 100r pur & red	60	60
B6	SP2	300r + 100r ol brn & red	60	45
B7	SP2	700r + 100r turq bl & red	7.25	4.75
		Nos. B5-B7 (3)	8.45	5.80

3rd Pan-American Red Cross Conference. Exist imperf.

Three Wise Men and Star of Bethlehem — SP3

Angel and Child — SP4

Southern Cross and Child — SP5

Mother and Child — SP6

Perf. 10½
1939, Dec. 20 Litho. Wmk. 249

B8	SP3	100r + 100r chlky bl & bl blk	32	32
a.		Horiz. or vert. pair, imperf. between	30.00	
B9	SP4	200r + 100r brt grnsh bl	65	65
a.		Horizontal pair, imperf. between	30.00	
B10	SP5	400r + 200r ol grn & ol	65	16
B11	SP6	1200r + 400r crim & brn red	3.25	1.00
a.		Vertical pair, imperf. between	30.00	
		Nos. B8-B11 (4)	4.87	2.13

The surtax was distributed to charitable institutions.
For surcharges see Nos. C55-C59.

AIR POST STAMPS

Nos. O14-O29 Surcharged

SERVIÇO AEREO 200 Rs.

1927, Dec. 28 Unwmk. *Perf. 12*

C1	O2	50r on 10r	15	15
a.		Inverted surcharge	225.00	
b.		Top ornaments missing	40.00	
C2	O2	200r on 1000r	1.40	2.75
a.		Double surcharge	210.00	
C3	O2	200r on 2000r	1.40	4.75
a.		Double surcharge	210.00	
C4	O2	200r on 5000r	1.00	1.00
a.		Double surcharge	200.00	
b.		Double surcharge, one inverted	210.00	
c.		Triple surcharge	275.00	
C5	O2	300r on 500r	1.00	1.00
C6	O2	300r on 600r	40	32
b.		Pair, one without surch.		
C6A	O2	500r on 10r	325.00	375.00
C7	O2	500r on 50r	1.00	32
a.		Double surcharge	225.00	225.00
C8	O2	1000r on 20r	60	15
a.		Double surcharge	200.00	*175.00*
C9	O2	2000r on 100r	1.65	1.10
a.		Pair, one without surcharge	675.00	
C10	O2	2000r on 200r	1.65	1.10
C11	O2	2000r on 10,000r	1.40	40
C12	O2	5000r on 20,000r	2.50	2.50
C13	O2	5000r on 50,000r	2.50	2.50
C14	O2	5000r on 100,000r	14.00	17.00
C15	O2	10,000r on 500,000r	17.00	12.00
C16	O2	10,000r on 1,000,000r	13.00	13.00
		Nos. C1-C6,C7-C16 (16)	60.65	60.04

Nos. C1, C1b, C7, C8 and C9 have small diamonds printed over the numerals in the upper corners.

Monument to de Gusmao — AP1

Santos-Dumont's Airship — AP2

Augusto Severo's Airship "Pax" — AP3

Santos-Dumont's Biplane "14 Bis" — AP4

Ribeiro de Barros's Seaplane "Jahu" — AP5

Perf. 11, 12½x13, 13x13½
1929 Typo. Wmk. 206

C17	AP1	50r bl grn	25	20
C18	AP2	200r red	1.25	20
C19	AP3	300r brt bl	1.50	20
C20	AP4	500r red vio	2.00	20
C21	AP5	1000r org brn	6.00	40
		Nos. C17-C21 (5)	11.00	1.20

See #C32-C36. For surcharges see #C26-C27.

Bartholomeu de Gusmao AP6

Augusto Severo AP7

Alberto Santos-Dumont — AP8

Perf. 9, 11 and Compound
1929-30 Engr. Wmk. 101

C22	AP6	2000r lt grn ('30)	6.75	25
C23	AP7	5000r carmine	6.75	1.00
C24	AP8	10,000r ol grn	6.75	1.25
		Nos. C22-C24 (3)	20.25	2.50

Nos. C23-C24 exist imperf.
See Nos. C37, C40.

Allegory: Airmail Service between Brazil and the US — AP9

1929 Typo. Wmk. 206

C25	AP9	3000r violet	7.50	65

Exists imperf. See Nos. C38, C41. For surcharge see No. C28.

Nos. C18-C19 Surcharged in Blue or Red

ZEPPELIN 2$500

1931, Aug. 16 *Perf. 12½x13½*

C26	AP2	2500r on 200r (Bl)	15.00	17.00
C27	AP3	5000r on 300r (R)	17.00	21.00

No. C25 Surcharged **2.500 REIS**

1931, Sept. 2 *Perf. 11*

C28	AP9	2500r on 3000r vio	12.50	*12.50*
a.		Inverted surcharge	150.00	
b.		Surch. on front and back	150.00	

Regular Issues of 1928-29 Surcharged

ZEPPELIN 3$500

1932, May Wmk. 101 *Perf. 11, 11½*

C29	A89	3500r on 5000r gray lil	15.00	17.50
C30	A72	7000r on 10,000r rose	15.00	20.00
b.		Horiz. pair, imperf. between	*750.00*	

Imperforates
Since 1933, imperforate or partly perforated sheets of nearly all of the airmail issues have become available.

Flag and Airplane — AP10

Wmk. 222
1933, June 7 Typo. *Perf. 11*

C31	AP10	3500r grn, yel & dk bl	2.50	85

See Nos. C39, C42.

1934 Wmk. 222

C32	AP1	50r bl grn	1.00	1.00
C33	AP2	200r red	1.25	60
C34	AP3	300r brt bl	2.50	1.25
C35	AP4	500r red vio	1.25	50
C36	AP5	1000r org brn	3.00	40
		Nos. C32-C36 (5)	9.00	3.75

1934 Wmk. 236 Engr. *Perf. 12x11*
Thick Laid Paper

C37	AP6	2000r lt grn	3.00	1.00

Types of 1929, 1933
Perf. 11, 11½, 12
1937-40 Typo. Wmk. 249

C38	AP9	3000r violet	14.00	1.50
C39	AP10	3500r grn, yel & dk bl	1.50	1.25
		Engr.		
C40	AP7	5000r ver ('40)	3.50	60
		Nos. C38-C40 (3)	19.00	3.35

Watermark note after No. 501 also applies to No. C40.

Types of 1929-33
Perf. 11, 11½x12
1939-40 Typo. Wmk. 256

C41	AP9	3000r violet	1.00	50
C42	AP10	3500r bl, dl grn & yel ('40)	75	40

Map of the Western Hemisphere Showing Brazil AP11

1941, Jan. 14 Engr. *Perf. 11*

C43	AP11	1200r dark brown	1.50	50

5th general census of Brazil.

No. 506A Overprinted in Carmine

AÉREO "10 Nov." 937-941

1941, Nov. 10 Wmk. 264 *Rouletted*

C45	A180	5400r slate grn	1.50	1.00
a.		Overprint inverted	140.00	

President Varges' new constitution, 4th anniv.

Nos. 506A and 508 Surcharged in Black

AÉREO "10 Nov." 937-942 Cr.$ 5,40

1942, Nov. 10 Wmk. 264

C47	A180	5.40cr on 5400r sl grn	1.50	1.00
a.		Wmk. 249	40.00	50.00
b.		Surcharge inverted	60.00	75.00

President Vargas' new constitution, 5th anniv.
The status of No. C47a is questioned.

Southern Cross and Arms of Paraguay AP12

Perf. 12½
1943, May 11 Engr. Wmk. 270

C48	AP12	1.20cr lt gray blue	1.00	50

Issued in commemoration of the visit of President Higinio Morinigo of Paraguay.

Map of South America — AP13

1943, June 30 Wmk. 271 *Perf. 12½*

C49	AP13	1.20cr multi	1.00	50

Visit of President Penaranda of Bolivia.

Numeral of Value — AP14

1943, Aug. 7

C50	AP14	1cr blk & dull yel	2.00	1.50
a.		Double impression	30.00	
C51	AP14	2cr blk & pale grn	2.75	1.50
a.		Double impression	40.00	
C52	AP14	5cr blk & pink	3.25	2.00
		Nos. C50-C52 (3)	8.00	5.00

Centenary of Brazil's first postage stamps.

Souvenir Sheet

AP15

Without Gum *Imperf.*

C53 AP15	Sheet of three	35.00	35.00
a.	1cr black & dull yellow	10.00	10.00
b.	2cr black & pale green	10.00	10.00
c.	5cr black & pink	10.00	10.00

100th anniv. of the 1st postage stamps of Brazil and the 2nd Phil. Exposition (Brapex). Printed in panes of 6 sheets, perforated 12½ between. Each sheet is perforated on two or three sides. Size approximately 155x155mm.

Law Book — AP16

1943, Aug. 13 *Perf. 12½*

C54 AP16 1.20cr rose & lil rose 40 20

2nd Inter-American Conf. of Lawyers.

AÉREO

No. B10 Surcharged in Red, Carmine or Black **20 Cts.**

1944, Jan. 3 Wmk. 249 *Perf. 10½*

C55 SP5	20c on 400r+200r (R)	42	35
C56 SP5	40c on 400r+200r (Bk)	75	25
C57 SP5	60c on 400r+200r (C)	75	18
C58 SP5	1cr on 400r+200r (Bk)	1.00	22
C59 SP5	1.20cr on 400r+200r (C)	1.25	22
	Nos. C55-C59 (5)	4.17	1.22

No. C59 is known with surcharge in black but its status is questioned.

Bartholomeu de Gusmao and the "Aerostat" — AP17

Wmk. 268

1944, Oct. 23 Engr. *Perf. 12*

C60 AP17 1.20cr rose car 35 15

Week of the Wing.

L. L. Zamenhof AP18

1945, Apr. 16 Litho. *Perf. 11*

C61 AP18 1.20cr dl brn 35 25

Esperanto Congress held in Rio, Apr. 14-22.

Map of South America — AP19

Baron of Rio Branco — AP20

1945, Apr. 20

C62 AP19	1.20cr gray brn	32	25
C63 AP20	5cr rose lil	95	40

Centenary of the birth of José Maria de Silva Paranhos, Baron of Rio Branco.

Dove and Flags of American Republics AP21

Perf. 12x11

1947, Aug. 15 Engr. Unwmk.

C64 AP21 2.20cr dk bl grn 30 25

Inter-American Defense Conference at Rio de Janeiro August-September, 1947.

Santos-Dumont Monument, St. Cloud, France — AP22

Bay of Rio de Janeiro and Rotary Emblem — AP23

1947, Nov. 15 Typo. *Perf. 11x12*

C65 AP22 1.20cr org brn & ol 30 25

Issued to commemorate the Week of the Wing and to honor the Santos-Dumont monument which was destroyed in World War II.

Catalogue values for unused stamps in this section, from this point to the end of the section, are for Never Hinged items.

1948, May 16 Engr. *Perf. 11*

C66 AP23	1.20cr deep claret	50	40
C67 AP23	3.80cr dull violet	1.00	40

39th convention of Rotary International, Rio de Janeiro, May 1948.

Hotel Quitandinha, Petropolis AP24

1948, July 10 Litho. Wmk. 267

C68 AP24	1.20cr org brn	25	25
C69 AP24	3.80cr violet	48	30

International Exposition of Industry and Commerce, Petropolis, 1948.

Musician and Singers AP25

1948, Aug. 13 Engr. Unwmk.

C70 AP25 1.20cr blue 30 16

National School of Music, cent.

Luis Batlle Berres AP26

1948, Sept. 2 Typo.

C71 AP26 1.70cr blue 20 16

Visit of President Luis Batlle Berres of Uruguay, September, 1948.

Merino Ram — AP27

1948, Oct. 10 Wmk. 267 *Perf. 12x11*

C72 AP27 1.20cr dp org 50 30

Intl. Livestock Exposition at Bagé.

Eucharistic Congress Seal — AP28

Unwmk.

1948, Oct. 23 Engr. *Perf. 11*

C73 AP28 1.20cr dk car rose 30 30

5th Natl. Eucharistic Cong., Porto Alegre, Oct. 24-31.

Souvenir Sheet

AP28a

1948, Dec. 14 Engr. *Imperf.*

Without Gum

C73A AP28a Sheet of 3 50.00 65.00

No. C73A contains one each of Nos. 674-676. Issued in honor of President Eurico Gasper Dutra and the armed forces. Exists both with and without number on back. Measures 130x75mm.

Church of Prazeres, Guararapes — AP29

Perf. 11½x12

1949, Feb. 15 Litho. Wmk. 267

C74 AP29 1.20cr pink 1.50 75

Second Battle of Guararapes, 300th anniv.

Thomé de Souza Meeting Indians — AP30

Perf. 11x12

1949, Mar. 29 Engr. Unwmk.

C75 AP30 1.20cr blue 20 16

Founding of the City of Salvador, 400th anniv.

A souvenir folder, issued with No. C75, has an engraved 20cr red brown postage stamp portraying John III printed on it, and a copy of No. C75 affixed to it and postmarked. Paper is laid, and size of folder front is 100x150mm. Value, $5.

Franklin D. Roosevelt AP31

1949, May 20 Unwmk. *Imperf.*

C76 AP31	3.80cr deep blue	60	60
a.	Souvenir sheet	12.00	15.00

No. C76a measures 85x110mm, with deep blue inscriptions in upper and lower margins. It also exists with papermaker's watermark.

Joaquim Nabuco (1849-1910), Lawyer and Writer — AP32

1949, Aug. 30 *Perf. 12*

C77 AP32	3.80cr rose lilac	40	32
a.	Wmk. 256, imperf.	25.00	

Maracanã Stadium AP33

Soccer Player and Flag — AP34

Perf. 11x12, 12x11

1950, June 24 Litho. Wmk. 267

C78 AP33	1.20cr ultra & salmon	95	40
C79 AP34	5.80cr bl, yel grn & yel	2.75	50

4th World Soccer Championship, Rio.

Symbolical of Brazilian Population Growth — AP35

1950, July 10 *Perf. 12x11*

C80 AP35 1.20cr red brn		30	15

Issued to publicize the 6th Brazilian census.

J. B. Marcelino Champagnat — AP36

1956, Sept. 8 **Engr.** *Perf. 11½*

C81 AP36 3.30cr rose lilac		30	15

50th anniversary of the arrival of the Marist Brothers in Northern Brazil.

Santos-Dumont's 1906 Plane — AP37

1956, Oct. 16 **Photo.**

C82 AP37	3cr dk bl grn	85	30
a.	Souv. sheet of 4, #C82b	6.00	6.00
b.	3cr dark carmine	1.50	90
C83 AP37	3.30cr brt ultra	20	15
C84 AP37	4cr dp claret	40	15
C85 AP37	6.50cr red brn	15	15
C86 AP37	11.50cr org red	85	35
Nos. C82-C86 (5)		2.45	1.10

1st flight by Santos-Dumont, 50th anniv. No. C82b issued Oct. 14, 1956.

Lord Baden-Powell — AP38

1957, Aug. 1 **Unwmk.**

Granite Paper

C87 AP38 3.30cr deep red lilac		25	15

Centenary of the birth of Lord Baden-Powell, founder of the Boy Scouts.

UN Emblem, Soldier and Map of Suez Canal Area — AP39

Perf. 11½

1957, Oct. 24 **Wmk. 267** **Engr.**

C88 AP39 3.30cr dk blue		25	18

Brazilian contingent of the UN Emergency Force.

Basketball Player — AP40

1959, May 30 **Photo.** *Perf. 11½*

C89 AP40 3.30cr brt red brn & bl		25	15

Brazil's victory in the World Basketball Championships of 1959.

Symbol of Flight — AP41

1959, Oct. 21 **Wmk. 267**

C90 AP41 3.30cr dp ultra		16	15

Issued to publicize Week of the Wing.

Caravelle AP42

1959, Dec. 18 *Perf. 11½*

C91 AP42 6.50cr ultra		16	15

Inauguration of Brazilian jet flights.

Pres. Adolfo Lopez Mateos AP43

Pres. Dwight D. Eisenhower AP44

1960, Jan. 19 **Photo.** **Wmk. 267**

C92 AP43 6.50cr brown		16	15

Issued to commemorate the visit of President Adolfo Lopez Mateos of Mexico.

1960, Feb. 23 *Perf. 11½*

C93 AP44 6.50cr dp org		16	15

Visit of Pres. Dwight D. Eisenhower.

World Refugee Year Emblem — AP45

Tower at Brasilia — AP46

1960, Apr. 7 **Wmk. 268**

C94 AP45 6.50cr blue		16	15

WRY, July 1, 1959-June 30, 1960.

Type of Regular Issue and AP46

Designs: 3.30cr, Square of the Three Entities. 4cr, Cathedral. 11.50cr, Plan of Brasilia.

Perf. 11x11½, 11½x11

1960, Apr. 21 **Photo.** **Wmk. 267**

C95 A436	3.30cr violet	15	15
C96 A436	4cr blue	75	15
C97 AP46	6.50cr rose car	15	15
C98 A436	11.50cr brown	15	15
Nos. C95-C98 (4)		1.20	
Set value			40

Inauguration of Brazil's new capital, Brasilia, Apr. 21, 1960.

Chrismon and Oil Lamp AP47

1960, May 16 *Perf. 11x11½*

C99 AP47 3.30cr lil rose		15	15

7th Natl. Eucharistic Congress at Curitiba.

Cross, Sugarloaf Mountain and Emblem AP48

1960, July 1 **Wmk. 267**

C100 AP48 6.50cr brt bl		15	15

10th Cong. of the World Baptist Alliance, Rio.

Boy Scout — AP49

Caravel — AP50

1960, July 23 *Perf. 11½x11*

C101 AP49 3.30cr org ver		15	15

Boy Scouts of Brazil, 50th anniversary.

1960, Aug. 5 **Engr.** **Wmk. 268**

C102 AP50 6.50cr black		15	15

Prince Henry the Navigator, 500th birth anniv.

Maria E. Bueno AP51

1960, Dec. 15 **Photo.** *Perf. 11x11½*

C103 AP51 60cr pale brn		15	15

Victory at Wimbledon of Maria E. Bueno, women's singles tennis champion.

War Memorial, Sugarloaf Mountain and Allied Flags AP52

1960, Dec. 22 **Wmk. 268**

C104 AP52 3.30cr lilac rose		15	15

Reburial of Brazilian servicemen of WW II.

Power Line and Map AP53

Malaria Eradication Emblem AP54

1961, Jan. 20 *Perf. 11½x11*

C105 AP53 3.30cr lilac rose		15	15

Inauguration of Three Marias Dam and hydroelectric station in Minas Gerais.

1962, May 24 **Wmk. 267** **Engr.**

C106 AP54 21cr blue		15	15

WHO drive to eradicate malaria.

F. A. de Varnhagen — AP55

1966, Feb. 17 **Photo.** **Wmk. 267**

C107 AP55 45cr red brown		18	15

Francisco Adolfo de Varnhagen, Viscount of Porto Seguro (1816-1878), historian and diplomat.

Map of the Americas and Alliance for Progress Emblem AP56

1966, Mar. 14 *Perf. 11x11½*

C108 AP56 120cr grnsh bl & vio bl		40	15

5th anniv. of the Alliance for Progress.

A souvenir card contains one impression of No. C108, imperf. Size: 113x160mm.

Nun and Globe — AP57

Face of Jesus from Shroud of Turin — AP58

1966, Mar. 25 **Photo.** *Perf. 11½x11*

C109 AP57 35cr violet		18	15

Centenary of the arrival of the teaching Sisters of St. Dorothea.

1966, June 3 **Photo.** **Wmk. 267**

C110 AP58 45cr brown org		20	15

Issued to commemorate Vatican II, the 21st Ecumenical Council of the Roman Catholic Church, Oct. 11, 1962-Dec. 8, 1965.

A souvenir card contains one impression of No. C110, imperf. Size: 100x39mm.

Admiral Mariz e Barros
AP59

"Youth" by Eliseu Visconti
AP60

1966, June 13 Photo. Wmk. 267

C111 AP59 35cr red brown 16 15

Death centenary of Admiral Antonio Carlos Mariz e Barros, who died in the Battle of Itaperu.

1966, July 31 *Perf. 11½x11*

C112 AP60 120cr red brown 40 20

Birth centenary of Eliseu Visconti, painter.

SPECIAL DELIVERY STAMPS

No. 191 Surcharged **1000 REIS EXPRESSO**

1930 Unwmk. *Perf. 12*

E1 A62 1000r on 200r dp bl 3.00 1.50
a. Inverted surcharge 500.00

POSTAGE DUE STAMPS

D1

D2

1889 Unwmk. Typo. *Rouletted*

J1	D1	10r carmine	1.05	52
J2	D1	20r carmine	1.25	90
J3	D1	50r carmine	2.50	1.40
J4	D1	100r carmine	1.40	70
J5	D1	200r carmine	22.50	7.00
J6	D1	300r carmine	2.75	3.50
J7	D1	500r carmine	2.75	3.50
J8	D1	700r carmine	5.25	5.00
J9	D1	1000r carmine	5.25	5.00
		Nos. J1-J9 (9)	44.70	27.52

Counterfeits are common.

1890

J10	D1	10r orange	38	15
J11	D1	20r ultra	60	15
J12	D1	50r olive	75	15
J13	D1	200r magenta	2.25	24
J14	D1	300r bl grn	1.50	50
J15	D1	500r slate	1.90	1.75
J16	D1	700r purple	2.75	3.75
J17	D1	1000r dk vio	3.75	3.00
		Nos. J10-J17 (8)	13.88	9.69

Perf. 11 to 11½, 12½ to 14 and Compound

1895-1901

J18	D2	10r dk bl ('01)	80	40
J19	D2	20r yel grn	8.00	2.50
J20	D2	50r yel grn ('01)	6.00	2.75
J21	D2	100r brick red	6.25	32
J22	D2	200r violet	4.00	20
a.		200r gray lilac ('98)	10.00	1.25
J23	D2	300r dl bl	2.75	1.65
J24	D2	2000r brown	8.00	8.00
		Nos. J18-J24 (7)	35.80	15.82

1906 Wmk. 97

J25 D2 100r brick red 6.50 2.50

Wmk. (97? or 98?)

J26 D2 200r violet 6.00 1.00
a. Wmk. 97 275.00 85.00
b. Wmk. 98 10.00 45.00

D3

D4

1906-10 Unwmk. Engr. *Perf. 12*

J28	D3	10r slate	15	15
J29	D3	20r brt vio	15	15
J30	D3	50r dk grn	20	15
J31	D3	100r carmine	1.50	50
J32	D3	200r dp bl	80	25
J33	D3	300r gray blk	30	50
J34	D3	400r ol grn	80	75
J35	D3	500r dk vio	30.00	30.00
J36	D3	600r vio ('10)	1.00	*2.50*
J37	D3	700r red brn	25.00	25.00
J38	D3	1000r red	1.25	*2.50*
J39	D3	2000r green	4.00	5.00
J40	D3	5000r choc ('10)	1.25	*12.00*
		Nos. J28-J40 (13)	66.40	79.45

Perf. 12½, 11, 11x10½

1919-23 Typo.

J41	D4	5r red brn	15	22
J42	D4	10r violet	22	22
J43	D4	20r ol gray	18	15
J44	D4	50r grn ('23)	18	18
J45	D4	100r red	1.05	90
J46	D4	200r blue	5.00	1.40
J47	D4	400r brn ('23)	1.25	1.25
		Nos. J41-J47 (7)	8.03	4.32

Perf. 12½, 12½x13½

1924-35 Wmk. 100

J48	D4	5r red brn	25	20
J49	D4	100r red	75	30
J50	D4	200r slate bl ('29)	1.00	50
J51	D4	400r dp brn ('29)	1.50	1.00
J52	D4	600r dk vio ('29)	1.75	1.10
J53	D4	600r org ('35)	75	50
		Nos. J48-J53 (6)	6.00	3.60

1924 Wmk. 193 *Perf. 11x10½*

J54	D4	100r red	40.00	40.00
J55	D4	200r slate blue	5.00	5.00

Perf. 11x10½, 13x13½

1925-27 Wmk. 101

J56	D4	20r olive gray	18	15
J57	D4	100r red	1.05	28
J58	D4	200r slate blue	3.25	35
J59	D4	400r brown	1.75	1.25
J60	D4	600r dk vio	4.25	2.50
		Nos. J56-J60 (5)	10.48	4.53

Wmk. E U BRASIL Multiple (218)

1929-30 *Perf. 12½x13½*

J61	D4	100r light red	25	20
J62	D4	200r blue black	40	25
J63	D4	400r brown	40	25
J64	D4	1000r myrtle green	75	50
		Nos. J61-J64 (4)	1.80	1.20

Perf. 11, 12½x13, 13

1931-36 Wmk. 222

J65	D4	10r lt vio ('35)	15	15
J66	D4	20r blk ('33)	16	15
J67	D4	50r bl grn ('35)	24	20
J68	D4	100r rose red ('35)	24	20
J69	D4	200r sl bl ('35)	40	28
J70	D4	400r blk brn ('35)	2.00	2.00
J71	D4	600r dk vio	32	20
J72	D4	1000r myr grn	48	32
J73	D4	2000r brn ('36)	80	80
J74	D4	5000r indigo ('36)	1.25	1.00
		Nos. J65-J74 (10)	6.04	5.30

1938 Wmk. 249 *Perf. 11*

J75 D4 200r slate blue 2.00 75

1940 Typo. Wmk. 256

J76	D4	10r light violet	50	50
J77	D4	20r black	50	50
J79	D4	100r rose red	50	50
J80	D4	200r myrtle green	50	50
		Nos. J76-J80 (4)	2.00	2.00

1942 Wmk. 264

J81	D4	10r lt vio	15	15
J82	D4	20r ol blk	15	15
J83	D4	50r lt bl grn	15	15
J84	D4	100r vermilion	40	30
J85	D4	200r gray bl	40	30
J86	D4	400r claret	40	30
J87	D4	600r rose vio	30	20
J88	D4	1000r dk bl grn	30	20
J89	D4	2000r dp yel brn	75	50
J90	D4	5000r indigo	40	30
		Nos. J81-J90 (10)	3.40	2.55

1949 Wmk. 268

J91	D4	10c pale rose lilac	4.00	3.25
J92	D4	20r black	25.00	25.00

No. J92 exists in shades of gray ranging to gray olive.

OFFICIAL STAMPS

Pres. Affonso Penna — O1

Pres. Hermes da Fonseca — O2

Unwmk.

1906, Nov. 15 Engr. *Perf. 12*

O1	O1	10r org & grn	15	15
O2	O1	20r org & grn	25	15
O3	O1	50r org & grn	85	15
O4	O1	100r org & grn	25	15
O5	O1	200r org & grn	45	15
O6	O1	300r org & grn	1.25	30
O7	O1	400r org & grn	3.25	65
O8	O1	500r org & grn	1.40	50
O9	O1	700r org & grn	2.50	2.00
O10	O1	1000r org & grn	1.75	75
O11	O1	2000r org & grn	2.10	90
O12	O1	5000r org & grn	4.50	90
O13	O1	10,000r org & grn	5.50	50
		Nos. O1-O13 (13)	24.20	7.25

The portrait is the same but the frame differs for each denomination of this issue.

1913, Nov. 15

Center in Black

O14	O2	10r gray	22	15
O15	O2	20r ol grn	22	15
O16	O2	50r gray	25	15
O17	O2	100r ver	35	15
O18	O2	200r blue	52	18
O19	O2	500r orange	1.75	42
O20	O2	600r violet	2.75	65
O21	O2	1000r blk brn	3.50	52
O22	O2	2000r red brn	4.50	52
O23	O2	5000r brown	5.50	70
O24	O2	10,000r black	8.50	2.75
O25	O2	20,000r blue	21.00	21.00
O26	O2	50,000r green	32.50	25.00
O27	O2	100,000r org red	105.00	105.00
O28	O2	500,000r brown	165.00	175.00
O29	O2	1,000,000r dk brn	175.00	190.00
		Nos. O14-O29 (16)	526.56	522.34

The portrait is the same on all denominations of this series but there are eight types of the frame.

Pres. Wenceslau Braz — O3

Perf. 11, 11½

1919, Apr. 11 Wmk. 100

O30	O3	10r olive green	40	1.00
O31	O3	50r green	50	50
O32	O3	100r rose red	75	40
O33	O3	200r dull blue	1.00	40
O34	O3	500r orange	6.50	7.50
		Nos. O30-O34 (5)	9.15	9.80

The official decree called for eleven stamps in this series but only five were issued.
For surcharges see Nos. 293-297.

NEWSPAPER STAMPS

N1

Rouletted

1889, Feb. 1 Unwmk. Litho.

P1	N1	10r yellow	2.00	2.10
a.		Pair, imperf. between	87.50	125.00
P2	N1	20r yellow	4.25	5.00
P3	N1	50r yellow	7.00	4.25
P4	N1	100r yellow	2.75	2.10
P5	N1	200r yellow	2.10	1.05
P6	N1	300r yellow	2.10	1.05
P7	N1	500r yellow	12.50	5.50
P8	N1	700r yellow	2.10	7.00
P9	N1	1000r yellow	2.10	7.00
		Nos. P1-P9 (9)	36.90	35.05

For surcharges see Nos. 125-127.

1889, May 1

P10	N1	10r olive	30	15
P11	N1	20r green	30	15
P12	N1	50r brn yel	40	15
P13	N1	100r violet	85	60
P14	N1	200r black	75	60
P15	N1	300r carmine	5.00	5.00
P16	N1	500r green	25.00	25.00
P17	N1	700r ultra	12.50	15.00
P18	N1	1000r brown	5.00	9.00
		Nos. P10-P18 (9)	50.10	55.65

For surcharges see Nos. 128-135.

N2

N3

White Wove Paper Thin to Thick

Perf. 11 to 11½, 12½ to 14 and 12½ to 14x11 to 11½

1890 Typo.

P19	N2	10r blue	7.00	5.00
a.		10r ultramarine	7.00	5.00
P20	N2	20r emerald	20.00	7.50
P21	N2	100r violet	8.00	4.50
		Nos. P19-P21 (3)	35.00	17.00

For surcharge see No. 137.

1890-93

P22	N3	10r blue	35	18
a.		10r ultramarine	90	35
P23	N3	10r ultra, *buff*	70	35
P24	N3	20r green	70	42
a.		20r emerald	90	52
P25	N3	50r yel grn ('93)	4.25	2.75
		Nos. P22-P25 (4)	6.00	3.70

For surcharges see Nos. 136, 138-139.

POSTAL TAX STAMPS

Icarus from the Santos-Dumont Monument at St. Cloud, France — PT1

Perf. 13½x12½, 11

1933, Oct. 1 Typo. Wmk. 222

RA1 PT1 100r deep brown 50 15

Honoring the Brazilian aviator, Santos-Dumont. Its use was obligatory as a tax on all correspondence sent to countries in South America, the US and Spain. Its use on correspondence to other countries was optional. The funds obtained were used for the construction of airports throughout Brazil.

Catalogue values for unused stamps in this section, from this point to the end of the section, are for Never Hinged items.

Father Joseph Damien and Children
PT2

Perf. 12x11

1952, Nov. 24 Litho. Wmk. 267

RA2 PT2 10c yel brn 25 15

1953, Nov. 30

RA3 PT2 10c yel grn 25 15

Father Bento Dias Pacheco
PT3

Eunice Weaver
PT4

1954, Nov. 22 Photo. *Perf. 11½*

RA4 PT3 10c vio bl 20 15

1955-66, Nov. 24

RA5 PT3 10c dk car rose 20 15
RA6 PT3 10c org red ('57) 20 15
RA7 PT3 10c dp emer ('58) 15 15
RA8 PT3 10c red lilac ('61) 15 15
RA9 PT3 10c choc ('62) 15 15
RA10 PT3 10c slate ('63) 15 15
RA11 PT3 2cr dp mag ('64) 15 15
RA12 PT3 2cr violet ('65) 15 15
RA13 PT3 2cr orange ('66) 15 15
Set value 95

1968, Nov. 25

RA14 PT3 5c brt yel grn 1.25 75

1969, Nov. 28

RA15 PT3 5c deep plum 50 25

1971, Nov. 24

RA16 PT4 10c slate green 1.00 40

1973, Nov. 24

RA17 PT4 10c brt rose lil ('73) 20 15

Father Nicodemos
PT5

Father Vicente Borgard (1888-1977)
PT6

1975, Nov. 24 Litho. Unwmk.

RA18 PT5 10c sepia 20 15

1983, Nov. 24 Photo. *Perf. 11½*

RA19 PT6 10cr brown 60 60

Father Bento Dias Pacheco — PT7

Father Santiago Uchoa — PT8

1984, Nov. 24 Photo. *Perf. 11½*

RA20 PT7 30cr deep blue 15 15

1985, Nov. 24 Litho.

RA21 PT7 100cr lake 15 15

1986, Nov. 24 Litho.

RA22 PT7 10c gray brown 15 15

1987, Nov. 24 Photo.

RA23 PT7 30c sage green 15 15

1988, Nov. 24 Litho.

RA24 PT8 1.30cz dull red brn 15 15

See No. RA29.

Fr. Joseph Damien — PT9

1989-92 Photo. *Perf. 11½*

RA25 PT9 2c deep lilac rose 15 15
RA26 PT9 50c blue 15 15

Perf. 12½

RA27 PT9 3cr green 15 15
RA28 PT9 30cr brown 15 15
Set value 20 20

Issue dates: 2c, Nov. 24. 50c, Nov. 24, 1990. 3cr, Nov. 24, 1991. 30cr, Nov. 24, 1992.

Use of Nos. RA2-RA29 was required for one week. The tax was for the care and treatment of lepers.

Father Santiago Uchoa Type of 1988

1993, Nov. 24 Photo. *Perf. 12½*

RA29 PT8 50c blue 15 15

The tax was for the care and treatment of lepers.

Use of Nos. RA2-RA29 was required for one week. The tax was for the care and treatment of lepers.

POSTAL TAX SEMI-POSTAL STAMP

Catalogue values for unused stamps in this section are for Never Hinged items.

Icarus — PTSP1

Wmk. 267

1947, Nov. 15 Typo. *Perf. 11*

RAB1 PTSP1 40c + 10c brt red 35 20
a. Pair, imperf. between *350.00*

Aviation Week, November 15-22, 1947, and compulsory on all domestic correspondence during that week.

BULGARIA

LOCATION — Southeastern Europe bordering on the Black Sea on the east and the Danube River on the north
GOVT. — Republic
AREA — 42,823 sq. mi.
POP. — 8,929,332 (1983)
CAPITAL — Sofia

In 1885 Bulgaria, then a principality under the suzerainty of the Sultan of Turkey, was joined by Eastern Rumelia. Independence from Turkey was obtained in 1908.

100 Centimes = 1 Franc
100 Stotinki = 1 Lev (1881)

Catalogue values for unused stamps in this country are for Never Hinged items, beginning with Scott 293 in the regular postage section, Scott B1 in the semi-postal section, Scott C15 in the airpost section, Scott CB1 in the airpost semi-postal section, Scott E1 in the special delivery section, Scott J47 in the postage due section, Scott O1 in the officials section, and Scott Q1 in the parcel post section.

Lion of Bulgaria
A1 A2 A3

Perf. 14½x15

1879, June 1 Wmk. 168 Typo.

Laid Paper

1 A1 5c black & yel 65.00 18.00
2 A1 10c black & grn 250.00 60.00
3 A1 25c black & vio 175.00 15.00
a. Imperf.
4 A1 50c black & blue 250.00 50.00
5 A2 1fr black & red 50.00 17.50

1881, June 10

6 A3 3s red & silver 12.50 2.50
7 A3 5s black & org 15.00 2.50
a. Background inverted *1,750.*
8 A3 10s black & grn 65.00 6.50
9 A3 15s red & grn 60.00 6.50
10 A3 25s black & vio 250.00 30.00
11 A3 30s blue & fawn 17.50 6.50

1882, Dec. 4

12 A3 3s orange & yel 1.00 50
a. Background inverted *2,750. 1,400.*
13 A3 5s green & pale green 6.00 50
a. 5s rose & pale rose (error) *1,600. 1,300.*
14 A3 10s rose & pale rose 8.00 75
15 A3 15s red vio & pale lil 6.00 40
16 A3 25s blue & pale blue 6.00 50
17 A3 30s violet & grn 6.00 75
18 A3 50s blue & pink 6.00 75
Nos. 12-18 (7) 39.00 4.15

See Nos. 207-210, 286.

A4

A5

Surcharged in Black, Carmine or Vermilion

1884, May 1

Typo. Surcharge

19 A4 3s on 10s rose (Bk) 95.00 30.00
20 A4 5s on 30s blue & fawn (C) 95.00 45.00
20A A4 5s on 30s bl & fawn (Bk) *1,750. 1,750.*
21 A5 15s on 25s blue (C) 140.00 40.00

On some values the surcharge may be found inverted or double.

1885, June

Litho. Surcharge

21B A4 3s on 10s rose (Bk) 45.00 27.50
21C A4 5s on 30s bl & fawn (V) 50.00 35.00
21D A5 15s on 25s blue (V) 70.00 45.00
22 A5 50s on 1fr blk & red (Bk) 190.00 125.00

Forgeries of Nos. 19-22 are plentiful.

Word below left star in oval has 5 letters — A6

Third letter below left star is "A" — A7

1885, May 25

23 A6 1s gray vio & pale gray 12.00 5.00
24 A7 2s sl grn & pale gray 12.00 4.00

Word below left star has 4 letters — A8

Third letter below left star is "b" with cross-bar in upper half — A9

A10

1886-87

25 A8 1s gray vio & pale gray 1.00 20
26 A9 2s sl grn & pale gray 1.00 20
27 A10 1 l black & red ('87) 27.50 3.00
Nos. 25-27 (3) 29.50 3.40

For surcharge see No. 40.

A11

Perf. 10½, 11, 11½, 13, 13½

1889 Wove Paper Unwmk.

28 A11 1s lilac 16 15
29 A11 2s gray 60 15
30 A11 3s bister brown 40 15
31 A11 5s yellow green 25 15
a. Vert. pair, imperf. btwn.
32 A11 10s rose 1.10 15
33 A11 15s orange 65 15
34 A11 25s blue 1.00 15
35 A11 30s dk brown 8.75 15
36 A11 50s green 60 32
37 A11 1 l orange red 52 38
Nos. 28-37 (10) 14.03
Set value 1.50

The 10s orange is a proof.

Nos. 28-34 are known imperforate. Value, set $225.

See Nos. 39, 41-42. For overprints and surcharges see Nos. 38, 55-56, 77-81, 113.

No. 35 Surcharged in Black **15**

1892, Jan. 26

38 A11 15s on 30s brn 10.00 1.00
a. Inverted surcharge *70.00 52.50*

1894 *Perf. 10½, 11, 11½*

Pelure Paper

39 A11 10s red 7.00 50
a. Imperf. *57.50*

No. 26 Surcharged in Red **01**

Wmk. Wavy Lines (168)

1895, Oct. 25 *Perf. 14½x15*

Laid Paper

40 A9 1s on 2s 75 20
a. Inverted surcharge *6.00 5.00*
b. Double surcharge *62.50 62.50*
c. Pair, one without surcharge *125.00 125.00*

This surcharge on No. 24 is a proof.

Wmk. Coat of Arms in the Sheet

1896, Apr. 30 *Perf. 11½, 13*

Wove Paper

41 A11 2 l rose & pale rose 2.00 1.50
42 A11 3 l black & buff 3.50 3.00

Coat of Arms — A14

Cherry Wood Cannon — A15

1896, Feb. 2 *Perf. 13*

43 A14 1s blue green 32 15
44 A14 5s dark blue 32 15
45 A14 15s purple 50 18
46 A14 25s red 4.75 85
Nos. 43-46 (4) 5.89 1.33

Baptism of Prince Boris.

Examples of Nos. 41-46 from sheet edges show no watermark.

Nos. 43, 45-46 were also printed on rough unwatermarked paper.

1901, Apr. 20 Litho. Unwmk.

53 A15 5s carmine 1.25 90
54 A15 15s yellow green 1.25 90

Insurrection of Independence in April, 1876, 25th anniversary.

Exist imperf. Forgeries exist.

Nos. 30 and 36 Surcharged in Black

5

1901, Mar. 24 Typo.

55	A11	5s on 3s bister brn	1.75	75
a.		Inverted surcharge	42.50	42.50
b.		Pair, one without surcharge	70.00	70.00
56	A11	10s on 50s green	2.25	75
a.		Inverted surcharge	50.00	50.00
b.		Pair, one without surcharge	70.00	70.00

Tsar Ferdinand A17

Fighting at Shipka Pass A18

ONE LEV:

Type I - The numerals in the upper corners have, at the top, a sloping serif on the left side and a short straight serif on the right.

Type II - The numerals in the upper corners are of ordinary shape without the serif at the right.

1901-05 Typo. *Perf. 12½*

57	A17	1s vio & gray blk	15	15
58	A17	2s brnz grn & ind	15	15
a.		Imperf.		
59	A17	3s orange & ind	15	15
60	A17	5s emerald & brn	2.25	15
61	A17	10s rose & blk	1.50	15
62	A17	15s claret & gray blk	65	15
63	A17	25s blue & blk	65	15
64	A17	30s bis & gray blk	15.00	15
65	A17	50s dk blue & brn	80	15
66	A17	1 l red org & brnz grn, type I	2.00	15
67	A17	1 l brn red & brnz grn, II ('05)	45.00	1.75
68	A17	2 l carmine & blk	4.00	85
69	A17	3 l slate & red brn	5.00	1.90
		Nos. 57-69 (13)	77.30	
		Set value		4.50

For surcharges see Nos. 73, 83-85, 87-88.

1902, Aug. 29 Litho. *Perf. 11½*

70	A18	5s lake	1.00	35
71	A18	10s blue green	1.00	35
72	A18	15s blue	5.25	1.65
		Nos. 70-72 (3)	7.25	2.35

Battle of Shipka Pass, 1877.

Imperf. copies are proofs.

Excellent forgeries of Nos. 70 to 72 exist.

No. 62 Surcharged in Black **10**

1903, Oct. 1 *Perf. 12½*

73	A17	10s on 15s	5.00	35
a.		Inverted surcharge	57.50	50.00
b.		Double surcharge	57.50	50.00
c.		Pair, one without surcharge	100.00	100.00
d.		10s on 10s rose & blk	250.00	250.00

Ferdinand in 1887 and 1907 — A19

1907, Aug. 12 Litho. *Perf. 11½*

74	A19	5s deep green	9.00	90
75	A19	10s red brown	16.00	90
76	A19	25s deep blue	24.00	1.75
		Nos. 74-76 (3)	49.00	3.55

Accession to the throne of Ferdinand I, 20th anniversary.

Nos. 74-76 imperf. are proofs. Nos. 74-76 exist in pairs imperforate between.

Stamps of 1889 Overprinted **1909**

1909

77	A11	1s lilac	1.00	50
a.		Inverted overprint	21.00	17.50
b.		Double overprint, one inverted	25.00	25.00
78	A11	5s yellow green	1.00	50
a.		Inverted overprint	25.00	25.00
b.		Double overprint	25.00	25.00

With Additional Surcharge **5** or **10**

79	A11	5s on 30s brown (Bk)	1.50	18
a.		"5" double		
b.		"1990" for "1909"	700.00	550.00
80	A11	10s on 15s org (Bk)	1.50	40
a.		Inverted surcharge	17.50	17.50
b.		"1909" omitted	27.50	27.50
81	A11	10s on 50s dk grn (R)	1.50	40
a.		"1990" for "1909"	100.00	100.00
b.		Black surcharge	52.50	52.50

Nos. 62 & 64 Surcharged with Value Only

83	A17	5s on 15s (Bl)	1.75	60
a.		Inverted surcharge	21.00	21.00
84	A17	10s on 15s (Bl)	4.50	40
a.		Inverted surcharge	21.00	21.00
85	A17	25s on 30s (R)	5.75	90
a.		Double surcharge	70.00	70.00
b.		"2" of "25" omitted	87.50	87.50
c.		Blue surcharge	275.00	175.00

1910

Nos. 59 and 62 Surcharged in Blue

5

1910, Oct.

87	A17	1s on 3s	3.50	75
a.		"1910" omitted	21.00	
88	A17	5s on 15s	1.50	50

Tsar Assen's Tower (Crown over lion) A20

Tsar Ferdinand A21

City of Trnovo A22

Tsar Ferdinand A23

Ferdinand A24

Isker River A25

Ferdinand A26

Rila Monastery (Crown at UR) A27

Tsar and Princes — A28

Ferdinand in Robes of Ancient Tsars — A29

Monastery of Holy Trinity — A30

View of Varna — A31

1911, Feb. 14 Engr. *Perf. 12*

89	A20	1s myrtle green	16	15
90	A21	2s car & blk	16	15
91	A22	3s lake & blk	40	15
92	A23	5s green & blk	1.00	15
93	A24	10s dp red & blk	1.40	15
94	A25	15s brown bister	2.50	15
95	A26	25s ultra & blk	50	15
96	A27	30s blue & blk	6.75	16
97	A28	50s ocher & blk	16.00	22
a.		Center inverted		2,250.
98	A29	1 l chocolate	6.00	28
99	A30	2 l dull pur & blk	1.65	90
100	A31	3 l blue vio & blk	6.75	3.00
		Nos. 89-100 (12)	43.27	5.61

See Nos. 114-120, 161-162. For overprints and surcharges see Nos. 104-112, 188, B8, Greece N167-N178, N182-N187, Thrace 16-21, Romania 2N1-2N4.

Tsar Ferdinand — A32

1912, Aug. 2 Typo. *Perf. 12½*

101	A32	5s olive green	2.25	70
a.		5s pale green	250.00	110.00
102	A32	10s claret	3.50	1.50
103	A32	25s slate	5.00	1.75
		Nos. 101-103 (3)	10.75	3.95

25th year of reign of Tsar Ferdinand.

ОСВОБ. ВОЙНА

Nos. 89-95 Overprinted in Various Colors

1912-1913

1913, Aug. 6 Engr.

104	A20	1s myrtle grn (C)	15	15
105	A21	2s car & blk (Bl)	15	15
107	A22	3s lake & blk (Bl Bk)	18	15
108	A23	5s grn & blk (R)	15	15
109	A24	10s dp red & blk (Bk)	28	15
110	A25	15s brown bis (G)	55	26
111	A26	25s ultra & blk (R)	2.75	38
		Nos. 104-111 (7)	4.21	
		Set value		1.00

Victory over the Turks in Balkan War of 1912-1913.

10 СТ.

No. 95 Surcharged in Red

1915, July 6

112	A26	10s on 25s	50	15

No. 28 Surcharged in Green **3 СТОТИНКИ**

113	A11	3s on 1s lilac	3.50	4.50

Types of 1911 Re-engraved

1915, Nov. 7 *Perf. 11½, 14*

114	A20	1s dk bl grn	15	15
115	A23	5s grn & brn vio	1.40	15
116	A24	10s red brn & brnsh blk	22	15
117	A25	15s olive green	22	15
118	A26	25s indigo & blk	22	15
119	A27	30s ol grn & red brn	22	15
120	A29	1 l dark brown	32	28
		Nos. 114-120 (7)	2.75	
		Set value		55

Widths: No. 114 is 19½mm; No. 89, 18½mm. No. 118 is 19¼mm; No. 95, 18¼mm. No. 120 is 20mm; No. 98, 19mm. The re-engraved stamps also differ from the 1911 issue in many details of design. Nos. 114-120 exist imperforate.

The 5s and 10s exist perf. 14x11½.

For Nos. 114-116 and 118 overprinted with Cyrillic characters and "1916-1917," see Romania Nos. 2N1-2N4.

Coat of Arms — A33

Peasant and Bullock — A34

Soldier and Mt. Sonichka — A35

View of Nish — A36

Town and Lake Okhrida — A37

Demir-Kapiya (Iron Gate) — A37a

View of Gevgeli — A38

Perf. 11½, 12½x13, 13x12½

1917-19 Typo.

122	A33	5s green	28	15
123	A34	15s slate	15	15
124	A35	25s blue	15	15
125	A36	30s orange	15	15
126	A37	50s violet	52	28
126A	A37a	2 l brn org ('19)	52	35
127	A38	3 l claret	80	75
		Nos. 122-127 (7)	2.57	1.98

Liberation of Macedonia. A 1 l dark green was prepared but not issued. Value $1.65.

For surcharges see Nos. B9-B10, B12.

View of Veles — A39

Monastery of St. Clement at Okhrida — A40

1918 *Perf. 13x14*

128	A39	1s gray	15	15
129	A40	5s green	15	15
		Set value	15	15

Tsar Ferdinand
A41

Plowing with Oxen
A42

1918, July 1 ***Perf. 12½x13***

130	A41	1s dark green	15	15
131	A41	2s dark brown	15	15
132	A41	3s indigo	30	16
133	A41	10s brown red	30	16
		Set value	75	50

30th anniversary of Tsar Ferdinand's accession to the throne.

1919 ***Perf. 13½x13***

134	A42	1s gray	15	15

Sobranye
Palace — A43

Tsar Boris
III — A44

1919 ***Perf. 11½x12, 12x11½***

135	A43	1s black	15	15
137	A43	2s olive green	15	15
		Set value	15	15

For surcharges see Nos. 186, B1.

1919, Oct. 3

138	A44	3s orange brn	15	15
139	A44	5s green	15	15
140	A44	10s rose red	15	15
141	A44	15s violet	15	15
142	A44	25s deep blue	15	15
143	A44	30s chocolate	18	15
144	A44	50s yellow brn	18	15
		Set value	65	35

1st anniv. of enthronement of Tsar Boris III.
Nos. 135-144 exist imperforate.
For surcharges see Nos. 187, B2-B7.

Birthplace of Vazov at Sopot and Cherrywood Cannon — A47

"The Bear Fighter"-a Character from "Under the Yoke" — A48

Ivan Vazov in 1870 and 1920 — A49

Vazov — A50

The Monk
Paisii — A52

Homes of Vazov at Plovdiv and Sofia — A51

1920, Oct. 20 **Photo.** ***Perf. 11½***

147	A47	30s brown red	15	15
148	A48	50s dark green	15	15
149	A49	1 l drab	22	28
150	A50	2 l light brown	60	60
151	A51	3 l black violet	95	65
152	A52	5 l deep blue	1.10	80
		Nos. 147-152 (6)	3.17	2.63

70th birthday of Ivan Vazov (1850-1921), Bulgarian poet and novelist.
Several values of this series exist imperforate and in pairs imperforate between.

Tsar Ferdinand
A53 A54

Mt.
Shar — A55

Bridge over Vardar
River — A56

View of
Ohrid — A57

Perf. 13x14, 14x13

1921, June 11 **Typo.**

153	A53	10s claret	15	15
154	A54	10s claret	15	15
155	A55	10s claret	15	15
156	A56	10s rose lil	15	15
157	A57	20s blue	28	16
		Set value	55	36

Nos. 153-157 were intended to be issued in 1915 to commemorate the liberation of Macedonia. They were not put in use until 1921. A 50s violet was prepared but never placed in use. Value $1.75.

View of
Sofia — A58

"The Liberator," Monument to Alexander II
A59

Monastery at Shipka
Pass — A62

Tsar Boris
III — A63

Harvesting
Grain — A64

Tsar Assen's Tower (No crown over lion) — A65

Rila Monastery (Rosette at upper right) — A66

1921-23 **Engr.** ***Perf. 12***

158	A58	10s blue gray	15	15
159	A59	20s deep green	15	15
160	A63	25s blue grn ('22)	15	15
161	A22	50s orange	15	15
162	A22	50s dk blue ('23)	2.50	2.50
163	A62	75s dull vio	15	15
164	A62	75s dp blue ('23)	30	15
165	A63	1 l carmine	30	16
166	A63	1 l dp blue ('22)	30	15
167	A64	2 l brown	32	15
168	A65	3 l brown vio	38	15
169	A66	5 l lt blue	2.50	32
170	A63	10 l violet brn	6.75	1.10
		Nos. 158-170 (13)	14.10	5.43

For surcharge see No. 189.

Bourchier in Bulgarian Costume
A67

James David Bourchier
A68

View of Rila Monastery
A69

1921, Dec. 31

171	A67	10s red orange	15	15
172	A67	20s orange	15	15
173	A68	30s dp gray	15	15
174	A68	50s bluish gray	15	15
175	A68	1 l dull vio	18	15
176	A69	1½ l olive grn	18	15
177	A69	2 l deep green	18	15
178	A69	3 l Prus blue	45	20
179	A69	5 l red brown	85	35
		Set value	2.00	1.00

Death of James D. Bourchier, Balkan correspondent of the London Times.
For surcharges see Nos. B13-B16.

Postage Due Stamps of 1919-22 Surcharged

a **10 СТОТИНКИ**

1924

182	D6	20s on 20s yellow	15	15
183	D6	20s on 5s gray grn	15	15
a.		20s on 5s emerald	7.00	7.00
184	D6	20s on 10s violet	15	15
185	D6	20s on 30s orange	15	15
		Set value	35	35

Nos. 182 to 185 were used for ordinary postage.

Regular Issues of 1919-23 Surcharged in Blue or Red:

1 ЛЕВЪ **3 ЛЕВА**

186	A43 (a)	10s on 1s black (R)	15	15
187	A44 (b)	1 l on 5s emer (Bl)	15	15
188	A22 (c)	3 l on 50s dk bl (R)	20	15
189	A63 (b)	6 l on 1 l car (Bl)	60	20
		Set value	1.10	60

The surcharge of No. 188 comes in three types: normal, thick and thin.
Nos. 182, 184-189 exist with inverted surcharge.

Lion of Bulgaria
A70 A71

Tsar Boris
III — A72

New Sofia
Cathedral — A73

Harvesting — A74

1925 **Typo.** ***Perf. 13, 11½***

191	A70	10s red & bl, *pink*	15	15
192	A70	15s car & org, *blue*	15	15
193	A70	30s blk & buff	15	15
a.		Cliche of 15s in plate of 30s		
194	A71	50s choc, *green*	15	15
195	A72	1 l dull green	48	15
196	A73	2 l dk grn & buff	1.10	15
197	A74	4 l lake & yellow	1.10	15
		Set value	2.90	50

Several values of this series exist imperforate and in pairs imperforate between.
See #199, 201. For overprint see #C2.

Cathedral of Sveta Nedelya, Sofia, Ruined by Bomb — A75

1926 ***Perf. 11½***

198	A75	50s gray black	15	15

A76

A77

Type A72 Re-engraved. (Shoulder at left does not touch frame)

1926

199	A76	1 l gray	45	15
a.		1 l green	45	15
201	A76	2 l olive brown	52	15

Center Embossed

202	A77	6 l dp bl & pale lemon	1.10	15
203	A77	10 l brn blk & brn org	4.00	75
		Nos. 199-203 (4)	6.07	
		Set value		1.00

For overprints see Nos. C1, C3-C4.

Christo Botev — A78

Tsar Boris III — A79

1926, June 2

204 A78	1 l olive green		32	15
205 A78	2 l slate violet		90	15
206 A78	4 l red brown		90	35
	Nos. 204-206 (3)		2.12	
	Set value			49

Botev (1847-76), Bulgarian revolutionary and poet.

Lion Type of 1881

1927-29 *Perf. 13*

207 A3	10s dk red & drab		15	15
208 A3	15s blk & org ('29)		15	15
209 A3	30s dk bl & bis brn ('28)		15	15
a.	30s indigo & buff		15	15
210 A3	50s blk & rose red ('28)		15	15
	Set value		35	25

1928, Oct. 3 *Perf. 11½*

211 A79	1 l olive green		90	15
212 A79	2 l deep brown		1.00	15
	Set value			15

St. Clement — A80

Konstantin Miladinov — A81

George S. Rakovski A82

Drenovo Monastery A83

Paisii — A84

Tsar Simeon — A85

Lyuben Karavelov A86

Vassil Levski A87

Georgi Benkovski A88

Tsar Alexander II A89

1929, May 12

213 A80	10s dk violet		15	15
214 A81	15s violet brn		15	15
215 A82	30s red		15	15
216 A83	50s olive grn		25	15
217 A84	1 l orange brn		60	15
218 A85	2 l dk blue		70	15
219 A86	3 l dull green		1.50	45
220 A87	4 l olive brown		2.50	22
221 A88	5 l brown		1.50	35
222 A89	6 l Prus green		2.25	90
	Nos. 213-222 (10)		9.75	2.82

Millenary of Tsar Simeon and 50th anniv. of the liberation of Bulgaria from the Turks.

Royal Wedding Issue

Tsar Boris and Fiancee, Princess Giovanna A90

Queen Ioanna and Tsar Boris — A91

1930, Nov. 12 *Perf. 11½*

223 A90	1 l green		25	24
224 A91	2 l dull violet		22	32
225 A90	4 l rose red		22	32
226 A91	6 l dark blue		25	38
	Nos. 223-226 (4)		94	1.26

Fifty-five copies of a miniature sheet incorporating one each of Nos. 223-226 were printed and given to royal, governmental and diplomatic personages.

Tsar Boris III

A92 A93

Perf. 11½, 12x11½, 13

1931-37 **Unwmk.**

227 A92	1 l blue green		25	15
228 A92	2 l carmine		40	15
229 A92	4 l red org ('34)		75	15
230 A92	4 l yel org ('37)		20	15
231 A92	6 l deep blue		70	15
232 A92	7 l dp bl ('37)		20	15
233 A92	10 l slate blk		8.75	70
234 A92	12 l lt brown		40	18
235 A92	14 l lt brn ('37)		28	22
236 A93	20 l claret & org brn		1.00	45
	Nos. 227-236 (10)		12.93	
	Set value			2.00

Nos. 230-233 and 235 have outer bars at top and bottom as shown on cut A92; Nos. 227-229 and 234 are without outer bars.

See Nos. 251, 279-280, 287. For surcharge see No. 252.

Balkan Games Issues

Gymnast — A95

Soccer — A96

Riding — A97

Swimmer A100

"Victory" A101

Designs: 6 l, Fencing. 10 l, Bicycle race.

1931, Sept. 18 *Perf. 11½*

237 A95	1 l lt green		85	50
238 A96	2 l garnet		85	50
239 A97	4 l carmine		1.90	75
240 A95	6 l Prus blue		4.00	1.25
241 A95	10 l red org		9.50	3.75
242 A100	12 l dk blue		32.50	7.50
243 A101	50 l olive brn		30.00	22.50
	Nos. 237-243 (7)		79.60	36.75

1933, Jan. 5

244 A95	1 l blue grn		1.10	95
245 A96	2 l blue		1.90	95
246 A97	4 l brn vio		2.50	1.10
247 A95	6 l brt rose		4.75	1.65
248 A95	10 l olive brn		26.00	9.00
249 A100	12 l orange		55.00	18.00
250 A101	50 l red brown		100.00	82.50
	Nos. 244-250 (7)		191.25	114.15

Nos. 244-250 were sold only at the philatelic agency.

Boris Type of 1931

Outer Bars at Top and Bottom Removed

1933 *Perf. 13*

251 A92	6 l deep blue		80	15

Type of 1931 Surcharged in Blue **2**

1934

252 A92	2 (l) on 3 l ol brn		4.00	25

Soldier Defending Shipka Pass A102

Shipka Battle Memorial A103

Color-Bearer A104

Veteran of the War of Liberation, 1878 A105

Widow and Orphans — A106

Perf. 10½, 11½

1934, Aug. 26 **Wmk. 145**

253 A102	1 l green		45	38
254 A103	2 l pale red		45	24
255 A104	3 l bister brn		1.40	1.25
256 A105	4 l dk carmine		1.25	60
257 A104	7 l dk blue		2.25	2.00
258 A106	14 l plum		6.00	5.75
	Nos. 253-258 (6)		11.80	10.22

Shipka Pass Battle memorial unveiling.

An unwatermarked miniature sheet incorporating one each of Nos. 253-258 was put on sale in 1938 in five cities at a price of 8,000 leva. Printing: 100 sheets.

1934, Sept. 21

259 A102	1 l bright green		45	38
260 A103	2 l dull orange		45	24
261 A104	3 l yellow		1.40	1.25
262 A105	4 l rose		1.25	60
263 A104	7 l blue		2.25	2.00
264 A106	14 l olive bister		6.00	5.75
	Nos. 259-264 (6)		11.80	10.22

An unwatermarked miniature sheet incorporating one each of Nos. 259-263 was issued.

Velcho A. Djamjiyata A108

Capt. G. S. Mamarchev A109

1935, May 5 *Perf. 11½*

265 A108	1 l deep blue		95	25
266 A109	2 l maroon		95	28

Centenary of a Bulgarian uprising against the Turks.

Soccer Game — A110

Cathedral of Alexander Nevski — A111

Soccer Team — A112

Symbolical of Victory — A113

Player and Trophy — A114

The Trophy — A115

1935, June 14

267	A110	1 l green	1.10	90
268	A111	2 l blue gray	2.50	1.40
269	A112	4 l crimson	4.00	2.00
270	A113	7 l brt blue	7.75	2.50
271	A114	14 l orange	7.75	3.25
272	A115	50 l lilac brn	60.00	52.50
		Nos. 267-272 (6)	83.10	62.55

5th Balkan Soccer Tournament.

Gymnast on Parallel Bars — A116

Youth in "Yunak" Costume — A117

Girl in "Yunak" Costume A118

Pole Vaulting A119

Stadium, Sofia — A120

Yunak Emblem — A121

1935, July 10

273	A116	1 l green	1.90	1.10
274	A117	2 l lt blue	2.50	1.10
275	A118	4 l carmine	5.00	2.25
276	A119	7 l dk blue	5.00	3.00
277	A120	14 l dk brown	5.00	3.00
278	A121	50 l red	55.00	42.50
		Nos. 273-278 (6)	74.40	52.95

8th tournament of the Yunak Gymnastic Organization at Sofia, July 12-14.

Boris Type of 1931

1935 Wmk. 145 ***Perf. 12½, 13***

279	A92	1 l green	30	15
280	A92	2 l carmine	20.00	15
		Set value		15

Janos Hunyadi A122

King Ladislas Varnenchik A123

Varna Memorial — A124

King Ladislas III — A125

Battle of Varna, 1444 — A126

1935, Aug. 4 ***Perf. 10½, 11½***

281	A122	1 l brown org	1.10	75
282	A123	2 l maroon	1.10	75
283	A124	4 l vermilion	5.50	3.75
284	A125	7 l dull blue	2.50	1.25
285	A126	14 l green	2.50	1.25
		Nos. 281-285 (5)	12.70	7.75

Battle of Varna, and the death of the Polish King, Ladislas Varnenchik (1424-44).

Lion Type of 1881

1935 Wmk. 145 ***Perf. 13***

286	A3	10s dk red & drab	70	15

Boris Type of 1933

Outer Bars at Top and Bottom Removed

1935

287	A92	6 l gray blue	60	15

Dimitr Monument A127

Haji Dimitr A128

Haji Dimitr and Stefan Karaja — A129

Taking the Oath — A130

Birthplace of Dimitr — A131

1935, Oct. 1 Unwmk. ***Perf. 11½***

288	A127	1 l green	1.25	35
289	A128	2 l brown	1.75	70
290	A129	4 l car rose	3.50	2.50
291	A130	7 l blue	4.50	3.50
292	A131	14 l orange	4.50	3.50
		Nos. 288-292 (5)	15.50	10.55

67th anniv. of the death of the Bulgarian patriots, Haji Dimitr and Stefan Karaja.

Catalogue values for unused stamps in this section, from this point to the end of the section, are for Never Hinged items.

A132

A133

1936-39 ***Perf. 13x12½, 13***

293	A132	10s red org ('37)	15	15
294	A132	15s emerald	15	15
295	A133	30s maroon	15	15
296	A133	30s yel brn ('37)	15	15
297	A133	30s Prus bl ('37)	15	15
298	A133	50s ultra	15	15
299	A133	50s dk car ('37)	20	15
300	A133	50s sl grn ('39)	15	15
		Set value	1.00	50

Meteorological Station, Mt. Moussalla — A134

Peasant Girl — A135

Town of Nessebr A136

1936, Aug. 16 Photo. ***Perf. 11½***

301	A134	1 l purple	1.40	65
302	A135	2 l ultra	1.40	60
303	A136	7 l dark blue	3.75	1.50
		Nos. 301-303 (3)	6.55	2.75

4th Geographical & Ethnographical Cong., Sofia, Aug. 1936.

Sts. Cyril and Methodius A137

Displaying the Bible to the People A138

1937, June 2

304	A137	1 l dk green	22	15
305	A137	2 l dk plum	22	15
306	A138	4 l vermilion	45	22
307	A137	7 l dk blue	1.75	1.10
308	A138	14 l rose red	1.75	1.10
		Nos. 304-308 (5)	4.39	2.72

Millennium of Cyrillic alphabet.

Princess Marie Louise — A139

Tsar Boris III — A140

1937, Oct. 3

310	A139	1 l yellow green	35	15
311	A139	2 l brown red	26	15
312	A139	4 l scarlet	35	15
		Nos. 310-312 (3)	96	
		Set value		30

Issued in honor of Princess Marie Louise.

1937, Oct. 3

313	A140	2 l brown red	35	15

19th anniv. of the accession of Tsar Boris III to the throne. See No. B11.

National Products Issue

Peasants Bundling Wheat A141

Sunflower A142

Wheat — A143

Chickens and Eggs — A144

Cluster of Grapes — A145

Rose and Perfume Flask — A146

Strawberries A147

Girl Carrying Grape Clusters A148

Rose — A149

Tobacco Leaves — A150

1938 ***Perf. 13***

316	A141	10s orange	15	15
317	A141	10s red org	15	15
318	A142	15s brt rose	30	15
319	A142	15s deep plum	30	15
320	A143	30s golden brn	15	15
321	A143	30s copper brn	15	15
322	A144	50s black	15	15
323	A144	50s indigo	15	15
324	A145	1 l yel grn	65	15
325	A145	1 l green	65	15
326	A146	2 l rose pink	60	15
327	A146	2 l rose brn	60	15
328	A147	3 l dp red lil	1.25	15
329	A147	3 l brn lake	1.25	15
330	A148	4 l plum	80	15
331	A148	4 l golden brn	80	15
332	A149	7 l vio blue	1.50	55
333	A149	7 l dp blue	1.50	55
334	A150	14 l dk brown	2.25	90
335	A150	14 l red brn	2.25	90
		Nos. 316-335 (20)	15.60	
		Set value		4.00

Several values of this series exist imperforate.

Crown Prince Simeon A151 A153

Designs: 2 l, Same portrait as 1 l, value at lower left. 14 l, similar to 4 l, but no wreath.

1938, June 16

336	A151	1 l brt green	15	15
337	A151	2 l rose pink	15	15
338	A153	4 l dp orange	16	15
339	A151	7 l ultra	80	38
340	A153	14 l dp brown	80	38
		Nos. 336-340 (5)	2.06	
		Set value		90

First birthday of Prince Simeon.

Tsar Boris III
A155 A156

Various Portraits of Tsar.

1938, Oct. 3

341 A155	1 l lt green		15	15
342 A156	2 l rose brown		60	15
343 A156	4 l golden brn		15	15
344 A156	7 l brt ultra		30	22
345 A156	14 l deep red lilac		35	26
	Nos. 341-345 (5)		1.55	
	Set value			65

20th anniversary, reign of Tsar Boris III.

Early Locomotive A160

Designs: 2 l, Modern locomotive. 4 l, Train crossing bridge. 7 l, Tsar Boris in cab.

1939, Apr. 26

346 A160	1 l yel green	20	15
347 A160	2 l copper brn	20	15
348 A160	4 l red orange	1.40	16
349 A160	7 l dark blue	3.25	85
	Nos. 346-349 (4)	5.05	1.31

50th anniv. of Bulgarian State Railways.

Post Horns and Arrows — A164

Central Post Office, Sofia — A165

1939, May 14 **Typo.**

350 A164	1 l yellow grn	16	15
351 A165	2 l brt carmine	24	15
	Set value		15

60th anniversary of the establishment of the postal system.

Gymnast on Bar — A166

Yunak Emblem — A167

Discus Thrower — A168

Athletic Dancer — A169

Weight Lifter — A170

1939, July 7 **Photo.**

352 A166	1 l yel grn & pale grn	35	15
353 A167	2 l brt rose	35	15
354 A168	4 l brn & gldn brn	52	22
355 A169	7 l dk bl & bl	1.25	65
356 A170	14 l plum & rose vio	5.50	2.75
	Nos. 352-356 (5)	7.97	3.92

9th tournament of the Yunak Gymnastic Organization at Sofia, July 4-8.

Tsar Boris III — A171

Bulgaria's First Stamp — A172

1940-41 **Typo.**

356A A171	1 l dl grn ('41)	80	15
357 A171	2 l brt crimson	20	15
	Set value		15

1940, May 19 **Photo.** ***Perf. 13***

Design: 20 l, Similar design, scroll dated "1840-1940."

358 A172	10 l olive black	1.25	85
359 A172	20 l indigo	1.25	85

Cent. of 1st postage stamp. Exist imperf.

Peasant Couple and Tsar Boris — A174

Flags over Wheat Field and Tsar Boris — A175

Tsar Boris and Map of Dobrudja A176

1940, Sept. 20

360 A174	1 l slate green	15	15
361 A175	2 l rose red	15	15
362 A176	4 l dark brown	15	15
363 A176	7 l dark blue	60	32
	Nos. 360-363 (4)	1.05	
	Set value		50

Return of Dobrudja from Romania.

Fruit A177

Bees and Flowers A178

Plowing A179

Shepherd and Sheep A180

Tsar Boris III — A181

Perf. 10, 10½x11½, 11½, 13

1940-44 **Typo.** **Unwmk.**

364 A177	10s red orange	15	15
365 A178	15s blue	15	15
366 A179	30s olive brn ('41)	15	15
367 A180	50s violet	15	15
368 A181	1 l brt green	15	15
369 A181	2 l rose car	15	15
370 A181	4 l red orange	15	15
371 A181	6 l red vio ('44)	28	15
372 A181	7 l blue	28	15
373 A181	10 l blue grn ('41)	30	15
	Set value	1.50	55

See Nos. 373A-377, 440. For overprints see Nos. 455-463, C31-C32.

1940-41 **Wmk. 145** ***Perf. 13***

373A A180	50s vio ('41)	15	15
374 A181	1 l brt grn	15	15
375 A181	2 l rose car	18	15
376 A181	7 l dull blue	45	15
377 A181	10 l blue green	65	15
	Nos. 373A-377 (5)	1.58	
	Set value		35

Watermarked vertically or horizontally.

P. R. Slaveikov A182

Sofronii, Bishop of Vratza A183

Saint Ivan Rilski — A184

Martin S. Drinov — A185

Monk Khrabr — A186

Kolio Ficheto — A187

1940, Sept. 23 **Photo.** **Unwmk.**

378 A182	1 l brt bl grn	15	15
379 A183	2 l brt carmine	15	15
380 A184	3 l dp red brn	15	15
381 A185	4 l red orange	15	15
382 A186	7 l deep blue	1.00	60
383 A187	10 l dp red brn	1.50	85
	Nos. 378-383 (6)	3.10	
	Set value		1.65

Issued in commemoration of the liberation of Bulgaria from the Turks in 1878.

Johannes Gutenberg A188

N. Karastoyanov, 1st Bulgarian Printer A189

1940, Dec. 16

384 A188	1 l slate green	15	15
385 A189	2 l orange brown	15	15
	Set value	25	15

500th anniv. of the invention of the printing press and 100th anniv. of the 1st Bulgarian printing press.

Christo Botev — A190

Monument to Botev — A192

Botev with his Insurgent Band — A191

1941, May 3

386 A190	1 l dark blue green	15	15
387 A191	2 l crimson rose	20	15
388 A192	3 l dark brown	65	32
	Nos. 386-388 (3)	1.00	
	Set value		42

Issued in honor of Christo Botev, patriot and poet.

Palace of Justice, Sofia — A193

Designs: 20 l, Workers' hospital. 50 l, National Bank.

1941-43 **Engr.** ***Perf. 11½***

389 A193	14 l lt gray brn ('43)	20	15
390 A193	20 l gray grn ('43)	38	16
391 A193	50 l lt bl gray	1.90	1.25
	Nos. 389-391 (3)	2.48	1.56

Macedonian Woman — A196

City of Okhrida — A200

Outline of Macedonia and Tsar Boris III A197

View of Aegean Sea — A198

Poganovski Monastery A199

1941, Oct. 3		Photo.	*Perf. 13*	
392	A196	1 l slate grn	15	15
393	A197	2 l crimson	15	15
394	A198	2 l red org	15	15
395	A199	4 l org brn	15	15
396	A200	7 l dp gray bl	38	28
		Set value	65	50

Issued to commemorate the acquisition of Macedonian territory from neighboring countries.

Peasant Working in a Field — A201

Designs: 15s, Plowing. 30s, Apiary. 50s, Women harvesting fruit. 3 l, Shepherd and sheep. 5 l, Inspecting cattle.

1941-44				
397	A201	10s dk violet	15	15
398	A201	10s dk blue	15	15
399	A201	15s Prus blue	15	15
400	A201	15s dk ol brn	15	15
401	A201	30s red orange	15	15
402	A201	30s dk slate grn	15	15
403	A201	50s blue vio	15	15
404	A201	50s red lilac	15	15
405	A201	3 l henna brn	42	25
406	A201	3 l dk brn ('44)	1.40	1.10
407	A201	5 l sepia	52	48
408	A201	5 l vio bl ('44)	1.40	1.10
		Set value	4.00	3.25

Girls Singing — A207

Boys in Camp — A208

Raising Flag — A209

Folk Dancers — A211

Camp Scene — A210

1942, June 1			Photo.	
409	A207	1 l dk bl grn	15	15
410	A208	2 l scarlet	15	15
411	A209	4 l olive gray	15	15
412	A210	7 l deep blue	16	15
413	A211	14 l fawn	32	22
		Nos. 409-413 (5)	93	
		Set value		45

National "Work and Joy" movement.

Wounded Soldier — A212

Soldier's Farewell — A213

Designs: 4 l, Aiding wounded soldier. 7 l, Widow and orphans at grave. 14 l, Tomb of Unknown Soldier. 20 l, Queen Ioanna visiting wounded.

1942, Sept. 7				
414	A212	1 l slate grn	15	15
415	A213	2 l brt rose	15	15
416	A213	4 l yel org	15	15
417	A213	7 l dark blue	15	15
418	A213	14 l brown	15	15
419	A213	20 l olive blk	22	15
		Set value	75	36

Issued to aid war victims. No. 419 was printed in sheets of 50, alternating with 50 labels.

Legend of Kubrat — A218

Cavalry Charge — A219

Designs: 30s, Rider of Madara. 50s, Christening of Boris I. 1 l, School, St. Naum. 2 l, Crowning of Tsar Simeon by Boris I. 3 l, Golden era of Bulgarian literature. 4 l, Sentencing of the Bogomil Basil. 5 l, Proclamation of 2nd Bulgarian Empire. 7 l, Ivan Assen II at Trebizond. 10 l, Deporting the Patriarch Jeftimi. 14 l, Wandering minstrel. 20 l, Monk Paisii. 30 l, Monument, Shipka Pass.

1942, Oct. 12				
420	A218	10s bluish blk	15	15
421	A219	15s Prus grn	15	15
422	A219	30s dk rose vio	15	15
423	A219	50s indigo	15	15
424	A219	1 l slate grn	15	15
425	A219	2 l crimson	15	15
426	A219	3 l brown	15	15
427	A219	4 l orange	15	15
428	A219	5 l grnsh blk	15	15
429	A219	7 l dk blue	15	15
430	A219	10 l brown blk	15	15
431	A219	14 l olive blk	15	15
432	A219	20 l henna brn	42	28
433	A219	30 l black	70	42
		Set value	2.00	1.25

Tsar Boris III — A234

Designs: Various portraits of Tsar.

Perf. 13, Imperf.

1944, Feb. 28		Photo.	Wmk. 275	
		Frames in Black		
434	A234	1 l olive grn	15	15
435	A234	2 l red brown	16	15
436	A234	4 l brown	20	15
437	A234	5 l gray vio	28	16
438	A234	7 l slate blue	28	16
		Nos. 434-438 (5)	1.07	
		Set value		52

Tsar Boris III (1894-1943).

Tsar Simeon II — A239

Perf. 11½, 13

1944, June 12		Typo.	Unwmk.	
439	A239	3 l red orange	25	15

Shepherd Type of 1940

1944				
440	A180	50s yellow green	20	15

Parcel Post Stamps of 1944 Overprinted in Black or Orange

ВСИЧКО
ЗА
ФРОНТА

1945, Jan. 25			*Perf. 11½*	
448	PP5	1 l dk carmine	15	15
449	PP5	7 l rose lilac	15	15
450	PP5	20 l org brn	15	15
451	PP5	30 l dk brn car	15	15
452	PP5	50 l red orange	25	15
453	PP5	100 l blue (O)	60	16

Overprint reads: "Everything for the Front."

No. 448 with Additional Surcharge of New Value in Black

454	PP5	4 l on 1 l dk car	15	15
		Nos. 448-454 (7)	1.60	
		Set value		45

Nos. 368 to 370 Overprinted in Black

СЪБИРАЙТЕ
СТАРО
ЖЕЛЪЗО

1945, Mar. 15			*Perf. 11½, 13*	
455	A181	1 l brt green	25	15
456	A181	2 l rose carmine	40	15
457	A181	4 l red orange	60	15

Overprint reads: "Collect old iron."

Overprinted in Black

СЪБИРАЙТЕ
ХАРТИЕНИ
ОТПАДЪЦИ

458	A181	1 l brt green	25	15
459	A181	2 l rose carmine	40	15
460	A181	4 l red orange	60	15

Overprint reads: "Collect discarded paper."

Overprinted in Black

СЪБИРАЙТЕ
ВСЪКАКВИ
ПАРЦАЛИ

461	A181	1 l brt green	25	15
462	A181	2 l rose carmine	40	15
463	A181	4 l red orange	60	15
		Nos. 455-463 (9)	3.75	
		Set value		40

Overprint reads: "Collect all kinds of rags."

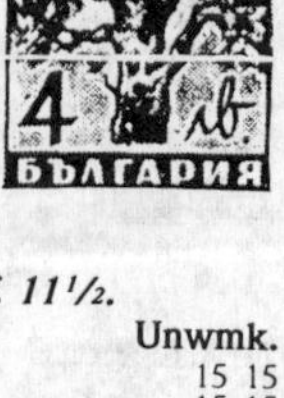

Oak Tree — A245

Imperf., Perf. 11½.

1945		Litho.	Unwmk.	
464	A245	4 l vermilion	15	15
465	A245	10 l blue	15	15

Imperf

466	A245	50 l brown lake	15	15
		Set value	25	25

Slav Congress, Sofia, March, 1945.

A246

A247

A248

A249

A251

A252

A253

A254

Two types of 2 l and 4 l: Type I. Large crown close to coat of arms. Type II. Smaller crown standing high.

1945-46		Photo.	*Perf. 13*	
469	A246	30s yellow grn	15	15
470	A247	50s peacock grn	15	15
471	A248	1 l dk green	15	15
472	A249	2 l choc (I)	15	15
a.		Type II	15	15
473	A249	4 l dk blue (I)	15	15
a.		Type II	15	15
475	A251	5 l red violet	15	15
476	A251	9 l slate gray	15	15
477	A252	10 l Prus blue	15	15
478	A253	15 l brown	15	15
479	A254	20 l carmine	20	15
480	A254	20 l gray blk	20	15
		Set value	1.00	55

Breaking Chain — A255

1 Lev Coin — A256

Water Wheel — A257

Coin and Symbols of Agriculture and Industry — A258

1945, June 4		Unwmk. Litho.	*Imperf.*	
		Laid Paper		
481	A255	50 l brn red, *pink*	15	15
482	A255	50 l org, *pink*	15	15
483	A256	100 l gray bl, *pink*	20	15
484	A256	100 l brn, *pink*	20	15
485	A257	150 l dk ol gray, *pink*	35	18
486	A257	150 l dl car, *pink*	35	18
487	A258	200 l dp bl, *pink*	50	30
488	A258	200 l ol grn, *pink*	50	30
		Nos. 481-488 (8)	2.40	
		Set value		1.25

Souvenir Sheets

489	Sheet of 4	3.00	1.75
a.	A255 50 l violet blue	30	18
b.	A256 100 l violet blue	30	18
c.	A257 150 l violet blue	30	18
d.	A258 200 l violet blue	30	18
490	Sheet of 4	3.00	1.75
a.	A255 50 l brown orange	30	18
b.	A256 100 l brown orange	30	18
c.	A257 150 l brown orange	30	18
d.	A258 200 l brown orange	30	18

Publicizing Bulgaria's Liberty Loan.

Olive Branch — A260

1945, Sept. 1 **Typo.** ***Perf. 13***

491	A260 10 l org brn & yel grn	15	15
492	A260 50 l dull red & dp grn	25	15
	Set value	31	20

Victory of Allied Nations, World War II.

September 9, 1944 — A261

Numeral, Broken Chain — A262

1945, Sept. 7

493	A261 1 l gray green	15	15
494	A261 4 l deep blue	15	15
495	A261 5 l rose lilac	15	15
496	A262 10 l lt blue	15	15
497	A262 20 l brt car	18	15
498	A261 50 l brt bl grn	42	20
499	A261 100 l orange brn	48	35
	Set value	1.25	80

1st anniv. of Bulgaria's liberation.

Old Postal Savings Emblem — A263

Child Putting Coin in Bank — A265

First Bulgarian Postal Savings Stamp — A264

Postal Savings Building, Sofia — A266

1946, Apr. 12

500	A263 4 l brown org	15	15
501	A264 10 l dk olive	15	15
502	A265 20 l ultra	15	15
503	A266 50 l slate gray	52	52
	Set value	75	66

50th anniv. of Bulgarian Postal Savings.

Refugee Children — A267

Nurse Assisting Wounded Soldier — A269

Wounded Soldier — A268

Design: 35 l, 100 l, Red Cross hospital train.

1946, Apr. 4

Cross in Carmine

504	A267 2 l dk olive	15	15
505	A268 4 l violet	15	15
506	A267 10 l plum	15	15
507	A268 20 l ultra	15	15
508	A269 30 l brown org	15	15
509	A268 35 l gray blk	15	15
510	A269 50 l violet brn	22	18
511	A268 100 l gray brn	70	60
	Set value	1.50	1.15

See Nos. 553 to 560.

Advancing Troops A271

Grenade Thrower A272

Attacking Planes — A274

Designs: 5 l, Horse-drawn cannon. 9 l, Engineers building pontoon bridge. 10 l, 30 l, Cavalry charge. 40 l, Horse-drawn supply column. 50 l, Motor transport column. 60 l, Infantry, tanks and planes.

1946, Aug. 9 **Typo.** **Unwmk.**

512	A271 2 l dk red vio	15	15
513	A272 4 l dk gray	15	15
514	A271 5 l dk org red	15	15
515	A274 6 l black brn	15	15
516	A271 9 l rose lilac	15	15
517	A271 10 l dp violet	15	15
518	A271 20 l dp blue	24	15
519	A271 30 l red org	24	15
520	A271 40 l dk ol bis	30	16
521	A271 50 l dk green	30	16
522	A271 60 l red brown	42	28
	Set value	1.85	1.10

Bulgaria's participation in World War II.

Arms of Russia and Bulgaria A279

Lion Rampant A280

1946, May 23

523	A279 4 l red orange	15	15
525	A279 20 l turq green	22	15
	Set value	30	21

Congress of the Bulgarian-Soviet Association, May 1946. The 4 l exists in dk car rose and 20 l in blue, value, set $7.

1946, May 25 ***Imperf.***

526	A280 20 l blue	30	22

Day of the Postage Stamp, May 26, 1946.

Alekandr Stamboliski A281

Flags of Albania, Romania, Bulgaria and Yugoslavia A282

1946, June 13 ***Perf. 12***

527	A281 100 l red orange	4.00	1.90

23rd anniversary of the death of Alekandr Stamboliski, agrarian leader.

1946, July 6 ***Perf. 11½***

528	A282 100 l black brown	75	50

1946 Balkan Games.

Sheet of 100 arranged so that all stamps are tete beche vert. and horiz., except 2 center rows in left pane which provide 10 vert. pairs that are not tete beche vert.

St. Ivan Rilski — A283

A286

A284

A285

Views of Rila Monastery A287

1946, Aug. 26

529	A283 1 l red brown	15	15
530	A284 4 l black brn	15	15
531	A285 10 l dk green	15	15
532	A286 20 l dp blue	18	15
533	A287 50 l dk red	80	50
	Set value	1.25	70

Millenary of Rila Monastery.

People's Republic

A288

1946, Sept. 15 **Typo.**

534	A288 4 l brown lake	15	15
535	A288 20 l dull blue	15	15
536	A288 50 l olive bister	18	16
	Set value	30	26

No. 535 is inscribed "BULGARIA" in Latin characters.

Referendum of Sept. 8, 1946, resulting in the establishment of the Bulgarian People's Republic.

Partisan Army — A289

Snipers — A290

Soldiers: Past and Present — A291

Design: 30 l, Partisans advancing.

1946, Dec. 2

537	A289 1 l violet brn	15	15
538	A290 4 l dull grn	15	15
539	A291 5 l chocolate	15	15
540	A290 10 l crimson	15	15
541	A289 20 l ultra	24	15
542	A290 30 l olive bister	24	15
543	A291 50 l black	28	22
	Set value	1.00	66

Relief Worker and Children — A294

Child with Gift Parcels — A295

Waiting for Food Distribution A296

Mother and Child A297

1946, Dec. 30

545	A294 1 l dk vio brn	15	15
546	A295 4 l brt red	15	15
547	A295 9 l olive bis	15	15
548	A294 10 l slate gray	15	15
549	A296 20 l ultra	15	15
550	A297 30 l dp brn org	15	15
551	A296 40 l maroon	18	15
552	A294 50 l peacock grn	32	28
	Set value	90	72

"Bulgaria" is in Latin characters on No. 548.

Red Cross Types of 1946

1947, Jan. 31

Cross in Carmine

553	A267	2 l olive bister	15	15
554	A268	4 l olive black	15	15
555	A267	10 l blue grn	15	15
556	A268	20 l brt blue	15	15
557	A269	30 l yellow grn	30	22
558	A268	35 l grnsh gray	32	24
559	A269	50 l henna brn	48	35
560	A268	100 l dark blue	70	50
		Nos. 553-560 (8)	2.40	1.91

Laurel Branch, Allied and Bulgarian Emblems — A298

Dove of Peace — A299

1947, Feb. 28

561	A298	4 l olive	15	15
562	A299	10 l brown red	15	15
563	A299	20 l deep blue	18	16
		Set value	30	26

Return to peace at the close of World War II. "Bulgaria" in Latin characters on No. 563.

A302

Guerrilla Fighters
A303 A304

1947, Jan. 21 ***Perf. 11½***

567	A302	10 l choc & brn org	32	16
568	A303	20 l dk bl & bl	32	16
569	A304	70 l dp claret & rose	18.00	8.00
		Nos. 567-569 (3)	18.64	8.32

Issued to honor the anti-fascists.

Hydroelectric Station — A305

Miner
A306

Symbols of Industry
A307

Tractor — A308

1947, Aug. 6

570	A305	4 l olive green	15	15
571	A306	9 l red brown	15	15
572	A307	20 l deep blue	18	18
573	A308	40 l olive brown	42	28
		Nos. 570-573 (4)	90	
		Set value		50

Exhibition Building
A309

Former Home of Alphonse de Lamartine
A310

Symbols of Agriculture and Horticulture — A311

Perf. 11x11½, 11½x11

1947, Aug. 31 **Litho.** **Unwmk.**

574	A309	4 l scarlet	15	15
575	A310	9 l brown lake	15	15
576	A311	20 l brt ultra	20	15
		Set value	31	18

Plovdiv Intl. Fair, 1947. See No. C54.

Basil Evstatiev Aprilov — A312

1947, Oct. 19 **Photo.** ***Perf. 11***

577	A312	40 l brt ultra	35	18

Cent. of the death of Basil Evstatiev Aprilov, educator and historian. See No. 603.

Bicycle Race — A313

Basketball
A314

Chess
A315

Balkan Games: 20 l, Soccer players. 60 l, Four flags of participating nations.

1947, Sept. 29 **Typo.** ***Perf. 11½***

578	A313	2 l plum	18	15
579	A314	4 l dk olive grn	18	15
580	A315	9 l orange brn	42	15
581	A315	20 l brt ultra	80	18
582	A315	60 l violet brn	1.65	75
		Nos. 578-582 (5)	3.23	1.38

People's Theater, Sofia
A316

National Assembly
A317

Central Post Office, Sofia
A318

Presidential Mansion
A319

1947-48 **Typo.** ***Perf. 12½***

583	A316	50s yellow grn	15	15
584	A317	50s yellow grn	15	15
585	A318	1 l green	15	15
586	A319	1 l green	15	15
587	A316	2 l brown lake	15	15
588	A317	2 l lt brown	15	15
589	A316	4 l deep blue	15	15
590	A317	4 l deep blue	15	15
591	A316	9 l carmine	35	15
592	A317	20 l deep blue	75	30
		Set value	1.50	75

On Nos. 583-592 inscription reads "Bulgarian Republic." No. 592 is inscribed in Latin characters.

Redrawn

НАРОДНА

added to inscription

593	A318	1 l green	15	15
594	A318	2 l brown lake	15	15
595	A318	4 l deep blue	15	15
		Set value	25	15

Cyrillic inscription beneath design on Nos. 593-595 reads "Bulgarian People's Republic".

Geno Kirov — A320

Actors' Portraits: 1 l, Zlatina Nedeva. 2 l, Ivan Popov. 3 l, Athanas Kirchev. 4 l, Elena Snejina. 5 l, Stoyan Bachvarov.

Perf. 10½

1947, Dec. 8 **Unwmk.** **Litho.**

596	A320	50s bister brn	15	15
597	A320	1 l lt blue grn	15	15
598	A320	2 l slate green	15	15
599	A320	3 l dp blue	15	15
600	A320	4 l scarlet	15	15
601	A320	5 l red brown	15	15
		Set value, #596-601, B22-B26	1.60	1.00

National Theater, 50th anniversary.

Merchant Ship "Fatherland" — A321

1947, Dec. 19

602	A321	50 l Prus bl, *cream*	45	15

B. E. Aprilov — A322

Worker — A323

1948, Feb. 19 ***Perf. 11***

603	A322	4 l brn car, *cream*	15	15

Centenary of the death of Basil Evstatiev Aprilov, educator and historian.

1948, Feb. 29 **Photo.** ***Perf. 11½x12***

604	A323	4 l dp blue, *cream*	15	15

2nd Bulgarian Workers' Congress.

Self-education — A324

Accordion Player — A325

Factory Recess
A326

Girl Throwing Basketball
A327

1948, Mar. 31 **Photo.**

605	A324	4 l red	15	15
606	A325	20 l deep blue	15	15
607	A326	40 l dull green	20	15
608	A327	60 l brown	60	35
		Nos. 605-608 (4)	1.10	
		Set value		60

Nicholas Vaptzarov — A328

Portraits: 9 l, P. K. Iavorov. 15 l, Christo Smirnenski. 20 l, Ivan Vazov. 45 l, P. R. Slaveikov.

1948, May 18 **Litho.** ***Perf. 11***

Cream Paper

611	A328	4 l brt ver	15	15
612	A328	9 l lt brown	15	15
613	A328	15 l claret	15	15
614	A328	20 l deep blue	15	15
615	A328	45 l green	32	32
		Set value	60	56

Soviet Soldier — A329

Civilians Offering Gifts to Soldiers — A330

Designs: 20 l, Soldiers, 1878 and 1944. 60 l, Stalin and Spasski Tower.

1948, July 5 **Photo.**

Cream Paper

616	A329	4 l brown org	15	15
617	A330	10 l olive grn	15	15
618	A330	20 l dp blue	15	15
619	A329	60 l olive brn	42	35
		Set value	62	52

The Soviet Army.

Demeter Blagoev — A331

Monument to Bishop Andrey — A332

Designs: 9 l, Gabriel Genov. 60 l, Marching youths.

1948, Sept. 6 **Litho.**

Cream Paper

620	A331	4 l dk brown	15	15
621	A331	9 l brown org	15	15
622	A332	20 l dp blue	15	15
623	A332	60 l brown	52	42
		Set value	69	58

No. 623 is inscribed in Cyrillic characters.
Natl. Insurrection of 1923, 25th anniv.

Christo Smirnenski A333

Battle of Grivitza, 1877 A334

1948, Oct. 2 **Photo.** ***Perf. 11½***

Cream Paper

624	A333	4 l blue	15	15
625	A333	16 l red brown	16	15
		Set value	25	15

Christo Smirnenski, poet, 1898-1923.

1948, Nov. 1

626	A334	20 l blue	15	15

Issued to publicize Romanian-Bulgarian friendship. See Nos. C56-C57.

Bath, Gorna Banya — A335

Bath, Bankya — A336

Mineral Bath, Sofia A337

Maliovitza A338

1948-49 **Typo.** ***Perf. 12½***

627	A335	2 l red brown	15	15
628	A336	3 l red orange	15	15
629	A337	4 l deep blue	15	15
630	A338	5 l violet brown	15	15
631	A336	10 l red violet	15	15
632	A338	15 l olive grn ('49)	20	15
633	A335	20 l deep blue	75	16
		Nos. 627-633 (7)	1.70	
		Set value		50

Latin characters on No. 633. See No. 653.

Emblem of the Republic — A339

1948-50

634	A339	50s red orange	15	15
634A	A339	50s org brn ('50)	15	15
635	A339	1 l green	15	15
636	A339	9 l black	15	15
		Set value	30	20

Botev's Birthplace, Kalofer — A340

Christo Botev — A341

Designs: 9 l, Steamer "Radetzky." 15 l, Kalofer village. 20 l, Botev in uniform. 40 l, Botev's mother. 50 l, Pen, pistol and wreath.

Perf. 11x11½, 11½

1948, Dec. 21 **Photo.**

Cream Paper

638	A340	1 l dk green	15	15
639	A341	4 l violet brn	15	15
640	A340	9 l violet	15	15
641	A340	15 l brown	15	15
642	A341	20 l blue	16	15
643	A340	40 l red brown	25	16
644	A341	50 l olive blk	35	22
		Set value	1.00	65

Botev, Bulgarian natl. poet, birth cent.

Lenin — A342

Lenin Speaking — A343

1949, Jan. 24 **Unwmk.** ***Perf. 11½***

Cream Paper

645	A342	4 l brown	15	15
646	A343	20 l brown red	30	18
		Set value		23

25th anniversary of the death of Lenin.

Road Construction A344

Designs: 5 l, Tunnel construction. 9 l, Locomotive. 10 l, Textile worker. 20 l, Female tractor driver. 40 l, Workers in truck.

1949, Apr. 6 ***Perf. 10½***

Inscribed: "CHM"

Cream Paper

647	A344	4 l dark red	15	15
648	A344	5 l dark brown	15	15
649	A344	9 l dk slate grn	22	15
650	A344	10 l violet	25	15
651	A344	20 l dull blue	60	38
652	A344	40 l brown	95	55
		Nos. 647-652 (6)	2.32	
		Set value		1.28

Issued to honor the Workers' Cultural Brigade.

Type of 1948
Redrawn
Country Name and "POSTA" in Latin Characters

1949 **Typo.** ***Perf. 12½***

653	A337	20 l deep blue	55	15

Miner — A345

1949 ***Perf. 11x11½***

654	A345	4 l dark blue	20	15

A347

Prime Minister George Dimitrov, 1882-1949 — A348

1949, July 10 **Photo.**

656	A347	4 l red brown	22	15
657	A348	20 l dark blue	52	16
		Set value		21

Power Station — A349

Grain Towers — A350

Farm Machinery A351

Tractor Parade A352

Agriculture and Industry — A353

1949, Aug. 5 ***Perf. 11½x11, 11x11½***

658	A349	4 l olive green	15	15
659	A350	9 l dark red	15	15
660	A351	15 l purple	18	15
661	A352	20 l blue	55	38
662	A353	50 l orange brn	1.75	85
		Nos. 658-662 (5)	2.78	1.68

Bulgaria's Five Year Plan.

Grenade and Javelin Throwers A354

Hurdlers A355

Motorcycle and Tractor — A356

Boy and Girl Athletes — A357

1949, Sept. 5

663	A354	4 l brown orange	30	15
664	A355	9 l olive green	60	22
665	A356	20 l violet blue	1.25	65
666	A357	50 l red brown	3.00	1.25
		Nos. 663-666 (4)	5.15	2.27

Frontier Guards
A358 A359

1949, Oct. 31

667	A358	4 l chestnut brn	15	15
668	A359	20 l gray blue	60	26
		Set value		31

See No. C60.

George Dimitrov A360

Allegory of Labor A361

Laborers of Both Sexes — A362

Workers and Flags of Bulgaria and Russia — A363

Perf. 11½

1949, Dec. 13 **Photo.** **Unwmk.**

669	A360	4 l orange brn	15	15
670	A361	9 l purple	18	15
671	A362	20 l dull blue	32	22
672	A363	50 l red	65	45
		Nos. 669-672 (4)	1.30	
		Set value		77

Joseph V. Stalin — A364

Stalin and Dove — A365

1949, Dec. 21

673 A364	4 l deep orange	20	15
674 A365	40 l rose brown	60	32
	Set value		37

70th anniv. of the birth of Joseph V. Stalin.

Kharalamby Stoyanov — A366

Communications Strikers — A368

Railway Strikers — A367

1950, Feb. 15

675 A366	4 l yellow brown	15	15
676 A367	20 l violet blue	22	15
677 A368	60 l brown olive	60	38
	Nos. 675-677 (3)	97	
	Set value		50

30th anniv. (in 1949) of the General Railway and Postal Employees' Strike of 1919.

Miner — A369

Locomotive — A370

Shipbuilding A371

Tractor A372

Stalin Central Heating Plant — A374

Textile Worker — A375

Farm Machinery A373

1950-51 *Perf. 11½, 13*

678	A369	1 l olive	15	15
679	A370	2 l gray blk	15	15
680	A371	3 l gray blue	20	15
681	A372	4 l dk blue grn	1.75	52
682	A373	5 l henna brn	40	15
682A	A373	9 l gray blk ('51)	20	15
683	A374	10 l dp plum ('51)	28	15
684	A375	15 l dk car ('51)	40	15
685	A375	20 l dk blue ('51)	70	40
		Nos. 678-685 (9)	4.23	
		Set value		1.30

No. 685 is inscribed in Latin characters.
See Nos. 750-751A.

Vassil Kolarov (1877-1950) — A377

1950, Mar. 6 *Perf. 11½*

Size: 21½x31½mm

686 A377	4 l red brown	15	15

Size: 27x39½mm

687 A377	20 l violet blue	26	22
	Set value	31	27

No. 687 has altered frame and is inscribed in Latin characters.

Stanislav Dospevski, Self-portrait A378

King Kaloyan and Desislava A379

Plowman Resting, by Christo Stanchev A380

Statue of Dimtcho Debelianov, by Ivan Lazarov A381

"Harvest," by V. Dimitrov A382

Design: 9 l, Nikolai Pavlovich, self-portrait.

1950, Apr. 15 *Perf. 11½*

688	A378	1 l dk olive grn	32	15
689	A379	4 l dk red	90	22
690	A378	9 l chocolate	90	22
691	A380	15 l brown	1.50	25
692	A380	20 l deep blue	2.00	80
693	A381	40 l red brown	2.75	1.25
694	A382	60 l deep orange	4.00	1.65
		Nos. 688-694 (7)	12.37	4.54

Latin characters on No. 692.

Ivan Vazov (1850-1921), Poet and Birthplace A383

1950, June 26

695 A383	4 l olive green	15	15

Road Building — A384

Men of Three Races and "Stalin" Flag — A385

Perf. 11½x11, 11x11½

1950, Sept. 19

696 A384	4 l brown red	15	15
697 A385	20 l violet blue	32	16
	Set value	40	21

2nd National Peace Conference.

Molotov, Kolarov, Stalin and Dimitrov — A386

Spasski Tower and Flags — A387

Russian and Bulgarian Women — A388

Loading Russian Ship — A389

Perf. 11½

1950, Oct. 10 **Unwmk.** **Photo.**

698 A386	4 l brown	15	15
699 A387	9 l rose carmine	15	15
700 A388	20 l gray blue	20	15
701 A389	50 l dk grnsh blue	1.10	45
	Nos. 698-701 (4)	1.60	
	Set value		67

2nd anniversary of the Soviet-Bulgarian treaty of mutual assistance.

St. Constantine Sanatorium — A390

Designs: 2 l, 10 l, Children at seashore. 5 l, Rest home.

1950 **Typo.**

702 A390	1 l dark green	15	15
703 A390	2 l carmine	15	15
704 A390	5 l deep orange	16	15
705 A390	10 l deep blue	42	22
	Set value	75	42

Originally prepared in 1945 as "Sunday Delivery Stamps," this issue was released for ordinary postage in 1950.

Runners — A393

1950, Aug. 21 **Photo.** *Perf. 11*

706 A393	4 l shown	15	15
707 A393	9 l Cycling	15	15
708 A393	20 l Shot put	20	20
709 A393	40 l Volleyball	42	42
	Nos. 706-709 (4)	92	92

Marshal Fedor I. Tolbukhin A394

Natives Greeting Tolbukhin A395

Perf. 11½x11, 11x11½

1950, Dec. 10 **Photo.** **Unwmk.**

710 A394	4 l claret	15	15
711 A395	20 l dk blue	35	18
	Set value		24

The return of Dobrich and part of the province of Dobruja from Romania to Bulgaria.

Dimitrov's Birthplace A396

George Dimitrov
A397 A398

Various Portraits, Inscribed:

Г.ДИМИТРОВ

Design: 2 l, Dimitrov Museum, Sofia.

1950, July 2 *Perf. 10½*

712	A396	50s olive grn	15	15
713	A397	50s brown	15	15
714	A397	1 l redsh brn	22	15
715	A396	2 l gray	22	15
716	A397	4 l claret	40	15
717	A397	9 l red brown	60	25
718	A398	10 l brown red	65	35
719	A396	15 l olive gray	65	35
720	A396	20 l dark blue	1.75	55
		Nos. 712-720,C61 (10)	7.79	
		Set value		2.90

1st anniversary of the death of George Dimitrov, statesman. No. 720 is inscribed in Latin characters.

A. S. Popov — A400

1951, Feb. 10

722 A400	4 l red brown	20	15
723 A400	20 l dark blue	55	15
	Set value		24

No. 723 is inscribed in Latin characters.

Arms of Bulgaria
A401 A402

1950 Unwmk. Typo. *Perf. 13*

724 A401	2 l dk brown	15	15
725 A401	3 l rose	15	15
726 A402	5 l carmine	15	15
727 A402	9 l aqua	15	15
	Set value	31	20

Nos. 724-727 were prepared in 1947 for official use but were issued as regular postage stamps Oct. 1, 1950.

Heroes Chankova, Antonov-Malchik, Dimitrov and Dimitrova — A403

Stanke Dimitrov-Marek
A404

George Kirkov
A405

George Dimitrov at Leipzig — A406

Natcho Ivanov and Avr. Stoyanov — A407

Portraits: 9 l, Anton Ivanov. 15 l, Christo Michailov.

1951, Mar. 25 Photo. *Perf. 11½*

728 A403	1 l red violet	15	15
729 A404	2 l dk red brn	15	15
730 A405	4 l car rose	15	15
731 A405	9 l orange brn	45	15
732 A405	15 l olive brn	80	22
733 A406	20 l dark blue	1.10	55
734 A407	50 l olive gray	2.50	90
	Nos. 728-734 (7)	5.30	2.27

First Bulgarian Tractor
A408

First Steam Roller — A409

First Truck — A410

Bulgarian Embroidery — A411

Designs: 15 l, Carpet. 20 l, Tobacco and roses. 40 l, Fruits.

Perf. 11x10½

1951, Mar. 30 Photo. Unwmk.

735 A408	1 l olive brn	18	15
736 A409	2 l violet	28	15
737 A410	4 l red brown	50	15
738 A411	9 l purple	70	15
739 A409	15 l deep plum	1.00	28
740 A411	20 l violet blue	1.50	32
741 A410	40 l deep green	2.50	65

Perf. 13

Size: 23x18½mm

742 A408	1 l purple	15	15
743 A409	2 l Prus green	28	15
744 A410	4 l red brown	28	15
	Nos. 735-744 (10)	7.37	
	Set value		1.70

See Nos. 894, 973. For surcharge see No. 973.

Turkish Attack on Mt. Zlee Dol
A412

Designs: 4 l, Georgi Benkovski speaking to rebels. 9 l, Cherrywood cannon of 1876 and Russian cavalry, 1945. 20 l, Rebel, 1876 and partisan, 1944. 40 l, Benkovski and Dimitrov.

1951, May 3 *Perf. 10½*

Cream Paper

745 A412	1 l redsh brown	16	15
746 A412	4 l dark green	16	15
747 A412	9 l violet brown	50	28
748 A412	20 l deep blue	65	48
749 A412	40 l dark red	1.00	70
	Nos. 745-749 (5)	2.47	1.76

75th anniv. of the "April" revolution.

Industrial Types of 1950

1951 *Perf. 13*

750 A369	1 l violet	15	15
751 A370	2 l dk brown	15	15
751A A372	4 l dk yel grn	75	15
	Nos. 750-751A (3)	1.05	
	Set value		17

Demeter Blagoev Addressing 1891 Congress at Busludja — A413

1951 Photo. *Perf. 11*

752 A413	1 l purple	24	15
753 A413	4 l dark green	35	15
754 A413	9 l deep claret	60	32
	Nos. 752-754 (3)	1.19	
	Set value		50

60th anniversary of the first Congress of the Bulgarian Social-Democratic Party.

See Nos. 1174-1176.

Day Nursery — A414

Designs: 4 l, Model building construction. 9 l, Playground. 20 l, Children's town.

1951, Oct. 10 Unwmk.

755 A414	1 l brown	15	15
756 A414	4 l deep plum	20	15
757 A414	9 l blue green	60	22
758 A414	20 l deep blue	1.00	55
	Nos. 755-758 (4)	1.95	1.07

Children's Day, Sept. 25, 1951.

Order of Labor
A415 A416

1952, Feb. 1 *Perf. 13*

Reverse of Medal

759 A415	1 l red brown	15	15
760 A415	4 l blue green	15	15
761 A415	9 l dark blue	28	15

Obverse of Medal

762 A416	1 l carmine	15	15
763 A416	4 l green	15	15
764 A416	9 l purple	28	15
	Set value	85	32

No. 764 has numeral at lower left and different background.

Workers and Symbols of Industry — A417

Design: 4 l, Flags, Dimitrov, Chervenkov.

1951, Dec. 29 *Perf. 11*

Inscribed: "16 XII 1951"

765 A417	1 l olive black	15	15
766 A417	4 l chocolate	16	15
	Set value	25	15

Third Congress of Bulgarian General Workers' Professional Union.

Dimitrov and Chemical Works — A418

George Dimitrov and V. Chervenkov
A419

Portrait: 80s, Dimitrov.

Unwmk.

1952, June 18 Photo. *Perf. 11*

767 A418	16s brown	35	22
768 A419	44s brown carmine	52	25
769 A418	80s brt blue	1.10	52
	Nos. 767-769 (3)	1.97	99

70th anniv. of the birth of George Dimitrov.

Vassil Kolarov Dam — A420

Republika Power Station — A421

1952, May 16 *Perf. 13*

770 A420	4s dark green	15	15
771 A420	12s purple	15	15
772 A420	16s red brown	15	15
773 A420	44s rose brown	50	15
774 A420	80s brt blue	1.65	18
	Nos. 770-774 (5)	2.60	
	Set value		40

No. 774 is inscribed in Latin characters.

1952, June 30 *Perf. 13, Pin Perf.*

775 A421	16s dark brown	20	15
776 A421	44s magenta	75	15
	Set value		20

Nikolai I. Vapzarov — A422

Designs: Various portraits.

1952, July 23 *Perf. 10½*

777 A422	16s rose brown	16	15
778 A422	44s dk red brn	65	16
779 A422	80s dk olive brn	1.40	52
	Nos. 777-779 (3)	2.21	83

10th anniversary of the death of Nikolai I. Vapzarov, poet and revolutionary.

Dimitrov and Youth Conference — A423

Designs: 16s, Resistance movement incident. 44s, Frontier guards and industrial scene. 80s, George Dimitrov and young workers.

1952, Sept. 1 *Perf. 11x11½*

780 A423	2s brown carmine	15	15
781 A423	16s purple	20	15
782 A423	44s dark green	52	28
783 A423	80s dark brown	1.10	60
	Nos. 780-783 (4)	1.97	1.18

40th anniv. of the founding conference of the Union of Social Democratic Youth.

Assault on the Winter Palace — A424

Designs: 8s, Volga-Don Canal. 16s, Symbols of world peace. 44s, Lenin and Stalin. 80s, Himlay hydroelectric station.

Perf. 11½

1952, Nov. 6 Unwmk. Photo.

Dated: "1917-1952"

784 A424	4s red brown	15	15
785 A424	8s dark green	15	15
786 A424	16s dark blue	15	15
787 A424	44s brown	32	18
788 A424	80s olive brown	75	35
	Nos. 784-788 (5)	1.52	
	Set value		70

35th anniv. of the Russian revolution.

Vassil Levski — A425

Design: 44s, Levski and comrades.

1953, Feb. 19 Cream Paper *Perf. 11*

789 A425 16s brown 15 15
790 A425 44s brown blk 25 15
Set value 15

80th anniv. of the death of Levski, patriot.

Ferrying Artillery and Troops into Battle A426

Soldier A427

Mother and Children A428

Designs: 44s, Victorious soldiers. 80s, Soldier welcomed. 1 l, Monuments.

1953, Mar. 3 *Perf. 10½*

791 A426 8s Prus green 16 15
792 A427 16s dp brown 22 15
793 A426 44s dk slate grn 42 15
794 A426 80s dull red brn 85 20
795 A426 1 l black 1.10 32
Nos. 791-795 (5) 2.75
Set value 70

75th anniversary of Bulgaria's independence from Turkey.

1953, Mar. 9

796 A428 16s slate green 15 15
797 A428 16s bright blue 15 15
Set value 25 15

Women's Day.

Woodcarvings at Rila Monastery
A429 A430

Designs: 12s, 16s, 28s, Woodcarvings, Rila Monastery. 44s, Carved Ceilings, Trnovo. 80s, 1 l, 4 l, Carvings, Pasardjik.

1953 Unwmk. Photo. *Perf. 13*

798 A429 2s gray brown 15 15
799 A430 8s dk slate grn 15 15
800 A430 12s brown 15 15
801 A430 16s rose lake 24 15
802 A429 28s dk olive grn 32 15
803 A430 44s dk brown 50 15
804 A430 80s ultra 85 15
805 A430 1 l violet blue 1.75 22
806 A430 4 l rose lake 3.50 90
Nos. 798-806 (9) 7.61
Set value 1.55

Karl Marx A431

"Das Kapital" A432

1953, Apr. 30 *Perf. 10½*

807 A431 16s bright blue 15 15
808 A432 44s deep brown 32 18
Set value 25

70th anniversary of the death of Karl Marx.

Labor Day Parade — A433

Joseph V. Stalin — A434

1953, Apr. 30 *Perf. 13*

809 A433 16s brown red 15 15

Labor Day, May 1, 1953.

1953, May 23 *Perf. 13x13½*

810 A434 16s dark gray 20 15
811 A434 16s dark brown 20 15
Set value 15

Death of Joseph V. Stalin, Mar. 5, 1953.

Georgi Delchev — A435

Battle Scene — A436

Peasants Attacking Turkish Troops — A437

1953, Aug. 8 *Perf. 13*

812 A435 16s dark brown 15 15
813 A436 44s purple 30 15
814 A437 1 l deep claret 45 16
Nos. 812-814 (3) 90
Set value 35

50th anniv. of the Ilinden Revolt (#812, 814) and the Preobrazhene Revolt (#813).

Soldier and Rebels — A438

Design: 44s, Soldier guarding industrial construction.

1953, Sept. 18

815 A438 16s deep claret 15 15
816 A438 44s greenish blue 35 15
Set value 17

Army Day.

George Dimitrov and Vassil Kolarov — A439

Demeter Blagoev — A440

Designs: 16s, Citizens in revolt. 44s, Attack.

1953, Sept. 22

817 A439 8s olive gray 15 15
818 A439 16s dk red brn 18 15
819 A439 44s cerise 45 18
Nos. 817-819 (3) 78
Set value 28

September Revolution, 30th anniversary.

1953, Sept. 21

Portraits: 44s, G. Dimitrov and D. Blagoev.

820 A440 16s brown 25 15
821 A440 44s red brown 38 15
Set value 17

50th anniversary of the formation of the Social Democratic Party.

Railway Viaduct — A441

Pouring Molten Metal — A442

Designs: 16s, Welder and storage tanks. 80s, Harvesting machine.

1953, Oct. 17

826 A441 8s brt blue 15 15
827 A441 16s grnsh blk 15 15
828 A442 44s brown red 28 15
829 A441 80s orange 45 28
Nos. 826-829 (4) 1.03
Set value 50

Month of Bulgarian-Russian friendship.

Belladonna A443

Kolarov Library, Sofia A444

Medicinal Flowers: 4s, Jimson weed. 8s, Sage. 12s, Dog rose. 16s, Gentian. 20s, Poppy. 28s, Peppermint. 40s, Bear grass. 44s, Coltsfoot. 80s, Cowslip. 1 l, Dandelion. 2 l, Foxglove.

1953 Unwmk. Photo. *Perf. 13*
White or Cream Paper

830 A443 2s dull blue 15 15
831 A443 4s brown org 15 15
832 A443 8s blue grn 15 15
833 A443 12s brown org 15 15
834 A443 12s blue grn 15 15
835 A443 16s violet blue 15 15
836 A443 16s dp red brn 15 15
837 A443 20s car rose 15 15
838 A443 28s dk gray grn 30 15
839 A443 40s dark blue 35 18
840 A443 44s brown 35 18
841 A443 80s yellow brn 60 35
842 A443 1 l henna brn 2.25 48
843 A443 2 l purple 3.75 1.25
a. Souvenir sheet 27.50 20.00
Nos. 830-843 (14) 8.80
Set value 2.95

No. 843a contains 12 stamps, one of each denomination above, printed in dark green. Size: 161x172mm. Sold for 6 leva.

1953, Dec. 16

854 A444 44s brown 25 15

75th anniversary of the founding of the Kolarov Library, Sofia.

Singer and Accordionist A445

Lenin and Stalin A446

1953, Dec. 26

855 A445 16s shown 15 15
856 A445 44s Dancers 18 15
Set value 25 17

1954, Mar. 13

Designs: 44s, Lenin statue. 80s, Lenin mausoleum, Moscow. 1 l, Lenin.

Cream Paper

857 A446 16s brown 20 15
858 A446 44s rose brown 26 15
859 A446 80s blue 42 15
860 A446 1 l dp olive grn 60 26
Nos. 857-860 (4) 1.48
Set value 50

30th anniversary of the death of Lenin.

Demeter Blagoev and Followers A447

Design: 44s, Blagoev at desk.

1954, Apr. 28

Cream Paper

861 A447 16s dp red brn 15 15
862 A447 44s black brn 32 15
Set value 15

30th anniv. of the death of Demeter Blagoev.

George Dimitrov A448

Dimitrov and Refinery A449

1954, June 11

863 A448 44s lake, *cream* 22 15
864 A449 80s brown, *cream* 65 15
Set value 15

5th anniv. of the death of George Dimitrov.

Train Leaving Tunnel — A450

1954, July 30

865	A450	44s dk grn, *cream*	60	15
866	A450	44s blk brn, *cream*	60	15
		Set value		20

Day of the Railroads, Aug. 1, 1954.

Miner at Work — A451

1954, Aug. 19

867	A451	44s grnsh blk, *cream*	20	15

Miners' Day.

Academy of Science — A452

1954, Oct. 27

868	A452	80s black, *cream*	55	18

85th anniversary of the foundation of the Bulgarian Academy of Science.

Horsemanship A454

16s, 44s, 2 l, vert.

1954, Dec. 21

869	A454	16s Gymnastics	52	16
870	A454	44s Wrestling	60	20
871	A454	80s shown	1.25	55
872	A454	2 l Skiing	3.00	1.65
		Nos. 869-872 (4)	5.37	2.56

Welcoming Liberators — A455

Soldier's Return — A456

Designs: 28s, Refinery. 44s, Dimitrov and Workers. 80s, Girl and boy. 1 l, George Dimitrov.

1954, Oct. 4

Cream Paper

873	A455	12s brown car	15	15
874	A456	16s dp carmine	15	15
875	A455	28s indigo	15	15
876	A455	44s redsh brn	15	15
877	A456	80s deep blue	55	25
878	A456	1 l dark green	55	25
		Set value	1.40	70

10th anniversary of Bulgaria's liberation.

Recreation at Workers' Rest Home — A457

Metal Worker and Furnace — A458

Portraits: 80s, Dimitrov, Blagoev, and Kirkov.

Unwmk.

1954, Dec. 28 Photo. *Perf. 13*

Cream Paper

879	A457	16s dark green	16	15
880	A458	44s brown orange	16	15
881	A457	80s dp violet blue	42	20
		Nos. 879-881 (3)	74	
		Set value		30

50th anniversary of Bulgaria's trade union movement.

Geese — A459

Designs: 4s, Chickens. 12s, Hogs. 16s, Sheep. 28s, Telephone building. 44s, Communist party headquarters. 80s, Apartment buildings. 1 l, St. Kiradgieff Mills.

1955-56

882	A459	2s dk blue grn	16	15
883	A459	4s olive green	28	15
884	A459	12s dk red brn	42	15
885	A459	16s brown orange	65	15
886	A459	28s violet blue	32	15
887	A459	44s lil red, *cream*	60	15
a.		44s brown red	4.50	15
888	A459	80s dk red brown	75	15
889	A459	1 l dk blue green	1.50	16
		Nos. 882-889 (8)	4.68	
		Set value		56

Issued: #887, 4/20/56; others, 2/19/55.

Textile Worker — A460

Mother and Child — A461

Design: 16s, Woman feeding calf.

1955, Mar. 5

890	A460	12s dark brown	15	15
891	A460	16s dark green	15	15
892	A461	44s dk car rose	50	15
893	A461	44s blue	50	15
		Nos. 890-893 (4)	1.30	
		Set value		26

Women's Day, Mar. 8, 1955.

No. 744 Surcharged in Blue

1955, Mar. 8 ***Perf. 13***

894	A410	16s on 4 l red brown	45	15

May Day Demonstration of Workers A462

Sts. Cyril and Methodius A463

Design: 44s, Three workers and globe.

1955, Apr. 23 **Photo.**

895	A462	16s car rose	15	15
896	A462	44s blue	30	15
		Set value		15

Labor Day, May 1, 1955.

1955, May 21

Designs: 8s, Paisii Hilendarski. 16s, Nicolas Karastoyanov's printing press. 28s, Christo Botev. 44s, Ivan Vazov. 80s, Demeter Blagoev and socialist papers. 2 l, Blagoev printing plant, Sofia.

Cream Paper

897	A463	4s deep blue	15	15
898	A463	8s olive	15	15
899	A463	16s black	15	15
900	A463	28s henna brn	16	15
901	A463	44s brown	32	15
902	A463	80s rose red	50	16
903	A463	2 l black	1.50	42
		Nos. 897-903 (7)	2.93	
		Set value		80

Creation of the Cyrillic alphabet, 1100th anniv. Latin lettering at bottom on #901-903.

Sergei Rumyantzev A464

Mother and Children A465

Portraits: 16s, Christo Jassenov. 44s, Geo Milev.

1955, June 30 Unwmk. *Perf. 13*

Cream Paper

904	A464	12s orange brn	16	15
905	A464	16s lt brown	16	15
906	A464	44s grnsh blk	42	15
		Nos. 904-906 (3)	74	
		Set value		24

30th anniv. of the deaths of Sergei Rumyanchev, Christo Jassenov and Geo Milev. Latin lettering at bottom of No. 906.

1955, July 30

907	A465	44s brn car, *cream*	30	15

World Congress of Mothers in Lausanne, 1955.

Young People of Three Races — A466

Friedrich Engels and Book — A467

1955, July 30

908	A466	44s blue, *cream*	30	15

5th World Festival of Youth in Warsaw, July 31-Aug. 14.

1955, July 30

909	A467	44s brown	30	15

60th anniv. of the death of Friedrich Engels.

Entrance to Fair, 1892 — A468

Statuary Group at Fair, 1955 — A469

Designs: 44s, "Fruit of our Land." 80s, Woman holding Fair emblem.

1955, Aug. 31

Cream Paper

910	A468	4s deep brown	15	15
911	A469	16s dk car rose	15	15
912	A468	44s olive blk	20	15
913	A469	80s deep blue	45	15
		Set value	80	32

16th International Plovdiv Fair. Latin lettering on Nos. 912-913.

Friedrich von Schiller — A470

Portraits: 44s, Adam Mickiewicz. 60s, Hans Christian Andersen. 80s, Baron de Montesquieu. 1 l, Miguel de Cervantes. 2 l, Walt Whitman.

1955, Oct. 31

Cream Paper

914	A470	16s brown	15	15
915	A470	44s brown red	38	15
916	A470	60s Prus blue	60	15
917	A470	80s black	60	15
918	A470	1 l rose violet	1.40	32
919	A470	2 l olive green	1.90	50
		Nos. 914-919 (6)	5.03	
		Set value		1.05

Various anniversaries of famous writers. Nos. 918 and 919 are issued in sheets alternating with labels without franking value. The labels show title pages for Leaves of Grass and Don Quixote in English and Spanish, respectively. Latin lettering on #915-919.

Karl Marx Industrial Plant — A471

Friendship Monument — A472

I. V. Michurin — A473

Designs: 4s, Alekandr Stamboliski Dam. 16s, Bridge over Danube. 1 l, Vladimir V. Mayakovsky.

1955, Dec. 1 **Unwmk.**

920	A471	2s slate blk	15	15
921	A471	4s deep blue	15	15
922	A471	16s dk blue grn	15	15
923	A472	44s red brown	15	15
924	A473	80s dark green	25	15
925	A473	1 l gray blk	38	15
		Set value	90	45

Russian-Bulgarian friendship.

Library Seal — A474

Krusto Pishurka — A475

Portrait: 44s, Bacho Kiro.

1956, Feb. 10 ***Perf. 11x10½***

926	A474	12s car lake, *cream*	15	15
927	A475	16s dp brn, *cream*	15	15
928	A475	44s slate blk, *cream*	22	15
		Set value	33	17

100th anniversary of the National Library. Latin lettering at bottom of No. 928.

Canceled to Order

Beginning about 1956, some issues were sold in sheets canceled to order. Values in second column when much less than unused are for "CTO" copies. Postally used stamps are valued at slightly less than, or the same as, unused.

Quinces — A476

Cherrywood Cannon — A477

Designs: 8s, Pears. 16s, Apples. 44s, Grapes.

1956	**Photo.**		***Perf. 13***	
929	A476	4s carmine	75	15
930	A476	8s blue green	32	15
931	A476	16s lilac rose	80	15
932	A476	44s deep violet	80	16
		Nos. 929-932 (4)	2.67	
		Set value		32

Latin lettering on #932. See #964-967. For surcharge see #1364.

1956, Apr. 28			***Perf. 11x10½***	
933	A477	16s shown	15	15
934	A477	44s Cavalry attack	22	15
		Set value		15

April Uprising against Turkish rule, 80th anniv.

Demeter Blagoev (1856-1924), Writer, Birthplace A478

Cherries A479

1956, May 30			***Perf. 11***	
935	A478	44s Prus blue	25	15

1956	**Unwmk.**		***Perf. 13***	
936	A479	2s shown	15	15
937	A479	12s Plums	15	15
938	A479	28s Peaches	18	15
939	A479	80s Strawberries	55	20
		Nos. 936-939 (4)	1.03	
		Set value		35

Latin lettering on No. 939.

Gymnastics A480

Pole Vaulting A481

Designs: 12s, Discus throw. 44s, Soccer, 80s, Basketball. 1 l, Boxing.

Perf. 11x10½, 10½x11

1956, Aug. 29				
940	A480	4s brt ultra	15	15
941	A480	12s brick red	15	15
942	A481	16s yellow brn	32	16
943	A481	44s dark green	48	25
944	A480	80s dark red brn	1.00	50
945	A481	1 l deep magenta	1.65	65
		Nos. 940-945 (6)	3.75	1.86

Latin lettering on Nos. 943-945.
16th Olympic Games at Melbourne, Nov. 22-Dec. 8, 1956.

Tobacco, Rose and Distillery A482

People's Theater A483

1956, Sept. 1			***Perf. 13***	
946	A482	44s deep carmine	38	16
947	A482	44s olive green	38	16

17th International Plovdiv Fair.

1956, Nov. 16			**Unwmk.**	

Design: 44s, Dobri Woinikoff and Sawa Dobroplodni, dramatists.

948	A483	16s dull red brown	15	15
949	A483	44s dark blue green	22	15
		Set value		15

Bulgarian Theater centenary.

Benjamin Franklin A484

Cyclists, Palms and Pyramids A485

Portraits: 20s, Rembrandt. 40s, Mozart. 44s, Heinrich Heine. 60s, Shaw. 80s, Dostoevski. 1 l, Ibsen. 2 l, Pierre Curie.

1956, Dec. 29				
950	A484	16s dark olive grn	15	15
951	A484	20s brown	18	15
952	A484	40s dark car rose	18	15
953	A484	44s dark violet brn	22	15
954	A484	60s dark slate	32	15
955	A484	80s dark brown	45	15
956	A484	1 l bluish grn	80	30
957	A484	2 l Prus green	1.75	52
		Nos. 950-957 (8)	4.05	
		Set value		1.20

Great personalities of the world.

1957, Mar. 6	**Photo.**		***Perf. 10½***	
958	A485	80s henna brown	50	25
959	A485	80s Prus green	50	25

Fourth Egyptian bicycle race.

Woman Technician — A486

"New Times" Review — A487

Designs: 16s, Woman and children. 44s, Woman feeding chickens.

1957, Mar. 8				
960	A486	12s deep blue	15	15
961	A486	16s henna brown	15	15
962	A486	44s slate green	30	15
		Set value	40	17

Women's Day. Latin lettering on 44s.

1957, Mar. 8			**Unwmk.**	
963	A487	16s deep carmine	20	15

60th anniversary of the founding of the "New Times" review.

Fruit Type of 1956.

Designs: 4s, Quinces. 8s, Pears. 16s, Apples. 44s, Grapes.

1957	**Photo.**		***Perf. 13***	
964	A476	4s yellow green	15	15
965	A476	8s brown orange	15	15
966	A476	16s rose red	15	15
967	A476	44s orange yellow	40	15
		Set value	62	35

Latin lettering on #967. For surcharge see #1364.

Sts. Cyril and Methodius A488

Basketball A489

1957, May 22			***Perf. 11***	
968	A488	44s olive grn & buff	50	15

Centenary of the first public veneration of Sts. Cyril and Methodius, inventors of the Cyrillic alphabet.

1957, June 20	**Photo.**		***Perf. 10½x11***	
969	A489	44s dark green	95	30

10th European Basketball Championship at Sofia.

Dancer and Spasski Tower, Moscow — A490

1957, July 18			***Perf. 13***	
970	A490	44s blue	30	15

Sixth World Youth Festival in Moscow.

George Dimitrov (1882-1949) — A491

1957, July 18				
971	A491	44s deep carmine	50	15

Vassil Levski — A492

1957, July 18			***Perf. 11***	
972	A492	44s grnsh black	30	15

120th anniversary of the birth of Vassil Levski, patriot and national hero.

No. 742 Surcharged in Carmine

1957	**Unwmk.**		***Perf. 13***	
973	A408	16s on 1 l purple	15	15

Trnovo and Lazarus L. Zamenhof A493

1957, July 27				
974	A493	44s slate green	50	15

50th anniv. of the Bulgarian Esperanto Society and the 70th anniv. of Esperanto.
For surcharge see No. 1235.

Bulgarian Veteran of 1877 War and Russian Soldier — A494

Design: 44s, Battle of Shipka Pass.

1957, Aug. 13				
975	A494	16s dk blue grn	15	15
976	A494	44s brown	32	15
		Set value		15

80th anniversary of Bulgaria's liberation from the Turks. Latin lettering on No. 976.

Woman Planting Tree — A495

Red Deer in Forest — A496

Designs: 16s, Dam, lake and forest. 44s, Plane over forest. 80s, Fields on edge of forest.

1957, Sept. 16	**Photo.**		***Perf. 13***	
977	A495	2s deep green	15	15
978	A496	12s dark brown	15	15
979	A496	16s Prus blue	15	15
980	A496	44s Prus green	22	15
981	A496	80s yellow green	42	15
		Set value	90	45

Latin lettering on Nos. 980 and 981.

Lenin — A497

Designs: 16s, Cruiser "Aurora." 44s, Dove over map of communist area. 60s, Revolutionaries and banners. 80s, Oil refinery.

1957, Oct. 29			***Perf. 11***	
982	A497	12s chocolate	16	15
983	A497	16s Prus green	32	15
984	A497	44s deep blue	65	15
985	A497	60s dk car rose	75	15
986	A497	80s dark green	1.25	22
		Nos. 982-986 (5)	3.13	
		Set value		54

40th anniv. of the Communist Revolution.
Latin lettering on Nos. 984-985.

Globes
A498

1957, Oct. 4 *Perf. 13*

987 A498 44s Prus blue	30	15

4th Intl. Trade Union Cong., Leipzig, Oct. 4-15.

Vassil Kolarov Hotel
A499

Bulgarian Health Resorts: 4s, Skis and Pirin Mountains. 8s, Old house at Koprivspitsa. 12s, Rest home at Velingrad. 44s, Momin-Prochod Hotel. 60s, Nesebr Hotel, shoreline and peninsula. 80s, Varna beach scene. 1 l, Hotel at Varna.

1958 **Photo.** *Perf. 13*

988 A499 4s blue	15	15
989 A499 8s orange brn	15	15
990 A499 12s dk green	15	15
991 A499 16s green	15	15
992 A499 44s dk blue grn	15	15
993 A499 60s deep blue	18	15
994 A499 80s fawn	28	15
995 A499 1 l dk red brn	35	18
Set value	1.14	62

Latin lettering on 44s, 60s, 80s, and 1 l.
Issue dates: #991-994, Jan. 20. Others, July 5.
For surcharge see No. 1436.

Mikhail I. Glinka — A500

Portraits: 16s, Jan A. Komensky (Comenius). 40s, Carl von Linné. 44s, William Blake. 60s, Carlo Goldoni. 80s, Auguste Comte.

1957, Dec. 30

996 A500 12s dark brown	20	15
997 A500 16s dark green	20	15
998 A500 40s Prus blue	20	15
999 A500 44s maroon	20	15
1000 A500 60s orange brown	75	15
1001 A500 80s deep plum	2.50	90
Nos. 996-1001 (6)	4.05	
Set value		1.25

Famous men of other countries. Latin lettering on Nos. 999-1001.

Young Couple, Flag, Dimitrov
A501

People's Front Salute
A502

1957, Dec. 28 *Perf. 11*

1002 A501 16s carmine rose	15	15

10th anniversary of Dimitrov's Union of the People's Youth.

1957, Dec. 28

1003 A502 16s dk violet brn	15	15

15th anniversary of the People's Front.

Hare — A503

Animals: 12s, Red deer (doe), vert. 16s, Red deer (stag). 44s, Chamois. 80s, Brown bear. 1 l, Wild boar.

Perf. 10½

1958, Apr. 5 **Unwmk.** **Photo.**

1004 A503 2s lt & dk ol grn	15	15
1005 A503 12s sl grn & red brn	18	15
1006 A503 16s bluish grn & dk red brn	20	15
1007 A503 44s blue & brown	24	15
1008 A503 80s bis & dk brn	75	25
1009 A503 1 l stl bl & dk brn	1.00	22
Nos. 1004-1009 (6)	2.52	
Set value		55

Value, imperf. set $4.

Marx and Lenin
A504

Designs: 16s, Marchers and flags. 44s, Lenin blast furnaces.

1958, July 2 *Perf. 11*

1010 A504 12s dark brown	16	15
1011 A504 16s dark carmine	20	15
1012 A504 44s dark blue	85	15
Nos. 1010-1012 (3)	1.21	
Set value		20

Bulgarian Communist Party, 7th Congress.

Wrestlers — A505

1958, June 20 *Perf. 10½*

1013 A505 60s dk carmine rose	65	35
1014 A505 80s deep brown	1.10	55

World Wrestling Championship, Sofia.

Chessmen and Globe
A506

Perf. 10½

1958, July 18 **Unwmk.** **Photo.**

1015 A506 80s grn & yel grn	2.50	80

5th World Students' Chess Games, Varna.

Conference Emblem
A507

1958, Sept. 24

1016 A507 44s blue	40	15

World Trade Union Conference of Working Youth, Prague, July 14-20.

Swimmer
A508

1958 Students' Games: 28s, Dancer, vert. 44s, Volleyball, vert.

1958, Sept. 19 *Perf. 11x10½*

1017 A508 16s brt blue	15	15
1018 A508 28s brown orange	22	15
1019 A508 44s brt green	30	15
Nos. 1017-1019 (3)	67	
Set value		35

Onions — A509

Vegetables: 12s, Garlic. 16s, Peppers. 44s, Tomatoes. 80s, Cucumbers. 1 l, Eggplant.

1958, Sept. 20 *Perf. 13*

1020 A509 2s orange brown	15	15
1021 A509 12s Prus blue	15	15
1022 A509 16s dark green	15	15
1023 A509 44s deep carmine	16	15
1024 A509 80s deep green	40	15
1025 A509 1 l brt purple	60	15
Nos. 1020-1025 (6)	1.61	
Set value		38

See No. 1072. Value, imperf. set $4.

Plovdiv Fair Building
A510

1958, Sept. 14 **Unwmk.** *Perf. 11*

1026 A510 44s deep carmine	40	15

18th International Plovdiv Fair.

Attack — A511

Design: 44s, Fighter dragging wounded man.

1958, Sept. 23 **Photo.** *Perf. 11*

1027 A511 16s orange ver	15	15
1028 A511 44s lake	35	15
Set value		15

35th anniv. of the September Revolution.

Emblem, Brussels Fair — A512

1958, Oct. 13 *Perf. 11*

1029 A512 1 l blk & brt blue	4.75	1.25

Brussels World's Fair, Apr. 17-Oct. 19. Exists imperf.

Runner at Finish Line — A513

Woman Throwing Javelin
A514

Sports: 60s, High jumper. 80s, Hurdler. 4 l, Shot putter.

1958, Nov. 30

1030 A513 16s red brn, *pnksh*	35	15
1031 A514 44s olive, *yelsh*	35	15
1032 A514 60s dk bl, *bluish*	65	20
1033 A514 80s dp grn, *grnsh*	85	20
1034 A513 4 l dp rose cl, *pnksh*	5.50	1.40
Nos. 1030-1034 (5)	7.70	2.10

1958 Balkan Games.
Latin lettering on Nos. 1032-1033.

Christo Smirnenski — A515

1958, Dec. 22

1035 A515 16s dark carmine	15	15

60th anniversary of the birth of Christo Smirnenski, poet, 1898-1923.

Girls Harvesting — A516

Girl Tending Calves
A517

Designs: 16s, Boy and girl laborers. 40s, Boy pushing wheelbarrow. 44s, Headquarters building.

1959, Nov. 29 **Photo.**

1036 A516 8s dk olive green	15	15
1037 A517 12s redsh brown	15	15
1038 A516 16s violet brown	15	15
1039 A517 40s Prus blue	15	15
1040 A516 44s deep carmine	60	15
Set value	95	34

4th Congress of Dimitrov's Union of People's Youth.

The values of stamps in very fine to superb condition are greater than catalogue value.

UNESCO Building, Paris
A518

1959, Mar. 28 Unwmk. *Perf. 11*

1041	A518 2 l dp red lilac, *cream*	1.25	1.00

Opening of UNESCO Headquarters, Paris, Nov. 3, 1958. Value imperf. $2.50

Skier — A519

Soccer Players — A520

1959, Mar. 28 *Perf. 11*

1042	A519 1 l blue, *cream*	90	50

Forty years of skiing in Bulgaria.

1959, Mar. 25

1043	A520 2 l chestnut, *cream*	1.25	65

1959 European Youth Soccer Championship.

Russian Soldiers Installing Telegraph Wires — A521

First Bulgarian Postal Coach
A522

Designs: 60s, Stamp of 1879. 80s, First Bulgarian automobile. 1 l, Television tower. 2 l, Strike of railroad and postal workers, 1919.

1959, May 4

1044	A521	12s dk grn & cit	15	15
1045	A522	16s deep plum	15	15
1046	A521	60s dk brn & yel	32	15
1047	A522	80s hn brn & sal	45	15
1048	A521	1 l blue	60	16
1049	A522	2 l dk red brown	1.65	80
		Nos. 1044-1049 (6)	3.32	
		Set value		1.25

80th anniv. of the Bulgarian post. Latin lettering on Nos. 1046-1049.

Two imperf. souvenir sheets exist with olive borders and inscriptions. One contains one copy of No. 1046 in black & ocher, and measures 92x121mm. The other sheet contains one copy each of Nos. 1044-1045 and 1047-1048 in changed colors: 12s, olive green & ocher; 16s, deep claret & ocher; 80s, dark red & ocher; 1 l, olive & ocher. Each sheet sold for 5 leva. Value, each $22.50.

Great Tits
A523

Birds: 8s, Hoopoe. 16s, Great spotted woodpecker, vert. 45s, Gray partridge, vert. 60s, Rock partridge. 80s, European cuckoo.

1959, June 30 Photo.

1050	A523	2s olive & sl grn	15	15
1051	A523	8s dp orange & blk	15	15
1052	A523	16s chestnut & dk brn	22	15
1053	A523	45s brown & blk	28	15
1054	A523	60s dp blue & gray	65	15
1055	A523	80s dp bl grn & gray	1.10	18
		Nos. 1050-1055 (6)	2.55	
		Set value		55

Bagpiper — A524

Designs: 12s, Acrobats. 16s, Girls exercising with hoops. 20s, Male dancers. 80s, Ballet dancers. 1 l, Ceramic pitcher. 16s, 20s, 80s are horizontal.

1959, Aug. 29 Unwmk. *Perf. 11*
Surface-colored Paper

1056	A524	4s dk olive	15	15
1057	A524	12s scarlet	15	15
1058	A524	16s maroon	15	15
1059	A524	20s dk blue	25	15
1060	A524	80s brt green	52	26
1061	A524	1 l brown org	95	42
		Nos. 1056-1061 (6)	2.17	
		Set value		1.00

7th International Youth Festival, Vienna. Latin inscriptions on Nos. 1060-1061.

Partisans in Truck
A525

Designs: 16s, Partisans and soldiers shaking hands. 45s, Refinery. 60s, Tanks. 80s, Harvester. 1.25 l, Children with flag, vert.

1959, Sept. 8

1062	A525	12s red & Prus grn	15	15
1063	A525	16s red & dk pur	15	15
1064	A525	45s red & int bl	15	15
1065	A525	60s red & ol grn	15	15
1066	A525	80s red & brn	26	15
1067	A525	1.25 l red & dp brn	65	38
		Set value	1.20	75

15th anniversary of Bulgarian liberation.

Soccer
A526

1959, Oct. 10 Unwmk. *Perf. 11*

1068	A526 1.25 l dp green, *yel*	3.50	2.00

50 years of Bulgarian soccer.

Set exists imperf. in changed colors. Value $7.50 unused, $4 canceled.

Batak Defenders
A527

1959, Aug. 8

1069	A527 16s deep claret	20	15

300th anniv. of the settlement of Batak.

Post Horn and Letter — A528

Bird-shaped Lyre — A529

Design: 1.25 l, Dove and letter.

1959, Nov. 23

1070	A528	45s emerald & blk	30	15
1071	A528	1.25 l lt blue, red & blk	50	20
		Set value		27

Intl. Letter Writing Week Oct. 5-11.

Type of 1958 Surcharged "45 CT." in Dark Blue

Design: Tomatoes.

1959 Photo. *Perf. 13*

1072	A509 45s on 44s scarlet	55	15

1960, Feb. 23 Unwmk. *Perf. 10½*

1073	A529	80s shown	40	15
1074	A529	1.25 l Lyre	70	18
		Set value		27

50th anniv. of Bulgaria's State Opera.

N. I. Vapzarov — A530

Parachute and Radio Tower — A531

1959, Dec. 14 *Perf. 11*

1075	A530 80s yel grn & red brn	35	15

Vapzarov, poet and patriot, 50th birth anniv.

1959, Dec. 3 Photo.

1076	A531 1.25 l dp grnsh bl & yel	1.25	45

Third Congress of Voluntary Participants in Defense.

Cotton Picker — A532

Harvester Combine — A533

Designs: 2s, Kindergarten. 4s, Woman doctor and child. 10s, Woman milking cow. 12s, Woman holding tobacco leaves. 15s, Woman working loom. 16s, Stalin textile mill, Dimitrovgrad. 25s, Rural electrification. 28s, Woman picking sunflowers. 40s, "Cold-well" hydroelectric dam. 45s, Miner. 60s, Foundry worker. 80s. Woman harvesting grapes. 1 l, Worker and peasant with cogwheel. 1.25 l, Industrial worker. 2 l, Party leader.

1959-61 Photo. *Perf. 13*

1077	A533	2s brown org ('60)	15	15
1077A	A532	4s gldn brn ('61)	15	15
1078	A532	5s dk green	15	15
1079	A533	10s red brn ('61)	15	15
1080	A532	12s red brown	15	15
1081	A532	15s red lil ('60)	15	15
1082	A533	16s dp vio ('60)	15	15
1083	A533	20s orange	15	15
1084	A532	25s brt blue ('60)	15	15
1085	A532	28s brt green	18	15
1086	A533	40s brt grnsh bl	30	15
1087	A532	45s choc ('60)	22	15
1088	A533	60s scarlet	42	15
1089	A532	80s ol ('60)	50	15
1090	A532	1 l maroon	50	15
1090A	A533	1.25 l dull bl ('61)	1.75	30
1091	A532	2 l dp car ('60)	1.10	22
		Nos. 1077-1091 (17)	6.32	
		Set value		1.25

Early completion of the 5-year plan (in 1959).

L. L. Zamenhof — A534

Path of Lunik 3 — A535

1959, Dec. 5 Unwmk. *Perf. 11*

1092	A534 1.25 l dk grn & yel grn	75	38

Lazarus Ludwig Zamenhof (1859-1917), inventor of Esperanto.

1960, Mar. 28 *Perf. 11*

1093	A535 1.25 l Prus bl & brt yel	3.50	1.90

Flight of Lunik 3 around moon. Value, imperf. $5

Skier
A536

1960, Apr. 15 Litho.

1094	A536 2 l ultra, blk & brn	95	35

8th Winter Olympics, Squaw Valley, CA, Feb. 18-29. Value, imperf. $2 unused, $1 canceled.

Vela Blagoeva — A537

Portraits: 28s, Anna Maimunkova. 45s, Vela Piskova. 60s, Rosa Luxemburg. 80s, Klara Zetkin. 1.25 l, N. K. Krupskaya.

1960, Apr. 27 Photo. *Perf. 11*

1095	A537	16s rose & red brn	15	15
1096	A537	28s citron & olive	15	15
1097	A537	45s ol grn & sl grn	20	15
1098	A537	60s lt bl & Prus bl	20	15
1099	A537	80s red org & dp brn	35	15
1100	A537	1.25 l dull yel & olive	60	18
		Nos. 1095-1100 (6)	1.65	
		Set value		50

International Women's Day, Mar. 8, 1960.

Lenin — A538

1960, May 12

1101	A538	16s shown	50	15
1102	A538	45s Lenin sitting	1.10	16

90th anniversary of the birth of Lenin.

A539

A541

1960, June 3 *Perf. 11*

1103 A539 1.25 l yel & slate grn 85 35

Seventh European Women's Basketball championships.

1960, June 29 **Litho.**

1105 A541 16s Parachutist 55 30
1106 A541 1.25 l Parachutes 1.50 45

5th International Parachute Championships.

Yellow Gentian — A542

Flowers: 5s, Tulips. 25s, Turk's-cap lily. 45s, Rhododendron. 60s, Lady's-slipper. 80s, Violets.

1960, July 27 **Photo.** *Perf. 11*

1107 A542 2s beige, grn & yel 15 15
1108 A542 5s yel grn, grn & car rose 15 15
1109 A542 25s pink, grn & org 20 15
1110 A542 45s pale lil, grn & rose lil 35 15
1111 A542 60s yel, grn & org 75 15
1112 A542 80s gray, grn & vio bl 90 22
Nos. 1107-1112 (6) 2.50
Set value 55

Soccer A543

Sports: 12s, Wrestling. 16s, Weight lifting. 45s, Woman gymnast. 80s, Canoeing. 2 l, Runner.

1960, Aug. 29 **Unwmk.** *Perf. 11*

Athletes' Figures in Pink

1113 A543 8s brown 15 15
1114 A543 12s violet 15 15
1115 A543 16s Prus blue 15 15
1116 A543 45s deep plum 18 15
1117 A543 80s blue 30 15
1118 A543 2 l deep green 1.25 35
Set value 2.00 75

17th Olympic Games, Rome, Aug. 25-Sept. 11.
Value, set imperf. in changed colors, $3.50.

Globes A544

Unwmk.

1960, Oct. 12 **Photo.** *Perf. 11*

1125 A544 1.25 l blue & ultra 50 20

15th anniversary of the World Federation of Trade Unions.

Alexander Popov — A545

1960, Oct. 12

1126 A545 90s blue & blk 75 15

Centenary of the birth of Alexander Popov, radio pioneer.

Bicyclists A546

1960, Sept. 22

1127 A546 1 l yel, red org & blk 90 45

The 10th Tour of Bulgaria Bicycle Race.

Jaroslav Vésin — A547

1960, Nov. 22 **Unwmk.** *Perf. 11*

1128 A547 1 l brt cit & ol grn 2.75 65

Birth centenary of Jaroslav Vesin, painter.

UN Headquarters A548

Costume of Kyustendil A549

1961, Jan. 14 **Photo.** *Perf. 11*

1129 A548 1 l brown & yel 1.00 45
a. Souvenir sheet 4.00 2.75

15th anniv. of the UN. #1129 sold for 2 l.
Value, imperf. $3.50.
No. 1129a sold for 2.50 l and contains one copy of No. 1129, imperf, in dark olive and pink.

1961, Jan. 28

Designs (Regional Costumes): 16s, Pleven. 28s, Sliven. 45s, Sofia. 60s, Rhodope. 80s, Karnobat.

1130 A549 12s sal, sl grn & yel 15 15
1131 A549 16s pale lil, brn vio & buff 15 15
1132 A549 28s pale grn, sl grn & rose 15 15
1133 A549 45s blue & red 30 15
1134 A549 60s grnsh bl, Prus bl & yel 48 15
1135 A549 80s yel, sl grn & pink 60 26
Nos. 1130-1135 (6) 1.83
Set value 60

Theodor Tiro (Fresco) A550

Designs: 60s, Boyana Church. 1.25 l, Duchess of Dessislava (fresco).

1961, Jan. 28 **Photo.**

1136 A550 60s yel grn, blk & grn 50 15
1137 A550 80s yel, sl grn & org 50 15
1138 A550 1.25 l yel grn, hn brn & buff 1.00 22
Nos. 1136-1138 (3) 2.00
Set value 40

700th anniv. of murals in Boyana Church.

Clock Tower, Vratsa — A551

Wooden Jug — A552

Designs: 12s, Clock tower, Bansko. 20s, Anguchev House, Mogilitsa. 28s, Oslekov House, Koprivspitsa, horiz. 40s, Pasha's house. Melnik, horiz. 45s, Lion sculpture. 60s, Man on horseback, Madara. 80s, Fresco, Bratchkovo monastery. 1 l, Tsar Assen coin.

1961, Feb. 25 **Unwmk.** *Perf. 11*

Denomination and Stars in Vermilion

1139 A551 8s olive grn 15 15
1140 A551 12s lt violet 15 15
1141 A552 16s dk red brn 15 15
1142 A551 20s brt blue 15 15
1143 A551 28s grnsh blue 15 15
1144 A551 40s red brown 15 15
1145 A552 45s olive gray 16 15
1146 A552 60s slate 32 15
1147 A552 80s dk olive gray 55 15
1148 A552 1 l green 70 16
Set value 2.25 65

Capercaillie — A553

Birds: 4s, Dalmatian pelican. 16s, Ringnecked pheasant. 80s, Great bustard. 1 l, Lammergeier. 2 l, Hazel hen.

1961, Mar. 31

1149 A553 2s blk, sal & Prus grn 15 15
1150 A553 4s blk, yel grn & org 15 15
1151 A553 16s brn, lt grn & org 15 15
1152 A553 80s brn, bluish grn & yel 35 15
1153 A553 1 l blk, lt bl & yel 65 15
1154 A553 2 l brn, bl & yel 1.65 55
Nos. 1149-1153 (5) 1.45
Set value 1.00

Radio Tower and Winged Anchor — A554

1961, Apr. 1 **Unwmk.** *Perf. 11*

1155 A554 80s brt green & blk 45 20

50th anniv. of the Transport Workers' Union.

T. G. Shevchenko — A555

Water Polo — A556

1961, Apr. 27

1156 A555 1 l olive & blk 2.50 65

Centenary of the death of Taras G. Shevchenko, Ukrainian poet.

1961, May 15

Designs: 5s, Tennis. 16s, Fencing. 45s, Throwing the discus. 1.25 l, Sports Palace. 2 l, Basketball. 5 l, Sports Palace, different view. 5s, 16s, 45s and 1.25 l, are horizontal.

Black Inscriptions

1157 A556 4s lt ultra 15 15
1158 A556 5s orange ver 15 15
1159 A556 16s olive grn 15 15
1160 A556 45s dull blue 15 15
1161 A556 1.25 l yellow brn 60 18
1162 A556 2 l lilac 85 40
Nos. 1157-1162 (6) 2.05
Set value 75

Souvenir Sheet

Imperf

1163 A556 5 l yel grn, dl bl & yel 7.50 6.50

1961 World University Games, Sofia, Aug. 26-Sept. 3.
Value, Nos. 1157-1162 in changed colors, imperf. $4.50.

Monk Seal A557

Black Sea Fauna: 12s, Jellyfish. 16s, Dolphin. 45s, Black Sea sea horse, vert. 1 l, Starred sturgeon. 1.25 l, Thornback ray.

1961, June 19 *Perf. 11*

1164 A557 2s green & blk 15 15
1165 A557 12s Prus grn & pink 15 15
1166 A557 16s ultra & vio bl 15 15
1167 A557 45s lt blue & brn 28 15
1168 A557 1 l yel grn & Prus grn 65 20
1169 A557 1.25 l lt vio bl & red brn 1.10 35
Nos. 1164-1169 (6) 2.48
Set value 90

Hikers — A558

Designs: 4s, "Sredetz" hostel, horiz. 16s, Tents. 1.25 l, Mountain climber.

1961, Aug. 25 **Litho.** *Perf. 11*

1170 A558 4s yel grn, yel & blk 15 15
1171 A558 12s lt bl, cr & blk 15 15
1172 A558 16s green, cr & blk 15 15
1173 A558 1.25 l bister, cr & blk 45 15
Set value 65 30

"Know Your Country" campaign.

Demeter Blagoev Addressing 1891 Congress at Busludja — A559

1961, Aug. 5 **Photo.**

1174 A559 45s dk red & buff		20	15
1175 A559 80s blue & pink		30	15
1176 A559 2 l dk brn & pale citron		75	25
Nos. 1174-1176 (3)		1.25	55

70th anniversary of the first Congress of the Bulgarian Social-Democratic Party.

The Golden Girl — A560

Fairy Tales: 8s, The Living Water. 12s, The Golden Apple. 16s, Krali-Marko, hero. 45s, Samovila-Vila, Witch. 80s, Tom Thumb.

1961, Oct. 10 **Unwmk.** ***Perf. 11***

1177 A560 2s blue, blk & org	18	15
1178 A560 8s rose lil, blk & gray	24	15
1179 A560 12s bl grn, blk & pink	24	15
1180 A560 16s red, blk, bl & gray	38	15
1181 A560 45s ol grn, blk & pink	75	22
1182 A560 80s ocher, blk & dk car	1.10	28
Nos. 1177-1182 (6)	2.89	
Set value		80

Caesar's Mushroom A561

Miladinov Brothers and Title Page A562

Designs: Various mushrooms.

1961, Dec. 20 **Photo.** ***Perf. 11***

Denominations in Black

1183 A561 2s lemon & red	15	15
1184 A561 4s ol grn & red brn	15	15
1185 A561 12s bister & red brn	15	15
1186 A561 16s lilac & red brn	15	15
1187 A561 45s car rose & yel	15	15
1188 A561 80s brn org & sep	18	15
1189 A561 1.25 l vio & dk brn	40	18
1190 A561 2 l org brn & brn	70	40
Set value	1.55	1.00

Value, denomination in dark grn, imperf. set $5 unused, $1.75 canceled.

1961, Dec. 21 **Unwmk.** ***Perf. 10½***

1191 A562 1.25 l olive & blk	60	20

Centenary of the publication of "Collected Folksongs" by the Brothers Miladinov, Dimitri and Konstantin.

Nos. 1079-1085, 1087, 992, 1023, 1090-1091 and 806 Surcharged with New Value in Black, Red or Violet

1962, Jan. 1

1192 A533 1s on 10s red brown	15	15
1193 A532 1s on 12s red brown	15	15
1194 A532 2s on 15s red lilac	15	15
1195 A533 2s on 16s dp vio (R)	15	15
1196 A533 2s on 20s orange	15	15
a. "2 CT." on 2 lines	15	15
1197 A532 3s on 25s brt bl (R)	15	15
a. Black surcharge	7.00	4.00
1198 A532 3s on 28s brt grn (R)	15	15
1199 A532 5s on 45s chocolate	15	15
1200 A499 5s on 44s dk bl grn (R)	15	15
1201 A509 5s on 44s dp car (V)	15	15
1202 A532 10s on 1 l maroon	25	15
1203 A532 20s on 2 l dp car	70	22
1204 A430 40s on 4 l rose lake (V)	1.50	48
Nos. 1192-1204 (13)	3.95	
Set value		1.30

Freighter "Varna" A563

Designs: 5s, Tanker "Komsomoletz." 20s, Liner "G. Dimitrov."

1962, Mar. 1 **Photo.** ***Perf. 10½***

1205 A563 1s lt grn & brt bl	15	15
1206 A563 5s lt blue & grn	18	15
1207 A563 20s gray bl & grnsh bl	70	16
Nos. 1205-1207 (3)	1.03	
Set value		26

Dimitrov Working as Printer — A564

Roses — A565

Design: 13s, Griffin, emblem of state printing works.

1962, Mar. 19 **Unwmk.**

1208 A564 2s ver, blk & yel	15	15
1209 A564 13s red org, blk & yel	42	15
Set value	50	15

80th anniversary (in 1961) of the George Dimitrov state printing works.

1962, Mar. 28

Various Roses in Natural Colors

1210 A565 1s deep violet	15	15
1211 A565 2s salmon & dk car	15	15
1212 A565 3s gray & car	15	15
1213 A565 4s dark green	16	15
1214 A565 5s ultra	22	15
1215 A565 6s bluish grn & dk car	48	15
1216 A565 8s citron & car	1.10	18
1217 A565 13s blue	2.25	60
Nos. 1210-1217 (8)	4.66	
Set value		1.15

For overprint and surcharges see Nos. 1281-1283.

Malaria Eradication Emblem and Mosquito A566

Design: 20s, Malaria eradication emblem.

1962, Apr. 19

1218 A566 5s org brn, yel & blk	40	15
1219 A566 20s emerald, yel & blk	85	35

WHO drive to eradicate malaria.
Value, imperf. $2.50 unused, $1.50 canceled.

Lenin and First Issue of Pravda A567

1962, May 4 **Unwmk.** ***Perf. 10***

1220 A567 5s deep rose & slate	50	15

50th anniversary of Pravda, Russian newspaper founded by Lenin.

Blackboard and Book — A568

1962, May 21 **Photo.**

1221 A568 5s Prus bl, blk & yel	25	15

The 1962 Teachers' Congress.

Soccer Player and Globe — A569

1962, May 26 ***Perf. 10½***

1222 A569 13s brt grn, blk & lt brn	65	25

World Soccer Championship, Chile, May 30-June 17. Value, imperf. in changed colors, $2.50 unused, $1.65 canceled.

George Dimitrov A570

1962, June 18 **Photo.**

1223 A570 2s dark green	20	15
1224 A570 5s turq blue	40	15
Set value		15

80th anniv. of the birth of George Dimitrov (1882-1949), communist leader and premier of the Bulgarian Peoples' Republic.

Bishop — A571

1962, July 7 **Unwmk.** ***Perf. 10½***

1225 A571 1s shown	15	15
1226 A571 2s Rook	15	15
1227 A571 3s Queen	15	15
1228 A571 13s Knight	65	22
1229 A571 20s Pawn	1.10	42
Nos. 1225-1229 (5)	2.20	
Set value		95

15th Chess Olympics, Varna. Nos. 1225-1229 were also issued imperf. in changed colors.

An imperf. souvenir sheet contains one 20s horizontal stamp showing five chessmen. Size: 75x66mm.

Rila Mountain A572

Designs: 2s, Pirin mountain. 6s, Nesebr, Black Sea. 8s, Danube. 13s, Vidin Castle. 1 l, Rhodope mountain.

1962-63 ***Perf. 13***

1230 A572 1s dk blue grn	15	15
1231 A572 2s blue	15	15
1232 A572 6s grnsh blue	15	15
1233 A572 8c lilac	16	15
1234 A572 13s yellow grn	38	15
1234A A572 1 l dp green ('63)	3.25	30
Nos. 1230-1234A (6)	4.24	
Set value		58

No. 974 Surcharged in Red

XXXV КОНГРЕС
1962

13 =

1962, July 14 ***Perf. 13***

1235 A493 13s on 44s slate grn	2.25	80

25th Bulgarian Esperanto Congress, Burgas, July 14-16.

Girl and Festival Emblem A573

Design: 5s, Festival emblem.

1962, Aug. 18 **Photo.** ***Perf. 10½***

1236 A573 5s green, lt bl & pink	20	15
1237 A573 13s lilac, lt bl & gray	35	15
Set value		15

8th Youth Festival for Peace and Friendship, Helsinki, July 28-Aug. 6, 1962.

Parnassius Apollo A574

1962, Sept. 13

Various Butterflies in Natural Colors

1238 A574 1s pale cit & dk grn	15	15
1239 A574 2s rose & brown	15	15
1240 A574 3s buff & red brn	15	15
1241 A574 4s gray & brown	15	15
1242 A574 5s lt gray & brn	16	15
1243 A574 6s gray & black	18	15
1244 A574 10s pale grn & blk	1.25	25
1245 A574 13s buff & red brn	1.90	40
Nos. 1238-1245 (8)	4.09	
Set value		1.00

Planting Machine A575

Designs: 2s, Electric locomotive. 3s, Blast furnace. 13s, Blagoev and Dimitrov and Communist flag.

1962, Nov. 1 ***Perf. 11½***

1246 A575 1s bl grn & dk ol grn	15	15
1247 A575 2s bl & Prus bl	15	15
1248 A575 3s carmine & brn	18	15
1249 A575 13s plum, red & blk	55	20
Nos. 1246-1249 (4)	1.03	
Set value		45

Bulgarian Communist Party, 8th Congress.

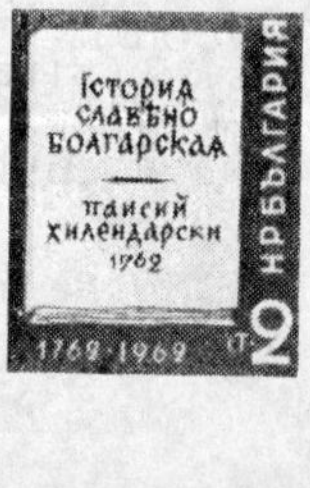

Title Page of "Slav-Bulgarian History" — A576

Paisii Hilendarski Writing History — A577

1962, Dec. 8 Unwmk. *Perf. 10½*

1250	A576	2s olive grn & blk		15	15
1251	A577	5s brown org & blk		15	15
		Set value		25	20

200th anniv. of "Slav-Bulgarian History."

Aleco Konstantinov (1863-1897), Writer — A578

1963, Mar. 5 Photo. *Perf. 11½*

1252	A578	5s red, grn & blk	25	15

Printed with alternating red brown and black label showing Bai Ganu, hero from Konstantinov's books.

A579

Sofia University — A580

Designs: No. 1255, Levski Stadium, Sofia. No. 1256, Arch, Nissaria. No. 1257, Parachutist.

1963, Feb. 20 Unwmk. *Perf. 10*

1253	A579	1s brown red	15	15
1254	A580	1s red brown	15	15
1255	A580	1s blue green	15	15
1256	A580	1s dark green	15	15
1257	A580	1s brt blue	15	15
		Set value	25	25

Vassil Levski — A581

Boy, Girl and Dimitrov — A582

1963, Apr. 11 Photo.

1258	A581	13s grnsh blue & buff	75	25

90th anniversary of the death of Vassil Levski, revolutionary leader in the fight for liberation from the Turks.

1963, Apr. 25 Unwmk. *Perf. 11½*

Design: 13s, Girl with book and boy with hammer.

1259	A582	2s org, ver, red brn & blk	15	15
1260	A582	13s bluish grn, brn & blk	42	15
		Set value		20

10th Congress of Dimitrov's Union of the People's Youth.

Red Squirrel — A583

Sun Coast Promenade — A584

Animals: 2s, Hedgehog. 3s, European polecat. 5s, Pine marten. 13s, Badger. 20s, Otter. 2s, 3s, 13s, horiz.

1963, Apr. 30

Red Numerals

1261	A583	1s grn & brn, *grnsh*	15	15
1262	A583	2s grn & blk, *yel*	15	15
1263	A583	3s grn & brn, *bis*	15	15
1264	A583	5s vio & red brn, *lil*	20	15
1265	A583	13s red brn & blk, *pink*	80	16
1266	A583	20s blk & brn, *blue*	1.25	20
		Nos. 1261-1266 (6)	2.70	
		Set value		60

1963, Mar. 12 Unwmk. *Perf. 13*

Black Sea Resorts: 2s, 3s, 13s, Views of Gold Sand. 5s, 20s, Sun Coast.

1267	A584	1s blue	15	15
1268	A584	2s vermilion	26	15
1269	A584	2s car rose	38	15
1270	A584	3s ocher	18	15
1271	A584	5s lilac	18	15
1272	A584	13s blue green	52	15
1273	A584	20s green	95	20
		Nos. 1267-1273 (7)	2.62	
		Set value		53

Freestyle Wrestling — A585

Design: 20s, Freestyle wrestling, horiz.

1963, May 31 *Perf. 11½*

1274	A585	5s yel bister & blk	16	15
1275	A585	20s org brn & blk	80	18
		Set value		24

15th International Freestyle Wrestling Competitions, Sofia.

"Women for Peace" A586

1963, June 24 Unwmk. *Perf. 11½*

1276	A586	20s blue & blk	60	15

World Congress of Women, Moscow, June 24-29.

Esperanto Emblem and Arms of Sofia — A587

Moon, Earth and Lunik 4 — A588

1963, June 29 Photo.

1277	A587	13s multicolored	60	15

48th World Esperanto Congress, Sofia, Aug. 3-10.

1963, July 22

Designs: 2s, Radar equipment. 3s, Satellites and moon.

1278	A588	1s ultra	15	15
1279	A588	2s red lilac	15	15
1280	A588	3s greenish blue	15	15
		Set value	25	15

Russia's rocket to the moon, Apr. 2, 1963.

= MOSTRA EUROPEISTICA-1963 13 RICCIONE

Nos. 1211-1212 and 1215 Overprinted or Surcharged in Green, Ultramarine or Black

1963, Aug. 31 *Perf. 10½*

1281	A565	2s (G)	25	15
1282	A565	5s on 3s (U)	38	15
1283	A565	13s on 6s	70	22
		Nos. 1281-1283 (3)	1.33	
		Set value		40

Intl. Stamp Fair, Riccione, Aug. 31.

Women's Relay Race A589

Designs: 2s, Hammer thrower. 3s, Women's long jump. 5s, Men's high jump. 13s, Discus thrower.

Perf. 11½

1963, Sept. 13 Photo. Unwmk.

Flags in National Colors

1284	A589	1s slate green	15	15
1285	A589	2s purple	15	15
1286	A589	3s Prus blue	16	15
1287	A589	5s maroon	45	30
1288	A589	13s chestnut brn	1.65	1.25
		Nos. 1284-1288 (5)	2.56	2.00

Balkan Games. A multicolored, 50s, imperf. souvenir sheet shows design of women's relay race. Size: 74x70mm.

"Slav-Bulgarian History" — A590

1963, Sept. 19 *Perf. 10½*

1289	A590	5s sal pink, slate & yel	20	15

5th International Slavic Congress.

Revolutionists A591

Christo Smirnenski A592

1963, Sept. 22 *Perf. 11½*

1290	A591	2s brt red & blk	15	15

40th anniversary of the September Revolution.

1963, Oct. 28 *Perf. 10½*

1291	A592	13s pale lilac & indigo	45	15

Christo Smirnenski, poet, 65th birth anniv.

Columbine A593

Horses A594

1963, Oct. 9 Photo. *Perf. 11½*

1292	A593	1s shown	15	15
1293	A593	2s Edelweiss	15	15
1294	A593	3s Primrose	15	15
1295	A593	5s Water lily	15	15
1296	A593	6s Tulips	16	15
1297	A593	8s Larkspur	30	15
1298	A593	10s Alpine clematis	70	16
1299	A593	13s Anemone	1.25	25
		Nos. 1292-1299 (8)	3.01	
		Set value		90

1963, Dec. 28 Unwmk. *Perf. 10½*

Designs: 2s, Charioteer and chariot. 3s, Trumpeters. 5s, Woman carrying tray with food. 13s, Man holding bowl. 20s, Woman in armchair. Designs are from a Thracian tomb at Kazanlik.

1300	A594	1s gray, org & dk red	15	15
1301	A594	2s gray, ocher & pur	15	15
1302	A594	3s gray, dl yel & sl grn	15	15
1303	A594	5s pale grn, ocher & brn	15	15
1304	A594	13s pale grn, bis & blk	42	15
1305	A594	20s pale grn, org & dk car	75	30
		Set value	1.50	75

World Map and Emblem A595

Designs: 2s, Blood transfusion. 3s, Nurse bandaging injured wrist. 5s, Red Cross nurse. 13s, Henri Dunant.

1964, Jan. 27 *Perf. 10½*

1306	A595	1s lem, blk & red	15	15
1307	A595	2s ultra, blk & red	15	15
1308	A595	3s gray, sl, blk & red	15	15
1309	A595	5s brt bl, blk & red	15	15
1310	A595	13s org yel, blk & red	42	15
		Set value	80	32

Centenary of International Red Cross.

Speed Skating A596

Sports: 2s, 50s, Women's figure skating. 3s, Cross-country skiing. 5s, Ski jump. 10s, Ice hockey goalkeeper. 13s, Ice hockey players.

1964, Feb. 21 Unwmk. *Perf. 10½*

1311	A596	1s grnsh bl, ind & ocher	15	15
1312	A596	2s brt pink, ol grn & dk sl grn	15	15
1313	A596	3s dl grn, dk grn & brn	15	15
1314	A596	5s bl, blk & yel brn	18	15
1315	A596	10s gray, org & blk	40	18
1316	A596	13s lil, blk & lil rose	70	28
		Nos. 1311-1316 (6)	1.73	
		Set value		60

Miniature Sheet

Imperf

1317	A596	50s gray, Prus grn & pink	3.75	3.00

9th Winter Olympic Games, Innsbruck, Jan. 29-Feb. 9, 1964.

Mask of Nobleman, 2nd Century — A597

Designs: 2s, Thracian horseman. 3s, Ceramic jug. 5s, Clasp and belt. 6s, Copper kettle. 8s, Angel. 10s, Lioness. 13s, Scrub woman, contemporary sculpture.

1964, Mar. 14 Photo. *Perf. 10½*
Gray Frame

1318 A597 1s dp green & red 15 15
1319 A597 2s ol gray & red 15 15
1320 A597 3s bister & red 15 15
1321 A597 5s indigo & red 16 15
1322 A597 6s org brn & red 22 15
1323 A597 8s brn red & red 38 15
1324 A597 10s olive & red 42 15
1325 A597 13s gray ol & red 65 22
Nos. 1318-1325 (8) 2.28
Set value 75

2,500 years of Bulgarian art.

"The Unborn Maid" A598

Fairy Tales: 2s, Grandfather's Glove. 3s, The Big Turnip. 5s, The Wolf and the Seven Kids. 8s, Cunning Peter. 13s, The Wheat Cake.

1964, Apr. 17 Unwmk. *Perf. 10½*

1326 A598 1s bl grn, red & org brn 15 15
1327 A598 2s ultra, ocher & blk 15 15
1328 A598 3s cit, red & blk 15 15
1329 A598 5s dp rose, brn & blk 15 15
1330 A598 8s yel grn, red & blk 20 15
1331 A598 13s lt vio bl, grn & blk 70 18
Set value 1.25 46

Ascalaphus Otomanus A599

Insects: 2s, Nemoptera coa., vert. 3s, Saga natalia (grasshopper). 5s, Rosalia alpina, vert. 13s, Anisoplia austriaca, vert. 20s, Scolia flavitrons.

1964, May 16 Photo. *Perf. 11½*

1332 A599 1s brn org, yel & blk 15 15
1333 A599 2s dl bl grn, bis & blk 15 15
1334 A599 3s gray, grn & blk 15 15
1335 A599 5s lt ol grn, blk & vio 15 15
1336 A599 13s vio, bis & blk 55 16
1337 A599 20s gray bl, yel & blk 85 28
Nos. 1332-1337 (6) 2.00
Set value 75

Soccer — A600

Designs: 13s, Women's volleyball. 60s, Map of Europe and European Women's Volleyball Championship Cup (rectangular, size: 60x69mm).

1964, June 8 Unwmk. *Perf. 11½*

1338 A600 2s bl, dk bl, ocher & red 15 15
1339 A600 13s bl, dk bl, ocher & red 52 22
Set value 30

Miniature Sheet
Imperf

1340 A600 60s ultra, ocher, red & gray 3.00 2.25

Levski Physical Culture Assoc., 50th anniv.

Peter Beron and Title Page of Primer A601

1964, June 22 *Perf. 11½*

1341 A601 20s red brn & dk brn, *grysh* 1.00 60

140th anniversary of the publication of the first Bulgarian primer.

Robert Stephenson's "Rocket" Locomotive, 1825 — A602

Designs: 2s, Modern steam locomotive. 3s, Diesel locomotive. 5s, Electric locomotive. 8s, Freight train on bridge. 13s, Diesel locomotive and tunnel.

1964, July 1 Photo. *Perf. 11½*

1342 A602 1s multicolored 15 15
1343 A602 2s multicolored 15 15
1344 A602 3s multicolored 15 15
1345 A602 5s multicolored 15 15
1346 A602 8s multicolored 32 15
1347 A602 13s multicolored 80 20
Nos. 1342-1347 (6) 1.72
Set value 50

German Shepherd A603

1964, Aug. 22 Photo.

1348 A603 1s shown 15 15
1349 A603 2s Setter 15 15
1350 A603 3s Poodle 15 15
1351 A603 4s Pomeranian 16 15
1352 A603 5s St. Bernard 20 15
1353 A603 6s Terrier 26 15
1354 A603 10s Pointer 1.40 22
1355 A603 13s Dachshund 2.75 42
Nos. 1348-1355 (8) 5.22
Set value 90

Partisans — A604

Designs: 2s, People welcoming Soviet army. 3s, Russian aid to Bulgaria. 4s, Blast furnace, Kremikovski. 5s, Combine. 6s, Peace demonstration. 8s, Sentry. 13s, Demeter Blagoev and George Dimitrov.

1964, Sept. 9 Unwmk. *Perf. 11½*
Flag in Red

1356 A604 1s lt & dp ultra 15 15
1357 A604 2s ol bis & dp ol 15 15
1358 A604 3s rose lil & mar 15 15
1359 A604 4s lt vio & vio 15 15
1360 A604 5s org & red brn 15 15
1361 A604 6s bl & dp bl 15 15
1362 A604 8s lt grn & grn 20 15
1363 A604 13s fawn & red brn 42 15
Set value 1.00 50

20th anniv. of People's Government of Bulgaria.

No. 967 Surcharged

м м панаир
ПЛОВДИВ - 1964
ST 20

1964, Sept. 13 *Perf. 13*

1364 A476 20s on 44s org yel 1.00 35

International Plovdiv Fair.

Gymnast on Parallel Bars A606

Vratcata Mountain Road A607

Sports: 2s, Long jump. 3s, Woman diver. 5s, Soccer. 13s, Women's volleyball. 20s, Wrestling.

1964, Oct. 10 *Perf. 11½*

1366 A606 1s pale grn, grn & red 15 15
1367 A606 2s pale vio, vio bl & red 15 15
1368 A606 3s bl grn, brn & red 15 15
1369 A606 5s pink, pur & red 16 15
1370 A606 13s bl, Prus grn & red 52 15
1371 A606 20s yel, grn & red 90 22
Set value 1.75 60

18th Olympic Games, Tokyo. Oct. 10-25. See No. B27.

1964, Oct. 26 Photo. *Perf. 12½x13*

Bulgarian Views: 2s, Ritlite mountain road. 3s, Pines, Malovica peak. 4s, Pobitite rocks. 5s, Erkupria. 6s, Rhodope mountain road.

1372 A607 1s dk slate grn 15 15
1373 A607 2s brown 15 15
1374 A607 3s grnsh blue 15 15
1375 A607 4s dk red brn 15 15
1376 A607 5s deep green 20 15
1377 A607 6s blue violet 30 15
Set value 80 35

Mail Coach, Plane and Rocket A608

1964, Oct. 3 Unwmk. *Perf. 11½*

1378 A608 20s greenish blue 1.25 48

First national stamp exhibition, Sofia, Oct. 3-18. Issued in sheets of 12 stamps and 12 labels (woman's head and inscription, 5x5) arranged around one central label showing stylized bird design.

Students Holding Book — A609

1964, Dec. 30 Photo.

1379 A609 13s lt blue & blk 45 15

8th Intl. Students' Congress, Sofia.

500-Year-Old Walnut Tree at Golemo Drenovo A610

Designs: Various old trees.

1964, Dec. 28

1380 A610 1s blk, buff & cl brn 15 15
1381 A610 2s blk, pink & dp cl 15 15
1382 A610 3s blk, yel & dk brn 15 15
1383 A610 4s blk, lt bl & Prus bl 15 15
1384 A610 10s blk, pale grn & grn 22 15
1385 A610 13s blk, pale bis & dk ol grn 42 15
Set value 84 42

Soldiers' Monument — A611

1965, Jan. 1 Unwmk.

1386 A611 2s red & black 20 15

Bulgarian-Soviet friendship.

Olympic Medal Inscribed "Olympic Glory" — A612

1965, Jan. 27 Photo. *Perf. 11½*

1387 A612 20s org brn, gold & blk 60 16

Bulgarian victories in the 1964 Olympic Games.

"Victory Over Fascism" A613

Design: 13s, "Fight for Peace" (dove and globe).

1965, Apr. 16 *Perf. 11½*

1388 A613 5s gray, blk & ol bis 15 15
1389 A613 13s gray, blk & blue 26 16
Set value 21

20th anniv. of victory over Fascism, May 9, 1945.

Vladimir M. Komarov and Section of Globe — A614

Designs: 2s, Konstantin Feoktistov. 5s, Boris B. Yegorov. 13s, Komarov, Feoktistov and Yegorov. 20s, Spaceship Voskhod.

1965, Feb. 15 **Photo.**

1390	A614	1s pale lil & dk bl	15	15
1391	A614	2s lt bl, ind & dl vio	15	15
1392	A614	5s pale grn, grn & ol grn	15	15
1393	A614	13s pale pink, dp rose & mar	42	15
1394	A614	20s lt bl, vio bl, grnsh bl & yel	75	16
		Nos. 1390-1394 (5)	1.62	
		Set value		42

Russian 3-man space flight, Oct. 12-13, 1964.

Imperfs. in changed colors. Four low values se-tenant. Value, set $2 unused, $1 canceled.

Bullfinch — A615

Birds: 2s, European golden oriole. 3s, Common rock thrush. 5s, Barn swallow. 8s, European roller. 10s, European goldfinch. 13s, Rosy pastor starling. 20s, Nightingale.

1965, Apr. 20 Unwmk. *Perf. 11½*

Birds in Natural Colors

1395	A615	1s blue green	15	15
1396	A615	2s rose lilac	15	15
1397	A615	3s rose	15	15
1398	A615	5s brt blue	15	15
1399	A615	8s citron	32	15
1400	A615	10s gray	1.10	15
1401	A615	13s lt vio blue	1.10	18
1402	A615	20s emerald	2.25	35
		Nos. 1395-1402 (8)	5.37	
		Set value		88

Black Sea Fish — A616

1965, June 10 Photo. *Perf. 11½*

Gray Frames

1403	A616	1s Sting ray	15	15
1404	A616	2s Belted bonito	15	15
1405	A616	3s Hogfish	15	15
1406	A616	5s Gurnard	18	15
1407	A616	10s Scad	75	16
1408	A616	13s Turbot	1.10	26
		Nos. 1403-1408 (6)	2.48	
		Set value		64

Plane, Bus, Train, Ship and Whale — A617

1965, Apr. 30

1409	A617	13s multicolored	45	15

4th Intl. Conf. of Transport, Dock and Fishery Workers, Sofia, May 10-14.

ITU Emblem and Communications Symbols — A618

1965, May 17

1410	A618	20s multicolored	65	30

Centenary of the ITU.

Col. Pavel Belyayev and Lt. Col. Alexei Leonov A619

Design: 20s, Leonov floating in space.

1965, May 20 Unwmk.

1411	A619	2s gray, dull bl & dk brn	15	20
1412	A619	20s multicolored	1.00	45

Space flight of Voskhod 2 and the first man floating in space, Lt. Col. Alexei Leonov.

ICY Emblem — A620

1965, May 15 Photo.

1413	A620	20s orange, olive & blk	65	15

International Cooperation Year, 1965.

Corn A621

Marx and Lenin A622

1965, Apr. 1 *Perf. 12½x13*

1414	A621	1s shown	15	15
1415	A621	2s Wheat	15	15
1416	A621	3s Sunflowers	15	15
1417	A621	4s Sugar beet	15	15
1418	A621	5s Clover	15	15
1419	A621	10s Cotton	42	15
1420	A621	13s Tobacco	60	15
		Set value	1.40	42

1965, June *Perf. 10½*

1421	A622	13s red & dk brn	65	15

6th Conference of Postal Ministers of Communist Countries, Peking, June 21-July 15.

Film and UNESCO Emblem A623

1965, June 30

1422	A623	13s dp bl, blk & lt gray	50	15

Balkan Film Festival, Varna.

Ballerina — A624

1965, July 10 Photo.

1423	A624	5s dp lil rose & blk	60	25

2nd Intl. Ballet Competition, Varna.

Map of Balkan Peninsula and Dove with Letter — A625

Col. Pavel Belyayev and Lt. Col. Alexei Leonov — A626

Designs: 2s, Sailboat and modern buildings. 3s, Fish and plants. 13s, Symbolic sun and rocket. 40s, Map of Balkan Peninsula and dove with letter (like 1s).

1965, July 23-Aug. 7 *Perf. 10½*

1424	A625	1s sil, dp ultra & yel	15	15
1425	A625	2s sil, pur & yel	15	15
1426	A625	3s gold, grn & yel	15	15
1427	A625	13s gold, hn brn & yel	55	50
1428	A626	20s sil, bl & brn	70	55
		Nos. 1424-1428 (5)	1.70	
		Set value		1.25

Miniature Sheet

Imperf

1429	A625	40s gold & brt bl	1.75	1.00

Balkanphila 1965 Philatelic Exhibition, Varna, Aug. 7-15, and visit of Russian astronauts Belyayev and Leonov. The 20s and 40s were issued Aug. 7.

Value, No. 1428 imperf. in changed colors, 90 cents.

Woman Gymnast — A627

Designs: 2s, Woman gymnast on parallel bars. 3s, Weight lifter. 5s, Automobile and chart. 10s, Women basketball players. 13s, Automobile and map of rally.

1965, Aug. 14 *Perf. 10½*

1430	A627	1s crim, brn & blk	15	15
1431	A627	2s rose vio, dp cl & blk	15	15
1432	A627	3s dp car, brn & blk	15	15
1433	A627	5s fawn, red brn & blk	15	15
1434	A627	10s dp lil rose, dp cl & blk	52	15
1435	A627	13s lilac, claret & blk	65	16
		Set value	1.45	48

Sports events in Bulgaria during May-June, 1965.

No. 989 Surcharged

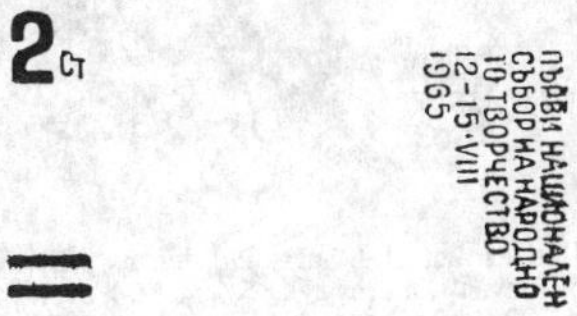

1965, Aug. 12 *Perf. 13*

1436	A499	2s on 8s orange brn	75	26

1st Natl. Folklore Competition, Aug. 12-15.

Escaping Prisoners A628

Fruit A629

1965, July 23 *Perf. 10½*

1437	A628	2s slate	20	15

40th anniversary of the escape of political prisoners from Bolshevik Island.

1965, July 1 *Perf. 13*

1438	A629	1s Apples	15	15
1439	A629	2s Grapes	15	15
1440	A629	3s Pears	15	15
1441	A629	4s Peaches	15	15
1442	A629	5s Strawberries	20	15
1443	A629	6s Walnuts	32	15
		Set value	75	34

Horsemanship — A630

1965, Sept. 30 Unwmk. *Perf. 10½*

1444	A630	1s Dressage	15	15
1445	A630	2s Three-day test	15	15
1446	A630	3s Jumping	15	15
1447	A630	5s Race	15	15
1448	A630	10s Steeplechase	75	20
1449	A630	13s Hurdle race	1.40	28
		Nos. 1444-1449 (6)	2.75	
		Set value		75

See No. B28.

Smiling Children — A631

Designs: 2s, Two girl Pioneers. 3s, Bugler. 5s, Pioneer with model plane. 8s, Two singing girls in national costume. 13s, Running boy.

1965, Oct. 24 Photo.

1450	A631	1s dk bl grn & yel grn	15	15
1451	A631	2s vio & deep rose	15	15
1452	A631	3s olive & lemon	15	15
1453	A631	5s dp blue & bister	15	15
1454	A631	8s olive bister & org	28	15
1455	A631	13s rose car & vio	65	24
		Set value	1.25	60

Dimitrov Pioneer Organization.

U-52 Plane over Trnovo
A632

Designs: 2c, IL-14 over Plovdiv. 3s, Mi-4 Helicopter over Dimitrovgrad. 5s, Tu-104 over Ruse. 13s, IL-18 over Varna. 20s, Tu-114 over Sofia.

1965, Nov. 25 *Perf. 10½*

1456	A632	1s gray, blue & red	15	15
1457	A632	2s gray, lilac & red	15	15
1458	A632	3s gray, grnsh bl & red	15	15
1459	A632	5s gray, orange & red	15	15
1460	A632	13s gray, bister & red	70	15
1461	A632	20s gray, lt grn & red	1.00	28
		Set value	2.00	60

Development of Bulgarian Civil Air Transport.

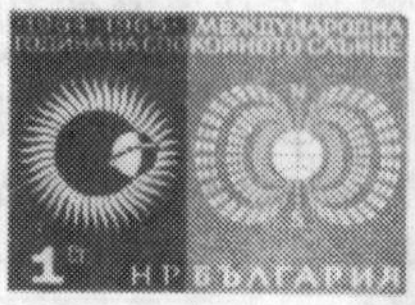

IQSY Emblem, and Earth Radiation Zones
A633

Designs (IQSY Emblem and): 2s, Sun with corona. 13s, Solar eclipse.

1965, Dec. 15 **Photo.** *Perf. 10½*

1462	A633	1s grn, yel & ultra	15	15
1463	A633	2s yel, red lil & red	15	15
1464	A633	13s bl, yel & blk	32	15
		Set value	42	24

International Quiet Sun Year, 1964-65.

"North and South Bulgaria"
A634

"Martenitsa" Emblem
A635

1965, Dec. 6

1465 A634 13s brt yel grn & blk 50 25

Union of North and South Bulgaria, cent.

1966, Jan. 10 **Photo.** *Perf. 10½*

"Spring" in Folklore: 2s, Drummer. 3s, Bird ornaments. 5s, Dancer "Lazarka." 8s, Vase with flowers. 13s, Bagpiper.

1466	A635	1s rose lil, vio bl & gray	15	15
1467	A635	2s gray, blk & crim	15	15
1468	A635	3s red, vio & gray	15	15
1469	A635	5s lil, blk & crim	15	15
1470	A635	8s rose lil, brn & pur	22	15
1471	A635	13s bl, blk & rose lil	50	20
		Set value	1.00	50

Church of St. John the Baptist, Nessebr
A636

Designs: 1s, Christ, fresco from Bojana Church. 2s, Ikon "Destruction of Idols," horiz. 3s, Bratchkovo Monastery. 4s, Zemen Monastery, horiz. 13s, Nativity, ikon from Arbanassi. 20s, Ikon "Virgin and Child," 1342.

1966, Feb. 25 **Litho.** *Perf. 11½*

1472	A636	1s gray & multi	*3.50*	*1.25*
1473	A636	2s gray & multi	25	15
1474	A636	3s multicolored	25	15
1475	A636	4s multicolored	25	15
1476	A636	5s multicolored	25	15
1477	A636	13s gray & multi	50	15
1478	A636	20s multicolored	95	35
		Nos. 1472-1478 (7)	*5.95*	*2.35*

2,500 years of art in Bulgaria.

Georgi Benkovski and T. Kableshkov
A637

Designs: 1s, Proclamation of April Uprising, Koprivstitsa. 3s, Dedication of flag, Panaguriste. 5s, V. Petleshkov and Z. Dyustabanov. 10s, Botev landing at Kozlodui. 13s, P. Volov and Ilarion Dragostinov.

1966, Mar. 3 **Photo.** *Perf. 10½*

Center in Black

1479	A637	1s red brn & gold	15	15
1480	A637	2s brt red & gold	15	15
1481	A637	3s ol grn & gold	15	15
1482	A637	5s steel bl & gold	15	15
1483	A637	10s brt rose lil & gold	20	15
1484	A637	13s lt vio & gold	48	15
		Set value	95	34

90th anniv. of the April Uprising against the Turks.

Sofia Zoo Animals
A638

1966, May 23 **Litho.**

1485	A638	1s Elephant	15	15
1486	A638	2s Tiger	15	15
1487	A638	3s Chimpanzee	15	15
1488	A638	4s Siberian ibex	18	15
1489	A638	5s Polar bear	25	15
1490	A638	8s Lion	25	15
1491	A638	13s Bison	80	20
1492	A638	20s Kangaroo	1.50	30
		Nos. 1485-1492 (8)	3.43	
		Set value		85

WHO Headquarters, Geneva — A639

1966, May 3 **Photo.**

1493 A639 13s dp blue & silver 60 25

Inauguration of the WHO Headquarters, Geneva.

Worker
A640

1966, May 9 **Photo.** *Perf. 10½*

1494 A640 20s gray & rose 65 15

Sixth Trade Union Congress.

Yantra River Bridge, Biela — A641

Designs: No. 1496, Maritsa River Bridge, Svilengrad. No. 1497, Fountain, Samokov. No. 1498, Ruins of Fort, Kaskovo. 8s, Old Fort, Ruse. 13s, House, Gabrovo.

1966, Feb. 10 **Photo.** *Perf. 13*

1495	A641	1s Prus blue	15	15
1496	A641	1s brt green	15	15
1497	A641	2s olive green	15	15
1498	A641	2s dk red brown	15	15
1499	A641	8s red brown	25	15
1500	A641	13s dark blue	42	15
		Set value	95	36

Souvenir Sheet

Moon Allegory — A642

1966, Apr. 29 *Imperf.*

1501 A642 60s blk, plum & sil 2.50 1.25

1st Russian soft landing on the moon by Luna 9, Feb. 3, 1966.

Steamer Radetzky and Bugler
A643

1966, May 28 *Perf. 10½*

1502 A643 2s multicolored 15 15

90th anniv. of the participation of the Danube steamer Radetzky in the uprising against the Turks.

Standard Bearer Nicola Simov-Kuruto
A644

1966, May 30

1503 A644 5s bis, grn & ol 25 15

Hero of the Turkish War.

UNESCO Emblem — A645

1966, June 8

1504 A645 20s gold, blk & ver 60 16

20th anniv. of UNESCO.

Youth Federation Badge — A646

1966, June 6 **Photo.** *Perf. 10½*

1505 A646 13s silver, bl & blk 40 15

7th Assembly of the Intl. Youth Federation.

Soccer — A647

Designs: Various soccer scenes. 50s, Jules Rimet Cup.

1966, June 27

1506	A647	1s gray, yel brn & blk	15	15
1507	A647	2s gray, crim & blk	15	15
1508	A647	5s gray, ol bis & blk	15	15
1509	A647	13s gray, ultra & blk	35	15
1510	A647	20s gray, Prus bl & blk	60	20
		Nos. 1506-1510 (5)	1.40	
		Set value		45

Miniature Sheet

Imperf

1511 A647 50s gray, dp lil rose & gold 2.25 1.50

World Soccer Cup Championship, Wembley, England, July 11-30. Size of No. 1511: 60x64mm.

Woman Javelin Thrower — A648

Designs: No. 1513, Runner. No. 1514, Young man and woman carrying banners, vert.

1966 **Photo.** *Perf. 10½*

1512	A648	2s grn, yel & ver	15	15
1513	A648	13s dp grn, yel & sal pink	40	15
1514	A648	13s bl, lt bl & salmon	40	15
		Nos. 1512-1514 (3)	95	
		Set value		26

Nos. 1512-1513: 3rd Spartacist Games; issued Aug. 10. No. 1514: 3rd congress of the Bulgarian Youth Federation; issued May 25.

Wrestlers Nicolas Petrov and Dan Kolov — A649

1966, July 29

1515 A649 13s bis brn, dk brn & lt ol grn 40 20

3rd International Wrestling Championships.

Map of Balkan Countries, Globe and UNESCO Emblem — A650

1966, Aug. 26 *Perf. 10½x11½*

1516 A650 13s ultra, lt grn & pink 40 15

First Congress of Balkanologists.

Children with Building Blocks — A651

Designs: 2s, Bunny and teddy bear with book. 3s, Children as astronauts. 13s, Children with pails and shovel.

1966, Sept. 1 *Perf. 10½*

1517	A651	1s	dk car, org & blk	15	15
1518	A651	2s	emerald, blk & red brn	15	15
1519	A651	3s	ultra, org & blk	15	15
1520	A651	13s	blue, rose & blk	60	15
			Set value	80	29

Children's Day.

Yuri A. Gagarin and Vostok 1 — A652

Designs: 2s, Gherman S. Titov, Vostok 2. 3s, Andrian G. Nikolayev, Pavel R. Popovich, Vostoks 3 & 4. 5s, Valentina Tereshkova, Valeri Bykovski, Vostoks 5 & 6. 8s, Vladimir M. Komarov, Boris B. Yegorov, Konstantin Feoktistov, Voskhod 1. 13s, Pavel Belyayev, Alexei Leonov, Voskhod 2.

1966, Sept. 29 Photo. *Perf. 11½x11*

1521	A652	1s	slate & gray	15	15
1522	A652	2s	plum & gray	15	15
1523	A652	3s	yel brn & gray	15	15
1524	A652	5s	brn red & gray	15	15
1525	A652	8s	ultra & gray	15	15
1526	A652	13s	Prus bl & gray	48	15
			Set value, #1521-1526, B29	1.90	72

Russian space explorations.

St. Clement, 14th Century Wood Sculpture — A653

1966, Oct. 27 Photo. *Perf. 11½x11*

1527	A653	5s	red, buff & brn	20	15

1050th anniversary of the birth of St. Clement of Ochrida.

Metodi Shatorov A654

Portraits: 3s, Vladimir Trichkov. 5s, Valcho Ivanov. 10s, Raiko Daskalov. 13s, General Vladimir Zaimov.

1966, Nov. 8 *Perf. 11x11½*

Gold Frame, Black Denomination

1528	A654	2s	crimson & bl vio	15	15
1529	A654	3s	magenta & blk	15	15
1530	A654	5s	car rose & dk bl	15	15
1531	A654	10s	orange & olive	28	15
1532	A654	13s	red & brown	40	15
			Set value	90	32

Fighters against fascism.

George Dimitrov — A655

Steel Worker — A656

1966, Nov. 14 Photo. *Perf. 11½x11*

1533	A655	2s	magenta & blk	15	15
1534	A656	20s	fawn, gray & blk	70	15
			Set value		17

Bulgarian Communist Party, 9th Congress.

Deer's Head Drinking Cup A667

Gold Treasure: 2s, 6s, 10s, Various Amazon's head jugs. 3s, Ram's head cup. 5s, Circular plate. 8s, Deer's head cup. 13s, Amphora. 20s, Ram drinking horn.

1966, Nov. 28 *Perf. 12x11½*

Vessels in Gold and Brown; Black Inscriptions

1535	A667	1s	gray & violet	15	15
1536	A667	2s	gray & green	15	15
1537	A667	3s	gray & dk bl	15	15
1538	A667	5s	gray & red brn	15	15
1539	A667	6s	gray & Prus bl	15	15
1540	A667	8s	gray & brn ol	85	15
1541	A667	10s	gray & sepia	85	18
1542	A667	13s	gray & dk vio bl	85	28
1543	A667	20s	gray & vio brn	95	32
			Nos. 1535-1543 (9)	4.25	
			Set value		1.25

The gold treasure from the 4th century B.C. was found near Panagyurishte in 1949.

Tourist House, Bansko — A668

Tourist Houses: No. 1545, Belogradchik. No. 1546, Triavna. 20s, Rila.

1966, Nov. 29 Photo. *Perf. 11x11½*

1544	A668	1s	dark blue	15	15
1545	A668	2s	dark green	15	15
1546	A668	2s	brown red	15	15
1547	A668	20s	lilac	42	15
			Set value	65	25

Decorated Tree — A669

Design: 13s, Jug with bird design.

1966, Dec. 12 *Perf. 11*

1548	A669	2s	grn, pink & gold	18	15
1549	A669	13s	brn lake, rose, emer & gold	38	15
			Set value		15

New Year, 1967.

Pencho Slavikov, Author — A670

Dahlia — A671

Portraits: 2s, Dimcho Debeljanov, author. 3s, P. H. Todorov, author. 5s, Dimitri Dobrovich, painter. 8s, Ivan Markvichka, painter. 13s, Ilya Bezhkov, painter.

1966, Dec. 15 *Perf. 10½x11*

1550	A670	1s	blue, olive & org	15	15
1551	A670	2s	orange, brn & gray	15	15
1552	A670	3s	olive, bl & org	15	15
1553	A670	5s	gray, red brn & org	15	15
1554	A670	8s	lilac, dk gray & bl	30	15
1555	A670	13s	blue, vio & lil	38	15
			Set value	95	34

1966, Dec. 29

Flowers: No. 1557, Clematis. No. 1558, Foxglove. No. 1559, Narcissus. 3s, Snowdrop. 5s, Petunia. 13s, Tiger lily. 20s, Bellflower.

Flowers in Natural Colors

1556	A671	1s	gray & lt brn	15	15
1557	A671	1s	gray & dull bl	15	15
1558	A671	2s	gray & dull lil	15	15
1559	A671	2s	gray & brown	15	15
1560	A671	3s	gray & dk grn	16	15
1561	A671	5s	gray & dp ultra	22	15
1562	A671	13s	gray & brown	60	15
1563	A671	20s	gray & ultra	95	15
			Nos. 1556-1563 (8)	2.53	
			Set value		55

Ringnecked Pheasant A672

Game: 2s, Rock partridge. 3s, Gray partridge. 5s, Hare. 8s, Roe deer. 13s, Red deer.

1967, Jan. 28 *Perf. 11x10½*

1564	A672	1s	lt ultra, dk brn & ocher	15	15
1565	A672	2s	pale yel grn & dk grn	15	15
1566	A672	3s	lt bl, blk & cr	16	15
1567	A672	5s	lt grn & blk	16	15
1568	A672	8s	pale bl, dk brn & ocher	70	15
1569	A672	13s	bl & dk brn	1.25	25
			Nos. 1564-1569 (6)	2.57	
			Set value		60

Bulgaria No. 1, 1879 — A673

Thracian Coin, 6th Century, B.C. — A674

1967, Feb. 4 Photo. *Perf. 10½*

1570	A673	10s	emerald, blk & yel	75	22

Bulgarian Philatelic Union, 10th Congress.

1967, Mar. 30 *Perf. 11½x11*

Coins: 2s, Macedonian tetradrachma, 2nd cent. B.C. 3s, Tetradrachma of Odessus, 2nd cent. B.C. 5s, Philip II of Macedonia, 4th cent., B.C. 13s, Thracian King Seuthus VII, 4th cent., B.C., obverse and reverse. 20s, Apollonian coin, 5th cent., B.C., obverse and reverse.

Size: 25x25mm

1571	A674	1s	brn, blk & sil	15	15
1572	A674	2s	red lil, blk & sil	15	15
1573	A674	3s	grn, blk & sil	15	15
1574	A674	5s	brn org, blk & sil	16	15

Size: 37½x25mm

1575	A674	13s	brt bl, blk & brnz	70	24
1576	A674	20s	vio, blk & sil	1.25	45
			Nos. 1571-1576 (6)	2.56	
			Set value		88

Partisans Listening to Radio — A675

Design: 20s, George Dimitrov addressing crowd and Bulgarian flag.

1967, Apr. 20 *Perf. 11x11½*

1577	A675	1s	red, gold, buff & sl grn	15	15
1578	A675	20s	red, gold, dl red, grn & blk	55	15
			Set value		17

25th anniversary of the Union of Patriotic Front Organizations.

Nikolas Kofardjiev A676

Portraits: 2s, Petko Napetov. 5s, Petko D. Petkov. 10s, Emil Markov. 13s, Traitcho Kostov.

1967, Apr. 24 *Perf. 11½x11*

1579	A676	1s	brn red, gray & blk	15	15
1580	A676	2s	ol grn, gray & blk	15	15
1581	A676	5s	brn, gray & blk	15	15
1582	A676	10s	dp bl, gray & blk	20	15
1583	A676	13s	mag, gray & blk	42	15
			Set value	85	30

Fighters against fascism.

Symbolic Flower and Flame — A677

1967, May 18 Photo. *Perf. 11x11½*

1584	A677	13s	gold, yel & lt grn	45	15

First Cultural Congress, May 18-19.

Gold Sand Beach and ITY Emblem A678

Designs: 20s, Hotel, Pamporovo. 40s, Nessebr Church.

1967, June 12 Photo. *Perf. 11x11½*

1585	A678	13s	ultra, yel & blk	28	15
1586	A678	20s	Prus bl, blk & buff	42	15
1587	A678	40s	brt grn, blk & ocher	1.00	28
			Nos. 1585-1587 (3)	1.70	58

International Tourist Year, 1967.

Angora Cat — A679

Cats: 2s, Siamese, horiz. 3s, Abyssinian. 5s, Black European. 13s, Persian, horiz. 20s, Striped domestic.

Perf. 11½x11, 11x11½

1967, June 19

1588	A679	1s	dl vio, dk brn & buff	15	15
1589	A679	2s	ol, sl & brt bl	15	15
1590	A679	3s	dull blue & brn	15	15
1591	A679	5s	grn, blk & yel	20	15
1592	A679	13s	dl red brn, sl & org	90	15
1593	A679	20s	gray grn, brn & buff	1.65	25
			Nos. 1588-1593 (6)	3.20	
			Set value		56

Scene from Opera "The Master of Boyana" by K. Iliev — A680

Songbird on Keyboard — A681

1967, June 19

1594	A680	5s gray, vio bl & dp car	38	15
1595	A681	13s gray, dp car & dk bl	1.10	15
		Set value		15

3rd Intl. Competition for Young Opera Singers.

George Kirkov (1867-1919), Revolutionist A682

1967, June 24 *Perf. 11x11½*

1596	A682	2s rose red & dk brn	15	15

Symbolic Tree and Stars — A683

1967, July 28 Photo. *Perf. 11½x11*

1597	A683	13s dp bl, car & blk	30	15

11th Congress of Dimitrov's Union of the People's Youth.

Roses and Distillery A684

Designs: No. 1599, Chick and incubator. No. 1600, Cucumbers and hothouse. No. 1601, Lamb and sheep farm. 3s, Sunflower and oil mill. 4s, Pigs and pig farm. 5s, Hops and hop farm. 6s, Corn and irrigation system. 8s, Grapes and Bolgar tractor. 10s, Apples and cultivated tree. 13s, Bees and honey. 20s, Bee, blossoms and beehives.

1967 *Perf. 11x11½*

1598	A684	1s multicolored	15	15
1599	A684	1s dk car, yel & blk	15	15
1600	A684	2s vio, lt grn & blk	15	15
1601	A684	2s brt grn, gray & blk	15	15
1602	A684	3s yel grn, yel & blk	15	15
1603	A684	4s brt pur, yel & blk	15	15
1604	A684	5s ol bis, yel grn & blk	15	15
1605	A684	6s ol, brt grn & blk	15	15
1606	A684	8s grn, bis & blk	15	15
1607	A684	10s multicolored	25	15
1608	A684	13s grn, bis brn & blk	42	15
1609	A684	20s grnsh bl, brt pink & blk	55	15
		Set value	2.00	80

Issue dates: Nos. 1598-1601, 1607, 1609, July 15; Nos. 1602-1606, 1608, July 24.

Map of Communist Countries, Spasski Tower A685

Designs: 2s, Lenin speaking to soldiers. 3s, Fighting at Wlodaja, 1918. 5s, Marx, Engels and Lenin. 13s, Oil refinery. 20s, Molniya communication satellite.

1967, Aug. 25 *Perf. 11*

1610	A685	1s multicolored	15	15
1611	A685	2s magenta & olive	15	15
1612	A685	3s magenta & dull vio	15	15
1613	A685	5s magenta & red	15	15
1614	A685	13s magenta & ultra	25	15
1615	A685	20s magenta & blue	45	15
		Set value	1.10	50

50th anniv. of the Russian October Revolution.

Rod, "Fish" and Varna — A686

1967, Aug. 29 Photo. *Perf. 11*

1616	A686	10s multicolored	35	15

7th World Angling Championships, Varna.

Skiers and Winter Olympics' Emblem — A687

Sports and Emblem: 2s, Ski jump. 3s, Biathlon. 5s, Ice hockey. 13s, Figure skating couple.

1967, Sept. 20 Photo. *Perf. 11*

1617	A687	1s dk bl grn, red & blk	15	15
1618	A687	2s ultra, blk & ol	15	15
1619	A687	3s vio brn, bl & blk	15	15
1620	A687	5s green, yel & blk	15	15
1621	A687	13s vio bl, blk & buff	35	15
		Nos. 1617-1621,B31 (6)	2.05	
		Set value		50

10th Winter Olympic Games, Grenoble, France, Feb. 6-18, 1968.

Mountain Peaks — A688

1967, Sept. 25 Engr. *Perf. 11½*

1622	A688	1s Bogdan	15	15
1623	A688	2s Czerny	15	15
1624	A688	3s Ruen, vert.	15	15
1625	A688	5s Persenk	15	15
1626	A688	10s Botev	15	15
1627	A688	13s Rila, vert.	25	15
1628	A688	20s Vihren	55	15
		Set value	1.25	50

George Rakovski A689

1967, Oct. 20 Photo. *Perf. 11*

1629	A689	13s yellow grn & blk	40	15

Centenary of the death of George Rakovski, revolutionary against Turkish rule.

Yuri A. Gagarin, Valentina Tereshkova and Alexei Leonov — A690

Designs: 2s, Lt. Col. John H. Glenn, Jr., and Maj. Edward H. White. 5s, Earth and Molniya 1. 10s, Gemini 6 and 7. 13s, Luna 13 moon probe. 20s, Gemini 10 and Agena rocket.

1967, Nov. 25

1630	A690	1s Prus bl, blk & yel	15	15
1631	A690	2s dl bl, blk & dl yel	15	15
1632	A690	5s vio bl, grnsh bl & blk	15	15
1633	A690	10s dk bl, blk & red	35	15
1634	A690	13s grnsh bl, brt yel & blk	55	15
1635	A690	20s dl bl, blk & red	75	20
		Nos. 1630-1635 (6)	2.10	
		Set value		50

Achievements in space exploration.

View of Trnovo — A691

Various Views of Trnovo.

1967, Dec. 5 Photo. *Perf. 11*

1636	A691	1s multicolored	15	15
1637	A691	2s multicolored	15	15
1638	A691	3s multicolored	15	15
1639	A691	5s multicolored	16	15
1640	A691	13s multicolored	32	15
1641	A691	20s multicolored	50	15
		Nos. 1636-1641 (6)	1.43	
		Set value		46

Restoration of the ancient capital Veliko Trnovo.

Ratchenitza Folk Dance, by Ivan Markvichka — A692

1967, Dec. 9

1642	A692	20s gold & gray green	1.00	80

Belgo-Bulgarian Philatelic Exposition, Brussels, Dec. 9-10. Printed in sheets of 8 stamps and 8 labels.

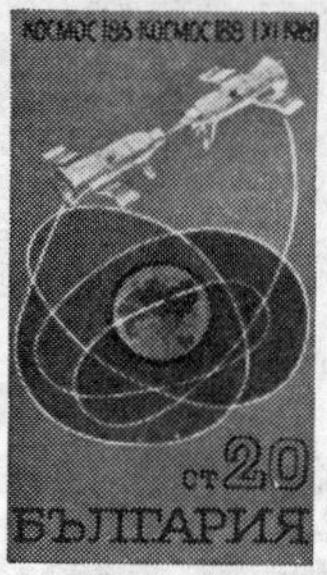

Cosmos 186 and 188 Docking — A693

Design: 40s, Venus 4 and orbits around Venus, horiz.

1968, Jan.

1643	A693	20s vio, gray & pink	55	15
1644	A693	40s multicolored	1.00	24

Docking maneuvers of the Russian spaceships Cosmos 186 and Cosmos 188, Nov. 1, 1967, and the flight to Venus of Venus 4, June 12-Nov. 18, 1967.

Crossing the Danube, by Orenburgski A694

Paintings: 2s, Flag of Samara, by J. Veschin, vert. 3s, Battle of Pleven by Orenburgski. 13s, Battle of Orlovo Gnezdo, by N. Popov, vert. 20s, Welcome for Russian Soldiers, by D. Gudienov.

1968, Jan. 25 Photo. *Perf. 11*

1645	A694	1s gold & dk green	15	15
1646	A694	2s gold & dk blue	15	15
1647	A694	3s gold & chocolate	15	15
1648	A694	13s gold & dk vio	32	15
1649	A694	20s gold & Prus grn	48	18
		Set value	95	45

90th anniv. of the liberation from Turkey.

Shepherds, by Zlatyn Boyadjiev — A695

Paintings: 2s, Wedding dance, by V. Dimitrov, vert. 3s, Partisans' Song, by Ilya Petrov. 5s, Portrait of Anna Penchovich, by Nikolai Pavlovich, vert. 13s, Self-portrait, by Zachary Zograf, vert. 20s, View of Old Plovdiv, by T. Lavrenov. 60s, St. Clement of Ochrida, by A. Mitov.

1967, Dec. Litho. *Perf. 11½*

Size: 45x38mm, 38x45mm

1650	A695	1s gray & multi	15	15
1651	A695	2s gray & multi	15	15

Size: 55x35mm

1652	A695	3s gray & multi	22	15

Size: 38x45mm, 45x38mm

1653	A695	5s gray & multi	40	15
1654	A695	13s gray & multi	90	22
1655	A695	20s gray & multi	1.25	40
		Nos. 1650-1655 (6)	3.07	
		Set value		88

Miniature Sheet

Size: 65x84mm

Imperf

1656	A695	60s multicolored	3.25	1.90

Marx Statue, Sofia — A696

Maxim Gorky — A697

1968, Feb. 20 Photo. *Perf. 11*

1657	A696	13s black & red	35	15

150th anniversary of birth of Karl Marx.

1968, Feb. 20

1658	A697	13s ver & grnsh blk	40	15

Maxim Gorky (1868-1936), Russian writer.

Folk Dancers — A698

Designs: 5s, Runners. 13s, Doves. 20s, Festival poster, (head, flowers and birds). 40s, Globe and Bulgaria No. 1 under magnifying glass.

1968, Mar. 20

1659	A698	2s multicolored	15	15
1660	A698	5s multicolored	15	15
1661	A698	13s multicolored	22	15
1662	A698	20s multicolored	48	20
1663	A698	40s multicolored	1.10	40
		Nos. 1659-1663 (5)	2.10	
		Set value		80

9th Youth Festival for Peace and Friendship, Sofia, July 28-Aug. 6.

Bellflower — A699

1968, Apr. 25 *Perf. 11*

1664	A699	1s shown	15	15
1665	A699	2s Gentian	15	15
1666	A699	3s Crocus	15	15
1667	A699	5s Iris	16	15
1668	A699	10s Dog-tooth violet	20	15
1669	A699	13s Sempervivum	70	15
1670	A699	20s Dictamnus	95	22
		Nos. 1664-1670 (7)	2.46	
		Set value		60

"The Unknown Hero," Tale by Ran Bosilek A700

Design: 20s, The Witch and the Young Man (Hans Christian Andersen fairy tale.)

1968, Apr. 25 Photo. *Perf. 10½*

1671	A700	13s black & multi	35	15
1672	A700	20s black & multi	52	20

Bulgarian-Danish Philatelic Exhibition.

Memorial Church, Shipka — A701

Steeplechase — A702

1968, May 3

1673	A701	13s multicolored	60	20

Bulgarian Stamp Exhibition in Berlin.

1968, June 24 Photo. *Perf. 10½*

Designs (Olympic Rings and): 1s, Gymnast on bar. 3s, Fencer. 10s, Boxer. 13s, Woman discus thrower.

1674	A702	1s red & black	15	15
1675	A702	2s gray, blk & rose brn	15	15
1676	A702	3s magenta, gray & blk	15	15
1677	A702	10s grnsh bl, blk & lem	15	15
1678	A702	13s vio bl, gray & pink	55	18
		Nos. 1674-1678,B33 (6)	2.15	
		Set value		75

19th Olympic Games, Mexico City, Oct. 12-27.

Battle of Buzluja A703

Design: 13s, Haji Dimitr and Stefan Karaja.

1968, July 1

1679	A703	2s silver & red brn	15	15
1680	A703	13s gold & sl grn	32	15
		Set value	40	17

Centenary of the death of the patriots Haji Dimitr and Stefan Karaja.

Lakes of Smolian — A704

Sofia Zoo, Cent. — A705

Bulgarian Scenes: 2s, Ropotamo Lake. 3s, Erma-Idreloto mountain pass. 8s, Isker River dam. 10s, Slanchev Breg (sailing ship). 13s, Cape Caliacra. 40s, Old houses, Sozopol. 2 l, Chudnite Skali ("Strange Mountains").

1968 Photo. *Perf. 13*

1681	A704	1s Prus green	15	15
1682	A704	2s dark green	15	15
1683	A704	3s dark brown	15	15
1684	A704	8s olive green	15	15
1685	A704	10s redsh brown	15	15
1686	A704	13s dk olive grn	22	15
1687	A704	40s Prus blue	60	24
1688	A704	2 l sepia	3.75	85
		Nos. 1681-1688 (8)	5.32	
		Set value		1.40

1968, July 29 *Perf. 10½*

1689	A705	1s Cinereous vulture	15	15
1690	A705	2s Crowned crane	15	15
1691	A705	3s Zebra	22	15
1692	A705	5s Leopard	38	15
1693	A705	13s Indian python	70	15
1694	A705	20s African crocodile	1.25	30
		Nos. 1689-1694 (6)	2.85	
		Set value		75

Human Rights Flame — A706

1968, July 8

1695	A706	20s dp blue & gold	60	15

International Human Rights Year, 1968.

Congress Hall, Varna, and Emblem A707

1968, Sept. 17 Photo. *Perf. 10½*

1696	A707	20s bister, grn & red	50	15

56th International Dental Congress, Varna.

Flying Swans — A708

Rose A709

Stag Beetle A710

Designs: 2s, Jug. 20s, Five Viking ships.

1968 Photo. *Perf. 10½*

1697	A709	2s green & ocher	75	50
1698	A708	5s dp blue & gray	75	50
1699	A709	13s dp plum & lil rose	75	50
1700	A708	20s dp vio & gray	75	50
		Nos. 1697-1700 (4)	3.00	2.00

Cooperation with the Scandinavian countries. Nos. 1697 and 1700 are printed with connecting label showing bridge made of flags of Scandinavian countries.

Issue dates: 5s, 13s, Sept. 12. Others, Nov. 22.

Perf. 12½x13, 13x12½

1968, Aug. 26

Insects: No. 1702, Ground beetle (Procerus scabrosus). No. 1703, Ground beetle (Calosoma sycophania). No. 1704, Scarab beetle, horiz. No. 1705, Saturnid moth, horiz.

1701	A710	1s brown olive	15	15
1702	A710	1s dark blue	15	15
1703	A710	1s dark green	15	15
1704	A710	1s orange brown	15	15
1705	A710	1s magenta	15	15
		Set value	30	25

Turks Fighting Insurgents, 1688 A711

1968, Aug. 22 *Perf. 10½*

1706	A711	13s multicolored	45	15

280th anniversary of the Tchiprovtzi insurrection.

Christo Smirnenski (1898-1923), Poet — A712

1968, Sept. 28 Litho. *Perf. 10½*

1707	A712	13s gold, red org & blk	40	15

Dalmatian Pelican A713

Birds: 2s, Little egret. 3s, Crested grebe. 5s, Common tern. 13s, European spoonbill. 20s, Glossy ibis.

1968, Oct. 28 Photo.

1708	A713	1s silver & multi	15	15
1709	A713	2s silver & multi	15	15
1710	A713	3s silver & multi	15	15
1711	A713	5s silver & multi	15	15
1712	A713	13s silver & multi	52	15
1713	A713	20s silver & multi	1.10	32
		Nos. 1708-1713 (6)	2.22	
		Set value		65

Srebirna wild life reservation.

Carrier Pigeon A714

1968, Oct. 19

1714	A714	20s emerald	70	25
a.		Sheet of 4 + labels	5.00	1.65

2nd Natl. Stamp Exhib. in Sofia, Oct. 25-Nov. 15. No. 1714a contains 4 No. 1714 and 5 labels.

Man and Woman from Lovetch — A715

Regional Costumes: 1s, Silistra. 3s, Jambol. 13s, Chirpan. 20s, Razgrad. 40s, Ihtiman.

1968, Nov. 20 Litho. *Perf. 13½*

1715	A715	1s dp org & multi	15	15
1716	A715	2s Prus bl & multi	15	15
1717	A715	3s multicolored	16	15
1718	A715	13s multicolored	28	15
1719	A715	20s multicolored	55	25
1720	A715	40s green & multi	1.40	45
		Nos. 1715-1720 (6)	2.69	
		Set value		1.00

Buying Sets
It is often less expensive to purchase complete sets than individual stamps that make up the set. Set values are provided for many such sets.

St. Arsenius A716

Designs (10th century Murals and Icons): 2s, Procession with relics of St. Ivan Rilsky, horiz. 3s, St. Michael Torturing the Soul of the Rich Man. 13s, St. Ivan Rilski. 20s, St. John. 40s, St. George. 1 l, Procession meeting relics of St. Ivan Rilsky, horiz.

Perf. 11½x12½, 12½x11½

1968, Nov. 25 **Photo.**

1721	A716	1s gold & multi	15	15
1722	A716	2s gold & multi	15	15
1723	A716	3s gold & multi	15	15
1724	A716	13s gold & multi	42	16
1725	A716	20s gold & multi	95	28
1726	A716	40s gold & multi	1.40	60
		Nos. 1721-1726 (6)	3.22	
		Set value		1.25

Souvenir Sheet

Imperf

1727	A716	1 l gold & multi	3.75	2.75

Millenium of Rila Monastery. No. 1727 also: Sofia 1969 Intl. Phil. Exhib., May 31-June 8, 1969. No. 1727 contains one stamp, size: 57x51mm.

Medlar A717

Herbs: No. 1729, Camomile. 2s, Lily-of-the-valley. 3s, Belladonna. 5s, Mallow. 10s, Buttercup. 13s, Poppies. 20s, Thyme.

1969, Jan. 2 **Litho.** ***Perf. 10½***

1728	A717	1s black, grn & org red	15	15
1729	A717	1s black, grn & yel	15	15
1730	A717	2s black, emer & grn	15	15
1731	A717	3s black & multi	15	15
1732	A717	5s black & multi	15	15
1733	A717	10s black, grn & yel	16	15
1734	A717	13s black & multi	30	15
1735	A717	20s black, lil & grn	65	15
		Set value	1.50	60

Silkworms and Spindles A718

Designs: 2s, Silkworm, cocoons and pattern. 3s, Cocoons and spinning wheel. 5s, Cocoons, woof-and-warp diagram. 13s, Silk moth, Cocoon and spinning frame. 20s, Silk moth, eggs and shuttle.

1969, Jan. 30 **Photo.** ***Perf. 10½***

1736	A718	1s bl, grn, sl & blk	15	15
1737	A718	2s dp car, sil & blk	15	15
1738	A718	3s Prus bl, sil & blk	15	15
1739	A718	5s pur, ver, sil & blk	15	15
1740	A718	13s red lil, ocher, sil & blk	25	15
1741	A718	20s grn, org, sil & blk	45	15
		Set value	95	45

Bulgarian silk industry.

Attack and Capture of Emperor Nicephorus — A719

Sts. Cyril and Methodius, Mural, Troian Monastery — A720

Designs (Manasses Chronicle): No. 1742, Death of Ivan Asen. 3s, Khan Kroum feasting after victory. No. 1748, Invasion of Bulgaria by Prince Sviatoslav of Kiev. No. 1750, Russian invasion and campaigns of Emperor John I Zimisces, c. 972 A.D. 40s, Tsar Ivan Alexander, Jesus and Constantine Manasses.

Horizontal designs: No. 1743, Kings Nebuchadnezzar, Balthazar, Darius and Cyrus. No. 1745, Kings Cambyses, Gyges and Darius. 5s, King David and Tsar Ivan Alexander. No. 1749, Persecution of Byzantine army after battle of July 26, 811. No. 1751, Christening of Bulgarian Tsar Boris, 865. 60s, Arrival of Tsar Simeon in Constantinople and his succeeding surprise attack on that city.

1969 **Photo.** ***Perf. 14x13½, 13½x14***

1742	A719	1s multicolored	15	15
1743	A719	1s multicolored	15	15
1744	A719	2s multicolored	15	15
1745	A719	2s multicolored	15	15
1746	A719	3s multicolored	15	15
1747	A719	5s multicolored	15	15
1748	A719	13s multicolored	38	15
1749	A719	13s multicolored	38	15
1750	A719	20s multicolored	80	15
1751	A719	20s multicolored	80	15
1752	A719	40s multicolored	1.25	38
1753	A719	60s multicolored	2.25	42
		Nos. 1742-1753 (12)	6.76	
		Set value		1.50

1969, Mar. 23

1754	A720	28s gold & multi	75	45

Post Horn — A721

Designs: 13s, Bulgaria Nos. 1 and 534. 20s, Street fighting at Stackata, 1919.

1969, Apr. 15 **Photo.** ***Perf. 10½***

1755	A721	2s green & yel	15	15
1756	A721	13s multicolored	40	15
1757	A721	20s dk bl & lt bl	48	18
		Nos. 1755-1757 (3)	1.03	
		Set value		35

90th anniversary of the Bulgarian postal administration.

The Fox and the Rabbit A722

Children's Drawings: 2s, Boy reading to wolf and fox. 13s, Two birds and cat singing together.

1969, Apr. 21

1758	A722	1s emer, org & blk	15	15
1759	A722	2s org, lt bl & blk	15	15
1760	A722	13s lt bl, ol & blk	38	15
		Set value	50	25

Issued for Children's Week.

ILO Emblem — A723

1969, Apr. 28

1761	A723	13s dull grn & blk	30	15

50th anniv. of the ILO.

St. George and SOFIA 69 Emblem — A724

Designs: 2s, Virgin Mary and St. John Bogoslov. 3s, Archangel Michael. 5s, Three Saints. 8s, Jesus Christ. 13s, Sts. George and Dimitrie. 20s, Christ, the Almighty. 40s, St. Dimitrie. 60s, The 40 Martyrs. 80s, The Transfiguration.

1969, Apr. 30 ***Perf. 11x12***

1762	A724	1s gold & multi	15	15
1763	A724	2s gold & multi	15	15
1764	A724	3s gold & multi	15	15
1765	A724	5s gold & multi	15	15
1766	A724	8s gold & multi	16	15
1767	A724	13s gold & multi	32	15
1768	A724	20s gold & multi	65	22
1769	A724	40s gold & multi	1.40	42
a.		Sheet of 4	5.75	5.00
1770	A724	60s gold & multi	1.75	85
1771	A724	80s gold & multi	2.75	1.00
		Nos. 1762-1771 (10)	7.63	
		Set value		3.00

Old Bulgarian art from the National Art Gallery. No. 1769a contains 4 of No. 1769 with center gutter showing Alexander Nevski Shrine. See note on SOFIA 69 after Nos. C112-C120.

St. Cyril Preaching — A725

Design: 28s, St. Cyril and followers.

1969, June 20 **Litho.** ***Perf. 10½***

1772	A725	2s sil, grn & red	16	15
1773	A725	28s sil, dk bl & red	75	22
		Set value		27

St. Cyril (827-869), apostle to the Slavs, inventor of Cyrillic alphabet. Issued in sheets of 25 with se-tenant labels; Cyrillic inscription on label of 2s, Glagolitic inscription on label of 28s.

St. Sophia Church — A726

Sofia Through the Ages: 1s, Roman coin with inscription "Ulpia Serdica." 2s, Roman coin with Aesculapius Temple. 4s, Bojana Church. 5s, Sobranic Parliament. 13s, Vasov National Theater. 20s, Alexander Nevski Shrine. 40s, Clement Ochrida University. 1 l, Coat of arms.

1969, May 25 ***Perf. 13x12½***

1774	A726	1s gold & blue	15	15
1775	A726	2s gold & ol grn	15	15
1776	A726	3s gold & red brn	15	15
1777	A726	4s gold & purple	15	15
1778	A726	5s gold & plum	15	15
1779	A726	13s gold & brt grn	28	15
1780	A726	20s gold & vio bl	45	15
1781	A726	40s gold & dp car	1.10	25
		Nos. 1774-1781 (8)	2.58	
		Set value		75

Souvenir Sheet

Imperf

1782	A726	1 l grn, gold & red	2.25	2.00

Historic Sofia in connection with the International Philatelic Exhibition, Sofia, May 31-June 8.

No. 1782 contains one stamp (size: 43½x43½mm). Emblems of 8 preceding philatelic exhibitions in metallic ink in margin; gold inscription.

No. 1782 was overprinted in green "IBRA 73" and various symbols, and released May 4, 1973, for the Munich Philatelic Exhibition. The overprint also exists in gray.

St. George — A727

1969, June 9 **Litho.** ***Perf. 11½***

1783	A727	40s sil, blk & pale rose	1.25	50

38th FIP Congress, June 9-11.

Hand Planting Sapling A728

1969, Apr. 28 **Photo.** ***Perf. 11***

1784	A728	2s ol grn, blk & lilac	15	15

25 years of the reforestation campaign.

Partisans A729

Designs: 2s, Combine harvester. 3s, Dam. 5s, Flutist and singers. 13s, Factory. 20s, Lenin, Dimitrov, Russian and Bulgarian flags.

1969, Sept. 9

1785	A729	1s blk, pur & org	15	15
1786	A729	2s blk, ol bis & org	15	15
1787	A729	3s blk, bl grn & org	15	15
1788	A729	5s blk, brn red & org	15	15
1789	A729	13s blk, bl & org	30	15
1790	A729	20s blk, brn & org	50	15
		Set value	1.10	45

25th anniversary of People's Republic.

Women Gymnasts A730

1969, Sept. Photo. *Perf. 11*
1791 A730 2s shown 15 15
1792 A730 20s Wrestlers 42 22
Set value 30

Third National Spartakiad.

Tchanko Bakalov Tcherkovski, Poet. Birth Cent. — A731

1969, Sept.
1793 A731 13s multicolored 35 15

Woman Gymnast A732

Designs: 2s, Two women with hoops. 3s, Woman with hoop. 5s, Two women with spheres.

1969, Oct.
Gymnasts in Light Gray
1794 A732 1s green & dk blue 15 15
1795 A732 2s blue & dk blue 15 15
1796 A732 3s emer & sl grn 15 15
1797 A732 5s orange & pur 15 15
Set value, #1794-1797, B35-B36 1.45 70

World Championships for Artistic Gymnastics, Varna.

The Priest Rilski, by Zachary Zograf — A733

Paintings from the National Art Gallery. 2s, Woman at Window, by Vasil Stoilov. 3s, Workers at Rest, by Nenko Balkanski, horiz. 4s, Woman Dressing (Nude), by Ivan Nenov. 5s, Portrait of a Woman, by N. Pavlovich. 13s, Falstaff, by Duzunov Kr. Sarafov. No. 1804, Portrait of a Woman, by N. Mihajlov, horiz. No. 1805, Workers at Mealtime, by Stojan Sotirov, horiz. 40s, Self-portrait, by Tcheno Togorov.

Perf. 11½x12, 12x11½
1969, Nov. 10
1798 A733 1s gold & multi 15 15
1799 A733 2s gold & multi 15 15
1800 A733 3s gold & multi 15 15
1801 A733 4s gold & multi 15 15
1802 A733 5s gold & multi 15 15
1803 A733 13s gold & multi 32 15
1804 A733 20s gold & multi 70 22
1805 A733 20s gold & multi 70 22
1806 A733 40s gold & multi 1.40 60
Nos. 1798-1806 (9) 3.87
Set value 1.50

Roman Bronze Wolf A734

Design: 2s, Roman statue of woman, found at Silistra, vert.

1969, Oct. Photo. *Perf. 11*
1807 A734 2s sil, ultra & gray 15 15
1808 A734 13s sil, dk grn & gray 42 15
Set value 17

City of Silistra's 1,800th anniversary.

Worker and Factory — A735

1969 *Perf. 13*
1809 A735 6s ultra & blk 15 15

25th anniversary of the factory militia.

European Hake — A736

Designs: No. 1811, Deep-sea fishing trawler. Fish: 2s, Atlantic horse mackerel. 3s, Pilchard. 5s, Dentex macrophthalmus. 10s, Chub mackerel. 13s, Otolithes macrognathus. 20s, Lichia vadigo.

1969 *Perf. 11*
1810 A736 1s ol grn & blk 15 15
1811 A736 1s ultra, ind & gray 15 15
1812 A736 2s lilac & blk 15 15
1813 A736 3s vio bl & blk 15 15
1814 A736 5s rose cl, pink & blk 24 15
1815 A736 10s gray & blk 48 15
1816 A736 13s ver, sal & blk 70 15
1817 A736 20s ocher & black 1.25 18
Nos. 1810-1817 (8) 3.27
Set value 58

Marin Drinov A737

1969, Nov. 10 Litho. *Perf. 11*
1818 A737 20s black & red org 35 15

Centenary of the Bulgarian Academy of Science, founded by Marin Drinov.

Trapeze Artists A738

Pavel Bania Sanatorium A739

Circus Performers: 2s, Jugglers. 3s, Jugglers with loops. 5s, Juggler and bear on bicycle. 13s, Woman and performing horse. 20s, Musical clowns.

1969 Photo. *Perf. 11*
1819 A738 1s dk blue & multi 15 15
1820 A738 2s dk green & multi 15 15
1821 A738 3s dk violet & multi 15 15
1822 A738 5s multicolored 15 15
1823 A738 13s multicolored 30 15
1824 A738 20s multicolored 55 20
Set value 1.10 50

1969, Dec. Photo. *Perf. 10½-14*

Health Resorts: 5s, Chisar Sanatorium. 6s, Kotel Children's Sanatorium. 20s, Narechen Polyclinic.

1825 A739 2s blue 15 15
1826 A739 5s ultra 15 15
1827 A739 6s green 15 15
1828 A739 20s emerald 32 15
Set value 65 22

G. S. Shonin, V. N. Kubasov and Spacecraft — A740

Designs: 2s, A. V. Filipchenko, V. N. Volkov, V. V. Gorbatko and spacecraft. 3s, Vladimir A. Shatalov, Alexei S. Yeliseyev and spacecraft. 28s, Three spacecraft in orbit.

1970, Jan. Photo. *Perf. 11*
1829 A740 1s rose car, ol grn & blk 15 15
1830 A740 2s bl, dl cl & blk 15 15
1831 A740 3s grnsh bl, vio & blk 15 15
1832 A740 28s vio bl, lil rose & lt bl 70 16
Set value 90 31

Russian space flights of Soyuz 6, 7 and 8, Oct. 11-13, 1969.

Khan Krum and Defeat of Emperor Nicephorus, 811 — A741

Bulgarian History: 1s, Khan Asparuch and Bulgars crossing the Danube (679). 3s, Conversion of Prince Boris to Christianity, 865. 5s, Tsar Simeon and battle of Akhelo, 917. 8s, Tsar Samuel defeating the Byzantines, 976. 10s, Tsar Kaloyan defeating Emperor Baldwin, 1205. 13s, Tsar Ivan Assen II defeating Greek King Theodore Komnine, 1230. 20s, Coronation of Tsar Ivailo, 1277.

1970, Feb. *Perf. 10½*
1833 A741 1s gold & multi 15 15
1834 A741 2s gold & multi 15 15
1835 A741 3s gold & multi 15 15
1836 A741 5s gold & multi 15 15
1837 A741 8s gold & multi 18 15
1838 A741 10s gold & multi 30 15
1839 A741 13s gold & multi 40 15
1840 A741 20s gold & multi 70 15
Nos. 1833-1840 (8) 2.18
Set value 56

See Nos. 2126-2133.

Bulgarian Pavilion, EXPO '70 — A742

1970 *Perf. 12½*
1841 A742 20s brown, sil & org 75 50

EXPO '70 International Exposition, Osaka, Japan, Mar. 15-Sept. 13, 1970.

Soccer A743

Designs: Various views of soccer game.

1970, Mar. 4 Photo. *Perf. 12½*
1842 A743 1s blue & multi 15 15
1843 A743 2s rose car & multi 15 15
1844 A743 3s ultra & multi 15 15
1845 A743 5s green & multi 15 15
1846 A743 20s emerald & multi 55 15
1847 A743 40s red & multi 1.25 28
Nos. 1842-1847 (6) 2.40
Set value 65

9th World Soccer Championships for the Jules Rimet Cup, Mexico City, May 30-June 21, 1970. See No. B37.

Lenin (1870-1924) A744

1970, Apr. 22
1848 A744 2s shown 15 15
1849 A744 13s Portrait 32 15
1850 A744 20s Writing 70 15
Nos. 1848-1850 (3) 1.17
Set value 26

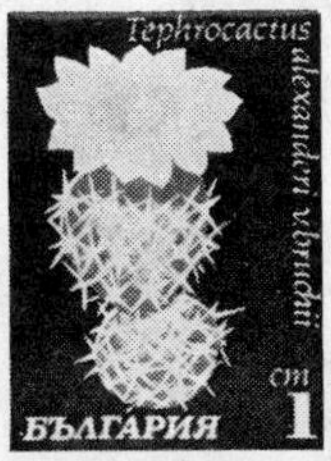

Tephrocactus Alexanderi V. Bruchii — A745

Cacti: 2s, Opuntia drummondii. 3s, Hatiora cilindrica. 5s, Gymnocalycium vatteri. 8s, Helianthocereus grandiflorus. 10s, Neochilenia andreaeana. 13s, Peireskia vargasii v. longispina. 20s, Neobesseya rosiflora.

1970 Photo. *Perf. 12½*
1851 A745 1s multicolored 15 15
1852 A745 2s dk green & multi 15 15
1853 A745 3s multicolored 15 15
1854 A745 5s blue & multi 15 15
1855 A745 8s brown & multi 28 15
1856 A745 10s vio bl & multi 1.00 16
1857 A745 13s brn red & multi 1.00 16
1858 A745 20s purple & multi 1.40 32
Nos. 1851-1858 (8) 4.28
Set value 1.00

Rose — A746

Designs: Various Roses.

1970, June 8 Litho. *Perf. 13½*
1859 A746 1s gray & multi 15 15
1860 A746 2s gray & multi 15 15
1861 A746 3s gray & multi 15 15
1862 A746 4s gray & multi 15 15
1863 A746 5s gray & multi 15 15
1864 A746 13s gray & multi 16 15
1865 A746 20s gray & multi 1.10 25
1866 A746 28s gray & multi 1.90 42
Nos. 1859-1866 (8) 3.91
Set value 1.10

Gold Bowl — A747

Designs: Various bowls and art objects from Gold Treasure of Thrace.

1970, June 15 — Photo. — *Perf. 12½*

1867 A747 1s blk, bl & gold 15 15
1868 A747 2s blk, lt vio & gold 15 15
1869 A747 3s blk, ver & gold 15 15
1870 A747 5s blk, yel grn & gold 15 15
1871 A747 13s blk, org & gold 70 15
1872 A747 20s blk, lil & gold 85 18
Nos. 1867-1872 (6) 2.15
Set value 50

EXPO Emblem, Rose and Bulgarian Woman — A748

Designs (EXPO Emblem and): 2s, Three women. 3s, Woman and fruit. 28s, Dancers. 40s, Mt. Fuji and pavilions.

1970, June 20

1873 A748 1s gold & multi 15 15
1874 A748 2s gold & multi 15 15
1875 A748 3s gold & multi 15 15
1876 A748 28s gold & multi 70 22
Nos. 1873-1876 (4) 1.15
Set value 45

Miniature Sheet

Imperf

1877 A748 40s gold & multi 1.00 60

EXPO '70 International Exposition, Osaka, Japan, Mar. 15-Sept. 13. No. 1877 contains one stamp with simulated perforations.

Ivan Vasov — A749

1970, Aug. 1 — Photo. — *Perf. 12½*

1878 A749 13s violet blue 40 15

120th anniv. of the birth of Ivan Vasov, author.

UN Emblem — A750

1970, Aug. 1

1879 A750 20s Prus bl & gold 50 20

25th anniversary of the United Nations.

George Dimitrov A751

Retriever A752

1970, Aug.

1880 A751 20s blk, gold & org 60 15

70th anniv. of BZNC (Bulgarian Communist Party).

1970 — Photo. — *Perf. 12½*

Dogs: 1s, Golden retriever, horiz. 3s, Great Dane. 4s, Boxer. 5s, Cocker spaniel. 13s, Doberman pinscher. 20s, Scottish terrier. 28s, Russian greyhound, horiz.

1881 A752 1s multicolored 15 15
1882 A752 2s multicolored 15 15
1883 A752 3s multicolored 15 15
1884 A752 4s multicolored 15 15
1885 A752 5s multicolored 15 15
1886 A752 13s multicolored 52 15
1887 A752 20s multicolored 1.10 26
1888 A752 28s multicolored 1.65 32
Nos. 1881-1888 (8) 4.02
Set value 94

Volleyball — A753

Designs: No. 1890, Two women players. No. 1891, Woman player. No. 1892, Man player.

1970, Sept. — Photo. — *Perf. 12½*

1889 A753 2s dk red brn, bl & blk 15 15
1890 A753 2s ultra, org & blk 15 15
1891 A753 20s Prus bl, yel & blk 48 15
1892 A753 20s grn, yel & blk 48 15
Nos. 1889-1892 (4) 1.26
Set value 34

World Volleyball Championships.

Enrico Caruso and "I Pagliacci" by Ruggiero Leoncavallo — A754

Opera Singers and Operas: 2s, Christina Morfova and "The Bartered Bride" by Bedrich Smetana. 3s, Peter Reitchev and "Tosca" by Giacomo Puccini. 10s, Svetana Tabakova and "The Flying Dutchman" by Richard Wagner. 13s, Katia Popova and "The Masters" by Paroshkev Hadjev. 20s, Feodor Chaliapin and "Boris Godunov" by Modest Musorgski.

1970, Oct. 15 — Photo. — *Perf. 14*

1893 A754 1s black & multi 15 15
1894 A754 2s black & multi 15 15
1895 A754 3s black & multi 15 15
1896 A754 10s black & multi 20 15
1897 A754 13s black & multi 28 16
1898 A754 20s black & multi 1.00 25
Nos. 1893-1898 (6) 1.93
Set value 80

Honoring opera singers in their best roles.

Ivan Assen II Coin — A755

Coins from 14th Century with Ruler's Portrait: 2s, Theodor Svetoslav. 3s, Mikhail Chichman. 13s, Ivan Alexander and Mikhail Assen. 20s, Ivan Sratsimir. 28s, Ivan Chichman (initials).

1970, Nov. — *Perf. 12½*

1899 A755 1s buff & multi 15 15
1900 A755 2s gray & multi 15 15
1901 A755 3s multicolored 15 15
1902 A755 13s multicolored 22 15
1903 A755 20s lt blue & multi 60 15
1904 A755 28s multicolored 85 22
Nos. 1899-1904 (6) 2.12
Set value 65

Fire Protection A756

1970 — Litho. — *Perf. 12½*

1905 A756 1s Fireman 15 15
1906 A756 3s Fire engine 15 15
Set value 20 15

Bicyclists — A757

Congress Emblem — A758

1970 — Photo.

1907 A757 20s grn, yel & pink 50 20

20th Bulgarian bicycle race.

1970

1908 A758 13s gold & multi 35 15

7th World Congress of Sociology, Varna, Sept. 14-19.

Ludwig van Beethoven — A759

Friedrich Engels — A760

1970

1909 A759 28s lil rose & dk bl 90 40

Beethoven (1770-1827), composer.

1970 — Photo. — *Perf. 12½*

1910 A760 13s ver, tan & brn 30 15

Friedrich Engels (1820-1895), German socialist, collaborator of Karl Marx.

Miniature Sheets

Luna 16 A761

Russian moon mission: 80s, Lunokhod 1, unmanned vehicle on moon, horiz.

1970 — Photo. — *Imperf.*

1911 A761 80s plum, sil, blk & bl 2.00 2.00
1912 A761 1 l vio bl, sil & red 4.00 2.75

No. 1911 , Lunokhod 1, Nov. 10-17. No. 1912, Luna 16 mission, Sept. 12-24.
Issue dates: 80s, Dec. 18; 1 l, Nov. 10.

Snowflake A762

1970, Dec. 15 — Photo. — *Perf. 12½x13*

1913 A762 2s ultra & multi 15 15

New Year 1971.

Birds and Flowers A763

Folk Art: 2s, Bird and flowers. 3s, Flying birds. 5s, Birds and flowers. 13s, Sun. 20s, Tulips and pansies.

1971, Jan. 25 — *Perf. 12½x13½*

1914 A763 1s multicolored 15 15
1915 A763 2s multicolored 15 15
1916 A763 3s multicolored 15 15
1917 A763 5s multicolored 15 15
1918 A763 13s multicolored 16 15
1919 A763 20s multicolored 55 15
Set value 95 40

Spring 1971.

Girl, by Zeko Spiridonov A764

Modern Bulgarian Sculpture: 2s, Third Class (people looking through train window), by Ivan Funev. 3s, Bust of Elin Pelin, by Marko Markov. 13s, Bust of Nina, by Andrej Nikolov. 20s, Monument to P. K. Yavorov (kneeling woman), by Ivan Lazarov. 28s, Engineer, by Ivan Funev. 1 l, Refugees, by Sekul Krimov, horiz.

1971, Feb. — *Perf. 12½*

1920 A764 1s gold & vio 15 15
1921 A764 2s gold & dk ol grn 15 15
1922 A764 3s gold & rose brn 15 15
1923 A764 13s gold & dk grn 30 15

15-Cent Minimum Value
The minimum value for a single stamp is 15 cents. This value reflects the costs of handling inexpensive stamps.

1924 A764 20s gold & red brn 52 15
1925 A764 28s gold & dk brn 80 20
Nos. 1920-1925 (6) 2.07
Set value 65

Souvenir Sheet

Imperf

1926 A764 1 l gold, dk brn & buff 2.00 1.75

Runner A765

Design: 20s, Woman putting the shot.

1971, Mar. 13 Photo. *Perf. 12½x13*

1927 A765 2s brown & multi 15 15
1928 A765 20s dp grn, org & blk 90 22
Set value 30

2nd European Indoor Track and Field Championships.

Bulgarian Secondary School, Bolgrad — A766

Educators: 20s, Dimiter Mitev, Prince Bogoridi and Sava Radoulov.

1971, Mar. 16 *Perf. 12½*

1929 A766 2s silver, brn & grn 15 15
1930 A766 20s silver, brn & vio 52 15
Set value 20

First Bulgarian secondary school, 1858, in Bolgrad, USSR.

Communards — A767

1971, Mar. 18 Photo. *Perf. 12½x13*

1931 A767 20s rose mag & blk 50 20

Centenary of the Paris Commune.

Dimitrov Facing Goering, Quotation, FIR Emblem A768

1971, Apr. 11 *Perf. 12½*

1932 A768 2s grn, gold, blk & red 15 15
1933 A768 13s plum, gold, blk & red 70 15
Set value 15

International Federation of Resistance Fighters (FIR), 20th anniversary.

George S. Rakovski (1821-1867), Revolutionary Against Turkish Rule — A769

1971, Apr. 14

1934 A769 13s olive & blk brn 30 15

Edelweiss Hotel, Borovets — A770

Designs: 2s, Panorama Hotel, Pamporovo. 4s, Boats at Albena, Black Sea. 8s, Boats at Rousalka. 10s, Shtastlivetsa Hotel, Mt. Vitosha.

1971 *Perf. 13*

1935 A770 1s brt green 15 15
1936 A770 2s olive gray 15 15
1937 A770 4s brt blue 15 15
1938 A770 8s blue 15 15
1939 A770 10s bluish green 25 15
Set value 65 30

Technological Progress — A771

Designs: 1s, Mason with banner, vert. 13s, Two men and doves, vert.

1971, Apr. 20 Photo. *Perf. 12½*

1940 A771 1s gold & multi 15 15
1941 A771 2s gray blue & multi 15 15
1942 A771 13s lt green & multi 52 16
Set value 70 30

10th Cong. of Bulgarian Communist Party.

Panayot Pipkov and Anthem A772

1971, May 20

1943 A772 13s sil, blk & brt grn 45 15

Panayot Pipkov, composer, birth cent.

Mammoth A773

Prehistoric Animals: 2s, Bear, vert. 3s, Hipparion (horse). 13s, Platybelodon. 20s, Dinotherium, vert. 28s, Saber-tooth tiger.

1971, May 29 *Perf. 12½*

1944 A773 1s dull bl & multi 15 15
1945 A773 2s lilac & multi 15 15
1946 A773 3s multicolored 15 15
1947 A773 13s multicolored 48 15
1948 A773 20s dp grn & multi 80 18
1949 A773 28s multicolored 1.40 28
Nos. 1944-1949 (6) 3.13
Set value 75

Khan Asparuch Crossing Danube, 679 A.D., by Boris Angelushev — A774

Historical Paintings: 3s, Reception at Trnovo, by Ilya Petrov. 5s, Chevartov's Troops at Benkovsky, by P. Morozov. 8s, Russian Gen. Gurko and People in Sofia, 1878, by D. Gudjenko. 28s, People Greeting Red Army, by S. Venov.

1971, Mar. 6 *Perf. 13½x14*

1950 A774 2s gold & multi 15 15
1951 A774 3s gold & multi 15 15
1952 A774 5s gold & multi 16 15
1953 A774 8s gold & multi 32 15
a. Souv. sheet of 4, #1950-1953 1.00 50
1954 A774 28s gold & multi 2.75 85
Nos. 1950-1954 (5) 3.53
Set value 1.20

In 1973, No. 1953a was surcharged 1 lev and overprinted "Visitez la Bulgarie," airline initials and emblems, and, on the 5s stamp, "Par Avion."

Freed Black, White and Yellow Men — A775

1971, May 20 Photo. *Perf. 12½*

1955 A775 13s blue, blk & yel 35 15

Intl. Year against Racial Discrimination.

Map of Europe, Championship Emblem — A776

"XXX" Supporting Barbell — A777

1971, June 19

1956 A776 2s lt blue & multi 15 15
1957 A777 13s yellow & multi 60 18
Set value 65 25

30th European Weight Lifting Championships, Sofia, June 19-27.

Facade, Old House, Koprivnica A778

Designs: Decorated facades of various old houses in Koprivnica.

1971, July 10 Photo. *Perf. 12½*

1958 A778 1s green & multi 15 15
1959 A778 2s brown & multi 15 15
1960 A778 6s violet & multi 15 15
1961 A778 13s dk red & multi 42 15
Set value 65 30

Frontier Guard and German Shepherd A779

1971, July 31 *Perf. 13*

1962 A779 2s green & ol grn 15 15

25th anniversary of the Frontier Guards.

Congress of Busludja, Bas-relief — A780

1971, July 31 *Perf. 12½*

1963 A780 2s dk red & ol grn 15 15

80th anniversary of the first Congress of the Bulgarian Social Democratic party.

Young Woman, by Ivan Nenov — A781

Paintings: 2s, Lazarova in Evening Gown, by Stefan Ivanov. 3s, Performer in Dress Suit, by Kyril Zonev. 13s, Portrait of a Woman, by Detchko Uzunov. 20s, Woman from Kalotina, by Vladimir Dimitrov. 40s, Gorjanin (Mountain Man), by Stoyan Venev.

1971, Aug. 2 *Perf. 14x13½*

1964 A781 1s green & multi 15 15
1965 A781 2s green & multi 15 15
1966 A781 3s green & multi 15 15
1967 A781 13s green & multi 38 15
1968 A781 20s green & multi 75 30
1969 A781 40s green & multi 1.65 45
Nos. 1964-1969 (6) 3.23
Set value 1.00

National Art Gallery.

Wrestlers A782

Designs: 13s, Wrestlers.

1971, Aug. 27 *Perf. 12½*

1970 A782 2s green, blk & bl 15 15
1971 A782 13s red org, blk & bl 48 15
Set value 20

European Wrestling Championships.

Young Workers
A783

Post Horn Emblem
A784

1971 Photo. *Perf. 13*

1972 A783 2s dark blue	15	15

25th anniv. of the Young People's Brigade.

1971, Sept. 15 *Perf. 12½*

1973 A784 20s dp green & gold	45	20

8th meeting of postal administrations of socialist countries, Varna.

FEBS Waves Emblem — A785

1971, Sept. 20

1974 A785 13s black, red & mar	50	20

7th Congress of European Biochemical Association (FEBS), Varna.

Statue of Republic — A786

Design: 13s, Bulgarian flag.

1971, Sept. 20 *Perf. 13x12½*

1975 A786 2s gold, yel & dk red	15	15
1976 A786 13s gold, grn & red	38	20
Set value	45	25

Bulgarian People's Republic, 25th anniv.

Cross Country Skiing and Winter Olympics Emblem
A787

Sport and Winter Olympics Emblem: 2s, Downhill skiing. 3s, Ski jump and skiing. 4s, Women's figure skating. 13s, Ice hockey. 28s, Slalom skiing. 1 l, Torch and stadium.

1971, Sept. 25 *Perf. 12½*

1977 A787 1s dk green & multi	15	15
1978 A787 2s vio blue & multi	15	15
1979 A787 3s ultra & multi	15	15
1980 A787 4s dp plum & multi	15	15
1981 A787 13s dk blue & multi	40	15
1982 A787 28s multicolored	90	35
Set value	1.50	75

Miniature Sheet

Imperf

1983 A787 1 l multicolored	3.50	1.65

11th Winter Olympic Games, Sapporo, Japan, Feb. 3-13, 1972.

Factory, Botevgrad
A788

Industrial Buildings: 2s, Petro-chemical works, Pleven, vert. 10s, Chemical works, Vratsa. 13s, Maritsa-Istok Power Station, Dimitrovgrad. 40s, Electronics works, Sofia.

1971 Photo. *Perf. 13*

1984 A788 1s violet	15	15
1985 A788 2s orange	15	15
1986 A788 10s deep purple	18	15
1987 A788 13s lilac rose	22	15
1988 A788 40s deep brown	70	15
Nos. 1984-1988 (5)	1.40	
Set value		32

UNESCO Emblem
A789

1971, Nov. 4 *Perf. 12½*

1989 A789 20s lt bl, blk, gold & red	45	15

25th anniv. of UNESCO.

Soccer Player, by Kyril Zonev (1896-1971)
A790

Paintings by Kyril Zonev: 2s, Landscape, horiz. 3s, Self-portrait. 13s, Lilies. 20s, Landscape, horiz. 40s, Portrait of a Young Woman.

1971, Nov. 10 *Perf. 11x12*

1990 A790 1s gold & multi	15	15
1991 A790 2s gold & multi	15	15
1992 A790 3s gold & multi	15	15
1993 A790 13s gold & multi	22	15
1994 A790 20s gold & multi	85	24
1995 A790 40s gold & multi	1.25	35
Nos. 1990-1995 (6)	2.77	
Set value		85

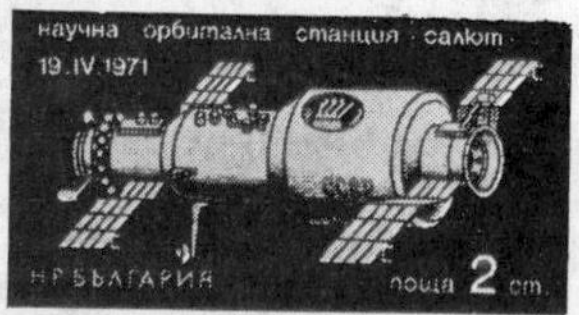

Salyut Space Station — A791

Astronauts Dobrovolsky, Volkov and Patsayev — A792

Designs: 13s, Soyuz 11 space transport. 40s, Salyut and Soyuz 11 joined.

1971, Dec. 20 *Perf. 12½*

1996 A791 2s dk grn, yel & red	15	15
1997 A791 13s multicolored	22	16
1998 A791 40s dk blue & multi	1.25	40
Nos. 1996-1998 (3)	1.62	71

Souvenir Sheet

Imperf

1999 A792 80s multicolored	2.00	1.50

Salyut-Soyuz 11 space mission, and in memory of the Russian astronauts Lt. Col. Georgi T. Dobrovolsky, Vladislav N. Volkov and Victor I. Patsayev, who died during the Soyuz 11 space mission, June 6-30, 1971.

Oil Tanker Vihren
A793

1972, Jan. 8 Photo. *Perf. 12½*

2000 A793 18s lil rose, vio & blk	75	25

Bulgarian shipbuilding industry.

Goce Delchev
A794

Portraits: 5s, Jan Sandanski. 13s, Damjan Gruev.

1972, Jan. 21 Photo. *Perf. 12½*

2001 A794 2s brick red & blk	15	15
2002 A794 5s green & blk	15	15
2003 A794 13s lemon & blk	35	15
Set value	50	22

Centenary of the births of Bulgarian patriots Delchev (1872-1903) and Sandanski, and of Macedonian Gruev (1871-1906).

Gymnast with Ball, Medals — A795

Designs: 18s, Gymnast with hoop, and medals. 70s, Gymnasts with hoops, and medals.

1972, Feb. 10

2004 A795 13s multicolored	42	15
2005 A795 18s multicolored	55	16
Set value		25

Miniature Sheet

Imperf

2006 A795 70s multicolored	2.25	2.00

5th World Women's Gymnastic Championships, Havana, Cuba.

View of Melnik, by Petar Mladenov — A796

Paintings from National Art Gallery: 2s, Plower, by Pencho Georgiev. 3s, Funeral, by Alexander Djendov. 13s, Husband and Wife, by Vladimir Dimitrov. 20s, Nursing Mother, by Nenko Balkanski. 40s, Paisii Hilendarski Writing History, by Koio Denchev.

1972, Feb. 20 *Perf. 13½x14*

2007 A796 1s green & multi	15	15
2008 A796 2s green & multi	15	15
2009 A796 3s green & multi	15	15
2010 A796 13s green & multi	42	15
2011 A796 20s green & multi	75	20
2012 A796 40s green & multi	1.25	35
Nos. 2007-2012 (6)	2.87	
Set value		90

Paintings from National Art Gallery.

Worker — A797

1972, Mar. 7 *Perf. 12½*

2013 A797 13s silver & multi	20	15

7th Bulgarian Trade Union Congress.

Singing Harvesters
A798

Designs: Paintings by Vladimir Dimitrov.

Perf. 11½x12, 12x11½

1972, Mar. 31

2014 A798 1s shown	15	15
2015 A798 2s Harvester	15	15
2016 A798 3s Women Diggers	15	15
2017 A798 13s Fabric Dyers	35	15
2018 A798 20s "My Mother"	70	15
2019 A798 40s Self-portrait	1.40	32
Nos. 2014-2019 (6)	2.90	
Set value		80

Vladimir Dimitrov, painter, 90th birth anniv.

"Your Heart is your Health" — A799

St. Mark's Basilica and Wave — A800

1972, Apr. 30 *Perf. 12½*

2020 A799 13s red, blk & grn	70	30

World Health Day.

1972, May 6 *Perf. 13x12½*

Design: 13s, Ca' D'Oro and wave.

2021 A800 2s ol grn, bl grn & lt bl	15	15
2022 A800 13s red brn, vio & lt grn	52	18
Set value	60	25

UNESCO campaign to save Venice.

Dimitrov in Print Shop, 1901 — A801

Designs: Life of George Dimitrov.

1972, May 8 Photo. *Perf. 12½*

2023 A801 1s shown 15 15
2024 A801 2s Dimitrov as leader of 1923 uprising 15 15
2025 A801 3s Leipzig trial, 1933 15 15
2026 A801 5s As Communist functionary, 1935 15 15
2027 A801 13s As leader and teacher, 1948 15 15
2028 A801 18s Addressing youth rally, 1948 42 15
2029 A801 28s With Pioneers, 1948 65 16
2030 A801 40s Mausoleum 1.00 32
2031 A801 80s Portrait 2.75 45
a. Souvenir sheet 4.25 2.50
Nos. 2023-2031 (9) 5.57 1.83

90th anniversary of the birth of George Dimitrov (1882-1949), communist leader.

No. 2031a contains one imperf. stamp similar to No. 2031, but in different colors.

Value, No. 2031 imperf. in slightly changed colors, $5.

Paisii Hilendarski — A802

Design: 2s, Flame and quotation.

1972, May 12

2032 A802 2s gold, grn & brn 15 15
2033 A802 13s gold, grn & brn 50 15
Set value 15

Paisii Hilendarski (1722-1798), monk, writer of Bulgarian-Slavic history.

Canoeing, Motion and Olympic Emblems — A803

Designs (Motion and Olympic emblems and): 2s, Gymnastics. 3s, Swimming, women's. 13s, Volleyball. 18s, Jumping. 40s, Wrestling. 80s, Stadium and sports.

1972, June 25

Figures of Athletes in Silver & Black

2034 A803 1s lt blue & multi 15 15
2035 A803 2s orange & multi 15 15
2036 A803 3s multicolored 15 15
2037 A803 13s yellow & multi 15 15
2038 A803 18s multicolored 42 18
2039 A803 40s pink & multi 1.25 30
Nos. 2034-2039 (6) 2.27
Set value 75

Miniature Sheet

Imperf

Size: 62x60mm

2040 A803 80s gold, ver & yel 1.75 1.00

20th Olympic Games, Munich, Aug. 26-Sept. 11.

Angel Kunchev A804

1972, June 30 Photo. *Perf. 12½*

2041 A804 2s mag, dk pur & gold 15 15

Centenary of the death of Angel Kunchev, patriot and revolutionist.

Zlatni Pyassatsi — A805

1972, Sept. 16

2042 A805 1s shown 15 15
2043 A805 2s Drouzhba 15 15
2044 A805 3s Slunchev Bryag 15 15
2045 A805 13s Primorsko 15 15
2046 A805 28s Roussalka 60 24
2047 A805 40s Albena 85 30
Nos. 2042-2047 (6) 2.05
Set value 80

Bulgarian Black Sea resorts.

Bronze Medal, Olympic Emblems, Canoeing A806

Designs (Olympic Emblems and): 2s, Silver medal, broad jump. 3s, Gold medal, boxing. 18s, Gold medal, wrestling. 40s, Gold medal, weight lifting.

1972, Sept. 29

2048 A806 1s Prus bl & multi 15 15
2049 A806 2s dk green & multi 15 15
2050 A806 3s orange brn & multi 15 15
2051 A806 18s olive & multi 50 16
2052 A806 40s multicolored 1.00 30
Nos. 2048-2052 (5) 1.95
Set value 65

Bulgarian victories in 20th Olympic Games. For overprint see No. 2066.

Stoj Dimitrov — A807

Resistance Fighters: 2s, Cvetko Radoinov. 3s, Bogdan Stivrodski. 5s, Mirko Laiev. 13s, Nedelyo Nikolov.

1972, Oct. 30 Photo. *Perf. 12½x13*

2053 A807 1s olive & multi 15 15
2054 A807 2s multicolored 15 15
2055 A807 3s multicolored 15 15
2056 A807 5s multicolored 15 15
2057 A807 13s multicolored 28 15
Set value 60 30

"50 Years USSR" A808

1972, Nov. 3 Photo. *Perf. 12½x13*

2058 A808 13s gold, red & yel 35 15

50th anniversary of Soviet Union.

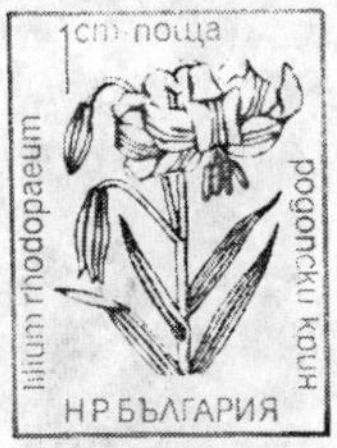

Turk's-cap Lily — A809

Protected Plants: 2s, Gentian. 3s, Sea daffodil. 4s, Globe flower. 18s, Primrose. 23s, Pulsatilla vernalis. 40s, Snake's-head.

1972, Nov. 25 *Perf. 12½*

Flowers in Natural Colors

2059 A809 1s olive bister 15 15
2060 A809 2s olive bister 15 15
2061 A809 3s olive bister 15 15
2062 A809 4s olive bister 15 15
2063 A809 18s olive bister 28 15
2064 A809 23s olive bister 75 20
2065 A809 40s olive bister 1.40 35
Nos. 2059-2065 (7) 3.03
Set value 90

No. 2052 Overprinted in СВЕТОВЕН ПЪРВЕНЕЦ Red

1972, Nov. 27

2066 A806 40s multicolored 95 24

Bulgarian weight lifting Olympic gold medalists.

Dobri Chintulov — A810

1972, Nov. 28 Photo. *Perf. 12½*

2067 A810 2s gray, dk & lt grn 20 15

Dobri Chintulov, writer, 150th birth anniversary.

Forehead Band — A811

Designs (14th-19th Century Jewelry): 2s, Belt buckles. 3s, Amulet. 8s, Pendant. 23s, Earrings. 40s, Necklace.

1972, Dec. 27 Engr. *Perf. 14x13½*

2068 A811 1s red brn & blk 15 15
2069 A811 2s emerald & blk 15 15
2070 A811 3s Prus bl & blk 15 15
2071 A811 8s dk red & blk 15 15
2072 A811 23s red org & multi 50 20
2073 A811 40s violet & blk 1.10 42
Set value 1.90 90

Skin Divers A812

Designs: 2s, Shelf-1 underwater house and divers. 18s, Diving bell and diver, vert. 40s, Elevation balloon and divers, vert.

1973, Jan. 24 Photo. *Perf. 12½*

2074 A812 1s lt bl, blk & yel 15 15
2075 A812 2s blk, bl & org yel 15 15
2076 A812 18s blk, Prus bl & dl org 42 15
2077 A812 40s blk, ultra & bister 95 30
Nos. 2074-2077 (4) 1.67
Set value 54

Bulgarian deep-sea research in the Black Sea.

A souvenir sheet of four contains imperf. 20s stamps in designs of Nos. 2074-2077 with colors changed. Sold for 1 l. Value $3.50 unused, $3 canceled.

Execution of Levski, by Boris Angelushev — A813

Design: 20s, Vassil Levski, by Georgi Danchev.

1973, Feb. 19 *Perf. 13x12½*

2078 A813 2s dull rose & Prus grn 15 15
2079 A813 20s dull grn & brn 90 18
Set value 23

Centenary of the death of Vassil Levski (1837-1873), patriot, executed by the Turks.

Kukersky Mask, Elhovo Region A814

Nicolaus Copernicus A815

Kukersky Masks at pre-Spring Festival: 2s, Breznik. 3s, Hissar. 13s, Radomir. 20s, Karnobat. 40s, Pernik.

1973, Feb. 26 *Perf. 12½*

2080 A814 1s dp rose & multi 15 15
2081 A814 2s emerald & multi 15 15
2082 A814 3s violet & multi 15 15
2083 A814 13s multicolored 35 15
2084 A814 20s multicolored 38 15
2085 A814 40s multicolored 2.25 1.10
Nos. 2080-2085 (6) 3.43
Set value 1.45

1973, Mar. 21 Photo. *Perf. 12½*

2086 A815 28s ocher, blk & cl 1.25 60

500th anniversary of the birth of Nicolaus Copernicus (1473-1543), Polish astronomer.

Vietnamese Worker and Rainbow — A816

1973, Apr. 16

2087 A816 18s lt blue & multi	35	15

Peace in Viet Nam.

A817

A818

Wild flowers.

1973, May Photo. *Perf. 13*

2088 A817 1s Poppy	15	15
2089 A817 2s Daisy	15	15
2090 A817 3s Peony	15	15
2091 A817 13s Centaury	25	15
2092 A817 18s Corn cockle	2.75	1.10
2093 A817 28s Ranunculus	60	22
Nos. 2088-2093 (6)	4.05	
Set value		1.50

1973, June 2

2094 A818 2s pale grn, buff & brn	15	15
2095 A818 18s pale brn, gray & grn	65	42

Christo Botev (1848-1876), poet.

“Suffering Worker” — A819

Design: 1s, Asen Halachev and revolutionists.

1973, June 6 Photo. *Perf. 13*

2096 A819 1s gold, red & blk	15	15
2097 A819 2s gold, org & dk brn	15	15
Set value	15	15

50th anniversary of Pleven uprising.

Muskrat A820

Perf. 12½x13, 13x12½

1973, June 29 Litho.

2098 A820 1s shown	15	15
2099 A820 2s Racoon	15	15
2100 A820 3s Mouflon, vert.	15	15
2101 A820 12s Fallow deer, vert.	22	15
2102 A820 18s European bison	50	15
2103 A820 40s Elk	2.50	1.00
Nos. 2098-2103 (6)	3.67	
Set value		1.35

Aleksandr Stamboliski A821

1973, June 14 Photo. *Perf. 12½*

2104 A821 18s dp brown & org	35	18
a. 18s orange	2.50	75

Aleksandr Stamboliski (1879-1923), leader of Peasants' Party and premier.

Trade Union Emblem — A822

Stylized Sun, Olympic Rings — A823

1973, Aug. 27 Photo. *Perf. 12½*

2105 A822 2s yellow & multi	15	15

8th Congress of World Federation of Trade Unions, Varna, Oct. 15-22.

1973, Aug. 29 *Perf. 13*

Designs: 28s, Emblem of Bulgarian Olympic Committee and Olympic rings. 80s, Soccer, emblems of Innsbruck and Montreal 1976 Games, horiz.

2106 A823 13s multicolored	70	32
2107 A823 28s multicolored	1.25	40

Souvenir Sheet

2108 A823 80s multicolored	3.25	1.75

Olympic Congress, Varna. No. 2108 contains one stamp. It also exists imperf.; also with violet margin, imperf.

Revolutionists with Communist Flag — A824

Designs: 5s, Revolutionists on flatcar blocking train. 13s, Raising Communist flag, vert. 18s, George Dimitrov and Vassil Kolarov.

1973, Sept. 22 Photo. *Perf. 12½*

2109 A824 2s magenta & multi	15	15
2110 A824 5s magenta & multi	15	15
2111 A824 13s magenta & multi	30	15
2112 A824 18s magenta & multi	85	32
Nos. 2109-2112 (4)	1.45	
Set value		50

50th anniv. of the September Revolution.

Warrior Saint — A825

Murals from Boyana Church: 1s, Tsar Kaloyan and 2s, his wife Dessislava. 5s, “St. Wystratti.” 10s, Tsar Constantine Assen. 13s, Deacon Laurentius. 18s, Virgin Mary. 20s, St. Ephraim. 28s, Jesus. 80s, Jesus in the Temple, horiz.

1973, Sept. 24

2113 A825 1s gold & multi	15	15
2114 A825 2s gold & multi	15	15
2115 A825 3s gold & multi	15	15
2116 A825 5s gold & multi	15	15
2117 A825 10s gold & multi	35	15
2118 A825 13s gold & multi	45	15
2119 A825 18s gold & multi	70	15
2120 A825 20s gold & multi	95	18
2121 A825 28s gold & multi	3.50	35
Nos. 2113-2121 (9)	6.55	
Set value		1.00

Miniature Sheet

Imperf

2122 A825 80s gold & multi	3.75	2.25

No. 2122 contains one stamp with simulated perforations.

Christo Smirnenski — A826

1973, Sept. 29 Photo. *Perf. 12½*

2123 A826 1s multicolored	15	15
2124 A826 2s vio blue & multi	18	15
Set value	25	15

75th anniversary of the birth of Christo Smirnenski (1898-1923), poet.

Human Rights Flame — A827

1973, Oct. 10

2125 A827 13s dk blue, red & gold	30	16

25th anniversary of the Universal Declaration of Human Rights.

Type of 1970

History of Bulgaria: 1s, Tsar Theodor Svetoslav receiving Byzantine envoys. 2s, Tsar Mihail Shishman's army in battle with Byzantines. 3s, Tsar Ivan Alexander's victory at Russocastro. 4s, Patriarch Euthimius at the defense of Turnovo. 5s, Tsar Ivan Shishman leading horsemen against the Turks. 13s, Momchil attacking Turks at Umour. 18s, Tsar Ivan Stratsimir meeting King Sigismund's crusaders. 28s, The Boyars Balik, Theodor and Dobrotitsa, meeting ship bringing envoys from Anne of Savoy.

1973, Oct. 23 *Perf. 13*

Silver and Black Vignettes

2126 A741 1s olive bister	15	15
2127 A741 2s Prus blue	15	15
2128 A741 3s lilac	15	15
2129 A741 4s green	15	15
2130 A741 5s violet	15	15
2131 A741 13s orange & brn	22	15
2132 A741 18s olive green	40	18
2133 A741 28s yel brn & brn	1.10	48
Nos. 2126-2133 (8)	2.47	
Set value		1.25

Finn Class — A828

Sailboats: 2s, Flying Dutchman. 3s, Soling class. 13s, Tempest class. 20s, Class 470. 40s, Tornado class.

1973, Oct. 29 Litho. *Perf. 13*

2134 A828 1s ultra & multi	15	15
2135 A828 2s green & multi	15	15
2136 A828 3s dk blue & multi	15	15
2137 A828 13s dull vio & multi	28	15
2138 A828 20s gray bl & multi	60	32
2139 A828 40s dk blue & multi	2.50	2.00
Nos. 2134-2139 (6)	3.83	2.92

Value, set imperf. in changed colors, $10.

Village, by Bencho Obreshkov — A829

Paintings: 2s, Mother and Child, by Stoyan Venev. 3s, Rest (woman), by Tsenko Boyadjiev. 13s, Flowers in Vase, by Sirak Skitnik. 18s, Meri Kuneva (portrait), by Ilya Petrov. 40s, Winter in Plovdiv, by Zlatyu Boyadjiev. 13s, 18s, 40s, vert.

Perf. 12½x12, 12x12½

1973, Nov. 10

2140 A829 1s gold & multi	15	15
2141 A829 2s gold & multi	15	15
2142 A829 3s gold & multi	15	15
2143 A829 13s gold & multi	22	15
2144 A829 18s gold & multi	42	20
2145 A829 40s gold & multi	2.25	75
Nos. 2140-2145 (6)	3.34	
Set value		1.20

Souvenir Sheet

Paintings by Stanislav Dospevski: a, Domnica Lambreva. b, Self-portrait. Both vert.

2146 Sheet of 2	2.75	1.75
a. A829 50s gold & multi	70	52
b. A829 50s gold & multi	70	52

Bulgarian paintings. No. 2146 commemorates the 150th birth anniv. of Stanislav Dospevski.

Souvenir Sheet

Soccer A830

1973, Dec. 10 Photo. *Perf. 13*

2147 A830 28s multicolored	4.00	3.50

No. 2147 sold for 1 l. Exists overprinted for Argentina 78.

Angel and Ornaments — A831

Designs: 1s, Attendant facing right. 2s, Passover table and lamb. 3s, Attendant facing left. 8s, Abraham and ornaments. 13s, Adam and Eve. 28s, Expulsion from Garden of Eden.

1974, Jan. 21 Photo. *Perf. 13*

2148 A831	1s fawn, yel & brn	15	15
2149 A831	2s fawn, yel & brn	15	15
2150 A831	3s fawn, yel & brn	15	15
a.	Strip of 3, #2148-2150	25	20
2151 A831	5s slate grn & yel	15	15
2152 A831	8s slate grn & yel	20	15
a.	Pair, #2151-2152	30	25
2153 A831	13s lt brown, yel & ol	28	24
2154 A831	28s lt brown, yel & ol	52	32
a.	Pair, #2153-2154	80	35
	Set value	1.28	1.00

Woodcarvings from Rozhen Monastery, 19th century.

Lenin, by N. Mirtchev — A832

Design: 18s, Lenin visiting Workers, by W. A. Serov.

1974, Jan. 28 Litho. *Perf. 12½x12*

2155 A832	2s ocher & multi	15	15
2156 A832	18s ocher & multi	48	22
	Set value		30

50th anniversary of the death of Lenin.

1974, Jan. 28

Design: Demeter Blagoev at Rally, by G. Kowachev.

2157 A832	2s multicolored	15	15

50th anniversary of the death of Demeter Blagoev, founder of Bulgarian Communist Party.

Domestic Animals A833

1974, Feb. 1 Photo. *Perf. 13*

2158 A833	1s Sheep	15	15
2159 A833	2s Goat	15	15
2160 A833	3s Pig	15	15
2161 A833	5s Cow	16	15
2162 A833	13s Buffalo cow	30	15
2163 A833	20s Horse	80	28
	Nos. 2158-2163 (6)	1.71	
	Set value		75

Comecon Emblem A834

1974, Feb. 11 Photo. *Perf. 13*

2164 A834	13s silver & multi	40	15

25th anniversary of the Council of Mutual Economic Assistance.

Soccer — A835

Designs: Various soccer action scenes.

1974, Mar. Photo. *Perf. 13*

2165 A835	1s dull green & multi	15	15
2166 A835	2s brt green & multi	15	15
2167 A835	3s slate grn & multi	15	15
2168 A835	13s olive & multi	15	20
2169 A835	28s blue grn & multi	65	42
2170 A835	40s emerald & multi	1.50	70
	Nos. 2165-2170 (6)	2.75	1.77

Souvenir Sheet

2171 A835	1 l green & multi	3.00	1.65

World Soccer Championship, Munich, June 13-July 7. No. 2171 exists imperf.

Salt Production A836

Children's Paintings: 1s, Cosmic Research for Peaceful Purposes. 3s, Fire Dancers. 28s, Russian-Bulgarian Friendship (train and children). 60s, Spring (birds).

1974, Apr. 15 Photo. *Perf. 13*

2172 A836	1s lilac & multi	15	15
2173 A836	2s lt green & multi	15	15
2174 A836	3s blue & multi	15	15
2175 A836	28s slate & multi	1.75	95
	Nos. 2172-2175 (4)	2.20	1.40

Souvenir Sheet

Imperf

2176 A836	60s blue & multi	2.25	1.75

Third World Youth Philatelic Exhibition, Sofia, May 23-30. No. 2176 contains one stamp with simulated perforations.

Folk Singers — A837

Designs: 2s, Folk dancers (men). 3s, Bagpiper and drummer. 5s, Wrestlers. 13s, Runners (women). 18s, Gymnast.

1974, Apr. 25 *Perf. 13*

2178 A837	1s vermilion & multi	15	15
2179 A837	2s orange brn & multi	15	15
2180 A837	3s brn red & multi	15	15
2181 A837	5s blue & multi	15	15
2182 A837	13s ultra & multi	75	24
2183 A837	18s violet bl & multi	42	15
	Set value	1.45	58

4th Amateur Arts and Sports Festival

Flowers A838

1974, May Photo. *Perf. 13*

2184 A838	1s Aster	15	15
2185 A838	2s Petunia	15	15
2186 A838	3s Fuchsia	15	15
2187 A838	18s Tulip	28	15
2188 A838	20s Carnation	60	22
2189 A838	28s Pansy	1.65	55
	Nos. 2184-2189 (6)	2.98	
	Set value		1.10

Souvenir Sheet

2190 A838	80s Sunflower	1.75	85

Automobiles and Emblems A839

1974, May 15 Photo. *Perf. 13*

2191 A839	13s multicolored	30	15

International Automobile Federation (FIA) Spring Congress, Sofia, May 20-24.

Old and New Buildings, UNESCO Emblem A840

1974, June 15

2192 A840	18s multicolored	30	15

UNESCO Executive Council, 94th Session, Varna.

Postrider A841

Designs: 18s, First Bulgarian mail coach. 28s, UPU Monument, Bern.

1974, Aug. 5

2193 A841	2s ocher, blk & vio	15	15
2194 A841	18s ocher, blk & grn	38	15
	Set value	45	19

Souvenir Sheet

2195 A841	28s ocher, blk & bl	2.00	1.50

UPU cent. No. 2195 exists imperf.

Pioneer and Komsomol Girl — A842

Designs: 2s, Pioneer and birds. 60s, Emblem with portrait of George Dimitrov.

1974, Aug. 12

2196 A842	1s green & multi	15	15
2197 A842	2s blue & multi	15	15
	Set value	15	15

Souvenir Sheet

2198 A842	60s red & multi	1.65	1.10

30th anniversary of Dimitrov Pioneer Organization, Septemvrilche.

"Bulgarian Communist Party" — A843

Symbolic Designs: 2s, Russian liberators. 5s, Industrialization. 13s, Advanced agriculture and husbandry. 18s, Scientific and technical progress.

1974, Aug. 20

2199 A843	1s blue gray & multi	15	15
2200 A843	2s blue gray & multi	15	15
2201 A843	5s gray & multi	15	15
2202 A843	13s gray & multi	26	15
2203 A843	18s gray & multi	35	15
	Set value	85	30

30th anniversary of the People's Republic.

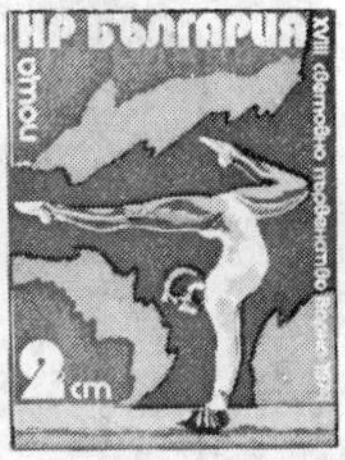

Gymnast on Parallel Bars — A844

Design: 13s, Gymnast on vaulting horse.

1974, Oct. 18 Photo. *Perf. 13*

2204 A844	2s multicolored	15	15
2205 A844	13s multicolored	28	20
	Set value	35	25

18th Gymnastic Championships, Varna.

Souvenir Sheet

Symbols of Peace — A845

1974, Oct. 29 Photo. *Perf. 13*

2206 A845	Sheet of 4	2.50	1.10
a.	13s Doves	18	15
b.	13s Map of Europe	18	15
c.	13s Olive Branch	18	15
d.	13s Inscription	18	15

1974 European Peace Conference. "Peace" in various languages written on Nos. 2206a-2206c. Sold for 60s. Exists imperf.

Nib and Envelope — A846

1974, Nov. 20

2207 A846	2s yellow, blk & grn	15	15

Introduction of postal zone numbers.

Flowers A847

1974, Dec. 5

2208 A847	2s emerald & multi	15	15

St. Todor, Ceramic Icon — A848

Fruit Tree Blossoms — A849

Designs: 2s, Medallion, Veliko Turnovo. 3s, Carved capital. 5s, Silver bowl. 8s, Goblet. 13s, Lion's head finial. 18s, Gold plate with Cross. 28s, Breastplate with eagle.

1974, Dec. 18 Photo. *Perf. 13*

2209	A848	1s orange & multi	15	15
2210	A848	2s pink & multi	15	15
2211	A848	3s blue & multi	15	15
2212	A848	5s lt vio & multi	15	15
2213	A848	8s brown & multi	15	15
2214	A848	13s multicolored	22	15
2215	A848	18s red & multi	32	16
2216	A848	28s ultra & multi	1.00	60
		Set value	1.90	1.25

Art works from 9th-12th centuries.

1975, Jan. Photo. *Perf. 13*

2217	A849	1s Apricot	15	15
2218	A849	2s Apple	15	15
2219	A849	3s Cherry	15	15
2220	A849	19s Pear	28	15
2221	A849	28s Peach	70	25
		Set value	1.10	50

Tree and Book A850

1975, Mar. 25 Photo. *Perf. 13*

2222	A850	2s gold & multi	15	15

Forestry High School, 50th anniversary.

Souvenir Sheet

Farmers' Activities (Woodcuts) — A851

1975, Mar. 25

2223	A851	Sheet of 4	80	48

a. 2s Farmer with ax and flag
b. 5s Farmers on guard
c. 13s Dancing couple
d. 18s Woman picking fruit

Bulgarian Agrarian Peoples Union, 75th anniversary.

Michelangelo, Self-portrait A852

Designs: 13s, Night, horiz. 18s, Day, horiz. Both designs after sculptures from Medici Tomb, Florence.

1975

2224	A852	2s plum & dk blue	15	15
2225	A852	13s vio bl & plum	24	15
2226	A852	18s brown & green	52	15
		Nos. 2224-2226 (3)	91	
		Set value		30

Souvenir Sheet

2227	A852	2s olive & red	1.25	1.25

Michelangelo Buonarotti (1475-1564), Italian sculptor, painter and architect. No. 2227 issued to publicize ARPHILA 75 Intl. Phil. Exhib., Paris, June 6-16. Sheet sold for 60s.

Issue dates: Nos. 2224-2226, Mar. 28. No. 2227, Mar. 31.

Souvenir Sheet

Spain No. 1 and España 75 Emblem A853

1975, Apr. 4

2228	A853	40s multicolored	3.75	3.00

Espana 75 International Philatelic Exhibition, Madrid, Apr. 4-13.

Gabrov Costume — A854

Regional Costumes: 3s, Trnsk. 5s, Vidin. 13s, Gocedelchev. 18s, Risen.

1975, Apr. Photo. *Perf. 13*

2229	A854	2s blue & multi	15	15
2230	A854	3s emerald & multi	15	15
2231	A854	5s orange & multi	15	15
2232	A854	13s olive & multi	35	15
2233	A854	18s multicolored	80	24
		Nos. 2229-2233 (5)	1.60	
		Set value		50

Red Star and Arrow — A855

Standard Kilogram and Meter — A856

Design: 13s, Dove and broken sword.

1975, May 9

2234	A855	2s red, blk & gold	15	15
2235	A855	13s blue, blk & gold	32	15
		Set value	37	19

Victory over Fascism, 30th anniversary.

1975, May 9 *Perf. 13x13½*

2236	A856	13s silver, lil & blk	35	15

Cent. of Intl, Meter Convention, Paris, 1875.

IWY Emblem, Woman's Head — A857

Ivan Vasov — A858

1975, May 20 Photo. *Perf. 13*

2237	A857	13s multicolored	35	15

International Women's Year 1975.

1975, May

Design: 13s, Ivan Vasov, seated.

2238	A858	2s buff & multi	15	15
2239	A858	13s gray & multi	32	15
		Set value	40	15

125th birth anniversary of Ivan Vasov.

Nikolov and Sava Kokarechkov — A859

Designs: 2s, Mitko Palaouzov and Ivan Vassilev. 5s, Nicolas Nakev and Stevtcho Kraychev. 13s, Ivanka Pachkoulova and Detelina Mintcheva.

1975, May 30

2240	A859	1s multicolored	15	15
2241	A859	2s multicolored	15	15
2242	A859	5s multicolored	15	15
2243	A859	13s multicolored	28	15
		Set value	50	35

Teen-age resistance fighters, killed during World War II.

Mother Feeding Child, by John E. Millais — A861

Etchings: 2s, The Dead Daughter, by Goya. 3s, Reunion, by Beshkov. 13s, Seated Nude, by Renoir. 20s, Man in a Fur Hat, by Rembrandt. 40s, The Dream, by Daumier, horiz. 1 l, Temptation, by Dürer.

Photogravure and Engraved

1975, Aug. *Perf. 12x11½, 11½x12*

2248	A861	1s yel grn & multi	15	15
2249	A861	2s orange & multi	15	15
2250	A861	3s lilac & multi	15	15
2251	A861	13s lt blue & multi	26	15
2252	A861	20s ocher & multi	40	18
2253	A861	40s rose & multi	1.10	28
		Set value	1.95	70

Souvenir Sheet

2254	A861	1 l emerald & multi	2.00	1.25

World Graphics Exhibition.

Letter "Z" from 12th Century Manuscript A862

Initials from Illuminated Manuscripts: 2s, "B" from 17th cent. prayerbook. 3s, "V" from 16th cent. Bouhovo Gospel. 8s, "B" from 14th cent. Turnovo collection. 13s, "V" from Dobreisho's Gospel, 13th cent. 18s, "E" from 11th cent. Enina book of the Apostles.

1975, Aug. Litho. *Perf. 11½*

2255	A862	1s multicolored	15	15
2256	A862	2s multicolored	15	15
2257	A862	3s multicolored	15	15
2258	A862	8s multicolored	15	15
2259	A862	13s multicolored	25	15
2260	A862	18s multicolored	65	16
		Set value	1.25	50

Bulgarian art.

Whimsical Globe — A863

1975, Aug. Photo. *Perf. 13*

2261	A863	2s multicolored	15	15

Festival of Humor and Satire.

Lifeboat Dju IV and Gibraltar-Cuba Route — A864

1975, Aug. 5 Photo. *Perf. 13*

2262 A864 13s multicolored 25 15

Oceanexpo 75, 1st Intl. Ocean Exhib., Okinawa, July 20, 1975-Jan. 18, 1976.

Sts. Cyril and Methodius A865

Sts. Constantine and Helena A866

St. Sophia Church, Sofia, Woodcut by V. Zahriev — A867

1975, Aug. 21

2263 A865 2s ver, yel & brn 15 15
2264 A866 13s green, yel & brn 25 15
Set value 30 20

Souvenir Sheet

2265 A867 50s orange & multi 1.25 80

Balkanphila V, philatelic exhibition, Sofia, Sept. 27-Oct. 5.

Peace Dove and Map of Europe — A868

1975, Nov. Photo. *Perf. 13*

2266 A868 18s ultra, rose & yel 45 22

European Security and Cooperation Conference, Helsinki, Finland, July 30-Aug. 1. No. 2266 printed in sheets of 5 stamps and 4 labels, arranged checkerwise.

Acherontia Atropos A869

Designs: Moths.

1975 Photo. *Perf. 13*

2267 A869 1s *shown* 15 15
2268 A869 2s *Daphnis nerii* 15 15
2269 A869 3s *Smerinthus ocellata* 15 15
2270 A869 10s *Deilephila nicea* 20 15
2271 A869 13s *Choerocampa elpenor* 24 15
2272 A869 18s *Macroglossum fuciformis* 90 24
Set value 1.50 53

Soccer Player — A870

1975, Sept. 21

2273 A870 2s multicolored 15 15

8th Inter-Toto (soccer pool) Soccer Championships, Varna.

Constantine's Rebellion Against the Turks, 1403 — A871

Designs (Woodcuts): 2s, Campaign of Vladislav III, 1443-1444. 3s, Battles of Turnovo, 1598 and 1686. 10s, Battle of Liprovsko, 1688. 13s, Guerrillas, 17th century. 18s, Return of exiled peasants.

1975, Nov. 27 Photo. *Perf. 13*

2274 A871 1s bister, grn & blk 15 15
2275 A871 2s blue, car & blk 15 15
2276 A871 3s yellow, lil & blk 15 15
2277 A871 10s orange, grn & blk 16 15
2278 A871 13s green, lil & blk 22 15
2279 A871 18s pink, grn & blk 45 18
Set value 1.00 45

Bulgarian history.

Red Cross and First Aid — A872

Design: 13s, Red Cross and dove.

1975, Dec. 1

2280 A872 2s red brn, red & blk 15 15
2281 A872 13s bl grn, red & blk 22 15
Set value 30 15

90th anniversary of Bulgarian Red Cross.

Egyptian Galley A873

Historic Ships: 2s, Phoenician galley. 3s, Greek trireme. 5s, Roman galley. 13s, Viking longship. 18s, Venetian galley.

1975, Dec. 15 Photo. *Perf. 13*

2282 A873 1s multicolored 15 15
2283 A873 2s multicolored 15 15
2284 A873 3s multicolored 15 15
2285 A873 5s multicolored 15 15
2286 A873 13s multicolored 32 15
2287 A873 18s multicolored 60 16
Set value 1.25 46

See Nos. 2431-2436, 2700-2705.

Souvenir Sheet

Ethnographical Museum, Plovdiv — A874

1975, Dec. 17

2288 Sheet of 3 4.50 2.50
a. A874 80s green, yellow & dark brown 1.25 65

European Architectural Heritage Year. No. 2288 contains 3 stamps and 3 labels showing stylized bird.

Dobri Hristov — A875

1975, Dec. *Perf. 13*

2289 A875 5s brt green, yel & brn 15 15

Dobri Hristov, musician, birth centenary.

United Nations Emblem — A876

1975, Dec.

2290 A876 13s gold, blk & mag 20 15

United Nations, 30th anniversary.

Glass Ornaments A877

Design: 13s, Peace dove, decorated ornament.

1975, Dec. 22 Photo. *Perf. 13*

2291 A877 2s brt violet & multi 15 15
2292 A877 13s gray & multi 20 15
Set value 25 15

New Year 1976.

Downhill Skiing — A878

Designs (Winter Olympic Games Emblem and): 2s, Cross country skier, vert. 3s, Ski jump. 13s, Biathlon, vert. 18s, Ice hockey, vert. 23s, Speed skating, vert. 80s, Figure skating, pair, vert.

1976, Jan. 30 *Perf. 13½*

2293 A878 1s silver & multi 15 15
2294 A878 2s silver & multi 15 15
2295 A878 3s silver & multi 15 15
2296 A878 13s silver & multi 22 15
2297 A878 18s silver & multi 32 15
2298 A878 23s silver & multi 80 30
Set value 1.50 68

Souvenir Sheet

2299 A878 80s silver & multi 1.65 1.10

12th Winter Olympic Games, Innsbruck, Austria, Feb. 4-15.

Electric Streetcar, Sofia, 1976 — A879

Design: 13s, Streetcar and trailer, 1901.

1976, Jan. 12 Photo. *Perf. 13½x13*

2300 A879 2s gray & multi 15 15
2301 A879 13s gray & multi 38 15
Set value 15

75th anniversary of Sofia streetcars.

Stylized Bird — A880

Designs: 5s, Dates "1976" and "1956" and star. 13s, Hammer and sickle. 50s, George Dimitrov.

1976, Mar. 1 *Perf. 13*

2302 A880 2s gold & multi 15 15
2303 A880 5s gold & multi 15 15
2304 A880 13s gold & multi 25 15
Set value 45 18

Souvenir Sheet

2305 A880 50s gold & multi 1.00 45

11th Bulgarian Communist Party Congress.

A. G. Bell and Telephone, 1876 A881

1976, Mar. 10

2306 A881 18s dk brn, yel & ocher 25 15

Centenary of first telephone call by Alexander Graham Bell, Mar. 10, 1876.

Mute Swan — A882

Waterfowl: 2s, Ruddy shelduck. 3s, Common shelduck. 5s, Garganey teal. 13s, Mallard. 18s, Red-crested pochard.

1976, Mar. 27 Litho. *Perf. 11½*

2307 A882 1s vio bl & multi 15 15
2308 A882 2s yel grn & multi 15 15
2309 A882 3s blue & multi 15 15
2310 A882 5s multicolored 22 15
2311 A882 13s purple & multi 65 15
2312 A882 18s green & multi 90 15
Nos. 2307-2312 (6) 2.22
Set value 40

Guerrillas — A883

Designs (Woodcuts by Stoev): 2s, Peasants with rifle and proclamation. 5s, Raina Knaginia with horse and guerrilla. 13s, Insurgents with cherrywood cannon.

1976, Apr. 5 Photo. *Perf. 13*

2313	A883	1s multicolored	15	15
2314	A883	2s multicolored	15	15
2315	A883	5s multicolored	15	15
2316	A883	13s multicolored	24	15
		Set value	45	23

Centenary of uprising against Turkey.

Guard and Dog A884

Design: 13s, Men on horseback, observation tower.

1976, May 15

2317	A884	2s multicolored	15	15
2318	A884	13s multicolored	20	15
		Set value	25	15

30th anniversary of Border Guards.

Construction Worker — A885

1976, May 20

2319	A885	2s multicolored	15	15

Young Workers Brigade, 30th anniversary.

Busludja, Bas-relief — A886

AES Complex — A887

Design: 5s, Memorial building.

1976, May 28 Photo. *Perf. 13*

2320	A886	2s green & multi	15	15
2321	A886	5s violet bl & multi	15	15
		Set value	20	15

First Congress of Bulgarian Social Democratic Party, 85th anniversary.

1976, Apr. 7

Designs: 8s, Factory. 10s, Apartment houses. 13s, Refinery. 20s, Hydroelectric station.

2322	A887	5s green	15	15
2323	A887	8s maroon	16	15
2324	A887	10s green	20	15
2325	A887	13s violet	32	15
2326	A887	20s brt green	42	15
		Nos. 2322-2326 (5)	1.25	
		Set value		32

Five-year plan accomplishments.

Children Playing Around Table — A888

Designs (Kindergarten Children): 2s, with doll carriage and hobby horse. 5s, playing ball. 23s, in costume.

1976, June 15

2327	A888	1s green & multi	15	15
2328	A888	2s yellow & multi	15	15
2329	A888	5s lilac & multi	15	15
2330	A888	23s rose & multi	42	15
		Set value	65	29

Demeter Blagoev — A889

Christo Botev — A890

1976, May 28

2331	A889	13s bluish blk, red & gold	25	15

Demeter Blagoev (1856-1924), writer, political leader, 120th birth anniversary.

1976, May 25

2332	A890	13s ocher & slate grn	25	15

Christo Botev (1848-1876), poet, death centenary. Printed se-tenant with yellow green and ocher label, inscribed with poem.

Boxing, Montreal Olympic Emblem — A891

Belt Buckle — A892

Designs (Montreal Olympic Emblem): 1s, Wrestling, horiz. 3s, 1 l, Weight lifting. 13s, One-man kayak. 18s, Woman gymnast. 28s, Woman diver. 40s, Woman runner.

1976, June 25

2333	A891	1s orange & multi	15	15
2334	A891	2s multicolored	15	15
2335	A891	3s lilac & multi	15	15
2336	A891	13s multicolored	18	15
2337	A891	18s multicolored	28	15
2338	A891	28s blue & multi	38	16
2339	A891	40s lemon & multi	75	30
		Set value	1.75	75

Souvenir Sheet

2340	A891	1 l orange & multi	1.65	1.10

21st Olympic Games, Montreal, Canada, July 17-Aug. 1.

1976, July 30 Photo. *Perf. 13*

Thracian Art (8th-4th Centuries): 2s, Brooch. 3s, Mirror handle. 5s, Helmet cheek cover. 13s, Gold ornament. 18s, Lion's head (harness decoration). 20s, Knee guard. 28s, Jeweled pendant.

2341	A892	1s brown & multi	15	15
2342	A892	2s blue & multi	15	15
2343	A892	3s multicolored	15	15
2344	A892	5s claret & multi	15	15
2345	A892	13s purple & multi	24	15
2346	A892	18s multicolored	32	15
2347	A892	20s multicolored	42	15
2348	A892	28s multicolored	60	18
		Set value	1.85	68

Composite of Bulgarian Stamp Designs A893

1976, June 5

2349	A893	50s red & multi	1.65	65

International Federation of Philately (F.I.P.), 50th anniversary and 12th Congress.

Partisans at Night, by Ilya Petrov — A894

Paintings: 5s, Old Town, by Tsanko Lavenov. 13s, Seated Woman, by Petrov, vert. 18s, Seated Boy, by Petrov, vert. 28s, Old Plovdiv, by Lavenov, vert. 80s, Ilya Petrov, self-portrait, vert.

1976, Aug. 11 Photo. *Perf. 14*

2350	A894	2s multicolored	15	15
2351	A894	5s multicolored	15	15
2352	A894	13s ultra & multi	32	15
2353	A894	18s multicolored	45	15
2354	A894	28s multicolored	65	18
		Nos. 2350-2354 (5)	1.72	
		Set value		45

Souvenir Sheet

2354A	A894	80s multicolored	1.25	95

Souvenir Sheet

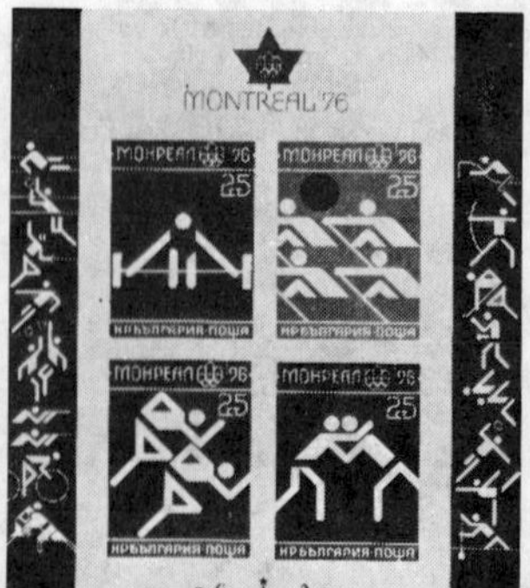

Olympic Sports and Emblems — A895

1976, Sept. 6 Photo. *Perf. 13*

2355	A895	Sheet of 4	1.65	1.00
a.		25s Weight Lifting	35	18
b.		25s Rowing	35	18
c.		25s Running	35	18
d.		25s Wrestling	35	18

Medalists, 21st Olympic Games, Montreal.

Souvenir Sheet

Fresco and UNESCO Emblem — A896

1976, Dec. 3

2356	A896	50s red & multi	1.25	55

UNESCO, 30th anniv.

"The Pianist" by Jendov — A897

Fish and Hook — A898

Designs (Caricatures by Jendov): 5s, Imperialist "Trick or Treat." 13s, The Leader, 1931.

1976, Sept. 30 Photo. *Perf. 13*

2357	A897	2s green & multi	15	15
2358	A897	5s purple & multi	15	15
2359	A897	13s magenta & multi	32	15
		Set value	50	18

Alex Jendov (1901-1953), caricaturist.

1976, Sept. 21 Photo. *Perf. 13*

2360	A898	5s multicolored	15	15

World Sport Fishing Congress, Varna.

St. Theodore A899

Frescoes: 3s, St. Paul. 5s, St. Joachim. 13s, Melchizedek. 19s, St. Porphyrius. 28s, Queen. 1 l, The Last Supper.

1976, Oct. 4 Litho. *Perf. 12x12½*

2361	A899	2s gold & multi	15	15
2362	A899	3s gold & multi	15	15
2363	A899	5s gold & multi	15	15
2364	A899	13s gold & multi	32	15
2365	A899	19s gold & multi	35	15
2366	A899	28s gold & multi	65	20
		Set value	1.50	56

Miniature Sheet

Perf. 12

2367	A899	1 l gold & multi	1.50	95

Zemen Monastery frescoes, 14th cent.

Document — A900

1976, Oct. 5
2368 A900 5s multicolored 15 15

State Archives, 25th anniversary.

Cinquefoil — A901

1976, Oct. 14 Photo. *Perf. 13*

2369	A901	1s Chestnut	15	15
2370	A901	2s shown	15	15
2371	A901	5s Holly	15	15
2372	A901	8s Yew	15	15
2373	A901	13s Daphne	32	15
2374	A901	23s Judas tree	60	18
		Set value	1.25	46

Dimitri Polianov — A902

1976, Nov. 19
2375 A902 2s dk purple & ocher 15 15

Dimitri Polianov (1876-1953), poet.

Christo Botev, by Zlatyu Boyadjiev A903

Paintings: 2s, Partisan Carrying Cherrywood Cannon, by Ilya Petrov. 3s, "Necklace of Immortality" (man's portrait), by Detchko Uzunov. 13s, "April 1876," by Georgi Popoff. 18s, Partisans, by Stoyan Venev. 60s, The Oath, by Svetlin Ruseff.

1976, Dec. 8

2376	A903	1s bister & multi	15	15
2377	A903	2s bister & multi	15	15
2378	A903	3s bister & multi	15	15
2379	A903	13s bister & multi	24	15
2380	A903	18s bister & multi	35	15
		Set value	80	32

Souvenir Sheet

Imperf

2381 A903 60s gold & multi 95 55

Uprising against Turkish rule, centenary.

"Pollution" and Tree A904

Design: 18s, "Pollution" obscuring sun.

1976, Nov. 10 *Perf. 13*

2382	A904	2s ultra & multi	15	15
2383	A904	18s blue & multi	30	15
		Set value	35	15

Protection of the environment.

Congress Emblem — A904a

Flags — A904b

1976, Nov. 28 Photo. *Perf. 13*

2384	A904a	2s multicolored	15	15
2384A	A904b	13s multicolored	26	15
		Set value		15

33rd BSIS Cong. (Bulgarian Socialist Party).

Tobacco Workers, by Stajkov A905

Paintings by Stajkov: 2s, View of Melnik. 13s, Shipbuilder.

1976, Dec. 16 Photo. *Perf. 13*

2385	A905	1s multicolored	15	15
2386	A905	2s multicolored	15	15
2387	A905	13s multicolored	28	15
		Set value	38	20

Veselin Stajkov (1906-1970), painter.

Snowflake A906

1976, Dec. 20
2388 A906 2s silver & multi 15 15

New Year 1977.

Zachary Stoyanov (1851-1889), Historian — A907

1976, Dec. 30
2389 A907 2s multicolored 15 15

Bronze Coin of Septimus Severus — A908

Roman Coins: 2s, 13s, 18s, Bronze coins of Caracalla, diff. 23s, Copper coin of Diocletian.

1977, Jan. 28 Photo. *Perf. 13½x13*

2390	A908	1s gold & multi	15	15
2391	A908	2s gold & multi	15	15
2392	A908	13s gold & multi	20	15
2393	A908	18s gold & multi	26	15
2394	A908	23s gold & multi	45	20
		Set value	1.00	52

Coins struck in Serdica (modern Sofia).

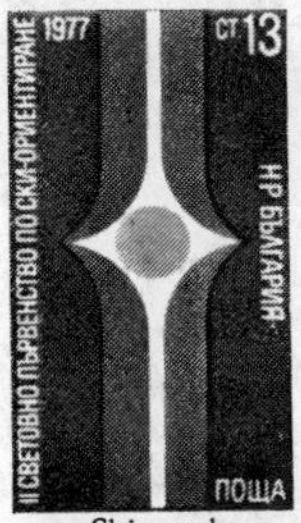

Skis and Compass — A909

Tourist Congress Emblem — A910

1977, Feb. 14 *Perf. 13*
2395 A909 13s ultra, red & lt bl 25 15

2nd World Ski Orienteering Championships.

1977, Feb. 24 Photo. *Perf. 13*
2396 A910 2s multicolored 15 15

5th Congress of Bulgarian Tourist Organization.

Bellflower — A911

Designs: Various bellflowers.

1977, Mar. 2

2397	A911	1s yellow & multi	15	15
2398	A911	2s rose & multi	15	15
2399	A911	3s lt blue & multi	15	15
2400	A911	13s multicolored	30	15
2401	A911	43s yellow & multi	1.10	28
		Set value	1.50	50

Vasil Kolarov — A912

Union Congress Emblem — A913

1977, Mar. 21 Photo. *Perf. 13*
2402 A912 2s blue & black 15 15

Vasil Kolarov (1877-1950), politician.

1977, Mar. 25
2403 A913 2s multicolored 15 15

8th Bulgarian Trade Union Cong., Apr. 4-7.

Wolf A914

Wild Animals: 2s, Red fox. 10s, Weasel. 13s, European wildcat. 23s, Jackal.

1977, May 16 Litho. *Perf. 12½x12*

2404	A914	1s multicolored	15	15
2405	A914	2s multicolored	15	15
2406	A914	10s multicolored	18	15
2407	A914	13s multicolored	35	15
2408	A914	23s multicolored	60	18
		Nos. 2404-2408 (5)	1.43	
		Set value		40

Diseased Knee — A915

1977, Mar. 31 Photo. *Perf. 13*
2409 A915 23s multicolored 40 15

World Rheumatism Year.

Writers' Congress Emblem A916

1977, June 7
2410 A916 23s lt bl & yel grn 65 20

International Writers Congress: "Peace, the Hope of the Planet." No. 2410 printed in sheets of 8 stamps and 4 labels with signatures of participating writers.

Old Testament Trinity, Sofia, 16th Century A917

Icons: 1s, St. Nicholas, Nessebur, 13th cent. 3s, Annunciation, Royal Gates, Veliko Turnovo, 16th cent. 5s, Christ Enthroned, Nessebur, 17th cent. 13s, St. Nicholas, Elena, 18th cent. 23s, Presentation of the Virgin, Rila Monastery, 18th cent. 35s, Virgin and Child, Tryavna, 19th cent. 40s, St. Demetrius on Horseback, Provadia, 19th cent. 1 l, The 12 Holidays, Rila Monastery, 18th cent.

1977, May 10 Photo. *Perf. 13*

2411	A917	1s black & multi	15	15
2412	A917	2s green & multi	15	15
2413	A917	3s brown & multi	15	15
2414	A917	5s blue & multi	15	15
2415	A917	13s olive & multi	30	15
2416	A917	23s maroon & multi	50	15
2417	A917	35s green & multi	80	25
2418	A917	40s dp ultra & multi	1.10	38
		Nos. 2411-2418 (8)	3.30	
		Set value		1.00

Miniature Sheet

Imperf

2419 A917 1 l gold & multi 2.25 1.10

Bulgarian icons. See Nos. 2615-2619.

Souvenir Sheet

St. Cyril A918

1977, June 7 Photo. *Perf. 13*

2420 A918 1 l gold & multi 1.75 90

1150th anniversary of the birth of St. Cyril (827-869), reputed inventor of Cyrillic alphabet.

Congress Emblem — A919

1977, May 9

2421 A919 2s red, gold & grn 15 15

13th Komsomol Congress.

Newspaper Masthead A920

1977, June 3 Photo. *Perf. 13*

2422 A920 2s multicolored 15 15

Cent. of Bulgarian daily press and 50th anniv. of Rabotnichesko Delo newspaper.

Patriotic Front Emblem — A921

Weight Lifting — A922

1977, May 26

2423 A921 2s gold & multi 15 15

8th Congress of Patriotic Front.

1977, June 15

2424 A922 13s dp brown & multi 25 15

European Youth Weight Lifting Championships, Sofia, June.

Women Basketball Players — A923

1977, June 15 *Perf. 13*

2425 A923 23s multicolored 50 18

7th European Women's Basketball Championships.

Wrestling — A924

Designs (Games Emblem and): 13s, Running. 23s, Basketball. 43s, Women's gymnastics.

1977, Apr. 15

2426 A924 2s multicolored 15 15
2427 A924 13s multicolored 20 15
2428 A924 23s multicolored 38 15
2429 A924 43s multicolored 70 26
Nos. 2426-2429 (4) 1.43
Set value 50

UNIVERSIADE '77, University Games, Sofia, Aug. 18-27.

TV Tower, Berlin — A925

1977, Aug. 12 Litho. *Perf. 13*

2430 A925 25s blue & dk blue 50 16

SOZPHILEX 77 Philatelic Exhibition, Berlin, Aug. 19-28.

Ship Type of 1975

Historic Ships: 1s, Hansa cog. 2s, Santa Maria, caravelle. 3s, Golden Hind, frigate. 12s, Santa Catherina, carrack. 13s, La Corone, galleon. 43s, Mediterranean galleass.

1977, Aug. 29 Photo. *Perf. 13*

2431 A873 1s multicolored 15 15
2432 A873 2s multicolored 15 15
2433 A873 3s multicolored 15 15
2434 A873 12s multicolored 25 15
2435 A873 13s multicolored 25 15
2436 A873 43s multicolored 1.00 26
Set value 1.65 52

Ivan Vasov National Theater — A926

Buildings, Sofia: 13s, Party Headquarters. 23s, House of the People's Army. 30s, Clement Ochrida University. 80s, National Gallery. 1 l, National Assembly.

1977, Aug. 30 Photo. *Perf. 13*

2437 A926 12s red, *gray* 18 15
2438 A926 13s red brn, *gray* 18 15
2439 A926 23s blue, *gray* 30 15
2440 A926 30s olive, *gray* 40 15
2441 A926 80s violet, *gray* 1.10 42
2442 A926 1 l claret, *gray* 1.40 52
Nos. 2437-2442 (6) 3.56 1.54

Map of Europe A927

1977, June 10

2443 A927 23s brown, bl & grn 40 18

21st Congress of the European Organization for Quality Control, Varna.

Union of Earth and Water, by Rubens A928

Rubens Paintings: 23s, Venus and Adonis. 40s, Pastoral Scene (man and woman). 1 l, Portrait of a Lady in Waiting.

1977, Sept. 23 Litho. *Perf. 12*

2444 A928 13s gold & multi 45 15
2445 A928 23s gold & multi 65 15
2446 A928 40s gold & multi 1.10 25
Nos. 2444-2446 (3) 2.20
Set value 44

Souvenir Sheet

2447 A928 1 l gold & multi 2.50 1.65

Peter Paul Rubens (1577-1640).

George Dimitrov A929

1977, June 17 Photo. *Perf. 13*

2448 A929 13s red & deep claret 35 15

George Dimitrov (1882-1947).

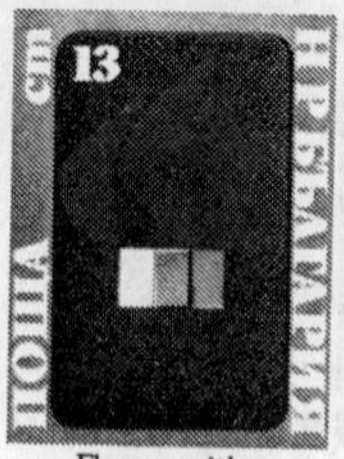

Flame with Star — A930

Smart Pete on Donkey, by Ilya Beshkov — A931

1977, May 17

2449 A930 13s gold & multi 25 15

3rd Bulgarian Culture Congress.

1977, May 19

2450 A931 2s multicolored 15 15

11th National Festival of Humor and Satire Gabrovo.

Elin Pelin — A932

Dr. Pirogov — A934

13th Canoe World Championships — A933

Albena, Black Sea A933a

Writers: 2s, Pelin (Dimitur Ivanov Stojanov, (1877-1949). 5s, Peju K. Jaworov (1878-1914). Artists: 13s, Boris Angelushev (1902-1966), 23s, Ceno Todorov (Ceno Todorov Dikov, 1877-1953). Each printed with label showing scenes from authors' works or illustrations by the artists.

1977, Aug. 26 Photo. *Perf. 13*

2451 A932 2s gold & brown 15 15
2452 A932 5s gold & gray grn 15 15
2453 A932 13s gold & claret 22 15
2454 A932 23s gold & blue 45 15
Set value 80 28

1977, Sept. 1 Photo. *Perf. 13*

2455 A933 2s shown 15 15
2456 A933 23s 2-man canoe 42 18
Set value 25

1977, Oct. 5 Photo. *Perf. 13*

2456A A933a 35s shown 65 25
2456B A933a 43s Rila Monastery 80 30

Sheet contains 4 each plus label.

1977, Oct. 14 Photo. *Perf. 13*

2457 A934 13s olive, ocher & brown 25 15

Centenary of visit by Russian physician N. J. Pirogov during war of liberation from Turkey.

Peace Decree, 1917
A935

Old Soldier with Grandchild
A936

Designs: 13s, Lenin, 1917. 23s, "1917" as a flame.

1977, Oct. 21

2458 A935 2s black, buff & red 15 15
2459 A935 13s multicolored 24 15
2460 A935 23s multicolored 45 15
Nos. 2458-2460 (3) 84
Set value 30

60th anniv. of Russian October Revolution.

1977, Sept. 30

Designs (Festival Posters): 13s, "The Bugler." 23s, Liberation Monument, Sofia (detail). 25s, Samara flag.

2461 A936 2s multicolored 15 15
2462 A936 13s multicolored 25 15
2463 A936 23s multicolored 42 15
2464 A936 25s multicolored 52 22
Nos. 2461-2464 (4) 1.34
Set value 50

Liberation from Turkish rule, centenary.

Souvenir Sheet

Games' and Sports Emblems — A937

1977, Aug. 10 Photo. ***Perf.*** ***13½x13***

2465 A937 1 l multicolored 1.50 1.25

University Games '77, Sofia.

Conference Building — A938

1977, Sept. 12 ***Perf. 13½***

2466 A938 23s multicolored 40 18

64th Interparliamentary Union Conference, Sofia.

Bulgarian Worker's Newspaper, Anniversaries
A939

1977, Sept. 12 Photo. ***Perf. 13***

2467 A939 2s yel grn, blk & red 15 15

Ornament
A940

New Year 1978: 13s, Different ornament.

1977, Dec. 1

2468 A940 2s gold & multi 15 15
2469 A940 13s silver & multi 26 15
Set value 15

Railroad Bridge — A941

1977, Nov. 9

2470 A941 13s green, yel & gray 30 15

Transport Organization, 50th anniversary.

A942

A943

1977, Nov. 15

2471 A942 8s gold & vio brn 15 15

Petko Ratchev Slaveikov (1827-95), poet, birth sesquicentennial. No. 2471 printed in sheets of 8 stamps and 8 labels in 4 alternating vertical rows.

1978, Jan. 30 Photo. ***Perf. 13***

Designs: 23s, Soccer player and Games' emblem. 50s, Soccer players.

2472 A943 13s multicolored 24 15
2473 A943 23s multicolored 45 15
Set value 19

Souvenir Sheet

2474 A943 50s ultra & multi 1.00 85

11th World Cup Soccer Championship, Argentina, June 1-25.

Todor Zhivkov and Leonid I. Brezhnev — A944

Ostankino Tower, Moscow, Bulgarian Post Emblem — A945

1977, Sept. 7 Photo. ***Perf. 13***

2475 A944 18s gold, car & brn 30 15

Bulgarian-Soviet Friendship. No. 2475 issued in sheets of 3 stamps and 3 labels.

1978, Mar. 1

2476 A945 13s multicolored 25 15

20th anniversary of the Comecon Postal Organization (Council of Mutual Economic Assistance).

Leo Tolstoy — A946

Shipka Pass Monument — A947

Portraits: 5s, Fedor Dostoevski. 13s, Ivan Sergeevich Turgenev. 23s, Vasili Vasilievich Vershchagin. 25s, Giuseppe Garibaldi. 35s, Victor Hugo.

1978, Mar. 28 Photo. ***Perf. 13***

2477 A946 2s yellow & dk grn 15 15
2478 A946 5s lemon & brown 15 15
2479 A946 13s tan & sl grn 22 15
2480 A946 23s gray & vio brn 35 15
2481 A946 25s yel grn & blk 40 15
2482 A946 35s lt bl & vio bl 80 38
Nos. 2477-2482 (6) 2.07
Set value 73

Souvenir Sheet

2483 A947 50s multicolored 80 60

Bulgaria's liberation from Ottoman rule, cent.

Bulgarian and Russian Colors
A948

1978, Mar. 18

2484 A948 2s multicolored 15 15

30th anniv. of Russo-Bulgarian co-operation.

Heart and WHO Emblem
A949

1978, May 12

2485 A949 23s gray, red & org 32 15

World Health Day, fight against hypertension.

Goddess
A950

Ceramics (2nd-4th Centuries) and Exhibition Emblem: 5s, Mask of bearded man. 13s, Vase. 23s, Vase. 35s, Head of Silenus. 53s, Cock.

1978, Apr. 26

2486 A950 2s green & multi 15 15
2487 A950 5s multicolored 15 15
2488 A950 13s multicolored 26 15
2489 A950 23s multicolored 48 16
2490 A950 35s multicolored 75 24
2491 A950 53s carmine & multi 1.25 32
Nos. 2486-2491 (6) 3.04
Set value 90

Philaserdica Philatelic Exhibition.

Nikolai Roerich, by Svyatoslav Roerich — A951

"Mind and Matter," by Andrei Nikolov — A952

1978, Apr. 5

2492 A951 8s multicolored 16 15
2493 A952 13s multicolored 28 15
Set value 15

Nikolai K. Roerich (1874-1947) and Andrei Nikolov (1878-1959), artists.

Bulgarian Flag and Red Star — A953

1978, Apr. 18

2494 A953 2s vio blue & multi 15 15

Bulgarian Communist Party Congress.

Young Man, by Albrecht Dürer
A954

Paintings: 23s, Bathsheba at Fountain, by Rubens. 25s, Portrait of a Man, by Hans Holbein the Younger. 35s, Rembrandt and Saskia, by Rembrandt. 43s, Lady in Mourning, by Tintoretto. 60s, Old Man with Beard, by Rembrandt. 80s, Knight in Armor, by Van Dyck.

1978, June 19 Photo. ***Perf. 13***

2495 A954 13s multicolored 16 15
2496 A954 23s multicolored 30 15
2497 A954 25s multicolored 32 15
2498 A954 35s multicolored 45 15
2499 A954 43s multicolored 55 20
2500 A954 60s multicolored 85 26
2501 A954 80s multicolored 1.10 38
Nos. 2495-2501 (7) 3.73
Set value 1.18

Dresden Art Gallery paintings.

Doves and Festival Emblem — A955

1978, May 31

2502 A955 13s multicolored 25 15

11th World Youth Festival, Havana, July 28-Aug. 5.

Fritillaria Stribrnyi — A956

Rare Flowers: 2s, Fritillaria drenovskyi. 3s, Lilium rhodopaeum. 13s, Tulipa urumoffii. 23s, Lilium jankae. 43s, Tulipa rhodopaea.

1978, June 27

2503 A956	1s multicolored		15	15
2504 A956	2s multicolored		15	15
2505 A956	3s multicolored		15	15
2506 A956	13s multicolored		26	15
2507 A956	23s multicolored		45	15
2508 A956	43s multicolored		90	30
Nos. 2503-2508 (6)			2.06	
Set value				67

Yacht Cor Caroli and Map of Voyage A957

1978, May 19 **Photo.** ***Perf. 13***

2509 A957 23s multicolored 50 18

First Bulgarian around-the-world voyage, Capt. Georgi Georgiev, Dec. 20, 1976-Dec. 20, 1977.

Market, by Naiden Petkov — A958

Views of Sofia: 5s, Street, by Emil Stoichev. 13s, Street, by Boris Ivanov. 23s, Tolbukhin Boulevard, by Nikola Tanev. 35s, National Theater, by Nikola Petrov. 53s, Market, by Anton Mitov.

1978, Aug. 28 **Litho.** ***Perf. 12½x12***

2510 A958	2s multicolored	15	15
2511 A958	5s multicolored	15	15
2512 A958	13s multicolored	18	15
2513 A958	23s multicolored	30	15
2514 A958	35s multicolored	52	18
2515 A958	53s multicolored	85	28
Nos. 2510-2515 (6)		2.15	
Set value			72

Miniature Sheet

Sleeping Venus, by Giorgione — A959

1978, Aug. 7 **Photo.** ***Imperf.***

2516 A959 1 l multicolored 2.00 85

View of Varna — A960

1978, July 13 **Photo.** ***Perf. 13***

2517 A960 13s multicolored 25 15

63rd Esperanto Cong., Varna, July 29-Aug. 5.

Black Woodpecker — A961

Woodpeckers: 2s, Syrian. 3s, Three-toed. 13s, Middle spotted. 23s, Lesser spotted. 43s, Green.

1978, Sept. 1

2518 A961	1s multicolored	15	15
2519 A961	2s multicolored	15	15
2520 A961	3s multicolored	15	15
2521 A961	13s multicolored	26	15
2522 A961	23s multicolored	42	15
2523 A961	43s multicolored	1.10	24
Set value		1.95	58

"September 1923" A962

1978, Sept. 5

2524 A962 2s red & brn 25 15

55th anniversary of September uprising.

Souvenir Sheet

National Theater, Sofia A963

Photogravure and Engraved

1978, Sept. 1 ***Perf. 12x11½***

2525	Sheet of 4	2.50	1.00
a.	A963 40s shown	60	16
b.	A963 40s Festival Hall, Sofia	60	16
c.	A963 40s Charles Bridge, Prague	60	16
d.	A963 40s Belvedere Palace, Prague	60	16

PRAGA '78 and PHILASERDICA '79 Philatelic Exhibitions.

Black and White Hands, Human Rights Emblem — A964

1978, Oct. 3 **Photo.** ***Perf. 13x13½***

2526 A964 13s multicolored 25 15

Anti-Apartheid Year.

Gotse Deltchev — A965

Bulgarian Calculator — A966

1978, Aug. 1 **Photo.** ***Perf. 13***

2527 A965 13s multicolored 25 15

Gotse Deltchev (1872-1903), patriot.

1978, Sept. 3

2528 A966 2s multicolored 15 15

International Sample Fair, Plovdiv.

Guerrillas — A967

1978, Aug. 1

2529 A967 5s blk & rose red 15 15

75th anniversary of the Ilinden and Preobrazhene revolts.

"Pipe Line" and Flags A968

1978, Oct. 3

2530 A968 13s multicolored 25 15

Construction of gas pipe line from Orenburg to Russian border.

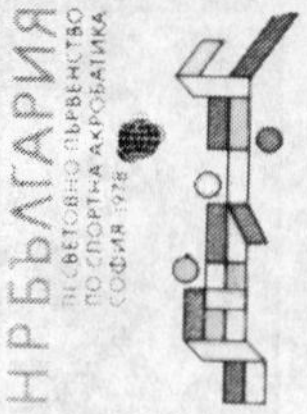

A969

A970

1978, Oct. 4 ***Perf. 13x13½***

2531 A969 13s Three acrobats 25 15

3rd World Acrobatic Championships, Sofia, Oct. 6-8.

1978, Sept. 18 **Photo.** ***Perf. 13***

2532 A970 2s dp claret & ocher 15 15

Christo G. Danov (1828-1911), 1st Bulgarian publisher. No. 2532 printed with se-tenant label showing early printing press.

Insurgents, by Todor Panajotov A971

1978, Sept. 20

2533 A971 2s multicolored 15 15

Vladaja mutiny, 60th anniversary.

A972

A973

1978, Oct. 11 **Photo.** ***Perf. 13***

2534 A972 13s dk brn & org red 25 15

Salvador Allende (1908-1973), president of Chile.

1978, Oct. 18

2535 A973 23s Human Rights flame 50 20

Universal Declaration of Human Rights, 30th anniversary.

A974

A975

Burgarian Paintings: 1s, Levski and Matei Mitkaloto, by Kalina Tasseva. 2s, "Strength for my Arm" by Zlatyu Boyadjiev. 3s, Rumena, woman military leader, by Nikola Mirchev, horiz. 13s, Kolju Ficeto, by Elza Goeva. 23s, Family, National Revival Period, by Naiden Petkov.

Perf. 12x12½, 12½x12

1978, Oct. 25 **Litho.**

2536 A974	1s multicolored	15	15
2537 A974	2s multicolored	15	15
2538 A974	3s multicolored	15	15

2539	A974	13s multicolored	24	15
2540	A974	23s multicolored	42	15
		Set value	85	30

1300th anniversary of Bulgaria (in 1981).

Designs: a, Tourism building, Plovdiv. b, Chrelo Tower, Rila Cloister.

1978, Nov. 1 Photo. *Perf. 13*

Souvenir Sheet

2541	Sheet of 5 + label	4.00	2.00
a.	A975 43s multicolored	70	28
b.	A975 43s multicolored	70	28

Conservation of European architectural heritage. No. 2541 contains 3 No. 2541a & 2 No. 2541b.

Ferry, Map of Black Sea with Route A976

1978, Nov. 1 Photo. *Perf. 13*

2542 A976 13s multicolored 25 15

Opening of Ilychovsk-Varna Ferry.

Bird, from Marble Floor, St. Sofia Church — A977

1978, Nov. 20

2543 A977 5s multicolored 15 15

3rd Bulgaria '78, National Philatelic Exhibition, Sofia. Printed se-tenant with label showing emblems of Bulgaria '78 and Philaserdica '79.

Initial, 13th Century Gospel — A978

Designs: 13s, St. Cyril, miniature, 1567. 23s, Book cover, 16th century. 80s, St. Methodius, miniature, 13th century.

1978, Dec. 15 Photo. *Perf. 13*

2544	A978	2s multicolored	15	15
2545	A978	13s multicolored	20	15
2546	A978	23s multicolored	35	15
		Nos. 2544-2546 (3)	70	
		Set value		24

Souvenir Sheet

2547 A978 80s multicolored 1.25 1.00

Cent. of the Cyril and Methodius Natl. Library.

Bulgaria No. 53 A979

Bulgarian Stamps: 13s, No. 534. 23s, No. 968. 35s, No. 1176, vert. 53s, No. 1223, vert. 1 l, No. 1.

1978, Dec. 30

2548	A979	2s ol grn & red	15	15
2549	A979	13s ultra & rose car	18	15
2550	A979	23s rose lil & ol grn	32	15
2551	A979	35s brt bl & blk	48	20
2552	A979	53s ver & sl grn	90	32
		Nos. 2548-2552 (5)	2.03	
		Set value		74

Souvenir Sheet

2553 A979 1 l multicolored 1.50 1.25

Philaserdica '79, International Philatelic Exhibition, Sofia, May 18-27, 1979, and centenary of Bulgarian stamps. No. 2553 exists imperf. See Nos. 2560-2564.

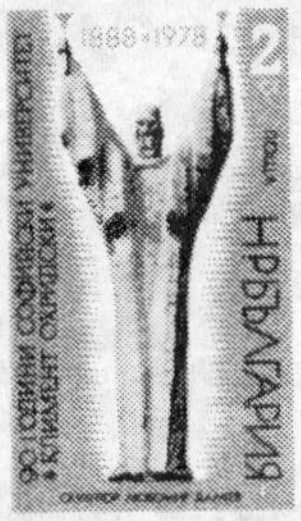

St. Clement of Ochrida — A980

1978, Dec. 8

2554 A980 2s multicolored 15 15

Clement of Ochrida University, 90th anniv.

Ballet Dancers A981

1978, Dec. 22

2555 A981 13s multicolored 30 15

Bulgarian ballet, 50th anniversary.

Nikola Karastojanov A982

1978, Dec. 12

2556 A982 2s multicolored 15 15

Nikola Karastojanov (1778-1874), printer. No. 2556 printed se-tenant with label showing printing press.

Christmas Tree Made of Birds A983

1978, Dec. 22

2557	A983	2s shown	15	15
2558	A983	13s Post horn	20	15
		Set value	25	15

New Year 1979.

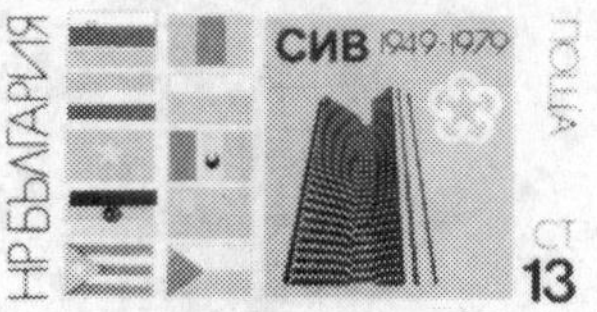

COMECON Building, Moscow, Members' Flags — A984

1979, Jan. 25 Photo. *Perf. 13*

2559 A984 13s multicolored 25 15

Council for Mutual Economic Aid (COMECON), 30th anniversary.

Philaserdica Type of 1978

Designs as Before

1979, Jan. 30

2560	A979	2s brt bl & red	15	15
2561	A979	13s grn & dk car	18	15
2562	A979	23s org brn & multi	32	15
2563	A979	35s dl red & blk	50	22
2564	A979	53s vio & dk ol	90	35
		Nos. 2560-2564 (5)	2.05	
		Set value		78

Philaserdica '79.

Bank Building, Commemorative Coin — A985

1979, Feb. 13

2565 A985 2s yel, gray & sil 15 15

Centenary of Bulgarian People's Bank.

Aleksandr Stamboliski A986

1979, Feb. 28

2566 A986 2s orange & dk brn 15 15

Aleksandr Stamboliski (1879-1923), leader of peasant's party and premier.

Flower with Child's Face, IYC Emblem — A987

1979, Mar. 8

2568 A987 23s multicolored 40 15

International Year of the Child.

Stylized Heads, World Association Emblem — A988

1979, Mar. 20

2569 A988 13s multicolored 25 15

8th World Cong. for the Deaf, Varna, June 20-27.

"75" and Trade Union Emblem — A989

1979, Mar. 20

2570 A989 2s slate grn & org 15 15

75th anniversary of Bulgarian Trade Unions.

Souvenir Sheet

Sculptures in Sofia — A990

Designs: 2s, Soviet Army Monument (detail). 5s, Mother and Child, Central Railroad Station. 13s, 23s, 25s, Bas-relief from Monument of the Liberators.

1979, Apr. 2 Photo. *Perf. 13*

2571	A990 Sheet of 5 + label	1.25	60
a.	2s multicolored	15	
b.	5s multicolored	15	
c.	13s multicolored	22	
d.	23s multicolored	38	
e.	25s multicolored	48	

Centenary of Sofia as capital.

Rocket Launch, Space Flight Emblems — A991

Designs (Intercosmos and Bulgarian-USSR Flight Emblems and): 25s, Link-up, horiz. 35s, Parachute descent. 1 l, Globe, emblems and orbit, horiz.

1979, Apr. 11

2572	A991	12s multicolored	20	15
2573	A991	25s multicolored	45	15
2574	A991	35s multicolored	60	22
		Nos. 2572-2574 (3)	1.25	52

Souvenir Sheet

2575 A991 1 l multicolored 1.50 75

1st Bulgarian cosmonaut on Russian space flight.

A slightly larger imperf. sheet similar to No. 2575 with control numbers at bottom and rockets at sides exists.

Nicolai Rukavishnikov — A992

Design: 13s, Rukavishnikov and Soviet cosmonaut Georgi Ivanov.

1979, May 14 Photo. *Perf. 13*

2576	A992	2s multicolored	15	15
2577	A992	13s multicolored	32	15
		Set value	40	15

Col. Nicolai Rukavishnikov, first Bulgarian astronaut.

Souvenir Sheet

Thracian Gold-leaf Collar — A993

1979, May 16

2578	A993	1 l multicolored	2.00	1.50

48th International Philatelic Federation Congress, Sofia, May 16-17.

Post Horn, Carrier Pigeon, Jet, Globes and UPU Emblem — A994

Designs (Post Horn, Globes and ITU Emblem): 5s, 1st Bulgarian and modern telephones. 13s, Morse key and teleprinter. 23s, Old radio transmitter and radio towers. 35s, Bulgarian TV tower and satellite. 50s, Ground receiving station

1979, May 8 *Perf. 13½x13*

2579	A994	2s multicolored	15	15
2580	A994	5s multicolored	15	15
2581	A994	13s multicolored	20	15
2582	A994	23s multicolored	38	15
2583	A994	35s multicolored	60	22
		Nos. 2579-2583 (5)	1.48	
		Set value		48

Souvenir Sheet

Perf. 13

2584	A994	50s vio, blk & gray	1.00	65

Intl. Telecommunications Day and cent. of Bulgarian Postal & Telegraph Services. Size of stamp in #2584: 39x28mm. #2584 exists imperf.

Hotel Vitosha-New Otani — A996

1979, May 20

2586	A996	2s ultra & pink	15	15

Philaserdica '79 Day.

Horseman Receiving Gifts, by Karellia and Boris Kuklievi A997

1979, May 23

2587	A997	2s multicolored	15	15

Bulgarian-Russian Friendship Day.

A998

A999

Design: Man on Donkey, by Boris Angeloushev.

1979, May 23 Photo. *Perf. 13½*

2588	A998	2s multicolored	15	15

12th National Festival of Humor and Satire, Gabrovo.

Lithographed and Engraved

1979, May 31 *Perf. 14x13½*

Durer Engravings: 13s, Four Women. 23s, Three Peasants. 25s, The Cook and his Wife. 35s, Portrait of Helius Eobanus Hessus. 80s, Rhinoceros, horiz.

2589	A999	13s multicolored	24	15
2590	A999	23s multicolored	40	15
2591	A999	25s multicolored	45	15
2592	A999	35s multicolored	65	18
		Nos. 2589-2592 (4)	1.74	
		Set value		49

Souvenir Sheet

Imperf

2593	A999	80s multicolored	1.50	1.25

Albrecht Durer (1471-1528), German engraver and painter.

R. Todorov (1879-1916) A1000

Bulgarian Writers: No. 2595, Dimitri Dymov (1909-1966). No. 2596, S. A. Kostov (1879-1939).

1979, June 26 Photo. *Perf. 13*

2594	A1000	2s multicolored	15	15
2595	A1000	2s slate grn & yel grn	15	15
2596	A1000	2s dp claret & yel	15	15
		Set value	25	15

Nos. 2594-2596 each printed se-tenant with label showing title page or character from writer's work.

Moscow '80 Emblem, Runners — A1001

Moscow '80 Emblem and: 13s, Pole vault, horiz. 25s, Discus. 35s, Hurdles, horiz. 43s, High jump, horiz. 1 l, Long jump.

1979, May 15 *Perf. 13*

2597	A1001	2s multicolored	15	15
2598	A1001	13s multicolored	20	15
2599	A1001	25s multicolored	40	15
2600	A1001	35s multicolored	80	24
2601	A1001	43s multicolored	1.00	30
2602	A1001	1 l multicolored	2.25	65
		Nos. 2597-2602 (6)	4.80	1.64

Souvenir Sheet

2602A	A1001	2 l multicolored	6.00	3.25

22nd Summer Olympic Games, Moscow, July 19-Aug. 3, 1980.

Rocket — A1002

Designs: 5s, Flags of USSR and Bulgaria. 13s, "35."

1979, Sept. 4 Photo.

2603	A1002	2s multicolored	15	15
2604	A1002	5s multicolored	15	15
2605	A1002	13s multicolored	18	15
		Set value	30	18

35th anniversary of liberation.

Moscow '80 Emblem, Gymnast A1003

Designs: Moscow '80 Emblem and gymnasts. 13s horiz.

1979, July 31 Photo. *Perf. 13*

2606	A1003	2s multicolored	15	15
2607	A1003	13s multicolored	20	15
2608	A1003	25s multicolored	48	15
2609	A1003	35s multicolored	75	22
2610	A1003	43s multicolored	1.00	25
2611	A1003	1 l multicolored	2.25	80
		Nos. 2606-2611 (6)	4.83	1.72

Souvenir Sheet

2612	A1003	2 l multicolored	6.00	3.25

22nd Summer Olympic Games, Moscow, July 19-Aug. 3, 1980.

A1004

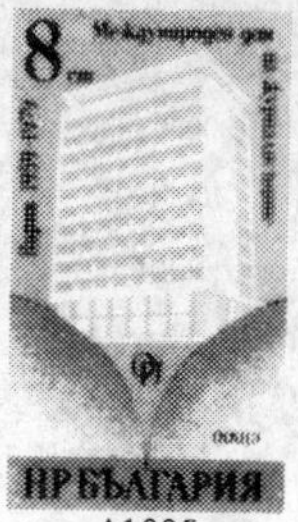

A1005

1979, July 8 Photo. *Perf. 13*

2613	A1004	13s ultra & blk	18	15

Theater Institute, 18th Congress.

1979, July 17

2614	A1005	8s multicolored	15	15

Journalists' Vacation House, Varna, 20th Anniv.

Icon Type of 1977

Virgin and Child by: 13s, 23s, Nesebar, 16th cent., diff. 35s, 43s, Sozopol, 16th cent., diff. 53s, Samokov, 19th cent. Inscribed 1979.

1979, Aug. 7 Litho. *Perf. 12½*

2615	A917	13s multicolored	20	15
2616	A917	23s multicolored	35	15
2617	A917	35s multicolored	50	15
2618	A917	43s multicolored	60	16
2619	A917	53s multicolored	85	24
		Nos. 2615-2619 (5)	2.50	
		Set value		69

A1006

A1007

1979, Aug. 9 Photo. *Perf. 13x13½*

2620	A1006	2s Anton Besenschek	15	15

Bulgarian stenography centenary.

1979, Aug. 28 *Perf. 13*

2621	A1007	2s multicolored	15	15

Bulgarian Alpine Club, 50th anniv.

Public Health Ordinance A1008

1979, Aug. 31 *Perf. 13½*

2622	A1008	2s multicolored	15	15

Public Health Service centenary. No. 2622 printed with label showing Dimitar Mollov, founder.

Isotope Measuring Device — A1009

1979, Sept. 8 *Perf. 13½x13*

2623	A1009	2s multicolored	15	15

International Sample Fair, Plovdiv.

Games' Emblem — A1010

1979, Sept. 20 *Perf. 13*

2624	A1010	5s multicolored	15	15

Universiada '79, World University Games, Mexico City, Sept.

Sofia Locomotive Sports Club, 50th Anniversary — A1011

1979, Oct. 2

2625	A1011	2s blue & org red	15	15

Ljuben Karavelov (1837-1879), Poet and Freedom Fighter — A1012

1979, Oct. 4 **Photo.** *Perf. 13*

2626	A1012	2s blue & slate grn	15	15

A1013

A1014

1979, Oct. 20

2627	A1013	2s Biathlon	15	15
2628	A1013	13s Speed skating	22	15
2629	A1013	23s Downhill skiing	38	15
2630	A1013	43s Luge	75	22
		Nos. 2627-2630 (4)	1.50	
		Set value		44

Souvenir Sheet

Imperf

2631	A1013	1 l Slalom	1.75	1.10

13th Winter Olympic Games, Lake Placid, NY, Feb. 12-24.

1979, Oct. 31 *Perf. 14*

Decko Uzunov, 80th Birthday: 12s, Apparition in Red. 13s, Woman from Thrace. 23s, Composition.

2632	A1014	12s multicolored	24	15
2633	A1014	13s multicolored	24	15
2634	A1014	23s multicolored	38	15
		Nos. 2632-2634 (3)	86	
		Set value		22

Swimming, Moscow '80 Emblem A1016

1979, Nov. 30 **Photo.** *Perf. 13*

2636	A1016	2s Two-man kayak, vert.	15	15
2637	A1016	13s Swimming, vert.	18	15
2638	A1016	25s shown	40	15
2639	A1016	35s One-man kayak	80	20
2640	A1016	43s Diving, vert	1.00	40
2641	A1016	1 l Diving, vert. (diff.)	2.25	70
		Nos. 2636-2641 (6)	4.78	1.75

Souvenir Sheet

2642	A1016	2 l Water polo, vert.	6.00	3.25

22nd Summer Olympic Games, Moscow, July 19-Aug. 3, 1980.

Nikola Vapzarov A1017

1979, Dec. 7 **Photo.** *Perf. 13*

2643	A1017	2s claret & rose	15	15

Vapzarov (1909-1942), poet and freedom fighter. No. 2643 printed with label showing smokestacks.

The First Socialists, by Bojan Petrov — A1018

Paintings: 13s, Demeter Blagoev Reading Newspaper, by Demeter Gjudshenov, 1892. 25s, Workers' Party March, by Sotir Sotirov, 1917. 35s, Dawn in Plovdiv, by Johann Leviev, vert.

Perf. 12½x12, 12x12½

1979, Dec. 10 **Litho.**

2644	A1018	2s multicolored	15	15
2645	A1018	13s multicolored	22	15
2646	A1018	25s multicolored	38	15
2647	A1018	35s multicolored	55	15
		Nos. 2644-2647 (4)	1.30	
		Set value		36

Sharpshooting, Moscow '80 Emblem — A1019

1979, Dec. 22 **Photo.** *Perf. 13*

2648	A1019	2s shown	15	15
2649	A1019	13s Judo, horiz.	20	15
2650	A1019	25s Wrestling, horiz.	40	16
2651	A1019	35s Archery	80	25
2652	A1019	43s Fencing, horiz.	1.00	50
2653	A1019	1 l Fencing	2.25	90
		Nos. 2648-2653 (6)	4.80	2.11

Souvenir Sheet

2654	A1019	2 l Boxing	6.00	4.00

Procession with Relics, 11th Century Fresco A1020

Frescoes of Sts. Cyril and Methodius, St. Clement's Basilica, Rome: 13s, Reception by Pope Hadrian II. 23s, Burial of Cyril the Philosopher, 18th century. 25s, St. Cyril. 35s, St. Methodius.

1979, Dec. 25

2655	A1020	2s multicolored	15	15
2656	A1020	13s multicolored	24	15
2657	A1020	23s multicolored	42	15
2658	A1020	25s multicolored	45	15
2659	A1020	35s multicolored	65	18
		Nos. 2655-2659 (5)	1.91	
		Set value		48

Bulgarian Television Emblem A1021

1979, Dec. 29 *Perf. 13½*

2660	A1021	5s violet bl & lt bl	15	15

Bulgarian television, 25th anniversary. No. 2660 printed with label showing Sofia television tower.

Doves in Girl's Hair A1022

Design: 2s, Children's heads, mosaic, vert.

1979 *Perf. 13*

2661	A1022	2s multicolored	15	15
2662	A1022	13s multicolored	16	15
		Set value	25	15

International Year of the Child. Issue dates: 2s, July 17; 13s, Dec. 14.

Puppet on Horseback, IYC Emblem — A1023

Thracian Rider, Votive Tablet, 3rd Century — A1024

1980, Jan. 22 **Photo.** *Perf. 13*

2663	A1023	2s multicolored	15	15

UNIMA, Intl. Puppet Theater Organization, 50th anniv. (1979); Intl. Year of the Child (1979).

1980, Jan. 29 **Photo.** *Perf. 13x13½*

National Archaeological Museum Centenary; 13s, Deines stele, 5th century B.C.

2664	A1024	2s brown & gold	15	15
2665	A1024	13s multicolored	20	15
		Set value	25	15

Dimitrov Meeting Lenin in Moscow, by Alexander Poplilov A1026

1980, Mar. 28 *Perf. 12x12½*

2667	A1026	13s multicolored	20	15

Lenin, 110th birth anniversary.

A1027

A1027a

Circulatory system, lungs enveloped in smoke.

1980, Apr. 7 *Perf. 13*

2668	A1027	5s multicolored	15	15

World Health Day fight against cigarette smoking.

1980, Apr. 10 **Photo.** *Perf. 13*

2669	A1027a	2s Basketball	15	15
2670	A1027a	13s Soccer	18	15
2671	A1027a	25s Hockey	40	15
2672	A1027a	35s Cycling	80	20
2673	A1027a	43s Handball	1.00	40
2674	A1027a	1 l Volleyball	2.25	70
		Nos. 2669-2674 (6)	4.78	1.75

Souvenir Sheet

2675	A1027a	2 l Weightlifting	6.00	4.25

Foreign postal stationery (stamped envelopes, postal cards and air letter sheets) is beyond the scope of this catalogue.

Souvenir Sheet

Intercosmos Emblem, Cosmonauts — A1028

1980, Apr. 22 *Perf. 12*
2676 A1028 50s multicolored 1.00 45

Intercosmos cooperative space program.

Penio Penev (1930-1959), Poet — A1029

1980, Apr. 22 **Photo.** *Perf. 13*
2677 A1029 5s multicolored 15 15

Se-tenant with label showing quote from author's work.

Penny Black — A1030

1980, Apr. 24 *Perf. 13*
2678 A1030 25s dark red & sepia 60 45

London 1980 International Stamp Exhibition, May 6-14; printed se-tenant with label showing Rowland Hill between every two stamps.

Demeter H. Tchorbadjiiski, Self-portrait — A1031

1980, Apr. 29

2679 A1031	5s	shown	15	15
2680 A1031	13s	"Our People"	18	15
		Set value		25 15

Nikolai Giaurov — A1032

Raising Red Flag Reichstag Building, Berlin — A1033

1980, Apr. 30
2681 A1032 5s multicolored 15 15

Nikolai Giaurov (b. 1930), opera singer; printed se-tenant with label showing Boris Godunov.

1980, May 6 *Perf. 13x13½*

Armistice, 35th Anniversary: 13s, Soviet Army memorial, Berlin-Treptow.

2682 A1033	5s	multicolored	15	15
2683 A1033	13s	multicolored	18	15
		Set value	25	15

Numeral — A1034

1979 *Perf. 14*

2684 A1034	2s	ultra	15	15
2685 A1034	5s	rose car	15	15
		Set value	20	15

A1034a

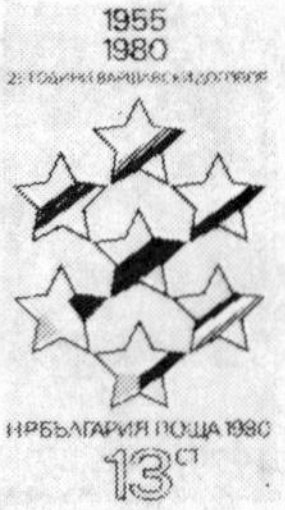

A1035

1980, May 12 **Photo.** *Perf. 13*
2685A A1034a 5s multicolored 15 15

75th Anniv. of Teachers' Union.

1980, May 14 **Photo.** *Perf. 13*
2686 A1035 13s multicolored 20 15

Warsaw Pact, 25th anniv.

A1036

A1037

Statues.

1980, June 10

2687 A1036	2s	multicolored	15	15
2688 A1036	13s	multicolored	18	15
2689 A1036	25s	multicolored	40	15
2690 A1036	35s	multicolored	80	30
2691 A1036	43s	multicolored	1.00	60
2692 A1036	1 l	multicolored	2.25	1.10
		Nos. 2687-2692 (6)	4.78	2.45

Souvenir Sheet

2693 A1036 2 l multicolored 6.00 3.25

22nd Summer Olympic Games, Moscow, July 19-Aug. 3.

1980, Sept. **Photo.** *Perf. 13*
2694 A1037 13s multicolored 25 15

10th Intl. Ballet Competition, Varna.

Hotel Europa, Sofia A1038

Hotels: No. 2696, Bulgaria, Burgas, vert. No. 2697, Plovdiv, Plovdiv. No. 2698, Riga, Russe, vert. No. 2699, Varna, Djuba.

1980, July 11

2695 A1038	23s	lt ultra & multi	30	15
2696 A1038	23s	orange & multi	30	15
2697 A1038	23s	gray & multi	30	15
2698 A1038	23s	blue & multi	30	15
2699 A1038	23s	yellow & multi	30	15
		Nos. 2695-2699 (5)	1.50	
		Set value		60

See No. 2766.

Ship Type of 1975

Ships of 16th, 17th Centuries: 5s, Christ of Lubeck, galleon. 8s, Roman galley. 13s, Eagle, Russian galleon. 23s, Mayflower. 35s, Maltese galley. 53s, Royal Louis, galleon.

1980, July 14

2700 A873	5s	multicolored	15	15
2701 A873	8s	multicolored	15	15
2702 A873	13s	multicolored	25	15
2703 A873	23s	multicolored	45	18
2704 A873	35s	multicolored	70	20
2705 A873	53s	multicolored	1.10	35
		Nos. 2700-2705 (6)	2.80	
		Set value		92

Int'l Year of the Child, 1979 — A1040

Designs: Children's drawings and IYC emblem. 43s, Tower. 5s, 25s, 43s, vert.

1980 **Litho.** *Perf. 12½x12, 12x12½*

2708 A1040	3s	multicolored	15	15
2709 A1040	5s	multicolored	15	15
2710 A1040	8s	multicolored	15	15
2711 A1040	13s	multicolored	20	15
2712 A1040	25s	multicolored	38	15
2713 A1040	35s	multicolored	52	15
2714 A1040	43s	multicolored	65	18
		Nos. 2708-2714 (7)	2.20	
		Set value		64

Helicopter, Missile Transport, Tank — A1041

1980, Sept. 23 **Photo.** *Perf. 13*

2715 A1041	3s	shown	15	15
2716 A1041	5s	Jet, radar, rocket	15	15
2717 A1041	8s	Helicopter, ships	16	15
		Set value	35	15

Bulgarian People's Army, 35th anniversary.

St. Anne, by Leonardo da Vinci A1042

Da Vinci Paintings: 8s, 13s, Annunciation (diff.). 25s, Adoration of the Kings. 35s, Lady with the Ermine. 50s, Mona Lisa.

1980, Nov.

2718 A1042	5s	multicolored	15	15
2719 A1042	8s	multicolored	15	15
2720 A1042	13s	multicolored	20	15
2721 A1042	25s	multicolored	38	15
2722 A1042	35s	multicolored	55	18
		Nos. 2718-2722 (5)	1.43	
		Set value		45

Souvenir Sheet

Imperf

2723 A1042 50s multicolored 1.00 35

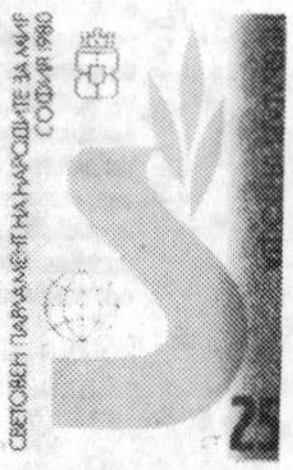

International Peace Conference, Sofia — A1043

1980, Sept. 4 **Photo.** *Perf. 13*
2724 A1043 25s multicolored 35 15

Jordan Jowkov (1880-1937), Writer — A1044

1980, Sept. 19
2725 A1044 5s multicolored 15 15

Se-tenant with label showing scene from Jowkov's work.

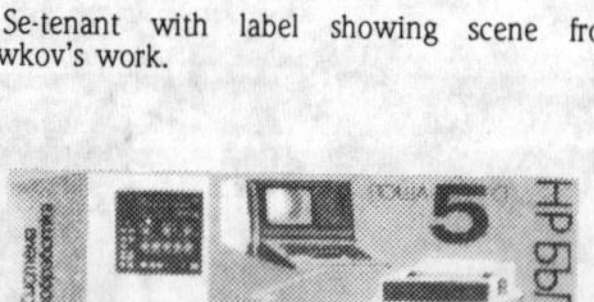

International Samples Fair, Plovdiv — A1045

1980, Sept. 24 *Perf. 13½x13*
2726 A1045 5s multicolored 15 15

15-Cent Minimum Value
The minimum catalogue value is 15 cents. Separating se-tenant pieces into individual stamps does not increase the value of the stamps since demand for the separated stamps may be small.

Blooming Cacti — A1045a

1980, Nov. 4 Photo. *Perf. 13*

2726A A1045a 5s multicolored 15 15
2726B A1045a 13s multicolored 20 15
2726C A1045a 25s multicolored 42 16
2726D A1045a 35s multicolored 60 25
2726E A1045a 53s multicolored 1.00 32
Nos. 2726A-2726E (5) 2.37 1.03

Souvenir Sheet

25th Anniv. of Bulgarian UN Membership — A1045b

1980, Nov. 25

2726F A1045b 60s multicolored 2.25 2.00

World Ski Racing Championship, Velingrad — A1046

1981, Jan. 17 Photo. *Perf. 13*

2727 A1046 43s multicolored 60 22

Hawthorn — A1047 Slalom — A1048

Designs: Medicinal herbs.

1981, Jan.

2728 A1047 3s shown 15 15
2729 A1047 5s St. John's wort 15 15
2730 A1047 13s Common elder 20 15
2731 A1047 25s Blackberries 38 15
2732 A1047 35s Lime 55 20
2733 A1047 43s Wild briar 65 24
Nos. 2728-2733 (6) 2.08
Set value 75

1981, Feb. 27 Photo. *Perf. 13*

2734 A1048 43s multicolored 60 25

Evian Alpine World Ski Cup Championship, Borovets.

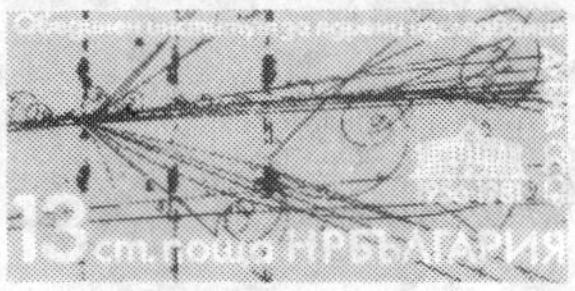

Nuclear Traces, Research Institute — A1049

1981, Mar. 10 *Perf. 13½x13*

2735 A1049 13s gray & blk 20 15

Nuclear Research Institute, Dubna, USSR, 25th anniversary.

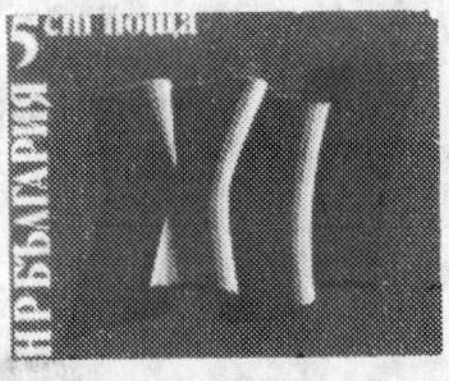

Congress Emblem A1050

1981, Mar. 12 *Perf. 13½*

2736 A1050 5s shown 15 15
2737 A1050 13s Stars 20 15
2738 A1050 23s Teletape 35 15
Nos. 2736-2738 (3) 70
Set value 24

Souvenir Sheet

2739 A1050 50s Demeter Blagoev, George Dimitrov 80 48

12th Bulgarian Communist Party Congress. Nos. 2736-2738 each printed se-tenant with label.

Paintings by Zachary Zograf — A1050a

1981, Mar. 23 Photo. *Perf. 12x12½*

2739A A1050a 5s multicolored 15 15
2739B A1050a 13s multicolored 22 15
2739C A1050a 23s multicolored 42 15
2739D A1050a 25s multicolored 48 15
2739E A1050a 35s multicolored 70 18
Nos. 2739A-2739E (5) 1.97
Set value 55

Nos. 2739A-2739C are vert.

EXPO '81, Plovdiv A1050b

1981, Apr. 7

2739F A1050b 5s multicolored 15 15
2739G A1050b 8s multicolored 15 15
2739H A1050b 13s multicolored 25 15
2739J A1050b 25s multicolored 45 15
2739K A1050b 53s multicolored 1.00 24
Nos. 2739F-2739K (5) 2.00
Set value 55

Centenary of Bulgarian Shipbuilding — A1050c

1981, Apr. 15 Photo. *Perf. 13*

2739L A1050c 35s Georgi Dimitrov, liner 55 20
2739M A1050c 43s 5th from RMS, freighter 65 25
2739N A1050c 53s Khan Asparuch, tanker 80 28
Nos. 2739L-2739N (3) 2.00 73

Arabian Horse A1051

1980, Nov. 27 Litho. *Perf. 12½x12*

2740 A1051 3s multicolored 15 15
2741 A1051 5s multicolored 15 15
2742 A1051 13s multicolored 30 15
2743 A1051 23s multicolored 45 15
2744 A1051 35s multicolored 75 20
Nos. 2740-2744 (5) 1.80
Set value 48

Vassil Stoin, Ethnologist, Birth Centenary — A1052

1980, Dec. 5 Photo. *Perf. 13½x13*

2745 A1052 5s multicolored 15 15

12th Bulgarian Communist Party Congress — A1052a

1980, Dec. 26 Photo. *Perf. 13x13½*

2745A A1052a 5s Party symbols 15 15

New Year A1053

1980, Dec. 8 *Perf. 13*

2746 A1053 5s shown 15 15
2747 A1053 13s Cup, date 18 15
Set value 25 15

Culture Palace, Sofia A1053a

1981, Mar. 13 Photo. *Perf. 13*

2747A A1053a 5s multicolored 15 15

Vienna Hofburg Palace A1054

1981, May 15 Photo. *Perf. 13*

2748 A1054 35s multicolored 45 18

WIPA 1981 Intl. Philatelic Exhibition, Vienna, May 22-31.

34th Farmers' Union Congress A1055

1981, May 18 *Perf. 13½*

2749 A1055 5s shown 15 15
2750 A1055 8s Flags 15 15
2751 A1055 13s Flags, diff. 20 15
Set value 40 18

Wild Cat A1056

1981, May 27

2752 A1056 5s shown 15 15
2753 A1056 13s Boar 22 15
2754 A1056 23s Mouflon 40 15
2755 A1056 25s Mountain goat 45 15
2756 A1056 35s Stag 60 18
2757 A1056 53s Roe deer 1.00 26
Nos. 2752-2757 (6) 2.82
Set value 82

Souvenir Sheet

Perf. 13½x13

2758 A1056 1 l Stag, diff. 1.65 85

EXPO '81 Intl. Hunting Exhibition, Plovdiv. Nos. 2752-2757 each se-tenant with labels showing various hunting rifles. No. 2758 contains one stamp, size: 48½x39mm.

25th Anniv. of UNESCO Membership A1057

1981, June 11 *Perf. 13*

2759 A1057 13s multicolored 20 15

Hotel Type of 1980

1981, July 13 Photo. *Perf. 13*

2766 A1038 23s Veliko Tirnovo Hotel 35 15

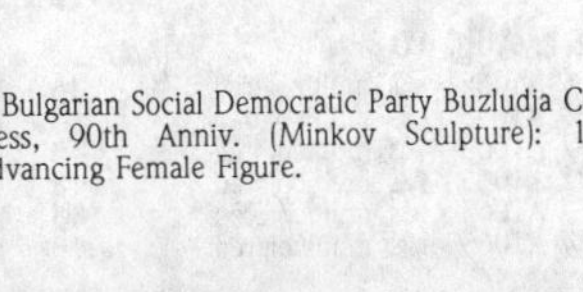

Flying Figure, Sculpture by Velichko Minekov — A1059

Bulgarian Social Democratic Party Buzludja Congress, 90th Anniv. (Minkov Sculpture): 13s, Advancing Female Figure.

1981, July 16 *Perf. 13½*

2767 A1059	5s multicolored		15	15
2768 A1059	13s multicolored		18	15
	Set value		25	15

Kukeri, by Georg Tschapkanov A1060

Statistics Office Centenary A1061

1981, May 28 **Photo.** *Perf. 13*

2769 A1060	5s multicolored	15	15

13th Natl. Festival of Humor and Satire.

1981, June 9

2770 A1061	5s multicolored	15	15

Gold Dish A1063

Designs: Goldsmiths' works, 7th-9th cent.

1981, July 21

2772 A1063	5s multicolored	15	15
2773 A1063	13s multicolored	20	15
2774 A1063	23s multicolored	35	22
2775 A1063	25s multicolored	40	25
2776 A1063	35s multicolored	55	35
2777 A1063	53s multicolored	90	38
	Nos. 2772-2777 (6)	2.55	1.50

35th Anniv. of Frontier Force — A1064

1981, July 28 *Perf. 13½x13*

2778 A1064	5s multicolored	15	15

1300th Anniv. of First Bulgarian State — A1065

Designs: No. 2779, Sts. Cyril and Methodius. No. 2780, 9th cent. bas-relief. 8s, Floor plan, Round Church, Preslav, 10th cent. 12s, Four Evangelists of King Ivan Alexander, miniature, 1356. No. 2783, King Ivan Asen II memorial column. No. 2784, Warriors on horseback. 16s, April uprising, 1876. 23s, Russian liberators, Tirnovo. 25s, Social Democratic Party founding, 1891. 35s, September uprising, 1923. 41s, Fatherland Front. 43s, Prime Minister George Dimitrov, 5th Communist Party Congress, 1948. 50s, Lion, 10th cent. bas-relief. 53s, 10th Communist Party Congress. 55s, Kremikovski Metalurgical Plant. 1 l, Brezhnev, Gen. Todor Zhivkov.

1981, Aug. 10

2779 A1065	5s multicolored	15	15
2780 A1065	5s multicolored	15	15
2781 A1065	8s multicolored	15	15
2782 A1065	12s multicolored	18	15
2783 A1065	13s multicolored	18	15
2784 A1065	13s multicolored	18	15
2785 A1065	16s multicolored	22	15
2786 A1065	23s multicolored	30	15
2787 A1065	25s multicolored	35	15
2788 A1065	35s multicolored	48	20
2789 A1065	41s multicolored	55	22
2790 A1065	43s multicolored	60	24
2791 A1065	53s multicolored	75	30
2792 A1065	55s multicolored	75	30
	Nos. 2779-2792 (14)	4.99	
	Set value		2.00

Souvenir Sheets

2793 A1065	50s multicolored	90	55
2794 A1065	1 l multicolored	1.90	1.10

European Volleyball Championship A1066

1981, Sept. 16 *Perf. 13*

2795 A1066	13s multicolored	20	15

Pegasus, Bronze Sculpture (Word Day) — A1067

World Food Day — A1068

1981, Oct. 2

2796 A1067	5s olive & cream	15	15

1981, Oct. 16

2797 A1068	13s multicolored	16	15

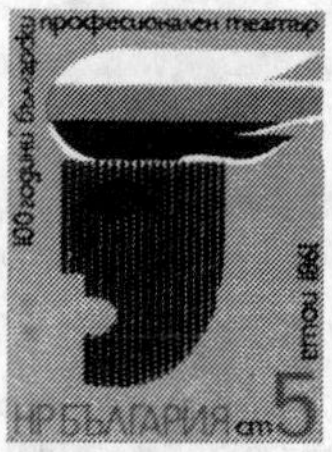

Professional Theater Centenary A1069

1981, Oct. 30

2798 A1069	5s multicolored	15	15

Anti-Apartheid Year — A1070

1981, Dec. 2

2799 A1070	5s multicolored	15	15

Espana '82 World Cup Soccer — A1071

Designs: Various soccer players.

1981, Dec.

2800 A1071	5s multicolored	15	15
2801 A1071	13s multicolored	24	18
2802 A1071	43s multicolored	70	24
2803 A1071	53s multicolored	95	35
	Nos. 2800-2803 (4)	2.04	92

Heritage Day A1072

1981, Nov. 21 **Photo.** *Perf. 13*

2804 A1072	13s multicolored	20	15

Souvenir Sheet

2804A A1072	60s multicolored	4.25	1.10

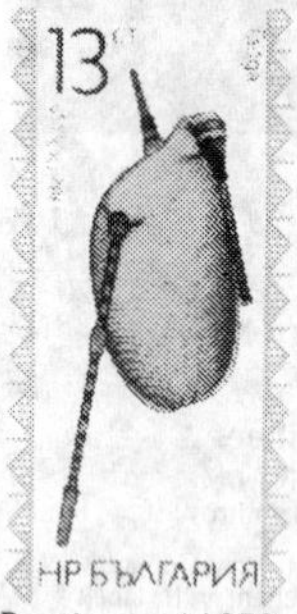

Bagpipe — A1073

Public Libraries and Reading Rooms, 125th Anniv — A1074

1982, Jan. 14

2805 A1073	13s shown	20	15
2806 A1073	25s Flutes	40	18
2807 A1073	30s Rebec	50	20
2808 A1073	35s Flute, recorder	55	24
2809 A1073	44s Mandolin	75	30
	Nos. 2805-2809 (5)	2.40	1.07

1982, Jan. 20

2810 A1074	5s dk grn	15	15

Souvenir Sheet

Intl. Decade for Women (1975-1985) — A1075

1982, Mar. 8

2811 A1075	1 l multicolored	1.65	1.00

New Year 1982 A1076

1981, Dec. 22 **Photo.** *Perf. 13*

2812 A1076	5s Ornament	15	15
2813 A1076	13s Ornament, diff.	18	15
	Set value	25	15

The Sofia Plains, by Nicolas Petrov (1881-1916) — A1077

1982, Feb. 10 *Perf. 12½*

2814 A1077	5s shown	15	15
2815 A1077	13s Girl Embroidering	20	15
2816 A1077	30s Fields of Peshtera	48	20
	Nos. 2814-2816 (3)	83	
	Set value		33

25th Anniv. of UNICEF (1981) — A1078

Mother and Child Paintings.

1982, Feb. 25 *Perf. 14*

2817 A1078	53s Vladimir Dimitrov	80	32
2818 A1078	53s Basil Stoilov	80	32
2819 A1078	53s Ivan Milev	80	32
2820 A1078	53s Liliana Russeva	80	32
	Nos. 2817-2820 (4)	3.20	1.28

Figures, by Vladamir Dimitrov (1882-1961) — A1079

1982, Mar. 8 **Litho.**

2821 A1079	5s shown	15	15
2822 A1079	8s Landscape	15	15
2823 A1079	13s View of Istanbul	22	15
2824 A1079	25s Harvesters, vert.	42	16
2825 A1079	30s Woman in a Landscape, vert.	50	20
2826 A1079	35s Peasant Woman, vert.	60	25
	Nos. 2821-2826 (6)	2.04	
	Set value		78

Souvenir Sheet

2827 A1079	50s Self-portrait	80	65

No. 2827 contains one stamp, size: 54x32mm.

Trade Union Congress A1080

1982, Apr. 8 **Photo.** *Perf. 13½*

2828 A1080	5s Dimitrov reading union paper	15	15
2829 A1080	5s Culture Palace	15	15
	Set value	25	15

#2828-2829 se-tenant with label showing text.

Marsh Snowdrop — A1081

Designs: Medicinal plants.

1982, Apr. 10 Photo. *Perf. 13*

2830 A1081 3s shown 15 15
2831 A1081 5s Chicory 15 15
2832 A1081 8s Chamaenerium angustifolium 15 15
2833 A1081 13s Solomon's seal 25 15
2834 A1081 25s Violets 50 20
2835 A1081 35s Centaury 70 26
Nos. 2830-2835 (6) 1.90
Set value 70

Cosmonauts' Day — A1082

1982, Apr. 12 *Perf. 13½*

2836 A1082 13s Salyut-Soyuz link-up 20 15

Se-tenant with label showing K.E. Tsiolkovsky (space pioneer).

Souvenir Sheet

SOZFILEX Stamp Exhibition — A1083

1982, May 7 *Perf. 13*

2837 A1083 50s Dimitrov, emblems 80 45

14th Komsomol Congress (Youth Communists) — A1084

1982, May 25

2838 A1084 5s multicolored 15 15

PHILEXFRANCE '82 Intl. Stamp Exhibition, Paris, June 11-21 — A1085

1982, May 28

2839 A1085 42s France #1, Bulgaria #1 65 25

19th Cent. Fresco A1086

Designs: Various floral pattern frescoes.

1982, June 8 *Perf. 11½*

2840 A1086 5s red & multi 15 15
2841 A1086 13s green & multi 20 15
2842 A1086 25s violet & multi 38 16
2843 A1086 30s ol grn & multi 45 22
2844 A1086 42s blue & multi 65 26
2845 A1086 60s brown & multi 95 42
Nos. 2840-2845 (6) 2.78 1.36

Souvenir Sheet

George Dimitrov (1882-1949), First Prime Minister — A1087

1982, June 15 *Perf. 13*

2846 A1087 50s multicolored 80 45

9th Congress of the National Front — A1088

1982, June 21 Photo. *Perf. 13*

2847 A1088 5s Dimitrov 15 15

35th Anniv. of Balkan Bulgarian Airline A1089

1982, June 28 *Perf. 13½x13*

2848 A1089 42s multicolored 65 26

A1090

A1091

1982, July 15 *Perf. 13*

2849 A1090 13s multicolored 25 15

Nuclear disarmament.

1982, July Photo. *Perf. 13*

2850 A1091 5s multicolored 15 15
2851 A1091 13s multicolored 18 15
Set value 25 15

Souvenir Sheet

2852 A1091 1 l multicolored 1.50 75

Ludmila Zhivkova (b. 1942), artist.

5th Congress of Bulgarian Painters — A1092

1982, July 27 *Perf. 13½*

2853 A1092 5s multicolored 20 15

Se-tenant with label showing text.

Flag of Peace Youth Assembly — A1093

Various children's drawings.

1982, Aug. 10 *Perf. 14*

2853A A1093 3s multicolored 15 15
2853B A1093 5s multicolored 15 15
2853C A1093 8s multicolored 15 15
2853D A1093 13s multicolored 22 15
Set value 46 23

Souvenir Sheet

Perf. 14, Imperf.

2853E A1093 50s In balloon 3.00 35

See Nos. 2864-2870, 3052-3058, 3321-3327.

10th Anniv. of UN Conference on Human Environment, Stockholm — A1093a

1982, Nov. 10 *Perf. 13*

2854 A1093a 13s dk blue & grn 20 15

A1094

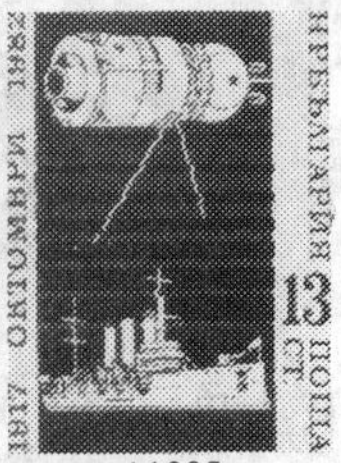

A1095

Designs: No. 2855, Park Hotel Moskva, Sofia. No. 2856, Tchernomore, Varna.

1982, Oct. 20 Photo. *Perf. 13*

2855 A1094 32s lt blue & multi 42 18
2856 A1094 32s pink & multi 42 18

1982, Nov. 4

2857 A1095 13s Cruiser Aurora, Sputnik II 16 15

October Revolution, 65th anniv.

60th Anniv. of Institute of Communications A1096

1982, Dec. 9

2858 A1096 5s ultra 15 15

60th Anniv. of USSR A1097

1982, Dec. 9

2859 A1097 13s multicolored 18 15

The Piano, by Pablo Picasso (1881-1973) A1098

Perf. 11½x12½

1982, Dec. 24 Litho.

2860 A1098 13s shown 20 15
2861 A1098 30s Portrait of Jacqueline 40 18
2862 A1098 42s Maternity 60 26
Nos. 2860-2862 (3) 1.20 59

Souvenir Sheet

2863 A1098 1 l Self-portrait 1.50 75

Children's Drawings Type of 1982

Various children's drawings. 8s, 13s, 50s vert.

1982, Dec. 28 *Perf. 14*

2864 A1093 3s multicolored 15 15
2865 A1093 5s multicolored 15 15
2866 A1093 8s multicolored 15 15
2867 A1093 13s multicolored 20 15
2868 A1093 25s multicolored 35 15
2869 A1093 30s multicolored 40 18
Nos. 2864-2869 (6) 1.40
Set value 56

Souvenir Sheet

Perf. 14, Imperf.

2870 A1093 50s Shaking hands 2.50 35

New Year
A1100

1982, Dec. 28 Photo. *Perf. 13*
2872 A1100 5s multicolored 15 15
2873 A1100 13s multicolored 18 15
Set value 25 15

A1101

A1102

1982, Dec. 28
2874 A1101 25s Robert Koch 38 15
2875 A1101 30s Simon Bolivar 42 18
2876 A1101 30s Rabindranath Tagore (1861-1941) 42 18
Nos. 2874-2876 (3) 1.22 51

No. 2874 also for TB bacillus cent.

1983, Jan. 10 Photo. *Perf. 13x13½*
2877 A1102 5s olive & brown 15 15

Vassil Levski (1837-73), revolutionary.

Universiade Games — A1103

1983, Feb. 15 *Perf. 13*
2878 A1103 30s Downhill skiing 35 18

Fresh-water Fish — A1104

1983, Mar. 24 Photo. *Perf. 13½x13*
2879 A1104 3s Pike 15 15
2880 A1104 5s Sturgeon 15 15
2881 A1104 13s Chub 20 15
2882 A1104 25s Perch 38 15
2883 A1104 30s Catfish 42 18
2884 A1104 42s Trout 55 24
Nos. 2879-2884 (6) 1.85
Set value 75

Karl Marx (1818-1883)
A1105

1983, Apr. 5 *Perf. 13x13½*
2885 A1105 13s multicolored 20 15

Jaroslav Hasek (1883-1923) — A1106

1983, Apr. 20 Photo. *Perf. 13*
2886 A1106 13s multicolored 20 15

Martin Luther (1483-1546)
A1107

1983, May 10
2887 A1107 13s multicolored 20 15

55th Anniv. of Komsomol Youth Movement — A1108

1983, May 13
2888 A1108 5s "PMC" 15 15

A1109

A1111

National costumes.

1983, May 17 Litho. *Perf. 14*
2889 A1109 5s Khaskovo 15 15
2890 A1109 8s Pernik 15 15
2891 A1109 13s Burgas 20 15
2892 A1109 25s Tolbukhin 38 15
2893 A1109 30s Blagoevgrad 40 15
2894 A1109 42s Topolovgrad 55 22
Nos. 2889-2894 (6) 1.83
Set value 68

1983, May 20

6th Intl. Satire and Humor Biennial, Gabrovo: Old Man Feeding Chickens.

2900 A1111 5s multicolored 15 15

Christo Smirnensky (1898-1983), Poet — A1112

1983, May 25
2901 A1112 5s multicolored 15 15

17th Intl. Geodesists' Congress — A1113

1983, May 27
2902 A1113 30s Emblem 45 20

Interarch '83 Architecture Exhibition, Sofia — A1114

1983, June 6
2903 A1114 30s multicolored 45 20

8th European Chess Championships, Plovdiv — A1115

1983, June 20 Photo. *Perf. 13*
2904 A1115 13s Chess pieces, map of Europe 20 15

Souvenir Sheet

BRASILIANA '83 Philatelic Exhibition — A1116

1983, June 24
2905 A1116 1 l Brazilian and Bulgarian stamps 1.50 95

Social Democratic Party Congress of Russia, 80th Anniv.
A1118

Design: Lenin addressing congress.

1983, July 29 Photo. *Perf. 13*
2907 A1118 5s multicolored 15 15

Ilinden-Preobrazhensky Insurrection, 80th Anniv. — A1119

1983, July 29
2908 A1119 5s Gun, dagger, book 15 15

Institute of Mining and Geology, Sofia, 30th Anniv. — A1120

1983, Aug. 10
2909 A1120 5s multicolored 15 15

60th Anniv. of September 1923 Uprising — A1121

1983, Aug. 19
2910 A1121 5s multicolored 15 15
2911 A1121 13s multicolored 18 15
Set value 25 15

Angora Cat
A1123

1983, Sept. 26 *Perf. 13*
2917 A1123 5s shown 15 15
2918 A1123 13s Siamese 22 15
2919 A1123 20s Abyssinian, vert. 38 15
2920 A1123 25s Persian 45 18
2921 A1123 30s European, vert. 55 22
2922 A1123 42s Indochinese 75 30
Nos. 2917-2922 (6) 2.50 1.15

Animated Film Festival — A1124

1983, Sept. 15 Photo. *Perf. 14x13½*
2923 A1124 5s Articulation layout 15 15

Trevethick's Engine, 1804 — A1125

Locomotives: 13s, Blenkinsop's Prince Royal, 1810. 42s, Hedley's Puffing Billy, 1812. 60s, Adler (first German locomotive), 1835.

1983, Oct. 20 *Perf. 13*

2924	A1125	5s multicolored	15	15
2925	A1125	13s multicolored	32	15
2926	A1125	42s multicolored	95	30
2927	A1125	60s multicolored	1.40	42
		Nos. 2924-2927 (4)	2.82	
		Set value		84

See Nos. 2983-2987.

Souvenir Sheet

Liberation Monument, Plovdiv — A1126

1983, Nov. 4

2928 A1126 50s multicolored 80 60

Philatelic Federation, 90th anniv.

Sofia Opera, 75th Anniv. — A1127

Composers' Assoc., 50th Anniv. — A1128

1983, Dec. 2 *Perf. 13x13½*

2929 A1127 5s Mask, lyre, laurel 15 15

1983, Dec. 5

Composers: 5s, Ioan Kukuzel (14th cent.) 8s, Atanasov. 13s, Petko Stainov. 20s, Veselin Stodiov. 25s, Liubomir Pipkov. 30s, Pancho Vladigerov. Se-tenant with labels showing compositions.

2930	A1128	5s multicolored	15	15
2931	A1128	8s multicolored	15	15
2932	A1128	13s multicolored	18	15
2933	A1128	20s multicolored	30	15
2934	A1128	25s multicolored	38	16
2935	A1128	30s multicolored	48	20
		Nos. 2930-2935 (6)	1.64	
		Set value		65

New Year 1984 A1129

1983, Dec. 10 *Perf. 13*

2936 A1129 5s multicolored 15 15

Angelo Donni, by Raphael — A1130

1983, Dec. 22 *Perf. 14*

2937	A1130	5s shown	15	15
2938	A1130	13s Cardinal	20	15
2939	A1130	30s Baldassare Castiglioni	45	20
2940	A1130	42s Donna Belata	68	30
		Nos. 2937-2940 (4)	1.48	
		Set value		62

Souvenir Sheet

2941 A1130 1 l Sistine Madonna 1.65 1.25

Bat, World Wildlife Emblem A1131

Various bats and rodents.

1983, Dec. 30 *Perf. 13*

2942	A1131	12s multicolored	16	15
2943	A1131	13s multicolored	18	15
2944	A1131	20s multicolored	28	15
2945	A1131	30s multicolored	45	22
2946	A1131	42s multicolored	65	30
		Nos. 2942-2946 (5)	1.72	
		Set value		79

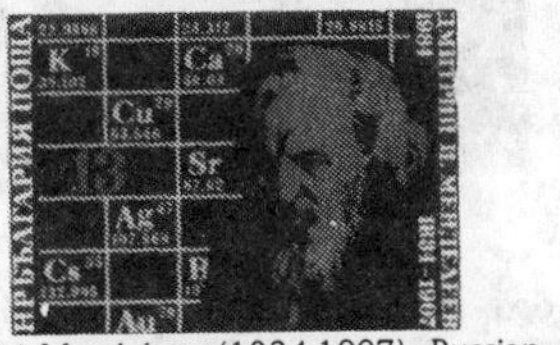

Dmitri Mendeleev (1834-1907), Russian Chemist — A1132

1984, Mar. 14

2947 A1132 13s multicolored 22 15

Ljuben Karavelov, Poet and Freedom Fighter, Birth Sesquicentenary A1133

1984, Jan. 31 *Perf. 13x13½*

2948 A1133 5s multicolored 15 15

Tanker Gen. V.I. Zaimov A1137

1984, Mar. 22 *Perf. 13½*

2959	A1137	5s shown	15	15
2960	A1137	13s Mesta	22	15
2961	A1137	25s Veleka	42	16
2962	A1137	32s Ferry	52	22
2963	A1137	42s Cargo ship Rossen	70	28
		Nos. 2959-2963 (5)	2.01	
		Set value		78

Souvenir Sheet

World Cup Soccer Commemorative of 1982, Spain No. 2281 — A1137a

1984, Apr. 18 **Photo.** *Perf. 13x13½*

2963A A1137a 2 l multicolored 3.00 2.50

ESPANA '84.

Dove with Letter over Globe — A1138

Berries — A1139

1984, Apr. 24 *Perf. 13*

2964 A1138 5s multicolored 15 15

World Youth Stamp Exhibition, Pleven, Oct. 5-11.

1984, May 5

2965	A1139	5s Cherries	15	15
2966	A1139	8s Strawberries	15	15
2967	A1139	13s Blackberries	20	15
2968	A1139	20s Raspberries	35	15
2969	A1139	42s Currants	70	32
		Nos. 2965-2969 (5)	1.55	
		Set value		62

A1140

A1142

1984, May 23

2970 A1140 13s Athlete, doves 20 15

6th Republican Spartikiade games,

1984, June 12

2972 A1142 5s Folk singer, drum 15 15

6th amateur art festival.

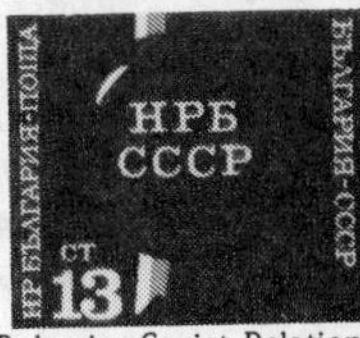

Bulgarian-Soviet Relations, 50th Anniv. — A1143

1984, June 27

2973 A1143 13s Initialed seal 15 15

Doves and Pigeons — A1144

1984, July 6 **Litho.** *Perf. 14*

2974	A1144	5s Rock dove	15	15
2975	A1144	13s Stock dove	20	15
2976	A1144	20s Wood pigeon	35	15
2977	A1144	30s Turtle dove	48	20
2978	A1144	42s Domestic pigeon	70	28
		Nos. 2974-2978 (5)	1.88	
		Set value		74

1st Natl. Communist Party Congress, 60th Anniv. — A1145

1984, May 18 **Photo.** *Perf. 13½x13*

2979 A1145 5s multicolored 15 15

Souvenir Sheet

Intl. Stamp Exhibition, Essen, May 26-31 — A1146

Europa Conference stamps: No. 2980a, 1980. No. 2980b, 1981.

1984, May 22 *Perf. 13x13½*

2980	A1146	Sheet of 2	*12.00*	*10.00*
a.-b.		1.50 l multi	*6.00*	*5.00*

Mount Everest — A1147

1984, May 31 *Perf. 13*
2981 A1147 5s multicolored 15 15

1st Bulgarian Everest climbing expedition, Apr. 20-May 9.

Souvenir Sheet

UPU Congress, Hamburg — A1148

1984, June 11 *Perf. 13½x13*
2982 A1148 3 l Sailing ship *12.00 10.00*

Locomotives Type of 1983

1984, July 31 *Perf. 13*
2983 A1125 13s Best Friend of Charleston, 1830, US 24 15
2984 A1125 25s Saxonia, 1836, Dresden 42 25
2985 A1125 30s Lafayette, 1837, US 52 30
2986 A1125 42s Borsig, 1841, Germany 75 42
2987 A1125 60s Philadelphia, 1843, Austria 1.10 65
Nos. 2983-2987 (5) 3.03 1.77

September 9 Revolution, 40th Anniv. — A1149

1984, Aug. 4
2988 A1149 5s K, production quality emblem 15 15
2989 A1149 20s Victory Monument, Sofia 35 20
2990 A1149 30s Star, "9" 55 30
Nos. 2988-2990 (3) 1.05
Set value 55

Paintings by Nenko Balkanski (1907-1977) — A1150

1984, Sept. 17 *Perf. 14*
2991 A1150 5s Boy Playing Harmonica, vert. 15 15
2992 A1150 30s A Paris Window, vert. 55 30
2993 A1150 42s Double Portrait 80 42
Nos. 2991-2993 (3) 1.50 87

Souvenir Sheet

2994 A1150 1 l Self-portrait, vert. 1.75 1.25

MLADPOST '84 International Youth Stamp Exhibition, Pleven — A1151

Buildings in Pleven: 5s, Mausoleum to Russian soldiers, 1877-78 Russo-Turkish War. 13s, Panorama Building.

1984, Sept. 20 *Perf. 13*
2995 A1151 5s multicolored 15 15
2996 A1151 13s multicolored 28 15
Set value 19

Septembrist Young Pioneers Org., 40th Anniv. A1152

1984, Sept. 21 Photo. *Perf. 13*
2997 A1152 5s multicolored 15 15

Nikola Vapzarov A1153

1984, Oct. 2
2998 A1153 5s maroon & pale yel 15 15

Natl. Soccer, 75th Anniv. A1154

1984, Oct. 3
2999 A1154 42s multicolored 75 42

Souvenir Sheet

MLADPOST '84 — A1155

1984, Oct. 5 Photo. *Perf. 13*
3000 A1155 50s multicolored 1.00 50

Bridges and Maps — A1156

1984, Oct. 5 Photo. *Perf. 13½x13*
3001 A1156 5s Devil's Bridge, Arda River 15 15
3002 A1156 13s Koljo-Fitscheto, Bjala 28 15
3003 A1156 30s Asparuchow, Warna 65 32
3004 A1156 42s Bebresch Highway Bridge, Botevgrad 90 45
Nos. 3001-3004 (4) 1.98 1.07

Intl. Olympic Committee, 90th Anniv. A1158

1984, Oct. 24 Photo. *Perf. 13*
3007 A1158 13s multicolored 25 15

A1159

A1160

Pelecanus crispus.

1984, Nov. 2
3008 A1159 5s Adult, young 15 15
3009 A1159 13s Two adults 28 15
3010 A1159 20s Adult in water 40 20
3011 A1159 32s In flight 65 32
Nos. 3008-3011 (4) 1.48 82

World Wildlife Fund.

1984, Nov. 2
3012 A1160 5s multicolored 15 15

Anton Ivanov (1884-1942), labor leader.

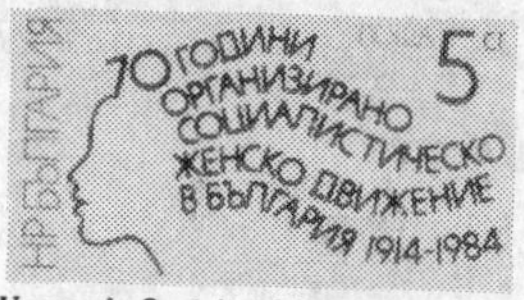

Women's Socialist Movement, 70th Anniv. — A1161

1984, Nov. 9
3013 A1161 5s multicolored 15 15

Telecommunication Towers — A1162

1984, Nov. 23
3014 A1162 5s Snezhanka 15 15
3015 A1162 1 l Orelek 1.90 1.00

Snowflakes, New Year 1985 — A1163

1984, Dec. 5
3016 A1163 5s Doves, posthorns 15 15
3017 A1163 13s Doves, blossom 22 15
Set value 30 19

Paintings by Stoyan Venev (b. 1904) — A1164

1984, Dec. 10 Litho.
3018 A1164 5s September Nights 15 15
3019 A1164 30s Man with Three Medals 48 30
3020 A1164 42s The Best 70 42
Nos. 3018-3020 (3) 1.33 87

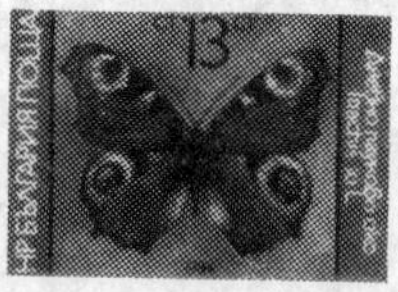

Butterflies A1165

1984, Dec. 14 *Perf. 11½*
3021 A1165 13s Inachis io 25 15
3022 A1165 25s Papilio machaon 42 25
3023 A1165 30s Brintesia circe 52 30
3024 A1165 42s Anthocaris cardamines 75 42
3025 A1165 60s Vanessa atalanta 1.00 60
Nos. 3021-3025 (5) 2.94 1.72

Souvenir Sheet

3026 A1165 1 l Limenitis populi 2.00 1.00

A1166

A1167

1984, Dec. 18 Photo. *Perf. 13x13½*

3027 A1166	13s	multicolored	25	15

Cesar Augusto Sandino (1895-1934), Nicaraguan freedom fighter.

1984, Dec. 28 Litho. *Perf. 14*

3028 A1167	5s	The Three Graces	15	15
3029 A1167	13s	Cupid and the Graces	28	15
3030 A1167	30s	Original Sin	55	30
3031 A1167	42s	La Fornarina	80	42
		Nos. 3028-3031 (4)	1.78	1.02

Souvenir Sheet

3032 A1167	1 l	Galatea	2.00	1.00

Raphael, 500th birth anniv. (1983).

Cruise Ship Sofia, Maiden Voyage — A1168

1984, Dec. 29 Photo. *Perf. 13*

3033 A1168	13s	blue, dk bl & yel	25	15

Predators A1170

1985, Jan. 17

3035 A1170	13s	Conepatus leuconotus	25	15
3036 A1170	25s	Prionodon linsang	42	25
3037 A1170	30s	Ictonix striatus	52	30
3038 A1170	42s	Hemigalus derbyanus	75	42
3039 A1170	60s	Galidictis fasciata	1.00	60
		Nos. 3035-3039 (5)	2.94	1.72

Nikolai Liliev (1885-1960), Poet, UNESCO Emblem — A1171

1985, Jan. 25

3040 A1171	30s	multicolored	50	30

Zviatko Radojnov (1895-1942), Labor Leader — A1172

1985, Jan. 29

3041 A1172	5s	dk red & dk brn	15	15

Dr. Assen Zlatarov (1885-1936), Chemist — A1173

1985, Feb. 14

3042 A1173	5s	multicolored	15	15

Souvenir Sheet

Akademik, Research Vessel — A1174

1985, Mar. 1

3043 A1174	80s	multicolored	1.25	80

UNESCO Intl. Oceanographic Commission, 25th anniv.

Souvenir Sheet

Lenin — A1175

1985, Mar. 12

3044 A1175	50s	multicolored	85	50

A1176

A1177

1985, Mar. 19

3045 A1176	13s	multicolored	25	15

Warsaw Treaty Org., 30th anniv.

1985, Mar. 25

Composers.

3046 A1177	42s	Bach	75	42
3047 A1177	42s	Mozart	75	42
3048 A1177	42s	Tchaikovsky	75	42
3049 A1177	42s	Mussorgsky	75	42
3050 A1177	42s	Verdi	75	42
3051 A1177	42s	Tenev	75	42
		Nos. 3046-3051 (6)	4.50	2.52

Children's Drawings Type of 1982

Inscribed 1985. Various children's drawings.

1985, Mar. 26 Litho. *Perf. 14*

3052 A1093	5s	multicolored	15	15
3053 A1093	8s	multicolored	15	15
3054 A1093	13s	multicolored	24	15
3055 A1093	20s	multicolored	35	20
3056 A1093	25s	multicolored	42	25
3057 A1093	30s	multicolored	52	30
		Nos. 3052-3057 (6)	1.83	1.20

Souvenir Sheet

3058 A1093	50s	Children dancing, vert.	1.00	50

3rd Flag of Peace Intl. Assembly, Sofia. No. 3058 exists imperf. with blue control number, same value.

St. Methodius, 1100th Death Anniv. — A1179

1985, Apr. 6 Photo. *Perf. 13*

3059 A1179	13s	multicolored	25	15

Victory Parade, Moscow, 1945 A1180

Designs: 13s, 11th Infantry on parade, Sofia. 30s, Soviet soldier, orphan. 50s, Soviet flag-raising, Berlin.

1985, Apr. 30 *Perf. 13½*

3060 A1180	5s	multicolored	15	15
3061 A1180	13s	multicolored	24	15
3062 A1180	30s	multicolored	52	30
		Nos. 3060-3062 (3)	91	
		Set value		50

Souvenir Sheet

Perf. 13

3063 A1180	50s	multicolored	1.00	50

Defeat of Nazi Germany, end of World War II, 40th anniv. Nos. 3060-3062 printed se-tenant with labels picturing Soviet (5s, 30s) and Bulgarian medals of honor.

7th Intl. Humor and Satire Biennial A1181

1985, Apr. 30 *Perf. 13½*

3064 A1181	13s	yel, sage grn & red	25	15

No. 3064 printed se-tenant with label picturing Gabrovo Cat emblem.

Intl. Youth Year — A1182

1985, May 21 *Perf. 13*

3065 A1182	13s	multicolored	25	15

Ivan Vasov (1850-1921), Poet — A1183

1985, May 30 *Perf. 13½*

3066 A1183	5s	tan & sepia	15	15

No. 3066 printed se-tenant with label picturing Vasov's birthplace in Sopot.

Soviet War Memorial, Haskovo City Arms A1184

1985, June 1 *Perf. 13*

3067 A1184	5s	multicolored	15	15

Haskovo millennium.

12th World Youth Festival, Moscow — A1185

1985, June 25

3068 A1185	13s	multicolored	25	15

The Scott Catalogue value is a retail value; that is, what you could expect to pay for the stamp in a grade of Fine-Very Fine. The value listed reflects recent actual dealer selling prices.

Indira Gandhi (1917-1984), Prime Minister of India — A1186

1985, June 26

3069	A1186	30s org yel, sep & ver	60	30

Vasil Aprilov, Founder — A1187

1985, June 30

3070	A1187	5s multicolored	15	15

1st secular school, Gabrovo, 150th anniv.

INTERSTENO '85 — A1188

1985, June 30

3071	A1188	13s multicolored	25	15

Congress for the Intl. Union of Stenographers and Typists, Sofia.

Alexander Nevski Cathedral A1189

1985, July 9

3072	A1189	42s multicolored	80	42

World Tourism Org., general assembly, Sofia.

UN, 40th Anniv. A1190

1985, July 16

3073	A1190	13s multicolored	25	15

A1191

Roses — A1192

1985, July 16

3074	A1191	13s multicolored	25	15

Admission of Bulgaria to UN, 30th anniv.

1985, July 20 **Litho.**

3075	A1192	5s Rosa damascena	15	15
3076	A1192	13s Rosa trakijka	24	15
3077	A1192	20s Rosa radiman	35	20
3078	A1192	30s Rosa marista	50	30
3079	A1192	42s Rosa valentina	75	42
3080	A1192	60s Rosa maria	1.00	60
a.		Min. sheet of 6, #3075-3080	3.50	2.00
		Nos. 3075-3080 (6)	2.99	1.82

Helsinki Conference, 10th Anniv. — A1193

1985, Aug. 1 **Photo.**

3081	A1193	13s multicolored	25	15

European Swimming Championships, Sofia — A1194

1985, Aug. 2 **Litho.** ***Perf. 12½***

3082	A1194	5s Butterfly stroke	15	15
3083	A1194	13s Water polo, vert.	25	15
3084	A1194	42s Diving, vert.	80	42
3085	A1194	60s Synchronized swimming	1.10	50
		Nos. 3082-3085 (4)	2.30	1.22

The 60s exists with central design inverted.

Natl. Tourism Assoc., 90th Anniv. A1195

1985, Aug. 15 **Photo.** ***Perf. 13***

3086	A1195	5s multicolored	15	15

1986 World Cup Soccer Championships, Mexico — A1196

Various soccer plays. Nos. 3087-3090 vert.

1985, Aug. 29 ***Perf. 13***

3087	A1196	5s multicolored	15	15
3088	A1196	13s multicolored	28	15
3089	A1196	30s multicolored	60	30
3090	A1196	42s multicolored	85	42
		Nos. 3087-3090 (4)	1.88	1.02

Souvenir Sheet

3091	A1196	1 l multicolored	2.00	1.00

Union of Eastern Rumelia and Bulgaria, 1885 — A1197

1985, Aug. 29 ***Perf. 14x13½***

3092	A1197	5s multicolored	15	15

Computer Design Portraits — A1198

1985, Sept. 23 ***Perf. 13***

3093	A1198	5s Boy	15	15
3094	A1198	13s Youth	24	15
3095	A1198	30s Cosmonaut	52	30
		Nos. 3093-3095 (3)	91	
		Set value		50

Intl. Exhibition of the Works of Youth Inventors, Plovdiv.

St. John the Baptist Church, Nessebar — A1199

Natl. restoration projects: 13s, Tyrant Hreljo Tower, Rila Monastery. 35s, Soldier, fresco, Ivanovo Rock Church. 42s, Archangel Gabriel, fresco, Bojana Church. 60s, Thracian Woman, fresco, Tomb of Kasanlak, 3rd century B.C. 1 l, The Horseman of Madara, bas-relief.

1985, Sept. 25 **Litho.** ***Perf. 12½***

3096	A1199	5s multicolored	15	15
3097	A1199	13s multicolored	22	15
3098	A1199	35s multicolored	60	32
3099	A1199	42s multicolored	75	40
3100	A1199	60s multicolored	1.10	60
		Nos. 3096-3100 (5)	2.82	1.62

Souvenir Sheet

Imperf

3101	A1199	1 l multicolored	1.75	1.00

UNESCO, 40th anniv.

Souvenir Sheet

Ludmila Zhishkova Cultural Palace, Sofia — A1200

1985, Oct. 8 ***Perf. 13***

3102	A1200	1 l multicolored	1.75	1.00

UNESCO 23rd General Assembly, Sofia.

Colosseum, Rome A1201

1985, Oct. 15 **Photo.** ***Perf. 13½***

3103	A1201	42s multicolored	75	42

ITALIA '85. No. 3103 printed se-tenant with label picturing the exhibition emblem.

Souvenir Sheet

Cultural Congress, Budapest — A1202

Designs: No. 3104a, St. Cyril, patron saint of Europe. No. 3104b, Map of Europe. No. 3104c, St. Methodius, patron saint of Europe.

Perf. 13, 13 Vert. (#3104b)

1985, Oct. 22 **Photo.**

3104	A1202	Sheet of 3	2.75	1.50
a.-c.		50s, any single	90	50

Helsinki Congress, 10th anniv.

Flowers — A1203

1985, Oct. 22 Photo. *Perf. 13x13¹/₂*

3105	A1203	5s Gladiolus hybridy	15	15
3106	A1203	5s Iris germanica	15	15
3107	A1203	5s Convolvulus tricolor	15	15
		Set value	25	15

See Nos. 3184-3186.

Historic Sailing Ships A1204

1985, Oct. 28 Photo. *Perf. 13*

3108	A1204	5s Dutch	15	15
3109	A1204	12s Sea Sovereign, Britain	22	15
3110	A1204	20s Mediterranean	35	20
3111	A1204	25s Royal Prince, Britain	45	25
3112	A1204	42s Mediterranean	75	42
3113	A1204	60s British battleship	1.10	60
		Nos. 3108-3113 (6)	3.02	1.77

Souvenir Sheet

PHILATELIA '85, Cologne — A1205

Designs: a, Cologne Cathedral. b, Alexander Nevski Cathedral, Sofia.

1985, Nov. 4 *Imperf.*

3114	A1205	Sheet of 2	1.25	65
a.-b.		30s, any single	60	30

Conspiracy to Liberate Bulgaria from Turkish Rule, 150th Anniv. — A1206

Freedom fighters and symbols: No. 3115, Georgi Stojkov Rakowski (1820-1876). No. 3116, Batscho Kiro (1835-1876). No. 3117, Sword, Bible and hands.

1985, Nov. 6 *Perf. 13*

3115	A1206	5s multicolored	15	15
3116	A1206	5s multicolored	15	15
3117	A1206	13s multicolored	22	15
		Set value	40	22

Liberation from Byzantine Rule, 800th Anniv. A1207

Paintings: 5s, The Revolt 1185, by G. Bogdanov. 13s, The Revolt 1185, by Alexander Tersiev. 30s, Battle Near Klokotnitza, by B. Grigorov and M. Ganowski. 42s, Velika Tarnovo Town Wall, by Zanko Lawrenov. 1 l, St. Dimitriev Church, 12th cent.

1985, Nov. 15 Litho.

3118	A1207	5s multicolored	15	15
3119	A1207	13s multicolored	22	15
3120	A1207	30s multicolored	52	30
3121	A1207	42s multicolored	75	42
		Nos. 3118-3121 (4)	1.64	1.02

Souvenir Sheet

Imperf

3122	A1207	1 l multicolored	2.00	1.00

Souvenir Sheet

BALKANPHILA '85 — A1208

1985, Nov. 29 Photo. *Perf. 13*

3123	A1208	40s Dove, posthorn	75	40

Intl. Post and Telecommunications Development Program — A1209

1985, Dec. 2

3124	A1209	13s multicolored	25	15

Anton Popov (1915-1942), Freedom Fighter — A1210

1985, Dec. 11 Photo. *Perf. 13*

3125	A1210	5s lake	15	15

New Year 1986 A1211

1985, Dec. 11 Photo. *Perf. 13*

3126	A1211	5s Doves, snowflake	15	15
3127	A1211	13s Doves	22	15
		Set value	30	19

Hunting Dogs and Prey — A1212

Designs: 5s, Pointer and partridge. 8s, Irish setter and pochard. 13s, English setter and mallard. 20s, Cocker spaniel and woodcock. 25s, German pointer and rabbit. 30s, Balkan hound and boar. 42s, Shorthaired dachshund and fox.

1985, Dec. 27 Litho. *Perf. 13x12¹/₂*

3128	A1212	5s multicolored	15	15
3129	A1212	8s multicolored	16	15
3130	A1212	13s multicolored	28	15
3131	A1212	20s multicolored	40	20
3132	A1212	25s multicolored	50	25
3133	A1212	30s multicolored	60	30
3134	A1212	42s multicolored	85	42
		Nos. 3128-3134 (7)	2.94	1.62

Intl. Year of the Handicapped — A1213

1985, Dec. 30 Photo. *Perf. 13*

3135	A1213	5s multicolored	15	15

George Dimitrov (1882-1949) — A1214

1985, Dec. 30 Photo. *Perf. 13*

3136	A1214	13s brn lake	25	15

7th Intl. Communist Congress, Moscow.

UN Child Survival Campaign — A1215

1986, Jan. 21 Photo. *Perf. 13*

3137	A1215	13s multicolored	25	15

UNICEF, 40th anniv.

Demeter Blagoev (1856-1924) — A1216

1986, Jan. 28 Photo. *Perf. 13*

3138	A1216	5s dk lake, car & dk red	15	15

Intl. Peace Year — A1217

1986, Jan. 31 *Perf. 13¹/₂*

3139	A1217	5s multicolored	15	15

Orchids — A1218

1986, Feb. 12 Litho. *Perf. 13x12¹/₂*

3140	A1218	5s Dactylorhiza romana	15	15
3141	A1218	13s Epipactis palustris	22	15
3142	A1218	30s Ophrys cornuta	52	30
3143	A1218	32s Limodorum abortivum	55	32
3144	A1218	42s Cypripedium calceolus	75	42
3145	A1218	60s Orchis papilionacea	1.10	60
a.		Min. sheet of 6, #3140-3145	3.50	2.00
		Nos. 3140-3145 (6)	3.29	1.94

Hares and Rabbits A1219

1986, Feb. 24 *Perf. 12¹/₂x12*

3146	A1219	5s multicolored	15	15
3147	A1219	25s multicolored	45	25
3148	A1219	30s multicolored	55	30
3149	A1219	32s multicolored	60	32
3150	A1219	42s multicolored	75	42
3151	A1219	60s multicolored	1.00	60
		Nos. 3146-3151 (6)	3.50	2.04

Bulgarian Eagle, Newspaper, 140th Anniv. — A1220

Design: Front page of first issue and Ivan Bogorov, journalist.

1986, Feb. 2 Photo. *Perf. 13*

3152	A1220	5s multicolored	15	15

Souvenir Sheet

Halley's Comet A1221

Comet's orbit in the Solar System: a, 1980. b, 1910-86. c, 1916-70. d, 1911.

1986, Mar. 7 *Perf. 13¹/₂x13*

3153		Sheet of 4	1.75	1.25
a.-d.	A1221	25s, any single	42	30

A1222

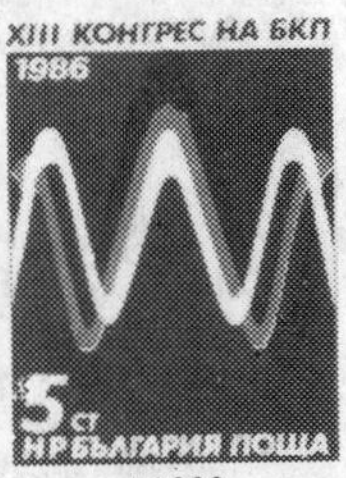

A1223

1986, Mar. 12 *Perf. 13x13¹/₂*

3154	A1222	5s dp bl & bl	15	15

Vladimir Bachev (1935-1967), poet.

1986, Mar. 17 *Perf. 13*

3155 A1223 5s Wavy lines 15 15
3156 A1223 8s Star 15 15
3157 A1223 13s Worker 24 15
Set value 45 27

Souvenir Sheet

Imperf

3158 A1223 50s Scaffold, flags 90 50

13th Natl. Communist Party Congress.

Souvenir Sheet

1st Manned Space Flight, 25th Anniv. — A1224

Designs: a, Vostok I, 1961. b, Yuri Gagarin (1934-68), Russian cosmonaut.

1986, Mar. 28 *Perf. 13½x13*

3159 Sheet of 2 1.75 1.00
a.-b. A1224 50s, any single 1.00 50

April Uprising against the Turks, 110th Anniv. — A1225

Monuments: 5s, 1876 Uprising monument, Panagjuriste. 13s, Christo Botev, Vraca.

1986, Mar. 30 *Perf. 13*

3160 A1225 5s multicolored 15 15
3161 A1225 13s multicolored 26 15
Set value 20

A1225a

Levsky-Spartak Sports Club, 75th Anniv. — A1226

1986 *Perf. 13*

3161A A1225a 5s multicolored 15 15

Souvenir Sheet

Imperf

3162 A1226 50s Rhythmic gymnastics 80 50

Issue dates: 5s, Dec. 50s, May 12.

A1227 A1228

1986, May 19 *Perf. 13*

3163 A1227 5s Congress emblem 15 15
3164 A1227 8s Emblem on globe 15 15
3165 A1227 13s Flags 24 15
Set value 45 27

35th Congress of Bulgarian farmers, Sofia.

1986, May 27 *Perf. 13x13½*

3166 A1228 13s multicolored 25 15

Conference of Transport Ministers from Socialist Countries.

17th Intl. Book Fair, Sofia — A1229

1986, May 28

3167 A1229 13s blk, brt red & grysh blk 25 15

1986 World Cup Soccer Championships, Mexico — A1230

Various soccer plays; attached labels picture Mexican landmarks.

1986, May 30 *Perf. 13½*

3168 A1230 5s multi, vert. 15 15
3169 A1230 13s multicolored 25 15
3170 A1230 20s multicolored 35 20
3171 A1230 30s multicolored 55 30
3172 A1230 42s multicolored 75 42
3173 A1230 60s multi, vert. 1.10 60
Nos. 3168-3173 (6) 3.15 1.82

Souvenir Sheet

Perf. 13

3174 A1230 1 l Azteca Stadium 1.75 1.00

Treasures of Preslav — A1231

Gold artifacts: 5s, Embossed brooch. 13s, Pendant with pearl cross, vert. 20s, Crystal and pearl pendant. 30s, Embossed shield. 42s, Pearl and enamel pendant, vert. 60s, Enamel shield.

1986, June 7 *Perf. 13½x13, 13x13½*

3175 A1231 5s multicolored 15 15
3176 A1231 13s multicolored 25 15
3177 A1231 20s multicolored 35 20
3178 A1231 30s multicolored 55 30
3179 A1231 42s multicolored 75 42
3180 A1231 60s multicolored 1.00 60
Nos. 3175-3180 (6) 3.05 1.82

World Fencing Championships, Sofia, July 25-Aug. 3 — A1232

1986, July 25 **Photo.** *Perf. 13*

3181 A1232 5s Head cut, lunge 15 15
3182 A1232 13s Touche 25 15
3183 A1232 25s Lunge, parry 45 25
Nos. 3181-3183 (3) 85
Set value 44

Flower Type of 1985

1986, July 29 *Perf. 13x13½*

3184 A1203 8s Ipomoea tricolor 15 15
3185 A1203 8s Anemone coronaria 15 15
3186 A1203 32s Lilium auratum 55 32
Nos. 3184-3186 (3) 85
Set value 48

A1233 A1234

1986, Aug. 25

3187 A1233 42s sep, sal brn & lake 75 42

STOCKHOLMIA '86. No. 3187 printed in sheets of 3 + 3 labels picturing folk art.

Miniature Sheet

Environmental Conservation: a, Ciconia ciconia. b, Nuphar lutea. c, Salamandra salamandra. d, Nymphaea alba.

1986, Aug. 25 **Litho.** *Perf. 14*

3188 Sheet of 4 + label 2.00 90
a.-d. A1234 30s any single 50 22

No. 3188 contains center label picturing the oldest oak tree in Bulgaria, Granit Village.

Natl. Arms, Building of the Sobranie — A1235

1986, Sept. 13 **Photo.** *Perf. 13*

3189 A1235 5s Prus grn, yel grn & red 15 15

People's Republic of Bulgaria, 40th anniv.

15th Postal Union Congress — A1236

1986, Sept. 24

3190 A1236 13s multicolored 25 15

Natl. Youth Brigade Movement, 40th Anniv. A1237

Intl. Organization of Journalists, 10th Congress A1238

1986, Oct. 4

3191 A1237 5s multicolored 15 15

1986, Oct. 13

3192 A1238 13s blue & dark blue 25 15

Sts. Cyril and Methodius, Disciples A1239

1986, Oct. 23 *Perf. 13½*

3193 A1239 13s dark brown & buff 25 15

Sts. Cyril and Methodius in Bulgaria, 1100th anniv. No. 3193 printed se-tenant with inscribed label.

Telephones in Bulgaria, Cent. A1240

1986, Nov. 5 *Perf. 13*

3194 A1240 5s multicolored 15 15

World Weight Lifting Championships — A1241

1986, Nov. 6

3195 A1241 13s multicolored 25 15

Ships A1242

1986, Nov. 20

3196 A1242 5s King of Prussia 15 15
3197 A1242 13s East Indiaman, 18th cent. 25 15
3198 A1242 25s Shebek, 18th cent. 45 25
3199 A1242 30s St Paul 55 30
3200 A1242 32s Topsail schooner, 18th cent. 60 32
3201 A1242 42s Victory 80 42
Nos. 3196-3201 (6) 2.80 1.59

Souvenir Sheet

European Security and Cooperation Congress, Vienna — A1243

Various buildings and emblems: a, Bulgaria. b, Austria. c, Donau Park, UN.

Perf. 13, Imperf. x13 (#3202b)

1986, Nov. 27

3202	Sheet of 3	3.00	1.50
a.-c.	A1243 50s any single	1.00	50

Exists imperf. bearing control number.

Rogozen Thracian Pitchers A1244

1986, Dec. 5 ***Perf. 13***

3203 A1244	10s	Facing left	18	15
3204 A1244	10s	Facing right	18	15
		Set value		20

Union of Bulgarian Philatelists, 14th Congress. Nos. 3203-3204 printed se-tenant with labels picturing carved figures on pitchers in blocks of 4.

New Year 1987 A1245

1986, Dec. 9

3205 A1245	5s	shown	15	15
3206 A1245	13s	Snow flakes	26	15
		Set value		19

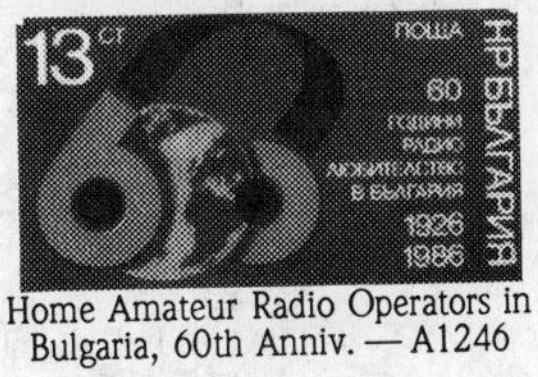

Home Amateur Radio Operators in Bulgaria, 60th Anniv. — A1246

1986, Dec. 10

3207 A1246	13s multicolored	25	15

Miniature Sheet

Paintings by Bulgarian Artists — A1247

Designs: a, Red Tree, by Danail Dechev (1891-1962). b, Troopers Confront Two Men, by Ilya Beshkov (1901-58). c, View of Melnik, by Veselin Stajkov (1906-70). d, View of Houses through Trees, by Kyril Zonev (1896-1961).

1986, Dec. 10 **Litho.** ***Perf. 14***

3208	Sheet of 4	2.25	1.10
a.-b.	A1247 25s any single	50	25
c.-d.	A1247 30s any single	60	30

Sofia Academy of Art, 90th anniv.

Augusto Cesar Sandino (1893-1934), Nicaraguan Revolutionary, and Flag — A1248

1986, Dec. 16 **Photo.** ***Perf. 13***

3209 A1248	13s multicolored	25	15

Sandinista movement in Nicaragua, 25th anniv.

Smoyan Mihylovsky (b. 1856), Writer — A1249

Ran Bossilek (b. 1886) — A1250

Title Page from Bulgarian Folk Songs of the Miladinov Brothers — A1251

Annivs. and events: No. 3211, Pentcho Slaveyckov (b. 1861), writer. No. 3212, Nickola Atanassov (b. 1886), musician.

1986, Dec. 17

3210 A1249	5s multicolored	15	15
3211 A1249	5s multicolored	15	15
3212 A1249	8s multicolored	16	15
3213 A1250	8s multicolored	16	15
3214 A1251	10s multicolored	20	15
	Nos. 3210-3214 (5)	82	
	Set value		36

A1252

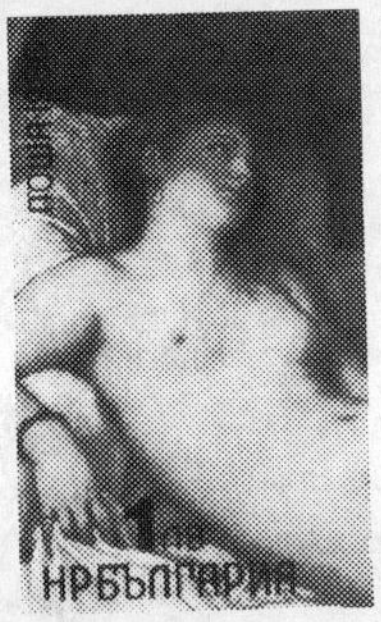

Paintings by Titian — A1253

Various portraits.

1986, Dec. 23 **Litho.** ***Perf. 14***

3215 A1252	5s	multicolored	15	15
3216 A1252	13s	multicolored	28	15
3217 A1252	20s	multicolored	40	20
3218 A1252	30s	multicolored	60	30
3219 A1252	32s	multicolored	65	32
3220 A1252	42s	multicolored	85	42
a.		Min. sheet of 6, #3215-3220	3.00	1.50
		Nos. 3215-3220 (6)	2.93	1.54

Souvenir Sheet

3221 A1253	1 l multicolored	2.25	1.00

Rayko Daskalov (b. 1886), Politician A1254

1986, Dec. 23 **Photo.** ***Perf. 13***

3222 A1254	5s deep claret	15	15

Sports Cars — A1255

1986, Dec. 30 **Litho.** ***Perf. 13½***

3223 A1255	5s	1905 Fiat	15	15
3224 A1255	10s	1928 Bugatti	18	15
3225 A1255	25s	1936 Mercedes	45	25
3226 A1255	32s	1952 Ferrari	55	32
3227 A1255	40s	1985 Lotus	70	40
3228 A1255	42s	1986 McLaren	75	42
		Nos. 3223-3228 (6)	2.78	1.69

Varna Railway Inauguration, 120th Anniv. — A1257

1987, Jan. 19 **Photo.**

3229 A1257	5s multicolored	15	15

Dimcho Debelianov (1887-1916), Poet — A1258

1987, Jan. 20 **Photo.** ***Perf. 13***

3230 A1258	5s blue, dull yel & dp blue	15	15

L.L. Zamenhof, Creator of Esperanto A1259

1987, Feb. 12

3231 A1259	13s multicolored	15	15

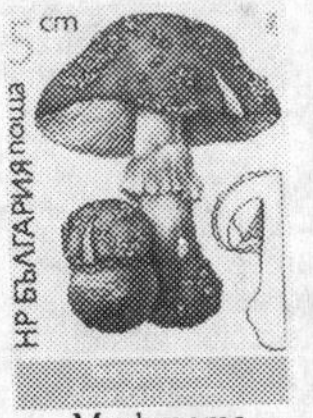

Mushrooms A1260

10th Natl. Trade Unions Congress A1261

1987, Feb. 6 **Litho.** ***Perf. 11½***

3232 A1260	5s	Amanita rubescens	15	15
3233 A1260	20s	Boletus regius	50	30
3234 A1260	30s	Leccinum aurantiacum	70	45
3235 A1260	32s	Coprinus comatus	75	48
3236 A1260	40s	Russula vesca	1.00	60
3237 A1260	60s	Cantharellus cibarius	1.40	90
a.		Min. sheet of 6, #3232-3237	5.25	
		Nos. 3232-3237 (6)	4.50	2.88

1987, Mar. 20 **Photo.** ***Perf. 13***

3238 A1261	5s dark red & violet	15	15

Rogozen Thracian Treasure A1262

Embossed and gilded silver artifacts: 5s, Plate, Priestess Auge approaching Heracles. 8s, Pitcher, lioness attacking stag. 20s, Plate, floral pattern. 30s, Pitcher, warriors on horseback dueling. 32s, Urn, decorative pattern. 42s, Pitcher (not gilded), winged horses.

1987, Mar. 31

3239 A1262	5s multicolored	15	15
3240 A1262	8s multicolored	20	15
3241 A1262	20s multicolored	48	30
3242 A1262	30s multicolored	70	45
3243 A1262	32s multicolored	75	48
3244 A1262	42s multicolored	1.00	62
	Nos. 3239-3244 (6)	3.28	2.15

Miniature Sheet

Modern Architecture — A1263

Designs: a, Ludmila Zhivkova conf. center, Varna. b, Ministry of Foreign Affairs, Sofia. c, Interpred Building, Sofia. d, Hotel, Sandanski.

1987, Apr. 7 *Perf. 13¹/₂x13*
3245 Sheet of 4 3.00 1.80
a.-d. A1263 30s any single 90 45

Exists imperf. with black control number.

European Freestyle Wrestling Championships A1264

1987, Apr. 22 *Perf. 13*
3246 A1264 5s multicolored 15 15
3247 A1264 13s multi, diff. 38 18

CAPEX '87, Toronto A1265

1987, Apr. 24
3248 A1265 42s multicolored 1.00 42

10th Congress of the Natl. Front — A1266

1987, May 11
3249 A1266 5s multicolored 15 15

15th Communist Youth Congress A1267

1987, May 13
3250 A1267 5s George Dimitrov 15 15

8th Intl. Humor and Satire Biennial, Gabrovo — A1268

1987, May 15 *Perf. 13x13¹/₂*
3251 A1268 13s multicolored 35 15

13th World Rhythmic Gymnastics Championships, Varna — A1269

Gymnasts.

1987, Aug. 5 **Photo.** *Perf. 13*
3252 A1269 5s Maria Gigova 15 15
3252A A1269 8s Iliana Raeva 18 15
3252B A1269 13s Anelia Ralenkova 28 16
3252C A1269 25s Pilyana Georgieva 55 32
3252D A1269 30s Lilia Ignatova 65 38
3252E A1269 42s Bianca Panova 90 52
Nos. 3252-3252E (6) 2.71 1.68

Souvenir Sheet

Perf. 13x13¹/₂

3252F A1269 1 l Neshka Robeva, coach 2.25 1.50

Exists imperf. with black control number.

Vassil Kolarov — A1270

1987, June 3 *Perf. 13*
3253 A1270 5s dark red, yel & dark blue 15 15

Stela Blagoeva (b. 1887) — A1271

1987, June 4
3254 A1271 5s pink & sepia 15 15

Rabotnichesko Delo Newspaper, 60th Anniv. — A1272

1987, May 28
3255 A1272 5s black & lake 15 15

Deer A1273

1987, June 23 **Litho.**
3256 A1273 5s Capreolus capreolus, vert. 15 15
3257 A1273 10s Alces alces 25 15
3258 A1273 32s Dama dama, vert. 75 25
3259 A1273 40s Cervus nippon, vert. 1.10 30
3260 A1273 42s Cervus elaphus 1.10 32
3261 A1273 60s Rangifer tarandus, vert. 1.40 45
a. Min. sheet of 6, #3256-3261, imperf. 5.50 2.85
Nos. 3256-3261 (6) 4.75 1.62

Vassil Levski (1837-73) A1274

Various portraits.

1987, June 19 **Photo.**
3262 A1274 5s red brn & dark grn 15 15
3263 A1274 13s dark grn & red brn 35 20
Set value 26

Namibia Day A1275

1987, July 8
3264 A1275 13s org, blk & dark red 30 20

Georgi Kirkov (1867-1919), Revolutionary A1276

1987, July 17 *Perf. 13x13¹/₂*
3265 A1276 5s claret & deep claret 15 15

Bees and Plants — A1277

1987, July 29 **Litho.** *Perf. 13*
3266 A1277 5s Phacelia tanacetifolia 15 15
3267 A1277 10s Helianthus annuus 25 15
3268 A1277 30s Robinia pseudoacacia 75 45
3269 A1277 32s Lavandula vera 80 48
3270 A1277 42s Tilia parvifolia 1.10 62
3271 A1277 60s Onobrychis sativa 1.50 90
a. Min. sheet of 6, #3266-3271 5.00 2.75
Nos. 3266-3271 (6) 4.55 2.75

BULGARIA '89 — A1278

1987, Sept. 3 *Perf. 13¹/₂x13*
3272 A1278 13s No. 1 40 20

HAFNIA '87 — A1279

1987, Sept. 8 *Perf. 13*
3273 A1279 42s multicolored 1.00 62

No. 3273 issued in sheets of 3 plus 2 labels picturing emblems of the HAFNIA '87 and BULGARIA '89 exhibitions, and 1 label with background similar to Denmark Type A32 with castle instead of denomination.

Portrait of a Girl, by Stefan Ivanov — A1280

Paintings in the Sofia City Art Galler: 8s, Grape-gatherer, by Bencho Obreshkov. 20s, Portrait of a Lady with a Hat, by David Perets. 25s, Listeners of Marimba, by Kiril Tsonev. 32s, Boy with an Harmonica, by Nenko Balkanski. 60s, Rumyana, by Vasil Stoilov.

1987, Sept. 15 **Litho.** *Perf. 14*
3274 A1280 5s shown 15 15
3275 A1280 8s multicolored 22 15
3276 A1280 20s multicolored 52 30
3277 A1280 25s multicolored 65 38
3278 A1280 32s multicolored 85 48
3279 A1280 60s multicolored 1.50 90
Nos. 3274-3279 (6) 3.89 2.36

Intl. Atomic Energy Agency, 30th Anniv. A1281

1987, Sept. 15 **Photo.** *Perf. 13¹/₂x13*
3280 A1281 13s red, lt blue & emer 35 20

Songbirds A1282

1987, Oct. 12 Litho. *Perf. 12½x12*

3281	A1282	5s	Troglodytes troglodytes	15	15
3282	A1282	13s	Emberiza citrinella	35	16
3283	A1282	20s	Sitta europaea	55	25
3284	A1282	30s	Turdus merula	80	35
3285	A1282	42s	Coccothraustes coccothraustes	1.10	50
3286	A1282	60s	Cinclus cinclus	1.50	75
a.			Min. sheet of 6, #3281-3286	5.00	2.25
			Nos. 3281-3286 (6)	4.45	2.16

Balkan War, 75th Anniv. A1283

1987, Sept. 15 Photo. *Perf. 13½*

3287	A1283	5s	buff, blk & brt org	15	15

Newspaper Anniversaries — A1283a

1987, Sept. 24 Photo. *Perf. 13*

3287A	A1283a	5s	multicolored	15	15

Rabotnik 95th anniv., *Rabotnicheski Vstnik* 90th anniv. and *Rabotnichesko Delo* 60th anniv.

October Revolution, Russia, 70th Anniv. A1284

Lenin and: 5s, Revolutionary. 13s, Cosmonaut.

1987, Oct. 27 Photo. *Perf. 13*

3288	A1284	5s	rose brn & red org	15	15
3289	A1284	13s	brt ultra & red org	35	20
			Set value		26

1988 Winter Olympics, Calgary — A1285

1987, Oct. 27 Litho. *Perf. 13x13½*

3290	A1285	5s	Biathlon	15	15
3291	A1285	13s	Slalom	38	20
3292	A1285	30s	Women's figure skating	85	45
3293	A1285	42s	4-Man bobsled	1.10	62
			Nos. 3290-3293 (4)	2.48	1.42

Souvenir Sheet

3294	A1285	1 l	Ice hockey	2.75	1.50

No. 3294 exists imperf.

Souvenir Sheet

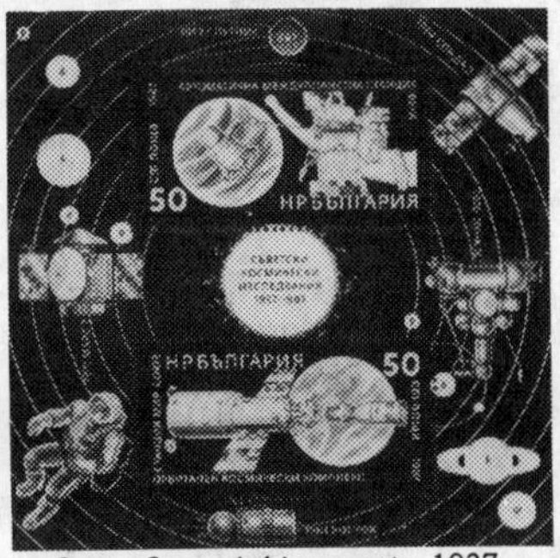

Soviet Space Achievements, 1937-87 — A1286

Designs: No. 3295a, Vega probe. No. 3295b, Mir-Soyuz Space Station.

1987, Dec. 24 Photo. *Perf. 13½x13*

3295	A1286		Sheet of 2	2.75	1.50
a.-b.			50s any single	1.25	75

Exists imperf.

New Year 1988 A1287

Sofia stamp exhibition emblem within folklore patterns.

1987, Dec. 25 *Perf. 13*

3296	A1287	5s	multicolored	15	15
3297	A1287	13s	multi, diff.	35	20
			Set value		26

Souvenir Sheet

European Security Conferences A1288

Conferences held in Helsinki, 1973, and Vienna, 1987: a, Helsinki Conf. Center. b, Map of Europe. c, Vienna Conf. Center.

Perf. 13x13½ on 2 or 4 Sides

1987, Dec. 30

3298			Sheet of 3	4.00	3.00
a.-c.	A1288		50s any single	1.50	75

Exists imperf.

A1289

A1290

1988, Jan. 20

3299	A1289	5s	multicolored	15	15

Christo Kabaktchiev (b. 1878), party leader.

1988, Jan. 25 Litho. *Perf. 12*

Marine flowers.

3300	A1290	5s	Scilla bythynica	15	15
3301	A1290	10s	Geum rhodopaeum	24	15
3302	A1290	13s	Caltha polypetala	32	20
3303	A1290	25s	Nymphoides peltata	60	38
3304	A1290	30s	Cortusa matthioli	75	45
3305	A1290	42s	Stratiotes aloides	1.00	62
a.			Min. sheet of 6, #3300-3305	3.50	2.00
			Nos. 3300-3305 (6)	3.06	1.95

Liberation of Bulgaria, 110th Anniv. A1291

1988, Feb. 15 Photo. *Perf. 13*

3306	A1291	5s	Officer, horse	15	15
3307	A1291	13s	Soldiers	35	20
			Set value		26

8th Intl. Civil Servants Congress, Sofia A1292

1988, Mar. 22 Photo. *Perf. 13*

3308	A1292	13s	multicolored	30	16

State Railways, Cent. — A1293

Locomotives: 5s, Jantra, 1888. 13s, Christo Botev, 1905. 25s, 0-10-1, 1918. 32s, 4-12-1 heavy duty, 1943. 42s, Diesel, 1964. 60s, Electric, 1979.

1988, Mar. 25 Litho. *Perf. 11*

3309	A1293	5s	multicolored	15	15
3310	A1293	13s	multicolored	28	16
3311	A1293	25s	multicolored	52	30
3312	A1293	32s	multicolored	70	40
3313	A1293	42s	multicolored	95	52
3314	A1293	60s	multicolored	1.25	72
a.			Min. sheet of 6, #3309-3314	4.00	2.00
			Nos. 3309-3314 (6)	3.85	2.25

Ivan Nedyalkov (1880-1925) A1294

Postal workers, heroes of socialism: 8s, Delcho Spasov (1918-43). 10s, Nikola Ganchev (1915-43). 13s, Ganka Stoyanova Rasheva (1921-44).

1988, Mar. 31 Photo. *Perf. 13½x13*

3315	A1294	5s	buff & dark rose brn	15	15
3316	A1294	8s	pale ultra & violet blue	16	15
3317	A1294	10s	pale olive grn & olive grn	22	15
3318	A1294	13s	pale pink & lake	26	16
			Nos. 3315-3318 (4)	79	
			Set value		44

Georgi Traikov (b. 1898), Statesman A1295

Intl. Red Cross and Red Crescent Organizations, 125th Annivs. A1296

1988, Apr. 8 Litho. *Perf. 13x13½*

3319	A1295	5s	orange & brn	15	15

1988, Apr. 26 Photo. *Perf. 13*

3320	A1296	13s	multicolored	25	16

Children's Drawings Type of 1982

Designs: 5s, Girl wearing a folk costume, vert. 8s, Painter at easel, vert. 13s, Children playing. 20s, Ringing bells for peace. 32s, Accordion player, vert. 42s, Cosmonaut, vert. 50s, Assembly emblem.

1988, Apr. 28 Litho. *Perf. 14*

3321	A1093	5s	multicolored	15	15
3322	A1093	8s	multicolored	18	15
3323	A1093	13s	multicolored	28	16
3324	A1093	20s	multicolored	42	25
3325	A1093	32s	multicolored	65	40
3326	A1093	42s	multicolored	90	52
			Nos. 3321-3326 (6)	2.58	1.63

Souvenir Sheet

3327	A1093	50s	multicolored	1.00	62

4th Intl. Children's Assembly, Sofia. No. 3327 exists imperf.

Karl Marx A1297

1988, May 5 *Perf. 13*

3328	A1297	13s	multicolored	30	16

Birds — A1297a

1988, May 6 Litho. *Perf. 13x13½*

3328A	A1297a	5s	*Ciconia ciconia*	15	15
3328B	A1297a	5s	*Larus argentatus*	15	15
3328C	A1297a	8s	*Ardea cinerea*	18	15
3328D	A1297a	8s	*Corvus corone cornix*	18	15
3328E	A1297a	10s	*Accipiter gentilis*	22	15
3328F	A1297a	42s	*Bubo bubo*	90	50
			Nos. 3328A-3328F (6)	1.78	
			Set value		94

Dated 1987.

Sofia Zoo, Cent. A1298

1988, May 20

3329	A1298	5s	Loxodonta africana	15	15
3330	A1298	13s	Ceratotherium simum	25	16
3331	A1298	25s	Lycaon pictus	50	30

3332 A1298 30s Pelecanus onocrotalus 65 36
3333 A1298 32s Bucorvus abissinicus 70 40
3334 A1298 42s Nyctea scandiaca 90 52
a. Min. sheet of 6, #3329-3334 3.60 1.80
Nos. 3329-3334 (6) 3.15 1.89

FINLANDIA '88 — A1299

1988, June 7
3335 A1299 30s Finland No. 1 70 35

No. 3335 printed in miniature sheets of 3 plus 3 labels picturing skyline, SOFIA '89 and FINLANDIA '88 exhibition emblems.
Exists imperf.

2nd Joint USSR-Bulgaria Space Flight — A1300

1988, June 7
3336 A1300 5s shown 15 15
3337 A1300 13s Rocket, globe 30 16
Set value 22

EXPO '91, Plovdiv — A1301

1988, June 7 *Perf. 13¹/₂x13*
3338 A1301 13s multicolored 30 16

1988 European Soccer Championships — A1302

1988, June 10 *Perf. 13*
3339 A1302 5s Corner kick 15 15
3340 A1302 13s Heading the ball 25 16
3341 A1302 30s Referee, player 55 36
3342 A1302 42s Player holding trophy 85 55
Nos. 3339-3342 (4) 1.80 1.22

Souvenir Sheet

3343 A1302 1 l Stadium 2.25 1.25

Paintings by Dechko Usunov (1899-1986) A1303

Designs: 5s, *Portrait of a Young Girl.* 13s, *Portrait of Maria Wassilewa.* 30s, *Self-portrait.*

1988, June 14 *Perf. 13x13¹/₂*
3344 A1303 5s multicolored 15 15
3345 A1303 13s multicolored 32 16
3346 A1303 30s multicolored 72 36
Nos. 3344-3346 (3) 1.19 67

Souvenir Sheet

1st Woman in Space, 25th Anniv. — A1304

1988, June 16 *Perf. 13¹/₂x13*
3347 A1304 1 l multicolored 2.50 1.50

Valentina Tereshkova's flight, June 16-19, 1963.

Kurdzhali Region Religious Art — A1305

Designs: 5s, *St. John the Baptist,* 1592. 8s, *St. George Slaying the Dragon,* 1841.

1988, June 27 *Perf. 13x13¹/₂*
3348 A1305 5s multicolored 15 15
3349 A1305 8s multicolored 20 15
Set value 16

1988 Summer Olympics, Seoul — A1306

1988, July 25 **Litho.** *Perf. 13*
3350 A1306 5s High jump 15 15
3351 A1306 13s Weight lifting 28 16
3352 A1306 30s Greco-Roman wrestling 65 38
3353 A1306 42s Rhythmic gymnastics 90 52
Nos. 3350-3353 (4) 1.98 1.21

Souvenir Sheet

3354 A1306 1 l Volleyball 2.50 1.25

No. 3354 exists imperf.

Dimitr and Karaja A1307

1988, July 25 **Litho.** *Perf. 13*
3355 A1307 5s blk, dark olive bister & grn 15 15

120th anniv. of the deaths of Haji Dimitr and Stefan Karaja, patriots killed during the Balkan Wars.

Problems of Peace and Socialism, 30th Anniv. A1308

1988, July 26 **Photo.**
3356 A1308 13s multicolored 25 16

Paintings in the Ludmila Zhivkova Art Gallery — A1309

Paintings: No. 3357, *Harbor, Algiers,* by Albermarke (1875-1947). No. 3358, *Portrait of Ermin David in the Studio,* by Jul Pasken (1885-1930). No. 3359, *Madonna with Child and Sts. Sebastian and Roko,* by Giovanni Rosso (1494-1540). No. 3360, *The Barren Tree,* by Roland Udo (1879-1982).

1988, July 27 **Litho.** *Perf. 14*
3357 A1309 30s multicolored 65 38
3358 A1309 30s multicolored 65 38
3359 A1309 30s multicolored 65 38
3360 A1309 30s multicolored 65 38
Nos. 3357-3360 (4) 2.60 1.52

St. Clement of Ohrid University, Sofia, 100th Anniv. A1310

1988, Aug. 22 *Perf. 13*
3361 A1310 5s blk & pale yel 15 15

PRAGA '88 A1311

1988, Aug. 22
3362 A1311 25s Czechoslovakia #2 in vermilion 60 30

Printed in miniature sheets of 3 plus 3 labels picturing skyline, PRAGA '88 and SOFIA '89 exhibition emblems.
Exists imperf.

OLYMPHILEX '88 — A1312

1988, Sept. 1
3363 A1312 62s Korea No. 1 1.25 75

Printed in miniature sheets of 3 plus 3 labels picturing skyline, OLYMPHILEX '88 and SOFIA '89 exhibition emblems.
Exists imperf.

A1313

A1314

1988, Sept. 15
3364 A1313 5s deep blue, lt blue & red 15 15

Kremikovtsi steel mill, 25th anniv.

1988, Sept. 16 *Perf. 13¹/₂x13*
3365 A1314 13s dark red & ultra 25 16

80th Interparliamentary Conference.

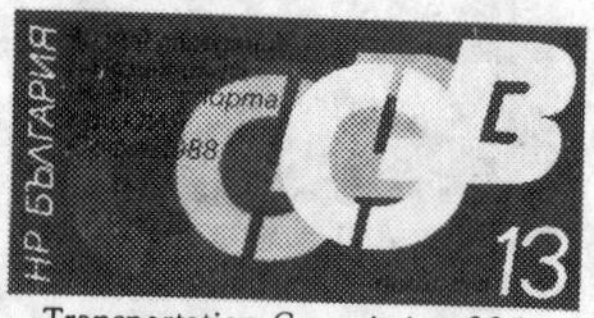

Transportation Commission 80th Congress — A1315

1988, Oct. 17
3366 A1315 13s deep lil rose & blk 25 16

Kurdzhali Region Artifacts A1316

Designs: 5s, Earthenware bowl, 13th-14th cent. 8s, Medieval fortification, Gorna Krepost Village, vert.

1988, Sept. 20 *Perf. 13*
3367 A1316 5s multicolored 15 15
3368 A1316 8s multicolored 20 15
Set value 16

Chiprovo Uprising, 300th Anniv. — A1317

1988, Sept. 23
3369 A1317 5s multicolored 15 15

Bears A1318

1988, Sept. 26 *Perf. 12¹/₂*
3370 A1318 5s *Ursus arctos* 15 15
3371 A1318 8s *Thalassarctos maritimus* 18 15
3372 A1318 13s *Melursus ursinus* 30 16
3373 A1318 20s *Helarctos malayanus* 45 25
3374 A1318 32s *Selenarctos thibetanus* 70 40
3375 A1318 42s *Tremarctos ornatus* 95 52
a. Min. sheet of 6, #3370-3375 3.00 1.50
Nos. 3370-3375 (6) 2.73 1.63

ECOFORUM for Peace — A1319

1988, Oct. 29 *Perf. 13*
3376 A1319 20s multicolored 50 25

PLOVDIV '88 A1320

Design: Amphitheater ruins, PRAGA '88 and PLOVDIV '88 emblems.

1988, Nov. 2
3377 A1320 5s multicolored 15 15

Exists in imperf. sheet of six.

Radio & Television Authority, 25th Anniv. — A1321

1988, Nov. 17 **Litho.** *Perf. 13*
3378 A1321 5s multicolored 15 15

BULGARIA '89 A1321a

1988, Nov. 22 **Litho.** *Perf. 13*
3379 A1321a 42s No. 1 1.10 58

Printed in miniature sheets of 3+3 labels picturing exhib. emblem and conf. center.
Exists imperf.

Souvenir Sheet

Danube Cruise Excursion Industry, 40th Anniv. — A1321b

1988, Nov. 25 *Perf. 13½x13*
3380 Sheet of 2 4.75 2.75
a. A1321b 1 l *Russia* 2.50 1.35
b. A1321b 1 l *Aleksandr Stamboliski* 2.50 1.35

Traffic Safety A1321c

1988, Nov. 28
3381 A1321c 5s multicolored 15 15

New Year 1989 — A1321d

1988, Dec. 20 *Perf. 13*
3382 A1321d 5s shown 15 15
3383 A1321d 13s multi, diff. 35 25

Hotels in Winter A1322

1988, Dec. 19 **Litho.** *Perf. 13½x13*
3384 A1322 5s shown 15 15
3385 A1322 8s multi, diff. 18 15
3386 A1322 13s multi, diff. 28 16
3387 A1322 30s multi, diff. 70 38
Nos. 3384-3387 (4) 1.31
Set value 70

Souvenir Sheet

Soviet Space Shuttle *Energija-Buran* — A1322a

1988, Dec. 28 *Perf. 13½x13*
3387A A1322a 1 l dark blue 2.75 1.50

BULGARIA '89 — A1322b

Traditional modes of postal conveyance.

1988, Dec. 29 *Perf. 13½x13*
3387B A1322b 25s Mail coach 50 30
3387C A1322b 25s Biplane 50 30
3387D A1322b 25s Truck 50 30
3387E A1322b 25s Steam packet 50 30
Nos. 3387B-3387E (4) 2.00 1.20

Philatelic Exhibitions A1323

1989 **Litho.** *Perf. 13*
3388 A1322 42s France No. 1 1.00 52
3389 A1322 62s India No. 200 1.50 78

BULGARIA '89 and PHILEXFRANCE '89 (42s) or INDIA '89 (62s).

Issue dates: 42s, Feb. 23; 62s, Jan. 14. Nos. 3388-3389 printed in miniature sheets of 3 plus 3 labels picturing skylines, BULGARIA '89 and PHILEXFRANCE or INDIA exhibition labels. Exist imperf.

Exist in sheet of four also.

Souvenir Sheet

Universiade Winter Games, Sofia — A1324

Designs: a, Downhill skiing. b, Ice hockey. c, Cross-country skiing. d, Speed skating.

1989, Jan. 30 **Litho.** *Imperf.*
Simulated Perforations
3390 Sheet of 4 2.25 1.25
a.-d. A1324 25s multicolored 55 30

No. 3390 exists imperf. without simulated perforations and containing black control number.

Humor and Satire Festival, Gabrovo A1325

1989, Feb. 7 *Perf. 13½x13*
3391 A1325 13s Don Quixote 30 16

Endangered Plant Species — A1326

1989, Feb. 22 *Perf. 13x13½*
3392 A1326 5s *Ramonda serbica* 15 15
3393 A1326 10s *Paeonia maskula* 20 15
3394 A1326 25s *Viola perinensis* 50 30
3395 A1326 30s *Dracunculus vulgaris* 60 35
3396 A1326 42s *Tulipa splendens* 85 50
3397 A1326 60s *Rindera umbellata* 1.25 70
a. Min. sheet of 6, #3392-3397 4.00 2.50
Nos. 3392-3397 (6) 3.55 2.15

World Wildlife Fund A1327

Bats.

1989, Feb. 27 *Perf. 13*
3398 A1327 5s *Nyctalus noctula* 15 15
3399 A1327 13s *Rhinolophus ferrumequinum* 30 15
3400 A1327 30s *Myotis myotis* 70 35
3401 A1327 42s *Vespertilio murinus* 1.00 50
a. Min. sheet of 4, #3398-3401 2.25 1.25
Nos. 3398-3401 (4) 2.15 1.15

Aleksandr Stamboliski (1879-1923), Premier — A1328

1989, Mar. 1 *Perf. 13½x13*
3402 A1328 5s brt org & blk 15 15

Souvenir Sheet

Soviet-Bulgarian Joint Space Flight, 10th Anniv. — A1329

Designs: a, Liftoff. b, Crew.

1989, Apr. 10 *Perf. 13*
3403 A1329 Sheet of 2 2.25 1.25
a.-b. 50s any single 1.10 62

Exists imperf.

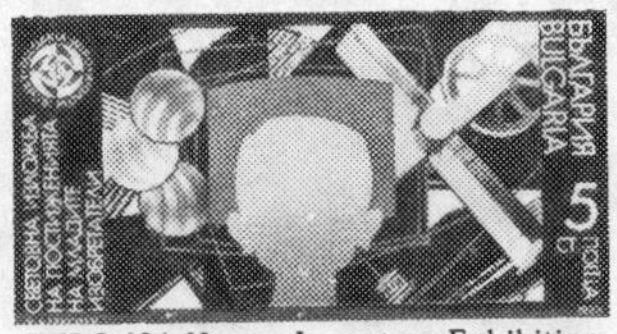

EXPO '91 Young Inventors Exhibition, Plovdiv — A1330

1989, Apr. 20 *Perf. 13½x13*
3404 A1330 5s multicolored 15 15

Petko Enev (b. 1889) A1331

Stanke Dimitrov Marek (b. 1889) — A1332

Perf. 13½x13, 13x13½
1989, Apr. 28
3405 A1331 5s scarlet & black 15 15
3406 A1332 5s scarlet & black 15 15
Set value 15

Icons
A1333

Photocopier
A1334

Paintings by Bulgarian artists: No. 3407, Archangel Michael, by Dimiter Molerov. No. 3408, Mother and Child, by Toma Vishanov. No. 3409, St. John, by Vishanov. No. 3410, St. Dimitri, by Ivan Terziev.

1989, Apr. 28 *Perf. 13x13½*

3407 A1333 30s multicolored 65 35
3408 A1333 30s multicolored 65 35
3409 A1333 30s multicolored 65 35
3410 A1333 30s multicolored 65 35
Nos. 3407-3410 (4) 2.60 1.40

Nos. 3408, 3410 exist in sheets of four. Nos. 3407-3410 exist in souvenir sheets of four and together in one sheet of four, imperf.

1989, May 5

3411 A1334 5s shown 15 15
3412 A1334 8s Computer 18 15
3413 A1334 35s Telephone 80 45
3414 A1334 42s Dish receiver 90 52
Nos. 3411-3414 (4) 2.03 1.27

Bulgarian Communications, 110th anniv. Nos. 3411-3413 exist in imperf. sheets of six.

Souvenir Sheet

58th FIP Congress — A1335

1989, May 22

3415 A1335 1 l Charioteer 2.00 1.00

Exists imperf.

1st Communist Party Congress in Bulgaria, 70th Anniv. — A1336

Famous Men — A1337

1989, June 15

3416 A1336 5s mar, black & dark red 15 15

1989

Portraits: No. 3417, Ilya Blaskov. No. 3418, Sofronii, Bishop of Vratza. No. 3419, Vassil Aprilov (b. 1789), educator, historian. No. 3420, Christo Jassenov (1889-1925). 10s, Stoyan Zagorchinov (1889-1969).

3417 A1337 5s black & gray olive 15 15
3418 A1337 5s blk, brn blk & pale green 15 15
3419 A1337 8s lt blue, blk & vio blk 28 15
3420 A1337 8s tan, blk & dark red brown 22 15
3421 A1337 10s blk, pale pink & gray blue 28 15
Nos. 3417-3421 (5) 1.08
Set value 50

Issued: #3417-3418, June 15; #3419, Aug. 1; #3420, Sept. 25; 10s, Aug. 5.

French Revolution, Bicent. — A1338

1989, June 26 *Perf. 13½x13*

3422 A1338 13s Anniv. emblem 26 15
3423 A1338 30s Jean-Paul Marat 60 35
3424 A1338 42s Robespierre 85 50
Nos. 3422-3424 (3) 1.71 1.00

7th Army Games A1339

1989, June 30 *Perf. 13*

3425 A1339 5s Gymnast 15 15
3426 A1339 13s Equestrian 28 16
3427 A1339 30s Running 65 38
3428 A1339 42s Shooting 95 52
Nos. 3425-3428 (4) 2.03 1.21

22nd World Canoe and Kayak Championships, Plovdiv — A1340

1989, Aug. 11 **Litho.** *Perf. 13*

3429 A1340 13s Woman paddling 28 15
3430 A1340 30s Man rowing 60 25

Photography, 150th Anniv. — A1341

1989, Aug. 29 *Perf. 13½x13*

3431 A1341 42s blk, buff & yellow 85 45

September 9 Revolution, 45th Anniv. — A1342

1989, Aug. 30 *Perf. 13*

3432 A1342 5s Revolutionaries 15 15
3433 A1342 8s Couple embracing 16 15
3434 A1342 13s Faces in a crowd 25 16
Nos. 3432-3434 (3) 56
Set value 32

Natural History Museum, Cent. A1343

1989, Aug. 31

3435 A1343 13s multicolored 30 16

Postal Workers Killed in World War II — A1343a

Designs: 5s, L.D. Dardjikov. 8s, I.B. Dobrev. 10s, N.P. Antonov.

1989, Sept. 22 **Litho.** *Perf. 13*

3436 A1343a 5s multicolored 15 15
3437 A1343a 8s multicolored 18 15
3438 A1343a 13s multicolored 32 18
Nos. 3436-3438 (3) 65
Set value 34

12th Shipping Unions Congress (FIATA) A1344

1989, Sept. 25 **Litho.** *Perf. 13½x13*

3439 A1344 42s light blue & dark blue 85 45

Jawaharlal Nehru, 1st Prime Minister of Independent India — A1346

1989, Oct. 10

3440 A1346 13s blk, pale yel & brn 32 16

Souvenir Sheet

European Ecology Congress — A1347

1989, Oct. 12 *Perf. 13*

3441 A1347 Sheet of 2 3.50 1.75
a. 50s multicolored 1.20 60
b. 1 l multicolored 2.25 1.15

Snakes A1368

1989, Oct. 20 **Litho.** *Perf. 13*

3491 A1368 5s *Eryx jaculus turcicus* 15 15
3492 A1368 10s *Elaphe longissima* 22 15
3493 A1368 25s *Elaphe situla* 55 30
3494 A1368 30s *Elaphe quatuorlineata* 65 35
3495 A1368 42s *Telescopus fallax* 90 50
3496 A1368 60s *Coluber rubriceps* 1.25 70
a. Min. sheet of 6, #3491-3496 4.00 2.05
Nos. 3491-3496 (6) 3.72 2.15

Intl. Youth Science Fair, Plovdiv, 1989 — A1369

1989, Nov. 4

3497 A1369 13s multicolored 25 15

1990 World Soccer Championships, Italy — A1370

Various athletes: No. 3502a, Athletes facing right. No. 3502b, Athletes facing left.

1989, Dec. 1

3498 A1370 5s shown 15 15
3499 A1370 13s multi, diff. 30 15
3500 A1370 30s multi, diff. 70 35
3501 A1370 42s multi, diff. 98 50
Nos. 3498-3501 (4) 2.13 1.15

Souvenir Sheet

3502 Sheet of 2 2.30 1.15
a.-b. A1370 50s any single 1.15 57

Air Sports A1371

1989, Dec. 8

3503	A1371	5s Glider planes	15	15
3504	A1371	13s Hang glider	30	15
3505	A1371	30s Sky diving	70	35
3506	A1371	42s Three sky divers	98	50
		Nos. 3503-3506 (4)	2.13	1.15

82nd General conference of the FAI, Varna.

Traffic Safety A1372

1989, Dec. 12

3507	A1372	5s multicolored	15	15

New Year 1990 — A1373

1989, Dec. 25 Litho. *Perf. 13*

3508	A1373	5s Santa's sleigh	15	15
3509	A1373	13s Snowman	32	16

Cats — A1374

Designs: No. 3510, Persian. No. 3511, Tiger. 8s, Tabby. No. 3513, Himalayan. No. 3514, Persian, diff. 13s, Siamese. Nos. 3511 and 3514-3515 vert.

Perf. 13½x13, 13x13½

1989, Dec. 26 Background Color

3510	A1374	5s gray	15	15
3511	A1374	5s yellow	15	15
3512	A1374	8s orange	20	15
3513	A1374	10s blue	24	15
3514	A1374	10s brown orange	24	15
3515	A1374	13s red	30	15
		Nos. 3510-3515 (6)	1.28	
		Set value		61

Explorers and Their Ships A1375

1990, Jan. 17 *Perf. 13*

3516	A1375	5s Christopher Columbus	15	15
3517	A1375	8s Vasco da Gama	20	15
3518	A1375	13s Fernando Magellan	30	15
3519	A1375	32s Sir Francis Drake	78	38
3520	A1375	42s Henry Hudson	1.00	50
3521	A1375	60s James Cook	1.45	72
a.		Min. sheet of 6, #3516-3521	3.85	1.90
		Nos. 3516-3521 (6)	3.88	2.05

Natl. Esperanto Movement, Cent. — A1376

1990, Feb. 23 Litho. *Perf. 13*

3522	A1376	10s multicolored	25	15

Paintings by Foreign Artists in the Natl. Museum — A1377

Artists: No. 3523, Suzanna Valadon (1867-1938). No. 3524, Maurice Brianchon (1899-1978). No. 3525, Moise Kisling (1891-1953). No. 3526, Giovanni Beltraffio (1467-1516).

1990, Mar. 23 *Perf. 14*

3523	A1377	30s multicolored	65	38
3524	A1377	30s multicolored	65	38
3525	A1377	30s multicolored	65	38
3526	A1377	30s multicolored	65	38
		Nos. 3523-3526 (4)	2.60	1.52

1990 World Soccer Championships, Italy — A1378

Various athletes.

1990, Mar. 26 *Perf. 13*

3527	A1378	5s multicolored	15	15
3528	A1378	13s multi, diff.	28	15
3529	A1378	30s multi, diff.	70	38
3530	A1378	42s multi, diff.	95	50
		Nos. 3527-3530 (4)	2.08	1.18

Souvenir Sheet

3531		Sheet of 2	2.25	1.20
a.	A1378	50s Three players	1.10	60
b.	A1378	50s Two players	1.10	60

Bavaria No. 1 A1379

1990, Apr. 6 Litho. *Perf. 13*

3532	A1379	42s ver & blk	1.00	50

ESSEN '90, Germany, Apr. 12-22. No. 3532 printed in sheets of 3 + 3 labels.

Souvenir Sheet

Penny Black, 150th Anniv. A1380

1990, Apr. 10

3533		Sheet of 2	2.25	1.20
a.	A1380	50s Great Britain #1	1.10	60
b.	A1380	50s Sir Rowland Hill	1.10	60

Cooperative Farming in Bulgaria, Cent. — A1381

1990, Apr. 17

3534	A1381	5s multicolored	15	15

Dimitar Chorbadjiski-Chudomir (1890-1967) — A1382

1990, Apr. 24

3535	A1382	5s multicolored	15	15

Labor Day, Cent. — A1383

1990, May 1 *Perf. 13x13½*

3536	A1383	10s multicolored	25	15

ITU, 125th Anniv. — A1384

1990, May 13 Litho. *Perf. 13½x13*

3537	A1384	20s blue, red & black	45	24

Belgium No. 1 A1385

1990, May 23 *Perf. 13*

3538	A1385	30s multicolored	75	38

Belgica '90. No. 3538 printed in sheets of 3 + 3 labels.

Lamartine (1790-1869), French Poet — A1386

1990, June 15 *Perf. 13½x13*

3539	A1386	20s multicolored	45	25

Dinosaurs — A1387

1990, June 19 *Perf. 12½*

3540	A1387	5s Brontosaurus	15	15
3541	A1387	8s Stegosaurus	20	15
3542	A1387	13s Edaphosaurus	32	16
3543	A1387	25s Rhamphorhynchus	62	30
3544	A1387	32s Protoceratops	80	40
3545	A1387	42s Triceratops	1.05	55
a.		Min. sheet of 6, #3540-3545	3.25	1.60
		Nos. 3540-3545 (6)	3.14	1.71

1992 Summer Olympic Games, Barcelona — A1388

1990, July 13 *Perf. 13½x13*

3546	A1388	5s Swimming	15	15
3547	A1388	13s Handball	32	16
3548	A1388	30s Hurdling	75	38
3549	A1388	42s Cycling	1.05	55
		Nos. 3546-3549 (4)	2.27	1.24

Souvenir Sheet

3550		Sheet of 2	2.50	1.25
a.	A1388	50s Tennis, forehand	1.25	62
b.	A1388	50s Tennis, backhand	1.25	62

Butterflies A1389

1990, Aug. 8 Litho. *Perf. 13*

3551	A1389	5s Zerynthia Polyxena	15	15
3552	A1389	10s Panaxia quadripunctaria	22	15
3553	A1389	20s Proserpinus proserpina	45	24
3554	A1389	30s Hyles lineata	65	36
3555	A1389	42s Thecla betulae	95	55
3556	A1389	60s Euphydryas cynthia	1.25	72
a.		Min. sheet of 6, #3551-3556	4.00	2.10
		Nos. 3551-3556 (6)	3.67	2.17

Airplanes — A1390

1990, Aug. 30 Litho. *Perf. 13½x13*

3557	A1390	5s Airbus A-300	15	15
3558	A1390	10s Tu-204	18	15
3559	A1390	25s Concorde	42	30
3560	A1390	30s DC-9	52	36
3561	A1390	42s Il-86	75	55
3562	A1390	60s Boeing 747	1.00	72
a.		Min. sheet of 6, #3557-3562	3.25	2.15
		Nos. 3557-3562 (6)	3.02	2.23

Exarch Joseph I (1840-1915), Religious Leader — A1391

1990, Sept. 27 *Perf. 13*

3563 A1391 5s blk, pur & grn		15	15

Intl. Traffic Safety Year A1392

1990, Oct. 9 **Litho.** *Perf. 13*

3564 A1392 5s multicolored		15	15

Olymphilex '90, Varna — A1393

1990, Oct. 16 *Perf. 13x13½*

3565 A1393	5s Shot put	15	15
3566 A1393	13s Discus	25	15
3567 A1393	42s Hammer throw	90	55
3568 A1393	60s Javelin	1.25	72
a.	Souv. sheet of 4, #3565-3568, imperf.	12.00	1.50
	Nos. 3565-3568 (4)	2.55	1.57

Space Exploration — A1394

Designs: 5s, Sputnik, 1957, USSR. 8s, Vostok, 1961, USSR. 10s, Voshkod 2, 1965, USSR. 20s, Apollo-Soyuz, 1975, US-USSR. 42s, Space Shuttle Columbia, 1981, US. 60s, Galileo, 1989-1996, US. 1 l, Apollo 11 Moon landing, 1969, US.

1990, Oct. 22 *Perf. 13½x13*

3569 A1394	5s multicolored	15	15
3570 A1394	8s multicolored	16	15
3571 A1394	10s multicolored	20	15
3572 A1394	20s multicolored	40	24
3573 A1394	42s multicolored	90	55
3574 A1394	60s multicolored	1.25	72
	Nos. 3569-3574 (6)	3.06	1.96

Souvenir Sheet

3575 A1394	1 l multicolored	2.75	1.50

St. Clement of Okhrida — A1395

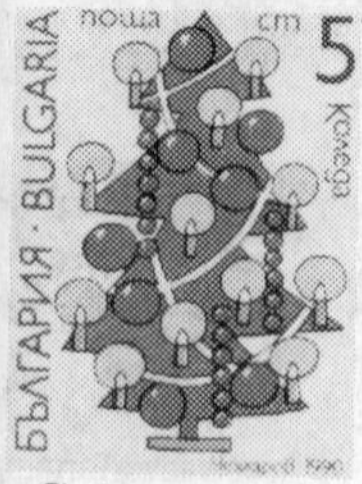

Christmas — A1396

1990, Nov. 29 **Litho.** *Perf. 13*

3576 A1395 5s multicolored		15	15

1990, Dec. 25 **Litho.** *Perf. 13*

3577 A1396	5s Christmas tree	15	15
3578 A1396	20s Santa Claus	40	24
	Set value		30

European Figure Skating Championships, Sofia — A1397

1991, Jan. 18 *Perf. 13½x13*

3579 A1397 15s multicolored		35	18

Farm Animals — A1398

1991 *Perf. 14x13½*

3581 A1398	20s Sheep	30	18
3582 A1398	25s Goose	35	22
3583 A1398	30s Hen, chicks	42	28
3584 A1398	40s Horse	55	35
3585 A1398	62s Goat	85	55
3586 A1398	86s Sow	1.25	75
3587 A1398	95s Goat	70	42
3588 A1398	1 l Donkey	1.40	90
3589 A1398	2 l Bull	2.75	1.75
3590 A1398	5 l Turkey	7.00	4.25
3591 A1398	10 l Cow	14.00	8.50
	Nos. 3581-3591 (11)	29.57	18.15

Issued: 20s, 25s, 40s, 86s, 1 l, Aug. 21; 10 l, Feb. 22; 95s, May 5, 1992; others, Feb. 11, 1991.

Mushrooms A1399

1991, Mar. 19 *Perf. 12½x13*

3597 A1399	5s Amanita phalloides	15	15
3598 A1399	10s Amanita verna	16	15
3599 A1399	20s Amanita pantherina	32	18
3600 A1399	32s Amanita muscaria	55	30
3601 A1399	42s Gyromitra esculenta	70	38
3602 A1399	60s Boletus satanas	95	55
a.	Min. sheet of 6, #3597-3602	3.00	1.50
	Nos. 3597-3602 (6)	2.83	1.71

French Impressionists A1400

Designs: 20s, Good Morning, by Gauguin. 43s, Madame Dobini, by Degas. 62s, Peasant Woman, by Pissarro. 67s, Woman with Black Hair, by Manet. 80s, Blue Vase, by Cezanne. 2 l, Jeanny Samari, by Renoir. 3 l, Self portrait, by Van Gogh.

1991, Apr. 1 *Perf. 13*

3603 A1400	20s multicolored	22	18
3604 A1400	43s multicolored	50	38
3605 A1400	62s multicolored	70	55
3606 A1400	67s multicolored	80	60
3607 A1400	80s multicolored	1.00	75
3608 A1400	2 l multicolored	2.25	1.75
	Nos. 3603-3608 (6)	5.47	4.21

Miniature Sheet

3609 A1400	3 l multicolored	4.50	2.65

Swiss Confederation, 700th Anniv. — A1401

1991, Apr. 11

3610 A1401 62s multicolored		90	55

Philatelic Review, Cent. — A1402

1991, May 7 **Litho.** *Perf. 13*

3611 A1402 30s multicolored		45	25

Europa — A1403

1991, May 10 *Perf. 13x13½*

3612 A1403	43s Meteosat	70	38
3613 A1403	62s Ariane rocket	1.00	55

Horses A1404

1991, May 21 *Perf. 13x12½*

3614 A1404	5s Przewalski's horse	15	15
3615 A1404	10s Tarpan	16	15
3616 A1404	25s Arabian	40	22
3617 A1404	35s Arabian	55	32
3618 A1404	42s Shetland pony	65	38
3619 A1404	60s Draft horse	90	55
a.	Min. sheet of 6, #3614-3619	3.00	1.65
	Nos. 3614-3619 (6)	2.81	1.77

EXPO 91, Plovdiv — A1405

1991, June 6 **Litho.** *Perf. 13½x13*

3620 A1405 30s multicolored		45	28

Wolfgang Amadeus Mozart A1406

1991, July 2 *Perf. 13*

3621 A1406 62s multicolored		95	55

Space Shuttle Missions, 10th Anniv. A1407

1991, July 23 **Litho.** *Perf. 13*

3622 A1407	12s Columbia	16	15
3623 A1407	32s Challenger	45	30
3624 A1407	50s Discovery	70	45
3625 A1407	86s Atlantis, vert.	1.25	75
3626 A1407	1.50 l Buran, vert.	2.25	1.30
3627 A1407	2 l Atlantis, diff., vert.	2.75	1.75
	Nos. 3622-3627 (6)	7.56	4.70

Souvenir Sheet

3628 A1407	3 l US shuttle, earth	4.50	2.65

1992 Winter Olympics, Albertville — A1408

1991, Aug. 7 **Litho.** *Perf. 13x13½*

3629 A1408	30s Luge	40	28
3630 A1408	43s Slalom skiing	52	38
3631 A1408	67s Ski jumping	85	60
3632 A1408	2 l Biathlon	2.50	1.75
	Nos. 3629-3632 (4)	4.27	3.01

Souvenir Sheet

3633 A1408	3 l Two-man bobsled	4.50	2.65

Sheraton Sofia Hotel Balkan A1409

1991, Sept. 6 Litho. *Perf. 13*

3634	A1409	62s multicolored	1.10	55
a.		Sheet of 3 + 3 labels	3.30	1.65

Dogs — A1410

1991, Oct. 11 *Perf. 13x13½*

3635	A1410	30s Japanese	52	26
3636	A1410	43s Chihuahua	75	38
3637	A1410	62s Pinscher	1.10	55
3638	A1410	80s Yorkshire terrier	1.40	70
3639	A1410	1 l Chinese	1.75	90
3640	A1410	3 l Pug	5.25	2.65
a.		Min. sheet of 6, #3635-3640	10.80	5.45
		Nos. 3635-3640 (6)	10.77	5.44

Cologne '91, Intl. Philatelic Exhibition A1411

1991, Oct. 21 *Perf. 13*

3641	A1411	86s multicolored	1.50	75

Printed in sheets of 3 + 3 labels.

Souvenir Sheet

Brandenburg Gate, Bicent. — A1412

1991, Oct. 23

3642	A1412	4 l multicolored	7.00	3.50

Exists imperf.

Phila Nippon '91 A1413

1991, Nov. 11

3643	A1413	62s Japan #1	1.10	55

Printed in miniature sheets of 3 + 3 labels.

Bulgarian Railroad, 125th Anniv. — A1414

1991, Nov. 30

3644	A1414	30s Locomotive	55	28
3645	A1414	30s Passenger car	55	28

Medicinal Plants A1415

Designs: 30s, Pulsatilla vernalis. 40s, Pulsatilla pratensis. 55s, Pulsatilla halleri. 60s, Aquilegia nigricans. 1 l, Hippophae rhamnoides. 2 l, Ribes nigrum.

1991, Nov. 20 Litho. *Perf. 13*

3646	A1415	30s +15s label	78	38
3647	A1415	40s multicolored	70	35
3648	A1415	55s multicolored	95	48
3649	A1415	60s multicolored	1.05	58
3650	A1415	1 l multicolored	1.75	90
3651	A1415	2 l multicolored	3.50	1.75
a.		Min. sheet of 6, #3646-3651	8.75	4.45
		Nos. 3646-3651 (6)	8.73	4.44

No. 3646 printed se-tenant with label. No. 3651a sold for 5 l, but does not contain the 15s label printed with No. 3646.

Basketball, Cent. A1416

1991, Dec. 6 *Perf. 13½x13*

3652	A1416	43s Ball below rim	75	38
3653	A1416	62s Ball at rim	1.10	55
3654	A1416	90s Ball in cylinder	1.60	80
3655	A1416	1 l Ball in basket	1.75	90
		Nos. 3652-3655 (4)	5.20	2.63

El Greco, 450th Birth Anniv. — A1417

Paintings: 43s, Christ Carrying the Cross. 50s, Holy Family with St. Anne. 60s, St. John the Evangelist and St. John the Baptist. 62s, St. Andrew and St. Francis. 1 l, Holy Family with St. Mary Magdalene. 2 l, Cardinal Nino de Guevara. 3 l, Holy Family with St. Anne (detail).

1991, Dec. 13 *Perf. 13*

3656	A1417	43s multicolored	75	38
3657	A1417	50s multicolored	90	45
3658	A1417	60s multicolored	1.05	52
3659	A1417	62s multicolored	1.10	55
3660	A1417	1 l multicolored	1.75	90
3661	A1417	2 l multicolored	3.50	1.75
		Nos. 3656-3661 (6)	9.05	4.55

Souvenir Sheet

3662	A1417	3 l multicolored	5.25	2.65

No. 3662 contains one 43x53mm stamp.

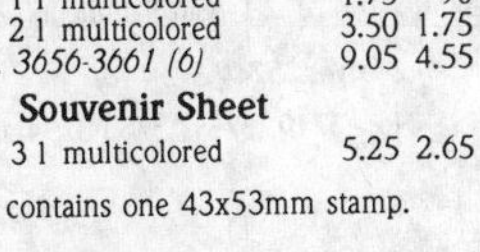

Christmas A1418

1991, Dec. 18

3663	A1418	30s Snowman, candle, bell, heart	55	28
3664	A1418	62s Star, angel, flower, house, tree	1.10	55

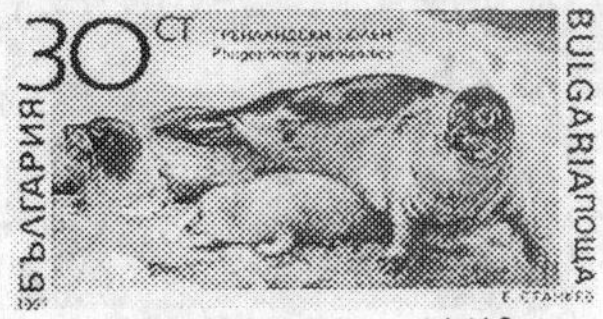

Marine Mammals — A1419

Designs: 30s, Phogophoca graenlandica. 43s, Orcinus orca. 62s, Odobenus rosmarus. 68s, Tursiops truncatus. 1 l, Monachus monachus. 2 l, Phocaena phocaena.

1991, Dec. 24

3665	A1419	30s multicolored	52	26
3666	A1419	43s multicolored	75	38
3667	A1419	62s multicolored	1.10	55
3668	A1419	68s multicolored	1.20	60
3669	A1419	1 l multicolored	1.75	90
3670	A1419	2 l multicolored	3.50	1.75
a.		Min. sheet of #3665-3670	8.85	4.45
		Nos. 3665-3670 (6)	8.82	4.44

Settlement of Jews in Bulgaria, 500th Anniv. — A1420

1992, Mar. 5 Litho. *Perf. 13*

3671	A1420	1 l multicolored	1.75	90

Gioacchino Rossini (1792-1868), Composer — A1421

1992, Mar. 11

3672	A1421	50s multicolored	88	45

Plovdiv Fair, Cent. A1422

1992, Mar. 25

3673	A1422	1 l buff & black	1.75	90

Fiat Croma — A1423

Automobiles.

1992, Mar. 26 *Perf. 13½x13*

3674	A1423	30s Volvo 740	52	26
3675	A1423	45s Ford Escort	80	40
3676	A1423	50s shown	90	45
3677	A1423	50s Mercedes 600	90	45
3678	A1423	1 l Peugeot 605	1.75	90
3679	A1423	2 l BMW 316	3.50	1.75
		Nos. 3674-3679 (6)	8.37	4.21

Francisco de Orellana — A1424

Explorers: No. 3681, Vespucci. No. 3682, Magellan. No. 3683, Gonzalo Jimenez de Quesada (1500-1579). 2 l, Drake. 3 l, Pedro de Valdivia (1500-1553). 4 l, Columbus.

1992, Apr. 22 Litho. *Perf. 13*

3680	A1424	50s multicolored	45	22
3681	A1424	50s multicolored	45	22
3682	A1424	1 l multicolored	90	45
3683	A1424	1 l multicolored	90	45
3684	A1424	2 l multicolored	1.80	90
3685	A1424	3 l multicolored	2.70	1.35
		Nos. 3680-3685 (6)	7.20	3.59

Souvenir Sheet

3686	A1424	4 l multicolored	3.50	1.75

Granada '92 A1425

1992, Apr. 23

3687	A1425	62s multicolored	55	28

No. 3687 printed in sheets of 3 + 3 labels.

Discovery of America, 500th Anniv. A1426

1992, Apr. 24

3688	A1426	1 l Ships, map	90	45
3689	A1426	2 l Columbus, ship	1.80	90
a.		Pair, #3688-3689	2.60	1.30

Europa.

SOS Children's Village A1427

1992, June 15 Litho. *Perf. 13*

3690	A1427	1 l multicolored	90	45

1992 Summer Olympics, Barcelona A1428

1992, July 15 *Perf. 13½x13*

3691	A1428	50s Swimming	45	22
3692	A1428	50s Long jump	45	22
3693	A1428	1 l High jump	90	45
3694	A1428	3 l Gymnastics	2.70	1.35
		Nos. 3691-3694 (4)	4.50	2.24

Souvenir Sheet

Perf. 13x13½

3695	A1428	4 l Torch, vert.	3.60	1.80

Motorcycles A1429

Designs: 30s, 1902 Laurin & Klement. No. 3697, 1928 Puch 200 Luxus. No. 3698, 1931 Norton CS1. 70s, 1950 Harley Davidson. 1 l, 1986 Gilera SP 01. 2 l, 1990 BMW K1.

1992, July 30 *Perf. 13*

3696	A1429	30s multicolored	28	15
3697	A1429	50s multicolored	45	22
3698	A1429	50s multicolored	45	22
3699	A1429	70s multicolored	62	30
3700	A1429	1 l multicolored	90	45
3701	A1429	2 l multicolored	1.80	90
		Nos. 3696-3701 (6)	4.50	2.24

Genoa '92 Intl. Philatelic Exhibition A1430

1992, Sept. 18 *Perf. 13*

3702	A1430	1 l multicolored	90	45

Issued: This is a developing set. Numbers may change.

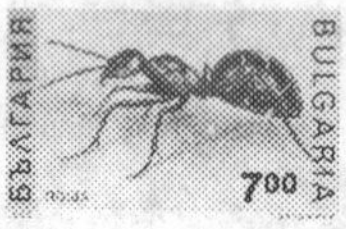

Insects — A1431

1992 Litho. *Perf. 14x13½*

3710	A1431	1 l Dragonfly	*15*
3711	A1431	2 l Mayfly	*22*
3712	A1431	3 l Locust	*32*
3713	A1431	4 l Stag beetle	*45*
3714	A1431	5 l Carrion beetle	*55*
3715	A1431	7 l Ant	*75*
3718	A1431	20 l Bee	*2.25*
3718A	A1431	50 l Praying mantis	*5.75*
		Nos. 3710-3718A (8)	*10.44*

Issued: 7, 20 l, Sept. 25; 3, 50 l, Nov. 30; 1, 2, 4, 5 l, Dec. 15, 1993.
This is a developing set. Numbers may change.

Based on available currency exchange rates the face value of No. 3718A is about $2. It appears that Bulgarian stamps are appearing in the market at significantly higher prices.

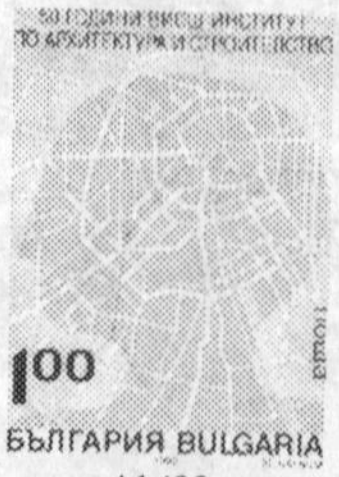

A1432

A1433

1992, Sept. 30 *Perf. 13*

3719	A1432	1 l blk, pink & rose	90	45

Higher Institute of Architecture and Building, 50th anniv.

1992, Oct. 16 Litho. *Perf. 13*

Trees: No. 3720, Quercus mestensis. No. 3721, Aesculus hippocastanum. No. 3722, Quercus thracica. No. 3723, Pinus peuce. 2 l, Acer heldreichii. 3 l, Pyrus bulgarica.

3720	A1433	50s multicolored	45	22
3721	A1433	50s multicolored	45	22
3722	A1433	1 l multicolored	90	45
3723	A1433	1 l multicolored	90	45
3724	A1433	2 l multicolored	1.80	90
3725	A1433	3 l multicolored	2.70	1.35
		Nos. 3720-3725 (6)	7.20	3.59

Ethnographical Museum, Cent. — A1434

1992, Oct. 23

3726	A1434	1 l multicolored	90	45

Tanker Bulgaria — A1435

1992, Oct. 30 Litho. *Perf. 13*

3727	A1435	30s Freighter Bulgaria	28	15
3728	A1435	50s Castor	45	22
3729	A1435	1 l Hero of Sevastopol	90	45
3730	A1435	2 l shown	1.80	90
3731	A1435	2 l Aleko Constantinov	1.80	90
3732	A1435	3 l Varna	2.70	1.35
		Nos. 3727-3732 (6)	7.93	3.97

Bulgarian Merchant Fleet, Cent.

Bulgaria, Member of the Council of Europe — A1436

1992, Nov. 6 Litho. *Perf. 13*

3733	A1436	7 l multicolored	6.30	3.15

Souvenir Sheet

4th World Congress of Popular Sports, Varna — A1437

1992, Nov. 17 Litho. *Perf. 13*

3734	A1437	4 l multicolored	*4.00*

Christmas A1438

1992, Dec. 1 *Perf. 13½x13*

3735	A1438	1 l Santa Claus	*75*
3736	A1438	7 l Madonna & Child	*5.25*

Wild Cats — A1439

1992, Dec. 18 Litho. *Perf. 13*

3737	A1439	50s Panthera pardus	*38*
3738	A1439	50s Acinonyx jubatus	*38*
3739	A1439	1 l Panthera onca	*75*
3740	A1439	2 l Panthera tigris	*1.50*
3741	A1439	2 l Felis concolor	*1.50*
3742	A1439	3 l Panthera leo	*2.25*
		Nos. 3737-3742 (6)	*6.76*

Sports A1440

1992, Dec. 18

3743	A1440	50s Baseball	*38*
3744	A1440	50s Cricket	*38*
3745	A1440	1 l Polo	*75*
3746	A1440	1 l Harness racing	*75*
3747	A1440	2 l Field hockey	*1.50*
3748	A1440	3 l Football	*2.25*
		Nos. 3743-3748 (6)	*6.01*

Owls A1441

1992, Dec. 23

3749	A1441	30s Aegolius funereus	*25*
3750	A1441	50s Strix aluco	*38*
3751	A1441	1 l Asio otus	*75*
3752	A1441	2 l Otus scops	*1.50*
3753	A1441	2 l Asio flammeus	*1.50*
3754	A1441	3 l Tyto alba	*2.25*
		Nos. 3749-3754 (6)	*6.63*

Nos. 3749, 3751, 3753-3754 are vert.

Paintings Depicting History of Bulgaria A1442

Artists: 50s, Dimiter Gyudzhenov. 1 l, 3 l, Nikolai Pavlovich. 2 l, Dimiter Panchev. 4 l, Mito Ganovski.

1992, Dec. 28

3755	A1442	50s multicolored	*38*
3756	A1442	1 l multicolored	*75*
3757	A1442	2 l multicolored	*1.50*
3758	A1442	3 l multicolored	*2.25*
		Nos. 3755-3758 (4)	*4.88*

Souvenir Sheet

3759	A1442	4 l multicolored, vert.	3.00

Archeological Museum, Cent. — A1443

1993 World Biathlon Championships, Borovetz — A1444

1993, Jan. 1 Litho. *Perf. 13x13½*

3760	A1443	1 l multicolored	*75*

1993, Feb. 5

3761	A1444	1 l Woman aiming rifle	*75*
3762	A1444	7 l Skiing	*5.25*

Neophit Rilski, Birth Bicent. A1445

1993, Apr. 22 Litho. *Perf. 13½x13*

3763	A1445	1 l henna brn & ol bis	*75*

Contemporary Art — A1446

Europa: 3 l, Sculpture of centaur, by Georgi Chapkinov. 8 l, Painting of geometric forms, by D. Bujukliski.

1993, Apr. 29 *Perf. 13x13½*

3764	A1446	3 l multicolored	*2.25*
3765	A1446	8 l multicolored	*6.00*

Fish A1447

1993, June 29 Litho. *Perf. 13*

3766	A1447	1 l C.a.j. bicaudatus	*75*
3767	A1447	2 l Mollienesia velifera	*1.50*
3768	A1447	3 l Aphyosemion bivittatum	*2.25*
3769	A1447	3 l Pterophyllum eimekei	*2.25*
3770	A1447	4 l Symphysodon discus	*3.00*
3771	A1447	8 l Trichogaster leeri	*6.00*
		Nos. 3766-3771 (6)	*15.75*

Fruit — A1448

1993, July 8 *Perf. 13x13½*

3772	A1448	1 l Malus domestica	*75*
3773	A1448	2 l Pyrus sativa	*1.50*
3774	A1448	2 l Persica vulgaris	*1.50*
3775	A1448	3 l Cydonia oblonga	*2.25*

3776 A1448 5 l Punica granatum *3.75*
3777 A1448 7 l Ficus carica *5.25*
Nos. 3772-3777 (6) *15.00*

Claudio Monteverdi (1567-1643), Composer
A1449

1993, July 20 Litho. *Perf. 13¹/₂x13*
3778 A1449 1 l multicolored *75*

17th World Summer Games for the Deaf
A1450

1993, July 20 *Perf. 13*
3779 A1450 1 l shown *75*
3780 A1450 2 l Swimming *1.50*
3781 A1450 3 l Cycling *2.25*
3782 A1450 4 l Tennis *3.00*
Nos. 3779-3782 (4) *7.50*

Souvenir Sheet

3783 A1450 5 l Soccer

Miniature Sheet

A1451

Council of Preslav, Cyrillic Alphabet in Bulgaria, 1100th Anniv.: a, Baptism of Christian convert. b, Tsar Boris I (852-889). c, Tsar Simeon (893-927). d, Battle between Bulgarians and Byzantines.

1993, Sept. 16 Litho. *Perf. 13¹/₂x13*
3784 A1451 5 l Sheet of 4, #a.-d. *3.50*

Alexander of Battenberg (1857-93), Prince of Bulgaria — A1452

1993, Sept. 23 *Perf. 13x13¹/₂*
3785 A1452 3 l multicolored *50*

Peter I. Tchaikovsky (1840-93)
A1453

1993, Sept. 30 *Perf. 13¹/₂x13*
3786 A1453 3 l multicolored *50*

Small Arms
A1454

Isaac Newton (1643-1725)
A1455

1993, Oct. 22 Litho. *Perf. 13¹/₂x14*
3787 A1454 1 l Crossbow, 16th cent. *18*
3788 A1454 2 l Pistol, 18th cent. *35*
3789 A1454 3 l Luger, 1908 *50*
3790 A1454 3 l Pistol, 1873 *50*
3791 A1454 5 l Rifle, 1938 *85*
3792 A1454 7 l Kalashnikov, 1947 *1.25*
Nos. 3787-3792 (6) *3.63*

1993, Oct. 29 *Perf. 13¹/₂x13*
3793 A1455 1 l multicolored *18*

Organized Philately in Bulgaria, Cent.
A1456

1993, Nov. 16
3794 A1456 1 l multicolored *18*

Ecology
A1457

1993, Nov. 17
3795 A1457 1 l shown *18*
3796 A1457 7 l Ecology *1.25*

Game Animals
A1458

1993, Nov. 25
3797 A1458 1 l Anas platrhynchos *18*
3798 A1458 1 l Phasianus colchicus *18*
3799 A1458 2 l Vulpes vulpes *35*
3800 A1458 3 l Capreolus capreolus *50*
3801 A1458 6 l Lepus europaeus *1.00*
3802 A1458 8 l Sus scrofa *1.40*
Nos. 3797-3802 (6) *3.61*

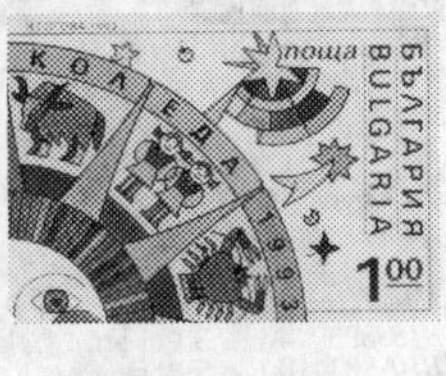

Christmas
A1459

Signs of Zodiac on sundial: No. 3803a, Taurus, Gemini, Cancer. b, Libra, Virgo, Leo.
No. 3804a, Aquarius, Pisces, Aries. b, Capricorn, Sagittarius, Scorpio.

1993, Dec. 1
3803 A1459 1 l Pair, #a.-b. *35*
3804 A1459 7 l Pair, #a.-b. *2.50*

When placed together, Nos. 3803-3804 form a complete sundial.

Regional Folk Costumes for Men
A1460 A1461

1993, Dec. 16 Litho. *Perf. 13¹/₂x14*
3805 A1460 1 l Sofia *15*
3806 A1461 1 l Plovdiv *15*
3807 A1460 2 l Belogradchik *22*
3808 A1460 3 l Shumen *32*
3809 A1461 3 l Oryakhovitsa *32*
3810 A1461 8 l Kurdzhali *90*
Nos. 3805-3810 (6) *2.06*

1994 Winter Olympics, Lillehammer
A1462

1994, Feb. 8 *Perf. 13*
3811 A1462 1 l Freestlye skiing *15*
3812 A1462 2 l Speed skating *22*
3813 A1462 3 l 2-Man luge *32*
3814 A1462 4 l Hockey *45*
Nos. 3811-3814 (4) *1.14*

Souvenir Sheet

3815 A1462 5 l Downhill skiing *55*

Nikolai Pavlovich (1835-94)
A1463

1994, Feb. 16 *Perf. 13¹/₂x13*
3816 A1463 3 l multicolored *32*

Dinosaurs
A1464

1994, Apr. 27 Litho. *Perf. 13*
3817 A1464 2 l Plesiosaurus *15*
3818 A1464 3 l Iguanodon *15*
3819 A1464 3 l Archaeopteryx *15*
3820 A1464 4 l Edmontonia *16*
3821 A1464 5 l Styracosaurus *20*
3822 A1464 7 l Tyrannosaurus Rex *28*
Nos. 3817-3822 (6) *1.09*

1994 World Cup Soccer Championships, US — A1465

Players in championships of : 3 l, Chile, 1962. 6 l, England, 1966. 7 l, Mexico, 1970. 9 l, West Germany, 1974. No. 3827a, Mexico, 1986, vert. b, US, 1994.

1994, Apr. 28
3823 A1465 3 l multicolored *15*
3824 A1465 6 l multicolored *22*
3825 A1465 7 l multicolored *28*
3826 A1465 9 l multicolored *35*
Nos. 3823-3826 (4) *1.00*

Souvenir Sheet

3827 A1465 5 l Sheet of 2, #a.-b. *40*

See No. 3851.

European Discoveries
A1466

Europa: 3 l, Axis of symmetry. 15 l, Electrocardiogram.

1994, Apr. 29 Litho. *Perf. 13¹/₂*
3828 A1466 3 l multicolored *15*
3829 A1466 15 l multicolored *60*

Boris Hristov (1914-93) — A1467

1994, May 18 Litho. *Perf. 13*
3830 A1467 3 l brown & bister *15*

Cricetus Cricetus — A1468

Designs: 3 l, In nest. 7 l, Emerging from burrow. 10 l, Standing on hind legs. 15 l, Finding berry.

1994, Sept. 23 Litho. *Perf. 13*
3831 A1468 3 l multicolored *15*
3832 A1468 7 l multicolored *28*
3833 A1468 10 l multicolored *40*
3834 A1468 15 l multicolored *60*
Nos. 3831-3834 (4) *1.43*

World Wildlife Fund.

Space Program — A1469

Intl. Olympic Committee, Cent. — A1470

1994, Nov. 4 Litho. *Perf. 13*
3835 A1469 3 l multicolored 15

1994, Nov. 7
3836 A1470 3 l multicolored 15

Icons A1471

Christmas A1472

1994, Nov. 24 Litho. *Perf. 13x13½*
3837 A1471 2 l Christ 15
3838 A1471 3 l Christ, the healer 15
3839 A1471 5 l Crucifixion 16
3840 A1471 7 l Archangel Michael 22
3841 A1471 8 l Sts. Cyril, Methodius 25
3842 A1471 15 l Madonna & Child 45
Nos. 3837-3842 (6) 1.38

1994, Dec. 1
3843 A1472 3 l Ancient coin 20
3844 A1472 15 l Coin, diff. 1.00

Roses A1473

1994, Dec. 12 *Perf. 13*
Color of Rose
3845 A1473 2 l yellow 15
3846 A1473 3 l rose red 15
3847 A1473 5 l white 16
3848 A1473 7 l salmon 22
3849 A1473 10 l carmine 32
3850 A1473 15 l orange & yellow 45
Nos. 3845-3850 (6) 1.45

No. 3827 with Additional Inscription in Sheet Margin

БЪЛГАРИЯ - С БРОНЗОВИ МЕДАЛИ

1994, Dec. 15 Litho. *Perf. 13*
3851 A1465 5 l Sheet of 2, #a.-b. 40

Trams A1474

1994, Dec. 29
3852 A1474 1 l Model 1912 15
3853 A1474 2 l Model 1928 15
3854 A1474 3 l Model 1931 15
3855 A1474 5 l Model 1942 16
3856 A1474 8 l Model 1951 25
3857 A1474 10 l Model 1961 32
Set value 88

SEMI-POSTAL STAMPS

Catalogue values for unused stamps in this section are for Never Hinged items.

Regular Issues of 1911-20 Surcharged:

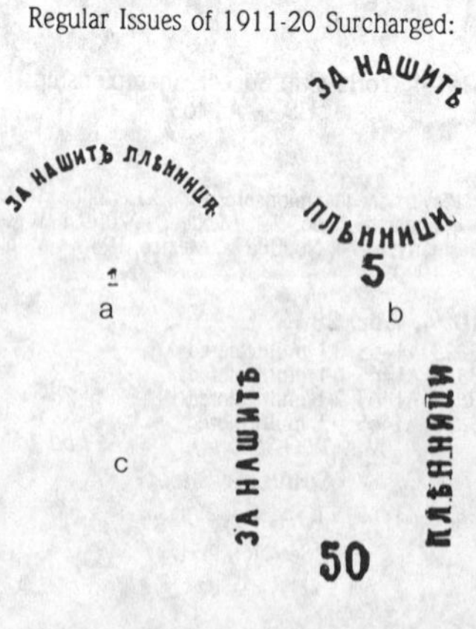

Perf. 11½x12, 12x11½
1920, June 20 Unwmk.
B1 A43 (a) 2s + 1s ol grn 15 15
B2 A44 (b) 5s + 2½s grn 15 15
B3 A44 (b) 10s + 5s rose 15 15
B4 A44 (b) 15s + 7½s vio 15 15
B5 A44 (b) 25s + 12½s dp bl 15 15
B6 A44 (b) 30s + 15s choc 15 15
B7 A44 (b) 50s + 25s yel brn 15 15
B8 A29 (c) 1 l + 50s dk brn 15 15
B9 A37a (a) 2 l + 1 l brn org 24 24
B10 A38 (a) 3 l + 1½ l claret 55 42
Set value 1.50 1.10

Surtax aided ex-prisoners of war. Value, Nos. B1-B7 imperf., $7.75.

Tsar Boris Type of 1937
Souvenir Sheet

1937, Nov. 22 Photo. *Imperf.*
B11 A140 2 l + 18 l ultra 4.50 2.50

19th anniv. of the accession of Tsar Boris III to the throne.

Stamps of 1917-21 Surcharged in Black

Наводнението
1939
1+1
лева

1939, Oct. 22 *Perf. 12½, 12*
B12 A34 1 l + 1 l on 15s slate 15 15
B13 A69 2 l + 1 l on 1½ l ol grn 15 15
B14 A69 4 l + 2 l on 2 l dp grn 18 15
B15 A69 7 l + 4 l on 3 l Prus bl 50 28
B16 A69 14 l + 7 l on 5 l red brn 85 48
Nos. B12-B16 (5) 1.83
Set value 1.00

Surtax aided victims of the Sevlievo flood. The surcharge on #B13-B16 omits "leva."

Map of Bulgaria — SP2

1947, June 6 Typo. *Perf. 11½*
B17 SP2 20 l + 10 l dk brn red & grn 45 30

30th Jubilee Esperanto Cong., Sofia, 1947.

Postman — SP3

Radio Towers — SP6

Designs: 10 l+5 l, Lineman. 20 l+10 l, Telephone operators.

1947, Nov. 5
B18 SP3 4 l + 2 l ol brn 15 15
B19 SP3 10 l + 5 l brt red 15 15
B20 SP3 20 l + 10 l dp ultra 15 15
B21 SP6 40 l + 20 l choc 70 55
Nos. B18-B21 (4) 1.15
Set value 80

Christo Ganchev — SP7

Actors' Portraits: 10 l+6 l, Adriana Budevska. 15 l+7 l, Vasil Kirkov. 20 l+15 l, Sava Ognianov. 30 l+20 l, Krostyu Sarafov.

1947, Dec. 8 Litho. *Perf. 10½*
B22 SP7 9 l + 5 l Prus grn 15 15
B23 SP7 10 l + 6 l car lake 20 15
B24 SP7 15 l + 7 l rose vio 20 15
B25 SP7 20 l + 15 l ultra 20 15
B26 SP7 30 l + 20 l vio brn 48 30
Nos. B22-B26 (5) 1.23
Set value 73

National Theater, 50th anniversary.

Souvenir Sheet

Olympic Emblem — SP8

1964, Oct. 10 Litho. *Imperf.*
B27 SP8 40s + 20s bis, red & bl 2.75 1.40

18th Olympic Games, Tokyo, Oct. 10-25.

Horsemanship Type of 1965
Miniature Sheet

1965, Sept. 30 Photo. *Imperf.*
B28 A630 40s + 20s Hurdle race 2.00 1.00

Space Exploration Type of 1966

Designs: 20s+10s, Yuri A. Gagarin, Alexei Leonov and Valentina Tereshkova. 30s+10s, Rocket and globe.

1966, Sept. 29 Photo. *Perf. 11½x11*
B29 A652 20s + 10s pur & gray 1.00 35

Miniature Sheet
B30 A652 30s + 10s gray, fawn & blk 2.00 95

Winter Olympic Games Type of 1967

Sports and Emblem: 20s+10s, Slalom. 40s+10s, Figure skating couple.

1967, Sept. Photo. *Perf. 11*
B31 A687 20s + 10s multi 1.10 28

Souvenir Sheet
Imperf
B32 A687 40s + 10s multi 2.00 85

Type of Olympic Games Issue, 1968

Designs: 20s+10s, Rowing. 50s+10s, Stadium, Mexico City, and communications satellite.

1968, June 24 Photo. *Perf. 10½*
B33 A702 20s + 10s vio bl, gray & pink 1.00 32

Miniature Sheet
Imperf
B34 A702 50s + 10s gray, blk & Prus bl 2.25 1.50

Sports Type of Regular Issue, 1969

Designs: 13s+5s, Woman with ball. 20s+10s, Acrobatic jump.

1969, Oct. Photo. *Perf. 11*
Gymnasts in Light Gray
B35 A732 13s + 5s brt rose & vio 40 15
B36 A732 20s + 10s cit & bl grn 70 30

Miniature Sheet

Soccer Ball — SP9

1970, Mar. 4 **Photo.** ***Imperf.***

B37 SP9	80s + 20s multi	2.25	1.40

9th World Soccer Championships for the Jules Rimet Cup, Mexico City, May 30-June 21, 1970.

Souvenir Sheet

Yuri A. Gagarin — SP10

1971, Apr. 12 **Photo.** ***Imperf.***

B38 SP10	40s + 20s multi	2.00	1.10

10th anniversary of the first man in space.

SP11

SP12

Bulgarian lion, magnifying glass, stamp tongs

1971, July 10 **Photo.** ***Perf. 12½***

B39 SP11	20s + 10s brn org, blk & gold	90	40

11th Congress of Bulgarian Philatelists, Sofia, July, 1971.

1989, Nov. 10 **Litho.** ***Perf. 13x13½***

Toys: a, Skateboarding. b, Doll, ball. c, Rope. d, Train set.

Souvenir Sheet

B40	Sheet of 4	2.75	1.40
a.-d.	SP12 30s +15s any single	65	35

For the benefit of the Children's Foundation.

AIR POST STAMPS

Regular Issues of 1925-26 Overprinted in Various Colors

1927-28 **Unwmk.** ***Perf. 11½***

C1 A76	2 l ol (R) ('28)	1.10	70
C2 A74	4 l lake & yel (Bl)	1.10	70
C3 A77	10 l brn blk & brn org (G) ('28)	17.00	13.00

Overprinted Vertically and Surcharged with New Value

C4 A77	1 l on 6 l dp bl & pale lem (C)	1.10	70
a.	Inverted surcharge	*325.00*	*275.00*
b.	Pair, one without surcharge	*425.00*	
	Nos. C1-C4 (4)	20.30	15.10

Nos. C2-C4 overprinted in changed colors were not issued, value set $10.50.

Dove Delivering Message — AP1

Junkers Plane, Rila Monastery — AP2

1931, Oct. 28 **Typo.**

C5 AP1	1 l dk green	18	15
C6 AP1	2 l maroon	18	15
C7 AP1	6 l dp blue	28	20
C8 AP1	12 l carmine	28	30
C9 AP1	20 l dk violet	70	55
C10 AP1	30 l dp orange	1.10	1.25
C11 AP1	50 l orange brn	2.25	1.40
	Nos. C5-C11 (7)	4.97	4.00

Counterfeits exist. See Nos. C15-C18.

1932, May 9

C12 AP2	18 l blue grn	14.00	11.00
C13 AP2	24 l dp red	14.00	11.00
C14 AP2	28 l ultra	14.00	11.00
	Nos. C12-C14 (3)	42.00	33.00

Catalogue values for unused stamps in this section, from this point to the end of the section, are for Never Hinged items.

1938, Dec. 27

C15 AP1	1 l violet brown	24	15
C16 AP1	2 l green	18	15
C17 AP1	6 l deep rose	70	28
C18 AP1	12 l peacock blue	85	32
	Nos. C15-C18 (4)	1.97	90

Counterfeits exist.

Mail Plane — AP3

Plane over Tsar Assen's Tower — AP4

Designs: 4 l, Plane over Bachkovski Monastery. 6 l, Bojurishte Airport, Sofia. 10 l, Plane, train and motorcycle. 12 l, Planes over Sofia Palace. 16 l, Plane over Pirin Valley. 19 l, Plane over Rila Monastery. 30 l, Plane and Swallow. 45 l, Plane over Sofia Cathedral. 70 l, Plane over Shipka Monument. 100 l, Plane and Royal Cipher.

1940, Jan. 15 **Photo.** ***Perf. 13***

C19 AP3	1 l dk green	15	15
C20 AP4	2 l crimson	1.10	15
C21 AP4	4 l red orange	15	15
C22 AP3	6 l dp blue	20	15
C23 AP4	10 l dk brown	30	15
C24 AP3	12 l dull brown	52	18
C25 AP3	16 l brt bl vio	55	24
C26 AP3	19 l sapphire	75	32
C27 AP4	30 l rose lake	1.10	48
C28 AP4	45 l gray violet	2.75	95
C29 AP4	70 l rose pink	2.75	1.25
C30 AP4	100 l dp slate bl	9.00	3.75
	Nos. C19-C30 (12)	19.32	7.92

Nos. 368 and 370 Overprinted in Black

1945, Jan. 26

C31 A181	1 l bright green	15	15
C32 A181	4 l red orange	15	15
	Set value	18	15

A similar overprint on Nos. O4, O5, O7 and O8 was privately applied.

Type of Parcel Post Stamps of 1944 Surcharged or Overprinted in Various Colors

Imperf

C37 PP5	10 l on 100 l dl yel (Bl)	18	15
C38 PP5	45 l on 100 l dl yel (C)	28	15
C39 PP5	75 l on 100 l dl yel (G)	38	25
C40 PP5	100 l dl yel (V)	70	35
	Nos. C37-C40 (4)	1.54	90

Plane and Sun — AP16

Pigeon with Letter — AP17

Plane, Letter — AP18

Wings, Posthorn — AP19

Winged Letter — AP20

Plane, Sun — AP21

Pigeon, Posthorn — AP22

Mail Plane — AP23

Conventionalized Figure Holding Pigeon — AP24

1946, July 15 **Litho.** ***Perf. 13***

C41 AP16	1 l dull lilac	15	15
C42 AP16	2 l slate gray	15	15
C43 AP17	4 l violet blk	15	15
C44 AP18	6 l blue	15	15
C45 AP19	10 l turq green	15	15
C46 AP19	12 l yellow brn	15	15
C47 AP20	16 l rose violet	15	15
C48 AP19	19 l carmine	15	15
C49 AP21	30 l orange	15	15
C50 AP22	45 l lt ol grn	18	15
C51 AP22	75 l red brown	24	15
C52 AP23	100 l slate blk	65	24
C53 AP24	100 l red	65	24
	Set value	2.50	1.25

No. C47 exists imperf. Value $90.

People's Republic

Plane over Plovdiv AP25

1947, Aug. 31 **Photo.** ***Imperf.***

C54 AP25	40 l dull olive grn	60	50

Plovdiv International Fair, 1947.

Baldwin's Tower — AP26

1948, May 23 **Litho.** ***Perf. 11½***

C55 AP26	50 l ol brn, *cr*	75	60

Stamp Day and the 10th Congress of Bulgarian Philatelic Societies, June 1948.

Romanian and Bulgarian Parliament Buildings AP27

Romanian and Bulgarian Flags, Bridge over Danube AP28

1948, Nov. 3 **Photo.**

C56 AP27	40 l ol gray, *cr*	22	15
C57 AP28	100 l red vio, *cr*	52	32

Romanian-Bulgarian friendship.

Mausoleum of Pleven — AP29

1949, June 26

C58 AP29	50 l brown	2.00	1.25

7th Congress of Bulgarian Philatelic Associations, June 26-27, 1949.

Symbols of the UPU — AP30

Frontier Guard and Dog — AP31

1949, Oct. 10 ***Perf. 11½***

C59 AP30	50 l violet blue	1.50	75

75th anniv. of the UPU.

1949, Oct. 31

C60 AP31	60 l olive black	1.25	90

Dimitrov Mausoleum AP32

1950, July 3 *Perf. 10½*

C61 AP32 40 l olive brown 3.00 1.10

1st anniv. of the death of George Dimitrov.

Belogradchic Rocks — AP33

Air View of Plovdiv Fair — AP34

Designs: 16s, Beach, Varna. 20s, Harvesting grain. 28s, Rila monastery. 44s, Studena dam. 60s, View of Dimitrovgrad. 80s, View of Trnovo. 1 l, University building, Sofia. 4 l, Partisans' Monument.

1954, Apr. 1 **Unwmk.** *Perf. 13*

C62 AP33	8s olive black		15	15
C63 AP34	12s rose brown		15	15
C64 AP33	16s brown		15	15
C65 AP33	20s brn red, *cream*		15	15
C66 AP33	28s dp bl, *cream*		18	15
C67 AP33	44s vio brn, *cream*		18	15
C68 AP33	60s red brn, *cream*		26	15
C69 AP34	80s dk grn, *cream*		26	18
C70 AP33	1 l dk bl grn, *cream*		1.25	35
C71 AP34	4 l deep blue		3.00	80
	Nos. C62-C71 (10)		5.73	2.38

Glider on Mountainside AP35

Designs: 60s, Glider over airport. 80s, Three gliders.

1956, Oct. 15 **Photo.**

C72 AP35	44s brt blue	16	15
C73 AP35	60s purple	30	15
C74 AP35	80s dk blue grn	48	15
	Nos. C72-C74 (3)	94	
	Set value		31

30th anniv. of glider flights in Bulgaria.

Passenger Plane AP36

1957, May 21 **Unwmk.** *Perf. 13*

C75 AP36 80s deep blue 60 32

10th anniv. of civil aviation in Bulgaria.

Sputnik 3 over Earth — AP37

1958, Nov. 28 *Perf. 11*

C76 AP37 80s brt grnsh blue 3.00 2.25

International Geophysical Year, 1957-58. Value, imperf. $7.50.

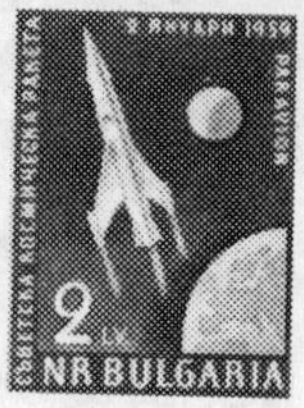

Lunik 1 Leaving Earth for Moon — AP38

1959, Feb. 28 *Perf. 10½*

C77 AP38 2 l brt blue & ocher 3.00 2.75

Launching of 1st man-made satellite to orbit moon. Value, imperf. in slightly different colors, $7.50 unused, $5.25 canceled.

Statue of Liberty and Tu-110 Airliner AP39

Perf. 10½

1959, Nov. 11 **Photo.** **Unwmk.**

C78 AP39 1 l violet bl & pink 1.75 1.50

Visit of Khrushchev to US. Value, imperf. $5.

Lunik 2 and Moon — AP40

1960, June 23 **Litho.** *Perf. 11*

C79 AP40 1.25 l blue, blk & yel 3.50 1.65

Russian rocket to the Moon, Sept. 12, 1959.

Sputnik 5 and Dogs Belka and Strelka AP41

1961, Jan. 14 **Photo.** *Perf. 11*

C80 AP41 1.25 l brt grnsh bl & org 4.00 2.50

Russian rocket flight of Aug. 19, 1970.

Maj. Yuri A. Gagarin and Vostok 1 AP42

1961, Apr. 26 **Unwmk.**

C81 AP42 4 l grnsh bl, blk & red 2.50 1.50

First manned space flight, Apr. 12, 1961.

Soviet Space Dogs — AP43

1961, June 28 *Perf. 11*

C82 AP43 2 l slate & dk car 2.00 1.00

Venus-bound Rocket — AP44

1961, June 28

C83 AP44 2 l brt bl, yel & org 4.00 2.50

Issued to commemorate the Soviet launching of the Venus space probe, Feb. 12, 1961.

Maj. Gherman Titov — AP45

Design: 1.25 l, Spaceship Vostok 2.

1961, Nov. 20 **Photo.** *Perf. 11x10½*

C84 AP45	75s dk ol grn & gray grn	1.75	1.25
C85 AP45	1.25 l vio bl, lt bl & pink	2.25	1.75

1st manned space flight around the world, Maj. Gherman Titov of Russia, Aug. 6-7, 1961.

Iskar River Narrows — AP46

Designs: 2s, Varna and sailboat. 3s, Melnik. 10s, Trnovo. 40s, Pirin mountains.

1962, Feb. 3 **Unwmk.** *Perf. 13*

C86 AP46	1s bl grn & gray bl	15	15
C87 AP46	2s blue & pink	15	15
C88 AP46	3s brown & ocher	22	15
C89 AP46	10s black & lemon	45	15
C90 AP46	40s dk green & green	1.10	28
	Nos. C86-C90 (5)	2.07	
	Set value		48

Ilyushin Turboprop Airliner AP47

1962, Aug. 18 *Perf. 11*

C91 AP47 13s blue & black 60 25

15th anniversary of TABSO airline.

Konstantin E. Tsiolkovsky and Rocket Launching AP48

Design: 13s, Earth, moon and rocket on future flight to the moon.

1962, Sept. 24 *Perf. 11*

C92 AP48	5s dp green & gray	1.90	85
C93 AP48	13s ultra & yellow	1.10	35

13th meeting of the International Astronautical Federation.

Maj. Andrian G. Nikolayev — AP49

Designs: 2s, Lt. Col. Pavel R. Popovich. 40s, Vostoks 3 and 4 in orbit.

1962, Dec. 9 **Photo.** **Unwmk.**

C94 AP49	1s bl, sl grn & blk	15	15
C95 AP49	2s bl grn, grn & blk	24	15
C96 AP49	40s dk bl grn, pink & blk	1.65	85
	Nos. C94-C96 (3)	2.04	1.15

First Russian group space flight of Vostoks 3 and 4, Aug. 12-15, 1962.

Spacecraft "Mars 1" Approaching Mars — AP50

Design: 13s, Rocket launching spacecraft, Earth, Moon and Mars.

1963, Feb. 25 **Unwmk.** *Perf. 11*

C97 AP50	5s multicolored	50	28
C98 AP50	13s multicolored	1.00	45

Launching of the Russian spacecraft "Mars 1," Nov. 1, 1962.

Lt. Col. Valeri F. Bykovski AP51

Designs: 2s, Lt. Valentina Tereshkova. 5s, Globe and trajectories.

1963, Aug. 26 **Unwmk.** *Perf. 11½*

C99 AP51	1s pale vio & Prus bl	15	15
C100 AP51	2s citron & red brn	15	15
C101 AP51	5s rose & dk red	15	15
	Set value	24	15

The space flights of Valeri Bykovski, June 14-19, and Valentina Tereshkova, first woman cosmonaut, June 16-19, 1963. An imperf. souvenir sheet contains one 50s stamp showing Spasski tower and globe in lilac and red brown. Light blue border with red brown inscription. Size: 77x67mm. Value $2.50. See No. CB3.

Nos. C99-C100 Surcharged in Magenta or Green

1964, Aug. 22

C102 AP51	10s on 1s (M)	32	18
C103 AP51	20s on 2s	65	22

International Space Exhibition in Riccione, Italy. Overprint in Italian on No. C103.

St. John's Monastery, Rila — AP52

Design: 13s, Notre Dame, Paris; French inscription.

1964, Dec. 22 Photo. *Perf. 11½*

C104 AP52	5s pale brn & blk	18	15
C105 AP52	13s lt ultra & sl bl	65	20
	Set value		27

The philatelic exhibition at St. Ouen (Seine) organized by the Franco-Russian Philatelic Circle and philatelic organizations in various People's Democracies.

Paper Mill, Bukijovtz AP53

Designs: 10s, Metal works, Plovdiv. 13s, Metal works, Kremikovtsi. 20s, Oil refinery, Stara-Zagora. 40s, Fertilizer plant, Stara-Zagora. 1 l, Rest home, Meded.

1964-68 Unwmk. *Perf. 13*

C106 AP53	8s grnsh blue	15	15
C107 AP53	10s red lilac	15	15
C108 AP53	13s brt violet	22	15
C109 AP53	20s slate blue	70	15
C110 AP53	40s dk olive grn	1.10	18
C111 AP53	1 l red ('68)	1.90	32
	Nos. C106-C111 (6)	4.22	
	Set value		75

Issue dates: 1 l, May 6. Others, Dec. 7.

Three-master — AP54

Veliko Turnovo — AP55

Means of Communication: 2s, Postal coach. 3s, Old steam locomotive. 5s, Early cars. 10s, Montgolfier balloon. 13s, Early plane. 20s, Jet planes. 40s, Rocket and satellites. 1 l, Postrider.

1969, Mar. 31 Photo. *Perf. 13x12½*

C112 AP54	1s gray & multi	15	15
C113 AP54	2s gray & multi	15	15
C114 AP54	3s gray & multi	15	15
C115 AP54	5s gray & multi	15	15
C116 AP54	10s gray & multi	15	15
C117 AP54	13s gray & multi	25	15
C118 AP54	20s gray & multi	50	22
C119 AP54	40s gray & multi	90	38
	Set value	2.00	1.00

Miniature Sheet

Imperf

C120 AP54	1 l gold & org	2.25	1.50

SOFIA 1969 Philatelic Exhibition, Sofia, May 31-June 8.

1973, July 30 Photo. *Perf. 13*

Designs: Historic buildings in various cities.

C121 AP55	2s shown	15	15
C122 AP55	13s Roussalka	25	15
C123 AP55	20s Plovdiv	1.50	80
C124 AP55	28s Sofia	65	18
	Nos. C121-C124 (4)	2.55	1.28

Aleksei A. Leonov and Soyuz AP56

Designs: 18s, Thomas P. Stafford and Apollo. 28s, Apollo and Soyuz over earth. 1 l, Apollo Soyuz link-up.

1975, July 15

C125 AP56	13s blue & multi	30	15
C126 AP56	18s purple & multi	40	15
C127 AP56	28s multicolored	1.00	28
	Nos. C125-C127 (3)	1.70	
	Set value		38

Souvenir Sheet

C128 AP56	1 l violet & multi	2.00	1.25

Apollo Soyuz space test project (Russo-American cooperation), launching July 15; link-up July 17.

Balloon Over Plovdiv — AP57

1977, Sept. 3

C129 AP57	25s yellow, brn & red	50	20

Alexei Leonov Floating in Space — AP58

Designs: 25s, Mariner 6, US spacecraft. 35s, Venera 4, USSR Venus probe.

1977, Oct. 14 Photo. *Perf. 13½*

C130 AP58	12s multicolored	20	15
C131 AP58	25s multicolored	42	15
C132 AP58	35s multicolored	60	22
	Nos. C130-C132 (3)	1.22	52

Space era, 20 years.

TU-154, Balkanair Emblem — AP59

1977 *Perf. 13*

C133 AP59	35s ultra & multi	75	35

30th anniv. of Bulgarian airline, Balkanair. Issued in sheets of 6 stamps + 3 labels (in lilac) with inscription and Balkanair emblem.

Baba Vida Fortress AP60

Design: 35s, Peace Bridge, connecting Rousse, Bulgaria, with Giurgiu, Romania.

1978 Photo. *Perf. 13*

C134 AP60	25s multicolored	40	40
C135 AP60	35s multicolored	55	55

The Danube, European Intercontinental Waterway. Issued in sheets containing 5 each of Nos. C134-C135 and 2 labels, one showing course of Danube, the other hydrofoil and fish.

Red Cross AP61

1978, Mar. Photo. *Perf. 13*

C136 AP61	25s multicolored	50	16

Centenary of Bulgarian Red Cross.

Clock Tower, Byalla Cherkva — AP62

1979, June 5 Litho. *Perf. 12x12½*

C137 AP62	13s shown	16	15
C138 AP62	23s Botevgrad	30	15
C139 AP62	25s Pazardgick	32	15
C140 AP62	35s Grabovo	42	18
C141 AP62	53s Tryavna	75	30
	Nos. C137-C141 (5)	1.95	93

1980, Oct. 22 Photo. *Perf. 12x12½*

C142 AP62	13s Bjala	20	15
C143 AP62	23s Rasgrad	35	22
C144 AP62	25s Karnabat	40	18
C145 AP62	35s Serlievo	52	25
C146 AP62	53s Berkovitza	80	35
	Nos. C142-C146 (5)	2.27	1.15

15th World Parachute Championships, Kazanluk — AP63

1980

C147 AP63	13s shown	20	15
C148 AP63	25s Parachutist	40	15
	Set value		21

DWVY-1 Aircraft — AP64

1981, June 27 Litho. *Perf. 12½*

C149 AP64	5s shown	15	15
C150 AP64	12s LAS-7	20	15
C151 AP64	25s LAS-8	40	15
C152 AP64	35s DAR-1	52	20
C153 AP64	45s DAR-3	70	26
C154 AP64	55s DAR-9	88	32
	Nos. C149-C154 (6)	2.85	1.23

Women in Space, 20th Anniv. — AP65

1983, June 28

C155	Sheet of 2	1.50	1.00
a.	AP65 50s Valentina Tereshkova	75	50
b.	AP65 50s Svetlana Savitskaya	75	50

World Communications Year — AP66

1983, July 20 Photo. *Perf. 13*

C156 AP66	5s TV tower, Tolbukhin	15	15
C157 AP66	13s Postwoman	25	15
C158 AP66	30s TV tower, Mt. Botev	60	30
a.	Strip of 3, #C156-C158	95	50
	Nos. C156-C158 (3)	1.00	
	Set value		47

Emblems of World Communications Year, Bulgarian Post, UPU and ITU on attached margins.

Souvenir Sheet

Geophysical Map of the Moon, Russia's Luna I, II and III Satellites — AP67

1984, Oct. 24 Photo. *Perf. 13*

C159 AP67	1 l multicolored	2.00	1.00

Conquest of Space.

Intl. Civil Aviation Org., 40th Anniv. — AP68

1984, Dec. 21 Photo. *Perf. 13*

C160 AP68	42s Balkan Airlines jet	85	42

Balkan Airlines — AP69

Design: Helicopter MU-8, passenger jet TU-154 and AN-21 transport plane.

1987, Aug. 25 Photo.

C161 AP69	25s multicolored	75	35

2nd Joint Soviet-Bulgarian Space Flight — AP70

Cosmonauts: A. Aleksandrov, A. Solovov and V. Savinich.

1989, June 7 Litho. *Perf. 13½x13*

C162 AP70 13s multicolored	35	18

AIR POST SEMI-POSTAL STAMPS

Catalogue values for unused stamps in this section are for Never Hinged items.

Statue of Liberty, Plane and Bridge — SPAP1

Perf. 11½.

1947, May 24 Unwmk. Litho.

CB1 SPAP1 70 l + 30 l red brn	95	95

5th Philatelic Congress, Trnovo, and CIPEX, NYC, May, 1947.

Bulgarian Worker SPAP2

1948, Feb. 28 Photo. *Perf. 12x11½.*

CB2 SPAP2 60 l hn brn, *cr*	45	35

2nd Bulgarian Workers' Congress, and sold by subscription only, at a premium of 16 l over face value.

Type of Air Post Stamps, 1963

Design: Valeri Bykovski and Valentina Tereshkova.

1963, Aug. 26 Unwmk. *Perf. 11½*

CB3 AP51 20s + 10s pale bluish grn & dk grn	1.25	45

See note after No. C101.

SPECIAL DELIVERY STAMPS

Catalogue values for unused stamps in this section are for Never Hinged items.

Postman on Bicycle — SD1

Mail Car — SD2

Postman on Motorcycle — SD3

1939 Unwmk. Photo. *Perf. 13*

E1 SD1 5 l deep blue	60	15
E2 SD2 6 l copper brn	24	15
E3 SD3 7 l golden brn	35	15
E4 SD2 8 l red orange	60	15
E5 SD1 20 l bright rose	1.25	38
Nos. E1-E5 (5)	3.04	98

POSTAGE DUE STAMPS

D1

D2

Large Lozenge Perf. 5½ to 6½

1884 Typo. Unwmk.

J1 D1 5s orange	150.00	15.00
J2 D1 25s lake	75.00	10.00
J3 D1 50s blue	12.00	5.00
Nos. J1-J3 (3)	237.00	30.00

1886 *Imperf.*

J4 D1 5s orange	75.00	2.50
J5 D1 25s lake	120.00	2.50
J6 D1 50s blue	5.00	2.75
Nos. J4-J6 (3)	200.00	7.75

1887 *Perf. 11½*

J7 D1 5s orange	9.50	1.00
J8 D1 25s lake	9.50	1.00
J9 D1 50s blue	3.50	1.00
Nos. J7-J9 (3)	22.50	3.00

Same, Redrawn

24 horizontal lines of shading in upper part instead of 30 lines

1892 *Perf. 10½, 11½*

J10 D1 5s orange	7.50	1.25
J11 D1 25s lake	7.50	1.25

1893

Pelure Paper

J12 D2 5s orange	10.00	3.50

D3

D4

1895 *Imperf.*

J13 D3 30s on 50s blue	7.00	2.00

Perf. 10½, 11½

J14 D3 30s on 50s blue	7.00	2.00

Wmk. Coat of Arms in the Sheet

1896 *Perf. 13*

J15 D4 5s orange	3.00	75
J16 D4 10s purple	2.00	75
J17 D4 30s green	1.40	45
Nos. J15-J17 (3)	6.40	1.95

Nos. J15-J17 are also known on unwatermarked paper from the edges of sheets.

In 1901 a cancellation, "T" in circle, was applied to Nos. 60-65 and used provisionally as postage dues.

D5

D6

1901-04 Unwmk. *Perf. 11½*

J19 D5 5s dl rose	20	15
J20 D5 10s yel grn	42	15
J21 D5 20s dl bl ('04)	3.25	16
J22 D5 30s vio brn	35	16
J23 D5 50s org ('02)	5.50	4.00
Nos. J19-J23 (5)	9.72	4.62

Nos. J19-J23 exist imperf. and in pairs imperf. between. Value, imperf., $250.

1915 Unwmk. *Perf. 11½*

Thin Semi-Transparent Paper

J24 D6 5s green	15	15
J25 D6 10s purple	20	15
J26 D6 20s dl rose	20	15
J27 D6 30s dp org	1.10	20
J28 D6 50s dp bl	35	17
Nos. J24-J28 (5)	2.00	
Set value		52

1919-21 *Perf. 11½, 12x11½*

J29 D6 5s emerald	15	15
a. 5s gray green ('21)	30	15
J30 D6 10s violet	15	15
J31 D6 20s salmon	15	15
a. 20s yellow	15	15
J32 D6 30s orange	15	15
a. 30s red orange ('21)	65	65
J33 D6 50s blue	15	15
J34 D6 1 l emerald ('21)	18	15
J35 D6 2 l rose ('21)	18	15
J36 D6 3 l brown org ('21)	30	15
Set value	1.16	42

Stotinki values of the above series surcharged 10s or 20s were used as ordinary postage stamps. See Nos. 182-185.

The 1919 printings are on thicker white paper with clean-cut perforations, the 1921 printings on thicker grayish paper with rough perforations.

Most of this series exist imperforate and in pairs imperforate between.

Heraldic Lion — D7

Lion of Trnovo — D8

National Arms

D9 D10

1932, Aug. 15

Thin Paper

J37 D7 1 l olive bister	24	20
J38 D7 2 l rose brown	24	20
J39 D7 6 l brown violet	75	35
Nos. J37-J39 (3)	1.23	75

1933, Apr. 10

J40 D8 20s dk brn	15	15
J41 D8 40s dp bl	15	15
J42 D8 80s car rose	15	15
J43 D9 1 l org brn	24	18
J44 D9 2 l olive	30	25
J45 D9 6 l dl vio	15	15
J46 D9 14 l ultra	24	15
Set value	1.00	78

Catalogue values for unused stamps in this section, from this point to the end of the section, are for Never Hinged items.

1947, June Typo. *Perf. 10½*

J47 D10 1 l chocolate	15	15
J48 D10 2 l deep claret	15	15
J49 D10 8 l deep orange	15	15
J50 D10 20 l blue	22	15
Set value	42	25

Arms of the People's Republic — D11

1951 *Perf. 11½x10½*

J51 D11 1 l chocolate	15	15
J52 D11 2 l claret	15	15
J53 D11 8 l red orange	22	15
J54 D11 20 l deep blue	60	32
Set value	92	52

OFFICIAL STAMPS

Catalogue values for unused stamps in this section are for Never Hinged items.

Bulgarian Coat of Arms

O1 O2

1942 Unwmk. Typo. *Perf. 13*

O1 O1 10s yel grn	15	15
O2 O1 30s red	15	15
O3 O1 50s bister	15	15
O4 O2 1 l vio bl	15	15
O5 O2 2 l dk grn	15	15
O6 O2 3 l lilac	15	15
O7 O2 4 l rose	15	15
O8 O2 5 l carmine	16	15
Set value	65	40

1944 *Perf. 10½x11½*

O9 O2 1 l blue	20	15
O10 O2 2 l brt red	20	15

Lion Rampant

O3 O4

O5

1945 *Imperf.*

O11 O5 1 l pink	15	15

Perf. 10½x11½, Imperf.

O12 O3 2 l blue green	15	15
O13 O4 3 l bister brown	15	15
O14 O4 4 l light ultra	15	15
O15 O5 5 l brown lake	15	15
Set value	25	25

In 1950, four stamps prepared for official use were issued as regular postage stamps. See Nos. 724-727.

PARCEL POST STAMPS

Catalogue values for unused stamps in this section are for Never Hinged items.

Weighing Packages — PP1

Parcel Post — PP2

Designs: 3 l, 8 l, 20 l, Parcel post truck. 4 l, 6 l, 10 l, Motorcycle.

Perf. 12½x13½, 13½x12½

1941-42 Photo. Unwmk.

Q1 PP1 1 l slate grn	15	15
Q2 PP2 2 l crimson	15	15
Q3 PP2 3 l dull brn	15	15
Q4 PP2 4 l red org	15	15
Q5 PP1 5 l deep blue	15	15

Q6	PP1	5 l slate grn ('42)	15	15
Q7	PP2	6 l red vio	15	15
Q8	PP2	6 l henna brn ('42)	15	15
Q9	PP1	7 l dark blue	15	15
Q10	PP1	7 l dk brn ('42)	15	15
Q11	PP2	8 l brt bl grn	15	15
Q12	PP2	8 l green ('42)	15	15
Q13	PP2	9 l olive gray	15	15
Q14	PP2	9 l dp olive ('42)	15	15
Q15	PP2	10 l orange	15	15
Q16	PP2	20 l gray vio	42	15
Q17	PP2	30 l dull blk	55	15
Q18	PP2	30 l sepia ('42)	50	15
		Set value	2.50	1.00

Arms of Bulgaria — PP5

1944 Litho. *Imperf.*

Q21	PP5	1 l dk carmine	15	15
Q22	PP5	3 l blue grn	15	15
Q23	PP5	5 l dull bl grn	15	15
Q24	PP5	7 l rose lilac	15	15
Q25	PP5	10 l deep blue	15	15
Q26	PP5	20 l orange brn	15	15
Q27	PP5	30 l dk brn car	15	15
Q28	PP5	50 l red orange	30	15
Q29	PP5	100 l blue	52	22
		Set value	1.30	75

For overprints and surcharges see Nos. 448-454, C37-C40.

POSTAL TAX STAMPS

The use of stamps Nos. RA1 to RA18 was compulsory on letters, etc., to be delivered on Sundays and holidays. The money received from their sale was used toward maintaining a sanatorium for employees of the post, telegraph and telephone services.

View of Sanatorium PT1

Sanatorium, Peshtera PT2

1925-29 Unwmk. Typo. *Perf. 11½*

RA1	PT1	1 l blk, *grnsh bl*	2.75	15
RA2	PT1	1 l chocolate ('26)	2.75	15
RA3	PT1	1 l orange ('27)	3.00	15
RA4	PT1	1 l pink ('28)	4.50	15
RA5	PT1	1 l vio, *pnksh* ('29)	4.25	15
RA6	PT2	2 l blue green	35	15
RA7	PT2	2 l violet ('27)	35	16
RA8	PT2	5 l deep blue	3.00	80
RA9	PT2	5 l rose ('27)	3.75	40
		Nos. RA1-RA9 (9)	24.70	2.26

St. Constantine Sanatorium PT3

1930-33

RA10	PT3	1 l red brn & ol grn	4.00	16
RA11	PT3	1 l ol grn & yel ('31)	50	16
RA12	PT3	1 l red vio & ol brn ('33)	50	16
		Nos. RA10-RA12 (3)	5.00	48

Trojan Rest Home — PT4

Sanatorium PT5

1935 Wmk. 145 *Perf. 11, 11½*

RA13	PT4	1 l choc & red org	32	15
RA14	PT4	1 l emer & indigo	32	15
RA15	PT5	5 l red brn & indigo	1.40	35
		Nos. RA13-RA15 (3)	2.04	
		Set value		51

St. Constantine Sanatorium PT6

Designs: 2 l, Children at seashore. 5 l, Rest home.

1941 Unwmk. Photo. *Perf. 13*

RA16	PT6	1 l dark olive green	15	15
RA17	PT6	2 l red orange	15	15
RA18	PT6	5 l deep blue	30	15
		Set value	50	22

See Nos. 702-705 for same designs in smaller size issued as regular postage.

BURKINA FASO

Upper Volta

LOCATION — Northwestern Africa, north of Ghana
GOVT. — Republic
AREA — 105,869 sq. mi.
POP. — 6,695,500 (est. 1984)
CAPITAL — Ouagadougou

In 1919 the French territory of Upper Volta was detached from the southern section of Upper Senegal and Niger and made a separate colony. In 1933 the colony was divided among its neighbors: French Sudan, Ivory Coast, and Niger Territory. The Republic of Upper Volta was proclaimed December 11, 1958; the name was changed to Burkina Faso on August 4, 1984.

100 Centimes = 1 Franc

Catalogue values for unused stamps in this country are for Never Hinged items, beginning with Scott 70 in the regular postage section, Scott B1 in the semi-postal section, Scott C1 in the airpost section, Scott J21 in the postage due section, and Scott O1 in the official section.

Stamps and Types of Upper Senegal and Niger, 1914-17, Overprinted in Black or Red **HAUTE-VOLTA**

1920-28 Unwmk. *Perf. 13½x14*

1	A4	1c brn vio & vio	15	15
2	A4	2c gray & brn vio (R)	15	15
3	A4	4c blk & bl	15	15
4	A4	5c yel grn & bl grn	25	15
5	A4	5c ol brn & dk brn ('22)	15	15
6	A4	10c red org & rose	38	32
7	A4	10c yel grn & bl grn ('22)	15	15
8	A4	10c claret & bl ('25)	22	22
a.		Overprint omitted	80.00	
9	A4	15c choc & org	38	28
10	A4	20c brn vio & blk (R)	55	50
11	A4	25c ultra & bl	55	28
12	A4	25c blk & bl grn ('22)	40	40
a.		Overprint omitted	65.00	
13	A4	30c ol brn & brn (R)	90	62
14	A4	30c red org & rose ('22)	35	35
15	A4	30c vio & brn red ('25)	35	35
16	A4	30c dl grn & bl grn ('27)	60	45
17	A4	35c car rose & vio	40	28
18	A4	40c gray & car rose	40	32
19	A4	45c bl & brn (R)	32	20
20	A4	50c blk & grn	1.40	1.00
21	A4	50c ultra & bl ('22)	15	15
22	A4	50c red org & bl ('25)	35	35
23	A4	60c org red ('26)	15	15
24	A4	65c bis & pale bl ('28)	60	45
25	A4	75c org & brn	28	28
26	A4	1fr brn & brn vio	55	40
27	A4	2fr grn & bl	80	60
28	A4	5fr vio & blk (R)	2.00	1.60
		Nos. 1-28 (28)	13.08	10.45

No. 9 Surcharged in Various Colors **0,01 ═ 0,01**

1922

29	A4	0,01c on 15c (Bk)	40	40
a.		Double surcharge	50.00	50.00
30	A4	0,02c on 15c (Bl)	40	40
31	A4	0,05c on 15c (R)	40	40
		Nos. 29-31 (3)	1.20	1.20

Type of 1920 Surcharged **60 ═ 60**

1922

32	A4	60c on 75c vio, *pnksh*	35	35

Stamps and Types of 1920 Surcharged with New Value and Bars

1924-27

33	A4	25c on 2fr grn & bl	40	40
34	A4	25c on 5fr vio & blk	40	40
35	A4	65c on 45c bl & brn ('25)	45	45
36	A4	85c on 75c org & brn ('25)	62	62
37	A4	90c on 75c brn red & sal pink ('27)	65	65
38	A4	1.25fr on 1fr dp bl & lt bl (R) ('26)	40	40
39	A4	1.50fr on 1fr dp bl & ultra ('27)	1.10	1.10
40	A4	3fr on 5fr dl red & brn org ('27)	1.40	1.40
41	A4	10fr on 5fr ol grn & lil rose ('27)	6.50	6.50
42	A4	20fr on 5fr org brn & vio ('27)	9.00	9.00
		Nos. 33-42 (10)	20.92	20.92

Hausa Chief — A5

Hausa Woman — A6

Hausa Warrior A7

1928 Typo. *Perf. 13½x14*

43	A5	1c indigo & grn	15	15
44	A5	2c brn & lil	15	15
45	A5	4c blk & yel	15	15
46	A5	5c indigo & gray bl	16	16
47	A5	10c indigo & pink	45	45
48	A5	15c brn & bl	80	80
49	A5	20c brn & grn	80	80
50	A6	25c brn & yel	1.00	1.00
51	A6	30c dp grn & grn	1.00	1.00
52	A6	40c blk & pink	1.00	1.00
53	A6	45c brn & blue	1.00	1.00
54	A6	50c blk & grn	1.00	1.00
55	A6	65c indigo & bl	1.40	1.40
56	A6	75c blk & lil	1.00	1.00
57	A6	90c brn red & lil	1.00	1.00

Perf. 14x13½

58	A7	1fr brn & grn	1.00	1.00
59	A7	1.10fr indigo & lil	1.00	1.00
60	A7	1.50fr ultra & grysh	1.60	1.60
61	A7	2fr blk & bl	1.90	1.90
62	A7	3fr brn & yel	2.00	2.00
63	A7	5fr brn & lil	2.00	2.00
64	A7	10fr blk & grn	8.00	8.00
65	A7	20fr blk & pink	12.00	12.00
		Nos. 43-65 (23)	40.56	40.56

Colonial Exposition Issue

Common Design Types

1931 Engr. *Perf. 12½*

Country Name Typo. in Black

66	CD70	40c dp grn	1.50	1.50
67	CD71	50c violet	1.50	1.50
68	CD72	90c red org	1.50	1.50
69	CD73	1.50fr dull blue	2.00	2.00
		Nos. 66-69 (4)	6.50	6.50

Common Design Types pictured in section at front of book.

Catalogue values for unused stamps in this section, from this point to the end of the section, are for Never Hinged items.

Republic

President Ouezzin Coulibaly — A8

Deer Mask and Deer — A9

1959 Unwmk. Engr. *Perf. 13*

70	A8	25fr black & mag	25	15

1st anniv. of the proclamation of the Republic; Ouezzin Coulibaly, Council President, who died in December, 1958.

Imperforates
Most Upper Volta stamps from 1959 onward exist imperforate in issued and trial colors, and also in small presentation sheets in issued colors.

1960

Animal Masks: 1fr, 2fr, 4fr, Wart hog. 5fr, 6fr, 8fr, Monkey. 10fr, 15fr, 20fr, Buffalo. 25fr, Coba (antelope). 30fr, 40fr, 50fr, Elephant. 60fr, 85fr, Secretary bird.

71	A9	30c rose & vio	15	15
72	A9	40c buff & dp cl	15	15
73	A9	50c bl grn & gray ol	15	15
74	A9	1fr red, blk & red brn	15	15
75	A9	2fr emer, yel grn & dk grn	15	15
76	A9	4fr bl, vio & ind	15	15
77	A9	5fr ol bis, red & brn	15	15
78	A9	6fr grnsh bl & vio brn	15	15
79	A9	8fr org & red brn	15	15
80	A9	10fr lt yel grn & plum	15	15
81	A9	15fr org, ultra & brn	15	15
82	A9	20fr green & ultra	22	15
83	A9	25fr bl, emer & dp cl	25	15
84	A9	30fr dk bl grn, blk & brn	30	15
85	A9	40fr ultra, ind & dk car	38	15
86	A9	50fr brt pink, brn & grn	42	18
87	A9	60fr org brn & bl	55	25
88	A9	85fr gray ol & dk bl	80	32
		Set value	3.60	1.80

C.C.T.A. Issue

Common Design Type

1960 Engr. *Perf. 13*

89	CD106	25fr vio bl & slate	35	35

Values quoted in this catalogue are for stamps graded Fine-Very Fine and with no faults. An illustrated guide to grade is provided in the "Catalogue Information" section of the Introduction.

Emblem of the Entente — A9a

Pres. Maurice Yameogo — A10

1960 Photo. *Perf. 13x13¹/₂*
90 A9a 25fr multicolored 40 35

Council of the Entente.

1960, May 1 Engr. *Perf. 13*
91 A10 25fr dk vio brn & slate 25 16

Flag, Village and Couple — A11

1960, Aug. 5 Unwmk. *Perf. 13*
92 A11 25fr red brn, blk & red 35 25

Proclamation of independence, Aug. 5, 1960.

World Meteorological Organization Emblem — A12

1961, May 4
93 A12 25fr blk, bl & red 30 25

First World Meteorological Day.

Arms of Republic — A13

1961, Dec. 8 Photo. *Perf. 12x12¹/₂*
94 A13 25fr multicolored 25 25

The 1961 independence celebrations.

WMO Emblem, Weather Station and Sorghum Grain — A14

1962, Mar. 23 Unwmk. *Perf. 13*
95 A14 25fr dk bl, emer & brn 30 25

UN 2nd World Meteorological Day, Mar. 23.

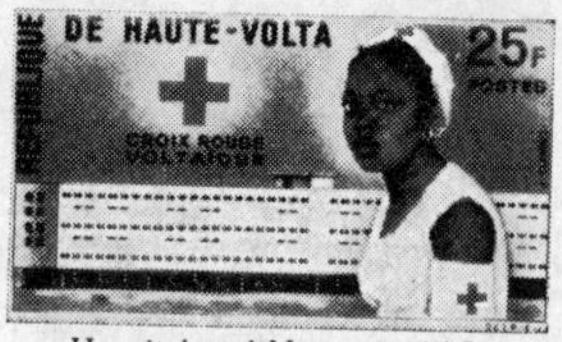
Hospital and Nurse — A15

1962, June 23 *Perf. 13x12*
96 A15 25fr multicolored 35 35

Founding of Upper Volta Red Cross.

Buffalos at Water Hole — A16

Designs: 10fr, Lions, horiz. 15fr, Defassa waterbuck. 25fr, Arly reservation, horiz. 50fr, Diapaga reservation, horiz. 85fr, Buffon's kob.

Perf. 12¹/₂x12, 12x12¹/₂
1962, June 30 Engr.

97	A16	5fr sepia, bl & grn	15	15
98	A16	10fr red brn, grn & yel	16	15
99	A16	15fr sepia, grn & yel	25	16
100	A16	25fr vio brn, bl & grn	45	20
101	A16	50fr vio brn, bl & grn	80	55
102	A16	85fr red brn, bl & grn	1.20	80
		Nos. 97-102 (6)	3.01	2.01

Abidjan Games Issue
Common Design Type

Designs: 20fr, Soccer. 25fr, Bicycling. 85fr, Boxing. All horiz.

1962, July 21 Photo. *Perf. 12¹/₂x12*

103	CD109	20fr multicolored	25	18
104	CD109	25fr multicolored	30	25
105	CD109	85fr multicolored	60	40
		Nos. 103-105 (3)	1.15	83

African-Malgache Union Issue
Common Design Type

1962, Sept. 8 Unwmk.
106 CD110 30fr red, bluish grn & gold 70 65

Weather Map and UN Emblem A17

1963, Mar. 23 *Perf. 12x12¹/₂*
107 A17 70fr multicolored 60 45

3rd World Meteorological Day, Mar. 23.

Friendship Games, Dakar, Apr. 11-21 — A18

1963, Apr. 11 Engr. *Perf. 13*

108	A18	20fr Basketball	22	15
109	A18	25fr Discus	25	15
110	A18	50fr Judo	55	25
		Nos. 108-110 (3)	1.02	55

Amaryllis A19

Flowers: 50c, Hibiscus. 1fr, Oldenlandia grandiflora. 1.50fr, Rose moss (portulaca). 2fr, Tobacco. 4fr, Morning glory. 5fr, Striga senegalensis. 6fr, Cowpea. 8fr, Lepidagathis heudelotiana. 10fr, Spurge. 25fr, Argyreia nervosa. 30fr, Rangoon creeper. 40fr, Water lily. 50fr, White plumeria. 60fr, Crotalaria retusa. 85fr, Hibiscus. Nos. 111-119 are vert.

1963 Photo.

111	A19	50c multicolored	15	15
112	A19	1fr multicolored	15	15
113	A19	1.50fr multicolored	15	15
114	A19	2fr multicolored	15	15
115	A19	4fr multicolored	15	15
116	A19	5fr multicolored	15	15
117	A19	6fr multicolored	15	15
118	A19	8fr multicolored	15	15
119	A19	10fr multicolored	16	15
120	A19	15fr multicolored	20	15
121	A19	25fr multicolored	30	16
122	A19	30fr multicolored	35	20
123	A19	40fr multicolored	40	30
124	A19	50fr multicolored	55	38
125	A19	60fr multicolored	65	42
126	A19	85fr multicolored	90	55
		Set value	4.00	2.75

Centenary Emblem and Globe — A20

Scroll — A21

1963, Oct. 21 Unwmk. *Perf. 12*
127 A20 25fr multicolored 50 40

Centenary of International Red Cross.

1963, Dec. 10 Photo. *Perf. 13x12¹/₂*
128 A21 25fr dp claret, gold & bl 30 20

15th anniv. of the Universal Declaration of Human Rights.

Sound Wave Patterns A22

1964, Jan. 16 *Perf. 12¹/₂x13*
129 A22 25fr multicolored 25 20

Upper Volta's admission to the ITU.

Barograph and WMO Emblem A23

1964, Mar. 23 Engr. *Perf. 13*
130 A23 50fr dk car rose, grn & bl 55 40

4th World Meteorological Day, Mar. 23.

World Connected by Letters and Carrier Pigeon — A24

Design: 60fr, World connected by letters and jet plane.

1964, Mar. 29 Photo. *Perf. 13x12*
131 A24 25fr gray brn & ultra 25 20
132 A24 60fr gray brn & org 60 42

Upper Volta's admission to the UPU.

IQSY Emblem and Seasonal Allegories — A25

1964, Aug. 17 Engr. *Perf. 13*
133 A25 30fr grn, ocher & car 35 25

International Quiet Sun Year.

Cooperation Issue
Common Design Type

1964, Nov. 7 Unwmk. *Perf. 13*
134 CD119 70fr dl bl grn, dk brn & car 65 42

Hotel Independance, Ouagadougou A26

1964, Dec. 11 Litho. *Perf. 12¹/₂x13*
135 A26 25fr multicolored 1.00 35

Pigmy Long-tailed Sunbird — A27

Comoe Waterfall — A28

1965, Mar. 1 Photo. *Perf. 13x12¹/₂*
Size: 22x36mm

136	A27	10fr shown	20	16
137	A27	15fr Olive-bellied Sunbird	25	20
138	A27	20fr Splendid Sunbird	40	25
		Nos. 136-138 (3)	85	61

See No. C20.

1965 Engr. *Perf. 13*

Design: 25fr, Great Waterfall of Banfora, horiz.

139	A28	5fr yel grn, bl & red brn	15	15
140	A28	25fr dk red, brt bl & grn	25	16
		Set value		23

Soccer — A29

Abraham Lincoln — A30

Designs: 25fr, Boxing gloves and ring. 70fr, Tennis rackets, ball and net.

1965, July 15 Unwmk. *Perf. 13*

141	A29	15fr brn, red & dk grn	16	15
142	A29	25fr pale org, bl & brn	28	18
143	A29	70fr dk car & brt grn	60	32
		Nos. 141-143 (3)	1.04	65

1st African Games, Brazzaville, July 18-25.

1965, Nov. 3 Photo. *Perf. 13x12½*

144 A30 50fr green & multi 50 38

Centenary of death of Abraham Lincoln.

Pres. Maurice Yameogo — A31

1965, Dec. 11 Photo. *Perf. 13x12½*

145 A31 25fr multicolored 25 16

Mantis A32

Wart Hog A33

Headdress A34

1966 *Perf. 13x12½, 12½x13*

146	A33	1fr Nemopistha imperatrix	15	15
147	A33	2fr Ball python	15	15
148	A32	3fr shown	15	15
149	A32	4fr Grasshopper	15	15
150	A33	5fr shown	15	15
151	A32	6fr Scorpion	15	15
152	A33	8fr Green monkey	15	15
153	A32	10fr Dromedary	15	15
154	A33	15fr Leopard	20	15
155	A32	20fr Cape buffalo	22	16
156	A33	25fr Hippopotamus	30	16
157	A32	30fr Agama lizard	38	20
158	A33	45fr Common puff adder	55	22
159	A33	50fr Chameleon	60	35
160	A33	60fr Ugada limbata	70	42
161	A33	85fr Elephant	90	50
		Nos. 146-161 (16)	5.05	
		Set value		2.65

1966, Apr. 9 Photo. *Perf. 13x12½*

Designs: 25fr, Plumed headdress. 60fr, Male dancer.

162	A34	20fr yel grn, choc & red	20	15
163	A34	25fr multicolored	25	16
164	A34	60fr org, dk brn & red	60	35
		Nos. 162-164 (3)	1.05	66

Intl. Negro Arts Festival, Dakar, Senegal, Apr. 1-24.

Pô Church A35

Design: No. 166, Bobo-Dioulasso Mosque.

1966, Apr. 15 *Perf. 12½x13*

165	A35	25fr multicolored	22	16
166	A35	25fr bl, cr & red brn	22	16

The Red Cross Helping the World — A36

1966, June Photo. *Perf. 13x12½*

167 A36 25fr lemon, blk & car 22 15

Issued to honor the Red Cross.

Boy Scouts in Camp — A37

Design: 15fr, Two Scouts on a cliff exploring the country.

1966, June 15 *Perf. 12½x13*

168	A37	10fr multicolored	15	15
169	A37	15fr blk, bis brn, & dl yel	16	15
		Set value		17

Issued to honor the Boy Scouts.

Cow Receiving Injection A38

1966, Aug. 16 Photo. *Perf. 12½x13*

170 A38 25fr yel, blk & bl 25 20

Campaign against cattle plague.

Plowing with Donkey A39

Design: 30fr, Crop rotation, Kamboince Experimental Station.

1966, Sept. 15 Photo. *Perf. 12½x13*

171	A39	25fr multicolored	22	15
172	A39	30fr multicolored	25	16

Natl. and rural education; 3rd anniv. of the Kamboince Experimental Station (No. 172).

UNESCO Emblem and Map of Africa — A40

UNICEF Emblem and Children A41

1966, Dec. 10 Engr. *Perf. 13*

173	A40	50fr brt bl, blk & red	50	25
174	A41	50fr dk vio, dp lil & dk red	50	25

20th anniv. of UNESCO and of UNICEF.

Arms of Upper Volta — A42

Symbols of Agriculture, Industry, Men and Women — A43

1967, Jan. 2 Photo. *Perf. 12½x13*

175 A42 30fr multicolored 22 15

Europafrica Issue

1967, Feb. 4 Photo. *Perf. 12½*

176 A43 60fr multicolored 50 30

Scout Handclasp and Jamboree Emblem A44

Design: 5fr, Jamboree emblem and Scout holding hat.

1967, June 8 Photo. *Perf. 12½x13*

177	A44	5fr multicolored	20	15
178	A44	20fr multicolored	55	40

12th Boy Scout World Jamboree, Farragut State Park, Idaho, Aug. 1-9. See No. C41.

Bank Book and Hands with Coins — A45

1967, Aug. 22 Engr. *Perf. 13*

179 A45 30fr sl grn, ocher & ol 25 15

National Savings Bank.

Mailman on Bicycle — A46

1967, Oct. 15 Engr. *Perf. 13*

180 A46 30fr dk bl, emer & brn 30 16

Stamp Day.

Monetary Union Issue

Common Design Type

1967, Nov. 4 Engr. *Perf. 13*

181 CD125 30fr dk vio & dl bl 25 15

View of Nizier — A47

Designs (Olympic Emblem and): 50fr, Les Deux-Alps, vert. 100fr, Ski lift and view of Villard-de-Lans.

1967, Nov. 28

182	A47	15fr brt bl, grn & brn	16	15
183	A47	50fr brt bl & slate grn	45	20
184	A47	100fr brt bl, grn & red	90	45
		Nos. 182-184 (3)	1.51	80

10th Winter Olympic Games, Grenoble, France, Feb. 6-18, 1968.

White and Black Men Holding Human Rights Emblem A48

1968, Jan. 2 Photo. *Perf. 12½x13*

185	A48	20fr brt bl, gold & dp car	20	15
186	A48	30fr grn, gold & dp car	30	16

International Human Rights Year.

Administration School and Student — A49

1968, Feb. 2 Engr. *Perf. 13*

187 A49 30fr ol bis, Prus bl & brt grn 25 15

National School of Administration.

WHO Emblem and Sick People — A50

1968, Apr. 7 Engr. *Perf. 13*

188	A50	30fr ind, brt bl & car rose	30	16
189	A50	50fr brt bl, sl grn & lt brn	45	22

WHO, 20th anniversary.

Telephone Office, Bobo-Dioulasso — A51

1968, Sept. 30 Photo. *Perf. 12½x12*

190 A51 30fr multicolored 28 15

Opening of the automatic telephone office in Bobo-Dioulasso.

Weaver A52

1968, Oct. 30 Engr. *Perf. 13*

Size: 36x22mm

191 A52 30fr mag, brn & ocher 30 16

See No. C58.

Grain Pouring over World, Plower and FAO Emblem — A53

1969, Jan. 7 **Engr.** ***Perf. 13***
192 A53 30fr sl, vio bl & mar 25 15

UNFAO world food program.

Automatic Looms and ILO Emblem A54

1969, Mar. 15 **Engr.** ***Perf. 13***
193 A54 30fr brt grn, mar & ind 25 15

ILO, 50th anniversary.

Smith — A55

1969, Apr. 3 **Engr.** ***Perf. 13***
Size: 36x22mm
194 A55 5fr magenta & blk 15 15

See No. C64.

Blood Donor — A56

1969, May 15 **Engr.** ***Perf. 13***
195 A56 30fr blk, bl & car 25 16

League of Red Cross Societies, 50th anniv.

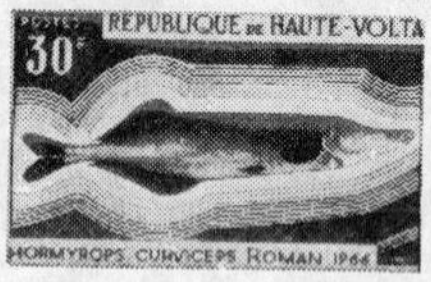

Nile Pike — A57

Fish: 20fr, Nannocharax gobioides. 25fr, Hemigrammocharax polli. 55fr, Alestes luteus. 85fr, Micralestes voltae.

1969 **Engr.** ***Perf. 13***
Size: 36x22mm
196 A57 20fr brt bl, brn & yel 32 20
197 A57 25fr sl, brn & dk brn 32 20
198 A57 30fr dk olive & blk 45 25
199 A57 55fr dk grn, yel & ol 60 42
200 A57 85fr sl brn & pink 1.25 90
Nos. 196-200,C66-C67 (7) 5.24 3.01

Development Bank Issue
Common Design Type

1969, Sept. 10 **Engr.** ***Perf. 13***
201 CD130 30fr sl grn, grn & ocher 22 15

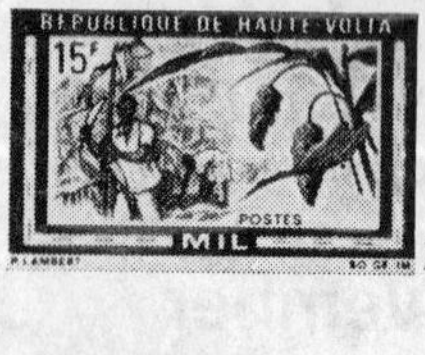

Millet — A58

Design: 30fr, Cotton.

1969, Oct. 30 **Photo.** ***Perf. 12½x13***
202 A58 15fr dk brn, grn & yel 16 15
203 A58 30fr dp cl & brt bl 30 16

See Nos. C73-C74.

ASECNA Issue
Common Design Type

1969, Dec. 12 **Engr.** ***Perf. 13***
204 CD132 100fr brown 80 50

Niadale Mask — A59

Carvings from National Museum: 30fr, Niaga. 45fr, Man and woman, Iliu Bara. 80fr, Karan Weeba figurine.

1970, Mar. 5 **Engr.** ***Perf. 13***
207 A59 10fr dk car rose, org & dk brn 15 15
209 A59 30fr dk brn, brt vio & grnsh bl 22 15
211 A59 45fr yel grn, brn & bl 32 15
212 A59 80fr pur, rose lil & brn 60 25
Nos. 207-212 (4) 1.29
Set value 55

African Huts and European City — A60

1970, Apr. 25 **Engr.** ***Perf. 13***
213 A60 30fr dk brn, red & bl 25 15

Issued for Linked Cities' Day.

Mask for Nebwa Gnomo Dance — A61

Designs: 8fr, Cauris dancers, vert. 20fr, Gourmantchés dancers, vert. 30fr, Larllé dancers.

1970, May 7 **Photo.** ***Perf. 13***
214 A61 5fr lt brn, vio bl & blk 15 15
215 A61 8fr org brn, car & blk 15 15
216 A61 20fr dk brn, sl grn & ocher 16 15
217 A61 30fr dp car, dk gray & brn 25 15
Set value 58 36

Education Year Emblem, Open Book and Pupils — A62

Design: 90fr, Education Year emblem, telecommunication and education symbols.

1970, May 14 ***Perf. 12½x12***
218 A62 40fr black & multi 35 20
219 A62 90fr olive & multi 65 35

International Education Year.

UPU Headquarters Issue

Abraham Lincoln, UPU Headquarters and Emblem — A63

1970, May 20 **Engr.** ***Perf. 13***
220 A63 30fr dk car rose, ind & red brn 30 16
221 A63 60fr dk bl grn, vio & red brn 50 25

See note after CD133, Common Design section.

Ship-building Industry A64

Designs: 45fr, Chemical industry. 80fr, Electrical industry.

1970, June 15
222 A64 15fr brt pink, red brn & blk 15 15
223 A64 45fr emer, dp bl & blk 35 20
224 A64 80fr red brn, claret & blk 65 35
Nos. 222-224 (3) 1.15 70

Hanover Fair.

Cattle Vaccination A65

1970, June 30 **Photo.** ***Perf. 13***
225 A65 30fr Prus bl, yel & sep 30 15

National Veterinary College.

Vaccination and Red Cross — A66

1970, Aug. 28 **Engr.** ***Perf. 12½x13***
226 A66 30fr choc & car 25 16

Issued for the Upper Volta Red Cross.
For surcharge see No. 252.

Europafrica Issue

Nurse with Child, by Frans Hals — A67

Paintings: 30fr, Courtyard of a House in Delft, by Pieter de Hooch. 150fr, Christina of Denmark, by Hans Holbein. 250fr, Courtyard of the Royal Palace at Innsbruck, Austria, by Albrecht Dürer.

1970, Sept. 25 **Litho.** ***Perf. 13x14***
227 A67 25fr multicolored 22 15
228 A67 30fr multicolored 30 16
229 A67 150fr multicolored 1.40 65
230 A67 250fr multicolored 2.00 1.00
Nos. 227-230 (4) 3.92 1.96

Citroen — A68

Design: 40fr, Old and new Citroen cars.

1970, Oct. 16 **Engr.** ***Perf. 13***
231 A68 25fr ol brn, mar & sl grn 22 15
232 A68 40fr brt grn, plum & sl 40 20

57th Paris Automobile Salon.

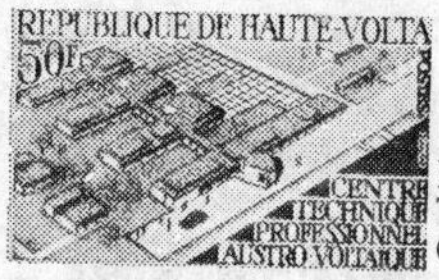

Professional Training Center — A69

1970, Dec. 10 **Engr.** ***Perf. 13***
233 A69 50fr grn, bis & brn 38 16

Opening of Professional Training Center under joint sponsorship of Austria and Upper Volta.

Upper Volta Arms and Soaring Bird — A70

1970, Dec. 10 **Photo.**
234 A70 30fr lt blue & multi 22 15

Tenth anniversary of independence, Dec. 11.

Political Maps of Africa — A71

1970, Dec. 14 **Litho.** ***Perf. 13½***
235 A71 50fr multicolored 40 20

10th anniv. of the declaration granting independence to colonial territories and countries.

Beingolo Hunting Horn — A72

Musical Instruments: 15fr, Mossi guitar, vert. 20fr, Gourounsi flutes, vert. 25fr, Lunga drums.

1971, Mar. 1 **Engr.** ***Perf. 13***
236 A72 5fr blue, brn & car 15 15
237 A72 15fr green, crim rose & brn 15 15
238 A72 20fr car rose, bl & gray 16 15
239 A72 25fr brt grn, red brn & ol gray 20 15
Nos. 236-239 (4) 66
Set value 37

Voltaphilex I, National Phil. Exhibition.

Four Races — A73

1971, Mar. 21 **Engr.** ***Perf. 13***
240 A73 50fr rose cl, lt grn & dk brn 40 22

Intl. year against racial discrimination.

Telephone and Globes — A74

1971, May 17 **Engr.** ***Perf. 13***
241 A74 50fr brn, gray & dk pur 40 20

3rd World Telecommunications Day.

Cane Field Worker, Banfora Sugar Mill — A75

Cotton and Voltex Mill Emblem — A76

1971, June 24 **Photo.** ***Perf. 13***
242 A75 10fr multicolored 15 15
243 A76 35fr multicolored 25 15
Set value 19

Industrial development.

Gonimbrasia Hecate A77

Butterflies and Moths: 2fr, Hamanumida daedalus. 3fr, Ophideres materna. 5fr, Danaus chyrsippus. 40fr, Hypolimnas misippus. 45fr, Danaus petiverana.

1971, June 30
244 A77 1fr blue & multi 15 15
245 A77 2fr lt lilac & multi 15 15
246 A77 3fr multicolored 15 15
247 A77 5fr gray & multi 15 15
248 A77 40fr ocher & multi 60 35
249 A77 45fr multicolored 80 50
Set value 1.65 1.10

Kabuki Actor — A78

Design: 40fr, African mask and Kabuki actor.

1971, Aug. 12 **Photo.** ***Perf. 13***
250 A78 25fr multicolored 20 15
251 A78 40fr multicolored 30 15
Set value 24

Philatokyo 71, Philatelic Exposition, Tokyo, Apr. 19-29.

No. 226 Surcharged

1971 **Engr.** ***Perf. 12½x13***
252 A66 100fr on 30fr choc & car 65 40

10th anniversary of Upper Volta Red Cross.

Seed Preparation A79

Designs: 75fr, Old farmer with seed packet, vert. 100fr, Farmer in rice field.

1971, Sept. 30 **Photo.** ***Perf. 13***
253 A79 35fr ocher & multi 22 15
254 A79 75fr lt blue & multi 50 20
255 A79 100fr brown & multi 65 35
Nos. 253-255 (3) 1.37 70

National campaign for seed protection.

Outdoor Classroom A80

Design: 50fr, Mother learning to read.

1971, Oct. 14
256 A80 35fr multicolored 22 15
257 A80 50fr multicolored 38 16

Women's education.

Joseph Dakiri, Soldiers Driving Tractors — A81

Children and UNICEF Emblem — A84

Spraying Lake, Fly, Man Leading Blind Women A82

Design: 40fr, Dakiri and soldiers gathering harvest.

1971, Oct. 13 ***Perf. 12x12½***
258 A81 15fr blk, yel & red brn 15 15
259 A81 40fr blue & multi 25 16

Joseph Dakiri (1938-1971), inaugurator of the Army-Aid-to-Agriculture Program.

1971, Nov. 26 **Photo.** ***Perf. 13***
260 A82 40fr dk brn, yel & bl 25 16

Drive against onchocerciasis, roundworm infestation.

For surcharge see No. 295.

1971, Dec. 11 ***Perf. 13***
262 A84 45fr red, bis & blk 35 16

UNICEF, 25th anniv.

Peulh House — A85

Upper Volta Houses: 20fr, Gourounsi house. 35fr, Mossi houses. 45fr, Bobo house, vert. 50fr, Dagari house, vert. 90fr, Bango house, interior.

Perf. 13x13½, 13½x13

1971-72 **Photo.**
263 A85 10fr ver & multi 15 15
264 A85 20fr multicolored 16 15
265 A85 35fr brt grn & multi 22 15
266 A85 45fr multi ('72) 35 16
267 A85 50fr multi ('72) 40 20
268 A85 90fr multi ('72) 60 35
Nos. 263-268 (6) 1.88 1.16

Town Halls of Bobo-Dioulasso and Chalons-sur-Marne — A86

1971, Dec. 23 ***Perf. 13x12½***
269 A86 40fr yellow & multi 25 15

Kinship between the cities of Bobo-Dioulasso, Upper Volta, and Chalons-sur-Marne, France.

Louis Armstrong — A87

1972, May 17 ***Perf. 14x13***
270 A87 45fr multicolored 45 25

Black musician. See No. C104.

Red Crescent, Cross and Lion Emblems A88

1972, June 23 ***Perf. 13x14***
271 A88 40fr yellow & multi 35 16

World Red Cross Day. See No. C105.

Coiffure of Peulh Woman — A89

Designs: Various hair styles.

1972, July 23 **Litho.** ***Perf. 13***
272 A89 25fr blue & multi 20 15
273 A89 35fr emerald & multi 22 15
274 A89 75fr yellow & multi 45 18
Nos. 272-274 (3) 87
Set value 38

Classroom A90

Designs: 15fr, Clinic. 20fr, Factory. 35fr, Cattle. 40fr, Plowers. 85fr, Road building machinery.

1972, Oct. 30 **Engr.** ***Perf. 13***
275 A90 10fr sl grn, lt grn & choc 15 15
276 A90 15fr brt grn, brn org & brn 15 15
277 A90 20fr bl, lt brn & grn 15 15
278 A90 35fr grn, brn & brt bl 18 15
279 A90 40fr choc, pink & sl grn 22 16
Nos. 275-279,C106 (6) 1.30
Set value 75

2nd Five-Year Plan.

West African Monetary Union Issue
Common Design Type

1972, Nov. 2
280 CD136 40fr brn, bl & gray 25 15

Lottery Office and Emblem — A91

1972, Nov. 6 **Litho.**
281 A91 35fr multicolored 22 15

5th anniversary of National Lottery.

Domestic Animals — A92

1972, Dec. 4 **Litho.** ***Perf. 13½x12½***
282 A92 5fr Donkeys 15 15
283 A92 10fr Geese 15 15
284 A92 30fr Goats 20 15
285 A92 50fr Cow 35 15
286 A92 65fr Dromedaries 42 20
Nos. 282-286 (5) 1.27
Set value 52

Mossi Woman's Hair Style, and Village — A93

1973, Jan. 24 **Engr.** ***Perf. 13***
287 A93 5fr slate grn, org & choc 15 15
288 A93 40fr bl, org & chocolate 22 15
Set value 27 19

Eugene A. Cernan and Lunar Module A94

Designs: 65fr, Ronald E. Evans and splashdown. 100fr, Capsule, in orbit and interior, horiz. 150fr, Harrison H. Schmitt and lift-off. 200fr, Conference and moon-buggy. 500fr, Moon-buggy and capsule, horiz.

Perf. 12½x13½, 13½x12½

1973, Mar. 29 **Litho.**

289 A94	50fr multi	32	16
290 A94	65fr multi	38	18
291 A94	100fr multi	60	30
292 A94	150fr multi	90	45
293 A94	200fr multi	1.25	60
	Nos. 289-293 (5)	3.45	1.69

Souvenir Sheet

294 A94 500fr multi 3.50 1.60

Apollo 17 moon mission.

No. 260 Surcharged in Red

O. M. S.
25ᵉ Anniversaire
45F

1973, Apr. 7 **Photo.** ***Perf. 13***

295 A82 45fr on 40fr multi 25 16

WHO, 25th anniversary.

Scout Bugler — A95

1973, July 18 **Litho.** ***Perf. 12½x13***

296 A95	20fr multicolored	15	15
	Nos. 296,C160-C163 (5)	3.30	1.70

African Postal Union Issue
Common Design Type

1973, Sept. 12 **Engr.** ***Perf. 13***

297 CD137 100fr brt red, mag & dl yel 65 25

Pres. Kennedy, Saturn 5 on Assembly Trailer — A96

Pres. John F. Kennedy (1917-1963) and: 10fr, Atlas rocket carrying John H. Glenn. 30fr, Titan 2 rocket and Gemini 3 capsule.

1973, Sept. 12 **Litho.** ***Perf. 12½x13***

298 A96	5fr multicolored	15	15
299 A96	10fr multicolored	15	15
300 A96	30fr multicolored	20	15
	Nos. 298-300,C167-C168 (5)	3.90	2.10

Cross-examination — A97

Designs: 65fr, "Diamond Ede." 70fr, Forensic Institute. 150fr, Robbery scene.

1973, Sept. 15 ***Perf. 13x12½***

301 A97	50fr multicolored	32	16
302 A97	65fr multicolored	38	18
303 A97	70fr multicolored	40	20
304 A97	150fr multicolored	90	45
	Nos. 301-304 (4)	2.00	99

Interpol, 50th anniversary. See No. C170.

Market Place, Ouagadougou — A98

Design: 40fr, Swimming pool, Hotel Independence.

1973, Sept. 30

305 A98	35fr multicolored	22	15
306 A98	40fr multicolored	25	15

Tourism. See Nos. C171-C172.

Protestant Church — A99

Design: 40fr, Ouahigouya Mosque.

1973, Sept. 28 ***Perf. 13x12½***

307 A99	35fr multicolored	22	15
308 A99	40fr multicolored	25	15

Houses of worship. See No. C173.

Kiembara Dancers A100

Design: 40fr, Dancers.

1973, Nov. 30 **Litho.** ***Perf. 12½x13***

309 A100	35fr multicolored	22	15
310 A100	40fr multicolored	25	15

Folklore. See Nos. C174-C175.

Yuri Gagarin and Aries — A101

Famous Men and their Zodiac Signs: 10fr, Lenin and Taurus. 20fr, John F. Kennedy, rocket and Gemini. 25fr, John H. Glenn, orbiting capsule and Cancer. 30fr, Napoleon and Leo. 50fr, Goethe and Virgo. 60fr, Pelé and Libra. 75fr, Charles de Gaulle and Scorpio. 100fr, Beethoven and Sagittarius. 175fr, Conrad Adenauer and Capricorn. 200fr, Edwin E. Aldrin, Jr. (Apollo XI) and Aquarius. 250fr, Lord Baden-Powell and Pisces.

1973, Dec. 15 **Litho.** ***Perf. 13x14***

311 A101	5fr multicolored	15	15
312 A101	10fr multicolored	15	15
313 A101	20fr multicolored	15	15
314 A101	25fr multicolored	15	15
315 A101	30fr multicolored	16	15
316 A101	50fr multicolored	30	15
317 A101	60fr multicolored	38	18
318 A101	75fr multicolored	42	20
319 A101	100fr multicolored	60	30
320 A101	175fr multicolored	1.10	55
321 A101	200fr multicolored	1.20	55
322 A101	250fr multicolored	1.50	70
	Nos. 311-322 (12)	6.26	3.38

See Nos. C176-C178.

Rivera with Italian Flag and Championship '74 Emblem — A102

Design: 40fr, World Cup, soccer ball, World Championship '74 emblem and Pelé with Brazilian flag.

1974, Jan. 15 ***Perf. 13x12½***

323 A102	5fr multicolored	15	15
324 A102	40fr multicolored	25	15
	Nos. 323-324,C179-C181 (5)	3.15	1.70

10th World Cup Soccer Championship, Munich, June 13-July 7.

Charles de Gaulle A103

Designs: 40fr, De Gaulle memorial. 60fr, Pres. Charles de Gaulle.

1974, Feb. 4 **Litho.** ***Perf. 12½x13***

325 A103	35fr multicolored	20	15
326 A103	40fr multicolored	20	15
327 A103	60fr multicolored	35	16
	Nos. 325-327,C183 (4)	2.75	1.46

Gen. Charles de Gaulle (1890-1970), president of France. Nos. 325-327 printed se-tenant. See No. C184.

N'Dongo and Cameroun Flag — A104

World Cup, Emblems and: 20fr, Kolev and Bulgarian flag. 50fr, Keita and Mali flag.

1974, Mar. 19

328 A104	10fr multicolored	15	15
329 A104	20fr multicolored	15	15
330 A104	50fr multicolored	35	16
	Nos. 328-330,C185-C186 (5)	2.90	1.59

10th World Cup Soccer Championship, Munich, June 13-July 7.

Map and Flags of Members A105

1974, May 29 **Photo.** ***Perf. 13x12½***

331 A105 40fr blue & multi 22 15

15th anniversary of the Council of Accord.

UPU Emblem and Mail Coach — A106

UPU emblem and: 40fr, Steamship. 85fr, Mailman.

1974, July 23 **Litho.** ***Perf. 13½***

332 A106	35fr multicolored	22	15
333 A106	40fr multicolored	25	15
334 A106	85fr multicolored	55	28
	Nos. 332-334,C189-C191 (6)	4.02	2.08

Universal Postal Union centenary.
For overprints see #339-341, C197-C200.

Soccer Game, Winner Italy, in France, 1938 — A107

World Cup, Game and Flags: 25fr, Uruguay, in Brazil, 1950. 50fr, East Germany, in Switzerland, 1954.

1974, Sept. 2 **Litho.** ***Perf. 13½***

335 A107	10fr multicolored	15	15
336 A107	25fr multicolored	16	15
337 A107	50fr multicolored	35	16
	Nos. 335-337,C193-C195 (6)	4.66	2.41

World Cup Soccer winners.

Map and Farm Woman — A108

1974, Oct. 2 **Litho.** ***Perf. 13x12½***

338 A108 35fr yellow & multi 20 15

Kou Valley Development.

Nos. 332-334 Overprinted in Red "100e ANNIVERSAIRE DE L'UNION POSTALE UNIVERSELLE / 9 OCTOBRE 1974"

1974, Oct. 9

339	A106	35fr multicolored	22	15
340	A106	40fr multicolored	25	15
341	A106	85fr multicolored	55	28
		Nos. 339-341,C197-C199 (6)	5.07	2.58

Universal Postal Union centenary.

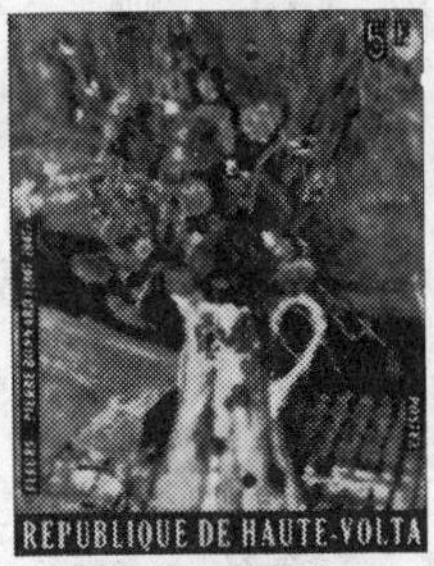

Flowers, by Pierre Bonnard A109

Flower Paintings by: 10fr, Jan Brueghel. 30fr, Jean van Os. 50fr, Van Brussel.

1974, Oct. 31 Litho. ***Perf. 12½x13***

342	A109	5fr multicolored	15	15
343	A109	10fr multicolored	15	15
344	A109	30fr multicolored	16	15
345	A109	50fr multicolored	25	15
		Nos. 342-345,C201 (5)	2.71	
		Set value		1.30

Churchill as Officer of India Hussars — A110

Churchill: 75fr, As Secretary of State for Interior. 100fr, As pilot. 125fr, meeting with Roosevelt, 1941. 300fr, As painter. 450fr, and "HMS Resolution."

1975, Jan. 11 ***Perf. 13½***

346	A110	50fr multicolored	30	15
347	A110	75fr multicolored	42	20
348	A110	100fr multicolored	55	28
349	A110	125fr multicolored	70	38
350	A110	300fr multicolored	1.60	80
		Nos. 346-350 (5)	3.57	1.81

Souvenir Sheet

351	A110	450fr multicolored	2.50	1.25

Sir Winston Churchill, birth centenary.

US No. 619 and Minutemen — A111

US Stamps: 40fr, #118 and Proclamation of Independence. 75fr, #798 and Signing the Constitution. 100fr, #703 and Surrender at Yorktown. 200fr, #1003 and George Washington. 300fr, #644 and Surrender of Burgoyne at Saratoga. 500fr, #63, 68, 73, 157, 179, 228 and 1483a.

1975, Feb. 17 Litho. ***Perf. 11***

352	A111	35fr multicolored	20	15
353	A111	40fr multicolored	22	15
354	A111	75fr multicolored	42	20
355	A111	100fr multicolored	55	28
356	A111	200fr multicolored	1.20	55
357	A111	300fr multicolored	1.60	80
		Nos. 352-357 (6)	4.19	2.13

Souvenir Sheet

Imperf

358	A111	500fr multicolored	3.00	1.50

American Bicentennial.

"Atlantic" No. 2670, 1904-12 — A112

Locomotives from Mulhouse, France, Railroad Museum: 25fr, No. 2029, 1882. 50fr, No. 2129, 1882.

1975, Feb. 28 Litho. ***Perf. 13x12½***

359	A112	15fr multicolored	15	15
360	A112	25fr multicolored	16	15
361	A112	50fr multicolored	35	16
		Nos. 359-361,C203-C204 (5)	2.71	1.46

French Flag and Renault Petit Duc, 1910 — A113

Flags and Old Cars: 30fr, US and Ford Model T, 1909. 35fr, Italy and Alfa Romeo "Le Mans," 1931.

1975, Apr. 6 ***Perf. 14x13½***

362	A113	10fr multicolored	15	15
363	A113	30fr multicolored	20	15
364	A113	35fr multicolored	22	15
		Nos. 362-364,C206-C207 (5)	2.97	1.60

Washington and Lafayette — A114

American Bicentennial: 40fr, Washington reviewing troops at Valley Forge. 50fr, Washington taking oath of office.

1975, May 6 Litho. ***Perf. 14***

365	A114	30fr multicolored	20	15
366	A114	40fr multicolored	25	15
367	A114	50fr multicolored	35	16
		Nos. 365-367,C209-C210 (5)	4.20	2.11

Souvenir Sheet

367A	A114	500fr multicolored	3.50	1.60

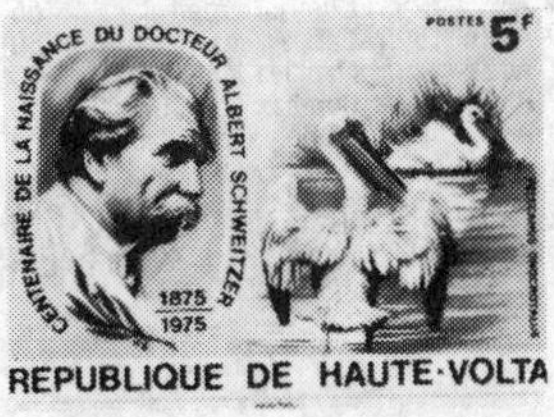

Schweitzer and Pelicans — A115

Design: 15fr, Albert Schweitzer and bateleur eagle.

1975, May 25 Litho. ***Perf. 13½***

368	A115	5fr multicolored	15	15
369	A115	15fr multicolored	15	15
		Nos. 368-369,C212-C214 (5)	3.90	2.00

Albert Schweitzer, birth centenary.

Apollo and Soyuz Orbiting Earth — A116

Design: 50fr, Apollo and Soyuz near link-up.

1975, July 18

370	A116	40fr multicolored	25	15
371	A116	50fr multicolored	35	16
		Nos. 370-371,C216-C218 (5)	4.65	2.31

Apollo-Soyuz space test project, Russo-American cooperation, launched July 15, link-up July 17.

Maria Picasso Lopez, Artist's Mother A117

Paintings by Pablo Picasso (1881-1973): 60fr, Self-portrait. 90fr, First Communion.

1975, Aug. 7

372	A117	50fr multicolored	35	16
373	A117	60fr multicolored	40	20
374	A117	90fr multicolored	60	30
		Nos. 372-374,C220-C221 (5)	4.60	2.36

Expo '75 Emblem and Tanker, Idemitsu Maru — A118

Oceanographic Exposition, Okinawa: 25fr, Training ship, Kaio Maru. 45fr, Firefighting ship, Hiryu. 50fr, Battleship, Yamato. 60fr, Container ship, Kamakura Maru.

1975, Sept. 26 Litho. ***Perf. 11***

375	A118	15fr multicolored	15	15
376	A118	25fr multicolored	16	15
377	A118	45fr multicolored	30	15
377A	A118	50fr multicolored	35	16
378	A118	60fr multicolored	40	20
		Nos. 375-378,C223 (6)	2.11	1.19

Woman, Globe and IWY Emblem — A119

1975, Nov. 20 Photo. ***Perf. 13***

379	A119	65fr multicolored	38	22

International Women's Year.

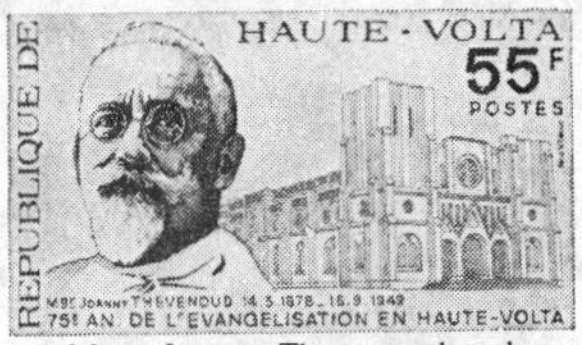

Msgr. Joanny Thevenoud and Cathedral — A120

Design: 65fr, Father Guillaume Templier and Cathedral.

1975, Nov. 20 Engr. ***Perf. 13x12½***

380	A120	55fr grn, blk & dl red	20	15
381	A120	65fr blk, org & dl red	26	16

75th anniv. of the Evangelization of Upper Volta.

Farmer's Hat, Hoe and Emblem A121

1975, Dec. 10 Photo. ***Perf. 13x13½***

382	A121	15fr buff & multi	15	15
383	A121	50fr lt green & multi	18	15
		Set value	24	16

Development of the Volta valleys.

Sledding and Olympic Emblem — A122

Innsbruck Background, Olympic Emblem and: 45fr, Figure skating. 85fr, Skiing.

1975, Dec. 16 Litho. ***Perf. 13½***

384	A122	35fr multicolored	18	15
385	A122	45fr multicolored	22	15
386	A122	85fr multicolored	45	22
		Nos. 384-386,C225-C226 (5)	2.90	1.52

12th Winter Olympic Games, Innsbruck, Austria, Feb. 4-15, 1976.

Gymnast and Olympic Emblem — A123

Olympic Emblem and: 50fr, Sailing. 100fr, Soccer.

1976, Mar. 17

387	A123	40fr multicolored	20	15
388	A123	50fr multicolored	25	15
389	A123	100fr multicolored	55	28
		Nos. 387-389,C228-C229 (5)	2.40	1.26

21st Olympic Games, Montreal, Canada, July 17-Aug. 1.

The lack of a value for a listed item does not necessarily indicate rarity.

Olympic Emblem and Sprinters A124

Olympic Emblem and: 55fr, Equestrian. 75fr, Hurdles.

1976, Mar. 25 Litho. *Perf. 11*

390 A124 30fr multicolored 16 15
391 A124 55fr multicolored 30 15
392 A124 75fr multicolored 42 20
Nos. 390-392,C231-C232 (5) 2.63 1.38

21st Olympic Games, Montreal.
For overprints see #420-422, C245-C247.

Blind Woman and Man — A125

1976, Apr. 7 Engr. *Perf. 13*

393 A125 75fr dk brn, grn & org 40 25
394 A125 250fr dk brn, ocher & org 1.40 80

Drive against onchocerciasis, roundworm infestation.

"Deutschland" over Friedrichshafen — A126

Airships: 40fr, "Victoria Louise" over sailing ships. 50fr, "Sachsen" over German countryside.

1976, May 11 Litho. *Perf. 11*

395 A126 10fr multicolored 70 15
396 A126 40fr multicolored 25 15
397 A126 50fr multicolored 35 16
Nos. 395-397,C234-C236 (6) 5.35 2.46

75th anniversary of the Zeppelin.

Viking Lander and Probe on Mars — A127

Viking Mars project: 55fr, Viking orbiter in flight. 75fr, Titan rocket start for Mars, vert.

1976, June 24 *Perf. 13½*

398 A127 30fr multicolored 15 15
399 A127 55fr multicolored 22 15
400 A127 75fr multicolored 32 16
Nos. 398-400,C238-C239 (5) 3.19 1.71

World Map, Arms of Upper Volta — A128

Design: 100fr, World map, arms and dove.

1976, Aug. 19 Litho. *Perf. 12½*

401 A128 55fr brown & multi 22 16
402 A128 100fr blue & multi 42 30

5th Summit Conference of Non-aligned Countries, Colombo, Sri Lanka, Aug. 9-19.

Bicentennial, Interphil 76 Emblems and Washington at Battle of Trenton — A129

Design: 90fr, Bicentennial, Interphil 76 emblems and Seat of Government, Pennsylvania.

1976, Sept. 30 *Perf. 13½*

403 A129 60fr multicolored 40 16
404 A129 90fr multicolored 55 22
Nos. 403-404,C241-C243 (5) 5.00 2.38

American Bicentennial, Interphil 76, Philadelphia, Pa., May 29-June 6.

UPU and UN Emblems — A130

1976, Dec. 8 Engr. *Perf. 13*

405 A130 200fr red, ol & bl 1.00 60

UN Postal Administration, 25th anniv.

Arms of Tenkodogo A131

Bronze Statuette A132

Coats of Arms: 20fr, 100fr, Ouagadougou.

1977, May 2 Litho. *Perf. 13*

406 A131 10fr multicolored 15 15
407 A131 20fr multicolored 15 15
408 A131 65fr multicolored 35 25
409 A131 100fr multicolored 55 40
Nos. 406-409 (4) 1.20
Set value 78

1977, June 13 Photo. *Perf. 13*

Design: 65fr, Woman with bowl, bronze.

410 A132 55fr multicolored 30 20
411 A132 65fr multicolored 35 20

#410-411 issued in sheets and coils with black control number on every 5th stamp.

Granaries — A133

Handbags — A134

1977, June 20 Photo. *Perf. 13½x13*

412 A133 5fr Samo 15 15
413 A133 35fr Boromo 20 15
414 A133 45fr Banfora 22 15
415 A133 55fr Mossi 30 20
Nos. 412-415 (4) 87
Set value 50

1977, June 20

416 A134 30fr Gouin 16 15
417 A134 40fr Bissa 20 15
418 A134 60fr Lobi 35 20
419 A134 70fr Mossi 38 22
Nos. 416-419 (4) 1.09 72

Nos. 390-392 Overprinted in Gold:
a. VAINQUEUR 1976 / LASSE VIREN / FINLANDE
b. VAINQUEUR 1976 / ALWIN SCHOCKEMOHLE / R.F.A.
c. VAINQUEUR 1976 / JOHANNA SCHALLER / R.D.A.

1977, July 4 Litho. *Perf. 11*

420 A124 (a) 30fr multicolored 16 15
421 A124 (b) 55fr multicolored 30 15
422 A124 (c) 75fr multicolored 40 20
Nos. 420-422,C245-C246 (5) 3.26 1.65

Winners, 21st Olympic Games.

Crinum Ornatum — A135

Haemanthus Multiflorus — A136

Hannoa Undulata — A137

Designs: Flowers, flowering branches and wild fruits. 175fr, 300fr, horiz.

1977 Litho. *Perf. 12½*

423 A137 2fr Cordia myxa 15 15
424 A137 3fr Opilia celtidifolia 15 15
425 A135 15fr shown 15 15
426 A136 25fr shown 15 15
427 A137 50fr shown 25 20
428 A135 90fr Cochlospermum planchonii 45 35
429 A135 125fr Clitoria ternatea 65 50
430 A136 150fr Cassia alata 80 60
431 A136 175fr Nauclea latifolia 90 65
432 A136 300fr Bombax costatum 1.60 1.20
433 A135 400fr Eulophia cucullata 2.00 1.60
Nos. 423-433 (11) 7.25 5.70

Issued: 25fr, 150fr, 175fr, 300fr, Aug. 1; 2fr, 3fr, 50fr, Aug. 8; 15fr, 90fr, 125fr, 400fr, Aug. 23.

De Gaulle and Cross of Lorraine A138

Designs: 200fr, King Baudouin of Belgium.

1977, Aug. 16 *Perf. 13½x14*

434 A138 100fr multicolored 55 22
435 A138 200fr multicolored 1.10 42

Elizabeth II — A139

Designs: 300fr, Elizabeth II taking salute. 500fr, Elizabeth II after Coronation.

1977, Aug. 16

436 A139 200fr multicolored 80 32
437 A139 300fr multicolored 1.20 50

Souvenir Sheet

438 A139 500fr multicolored 2.00 90

25th anniv. of reign of Queen Elizabeth II.
For overprints see Nos. 478-480.

Lottery Tickets, Cars and Map of Upper Volta in Flag Colors — A140

1977, Sept. 16 Photo. *Perf. 13*

439 A140 55fr multicolored 30 22

10th anniversary of National Lottery.

Selma Lagerlof, Literature — A141

Nobel Prize Winners: 65fr, Guglielmo Marconi, physics. 125fr, Bertrand Russell, literature. 200fr, Linus C. Pauling, chemistry. 300fr, Robert Koch, medicine. 500fr, Albert Schweitzer, peace.

1977, Sept. 22 Litho. *Perf. 13½*

440 A141 55fr multicolored 30 15
441 A141 65fr multicolored 38 16
442 A141 125fr multicolored 65 25
443 A141 200fr multicolored 1.10 42
444 A141 300fr multicolored 1.60 65
Nos. 440-444 (5) 4.03 1.63

Souvenir Sheet

445 A141 500fr multicolored 2.50 1.20

The Three Graces, by Rubens
A142

Paintings by Peter Paul Rubens (1577-1640): 55fr, Heads of Black Men, horiz. 85fr, Bathsheba at the Fountain. 150fr, The Drunken Silenus. 200fr, 300fr, Life of Maria de Medicis, diff.

1977, Oct. 19 — Litho. — *Perf. 14*

446	A142	55fr multicolored	30	15
447	A142	65fr multicolored	38	16
448	A142	85fr multicolored	45	22
449	A142	150fr multicolored	80	40
450	A142	200fr multicolored	1.10	45
451	A142	300fr multicolored	1.60	60
		Nos. 446-451 (6)	4.63	1.98

Lenin in His Office
A143

Designs: 85fr, Lenin Monument, Kremlin. 200fr, Lenin with youth. 500fr, Lenin and Leonid Brezhnev.

1977, Oct. 28 — Litho. — *Perf. 12*

452	A143	10fr multicolored	15	15
453	A143	85fr multicolored	45	25
454	A143	200fr multicolored	1.10	65
455	A143	500fr multicolored	2.50	1.60
		Nos. 452-455 (4)	4.20	2.65

Russian October Revolution, 60th anniv.

Stadium and Brazil No. C79 — A144

Stadium and: 65fr, Brazil #1144. 125fr, Gt. Britain #458. 200fr, Chile #340. 300fr, Switzerland #350. 500fr, Germany #1147.

1977, Dec. 30 — Litho. — *Perf. 13½*

456	A144	55fr multicolored	30	15
457	A144	65fr multicolored	38	16
458	A144	125fr multicolored	65	25
459	A144	200fr multicolored	1.10	42
460	A144	300fr multicolored	1.60	65
		Nos. 456-460 (5)	4.03	1.63

Souvenir Sheet

461	A144	500fr multicolored	2.50	1.20

11th World Cup Soccer Championship, Argentina. For overprints see Nos. 486-491.

Jean Mermoz and Seaplane — A145

History of Aviation: 75fr, Anthony H. G. Fokker. 85fr, Wiley Post. 90fr, Otto Lilienthal, vert. 100fr, Concorde. 500fr, Charles Lindbergh and "Spirit of St. Louis."

1978, Jan. 2 — Litho. — *Perf. 13½*

462	A145	65fr multicolored	38	16
463	A145	75fr multicolored	40	20
464	A145	85fr multicolored	45	20
465	A145	90fr multicolored	50	20
466	A145	100fr multicolored	55	22
		Nos. 462-466 (5)	2.28	98

Souvenir Sheet

467	A145	500fr multicolored	2.50	1.25

Crataeva Religiosa — A146

1978, Feb. 28 — Litho. — *Perf. 12½*

468	A146	55fr shown	30	22
469	A146	75fr Fig tree	40	30

Souvenir Sheet

Virgin and Child, by Rubens
A147

1978, May 24 — Litho. — *Perf. 13½x14*

470	A147	500fr multicolored	2.50	1.20

Peter Paul Rubens (1577-1640).

Antenna and ITU Emblem
A148

1978, May 30 — *Perf. 13*

471	A148	65fr silver & multi	38	16

10th World Telecommunications Day.

Fetish Gate of Bobo — A149

1978, July 10 — Litho. — *Perf. 13½*

472	A149	55fr shown	30	15
473	A149	65fr Mossi fetish	38	16

Capt. Cook and "Endeavour" — A150

Capt. James Cook (1728-1779) and: 85fr, Death on Hawaiian beach. 250fr, Navigational instruments. 350fr, "Resolution."

1978, Sept. 1 — Litho. — *Perf. 14½*

474	A150	65fr multicolored	38	16
475	A150	85fr multicolored	45	20
476	A150	250fr multicolored	1.40	65
477	A150	350fr multicolored	1.90	80
		Nos. 474-477 (4)	4.13	1.81

Nos. 436-438 Overprinted Vertically in Silver: "ANNIVERSAIRE DU COURONNEMENT 1953-1978"

1978, Oct. 24 — Litho. — *Perf. 13½x14*

478	A139	200fr multicolored	1.10	42
479	A139	300fr multicolored	1.60	65

Souvenir Sheet

480	A139	500fr multicolored	2.50	1.20

25th anniversary of Coronation of Queen Elizabeth II. Overprint in 3 lines on 200fr, in 2 lines on 300fr and 500fr.

#478-480 exist with overprint in metallic red.

Trent Castle, by Dürer
A151

Paintings by Albrecht Durer (1471-1528): 150fr, Virgin and Child with St. Anne, vert. 250fr, Sts. George and Eustachius, vert. 350fr, Hans Holzschuher, vert.

Perf. 14x13½, 13½x14

1978, Nov. 20 — Litho.

481	A151	65fr multicolored	38	16
482	A151	150fr multicolored	80	38
483	A151	250fr multicolored	1.40	65
484	A151	350fr multicolored	1.90	65
		Nos. 481-484 (4)	4.48	1.84

Human Rights Emblem
A152

1978, Dec. 10 — Litho. — *Perf. 12½*

485	A152	55fr multicolored	30	15

Universal Declaration of Human Rights, 30th anniv.

Nos. 456-461 Overprinted in Silver
a, VAINQUEURS 1950 URUGUAY / 1978 / ARGENTINE
b, VAINQUEURS 1970 BRESIL / 1978 ARGENTINE
c, VAINQUEURS 1966 GRANDE BRETAGNE / 1978 ARGENTINE
d, VAINQUEURS / 1962 BRESIL / 1978 ARGENTINE
e, VAINQUEURS 1954 ALLEMAGNE (RFA) / 1978 ARGENTINE
f, VAINQUEURS 1974 ALLEMAGNE (RFA) / 1978 ARGENTINE

1979, Jan. 4 — Litho. — *Perf. 13½*

486	A144(a)	55fr multicolored	30	15
487	A144(b)	65fr multicolored	38	16
488	A144(c)	125fr multicolored	65	25
489	A144(d)	200fr multicolored	1.10	40
490	A144(e)	300fr multicolored	1.60	65
		Nos. 486-490 (5)	4.03	1.61

Souvenir Sheet

491	A144(f)	500fr multicolored	2.50	1.20

Winners, World Soccer Cup Championships 1950-1978.

Radio Station
A153

Design: 65fr, Mail plane at airport.

1979, Mar. 30 — Litho. — *Perf. 12½*

492	A153	55fr multicolored	30	15
493	A153	65fr multicolored	38	16

Post and Telecommunications Org., 10th anniv.

Teacher and Pupils, IYC Emblem — A154

1979, Apr. 9 — *Perf. 13½*

494	A154	75fr multicolored	40	20

International Year of the Child.

Telecommunications
A155

1979, May 17 — Litho. — *Perf. 13*

495	A155	70fr multicolored	45	20

11th Telecommunications Day.

Basketmaker and Upper Volta No. 111 — A156

Design: No. 497, May of Upper Volta, Concorde, truck and UPU emblem.

1979, June 8 — Photo.

496	A156	100fr multicolored	65	35
497	A156	100fr multicolored	65	35

Philexafrique II, Libreville, Gabon, June 8-17. Nos. 496, 497 each printed in sheets of 10 and 5 labels showing exhibition emblem.

Synodontis Voltae
A157

Fresh-water Fish: 50fr, Micralestes comoensis. 85fr, Silurus.

1979, June 10 Litho. *Perf. 12½*

498 A157 20fr multicolored 15 15
499 A157 50fr multicolored 35 16
500 A157 85fr multicolored 55 30
Nos. 498-500 (3) 1.05 61

Rowland Hill, Train and Upper Volta No. 60 — A158

Sir Rowland Hill (1795-1879), originator of penny postage, Trains and Upper Volta Stamps: 165fr, #59. 200fr, #57. 300fr, #56. 500fr, #55.

1979, June Litho. *Perf. 13½*

501 A158 65fr multicolored 42 20
502 A158 165fr multicolored 1.10 55
503 A158 200fr multicolored 1.40 65
504 A158 300fr multicolored 2.00 1.00
Nos. 501-504 (4) 4.92 2.40

Souvenir Sheet

505 A158 500fr multicolored 3.50 1.60

Wildlife Fund Emblem and Protected Animals — A159

1979, Aug. 30 Litho. *Perf. 14½*

506 A159 30fr Waterbuck 20 15
507 A159 40fr Roan antelope 25 15
508 A159 60fr Caracal 40 20
509 A159 100fr African bush elephant 65 35
510 A159 175fr Hartebeest 1.20 55
511 A159 250fr Leopard 1.60 80
Nos. 506-511 (6) 4.30 2.20

Adult Students and Teacher — A160

Design: 55fr, Man reading book, vert.

Perf. 12½x13, 13x12½

1979, Sept. 8

512 A160 55fr multicolored 38 18
513 A160 250fr multicolored 1.60 85

World Literacy Day.

Map of Upper Volta, Telephone Receiver and Lines, Telecom Emblem — A161

1979, Sept. 20 *Perf. 13x12½*

514 A161 200fr multicolored 1.40 65

3rd World Telecommunications Exhibition, Geneva, Sept. 20-26.

King Vulture — A162

1979, Oct. 26 Litho. *Perf. 13*

515 A162 5fr shown 15 15
516 A162 10fr Hoopoe 15 15
517 A162 15fr Bald vulture 15 15
518 A162 25fr Herons 16 15
519 A162 35fr Ostrich 22 15
520 A162 45fr Crowned crane 30 15
521 A162 125fr Eagle 80 40
Nos. 515-521 (7) 1.93
Set value 90

Control Tower, Emblem, Jet — A163

1979, Dec. 12 Photo. *Perf. 13x12½*

522 A163 65fr multicolored 42 20

ASECNA (Air Safety Board), 20th anniv.

Central Bank of West African States — A164

1979, Dec. 28 Litho. *Perf. 12½*

523 A164 55fr multicolored 38 18

Eugene Jamot, Map of Upper Volta, Tsetse Fly — A165

1979, Dec. 28 *Perf. 13x13½*

524 A165 55fr multicolored 38 18

Eugene Jamot (1879-1937), discoverer of sleeping sickness cure.

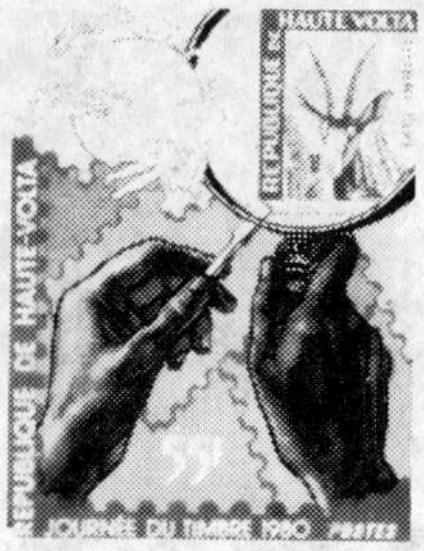

UPU Emblem, Upper Volta Type D4 under Magnifier
A166

1980, Feb. 26 Litho. *Perf. 12½x13*

525 A166 55fr multicolored 38 18

Stamp Day.

World Locomotive Speed Record, 25th Anniversary
A167

1980, Mar. 30 Litho. *Perf. 12½*

526 A167 75fr multicolored 50 25
527 A167 100fr multicolored 65 35

Pres. Sangoule Lamizana, Pope John Paul II, Cardinal Pau Zoungrana, Map of Upper Volta — A168

1980, May 10 Litho. *Perf. 12½*

528 A168 65fr shown 42 20

Size: 21x36mm

529 A168 100fr Pope John Paul II 65 35

Visit of Pope John Paul II to Upper Volta.

A169

A170

1980, May 17 *Perf. 13x12½*

530 A169 50fr multicolored 35 16

12th World Telecommunications Day.

1980, June 12 Litho. *Perf. 13*

531 A170 65fr Sun and earth 42 20
532 A170 100fr Solar energy 65 35

Downhill Skiing, Lake Placid '80 Emblem
A171

1980, June 26 *Perf. 14½*

533 A171 65fr shown 35 16
534 A171 100fr Women's downhill 55 30
535 A171 200fr Figure skating 1.25 55
536 A171 350fr Slalom, vert. 1.90 1.00
Nos. 533-536 (4) 4.05 2.01

Souvenir Sheet

537 A171 500fr Speed skating 3.50 1.60

12th Winter Olympic Game Winners, Lake Placid, NY, Feb. 12-24.

Map of Europe and Africa, Jet — A172

Hand Holding Back Sand Dune — A173

Europafrica Issue

1980, July 14 Litho. *Perf. 13*

538 A172 100fr multicolored 65 35

1980, July 18

Operation Green Sahel: 55fr, Hands holding seedlings.

539 A173 50fr multicolored 35 16
540 A173 55fr multicolored 38 20

Gourmantche Chief Initiation — A174

1980, Sept. 12 Litho. *Perf. 14*

541 A174 30fr shown 20 15
542 A174 55fr Moro Naba, Mossi Emperor 38 18
543 A174 65fr Princess Guimbe Ouattara, vert. 42 20
Nos. 541-543 (3) 1.00 53

A175

A176

Gourounsi mask, conference emblem.

1980, Oct. 6 *Perf. 13½x13*

544 A175 65fr multicolored 42 20

World Tourism Conf., Manila, Sept. 27.

1980, Nov. 5 Litho. *Perf. 12½*

545 A176 55fr Agriculture 38 18
546 A176 65fr Transportation 42 20
547 A176 75fr Dam, highway 50 25
548 A176 100fr Industry 65 35
Nos. 545-548 (4) 1.95 98

West African Economic Council, 5th anniv.

20th Anniv. of Independence — A177

1980, Dec. 11 *Perf. 13*

540 A177 500fr multicolored	3.50	1.60

Madonna and Child, by Raphael — A178

West African Postal Union, 5th Anniv. — A179

Christmas: Paintings of Madonna and Child, by Raphael.

1980, Dec. 22 *Perf. 12½*

550 A178 60fr multicolored	40	20
551 A178 150fr multicolored	1.00	50
552 A178 250fr multicolored	1.60	80
Nos. 550-552 (3)	3.00	1.50

1980, Dec. 24 Photo. *Perf. 13½*

553 A179 55fr multicolored	38	20

Dung Beetle — A180

Perf. 13x13½, 13½x13

1981, Mar. 10 **Litho.**

554 A180 5fr shown	15	15
555 A180 10fr Crickets	15	15
556 A180 15fr Termites	15	15
557 A180 20fr Praying mantis, vert.	15	15
558 A180 55fr Emperor moth	38	25
559 A180 65fr Locust, vert.	42	20
Set value	1.15	65

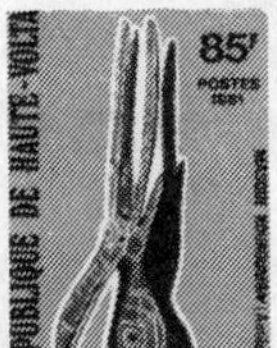

Antelope Mask, Kouroumba — A181

Designs: Various ceremonial masks.

1981, Mar. 20 Litho. *Perf. 13*

560 A181 45fr multicolored	26	15
561 A181 55fr multicolored	32	16
562 A181 85fr multicolored	48	25
563 A181 105fr multicolored	60	30
Nos. 560-563 (4)	1.66	86

Notre Dame of Kologh' Naba College, 25th Anniv. A182

1981, Mar. 30

564 A182 55fr multicolored	32	18

Heinrich von Stephan, UPU Founder, Birth Sesquicentennial — A183

1981, May 4 Litho. *Perf. 13*

565 A183 65fr multicolored	35	18

13th World Telecommunications Day — A184

1981, May 17 *Perf. 13½x13*

566 A184 90fr multicolored	52	25

Diesel Train, Abidjan-Niger Railroad A185

Designs: Trains.

1981, July 6 Litho. *Perf. 13*

567 A185 25fr shown	16	15
568 A185 30fr Gazelle	20	15
569 A185 40fr Belier	25	15
Nos. 567-569 (3)	61	
Set value		32

Tree Planting Month — A186

1981, July 15

570 A186 70fr multicolored	45	22

Natl. Red Cross, 20th Anniv. A187

1981, July 31 *Perf. 12½x13*

571 A187 70fr multicolored	45	22

Intl. Year of the Disabled — A188

1981, Aug. 20 Litho. *Perf. 13x12½*

572 A188 70fr multicolored	45	22

View of Koudougou A189

1981, Sept. 3 Litho. *Perf. 12½*

573 A189 35fr shown	22	15
574 A189 45fr Toma	30	15
575 A189 85fr Volta Noire	55	28
Nos. 573-575 (3)	1.07	58

World Food Day A190

1981, Oct. 16 *Perf. 13*

576 A190 90fr multicolored	60	30

Elephant A191

Designs: Various protected species.

1981, Oct. 21 Photo. *Perf. 14*

577 A191 5fr multicolored	15	15
578 A191 15fr multicolored	15	15
579 A191 40fr multicolored	25	15
580 A191 60fr multicolored	40	20
581 A191 70fr multicolored	45	22
Nos. 577-581 (5)	1.40	
Set value		65

Fight Against Apartheid — A192

Mangoes — A193

1981, Dec. 9 Litho. *Perf. 12½*

582 A192 90fr red orange	60	30

Perf. 13x13½, 13½x13

1981, Dec. 15

583 A193 20fr Papayas, horiz.	15	15
584 A193 35fr Fruits, vegetables, horiz.	22	15
585 A193 75fr shown	50	25
586 A193 90fr Melons, horiz.	60	30
Nos. 583-586 (4)	1.47	85

Guinea Hen — A194

West African Rice Development Assoc., 10th Anniv. — A195

Designs: Breeding animals. 10fr, 25fr, 70fr, 250fr, 300fr horiz.

1981, Dec. 22 *Perf. 13*

587 A194 10fr Donkey	15	15
588 A194 25fr Pig	16	15
589 A194 70fr Cow	45	22
590 A194 90fr shown	60	30
591 A194 250fr Rabbit	1.60	80
Nos. 587-591 (5)	2.96	1.62

Souvenir Sheet

592 A194 300fr Sheep	2.00	1.00

1981, Dec. 29

593 A195 90fr multicolored	60	30

20th Anniv. of World Food Program — A196

1982, Jan. 18

594 A196 50fr multicolored	35	16

Traditional Houses — A197

1982, Apr. 23 Litho. *Perf. 12½*

595 A197 30fr Morhonaba Palace, vert.	20	15
596 A197 70fr Bobo	45	22
597 A197 100fr Gourounsi	65	35
598 A197 200fr Peulh	1.40	65
599 A197 250fr Dagari	1.60	80
Nos. 595-599 (5)	4.30	2.17

14th World Telecommunications Day — A198

1982, May 17

600 A198 125fr multicolored	85	40

Water Lily — A199

25th Anniv. of Cultural Aid Fund — A201

African Postal Union A200

1982, Sept. 22 *Perf. 13x12½*

601	A199	25fr	shown	15	15
602	A199	40fr	Kapoks	20	15
603	A199	70fr	Frangipani	35	18
604	A199	90fr	Cochlospermum planchonii	60	22
605	A199	100fr	Cotton	50	25
			Nos. 601-605 (5)	1.80	95

1982, Oct. 7

606	A200	70fr	multicolored	45	22
607	A200	90fr	multicolored	60	30

1982, Nov. 10 *Perf. 12½x13*

608	A201	70fr	multicolored	45	22

Map, Hand Holding Grain, Steer Head — A202

1982 *Perf. 12½*

609	A202	90fr	multicolored	60	30

Traditional Hairstyle A203

1983, Jan. **Litho.** *Perf. 12½*

610	A203	90fr	lt green & multi	52	25
611	A203	120fr	lt blue & multi	70	35
612	A203	170fr	pink & multi	95	48
			Nos. 610-612 (3)	2.17	1.08

For overprints see Nos. 884-886.

8th Film Festival, Ouagadougou — A204

1983, Feb. 10 **Litho.** *Perf. 13x12½*

613	A204	90fr	Scene	60	30
614	A204	500fr	Filmmaker Dumarou Ganda	3.50	1.60

UN Intl. Drinking Water and Sanitation Decade, 1981-90 — A205

1983, Apr. 21 **Litho.** *Perf. 13½x13*

615	A205	60fr	Water drops	40	20
616	A205	70fr	Carrying water	45	22

Manned Flight Bicentenary A206

Portraits and Balloons: 15fr, J.M. Montgolfier, 1783. 25fr, Etienne Montgolfier's balloon, 1783, Pilatre de Rozier. 70fr, Charles & Roberts flight, 1783, Jacques Charles. 90fr, Flight over English Channel, John Jeffries. 100fr, Testu-Brissy's horseback flight, Wilhemine Reichardt. 250fr, Andree's Spitzbergen flight, 1897, S.A. Andree. 300fr, Piccard's stratosphere flight, 1931, August Piccard.

1983, Apr. 15 **Litho.** *Perf. 13½*

617	A206	15fr	multicolored	15	15
618	A206	25fr	multicolored	16	15
619	A206	70fr	multicolored	45	22
620	A206	90fr	multicolored	60	30
621	A206	100fr	multicolored	65	35
622	A206	250fr	multicolored	1.60	80
			Nos. 617-622 (6)	3.61	1.97

Souvenir Sheet

623	A206	300fr	multicolored	2.00	1.00

No. 623 contains one stamp 38x47mm. Nos. 621-623 airmail.

World Communications Year — A207

1983, May 26 **Litho.** *Perf. 12½*

624	A207	30fr	Man reading letter	16	15
625	A207	35fr	Like No. 624	18	15
626	A207	45fr	Aircraft over stream	25	15
627	A207	90fr	Girl on telephone	50	25
			Nos. 624-627 (4)	1.09	
			Set value		55

Fishing Resources A208

1983, July 28 **Litho.** *Perf. 13*

628	A208	20fr	Synadontis gambiensis	15	15
629	A208	30fr	Palmotochromis	15	15
630	A208	40fr	Boy fishing, vert.	15	15
631	A208	50fr	Fishing with net	16	15
632	A208	75fr	Fishing with basket	25	15
			Set value	72	37

Anti-deforestation — A209

1983, Sept. 13 **Litho.** *Perf. 13*

633	A209	10fr	Planting saplings	15	15
634	A209	50fr	Tree nursery	16	15
635	A209	100fr	Prevent forest fires	35	16
636	A209	150fr	Woman cooking	50	25
637	A209	200fr	Prevent felling, vert.	65	35
			Nos. 633-637 (5)	1.81	
			Set value		88

Fresco Detail, by Raphael — A210

Paintings: 120fr, Self-portrait, by Pablo Picasso, 1901, vert. 185fr, Self-portrait at the palette, by Manet, 1878, vert. 350fr, Fresco Detail, diff., by Raphael. 500fr, Goethe, by George Oswald May, 1779, vert.

1983, Nov. **Litho.** *Perf. 13*

638	A210	120fr	multicolored	40	20
639	A210	185fr	multicolored	62	32
640	A210	300fr	multicolored	1.00	50
641	A210	350fr	multicolored	1.20	60
642	A210	500fr	multicolored	1.60	80
			Nos. 638-642 (5)	4.82	2.42

25th Anniv. of the Republic A211

1983, Dec. 9 **Litho.** *Perf. 14*

643	A211	90fr	Arms	30	15
644	A211	500fr	Family, flag	1.60	80

A212

Scouting — A213

1984, May 29 **Litho.** *Perf. 12½*

645	A212	90fr	multicolored	30	15
646	A212	100fr	multicolored	35	16

Council of Unity, 25th anniv.

1984, June 15 **Litho.** *Perf. 13½*

647	A213	25fr	Polystictus leoninus	15	15
648	A213	185fr	Pterocarpus Lucens	90	45
649	A213	200fr	Phlebopus colossus sudanicus	1.10	50
650	A213	250fr	Cosmos sulphureus	1.25	62
651	A213	300fr	Trametes versicolor	1.50	80
652	A213	400fr	Ganoderma lucidum	2.00	1.10
			Nos. 647-652 (6)	6.90	3.62

Souvenir Sheet

653	A213	600fr	Leucocoprinus cepaestipes	3.25	1.60

Nos. 651-653 are airmail. For overprints see Nos. 669-674.

Wildlife A214

Wildlife — A215

1984, July 19

654	A214	15fr	Cheetah, four cubs	15	15
655	A214	35fr	Two adults	15	15
656	A214	90fr	One adult	35	16
657	A214	120fr	Cheetah, two cubs	45	22
658	A214	300fr	Baboons	1.20	55
659	A214	400fr	Vultures	1.50	80
			Nos. 654-659 (6)	3.80	2.03

Souvenir Sheet

660	A215	1000fr	Antelopes	4.00	1.90

World Wildlife Fund (Nos. 654-567); Rotary Intl. (Nos. 658, 660); Natl. Boy Scouts (No. 659). Nos. 658-660 are airmail.

Sailing Ships and Locomotives — A216

1984, Aug. 14 *Perf. 12½*

661	A216	20fr	Maiden Queen	15	15
662	A216	40fr	CC 2400 ch	16	15
663	A216	60fr	Scawfell	22	15
664	A216	100fr	PO 1806	38	18
665	A216	120fr	Harbinger	45	22
666	A216	145fr	Livingstone	55	28
667	A216	400fr	True Briton	1.50	80
668	A216	450fr	Pacific C51	1.60	85
			Nos. 661-668 (8)	5.01	2.78

Natl. Defense — A216a

Design: 120fr, Capt. Sankara, crowd, horiz.

1984, Nov. 21 **Litho.** *Perf. 13½*

668A	A216a	90fr	multicolored		
668B	A216a	120fr	multicolored		

Burkina Faso

Nos. 647-652 Ovptd. with Two Bars and "BURKINA FASO"

1985, Mar. 5 **Litho.** *Perf. 13½*

669	A213	25fr	multicolored	15	15
670	A213	185fr	multicolored	55	25
671	A213	200fr	multicolored	60	30
672	A213	250fr	multicolored	75	38
673	A213	300fr	multicolored	90	45
674	A213	400fr	multicolored	1.20	60
			Nos. 669-674 (6)	4.15	2.13

A217

Designs: 5fr, 120fr, Flag. 15fr, 150fr, Natl. Arms, vert. 90fr, 185fr, Map.

1985, Mar. 8 Litho. *Perf. 12½*

675 A217 5fr multicolored
676 A217 15fr multicolored
677 A217 90fr multicolored
678 A217 120fr multicolored
679 A217 150fr multicolored
680 A217 185fr multicolored

Nos. 678-680 are airmail.

1986 World Cup Soccer Championships, Mexico — A218

A219

Various soccer plays and Aztec artifacts.

1985, Apr. 20 Litho. *Perf. 13*

681 A218 25fr multicolored 15 15
682 A218 45fr multicolored 16 15
683 A218 90fr multicolored 35 16
684 A218 100fr multicolored 38 18
685 A218 150fr multicolored 55 25
686 A218 200fr multicolored 70 38
687 A218 250fr multicolored 90 45
Nos. 681-687 (7) 3.19 1.72

Souvenir Sheet

688 A219 500fr multicolored 1.90 1.20

Nos. 681-685 vert. No. 684-688 are airmail.

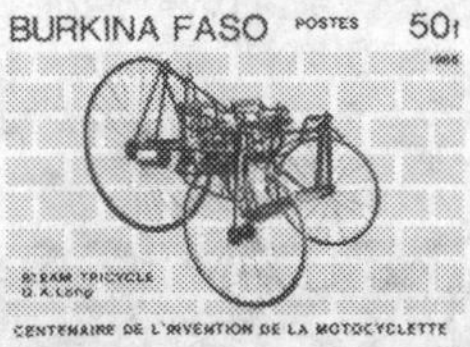

Motorcycle, Cent. — A220

1985, May 26

689 A220 50fr Steam tricycle, G.A. Long 18 15
690 A220 75fr Pope 28 15
691 A220 80fr Manet-90 30 15
692 A220 100fr Ducati 38 18
693 A220 150fr Jawa 55 28
694 A220 200fr Honda 70 38
695 A220 250fr B.M.W. 90 45
Nos. 689-695 (7) 3.29 1.74

Nos. 692-695 are airmail.

Reptiles A221

1985, June 20

696 A221 5fr Chamaeleon dilepis 15 15
697 A221 15fr Agama stellio 15 15
698 A221 35fr Lacerta Lepida 15 15
699 A221 85fr Hiperolius marmoratus 32 16
700 A221 100fr Echis leucogaster 38 18
701 A221 150fr Kinixys erosa 55 28
702 A221 250fr Python regius 90 45
Nos. 696-702 (7) 2.60
Set value 1.24

#696-697 vert. #700-702 are airmail.

British Queen Mother, 85th Birthday A222

1985, June 21 *Perf. 13½*

703 A222 75fr On pony bobs 22 15
704 A222 85fr Wedding, 1923 25 15
705 A222 500fr Holding infant Elizabeth, 1926 1.60 80
706 A222 600fr Coronation of King George VI, 1937 1.90 90
Nos. 703-706 (4) 3.97 2.00

Souvenir Sheet

707 A222 1000fr Christening of Prince William, 1982 3.25 1.60

Nos. 705-707 are airmail.

Vintage Autos and Aircraft — A223

1985, June 21

708 A223 5fr Benz Victoria, 1893 15 15
709 A223 25fr Peugeot 174, 1927 15 15
710 A223 45fr Louis Bleriot 16 15
711 A223 50fr Breguet 14 20 15
712 A223 500fr Bugatti Coupe Napoleon T41 Royale 1.90 90
713 A223 500fr Airbus A300-P4 1.90 90
714 A223 600fr Mercedes-Benz 540K, 1938 2.25 1.20
715 A223 600fr Airbus A300B 2.25 1.20
Nos. 708-715 (8) 8.96 4.80

Souvenir Sheet

716 A223 1000fr Louis Bleriot, Karl Benz 4.00 1.90

Automobile, cent. Nos. 712-716 are airmail.

Audubon Birth Bicent. A224

Illustrations of No. American bird species by Audubon and scouting trefoil.

1985, June 21

717 A224 60fr Aix sponsa 22 15
718 A224 100fr Mimus polyglotos 38 18
719 A224 300fr Icterus galbula 1.20 60
720 A224 400fr Sitta carolinensis 1.50 80
721 A224 500fr Asyndesmus lewis 1.50 90
722 A224 600fr Buteo cagopus 2.25 1.10
Nos. 717-722 (6) 7.05 3.73

Souvenir Sheet

723 A224 1000fr Columba leucocephala 4.00 1.90

Nos. 721-723 are airmail.

ARGENTINA '85, Buenos Aires — A225

Various equestrians.

1985, July 5 *Perf. 13*

724 A225 25fr Gaucho, piebald 15 15
725 A225 45fr Horse and rider, Andes Mountains 16 15
726 A225 90fr Rodeo 32 16
727 A225 100fr Hunting gazelle 38 18
728 A225 150fr Gauchos, 3 horses 55 25
729 A225 200fr Rider beside mount 70 35
730 A225 250fr Contest 90 42
Nos. 724-730 (7) 3.16 1.66

Souvenir Sheet

731 A225 500fr Foal 1.90 70

Nos. 727-731 are airmail.

Locomotives — A226

1985, July 23

732 A226 50fr 105-30 electric, tank wagon 18 15
733 A226 75fr Diesel shunting locomotive 25 15
734 A226 80fr Diesel locomotive 28 15
735 A226 100fr Diesel railcar 38 18
736 A226 150fr No. 6093 55 25
737 A226 200fr No. 105 diesel railcar 70 35
738 A226 250fr Diesel, passenger car 90 42
Nos. 732-738 (7) 3.24 1.65

Nos. 735-738 are airmail.

Artifacts — A227

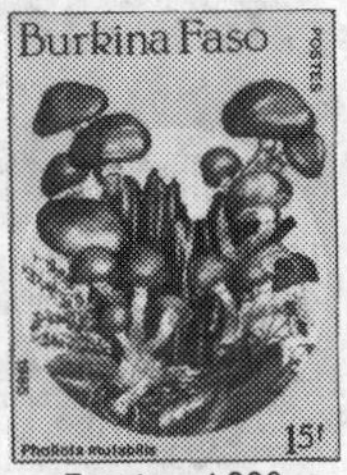

Fungi — A228

1985, July 27 *Perf. 13x12½*

739 A227 10fr 4-legged jar, Tikare 15 15
740 A227 40fr Lidded pot with bird handles, P. Bazega 15 15
741 A227 90fr Mother and child, bronze statue, Ouagadougou 35 16
742 A227 120fr Drummer, bronze statue, Ouagadougou 42 20
Nos. 739-742 (4) 1.07
Set value 48

No. 742 is airmail.

1985, Aug. 8 *Perf. 13*

743 A228 15fr Philiota mutabilis 15 15
744 A228 20fr Hypholoma (nematoloma) fasciculare 15 15
745 A228 30fr Ixocomus granulatus 15 15
746 A228 60fr Agaricus campestris 22 15
747 A228 80fr Trachypus scaber 30 15
748 A228 150fr Armillaria mellea 55 25
749 A228 250fr Marasmius scorodonius 90 42
Nos. 743-749 (7) 2.42
Set value 1.05

Nos. 748 is airmail.

ITALIA '85 — A228a

Paintings by Botticelli: 25fr, Virgin and Child. 45fr, Portrait of a Man. 90fr, Mars and Venus. 100fr, Birth of Venus. 150fr, Allegory of the Calumny. 200fr, Pallas and the Centaur. 250fr, Allegory of Spring. 500fr, The Virgin of Melagrana.

1985, Oct. 25 Litho. *Perf. 12½x13*

749A A228a 25fr multicolored 15 15
749B A228a 45fr multicolored 22 15
749C A228a 90fr multicolored 45 22
749D A228a 100fr multicolored 50 25
749E A228a 150fr multicolored 70 38
749F A228a 200fr multicolored 1.00 50
749G A228a 250fr multicolored 1.25 60
Nos. 749A-749G (7) 4.27 2.25

Souvenir Sheet

749H A228a 500fr multicolored 2.50 1.25

No. 749D-749H are airmail.

Intl. Red Cross in Burkina Faso, 75th Anniv. A229

1985, Nov. 10

750 A229 40f Helicopter 15 15
751 A229 85fr Ambulance 30 15
752 A229 150fr Henri Dunant 55 25
753 A229 250fr Physician, patient 90 42
Nos. 750-753 (4) 1.90 97

Nos. 752-753 are vert. and airmail.

Child Survival — A230

1986, Jan. 6

754 A230 90fr Breast-feeding 48 25

Dated 1985.

Dodo Carnival A231

1986, Jan. 6 *Perf. 12½*

755 A231 20fr Three children, drummer 15 15
756 A231 25fr Lion, 4 dancers 15 15
757 A231 40fr Two dancers, two drummers 22 15
758 A231 45fr Three dancers 25 15
759 A231 90fr Zebra, ostrich, dancers 48 25
760 A231 90fr Elephant, dancer 48 25
Nos. 755-760 (6) 1.73
Set value 86

Dated 1985.

Christopher Columbus (1451-1506) — A232

Columbus: 250fr, At Court of King of Portugal, the Nina. 300fr, Using astrolabe, the Santa Maria. 400fr, Imprisonment at Hispanola, 1500, the Santa Maria. 450fr, At San Salvador, 1492, the Pinta. 1000fr, Fleet departing Palos harbor, 1492.

1986, Feb. 10 *Perf. 13½*

761	A232	250fr multicolored	1.35	68
762	A232	300fr multicolored	1.65	82
763	A232	400fr multicolored	2.25	1.15
764	A232	450fr multicolored	2.50	1.25
		Nos. 761-764 (4)	7.75	3.90

Souvenir Sheet

765 A232 1000fr multicolored 5.50 2.75

Nos. 764-765 are airmail. Dated 1985.

Railroad Construction — A233

1986, Feb. 10

766	A233	90fr Man, woman carrying rail	50	25
767	A233	120fr Laying rails	65	32
768	A233	185fr Diesel train on new tracks	1.00	50
769	A233	500fr Adler locomotive, 1835	2.75	1.40
		Nos. 766-769 (4)	4.90	2.47

Souvenir Sheet

770 A233 1000fr Electric train, Series 290 diesel 5.00 2.75

German Railways, sesquicentennial. Nos. 769-770 are airmail. Dated 1985.

Intl. Peace Year — A234

World Health by the Year 2000 — A235

1986, Oct. 10 **Photo.** *Perf. 12½x13*

771 A234 90fr blue 1.10 55

1986, Aug. 8 **Litho.** *Perf. 13*

Designs: 100fr, Primary care medicine. 150fr, Mass inoculations.

772 A235 90fr multicolored 65 32

Size: 26x30mm

Perf. 12½x13

773	A235	100fr multicolored	72	35
774	A235	120fr multicolored	85	42
		Nos. 772-774 (3)	2.22	1.09

Insects — A236

World Post Day — A237

1986, Sept. 10 **Litho.** *Perf. 12½x13*

775	A236	15fr Phryneta aurocinta	15	15
776	A236	20fr Sternocera interrupta	18	15
777	A236	40fr Prosoprocera lactator	36	18
778	A236	45fr Gonimbrasia hecate	42	20
778A	A236	85fr Charaxes epijasius	78	36
		Nos. 775-778A (5)	1.89	1.04

1986, Oct. 9 *Perf. 13*

779 A237 120fr multicolored 68 35

UN Child Survival Campaign — A238

Designs: 30fr, Mother feeding child. 90fr, Nurse vaccinating child.

1986, Oct. 8 **Litho.** *Perf. 11½x12*

780 A238 30fr multicolored
782 A238 90fr multicolored

Numbers have been reserved for 60fr and 120fr stamps in this set.

Mammals A239

Designs: 50fr, Warthog. 65fr, Hyena. 90fr, Antelope. 100fr, Gazelle. 120fr, Bushbuck. 145fr, Kudu. 500fr, Gazelle, diff.

1986, Nov. 3 **Litho.** *Perf. 13x12½*

784	A239	50fr multicolored
784A	A239	65fr multicolored
784B	A239	90fr multicolored
784C	A239	100fr multicolored
784D	A239	120fr multicolored
784E	A239	145fr multicolored
784F	A239	500fr multicolored

Traditional Dances — A240

Designs: 10fr, Namende. 25fr, Mouhoun. 90fr, Houet. 105fr, Seno. 120fr, Ganzourgou.

1986, Nov. 3 **Litho.** *Perf. 12½x13*

785	A240	10fr multicolored
785A	A240	25fr multicolored
785B	A240	90fr multicolored
785C	A240	105fr multicolored
785D	A240	120fr multicolored

Hairstyles — A241

1986, Nov. 4 **Litho.** *Perf. 12½x13*

788	A241	35fr Peul	28	15
789	A241	75fr Dafing	60	30
790	A241	90fr Peul, diff.	70	35
791	A241	120fr Mossi	95	48
792	A241	185fr Peul, diff.	1.50	75
		Nos. 788-792 (5)	4.03	2.03

10th African Film Festival — A242

Intl Women's Day — A243

1987, Feb. 21 **Litho.** *Perf. 12x12½*

793 A242 90fr Maps, cameras
794 A242 120fr Jolson, cameramen
795 A242 185fr Charlie Chaplin

60th Anniv. of the film *The Jazz Singer* (120fr); 10th anniv. of the death of Charlie Chaplin (185fr).

1987, Mar. 8 *Perf. 13½*

796 A243 90fr multicolored

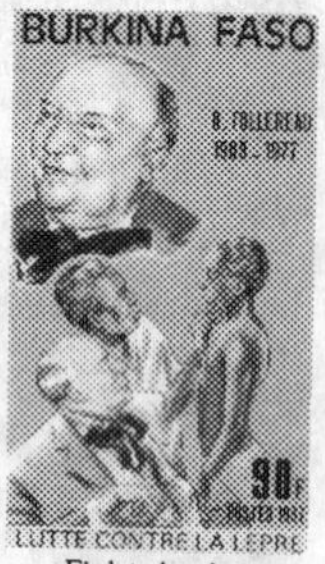

Flora — A244

Fight Against Leprosy — A245

1987, June 6 **Litho.** *Perf. 12½x13*

797	A244	70fr Calotropis procera	48	24
798	A244	75fr Acacia seyal	52	25
799	A244	85fr Parkia biglobosa	60	30
800	A244	90fr Sterospernum kunthianum	62	30
801	A244	100fr Dichrostachys cinerea	70	35
802	A244	300fr Combretum paniculatum	2.10	1.05
		Nos. 797-802 (6)	5.02	2.49

1987, Aug. 6 *Perf. 13*

Raoul Follereau (1903-1977) and: 90fr, Doctors examining African youth. 100fr, Laboratory research. 120fr, Gerhard Hansen (1841-1912), microscope, bacillus under magnification. 300fr, Follereau embracing cured leper.

803	A245	90fr multicolored	62	30
804	A245	100fr multicolored	70	35
805	A245	120fr multicolored	85	42
806	A245	300fr multicolored	2.10	1.05
		Nos. 803-806 (4)	4.27	2.12

World Environment Day — A246

1987, Aug. 18 **Litho.** *Perf. 13x12½*

807	A246	90fr shown	68	35
808	A246	145fr Emblem, huts	1.10	55

Pre-Olympic Year — A247

1987, Aug. 31 *Perf. 12½*

809	A247	75fr High jump	55	28
810	A247	85fr Tennis, vert.	62	30
811	A247	90fr Ski jumping	68	35
812	A247	100fr Soccer	75	38
813	A247	145fr Running	1.10	55
814	A247	350fr Pierre de Coubertin, tennis, vert.	2.60	1.30
		Nos. 809-814 (6)	6.30	3.16

Pierre de Coubertin (1863-1937).

World Post Day — A248

1987, Oct. 5 **Litho.** *Perf. 12½x13*

815 A248 90fr multicolored

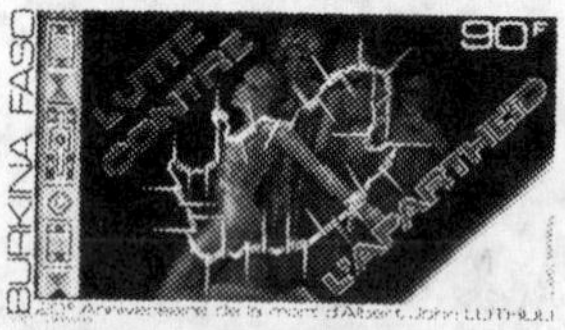

Fight Against Apartheid — A249

1987, Nov. 11 **Litho.** *Perf. 13*

816	A249	90fr shown	1.00	50
817	A249	100fr Luthuli, book, 1962	1.10	55

Albert John Luthuli (1898-1967), South African reformer, author and 1960 Nobel Peace Prize winner. No. 817 incorrectly inscribed "1899-1967."

Traditional Costumes — A250

1987, Dec. 4 **Litho.** *Perf. 11½x12*

820 A250 90fr Mossi
821 A250 200fr Senoufo

Numbers have been reserved for 10fr, 30fr and 500fr stamps in this set.

Traditional Musical Instruments A251

Perf. 12x11½, 11½x12

1987, Dec. 4 **Litho.**
823 A251 20fr Xylophone 18 15
824 A251 25fr 3-Stringed lute, vert. 22 15
825 A251 35fr Zither 30 15
826 A251 90fr Conical drum 78 40
827 A251 1000fr Calabash drum, vert. 8.50 4.25
Nos. 823-827 (5) 9.98 5.10

Intl. Year of Shelter for the Homeless — A252

1987, Dec. 4 **Litho.** ***Perf. 13***
828 A252 90fr multicolored 65 32

Five-year Natl. Development Plan — A253

1987, Dec. 15 ***Perf. 13½***
829 A253 40fr Small businesses 30 15
830 A253 55fr Agriculture 40 20
831 A253 60fr Constructing schools 45 22
832 A253 90fr Transportation and communications 65 32
833 A253 100fr Literacy 72 35
834 A253 120fr Animal husbandry 88 45
Nos. 829-834 (6) 3.40 1.69

World Health Organization, 40th Anniv. — A254

1988, Mar. 31 **Litho.** ***Perf. 12½x13***
835 A254 120fr multicolored 78 40

1988 Summer Olympics, Seoul — A255

1988, May 5 ***Perf. 13x12½***
836 A255 30fr shown 20 15
837 A255 160fr Torch, vert. 1.05 52
838 A255 175fr Soccer 1.15 58
839 A255 235fr Volleyball, vert. 1.50 75
840 A255 450fr Basketball, vert. 2.90 1.45
Nos. 836-840 (5) 6.80 3.45

Souvenir Sheet

Perf. 12½x13

841 A255 500fr Runners 3.25 1.65

No. 841 contains one stamp, size: 40x52mm plus two labels.

Ritual Masks A256

1988, May 30 **Litho.** ***Perf. 13***
842 A256 10fr Epervier, Houet 15 15
843 A256 20fr Jeunes Filles, Oullo 15 15
844 A256 30fr Bubale, Houet 20 15
845 A256 40fr Forgeron, Mouhoun 28 15
846 A256 120fr Nounouma, Ouri 80 40
847 A256 175fr Chauve-souris, Ouri 1.20 60
Nos. 842-847 (6) 2.78
Set value 1.35

Nos. 842-846 vert.

Handicrafts A257

1988, Aug. 22 **Litho.** ***Perf. 13½***
848 A257 5fr Kieriebe ceramic pitcher, vert. 15 15
849 A257 15fr Mossi basket 15 15
850 A257 25fr Gurunsi chair 18 15
851 A257 30fr Bissa basket 20 15
852 A257 45fr Ougadougou leather box 35 18
853 A257 85fr Ougadougou bronze statue, vert. 68 35
854 A257 120fr Ougadougou leather valise 80 40
Nos. 848-854 (7) 2.51
Set value 1.20

World Post Day — A258

1988, Oct. 9 **Litho.** ***Perf. 13***
855 A258 120fr multicolored 80 40

Aquatic Fauna — A259

1988, Oct. 31 ***Perf. 12***
856 A259 70fr Angler martin 48 25
857 A259 100fr Mormyrus rume 68 35
858 A259 120fr Frog 80 40
859 A259 160fr Duck 1.10 55
Nos. 856-859 (4) 3.06 1.55

Civil Rights and Political Activists A260

Designs: 80fr, Mohammed Ali Jinnah (1876-1948), 1st Governor General of Pakistan. 120fr, Mahatma Gandhi (1869-1948), India. 160fr, John F. Kennedy. 235fr, Martin Luther King, Jr.

1988, Nov. 22 **Litho.** ***Perf. 14***
860 A260 80fr multicolored 52 25
861 A260 120fr multicolored 78 40
862 A260 160fr multicolored 1.00 50
863 A260 235fr multicolored 1.50 75
Nos. 860-863 (4) 3.80 1.90

A261

A262

Christmas: Stained-glass windows.

1988, Dec. 2 ***Perf. 12***
864 A261 120fr Adoration of the shepherds 78 40
865 A261 160fr Adoration of the Magi 1.00 50
866 A261 450fr Madonna and child 2.90 1.45
867 A261 1000fr Flight into Egypt 6.35 3.15
Nos. 864-867 (4) 11.03 5.50

1989, Feb. 25 **Litho.** ***Perf. 14***
868 A262 75fr shown 24 15
869 A262 500fr Ababacar Makharam 1.60 80
870 A262 500fr Jean Tchissoukou 1.60 80
871 A262 500fr Paulin Vieyra 1.60 80
Nos. 868-871 (4) 5.04 2.55

Souvenir Sheet

872 Sheet of 3 9.00 4.50
a.-c. A262 500fr like #869-871, inscribed in gold 3.00 1.50

Panafrican Film Festival (FESPACO), 20th anniv. Nos. 869-872 are airmail.

World Fight Against AIDS A263

1989, Apr. 7 **Litho.** ***Perf. 13***
873 A263 120fr multicolored 78 40

Council for Rural Development, 30th Anniv. A264

1989, May 3 **Litho.** ***Perf. 15x14***
874 A264 75fr multicolored 48 25

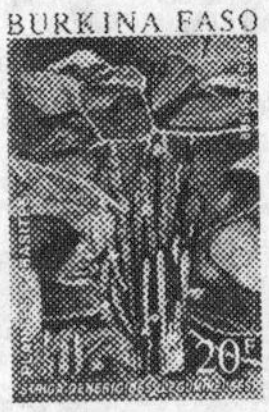

Parasitic Plants — A265

Legumes and cereals.

1989, Oct. 9 **Litho.** ***Perf. 11½***

Granite Paper

875 A265 20fr *Striga generiodes* 15 15
876 A265 50fr *Striga hermonthica* 32 16
877 A265 235fr *Striga aspera* 1.50 78
878 A265 450fr *Alectra vogelii* 3.00 1.50
Nos. 875-878 (4) 4.97 2.59

Dogs A266

1989, Oct. 9 ***Perf. 15x14½***
879 A266 35fr Sahel 24 15
880 A266 50fr Puppy 35 18
881 A266 60fr Hunting dog 40 20
882 A266 350fr Guard dog 2.30 1.15
Nos. 879-882 (4) 3.29 1.68

Solidarity with the Palestinian People — A267

1989, Nov. 15 ***Perf. 13***
883 A267 120fr Monument, Place de la Palestine 80 40

Nos. 610-612 Overprinted

1988, Dec. 21 **Litho.** ***Perf. 12½***
884 A203 90fr multicolored 62 30
885 A203 120fr multicolored 85 42
886 A203 170fr multicolored 1.20 60
Nos. 884-886 (3) 2.67 1.32

Visit of Pope John Paul II — A268

1990, Jan. 1 **Litho.** ***Perf. 15x14***
887 A268 120fr Our Lady of Yagma 85 42
888 A269 160fr Pope, crowd 1.20 60

150th Anniv. of the Postage Stamp A269

1990, Mar. 20 **Litho.** ***Perf. 15x14***
889 A269 120fr multicolored 1.00 50

Souvenir Sheet

Perf. 14x15

890 A269 500fr Penny Black, ship 4.00 2.00

Stamp World London '90.

World Cup Soccer Championships, Italy — A270

1990, Apr. 26 Litho. *Perf. 11½*
891 A270 30fr multicolored 22 15
892 A270 150fr multi, diff. 1.10 55

Souvenir Sheet

893 A270 1000fr multi, horiz. 7.25 3.65

Intl. Literacy Year — A271

1990, July 10 Litho. *Perf. 13*
894 A271 40fr multicolored 28 15
895 A271 130fr multicolored 90 45

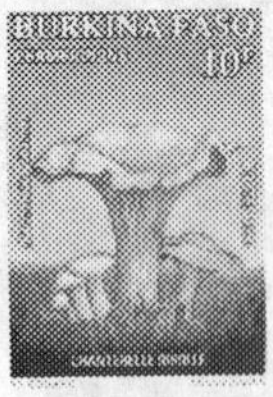

Mushrooms — A272

1990, May 17 Litho. *Perf. 11½*
896 A272 10fr Cantharellus cibarius 15 15
897 A272 15fr Psalliota bispora 15 15
898 A272 60fr Amanita caesarea 48 24
899 A272 190fr Boletus badius 1.50 75
a. Souv. sheet of 4, #896-899 2.18 1.10
Nos. 896-899 (4) 2.28
Set value 1.10

Intl. Exposition of Handicrafts — A273

1990, Sept. 25 Litho. *Perf. 13*
900 A273 35fr Masks, fans, vert. 30 15
901 A273 45fr shown 40 20
902 A273 270fr Rattan chair, vert. 2.35 1.20
Nos. 900-902 (3) 3.05 1.55

Gen. Charles de Gaulle (1890-1970) A274

1990, Nov. 22 Litho. *Perf. 13*
903 A274 200fr multicolored 1.75 90

Minerals A275

1991, Feb. 4 Litho. *Perf. 15x14*
904 A275 20fr Quartz 15 15
905 A275 50fr Granite 40 20
906 A275 280fr Amphibolite 2.25 1.12
Nos. 904-906 (3) 2.80 1.47

African Film Festival — A276

Fight Against Drugs — A277

1991, Feb. 20 *Perf. 11½*
907 A276 150fr multicolored 1.20 60

Souvenir Sheet

908 A276 1000fr Award 8.00 4.00

1991, Feb. 20
909 A277 130fr multicolored 1.05 55

Samuel F.B. Morse (1791-1872), Inventor — A278

1991, May 17 Litho. *Perf. 13*
910 A278 200fr multicolored 1.60 80

Native Girl — A279

Flowers — A280

1991-93 Litho. *Perf. 14½x15*
911 A279 5fr gray & multi 15 15
912 A279 10fr yellow & multi 15 15
913 A279 25fr lilac rose & multi 15 15
914 A279 50fr red lilac & multi 28 15
915 A279 130fr blue & multi 1.10 55
916 A279 150fr multicolored 1.20 60
920 A279 200fr multicolored 1.60 80
922 A279 330fr orange & multi 2.75 1.40
Nos. 911-922 (8) 7.38 3.95

Issued: 150fr, 200fr, 6/20/91; 130fr, 330fr, 1/15/93; 5-50fr, 1994.
This is an expanding set. Numbers may change.

1991, July 31 Litho. *Perf. 11½*
926 A280 5fr Grewia tenax 15 15
927 A280 15fr Hymenocardia acide 15 15
928 A280 60fr Cassia sieberiana, vert. 48 24
929 A280 100fr Adenium obesum 78 40
930 A280 300fr Mitragyna inermis 2.40 1.20
Nos. 926-930 (5) 3.96 2.14

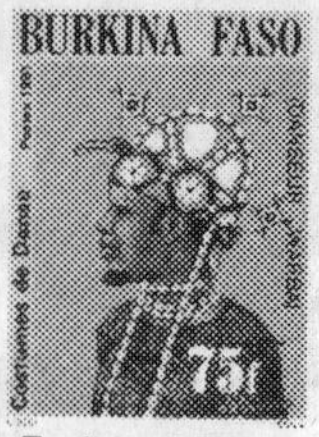

Traditional Dance Costumes — A281

World Post Day — A282

1991, Aug. 20 *Perf. 12½*
931 A281 75fr Warba 60 30
932 A281 130fr Wiskamba 1.05 52
933 A281 280fr Pa-zenin 2.20 1.10
Nos. 931-933 (3) 3.85 1.92

1991, Oct. 9 *Perf. 13½*
934 A282 130fr multicolored 1.05 52

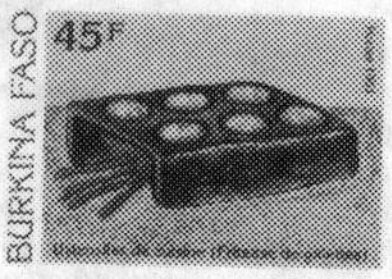

Cooking Utensils A283

1992, Jan. 8 Litho. *Perf. 11½*
935 A283 45fr Pancake fryer 35 18
936 A283 130fr Cooking pot, vert. 1.00 50
937 A283 310fr Mortar & pestle, vert. 2.40 1.20
938 A283 500fr Ladle, calabash 4.00 2.00
Nos. 935-938 (4) 7.75 3.88

1992 African Soccer Championships, Senegal — A284

1992, Jan. 17 *Perf. 13½*
939 A284 50fr Yousouf Fofana 40 20
940 A284 100fr Francois-Jules Bocande 78 40

Souvenir Sheet
Perf. 13x12½

941 A284 500fr Trophy 4.00 2.00

UN Decade For the Handicapped A285

1992, Mar. 31 Litho. *Perf. 12½*
942 A285 100fr multicolored 85 42

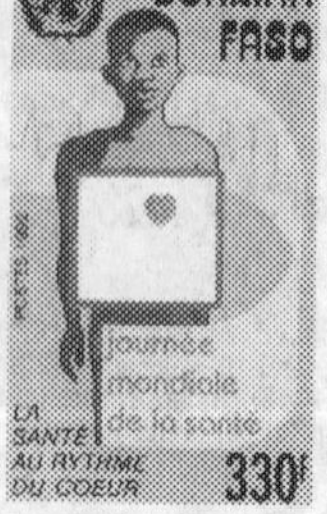

World Health Day — A286

1992, Apr. 7 *Perf. 13*
943 A286 330fr multicolored 2.70 1.35

Discovery of America, 500th Anniv. A287

1992, Aug. 12 Litho. *Perf. 12½*
944 A287 50fr Columbus, Santa Maria 42 22
945 A287 150fr Ships, natives 1.25 65

Souvenir Sheet

946 A287 350fr Map 3.00 1.50

Genoa '92. No. 946 contains one 52x31mm stamp.

Insects — A288

1992, Aug. 17 *Perf. 15x14*
947 A288 20fr Dysdercus voelkeri 18 15
948 A288 40fr Rhizopertha dominica 35 18
949 A288 85fr Orthetrum microstigma 75 35
950 A288 500fr Apis mellifera 4.25 2.25
Nos. 947-950 (4) 5.53 2.93

Christmas — A289

Designs: 10fr, Boy, creche. 130fr, Children decorating creche. 1000fr, Boy holding painting of Madonna and Child.

1992, Dec. 21 Litho. *Perf. 11½*
951 A289 10fr multicolored 15 15
952 A289 130fr multicolored 1.00 50
953 A289 1000fr multicolored 8.00 4.00
Nos. 951-953 (3) 9.15 4.65

Invention of the Diesel Engine, Cent. A290

1993, Jan. 25 Litho. *Perf. 11½*
954 A290 1000fr multicolored 8.00 4.00

The date of issue is in question.

Paris '94, Philatelic Exhibition A291

1993, July 15
955 A291 400fr multicolored 3.50 1.75
956 A291 650fr multi, diff. 5.50 2.75

African Film Festival — A292

Birds — A293

Designs: 250fr, Monument to the cinema. 750fr, M. Douta (1919-1991), comedian, horiz.

Perf. 11½x12, 12x11½

1993, Feb. 16 **Litho.**

957 A292 250fr multicolored 2.00 1.00
958 A292 750fr multicolored 6.00 3.00

1993, Mar. 31 *Perf. 11½x12*

Designs: 100fr, Mycteria ibis. 200fr, Leptoptilos crumeniferus. 500fr, Ephippiorhynchus senegalensis.

959 A293 100fr multicolored 80 40
960 A293 200fr multicolored 1.60 80
961 A293 500fr multicolored 4.00 2.00
a. Souvenir sheet of 3, #959-961 9.60 4.80
Nos. 959-961 (3) 6.40 3.20

No. 961a sold for 1200fr.

1994 World Cup Soccer Championships, US — A294

1993, Apr. 8 *Perf. 15*

962 A294 500fr shown 4.00 2.00
963 A294 1000fr Players, US flag 8.00 4.00

Fruit Trees — A295

Designs: 150fr, Saba senegalensis, vert. 300fr, Butyrospermum parkii. 600fr, Adansonia digitata, vert.

1993, June 2 **Litho.** *Perf. 11½*

964 A295 150fr multicolored 1.25 65
965 A295 300fr multicolored 2.50 1.25
966 A295 600fr multicolored 5.00 2.50
Nos. 964-966 (3) 8.75 4.40

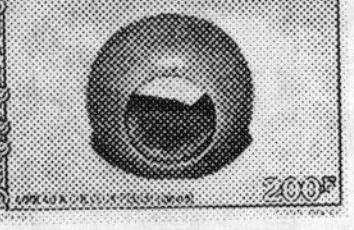

Traditional Jewelry — A296

1993, Sept. 25 **Litho.** *Perf. 11½*

967 A296 200fr Ring for hair 1.65 85
968 A296 250fr Agate necklace, vert. 2.00 1.00
969 A296 500fr Bracelet 4.00 2.00
Nos. 967-969 (3) 7.65 3.85

Gazella Rufifrons A297

1993, Dec. 10 **Litho.** *Perf. 14½*

970 A297 30fr shown 25 15
971 A297 40fr Two facing left 32 16
972 A297 60fr Two standing 50 25
973 A297 100fr Young gazelle 80 40
a. Souvenir sheet, #970-973 3.25 1.65
Nos. 970-973 (4) 1.87 96

World Wildlife Fund (#970-973). No. 973a sold for 400fr.

Kingfishers — A298

1994, Mar. 8 **Litho.** *Perf. 11½*

974 A298 600fr Halcyon senegalensis 2.00 1.00
975 A298 1200fr Halcyon chelicuti 4.25 2.25

Souvenir Sheet

976 A298 2000fr Ceyx picta 7.00 3.50

1994 World Cup Soccer Championships, US — A299

1994, Mar. 28

977 A299 1000fr Players, US map 3.50 1.75
978 A299 1800fr Soccer ball, players 6.50 3.25
a. Souvenir sheet of 1 7.00 3.50

No. 978a sold for 2000fr.

First Manned Moon Landing, 25th Anniv. — A300

1994 **Litho.** *Perf. 11½*

979 A300 750fr Astronaut, flag 3.75 1.90
980 A300 750fr Lunar module, earth 3.75 1.90
a. Pair, #979-980 7.50 3.75

No. 980a is a continuous design.

First Stamp Exhibition, Paris, 1994 A301

1994

981 A301 1500fr Dogs 7.75 3.75
a. Souvenir sheet of 1 7.75 3.75

See French West Africa Nos. 67, 84 for additional stamps inscribed "Haute Volta" and "Afrique Occidentale Francaise."

SEMI-POSTAL STAMPS

Catalogue values for unused stamps in this section are for Never Hinged items.

Anti-Malaria Issue
Common Design Type

Perf. 12½x12

1962, Apr. 7 **Engr.** **Unwmk.**

B1 CD108 25fr + 5fr red org 50 50

Freedom from Hunger Issue
Common Design Type

1963, Mar. 21 *Perf. 13*

B2 CD112 25fr + 5fr dk grn, bl & brn 50 50

AIR POST STAMPS

Catalogue values for unused stamps in this section are for Never Hinged items.

Plane over Map Showing Air Routes — AP1

Designs: 200fr, Plane at airport, Ouagadougou. 500fr, Champs Elysees, Ouagadougou.

Unwmk.

1961, Mar. 4 **Engr.** *Perf. 13*

C1 AP1 100fr multicolored 85 28
C2 AP1 200fr multicolored 1.65 55
C3 AP1 500fr multicolored 4.00 1.50
Nos. C1-C3 (3) 6.50 2.33

Air Afrique Issue
Common Design Type

1962, Feb. 17

C4 CD107 25fr brt pink, dk pur & lt grn 30 18

UN Emblem and Upper Volta Flag — AP2

Perf. 13½x12½

1962, Sept. 22 **Photo.**

C5 AP2 50fr multicolored 42 22
C6 AP2 100fr multicolored 85 48

Admission to UN, second anniversary.

Post Office, Ouagadougou — AP3

1962, Dec. 11 *Perf. 13x12*

C7 AP3 100fr multicolored 75 42

Jet Over Map AP4

1963, June 24

C8 AP4 200fr multicolored 1.65 65

First jet flight, Ouagadougou to Paris.
For surcharge see No. C10.

African Postal Union Issue
Common Design Type

1963, Sept. 8 **Unwmk.** *Perf. 12½*

C9 CD114 85fr dp vio, ocher & red 70 48

No. C8 Surcharged in Red

AIR AFRIQUE
19-11-63
50F

1963, Nov. 19 *Perf. 13x12*

C10 AP4 50fr on 200fr multi 52 42

See note after Mauritania No. C26.

Europafrica Issue
Common Design Type

Design: 50fr, Sunburst and Europe linked with Africa.

1964, Jan. 6 *Perf. 12x13*

C11 CD116 50fr multicolored 75 52

Ramses II, Abu Simbel — AP5

Greek Sculptures — AP6

1964, Mar. 8 **Engr.** *Perf. 13*

C12 AP5 25fr dp green & choc 35 30
C13 AP5 100fr brt bl & brn 1.40 1.20

UNESCO world campaign to save historic monuments of Nubia.

1964, July 1 **Unwmk.** *Perf. 13*

C14 AP6 15fr Greek Portrait Head 20 15
C15 AP6 25fr Seated boxer 25 20
C16 AP6 85fr Victorious athlete 80 60
C17 AP6 100fr Venus of Milo 1.10 70
a. Min. sheet of 4, #C14-C17 3.50 3.50
Nos. C14-C17 (4) 2.35 1.65

18th Olympic Games, Tokyo, Oct. 10-25.

West African Gray Woodpecker AP7

President John F. Kennedy (1917-1963) AP8

1964, Oct. 1 **Engr.** *Perf. 13*

C18 AP7 250fr multicolored 2.75 1.90

1964, Nov. 25 **Photo.** *Perf. 12½*

C19 AP8 100fr orange, brn & lil 70 70
a. Souvenir sheet of 4 4.50 4.50

Bird Type of Regular Issue, 1965

1965, Mar. 1 **Photo.** *Perf. 13*

Size: 27x48mm

C20 A27 500fr Abyssinian roller 5.50 2.50

Earth and Sun
AP9

1965, Mar. 23 **Engr.**
C21 AP9 50fr multicolored 45 16

5th World Meteorological Day.

Hughes Telegraph, ITU Emblem and Dial Telephone — AP10

1965, May 17 **Unwmk.** ***Perf. 13***
C22 AP10 100fr red, sl grn & bl grn 80 40

ITU, centenary.

Intl. Cooperation Year — AP10a

1965, June 21 **Photo.** ***Perf. 13***
C23 AP10a 25fr multicolored 20 15
C24 AP10a 100fr multicolored 55 26
a. Min. sheet, 2 each #C23-C24 1.90 1.90

Sacred Sabou Crocodile — AP11

1965, Aug. 9 **Engr.** ***Perf. 13***
C25 AP11 60fr shown 60 30
C26 AP11 85fr Lion, vert. 80 42

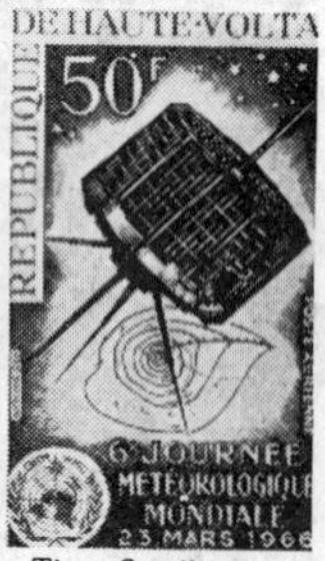

Early Bird Satellite over Globe — AP12

Tiros Satellite and Weather Map — AP13

1965, Sept. 15 **Unwmk.** ***Perf. 13***
C27 AP12 30fr brt bl, brn & brn red 28 16

Space communications.

1966, Mar. 23 **Engr.** ***Perf. 13***
C28 AP13 50fr dk car, brt bl & blk 40 28

6th World Meteorological Day.

FR-1 Satellite over Ouagadougou Space Tracking Station
AP14

1966, Apr. 28 ***Perf. 13***
C29 AP14 250fr mag, ind & org brn 2.00 90

Inauguration of WHO Headquarters, Geneva — AP15

1966, May 3 **Photo.**
C30 AP15 100fr yel, blk & bl 80 45

Air Afrique Issue
Common Design Type

1966, Aug. 31 **Photo.** ***Perf. 13***
C31 CD123 25fr tan, blk & yel grn 30 15

Sir Winston Churchill, British Lion and "V" Sign — AP16

1966, Nov. 5 **Engr.** ***Perf. 13***
C32 AP16 100fr sl grn & car rose 1.00 55

Sir Winston Spencer Churchill (1874-1965), statesman and WWII leader.

Pope Paul VI, Peace Dove, UN General Assembly and Emblem — AP17

1966, Nov. 5
C33 AP17 100fr dk blue & pur 1.00 55

Pope Paul's appeal for peace before the UN General Assembly, Oct. 4, 1965.

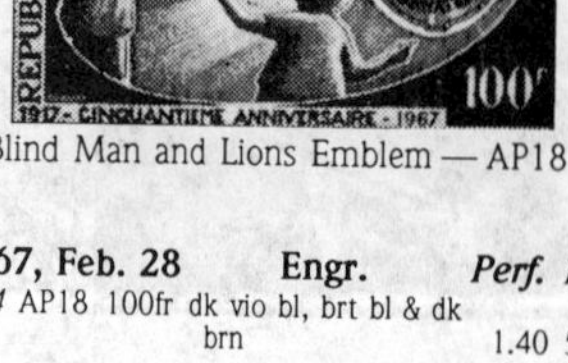

Blind Man and Lions Emblem — AP18

1967, Feb. 28 **Engr.** ***Perf. 13***
C34 AP18 100fr dk vio bl, brt bl & dk brn 1.40 55

50th anniversary of Lions Intl.

UN Emblem and Rain over Landscape — AP19

Diamant Rocket — AP20

1967, Mar. 23 **Engr.** ***Perf. 13***
C35 AP19 50fr ultra, dk grn & bl grn 50 22

7th World Meteorological Day.

1967, Apr. 18 **Engr.** ***Perf. 13***

French Spacecraft: 20fr, FR-1 satellite, horiz. 30fr, D1-C satellite. 100fr, D1-D satellite, horiz.

C36 AP20 5fr brt bl, sl grn & org 15 15
C37 AP20 20fr lilac & slate blue 20 15
C38 AP20 30fr red brn, brt bl & emer 32 16
C39 AP20 100fr emer & dp claret 90 45
Nos. C36-C39 (4) 1.57 91

For overprint see No. C69.

Albert Schweitzer (1875-1965), Medical Missionary and Organ Pipes — AP21

1967, May 12 **Engr.** ***Perf. 13***
C40 AP21 250fr claret & blk 1.75 95

World Map and 1967 Jamboree Emblem — AP22

1967, June 8 **Photo.**
C41 AP22 100fr multicolored 1.00 55

12th Boy Scout World Jamboree, Farragut State Park, Idaho, Aug. 1-9.

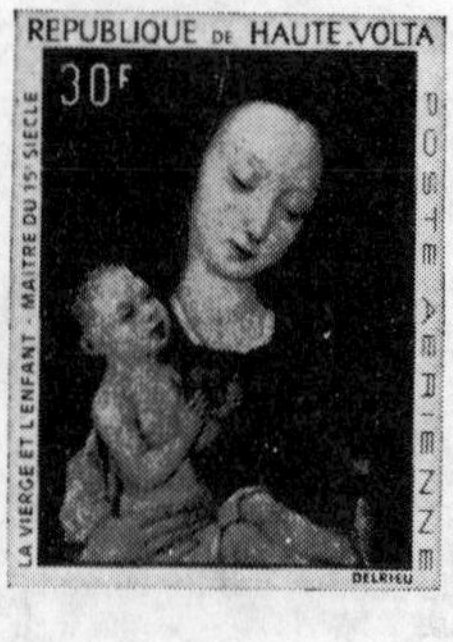

Madonna and Child, 15th Century
AP23

Paintings: 20fr, Still life by Paul Gauguin. 50fr, Pietà, by Dick Bouts. 60fr, Anne of Cleves, by Hans Holbein the Younger. 90fr, The Money Lender and his Wife, by Quentin Massys (38x40mm). 100fr, Blessing of the Risen Christ, by Giovanni Bellini. 200fr, The Handcart, by Louis Le Nain, horiz. 250fr, The Four Evangelists, by Jacob Jordaens.

Perf. 12½x12, 12x12½, 13½ (90fr)

1967-68 **Photo.**
C42 AP23 20fr multi ('68) 25 15
C43 AP23 30fr multicolored 30 15
C44 AP23 50fr multicolored 50 25
C45 AP23 60fr multi ('68) 60 25
C46 AP23 90fr multi ('68) 85 42
C47 AP23 100fr multicolored 1.00 38
C48 AP23 200fr multi ('68) 2.00 70
C49 AP23 250fr multicolored 2.75 1.00
Nos. C42-C49 (8) 8.25 3.30

See Nos. C70-C72.

African Postal Union Issue, 1967
Common Design Type

1967, Sept. 9 **Engr.** ***Perf. 13***
C50 CD124 100fr brn red, dp bl & bl grn 80 35

Caravelle "Ouagadougou" — AP24

1968, Feb. 29 **Engr.** ***Perf. 13***
C51 AP24 500fr bl, dp cl & blk 3.75 1.40

WMO Emblem, Sun, Rain, Wheat — AP25

1968, Mar. 23 **Engr.** ***Perf. 13***
C52 AP25 50fr dk red, ultra & gray grn 45 22

8th World Meteorological Day.

Europafrica Issue

Clove Hitch — AP25a

1968, July 20 **Photo.** ***Perf. 13***
C53 AP25a 50fr yel bis, blk & dk red 40 20

See note after Niger No. C89.

Vessel in Form of Acrobat with Bells, Colima Culture — AP26

Mexican Sculptures: 30fr, Ballplayer, Veracruz, vert. 60fr, Javelin thrower, Colima, vert. 100fr, Seated athlete with cape, Jalisco.

1968, Oct. 14 **Engr.** ***Perf. 13***
C54 AP26 10fr dk red, ocher & choc 15 15
C55 AP26 30fr bl grn, brt grn & dk brn 22 15
C56 AP26 60fr ultra, ol & mar 45 22
C57 AP26 100fr brt grn, bl & mar 65 35
Nos. C54-C57 (4) 1.47 87

19th Olympic Games, Mexico City, Oct. 12-27.

Artisan Type of Regular Issue

1968, Oct. 30 Engr. *Perf. 13*
Size: 48x27mm

C58 A52 100fr Potter 70 32

PHILEXAFRIQUE Issue

Too Late or The Letter, by Armand Cambon AP27

1968, Nov. 22 Photo. *Perf. 12½*

C59 AP27 100fr multicolored 1.00 75

PHILEXAFRIQUE, Phil. Exhib., Abidjan, Feb. 14-23, 1969. Printed with alternating rose claret label.

Albert John Luthuli — AP28

Design: No. C61, Mahatma Gandhi.

1968, Dec. 16 Photo. *Perf. 12½*

C60 AP28 100fr dk grn, yel grn & blk 75 40
C61 AP28 100fr dk grn, yel & blk 75 40
a. Min. sheet, 2 each #C60-C61 3.00 3.00

Exponents of non-violence.

2nd PHILEXAFRIQUE Issue
Common Design Type

Design: 50fr, Upper Volta No. 59, dancers and musicians.

1969, Feb. 14 Engr. *Perf. 13*

C62 CD128 50fr pur, bl car & brn 55 55

Weather Sonde, WMO Emblem, Mule and Cattle in Irrigated Field — AP29

1969, Mar. 24 Engr. *Perf. 13*

C63 AP29 100fr dk brn, brt bl & grn 90 50

9th World Meteorological Day.

Artisan Type of Regular Issue

Design: 150fr, Basket weaver.

1969, Apr. 3 Engr. *Perf. 13*
Size: 48x27mm

C64 A55 150fr brn, bl & blk 1.20 60

Lions Emblem, Eye and Blind Man — AP30

1969, Apr. 30 Photo.

C65 AP30 250fr red & multi 2.50 1.00

12th Congress of District 403 of Lions Intl., Ouagadougou, May 2-3.

Fish Type of Regular Issue

Designs: 100fr, Phenacogrammus pabrensis. 150fr, Upside-down catfish.

1969 Engr. *Perf. 13*
Size: 48x27mm

C66 A57 100fr slate, pur & yel 90 42
C67 A57 150fr org brn, gray & sl 1.40 62

Earth and Astronaut — AP31

Embossed on Gold Foil

1969 *Die-cut Perf. 10½x10*

C68 AP31 1000fr gold 8.25 8.25

Apollo 8 mission, which put the first man into orbit around the moon, Dec. 21-27, 1968.

No. C39 Overprinted in red with Lunar Landing Module and: "L'HOMME SUR LA LUNE / JUILLET 1969 / APOLLO 11"

1969, July 25 Engr. *Perf. 13*

C69 AP20 100fr emer & dp cl 2.25 1.90

See note after Mali No. C80.

Painting Type of 1967-68

Paintings: 50fr, Napoleon Crossing Great St. Bernard Pass, by Jacques Louis David. 150fr, Napoleon Awarding the First Cross of the Legion of Honor, by Jean-Baptiste Debret. 250fr, Napoleon Before Madrid, by Carle Vernet.

1969, Aug. 18 Photo. *Perf. 12½x12*

C70 AP23 50fr carmine & multi 45 35
C71 AP23 150fr violet & multi 1.10 80
C72 AP23 250fr green & multi 2.25 1.40
Nos. C70-C72 (3) 3.80 2.55

Napoleon Bonaparte (1769-1821).

Agriculture Type of Regular Issue

1969, Oct. 30 Photo. *Perf. 12½x13*
Size: 47½x27mm

C73 A58 100fr Peanuts 75 28
C74 A58 200fr Rice 1.65 55

AP32

AP33

Tree of Life, symbols of science, agriculture and industry.

1969, Nov. 21 Photo. *Perf. 12x13*

C75 AP32 100fr multicolored 65 35

See note after Mauritania No. C28.

1970, Apr. 22 Photo. *Perf. 12½*

Designs: 20fr, Lenin. 100fr, Lenin Addressing Revolutionaries in Petrograd, by V. A. Serov, horiz.

C76 AP33 20fr ocher & brn 15 15
C77 AP33 100fr blk, lt grn & red 65 38

Lenin (1870-1924), Russian communist leader.

Pres. Roosevelt with Stamp Collection — AP34

Design: 10fr, Franklin Delano Roosevelt, vert.

1970, June 4 Photo. *Perf. 12½*

C78 AP34 10fr dk brn, emer & red brn 15 15
C79 AP34 200fr vio bl, gray & dk car 1.40 45
Set value 50

Soccer Game and Jules Rimet Cup — AP35

Design: 100fr, Goalkeeper catching ball and globe.

1970, June 4 Engr. *Perf. 13*

C80 AP35 40fr ol, brt grn & brn 40 20
C81 AP35 100fr blk, lil, brn & grn 90 40

9th World Soccer Championships for the Jules Rimet Cup, Mexico City, May 30-June 21, 1970.

EXPO Emblem, Monorail and "Cranes at the Seashore" — AP36

UN Emblem, Dove and Star — AP37

Design: 150fr, EXPO emblem, rocket, satellites and "Geisha."

1970, Aug. 7 Photo. *Perf. 12½*

C82 AP36 50fr multicolored 35 16
C83 AP36 150fr green & multi 1.00 60

Issued to publicize EXPO '70 International Exhibition, Osaka, Japan, Mar. 15-Sept. 13.

1970, Oct. 2 Engr. *Perf. 13*

Design: 250fr, UN emblem and doves, horiz.

C84 AP37 60fr dk bl, bl & grn 40 20
C85 AP37 250fr dk red brn, vio bl & ol 1.60 65

25th anniversary of the United Nations.

Holy Family AP38

Silver Embossed

1970, Nov. 27 *Die-Cut Perf. 10*

C86 AP38 300fr silver 2.50 2.50

Gold Embossed

C87 AP38 1000fr gold 9.00 9.00

Christmas.

Family and Upper Volta Flag — AP39

Gamal Abdel Nasser — AP41

UN "Key to a Free World" — AP40

Litho.; Gold Embossed

1970, Dec. 10 *Perf. 12½*

C88 AP39 500fr gold, blk & red 2.50 1.50

10th anniversary of independence, Dec. 11.

1970, Dec. 14 Engr. *Perf. 13*

C89 AP40 40fr red, bister & blue 35 16

UN Declaration of Independence for Colonial Peoples, 10th anniv.

1971, Jan. 30 Photo. *Perf. 12½*

C90 AP41 100fr green & multi 65 30

Nasser (1918-1970), president of Egypt.

Herons, Egyptian Art, 1354 — AP42

Design: 250fr, Page from Koran, Egypt, 1368-1388, vert.

1971, May 13 Photo. *Perf. 13*

C91 AP42 100fr multicolored 55 25
C92 AP42 250fr multicolored 1.40 70

Olympic Rings and Various Sports — AP43

1971, June 10 Engr. *Perf. 13*

C93 AP43 150fr vio bl & red 1.00 60

Pre-Olympic Year.

Boy Scout and Buildings — AP44

1971, Aug. 12 Photo. *Perf. 12½*

C94 AP44 45fr multicolored 35 16

13th Boy Scout World Jamboree, Asagiri Plain, Japan, Aug. 2-10.

De Gaulle, Map of Upper Volta, Cross of Lorraine — AP45

Charles de Gaulle — AP46

1971, Nov. 9 Photo. *Perf. 13x12*

C95 AP45 40fr lt brn, grn & blk 40 35

Lithographed; Gold Embossed

Perf. 12½

C96 AP46 500fr gold & grn 4.00 3.75

Gen. Charles de Gaulle (1890-1970), president of France.

African Postal Union Issue, 1971

Common Design Type

Design: 100fr, Mossi dancer and UAMPT building, Brazzaville, Congo.

1971, Nov. 13 Photo. *Perf. 13x13½*

C97 CD135 100fr bl & multi 65 35

> ***Set Values***
> *A 15-cent minimum now applies to individual stamps and sets. Where the 15-cent minimum per stamp would increase the value of a set beyond retail, there is a "Set Value" notation giving the retail value of the set.*

Gen. Sangoule Lamizana — AP47

Kabuki Actor and Ice Hockey — AP48

1971, Dec. 11 *Perf. 12½*

C98 AP47 35fr sep, blk, gold & ultra 22 15

Inauguration of 2nd Republic of Upper Volta.

1972, Feb. 15 Engr. *Perf. 13*

C99 AP48 150fr red, bl & pur 1.00 60

11th Winter Olympic Games, Sapporo, Japan, Feb. 3-13.

Music, by Pietro Longhi AP49

Design: 150fr, Gondolas and general view, by Ippolito Caffi, horiz.

1972, Feb. 28 Photo. *Perf. 13*

C100 AP49 100fr gold & multi 65 35

C101 AP49 150fr gold & multi 1.10 40

UNESCO campaign to save Venice.

Running and Olympic Rings — AP50

Design: 200fr, Discus and Olympic rings.

1972, May 5 Engr. *Perf. 13*

C102 AP50 65fr dp bl, brn & grn 35 15

C103 AP50 200fr dp bl & brn 1.10 35

a. Min. sheet of 2, #C102-C103 1.65 1.65

20th Olympic Games, Munich, Aug. 26-Sept. 10.

Musician Type of Regular Issue

Design: 500fr, Jimmy Smith and keyboard.

1972, May 17 Photo. *Perf. 14x13*

C104 A87 500fr green & multi 4.00 1.90

Red Crescent Type of Regular Issue

1972, June 23 *Perf. 13x14*

C105 A88 100fr yellow & multi 65 25

2nd Plan Type of Regular Issue

Design: 85fr, Road building machinery.

1972, Oct. 30 Engr. *Perf. 13*

C106 A90 85fr brick red, bl & blk 45 22

Presidents Pompidou and Lamizana — AP51

Design: 250fr, Presidents Pompidou and Lamizana, different design.

1972, Nov. 20 Photo. *Perf. 13*

Size: 48x37mm

C107 AP51 40fr gold & multi 45 35

Photogravure; Gold Embossed

Size: 56x36mm

C108 AP51 250fr yel grn, dk grn & gold 2.50 2.50

Visit of Pres. Georges Pompidou of France, Nov. 1972.

Skeet-shooting, Scalzone, Italy — AP52

Gold-medal Winners: 40fr, Pentathlon, Peters, Great Britain. 45fr, Dressage, Meade, Great Britain. 50fr, Weight lifting, Talts, USSR. 60fr, Boxing, lightweight, Seales, US 65fr, Fencing, Ragno-Lonzi, Italy. 75fr, Gymnastics, rings, Nakayama, Japan. 85fr, Gymnastics, Touritcheva, USSR. 90fr, 110m high hurdles, Milburn, US 150fr, Judo, Kawaguchi, Japan. 200fr, Sailing, Finn class, Maury, France. 250fr, Swimming, Spitz, US (7 gold). 300fr, Women's high jump, Meyfarth, West Germany. 350fr, Field Hockey, West Germany. 400fr, Javelin, Wolfermann, West Germany. No. C124, Women's diving, King, US No. C125, Cycling, Morelon, France. No. C126, Individual dressage, Linsenhoff, West Germany.

1972-73 Litho. *Perf. 12½*

C109 AP52 35fr multi ('73) 18 15
C110 AP52 40fr multicolored 20 15
C111 AP52 45fr multi ('73) 22 15
C112 AP52 50fr multi ('73) 25 15
C113 AP52 60fr multi ('73) 30 15
C114 AP52 65fr multicolored 35 16
C115 AP52 75fr multi ('73) 40 20
C116 AP52 85fr multicolored 42 20
C117 AP52 90fr multi ('73) 45 22
C118 AP52 150fr multi ('73) 80 40
C119 AP52 200fr multicolored 1.10 50
C120 AP52 250fr multi ('73) 1.40 65
C121 AP52 300fr multicolored 1.60 80
C122 AP52 350fr multi ('73) 1.90 90
C123 AP52 400fr multi ('73) 2.00 1.10
Nos. C109-C123 (15) 11.57 5.88

Souvenir Sheets

C124 AP52 500fr multicolored 2.25 1.60
C125 AP52 500fr multi ('73) 2.25 1.60
C126 AP52 500fr multi ('73) 2.25 1.60

20th Olympic Games, Munich.

Nativity, by Della Notte — AP53

Christmas: 200fr, Adoration of the Kings, by Albrecht Dürer.

1972, Dec. 23 Photo. *Perf. 13*

C127 AP53 100fr gold & multi 50 22
C128 AP53 200fr gold & multi 1.10 65

Madonna and Child, by Albrecht Dürer — AP54

Christmas: 75fr, Virgin Mary, Child and St. John, by Joseph von Führich. 100fr, The Virgin of Grand Duc, by Raphael. 125fr, Holy Family, by David. 150fr, Madonna and Child, artist unknown. 400fr, Flight into Egypt, by Gentile da Fabriano, horiz.

1973, Mar. 22 Litho. *Perf. 12½x13*

C129 AP54 50fr multi 35 16
C130 AP54 75fr multi 50 25
C131 AP54 100fr multi 65 35
C132 AP54 125fr multi 80 40
C133 AP54 150fr multi 1.00 50
Nos. C129-C133 (5) 3.30 1.66

Souvenir Sheet

C134 AP54 400fr multi 2.50 1.40

Manned Lunar Buggy on Moon — AP55

Moon Exploration: 65fr, Lunakhod, Russian unmanned vehicle on moon. 100fr, Lunar module returning to orbiting Apollo capsule. 150fr, Apollo capsule in moon orbit. 200fr, Space walk. 250fr, Walk in Sea of Tranquillity.

1973, Apr. 30 Litho. *Perf. 13x12½*

C135 AP55 50fr multi 35 16
C136 AP55 65fr multi 42 20
C137 AP55 100fr multi 65 35
C138 AP55 150fr multi 1.00 50
C139 AP55 200fr multi 1.40 65
Nos. C135-C139 (5) 3.82 1.86

Souvenir Sheet

C140 AP55 250fr multi 1.60 80

Giraffes AP56

African Wild Animals: 150fr, Elephants. 200fr, Leopard, horiz. 250fr, Lion, horiz. 300fr, Rhinoceros, horiz. 500fr, Crocodile, horiz.

Perf. 12½x13, 13x12½

1973, May 3 Litho.

C141 AP56 100fr multi 65 35
C142 AP56 150fr multi 1.00 50
C143 AP56 200fr multi 1.40 65
C144 AP56 250fr multi 1.60 80
C145 AP56 500fr multi 3.50 1.60
Nos. C141-C145 (5) 8.15 3.90

Souvenir Sheet

C146 AP56 300fr multi 2.00 1.00

Europafrica Issue

Girl Reading Letter, by Jan Vermeer AP57

Paintings: 65fr, Portrait of a Lady, by Roger van der Weyden. 100fr, Young Lady at her Toilette, by Titian. 150fr, Jane Seymour, by Hans Holbein. 200fr, Mrs. Williams, by John Hoppner. 250fr, Milkmaid, by Jean-Baptiste Greuze.

1973, June 7 Litho. ***Perf. 12½x13***

C147	AP57	50fr multi	35	16
C148	AP57	65fr multi	42	20
C149	AP57	100fr multi	65	35
C150	AP57	150fr multi	1.00	50
C151	AP57	200fr multi	1.40	65
		Nos. C147-C151 (5)	3.82	1.86

Souvenir Sheet

C152	AP57	250fr multi	1.60	80

For overprint see No. C165-C166.

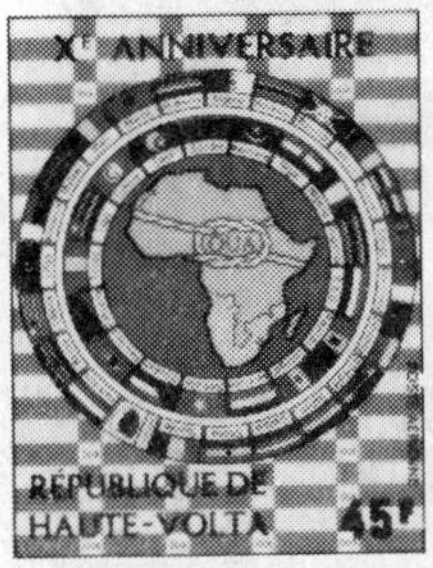

Africa Encircled by OAU Flags — AP58

1973, June 7

C153	AP58	45fr multi	30	15

10th anniv. of Org. for African Unity.

Locomotive "Pacific" 4546, 1908 — AP59

Locomotives from Railroad Museum, Mulhouse, France: 40fr, No. 242, 1927. 50fr, No. 2029, 1882. 150fr, No. 701, 1885-92. 250fr, "Coupe-Vent" No. C145, 1900. 350fr, Buddicomb No. 33, Paris to Rouen, 1884.

1973, June 30 ***Perf. 13x12½***

C154	AP59	10fr multi	15	15
C155	AP59	40fr multi	25	15
C156	AP59	50fr multi	35	16
C157	AP59	150fr multi	1.00	50
C158	AP59	250fr multi	1.60	80
		Nos. C154-C158 (5)	3.35	1.76

Souvenir Sheet

C159	AP59	350fr multi	2.25	1.20

Boy Scout Type of 1973

Boy Scouts: 40fr, Flag signaling. 75fr, Skiing. 150fr, Cooking. 200fr, Hiking. 250fr, Studying stars.

1973, July 18 Litho. ***Perf. 12½x13***

C160	A95	40fr multi	25	15
C161	A95	75fr multi	50	25
C162	A95	150fr multi	1.00	50
C163	A95	200fr multi	1.40	65
		Nos. C160-C163 (4)	3.15	1.55

Souvenir Sheet

C164	A95	250fr multi	1.60	80

Nos. C148 and C150 Surcharged in Silver New Value and "SECHERESSE / SOLIDARITE AFRICAINE / ET INTERNATIONALE"

1973, Aug. 16

C165	AP57	100fr on 65fr multi	65	35
C166	AP57	200fr on 150fr multi	1.40	65

Drought relief.

Kennedy Type, 1973

John F. Kennedy and: 200fr, Firing Saturn 1 rocket, Apollo program. 300fr, First NASA manned space capsule. 400fr, Saturn 5 countdown.

1973, Sept. 12 Litho. ***Perf. 12½x13***

C167	A96	200fr multi	1.40	65
C168	A96	300fr multi	2.00	1.00

Souvenir Sheet

C169	A96	400fr multi	2.50	1.40

10th death anniv. of Pres John F. Kennedy.

Interpol Type of 1973
Souvenir Sheet

Design: Victim in city street.

1973, Sept. 15 ***Perf. 13x12½***

C170	A97	300fr multi	2.00	1.00

Tourism Type of 1973

1973, Sept. 30

C171	A98	100fr Waterfalls	65	35

Souvenir Sheet

C172	A98	275fr Elephant	1.90	90

House of Worship Type of 1973

Design: Cathedral of the Immaculate Conception.

1973, Sept. 28

C173	A99	200fr multi	1.40	65

Folklore Type of 1973

Designs: 100fr, 225fr, Bobo masked dancers, diff.

1973, Nov. 30 Litho. ***Perf. 12½x13***

C174	A100	100fr multi	65	35
C175	A100	225fr multi	1.50	70

Zodiac Type of 1973
Souvenir Sheets

Zodiacal Light and: #C176, 1st 4 signs of Zodiac. #C177, 2nd 4 signs. #C178, Last 4 signs.

1973, Dec. 15 ***Perf. 13x14***

C176	A101	250fr multi	1.60	80
C177	A101	250fr multi	1.60	80
C178	A101	250fr multi	1.60	80

Nos. C176-C178 have multicolored margin showing night sky and portraits: No. C176, Louis Armstrong; No. C177, Mahatma Gandhi; No. C178, Martin Luther King.

Soccer Championship Type, 1974

Championship '74 emblem and: 75fr, Gento, Spanish flag. 100fr, Bereta, French flag. 250fr, Best, British flag. 400fr, Beckenbauer, West German flag.

1974, Jan. 15 Litho. ***Perf. 13x12½***

C179	A102	75fr multi	50	25
C180	A102	100fr multi	65	35
C181	A102	250fr multi	1.60	80
		Nos. C179-C181 (3)	2.75	1.40

Souvenir Sheet

C182	A102	400fr multi	2.50	1.40

De Gaulle Type, 1974

Designs: 300fr, De Gaulle and Concorde, horiz. 400fr, De Gaulle and French space shot.

Perf. 13x12½, 12½x13

1974, Feb. 4 Litho.

C183	A103	300fr multi	2.00	1.00

Souvenir Sheet

C184	A103	400fr multi	2.50	1.40

Soccer Cup Championship Type, 1974

World Cup, Emblems and: 150fr, Brindisis, Argentinian flag. No. C186, Kenko, Zaire flag. No. C187, Streich, East German flag. 400fr, Cruyff, Netherlands flag.

1974, Mar. 19 ***Perf. 12½x13***

C185	A104	150fr multi	75	38
C186	A104	300fr multi	1.50	75

Souvenir Sheets

C187	A104	300fr multi	1.50	75
C188	A104	400fr multi	2.00	1.00

UPU Type, 1974

UPU Emblem and: 100fr, Dove carrying mail. 200fr, Air Afrique 707. 300fr, Dish antenna. 500fr, Telstar satellite.

1974, July 23 ***Perf. 13½***

C189	A106	100fr multi	50	25
C190	A106	200fr multi	1.00	50
C191	A106	300fr multi	1.50	75
		Nos. C189-C191 (3)	3.00	1.50

Souvenir Sheet

C192	A106	500fr multi	2.50	1.25

For overprint see No. C197-C200.

Soccer Cup Winners Type, 1974

World Cup, Game and Flags: 150fr, Brazil, in Sweden, 1958. 200fr, Brazil, in Chile, 1962. 250fr, Brazil, in Mexico, 1970. 450fr, England, in England, 1966.

1974, Sept. 2

C193	A107	150fr multi	1.00	50
C194	A107	200fr multi	1.40	65
C195	A107	250fr multi	1.60	80
		Nos. C193-C195 (3)	4.00	1.95

Souvenir Sheet

C196	A107	450fr multi	3.00	1.50

Nos. C189-C192 Overprinted in Red "100e ANNIVERSAIRE DE L'UNION POSTALE UNIVERSELLE / 9 OCTOBRE 1974"

1974, Oct. 9

C197	A106	100fr multi	65	35
C198	A106	200fr multi	1.40	65
C199	A106	300fr multi	2.00	1.00
		Nos. C197-C199 (3)	4.05	2.00

Souvenir Sheet

C200	A106	500fr multi	3.00	1.40

Universal Postal Union, centenary.

Flower Type of 1974

Flower Paintings by: 300fr, Auguste Renoir. 400fr, Carl Brendt.

1974, Oct. 31 Litho. ***Perf. 12½x13***

C201	A109	300fr multi	2.00	1.00

Souvenir Sheet

C202	A109	400fr multi	2.50	1.40

Locomotive Type of 1975

Locomotives from Railroad Museum, Mulhouse, France: 100fr, Crampton No. 80, 1852. 200fr, No. 701, 1885-92. 300fr, "Forquenot," 1882.

1975, Feb. 28 Litho. ***Perf. 13x12½***

C203	A112	100fr multi	65	35
C204	A112	200fr multi	1.40	65

Souvenir Sheet

C205	A112	300fr multi	2.00	1.00

Old Cars Type, 1975

Flags and Old Cars: 150fr, Germany and Mercedes-Benz, 1929. 200fr, Germany and Maybach, 1936. 400fr, Great Britain and Rolls Royce Silver Ghost, 1910.

1975, Apr. 6 ***Perf. 14x13½***

C206	A113	150fr multi	1.00	50
C207	A113	200fr multi	1.40	65

Souvenir Sheet

C208	A113	400fr multi	2.50	1.40

American Bicentennial Type of 1975

American Bicentennial: 200fr, Washington crossing Delaware. 300fr, Hessians Captured at Trenton.

1975, May 6 Litho. ***Perf. 14***

C209	A114	200fr multi	1.40	65
C210	A114	300fr multi	2.00	1.00

Schweitzer Type of 1975

Albert Schweitzer and: 150fr, Toucan. 175fr, Vulturine guinea fowl. 200fr, King vulture. 450fr, Crested corythornis.

1975, May 25 Litho. ***Perf. 13½***

C212	A115	150fr multi	1.00	50
C213	A115	175fr multi	1.20	55
C214	A115	200fr multi	1.40	65
		Nos. C212-C214 (3)	3.60	1.70

Souvenir Sheet

C215	A115	450fr multi	3.00	1.50

Apollo Soyuz Type of 1975

Designs: 100fr, Apollo and Soyuz near link-up. 200fr, Cosmonauts Alexei Leonov and Valeri Kubasov. 300fr, Astronauts Donald K. Slayton, Vance Brand and Thomas P. Stafford. 500fr, Apollo Soyuz emblem, US and USSR flags.

1975, July 18 Litho. ***Perf. 13½***

C216	A116	100fr multi	65	35
C217	A116	200fr multi	1.40	65
C218	A116	300fr multi	2.00	1.00
		Nos. C216-C218 (3)	4.05	2.00

Souvenir Sheet

C219	A116	500fr multi	3.50	1.60

Picasso Type of 1975

Picasso Paintings: 150fr, El Prado, horiz. 350fr, Couple in Patio. 400fr, Science and Charity.

1975, Aug. 7

C220	A117	150fr multi	1.00	50
C221	A117	350fr multi	2.25	1.20

Souvenir Sheet

C222	A117	400fr multi	2.50	1.40

EXPO '75 Type of 1975

Expo '75 emblem and: 150fr, Passenger liner Asama Maru. 300fr, Future floating city Aquapolis.

1975, Sept. 26 Litho. ***Perf. 11***

C223	A118	150fr multi	75	38

Souvenir Sheet
Perf. 13½

C224	A118	300fr multi	1.50	75

Winter Olympic Games Type of 1975

Innsbruck Background, Olympic Emblem and: 100fr, Ice hockey. 200fr, Ski jump. 300fr, Speed skating.

1975, Dec. 15 ***Perf. 13½***

C225	A122	100fr multi	65	35
C226	A122	200fr multi	1.40	65

Souvenir Sheet

C227	A122	300fr multi	2.00	1.00

Olympic Games Type of 1976

Olympic Emblem and: 125fr, Heavyweight judo. 150fr, Weight lifting. 500fr, Sprint.

1976, Mar. 17 Litho. ***Perf. 13½***

C228	A123	125fr multi	65	30
C229	A123	150fr multi	75	38

Souvenir Sheet

C230	A123	500fr multi	2.50	1.25

Summer Olympic Games Type of 1976

Olympic emblem and: 150fr, Pole vault. 200fr, Gymnast on balance beam. 500fr, Two-man sculls.

1976, Mar. 25 ***Perf. 11***

C231	A124	150fr multi	75	38
C232	A124	200fr multi	1.00	50

Souvenir Sheet

C233	A124	500fr multi	2.50	1.25

For overprint see No. C245-C247.

Zeppelin Type of 1976

Airships: 100fr, Graf Zeppelin over Swiss Alps. 200fr, LZ-129 over city. 300fr, Graf Zeppelin. 500fr, Zeppelin over Bodensee.

1976, May 11

C234	A126	100fr multi	65	35
C235	A126	200fr multi	1.40	65
C236	A126	300fr multi	2.00	1.00
		Nos. C234-C236 (3)	4.05	2.00

Souvenir Sheet

C237	A126	500fr multi	3.50	1.60

Viking Mars Type of 1976

Designs: 200fr, Viking lander assembly. 300fr, Viking orbiter in descent on Mars. 450fr, Viking in Mars orbit.

1976, June 24 Litho. ***Perf. 13½***

C238	A127	200fr multi	1.00	50
C239	A127	300fr multi	1.50	75

Souvenir Sheet

C240	A127	450fr multi	2.25	1.10

American Bicentennial Type of 1976

Bicentennial and Interphil '76 Emblems and: 100fr, Siege of Yorktown. 200fr, Battle of Cape St. Vincent. 300fr, Peter Francisco's bravery. 500fr, Surrender of the Hessians.

1976, Sept. 30 Litho. *Perf. 13½*

C241 A129 100fr multi 65 35
C242 A129 200fr multi 1.40 65
C243 A129 300fr multi 2.00 1.00
Nos. C241-C243 (3) 4.05 2.00

Souvenir Sheet

C244 A129 500fr multi 3.50 1.60

Nos. C231-C233 Overprinted in Gold:

a. VAINQUEUR 1976 / TADEUSZ SLUSARSKI / POLOGNE

b. VAINQUEUR 1976 / NADIA COMANECI / ROUMANIE

c. VAINQUEUR 1976 / FRANK ET ALF HANSEN / NORVEGE

1976, July 4 Litho. *Perf. 11*

C245 A124(a) 150fr multi 1.00 50
C246 A124(b) 200fr multi 1.40 65

Souvenir Sheet

C247 A124(c) 500fr multi 3.50 1.60

Winners, 21st Olympic Games.

UPU Emblem over Globe — AP60

1978, Aug. 8 Litho. *Perf. 13*

C248 AP60 350fr multi 2.25 1.50

Congress of Paris, establishing UPU, cent.

Jules Verne, Apollo 11 Emblem, Footprint on Moon, Neil Armstrong — AP61

Space Conquest: 50fr, Yuri Gagarin and moon landing. 100fr, Montgolfier hot air balloon and memorial medal, 1783; Bleriot's monoplane, 1909.

1978, Sept. 27 Litho. *Perf. 13x12½*

C249 AP61 50fr multi 35 16
C250 AP61 60fr multi 40 20
C251 AP61 100fr multi 65 35
Nos. C249-C251 (3) 1.40 71

Anti-Apartheid Year — AP62

1978, Oct. 12 Litho. *Perf. 13*

C252 AP62 100fr blue & multi 65 35

Philexafrique II-Essen Issue

Common Design Types

Designs: #C253, Hippopotamus and Upper Volta #C18. #C254, Hummingbird and Hanover #1.

1978, Nov. 1 Litho. *Perf. 12½*

C253 CD138 100fr multi 65 35
C254 CD139 100fr multi 65 35

Nos. C253-C254 printed se-tenant.

Sun God Horus with Sun — AP63

Jules Verne and Balloon — AP64

Design: 300fr, Falcon with cartouches and UNESCO emblem.

1978, Dec. 4

C255 AP63 200fr multi 1.40 65
C256 AP63 300fr multi 2.00 1.00

UNESCO Campaign to safeguard monuments at Philae.

1978, Dec. 10 Engr. *Perf. 13*

C257 AP64 200fr multi 1.40 65

Verne (1828-1905), science fiction writer.

Bicycling, Olympic Rings AP65

Designs: Bicycling scenes.

1980 *Perf. 14½*

C258 AP65 65fr multi 65 32
C259 AP65 150fr multi, vert. 1.00 50
C260 AP65 250fr multi 1.60 80
C261 AP65 350fr multi 2.25 1.20
Nos. C258-C261 (4) 5.50 2.82

Souvenir Sheet

C262 AP65 500fr multi 3.50 1.60

22nd Summer Olympic Games, Moscow, July 19-Aug. 3.

Nos. C258-C262 Overprinted with Name of Winner and Country

1980, Nov. 22 Litho. *Perf. 14½*

C263 AP65 65fr multi 42 20
C264 AP65 150fr multi 1.00 50
C265 AP65 250fr multi 1.60 80
C266 AP65 350fr multi 2.25 1.20
Nos. C263-C266 (4) 5.27 2.70

Souvenir Sheet

C267 AP65 500fr multi 3.50 1.60

1982 World Cup — AP66

Designs: Various soccer players.

1982, June 22 Litho. *Perf. 13½*

C268 AP66 70fr multi 45 22
C269 AP66 90fr multi 60 30
C270 AP66 150fr multi 1.00 50
C271 AP66 300fr multi 2.00 1.00
Nos. C268-C271 (4) 4.05 2.02

Souvenir Sheet

C272 AP66 500fr multi 3.50 1.60

Anniversaries and Events — AP67

1983, June Litho. *Perf. 13½*

C273 AP67 90fr Space Shuttle 30 15
C274 AP67 120fr World Soccer Cup 40 20
C275 AP67 300fr Cup, diff. 1.00 50
C276 AP67 450fr Royal Wedding 1.50 70
Nos. C273-C276 (4) 3.20 1.55

Souvenir Sheet

C277 AP67 500fr Prince Charles, Lady Diana 1.60 1.60

Pre-Olympics, 1984 Los Angeles AP68

1983, Aug. 1 Litho. *Perf. 13*

C278 AP68 90fr Sailing 30 15
C279 AP68 120fr Type 470 40 20
C280 AP68 300fr Wind surfing 1.00 50
C281 AP68 400fr Wind surfing, diff. 1.40 65
Nos. C278-C281 (4) 3.10 1.50

Souvenir Sheet

C282 AP68 520fr Soling Class, Wind surfing 1.60 1.60

Christmas AP69

Rubens Paintings.

1983 Litho. *Perf. 13*

C283 AP69 120fr Adoration of the Shepherds 40 20
C284 AP69 350fr Virgin of the Garland 1.20 60
C285 AP69 500fr Adoration of the Kings 1.60 80
Nos. C283-C285 (3) 3.20 1.60

1984 Summer Olympics — AP70

1984, Mar. 26 Litho. *Perf. 12½*

C286 AP70 90fr Handball, vert. 30 15
C287 AP70 120fr Volleyball, vert. 40 20
C288 AP70 150fr Handball, diff. 50 25
C289 AP70 250fr Basketball 80 42
C290 AP70 300fr Soccer 1.00 50
Nos. C286-C290 (5) 3.00 1.52

Souvenir Sheet

C291 AP70 500fr Volleyball, diff. 1.60 80

Local Birds AP71

1984, May 14 Litho. *Perf. 12½*

C292 AP71 90fr Phoenicopterus roseus 30 15
C293 AP71 185fr Choriotis kori, vert. 62 32
C294 AP71 200fr Buphagus erythrorhynchus, vert. 65 35
C295 AP71 300fr Bucorvus leadbeateri 1.00 50
Nos. C292-C295 (4) 2.57 1.32

AP72

Famous Men — AP73

Designs: 5fr, Houari Boumediene (1927-1978), president of Algeria 1965-78. 125fr, Gottlieb Daimler (1834-1900), German automotive pioneer, and 1886 Daimler. 250fr, Louis Bleriot (1872-1936), French aviator, first to fly the English Channel in a heavier-than-air craft. 300fr, Abraham Lincoln. 400fr, Henri Dunant (1828-1910), founder of the Red Cross. 450fr, Auguste Piccard (1884-1962), Swiss physicist, inventor of the bathyscaphe Trieste, 1948. 500fr, Robert Baden-Powell (1856-1941), founder of Boy Scouts. 600fr, Anatoli Karpov, Russian chess champion. 1000fr, Paul Harris (1868-1947), founder of Rotary Intl.

1984, May 21 Litho. *Perf. 13½*

C296 AP72 5fr multi 15 15
C297 AP72 125fr multi 50 25
C298 AP72 250fr multi 1.00 50
C299 AP72 300fr multi 1.20 60
C300 AP72 400fr multi 1.60 80
C301 AP72 450fr multi 1.90 90
C302 AP72 500fr multi 2.00 1.00
C303 AP72 600fr multi 2.25 1.20
Nos. C296-C303 (8) 10.60 5.40

Souvenir Sheet

C304 AP73 1000fr multi 4.00 2.00

No. C304 contains one 51x30mm stamp.

Burkina Faso

Butterflies — AP73a

1984, May 23 *Perf. 13½*

C305 AP73a 10fr Graphium pylades 15 15
C306 AP73a 120fr Hypolimnas misippus 50 22
C307 AP73a 400fr Danaus chrysippus 1.60 80
C308 AP73a 450fr Papilio demodocus 1.90 90
Nos. C305-C308 (4) 4.15 2.07

Philexafrica '85, Lome — AP74

1985, May 20 Litho. *Perf. 13*

C309	AP74	200fr Solar & wind energy	55	25
C310	AP74	200fr Children	55	25

Nos. C309-C310 se-tenant with center label picturing a map of Africa or the exhibition emblem.

PHILEXAFRICA '85, Lome — AP75

National development: No. C311, Youth. No. C312, Communications and transportation.

1985, Nov. 16 Litho. *Perf. 13*

C311	AP75	250fr multi	90	45
C312	AP75	250fr multi	90	45

Intl. Youth Year (No. C311). Nos. C311-C312 printed se-tenant with center label picturing PHILEXAFRICA '85 emblem or outline map of Africa.

French Revolution, Bicent. — AP76

Illustration reduced.

Designs: 150fr, *Oath of the Tennis Court,* by David. 200fr, *Storming of the Bastille,* by Thevenin. 600fr, *Rouget de Lisle Singing La Marseillaise,* by Pils.

1989, May 3 Litho. *Perf. 13*

C313	AP76	150fr multi	90	45
C314	AP76	200fr multi	1.20	60
C315	AP76	600fr multi	3.60	1.80
		Nos. C313-C315 (3)	5.70	2.85

PHILEXFRANCE '89. Printed se-tenant with label containing the exhibition emblem.

POSTAGE DUE STAMPS

Postage Due Stamps of Upper Senegal and Niger, 1914, Overprinted in Black or Red

HAUTE-VOLTA

1920 Unwmk. *Perf. 14x13¹/₂*

J1	D2	5c green	28	28
J2	D2	10c rose	28	28
J3	D2	15c gray	28	28
J4	D2	20c brown (R)	35	35
J5	D2	30c blue	40	40
J6	D2	50c black (R)	62	62
J7	D2	60c orange	62	62
J8	D2	1fr violet	80	80
		Nos. J1-J8 (8)	3.63	3.63

Type of 1914 Issue Surcharged **2F.**

1927

J9	D2	2fr on 1fr lilac rose	2.00	2.00
J10	D2	3fr on 1fr orange brn	2.25	2.25

D3

Red-fronted Gazelle — D4

1928 Typo.

J11	D3	5c green	28	28
J12	D3	10c rose	28	28
J13	D3	15c dark gray	40	40
J14	D3	20c dark brown	40	40
J15	D3	30c dark blue	45	45
J16	D3	50c black	1.60	1.60
J17	D3	60c orange	2.00	2.00
J18	D3	1fr dull violet	3.25	3.25
J19	D3	2fr lilac rose	6.00	6.00
J20	D3	3fr orange brn	6.25	6.25
		Nos. J11-J20 (10)	20.91	20.91

Catalogue values for unused stamps in this section, from this point to the end of the section, are for Never Hinged items.

Republic

1962, Jan. 31 *Perf. 14x13¹/₂*

Denomination in Black

J21	D4	1fr bright blue	15	15
J22	D4	2fr orange	15	15
J23	D4	5fr brt vio blue	15	15
J24	D4	10fr red lilac	20	20
J25	D4	20fr emerald	45	45
J26	D4	50fr rose red	1.10	1.10
		Nos. J21-J26 (6)	2.20	2.20

OFFICIAL STAMPS

Catalogue values for unused stamps in this section are for Never Hinged items.

Elephant O1

Perf. 12¹/₂

1963, Feb. 1 Unwmk. Photo.

Center in Sepia

O1	O1	1fr red brown	15	15
O2	O1	5fr yel green	15	15
O3	O1	10fr deep vio	18	18
O4	O1	15fr red org	22	22
O5	O1	25fr brt rose lilac	32	32
O6	O1	50fr brt green	50	50
O7	O1	60fr brt red	65	65
O8	O1	85fr dk slate grn	1.00	1.00
O9	O1	100fr brt blue	1.65	1.65
O10	O1	200fr bright rose	2.75	2.75
		Nos. O1-O10 (10)	7.57	7.57

BURUNDI

LOCATION — Central Africa, adjoining the ex-Belgian Congo Republic, Rwanda and Tanzania

GOVT. — Republic

AREA — 10,759 sq. mi.

POP. — 4,920,000 (est. 1983)

CAPITAL — Bujumbura

Burundi was established as an independent country on July 1, 1962. With Rwanda, it had been a UN trusteeship territory (Ruanda-Urundi) administered by Belgium. A military coup overthrew the monarchy November 28, 1966.

100 Centimes = 1 Franc

Catalogue values for all unused stamps in this country are for Never Hinged items.

Flower Issue of Ruanda-Urundi, 1953 Overprinted:

Royaume
du

Burundi

Perf. 11¹/₂

1962, July 1 Unwmk. Photo.

Flowers in Natural Colors

1	A27	25c dk grn & dull org	15	15
2	A27	40c green & salmon	15	15
3	A27	60c blue grn & pink	20	15
4	A27	1.25fr dk green & blue	7.00	6.50
5	A27	1.50fr vio & apple grn	30	25
6	A27	5fr dp plum & lt bl grn	42	30
7	A27	7fr dk green & fawn	85	55
8	A27	10fr dp plum & pale ol	1.20	85
		Nos. 1-8 (8)	10.27	8.90

Animal Issue of Ruanda-Urundi, 1959-61 with Similar Overprint or Surcharge in Black or Violet Blue

Size: 23x33mm, 33x23mm

9	A29	10c brn, crim & blk brn	15	15
10	A30	20c gray, ap grn & blk	15	15
11	A29	40c mag, blk & gray grn	15	15
12	A30	50c grn, org yel & brn	15	15
a.		Larger overprint and bar	15	15
13	A29	1fr brn, ultra & blk	15	15
14	A30	1.50fr blk, gray & org (VB)	15	15
15	A29	2fr grnsh bl, ind & brn	15	15
16	A30	3fr brn, dp car & blk	15	15
17	A30	3.50fr on 3fr brn, dp car & blk	15	15
18	A30	4fr on 10fr multi ("XX" 6mm wide)	15	15
a.		"XX" 4mm wide	45	45
19	A30	5fr multicolored	15	15
20	A30	6.50fr red, org yel & brn	25	18
21	A30	8fr bl, mag & blk	30	22
a.		Violet blue overprint	65	65
22	A30	10fr multicolored	30	30

Size: 45x26¹/₂mm

23	A30	20fr multicolored	65	65
24	A30	50fr multi (ovpt. bars 2mm wide)	1.25	1.10
a.		Overprint bars 4mm wide	1.90	1.10
		Set value	3.65	3.35

On No. 12a, "Burundi" is 13mm long; bar is continuous line across sheet. On No. 12, "Burundi" is 10mm; bar is 29mm. No. 12a was issued in 1963.

Two types of overprint exist on 10c, 40c, 1fr and 2fr: I, "du" is below "me"; bar 22¹/₂mm. II, "du" below "oy"; bar 20mm.

The 50c and 3fr exist in two types, besides the larger 50c overprint listed as No. 12: I, "du" is closer to "Royaume" than to "Burundi"; bar is less than 29mm; wording is centered above bar. II, "du" is closer to "Burundi"; bar is more than 30mm; wording is off-center leftward.

King Mwami Mwambutsa IV and Royal Drummers — A1

Flag and Arms of Burundi — A2

Design: 2fr, 8fr, 50fr, Map of Burundi and King.

Unwmk.

1962, Sept. 27 Photo. *Perf. 14*

25	A1	50c dull rose car & dk brn	15	15
26	A2	1fr dk green, red & emer	15	15
27	A1	2fr brown ol & dk brn	15	15
28	A1	3fr vermilion & dk brn	22	15
29	A2	4fr Prus blue, red & emer	18	15
30	A1	8fr violet & dk brn	32	15
31	A1	10fr brt green & dk brn	50	15
32	A2	20fr brown, red & emer	1.25	20
33	A1	50fr brt pink & dk brn	2.25	40
		Nos. 25-33 (9)	5.17	
		Set value		1.00

Burundi's independence, July 1, 1962.

See Nos. 47-50. For overprints see Nos. 45-46, 51-52.

Ruanda-Urundi Nos. 151-152 Surcharged:

HOMMAGE A
DAG HAMMARSKJÖLD
3⁵⁰F
ROYAUME DU BURUNDI

Photogravure, Surcharge Engraved

1962, Oct. 31 *Perf. 11¹/₂*

Inscription in French

34	A31	3.50fr on 3fr ultra & red	15	15
35	A31	6.50fr on 3fr ultra & red	20	15
36	A31	10fr on 3fr ultra & red	30	25

Inscription in Flemish

37	A31	3.50fr on 3fr ultra & red	15	15
38	A31	6.50fr on 3fr ultra & red	20	15
39	A31	10fr on 3fr ultra & red	30	25
		Nos. 34-39 (6)	1.30	1.10

Dag Hammarskjold, Secretary General of the United Nations, 1953-61.

King Mwami Mwambutsa IV, Map of Burundi and Emblem — A3

1962, Dec. 10 Photo. *Perf. 14*

40	A3	8fr yel, bl grn & blk brn	65	15
41	A3	50fr gray grn, bl grn & blk brn	1.75	35

WHO drive to eradicate malaria.

Stamps of type A3 without anti-malaria emblem are listed as Nos. 27, 30 and 33.

Sowing Seed over Africa — A4

1963, Mar. 21 *Perf. 14x13*

42 A4 4fr olive & dull pur 15 15
43 A4 8fr dp org & dull pur 15 15
44 A4 15fr emerald & dull pur 20 15
Set value 41 30

FAO "Freedom from Hunger" campaign.

Nos. 27 and 33 Overprinted in Dark Green

1963, June 19 **Unwmk.** *Perf. 14*

45 A1 2fr brn olive & dk brn 1.65 1.25
46 A1 50fr brt pink & dk brn 1.90 1.25

Conquest and peaceful use of outer space.

Types of 1962 Inscribed: "Premier Anniversaire" in Red or Magenta

1963, July 1 **Photo.**

47 A2 4fr olive, red & emer (R) 15 15
48 A1 8fr orange & dk brn (M) 15 15
49 A1 10fr lilac & dk brn (M) 20 15
50 A2 20fr gray, red & emer (R) 40 25
Nos. 47-50 (4) 90
Set value 50

First anniversary of independence.

Nos. 26 and 32 Surcharged in Brown

1963, Sept. 24 **Unwmk.** *Perf. 14*

51 A2 6.50fr on 1fr multi 38 15
52 A2 15fr on 20fr multi 75 25

Red Cross Flag over Globe with Map of Africa — A5

1963, Sept. 26 *Perf. 14x13*

53 A5 4fr emer, car & gray 15 15
54 A5 8fr brn ol, car & gray 25 15
55 A5 10fr blue, car & gray 38 18
56 A5 20fr lilac, car & gray 75 30
Nos. 53-56 (4) 1.53 78

Centenary of International Red Cross.
See No. B7.

"1962", Arms of Burundi, UN and UNESCO Emblems A6

UN Agency Emblems: 8fr, ITU. 10fr, World Meteorological Organization. 20fr, UPU. 50fr, FAO.

1963, Nov. 4 **Unwmk.** *Perf. 14*

57 A6 4fr yel, ol grn & blk 15 15
58 A6 8fr pale lil, Prus bl & blk 15 15
59 A6 10fr blue, lil & blk 20 15
60 A6 20fr yel grn, grn & blk 35 15
61 A6 50fr yel, red brn & blk 90 30
a. Souvenir sheet of 2 3.00 3.00
Nos. 57-61 (5) 1.75
Set value 65

1st anniv. of Burundi's admission to the UN. No. 61a contains two imperf. stamps with simulated perforations similar to Nos. 60-61. The 20fr stamp shows the FAO and the 50fr the WMO emblems.

UNESCO Emblem, Scales and Map — A7

Designs: 3.50fr, 6.50fr, Scroll, scales and "UNESCO." 10fr, 20fr, Abraham Lincoln, broken chain and scales.

1963, Dec. 10 **Litho.** *Perf. 14x13½*

62 A7 50c pink, lt bl & blk 15 15
63 A7 1.50fr org, lt bl & blk 15 15
64 A7 3.50fr fawn, lt grn & blk 15 15
65 A7 6.50fr lt vio, lt grn & blk 18 15
66 A7 10fr blue, bis & blk 30 15
67 A7 20fr pale brn, ocher, bl & blk 60 18
Set value 1.25 55

15th anniv. of the Universal Declaration of Human Rights and the cent. of the American Emancipation Proclamation (Nos. 66-67).

Ice Hockey — A8

Impala — A9

Designs: 3.50fr, Women's figure skating. 6.50fr, Torch. 10fr, Men's speed skating. 20fr, Slalom.

Unwmk.

1964, Jan. 25 **Photo.** *Perf. 14*

68 A8 50c olive, blk & gold 15 15
69 A8 3.50fr lt brown, blk & gold 15 15
70 A8 6.50fr pale gray, blk & gold 38 15
71 A8 10fr gray, blk & gold 50 15
72 A8 20fr tan, blk & gold 1.00 32
Nos. 68-72 (5) 2.18
Set value 65

Issued to publicize the 9th Winter Olympic Games, Innsbruck, Jan. 29-Feb. 9, 1964.

A souvenir sheet contains two stamps (10fr+5fr and 20fr+5fr) in tan, black and gold.

Canceled to Order

Starting about 1964, values in the used column are for "canceled to order" stamps. Postally used copies sell for much more.

1964 **Litho.** *Perf. 14x13, 13x14*

Animals: 1fr, 5fr, Hippopotamus, horiz. 1.50fr, 10fr, Giraffe. 2fr, 8fr, Cape buffalo, horiz. 3fr, 6.50fr, Zebra, horiz. 3.50fr, 15fr, Defassa waterbuck. 20fr, Cheetah. 50fr, Elephant. 100fr, Lion.

Size: 21½x35mm, 35x21½mm

73 A9 50c multi 15 15
74 A9 1fr multi 15 15
75 A9 1.50fr multi 15 15
76 A9 2fr multi 15 15
77 A9 3fr multi 18 15
78 A9 3.50fr multi 20 15

Size: 26x42mm, 42x26mm

79 A9 4fr multi 22 15
80 A9 5fr multi 28 15
81 A9 6.50fr multi 32 15
82 A9 8fr multi 40 15
83 A9 10fr multi 50 15
84 A9 15fr multi 65 18

Perf. 14

Size: 53x33mm

85 A9 20fr multi 85 20
86 A9 50fr multi 2.25 32
87 A9 100fr multi 4.00 65
Nos. 73-87,C1-C7 (22) 13.12
Set value 2.80

Burundi Dancer — A10

Designs: Various Dancers and Drummers.

Unwmk.

1964, Aug. 21 **Litho.** *Perf. 14*

Dancers Multicolored

88 A10 50c gold & emerald 15 15
89 A10 1fr gold & vio blue 15 15
90 A10 4fr gold & brt blue 15 15
91 A10 6.50fr gold & red 20 15
92 A10 10fr gold & brt blue 30 15
93 A10 15fr gold & emerald 45 15
94 A10 20fr gold & red 65 22
a. Souvenir sheet of 3, #92-94 1.50 1.50
Nos. 88-94 (7) 2.05
Set value 73

1965, Sept. 10

Dancers Multicolored

88a A10 50c silver & emerald 15 15
89a A10 1fr silver & violet blue 15 15
90a A10 4fr silver & bright blue 15 15
91a A10 6.50fr silver & red 15 15
92a A10 10fr silver & bright blue 18 15
93a A10 15fr silver & emerald 20 18
94b A10 20fr silver & red 30 30
c. Souvenir sheet of 3, #92a-94b 1.50 1.50
Set value 95 80

New York World's Fair, 1964-65.

Pope Paul VI and King Mwami Mwambutsa IV — A11

22 Sainted Martyrs — A12

Designs: 4fr, 14fr, Pope John XXIII and King Mwami.

1964, Nov. 12 **Photo.** *Perf. 12*

95 A11 50c brt bl, gold & red brn 15 15
96 A12 1fr mag, gold & slate 15 15
97 A11 4fr pale rose lil, gold & brn 18 15
98 A12 8fr red, gold & brn 18 15
99 A11 14fr lt grn, gold & brn 42 15
100 A11 20fr red brn, gold & grn 65 30
Nos. 95-100 (6) 1.73
Set value 68

Issued to commemorate the canonization of 22 African martyrs, Oct. 18, 1964.

Shot Put — A13

African Purple Gallinule — A14

Sports: 1fr, Discus. 3fr, Swimming, horiz. 4fr, Running. 6.50fr, Javelin, woman. 8fr, Hurdling, horiz. 10fr, Broad jump, horiz. 14fr, Diving, woman. 18fr, High jump, horiz. 20fr, Vaulting, horiz.

1964, Nov. 18 **Litho.** *Perf. 14*

101 A13 50c olive & multi 15 15
102 A13 1fr brt pink & multi 15 15
103 A13 3fr multi 15 15
104 A13 4fr multi 15 15
105 A13 6.50fr multi 15 15
106 A13 8fr lt bl & multi 16 15
107 A13 10fr multi 20 15
108 A13 14fr multi 26 15
109 A13 18fr bister & multi 32 18
110 A13 20fr gray & multi 35 22
Set value 1.60 95

18th Olympic Games, Tokyo, Oct. 10-25, 1964. See No. B8.

1965 **Unwmk.** *Perf. 14*

Birds: 1fr, 5fr, Little bee eater. 1.50fr, 6.50fr, Secretary bird. 2fr, 8fr, Yellow-billed stork. 3fr, 10fr, Congo peacock. 3.50fr, 15fr, African anhinga. 20fr, Saddle-billed stork. 50fr, Abyssinian ground hornbill. 100fr, Crowned crane.

Birds in Natural Colors

Size: 21x35mm

111 A14 50c tan, grn & blk 15 15
112 A14 1fr pink, mag & blk 15 15
113 A14 1.50fr blue & blk 15 15
114 A14 2fr yel grn, dk grn & blk 15 15
115 A14 3fr yellow, brn & blk 15 15
116 A14 3.50fr yel grn, dk grn & blk 15 15

Size: 26x43mm

117 A14 4fr tan, grn & blk 15 15
118 A14 5fr pink, mag & blk 15 15
119 A14 6.50fr blue & blk 15 15
120 A14 8fr yel grn, dk grn & blk 15 15
121 A14 10fr yel, brn & blk 20 15
122 A14 15fr yel grn, dk grn & blk 38 15

Size: 33x53mm

123 A14 20fr rose lilac & blk 50 30
124 A14 50fr yellow, brn & blk 1.25 20
125 A14 100fr green, yel & blk 2.75 40
Nos. 111-125 (15) 6.58
Set value 1.50

Issue dates: Nos. 111-116, Mar. 31. Nos. 117-122, Apr. 16. Nos. 123-125, Apr. 30.

For overprints see #174-184, C35A-C35I.

Relay Satellite and Morse Key — A15

Designs: 3fr, Telstar and old telephone handpiece. 4fr, Relay satellite and old wall telephone. 6.50fr, Orbiting Geophysical Observatory and radar screen. 8fr, Telstar II and headphones. 10fr, Sputnik II and radar aerial. 14fr, Syncom and transmission aerial. 20fr, Interplanetary Explorer and tracking aerial.

1965, July 3 **Litho.** ***Perf. 13***

126 A15	1fr	multi	15	15
127 A15	3fr	multi	15	15
128 A15	4fr	multi	15	15
129 A15	6.50fr	multi	15	15
130 A15	8fr	multi	15	15
131 A15	10fr	multi	18	15
132 A15	14fr	multi	25	15
133 A15	20fr	multi	30	18
		Set value	1.10	74

Cent. of the ITU. Perf. and imperf. souv. sheets of 2 contain Nos. 131, 133. Size: 120x86mm. Value, both sheets, $7.50.

Globe and ICY Emblem — A16

Designs: 4fr, Map of Africa and UN development emblem. 8fr, Map of Asia and Colombo Plan emblem. 10fr, Globe and UN emblem. 18fr, Map of the Americas and Alliance for Progress emblem. 25fr, Map of Europe and EUROPA emblems. 40fr, Map of Outer Space and satellite with UN wreath.

1965, Oct. 1 **Litho.** ***Perf. 13***

134 A16	1fr	ol green & multi	15	15
135 A16	4fr	dull blue & multi	15	15
136 A16	8fr	pale yellow & multi	15	15
137 A16	10fr	lilac & multi	16	15
138 A16	18fr	salmon & multi	25	15
139 A16	25fr	gray & multi	50	15
140 A16	40fr	blue & multi	75	16
a.		Souvenir sheet of 3, #138-140	1.65	1.65
		Nos. 134-140 (7)	2.11	
		Set value		70

International Cooperation Year.

Protea
A17

Flowers: 1fr, 5fr, Crossandra. 1.50fr, 6.50fr, Ansellia. 2fr, 8fr, Thunbergia. 3fr, 10fr, Schizoglossum. 3.50fr, 15fr, Dissotis. 4fr, 20fr, Protea. 50fr, Gazania. 100fr, Hibiscus. 150fr, Markhamia.

1966 **Unwmk.** ***Perf. 13½***

Size: 26x26mm

141 A17	50c	multi	15	15
142 A17	1fr	multi	15	15
143 A17	1.50fr	multi	15	15
144 A17	2fr	multi	15	15
145 A17	3fr	multi	15	15
146 A17	3.50fr	multi	15	15

Size: 31x31mm

147 A17	4fr	multi	15	15
148 A17	5fr	multi	15	15
149 A17	6.50fr	multi	15	15
150 A17	8fr	multi	15	15
151 A17	10fr	multi	15	15
152 A17	15fr	multi	30	15

Size: 39x39mm

153 A17	20fr	multi	38	15
154 A17	50fr	multi	1.00	25
155 A17	100fr	multi	1.90	38
156 A17	150fr	multi	2.75	55
		Nos. 141-156,C17-C25 (25)	12.02	
		Set value		3.00

Issue dates: Nos. 141-147, Feb. 28; Nos. 148-153, May 18; Nos. 154-156, June 15.
For overprints see Nos. 159-173, C27-C35.

Souvenir Sheets

Allegory of Prosperity and Equality Tapestry by Peter Colfs — A18

1966, Nov. 4 **Litho.** ***Perf. 13½***

157 A18		Sheet of 7 (1.50fr)	65	25
158 A18		Sheet of 7 (4fr)	1.65	65

20th anniv. of UNESCO. Each sheet contains 6 stamps showing a reproduction of the Colfs tapestry from the lobby of the General Assembly Building, NYC, and one stamp with the UNESCO emblem plus a label. The labels on Nos. 157-158 and C26 are inscribed in French or English. The 3 sheets with French inscription have light blue marginal border. The 3 sheets with English inscription have pink border. See No. C26.

Republic

Nos. 141-152, 154-156 Overprinted

REPUBLIQUE
DU
BURUNDI

1967 **Litho.** ***Perf. 13½***

Size: 26x26mm

159 A17	50c	multi	15	15
160 A17	1fr	multi	15	15
161 A17	1.50fr	multi	15	15
162 A17	2fr	multi	15	15
163 A17	3fr	multi	15	15
164 A17	3.50fr	multi	15	15

Size: 31x31mm

165 A17	4fr	multi	80	30
166 A17	5fr	multi	16	15
167 A17	6.50fr	multi	20	15
168 A17	8fr	multi	25	15
169 A17	10fr	multi	32	15
170 A17	15fr	multi	38	15

Size: 39x39mm

171 A17	50fr	multi	3.75	1.25
172 A17	100fr	multi	6.25	2.50
173 A17	150fr	multi	5.00	2.25
		Nos. 159-173,C27-C35 (24)	29.24	
		Set value		9.59

Nos. 111, 113, 116, 118-125 Overprinted "REPUBLIQUE DU BURUNDI" and Horizontal Bar

1967 **Litho.** ***Perf. 14***

Birds in Natural Colors

Size: 21x35mm

174 A14	50c	multi	1.25	65
175 A14	1.50fr	blue & black	15	15
176 A14	3.50fr	multi	15	15

Size: 26x43mm

177 A14	5fr	multi	15	15
178 A14	6.50fr	blue & black	15	15
179 A14	8fr	multi	18	15
180 A14	10fr	yel, brn & blk	32	15
181 A14	15fr	multi	65	15

Size: 33x53mm

182 A14	20fr	multi	2.00	38
183 A14	50fr	multi	4.00	1.40
184 A14	100fr	multi	6.00	2.75
		Nos. 174-184 (11)	15.00	6.23

Haplochromis Multicolor — A19

Various Tropical Fish.

1967 **Photo.** ***Perf. 13½***

Size: 42x19mm

186 A19	50c	multi	15	15
187 A19	1fr	multi	15	15
188 A19	1.50fr	multi	15	15
189 A19	2fr	multi	15	15
190 A19	3fr	multi	15	15
191 A19	3.50fr	multi	15	15

Size: 50x25mm

192 A19	4fr	multi	16	15
193 A19	5fr	multi	20	15
194 A19	6.50fr	multi	25	15
195 A19	8fr	multi	28	15
196 A19	10fr	multi	32	15
197 A19	15fr	multi	50	15

Size: 59x30mm

198 A19	20fr	multi	65	15
199 A19	50fr	multi	1.40	18
200 A19	100fr	multi	3.00	30
201 A19	150fr	multi	4.25	45
		Nos. 186-201,C46-C54 (25)	17.27	
		Set value		2.50

Issue Dates: Nos. 186-191, Apr. 4; Nos. 192-197, Apr. 28; Nos. 198-201, May 18.

Ancestor Figures, Ivory Coast — A20

African Art: 1fr, Seat of Honor, Southeast Congo. 1.50fr, Antelope head, Aribinda Region. 2fr, Buffalo mask, Upper Volta. 4fr, Funeral figures, Southwest Ethiopia.

1967, June 5 **Photo.** ***Perf. 13½***

202 A20	50c	silver & multi	15	15
203 A20	1fr	silver & multi	15	15
204 A20	1.50fr	silver & multi	15	15
205 A20	2fr	silver & multi	15	15
206 A20	4fr	silver & multi	15	15
		Set value, #202-206, C36-C40	1.30	80

Scouts on Hiking Trip — A21

Designs: 1fr, Cooking at campfire. 1.50fr, Lord Baden-Powell. 2fr, Boy Scout and Cub Scout giving Scout sign. 4fr, First aid.

1967, Aug. 9 **Photo.** ***Perf. 13½***

207 A21	50c	silver & multi	15	15
208 A21	1fr	silver & multi	15	15
209 A21	1.50fr	silver & multi	15	15
210 A21	2fr	silver & multi	15	15
211 A21	4fr	silver & multi	15	15
		Set value, #207-211, C41-C45	2.00	90

60th anniv. of the Boy Scouts and the 12th Boy Scout World Jamboree, Farragut State Park, Idaho, Aug. 1-9.

The Gleaners, by Francois Millet A22

Paintings Exhibited at EXPO '67: 8fr, The Water Carrier of Seville, by Velazquez. 14fr, The Triumph of Neptune and Amphitrite, by Nicolas Poussin. 18fr, Acrobat Standing on a Ball, by Picasso. 25fr, Marguerite van Eyck, by Jan van Eyck. 40fr, St. Peter Denying Christ, by Rembrandt.

1967, Oct. 12 **Photo.** ***Perf. 13½***

212 A22	4fr	multi	15	15
213 A22	8fr	multi	18	15
214 A22	14fr	multi	25	15
215 A22	18fr	multi	32	15
216 A22	25fr	multi	50	18
217 A22	40fr	multi	75	25
a.		Souvenir sheet of 2, #216-217	1.25	1.00
		Nos. 212-217 (6)	2.15	
		Set value		69

EXPO '67 International Exhibition, Montreal, Apr. 28-Oct. 27. Printed in sheets of 10 stamps and 2 labels inscribed in French or English. No. 217a exists imperf.

Place de la Revolution and Pres. Michel Micombero — A23

Designs: 5fr, President Michel Micombero and flag. 14fr, Formal garden and coat of arms. 20fr, Modern building and coat of arms.

1967, Nov. 23 ***Perf. 13½***

218 A23	5fr	multi	15	15
219 A23	14fr	multi	20	15
220 A23	20fr	multi	30	15
221 A23	30fr	multi	45	22
		Nos. 218-221 (4)	1.10	
		Set value		47

First anniversary of the Republic.

Madonna by Carlo Crivelli — A24

Designs: 1fr, Adoration of the Shepherds by Juan Bautista Mayno. 4fr, Holy Family by Anthony Van Dyck. 14fr, Nativity by Maitre de Moulins.

1967, Dec. 7 **Photo.** ***Perf. 13½***

222 A24	1fr	multi	15	15
223 A24	4fr	multi	15	15
224 A24	14fr	multi	25	15
225 A24	26fr	multi	60	25
		Nos. 222-225 (4)	1.15	
		Set value		50

Christmas 1967.

Printed in sheets of 25 and one corner label inscribed "Noel 1967" and giving name of painting and painter.

Slalom — A25

Designs: 10fr, Ice hockey. 14fr, Women's skating. 17fr, Bobsled. 26fr, Ski jump. 40fr, Speed skating. 60fr, Hand holding torch, and Winter Olympics emblem.

1968, Feb. 16 Photo. *Perf. 13½*

226 A25	5fr silver & multi		15	15
227 A25	10fr silver & multi		20	15
228 A25	14fr silver & multi		25	15
229 A25	17fr silver & multi		30	15
230 A25	26fr silver & multi		50	15
231 A25	40fr silver & multi		75	15
232 A25	60fr silver & multi		1.25	20
	Nos. 226-232 (7)		3.40	
	Set value			60

Issued to publicize the 10th Winter Olympic Games, Grenoble, France, Feb. 6-18. Issued in sheets of 10 stamps and label.

The Lacemaker, by Vermeer A26

Paintings: 1.50fr, Portrait of a Young Man, by Botticelli. 2fr, Maja Vestida, by Goya, horiz.

1968, Mar. 29 Photo. *Perf. 13½*

233 A26	1.50fr gold & multi	15	15
234 A26	2fr gold & multi	15	15
235 A26	4fr gold & multi	15	15
	Nos. 233-235,C59-C61 (6)	1.80	
	Set value		69

Issued in sheets of 6.

Moon Probe — A27

Designs: 6fr, Russian astronaut walking in space. 8fr, Weather satellite. 10fr, American astronaut walking in space.

1968, May 15 Photo. *Perf. 13½*

Size: 35x35mm

236 A27	4fr silver & multi	15	15
237 A27	6fr silver & multi	15	15
238 A27	8fr silver & multi	20	15
239 A27	10fr silver & multi	22	15
	Nos. 236-239,C62-C65 (8)	2.42	
	Set value		65

Issued to publicize peaceful space explorations.

A souvenir sheet contains one 25fr stamp in Moon Probe design and one 40fr in Weather Satellite design. Stamp size: 41x41mm. Value $2. Sheet exists imperf. Price $3.

Salamis Aethiops — A28

Butterflies: 1fr, 5fr, Graphium ridleyanus. 1.50fr, 6.50fr, Cymothoe. 2fr, 8fr, Charaxes eupale. 3fr, 10fr, Papilio bromius. 3.50fr, 15fr, Teracolus annae. 20fr, Salamis aethiops. 50fr, Papilio zonobia. 100fr, Danais chrysippus. 150fr, Salamis temora.

1968

Size: 30x33½mm

240 A28	50c gold & multi	15	15
241 A28	1fr gold & multi	15	15
242 A28	1.50fr gold & multi	15	15
243 A28	2fr gold & multi	15	15
244 A28	3fr gold & multi	15	15
245 A28	3.50fr gold & multi	15	15

Size: 33½x37½mm

246 A28	4fr gold & multi	15	15
247 A28	5fr gold & multi	15	15
248 A28	6.50fr gold & multi	28	15
249 A28	8fr gold & multi	32	15
250 A28	10fr gold & multi	38	15
251 A28	15fr gold & multi	45	15

Size: 41x46mm

252 A28	20fr gold & multi	75	15
253 A28	50fr gold & multi	1.50	15
254 A28	100fr gold & multi	2.50	28
255 A28	150fr gold & multi	3.75	40
	Nos. 240-255,C66-C74 (25)	16.26	
	Set value		2.25

Issue dates: Nos. 240-245, June 7; Nos. 246-251, June 28. Nos. 252-255, July 19.

Women, Along the Manzanares, by Goya — A29

Paintings: 7fr, The Letter, by Pieter de Hooch. 11fr, Woman Reading a Letter, by Gerard Terborch. 14fr, Man Writing a Letter, by Gabriel Metsu.

1968, Sept. 30 Photo. *Perf. 13½*

256 A29	4fr multi	15	15
257 A29	7fr multi	15	15
258 A29	11fr multi	20	15
259 A29	14fr multi	30	15
	Nos. 256-259,C84-C87 (8)	2.74	
	Set value		80

International Letter Writing Week.

Soccer — A30

Designs: 7fr, Basketball. 13fr, High jump. 24fr, Relay race. 40fr, Javelin.

1968, Oct. 24

260 A30	4fr gold & multi	15	15
261 A30	7fr gold & multi	15	15
262 A30	13fr gold & multi	18	15
263 A30	24fr gold & multi	35	15
264 A30	40fr gold & multi	60	30
	Nos. 260-264,C88-C92 (10)	3.98	
	Set value		1.25

19th Olympic Games, Mexico City, Oct. 12-27. Printed in sheets of 8.

Virgin and Child, by Fra Filippo Lippi — A31

Paintings: 5fr, The Magnificat, by Sandro Botticelli. 6fr, Virgin and Child, by Albrecht Durer. 11fr, Madonna del Gran Duca, by Raphael.

1968, Nov. 26 Photo. *Perf. 13½*

265 A31	3fr multi	15	15
266 A31	5fr multi	15	15
267 A31	6fr multi	15	15
268 A31	11fr multi	22	15
a.	Souvenir sheet of 4, #265-268	1.00	1.00
	Nos. 265-268,C93-C96 (8)	1.72	
	Set value		75

Christmas 1968. For overprints see Nos. 272-275, C100-C103.

WHO Emblem and Map of Africa — A32

1969, Jan. 22

269 A32	5fr gold, dk grn & yel	15	15
270 A32	6fr gold, vio & ver	15	15
271 A32	11fr gold, pur & red lil	22	15
	Nos. 269-271 (3)	52	
	Set value		21

20th anniv. of WHO in Africa.

Nos. 265-268 Overprinted in Silver

1969, Feb. 17 Photo. *Perf. 13½*

272 A31	3fr multi	15	15
273 A31	5fr multi	15	15
274 A31	6fr multi	15	15
275 A31	11fr multi	22	15
	Nos. 272-275,C100-C103 (8)	2.00	
	Set value		85

Man's 1st flight around the moon by the US spacecraft Apollo 8, Dec. 21-27, 1968.

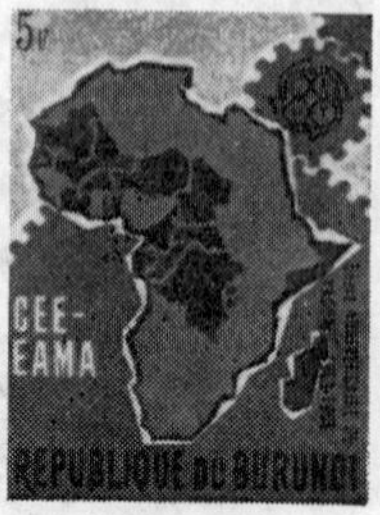

Map of Africa, and CEPT Emblem — A33

Designs: 14fr, Plowing with tractor. 17fr, Teacher and pupil. 26fr, Maps of Europe and Africa and CEPT (Conference of European Postal and Telecommunications Administrations) emblem, horiz.

1969, Mar. 12 Photo. *Perf. 13*

276 A33	5fr multi	15	15
277 A33	14fr multi	20	15
278 A33	17fr multi	25	15
279 A33	26fr multi	32	15
	Nos. 276-279 (4)	92	
	Set value		35

5th anniv. of the Yaounde (Cameroun) Agreement, creating the European and African-Malgache Economic Community.

Resurrection, by Gaspard Isenmann A34

Paintings: 14fr, Resurrection by Antoine Caron. 17fr, Noli me Tangere, by Martin Schongauer. 26fr, Resurrection, by El Greco.

1969, Mar. 24

280 A34	11fr gold & multi	15	15
281 A34	14fr gold & multi	20	15
282 A34	17fr gold & multi	25	15
283 A34	26fr gold & multi	38	15
a.	Souvenir sheet of 4, #280-283	1.50	1.50
	Nos. 280-283 (4)	98	
	Set value		34

Easter 1969.

Potter — A35

Designs (ITU Emblem and): 5fr, Farm workers. 7fr, Foundry worker. 10fr, Woman testing corn crop.

1969, May 17 Photo. *Perf. 13½*

284 A35	3fr multicolored	15	15
285 A35	5fr multicolored	15	15
286 A35	7fr multicolored	15	15
287 A35	10fr multicolored	20	15
	Set value	51	25

50th anniv. of the ILO.

Industry and Bank's Emblem A36

Designs (African Development Bank Emblem and): 17fr, Communications. 30fr, Education. 50fr, Agriculture.

1969, July 29 Photo. *Perf. 13½*

288 A36	10fr gold & multi	18	15
289 A36	17fr gold & multi	30	15
290 A36	30fr gold & multi	50	15
291 A36	50fr gold & multi	80	25
a.	Souvenir sheet of 4, #288-291	1.90	1.90
	Nos. 288-291 (4)	1.78	
	Set value		55

5th anniversary of the African Development Bank.

Girl Reading Letter, by Vermeer A37

Paintings: 7fr, Graziella (young woman), by Auguste Renoir. 14fr, Woman writing a letter, by Gerard Terborch. 26fr, Galileo Galilei, painter unknown. 40fr, Ludwig van Beethoven, painter unknown.

1969, Oct. 24 Photo. *Perf. 13½*

292	A37	4fr multicolored	15	15
293	A37	7fr multicolored	15	15
294	A37	14fr multicolored	32	15
295	A37	26fr multicolored	55	15
296	A37	40fr multicolored	75	20
a.		Souvenir sheet of 2, #295-296	1.75	1.75
		Nos. 292-296 (5)	1.92	
		Set value		52

Intl. Letter Writing Week, Oct. 7-13.

Rocket Launching A38

Moon Landing: 6.50fr, Rocket in space. 7fr, Separation of landing module from capsule. 14fr, 26fr, Landing module landing on moon. 17fr, Capsule in space. 40fr, Neil A. Armstrong leaving landing module. 50fr, Astronaut on moon.

1969, Nov. 6 Photo. *Perf. 13½*

297	A38	4fr blue & multi	15	15
298	A38	6.50fr vio blue & multi	22	15
299	A38	7fr vio blue & multi	22	15
300	A38	14fr black & multi	35	20
301	A38	17fr vio blue & multi	55	25
		Nos. 297-301,C104-C106 (8)	3.64	1.95

Souvenir Sheet

302		Sheet of 3	3.00	3.00
a.	A38	26fr multicolored	50	50
b.	A38	40fr multicolored	75	75
c.	A38	50fr multicolored	1.00	1.00

See note after Algeria No. 427.

Madonna and Child, by Rubens — A39

Paintings: 6fr, Madonna and Child with St. John, by Giulio Romano. 10fr, Magnificat Madonna, by Botticelli.

1969, Dec. 2 Photo.

303	A39	5fr gold & multi	15	15
304	A39	6fr gold & multi	15	15
305	A39	10fr gold & multi	25	15
a.		Souvenir sheet of 3, #303-305	75	75
		Nos. 303-305,C107-C109 (6)	2.33	
		Set value		65

Christmas 1969.

Sternotomis Bohemani A40

Designs: Various Beetles and Weevils.

1970 *Perf. 13½*

Size: 39x28mm

306	A40	50c multicolored	15	15
307	A40	1fr multicolored	15	15
308	A40	1.50fr multicolored	15	15
309	A40	2fr multicolored	15	15
310	A40	3fr multicolored	15	15
311	A40	3.50fr multicolored	15	15

Size: 46x32mm

312	A40	4fr multicolored	15	15
313	A40	5fr multicolored	15	15
314	A40	6.50fr multicolored	15	15
315	A40	8fr multicolored	20	15
316	A40	10fr multicolored	25	15
317	A40	15fr multicolored	38	15

Size: 52x36mm

318	A40	20fr multicolored	50	15
319	A40	50fr multicolored	1.00	18
320	A40	100fr multicolored	1.90	35
321	A40	150fr multicolored	2.75	50
		Nos. 306-321,C110-C118 (25)	19.11	
		Set value		2.85

Issue dates: Nos. 306-313, Jan. 20; Nos. 314-318, Feb. 17; Nos. 319-321, Apr. 3.

Jesus Condemned to Death — A41

Stations of the Cross, by Juan de Aranoa y Carredano: 1.50fr, Jesus carries His Cross. 2fr, Jesus falls the first time. 3fr, Jesus meets His mother. 3.50fr, Simon of Cyrene helps carry the cross. 4fr, Veronica wipes the face of Jesus. 5fr, Jesus falls the second time.

1970, Mar. 16 Photo. *Perf. 13½*

322	A41	1fr gold & multi	15	15
323	A41	1.50fr gold & multi	15	15
324	A41	2fr gold & multi	15	15
325	A41	3fr gold & multi	15	15
326	A41	3.50fr gold & multi	15	15
327	A41	4fr gold & multi	15	15
328	A41	5fr gold & multi	15	15
a.		Souv. sheet of 7, #322-328 + label	60	60
		Set value, #322-328, C119-C125	2.60	1.15

Easter 1970.

Parade and EXPO '70 Emblem — A42

Designs (EXPO '70 Emblem and): 6.50fr, Aerial view. 7fr, African pavilions. 14fr, Pagoda, vert. 26fr, Recording pavilion and pool. 40fr, Tower of the Sun, vert. 50fr, Flags of participating nations.

1970, May 5 Photo. *Perf. 13½*

329	A42	4fr gold & multi	15	15
330	A42	6.50fr gold & multi	15	15
331	A42	7fr gold & multi	15	15
332	A42	14fr gold & multi	22	15
333	A42	26fr gold & multi	38	15
334	A42	40fr gold & multi	55	15
335	A42	50fr gold & multi	80	20
		Nos. 329-335 (7)	2.40	
		Set value		65

EXPO '70 Intl. Exhibition, Osaka, Japan, Mar. 15-Sept. 13, 1970. See No. C126.

White Rhinoceros — A43

Designs, FAUNA: Camel, dromedary, okapi, addax, Burundi cow (2 stamps of each animal in 2 different poses). MAP OF THE NILE: Delta and pyramids, dhow, cataract, Blue Nile and crowned crane, Victoria Nile and secretary bird, Lake Victoria and source of Nile on Mt. Gikizi.

1970, July 8 Photo. *Perf. 13½*

336		Sheet of 18	7.00	1.50
a.		A43 7fr any single	38	15

Issued in sheets of 18 (3x6) stamps of different designs, to publicize the southernmost source of the Nile on Mt. Gikizi in Burundi. See No. C127.

Winter Wren, Firecrest, Skylark and Crested Lark — A44

Birds: 2fr, 3.50fr and 5fr, vertical; others horizontal.

1970, Sept. 30 Photo. *Perf. 13½*

Stamp Size: 44x33mm

337	A44	Block of 4	38	15
a.		2fr Northern shrike	15	
b.		2fr European starling	15	
c.		2fr Yellow wagtail	15	
d.		2fr Bank swallow	15	
338	A44	Block of 4	55	15
a.		3fr Winter wren	15	
b.		3fr Firecrest	15	
c.		3fr Skylark	15	
d.		3fr Crested lark	15	
339	A44	Block of 4	75	15
a.		3.50fr Woodchat shrike	18	
b.		3.50fr Common rock thrush	18	
c.		3.50fr Black redstart	18	
d.		3.50fr Ring ouzel	18	
340	A44	Block of 4	80	15
a.		4fr European Redstart	20	
b.		4fr Hedge sparrow	20	
c.		4fr Gray wagtail	20	
d.		4fr Meadow pipit	20	
341	A44	Block of 4	1.00	15
a.		5fr Eurasian hoopoe	25	
b.		5fr Pied flycatcher	25	
c.		5fr Great reed warbler	25	
d.		5fr Eurasian kingfisher	25	
342	A44	Block of 4	1.25	15
a.		6.50fr House martin	30	
b.		6.50fr Sedge warbler	30	
c.		6.50fr Fieldfare	30	
d.		6.50fr European Golden oriole	30	
		Nos. 337-342,C132-C137 (12)	23.63	3.25

Nos. 337-342 are printed in sheets of 16 containing 4 blocks of 4.

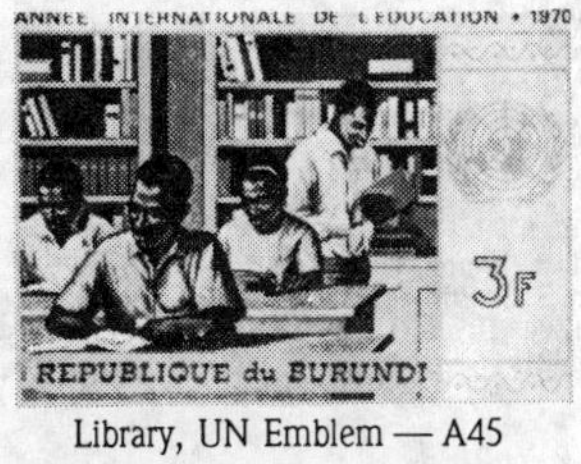

Library, UN Emblem — A45

Designs: 5fr, Students taking test, and emblem of University of Bujumbura. 7fr, Students in laboratory and emblem of Ecole Normale Superieure of Burundi. 10fr, Students with electron-microscope and Education Year emblem.

1970, Oct. 23

343	A45	3fr gold & multi	15	15
344	A45	5fr gold & multi	15	15
345	A45	7fr gold & multi	15	15
346	A45	10fr gold & multi	15	15
		Set value	41	20

Issued for International Education Year.

Pres. and Mrs. Michel Micombero — A46

Designs: 7fr, Pres. Michel Micombero and Burundi flag. 11fr, Pres. Micombero and Revolution Memorial.

1970, Nov. 28 Photo. *Perf. 13½*

347	A46	4fr gold & multi	15	15
348	A46	7fr gold & multi	15	15
349	A46	11fr gold & multi	20	15
a.		Souvenir sheet of 3	50	50
		Set value	40	20

4th anniv. of independence. No. 349a contains 3 stamps similar to Nos. 347-349, but inscribed "Poste Aerienne." Exists imperf.

See Nos. C140-C142.

Lenin with Delegates A47

Designs (Lenin, Paintings): 5fr, addressing crowd. 6.50fr, with soldier and sailor. 15fr, speaking from balcony. 50fr, Portrait.

1970, Dec. 31 Photo. *Perf. 13½*

Gold Frame

350	A47	3.50fr dk red brown	15	15
351	A47	5fr dk red brown	15	15
352	A47	6.50fr dk red brown	15	15
353	A47	15fr dk red brown	32	15
354	A47	50fr dk red brown	1.10	18
		Nos. 350-354 (5)	1.87	
		Set value		46

Lenin's birth centenary (1870-1924).

Lion — A48

1971, Mar. 19 Photo. *Perf. 13½*

Size: 38x38mm

355		Strip of 4	20	15
a.	A48	1fr Lion	15	
b.	A48	1fr Cape buffalo	15	
c.	A48	1fr Hippopotamus	15	
d.	A48	1fr Giraffe	15	
356		Strip of 4	24	15
a.	A48	2fr Hartebeest	15	
b.	A48	2fr Black rhinoceros	15	
c.	A48	2fr Zebra	15	
d.	A48	2fr Leopard	15	
357		Strip of 4	32	15
a.	A48	3fr Grant's gazelles	15	
b.	A48	3fr Cheetah	15	
c.	A48	3fr African white-backed vultures	15	
d.	A48	3fr Johnston's okapi	15	

358	Strip of 4	50	20
a.	A48 5fr Chimpanzee	15	
b.	A48 5fr Elephant	15	
c.	A48 5fr Spotted hyenas	15	
d.	A48 5fr Beisa	15	
359	Strip of 4	65	42
a.	A48 6fr Gorilla	15	
b.	A48 6fr Gnu	15	
c.	A48 6fr Wart hog	15	
d.	A48 6fr Cape hunting dog	15	
360	Strip of 4	1.40	45
a.	A48 11fr Sable antelope	32	
b.	A48 11fr Caracal lynx	32	
c.	A48 11fr Ostriches	32	
d.	A48 11fr Bongo	32	
	Nos. 355-360,C146-C151 (12)	15.31	3.31

For overprints and surcharges see Nos. C152, CB15-CB18.

The Resurrection, by Il Sodoma — A49

Paintings: 6fr, Resurrection, by Andrea del Castagno. 11fr, Noli me Tangere, by Correggio.

1971, Apr. 2

361 A49	3fr gold & multi	15	15
362 A49	6fr gold & multi	15	15
363 A49	11fr gold & multi	28	15
a.	Souvenir sheet of 3, #361-363	60	60
	Nos. 361-363,C143-C145 (6)	1.30	
	Set value		46

Easter 1971. No. 363a exists imperf.

Young Venetian Woman, by Dürer — A50

Dürer Paintings: 11fr, Hieronymus Holzschuher. 14fr, Emperor Maximilian I. 17fr, Holy Family, from Paumgartner Altar. 26fr, Haller Madonna. 31fr, Self-portrait, 1498.

1971, Sept. 20

364 A50	6fr multicolored	15	15
365 A50	11fr multicolored	22	15
366 A50	14fr multicolored	38	15
367 A50	17fr multicolored	45	22
368 A50	26fr multicolored	65	35
369 A50	31fr multicolored	80	40
a.	Souvenir sheet of 2, #368-369	1.60	1.60
	Nos. 364-369 (6)	2.65	1.42

International Letter Writing Week. Albrecht Dürer (1471-1528), German painter and engraver. No. 369a exists imperf.

Nos. 364-369, 369a Overprinted in Black and Gold: "VIème CONGRES / DE L'INSTITUT INTERNATIONAL / DE DROIT D'EXPRESSION FRANCAISE"

1971, Oct. 8

370 A50	6fr multicolored	15	15
371 A50	11fr multicolored	22	15
372 A50	14fr multicolored	28	15
373 A50	17fr multicolored	35	15
374 A50	26fr multicolored	50	15
375 A50	31fr multicolored	65	18
a.	Souvenir sheet of 2	1.25	1.25
	Nos. 370-375 (6)	2.15	
	Set value		62

6th Congress of the International Legal Institute of the French-speaking Area, Bujumbura, Aug. 10-19.

Madonna and Child, by Il Perugino — A51

Paintings of the Madonna and Child by: 5fr, Andrea del Sarto. 6fr, Luis de Morales.

1971, Nov. 2 Photo. *Perf. 13½*

376 A51	3fr dk green & multi	15	15
377 A51	5fr dk green & multi	15	15
378 A51	6fr dk green & multi	15	15
a.	Souvenir sheet of 3, #376-378	38	38
	Nos. 376-378,C153-C155 (6)	1.55	
	Set value		62

Christmas 1971. No. 378a exists imperf.
For surcharges see #B49-B51, CB19-CB21.

Lunar Orbiter — A52

Designs: 11fr, Vostok. 14fr, Luna 1. 17fr, Apollo 11 astronaut on moon. 26fr, Soyuz 11. 40fr, Lunar Rover (Apollo 15).

1972, Jan. 15

379 A52	6fr gold & multi	18	15
380 A52	11fr gold & multi	22	15
381 A52	14fr gold & multi	28	15
382 A52	17fr gold & multi	40	20
383 A52	26fr gold & multi	40	32
384 A52	40fr gold & multi	62	32
a.	Souvenir sheet of 6	2.25	2.25
	Nos. 379-384 (6)	2.10	1.29

Conquest of space. See No. C156.
No. 384a contains one each of Nos. 379-384 inscribed "APOLLO 16."

Slalom and Sapporo '72 Emblem — A53

Designs (Sapporo '72 Emblem and): 6fr, Figure skating, pairs. 11fr, Figure skating, women's. 14fr, Ski jump. 17fr, Ice hockey. 24fr, Speed skating, men's. 26fr, Snow scooter. 31fr, Downhill skiing. 50fr, Bobsledding.

1972, Feb. 3

385 A53	5fr silver & multi	15	15
386 A53	6fr silver & multi	15	15
387 A53	11fr silver & multi	18	15
388 A53	14fr silver & multi	22	15
389 A53	17fr silver & multi	28	15
390 A53	24fr silver & multi	38	15
391 A53	26fr silver & multi	40	15
392 A53	31fr silver & multi	50	15
393 A53	50fr silver & multi	80	20
	Nos. 385-393 (9)	3.06	
	Set value		82

11th Winter Olympic Games, Sapporo, Japan, Feb. 3-13. Printed in sheets of 12. See No. C157.
Issue dates: Nos. 385-390, Feb. 1; Nos. 391-393, Feb. 21.

Ecce Homo, by Quentin Massys — A54

Paintings: 6.50fr, Crucifixion, by Rubens. 10fr, Descent from the Cross, by Jacopo da Pontormo. 18fr, Pieta, by Ferdinand Gallegos. 27fr, Trinity, by El Greco.

1972, Mar. 20 Photo. *Perf. 13½*

394 A54	3.50fr gold & multi	15	15
395 A54	6.50fr gold & multi	15	15
396 A54	10fr gold & multi	15	15
397 A54	18fr gold & multi	25	15
398 A54	27fr gold & multi	65	15
a.	Souv. sheet of 5, #394-398 + label	1.50	1.25
	Nos. 394-398 (5)	1.35	
	Set value		42

Easter 1972. Printed in sheets of 8 with label. No. 398a exists imperf.

Gymnastics, Olympic Rings and "Motion" A55

1972, May 19

399 A55	5fr shown	15	15
400 A55	6fr Javelin	15	15
401 A55	11fr Fencing	22	15
402 A55	14fr Bicycling	25	15
403 A55	17fr Pole vault	32	15
	Nos. 399-403,C158-C161 (9)	2.94	
	Set value		95

Souvenir Sheet

404	Sheet of 2	1.75	1.25
a.	A55 31fr Discus	45	45
b.	A55 40fr Soccer	60	60

20th Olympic Games, Munich, Aug. 26-Sept. 11.

Prince Rwagasore, Pres. Micombero, Burundi Flag, Drummers A56

Designs: 7fr, Rwagasore, Micombero, flag, map of Africa, globe. 13fr, Micombero, flag, globe.

1972, Aug. 24 Photo. *Perf. 13½*

405 A56	5fr silver & multi	15	15
406 A56	7fr silver & multi	15	15
407 A56	13fr silver & multi	22	15
a.	Souvenir sheet of 3, #405-407	50	
	Nos. 405-407,C162-C164 (6)	1.52	
	Set value		52

10th anniversary of independence.

Madonna and Child, by Andrea Solario — A57

Paintings of the Madonna and Child by: 10fr, Raphael. 15fr, Botticelli.

1972, Nov. 2

408 A57	5fr lt blue & multi	15	15
409 A57	10fr lt blue & multi	15	15
410 A57	15fr lt blue & multi	22	15
a.	Souvenir sheet of 3, #408-410	50	
	Nos. 408-410,C165-C167 (6)	1.80	
	Set value		56

Christmas 1972. Sheets of 20 stamps + label.
For surcharges see #B56-B58, CB26-CB28.

Platycoryne Crocea — A58

1972

Size: 33x33mm

411 A58	50c *shown*	15	15
412 A58	1fr *Cattleya trianaei*	15	15
413 A58	2fr *Eulophia cucullata*	15	15
414 A58	3fr *Cymbidium hamsey*	15	15
415 A58	4fr *Thelymitra pauciflora*	15	15
416 A58	5fr *Miltassia*	15	15
417 A58	6fr *Miltonia*	15	15

Size: 38x38mm

418 A58	7fr Like 50c	15	15
419 A58	8fr Like 1fr	15	15
420 A58	9fr Like 2fr	15	15
421 A58	10fr Like 3fr	18	15
	Set value, #411-421, C168-C174	3.25	1.20

Orchids. Issue dates: Nos. 411-417, Nov. 6; Nos. 418-421, Nov. 29.

Henry Morton Stanley — A59

Designs: 7fr, Porters, Stanley's expedition. 13fr, Stanley entering Ujiji.

1973, Mar. 19 Photo. *Perf. 13½*

422 A59	5fr gold & multi	15	15
423 A59	7fr gold & multi	15	15
424 A59	13fr gold & multi	20	15
	Nos. 422-424,C175-C177 (6)	1.40	
	Set value		48

Exploration of Africa by David Livingstone (1813-1873) and Henry Morton Stanley (John Rowlands; 1841-1904).

Crucifixion, by Roger van der Weyden — A60

Easter (Paintings): 5fr, Flagellation of Christ, by Caravaggio. 13fr, The Burial of Christ, by Raphael.

1973, Apr. 10

425 A60	5fr gold & multi	15	15
426 A60	7fr gold & multi	15	15
427 A60	13fr gold & multi	20	15
a.	Souvenir sheet of 3, #425-427	60	60
	Nos. 425-427,C178-C180 (6)	1.63	
	Set value		46

INTERPOL Emblem, Flag — A61

Design: 10fr, INTERPOL flag and emblem. 18fr, INTERPOL Headquarters and emblem.

1973, May 19 Photo. *Perf. 13½*

428 A61	5fr silver & multi	15	15
429 A61	10fr silver & multi	15	15
430 A61	18fr silver & multi	28	15
	Nos. 428-430,C181-C182 (5)	1.46	
	Set value		59

50th anniversary of International Criminal Police Organization (INTERPOL).

Signs of the Zodiac, Babylon — A62

Designs: 5fr, Greek and Roman gods representing planets. 7fr, Ptolemy (No. 433a) and Ptolemaic solar system. 13fr, Copernicus (No. 434a) and heliocentric system.
a, UL. b, UR. c, LL. d, LR.

1973, July 27 Photo. *Perf. 13½*

431 A62	3fr Block of 4, #a.-d.	20	15
432 A62	5fr Block of 4, #a.-d.	25	15
433 A62	7fr Block of 4, #a.-d.	32	15
434 A62	13fr Block of 4, #a.-d.	75	20
e.	Souvenir sheet of 4, #431-434	2.75	1.40
	Nos. 431-434,C183-C186 (8)	9.32	2.50

500th anniversary of the birth of Nicolaus Copernicus (1473-1543), Polish astronomer.

Flowers and Butterflies — A63

Designs: Each block of 4 contains 2 flower and 2 butterfly designs. The 1fr, 2fr, 5fr and 11fr have flower designs listed as "a" and "d" numbers, butterflies as "b" and "c" numbers; the arrangement is reversed for the 3fr and 6fr.

1973, Sept. 3 Photo. *Perf. 13*
Stamp Size: 34x41½mm

435 A63	Block of 4	20	15
a.	1fr *Protea cynaroides*	15	15
b.	1fr *Precis octavia*	15	15
c.	1fr *Epiphora bauhiniae*	15	15
d.	1fr *Gazania longiscapa*	15	15
436 A63	Block of 4	20	15
a.	2fr *Kniphofia*	15	15
b.	2fr *Cymothoe coccinata*	15	15
c.	2fr *Nudaurelia zambesina*	15	15
d.	2fr *Freesia refracta*	15	15
437 A63	Block of 4	24	15
a.	3fr *Calotis eupompe*	15	15
b.	3fr *Narcissus*	15	15
c.	3fr *Cineraria hybrida*	15	15
d.	3fr *Cyrestis camillus*	15	15
438 A63	Block of 4	40	15
a.	5fr *Iris tingitana*	15	15
b.	5fr *Pappilio demodocus*	15	15
c.	5fr *Catopsilia avelaneda*	15	15
d.	5fr *Nerine sarniensis*	15	15
439 A63	Block of 4	50	20
a.	6fr *Hypolimnas dexithea*	15	15
b.	6fr *Zantedeschia tropicalis*	15	15
c.	6fr *Sandersonia aurantiaca*	15	15
d.	6fr *Drurya antimachus*	15	15
440 A63	Block of 4	1.00	22
a.	11fr *Nymphaea capensis*	25	15
b.	11fr *Pandoriana pandora*	25	15
c.	11fr *Precis orythia*	25	15
d.	11fr *Pelargonium domestica*	25	15
	Nos. 435-440,C187-C192 (12)	22.04	3.52

Virgin and Child, by Giovanni Bellini — A64

Virgin and Child by: 10fr, Jan van Eyck. 15fr, Giovanni Boltraffio.

1973, Nov. 13 Photo. *Perf. 13*

441 A64	5fr gold & multi	15	15
442 A64	10fr gold & multi	15	15
443 A64	15fr gold & multi	22	15
a.	Souvenir sheet of 3, #441-443	50	50
	Nos. 441-443,C193-C195 (6)	1.80	
	Set value		52

Christmas 1973.
For surcharges see #B59-B61, CB29-CB31.

Pietá, by Paolo Veronese — A65

Paintings: 10fr, Virgin and St. John, by van der Weyden. 18fr, Crucifixion, by van der Weyden. 27fr, Burial of Christ, by Titian. 40fr, Pietá, by El Greco.

1974, Apr. 19 Photo. *Perf. 14x13½*

444 A65	5fr gold & multi	15	15
445 A65	10fr gold & multi	15	15
446 A65	18fr gold & multi	28	15
447 A65	27fr gold & multi	42	15
448 A65	40fr gold & multi	65	15
a.	Souvenir sheet of 5, #444-448	1.65	1.65
	Nos. 444-448 (5)	1.65	
	Set value		46

Easter 1974.

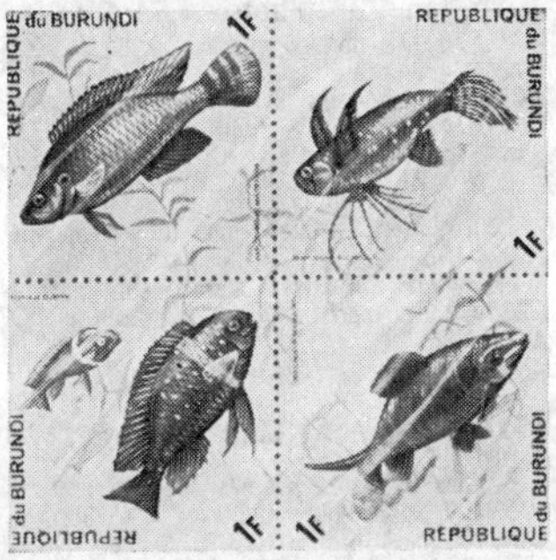

Fish — A66

1974, May 30 Photo. *Perf. 13*
Stamp Size: 35x35mm

449 A66	Block of 4	20	20
a.	1fr *Haplochromis multicolor*	15	15
b.	1fr *Pantodon buchholzi*	15	15
c.	1fr *Tropheus duboisi*	15	15
d.	1fr *Distichodus sexfasciatus*	15	15
450 A66	Block of 4	20	15
a.	2fr *Pelmatochromis kribensis*	15	15
b.	2fr *Nannaethiops tritaeniatus*	15	15
c.	2fr *Polycentropsis abbreviata*	15	15
d.	2fr *Hemichromis bimaculatus*	15	15
451 A66	Block of 4	20	20
a.	3fr *Ctenopoma acutirostre*	15	15
b.	3fr *Synodontis angelicus*	15	15
c.	3fr *Tilapia melanopleura*	15	15
d.	3fr *Aphyosemion bivittatum*	15	15
452 A66	Block of 4	32	15
a.	5fr *Monodactylus argenteus*	15	15
b.	5fr *Zanclus canescens*	15	15
c.	5fr *Pygoplites diacanthus*	15	15
d.	5fr *Cephalopholis argus*	15	15
453 A66	Block of 4	38	15
a.	6fr *Priacanthus arenatus*	15	15
b.	6fr *Pomacanthus arcuatus*	15	15
c.	6fr *Scarus guacamaia*	15	15
d.	6fr *Zeus faber*	15	15
454 A66	Block of 4	65	20
a.	11fr *Lactophrys quadricornis*	16	15
b.	11fr *Balistes vetula*	16	15
c.	11fr *Acanthurus bahianus*	16	15
d.	11fr *Holocanthus ciliaris*	16	15
	Nos. 449-454,C207-C212 (12)	12.25	2.65

Soccer and Cup A67

Designs: Various soccer scenes and cup.

1974, July 4 Photo. *Perf. 13*

455 A67	5fr gold & multi	15	
456 A67	6fr gold & multi	15	
457 A67	11fr gold & multi	16	
458 A67	14fr gold & multi	22	
459 A67	17fr gold & multi	25	
a.	Souvenir sheet of 3	1.40	
	Nos. 455-459,C196-C198 (8)	2.23	

World Soccer Championship, Munich, June 13-July 7. No. 459a contains 3 stamps similar to Nos. C196-C198 without "Poste Aerienne."
Nos. 455-459 and 459a exist imperf.

Flags over UPU Headquarters, Bern — A68

Designs: No. 461, G.P.O., Bujumbura. No. 462, Mailmen ("11F" in UR). No. 463, Mailmen ("11F" in UL). No. 464, UPU emblem. No. 465, Means of transportation. No. 466, Pigeon over globe showing Burundi. No. 467, Swiss flag, pigeon over map showing Bern.

1974, July 23

460 A68	6fr gold & multi	18	
461 A68	6fr gold & multi	18	
462 A68	11fr gold & multi	30	
463 A68	11fr gold & multi	30	
464 A68	14fr gold & multi	38	
465 A68	14fr gold & multi	38	
466 A68	17fr gold & multi	45	
467 A68	17fr gold & multi	50	
a.	Souvenir sheet of 8, #460-467	2.75	
	Nos. 460-467,C199-C206 (16)	9.97	
	Set, used		1.00

Cent. of UPU. Stamps of same denomination printed se-tenant (continuous design).

St. Ildefonso Writing Letter, by El Greco — A69

Paintings: 11fr, Lady Sealing Letter, by Chardin. 14fr, Titus at Desk, by Rembrandt. 17fr, The Love Letter, by Vermeer. 26fr, The Merchant G. Gisze, by Holbein. 31fr, Portrait of Alexandre Lenoir, by David.

1974, Oct. 1 Photo. *Perf. 13*

468 A69	6fr gold & multi	15	
469 A69	11fr gold & multi	16	
470 A69	14fr gold & multi	22	
471 A69	17fr gold & multi	25	
472 A69	26fr gold & multi	40	
473 A69	31fr gold & multi	45	
a.	Souvenir sheet of 2, #472-473	1.10	
	Nos. 468-473 (6)	1.63	

International Letter Writing Week, Oct. 6-12. No. 473a exists imperf.

Virgin and Child, by Bernaert van Orley — A70

Paintings of the Virgin and Child: 10fr, by Hans Memling. 15fr, by Botticelli.

1974, Nov. 7 Photo. *Perf. 13*

474 A70	5fr gold & multi	15	
475 A70	10fr gold & multi	15	
476 A70	15fr gold & multi	22	
a.	Souvenir sheet of 3, #474-476	50	
	Nos. 474-476,C213-C215 (6)	1.80	

Christmas 1974. Sheets of 20 stamps and one label. No. 476a exists imperf.

Apollo-Soyuz Space Mission and Emblem — A71

1975, July 10 Photo. *Perf. 13*

477 A71	Block of 4	80	
a.	26fr A.A. Leonov, V.N. Kubasov, Soviet flag	20	
b.	26fr Soyuz and Soviet flag	20	
c.	26fr Apollo and American flag	20	
d.	26fr D.K. Slayton, V.D. Brand, T.P. Stafford, American flag	20	

478 A71 Block of 4 — 1.25
a. 31fr Apollo-Soyuz link-up — 28
b. 31fr Apollo, blast-off — 28
c. 31fr Soyuz, blast-off — 28
d. 31fr Kubasov, Leonov, Slayton, Brand, Stafford — 28
Nos. 477-478,C216-C217 (4) — 4.35

Apollo Soyuz space test project (Russo-American cooperation), launching July 15; link-up, July 17.

Addax — A72

1975, July 31 Photo. *Perf. 13½*

479 Strip of 4 — 20
a. A72 1fr shown — 15
b. A72 1fr Roan antelope — 15
c. A72 1fr Nyala — 15
d. A72 1fr White rhinoceros — 15
480 Strip of 4 — 20
a. A72 2fr Mandrill — 15
b. A72 2fr Eland — 15
c. A72 2fr Salt's dik-dik — 15
d. A72 2fr Thomson's gazelles — 15
481 Strip of 4 — 20
a. A72 3fr African small-clawed otter — 15
b. A72 3fr Reed buck — 15
c. A72 3fr Indian civet — 15
d. A72 3fr Cape buffalo — 15
482 Strip of 4 — 35
a. A72 5fr White-tailed gnu — 15
b. A72 5fr African wild asses — 15
c. A72 5fr Black-and-white colobus monkey — 15
d. A72 5fr Gerenuk — 15
483 Strip of 4 — 36
a. A72 6fr Dama gazelle — 15
b. A72 6fr Black-backed jackal — 15
c. A72 6fr Sitatungas — 15
d. A72 6fr Zebra antelope — 15
484 Strip of 4 — 65
a. A72 11fr Fennec — 16
b. A72 11fr Lesser kudus — 16
c. A72 11fr Blesbok — 16
d. A72 11fr Serval — 16
Nos. 479-484,C218-C223 (12) — 12.61

For overprints see Nos. C224-C227.

Jonah, by Michelangelo — A73

Designs: Paintings from Sistine Chapel.

1975, Dec. 3 Photo. *Perf. 13*

485 A73 5fr shown — 15
486 A73 5fr Libyan Sybil — 15
487 A73 13fr Prophet Isaiah — 20
488 A73 13fr Delphic Sybil — 20
489 A73 27fr Daniel — 40
490 A73 27fr Cumaean Sybil — 40
a. Souvenir sheet of 6, #485-490 — 2.00
Nos. 485-490,C228-C233 (12) — 5.10

Michelangelo Buonarotti (1475-1564), Italian sculptor, painter and architect. Stamps of same denominations printed se-tenant in sheets of 18 stamps and 2 labels.
For surcharges see Nos. B65-B70, CB35-CB40.

Speed Skating — A74

Basketball — A75

Designs (Innsbruck Games Emblem and): 24fr, Figure skating, women's. 26fr, Two-man bobsled. 31fr, Cross-country skiing.

1976, Jan. 23 Photo. *Perf. 14x13½*

491 A74 17fr dp bl & multi — 30
492 A74 24fr multi — 45
493 A74 26fr multi — 48
494 A74 31fr plum & multi — 55
a. Souvenir sheet of 3 — 2.25
Nos. 491-494,C234-C236 (7) — 3.70

12th Winter Olympic Games, Innsbruck, Austria, Feb. 4-15.
No. 494a contains 3 stamps similar to Nos. C234-C236, perf. 13½, without "POSTE AERIENNE."

1976, May 3 Litho. *Perf. 13½*

Designs (Montreal Games Emblem and): Nos. 496, 499, 503b, Pole vault. Nos. 497, 500, 503d, Running. Nos. 498, 501, 503a, Soccer. No. 502, 503c, Basketball.

495 A75 14fr blue & multi — 25
496 A75 14fr olive & multi — 25
497 A75 17fr magenta & multi — 30
498 A75 17fr vermilion & multi — 30
499 A75 28fr olive & multi — 48
500 A75 28fr magenta & multi — 48
501 A75 40fr vermilion & multi — 70
502 A75 40fr blue & multi — 70
Nos. 495-502,C237-C242 (14) — 7.20

Souvenir Sheet

503 Sheet of 4 — 1.65
a. A75 14fr red & multi — 22
b. A75 17fr olive & multi — 25
c. A75 28fr blue & multi — 40
d. A75 40fr magenta & multi — 60

21st Olympic Games, Montreal, Canada, July 17-Aug. 1. Stamps of same denomination printed se-tenant in sheets of 20.

Virgin and Child, by Dirk Bouts — A76

Virgin and Child by: 13fr, Giovanni Bellini. 27fr, Carlo Crivelli.

1976, Oct. 18 Photo. *Perf. 13½*

504 A76 5fr gold & multi — 15
505 A76 13fr gold & multi — 20
506 A76 27fr gold & multi — 40
a. Souvenir sheet of 3, #504-506 — 75
Nos. 504-506,C250-C252 (6) — 2.05

Christmas 1976. Sheets of 20 stamps and descriptive label.
For surcharges see #B71-B73, CB41-CB43.

St. Veronica, by Rubens A77

Paintings by Rubens: 21fr, Christ on the Cross. 27fr, Descent from the Cross. 35fr, The Deposition.

1977, Apr. 5 Photo. *Perf. 13*

507 A77 10fr gold & multi — 15
508 A77 21fr gold & multi — 32
509 A77 27fr gold & multi — 40
510 A77 35fr gold & multi — 55
a. Souvenir sheet of 4 — 1.50
Nos. 507-510 (4) — 1.42

Easter 1977. Sheets of 30 stamps and descriptive label. No. 510a contains 4 stamps similar to Nos. 507-510 inscribed "POSTE AERIENNE."

Alexander Graham Bell — A78

Intelsat Satellite, Modern and Old Telephones — A79

Designs: No. 513, Switchboard operator, c. 1910, and wall telephone. No. 514, Intelsat and radar. No. 515, A.G. Bell and first telephone. No. 516, Satellites around globe and videophone.

1977, May 17 Photo. *Perf. 13*

511 A78 10fr multi — 15
512 A79 10fr multi — 15
513 A78 17fr multi — 15
514 A79 17fr multi — 15
515 A78 26fr multi — 22
516 A79 26fr multi — 22
Nos. 511-516,C253-C256 (10) — 1.84

Centenary of first telephone call by Alexander Graham Bell, Mar. 10, 1876. Stamps of same denomination printed se-tenant in sheets of 32.

Buffon's Kob — A80

1977, Aug. 22 Photo. *Perf. 14x14½*

517 Strip of 4 — 20
a. A80 2fr shown — 15
b. A80 2fr Marabous — 15
c. A80 2fr Brindled gnu — 15
d. A80 2fr River hog — 15
518 Strip of 4 — 35
a. A80 5fr Zebras — 15
b. A80 5fr Shoebill — 15
c. A80 5fr Striped hyenas — 15
d. A80 5fr Chimpanzee — 15
519 Strip of 4 — 48
a. A80 8fr Flamingos — 15
b. A80 8fr Nile crocodiles — 15
c. A80 8fr Green mamba — 15
d. A80 8fr Greater kudus — 15
520 Strip of 4 — 70
a. A80 11fr Hyrax — 16
b. A80 11fr Cobra — 16
c. A80 11fr Jackals — 16
d. A80 11fr Verreaux's eagles — 16
521 Strip of 4 — 1.40
a. A80 21fr Honey badger — 32
b. A80 21fr Harnessed antelopes — 32
c. A80 21fr Secretary bird — 32
d. A80 21fr Klipspringer — 32
522 Strip of 4 — 1.40
a. A80 27fr African big-eared fox — 35
b. A80 27fr Elephants — 35
c. A80 27fr Vulturine guineafowl — 35
d. A80 27fr Impalas — 35
Nos. 517-522,C258-C263 (12) — 20.68

The Goose Girl, by Grimm — A81

Fairy Tales: 5fr, by Grimm Brothers. 11fr, by Aesop. 14fr, by Hans Christian Andersen. 17fr, by Jean de La Fontaine. 26fr, English fairy tales.

1977, Sept. 14 *Perf. 14*

523 Block of 4 — 38
a. A81 5fr shown — 15
b. A81 5fr The Two Wanderers — 15
c. A81 5fr The Man of Iron — 15
d. A81 5fr Snow White and Rose Red — 15
524 Block of 4 — 85
a. A81 11fr The Quarreling Cats — 20
b. A81 11fr The Blind and the Lame — 20
c. A81 11fr The Hermit and the Bear — 20
d. A81 11fr The Fox and the Stork — 20
525 Block of 4 — 1.00
a. A81 14fr The Princess and the Pea — 25
b. A81 14fr The Old Tree Mother — 25
c. A81 14fr The Ice Maiden — 25
d. A81 14fr The Old House — 25
526 Block of 4 — 1.25
a. A81 17fr The Oyster and the Suitors — 30
b. A81 17fr The Wolf and the Lamb — 30
c. A81 17fr Hen with the Golden Egg — 30
d. A81 17fr The Wolf as Shepherd — 30
527 Block of 4 — 2.00
a. A81 26fr Three Heads in the Well — 50
b. A81 26fr Mother Goose — 50
c. A81 26fr Jack and the Beanstalk — 50
d. A81 26fr Alice in Wonderland — 50
Nos. 523-527 (5) — 5.48

Security Council Chamber, UN Nos. 28, 46, 37, C7 — A82

Designs (UN Stamps and): 8fr, UN General Assembly, interior. 21fr, UN Meeting Hall.

1977, Oct. 10 Photo. *Perf. 13½*

528 A82 Block of 4 — 65
a. 8fr No. 25 — 15
b. 8fr No. C5 — 15
c. 8fr No. 23 — 15
d. 8fr No. 2 — 15
529 A82 Block of 4 — 75
a. 10fr No. 28 — 18
b. 10fr No. 46 — 18
c. 10fr No. 37 — 18
d. 10fr No. C7 — 18
530 A82 Block of 4 — 1.50
a. 21fr No. 45 — 35
b. 21fr No. 42 — 35
c. 21fr No. 17 — 35
d. 21fr No. 13 — 35
e. Souvenir sheet of 3 — 65
Nos. 528-530,C264-C266 (6) — 10.05

25th anniv. (in 1976) of the UN Postal Administration. No. 530e contains 8fr in design of No. 529d, 10fr in design of No. 530b, 21fr in design of No. 528c.

Virgin and Child — A83

Designs: Paintings of the Virgin and Child.

1977, Oct. 31 Photo. *Perf. 14x13*

531 A83 5fr By Meliore Toscano — 15
532 A83 13fr By J. Lombardos — 20
533 A83 27fr By Emmanuel Tzanes, 1610-1680 — 40
a. Souvenir sheet of 3, #531-533 — 75
Nos. 531-533,C267-C269 (6) — 2.11

Christmas 1977. Sheets of 24 stamps with descriptive label.
For surcharges see #B74-B76, CB44-CB46.

Cruiser Aurora, Russia Nos. 211, 303, 1252, 187 — A84

Designs (Russian Stamps and): 8fr, Kremlin, Moscow. 11fr, Pokrovski Cathedral, Moscow. 13fr, Labor Day parade, 1977 and 1980 Olympic Games emblem.

1977, Nov. 14 Photo. *Perf. 13*

534 A84 Block of 4 38
 a. 5fr No. 211 15
 b. 5fr No. 303 15
 c. 5fr No. 1252 15
 d. 5fr No. 187 15
535 A84 Block of 4 65
 a. 8fr No. 856 15
 b. 8fr No. 1986 15
 c. 8fr No. 908 15
 d. 8fr No. 2551 15
536 A84 Block of 4 85
 a. 11fr No. 3844b 20
 b. 11fr No. 3452 20
 c. 11fr No. 3382 20
 d. 11fr No. 3837 20
537 A84 Block of 4 1.00
 a. 13fr No. 4446 25
 b. 13fr No. 3497 25
 c. 13fr No. 2926 25
 d. 13fr No. 2365 25
 Nos. 534-537 (4) 2.88

60th anniv. of Russian October Revolution.

Ship at Dock, Arms and Flag — A85

Burundi Arms and Flag and: 5fr, Men at lathes. 11fr, Male leopard dance. 14fr, Coffee harvest. 17fr, Government Palace.

1977, Nov. 25 Photo. *Perf. 13½*

538 A85 1fr sil & multi 15
539 A85 5fr sil & multi 15
540 A85 11fr sil & multi 16
541 A85 14fr sil & multi 20
542 A85 17fr sil & multi 25
 Set value 74

15th anniversary of independence.

A86

A87

Paintings of the Virgin and Child by: 13fr, Rubens. 17fr, Solario. 27fr, Tiepolo. 31fr, Gerard David. 40fr, Bellini.

1979, Feb. Photo. *Perf. 14x13*

543 A86 13fr multi 20
544 A86 17fr multi 25
545 A86 27fr multi 40
546 A86 31fr multi 48
547 A86 40fr multi 60
 Nos. 543-547 (5) 1.93

Christmas 1978. See No. C270.

1979 Photo. *Perf. 13½x13*

548 A87 1fr *Abyssinian hornbill* 15
549 A87 2fr *Snakebird* 15
550 A87 3fr *Melittophagus pusillus* 15
551 A87 5fr *Flamingo* 15
552 A87 8fr *Afropavo congenis* 15
553 A87 10fr *Gallinule* 18
554 A87 20fr *Martial eagle* 32
555 A87 27fr *Ibis* 42
556 A87 50fr *Saddle-billed stork* 85
 Nos. 548-556,C273-C281 (18) 6.96

Mother and Infant, IYC Emblem A88

IYC Emblem and: 20fr, Infant. 27fr, Girl with doll. 50fr, Children in Children's Village.

1979, July 19 Photo. *Perf. 14*

557 A88 10fr multi 15
558 A88 20fr multi 25
559 A88 27fr multi 32
560 A88 50fr multi 55
 Nos. 557-560 (4) 1.27

Intl. Year of the Child. See No. B82.

A89

A90

Virgin and Child by: 20fr, del Garbo. 27fr, Giovanni Penni. 31fr, G. Romano. 50fr, Jacopo Bassano.

1979, Oct. 12

561 A89 20fr multi 30
562 A89 27fr multi 40
563 A89 31fr multi 48
564 A89 50fr multi 75
 Nos. 561-564,B83-B86 (8) 3.95

Christmas 1979. See Nos. C271, CB48.

1979, Nov. 6

Designs: 20fr, Rowland Hill, Penny Black.
Stamps of Burundi: 27fr, German East Africa Nos. 17, N17. 31fr, Nos. 4, 24. 40fr, Nos. 29, 294. 60fr, Heinrich von Stephan, Nos. 464-465.

565 A90 20fr multi 30
566 A90 27fr multi 40
567 A90 31fr multi 48
568 A90 40fr multi 60
569 A90 60fr multi 90
 Nos. 565-569 (5) 2.68

Sir Rowland Hill (1795-1879), originator of penny postage. See No. C272.

A91

1980, Oct. 24 Photo. *Perf. 13x13½*

570 A91 20fr 110-meter hurdles 38
571 A91 20fr Hurdles, Thomas Munkelt 38
572 A91 20fr Hurdles, R.D.A. 38
573 A91 30fr Discus 55
574 A91 30fr Discus, V. Rasshchupkin 55
575 A91 30fr Discus, U.R.S.S. 55
576 A91 40fr Soccer, Tchecoslovaquie 75
577 A91 40fr "Football" 75
578 A91 40fr shown 75
 Nos. 570-578 (9) 5.04

22nd Summer Olympic Games, Moscow, July 19-Aug. 3. Stamps of same denomination se-tenant.

Virgin and Child, by Mainardi — A92

Christmas 1980 (Paintings): 30fr, Holy Family, by Michelangelo. 40fr, Virgin and Child, by di Cosimo. 45fr, Holy Family, by Fra Bartolomeo.

1980, Dec. 12 Photo. *Perf. 13½x13*

579 A92 10fr multi 15
580 A92 30fr multi 30
581 A92 40fr multi 42
582 A92 45fr multi 45
 Nos. 579-582,B87-B90 (8) 2.71

UPRONA Party National Congress, 1979 — A93

1980, Dec. 29 *Perf. 14x13½*

583 A93 10fr multi 15
584 A93 40fr multi 60
585 A93 45fr multi 65
 Nos. 583-585 (3) 1.40

Johannes Kepler, Dish Antenna A94

1981, Feb. 12 *Perf. 14*

586 A94 10fr shown 15
587 A94 40fr Satellite 60
588 A94 45fr Satellite, diff. 65
 a. Souvenir sheet of 3, #586-588 1.50
 Nos. 586-588 (3) 1.40

350th death anniv. of Johannes Kepler and 1st earth satellite station in Burundi.

Lion A95

1983, Apr. 22 Photo. *Perf. 13*

589 A95 2fr shown 15
590 A95 3fr Giraffes 15
591 A95 5fr Rhinoceros 15
592 A95 10fr Water buffalo 15
593 A95 20fr Elephant 30
594 A95 25fr Hippopotamus 38
595 A95 30fr Zebra 45
596 A95 50fr Warthog 75
597 A95 60fr Oryx 90
598 A95 65fr Wild dog 1.00
599 A95 70fr Leopard 1.10
600 A95 75fr Wildebeest 1.25
601 A95 85fr Hyena 1.75
 Nos. 589-601 (13) 8.48

Nos. 589-601 Overprinted in Silver with World Wildlife Fund Emblem

1983 Photo. *Perf. 13*

589a A95 2fr multi 15
590a A95 3fr multi 15
591a A95 5fr multi 15
592a A95 10fr multi 15
593a A95 20fr multi 30
594a A95 25fr multi 38
595a A95 30fr multi 45
596a A95 50fr multi 75
597a A95 60fr multi 90
598a A95 65fr multi 1.00
599a A95 70fr multi 1.10
600a A95 75fr multi 1.15
601a A95 85fr multi 1.25
 Nos. 589a-601a (13) 7.88

20th Anniv. of Independence, July 1, 1982 — A96

Flags, various arms, map or portrait.

1983 *Perf. 14*

602 A96 10fr multi 15
603 A96 25fr multi 38
604 A96 30fr multi 45
605 A96 50fr multi 75
606 A96 65fr multi 1.00
 Nos. 602-606 (5) 2.73

Christmas 1983 — A97

Virgin and Child paintings: 10fr, by Luca Signorelli (1450-1523). 25fr, by Esteban Murillo (1617-1682). 30fr, by Carlo Crivelli (1430-1495). 50fr, by Nicolas Poussin (1594-1665).

1983, Oct. 3 Litho. *Perf. 14½x13½*

607 A97 10fr multi 15
608 A97 25fr multi 38
609 A97 30fr multi 45
610 A97 50fr multi 75
 Nos. 607-610,B91-B94 (8) 3.52

See Nos. C285, CB50.

Butterflies A98

1984, June 29 Photo. *Perf. 13*

611 A98 5fr Cymothoe coccinata 15
612 A98 5fr Papilio zalmoxis 15
613 A98 10fr Asterope pechueli 25
614 A98 10fr Papilio antimachus 25
615 A98 30fr Papilio hesperus 70
616 A98 30fr Bebearia mardania 70
617 A98 35fr Euphaedra neophron 85
618 A98 35fr Euphaedra perseis 85
619 A98 65fr Euphaedra imperialis 1.50
620 A98 65fr Pseudocraea striata 1.50
 Nos. 611-620 (10) 6.90

Stamps of the same denomination printed horizontally se-tenant.
For surcharges see Nos. 654D-654E.

19th UPU Congress, Hamburg A99

UPU emblem and: 10fr, German East Africa, Nos. 17, N17. 30fr, Nos. 4, 24. 35fr, Nos. 294, 595. 65fr, Dr. Heinrich von Stephan, Nos. 464-465.

1984, July 14 Litho. *Perf. 13x13½*

621	A99	10fr	multi	15
622	A99	30fr	multi	45
623	A99	35fr	multi	50
624	A99	65fr	multi	1.00
			Nos. 621-624 (4)	2.10

See No. C286.

1984 Summer Olympics A100

Gold medalists: 10fr, Jesse Owens, US, track and field, Berlin, 1936. 30fr, Rafer Johnson, US, decathlon, 1960. 35fr, Bob Beamon, US, long jump, 1968. 65fr, Kipchoge Keino, Kenya, 3000-meter steeplechase, 1972.

1984, Aug. 6 *Perf. 13½x13*

625	A100	10fr	multi	25
626	A100	30fr	multi	70
627	A100	35fr	multi	85
628	A100	65fr	multi	1.50
			Nos. 625-628 (4)	3.30

See No. C287.

Christmas 1984 — A101

Paintings: 10fr, Rest During the Flight into Egypt, by Murillo (1617-1682). 25fr, Virgin and Child, by R. del Garbo. 30fr, Virgin and Child, by Botticelli (1445-1510). 50fr, The Adoration of the Shepherds, by Giacomo da Bassano (1517-1592).

1984, Dec. 15 *Perf. 13½*

629	A101	10fr	multi	15
630	A101	25fr	multi	38
631	A101	30fr	multi	45
632	A101	50fr	multi	75
			Nos. 629-632,B95-B98 (8)	3.52

See Nos. C288, CB51.

Flowers — A102

1986, July 31 Photo. *Perf. 13x13½*

633	A102	2fr	Thunbergia	15
634	A102	3fr	Saintpaulia	15
635	A102	5fr	Clivia	15
636	A102	10fr	Cassia	15
637	A102	20fr	Strelitzia	16
638	A102	35fr	Gloriosa	28
			Nos. 633-638,C289-C294 (12)	5.54

Intl. Peace Year — A103

1986, May 1 Litho. *Perf. 14*

639	A103	10fr	Rockets as housing	15
640	A103	20fr	Atom as flower	18
641	A103	30fr	Handshake	28
642	A103	40fr	Globe, chicks	35
a.			Souvenir sheet of 4, #639-642	90
			Nos. 639-642 (4)	96

No. 642a exists imperf.

Great Lake Nations Economic Community (CEPGI), 10th Anniv. — A104

Outline maps of Lake Tanganyika, CEPGI emblem and: 5fr, Aviation. 10fr, Agriculture. 15fr, Industry. 25fr, Electrification. 35fr, Flags of Burundi, Rwanda and Zaire.

1986, May 1 Photo. *Perf. 13½x14½*

643	A104	5fr	multi	15
644	A104	10fr	multi	15
645	A104	15fr	multi	20
646	A104	25fr	multi	32
647	A104	35fr	multi	45
a.			Souv. sheet of 5, #643-647 + label	1.25
			Nos. 643-647 (5)	1.27

Intl. Year of Shelter for the Homeless A105

1987, June Litho. *Perf. 14*

648	A105	10fr	Hovel	28
649	A105	20fr	Drain pipe shelter	55
650	A105	80fr	Shoveling sand	2.15
651	A105	150fr	Children, house model	4.00
a.			Souvenir sheet of 4, #648-651	7.00
			Nos. 648-651 (4)	6.98

A106

A107

1987(?) Litho. *Perf. 14*

652	A106	5fr	shown	15
653	A106	20fr	Skull, lungs	30
654	A106	80fr	Cigarette, face	1.25
			Nos. 652-654 (3)	1.70

WHO Anti-smoking campaign.

Nos. 615-616 Surcharged **80f**

1989 Photo. *Perf. 13*

654D	A98	80fr	on 30fr #615	
654E	A98	80fr	on 30fr #616	

Numbers have been reserved for additional values in this set.

1990 Litho. *Perf. 14*

655	A107	5fr	red lil & multi	15
656	A107	10fr	blue & multi	24
657	A107	20fr	gray & multi	48
658	A107	30fr	ol grn & multi	72
659	A107	50fr	brt blue & multi	1.20
660	A107	80fr	grn bl & multi	1.95
a.			Souv. sheet of 6, #655-660, perf. 13½	4.75
			Nos. 655-660 (6)	4.74

Visit of Pope John Paul II.

Animals A108

1991, Oct. 4 Litho. *Perf. 14*

661	A108	5fr	Hippopotamus	15
662	A108	10fr	Chickens	15
663	A108	20fr	Lion	32
664	A108	30fr	Elephant	48
665	A108	50fr	Guinea fowl	80
666	A108	80fr	Crocodile	1.25
a.			Souv. sheet of 6, #661-666, perf. 13½	3.15
			Nos. 661-666,C298-C301 (10)	12.95

No. 666a exists imperf.

Flowers — A108a

1992, June 2 Litho. *Perf. 14*

666B	A108a	15fr	Impatiens petersiana	40
666C	A108a	20fr	Lachenalia aloides	50
666D	A108a	30fr	Nymphaea lotus	80
666E	A108a	50fr	Clivia miniata	1.30
f.			Souvenir sheet of 4, #666B-666E, perf. 13½	3.00
			Nos. 666B-666E (4)	3.00

A109

Native Music and Dancing A110

Designs: 15fr, Native drummer. 30fr, Two dancers. 115fr, Drummers. 200fr, Five dancers.

1992, Apr. 2 Litho. *Perf. 14*

667	A109	15fr	multicolored	25
668	A109	30fr	multicolored	48
669	A110	115fr	multicolored	1.80
670	A110	200fr	multicolored	3.10
a.			Souvenir sheet	5.65
			Nos. 667-670 (4)	5.63

No. 670a contains one each of Nos. 667-668, perf. 13x13½, and Nos. 669-670, perf. 13½x13.

Independence, 30th Anniv. — A111

Designs: 30fr, 140fr, People with flag. 85fr, 115fr, Natl. flag. 110fr, 200fr, Monument, vert. 120fr, 250fr, Map, vert.

1992, June 30 Litho. *Perf. 15*

671	A111	30fr	multicolored	35
672	A111	85fr	multicolored	1.00
673	A111	110fr	multicolored	1.25
674	A111	115fr	multicolored	1.35
675	A111	120fr	multicolored	1.40
676	A111	140fr	multicolored	1.65
677	A111	200fr	multicolored	2.35
678	A111	250fr	multicolored	3.00
			Nos. 671-678 (8)	12.35

Discovery of America, 500th Anniv. A112

Columbus' fleet, globe and: 200fr, Pre-Columbian artifacts. 400fr, Fruits and vegetables.

1992, Oct. 12 Litho. *Perf. 15*

679	A112	200fr	multicolored	3.00
680	A112	400fr	multicolored	6.25

Felis Serval A113

1992, Oct. 16

681	A113	30fr	shown	48
682	A113	130fr	Two seated	2.00
683	A113	200fr	One standing, one lying	3.10
684	A113	220fr	Two faces	3.40
			Nos. 681-684 (4)	8.98

World Wildlife Fund.

Mushrooms A114

1992 Summer Olympics, Barcelona A115

Designs: 10fr, Russula ingens. 15fr, Russula brunneorigida. 20fr, Amanita zambiana. 30fr, Russula subfistulosa. 75fr, 85fr, Russula meleagris. 100fr, Russula immaculata. 110fr, like #685. 115fr, like #686. 120fr, 130fr, Russula sejuncta. 250fr, Afroboletus luteolus.

1992-93 *Perf. 11½x12*

Granite Paper

685	A114	10fr	multicolored	15
686	A114	15fr	multicolored	24
687	A114	20fr	multicolored	32
688	A114	30fr	multicolored	48
689	A114	75fr	multicolored	1.15
690	A114	85fr	multicolored	1.35
691	A114	100fr	multicolored	1.55
691A	A114	110fr	multicolored	1.65
691B	A114	115fr	multicolored	1.75
692	A114	120fr	multicolored	1.90

693 A114 130fr multicolored 2.00
694 A114 250fr multicolored 3.75
Nos. 685-694 (12) 16.29

Issued: 110fr, 115fr, 1993; others, 9/30/92.

1992, Nov. 6 ***Perf. 15***

695 A115 130fr Runners 2.00
696 A115 500fr Hurdler 7.75

A116

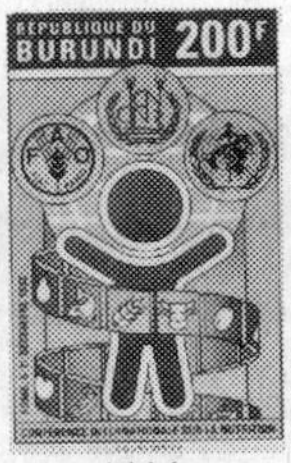

A116a

Christmas (Details of Adoration of the Kings, by Gentile da Fabriano): a, 100fr, Crowd, horses. b, 130fr, Kings. c, 250fr, Nativity scene.

1992, Dec. 7 Litho. ***Perf. 11½***

697 A116 Strip of 3, #a.-c. 5.25
d. Souvenir sheet of 3, #697a-697c 6.50

Nos. 697a-697c have white border. No. 697d has continuous design and sold for 580fr.

1992, Dec. 5 Litho. ***Perf. 15***

Designs: 200fr, Emblems. 220fr, Profile of person made from fruits and vegetables.

697E A116a 200fr multicolored 5.25
697F A116a 220fr multicolored 5.75

Intl. Conference on Nutrition, Rome.

European Common Market A117

Designs: 130fr, Flags, stars. 500fr, Europe, Africa, clasped hands, stars.

1993, Mar. 29 Litho. ***Perf. 15***

698 A117 130fr multicolored 1.50
699 A117 500fr multicolored 5.75

1994 World Cup Soccer Championships, US — A118

Players, stadium, US flag and: 130fr, Statue of Liberty. 200fr, Golden Gate Bridge.

1993, July 5 Litho. ***Perf. 15***

700 A118 130fr multicolored 1.50
701 A118 200fr multicolored 2.30

Traditional Musical Instruments A119

1993, Apr. 30 Litho. ***Perf. 15***

702 A119 200fr Indonongo 2.30
703 A119 220fr Ingoma 2.50
704 A119 250fr Ikembe 2.75
705 A119 300fr Umuduri 3.50
Nos. 702-705 (4) 11.05

A120

A121

1993, June 4 Litho. ***Perf. 11½***

706 A120 130fr Papilio bromius 1.50
707 A120 200fr Charaxes eupale 2.25
708 A120 250fr Cymothoe caenis 2.75
709 A120 300fr Graphium ridleyanus 3.50
a. Souvenir sheet of 4, #706-709 11.50
Nos. 706-709 (4) 10.00

No. 709a sold for 980fr.

1993, Dec. 9 ***Perf. 14***

710 A121 100fr Cattle 1.10
711 A121 120fr Sheep 1.40
712 A121 130fr Pigs 1.50
713 A121 250fr Goats 2.75
Nos. 710-713 (4) 6.75

Christmas — A122

Rock Stars — A123

Natives adoring Christ Child: a, 100fr, Woman carrying baby, two people kneeling. b, 130fr, With Christ Child. 250fr, c, Woman carrying baby, three other people.

1993, Dec. 10 ***Perf. 11½***

714 A122 Strip of 3, #a.-c. 5.00
d. Souvenir sheet of 3, #714a-714c 6.00

Nos. 714a-714c have white border. No. 714d has continuous design and sold for 580fr.

1994 Litho. ***Perf. 15***

715 A123 60fr Elvis Presley 65
716 A123 115fr Mick Jagger 1.25
717 A123 120fr John Lennon 1.25
718 A123 200fr Michael Jackson 2.25
a. Souvenir sheet, #715-718 6.50
Nos. 715-718 (4) 5.40

No. 718a sold for 600fr.

SEMI-POSTAL STAMPS

Prince Louis Rwagasore — SP1

Prince and Stadium SP2

Design: 1.50fr+75c, 6.50fr+3fr, Prince and memorial monument.

Perf. 14x13, 13x14

1963, Feb. 15 Photo. Unwmk.

B1 SP1 50c + 25c brt vio 15 15
B2 SP2 1fr + 50c red org & dk bl 15 15
B3 SP2 1.50fr + 75c lem & dk vio 15 15
B4 SP1 3.50fr + 1.50fr lil rose 15 15
B5 SP2 5fr + 2fr rose pink & dk bl 15 15
B6 SP2 6.50fr + 3fr gray ol & dk vio 15 15
Set value 50 39

Issued in memory of Prince Louis Rwagasore (1932-61), son of King Mwami Mwambutsa IV and Prime Minister. The surtax was for the stadium and monument in his honor.

Red Cross Type of Regular Issue
Souvenir Sheet

1963, Sept. 26 Litho. ***Imperf.***

B7 Sheet of 4 2.00 2.00
a. A5 4fr + 2fr fawn, red & black 32 32
b. A5 8fr + 2fr green, red & black 38 38
c. A5 10fr + 2fr gray, red & black 42 42
d. A5 20fr + 2fr ultra, red & black 65 65

Surtax for Red Cross work in Burundi.

Olympic Type of Regular Issue
Souvenir Sheet

Designs: 18fr+2fr, Hurdling, horiz. 20fr+5fr, Vaulting, horiz.

1964, Nov. 18 ***Perf. 13½***

B8 Sheet of 2 3.00 2.75
a. A13 18fr + 2fr yel grn & multi 1.25 1.00
b. A13 20fr + 5fr brt pink & multi 1.25 1.00

Scientist with Microscope and Map of Burundi — SP3

Lithographed and Photogravure

1965, Jan. 28 Unwmk. ***Perf. 14½***

B9 SP3 2fr + 50c multi 15 15
B10 SP3 4fr + 1.50fr multi 15 15
B11 SP3 5fr + 2.50fr multi 20 15
B12 SP3 8fr + 3fr multi 25 15
B13 SP3 10fr + 5fr multi 38 16
Nos. B9-B13 (5) 1.13
Set value 47

Souvenir Sheet

Perf. 13x13½

B14 SP3 10fr + 10fr multi 85 85

Issued for the fight against tuberculosis.

Coat of Arms, 10fr Coin, Reverse SP4

Designs (Coins of Various Denominations): 4fr+50c, 8fr+50c, 15fr+50c, 40fr+50c, King Mwambutsa IV, obverse.

Lithographed; Embossed on Gilt Foil

1965, Aug. 9 ***Imperf.***

Diameter: 39mm

B15 SP4 2fr + 50c crim & org 15 15
B16 SP4 4fr + 50c ultra & ver 15 15

Diameter: 45mm

B17 SP4 6fr + 50c org & gray 15 15
B18 SP4 8fr + 50c bl & mag 15 15

Diameter: 56mm

B19 SP4 12fr + 50c lt grn & red lil 25 25
B20 SP4 15fr + 50c yel grn & lt lil 30 30

Diameter: 67mm

B21 SP4 25fr + 50c vio bl & buff 50 50
B22 SP4 40fr + 50c brt pink & red brn 75 75
Nos. B15-B22 (8) 2.40 2.40

Stamps are backed with patterned paper in blue, orange and pink engine-turned design.

Prince Louis Rwagasore and Pres. John F. Kennedy SP5

Designs: 4fr+1fr, 20fr+5fr, Prince Louis and memorial. 20fr+2fr, 40fr+5fr, Pres. John F. Kennedy and library shelves. 40fr+2fr, King Mwambutsa IV at Kennedy grave, Arlington, vert.

1966, Jan. 21 Photo. ***Perf. 13½***

B23 SP5 4fr + 1fr gray bl & dk brn 15 15
B24 SP5 10fr + 1fr pale grn, ind & brn 18 15
B25 SP5 20fr + 2fr lil & dp grn 38 15
B26 SP5 40fr + 2fr gray grn & dk brn 65 15
Nos. B23-B26 (4) 1.36
Set value 28

Souvenir Sheet

B27 Sheet of 2 1.50 1.00
a. SP5 20fr + 5fr gray bl & dk brn 50 45
b. SP5 40fr + 5fr lilac & deep grn 75 50

Issued in memory of Prince Louis Rwagasore and President John F. Kennedy.

Republic

Winston Churchill and St. Paul's, London SP6

Designs: 15fr+2fr, Tower of London and Churchill. 20fr+3fr, Big Ben and Churchill.

1967, Mar. 23 Photo. ***Perf. 13½***

B28 SP6 4fr + 1fr multi 15 15
B29 SP6 15fr + 2fr multi 35 15
B30 SP6 20fr + 3fr multi 45 18
Nos. B28-B30 (3) 95
Set value 33

Issued in memory of Sir Winston Churchill (1874-1965), statesman and World War II leader.

A souvenir sheet contains one airmail stamp, 50fr+5fr, with Churchill portrait centered. Size: 80x80mm. Exists perf. and imperf. Value, each sheet, $3.50.

Nos. B28-B30 Overprinted

LIONS INTERNATIONAL 1917 1967

1967, July 14 Photo. ***Perf. 13½***

B31 SP6 4fr + 1fr multi 15 15
B32 SP6 15fr + 2fr multi 42 20
B33 SP6 20fr + 3fr multi 65 30
Nos. B31-B33 (3) 1.22 65

50th anniversary of Lions International.

Exist with dates transposed.

The souvenir sheets described below No. B30 also received this Lions overprint. Value, each $3.50.

Blood Transfusion and Red Cross — SP7

Designs: 7fr+1fr, Stretcher bearers and wounded man. 11fr+1fr, Surgical team. 17fr+1fr, Nurses tending blood bank.

1969, June 26 Photo. ***Perf. 13½***

B34 SP7 4fr + 1fr multi 15 15
B35 SP7 7fr + 1fr multi 15 15
B36 SP7 11fr + 1fr multi 30 15
B37 SP7 17fr + 1fr multi 32 15
Nos. B34-B37,CB9-CB11 (7) 2.50
Set value 68

League of Red Cross Societies, 50th anniv.

Pope Paul VI and Map of Africa — SP8

Designs: 3fr+2fr, 17fr+2fr, Pope Paul VI, vert. 10fr+2fr, Flag made of flags of African Nations. 14fr+2fr, View of St. Peter's, Rome. 40fr+2fr, 40fr+5fr, Martyrs of Uganda. 50fr+2fr, 50fr+5fr, Pope on Throne. All designs include portrait of Pope Paul VI.

1969, Sept. 12 Photo. *Perf. 13½*

B38 SP8	3fr + 2fr multi	15	15
B39 SP8	5fr + 2fr multi	15	15
B40 SP8	10fr + 2fr multi	30	15
B41 SP8	14fr + 2fr multi	42	15
B42 SP8	17fr + 2fr multi	50	15
B43 SP8	40fr + 2fr multi	1.00	18
B44 SP8	50fr + 2fr multi	1.10	20
	Nos. B38-B44 (7)	3.62	
	Set value		66

Souvenir Sheet

B45	Sheet of 2	2.00	1.75
a.	SP8 40fr + 5fr multi	90	75
b.	SP8 50fr + 5fr multi	1.00	90

Visit of Pope Paul VI to Uganda, July 31-Aug. 2.

"La Polenta," by Pietro Longhi SP10

Designs: 3fr+1fr, Archangel Michael, Byzantine icon from St. Mark's 6fr+1fr, "Gossip," by Pietro Longhi. 11fr+1fr, "Diana's Bath," by Giovanni Batista Pittoni. All stamps inscribed UNESCO.

1971, Dec. 27

B52 SP10	3fr + 1fr gold & multi	15	15
B53 SP10	5fr + 1fr gold & multi	15	15
B54 SP10	6fr + 1fr gold & multi	18	15
B55 SP10	11fr + 1fr gold & multi	30	15
a.	Souvenir sheet of 4	75	50
	Nos. B52-B55,CB22-CB25 (8)	2.26	
	Set value		75

The surtax was for the UNESCO campaign to save the treasures of Venice. No. B55a contains 4 stamps similar to Nos. B52-B55, but with 2fr surtax. Sheet exists imperf.

Nos. 408-410 Surcharged "+1F" in Silver

1972, Dec. 12 Photo. *Perf. 13½*

B56 A57	5fr + 1fr multi	15	15
B57 A57	10fr + 1fr multi	22	15
B58 A57	15fr + 1fr multi	32	15
a.	Souvenir sheet of 3	75	70
	Nos. B56-B58,CB26-CB28 (6)	2.02	
	Set value		60

Christmas 1972. No. B58a contains 3 stamps similar to Nos. B56-B58, but with 2fr surtax.

Nos. 441-443 Surcharged "+1F" in Silver

1973, Dec. 14 Photo. *Perf. 13*

B59 A64	5fr + 1fr multi	15	15
B60 A64	10fr + 1fr multi	20	15
B61 A64	15fr + 1fr multi	30	15
a.	Souvenir sheet of 3	65	65
	Nos. B59-B61,CB29-CB31 (6)	1.93	
	Set value		60

Christmas 1973. No. B61a contains 3 stamps similar to Nos. B59-B61 with 2fr surtax each.

Christmas Type of 1974

1974, Dec. 2 Photo. *Perf. 13*

B62 A70	5fr + 1fr multi	15	15
B63 A70	10fr + 1fr multi	20	15
B64 A70	15fr + 1fr multi	30	18
a.	Souvenir sheet of 3	75	75
	Nos. B62-B64,CB32-CB34 (6)	2.17	1.40

No. B64a contains 3 stamps similar to Nos. B62-B64 with 2fr surtax each.

Nos. 485-490 Surcharged "+ 1F" in Silver and Black

1975, Dec. 22 Photo. *Perf. 13*

B65 A73	5fr + 1fr #485	15	
B66 A73	5fr + 1fr #486	15	
B67 A73	13fr + 1fr #487	28	
B68 A73	13fr + 1fr #488	28	
B69 A73	27fr + 1fr #489	50	
B70 A73	27fr + 1fr #490	50	
a.	Souvenir sheet of 6	2.50	
	Nos. B65-B70,CB35-CB40 (12)	5.16	

Michelangelo Buonarroti (1475-1564), 500th birth anniversary. No. B70a contains 6 stamps similar to Nos. B65-B70 with 2fr surcharge each.

Nos. 504-506 Surcharged "+1f" in Silver and Black

1976, Nov. 25 Photo. *Perf. 13½*

B71 A76	5fr + 1fr multi	15	
B72 A76	13fr + 1fr multi	22	
B73 A76	27fr + 1fr multi	42	
a.	Souvenir sheet of 3	85	
	Nos. B71-B73,CB41-CB43 (6)	2.19	

Christmas 1976. No. B73a contains 3 stamps similar to Nos. B71-B73 with 2fr surtax each.

Virgin and Child, by Albrecht Dürer — SP9

Christmas (Paintings): 11fr+1fr, Madonna of the Eucharist, by Sandro Botticelli. 20fr+1fr, Holy Family, by El Greco.

1970, Dec. 14 Photo. *Perf. 13½*

Gold Frame

B46 SP9	6.50fr + 1fr multi	15	15
B47 SP9	11fr + 1fr multi	22	15
B48 SP9	20fr + 1fr multi	42	15
a.	Souvenir sheet of 3B46-B48	90	90
	Nos. B46-B48,CB12-CB14 (6)	2.14	
	Set value		70

Nos. 376-378 Surcharged in Gold and Black

1971, Nov. 27

B49 A51	3fr + 1fr multi	15	15
B50 A51	5fr + 1fr multi	15	15
B51 A51	6fr + 1fr multi	18	15
a.	Souvenir sheet of 3	55	55
	Nos. B49-B51,CB19-CB21 (6)	1.78	
	Set value		56

UNICE, 25th anniv. #B51a contains 3 stamps similar to #B49-B51 with 2fr surtax each.

Nos. 531-533 Surcharged "+1fr" in Silver and Black

1977 Photo. *Perf. 14x13*

B74 A83	5fr + 1fr multi	15	
B75 A83	13fr + 1fr multi	22	
B76 A83	27fr + 1fr multi	42	
a.	Souvenir sheet of 3	85	
	Nos. B74-B76,CB44-CB46 (6)	2.17	

Christmas 1977. No. B76a contains 3 stamps similar to Nos. B74-B76 with 2fr surtax each.

Christmas Type of 1979

1979, Feb. Photo. *Perf. 14x13*

B77 A86	13fr + 1fr multi	22	
B78 A86	17fr + 1fr multi	28	
B79 A86	27fr + 1fr multi	42	
B80 A86	31fr + 1fr multi	50	
B81 A86	40fr + 1fr multi	60	
	Nos. B77-B81 (5)	2.02	

IYC Type of 1979

1979, July 19 Photo. *Perf. 14*

B82	Sheet of 4	1.25	1.00
a.	A88 10fr + 2fr like #557	15	15
b.	A88 20fr + 2fr like #558	24	15
c.	A88 27fr + 2fr like #559	28	20
d.	A88 50fr + 2fr like #560	55	32

Christmas Type of 1979

1979, Dec. 10 Photo. *Perf. 13½*

B83 A89	20fr + 1fr like #561	32	
B84 A89	27fr + 1fr like #562	42	
B85 A89	31fr + 1fr like #563	48	
B86 A89	50fr + 2fr like #564	80	
	Nos. B83-B86 (4)	2.02	

Christmas Type of 1980

1981, Jan. 16 Photo. *Perf. 13½x13*

B87 A92	10fr + 1fr like #579	15	
B88 A92	30fr + 1fr like #580	32	
B89 A92	40fr + 1fr like #581	42	
B90 A92	50fr + 1fr like #582	50	
	Nos. B87-B90 (4)	1.39	

Christmas Type of 1983

1983, Nov. 2 Litho. *Perf. 14½x13½*

B91 A97	10fr + 1fr like #607	16	
B92 A97	25fr + 1fr like #608	40	
B93 A97	30fr + 1fr like #609	48	
B94 A97	50fr + 1fr like #610	75	
	Nos. B91-B94 (4)	1.79	

Christmas Type of 1984

1984, Dec. 15 *Perf. 13½*

B95 A101	10fr + 1fr like #629	16	
B96 A101	25fr + 1fr like #630	40	
B97 A101	30fr + 1fr like #631	48	
B98 A101	50fr + 1fr like #632	75	
	Nos. B95-B98 (4)	1.79	

AIR POST STAMPS

Animal Type of Regular Issue

Animals: 6fr, Zebra. 8fr, Cape buffalo (bubalis). 10fr, Impala, vert. 14fr, Hippopotamus. 15fr, Defassa waterbuck, vert. 20fr, Cheetah. 50fr, Elephant.

Unwmk.

1964, July 2 Litho. *Perf. 14*

Size: 42x21mm, 21x42mm

C1 A9	6fr multi	15	15
C2 A9	8fr multi	16	15
C3 A9	10fr multi	22	15
C4 A9	14fr multi	30	15
C5 A9	15fr multi	32	15

Size: 53x32½mm

C6 A9	20fr multi	42	15
C7 A9	50fr multi	1.10	38
	Nos. C1-C7 (7)	2.67	
	Set value		85

Bird Type of Regular Issue

Birds: 6fr, Secretary bird. 8fr, African anhinga. 10fr, African peacock. 14fr, Bee eater. 15fr, Yellow-billed stork. 20fr, Saddle-billed stork. 50fr, Abyssinian ground hornbill. 75fr, Martial eagle. 130fr, Lesser flamingo.

1965, June 10 Litho. *Perf. 14*

Size: 26x43mm

C8 A14	6fr multi	15	15
C9 A14	8fr multi	15	15
C10 A14	10fr multi	20	15
C11 A14	14fr multi	25	15
C12 A14	15fr multi	30	15

Size: 33x53mm

C13 A14	20fr multi	35	15
C14 A14	50fr multi	90	20
C15 A14	75fr multi	1.25	25
C16 A14	130fr multi	2.25	38
	Nos. C8-C16 (9)	5.80	
	Set value		1.15

For overprints see Nos. C35A-C35I.

Flower Type of Regular Issue

Flowers: 6fr, Dissotis. 8fr, Crossandra. 10fr, Ansellia. 14fr, Thunbergia. 15fr, Schizoglossum. 20fr, Gazania. 50fr, Protea. 75fr, Hibiscus. 130fr, Markhamia.

1966, Oct. 10 Unwmk. *Perf. 13½*

Size: 31x31mm

C17 A17	6fr multi	15	15
C18 A17	8fr multi	15	15
C19 A17	10fr multi	18	15
C20 A17	14fr multi	22	15
C21 A17	15fr multi	22	15

Size: 39x39mm

C22 A17	20fr multi	22	15
C23 A17	50fr multi	60	18
C24 A17	75fr multi	80	22
C25 A17	130fr multi	1.50	32
	Nos. C17-C25 (9)	4.04	
	Set value		1.10

For overprints see Nos. C27-C35.

Tapestry Type of Regular Issue

Souvenir Sheet

1966, Nov. 4 Unwmk. *Perf. 13½*

C26 A18	Sheet of 7 (14fr)	1.25	65

See note after No. 158.

Republic

Nos. C17-C25 Overprinted

1967 Litho. *Perf. 13½*

Size: 31x31mm

C27 A17	6fr multi	20	15
C28 A17	8fr multi	22	15
C29 A17	10fr multi	25	15
C30 A17	14fr multi	48	15
C31 A17	15fr multi	48	15

Size: 39x39mm

C32 A17	20fr multi	70	18
C33 A17	50fr multi	1.90	50
C34 A17	75fr multi	3.00	50
C35 A17	130fr multi	4.00	1.10
	Nos. C27-C35 (9)	11.23	3.03

Nos. C8-C16 Overprinted "REPUBLIQUE / DU / BURUNDI" and Horizontal Bar

1967 Litho. *Perf. 14*

Size: 26x43mm

C35A A14	6fr multi	*15*
C35B A14	8fr multi	*18*
C35C A14	10fr multi	*20*
C35D A14	14fr multi	*30*
C35E A14	15fr multi	*48*

Size: 33x53mm

C35F A14	20fr multi	*75*
C35G A14	50fr multi	*1.90*
C35H A14	75fr multi	*3.00*
C35I A14	130fr multi	*3.50*
	Nos. C35A-C35I (9)	*10.46*

African Art Type of Regular Issue

African Art: 10fr, Spirit of Bakutu figurine, Equatorial Africa. 14fr, Pearl throne of Sultan of the Bamum, Cameroun. 17fr, Bronze head of Mother Queen of Benin, Nigeria. 24fr, Statue of 109th Bakouba king, Kata-Mbula, Central Congo. 26fr, Baskets and lances, Burundi.

1967, June 5 Photo. *Perf. 13½*

C36 A20	10fr gold & multi	15	15
C37 A20	14fr gold & multi	15	15
C38 A20	17fr gold & multi	15	15
C39 A20	24fr gold & multi	22	15
C40 A20	26fr gold & multi	42	25
	Nos. C36-C40 (5)	1.09	
	Set value		55

Boy Scout Type of Regular Issue

Designs: 10fr, Scouts on hiking trip. 14fr, Cooking at campfire. 17fr, Lord Baden-Powell. 24fr, Boy Scout and Cub Scout giving Scout sign. 26fr, First aid.

1967, Aug. 9 *Perf. 13½*

C41 A21	10fr gold & multi	15	15
C42 A21	14fr gold & multi	22	15
C43 A21	17fr gold & multi	28	15
C44 A21	24fr gold & multi	42	18
C45 A21	26fr gold & multi	70	18
	Nos. C41-C45 (5)	1.77	
	Set value		66

A souvenir sheet of 2 contains one each of Nos. C44-C45 and 2 labels in the designs of Nos. 208-209 with commemorative inscriptions was issued Jan. 8, 1968. Size: 100x100mm

Fish Type of Regular Issue

Designs: Various Tropical Fish

1967, Sept. 8 **Photo.** *Perf. 13½*

Size: 50x23mm

C46 A19	6fr multi	15	15
C47 A19	8fr multi	16	15
C48 A19	10fr multi	18	15
C49 A19	14fr multi	25	15
C50 A19	15fr multi	25	15

Size: 58x27mm

C51 A19	20fr multi	32	15
C52 A19	50fr multi	80	15
C53 A19	75fr multi	1.25	16
C54 A19	130fr multi	2.00	26
	Nos. C46-C54 (9)	5.36	
	Set value		80

Boeing 707 of Air Congo and ITY Emblem — AP1

Designs: 14fr, Boeing 727 of Sabena over lake. 17fr, Vickers VC10 of East African Airways over lake. 26fr, Boeing 727 of Sabena over airport.

1967, Nov. 3 **Photo.** *Perf. 13*

C55 AP1	10fr blk, yel brn & sil	15	15
C56 AP1	14fr blk, org & sil	20	15
C57 AP1	17fr blk, brt bl & sil	25	15
C58 AP1	26fr blk, brt rose lil & sil	42	15
	Nos. C55-C58 (4)	1.02	
	Set value		38

Opening of the jet airport at Bujumbura and for International Tourist Year, 1967.

Paintings Type of Regular Issue

Paintings: 17fr, Woman with Cat, by Renoir. 24fr, The Jewish Bride, by Rembrandt, horiz. 26fr, Pope Innocent X, by Velazquez.

1968, Mar. 29 **Photo.** *Perf. 13½*

C59 A26	17fr multi	35	15
C60 A26	24fr multi	45	18
C61 A26	26fr multi	55	20
	Nos. C59-C61 (3)	1.35	53

Issued in sheets of 6.

Space Type of Regular Issue

Designs: 14fr, Moon Probe. 18fr, Russian astronaut walking in space. 25fr, Weather satellite. 40fr, American astronaut walking in space.

1968, May 15 **Photo.** *Perf. 13½*

Size: 41x41mm

C62 A27	14fr sil & multi	25	15
C63 A27	18fr sil & multi	30	15
C64 A27	25fr sil & multi	45	15
C65 A27	40fr sil & multi	70	18
	Nos. C62-C65 (4)	1.70	
	Set value		42

Butterfly Type of Regular Issue

Butterflies: 6fr, Teracolus annae. 8fr, Graphium ridleyanus. 10fr, Cymothoe. 14fr, Charaxes eupale. 15fr, Papilio bromius. 20fr, Papilio zenobia. 50fr, Salamis aethiops. 75fr, Danais chrysippus. 130fr, Salamis temora.

1968, Sept. 9 **Photo.** *Perf. 13½*

Size: 38x42mm

C66 A28	6fr gold & multi	15	15
C67 A28	8fr gold & multi	15	15
C68 A28	10fr gold & multi	18	15
C69 A28	14fr gold & multi	20	15
C70 A28	15fr gold & multi	20	15

Size: 44x49mm

C71 A28	20fr gold & multi	30	15
C72 A28	50fr gold & multi	70	15
C73 A28	75fr gold & multi	1.25	15
C74 A28	130fr gold & multi	2.00	20
	Nos. C66-C74 (9)	5.13	
	Set value		72

Painting Type of Regular Issue

Paintings: 17fr, The Letter, by Jean H. Fragonard. 26fr, Young Woman Reading Letter, by Jan Vermeer. 40fr, Lady Folding Letter, by Elisabeth Vigée-Lebrun. 50fr, Mademoiselle Lavergne, by Jean Etienne Liotard.

1968, Sept. 30 **Photo.** *Perf. 13½*

C84 A29	17fr multi	22	15
C85 A29	26fr multi	42	15
C86 A29	40fr multi	60	15
C87 A29	50fr multi	70	18
	Nos. C84-C87 (4)	1.94	
	Set value		48

Olympic Games Type of 1968

Designs: 10fr, Shot put. 17fr, Running. 26fr, Hammer throw. 50fr, Hurdling. 75fr, Broad jump.

1968, Oct. 24

C88 A30	10fr gold & multi	15	15
C89 A30	17fr gold & multi	22	15
C90 A30	26fr gold & multi	38	15
C91 A30	50fr gold & multi	70	20
C92 A30	75fr gold & multi	1.10	30
	Nos. C88-C92 (5)	2.55	
	Set value		70

Christmas Type of 1968

Paintings: 10fr, Virgin and Child, by Correggio. 14fr, Nativity, by Federigo Baroccio. 17fr, Holy Family, by El Greco. 26fr, Adoration of the Magi, by Maino.

1968, Nov. 26 **Photo.** *Perf. 13½*

C93 A31	10fr multi	15	15
C94 A31	14fr multi	22	15
C95 A31	17fr multi	28	15
C96 A31	26fr multi	40	15
a.	Souv. sheet of 4, #C93-C96	1.10	
	Nos. C93-C96 (4)	1.05	
	Set value		45

For overprints see Nos. C100-C103.

Human Rights Flame, Hand and Globe — AP2

1969, Jan. 22

C97 AP2	10fr multi	15	15
C98 AP2	14fr multi	22	15
C99 AP2	26fr lil & multi	40	15
	Nos. C97-C99 (3)	77	
	Set value		22

International Human Rights Year, 1968.

Nos. C93-C96 Overprinted in Silver

1969, Feb. 17 **Photo.** *Perf. 13½*

C100 A31	10fr multi	20	15
C101 A31	14fr multi	28	15
C102 A31	17fr multi	35	15
C103 A31	26fr multi	50	22
	Nos. C100-C103 (4)	1.33	67

Man's 1st flight around the moon by the US spacecraft Apollo 8, Dec. 21-27, 1968.

Moon Landing Type of 1969

Designs: 26fr, Neil A. Armstrong leaving landing module. 40fr, Astronaut on moon. 50fr, Splashdown in the Pacific.

1969, Nov. 6 **Photo.** *Perf. 13½*

C104 A38	26fr gold & multi	50	25
C105 A38	40fr gold & multi	75	38
C106 A38	50fr gold & multi	90	42
	Nos. C104-C106 (3)	2.15	1.05

Christmas Type of 1969

Paintings: 17fr, Madonna and Child, by Benvenuto da Garofalo. 26fr, Madonna and Child, by Jacopo Negretti. 50fr, Madonna and Child, by Il Giorgione. All horizontal.

1969, Dec. 2 **Photo.**

C107 A39	17fr gold & multi	38	15
C108 A39	26fr gold & multi	50	15
C109 A39	50fr gold & multi	90	28
a.	Souv. sheet of 3, #C107-C109	1.90	1.50
	Nos. C107-C109 (3)	1.78	
	Set value		48

Insect Type of Regular Issue

Designs: Various Beetles and Weevils.

1970 *Perf. 13½*

Size: 46x32mm

C110 A40	6fr gold & multi	15	15
C111 A40	8fr gold & multi	15	15
C112 A40	10fr gold & multi	18	15
C113 A40	14fr gold & multi	25	15
C114 A40	15fr gold & multi	30	15

Size: 52x36mm

C115 A40	20fr gold & multi	1.00	15
C116 A40	50fr gold & multi	2.00	25
C117 A40	75fr gold & multi	3.00	25
C118 A40	130fr gold & multi	3.75	40
	Nos. C110-C118 (9)	10.78	
	Set value		1.20

Issue dates: Nos. C110-C115, Jan. 20. Nos. C116-C118, Feb. 27.

Easter Type of 1970

Stations of the Cross, by Juan de Aranoa y Carredano: 8fr, Jesus meets the women of Jerusalem. 10fr, Jesus falls a third time. 14fr, Jesus stripped. 15fr, Jesus nailed to the cross. 18fr, Jesus dies on the cross. 20fr, Descent from the cross. 50fr, Jesus laid in the tomb.

1970, Mar. 16 **Photo.** *Perf. 13½*

C119 A41	8fr gold & multi	15	15
C120 A41	10fr gold & multi	15	15
C121 A41	14fr gold & multi	22	15
C122 A41	15fr gold & multi	25	15
C123 A41	18fr gold & multi	28	15
C124 A41	20fr gold & multi	30	15
C125 A41	50fr gold & multi	70	30
a.	Souv. sheet of 7, #C119-C125 + label	2.25	1.75
	Nos. C119-C125 (7)	2.05	
	Set value		84

EXPO '70 Type of Regular Issue Souvenir Sheet

Designs: 40fr, Tower of the Sun, vert. 50fr, Flags of participating nations, vert.

1970, May 5 **Photo.** *Perf. 13½*

C126	Sheet of 2	1.40	1.40
a.	A42 40fr multi	50	50
b.	A42 50fr multi	60	60

Rhinoceros Type of Regular Issue

Designs, FAUNA: Camel, dromedary, okapi, rhinoceros, addax, Burundi cow (2 stamps of each animal in 2 different poses). MAP OF THE NILE: Delta and pyramids, dhow, cataract, Blue Nile and crowned crane, Victoria Nile and secretary bird, Lake Victoria and source of Nile on Mt. Gikizi.

1970, July 8 **Photo.** *Perf. 13½*

C127	Sheet of 18	5.25	
a.	A43 14fr any single	28	15

Issued in sheets of 18 (3x6) stamps of different designs, to publicize the southernmost source of the Nile on Mt. Gikizi in Burundi.

UN Emblem and Headquarters, NYC — AP3

25th Anniv. of the UN (UN Emblem and): 11fr, Security Council and mural by Per Krohg. 26fr, Pope Paul VI and U Thant. 40fr, Flags in front of UN Headquarters, NYC.

1970, Oct. 23 **Photo.** *Perf. 13½*

C128 AP3	7fr gold & multi	15	15
C129 AP3	11fr gold & multi	18	15
C130 AP3	26fr gold & multi	40	15
C131 AP3	40fr gold & multi	60	15
a.	Souvenir sheet of 2	1.10	90
	Nos. C128-C131 (4)	1.33	
	Set value		30

No. C131a contains 2 stamps similar to Nos. C130-C131 but without "Poste Aerienne". Exists imperf.

Bird Type of Regular Issue

Birds: 8fr, 14fr, 30fr, vertical; 10fr, 20fr, 50fr, horizontal.

1970 **Photo.** *Perf. 13½*

Stamp size: 52x44mm

C132 A44	Block of 4	1.25	15
a.	8fr Northern shrike	30	15
b.	8fr European starling	30	15
c.	8fr Yellow wagtail	30	15
d.	8fr Bank swallow	30	15
C133 A44	Block of 4	1.50	18
a.	10fr Winter wren	35	15
b.	10fr Firecrest	35	15
c.	10fr Skylark	35	15
d.	10fr Crested lark	35	15
C134 A44	Block of 4	1.90	25
a.	14fr Woodchat shrike	45	15
b.	14fr Common rock thrush	45	15
c.	14fr Black redstart	45	15
d.	14fr Ring ouzel	45	15
C135 A44	Block of 4	3.00	32
a.	20fr European redstart	70	15
b.	20fr Hedge sparrow	70	15
c.	20fr Gray wagtail	70	15
d.	20fr Meadow pipit	70	15
C136 A44	Block of 4	4.25	55
a.	30fr Eurasian hoopoe	1.00	15
b.	30fr Pied flycatcher	1.00	15
c.	30fr Great reed warbler	1.00	15
d.	30fr Eurasian kingfisher	1.00	15
C137 A44	Block of 4	7.00	90
a.	50fr House martin	1.75	20
b.	50fr Sedge warbler	1.75	20
c.	50fr Fieldfare	1.75	20
d.	50fr European Golden oriole	1.75	20
	Nos. C132-C137 (6)	18.90	2.35

Nos. C132-C137 are printed in sheets of 16 containing 4 blocks of 4.

Queen Fabiola and King Baudouin of Belgium AP4

Designs: 20fr, Pres. Michel Micombero and King Baudouin. 40fr, Pres. Micombero and coats of arms of Burundi and Belgium.

1970, Nov. 28 **Photo.** *Perf. 13½*

C140 AP4	6fr multicolored	15	15
C141 AP4	20fr multicolored	45	15
C142 AP4	40fr multicolored	90	30
a.	Souvenir sheet of 3	1.50	1.50
	Nos. C140-C142 (3)	1.50	
	Set value		50

Visit of the King and Queen of Belgium. No. C142a contains 3 stamps similar to Nos. C140-C142, but without "Poste Aerienne." No. C142a exists imperf.

Easter Type of Regular Issue

Paintings of the Resurrection: 14fr, by Louis Borrassá. 17fr, Piero della Francesca. 26fr, Michel Wohlgemuth.

1971, Apr. 2 **Photo.** *Perf. 13½*

C143 A49	14fr gold & multi	20	15
C144 A49	17fr gold & multi	22	15
C145 A49	26fr gold & multi	30	15
a.	Souv. sheet of 3, #C143-C145	1.00	75
	Nos. C143-C145 (3)	72	
	Set value		29

Easter 1971. No. C145a sheet exists imperf.

Animal Type of Regular Issue

1971 Photo. *Perf. 13½*
Size: 44x44mm

C146 Strip of 4 1.00 15
a. A48 10fr Lion 22 15
b. A48 10fr Cape buffalo 22 15
c. A48 10fr Hippopotamus 22 15
d. A48 10fr Giraffe 22 15
C147 Strip of 4 1.50 22
a. A48 14fr Hartebeest 35 15
b. A48 14fr Black rhinoceros 35 15
c. A48 14fr Zebra 35 15
d. A48 14fr Leopard 35 15
C148 Strip of 4 1.75 25
a. A48 17fr Grant's gazelles 40 15
b. A48 17fr Cheetah 40 15
c. A48 17fr African white-backed vultures 40 15
d. A48 17fr Johnston's okapi 40 15
C149 Strip of 4 2.25 32
a. A48 24fr Chimpanzee 50 15
b. A48 24fr Elephant 50 15
c. A48 24fr Spotted Hyenas 50 15
d. A48 24fr Beisa 50 15
C150 Strip of 4 2.50 40
a. A48 26fr Gorilla 55 15
b. A48 26fr Gnu 55 15
c. A48 26fr Warthog 50 15
d. A48 26fr Cape hunting dog 55 15
C151 Strip of 4 3.00 45
a. A48 31fr Sable antelope 70 15
b. A48 31fr Caracal lynx 70 15
c. A48 31fr Ostriches 70 15
d. A48 31fr Bongo 70 15
Nos. C146-C151 (6) 12.00 1.79

For overprint and surcharges see Nos. C152, CB15-C18.

No. C146 Overprinted in Gold and Black

LUTTE CONTRE LE RACISME ET
LA DISCRIMINATION RACIALE

1971, July 20 Photo. *Perf. 13½*

C152 Strip of 4 60 15
a. A48 10fr Lion 15 15
b. A48 10fr Cape buffalo 15 15
c. A48 10fr Hippopotamus 15 15
d. A48 10fr Giraffe 15 15

Intl. Year Against Racial Discrimination.

Christmas Type of Regular Issue

Paintings of the Madonna and Child by: 14fr, Cima de Conegliano. 17fr, Fra Filippo Lippi. 31fr, Leonardo da Vinci.

1971, Nov. 2 Photo. *Perf. 13½*

C153 A51 14fr red & multi 28 15
C154 A51 17fr red & multi 32 15
C155 A51 31fr red & multi 50 20
a. Souv. sheet of 3, #C153-C155 1.10 1.10
Nos. C153-C155 (3) 1.10 50

Christmas 1971. No. C155a exists imperf.
For surcharges see Nos. CB19-CB21.

Spacecraft Type of Regular Issue
Souvenir Sheet

1972, Jan. 15 Photo. *Perf. 13½*

C156 Sheet of 6 1.50 1.00
a. A52 6fr Lunar Orbiter 15 15
b. A52 11fr Vostok 15 15
c. A52 14fr Luna I 18 15
d. A52 17fr Apollo 11 astronaut on moon 22 15
e. A52 26fr Soyuz 11 35 18
f. A52 40fr Lunar rover (Apollo 15) 50 25

Sapporo '72 Type of Regular Issue
Souvenir Sheet

Designs (Sapporo '72 Emblem and): 26fr, Snow scooter. 31fr, Downhill skiing. 50fr, Bobsledding.

1972, Feb. 3

C157 Sheet of 3 1.50 1.25
a. A53 26fr silver & multi 35 25
b. A53 31fr silver & multi 40 30
c. A53 50fr silver & multi 65 40

No. C157 contains 3 stamps, arranged vertically.

Olympic Games Type of 1972

1972, July 24 Photo. *Perf. 13½*

C158 A55 24fr Weight lifting 35 15
C159 A55 26fr Hurdles 40 15
C160 A55 31fr Discus 50 15
C161 A55 40fr Soccer 60 20
Nos. C158-C161 (4) 1.85 65

Independence Type of 1972

Designs: 15fr, Prince Rwagasore, Pres. Micombero, Burundi flag, drummers. 18fr, Rwagasore, Micombero, flag, map of Africa, globe. 27fr, Micombero, flag, globe.

1972, Aug. 24 Photo. *Perf. 13½*

C162 A56 15fr gold & multi 25 15
C163 A56 18fr gold & multi 30 15
C164 A56 27fr gold & multi 45 15
a. Souv. sheet of 3, #C162-C164 1.10 1.10
Nos. C162-C164 (3) 1.00
Set value 34

Christmas Type of 1972

Paintings of the Madonna and Child by: 18fr, Sebastiano Mainardi. 27fr, Hans Memling. 40fr, Lorenzo Lotto.

1972, Nov. 2 Photo. *Perf. 13½*

C165 A57 18fr dk car & multi 28 15
C166 A57 27fr dk car & multi 40 15
C167 A57 40fr dk car & multi 60 18
a. Souv. sheet of 3, #C165-C167 1.40 1.40
Nos. C165-C167 (3) 1.28
Set value 39

For surcharges see Nos. CB26-CB28.

Orchid Type of Regular Issue

1973, Jan. 18 Photo. *Perf. 13½*
Size: 38x38mm

C168 A58 13fr *Thelymitra pauciflora* 22 15
C169 A58 14fr *Miltassia* 22 15
C170 A58 15fr *Miltonia* 25 15
C171 A58 18fr *Platycoryne crocea* 28 15
C172 A58 20fr *Cattleya trinaei* 30 15
C173 A58 27fr *Eulophia cucullata* 42 15
C174 A58 36fr *Cymbidium hamsey* 55 15
Nos. C168-C174 (7) 2.24
Set value 59

African Exploration Type of 1973

Designs: 15fr, Livingstone writing his diary. 18fr, "Dr. Livingstone, I presume." 27fr, Livingstone and Stanley discussing expedition.

1973, Mar. 19 Photo. *Perf. 13½*

C175 A59 15fr gold & multi 22 15
C176 A59 18fr gold & multi 28 15
C177 A59 27fr gold & multi 40 15
a. Souv. sheet of 3 1.10 1.10
Nos. C175-C177 (3) 90
Set value 31

#C177a contains 3 stamps similar to #C175-C177, but without "Poste Aerienne."

Easter Type of 1973

Paintings: 15fr, Christ at the Pillar, by Guido Reni. 18fr, Crucifixion, by Mathias Grunewald. 27fr, Descent from the Cross, by Caravaggio.

1973, Apr. 10

C178 A60 15fr gold & multi 28 15
C179 A60 18fr gold & multi 35 15
C180 A60 27fr gold & multi 50 15
a. Souv. sheet of 3, #C178-C180 1.25 1.25
Nos. C178-C180 (3) 1.13
Set value 30

INTERPOL Type of Regular Issue

Designs: 27fr, INTERPOL emblem and flag. 40fr, INTERPOL flag and emblem.

1973, May 19 Photo. *Perf. 13½*

C181 A61 27fr gold & multi 40 16
C182 A61 40fr gold & multi 48 20

Copernicus Type of Regular Issue

Designs: 15fr, Copernicus (C183a), Earth, Pluto, and Jupiter. 18fr, Copernicus (No. C184a), Venus, Saturn, Mars. 27fr, Copernicus (No. C185a), Uranus, Neptune, Mercury. 36fr, Earth and various spacecrafts.
a, UL. b, UR. c, LL. d, LR.

1973, July 27 Photo. *Perf. 13½*

C183 A62 15fr Block of 4, #a.-d. 1.40 30
C184 A62 18fr Block of 4, #a.-d. 1.65 35
C185 A62 27fr Block of 4, #a.-d. 2.00 50
C186 A62 36fr Block of 4, #a.-d. 2.75 70
e. Souv. sheet of 4, #C183-C186 7.00 7.00
Nos. C183-C186 (4) 7.80 1.85

Flower-Butterfly Type of 1973

Designs: Each block of 4 contains 2 flower and 2 butterfly designs. The 10fr, 14fr, 24fr and 31fr have flower designs listed as "a" and "d" numbers, butterflies as "b" and "c" numbers; the arrangement is reversed for the 17fr and 26fr.

1973, Sept. 28 Photo. *Perf. 13*
Stamp Size: 35x45mm

C187 A63 Block of 4 2.00 20
a. 10fr *Protea cynaroides* 45 15
b. 10fr *Precis octavia* 45 15
c. 10fr *Epiphora bauhiniae* 45 15
d. 10fr *Cazania longiscapa* 45 15
C188 A63 Block of 4 2.50 28
a. 14fr *Kniphofia* 60 15
b. 14fr *Cymothoe coccinata* 60 15
c. 14fr *Nudaurelia zambesina* 60 15
d. 14fr *Freesia refracta* 60 15
C189 A63 Block of 4 3.00 32
a. 17fr *Calotis eupompe* 70 15
b. 17fr *Narcissus* 70 15
c. 17fr *Cineraria hybrida* 70 15
d. 17fr *Cyrestis camillus* 70 15
C190 A63 Block of 4 3.50 50
a. 24fr *Iris tingitana* 85 15
b. 24fr *Papilio demodocus* 85 15
c. 24fr *Catopsilia avelaneda* 85 15
d. 24fr *Nerine sarniensis* 85 15
C191 A63 Block of 4 4.00 55
a. 26fr *Hypolimnas dexithea* 1.00 15
b. 26fr *Zantedeschia tropicalis* 1.00 15
c. 26fr *Sandersonia aurantiaca* 1.00 15
d. 26fr *Drurya antimachus* 1.00 15
C192 A63 Block of 4 4.50 65
a. 31fr *Nymphaea capensis* 1.10 15
b. 31fr *Pandoriana pandora* 1.10 15
c. 31fr *Precis orythia* 1.10 15
d. 31fr *Pelargonium domestica* 1.10 15
Nos. C187-C192 (6) 19.50 2.50

Christmas Type of 1973

Virgin and Child by: 18fr, Raphael. 27fr, Pietro Perugino. 40fr, Titian.

1973, Nov. 19

C193 A64 18fr gold & multi 28 15
C194 A64 27fr gold & multi 40 15
C195 A64 40fr gold & multi 60 16
a. Souv. sheet of 3, #C193-C195 1.40 1.40
Nos. C193-C195 (3) 1.28
Set value 36

For surcharges see Nos. CB239-CB31.

Soccer Type of Regular Issue

Designs: Various soccer scenes and cup.

1974, July 4 Photo. *Perf. 13*

C196 A67 20fr gold & multi 30
C197 A67 26fr gold & multi 40
C198 A67 40fr gold & multi 60
Nos. C196-C198 (3) 1.30

For souvenir sheet see No. 459a.

UPU Type of 1974

Designs: No. C199, Flags over UPU Headquarters, Bern. No. C200, G.P.O., Usumbura. No. C201, Mailmen ("26F" in UR). No. C202, Mailmen ("26F" in UL). No. C203, UPU emblem. No. C204, Means of transportation. No. C205, Pigeon over globe showing Burundi. No. C206, Swiss flag, pigeon over map showing Bern.

1974, July 23

C199 A68 24fr gold & multi 65
C200 A68 24fr gold & multi 65
C201 A68 26fr gold & multi 75
C202 A68 26fr gold & multi 75
C203 A68 31fr gold & multi 1.00
C204 A68 31fr gold & multi 1.00
C205 A68 40fr gold & multi 1.25
C206 A68 40fr gold & multi 1.25
a. Souv. sheet of 8, #C199-C206 7.50
Nos. C199-C206 (8) 7.30

Stamps of same denomination printed setenant (continuous design) in sheets of 40.

Fish Type of 1974

1974, Sept. 9 Photo. *Perf. 13*
Size: 35x35mm

C207 A66 Block of 4 1.00 15
a. 10fr *Haplochromis multicolor* 25 15
b. 10fr *Pantodon buchholzi* 25 15
c. 10fr *Tropheus duboisi* 25 15
d. 10fr *Distichodus sexfasciatus* 25 15
C208 A66 Block of 4 1.25 20
a. 14fr *Pelmatochromis kribensis* 30 15
b. 14fr *Nannaethiops tritaeniatus* 30 15
c. 14fr *Polycentropsis abbreviata* 30 15
d. 14fr *Hemichromis bimaculatus* 30 15
C209 A66 Block of 4 1.65 20
a. 17fr *Ctenopoma acutirostre* 38 15
b. 17fr *Synodontis angelicus* 38 15
c. 17fr *Tilapia melanopleura* 38 15
d. 17fr *Aphyosemion bivittatum* 38 15
C210 A66 Block of 4 1.90 30
a. 24fr *Monodactylus argenteus* 45 15
b. 24fr *Zanclus canescens* 45 15
c. 24fr *Pygoplites diacanthus* 45 15
d. 24fr *Cephalopholis argus* 45 15
C211 A66 Block of 4 2.00 35
a. 26fr *Priacanthus arenatus* 50 15
b. 26fr *Pomacanthus arcutus* 50 15
c. 26fr *Scarus guacamaia* 50 15
d. 26fr *Zeus faber* 50 15
C212 A66 Block of 4 2.50 40
a. 31fr *Lactophrys quadricornis* 60 15
b. 31fr *Balistes vetula* 60 15
c. 31fr *Acanthurus bahianus* 60 15
d. 31fr *Holocanthus ciliaris* 60 15
Nos. C207-C212 (6) 10.30 1.60

Christmas Type of 1974

Paintings of the Virgin and Child: 18fr, by Hans Memling. 27fr, by Filippino Lippi. 40fr, by Lorenzo di Gredi.

1974, Nov. 7 Photo. *Perf. 13*

C213 A70 18fr gold & multi 28 22
C214 A70 27fr gold & multi 40 32
C215 A70 40fr gold & multi 60 48
a. Souv. sheet of 3, #C213-C215 1.50 1.50
Nos. C213-C215 (3) 1.28 1.02

Christmas 1974. Sheets of 20 stamps and one label. No. C215a exists imperf.

Apollo-Soyuz Type of 1975

1975, July 10 Photo. *Perf. 13*

C216 A71 Block of 4 90
a. 27fr A.A. Leonov, V.N. Kubasov, Soviet flag 22
b. 27fr Soyuz and Soviet flag 22
c. 27fr Apollo and American flag 22
d. 27fr Slayton, Brand, Stafford, American flag 22
C217 A71 Block of 4 1.40
a. 40fr Apollo-Soyuz link-up 32
b. 40fr Apollo, blast-off 32
c. 40fr Soyuz, blast-off 32
d. 40fr Kubasov, Leonov, Slayton, Brand, Stafford 32

Nos. C216-C217 are printed in sheets of 32 containing 8 blocks of 4.

Animal Type of 1975

1975, Sept. 17 Photo. *Perf. 13½*

C218 Strip of 4 90
a. A72 10fr Addax 22
b. A72 10fr Roan antelope 22
c. A72 10fr Nyala 22
d. A72 10fr White rhinoceros 22
C219 Strip of 4 1.25
a. A72 14fr Mandrill 30
b. A72 14fr Eland 30
c. A72 14fr Salt's dik-dik 30
d. A72 14fr Thomson's gazelles 30
C220 Strip of 4 1.50
a. A72 17fr African small-clawed otter 35
b. A72 17fr Reed buck 35
c. A72 17fr Indian civet 35
d. A72 17fr Cape buffalo 35
C221 Strip of 4 2.00
a. A72 24fr White-tailed gnu 50
b. A72 24fr African wild asses 50
c. A72 24fr Black-and-white colobus monkey 50
d. A72 24fr Gerenuk 50
C222 Strip of 4 2.25
a. A72 26fr Dama gazelle 55
b. A72 26fr Black-backed jackal 55
c. A72 26fr Sitatungas 55
d. A72 26fr Zebra antelope 55
C223 Strip of 4 2.75
a. A72 31fr Fennec 65
b. A72 31fr Lesser kudus 65
c. A72 31fr Blesbok 65
d. A72 31fr Serval 65
Nos. C218-C223 (6) 10.65

Nos. C218-C219 Overprinted in Black and Silver with IWY Emblem and: "ANNEE INTERNATIONALE / DE LA FEMME"

1975, Nov. 19 Photo. *Perf. 13½*

C224 Strip of 4 60 15
a. A72 10fr Addax 15 15
b. A72 10fr Roan antelope 15 15
c. A72 10fr Nyala 15 15
d. A72 10fr White rhinoceros 15 15
C225 Strip of 4 80 20
a. A72 14fr Mandrill 20 15
b. A72 14fr Oryx 20 15
c. A72 14fr Dik-dik 20 15
d. A72 14fr Thomson's gazelles 20 15

International Women's Year 1975.

Nos. C222-C223 Overprinted in Black and Silver with UN Emblem and: "30ème ANNIVERSAIRE DES/ NATIONS UNIES"

1975, Nov. 19

C226 Strip of 4 1.65 30
a. A72 26fr Dama gazelle 38 15
b. A72 26fr Wild dog 38 15
c. A72 26fr Sitatungas 38 15
d. A72 26fr Striped duiker 38 15
C227 Strip of 4 1.90 32
a. A72 31fr Fennec 45 15
b. A72 31fr Lesser kudus 45 15
c. A72 31fr Blesbok 45 15
d. A72 31fr Serval 45 15

United Nations, 30th anniversary.

Michelangelo Type of 1975

Designs: Paintings from Sistine Chapel.

1975, Dec. 3 Photo. *Perf. 13*

C228 A73 18fr Zachariah 35
C229 A73 18fr Joel 35
C230 A73 31fr Erythrean Sybil 65
C231 A73 31fr Prophet Ezekiel 65
C232 A73 40fr Persian Sybil 80
C233 A73 40fr Prophet Jeremiah 80
a. Souv. sheet of 6, #C228-C233 3.75
Nos. C228-C233 (6) 3.60

Stamps of same denominations printed se-tenant in sheets of 18 stamps and 2 labels.
For surcharges see Nos. CB35-CB40.

Olympic Games Type, 1976

Designs (Olympic Games Emblem and): 18fr, Ski jump. 36fr, Slalom. 50fr, Ice hockey.

1976, Jan. 23 Photo. *Perf. 14x13½*
C234 A74 18fr ol brn & multi 32
C235 A74 36fr grn & multi 70
C236 A74 50fr pur & multi 90
a. Souvenir sheet of 4 2.00
Nos. C234-C236 (3) 1.92

No. C236a contains 4 stamps similar to Nos. 491-494, perf. 13½, inscribed "POSTE AERIENNE."

Hurdles — AP5

Designs (Montreal Games Emblem and): Nos. C238, C241, C243b, High jump. Nos. C239, C242, C243a, Athlete on rings. No. C240, C243c, Hurdles.

1976, May 3 Litho. *Perf. 13½*
C237 AP5 27fr grn & multi 42
C238 AP5 27fr dk bl & multi 42
C239 AP5 31fr ocher & multi 55
C240 AP5 31fr grn & multi 55
C241 AP5 50fr dk bl & multi 90
C242 AP5 50fr ocher & multi 90
Nos. C237-C242 (6) 3.74

Souvenir Sheet

C243 Sheet of 3 1.75
a. AP5 27fr ocher & multi .38
b. AP5 31fr dk bl & multi .45
c. AP5 50fr grn & multi .75

21st Olympic Games, Montreal, Canada, July 17-Aug. 1. Stamps of same denomination printed se-tenant in sheets of 20.

Battle of Bunker Hill, by John Trumbull
AP6 AP7

Paintings: 26fr, Franklin, Jefferson and John Adams. 36fr, Declaration of Independence, by John Trumbull.

1976, July 16 Photo. *Perf. 13*
C244 AP6 18fr gold & multi 35
C245 AP7 18fr gold & multi 35
C246 AP6 26fr gold & multi 45
C247 AP7 26fr gold & multi 45
C248 AP6 36fr gold & multi 75
C249 AP7 36fr gold & multi 75
a. Souv. sheet of 6, #C244-C249 3.25
Nos. C244-C249 (6) 3.10

American Bicentennial. Stamps of same denomination printed se-tenant in sheets of 50.

Christmas Type of 1976

Paintings: 18fr, Virgin and Child with St. Anne, by Leonardo da Vinci. 31fr, Holy Family with Lamb, by Raphael. 40fr, Madonna of the Basket, by Correggio.

1976, Oct. 18 Photo. *Perf. 13½*
C250 A76 18fr gold & multi 25
C251 A76 31fr gold & multi 45
C252 A76 40fr gold & multi 60
a. Souv. sheet of 3, #C250-C252 1.40
Nos. C250-C252 (3) 1.30

Christmas 1976. Sheets of 20 stamps and descriptive label.
For surcharges see Nos. CB41-CB43.

A.G. Bell Type of 1977

Designs: 10fr, A.G. Bell and first telephone. Nos. C253, 17fr, A.G. Bell speaking into microphone. Nos. C254, C257e, Satellites around globe and videophone. No. C255, Switchboard operator, c.1910, and wall telephone. Nos. C256, 26fr, Intelsat satellite, modern and old telephones. No. C257c, Intelsat and radar.

1977, May 17 Photo. *Perf. 13*
C253 A78 18fr multi 15
C254 A79 18fr multi 15
C255 A78 36fr multi 25
C256 A79 36fr multi 25
C257 Sheet of 5 1.75 1.00
a. A78 10fr multi .15 .15
b. A78 17fr multi .25 .15
c. A79 18fr multi .25 .15
d. A79 26fr multi .40 .22
e. A79 36fr multi .52 .25

No. C257 contains 3 postage (10fr, 17fr, 26fr) and 2 air post stamps (18fr, 36fr).

Animal Type of 1977

1977, Aug. 22 Photo. *Perf. 14x14½*
C258 Strip of 4 80
a. A80 9fr Buffon's kob .20
b. A80 9fr Marabous .20
c. A80 9fr Brindled gnu .20
d. A80 9fr River hog .20
C259 Strip of 4 1.10
a. A80 13fr Zebras .25
b. A80 13fr Shoebill .25
c. A80 13fr Striped hyenas .25
d. A80 13fr Chimpanzee .25
C260 Strip of 4 2.25
a. A80 30fr Flamingos .55
b. A80 30fr Nile Crocodiles .55
c. A80 30fr Green mamba .55
d. A80 30fr Greater kudus .55
C261 Strip of 4 2.75
a. A80 35fr Hyrax .65
b. A80 35fr Cobra .65
c. A80 35fr Jackals .65
d. A80 35fr Verreaux's eagles .65
C262 Strip of 4 4.25
a. A80 54fr Honey badger 1.00
b. A80 54fr Harnessed antelopes 1.00
c. A80 54fr Secretary bird 1.00
d. A80 54fr Klipspringer 1.00
C263 Strip of 4 5.00
a. A80 70fr African big-eared fox 1.25
b. A80 70fr Elephants 1.25
c. A80 70fr Vulturine guineafowl 1.25
d. A80 70fr Impalas 1.25
Nos. C258-C263 (6) 16.15

UN Type of 1977

Designs (UN Stamps and): 24fr, UN buildings by night. 27fr, UN buildings and view of Manhattan. 35fr, UN buildings by day.

1977, Oct. 10 Photo. *Perf. 13½*
C264 A82 Block of 4 1.90
a. 24fr No. 77 .45
b. 24fr No. 78 .45
c. 24fr No. 40 .45
d. 24fr No. 32 .45
C265 A82 Block of 4 2.00
a. 27fr No. 50 .50
b. 27fr No. 21 .50
c. 27fr No. 30 .50
d. 27fr No. 44 .50
C266 A82 Block of 4 3.25
a. 35fr No. C6 .75
b. 35fr No. 105 .75
c. 35fr No. 4 .75
d. 35fr No. 1 .75
e. Souvenir sheet of 3 1.40
Nos. C264-C266 (3) 7.15

No. C266e contains 24fr in design of No. C265b, 27fr in design of No. C266a, 35fr in design of No. C264c.

Christmas Type of 1977

Designs: Paintings of the Virgin and Child.

1977, Oct. 31 Photo. *Perf. 14x13*
C267 A83 18fr Master of Moulins 28
C268 A83 31fr Workshop of Lorenzo de Credi 48
C269 A83 40fr Palma Vecchio 60
a. Souv. sheet of 3, #C267-C269 1.50
Nos. C267-C269 (3) 1.36

Sheets of 24 stamps and descriptive label.
For surcharges see Nos. CB44-CB46.

Christmas 1978 Type of 1979
Souvenir Sheet

1979, Feb. Photo. *Perf. 14x13½*
C270 Sheet of 5 2.00
a. A86 13fr like #543 .20
b. A86 17fr like #544 .25
c. A86 27fr like #545 .40
d. A86 31fr like #546 .48
e. A86 40fr like #547 .60

Christmas Type of 1979
Souvenir Sheet

1979, Oct. 12 *Perf. 13½*
C271 Sheet of 4 2.00 1.25
a. A89 20fr like #561 .30 .16
b. A89 27fr like #562 .40 .22
c. A89 31fr like #563 .48 .28
d. A89 50fr like #564 .75 .42

Hill Type of 1979
Souvenir Sheet

1979, Nov. 6
C272 Sheet of 5 3.50 1.75
a. A90 20fr like #565 .40 .16
b. A90 27fr like #566 .55 .22
c. A90 31fr like #567 .60 .28
d. A90 40fr like #568 .80 .35
e. A90 50fr like #569 1.00 .50

Sir Rowland Hill (1795-1879), originator of penny postage.

Bird Type of 1979

1979 Photo. *Perf. 13½x13*
C273 A87 6fr like #548 15
C274 A87 13fr like #549 20
C275 A87 18fr like #550 28
C276 A87 26fr like #551 38
C277 A87 31fr like #552 48
C278 A87 36fr like #553 55
C279 A87 40fr like #554 60
C280 A87 54fr like #555 80
C281 A87 70fr like #556 1.00
Nos. C273-C281 (9) 4.44

Olympic Type of 1980
Souvenir Sheet

1980, Oct. 24 Photo. *Perf. 13½*
C282 Sheet of 9 4.25
a. A91 20fr like #570 .30
b. A91 20fr like #571 .30
c. A91 20fr like #572 .30
d. A91 30fr like #573 .45
e. A91 30fr like #574 .45
f. A91 30fr like #575 .45
g. A91 40fr like #576 .60
h. A91 40fr like #577 .60
i. A91 40fr like #578 .60

22nd Summer Olympic Games, Moscow, July 19-Aug. 3.

Christmas Type of 1980
Souvenir Sheet

1980, Dec. 12 Photo. *Perf. 13½x13*
C283 Sheet of 4 1.90 1.40
a. A92 10fr like #579 .15 .15
b. A92 30fr like #580 .45 .30
c. A92 40fr like #581 .60 .40
d. A92 45fr like #582 .65 .45

UPRONA Type of 1980
Souvenir Sheet

1980, Dec. 29 *Perf. 14½x13½*
C284 Sheet of 3 1.50
a. A93 10fr like #583 .15
b. A93 40fr like #584 .60
c. A93 45fr like #585 .65

Christmas Type of 1983
Souvenir Sheet

1983, Oct. 3 Litho. *Perf. 14½x13½*
C285 Sheet of 4 1.75
a. A97 10fr like #607 .15
b. A97 25fr like #608 .38
c. A97 30fr like #609 .45
d. A97 50fr like #610 .75

UPU Congress Type of 1984
Souvenir Sheet

1984, July 14 *Perf. 13x13½*
C286 Sheet of 4 2.25
a. A99 10fr like #621 .15
b. A99 30fr like #622 .45
c. A99 35fr like #623 .50
d. A99 65fr like #624 1.00

Summer Olympics Type of 1984
Souvenir Sheet

1984, Aug. 6 *Perf. 13½x13*
C287 Sheet of 4 2.25
a. A100 10fr like #625 .15
b. A100 30fr like #626 .45
c. A100 35fr like #627 .50
d. A100 65fr like #628 1.00

Christmas Type of 1984
Souvenir Sheet

1984, Dec. 15 *Perf. 13½*
C288 Sheet of 4 1.75
a. A101 10fr like #629 .15
b. A101 25fr like #630 .38
c. A101 30fr like #631 .45
d. A101 50fr like #632 .75

Flower Type of 1986 with Dull Lilac Border

1986, July 31 Photo. *Perf. 13x13½*
C289 A102 70fr like #633 55
C290 A102 75fr like #634 60
C291 A102 80fr like #635 65
C292 A102 85fr like #636 70
C293 A102 100fr like #637 80
C294 A102 150fr like #638 1.20
Nos. C289-C294 (6) 4.50

Animal Type of 1991

1992, June 2 Litho. *Perf. 14*
C298 A108 100fr M. nemestrina 1.55
C299 A108 115fr Equus grevyi 1.75
C300 A108 200fr Long horn cattle 3.10
C301 A108 220fr Pelecanus onocrotalus 3.40
a. Souvenir sheet of 4, #C298-C301, perf. 13½ 10.00
Nos. C298-C301 (4) 9.80

AIR POST SEMI-POSTAL STAMPS

Coin Type of Semi-Postal Issue

Designs (Coins of Various Denominations): 3fr+1fr, 11fr+1fr, 20fr+1fr, 50fr+1fr, Coat of Arms, reverse. 5fr+1fr, 14fr+1fr, 30fr+1fr, 100fr+1fr, King Mwambutsa IV, obverse.

Lithographed; Embossed on Gilt Foil
1965, Nov. 15 *Imperf.*

Diameter: 39mm

CB1 SP4 3fr + 1fr lt & dk vio 15 15
CB2 SP4 5fr + 1fr pale grn & red 15 15

Diameter: 45mm

CB3 SP4 11fr + 1fr org & lilac 25 25
CB4 SP4 14fr + 1fr red & emer 30 30

Diameter: 56mm

CB5 SP4 20fr + 1fr ultra & blk 40 40
CB6 SP4 30fr + 1fr dp org & mar 60 60

Diameter: 67mm

CB7 SP4 50fr + 1fr bl & vio bl 1.00 1.00
CB8 SP4 100fr + 1fr rose & dp cl 2.25 2.25
Nos. CB1-CB8 (8) 5.10 5.10

Stamps are backed with patterned paper in blue, orange, and pink engine-turned design.

Red Cross Type of Semi-Postal Issue

Designs: 26fr+3fr, Laboratory. 40fr+3fr, Ambulance and thatched huts. 50fr+3fr, Red Cross nurse with patient.

1969, June 26 Photo. *Perf. 13½*
CB9 SP7 26fr + 3fr multi 38 15
CB10 SP7 40fr + 3fr multi 55 15
CB11 SP7 50fr + 3fr multi 65 20
Nos. CB9-CB11 (3) 1.58 50

Perf. and imperf. souvenir sheets exist containing 3 stamps similar to Nos. CB9-CB11, but without "Poste Aerienne." Size: 90½x97mm

Christmas Type of Semi-Postal Issue

Paintings: 14fr+3fr, Virgin and Child, by Velázquez. 26fr+3fr, Holy Family, by Joos van Cleve. 40fr+3fr, Virgin and Child, by Rogier van der Weyden.

1970, Dec. 14 Photo. *Perf. 13½*
CB12 SP9 14fr + 3fr multi 25 15
CB13 SP9 26fr + 3fr multi 45 15
CB14 SP9 40fr + 3fr multi 65 20
a. Souv. sheet of 3, #CB12-CB14 1.50 1.50
Nos. CB12-CB14 (3) 1.35 50

No. C147 Surcharged in Gold and Black

1971, Aug. 9 Photo. *Perf. 13½*
CB15 Strip of 4 80 20
a. A48 14fr+2fr Hartebeest .20 .15
b. A48 14fr+2fr Black rhinoceros .20 .15
c. A48 14fr+2fr Zebra .20 .15
d. A48 14fr+2fr Leopard .20 .15

UNESCO campaign against illiteracy.

No. C148 Surcharged in Gold and Black

1971, Aug. 9

CB16 Strip of 4 1.00 20
a. A48 17fr+1fr Grant's gazelles 22 15
b. A48 17fr+1fr Cheetah 22 15
c. A48 17fr+1fr African white-backed vultures 22 15
d. A48 17fr+1fr Johnston's okapi 22 15

International help for refugees.

Nos. C150-C151 Surcharged in Black and Gold

a

b

1971, Aug. 16

CB17 Strip of 4 2.25 45
a. A48(a) 26fr+1fr Gorilla 55 15
b. A48(a) 26fr+1fr Gnu 55 15
c. A48(a) 26fr+1fr Warthog 55 15
d. A48(a) 26fr+1fr Cape hunting dog 55 15
CB18 Strip of 4 3.00 60
a. A48(b) 31fr+1fr Sable antelope 75 15
b. A48(b) 31fr+1fr Caracal lynx 75 15
c. A48(b) 31fr+1fr Ostriches 75 15
d. A48(b) 31fr+1fr Bongo 75 15

75th anniv. of modern Olympic Games (#CB17); Olympic Games, Munich, 1972 (#CB18).

Nos. C153-C155 Surcharged

1971, Nov. 27 Photo. *Perf. 13½*

CB19 A51 14fr + 1fr multi 32 15
CB20 A51 17fr + 1fr multi 38 15
CB21 A51 31fr + 1fr multi 60 16
Nos. CB19-CB21 (3) 1.30
Set value 34

25th anniv. of UNICEF.

Casa D'Oro, Venice
SPAP1

Views in Venice: 17fr+1fr, Doge's Palace. 24fr+1fr, Church of Sts. John and Paul. 31fr+1fr, Doge's Palace and Piazzetta at Feast of Ascension, by Canaletto.

1971, Dec. 27

CB22 SPAP1 10fr + 1fr multi 16 15
CB23 SPAP1 17fr + 1fr multi 32 15
CB24 SPAP1 24fr + 1fr multi 45 15
CB25 SPAP1 31fr + 1fr multi 55 16
a. Souvenir sheet of 4 1.50 1.50
Nos. CB22-CB25 (4) 1.48
Set value 50

Surtax for the UNESCO campaign to save the treasures of Venice. No. CB25a contains 4 stamps similar to Nos. CB22-CB25, but with 2fr surtax.

Nos. C165-C167, C193-C195 Surcharged "+1F" in Silver

1972, Dec. 12 Photo. *Perf. 13½*

CB26 A57 18fr + 1fr multi 28 15
CB27 A57 27fr + 1fr multi 45 15
CB28 A57 40fr + 1fr multi 60 18
a. Souvenir sheet of 3 1.50 1.50
Nos. CB26-CB28 (3) 1.33
Set value 38

Christmas 1972. No. CB28a contains 3 stamps similar to Nos. CB26-CB28 but with 2fr surtax.

1973, Dec. 14 Photo. *Perf. 13*

CB29 A64 18fr + 1fr multi 28 15
CB30 A64 27fr + 1fr multi 40 15
CB31 A64 40fr + 1fr multi 60 20
a. Souvenir sheet of 3 1.50 1.50
Nos. CB29-CB31 (3) 1.28
Set value 40

Christmas 1973. No. CB31 contains 3 stamps similar to Nos. CB29-CB31 with 2fr surtax each.

Christmas Type of 1974

1974, Dec. 2 Photo. *Perf. 13*

CB32 A70 18fr + 1fr multi 32 20
CB33 A70 27fr + 1fr multi 50 30
CB34 A70 40fr + 1fr multi 70 42
a. Souvenir sheet of 3 1.75 1.75
Nos. CB32-CB34 (3) 1.52

Christmas 1974. No. CB34a contains 3 stamps similar to Nos. CB32-CB34 with 2fr surtax.

Nos. C228-C233 Surcharged "+ 1F" in Silver and Black

1975, Dec. 22 Photo. *Perf. 13*

CB35 A73 18fr + 1fr #C228 35
CB36 A73 18fr + 1fr #C229 35
CB37 A73 31fr + 1fr #C230 55
CB38 A73 31fr + 1fr #C231 55
CB39 A73 40fr + 1fr #C232 75
CB40 A73 40fr + 1fr #C233 75
a. Souvenir sheet of 6 4.25
Nos. CB35-CB40 (6) 3.30

Michelangelo Buonarroti (1475-1564). No. CB40a contains 6 stamps similar to Nos. CB35-CB40 with 2fr surtax each.

Nos. C250-C252 Surcharged "+1f" in Silver and Black

1976, Nov. 25 Photo. *Perf. 13½*

CB41 A76 18fr + 1fr multi 30
CB42 A76 31fr + 1fr multi 50
CB43 A76 40fr + 1fr multi 60
a. Souvenir sheet of 3 1.50
Nos. CB41-CB43 (3) 1.40

Christmas 1976. No. CB43a contains 3 stamps similar to Nos. CB41-CB43 with 2fr surtax each.

Nos. C267-C269 Surcharged "+1fr" in Silver and Black

1977 Photo. *Perf. 14x13*

CB44 A83 18fr + 1fr multi 28
CB45 A83 31fr + 1fr multi 50
CB46 A83 40fr + 1fr multi 60
a. Souvenir sheet of 3 1.50
Nos. CB44-CB46 (3) 1.38

Christmas 1977. No. CB46a contains 3 stamps similar to Nos. CB44-CB46 with 2fr surtax each.

Christmas 1978 Type
Souvenir Sheet

1979, Feb. Photo. *Perf. 14x13*

CB47 Sheet of 5 3.00
a. A86 13fr + 2fr multi 30
b. A86 17fr + 2fr multi 36
c. A86 27fr + 2fr multi 55
d. A86 31fr + 2fr multi 70
e. A86 40fr + 2fr multi 85

Christmas Type of 1979
Souvenir Sheet

1979, Dec. 10 Photo. *Perf. 13½*

CB48 Sheet of 4 2.75
a. A89 20fr + 2fr like #561 45
b. A89 27fr + 2fr like #562 55
c. A89 31fr + 2fr like #563 70
d. A89 50fr + 2fr like #564 1.00

Christmas Type of 1980
Souvenir Sheet

1981, Jan. 16 Photo. *Perf. 13½x13*

CB49 Sheet of 4 2.50
a. A92 10fr + 2fr like #579 20
b. A92 30fr + 2fr like #580 55
c. A92 40fr + 2fr like #581 75
d. A92 50fr + 2fr like #582 90

Christmas Type of 1983
Souvenir Sheet

1983, Nov. 2 Litho. *Perf. 14½x13½*

CB50 Sheet of 4 1.90
a. A97 10fr + 2fr like #607 16
b. A97 25fr + 2fr like #608 38
c. A97 30fr + 2fr like #609 50
d. A97 50fr + 2fr like #610 75

Christmas Type of 1984
Souvenir Sheet

1984, Dec. 15 *Perf. 13½*

CB51 Sheet of 4 1.90
a. A101 10fr + 2fr like #629 16
b. A101 25fr + 2fr like #630 38
c. A101 30fr + 2fr like #631 50
d. A101 50fr + 2fr like #632 1.00

CAMBODIA

Khmer Republic

LOCATION — Southern Indo-China
GOVT. — Republic
AREA — 69,866 sq. mi.
POP. — 7,640,000 (est. 1974)
CAPITAL — Phnom Penh

Before 1951, Cambodia used stamps of Indo-China. In October, 1970, the Kingdom of Cambodia became the Khmer Republic.

From 1978 to 1980 money was abolished.

100 Cents = 1 Piaster
100 Cents = 1 Riel (1955)

Imperforates

Most Cambodia stamps exist imperforate in issued and trial colors, and also in small presentation sheets in issued colors.

Catalogue values for all unused stamps in this country are for Never Hinged items.

Apsaras — A1

King Norodom Sihanouk — A3

Enthronement Hall — A2

1951-52 Unwmk. Engr. *Perf. 13*

1 A1 10c dk blue green 42 42
2 A1 20c cl & org brn 25 16
3 A1 30c pur & indigo 25 16
4 A1 40c ultra & brt bl grn 25 16
5 A2 50c dk grn & dk ol grn 25 16
6 A3 80c bl blk & dk bl grn 52 52
7 A2 1pi indigo & purple 65 65
8 A3 1.10pi dp car & brt red 65 65
9 A3 1.50pi blk brn & red brn ('51) 80 65
10 A1 1.50pi dp car & cerise 80 65
11 A2 1.50pi indigo & dp ultra 80 70
12 A3 1.90pi indigo & dp ultra 1.10 1.00
13 A2 2pi dp car & org brn 1.00 70
14 A3 3pi dp car & org brn 1.40 1.00
15 A1 5pi indigo & purple 5.75 3.00
a. Souvenir sheet of 1 18.00
16 A2 10pi purple & indigo 11.00 5.75
a. Souvenir sheet of 1 18.00
17 A3 15pi dk purple & purple 16.00 7.75
a. Souvenir sheet of 1 21.00
Nos. 1-17 (17) 41.89 24.08

Nos. 15a, 16a, 17a sold in a booklet for 30pi.
For surcharges see Nos. B1-B4.

Phnom Daun Penh — A4

East Gate, Angkor Thom — A5

Arms of Cambodia — A6

Methods of Mail Transport — A7

1954-55 Unwmk. *Perf. 13*

18 A4 10c rose carmine 15 15
a. Souvenir sheet of 5 ('55) 17.50
19 A4 20c dark green 15 15
20 A4 30c indigo 15 15
21 A4 40c dark purple 15 15
22 A4 50c dk violet brn 15 15
23 A5 70c chocolate 16 16
a. Souvenir sheet of 5 ('55) 21.00
24 A5 1pi red violet 16 16
25 A5 1.50pi red 16 16
26 A6 2pi rose red 28 28
a. Souvenir sheet of 5 ('55) 21.00
27 A6 2.50pi green 45 45
28 A7 2.50pi blue green 60 45
a. Souvenir sheet of 5 ('55) 21.00
29 A6 3pi ultra 65 55
30 A7 4pi black brown 75 75
31 A6 4.50pi purple 90 75
32 A7 5pi rose red 90 75
33 A6 6pi chocolate 1.10 75
34 A7 10pi purple 1.10 1.10
35 A7 15pi deep blue 1.65 1.40
36 A5 20pi ultra 3.25 1.75
37 A5 30pi blue green 4.50 4.00
Nos. 18-37 (20) 17.36 14.21

The four souvenir sheets each contain five different stamps: No. 18a (10c, 20c, 30c, 40c, 50c); No. 23a (70c, 1pi, 1.50pi, 20pi, 30pi); No. 26a (2pi, 2.50pi green, 3pi, 4.50pi, 6pi); No. 28a (2.50pi blue green, 4pi, 5pi. 10pi, 15pi). Size of Nos. 18a, 26a and 28a: 120x120mm. Size of No. 23a: 160x92mm.

For overprints see Nos. 99-100.

King Norodom Suramarit
A8

King Norodom Suramarit and Queen Kossamak Nearirat Serey Vathana
A9

Portraits: 50c (No. 39), 2.50r, 4r, 6r, 15r, Queen Kossamak Nearirat Serey Vathana.

Perf. 14x13(A8), 13(A9)

1955, Nov. 24 Engr. Unwmk.

38 A8 50c violet 15 15
39 A8 50c indigo 15 15
40 A8 1r car lake 15 15
41 A9 1.50r dk brown 30 30
42 A9 2r black & indigo 30 25
43 A8 2r dp ultra 20 30
44 A8 2.50r dk vio brn 30 30
45 A9 3r brn org & car 30 30
46 A8 4r dark green 48 48
47 A9 5r blk & dk grn 48 48
48 A8 6r deep plum 70 60
49 A8 7r dark brown 85 60
50 A9 10r brn car & vio 70 70
51 A8 15r purple 1.25 90
52 A8 20r deep green 1.65 1.40
Nos. 38-52 (15) 7.96 7.06

Coronation of King Norodom Suramarit and Queen Kossamak Nearirat Serey Vathana.

See Nos. 74-75. For surcharge see No. 122.

King Norodom Suramarit
A10

Prince Sihanouk, Globe and Flags
A11

Portrait: 3r, 5r, 50r, Queen Kossamak Nearirat Serey Vathana.

1956, Mar. 8 *Perf. 13*

53	A10	2r dark red	90	90
54	A10	3r dark blue	1.25	1.25
55	A10	5r yellow green	1.90	1.90
56	A10	10r dark green	4.75	4.75
57	A10	30r dark violet	10.50	10.50
58	A10	50r rose lilac	21.00	21.00
		Nos. 53-58 (6)	40.30	40.30

Coronation of King Norodom Suramarit and Queen Kossamak Nearirat Serey Vathana.

1957, Mar. 1

59	A11	2r green, ultra & car	42	30
60	A11	4.50r ultra	42	30
61	A11	8.50r carmine	42	30
		Nos. 59-61 (3)	1.26	90

Cambodia's admission to the UN, 1st anniv. (in 1956).

Type of Semi-Postal Stamps, 1957

1957, May 12 **Unwmk.** *Perf. 13*

62	SP1	1.50r vermilion	38	38
63	SP1	6.50r bluish violet	50	50
64	SP1	8r dark green	50	50
		Nos. 62-64 (3)	1.38	1.38

2500th anniv. of the birth of Buddha.

King Ang Duong
A12

1958, Mar. 4

65	A12	1.50r purple & brown	15	15
66	A12	5r olive gray & olive	32	22
67	A12	10r claret & dull brn	55	42
a.		Souvenir sheet of 3, #65-67	2.25	2.25
		Nos. 65-67 (3)	1.02	79

King Ang Duong (1795-1860).
No. 67a sold for 25r.

King Norodom I — A13

1958-59 **Engr.** *Perf. 12½x13*

68	A13	2r ultra & olive	22	22
69	A13	6r orange & sl grn	52	52
70	A13	15r green & ol gray	75	75
a.		Souv. sheet of 3, #68-70 ('59)	2.25	2.25
		Nos. 68-70 (3)	1.49	1.49

King Norodom I (1835-1904).
No. 70a sold for 32r.
Issue dates: Nos. 68-70, Nov. 3, 1958. No. 70a, Jan. 31, 1959.
For surcharge see No. 184.

Children of the World — A14

1959, Dec. 9 **Unwmk.** *Perf. 13*

71	A14	20c rose violet	15	15
72	A14	50c blue	15	15
73	A14	80c rose carmine	18	18
		Set value	35	35

Issued to promote friendship among the children of the world.
For surcharges see Nos. 115, B8-B10.

Nos. 49 and 52 with Black Border

1960 *Perf. 14x13*

74	A8	7r dk brown & blk	80	80
75	A8	20r dp green & blk	80	80

Death of King Norodom Suramarit.

Port of Sihanoukville, Prince Sihanouk and Serpent Naga — A15

20r (double size)

1960, Apr. *Perf. 13x12½*

76	A15	2r carmine & sepia	24	24
a.		Cambodian 20r	85	85
77	A15	5r ultra & dp brown	24	24
a.		Cambodian 20r	1.10	1.10
78	A15	20r lilac & dk blue	90	90
		Nos. 76-78 (3)	1.38	1.38

Opening of the port of Sihanoukville. By error the denomination in Cambodian on the 2r and 5r was engraved as 20r; it was corrected later.

Ceremonial Plow — A16

1960 *Perf. 12*

79	A16	1r magenta	28	28
80	A16	2r brown	28	28
81	A16	3r bluish green	28	28
		Nos. 79-81 (3)	84	84

Feast of the Sacred Furrow.

Fight Against Illiteracy A17

Water Conservation, Dam at Chhouksar A18

Dove, Factory and Books — A19

Buddhist Ceremony — A20

Works of Sangkum: 6r, Workman and house. 10r, Woman in rice field.

1960, Sept. 1 **Engr.** *Perf. 13*

82	A17	2r dk grn, brn & dk bl	15	15
a.		Souvenir sheet of 3	2.00	2.00
83	A18	3r brown & green	26	22
a.		Souvenir sheet of 3	2.00	2.00
84	A19	4r rose car, vio & grn	26	25
85	A17	6r brown, org & grn	35	30
86	A17	10r ultra, grn & bis	70	65
87	A20	25r dk car, red & mag	1.65	1.25
		Nos. 82-87 (6)	3.37	2.82

No. 82a contains one each of Nos. 82, 85 and 87, and sold for 42r. No. 83a contains one each of Nos. 83, 84 and 86, and sold for 23r. Nos. 82a-83a were issued Dec. 5, 1960.

Cambodian Flag and Dove
A21

Frangipani
A22

1960, Dec. 24 **Engr.** *Perf. 13*

Flag in Ultramarine and Red

88	A21	1.50r brown & green	18	18
89	A21	5r orange red	25	25
90	A21	7r green & ultra	65	65
a.		Souvenir sheet of 3, #88-90	2.00	2.00
b.		Souvenir sheet of 3 (colors changed)	4.00	4.00
		Nos. 88-90 (3)	1.08	1.08

Peace propaganda. No. 90a sold for 16r. No. 90b contains one of each denomination with colors changed to: 1.50r orange red, 5r green & ultramarine, 7r brown & green and sold for 20r.

1961, July 1 **Unwmk.** *Perf. 13*

91	A22	2r shown	24	24
92	A22	5r Oleander	40	40
93	A22	10r Amaryllis	80	80
a.		Souvenir sheet of 3, #91-93	3.00	3.00
		Nos. 91-93 (3)	1.44	1.44

No. 93a sold for 20r.

Krishna in Chariot, Khmer Frieze — A23

1961-63 **Typo.** *Perf. 14x13½*

94	A23	1r lilac	15	15
94A	A23	2r blue ('63)	90	55
95	A23	3r emerald	18	18
96	A23	6r orange	35	18
a.		Souvenir sheet of 3	5.00	5.00
		Nos. 94-96 (4)	1.58	1.06

Issued to honor Cambodian armed forces.
No. 94A issued in coils. No. 96a contains one each of Nos. 94, 95, 96. Sold for 12r.

Independence Monument
A24

1961, Nov. 9 **Engr.** *Perf. 13x12½*

97	A24	2r green	25	25
98	A24	4r gray brown	25	25
a.		Souvenir sheet of 2, #97-98	90	90
		Nos. 97-98,C15-C17 (5)	5.30	4.17

10th anniv. of Independence.
For surcharge see No. 116.

Nos. 27 and 31 Overprinted in Red:
"VIe CONFERENCE MONDIALE BOUDDIQUE 12-11-1961"

1961, Nov. 11 *Perf. 13*

99	A6	2.50pi green	32	32
100	A6	4.50pi purple	52	52

Sixth World Conference of Buddhism.

Highway (American Aid) — A25

Foreign Aid: 2r, Power station (Czech aid). 4r, Textile factory (Chinese aid). 5r, Hospital (Russian aid). 6r, Airport (French aid).

1961, Dec. **Engr.** *Perf. 13*

101	A25	2r org & rose car	15	15
102	A25	3r bl, grn & org brn	22	15
103	A25	4r dl bl, org brn & mag	24	15
104	A25	5r dl grn & lil rose	28	24
105	A25	6r dk bl & org brn	42	28
a.		Souvenir sheet of 5, #101-105	2.25	2.25
		Nos. 101-105 (5)	1.31	97

Malaria Eradication Emblem — A26

1962, Apr. 7 **Unwmk.** *Perf. 13*

106	A26	2r magenta & brown	18	15
107	A26	4r green & dk brown	28	24
108	A26	6r violet & olive bister	35	28
		Nos. 106-108 (3)	81	67

WHO drive to eradicate malaria.
For surcharges see Nos. B11-B12.

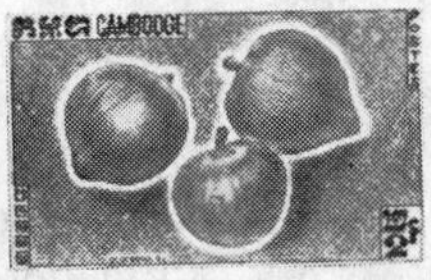

Fruits — A27

1962, June 4 **Engr.**

109	A27	2r Turmeric	28	24
110	A27	4r Cinnamon	28	24
111	A27	6r Mangosteens	45	38
a.		Souvenir sheet of 3, #109-111	1.40	1.40
		Nos. 109-111 (3)	1.01	86

Nos. 111a sold for 15r.

Pineapples — A28

1962 **Unwmk.** *Perf. 13*

112	A28	2r shown	32	28
113	A28	5r Sugar cane	45	32
114	A28	9r Sugar palms	65	45
		Nos. 112-114 (3)	1.42	1.05

No. 73 Surcharged

1962, Nov. 9 *Perf. 13*

115	A14	50c on 80c rose car	32	32

No. 97 Surcharged with New Value in Red and Overprinted in Black with Two Bars and: "INAUGURATION / DU / MONUMENT"

1962

116 A24 3r on 2r green 16 15

Dedication of Independence Monument.

Corn, Rice and FAO Emblem A29

1963, Mar. 21 **Engr.** ***Perf. 13***

117 A29 3r multicolored 38 30
118 A29 6r org red, vio bl & ocher 38 30

FAO "Freedom from Hunger" campaign.

Preah Vihear, Ancient Temple — A30

Tonsay Lake — A31

1963, June 15 ***Perf. 12½x13***

119 A30 3r claret, brown & sl grn 18 18
120 A30 6r orange, sl grn & grnsh blk 40 30
121 A30 15r blue, choc & green 75 70
Nos. 119-121 (3) 1.33 1.18

Return by Thailand of Preah Vihear on the Mekong River.
For overprint see No. 176.

No. 44 Surcharged with New Value and Bars

1963 **Engr.** ***Perf. 14x13***

122 A8 3r on 2½r dk violet brn 32 32

Perf. 12x12½, 12½x12

1963, Aug. 1 **Photo.**

Designs: 7r, Popokvil Falls. 20r, Beach, horiz.

123 A31 3r multicolored 16 16
124 A31 7r multicolored 35 24
125 A31 20r multicolored 95 52
Nos. 123-125 (3) 1.46 92

UNESCO Emblem, Scales and Globe — A32

1963, Dec. 10 **Engr.** ***Perf. 13***

126 A32 1r vio bl, rose cl & grn 18 18
127 A32 3r yel grn, vio bl & rose cl 30 30
128 A32 12r rose cl, yel grn & vio bl 65 65
Nos. 126-128 (3) 1.13 1.13

15th anniversary of the Universal Declaration of Human Rights.
For surcharge see No. 183.

Kouprey A33

1964, Mar. 3 **Unwmk.** ***Perf. 13***

129 A33 50c grn, dk brn & org brn 15 15
130 A33 3r org, brn, dk brn & grn 22 22
131 A33 6r blue, dk brn & grn 35 28
Nos. 129-131 (3) 72 65

Black-billed Magpie — A34

1964, May 2 **Engr.** ***Perf. 13***

132 A34 3r shown 15 15
133 A34 6r Kingfisher 55 32
134 A34 12r Gray heron 90 80
Nos. 132-134 (3) 1.60 1.27

For overprint and surcharge see Nos. 303, B16.

Emblem of Royal Cambodian Airline A35

1964 **Unwmk.** ***Perf. 13x12½***

135 A35 1.50r rose car & purple 18 18
136 A35 3r ver & dk blue 24 18
137 A35 7.50r ultra & car 60 42
Nos. 135-137 (3) 1.02 78

8th anniv. of the Royal Cambodian Airline.

Prince Norodom Sihanouk — A36

1964 **Engr.** ***Perf. 12½x13***

138 A36 2r purple 15 15
139 A36 3r red brown 20 18
140 A36 10r dark blue 55 48
Nos. 138-140 (3) 90 81

10th anniv. of the Sangkum (political party).
For overprints see Nos. 144-145.

Woman Weaver A37

Khmer Handicrafts: 3r, Metal worker. 5r, Basket maker.

1965, Feb. 1 ***Perf. 13x12½***

141 A37 1r multicolored 15 15
142 A37 3r red lil, red brn & gray ol 24 18
143 A37 5r green, dk brn & car 28 22
Nos. 141-143 (3) 67 55

Nos. 139-140 Overprinted in Black or Red: "CONFERENCE / DES PEUPLES / INDOCHINOIS"

1965, Mar. 1 ***Perf. 12½x13***

144 A36 3r red brown 28 28
145 A36 10r dark blue (R) 45 28

Conference of the people of Indo-China.

ITU Emblem, Old and New Communication Equipment — A38

1965, May 17 **Engr.** ***Perf. 13***

146 A38 3r green & ol bister 24 24
147 A38 4r red & blue 30 24
148 A38 10r violet & rose lilac 52 45
Nos. 146-148 (3) 1.06 93

Centenary of the ITU.

Cotton Plant — A39

Designs: 3r, Peanut plant. 7.50r, Coconut palm.

1965, Aug. 2 ***Perf. 12½x13***

149 A39 1.50r orange, sl grn & pur 20 20
150 A39 3r blue, yel, grn & brn 32 32
151 A39 7.50r orange brn & sl grn 60 60
Nos. 149-151 (3) 1.12 1.12

Preah Ko Temple, Rolouoh — A40

Temples at Angkor: 5r, Baksei Chamkrong, Rolouoh. 7r, Banteay Srei (Citadel of Women). 9r, Angkor Wat. 12r, Bayon, Angkor Thom.

1966, Feb. 1 **Engr.** ***Perf. 13***

152 A40 3r gray ol, sal & dl grn 40 22
153 A40 5r lil, dk grn & redsh brn 50 32
154 A40 7r dk grn, redsh brn & bis 55 40
155 A40 9r vio bl, pur & dk grn 75 50
156 A40 12r dk grn, rose car & ver 90 65
Nos. 152-156 (5) 3.10 2.09

For overprints see Nos. 172-175, 177.

WHO Headquarters, Geneva A41

1966, July 1 **Photo.** ***Perf. 12½x13***
WHO Emblem in Blue and Yellow

157 A41 2r black & pale rose 18 15
158 A41 3r black & yel grn 20 18
159 A41 5r black & lt bl 28 20
Nos. 157-159 (3) 66 53

Inauguration of WHO Headquarters, Geneva.

Tree Planting — A42

UNESCO Emblem — A43

1966, July 22 **Engr.** ***Perf. 12½x13***

160 A42 1r brn, dull brn & brt grn 15 15
161 A42 3r org, dull brn & brt grn 20 18
162 A42 7r gray, dull brn & brt grn 45 26
Nos. 160-162 (3) 80 59

Issued for Arbor Day.

1966 **Photo.** ***Perf. 13***

163 A43 3r multicolored 28 25
164 A43 7r multicolored 50 25

20th anniv. of UNESCO.

Wrestlers and Games' Emblem A44

GANEFO Games (Games Emblem and): 3r, Stadium, Phnom Penh. 7r, Swordsmen. 10r, Indian club swingers. Bas-reliefs from Angkor Wat.

1966, Nov. 25 **Engr.** ***Perf. 13***

165 A44 3r violet blue 18 15
166 A44 4r green 20 15
167 A44 7r dk car rose 30 18
168 A44 10r dark brown 42 26
Nos. 165-168 (4) 1.10 74

Indian Wild Boar — A45

Perf. 13x12½, 12½x13

1967, Feb. 20 **Engr.**

169 A45 3r shown 18 15
170 A45 5r Muntjac, vert. 24 15
171 A45 7r Elephant 38 20
Nos. 169-171 (3) 80 50

Nos. 152-153, 155-156 and 121 Overprinted in Red: "ANNEE INTERNATIONALE DU TOURISME 1967"

1967, Apr. 27 **Engr.** ***Perf. 13***

172 A40 3r multicolored 25 25
173 A40 5r multicolored 35 25
174 A40 9r multicolored 55 50
175 A40 12r multicolored 65 65
176 A30 15r multicolored 70 70
Nos. 172-176 (5) 2.50 2.35

International Tourist Year, 1967.

No. 154 Overprinted in Red: "MILLENAIRE / DE BANTEAY SREI / 967-1967"

1967, Apr. 27

177 A40 7r multicolored 65 40

Banteay Srei Temple at Angkor, millennium.

Royal Ballet Dancer — A46

Various Dancers

1967, June **Engr.** ***Perf. 13***

178 A46 1r orange 15 15
179 A46 3r Prus blue 22 18
180 A46 5r ultra 32 25
181 A46 7r carmine rose 45 42
182 A46 10r multicolored 70 50
Nos. 178-182 (5) 1.84 1.50

Cambodian Royal Ballet.

Nos. 128 and 70 Surcharged in Red

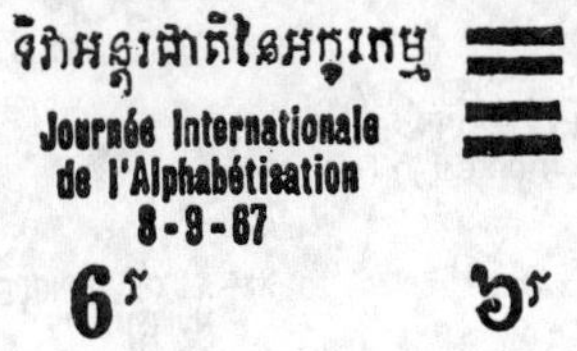

1967, Sept. 8 **Engr.**

183 A32 6r on 12r multi 42 32
184 A13 7r on 15r grn & olive gray 50 38

Intl. Literacy Day, Sept. 8. The surcharge on #184 is adapted to fit the shape of the stamp.

Symbolic Water Cycle — A47

1967, Nov. 1 **Typo.** ***Perf. 13x14***

185 A47 1r black, bl & org 15 15
186 A47 6r lilac, lt bl & org 30 20
187 A47 10r dk blue, emer & org 50 30
Nos. 185-187 (3) 95 65

Hydrological Decade (UNESCO), 1965-74.

Royal University, Kompong Cham — A48

Designs: 6r, Engineering School, Phnom Penh. 9r, University Center, Sangkum Reastr Niyum.

1968, Mar. 1 **Engr.** ***Perf. 13***

188 A48 4r violet bl & multi 20 20
189 A48 6r slate & multi 30 30
190 A48 9r Prus blue & multi 42 30
Nos. 188-190 (3) 92 80

Vaccination and WHO Emblem A49

WHO, 20th Anniv.: 7r, Malaria control and WHO emblem (man spraying DDT).

1968, July 8 **Engr.** ***Perf. 13***

191 A49 3r ultramarine 20 16
192 A49 7r deep blue 40 28

Stadium, Mexico City — A50

1968, Oct. 12 **Engr.** ***Perf. 13***

193 A50 1r shown 15 15
194 A50 2r Wrestling 16 15
195 A50 3r Bicycling 28 18
196 A50 5r Boxing, vert. 32 28
197 A50 7.50r Torch bearer, vert. 40 32
Nos. 193-197 (5) 1.31 1.08

Issued to commemorate the 19th Olympic Games, Mexico City, Oct. 12-27.

Red Cross Team — A51

1968, Nov. 1 **Engr.** ***Perf. 13***

198 A51 3r Prus bl, grn & red 40 18

Issued to honor the Cambodian Red Cross.

Prince Norodom Sihanouk A52

Design: 8r, Soldiers wading through swamp.

1968, Nov. 9

199 A52 7r emer, ultra & pur 35 20
200 A52 8r bl, grn & dp brn 40 20

15th anniversary of independence.

Human Rights Flame and Prince Sihanouk A53

1968, Dec. 10 **Engr.** ***Perf. 13***

201 A53 3r blue 20 15
202 A53 5r brt plum 32 20
203 A53 7r multicolored 42 24
Nos. 201-203 (3) 94 59

International Human Rights Year.

ILO Emblem A54

1969, May 1 **Engr.** ***Perf. 13***

204 A54 3r ultra 18 15
205 A54 6r dp carmine 28 18
206 A54 9r blue green 42 25
Nos. 204-206 (3) 88 58

ILO, 50th anniversary.

Globe, Red Cross, Crescent, Lion and Sun Emblems A55

1969, May 8

207 A55 1r blue, red & yel 15 15
208 A55 3r sl grn, red & vio brn 15 15
209 A55 10r brt lil, red & brn 40 20
Nos. 207-209 (3) 70 50

50th anniv. of the League of Red Cross Societies.

Papilio Oeacus A56

Butterflies: 4r, Papilio agamenon. 8r, Danaus plexippus.

1969, Oct. 10 **Engr.** ***Perf. 13***

210 A56 3r lilac, blk & yel 40 16
211 A56 4r ver, blk & grn 55 22
212 A56 8r yel grn, dk brn & org 80 30
Nos. 210-212 (3) 1.75 68

Map of Cambodia and Diesel Engine A57

Designs: Various railroad stations and trains.

1969, Nov. 27 **Engr.** ***Perf. 13***

213 A57 3r multicolored 45 16
214 A57 6r slate grn & lt brn 60 22
215 A57 8r black 80 30
216 A57 9r dk green & blue 1.00 30
Nos. 213-216 (4) 2.85 98

Issued to publicize the new rail link between Phnom Penh and Sihanoukville.

Fish — A58

1970, Jan. 29 **Photo.** ***Perf. 13***

217 A58 3r Tripletail 25 15
218 A58 7r Sleeper goby 42 18
219 A58 9r Snakehead 60 22
Nos. 217-219 (3) 1.27 55

Wat Maniratanaram — A59

Monasteries: 2r, Wat Tepthidaram, vert. 6r, Wat Patumavati. 8r, Wat Unnalom.

1970, Apr. 29 **Photo.** ***Perf. 13***

220 A59 2r multicolored 15 15
221 A59 3r multicolored 20 15
222 A59 6r multicolored 30 20
223 A59 8r multicolored 42 25
Nos. 220-223 (4) 1.07
Set value 65

UPU Headquarters and Monument, Bern — A60

1970, May 20

224 A60 1r green & multi 15 15
225 A60 3r scarlet & multi 15 15
226 A60 4r dp blue & multi 15 15
227 A60 10r brown & multi 15 15
Set value 45 38

New UPU Headquarters in Bern.

Open Book and Satellite Earth Receiving Station — A61

1970, May 17 **Photo.** ***Perf. 13***

228 A61 3r dk vio bl & multi 15 15
229 A61 4r sl grn & multi 15 15
230 A61 9r brn ol & multi 15 15
Set value 32 24

World Telecommunications Day.

Nelumbium Speciosum A62

Flowers: 4r, Eichhornia crassipes. 13r, Nymphea lotus.

1970, Aug. 17 **Photo.** ***Perf. 13***

231 A62 3r multicolored 15 15
a. Cambodian and Arabic 3's transposed 65
232 A62 4r multicolored 15 15
233 A62 13r multicolored 16 15
Set value 32 32

Elephant God, Basrelief at Banteay Srei — A63

1970, Sept. 21 **Engr.** ***Perf. 13***

234 A63 3r lil rose & dp grn 15 15
235 A63 4r bl grn, grn & lil rose 15 15
236 A63 7r bl grn, dk brn & grn 15 15
Set value 32 20

Issued for World Meteorological Day.

Khmer Republic

Globe, Rocket, Dove and UN Emblem A64

1970, Nov. 9 **Photo.** ***Perf. 12½x12***

237 A64 3r black & multi 15 15
238 A64 5r brown red & multi 15 15
239 A64 10r dp violet & multi 15 15
Set value 32 22

25th anniversary of the United Nations.

Education Year Emblem A65

1970, Nov. 9 **Engr.** ***Perf. 13x12½***

240 A65 1r blue 15 15
241 A65 3r brt rose lilac 15 15
242 A65 8r blue green 16 15
Set value 32 20

Issued for International Education Year.

Chuon-Nath — A66

1971, Jan. 27 **Photo.** ***Perf. 13***

243 A66	3r ol grn & multi	15	15
244 A66	8r purple & multi	15	15
245 A66	9r violet & multi	15	15
	Set value	38	26

In memory of Chuon-Nath (1883-1969), Cambodian language expert.
For surcharge see No. 322.

Soldiers in Battle — A67

1971, Mar. 18 **Photo.** ***Perf. 13***

246 A67	1r gray & multi	15	15
247 A67	3r bister & multi	15	15
248 A67	10r blue & multi	35	16
	Set value	50	28

National territorial defense.
For overprint see No. 321.

UN Emblem, Men of Four Races — A68

1971, Mar. 21

249 A68	3r blue & multi	15	15
250 A68	7r green & multi	15	15
251 A68	8r brt rose & multi	15	15
	Set value	32	25

Intl. year against racial discrimination.

General Post Office, Phnom Penh — A69

1971, Apr. 19

252 A69	3r blue & multi	15	15
253 A69	9r lilac rose & multi	35	15
254 A69	10r black & multi	38	16
	Nos. 252-254 (3)	88	
	Set value		37

Symbolic Globe and Waves A70

Design: 7r, 8r, ITU emblem and waves.

1971, May 17 **Photo.** ***Perf. 13***

255 A70	3r green, blk & bl	15	15
256 A70	4r yellow & multi	15	15
257 A70	7r lilac, blk & red	15	15
258 A70	8r sal pink, blk & red	15	15
	Set value	45	32

3rd World Telecommunications Day.

Erythrina Indica — A71

Wild Flowers: 3r, Bauhinia variegata. 6r, Butea frondosa. 10r, Lagerstroemia floribunda, vert.

1971, July 5 ***Perf. 13x12½, 12½x13***

259 A71	2r lt ultra & multi	15	15
260 A71	3r yel grn & multi	15	15
261 A71	6r blue & multi	15	15
262 A71	10r brown & multi	20	16
	Set value	44	35

Khmer Coat of Arms — A72

Flag and Square of the Republic — A73

1971, Oct. 9 **Engr.** ***Perf. 13***

263 A72	3r brt grn & bis	15	15
264 A73	3r purple & multi	15	15
265 A73	4r dp claret & multi	15	15
266 A72	8r orange & bis	15	15
267 A72	10r lt brn & bis	15	15
a.	Souv. sheet of 3, #263, 266-267	80	80
268 A73	10r slate grn & multi	15	15
a.	Souv. sheet of 3, #264-265, 268	65	65
	Set value	62	45

1st anniv. of the Republic. No. 267a sold for 25r. No. 268a sold for 20r.
For overprints and surcharges see Nos. 301-302, B13-B14.

UNICEF Emblem — A74

1971, Dec. 11

269 A74	3r black brown	15	15
270 A74	5r ultra	15	15
271 A74	9r dk pur & brn red	18	15
	Set value	38	26

25th anniv. of UNICEF.

Book Year Emblem A75

1972, Feb. 7

272 A75	3r blue, grn & vio	15	15
273 A75	8r violet, grn & bl	22	15
274 A75	9r emerald & multi	28	15
a.	Souvenir sheet of 3, #272-274	95	95
	Nos. 272-274 (3)	65	
	Set value		40

Intl. Book Year. No. 274a sold for 23r.

Lion of St. Mark — A76

Designs: 5r, Waves engulfing St. Mark's Basilica. 10r, Bridge of Sighs, vert.

1972, Feb. 7 **Engr.** ***Perf. 13***

275 A76	3r lil rose & org brn	15	15
276 A76	5r yel grn & org brn	15	15
277 A76	10r org brn, bl & yel grn	24	18
a.	Souvenir sheet of 3, #275-277	1.10	1.10
	Set value	45	32

UNESCO campaign to save Venice. No. 277a sold for 23r.

UN Emblem A77

1972, Mar. 28

278 A77	3r deep carmine	15	15
279 A77	6r deep blue	15	15
280 A77	9r deep orange	15	15
a.	Souvenir sheet of 3, #278-280	60	60
	Set value	31	25

25th anniv. UN Economic Commission for Asia and the Far East (ECAFE). No. 280a sold for 23r.

Dancing Apsarases A78

"UIT" A79

1972, May 5 **Engr.** ***Perf. 13***

281 A78	1r golden brn	15	15
282 A78	3r violet	15	15
283 A78	7r rose claret	15	15
284 A78	8r olive brn	15	15
285 A78	9r blue grn	15	15
286 A78	10r ultra	16	15
287 A78	12r purple	20	16
288 A78	14r Prus blue	28	18
	Set value	1.15	90

1972, May 17 **Litho.**

289 A79	3r blk, yel & grnsh bl	15	15
290 A79	9r blk, dp lil rose & bl grn	16	15
291 A79	14r blk, brn & bl grn	22	16
	Nos. 289-291 (3)	53	
	Set value		30

4th World Telecommunications Day.

"Human Environment" — A80

1972, June 5 **Engr.**

292 A80	3r org, plum & grn	15	15
293 A80	12r brt grn & plum	32	22
294 A80	15r plum & brt grn	42	30
a.	Souvenir sheet of 3, #292-294	1.65	1.65
	Nos. 292-294 (3)	89	
	Set value		58

UN Conf. on Human Environment, Stockholm, June 5-16. No. 294a sold for 35r.
For overprints and surcharges see Nos. 304-305, B15, B17.

Javan Rhinoceros A81

1972, Aug. 1 **Engr.** ***Perf. 13***

295 A81	3r shown	15	15
296 A81	4r Serow	15	15
297 A81	6r Malayan sambar	15	15
298 A81	7r Banteng	15	15
299 A81	8r Water buffalo	15	15
300 A81	10r Gaur	15	15
	Set value	50	32

Nos. 263, 267, 134, 293, 294 Overprinted in Red

1972, Sept. 9 **Engr.** ***Perf. 13***

301 A72	3r brt grn & bis	22	15
302 A72	10r orange & bis	45	22
303 A34	12r multicolored	70	24
304 A80	12r brt grn & plum	70	24
305 A80	15r plum & brt grn	85	38
	Nos. 301-305 (5)	2.92	1.23

20th Olympic Games, Munich, Aug. 26-Sept. 11.

Raising Khmer Flag — A82

1972, Oct. 9 **Photo.** ***Perf. 12½x13***

306 A82	3r multicolored	15	15
307 A82	5r brt rose & multi	15	15
308 A82	9r yel grn & multi	15	15
	Set value	32	24

2nd anniversary of the establishment of the Khmer Republic.
For surcharge see No. 323.

Stupa and Crest — A83

Apsaras — A84

1973, May 12 **Engr.** ***Perf. 13***

309 A83	3r ocher & multi	15	15
310 A83	12r yel grn & multi	15	15
311 A83	14r blue & multi	20	15
a.	Souvenir sheet of 3, #309-311	80	80
	Set value	39	32

New Constitution. No. 311a sold for 34r.

1973, July 23 **Engr.** ***Perf. 13***

Sculptures from Angkor Wat: 8r, 10r, Devata (different).

312 A84	3r brown black	15	15
313 A84	8r Prus green	15	15
314 A84	10r olive bister	15	15
a.	Souvenir sheet of 3, #312-314	60	60
	Set value	25	25

No. 314a sold for 25r.

INTERPOL Emblem — A85

Marshal Lon Nol — A86

1973, Oct. 2 Engr. *Perf. 13*

315 A85	3r green & multi	15	15
316 A85	7r red brn & multi	15	15
317 A85	10r olive & multi	15	15
a.	Souvenir sheet of 3, #315-317	75	75
	Set value	38	27

50th anniv. of the Intl. Criminal Police Org. No. 317a sold for 30r.

1973, Oct. 9

318 A86	3r lt grn, blk & brn	15	15
319 A86	8r brown, ol & blk	16	15
320 A86	14r black & brn	28	16
a.	Souvenir sheet of 3	1.00	1.00
	Nos. 318-320 (3)	59	
	Set value		31

Marshal Lon Nol, 1st pres. of the Republic. No. 320a contains stamps similar to Nos. 318-320 in changed colors. Sold for 50r.

Nos. 248, 243 and 307 Surcharged with New Value, 2 Bars and Overprinted in Red or Silver: "4th ANNIVERSAIRE/DE LA REPUBLIQUE"

1974 Photo. *Perf. 13, 12½x13*

321 A67	10r multi (R)	15	15
322 A66	50r on 3r multi	15	15
323 A82	100r on 5r multi	30	20
	Set value	49	35

4th anniversary of independence.

Copernicus and "Nerva" — A87

Designs: Copernicus, various spacecraft and events.

1974, Sept. 10 Litho. *Perf. 13*

324 A87	1r shown		
325 A87	5r Mariner II		
326 A87	10r Apollo		
327 A87	25r Telstar		
328 A87	50r Space walk		
329 A87	100r Moon landing		
330 A87	150r Separation of space-ship and module		
	Nos. 324-330, C32-C33(9)	15.00	15.00

500th anniversary of the birth of Nicolaus Copernicus (1473-1543), Polish astronomer.

Carrier Pigeon and UPU Emblem — A88

Design: 60r, Sailing ship and UPU emblem.

1974, Nov. 2

331 A88	10r multicolored	15	15
332 A88	60r multicolored	16	15
	Set value	21	15

Cent. of UPU. A souvenir sheet containing one No. 332 exists. See No. C34.

1976 Summer Olympics, Montreal (ancient and modern sports), set of nine, 1, 5, 10, 25, airmail 50, 100, 150, 200, 250r, plus 9 imperf. souv. sheets and 9 souv. sheets with simulated perfs., 2 perf. souv. sheets (200r, 250r), and 2 gold foil 1200r airmail, issued Jan. 2, 1975. Nos. 7501-7531.

World Cup Soccer Championships, set of nine, 1, 5, 10, 25r, airmail 50, 100, 150, 200, 250r, plus 9 imperf. souv. sheets and 9 souv. sheets with simulated perfs., 2 perf. souv. sheets (200r, 250r), and gold foil 1200r airmail and airmail souv. sheet, issued Feb. 13, 1975. Nos. 7532-7562.

UPU Cent. (2nd issue), set of nine, 15, 20, 70, 160, 180, 235r, airmail 500, 1000, 2000r, plus 9 imperf. souv. sheets and 9 souv. sheets with simulated perfs., 2 perf. souv. sheets (1000r, 2000r), 2 gold foil embossed perf. and imperf. 1000r airmail (train and plane) and 1200r airmail souv. sheet (Chinese junks), issued Apr. 12, 1975. Nos. 7563-7594.

SEMI-POSTAL STAMPS

Nos. 8, 12, 14 and 15 Surcharged in Black

+60c
AIDE A L'ÉTUDIANT

1952, Oct. 20 Unwmk. *Perf. 13*

B1 A3	1.10pi + 40c	3.00	3.00
B2 A3	1.90pi + 60c	3.00	3.00
B3 A3	3pi + 1pi	3.00	3.00
B4 A1	5pi + 2pi	3.00	3.00
	Nos. B1-B4 (4)	12.00	12.00

Preah Stupa — SP1

1957, Mar. 15 Engr. *Perf. 13*

B5 SP1	1.50r + 50c ind, ol & red	50	50
B6 SP1	6.50r + 1.50r red lil, ol & red	80	80
B7 SP1	8r + 2r bl, ol & red	1.25	1.25
	Nos. B5-B7 (3)	2.55	2.55

2500th anniv. of the birth of Buddha. See Nos. 62-64.

Type of Regular Issue, 1959, with Red Typographed Surcharge

+ 0,30

1959, Dec. 9

B8 A14	20c + 20c rose vio	15	15
B9 A14	50c + 30c blue	15	15
B10 A14	80c + 50c rose car	18	18
	Set value	38	38

The surtax was for the Red Cross.

Nos. 107-108 Surcharged and Overprinted in Red: "1863-1963 CENTENAIRE DE LA CROIX ROUGE"

1963, Oct. 1 Unwmk. *Perf. 13*

B11 A26	4r + 40c grn & dk brn	50	50
B12 A26	6r + 60c vio & ol bis	65	65

Centenary of International Red Cross.

+U +2

Nos. 263, 267, 293-294, 134 Surcharged in Red

SECOURS AUX VICTIMES DE GUERRE

1972, Nov. 15 Engr. *Perf. 13*

B13 A72	3r + 2r multi	20	20
B14 A72	10r + 6r multi	35	28
B15 A80	12r + 7r multi	50	30
B16 A34	12r + 7r multi	50	30
B17 A80	15r + 8r multi	75	60
	Nos. B13-B17 (5)	2.30	1.68

Surtax was for war victims. Surcharge arranged differently on Nos. B15-B17.

AIR POST STAMPS

Kinnari — AP1

Unwmk.

1953, Apr. 16 Engr. *Perf. 13*

C1 AP1	50c dp green	35	35
a.	Souv. sheet of 4, #C1, C3, C5, C9	37.50	37.50
C2 AP1	3pi red brown	45	38
a.	Souv. sheet of 3, #C2, C4, C8	37.50	37.50
C3 AP1	3.30pi rose vio	65	42
C4 AP1	4pi dk brn & dp bl	80	42
C5 AP1	5.10pi brn, red & org	1.00	65
C6 AP1	6.50pi dk brn & lil rose	1.00	1.00
a.	Souv. sheet of 2, #C6-C7	37.50	37.50
C7 AP1	9pi lil rose & dp grn	1.40	1.40
C8 AP1	11.50pi multi	2.75	2.00
C9 AP1	30pi dk brn, bl grn & org	3.75	2.25
	Nos. C1-C9 (9)	12.15	8.87

No. C1a sold for 50pi, No. C2a for 25pi, No. C6a for 20pi.

AP2

1957, Dec. 11

C10 AP2	50c maroon	15	15
C11 AP2	1r emerald	20	15
C12 AP2	4r ultra	90	60
C13 AP2	50r car rose	4.50	3.75
C14 AP2	100r grn, bl & car	7.50	5.50
a.	Souv. sheet of 5, #C10-C14	16.00	16.00
	Nos. C10-C14 (5)	13.25	10.15

No. C14a sold for 160r.

Independence Type of 1961

1961, Nov. 9 *Perf. 13x12½*

C15 A24	7r multicolored	65	32
C16 A24	30r grn, car & ultra	1.40	1.10
C17 A24	50r ind, grn & ol	2.75	2.25
a.	Souv. sheet of 3, #C15-C17	6.00	6.00
	Nos. C15-C17 (3)	4.80	3.67

No. C15 Surcharged with New Value in Red and Overprinted in Black with Two Bars and: "INAUGURATION DU MONUMENT"

1962, Nov. 9

C18 A24	12r on 7r multi	1.10	90

Dedication of Independence Monument.

Hanuman, Monkey God — AP3

1964, Sept. 1 Engr. *Perf. 13*

C19 AP3	5r multicolored	42	25
C20 AP3	10r ol bis, lil rose & grn	55	26
C21 AP3	20r vio, bl & ol bis	80	52
C22 AP3	40r bl, ol bis & dk bl	1.75	95
C23 AP3	80r multicolored	3.00	2.50
	Nos. C19-C23 (5)	6.52	4.48

Nos. C19-C22 Surcharged in Red

12 ₹
JEUX
OLYMPIQUES
TOKYO-1964

1964, Oct.

C24 AP3	3r on 5r multi	32	30
C25 AP3	6r on 10r multi	50	45
C26 AP3	9r on 20r multi	65	60
C27 AP3	12r on 40r multi	1.00	85
	Nos. C24-C27 (4)	2.47	2.20

18th Olympic Games, Tokyo, Oct. 10-25.

1972 Summer Olympics, Munich, set of 4 gold foil 900r airmail, and 2 souv. sheets of 2, issued Nov. 2, 1972. Nos. 72C01-72C06.

Apollo 16, set of 2 gold foil 900r airmail, and souv. sheet of 2, perf., imperf., issued Nov. 2, 1972. Nos. 72C07-72C09.

Garuda, 12th Century, Angkor Thom — AP4

1973, Jan. 18 Engr. *Perf. 13*

C28 AP4	3r carmine	15	15
C29 AP4	30r violet blue	55	40
C30 AP4	50r dull purple	90	65
C31 AP4	100r dull green	1.90	1.10
	Nos. C28-C31 (4)	3.50	2.30

World Cup Soccer Championships, set of 4 gold foil 900r airmail, issued Nov. 19, 1973. Nos. 73C01-73C04.

John F. Kennedy and Apollo 11 Astronauts on Moon, set of 2 gold foil 110r airmail, and souv. sheet of two, issued Feb. 18, 1974. Nos. 74C01-74C03.

Copernicus Type of 1974

Designs: 200r, Copernicus and Skylab III. 250r, Copernicus, Concorde and solar eclipse.

1974, Sept. 10 Litho. *Perf. 13*

C32 A87	200r multi		
C33 A87	250r multi		

A souvenir sheet containing No. C32 is perf., size 110x82mm. A souvenir sheet containing No. C33 is imperf., size 83x111mm.

Copernicus, gold foil 1200r airmail, and 1200r souv. sheet, issued Sept. 10, 1974. Nos. 74C04-74C05.

UPU Type of 1974

Design: 700r, Rocket, globe and UPU emblem.

1974, Nov. 2

C34 A88	700r gold & multi	1.75	1.25

A souvenir sheet of one exists.

UPU Cent. , set of 2 gold foil 1200r airmail, and 2 souv. sheets of 1, issued Nov. 2, 1974. Nos. 74C06-74C09.

POSTAGE DUE STAMPS

D1

Frieze, Angkor Wat — D2

1957 Unwmk. Typo. *Perf. 13½*
Denomination in Black

J1 D1 10c ver & pale blue 15 15
J2 D1 50c ver & pale blue 15 15
J3 D1 1r ver & pale blue 18 18
J4 D1 3r ver & pale blue 28 28
J5 D1 5r ver & pale blue 50 50
Nos. J1-J5 (5) 1.26 1.26

1974, Feb. 18 Engr. *Perf. 12½x13*
J6 D2 2r ocher 15 15
J7 D2 6r green 15 15
J8 D2 8r deep carmine 15 15
J9 D2 10r violet blue 24 15
Set value 55 36

CAMEROUN

(Kamerun)

LOCATION — On the west coast of Africa, north of the equator
GOVT. — Republic
AREA — 456,054 sq. mi.
POP. — 9,060,000 (est. 1983)
CAPITAL — Yaounde

Before World War I, Cameroun (Kamerun) was a German Protectorate. It was occupied during the war by Great Britain and France and in 1922 was mandated to these countries by the League of Nations. The French-mandated part became the independent State of Cameroun on January 1, 1960. The Southern Cameroons, a United Kingdom Trust Territory, joined this state to form the Federal Republic of Cameroun on October 1, 1961. The name was changed to United Republic of Cameroon on May 20, 1972.

Stamps of Southern Cameroons are listed under Cameroons in Volume 1.

100 Pfennig = 1 Mark
12 Pence = 1 Shilling
100 Centimes = 1 Franc

Catalogue values for unused stamps in this country are for Never Hinged items, beginning with Scott 281A in the regular postage section, Scott B13A in the semi-postal section, Scott C1 in the airpost section, Scott J24 in the postage due section, and Scott M1 in the military stamp section.

Watermark

Wmk. 125-Lozenges

Issued under German Dominion

A1

A2

Stamps of Germany, 1889-1900, Overprinted in Black

1897 Unwmk. *Perf. 13½x14½*
1 A1 3pf yel brn 8.00 10.00
a. 3pf red brown 19.00 35.00
b. 3pf dark brown 10.00 *25.00*
2 A1 5pf green 4.00 2.25
3 A2 10pf carmine 2.75 2.75
4 A2 20pf ultra 3.00 4.25
5 A2 25pf orange 14.00 22.50
6 A2 50pf red brn 11.00 19.00
Nos. 1-6 (6) 42.75 60.75

Kaiser's Yacht "Hohenzollern"
A3 A4

1900 Unwmk. Typo. *Perf. 14*
7 A3 3pf brown 90 90
8 A3 5pf green 11.00 50
9 A3 10pf carmine 30.00 75
10 A3 20pf ultra 20.00 1.50
11 A3 25pf org & blk, *yel* 90 *3.50*
12 A3 30pf org & blk, *sal* 1.25 *2.75*
13 A3 40pf lake & blk 1.25 *2.75*
14 A3 50pf pur & blk, *sal* 1.25 *3.25*
15 A3 80pf lake & blk, *rose* 1.75 *6.50*

Engr. *Perf. 14½x14*
16 A4 1m carmine 40.00 37.50
17 A4 2m blue 4.50 *35.00*
18 A4 3m blk vio 4.50 *60.00*
19 A4 5m slate & car 90.00 *200.00*
Nos. 7-19 (13) 207.30 *354.90*

1905-18 Wmk. 125 Typo.
20 A3 3pf brown ('18) 50
21 A3 5pf green ('06) 55 1.10
b. Bklt. pane of 6, 2 #21 + 4 #22 52.50
c. Booklet pane of 5 + label 250.00
22 A3 10pf carmine 55 55
b. Booklet pane of 5 + label 375.00
23 A3 20pf ultra ('14) 1.50 *140.00*
24 A4 1m car ('15) 1.50
25 A4 5m sl & car ('13) 14.00 *3,500.*
Nos. 20-25 (6) 18.60

The 3pf and 1m were not placed in use.

Issued under British Occupation

Stamps of German Cameroun Surcharged **C. E. F. ½ d.**

Wmk. Lozenges (125) (#54-56, 65); Unwmk. (Other Values)
1915 *Perf. 14, 14½*
Blue Surcharge
53 A3 ½p on 3pf brn 6.00 *11.00*
54 A3 ½p on 5pf grn 2.50 *5.00*
a. Double surcharge 400.00 *300.00*
b. Black surcharge 8.00 *10.00*
55 A3 1p on 10pf car 2.50 *5.00*
a. "1" with thin serifs 10.50 *13.00*
b. Double surcharge 175.00 *175.00*
c. Black surcharge 22.50 *30.00*
d. As "c," "1" with thin serifs 60.00 *70.00*

Black Surcharge
56 A3 2p on 20pf ultra 2.75 *10.00*
57 A3 2½p on 25pf org & blk, *yel* 12.00 21.00
a. Double surcharge *3,500.*
58 A3 3p on 30pf org & blk, *sal* 9.00 *21.00*
59 A3 4p on 40pf lake & blk 9.00 *21.00*
60 A3 6p on 50pf pur & blk, *sal* 9.00 *21.00*
61 A3 8p on 80pf lake & blk, *rose* 9.00 *21.00*

Surcharged **C. E. F. 1s.**

62 A4 1sh on 1m car 140.00 *275.00*
a. "S" inverted 650.00 *1,000.*
63 A4 2sh on 2m bl 140.00 *275.00*
a. "S" inverted 650.00 *1,000.*
64 A4 3sh on 3m blk vio 140.00 *275.00*
a. "S" inverted 650.00 *1,000.*
b. Double surcharge *4,000.*
65 A4 5sh on 5m sl & car 140.00 *275.00*
a. "S" inverted 650.00 *1,000.*
Nos. 53-65 (13) 621.75 *1,236.*

The letters "C. E. F." are the initials of "Cameroons Expeditionary Force."

Numerous overprint varieties exist for Nos. 53-65.

Counterfeits exist of Nos. 54a, 54b.

Issued under French Occupation

Stamps of Gabon, 1910, Overprinted

Corps Expéditionnaire Franco-Anglais CAMEROUN

1915 Unwmk. *Perf. 13½x14*
101 A10 10c red & car 16.00 6.00
102 A13 1c choc & org 50.00 15.00
103 A13 2c blk & choc 70.00 40.00
104 A13 4c vio & dp bl 70.00 42.50
105 A13 5c ol gray & grn 16.00 6.00
105A A13 10c red & car *10,500.* *11,000.*
106 A13 20c ol brn & dk vio 82.50 80.00
107 A14 25c dp bl & choc 32.50 10.00
108 A14 30c gray blk & red 82.50 75.00
109 A14 35c dk vio & grn 25.00 10.00
a. Double overprint 900.00 900.00
110 A14 40c choc & ultra 82.50 75.00
111 A14 45c car & vio 90.00 75.00
112 A14 50c bl grn & gray 90.00 80.00
113 A14 75c org & choc 125.00 80.00
114 A15 1fr dk brn & bis 110.00 90.00
115 A15 2fr car & brn 140.00 110.00
Nos. 101-105,106-115 (15) 1,082. 794.50

The overprint is vertical, reading up, on #101-106, 114-115, and horizontal on #107-113.

Stamps of Middle Congo, Issue of 1907, Overprinted **Occupation Francaise du Cameroun**

1916 Unwmk.
116 A1 1c ol gray & brn 37.50 37.50
117 A1 2c vio & brn 50.00 45.00
118 A1 4c bl & brn 50.00 45.00
119 A1 5c dk grn & bl 12.00 11.00
120 A2 35c vio brn & bl 50.00 37.50
121 A2 45c vio & red 35.00 30.00

The overprint is horiz. on Nos. 116-119, and vert., reading down, on Nos. 120-121.

Same Overprint On Stamps of French Congo, 1900

Wmk. Branch of Thistle (122)
122 A4 15c dl vio & ol grn 50.00 47.50
a. Inverted overprint 70.00 70.00

Wmk. Branch of Rose Tree (123)
123 A5 20c yel grn & org 65.00 47.50
124 A5 30c car rose & org 45.00 27.50
125 A5 40c org brn & brt grn 27.50 26.00
126 A5 50c gray vio & lil 45.00 27.50
127 A5 75c red vio & org 45.00 27.50

Wmk. Branch of Olive (124)
128 A6 1fr gray lil & ol 55.00 35.00
129 A6 2fr car & brn 55.00 35.00
Nos. 116-129 (14) 622.00 479.50

The overprint is horiz. on No. 122; vert., reading down or up, on Nos. 123-129.

Values are for copies centered in the grade of fine.

Counterfeits exist of Nos. 101-129.

Stamps of Middle Congo, Issue of 1907 Overprinted **CAMEROUN Occupation Française**

1916-17 Unwmk.
130 A1 1c ol gray & brn 15 15
131 A1 2c vio & brn 15 15
132 A1 4c bl & brn 15 15
133 A1 5c dk grn & bl 15 15
134 A1 10c car & bl 50 28
135 A1 15c brn vio & rose ('17) 50 22
136 A1 20c brn & bl 28 16
137 A2 25c bl & grn 35 22
a. Triple overprint 300.00
138 A2 30c scar & grn 20 20
a. Double overprint 200.00
139 A2 35c vio brn & bl 35 25
140 A2 40c dl grn & brn 65 28
141 A2 45c vio & red 65 32
142 A2 50c bl grn & red 65 40
143 A2 75c brn & bl 70 40
144 A3 1fr dp grn & vio 60 40
145 A3 2fr vio & gray grn 4.00 2.25
146 A3 5fr bl & rose 4.50 3.00
Nos. 130-146 (17) 14.53 8.98

Nos. 130-146 exist on ordinary paper and, with the exception of No. 135, on chalk surfaced paper. Nos. 137-146 are known with inverted "S" in "Francaise."

On Nos. 137-146 there is 7mm between "Cameroun" and "Occupation."

Provisional French Mandate

Types of Middle Congo, 1907, Overprinted **CAMEROUN**

1921
147 A1 1c ol grn & org 15 15
148 A1 2c brn & rose 15 15
149 A1 4c gray & lt grn 15 15
150 A1 5c dl red & org 15 15
a. Double overprint 450.00
151 A1 10c bl grn & lt grn 18 16
152 A1 15c bl & org 18 16
153 A1 20c red brn & ol 22 16
154 A2 25c sl & org 22 16
155 A2 30c rose & ver 25 16
156 A2 35c gray & ultra 32 30
157 A2 40c ol grn & org 25 22
158 A2 45c brn & rose 25 16
159 A2 50c bl & ultra 25 22
160 A2 75c red brn & lt grn 32 22
161 A3 1fr sl & org 75 60
162 A3 2fr ol grn & rose 2.50 2.00
163 A3 5fr dl red & gray 3.25 3.00
Nos. 147-163 (17) 9.54 8.12

The 2c, 4c, 15c, 25c and 50c exist with overprint omitted.

Nos. 152, 162, 163, 158, 160 Surcharged with New Value and Bars

1924-25
164 A1 25c on 15c bl & org ('25) 30 30
165 A3 25c on 2fr ol grn & rose 30 30
166 A3 25c on 5fr red & gray 38 38
a. Pair, one without new value and bars
167 A2 65c on 45c brn & rose ('25) 75 75
168 A2 85c on 75c red brn & lt grn ('25) 75 75
Nos. 164-168 (5) 2.48 2.48

French Mandate

Herder and Cattle Crossing Sanaga River — A5

Tapping Rubber Tree — A6

Rope Suspension Bridge — A7

1925-38 Typo. *Perf. 14x13½*
170 A5 1c ol grn & brn vio, *lav* 15 15
171 A5 2c rose & grn, *grnsh* 15 15
172 A5 4c bl & blk 15 15
173 A5 5c org & red vio, *lav* 15 15
174 A5 10c red brn & org, *yel* 15 15
175 A5 15c sl grn & grn 15 15
176 A5 15c lil & red ('27) 35 25

Perf. 13½x14
177 A6 20c ol brn & red brn 16 15
178 A6 20c grn ('26) 16 15
179 A6 20c brn red & ol brn ('27) 20 15
180 A6 25c lt grn & blk 35 15

181	A6	30c bluish grn & ver	16	15
182	A6	30c dk grn & grn ('27)	20	15
183	A6	35c brn & blk	16	15
184	A6	35c dl grn & grn ('38)	60	32
185	A6	40c org & vio	65	40
186	A6	45c dp rose & cer	16	15
187	A6	45c vio & org brn ('27)	1.00	70
188	A6	50c lt grn & cer	16	15
189	A6	55c ultra & car ('38)	65	55
190	A6	60c red vio & blk	16	15
191	A6	60c brn red ('26)	15	15
192	A6	65c ind & brn	15	15
193	A6	75c ind & dp bl	28	20
194	A6	75c org brn & red vio ('27)	28	16
195	A6	80c car & brn ('38)	60	40
196	A6	85c dp rose & bl	35	16
197	A6	90c brn red & cer ('27)	1.00	55

Perf. 14x13½

198	A7	1fr indigo & brn	42	28
199	A7	1fr dl bl ('26)	22	20
200	A7	1fr ol brn & red vio ('27)	40	22
201	A7	1fr grn & dk brn ('29)	65	45
202	A7	1.10fr rose red & dk brn ('28)	1.60	1.25
203	A7	1.25fr gray & dp bl ('33)	2.50	1.40
204	A7	1.50fr dl bl ('27)	38	20
205	A7	1.75fr brn & org ('33)	50	38
206	A7	1.75fr dk bl & lt bl ('38)	50	32
207	A7	2fr dl grn & brn org	80	35
208	A7	3fr ol brn & red vio ('27)	2.50	60
209	A7	5fr brn & blk, *bluish*	1.25	60
a.		Cliché of 2fr in plate of 5fr	*900.00*	
210	A7	10fr org & vio ('27)	5.00	2.50
211	A7	20fr rose & ol grn ('27)	8.00	4.50
		Nos. 170-211 (42)	33.55	19.64

Shades exist for several values.

For overprints and surcharge see Nos. 212, 264, 276, 278, 279, B7-B9, B21.

No. 199 Surcharged with New Value and Bars in Red

1926

212	A7	1.25fr on 1fr dull blue	22	22

Common Design Types pictured in section at front of book.

Colonial Exposition Issue

Common Design Types

Name of Country in Black

1931 Engr. *Perf. 12½*

213	CD70	40c dp grn	1.40	1.25
214	CD71	50c violet	2.00	1.75
215	CD72	90c red org	2.00	1.75
216	CD73	1.50fr dl bl	2.50	2.25
		Nos. 213-216 (4)	7.90	7.00

Paris International Exposition Issue

Common Design Types

1937 *Perf. 13*

217	CD74	20c dp vio	65	65
218	CD75	30c dk grn	60	60
219	CD76	40c car rose	60	60
220	CD77	50c dk brn	60	60
221	CD78	90c red	65	65
222	CD79	1.50fr ultra	65	65
		Nos. 217-222 (6)	3.75	3.75

French Colonial Art Exhibition

Common Design Type

Souvenir Sheet

1937 *Imperf.*

222A	CD77	3fr org red & blk	2.25	2.25

New York World's Fair Issue

Common Design Type

1939 *Perf. 12½x12*

223	CD82	1.25fr car lake	60	60
224	CD82	2.25fr ultra	60	60

For overprints and surcharges see Nos. 280-281, B14-B17, B23, B25.

Mandara Woman — A19

Falls on M'bam River near Banyo — A20

Elephants A21

Man in Yaré — A22

1939-40 Engr. *Perf. 13*

225	A19	2c blk brn	15	15
226	A19	3c magenta	15	15
227	A19	4c dp ultra	15	15
228	A19	5c red brn	15	15
229	A19	10c dp bl grn	15	15
230	A19	15c rose red	15	15
231	A19	20c plum	15	15
232	A20	25c blk brn	20	20
233	A20	30c dk red	20	16
234	A20	40c ultra	28	25
235	A20	45c slate green	80	65
236	A20	50c brn car	28	20
237	A20	60c pck bl	32	22
238	A20	70c plum	1.10	1.00
239	A21	80c Prus bl	80	70
240	A21	90c Prus bl	42	25
241	A21	1fr car rose	60	32
242	A21	1fr choc ('40)	60	28
243	A21	1.25fr car rose	1.60	1.10
244	A21	1.40fr org red	60	45
245	A21	1.50fr chocolate	45	35
246	A21	1.60fr blk brn	80	80
247	A21	1.75fr dk bl	42	28
248	A21	2fr dk grn	50	42
249	A21	2.25fr dk bl	42	28
250	A21	2.50fr brt red vio	60	42
251	A21	3fr dk vio	35	22
252	A22	5fr blk brn	42	28
253	A22	10fr brt red vio	80	65
254	A22	20fr dk grn	1.40	1.00
		Nos. 225-254 (30)	15.01	11.53

For overprints and surcharges see Nos. 255-263, 265-275, 277, 278A, 279A, B10-B13, B22, B24.

Stamps of 1925-40 Overprinted in Black or Orange "CAMEROUN FRANCAIS 27.8.40."

1940 *Perf. 14x13½, 13½x14, 13*

255	A19	2c blk brn (O)	28	28
256	A19	3c magenta	28	28
257	A19	4c dp ultra (O)	35	35
258	A19	5c red brn	1.10	1.10
259	A19	10c dp bl grn (O)	28	28
260	A19	15c rose red	42	42
260A	A19	20c plum (O)	3.25	2.50
261	A20	25c blk brn	35	28
b.		Inverted overprint	110.00	110.00
261A	A20	30c dk red	3.00	2.25
262	A20	40c ultra	1.50	1.00
263	A20	45c slate green	1.10	80
264	A6	50c lt grn & cer	60	28
a.		Inverted overprint	125.00	
265	A20	60c pck bl	1.50	1.00
266	A20	70c plum	55	55
267	A21	80c Prus bl (O)	1.50	1.25
268	A21	90c Prus bl (O)	38	38
269	A21	1.25fr car rose	55	35
270	A21	1.40fr org red	80	60
271	A21	1.50fr chocolate	35	35
272	A21	1.60fr blk brn (O)	60	35
273	A21	1.75fr dk bl (O)	80	80
274	A21	2.25fr dk bl (O)	42	42
275	A21	2.50fr brt red vio	42	42
276	A7	5fr brn & blk, *bluish*	5.75	4.25
277	A22	5fr blk brn	6.25	5.75
278	A7	10fr org & vio	8.00	5.75
278A	A22	10fr brt red vio	16.00	12.00
279	A7	20fr rose & ol grn	17.50	14.00
279A	A22	20fr dk grn	100.00	90.00

Same Overprint on Stamps of 1939

Perf. 12½x12

280	CD82	1.25fr car lake	1.50	1.50
281	CD82	2.25fr ultra	1.50	1.50
		Nos. 255-281 (31)	176.88	151.04

Issued to note Cameroun's affiliation with General de Gaulle's "Free France" movement.

Numerous overprint varieties exist.

Catalogue values for unused stamps in this section, from this point to the end of the section, are for Never Hinged items.

Cattle Fording Sanaga River and Marshal Petain A22a

1941 Engr. *Perf. 12½x12*

281A	A22a	1fr green	42	
281B	A22a	2.50fr dark blue	42	

Nos. 281A-281B were issued by the Vichy government, and were not placed on sale in Cameroun.

Lorraine Cross and Joan of Arc Shield — A23

1941 Photo. *Perf. 14x14½*

282	A23	5c brown	15	15
283	A23	10c dk bl	15	15
284	A23	25c emerald	15	15
285	A23	30c dp org	15	15
286	A23	40c dk slate green	15	15
287	A23	80c red brn	15	15
288	A23	1fr dp red lil	15	15
289	A23	1.50fr brt red	15	15
290	A23	2fr gray blk	20	15
291	A23	2.50fr brt ultra	22	15
292	A23	4fr dl vio	42	35
293	A23	5fr bister	45	42
294	A23	10fr dp brn	50	42
295	A23	20fr dp grn	1.00	65
		Set value	3.20	2.40

For surcharges see Nos. 297A-303.

Eboue Issue

Common Design Type

1945 Unwmk. Engr. *Perf. 13*

296	CD91	2fr black	20	20
297	CD91	25fr Prus grn	65	65

Nos. 282, 284, 291 Surcharged with New Values and Bars in Red, Carmine or Black

1946 *Perf. 14x14½*

297A	A23	50c on 5c (R)	16	16
298	A23	60c on 5c (R)	25	25
a.		Inverted surcharge	60.00	
299	A23	70c on 5c (R)	25	25
300	A23	1.20fr on 5c (C)	25	25
301	A23	2.40fr on 25c	20	20
302	A23	3fr on 25c	40	40
302A	A23	4.50fr on 25c	65	65
303	A23	15fr on 2.50fr (C)	65	65
		Nos. 297A-303 (8)	2.81	2.81

Zebu and Herder A25

Tikar Women — A26

Porters Carrying Bananas — A27

Bowman — A28

Lamido Horsemen — A29

Farmer — A30

1946 Engr. *Perf. 12½x12, 12x12½*

304	A25	10c bl grn	15	15
305	A25	30c brn org	15	15
306	A25	40c brt ultra	15	15
307	A26	50c ol brn	15	15
308	A26	60c dp plum	15	15
309	A26	80c chnt brn	20	15
310	A27	1fr org red	15	15
311	A27	1.20fr dp grn	25	16
312	A27	1.50fr dk car	80	60
313	A28	2fr black	15	15
314	A28	3fr dk car	15	15
314A	A28	3.60fr red brn	42	32
315	A28	4fr dp bl	20	15
316	A29	5fr brn car	42	15
317	A29	6fr ultra	42	15
318	A29	10fr slate green	45	15
319	A30	15fr grnsh bl	70	32
320	A30	20fr dk grn	80	22
321	A30	25fr black	1.10	45
		Nos. 304-321 (19)	6.96	
		Set value		2.95

Shades exist for most values.

For surcharges see Nos. 343-344, 346.

Imperforates

Most Cameroun stamps from 1952 onward exist imperforate in issued and trial colors, and also in small presentation sheets in issued colors.

Military Medal Issue

Common Design Type

Engraved and Typographed

1952 Unwmk. *Perf. 13*

322	CD101	15fr multi	2.50	1.60

Porters Carrying Bananas — A32

Picking Coffee Beans — A33

1954 Engr.

323	A32	8fr red vio, org brn & vio bl	35	16
324	A32	15fr brn red, yel & blk brn	60	28
325	A33	40fr blk brn, org brn & lil rose	60	28
		Nos. 323-325 (3)	1.55	72

FIDES Issue

Common Design Type

Designs: 5fr, Plowmen. 15fr, Wouri bridge. 20fr, Technical instruction. 25fr, Mobile medical station.

1956 Unwmk. *Perf. 13*

326	CD103	5fr org brn & dk brn	35	25
327	CD103	15fr aqua, slate & blk	60	40
328	CD103	20fr grnsh bl & dp ultra	60	40
329	CD103	25fr dp ultra	80	60
		Nos. 326-329 (4)	2.35	1.65

For surcharges see Nos. 345, 347.

Coffee Issue

Coffee — A35

1956 Engr. ***Perf. 13***
330 A35 15fr car & brt red 50 25

For surcharge see No. 348.

Autonomous Government

Flag and Woman Holding Child — A36

1958
331 A36 20fr multi 30 15

Anniv. of the installation of the 1st autonomous government of Cameroun.

Men Looking to the Sun — A37

1958
332 A37 20fr sepia & brn red 35 25

10th anniv. of the signing of the Universal Declaration of Human Rights.

Flower Issue
Common Design Type

Design: 20fr, Randia malleifera.

1959 Photo. ***Perf. 12½x12***
333 CD104 20fr dp grn, yel & rose 25 15

Loading Bananas A38

Harvesting Bananas — A39

1959 Engr. ***Perf. 13***
334 A38 20fr dk grn & org 20 15
335 A39 25fr maroon & slate grn 25 15
Set value 15

For surcharge see No. 349.

Buying Sets
It is often less expensive to purchase complete sets than individual stamps that make up the set. Set values are provided for many such sets.

Independent State

Map and Flag of Cameroun — A40

Prime Minister Ahmadou Ahidjo — A41

1960 Unwmk. Engr. ***Perf. 13***
336 A40 20fr multi 25 15
337 A41 25fr blk, grn & pale lem 30 15
Set value 17

Declaration of independence, Jan. 1, 1960.
For surcharge see No. 350.

Uprooted Oak Emblem A42

1960
338 A42 30fr red brn, ultra & yel grn 40 38

Issued to publicize World Refugee Year, July 1, 1959-June 30, 1960.
For surcharge see No. 351.

C.C.T.A. Issue
Common Design Type

1960
339 CD106 50fr dull claret & slate 65 40

UN Headquarters, NYC, and Flag — A43

1961, May 20 ***Perf. 13***
Flag in Green, Red and Yellow
340 A43 15fr grn, dk bl & brn 25 22
341 A43 25fr dk bl & grn 30 22
342 A43 85fr red, dk bl & vio brn 90 80
Nos. 340-342 (3) 1.45 1.24

Cameroun's admission to the UN, Sept. 20, 1960.

Federal Republic

Stamps of 1946-60 Surcharged in Red or Black:

REPUBLIQUE
FEDERALE
2 d

Two types of 2sh6p:
I- Large figures. "2/6" measures 8x3¾mm
II- Small figures. "2/6" measures 6x2½mm

1961, Oct. 1 Engr. ***Perf. 12x12½, 13***
343 A27 ½p on 1fr (#310) 16 16
344 A28 1p on 2fr (#313) 22 16
345 CD103 1½p on 5fr (#326) 22 16
346 A29 2p on 10fr (#318) 25 20
347 CD103 3p on 15fr (#327) 30 22
348 A35 4p on 15fr (Bk) (#330) 40 30
349 A38 6p on 20fr (#334) 50 35
350 A41 1sh on 25fr (#337) 1.00 80
351 A42 2sh6p on 30fr (#338) (I) 1.60 1.60
a. Type II 4.25 4.25
Nos. 343-351 (9) 4.65 3.95

Issued for use in the former United Kingdom Trust Territory of Southern Cameroons.
The "Republique Federale" overprint is in one line on Nos. 345, 347-349, in two vertical lines on No. 350. See Nos. C38-C40.

President Ahidjo and Prime Minister Foncha A45

1962, Jan. 1 Unwmk. Engr. ***Perf. 13***
352 A45 20fr vio & choc 5.00 4.25
353 A45 25fr dk grn & brn 8.00 6.50
354 A45 60fr car & dl grn 22.50 20.00
Nos. 352-354 (3) 35.50 30.75

Same Surcharged for Use in Southern Cameroons

3 d

355 A45 3p on 20fr 90.00 90.00
356 A45 6p on 25fr 90.00 90.00
357 A45 2sh6p on 60fr 90.00 90.00
Nos. 355-357 (3) 270.00 270.00

Reunification of the former French and British Sections of Cameroun. It is reported that Nos. 352-357 were withdrawn after a few days and destroyed.

Canceled to Order
Many Cameroun stamps from 1962 onward are available c-t-o. Values are for postally used copies. C-t-o copies sell for less.

Mustache Monkey A46

Designs: 1fr, 4fr, Elephant, Ntem Falls. 1.50fr, 3fr, Buffon's kob, Dschang. 2fr, 5fr, Hippopotamus. 6fr, 15fr, Mustache monkey. 8fr, 30fr, Manatee, Lake Ossa. 10fr, 25fr, Buffalo, Batouri. 20fr, 40fr, Giraffes, Waza Reservation, vert.

1962 Unwmk. Engr. ***Perf. 12***
358 A46 50c brn, brt grn & bl 15 15
359 A46 1fr gray brn, bl grn & org 15 15
360 A46 1.50fr brn, lt grn & sl grn 15 15
361 A46 2fr dk gray, grnsh bl & grn 15 15
362 A46 3fr brn, org & lil rose 15 15
363 A46 4fr brn, yel grn & bl grn 15 15
364 A46 5fr gray brn, grn & sal 15 15
365 A46 6fr brn, yel & bl 15 15
366 A46 8fr dk bl, red & grn 16 15
367 A46 10fr ol blk, org & brt bl 16 15
368 A46 15fr brn, Prus bl & bl 20 15
369 A46 20fr brn & gray 25 15
370 A46 25fr red brn, grn & yel 40 20
371 A46 30fr blk, org & bl 60 25
372 A46 40fr dp cl, yel grn & blk 80 40
Set value 3.20 1.50

See Nos. 396-397.

African and Malagasy Union Issue
Common Design Type

1962, Sept. 8 Photo. ***Perf. 12½x12***
373 CD110 30fr multi 65 45

Village and Map of Cameroun A48

Designs: 20fr, 25fr, Sun rising over city. 50fr, Hands holding scroll.

1962, Oct. 1 Engr. ***Perf. 13***
374 A48 9fr pur, ol & dk brn 15 15
375 A48 18fr grn, org brn & dk bl 22 16
376 A48 20fr lil rose, ol bis & ind 22 16
377 A48 25fr bl, red org & sep 35 20
378 A48 50fr dk red, sep & bl 65 50
Nos. 374-378 (5) 1.59 1.17

1st anniv. of the reunification of Cameroun.

"School under the Trees" — A49

1962, Nov. 5 Photo. ***Perf. 12x12½***
379 A49 20fr ver, emer & yel 25 15

Literacy and popular education campaign.

Telstar and Globe — A50

1963, Feb. 9 Engr. ***Perf. 13***
Size: 36x22mm
380 A50 1fr dk bl, olive & pur 15 15
381 A50 2fr dk bl, claret & grn 15 15
382 A50 3fr dk grn, ol & dp cl 15 15
383 A50 25fr grn, dp cl & brt bl 45 40
Set value 63 58

1st TV connection of the US and Europe through the Telstar satellite, July 11-12, 1962. See No. C45.

High Frequency Transmission Station, Mt. Bankolo — A51

Design: 20fr, Station and wiring plan.

1963, May 18 Photo. ***Perf. 12x12½***
384 A51 15fr multi 16 15
385 A51 20fr multi 22 16

Issued to publicize the high frequency telegraph connection Douala-Yaoundé. See No. C46.

"Yaoundé-Regional Center of Textbook Production" — A52

1963, Aug. 10 Unwmk. ***Perf. 12½***
386 A52 20fr emer, blk & red 22 15
387 A52 25fr org, blk & red 30 16
388 A52 100fr gold, blk & red 1.10 65
Nos. 386-388 (3) 1.62 96

UNESCO regional center for the production of school books at Yaounde.

Pres. Ahmadou Ahidjo and Flag — A53

Design: 18fr, Flag and map of Cameroun.

1963, Oct. 1 *Perf. 12x12½*

Flag in Green, Red and Yellow

389 A53 9fr grn, bl & dk brn 15 15
390 A53 18fr grn, bl & lil 20 16
391 A53 20fr grn, blk & yel grn 22 20
Nos. 389-391 (3) 57 51

Second anniversary of reunification.

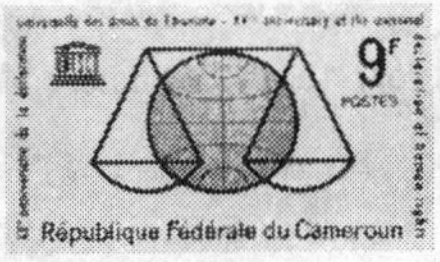

Scales, Globe, UNESCO Emblem A54

1963, Dec. 10 Photo. *Perf. 12½x12*

392 A54 9fr ultra, blk & sal 15 15
393 A54 18fr brt yel grn, blk & rose red 20 15
394 A54 25fr rose red, blk & brt yel grn 25 20
395 A54 75fr yel, blk & ultra 90 50
Nos. 392-395 (4) 1.50 1.00

15th anniversary of the Universal Declaration of Human Rights.

Animal Type of 1962

Design: 10fr, 25fr, Lion, Waza National Park, North Cameroun.

1964, June 20 Engr. *Perf. 13*

396 A46 10fr red brn, bis & grn 16 15
397 A46 25fr grn & bis 35 16
Set value 23

Soccer Game in Stadium A55

Designs: 18fr, Pile of sports equipment. 30fr, Stadium (outside), flags and map of Africa.

1964, July 11 Engr. *Perf. 13*

398 A55 10fr grn, bl & red brn 15 15
399 A55 18fr car, grn & vio 20 15
400 A55 30fr blk, dk bl & org brn 35 20
Nos. 398-400 (3) 70
Set value 41

Tropics Cup Games, Yaounde, July 11-19.

Europafrica Issue, 1964

Common Design Type and

Palace of Justice, Yaounde — A56

Design: 40fr, Emblems of Science, Agriculture, Industry and Education and two sunbursts.

1964, July 20 Photo. *Perf. 12x13*

401 A56 15fr multi 35 25
402 CD116 40fr multi 65 60

1st anniv. of the economic agreement between the European Economic Community and the African and Malgache Union.

Hurdling and Olympic Flame — A57

Design: 10fr, Runners, vert.

1964, Oct. 10 Engr. *Perf. 13*

403 A57 9fr red, yel grn & blk 60 40
404 A57 10fr red, vio & ol gray 60 40

18th Olympic Games, Tokyo, Oct. 10-25. See Nos. C49, C49a.

Bamileke Dance Dress — A58

Ntem Falls, Ebolowa Region — A59

Designs: 18fr, Dance mask, Bamenda region. 25fr, Fulani horseman, North Cameroun, horiz.

1964 Unwmk. *Perf. 13*

405 A58 9fr red, yel grn & bl 15 15
406 A58 18fr bl, red & brn 20 15
407 A59 20fr dk car, grn & ol 22 15
408 A58 25fr dk brn, org & car 30 20
Nos. 405-408 (4) 87 65

See No. C50.

Cooperation Issue

Common Design Type

1964, Nov. 7 Engr.

409 CD119 18fr dk bl, yel grn & dk brn 22 15
410 CD119 30fr red brn, bl grn & dk brn 40 16

Memorial Stone — A60

Diesel Train — A61

1965, Jan. 1 Engr. *Perf. 13*

411 A60 12fr bl, indigo & grn 16 15

Typo. *Perf. 14x13*

412 A61 20fr rose car, yel & grn 25 15
Set value 24

Laying of the 1st rail of the Mbanga-Kumba Railroad, Mar. 28, 1964.

Red Cross Station and Ambulance A62

Design: 50fr, Red Cross nurse and infant, vert.

1965, May 8 Engr. *Perf. 13*

413 A62 25fr car, sl grn & ocher 30 16
414 A62 50fr gray, red & red brn 60 30

Issued for the Cameroun Red Cross.

Coins Inserted in Map of Cameroun, and Bankbook — A63

Savings Bank Building — A64

Design: 20fr, Bankbook and coins inserted in cacao pod-shaped bank, horiz.

1965, June 10

Size: 22x37mm

415 A63 9fr grn, red & org 15 15

Size: 48x27mm, 27x48mm

416 A64 15fr choc, ultra & grn 20 16
417 A63 20fr ocher, brt grn & brn 22 20
Nos. 415-417 (3) 57 51

Federal Postal Savings Banks.

Soccer Players and Africa Cup — A65

Unwmk.

1965, June 26 Engr. *Perf. 13*

418 A65 9fr car, brn & yel 15 15
419 A65 20fr car, sl bl & yel 22 16

Cameroun Oryx Club, winner of the club champions' Africa Cup, February 1965.

Symbolic Map of Europe and Africa — A66

Designs: 40fr, Delegates around conference table.

1965, July 20 Photo. *Perf. 12x12½*

420 A66 5fr car, blk & lil 15 15
421 A66 40fr brn, buff, grn & ultra 45 35

2nd, anniv. of the economic agreement between the European Economic Community and the African and Malgache Union.

UPU Monument, Bern — A67

1965, July 26 Engr. *Perf. 13*

422 A67 30fr blk & red 40 25

Cameroun's admission to the UPU, 5th anniv.

ICY Emblem — A68

1965, Sept. 11 Unwmk. *Perf. 13*

423 A68 10fr dk bl & car rose 16 16

Issued for the International Cooperation Year, 1964-65. See No. C57.

Pres. Ahidjo and Government House — A69

Design: 9fr, 20fr, Pres. Ahidjo and Government House, vert.

Perf. 12x12½, 12½x12

1965, Oct. 1 Photo. Unwmk.

424 A69 9fr multi 15 15
425 A69 18fr multi 20 15
426 A69 20fr multi 22 15
427 A69 25fr multi 30 16
Nos. 424-427 (4) 87
Set value 50

Reelection of Pres. Ahmadou Ahidjo.

National Tourist Office, Yaoundé A70

Designs: 9fr, Pouss Musgum houses. 18fr, Great Calao's dance (North Cameroun). 20fr, Gate of Sultan's Palace, Foumban, vert.

1965 Engr. *Perf. 13*

428 A70 9fr brn, rose red & grn 15 15
429 A70 18fr brt bl, brn & grn 20 16
430 A70 20fr bl, brn & choc 22 15
431 A70 25fr mar, emer & gray 22 15
Nos. 428-431 (4) 79 61

See No. C58.

Mountain Hotel, Buea — A71

Designs: 20fr, Hotel of the Deputies, Yaoundé. 35fr, Dschang Health Center.

1966

432 A71 9fr sl grn, rose cl & brn 15 15
433 A71 20fr brt bl, sl grn & blk 22 15
434 A71 35fr brn, sl grn & car 40 30
Nos. 432-434,C63-C69 (10) 5.68 3.26

Bas-relief, Foumban A72

Designs: 18fr, Ekoi mask, vert. 20fr, Mother and child, carving, Bamiléké, vert. 25fr, Ceremonial stool, Bamoun.

1966, Apr. 15 **Unwmk.**

435 A72	9fr red & blk	16	15
436 A72	18fr brt grn, org brn & choc	22	16
437 A72	20fr brt bl, red brn & pur	30	16
438 A72	25fr pur & dk brn	35	20
	Nos. 435-438 (4)	1.03	67

Intl. Negro Arts Festival, Dakar, Senegal, Apr. 1-24.

New WHO Headquarters, Geneva A73

1966, May 3 **Photo.** ***Perf. 12½x13***

439 A73	50fr ultra, red brn & yel	60	35

ITU Headquarters, Geneva A74

1966, May 3 **Photo.** ***Perf. 12½x13***

440 A74	50fr ultra & yel	60	35

Phaeomeria Magnifica — A75

"6" and Men Dancing around UN Emblem — A76

Flowers: 18fr, Hibiscus (rose of China). 20fr, Mountain rose.

1966, May 20 ***Perf. 12x12½***

Flowers in Natural Colors

Size: 22x36mm

441 A75	9fr red brn	15	15
442 A75	18fr green	20	15
443 A75	20fr dk grn	22	15
	Nos. 441-443,C70-C72 (6)	2.42	
	Set value		76

See No. 469.

1966, Sept. 20 **Engr.** ***Perf. 13***

Design: 50fr, UN General Assembly, horiz.

444 A76	50fr ultra, grn & vio brn	60	15
445 A76	100fr red brn, grn & ultra	1.10	50

6th anniv. of Cameroun's admission to the UN.

Prime Minister's Residence, Buea — A77

Designs (Prime Minister's Residences): 18fr, at Yaoundé, front view. 20fr, at Yaoundé, side view. 25fr, at Buea, front view.

1966, Oct. 1 **Photo.**

446 A77	9fr multi	15	15
447 A77	18fr multi	20	15
448 A77	20fr multi	22	15
449 A77	25fr multi	25	16
	Nos. 446-449 (4)	82	
	Set value		46

5th anniversary of re-unification.

Learning to Write and UNESCO Emblem A78

Design: No. 451, Children's heads and UNICEF emblem.

1966, Nov. 24 **Engr.** ***Perf. 13***

450 A78	50fr red lil, bl & brn	60	30
451 A78	50fr red lil, blk & brt bl	60	30

20th anniv. of UNESCO, 20th anniv. of UNICEF.

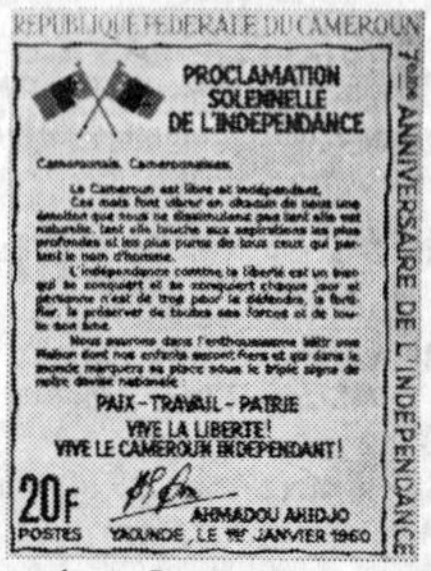

Independence Proclamation — A79

1967, Jan. 1 **Engr.** ***Perf. 13***

452 A79	20fr grn, red & yel	30	22

7th anniversary of independence.

Map of Africa and Madagascar, Railroad Tracks and Symbols — A80

Design: 25fr, Map of Africa and Madagascar and train.

1967, Feb. 21 **Photo.** ***Perf. 13***

453 A80	20fr multi	22	16
454 A80	25fr multi	30	16

5th Conf. of African and Madagascan Railroad Technicians.

Lions Emblem and Forest — A81

Design: 100fr, Lions emblem and palms.

1967, Mar. 3

455 A81	50fr multi	60	35
456 A81	100fr multi	1.10	65

Lions International, 50th anniversary.

Jet and I.C.A.O. Emblem — A82

Dove and I.A.E.A. Emblem A83

Perf. 13x12½, 12½x13

1967, Mar. 15 **Photo.**

457 A82	50fr ultra, lt bl, brn & gold	60	35
458 A83	50fr ultra & emer	60	35

UN agencies: No. 457, the ICAO; No. 458, the Intl. Atomic Energy Agency.

Rotary International Emblem A84

1967, Apr. 17 **Photo.** ***Perf. 12½***

459 A84	25fr crim, vio bl & gold	30	16

10th anniversary of the Douala, Cameroun, branch of Rotary International.

Pomelo — A85

Bird-of-Paradise Flower — A86

1967, May 10 **Photo.** ***Perf. 12x12½***

460 A85	1fr shown	15	15
461 A85	2fr Papaya	15	15
462 A85	3fr Custard apple	15	15
463 A85	4fr Breadfruit	15	15
464 A85	5fr Coconut	15	15
465 A85	6fr Mango	15	15
466 A85	8fr Avacado	16	15
467 A85	10fr Pineapple	20	15
468 A85	30fr Bananas	45	20
	Set value	1.30	65

For surcharges see Nos. 550, 593.

1967, June 22 **Photo.** ***Perf. 12x12½***

Size: 22x36mm

469 A86	15fr lt bl & multi	16	15

Sanaga Falls and ITY Emblem — A87

1967, Aug. 14 **Photo.** ***Perf. 13x12½***

470 A87	30fr multi	35	20

Issued for International Tourist Year 1967.

Art of Cameroun: Coconut Harvest A88

Designs (Carved Bas-relief): 20fr, Lion hunt. 30fr, Women carrying baskets. 100fr, Carved chest.

1967, Sept. 22 ***Perf. 12½x13***

471 A88	10fr brn, bl & car	15	15
472 A88	20fr brn, yel & grn	22	15
473 A88	30fr emer, brn & car	35	15
474 A88	100fr red org, brn & emer	1.10	45
	Nos. 471-474 (4)	1.82	90

Coat of Arms — A89

1968, Jan. 1 **Litho.** ***Perf. 12½x13***

475 A89	30fr gold & multi	40	20

Spiny Lobster A90

Designs (Fish and Crustaceans): 10fr, River crayfish. 15fr, Nile mouth-breeder. 20fr, Sole. 25fr, Common pike. 30fr, Crab. 40fr, Spadefish, vert. 50fr, Shrimp, vert. 55fr, African snakehead. 60fr, Threadfin.

1968, July 25 **Engr.** ***Perf. 13***

476 A90	5fr brn, vio bl & dl grn	15	15
477 A90	10fr ultra, brn ol & slate	15	15
478 A90	15fr sal, red lil & sepia	15	15
479 A90	20fr red brn, dp bl & sep	16	15
480 A90	25fr lt brn, emer & slate	25	15
481 A90	30fr mag, dk bl & dk brn	35	15
482 A90	40fr slate bl & org	40	15
483 A90	50fr emer, gray & rose car	50	20
484 A90	55fr lt brn, Prus bl & dk brn	60	25
485 A90	60fr brn, bl grn & indigo	65	35
	Nos. 476-485 (10)	3.36	
	Set value		1.35

Tanker, Refinery and Map of Area Served — A91

1968, July 30 **Photo.** ***Perf. 12½***

486 A91 30fr multi 30 15

Issued to commemorate the opening of the Port Gentil (Gabon) Refinery, June 12, 1968.

Human Rights Flame — A92

1968, Sept. 14 **Photo.** ***Perf. 12½x13***

487 A92 15fr blue & salmon 16 15

International Human Rights Year. See No. C110.

Pres. Ahmadou Ahidjo A93

1969, Apr. 10 **Photo.** ***Perf. 12½x12***

488 A93 30fr car & multi 30 15

Chocolate Vat — A94

Designs: 30fr, Chocolate factory. 50fr, Candy making, vert.

1969, Apr. 24 **Engr.** ***Perf. 13***

489 A94 15fr red brn, ind & choc 16 15
490 A94 30fr grn, blk & red brn 30 15
491 A94 50fr brn & multi 50 20
Nos. 489-491 (3) 96
Set value 40

Cameroun chocolate industry.

Fertility Symbol, Abbia — A95

Diesel Train on Bridge — A96

Art and Folklore from Abbia: 10fr, Two toucans, horiz. 15fr, Forest symbol. 30fr, Vulture attacking monkey, horiz. 70fr, Oliphant player.

1969, May 30 **Engr.** ***Perf. 13***

492 A95 5fr ultra, Prus bl & brt rose lil 15 15
493 A95 10fr bl, ol gray & org 15 15
494 A95 15fr ultra, dk red & blk 15 15
495 A95 30fr brt bl, lem & grn 30 15
496 A95 70fr brt bl, dk grn & ver 70 35
Nos. 492-496 (5) 1.45
Set value 65

Perf. 12½x13, 13x12½

1969, July 11 **Photo.**

Design: 30fr, Kumba Railroad station, horiz.

497 A96 30fr bl & multi 30 15
498 A96 50fr blk & multi 60 25

Opening of Mbanga-Kumba Railroad.

Development Bank Issue
Common Design Type

1969, Sept. 10 **Engr.** ***Perf. 13***

499 CD130 30fr vio bl, grn & ocher 35 15

African Development Bank, 5th anniv.

ASECNA Issue
Common Design Type

1969, Dec. 12 **Engr.** ***Perf. 13***

500 CD132 100fr slate grn 1.00 60

Red Sage — A99

Design: 30fr, Passionflower.

1970, Mar. 24 **Photo.** ***Perf. 12x12½***
Size: 22x36½mm

501 A99 15fr yel grn & multi 16 15
502 A99 30fr multi 25 15
Set value 20

See Nos. C140-C141.

UPU Headquarters Issue
Common Design Type

1970, May 20 **Engr.** ***Perf. 13***

503 CD133 30fr bl, pur & grn 30 15
504 CD133 50fr gray, red & bl 50 16

Brewery A100

Design: 30fr, Cellar with barrels.

1970, July 9 **Engr.** ***Perf. 13***

505 A100 15fr brn, gray & dk grn 15 15
506 A100 30fr bl grn, dk brn & brn red 25 15
Set value 20

Cameroun brewing industry.

Ozila Dancers — A101

Cameroun Doll — A102

Design: 50fr, Ozila dancer and drummer.

1970, Oct. 19 **Engr.** ***Perf. 13***

507 A101 30fr multi 25 15
508 A101 50fr red & multi 50 20

1970, Nov. 2

Designs: 15fr, Doll in short skirt. 30fr, Doll with basket on back.

509 A102 10fr car & multi 15 18
510 A102 15fr dk grn & multi 18 15
511 A102 30fr brn red & multi 35 15
Nos. 509-511 (3) 68
Set value 32

Cogwheels and Grain A103

1970, Feb. 9 **Photo.** ***Perf. 13***

512 A103 30fr multi 25 15

Europafrica Economic Conference.

Federal University, Yaoundé A104

1971, Jan. 19 **Engr.**

513 A104 50fr multi 40 15

Inauguration of Federal University at Yaoundé.

Presidents Ahidjo and Pompidou, Flags of Cameroun and France — A105

1971, Feb. 9 **Photo.** ***Perf. 13***

514 A105 30fr multi 40 35

Visit of Georges Pompidou, Pres. of France.

Young People, Globe, Map of Cameroun A106

1971, Feb. 11

515 A106 30fr blue & multi 22 15

Fifth National Youth Festival, Feb. 11.

Gerbera Hybrida — A107

Men of Four Races — A108

Designs: 40fr, Opuntia polyantha (cactus). 50fr, Hemerocallis hybrida (lily).

1971, Mar. 14 **Photo.**

516 A107 20fr multicolored 18 15
517 A107 40fr green & multi 30 15
518 A107 50fr blue & multi 40 15
Nos. 516-518 (3) 88
Set value 36

1971, Mar. 21 ***Perf. 13x12½***

Design: 30fr, Hands and globe.

519 A108 20fr green & multi 18 15
520 A108 30fr ultra & multi 25 15
Set value 15

Intl. year against racial discrimination.

Crowned Cranes at Waza Camp A109

Designs: 20fr, Canoe on Sanaga River. 30fr, Sanaga River.

1971, Apr. 9. **Engr.** ***Perf. 13***

521 A109 10fr red, grn & blk 15 15
522 A109 20fr dk grn, brn & red 18 15
523 A109 30fr red, dk grn & brt bl 22 15
Nos. 521-523 (3) 55
Set value 18

International Court, The Hague A110

1971, June 14 **Engr.** ***Perf. 13***

524 A110 50fr ultra, org brn & sl grn 40 16

25th anniversary of the International Court in The Hague, Netherlands.

Liana Bridge — A111

Bamoun Horseman — A113

Local Market A112

1971, Aug. 16 **Photo.** ***Perf. 13***

525 A111 40fr multi 35 15
526 A112 45fr multi 38 15

1971, Sept. 18

African Art: 15fr, Animal fetish statuette.

527 A113 10fr brown & yellow 15 15
528 A113 15fr dp brn & org yel 15 15
Set value 20 15

Communications Satellite and Globe — A114

1971, Oct. 14 *Perf. 13x12½*
529 A114 40fr Prus bl, sl grn & org 30 15

Pan-African telecommunications system.

UNICEF Emblem A115

Design: 50fr, UNICEF emblem and grain, vert.

1971, Dec. 11 **Engr.** *Perf. 13*
530 A115 40fr sl grn, bl grn & plum 40 20
531 A115 50fr dp bl, dk red & lt grn 60 25

25th anniv. of UNICEF.

Houses from South-Central Region A116

Design: 15fr, Adamaua round houses.

1972, Jan. 15 **Photo.** *Perf. 13*
532 A116 10fr dk blue & multi 15 15
533 A116 15fr black & multi 15 15
Set value 21 15

Giraffe — A117

Designs: 5fr, Home industries. 10fr, Smith, horiz. 15fr, Women carrying burdens.

Perf. 13x13½, 13½x13
1972, Feb. 18 **Litho.**
534 A117 2fr multicolored 15 15
535 A117 5fr black, org & red 15 15
536 A117 10fr multicolored 15 15
537 A117 15fr multicolored 16 15
Set value 43 22

Youth Day 1972.

Soccer Players and Field A118

Designs: 20fr, African Soccer Cup, vert. 45fr, Team captains shaking hands, vert.

1972, Feb. 22 *Perf. 13½*
538 A118 20fr gray & multi 16 15
539 A118 40fr gray & multi 35 20
540 A118 45fr yellow & multi 40 22
Nos. 538-540 (3) 91 57

African Soccer Cup, Yaoundé, Feb. 23-Mar. 5.

Government Building, Yaoundé, and Laurel A119

1972, Apr. 6 **Photo.** *Perf. 12½x12*
541 A119 40fr multicolored 22 15

110th session of Inter-Parliamentary Council, Yaoundé, Apr. 1972.

"Fantasia," North Cameroun A120

Bororo Woman — A121

Design: 40fr, Boat on Wouri River and Mt. Cameroun.

Perf. 13x12½, 12½x13
1972, Apr. 24
542 A120 15fr dk vio & multi 16 15
543 A121 20fr multicolored 16 15
544 A120 40fr multicolored 25 15
Nos. 542-544 (3) 57
Set value 28

Chemical Apparatus A122

1972, May 15 **Engr.** *Perf. 13*
545 A122 40fr lilac, red & grn 22 15

President Ahmadou Ahidjo Prize.

United Republic

Solanum Macranthum A123

Design: 45fr, Wax plant.

1972, July 20 **Photo.** *Perf. 13*
546 A123 40fr multicolored 25 15
547 A123 45fr yellow & multi 28 15

Charaxes Ameliae A124

Design: 45fr, Papilio tynderaeus.

1972, Aug. 20 **Photo.** *Perf. 13*
548 A124 40fr bl, dk bl & gold 35 16
549 A124 45fr lt grn, blk & gold 38 20

No. 468 Surcharged

40 F

1972, Aug. 30 **Photo.** *Perf. 12x12½*
550 A85 40fr on 30fr multi 25 15

Resurrection Lily — A125

Great Blue Touraco — A126

Flowers: 45fr, Candlestick cassia. 50fr, Amaryllis.

1972, Sept. 16 *Perf. 13*
551 A125 40fr lt green & multi 25 15
552 A125 45fr multicolored 30 16
553 A125 50fr lt blue & multi 38 20
Nos. 551-553 (3) 93 51

Perf. 12½x13, 13x12½
1972, Nov. 20 **Litho.**

Design: 45fr, Red-faced lovebirds, horiz.

554 A126 10fr yellow & multi 15 15
555 A126 45fr yellow & multi 30 15
Set value 19

Cotton (North) — A127

Designs: 10fr, Cacao (south central). 15fr, Logging (southeast and southern coast). 20fr, Coffee (west). 45fr, Tea (northwest and southwest).

1973, Mar. 26 **Photo.** *Perf. 12½x13*
556 A127 5fr black & multi 15 15
557 A127 10fr black & multi 15 15
558 A127 15fr black & multi 15 15
559 A127 20fr black & multi 15 15
560 A127 45fr black & multi 30 15
Set value 60 40

Third 5-Year Plan.
For surcharge see No. 568.

Flag and Map of Cameroun, Pres. Ahidjo and No. 331 — A128

Design: 20fr, Proclamation of independence, Pres. Ahidjo and No. 336.

1973, May 20 **Engr.** *Perf. 13*
561 A128 10fr ultra & multi 15 15
562 A128 20fr multicolored 15 15
Set value 21 15

First anniversary of the United Republic of Cameroun. See Nos. C200-C201.

Bamoun Mask — A129

Dr. Hansen — A130

Designs: Various Bamoun masks.

1973, July 10 **Engr.** *Perf. 13*
563 A129 5fr green, brn & blk 15 15
564 A129 10fr lilac, brn & blk 15 15
565 A129 45fr red, brn & blk 22 15
566 A129 100fr ultra, brn & blk 55 35
Set value 89 59

1973, July 25 **Engr.** *Perf. 13*
567 A130 45fr multicolored 25 15

Centenary of the discovery by Dr. Armauer G. Hansen of the Hansen bacillus, the cause of leprosy.

No. 556 Surcharged with New Value, 2 Bars, and Overprinted in Ultramarine: "SECHERESSE/SOLIDARITE AFRICAINE"

1973, Aug. 16 **Photo.** *Perf. 12½x13*
568 A127 100fr on 5fr multi 55 40

African solidarity in drought emergency.

Dancers, South West Africa — A131

WMO Emblem — A132

Designs: Southwest African dances.

1973, Aug. 17 *Perf. 13*
569 A131 10fr multi 15 15
570 A131 25fr multi 15 15
571 A131 45fr multi 30 15
Set value 49 29

1973, Sept. 1 **Engr.** *Perf. 13*
572 A132 45fr green & ultra 25 16

Cent. of intl. meteorological cooperation.

Garoua Party Headquarters — A133

1973, Sept. 1 **Photo.**
573 A133 40fr multicolored 25 16

7th anniv. of Cameroun National Union.

African Postal Union Issue, 1973
Common Design Type

1973, Sept. 12 **Engr.**
574 CD137 100fr brt bl, bl & sl grn 60 40

Avocados — A135

1973, Sept. 20
575 A135 10fr shown 15 15
576 A135 20fr Mangos 16 15
577 A135 45fr Plums 30 15
578 A135 50fr Custard apple 42 16
Nos. 575-578 (4) 1.03
Set value 44

Kirdi Village A136

Views: 45fr, Mabas village. 50fr, Fishing village.

1973, Oct. 25 **Engr.** ***Perf. 13***
579 A136 15fr black, bis & grn 15 15
580 A136 45fr magenta, brn & org 30 16
581 A136 50fr green, blk & org 35 20
Nos. 579-581 (3) 80 51

Handshake on Map of Africa — A137

1974, May 15 **Engr.** ***Perf. 12½x13***
582 A137 40fr carmine & multi 22 15
583 A137 45fr indigo & multi 25 15

10th anniversary of the Organization for African Unity.

Spinning Mill — A138

1974, May 25 **Engr.** ***Perf. 13x12½***
584 A138 45fr multicolored 25 16

CICAM Industrial Complex.

Carved Panel from Bilinga A139

Cameroun Art (Carvings): 40fr, Detail from Bubinga chair. 45fr, Detail Acajou Ngollon panel.

1974, May 30
585 A139 10fr brt grn & ocher 15 15
586 A139 40fr red & brown 22 15
587 A139 45fr blue & rose brn 25 16
Nos. 585-587 (3) 62
Set value 35

Zebu — A140

1974, June 1 ***Perf. 13½***
588 A140 40fr multicolored 22 15

North Cameroun cattle raising. See No. C210.

Laying Rail Section A141

Designs: 5fr, Map showing line Yaoundé to Ngaoundéré, vert. 40fr, Welding rail joint, vert. 100fr, Train on Djerem River Bridge.

Perf. 12½x13, 13x12½
1974, June 10 **Engr.**
589 A141 5fr multi 15 15
590 A141 20fr multi 15 15
591 A141 40fr multi 22 15
592 A141 100fr multi 50 42
Nos. 589-592 (4) 1.02
Set value 68

Opening of Yaoundé-Ngaoundéré railroad line. For surcharge see No. 596.

No. 466 Surcharged

1974, June 1 **Photo.** ***Perf. 12x12½***
593 A85 40fr on 8fr multi 25 15

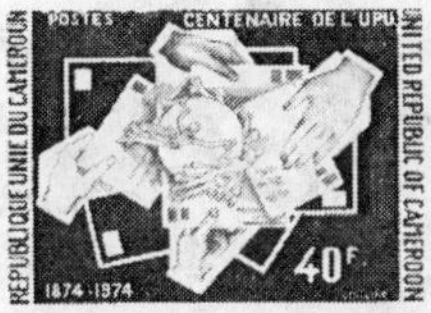

UPU Emblem, Hands Holding Letters A142

1974, Oct. 8 **Engr.** ***Perf. 13***
594 A142 40fr multicolored 20 15

Cent. of the UPU. See Nos. C218-C219.

Presidents and Flags of Cameroun, CAR, Congo, Gabon and Meeting Center — A143

1974, Dec. 8 **Photo.** ***Perf. 13***
595 A143 40fr gold & multi 22 15

10th anniversary of Central African Customs and Economic Union (Union Douanière et Economique de l'Afrique Centrale, UDEAC). See No. C223.

= 100F

No. 589 Surcharged in Violet Blue

10 DECEMBRE
1974

1974, Dec. 10 **Engr.** ***Perf. 12½x13***
596 A141 100fr on 5fr multi 55 45

Virgin of Autun, 15th Century Sculpture A144

Christmas: 45fr, Virgin and Child, by Luis de Morales (c. 1509-1586).

1974, Dec. 20 **Photo.** ***Perf. 13***
597 A144 40fr gold & multi 22 16
598 A144 45fr gold & multi 25 20

Tropical Plants — A145

1975, Mar. 10 **Photo.** ***Perf. 13***
599 A145 5fr Cockscomb 15 15
600 A145 40fr Costus spectabilis 22 15
601 A145 45fr Mussaenda erythrophylla 25 16
Set value 52 35

Fishing by Night — A146

1975, Apr. 1 **Engr.** ***Perf. 13***
602 A146 40fr shown 22 15
603 A146 45fr Fishing by day 25 16

Afo Akom Statue and Chief's Stool — A147

Tree Fungus — A148

1975, Apr. 1 **Photo.**
604 A147 40fr multi 20 15
605 A147 45fr multi 22 15
606 A147 200fr multi 1.10 75
Nos. 604-606 (3) 1.52 1.05

1975, Apr. 14
607 A148 15fr shown 15 15
608 A148 40fr Chrysalis 25 15
Set value 22

Ministry of Posts and Telecommunications — A149

1975, July 21 **Engr.** ***Perf. 13***
609 A149 40fr brn, grn & Prus bl 22 16
610 A149 45fr Prus bl, brn & grn 25 20

Presbyterian Church, Elat — A150

Designs: No. 612, Foumban Mosque. 45fr, Catholic Church, Ngaoundere.

1975, Aug. 20 **Engr.** ***Perf. 13***
611 A150 40fr multi 20 15
612 A150 40fr multi 20 15
613 A150 45fr multi 25 16
Nos. 611-613 (3) 65 46

Plowing A151

Design: No. 615, Corn harvest, vert.

Perf. 13x12½, 12½x13
1975, Dec. 15 **Photo.**
614 A151 40fr deep green & multi 20 15
615 A151 40fr deep green & multi 20 15

Green revolution.

Zamengoe Satellite Monitoring Station — A152

1976, May 20 **Litho.** ***Perf. 13***
616 A152 40fr shown 20 16
617 A152 100fr Radar, vert. 60 40

Porcelain Rose — A153

Design: 50fr, Flower of North Cameroun.

1976, July 20 **Litho.** ***Perf. 12½***
618 A153 40fr multicolored 20 15
619 A153 50fr multicolored 25 16

Leopard Dance — A154

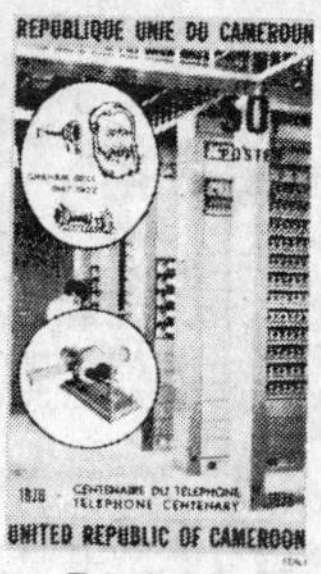

Telephone Exchange — A155

1976, Sept. 15 Litho. *Perf. 12*

620 A154 40fr gray & multi		20	16

See Nos. C233-C234.

1976, Oct. 5 ***Perf. 13***

621 A155 50fr multicolored		30	20

Centenary of first telephone call by Alexander Graham Bell, Mar. 10, 1876.

Young Men Building House — A156

Design: 45fr, Young women working in field.

1976, Oct. 10 Litho. *Perf. 12*

622 A156 40fr multicolored		20	16
623 A156 45fr multicolored		25	16

10th National Youth Day.

Konrad Adenauer (1876-1967), German Chancellor, Cologne Cathedral — A157

1976, Oct. 20

624 A157 100fr multicolored		60	40

Party Headquarters, Douala — A158

Design: No. 626, Party Headquarters, Yaoundé.

1976, Dec. 28 Litho. *Perf. 12*

625 A158 50fr orange & multi		25	20
626 A158 50fr blue & multi		25	20

10th anniv. of the Cameroun National Union.

Bamoun Copper Pipe — A159

Ostrich — A160

1977, Feb. 4 Litho. *Perf. 12½*

627 A159 50fr multicolored		25	20

2nd World Black and African Festival, Lagos, Nigeria, Jan. 15-Feb. 12. See No. C239.

1977, Mar. 20 Litho. *Perf. 12*

628 A160 30fr shown		16	15
629 A160 50fr Crowned cranes		25	16

Cameroun No. 609 and Switzerland No. 3L1 — A161

1977, June 5 Litho. *Perf. 12*

630 A161 50fr multicolored		25	20

Jufilex Philatelic Exhibition, Bern, Switzerland. See Nos. C252-C253.

Winter Olympics 1976, set of five, 40, 50fr, airmail 140, 200, 350fr, and airmail souv. sheet, 500fr, issued Aug. 10, 1977. Nos. 7701-7706.

Apollo-Soyuz, set of five, 40, 60fr, airmail 100, 250, 350fr, and airmail souv. sheet, 500fr, issued Aug. 10, 1977. Nos. 7707-7712.

No. 617 Overprinted in French and English in Red: "To the Welfare of the / families of martyrs and / freedom fighters of Palestine."

1977, Aug. 22 Litho. *Perf. 13*

635 A152 100fr multicolored		60	40

Palestinian fighters and their families.

Chairman Mao and Great Wall — A164

1977, Sept. 9 Engr. *Perf. 13*

636 A164 100fr olive & brown		60	40

Mao Tse-tung (1893-1976), Chinese communist leader, first death anniversary.

Nativity, by Albrecht Altdorfer A165

Design: 50fr, Madonna of the Grand Duke, by Raphael.

1977, Dec. 15 Litho. *Perf. 12½x12*

637 A165 30fr multicolored		16	15
638 A165 50fr multicolored		25	20

Christmas 1977. See Nos. C264-C265.

Gazelle and Rotary Emblem — A166

Pres. Ahidjo, Flag and Map of Cameroun — A167

1978, Feb. 11 Litho. *Perf. 12*

639 A166 50fr orange & multi		25	20

Rotary Club of Yaounde, 20th anniversary.

1978, Apr. 3 Litho. *Perf. 12½*

640 A167 50fr multicolored		25	15

New flag of Cameroun. See No. C266.

Cardioglossa Escalerae A168

Design: 60fr, Cardioglossa elegans.

1978, Apr. 5

641 A168 50fr multicolored		25	16
642 A168 60fr multicolored		35	22

See No. C267.

Jules Verne and "From Earth to Moon" — A169

1978, Oct. 10 Litho. *Perf. 12*

643 A169 250fr multicolored		1.60	1.40

Jules Verne (1828-1905), science fiction writer, birth sesquicentennial. See No. C276.

Hypolimnas Salmacis Drury — A170

Butterflies: 25fr, Euxanthe trajanus ward. 30fr, Euphaedra cyparissa cramer.

1978, Oct. 15

644 A170 20fr multi		15	15
645 A170 25fr multi		16	15
646 A170 30fr multi		20	15
Nos. 644-646 (3)		51	45

Men Planting Seedlings — A171

Carved Bamun Drum — A172

1978, Oct. 30 ***Perf. 12½***

647 A171 10fr multi		15	15
648 A171 15fr multi		15	15
Set value		17	15

Green barrier against the desert.

1978, Nov. 20 Litho. *Perf. 12½*

Designs: 60fr, String instrument (Gueguerou) horiz.

649 A172 50fr multi		35	20
650 A172 60fr multi		40	25

See No. C277.

Pres. Ahidjo, Giscard D'Estaing, Flags of Cameroun and France — A173

1979, Feb. 8 Photo. *Perf. 13*

651 A173 60fr multi		40	25

Visit of Pres. Valery Giscard D'Estaing of France to Cameroun.

Human Rights Emblem, Globe, Scroll and African — A174

1979, Feb. 11 Litho. *Perf. 12x12½*

652 A174 5fr multi		15	15

Universal Declaration of Human Rights, 30th anniversary (in 1978). See No. C278.
See No. 803.

Boy and Girl Greeting Sun — A175

1979, Aug. 15 Litho. *Perf. 12*

653 A175 50fr multi	35	20

International Year of the Child.

Protected Animals A176

Nos. 655, 658 vert.

1979, Sept. 20 *Perf. 12½*

654 A176 50fr Rhinoceros	35	20
655 A176 60fr Giraffe	40	25
656 A176 60fr Gorilla	40	25
657 A176 100fr Leopard	65	40
658 A176 100fr Elephant	65	40
Nos. 654-658 (5)	2.45	1.50

Eugene Jamot, Map of Cameroun, Tsetse Fly — A177

1979, Nov. 5 Engr. *Perf. 13*

659 A177 50fr multi	35	20

Eugene Jamot (1879-1937), discoverer of sleeping sickness cure.

Annunciation, by Fra Filippo Lippi — A178

Paintings; 50fr, Rest During the Flight to Egypt, c. 1620. No. 622, Flight into Egypt, by Jan Joest, No. 663, Nativity, by Joest. 100fr, Nativity, by Botticelli.

1979, Dec. 6 Litho. *Perf. 12½x12*

660 A178 10fr multi	15	15
661 A178 50fr multi	38	22
662 A178 60fr multi	42	30
663 A178 60fr multi	42	30
a. Pair, #662-663	85	65
664 A178 100fr multi	70	42
Nos. 660-664 (5)	2.07	1.39

Christmas 1979.

Piper Capense A179

Medicinal Plants: 60fr, Bracken fern.

1979, Dec. 15 Litho. *Perf. 12½*

665 A179 50fr multi	35	20
666 A179 60fr multi	40	25

Pres. Ahidjo, Cameroun Map, Arms and No. 331 — A180

1980, Feb. 12 Litho. *Perf. 12½*

667 A180 50fr multi	35	20

Independence, 20th anniversary.

Congress Building, Bafoussam A181

1980, Feb. 12

668 A181 50fr multi	35	20

Cameroun National Union, 3rd Ordinary Congress, Bafoussam, Feb. 12-17.

Rotary Emblem, Map of Cameroun — A182

Rotary Intl., 75th Anniv.: #670, Anniv. emblem.

1980, Mar. 15 Litho. *Perf. 12½*

669 A182 200fr multi	1.40	80
670 A182 200fr multi	1.40	80
a. Souvenir sheet of 2, #669-670	2.75	1.60

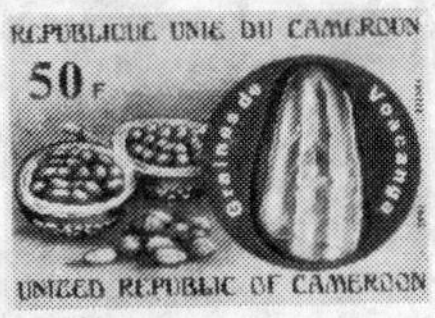

Voacanga Medicinal Beans A183

1980, Dec. 3 Litho. *Perf. 12½*

671 A183 50fr shown	35	20
672 A183 60fr Voacanga tree, vert.	40	25
673 A183 100fr Voacanga flower, vert.	65	40
Nos. 671-673 (3)	1.40	85

Violet Mellowstone A184

1980, Dec. 5

674 A184 50fr shown	40	20
675 A184 60fr Patula	45	25
676 A184 100fr Cashmere bouquet	80	40
Nos. 674-676 (3)	1.65	85

Occupation of Mecca by Mohammed, 1350th Anniversary — A185

1980, Dec. 9

677 A185 50fr multi	50	30

African Slender-snouted Crocodile (Endangered Species) — A186

1980, Dec. 24

678 A186 200fr shown	1.60	80
679 A186 300fr Buffon's antelope, vert.	2.00	1.20

Bororo Girls and Roumsiki Peaks — A187

1980, Dec. 29

680 A187 50fr shown	35	20
681 A187 60fr Dschang tourist center	40	25

Banana Tree A188

1981, Feb. 5

682 A188 50fr shown	50	30
683 A188 60fr Cattle, vert.	60	40

Girl on Crutches — A189

1981, Feb. 20 Litho. *Perf. 12½*

684 A189 60fr shown	40	25
685 A189 150fr Boy in motorized wheelchair	1.00	65

International Year of the Disabled.

Air Terminal, Douala Airport — A190

1981, Apr. 4 Litho. *Perf. 12½*

686 A190 100fr shown	75	55
687 A190 200fr Boeing 747	1.65	1.10
688 A190 300fr Douala Intl. Airport	2.50	1.65
Nos. 686-688 (3)	4.90	3.30

Cameroun Airlines, 10th anniv.

Pres. Ahidjo Presenting Trophy to Canon Soccer Team — A191

1981, Apr. 20

689 A191 60fr shown	60	40
690 A191 60fr Union team captain	60	40

1979 African Soccer Cup champions.

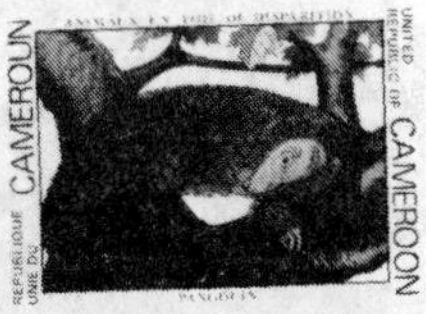

Scaly Anteater A192

Designs: Endangered species.

1981, July 20 Litho. *Perf. 12½*

691 A192 50fr Moutourou	35	20
692 A192 50fr Tortoise	35	20
693 A192 100fr shown	65	40
Nos. 691-693 (3)	1.35	80

Prince Charles and Lady Diana, St. Paul's Cathedral — A193

1981, July 29 Litho. *Perf. 12½*

694 A193 500fr shown	3.00	2.00
695 A193 500fr Couple, royal coach	3.00	2.00
a. Souvenir sheet of 2, #694-695	6.00	4.00

Royal wedding.

Bafoussam-Bamenda Highway — A194

1981, Sept. 10 **Litho.** ***Perf. 12½***

696 A194 50fr multi 35 20

Freighter Cam Iroko (Cameroun Shipping Line) A195

1981, Sept. 25

697 A195 60fr multi 60 40

20th Anniv. of Reunification A196

1981, Oct. 10 ***Perf. 12½x13***

698 A196 50fr multi 35 20

Medicinal Plants — A197

1981, Dec. 31 **Litho.** ***Perf. 12½***

699 A197 60fr Voacanga thouarsii 40 25
700 A197 70fr Cassia alata 45 30

Easter 1982 — A198

Paintings: 100fr, Christ in the Garden of Olives, by Delacroix. 200fr, Descent from the Cross, by Giotto. 250fr, Pieta in the Countryside, by Bellini.

1982, Apr. 10 **Litho.** ***Perf. 13***

701 A198 100fr multi 55 35
702 A198 200fr multi 1.00 65
703 A198 250fr multi 1.40 90
Nos. 701-703 (3) 2.95 1.90

PHILEXFRANCE '82 Stamp Exhibition, Paris, June 11-21 — A199

1982, Apr. 25 ***Perf. 12***

704 A199 90fr multi 60 40

Snakeskin Handbag — A200

1982, Apr. 30 ***Perf. 12½***

705 A200 60fr shown 40 25
706 A200 70fr Clay water jug 45 35

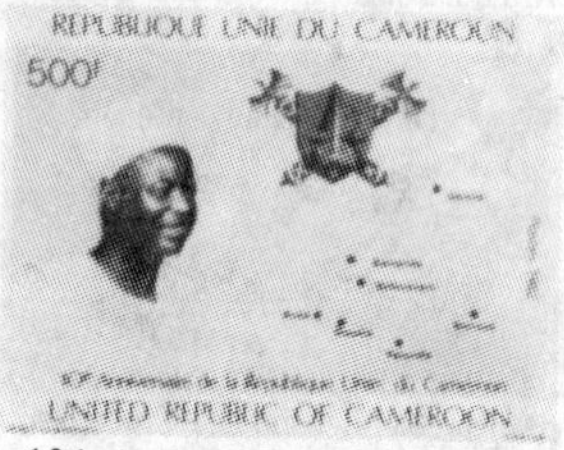

10th Anniv. of Republic — A201

1982, May 20 ***Perf. 13***

707 A201 500fr multi 3.50 2.00

Town Hall, Douala — A202

1982, June 15 **Litho.** ***Perf. 12½***

708 A202 40fr shown 25 20
709 A202 60fr Yaounde 40 25

See Nos. 730-731, 757-758, 790-791, 867.

1982 World Cup — A203

1982, July 10 ***Perf. 13***

710 A203 100fr Natl. team 65 42
711 A203 200fr Semi-finalists 1.40 80
712 A203 300fr Players, vert. 2.00 1.25
713 A203 400fr Natl. team 2nd lineup 2.50 1.60
a. Souvenir sheet of 2, #713 6.00 3.50
Nos. 710-713 (4) 6.55 4.07

Partridge — A204

1982 ***Perf. 12½x13***

714 A204 10fr shown 15 15
715 A204 15fr Turtle dove 15 15
716 A204 20fr Swallow 15 15
717 A204 200fr Bongo antelope 1.40 80
718 A204 300fr Black colobus 2.00 1.25
Nos. 714-718 (5) 3.85 2.50

Issued: 200fr, 300fr, July 20; others Aug. 10.
See No. 804.

Scouting Year — A205

1982, Sept. 30 **Litho.** ***Perf. 13x12½***

719 A205 200fr Campfire 1.10 80
720 A205 400fr Baden-Powell 2.25 1.60

25th Anniv. of the Presbyterian Church in Cameroun A206

Perf. 13x12½, 12½x13

1982, Oct. 30

721 A206 45fr Buea Chapel 22 15
722 A206 60fr Nyasoso Chapel, vert. 30 20

ITU Plenipotentiaries Conference, Nairobi, Sept. — A207

1982, Oct. 5 **Litho.** ***Perf. 12½x13***

723 A207 70fr multi 35 22

Italy's Victory in 1982 World Cup — A208

1982, Nov. ***Perf. 13***

724 A208 500fr multi 4.00 2.00
725 A208 1000fr multi 7.00 4.00

30th Anniv. of Customs Cooperation Council — A209

1983, Jan. 10 ***Perf. 12½x13***

726 A209 250fr Emblem 1.40 80
727 A209 250fr Headquarters, Brussels 1.40 80

2nd Yaoundé Medical Conference — A210

1983, Jan. 23 **Litho.** ***Perf. 13***

728 A210 60fr grn & multi 45 20
729 A210 70fr brn & multi 55 22

City Hall Type of 1982

1983, Feb. 25 **Litho.** ***Perf. 12½***

730 A202 60fr Bafoussam 40 25
731 A202 70fr Garoua 45 30

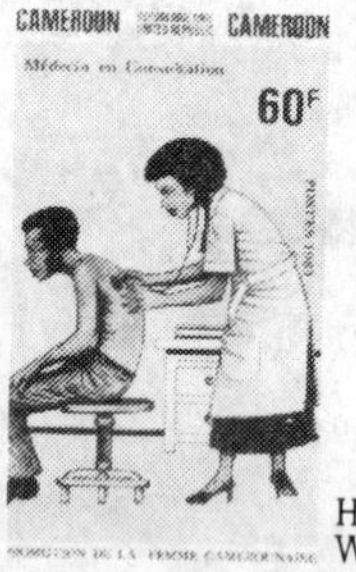

Homage to Women — A211

1983, Apr. 25 **Litho.** ***Perf. 12½***

733 A211 60fr Nurse 40 20
734 A211 70fr Lawyer 45 22

11th Anniv. of Independence — A212

Flag and Pres. Paul Biya.

1983, May 18 **Litho.** ***Perf. 13***

735 A212 60fr dk grn & multi 40 25
736 A212 70fr dk bl & multi 45 30

25th Anniv. of Intl. Maritime Org. — A213

1983, May 23 ***Perf. 13x12½***

737 A213 500fr multi 2.50 1.50

Eagle — A214

1983, June 15 Litho. *Perf. 12½x13*

738	A214 25fr	shown	16	15
739	A214 30fr	Sparrowhawk	20	15
740	A214 50fr	Purple heron	35	20
		Nos. 738-740 (3)	71	50

See Nos. 798-800, 873, 882, 886.

A215

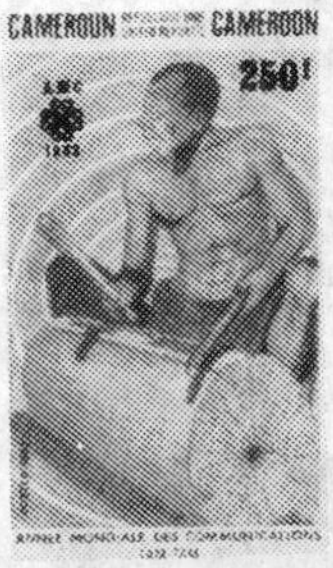

A216

1983, July 25 Litho. *Perf. 12*

741	A215 60fr	Pearl mask, by Wery-Nwen-Nto, 1899	40	25
742	A215 70fr	Basket with lid	45	30

1983, Aug. 20 Litho. *Perf. 12*

743	A216 90fr	Mobile Post Office, horiz	30	20
744	A216 150fr	Telegraph Operator	50	35
745	A216 250fr	Tom-Tom	80	55
		Nos. 743-745 (3)	1.60	1.10

World Communications Year.

Endangered Species — A217

1983, Sept. 22 *Perf. 12*

746	A217 200fr	Civet Cat	80	42
747	A217 200fr	Gorilla, vert	80	42
748	A217 350fr	Cobaya, vert	1.40	80
		Nos. 746-748 (3)	3.00	1.64

See No. 887.

Lake Tizon A218

1983, Nov. 25 Litho. *Perf. 13*

749	A218 60fr	shown	20	15
750	A218 70fr	Mt. Cameroon	22	16

Human Rights Declaration, 35th Anniv — A219

1983, Dec. 20 Litho. *Perf. 12½x13*

751	A219 60fr	multi	20	15
752	A219 70fr	multi	22	16

Christmas 1983 — A220

Designs: 60fr, Christmas tree. 200fr, Stained glass window, Yaoundé Cathedral. No. 755, Rest during Flight into Egypt, by Philipp Otto Runge. No. 756, Angel of the Annunciation. 60fr, 200fr, No. 756 vert.

1983, Dec. 20 Litho. *Perf. 12½*

753	A220 60fr	multi	22	15
754	A220 200fr	multi	80	50
755	A220 500fr	multi	2.00	1.20
756	A220 500fr	multi	2.00	1.20
a.		Souvenir sheet of 3, #754-756	5.00	3.25
		Nos. 753-756 (4)	5.02	3.05

City Hall Type of 1982

1984, Apr. 20 Litho. *Perf. 12½*

757	A202 60fr	Bamenda	30	20
758	A202 70fr	Mbalmayo	35	22

Catholic Church, Zoetele — A221

1984, July 25 Litho. *Perf. 13*

759	A221 60fr	shown	30	22
760	A221 70fr	Protestant Church, Yaounde	35	25

Endangered Species — A222

1984, Aug. 15

761	A222 250fr	Wild pig	1.00	65
762	A222 250fr	Deer	1.00	65

1984, Oct. 10 Litho. *Perf. 13½*

763	A222 60fr	Nightingale	18	15
764	A222 60fr	Vultures	18	15

See No. 883.

Bamenda Farming Fair — A223

1984, Dec. 10 Litho. *Perf. 13*

765	A223 60fr	Corn	28	20
766	A223 70fr	Cattle	32	22
767	A223 300fr	Potatoes	1.35	90
		Nos. 765-767 (3)	1.95	1.32

International Civil Aviation Organization, 40th Anniv. — A224

1984, Dec. 20 Litho. *Perf. 12½*

768	A224 200fr	Icarus	90	60
769	A224 200fr	ICAO emblem, vert.	90	60
770	A224 300fr	Boeing 747	1.35	90
771	A224 300fr	Solar Princess painting	1.35	90
		Nos. 768-771 (4)	4.50	3.00

Olymphilex '85, Lausanne — A225

Wmk. CARTOR

1985, Apr. 5 Photo. *Perf. 13*

772	A225 150fr	Wrestlers, exhibition emblem	42	42

Domestic Musical Instruments — A226

1985, Apr. 23 *Perf. 13½*

773	A226 60fr	Balafons (xylophone)	16	16
774	A226 70fr	Guitar	20	20
775	A226 100fr	Flute	28	28
		Nos. 773-775 (3)	64	64

INTELSAT Org., 20th Anniv. — A227

1985, May 8 *Perf. 13*

776	A227 125fr	Intelsat V	35	35
777	A227 200fr	Intelcam, Yaounde	60	60

New York Headquarters A228

UN, 40th Anniv.

1985, May 30

778	A228 250fr	multi	1.10	1.10
779	A228 500fr	multi	2.25	2.25

Pres. Mitterand, Biya — A229

1985, June 20

780	A229 60fr	multi	20	20
781	A229 70fr	multi	22	22

Visit of Pres. Mitterand of France.

UNICEF A230

UN Infant Survival Campaign A231

1985, July 15

782	A230 60fr	multi	20	20
783	A231 300fr	multi	1.00	1.00

Visit of Pope John Paul II, Aug. 10-14 — A232

1985, Aug. 9 *Perf. 13x12½*

784	A232 60fr	Pope, papal arms	20	20
785	A232 70fr	Pope, crosier	22	22

Size: 60x40mm

786 A232 300fr Pres. Biya, John Paul II 90 90
a. Souv. sheet of 3, #784-786 1.40 1.40
Nos. 784-786 (3) 1.32 1.32

Landscapes — A233

1985, July 25 Litho. *Perf. 12½*

787 A233 60fr Lake Barumbi, Kumba 16 16
788 A233 70fr Bonando Pygmy Village, Doume 18 18
789 A233 150fr Cameroun River 40 40
Nos. 787-789 (3) 74 74

City Hall Type of 1982

1985, July 30

790 A202 60fr Ngaoundere 16 16
791 A202 60fr D'Ebolowa 16 16

Wildlife — A234

Wood Sculptures — A235

1985, Aug. 20 *Perf. 13½*

792 A234 125fr Porcupine 38 38
793 A234 200fr Squirrel 60 60
794 A234 350fr Hedgehog 1.10 1.10
Nos. 792-794 (3) 2.08 2.08

1985, Sept. 15

795 A235 60fr Mask 20 20
796 A235 70fr Mask, diff. 22 22
797 A235 100fr Wood bas-relief, horiz. 30 30
Nos. 795-797 (3) 72 72

Bird Type of 1983
Inscribed Republic of Cameroon

1985, Nov. 10

798 A214 140fr Toucans 50 50
799 A214 150fr Rooster 55 55
800 A214 200fr Red-throated bee-eater 70 70
Nos. 798-800 (3) 1.75 1.75

See No. 873. For surcharge see No. 871.

American Peace Corps in Cameroun, 25th Anniv. — A237

1986, Jan. 1 Litho. *Perf. 12½*

801 A237 70fr multi 38 38
802 A237 100fr multi 55 55

Stamps of 1979-1982 Redrawn

1986, Mar. *Perf. 13, 13½*

803 A174 5fr multi 15 15
804 A204 10fr multi 15 15
Set value 15 15

Nos. 803-804 inscribed "Republic of Cameroon" instead of "United Republic of Cameroon."

Easter — A238

Insects — A239

Paintings: 210fr, Head of the Virgin, by Pierre-Paul Prud'Hon (1758-1823). 350fr, The Stoning of St. Steven, by Van Scorel (1495-1562).

1986, Apr. 15 *Perf. 13½*

805 A238 210fr multi 1.15 1.15
806 A238 350fr multi 1.90 1.90

1986, Apr. 20

807 A239 70fr Honeybee 38 38
808 A239 70fr Dragonfly 38 38
809 A239 100fr Grasshopper 55 55
Nos. 807-809 (3) 1.31 1.31

Nos. 808-809 horiz.

Flags, Conference Center — A240

1986, Apr. 25 Litho. *Perf. 13*

810 A240 100fr Map, vert. 55 55
811 A240 175fr shown 95 95

Conference of Ministers of the Economic Commission for Africa, Apr. 9-29.

Statues — A241

1986, July 5 Litho. *Perf. 13½*

812 A241 70fr Bronze earth mother 40 40
813 A241 100fr Wood funerary figure 60 60
814 A241 130fr Wood equestrian figure 80 80
Nos. 812-814 (3) 1.80 1.80

Queen Elizabeth II, 60th Birthday — A242

1986, July 15 Litho. *Perf. 13*

815 A242 100fr Elizabeth 60 60
816 A242 175fr Elizabeth, Pres. Biya 1.10 1.10
817 A242 210fr Elizabeth, diff. 1.25 1.25
Nos. 815-817 (3) 2.95 2.95

Natl. Democratic Party, 1st Anniv. — A243

1986, July 25 *Perf. 12½*

818 A243 70fr Party headquarters, Bamenda 40 40
819 A243 70fr Pres. Biya, vert. 40 40
820 A243 100fr Presidential address, vert. 60 60
Nos. 818-820 (3) 1.40 1.40

Kwem Mask Dancers of the Northeast — A244

1986, Aug. 1 *Perf. 13½*

821 A244 100fr multi 60 60
822 A244 130fr multi 80 80

Endangered Species A245

1986, Aug. 20

823 A245 300fr Varanus niloticus 1.75 1.75
824 A245 300fr Panthera pardus 1.75 1.75

For surcharge see No. 872.

A246

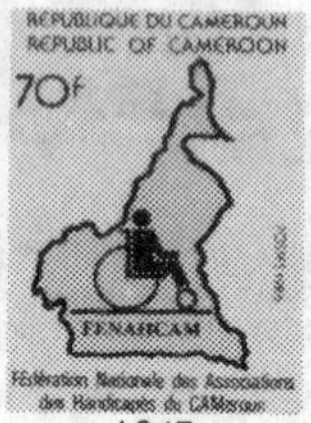

A247

Intl. Peace Year: 175fr, 200fr, Desmond Tutu, South Africa, Nobel Peace Prize winner. 250fr, UN and IPY emblems.

1986, Sept. 7 Litho. *Perf. 13½*

825 A246 175fr multi 1.10 1.10
826 A246 200fr multi 1.25 1.25
827 A246 250fr multi 1.50 1.50
Nos. 825-827 (3) 3.85 3.85

1986, Oct. 30 Litho. *Perf. 13½*

828 A247 70fr multi 40 40

Natl. Federation of Associations for the Handicapped.

A248

A249

1986, Nov. 9

829 A248 70fr Family under umbrella 40 40
830 A248 100fr Child immunization 55 55

African Vaccination Year.

1986, Dec. 20 Litho. *Perf. 13½*

831 A249 70fr Afforestation map 40 40
832 A249 100fr Hands, seedling 55 55

Arbor Day.

Agricultural Development — A250

1986, Dec. 24

833 A250 70fr ONCPB seminar 40 40
834 A250 70fr Coconut farming, Dibombari 40 40
835 A250 200fr Pineapple farm 1.10 1.10
Nos. 833-835 (3) 1.90 1.90

Insects Destructive to Agriculture A251

1987, Sept. 25 Litho. *Perf. 13½*

836 A251 70fr Antestiopsis lineaticollis intricata 50 50
837 A251 100fr Distantiella theobroma 72 72

4th African Games, Nairobi — A252

1987, Oct. 1 *Perf. 12½*

838 A252 100fr Shot put 72 72
839 A252 140fr Pole vault 1.00 1.00

Maroua Agricultural Show — A253

1988, Jan. 6

840 A253 70fr Millet field 50 50
841 A253 100fr Cotton 72 72
842 A253 150fr Cattle 1.10 1.10
Nos. 840-842 (3) 2.32 2.32

World Wildlife Fund — A254

Baboons, *Papio leucophaeus.*

1988, Apr. 25 **Litho.** *Perf. 13*
843 A254 30fr Adult 22 22
844 A254 40fr Adult grooming young 30 30
845 A254 70fr Baboon on branch 50 50
846 A254 100fr Adult carrying young 72 72
Nos. 843-846 (4) 1.74 1.74

Interparliamentary Union, Cent. — A255

1989 **Litho.** *Perf. 13½*
847 A255 50fr Natl. Assembly 32 32

World Cup Soccer Championships, Italy — A256

1990, Oct. 27 **Litho.** *Perf. 11½*
Granite Paper
848 A256 200fr shown 1.15 1.15
849 A256 250fr Players, diff. 1.45 1.45
850 A256 250fr Goalkeeper, flags 1.45 1.45
851 A256 300fr Team 1.70 1.70
a. Souv. sheet of 4, #848-851 7.60 7.60
Nos. 848-851 (4) 5.75 5.75

Roger Milla, World Cup Soccer Player — A257

1990, July 4 **Litho.** *Perf. 11½*
Granite Paper
852 A257 500fr multicolored 4.00 4.00
a. Souv. sheet of 1 4.00 4.00

Agriculture A258

Designs: 70fr, Treating cacao plants. 100fr, Sheep.

1990, Dec. 1 **Litho.** *Perf. 13½*
853 A258 70fr multicolored 55 55
854 A258 100fr multicolored 80 80
a. Sheet of 2, #853-854, perf. 12½ 1.35 1.35

UN Development Program, 40th Anniv. A259

1990, Dec. 31 **Litho.** *Perf. 13½*
855 A259 50fr multicolored 40 40

Intl. Literacy Year — A260

1990, Dec. 31
856 A260 200fr bl, blk, & lt bl 1.60 1.60

Independence, 30th Anniv. — A261

1991, Jan. 1 *Perf. 13*
857 A261 150fr shown 1.20 1.20
858 A261 1000fr Flag, Palace, #336 7.90 7.90
a. Souv. sheet. of 2, #857-858 9.10 9.10

Fight Against AIDS — A262

1991, Jan. 15
859 A262 15fr Hearts, map, vert. 15 15
860 A262 25fr shown 20 20

See Nos. 884-885.

Birds A263

Designs: Nos. 861, 864, Pie grieche, vert. Nos. 862, 863, Picathartes chauve.

1991, May 3 **Litho.** *Perf. 13½*
861 A263 70fr grn & multi 55 55
862 A263 70fr bl & multi 55 55
863 A263 300fr blk & multi 2.40 2.40
864 A263 350fr blk & multi 2.75 2.75
a. Souv. sheet of 2, #863-864 5.25 5.25
Nos. 861-864 (4) 6.25 6.25

Wild Animals A264

1991, May 8 *Perf. 13½*
865 A264 125fr Elephant 1.00 1.00
866 A264 250fr Water buffalo 2.00 2.00
a. Souvenir sheet of 2, #865-866, perf. 12½ 3.00 3.00

City Hall Type of 1982 Redrawn

1991 *Perf. 13*
867 A202 40fr multi 25 20

No. 867 inscribed "Republic of Cameroon" instead of "United Republic of Cameroon."

Cameroun Catholic Church, Cent. (in 1990) A265

1991, Dec. 8 **Litho.** *Perf. 13½*
868 A265 125fr Mvolye church 1.00 1.00
869 A265 250fr Akono church 2.00 2.00
a. Souvenir sheet of 2, #868-869 perf. 12½x13 3.00 3.00

Intl. Savings Banks Institute, 7th Meeting of the African Group A266

1991, Dec. 9
870 A266 250fr multicolored 2.00 2.00
a. Souv. sheet of 1, perf. 12½x13 2.00 2.00

Nos. 799 & 824 Surcharged

20 F **70 F**

1992 *Perf. 13½*
871 A214 20fr on 150fr #799 16 16
872 A245 70fr on 300fr #824 55 55

Bird Type of 1983

1992 **Litho.** *Perf. 13½*
873 A214 125fr like #800 95 95

Dated 1985.

Cameroun Soccer League — A267

Designs: 125fr, Mbappe Mbappe Samuel (1936-1985), soccer player, vert. 250fr, Linafoote League emblem, vert. 400fr, Linafoote emblem, diff. 500fr, Stadium.

1992, Aug. *Perf. 11½*
874 A267 125fr multicolored 95 95
875 A267 250fr multicolored 1.90 1.90
876 A267 400fr multicolored 3.00 3.00
877 A267 500fr multicolored 3.75 3.75
Nos. 874-877 (4) 9.60 9.60

Discovery of America, 500th Anniv. A268

Columbus and: 125fr, Fleet of ships. 250fr, Landing in New World. 400fr, Meeting with natives. 500fr, Map, ships.

1992, Aug.
878 A268 125fr multicolored 95 95
879 A268 250fr multicolored 1.90 1.90
880 A268 400fr multicolored 3.00 3.00
881 A268 500fr multicolored 3.75 3.75
Nos. 878-881 (4) 9.60 9.60

Types of 1983-84 Redrawn and Inscribed "Republic of Cameroon"

1992 **Litho.** *Perf. 13½*
882 A214 200fr like #739 1.45 1.45
883 A222 350fr like #763 2.55 2.55

AIDS Type of 1991

1993 **Litho.** *Perf. 13½*
884 A262 100fr like #859 70 70
885 A262 175fr like #860 1.20 1.20

Types of 1983 Redrawn and Inscribed "Republic of Cameroon"

886 A214 370fr like #738 2.55 2.55
Perf. 13
887 A217 410fr like #746 2.85 2.85

1994 World Cup Soccer Championships, US — A270

Designs: 125fr, Pres. Paul Biya holding soccer ball, lion. 250fr, Logo, lion, player, map. 450fr, Players, globe, World Cup, flag. 500fr, US eagle, Cameroun lion, soccer ball.

1994 **Litho.** *Perf. 13*
890 A270 125fr multicolored 48 48
891 A270 250fr multicolored 95 95
892 A270 450fr multicolored 1.75 1.75
893 A270 500fr multicolored 1.90 1.90
a. Min. sheet of 4, #890-893 5.00 5.00
Nos. 890-893 (4) 5.08 5.08

SEMI-POSTAL STAMPS

Curie Issue
Common Design Type

1938 **Unwmk.** *Perf. 13*
B1 CD80 1.75fr + 50c brt ultra 3.00 2.50

French Revolution Issue
Common Design Type

Photogravure; Name and Value Typographed in Black

1939
B2 CD83 45c + 25c grn 3.50 3.50
B3 CD83 70c + 30c brn 3.50 3.50
B4 CD83 90c + 35c red org 3.50 3.50
B5 CD83 1.25fr + 1fr rose pink 3.75 3.75
B6 CD83 2.25fr + 2fr bl 4.25 4.25
Nos. B2-B6 (5) 18.50 18.50

Stamps of 1925-33 Surcharged in Black

OEUVRES DE GUERRE

+ 2 frs.

1940 *Perf. 14x13½*
B7 A7 1.25fr + 2fr gray & dp bl 5.00 5.00
B8 A7 1.75fr + 3fr brn & org 5.00 5.00
B9 A7 2fr + 5fr dl grn & brn org 5.00 5.00
Nos. B7-B9 (3) 15.00 15.00

The surtax was used for war relief work.

Regular Stamps of 1939 Surcharged in Black

+ 5 Frs.
SPITFIRE

1940 *Perf. 13*
B10 A20 25c + 5fr blk brn 50.00 47.50
B11 A20 45c + 5fr slate grn 50.00 47.50
B12 A20 60c + 5fr pck bl 60.00 55.00
B13 A20 70c + 5fr plum 60.00 55.00
Nos. B10-B13 (4) 220.00 205.00

The surtax was used to purchase Spitfire planes for the Free French army.

Catalogue values for unused stamps in this section, from this point to the end of the section, are for Never Hinged items.

Common Design Type and

Military Doctor SP2

Cameroun Militiaman — SP4

1941 **Photo.** *Perf. 13½*

B13A	SP2	1fr + 1fr red	50
B13B	CD86	1.50fr + 3fr mar	50
B13C	SP4	2.50fr + 1fr dk bl	50
		Nos. B13A-B13C (3)	1.50

Nos. B13A-B13C were issued by the Vichy government, and were not placed on sale in Cameroun.

Nos. 281A-281B were surcharged "OEUVRES COLONIALES" and surtax (including change of denomination of the 2.50fr to 50c). These were issued in 1944 by the Vichy government, and not placed on sale in Cameroun.

New York World's Fair Stamps, 1939 Surcharged in Black

+
SPITFIRE 10fr.
Général de GAULLE

1941 *Perf. 12½x12*

B14	CD82	1.25fr + 10fr car lake	42.50	37.50
B15	CD82	2.25fr + 10fr ultra	42.50	37.50

New York World's Fair Stamps, 1939, Surcharged in Black or Blue

+ 10 Frs.
AMBULANCE
LAQUINTINIE

1941

B16	CD82	1.25fr + 10fr car lake (Bl)	7.50	6.00
B17	CD82	2.25fr + 10fr ultra (Bk)	7.50	6.00

The surtax was used to purchase ambulances for the Free French army.

Regular Stamps of 1933-39 Surcharged in Black

Valmy
+ 100 frs.

1943 *Perf. 14x13½, 13, 12½x12*

B21	A7	1.25fr + 100 gray & dp bl	3.75	3.75
B22	A21	1.25fr + 100fr car rose	3.75	3.75
B23	CD82	1.25fr + 100fr car lake	3.75	3.75
B24	A21	1.50fr + 100fr choc	3.75	3.75
B25	CD82	2.25fr + 100fr ultra	3.75	3.75
		Nos. B21-B25 (5)	18.75	18.75

Red Cross Issue

Common Design Type

1944 **Photo.** *Perf. 14½x14*

B28	CD90	5fr + 20fr rose	75	65

The surtax was for the French Red Cross and national relief.

Tropical Medicine Issue

Common Design Type

1950 **Engr.** *Perf. 13*

B29	CD100	10fr + 2fr dk bl grn & dk grn	1.60	1.60

The surtax was for charitable work.

Independent State

Map and Flag — SP7

Unwmk.

1961, Mar. 25 **Engr.** *Perf. 13*

B30	SP7	20fr + 5fr grn, car & yel	42	42
B31	SP7	25fr + 10fr multi	50	50
B32	SP7	30fr + 15fr car, yel & grn	70	70
		Nos. B30-B32 (3)	1.62	1.62

The surtax was for the Red Cross.

Federal Republic

Map of Cameroun, Lions Emblem and Physician Helping Leper — SP8

1962, Jan. 28

B33	SP8	20fr + 5fr multi	40	40
B34	SP8	25fr + 10fr multi	45	45
B35	SP8	50fr + 15fr multi	80	80
		Nos. B33-B35 (3)	1.65	1.65

Issued for leprosy relief work.

Anti-Malaria Issue

Common Design Type

1962, Apr. 7 *Perf. 12½x12*

B36	CD108	25fr + 5fr rose lilac	50	45

WHO drive to eradicate malaria.

Freedom from Hunger Issue

Common Design Type

1963, Mar. 21 **Engr.** *Perf. 13*

B37	CD112	18fr + 5fr multi	42	35
B38	CD112	25fr + 5fr multi	55	40

Antelopes — SP9

Designs: 125fr+10fr, Ourebia ourebi. 250fr+20fr, Kobus defassa.

1991, Apr. 30 **Litho.** *Perf. 13½x13*

B39	SP9	125fr + 10fr multi	1.15	1.15
B40	SP9	250fr + 20fr multi	2.30	2.30
a.		Souvenir sheet of 2, #B39-B40, perf. 12½	3.45	3.45

AIR POST STAMPS

Catalogue values for unused stamps in this section are for Never Hinged items.

Common Design Type

1942 **Unwmk.** **Photo.** *Perf. 14½x14*

C1	CD87	1fr dk org	15	15
C2	CD87	1.50fr brt red	15	15
C3	CD87	5fr brn red	15	15
C4	CD87	10fr black	25	25
C5	CD87	25fr ultra	30	30
C6	CD87	50fr dk grn	42	42
C7	CD87	100fr plum	60	60
		Nos. C1-C7 (7)	2.02	2.02

Victory Issue

Common Design Type

1946, May 8 **Engr.** *Perf. 12½*

C8	CD92	8fr dk vio brn	25	25

European victory of the Allied Nations in WWII.

Chad to Rhine Issue

Common Design Types

1946, June 6

C9	CD93	5fr dk bl grn	35	35
C10	CD94	10fr dk rose vio	35	35
C11	CD95	15fr red	40	40
C12	CD96	20fr brt bl	40	40
C13	CD97	25fr org red	50	50
C14	CD98	50fr gray	62	62
		Nos. C9-C14 (6)	2.62	2.62

Plane and Map — AP9

Seaplane Alighting — AP10

Plane and Freighters AP11

1946 **Photo.** *Perf. 13, 13½*

C15	AP9	25c brn red	15	15
C16	AP9	50c green	15	15
C17	AP9	1fr brt vio	15	15
C18	AP10	2fr ol grn	15	15
C19	AP10	3fr chocolate	15	15
C20	AP10	4fr dp ultra	15	15
C21	AP10	6fr bl grn	15	15
C22	AP10	7fr brt vio	15	15
C23	AP10	12fr orange	1.75	1.75
C24	AP10	20fr crimson	42	42
C25	AP11	50fr dk ultra	45	45
		Nos. C15-C25 (11)	3.82	3.82

Nos. C15 to C25 were "issued" in 1941 in France by the Vichy Government, but were not sold in Cameroun until 1946.

V8

This 100fr stamp and eight denominations of types AP9, AP10 and AP11 without "RF" monogram were issued by the Vichy Government in 1943-44, but were not on sale in Cameroun.

Birds over Mountains — AP12

Cavalry and Plane — AP13

Warrior, Dance Mask and Nose of Plane — AP14

Perf. 12½

1947, Feb. 10 **Unwmk.** **Engr.**

C26	AP12	50fr dk grn	60	35
C27	AP13	100fr brn red	1.25	20
C28	AP14	200fr black	2.50	60
		Nos. C26-C28 (3)	4.35	1.15

UPU Issue

Common Design Type

1949, July *Perf. 13*

C29	CD99	25fr multi	1.75	1.50

Humsiki Peak — AP16

1953, Feb. 16

C30	AP16	500fr grnsh blk, dk vio & vio bl	6.50	1.40

For surcharge see No. C40.

Edéa Dam and Sacred Ibis — AP17

1953, Nov. 18

C31	AP17	15fr choc, brn lake & ultra	80	35

Issued to publicize the official dedication of Edea Dam on the Sanaga River.

Liberation Issue

Common Design Type

1954, June 6

C32	CD102	15fr dk grnsh bl & bl grn	1.50	1.10

Dr. Eugene Jamot, Research Laboratory and Tsetse Flies — AP19

1954, Nov. 29

C33	AP19	15fr dk grn, ind & dk brn	90	80

75th anniv. of the birth of Dr. Eugene Jamot.

Logging — AP20

Designs: 100fr, Giraffes. 200fr, Port of Douala.

1955, Jan. 24

C34 AP20 50fr ol grn, brn & vio brn 45 15
C35 AP20 100fr grnsh bl, brn & dk brn 1.40 20
C36 AP20 200fr dk grn, choc & dp ultra 1.75 35
Nos. C34-C36 (3) 3.60 70

For surcharges see Nos. C38-C39.

Federal Republic
Air Afrique Issue
Common Design Type
Unwmk.

1962, Feb. 17 Engr. *Perf. 13*

C37 CD107 25fr mar, pur & lt grn 40 38

Nos. C35-C36 and C30 Surcharged in Red with New Value, Bars and: "REPUBLIQUE FEDERALE"

Two types of 5sh:
I - "5/-" measures 6½x4mm.
II - "5/" measures 3¾x3mm, No dash after diagonal line.

Three types of 10sh:
I - "10/-" measures 9x3¾mm.
II - "10/-" measures 7x2½-3mm.
III - "1" of "10/" vertically in line with last "E" of "FEDERALE".

Two types of £1:
I - "REPUBLIQUE / FEDERALE" 17¼mm wide.
II - "REPUBLIQUE / FEDERALE" 22mm wide.

1961, Oct. 1 Engr. *Perf. 13*

C38 AP20 5sh on 100fr (I) 2.50 2.50
a. Type II 6.50 6.50
C39 AP20 10sh on 200fr (I) 5.50 5.50
a. Type II 22.50 22.50
b. Type III 8.00 8.00
C40 AP16 £1 on 500fr (I) 10.00 10.00
a. Type II 15.00 15.00
Nos. C38-C40 (3) 18.00 18.00

Issued for use in the former United Kingdom Trust Territory of Southern Cameroons.

Kapsikis Mokolo — AP21

Designs: 50fr, Cocotieres Hotel, Douala. 100fr, Cymothoe sangaris butterflies. 200fr, Ostriches, Waza Reservation.

1962, June 15

C41 AP21 50fr sl grn, bl & dl red 50 30
C42 AP21 100fr multicolored 1.10 40
C43 AP21 200fr dk grn, blk & bis 2.25 65
C44 AP21 500fr vio brn, bl & ocher 5.00 1.60
Nos. C41-C44 (4) 8.85 2.95

Telstar Type of Regular Issue

1963, Feb. 9
Size: 48x27mm

C45 A50 100fr dk grn & red brn 1.10 65

See note after No. 383.

Edéa Relay Station — A22

1963, May 18 Photo. *Perf. 12x12½*

C46 AP22 100fr multicolored 1.10 65

Issued to publicize the high frequency telegraph connection Douala-Yaoundé.

African Postal Union Issue
Common Design Type

1963, Sept. 8 Unwmk. *Perf. 12½*

C47 CD114 85fr ultra, ocher & red 1.10 1.00

Air Afrique Issue, 1963
Common Design Type

1963, Nov. 19 *Perf. 13x12*

C48 CD115 50fr pink, gray, blk & grn 60 40

Olympic Games Type of 1964

Design: 300fr, Greco-Roman wrestlers (ancient).

1964, Oct. 10 Engr. *Perf. 13*

C49 A57 300fr red, dk brn & dl grn 3.50 2.00
a. Sheet of 3, #403-404, C49 4.25 4.25

Kribi Port — AP25

1964, Oct. 26 Unwmk. *Perf. 13*

C50 AP25 50fr red brn, ultra & grn 60 35

Black Rhinoceros — AP26

1965, Dec. 15 Engr. *Perf. 13*

C51 AP26 250fr brn red, grn & dk brn 3.00 1.10

Pres. John F. Kennedy — AP27

1964, Dec. 8 Photo. *Perf. 12½*

C52 AP27 100fr grn, yel grn & brn 1.10 1.10
a. Souvenir sheet of 4 4.50 4.50

Pres. John F. Kennedy (1917-63).

Abraham Lincoln — AP28

1965, Apr. 20 Unwmk. *Perf. 13*

C53 AP28 100fr multicolored 1.10 80

Abraham Lincoln, death centenary.

Syncom Satellite and ITU Emblem — AP29

1965, May 17 Engr.

C54 AP29 70fr red, dk bl, & blk 80 60

Cent. of the ITU.

Sir Winston Spencer Churchill, Statesman and World War II Leader — AP30

Design: 18fr, Churchill, battleship and oak leaves with acorns.

Perf. 13x12½

1965, May 28 Photo. Unwmk.

C55 AP30 12fr multicolored 65 50
C56 AP30 18fr multicolored 65 50
a. Strip of 2, #C55-C56 + label 1.60 1.40

ICY Type of Regular Issue

1965, Sept. 11 Engr. *Perf. 13*

C57 A68 100fr dk red & dk bl 1.10 70

Racing Boat, Sanaga River, Edéa — AP31

1965, Oct. 27 Unwmk. *Perf. 13*

C58 AP31 50fr brn, dk grn & sl 60 35

Edward H. White Floating in Space and Gemini IV — AP32

Designs: 50fr, Vostok 6. 200fr, Gemini V and REP (rendezvous evaluation pod). 500fr, Gemini VI & VII rendezvous.

1966, Mar. 30 Engr. *Perf. 13*

C59 AP32 50fr car rose & dk sl grn 60 35
C60 AP32 100fr red lil & vio bl 1.10 65
C61 AP32 200fr ultra & dk pur 2.00 1.40
C62 AP32 500fr brt bl & indigo 5.50 3.00
Nos. C59-C62 (4) 9.20 5.40

Man's conquest of space.

Hotel Type of Regular Issue

1966

Designs: 18fr, Mountain Hotel, Buea. 25fr, Hotel Akwa Palace, Douala. 50fr, Terminus Hotel, Yaoundé. 60fr, Imperial Hotel, Yaoundé. 85fr, Independence Hotel, Yaoundé. 100fr, Hunting Lodge, Mora, vert. 150fr, Boukarous (round huts), Waza Camp.

C63 A71 18fr sl grn, brt bl & blk 16 15
C64 A71 25fr car, ultra & sl 25 16
C65 A71 50fr choc, grn & ocher 60 35
C66 A71 60fr choc, grn & brt bl 60 35
C67 A71 85fr dk car rose, dl bl & grn 80 50
C68 A71 100fr brn, grn & sl 1.10 50
C69 A71 150fr brn, dl bl & ocher 1.40 65
Nos. C63-C69 (7) 4.91 2.66

Issue dates: Nos. C63-C64, Apr. 6; Nos. C65-C69, June 4.

Flower Type of Regular Issue

Flowers: 25fr, Hibiscus mutabilis. 50fr, Delonix regia. 100fr, Bougainvillea.

1966, May 20 Photo. *Perf. 12½*
Flowers in Natural Colors
Size: 26x45mm

C70 A75 25fr slate green 25 15
C71 A75 50fr brt grnsh bl 50 15
C72 A75 100fr gold 1.10 25
Nos. C70-C72 (3) 1.85 55

Military Police — AP33

Design: 25fr, "Army," soldier, tanks and parachutes. 60fr, "Navy," and "Vigilante." 100fr, "Air Force," plane.

1966, June 21 Engr. *Perf. 13*

C73 AP33 20fr vio bl, org brn & dl pur 20 15
C74 AP33 25fr dk grn, dl pur & brn 25 16
C75 AP33 60fr bl grn, bl & ind 65 30
C76 AP33 100fr brn, Prus bl & car rose 1.10 65
Nos. C73-C76 (4) 2.20 1.26

Issued to honor Cameroun's armed forces.

Wembley Stadium, London — AP34

1966, July 20

C77 AP34 50fr shown 55 25
C78 AP34 200fr Soccer 2.00 1.10

8th World Cup Soccer Championship, Wembley, England, July 11-30.

Air Afrique Issue, 1966
Common Design Type

1966, Aug. 31 Photo. *Perf. 13*

C79 CD123 25fr red lil, blk & gray 25 15

Yaoundé Cathedral — AP35

Designs: 18fr, Buea Cathedral. 30fr, Orthodox Church, Yaoundé. 60fr, Mosque, Garoua.

1966, Dec. 19 Engr. *Perf. 13*

C80 AP35 18fr choc, bl & grn 20 16
C81 AP35 25fr brn, grn & brt vio 25 16
C82 AP35 30fr lil, grn & dl red 30 20
C83 AP35 60fr mar, brt grn & grn 65 35
Nos. C80-C83 (4) 1.40 87

Pioneer A and Moon — AP36

1967, Apr. 30 Engr. *Perf. 13*

C84 AP36 25fr shown 25 16
C85 AP36 50fr Ranger 6 60 35
C86 AP36 100fr Luna 9 1.10 65
C87 AP36 250fr Luna 10 2.50 2.00
Nos. C84-C87 (4) 4.45 3.16

"Conquest of the Moon."

Flower Type of Regular Issue

Flowers: 200fr, Thevetia Peruviana. 250fr, Amaryllis.

1967, June 22 Photo. *Perf. 12½*
Size: 26x46mm

C88 A86 200fr multi 2.00 90
C89 A86 250fr multi 2.50 1.10

African Postal Union Issue, 1967
Common Design Type

1967, Sept. 9 Engr. *Perf. 13*

C90 CD124 100fr red brn, Prus bl & brt lil 1.10 65

Skis, Ice Skates, Olympic Flame and Emblem — AP38

1967, Oct. 11 Engr. *Perf. 13*

C91 AP38 30fr ultra & sepia 40 20

Issued to publicize the 10th Winter Olympic Games, Grenoble, Feb. 6-8, 1968.

Cameroun Exhibit, EXPO '67 — AP39

Designs: 100fr, Bangwa house poles carved with ancestor figures. 200fr, Canadian Pavilions.

1967, Oct. 18

C92 AP39 50fr mag, ol & maroon 50 22
C93 AP39 100fr dk grn, mar & dk brn 1.10 55
C94 AP39 200fr brn, lil rose & sl grn 2.25 1.10
Nos. C92-C94 (3) 3.85 1.87

EXPO '70, International Exhibition, Montreal, Apr. 28-Oct. 27, 1967.

See note after No. C116 regarding 1969 moon overprint.

Konrad Adenauer (1876-1967), Chancellor of West Germany (1949-63) and Cologne Cathedral — AP40

Design: 70fr, Adenauer and Chancellery, Bonn.

1967, Dec. 1 Photo. *Perf. 12½*

C95 AP40 30fr multi 35 20
C96 AP40 70fr multi 80 40
a. Strip of 2, #C95-C96 + label 1.20 65

Pres. Ahidjo, King Faisal and View of Mecca — AP41

Design: 60fr, Pres. Ahidjo, Pope Paul VI and view of Rome.

1968, Feb. 18 Photo. *Perf. 12½*

C97 AP41 30fr multi 30 16
C98 AP41 60fr multi 60 30

Issued to commemorate President Ahidjo's Pilgrimage to Mecca and visit to Rome.

Earth on Television Transmitted by Explorer VI — AP42

Designs: 30fr, Molniya spacecraft. 40fr, Earth on television screen transmitted by Molniya.

1968, Apr. 20 Engr. *Perf. 13*

C99 AP42 20fr multi 20 15
C100 AP42 30fr multi 30 16
C101 AP42 40fr multi 40 20
Nos. C99-C101 (3) 90 51

Telecommunication by satellite.

Forge — AP43 Boxing — AP44

Designs: No. C103, Tea harvest. No. C104, Trans-Cameroun railroad (diesel train emerging from tunnel). 40fr, Rubber harvest. 60fr, Douala Harbor, horiz.

1968, June 5 Engr. *Perf. 13*

C102 AP43 20fr red brn, dk grn & ind 20 15
C103 AP43 30fr dk brn, grn & ultra 30 16
C104 AP43 30fr ind, sl grn & bis brn 30 16
C105 AP43 40fr ol bis, dk grn & bl grn 35 20
C106 AP43 60fr ultra, dk brn & sl 60 40
Nos. C102-C106 (5) 1.75 1.07

Issued to publicize the Second Economic Development Five-Year Plan.

1968, Aug. 19 Engr. *Perf. 13*

Design: 50fr, Long jump. 60fr, Athlete on rings.

C107 AP44 30fr brt grn, dk grn & choc 30 16
C108 AP44 50fr brt grn, brn red & choc 50 30
C109 AP44 60fr brt grn, ultra & choc 60 35
a. Min. sheet of 3, #C107-C109 1.50 1.50
Nos. C107-C109 (3) 1.40 81

19th Olympic Games, Mexico City, Oct. 12-27.

Human Rights Type of Regular Issue

1968, Sept. 14 Photo. *Perf. 12½x13*

C110 A92 30fr grn & brt pink 25 15

Martin Luther King, Jr. — AP45

Portraits: No. C112, Mahatma Gandhi and map of India. 40fr, John F. Kennedy. 60fr, Robert F. Kennedy. No. C115, Rev. Martin Luther King, Jr. No. C116, Mahatma Gandhi.

1968, Dec. 5 Photo. *Perf. 12½*

C111 AP45 30fr bl & blk 35 20
C112 AP45 30fr multi 35 20
C113 AP45 40fr pink & blk 40 25
C114 AP45 60fr bluish lil & blk 60 40
C115 AP45 70fr yel grn & blk 65 45
a. Souvenir sheet of 4, #C112-C115 2.00 2.00
C116 AP45 70fr multi 65 45
Nos. C111-C116 (6) 3.00 1.95

Issued to honor exponents of non-violence. The 2 King stamps (Nos. C111 and C115), the 2 Gandhi stamps (Nos. C112 and C116) and the 2 Kennedy stamps (Nos. C113-C114) are each printed as triptychs with a descriptive label between.

In 1969 Nos. C111-C116 and C94 were overprinted in carmine capitals: "Premier Homme / sur la Lune / 20 Juillet 1969" and "First Man / Landing on Moon / 20 July 1969".

PHILEXAFRIQUE Issue

The Letter, by Armand Cambon AP46

1968, Dec. 10

C117 AP46 100fr multi 1.10 80

PHILEXAFRIQUE, Philatelic Exhibition in Abidjan, Feb. 14-23, 1969. Printed with alternating light green label.

2nd PHILEXAFRIQUE Issue
Common Design Type

Design: 50fr, Cameroun No. 199 and Wouri Bridge.

1969, Feb. 14 Engr. *Perf. 13*

C118 CD128 50fr multi 55 55

Caladium Bicolor — AP47

Flowers: 50fr, Aristolochia elegans. 100fr, Gloriosa simplex.

1969, May 14 Photo. *Perf. 12½*

C119 AP47 30fr lil & multi 30 20
C120 AP47 50fr grn & multi 60 35
C121 AP47 100fr brn & multi 1.00 55
Nos. C119-C121 (3) 1.90 1.10

3rd Intl. Flower Show, Paris, Apr. 23-Oct. 5.

Douala Post Office — AP48

Designs: 50fr, Buèa Post Office. 100fr, Bafoussam Post Office.

1969, June 19 Engr. *Perf. 13*

C122 AP48 30fr grn, vio bl & brn 22 15
C123 AP48 50fr sl, emer & red brn 45 25
C124 AP48 100fr dk brn, brt grn & brn 90 50
Nos. C122-C124 (3) 1.57 90

Coronation of Napoleon I, by Jacques Louis David — AP49

Napoleon Crossing Saint Bernard, after J. L. David — AP50

1969, July 4 Photo. *Perf. 12x12½*

C125 AP49 30fr vio bl & multi 50 20

Die-cut Perf. 10

Embossed on Gold Foil

C126 AP50 1000fr gold 16.00 16.00

Bicentenary of birth of Napoleon I.

William E. B. Du Bois (1868-1963), American Writer — AP51

Portraits: 15fr, Dr. Price Mars, Haiti (1876-1969). No. C128, Aimé Cesaire, Martinique (1913-). No. C130, Langston Hughes, US (1902-1967). No. C131, Marcus Garvey, Jamaica (1887-1940). 100fr, René Maran, Martinique (1887-1960).

1969, Sept. 25 Photo. *Perf. 12½*

C127 AP51 15fr lt bl & blk 15 15
C128 AP51 30fr lem & blk 25 15
C129 AP51 30fr rose brn & blk 25 15
C130 AP51 50fr gray & blk 42 22
C131 AP51 50fr emer & blk 42 22
C132 AP51 100fr yel & blk 90 60
a. Min. sheet of 6, #C127-C132 2.50 2.50
Nos. C127-C132 (6) 2.39 1.49

Issued to honor Negro writers.

ILO Emblem — AP52

1969, Oct. 29 Photo. *Perf. 13*

C133 AP52 30fr blk, bl grn & gray 35 15
C134 AP52 50fr blk, dp lil rose & gray 60 25

50th anniv. of the ILO.

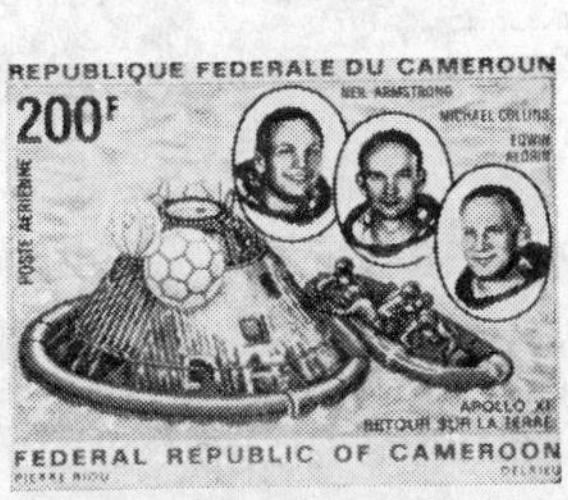

Armstrong, Collins and Aldrin Splashdown in the Pacific — AP53

Design: 500fr, Landing module and Neil A. Armstrong's first step on moon.

1969, Nov. 29 Photo. *Perf. 12½*

C135 AP53 200fr multi 2.50 1.25
C136 AP53 500fr multi 5.50 2.25

See note after Algeria No. 427.

Pres. Ahidjo, Arms and Map of Cameroun — AP54

Embossed on Gold Foil

1970, Jan. 1 *Die-cut Perf. 10*

C137 AP54 1000fr gold & multi 8.25 8.25

10th anniversary of independence.

Hotel Mont Fébé, Yaoundé — AP55

1970, Jan. 15 Engr. *Perf. 13*

C138 AP55 30fr lt brn, sl grn & gray 35 15

Lenin — AP56

1970, Jan. 25 Photo. *Perf. 12½*

C139 AP56 50fr org & blk 45 25

Plant Type of Regular Issue

Designs: 50fr, Cleome speciosa (caper). 100fr, Mussaenda erythrophylla (madder).

1970, Mar. 24 Photo. *Perf. 12½*

Size: 26x46mm

C140 A99 50fr blk & multi 40 25
C141 A99 100fr multi 80 40

Map of Africa and Lions Emblem Pinpointing Yaoundé — AP57

1970, May 2 Photo. *Perf. 12½*

C142 AP57 100fr multi 1.00 50

13th Lions International Congress of District 13, Yaoundé, May 2, 1970.

UN Emblem and Doves — AP58

Design: 50fr, UN emblem and dove, vert.

1970, June 26 Engr. *Perf. 13*

C143 AP58 30fr brn & org 25 16
C144 AP58 50fr Prus bl & sl bl 42 22

25th anniversary of the United Nations.

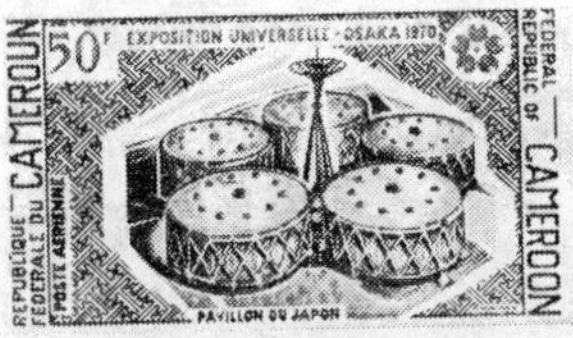

Japanese Pavilion and EXPO Emblem — AP59

Designs (EXPO Emblem and): 100fr, Map of Japan, vert. 150fr, Australian pavilion.

1970, Aug. 1 Engr. *Perf. 13*

C145 AP59 50fr ind, lt grn & ver 42 22
C146 AP59 100fr bl, lt grn & red 1.00 42
C147 AP59 150fr choc, bl & gray 1.40 65
Nos. C145-C147 (3) 2.82 1.29

EXPO '70 International Exhibition, Osaka, Japan, Mar. 15-Sept. 13.

Charles de Gaulle — AP60

Pelé and Team — AP61

Design: 200fr, de Gaulle in unifrom.

1970, Aug. 27

C148 AP60 100fr grn, vio bl & ol brn 1.00 50
C149 AP60 200fr ol brn, vio bl & grn 2.00 90
a. Strip of 2, #C148-C149 + label 3.50 1.60

Rallying of the Free French, 30th anniv. For overprints see Nos. C159-C160.

1970, Oct. 14 Photo. *Perf. 12½*

Designs: 50fr, Aztec Stadium, Mexico City, horiz. 100fr, Mexican soccer team, horiz.

C150 AP61 50fr multi 50 22
C151 AP61 100fr multi 1.00 50
C152 AP61 200fr multi 2.00 1.00
Nos. C150-C152 (3) 3.50 1.72

9th World Soccer Championships for the Jules Rimet Cup, Mexico City, May 30-June 21, and the final victory of Brazil over Italy.

Ludwig van Beethoven (1770-1827), Composer — AP62

1970, Nov. 23 Engr. *Perf. 13*

C153 AP62 250fr multi 2.00 1.00

Christ at Emmaus, by Rembrandt — AP63

Design: 150fr, The Anatomy Lesson, by Rembrandt.

1970, Dec. 5 Photo. *Perf. 12x12½*

C154 AP63 70fr grn & multi 55 25
C155 AP63 150fr multi 1.20 60

Charles Dickens — AP64

Designs: 50fr, Scenes from David Copperfield. 100fr, Dickens holding quill.

1970, Dec. 22 *Perf. 13*

C156 AP64 40fr blk & rose 35 16
C157 AP64 50fr bis & multi 40 20
C158 AP64 100fr rose & multi 80 40
a. Strip of 3, #C156-C158 1.75 1.00

Charles Dickens (1812-1870), English novelist.

De Gaulle Type of 1970 Overprinted with Black Border and: "IN MEMORIAM / 1890-1970"

1971, Jan. 15 Engr. *Perf. 13*

C159 AP60 100fr vio bl, emer & brn red 80 40
C160 AP60 200fr brn red, emer & vio bl 1.60 80

In memory of Gen. Charles de Gaulle (1890-1970), President of France.

Timber Storage, Douala — AP65

Designs (Industrialization): 70fr, ALUCAM aluminum plant, Edea, vert. 100fr, Mbakaou Dam.

1971, Feb. 14 Engr. *Perf. 13*

C161 AP65 40fr dk red, bl grn & ol brn 35 15
C162 AP65 70fr ol brn, sl grn & brt bl 55 25
C163 AP65 100fr Prus bl, yel grn & red brn 80 40
Nos. C161-C163 (3) 1.70 80

Relay Race — AP66

Designs: 50fr, Torch bearer, vert. 100fr, Discus.

1971, Apr. 24 Engr. *Perf. 13*

C164 AP66	30fr dk brn, ver & ind	25	15
C165 AP66	50fr blk, bl & choc	45	22
C166 AP66	100fr multi	80	35
	Nos. C164-C166 (3)	1.50	72

75th anniv. of revival of Olympic Games.

Fishing Trawler — AP67

Designs: 40fr, Local fishermen, Northern Cameroun. 70fr, Fishing harbor, Douala. 150fr, Shrimp boats, Douala.

1971, May 14 Engr. *Perf. 13*

C167 AP67	30fr lt brn, bl & grn	22	15
C168 AP67	40fr sl grn, bl & dk brn	30	16
C169 AP67	70fr dk brn, bl & red org	60	25
C170 AP67	150fr multi	1.20	60
	Nos. C167-C170 (4)	2.32	1.16

Cameroun fishing industry.

Cameroun No. 123 and War Memorial, Yaoundé — AP68

Designs (Cameroun Stamps): 25fr, No. C33 and Jamot memorial. 40fr, No. 431 and government buildings, Yaoundé. 50fr, No. 19 and Imperial German postal emblem. 100fr, No. 101 and World War II memorial.

1971, Aug. 1 Engr. *Perf. 13*

C171 AP68	20fr grn, ocher & dk brn	16	15
C172 AP68	25fr dk brn, vio bl & sl grn	20	15
C173 AP68	40fr grn, mar & sl	30	16
C174 AP68	50fr dk brn, blk & ver	40	20
C175 AP68	100fr mar, sl grn & org	80	40
	Nos. C171-C175 (5)	1.86	1.06

PHILATECAM 1971 Philatelic Exhibition.

Cameroun Flag, Pres. Ahidjo and Reunification Highway — AP69

Typographed, Silk Screen, Embossed

1971, Oct. 1 *Perf. 12½*

C176 AP69	250fr gold & multi	2.50	2.00

PHILATECAM Philatelic Exhibition, Yaoundé-Douala.

African Postal Union Issue, 1971

Common Design Type

1971, Nov. 13 Photo. *Perf. 13x13½*

C177 CD135	100fr bl & multi	90	42

Annunciation, by Fra Angelico — AP71

Christmas (Paintings): 45fr, Virgin and Child, by Andrea del Sarto. 150fr, Christ Child with Lamb, detail from Holy Family, by Raphael, vert.

Perf. 13x13½, 13½x13

1971, Dec. 19

C178 AP71	40fr multi	25	15
C179 AP71	45fr multi	40	20
C180 AP71	150fr multi	1.40	60
	Nos. C178-C180 (3)	2.05	95

Cameroun Airlines Emblem AP72

1972, Feb. 2 Photo. *Perf. 12½x12*

C181 AP72	50fr lt bl & multi	40	20

Inauguration of Cameroun Airlines.

Doge's Palace, by Ippolito Caffi — AP73

Paintings: 100fr, 200fr, Details from "Regatta on the Grand Canal," by School of Canaletto.

1972 Photo. *Perf. 13*

C182 AP73	40fr gold & multi	35	16
C183 AP73	100fr gold & multi	80	40
C184 AP73	200fr gold & multi	1.60	80
	Nos. C182-C184 (3)	2.75	1.36

UNESCO campaign to save Venice.

Cosmonauts Patsayev, Dobrovolsky and Volkov — AP74

1972, May 1 Photo. *Perf. 13x13½*

C185 AP74	50fr multi	40	16

Salute-Soyuz 11 space mission, and in memory of the Russian cosmonauts Victor I. Patsayev, Georgi T. Dobrovolsky and Vladislav N. Volkov, who died during Soyuz 11 space mission, June 6-30, 1971.

UN Headquarters, Chinese Flag and Gate of Heavenly Peace AP75

1972, May 19 *Perf. 13*

C186 AP75	50fr blk, scar & gold	35	16

Admission of People's Republic of China to UN.

United Republic

Olympic Rings, Swimming AP76

Designs (Olympic Rings and): No. C188, Boxing, vert. 200fr, Equestrian.

1972, Aug. 1 Engr. *Perf. 13*

C187 AP76	50fr lake & slate grn	40	20
C188 AP76	50fr choc & slate	40	20
C189 AP76	200fr cl, gray & dk brn	1.50	70
a.	Min. sheet of 3	2.25	2.25
	Nos. C187-C189 (3)	2.30	1.10

20th Olympic Games, Munich, Aug. 26-Sept. 11. No. C189a contains stamps similar to Nos. C187-C189, but in changed colors. The 50fr (swimming) is Prussian blue, violet & brown; the 50c (boxing) lilac, Prussian blue & brown; the 200fr, Prussian blue & brown.

Nos. C187-C189 Overprinted in Red or Black

NATATION MARK SPITZ
MEDAILLES D'OR
a

SUPER WELTER
KOTTYSCH
MEDAILLE D'OR
b

CONCOURS COMPLET
MEADE
MEDAILLE D'OR
c

1972, Oct. 23 Engr. *Perf. 13*

C190 AP76(a)	50fr (R)	40	20
C191 AP76(b)	50fr	40	20
C192 AP76(c)	200fr	1.60	80
	Nos. C190-C192 (3)	2.40	1.20

Gold Medal Winners in 20th Olympic Games: Mark Spitz, US, swimming (#C190); Dieter Kottysch, West Germany, light middleweight boxing (#C191); Richard Meade, Great Britain, 3-day equestrian (#C192).

Madonna with Angels, by Cimabue AP77

Christmas: 140fr, Madonna of the Rose Arbor, by Stefan Lochner.

1972, Dec. 21 Photo. *Perf. 13*

C193 AP77	45fr gold & multi	40	20
C194 AP77	140fr gold & multi	90	45

St. Teresa, the Little Flower — AP78

Design: 100fr, Lisieux Cathedral and St. Teresa.

1973, Jan. 2 Engr.

C195 AP78	45fr vio bl, pur & mar	35	16
C196 AP78	100fr mag, ultra & brn	65	38

Centenary of the birth of St. Teresa of Lisieux (1873-1897), Carmelite nun.

African Unity Hall, Addis Ababa and Emperor Haile Selassie — AP79

1973, Mar. 14 Photo. *Perf. 13*

C197 AP79	45fr yellow & multi	25	16

80th birthday of Emperor Haile Selassie of Ethiopia.

Corn, Grain, Healthy and Starving People — AP80

1973, Apr. 10 Typo. *Perf. 13*

C198 AP80	45fr multi	25	15

World Food Program, 10th anniversary.

Hearts and Blood Vessels — AP81

Scout Emblem and Flags — AP82

1973, May 5 Engr.

C199 AP81	50fr dk car rose & dk vio bl	25	16

"Your Heart is Your Health" and for the 25th anniv. of the WHO.

Type of Regular Issue

Designs: 45fr, Map of Cameroun, Pres. Ahidjo and No. C176. 70fr, National colors and commemorative inscriptions.

1973, May 20 Engr. *Perf. 13*

C200 A128	45fr grn & multi	25	16
C201 A128	70fr red & multi	40	25

1973, July 31 Typo. *Perf. 13*

C202 AP82	40fr multi	25	16
C203 AP82	45fr multi	30	20
C204 AP82	100fr multi	60	42
	Nos. C202-C204 (3)	1.15	78

Cameroun's admission to the World Scout Conference, Mar. 26, 1971.

African Weeks Issue

Head and City Hall, Brussels — AP83

1973, Sept. 17 Engr. *Perf. 13*
C205 AP83 40fr dp brn & rose claret 25 16

African Weeks, Brussels, Sept. 15-30.

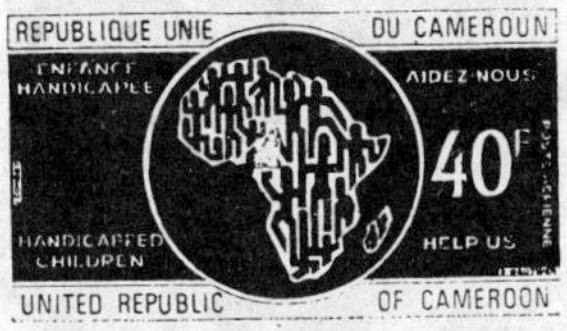

Map of Africa with Cameroun — AP84

1973, Sept. 29 Engr. *Perf. 13*
C206 AP84 40fr blk, red & grn 35 16

Help for handicapped children.

Zamengoe Radar Station AP85

1973, Dec. 8 Engr. *Perf. 13*
C207 AP85 100fr bl, lt brn & grn 60 40

Chancellor Rolin Madonna, by Van Eyck — AP86

Christmas: 140fr, Nativity, by Federigo Barocci.

1973, Dec. 11 Photo. *Perf. 13*
C208 AP86 45fr gold & multi 30 20
C209 AP86 140fr gold & multi 1.00 70

Zebu Type of 1974

1974, June 1 Litho. *Perf. 13*
C210 A140 45fr Zebu herd 25 15

Churchill and Union Jack — AP87

1974, July 10 Engr. *Perf. 13*
C211 AP87 100fr blk, bl & red 60 40

Winston Churchill (1874-1965).

Soccer, Arms of Frankfurt, Dortmund, Gelsenkirchen and Stuttgart — AP88

Designs: 100fr, Soccer and arms of Berlin, Hamburg, Hanover and Düsseldorf. 200fr, Soccer cup and game.

1974, Aug. 5 Photo. *Perf. 13*
C212 AP88 45fr gray, sl & org 25 15
C213 AP88 100fr gray, sl & org 60 40
C214 AP88 200fr org, slate & bl 1.10 65
a. Strip of 3, Nos. C212-C214 2.00 1.40

World Cup Soccer Championship, Munich, June 13-July 7.

Nos. C212-C214 Overprinted in Dark Blue: "7th JULY 1974 / R.F.A. 2 HOLLANDE 1 / 7 JUILLET 1974"

1974, Sept. 16 Photo. *Perf. 13*
C215 AP88 45fr multi 25 16
C216 AP88 100fr multi 60 42
C217 AP88 200fr multi 1.10 80
a. Strip of 3, Nos. C215-C217 2.25 1.50

World Cup Soccer Championship, 1974, victory of German Federal Republic.

UPU Type of 1974

Designs: 100fr, Cameroun No. 503. 200fr, Cameroun No. C29.

1974, Oct. 8 Engr. *Perf. 13*
C218 A142 100fr blue & multi 42 32
C219 A142 200fr red & multi 80 60

Copernicus and Planets Circling Sun — AP89

1974, Oct. 15 Engr. *Perf. 13*
C220 AP89 250fr multi 1.40 1.00

500th anniversary of the birth of Nicolaus Copernicus (1473-1543), Polish astronomer.

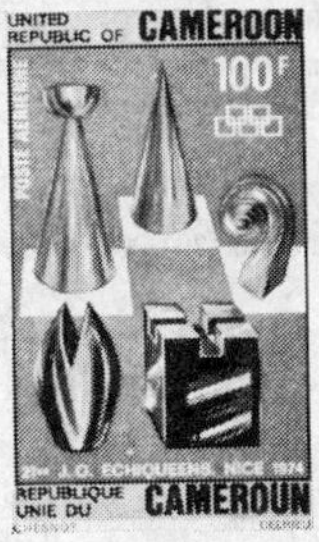

21st Chess Olympiad, Nice, France, June 6-30 — AP90

1974, Nov. 3 Photo. *Perf. 13x12½*
C221 AP90 100fr Chess pieces 50 40

Mask and ARPHILA Emblem — AP91

1974, Nov. 30 Engr. *Perf. 13*
C222 AP91 50fr choc & mag 25 16

ARPHILA 75, Paris, June 6-16, 1975.

Presidents and Flags of Cameroun, CAR, Gabon and Congo — AP92

1974, Dec. 8 Photo.
C223 AP92 100fr gold & multi 55 40

See note after No. 595.

Man Landing on Moon — AP93

1974, Dec. 15 Engr.
C224 AP93 200fr brn, bl & car 1.10 80

5th anniv. of man's 1st landing on the moon.

Charles de Gaulle and Félix Eboué — AP94

1975, Feb. 24 Typo. *Perf. 13*
C225 AP94 45fr multi 35 16
C226 AP94 200fr multi 1.40 80

Felix A. Eboué (1884-1944), Governor of Chad, first colonial governor to join Free French in WWII, 30th death anniversary.

Marquis de Lafayette — AP95

American Bicentennial: 140fr, Washington and soldiers. 500fr, Franklin and Independence Hall.

1975, Oct. 20 Engr. *Perf. 13*
C227 AP95 100fr vio bl & multi 55 40
C228 AP95 140fr brn & multi 70 60
C229 AP95 500fr grn & multi 2.50 1.60
Nos. C227-C229 (3) 3.75 2.60

The Burning Bush, by Nicolas Froment AP96

Painting: 500fr, Adoration of the Kings, by Gentile da Fabriano, horiz.

1975, Dec. 25 Photo. *Perf. 13*
C230 AP96 50fr gold & multi 35 16
C231 AP96 500fr gold & multi 3.25 1.60

Christmas 1975.

Concorde and Route: Paris-Dakar-Rio de Janeiro — AP97

1976, July 20 Litho. *Perf. 13*
C232 AP97 500fr lt bl & multi 3.00 1.60
a. Souvenir sheet of 1 3.75 3.75

1st commercial flight of supersonic jet Concorde from Paris to Rio de Janeiro, Jan. 21. No. C232a sold for 600fr.

For overprint see No. C263.

Dance Type of 1976

Designs: 50fr, Dancers and drummer. 100fr, Woman dancer.

1976, Sept. 15 Litho. *Perf. 12*
C233 A154 50fr gray & multi 25 20
C234 A154 100fr gray & multi 55 35

Virgin and Child, by Giovanni Bellini — AP98

Paintings: 30fr, Adoration of the Shepherds, by Le Brun. 60fr, Adoration of the Kings, by Rubens. 500fr, The Newborn, by Georges de la Tour.

1976, Dec. 15 Litho. *Perf. 12½*
C235 AP98 30fr gold & multi 16 15
C236 AP98 60fr gold & multi 35 22
C237 AP98 70fr gold & multi 38 25
C238 AP98 500fr gold & multi 2.50 1.60
a. Souv. sheet of 4, #C235-C238 3.75 3.75
Nos. C235-C238 (4) 3.39 2.22

Christmas 1976.

Festival Type of 1977

Design: 60fr, Traditional Chief on his throne, sculpture.

1977, Feb. 4 Litho. *Perf. 12½*
C239 A159 60fr multi 35 22

Crucifixion, by Matthias Grunewald — AP99

Paintings: 125fr, Christ on the Cross, by Velazquez, vert. 150fr, The Deposition, by Titian.

1977, Apr. 2 Litho. *Perf. 12½*

C240 AP99 50fr gold & multi 25 20
C241 AP99 125fr gold & multi 65 40
C242 AP99 150fr gold & multi 80 55
a. Souv. sheet of 3, #C240-C242, perf. 12 1.75 1.75
Nos. C240-C242 (3) 1.70 1.15

Easter 1977. No. C242a sold for 350fr.

Lions Emblem, Map of Africa — AP100

Rotary Emblem — AP101

1977, Apr. 29 Litho. *Perf. 12½*

C243 AP100 250fr multi 1.40 1.00

Lions Club of Douala, 19th Cong., Apr. 29-30.

1977, May 18

C244 AP101 60fr multi 35 22

Rotary Club of Douala, 20th anniversary.

Antoine de Saint-Exupéry AP102

Charles Lindbergh and Spirit of St. Louis — AP103

Designs: 50fr, Jean Mermoz and his plane. 80fr, Maryse Bastié and her plane. 100fr, Sikorsky S-43. 300fr, Concorde.

1977, May 20 Engr. *Perf. 13*

C245 AP103 50fr org & bl 25 20
C246 AP102 60fr mag & org 35 22
C247 AP103 80fr mag & bl 40 30
a. Souvenir sheet of 3, #C245-C247 1.10 1.10
C248 AP103 100fr grn & yel 55 40
C249 AP103 300fr multi 1.60 1.25
C250 AP103 500fr multi 2.50 1.75
a. Souvenir sheet of 3, #C248-C250 6.00 6.00
Nos. C245-C250 (6) 5.65 4.12

Aviation pioneers and events. No. C247a sold for 200fr. No. C250a sold for 1000fr.

For overprint see No. C262.

Sassenage Castle, Grenoble — AP104

1977, May 21 Litho. *Perf. 12½*

C251 AP104 70fr multi 40 25

10th anniv. of Intl. French Language Council.

Jufilex Type of 1977

Designs: 70fr, Switzerland (Zurich) No. 1L1 and Cameroun No. 16. 100fr, Switzerland (Geneva) No. 2L1 and Cameroun No. 254.

1977, June 5 Litho. *Perf. 12*

C252 A161 70fr multi 40 25
C253 A161 100fr multi 55 40

Diseased Knee, WHO Emblem AP105

1977, Oct. 15 Engr. *Perf. 13*

C260 AP105 70fr multi 40 25

World Rheumatism Year.

Nos. C249 and C232 Overprinted in Red: "PREMIER VOL PARIS-NEW YORK /FIRST FLIGHT PARIS-NEW YORK / 22 Nov. 1977-22nd Nov. 1977"

Engraved, Lithographed

1977, Nov. 22 *Perf. 13*

C262 AP103 300fr multi 1.60 1.20
C263 AP97 500fr multi 2.50 2.00

Concorde, 1st commercial flight Paris to NY.

Christmas Type of 1977

Paintings: 60fr, Virgin and Child with 4 Saints, by Bellini, horiz. 400fr, Adoration of the Shepherds, by George de la Tour, horiz.

1977, Dec. 15 Litho. *Perf. 12x12½*

C264 A165 60fr multi 35 22
C265 A165 400fr multi 2.25 1.75

Flag Type of 1978

Design: 60fr, New flag, Pres. Ahidjo and spear.

1978, Apr. 3 Litho. *Perf. 12½*

C266 A167 60fr multi 35 16

Frog Type of 1978

Design: 100fr, Cardioglossa trifasciata.

1978, Apr. 5

C267 A168 100fr multi 60 40

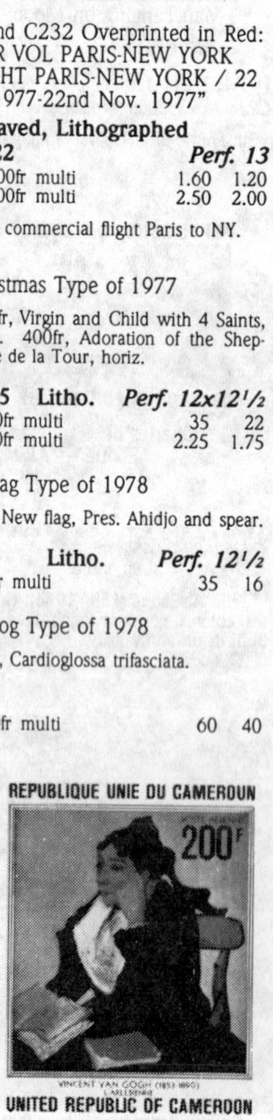

L'Arlesienne, by Van Gogh AP106

Painting: No. C269, Burial of Christ, by Albrecht Dürer.

1978, May 15 Litho. *Perf. 12½*

C268 AP106 200fr multi 1.40 1.10
C269 AP106 200fr multi 1.40 1.10

Leprosy Distribution on World Map, Raoul Follereau — AP107

1978, June 6 Litho. *Perf. 12*

C270 AP107 100fr multi 65 55

25th World Leprosy Day.

Capt. Cook and Siege of Quebec — AP108

Design: 250fr, Capt. Cook, Adventure and Resolution, map of voyages.

1978, July 26 Engr. *Perf. 13*

C271 AP108 100fr multi 65 55
C272 AP108 250fr multi 1.60 1.40

Capt. James Cook (1728-1779), explorer.

Argentine Soccer Team, Coat of Arms and Rimet Cup — AP109

Designs: 200fr, Two soccer players, vert. 1000fr, Soccer ball illuminating world map, vert.

1978, Sept. 1 Litho. *Perf. 13*

C273 AP109 100fr multi 65 55
C274 AP109 200fr multi 1.40 1.10
C275 AP109 1000fr multi 6.50 5.50
Nos. C273-C275 (3) 8.55 7.15

11th World Cup Soccer Championship, Argentina, June 1-25.

Jules Verne Type of 1978

Design: 400fr, Jules Verne and "20,000 Leagues Under the Sea," horiz.

1978, Oct. 10 Litho. *Perf. 12*

C276 A169 400fr multi 2.50 2.00

Musical Instrument Type of 1978

Design: 100fr, Man playing Mvet zither.

1978, Nov. 20 Litho. *Perf. 12½*

C277 A172 100fr multi 65 40

Human Rights Type of 1979

1979, Feb. 11 Litho. *Perf. 12x12½*

C278 A174 500fr multi 3.50 2.50

Lions Emblem, Map of District 403 — AP110

1979, Apr. 26 Litho. *Perf. 12½*

C279 AP110 60fr multi 40 25

21st Congress of Lions Club of Yaoundé.

Penny Black, Hill, Cameroun No. 9 — AP111

1979, Aug. 30 Engr. *Perf. 13*

C280 AP111 100fr multi 65 40

Sir Rowland Hill (1795-1879), originator of penny postage.

"TELECOM 79" — AP112

Pope Paul VI — AP113

1979, Sept. 26 Litho. *Perf. 13x12½*

C281 AP112 100fr multi 65 40

3rd World Telecommunications Exhibition, Geneva, Sept. 20-26.

1979, Oct. 23 Engr. *Perf. 12½x13*

C282 AP113 100fr shown 65 42
C283 AP113 100fr John Paul I 65 42
C284 AP113 100fr John Paul II 65 42
Nos. C282-C284 (3) 1.95 1.26

"Double Eagle" over French Coastline AP114

Design: No. C286, Balloonists and balloon.

1979, Dec. 15 Litho. *Perf. 12½*

C285 AP114 500fr multi 4.00 2.25
C286 AP114 500fr multi 4.00 2.25

First Transatlantic balloon crossing.

100-Meter Race — AP115

Designs: 150fr, Figure skating pairs. 200fr, Javelin. 300fr, Wrestling.

1980, Dec. 18 Litho. *Perf. 12½*

C287 AP115	100fr yel brn & brn		80	48
C288 AP115	150fr bl & brn		1.25	70
C289 AP115	200fr grn & brn		1.60	1.00
C290 AP115	300fr red & brn		2.50	1.40
	Nos. C287-C290 (4)		6.15	3.58

22nd Summer Olympic Games, Moscow, July 19-Aug. 3; 13th Winter Olympic Games, Lake Placid, Feb. 12-24 (150fr).

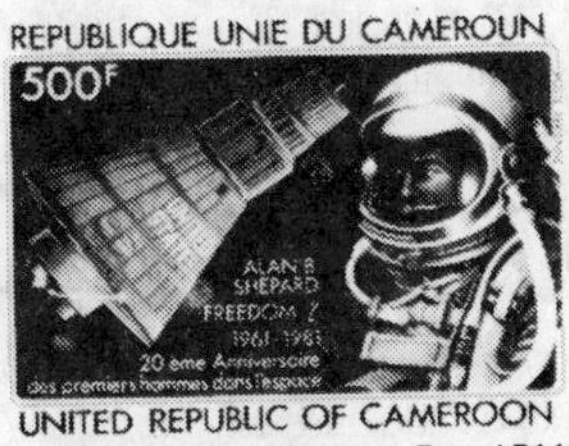

Alan Shepard and Freedom 7 — AP116

1981, Sept. 15 Litho. *Perf. 12½*

C291 AP116	500fr shown	6.00	4.00
C292 AP116	500fr Yuri Gagarin, Vostok I	6.00	4.00

Manned space flight, 20th anniv.

4th African Scouting Conference, Abidjan, June — AP117

1981, Oct. 5

C293 AP117	100fr Emblem, salute, badge	65	42
C294 AP117	500fr Scout saluting	3.50	2.00

Guernica (detail), by Pablo Picasso (1881-1973) — AP118

Design: No. C296, Landscape, by Paul Cezanne (1839-1906).

1981, Nov. 10 Litho. *Perf. 12½*

C295 AP118	500fr multi	3.50	2.00
C296 AP118	500fr multi	3.50	2.00

Christmas 1981 — AP119

Designs: 50fr, Virgin and Child, by Froment, vert. 60f, San Zeno Altarpiece, by Mantegna, vert. 400fr, Flight into Egypt, by Giotto.

1981, Dec. 1 Litho. *Perf. 12½*

C297 AP119	50fr multi	40	25
C298 AP119	60fr multi	48	32
C299 AP119	400fr multi	3.25	2.00
a.	Souv. sheet of 3, #C297-C299, perf. 13x13½	4.25	2.75
	Nos. C297-C299 (3)	4.13	2.57

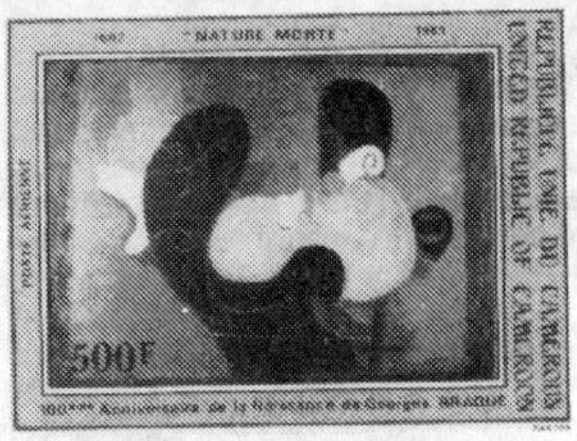

Still Life, by Georges Braque (1882-1963) — AP120

Paintings: No. C301, Olympia, by Edouard Manet (1832-1883).

1982, Dec. 5 Litho. *Perf. 13*

C300 AP120	500fr multi	3.00	2.00
C301 AP120	500fr multi	3.00	2.00

Pres. John F. Kennedy (1917-63) — AP121

Lions District 403 (Douala), 2nd Convention, May — AP122

1983, Mar. 15 Litho. *Perf. 13*

C302 AP121	500fr multi	3.50	2.00

1983, May 5 Litho. *Perf. 12½*

C303 AP122	70fr multi	40	30
C304 AP122	150fr multi	90	65

Jeanne of Aragon by Raphael AP123

Design: No. C306, Massacre of Scio by Delacroix.

1983, Oct. 15 Litho. *Perf. 13*

C305 AP123	500fr multi	2.00	1.00
C306 AP123	500fr multi	2.00	1.00

Easter 1984 — AP124

Designs: 200fr, Pieta, by G. Hernandez. 500fr, Martyrdom of St. John the Evangelist, by C. Le Brun.

1984, Mar. 30 Litho. *Perf. 13*

C307 AP124	200fr multi	75	50
C308 AP124	500fr multi	2.00	1.40
a.	Souv. sheet of 2, #C307-C308	3.00	2.00

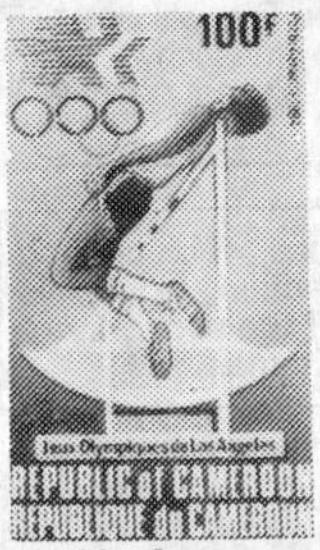

1984 Summer Olympics — AP125

European Soccer Championship, June 12-27 — AP126

1984, Apr. 30 *Perf. 12½*

C309 AP125	100fr High jump	35	22
C310 AP125	150fr Volleyball	50	32
C311 AP125	250fr Handball	80	55
C312 AP125	500fr Bicycling	1.60	1.10
	Nos. C309-C312 (4)	3.25	2.19

See Nos. C321-C324.

1984, June 5 Litho. *Perf. 12½*

C313 AP126	250fr Player in red shorts	1.00	65
C314 AP126	250fr Yellow shorts	1.00	65
C315 AP126	500fr Players	2.00	1.25
a.	Souvenir sheet of 3	4.00	2.75
	Nos. C313-C315 (3)	4.00	2.55

No. C315a contains Nos. C313-C315 in changed panel colors.

Presidential Oath — AP127

1984 Litho. *Perf. 13*

C316 AP127	60fr French inscription	20	15
a.	English inscription	20	15
C317 AP127	70fr French inscription	22	15
a.	English inscription	22	15
C318 AP127	200fr French inscription	60	40
a.	English inscription	60	40
	Nos. C316-C318 (3)	1.02	70

Issue dates: French, Sept. 15; English, Nov.

Famous Men — AP128

Paintings: No. C316, Diana in the Bath, by Watteau (1684-1721). No. C317, Portrait of Diderot (1713-1784).

1984, Sept. 20 Litho. *Perf. 13*

C319 AP128	500fr Watteau	1.50	1.00
C320 AP128	500fr Diderot, vert.	1.50	1.00

Nos. C309-C312 in Changed Colors with Added Inscriptions

100fr: MOEGENBURG (R.F.A.) 11-08-84

150fr: U.S.A. 11-08-84

250fr: YOUGOSLAVIE 9-08-84

500fr: GORSKI (U.S.A.) 3-08-84

1984, Sept. 25 Litho. *Perf. 12½*

C321 AP125	100fr multi	30	20
C322 AP125	150fr multi	45	30
C323 AP125	250fr multi	70	55
C324 AP125	500fr multi	1.50	1.00
	Nos. C321-C324 (4)	2.95	2.05

Moon Landing, 15th Anniv. — AP129

1984, Nov. 15 Litho. *Perf. 12½*

C325 AP129	500fr Neil Armstrong	1.50	1.00
C326 AP129	500fr Apollo 12 launching	1.50	1.00

Louis Pasteur (1822-1895), Chemist, Microbiologist — AP130

Designs: No. 328, Mourning Woman (detail), Mausoleum of Henri Claude d'Harcourt, by sculptor Jean Baptiste Pigalle (1714-1785).

1985, Oct. 10 Litho. *Perf. 13*

C327 AP130	500fr multi	2.00	2.00
C328 AP130	500fr multi	2.00	2.00

Christmas AP131

Designs: 250fr, Children's gifts. 300fr, Akono Church. 400fr, Holy Family and drummer boy. 500fr, The Virgin with the Blue Diadem, by Raphael.

1985, Dec. 20 Litho. *Perf. 13*

C329 AP131	250fr multi	90	90
C330 AP131	300fr multi	1.10	1.10
C331 AP131	400fr multi	1.50	1.50
C332 AP131	500fr multi	2.00	2.00
	Nos. C329-C332 (4)	5.50	5.50

1986 World Cup Soccer Championships, Mexico — AP132

1986 *Perf. 13½*

C333 AP132	250fr Argentina, winner	1.40	1.40
C334 AP132	300fr Stadium	1.65	1.65
C335 AP132	400fr Mexican team	2.25	2.25
	Nos. C333-C335 (3)	5.30	5.30

Famous Men — AP133

Designs: No. C336, Pierre Curie (1859-1906), chemist, atom, and elements. No. C337, Jean Mermoz (1901-1936), aviator, and aircraft.

1986, Sept. 10 Litho. *Perf. 12½*

C336	AP133	500fr multi	2.75	2.75
C337	AP133	500fr multi	2.75	2.75

AIR POST SEMI-POSTAL STAMPS

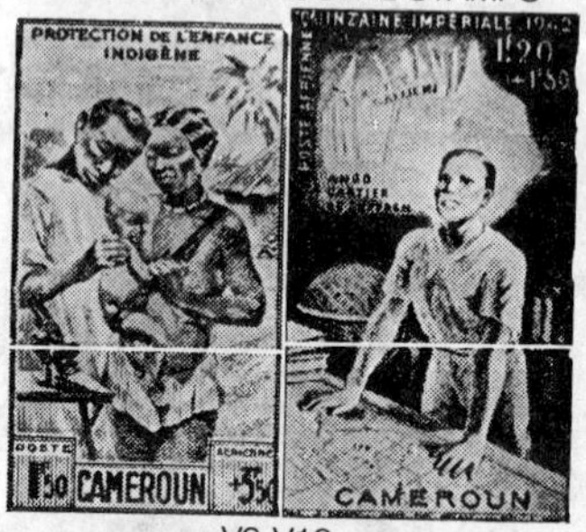

V9-V10

Stamps of the designs shown above were issued in 1942 by the Vichy Government, but were not placed on sale in Cameroun.

POSTAGE DUE STAMPS

Man Felling Tree — D1

Perf. 14x13½

1925-27 Unwmk. Typo.

J1	D1	2c lt bl & blk	15	15
J2	D1	4c ol bis & red vio	15	15
J3	D1	5c vio & blk	20	20
J4	D1	10c red & blk	20	20
J5	D1	15c gray & blk	25	25
J6	D1	20c olive grn & blk	30	30
J7	D1	25c yel & blk	35	35
J8	D1	30c blue & org	40	40
J9	D1	50c brn & blk	50	50
J10	D1	60c bl grn & rose red	60	60
J11	D1	1fr dl red & grn, *grnsh*	80	80
J12	D1	2fr red & vio ('27)	1.50	1.50
J13	D1	3fr org brn & ultra ('27)	2.25	2.25
		Nos. J1-J13 (13)	7.65	7.65

Shades occur for several values.

Carved Figures — D2

D3

1939 Engr. *Perf. 14x13*

J14	D2	5c brt red vio	15	15
J15	D2	10c Prus blue	35	35
J16	D2	15c car rose	15	15
J17	D2	20c blk brn	15	15
J18	D2	30c ultra	15	15
J19	D2	50c dk grn	15	15
J20	D2	60c brn vio	15	15
J21	D2	1fr dk vio	30	30
J22	D2	2fr org red	55	55
J23	D2	3fr dark blue	80	80
		Set value	2.50	2.50

A 10c stamp, type D2, without "RF" was issued in 1944 by the Vichy Government, but was not placed on sale in Cameroun.

Catalogue values for unused stamps in this section, from this point to the end of the section, are for Never Hinged items.

1947 Unwmk. *Perf. 13*

J24	D3	10c dark red	15	15
J25	D3	30c dp org	15	15
J26	D3	50c grnsh blk	15	15
J27	D3	1fr dark car	15	15
J28	D3	2fr dp yel grn	20	20
J29	D3	3fr dp red lil	22	22
J30	D3	4fr dp ultra	22	22
J31	D3	5fr red brn	25	25
J32	D3	10fr peacock bl	40	40
J33	D3	20fr sepia	65	65
		Set value	2.15	2.15

Federal Republic

Hibiscus — D4

Flowers: No. J35, Erythrine. No. J36, Plumeria lutea. No. J37, Ipomoea. No. J38, Hoodia gordonii. No. J39, Grinum. No. J40, Ochna. No. J41, Gloriosa. No. J42, Costus spectabilis. No. J43, Bougainvillea spectabilis. No. J44, Delonix regia. No. J45, Haemanthus. No. J46, Ophthalmophyllum. No. J47, Titanopsis. No. J48, Amorphophallus. No. J49, Zingiberacee.

Unwmk.

1963, Apr. 10 Engr. *Perf. 11*

J34	D4	50c car, bl, grn & yel	15	15
J35	D4	50c car, bl, grn & yel	15	15
J36	D4	1fr mag, grn & yel	15	15
J37	D4	1fr mag, grn & yel	15	15
J38	D4	1.50fr dk grn, lil & yel	15	15
J39	D4	1.50fr dk grn, lil & yel	15	15
J40	D4	2fr org ver, yel & grn	15	15
J41	D4	2fr org ver, yel & grn	15	15
J42	D4	5fr mag, grn & yel	15	15
J43	D4	5fr mag, grn & yel	15	15
J44	D4	10fr crim, grn & yel	22	22
J45	D4	10fr crim, grn & yel	22	22
J46	D4	20fr grn, yel & lil	45	45
J47	D4	20fr grn, yel & lil	45	45
J48	D4	40fr lilac & yel	80	80
J49	D4	40fr lilac & yel	80	80
		Set value	3.50	3.50

The two types of each denomination in Nos. J34-J49 were printed tête bêche, se-tenant at the base.

MILITARY STAMP

Catalogue values for unused stamps in this section are for Never Hinged items.

M1

1963, July 1 Unwmk. *Perf. 13*

M1	M1	rose claret	1.50	1.50

CAPE JUBY

LOCATION — Northwest coast of Africa in Spanish Sahara
GOVT. — Spanish administration
AREA — 12,700 sq. mi.
POP. — 9,836
CAPITAL — Villa Bens (Cape Juby)

By agreement with France, Spain's Sahara possessions were extended to include Cape Juby and in 1916 Spanish troops occupied the territory. It is attached for administrative purposes to Spanish Sahara.

100 Centimos = 1 Peseta

Stamps of Rio de Oro, 1914 Surcharged in Violet, Red or Green

CABO JUBI
5
CÉNTIMOS

1916 Unwmk. *Perf. 13*

1	A6	5c on 4p rose (V)	65.00	11.00
2	A6	10c on 10p dl vio (R)	24.50	11.00
3	A6	15c on 50c dk brn (G)	32.50	20.50
4	A6	15c on 50c dk brn (R)	24.00	11.00
5	A6	40c on 1p red vio (G)	50.00	25.00
6	A6	40c on 1p red vio (R)	40.00	14.00
		Nos. 1-6 (6)	236.00	92.50

Nos. 1-6 exist with inverted surcharge. Same values.

Stamps of Spain, 1876-1917, Overprinted in Red or Black

CABO JUBY

1919 *Imperf.*

7	A21	¼c bl grn (R)	15	15

Perf. 13x12½, 14

8	A46	2c dk brn (Bk)	15	15
a.		Double overprint	15.00	6.75
b.		Double overprint (Bk + R)	40.00	27.50
9	A46	5c grn (R)	35	15
a.		Double overprint	15.00	6.75
b.		Inverted overprint	21.50	14.00
10	A46	10c car (Bk)	42	15
a.		Double overprint (Bk + R)	40.00	27.50
11	A46	15c ocher (Bk)	2.00	15
b.		Double overprint	15.00	6.75
c.		Red control #	3.00	3.00
d.		As "c," inverted overprint	11.00	
12	A46	20c ol grn (R)	11.00	2.00
13	A46	25c dp bl (R)	1.75	20
a.		Double overprint	15.00	6.75
14	A46	30c bl grn (R)	1.75	25
15	A46	40c rose (Bk)	1.75	25
16	A46	50c sl bl (R)	2.00	25
17	A46	1p lake (Bk)	6.00	2.00
18	A46	4p dp vio (R)	22.50	9.25
19	A46	10p org (Bk)	32.50	10.00
		Nos. 7-19 (13)	82.32	24.95

Nos. 8-19 have blue control number on back. Nos. 8-13, 15, 17-19 exist imperf.

Same on Stamps of Spain, 1920-21

1922 *Imperf.*

20	A47	1c blue green (R)	15.00	8.50

Engr. *Perf. 13x12½*

Blue Control Number on Back

23	A46	20c violet	100.00	32.50

A 2c exists, value $150.

Same on Stamps of Spain, 1922-23

1925 *Perf. 13½x13*

25	A49	5c red vio	3.50	1.65
26	A49	10c bl grn	10.50	1.65
28	A49	20c violet	22.50	5.25
		Nos. 25-28 (3)	36.50	8.55

Exists on Spain No. 331, 2c olive green. Value $150 unused.

Seville-Barcelona Exposition Issue

Stamps of Spain, 1929, Overprinted in Red or Blue

CABO JUBY

1929 *Perf. 11*

29	A52	5c rose lake (Bl)	15	15
30	A53	10c green (R)	15	15
31	A50	15c Prus bl (R)	15	15
32	A51	20c pur (R)	15	15
33	A50	25c brt rose (Bl)	15	15
34	A52	30c blk brn (Bl)	20	25
35	A53	40c dk bl (R)	20	25
36	A51	50c dp org (Bl)	32	40
37	A52	1p bl blk (R)	9.25	5.75
38	A53	4p dp rose (Bl)	11.50	11.50
39	A53	10p brn (Bl)	11.50	8.25
		Nos. 29-39 (11)	33.72	27.15

Stamps of Spanish Morocco, 1928-33, Overprinted in Black or Red

Cabo Juby

1934 *Perf. 14*

40	A7	1c brt rose (Bk)	20	24
41	A2	2c dk vio (R)	1.90	28
42	A2	5c dp bl (R)	1.90	40
43	A2	10c dk grn (Bk)	4.25	75
43A	A10	10c dk grn (R)	1.40	1.10
44	A2	15c org brn (Bk)	9.50	3.50
45	A7	20c sl grn (R)	4.00	2.25
46	A3	25c cop red (Bk)	1.90	1.90
47	A10	30c red brn (Bk)	4.00	2.25
48	A13	40c dp bl (R)	13.00	8.50
49	A13	50c red org (Bk)	25.00	13.00
50	A4	1p yel grn (Bk)	15.00	7.50
51	A5	2.50p red vio (Bk)	35.00	16.00
52	A6	4p ultra (R)	45.00	21.00

No. 43A and 1c, 20c, 30c, 40c, 50c, with control numbers.

Same Overprint in Black on Stamp of Spanish Morocco, 1932

53	A2	1c car rose ("Ct")	85	40
		Nos. 40-53 (15)	162.90	79.07

Stamps of Spanish Morocco, 1933-35, Overprinted in Black, Blue or Red

CABO JUBY

1935-36

54	A8	2c grn (R)	32	15
55	A9	5c mag (Bk)	1.40	15
55A	A10	10c dk grn (R) ('36)	7.50	1.40
56	A11	15c yel (Bl)	3.00	90
57	A12	25c crim (Bk)	25.00	1.50
58	A8	1p sl blk (R)	4.50	2.25
59	A9	2.50p brn (Bl)	18.00	8.50
60	A11	4p yel grn (R)	24.00	10.00
61	A12	5p blk (R)	24.00	13.00
		Nos. 54-61 (9)	107.72	37.85

Same Overprint in Black or Red on Stamps of Spanish Morocco, 1935

1935 *Perf. 13½*

62	A14	25c vio (R)	2.25	1.00
63	A15	30c crim (Bk)	2.25	85
64	A14	40c org (Bk)	3.00	1.00
65	A15	50c brt bl (R)	6.00	1.00
66	A14	60c dk bl grn (R)	7.25	2.25
67	A15	2p brn lake (Bk)	40.00	14.00

Same Overprint on Stamps of Spanish Morocco, 1933

Perf. 13½, 14

68	A7	1c brt rose (Bk)	15	15

Perf. 14

69	A7	20c slate grn (R)	3.00	1.50
		Nos. 62-69 (8)	63.90	21.75

Same Overprint on Stamps of Spanish Morocco, 1937

1937 *Perf. 13½*

70	A21	1c dk bl (Bk)	16	15
71	A21	2c org brn (Bk)	16	15
72	A21	5c cer (Bk)	16	15
73	A21	10c emer (Bk)	16	15
74	A21	15c brt bl (Bk)	20	15
75	A21	20c red brn (Bk)	20	15
76	A21	25c mag (Bk)	20	15
77	A21	30c red org (Bk)	20	15
78	A21	40c org (Bk)	70	42
79	A21	50c ultra (R)	70	42
80	A21	60c yel grn (Bk)	70	42
81	A21	1p bl vio (Bk)	70	42
82	A21	2p Prus bl (Bk)	37.50	35.00
83	A21	2.50p gray blk (R)	37.50	35.00
84	A21	4p dk brn (Bk)	37.50	35.00
85	A22	10p vio blk (R)	37.50	35.00
		Nos. 70-85 (16)	154.24	142.88

1st Year of the Revolution.

Same Overprint in Black on Types of Spanish Morocco, 1939

Designs: 5c, Spanish quarter. 10c, Moroccan quarter. 15c, Street scene, Larache. 20c, Tetuan.

1939 Photo. *Perf. 13½*

86	A25	5c vermilion	40	30
87	A25	10c deep green	40	30
88	A25	15c brown lake	40	35
89	A25	20c bright blue	40	35
		Nos. 86-89 (4)	1.60	1.30

Same Overprint in Black or Red on Stamps of Spanish Morocco, 1940

1940 *Perf. 11½x11*

90	A26	1c dk brn (Bk)	15	15
91	A27	2c ol grn (R)	15	15
92	A28	5c dk bl (R)	15	15
93	A29	10c dk red lil (Bk)	15	15
94	A30	15c dk grn (R)	15	15
95	A31	20c pur (R)	15	15
96	A32	25c blk brn (R)	15	15
97	A33	30c brt grn (Bk)	15	15
98	A34	40c slate grn (R)	48	15
99	A35	45c org ver (Bk)	48	15
100	A36	50c brn org (Bk)	48	15
101	A37	70c saph (R)	1.25	48
102	A38	1p ind & brn (Bk)	2.75	48
103	A39	2.50p choc & dk grn (Bk)	7.00	3.25
104	A40	5p dk cer & sep (Bk)	7.00	3.25
105	A41	10p dk ol grn & brn org (Bk)	18.00	12.50
		Nos. 90-105 (16)	38.64	21.61

Imperfs exist.

Stamps of Spanish Morocco, 1944. Overprinted in Black or Red — **CABO JUBY**

1944, Oct. 2 **Unwmk.** *Perf. 12½*

106	A47	1c choc & lt bl	15	15
107	A48	2c slate grn & lt grn	15	15
108	A49	5c choc & grnsh blk (R)	15	15
109	A50	10c brt ultra & red org	15	15
110	A51	15c sl grn & lt grn	15	15
111	A52	20c dp cl & blk (R)	15	15
112	A53	25c lt bl & choc	15	15
113	A47	30c yel grn & brt ultra (R)	15	15
114	A48	40c choc & red vio	15	15
115	A49	50c brt ultra & red brn	15	15
116	A50	75c yel grn & brt ultra (R)	60	25
117	A51	1p brt ultra & choc	60	25
118	A52	2.50p blk & brt ultra (R)	1.65	1.25
119	A53	10p sal & gray blk (R)	11.50	9.25
		Nos. 106-119 (14)	15.85	12.50

Same Overprint on Stamps of Spanish Morocco, 1946

1946, Mar. *Perf. 10½x10*

120	A54	1c pur & brn	15	15
121	A55	2c dk Prus grn & vio blk (R)	15	15
122	A54	10c dp org vio bl	15	15
123	A55	15c dk bl & bl grn	15	15
124	A54	25c yel grn & ultra	15	15
125	A56	40c dk bl & brn (R)	15	15
126	A55	45c blk & rose	15	15
127	A57	1p dk Prus grn & dp bl	65	30
128	A58	2.50p dp org & grnsh gray (R)	2.00	1.50
129	A59	10p dk bl & gray (R)	6.50	4.50
		Nos. 120-129 (10)	10.20	7.35

Same Overprint in Carmine, Black or Brown on Stamps of Spanish Morocco, 1948

1948, Jan. 1 *Perf. 10, 10x10½*

130	A64	2c pur & brn	15	15
131	A65	5c dp claret & vio	15	15
132	A66	15c brt ultra & bl grn (Bk)	15	15
133	A67	25c blk & Prus grn	15	15
134	A65	35c brt ultra & gray blk	15	15
135	A68	50c red & vio (Br)	15	15
136	A66	70c dk gray grn & ultra (Bk)	15	15
137	A67	90c cer & dk gray grn (Bk)	15	15
138	A68	1p brt ultra & vio (Br)	18	18
139	A64	2.50p vio brn & sl grn	75	45
140	A69	10p blk & dp ultra	2.50	1.90
		Set value	4.05	3.15

SEMI-POSTAL STAMPS

Types of Semi-Postal Stamps of Spain, 1926, Overprinted — **CABO-JUBY**

1926 **Unwmk.** *Perf. 12½, 13*

B1	SP1	1c orange	5.50	3.00
B2	SP2	2c rose	5.50	3.00
B3	SP3	5c blk brn	1.50	1.25
B4	SP4	10c dk grn	1.00	1.00
B5	SP1	15c dk vio	1.00	1.00
B6	SP4	20c vio brn	1.00	1.00
B7	SP5	25c dp car	1.00	1.00
B8	SP1	30c ol grn	1.00	1.00
B9	SP3	40c ultra	1.00	1.00
B10	SP2	50c red brn	1.00	1.00
B11	SP4	1p vermilion	1.00	1.00
B12	SP3	4p bister	1.00	1.00
B13	SP5	10p lt vio	1.00	1.00
		Nos. B1-B13 (13)	22.50	17.25

Nos. B12-B13 surcharged "Alfonso XIII" and new value are listed as Spain Nos. B68-B69. See Spain No. B6a.

AIR POST STAMPS

Spanish Morocco, Nos. C1 to C10 Overprinted "CABO JUBY" as on #54-61

1938, June 1 **Unwmk.** *Perf. 13½*

C1	AP1	5c brown	15	15
C2	AP1	10c brt grn	15	15
C3	AP1	25c crimson	15	15
C4	AP1	40c light blue	1.50	65
C5	AP2	50c brt mag	15	15
C6	AP2	75c dk bl	15	15
C7	AP1	1p sepia	15	15
C8	AP1	1.50p dp vio	85	32
C9	AP1	2p dp red brn	2.00	85
C10	AP1	3p brn blk	5.25	2.75
		Nos. C1-C10 (10)	10.50	5.47

Strait of Gibraltar — AP3

Designs: 5c, Ketama landscape. 10c, Mosque, Tangier. 15c, Velez. 90c, Sanjurjo.

1942, Apr. 1 **Photo.** *Perf. 12½*

C11	AP3	5c deep blue	15	15
C12	AP3	10c org brn	15	15
C13	AP3	15c grnsh blk	15	15
C14	AP3	90c dk rose	40	22
C15	AP3	5p black	1.50	85
		Nos. C11-C15 (5)	2.35	
		Set value		1.20

SPECIAL DELIVERY STAMPS

Special Delivery Stamp of Spain Ovptd. "CABO JUBY" as on #7-28

1919 **Unwmk.** *Perf. 14*

E1	SD1	20c red (Bk)	1.25	75
b.		Double overprint	21.00	12.50

Spanish Morocco No. E4 Overprinted "CABO JUBY" as on Nos. 40-52 in Red

1934

E2 SD2 20c black 4.25 4.00

Spanish Morocco No. E5 Overprinted "CABO JUBY" as on Nos. 54-61

1935

E3 SD3 20c vermilion 2.25 65

Same Ovpt. on Spanish Morocco, No. E6

1937 *Perf. 13½*

E4 SD4 20c bright carmine 60 35

1st Year of the Revolution.

Same Ovpt. on Spanish Morocco, No. E8

1940 *Perf. 11½x11*

E5 SD5 25c scarlet 30 20

SEMI-POSTAL SPECIAL DELIVERY STAMP

Type of Semi-Postal Special Delivery Stamp of Spain, 1926, Overprinted "CABO-JUBY" as on Nos. B1-B13

1926 **Unwmk.** *Perf. 12½, 13*

EB1 SPSD1 20c ultra & black 1.50 1.10

CAPE VERDE

LOCATION — A group of 10 islands and five islets in the Atlantic Ocean, about 500 miles due west of Senegal.

GOVT. — Republic

AREA — 1,557 sq. mi.

POP. — 296,093 (1980)

CAPITAL — Praia

The Portuguese territory of Cape Verde became independent on July 5, 1975.

1000 Reis = 1 Milreis

100 Centavos = 1 Escudo (1913)

Catalogue values for unused stamps in this country are for Never Hinged items, beginning with Scott 268 in the regular postage section, Scott J31 in the postage due section, and Scott RA6 in the postal tax section.

Crown of Portugal — A1

King Luiz — A2

Perf. 12½, 13½

1877 **Unwmk.** **Typo.**

1	A1	5r black	1.10	1.00
2	A1	10r yellow	12.00	7.00
3	A1	20r bister	1.00	1.00
4	A1	25r rose	1.00	1.00
a.		Perf. 13½	5.75	4.00
5	A1	40r blue	40.00	20.00
a.		Cliche of Mozambique in Cape Verde plate, in pair with #5	700.00	500.00
b.		As "a," perf. 13½	1,500.	1,500.
6	A1	50r green	40.00	22.50
7	A1	100r lilac	4.25	1.50
8	A1	200r orange	1.75	1.50
a.		Perf. 13½	5.75	4.00
9	A1	300r brown	1.65	1.50
		Nos. 1-9 (9)	102.75	57.00

1881-85

10	A1	10r green	1.10	90
11	A1	20r carmine ('85)	2.25	1.50
a.		Perf. 13½	30.00	22.50
12	A1	25r violet ('85)	1.65	1.25
13	A1	40r yellow buff	1.10	90
a.		Imperf.	75	
b.		Cliche of Mozambique in Cape Verde plate, in pair with #13	50.00	50.00
c.		As "b," imperf.	25.00	
14	A1	50r blue	3.25	2.25
		Nos. 10-14 (5)	9.35	6.80

Reprints of the 1877-85 issues are on smooth white chalky paper, ungummed, and on thin white paper with shiny white gum. They are perf 13½.

1886 **Embossed** *Perf. 12½, 13½*

Chalk-Surfaced Paper

15	A2	5r black	2.25	1.50
16	A2	10r green	2.50	1.75
17	A2	20r carmine	3.50	2.50
a.		Perf. 13½	4.50	3.50
18	A2	25r violet	3.50	1.50
19	A2	40r chocolate	5.50	2.00
a.		Perf. 13½	6.25	4.00
20	A2	50r blue	4.75	1.75
21	A2	100r yel brown	4.25	2.25
22	A2	200r gray lilac	9.50	6.50
23	A2	300r orange	12.50	9.50
		Nos. 15-23 (9)	48.25	29.25

The 25, 50 and 100r have been reprinted in aniline colors with clean-cut Perf. 13½.

For surcharges see Nos. 59-67, 184-187.

King Carlos

A3 A4

Perf. 11½, 12½, 13½

1894-95 **Typo.**

24	A3	5r orange	90	60
25	A3	10r redsh violet	90	70
26	A3	15r chocolate	1.50	1.00
a.		Perf. 12½	100.00	67.50
27	A3	20r lavender	1.90	1.25
28	A3	25r dp green	1.90	1.40
a.		Perf. 12½	2.75	2.00
29	A3	50r lt blue	1.50	1.40
a.		Perf. 13½	6.50	2.00
30	A3	75r carmine ('95)	6.25	3.75
a.		Perf. 13½	17.50	10.50
31	A3	80r yel grn ('95)	7.75	5.00
a.		Perf. 13½	16.00	12.50
32	A3	100r brn, *buff* ('95)	5.25	1.50
a.		Perf. 12½	37.50	14.00
33	A3	150r car, *rose* ('95)	10.50	7.75
a.		Perf. 12½	100.00	80.00
b.		Perf. 11½	35.00	25.00
34	A3	200r dk blue, *lt blue* ('95)	8.75	5.50
a.		Perf. 12½	90.00	75.00
35	A3	300r dk blue, *sal* ('95)	15.00	9.50
		Nos. 24-35 (12)	62.10	39.35

For surcharges see Nos. 68-78, 137, 189-193, 201-205.

1898-1903 *Perf. 11½*

Name and Value in Black except 500r

36	A4	2½r gray	20	15
37	A4	5r orange	20	15
38	A4	10r lt green	45	15
39	A4	15r brown	2.50	1.00
40	A4	15r gray green ('03)	90	70
41	A4	20r gray violet	1.00	35
42	A4	25r sea green	2.25	70
a.		Perf. 12½	52.50	30.00
43	A4	25r carmine ('03)	55	16
44	A4	50r dark blue	2.25	60
45	A4	50r brown ('03)	1.75	1.40
46	A4	65r slate blue ('03)	12.00	*16.00*
47	A4	75r rose	4.25	2.00
48	A4	75r lilac ('03)	1.50	1.25
49	A4	80r violet	3.75	2.50
50	A4	100r dk blue, *blue*	1.25	75
51	A4	115r org brn, *pink* ('03)	8.00	*10.00*
52	A4	130r brown, *straw* ('03)	8.00	*10.00*
53	A4	150r brown, *straw*	6.00	4.25
54	A4	200r red vio, *pnksh*	1.75	1.40
55	A4	300r dk blue, *rose*	6.25	2.50
56	A4	400r dull blue, *straw* ('03)	5.25	4.25
57	A4	500r blk & red, *blue* ('01)	5.25	2.50
58	A4	700r violet, *yelsh* ('01)	14.00	8.75
		Nos. 36-58 (23)	89.30	71.51

For overprints and suecharges see Nos. 80-99, 139, 200.

Regular Issues Surcharged in Red or Black — **65 RÉIS**

Two spacing types of surcharge. See note above Angola No. 61.

On Issue of 1886

1902, Dec. 1 *Perf. 12½, 13½*

59	A2	65r on 5r black (R)	3.00	2.50
60	A2	65r on 200r gray lilac	3.00	2.50
61	A2	65r on 300r orange	3.00	2.50
62	A2	115r on 10r green	3.00	2.75
63	A2	115r on 20r rose	3.00	2.75
a.		Perf. 13½	27.50	18.00
64	A2	130r on 50r blue	3.00	2.50
65	A2	130r on 100r brown	3.00	2.50
66	A2	400r on 25r violet	1.50	1.25
67	A2	400r on 40r choc	2.50	2.00
a.		Perf. 13½	27.50	22.50

On Issue of 1894

Perf. 11½, 12½, 13½

68	A3	65r on 10r red violet	4.75	3.00
69	A3	65r on 20r lavender	4.50	2.50
70	A3	65r on 100r brown, *buff*	4.50	3.00
a.		Perf 12½	12.00	10.00
71	A3	115r on 5r orange	2.50	1.90
a.		Inverted surcharge	40.00	40.00
72	A3	115r on 25r blue grn	2.50	1.90
a.		Perf. 11½	14.00	6.00
73	A3	115r on 150r car, *rose*	4.50	3.75
a.		Perf. 13½	20.00	12.00
74	A3	130r on 75r car	2.50	2.00
a.		Perf. 13½	25.00	22.50
75	A3	130r on 80r yel grn	2.25	2.00
76	A3	130r on 200r dk blue, *blue*	3.00	1.90
77	A3	400r on 50r lt blue	3.00	2.50
a.		Inverted surcharge	65.00	55.00
b.		Perf. 13½	40.00	32.50
78	A3	400r on 300r dk blue, *sal*	1.50	1.10

On Newspaper Stamp of 1893

79	N1	400r on 2½r brown	1.25	1.10
a.		Inverted surcharge	25.00	
b.		Perf. 12½	30.00	20.00
		Nos. 59-79 (21)	61.75	47.90

Reprints of Nos. 59, 66, 67, and 77 have shiny white gum and clean-cut perforation 13½.

For overprint and surcharge see #137, 205-206.

Overprinted in Black On Nos. 39, 42, 44, 47 — **PROVISORIO**

1902-03 *Perf. 11½*

80 A4 15r brown	1.50	75
81 A4 25r sea green	1.50	75
82 A4 50r blue ('03)	1.75	1.00
83 A4 75r rose ('03)	2.25	1.40
a. Inverted overprint	40.00	40.00
Nos. 80-83 (4)	7.00	3.90

For overprint see No. 139.

No. 46 Surcharged in Black

50 RÉIS

1905, July 1

84 A4 50r on 65r slate blue	1.50	1.50

Stamps of 1898-1903 Overprinted in Carmine or Green

REPUBLICA

1911, Aug. 20

85 A4 2½r gray	20	15
86 A4 5r orange	20	15
87 A4 10r lt green	60	52
88 A4 15r gray green	35	20
89 A4 20r gray violet	65	65
90 A4 25r carmine (G)	65	32
91 A4 50r brown	4.00	2.75
92 A4 75r red lilac	85	50
93 A4 100r dk blue, *blue*	85	60
94 A4 115r org brn, *pink*	45	*1.25*
95 A4 130r brown, *straw*	45	*1.25*
96 A4 200r red vio, *pnksh*	3.25	3.25
97 A4 400r dull bl, *straw*	1.25	1.25
98 A4 500r blk & red, *bl*	1.50	1.10
99 A4 700r violet, *straw*	1.50	1.10
Nos. 85-99 (15)	16.75	15.04

King Manuel II — A5

Overprinted in Carmine or Green

1912 *Perf. 11½x12*

100 A5 2½r violet	15	*1.25*
101 A5 5r black	15	15
102 A5 10r gray grn	15	15
103 A5 20r carmine (G)	1.25	70
104 A5 25r vio brown	25	15
105 A5 50r dk blue	2.00	1.65
106 A5 75r bister brn	45	32
107 A5 100r brown, *lt grn*	45	32
108 A5 200r dk green, *sal*	70	60
109 A5 300r black, *azure*	70	60

Perf. 14½x15

110 A5 400r black & blue	2.00	1.65
111 A5 500r ol grn & vio brn	2.00	1.65
Nos. 100-111 (12)	10.25	9.19

Vasco da Gama Issue of Various Portuguese Colonies

Common Design Types CD20-CD27 Surcharged

REPUBLICA
CABO VERDE
¼ C.

On Stamps of Macao

1913, Feb. 13 *Perf. 12½ to 16*

112 ¼c on ½a blue grn	1.10	1.10
113 ½c on 1a red	1.10	1.10
114 1c on 2a red violet	1.10	1.10
115 2½c on 4a yel grn	1.10	1.10
116 5c on 8a dk blue	5.00	5.00
117 7½c on 12a vio brn	4.00	4.00
118 10c on 16a bister brn	2.50	2.50
119 15c on 24a bister	4.00	3.00
Nos. 112-119 (8)	19.90	18.90

On Stamps of Portuguese Africa
Perf. 14 to 15

120 ¼c on 2½r bl grn	85	85
121 ½c on 5r red	85	85
122 1c on 10r red vio	85	85
123 2½c on 25r yel grn	85	85
124 5c on 50r dk blue	1.50	1.50
125 7½c on 75r vio brn	2.00	2.00
126 10c on 100r bis brn	1.75	1.75
127 15c on 150r bister	2.50	2.50
Nos. 120-127 (8)	11.15	11.15

On Stamps of Timor

128 ¼c on ½a bl grn	1.10	1.10
129 ½c on 1a red	1.10	1.10
130 1c on 2a red vio	1.10	1.10
131 2½c on 4a yel grn	1.10	1.10
132 5c on 8a dk blue	3.75	3.75
133 7½c On 12a vio brn	3.75	3.75
134 10c on 16a bis brn	2.25	2.25
135 15c on 24a bister	2.75	2.75
Nos. 128-135 (8)	16.90	16.90
Nos. 112-135 (24)	47.95	46.95

For surcharges see Nos. 197-198.

No. 75 Overprinted in Red

REPUBLICA

1913 *Perf. 11½, 12½, 13½*

137 A3 130r on 80r yel grn	2.50	2.00

Nos. 73 and 76 overprinted but not issued. Values, $10, $12.

Same Overprint on No. 83 in Green

1914 *Perf. 12*

139 A4 75r rose	2.50	2.00
a. "PROVISORIO" double (G and R)	45.00	40.00

Ceres — A6

Perf. 11½, 12x11½, 15x14

1914-26 **Typo.**

Name and Value in Black

144 A6 ¼c olive brn	15	15
a. Imperf.		
145 A6 ½c black	15	15
146 A6 1c blue grn	80	75
147 A6 1c yel grn ('22)	15	15
148 A6 1½c lilac brown	15	15
149 A6 2c carmine	15	15
150 A6 2c gray ('26)	25	*5.00*
151 A6 2½c lt violet	15	15
152 A6 3c org ('22)	30	25
153 A6 4c rose ('22)	15	*1.65*
154 A6 4½c gray ('22)	15	*5.00*
155 A6 5c deep blue	75	45
156 A6 5c brt blue ('22)	15	15
157 A6 6c lilac ('22)	15	*2.75*
158 A6 7c ultra ('22)	15	*2.75*
159 A6 7½c yel brn	15	*1.00*
160 A6 8c slate	40	30
161 A6 10c orange brn	15	15
162 A6 12c blue grn ('22)	35	25
163 A6 15c plum	6.50	6.00
164 A6 15c brn rose ('22)	25	15
165 A6 20c yel grn	20	15
166 A6 24c ultra ('26)	1.40	*1.40*
167 A6 25c choc ('26)	1.40	1.40
168 A6 30c brown, *grn*	3.50	3.50
169 A6 30c gray grn ('22)	35	25
170 A6 40c brown, *pink*	3.75	3.75
171 A6 40c turq blue ('22)	90	22
172 A6 50c orange, *sal*	3.75	3.75
173 A6 50c violet ('26)	1.40	30
174 A6 60c dk blue ('22)	1.40	45
175 A6 60c rose ('26)	1.25	45
176 A6 80c brt rose ('22)	2.50	1.10
177 A6 1e green, *blue*	3.75	3.75
178 A6 1e rose ('22)	3.75	2.25
179 A6 1e dp blue ('26)	3.00	1.50
180 A6 2e dk violet ('22)	3.75	2.00
181 A6 5e buff ('26)	6.75	4.75
182 A6 10e pink ('26)	13.00	9.00
183 A6 20e pale turq ('26)	37.50	18.00
Nos. 144-183 (40)	104.85	85.47

For surcharge see No. 214.

Provisional Issue of 1902 Overprinted in Carmine

REPUBLICA

1915 *Perf. 11½, 12½, 13½*

184 A2 115r on 10r green	1.75	1.75
a. Perf. 13½	15.00	15.00
185 A2 115r on 20r rose	1.25	1.25
a. Perf. 13½	15.00	15.00
186 A2 130r on 50r blue	1.10	1.10
187 A2 130r on 100r brown	70	70
188 A3 115r on 5r orange	50	38
a. Inverted overprint	30.00	
189 A3 115r on 25r blue grn	70	65
a. Perf. 11½	15.00	15.00
190 A3 115r on 150r car, *rose*	50	32
191 A3 130r on 75r carmine	85	85
192 A3 130r on 80r yel grn	70	70
a. Inverted overprint	30.00	
193 A3 130r on 200r bl, *bl*	85	85
a. Perf. 12½	40.00	32.50
Nos. 184-193 (10)	8.90	8.55

War Tax Stamps of Portuguese Africa Surcharged

CABO VERDE
CORREIOS
½ C.

1921, Feb. 3 *Perf. 15x14, 11½*

194 WT1 ¼c on 1c green	22	22
195 WT1 ½c on 1c green	40	28
a. "1/2" instead of "½" as shown	10.00	10.00
196 WT1 1c green	40	28

Nos. 127 and 126 Surcharged

2 C.

Perf. 14 to 15

197 CD27 2c on 15c on 150r	1.00	1.00
198 CD26 4c on 10c on 100r	1.25	1.00
a. On No. 118 (error)	150.00	150.00

The 4c surcharge also exists on No. 134.

No. 50 Surcharged

6 C.
REPUBLICA

Perf. 12

200 A4 6c on 100r dk bl, *bl*	1.25	1.25
a. No accent on "U" of surcharge	12.50	8.00
Nos. 194-200 (6)	4.52	4.03

No. 200 has an accent on the "U" of the surcharge.

Stamps of 1913-15 Surcharged

$04

1922, Apr. *Perf. 11½, 12½, 13½*

On No. 137

201 A3 4c on 130r on 80r	1.25	1.25

On Nos. 191-193

202 A3 4c on 130r on 75r	1.65	1.65
203 A3 4c on 130r on 80r	1.25	1.25
204 A3 4c on 130r on 200r	85	60
a. Perf. 12½	15.00	15.00
Nos. 201-204 (4)	5.00	4.75

Surcharge of Nos. 201-204 with smaller $ occurs once in sheet of 28. Value eight times normal.

Nos. 78-79 Surcharged

República
40 C.

1925 *Perf. 13½, 11½*

205 A3 40c on 400r on 300r	60	55
206 N1 40c on 400r on 2½r	40	45

No. 176 Surcharged

70 C.

1931, Nov. *Perf. 12x11½*

214 A6 70c on 80c brt rose	2.75	1.40

Ceres — A7

1934, May 1 **Wmk. 232**

215 A7 1c bister	15	*1.25*
216 A7 5c olive brown	15	15
217 A7 10c violet	16	15
218 A7 15c black	18	15
219 A7 20c gray	22	15
220 A7 30c dk green	28	15
221 A7 40c red org	38	20
222 A7 45c brt blue	75	42
223 A7 50c brown	70	40
224 A7 60c olive grn	70	40
225 A7 70c brown org	70	40
226 A7 80c emerald	70	40
227 A7 85c deep rose	2.25	2.00
228 A7 1e maroon	1.75	55
229 A7 1.40e dk blue	3.00	2.25
230 A7 2e dk violet	3.50	1.75
231 A7 5e apple green	12.50	4.00
232 A7 10e olive bister	21.00	9.50
233 A7 20e orange	45.00	30.00
Nos. 215-233 (19)	94.07	54.27

For surcharge see No. 256.

Vasco da Gama Issue
Common Design Types

1938 **Unwmk.** *Perf. 13½x13*

Name and Value in Black

234 CD34 1c gray green	15	*70*
235 CD34 5c orange brn	15	*70*
236 CD34 10c dk carmine	15	15
237 CD34 15c dk vio brn	52	30
238 CD34 20c slate	20	16
239 CD35 30c rose vio	35	16
240 CD35 35c brt green	35	20
241 CD35 40c brown	35	16
242 CD35 50c brt red vio	35	16
243 CD36 60c gray blk	60	28
244 CD36 70c brown vio	60	20
245 CD36 80c orange	60	20
246 CD36 1e red	60	16
247 CD37 1.75e blue	1.10	42
248 CD37 2e dk blue grn	1.75	70
249 CD37 5e ol grn	4.50	1.40
250 CD38 10e blue vio	6.25	1.40
251 CD38 20e red brown	16.00	3.50
Nos. 234-251 (18)	34.57	10.95

For surcharges see #255, 271-276, 288-292.

Outline Map of Africa — A8

1939, June 23 **Litho.** *Perf. 11½x12*

252 A8 80c vio, *pale rose*	2.00	1.40
253 A8 1.75e blue, *pale bl*	10.00	7.00
254 A8 20e brown, *buff*	35.00	25.00
Nos. 252-254 (3)	47.00	33.40

Visit of the President of Portugal in 1939.

Nos. 239 and 221 Surcharged with New Value and Bars in Black

1948 **Unwmk.** *Perf. 13½x13*

255 CD35 10c on 30c rose violet	90	1.25

Perf. 12x11½
Wmk. 232

256 A7 25c on 40c red orange	1.00	1.25

Machado Pt., Sao Vicente — A9

Brava Creek, Sao Nicoláo — A10

Designs: 10c, Ribeira Grande. 1e, Harbor, Sao Vicente. 1.75e, Mindelo, distant view. 2e, Joao de Evora Beach. 5e, Mindelo. 10e, Volcano, Fire Island. 20e, Mt. Paul.

Perf. 14½

1948, Oct. 1 Litho. Unwmk.

257	A9	5c vio brn & bis	18	18
258	A9	10c ol grn & pale grn	18	15
259	A10	50c mag & lil rose	35	15
260	A10	1e brn vio & rose lil	1.25	60
261	A10	1.75e ultra & grnsh bl	1.50	1.10
262	A10	2e dk brn & buff	7.25	90
263	A10	5e ol grn & yel	10.50	4.25
264	A10	10e red & cream	13.00	7.25
265	A10	20e dk vio & bis	32.50	12.00
		Nos. 257-265 (9)	66.71	26.58

Common Design Types pictured in section at front of book

Lady of Fatima Issue
Common Design Type

1948, Dec.

266	CD40	50c dark blue	5.00	3.00

UPU Symbols — A10a

1949, Oct. *Perf. 14*

267	A10a	1e red vio & pink	2.00	2.00

UPU, 75th anniversary.

Catalogue values for unused stamps in this section, from this point to the end of the section, are for Never Hinged items.

Holy Year Issue
Common Design Types

1950, May *Perf. 13x13½*

268	CD41	1e orange brown	35	30
269	CD42	2e slate	1.75	1.10

Holy Year Conclusion Issue
Common Design Type

1951, Oct. Unwmk. *Perf. 14*

270	CD43	2e purple & lilac	75	60

Nos. 240, 244-245, 247, 250 Surcharged with New Value and Bars

Perf. 13½x13

1951, May 21 Unwmk.

271	CD35	10c on 35c	28	*1.00*
272	CD36	20c on 70c	42	*1.00*
273	CD36	40c on 70c	1.00	*1.40*
274	CD36	50c on 80c	1.75	*2.00*
275	CD37	1e on 1.75e	2.00	*2.75*
276	CD38	2e on 10e	3.50	*5.25*
a.		1e on 10e	225.00	175.00
		Nos. 271-276 (6)	8.95	*13.40*

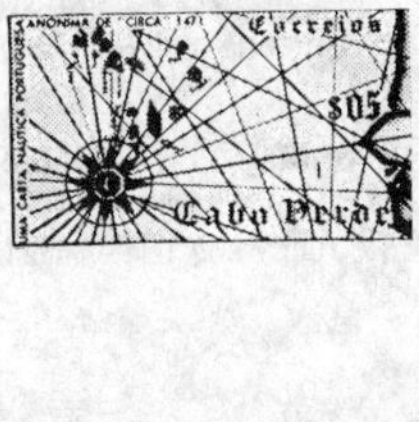

Map of Cape Verde Islands, 1502 — A11

Vicente Dias and Gonçalo de Cintra — A12

Portraits: 30c, Diogo Alfonso and Alvaro Fernandes. 50c, Lançarote and Soeiro da Costa. 1e, Diogo Gomes and Antonio da Nola. 2e, Prince Fernando and Prince Henry the Navigator. 3e, Antao Gonçalves and Dinis Dias. 5e, Alfonso Goncalves Baldaia and Joao Fernandes. 10e, Dinis Eanes da Gra and Alvaro de Freitas. 20e, Map of Cape Verde Islands, 1502.

1952, Feb. 24 *Perf. 14*

277	A11	5c multicolored	15	15
278	A12	10c multicolored	15	15
279	A12	30c multicolored	15	15
280	A12	50c multicolored	15	15
281	A12	1e multicolored	20	15
282	A12	2e multicolored	60	15
283	A12	3e multicolored	3.50	55
284	A12	5e multicolored	1.75	30
285	A12	10e multicolored	2.75	65
286	A11	20e multicolored	6.00	85
		Nos. 277-286 (10)	15.40	3.25

Medical Congress Issue
Common Design Type

Design: Hypodermic Injection.

1952, June *Perf. 13½*

287	CD44	20c ol grn & dk brn	40	30

No. 247 Surcharged with New Values and "X" in Black

1952, Jan. 25 *Perf. 13½x13*

288	CD37	10c on 1.75e	1.50	1.10
289	CD37	20c on 1.75e	1.50	1.10
290	CD37	50c on 1.75e	5.00	3.50
291	CD37	1e on 1.75e	75	45
292	CD37	1.50e on 1.75e	75	45
		Nos. 288-292 (5)	9.50	6.60

Facade of Jeronymos Convent — A13

Perf. 13½

1953, Jan. Unwmk. Litho.

293	A13	10c brn & pale olive	15	15
294	A13	50c purple & fawn	25	15
295	A13	1e dark green & fawn	65	42
		Nos. 293-295 (3)	1.05	72

Exhibition of Sacred Missionary Art held at Lisbon in 1951.

Stamp of Portugal and Arms of Colonies — A13a

1953 Photo.

296	A13a	50c multicolored	75	40

Centenary of Portuguese stamps.

Sao Paulo Issue
Common Design Type

1954 Litho. *Perf. 13½*

297	CD46	1e grn, cream & gray	35	15

Belem Tower, Lisbon, and Colonial Arms — A14

Arms of Praia — A15

1955, May 15 Litho. *Perf. 13½*

298	A14	1e multicolored	30	20
299	A14	1.60e buff & multi	50	30

Visit of Pres. Francisco H. C. Lopes.

1958, June 14 *Perf. 12x11½*

300	A15	1e multicolored	30	16
301	A15	2.50e pink & multi	60	20

Centenary of city of Praia.

Fair Emblem, Globe and Arms — A15a

1958 *Perf. 12x11½*

302	A15a	2e multicolored	45	30

World's Fair, Brussels, Apr. 17-Oct. 19.

Tropical Medicine Congress Issue
Common Design Type

1958, Sept. 5 *Perf. 13½*

303	CD47	3e Aloe vera	2.00	1.25

Prince Henry — A16

Antonio da Nola — A17

1960, June 25 Litho. *Perf. 13½*

304	A16	2e multicolored	30	15

500th anniv. of the death of Prince Henry the Navigator.

1960, Oct. Unwmk. *Perf. 14½*

Design: 2.50e, Diogo Gomes.

305	A17	1e multicolored	35	24
306	A17	2.50e multicolored	80	50

Discovery of Cape Verde, 500th anniv.

School Children — A18

1960

307	A18	2.50e multicolored	65	30

10th anniv. of the Commission for Technical Cooperation in Africa South of the Sahara (C.C.T.A.).

Arms of Praia — A19

Designs: Arms of various cities and towns of Cape Verde.

1961, July Litho. *Perf. 13½*

308	A19	5c shown	15	15
309	A19	15c Nova Sintra	15	15
310	A19	20c Ribeira Brava	15	15
311	A19	30c Assomada	15	15
312	A19	1e Maio	40	15
313	A19	2e Mindelo	32	15
314	A19	2.50e Santa Maria	60	15
315	A19	3e Pombas	1.10	20
316	A19	5e Sal-Rei	1.10	20
317	A19	7.50e Tarrafal	65	25
318	A19	15e Maria Pia	1.10	40
319	A19	30e San Felipe	2.25	85
		Nos. 308-319 (12)	8.12	
		Set value		2.45

Sports Issue
Common Design Type

Sports: 50c, Javelin. 1e, Discus. 1.50e, Cricket. 2.50e, Boxing. 4.50e, Hurdling. 12.50e, Golf.

1962, Jan. 18 *Perf. 13½*

320	CD48	50c lt brown	15	15
321	CD48	1e lt green	52	18
322	CD48	1.50e lt blue grn	30	15
323	CD48	2.50e pale vio bl	45	22
324	CD48	4.50e orange	75	45
325	CD48	12.50e beige	1.65	1.10
		Nos. 320-325 (6)	3.82	2.25

Anti-Malaria Issue
Common Design Type

Design: Anopheles pretoriensis.

1962 Litho. *Perf. 13½*

326	CD49	2.50e multicolored	60	42

Airline Anniversary Issue
Common Design Type

1963, Oct. Unwmk. *Perf. 14½*

327	CD50	2.50e gray & multi	40	25

National Overseas Bank Issue
Common Design Type

Design: 1.50e, Jose da Silva Mendes Leal.

1964, May 16 *Perf. 13½*

328	CD51	1.50e multicolored	40	32

ITU Issue
Common Design Type

1965, May 17 Litho. *Perf. 14½*

329	CD52	2.50e buff & multi	1.00	65

Militia Drummer, 1806 — A20

Designs: 1e, Soldier, Militia, 1806. 1.50e, Grenadier officer, 1833. 2.50e, Grenadier, 1833. 3e, Cavalry officer, 1834. 4e, Grenadier, 1835. 5e, Artillery officer, 1848. 10e, Drum major, infantry, 1856.

1965, Dec. 1 Litho. *Perf. 14½*

330	A20	50c multicolored	15	15
331	A20	1e multicolored	20	15
332	A20	1.50e multicolored	30	15
333	A20	2.50e multicolored	65	15
334	A20	3e multicolored	1.10	25
335	A20	4e multicolored	75	25
336	A20	5e multicolored	75	30
337	A20	10e multicolored	1.40	1.00
		Nos. 330-337 (8)	5.30	2.40

National Revolution Issue
Common Design Type

Design: 1e, Dr. Adriano Moreira School and Health Center.

1966, May 28 **Litho.** ***Perf. 12***

338	CD53	1e multicolored	30	30

Navy Club Issue
Common Design Type

Designs: 1e, Capt. Fontoura da Costa and gunboat Mandovy. 1.50e, Capt. Carvalho Araujo and minesweeper Augusto Castilho.

1967, Jan. 31 **Litho.** ***Perf. 13***

339	CD54	1e multicolored	48	24
340	CD54	1.50e multicolored	80	32

Virgin Mary Statue — A21

Pres. Rodrigues Thomaz — A22

1967, May 13 **Litho.** ***Perf. 12½x13***

341	A21	1e multicolored	20	15

50th anniv. of the apparition of the Virgin Mary to 3 shepherd children at Fatima.

1968, Feb. 9 **Litho.** ***Perf. 13½***

342	A22	1e multicolored	20	20

Issued to commemorate the 1968 visit of Pres. Americo de Deus Rodrigues Thomaz.

Cabral Issue

Pedro Alvares Cabral — A23

Design: 1e, Cantino's world map, 1502, horiz.

1968, Apr. 22 **Litho.** ***Perf. 14***

343	A23	1e multicolored	70	30
344	A23	1.50e multicolored	80	30

See note after Angola No. 545.
For overprint see No. 365.

Sao Vicente Harbor — A24

Physic Nut — A25

Designs: 1.50e, Peanut plant. 2.50e, Castor-oil plant. 3.50e, Yams. 4e, Date palm. 4.50e, Guavas. 5e, Tamarind. 10e, Bitter cassava. 30e, Woman carrying fruit baskets.

1968, Oct. 15 **Litho.** ***Perf. 14***

345	A24	50c multicolored	15	15
346	A25	1e multicolored	15	15
347	A25	1.50e multicolored	15	15
348	A25	2.50e multicolored	15	15
349	A25	3.50e multicolored	20	15
350	A25	4e multicolored	20	15
351	A25	4.50e multicolored	25	15
352	A25	5e multicolored	25	15
353	A25	10e multicolored	52	22
354	A25	30e multicolored	2.00	85
		Nos. 345-354 (10)	4.02	
		Set value		1.75

For overprint see No. 372.

Admiral Coutinho Issue
Common Design Type

Design: 30c, Adm. Coutinho and map showing route of first flight from Lisbon to Rio de Janeiro, vert.

1969, Feb. 17 **Litho.** ***Perf. 14***

355	CD55	30c multicolored	15	15

For surcharge see No. 388.

Vasco da Gama — A26

King Manuel I — A27

Vasco da Gama Issue

1969, Aug. 29 **Litho.** ***Perf. 14***

356	A26	1.50e multicolored	15	15

Vasco da Gama (1469-1524), navigator.

Administration Reform Issue
Common Design Type

1969, Sept. 25 **Litho.** ***Perf. 14***

357	CD56	2e multicolored	15	15

King Manuel I Issue

1969, Dec. 1 **Litho.** ***Perf. 14***

358	A27	3e multicolored	25	15

500th anniv. of the birth of King Manuel I.

Marshal Carmona Issue
Common Design Type

Design: 2.50e, Antonio Oscar Carmona in marshal's uniform.

1970, Nov. 15 **Litho.** ***Perf. 14***

359	CD57	2.50e multi	25	15

Galleons on Sanaga River — A28

1972, May 25 **Litho.** ***Perf. 13***

360	A28	5e lilac rose & multi	25	15

4th centenary of the publication of The Lusiads by Luiz Camoens.

Olympic Games Issue
Common Design Type

Design: 4e, Basketball and boxing, Olympic emblem.

1972, June 20 ***Perf. 14x13½***

361	CD59	4e multicolored	25	15

Lisbon-Rio de Janeiro Flight Issue
Common Design Type

Design: "Lusitania" landing at San Vicente.

1972, Sept. 20 **Litho.** ***Perf. 13½***

362	CD60	3.50e multi	32	15

WMO Centenary Issue
Common Design Type

1973, Dec. 15 **Litho.** ***Perf. 13***

363	CD61	2.50e ultra & multi	32	15

For overprint see No. 387.

Mindelo Desalination Plant — A29

1974 **Litho.** ***Perf. 13½***

364	A29	4e multicolored	50	25

Opening of the Mindelo desalination plant.

Republic

No. 343 Overprinted: "INDEPENDENCIA / 5-Julho-75"

1975, Dec. 19 **Litho.** ***Perf. 14***

365	A23	1e multicolored	15	15

Proclamation of Independence.

Amilcar Cabral, Flag and Crowd — A30

1976, Jan. 20

366	A30	5e multicolored	32	15

3rd anniv. of the assassination of Amilcar Cabral (1924-73), revolutionary leader.

Rising Sun, Coat of Arms, Liberated People — A31

1976, July 5 **Litho.** ***Perf. 14***

367	A31	50c multicolored	15	15
368	A31	3e multicolored	30	15
369	A31	15e multicolored	85	40
370	A31	50e multicolored	2.75	1.25
a.		Miniature sheet of 4, #367-370	*12.00*	*12.00*
		Nos. 367-370 (4)	4.05	1.95

First anniversary of independence.

No. 351 Overprinted with Row of Stars and: "REPUBLICA / DE"

1976 **Litho.** ***Perf. 14***

372	A25	4.50e multi	2.00	1.50

Amilcar Cabral, Map and Flag of Cape Verde A32

1976, Sept. 19 ***Perf. 14***

373	A32	1e multicolored	15	15

Party of Intl. Action (PAICC), 20th anniv.

Electronic Tree and ITU Emblem — A33

Ashtray — A34

1977, May 17 **Litho.** ***Perf. 13½x13***

374	A33	5.50e multi	25	15

World Telecommunications Day.

1977, July 5 **Litho.** ***Perf. 14***

Carved Coconut Shells: 30c, Bell on stand. 50c, Lamp with Adam and Eve. 1e, Hollow shell with Nativity. 1.50e, Desk lamp. 5e, Jar. 10e, Jar with hinged cover. 20e, Tobacco jar with palms. 30e, Stringed instrument.

375	A34	20c lilac & multi	15	15
376	A34	30c rose & multi	15	15
377	A34	50c salmon & multi	15	15
378	A34	1e lt green & multi	15	15
379	A34	1.50e orange yel & multi	15	15
380	A34	5e gray & multi	25	15
381	A34	10e lt blue & multi	52	15
382	A34	20e yellow & multi	1.00	52
383	A34	30e rose lilac & multi	1.65	85
		Nos. 375-383 (9)	4.17	
		Set value		1.95

Cape Verde No. 1 and Coat of Arms — A35

Congress Emblem — A36

1977, Sept. 12 **Litho.** ***Perf. 13½***

384	A35	4e blue & multi	20	15
385	A35	8e lilac & multi	45	18
		Set value		26

Centenary of Cape Verde stamps.

1977, Nov. 15 ***Perf. 14***

386	A36	3.50e multi	20	15

African Party of Independence of Guinea-Bissau and Cape Verde (PAIGC), 3rd congress, Nov. 15-20.

No. 363 Overprinted with Row of Stars and: "REPUBLICA / DE"

1978, May 1 ***Perf. 12***

387	CD61	2.50e ultra & multi	20	15

No. 355 Surcharged with New Value and Bars

1978, May 1 ***Perf. 14***

388	CD55	3e on 30c multi	20	15

Antenna and ITU Emblem — A37

1978, May 17 **Litho.** ***Perf. 14***

389	A37	3.50e silver & multi	20	15

10th World Telecommunications Day.

Freighter Cabo Verde — A38

1978, June 25 Litho. *Perf. 14*

391 A38 1e multicolored 15 15

First ship of Cape Verde merchant marine.

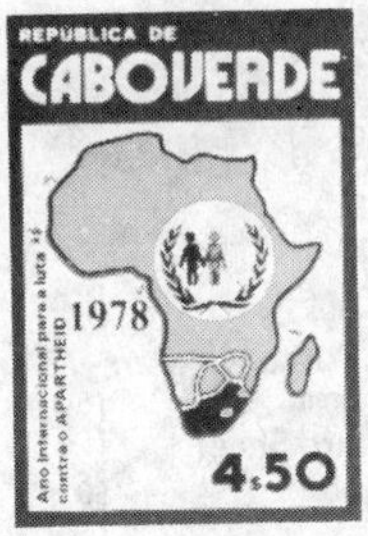

Map of Africa and Equality Emblem — A39

1978, June 21

392 A39 4.50e multi 25 15

Anti-Apartheid Year.

Human Rights Emblem — A40

1978, Dec. 10 Litho. *Perf. 14*

393 A40 1.50e multicolored 15 15
394 A40 2e multicolored 20 15
Set value 15

Universal Declaration of Human Rights, 30th anniversary.

Children and Balloons, IYC Emblem — A41

IYC Emblem and Child's Drawing: 3.50e, Children and flowers.

1979, June 1 Litho. *Perf. 14*

395 A41 1.50e multi 15 15
396 A41 3.50e multi 20 15
Set value 15

International Year of the Child.

Pindjiguiti Massacre Monument — A42

Natl. Youth Week — A42a

1979, Aug. 3 *Perf. 13*

397 A42 4.50e multi 25 15

Massacre of Pindjiguiti, 20th anniversary.

1979, Sept. 1 Litho. *Perf. 14*

397A A42a 3.50e Poster 45 15

Centenary of Mindelo — A43

1980, Apr. 23 Litho. *Perf. 12½*

398 A43 4e multicolored 20 15

Flag of Cape Verde — A44

Stylized Bird, "V" — A45

1980 Litho. *Perf. 12½*

399 A44 4e multicolored 20 15
400 A45 4e multicolored 20 15
401 A45 7e multicolored 40 15
402 A45 11e multicolored 60 20
Nos. 399-402 (4) 1.40
Set value 52

5th anniversary of independence.
No. 399 issued June 1, others July 5.

1980 Natl. Census — A45a

1980, May 13

402A A45a 3.50e multi 45
402B A45a 4.50e multi 60

Running — A46

1980, June 6

403 A46 1e shown 15 15
404 A46 2.50e Boxing 15 15
405 A46 3e Basketball 15 15
406 A46 4e Volleyball 20 15
407 A46 20e Swimming 1.10 25
408 A46 50e Tennis 2.75 65
Nos. 403-408 (6) 4.50 1.50

Souvenir Sheet

Perf. 13

409 A46 30e Soccer, horiz. 6.50

22nd Summer Olympic Games, Moscow, July 19-Aug. 3.

Thunnus Alalunga A47

1980, Nov. 11 Litho. *Perf. 13*

410 A47 50c shown 15 15
411 A47 4.50e Trachurus trachurus 20 15
412 A47 8e Muraena helena 40 15
413 A47 10e Corvina nigra 52 15
414 A47 12e Katsuwonus pelamis 65 20
415 A47 50e Prionace glauca 2.75 65
Nos. 410-415 (6) 4.67 1.45

Lochnera Rosea — A48

1980, Dec. 29

416 A48 50c shown 15 15
417 A48 4.50e Poinciana regia-bojer 20 15
418 A48 8e Mirabilis jalapa 40 15
419 A48 10e Nerium oleander 52 15
420 A48 12e Bougainvillia litoralis 65 20
421 A48 30e Hibiscus 1.65 40
Nos. 416-421 (6) 3.57 1.20

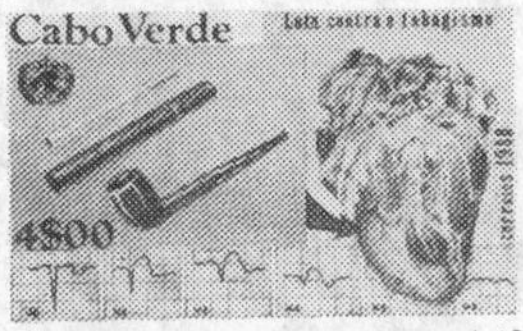

WHO Anti-smoking Campaign — A48a

1980, Sept. 19 *Perf. 12½*

421A A48a 4e multicolored 52
421B A48a 7e multicolored 90

Arca Verde A49

1980, Nov. 30 Litho. *Perf. 12½x12*

422 A49 3e shown 15 15
423 A49 5.50e Ilha do Maio 25 15
424 A49 7.50e Ilha de Komo 40 15
425 A49 9e Boa Vista 45 15
426 A49 12e Santo Antao 65 20
427 A49 30e Santiago 1.65 40
Nos. 422-427 (6) 3.55 1.20

Hand-woven Bag, Map — A49a

Various hand-woven articles. 10e, vert.

1978, May 21 Litho. *Perf. 14*

427A A49a 50c multi 15
427B A49a 1.50e multi 20
427C A49a 2e multi 25
427D A49a 3e multi 40
427E A49a 10e multi 1.25
Nos. 427A-427E (5) 2.25

Desert Erosion Prevention Campaign A50

1981, Mar. 30 Litho. *Perf. 13*

428 A50 4.50e multi 25 15
429 A50 10.50e multi 52 20

6th Anniv. of Constitution — A51

1981, Apr. 15

430 A51 4.50e multicolored 25 15

Souvenir Sheet

Austria No. B336 — A52

1981, May 18

431 A52 50e multicolored 2.50

WIPA '81 Philatelic Exhibition, Vienna, Austria, May 22-31.

Antenna — A53

1981, Aug. 25 Litho. *Perf. 12½*

432 A53 4.50e shown 25 15
433 A53 8e Dish antenna 40 15
434 A53 20e Dish antenna, diff. 1.10 32
Nos. 432-434 (3) 1.75 62

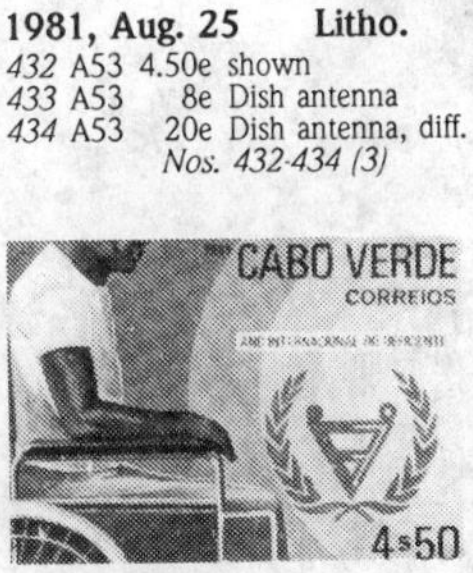

Intl. Year of the Disabled A54

1981, Dec. 25 Litho. *Perf. 12½*

435 A54 4.50e multicolored 20 15

Purple Gallinule
A55

1981, Dec. 30

436 A55	1e	Egret, vert.	15	15
437 A55	4.50e	Barn owl, vert.	20	15
438 A55	8e	Passerine, vert.	35	15
439 A55	10e	shown	40	15
440 A55	12e	Guinea fowl	45	15
		Nos. 436-440 (5)	1.55	
		Set value		49

Souvenir Sheet
Perf. 13

441 A55	50e	Razo Isld. lark	2.00	1.25

No. 441 contains 31x39mm one stamp.

CILSS Congress, Praia, Jan. 17 — A56

1982, Jan. 17 ***Perf. 13x12½***

442 A56	11.50e	multicolored	42	20

Amilcar Cabral Soccer Championship — A57

Designs: Soccer players and flags.

1982, Feb. 10 **Litho.** ***Perf. 12½***

443 A57	4.50e	multicolored	20	15
444 A57	7.50e	multicolored	30	15
445 A57	11.50e	multicolored	50	15
		Nos. 443-445 (3)	1.00	
		Set value		32

1982 World Cup — A58

Designs: Soccer players and ball.

1982, Apr. 25

446 A58	1.50e	multi	15	15
447 A58	4.50e	multi	20	15
448 A58	8e	multi	35	15
449 A58	10.50e	multi	40	15
450 A58	12e	multi	45	15
451 A58	20e	multi	85	20
		Nos. 446-451 (6)	2.40	
		Set value		71

Souvenir Sheet

452 A58	50e	multi	2.00	1.25

First Anniv. of Women's Organization — A59

1982, Apr. 15 **Litho.** ***Perf. 12½x12***

453 A59	4.50e	Marching	20	15
454 A59	8e	Farming	35	15
455 A59	12e	Child care	50	15
		Nos. 453-455 (3)	1.05	
		Set value		32

Estaleiros Navais Port, St. Vincent — A59a

1982, July 5 **Litho.** ***Perf. 13x12½***

455A A59a	10.50e	multi	40

Natl. independence, 7th anniv.

Return of Barque Morrissey-Ernestina — A60

1982, July 5 **Litho.** ***Perf. 13***

456 A60	12e	multi	50

Butterflies
A61

1982, July 27 **Litho.**

457 A61	2e	Hypolimnas misippus	15
458 A61	4.50e	Melanitis lede	15
459 A61	8e	Catopsilia florella	20
460 A61	10.50e	Colias electo	22
461 A61	11.50e	Danaus chrysippus	30
462 A61	12e	Papilio demodecus	32
		Nos. 457-462 (6)	1.34

Francisco Xavier da Cruz (1905-1958), Composer — A62

Design: 14e, Eugenio Tavares (1867-1930), poet.

1983, Feb. 20 **Litho.** ***Perf. 13***

463 A62	7e	multi	18
464 A62	14e	multi	35

World Communications Year — A63

1983, Oct. 10 **Litho.**

465 A63	13e	multicolored	32

Local Seashells — A64

1983, Nov. 30 ***Perf. 13½***

466 A64	50c	Conus ateralbus	15
467 A64	1e	Conus decoratus	15
468 A64	3e	Conus salreiensis	15
469 A64	10e	Conus verdensis	25
470 A64	50e	Conus cuneolus	1.25
		Nos. 466-470 (5)	1.95

40th Anniv. of Intl. Civil Aviation Org.
A65

Airplanes: 50c, Ogma-Auster D5/160, 1966. 2e, De Havilland DH-104 Dove, 1945. 10e, Hawker Siddeley 748-200, 1972. 13e, De Havilland Dragon Rapide, 1945. 20e, De Havilland Twin Otter, 1977. 50e, Britten-Norman Islander, 1971.

1984, Feb. 15 **Litho.**

471 A65	50c	multicolored	15
472 A65	2e	multicolored	15
473 A65	10e	multicolored	25
474 A65	13e	multicolored	32
475 A65	20e	multicolored	52
476 A65	50e	multicolored	1.25
		Nos. 471-476 (6)	2.64

Amilcar Cabral — A66

1983, Jan. 17 **Litho.** ***Perf. 14½***

477 A66	7e	multi	15
478 A66	10.50e	multi	22
a.		Souvenir sheet of 2, #477-478	75

Amilcar Cabral Symposium, Jan. 17-20. No. 478a sold for 30e.

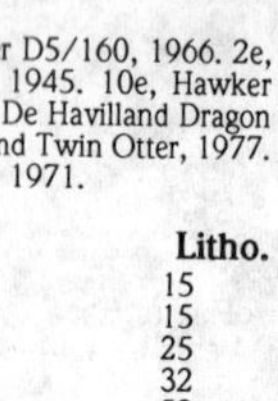

Christianity in Cape Verde, 450th Anniv. — A67

1983, Dec. 10 **Photo.** ***Perf. 14½***

479 A67	7e	Cross overshadowing islands	30

Natl. Solidarity Campaign — A68

1984, Sept. 12 ***Perf. 13½***

480 A68	6.50e	multi	15
481 A68	13.50e	multi	35

2nd Conference of Natl. Women's Orgs., Mar. 23-27 — A69

1985, Mar. 27 **Litho.** ***Perf. 13½***

482 A69	8e	multicolored	15

Miniature Sheet

483 A69	30e	multicolored	50

Natl. Independence, 10th Anniv. — A70

1985, July 5 **Litho.** ***Perf. 14***

484 A70	8c	multicolored	18
485 A70	12e	multicolored	28

Intl. Year of the Child — A71

1985, Sept. 12 **Litho.** ***Perf. 14***

486 A71	12e	multicolored	50

Vapor, by Hundertwasser
A72

Photogravure and Engraved

1986, Apr. 25 ***Perf. 14***

Black Surcharge

487 A72	30e	on 10e multi	75

Souvenir Sheets
Background Color

488	Sheet of 4	4.50
a.	A72 50e yellow & multi	1.10
489	Sheet of 4	4.50
a.	A72 50e red & multi	1.10
490	Sheet of 4	4.50
a.	A72 50e green & multi	1.10

No. 487 not issued without surcharge.

World Wildlife Fund — A73

Perf. 13½x14½

1986, June 15 **Litho.**

491 A73 8e Mabuya vaillanti 18
492 A73 10e Tarentola gigas brancoensis 22
493 A73 15e Tarentola gigas gigas 32
494 A73 30e Hemidactylus bouvieri 75
Nos. 491-494 (4) 1.47

Souvenir Sheet

495 Sheet of 2 2.25
a. A73 50e Mabuya vaillanti 1.10
b. A73 50e Hemidactylus bouvieri 1.10

No. 495 printed with center label picturing progress union emblem. Nos. 495a-495b printed without WWF emblem.

World Food Day — A74

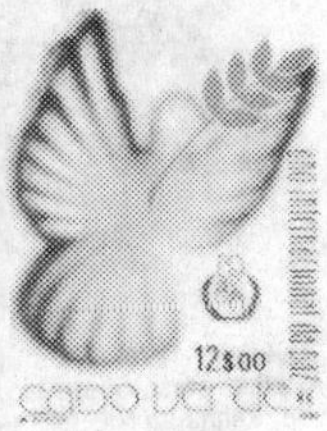
Intl. Peace Year — A75

1986, June 20 *Perf. 14*

496 A74 8e Cauldron 18
497 A74 12e Mortar & pestle 28
498 A74 15e Quern stone 32
Nos. 496-498 (3) 78

1986, Dec. 24 **Litho.** *Perf. 14*

499 A75 12e multicolored 28
500 A75 30e multicolored 75

Natl. Child Survival Campaign A76

1987, Mar. 27 **Litho.** *Perf. 14*

501 A76 8e multicolored 18
502 A76 10e multicolored 22
503 A76 12e multicolored 28
504 A76 16e multicolored 35
505 A76 100e multicolored 2.25
Nos. 501-505 (5) 3.28

Tourism A77

1987, May 17

506 A77 1e Bay, Mindelo 15
507 A77 2.50e Hill country 15
508 A77 5e Mountain peak 15
509 A77 8e Monument 15
510 A77 10e Mountain peaks 20
511 A77 12e Beached boats 24
512 A77 100e Harbor 2.00
Nos. 506-512 (7) 3.04

Ships — A78

1987, Aug. 3 *Perf. 13½x14½*

513 A78 12e Carvalho, 1937 24
514 A78 16e Nauta, 1943 32
515 A78 50e Maria Sony, 1911 1.10
Nos. 513-515 (3) 1.66

Souvenir Sheet

516 Sheet of 2 2.75
a. A78 60e Madalan, 1928 1.25

Crop Protection A80

1988, May 9 **Litho.** *Perf. 13½*

518 A80 50c Identification of insect plague 15
519 A80 2e Use of insecticides 15
520 A80 9e Import of parasites 30
521 A80 13e Import of predators 45
522 A80 16e Locust 55
523 A80 19e Estimation of crop loss 65
Nos. 518-523 (6) 2.25

Souvenir Sheet

524 A80 50e Agricultural Research Institute 1.70

Maps — A81

1988, July 5 **Litho.** *Perf. 14*

525 A81 1e Dutch, 17th cent. 15
526 A81 2.50e Belgian, 18th cent. 15
527 A81 4.50e French, 18th cent. 16
528 A81 9.50e English, 18th cent. 32
529 A81 19.50e English, 19th cent. 68
530 A81 20e French, 18th cent., vert. 70
Nos. 525-530 (6) 2.16

Churches A82

Designs: 5e, St. Amaro Abade, Tarrafal, Santiago Is. 8e, Our Lady of the Light, Maio Is. 10e, Nazarene, Praia, Santiago Is. 12e, Our Lady of Rosa'rio, Sao Nicolau Is. 15e, Nazarene, Mindelo, Sao Vicente Is. 20e, Our Lady of Grace, Praia, Santiago Is.

1988, Aug. 15 *Perf. 13½x14½*

531 A82 5e multicolored 18
532 A82 8e multicolored 28
533 A82 10e multicolored 35
534 A82 12e multicolored 42
535 A82 15e multicolored 52
536 A82 20e multicolored 70
Nos. 531-536 (6) 2.45

Water Conservation A83

1988, Sept. 26 **Litho.** *Perf. 14*

537 A83 12e multicolored 42

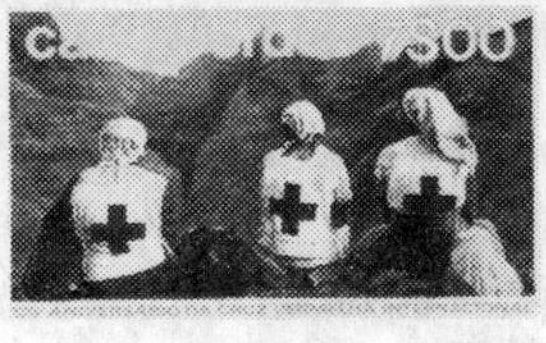
Intl. Red Cross, 125th Anniv. A84

1988, Oct. 20

538 A84 7e multi 24

3rd Communist Party (PAICV) Congress — A85

Portrait of Pres. Pereira, PAICV secretary-general, and: 7e, S. Jorginho Vocational Training Center. 10.50e, UN Secretary-General Perez de Cuellar. 30e, 100e, Star and text.

Perf. 14½x13½

1988, Nov. 25 **Litho.**

539 A85 7e multi 22
540 A85 10.50e multi 35
541 A85 30e multi 95
Nos. 539-541 (3) 1.52

Souvenir Sheet

542 A85 100e multi 3.10

1988 Summer Olympics, Seoul — A86

1988, Dec. 26

543 A86 12e shown 38
544 A86 15e Tennis 48
545 A86 20e Soccer 62
546 A86 30e Boxing 95
Nos. 543-546 (4) 2.43

Souvenir Sheet

547 A86 50e Long jump 1.55

2nd JAAC-CV Congress, Sept. 7-12 — A87

1989, Apr. 7 **Litho.** *Perf. 14*

548 A87 30e Hot air balloon 1.00

Liberty Guiding the People — A88

Relief, Arc de Triomphe — A89

1989, July 7 **Litho.** *Perf. 14*

549 A88 20e multicolored 58
550 A88 24e multicolored 70
551 A88 25e multicolored 72
Nos. 549-551 (3) 2.00

Souvenir Sheet

Perf. 14½x13½

552 A89 100e multicolored 3.00

French revolution, bicent.

Interparliamentary Union, Cent. — A90

1989, Sept. 18 **Litho.** *Perf. 14*

553 A90 2e shown 15
554 A90 4e Dove 15
555 A90 13e Natl. Assembly Bldg. 32
Set value 46

Traditional Ceramics A91

1989, Nov. 13 **Litho.** *Perf. 13½*

Panel Colors

556 A91 13e lilac 32
557 A91 20e red, vert. 50
558 A91 24e brown 60
559 A91 25e orange, vert. 62
Nos. 556-559 (4) 2.04

Outdoor Toys — A92

1989, Dec. 23

560 A92 1e Yellow truck 15
561 A92 6e Car 15
562 A92 8e White truck 20
563 A92 11.50e Trucks 28
564 A92 18e Scooter 45
565 A92 100e Boat 2.50
Nos. 560-565 (6) 3.73

Visit of Pope John Paul II — A93

1990, Jan. 25

566 A93 13e blue & multi 32
567 A93 25e violet & multi 62

Souvenir Sheet

568 A93 200e multi, diff. 5.00

Turtles — A94

1990, May 17 Litho. *Perf. 13½*

569 A94 50c Chelonia mydas 15
570 A94 1e Dermochelys coriacea 15
571 A94 5e Lepidochelys olivacea 15
572 A94 10e Caretta caretta 28
573 A94 42e Eretmochelys imbricata 1.20
Nos. 569-573 (5) 1.93

Women's Congress A95

1990, Aug. 13

574 A95 9e multicolored 25

A96

A97

Various drawings of soccer players in action.

1990, Aug. 7

575 A96 4e multicolored 15
576 A96 7.50e multicolored 20
577 A96 8e multicolored 22
578 A96 100e multicolored 2.80
Nos. 575-578 (4) 3.37

Souvenir Sheet

579 A96 100e multi, diff. 2.80

World Cup Soccer Championships, Italy.

1990, Oct. 15 *Perf. 11½*

Vaccinations: 5e, Emile Roux (1853-1933), diphtheria. 13e, Robert Koch (1843-1910), tuberculosis. 20e, Gaston Ramon (1886-1963), tetanus. 24e, Jonas Salk (1914-), polio.

Granite Paper

580 A97 5e multicolored 15
581 A97 13e multicolored 38
582 A97 20e multicolored 60
583 A97 24e multicolored 70
Nos. 580-583 (4) 1.83

Intl. Literacy Year — A98

Designs: 3e, Adult literacy class. 15e, Teacher holding flash card, children. 19e, Teacher, student at blackboard.

1990, Sept. 28

Granite Paper

584 A98 2e shown 15
585 A98 3e multicolored 15
586 A98 15e multicolored 40
587 A98 19e multicolored 55
Nos. 584-587 (4) 1.25

Traditional Fairy Tales — A99

1990, Dec. 20 Litho. *Perf. 12½*

588 A99 50c shown 15
589 A99 2.50e Man catching mermaid 15
590 A99 12e Woman, snake 42
591 A99 25e Man, eggs, woman 90
Nos. 588-591 (4) 1.62

Fight Against AIDS — A100

1991, Feb. 20 Litho. *Perf. 14*

Granite Paper

592 A100 13e multicolored 50
593 A100 24e multi, diff. 90

Fishing — A101

Designs: 24e, Man removing hook from fish. 25e, Fishing boats. 50e, Two men long-line fishing.

1991, Apr. 23 Litho. *Perf. 11½*

594 A101 10e multicolored 32
595 A101 24e multicolored 78
596 A101 25e multicolored 80
597 A101 50e multicolored 1.60
Nos. 594-597 (4) 3.50

Medicinal Plants — A102

Designs: 10e, Lavandula rotundifolia. 15e, Micromeria forbesii. 21e, Sarcostemma daltonii. 24e, Periploca chevalieri. 30e, Echium hypertropicum. 35e, Erysimum caboverdeanum.

1991, July 5 Litho. *Perf. 11½*

598 A102 10e multicolored 30
599 A102 15e multicolored 45
600 A102 21e multicolored 65
601 A102 24e multicolored 70
602 A102 30e multicolored 90
603 A102 35e multicolored 1.05
Nos. 598-602 (5) 3.00

Landmarks in Old Ribeira Grande on Santiago Island A103

Designs: 12.50e, Church of Our Lady of the Rosary, 1495. 15e, Ruins of the Cathedral, 1556. 20e, Fortress of San Felipe, 1587. 30e, Ruins of the Convent of St. Francis, 1642. 100e, Pillory, 1520, vert.

1991, June 25 Litho. *Perf. 11½*

604 A103 12.50e multicolored 40
605 A103 15e multicolored 45
606 A103 20e multicolored 60
607 A103 30e multicolored 90
Nos. 604-607 (4) 2.35

Souvenir Sheet

608 A103 100e multicolored 3.00

Musical Instruments — A104

1991, Oct. 9 Litho. *Perf. 11½*

609 A104 10e 6-string guitar 30
610 A104 20e Violin 60
611 A104 29e 5-string guitar 90
612 A104 47e Cimba 1.50
Nos. 609-612 (4) 3.30

Souvenir Sheet

613 A104 60e Accordion, horiz. 1.90

Christmas A105

1991, Dec. 20 Litho. *Perf. 11½*

614 A105 31e Nativity scene 1.00
615 A105 50e Nativity scene, diff. 1.65

Discovery of America, 500th Anniv. A106

1992, Mar. 31 Litho. *Perf. 11½*

616 A106 40e shown 1.30
617 A106 40e Columbus on ship 1.30
a. Pair, #616-617 2.60

Souvenir Sheet

618 A106 Sheet of 2 5.00

Stamps in No. 618 are smaller, without white border and "Luis Duran" and "Courvoisier" inscriptions. No. 618 was printed in continuous design and sold for 150e.

Souvenir Sheet

Granada '92 — A107

1992, Apr.24 *Perf. 11½*

619 A107 50e multicolored 5.00

No. 619 sold for 150e.

Tropical Fruits A108

1992, Feb. 29 *Perf. 12x11½*

620 A108 16e Syzygium jambos 50
621 A108 25e Mangifera indica 80
622 A108 31e Anacardium occidentale 1.00
623 A108 32e Persea americana 1.05
Nos. 620-623 (4) 3.35

1992 Summer Olympics, Barcelona — A109

1992, June 30 Litho. *Perf. 13½*

624 A109 16e Women's javelin 60
625 A109 20e Weight lifting 75
626 A109 32e Women's pole vault 1.25
627 A109 40e Women's shot put 1.50
Nos. 624-627 (4) 4.10

Souvenir Sheet

628 A109 100e Women's gymnastics 3.80

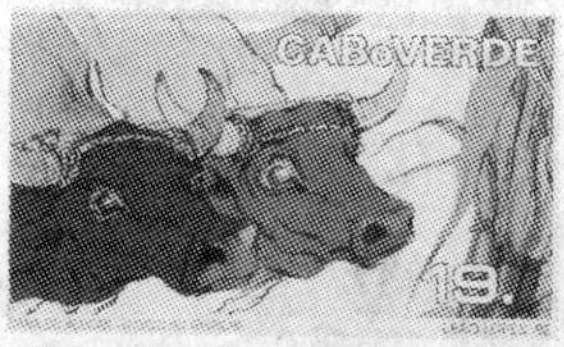

Sugar Cane Production — A110

Designs: 19e, Oxen, sugar cane. 20e, Oxen yoked to press. 37e, Man placing cane inside press. 38e, Refining process.

1992, Nov. Litho. *Perf. 11*

629 A110 19e multicolored 58
630 A110 20e multicolored 65
631 A110 37e multicolored 1.15
632 A110 38e multicolored 1.18
Nos. 629-632 (4) 3.56

Domestic Animals A111

1992, Nov. *Perf. 13½*

633 A111 16e Cat 48
634 A111 31e Chickens 95
635 A111 32e Dog, vert. 1.00
636 A111 50e Horse 1.55
Nos. 633-636 (4) 3.98

Corals A112

1993, Apr. 29 Litho. *Perf. 11½*

637 A112 5e Tubastrea aurea 15
638 A112 31e Corallium rubrum 90
639 A112 37e Porites porites 1.10
640 A112 50e Millepora alcicornis 1.50
Nos. 637-640 (4) 3.65

Treaty of Tordesillas, 500th Anniv. (in 1994) A113

Designs: No. 641, King Ferdinand, Queen Isabella of Spain, Pope Alexander VI. No. 642, Pope Julius II, King John II of Portugal. No. 643, Astrolabe, treaty signing. No. 644, Compass rose, map.

1993, Aug. 1 Litho. *Perf. 12x11½*

641 A113 37e multicolored 1.00
642 A113 37e multicolored 1.00
a. Pair, #641-642 2.00
643 A113 38e multicolored 1.05
644 A113 38e multicolored 1.05
a. Pair, #643-644 2.10
Nos. 641-644 (4) 4.10

Souvenir Sheet

Santiago Island, 1806 — A114

1993, July 30 *Perf. 13½*
645 A114 100e multicolored 2.75

Brasiliana '93.

Lobsters — A115

1993, Sept. 29 Litho. *Perf. 11½*
646 A115 2e Palinurus charlestoni 15
647 A115 10e Panulirus echinatus 15
648 A115 17e Panulirus regius 25
649 A115 38e Scyllarides latus 60
Nos. 646-649 (4) 1.15

Souvenir Sheet

650 A115 100e Panulirus regius, diff. 1.50

No. 650 contains one 51x36mm stamp.

Birds
A116

1993, Oct. 29 Litho. *Perf. 12x11½*
651 A116 10e Calonectris edwardsii 28
652 A116 30e Sula leucogaster 85
653 A116 40e Fregata magnificens 1.10
Nos. 651-653 (3) 2.23
a. Souvenir sheet of 1 4.25
654 A116 41e Phaeton aethereus 1.25

Hong Kong '94 (#653a).
No. 653a sold for 150e.

Flowers
A117

1993, Dec. 16 Litho. *Perf. 12x11½*
655 A117 5e Rosa alexandra 15
656 A117 30e Strelitzia reginae 90
657 A117 37e Dianthus barbatus 1.10
658 A117 50e Dahlia 1.50
Nos. 655-658 (4) 3.65

1994 World Cup Soccer Championships, US — A118

Players, US flag, and: 1e, Giant's Stadium, New Jersey. 20e, Rose Bowl Stadium, Pasadena. 37e, Foxboro Stadium, Boston. 38e, Silverdome, Pontiac. 100e, RFK Stadium, Washington DC.

1994, May 31 Litho. *Perf. 11½*
659 A118 1e multicolored 15
660 A118 20e multicolored 55
661 A118 37e multicolored 1.00
662 A118 38e multicolored 1.10
Nos. 659-662 (4) 2.80

Souvenir Sheet

663 A118 100e multicolored 2.75

Prince Henry the Navigator (1394-1460) — A119

Illustration reduced.

1994, Mar. 4 Litho. *Perf. 12*
664 A119 37e multicolored 1.10

See Brazil #2463, Macao #719, Portugal #1987.

Sharks
A120

1994 Litho. *Perf. 12x11½*
665 A120 21e Eugomphodus taurus 60
666 A120 27e Carcharhinus limbatus 80
667 A120 37e Rhiniodon typus 1.10
668 A120 38e Etmopterus spinax 1.10
Nos. 665-668 (4) 3.60

Bananas
A121

1994 Litho. *Perf. 11½*
669 A121 12e Prata, vert. 35
670 A121 16e Pao 48
671 A121 30e Ana roberta, vert. 90
672 A121 40e Roxa, vert. 1.25
Nos. 669-672 (4) 2.98

AIR POST STAMPS

Common Design Type
Name and Value in Black
Perf. 13½x13

1938, July 26 Unwmk.
C1 CD39 10c scarlet 35 28
C2 CD39 20c purple 35 28
C3 CD39 50c orange 35 28
C4 CD39 1e ultra 35 28
C5 CD39 2e lilac brown 60 52
C6 CD39 3e dk green 1.65 1.40
C7 CD39 5e red brown 3.50 1.40
C8 CD39 9e rose carmine 5.75 3.00
C9 CD39 10e magenta 8.25 4.50
Nos. C1-C9 (9) 21.15 11.94

No. C7 exists with overprint "Exposicao Internacional de Nova York, 1939-1940" and Trylon and Perisphere.

POSTAGE DUE STAMPS

D1

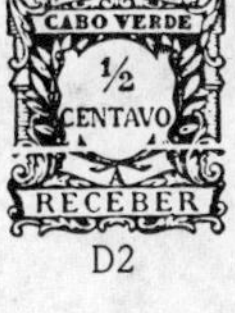

D2

1904 Unwmk. Typo. *Perf. 12*
J1 D1 5r yellow grn 20 40
J2 D1 10r slate 20 40
J3 D1 20r yellow brn 40 55
J4 D1 30r red orange 65 75
J5 D1 50r gray brown 40 75
J6 D1 60r red brown 5.00 5.00
J7 D1 100r lilac 95 1.50
J8 D1 130r dull blue 95 1.50
J9 D1 200r carmine 1.10 2.50
J10 D1 500r dull violet 3.25 4.75
Nos. J1-J10 (10) 13.10 18.10

Overprinted in Carmine or Green

1911
J11 D1 5r yellow grn 15 15
J12 D1 10r slate 16 15
J13 D1 20r yellow brn 16 15
J14 D1 30r orange 16 15
J15 D1 50r gray brown 16 15
J16 D1 60r red brown 35 28
J17 D1 100r lilac 45 28
J18 D1 130r dull blue 75 35
J19 D1 200r carmine (G) 1.25 52
J20 D1 500r dull violet 1.50 1.25
Nos. J11-J20 (10) 5.09 3.43

1921 *Perf. 11½*
J21 D2 ½c yellow grn 15 18
J22 D2 1c slate 15 18
J23 D2 2c red brown 15 18
J24 D2 3c orange 15 18
J25 D2 5c gray brown 15 18
J26 D2 6c lt brown 15 15
J27 D2 10c red violet 15 15
J28 D2 13c dull blue 30 55
J29 D2 20c carmine 30 55
J30 D2 50c gray 95 1.10
Set value 2.10 3.25

Catalogue values for unused stamps in this section, from this point to the end of the section, are for Never Hinged items.

Common Design Type
Photogravure and Typographed
1952 Unwmk. *Perf. 14*
Numeral in Red, Frame Multicolored
J31 CD45 10c chocolate 15 15
J32 CD45 30c black brown 15 15
J33 CD45 50c dark blue 15 15
J34 CD45 1e dark blue 20 20
J35 CD45 2e red brown 20 20
J36 CD45 5e olive green 40 40
Nos. J31-J36 (6) 1.25 1.25

NEWSPAPER STAMP

N1

1893 Typo. Unwmk. *Perf. 11½*
P1 N1 2½r brown 60 40
a. Perf. 12½ 3.00 3.00
b. Perf. 13½ 5.25 3.00

For surcharges see Nos. 79, 206.

POSTAL TAX STAMPS

Pombal Issue
Common Design Types
1925 Unwmk. Engr. *Perf. 12½*
RA1 CD28 15c dull vio & blk 40 40
RA2 CD29 15c dull vio & blk 40 40
RA3 CD30 15c dull vio & blk 40 40

St. Isabel — PT1

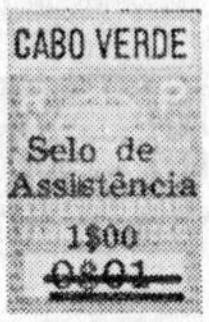

PT2

1948 Litho. *Perf. 11*
RA4 PT1 50c dark green 1.90 1.25
RA5 PT1 1e henna brown 3.50 2.50

Catalogue values for unused stamps in this section, from this point to the end of the section, are for Never Hinged items.

No. RA5 Surcharged with New Value and Bars

1959
RA6 PT1 50c on 1e henna brown 1.00 50

Perf. 14

RA7 PT1 50c carmine rose 1.10 52
RA8 PT1 1e blue 1.10 52

St. Isabel Type Redrawn
1967-72 Litho. *Perf. 14*
RA9 PT1 30c (blue panel) 15 15
RA10 PT1 50c (lilac rose panel) 50 50
RA11 PT1 50c (red panel) ('72) *3.25 3.25*
RA12 PT1 1e (brn panel) 60 60
RA13 PT1 1e (red lilac panel) ('72) *3.25 3.25*
Nos. RA9-RA13 (5) 7.75 7.75

Nos. RA9-RA13 are inscribed "ASSISTENCIA" in large letters in bottom panel and "PORTUGAL" and "CABO VERDE" in small letters in upper left corner.

Revenue Stamps Surcharged in Green, Blue or Black
1967-72 Typo. *Perf. 12*
Black "CABO VERDE" & Value
Pale Green Burelage
RA14 PT2 50c on 1c org (Bl) ('71) 1.00 60
a. Black surcharge ('68?) *7.50 8.75*
RA15 PT2 50c on 2c org (Bk) ('69) *17.50 17.50*
c. Inverted surcharge
RA16 PT2 50c on 3c org (G) ('72) 1.50 60
RA17 PT2 50c on 5c org (G) ('72) 70 60
RA18 PT2 50c on 10c org (G) ('71) 85 85
RA19 PT2 1e on 1c org (Bk) 4.50 4.00
RA20 PT2 1e on 2c org (G) ('71) 1.65 1.65
a. Blue surcharge ('71) 1.10 60
b. Black surcharge 3.50 3.00
Nos. RA14-RA20 (7) *27.70 25.80*

POSTAL TAX DUE STAMPS

Pombal Issue
Common Design Types
1925 Unwmk. *Perf. 12½*
RAJ1 CD31 30c dull vio & blk 45 45
RAJ2 CD32 30c dull vio & blk 45 45
RAJ3 CD33 30c dull vio & blk 45 45

Cape Verde stamps can be mounted in the Scott annual Portugal supplement.

CAROLINE ISLANDS

LOCATION — A group of about 549 small islands in the West Pacific Ocean, north of the Equator.
GOVT. — Former German colony
AREA — 550 sq. mi.
POP. — 40,000 (approx. 1915)

100 Pfennig = 1 Mark

Watermark

Wmk. 125-Lozenges

Stamps of Germany 1889-90 Overprinted in Black

Karolinen

Overprinted at 56 degree Angle

1900	Unwmk.	*Perf. 13½x14½*		
1	A9	3pf dk brown	7.75	9.00
2	A9	5pf green	9.50	9.00
3	A10	10pf carmine	11.00	11.00
4	A10	20pf ultra	13.00	15.00
5	A10	25pf orange	35.00	35.00
6	A10	50pf red brown	35.00	35.00
		Nos. 1-6 (6)	111.25	114.00

1899

Overprinted at 48 degree Angle

1a	A9	3pf light brown	400.00	575.00
2a	A9	5pf green	500.00	500.00
3a	A10	10pf carmine	50.00	125.00
4a	A10	20pf ultra	50.00	125.00
5a	A10	25pf orange	*1,000.*	*2,250.*
6a	A10	50pf red brown	*650.00*	*1,250.*

Kaiser's Yacht "Hohenzollern"
A3 A4

1900-10	Typo.	*Perf. 14*		
7	A3	3pf brown	55	*90*
8	A3	5pf green	55	*1.40*
9	A3	10pf carmine	55	*3.50*
a.		Half used as 5pf on cover, backstamped in Jaluit ('05)		*90.00*
10	A3	20pf ultra	75	*6.00*
a.		Half used as 10pf on cover ('10)		*6,250.*
11	A3	25pf org & blk, *yel*	1.00	*10.50*
12	A3	30pf org & blk, *sal*	1.00	*10.50*
13	A3	40pf lake & blk	1.00	*12.00*
14	A3	50pf pur & blk, *sal*	1.25	*12.50*
15	A3	80pf lake & blk, *rose*	1.75	*15.00*

Engr.		*Perf. 14½x14*		
16	A4	1m carmine	2.50	*45.00*
17	A4	2m blue	4.25	*60.00*
18	A4	3m black violet	6.25	*125.00*
19	A4	5m slate & carmine	105.00	425.00
		Nos. 7-19 (13)	126.40	

No. 9a is known as the "typhoon provisional" the stock of 5pf stamps having been destroyed during a typhoon. Covers (cards) without backstamp, value about $60.
Forged cancellations are found on #7-19.

No. 7 Handstamp Surcharged **5 Pf**

1910, July 12

20 A3 5pf on 3pf brown *4,750.*

Value is for stamp tied to cover. Stamps on piece sell for about one-third less.

1915-19	Wmk. 125	Typo.	
21	A3	3pf brown ('19)	60
22	A3	5pf green	9.00

Engr.

23	A4	5m slate & carmine	12.00
		Nos. 21-23 (3)	21.60

CASTELLORIZO

(Castelrosso)

LOCATION — A Mediterranean island in the Dodecanese group lying close to the coast of Asia Minor and about 60 miles east of Rhodes.
GOVT. — Former Italian Colony
AREA — 4 sq. mi.
POP. — 2,238 (1936)

Formerly a Turkish possession, Castellorizo was occupied by the French in 1915 and ceded to Italy after World War I.

25 Centimes = 1 Piaster
100 Centimes = 1 Franc

Used values in italics are for postally used copies. Stamps with CTO or fake cancels sell for about the same as hinged, unused stamps.

Issued under French Occupation

Stamps of French Offices in Turkey Overprinted

B. N. F.
CASTELLORIZO

1920	Unwmk.	*Perf. 14x13½*		
1	A2	1c gray	20.00	20.00
a.		Inverted overprint	40.00	40.00
b.		Double overprint	50.00	50.00
2	A2	2c vio brn	20.00	20.00
3	A2	3c red org	20.00	20.00
a.		Inverted overprint	40.00	40.00
4	A2	5c green	20.00	20.00
a.		Inverted overprint	40.00	40.00
5	A3	10c rose	22.50	22.50
6	A3	15c pale red	32.50	32.50
a.		Inverted overprint	55.00	55.00
7	A3	20c brn vio	35.00	35.00
8	A5	1pi on 25c blue	35.00	35.00
9	A3	30c lilac	35.00	35.00
10	A4	40c red & pale bl	55.00	55.00
a.		Inverted overprint	215.00	215.00
11	A6	2pi on 50c bis brn & lav	55.00	55.00
a.		Inverted overprint	215.00	215.00
12	A6	4pi on 1fr cl & ol grn	100.00	100.00
a.		Double overprint	225.00	225.00
b.		Inverted overprint	225.00	225.00
13	A6	20pi on 5fr dk bl & buff	300.00	300.00
a.		Double overprint	550.00	550.00
		Nos. 1-13 (13)	750.00	750.00

On Nos. 10-13 the overprint is placed vertically.
No. 1-9 were overprinted in blocks of 25. Position 4 had "CASTELLORIZO" inverted and Positions 8 and 18 had "CASTELLORISO". The later variety also occurred in the setting of the form for Nos. 10-13.
"B. N. F." are the initials of "Base Navale Francaise".

Overprinted in Black or Red

O. N. F.
Castellorizo

1920

On Stamps of French Offices in Turkey

14	A2	1c gray	9.25	9.25
15	A2	2c vio brn	9.25	9.25
16	A2	3c red org	10.50	10.50
17	A2	5c green (R)	10.50	10.50
19	A3	10c rose	10.50	10.50
20	A3	15c pale red	14.00	14.00
21	A3	20c brn vio	30.00	30.00
22	A5	1pi on 25c bl (R)	27.50	27.50
23	A3	30c lilac (R)	27.50	27.50
24	A4	40c red & pale bl	27.50	27.50
25	A6	2pi on 50c bis brn & lav	27.50	27.50
26	A6	4pi on 1fr claret & ol grn	30.00	30.00
28	A6	20pi on 5fr dk bl & buff	145.00	145.00
		Nos. 14-28 (13)	379.00	379.00

On Nos. 25, 26 and 28 the two lines of the overprint are set wider apart than on the lower values.
"O.N.F." are the initials of "Occupation Navale Francaise."
Overprint on 8pi on 2fr (#37), value $700.

On Stamps of France

30	A22	10c red	15.00	11.00
a.		Inverted overprint		60.00
31	A22	25c blue (R)	15.00	11.00
a.		Inverted overprint		60.00

This overprint exists on 8 other 1900-1907 denominations of France (5c, 15c, 20c, 30c, 40c, 50c, 1fr, 5fr). These are believed not to have been issued or postally used.

Stamps of France, 1900-1907, Handstamped in Black or Violet

O F
CASTELLORISO

1920				
33	A22	5c green	65.00	65.00
34	A22	10c red	65.00	65.00
35	A22	20c vio brn	65.00	65.00
36	A22	5c blue	65.00	65.00
37	A18	50c bis brn & lav	475.00	475.00
38	A18	1fr cl & ol grn (V)	475.00	475.00
		Nos. 33-38 (6)	1,210.	1,210.

Nos. 1-38 are considered speculative.
Forgeries of overprints on Nos. 1-38 exist. They abound of Nos. 33-38.
Stamps of French Offices in Turkey hand-stamped "Occupation Francaise Castellorizo" were made privately.

Issued under Italian Dominion

100 Centesimi = 1 Lira

Italian Stamps of 1906-20 Overprinted

CASTELROSSO

1922	Wmk. 140	*Perf. 14*		
51	A48	5c green	1.00	*3.00*
52	A48	10c claret	42	*3.00*
53	A48	15c slate	42	*3.00*
54	A50	20c brn org	42	*3.00*
a.		Double overprint	60.00	
55	A49	25c blue	42	*3.00*
56	A49	40c brown	8.75	3.00
57	A49	50c violet	8.75	3.00
58	A49	60c carmine	8.75	3.00
59	A49	85c chocolate	1.00	*4.00*
		Nos. 51-59 (9)	29.93	

Map of Castellorizo; Flag of Italy — A1

1923				
60	A1	5c gray green	20	*2.50*
61	A1	10c dull rose	20	*2.50*
62	A1	25c dull blue	20	*2.50*
63	A1	50c gray lilac	20	*2.50*
64	A1	1 l brown	20	*2.50*
		Nos. 60-64 (5)	1.00	

Italian Stamps of 1901-20 Overprinted

CASTELROSSO

1924				
65	A48	5c green	30	*10.00*
66	A48	10c claret	30	*10.00*
67	A48	15c slate	30	*10.00*
68	A50	20c brn orange	30	*10.00*
69	A49	25c blue	30	*10.00*
70	A49	40c brown	30	*10.00*
71	A49	50c violet	30	*10.00*
72	A49	60c carmine	30	*10.00*
a.		Double overprint	60.00	
73	A49	85c red brown	30	*10.00*
74	A46	1 l brn & green	30	*10.00*
		Nos. 65-74 (10)	3.00	

Ferrucci Issue

Types of Italian Stamps of 1930, Overprinted in Red or Blue

CASTELROSSO

1930		Wmk. Crowns (140)		
75	A102	20c violet	70	*1.25*
76	A103	25c dark green	70	*1.25*
77	A103	50c black	70	*1.25*
78	A103	1.25 l deep blue	70	*1.25*
79	A104	5 l + 2 l dp car (Bl)	3.00	*6.75*
		Nos. 75-79 (5)	5.80	

Garibaldi Issue

Types of Italian Stamps of 1932, Overprinted like Nos. 75-79 in Red or Blue

1932				
80	A138	10c brown	3.50	*7.25*
81	A138	20c red brn (Bl)	3.50	*7.25*
82	A138	25c dp grn	3.50	*7.25*
83	A138	30c bluish slate	3.50	*7.25*
84	A138	50c red vio (Bl)	3.50	*7.25*
85	A141	75c cop red (Bl)	3.50	*7.25*
86	A141	1.25 l dull blue	3.50	*7.25*
87	A141	1.75 l + 25c brn	3.50	*7.25*
88	A144	2.55 l + 50c org (Bl)	3.50	*7.25*
89	A145	5 l + 1 l dl vio	3.50	*7.25*
		Nos. 80-89 (10)	35.00	

CENTRAL AFRICA

LOCATION — Western Africa, north of equator
GOVT. — Empire
AREA — 241,313 sq. mi.
POP. — 2,610,000 (est. 1974)
CAPITAL — Bangui

The former French colony of Ubangi-Shari, a unit in French Equatorial Africa, proclaimed itself the Central African Republic Dec. 1, 1958. It became the Central African Empire Dec. 4, 1976. It became the Central African Republic again in 1979.

100 Centimes = 1 Franc

Catalogue values for all unused stamps in this country are for Never Hinged items.

Watermark

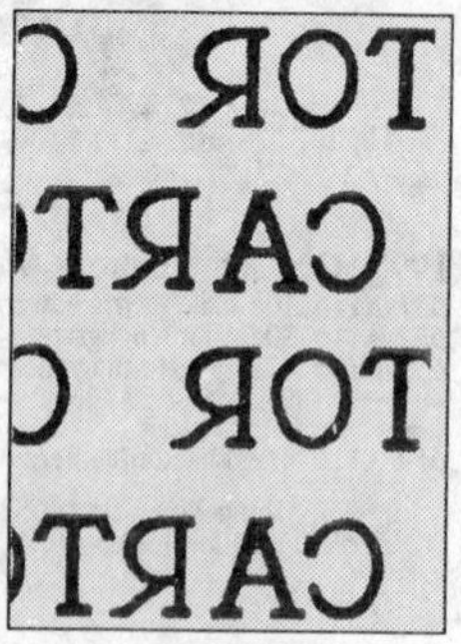

Wmk. 385

Central African Republic

Premier Barthélemy Boganda and Flag — A1

Design: 25fr, Barthélemy Boganda and flag, horiz.

Unwmk.

1959, Dec. 1	Engr.	*Perf. 13*		
1	A1	15fr multi	16	15
2	A1	25fr multi	25	15

1st anniv. of the Republic and honoring Premier Barthélemy Boganda (1910-59).
For overprints and surcharge see Nos. 12, 59, M1-M2.

Imperforates
Many stamps of Central African Republic exist imperforate in issued and trial colors, and also in small presentation sheets in issued colors.

C.C.T.A. Issue
Common Design Type

1960, May 21 Unwmk. ***Perf. 13***

3	CD106 50fr lt grn & dk bl	80	60

Dactyloceras Widenmanni A2

Designs: Various butterflies.

1960-61

4	A2	50c bl grn & dk red	15	15
5	A2	1fr multi	15	15
6	A2	2fr dk grn & brn	15	15
7	A2	3fr yel grn & dk red	15	15
8	A2	5fr multi	15	15
9	A2	10fr multi	15	15
10	A2	20fr multi	22	15
11	A2	85fr multi	90	55
		Set value	1.50	95

Issued: 50c-3fr, June 10, 1961, others, Sept. 3.

No. 2 Overprinted: "FETE NATIONALE 1-12-1960"

1960, Dec. 1

12	A1 25fr multi	70	70

National Holiday, Dec. 1, 1960.

Louis Pasteur and Pasteur Institute, Bangui — A3

1961, Feb. 25 Unwmk. ***Perf. 13***

13	A3 20fr multi	42	42

Opening of Pasteur Institute at Bangui.

Common Design Types pictured in section at front of book.

Flag, Map, and UN Emblem A4

1961, Mar. 4 Engr.

14	A4 15fr multi	15	15
15	A4 25fr multi	20	15
16	A4 85fr multi	65	55
	Nos. 14-16 (3)	1.00	85

Admission to the UN.

No. 15 Overprinted in Green: "FETE NATIONALE 1-12-61" and Star

1961, Dec. 1

17	A4 25fr multi	90	90

National Holiday, Dec. 1.

No. 16 Surcharged in Red Brown: "U.A.M. CONFERENCE DE BANGUI 25-27 Mars 1962"

1962, Mar. 25

18	A4 50fr on 85fr multi	80	80

Conf. of the African and Malgache Union at Bangui, Mar. 25-27.

Abidjan Games Issue
Common Design Type

1962, July 21 Photo. ***Perf. 12½x12***

19	CD109 20fr Hurdling	20	16
20	CD109 50fr Bicycling	55	38
	Nos. 19-20,C6 (3)	1.75	1.19

African-Malgache Union Issue
Common Design Type

1962, Sept. 8 Unwmk.

21	CD110 30fr multi	38	30

1st anniv. of the African and Malgache Union.

Pres. David Dacko — A5

Soldiers with Flag — A6

1962 ***Perf. 12***

22	A5 20fr multi	20	15
23	A5 25fr multi	22	15

For surcharge see No. 60.

1963, Aug. 13 Photo.

24	A6 20fr blk & multi	20	15

National Army, third anniversary.

Waves Around Globe — A6a

Design: 100fr, Orbit patterns around globe.

1963, Sept. 19 Unwmk. ***Perf. 12½***

25	A6a 25fr plum & grn	30	25
26	A6a 100fr org, bl & grn	1.10	1.00

Issued to publicize space communications.

Young Pioneers A7

1963, Oct. 14 Engr. ***Perf. 12½***

27	A7 50fr grnsh bl, vio bl & brn	45	35

Issued to honor Young Pioneers.

Boali Falls — A8

1963, Oct. 28 ***Perf. 13***

28	A8 30fr bl, grn & red brn	30	20

Colotis Evippe — A9

Designs: Various butterflies.

1963, Nov. 18 Photo. ***Perf. 12½x13***

29	A9	1fr multi	15	15
30	A9	3fr multi	15	15
31	A9	4fr multi	16	16
32	A9	60fr multi	65	65
		Nos. 29-32 (4)	1.11	1.11

For surcharge see No. 58.

UNESCO Emblem, Scales and Tree — A9a

1963, Dec. 10 ***Perf. 13***

33	A9a 25fr grn, ol & red brn	30	22

15th anniversary of the Universal Declaration of Human Rights.

Leaves and IQSY Emblem A10

1964, Apr. 20 Engr. ***Perf. 13***

34	A10 25fr org, Prus grn & bis	70	65

International Quiet Sun Year, 1964-65.

Child — A11

"All Men Are Men" — A12

Designs: Heads of Children.

1964, Aug. 13 Unwmk. ***Perf. 13***

35	A11	20fr multi	20	15
36	A11	25fr multi	22	16
37	A11	40fr multi	35	24
38	A11	50fr multi	50	28
a.		Miniature sheet of 4, #35-38	1.50	1.50
		Nos. 35-38 (4)	1.27	83

Cooperation Issue
Common Design Type

1964, Nov. 7 Engr.

39	CD119 25fr grn, mag & dk brn	30	20

1964, Dec. 1 Litho. ***Perf. 13x12½***

40	A12 25fr multi	28	15

Issued to publicize National Unity.

Putting Yoke on Oxen — A13

Designs: 50fr, Ox pulling harrow. 85fr, Team of oxen in field. 100fr, Hay wagon.

1965, Apr. 28 Engr. ***Perf. 13***

41	A13	25fr sl grn, sep & rose	25	20
42	A13	50fr sl grn, lt bl & brn	50	30
43	A13	85fr sl grn, bl, grn & red brn	80	50
44	A13	100fr multi	1.00	65
		Nos. 41-44 (4)	2.55	1.65

For surcharges see Nos. 63-64.

Telegraph Receiver by Pouget-Maisonneuve — A14

ITU cent.: 30fr, Chappe telegraph, vert. 50fr, Doignon regulator, vert. 85fr, Pouillet telegraph transcriber.

1965, May 17 Unwmk.

45	A14	25fr red, grn & ultra	25	20
46	A14	30fr lake & grn	35	22
47	A14	50fr car & vio	55	35
48	A14	85fr red lil & slate	80	55
		Nos. 45-48 (4)	1.95	1.32

"Health" A15

Designs: 25fr, "Clothes;" shuttle, cloth and women. 60fr, "Teaching;" student and school. 85fr, "Food;" mother feeding child, tractor in wheat field.

1965, June 10 Engr. ***Perf. 13***

49	A15	25fr ultra, brt grn & brn	25	20
50	A15	50fr ultra, brn & grn	50	35
51	A15	60fr grn, ultra & brn	60	42
52	A15	85fr multi	90	50
		Nos. 49-52 (4)	2.25	1.47

Issued to publicize the slogans and aims of "M.E.S.A.N." (Mouvement d'Evolution Sociale de l'Afrique Noire). See No. C30.

Caterpillars and Moth on Coffee Branch — A16

Designs: 3fr, Hawk moth and caterpillar on coffee leaves, horiz. 30fr, Platyedra moth and larvae on cotton plant.

1965, Aug. 25 Engr. ***Perf. 13***

53	A16	2fr dk pur, dp org & sl grn	15	15
54	A16	3fr blk, sl grn & red	15	15
55	A16	30fr red lil, red & sl grn	65	25
		Set value	75	35

Issued to publicize plant protection.

Boy Scout, Tents and Animals A17

Design: 25fr, Campfire and Scout emblem.

1965, Sept. 27 Unwmk. ***Perf. 13***

56	A17	25fr red org, bl & red lil	25	15
57	A17	50fr brn & Prus bl	55	38

Issued to honor the Boy Scouts.

Nos. 30, 1 and 22 Surcharged in Black or Brown

5 F

Engraved; Photogravure
Perf. 13, 12, 12½x13

1965, Aug. 26 **Unwmk.**

58 A9 2fr on 3fr multi 1.10 1.10
59 A1 5fr on 15fr multi 1.10 1.10
60 A5 10fr on 20fr multi (Br) 1.40 1.40
Nos. 58-60 (3) 3.60 3.60

The surcharges are adjusted to shape of stamps.

UN Emblem and Wheat — A18

1965, Oct. 16 **Engr.** ***Perf. 13***

61 A18 50fr ocher, sl grn & brt bl 60 40

FAO "Freedom from Hunger Campaign."

Diamond Cutter — A19

1966, Mar. 14 **Engr.** ***Perf. 13***

62 A19 25fr car rose, dk pur & brn 25 16

Nos. 43-44 Surcharged

5 F

1966, Feb.

63 A13 5fr on 85fr multi 16 16
64 A13 10fr on 100fr multi 30 30

Issue dates: 5fr, Feb. 17. 10fr, Feb. 15.

Statue of Mbaka Woman Porter — A20

WHO Headquarters, Geneva — A21

1966, Apr. 9 **Photo.** ***Perf. 13x12½***

65 A20 25fr multi 25 16

International Negro Arts Festival. Dakar, Senegal, Apr. 1-24.

1966, May 3 **Photo.** **Unwmk.**

66 A21 25fr pur, bl & yel 25 16

Inauguration of the WHO Headquarters, Geneva.

Eulophia Cucullata — A22

1966, May 16 **Photo.** ***Perf. 12x12½***
Orchids in Natural Colors

67 A22 2fr dk red 15 15
68 A22 5fr brn org & vio 15 15
69 A22 10fr bl grn & blk 15 15
70 A22 15fr lt grn & dk brn 16 15
71 A22 20fr dk grn 22 15
72 A22 25fr lt ultra & brn 30 15
Set value 90 55

Orchids: 5fr, Lissochilus horsfalii. 10fr, Tridactyle bicaudata. 15fr, Polystachya. 20fr, Eulophia alta. 25fr, Microcelia macrorrhynchium.

For surcharge see No. 78.

Congo Forest Mouse — A23

Rodents: 10fr, One-stripe mouse. 20fr, Dollman's tree mouse, vert.

1966, Sept. 15 **Photo.** ***Perf. 12½x12***

73 A23 5fr yel & multi 15 15
74 A23 10fr tan & multi 15 15
75 A23 20fr lt grn & multi 22 16
Set value 42 30

UNESCO Emblem — A24

Pres. Jean Bedel Bokassa — A25

1966, Dec. 5 **Photo.** ***Perf. 13***

76 A24 30fr multi 30 16

20th anniv. of UNESCO.

1967, Jan. 1 ***Perf. 12x12½***

77 A25 30fr yel grn, blk & bis brn 35 16

No. 72 Surcharged with New Value and "XX"

1967, May 8 **Photo.** ***Perf. 12x12½***

78 A22 10fr on 25fr multi 15 15

See No. C43.

Central Market, Bangui — A26

1967, Aug. 8 **Photo.** ***Perf. 12½x13***

79 A26 30fr multi 35 20

Safari Hotel, Bangui — A27

1967, Sept. 26 **Photo.** ***Perf. 12½x13***

80 A27 30fr multi 35 20

Leucocoprinus Africanus — A28

Various Mushrooms

1967, Oct. 3 **Engr.** ***Perf. 13***

81 A28 5fr dk brn, ol & ocher 15 15
82 A28 10fr dk brn, ultra & yel 15 15
83 A28 15fr dk brn, sl grn & yel 16 15
84 A28 30fr multi 40 16
85 A28 50fr multi 60 35
Nos. 81-85 (5) 1.46
Set value 78

Map, Radio Tower, Projector and People — A29

1967, Oct. 31

86 A29 30fr emer, ocher & ind 35 20

Radiovision service.

African Hair Style — A30

Various African Hair Styles.

1967, Nov. 7 **Engr.** ***Perf. 13***

87 A30 5fr ultra, dk brn & bis brn 15 15
88 A30 10fr car, dk brn & bis brn 15 15
89 A30 15fr dp grn, dk brn & bis brn 16 15
90 A30 20fr org, dk brn & bis brn 22 15
91 A30 30fr red lil, dk brn & bis brn 35 16
Nos. 87-91 (5) 1.03
Set value 48

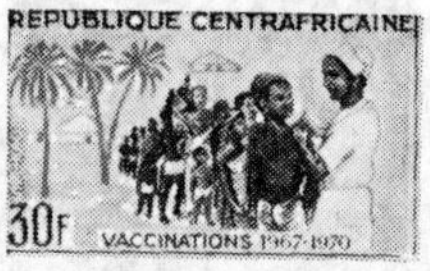

Nurse Vaccinating Children A31

1967, Nov. 14

92 A31 30fr dk red brn & brt grn 35 16

Vaccination campaign, 1967-70.

Douglas DC-3 — A32

1967, Nov. 24

93 A32 1fr shown 15 15
94 A32 2fr Beechcraft Baron 15 15
95 A32 5fr Douglas DC-4 15 15
Nos. 93-95,C47-C49 (6) 6.20 2.95

Pierced Stone, Kwe Tribe — A33

Designs: 30fr, Primitive dwelling at Toulou, horiz. 100fr, Megaliths, Bouar. 130fr, Rock painting (people), Toulou, horiz.

1967, Dec. 26 **Engr.** ***Perf. 13***

96 A33 30fr crim, ind & mar 35 20
97 A33 50fr ol brn, ocher & dk grn 55 25
98 A33 100fr dk brn, brt bl & brn 1.10 45
99 A33 130fr dk red, brn & dk grn 1.40 60
Nos. 96-99 (4) 3.40 1.50

6th Pan-African Prehistoric Cong., Dakar.

Tanker, Refinery and Map of Area Served — A33a

1968, July 30 **Photo.** ***Perf. 12½***

100 A33a 30fr multi 25 15

Issued to commemorate the opening of the Port Gentil (Gabon) Refinery, June 12, 1968.

Bulldozer Clearing Land — A34

Designs: 10fr, Baoule cattle. 20fr, 15,000-spindle spinning machine. No. 104, Automatic Diederichs looms. No. 105, Bulldozer.

1968, Oct. 1 **Engr.** ***Perf. 13***

101 A34 5fr blk, grn & dk brn 15 15
102 A34 10fr blk, pale grn & bis brn 15 15
103 A34 20fr grn, red brn & yel 20 15
104 A34 30fr brn, ol & ultra 35 15
105 A34 30fr ind, red brn & sl grn 35 15
Nos. 101-105 (5) 1.20
Set value 55

Issued to publicize "Operation Bokassa."

Bangui Mosque A35

1968, Oct. 14

106 A35 30fr grn, bl & ocher 30 15

Hunting Knife of Baya and Boufi Tribes — A36

Designs: 20fr, Hunting knife of Nzakara tribe. 30fr, Crossbow of Babinga and Babenzele (pygmy) tribes.

1968, Nov. 19 **Engr.** ***Perf. 13***

107 A36 10fr lem, Prus bl & ultra 15 15
108 A36 20fr ultra, dk ol & sl grn 20 15
109 A36 30fr sl grn, ultra & brn org 30 15
Nos. 107-109 (3) 65
Set value 32

"Ville de Bangui," 1958 — A37

River Boats: 30fr, "J. B. Gouandjia," 1968. 50fr, "Lamblin," 1944.

1968, Dec. 10 **Engr.** ***Perf. 13***
Size: 36x22mm

110 A37 10fr mag, brt grn & vio bl 15 15
111 A37 30fr bl, grn & brn 35 15
112 A37 50fr brn, sl & ol grn 60 25
Nos. 110-112,C62-C63 (5) 3.50 1.65

Woman Javelin Thrower — A38

Sport Designs: 10fr, Women runners. 15fr, Soccer.

1969, Mar. 18 Photo. *Perf. 13x12½*

113 A38 5fr multi 15 15
114 A38 10fr multi 15 15
115 A38 15fr multi 16 15
Nos. 113-115,C71-C72 (5) 1.96
Set value 80

BIT and ILO Emblems and Worker A39

1969, May 20 Photo. *Perf. 12½x13*

116 A39 30fr dp bl, grn & ol brn 25 15
117 A39 50fr dp car, grn & ol brn 50 22

50th anniv. of the ILO.

Pres. Bokassa — A40

Garayah — A41

1969, Dec. 1 Litho. *Perf. 13x13½*

118 A40 30fr ver & multi 25 15

ASECNA Issue

Common Design Type

1969, Dec. 12 Engr. *Perf. 13*

119 CD132 100fr dp bl 1.00 45

1970, Jan. 6 Engr. *Perf. 13*

Musical Instuments: 15fr, Ngombi (harp) horiz. 30fr, Xylophone, horiz. 50fr, Ndala (lute) horiz. 130fr, Gatta and babyon (drums).

120 A41 10fr yel grn, dk grn & ocher 15 15
121 A41 15fr bl grn, ocher & dk brn 16 15
122 A41 30fr mar, ocher & dk brn 30 15
123 A41 50fr rose car & ind 50 30
124 A41 130fr brt bl, brn & ol 1.40 45
Nos. 120-124 (5) 2.51 1.20

UPU Headquarters Issue

Common Design Type

1970, May 20 Engr. *Perf. 13*

125 CD133 100fr ultra, ver & red brn 65 35

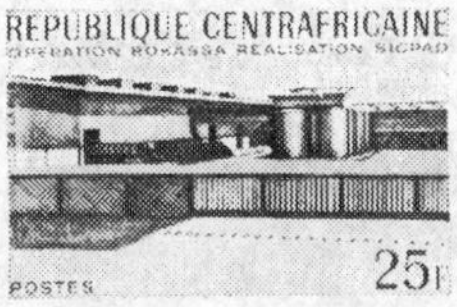

Loading Platform and Flour Storage Bins — A42

Designs: 50fr, Flour milling machinery. 100fr, View of mill.

1970, Feb. 24 Litho. *Perf. 14*

126 A42 25fr sl & multi 22 15
127 A42 50fr lil & multi 45 22
128 A42 100fr red & multi 90 50
Nos. 126-128 (3) 1.57 87

Inauguration of SICPAD (Société Industrielle Centrafricaine des Produits Alimentaires et Dérivés), a part of Operation Bokassa, Feb. 22, 1968.

Pres. Bokassa — A43

1970, Aug. 13 Litho. *Perf. 14*

129 A43 30fr multi 2.25 1.75
130 A43 40fr multi 3.25 2.25

Cheese Factory, Sarki — A44

Silk Worm — A45

Designs: 10fr, M'Bali Ranch. 20fr, Zebu, vert.

Perf. 13x13½, 13½x13

1970, Sept. 15

131 A44 5fr red & multi 15 15
132 A44 10fr red & multi 2.50 2.25
133 A44 20fr red & multi 42 30
134 A45 40fr red & multi 70 50
Nos. 131-134,C83 (5) 5.17 3.90

Issued to publicize Operation Bokassa, a national development plan.

Gnathonemus Monteiri — A46

River Fish: 20fr, Mormyrus proboscirostris. 30fr, Marcusenius wilverthi. 40fr, Gnathonemus elephas. 50fr, Gnathonemus curvirostris.

1971, Apr. 6 Photo. *Perf. 12½*

135 A46 10fr multi 15 15
136 A46 20fr multi 20 15
137 A46 30fr multi 35 16
138 A46 40fr multi 42 16
139 A46 50fr multi 55 25
Nos. 135-139 (5) 1.67 87

Berberati Cathedral A47

1971, July 20 Litho. *Perf. 13½*

140 A47 5fr grn & multi 15 15

New Roman Catholic Cathedral at Berberati.

Charles de Gaulle — A48

Gray Galago — A49

1971, Aug. 20 *Perf. 13½x13*

141 A48 100fr brt bl & multi 1.00 70

In memory of Gen. Charles de Gaulle (1890-1970), president of France.

1971, Oct. 25 Photo. *Perf. 13*

Designs: 40fr, Elegant galago. 100fr, Calabar potto, horiz. 150fr, Bosman's potto, horiz. 200fr, Oustalet's colobo, horiz.

142 A49 30fr pink & multi 35 25
143 A49 40fr lt bl & multi 50 35
144 A49 100fr multi 90 65
145 A49 150fr multi 1.50 80
146 A49 200fr multi 2.25 1.00
Nos. 142-146 (5) 5.50 3.05

Alan B. Shepard — A50

Designs: No. 148, Yuri Gagarin. No. 149, Edwin E. Aldrin, Jr. No. 150, Alexei Leonov. No. 151, Neil A. Armstrong on moon. No. 152, Lunokhod I on moon.

1971, Nov. 19 Litho. *Perf. 14*

147 A50 40fr vio & multi 35 16
148 A50 40fr vio & multi 35 16
149 A50 100fr multi 90 40
150 A50 100fr multi 90 40
151 A50 200fr red & multi 1.60 65
152 A50 200fr red & multi 1.60 65
Nos. 147-152 (6) 5.70 2.42

Space achievements of US and Russia.

"Operation Bokassa" and Pres. Bokassa A51

1971, Dec. 1 Photo. *Perf. 13*

153 A51 40fr red & multi 40 15

12th anniversary of independence.

Racial Equality Emblem A52

1971, Dec. 6 Litho.

154 A52 50fr multi 40 16

Intl. Year Against Racial Discrimination.

Bokassa School Emblem and Cadets — A53

Book Year Emblem — A54

1972, Jan. 1 Photo.

155 A53 30fr gold & multi 30 15

J. B. Bokassa Military School.

1972, Mar. 11 Photo. *Perf. 12½x13*

156 A54 100fr red brn, gold & org 70 42

International Book Year 1972.

"Your Heart is your Health" A55

1972, Apr. 7 Photo. *Perf. 13x12½*

157 A55 100fr yel, blk & car 70 42

World Health Day.

Red Cross Workers in Village — A56

1972, May 8 *Perf. 13*

158 A56 150fr multi 1.40 60

25th World Red Cross Day.

The Scott editorial staff regrettably cannot accept requests to identify, authenticate, or appraise stamps and postal markings.

Globe — A57

1972, May 17 **Litho.**

159	A57	50fr yel, blk & dp org	40 20

4th World Telecommunications Day.

Pres. and Mrs. Bokassa and Family A58

1972, May 28 ***Perf. 14***

160	A58	30fr yel & multi	25 15

Mother's Day. Mothers' gold medal awarded to Catherine Bokassa.

Pres. Bokassa Planting Cotton, Map of Africa — A59

1972, June 5 **Photo.** ***Perf. 13***

161	A59	40fr yel & multi	35 16

Operation Bokassa, a natl. development plan.

Postal Checking and Savings Center — A60

1972, June 21

162	A60	30fr yel org & multi	25 15

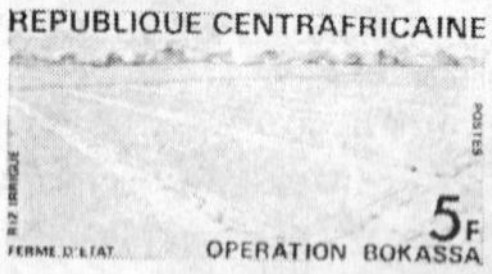

Irrigated Rice Fields A61

"Le Pacifique" Apartment House — A62

Designs: 25fr, Plowing rice field. No. 166, Swimming pool, Hotel St. Sylvestre. No. 167, Entrance, Hotel St. Sylvestre. No. 168, J. B. Bokassa University.

1972 **Litho.** ***Perf. 13x13½***

163	A61	5fr multi	15 15
164	A61	25fr multi	22 15

Engr. ***Perf. 13***

165	A62	30fr multi	22 15
166	A62	30fr multi	22 15
167	A62	40fr multi	30 16
168	A62	40fr multi	30 15
		Nos. 163-168 (6)	1.41
		Set value	65

Operation Bokassa. Issue dates: 5fr, 25fr, Nov. 10; No. 165, June 27; Nos. 166-167, Dec. 9; No. 168, Aug. 26.

Bull Chasing Woman on Clock Face — A63

Designs (Scenes Painted on Clock Faces): 10fr, Men and open cooking fire. 20fr, Fishermen. 30fr, Palms, monkeys and giraffe. 40fr, Warriors.

1972, July 31 **Photo.** ***Perf. 12½***

169	A63	5fr dk red & multi	15 15
170	A63	10fr brt bl & multi	15 15
171	A63	20fr grn & multi	16 15
172	A63	30fr yel & multi	30 15
173	A63	40fr vio & multi	35 20
		Set value	92 50

HORCEN Central African clock and watch factory.

Protestant Youth Center — A64

Design: 10fr, Postal runner carrying mail in cleft stick, vert.

1972, Aug. 12 ***Perf. 13***

174	A64	10fr multi	15 15
175	A64	20fr multi	16 15
		Nos. 174-175,C95-C98 (6)	3.66 1.82

Centraphilex 1972, Central African Philatelic Exhibition, Bangui.

Mail Truck — A65

1972, Oct. 23 **Photo.** ***Perf. 13***

176	A65	100fr ocher & multi	90 35

Universal Postal Union Day.

Mother Teaching Child to Write — A66

Central African Mothers: 10fr, Caring for infant. 15fr, Combing child's hair. 20fr, Teaching to read. 180fr, Nursing. 190fr, Teaching to walk.

1972, Dec. 27 ***Perf. 13½x13***

177	A66	5fr multi	15 15
178	A66	10fr lil & multi	15 15
179	A66	15fr dl org & multi	15 15
180	A66	20fr yel grn & multi	16 15
181	A66	180fr multi	1.50 50
182	A66	190fr pink & multi	1.50 70
		Nos. 177-182 (6)	3.61
		Set value	1.40

Farmer Carrying Sheaf — A67

1973, May 30 **Photo.** ***Perf. 13***

183	A67	50fr vio bl & multi	38 22

10th anniv. of the World Food Program.

Garcinia Punctata A68

African Flora: 20fr, Bertiera racemosa. 30fr, Corynanthe pachyceras. 40fr, Combretodendron africanum. 50fr, Xylopia Villosa, vert.

1973, June 8

184	A68	10fr pale bl & multi	15 15
185	A68	20fr multi	15 15
186	A68	30fr lt gray & multi	25 15
187	A68	40fr multi	25 20
188	A68	50fr multi	35 22
		Nos. 184-188 (5)	1.15
		Set value	64

For surcharge see No. 193.

Pygmy Chameleon A69

1973, June 26 **Photo.** ***Perf. 13***

189	A69	15fr multi	15 15

Caterpillar — A70

Designs: Various caterpillars.

1973, Aug. 6 **Photo.** ***Perf. 13***

190	A70	3fr multi	15 15
191	A70	5fr multi	15 15
192	A70	25fr multi	20 15
		Set value	30 20

For surcharge see No. 259.

No. 184 Surcharged with New Value, 2 Bars, and Overprinted in Red: "SECHERESSE SOLIDARITE AFRICAINE"

1973, Aug. 16

193	A68	100fr on 10fr multi	60 50

African solidarity in drought emergency.

African Postal Union Issue

Common Design Type

1973, Sept. 12 **Engr.** ***Perf. 13***

194	CD137	100fr dk brn, red org & ol	60 42

Pres. Bokassa and CAR Flag — A71

1973, Nov. 30 **Photo.** ***Perf. 12½***

195	A71	1fr brn & multi	15 15
196	A71	2fr pur & multi	15 15
197	A71	3fr vio bl & multi	15 15
198	A71	5fr ocher & multi	15 15
199	A71	10fr multi	15 15
200	A71	15fr org & multi	15 15
201	A71	20fr multi	15 15
202	A71	30fr dk grn & multi	20 15
203	A71	40fr dk brn & multi	25 20
		Set value, #195-203, C117-C118	1.95 1.40

INTERPOL Emblem A72

1973, Dec. 20 ***Perf. 13x12½***

204	A72	50fr yel & multi	35 25

50th anniv. of the Intl. Criminal Police Organization.

Catherine Bokassa Center — A73

Design: 40fr, Ambulance in front of Catherine Bokassa Center.

1974, Jan. 24 **Engr.** ***Perf. 13***

205	A73	30fr multi	16 15
206	A73	40fr multi	22 16

Catherine Bokassa Center for Mothers and Children.

Cigarette-making Machine — A74

Designs: 10fr, Cigarette in ashtray, and factory. 30fr, Hand lighting cigarette, and Administration Building.

1974, Jan. 29

207	A74	5fr slate grn & multi	15 15
208	A74	10fr slate grn & multi	15 15
209	A74	30fr slate grn & multi	16 15
		Set value	28 22

Publicity for Centra cigarettes.

"Communications" A75

1974, June 8 **Photo.** ***Perf. 12½x13***

210	A75	100fr multi	65 45

World Telecommunications Day.
For surcharge see No. 280.

People and WPY Emblem A76

1974, June 20 **Engr.** ***Perf. 13***

211 A76 100fr red, sl grn & brn 65 45

World Population Year.
For surcharge see No. 281.

Mother, Child, WHO Emblem — A77

1974, July 10

212 A77 100fr multi 65 30

26th anniv. of WHO.
For surcharge see No. 282.

Hoeing A78

Veterans' activities: 10fr, Battle scene ("yesterday"). 15fr, Pastoral scene ("today"). 20fr, Rice planting. 25fr, Storehouse. 40fr, Veterans Headquarters. Borders show tanks and tractors.

1974, Nov. 15 **Litho.** ***Perf. 13***

213 A78 10fr multi		15	15
214 A78 15fr multi		15	15
215 A78 20fr multi		15	15
216 A78 25fr multi		15	15
217 A78 30fr multi		16	15
218 A78 40fr multi		22	15
	Set value	80	46

For surcharges see Nos. 260, 265, 267.

Presidents and Flags of Cameroun, CAR, Congo, Gabon and Meeting Center — A79

1974, Dec. 8 **Photo.** ***Perf. 13***

219 A79 40fr gold & multi 25 15

See #C126 and note after Cameroun #595.
For surcharge see No. 272.

House in OCAM City — A80

Designs: Scenes in housing development, OCAM City.

1975, Feb. 1 **Photo.** ***Perf. 13***

220 A80 30fr multi		20	15
221 A80 40fr multi		25	15
222 A80 50fr multi		30	20
223 A80 100fr multi		60	42
	Nos. 220-223 (4)	1.35	92

For surcharges see Nos. 269, 273.

1975, Feb. 22

Designs: Cottage scenes in J. B. Bokassa "pilot village."

224 A80 25fr multi		15	15
225 A80 30fr multi		16	15
226 A80 40fr multi		25	15
	Nos. 224-226 (3)	56	
	Set value		32

For surcharges see Nos. 268, 270, 274.

Foreign Ministry A81

Television Station — A82

1975, Feb. 28 ***Perf. 13x12½***

227 A81 40fr multi 25 15

Perf. 13

228 A82 40fr multi 25 15

Public buildings, Bangui.
For surcharges see Nos. 275-276.

Bokassa's Saber — A83

Design: 40fr, Bokassa's baton.

1975, Feb. 22 **Photo.** ***Perf. 13***

229 A83 30fr dp bl & multi 16 15
230 A83 40fr vio bl & multi 22 15

Jean Bedel Bokassa, President for Life and Marshal of the Republic. See Nos. C127-C128. For surcharge see No. 286.

Traffic Signs — A84

1975, Mar. 20

231 A84 5fr Do Not Enter		15	15
232 A84 10fr Stop		15	15
233 A84 20fr No parking		15	15
234 A84 30fr School		15	15
235 A84 40fr Intersection		25	15
	Set value	60	42

For surcharges see Nos. 261, 277.

Buffon's Kob — A85

1975, June 24 **Photo.** ***Perf. 13***

236 A85 10fr shown		15	15
237 A85 15fr Wart hog		15	15
238 A85 20fr Waterbuck		15	15
239 A85 30fr Lion		20	15
	Set value	50	32

For surcharges see Nos. 262-263, 266, 271.

Crane Lifting Log onto Truck — A86

Designs: 10fr, Forest, vert. 15fr, Tree felling, vert. 100fr, Log pile. 150fr, Logs transported by raft. 200fr, Lumberyard.

1975, Nov. 28 **Engr.** ***Perf. 13***

240 A86 10fr multi		15	15
241 A86 15fr multi		15	15
242 A86 50fr multi		25	16
243 A86 100fr multi		50	38
244 A86 150fr multi		70	60
245 A86 200fr multi		1.00	70
	Nos. 240-245 (6)	2.75	2.14

Promotion of Central African wood.
For surcharges see Nos. 264, 279.

Women's Heads and Various Occupations — A87

1975, Dec. 10 **Photo.**

246 A87 40fr multi 22 15
247 A87 100fr multi 50 38

International Women's Year 1975.

Alexander Graham Bell — A88

1976, Mar. 25 **Litho.** ***Perf. 12½x13***

248 A88 100fr yel & blk 50 35

Centenary of first telephone call by Alexander Graham Bell, Mar. 10, 1876.
For surcharge see No. 283.

Satellite and ITU Emblem — A89

Design: No. 250, UPU emblem, various forms of mail transport.

1976 **Engr.** ***Perf. 13***

249 A89 100fr vio bl, cl & grn 50 35
250 A89 100fr car, grn & ocher 70 50

World Telecommunications Day (No. 249); Universal Postal Union Day (No. 250).
For surcharges see Nos. 284-285.

Soyuz on Launching Pad — A90

Design: 50fr, Apollo rocket.

1976, June 14 **Litho.** ***Perf. 14x13½***

251 A90 40fr multi 28 15
252 A90 50fr multi 38 16
Nos. 251-252,C135-C137 (5) 4.71 1.96

Apollo Soyuz space test project, Russo-American cooperation, launched July 15, link-up July 17, 1975.
For surcharges see Nos. 287, 290, C161, C168, C173, C177.

Drurya Antimachus — A91

Butterfly: 40fr, Argema mittrei, vert.

1976, Sept. 20 **Litho.** ***Perf. 12½***

253 A91 30fr ocher & multi		16	15
254 A91 40fr ultra & multi		22	15
	Set value		24

See Nos. C145-C146. For surcharge see No. 278.

Slalom, Piero Gros — A92

Design: 60fr, Karl Schnabel and Toni Innauer.

1976, Sept. 23 ***Perf. 13½***

255 A92 40fr multi 28 15
256 A92 60fr multi 42 22
Nos. 255-256,C147-C149 (5) 4.55 2.12

12th Winter Olympic Games winners, Innsbruck.
For surcharges see Nos. 288, 291, C164, C170, C174, C178.

Viking Components A93

Design: 60fr, Viking take-off.

1976, Dec.

257 A93 40fr multi 28 15
258 A93 60fr multi 42 20
Nos. 257-258,C151-C153 (5) 4.55 1.97

Viking Mars project.
For surcharges and overprints see Nos. 289, 292, 391-392, C165, C171, C175, C179.

Empire

Stamps of 1973-76 Overprinted with Bars and "EMPIRE CENTRAFRICAIN" in Black, Green, Violet Blue, Silver, Carmine, Brown or Red

Printing and Perforations as Before

1977, Mar.

259 A70	3fr (#190; B)	15	15
260 A78	10fr (#213;B)	15	15
261 A84	10fr (#232;VB)	15	15
262 A85	10fr (#236;C)	15	15
263 A85	15fr (#237;C)	15	15
264 A86	15fr (#241;B)	15	15
265 A78	20fr (#215;B)	15	15
266 A85	20fr (#238;C)	15	15
267 A78	25fr (#216;B)	16	15
268 A80	25fr (#224;B)	16	15
269 A80	30fr (#220;VB)	20	16

270 A80 30fr (#225;B) 20 16
271 A85 30fr (#239;C) 20 16
272 A79 40fr (#219;B) 22 20
273 A80 40fr (#221;VB) 25 20
274 A80 40fr (#226;B) 22 20
275 A81 40fr (#227;B & S) 22 20
276 A82 40fr (#228;B) 22 20
277 A84 40fr (#235;VB) 20 16
278 A91 40fr (#254;B) 20 16
279 A86 50fr (#242;Br) 30 22
280 A75 100fr (#210;B) 60 45
281 A76 100fr (#211;B) 60 45
282 A77 100fr (#212;G) 65 55
283 A88 100fr (#248;R) 65 55
284 A89 100fr (#249;B) 65 55
285 A89 100fr (#250;B) 65 55
Nos. 259-285 (27) 7.75 6.62

Stamps of 1975-76 Overprinted "EMPIRE CENTRAFRICAIN" in Black on Silver Panel

1977, Apr. 1
286 A83 40fr multi (#230) 20 16
287 A90 40fr multi (#251) 25 20
288 A92 40fr multi (#255) 20 16
289 A93 40fr multi (#257) 20 16
290 A90 50fr multi (#252) 35 22
291 A92 60fr multi (#256) 35 22
292 A93 60fr multi (#258) 35 22
Nos. 286-292 (7) 1.90 1.34

Pierre and Marie Curie A94

Design: 60fr, Wilhelm C. Roentgen.

1977, Apr. 1 Litho. *Perf. 13½*
293 A94 40fr multi 22 15
294 A94 60fr multi 40 20
Nos. 293-294,C180-C182 (5) 3.78 1.70

Nobel Prize winners.

Italy No. C42 and Faustine Temple, Rome — A95

Design: 60fr, Russia No. C12 and St. Basil's Cathedral, Moscow.

1977, Apr. 11 Litho. *Perf. 11*
295 A95 40fr multi 22 15
296 A95 60fr multi 40 20
Nos. 295-296,C184-C186 (5) 4.47 1.97

75th anniversary of the Zeppelin.

Lindbergh over Paris — A96

Designs: 60fr, Santos Dumont and "14 bis." 100fr, Bleriot and monoplane. 200fr, Roald Amundsen and "N24." 300fr, Concorde. 500fr, Lindbergh and Spirit of St. Louis.

1977, Sept. 30 Litho. *Perf. 13½*
297 A96 50fr multi 35 16
298 A96 60fr multi 40 20
299 A96 100fr multi 60 25
300 A96 200fr multi 1.25 50
301 A96 300fr multi 2.00 80
Nos. 297-301 (5) 4.60 1.91

Souvenir Sheet

302 A96 500fr multi 3.25 1.50

History of aviation, famous fliers.

Shot on Goal A97

Designs: 60fr, Heading ball in net. 100fr, Backfield defense. 200fr, Argentina '78 poster. 300fr, Mario Zagalo and stadium. 500fr, Ferenc Puskas.

1977, Nov. 18 Litho. *Perf. 13½*
303 A97 50fr multi 35 16
304 A97 60fr multi 40 20
305 A97 100fr multi 60 22
306 A97 200fr multi 1.25 50
307 A97 300fr multi 2.00 80
Nos. 303-307 (5) 4.60 1.88

Souvenir Sheet

308 A97 500fr multi 3.25 1.50

World Soccer Championships, Argentina, June 1-25, 1978.
For overprints see Nos. 370-375.

Emperor Bokassa I, Central African Flag — A98

1977, Dec. 4 Litho. *Perf. 13½*
309 A98 40fr multi 20 16
310 A98 60fr multi 35 22
311 A98 100fr multi 55 40
312 A98 150fr multi 80 60
Nos. 309-312,C188-C189 (6) 4.60 3.03

Coronation of Emperor Bokassa I, Dec. 4.

Lilium — A99

Electronic Tree, ITU Emblem — A100

1977 Litho. *Perf. 13½x14*
313 A99 5fr shown 15 15
314 A99 10fr Hibiscus 15 15
Set value 15 15

For overprints see Nos. 408-409.

1977
315 A100 100fr blk, org & brn 80 60

World Telecommunications Day.

Bible and People A101

1977 Litho. *Perf. 14x13½*
316 A101 40fr multi 25 15

Bible Week.

People and Rotary Emblem A102

1977
317 A102 60fr multi 40 20

Rotary Club of Bangui, 20th anniversary.

Holy Family, by Rubens — A103

Rubens Paintings: 150fr, Marie de Medicis. 200fr, Son of artist. 300fr, Neptune. 500fr, Marie de Medicis (different).

1978, Jan. 26
318 A103 60fr multi 40 20
319 A103 150fr multi 90 40
320 A103 200fr multi 1.25 55
321 A103 300fr multi 2.00 80
Nos. 318-321 (4) 4.55 1.95

Souvenir Sheet

322 A103 500fr gold & multi 3.25 1.50

Peter Paul Rubens (1577-1640).

Rhinoceros — A104

Endangered Animals and Wildlife Fund Emblem: 50fr, Slender-nosed crocodile. 60fr, Leopard, vert. 100fr, Giraffe, vert. 200fr, Elephant. 300fr, Gorilla, vert.

1978, Feb. 21 Litho. *Perf. 13½*
323 A104 40fr multi 22 15
324 A104 50fr multi 35 16
325 A104 60fr multi 40 20
326 A104 100fr multi 60 28
327 A104 200fr multi 1.25 55
328 A104 300fr multi 2.00 80
Nos. 323-328 (6) 4.82 2.14

Bokassa Sports Palace A105

Design: 60fr, Sports Palace, side view.

1978 *Perf. 14*
329 A105 40fr multi 20 16
330 A105 60fr multi 35 22

Automatic Telephone Exchange, Bangui A106

1978
331 A106 40fr multi 25 15
332 A106 60fr multi 40 20

Diligence and Satellite A107

Designs (UPU Emblem and): 50fr, Steam locomotive and communications via satellite. 60fr, Paddle-wheel steamer and ship-to-shore communication via satellite. 80fr, Old mail truck and satellite.

1978, May 17 *Perf. 13½*
333 A107 40fr multi 25 15
334 A107 50fr multi 35 16
335 A107 60fr multi 40 20
336 A107 80fr multi 55 25
Nos. 333-336,C191-C192 (6) 3.60 1.76

Century of progress of posts and telecommunications.

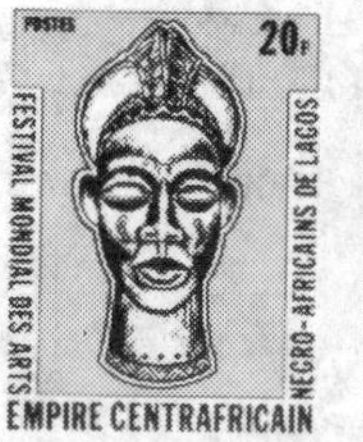

Mask A108

Capt. Cook on "Endeavour" A109

Designs: 30fr, Mask. 60fr, Women dancers, horiz. 100fr, Men dancers, horiz.

Perf. 13½x14, 14x13½
1978, July 11 Litho.
337 A108 20fr blk & yel 15 15
338 A108 30fr blk & brt bl 20 15
339 A108 60fr blk & multi 40 20
340 A108 100fr blk & multi 65 35
Nos. 337-340 (4) 1.40
Set value 72

Black-African World Arts Festival, Lagos.
For overprints see Nos. 411-412.

1978, Aug. 30 *Perf. 14½*

Designs: 60fr, Resolution off Hawaii, horiz. 200fr, Hawaiians welcoming Capt. Cook, horiz. 350fr, Masked rowers in Hawaiian boat, horiz.

341 A109 60fr multi 40 20
342 A109 80fr multi 55 25
343 A109 200fr multi 1.40 65
344 A109 350fr multi 2.25 1.10
Nos. 341-344 (4) 4.60 2.20

Capt. James Cook (1728-1779), explorer.

Dürer, Self-portrait A110

Dürer Paintings: 80fr, The Four Apostles. 200fr, Virgin and Child. 350fr, Emperor Maximilian I.

1978, Oct. 24 Litho. *Perf. 13½*

345 A110	60fr multi	40	20
346 A110	80fr multi	55	25
347 A110	200fr multi	1.40	65
348 A110	350fr multi	2.25	1.10
	Nos. 345-348 (4)	4.60	2.20

Albrecht Dürer (1471-1528), German painter.

Tutankhamen's Gold Mask — A111

Treasures of Tutankhamen: 60fr, King and Queen, gold back panel of throne. 80fr, Gilt folding chair. 100fr, King wearing crowns of Upper and Lower Egypt, painted wood sculpture. 120fr, Lion's head. 150fr, Tutankhamen, wood stature. 180fr, Gold throne. 250fr, Gold miniature coffin.

1978, Nov. 22

349 A111	40fr multi	25	15
350 A111	60fr multi	40	20
351 A111	80fr multi	55	25
352 A111	100fr multi	65	35
353 A111	120fr multi	80	40
354 A111	150fr multi	1.00	50
355 A111	180fr multi	1.20	60
356 A111	250fr multi	1.60	80
	Nos. 349-356 (8)	6.45	3.25

Tutankhamen, c. 1358 B.C., King of Egypt.

Lenin at Smolny Institute — A112

Designs: 60fr, 200fr, 300fr, Various Lenin portraits. 100fr, Ulyanov family, horiz. 150fr, Lenin, Cruiser "Aurora" and flag, horiz. 500fr, "Aurora" and star.

1978, Nov. *Perf. 14*

357 A112	40fr multi	25	15
358 A112	60fr multi	40	20
359 A112	100fr blk & gold	65	35
360 A112	150fr blk, gold & red	1.00	50
361 A112	200fr multi	1.40	65
362 A112	300fr multi	2.00	1.00
	Nos. 357-362 (6)	5.70	2.85

Souvenir Sheet

363 A112	500fr multi	3.50	

60th anniversary of the Soviet Union.

Catherine Bokassa — A113

Design: 60fr, Emperor Bokassa.

1978, Dec. 4 Litho. *Perf. 13*

364 A113	40fr multi	25	15
365 A113	60fr multi	40	20

1st anniv. of coronation. See No. C202.

Rowland Hill, Letter Scale and G.B. No. 1 — A114

Designs (Rowland Hill and): 50fr, US #1, mailman on bicycle. 60fr, Austria #P4, 19th cent. mailman. 80fr, Switzerland #2L1, postilion and mailcoach.

1978, Dec. 9 Litho. *Perf. 13½*

366 A114	40fr multi	25	15
367 A114	50fr multi	35	16
368 A114	60fr multi	40	20
369 A114	80fr multi	55	25
	Nos. 366-369,C203-C204 (6)	3.60	1.76

Sir Rowland Hill (1795-1879), originator of penny postage.

Nos. 303-307 Overprinted in Silver: "VAINQUEUR: ARGENTINE"

1978, Dec. 27

370 A97	50fr multi	35	16
371 A97	60fr multi	40	20
372 A97	100fr multi	65	35
373 A97	200fr multi	1.40	65
374 A97	300fr multi	2.00	1.00
	Nos. 370-374 (5)	4.80	2.36

Souvenir Sheet

No. 308 Overprinted in Silver: "ARGENTINE-PAYS BAS 3-1 / 25 juin 1978"

375 A97	500fr multi	3.50	1.60

Argentina's victory in World Cup Soccer Championship 1978.

Children Painting and Dutch Portrait — A115

Designs (UNICEF, Eagle Emblems and): 50fr, Eskimo children skiing, and ski jump. 60fr, Children with toy racing car, and Carl Benz with early car model. 80fr, Children launching rocket, and Intelsat.

1979, Mar. 6 Litho. *Perf. 13½*

376 A115	40fr multi	25	15
377 A115	50fr multi	35	16
378 A115	60fr multi	40	20
379 A115	80fr multi	55	25
	Nos. 376-379,C206-C207 (6)	3.60	1.76

International Year of the Child.

High Jump, Moscow '80 Emblem and "M" — A116

Designs (Moscow '80 Emblem, Various Sports and): 50fr, Bicycling and "O." 60fr, Weight lifting and "C." 80fr, Judo and "K."

1979, Mar. 16 Litho. *Perf. 13*

380 A116	40fr multi	22	15
381 A116	50fr multi	25	15
382 A116	60fr multi	32	16
383 A116	80fr multi	40	20
	Nos. 380-383,C209-C210 (6)	3.24	1.66

22nd Olympic Games, Moscow, July 19-Aug. 3, 1980. Background letters on Nos. 380-383, C209-C210 spell "Mockba." A 1500fr gold embossed stamp showing emblems and Discobolus exists.

Memorial, Bangui, Butterfly, Hibiscus — A117

Design: 150fr, Canoe, truck and letters.

1979, June 8 Litho. *Perf. 12x12½*

384 A117	60fr multi	32	16
385 A117	150fr multi	80	40

Philexafrique II, Libreville, Gabon, June 8-17. Nos. 384, 385 each printed in sheets of 10 with 5 labels showing exhibition emblem.

Schoolgirl A118

1979, July 25 Litho. *Perf. 12½x12*

386 A118	70fr multi	38	15

Intl. Bureau of Education, Geneva, 50th anniv.

Chicken A119

1979, Aug. *Perf. 13*

387 A119	10fr shown	15	15
388 A119	20fr Bull	15	15
389 A119	40fr Sheep	20	15
	Set value	35	20

National Husbandry Assoc. See No. C211.

Souvenir Sheet

Virgin and Child, by Dürer A120

1979, Aug. *Perf. 13½*

390 A120	500fr lt grn & dl red	2.75	1.25

Albrecht Dürer (1471-1528), German engraver and printer.

Nos. 257-258 Overprinted "ALUNISSAGE/APOLLO XI/ juillet/1969" and Emblem

1979, Nov. 11 Litho. *Perf. 13½*

391 A93	40fr multi	22	15
392 A93	60fr multi	32	16
	Nos. 391-392,C212-C214 (5)	3.79	1.91

Apollo 11 moon landing, 10th anniversary.

Girl and Rose A121

1979, Dec. 15

393 A121	30fr Butterfly and girl, vert.	16	15
394 A121	40fr shown	22	15
395 A121	60fr Hansel and Gretel, vert.	32	16
396 A121	200fr Cinderella	1.10	50
397 A121	250fr Mermaid, vert.	1.40	65
	Nos. 393-397 (5)	3.20	1.61

International Year of the Child.

Locomotive, US Type A27, Hill — A122

Locomotives, Hill and Stamps: 100fr, France #1. 150fr, Germany type A11. 250fr, Great Britain #32. 500fr, CAR #2.

1979, Dec. 20

398 A122	60fr multi	32	16
399 A122	100fr multi	55	25
400 A122	150fr multi	80	40
401 A122	250fr multi	1.40	65
	Nos. 398-401 (4)	3.07	1.46

Souvenir Sheet

402 A122	500fr multi	3.00	1.50

Sir Rowland Hill (1795-1879), originator of penny postage.

Basketball, Moscow '80 Emblem — A123

Pre-Olympic Year: Men's or women's basketball.

1979, Dec. 28 Litho. *Perf. 14½*

403 A123	50fr multi		25	15
404 A123	125fr multi		65	35
405 A123	200fr multi		1.10	55
406 A123	300fr multi		1.60	80
407 A123	500fr multi		2.75	1.40
	Nos. 403-407 (5)		6.35	3.25

For overprints see Nos. 425-429.

Nos. 313-314, 337-338 Overprinted "REPUBLIQUE CENTRAFRICAINE" in Black on Silver Panel and

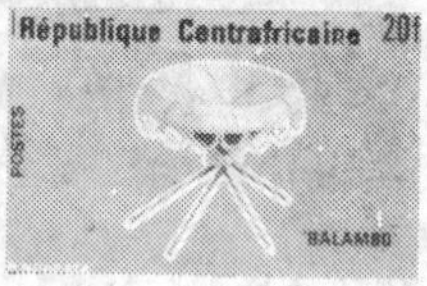

Balambo Chair — A124

Perf. 13½x14, 14x13½

1980, Mar. 20 Litho.

408 A99	5fr multi	15	15
409 A99	10fr multi	15	15
410 A124	20fr multi	15	15
411 A108	20fr multi	15	15
412 A108	30fr multi	16	15
	Set value	46	28

Viking Satellite A125

1980, Apr. 8 *Perf. 13½*

413 A125	40fr shown	20	15
414 A125	50fr Apollo-Soyuz	25	15
415 A125	60fr Voyager	32	16
416 A125	100fr European Space Agency emblem, flags	55	25
	Nos. 413-416,C221-C222 (6)	3.22	1.66

Walking, Olympic Medal, Moscow '80 Emblem — A126

1980, July 25 Litho. *Perf. 13½*

417 A126	30fr shown	16	15
418 A126	40fr Relay race	22	15
419 A126	70fr Running	38	16
420 A126	80fr High jump	42	22
	Nos. 417-420,C231-C232 (6)	2.53	1.33

For overprints see Nos. 462-465, C248-C250.

Agricultural Development A127

1980, Nov. 4 Litho. *Perf. 13½*

421 A127	30fr shown	16	15
422 A127	40fr Telecommunications	22	15
423 A127	70fr Engineering	38	16
424 A127	100fr Civil engineering	55	25
	Nos. 421-424,C234-C235 (6)	3.21	1.66

Europe-Africa cooperation.

Nos. 403-407 Overprinted with Medal and Country

1980, Nov. 12 *Perf. 14½*

425 A123	50fr multi	25	15
426 A123	125fr multi	65	35
427 A123	200fr multi	1.10	55
428 A123	300fr multi	1.60	80
429 A123	500fr multi	2.75	1.40
	Nos. 425-429 (5)	6.35	3.25

Virgin and Child, by Raphael A128

African Postal Union, 5th Anniversary A129

Christmas 1980: Virgin and Child paintings by Raphael.

1980, Dec. 20 *Perf. 12½*

430 A128	60fr multi	35	16
431 A128	150fr multi	80	40
432 A128	250fr multi	1.40	65
	Nos. 430-432 (3)	2.55	1.21

1980, Dec. 24 Photo. *Perf. 13½*

433 A129	70fr multi	38	16

Peruvian Soccer Team, Soccer Cup — A130

1981, Jan. 13 Litho. *Perf. 13½*

434 A130	10fr shown	15	15
435 A130	15fr Scotland	15	15
436 A130	20fr Mexico	15	15
437 A130	25fr Sweden	15	15
438 A130	30fr Austria	16	15
439 A130	40fr Poland	22	15
440 A130	50fr France	25	15
441 A130	60fr Italy	35	16
442 A130	70fr Germany	40	20
443 A130	80fr Brazil	42	22
	Nos. 434-443,C237-C238 (12)	4.05	
	Set value		1.90

ESPANA '82 World Cup Soccer Championship.

13th World Telecommunications Day — A131

1981, May 17 Litho. *Perf. 12½*

444 A131	150fr multi	80	40

Apollo 15 Crew on Moon A132

Space Exploration: Columbia space shuttle.

1981, June 10 Litho. *Perf. 14*

445 A132	100fr multi	55	25
446 A132	150fr multi	80	40
447 A132	200fr multi	1.10	55
448 A132	300fr multi	1.60	80
	Nos. 445-448 (4)	4.05	2.00

Souvenir Sheet

449 A132	500fr multi	2.75	1.40

Family of Acrobats with Monkey, by Picasso A133

Picasso Birth Centenary: 50fr, The Balcony. 80fr, The Artist's Son as Pierrot. 100fr, The Three Dancers.

1981, June 30 *Perf. 13½*

450 A133	40fr multi	22	15
451 A133	50fr multi	25	15
452 A133	80fr multi	42	22
453 A133	100fr multi	55	25
	Nos. 450-453,C245-C246 (6)	3.34	1.72

First Anniv. of Zimbabwe's Independence — A134

1981, July 9 Litho. *Perf. 12½*

454 A134	100fr multi	55	25
455 A134	150fr multi	80	40
456 A134	200fr multi	1.10	55
	Nos. 454-456 (3)	2.45	1.20

Prince Charles and Lady Diana — A135

1981, July, 24 *Perf. 14*

457 A135	75fr Charles	40	20
458 A135	100fr Diana	55	25
459 A135	150fr St. Paul's Cathedral	80	40
460 A135	175fr shown	90	45
	Nos. 457-460 (4)	2.65	1.30

Souvenir Sheet

461 A135	500fr Couple	2.75	1.40

Royal Wedding.
For overprints see Nos. 529-533.

Nos. 417-420 Overprinted with Event, Winner and Country in Gold

1981 Litho. *Perf. 13½*

462 A126	30fr multi	16	15
463 A126	40fr multi	22	15
464 A126	70fr multi	38	16
465 A126	80fr multi	42	22
	Nos. 462-465,C248-C249 (6)	2.53	1.33

Prince Charles and Lady Diana — A136

1981, Aug. 20 Litho. *Perf. 13½*

466 A136	40fr shown	22	15
467 A136	50fr Crowned Prince of Wales	25	15
468 A136	80fr Diana	42	22
469 A136	100fr Naval training	55	25
	Nos. 466-469,C251-C252 (6)	3.34	1.72

Royal wedding.

1906 Renault — A137

1981, Sept. 22 Litho. *Perf. 12½*

470 A137	20fr shown	15	15
471 A137	40fr Mercedes-Benz, 1937	22	15
472 A137	50fr Matra-Ford, 1969	25	15
473 A137	110fr Tazio Nuvolari, 1927	60	30
474 A137	150fr Jackie Stewart, 1965	80	40
	Nos. 470-474 (5)	2.02	1.15

Souvenir Sheet

Perf. 10

475 A137	450fr Finish line, 1914	2.50	1.40

Grand Prix of France, 75th anniv.

World Food Day — A138

1981, Oct. 16

476 A138	90fr multi	48	25
477 A138	110fr multi	60	30

Navigators and their Ships — A139

1981, Sept. 4 Litho. *Perf. 13½*

478 A139	40fr C.V. Rietschoten	22	15
479 A139	50fr M. Pajot	25	15
480 A139	60fr K. Jaworski	35	16
481 A139	80fr M. Birch	42	22
	Nos. 478-481,C254-C255 (6)	2.89	1.48

Downfall of Empire A140

1981, Oct. 6

482	A140	5fr Bayonet through crown	15	15
483	A140	10fr like #482	15	15
484	A140	25fr Victory holding map	15	15
485	A140	60fr like #484	35	16
486	A140	90fr Toppled Bokassa statue	48	24
487	A140	500fr like #486	2.75	1.40
		Nos. 482-487 (6)	4.03	2.25

Komba — A141

1981, Nov. 17

488	A141	50fr shown	25	15
489	A141	90fr Dodoro, horiz.	48	25
490	A141	140fr Kaya, horiz.	70	40
		Nos. 488-490 (3)	1.43	80

Central African States Bank — A142

1981, Dec. 12 Litho. *Perf. 12½x13*

491	A142	90fr multi	48	25
492	A142	110fr multi	60	30

Christmas 1981 — A143

Virgin and Child Paintings.

1981, Dec. 24

493	A143	50fr Fra Angelico, 1430	25	15
494	A143	60fr Cosimo Tura, 1484	35	16
495	A143	90fr Bramantino	50	25
496	A143	110fr Memling	45	22
		Nos. 493-496,C260-C261 (6)	3.35	1.73

Scouting Year — A144

1982, Jan. 13 *Perf. 12½*

497	A144	100fr Hiking	55	25
498	A144	150fr Scouts, horiz.	80	40
499	A144	200fr Hiking	1.10	55
500	A144	300fr Salute, flag, vert.	1.60	80
		Nos. 497-500 (4)	4.05	2.00

Souvenir Sheet

Perf. 13

501	A144	500fr Scout, Baden-Powell, vert.	2.75	1.40

Elephant — A145

1982, Jan. 22 *Perf. 13½*

502	A145	60fr shown	35	16
503	A145	90fr Giraffes	48	25
504	A145	100fr Addaxes	55	25
505	A145	110fr Okapi	60	30
		Nos. 502-505,C263-C264 (6)	6.33	3.16

Norman Rockwell Illustrations A146

1982, Feb. 17 *Perf. 13½x14*

506	A146	30fr Grandfather snowman	16	15
507	A146	60fr Croquet players	35	16
508	A146	110fr Women talking	60	30
509	A146	150fr Searching	80	40
		Nos. 506-509 (4)	1.91	1.01

AT 16 Dirigible A147

1982, Feb. 27 Litho. *Perf. 13½*

510	A147	5fr shown	15	15
511	A147	10fr Beyer-Garrat locomotive	15	15
512	A147	20fr Bugatti 24 "Royale," 1924	15	15
513	A147	110fr Vickers "Valentia," 1928	60	30
		Nos. 510-513,C266-C267 (6)	5.15	2.95

Bellvue Garden, by Edouard Manet — A148

Anniversaries: 400fr, Goethe, vert. #519-520, Princess Diana, 21st birthday, July 1, vert. 300fr, George Washington, vert.

1982, Apr. 6 Litho. *Perf. 13*

517	A148	200fr multi	1.10	55
517A	A148	300fr multi	1.60	80
518	A148	400fr multi	2.00	1.10
519	A148	500fr multi	2.75	1.40
		Nos. 517-519 (4)	7.45	3.85

Souvenir Sheet

520	A148	500fr multi	2.75	1.40

23rd Olympic Games, Los Angeles, 1984 — A149

1982, July 24 Litho. *Perf. 13½*

521	A149	5fr Soccer	15	15
522	A149	10fr Boxing	15	15
523	A149	20fr Running	15	15
524	A149	110fr Long jump	60	30
		Nos. 521-524,C269-C270 (6)	5.15	2.95

21st Birthday of Princess Diana — A150

Portraits.

1982, July 20 Litho. *Perf. 13½*

525	A150	5fr multi	15	15
526	A150	10fr multi	15	15
527	A150	20fr multi	15	15
528	A150	110fr multi	60	30
		Nos. 525-528,C272-C273 (6)	5.15	2.95

Nos. 457-461 Overprinted in Blue: "NAISSANCE ROYALE 1982"

1982, Aug. 20 *Perf. 14*

529	A135	75fr multi	40	20
530	A135	110fr multi	60	30
531	A135	150fr multi	80	40
532	A135	175fr multi	90	45
		Nos. 529-532 (4)	2.70	1.35

Souvenir Sheet

533	A135	500fr multi	2.75	1.40

Birth of Prince William of Wales, June 21.

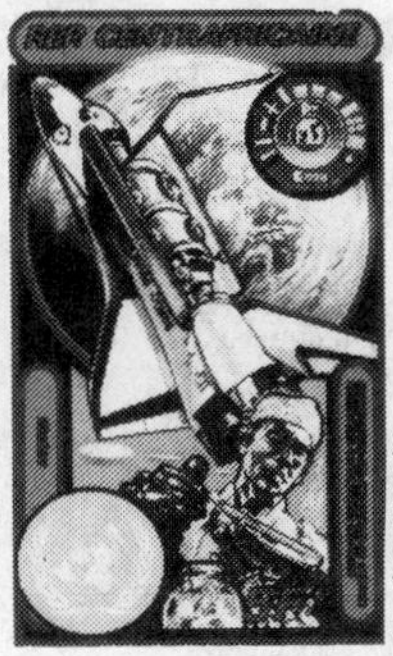

2nd UN Conference on Peaceful Uses of Outer Space, Vienna, Aug. 9-21 — A151

Various satellites and space scenes.

1982, Aug. 15 Litho. *Perf. 13½*

534	A151	5fr multi	15	15
535	A151	10fr multi	15	15
536	A151	20fr multi	15	15
537	A151	110fr multi	60	30
		Nos. 534-537,C277-C278 (6)	5.15	2.95

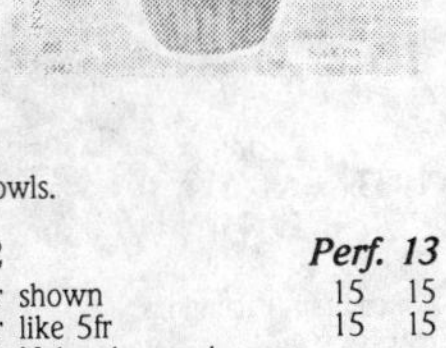

Sakpa Basket A152

Baskets and bowls.

1982, Sept. 2 *Perf. 13*

538	A152	5fr shown	15	15
539	A152	10fr like 5fr	15	15
540	A152	25fr Ngbenda gourd, vert.	15	15
541	A152	60fr like 25fr	32	16
542	A152	120fr Ta ti ngou jugs	65	35
543	A152	175fr Kangu bowls	1.10	55
544	A152	300fr Kolongo bowls, vert.	1.60	80
		Nos. 538-544 (7)	4.12	2.31

1982 World Cup Soccer Championships, Spain — A152a

Various soccer plays.

1982, Sept. Litho. *Perf. 13½x13*

Overprinted in Silver or Gold

545	A152a	60fr Italy, 1st, 2nd	16	15
546	A152a	150fr Poland, 3rd	40	20
547	A152a	300fr France, 4th	80	40
		Nos. 545-547 (3)	1.36	75

Souvenir Sheet

548	A152a	500fr Italy, 1st (G)	1.40	65

Not issued without overprint.

13th World UPU Day — A153

1982, Oct. 9

549	A153	60fr multi	32	16
550	A153	120fr multi	65	35

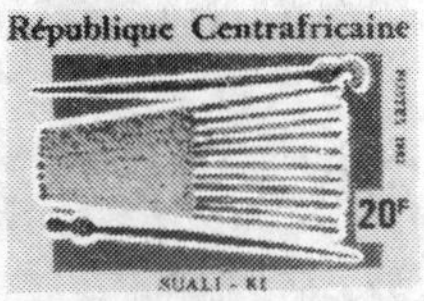

Comb and Hairpins A154

1982, Oct. 20 *Perf. 13x12½*

551	A154	20fr multi	15	15
552	A154	30fr multi	16	15
553	A154	60fr multi	32	16
554	A154	80fr multi	42	22
555	A154	120fr multi	65	35
		Nos. 551-555 (5)	1.70	
		Set value		85

Artist Pierre Ndarata and No.69 A155

1982, Oct. *Perf. 13*

556	A155	40fr Jean Tubind at easel, vert.	20	15
557	A155	70fr shown	38	18
558	A155	90fr like 70fr	48	25
559	A155	140fr like 40fr	90	42
		Nos. 556-559 (4)	1.96	1.00

TB Bacillus Centenary A156

1982, Nov. 30 *Perf. 13½x13*

560	A156	100fr vio & blk	55	25
561	A156	120fr red org & blk	65	35
562	A156	175fr bl & blk	1.10	55
		Nos. 560-562 (3)	2.30	1.15

10th Anniv. of UN Conference on Human Environment A157

1982, Dec. 8

563 A157 120fr multi	65	35
564 A157 150fr multi	80	40
565 A157 300fr multi	1.60	80
Nos. 563-565 (3)	3.05	1.55

Granary A158

1982, Dec. 15 *Perf. 13*

566 A158 60fr multi	32	16
567 A158 80fr multi	40	22
568 A158 120fr multi	65	35
569 A158 200fr multi	1.10	55
Nos. 566-569 (4)	2.47	1.28

A159

A160

1982, Dec.

570 A159 100fr multi	55	25
571 A159 120fr multi	65	35

ITU Plenipotentiaries Conf., Nairobi, Sept.

1983, Jan. 31 Litho. *Perf. 13½x13*

572 A160 5fr Modes of communication	15	15
573 A160 60fr like 5fr	35	16
574 A160 120fr Map, jet	65	35
575 A160 175fr like 120fr	1.10	55
Nos. 572-575 (4)	2.25	1.21

UN Decade for African Transportation and Communication, 1978-88.

Chess Champions — A161

Men and Chess Pieces: 5fr, Steinitz, first world champion, 1886. 10fr, Aaron Niemzovitch, castle. 20fr, Alexander Alekhine, knights. 110fr, Botvinnik. 300fr, Boris Spassky, glass pieces. 500fr, Bobby Fischer, king, knight. 600fr, Korchnoi, Karpov, pawn. No. 582A, Bobby Fischer. No. 582B, Reti, Larsen, Petrossian, and Mecking, horiz.

1983, Jan. 15

576 A161 5fr multi	15	15
577 A161 10fr multi	15	15
578 A161 20fr multi	15	15
579 A161 110fr multi	60	30
580 A161 300fr multi	1.60	80
581 A161 500fr multi	2.75	1.40
Nos. 576-581 (6)	5.40	2.95

Souvenir Sheet

582 A161 600fr multi	3.50	1.60

Litho. & Embossed
Perf. 13½
Size: 35x60mm

582A A161 1500fr gold & multi

Souvenir Sheet

582B A161 1500fr gold & multi

No. 582 contains one 56x33mm stamp, No. 582B one 35x60mm stamp. 300fr, 500fr, 600fr Nos. 581A and 582A airmail.

Marshal Tito (1892-1980) — A162

1983, Jan. 22

583 A162 20fr George Washington	15	15
a. Souvenir sheet	16	15
584 A162 110fr shown	60	30
a. Souvenir sheet	65	35
Set value		35

1982 World Cup Soccer Championships, Spain — A162a

Trophy, flags, scores, players: 5fr, Hamilton, Pezzey. 10fr, Borovski, Boniek. 20fr, Littbarski, Zamora. 110fr, Zico, Passarella. 300fr, Rossi, Smolarek. 500fr, Rummenigge, Giresse. 600fr, Rossi, Rummenigge. No. 584I, Platini. No. 584J, Rossi.

1983, Feb. 8 Litho. *Perf. 13½*

584B A162a 5fr multicolored	15	15
584C A162a 10fr multicolored	15	15
584D A162a 20fr multicolored	15	15
584E A162a 110fr multicolored	60	30
584F A162a 300fr multicolored	1.65	80
584G A162a 500fr multicolored	2.75	1.40
Nos. 584B-584G (6)	5.45	2.95

Souvenir Sheet

584H A162a 600fr multicolored	3.25	1.65

Litho. & Embossed

584I A162a 1500fr gold & multi

Souvenir Sheet

584J A162a 1500fr gold & multi

Nos. 584F-584J are airmail.

Easter 1983 — A163

Rembrandt Paintings.

1983, Apr. 16

585 A163 100fr Entombment	55	25
586 A163 300fr Crucifixion	1.60	80
587 A163 400fr Descent from the Cross	2.25	1.10
Nos. 585-587 (3)	4.40	2.15

Vintage Cars and their Makers A164

A164a

Designs: 10fr, Emile Levassor, Rene Panhard, 1895 car. 20fr, Henry Ford, 1896 car. 30fr, Louis Renault, 1899 car. 80fr, Ettore Bugatti, type 37, 1925. 400fr, Enzo Ferrari, 815 sport, 1940. 500fr, Ferdinand Porsche, 356 coupe, 1951. 600fr, Karl Benz, velocipede, 1886. No. 594A, F.H. Royce and C.S. Rolls, 1911 Rolls-Royce Silver Ghost. No. 594B, G. Daimler, 1900 Mercedes 35CV.

1983, June 3 Litho. *Perf. 13½*

588 A164 10fr multi	15	15
589 A164 20fr multi	15	15
590 A164 30fr multi	16	15
591 A164 80fr multi	42	22
592 A164 400fr multi	2.25	1.10
593 A164 500fr multi	2.75	1.40
Nos. 588-593 (6)	5.88	3.17

Souvenir Sheet

594 A164 600fr multi	3.50	1.60

Litho. & Embossed

594A A164a 1500fr gold & multi

Souvenir Sheet

594B A164a 1500fr gold & multi

Nos. 592-594B are airmail.

25th Anniv. of Intl. Maritime Org. — A165

1983, July 8 Litho. *Perf. 12½x13*

595 A165 40fr multi	22	15
596 A165 100fr multi	55	25

World Communications Year — A166

1983, July 22

597 A166 50fr multi	25	15
598 A166 130fr multi	65	35

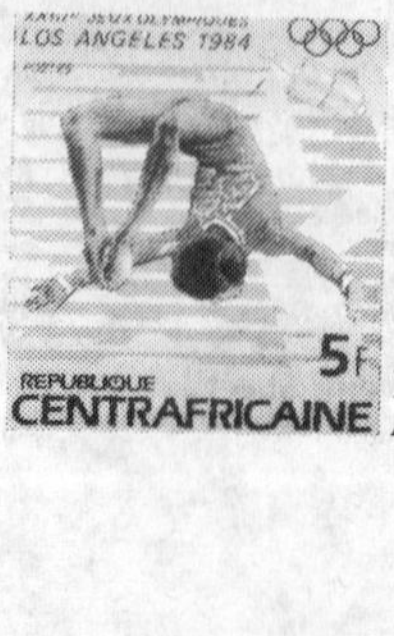

Pre-Olympics, Los Angeles — A167

1984 Summer Olympics, Los Angeles A167a

1983, Aug. 3 Litho. *Perf. 13*

599 A167 5fr Gymnast	15	15
600 A167 40fr Javelin throwing	22	15
601 A167 60fr Pole vault	32	16
602 A167 120fr Fencing	60	32
603 A167 200fr Cycling	1.10	55
604 A167 300fr Sailing	1.60	80
Nos. 599-604 (6)	3.99	2.13

Souvenir Sheet

605 A167 600fr Handball	3.50	1.60

Litho. & Embossed
Perf. 13½

605A A167a 1500fr Shot put

Souvenir Sheet

605B A167a 1500fr Dressage, horiz.

Nos. 603-605B are airmail.

Namibia Day — A168

1983, Sept. 16 Litho. *Perf. 13*

606 A168 100fr multi	55	25
607 A168 200fr multi	1.10	55

Manned Flight Bicentenary — A169

A169a

Designs: 50fr, J. Montgolfier and his balloon, 1783. 100fr, J.P. Blanchard, English Channel crossing, 1785. 200fr, L.-J. Gay-Lussac, 4000-meter balloon ascent, 1804. 300fr, Giffard and his dirigible, 1852. 400fr, Santos Dumont, dirigible, Eiffel Tower. 500fr, A. Laquot, captive observation balloon, 1914. 600fr, J.A. Charles, first gas balloon; G. Tissandier, dirigible, 1883. No. 614, Marquis d'Arlandes and Jean Francois Pilatre de Rozier, Montgolfier balloon. No. 614B, Ferdinand von Zeppelin, Graf Zeppelin, horiz.

1983, Sept. 30 Litho. *Perf. 13½*

608 A169 50fr multi	16	15
609 A169 100fr multi	35	16
610 A169 200fr multi	65	35
611 A169 300fr multi	1.00	50

612 A169 400fr multi 1.40 65
613 A169 500fr multi 1.60 80
Nos. 608-613 (6) 5.16 2.61

Souvenir Sheet

614 A169 600fr multi 2.00 1.00

Litho. & Embossed

614A A169a 1500fr gold & multi

Souvenir Sheet

614B A169a 1500fr gold & multi

Nos. 612-614B are airmail.

Black Rhinoceros and World Wildlife Emblem A170

Various black rhinoceroses.

1983, Nov. 14

615 A170 10fr multi 15 15
616 A170 40fr multi 15 15
617 A170 70fr multi 22 15
618 A170 180fr multi 60 30
Nos. 615-618,C291A-C292 (6) 4.72 2.55

UPU Day, World Communications Year — A171

1983, Nov. 2 Litho. *Perf. 13*

619 A171 205fr multi 1.10 55

2nd Anniv. of the Natl. Military Committee A172

Gen. Andre Kolingba, head of state.

1983, Sept. 1 *Perf. 12½*

620 A172 65fr sil & multi 22 15
621 A172 130fr gold & multi 42 22

Earth Satellite Receiving Station, Bangui M'Poko — A173

1983 *Perf. 13*

622 A173 130fr multi 42 20

Natl. Day of the Handicapped and the Elderly A174

1983, Dec. 20 Engr. *Perf. 13x12½*

623 A174 65fr vio & org 22 15
624 A174 130fr ultra & org 42 22
625 A174 205fr dk grn & org 70 35
Nos. 623-625 (3) 1.34 72

Fishing Resources A175

1983, Dec. 31 Litho. *Perf. 12½*

626 A175 25fr Breeding tank 15 15
627 A175 65fr Net fishing 22 15
628 A175 100fr Dam fishing 35 16
629 A175 130fr Still life with fish 42 22
630 A175 205fr Basket trap 70 35
Nos. 626-630 (5) 1.84 1.03

Wildlife Protection — A176

1984, Jan. 25 *Perf. 13*

631 A176 30fr Forest fire 15 15
632 A176 130fr Hunters 42 20
Set value 25

Packet Ship Pericles — A177

1984, June Litho. *Perf. 12½*

633 A177 65fr shown 22 15
634 A177 110fr CC-1500 locomotive 38 18
635 A177 120fr Three-master Pereire 40 20
636 A177 240fr PLM series 210, 1868 80 40
637 A177 250fr Admella 85 42
638 A177 350fr 231-726 locomotive, 1937 1.10 60
639 A177 400fr Royal William 1.40 65
640 A177 440fr Pacific S3/6, 1908 1.50 70
641 A177 500fr Great Britain 1.60 80
642 A177 500fr Henschel 151 series 45, 1937 1.60 80
Nos. 633-642 (10) 9.85 4.90

For overprints see Nos. 701-704.

J. W. Goethe, Scene from Faust A178

Designs: 100fr, Henri Dunant, Red Cross Founder, Battle of Solferino, 125th anniv. 200fr, Alfred Nobel, Nobel Foundation headquarters. 300fr, Lord Baden-Powell, World Scouting Jamboree, Alberta, 1983. 400fr, John F. Kennedy, first man on the Moon, 1969. 500fr, 600fr, wedding of Prince and Princess of Wales.

1984, Feb. 25 Litho. *Perf. 13½*

643 A178 50fr multi 16 15
644 A178 100fr multi 32 16
645 A178 200fr multi 65 35
646 A178 300fr multi 1.00 1.00
647 A178 400fr multi 1.25 60
648 A178 500fr multi 1.50 75
Nos. 643-648 (6) 4.88 3.01

Souvenir Sheet

649 A178 600fr multi 1.60 85

Nos. 647-649 are airmail.

Old Masters A179

Paintings: 50fr, Madonna and Child, by Raphael. 100fr, Madonna with Pear, by Durer. 200fr, Aldobrandini Madonna, by Raphael. 300fr, Madonna with Carnation, by Durer. 400fr, Virgin and Child, by Correggio. 500fr, La Bohemienne, by Modigliani. 600fr, Madonna and Child on the Throne, by Raphael.

1984, Mar. 30 Litho. *Perf. 13½*

650 A179 50fr multi 16 15
651 A179 100fr multi 32 16
652 A179 200fr multi 60 32
653 A179 300fr multi 1.00 50
654 A179 400fr multi 1.40 65
655 A179 500fr multi 1.60 80
Nos. 650-655 (6) 5.08 2.58

Miniature Sheet

656 A179 600fr multi 2.00 1.00

No. 656 contains 1 stamp, size 30x59mm. Nos. 654-656 are airmail.

Space — A180

1984, Aug. 6 Litho. *Perf. 13½*

657 A180 20fr Galileo, Ariane rocket 15 15
658 A180 70fr Piccard, X-15, balloon 22 15
659 A180 150fr Oberth, satellite 50 25
660 A180 205fr Einstein, satellites 70 38
661 A180 300fr Curie, Viking vehicle 1.00 50
662 A180 500fr Merbold, Spacelab 1.60 80
Nos. 657-662 (6) 4.17 2.23

Miniature Sheet

663 A180 600fr Armstrong, Apollo 11, horiz. 2.00 1.00

No. 663 contains 1 stamp, size: 42x36mm. 300fr, 500fr and 600fr are airmail.

Forestry Resources — A181

UNICEF — A182

1984, Oct. 9 Litho. *Perf. 13x12½*

664 A181 70fr Forest 22 15
665 A181 130fr Logging 42 20

1984, Oct. 27 Litho. *Perf. 13x12½*

666 A182 10fr Weighing child 15 15
667 A182 30fr Vaccinating child 15 15
668 A182 65fr Giving liquids 22 15
669 A182 100fr Balancing diet 35 16
Set value 72 38

Fishing Traps — A183

1984, Nov. 6 Litho. *Perf. 13*

670 A183 50fr Bangui-Kette 16 15
671 A183 80fr Mbres 25 15
672 A183 150fr Bangui-Kette 50 25
Nos. 670-672 (3) 91 55

Mushrooms A184

1984, Nov. 15 Litho. *Perf. 13½*

673 A184 5fr Leptoporus lignosus 15 15
674 A184 10fr Phlebopus sudanicus 15 15
675 A184 40fr Termitomyces letestui 15 15
676 A184 130fr Lepiota esculenta 35 16
677 A184 300fr Termitomyces aurantiacus 80 40
678 A184 500fr Termitomyces robustus 1.40 65
Nos. 673-678 (6) 3.00
Set value 1.35

Souvenir Sheet

679 A184 600fr Tricholoma- lobayensis 1.60 80

Nos. 677-679 are airmail.

1984 Winter Olympics, Sarajevo A184a

Gold medalists, communications satellite and events: 30fr, Gaetan Boucher, Canada, 1000 and 1500-meter speed skating. 90fr, W. Hoppe, R. Wetzig, D. Schauerhammer and A. Kirchner, German Democratic Republic, 4-man bobsled. 140fr, Paoletta Magoni, Italy, women's slalom. 200fr, Jayne Torvill and Christopher Dean, Great Britain, ice dancing. 400fr, Matti Nykaenen, Finland, 90-meter ski jumping. 500fr, USSR, ice hockey. 600fr, Bill Johnson, US, men's downhill.

1984, Nov. 30 Litho. *Perf. 13½*

679A A184a 30fr multi 15 15
679B A184a 90fr multi 30 15
679C A184a 140fr multi 42 20
679D A184a 200fr multi 65 35
679E A184a 400fr multi 1.40 65
679F A184a 500fr multi 1.60 80
Nos. 679A-679F (6) 4.52 2.30

Souvenir Sheet

679G A184a 600fr multi 2.00 1.00

Nos. 679E-679G are airmail.

Flowers — A185

1984, Nov. 22 Litho. *Perf. 13½*

680 A185 65fr Hibiscus 22 15
681 A185 130fr Canna Indica 42 22
682 A185 205fr Eichlornia Crassipes 70 35
Nos. 680-682 (3) 1.34 72

Economic Campaign — A186

1984, Dec. 3 Litho. *Perf. 13½*

683 A186 25fr Cotton planting 15 15
684 A186 40fr Selling cotton crop 15 15
685 A186 130fr Cotton market 42 22
Nos. 683-685 (3) 72
Set value 34

World Food Day A187

1984, Dec. 10 Litho. *Perf. 13½*

686 A187 205fr Picking corn 70 35

OLYMPHILEX '85 — A188

Publicity posters from previous Games and host city landmarks.

1985, Mar 18 Litho. *Perf. 13½*

687 A188 5fr Stockholm, 1912 15 15
688 A188 10fr Paris, 1924 15 15
689 A188 20fr London, 1948 15 15
690 A188 100fr Tokyo, 1964 45 22
691 A188 400fr Mexico 1.75 90
692 A188 500fr Munich, 1972 2.25 1.10
Nos. 687-692 (6) 4.90 2.67

Souvenir Sheet

693 A188 600fr Athens, 1896, Baron Pierre de Coubertin 3.00 1.50

Nos. 691-693 are airmail. No. 693 contains one 60x30mm stamp.

Anniversaries and Events A189

Queen Mother, 85th Birthday A189a

Famous men: 50fr, Abraham Lincoln, American Civil War soldiers. 90fr, Auguste Piccard (1884-1962), inventor, bathyscaphe Trieste. 120fr, Gottlieb Daimler (1834-1900), 1938 Mercedes Type 540. 200fr, Louis Bleriot (1872-1936), inventor, plane. 350fr, Anatoly Karpov, world chess champion. 400fr, Jean Henri Dunant (1828-1910), Red Cross founder, worker caring for wounded soldier.

1984, Dec. 22 Litho. *Perf. 13½*

694 A189 50fr multi 15 15
695 A189 90fr multi 25 15
696 A189 120fr multi 35 16
697 A189 200fr multi 55 25
698 A189 350fr multi 90 45
698A A189 400fr multi 1.10 60
Nos. 694-698A (6) 3.30 1.76

Nos. 698-698A are airmail.

Souvenir Sheet

1984 Litho. *Perf. 13½*

698B A189a 600fr multi 2.75 1.40

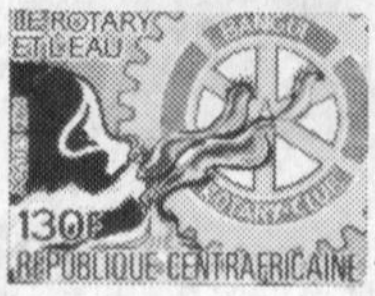

Bangui Rotary Club and Water — A190

1984, Dec. 29

699 A190 130fr multi 35 16
700 A190 205fr multi 60 28

Nos. 637-640, C302A Overprinted with Exhibitions in Red

1985, Mar. 13 Litho. *Perf. 12½*

701 A177 250fr Argentina '85, Buenos Aires 65 35
702 A177 350fr Tsukuba Expo '85 90 45
703 A177 400fr Italia '85, Rome 1.10 50
704 A177 440fr Mophila '85, Hamburg 1.25 60
Nos. 701-704 (4) 3.90 1.90

Souvenir Sheet

Perf. 13½x13

705 AP89 500fr Olymphilex '85, Lausanne 1.40 65

500fr airmail.

Beetles — A191

1985, Mar. Litho. *Perf. 13½*

706 A191 15fr Chelorrhina polyphemus 15 15
707 A191 20fr Fornasinius russus 15 15
708 A191 25fr Goliathus giganteus 15 15
709 A191 65fr Goliathus meleagris 16 15
Set value 33 23

Audubon Birth Bicentenary — A192

Illustrations of North American bird species by John Audubon.

1985, Mar. 25 Litho. *Perf. 13½*

710 A192 40fr Cyanocitta cristata 15 15
711 A192 80fr Caprimulgus carolinensis 20 15
712 A192 130fr Campephilus principales 35 16
713 A192 250fr Calocitta formosa 65 35
714 A192 300fr Coccizus minor, horiz. 80 40
715 A192 500fr Hirundo rustica, horiz. 1.40 65
Nos. 710-715 (6) 3.55 1.86

Souvenir Sheet

716 A192 600fr Dryocopus pileatus, horiz. 1.60 80

Nos. 714-716 are airmail.

Intl. Youth Year — A193

Famous children's book authors and scenes from their best-known novels: 100fr, The Jungle Book, 1894, by Kipling, vert. 200fr, Les Cavaliers, 1967, by Joseph Kessel (1898-1979). 300fr, Twenty-Thousand Leagues Under the Sea, 1873, by Verne. 400fr, The Adventures of Tom Sawyer, 1876, by Twain.

1985, Apr. Litho. *Perf. 13*

718 A193 100fr multi 25 15
719 A193 200fr multi 55 25
720 A193 300fr multi 80 40
721 A193 400fr multi 1.10 55
Nos. 718-721 (4) 2.70 1.35

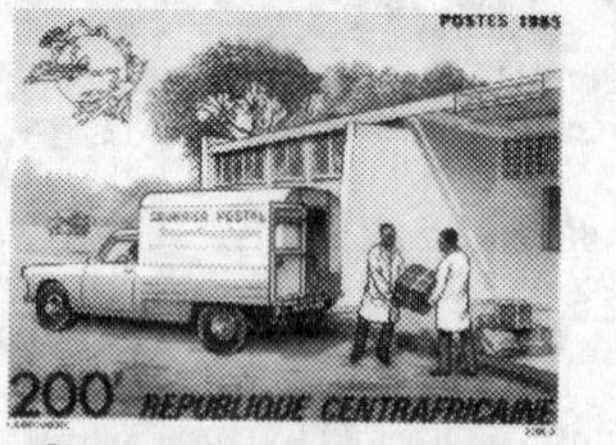

Philexafrica '85, Lome — A194

Designs: No. 722, UPU emblem, Postmen unloading parcel post van. No. 723, Exhibition emblem, scout troop.

1985, May 15 *Perf. 13x12½*

722 A194 200fr multi 55 25
723 A194 200fr multi 55 25

Nos. 722-723 se-tenant with center label picturing a map of Africa or the UAPT emblem.

Rabies Vaccine Cent., Louis Pasteur (1822-95), Chemist, Microbiologist — A195

Anniversaries and events: 200fr, Battle of Solferino, Founding of the Red Cross, 125th Anniv., Founder Jean-Henri Dunant (1828-1910), horiz. 300fr, Girl Guides, 75th anniv. 450fr, Elizabeth, the Queen Mother, 85th birthday. 500fr, Statue of Liberty, cent.

1985, June *Perf. 13*

724 A195 150fr multi 40 20
725 A195 200fr multi 55 25
726 A195 300fr multi 80 40
727 A195 450fr multi 1.20 60
728 A195 500fr multi 1.40 65
Nos. 724-728 (5) 4.35 2.10

15-Cent Minimum Value
The minimum value for a single stamp is 15 cents. This value reflects the costs of handling inexpensive stamps.

1986 World Cup Soccer Championships, Mexico — A196

Famous soccer players and match scenes.

1985, July 24 Litho. *Perf. 13½*

730 A196 5fr Pele 15 15
731 A196 10fr Tony Schumacher 15 15
732 A196 20fr Paolo Rossi 15 15
733 A196 350fr Kevin Keegan 1.10 60
734 A196 400fr Michel Platini 1.25 65
735 A196 500fr Karl Heinz Rummenigge 1.50 75
Nos. 730-735 (6) 4.30 2.45

Souvenir Sheet

736 A196 600fr Diego Armando Maradona 1.75 90

Nos. 734-736 are airmail.

Kotto Waterfalls A197

1985, July 27 Litho. *Perf. 13½*

737 A197 65fr multi 20 15
738 A197 90fr multi 25 15
739 A197 130fr multi 40 20
Nos. 737-739 (3) 85 50

State Visit of Pope John Paul II — A198

Portraits.

1985, Aug. 14

740 A198 65fr multi 20 15
741 A198 130fr multi 40 20

Natl. Economic Development Campaign — A199

Designs: 5fr, Troops plowing. 60fr, Soldier preparing field for planting, vert. 130fr, Planting cotton seeds, vert.

1985, Sept. 1 *Perf. 13*

742 A199 5fr multi 15 15
743 A199 60fr multi 18 15
744 A199 130fr multi 40 20
Nos. 742-744 (3) 73
Set value 35

Queen Mother, 85th Birthday — A200

1985, Sept. 16 Litho. *Perf. 13½*

745 A200 100fr Age 4, with brother 28 15
746 A200 200fr Duchess of York, 1923 52 25
747 A200 300fr Reviewing Irish Guards, 1928 80 42
748 A200 350fr Family portrait, 1936 90 45
749 A200 400fr George VI coronation, 1937 1.10 60
750 A200 500fr Wedding anniv., 1948 1.40 65
Nos. 745-750 (6) 5.00 2.52

Souvenir Sheet

751 A200 600fr Christening Prince Charles, 1948 1.60 80

Nos. 749-751 are airmail.

Dr. Rene Labusquiere (1919-1977), Promoter of Preventive Medicine A201

1985, Sept. 22 Litho. *Perf. 13½*

752 A201 10fr multi 15 15
753 A201 45fr multi 15 15
754 A201 110fr multi 30 15
Set value 47 27

Natl. Postal Service — A202

1985, Oct. 9 *Perf. 12½*

755 A202 15fr Loading mail van 15 15
756 A202 60fr Bangui P.O., van 20 15
757 A202 150fr Hdqtrs, Bangui, and vans 50 25
Nos. 755-757 (3) 85
Set value 40

Space Research A203

Designs: 40fr, Yuri Gagarin and Sergei Korolev, Soviet cosmonauts. 110fr, Nicolaus Copernicus, Cassini probe. 240fr, Galileo, Viking orbiter. 300fr, Theodor von Karman (1881-1963), American aeronautical engineer, and space shuttle recovering Palapa B satellite. 450fr, Percival Lowell (1855-1916), American astronomer, and Viking probe. 500fr, Dr. U. Merbold and orbiting space station project Colombo. 600fr, Apollo 11 Project, first step on Moon by Neil Armstrong.

1985, Oct. 31 Litho. *Perf. 13½*

758 A203 40fr multi 15 15
759 A203 110fr multi 40 22
760 A203 240fr multi 80 42
761 A203 300fr multi 1.10 60
762 A203 450fr multi 1.60 80
763 A203 500fr multi 1.75 90
Nos. 758-763 (6) 5.80 3.09

Souvenir Sheet

Imperf

764 A203 600fr multi 2.00 1.10

Nos. 762-764 are airmail.

Solar Energy Apparatus, Damara A204

1985, Nov. 4 Litho. *Perf. 13½*

765 A204 65fr multi 22 15
766 A204 130fr multi 45 22

Girl Guides Nature Study — A205

1985, Nov. 16 *Perf. 13*

767 A205 250fr shown 90 45
768 A205 250fr Ouaka Sugar Refinery 90 45

PHILEXAFRICA '85, Lome, Togo, Nov. 16-24. Nos. 767-768 se-tenant with center labels picturing map of Africa or UAPT emblem.

State Visit of Pres. Mitterand of France, Dec. 12-13 — A206

1985-86 Litho. *Perf. 13x12½*

769 A206 65fr multi 22 15
770 A206 130fr multi 45 22
770A A206 160fr multi ('86) 60 28
Nos. 769-770A (3) 1.27 65

Nos. 769-770 issued Dec. 12.

UN 40th Anniv., Central Africa Admission, 25th Anniv. — A207

1985, Dec. 18 *Perf. 13½*

771 A207 140fr multi 50 25

Intl. Youth Year A208

Designs: 40fr, Madonna with the Carnation, 1470, by Leonardo da Vinci. 80fr, Johann Sebastian Bach. 100fr, St. John at Patmos, 1619, by Velazquez. 250fr, The Erl King score, by Franz Schubert. 400fr, Portrait of Vicente Osorio de Moscoso, by Goya. 500fr, The Young Mozart Playing in Paris, 1764. 600fr, Woman in a Plumed Hat, 1901, by Picasso.

1985, Dec. 28

772 A208 40fr multi 15 15
773 A208 80fr multi 25 15
774 A208 100fr multi 35 18
775 A208 250fr multi 90 45
776 A208 400fr multi 1.40 65
777 A208 500fr multi 1.75 90
Nos. 772-777 (6) 4.80 2.48

Souvenir Sheet

778 A208 600fr multi 2.25 1.10

Nos. 776-778 are airmail.

Halley's Comet A209

Designs: 100fr, Edmond Halley, British astronomer. 200fr, Sir Isaac Newton's telescope and comet sighting. 300fr, Halley and Newton observing comet. 350fr, US probe. 400fr, Soviet probe plotting comet's perihelion. 500fr, Isodensity photograph of comet. 600fr, Comet, Earth, Sun and probe.

1985, Dec. 31

779 A209 100fr multi 35 18
780 A209 200fr multi 70 38
781 A209 300fr multi 1.10 60
782 A209 350fr multi 1.25 65
783 A209 400fr multi 1.40 65
784 A209 500fr multi 1.75 90
Nos. 779-784 (6) 6.55 3.36

Souvenir Sheet

785 A209 600fr multi 2.25 1.10

Nos. 783-785 are airmail.

Christopher Columbus A210

Various events leading to the discovery of America and beyond.

1986

786 A210 90fr Plotting course 32 16
787 A210 110fr Receiving blessing 40 20
788 A210 240fr Fleet in port 80 42
789 A210 300fr Trade with natives 1.10 60
790 A210 400fr Storm at sea 1.40 65
791 A210 500fr Fleet at sea 1.75 90
Nos. 779-784 (6) 6.55 3.36

Souvenir Sheet

792 A210 600fr Portrait 2.25 1.10

Nos. 790-792 are airmail.

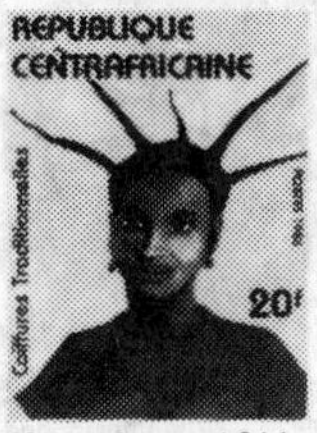

Hairstyles — A211

France- Central Africa Week — A212

1986, May 21 Litho. *Perf. 12½*

793 A211 20fr multi 15 15
794 A211 30fr multi 15 15
795 A211 65fr multi 16 15
796 A211 160fr multi 60 30
Nos. 793-796 (4) 1.06
Set value 48

1986, May 26

797 A212 40fr Communications, horiz. 15 15
798 A212 60fr Youth, horiz. 22 15
799 A212 100fr Basket maker 38 18
800 A212 130fr Bicycling 45 22
Nos. 797-800 (4) 1.20 70

Centrapalm Palm Oil — A213

Designs: 25fr, 65fr, Refinery, Bossongo, and palm tree. 120fr, 160fr, Refinery and palm tree, vert.

1986, Aug. 12 Litho. *Perf. 13½*

801 A213 25fr multi 15 15
802 A213 65fr multi 22 15
803 A213 120fr multi 50 25
804 A213 160fr multi 65 35
Nos. 801-804 (4) 1.52
Set value 77

Dogs and Cats A214

1986, Sept. 9

805 A214 10fr Pointer 15 15
806 A214 20fr Egyptian mau 15 15
807 A214 200fr Newfoundland 80 42
808 A214 300fr Borzoi 1.10 60
809 A214 400fr Persian red 1.60 80
Nos. 805-809 (5) 3.80 2.12

Souvenir Sheet

810 A214 500fr Spaniel, Burmese-Malayan 2.00 1.00

Nos. 808-810 are airmail.

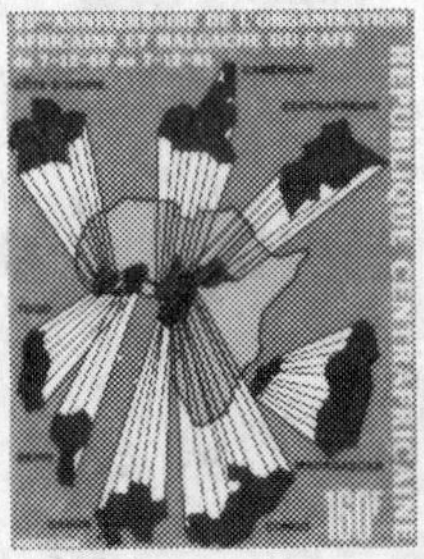

African Coffee Producers Organization, 25th Anniv. A215

1986, Sept. 25 Litho. *Perf. 13*

811 A215 160fr multi 60 30

1986 World Cup Soccer Championships, Mexico — A216

Satellites, final scores, World Cup and athletes: 30fr, Muller, Socrates. 110fr, Scifo, Ceulemans. 160fr, Stopyra, Platini. 350fr, Brehme, Schumacher. 450fr, Maradona. 500fr, Schumacher, Burruchaga.

1986, Nov. 12 *Perf. 13½*

812 A216 30fr multi 15 15
813 A216 110fr multi 40 20
814 A216 160fr multi 60 30
815 A216 350fr multi 1.40 65
816 A216 450fr multi 1.60 80
Nos. 812-816 (5) 4.15 2.10

Souvenir Sheet

817 A216 500fr multi 1.75 90

Nos. 816-817 are airmail.

US Anniversaries and Events — A217

Designs: 15fr, Judith Resnik. 25fr, Frederic Auguste Bartholdi. 70fr, Elvis Presley. 300fr, Ronald McNair. 450fr, Christa McAuliffe. 500fr, Challenger Astronauts: McAuliffe, Scobee, Smith, Resnik, Onizuka, McNair, Jarvis.

1986, Nov. 19

818 A217	15fr multi		15	15
819 A217	25fr multi		15	15
820 A217	70fr multi		25	15
821 A217	300fr multi		1.10	55
822 A217	450fr multi		1.60	80
	Nos. 818-822 (5)		3.25	1.80

Souvenir Sheet

823 A217	500fr multi		1.75	1.00

US space shuttle Challenger explosion; Statue of Liberty, cent. Nos. 822-823 are airmail.

For surcharges and overprint see Nos. 850-852.

Flora and Fauna A218

1986, May 30 Litho. *Perf. 13½*

824 A218	25fr	Allamanda neriifolia	15	15
825 A218	65fr	Taurotragus eurycerus	25	15
826 A218	160fr	Plumieria acuminata	60	30
827 A218	300fr	Acinonyx jubatus	1.10	40
828 A218	400fr	Eulophia erthoplata	1.50	70
829 A218	500fr	Leopard	1.75	90
		Nos. 824-829 (6)	5.35	2.60

Souvenir Sheet

830 A218	600fr	Derby's eland, eulophia cucullata	2.25	1.10

Nos. 824, 826, 828 vert. Nos. 828-830 are airmail. No. 830 contains one 51x30mm stamp.

Intl. Peace Year — A219

Air Africa, 25th Anniv. — A220

1986, Nov. 29

831 A219	160fr multi		60	30

1986, Dec. 15

832 A220	200fr multi		70	40

UNICEF, 40th Anniv. — A221

1986, Dec. 24

833 A221	15fr	shown	15	15
834 A221	130fr	Child immunization	45	22
835 A221	160fr	Youth, food, map	60	30
		Nos. 833-835 (3)	1.20	67

German Railways Sesquicentenary — A222

Inventors and locomotives: 40fr, Alfred de Glehn, Prussian Railways DH2 Green Elephant. 70fr, Rudolf Diesel, S3/6 No. 1829 Rheingold. 160fr, Carl Golsdorf, Trans-Europe Express train Type 103. 300fr, Wilhelm Schmidt, Beyer Garratt locomotive. 400fr, Monsieur de Bousquet, Series 3500 compound locomotive. 500fr, Werner von Siemens, 1980s electric locomotive.

1986, Dec. 31

836 A222	40fr multi		15	15
837 A222	70fr multi		25	15
838 A222	160fr multi		60	30
839 A222	300fr multi		1.10	40
840 A222	400fr multi		1.50	70
	Nos. 836-840 (5)		3.60	1.70

Souvenir Sheet

841 A222	500fr multi		1.75	1.00

Nos. 840-841 are airmail. No. 841 contains one 42x36mm stamp.

Agriculture Radio Project — A223

1986, Dec. 27 Litho. *Perf. 13½*

842 A223	170fr	shown	65	35
843 A223	265fr	Satellite communication	1.00	50

Pan-African Telecommunications Union congress, Dec. 7, 1986.

No. 842 exists in souvenir sheet of one.

Space — A224

Scientists and inventions: 25fr, Sir William Herschel (1738-1822), British astronomer, and Miranda satellite. 65fr, Wernher von Braun (1912-1977), American engineer, and Mars rover. 160fr, Rudolf Hanel, Mariner Mark II and Titan. 300fr, Patrick Baudry, Hermes shuttle and Eureka platform. 400fr, U. Keller, Halley's Comet and Giotto probe. 500fr, Wubbo Ockels, Ulf Merbold and Columbus European Space Station. 600fr, Wilhelm Obers (1758-1840) and Mariner Mark II surveying asteroids. No. 850 horiz.

1987, Jan. 27

844 A224	25fr multi		15	15
845 A224	65fr multi		38	20
846 A224	160fr multi		95	48
847 A224	300fr multi		1.75	90
848 A224	400fr multi		2.50	1.25
849 A224	500fr multi		3.00	1.50
	Nos. 844-849 (6)		8.73	4.48

Souvenir Sheet

850 A224	600fr multi		3.50	1.75

Nos. 848-850 are airmail.

No. 820 Surcharged

1987, Feb. 20 Litho. *Perf. 13½*

851 A217	485fr on 70fr Elvis Presley		2.75	1.40

Nos. 820 and 851 Ovptd. "Elvis PRESLEY / 1977-1987."

1987, Feb. 20 Litho. *Perf. 13½*

851A A217	70fr multi		55	28
851B A217	485fr on 70fr multi		2.75	1.40

1992 Barcelona Olympics A225

Athletes and landmarks or sights: 30fr, Soccer player, Lady with Umbrella fountain. 150fr, Judo, Barcelona Cathedral. 265fr, Cyclist, Church of the Holy Family, by Gaudi. 350fr, Gymnast, Tomb of Columbus. 495fr, Runner, human tower. 500fr, Swimmer, Statue of Columbus.

1987, June 4

852 A225	30fr multi		18	15
853 A225	150fr multi		82	40
854 A225	265fr multi		1.45	72
855 A225	350fr multi		1.90	95
856 A225	495fr multi		2.70	1.35
	Nos. 852-856 (5)		7.05	3.57

Souvenir Sheet

857 A225	500fr multi		2.75	1.40

Nos. 855-857 are airmail.

A226

1988 Winter Olympics, Calgary — A227

1987, June 26

858 A226	20fr	Two-man luge	15	15
859 A226	140fr	Cross-country skiing	78	40
860 A226	250fr	Women's figure skating	1.40	80
861 A226	300fr	Hockey	1.65	82
862 A226	400fr	Men's slalom	2.20	1.10
		Nos. 858-862 (5)	6.18	3.27

Souvenir Sheet

863 A227	500fr	Downhill skiing	2.75	1.35

Nos. 861-863 are airmail.

Intl. Peace Year — A228

1987, July 20

864 A228	50fr	dull ultra, sepia & blk	28	15
865 A228	160fr	lt olive green, sepia & blk	90	45

Butterflies A229

1987, Oct. 5 Litho. *Perf. 13½*

866 A229	100fr	Charaxes candiope	70	35
867 A229	120fr	Graphium leonidas	85	42
868 A229	130fr	Charaxes brutus	90	45
869 A229	160fr	Salamis aetiops	1.15	58
		Nos. 866-869 (4)	3.60	1.80

Pygmy Soccer Team from Nola — A230

1987, Nov. 30 Litho. *Perf. 13*

870 A230	90fr multi		65	32
871 A230	160fr multi		1.15	58

Integration of the pygmy people into Central African society.

Dinosaurs — A231

Perf. 14x13½, 13½x14

1988, Mar. 19 Litho.

872 A231	50fr	Brontosaurus	30	15
873 A231	65fr	Triceratops	40	20
874 A231	100fr	Ankylosaurus	60	30
875 A231	160fr	Stegosaurus	95	48
876 A231	200fr	Tyrannosaurus rex	1.20	60
877 A231	240fr	Corythosaurus	1.45	72
878 A231	300fr	Allosaurus	1.80	90
879 A231	350fr	Brachiosaurus	2.10	1.05
		Nos. 872-879 (8)	8.80	4.40

Nos. 876-879 vert.

Anniversaries and Events — A232

Designs: 40fr, Pres. James Madison and "We the People..." from the US Constitution. 160fr, Elizabeth II and Duke of Edinburgh . 200fr, Steffi Graf, tennis champion. 300fr, Garri Kasparov of Russia, 1985 world chess champion. 400fr, Boris Becker, 1985-86 Wimbledon champion. 500fr, Christoph

Willibald Gluck (1714-87), composer. Nos. 880-884 vert.

1988, Feb. 15 *Perf. 13½*

880	A232	40fr multi	24	15
881	A232	160fr multi	95	48
882	A232	200fr multi	1.20	60
883	A232	300fr multi	1.80	90
884	A232	400fr multi	2.40	1.20
		Nos. 880-884 (5)	6.59	3.33

Souvenir Sheet

885	A232	500fr multi	3.00	1.50

US Constitution bicentennial (40fr); 40th wedding anniv. of Elizabeth II and Prince Philip (160fr). Nos. 883-885 are airmail.

World Health Organization, 40th Anniv. — A233

1988, Apr. 7 **Litho.** *Perf. 13½*

886	A233	70fr multi	48	25
887	A233	120fr multi	80	40

Scout Ornithological Activities A234

Scouts and: 25fr, *Merops nubicus.* 170fr, *Euplectes hordeacea.* 300fr, *Ceryle rudis.* 400fr, *Estrilda bengala.* 450fr, *Kaupifalco monogrammicus.* 500fr, *Lamprotornis splendidus.*

1988, July 1 **Litho.** *Perf. 13½*

888	A234	25fr multi	18	15
889	A234	170fr multi	1.25	62
890	A234	300fr multi	2.25	1.15
891	A234	400fr multi	3.00	1.50
892	A234	450fr multi	3.40	1.70
		Nos. 888-892 (5)	10.08	5.12

Souvenir Sheet

893	A234	500fr multi	3.75	1.90

Nos. 891-893 are airmail.
For surcharges see Nos. 921-924.

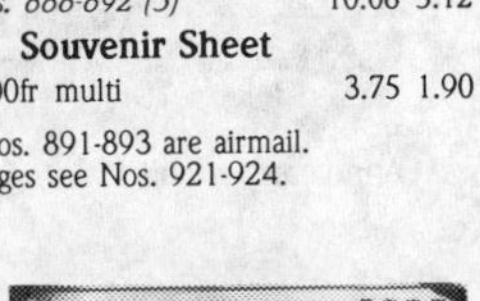

1988 Summer Olympics, Seoul A235

1988, Sept. 30

894	A235	150fr Running, vert.	1.15	58
895	A235	300fr Judo, vert.	2.25	1.15
896	A235	400fr Soccer, vert.	3.00	1.50
897	A235	450fr Tennis, vert.	3.40	1.70
		Nos. 894-897 (4)	9.80	4.93

Souvenir Sheet

898	A235	500fr Boxing	3.75	1.90

Nos. 896-898 are airmail.

1988 Winter Olympics, Calgary — A236

1988, Sept. 30 **Litho.** *Perf. 13½*

899	A236	170fr Cross-country skiing	1.25	62
900	A236	350fr Ice hockey	2.65	1.30
901	A236	400fr Downhill skiing	3.00	1.50
902	A236	450fr Freestyle	3.40	1.70
		Nos. 899-902 (4)	10.30	5.12

Souvenir Sheet

903	A236	500fr shown	3.75	1.90

Nos. 899-902 vert. Nos. 901-903 are airmail.

Natl. Arbor Day — A237

1988, July 16 **Litho.** *Perf. 13½*

904	A237	50fr Students planting trees	32	16
905	A237	100fr like 50fr	65	32
906	A237	130fr Forest (before and after)	85	42
		Nos. 904-906 (3)	1.82	90

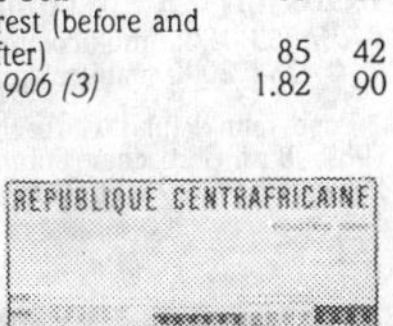

L'Amitie Hospital, 1st Anniv. — A238

1988, Nov. 30

907	A238	5fr shown	15	15
908	A238	60fr Aerial view	40	20
909	A238	160fr Front gate	1.05	52
		Nos. 907-909 (3)	1.60	87

A239

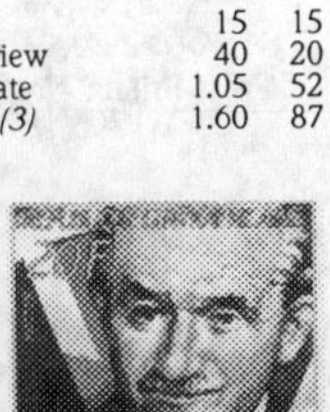
A240

Olympic Medalists, Seoul, 1988: 150fr, Kristine Otto, DDR, swimming. 240fr, Matt Biondi, US, swimming. 300fr, Florence Griffith-Joyner, US, running. 450fr, Pierre Durand, France, equestrian. 600fr, Carl Lewis, US, running.

1989, Apr. 1

910	A239	150fr multi	98	50
911	A239	240fr multi	1.55	78
912	A239	300fr multi	1.95	98
913	A239	450fr multi	2.95	1.45
a.		Souv. sheet of 4, #910-913		
		Nos. 910-913 (4)	7.43	3.71

Souvenir Sheet

914	A239	600fr multi	3.90	1.95

Nos. 913-914 airmail. No. 914 contains one 37x43mm stamp.

1989, Apr. 10 **Litho.** *Perf. 13½*

Transportation Innovations, Inventors: 20fr, Hebmuller and 1953 Volkswagen Beetle. 205fr, Werner von Siemens (1816-1892) and 1879 Locomotive B. 300fr, Dennis Conner, skipper of *Stars and Stripes*, winner of the 1988 America's Cup. 400fr, Andre Citroen (1878-1935) and 1955 Citroen-15 SIX. 450fr, Marc Seguin (1786-1875) and 1895 Decauville-Mallet 020-020. 750fr, Frederick S. Duesenberg (1876-1932), brother August, US flag and 1929 J Phaeton.

915	A240	20fr multi	15	15
916	A240	205fr multi	1.35	68
917	A240	300fr multi	1.95	98
918	A240	400fr multi	2.60	1.30
919	A240	450fr multi	2.90	1.45
		Nos. 915-919 (5)	8.95	4.56

Souvenir Sheet

920	A240	750fr multi	4.75	2.40

Nos. 919-920 airmail. No. 920 contains one 43x37mm stamp.

Nos. 889-892 Surcharged in Black or Silver

1988, Oct. 7 **Litho.** *Perf. 13½*

921	A234	30fr on 170fr No. 889 (B)	22	15
922	A234	70fr on 300fr No. 890	50	25
923	A234	160fr on 400fr No. 891	1.15	58
924	A234	200fr on 450fr No. 892	1.40	1.40
		Nos. 921-924 (4)	3.27	2.38

Nos. 923-924 are airmail.

PHILEXFRANCE '89, French Revolution Bicent. — A241

Designs: 200fr, Allegory in Honor of Liberty. 300fr, Declaration of Human Rights and Citizenship. 500fr, The Bastille, horiz.

1989, July 7 **Litho.** *Perf. 13*

925	A241	200fr multi	1.20	60
926	A241	300fr multi	1.75	88

Souvenir Sheet

927	A241	500fr multi	3.00	1.50

Nos. 925-926 printed se-tenant with center label picturing the exhibition emblem.

Souvenir Sheet

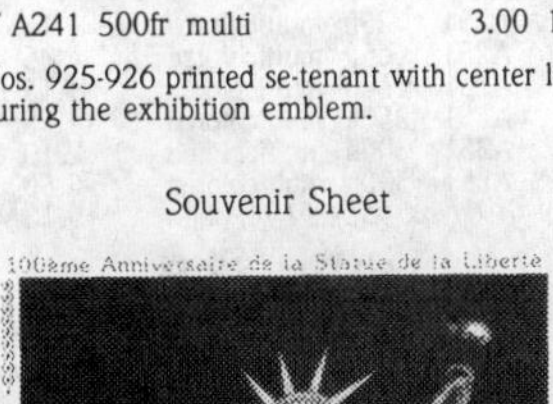

Statue of Liberty — A242

Designs: a, Crown and torch observatories lit at night. b, Working on statue's coiffure. c, Face and scaffolding. d, Workman sanding copper sheeting around the crown observatory. e, Re-opening ceremony, 1986. f, Crown observatory at night.

1989, July **Litho.** **Wmk. 385** *Perf. 13*

928		Sheet of 6	6.60	3.30
a.-c.		A242 150fr any single	95	48
d.-f.		A242 200fr any single	1.25	62

Statue of Liberty cent. (in 1986). Photograph of the statue is reversed.

M. Champagnat (1789-1840), Founder of the Marist Order — A243

1989 **Litho.** *Perf. 13½*

929	A243	15fr Madonna and child, map	15	15
930	A243	50fr Cross, Earth	32	16
931	A243	160fr shown	1.05	52
		Nos. 929-931 (3)	1.52	83

Nos. 929-930 vert.

Harvest Feast, Bambari A244

1989, Oct. 15

932	A244	100fr Produce	65	32
933	A244	160fr Ox plow	1.05	52

World Food Day — A245

1989, Oct. 16

934	A245	60fr Domestic animals	40	20
935	A245	240fr Arresting ivory poachers	1.50	75

French Revolution, Bicent. — A246

Battle scenes and leaders: 160fr, Brig.-Gen. Francois-Christophe Kellermann (1735-1820), Battle of Valmy, Sept. 22, 1792. 200fr, Minister of War Charles-Francois du Perier Dumouriez (1739-1823), Battle of Jemappes, Nov. 7, 1792. 500fr, Gen. Jean-Charles Pichegru (1761-1804), capture of the Dutch fleet, Jan. 22, 1795. 600fr, Gen. Louis-Lazare Hoche (1768-97), Battle of Quiberon Bay, July 21, 1795. 1000fr, Napoleon at the Battle of Rivoli Veronese, Jan. 15, 1797.

1989, Dec. 5 **Litho.** *Perf. 13½*

936	A246	160fr multicolored	1.05	52
937	A246	200fr multicolored	1.30	65
938	A246	500fr multicolored	1.65	82
939	A246	600fr multicolored	2.00	1.00
a.		Souvenir sheet of 4, #936-939	6.00	6.00
		Nos. 936-939 (4)	6.00	2.99

Souvenir Sheet

940	A246	1000fr multicolored	6.50	3.25

PHILEXFRANCE '89. Nos. 938-940 are airmail.
No. 936 is incorrectly inscribed "Francois-Etienne." Jemappes is incorrectly spelled on No. 937. No. 940 is incorrectly inscribed "January 14."

1990 World Cup Soccer Championships, Italy — A247

Various athletes and Italian landmarks: 20fr, Bell tower, Palermo Cathedral. 120fr, Trinity of the Mount, Rome. 160fr, St. Francis Church apse, Bologna. 200fr, Palace, Florence. 1000fr, Milan Cathedral.

1989, Dec. 23

941 A247	20fr multicolored	15	15
942 A247	120fr multicolored	78	40
943 A247	160fr multicolored	1.05	52
944 A247	200fr multicolored	1.30	65
	Nos. 941-944 (4)	3.28	1.72

Souvenir Sheet

945 A247	1000fr multicolored	6.50	3.25

Nos. 942 and 945 are airmail.

Save the Forests
A247a

1989 Litho. *Perf. 13½*

945A A247a	160fr multicolored	1.15	58

Town of Bangui, Cent. — A247b

Designs: 100fr, Governor's Palace, 1906. 160fr, Outpost. 200fr, A. Dolisie, founder of Bangui, vert. 1000fr, Signing of peace treaty between Michel Dolisie and Chief Gbembo, 1889, vert.

1989 Litho. *Perf. 13½*

945B A247b	100fr multicolored	75	38
945C A247b	160fr multicolored	1.20	60
945D A247b	200fr multicolored	1.50	75
945E A247b	1000fr multicolored	7.50	3.75
	Nos. 945B-945E (4)	10.95	5.48

Championship Team from Central Africa, 1987 — A248

1990, Feb. 23 Litho. *Perf. 13½*

946 A248	160fr Flag, players, trophy	1.15	58
947 A248	240fr shown	1.70	85
948 A248	500fr like 160fr	3.50	1.75
	Nos. 946-948 (3)	6.35	3.18

African Basketball Championships. Dated 1988. Nos. 946 and 948 vert.

A249

A250

1990, Feb. 23 Litho. *Perf. 13½*

949 A249	100fr multicolored	72	35
950 A249	130fr multicolored	92	45

Central Africa, winner of the 1987 African Basketball Cup Championships, Tunis. Dated 1989.

1990, Mar. 12 Litho. *Perf. 13½*

1992 Winter Olympics, Albertville: No. 955A, Slalom skier. No. 955B, Pairs figure skating.

951 A250	10fr Speed skating	15	15
952 A250	60fr Cross-country skiing	42	20
953 A250	500fr Slalom	3.50	1.75
954 A250	750fr Figure skating	5.25	2.60
	Nos. 951-954 (4)	9.32	4.70

Souvenir Sheet

955 A250	1000fr Downhill skiing	7.00	3.50

Litho. & Embossed

1990, Mar. 12 *Perf. 13½*

955A A250	1500fr gold & multi		

Souvenir Sheet

955B A250	1500fr gold & multi		

Nos. 953-955B are airmail. No. 955 contains one 36x42mm stamp.

Scout, *Euphaera eusemoides* A251

Boy scouts and butterflies: 65fr, *Cymothoe beckeri.* 160fr, *Pseudacraea clarki.* 250fr, *Charaxes castor.*300fr, *Euphaedra gausape.* 500fr, *Graphium ridleyanus.* 1000fr, *Euphaedra edwardsi.* No. 962A, Antanartia delius. No. 962B, Spotted flycatcher. No. 962C, Cymothoe sangaris.

1990, Mar. 26

956 A251	25fr multicolored	18	15
957 A251	65fr multicolored	45	22
958 A251	160fr multicolored	1.15	58
959 A251	250fr multicolored	1.75	88
960 A251	300fr multicolored	2.10	1.05
961 A251	500fr multicolored	3.50	1.75
	Nos. 956-961 (6)	9.13	4.63

Souvenir Sheet

962 A251	1000fr multicolored	7.00	3.50

Litho. & Embossed

Perf. 12½

962A A251	1500fr gold & multi		

Perf. 13½

962B A251	1500fr gold & multi		

Souvenir Sheet

962C A251	1500fr gold & multi		

Nos. 962A-962C are airmail. No. 962A exists in a souvenir sheet of 1.

1992 Summer Olympics, Barcelona A252

1990, Apr. 1 Litho. *Perf. 13½*

963 A252	10fr Javelin	15	15
964 A252	40fr Runner	28	15
965 A252	130fr Tennis	92	45
966 A252	240fr Hurdles	1.70	85
967 A252	400fr Yachting	2.85	1.45
968 A252	500fr Soccer	3.50	1.75
	Nos. 963-968 (6)	9.40	4.80

Souvenir Sheet

969 A252	1000fr Boxing	7.00	3.50

Nos. 963-965 vert. Nos. 967-969 are airmail.

Pres. Gorbachev, Pres. Bush — A253

Pres. Gorbachev, Pope John Paul II — A254

1990, July 27 Litho. *Perf. 13½*

970 A253	120fr multicolored	85	42
971 A254	200fr multicolored	1.45	72

Pope John Paul II-Gorbachev meeting Dec. 2, 1989. Bush-Gorbachev Summit Meeting Dec. 3, 1989. Nos. 970-971 exist in souvenir sheets of 1.

Great Britain No. 1, Sir Rowland Hill (1795-1879) — A255

1990, July 27

972 A255	130fr multicolored	90	45

No. 972 exists in a souvenir sheet of 1.

Events and Anniversaries — A256

Designs: 160fr, Galileo Probe to Jupiter. 240fr, Neil Armstrong, 1st man on moon. 250fr, Concorde, rapid-transit train, Rotary Intl. emblem.

1990, July 27 Litho. *Perf. 13½*

973 A256	160fr multicolored	1.15	58
974 A256	240fr multicolored	1.75	88
975 A256	250fr multicolored	1.80	90
	Nos. 973-975 (3)	4.70	2.36

Wildlife Protection A258

Design: 100fr, Declining elephant population, vert.

1991, Jan. 25 Litho. *Perf. 13½*

976 A258	15fr gold & multi	15	15
977 A258	60fr multicolored	45	22
978 A258	100fr multicolored	75	38
	Nos. 976-978 (3)	1.35	75

Eutropius A259

Design: 240fr, Distichodus.

1991, Jan. 26

979 A259	50fr multicolored	38	20
980 A259	160fr gold & multi	1.20	60
981 A259	240fr multicolored	1.80	90
	Nos. 979-981 (3)	3.38	1.70

Fight Against AIDS A260

Design: 120fr, Class speaker, vert.

1991, Jan. 24

982 A260	5fr gold & multi	15	15
983 A260	70fr multicolored	52	25
984 A260	120fr multicolored	90	45
	Nos. 982-984 (3)	1.57	85

Assumption of Power by Pres. Andre Kolingba, 10th Anniv. (in 1991) — A261

1992, Sept. 1 Litho. *Perf. 13x13½*

985 A261	160fr multicolored	1.35	65

Anniversaries and Events — A262

Designs: 80fr, Maybach Zeppelin, zeppelin airship, Count Ferdinand Zeppelin. 140fr, Child being comforted, Jean-Henri Dunant. 160fr, Benetton-Ford B 192, Michael Schumacher. 350fr, Konrad Adenauer signing Constitution of German Republic. 500fr, Pope John Paul II, mother and child, map. 600fr, Wolfgang Amadeus Mozart. 1000fr, Columbus at La Rabida, sailing ship, and building in Seville, Spain.

1992, Sept. 22 Litho. *Perf. 13½*

986 A262	80fr multicolored	58	28
987 A262	140fr multicolored	1.00	50
988 A262	160fr multicolored	1.15	58
989 A262	350fr multicolored	2.55	1.25
990 A262	500fr multicolored	3.65	1.80
991 A262	600fr multicolored	4.35	2.20
	Nos. 986-991 (6)	13.28	6.61

Souvenir Sheet

992 A262	1000fr multicolored	7.25	3.65

Count Zeppelin, 75th anniv. of death (#986). Jean-Henri Dunant, first recipient of Nobel Peace Prize, 90th anniv. (in 1991) (#987). Grand Prix of Monaco (#988). Brandenburg Gate, bicent (#989). Visit of Pope John Paul II to Africa (#990). Wolfgang Amadeus Mozart, bicent. of death (in 1991) (#991). Discovery of America, 500th anniv. and Expo '92, Seville (#992).

Nos. 990-992 are airmail. Nos. 986-991 exist in souvenir sheets of 1.

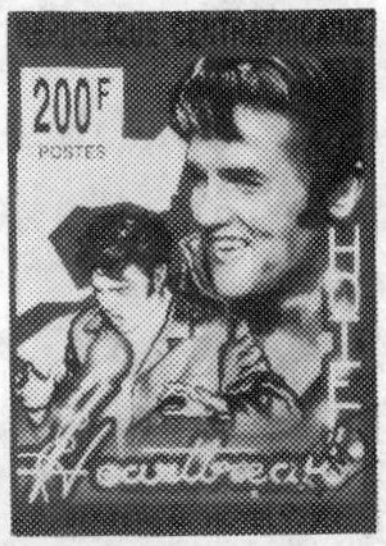
A264

Elvis Presley (1935-1977) A264a

Portrait of Presley, song or movie: 200fr, Heartbreak Hotel, 1956. 300fr, Love Me Tender, 1957. 400fr, Jailhouse Rock, 1957. 600fr, Harem Scarum, 1965.
1000fr, With guitar, at microphone.
No. 1001A, Holding microphone. No. 1001B, Playing guitar.

1993, July 12 Litho. *Perf. 13½*

997	A264	200fr multicolored		1.50	75
998	A264	300fr multicolored		2.25	1.15
999	A264	400fr multicolored		3.00	1.60
1000	A264	600fr multicolored		4.50	2.25
	Nos. 997-1000 (4)			11.25	5.75

Souvenir Sheet

1001 A264 1000fr multicolored 7.50 3.75

Litho. & Embossed

1001A A264a 1500fr gold & multi

Souvenir Sheet

1001B A264a 1500fr gold & multi

Nos. 1000-1001B are airmail. Nos. 997-1000 exist imperf. and in souvenir sheets of one. No. 1001 exists imperf.

Wedding of Japan's Crown Prince Naruhito and Masako Owada — A265

A265a

Designs: 50fr, Princess Masako, parents. 65fr, Crown Prince Naruhito, parents. 160fr, Princess Masako, Harvard University 450fr, Crown Prince Naruhito, Oxford University. 750fr, Crown Prince, Princess.

1993, July 12 Litho. *Perf. 13½*

1002	A265	50fr multicolored	38	18
1003	A265	65fr multicolored	48	24
1004	A265	160fr multicolored	1.20	60
1005	A265	450fr multicolored	3.40	1.70
	Nos. 1002-1005 (4)		5.46	2.72

Souvenir Sheet

1006 A265 750fr multicolored 5.75 2.80

Litho. & Embossed

1006A A265a 1500fr gold & multi

Nos. 1005-1006A are airmail. Nos. 1002-1005, 1006A exist imperf. and in souvenir sheets of one. No. 1006 exists imperf.

A266

1994 World Cup Soccer Championships, US — A266a

Designs show winning team, scenes from: 40fr, Amsterdam, 1928; Montevideo, 1930. 50fr, Rome, 1934; Paris, 1938. 60fr, Rio, 1950; Berne, 1954. 80fr, Stockholm, 1958; Santiago, 1962. 160fr, London, 1966; Mexico City, 1970. 200fr, Munich, 1974; Buenos Aires, 1978. 400fr, Madrid, 1982; Mexico City, 1986. 500fr, Rome, 1990; emblem for US competition, 1994.
1000fr, 1990 German team; 1994 US team.
No. 1015A, Pele, Brazil. No. 1015B, Gerd Muller, Germany.

1993, Oct. 9 Litho. *Perf. 13½*

1007	A266	40fr multicolored	30	15
1008	A266	50fr multicolored	38	18
1009	A266	60fr multicolored	45	22
1010	A266	80fr multicolored	60	30
1011	A266	160fr multicolored	1.20	60
1012	A266	200fr multicolored	1.50	75
1013	A266	400fr multicolored	3.00	1.50
1014	A266	500fr multicolored	3.75	1.90
	Nos. 1007-1014 (8)		11.18	5.60

Souvenir Sheet

1015 A266 1000fr multicolored 7.50 3.75

Litho. & Embossed

1015A A266a 1500fr gold & multi

Souvenir Sheet

1015B A266a 1500fr gol & multi

No. 1015 contains one 60x30mm stamp. Nos. 1007-1014 exist in souvenir sheets of one.
Nos. 1015A-1015B are airmail.

Miniature Sheets

Modern Olympic Games, Cent. (in 1996) — A267

Designs: No. 1016a, Ancient olympian. b, Baron de Coubertin, 1896. c, Charles Bennett, 1900. d, Etienne Desmarteau, 1904. e, Harry Porter, 1908. f, Patrick MacDonald, 1912. g, No games, 1916. h, Frank Loomis, 1920. i, Albert White, 1924.

No. 1017a, El Ouafi, 1928. b, Eddie Tolan, 1932. c, Jesse Owens, 1936. d, No games, 1940. e, No games, 1944. f, Tapio Rautavaara, 1948. g, Jean Boiteux, 1952. h, Petrus Kasterman, 1956. i, Sante Gaiardoni, 1960.

No. 1018a, Anton Geesink, 1964. b, Bob Beamon, 1968. c, Mark Spitz, 1972. d, Nadia Comaneci, 1976. e, Aleksandre Dityatin, 1980. f, J.F. Lamour, 1984. g, Pierre Durand, 1988. h, Michael Jordan, 1992. i, Soccer player, 1996.

1993 Litho. *Perf. 13½*

1016	A267	90fr Sheet of 9, #a.-i.	6.50	3.25
1017	A267	100fr Sheet of 9, #a.-i.	7.25	3.75
1018	A267	160fr Sheet of 9, #a.-i.	11.50	5.75

Miniature Sheet

Dinosaurs A268

Designs: No. 1019a, 25fr, Saltoposuchus. b, 25fr, Rhamphorhynchus. c, 25fr, Dimorphodon. d, 25fr, Archaeopteryx. e, 30fr, Compsognathus longipes. f, 30fr, Cryptocleidus oxoniensis. g, 30fr, Stegosaurus. h, 30fr, Cetiosaurus. i, 50fr, Brontosaurus. j, 50fr, Corythosaurus casuarius. k, 50fr, Styracosaurus. l, 50fr, Gorgosaurus. m, 500fr, Scolosaurus. n, 500fr, Trachodon. o, 500fr, Struthiomimus. p, 500fr, Tarbosaurus.
No. 1020, Tylosaur.

1993

1019 A268 Sheet of 16, #a.-p. 19.00 9.50

Souvenir Sheet

1020 A268 1000fr multicolored 7.75 3.75

No. 1020 is airmail and contains one 51x60mm stamp.

Biodiversity A269

Various fauna surrounding: 100fr, Man planting tree. 130fr, Man with local fauna, vert.

1993 Litho. *Perf. 13½*

1021	A269	100fr multicolored	38	18
1022	A269	130fr multicolored	50	25

M'Bali Dam — A270

1993, Jan. 14 Litho. *Perf. 13*

1023	A270	160fr shown	60	30
1024	A270	200fr Women, men with fish	75	38

Cooperation Council, 40th Anniv. A271

1993, Jan. 26

1025 A271 240fr multicolored 95 48

Intl. Conference on Nutrition, Rome — A272

1993, Apr. 1

1026	A272	90fr shown	35	16
1027	A272	140fr Fresh foods	55	28

University of Bangui A273

1993, Apr. 8

1028 A273 100fr multicolored 38 18

Dated 1992.

Environmental Development — A274

Designs: 160fr, Woman with vegetables, fruit. 240fr, Woman cooking food.

1993 Litho. *Perf. 13½*

1029	A274	160fr multicolored	60	30
1030	A274	240fr multicolored	90	45

Miniature Sheets

1994 Winter Olympics, Lillehammer A275

Past Winter Olympic champions: 1031a, Th. Haug, Nordic combined skiing, Chamonix, 1924. b, J. Heaton, 1-man sled, St. Moritz, 1928. c, B. Ruud, ski jumping, Lake Placid, 1932. d, I. Ballangrud, speed skating, Garmisch-Partenkirchen, 1936. e, G. Fraser, women's slalom skiing, St. Moritz, 1948. f, German 4-man bobsled, Oslo, 1952. g, USSR hockey team, Cortina D'Ampezzo, 1956. h, J. Vuarnet, downhill skiing, Squaw Valley, 1960.
No. 1032a, M. Goitschel, giant slalom, Innsbruck, 1964. b, Jean-Claude Killy, slalom skiing, Grenoble, 1968. c, U. Wehling, Nordic combined, Sapporo, 1972. d, Rodnina & Zaitsev, pairs figure skating, Innsbruck, 1976. e, E. Heiden, speed skating, Lake Placid, 1980. f, K. Witt, figure skating, Sarajevo, 1984. g, J. Mueller, luge, Calgary, 1988. h, E. Grospiron, freestyle skiing, Albertville, 1992. i, Speed skiing, Lillehammer, 1994.

1994 Litho. *Perf. 13½*

1031	A275	100fr Sheet of 8 + label	6.00	3.00
1032	A275	200fr Sheet of 9, #a.-i.	14.00	7.00

1994 Winter Olympics, Lillehammer — A276

Design: 1500fr, Women figure skaters.

1994	**Litho. & Embossed**	***Perf. 13½***
1033 A276 1500fr gold & multi		

#1033 is airmail & exists in a souvenir sheet of 1.

Flowers, Vegetables, Fruit, & Mushrooms A277

Flowers: No. 1034a, 25fr, Ansellia africana. b, 60fr, Polystachia bella. c, 90fr, Aerangis rhodosticta. d, 500fr, Angraecum eburneum.
Vegetables: No. 1035a, 30r, Yams. b, 65fr, Manioc. c, 100fr, Corn. d, 400fr, Sweet potato.
Fruits: No. 1036a, 40fr, Orange. b, 70fr, Banana. c, 160fr, Mango. d, 300fr, Coffee.
Mushrooms: No. 1037a, 50fr, Termitomyces schimperi. b, 80fr, Sympodia arborescens. c, 200fr, Phlebopus sudanicus. d, 600fr, Leucocoprinus africanus.

1994	**Litho.**	***Perf. 13½***	
1034 A277	Strip of 4, #a.-d.	5.00	2.50
1035 A277	Strip of 4, #a.-d.	4.50	2.25
1036 A277	Strip of 4, #a.-d.	4.25	2.00
1037 A277	Strip of 4, #a.-d.	7.00	3.50
e.	Sheet of 16, #1034-1037	21.00	10.50

Catholic Church in Africa, Cent. — A278

Designs: 130fr, Monsignor Augouard, founder of mission, St. Paul of the Rapids. 160fr, Monsignor Grandin, Abbe Boganda, first sacred ordainment, 1938. 240fr, Father Louis Godart, House of Charity, Bangui.

1994	**Litho.**	***Perf. 13½***	
1038 A278	130fr multicolored	52	25
1039 A278	160fr multicolored	65	32
1040 A278	240fr multicolored	95	48
	Nos. 1038-1040 (3)	2.12	1.05

Relics from Early Civilizations, Landmarks — A279

Designs: 10fr, Cabin-shaped cinerary urn, Rome. 25fr, Face of the secret denunciation, Venice, vert. 30fr, Statue of the Tetrarchs, Venice, vert. 50fr, Little cube-shaped building, Palermo, vert. 65fr, Frieze, The Alhambra, Granada, vert. 90fr, Grand Chateau, Bellinzona. 100fr, Museum D'Orsay, Paris, vert. 130fr, Granary, Galicia. 140fr, Mural, by Diego Rivera, Mexico, vert. 160fr, Guacamaya mask, Mexico, vert. 200fr, Ivory mask, Western Africa, vert. 240fr, La Sagrada Familia, Barcelona, vert. 260fr, Casbah of Amerhidil. 300fr, Gold aureus of Sulla, Rome, 82 BC. 400fr, Chimborazo volcano.

1994		***Perf. 13***	
1041-1055 A279	Set of 15	8.75	4.50

D-Day, 50th Anniv. — A280

Pegasus Bridge, June 6: No. 1056a, British troops crossing bridge, piper. b, Glider, British and German soldiers. c, German soldiers.
Operation COBRA, July 24: a, Tank, monument, soldiers. b, Bombers, soldiers, gun barrel. c, Tank, soldiers up close.

1994	**Litho.**	***Perf. 13½***	
1056 A280	600fr Strip of 3, #a.-c.	7.50	3.75
1057 A280	600fr Strip of 3, #a.-c.	7.50	3.75

Nos. 1056b, 1057b are 30x46mm. Nos. 1056-1057 are continuous designs.

SEMI-POSTAL STAMPS

Central African Republic Anti-Malaria Issue

Common Design Type

Perf. 12½x12

1962, Apr. 7	**Engr.**	**Unwmk.**	
B1 CD108	25fr + 5fr slate	45	45

WHO drive to eradicate malaria.

Freedom from Hunger Issue

Common Design Type

1963, Mar. 21		***Perf. 13***	
B2 CD112	25fr + 5fr multi	42	42

Guinea Fowl and Partridge SP1

Designs: 10fr+5fr, Yellow-backed duiker and snail. 20fr+5fr, Elephant, tortoise and hippopotamus playing tug-of-war. 30fr+10fr, Cuckoo and tortoise. 50fr+20fr, Patas monkey and leopard.

1971, Feb. 9	**Photo.**	***Perf. 12½x12***	
B3 SP1	5fr + 5fr multi	80	40
B4 SP1	10fr + 5fr multi	1.25	80
B5 SP1	20fr + 5fr multi	1.60	1.10
B6 SP1	30fr + 10fr multi	2.25	1.60
B7 SP1	50fr + 20fr multi	4.50	3.50
	Nos. B3-B7 (5)	10.40	7.40

Lengué Dancer — SP2

Dancers: 40fr+10fr, Le Lengué. 100fr+40fr, Teke. 140fr+40fr, Englabolo.

1971	**Litho.**	***Perf. 13***	
B8 SP2	20fr + 5fr multi	22	15
B9 SP2	40fr + 10fr multi	42	25
B10 SP2	100fr + 40fr multi	1.10	60
B11 SP2	140fr + 40fr multi	1.50	80
	Nos. B8-B11 (4)	3.24	1.80

AIR POST STAMPS

Central African Republic

Abyssinian Roller — AP1

Birds: 200fr, Gold Coast touraco. 500fr, African fish eagle.

Unwmk.

1960, Sept. 3	**Engr.**	***Perf. 13***	
C1 AP1	100fr vio bl, org brn & emer	1.00	42
C2 AP1	200fr multi	2.00	80
C3 AP1	500fr Prus bl, emer & red brn	5.00	2.00
	Nos. C1-C3 (3)	8.00	3.22

French Equatorial Africa No. C37 Surcharged in Red

1960, Dec. 15		***Perf. 13***	
C4 AP8	250fr on 500fr grnsh blk, blk & sl	4.25	4.25

17th Olympic Games, Rome, Aug. 25-Sept. 11.

Air Afrique Issue

Common Design Type

1962, Feb. 17	**Unwmk.**	***Perf. 13***	
C5 CD107	50fr vio, lt grn & red brn	50	45

Founding of Air Afrique airline.

Pole Vault — AP1a

1962, July 21	**Photo.**	***Perf. 12x12½***	
C6 AP1a	100fr grn, yel, brn & blk	1.00	65

Abidjan games.

Red-faced Lovebirds — AP2

1962-63	**Engr.**	***Perf. 13***	
C7 AP2	50fr Great blue touraco	50	22
C8 AP2	250fr shown ('63)	2.50	1.40

Issued: 50fr, Nov. 15; 250fr, Mar. 11, 1963.

Runner with Torch and Palm Branch — AP3

1962, Dec. 24			
C9 AP3	100fr gray grn, brn & car	1.00	65

Tropics Cup Games, Bangui, Dec. 24-31.

African Postal Union Issue

Common Design Type

1963, Sept. 8	**Photo.**	***Perf. 12½***	
C10 CD114	85fr emer, ocher & red	80	60

Sun Shining on Africa — AP4

1963, Nov. 9		***Perf. 13x12***	
C11 AP4	25fr bl, yel & vio bl	25	20

Issued for African unity.

Europafrica Issue

Common Design Type

1963, Nov. 30		***Perf. 12x13***	
C12 CD116	50fr ultra, yel & dk brn	90	70

Diesel Engine — AP5

Designs: Various Locomotives; 25fr, 50fr, vertical.

1963, Dec. 1	**Engr.**	***Perf. 13***	
C13 AP5	20fr brn, cl & dk grn	20	20
C14 AP5	25fr brn, bl & choc	25	20
C15 AP5	50r brn, red lil & vio	55	40
C16 AP5	100fr brn, grn & dl red brn	1.10	80
a.	Min. sheet of 4, #C13-C16	2.25	2.25
	Nos. C13-C16 (4)	2.10	1.60

Bangui-Douala railroad project.

Bangui Cathedral — AP6

1964, Jan. 21	**Unwmk.**	***Perf. 13***	
C17 AP6	100fr yel grn, org brn & bl	1.00	60

Radar Tracking Station and WMO Emblem — AP7

1964, Mar. 23 **Engr.** ***Perf. 13***

C18 AP7 50fr org brn, bl & pur	50	42

World Meteorological Day.

Map and Presidents of Chad, Congo, Gabon and Central African Republic — AP8

1964, June 23 **Photo.** ***Perf. 12½***

C19 AP8 100fr multi	1.00	65

5th anniversary of the Conference of Chiefs of State of Equatorial Africa.

Javelin Throwers — AP9

Designs: 50fr, Basketball game. 100fr, Four runners. 250fr, Swimmers, one in water.

1964, June 23 **Engr.** ***Perf. 13***

C20 AP9 25fr grn, dk brn & lt vio bl	25	15
C21 AP9 50fr blk, car & grn	50	25
C22 AP9 100fr grn, vio bl & dk brn	1.00	55
C23 AP9 250fr grn, blk & car	2.50	1.50
a. Min. sheet of 4, #C20-C23	4.25	4.25
Nos. C20-C23 (4)	4.25	2.45

18th Olympic Games, Tokyo, Oct. 10-25, 1964.

John F. Kennedy — AP10

1964, July 4 **Photo.** ***Perf. 12½***

C24 AP10 100fr lil, brn & blk	1.10	90
a. Min. sheet of 4	5.00	5.00

President John F. Kennedy.

Industrial Symbols, Maps of Africa and Europe — AP11

1964, Dec. 19 **Unwmk.** ***Perf. 13x12***

C25 AP11 50fr yel, org & grn	50	45

See note after Cameroun No. 402.

International Cooperation Year Emblem — AP12

1965, Jan. 2 ***Perf. 13***

C26 AP12 100fr red brn, yel & bl	1.00	60

International Cooperation Year.

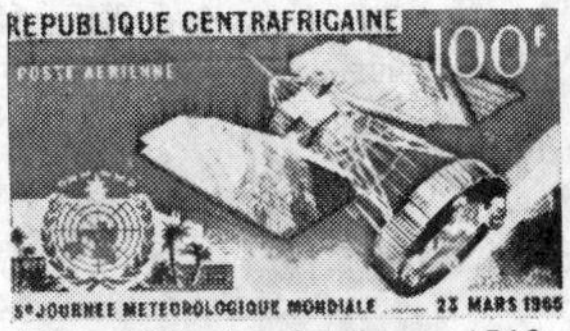

Nimbus Weather Satellite — AP13

1965, Mar. 23 **Engr.** ***Perf. 13***

C27 AP13 100fr org brn, ultra & blk	1.10	65

Fifth World Meteorological Day.

Lincoln and Statue of Liberty — AP14

1965, Apr. 15 **Photo.** ***Perf. 13***

C28 AP14 100fr bluish grn, ind & bis	1.10	60

Centenary of death of Abraham Lincoln.

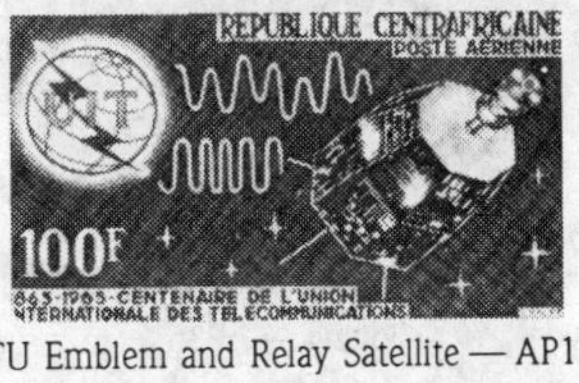

ITU Emblem and Relay Satellite — AP15

1965, May 17 **Engr.** ***Perf. 13***

C29 AP15 100fr dk grn vio bl & brn	1.10	60

Centenary of the ITU.

"Housing," New Home in Village — AP16

1965, June 10 **Unwmk.**

C30 AP16 100fr ultra, brn & sl grn	1.00	60

See note after No. 52.

Europafrica Issue

Tractor, Cotton Picker, Cotton, Sun and Emblem — AP17

1965, Nov. 7 **Photo.** ***Perf. 12x13***

C31 AP17 50fr multi	45	35

See note after Chad No. C11.

Mercury by Antoine Coysevox — AP18

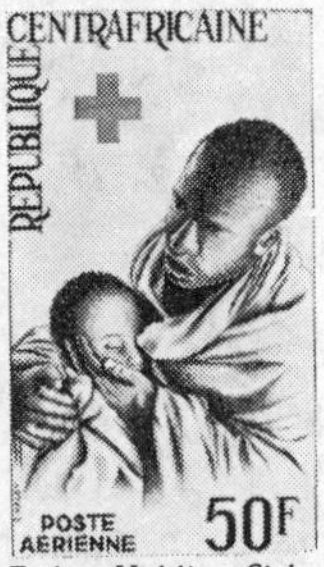

Father Holding Sick Child — AP19

1965, Dec. 5 **Engr.** ***Perf. 13***

C32 AP18 100fr red brn, bl & blk	1.10	65

5th anniv. of Central African Republic's admission to the UPU.

1965, Dec. 12

Design: 100fr, Mother and child.

C33 AP19 50fr dk bl, car & blk	50	35
C34 AP19 100fr red brn, red & brt grn	1.00	65

Issued to honor the Red Cross.

Air Afrique Issue
Common Design Type

1966, Aug. 31 **Photo.** ***Perf. 13***

C35 CD123 25fr bl, blk & lem	25	15

For surcharge see No. C43.

Surveyor Spacecraft on Moon — AP20

Designs: No. C37, Luna 9 on Moon and Earth. 200fr, Rocket take-off, Jules Verne's "From the Earth to the Moon."

1966, Oct. 24 **Photo.** ***Perf. 12x12½***

C36 AP20 130fr multi	1.40	80
C37 AP20 130fr multi	1.40	80
C38 AP20 200fr multi	2.00	1.20
a. Souv. sheet of 3, #C36-C38	5.50	5.50
Nos. C36-C38 (3)	4.80	2.80

Conquest of the Moon.
For surcharges see Nos. C58, C61.

Eugene A. Cernan, Gemini 9 and Agena Rocket — AP21

Design: No. C40, Pavel R. Popovich and rocket.

1966, Nov. 14 **Photo.** ***Perf. 13***

C39 AP21 50fr multi	50	22
C40 AP21 50fr multi	50	22

American and Russian astronauts.

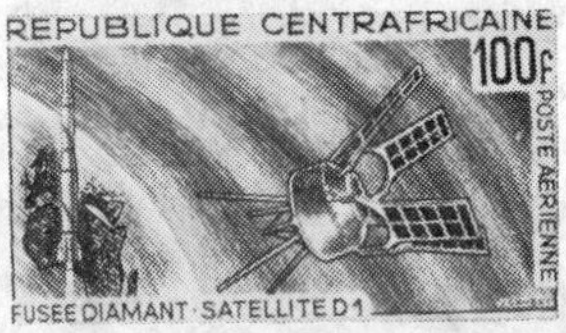

Diamant Rocket, D-1 Satellite and Globe with Map of Africa — AP22

1966, Nov. 14 **Engr.**

C41 AP22 100fr brt rose lil & brn	1.10	50

Issued to commemorate the launching of France's first satellite, Nov. 26, 1965, and the launching of the D-1 satellite, Feb. 17, 1966.

Exchange of Agricultural and Industrial Products between Africa and Europe — AP23

1966, Dec. 5 **Photo.** ***Perf. 12x13***

C42 AP23 50fr multi	50	30

See note after Gabon No. C46.

No. C35 Surcharged

XIX

1967, May 8 ***Perf. 13***

C43 CD123 5fr on 25fr multi	15	15

The surcharge obliterates the "2" of the original 25fr denomination.

DC-8F Over M'Poko Airport, Bangui — AP24

1967, July 3 **Engr.** ***Perf. 13***
C44 AP24 100fr sl, dk grn & brn 1.10 50

View of EXPO '67, Montreal — AP25

1967, July 17
C45 AP25 100fr vio bl, dk red brn & dk grn 1.00 45

International Exposition. EXPO '67, Montreal, Apr. 28-Oct. 27.

African Postal Union Issue, 1967
Common Design Type

1967, Sept. 9 **Engr.** ***Perf. 13***
C46 CD124 100fr brt grn, dk car rose & plum 1.00 45

Potez 25 TOE AP26

1967, Nov. 24 **Engr.** ***Perf. 13***
C47 AP26 100fr shown 75 30
C48 AP26 200fr Junkers 52 1.25 55
C49 AP26 500fr Caravelle 11R 3.75 1.65
Nos. C47-C49 (3) 5.75 2.50

For surcharges see Nos. C59-C60.

Presidents Boganda and Bokassa — AP27

1967, Dec. 1 **Photo.** ***Perf. 12½***
C50 AP27 130fr org, red, lt bl & blk 1.40 90

9th anniversary of the republic.

Pres. Jean Bedel Bokassa AP28

1968, Jan. 1 ***Perf. 12½x12***
C51 AP28 30fr multi 35 20

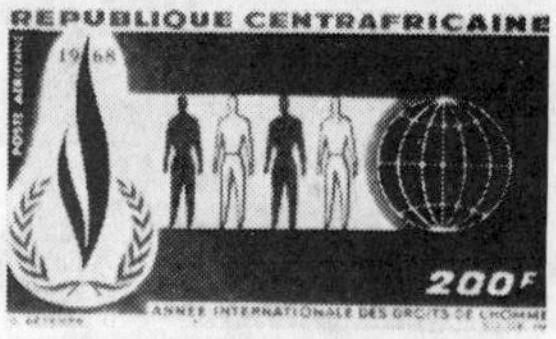

Human Rights Flame, Men and Globe — AP29

1968, Mar. 26 **Photo.** ***Perf. 13***
C52 AP29 200fr brt grn, vio & ver 2.00 1.00

International Human Rights Year.

Man, WHO Emblem and Tsetse Fly — AP30

1968, Apr. 8 **Engr.**
C53 AP30 200fr multi 2.00 1.00

20th anniv. of WHO.

Javelin Thrower — AP31

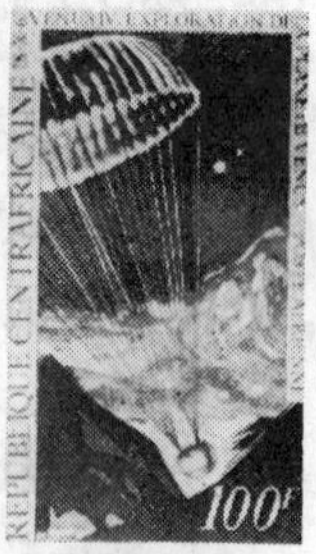

Space Probe Landing on Venus — AP32

1968, Apr. 16 **Engr.** ***Perf. 13***
C54 AP31 200fr shown 2.00 1.10
C55 AP31 200fr Downhill skier 2.00 1.10

The 1968 Olympic Games.

1968, Apr. 23
C56 AP32 100fr ultra, dk & brt grn 1.00 45

Venus exploration by Venus IV, Oct. 18, 1967.

Marie Curie and "Cancer Destroyed" — AP33

1968, Apr. 30
C57 AP33 100fr vio, brt bl & brn 1.00 45

Marie Curie (1867-1934), scientist.

Nos. C36-C37 and C47-C48 Surcharged with New Value

Photogravure; Engraved

1968, Sept. 16 ***Perf. 12x12½, 13***
C58 AP20 5fr on 130fr multi 15 15
C59 AP26 10fr on 100fr multi 15 15
C60 AP26 20fr on 200fr multi 20 15
C61 AP20 50fr on 130fr multi 55 38
Nos. C58-C61 (4) 1.05
Set value 58

On No. C58 the old denomination has been obliterated with "XIX," on No. C61 the obliteration is a rectangular bar. On Nos. C59-C60 the last zero of the old denomination has been obliterated with a black square.

River Boat Type of Regular Issue

Craft: 100fr, "Pie X," Bangui, 1894. 130fr, "Ballay," Bangui, 1891.

1968, Dec. 10 **Engr.** ***Perf. 13***
Size: 48x27mm
C62 A37 100fr bl, dk brn & ol 1.00 45
C63 A37 130fr brt pink, sl grn & slate 1.40 65

PHILEXAFRIQUE Issue

Mme. de Sévigné, French School, 17th Century AP34

1968, Dec. 17 **Photo.** ***Perf. 12½***
C64 AP34 100fr brn & multi 1.10 90

Issued to publicize PHILEXAFRIQUE, Philatelic Exhibition in Abidjan, Feb. 14-23. Printed with alternating brown label.

2nd PHILEXAFRIQUE Issue
Common Design Type

Design: 50fr, Ubangi-Shari No. J16, cotton field and Pres. Bokassa.

1969, Feb. 14 **Engr.** ***Perf. 13***
C65 CD128 50fr bis brn, blk & dk grn 60 60

Holocerina Angulata Aur. — AP35

Butterflies and Moths: 20fr, Nudaurelia dione fabr. 30fr, Eustera troglophylla hamp., vert. 50fr, Aurivillius aratus west. 100fr, Epiphora albida druce.

1969, Feb. 25 **Photo.**
C66 AP35 10fr yel & multi 15 15
C67 AP35 20fr vio & multi 20 15
C68 AP35 30fr multi 30 15
C69 AP35 50fr multi 60 25
C70 AP35 100fr multi 1.10 55
Nos. C66-C70 (5) 2.35 1.25

Boxing — AP36

1969, Mar. 18 **Photo.** ***Perf. 13***
C71 AP36 50fr shown 50 22
C72 AP36 100fr Basketball 1.00 40

Apollo 8 over Moonscape — AP37

1969, May 27 **Photo.** ***Perf. 13***
C73 AP37 200fr dp bl, gray & yel 2.00 90

US Apollo 8 mission, the 1st men in orbit around the moon, Dec. 21-27, 1968.

For overprint see No. C81.

Market Cross, Nuremberg, and Toys — AP38

1969, June 3
C74 AP38 100fr blk, brt rose lil & emer 1.00 65

Intl. Toy Fair in Nuremberg, Germany.

Napoleon as First Consul, by Anne-Louis Girodet-Trioson — AP39

Designs: 130fr, Napoleon meeting Emperor Francis II, by Antoine Jean Gros, horiz. 200fr, The Wedding of Napoleon and Marie-Louise, by Georges Rouget, horiz.

1969, Nov. 4 **Photo.** ***Perf. 12½***
C75 AP39 100fr multi 1.10 80
C76 AP39 130fr brn & multi 1.60 1.00
C77 AP39 200fr multi 2.75 2.00
Nos. C75-C77 (3) 5.45 3.80

Napoleon Bonaparte (1769-1821).

Pres. Bokassa, Map of Africa and Flag — AP40

Franklin Delano Roosevelt — AP41

1970, Jan. 1 ***Die-cut; Perf. 10½***
Embossed on Gold Foil
C78 AP40 2000fr gold 16.00 16.00

1970 **Litho.** ***Perf. 13½x14***
C79 AP41 100fr shown 90 55
C80 AP41 100fr Lenin 80 45

25th anniv. Roosevelt and cent. of the birth of Lenin.

Issue dates: #C79, Apr. 29; #C80. Apr. 22.

No. C73 Overprinted in Red:

ATTERRISSAGE
d'APOLLO 12
19 novembre 1969

1970, June 1 **Photo.** ***Perf. 13***
C81 AP37 200fr multi 5.50 4.25

Issued to commemorate the moon landing mission of Apollo 12, Nov. 14-24, 1969.

AP42

1970, Sept. 15 Litho. *Perf. 10*

C82 AP42 Pair + label 1.60 80
a. 100fr Dancer 80 35
b. 100fr Still life 80 35

Knokphila 70, 6th Intl. Phil. Exhib. at Knokke, Belgium, July 4-10. Imperf. between stamps and label.

Sericulture Type of Regular Issue

1970, Sept. 15 *Perf. 10*

C83 A45 140fr multi 1.40 70

C.A.R. Flag, EXPO Emblem and Pavilion — AP43

1970, Dec. 18 Litho. *Perf. 13½x13*

C84 AP43 200fr red & multi 1.75 90

Intl. Exposition EXPO '70, Osaka, Japan.

Soccer AP44

1970, Dec. 8 *Perf. 13x13½*

C85 AP44 200fr multi 1.75 90

World Soccer Championships, Mexico, May 30-June 21, 1970.

Dove AP45

1970, Dec. 31

C86 AP45 200fr bl, yel & blk 1.75 90

25th anniversary of the United Nations.

Presidents Mobutu, Bokassa, and Tombalbaye — AP46

1971, Jan. 10

C87 AP46 140fr multi 1.40 60

Return of Central African Republic to the United States of Central Africa which also includes Congo Democratic Republic and Chad.

Satellite over Globe — AP47

1971, May 17 Photo. *Perf. 12½*

C88 AP47 100fr multi 90 42

3rd World Telecommunications Day.

African Postal Union Issue, 1971

Common Design Type

Design: 100fr, Carved head and UAMPT building, Brazzaville, Congo.

1971, Nov. 13 Photo. *Perf. 13x13½*

C89 CD135 100fr bl & multi 90 42

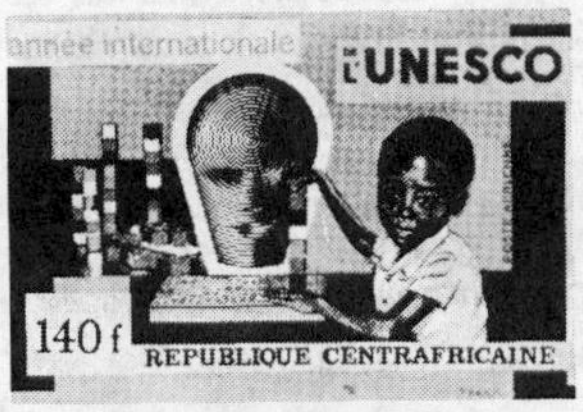

Child and Education Year Emblem — AP48

1971, Nov. 11 Litho. *Perf. 13x13½*

C90 AP48 140fr multi 1.10 50

25th anniv. of UNESCO.

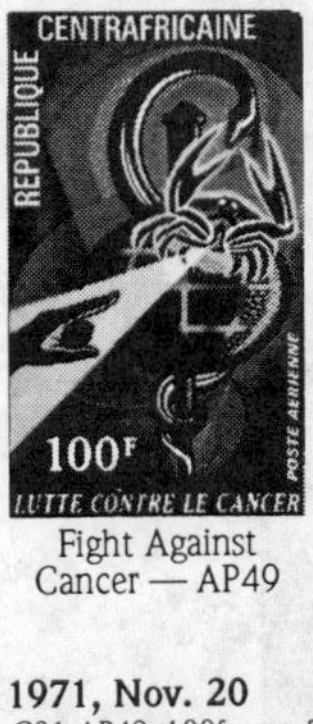

Fight Against Cancer — AP49

Gamal Abdel Nasser — AP50

1971, Nov. 20 Photo. *Perf. 12½*

C91 AP49 100fr grn & multi 90 40

1972, Jan. 15

C92 AP50 100fr dk red, blk & bister 80 40

In memory of Gamal Abdel Nasser (1918-1970), president of Egypt.

Olympic Rings and Boxing — AP51

Design: No. C94, Track and Olympic rings, vert.

1972, May 26 Engr. *Perf. 13*

C93 AP51 100fr brn org & sepia 1.00 40
C94 AP51 100fr green & violet 1.00 40
a. Miniature sheet of 2 2.00 2.00

20th Olympic Games, Munich, Aug. 26-Sept. 10. No. C94a contains 2 stamps similar to Nos. C93-C94, but in changed colors. The boxing stamp is red lilac and green, the track stamp ocher and red lilac.

For overprints see Nos. C100-C101.

Tiling's Mail Rocket, 1931, and Mailman — AP52

Designs: 50fr, DC-3 and mailman riding camel, vert. 150fr, Sirio satellite and rocket, vert. 200fr, Intelsat 4 and rocket.

1972, Aug. 12

C95 AP52 40fr bl, org & indigo 35 16
C96 AP52 50fr bl, brn & org 40 16
C97 AP52 150fr brn, org & gray 1.10 55
C98 AP52 200fr brn, bl & org 1.50 65
a. Souv. sheet of 4, #C95-C98 3.50 3.50
Nos. C95-C98 (4) 3.35 1.52

Centraphilex 1972, Central African Philatelic Exhibition, Bangui.

Europafrica Issue

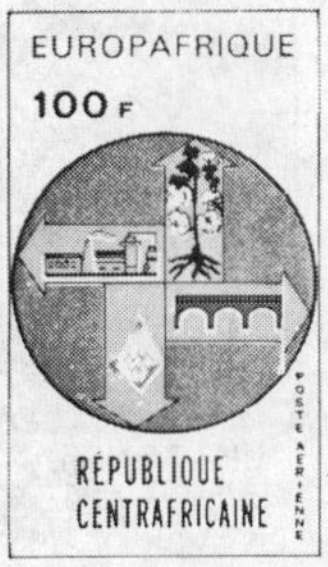

Arrows with Symbols of Agriculture and Industry — AP53

1972, Nov. 17 Litho. *Perf. 13*

C99 AP53 100fr multi 65 40

Nos. C93-C94, C94a Overprinted
a. POIDS-MOYEN / LEMECHEV MEDAILLE D'OR
b. LONGUER / WILLIAMS MEDAILLE D'OR

1972, Nov. 24 Engr.

C100 AP51 (a) 100fr 90 40
C101 AP51 (b) 100fr 90 40
a. Miniature sheet of 2 2.00 2.00

Gold Medal Winners in 20th Olympic Games: Viatscheslav Lemechev, USSR, middleweight boxing; Randy Williams, US, broad jump.

Lunar Rover and Module — AP54

1972, Dec. 18 Engr. *Perf. 13*

C102 AP54 100fr slate grn, bl & gray 80 42

Apollo 16 US moon mission, Apr. 15-27, 1972.

Virgin and Child, by Francesco Pesellino AP55

Christmas: 150fr, Adoration of the Child with St. John the Baptist and St. Romuald, by Fra Filippo Lippi.

1972, Dec. 25 Photo.

C103 AP55 100fr gold & multi 80 42
C104 AP55 150fr gold & multi 1.25 65

Parthenon, Athens, Spyridon Louis, Marathon, 1896 — AP56

Designs (Olympic Rings and): 40fr, Arc de Triomphe, Paris, H. Barrelet, single scull, 1900. 50fr, Old Courthouse and Western Arch, St. Louis, Myer Prinstein, triple jump, 1904. 100fr, Tower, London, Henry Taylor, swimming, 1908. 150fr, City Hall, Stockholm, Greco-Roman wrestling, 1912.

1972, Dec. 28 Engr.

C105 AP56 30fr brt grn, mag & brn 25 15
C106 AP56 40fr vio bl, emer & brn 35 15
C107 AP56 50fr car rose, vio bl & Prus bl 40 16
C108 AP56 100fr sl, red lil & brn 80 38
C109 AP56 150fr red lil, blk & Prus bl 1.25 60
Nos. C105-C109 (5) 3.05 1.44

Olympic Games 1896-1912.

WHO Emblem, Surgeon and Nurse — AP57

1973, Apr. 7 Photo. *Perf. 13*

C110 AP57 100fr multi 80 45

WHO, 25th anniv.

AP58

AP58a

1973, May 17 Litho. *Perf. 12½*
C111 AP58 200fr World map, arrows, waves 1.40 80

5th International Telecommunications Day.

1973, Sept. 17 Engr. *Perf. 13*

Head and City Hall, Brussels.

C112 AP58a 100fr pur, ocher & brn 80 45

African Weeks, Brussels, Sept. 15-30, 1973.

Europafrica Issue

Map of Central African Republic with Industry and Agriculture, Young Man — AP59

1973, Sept. 28 Engr. *Perf. 13*
C113 AP59 100fr sepia, grn & org 70 45

Carrier Pigeon with Letter and UPU Emblem — AP60

1973, Oct. 9 Photo.
C114 AP60 200fr multi 1.50 90

Universal Postal Union Day.

WMO Emblem, Weather Map — AP61

1973, Oct. 20 Engr. *Perf. 13*
C115 AP61 150fr brt ultra & sl grn 1.00 50

Cent. of intl. meteorological cooperation.

Copernicus, Heliocentric System — AP62

1973, Nov. 2 Photo.
C116 AP62 100fr gold & multi 75 45

500th anniversary of the birth of Nicolaus Copernicus (1473-1543), Polish astronomer.

Pres. Bokassa AP63

Pres. Bokassa — AP64

Rocket Launch and Apollo 17 Badge — AP65

1973, Nov. 30 Photo. *Perf. 12½*
C117 AP63 50fr multi 35 22
C118 AP64 100fr multi 65 45

1973, Dec. 15 Engr. *Perf. 13*

Designs: 65fr, Capsule over moonscape, horiz. 100fr, Moon landing, horiz. 150fr, Astronauts on moon. 200fr, Splashdown with parachutes and badge.

C119 AP65 50fr ver, gray grn & brn 35 25
C120 AP65 65fr dk brn, brn red & sl grn 40 35
C121 AP65 100fr ver, slate & choc 65 45
C122 AP65 150fr brn, ol & sl grn 90 65
C123 AP65 200fr red, bl & sl grn 1.40 90
Nos. C119-C123 (5) 3.70 2.60

Apollo 17 US moon mission, Dec. 7-19, 1972.

St. Teresa — AP66

UPU Emblem, Letter — AP67

1973, Dec. 25
C124 AP66 500fr vio bl & grnsh bl 3.50 2.00

St. Teresa of the Infant Jesus, the Little Flower (1873-1897), Carmelite nun.

1974, Oct. 9 Engr. *Perf. 13*
C125 AP67 500fr multi 3.50 2.25

Centenary of Universal Postal Union.
For surcharge see No. C159.

Presidents and Flags of Cameroun, CAR, Gabon and Congo — AP68

1974, Dec. 8 Photo. *Perf. 13*
C126 AP68 100fr gold & multi 60 42

See note after Cameroun No. 595.
For surcharge see No. C155.

Marshal Bokassa AP69

Design: 100fr, Bokassa in Marshal's uniform with cape.

1975, Feb. 22 Photo. *Perf. 13*
C127 AP69 50fr tan & multi 25 20
C128 AP69 100fr tan & multi 55 40

Jean Bedel Bokassa, President for Life and Marshal of the Republic.

Mask, Map of Africa, Arphila Emblem — AP70

Albert Schweitzer and Dugout, Lambarene — AP71

1975, Aug. 25 Engr. *Perf. 13*
C129 AP70 100fr brt bl, red brn & red 65 35

ARPHILA 75 International Philatelic Exhibition, Paris, June 6-16.
For surcharge see No. C156.

1975, Sept. 30 Engr. *Perf. 13*
C130 AP71 200fr blk, ultra & ol 1.40 65

Dr. Albert Schweitzer (1875-1965), medical missionary and musician.
For surcharge see No. C158.

Pres. Bokassa's Houseboat, Bow — AP72

Design: 40fr, Pres. Bokassa's houseboat, stern.

1976, Feb. 22 Litho. *Perf. 13*
C131 AP72 30fr multi 16 15
C132 AP72 40fr multi 22 15

Monument to Franco-CAR Cooperation AP73

Presidents and Flags of France and CAR — AP74

1976, Mar. 5
C133 AP73 100fr multi 55 35
C134 AP74 200fr multi 1.10 65

Official visit of Pres. Valery Giscard d'Estaing to Central African Republic, Mar. 5-8.
For surcharge see No. C157.

Apollo Soyuz Type, 1976

Designs: 100fr, Soyuz space ship. 200fr, Apollo space ship. 300fr, Astronauts and cosmonauts in cabin. 500fr, Apollo and Soyuz after link-up.

1976, June 14 Litho. *Perf. 14x13½*
C135 A90 100fr multi 65 25
C136 A90 200fr multi 1.40 60
C137 A90 300fr multi 2.00 80
Nos. C135-C137 (3) 4.05 1.65

Souvenir Sheet

C138 A90 500fr multi 3.25 1.50

For surcharges see #C161, C168, C173, C177.

French Hussar — AP75

Uniforms: 125fr, Scottish "Black Watch." 150fr, German dragoon. 200fr, British grenadier. 250fr, American ranger. 450fr, American dragoon.

1976, July 4 *Perf. 13½*
C139 AP75 100fr multi 60 20
C140 AP75 125fr multi 80 35
C141 AP75 150fr multi 1.00 40
C142 AP75 200fr multi 1.25 45
C143 AP75 250fr multi 1.50 60
Nos. C139-C143 (5) 5.15 2.00

Souvenir Sheet

C144 AP75 450fr multi 3.00 1.25

American Bicentennial.
For surcharges see Nos. C162, C166-C167, C169, C172, C176.

Acherontia Atropos — AP76

Design: 100fr, Papilio nireus and heniocha marnois.

1976, Sept. 20 Litho. *Perf. 12½*
C145 AP76 50fr multi 25 16
C146 AP76 100fr multi 55 35

For surcharges see Nos. C160, C163.

Olympic Winners Type, 1976

Designs: 100fr, Women's figure skating, Dorothy Hamill, vert. 200fr, Ice skating, Alexander Gorshkov and Ludmilla Pakhomova. 300fr, Men's figure skating, John Curry, vert. 500fr, Downhill skiing, Rosi Mittermaier, vert.

1976, Sept. 23 Litho. *Perf. 13½*

C147 A92 100fr multi 60 25
C148 A92 200fr multi 1.25 60
C149 A92 300fr multi 2.00 90
Nos. C147-C149 (3) 3.85 1.75

Souvenir Sheet

C150 A92 500fr multi 3.25 1.50

For surcharges see #C164, C170, C174, C178.

Viking Mars Type, 1976

Designs: 100fr, Phases of Mars landing. 200fr, Viking descending on Mars, horiz. 300fr, Viking probe. 500fr, Viking flight to Mars, horiz.

1976, Dec.

C151 A93 100fr multi 60 22
C152 A93 200fr multi 1.25 60
C153 A93 300fr multi 2.00 80
Nos. C151-C153 (3) 3.85 1.62

Souvenir Sheet

C154 A93 500fr multi 3.25 1.50

For surcharges and overprints see Nos. C165, C171, C175, C179, C212-C215.

Empire

Stamps of 1973-76 Overprinted with Bars and "EMPIRE CENTRAFRICAIN" in Black, Violet Blue or Gold

Printing and Perforations as Before

1977, Mar.

C155 AP68 100fr (#C126;B) 60 45
C156 AP70 100fr (#C129;VB) 60 45
C157 AP73 100fr (#C133;G) 60 45
C158 AP71 200fr (#C130;B) 1.40 1.00
C159 AP67 500fr (#C125;B) 3.75 2.75
Nos. C155-C159 (5) 6.95 5.10

No bar on No. C159.

Stamps of 1976 Overprinted "EMPIRE CENTRAFRICAIN" in Black on Silver Panel

1977, Apr. 1

C160 AP76 50fr (#C145) 35 20
C161 A90 100fr (#C135) 60 45
C162 AP75 100fr (#C139) 55 40
C163 AP76 100fr (#C146) 55 40
C164 A92 100fr (#C147) 55 40
C165 A93 100fr (#C151) 55 50
C166 AP75 125fr (#C140) 65 55
C167 AP75 150fr (#C141) 80 60
C168 A90 200fr (#C136) 1.40 1.00
C169 AP75 200fr (#C142) 1.10 80
C170 A92 200fr (#C148) 1.10 80
C171 A93 200fr (#C152) 1.10 80
C172 AP75 250fr (#C143) 1.40 1.00
C173 A90 300fr (#C137) 2.00 1.50
C174 A92 300fr (#C149) 1.60 1.25
C175 A93 300fr (#C153) 1.60 1.25
Nos. C160-C175 (16) 15.90 11.90

Souvenir Sheets

C176 AP75 450fr (#C144) 2.50 2.50
C177 A90 500fr (#C138) 2.75 2.75
C178 A92 500fr (#C150) 2.75 2.75
C179 A93 500fr (#C154) 2.75 2.75

Overprint on type AP75 is in upper and lower case letters.

Nobel Prize Type, 1977

Designs: 100fr, Rudyard Kipling. 200fr, Ernest Hemingway. 300fr, Luigi Pirandello. 500fr, Rabindranath Tagore.

1977, Apr. 1 Litho. *Perf. 13½*

C180 A94 100fr multi 65 22
C181 A94 200fr multi 1.25 60
C182 A94 300fr multi 2.00 80
Nos. C180-C182 (3) 3.90 1.62

Souvenir Sheet

C183 A94 500fr multi 3.25 1.50

Zeppelin Type of 1977

Designs: 100fr, Germany #C42 and North Pole. 200fr, Germany #C44 and Science and Industry Building, Chicago. 300fr, Germany #C35 and Brandenburg Gate, Berlin. 500fr, US #C14 and US Capitol, Washington, DC.

1977, Apr. 11 Litho. *Perf. 11*

C184 A95 100fr multi 60 22
C185 A95 200fr multi 1.25 60
C186 A95 300fr multi 2.00 80
Nos. C184-C186 (3) 3.85 1.62

Souvenir Sheet

C187 A95 500fr multi 3.25 1.50

75th anniversary of Zeppelin.

Bokassa Type of 1977

1977, Dec. 4 Litho. *Perf. 13½*

C188 A98 200fr multi 1.10 65
C189 A98 300fr multi 1.60 1.00
a. Souvenir sheet, 500fr 2.50 2.00

Coronation of Emperor Bokassa I, Dec. 4. No. C189a contains a horizontal stamp in similar design. A 2500fr gold embossed horizontal stamp in similar design exists.

Vaccination AP77

1977 Litho. *Perf. 14x13½*

C190 AP77 150fr multi 1.00 50

World Health Day.

Communications Type of 1978

Designs: 100fr, Balloon and spaceships docking in space. 200fr, Hydrofoil and Concorde. 500fr, Tom-tom and Zeppelin. No. C193A, Early postman and rider, UPU emblem, Concorde. No. C193B, Mail coach, dove, satellites.

1978, May 17 Litho. *Perf. 13½*

C191 A107 100fr multi 65 35
C192 A107 200fr multi 1.40 65

Souvenir Sheet

C193 A107 500fr multi 3.75 2.25

Cent. of progress of posts and telecommunications. No. C193 contains one 53x35mm stamp.

C193A A107 1500fr gold & multi
C193B A107 1500fr gold & multi

Nos. C193A-C193B exist imperf. No. C193A exists in a souvenir sheet of one. No. C193B contains one 57x39mm stamp.

Clement Ader and his Plane — AP78

Designs: 50fr, Wilbur and Orville Wright and plane. 60fr, John W. Alcock, Arthur W. Brown and plane. 100fr, Alan Cobham and plane 150fr, Claude Dornier and hydroplane. 500fr, Wilbur and Orville Wright and plane.

1978, Sept. 19 *Perf. 14*

C194 AP78 40fr multi 30 15
C195 AP78 50fr multi 38 16
C196 AP78 60fr multi 42 20
C197 AP78 100fr multi 70 35
C198 AP78 150fr multi 1.10 50
Nos. C194-C198 (5) 2.90 1.36

Souvenir Sheet

C199 AP78 500fr multi 3.75 1.75

History of aviation.

Philexafrique II-Essen Issue

Common Design Types

Designs: No. C200, Crocodile and CAR #C3. No. C201, Birds and Mecklenburg-Schwerin #1.

1978, Nov. 1 Litho. *Perf. 12½*

C200 CD138 100fr multi 65 35
C201 CD139 100fr multi 65 35

Nos. C200-C201 printed se-tenant.

Bokassa Type of 1978

Design: 150fr, Catherine and Jean Bedel Bokassa, horiz.

1978, Dec. 4 Litho. *Perf. 13*

C202 A113 150fr multi 1.00 50

First anniversary of coronation. A 1000fr gold embossed souvenir sheet showing Emperor Bokassa exists.

Rowland Hill Type of 1978

Designs (Rowland Hill and): 100fr, Mailman and Tuscany No. 23. 200fr, Balloon and France No. 1. 500fr, Central Africa Nos. 1-2.

1978, Dec. 27

C203 A114 100fr multi 65 35
C204 A114 200fr multi 1.40 65

Souvenir Sheet

C205 A114 500fr multi 3.50 1.60

Sir Rowland Hill (1795-1879), originator of penny postage. No. C205 contains one 37½x39mm stamp. 1500fr gold embossed stamp and souvenir sheet exist.

IYC Type of 1979

Designs (UNICEF, Eagle Emblems and): 100fr, Chinese girl flying kites and German Do-X flying boat, 1929. 200fr, Boys playing leapfrog, hurdler and Olympic emblem. 500fr, Child with abacus and Albert Einstein with his equation.

1979, Mar. 6 *Perf. 13½*

C206 A115 100fr multi 65 35
C207 A115 200fr multi 1.40 65

Souvenir Sheet

C208 A115 500fr multi 3.50 1.60

International Year of the Child. No. C208 contains one 56x33mm stamp. 1500fr gold embossed stamp and souvenir sheet exist.

Olympic Type of 1979

Designs (Moscow '80 Emblem, various Sports and): 100fr, Hurdles and "B". 200fr, Broad jump and "A".

1979, Mar. 16 Litho. *Perf. 13*

C209 A116 100fr multi 65 35
C210 A116 200fr multi 1.40 65

22nd Olympic Games, Moscow, July 19-Aug. 3, 1980. A 1500fr gold embossed souvenir sheet exists showing diver, runner and javelin.

National Husbandry Association Type

1979, Aug. Litho. *Perf. 13*

C211 A119 60fr Horse 32 16

Nos. C151-C154 Overprinted "ALUNISSAGE/APOLLO XI/ JUILLET 1969" and Emblem in Black or Silver

1979, Oct. Litho. *Perf. 14x13½*

C212 A93 100fr multi 55 25
C213 A93 200fr multi 1.10 55
C214 A93 300fr multi 1.60 80
Nos. C212-C214 (3) 3.25 1.60

Souvenir Sheet

C215 A93 500fr multi (S) 3.00 1.50

Apollo 11 moon landing, 10th anniversary.

Ski Jump, Lake Placid '80 Emblem — AP79

Lake Placid Emblem and: 100fr, Downhill skiing. 200fr, Hockey. 300fr, Slalom. 500fr, Bobsledding.

1979, Nov. 11 Litho. *Perf. 13½*

C216 AP79 60fr multi 32 16
C217 AP79 100fr multi 55 25
C218 AP79 200fr multi 1.10 55
C219 AP79 300fr multi 1.60 80
Nos. C216-C219 (4) 3.57 1.76

Souvenir Sheet

C220 AP79 500fr multi 3.00 1.50

13th Winter Olympics Games, Lake Placid, NY, Feb. 12-24, 1980.
For overprints see Nos. C224-C228.

Space Type of 1980

1980, Apr. 8 Litho. *Perf. 13½*

C221 A125 150fr Early satellites 80 40
C222 A125 200fr Space shuttle 1.10 55

Souvenir Sheet

C223 A125 500fr Apollo 11, Armstrong 2.75 1.40

Litho. & Embossed

1980, Apr. 8 Litho *Perf. 13½*

Size: 51x57mm

C223A A125 1500fr Armstrong, Apollo 11

Souvenir Sheet

C223B A125 1500fr Space shuttle, horiz.

C223A-C223B exist imperf. No. C223A exists in a souvenir sheet of one. No. C223B contains one 57x51mm stamp.

Nos. C216-C220 Overprinted:
a. VAINQUEUR / INNAVER / AUTRICHE
b. VAINQUEUR / MOSER-PROELL / AUTRICHE
c. VAINQUEUR / ETATS-UNIS
d. VAINQUEUR / STENMARK / SUEDE
e. VAINQUEURS / SCHAERER-BENZ / SUISSE

1980, May 12 Litho. *Perf. 13½*

C224 AP79 (a) 60fr multi 32 16
C225 AP79 (b) 100fr multi 55 25
C226 AP79 (c) 200fr multi 1.10 55
C227 AP79 (d) 300fr multi 1.60 80
Nos. C224-C227 (4) 3.57 1.76

Souvenir Sheet

C228 AP79 (e) 500fr multi 2.75 1.40

World Telecommunications Day — AP80

1980, June 26 Litho. *Perf. 12½*

C229 AP80 100fr multi 55 25
C230 AP80 150fr multi, vert. 80 40

Olympic Type of 1980

1980, July 25 Litho. *Perf. 13½*

C231 A126 100fr Boxing 55 25
C232 A126 150fr Hurdles 80 40

Souvenir Sheet

C233 A126 250fr Long jump 1.40 65

Litho. & Embossed

C233A A126 1500fr Relay race, diff.

Souvenir Sheet

C233B A126 1500fr Basketball, vert.

22nd Summer Olympic Games, Moscow, July 19-Aug. 3. No. C233 contains one 39x36mm stamp.
For overprints see Nos. C248-C250B.

Europe-Africa Type of 1980

1980, Nov. 4 Litho. *Perf. 13½*

C234 A127 150fr Meteorology 80 40
C235 A127 200fr Aviation 1.10 55

Souvenir Sheet

C236 A127 500fr Concorde jet 2.75 1.40

No. C236 contains one 41½x29mm stamp.

Litho. & Embossed

Size: 42x39mm

C236A A127 1500fr Boy Scouts

Souvenir Sheet

C236B A127 1500fr Concorde

Nos. C236A-C236B exist imperf. No. C236A exists in a souvenir sheet of one. No. C236B contains one 42x39mm stamp.

Soccer Type of 1981

1981, Jan. 13 Litho. *Perf. 13½*

C237 A130 100fr Netherlands 55 25
C238 A130 200fr Spain 1.10 55

Souvenir Sheet

C239 A130 500fr Argentina 2.75 1.40

Litho. & Embossed

Size: 57x39mm

C239A A130 1500fr Players, trophy

Souvenir Sheet

C239B A130 1500fr Players, trophy, diff.

Nos. C239A-C239B exist imperf. No. C239A exists in a souvenir sheet of one. No. C239B contains one 36x60mm stamp.

Jacob Wrestling with the Angel, by Rembrandt
AP81

Rembrandt Paintings: 90fr, Christ during the Storm. 150fr, Jeremiah Mourning the Destruction of Jerusalem. 250fr, Tobit Accusing Anne of Theft of a Goat. 500fr, Belshazzar's Feast, horiz.

1981, Feb. 20 *Perf. 12½*

C240 AP81 60fr multi 35 16
C241 AP81 90fr multi 45 22
C242 AP81 150fr multi 80 40
C243 AP81 250fr multi 1.40 65
Nos. C240-C243 (4) 3.00 1.43

Souvenir Sheet

C244 AP81 500fr multi 2.50 1.40

Picasso Type of 1981

Paintings: 150fr, Woman in Mirror with Self-portrait. 200fr, Woman Sleeping, The Dream. 500fr, Portrait of Maia (the Artist's Daughter). No. C247A, Two Women and Glasses, Picasso. No. C247B, Woman with Handbag, statue of standing woman, vert.

1981, June 30 **Litho.** *Perf. 13½*

C245 A133 150fr multi 80 40
C246 A133 200fr multi 1.10 55

Souvenir Sheet

C247 A133 500fr multi 2.75 1.40

No. C247 contains one 42x46mm stamp.

Litho. & Embossed
Size: 57x39mm

C247A A133 1500fr gold & multi

Souvenir Sheet

C247B A133 1500fr gold & multi

Nos. C247A-C247B exist imperf. No. C247A exists in a souvenir sheet of one. No. C247B contains one 39x58mm stamp.

Nos. C231-C233B Overprinted with Event, Winner and Country in Gold

1981 **Litho.** *Perf. 13½*

C248 A126 100fr multi 55 25
C249 A126 150fr multi 80 40

Souvenir Sheet

C250 A126 250fr multi 1.40 65

Litho. & Embossed

C250A A126 1500fr on #C233A

Souvenir Sheet

C250B A126 1500fr on #C233B

Royal Wedding Type of 1981

1981, Aug. 20 **Litho.** *Perf. 13½*

C251 A136 150fr Prince of Wales arms 80 40
C252 A136 200fr Palace 1.10 55

Souvenir Sheet

C253 A136 500fr St. Paul's Cathedral 2.75 1.40

No. C253 contains one 60x32mm stamp.

Litho. & Embossed
Size: 51x42mm

C253A A136 1500fr Diana, Charles

Souvenir Sheet

C253B A136 1500fr Charles, Diana, ship

Nos. C253A-C253B exist imperf. No. C253A exists in a souvenir sheet of one. No. C253B contains one 51x42mm stamp.

Navigator Type of 1981

1981, Sept. 4 **Litho.** *Perf. 13½*

C254 A139 100fr O. Kersauson 55 25
C255 A139 200fr Chichester 1.10 55

Souvenir Sheet

C256 A139 500fr A. Colas 2.75 1.40

Litho. & Embossed
Size: 51x42mm

C256A A139 1500fr Riguidel

Souvenir Sheet

C256B A139 1500fr Tabarly

Nos. C256A-C256B exist imperf. No. C256A exists in a souvenir sheet of one. No. C256B contains one 51x42mm stamp.

Lizard — AP82

1981, Oct. 30 *Perf. 12½x13*

C257 AP82 30fr shown 16 15
C258 AP82 60fr Snake 35 16
C259 AP82 110fr Crocodile 60 30
Nos. C257-C259 (3) 1.11 61

Christmas Type of 1981

1981, Dec. 24 *Perf. 13½*

C260 A143 140fr Correggio 70 40
C261 A143 200fr Gentileschi, 1610 1.10 55

Souvenir Sheet

C262 A143 500fr Holy Family, by Cranach 2.75 1.40

No. C262 contains one 41x50mm stamp.

Litho. & Embossed
Size: 30x60mm

C262A A143 1500fr Hans Memling, c. 1470

Souvenir Sheet

C262B A143 1500fr Fra Angelico, 1438

Nos. C262A-C262B exist imperf. No. C262A exists in a souvenir sheet of one. No. C262B contains one 30x60mm stamp.

Animal Type of 1982

1982, Jan. 22 **Litho.** *Perf. 13½*

C263 A145 300fr Mandrill 1.60 80
C264 A145 500fr Lion 2.75 1.40

Souvenir Sheet

C265 A145 600fr Nile crocodiles 3.50 1.60

No. C265 contains one 47x38mm stamp.

Litho. & Embossed
Size: 51x57mm

C265A A145 1500fr Leopard, Rotary emblem

Souvenir Sheet

C265B A145 1500fr Emblem, eagle, horiz.

Nos. C265A-C265B exist imperf. No. C265A exists in a souvenir sheet of one. No. C265B contains one 57x51mm stamp.

Transportation Type of 1982 and

AP82a

Designs: No. C267A, Space shuttle launch, horiz. No. C268A, Shuttle, space telescope.

1982, Feb. 27 **Litho.** *Perf. 13½*

C266 A147 300fr Savannah cargo ship 1.60 80
C267 A147 500fr Columbia space shuttle 2.50 1.40

Souvenir Sheet

C268 A147 600fr Spirit of Locomotion emblem 3.50 1.60

Litho. & Embossed

C268A AP82a 1500fr gold & multi

Souvenir Sheet

C268B AP82a 1500fr gold & multi

No. C268 contains one 39x43mm stamp. No. C268B contains one 51x42mm stamp.

Olympic Type of 1982

1982, July 24 **Litho.** *Perf. 13½*

C269 A149 300fr Diving 1.60 80
C270 A149 500fr Equestrian 2.50 1.40

Souvenir Sheet

C271 A149 600fr Basketball 3.50 1.60

No. C271 contains one 38x56mm stamp.

Diana Type of 1982

1982, July 20 **Litho.** *Perf. 13½*

C272 A150 300fr multi 1.60 80
C273 A150 500fr multi 2.50 1.40

Souvenir Sheet

C274 A150 600fr multi 3.50 1.60

No. C274 contains one 56x32mm stamp.

Christmas 1982 — AP83

Raphael Paintings.

1982, Dec. *Perf. 13*

C275 AP83 150fr Beautiful Gardener 80 40
C276 AP83 500fr Holy Family 2.50 1.40

Space Type of 1982

Designs: Various satellites and space scenes. No. C279A, European communications satellite, controller. No. C279B, Viking on Mars, vert.

1982, Aug. 15 **Litho.** *Perf. 13½*

C277 A151 300fr multi 1.60 80
C278 A151 500fr multi 2.50 1.40

Souvenir Sheet

C279 A151 600fr multi 3.50 1.60

Litho. & Embossed
Size: 60x36mm

C279A A151 1500fr gold & multi

Souvenir Sheet

C279B A151 1500fr gold & multi

Nos. C279A-C279B exist imperf. No. C279A exists in a souvenir sheet of one. No. C279B contains one 36x60mm stamp.

Birth of Prince William of Wales, June 21, 1982 — AP84

Designs: No. C281, Diana, William, Charles. No. 281B, Diana, William, vert.

1983, Jan. 22

C280 AP84 500fr Diana, William 2.50 1.40

Souvenir Sheet

C281 AP84 600fr Family 3.50 1.60

Litho. & Embossed

C281A AP84 1500fr gold & multi

Souvenir Sheet

C281B AP84 1500fr gold & multi

Manned Flight Bicentenary
AP85

1983, Apr.

C282 AP85 65fr Robert's & Hullin's balloon 35 16
C283 AP85 130fr John Wise's, 1859 70 35
C284 AP85 350fr Mail balloon, 1870 1.75 90
C285 AP85 400fr Dirigible Underberg 2.25 1.10
Nos. C282-C285 (4) 5.05 2.51

Souvenir Sheet

C286 AP85 500fr Montgolfiere, 1783 2.50 1.40

Pre-Olympics — AP86

Various equestrian events.

1983, July **Litho.** *Perf. 13*

C287 AP86 100fr multi 50 20
C288 AP86 200fr multi 1.00 45
C289 AP86 300fr multi 1.40 55
C290 AP86 400fr multi 1.75 90
Nos. C287-C290 (4) 4.65 2.10

Souvenir Sheet

C291 AP86 500fr multi 2.25 1.10

Endangered Animals, Rotary Emblem
AP87

1983, Nov. 14 **Litho.** *Perf. 13½*

C291A AP87 400fr Black rhinoceros, parrot, zebra, scouts 2.00 1.00
C292 AP87 500fr shown 1.60 80

Souvenir Sheet

C293 AP87 600fr Leopard 2.00 1.00

15th World Scout Jamboree, Alberta (400fr). No. C293 contains one 47x32mm stamp.

Christmas 1983 — AP88

Paintings: 130fr, Annunciation, by da Vinci. 205fr, Virgin of the Rocks, by da Vinci. 350fr, Adoration of the Shepherds, by Rubens. 500fr, Virgin and Child with Donor, by Rubens.

1984, Jan. 3 **Litho.** *Perf. 13*

C294 AP88 130fr multi 45 22
C295 AP88 205fr multi 70 35
C296 AP88 350fr multi 1.10 55
C297 AP88 500fr multi 1.60 80
Nos. C294-C297 (4) 3.85 1.92

1984 Summer Olympics — AP89

Various gymnastic and rhythmic gymnastic events. 65fr, 100fr, 205fr, 350fr vert.

1984, Mar. 13 Litho. *Perf. 13*

C298	AP89 65fr multi		22	15
C299	AP89 100fr multi		35	16
C300	AP89 130fr multi		42	22
C301	AP89 205fr multi		70	35
C302	AP89 350fr multi		1.10	60
	Nos. C298-C302 (5)		2.79	1.48

Souvenir Sheet

Perf. 13½x13

C302A	AP89 500fr Rhythmic formation	1.60	80

For overprint see No. 705.

Summer Olympics Winners AP90

1985, Jan. 7 Litho. *Perf. 14*

C303	AP90 60fr 400 meter relay	16	15
C304	AP90 140fr 400 meter hurdles	40	20
C305	AP90 300fr 5000 meter race	90	45
C306	AP90 440fr Decathlon	1.20	60
	Nos. C303-C306 (4)	2.66	1.40

Souvenir Sheet

C307	AP90 500fr 800 meter race, horiz.	1.40	65

Christmas 1984 — AP91

Paintings by Titian: 130fr, Virgin and Infant Jesus. 350fr, Virgin with Rabbit. 400fr, Virgin and Child.

1985, Jan. 17 Litho. *Perf. 13*

C308	AP91 130fr multi	38	20
C309	AP91 350fr multi	90	50
C310	AP91 400fr multi	1.10	60
	Nos. C308-C310 (3)	2.38	1.30

Audubon Bicentenary — AP92

1985, Jan. 25 Litho. *Perf. 13*

C311	AP92 60fr Otus asio	16	15
C312	AP92 110fr Coccizus minor, vert.	32	16
C313	AP92 200fr Zenaidura macroura, vert.	60	28
C314	AP92 500fr Aix sponsa	1.40	70
	Nos. C311-C314 (4)	2.48	1.29

Christmas 1985 — AP93

Religious paintings: 100fr, Virgin with Angels, by the Master of Burgo de Osma. 200fr, Nativity, by Louis Le Nain (1593-1648). 400fr, Virgin and Child with Dove, by Piero de Cosimo (1462-1521).

1985, Dec. 24 Litho. *Perf. 13*

C315	AP93 100fr multi	35	20
C316	AP93 200fr multi	70	38
C317	AP93 400fr multi	1.50	70
	Nos. C315-C317 (3)	2.55	1.28

Halley's Comet — AP94

1986, Mar. 8

C318	AP94 110fr Edmond Halley	40	20
C319	AP94 130fr Giotto probe	45	22
C320	AP94 200fr Comet, planet	70	38
C321	AP94 300fr Vega probe	1.10	55
C322	AP94 400fr Space shuttle	1.50	70
	Nos. C318-C322 (5)	4.15	2.05

Christmas AP95

Painting details: 250fr, Nativity, by Giotto. 440fr, Adoration of the Magi, by Botticelli, vert. 500fr, Nativity, by Giotto, diff.

1986, Dec. 24 Litho. *Perf. 13½*

C323	AP95 250fr multi	90	45
C324	AP95 440fr multi	1.60	80
C325	AP95 500fr multi	1.75	90
	Nos. C323-C325 (3)	4.25	2.15

Tennis at the 1988 Olympics — AP96

Various plays.

1986, Dec. 31 *Perf. 12½*

C326	AP96 150fr multi	55	25
C327	AP96 250fr multi, vert.	90	45
C328	AP96 440fr multi, vert.	1.60	80
C329	AP96 600fr multi	2.25	1.10
	Nos. C326-C329 (4)	5.30	2.60

1988 Summer Olympics, Seoul — AP97

1987, June 15 Litho. *Perf. 13*

C330	AP97 100fr Triple jump, vert.	55	28
C331	AP97 200fr High jump	1.10	55
C332	AP97 300fr Long jump	1.65	82
C333	AP97 400fr Pole vault, vert.	2.25	1.10
	Nos. C330-C333 (4)	5.55	2.75

Souvenir Sheet

C334	AP97 500fr High jump, diff.	2.75	1.40

1988 Summer Olympics, Seoul — AP98

Stamps on stamps and gymnasts: 90fr, No. C94, balance beam, vert. 200fr, No. C21, balance beam, diff. 300fr, No. C22, pommel horse. 400fr, No. C23, parallel bars. 500fr, No. C93, rings.

1988, July 26 Litho. *Perf. 13*

C335	AP98 90fr multi	58	30
C336	AP98 200fr multi	1.30	65
C337	AP98 300fr multi	1.90	95
C338	AP98 400fr multi	2.60	1.30
	Nos. C335-C338 (4)	6.38	3.20

Souvenir Sheet

C339	AP98 500fr multi	3.25	1.60

1st Moon Landing, 20th Anniv. AP99

1989, Aug. 4 Litho. *Perf. 13*

C340	AP99 40fr Apollo 11	25	15
C341	AP99 80fr Apollo 15	52	25
C342	AP99 130fr Apollo 16	85	42
C343	AP99 1000fr Apollo 17	6.40	3.20
	Nos. C340-C343 (4)	8.02	4.02

World Cup Soccer Championships, Italy — AP100

1990, July 7 Litho. *Perf. 13*

C344	AP100 5fr multicolored	15	15
C345	AP100 30fr multi, diff.	22	15
C346	AP100 500fr multi, diff.	3.75	1.90
C347	AP100 1000fr multi, diff.	7.50	3.75
	Nos. C344-C347 (4)	11.62	5.95

Charles de Gaulle (1890-1979) — AP101

1990, July 27 *Perf. 13½*

C348	AP101 500fr multicolored	3.50	1.75

No. C348 exists in a souvenir sheet of 1.

Don Mattingly, Baseball Player — AP102

Saturn V Rocket, Apollo 11 Astronauts AP103

Charles de Gaulle, Birth Cent. AP104

Design: No. C352, De Gaulle and Cross of Lorraine.

1990, July 27 Litho. *Perf. 13½*

C349	AP102 300fr multicolored	2.10	1.05

Souvenir Sheet

C350	AP103 1000fr multicolored	7.00	3.50

Litho. & Embossed

C351	AP104 1500fr gold & multi		

Souvenir Sheet

C352	AP104 1500fr gold & multi		

No. C351 exists in souvenir sheet of 1. For overprints see Nos. C355-C356.

Visit of Pope John Paul II to Africa AP105

Pope John Paul II and: No. C353, Mother Theresa, portrait. No. C354, Papal arms, globe.

1993 Litho. & Embossed *Perf. 13½*

C353	AP105	1500fr gold & multi	

Souvenir Sheet

C354	AP105	1500fr gold & multi	

No. C351 Ovptd. "6 JUIN / 1944"
No. C352 Ovptd. in Silver in Sheet Margin

1994 Litho. & Embossed *Perf. 13½*

C355	AP104	1500fr gold & multi	

Souvenir Sheet

C356	AP104	1500fr gold & multi	

Overprint on No. C356 contains map, soldiers and "50 eme ANNIVERSAIRE DU /DEBARQUEMENT." No. C355 exists in souvenir sheet of 1.

AIR POST SEMI-POSTAL STAMPS

Central African Republic

Isis of Kalabsha — SPAP1

Unwmk.

1964, Mar. 7 Engr. *Perf. 13*

CB1	SPAP1	25fr + 10fr multi	65	65
CB2	SPAP1	50fr + 10fr multi	1.00	1.00
CB3	SPAP1	100fr + 10fr multi	1.60	1.60
		Nos. CB1-CB3 (3)	3.25	3.25

UNESCO world campaign to save historic monuments in Nubia.

African Infants and Globe — SPAP2

1971, Dec. 11 Litho. *Perf. 13x13½*

CB4	SPAP2	140fr + 50fr multi	1.60	1.00

25th anniv. of UNICEF, and Children's Day.

POSTAGE DUE STAMPS

Central African Republic

Sternotomis Virescens — D1

Beetles: No. J2, Sternotomis gama. No. J3, Augosoma centaurus. No. J4, Phosphorus virescens and ceroplesis carabarica. No. J5, Cetoine scaraboidae. No. J6, Ceroplesis S.P. No. J7, Macrorhina S.P. No. J8, Cetoine scaraboidae. No. J9, Phryneta leprosa. No. J10, Taurina longiceps. No. J11, Monohamus griseoplagiatus. No. J12, Jambonus trifasciatus.

Unwmk.

1962, Oct. 15 Engr. *Perf. 11*

J1	D1	50c grn & dp org	15	15
J2	D1	50c grn & dp org	15	15
J3	D1	1fr blk, brn & lt grn	15	15
J4	D1	1fr blk, brn & lt grn	15	15
J5	D1	2fr blk, org & yel grn	15	15
J6	D1	2fr blk & red org	15	15
J7	D1	5fr brn, org & grn	15	15
J8	D1	5fr brn, org, grn & red	15	15
J9	D1	10fr blk, grn & brn	30	30
J10	D1	10fr blk, brn & grn	30	30
J11	D1	25fr blk, bl grn & brn	45	45
J12	D1	25fr blk, brn & bl grn	45	45
		Set value	2.10	2.10

Each two stamps of the same denomination are printed together in the sheet, se-tenant at the base.

Giant Anteater — D2

1985, Jan. 25 Litho. *Perf. 12½*

J13	D2	5fr multi	15	15
J14	D2	20fr multi	15	15
J15	D2	30fr multi	15	15
		Set value	22	15

MILITARY STAMPS

Central African Republic

No. 1 Overprinted **FM**

1962, Jan. 1 Unwmk. Engr. *Perf. 13*

M1	A1	bl, car, grn & yel	8.25	8.25

=

No. 1 Overprinted **FM**

1963

M2	A1	bl, car, grn & yel	9.00	9.00

OFFICIAL STAMPS

Central African Republic

Coat of Arms — O1

Imprint: "d'après G. RICHER SO.GE.IM."

Perf. 13x12½

1965-69 Litho. Unwmk.

Arms in Original Colors

O1	O1	1fr blk & brn org	15	15
O2	O1	2fr blk & violet	15	15
O3	O1	5fr blk & gray	15	15
O4	O1	10fr blk & green	18	15
O5	O1	20fr blk & red brn	30	22
O6	O1	30fr blk & emer ('69)	55	40
O7	O1	50fr blk & dk bl	65	55
O8	O1	100fr blk & bister	1.40	80
O9	O1	130fr blk & ver ('69)	2.00	1.60
O10	O1	200fr blk & claret	3.00	2.00
		Nos. O1-O10 (10)	8.53	6.17

Redrawn

Imprint: "d'après G. RICHER DELRIEU"

1971 Photo. *Perf. 12x12½*

Arms in Original Colors

O11	O1	5fr blk & gray	15	15
O12	O1	30fr blk & emer	30	18
O13	O1	40fr blk & dp claret	40	22
O14	O1	100fr blk & bister	90	45
O15	O1	140fr blk & lt bl	1.60	65
O16	O1	200fr blk & claret	2.25	1.10
		Nos. O11-O16 (6)	5.60	2.75

Empire

Nos. O11, O13-O16 Overprinted with Bar and "EMPIRE CENTRAFRICAIN"

1977 Litho. *Perf. 12x12½*

O17	O1	5fr multi	15	15
O18	O1	40fr multi	22	18
O19	O1	100fr multi	55	38
O20	O1	140fr multi	80	60
O21	O1	200fr multi	1.25	90
		Nos. O17-O21 (5)	2.97	2.21

Type of 1965 Inscribed: "EMPIRE CENTRAFRICAIN"

1978, July Litho. *Perf. 12½*

O22	O1	1fr multi	15	15
O23	O1	2fr multi	15	15
O24	O1	5fr multi	15	15
O25	O1	10fr multi	15	15
O26	O1	15fr multi	15	15
O27	O1	20fr multi	15	15
O28	O1	30fr multi	20	20
O29	O1	40fr multi	25	25
O30	O1	50fr multi	35	35
O31	O1	60fr multi	40	40
O32	O1	100fr multi	65	65
O33	O1	130fr multi	90	90
O34	O1	140fr multi	90	90
O35	O1	200fr multi	1.40	1.40
		Nos. O22-O35 (14)	5.95	5.95

CENTRAL LITHUANIA

LOCATION — North of Poland and east of Lithuania
CAPITAL — Vilnius

At one time Central Lithuania was a grand duchy of Lithuania but at the end of the 18th Century it fell under Russian rule. After World War I, Lithuania regained her sovereignty but certain areas were occupied by Poland. During the Russo-Polish war this territory was seized by Lithuania whose claim was promptly recognized by the Soviet Government. Under the leadership of the Polish General Zeligowski the territory was recaptured and it was during this occupation the stamps of Central Lithuania came into being. Subsequently the territory became a part of Poland.

100 Fennigi = 1 Markka

Coat of Arms — A1

Perf. 11½, Imperf.

1920-21 Typo. Unwmk.

1	A1	25f red	15	38
2	A1	25f dark grn ('21)	15	38
3	A1	1m blue	15	38
4	A1	1m dark brn ('21)	15	38
5	A1	2m violet	20	38
6	A1	2m orange ('21)	20	38
		Nos. 1-6 (6)	1.00	2.28

For surcharges see Nos. B1-B5.

Lithuanian Stamps of 1919 Surcharged in Blue or Black

Perf. 11½x12, 12½x11½, 14

1920, Nov. 23 Wmk. 145

13	A5	2m on 15sk lil	5.00	5.00
a.		Inverted surcharge	*125.00*	
14	A5	4m on 10sk red	5.00	5.00
a.		Inverted surcharge	*125.00*	
15	A5	4m on 20sk dl bl (Bk)	5.00	5.00
a.		Inverted surcharge	*125.00*	
16	A5	4m on 30sk buff	5.00	5.00
a.		Inverted surcharge	*125.00*	
17	A6	6m on 50sk lt grn	5.00	5.00
a.		4m on 50sk (error)	*125.00*	
b.		10m on 50sk (error)	*125.00*	
18	A6	6m on 60sk vio & red	5.00	5.00
a.		4m on 60sk (error)	*125.00*	
b.		10m on 60sk (error)	*125.00*	
19	A6	6m on 75sk bis & red	5.00	5.00
a.		4m on 75sk (error)	*125.00*	
b.		10m on 75sk (error)	*125.00*	
20	A8	10m on 1auk gray & red	7.50	7.50
a.		Inverted surcharge	*190.00*	
21	A8	10m on 3auk lt brn & red	250.00	275.00
22	A8	10m on 5auk bl grn & red	250.00	275.00
		Nos. 13-22 (10)	542.50	592.50

Reprints of Nos. 17a, 17b, 18a, 18b, 19a, 19b. Value, each $37.50.
Counterfeits of Nos. 21-22 exist.

Lithuanian Girl — A2

Warrior — A3

Holy Gate of Vilnius — A4

Tower and Cathedral, Vilnius — A5

Rector's Insignia — A6

Gen. Lucien Zeligowski — A7

Perf. 11½, Imperf.

1920 Litho. Unwmk.

23	A2	25f gray	15	30
24	A3	1m orange	15	30
25	A4	2m claret	25	65
26	A5	4m gray grn & buff	38	65
27	A6	6m rose & gray	75	80
28	A7	10m brown & yellow	1.25	1.90
		Nos. 23-28 (6)	2.93	4.60

For surcharges see Nos. B13-B14, B17-B19.

St. Anne's Church, Vilnius — A8

St. Stanislas Cathedral, Vilnius — A9

White Eagle, White Knight Vytis — A10

Queen Hedwig and King Ladislas II Jagello — A11

Coat of Arms of Vilnius A12

Poczobut Astronomical Observatory A13

Union of Lithuania and Poland — A14

Tadeusz Kosciuszko and Adam Mickiewicz A15

1921 *Perf. 13½, 14, Imperf.*

35	A8	1m dk gray & yel	25	38
36	A9	2m rose & green	25	38
37	A10	3m dark green	25	38
38	A11	4m brown & buff	25	38
39	A12	5m red brown	25	38
40	A13	6m slate & buff	25	50
41	A14	10m red vio & buff	62	85
42	A15	20m blk brn & buff	75	85
		Nos. 35-42 (8)	2.87	4.10

Peasant Girl Sowing — A16

White Eagle and Vytis — A17

Great Theater at Vilnius A18

Allegory: Peace and Industry A19

Gen. Zeligowski Entering Vilnius A20

Gen. Zeligowski A21

1921-22 *Perf. 11½, Imperf.*

53	A16	10m brown ('22)	2.50	2.75
54	A17	25m red & yel ('22)	2.50	2.50
55	A18	50m dk blue ('22)	2.75	2.75
56	A19	75m violet ('22)	3.75	3.75
57	A20	100m bl & bister	2.75	3.75
58	A21	150m ol grn & brn	3.00	3.75
		Nos. 53-58 (6)	17.25	19.25

Opening of the Natl. Parliament, Nos. 53-56; anniv. of the entry of General Zeligowski into Vilnius, Nos. 57-58.

SEMI-POSTAL STAMPS

Nos. 1-6 Surcharged in Black or Red

NA
ŚLĄSK
2 M.

1921 Unwmk. *Perf. 11½, Imperf.*

B1	A1	25f + 2m red (Bk)	60	1.00
B2	A1	25f + 2m dk green	60	1.00
B3	A1	1m + 2m blue	75	1.00
B4	A1	1m + 2m dk brown	75	1.00
B5	A1	2m + 2m violet	75	1.00
B6	A1	2m + 2m orange	75	1.00
		Nos. B1-B6 (6)	4.20	6.00

The surcharge means "For Silesia 2 marks." The stamps were intended to provide a fund to assist the plebiscite in Upper Silesia.

Nos. 25, 26 Surcharged:

✚ 1 (a) ✚ 1 M (b)

Perf. 11½, Imperf.

B13	A4 (a)	2m + 1(m) claret	1.50	1.75
B14	A5 (b)	4m + 1m gray green & buff	1.50	1.75

Nos. 25-26, 28 with inset 10M

Perf. 11½, Imperf.

B17	A4	2m + 1m claret	75	75
B18	A5	4m + 1m gray green & buff	75	75
B19	A7	10m + 2m brn & yel	75	75
		Nos. B13-B19 (5)	5.25	5.75

POSTAGE DUE STAMPS

University, Vilnius — D1

Castle Hill, Vilnius — D2

Castle Ruins, Troki — D3

Holy Gate, Vilnius — D4

St. Stanislas Cathedral — D5

St. Anne's Church, Vilnius — D6

1920-21 Unwmk. *Perf. 11½, Imperf.*

J1	D1	50f red violet	25	50
J2	D2	1m green	25	50
J3	D3	2m red violet	25	50
J4	D4	3m red violet	40	65
J5	D5	5m red violet	65	1.00
J6	D6	20m scarlet	2.00	2.25
		Nos. J1-J6 (6)	3.80	5.40

CHAD

(Tchad)

LOCATION — Central Africa, south of Libya
GOVT. — Republic
AREA — 495,572 sq. mi.
POP. — 5,122,000 (est. 1984)
CAPITAL — N'djamena

A former dependency of Ubangi-Shari, Chad became a separate French colony in 1920. In 1934, the colonies of Chad, Gabon, Middle Congo and Ubangi-Shari were grouped in a single administrative unit known as French Equatorial Africa, with the capital at Brazzaville. The Republic of Chad was proclaimed November 28, 1958.

100 Centimes = 1 Franc

Catalogue values for unused stamps in this country are for Never Hinged items, beginning with Scott 64 in the regular postage section, Scott B1 in the semi-postal section, Scott C1 in the air post section, Scott CB1 in the air post semi-postal section, Scott J23 in the postage due section, Scott M1 in the military stamp section, and Scott O1 in the officials section.

See French Equatorial Africa No. 190 for stamp inscribed "Tchad."

Types of Middle Congo, 1907-17, Overprinted **TCHAD**

Perf. 14x13½, 13½x14

1922 **Unwmk.**

1	A1	1c red & vio	15	15
a.		Overprint omitted	75.00	
2	A1	2c ol brn & sal	20	20
a.		Overprint omitted	125.00	
3	A1	4c ind & vio	28	28
4	A1	5c choc & grn	35	35
5	A1	10c dp grn & gray grn	60	60
6	A1	15c vio & red	80	80
7	A1	20c grn & vio	2.00	2.00
8	A2	25c ol brn & brn	3.75	3.75
9	A2	30c rose & pale rose	48	48
10	A2	35c dl bl & dl rose	90	90
11	A2	40c choc & grn	90	90
12	A2	45c vio & grn	90	90
13	A2	50c dk bl & pale bl	1.00	1.00
14	A2	60c on 75c vio, *pnksh*	1.60	1.60
a.		"TCHAD" omitted	125.00	
b.		"60" omitted	125.00	
15	A1	75c red & vio	90	90
16	A3	1fr indigo & sal	4.25	4.25
17	A3	2fr indigo & vio	6.75	6.75
18	A3	5fr ind & ol brn	5.75	5.75
		Nos. 1-18 (18)	31.56	31.56

Stamps of 1922 Overprinted in Various Colors:

AFRIQUE EQUATORIALE FRANÇAISE Nos. 19-28 — **AFRIQUE EQUATORIALE FRANÇAISE** Nos. 29-50

1924-33

19	A1	1c red & vio	15	15
a.		"TCHAD" omitted	75.00	
b.		Double overprint	65.00	
20	A1	2c ol brn & sal	15	15
a.		"TCHAD" omitted	75.00	
b.		Double overprint	80.00	
21	A1	4c ind & vio	15	15
a.		"TCHAD" omitted	400.00	
22	A1	5c choc & grn (Bl)	40	25
a.		"TCHAD" omitted	75.00	
23	A1	5c choc & grn	25	22
a.		"TCHAD" omitted	90.00	
24	A1	10c dp grn & gray grn (Bl)	25	22
25	A1	10c dp grn & gray grn	25	22
26	A1	10c red org & blk ('25)	18	18
27	A1	15c vio & red	25	22
28	A1	20c grn & vio	25	22
29	A2	25c ol brn & brn	25	22
30	A2	30c rose & pale rose	15	15
31	A2	30c gray & bl (R) ('25)	15	15
32	A2	30c dk grn & grn ('27)	40	40
a.		"Afrique Equatoriale Francaise" omitted	110.00	
33	A2	35c ind & dl rose	15	15
34	A2	40c choc & grn	40	40
a.		Dbl. overprint (R + Bk)	110.00	
35	A2	45c vio & grn	32	32
a.		Dbl. overprint (R + Bk)	110.00	
36	A2	50c dk bl & pale bl	32	32
a.		Inverted overprint	60.00	
37	A2	50c grn & vio ('25)	40	40
38	A2	65c org brn & bl ('28)	90	90
39	A2	75c red & vio	25	25
40	A2	75c dp bl & lt bl (R) ('25)	18	18
a.		"TCHAD" omitted	75.00	
41	A2	75c rose & dk brn ('28)	90	90
42	A2	90c brn red & pink ('30)	2.75	2.75
43	A3	1fr ind & salmon	60	60
44	A3	1.10fr dl grn & bl ('28)	90	90
45	A3	1.25fr org brn & lt bl ('33)	2.75	2.75
46	A3	1.50fr ultra & bl ('30)	2.75	2.75
47	A3	1.75fr ol brn & vio ('33)	20.00	20.00
48	A3	2fr ind & vio	1.00	90
49	A3	3fr red vio ('30)	4.00	4.00
50	A3	5fr ind & ol brn	1.00	90
		Nos. 19-50 (32)	42.80	42.27

Types of 1922 Overprinted like Nos. 29-50 and Surcharged with New Values

1924-27

51	A2	60c on 75c dk vio, *pnksh*	25	25
a.		"60" omitted	57.50	
52	A3	65c on 1fr brn & ol grn ('25)	65	65
53	A3	85c on 1fr brn & ol grn ('25)	65	65
54	A2	90c on 75c brn red & rose red ('27)	65	65
55	A3	1.25fr on 1fr dk bl & ultra (R) ('26)	18	18
a.		"Afrique Equatoriale Francaise" omitted	75.00	
56	A3	1.50fr on 1fr ultra & bl ('27)	65	65
57	A3	3fr on 5fr org brn & dl red ('27)	1.75	1.75
58	A3	10fr on 5fr ol grn & cer ('27)	4.50	4.50
59	A3	20fr on 5fr vio & ver ('27)	7.00	7.00
		Nos. 51-59 (9)	16.28	16.28

Colonial Exposition Issue
Common Design Types

1931 Engr. *Perf. 12½*

Name of Country in Black

60	CD70	40c deep green	1.75	1.75
61	CD71	50c violet	1.75	1.75
62	CD72	90c red orange	1.75	1.75
63	CD73	1.50fr dull blue	1.75	1.75
		Nos. 60-63 (4)	7.00	7.00

Catalogue values for unused stamps in this section, from this point to the end of the section, are for Never Hinged items.

Republic

"Birth of the Republic" A1

"Solidarity of the Community" A2

1959 Unwmk. Engr. *Perf. 13*

64	A1	15fr ultra, grn & maroon	15	15
65	A2	25fr dk grn & dp claret	25	15
		Set value		16

1st anniv. of the proclamation of the Republic.

Common Design Types pictured in section at front of book.

Imperforates
Most Chad stamps from 1959 onward exist imperforate in issued and trial colors, and also in small presentation sheets in issued colors.

C.C.T.A. Issue
Common Design Type

1960

66		CD106 50fr rose lil & dk pur	55	50

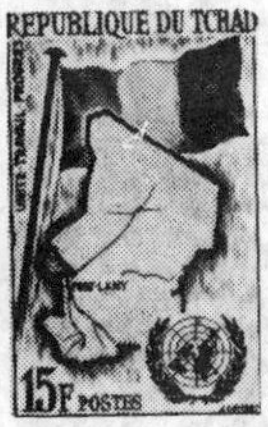

Flag and Map of Chad and UN Emblem — A3

Unwmk.

1961, Jan. 11 Engr. *Perf. 13*

Flag in blue, yellow and carmine

67	A3	15fr brn & dk bl	20	15
68	A3	25fr org brn & dk bl	25	15
69	A3	85fr slate grn & dk bl	80	45
		Nos. 67-69 (3)	1.25	75

Admission of Chad to United Nations.

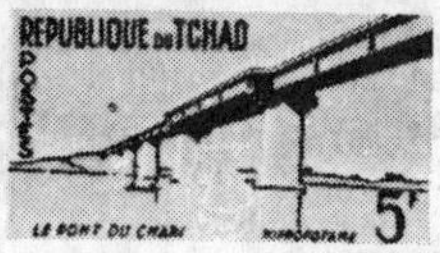

Chari Bridge and Hippopotamus — A4

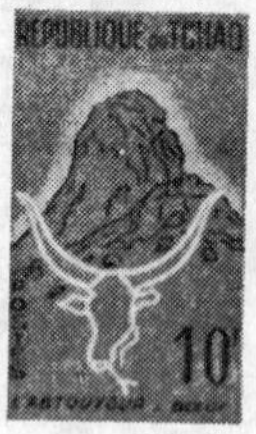

Abtouyoua Mountain and Ox — A5

Designs: 50c, Biltine and dorcas gazelle. 1fr, Logone and elephant. 2fr, Batha and lion. 3fr, Salamat and buffalo. 4fr, Ouaddai and Kudu. 15fr, Bessada and giant eland. 20fr, Tibesti mountains and mouflon. 25fr, Rocherg and antelope. 30fr, Kanem and cheetah. 60fr, Borkou and oryx. 85fr, Gorge of Archet and addax.

Perf. 13¹/₂x14, 14x13¹/₂

1961-62 **Typo.**

70	A5	50c yel grn & dk grn ('62)	15	15
71	A5	1fr bl grn & dk bl grn ('62)	15	15
72	A5	2fr dk red brn & blk ('62)	15	15
73	A5	3fr ocher & dl grn ('62)	15	15
74	A5	4fr dk crim & blk ('62)	15	15
75	A4	5fr yellow & blk	15	15
76	A5	10fr pink & blk	15	15
77	A5	15fr lilac & blk ('62)	16	15
78	A5	20fr red & blk	20	15
79	A5	25fr blue & blk ('62)	25	15
80	A5	30fr ultra & blk ('62)	35	15
81	A5	60fr yel & ol grn ('62)	60	20
82	A5	85fr org & blk	80	35
		Set value	2.75	1.30

First anniversary of Independence.
For overprint see No. M1.

Abidjan Games Issue
Common Design Type

1962, July 21 **Photo.** ***Perf. 12¹/₂x12***

83	CD109	20fr Relay race	20	15
84	CD109	50fr High jump	40	30

See No. C8.

African-Malgache Union Issue
Common Design Type

1962, Sept. 8 **Unwmk.**

85	CD110	30fr dk bl, bluish grn, red & gold	35	30

Pres. Ngarta Tombalbaye — A7

1963, Apr. 22 ***Perf. 12x12¹/₂***

86	A7	20fr multi	20	15
87	A7	85fr multi	80	30

Space Communciations Issue

Waves Around Globe — A8

Design: 100fr, Orbit patterns around globe.

Perf. 12¹/₂

1963, Sept. 19 **Unwmk.** **Photo.**

88	A8	25fr grn & pur	25	22
89	A8	100fr pink & ultra	1.00	70

Ancestral Mask — A9

Excavated Sao Art: 5fr, Clay weight. 25fr, Ancestral clay statuette. 60fr, Gazelle, bronze. 80fr, Bronze pectoral.

1963, Dec. 2 **Engr.** ***Perf. 13***

90	A9	5fr brt grn & red brn	15	15
91	A9	15fr gray, dl cl & red	16	15
92	A9	25fr dk bl & org brn	25	16
93	A9	60fr org brn & slate grn	60	25
94	A9	80fr org red & olive	80	25
		Nos. 90-94 (5)	1.96	
		Set value		80

UNESCO Emblem, Scales and Tree — A10

1963, Dec. 10

95	A10	25fr green & maroon	25	20

15th anniv. of the Universal Declaration of Human Rights.

Potter — A11

Perf. 12¹/₂

1964, Feb. 5 **Unwmk.** **Engr.**

96	A11	10fr shown	15	15
97	A11	30fr Boatmaker	30	15
98	A11	50fr Weaver	50	20
99	A11	85fr Smiths	55	35
		Nos. 96-99 (4)	1.50	85

Barograph and WMO Emblem A12

1964, Mar. 23 ***Perf. 13***

100	A12	50fr red lil, pur & ultra	55	30

Fourth World Meteorological Day.

Cotton — A13

Design: 25fr, Royal poinciana.

1964, Apr. 6 **Photo.** ***Perf. 12¹/₂x13***

101	A13	20fr multi	25	15
102	A13	25fr multi	25	15

Co-operation Issue
Common Design Type

1964, Nov. 7 **Engr.** ***Perf. 13***

103	CD119	25fr ver, dk bl & dk brn	25	20

National Guard and Map of Chad — A14

Design: 25fr, Infantry, flag and map, vert.

Perf. 12¹/₂x13, 13x12¹/₂

1964, Dec. 11 **Photo.**

104	A14	20fr multi	22	15
105	A14	25fr lt bl & multi	25	15

Issued to honor the army of Chad.

Aoudad or Barbary Sheep — A15

Animals: 10fr, Addax. 20fr, Oryx. 25fr, Derby's eland, vert. 30fr, Giraffe, buffalo and lion, Zakouma Park, vert. 85fr, Great kudu at water hole., vert.

Perf. 12¹/₂x12, 12x12¹/₂

1965, Jan. 11 **Unwmk.**

106	A15	5fr dk brn, ultra & yel	15	15
107	A15	10fr ultra, org & blk	15	15
108	A15	20fr multi	20	15
109	A15	25fr multi	25	15
110	A15	30fr multi	30	16
111	A15	85fr multi	80	42
		Nos. 106-111 (6)	1.85	
		Set value		95

Olsen Perforator A16

Designs: 60fr, Mildé telephone, vert. 100fr, Distributor of Baudot telegraph.

1965, May 17 **Engr.** ***Perf. 13***

112	A16	30fr multi	30	20
113	A16	60fr multi	60	40
114	A16	100fr multi	90	65
		Nos. 112-114 (3)	1.80	1.25

Cent. of the ITU.

Motorized Police — A17

Perf. 12¹/₂x12

1965, June 22 **Photo.** **Unwmk.**

115	A17	25fr ol, dk grn, gold & brn	25	16

Issued to honor the national police.

Guitar — A18

Musical Instruments from National Museum: 1fr, Drum and stool, vert. 3fr, Shoulder drums, vert. 15fr, Viol. 60fr, Harp, vert.

1965, Oct. 26 **Engr.** ***Perf. 13***

Size: 22x36mm, 36x22mm

116	A18	1fr car, emer & brn	15	15
117	A18	2fr red, brt lil & brn	15	15
118	A18	3fr red & sepia	15	15
119	A18	15fr red, ocher & sl grn	16	15
120	A18	60fr maroon & slate grn	60	25
		Nos. 116-120,C23 (6)	2.11	
		Set value		80

Head and Bowl — A19

WHO Headquarters, Geneva — A20

Sao Art: 20fr, Head. 60fr, Head with crown. 80fr, Circlet with human head. From excavations at Bouta Kebira and Gawi.

1966, Apr. 1 **Engr.** ***Perf. 13***

121	A19	15fr ol, choc & ultra	15	15
122	A19	20fr dk red, brn & bl grn	20	15
123	A19	60fr brt bl, choc & ver	60	35
124	A19	80fr brn org, grn & pur	80	40
		Nos. 121-124 (4)	1.75	1.05

Issued to publicize the International Negro Arts Festival, Dakar, Senegal, Apr. 1-24.

No. 86 Surcharged with New Value and Two Bars in Orange

1966, Apr. 15 **Photo.** ***Perf. 12x12¹/₂***

125	A7	25fr on 20fr multi	25	15

1966, May 3

126	A20	25fr car, lt ultra & yel	25	20
127	A20	32fr emer, ultra & yel	30	22

New WHO Headquarters, Geneva.

Staff of Mercury and Map of Africa — A21

1966, May 24 ***Perf. 12¹/₂x12***

128	A21	30fr multi	30	15

Central African Customs and Economic Union (Union Douaniere et Economique de l'Afrique Centrale, UDEAC).

Soccer Player — A22

Design: 60fr, Soccer player facing left.

1966, July 12 **Engr.** ***Perf. 13***

129	A22	30fr grn, bl grn & mar	30	16
130	A22	60fr dk bl, gray & car	60	35

8th World Cup Soccer Championship, Wembley, England, July 11-30.

Young Men, Flag and Emblem A23

1966, Aug. 11 **Photo.** ***Perf. 12¹/₂x13***

131	A23	25fr dk bl & multi	25	16

Chad Youth Movement.

Greek Columns and UNESCO Emblem — A24

1966, Aug. 23 **Engr.** ***Perf. 13***
132 A24 32fr sl bl, vio & car rose 35 20

20th anniv. of UNESCO.

Reconstructed Skull of Chadanthropus — A25

1966, Sept. 20 **Engr.** ***Perf. 13***
133 A25 30fr gray, red & ocher 30 15

Yves Coppens' discovery of Lake Chad man.

Stone Axe — A26

Prehistoric Tools: 30fr, Flint arrow head. 85fr, Bone harpoon. 100fr, Sandstone millstone with grinder.

1966, Dec. 11 **Engr.** ***Perf. 13***
134 A26 25fr dp bl, red & dk brn 22 15
135 A26 30fr brn, dp bl & blk 30 15
136 A26 85fr dk red, brt bl & brn 80 38
137 A26 100fr Prus grn, dk brn & bis brn 90 45
a. Miniature sheet of 4, #134-137 2.50 2.60
Nos. 134-137 (4) 2.22 1.13

Map of Chad and Various Sports — A27

1967, Apr. 10 **Photo.** ***Perf. 12x12½***
138 A27 25fr multi 25 16

Issued for Sports Day, Apr. 10, 1967.

Colotis Protomedia A28

Various Butterflies.

1967, May 23 **Photo.** ***Perf. 12½x12***
139 A28 5fr blue & multi 15 15
140 A28 10fr emerald & multi 15 15
141 A28 20fr orange & multi 20 15
142 A28 130fr red & multi 1.10 60
Nos. 139-142 (4) 1.60
Set value 87

WHO Headquarters, Brazzaville A29

1967, Sept. 23 **Photo.** ***Perf. 12½x13***
143 A29 30fr vio bl & multi 30 16

Opening of the Regional Office of the WHO, Brazzaville.

Jamboree Emblem and Boy Scouts — A30

Design: 32fr, Jamboree emblem and Boy Scout.

1967, Oct. 17 **Photo.** ***Perf. 12½x13***
144 A30 25fr multi 22 15
145 A30 32fr multi 35 16

12th Boy Scout World Jamboree, Farragut State Park, Idaho, Aug. 1-9.

Great Mills of Chad — A31

Design: 30fr, Lake reclamation project, grain fields.

1967, Nov. 14 **Engr.** ***Perf. 13***
146 A31 25fr brt bl, ind & sep 22 15
147 A31 30fr ultra, emer & ol brn 25 16

Economic development of Chad.

Woman and Harp Player — A32

Rock Paintings: 30fr, Giraffes. 50fr, Camel rider hunting ostrich.

1967, Dec. 19 **Engr.** ***Perf. 13***
Size: 36x22mm
148 A32 15fr bl, sal & mar 15 15
149 A32 30fr grnsh bl, sal & mar 30 16
150 A32 50fr emer, sal & mar 50 20
Nos. 148-150,C38-C39 (5) 3.20 1.53

Balloud expedition in the Ennedi Mountains. See Nos. 163-166.

Rotary Emblem — A33

Map of Chad, WHO Emblem, Well, Physicians, Mother and Child — A34

1968, Jan. 9 **Photo.** ***Perf. 13x12½***
151 A33 50fr multi 50 22

Rotary Club of Chad, 10th anniversary.

1968, Apr. 6 ***Perf. 13x12½***
152 A34 25fr multi 22 15
153 A34 32fr multi 35 20

20th anniv. of WHO.

"Water" Aiding Agriculture and Industry A35

1968, Apr. 23 **Engr.** ***Perf. 13***
154 A35 50fr grnsh bl, brn & brt grn 45 20

Hydrological Decade (UNESCO), 1965-74.

National Administration School — A36

1968, Aug. 20 **Engr.** ***Perf. 13***
155 A36 25fr sl, brn red & rose vio 22 15

Boy Learning to Write — A37

1968, Sept. 10
156 A37 60fr dk bl, dk brn & blk 50 22

Issued for National Literacy Day.

Cotton Harvest A38

Loom, Fort Archambault Factory — A39

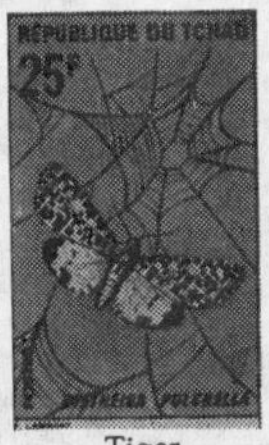

Tiger Moth — A40

1968, Sept. 24 **Engr.** ***Perf. 13***
157 A38 25fr Prus bl, choc & dk grn 22 15
158 A39 30fr brt grn, ol & ultra 30 15
Set value 24

Issued to publicize the cotton industry.

1968, Oct. 1 **Photo.**

Designs (Moths): 30fr, Owlet. 50fr, Saturnid (Gynanisa maja). 100fr, Saturnid (Epiphora bauhiniae).

159 A40 25fr multi 20 15
160 A40 30fr multi 25 15
161 A40 50fr multi 45 22
162 A40 100fr multi 80 35
Nos. 159-162 (4) 1.70 87

Rock Paintings Type of 1967

Rock Paintings: 2fr, Archers. 10fr, Costumes (4 women, 1 man). 20fr, Funeral vigil. 25fr, Dispute.

1968, Nov. 19 **Engr.** ***Perf. 13***
Size: 36x22mm
163 A32 2fr scar, salmon & brn 15 15
164 A32 10fr pur, salmon & dk red 15 15
165 A32 20fr grn, salmon & maroon 20 15
166 A32 25fr bl, salmon & maroon 25 15
Set value 60 34

Man and Human Rights Flame — A41

St. Paul — A42

1968, Dec. 10 **Engr.** ***Perf. 13***
167 A41 32fr grn, brt bl & red 35 20

International Human Rights Year.

1969, May 6 **Litho.** ***Perf. 12½x13***

Apostles: 1fr, St. Peter. 2fr, St. Thomas. 5fr, St. John the Evangelist. 10fr, St. Bartholomew. 20fr, St. Matthew. 25fr, St. James the Less. 30fr, St. Andrew. 40fr, St. Jude. 50fr, St. James the Greater. 85fr, St. Philip. 100fr, St. Simon.

168 A42 50c multi 15 15
169 A42 1fr multi 15 15
170 A42 2fr multi 15 15
171 A42 5fr multi 15 15
172 A42 10fr multi 15 15
173 A42 20fr multi 18 15
174 A42 25fr multi 22 15
175 A42 30fr multi 28 15
176 A42 40fr multi 40 16
177 A42 50fr multi 42 20
178 A42 85fr multi 65 40
179 A42 100fr multi 80 40
Set value 3.25 1.75

Jubilee Year of the Catholic Church in Chad. #168-179 printed se-tenant in sheets of 12 (4x3).

Tractors and Trucks — A43

1969, June 19 **Engr.** ***Perf. 13***
180 A43 32fr grn, red brn & ind 25 16

50th anniv. of the ILO.

Deborah Meyer, US, 200 Meter Freestyle — A44

Woman with Flowers, by Veneto — A45

Winners of 1968 Olympic Games: #182, Roland Matthes, East Germany, 100m backstroke. #183, Klaus DiBiasi, Italy, springboard diving. #184, Bruno Cipolla, Primo Baran and Renzo Sambo, Italy, pair with coxswain. #185, Annemarie Zimmermann and Rosewitha Esser, West Germany, women's kayak tandem. #186, Sailing, G.B. #187, Pierre Trentin, France, 1000 meter bicycling. #188, Pier Franco Vianelli, Italy, 196k bicycle road race. #189, Daniel Morelon and Pierre Trentin, France, tandem. #190, Daniel R. Rebillard, France, 4000m pursuit (bicycle). #191, Ingrid Becker, West Germany, pentathlon. #192, Jean J. Guyon, France, equestrian. #193, Olympic dressage team, West Germany. #194, Bernd Klinger, West Germany, small bore rifle. #195, Manfred Wolke, East Germany, welterweight. #196, Randy Matson, US, shot put. #197, Colette Besson, France, 400m run. #198, Mohammed Gammoudi, Tunisia, 5,000m run. #199, Tommie Smith, US, 200m run. #200, David Hemery, G.B., 200m hurdles. #201, Willie Davenport, US, 110m hurdles. #202, Bob Beamon, US, long jump. #203, Sawao Kato, Japan, all around gymnastics. #204, Dick Fosbury, US, high jump.

Paintings: #206, Holy Family, by Murillo, horiz. #207, Adoration of the Magi, by Rubens. #208, Portrait of an African Woman, by Bezombes. #209, Three Black Men, by Rubens. #210, Mother and Child, by Gauguin.

1969, June 30 Litho. *Perf. 12½x13*
181-204 A44 1fr set of 24 5.00 5.00

Perf. 12½x13, 13x12½
205-210 A45 1fr set of 6 1.25 1.25

Issued to stress the brotherhood of mankind.
For overprints see Nos. 244A-244F, 245A-245X.

Cochlospermum Tinctorium — A46

Flowers: 4fr, Parkia biglobosa. 10fr, Pancratium trianthum. 15fr, Morning glory.

1969, July 8 Photo. *Perf. 12½x13*
211 A46 1fr pink, yel & blk 15 15
212 A46 4fr dk grn, yel & red 15 15
213 A46 10fr dk grn, yel & gray 15 15
214 A46 15fr vio bl & multi 15 15
Set value 34 22

Meat Freezer, Farcha — A47

Design: 30fr, Cattle at Farcha slaughterhouse.

1969, Aug. 19 Engr. *Perf. 13*
215 A47 25fr sl grn, ocher & red brn 22 15
216 A47 30fr red brn, sl grn & gray 25 16

Economic development in Chad.

Development Bank Issue
Common Design Type

1969, Sept. 10
217 CD130 30fr dl red, grn & ocher 25 15

Tilapia Nilotica A48

Fish: 3fr, Citharinus latus. 5fr, Tetraodon fahaka strigosus. 20fr, Hydrocyon forskali.

1969, Nov. 25 Engr. *Perf. 13*
218 A48 2fr choc, grn & gray 15 15
219 A48 3fr gray, red & bl 15 15
220 A48 5fr ocher, blk & yel 15 15
221 A48 20fr blk, red & grn 22 15
Set value 39 27

ASECNA Issue
Common Design Type

1969, Dec. 12 Engr. *Perf. 13*
222 CD132 30fr orange 20 15

Pres. François Tombalbaye — A49

Lenin — A50

1970, Jan. 11 Litho. *Perf. 14*
223 A49 25fr multi 25 15

1970, Apr. 22 Photo. *Perf. 11½*
224 A50 150fr gold, blk & buff 1.10 65

Lenin (1870-1924), Russian communist leader.

UPU Headquarters Issue
Common Design Type

1970, May 20 Engr. *Perf. 13*
225 CD133 30fr dk red, pur & brn 25 15

During the 1970-73 period three different agents had entered into contracts to produce stamps with various officials of the Chad government, apparently including Pres. Tombalbaye. In June 1973, Tombalbaye declared that some of the stamps produced by these agents were not recognized by the Chad government but might be put on sale at a later date, and that other stamps produced and shipped to Chad were refused by the government. In July 1973, the Chad government announced that the stamps that were not recognized would be put on sale by the end of the year. We have no evidence that this actually happened.

Apollo Program A50a

Designs: 15fr, Apollo 11 in Lunar orbit. 25fr, Apollo 12 astronaut deploying lunar research equipment. 40fr, Astronaunt, lunar module on moon. 50fr, Astronauts Conrad and Bean in life raft after splashdown, horiz.

1970, June 12 Litho. *Perf. 12x12½*
225A A50a Strip of 3

Souvenir Sheet
Perf. 13½x13
225C A50a 50fr multicolored

No. 225C contains one 66x44mm stamp. No. 225C, 15fr, 25fr are airmail.

Expo '70, Japan — A50b

Japanese prints of women: 50c, by Kiyonaga. 1fr, by Utamaro. 2fr, from Heian period.

1970, June 12 Litho. *Perf. 12x12½*
225E A50b Strip of 3

For overprint see No. 239C.

Adult Education Class and UN Emblem A52

1970, June 16 Litho. *Perf. 14*
226 A52 100fr blue & multi 80 20

International Education Year.

Bull's Head, Symbols of Weather and Agriculture — A53

1970, July 22 Engr. *Perf. 13*
227 A53 50fr org, gray & grn 38 15

Issued for World Meteorological Day.

1970 World Cup Soccer Championships, Mexico City — A53a

Designs: 1fr, Three players, Italian flag. 4fr, Franz Beckenbauer, German flag. Nos. 227C, 227E, English players receiving World Cup trophy, 1966. No. 227D, Three players, Brazilian flag. No. 227F, Four players, "1970."

1970-71 Litho. *Perf. 12*
227A A53a 1fr multicolored
227B A53a 4fr multicolored
227C A53a 5fr multicolored
227D A53a 5fr multicolored

Embossed
Die Cut Perf 13
227E A53a 5fr gold

Souvenir Sheet
Litho.
Perf. 13½x13
227F A53a 15fr multicolored

No. 227F contains one 66x44mm stamp. Nos. 227D, 227F are airmail.
Issue dates: Nos. 227A-227D, 227F, July 2, 1970. No. 227E, Nov. 1, 1971.
For overprints see Nos. 267A-267E.

Christmas A53b

Virgin and Child by: 3fr, Solario. 25fr, Durer. 32fr, Fouquet.

1970, Aug. 19 Litho. *Perf. 12x12½*
227G A53b 3fr multicolored
227H A53b 25fr multicolored
227I A53b 32fr multicolored

No. 227I is airmail.

Ahmed Mangue, Minister of Education — A54

1970, Sept. 15 Litho. & Engr.
228 A54 100fr gold, car & blk 65 16

1972 Summer Olympics, Munich — A54a

Designs: No. 228A, 3fr, Horses pulling chariot. 8fr, Men running. 19fr, No. 228C, Woman hurdling. No. 228B, 20fr, Equestrian. 35fr, Woman diving. No. 228D, Woman diver in tuck position.

1970 Litho. *Perf. 12½x12*
228A A54a Strip of 3

Perf. 12x12½
228B A54a Pair + label

Embossed
Die Cut Perf 13
228C A54a 10fr gold

Souvenir Sheet
Litho.
Perf. 13½x13
228D A54a 40fr multicolored

19fr, 35fr, Nos. 228C-228D are airmail. No. 228D contains one 66x43mm stamp. Issue dates: Nos. 228A-228B, 228D, Sept. No. 228C, Oct. 14.
For overprints see Nos. 239D-239F.

Tanner — A55

Designs: 2fr, Cloth dyer, vert. 3fr, Camel turning oil press. 4fr, Water carrier. 5fr, Copper worker.

1970, Oct. 10 Engr. *Perf. 13*
229 A55 1fr ol brn, bl & brn 15 15
229A A55 2fr dk brn, ol & ind 15 15
229B A55 3fr pur, ol brn & rose car 15 15
229C A55 4fr choc, lem & bl grn 15 15
229D A55 5fr red, choc & sl grn 15 15
Set value 25 25

UN Emblem, Grain and Dove — A56

1970, Oct. 24 Photo. *Perf. 12x12½*
230 A56 32fr dk bl & multi 25 16

25th anniversary of United Nations.

OCAM Headquarters, Map of Africa, Stars — A57

1971, Jan. 23 Photo. *Perf. 12½x12*
231 A57 30fr dk grn & multi 25 16

OCAM (Organisation Commune Africaine, Malgache et Mauricienne) Summit Conference, N'djamena, Jan. 22-30.

Space Exploration — A57a

Illustration reduced.

1971, Feb. 16 Litho. *Perf. 13x13½*
231A A57a 8fr shown
231B A57a 10fr Apollo 11
231C A57a 35fr Soviet space station

Embossed
Die Cut Perf 13
231D A57a 8fr gold, like #231A
f. Sheet of 1, imperf.

Souvenir Sheet
Perf. 13½x13
231E A57a 40fr John F. Kennedy, Apollo spacecraft, vert.

Nos. 231C, 231E are airmail. No. 231f contains one 73x45mm stamp with same size design as No. 231D. No. 231E contains one 33x50mm stamp.
Nos. 231D, 231f probably were not available in Chad.

1972 Winter Olympics, Sapporo A57b

Paintings by Kiyonaga: 50c, Cherry Trees in Bloom, Tokyo. 1fr, Snowy Morning. 2fr, Sake Party.

1971 Litho. *Perf. 12x12½*
231G A57b 50c multicolored
231H A57b 1fr multicolored
231I A57b 2fr multicolored

Embossed
Die Cut Perf 13
231J A57b 2fr gold, like #231I
k. Sheet of 1, imperf.

Issue dates: Nos. 231G-231I, Feb. 16. Nos. 231J-231k, Nov. 1, 1971. No. 231k contains one 43x54mm stamp with same size design as No. 231I.
For overprints see Nos. 246A-246C.
Nos. 231J-231k probably were not available in Chad.

Portraits of French Royalty A57c

Designs: No. 232A, 25fr, The Dauphin (Louis XVII), by J.M. Vien the Younger. 32fr, Marie Antoinette, by E. Vigee-Lebrun. 60fr, Louis XVI, by J.S. Duplessis.
No. 232B, 25fr, Comtesse du Barry, by E. Vigee-Lebrun. 40fr, Louis XV, by M.Q. Delatour.
No. 232C, 40fr, Marie Antoinette, by Charpentier. 50fr, Louis XVI (Dauphin), by Michel Van Loo.
No. 232D, 35fr, Madame de Pompadour (detail), by Delatour. 70fr, Louis XV by Delatour.
No. 232E, 30fr, Madame de Pompadour (entire), by Delatour. 60fr, Marie Leszczynska, by Jean Marc Nattier. 80fr, Louis XV, by Van Loo.
No. 232F, 40fr, Duc D'Orleans as Regent, by 19th cent. French school. 200fr, Louis XIV, by H. Rigaud.
No. 232G, 100fr, Madame de Montespan, by Henry Gascard. 100fr, Madame de Maintenon, by Pierre Mignard.
No. 232H, 50fr, Colbert, by Claude Lefebvre. 200fr, Louis XIV, by J. Garnier.
No. 232J, 50fr, Marie Therese, by Mignard. 200fr, Louis XIV, by Marot.
No. 232K, 50fr, Marie de la Valliere, by English school. 200fr, Louis XIV, by French school.
No. 232L, 100fr, Giulio Cardinal Mazarin, by Mignard. 100fr, Anne of Austria, by Rubens.
No. 232M, 50fr, Vicomte de Turenne, by Champaigne. 200fr, Louis XIV as a Boy, by Mignard.
No. 232N, 100fr, Marquis de Cinq-Mars, by M. le Nain. 150fr, Cardinal Richelieu, by Champaigne.
No. 232P, 150fr, Anne of Austria, by Rubens, diff. 250fr, Louis XIII (detail), by Simon Vouet.
No. 232Q, 150fr, Marriage of Marie de Medicis (looking right), by Rubens. 150fr, Mirror image.
No. 232R, Duke of Sully, by Quesnel. Mirror image.
No. 232S, 150fr, Henry IV, by Rubens. 150fr, Marie de Medicis, by Rubens.
No. 232T, 200fr, Gabrielle d'Estrees, by unknown artist. 250fr, Henry IV, by French school, c. 1595.
No. 232U, 150fr, Jeanne d'Albret, by Francois Clouet. Marie de Medicis as a Girl, by Angelo Bronzino.
No. 232V, 200fr, Henry III, by Clouet. 250fr, Ambroise Pare, by 16th century French school.
No. 232W, 150fr, Catherine de Medicis, by Clouet. 250fr, Henry II, by Clouet.
No. 233A, 200fr, Elizabeth of Austria, by Clouet. Charles IX, by Clouet.
No. 233B, 200fr, Mary Stuart, by 16th cent. Scottish school. 300fr, Diane of Poitiers, by Fontainbleu school.
No. 233C, 200fr, Elizabeth of Valois, by Alonso S. Coello. 250fr, Francis, Duke of Alencon, by Clouet.
No. 233D, 150fr, Marguerite d'Angouleme, by Clouet. 300fr, Francis I, by Clouet.
No. 233E, 200fr, Francis I, by Titian. 300fr, Francis I as Dauphin, by Corneille of Lyon.
No. 233F, 100fr, Anne of Austria, by Coello. 250fr, Louis XIII, by Champaigne.
No. 233G, 200fr, Marie de Medicis, by Rubens, diff. 200fr, Marie de Medicis, Louis XIII, by Rubens.
No. 233H, 150fr, The Exchange of Princess Elizabeth of France and Princess Anne of Austria on the Andaye River, by Rubens. 250fr, Louis XIII of France and Navarre, by Vouet.
No. 233J, 250fr, Marie de Medicis, by Rubens, diff. 250fr, Henry IV, by Rubens.
No. 233K, Louis XV and the Dauphin at Battle of Fontenoy. No. 233L, The Grand Dauphin and his Family, by Mignard. No. 233M, Madame de Montespan, horiz. No. 233N, Madame de la Valliere and her Children. No. 233P, The Birth of Louis XIII at Fontainebleau, by Rubens. No. 233Q, Reconciliation of the Queen and Louis XIII, by Rubens. No. 233R, Henry IV Entrusting Regency to Marie de Medici, by Rubens. No. 233S, The Majority of Louis XIII, by Rubens. No. 233T, The Apotheosis of Henry IV and the Proclamation of Regency, by Rubens. No. 233U, Felicity of the Regency, by Rubens.

1971-73 Litho. *Perf. 12½x13*
232A A57c Strip of 3
232B A57c Pair
232C A57c Pair
232D A57c Pair
232E A57c Strip of 3
232F A57c Pair
232G A57c Pair
232H A57c Pair
232J A57c Pair
232K A57c Pair
232L A57c Pair
232M A57c Pair
232N A57c Pair
232P A57c Pair
232Q A57c Pair
232R A57c Pair
232S A57c Pair
232T A57c Pair
232U A57c Pair
232V A57c Pair
232W A57c Pair
233A A57c Pair
233B A57c Pair
233C A57c Pair
233D A57c Pair
233E A57c Pair
233F A57c Pair
233G A57c Pair
233H A57c Pair
233J A57c Pair

Souvenir Sheets
Perf. 13x13½, 13½x13, 13½
233K A57c 75fr multi
233L A57c 100fr multi
233M A57c 200fr multi
233N A57c 300fr multi
233P A57c 350fr multi
233Q A57c 400fr multi
233R A57c 400fr multi
233S A57c 400fr multi
233T A57c 400fr multi
233U A57c 500fr multi

Nos. 232A 60fr, 232B 40fr, 232C 50fr, 232D 70fr, 232E 80fr, 232F 200fr, 232G, 232H 200fr, 232J 200fr, 232K, 232L, 232M 200fr, 232N-233U are airmail.
Issue dates: 1971 - #232A, Feb. 24. #232B, Mar. 30. #232C, Mar. 4. #232D, 233K, Mar. 15. #232E, Apr. 12. #232F, 233L, Apr. 26. #232G, Aug. 10. #232H, Sept. 6. #232J, Sept. 23. #232K, Oct. 6. #232L, Oct. 26. #232M, Nov. 16. #232N, Nov. 20.
1972 - #232P, 233P, Jan. #232Q, 233M-233N, Feb. #233Q-233R, May. #232R, 233S, June 15. #232S, 233T, June 26. #232T, Aug. 8. #232U, Aug. 17. #232V, Aug. 30. #232W, 233U, Dec. 11. #233A, Dec. 18. #233B, Dec. 28.
1973 - #233C-233J.
Nos. 233K-233L, 233T-233U each contain one 37x62mm stamp. Nos. 233N, 233P each contain one 32x50mm stamp. No. 233M contains one 45x65mm stamp. Nos. 233Q-233R, 233U each contain one 65x45mm stamp.
Nos. 232Q-232V, 233G, 233J, 233R-233U and possibly 232P, 232W-233F, 233H probably were not available in Chad.

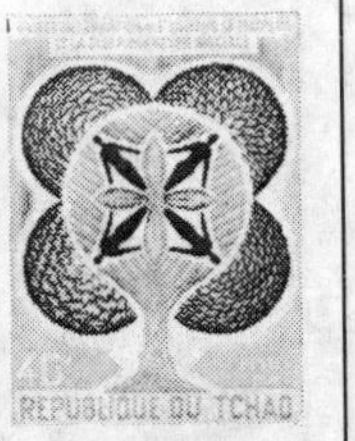

Symbolic Tree — A58

1971, Mar. 21 Engr. *Perf. 13*
236 A58 40fr bl grn, dk red & grn 35 16

Intl. year against racial discrimination.

Paintings of Flowers A58a

Designs: 1fr, The Three Graces (detail), by Rubens. 4fr, Imperial Bouquet, by Van Os. 5fr, Bouquet, by Jan Brueghel.

1971, Apr. 28 Litho. *Perf. 12x12½*
236A A58a Strip of 3

For overprint see No. 278A.

Summer Olympic Games — A58b

Designs: 15fr, Swimming, vert. 20fr, Women's relay races, vert. 25fr, Swimming, medals. 50fr, Running.

Perf. 12x12½, 12½x12
1971, Apr. 28 Litho.
236B A58b 15fr multicolored
236C A58b 20fr multicolored
236D A58b 25fr multicolored

Embossed
Perf. 13
236E A58b 25fr gold, like No. 236D

Souvenir Sheet
Litho.
Die Cut Perf 13
236F A58b 50fr multicolored

Nos. 236D-236F are airmail. No. 236F contains one 62x36mm stamp.
Issue dates: Nos. 236B-236D, 236F, Apr. 28. No. 236E, Nov. 1.
For overprints see Nos. 251A-251D.
No. 236E probably was not available in Chad.

Map of Africa, Radar Antenna A59

Designs (Map of Africa and): 40fr, Communications tower. 50fr, Communications satellite.

1971, May 17 Engr. *Perf. 13*
237 A59 5fr ultra, org & dk red 15 15
238 A59 40fr pur, emer & brn 25 15
239 A59 50fr dk red, blk & brn 40 20
Nos. 237-239 (3) 80
Set value 39

3rd World Telecommunications Day.

Apollo 11 — A59a

1971, July 5 Embossed *Perf. 13*
239A A59a 10fr gold
b. Sheet of 1, imperf.

No. 239b contains one 73x45mm stamp with same size design as No. 239A.
Nos. 239A-239b probably were not available in Chad.

No. 225E Ovptd. in Gold

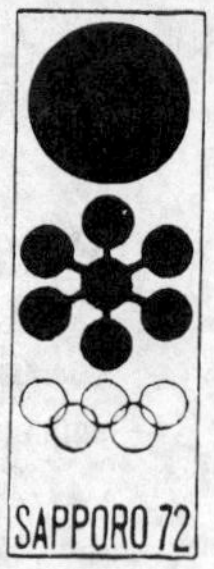

1971, July 17 Litho. *Perf. 12x12½*
239C A50b Strip of 3

1972 Winter Olympics, Sapporo.

Nos. 228A-228B, 228D Ovptd. with "MUNICH 72" and Olympic Rings in Gold

Perf. 12½x12, 12x12½

1971, Nov. 1 Litho.
239D A54a Strip of 3
239E A54a Pair + label

Souvenir Sheet

Perf. 13½x13

239F A54a 40fr on #228D

UNICEF Emblem and Children — A60

1971, Dec. 11 Engr. *Perf. 13*

240 A60 50fr Prus bl, emer & brt pink		40	20

25th anniv. of UNICEF.

Gorane Nangara Dancers A61

Dancers: 15fr, Girls' initiation dance, Yondo. 30fr, Women of M'Boum, vert. 40fr, Men of Sara Kaba, vert.

1971, Dec. 18 Litho. *Perf. 13*

241 A61 10fr blk & multi	15	15
242 A61 15fr brn org & multi	16	15
243 A61 30fr bl & multi	35	15
244 A61 40fr yel grn & multi	42	15
Nos. 241-244 (4)	1.08	
Set value		32

Nos. 205-210 Ovptd. in Gold

noël 1971

1971 Litho. *Perf. 12½x13, 13x12½*
244A-244F A45 1fr on #205-210

Nos. 244A-244F probably were not available in Chad.

Presidents Pompidou and Tombalbaye, Map with Paris and Fort Lamy — A62

1972, Jan. 25 Photo. *Perf. 13*

245 A62 40fr blue & multi	35	20

Visit of Pres. Georges Pompidou of France, Jan. 1972.

Nos. 181-204 Ovptd. with "MUNICH 72" and Olympic Rings in Gold

1972, Feb. 7 Litho. *Perf. 12½x13*
245A-245X A44 1fr on #181-204

Nos. 245A-245X probably were not available in Chad.

Nos. 231G-231I Ovptd. in Gold

a

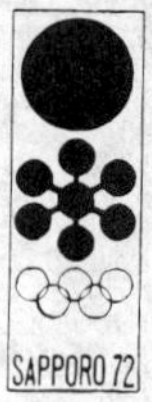

b

1972, Feb. Litho. *Perf. 12x12½*
246A A57b 50c Pair, #a.-b.
246B A57b 1fr Pair, #a.-b.
246C A57b 2fr Pair, #a.-b.

Nos. 246A-246C probably were not available in Chad.

President Tombalbaye A63

1972, Apr. 13 Litho. *Perf. 13*

247 A63 30fr multi	20	15
247A A63 40fr multi	25	15
Set value		24

See Nos. C112-C113.

Downhill Skiing — A64

Designs: 75fr, Women's figure skating. 150fr, Luge.

1972, Apr. 13 *Perf. 13½*

248 A64 25fr multi	16	15
249 A64 75fr multi	50	25
250 A64 150fr multi	1.00	50
Nos. 248-250,C114-C115 (5)	3.91	1.95

11th Winter Olympic Games, Sapporo, Japan.

Heart — A65

Gorrizia Dubiosa — A66

1972, Apr. 25 Engr. *Perf. 13*

251 A65 100fr purple, bl & car	80	16

"Your heart is your health," World Health Month.

Nos. 236B-236D, 236F Ovptd. with "MUNICH 72" and Olympic Rings in Gold

1972 Litho. *Perf. 12x12½, 12½x12*
251A A58b 15fr multicolored
251B A58b 20fr multicolored
251C A58b 25fr multicolored

Souvenir Sheet

Die Cut Perf 13

251D A58b 50fr multicolored

Nos. 251C-251D are airmail.

1972, May 6 Photo.

Insects: 2fr, Spider (argiope sector). 3fr, Silk spider (nephila senegalense). 4fr, Beetle (oryctes boas). 5fr, Dragonfly (hemistigma albipunctata).

252 A66 1fr green & multi	15	15
253 A66 2fr blue & multi	15	15
254 A66 3fr car rose & multi	15	15
255 A66 4fr yellow grn & multi	15	15
256 A66 5fr dp green & multi	15	15
Set value	25	25

Trains A66a

1972 Litho. *Perf. 12*
256A A66a 10fr Orient Express
256B A66a 40fr Osaka Express
256C A66a 50fr St. Germain
256D A66a 150fr Blue train
256E A66a 200fr Trans-Europe Express

Souvenir Sheet

256F A66a 300fr Rogers "Madison," 1855

No. 256F contains one 60x40mm stamp. See note before No. 225A.

Scout Greeting — A67

Designs: 70fr, Mountain climbing. 80fr, Canoeing.

1972, May 15 Photo.

257 A67 30fr multi	20	15
258 A67 70fr multi	45	22
259 A67 80fr multi	55	25
Nos. 257-259,C118-C119 (5)	2.55	1.50

Scout Jamboree.

Hurdles, Motion and Olympic Emblems A68

Motion and Olympic Emblems and: 130fr, Gymnast on rings. 150fr, Swimming. 300fr, Bicycling.

1972, June 9 Litho. *Perf. 13½*

260 A68 50fr blk & multi	40	15
261 A68 130fr blk & multi	90	25
262 A68 150fr blk & multi	1.20	30
Nos. 260-262 (3)	2.50	70

Souvenir Sheet

263 A68 300fr blk & multi	2.25	2.00

20th Olympic Games, Munich, Aug. 26-Sept. 10.

Ski Jump, Kasaya, Japan — A69

Designs: 75fr, Cross-country skiing, P. Tyldum, Sweden. 100fr, Figure-skating, pairs, L. Rodnina and A. Ulanov, USSR. 130fr, Men's speed skating, A. Schenk, Netherlands.

1972, June 15 *Perf. 14½*

264 A69 25fr gold & multi	16	15
265 A69 75fr gold & multi	50	25
266 A69 100fr gold & multi	65	35
267 A69 130fr gold & multi	90	42
Nos. 264-267,C130-C131 (6)	4.41	2.25

11th Winter Olympic Games, gold-medal winners. Nos. 264-267 exist se-tenant with label showing earth satellite.

Nos. 227A-227D, 227F Overprinted With Soccer Ball, "MUNICH 72" and Olympic Rings in Gold

1972 Litho. *Perf. 12*
267A A53a 1fr multicolored
267B A53a 4fr multicolored
267C A53a 5fr multicolored
267D A53a 5fr multicolored

Souvenir Sheet

Perf. 13½x13

267E A53a 15fr multicolored

Nos. 267D-267E are airmail.
Nos. 267A-267E probably were not available in Chad.

TV Tower and Weight-lifting — A70

Designs (TV Tower, Munich and): 40fr, Woman sprinter. 60fr, Soccer goalkeeper.

1972, Aug. 15 Litho. *Perf. 14½*

268	A70 20fr gold & multi	15	15
269	A70 40fr gold & multi	25	15
270	A70 60fr gold & multi	40	20
	Nos. 268-270,C135-C137 (6)	3.10	1.70

20th Summer Olympic Games, Munich. Nos. 268-270 exist se-tenant with label showing arms of Munich.

Domestic Animals A71

1972, Aug. 29 Engr. *Perf. 13*

271	A71 25fr Dromedary	22	15
272	A71 30fr Horse	25	15
273	A71 40fr Dog	35	15
274	A71 45fr Goat	38	15
	Nos. 271-274 (4)	1.20	
	Set value		42

For surcharge see No. 293.

Tobacco Cultivation A72

1972, Oct. 24 Engr. *Perf. 13*

275	A72 40fr shown	25	15
276	A72 50fr Plowing	35	16

Massa Warrior — A73

Design: 20fr, Moundang warrior.

1972, Nov. 15 Photo. *Perf. 14x13*

277	A73 15fr orange & multi	16	16
278	A73 20fr yellow & multi	20	16

No. 236A Overprinted "Noel 1972" in gold

1972 Litho. *Perf. 12x12½*

278A	A58a Strip of 3		

No. 228A probably was not available in Chad.

King Faisal and Pres. Tombalbaye — A74

1972, Nov. 17 Litho. *Perf. 13*

279	A74 100fr gold & multi	65	40

Visit of King Faisal of Saudi Arabia. See No. C143.

Gen. Gowon and Pres. Tombalbaye — A75

1972, Dec. 7

280	A75 70fr multi	50	25

Visit of Gen. Yakubu Gowon of Nigeria.

Olympic Emblem and 100-meter Sprint, Valeri Borzov, USSR — A76

Designs (Olympic Emblem and): 20fr, Shotput, Komar, Poland. 40fr, Hammer throw, Bondartchuk, USSR. 60fr, Discus, Danek, Czechoslovakia.

1972, Dec. 22 *Perf. 11*

281	A76 10fr multi	15	15
282	A76 20fr multi	15	15
283	A76 40fr multi	25	15
284	A76 60fr multi	40	20
	Nos. 281-284,C148-C149 (6)	3.40	1.95

20th Summer Olympic Games, winners.

Olympic Emblem and Fencing, Woyda, Poland — A77

Designs (Olympic Emblem and): 30fr, 3-day equestrian event, Richard Meade, Gt. Britain. 50fr, Two-man sculls, Brietzke-Mager, East Germany.

1972, Dec. 22

285	A77 20fr gold & multi	15	15
286	A77 30fr gold & multi	20	15
287	A77 50fr gold & multi	35	16
	Nos. 285-287,C151-C152 (5)	3.15	1.74

20th Summer Olympic Games, winners.

1972 Summer Olympics Gold Medalists — A77a

Designs: 20fr, Teofilo Stevenson, boxing, Cuba. 25fr, Yugoslavia, team handball. 30fr, M. Peters, pentathlon, Great Britain. 40fr, basketball, USSR. No. 287E, W. Ruska, judo, Netherlands. No. 287F, Women's gymnastics, Ludmila Tourischeva, USSR. 75fr, Men's volleyball, Japan. No. 287H, A. Scalzone, shooting, Italy. No. 287I, Soccer, Poland. 130fr, J. Williams, archery, US. No. 287K, A. Nakayama, men's rings, Japan. No. 287L, Field hockey, West Germany. 200fr, Vassily Alexeiev, weight lifting, USSR. 250fr, D. Morelon, cycling, France.

1972, Dec. 22 Litho. *Perf. 11½*

287A	A77a	20fr multicolored
287B	A77a	25fr multicolored
287C	A77a	30fr multicolored
287D	A77a	40fr multicolored
287E	A77a	50fr multicolored
287F	A77a	50fr multicolored
287G	A77a	75fr multicolored
287H	A77a	100fr multicolored
287I	A77a	100fr multicolored
287J	A77a	130fr multicolored
287K	A77a	150fr multicolored
287L	A77a	150fr multicolored

Souvenir Sheets

Perf. 15

287M	A77a	200fr multicolored
287N	A77a	250fr multicolored

Nos. 287G-287N are airmail.

Soviet Flag and Shield — A78

1972, Dec. 30 Litho. *Perf. 12*

288	A78 150fr red & multi	1.00	42

50th anniversary of the Soviet Union.

High Jump — A79

Designs (Games Emblem and): 125fr, Running. 200fr, Shot put. 250fr, Discus.

1973, Jan. 17 Litho. *Perf. 13½x13*

289	A79 50fr vio bl & multi	35	15
290	A79 125fr olive & multi	80	40
291	A79 200fr lilac & multi	1.40	65
	Nos. 289-291 (3)	2.55	1.20

Souvenir Sheet

292	A79 250fr brn & multi	2.00	2.00

2nd African Games, Lagos, Nigeria, Jan. 7-18.

Paintings with Musical Instruments — A79a

Details from Paintings: 30fr, Madeleine Playing her Lute, by unknown artist. 70fr, A Concert, by Lorenzo Costa. 100fr, Bass and Sheet Music, by Jean-Baptiste Oudry, horiz. 125fr, St. Cecilia and Angel, by Carlo Saraceni. 150fr, Woman Listening to Violinist, by Gabriel Metsu. 300fr, Still Life with Musical Instruments, by Pieter Claesz, horiz.

1973, Apr. Litho. *Perf. 11½*

292A	A79a	30fr multicolored
292B	A79a	70fr multicolored
292C	A79a	100fr multicolored
292D	A79a	125fr multicolored
292E	A79a	150fr multicolored

Souvenir Sheet

Perf. 15

292F	A79a	300fr multicolored

Nos. 292D-292F are airmail.

No. 271 Surcharged with New Value, 2 Bars, and Overprinted in Red: "SECHERESSE SOLIDARITE AFRICAINE"

1973, Aug. 16 Engr. *Perf. 13*

293	A71 100fr on 25fr multi	65	42

African solidarity in drought emergency.

African Postal Union Issue

Common Design Type

1973, Sept. 17 Engr. *Perf. 13*

294	CD137 100fr cl, sl grn & brn ol	65	40

Easter A79b

Details from paintings: 40fr, Christ on the Cross, by Lucas Cranach. 60fr, Supper in Emmaus, by Titian, horiz. 120fr, The Crucifixion, by Durer. 150fr, The Tribute, by Titian. 250fr, The Pieta, by Botticelli. 400fr, Entombment of Christ, by Gaspard Isenmann, horiz.

1973 Litho. *Perf. 11½*

294A	A79b	40fr multicolored
294B	A79b	60fr multicolored
294C	A79b	120fr multicolored
294D	A79b	150fr multicolored
294E	A79b	250fr multicolored

Souvenir Sheet

Perf. 15

294F	A79b	400fr multicolored

Nos. 294A, 294D-294F are airmail.

Animals A79c

1973 Litho. *Perf. 13½*

294G	A79c	20fr Sheep
294H	A79c	30fr Camels
294J	A79c	100fr Cats
294K	A79c	130fr Dogs
294L	A79c	150fr Horses

Nos. 294J-294L are airmail.

See note before No. 225A.

Christmas — A79d

Designs: 30fr, The Virgin and Infant Surrounded by Saints, by Lorenzo Lotto. 40fr, The Holy Family, by Tintoretto, vert. 55fr, Nativity Scene, by Martin Schongauer, vert. 60fr, Nativity Scene, by Federico Barocci, vert. 250fr, Adoration of the Magi, by Stephan Lochner, vert. 400fr, Epiphany, by Hans Memling.

1973 Litho. *Perf. 11½*

294M A79d 30fr multicolored
294N A79d 40fr multicolored
294P A79d 55fr multicolored
294Q A79d 60fr multicolored
294R A79d 250fr multicolored

Souvenir Sheet

Perf. 15

294S A79d 400fr multicolored

Nos. 294Q-294S are airmail.
See note before No. 225A.

Dinothrombium Tinctorium A80

Rotary Emblem A81

1974, Sept. 3 Photo. *Perf. 13*

295 A80 25fr *shown* 15 15
296 A80 30fr *Bupreste sternocera* 16 15
297 A80 40fr *Diptere hyperechia* 22 15
298 A80 50fr *Chrysis* 30 18
299 A80 100fr *Longicorn beetle* 60 25
300 A80 130fr *Spider* 75 35
Nos. 295-300 (6) 2.18 1.23

1975, Apr. 11 Typo. *Perf. 13*

301 A81 50fr multi 30 16

Rotary International, 70th anniversary.

Craterostigma Plantagineum A82

Flowers: 10fr, Tapinanthus globiferus. 15fr, Commelina forskalaei, vert. 20fr, Adenium obesum. 25fr, Yellow hibiscus. 30fr, Red hibiscus. 40fr, Kigelia africana.

1975, Sept. 25 Photo. *Perf. 13*

302 A82 5fr org & multi 15 15
303 A82 10fr gray bl & multi 15 15
304 A82 15fr yel grn & multi 15 15
305 A82 20fr lt brn & multi 15 15
306 A82 25fr lil & multi 15 15
307 A82 30fr bis & multi 15 15
308 A82 40fr ultra & multi 18 15
Set value 73 42

A. G. Bell, Satellite and Waves — A83

1976, June 10 Litho. *Perf. 12½*

309 A83 100fr bl, brn & ocher 48 30
310 A83 125fr lt grn, brn & ocher 60 38

Centenary of first telephone call by Alexander Graham Bell, Mar. 10, 1876.

Ice Hockey, USSR — A84

Design: 90fr, Ski jump, Karl Schnabl, Austria.

1976, June 21 *Perf. 14*

311 A84 60fr multi 35 18
312 A84 90fr multi 48 20

12th Winter Olympic Games, winners. See Nos. C178-C180.

High Hurdles A85

1976, July 12 Litho. *Perf. 13½*

313 A85 45fr multi 28 15

21st Summer Olympic Games, Montreal, Canada. See Nos. C187-C190.

Mars Landing and Viking Rocket — A86

Design (Mars Landing and): 90fr, Viking trajectory, Earth to Mars.

1976, July 23 *Perf. 14*

314 A86 45fr multi 25 15
315 A86 90fr multi 55 28
Nos. 314-315,C191-C193 (5) 4.30 1.90

Viking Mars project.
For overprints see Nos. 379-380.

Robert Koch, Medicine — A87

Design: 90fr, Anatole France, literature.

1976, Dec. 15

316 A87 45fr multi 30 15
317 A87 90fr multi 52 25
Nos. 316-317,C196-C198 (5) 4.57 1.97

Nobel Prize winners.

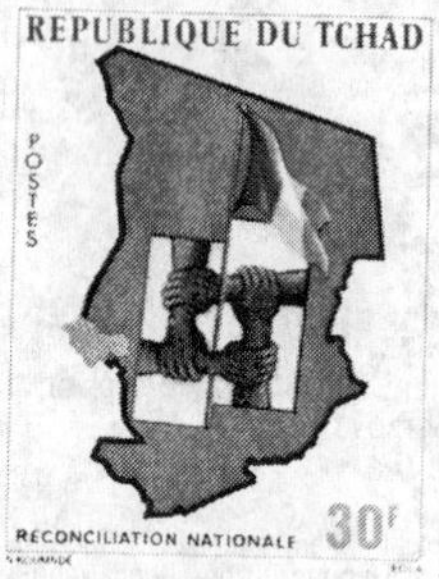

Map and Flag of Chad, Clasped Hands A88

Designs: 120fr, Map of Chad, people and various occupations.

1976, Sept. 15 Litho. *Perf. 12½x13*

318 A88 30fr multi 15 15
319 A88 60fr orange & multi 30 18
320 A88 120fr brown & multi 60 42
Nos. 318-320 (3) 1.05 75

National reconciliation.

Freed Political Prisoners — A89

Designs: 60fr, Parade of cadets.

1976, Sept. 25 Litho. *Perf. 12½*

321 A89 30fr bl & multi 15 15
322 A89 60fr blk & multi 30 18
323 A89 120fr red & multi 60 40
Nos. 321-323 (3) 1.05 73

Revolution of Apr. 13, 1975, 1st anniv.

Decorated Calabashes — A90

Designs: Various pyrographed calabashes.

1976, Nov. Litho. *Perf. 12½x13*

324 A90 30fr multi 15 15
325 A90 60fr multi 30 18
326 A90 120fr multi 60 40
Nos. 324-326 (3) 1.05 73

Germany No. C57 and Friedrichshafen, Germany — A91

1977, Mar. 30 *Perf. 14*

327 A91 100fr multi 60 25
Nos. 327,C206-C209 (5) 4.85 1.89

75th anniversary of the Zeppelin.

Elizabeth II in Coronation Regalia and Clergy — A92

Design: 450fr, Elizabeth II and Prince Philip.

1977, June 15 Litho. *Perf. 14x13½*

328 A92 250fr multi 1.75 45

Souvenir Sheet

329 A92 450fr multi 3.00 1.40

25th anniv. of the reign of Elizabeth II.
For overprints see Nos. 347-348.

Simon Bolivar — A93

Famous Personalities: 175fr, Joseph J. Roberts. No. 332, Queen Wihelmina of Netherlands. No. 333, Charles de Gaulle. 325fr, King Baudouin and Queen Fabiola of Belgium.

1977, June 15 *Perf. 13½x14*

330 A93 150fr multi 70 25
331 A93 175fr multi 80 30
332 A93 200fr multi 90 38
333 A93 200fr multi 90 38
334 A93 325fr multi 1.75 50
Nos. 330-334 (5) 5.05 1.81

Post and Telecommunications Emblem — A94

Map of Chad and Waves — A95

Society Emblem — A96

1977, Aug. 15 **Litho.** ***Perf. 13***
335 A94 30fr yel & blk 15 15

Perf. 12½
336 A95 60fr multi 30 18

Perf. 13½x13
337 A96 120fr multi 60 40
Nos. 335-337 (3) 1.05 73

Telecommunications (30fr); Natl. Telecommunications School, 10th anniv. (60fr); Intl. Telecommunication Soc. of Chad (120fr).

WHO Emblem and Man (Back Pain) — A97

World Rheumatism Year (WHO Emblem and): 60fr, Woman's head (neck pain; horiz.). 120fr, Leg (knee pain).

Perf. 12½x13, 13x12½
1977, Nov. 10 **Engr.**
338 A97 30fr multi 15 15
339 A97 60fr multi 30 18
340 A97 120fr multi 60 40
Nos. 338-340 (3) 1.05 73

World Cup Emblems and Saving a Goal — A98

Designs (Argentina '78, World Cup Emblems and): 60fr, Heading the ball. 100fr, Referee whistling a goal. 200fr, World Cup poster. 300fr, Pelé. 500fr, Helmut Schoen and Munich stadium.

1977, Nov. 25 **Litho.** ***Perf. 13½***
341 A98 40fr multi 22 15
342 A98 60fr multi 38 18
343 A98 100fr multi 55 25
344 A98 200fr multi 1.25 50
345 A98 300fr multi 1.90 75
Nos. 341-345 (5) 4.30 1.83

Souvenir Sheet
346 A98 500fr multi 3.00 1.10

World Cup Soccer Championship, Argentina '78.
For overprints see Nos. 359-364.

Nos. 328-329 Overprinted in Silver: "ANNIVERSAIRE DU COURONNEMENT 1953-1978"

1978, Sept. 13 ***Perf. 14x13½***
347 A92 250fr multi 1.25 60

Souvenir Sheet
348 A92 450fr multi 2.50 1.25

25th anniv. of coronation of Elizabeth II.

Abraham and Melchisedek, by Rubens — A99

Rubens Paintings: 120fr, Helene Fourment, vert. 200fr, David and the Elders of Israel. 300fr, Anne of Austria, vert. 500fr, Marie de Medicis, vert.

1978, Nov. 23 **Litho.** ***Perf. 13½***
349 A99 60fr multi 38 18
350 A99 120fr multi 75 38
351 A99 200fr multi 1.25 60
352 A99 300fr multi 1.90 95
Nos. 349-352 (4) 4.28 2.11

Souvenir Sheet
353 A99 500fr multi 3.50 1.75

Peter Paul Rubens (1577-1640).

Dürer Portrait A100

Dürer Paintings: 150fr, Jacob Muffel. 250fr, Young Woman. 350fr, Oswolt Krel.

1978, Nov. 23
354 A100 60fr multi 38 18
355 A100 150fr multi 90 50
356 A100 250fr multi 1.50 80
357 A100 350fr multi 2.25 1.10
Nos. 354-357 (4) 5.03 2.58

Head, Village and Fly — A101

1978, Nov. 28 ***Perf. 13***
358 A101 60f multi 38 18

National Health Day.

Nos. 341-346 Overprinted in Silver:
a. 1962 BRESIL-TCHECOSLOVAQUIE / 3-1
b. 1966 / GRANDE BRETAGNE / - ALLEMAGNE (RFA) / 4-2
c. 1970 BRESIL-ITALIE 4-1
d. 1974 ALLEMAGNE (RFA)- / PAYS BAS 2-1
e. 1978 / ARGENTINE -/ PAYS BAS / 3-1
f. ARGENTINE -PAYS BAS / 3-1

1978, Dec. 30 **Litho.** ***Perf. 13½***
359 A98(a) 40fr multi 22 15
360 A98(b) 60fr multi 38 18
361 A98(c) 100fr multi 55 32
362 A98(d) 200fr multi 1.25 60
363 A98(e) 300fr multi 1.90 95
Nos. 359-363 (5) 4.30 2.20

Souvenir Sheet
364 A98(f) 500fr multi 3.00 1.50

World Soccer Championship winners.

UPU Emblems, Camel Caravan, Satellites — A102

Design: 150fr, Obus woman and houses, Massa Territory, hibiscus.

1979, June 8 **Litho.** ***Perf. 12x12½***
365 A102 60fr multi 38 18
366 A102 150fr multi 90 50

Philexafrique II, Libreville, Gabon, June 8-17. Nos. 365, 366 each printed in sheets of 10 with 5 labels showing exhibition emblem.

Wildlife Fund Emblem and Gazelle A103

Protected Animals: 50fr, Addax. 60fr, Oryx antelope. 100fr, Cheetah. 150fr, Zebra. 300fr, Rhinoceros.

1979, Sept. 15 **Litho.** ***Perf. 14½***
367 A103 40fr multi 25 15
368 A103 50fr multi 32 15
369 A103 60fr multi 38 18
370 A103 100fr multi 60 32
371 A103 150fr multi 95 50
372 A103 300fr multi 1.90 95
Nos. 367-372 (6) 4.40 2.25

Souvenir Sheet

Holy Family, by Dürer A104

1979, Sept. 1 ***Perf. 13½***
373 A104 500fr brown & dull red 3.50 1.75

Boy and Handpainted Doors — A105

IYC Emblem and: 75fr, Oriental girl. 100fr, Caucasian girl, doves. 150fr, African boys. 250fr, Pencil and outlines of child's hands.

1979, Sept. 19 **Litho.** ***Perf. 13½***
374 A105 65fr multi 40 20
375 A105 75fr multi 48 25
376 A105 100fr multi 60 32
377 A105 150fr multi 95 48
Nos. 374-377 (4) 2.43 1.25

Souvenir Sheet
378 A105 20fr multi 1.90 95

Nos. 314-315 Overprinted "ALUNISSAGE/APOLLO XI/JUILLET 1969" and Emblem

1979, Nov. 26 **Litho.** ***Perf. 13½x14***
379 A86 45fr multi 28 15
380 A86 90fr multi 55 32
Nos. 379-380,C240-C242 (5) 4.18 2.19

Apollo 11 moon landing, 10th anniversary.

Ski Jump, Lake Placid '80 Emblem A106

Lake Placid '80 Emblem and: 20fr, Slalom, vert. 40fr, Biathlon, vert. 150fr, Women's slalom, vert. 350fr, Cross-country skiing. 500fr, Downhill skiing.

1979, Dec. 18 ***Perf. 14½***
381 A106 20fr multi 16 15
382 A106 40fr multi 30 15
383 A106 60fr multi 45 20
384 A106 150fr multi 1.10 55
385 A106 350fr multi 2.50 1.25
386 A106 500fr multi 3.75 1.75
Nos. 381-386 (6) 8.26 4.05

13th Winter Olympic Games, Lake Placid, NY, Feb. 12-24, 1980.

Jet over Map of Africa A107

1980, Feb. 20 **Litho.** ***Perf. 12½***
387 A107 15fr yellow & multi 15 15
388 A107 30fr blue & multi 20 15
389 A107 60fr red & multi 42 20
Nos. 387-389 (3) 77
Set value 35

ASECNA (Air Safety Board), 20th anniv.

1982 World Cup Soccer Championships, Spain — A108

1982 **Litho.** ***Perf. 13½***
390 A108 30fr Hungary 15 15
391 A108 40fr Italy 15 15
392 A108 50fr Algeria 15 15
393 A108 60fr Argentina 15 15
Nos. 390-393,C258-C259 (6) 1.60
Set value 75

21st Birthday of Princess Diana A109

1982, July 2 **Litho.** ***Perf. 13½***
395 A109 30fr 1961 18 15
396 A109 40fr 1965 25 15
397 A109 50fr 1967 32 15
398 A109 60fr 1975 38 18
Nos. 395-398,C260-C261 (6) 3.53 1.83

For overprints see Nos. 413-419B.

A110

1984 Summer Olympics, Los Angeles — A110a

Designs: No. 405A, Runner. No. 405B, Long jumper, vert.

1982, Aug. 2 Litho. *Perf. 13½*

399 A110 30fr Gymnast 18 15
400 A110 40fr Equestrian 25 15
401 A110 50fr Judo 32 15
402 A110 60fr High jump 38 18
403 A110 80fr Hurdles 50 25
404 A110 300fr Woman gymnast 1.90 95
Nos. 399-404 (6) 3.53 1.83

Souvenir Sheet

405 A110 500fr Relay race 3.25 1.50

For surcharge see No. C302.

1982, July 31 Litho. & Embossed

405A A110a 1500fr gold & multi

Souvenir Sheet

405B A110a 1500fr gold & multi

No. 405 contains one 56x39mm stamp. Nos. 403-405B airmail.

Scouting Year — A111

Boy Scouts, 75th Anniv. A111a

Scouts from various countries. No. 412A, Lord Robert Baden-Powell. No. 412B, Scouts at campsite, Baden-Powell, horiz.

1982, July 15

406 A111 30fr West Germany 18 15
407 A111 40fr Upper Volta 25 15
408 A111 50fr Mali 32 15
409 A111 60fr Scotland 38 18
410 A111 80fr Kuwait 50 25
411 A111 300fr Chad 1.90 95
Nos. 401-411 (11) 9.88 4.86

Souvenir Sheet

412 A111 500fr Chad, diff. 3.25 1.50

Litho. & Embossed

412A A111a 1500fr gold & multi

Souvenir Sheet

412B A111a 1500fr gold & multi

No. 412 contains one 53x35mm stamp. Nos. 410-412B airmail.

For overprints see Nos. 466-472B.

Nos. 395-398, C260-C262B Overprinted: "21 JUIN 1982 / WILLIAM ARTHUR PHILIP LOUIS/ PRINCE DE GALLES"

1982, Oct. 4 Litho. *Perf. 13½*

413 A109 30fr multi 18 15
414 A109 40fr multi 25 15
415 A109 50fr multi 32 15
416 A109 60fr multi 38 18
417 A109 80fr multi 50 25
418 A109 300fr multi 1.90 95
Nos. 413-418 (6) 3.53 1.83

Souvenir Sheet

419 A109 500fr multi 3.25 1.50

Litho. & Embossed

419A AP71b 1500fr on #C262A

Souvenir Sheet

419B AP71b 1500fr on #C262B

Birth of Prince William of Wales, June 21. Nos. 417-419B airmail.

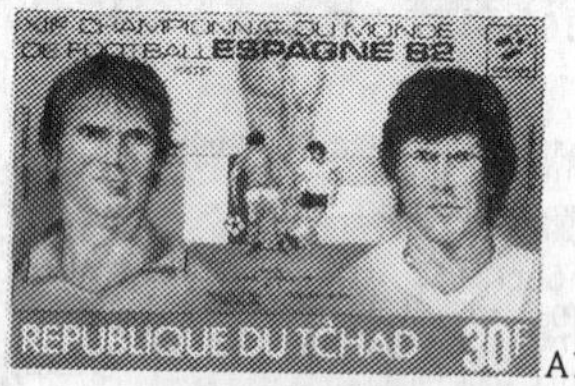

A112

1982 World Cup Soccer Championships, Spain — A112a

Various players and flags. No. 426A, Dino Zoff, Italy, holding World Cup trophy. No. 426B, Paolo Rossi, Italy, two players, trophy, horiz.

1982, Nov. 30

420 A112 30fr multi 18 15
421 A112 40fr multi 25 15
422 A112 50fr multi 32 15
423 A112 60fr multi 38 18
424 A112 80fr multi 50 25
425 A112 300fr multi 1.90 95
Nos. 420-425 (6) 3.53 1.83

Souvenir Sheet

426 A112 500fr multi 3.25 1.50

Litho. & Embossed

426A A112a 1500fr gold & multi

Souvenir Sheet

426B A112a 1500fr gold & multi

No. 426 contains one 56x32mm stamp. Nos. 424-426B airmail. For surcharge see No. C306.

A113

Chess Champions — A113a

Designs: No. 433A, Bobby Fischer. No. 433B, William Steinitz.

1982, Dec. 24

427 A113 30fr Philidor 18 15
428 A113 40fr Paul Morphy 25 15
429 A113 50fr Howard Staunton 32 15
430 A113 60fr Capablanca 38 18
431 A113 80fr Boris Spassky 50 25
432 A113 300fr Anatoly Karpov 1.90 95
Nos. 427-432 (6) 3.53 1.83

Souvenir Sheet

433 A113 500fr Victor Korchnoi 3.25 1.50

Litho. & Embossed

433A A113a 1500fr gold & multi

Souvenir Sheet

433B A113a 1500fr gold & multi

No. 433 contains one 53x35mm stamp. Nos. 431-433B airmail.

For overprints see Nos. 459-465.

2nd UN Conference on Peaceful Uses of Outer Space, Vienna, Aug. 9-21 — A114

A114a

Inventors and Satellites: 30fr, K.E. Tsiolkovsky, Soyuz. 40fr, R.H. Goddard, space telescope design. 50fr, Korolev, ultraviolet telescope. 60fr, von Braun, Columbia space shuttle. 80fr, Esnault Pelterie, Ariana rocket. 300fr, H. Oberth, orbital space station. 500fr, Pres. Kennedy, Apollo 11 badge, lunar rover. No. 440A, Sir Bernard Lovell, Viking I & II. No. 440B, Sir Isaac Newton, satellite TDF 1.

1983, Jan. 31 Litho. *Perf. 13½*

434 A114 30fr multi 18 15
435 A114 40fr multi 25 15
436 A114 50fr multi 32 15
437 A114 60fr multi 38 18
438 A114 80fr multi 50 25
439 A114 300fr multi 1.90 95
Nos. 434-439 (6) 3.53 1.83

Souvenir Sheet

440 A114 500fr multi 3.25 1.50

Litho. & Embossed

440A A114a 1500fr gold & multi

Souvenir Sheet

440B A114a 1500fr gold & multi

No. 440 contains one 42x50mm stamp. Nos. 438-440B airmail.

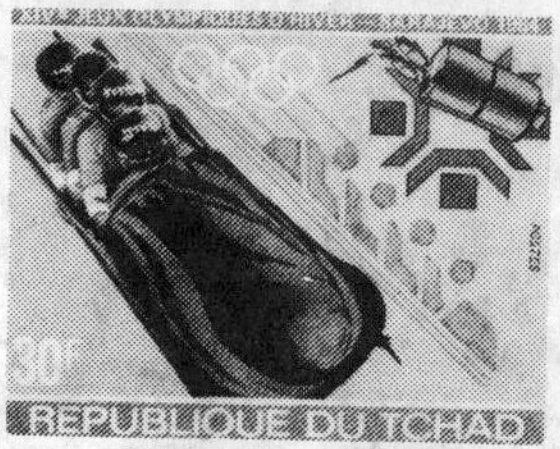

Bobsledding — A115

Woman Figure Skater A115a

Design: No. 447B, Slalom skier, horiz.

1983, Apr. 25 Litho. *Perf. 13½*

441 A115 30fr shown 15 15
442 A115 40fr Speed skating 18 15
443 A115 50fr Cross-country skiing 25 15
444 A115 60fr Hockey 32 18
445 A115 80fr Ski jumping 40 25
446 A115 300fr Downhill skiing 1.50 95
Nos. 441-446 (6) 2.80 1.83

Souvenir Sheet

447 A115 500fr Figure skating 2.50 1.50

Litho. & Embossed

447A A115a 1500fr gold & multi

Souvenir Sheet

447B A115a 1500fr gold & multi

14th Winter Olympic Games, Sarajevo, Yugoslavia, Feb. 8-19, 1984. Nos. 445-447B airmail. For surcharge see No. C298.

First Manned Balloon Flight, 200th Anniv. A116

Designs: 25fr, Hot air balloon, Montgolfier Brothers. 45fr, Captive balloon, Pilatre De Rozier. 50fr, First parachute descent, Jacques Garnerin. 60fr, Chelsea balloon, J.P. Blanchard.

1983, May 30 Litho. *Perf. 13½*

448 A116 25fr multi 15 15
449 A116 45fr multi 28 15
450 A116 50fr multi 32 15
451 A116 60fr multi 38 18
Nos. 448-451,C268-C269 (6) 2.43 1.26

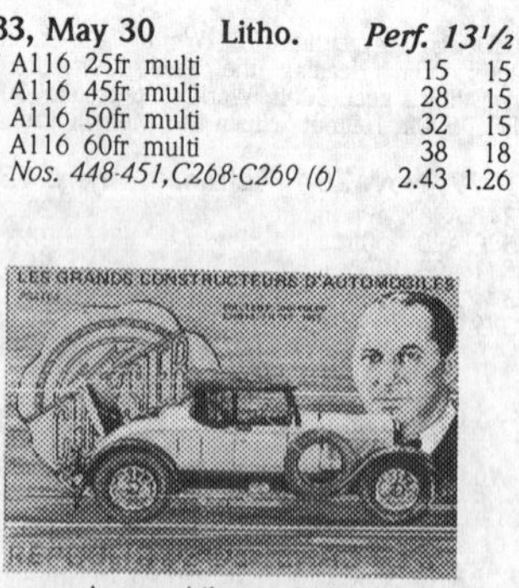

Automobiles — A116a

Automobiles and their builders: 25fr, 1927 Mercedes Type S, Gottlieb Daimler and Karl Benz. 45fr, 1913 Torpedo Martini Type GC 32-2, 6L, Friedrich Martini. 50fr, 1926 Chrysler "70," Walter P. Chrysler. 60fr, 1929 Alfa Romeo 6C 1750 Grand Sport, Nicola Romeo. 80fr, 1934 Phantom II Continental, Stewart Rolls and Henry Royce. 250fr, 1948 Talbot Lago, Lord Shrewsbury and Talbot.

1983, July 15 **Litho.** *Perf. 13½*

451A A116a 25fr multicolored
451B A116a 45fr multicolored
451C A116a 50fr multicolored
451D A116a 60fr multicolored
451E A116a 80fr multicolored
451F A116a 250fr multicolored

Nos. 451E-451F are airmail.

1984 Summer Olympics, Los Angeles — A117

A117a

1983, Nov. 15 **Litho.** *Perf. 13½*

452	A117	25fr Kayak	15	15
453	A117	45fr Long jump	15	15
454	A117	50fr Boxing	15	15
455	A117	60fr Discus	18	15
456	A117	80fr Running	25	15
457	A117	350fr Equestrian	1.10	55
		Nos. 452-457 (6)	1.98	
		Set value		94

Souvenir Sheet

458 A117 500fr Gymnastics 1.50 80

Litho. & Embossed

458A A117a 1500fr Hurdles

Souvenir Sheet

458B A117a 1500fr Equestrian, vert.

Nos. 456-458B are airmail.

Nos. 427-433 Overprinted: "60e ANNIVERSAIRE FEDERATION / MONDIALE D'ECHECS 1924-1984"

1983, Dec. 27 **Litho.** *Perf. 13½*

459 A113	30fr multi	15	15
460 A113	40fr multi	15	15
461 A113	50fr multi	15	15
462 A113	60fr multi	18	15
463 A113	80fr multi	25	15
464 A113	300fr multi	95	50
	Nos. 459-464 (6)	1.83	
	Set value		88

Souvenir Sheet

465 A113 500fr multi 1.50 80

World Chess Fedn., 60th anniv.

Nos. 406-412B Ovptd. with Emblem for the 15th World Scout Jamboree, Alberta, Canada, 1983

1983, Dec. 27 **Litho.** *Perf. 13½*

466 A111	30fr multi	15	15
467 A111	40fr multi	15	15
468 A111	50fr multi	15	15
469 A111	60fr multi	18	15
470 A111	80fr multi	25	15
471 A111	300fr multi	95	50
	Nos. 466-471 (6)	1.83	
	Set value		88

Souvenir Sheet

472 A111 500fr multi 1.50 80

Litho. & Embossed

472A A111a 1500fr on #412A

Souvenir Sheet

472B A111a 1500fr on #412B

Locomotive "Lady," 1879 A118

1984, Mar. 15

473 A118	50fr shown	15	15
474 A118	200fr Sailboat, Lake Chad	60	32
475 A118	300fr Graf Zeppelin	90	45
476 A118	350fr Renault desert transport, 1930	1.10	55
477 A118	400fr Bloch 120 monoplane	1.25	60
478 A118	500fr Air Africa DC-8	1.40	70
	Nos. 473-478 (6)	5.40	2.77

Souvenir Sheet

479 A118 600fr Intelsat V satellite 1.75 85

Nos. 477-479 airmail. For surcharge see No. 579.

Liberation, 2nd Anniv. — A119

Pres. Hissein Habre — A120

1984, June 6 *Perf. 12½*

480 A119 50fr multi 15 15

1984, June 18 *Perf. 12½x13*

481 A120 125fr multi 38 18

Anniversaries and Events — A121

Designs: 50fr, Pres. Habre, civil war martyrs. 200fr, Paul Harris, Rotary Intl. headquarters, Illinois. 300fr, Alfred Nobel, will establishing fund for Prizes. 350fr, Raphael, detail from Virgin with Child and St. John the Baptist. 400fr, Rembrandt, detail from The Holy Family. 500fr, J.W. Goethe, scene from Faust. 600fr, Rubens, detail from Helene Forement and Her Two Children.

1984, Jan. 16 **Litho.** *Perf. 13½*

482 A121	50fr multi	15	15
483 A121	200fr multi	55	32
484 A121	300fr multi	85	45
485 A121	350fr multi	1.10	55
486 A121	400fr multi	1.25	60
487 A121	500fr multi	1.40	70
	Nos. 482-487 (6)	5.30	2.77

Souvenir Sheet

488 A121 600fr multi 1.75 85

Nos. 486-488 are airmail.

Homage to Our Martyred Dead — A122

1984, Feb. 22 **Litho.** *Perf. 13½*

500 A122	50fr multi	15	15
501 A122	80fr multi	24	15
502 A122	120fr multi	35	18
503 A122	200fr multi	65	28
504 A122	250fr multi	80	40
	Nos. 500-504 (5)	2.19	1.16

#503-504 airmail. For surcharge see #C303.

World Communications Year — A123

1984, Feb. 29 **Litho.** *Perf. 13½*

505 A123	50fr sil & multi	15	15
506 A123	60fr sil & multi	18	15
507 A123	70fr sil & multi	20	15
508 A123	125fr sil & multi	38	18
509 A123	250fr sil & multi	80	40
	Nos. 505-509 (5)	1.71	
	Set value		83

#508-509 airmail. For surcharge see #C304.

Anniversaries and Events — A123a

Designs: 50fr, Durer, detail from Madonna of the Rosary. 200fr, Henri Dunant, Red Cross founder, Battle of Solferino. 300fr, Early telephone, Goonhilly Downs Satellite Station, Britain. 350fr, J.F. Kennedy, Neil Armstrong's first step on Moon, 1969. 400fr, Europe-Africa Satellite infrared photograph. 500fr, Prince Charles and Lady Diana. 600fr, Wedding photograph of Prince Charles and Lady Diana.

1984

510 A123a	50fr multi	15	15
511 A123a	200fr multi	55	28
512 A123a	300fr multi	85	45
513 A123a	350fr multi	1.10	52
514 A123a	400fr multi	1.25	55
515 A123a	500fr multi	1.50	80
a.	Souvenir sheet of one	2.25	1.10
	Nos. 510-515 (6)	5.40	2.75

Souvenir Sheet

516 A121 600fr multicolored

Nos. 514-516 are airmail. For surcharge see No. 578.

Development of Communications — A123b

Ships and locomotives.

1984, Aug. 1 **Litho.** *Perf. 12½*

517 A123b	90fr Indiaman, East India Co.	25	15
518 A123b	100fr Nord 701, 1885	28	15
519 A123b	125fr Vera Cruz	38	18
520 A123b	150fr Columbia, 1888	42	20
521 A123b	200fr Carlisle Castle	55	28
522 A123b	250fr Rete Mediterranea, 1900	80	40
523 A123b	300fr Britannia	85	45
524 A123b	350fr Mav 114	1.10	52
	Nos. 517-524 (8)	4.63	2.33

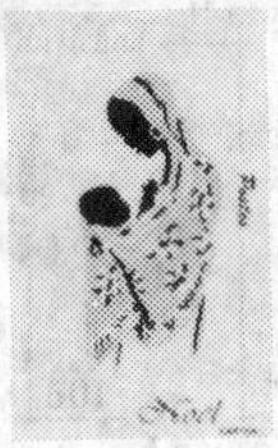
Christmas — A124

1984, Dec. 28 **Litho.** *Perf. 13*

525 A124	50fr lt bl & org brn	15	15
526 A124	60fr ver & org brn	15	15
527 A124	80fr emer & org brn	20	15
528 A124	85fr rose lil & org brn	22	15
529 A124	100fr org yel & org brn	25	15
530 A124	135fr dp bl vio & org brn	38	18
	Nos. 525-530 (6)	1.35	
	Set value		73

European Music Year A125

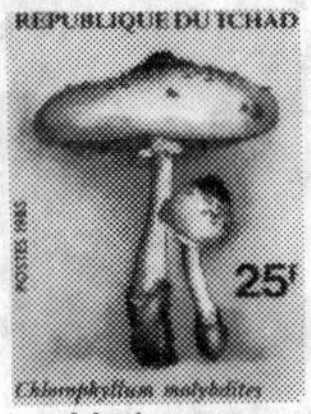

Mushrooms A126

Instruments.

1985, Apr. 30 **Litho.** *Perf. 12x12½*

531 A125	20fr Guitar	15	15
532 A125	25fr Harp	15	15
533 A125	30fr Xylophone	15	15
534 A125	50fr Shoulder drum	15	15
535 A125	70fr like #534	18	15
536 A125	80fr like #532	20	15
537 A125	100fr like #531	25	15
538 A125	250fr like #533	60	32
	Set value	1.50	84

1985, May 15 **Litho.** *Perf. 12½*

539 A126	25fr Chlorophyllum molybdites	15	15
540 A126	30fr Tulostoma volvulatum	15	15
541 A126	50fr Lentinus tuber-regium	15	15
542 A126	70fr like #541	18	15
543 A126	80fr Podaxis pistillaris	20	15
544 A126	100fr like #539	25	32
	Set value	88	66

Anniversaries and Events — A127

Designs: 25fr, Abraham Lincoln. 45fr, Henri Dunant, Geneva birthplace and red cross. 50fr, Gottlieb Daimler, 1887 Motor Carriage. 60fr, Louis Bleriot, Bleriot XI monoplane, 1909. 80fr, Paul Harris, Chicago site of Rotary Intl. founding. 350fr, Auguste Piccard, bathyscaphe Trieste, 1953. 600fr, Anatoly Karpov, 1981 world chess champion. 1500fr, Paul Harris.

1985, May 25 **Litho.** *Perf. 13½*

545 A127	25fr multi	15	15
546 A127	45fr multi	15	15
547 A127	50fr multi	15	15
548 A127	60fr multi	15	15
549 A127	80fr multi	22	15
550 A127	350fr multi	85	45
	Nos. 545-550 (6)	1.67	
	Set value		80

Souvenir Sheets

551 A127 600fr multi 1.75 85

Litho. & Embossed

551A A127 150fr multi

No. 551A contains one 130x90mm stamp. Nos. 548-551A are airmail.

Souvenir sheets of one exist for Nos. 545-551.

Intl. Youth Year — A128

1985, May 30 **Litho.** *Perf. 13*

552 A128 70fr Development levels, vert. 18 15
553 A128 200fr Globe 50 25

A129

3rd Anniv. of the Republic A130

Perf. 13, 12½x13

1985, June 7 **Litho.**

554 A129 70fr Hand, claw 18 15
555 A129 70fr Hands, map 18 15
556 A130 70fr Pres. Hissein Habre 18 15
557 A129 110fr like #554 28 15
558 A129 110fr like #555 28 15
559 A130 110fr like #556 28 15
Nos. 554-559 (6) 1.38
Set value 63

Audubon Birth Bicent. — A131 Mammals — A132

1985, July 20 **Engr.** *Perf. 13*

560 A131 70fr Stork 18 15
561 A131 110fr Ostrich 32 15
562 A131 150fr Marabou 45 22
563 A131 200fr Snake eagle 55 28
Nos. 560-563 (4) 1.50 80

Souvenir Sheet

564 A131 500fr like 200fr 1.40 70

1985, Oct. 1

565 A132 50fr Waterbuck 15 15
566 A132 70fr Kudus, horiz. 38 18
567 A132 250fr Shaggy mouflon 80 40
Nos. 565-567 (3) 1.33 73

Souvenir Sheet

568 A132 500fr White rhinoceros 1.75 85

UN, 40th Anniv. — A133

1985, Oct. 24

569 A133 200fr brt bl, red & brn 55 28

Chad Admission to UN, 25th Anniv. — A134

1985, Oct. 24

570 A134 300fr red, brt bl & yel 1.00 50

President's Visit to the Nation's Interior A135

1986, June 7 **Litho.** *Perf. 12½x13*

571 A135 100fr multi 45 22
572 A135 170fr multi 75 38
573 A135 200fr multi 90 45
Nos. 571-573 (3) 2.10 1.05

World Wildlife Fund — A136

Various mouflons, *Ammotragus lervia.*

1988, Nov. 10 **Litho.** *Perf. 13*

574 A136 25fr shown 18 15
575 A136 45fr Adult, young 30 15
576 A136 70fr Two adults, diff. 48 25
577 A136 100fr Adults, young 68 35
Nos. 574-577 (4) 1.64 90

Nos. 512 and 475 Surcharged

1989 **Litho.** *Perf. 13½*

578 A123a 170fr on 300fr #512
579 A118 240fr on 300fr #475

Liberation — A137

1989 *Perf. 11½x12*

580 A137 20fr multi 15 15
581 A137 25fr multi 15 15
582 A137 40fr multi 24 15
583 A137 100fr multi 60 30
584 A137 170fr multi 1.05 52
Nos. 580-584 (5) 2.19 1.27

Visit of Pope John Paul II — A138

Cathedral in Chad and: 20fr, 100fr, Pope holding crosier. 80fr, 170fr, Pope, diff.

1990, Jan. 30 **Litho.** *Perf. 13*

585 A138 20fr multicolored 15 15
586 A138 80fr multicolored 58 30
587 A138 100fr multicolored 70 35
588 A138 170fr multicolored 1.20 60
Nos. 585-588 (4) 2.63 1.40

Vaccinations A140

1991 **Photo.** *Perf. 11½*

Granite Paper

593 A140 30fr brown & multi 26 15
594 A140 100fr green & multi 90 45
595 A140 170fr vio & multi 1.50 75
596 A140 180fr blue & multi 1.60 80
597 A140 200fr red & multi 1.75 90
Nos. 593-597 (5) 6.01 3.05

A141

A142

1991 **Litho.**

598 A141 10fr green & multi 15 15
599 A141 20fr lilac & multi 18 15
600 A141 40fr yellow & multi 35 18
601 A141 70fr blue & multi 60 30
602 A141 130fr tan & multi 1.15 58
603 A141 200fr pink & multi 1.75 90
Nos. 598-603 (6) 4.18 2.26

Liberty and Democracy Day, Dec. 1, 1990.

1992, Nov. 15 **Litho.** *Perf. 11½*

604 A142 20fr bright yel & multi 15 15
605 A142 45fr golden yel & multi 35 18
606 A142 85fr pink & multi 68 35
607 A142 170fr blue & multi 1.35 68
608 A142 300fr gray & multi 2.35 1.20
Nos. 604-608 (5) 4.88 2.56

Doctors Without Borders, 20th anniv.

Campaign Against Illiteracy A143

1992, Nov. 30

609 A143 25fr yellow green & multi 20 15
610 A143 40fr golden yel & multi 32 15
611 A143 70fr pink & multi 55 28
612 A143 100fr lilac & multi 78 40
613 A143 180fr blue & multi 1.40 70
614 A143 200fr gray & multi 1.60 80
Nos. 609-614 (6) 4.85 2.48

Intl. Conference on Nutrition, Rome — A144

1992, Dec. 15

615 A144 10fr yellow & multi 15 15
616 A144 60fr pink & multi 48 24
617 A144 120fr yellow green & multi 95 48
618 A144 500fr blue & multi 4.00 2.00
Nos. 615-618 (4) 5.58 2.87

SEMI-POSTAL STAMPS

Catalogue values for unused stamps in this section are for Never Hinged items.

Anti-Malaria Issue
Common Design Type
Perf. 12½x12

1962, Apr. 7 **Engr.** **Unwmk.**

B1 CD108 25fr + 5fr orange 42 42

Freedom from Hunger Issue
Common Design Type

1963, Mar. 21 *Perf. 13*

B2 CD112 25fr + 5fr dk grn, dk bl & brn 42 42

Red Cross, Mother and Children — SP1

1974, Oct. 2 **Photo.** *Perf. 12½x13*

B3 SP1 30fr + 10fr multi 22 20

Red Cross of Chad, first anniversary.

AIR POST STAMPS

Catalogue values for unused stamps in this section are for Never Hinged items.

Olympic Games Issue
French Equatorial Africa No. C37
Surcharged in Red

XVII• OLYMPIADE 1960
REPUBLIQUE DU TCHAD
250F

Unwmk.

1960, Dec. 15 Engr. *Perf. 13*
C1 AP8 250fr on 500fr grnsh blk, blk & slate 6.00 6.00

17th Olympic Games, Rome, Aug. 25-Sept. 11. Surcharge 46mm wide; illustration reduced.

Red Bishops — AP1

Discus Thrower — AP2

Designs (birds in pairs): 100fr, Scarlet-chested sunbird. 200fr, African paradise flycatcher. 250fr, Malachite kingfisher. 500fr, Nubian carmine bee-eater.

1961-63 Unwmk. Engr. *Perf. 13*
C2 AP1 50fr dk grn, mag & blk 40 16
C3 AP1 100fr multi 1.00 45
C4 AP1 200fr multi 2.00 80
C5 AP1 250fr dk bl, grn & dp org ('63) 2.75 1.40
C6 AP1 500fr multi 6.00 2.50
Nos. C2-C6 (5) 12.15 5.31

Air Afrique Issue
Common Design Type

1962, Feb. 17 Unwmk. *Perf. 13*
C7 CD107 25fr lt bl, org brn & blk 25 15

Abidjan Games Issue

1962, July 21 Photo. *Perf. 12x12½*
C8 AP2 100fr brn, lt grn & blk 1.00 60

African Postal Union Issue
Common Design Type

1963, Sept. 8 Unwmk. *Perf. 12½*
C9 CD114 85fr dk bl, ocher & red 65 30

Air Afrique Issue, 1963
Common Design Type

1963, Nov. 19 *Perf. 13x12*
C10 CD115 50fr multi 60 40

Europafrica Issue
Common Design Type

1963, Nov. 30 Photo. *Perf. 12x13*
C11 CD116 50fr dp grn, yel & dk brn 50 38

Mail Truck and Broussard Plane — AP4

Unwmk.

1963, Dec. 16 Engr. *Perf. 13*
C12 AP4 100fr sl grn, ultra & red brn 1.00 35

The index in each volume of the Scott Catalogue contains many listings that help identify stamps.

Chiefs of State Issue

Map and Presidents of Chad, Congo, Gabon and Central African Republic AP4a

1964, June 23 Photo. *Perf. 12½*
C13 AP4a 100fr multi 90 42

See note after Central African Republic No. C19.

Europafrica Issue, 1964

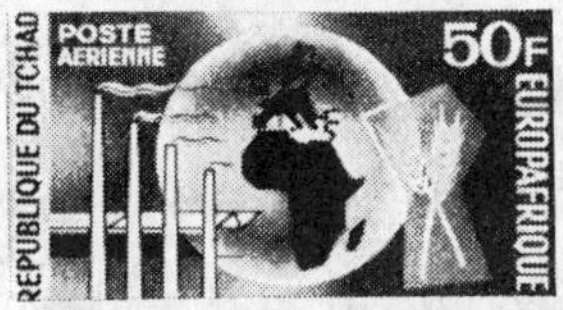

Globe and Emblems of Industry and Agriculture — AP5

1964, July 20 *Perf. 13x12*
C14 AP5 50fr brn, pur & dp org 42 30

See note after Cameroun No. 402.

Soccer — AP6

Designs: 50fr, Javelin throw, vert. 100fr, High jump, vert. 200fr, Runners.

1964, Aug. 12 Engr. *Perf. 13*
C15 AP6 25fr yel grn, sl grn & org brn 25 16
C16 AP6 50fr org brn, ind & brt bl 45 32
C17 AP6 100fr blk, red & brt grn 1.00 65
C18 AP6 200fr bis, blk & car 2.00 1.25
a. Min. sheet of 4, #C15-C18 3.75 3.75
Nos. C15-C18 (4) 3.70 2.38

18th Olympic Games, Tokyo, Oct. 10-25, 1964.

Communications Symbols — AP7

1964, Nov. 2 Litho. *Perf. 12½x13*
C19 AP7 25fr lil, dk brn & lt red brn 25 15

Pan-African and Malagasy Posts and Telecommunications Cong., Cairo, Oct. 24-Nov. 6.

President John F. Kennedy (1917-63) — AP8

1964, Nov. 3 Photo. *Perf. 12½*
C20 AP8 100fr multi 1.10 80
a. Souvenir sheet of 4 3.50 3.50

ICY Emblem — AP9

1965, July 5 Photo. *Perf. 13*
C21 AP9 100fr multi 1.00 60

International Cooperation Year, 1965.

Abraham Lincoln — AP10

1965, Sept. 7 Unwmk. *Perf. 13*
C22 AP10 100fr multi 1.00 60

Centenary of death of Abraham Lincoln.

Musical Instrument Type of Regular Issue

Design: 100fr, Xylophone (marimba).

1965, Oct. 26 Engr. *Perf. 13*
Size: 48x27mm
C23 A18 100fr ocher, brt bl & vio bl 90 30

Sir Winston Spencer Churchill (1874-1965) — AP11

1965, Nov. 23 Engr. *Perf. 13*
C24 AP11 50fr dk grn & blk 50 22

Dr. Albert Schweitzer and Outstretched Hands — AP12

1966, Feb. 15 Photo. *Perf. 12½*
C25 AP12 100fr multi 1.00 50

Dr. Albert Schweitzer (1875-1965), medical missionary, theologian and musician.

Air Afrique Issue, 1966
Common Design Type

1966, Aug. 31 Photo. *Perf. 13*
C26 CD123 30fr yel grn, blk & gray 30 16

White-throated Bee-eater — AP13

Birds: 50fr, Blue-eared glossy starling. 200fr, African pygmy kingfisher. 250fr, Red-throated bee-eater. 500fr, Little green bee-eater.

1966-67 Photo. *Perf. 13x12½*
C27 AP13 50fr gold & multi 35 16
C28 AP13 100fr bluish gray & multi 65 30
C29 AP13 200fr grnsh gray & multi 1.40 65
C30 AP13 250fr pale bl & multi 1.60 80
C31 AP13 500fr pale sal & multi 3.00 1.60
Nos. C27-C31 (5) 7.00 3.51

Issue dates: 100fr, 200fr, 500fr, Oct. 18, 1966. Others, Mar. 21, 1967.
For surcharges see Nos. C67-C69.

Congress Hall — AP14

1967, Jan. 5 Photo. *Perf. 12½*
C32 AP14 25fr multi 25 15

Opening of the new Congress Hall.

Breguet 19 Biplane — AP15

Planes: 30fr, Latécoère 631 hydroplane. 50fr, Douglas DC-3. 100fr, Piper Cherokee 6.

1967, Aug. 1 Engr. *Perf. 13*
C33 AP15 25fr sky bl, sl grn & lt brn 25 15
C34 AP15 30fr sky bl, indigo & grn 30 16
C35 AP15 50fr sky bl, ol bis & sl grn 50 25
C36 AP15 100fr dk bl, sl grn & dk red 1.00 50
Nos. C33-C36 (4) 2.05 1.06

First anniversary of Air Chad.

African Postal Union Issue, 1967
Common Design Type

1967, Sept. 9 Engr. *Perf. 13*
C37 CD124 100fr ol, brt pink & red brn 90 45

Rock Painting Type of Regular Issue

1967, Dec. 19 Engr. *Perf. 13*
Size: 48x27mm
C38 A32 100fr Masked dancers 1.00 42
C39 A32 125fr Rabbit hunt 1.25 60

Downhill Skiing — AP16

1968, Feb. 5 **Engr.** ***Perf. 13***
C40 AP16 30fr shown 30 16
C41 AP16 100fr Ski jump, vert. 1.00 60

10th Winter Olympic Games, Grenoble, France, Feb. 6-18.

Konrad Adenauer (1876-1967), Chancellor of West Germany (1949-63) — AP17

1968, Mar. 19 **Photo.** ***Perf. 12½***
C42 AP17 52fr grn, dk brn & lt lil 55 30
a. Souvenir sheet of 4 2.25 2.25

The Snake Charmer, by Henri Rousseau AP18

Design: 130fr, "War" by Henri Rousseau.

1968, May 14 **Photo.** ***Perf. 13½***
Size: 41x41mm
C43 AP18 100fr ultra & multi 1.00 40
Size: 48x35mm
Perf. 12½
C44 AP18 130fr brn & multi 1.10 55

Hurdlers — AP19

1968, Oct. 16 **Engr.** ***Perf. 13***
C45 AP19 32fr shown 35 15
C46 AP19 80fr Relay race 65 20

19th Olympic Games, Mexico City, Oct. 12-27.

PHILEXAFRIQUE Issue

The Actor Wolf (Bernard), by Jacques L. David AP20

1969, Jan. 15 **Photo.** ***Perf. 12½***
C47 AP20 100fr multi 95 55

PHILEXAFRIQUE, Philatelic Exhib. in Abidjan, Feb. 14-23. Printed with alternating label.

2nd PHILEXAFRIQUE Issue
Common Design Type

Design: 50fr, Chad No. J12 and Moundang Dancers.

1969, Feb. 14 **Engr.** ***Perf. 13***
C48 CD128 50fr red, brt bl, brn & grn 48 32

Gustav Nachtigal and Tibesti Gorge, 1869 — AP21

Design: No. C50, Heinrich Barth and Lake Chad, 1851.

1969, Feb. 17
C49 AP21 100fr vio bl, dk brn & brn 80 25
C50 AP21 100fr grn, pur & bl 80 25

German explorers Gustav Nachtigal (1834-85) and Heinrich Barth (1821-65), and state visit of the Pres. of West Germany Heinrich Lubke.

Apollo 8, Earth and Moon — AP22

1969, Apr. 10 **Photo.** ***Perf. 13***
C51 AP22 100fr multi 80 45

US Apollo 8 mission, the 1st men in orbit around the moon, Dec. 21-27, 1968.

Mahatma Gandhi — AP23

Portraits: No. C53, John F. Kennedy. No. C54, Dr. Martin Luther King, Jr. No. C55, Robert F. Kennedy.

1969, May 20 **Photo.** ***Perf. 12½***
C52 AP23 50fr blk & lt grn 42 25
C53 AP23 50fr blk & tan 42 25
C54 AP23 50fr blk & pink 42 25
C55 AP23 50fr blk & lt vio bl 42 25
a. Souvenir sheet of 4, #C52-C55 2.50 2.50
Nos. C52-C55 (4) 1.68 1.00

Issued to honor exponents of non-violence.

Presidents Tombalbaye and Mobutu, Map and Flags of Chad and Congo — AP24

Embossed on Gold Foil
1969 ***Die-cut; Perf. 13½***
C56 AP24 1000fr gold, dk bl & red 10.00 10.00

1st anniv. of the establishment of the Union of Central African States, comprising Chad, Congo Democratic Republic and Central African Republic.

Napoleon Visiting Hospital, by Alexandre Veron-Bellecourt — AP25

Paintings: 85fr, Battle of Wagram, by Horace Vernet. 130fr, Battle of Austerlitz, by Francois Pascal Gerard.

1969, July 23 **Photo.** ***Perf. 12x12½***
C57 AP25 30fr multi 38 28
C58 AP25 85fr multi 1.10 70
C59 AP25 130fr multi 1.90 1.10
Nos. C57-C59 (3) 3.38 2.08

Bicentenary of birth of Napoleon I.

Apollo 11 Issue

Astronaut on Moon — AP26

Embossed on Gold Foil
1969, Oct. 17 ***Die-cut; Perf. 13½***
C60 AP26 1000fr gold 10.00 10.00

See note after Algeria No. 427.

Village Life, by Goto Narcisse — AP27

Designs: No. C62, Women at the Market, by Iba N'Diaye. No. C63, Woman with Flowers, by Iba N'Diaye, vert.

1970 **Photo.** ***Perf. 12x12½, 12½x12***
C61 AP27 100fr multi 55 15
C62 AP27 250fr grn & multi 2.00 35
C63 AP27 250fr brn & multi 2.00 35
Nos. C61-C63 (3) 4.55 85

Issue dates: Mar. 17, 100fr; Aug. 28, #C62-C63.

Napoleon — AP27a

Designs: Nos. C63A, C63E, Napoleon II, Duke of Reichstadt, vert.
No. C63B, 10fr, Crossing the Grand St. Bernard, by David. 25fr, Emperor Napoleon, by Gerard. 32fr, Marriage of Napoleon and Marie Louise, by Rouget. 40fr, Napoleon after return from Elba, vert.

Perf. 12x12½, 12½x12
1970-71 **Litho.**
C63A AP27a 10fr multicolored
C63B AP27a Strip of 3

Embossed
Perf. 13
C63C AP27a 10fr gold
f. Sheet of 1, Imperf.

Souvenir Sheets
Litho.
Perf. 13x13½
C63D AP27a 40fr multicolored

Embossed
Imperf
C63E AP27a 10fr gold, like #C63A

#C63A is printed se-tenant with label. #C63D contains one 43x67mm stamp. #C63f contains one 53x42mm stamp with same size design as #C63B, 10fr. #C63E contains one 43x104mm stamp with same size design as #C63A.
No. C63E probably was not available in Chad.
Issue dates: No. C63B, June 12. Nos. C63A, C63D-C63E, Apr. 1971. No. C63C, Nov. 1, 1971.

EXPO Emblem and Osaka Print — AP28

Designs (EXPO Emblem and): 100fr, Tower of the Sun. 125fr, Osaka print (diff. design).

1970, June 30 **Engr.** ***Perf. 13***
C64 AP28 50fr bl, red brn & sl grn 42 15
C65 AP28 100fr red, yel grn & Prus bl 80 18
C66 AP28 125fr blk, dk red & bis 1.00 25
Nos. C64-C66 (3) 2.22 58

Issued to publicize EXPO '70 International Exhibition, Osaka, Japan, Mar. 15-Sept. 13.

1968 Summer Olympics, 1970 World Cup Soccer Championships, Mexico — AP28a

1970, July 1 **Litho.** ***Perf. 12½x12***
C66A AP28a 5fr Flags, soccer players

Souvenir Sheet
Perf. 13½x13
C66C AP28a 15fr Olympic torch, soccer player

No. C66A printed in sheets of 2 + 2 labels. No. C66C contains one 66x43mm stamp.
For overprints see Nos. C88A-C88B.

Nos. C28-C30 Surcharged in Carmine with New Value and Bars and Overprinted:
a. "APOLLO XI / 1er débarquement sur la lune/20 juillet 1969"
b. "APOLLO XII / Exploration de la lune / 19 Novembre 1969"
c. "APOLLO XIII / Exploit spatial / 11-17 avril 1970"

1970, July 9 **Photo.** ***Perf. 13x12½***
C67 AP13 (a) 50fr on 100fr multi 40 25
C68 AP13 (b) 100fr on 200fr multi 80 38
C69 AP13 (c) 125fr on 250fr multi 1.00 50
Nos. C67-C69 (3) 2.20 1.13

Space missions of Apollo 11, 12 and 13.

DC-8 "Fort Lamy" over Airport AP29

1970, Aug. 5 *Perf. 12½*

C70	AP29	30fr dk sl grn & multi	25	15

Souvenir Sheet

Apollo 12 AP29a

1970, Sept. **Embossed** ***Imperf.***

C70A	AP29a	25fr gold		

No. C70A probably was not available in Chad.

The Visitation, Venetian School, 15th Century AP30

Paintings, Venetian School: 25fr, Nativity, 15th century. 30fr, Virgin and Child, c. 1350.

1970, Dec. 15 **Photo.** ***Perf. 12½x12***

C71	AP30	20fr gold & multi	18	15
C72	AP30	25fr gold & multi	20	15
C73	AP30	30fr gold & multi	25	15
		Nos. C71-C73 (3)	63	45

Christmas 1970. See Nos. C105-C108.

Post Office Mauritius and Emblem AP31

1971, Jan. 23 **Engr.** ***Perf. 13***

C74	AP31	10fr shown	15	15
C75	AP31	20fr Tuscany #23	15	15
C76	AP31	30fr France #8	25	15
C77	AP31	60fr US #2	42	15
C78	AP31	80fr Japan #8	55	25
C79	AP31	100fr Saxony #1	80	28
a.		Souvenir sheet of 6, #C74-C79	3.25	3.25
		Nos. C74-C79 (6)	2.32	
		Set value		85

Publicity for PHILEXOCAM, philatelic exhibition, Fort Lamy, Jan. 23-30.

Gamal Abdel Nasser — AP32

1971, Feb. 16 **Photo.** ***Perf. 12½***

C80	AP32	75fr multi	48	15

In memory of Gamal Abdel Nasser (1918-1970), President of Egypt.

Presidents Mobutu, Bokassa and Tombalbaye — AP33

1971, Apr. 28 **Photo.** ***Perf. 13***

C81	AP33	100fr multi	65	32

Return of Central African Republic to the United States of Central Africa which also includes Congo Democratic Republic and Chad.

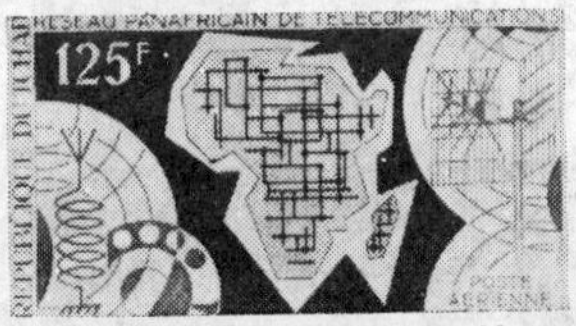

Map of Africa, Communications Network and Symbols — AP34

1971, May 17 **Engr.** ***Perf. 13***

C82	AP34	125fr ultra, sl grn & brn red	85	18

Pan-African telecommunications system.

Boys Around Campfire, Torii — AP35

1971, Aug. 24 **Photo.** ***Perf. 12½***

C83	AP35	250fr multi	1.75	55

13th Boy Scout World Jamboree, Asagiri Plain, Japan, Aug. 2-10.

White Egret AP36

1971, Sept. 28 **Photo.** ***Perf. 13x12½***

C84	AP36	1000fr blk, dk bl & ocher	6.25	4.50

Greek Marathon Runners — AP37

Designs: 45fr, Ancient Olympic Stadium. 75fr, Greek wrestlers. 130fr, Olympic Stadium, Athens, 1896.

1971, Oct. 5 ***Perf. 12½***

C85	AP37	40fr multi	32	15
C86	AP37	45fr multi	35	22
C87	AP37	75fr multi	52	25
C88	AP37	130fr multi	85	42
		Nos. C85-C88 (4)	2.04	1.04

75th anniv. of modern Olympic Games.

Nos. C66A, C66C Ovptd. in Gold

1971 **Litho.** ***Perf. 12½x12***

C88A	AP28a	5fr on #C66A		

Souvenir Sheet

Perf. 13½x13

C88B	AP28a	15fr on #C66C		

Overprint on No. C88B is 36mm long.

Duke Ellington — AP38

Charles de Gaulle — AP39

Portraits: 50fr, Sidney Bechet. 100fr, Louis Armstrong.

1971, Oct. 20 **Litho.** ***Perf. 13***

C89	AP38	50fr multi	40	15
C90	AP38	75fr lt bl & multi	55	28
C91	AP38	100fr multi	80	40
		Nos. C89-C91 (3)	1.75	83

Famous American jazz musicians.

Lithographed and Embossed

1971, Nov. 9 ***Perf. 12½***

Design: No. C93, Félix Eboué.

C92	AP39	200fr grn, yel grn & gold	2.50	2.50
C93	AP39	200fr bl, lt bl & gold	2.50	2.50
a.		Souv. sheet of 2, #C92-C93 + label	5.00	5.00

Charles de Gaulle (1890-1970), pres. of France.

African Postal Union Issue, 1971

Common Design Type

Design: 100fr, Sao antelope head and UAMPT building, Brazzaville, Congo.

1971, Nov. 13 **Photo.** ***Perf. 13x13½***

C94	CD135	100fr bl & multi	70	22

Apollo 15 Rocket AP40

Designs: 80fr, Apollo 15 capsule, horiz. 150fr, Lunar module on Moon, horiz. 250fr, Astronaut making tests. 300fr, Moon-buggy. No. C100, Successful splashdown, horiz. No. C101, Apollo 15 insignia.

1972, Jan. 5 **Litho.** ***Perf. 13½***

C95	AP40	40fr multi	20	15
C96	AP40	80fr multi	40	18
C97	AP40	150fr multi	75	38
C98	AP40	250fr multi	1.25	60
C99	AP40	300fr multi	1.50	75
C100	AP40	500fr multi	2.50	1.25
		Nos. C95-C100 (6)	6.60	3.31

Souvenir Sheet

C101	AP40	500fr multi	2.50	1.10

Apollo 15 moon landing.

Soyuz 2 Link-up — AP41

Designs: 30fr, Soyuz 2 on launching pad, vert. 50fr, No. C108, Cosmonauts in uniform. 200fr, V. I. Patsayev. No. C106, V. N. Volkov. 400fr, G. L. Dobrovolsky. No. C109, Three cosmonauts.

1972, Jan. 5 ***Perf. 13½x13***

C102	AP41	30fr multi	15	15
C103	AP41	50fr multi	25	15
C104	AP41	100fr multi	50	25
C105	AP41	200fr multi	1.00	50
C106	AP41	300fr multi	1.50	75
C107	AP41	400fr multi	2.25	1.00
		Nos. C102-C107 (6)	5.65	2.80

Souvenir Sheets

C108	AP41	300fr multi	1.90	95
C109	AP41	400fr multi	2.50	1.25

Soyuz 2 link-up project.

Bobsledding — AP42

Design: 100fr, Slalom.

1972, Feb. 24 **Engr.** ***Perf. 13***

C110	AP42	50fr Prus bl & rose red	38	15
C111	AP42	100fr red lil & slate grn	75	22

11th Winter Olympic Games, Sapporo, Japan, Feb. 3-13.

Pres. Tombalbaye Type, 1972

1972, Apr. 13 **Litho.** ***Perf. 13***

C112	A63	70fr multi	42	22
C113	A63	80fr multi	50	25

11th Winter Olympic Type, 1972

Designs: 130fr, Speed skating. No. C115, Ice hockey. No. C116, Ski jumping. 250fr, 4-man bobsled.

1972, Apr. 13 *Perf. 13½*

C114 A64 130fr multi 75 45
C115 A64 200fr multi 1.50 60

Souvenir Sheets

C116 A64 200fr multi 1.50 60
C117 A64 250fr multi 1.75 95

Scout Jamboree Type, 1972

Designs: 100fr, Cooking preparation. 120fr, Lord Baden Powell. 250fr, Hiking.

1972, May 15

C118 A67 100fr multi 60 38
C119 A67 120fr multi 75 50

Souvenir Sheet

C120 A67 250fr multi 1.50 95

Zebras — AP43

African wild animals: 30fr, Mandrills. 100fr, African elephants. 130fr, Gazelles. 150fr, Hippopotamuses. 200fr, Lion cub.

1972, May 15 **Litho.** *Perf. 13*

C121 AP43 20fr multi 15 15
C122 AP43 30fr multi 18 15
C123 AP43 100fr multi 60 32
C124 AP43 130fr multi 80 40
C125 AP43 150fr multi 95 50
Nos. C121-C125 (5) 2.68 1.52

Souvenir Sheet

C126 AP43 200fr multi 1.25 60

View of Venice, by Caffi — AP44

Paintings by Ippolito Caffi: 40fr, Sailing ship and Doge's Palace, vert. 140fr, Grand Canal, vert.

1972, May 23 **Photo.**

C127 AP44 40fr gold & multi 32 15
C128 AP44 45fr gold & multi 38 15
C129 AP44 140fr gold & multi 95 60
Nos. C127-C129 (3) 1.65 90

UNESCO campaign to save Venice.

11th Winter Olympic Winners Type, 1972

Designs: 150fr, Slalom, B. Cochran, US. 200fr, Women's figure skating, B. Schuba, Austria. 250fr, Ice hockey, USSR. 300fr, 2-man bobsled. W. Zimmerer and P. Utzschneider, West Germany.

1972, June 15 *Perf. 14½*

C130 A69 150fr gold & multi 95 48
C131 A69 200fr gold & multi 1.25 60

Souvenir Sheets

C132 A69 250fr gold & multi 1.25 80
C133 A69 300fr gold & multi 1.90 1.10

Nos. C130-C131 exist se-tenant with label showing earth satellite.

Daudet, "Tartarin de Tarascon," Book Year Emblem — AP45

1972, July 22 **Engr.** *Perf. 13*

C134 AP45 100fr dk red, lil & dk brn 75 18

Intl. Book Year, 1972, and to honor Alphonse Daudet (1840-1897), French writer.

20th Summer Olympics Type, 1972

Designs (TV Tower, Munich and): 100fr, Gymnast. 120fr, Pole vault. 150fr, Fencing. 250fr, Hammer throw. 300fr, Boxing.

1972, Aug. 15

C135 A70 100fr gold & multi 60 32
C136 A70 120fr gold & multi 75 38
C137 A70 150fr gold & multi 95 50
Nos. C135-C137 (3) 2.30 1.20

Souvenir Sheets

C138 A70 250fr gold & multi 1.75 90
C139 A70 300fr gold & multi 2.00 1.00

Nos. C135-C137 exist se-tenant with label showing arms of Munich.

Lunokhod on Moon — AP46

Russian moon missions: 100fr, Luna 16 on moon and rocket in flight, vert.

1972, Sept. 19

C140 AP46 100fr dk bl, pur & bis 75 32
C141 AP46 150fr slate, brn & lil 1.10 50

Farcha Laboratory, Cattle, Scientist — AP47

1972, Nov. 11 **Photo.** *Perf. 13*

C142 AP47 75fr yellow & multi 42 22

20th anniversary of the Farcha Laboratory for veterinary research.

King Faisal and Holy Kaaba, Mecca — AP48

1972, Nov. 17

C143 AP48 75fr multi 48 25

Visit of King Faisal of Saudi Arabia.

Christmas Type of 1970

Christmas: 40fr, Virgin and Child, by Giovanni Bellini. 75fr, Virgin and Child, by Dall'Occhio. 80fr, Nativity, by Fra Angelico, horiz. 95fr, Adoration of the Kings, by Il Perugino.

1972, Dec. 15 **Photo.** *Perf. 13*

C144 AP30 40fr gold & multi 32 15
C145 AP30 75fr gold & multi 55 15
C146 AP30 80fr gold & multi 60 18
C147 AP30 95fr gold & multi 65 25
Nos. C144-C147 (4) 2.12 73

Summer Olympic Winners Type, 1972

Designs (Olympic Emblems and): 150fr, Pole vault, Nordwig, East Germany. 250fr, Hurdles, Milburn, US 300fr, Javelin, Wolfermann, West Germany.

1972, Dec. 22

C148 A76 150fr multi 95 50
C149 A76 250fr multi 1.50 80

Souvenir Sheet

C150 A76 300fr multi 2.00 95

Summer Olympic Winners Type, 1972

Designs (Olympic Emblem and): 150fr, Dressage, Mancinelli, Italy. No. C152; Finn class sailing, Serge Maury, France. No. C153, Swimming, Mark Spitz.

1972, Dec. 22 **Litho.** *Perf. 11*

C151 A77 150fr gold & multi 95 48
C152 A77 250fr gold & multi 1.50 80

Souvenir Sheet

C153 A77 250fr multi 1.50 80

Copernicus and Solar System — AP49

1973, Mar. 31 **Engr.** *Perf. 13*

C154 AP49 250fr gray, mag & brn 1.75 95

500th anniversary of the birth of Nicolaus Copernicus (1473-1543), Polish astronomer.

Horses — AP49a

Details from paintings: 20fr, A Horse Frightened by Lightning, by Theordore Gericault. 60fr, The White Horse, by Paul Potter. 100fr, Mares and Foals, by George Stubbs. 150fr, Horse Head, by Theordore Gericault, vert. 500fr, The Carriage, by Vernet.

1973 **Litho.** *Perf. 11½*

C154A AP49a 20fr multicolored
C154B AP49a 60fr multicolored
C154C AP49a 100fr multicolored
C154D AP49a 150fr multicolored

Souvenir Sheet

Perf. 15

C154E AP49a 500fr multicolored

See note before No. 225A.

Airplanes — AP49b

1973 **Litho.** *Perf. 12*

C154F AP49b 5fr Fokker F VII/3M
C154G AP49b 25fr DH 89A Rapide
C154H AP49b 70fr Viscount
C154J AP49b 150fr Boeing 747
C154K AP49b 200fr Concorde

Souvenir Sheet

Perf. 12

C154L AP49b 350fr Concorde, diff.

Nos. C154L contains one 60x40mm stamp. See note before No. 225A.

Skylab over Africa — AP50

1974, Aug. 6 **Engr.** *Perf. 13*

C155 AP50 100fr shown 60 35
C156 AP50 150fr Skylab 85 48

Exploits of Skylab, US manned space station.

Soccer — AP51

Designs: 125fr, 150fr, Soccer players; 125fr, vert.

1974, Oct. 22 **Engr.** *Perf. 13*

C157 AP51 50fr dl red & choc 28 15
C158 AP51 125fr red & dp grn 65 40
C159 AP51 150fr grn & rose red 80 48
Nos. C157-C159 (3) 1.73 1.03

World Cup Soccer Championship, Munich, June 13-July 7.

Family and WPY Emblem — AP52

1974, Nov. 11

C160 AP52 250fr multi 1.50 95

World Population Year.

Mail Delivery by Canoe — AP53

UPU Cent.: 40fr, Diesel train. 100fr, Jet. 150fr, Spacecraft.

1974, Dec. 20 **Engr.** *Perf. 13*

C161 AP53 30fr car & multi 18 15
C162 AP53 40fr ultra & blk 22 15
C163 AP53 100fr brn, ultra & blk 55 35
C164 AP53 150fr grn, lil & ol 85 52
Nos. C161-C164 (4) 1.80 1.17

Women of Different Races, IWY Emblem — AP54

1975, June 25 Photo. *Perf. 13*

C165 AP54 250fr bl & multi	1.40	80

International Women's Year 1975.

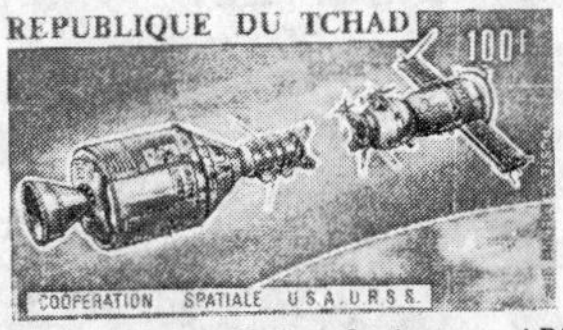

Apollo and Soyuz Before Link-up — AP55

Design: 130fr, Apollo and Soyuz after link-up.

1975, July 15 Engr. *Perf. 13*

C166 AP55 100fr ultra, choc & grn	60	32
C167 AP55 130fr vio bl, brn & grn	75	48

Apollo Soyuz space test project (Russo-American space cooperation), launching July 15; link-up July 17.

For overprints see Nos. C171-C172.

Soccer Player, View of Montreal — AP56

Designs (Olympic Rings, Montreal Skyline): 100fr, Discus thrower. 125fr, Runner.

1975, Oct. 14 Engr. *Perf. 13*

C168 AP56 75fr car & sl grn	42	25
C169 AP56 100fr car, choc & bl grn	60	32
C170 AP56 125fr brn, bl & car	80	50
Nos. C168-C170 (3)	1.82	1.07

Pre-Olympic Year 1975.

Nos. C166-C167 Overprinted: "JONCTION / 17 JUILLET 1975"

1975, Nov. 4 Engr. *Perf. 13*

C171 AP55 100fr multi	60	32
C172 AP55 130fr multi	75	42

Apollo-Soyuz link-up in space, July 17.

Stylized British and American Flags, "200" — AP57

1975, Dec. 5 Engr. *Perf. 13*

C173 AP57 150fr vio bl, car & ol bis	80	50

American Bicentennial.

Adoration of the Shepherds, by Murillo — AP58

Christmas (Paintings): 75fr, Adoration of the Shepherds, by Georges de La Tour. 80fr, Virgin and Child with Bible, by Rogier van der Weyden, vert. 100fr, Holy Family, by Raphael, vert.

1975, Dec. 15 Litho. *Perf. 13x12½*

C174 AP58 40fr yel & multi	25	15
C175 AP58 75fr yel & multi	42	25
C176 AP58 80fr yel & multi	50	25
C177 AP58 100fr yel & multi	60	28
Nos. C174-C177 (4)	1.77	93

12th Winter Olympic Winners Type, 1976

Designs: 250fr, 4-man bobsled, West Germany. 300fr, Speed skating, J. E. Storholt, Norway. 500fr, Downhill skiing, F. Klammer, Austria.

1976, June 21 *Perf. 14*

C178 A84 250fr multi	1.40	70
C179 A84 300fr multi	1.75	95

Souvenir Sheet

C180 A84 500fr multi	3.25	1.25

Paul Revere's Ride and Portrait by Copley — AP59

American Bicentennial: 125fr, Washington crossing Delaware. 150fr, Lafayette offering his services to America. 200fr, Rochambeau at Yorktown with Washington. 250fr, Franklin presenting Declaration of Independence. 400fr, Count de Grasse's victory at Cape Charles.

1976, July 4 Litho. *Perf. 14*

C181 AP59 100fr multi	60	32
C182 AP59 125fr multi	75	38
C183 AP59 150fr multi	85	42
C184 AP59 200fr multi	1.25	55
C185 AP59 250fr multi	1.90	60
Nos. C181-C185 (5)	5.35	2.27

Souvenir Sheet

C186 AP59 400fr multi	2.75	1.25

Summer Olympics Type, 1976

Designs: 100fr, Boxing. 200fr, Pole vault. 300fr, Shot put. 500fr, Sprint.

1976, July 12

C187 A85 100fr multi	50	32
C188 A85 200fr multi	1.25	55
C189 A85 300fr multi	1.90	70
Nos. C187-C189 (3)	3.65	1.57

Souvenir Sheet

C190 A85 500fr multi	2.50	1.25

Viking Mars Project Type, 1976

Designs (Mars Lander and): 100fr, Viking landing on Mars. 200fr, Capsule over Mars. 250fr, Lander over Mars. 450fr, Lander and probe.

1976, July 23 Litho. *Perf. 14*

C191 A86 100fr multi	60	32
C192 A86 200fr multi	1.40	55
C193 A86 250fr multi	1.50	60
Nos. C191-C193 (3)	3.50	1.47

Souvenir Sheet

C194 A86 450fr multi	2.75	1.25

For overprints see Nos. C240-C243.

Concorde — AP60

1976, Oct. 15 Litho. *Perf. 12½*

C195 AP60 250fr bl, blk & ver	1.25	38

First commercial flight of supersonic jet Concorde, Jan. 21.

Nobel Prize Type, 1976

Designs: 100fr, Albert Einstein, physics. 200fr, Dag Hammarskjold, peace. 300fr, Shinichiro Tomanaga, physics. 500fr, Alexander Fleming, medicine.

1976, Dec. 15

C196 A87 100fr multi	60	32
C197 A87 200fr multi	1.25	55
C198 A87 300fr multi	1.90	70
Nos. C196-C198 (3)	3.75	1.57

Souvenir Sheet

C199 A87 500fr multi	3.00	1.25

Adoration of the Shepherds, by Gerard van Honthorst — AP61

Christmas (Paintings): 30fr, Nativity, by Albrecht Altdorfer, vert. 60fr, Nativity, by Hans Holbein, vert. 150fr, Adoration of the Kings, by Gerard David.

1976, Dec. 22 Litho. *Perf. 12½*

C200 AP61 30fr gold & multi	15	15
C201 AP61 60fr gold & multi	32	18
C202 AP61 120fr gold & blk	60	38
C203 AP61 150fr gold & blk	75	42
Nos. C200-C203 (4)	1.82	1.13

Lesdiguières Bridge, by Jongkind — AP62

Design: 120fr, Sailing Ship and Boats, by Johan Barthold Jongkind (1819-1891).

1976, Dec. 27 Photo. *Perf. 13*

C204 AP62 100fr multi	50	28
C205 AP62 120fr multi	60	38

Centenary of impressionism.

Zeppelin Type of 1977

Designs: 125fr, Germany #C40, North Pole. 150fr, Germany #C45, Chicago department store. 175fr, Germany #C38 and scenes of NYC and London. 200fr, 500fr, US #C15, NYC.

1977, Mar. 30 *Perf. 11*

C206 A91 125fr multi	75	32
C207 A91 150fr multi	90	38
C208 A91 175fr multi	1.10	42
C209 A91 200fr multi	1.50	52
Nos. C206-C209 (4)	4.25	1.64

Souvenir Sheet

C210 A91 500fr multi	3.00	1.25

Sassenage Castle, Grenoble — AP63

1977, May 21 Litho. *Perf. 12½*

C211 AP63 100fr multi	50	28

Intl. French Language Council, 10th Anniv.

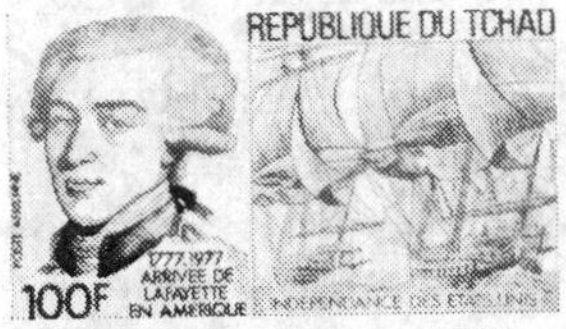

Lafayette and Ships — AP64

American Bicentennial: 120fr, Abraham Lincoln, eagle and flags, vert. 150fr, James Madison and family.

1977, July 30 Engr. *Perf. 13*

C212 AP64 100fr multi	50	38
C213 AP64 120fr multi	60	42
C214 AP64 150fr multi	75	55
Nos. C212-C214 (3)	1.85	1.35

Lindbergh and Spirit of St. Louis — AP65

Designs: 100fr, Concorde. 150fr, 200fr, 300fr, Various Lindbergh portraits and Spirit of St. Louis.

1977, Sept. 27

C215 AP65 100fr multi	50	38
C216 AP65 120fr multi	60	42
C217 AP65 150fr multi	75	55
C218 AP65 200fr multi	1.00	70
C219 AP65 300fr multi	1.50	1.00
Nos. C215-C219 (5)	4.35	3.05

Charles A. Lindbergh's solo transatlantic flight from NY to Paris, 50th anniv., and 1st supersonic transatlantic flight of Concorde.

For overprint see No. C227.

Mariner 10 — AP66

Spacecraft: 200fr, Lunokhod on moon, Luna 21. 300fr, Viking on Mars.

1977, Oct. 10 Engr. *Perf. 13*

C220 AP66 100fr multi	50	38
C221 AP66 200fr multi	1.00	75
C222 AP66 300fr multi	1.50	1.00
Nos. C220-C222 (3)	3.00	2.13

Running — AP67

1977, Oct. 24 Engr. *Perf. 13*

C223	AP67	30fr shown	15	15
C224	AP67	60fr Volleyball	32	22
C225	AP67	120fr Soccer	60	42
C226	AP67	125fr Basketball	60	48
		Nos. C223-C226 (4)	1.67	1.27

No. C215 Overprinted: "PARIS NEW-YORK / 22.11.77"

1977, Nov. 22

C227	AP65	100fr multi	50	38

Concorde, 1st commercial flight Paris to New York.

Virgin and Child, by Rubens AP68

Rubens Paintings: 60fr, Virgin and Child and Two Donors. 100fr, Adoration of the Shepherds. 125fr, Adoration of the Kings.

1977, Dec. 20 Litho. *Perf. 12½x12*

C228	AP68	30fr multi	15	15
C229	AP68	60fr multi	32	22
C230	AP68	100fr multi	50	38
C231	AP68	125fr multi	60	48
		Nos. C228-C231 (4)	1.57	1.23

Christmas 1977.

Antoine de Saint-Exupéry — AP69

Designs: 50fr, Wilbur and Orville Wright and Flyer. 80fr, Hugo Junkers and his plane. 100fr, Gen. Italo Balbo and his plane. 120fr, Concorde. 500fr, Wilbur and Orville Wright and Flyer.

1978, Oct. 25 Litho. *Perf. 13½*

C232	AP69	40fr multi	25	15
C233	AP69	50fr multi	32	15
C234	AP69	80fr multi	50	25
C235	AP69	100fr multi	60	32
C236	AP69	120fr multi	75	38
		Nos. C232-C236 (5)	2.42	1.25

Souvenir Sheet

C237	AP69	500fr multi	3.50	1.75

History of aviation and 75th anniversary of 1st powered flight.

Philexafrique II-Essen Issue
Common Design Types

Designs: No. C238, Rhinoceros and Chad No. C6. No. C239, Kingfisher and Mecklenburg-Strelitz No. 1.

1978, Nov. 1 *Perf. 12½*

C238	CD138	100fr multi	60	32
C239	CD139	100fr multi	60	32

Nos. C238-C239 printed se-tenant.

Nos. C191-C194 Overprinted "ALUNISSAGE/APOLLO XI/ JUILLET 1969"

1979, Nov. 26 Litho. *Perf. 13½x14*

C240	A86	100fr multi	60	32
C241	A86	200fr multi	1.25	60
C242	A86	250fr multi	1.50	80
		Nos. C240-C242 (3)	3.35	1.72

Souvenir Sheet

C243	A86	450fr multi	3.00	1.50

Apollo 11 moon landing, 10th anniversary.

Hurdles, Moscow '80 Emblem — AP70

Moscow '80 Emblem and: 30fr, Field hockey. 250fr, Swimming. 350fr, Running. 500fr, Yachting.

1979, Nov. 30 *Perf. 13½*

C244	AP70	15fr multi	15	15
C245	AP70	30fr multi	25	15
C246	AP70	250fr multi	1.90	80
C247	AP70	350fr multi	2.50	1.25
		Nos. C244-C247 (4)	4.80	2.35

Souvenir Sheet

C248	AP70	500fr multi	3.75	1.90

Pre-Olympic Year.
For overprints see Nos. C254-C255.

Austria Jubilee Issue of 1910, Canoe, Hill AP71

Hill, Stamps and Vessels: 100fr, US type A97, dhow. 200fr, France No. 21, Sidewheeler. 300fr, Holstein No. 16, ocean liner. 500fr, Chad No. J13, ocean liner.

1979, Dec. 3 *Perf. 14x13½*

C249	AP71	65fr multi	50	25
C250	AP71	100fr multi	65	32
C251	AP71	200fr multi	1.50	60
C252	AP71	300fr multi	2.25	95
		Nos. C249-C252 (4)	4.90	2.12

Souvenir Sheet

C253	AP71	500fr multi	3.75	1.90

Sir Rowland Hill (1795-1879), originator of penny postage.
For overprints see Nos. C256-C257.

Nos. C244-C245, C249-C250 Overprinted: "POSTES 1981" in Red or Overprinted and Surcharged Silver on Red

Perf. 13½, 14x13½

1981, Nov. 15 Litho.

C254	AP70	30fr on 15fr multi	18	15
C255	AP70	30fr multi	18	15
C256	AP71	60fr on 65fr multi	38	18
C257	AP71	60fr on 100fr multi	38	18
		Nos. C254-C257 (4)	1.12	66

Soccer Type of 1982 and

1982 World Cup Soccer Championships, Spain — AP71a

Design: No. C259C, Soccer players, ball, and trophy, vert.

1982 Litho. *Perf. 13½*

C258	A108	80fr Brazil	20	15
C259	A108	300fr W. Germany	80	42

Souvenir Sheet

C259A	A108	500fr like 300fr	1.40	70

Litho. & Embossed

C259B	AP71a	1500fr gold & multi		

Souvenir Sheet

C259C	AP71a	1500fr gold & multi		

No. C259A contains one 42x51mm stamp.
For surcharge see No. C305.

Diana Type of 1982 and

Princess Diana, 21st Birthday AP71b

Design: No. C262A, Portrait, horiz.

1982, July 2 Litho. *Perf. 13½*

C260	A109	80fr 1977	50	25
C261	A109	300fr 1980	1.90	95

Souvenir Sheet

C262	A109	500fr 1981	3.00	1.50

Litho. & Embossed

C262A	AP71b	1500fr gold & multi		

Souvenir Sheet

C262B	AP71b	1500fr gold & multi		

For overprints see Nos. 419A-419B.

Manned Flight Bicentenary AP72

Balloons: 100fr, Charles' and Roberts', 1783, vert. 200fr, J.P. Blanchard, Berlin, 1788, vert. 300fr, Charles Green, London, 1837. 400fr, Modern blimp. 500fr, Montgolfiere, 1783, vert.

1983, Apr. Litho. *Perf. 13*

C263	AP72	100fr multi	48	25
C264	AP72	200fr multi	95	48
C265	AP72	300fr multi	1.40	70
C266	AP72	400fr multi	1.90	95
		Nos. C263-C266 (4)	4.73	2.38

Souvenir Sheet

C267	AP72	500fr multi	3.00	1.50

Balloon Type and

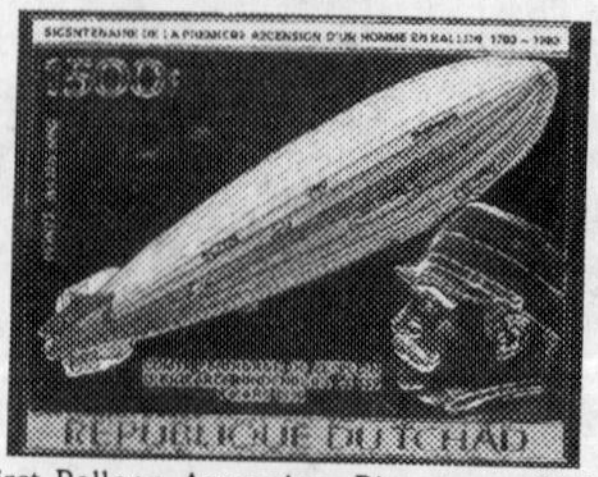

First Balloon Ascension, Bicent. — AP72a

Designs: 80fr, Steam Powered Airship, H. Giffard. 250fr, Graf Zeppelin; Airship L-1, 1st flight. 300fr, 1st Balloon Flight, Montgolfier and Rozier. No. C270A, Airship Hindenburg, Count Ferdinand von Zeppelin. No. C270B, Jean-Francois Pilatre de Rozier and Marquis d'Arlandes, first balloon ascension.

1983, May 30 Litho. *Perf. 13*

C268	A116	80fr multi	50	25
C269	A116	250fr multi	80	38

Souvenir Sheet

C270	A116	300fr multi	1.90	95

Litho. & Embossed

Perf. 13½

C270A	AP72a	1500fr gold & multi		

Souvenir Sheet

C270B	AP72a	1500fr gold & multi		

For surcharge see No. C299.

1984 Summer Olympics — AP73

Various kayak scenes.

1984, Mar. 1 Litho. *Perf. 13*

C271	AP73	100fr multi	28	15
C272	AP73	200fr multi	55	28
C273	AP73	300fr multi	85	42
C274	AP73	400fr multi	1.10	55
		Nos. C271-C274 (4)	2.78	1.40

Souvenir Sheet

C275	AP73	500fr multi	1.40	70

Natl. Goals — AP73a

Designs: Nos. C276, C278, Peace and reconciliation. Nos. C277, C279, Self-sufficiency in food production.

1983, Dec. 26 Litho. *Perf. 13½*

C276	AP73a	150fr multi	85	42
C277	AP73a	150fr multi	85	42
C278	AP73a	200fr multi	1.10	55
C279	AP73a	200fr multi	1.10	55
		Nos. C276-C279 (4)	3.90	1.94

For surcharges see Nos. C300-C301.

Paul P. Harris (1868-1947), Founder of Rotary Intl. — AP73b

Litho. & Embossed

1984, Jan. 16 *Perf. 13½*

C279B	AP73b	1500fr gold & multi		

IYY, PHILEXAFRICA '85 — AP74

1985, May 2 Litho. *Perf. 13*

C280	AP74	200fr	Boy scout, tree	50	25
C281	AP74	200fr	Air Chad Fokker 27	50	25

Printed se-tenant with center label.

IYY, PHILEXAFRICA Type of 1985

1985, Nov. 1 Litho. *Perf. 13x12½*

C283	AP74	250fr	Girl, Scout ceremony	85	42
C284	AP74	250fr	Communications and transportation	85	42

Nos. C283-C284 printed se-tenant with center labels picturing map of Africa or UAPT emblem.

ASCENA Airlines, 25th Anniv. — AP75

1985, Aug. 15 *Perf. 12½*

C285	AP75	70fr	bl & multi	18	15
C286	AP75	110fr	org & multi	28	15
C287	AP75	250fr	yel & multi	70	35
			Nos. C285-C287 (3)	1.16	65

Victor Hugo (1802-1885), French Novelist — AP76

Scene from Les Miserables.

1985, Nov. 24 Engr. *Perf. 13*

C288	AP76	70fr	org brn, chlky bl & dp brn	18	15
C289	AP76	110fr	lake, dk brn & dk grn	38	18
C290	AP76	250fr	brt org, blk & dk red	90	42
C291	AP76	300fr	dk red, cl & sl bl	1.00	52
			Nos. C288-C291 (4)	2.46	1.27

Christmas 1985 — AP77

1985, Dec. 22 Litho. *Perf. 13½*

C292	250fr	Adoration of the Magi	85	42

1988 Summer Olympics, Seoul — AP78

1988, June 1 Litho. *Perf. 13*

C293	AP78	100fr	400-Meter hurdles, vert.	65	32
C294	AP78	170fr	5000-Meter race	1.10	55
C295	AP78	200fr	Long jump	1.30	65
C296	AP78	600fr	Triple jump, vert.	3.85	1.95
			Nos. C293-C296 (4)	6.90	3.47

Souvenir Sheet

C297	AP78	750fr	10,000-Meter race, vert.	5.00	2.50

Stamps of 1982-84 Surcharged

1989 *Perfs. as Before*

C298	A115	100 on 300fr #446	
C299	A116	100 on 250fr #C269	
C300	AP73a	100 on 200fr #C278	
C301	AP73a	100 on 200fr #C279	
C302	A110	170 on 300fr #404	
C303	A122	170 on 200fr #503	
C304	A123	170 on 250fr #509	
C305	A108	170 on 300fr #C259	
C306	A112	240 on 300fr #425	

AIR POST SEMI-POSTAL STAMPS

Catalogue values for unused stamps in this section are for Never Hinged items.

Ramses II Battling the Hittites (from Abu Simbel) — SPAP1

Unwmk.

1964, Mar. 9 Engr. *Perf. 13*

CB1	SPAP1	10fr + 5fr	multi	22	20
CB2	SPAP1	25fr + 5fr	multi	35	25
CB3	SPAP1	50fr + 5fr	multi	65	60
			Nos. CB1-CB3 (3)	1.22	1.05

UNESCO world campaign to save historic monuments in Nubia.

Lions Emblem — SPAP2

1967, July 5 Photo. *Perf. 13*

CB4	SPAP2	50fr + 10fr	multi	60	22

50th anniv. of Lions Intl. and to publicize the Lions work for the blind.

POSTAGE DUE STAMPS

TCHAD

Postage Due Stamps of France Overprinted

A. E. F.

1928 Unwmk. *Perf. 14x13½*

J1	D2	5c	light blue	15	15
J2	D2	10c	gray brown	15	15
J3	D2	20c	olive green	16	16
J4	D2	25c	bright rose	30	30
J5	D2	30c	light red	38	38
J6	D2	45c	blue green	50	50
J7	D2	50c	brown violet	60	60
J8	D2	60c	yellow brown	65	65
J9	D2	1fr	red brown	65	65
J10	D2	2fr	orange red	2.25	2.25
J11	D2	3fr	bright violet	1.10	1.10
			Nos. J1-J11 (11)	6.89	6.89

Huts — D3

Canoe — D4

1930 Typo. *Perf. 14x13½, 13½x14*

J12	D3	5c	dp bl & olive	20	20
J13	D3	10c	dk red & brn	25	25
J14	D3	20c	grn & brn	45	45
J15	D3	25c	lt bl & brn	52	52
J16	D3	30c	bis brn & Prus bl	52	52
J17	D3	45c	Prus bl & olive	65	65
J18	D3	50c	red vio & brn	90	90
J19	D3	60c	gray lil & bl blk	1.25	1.25
J20	D4	1fr	bis brn & bl blk	1.25	1.25
J21	D4	2fr	vio & brn	2.50	2.50
J22	D4	3fr	dp red & brn	20.00	20.00
			Nos. J12-J22 (11)	28.49	28.49

In 1934 stamps of Chad were superseded by those of French Equatorial Africa.

Catalogue values for unused stamps in this section, from this point to the end of the section, are for Never Hinged items.

Republic

Rhinoceros — D5

Tibesti Pictographs: No. J24, Kudu. No. J25, Two antelopes. No. J26, Three antelopes. No. J27, Ostrich. No. J28, Horned bull. No. J29, Bull. No. J30, Wild swine. No. J31, Elephant. No. J32, Rhinoceros. No. J33, Warrior with spear and shield. No. J34, Masked archer.

Unwmk.

1962, Apr. 20 Engr. *Perf. 13*

J23	D5	50c	olive bister	15	15
J24	D5	50c	brown red	15	15
J25	D5	1fr	blue	15	15
J26	D5	1fr	green	15	15
J27	D5	2fr	vermilion	15	15
J28	D5	2fr	maroon	15	15
J29	D5	5fr	slate green	15	15
J30	D5	5fr	violet blue	15	15
J31	D5	10fr	brown	35	35
J32	D5	10fr	orange brown	35	35
J33	D5	25fr	carmine rose	80	80
J34	D5	25fr	violet	80	80
			Set value	2.95	2.95

The two designs of the same denomination are printed se-tenant.

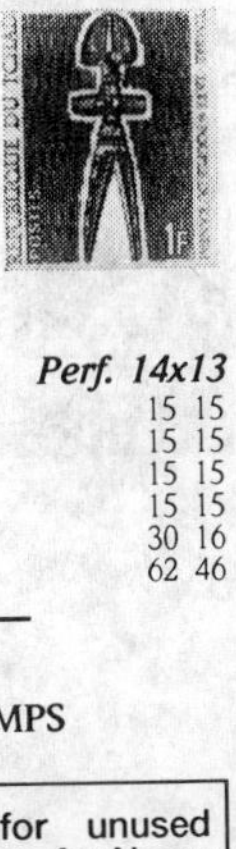
Dolls — D6

1969, Sept. 19 Engr. *Perf. 14x13*

J35	D6	1fr	Kanem	15	15
J36	D6	2fr	Kotoko	15	15
J37	D6	5fr	Leather	15	15
J38	D6	10fr	Kotoko	15	15
J39	D6	25fr	Guera	30	16
			Set value	62	46

MILITARY STAMPS

Catalogue values for unused stamps in this section are for Never Hinged items.

No. 78 Overprinted "F.M."

1965 Typo. *Perf. 14x13½*

M1	A5	20fr	red & black	100.00	100.00

Flag Bearer and Map of Chad — M1

1st Regiment Emblem — M2

1968 Unwmk. Litho. *Perf. 13x12½*

M2	M1	tan & multi	1.00	60

1972, Jan. 21 Photo. *Perf. 13*

M3	M2	blue & multi	42	25

OFFICIAL STAMPS

Catalogue values for unused stamps in this section are for Never Hinged items.

Flag and Map of Chad — O1

Perf. 13½x14

1966-71 Typo. Unwmk.

Flag in blue, yellow and carmine

O1	O1	1fr	light blue	15	15
O2	O1	2fr	gray	15	15
O3	O1	5fr	black	15	15
O4	O1	10fr	violet blue	15	15
O5	O1	25fr	orange	16	15
O6	O1	30fr	bright green	25	15
O7	O1	40fr	carmine ('71)	30	15
O8	O1	50fr	red lilac	40	16
O9	O1	85fr	green	60	30
O10	O1	100fr	brown	1.00	35
O11	O1	200fr	red	1.60	60
			Nos. O1-O11 (11)	4.91	
			Set value		1.90

CHILE

LOCATION — Southwest corner of South America
GOVT. — Republic
AREA — 292,135 sq. mi.
POP. — 11,682,260 (est. 1982)

15-Cent Minimum Value
The minimum catalogue value is 15 cents. Separating se-tenant pieces into individual stamps does not increase the value of the stamps since demand for the separated stamps may be small.

CAPITAL — Santiago

100 Centavos = 1 Peso

1000 Milésimos = 100 Centésimos = 1 Escudo (1960)

100 Centavos = 1 Peso (1975)

Catalogue values for unused stamps in this country are for Never Hinged items, beginning with Scott 257 in the regular postage section, Scott B3 in the semi-postal section, Scott C125 in the airpost section, and Scott CB1 in the airpost semi-postal section.

Values of early Chile stamps vary according to condition. Quotations for Nos. 1-14 are for fine to very fine copies. Very fine to superb specimens sell at much higher prices, and inferior or poor copies sell at reduced prices, depending on the condition of the individual specimen.

Pen cancellations are common on the 1862-67 issues. Such stamps sell for much less than the quoted values which are for those with hand-stamped postal cancellations.

Watermarks

a b c d

e f g

Wmk. 215- Small Star in Shield, Multiple

Christopher Columbus — A1

London Prints

1853 Wmk. b Engr. *Imperf.*

Blued Paper

1	A1	5c brown red	*350.00*	37.50
a.		White paper		62.50

Wmk. e

White Paper

2	A1	10c dp brt bl	*575.00*	80.00
a.		Blued paper		*450.00*
b.		Diag. half used as 5c on cover		*300.00*

Santiago Prints

Impressions Fine and Clear

1854 Wmk. b and e

White Paper

3	A1	5c pale red brn	325.00	32.50
a.		5c deep red brown	*350.00*	35.00
b.		5c chestnut	*575.00*	110.00
4	A1	5c burnt sienna	*1,050.*	165.00
a.		5c dull chocolate	*2,000.*	850.00
5	A1	10c deep blue	*875.00*	87.50
a.		10c slate blue		87.50
b.		10c greenish blue		850.00
c.		Half used as 5c on cover		400.00
6	A1	10c lt dl bl	*875.00*	87.50
a.		10c pale blue		87.50
b.		Diag. half used as 5c on cover		275.00

Litho.

7	A1	5c pale brown	*1,100.*	165.00
a.		5c red brown	*1,600.*	210.00

London Print

1855 Blued Paper Wmk. c Engr.

8	A1	5c brown red	125.00	8.75

Santiago Prints

Impressions Worn and Blurred

1856-62 Wmk. b and e

White Paper

9	A1	5c rose red ('58)	27.50	4.25
a.		5c carmine red ('62)	70.00	14.00
b.		5c orange red ('61)	175.00	105.00
c.		5c dull redsh brn ('57)	175.00	17.50
d.		Printed on both sides		*450.00*
e.		Double impression		
10	A1	10c deep blue	140.00	17.50
a.		10c sky blue ('57)	140.00	17.50
b.		10c light blue	140.00	17.50
c.		10c indigo blue	175.00	52.50
d.		Half used as 5c on cover		*125.00*

London Prints

1862 Wmk. a, f and g

11	A1	1c lemon yellow	21.00	27.50
a.		Double impression		*675.00*
12	A1	10c bright blue	35.00	6.00
a.		10c deep blue	35.00	6.00
b.		Blued paper	87.50	17.50
c.		Wmkd. "20" (error)	*5,000.*	*4,000.*
d.		Half used as 5c on cover		105.00
13	A1	20c green	52.50	32.50
a.		20c emerald		
		Nos. 11-13 (3)	108.50	66.00

Santiago Print

1865 Wmk. d

14	A1	5c rose red	21.00	8.75
a.		5c carmine red	25.00	8.75
b.		Printed on both sides	300.00	*210.00*
c.		Laid paper		*165.00*
d.		Double impression		*165.00*

The 5c rose red (shades) on unwatermaked paper, either wove or ribbed, and on paper watermarked Chilean arms in the sheet are reprints made about 1870.

No. 13 has been reprinted in the color of issue and in fancy colors, both from the original engraved plate and from lithographic transfers. The reprints are on paper without watermark or with watermark CHILE and Star.

A2

A3

1867 Unwmk. *Perf. 12*

15	A2	1c orange	12.50	1.75
		Pen cancellation		25
16	A2	2c black	16.00	2.75
		Pen cancellation		40
17	A2	5c red	12.50	90
		Pen cancellation		15
18	A2	10c blue	12.50	1.75
		Pen cancellation		25
19	A2	20c green	17.50	2.75
		Pen cancellation		35
		Nos. 15-19 (5)	71.00	9.90

Unused values for Nos. 15-19 are for stamps with original gum.

1877 *Rouletted*

20	A3	1c gray	1.75	90
21	A3	2c orange	10.50	2.75
22	A3	5c dull lake	12.50	70
23	A3	10c blue	10.50	1.75
a.		Diagonal half used as 5c on cover		
24	A3	20c green	11.00	2.75
		Nos. 20-24 (5)	46.25	8.85

The panel inscribed "CENTAVO" is straight on No. 22.

A4

A5

Columbus — A6

1878-99 *Rouletted*

25	A4	1c green ('81)	70	15
26	A4	2c rose ('81)	90	15
27	A5	5c dull lake ('78)	3.75	35
28	A5	5c ultra ('83)	90	15
29	A5	10c orange ('85)	1.40	28
a.		10c yellow	5.50	70
30	A5	15c dk grn ('92)	1.05	35
31	A5	20c gray ('86)	90	35
32	A5	25c org brn ('92)	1.40	35
33	A5	30c rose car ('99)	3.50	1.40
34	A5	50c lilac ('78)	35.00	7.00
35	A5	50c violet ('85)	1.65	70
36	A6	1p dk brn & blk ('92)	17.00	1.40
a.		Imperf. horiz. or vert., pair	90.00	
		Nos. 25-36 (12)	68.15	12.63

For surcharge and overprint see Nos. 50, O16.

Columbus

A7 A8

1894 Re-engraved

37	A7	1c blue green	70	15
38	A7	2c carmine lake	70	15

In type A4 there is a small colorless ornament at each side of the base of the numeral, above the "E" and "V" of "CENTAVO." In type A7 these ornaments are missing, the figure "1" is broader than in type A4 and the head of the figure "2" is formed by a curved line instead of a ball.

1900-01

Type I- There is a heavy shading of short horzontal lines below "Chile" and the adjacent ornaments.

Type II- There is practically no shading below "Chile" and the ornaments.

Type I

39	A8	1c yel grn	70	15
40	A8	2c brn rose	1.40	15
41	A8	5c dp bl	9.00	15
42	A8	10c violet	5.25	28
a.		Horizontal pair, imperf. between		
43	A8	20c gray	3.50	70
44	A8	30c dp org ('01)	4.25	70
45	A8	50c red brn	5.25	1.25
a.		Horiz. pair, imperf. btwn.	52.50	
		Nos. 39-45 (7)	29.35	3.38

Type II

46	A8	1c yel grn ('01)	70	15
47	A8	2c rose ('01)	70	15
48	A8	5c dull blue ('01)	3.50	15
a.		Printed on both sides		
49	A8	10c vio ('01)	4.25	35
		Nos. 46-49 (4)	9.15	80

For surcharge see No. 57.

Columbus

A9 A10

1900

Black Surcharge

50	A9	5c on 30c rose car	70	15
a.		Inverted surcharge	27.50	14.00
b.		Double surcharge	90.00	57.50
c.		Double surcharge, both invtd.	90.00	57.50
d.		Double surcharge, one invtd.	90.00	57.50
e.		Surcharged on front and back	90.00	57.50

1901-02 *Perf. 12*

51	A10	1c green	25	15
52	A10	2c carmine	35	15
53	A10	5c ultra	70	15
54	A10	10c red & blk	1.50	28
55	A10	30c vio & blk	5.25	28
56	A10	50c red org & blk	6.25	2.10
		Nos. 51-56 (6)	14.30	3.11

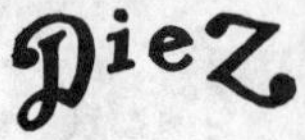

No. 44 Surcharged in Dark Blue

1903 *Rouletted*

57	A8	10c on 30c orange	1.75	35
a.		Inverted surcharge	17.50	10.50
b.		Double surcharge	21.00	10.50
c.		Double surch., one inverted	21.00	10.50
d.		Double surch., both invtd.	21.00	10.50
e.		Stamp design printed on both sides		

Pedro de Valdivia
A11

Coat of Arms
A12

A13

Telegraph Stamps Surcharged or Overprinted in Black

Type I - Animal at left has neither mane nor tail.
Type II - Animal at left has mane and tail.

1904 *Perf. 12*

58	A11	1c on 20c ultra	25	15
a.		Imperf. horiz., pair	35.00	35.00
b.		Inverted surcharge	42.50	42.50
59	A13	2c yel brn, I	25	15
a.		Inverted overprint	17.50	17.50
b.		Pair, one without overprint	42.50	42.50
60	A13	5c red, I	42	15
a.		Inverted overprint	17.50	17.50
c.		Pair, one without overprint	42.50	42.50
61	A13	10c ol grn, I	1.40	42
a.		Inverted overprint	42.50	42.50
		Nos. 58-61 (4)	2.32	87

Perf. 12½ to 16

62	A13	2c yel, brn, II	4.25	4.25
63	A11	3c on 5c brn red	42.50	37.50
a.		Inverted surcharge		
64	A12	3c on 1p brn, II	35	22
a.		Double surcharge	42.50	42.50
65	A13	5c red, II	7.00	7.00
a.		Inverted overprint		
66	A13	10c ol grn, II	16.00	9.00
67	A11	12c on 5c brn red	80	35
a.		No star at left of "Centavos"	1.75	1.05
b.		Inverted surcharge	35.00	35.00
c.		Double surcharge	42.50	42.50
		Nos. 62-67 (6)	70.90	58.32

Counterfeits exist of the overprint and surcharge varieties of Nos. 57-67.

For overprint see No. O12.

A14

A15

Columbus — A16

1905-09 *Perf. 12*

68	A14	1c green	22	15
69	A14	2c carmine	30	15
70	A14	3c yel brn	52	22
71	A14	5c ultra	52	15
72	A15	10c gray & blk	1.05	15
73	A15	12c lake & blk	5.00	1.75
74	A15	15c vio & blk	1.05	15
75	A15	20c org brn & blk	2.50	15
76	A15	30c bl grn & blk	3.25	22

77 A15 50c ultra & blk 3.50 22
78 A16 1p gold, grn & gray 10.50 9.00
Nos. 68-78 (11) 28.41 12.31

A 20c dull red and black, type A15, was prepared but not issued. Value $125. "Specimen" copies of Nos. 74, 76-78 exist, punched to prevent postal use.

For surcharges and overprints see Nos. 79-82, O9, O11-O15.

Nos. 73, 78 Surcharged in Blue or Red

ISLAS DE JUAN FERNANDEZ 5
a

ISLAS DE JUAN FERNANDEZ 10 Cts.
b

1910
79 A15 (a) 5c on 12c (Bl) 42 15
80 A16 (b) 10c on 1p (R) 1.05 28
81 A16 (b) 20c on 1p (R) 1.50 55
82 A16 (b) 1p (R) 2.75 1.05
Nos. 79-82 (4) 5.72 2.03

The 1p is overprinted "ISLAS DE JUAN FERNANDEZ" only. The use of these stamps throughout Chile was authorized.

Independence Centenary Issue

Oath of Independence
A17

Monument to O'Higgins
A26

Gen. Manuel Blanco Encalada — A29

Designs: 2c, Battle of Chacabuco. 3c, Battle of Roble. 5c, Battle of Maipu. 10c, Naval Engagement of "Lautaro" and "Esmeralda." 12c, Capturing the "Maria Isabel." 15c, First Sortie of Liberating Forces. 20c, Abdication of O'Higgins. 25c, Chile's First Congress. 50c, Monument to José M. Carrera. 1p, Monument to San Martin. 5p, Gen. José Ignacio Zenteno. 10p, Adm. Lord Thomas Cochrane.

1910

Center in Black
83 A17 1c dk green 25 15
a. Center inverted *7,000.*
84 A17 2c lake 25 15
85 A17 3c red brown 90 42
86 A17 5c dp blue 52 15
87 A17 10c gray brn 90 28
88 A17 12c vermilion 2.10 85
89 A17 15c slate 2.10 42
90 A17 20c red orange 2.75 70
91 A17 25c ultra 3.50 1.40
92 A26 30c violet 2.75 70
93 A26 50c olive grn 6.25 2.10
94 A26 1p yel org 14.00 5.25
95 A29 2p red 14.00 5.25
96 A29 5p yel grn 37.50 17.50
97 A29 10p dk violet 35.00 16.00
Nos. 83-97 (15) 122.77 51.32

Columbus
A32

De Valdivia
A33

Mateo de Toro Zambrano
A34

Bernardo O'Higgins
A35

Ramón Freire — A36

F. A. Pinto — A37

Joaquín Prieto — A38

Manuel Bulnes — A39

Manuel Montt — A40

José Joaquín Pérez — A41

Federico Errázuriz Zanartu — A42

Aníbal Pinto — A43

Designs: 2p, Domingo Santa María. 5p, José de Balmaceda. 10p, Federico Errázuriz Echaurren.

Outer backgrounds consist of horizontal and diagonal lines

1911 **Engr.** ***Perf. 12***
98 A32 1c dp green 22 15
99 A33 2c scarlet 22 15
100 A34 3c sepia 70 28
101 A35 5c dk blue 22 15
102 A36 10c gray & blk 70 15
a. Center inverted 1,000. 700.00
103 A37 12c carmine & blk 1.05 15
104 A38 15c violet & blk 85 15
a. Center inverted *1,000.*
105 A39 20c org red & blk 1.75 15
a. Center inverted 60.00 60.00
106 A40 25c lt blue & blk 2.10 52
107 A41 30c bis brn & blk 3.25 22
108 A42 50c myr grn & blk 3.75 22
109 A43 1p green & blk 7.00 28
110 A43 2p ver & blk 12.50 1.05
111 A43 5p ol grn & blk 45.00 7.00
112 A43 10p org yel & blk 37.50 5.50
Nos. 98-112 (15) 116.81 16.12

See Nos. 117, 121, 123, 127-128, 133-141, 143, 155A, 157-161, 165-169,171-172 and designs A47-A55, A57.. For overprints see Nos. C6, C6B-C6D, C7-C8, C10-C11, C13-C21, O19-O22, O24-O27, O30-O34, O40.

Columbus
A47

Toro Zambrano
A48

Freire
A49

O'Higgins
A50

1912-13 **Engr.** ***Perf. 12***
113 A47 2c scarlet 18 15
114 A48 4c black brn 24 15
115 A49 8c gray 1.00 15
116 A50 10c blue & blk 1.00 15
a. Center inverted 600.00 500.00
b. Imperf. horiz. or vert., pair 50.00
117 A37 14c car & blk 1.00 15
121 A38 40c violet & blk 4.50 42
123 A40 60c lt blue & blk 9.75 1.25
Nos. 113-123 (7) 17.67 2.42

See Nos. 125-126, 131, 164, 170, 173. For overprints see Nos. C6E, O18, O23, O28, O29.

Cochrane
A52

Columbus
A53

1915 **Engr.** ***Perf. 13½x14***
124 A52 5c slate blue 52 15
a. Imperf., pair 11.50

See Nos. 155, 162-163. For overprints see Nos. O17, O37.

1918
125 A49 8c slate 13.00 50

No. 125 is from a plate made in Chile to resemble No. 115. The top of the head is further from the oval, the spots of color enclosed in the figures "8" are oval instead of round, and there are many small differences in the design.

1921

Worn Plate
126 A49 8c gray 25.00 6.25

No. 126 differs from No. 125 in not having diagonal lines in the frame and only a few diagonal lines above the shoulders (due to wear), while No. 125 has diagonal lines in the oval up to the level of the forehead.

1915-25 **Typo.** ***Perf. 13½ to 14½***
127 A32 1c gray green 20 15
128 A33 2c red 20 15
129 A53 4c brown ('18) 30 15

Frame Litho.; Head Engr.
131 A50 10c bl & blk 1.25 15
a. 10c dark blue & black 1.25 15
b. Imperf., pair 110.00
c. Center inverted 325.00
133 A38 15c vio & blk 90 15
134 A39 20c org red & blk 1.65 15
a. 20c brown orange & blk 1.65 15
135 A40 25c dl bl & blk 60 15
136 A41 30c bis brn & blk 2.00 15
137 A42 50c dp grn & blk 2.00 15

Perf. 14
138 A43 1p grn & blk 9.00 18
139 A43 2p red & blk 10.50 15
a. 2p vermilion & black 32.50 60
140 A43 5p ol grn & blk ('20) 27.50 60
141 A43 10p org & blk ('25) 30.00 1.75
Nos. 127-141 (13) 86.10
Set value 3.35

The frames have crosshatching on the 15c, 20c, 30c, 2p, 5p and 10p. They have no crosshatching on the 10c, 25c, 50c and 1p.

Nos. 131a and 134a are printed from new head plates which give blacker and heavier impressions. No. 131a exists with; (a) frame litho., head engr.; (b) frame typo., head engr.; (c) frame typo., head litho. No. 134a is with frame typo., head engr.

A 4c stamp with portrait of Balmaceda and a 14c with portrait of Manuel de Salas were prepared but not placed in use. Both stamps were sent to the paper mill at Puente Alto for destruction. They were not all destroyed as some were privately preserved and sold.

Columbus
A54

Manuel Rengifo
A55

Types of 1915-20 Redrawn

1918-20 ***Perf. 13½x14½***
143 A32 1c gray grn ('20) 40 15
144 A54 4c brown 50 15

No. 143 has all the lines much finer and clearer than No. 127. The white shirt front is also much less shaded.

1921
145 A55 40c dk vio & blk 2.00 15

For overprints see Nos. C6A, C9.

Pan-American Congress Building — A56

Adm. Juan José Latorre — A57

1923, Apr. 25 **Typo.** ***Perf. 14½x14***
146 A56 2c red 16 15
147 A56 4c brown 16 15

Typo.; Center Engr.
148 A56 10c blue & blk 16 15
149 A56 20c orange & blk 40 15
150 A56 40c dl vio & blk 65 20
151 A56 1p green & blk 80 32
152 A56 2p red & blk 3.25 40
153 A56 5p dk grn & blk 11.50 3.00
Nos. 146-153 (8) 17.08 4.52

Fifth Pan-American Congress.

Typographed; Head Engraved
1927 ***Perf. 13½x14½***
154 A57 80c dk brn & blk 2.00 60

Types of 1915-25 Issues
Inscribed: "Chile Correos"
Perf. 13½x14½

1928-31 **Engr.** **Wmk. 215**
155 A52 5c slate blue 1.10 20

Frame Typo.; Center Engr.
155A A38 15c violet & blk *350.00*
156 A55 40c dk vio & blk 55 15
157 A42 50c dp grn & blk 2.00 15

Perf. 14
158 A43 1p green & blk 90 15
159 A43 2p red & blk 3.25 15
160 A43 5p ol grn & blk 7.25 25
161 A43 10p orange & blk 7.25 1.10
Nos. 155,156-161 (7) 22.30 2.15

Paper of #155-161 varies from thin to thick.

Types of 1915-25 Issues
Inscribed: "Correos de Chile"

1928 **Engr.** ***Perf. 13½x14½***
162 A52 5c deep blue 40 15

1929 **Litho.**
163 A52 5c light green 40 15

Frame Litho.; Center Engr.
164 A50 10c blue & blk 1.65 15
165 A38 15c violet & blk 1.90 15
166 A39 20c org red & blk 4.50 15
167 A40 25c blue & blk 85 15
168 A41 30c brown & blk 60 20
169 A42 50c dp grn & blk 50 15
Nos. 163-169 (7) 10.40
Set value 63

Redrawn

1929 Frame Typo.; Center Litho.

170 A50	10c blue & blk		2.00	15
171 A38	15c violet & blk		1.75	15
172 A39	20c org red & blk		2.75	16
	Nos. 170-172 (3)		6.50	
	Set value			35

1931 Unwmk.

173 A50	10c blue & blk	70	20

In the redrawn stamps the lines behind the portraits are heavier and completely fill the ovals. There are strong diagonal lines above the shoulders. On No. 170 the head is larger than on Nos. 164 and 173.

A58

Prosperity of Saltpeter Trade
A59 A60

Perf. 13½x14

1930, July 21 Litho. Wmk. 215

Size: 20x25mm

175 A58	5c yellow grn	35	15
176 A58	10c red brown	35	15
177 A58	15c violet	35	15
178 A59	25c deep gray	1.40	40
179 A60	70c dark blue	3.50	1.00

Perf. 14

Size: 24½x30mm

180 A60	1p dk gray grn	2.50	50
	Nos. 175-180 (6)	8.45	2.35

Cent. of the 1st shipment of saltpeter from Chile, July 21, 1830.

Manuel Bulnes
A61

Bernardo O'Higgins
A62

1931 ***Perf. 13½, 14***

181 A61	20c dark brown	90	15

For overprints see Nos. O35, O39.

1932

182 A62	10c deep blue	1.00	15

For overprints see Nos. O36, O38.

Mariano Egana — A63

Joaquin Tocornal — A64

1934 ***Perf. 13½x14***

183 A63	30c magenta	50	15

Perf. 14

184 A64	1.20p bright blue	90	20

Centenary of the constitution.

José Joaquín Pérez — A65

1934 ***Perf. 13½x14***

185 A65	30c bright pink	1.40	15

Atacama Desert — A66

Designs: 10c, Fishing boats. 20c, Coquito palms. 25c, Sheep. 30c, Mining. 40c, Lonquimay forest. 50c, Colliery at Port Lota. 1p, Shipping at Valparaiso. 1.20p, Puntiagudo volcano. 2p, Diego de Almagro. 5p, Cattle. 10p, Mining saltpeter.

Wmk. 215

1936, Mar. 1 Litho. ***Perf. 14***

186 A66	5c vermilion	22	15
187 A66	10c violet	15	15
188 A66	20c magenta	15	15
189 A66	25c grnsh blue	1.50	48
190 A66	30c lt green	15	15
191 A66	40c blk, *cream*	1.50	65
192 A66	50c bl, *bluish*	75	18

Engr.

193 A66	1p dk green	75	32
194 A66	1.20p dp blue	90	45
195 A66	2p dk brown	90	55
196 A66	5p copper red	2.50	1.50
197 A66	10p dk violet	6.00	5.25
	Nos. 186-197 (12)	15.47	9.98

400th anniv. of the discovery of Chile by Diego de Almagro.

Laja Waterfall — A78

Fishing in Chiloé — A84

Designs: 10c, Agriculture. 15c, Boldo tree. 20c, Nitrate Industry. 30c, Mineral spas. 40c, Copper mine. 50c, Mining. 1.80p, Osorno Volcano. 2p, Mercantile marine. 5p, Lake Villarrica. 10p, State railways.

Perf. 13½x14

1938-40 Litho. Wmk. 215

198 A78	5c brn car ('39)	18	15
199 A78	10c sal pink ('39)	18	15
200 A78	15c brn org ('40)	18	15
201 A78	20c light blue	18	15
202 A78	30c brt pink	18	15
203 A78	40c lt grn ('39)	18	15
204 A78	50c violet	18	15

Engr. ***Perf. 14***

205 A84	1p orange brn	18	15
206 A84	1.80p deep blue	45	22
207 A84	2p car lake	18	15
208 A84	5p dk slate grn	35	15
209 A84	10p rose vio ('40)	90	15
	Nos. 198-209 (12)	3.32	
	Set value		96

See Nos. 217-227. For surcharge and overprints see Nos. 253, O41-O66, O70-O71.

Map of the Americas — A89

Unwmk.

1940, Sept. 11 Litho. ***Perf. 14***

210 A89	40c dl grn & yel grn	15	15

Pan American Union, 50th anniversary.

Camilo Henríquez — A90

Founding of Santiago
A93

Designs: 40c, Pedro de Valdivia. 1.10p, Benjamin Vicuna Mackenna. 3.60p, Diego Barros Arana.

Perf. 14½x14, 14½

1941, Jan. 23 Engr. Wmk. 215

211 A90	10c car lake	16	15
212 A90	40c green	20	15
213 A90	1.10p red	90	50
214 A93	1.80p blue	90	50
215 A90	3.60p indigo	2.75	2.00
	Nos. 211-215 (5)	4.91	3.30

400th anniversary of Santiago.

Types of 1938

Perf. 13½x14

1942-46 Unwmk. Litho.

217 A78	10c sal pink ('43)	18	15
218 A78	15c brn org ('43)	18	15
219 A78	20c lt bl ('43)	18	15
220 A78	30c brt pink ('43)	20	15
221 A78	40c yel grn	70	15
222 A78	50c vio ('43)	18	15

Engr. ***Perf. 14***

223 A84	1p brn org	1.40	15
225 A84	2p car lake ('43)	18	15
226 A84	5p dk sl grn ('43)	45	15
227 A84	10p rose vio ('46)	70	15
	Nos. 217-227 (10)	4.35	
	Set value		70

Valentin Letelier
A95

University of Chile
A98

Designs: 40c, Andrés Bello. 90c, Manuel Bulnes. 1.80p, Manuel Montt.

1942, Nov. 1 ***Perf. 14x14½, 14 (1p)***

228 A95	30c rose red	18	15
229 A95	40c dp grn	18	15
230 A95	90c rose vio	1.00	90
231 A98	1p dp brn	70	50
232 A95	1.80p dk bl	2.00	1.75
	Nos. 228-232 (5)	4.06	3.45

University of Chile cent. See No. C89.

Manuel Bulnes — A100

Map Showing Strait of Magellan — A104

Designs: 30c, Juan Williams Wilson. 40c, Diego Duble Almeida. 1p, José Mardones.

1944, Mar. 2 Litho. ***Perf. 14***

233 A100	15c black	18	15
234 A100	30c dp rose	18	15
235 A100	40c yel grn	18	15
236 A100	1p brn car	85	15
237 A104	1.80p ultra	1.25	70
	Nos. 233-237 (5)	2.64	1.30

100th anniversary of the occupation of the Strait of Magellan.

Red Cross and Lamp of Life — A105

Serpent and Cup — A106

1944, Oct. 18 Unwmk.

238 A105	40c grn, red & blk	25	15
239 A106	1.80p ultra & red	60	35

80th anniv. of the Intl. Red Cross Soc.

Bernardo O'Higgins — A107

"Embrace of Maipú" (O'Higgins Joining San Martin)
A108

Designs: 40c, Abdication of O'Higgins. 1.80p, Battle of Rancagua.

1945 Engr. ***Perf. 14 (15c), 14½***

Center in Black

240 A107	15c carmine	18	15
241 A108	30c brown	25	15
242 A108	40c dp grn	25	15
243 A108	1.80p dk bl	1.25	80
	Nos. 240-243 (4)	1.93	1.25

Death of Bernardo O'Higgins in 1842, cent.

A111

A112

Proposed Columbus lighthouse.

Wmk. 215

1945, Sept. 10 Litho. ***Perf. 14***

244 A111	40c light green	20	15

Issued in honor of the discovery of America by Columbus and the Memorial Lighthouse to be erected in his memory.

1946 Engr.

245 A112	40c dk grn	15	15
246 A112	1.80p dk bl	15	15
	Set value		17

80th anniv. of the death of Andrés Bello, poet and educator.

Map Showing Chile's Claims of Antarctic Territory — A113

1947, May 12 Litho. *Perf. 14½*

247 A113 40c carmine 35 15
248 A113 2.50p deep blue 70 25

Eusebio Lillo and Ramon Carnicer A114

1947, Sept. 18 Engr.

249 A114 40c dark green 15 15

Centenary of national anthem.

Miguel de Cervantes Saavedra — A115

1947, Oct. 11 Wmk. 215

250 A115 40c dk carmine 20 15

400th anniv. of the birth of Cervantes, novelist, playwright and poet.

Arturo Prat Chacón and Iquique Naval Battle A116

1948, Dec. 24 *Perf. 14½*

251 A116 40c deep blue 18 15

Centenary of the birth of Arturo Prat Chacon, Chilean naval hero.

Bernardo O'Higgins — A117

Perf. 13½x14

1948 Wmk. 215 Litho.

252 A117 60c black 15 15

See No. 262. For surcharges see Nos. 266-267.

No. 203 Surcharged in Black

VEINTE
CTS.

1948

253 A78 20c on 40c lt grn 15 15

Chilean Pigeons — A118

FAUNA: a, Chilean Otter. c, Chilean pigeons. d, American skunk. f, Southern sea lions. g, Sugarcane borer moth. h, Emperor penguins. i, Bat. j, Chinchilla. k, Grant's stag beetle. l, Trevally (fish). m, Chilean slender lizard. o, Crested caracara. q, Red-gartered coot. r, Chilean guemal (deer). s, Spiny rock lobster. u, Tilefish. v, Praying mantis. x, Torrent duck. y, Red conger.

FLORA: b, Araucarian pine (monkey puzzle tree). e, Evening primrose. n, Chilean red bell flower. p, Loxodon (flower). t, Boldo tree. w, Coquito palm trees.

Wmk. 215

1948, Dec. 6 Litho. *Perf. 14*

254 A118 60c Block of 25 7.50
a.-y. any single 25 15
255 A118 2.60p Block of 25 10.00
a.-y. any single 35 25

Issued in panes of 100.

Cent. (in 1944) of the publication of the 1st volume of Claudio Gay's Natural History of Chile. See No. C124.

Catalogue values for unused stamps in this section, from this point to the end of the section, are for Never Hinged items.

Benjamin Vicuna Mackenna — A121

1949, Mar. 22 Engr. *Perf. 13½x14*

257 A121 60c deep blue 15 15

See No. C126.

Symbols of Arts and Crafts Education — A122

Heinrich von Stephan — A123

Design: 2.60p, Badge and book.

Unwmk.

1949, Nov. 11 Litho. *Perf. 14*

258 A122 60c lilac rose 18 15
259 A122 2.60p vio bl 42 35
Nos. 258-259,C127-C128 (4) 2.20 1.50

Cent. of the foundation of Chile's School of Arts and Crafts.

1950, Jan. 6 Engr.

260 A123 60c dp car 18 15
261 A123 2.50p dp bl 42 30
Nos. 260-261,C129-C130 (4) 1.45 1.05

UPU, 75th anniv.

O'Higgins Type of 1948

1950 Litho. *Perf. 13x14*

262 A117 60c black 15 15

For surcharge see No. 266.

San Martín — A124

Isabella I — A125

Wmk. 215

1951, Mar. 16 Engr. *Perf. 14*

263 A124 60c deep blue 15 15

Cent. of the death of Gen. José de San Martin. See No. C165.

1952, Mar. 20

264 A125 60c brt bl 15 15

500th anniv. of the birth of Queen Isabella I of Spain. See No. C166.

Bernardo O'Higgins A126

Mateo de Toro Zambrano A127

1952 Unwmk. Litho. *Perf. 13½x14*

265 A126 1p dk bl grn 15 15

See No. 275. For overprints see Nos. O67-O69.

Nos. 262 and 252 Surcharged "40 Ctvs." in Red

1952, Sept.

266 A117 40c on 60c black 15 15

Wmk. 215

267 A117 40c on 60c black 15 15
Set value 20 16

1953, Mar. 13 Wmk. 215

268 A127 80c green 15 15

See No. 285.

Valdivia Arms — A128

Old Fort — A129

Designs: 3p, Modern Valdivia. 5p, Street in ancient Valdivia.

1953, May *Perf. 14*

269 A128 1p brt ultra 35 15
270 A129 2p dl rose vio 35 15
271 A129 3p bl grn 45 20
272 A129 5p dp brn 45 20
Nos. 269-272,C167 (5) 2.60 95

4th centenary of the founding of Valdivia, capital of Valdivia province.

José Toribio Medina (1852-1930), Historian and Bibliographer A130

1953, June Engr. *Perf. 14½*

273 A130 1p brown 15 15
274 A130 2.50p dp bl 30 20

O'Higgins Type of 1952

Perf. 13½x14

1953, Oct. Wmk. 215 Litho.

275 A126 1p dk bl grn 15 15

For overprint see No. O69.

Stamp of 1853 — A131

1953, Oct. 15 Engr. *Perf. 14½*

276 A131 1p chocolate 20 15

Centenary of Chile's first postage stamps. Souvenir sheet including No. 276 is noted below No. C168.

Census Chart and Map — A132

1953, Nov. 5 Litho. *Perf. 13½x14*

277 A132 1p bl grn 15 15
278 A132 2.50p vio bl 20 15
279 A132 3p chocolate 30 20
280 A132 4p carmine 40 20
Nos. 277-280 (4) 1.05 70

12th general census of population and housing.

Arms of Angol — A133

Ignacio Domeyko — A134

1954, May 28 Unwmk. *Perf. 14*

281 A133 2p dp car 15 15

400th anniversary of the founding of Angol, capital of Malleco province.

1954, Aug. 16 Engr. *Perf. 13½x14*

282 A134 1p greenish blue 15 15

150th anniversary of the birth of Ignacio Domeyko (1802-89), mineralogist and educator. See No. C171.

Early Steam Locomotive A135

1954, Sept. 10 Wmk. 215 *Perf. 14½*

283 A135 1p red 15 15

Centenary (in 1951) of the first South American railroad. See No. C172.

Adm. Arturo Prat Chacón — A136

Arms of Viña del Mar — A137

1954 Unwmk. Litho. *Perf. 14*

284 A136 2p dk vio bl 15 15

75th anniv. of the naval Battle of Iquique.

Toro Zambrano Type of 1953

1954, Nov. 6 *Perf. 13½x14*

285 A127 80c green 15 15

1955, Mar. 5 Wmk. 215 *Perf. 14*

Design: 2p, Arms of Valparaiso.

286 A137 1p vio bl 15 15
287 A137 2p carmine 15 15
Set value 20 16

1st Intl. Phil. Exhib., Valparaiso, Mar. 1955.

Dr. Alejandro del Rio — A138

1955, May 24 *Perf. 13½x14*

288 A138 2p vio bl 15 15

14th Pan-American Sanitary Conference.

Christ of the Andes, Emblems of Chile, Argentina A139

1955, Aug. 31 Unwmk. *Perf. 14½*

289 A139 1p vio bl 15 15

Reciprocal visits of Presidents Juan D. Peron and Carlos Ibanez del Campo. See No. C173.

Manuel Rengifo — A140

Portraits: 5p, Mariano Egana. 50p, Diego Portales.

1955-56 Unwmk. *Perf. 14x14½*

290 A140 3p vio bl 15 15
291 A140 5p dk car rose 15 15
292 A140 50p rose lil ('56) 1.50 40
Nos. 290-292 (3) 1.80
Set value 56

Joaquin Prieto (1786-1854), soldier and political leader; president, 1831-41. See No. QRA1.

Jose M. Carrera — A141

Ramón Freire — A142

Portraits: 5p, Manuel Bulnes. 10p, Pres. Francisco A. Pinto. 50p, Manuel Montt.

Perf. 14x14½

1956-58 Unwmk. Litho.

293 A141 2p purple 15 15
293A A142 3p lt vio bl 15 15
294 A141 5p redsh brn (19½x23mm) 15 15
a. Size 19x22mm 15 15
295 A142 10p vio (19x22¼mm) 15 15
a. Perf. 13½x14 (19¼x22½mm) ('58) 50 15
296 A141 50p rose red 35 15
Set value 80 30

#294 has yellow gum; #294a, white gum.
For overprints see Nos. O72-O76.

Wmk. 215

297 A141 2p dl pur 15 15
298 A142 3p vio bl 15 15
Set value 20 16

Federico Santa Maria — A143

Gabriela Mistral — A144

Unwmk.

1957, Jan. 31 Engr. *Perf. 14*

299 A143 5p dk red brn 15 15

25th anniv. of the Federico Santa Maria Technical University. See Nos. C190-C191.
Souvenir sheet including No. 299 is noted below No. C191.

1958, Jan. 10

300 A144 10p red brn 15 15

Issued in honor of Gabriela Mistral, poet and educator. See No. C192.

Arms of Osorno — A145

Arms of Santiago — A146

Design: 50p, Garcia Hdo. de Mendoza.

1958, Mar. 23 Litho. *Perf. 14*

301 A145 10p carmine 15 15

Engr.

302 A145 50p green 30 15

400th anniversary of the founding of the city of Osorno, capital of Osorno province.
Souvenir sheet including No. 302 in red brown is noted below No. C193.

1958, Oct. 18 Unwmk. *Perf. 14*

303 A146 10p dk vio 15 15

Issued to publicize the National Philatelic Exposition, Santiago, Oct. 18-26.
Souvenir sheet including No. 303 in deep red is noted below No. C194.

Symbolical Savings Bank — A147

Modern Map of Antarctica — A148

1958, Dec. 18

304 A147 10p dk bl 15 15

Savings Bank for Public Employees, cent.

Souvenir sheet including No. 304 in violet is noted below No. C195.

1958, Aug. 28 Unwmk. *Perf. 14*

305 A148 40p rose car 15 15

IGY, 1957-1958. See No. C214.

Antarctic Map and "La Araucana" A149

Map of Strait of Magellan, 1588 A150

1958 Litho. *Perf. 14*

310 A149 10p vio bl 15 15

Engr.

311 A150 200p dl pur 2.00 1.10
Nos. 310-311,C199-C200 (4) 5.10 2.65

For overprint see No. O77.

Valdivia River Bridge — A153

1959, Feb. 9 Engr. *Perf. 14*

319 A153 40p green 20 15

Cent. of the German School in Valdivia and to publicize the Valdivia Phil. Exhib., Feb. 9-18.
Souvenir sheet including No. 319 is noted below No. C213.

Strait of Magellan, Map by Pedro Sarmiento de Gamboa, c. 1582 — A154

1959, Aug. 27 Litho.

320 A154 10p dull purple 15 15

400th anniv. of the Juan Ladrillero expedition to explore the Strait of Magellan, 1557-58. See No. C215.

Diego Barros Arana — A155

Henri Dunant — A156

1959, Aug. 27

321 A155 40p ultra 15 15

50th anniv. of the death of Diego Barros Arana (1830-1907), historian. See No. C216.

1959, Oct. 6 Unwmk. *Perf. 14*

322 A156 20p red & red brn 15 15

Centenary of the Red Cross idea. See No. C217.

Manuel Bulnes — A157

Francisco A. Pinto — A158

Choshuenco Volcano — A159

Designs: No. 326, Choshuenco volcano, redrawn. 5c, Manuel Montt. 10c, Maule River Valley. 20c, 1e, Inca Lake.

1960-67 Litho. *Perf. 13x14*

323 A157 5m bluish grn 15 15
324 A158 1c carmine 15 15

Perf. 14

Size: 29x25mm

325 A159 2c ultra ('61) 15 15

Perf. 14x13

Size: 23½x18mm

326 A159 2c ultra ('62) 15 15

Perf. 13x14

327 A157 5c blue 15 15

Perf. 14

Size: 29x25mm

328 A159 10c grn ('62) 20 15
329 A159 20c Prus bl ('62) 32 15
329A A159 1e bluish grn ('67) 40 20
Set value 1.20 65

On No. 325 "Volcan Choshuenco" is at upper left, below "Correos." On No. 326, it is at bottom, above "Centesimos."
For overprint and surcharge see #O79, RA1.

Refugee Family — A160

1960, Apr. 7 *Perf. 14½*

330 A160 1c green 15 15

WRY, July 1, 1959-June 30, 1960. A souvenir sheet is noted below No. C218.

Type of Air Post Issue, 1962, and

Arms of Chile A161

José M. Carrera — A162

Designs: No. 332, Palace of Justice. 5c, National Memorial. 10c, Manuel de Toro y Zambrano and Martinez de Rozas. 20c, Manuel de Salas and Juan Egana. 50c, Manuel Rodriguez and Juan Mackenna.

Wmk. 215 (#331, 1e); Unwmk.

1960-65 Engr. *Perf. 14½*

331 A161 1c maroon & sepia 16 15
332 A161 1c brn & claret ('62) 15 15
333 A162 5c grn & Prus grn ('61) 15 15
334 AP54 10c brn & vio brn ('64) 16 15
334A AP54 20c ind & bl grn ('65) 16 15

335 AP54 50c red brn & mar ('65) 28 15
336 A162 1e gray ol & brn 1.00 40
Nos. 331-336,C218A-C220D (14) 4.56
Set value 1.90

150th anniv. of the formation of the 1st Natl. Government. A souvenir sheet is noted below No. C220B. See No. C285.

Family — A163

Design: 10c, Various buildings.

Unwmk.

1960, Jan. 18 Litho. *Perf. 14*

337 A163 5c green 15 15
338 A163 10c brt vio 15 15
Set value 30 16

13th population census (No. 337) and 2nd housing census (No. 338).

Chamber of Deputies A164

1961, Aug. 14 Unwmk. *Perf. 14½*

339 A164 2c red brown 48 15

150th anniv. of the 1st National Congress. See No. C245.

Soccer Players and Globe A165

Design: 5c, Goalkeeper and stadium (vert.).

1962, May 30 Engr. *Perf. 14½*

340 A165 2c blue 16 15
341 A165 5c green 24 15
Set value 20

World Soccer Championship, Chile, May 30-June 17. Note on souvenir sheet follows No. C247.

Mother and Child — A166

Centenary Emblem — A167

1963, Mar. 21 Litho. *Perf. 14*

342 A166 3c maroon 15 15

FAO "Freedom from Hunger" campaign. See No. C248.

1963, Aug. 23 Unwmk. *Perf. 14*

343 A167 3c red & gray 15 15

Centenary of the Intl. Red Cross. See No.C249.

Fireman Carrying Woman — A168

Enrique Molina — A169

1963, Dec. 20 Unwmk. *Perf. 14*

344 A168 3c violet 15 15

Issued to commemorate the centenary of the Santiago Fire Brigade. See No. C250.

1964, Nov. 14 Litho. *Perf. 14*

Design: No. 346, Magr. Carlos Casanueva.

345 A169 4c bister brown 15 15
346 A169 4c rose claret 15 15
Set value, #345-346, C257-C258 42 25

Enrique Molina, founder of the University of Concepcion, and Msgr. Carlos Casanueva, rector of the Catholic University, 1920-53.

Easter Island Statue A170

Copihue, National Flower A171

Design: 30c, Robinson Crusoe.

1965-69 Litho. *Perf. 14x14½*

347 A170 6c rose lilac 15 15
347A A170 10c rose pink ('68) 15 15

Perf. 14

348 A171 15c yel grn & rose red 15 15
348A A171 20c yel grn & rose red ('69) 15 15

Perf. 14x14½

349 A170 30c rose claret 20 15
Set value 65 41

For surcharge see No. RA2.

Skier — A172

Lorenzo Sazie — A173

1965, Aug. 30 *Perf. 14*

350 A172 4c bl grn 15 15

World Skiing Championships, Chile, 1966.

1966, Feb. 9 Litho. *Perf. 14x14½*

351 A173 1e green 50 15

Issued to commemorate the centenary of the death of Dr. Lorenzo Sazie, dean of the Faculty of Medicine, University of Santiago.

German Riesco, President in 1901-1906 — A174

Portrait: 30c, Jorge Montt (1847-1922), president in 1891-1896.

1966 Unwmk. *Perf. 13x14*

354 A174 30c violet 15 15
355 A174 50c dl brn 15 15
Set value 20 15

William Wheelwright and S.S. Chile — A175

1966, Aug. 2 *Perf. 14½*

358 A175 10c ultra & lt bl 15 15

125th anniv. (in 1965) of the arrival of the paddle steamers "Chile" and "Peru." See No. C268.

Learning to Read — A176

1966, Aug. 13 Litho. *Perf. 14*

359 A176 10c red brn 15 15

Literacy campaign.

UN and ICY Emblems A177

1966, Oct. 28 Unwmk. *Perf. 14½*

360 A177 1e grn & brn 80 20

Intl. Cooperation Year, 1965. See No. C269.

Capt. Luis Pardo and Ship in Antarctica A178

1967, Jan. Litho. *Perf. 14½*

361 A178 20c turq bl 15 15

50th anniv. of the rescue of the Shackleton South Pole expedition by Capt. Luis Pardo of Chile. See No. C271.

Family — A179

Trees and Mountains — A180

1967, Apr. 13 Unwmk. *Perf. 14*

362 A179 10c magenta & blk 15 15

8th Intl. Conf. for Family Planning, Santiago, Apr. 1967. See No. C272.

1967, June 9 Litho. *Perf. 14½*

363 A180 10c bl grn & lt bl 15 15

Reforestation Campaign. See No. C274.

Lions Emblem — A181

1967, July 12 Litho. *Perf. 14*

364 A181 20c Prus bl & yel 15 15
Nos. 269-272,C167 (5) 2.60
Set value 25

50th anniv. of Lions Intl.

Chilean Flag A182

1967, Oct. 20 Unwmk. *Perf. 14½*

365 A182 80c crim & ultra 15 15

Natl, flag, 150th anniv. See No. C277.

José Maria Cardinal Caro — A183

1967, Dec. 4 Engr. *Perf. 14½*

366 A183 20c dp car 50 30

Centenary of the birth of José Maria Cardinal Caro, the first Chilean cardinal. See No. C279.

San Martin and O'Higgins A184

1968, Apr. 23 Litho. Unwmk.

367 A184 3e blue 15 15

Sesquicentennial of the Battles of Chacabuco and Maipu. See No. C280.

Farm Couple — A185

1968, June 18 *Perf. 14½*

368 A185 20c blk, org & grn 16 15

Agrarian reforms. See No. C281.

Juan I. Molina A186

1968, Aug. 27 **Litho.** ***Perf. 14½***
369 A186 2e red lilac 15 15

Issued to honor Juan I. Molina, educator and scientist. See No. C282.

Hand Holding Cogwheel — A187

1968, Sept. ***Perf. 14x14½***
370 A187 30c deep carmine 15 15

Fourth census of manufacturers.

Map of Chiloé Province, Sailing Ship and Coastal Vessel A188

1968, Oct. 7 ***Perf. 14½***
371 A188 30c ultra 15 15

Anniversaries of the founding of five towns in Chiloé Province. See No. C283.

Automobile Club Emblem — A189

1968, Nov. 10 **Engr.** ***Perf. 14½x14***
372 A189 1e car rose 15 15

40th anniversary of the Automobile Club of Chile. See No. C284.

Francisco Garcia Huidobro A190

Design: 5e, King Philip V of Spain.

1968, Dec. 31 **Litho.** ***Perf. 14½***
373 A190 2e pale rose & ultra 15 15
374 A190 5e brn & yel grn 15 15
Set value, #373-374, C288-C289 35 30

225th anniv. of the founding of the State Mint (Casa de Moneda de Chile).

Satellite and Radar Station A191

1969, May 20 **Litho.** ***Perf. 14½***
375 A191 30c blue 15 15

Inauguration of ENTEL-Chile, the 1st commercial satellite communications ground station, Longovilo.

See No. C290. For surcharge see No. 397.

Red Cross, Crescent and Lion and Sun Emblems A192

1969, Sept. **Litho.** ***Perf. 14½***
376 A192 2e vio bl & red 15 15

Issued to commemorate the 50th anniversary of the League of Red Cross Societies. See No. C291.

Rapel Hydroelectric Plant A193

1969, Nov. 18 **Litho.** ***Perf. 14½***
377 A193 40c green 15 15

See No. C292.

Col. Rodriguez Monument A194

1969, Nov. 24
378 A194 2e rose claret 15 15

150th anniversary of the death of Col. Manuel Rodriguez. See No. C293.

EXPO '70 Emblem — A195

1969, Dec. 2 **Litho.** ***Perf. 14***
379 A195 3e blue 15 15

Issued to publicize EXPO '70 International Exhibition, Osaka, Japan, March 15-Sept. 13, 1970. See No. C294.

Open Book A196

1969, Dec. 3 ***Perf. 14½***
380 A196 40c red brn 15 15

400th anniv. of the translation of the Bible into Spanish by Casiodoro de Reina. See No. C295.

Globes and ILO Emblem A197

1969, Dec. 17 ***Perf. 14½***
381 A197 1e grn & blk 15 15

ILO, 50th anniv. See No. C296.

Human Rights Flame A198

1969, Dec. 18
382 A198 4e blue & red 15 15

Human Rights Year, 1968. See No. C297.

Policarpo Toro and Easter Island A199

1970, Jan. 26 ***Perf. 14½***
383 A199 5e lilac 15 15

80th anniversary of the acquisition of Easter Island. See No. C298.

Sailing Ship and Arms of Valdivia A200

1970, Feb. 4 **Litho.** ***Perf. 14½***
384 A200 40c dk car 15 15

150th anniv. of the capture of Valdivia during Chile's war of independence by Thomas Cochrane (1775-1860), naval commander. See No. C299.

Paul Harris and Rotary Emblem — A201

1970, Mar. 18 **Litho.** ***Perf. 14***
385 A201 10e vio bl 15 15

Cent. of the birth of Paul Harris (1868-1947), founder of Rotary Intl. See No. C300.

Mahatma Gandhi — A202

Santo Domingo Church, Santiago, Chile — A203

1970, Apr. 1 **Litho.** ***Perf. 14½***
386 A202 40c bl grn 15 15

Issued to commemorate the centenary of the birth of Mohandas K. Gandhi (1869-1948), leader in India's fight for independence. See No. C301.

1970, Apr. 30 **Engr.**

Designs: 2e, Casa de Moneda de Chile, horiz. 3e, Pedro de Valdivia. 5e, Bridge, horiz. 10e, Ambrosio O'Higgins.

387 A203 2e vio brn 15 15
388 A203 3e dk red 15 15
389 A203 4e dk bl 15 15
390 A203 5e brown 15 15
391 A203 10e green 15 15
Set value 46 28

Exploration and development of Chile by Spanish explorers.

Education Year Emblem — A204

Virgin and Child — A205

1970, July 17 **Litho.** ***Perf. 14½***
392 A204 2e claret 15 15

Issued for International Education Year. See No. C302.

1970, July 28
393 A205 40c green 15 15

O'Higgins National Shrine at Maipu. See No. C303. For surcharge see No. 454.

Torch and Snake — A206

Copper Symbol, Chile Arms — A207

1970, Aug. 11
394 A206 40c claret & light blue 15 15

International Cancer Congress, Houston, Texas, May 22-29. See No. C304.

1970, Oct. 21 **Litho.** ***Perf. 14½***
395 A207 40c car & lt red brn 15 15

Nationalization of the copper industry. See No. C305. For surcharge see No. 459.

Dove and World Map A208

1970, Oct. 22
396 A208 3e rose magenta & pur 15 15

25th anniv. of the UN. See No. C306.

No. 375 Surcharged in Red

1970, Dec. 24 **Litho.** ***Perf. 14½***
397 A191 52c on 30c blue 15 15

Freighter and Ship's Wheel — A209

1971, Jan. 18 **Litho.** ***Perf. 14***
398 A209 52c dp car 15 15

National Maritime Commission. See No. C307.

Bernardo O'Higgins and Ship
A210

1971, Feb. 3 *Perf. 14½*

399 A210 5e grnsh bl & grn 15 15

150th anniv. of the expedition to liberate Peru from Spanish rule. See No. C309.

Youth, Girl and UN Emblem
A211

1971, Feb. 11 **Litho.** *Perf. 14½*

400 A211 52c dk bl & brn 15 15

1st meeting in Latin America of the Executive Council of UNICEF, Santiago, May 20-31, 1969. See No. C310.

Chilean Boy Scout Emblem — A212

1971, Feb. 10 *Perf. 14*

401 A212 1e grn & brn 15 15

Founding of Chilean Boy Scouts, 60th anniversary. See No. C311.

Satellite and Radar Station
A213

1971, May 25 **Litho.** *Perf. 14½*

402 A213 40c dl grn 15 15

First commercial Chilean satellite communications ground station, Longovilo. See No. C312.

Diver with Harpoon Gun
A214

1971, Sept. 1

403 A214 1.15e lt & dk grn 15 15
404 A214 2.35e vio bl & dp vio bl 15 15
Set value 15

10th World Championship of Underwater Fishing.

Ferdinand Magellan and Sailing Ship — A215

1971, Nov. 3

405 A215 35c lt vio & brn vio 15 15

450th anniversary of first trip through and discovery of the Strait of Magellan, Oct. 21-Nov. 28, 1520.

Dagoberto Godoy and Plane over Andes
A216

1971, Nov. 4

406 A216 1.15e bl & grn 15 15

First trans-Andean flight, Dec. 12, 1918.

Virgin of San Cristobal — A217

Chilean Flag and Congress Emblem
A218

Designs (Congress Emblem and): 4.35e, Church of San Francisco. 9.35e, Central post office, horiz. 18.35e, La Posada (Inn) del Corregidor, horiz.

1971

407 A217 1.15e dk bl 15 15
408 A218 2.35e ultra & car 15 15
409 A217 4.35e brn red 15 15
410 A217 9.35e violet 15 15
411 A217 18.35e lil rose 15 15
Set value 60 32

10th Congress of the Postal Union of the Americas and Spain, Santiago. Issue dates: 2.35e, 4.35e, Nov. 5; 1.15e, Nov. 11; 9.35e, Nov. 18; 18.35e, Nov. 19.

Observation Dome, Cerro el Tololo Observatory
A219

1971, Dec. 18

412 A219 1.95e lt & dk bl 15 15

Boeing 707 over Easter Island
A220

1971, Dec. 18

413 A220 2.35e dk brn & yel 15 15

Inauguration of regular flights: Santiago, Easter Island, Tahiti.

Alonso de Ercilla y Zuniga — A221

1972, Mar. 20 **Engr.** *Perf. 14*

414 A221 1e dk red 15 15

4th centenary (in 1969) of "La Araucana," by Alonso de Ercilla y Zuniga (1533-1596), Spanish author. See No. C313.

Map of Antarctica and Dog Sled
A222

1972, Mar. 20 **Litho.** *Perf. 14½x15*

415 A222 1.15e vio bl & blk 15 15
416 A222 3.50e bl grn & grn 15 15
Set value 22 16

10th anniversary (in 1971) of the Antarctic Treaty pledging peaceful uses of and scientific cooperation in Antarctica.
For surcharge see No. 630.

"Your Heart is your Health" — A223

1972, Apr. 2 **Litho.** *Perf. 14½*

417 A223 1.15e blk & car 15 15

World Health Day.
For surcharge see No. 631.

People and Statement by Pres. Allende
A224

Conference Hall and UN Emblem
A225

1972, Apr. 13 **Litho.** *Perf. 14½*

418 A224 35c dl grn & buff 15 15
419 A225 1.15e ultra & pur 15 15
420 A224 4e dk pur & pale rose 15 15
421 A225 6e org & vio bl 15 15
Nos. 418-421 (4) 60
Set value 34

3rd UN Conf. on Trade and Development (UNCTAD III), Santiago, Apr.-May 1972. Design A224 is perf. horiz. in the middle.

Soldier, 1822, Andes, Military College Emblem
A226

1972, June 9

422 A226 1.15e bl & yel 15 15

Sesquicentennial of Bernardo O'Higgins Military College.

Miner Holding Copper Ingot, Chilean Flag — A227

Sailing Ship — A228

1972, July 11 **Litho.** *Perf. 15x14½*

423 A227 1.15e bl & rose red 15 15
424 A227 5e bl, blk & rose red 15 15
Set value 18 15

Nationalization of copper industry.

1972, Aug. 4

425 A228 1.15e violet brown 15 15

Sesquicentennial of the Arturo Pratt Naval Training School.

Mt. Calan Observatory
A229

1972, Aug. 31 **Litho.** *Perf. 14½*

426 A229 50c ultra 15 15

University of Chile Mt. Calan Observatory.

Carrier Pigeon — A230

1972, Oct. 9 **Litho.** *Perf. 14½*

427 A230 1.15e red lilac & vio 15 15

Intl. Letter Writing Week, Oct. 9-15.

René Schneider and Army Flag — A231

1972, Oct. 25 *Perf. 14*

428 A231 2.30e multi 15 15

2nd anniv. of the death of Gen. René Schneider. No. 428 is perforated vertically in the middle.

Book and Young People
A232

1972, Oct. 31 *Perf. 14½*

429 A232 50c blk & dp org 15 15

International Book Year 1972.

Guitar and Earthen Jar — A233

Designs: 2.65e, Fish and produce. 3.50e, Stove, pots and rug, vert.

1972, Nov. 20 Litho. *Perf. 14½*

430 A233	1.15e red & blk		15	15
431 A233	2.65e ultra & rose lake		15	15
432 A233	3.50e red & red brn		15	15
	Set value		24	15

Tourism Year of the Americas.

José M. Carrera Before Execution — A234

Map of Antarctica, Flag at Base — A235

1973, Feb. 1 Litho. *Perf. 14½*

433 A234 2.30e lt ultra 15 15

Sesquicentennial of the death of José Miguel Carrera (1785-1821), Chilean revolutionist and dictator.

1973, Feb. 8

434 A235 10e ultra & red 15 15

25th anniversary of the Bernardo O'Higgins Antarctic Base.

Naval Air Service Emblem, Destroyer A236

La Silla Observatory A237

1973, Mar. 16 Litho. *Perf. 14½*

435 A236 20e brt bl & ocher 15 15

Chilean Naval Aviation, 50th anniversary.

1973, Apr. 25 Litho. *Perf. 14½*

436 A237 2.30e ultra & blk 15 15

INTERPOL Emblem — A238

Designs: 50e, Fingerprint over globe.

1973, Sept. 23 Litho. *Perf. 14½*

437 A238	30e bis & ultra	15	15
438 A238	50e blk & red	25	15
	Set value		16

50th anniversary of International Criminal Police Organization.

Grapes — A239

Chilean wine export: 100e, Globe inscribed "Chile Exporta Vino."

1973, Dec. 10 Litho. *Perf. 14½*

439 A239	20e buff & lilac	15	15
440 A239	100e blue & claret	15	15
	Set value	20	16

UPU Headquarters, Bern — A240

1974, Apr. 4

441 A240 500e on 45c green 15 15

UPU cent. No. 441 was not issued without dark green surcharge and overprint.

Bernardo O'Higgins, Armed Forces Emblems A241

1974, Apr. 11 Litho. *Perf. 14½*

442 A241	30e shown	15	15
443 A241	30e Soldiers with mortar	15	15
444 A241	30e Navy anti-aircraft gunners	15	15
445 A241	30e Pilot in cockpit	15	15
446 A241	30e Mounted policeman	15	15
	Set value	40	25

Honoring the Armed Forces.

Soccer Ball and Globe — A242

Traffic Police — A243

Design: 1000e, Soccer ball and stadium, horiz.

1974 Litho. *Perf. 14*

447 A242	500e dk red & org	15	15
448 A242	1000e bl & indigo	20	15
	Set value		15

World Cup Soccer Championship, Munich, June 13-July 7.

A souvenir sheet contains 2 imperf. stamps similar to Nos. 447-448, with blue marginal inscription. Printed on thin card. Size: 90x119mm.

Nos. 386, 355 Surcharged

1974, June Litho. *Perf. 14½*

449 A202 100e on 40c bl grn 15 15

Perf. 13x14

450 A174	300e on 50c dl brn	15	15
	Set value	20	15

1974, June 20 *Perf. 14½*

451 A243 30e red brn & grn 15 15

Traffic safety.

Santiago-Australia Air Service — A244

1974, Sept. 5 Litho. *Perf. 14½x14*

452 A244	Block of 4	1.00	50
a.	200e Easter Island turtle	20	15
b.	200e Polynesian dancer	20	15
c.	200e Map of Fiji Islands	20	15
d.	200e Kangaroo	20	15

Inauguration of air service by LAN (Chile's national airline) from Santiago to Easter Island, Tahiti, Fiji, Australia.

Globe Cut to Show Mantle and Core — A245

1974, Sept. 9 *Perf. 14x14½*

453 A245 500e red brn & org 15 15

International Volcanology Congress, Santiago, Sept. 9-14.

E°100

24 OCTUBRE 1974

INAUGURACION TEMPLO VOTIVO

No. 393 Surcharged in Brown

1974, Oct. 24 Litho. *Perf. 14½*

454 A205 100e on 40c green 15 15

Inauguration of the O'Higgins National Shrine at Maipu, Oct. 24, 1974.

Juan Fernandez Archipelago — A246

1974, Nov. 22 Litho. *Perf. 14½x14*

455 A246	Block of 4	75	50
a.	200e Robinson Crusoe Island	15	15
b.	200e Chonta palms	15	15
c.	200e Mountain goat	15	15
d.	200e Crayfish	15	15

400th anniversary of discovery of Juan Fernandez Archipelago.

O'Higgins and Bolivar A247

1974, Dec. 9 *Perf. 14½*

456 A247 100e red brn & buff 15 15

Sesquicentennial of the Battles of Junin and Ayacucho.

F. Vidal Gormaz and Institute Seal A248

Albert Schweitzer A249

1975, Jan. 22 Litho. *Perf. 14½*

457 A248 100e rose cl & bl 15 15

Centenary of the Naval Hydrographic Institute; F. Vidal Gormaz was first commandant.

1975, Apr. 7 Litho. *Perf. 14x14½*

458 A249 500e yel & red brn 15 15

Dr. Albert Schweitzer (1875-1965), medical missionary, birth centenary.

E° 70.-

Revalorizada 1975

No. 395 Surcharged in Red

1975, Apr. 7 *Perf. 14½*

459 A207 70e on 40c car & lt red brn 15 15

Volunteer Lifeboat Service — A250

1975, Apr. 15 Litho. *Perf. 14½x14*

460 A250	Block of 4	75	50
a.	150e Lighthouse	15	15
b.	150e Shipwreck	15	15
c.	150e Lifeboat	15	15
d.	150e Sailor reaching for life preserver	15	15

Valparaiso Volunteer Lifeboat service, 50th anniversary.

Frigate Lautaro A251

1975, May 21 Photo. & Engr.

461 A251	500e shown	25	15
462 A251	500e Corvette Baquedano	25	15
463 A251	500e Cruiser Chacabuco	25	15

464 A251	500e Brigantine Goleta Esmeralda		25	15
a.	Block of 4, #461-464		1.00	75
465 A251	800e like #461		30	18
466 A251	800e like #462		30	18
467 A251	800e like #463		30	18
468 A251	800e like #464		30	18
a.	Block of 4, #465-468		1.25	1.00
469 A251	1000e like #461		40	20
470 A251	1000e like #462		40	20
471 A251	1000e like #463		40	20
472 A251	1000e like #464		40	20
a.	Block of 4, #469-472		1.75	1.25
	Nos. 461-472 (12)		3.80	2.12

Shipwreck of training frigate Lautaro, 30th anniversary. Se-tenant in sheets of 25 (5x5) with 7 Lautaro stamps and 6 each of the others.

A souvenir card contains impressions of Nos. 469-472. Size: 118x150mm.

Happy Mother, by Alfredo Valenzuela P. — A252

Diego Portales, Finance Minister — A253

Paintings: No. 474, Young Girl, by Francisco Javier Mandiola. No. 475, Lucia Guzman, by Pedro Lira Rencoret. No. 476, Woman, by Magdalena Mira Mena.

1975, Oct. 13 Litho. *Perf. 14½*

473 A252	50c multi	15	15
474 A252	50c multi	15	15
475 A252	50c multi	15	15
476 A252	50c multi	15	15
	Nos. 473-476 (4)	60	60

International Women's Year 1975. Gray inscription on back, printed beneath gum, gives details about painting shown.

A souvenir card contains impressions of Nos. 473-476.

Inscribed D. Portales

1975-78 Litho. *Perf. 13x14*

477	A253	10c gray grn	15	15
478	A253	20c vio ('76)	15	15
479	A253	30c org ('76)	15	15
480	A253	50c lt brn	15	15
481	A253	1p blue	15	15
482	A253	1.50p ocher ('76)	15	15
483	A253	2p gray ('77)	15	15
483A	A253	2.50p citron ('78)	15	15
483B	A253	3.50p pnksh rose ('78)	20	15
484	A253	5p rose claret	20	15
		Set value	1.20	65

See Nos. 635-639.

Cochrane and Liberating Squadron, 1820 A254

Designs: No. 486, Capture of Valdivia, 1820. No. 487, Capture of Three-master Esmeralda, 1820. No. 488, Cruiser Cochrane, 1874. No. 489, Destroyer Cochrane, 1962.

1976, Jan. 6 *Perf. 14½*

485 A254	1p multi	15	15
486 A254	1p multi	15	15
487 A254	1p multi	15	15
488 A254	1p multi	15	15
489 A254	1p multi	15	15
a.	Strip of 5, #485-489	75	75
	Nos. 485-489 (5)	75	75

Lord Thomas Cochrane, first commander of Chilean Navy, birth bicentenary.

Flags of Chile and Bolivia A255

1976, May 25 Litho. *Perf. 14½*

490 A255	1.50p multi	20	15

Sesquicentennial of Bolivia's independence.

Lake of the Inca, OAS Emblem A256

1976, June 11

491 A256	1.50p multi	20	15

6th General Assembly of the Organization of American States.

George Washington — A257

1976, July

492 A257	5p multi	38	15

American Bicentennial.

Minerva and Academy Emblem A258

1976, July

493 A258	2.50p multi	15	15

Polytechnic Military Academy, 50th anniv.

Araucan Indian — A259

Designs: 2p, Condor with broken chain. 3p, Winged woman, symbolizing rebirth.

1976, Sept. 20 Litho. *Perf. 14½*

494 A259	1p bl & multi	15	15
495 A259	2p bl & multi	15	15
496 A259	3p yel & multi	25	20
a.	Strip of 3, #494-496	50	45

3rd anniversary of the Military Junta.

View, Antarctica A260

1977, Feb. 10 Litho. *Perf. 14½*

497 A260	2p multi	15	15

Visit of President Augusto Pinochet to Antarctica.

School Emblem, Planted Field — A261

Justice — A262

1977, Mar. 10 *Perf. 14½*

498 A261	2p multi	18	15

Cent. of advanced agricultural education.

1977, Mar. 30 Litho. *Perf. 14½*

499 A262	2p brn & slate	18	15

Supreme Court of Justice, sesquicentennial.

Eye with Globe, Caduceus A263

1977, Mar. 30 Litho. *Perf. 14½*

500 A263	2p multi	20	15

11th Pan-American Ophthalmological Cong.

Mounted Policeman — A264

Designs: No. 502, Policewoman with children. No. 503, Paine Peaks and Osorno Volcano, crossed rifle emblem. No. 504, Crossed rifle emblem, mounted and motorcycle policemen, helicopter and automobile, horiz.

1977, Apr. 27

501 A264	2p multi	15	15
502 A264	2p multi	15	15
503 A264	2p multi	15	15
504 A264	2p multi	15	15
	Nos. 501-504 (4)	60	60

Chilean police organization, 50th anniv.

Intelsat Satellite over Globe — A265

1977, May 17 Litho. *Perf. 14½*

505 A265	2p multi	18	18

World Telecommunications Day.

El Mercurio's First Front Page, Press and Ship A266

1977, July 5 Litho. *Perf. 14½*

506 A266	2p multi	18	18

El Mercurio de Valparaiso, first Chilean newspaper, 150th anniversary.

St. Francis, Birds and Cross A267

Science and Technology A268

1977, July 26 Litho. *Perf. 14½*

507 A267	5p multi	30	15

St. Francis of Assisi, 750th death anniv.

1977, Aug. 26 Litho. *Perf. 14½*

508 A268	4p multi	25	15

Young Mother Weaving — A269

Diego de Almagro — A270

Designs: No. 510, Handicapped boy in wheelchair and nurse. No. 511, Children dancing in circle, horiz. No. 512, Old man and home, horiz.

1977, Sept. 13 Litho. *Perf. 14½*

509 A269	5p multi	25	15
510 A269	5p multi	25	15
511 A269	10p multi	50	20
512 A269	10p multi	50	20
	Nos. 509-512 (4)	1.50	70

4th anniversary of Government Junta and social services of armed forces.

1977, Oct. 31 Engr. *Perf. 14½*

513 A270	5p rose & car	25	15

Diego de Almagro (1475-1538), leader of Spanish expedition to Chile.

Bell, Letters, Dove and Child
A271

1977, Dec. 12 Litho. *Perf. 14½*
514 A271 2.50p multi 15 15

Christmas 1977.

Loading Timber
A272

1978 Litho. *Perf. 15*
515 A272 10p multi 50 20
516 A272 20p multi 1.00 20

No. 516 inscribed "CORREOS," ship is flying Chilean flag.

Papal Arms and Globe
A273

University
A274

1978 Litho. *Perf. 14½*
521 A273 10p multi 50 20
522 A274 25p multi 1.25 30

World Peace Day (10p); Catholic University of Valparaiso, 50th anniversary (25p). Issue dates: 10p, July 28; 25p, July 31.

O'Higgins, by Gil de Castro — A275

1978, Aug. 20 Litho. *Perf. 15*
523 A275 10p multi 50 20

Bernardo O'Higgins (1778-1842), soldier and statesman.

Chacabuco Victory Monument
A276

1978, Sept. 11
524 A276 10p multi 50 20

160th anniversary of O'Higgins victory at Chacabuco, and 5th anniversary of military government.

Teacher Writing on Blackboard
A277

1978, Sept. 21
525 A277 15p multi 75 20

10th anniversary and 9th Reunion of Interamerican Council for Education, Science and Culture (C.I.E.C.C.), Sept. 21-29.

First National Fleet, by Thomas Somerscales — A278

Design: 30p, Last Moments of Rancagua Battle, by Pedro Subercaseaux.

1978 Litho. *Perf. 15*
526 A278 20p multi 1.00 20
527 A278 30p multi 1.50 35

Bernardo O'Higgins (1778-1842), soldier and statesman.
Issue dates: 20p, Oct. 9; 30p, Oct. 2.

San Martin-O'Higgins Medal, by Rene Thenot, 1942 — A279

1978, Oct. 20
528 A279 7p multi 35 15

José de San Martin and Bernardo O'Higgins, 200th birth anniversaries.

Council Emblem — A280

1978, Nov. 27 Litho. *Perf. 14½*
529 A280 50p multi 3.00 65

Intl. Council of Military Sports, 30th anniv.

Three Kings — A281

Virgin and Child — A282

1978, Dec. 14 Litho. *Perf. 14½*
530 A281 3p multi 15 15
531 A282 11p multi 60 28

Christmas 1978.

Philippi Brothers
A283

1978, Dec. 29 Litho. *Perf. 14½x15*
532 A283 3.50p multi 20 15

Bernardo E. Philippi (1811-1852) and Rodulfo A. Philippi (1808-1904), scientists and travelers.

No. 477 Surcharged in Bright Green

1979 Litho. *Perf. 13x14*
533 A253 3.50p on 10c gray grn 25 25

Flags of Chile and Salvation Army — A284

1979, Mar. 17 Litho. *Perf. 14½*
534 A284 10p multi 75 50

Salvation Army in Chile, 70th anniversary.

Pope Paul VI (1897-1978)
A285

1979, Mar. 30
535 A285 11p multi 80 50

Battle of Maipu Monument
A286

1979, Apr. 17 Litho. *Perf. 14½*
536 A286 8.50p multi 65 40

Bernardo O'Higgins (1778-1842), Liberator of Chile.

Naval Battles
A287

1979, May 21 Litho. *Perf. 14½*
537 A287 3.50p Angamos 35 20
538 A287 3.50p Iquique 35 20
539 A287 3.50p Punta Gruesa 35 20
Nos. 537-539 (3) 1.05 60

Centenary of victorious naval battles against Peru.

1903 Ambulance and Red Cross
A288

1979, June 29 Litho. *Perf. 14½*
540 A288 25p multi 1.50 90

75th anniversary of Chilean Red Cross.

Diego Portales — A289

1979-86 Litho. *Perf. 13½*

542	A289	1.50p ocher	15	15
543	A289	2p gray ('81)	15	15
544	A289	3.50p red	20	15
545	A289	4.50p bl grn ('81)	25	15
546	A289	5p rose cl	30	15
547	A289	6p emerald	35	20
548	A289	7p yel ('82)	30	20
549	A289	10p bl ('82)	45	20
550	A289	12p org ('86)	15	15
		Nos. 542-550 (9)	2.30	
		Set value		1.22

1.50p, 3.50p, 5p and 6p inscribed "D. Portales."

People and Flag — A290

1979, Aug. 28 Litho. *Perf. 14½*
551 A290 10p multi 60 35

Yugoslavian immigration, centenary.

Coat of Arms and Mt. Castillo
A290a

1979, Oct. 12 Litho. *Perf. 14½*
552 A290a 20p multi 1.20 75

Coyhaique 50th anniv.

IYC Emblem, Playground
A291

IYC Emblem, Children's Drawings: 11p, Girl and shadow, vert. 12p, Dancing.

1979, Oct. 9 *Perf. 14½*
553 A291 9.50p multi 60 35
554 A291 11p multi 65 40
555 A291 12p multi 70 40
Nos. 553-555 (3) 1.95 1.15

International Year of the Child.

Telecom 79 — A292

1979, Oct. 26 **Litho.** ***Perf. 14½***
556 A292 15p multi 90 50

3rd World Telecommunications Exhibition, Geneva, Sept. 20-26.

Puerto Williams, 25th Anniversary A293

1979, Nov. 21
557 A293 3.50p multi 20 15

Adoration of the Kings A294

1979, Dec. 4 **Litho.** ***Perf. 15***
558 A294 3.50p multi 20 15

Christmas 1979.

Rafael Sotomayor, Minister of War — A295

Military Heroes: No. 560, Erasmo Escala. No. 561, Emilio Sotomayor. No. 562, Eleuterio Ramirez

1979, Dec. 29 ***Perf. 13½***
559 A295 3.50p ocher & brn 20 15
560 A295 3.50p ocher & brn 20 15
561 A295 3.50p ocher & brn 20 15
562 A295 3.50p ocher & brn 20 15
a. Block of 4, #559-562 85 45

Bell UH-1 Rescue Helicopter at Tinguiririca Volcano, by S.O. Mococain — A296

Air Force, 50th Anniversary: No. 564, Flying boat Catalina Skua over Antarctic, by E.F. Alvarez. No. 565, F5-E Tiger II over Andes, by M.M. Barria.

1980, Mar. 21 **Litho.** ***Perf. 13½***
563 A296 3.50p shown 25 15
564 A296 3.50p Jet 25 15
565 A296 3.50p Sea plane 25 15
Nos. 563-565 (3) 75
Set value 36

The Death of Bueras, by Pedro Leon Carmona — A297

1980, Apr. 14 **Litho.** ***Perf. 13½***
566 A297 12p multi 70 40

Charge of Bueras, Battle of Maipo, 1818.

Rotary International, 75th Anniversary — A298

1980, Apr. 15
567 A298 10p multi 60 30

Gen. Manuel Baquedano, by Pedro Subercaseaux A299

Gen. Pedro Lagos, Battle Scene, by Subercaseaux — A300

Battle of Morro de Arica Centenary (Subercaseaux Paintings): No. 570, Commander Juan J. San Martin, battle scene.

1980, June 7 **Litho.** ***Perf. 13½***
568 A299 3.50p multi 20 15
569 A300 3.50p multi 20 15
570 A300 3.50p multi 20 15
Nos. 568-570 (3) 60
Set value 30

Score and Perez's Silhouette — A301

1980, June 27 **Litho.** ***Perf. 13½***
571 A301 6p multi 35 20

Osman Perez Freire (1880-1930), composer, and fragment from his song "Ay, Ay, Ay."

Mt. Gasherbrum II, Chilean Flag, Ice Pick — A302

1980, July 9
572 A302 15p multi 90 50

Chilean Himalayan expedition, June 1979.

"Charity," Stained-glass Window A303

1980, July 18
573 A303 10p multi 60 30

Daughters of Charity, 125th anniv. in Chile.

Condor, Colors of Chile A304

1980, Sept. 11 **Litho.** ***Perf. 13½***
574 A304 3.50p multi 20 15

17th anniversary of constitution.

Inca Child Mummy A305

Pablo Burchard, by Pedro Lira A306

1980, Sept. 14
575 A305 5p shown 30 15
576 A305 5p Claudio Gay 30 15
a. Pair, #575-576 + label 60 40

Natl. Museum of Natural History (founded by Claudio Gay, 1800-73) sesqui.

1980, Sept. 27 **Litho.** ***Perf. 13½***
577 A306 3.50p multi 20 15

Museum of Fine Art centenary (directed by Burchard, 1932).

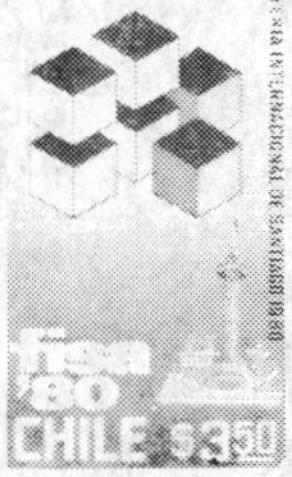

Santiago International Fair — A307

1980, Oct. 30
578 A307 3.50p multi 20 15

Nativity — A308

Christmas 1980: 3.50p, Family, vert.

1980, Nov. 25 **Litho.** ***Perf. 13½***
579 A308 3.50p multi 20 15
580 A308 10.50p multi 65 35

Infantryman 1879 — A309

Congress Emblem — A310

Designs: Pacific War period uniforms, 1879.

1980, Nov. 27
581 A309 3.50p shown 20 15
582 A309 3.50p Cavalry officer 20 15
583 A309 3.50p Artillery officer 20 15
584 A309 3.50p Engineer colonel 20 15
a. Block of 4, #581-584 85 45

See Nos. 606-609.

1980, Dec. 1
585 A310 11.50p multi 70 40

23rd International Congress of Military Medicine and Pharmacy.

Eradication of Hoof and Mouth Disease — A311

1981, Jan. 16 **Litho.** ***Perf. 13½***
586 A311 9.50p multi 45 15

Moai Statues, Easter Island A312

1981, Jan. 28 **Litho.** ***Perf. 13½***

587 A312	3.50p	shown	20	15
588 A312	3.50p	Robinson Crusoe Island	20	15
589 A312	10.50p	Penguins, Antarctic Territory	70	50
		Nos. 587-589 (3)	1.10	80

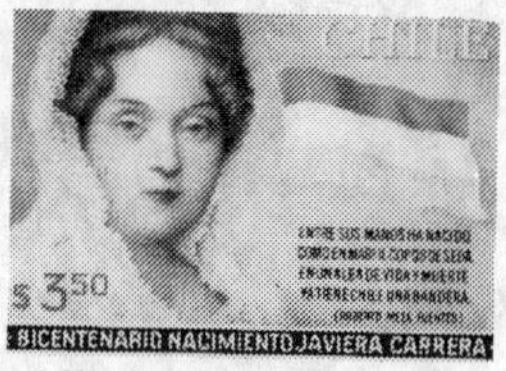

National Heroine Javiera Carrera, by O.M. Pizarro, Birth Bicentenary — A313

1981, Mar. 20

590 A313	3.50p	multi	16	15

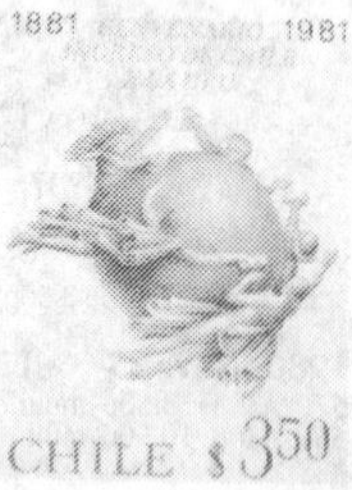

UPU Membership Centenary A314

1981, Apr. 1

591 A314	3.50p	multi	16	15

C130 Hercules Air Force Transport Plane Unloading Cargo — A315

1981, Apr. 21

592 A315	3.50p	multi	16	15

Lieutenant Marsh Air Force Base, first anniversary.

13th World Telecommunications Day — A316

1981, May 17 **Litho.** ***Perf. 13½***

593 A316	3.50p	multi	16	15

Arturo Prat Naval Base A317

1981, June 23 **Litho.** ***Perf. 13½***

594 A317	3.50p	multi	16	15

Capt. Jose Luis Araneda — A318

1981, June 26

595 A318	3.50p	multi	16	15

Battle of Sangrar centenary.

Philatelic Society of Chile, 90th Anniv. — A319

1981, July 29 **Litho.** ***Perf. 13½***

596 A319	4.50p	multi	20	15

Minister Recabarren and Chief Conuepan Giving Speeches, by Hector Robles Acuna — A320

1981, Aug. 7

597 A320	4.50p	multi	20	15

Temuco city centenary.

Exports — A321

1981, Aug. 31 **Litho.** ***Perf. 13½***

598 A321	14p	multi	65	35

Presidential Palace — A322

1981, Sept. 11

599 A322	4.50p	multi	20	15

Natl. liberation, 8th anniv.

St. Vincent de Paul, 400th Birth Anniv. — A323

1981, Sept. 27 **Litho.** ***Perf. 13½***

600 A323	4.50p	multi	25	15

Andres Bello, Statesman, Birth Bicentenary A324

1981, Sept. 29

601 A324	4.50p	Coin	25	15
602 A324	9.50p	Bust, books	50	20
603 A324	11.50p	Statue, arms	60	28
		Nos. 601-603 (3)	1.35	63

2nd Congress of South American Uniformed Police — A325

1981, Oct. 15

604 A325	4.50p	multi	25	15

World Food Day A326

1981, Oct. 16

605 A326	5.50p	multi	30	15

Uniform Type of 1980

1879 Parade Uniforms.

1981, Nov. 6 ***Perf. 13½***

606 A309	5.50p	Infantry private	30	15
607 A309	5.50p	Cadet	30	15
608 A309	5.50p	Cavalryman	30	15
609 A309	5.50p	Artilleryman	30	15
a.		Block of 4, #606-609	1.25	60
		Set value		48

Intl. Year of the Disabled — A327

1981, Nov. 11

610 A327	5.50p	multi	30	15

Christmas 1981 — A328

1981, Nov. 25

611 A328	5.50p	Nativity	30	15
612 A328	11.50p	Three Kings	60	28

50th Anniv. of Federico Santa Maria Technical University — A329

1981, Dec 1 **Litho.** ***Perf. 13½***

613 A329	5.50p	multi	30	15

Dario Salas (1881-1941), Educator — A330

1981, Dec. 4

614 A330	5.50p	multi	30	15

FIDA '82, 2nd Natl. Air Force Fair — A331

1982, Mar. 6 **Litho.** ***Perf. 13½***

615 A331	4.50p	multi	25	15

1982 Constitution — A332

1982, Mar. 11

616 A332	4.50p	Cardinal Caro, family	25	15
617 A332	11p	Diego Portales	65	25
618 A332	30p	Bernardo O'Higgins	1.80	60
		Nos. 616-618 (3)	2.70	1.00

Panamerican Institute of Geography and History, 12th General Assembly A333

1982, Mar. 22 Litho. *Perf. 13½*
619 A333 4.50p multi 25 15

American Air Forces Cooperation System — A334

1982, Apr. 12
620 A334 4.50p multi 25 15

Pedro Montt A335

Fish Exports A336

1982, Mar. 27
621 A335 4.50p light vio 25 15

1982, May 3 Litho. *Perf. 13½*
622 A336 20p multi 1.20 50

Scouting Year — A337

1982, May 21 Litho. *Perf. 13*
623 A337 Pair 50 20
a.-b. 4.50p, either single 25 15

Battle of Concepcion Centenary — A338

Designs: Chacabuco Regiment officers killed in battle.

1982, June 18 Litho. *Perf. 13½*
624 Block of 4 1.00 60
a. A338 4.50p I. Carrera Pinto 25 15
b. A338 4.50p A. Perez Canto 25 15
c. A338 4.50p J. Montt Salamanca 25 15
d. A338 4.50p L. Cruz Martinez 25 15

UN World Assembly on Aging, July 26-Aug 6 — A339

1982, Aug. 5
625 A339 4.50p multi 25 15

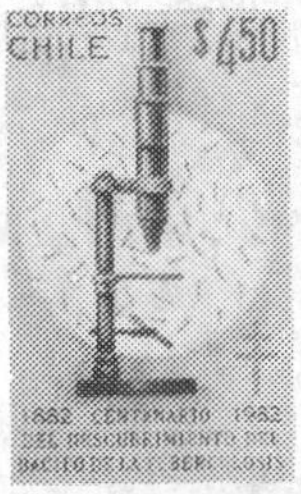

TB Bacillus Centenary — A340

1982, Aug. 31
626 A340 4.50p multi 20 15

9th Anniv. of National Liberation — A341

1982, Sept. 11 Litho. *Perf. 13½*
627 A341 4.50p multi 20 18

Christmas 1982 — A342

Children's drawings.

1982, Nov. 2
628 A342 10p multi 45 18
629 A342 25p multi, vert. 1.00 40

Nos. 416-417 Surcharged in Green or Black

1982, Nov. *Perf. 14½x15, 14½*
630 A222 1p on 3.50p bl grn & grn (G) 15 15
631 A223 2p on 1.15p blk & car 15 15
Set value 15 15

Marist Alumni, 9th World Congress — A342a

Design: 7p, Virgin Mary and Marcellus Champagnat (founder of Marist Brotherhood), stained glass window, Church of the Sacred Heart of Jesus, Barcelona.

1982, Nov. 11 Litho. *Perf. 13½*
631A A342a 7p multi 30 15

El Sur Newspaper Centenary A342b

1982, Nov. 15
631B A342b 7p Wooden handpress, masthead 30 15

110th Anniv. of South American Steamship Co. — A342c

1982, Dec. 20
631C A342c 7p Steamer Copiapo 30 15

60th Anniv. of Radio Club of Chile — A342d

1982, Dec. 29
631D A342d 7p multi 30 15

First Anniv. of Postal Agreement with Order of Malta — A343

1983, Mar. 30 Litho. *Perf. 13½*
632 A343 25p Arms of Order of Malta 1.00 25
633 A343 50p Chile 2.00 50
a. Pair, #632-633 3.00 75

D. Portales Type of 1975 Inscribed Diego Portales and:

Ramon Barros Luco A344

Juan Luis Sanfuentes A344a

1983-88 Litho. *Perf. 13½*

634	A344	1p	grnsh bl	15	15
635	A253	1p	chalky bl	15	15
636	A253	1.50p	ocher	15	15
637	A344	2p	dl vio ('84)	15	15
638	A253	2p	ol gray	15	15
639	A253	2.50p	lemon	15	15
641	A344	5p	crim rose	15	15
642	A344a	5p	red ('84)	15	15
643	A344	7p	ultra	28	15
644	A344a	9p	brn ('84)	22	15
645	A344a	9p	grn ('84)	22	15
646	A344	10p	black	25	15
646A	A344a	10p	gray ('84)	25	15
647	A344a	15p	ultra ('87)	15	15
648	A344a	20p	yel ('88)	20	15
b.			Booklet pane of 10	2.00	
			Set value	2.25	1.00

Nos. 644, 647, 648 inscribed "D.S. No. 20."
For surcharge see No. 779.

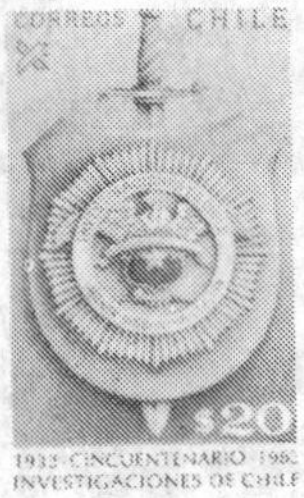

50th Anniv. of Bureau of Investigation — A345

1983, June 19 Litho. *Perf. 13½*
649 A345 20p multi 80 35

Antonio Cardinal Samore (1905-1983) — A346

1983, June 26
650 A346 30p multi 1.20 50

Centenary of Cliff Elevators in Valparaiso A347

1983, Aug. 19 Litho. *Perf. 13½*
651 A347 40p multi 1.00 40

Pucara de Quitor Settlement Ruins, San Pedro de Atacama — A348

Designs: No. 653, Llamas, rock painting, Rio Ibanez, Aisen. No. 654, Duck-shaped jug with human head, Diaguita cultures. No. 655, Puoko Tangata carved stone head, Easter Isld., vert.

1983, Aug. 26
652 A348 7p multi 20 20
653 A348 7p multi 20 20
654 A348 7p multi 20 20
655 A348 7p multi 20 20
Nos. 652-655 (4) 80 80

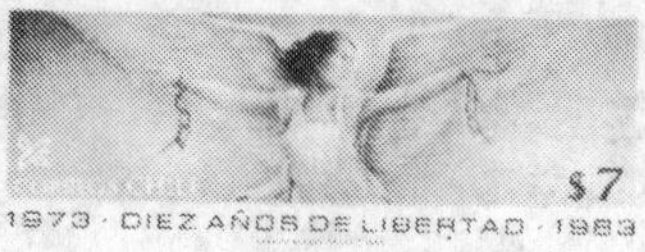

10th Anniv. of National Liberation — A349

1983, Sept. 11 Litho. *Perf. 13½*

656 A349 7p Angel with broken chains 18 15
657 A349 7p Couple, flag 18 15
658 A349 10p Family, torch 25 15
659 A349 40p Coat of arms, "10" 1.00 40
a. Strip of 4, #656-659 1.75 75
Set value 64

For surcharges see Nos. 669-670.

Famous Hondurans — A350

Designs: No. 660, Francisco Morazan (1792-1842), Advocate of United Central America. No. 661, Jose Cecilio Del Valle (1777-1834), Scholar and Leader of Pan Americanism.

1983, Oct. 3 Litho. *Perf. 13½*

660 A350 7p multi 18 15
661 A350 7p multi 18 15
Set value 16

World Communications Year A351 A352

1983, Oct. 13 Litho. *Perf. 13½*

662 A351 7p Central P.O. 18 15
663 A352 7p Challenger spaceship 18 15
a. Pair, #662-663 40 20

Christmas 1983 — A353

Childrens' Drawings: 10p Chilean Peasant, Hanny Chacon. 30p, Holy Family. Lucrecia Cardenas, vert.

1983, Nov. 14 Litho. *Perf. 13*

664 A353 10p multi 25 15
665 A353 30p multi 75 38

Design descriptions printed on back on top of gum.

State Railways Centenary — A354

Train Cars: a, Presidential coach, 1911. b, Service coach, 1910; tender, 1929. c, Locomotive Type 80, 1929.

1984, Jan. 4 Litho. *Perf. 13½*

666 Strip of 3 70 30
a.-c. A354 9p, any single 22 15

3rd Intl. Air Fair, Santiago, Mar. 3-11 — A355

1984, Jan. 31 Litho. *Perf. 13½*

667 A355 9p Flags, plane 22 15

20th Anniv. of Nuclear Energy Commission — A356

1984, Apr. 16 Litho. *Perf. 13*

668 A356 9p multi 22 15

Nos. 656-657 Surcharged in Purple

1984, June 11 Litho. *Perf. 13½*

669 A349 9p on 7p #656 18 15
670 A349 9p on 7p #657 18 15
a. Pair, #669-670 40 20

Antarctic Colonization — A357

1984, June 18

671 A357 15p Women's expedition 30 15
672 A357 15p Villa las Estrellas Station 30 15
673 A357 15p Scouts, flag, Air Force base 30 15
a. Strip of 3, #671-673 90 50

10th Anniv. of Regionalization — A358

Designs: a, Parinacota Church, Tarapaca. b, El Tatio geyser, Antofagasta. c, Copper mining, Atacama. d, Tololo Observatory, Coquimbo. e, Valparaiso Harbor, Valparaiso. f, Ahu Akivi head sculptures, Easter Isld. g, St. Francis Church, Santiago. h, El Hunique House, O'Higgins. i, Colburn Machicura Dam and Hydroelectric Power Station, Maule. j, Sta. Juana de Guadalcazar Fort, Bio-Bio. k, Indian woman, Araucania. l, Guar Isld. Church, Los Lagos. m, Main road, Gen. del Campo. n, Shepherds' Monument, Magellanes and Antarctic. o, Family, Villa las Estrellas Station, Antarctic.

1984, July 11

674 Sheet of 15 3.25 3.25
a.-o. A358 9p multi, any single 25 18

Capt. Pedro Sarmiento de Gamboa, Map, 1584 — A359

1984, July 31 Litho. *Perf. 13*

675 A359 100p multi 2.00 1.00

400th anniv. of Spanish presence in Straits of Magellan.

State Bank of Chile Centenary — A360

1984, Sept. 6 Litho. *Perf. 13½*

676 A360 35p Founder Antonio Varas de la Barra, coin 70 30

11th Anniv. of Liberation — A361

1984, Sept. 11

677 A361 20p Monument to O'Higgins 40 20

Circus Centenary — A362

1984, Sept. 28 Litho. *Perf. 13½*

678 A362 45p Clown 90 45

Endangered Species, World Wildlife Emblem — A363

1985, July Litho. *Perf. 13½*

679 A363 9p Chinchilla 18 15
680 A363 9p Blue whale 18 15
681 A363 9p Sea lions 18 15
682 A363 9p Chilean huemuls 18 15
a. Block of 4, #679-682 75 40
Set value 32

Christmas 1984 — A364

Children's drawings.

1984, Nov. 20 Litho. *Perf. 13½*

683 A364 9p Shepherds 18 15
684 A364 40p Bethlehem 80 40

Santiago University Planetarium Opening — A365

1984, Dec. 29

685 A365 10p multi 20 15

Flora and Fauna — A366

Wildlife: a, Conepatus chinga. b, Leucocoryne purpurea. c, Himantopus himantopus. d, Lutra felina. e, Balbisia peduncularis. f, Psittacus cyanalysias. g, Pudu pudu. h, Fuschia magellanica. i, Diuca diuca. j, Dusicyon griseus. k, Alstroemeria sierrae. l, Glaucidium nanum.

1985, Feb.

686 Block of 12 2.40 2.40
a.-l. A366 10p, Any single 20 15

American Airforces Cooperation System, 25th Anniv. — A367

1985, Mar. 26

687 A367 45p Emblem, flags 90 45

Chile-Argentina Peace Treaty — A368

1985, May 2 Litho. *Perf. 13½*

688 A368 20p Papal arms, flags 25 15

Fr. Joseph Kentenich (1885-1968), Founder, Intl. Schonstatt Movement of Catholic Laymen — A369

1985, May 19 Litho. *Perf. 13½*

689 A369 40p Portrait, La Florida Sanctuary, Santiago 48 24

Antarctic Treaty, 25th Anniv. A370

Resources, research: 15p, Krill, pack ice, map. 20p, Seismological Station, O'Higgins' Base. 35p, Georeception Station, dish receiver.

1985, June 21

690 A370 15p multi 18 15
691 A370 20p multi 24 15
692 A370 35p multi 42 20
Nos. 690-692 (3) 84
Set value 41

Canis Fulvipes — A371

Endangered wildlife: b, Phoenicoparrus jamesi. c, Fulica gigantea. d, Lutra provocax.

1985, Aug. 9 Litho. *Perf. 13½*
693 Block of 4 1.00 70
a.-d. A371 20p, any single 25 15

Intl. Youth Year A372

UN, 40th Anniv. A373

1985, Aug. 31
694 A372 15p multi 18 15
695 A373 15p multi 18 15
a. Pair, #694-695 40 25

Gen. Jose Miguel Carrera Verdugo (1785-1821) — A374

1985, Oct. 8 Litho. *Perf. 13½*
696 A374 40p multi 45 20

Farmer and Ox-drawn Hay Cart — A375

Folklore: b, Street photographer, wet plate camera. c, One-man band. d, Basket maker.

1985, Oct.
697 Block of 4 40 20
a.-d. A375 10p, any single 15 15

For surcharges see Nos. 770-771.

Christmas 1985 — A376

Holy Family — A376a

Winning children's drawings, 7th natl. design contest.

1985, Nov. 4
698 A376 15p Nativity 16 15
699 A376 100p Father Christmas, vert. 1.10 55

Nos. 698-699 inscribed in black on gummed side with child's name, age, school and region.

1985 Litho. *Perf. 13½*
699A A376a 10p buff & brn 15 15

For surcharge see No. 768.

16th Armed Forces Conference — A377

Designs: 20p, Cavalryman, Directorial Escort, 1818. 35p, Officer, Grand Guard, 1813.

1985, Nov. 15 Litho. *Perf. 13½*
700 A377 20p multi 22 15
701 A377 35p multi 38 20

Halley's Comet — A378

1985, Nov. 29 Litho. *Perf. 13½*
702 A378 45p multi 48 25
a. Souvenir sheet *4.00*

No. 702a exists imperf.

Natl. Solidarity Campaign — A379

1985
703 A379 5p red & blue 15 15

Campaign for Prevention of Forest Fires — A380

1985, Dec. 27
704 A380 40p Forest 45 25
705 A380 40p Fire destruction 45 25
a. Pair, #704-705 90 50

No. 705a has continuous design.

Dungeness Point Lighthouse, Straits of Magellan — A381

1986, Jan. 26
706 A381 45p shown 50 25
707 A381 45p Evangelistas Lighthouse 50 25
a. Pair, #706-707 1.00 50

No. 707a continuous design.

View of Santiago, Mackenna — A382

1986, Jan. 28
708 A382 30p multi 35 18

Benjamin Vicuna Mackenna (d. 1886), municipal superintendent of Santiago, 1872-1875.

Diego Portales, Natl. Crest, Text A382a

1986, Feb. Litho. *Perf. 13½*
708A A382a 12p on 3.50p multi 15 15

No. 708A not issued without surcharge.

1986 World Cup Soccer Championships, Mexico — A383

Host stadiums: 15p, Natl. Stadium, Chile, 1962. 20p, Aztec Stadium, Mexico, 1970. 35p, Maracana Stadium, Brazil, 1950. 50p, Wembley Stadium, Great Britain, 1966.

1986, Feb. 18
709 A383 15p multi 18 15
710 A383 20p multi 22 15
711 A383 35p multi 40 20
712 A383 50p multi 55 30
Nos. 709-712 (4) 1.35 80

Environmental Conservation — A384

1986, Feb. 28
713 A384 20p Water 24 15
714 A384 20p Air 24 15
715 A384 20p Soil 24 15
Nos. 713-715 (3) 72
Set value 36

Sailing Ship Santiaguillo, Flags — A385

1986, Mar. 20
716 A385 40p multi 48 25

Discovery of Valparaiso Bay, 450th anniv.

Interamerican Development Bank, 25th Anniv. — A386

1986, Apr. 9
717 A386 45p multi 55 25

St. Rosa de Lima (1586-1617), Sanctuary at Pelequen — A387

1986, Apr. 30 Litho. *Perf. 13½*
718 A387 15p multi 18 15

Moai Statues, Easter Is. — A388

1986, May 15
719 A388 60p Raraku Volcano 65 40
a. Souvenir sheet *1.15 1.15*
720 A388 100p Tongariki Ruins 1.10 75
a. Souvenir sheet *1.90 1.90*

AMERIPEX '86 — A389

1986, May 23
721 A389 100p multi 1.10 55

Historic Naval Ships A390

1986, May 30
722 A390 35p Schooner Ancud, 1843 38 20
723 A390 35p Armed merchantman Aguilar, 1830 38 20
724 A390 35p Corvette Esmeralda, 1856 38 20
725 A390 35p Frigate O'Higgins, 1834 38 20
a. Block of 4, #722-725 1.75 90

See Nos. 752-753.

Paintings by Juan Francisco Gonzalez (1853-1933) A391

1986, June 24

726 A391 30p Rush and Chrysanthemums 32 15
727 A391 30p Gate of La Serena 32 15

Exports — A392

Designs: a, Saltpeter. b, Iron. c, Copper. d, Molybdenum.

1986 Litho. *Perf. 13½*

728 A392 Block of 4 56 40
a.-d. 12p, any single 15 15

Antarctic Fauna — A393

Designs: a, Sterna vittata. b, Phalacrocorax atriceps. c, Aptenodytes forsteri. d, Catharacta lonnberg.

1986, July 16 Litho. *Perf. 13½*

729 Block of 4 1.80 1.25
a.-d. A393 40p, any single 45 25

Writers A394

Designs: No. 730, Pedro de Ona (1570-1643). No. 731, Vicente Huidobro (1893-1948).

1986, Aug. 19

730 A394 20p multi 22 15
731 A394 20p multi 22 15
a. Pair, #730-731 45 25

Has continuous design.

Military Academy, Cent. — A395

1986, Sept. 8 Litho. *Perf. 13½*

732 A395 45p Major-General, 1878 48 25
733 A395 45p Major, 1950 48 25
a. Pair, #732-733 1.00 50

Art A396

1986, Oct. 17 *Perf. 13½*

734 A396 30p Diaguita urn, duck jug 30 15
735 A396 30p Mapuche silver ornament, embroidery 30 15
a. Pair, #734-735 65 30

Christmas — A397

8th Natl. design contest-winning children's drawings.

1986, Nov. 19 Litho. *Perf. 13½*

736 A397 15p multi 16 15
737 A397 105p multi 1.10 55

Nos. 736-737 inscribed in black on gummed side with child's name, age, school and region.

Christmas A397a

Design: Shepherds see star, Bethlehem.

1986, Nov. Litho. *Perf. 13½*

737A A397a 12p multi 15 15

Intl. Peace Year — A398

1986, Nov. 26

738 A398 85p multi 88 45

Natl. Women Volunteers — A399

1986, Dec. 15 Litho. *Perf. 13½*

739 A399 15p multi 16 15

Crowning of Our Lady of Mt. Carmel, Patron of Chile, by Pius XI, 60th Anniv. — A400

1986, Dec. 19

740 A400 25p multi 28 15

Andean Railways Kitson-Meyer No. 59, 1907, Designed by Robert Sterling — A401

1987, Jan. 27 Litho. *Perf. 13½*

741 A401 95p multi 1.05 75

Arturo Prat Naval Base, Greenwich Island, the Antarctic, 40th Anniv. — A402

1987, Feb. 6

742 A402 100p Storage and power supplies 1.15 60
743 A402 100p Working and living quarters 1.15 60
a. Pair, #742-743 2.50 1.50

No. 743a has continuous design.

State Visit of Pope John Paul II, Apr. 1-6, 1987 A403

Pope John Paul II and: 20p, Christ the Redeemer statue. 25p, Votive Church, Maipu. 90p, Cross of the Seas, Straits of Magellan. 115p, Virgin of the Hill.

1987 Litho. *Perf. 13½*

744 A403 20p multi 20 15
745 A403 25p multi 25 15
746 A403 90p multi 90 45
747 A403 115p multi 1.25 65
a. Souv. sheet of one 2.50 2.50
747B A403 115p multi 1.25 65
Nos. 744-747B (5) 3.85 2.05

No. 747a sold for 250p.
No. 747B differs from No. 747 in that the Statue of the Virgin has a halo and Pope John Paul II is smiling.
Issue date: Nos. 744-747a, Apr. 6.

Los Carabineros (Natl. Guard), 60th Anniv. A404

World Youth Soccer Championships A405

1987, Apr. 21

748 A404 50p Cavalry showmanship 50 25
749 A404 50p Air-sea rescue 50 25
a. Pair, #748-749 1.00 50

1987, May 28

Designs: No. 750b, Concepcion Stadium, kick play. No. 750c, Antofagasta Stadium, dribbling the ball. No. 750d, Valparaiso Stadium, heading the ball.

750 Block of 4 1.80 1.25
a.-d. A405 45p any single 45 25

Souvenir Sheet

751 A405 45p Four players 1.50 1.50

No. 751 sold for 150p.

Naval Ships Type of 1986

1987, May 29

752 A390 60p Battleship Almirante Latorre, 1913 60 30
753 A390 60p Cruiser O'Higgins, 1936 60 30

Diego Portales (1793-1837), Finance Minister — A406

1987, June 16

754 A406 30p multi 30 15

Public Works Ministry, Cent. — A407

1987, June 26

755 A407 25p multi 25 15

Infantry School, Cent. A408

1987, July 9

756 A408 50p Entrance 50 25
757 A408 100p Soldiers, natl. flag 1.00 50

Miniature Sheet

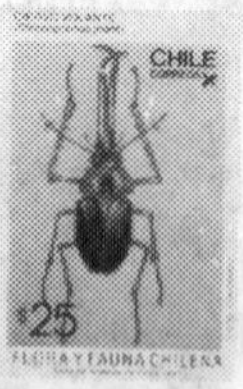

Flora and Fauna — A409

Designs: a, Chiasognathus granti. b, Calidris alba. c, Hippocamelus antisensis. d, Jubaea chilensis. e, Colias vauthieri. f, Pandion haliaetus. g, Cephalorhynchus commersonii. h, Austrocedrus chilensis. i, Jasus frontalis. j, Stephanoides fernandensis. k, Vicugna vicugna. l, Thyrsopteris elegans. m, Lithodes antarctica. n, Pterocnemia pennata. o, Lagidium viscacia. p, Cereus atacamensis.

1987, July 30

758 Sheet of 16 4.00 3.00
a.-p. A409 25p any single 25 15

Intl. Year of Shelter for the Homeless
A410

The Guitarist of Quinchamali
A411

1987, Aug. 6
759 A410 40p multi 40 20

1987, July **Litho.** ***Perf. 13½***

Legends and folk tales: b, El Caleuche. c, El Pihuychen. d, La Lola.

760 Block of 4 58 40
a.-d. A411 15p any single 15 15

Nos. 760a-760d exist ovptd. "D.S. No 20." in golden brown on back.
For surcharges see Nos. 812, 1104.

FISA '87, Santiago — A412

1987, Oct. 16 **Litho.** ***Perf. 13½***
761 A412 20p multi 18 15

25th Intl. agriculture and exports exhibition.

Rear Admiral Carlos Condell de la Haza (1843-1887), Naval Hero at the Battle of the Pacific — A413

1987, Nov. 7
762 A413 50p multi 45 22

Christmas 1987 — A414

COBRE '87, Intl. Conf. on Copper — A415

Children's drawings: 30p, Holy Family. 100p, Star Over Bethlehem, horiz.

1987, Nov. 13
763 A414 30p multi 28 15
764 A414 100p multi 90 45

1987, Nov. 23
765 A415 40p Foundry 35 15
a. Souv. sheet of one 1.35 1.35

No. 765 sold for 150p.

Natl. Antarctic Exploration Commission, 25th Anniv. — A415a

1987, Dec. 11 **Litho.** ***Perf. 13½***
765B A415a 45p multi 40 20

Ramon Freire Serrano (1787-1851), Chief of State
A416

To Smoke Is To Contaminate
A417

1987, Dec. 29 ***Perf. 13x13½***
766 A416 20p pale lil & rose claret 18 15

1987, Dec. **Litho.** ***Perf. 13½***
767 A417 15p blue & ver 15 15

Natl. Commission for the Control of Smoking.

$12

No. 699A Surcharged in Green

D.S.N°20

1987 **Litho.** ***Perf. 13½***
768 A376a 12p on 10p buff & brn 15 15

Christmas 1987 — A418

1987, Dec.
769 A418 15p ultra, org yel & blk 15 15
a. Bklt. pane of 10 4.00

No. 769a exists ovptd. "D.S. No 20." on back.

No. 697 Surcharged with New Value and 6 Bars in Rose Red and Black

1987, Dec.
770 Block of 4 48 30
a.-d. A375 12p on 10p, #697a-697d 15 15
771 Block of 4 58 40
a.-d. A375 15p on 10p, #697a-697d 15 15

St. John Bosco (1815-1888), Educator Canonized in 1934 — A419

1988, Jan. 29
772 A419 40p multi 38 20

20th Music Week, Frutillar
A420

1988, Jan. 27
773 A420 30p multi 28 15

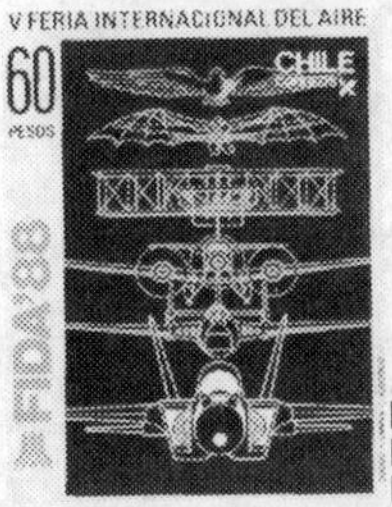

FIDA '88, 5th Intl. Aviation Fair — A421

1988, Mar. 4 **Litho.** ***Perf. 13½***
774 A421 60p dark blue & blue 48 25

1988 Summer Olympics, Seoul — A422

Flags of Chile and Korea, events: 50p, Shot put, pole vault, javelin. 100p, Swimming, cycling, running.

1988, Mar. 18 ***Perf. 13½***
775 A422 50p multi 40 20
776 A422 100p multi 80 40
a. Souv. sheet of 2, #775-776 2.00 2.00

No. 776a sold for 250p.

Natl. Agricultural Soc., 150th Anniv. — A423

1988, Apr. 8
777 A423 45p multi 35 18

Intl. Red Cross and Red Crescent Organizations, 125th Annivs. — A424

1988, May 10
778 A424 150p multi 1.10 60

$20

No. 645 Surcharged

DS Nº20

1988 **Litho.** ***Perf. 13½***
779 A344a 20p on 9p green 18 15

Easter Island Folk Art — A425

Designs: Nos. 780, 782, Carved wooden head from Kava Kava. Nos. 781, 783, Bird man stone carving from Tangata Manu.

1988, Apr. 1 **Litho.** ***Perf. 13½***
780 A425 20p brick red & blk 18 18
781 A425 20p brick red & blk 18 18
a. Bklt. pane, 6 #780, 4 #781 1.80
b. Pair, #780-781 40 40
782 A425 20p yel & blk 18 18
783 A425 20p yel & blk 18 18
a. Bklt. pane, 6 #782, 4 #783 1.80
b. Pair, #782-783 40 40
Nos. 780-783 (4) 72 72

Nos. 782-783 inscribed "D.S. No 20."
For surcharges see Nos. 813-816, 955-956.

Merino, Biplane, Jet Passenger Plane and Supersonic Fighter Plane — A426

1988, May 17 **Litho.** ***Perf. 13½***
784 A426 35p multi 32 15

Commodore Arturo Merino Benitez (b. 1888), aviation pioneer.

Naval Tradition
A427 A428

Designs: No. 785, Training ship *Esmeralda.* No. 786, Capt. Arturo Pratt, a stained-glass window in the Naval Museum, Valparaiso.

1988, May 23
785 A427 50p multi 45 22
786 A428 50p multi 45 22
a. Pair, #785-786 90 45

Pontifical Catholic University of Chile, Santiago, Cent. — A429

1988, June 21

787 A429 40p Papal and university arms 35 18

Locomotives — A430

1988, July 22 Litho. *Perf. 13½*

788 A430 60p Esslingen No. 3331 45 22
789 A430 60p North British No. 45 45 22
a. Souv. sheet of 2, #788-789, imperf. 1.35 1.35
b. Pair, #788-789 90 45

Arica-La Paz Railway, 75th anniv. (#788); Antofagasta Bolivia Railway, cent. (#789).

Jose Miguel Carrera Natl. Institute, 175th Anniv. — A431

1988, Aug. 10 Litho. *Perf. 13½*

790 A431 45p multi 40 20

Annexation of Easter Is., Cent. — A432

1988, Sept. 9

791 A432 50p Ship, officer 45 25
792 A432 50p Map, globe 45 25
a. Pair, #791-792 90 50
793 A432 100p Easter Is. folk dancers 90 50
794 A432 100p Stone ruins 90 50
a. Souv. sheet of 4, #791-794, imperf. 4.00 4.00
b. Pair, #793-794 2.00 1.25
Nos. 791-794 (4) 2.70 1.50

Miniature Sheet

Flowers — A433

Designs: a, *Chloraea chrysantha.* b, *Lapageria rosea.* c, *Nolana paradoxa.* d, *Rhodophiala advena.* e, *Schizanthus hookeri.* f, *Acacia caven.* g, *Cordia decandra.* h, *Leontochir ovallei.* i, *Alstroemeria pelegrina.* j, *Copiapoa cinerea.* k, *Salpiglossis sinuata.* l, *Leucocoryne coquimbensis.* m, *Eucryphia glutinosa.* n, *Calandrinia longiscapa.* o, *Desfontainia spinosa.* p, *Sophora macrocarpa.*

1988, Aug. 23 Litho. *Perf. 13½*

795 Sheet of 16 4.50 3.00
a.-p. A433 30p any single 28 15

First Domestic Airmail Route, 1919 — A434

1988, Oct. 11

796 A434 150p Clodomiro Figueroa Ponce's aircraft 1.35 65

Christmas 1988
A435 A436

Children's drawings: 35p, Nativity, by Paulette Thiers, age 8. 100p, Going to church, by Jose M. Lamas, age 9, horiz.

1988, Nov. 17

797 A435 20p rose lake & org yel 18 15
a. Bklt. pane of 10 1.80
798 A435 20p rose lake & org yel 18 15
a. Bklt. pane of 10 3.00
Set value 20
799 A436 35p multi 30 15
800 A436 100p multi 88 45
Nos. 797-800 (5) 1.54 1.10

No. 798 inscribed "D.S. No 20."

Artisans — A437

1988, Oct. 25 Litho. *Perf. 13½*

801 A437 25p Potter 22 15
802 A437 25p Weaver 22 15
a. Pair, #801-802 45 25

No. 802a has continuous design.

Natl. Philatelic Soc., Cent. — A438

1988, Nov. 24

803 A438 40p No. 38, cancellation 35 15

School Crossing Guards — A439

1988, Oct. 26

804 A439 45p multi 40 20

Commander and Battle Scene — A440 Battle Scene and Serviceman — A441

1989, Jan. 12 Litho. *Perf. 13½*

805 A440 50p Manuel Bulnes (1799-1866) 38 18
806 A441 50p Cavalryman 38 18
a. Pair, #805-806 80 40
807 A440 100p Roberto Simpson 75 42
808 A441 100p Seaman 75 42
a. Pair, #807-808 1.50 90
Nos. 805-808 (4) 2.26 1.20

Battles of 1839: Yungay (50p) and Casma (100p). Nos. 806a, 808a have continuous designs.

Municipal Annivs. — A442

Municipal coats of arms and: 30p, San Ambrosio Church. 35p, Craftsman sculpting marble. 45p, Laja Spring and falls.

1989, Jan. 20

809 A442 30p multi 28 15
810 A442 35p multi 32 16
811 A442 45p multi 42 20
Nos. 809-811 (3) 1.02 51

Founding of Vallenar, 200th anniv. (30p); founding of Combarbala, 200th anniv. (35p); founding of Los Angeles, 250th anniv. (45p).

Nos. 760a-760d and 780-783 Surcharged

$25
a

$25
b

1989, Mar. 20 Litho. *Perf. 13½*

812 Block of 4 88 60
a.-d. A411(a) 25p on 15p #760a-760d, any single 22 15
813 A425(b) 25p on 20p #780 22 15
814 A425(b) 25p on 20p #781 22 15
815 A425(b) 25p on 20p #782 20 15
816 A425(b) 25p on 20p #783 20 15
Nos. 812-816 (8) 1.72
Set value 1.00

Surcharge differs on Nos. 814, 816.
Issued: #812-814, Mar. 20. #815-816, Nov. 30.

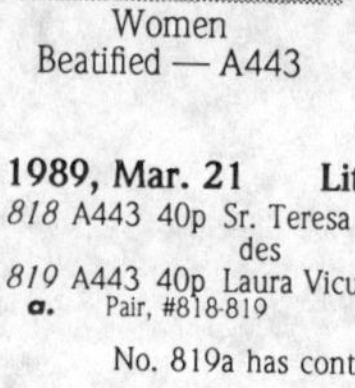

Women Beatified — A443

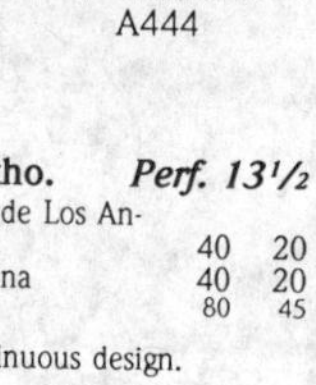

A444

1989, Mar. 21 Litho. *Perf. 13½*

818 A443 40p Sr. Teresa de Los Andes 40 20
819 A443 40p Laura Vicuna 40 20
a. Pair, #818-819 80 45

No. 819a has continuous design.

1989, Mar. 31

820 A444 100p Christopher Columbus 1.05 52
821 A444 100p Galleons 1.05 52
a. Pair, #820-821 2.25 1.50
b. Souvenir sheet of 2, #820-821 3.15 2.00
c. Souvenir sheet of 2, #820-821 3.15 2.00

EXFINA '89, Santiago. No. 821a has continuous design. No. 821b margin pictures Columbus's coat of arms and the Order of the Great Admiralty. No. 821c margin Nos. 55, 69, 18, 76, 37, 1, 20 and 98.

CORFO Development Corp., 50th Anniv. — A445

1989, Apr. 4

822 A445 60p Shipping 52 26
823 A445 60p Lumber 52 26
824 A445 60p Communication 52 26
825 A445 60p Coal 52 26
a. Block of 4, #822-825 2.25 1.25

Gabriela Mistral (1889-1957), Poet — A446

1989, Apr. 7 Litho. *Perf. 13½*

826 A446 30p Poet, steeple 25 15
827 A446 30p Poet, children 25 15
828 A446 30p Poet working 25 15
829 A446 30p Receiving Nobel Prize, 1945 25 15
a. Block of 4, #826-829 1.10 55

Exports — A447

Designs: Nos. 830, 832, Grapes. Nos. 831, 833, Apple.

1989, Apr. 19

830 A447 25p indigo & brt yel grn 22 15
831 A447 25p ver & brt yel grn 22 15
a. Bklt. pane, 5 each #830-831 2.20
b. Pair, #830-831 45 25
832 A447 25p indigo & pale yel org 22 15
833 A447 25p ver & pale yel org 22 15
a. Bklt. pane, 5 each #832-833 2.20
b. Pair, #832-833 45 25
Nos. 830-833 (4) 88
Set value 40

Nos. 832-833 inscribed "D.S. No 20."
See Nos. 861-864, 943-946. For surcharges see Nos. 956B-956C, 1085-1088.

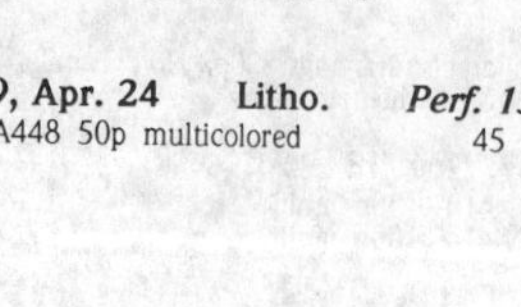

Military Justice Department, 150th Anniv. — A448

1989, Apr. 24 Litho. *Perf. 13½*

834 A448 50p multicolored 45 22

Monument to the Martyrs of Carabineros de Chile — A449

1989, Apr. 26
835 A449 35p multicolored 30 15

Surveyor and Penguins — A450

1989, May 29
836 A450 150p multi 1.25 60

Antarctic Research Institute expeditions, 25th anniv.

Naval Engineers, Cent. — A451

Designs: No. 837, Naval school. No. 838, Seamen in boiler room. No. 839, Ship, helicopter, submarine. No. 840, *Aquiles* launch, Asmar-Talcahuano.

1989, May 31
837 A451 45p multicolored 38 18
838 A451 45p multicolored 38 18
839 A451 45p multicolored 38 18
840 A451 45p multicolored 38 18
a. Block of 4, #837-840 1.60 75

Horse-drawn Carriage (Victoria), Vina del Mar — A452

Early transportation: 35p, Launch off Chiloe Is., vert. 40p, Cart, Cautin. 45p, Ferry, Rio Palena. 50p, Car transport, Lake Gral, Carretta. 60p, Incline railroad, Valparaiso. 100p, Cable car (funicular), Santiago.

1989-92 Litho. *Perf. 13½*
841 A452 30p black & orange 24 15
842 A452 60p black & lemon 48 24
842A A452 60p like No. 842 38 18
843 A452 100p black & brt yel grn 80 40

1989-91
844 A452 35p black & brt blue 25 15
845 A452 40p black & olive 30 15
846 A452 45p black & pale blue grn 32 16
846A A452 45p black & lt ol grn 32 16
847 A452 50p black & scarlet 35 18
Nos. 841-847 (9) 3.44 1.77

Nos. 842A, 846A inscribed DS No. 20.
Issue dates: Nos. 841-842, 843, May 22, 1989; No. 846A, Feb. 1, 1991; No. 842A, 1992; others, Aug. 1989.
For surcharge see No. 1002.
This is an expanding set. Numbers will change if necessary.

Export Type of 1989

Designs: Nos. 861, 863, Grapes. Nos. 862, 864, Apple.

1989, May 22
861 A447 5p dark blue & gray 15 15
862 A447 5p brt red, dark blue & gray 15 15
a. Pair, #861-862 15 15
863 A447 10p dark blue & gray 15 15
864 A447 10p brt red, dark blue & gray 15 15
a. Pair, #863-864 18 15
Set value 26 20

A453

A454

1989, Aug. 25 Litho. *Perf. 13½*
865 A453 250p multicolored 1.80 90
a. Souvenir sheet of 1 2.45 1.65

World Stamp Expo '89.

1989, Oct. 12

UPAE emblem and pre-Columbian peoples: 30p, Atacamena potter. 150p, Selk'nam-onas bow hunter.

866 A454 30p multicolored 22 15
867 A454 150p multicolored 1.05 52

Drawing by Christina Lopez — A455

1989, Nov. 20 Litho. *Perf. 13½*
868 A455 100p multicolored 68 32

Christmas.

Christmas Ornaments — A456

Designs: Nos. 869, 871, Balls. Nos. 870, 872, Bells.

1989
869 A456 25p dull green & org 20 15
870 A456 25p dull green & org 20 15
a. Bklt. pane, 5 each Nos. 869-870 2.00
b. Pair, #869-870 40 30
871 A456 25p dull green & ver 20 15
872 A456 25p dull green & ver 20 15
a. Bklt. pane, 5 each Nos. 871-872 2.00
b. Pair, #871-872 40 30
Nos. 869-872 (4) 80 60

Nos. 871-872 inscribed "D.S. No 20."

Miniature Sheet

Wildlife, Natl. Parks — A457

Designs: a, Vicuna, Lauca Park. b, Chilean flamingos, Salar de Surire. c, Cactus, La Chimba Reserve. d, Guanaco, Pan de Azucar Park. e, Song bird, Father Jorge Park. f, Terns, Rapa Nui Park. g, Ferret, La Campana Park. h, Duck, Rio Clarillo Park. i, Cypress tree, Rio de Los Cipreses Reserve. j, Black-headed swan, Laguna de Torca Reserve. k, Puma, Laguna del Laja Park. l, Araucaria tree, Villarrica Park. m, Flower, Vicente Perez Rosales Park. n, Lenga tree, Dos Lagunas. o, Sea lion, Laguna San Rafael Park. p, Rhea, Torres del Paine Park.

1990, Jan. 25
873 Sheet of 16 3.85 2.50
a.-p. A457 35p any single 24 15

1990 World Cup Soccer Championships, Italy — A458

1990, Feb. 23
874 A458 50p Cleated shoe 35 18
875 A458 50p Hand 35 18
876 A458 50p Soccer ball 35 18
877 A458 50p Athlete 35 18
a. Block of 4, #874-877 1.50 75

Natl. Air Force A459

Various aircraft: No. 878, Vickers Wibault. No. 879, Curtiss O1E Falcon. No. 880, Pitts S2A. No. 881, Extra 300.

1990, Mar. 16 Litho. *Perf. 13½*
878 A459 40p multicolored 28 15
879 A459 40p multicolored 28 15
880 A459 40p multicolored 28 15
881 A459 40p multicolored 28 15
a. Souvenir sheet of 4, #878-881 1.15 56
Nos. 878-881 (4) 1.12 60

FIDAE '90.

Discovery of America 500th Anniv. (in 1992)
A460 A461

Maps and 16th cent. men: No. 882, Incan. No. 883, Spanish infantryman.

1990, Apr. 20 Litho. *Perf. 13½*
882 A460 60p multicolored 42 20
883 A461 60p multicolored 42 20
a. Pair, #882-883 85 45

Port Cities A462

1990, Apr. 27
884 A462 40p Valparaiso 28 15
885 A462 40p San Vicente 28 15
a. Pair, #884-885 60 30

Democracy — A463

1990, June 8 Litho. *Perf. 13½*
886 A463 20p Sunrise 15 15
887 A463 30p Peace dove 22 15
888 A463 60p Pleasure 45 24
889 A463 100p Star 78 40
a. Souvenir sheet of 4, #886-889 2.40 1.20
Nos. 886-889 (4) 1.60 94

Equality — A464

1990, June 8
890 A464 45p multicolored 35 18
a. Souvenir sheet 60 30

No. 890a margin continues the design.

Naval Tradition — A465

Designs: No. 891, Transport ship Piloto Pardo. No. 892, Oceanographic research ship Yelcho.

1990, May 30 Litho. *Perf. 13½*
891 A465 50p multicolored 36 18
892 A465 50p multicolored 36 18
a. Pair, #891-892 72 36

Penny Black, 150th Anniv. — A466

1990, June 12
893 A466 250p Sir Rowland Hill 2.75 1.40
a. Souvenir sheet of 1 4.10 2.00

No. 893a margin continues the design.

Organization of American States, Cent. — A467

1990, June 21
894 A467 150p multicolored 1.00 50

Marine Resources — A468

Designs: a, Scallop. b, Clam. c, Swordfish. d, Crab. e, Fish. f, Baiting, processing.

1990, July 27 Litho. *Perf. 13½*
895 Block of 6 1.80 90
a.-f. A468 40p any single 30 15

Curimon Convent — A469

1990, Aug. 1

896 A469 50p multicolored		36	18

250th anniversary of San Felipe.

Environmental Protection — A470

1990, Sept. 1 Litho. *Perf. 13½*

897 A470 35p Aerosol propellants	24	15
898 A470 35p Deforestation	24	15
899 A470 35p Smokestacks	24	15
900 A470 35p Oil slick, shore	24	15
901 A470 35p Forest fire	24	15
a. Strip of 5, #897-901	1.20	60
b. Bklt. pane, 2 each #897-901	2.40	
Nos. 897-901 (5)	1.20	
Set value		60

Inscribed "D.S. No 20"

902 A470 35p Aerosol propellants	24	15
903 A470 35p Deforestation	24	15
904 A470 35p Smokestacks	24	15
905 A470 35p Oil slick, shore	24	15
906 A470 35p Forest fire	24	15
a. Strip of 5, #902-906	1.20	60
b. Bklt. pane, 2 each #902-906	2.40	
Nos. 902-906 (5)	1.20	
Set value		60

See Nos. 988-997.

Presidents of Chile — A471

1990, Sept. 4

912 A471 35p Salvador Allende	24	15
913 A471 35p Eduardo Frei	24	15
914 A471 40p Jorge Alessandri	30	15
915 A471 45p Gabriel Gonzalez V	35	18
916 A471 50p Juan Antonio Rios	38	20
917 A471 60p Pedro Aguirre Cerda	45	24
918 A471 70p Juan E. Montero	52	25
919 A471 80p Carlos Ibanez	60	30
920 A471 90p Emiliano Figueroa	70	35
921 A471 100p Arturo Alessandri	75	38
Nos. 912-921 (10)	4.53	2.35

Rodeos — A472

Designs: a, Rodeo ring. b, Men on horses. c, Man stopping horse. d, Men, horses, bull.

1990, Sept. 24

926 Block of 4	1.40	70
a.-d. A472 45p any single	35	18

Discovery of America, 500th Anniv. (in 1992) — A473

1990, Oct. 12 Litho. *Perf. 13½*

927 A473 30p Phoenicopterus chilensis	22	15
928 A473 150p Arctocephalus australis	1.10	55

King and Queen of Spain's Visit — A474

Design: No. 930, Arms of King Juan Carlos I, Chilean Arms.

1990, Oct. 18

929 A474 100p shown	75	38
930 A474 100p Denomination at LR	75	38
a. Pair, #929-930	1.50	76

Malleco Bridge, Cent. — A475

Design: #932, Boy waving at train on bridge.

1990, Oct. 26 Litho. *Perf. 13½*

931 A475 60p multicolored	85	42
932 A475 60p multicolored	85	42
a. Pair, #931-932	1.70	85

Chilean Antarctic Territorial Claims, 50th Anniv. — A476

Design: #934, Penguins, helicopter, camp.

1990, Nov. 6 *Perf. 13½*

933 A476 250p multicolored	1.80	90
934 A476 250p multicolored	1.80	90
a. Souvenir sheet of 2, #933-934	5.25	2.65

A477

Christmas — A478

1990, Nov. 20 Litho. *Perf. 13½*

935 A477 35p lt green & bl grn	25	15
a. Booklet pane of 10	2.50	
936 A477 35p dull org & bl grn	25	15
a. Booklet pane of 10	2.50	
937 A478 35p shown	25	15
938 A478 150p Underwater dwelling	1.10	55
Nos. 935-938 (4)	1.85	1.00

No. 936 inscribed "D.S. No.20."

National Congress — A479

1990, Dec. 21 Litho. *Perf. 13½*

939 A479 100p Congress chamber	75	38
940 A479 100p Early congressional session	75	38
a. Pair, #939-940	1.50	75

City of Santiago, 450th Anniv. — A480

1991, Feb. 7

941 A480 100p Colorado House	75	38
942 A480 100p Skyline	75	38
a. Pair, #941-942	1.50	75
b. Souvenir sheet of 2, #941-942	2.00	1.00

Exports Type of 1989

Designs: Nos. 943, 945, Grapes. Nos. 944, 946, Apple.

1991, Feb. 8 *Perf. 13½ on 3 Sides*

943 A447 45p indigo & brt pink	32	16
944 A447 45p vermilion & brt pink	32	16
a. Bklt. pane, 5 each #943-944	3.25	
945 A447 45p indigo & yel	32	16
946 A447 45p ver & yel	32	16
a. Bklt. pane, 5 each #945-946	3.25	
Nos. 943-946 (4)	1.28	64

Nos. 945-946 inscribed "D.S. No.20."
For surcharges see Nos. 1085-1088.

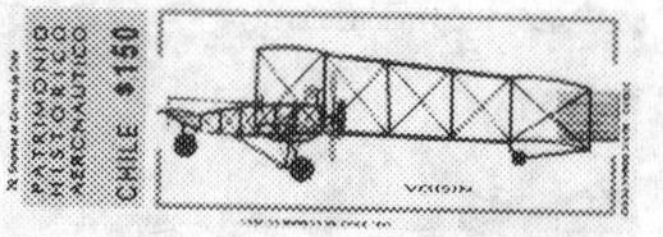

Historical Aircraft — A481

Designs: a, Voisin. b, S.E. 5a. c, Morane Saulnier MS 35. d, Consolidated PBY-5A/OA-10 Catalina. (Illustration reduced).

1991, Mar. 21 Litho. *Perf. 13½*

947 A481 150p Block of 4, #a.-d.	4.50	2.25

American Soccer Cup, Chile — A482

1991, Apr. 12 Litho. *Perf. 13½*

948 A482 100p shown	65	32
949 A482 100p Ball, goalie	65	32
a. Pair, #948-949	1.30	65

Coal Mining A483

Design: #951, Miners dumping cart of coal.

1991, Apr. 18

950 A483 200p shown	1.30	65
951 A483 200p multicolored	1.30	65
a. Pair, #950-951	2.60	1.30

Cultural Art — A484

Design: #953, Small sculptures, spurs, dish.

1991, Apr. 29

952 A484 90p shown	60	30
953 A484 90p multicolored	60	30
a. Pair, #952-953	1.20	60

Chilean Scientific Society, Cent. — A485

1991, Apr. 29

954 A485 45p blue grn & blk	30	15

Nos. 782-783 Surcharged

$45 ≡ a

$45 ≡ b

1991, Apr. 30

955 A425(a) 45p on 20p, #782	30	15
956 A425(b) 45p on 20p, #783	30	15
a. Pair, #955-956	60	30

Nos. 832-833 Surcharged $45 ≡

1991, May 6 Litho. *Perf. 13½*

956B A447 45p on 25p, #832	25	15
956C A447 45p on 25p, #833	25	15
d. Pair, #956B-956C	50	30

Santiago Cathedral A486

1991, May 9 Litho & Engr.

957 A486 300p red brn, sal & blk	2.00	1.00

World Telecommunications Day — A487

1991, May 17 Litho.

958 A487 90p multicolored	60	30

A488

A489

1991, May 23

959 A488 100p Pope Leo XIII 65 32

Rerum Novarum Encyclical, cent.

1991, May 28 Litho. *Perf. 13½*

Rescue of Shackleton Expedition, 75th anniv.: a, Lt. Luis Pardo, Sir Ernest Shackleton. b, Rescue ship, Yelcho. c, Sailor pointing to survivors. d, Shackleton's ship, Endurance.

960 A489 50p Block of 4, #a.-d. 1.30 65
e. Miniature sheet, #960 1.30

21st General Assembly of Organization of American States, Santiago — A490

1991, June 5

961 A490 70p multicolored 45 24

New Carabinero School — A491

1991, June 12

962 A491 50p multicolored 32 16

Natl. Merchant Marine Day — A492

1991, June 26

963 A492 45p black & red 30 15

11th Pan American Games, Havana — A493

1991, July 23

964 A493 100p Runners, torch, flags 65 32
965 A493 100p Cycling, running, basketball 65 32
a. Pair, #964-965 1.30 65

Founding of the City of Los Andes, Bicent. — A494

1991, July 29

966 A494 100p multicolored 65 32

Miniature Sheet

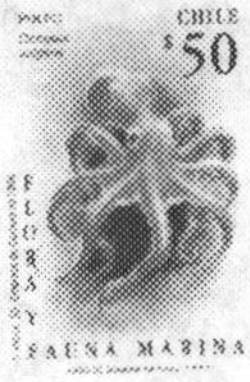

Marine Life — A495

Designs: No. 967a, Octopus vulgaris. b, Durvillaea antarctica. c, Paralichthys adspersus. d, Austromegabalanus psittacus. e, Concholepas concholepas. f, Cancer setosus. g, Lessonia nigrescens. h, Loxechinus albus. i, Homalaspis plana. j, Porphyra columbina. k, Oplegnathus insignis. l, Chorus giganteus. m, Rhynchocinetes typus. n, Engraulis ringens. o, Gracilaria spp. p, Pyura chilensis.

1991, Aug. 20 Litho. *Perf. 13½*

967 Sheet of 16 5.25 2.60
a.-p. A495 50p any single 32 16

1891 Revolution, Cent. — A496

Jose M. Balmaceda (1840-1891) and: No. 968, Machinery. No. 969, Teacher, students at Valentin Letelier School of Medicine.

1991, Aug. 29

968 A496 100p multicolored 65 32
969 A496 100p multicolored 65 32
a. Pair, #968-969 1.30 65

Chilean Art — A497

Paintings: 50p, Woman in Red, by Pedro Reszka. 70p, The Traveler, by Camilo Mori. 200p, Head of Child, by Benito Rebolledo. 300p, Boy Wearing a Fez, by A. Valenzuela Puelma.

1991, Sept. 26

970 A497 50p multicolored 32 16
971 A497 70p multicolored 45 24
972 A497 200p multicolored 1.30 65
973 A497 300p multicolored 1.95 95
Nos. 970-973 (4) 4.02 2.00

Antarctic Treaty, 30th Anniv. — A498

1991, Oct. 7 Litho. *Perf. 13½*

974 A498 80p shown 50 25
975 A498 80p Birds, sea life 50 25
a. Pair, #974-975 1.00 50

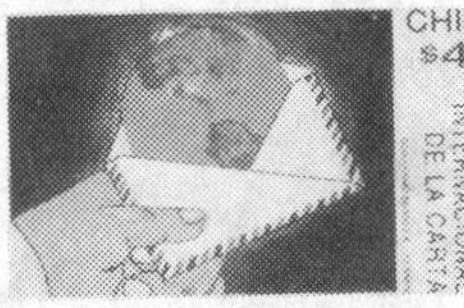

Intl. Letter Writing Week A499

1991, Oct. 9

976 A499 45p shown 30 15
977 A499 70p Envelope filled with people 45 22

America Issue A500

UPAEP emblem, sailing ships and: 150p, Navigator.

1991, Oct. 14

978 A500 50p multicolored 32 16
979 A500 150p multicolored 95 48

A501

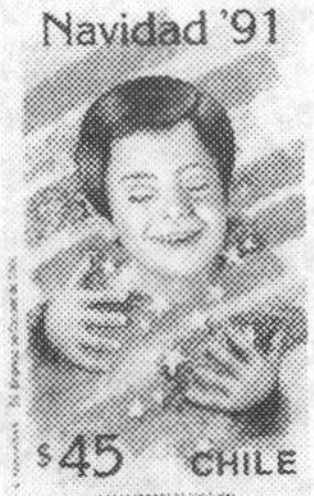

Christmas — A502

1991, Oct. 21

980 A501 45p blue hat 30 15
981 A501 45p red hat 30 15
a. Pair, #980-981 60 30
b. Souvenir sheet of 2, #980-981 1.25 1.25

Pablo Neruda, (1904-1973), Nobel Prize winner for literature, 1971. Nos. 981a has a continuous design.

1991, Nov. 4

982 A502 45p Boy with stars 30 15
983 A502 100p Girl with stars 65 32

Christmas

A503 A504

1991, Nov. 18 Litho. *Perf. 13½*

984 A503 45p violet & brt pink 28 15
985 A504 45p violet & brt pink 28 15
a. Pair, #984-985 56 15
b. Bklt. pane of 5 #985a 2.80
986 A503 45p violet & brt pink 28 15
987 A504 45p violet & brt pink 28 15
a. Pair, #986-987 56 15
b. Bklt. pane of 5 #987a 2.80
Nos. 984-987 (4) 1.12 60

Nos. 986-987 inscribed "D.S. No. 20."
For surcharges see Nos. 1016-1019.

Environmental Protection Type of 1990

1992, Jan. 28 Litho. *Perf. 13½*

988 A470 60p like #897, lem & blk 35 18
989 A470 60p like #898, lem & blk 35 18
990 A470 60p like #899, lem & blk 35 18
991 A470 60p like #900, lem & blk 35 18
992 A470 60p like #901, blk & lem 35 18
a. Strip of 5, #988-992 1.75 90
b. Bklt. pane, 2 each #988-992 3.50

Inscribed "D.S. No. 20"

993 A470 60p like #902, org & dk grn 35 18
994 A470 60p like #903, org & dk grn 35 18
995 A470 60p like #904, org & dk grn 35 18
996 A470 60p like #905, org & dk grn 35 18
997 A470 60p like #906, dk grn & org 35 18
a. Strip of 5, #993-997 1.75 90
b. Bklt. pane, 2 each #993-997 3.50
Nos. 988-997 (10) 3.50 1.80

Wolfgang Amadeus Mozart, Death Bicent. (in 1991) — A505

1992, Jan. 31

998 A505 60p shown 35 18
999 A505 200p Hands at piano 1.15 62
a. Sheet of 2, #998-999 2.30 1.50

FIDAE '92, Intl. Air and Space Fair — A506

1992, Mar. 5 Litho. *Perf. 13½*

1000 A506 60p multicolored 35 18

16th Population and Housing Census — A507

1992, Mar.

1001 A507 60p multicolored 35 18

No. 846 Surcharged in Red Brown **$60**

1992, Mar.

1002 A452 60p on 45p 35 18

Chilean Cities — A508

Cities' coat of arms and: 80p, Church of San Jose de Maipo. 90p, People making pottery. 100p, Lircunlauta House. 150p, Wine and lumber industries. 250p, Huilquilemu cultural center. (Illustration reduced).

1992, Apr. 10 Litho. *Perf. 13½*

1003 A508 80p multicolored 45 22
1004 A508 90p multicolored 52 26
1005 A508 100p multicolored 58 28
1006 A508 150p multicolored 88 45
1007 A508 250p multicolored 1.45 72
Nos. 1003-1007 (5) 3.88 1.93

80p, San Jose de Maipo, 200th anniv. 90p, Melipilla, 250th anniv. 100p, San Fernando, 250th anniv. 150p, Cauquenes, 250th anniv. 250p, Talca, 250th anniv.

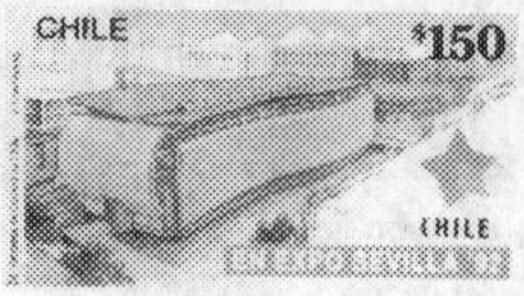

Expo '92, Seville A509

1992, Apr. 23

1008 A509 150p Pavilion 88 45
1009 A509 200p Iceberg 1.15 58
a. Sheet of 2, #1008-1009 *2.75 1.40*

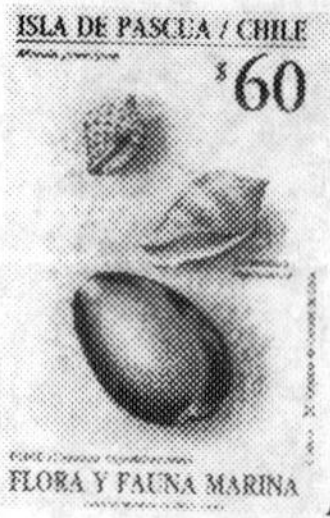

A510

Easter Island A511

Marine life: No. 1010a, Morula praecipua, Strombus maculatus, Cypraea caputdraconis. b, Codium pocockiae. c, Myripristis tiki. d, Sargassum skottsbergii. e, Pseudolabrus fuentesi. f, Pocillopora danae. g, Panulirus pascuensis. h, Tripneustes gratilla.

No. 1011b, Natives, airplane, petroglyph.

1992, June 9 Litho. *Perf. 13½*

1010 A510 60p Sheet of 8, #a.-h. 3.30 2.20
1011 A511 200p Pair, #a.-b. 2.75 1.40

Natl. Council of the Disabled — A512

Military Chiefs of Staff, 50th Anniv. — A513

1992, June 23

1012 A512 60p multicolored 42 20

1992, July 3

1013 A513 60p multicolored 42 20

Submarine Forces, 75th Anniv. — A514

Coat of arms and: 250p, Officer using periscope, control room.

1992, July 4

1014 A514 150p multicolored 95 48
1015 A514 250p multicolored 1.60 80

Nos. 984-987 Surcharged

1992, Aug. 11 Litho. *Perf. 13½*

1016 A503 60p on 45p No. 984 35 18
1017 A504 60p on 45p No. 985 35 18
a. Pair, #1016-1017 70 35
1018 A503 60p on 45p No. 986 35 18
1019 A504 60p on 45p No. 987 35 18
a. Pair, #1018-1019 70 35
Nos. 1016-1019 (4) 1.40 72

Nos. 1018-1019 inscribed "D.S. No. 20."

Emperor Penguins — A515

1992, Sept. 28 Litho. *Perf. 13½*

1020 A515 200p shown 1.15 55
1021 A515 250p Adults with young 1.40 70
a. Souvenir sheet of 2, #1020-1021 3.75 1.90

Central Post Office, Santiago, 1772 — A516

1992, Oct. 9

1022 A516 200p multicolored 1.15 58

Discovery of America, 500th Anniv. — A517

UPAEP emblem and: 200p, Calendar stone, astrolabe, Columbus. 250p, Church, map of Central and South America, sailing ship.

1992, Oct. 20

1023 A517 200p multicolored 1.15 58
1024 A517 250p multicolored 1.40 70

Radio Chile, 75th Anniv. A518

Bernardo O'Higgins (1778-1842) A519

1992, Oct. 22

1025 A518 250p multicolored 1.40 70

1992, Oct. 23

1026 A519 60p multicolored 35 18

Claudio Arrau, Pianist A520

1992, Nov. 12 Litho. *Perf. 13½*

1027 A520 150p As child 90 45
1028 A520 200p As adult 1.20 60
a. Souvenir sheet of 2, #1027-1028 2.40 1.20

Natl. Human Rights Day A521

1992, Dec. 10

1029 A521 100p multicolored 58 30
a. Souvenir sheet of 1 1.05 52

Christmas — A522

Designs: Nos. 1030, 1032, Denomination at LR. Nos. 1031, 1033, Denomination at LL.

1992, Dec. 12 Litho. *Perf. 13½*

1030 A522 60p buff & brown 32 16
1031 A522 60p buff & brown 32 16
a. Pair, #1030-1031 64 32
b. Booklet pane of 5 #1031a 3.25
1032 A522 60p buff & red 32 16
1033 A522 60p buff & red 32 16
a. Pair, #1032-1033 64 32
b. Booklet pane of 5 #1033a 3.25
Nos. 1030-1033 (4) 1.28 64

Nos. 1032-1033 inscribed "DS/20."

A523

A524

University of Chile, 150th Anniv.: a, Statue. b, Coat of arms, facade of building.

1992, Nov. 19 Litho. *Perf. 13½*

1034 A523 200p Pair, #a.-b. 2.30 1.15
c. Souvenir sheet of 1, #1034 2.30 1.15

Nos. 1034a-1034b have a continuous design.

1992, Dec. 12

1035 A524 70p black & yellow 42 22

23rd meeting of Latin American Energy Ministers.

Churches of Chile — A525

Designs: Nos. 1036, 1038, Achao. Nos. 1037, 1039, Castro.

1993, Mar. 1 Litho. *Perf. 13½*

1036 A525 70p black & pink 42 22
1037 A525 70p black & pink 42 22
a. Pair #1036-1037 84 44
b. Booklet pane of 5 #1037a 4.20

Inscribed "DS/20"

1038 A525 70p black & yellow 42 22
1039 A525 70p black & yellow 42 22
a. Pair, #1038-1039 84 44
b. Booklet pane of 5 #1039a 4.20
Nos. 1036-1039 (4) 1.68 88

See Nos. 1053-1060.

Arrival of the Jesuits, 400th Anniv. — A526

Canonization of St. Teresa of the Andes, 1993 — A527

1993 Litho. *Perf. 13½*

1040 A526 200p St. Ignatius of Loyola 1.15 58
a. Souvenir sheet of 1 1.45 72
1041 A527 300p St. Teresa of the Andes 1.75 90

Issue dates: 200p, Mar. 15. 300p, Mar. 31. No. 1040a sold for 250p.

World Festival of Theatre of the Nations — A528

Clotario Blest (1899-1990), Syndicalist — A530

Second Space Conference of the Americas — A529

1993, Apr. 22

1042 A528 250p multicolored 1.45 75

1993, Apr. 26

1043 A529 150p multicolored 90 45
a. Souvenir sheet of 1 2.10 1.05

No. 1043a sold for 350p.

1993, Apr. 30

1044 A530 70p multicolored 40 20

Intl. Labor Day.

Vicente Huidobro, Poet (1893-1948) — A531

1993, May 19 Litho. *Perf. 13½*

1045 A531 100p shown 58 30
1046 A531 100p Portrait, seated 58 30
a. Pair, #1045-1046 1.15 60

Antique Fire Engines A532

Designs: No. 1047, 1902 Watterous Engineering Co. Ltd., Canada. No. 1048, 1872 Merryweather, England.

1993, June 30 Litho. *Perf. 13½*

1047 A532 100p multicolored 55 28
1048 A532 100p multicolored 55 28
a. Souvenir sheet of 2, #1047-1048 2.25 1.10

No. 1048a sold for 400p.

Aircraft A533

Designs: No. 1049, Douglas B-26 Invader. No. 1050, Mirage M50 Panther. No. 1051, Sanchez Besa. No. 1052, Bell 47D1 helicopter.

1993, July 13

1049 A533 100p multicolored 55 28
1050 A533 100p multicolored 55 28
1051 A533 100p multicolored 55 28
1052 A533 100p multicolored 55 28
a. Block of 4, #1049-1052 2.10 1.15

Church Type of 1993

Designs: 10p, Chonchi. 20p, Vilupulli. 30p, Llau-llao. 40p, Dalcahue. 50p, Tenaun. 80p, Quinchao. 90p, Quehui. 100p, Nercon.

1993, July Litho. *Perf. 13½*

1053 A525 10p green & black 15 15
1054 A525 20p black & brown 15 15
1055 A525 30p black & vermilion 16 16
1056 A525 40p black & blue 22 22
1057 A525 50p black & green blue 28 28
1058 A525 80p black & buff 45 45
a. Booklet pane of 10 4.25
1059 A525 90p olive & black 50 50
1060 A525 100p gray violet & black 55 55
Nos. 1053-1060 (8) 2.46 2.46

Issued: No. 1058a, 1/1/94.
See No. 1093 for 80p black & violet.

Natl. Dance, "La Cueca" — A534

Paintings — A535

1993, Sept. 15 Litho. *Perf. 13½*

1061 A534 70p Cueca chilota 38 16
1062 A534 70p Cueca central 38 16
1063 A534 70p Cueca nortina 38 16
Nos. 1061-1063 (3) 1.14 48

1993, Sept. 28

Designs: 80p, Tarde Amanecer, by Mario Carreno, horiz. 90p, Summer, by Gracia Barrios, horiz. 150p, Figura Protegida, by Roser Bru. 200p, Tangueria-Valparaiso, by Nemesio Antunez, horiz.

1064 A535 80p multicolored 45 22
1065 A535 90p multicolored 50 25
1066 A535 150p multicolored 80 40
1067 A535 200p multicolored 1.10 55
Nos. 1064-1067 (4) 2.85 1.42

Chilean Mint, 250th Anniv. — A536

1993, Oct. 7 Litho. & Engr.

1068 A536 250p multicolored 1.40 70
a. Souvenir sheet of 1 1.75 90

Urban Transportation System, 25th Anniv. — A537

1993, Oct. 19 Litho.

1069 A537 80p multicolored 45 22

America Issue — A538

1993, Oct. 12 Litho. *Perf. 13½*

1070 A538 150p Cyanoliseus patagonus 80 40
1071 A538 200p Hippocamelus bisculcus 1.10 55

Chilean Possession of Straits of Magellan, 150th Anniv. — A539

1993, Oct. 21

1072 A539 100p multicolored 55 28

Naval Anniversaries — A540

1993, Oct. 27

1073 A540 80p Sailing ships 45 22
1074 A540 80p Schooner 45 22
1075 A540 80p Assault ship 45 22
1076 A540 80p Patrol boat 45 22
Nos. 1073-1076 (4) 1.80 88

Sailing of first naval squadron (#1073), Arturo Prat Naval Academy (#1074), Marine Corps (#1075), 175th anniversaries. Alejandro Navarette School for Cadets (#1076), 125th anniv.

Intl. Year of Indigenous Peoples — A541

1993, Nov. 24

1077 A541 100p multicolored 55 28

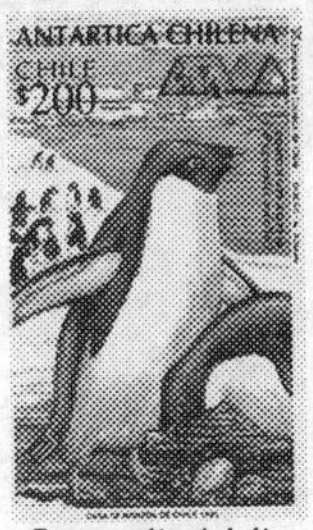

Christmas A542

Pygoscelis Adelie A543

1993, Dec. 1 Litho. *Perf. 13½*

1078 A542 70p tan & violet 35 18
a. Booklet pane of 10 3.50
1079 A542 70p green & blue 35 18
a. Booklet pane of 10 3.50

No. 1079 inscribed "DS/20."

1993, Dec. 3

1080 A543 200p Nesting 1.00 50
1081 A543 250p Adult, chicks 1.25 65
a. Souv. sheet of 2, #1080-1081, imperf. 2.25 1.25

Chilean Antarctica.
No. 1081a has simulated perfs.

Chilean Cities A544

1993, Dec. 15

1082 A544 80p Rancagua 38 20
1083 A544 80p Curico 38 20
1084 A544 80p Ancud 38 20
Nos. 1082-1084 (3) 1.14 60

Rancagua and Curico, 250th anniv. Ancud, 225th anniv.

Nos. 943-946 Surcharged $60

1993 Litho. *Perf. 13½ on 3 Sides*

1085 A447 60p on 45p, #943 32 16
1086 A447 60p on 45p, #944 32 16
a. Bklt. pane, 5 each #1085-1086 3.25
1087 A447 60p on 45p, #945 32 16
1088 A447 60p on 45p, #946 32 16
a. Bklt. pane, 5 each #1087-1088 3.25
Nos. 1085-1088 (4) 1.28 64

Nos. 1087-1088 inscribed "D.S. No. 20."

Intl. Year of the Family — A545

1994, Jan. 17 Litho. *Perf. 13½*

1089 A545 100p multicolored 48 25

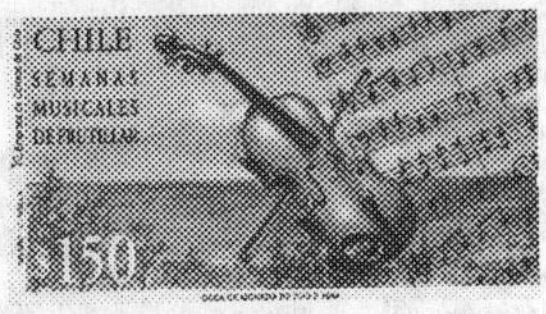

Musical Instruments — A546

Designs: a, Violin. b, Cello.

1994, Jan. 27 Litho. *Perf. 13½*

1091 A546 150p Pair, #a.-b. 1.40 70

Nos. 1091a-1091b have a continuous design.

Church Type of 1993

Design: No. 1090, Quinchao.

1994 Litho. *Perf. 13½*

1093 A525 80p black & violet 42 22

Issued: No. 1093, 1/1/94.
No. 1093 inscribed "DS/20."

Souvenir Sheet

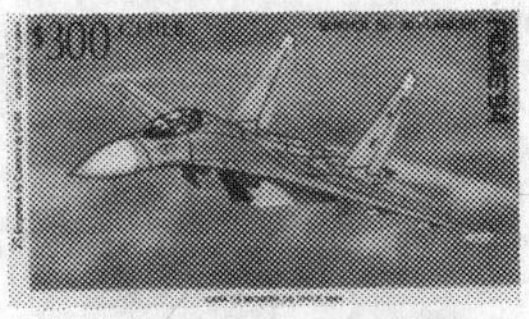

Natl. Aviation Museum, 50th Anniv. — A547

Aircraft: a, Sukhoi SU-30 Flanker. b, Vought-Sikorsky OS-2U3 Kingfisher. c, Lockheed F-117A Nighthawk. d, Northrop F-5E Tiger III.

1994, Mar. 17 Litho. *Perf. 13*

1102 A547 300p Sheet of 4, #a.-d. + 2 labels 6.00 3.00

Intl. Air and Space Fair, FIDAE '94.

College of Agronomy, 50th Anniv. — A548

1994, Apr. 28 Litho. *Perf. 13*

1103 A548 220p multicolored 1.10 55

No. 760 Surcharged

$80

1994, May 1 Litho. *Perf. 13½*

1104 Block of 4 1.50 75
a.-d. A411 80p on 15p any single 35 18

Concepcion University, 75th Anniv. — A549

Sections of mural, by Jorge Gonzalez Camarena: No. 1105, Cactus plant, skeletons. No. 1106, Flags, pillars, nude woman, faces. No. 1107, Flags, bodies, woman, soldier in armor. No. 1108, Women's faces, pipelines.

1994, May 14 Litho. *Perf. 13*

1105 A549	250p	multicolored	1.25	60
1106 A549	250p	multicolored	1.25	60
1107 A549	250p	multicolored	1.25	60
1108 A549	250p	multicolored	1.25	60
a.		Strip of 4, #1105-1108 + label	5.00	2.50

No. 1108a is a continuous design.

Chilean Antarctic Institute, 30th Anniv. — A550

Designs: No. 1109, Penguins, buildings. No. 1110, Buildings, coastal waters.

1994, May 31 *Perf. 13*

1109 A550	300p	multicolored	1.50	75
1110 A550	300p	multicolored	1.50	75
a.		Pair, #1109-1110	3.00	1.50

No. 1110a is a continuous design.

Antique Fire Engines A551

Designs: No. 1111, Merryweather steam pumper, England, 1869. No. 1112, Western lever pumper, US, 1863. No. 1113, Mieusset steam pumper, France, 1905. No. 1114, Merryweather pumper, England, 1903.

1994, July 19 Litho. *Perf. 13*

1111 A551	150p	multicolored	70	35
1112 A551	150p	multicolored	70	35
1113 A551	150p	multicolored	70	35
1114 A551	150p	multicolored	70	35
a.		Block of 4, #1111-1114	2.80	1.40

Javiera Carrera Girls' School, Cent. A552

1994, Aug. 10

1115 A552	200p	multicolored	95	48

Arms, Sights from Chilean Cities A553

Designs: 90p, Porvenir, cent. 100p, Villa Alemana, cent. 150p, Constitucion, bicent. 200p, Linares, bicent. 250p, Copiapo, 250th anniv. 300p, La Serena, 450th anniv.

1994, Aug. 26

1116 A553	90p	multicolored	42	20
1117 A553	100p	multicolored	48	24
1118 A553	150p	multicolored	70	35
1119 A553	200p	multicolored	95	48
1120 A553	250p	multicolored	1.20	60
1121 A553	300p	multicolored	1.50	75
		Nos. 1116-1121 (6)	5.25	2.62

Miniature Sheet of 8

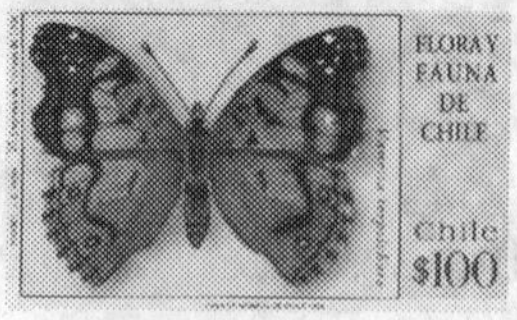

Butterflies — A554

Designs: a, Vanessa terpsichore. b, Hypsochila wagenknechti. c, Battus polydamas. d, Polythysana apollina. e, Satyridae. f, Tetraphloebia stellygera. g, Eroessa chilensis. h, Phoebis sennae.

1994, June 24 Litho. *Perf. 13*

1122 A554	100p	#a.-h.	4.25	4.25

20th Intl. Conference on Data Bases — A555

1994, Sept. 21 Litho. *Perf. 13½*

1123 A555	100p	multicolored	55	28

America Issue A556

Early postal transport vehicles: 80p, Van. 220p, DH-60-G, Gypsy Moth.

1994, Oct. 12

1124 A556	80p	multicolored	45	22
1125 A556	220p	multicolored	1.25	65

Beatification of Father Alberto Hurtado — A557

1994, Oct. 31 Litho. & Engr.

1126 A557	300p	multicolored	1.65	80

SEMI-POSTAL STAMPS

S. S. Abtao and Captain Policarpo Toro — SP1

S. S. Abtao and Brother Eugenio Eyraud SP2

Perf. 14½x15

1940, Mar. 1 Engr. Unwmk.

B1 SP1	80c + 2.20p	dk grn & lake	1.40	1.25
B2 SP2	3.60p + 6.40p	lake & dk grn	1.40	1.25
a.		Pair, #B1-B2	3.50	3.50

50th anniv. of Chilean ownership of Easter Is. Surtax used for charitable institutions.

Sheets containing 15 of each value, with 9 se-tenant pairs.

Catalogue values for unused stamps in this section, from this point to the end of the section, are for Never Hinged items.

Pedro de Valdivia — SP3

Portraits: 10c+10c, Jose Toribio Medina.

1961, Apr. 29 Photo. *Perf. 13x12½*

B3 SP3	5c + 5c	pale brn & sl grn	80	18
B4 SP3	10c + 10c	buff & vio blk	60	18

Printed without charge by the Spanish Mint as a gift to Chile. The surtax was to aid the 1960 earthquake victims and to increase teachers' salaries. See Nos. CB1-CB2.

No. 402 Surcharged in Dark Green

Eº 27 + 3

"Centenario de la Organización Meteorológica Mundial IMO-W-MO 1973"

1974, Mar. 25 Litho. *Perf. 14½*

B5 A213	27e + 3e on 40c	dl grn	15	15

Cent. of intl. meteorological cooperation.

The 3e surtax of Nos. B5-B10 was for modernization of the postal system.

No. 412 Surcharged in Dark Blue

Eº 27 + 3

"V Centenario del Nacimiento de Copérnico 1473 - 1973"

1974, Apr. 25 Litho. *Perf. 14½*

B6 A219	27e + 3e on 1.95e		15	15

500th anniversary of the birth of Nicolaus Copernicus (1473-1534), Polish astronomer.

No. 329A Surcharged

Eº 27 + 3

"Centenario de la ciudad de Viña del Mar 1874 - 1974"

1974, May 2 Litho. *Perf. 14*

B7 A159	27e + 3e on 1e	bluish grn	15	15

Centenary of the city of Vina del Mar.

No. 377 Surcharged

1974, June 7 Litho. *Perf. 14½*

B8 A193	47e + 3e on 40c	grn	15	15

Nos. 395 and 380 Surcharged in Red

1974

B9 A207	67e + 3e on 40c	multi	15	15
B10 A196	97e + 3e on 40c	red brn	15	15
		Set value	16	15

Issue dates: #B9, July 9; #B10, June 20.

AIR POST STAMPS

Correo Aéreo

2 pesos

Black Surcharge

Lithographed; Center Engraved

1927 Unwmk. *Perf. 13½x14*

Black Brown & Blue

C1	40c on 10c	225.00	25.00
C2	80c on 10c	225.00	40.00
C3	1.20p on 10c	225.00	40.00
C4	1.60p on 10c	225.00	40.00
C5	2p on 10c	225.00	40.00
	Nos. C1-C5 (5)	1,125.	185.00

Issued for air post service between Santiago and Valparaiso. The stamps picture Bernardo O'Higgins and are not known without surcharge.

Regular Issues of 1915-28 Overprinted or Surcharged in Black, Red or Blue

CORREO AEREO

Inscribed: "Chile Correos"

1928-29 *Perf. 13½x14, 14*

C6 A39	20c	brn org & blk (Bk)	35	20
C6A A55	40c	dk vio & blk (R)	35	15
C6B A43	1p	grn & blk (Bl)	1.00	50
C6C A43	2p	red & blk (Bl)	1.75	28
f.		2p ver & blk (Bl)	75.00	18.00
C6D A43	5p	ol grn & blk (Bl)	2.50	70
C6E A50	6p on 10c	dp bl & blk (R)	40.00	22.50
C7 A43	10p	org & blk (Bk) ('29)	8.50	2.75
C8 A43	10p	org & blk (Bl)	37.50	22.50
		Nos. C6-C8 (8)	91.95	49.58

On Nos. C6B to C6D, C7 and C8 the overprint is larger than on the other stamps of the issue.

Same Overprint or Surcharge on Nos. 155, 156, 158-161

Inscribed: "Chile Correos"

1928-32 Wmk. 215

C9 A55	40c	vio & blk (R)	42	22
C10 A43	1p	grn & blk (Bl)	1.25	35
C11 A43	2p	red & blk (Bl)	7.00	1.40
C12 A52	3p on 5c	sl bl (R)	27.50	20.00
C13 A43	5p	ol grn & blk (Bl)	5.25	1.40
C14 A43	10p	org & blk (Bk)	27.50	7.00
		Nos. C9-C14 (6)	68.92	30.37

Same Overprint on Nos. 166-169, 172 and 158 in Black or Red

Inscribed: "Correos de Chile"

1928-30

C15 A39	20c	(#166) ('29)	90	45
C16 A39	20c	(#172) ('30)	28	15
C17 A40	25c	bl & blk (R)	42	15
C18 A41	30c	brn & blk	25	15
a.		Double ovpt., one inverted	*250.00*	*250.00*
C19 A42	50c	dp grn & blk (R)	35	15
		Nos. C15-C19 (5)	2.20	1.05

Inscribed: "Chile Correos"

1932 *Perf. 13½x14, 14*

C21 A43	1p	yel grn & blk (Bk)	2.75	1.50

Condor on Andes — AP1a

Airplane Crossing Andes — AP3

Los Cerrillos Airport — AP2

1931 Litho. *Perf. 13½x14, 14½x14*

No.	Type	Description	Unused	Used
C22	AP1a	5c yellow grn	22	15
C23	AP1a	10c yellow brn	22	15
C24	AP1a	20c rose	22	15
C25	AP2	50c dark blue	1.05	40
C26	AP3	50c black brn	52	20
C27	AP3	1p purple	45	18
C28	AP3	2p blue blk	90	24
a.		2p bluish slate	90	24
C29	AP2	5p lt red	2.25	22
		Nos. C22-C29 (8)	5.83	1.69

For surcharges see Nos. C51-C53.

Airplane over City — AP4

Two Airplanes over Globe — AP9

Designs: 30c, 40c, 50c, Wings over Chile. 60c, Condor. 70c, Airplane and Star of Chile. 80c, Condor and Statue of Canpolican. 3p, 4p, 5p, Seaplane. 6p, 8p, 10p, Airplane. 20p, 30p, Airplane and Southern Cross. 40p, 50p, Airplane and symbols of space.

Perf. 13½x14

1934-39 Engr. Wmk. 215

No.	Type	Description	Unused	Used
C30	AP4	10c yel grn ('35)	25	15
C31	AP4	15c dk grn ('35)	35	20
C32	AP4	20c dp bl ('36)	20	15
C33	AP4	30c blk brn ('35)	20	15
C34	AP4	40c indigo ('38)	20	15
C35	AP4	50c dk brn ('36)	20	15
C36	AP4	60c vio blk ('35)	20	15
C37	AP4	70c blue ('35)	35	20
C38	AP4	80c ol blk ('35)	20	15

Perf. 14

No.	Type	Description	Unused	Used
C39	AP9	1p slate blk	20	15
C40	AP9	2p grnsh bl	20	15
C41	AP9	3p org brn ('35)	25	15
C42	AP9	4p brn ('35)	25	15
C43	AP9	5p org red	25	15
C44	AP9	6p yel brn ('35)	35	20
a.		6p brown ('39)	3.75	2.00
C45	AP9	8p grn ('35)	30	15
C46	AP9	10p brn lake	35	20
C47	AP9	20p olive	35	20
C48	AP9	30p gray blk	40	20
C49	AP9	40p gray vio	1.00	60
C50	AP9	50p brn vio	1.25	60
		Nos. C30-C50 (21)	7.30	4.35

Nos. C30-C50 have been re-issued in slightly different colors, with white gum. The first printings are considerably scarcer.

See Nos. C90-C107B, C148-C154.

Types of 1931 Surcharged in Black or Red

Perf. 13½x14, 14½x14

1940 Wmk. 215

No.	Type	Description	Unused	Used
C51	AP1a	80c on 20c lt rose	32	15
C52	AP2	1.60p on 5p lt red	2.25	70
C53	AP3	5.10p on 2p sl bl (R)	1.65	1.00
		Nos. C51-C53 (3)	4.22	1.85

The surcharge on #C52 measures 21½mm.

Plane and Weather Vane — AP14

Plane and Caravel — AP23

Designs (Plane and): 20c, Globe. 30c, Chilean flag. 40c, Star of Chile and Southern Cross. 50c, Mountains. 60c, Tree. 70c, Lakes. 80c, Shore. 90c, Sunrise. 2p, Compass. 3p, Telegraph lines. 4p, Rainbow. 5p, Factory. 10p, Snow-capped mountain.

1941-42 Wmk. 215 Litho. *Perf. 14*

No.	Type	Description	Unused	Used
C54	AP14	10c ol gray	15	15
C55	AP14	20c dp rose	15	15
C56	AP14	30c blue vio	15	15
C57	AP14	40c dl red brn	15	15
C58	AP14	50c red org ('42)	40	15
C59	AP14	60c dp green	15	15
C60	AP14	70c rose	30	22
C61	AP14	80c ultra ('42)	1.75	45
C62	AP14	90c dk brown	45	22
C63	AP23	1p brt blue	30	18
C64	AP23	2p rose lake	45	25
C65	AP23	3p dk bl grn & yel grn	65	50
C66	AP23	4p bl vio & buff	1.00	65
C67	AP23	5p dk org red ('42)	9.00	4.50
C68	AP23	10p gray grn & bl grn	5.00	3.50
		Nos. C54-C68 (15)	20.05	11.37

The 1p, dated "1541-1941", commemorates the 400th anniversary of Santiago.

1942-46 Unwmk.

No.	Type	Description	Unused	Used
C69	AP14	10c ultra ('43)	18	15
C70	AP14	10c rose lil ('45)	18	15
C71	AP14	20c dull grn ('43)	18	15
C72	AP14	20c cop brn ('45)	18	15
C73	AP14	30c dull vio ('44)	18	15
C74	AP14	30c ol blk ('45)	18	15
C75	AP14	40c red brn ('44)	35	15
C76	AP14	40c ultra ('45)	18	15
C77	AP14	50c rose ('43)	18	15
C78	AP14	50c org red ('45)	18	15
C79	AP14	60c orange	18	15
C79B	AP14	60c dp grn ('46)	18	15
C80	AP14	70c rose ('45)	50	32
C81	AP14	80c slate grn	18	15
C82	AP14	90c brown ('45)	50	32
C83	AP23	1p gray grn & lt bl ('43)	25	15
C84	AP23	2p org red ('43)	55	15
C85	AP23	3p dk pur & pale org ('43)	55	15
C86	AP23	4p bl grn & yel grn	55	28
C87	AP23	5p dk rose car ('43)	45	20
a.		5p dk car rose ('44)	20	15
C88	AP23	10p sapphire ('43)	55	28
		Nos. C69-C88 (21)	6.41	
		Set value		3.20

No. C83 is without dates "1541-1941." See Nos. C109-C123, C145-C147. For surcharges see Nos. C145-C147

Coat of Arms and Plane AP29

1942, Nov. 5 Engr. *Perf. 14½*

No.	Type	Description	Unused	Used
C89	AP29	100p car lake	25.00	20.00

University of Chile centenary.

Types of 1934-39

Perf. 13½x14

1944-55 Unwmk. Engr.

No.	Type	Description	Unused	Used
C90	AP4	10c yel grn ('55)	25	18
C92	AP4	20c deep blue	15	15
C93	AP4	30c black brn	15	15
C94	AP4	40c indigo	15	15
C95	AP4	50c dk brn ('47)	15	15
C96	AP4	60c slate vio	15	15
C97	AP4	70c blue ('48)	15	15
C98	AP4	80c olive blk	15	15

Perf. 14

No.	Type	Description	Unused	Used
C99	AP9	1p slate blk	15	15
C100	AP9	2p grnsh bl	25	15
C101	AP9	3p org brn ('45)	15	15
C102	AP9	4p brown	15	18
C103	AP9	5p org red	35	15
C104	AP9	6p yel brn ('46)	40	18
C105	AP9	8p green	40	15
C106	AP9	10p brn lake	1.10	15
C107	AP9	20p ol gray ('45)	70	15
a.		Imperf., pair	70.00	
C107B	AP9	50p rose vio ('50)	17.50	3.50
		Nos. C90-C107B (18)	22.45	
		Set value		5.40

Plane and Radio Tower — AP30

1945 Unwmk. Litho. *Perf. 14*

No.	Type	Description	Unused	Used
C108	AP30	1.60p brt violet	55	22

Types of 1941-42

1946-48 Wmk. 215

No.	Type	Description	Unused	Used
C109	AP14	10c rose lil ('47)	15	15
C110	AP14	20c dk red brn ('48)	15	15
C111	AP14	20c dull grn ('48)	1.50	30
C112	AP14	30c black ('48)	15	15
C113	AP14	40c ultra ('48)	15	15
C114	AP14	60c ol grn ('48)	15	15
C115	AP14	80c ol blk ('48)	15	15
C116	AP14	90c choc ('48)	20	15
C117	AP23	1p gray grn & lt bl ('48)	20	15
C118	AP30	1.60p brt violet	20	15
C119	AP30	1.80p brt vio ('48)	20	15
C119A	AP23	2p org red	38	15
C120	AP23	3p dk pur & pale org ('47)	1.50	30
C121	AP23	4p bl grn & yel grn ('48)	1.10	45
C122	AP23	5p rose car ('47)	75	22
C123	AP23	10p sapphire ('47)	95	22
		Nos. C109-C123 (16)	7.88	
		Set value		2.50

No. C117 is without dates "1541-1941."
For surcharges see Nos. C145, C147.

Flora anf Fauna Type of 1948

1948

No.	Type	Description	Unused	Used
C124	A118	3p Block of 25	25.00	
a.-y.		any single	60	60

Catalogue values for unused stamps in this section, from this point to the end of the section, are for Never Hinged items.

Air Line Emblem and Planes — AP32

1949 Wmk. 215 Litho. *Perf. 14*

No.	Type	Description	Unused	Used
C125	AP32	2p ultra	40	25

20th anniversary of the establishment of Chile's National Air Line.

Benjamin Vicuna Mackenna AP33

Factory, Badge and Book AP34

1949, Mar. 22 Engr. *Perf. 13½x14*

No.	Type	Description	Unused	Used
C126	AP33	3p dk car rose	25	15

Unwmk.

1949, Nov. 11 Litho. *Perf. 14*

Design: 10p, Column and cogwheel.

No.	Type	Description	Unused	Used
C127	AP34	5p green	60	40
C128	AP34	10p red brown	1.00	60

Centenary of the founding of Chile's School of Arts and Crafts.

Plane and Globe — AP35

1950, Jan. Engr.

No.	Type	Description	Unused	Used
C129	AP35	5p green	25	20
C130	AP35	10p red brown	60	40

75th anniv. of the UPU.

Plane over Snow-capped Mountain — AP36

Araucarian Pine and Plane — AP38

Plane and: 40c, Coast and Sunrise. 60c, Over fishing boat. 2p, Chilean flag. 3p, Dock crane. 4p, Above river. 5p, Blast furnace. 10p, Mountain lake. 20p, Cable cars.

Imprint: "Especies Valoradas-Chile"

1950-54 Wmk. 215 Litho. *Perf. 14*

No.	Type	Description	Unused	Used
C135	AP36	20c yel brn ('54)	20	15
C136	AP36	40c purple ('52)	20	15
C137	AP36	60c lt bl ('53)	1.50	75
C138	AP38	1p dull green	20	15
C139	AP38	2p brown red	20	15
C140	AP38	3p violet bl	20	15
C141	AP38	4p red org ('54)	20	15
C142	AP38	5p violet	20	15
C143	AP38	10p yel grn ('53)	25	15
C144	AP38	20p red brn ('54)	40	15
		Nos. C135-C144 (10)	3.55	
		Set value		1.65

See Nos. C155-C164, C207-C212.

Nos. C115, C81 and C116 Surcharged with New Value in Carmine or Black

1951-52 Wmk. 215

No.	Type	Description	Unused	Used
C145	AP14	40c on 80c ol blk (C) ('52)	20	15
		Unwmk.		
C146	AP14	40c on 80c sl grn (C) ('52)	5.00	3.50
		Wmk. 215		
C147	AP14	1p on 90c choc	20	15
		Nos. C145-C147 (3)	5.40	3.80

Types of 1934-39

1951-53 Unwmk. Engr. *Perf. 14*

No.	Type	Description	Unused	Used
C148	AP9	1p deep blue	16	15
C149	AP9	2p blue	28	15
C150	AP9	6p bis brn ('52)	45	16
C151	AP9	30p dk gray ('53)	4.00	60
C152	AP9	40p dk pur brn	12.00	1.65
C153	AP9	50p dark purple	20.00	6.50
		Nos. C148-C153 (6)	36.89	9.21
		Wmk. 215		
C154	AP13	50p dk pur ('52)	80	40

Types of 1950-54
Designs as Before
Imprint: "Especies Valoradas-Chile"

1951-55 Unwmk. Litho. *Perf. 14*

No.	Type	Description	Unused	Used
C155	AP36	20c yel brn ('54)	16	15
C156	AP36	40c purple	16	15
C157	AP36	60c lt blue ('53)	25	15
C158	AP38	1p dk bl grn ('55)	16	15
C159	AP38	2p brown red	16	15
C160	AP38	3p violet bl	16	15
C161	AP38	4p red org ('52)	28	16
C162	AP38	5p violet	28	16
C163	AP38	10p emerald	28	15
C164	AP38	20p brown	40	15
		Nos. C155-C164 (10)	2.29	
		Set value		1.05

San Martin Crossing Andes AP40

Perf. 14½

1951, Mar. 16 Wmk. 215 Engr.

No.	Type	Description	Unused	Used
C165	AP40	5p red violet	40	25

Gen. José de San Martín, death cent.

Isabella Type of Regular Issue, 1952.

1952, Mar. 21 *Perf. 14*

C166	A125	10p carmine	50	30

A souvenir card without franking value was issued for the Hispano-Chilean Philatelic Exhibition at Santiago, Oct. 12, 1969. It contains 2 imperf. stamps similar to Nos. 264 and C166-60c green and 10p rose red. Size: 115x137½mm.

Ancient Fortress — AP42

1953, Apr. 28

C167	AP42	10p brown car	1.00	25

4th centenary of the founding of Valdivia.

Stamp Centenary Type of 1953

1953, Oct. 15 Engr. *Perf. 14½*

C168	A131	100p dp grnsh bl	1.25	75

An imperf. souvenir sheet contains one each of Nos. 276 and C168, with inscriptions in black at top and bottom center. Sheet measures 178x229mm. It is stated that this sheet was not valid for postage.

Early Plane and Stylized Modern Version — AP44

Unwmk.

1954, May 26 Engr. *Perf. 14*

C170	AP44	3p deep blue	15	15

25th anniversary of the founding of Chile's National Air Line.

Domeyko Type of Regular Issue, 1954.

1954, Aug. 16 *Perf. 13½x14*

C171	A134	5p orange brown	20	15

Railroad Type of Regular Issue, 1954

1954, Sept. 10 Wmk. 215 *Perf. 14½*

C172	A135	10p dk purple	40	20

An imperforate souvenir sheet contains one each of Nos. 283 and C172. Size: 174x232mm. Value, $200.

Presidential Visits Type of 1955

1955, May 24

C173	A139	100p red	1.50	1.25

Jet Plane in Clouds — AP48

Comet Air Liner — AP49

Designs: 2p, Helicopter over bridge. 10p, Oil derricks and plane. 50p, Control tower and plane. 200p, Beechcraft monoplane. 500p, Douglas DC-6.

Perf. 14½x14, 14x13½ (AP49)

1955-56 Engr. Wmk. 215

C174	AP48	1p dp red lil ('56)	20	15
C175	AP48	2p pale brn ('56)	15	15
C176	AP48	10p bluish grn ('56)	15	15
C177	AP48	50p rose ('56)	60	25
C178	AP49	100p green	75	15
C179	AP49	200p dp ultra	5.00	70
C180	AP49	500p dk carmine	6.00	70
		Nos. C174-C180 (7)	12.85	2.25

Stamps similar to type AP49, but inscribed in escudo currency, are listed as type AP58.

1956-58 Unwmk.

Designs: 5p, Train and plane. 20p, Jet plane and Easter Island statue.

C183	AP48	5p violet	15	15
C184	AP48	10p grn ('57)	15	15
C185	AP48	20p ultra	15	15
C186	AP48	50p rose ('57)	15	15
C187	AP49	100p bl grn ('57)	40	15
a.		Lithographed ('60)	40	20
C188	AP49	200p dp ultra ('57)	50	15
C189	AP49	500p car ('58)	65	20
		Nos. C183-C189 (7)	2.15	
		Set value		70

Symbols of University Departments — AP50

Design: 100p, View of the University.

1956, Dec. 15 Unwmk. *Perf. 14½*

C190	AP50	20p green	25	15
C191	AP50	100p dk vio bl	1.00	60

25th anniversary of the Federico Santa Maria Technical University, Valparaiso.

A souvenir sheet contains one each of Nos. 299, C190-C191, imperf. It was not issued for postal use, though some served postally. Size: 127x160mm. Value, $25.

Mistral Type of Regular Issue, 1958

1958, Jan. 10 Engr. *Perf. 14*

C192	A144	100p green	20	15

Ambrosio O'Higgins — AP51

1958, Mar. 23

C193	AP51	100p lt blue	25	15

Founding of the city of Osorno, 500th anniv.

A souvenir sheet contains one each of Nos. 302 and C193, imperf. and printed in red brown. It was not issued for postal use, though some served postally. Size: 155x138mm. Value, $15.

Exhibition Type of Regular Issue

1958, Oct. 18 Unwmk.

C194	A146	50p dull green	15	15

A souvenir sheet contains one each of Nos. 303 and C194, imperf. and printed in deep red. It was not issued for postal use, though some served postally. Size: 188x220mm. Value, $15.

Bank Type of Regular Issue, 1958.

1958, Dec. 18 Engr. *Perf. 14*

C195	A147	50p redsh brown	15	15

A souvenir sheet contains one each of Nos. 304 and C195, printed in dull violet, imperf. It was not issued for postal use, though some served postally. Value, $150.

Antarctic Types of Regular Issue

1958 Litho. *Perf. 14*

C199	A149	20p violet	20	15

Engr.

C200	A150	500p dark blue	2.75	1.25

Symbols of Various Religions — AP52

Perf. 14½

1959, Jan. 23 Unwmk. Engr.

C206	AP52	50p dk car rose	15	15

10th anniversary of the Universal Declaration of Human Rights.

Types of 1950-54.

Imprint: "Casa de Moneda de Chile."

Designs: 50p, Plane silhouette over shore. 100p, Plane over map of Antarctica. 200p, Plane over natural arch rock.

1959 Litho. *Perf. 14*

C207	AP38	1p dk blue grn	60	35
a.		Wmk. 215	30.00	
C208	AP38	10p emerald	40	15
C209	AP38	20p red brown	25	15
C210	AP38	50p yellow grn	25	15
C211	AP38	100p car rose	25	15
C212	AP38	200p brt blue	40	15
		Nos. C207-C212 (6)	2.15	1.10

Carlos Anwandter — AP53

1959, June 18 Engr. *Perf. 14*

C213	AP53	20p rose carmine	20	15

Centenary of the German School in Valdivia, founded by Carlos Anwandter.

A souvenir sheet contains one each of Nos. 319 and C213, imperf. It was not issued for postal use, though some served postally. Value, $20.

IGY Type of Regular Issue, 1958.

1959, Aug. 28 Unwmk. *Perf. 14*

C214	A148	50p green	20	15

Ladrillero Type of Regular Issue

1959, Aug. 28 Litho.

C215	A154	50p green	20	15

Barros Arana Type of Regular Issue

1959, Aug. 28

C216	A155	100p purple	40	20

Red Cross Type of Regular Issue

1959, Oct. 6

C217	A156	50p red & blk	25	15

WRY Type of Regular Issue, 1960.

1960, Apr. 7 Unwmk. *Perf. 14½*

C218	A160	10c violet	25	15

A souvenir sheet contains two stamps similar to Nos. 330 and C218, the 1c printed in blue, the 10c airmail in maroon. The sheet is imperf., printed on thin cardboard. Size: 160x204mm. Value, $90.

Type of Regular Issue, 1960-62, and

José Agustín Eyzaguirre and José Miguel Infante AP54

Designs: 2c, Palace of Justice. 5c, National memorial. No. C220, Arms of Chile. No. C220A, José Gaspar Marin and J. Gregorio Argomedo. 50c, Archbishop J. I. Cienfuegos and Brother Camilo Henriquez. 1e, Bernardo O'Higgins.

1960-65 Unwmk. Engr. *Perf. 14½*

C218A	AP54	2c mar & gray vio ('62)	15	15
C219	A162	5c vio bl & dl pur ('61)	20	15

Wmk. 215

C220	A161	10c dk brn & red brn	20	15

Unwmk.

C220A	AP54	10c vio brn & brn ('64)	20	15
C220B	AP54	20c dk bl & dl pur ('64)	25	15
C220C	AP54	50c bl grn & ind ('65)	50	20
C220D	A162	1e dk red & red brn ('63)	1.00	40
		Nos. C218A-C220D (7)	2.50	
		Set value		1.10

150th anniv. of the formation of the 1st Natl. Government.

A souvenir sheet contains two airmail stamps: a 5c brown similar to No. C219 (National Memorial) and a 10c green, type A161. The sheet is imperf., printed on heavy paper with papermaker's watermark. Size: 120x168mm. Value, $30.

Map and Rotary Emblem — AP55

Unwmk.

1960, Dec. 1 Litho. *Perf. 14*

C221	AP55	10c blue	30	15

South American Rotary Regional Conference, Santiago, 1960.

A souvenir sheet contains one 10c maroon, type AP55, with brown marginal inscription. Size: 118x158mm. Value, $14.

The souvenir sheet was overprinted in green "El Mundo Unida Contra la Malaria" and the outline of a mosquito, and released in October, 1962. Value, $27.50.

Plane over Mountain Lake — AP56

Designs: 1m, Araucarian pine and plane. 2m, Chilean flag and plane. 3m, Plane and dock crane. 4m, Plane above river (vignette like AP39). 5m, Blast furnace. 2c, Plane over cable cars. 5c, Plane silhouette over shore. 10c, Plane over map of Antarctica. 20c, Plane over natural arch rock.

Imprint: "Casa de Moneda de Chile."

1960-62 Litho. *Perf. 14*

C222	AP56	1m orange	15	15
C223	AP56	2m yellow grn	15	15
C224	AP56	3m violet	15	15
C225	AP56	4m gray olive	15	15
C226	AP56	5m brt bl grn	15	15
C227	AP56	1c ultra	15	15
C228	AP56	2c red brn ('61)	22	15
C229	AP56	5c yel grn ('61)	1.25	15
C230	AP56	10c car rose ('62)	30	15
C231	AP56	20c brt bl ('62)	35	15
		Nos. C222-C231 (10)	3.02	
		Set value		70

Oil Derricks and Douglas DC-6 — AP57

Beechcraft Monoplane — AP58

Designs: 5m, Train and plane. 2c, Jet plane and Easter Island statue. 5c, Control tower and plane. 10c, Comet airliner. 50c, Douglas DC-6.

Perf. 14x13½

1960-67 Unwmk. Litho.

C234	AP57	5m red brown	15	15
C235	AP57	1c dull blue	15	15
C236	AP57	2c ultra ('62)	15	15
C237	AP57	5c rose red ('64)	15	15
C238	AP58	10c ultra ('67)	15	15
C239	AP58	20c car ('62)	15	15
C240	AP58	50c green ('63)	15	15
		Set value	44	36

Stamps similar to type AP58, but inscribed in peso ($) currency, are listed as type AP49.

Congress Type of Regular Issue.

1961, Oct. 5 *Perf. 14½*

C245	A164	10c gray green	75	25

Soccer Type of Regular Issue, 1962.

Designs: 5c, Goalkeeper and stadium, vert. 10c, Soccer players and globe.

1962, May 30 Unwmk. Engr.

C246	A165	5c rose lilac	15	15
C247	A165	10c dk carmine	25	15

A souvenir sheet of four contains one each of Nos. 340-341, C246-C247, imperf., with light brown marginal inscriptions. Size: 123x194mm. Sold for 7.50 escudos (face value, 22 centavos). Value, $5.

Hunger Type of Regular Issue.

Design: 20c, Mother with empty bowl, horiz.

1963, Mar. 21 Litho. *Perf. 14*
C248 A166 20c green 15 15

Red Cross Type of Regular Issue.

Design: 20c, Centenary emblem and plane silhouette, horiz.

1963, Sept. 6 Unwmk. *Perf. 14*
C249 A167 20c gray & red 15 15

Fire Engine of 1860's AP59

1963, Dec. 20 Litho. *Perf. 14½*
C250 AP59 30c red 15 15

Centenary of the Santiago Fire Brigade.

Western Hemisphere AP60

1964, Apr. 9 Unwmk. *Perf. 14½*
C254 AP60 4c ultra 15 15

Issued in memory of President John F. Kennedy and to honor the Alliance for Progress.

Battle of Rancagua AP61

1965, May 7 Engr. *Perf. 14½*
C255 AP61 5c dull grn & sepia 15 15

Battle of Rancagua, Oct. 7, 1814, 150th anniv.

ITU Emblem, Old and New Communication Equipment AP62

1965, May 7 Litho. *Perf. 14½x14*
C256 AP62 40c red & maroon 15 15

ITU centenary.

Portrait Type of 1964

Portraits: No. C257, Enrique Molina. No. C258, Msgr. Carlos Casanueva.

1965, June Litho. *Perf. 14*
C257 A169 60c brt violet 15 15
C258 A169 60c green 15 15
Set value 20 15

See note after No. 346.

Skier Type of Regular Issue 1965

Design: 20c, Skier, horiz.

1965, Aug. 30 Unwmk. *Perf. 14*
C259 A172 20c ultra 15 15

Fishing Boats, Angelmo Harbor AP63

Aviators' Monument AP64

1965
C260 AP63 40c brown 15 15

Perf. 14x14½
C262 AP64 1e car rose 15 15
Set value 15

Andrés Bello (1780?-1865), Venezuela-born Writer and Educator — AP65

1965, Nov. 29 Engr. Unwmk.
C263 AP65 10c dk car rose 15 15

Skiers — AP66

Basketball — AP67

1966, Apr. 6 Litho. *Perf. 14*
C264 AP66 4e dk bl & red brn 60 15

World Skiing Championships, Partillo, Aug. 1966.

1966, Apr. 28
C265 AP67 13c rose carmine 15 15

International Basketball Championships.

Slalom AP68

Perf. 14½x15
1966, July 20 Litho. Unwmk.
C266 AP68 75c rose car & lil 15 15
C267 AP68 3e ultra & lt bl 20 15
Set value 15

International Skiing Championships, Partillo, August 1966. A souvenir sheet of 2 contains imperf. stamps similar to Nos. C266-C267. No gum. Size: 109x140mm. Value $2.50.

Ship Type of Regular Issue

1966 Litho. *Perf. 14½*
C268 A175 70c Prus grn & yel grn 15 15

See note below No. 358.

ICY Type of Regular Issue

1966, Oct. 28 Unwmk. *Perf. 14½*
C269 A177 3e blue & carmine 40 20

A souvenir sheet of 2 contains imperf. stamps similar to Nos. 360 and C269. No gum. Size: 111x140mm. Value $2.25.

Chilean Flag and Ships — AP69

1966, Nov. 21 Litho. *Perf. 14*
C270 AP69 13c dull red brn 15 15

Centenary of the city of Antofagasta.

Pardo Type of Regular Issue

Design: 40c, Pardo and map of Chile's claim to Antarctica.

1967, Jan. 6 Unwmk. *Perf. 14½*
C271 A178 40c ultra 15 15

See note below No. 361.

Family Type of Regular Issue

1967, Apr. 13 Litho. *Perf. 14*
C272 A179 80c brt bl & blk 15 15

Ruben Dario and Title Page of "Azul" AP70

1967, May 15 Engr. *Perf. 14½*
C273 AP70 10c dark blue 15 15

Ruben Dario (pen name of Felix Ruben Garcia Sarmiento, 1867-1916), Nicaraguan poet, newspaper correspondent and diplomat.

Tree Type of Regular Issue

1967, June 9 Litho.
C274 A180 75c grn & pale rose 15 15

Lions Type of Regular Issue

1967 Litho. *Perf. 14*
C275 A181 1e purple & yel 15 15
C276 A181 5e blue & yel 80 15
Set value 20

A souvenir sheet without franking value contains 3 imperf. stamps, 20c, 1e and 5e, in violet blue and yellow. Size: 110x140mm. Value, $7.50.
Issue dates: 1e, July 12; 5e, Aug. 11.

Flag Type of Regular Issue

1967, Oct. 20 Unwmk. *Perf. 14½*
C277 A182 50c ultra & crimson 15 15

ITY Emblem AP71

1967, Nov. 22 Litho. *Perf. 14½*
C278 AP71 30c lt vio bl & blk 15 15

Issued for International Tourist Year, 1967.

Caro Type of Regular Issue, 1967.

1967, Dec. 4 Engr. *Perf. 14½*
C279 A183 40c violet 50 20

Type of Regular Issue, 1968

1968, Apr. 23 Litho. *Perf. 14½*
C280 A184 2e brt violet 15 15

Sesquicentennial of the Battles of Chacabuco and Maipu. A souvenir sheet of 2 contains imperf. stamps similar to Nos. 367 and C280. Value, $4. A second sheet exists with the 2e in green and the 3e in brown. Size: 139½x100mm. Value, $4.

Farm Type of Regular Issue

1968, June 18 Unwmk.
C281 A185 50c blk, org & grn 15 15

Juan I. Molina, Educator and Scientist AP72

1968, Aug. 27 Litho. *Perf. 14½*
C282 AP72 1e bright green 15 15

Map of Chiloé Province — AP73

British Crown and Map of Chile — AP74

Perf. 14½
1968, Oct. 7 Unwmk. Litho.
C283 AP73 1e rose claret 15 15

Anniversaries of the founding of five towns in Chiloé Province.

Auto Club Type of Regular Issue

1968, Nov. 10 Engr. *Perf. 14½x14*
C284 A189 5e ultra 20 15

1968, Nov. 12 Litho. *Perf. 14½*

Designs: 50c, Chilean coat of arms (horiz.; similar to type A161). 3e, British coat of arms, horiz.

C285 AP74 50c green & brn 20 15
C286 AP74 3e bl & org brn 15 15

Engr.

C287 AP74 5e purple & mag 20 15
Nos. C285-C287 (3) 55
Set value 28

Visit of Queen Elizabeth II of Great Britain, Nov. 11-18. A souvenir sheet of 3 contains imperf., lithographed stamps similar to Nos. C285-C287. Size: 124½x190mm. The souvenir sheet also publicizes the British-Chilean Philatelic Exhibition. Value, $8.

First Coin Minted in Chile and Coin Press AP75

Design: 1e, Chile No. 128.

1968, Dec. 31 Litho. *Perf. 14½*
C288 AP75 50c ocher & vio brn 15 15
C289 AP75 1e lt bl & dp org 15 15
Set value 20 15

225th anniversary of the founding of the State Mint (Casa de Moneda de Chile).
A souvenir sheet of 4 contains imperf. stamps similar to Nos. 373-374, C288-C289. Size: 150x119mm. Value, $2.

Satellite Type of Regular Issue

1969, May 20 Litho. *Perf. 14½*
C290 A191 2e rose lilac 15 15

Red Cross Type of Regular Issue

1969, Sept. Litho. *Perf. 14½*
C291 A192 5e black & red 15 15

A souvenir card contains 2 imperf. stamps similar to Nos. 376 and C291, with red marginal inscription. Size: 109x140mm. Value $3.

Dam Type of Regular Issue

1969, Nov. 18 Litho. *Perf. 14½*
C292 A193 3e blue 15 15

Rodriguez Type of Regular Issue

1969, Nov. 24
C293 A194 30c brown 15 15

EXPO '70 Type of Regular Issue

1969, Dec. 1 Litho. *Perf. 14*
C294 A195 5e red 15 15

Bible Type of 1969

1969, Dec. 2 *Perf. 14½*
C295 A196 1e green 15 15

ILO Type of Regular Issue

1969, Dec. 17 *Perf. 14½*
C296 A197 2e rose lil & blk 15 15

Human Rights Year Type of 1969

1969, Dec. 18
C297 A198 4e brown & red 15 15

A souvenir sheet of 2 contains imperf. stamps similar to Nos. 382 and C297. Size: 110x140mm. Value, $3.50.

Easter Island Type of 1970

1970, Jan. 26
C298 A199 50c dull grnsh bl 15 15

Ship Type of Regular Issue

1970, Feb. 4 Litho. *Perf. 14½*
C299 A200 2e deep ultra 20 15

Rotary Type of Regular Issue

1970, Mar. 18 Litho. *Perf. 14*
C300 A201 1e rose claret 15 15

Gandhi Type of Regular Issue

1970, Apr. 1 Litho. *Perf. 14½*
C301 A202 1e red brown 15 15

Education Year Type of 1970

1970, July 17 Litho. *Perf. 14½*
C302 A204 4e red brown 15 15

National Shrine Type of 1970

1970, July 28 Litho. *Perf. 14½*
C303 A205 1e ultra 15 15

Cancer Type of Regular Issue

1970, Aug. 11
C304 A206 2e brn & lt olive 15 15

A few copies are known inscribed "Correos de Chile" instead of "Correos Aereo Chile."

Copper Type of Regular Issue

1970, Oct. 21 Litho. *Perf. 14½*
C305 A207 3e grn & lt red brn 15 15

United Nations Type of 1970

1970, Oct. 22
C306 A208 5e dk car & grn 32 15

Freighter Type of Regular Issue

1971, Jan. 18 Litho. *Perf. 14*
C307 A209 5e lt red brown 15 15

No. C290 Surcharged in Red

1971, Jan. 21 Litho. *Perf. 14½*
C308 A191 52c on 2e rose lil 20 15

Liberation Type of Regular Issue

1971, Feb. 3 *Perf. 14½*
C309 A210 1e gray bl & brn 15 15

UNICEF Type of Regular Issue

1971, Feb. 11 Litho. *Perf. 14½*
C310 A211 2e blue & grn 15 15

Boy Scout Type of Regular Issue

1971, Feb. 10 *Perf. 14*
C311 A212 5c dk car & ol 15 15

Satellite Type of Regular Issue

1971, May 25 Litho. *Perf. 14½*
C312 A213 2e brown 15 15

De Ercilla Type of Regular Issue

1972, Mar. 20 Engr. *Perf. 14*
C313 A221 2e Prussian blue 15 15

A souvenir card contains impressions of Nos. 414 and C313 with black marginal inscription commemorating España 75 Philatelic Exhibition. Size: 165x220mm.

AIR POST SEMI-POSTAL STAMPS

Catalogue values for unused stamps in this section are for Never Hinged items.

Type of Semi-Postal Stamps, 1961

Portraits: 10c+10c, Alonso de Ercilla. 20c+20c, Gabriela Mistral.

Perf. 13x12½

1961, Apr. 29 Photo. Unwmk.
CB1 SP3 10c + 10c sal & choc 65 20
CB2 SP3 20c + 20c gray & dp cl 65 20

Printed without charge by the Spanish Mint as a gift to Chile. The surtax was to aid the 1960 earthquake victims and to increase teachers' salaries.

ACKNOWLEDGMENT OF RECEIPT STAMPS

AR1

1894 Unwmk. *Perf. 11½*
H1 AR1 5c brown 75 50
a. Imperf., pair 3.00

The black stamp of design similar to AR1 inscribed "Avis de Paiement" was prepared for use on notices of payment of funds but was not regularly issued.

POSTAGE DUE STAMPS

D1

D2

Handstamped

1894 Unwmk. *Perf. 13*
J1 D1 2c black, *straw* 10.00 4.75
J2 D1 4c black, *straw* 10.00 4.75
J3 D1 6c black, *straw* 10.00 4.75
J4 D1 8c black, *straw* 10.00 4.75
J5 D2 10c black, *straw* 10.00 4.75
J6 D1 16c black, *straw* 10.00 4.75
J7 D1 20c black, *straw* 10.00 4.75
J8 D1 30c black, *straw* 10.00 4.75
J9 D1 40c black, *straw* 10.00 4.75
Nos. J1-J9 (9) 90.00 42.75

J1a D1 2c black, *yellow* 42.50 40.00
J2a D1 4c black, *yellow* 35.00 27.50
J3a D1 6c black, *yellow* 25.50 24.00
J4a D1 8c black, *yellow* 10.00 8.50
J5a D2 10c black, *yellow* 10.00 8.50
J6a D1 16c black, *yellow* 10.00 8.50
J7a D1 20c black, *yellow* 10.00 8.50
J8a D1 30c black, *yellow* 10.00 8.50
J9a D1 40c black, *yellow* 10.00 8.50
Nos. J1a-J9a (9) 163.00 142.50

Counterfeits exist.

D3

1895 Litho. *Perf. 11*
J19 D3 1c red, *yellow* 5.00 2.00
J20 D3 2c red, *yellow* 5.00 2.00
J21 D3 4c red, *yellow* 4.00 2.00
J22 D3 6c red, *yellow* 5.00 2.00
J23 D3 8c red, *yellow* 3.00 2.00
J24 D3 10c red, *yellow* 3.00 3.00
J25 D3 20c red, *yellow* 3.00 1.50
J26 D3 40c red, *yellow* 3.00 2.00
J27 D3 50c red, *yellow* 3.00 2.00
J28 D3 60c red, *yellow* 6.00 3.00
J29 D3 80c red, *yellow* 6.00 4.00
J30 D3 1p red, *yellow* 6.00 4.00
Nos. J19-J30 (12) 52.00 29.50

Nos. J19-J30 were printed in sheets of 100 (10x10) containing all 12 denominations.
Counterfeits of Nos. J19-J42 exist.

1896 *Perf. 13½*
J31 D3 1c red, *straw* 60 35
J32 D3 2c red, *straw* 60 35
J33 D3 4c red, *straw* 75 35
J34 D3 6c red, *straw* 1.65 65
J35 D3 8c red, *straw* 75 40
J36 D3 10c red, *straw* 60 40
J37 D3 20c red, *straw* 60 40
J38 D3 40c red, *straw* 12.00 10.00
J39 D3 50c red, *straw* 12.00 10.00
J40 D3 60c red, *straw* 12.00 10.00
J41 D3 80c red, *straw* 12.00 10.00
J42 D3 100c red, *straw* 25.00 20.00
Nos. J31-J42 (12) 78.55 62.90

D4

D5

1898 *Perf. 13*
J43 D4 1c scarlet 35 30
J44 D4 2c scarlet 90 60
J45 D4 4c scarlet 35 30
J46 D4 10c scarlet 35 30
J47 D4 20c scarlet 35 30
Nos. J43-J47 (5) 2.30 1.80

1924 *Perf. 11½, 12½*
J48 D5 2c blue & red 75 60
J49 D5 4c blue & red 75 60
J50 D5 8c blue & red 75 60
J51 D5 10c blue & red 75 60
J52 D5 20c blue & red 75 35
J53 D5 40c blue & red 75 60
J54 D5 60c blue & red 75 60
J55 D5 80c blue & red 75 60
J56 D5 1p blue & red 1.00 75
J57 D5 2p blue & red 1.75 1.25
J58 D5 5p blue & red 1.75 1.25
Nos. J48-J58 (11) 10.50 7.80

Nos. J48-J58 were printed in sheets of 150 containing all 11 denominations, and in sheets of 50 containing the five lower denominations, providing various se-tenants.

All values of this issue exist imperforate, also with center inverted, but are not believed to have been regularly issued. Those with inverted centers sell for about 10 times normal stamps.

OFFICIAL STAMPS

For Domestic Postage

O1

Single-lined frame
Control number in violet

1907 Unwmk. *Imperf.*
O1 O1 dl bl, "CARTA" org 21.00 16.00
O2 O1 red, "OFICIO" bl 21.00 16.00
O3 O1 vio, "PAQUETE" red 21.00 16.00
O4 O1 org, *bl*, "EP" vio 21.00 16.00
Nos. O1-O4 (4) 84.00 64.00

The diagonal inscription in differing color indicates type of usage: CARTA for letters of ordinary weight; OFICIO, heavy letters to 100 grams; PAQUETE, parcels to 100 grams; E P (Encomienda Postal), heavier parcels; C (Certificado), as on No. O8, registration including postage.

Varieties include CARTA, PAQUETE and E P inverted, OFICIO omitted, etc.

Double-lined frame
Large control number in black

Perf. 11
O5 O1 bl, "CARTA" yel 7.50 6.50
O6 O1 red, "OFICIO" bl 7.50 5.00
O7 O1 brn, "PAQUETE" grn 7.50 5.00
O8 O1 grn, "C" red 110.00 80.00
Nos. O5-O8 (4) 132.50 96.50

Nos. O5-O8 exist in tête bêche pairs; with CARTA, OFICIO or PAQUETE double or inverted, and other varieties.

Counterfeits of Nos. O1-O8 exist.

For Foreign Postage

Regular Issues of 1892-1909 Overprinted in Red — a

On Stamps of 1904-09

1907 *Perf. 12*
O9 A14 1c green 7.50 7.50
a. Inverted overprint 17.50
O10 A12 3c on 1p brn 14.00 14.00
a. Inverted overprint 52.50
O11 A14 5c ultra 10.50 10.50
a. Inverted overprint 35.00
O12 A15 10c gray & blk 10.50 10.50
O13 A15 15c vio & blk 14.00 14.00
O14 A15 20c org brn & blk 14.00 14.00
O15 A15 50c ultra & blk 45.00 45.00

On Stamp of 1892

Rouletted
O16 A6 1p dk brn & blk 110.00 87.50
Nos. O9-O16 (8) 225.50 203.00

Counterfeits of Nos. O9-O16 exist.

Regular Issues of 1915-25 Overprinted in Red or Blue — b

OFICIAL

1926 *Perf. 13½x14, 14*
O17 A52 5c slate bl (R) 2.50 50
O18 A50 10c bl & blk (R) 4.00 75
O19 A39 20c org red & blk (Bl) 2.00 40
O20 A42 50c dp grn & blk (Bl) 2.00 40
O21 A43 1p grn & blk (R) 2.75 70
O22 A43 2p ver & blk (Bl) 4.00 1.00
Nos. O17-O22 (6) 17.25 3.75

Nos. O21 and O22 are overprinted vertically at each side.

Nos. O17 to O22 were for the use of the Biblioteca Nacional.

Regular Issue of 1915-25 Overprinted in Red — c

Servicio del

ESTADO

1928 *Perf. 13½x14, 14*
O23 A50 10c bl & blk 6.50 2.00
O24 A39 20c brn org & blk 3.00 1.00
O25 A40 25c dl bl & blk 7.50 1.00
O26 A42 50c dp grn & blk 4.00 1.00
O27 A43 1p grn & blk 5.00 1.50
Nos. O23-O27 (5) 26.00 6.50

The overprint on Nos. O23 to O26 is 16½mm high; on No. O27 it is 20mm.

Regular Issues of 1928-30 Overprinted in Red — d

Servicio del

ESTADO

On Stamp Inscribed: "Correos de Chile"

1930-31
O28 A50 10c bl & blk 3.00 1.50

Wmk. 215

On Stamps Inscribed: "Correos de Chile"
O29 A50 10c bl & blk 6.00 3.00
O30 A39 20c org red & blk 75 50
O31 A40 25c bl & blk 75 50
O32 A42 50c dp grn & blk 1.50 75

On Stamps Inscribed: "Chile Correos"
O33 A42 50c dp grn & blk 1.50 75
O34 A43 1p grn & blk 1.50 75
Nos. O28-O34 (7) 15.00 7.75

Same Overprint on No. 181

1933 ***Perf. 13½x14***

O35 A61 20c dk brn 75 25

Same Overprint in Red on No. 182

1935 **Wmk. 215**

O36 A62 10c deep blue 75 50

No. 163 Ovptd. Type "b" in Red
Inscribed: "Correos de Chile"

1934

O37 A52 5c lt grn 60 50

Overprint "b" on No. 182

1935

O38 A62 10c dp bl 50 50

Same Overprint in Black on No. 181

1936 **Wmk. 215** ***Perf. 13½x14***

O39 A61 20c dk brn 10.00 50

Overprint "b" in Red on No. 158

1938 ***Perf. 14***

O40 A43 1p grn & blk 2.50 1.00

Nos. 204 and 205 Overprinted Type "d" in Black

1939 ***Perf. 13½x14, 14***

O41 A78 50c violet 4.00 2.50
O42 A84 1p org brn 5.00 4.00

Stamps of 1938-40 Overprinted Type "b" in Black, Red or Blue

1940-46 ***Perf. 13½x14, 14***

O43 A78 10c sal pink ('45) 2.00 1.75
O44 A78 15c brn org 1.00 40
O45 A78 20c lt bl (R) ('42) 1.50 60
O46 A78 30c brn pink (Bl) 75 40
O47 A78 40c lt grn 75 40
O48 A78 50c vio ('45) 4.00 75
O49 A84 1p org brn ('42) 2.50 75
O50 A84 1.80p dp bl (R) ('45) 10.00 6.00
O51 A84 2p car lake ('42) 2.00 1.25
Nos. O43-O51 (9) 24.50 12.30

Overprint "b" in Black on Nos. 223, 225

Unwmk.

O58 A84 1p brn org 2.50 1.50
O59 A84 2p car lake ('46) 5.00 2.00

Regular Issues of 1938-43 Overprinted Diagonally in Carmine, Black or Blue — e

OFICIAL

Wmk. 215, Unwmkd.

1948-54 ***Perf. 13½x14, 14***

O60 A78 20c lt bl, #219 (C) 75 40
O61 A78 30c brt pink, #202 (Bl) ('54) 1.50 50
O62 A78 40c brt grn, #203 ('54) 2.50 1.25
O63 A78 50c vio #222 ('49) 75 40
O64 A84 1p org brn, #205 2.50 1.00
O65 A84 2p car lake, #207 ('54) 1.00 50
O66 A84 5p dk sl grn, #208 (C) ('51) 1.75 1.00
Nos. O60-O66 (7) 10.75 5.05

Overprint "e" Diagonally on Nos. 265 and 275 in Red or Black

Perf. 13½x14, 13x14

1953-55 **Wmk. 215, Unwmkd.**

O67 A126 1p dk bl grn, #265 (R) 1.00 50
O68 A126 1p dk bl grn, #265 (Bk) ('55) 75 50
O69 A126 1p dk bl grn, #275 (R) ('55) 75 50
Nos. O67-O69 (3) 2.50 1.50

Overprint "e" Horizontally on Nos. 207, 209 in Black or Blue

1955-56 **Wmk. 215** ***Perf. 14***

O70 A84 2p car lake ('56) 1.75 75
O71 A84 10p rose vio (Bl) 2.75 1.75

Overprint "e" Horizontally on Nos. 293-295 and Types of 1956 Regular Issue in Black or Red

1956 **Unwmk.** ***Perf. 14x14½***

O72 A141 2p purple 1.00 60
O73 A142 3p lt vio bl (R) 3.00 2.00
O74 A141 5p redsh brn 75 35
O75 A142 10p vio (19x22¼mm) (R) 3.00 1.75
a. Perf. 13½x14 (19½x22½mm) ('58) 50 40
O76 A141 50p rose red 2.50 1.00

No. 310 Overprinted in Red Vertically, Reading Down, Similar to Type "e"
Size of Overprint: 21x2½mm

1958 **Litho.** ***Perf. 14***

O77 A149 10p vio blue 200.00 30.00

Overprint "e" Horizontally on No. 327 in Red

1960 **Unwmk.** ***Perf. 13x14***

O79 A157 5c blue 1.75 70

POSTAL TAX STAMPS

Talca Issue.
A 10c blue postal tax stamp, inscribed "Bicentenario de Talca" and picturing a coat of arms, was issued in 1942. It was sold only in Talca and was required for a time on all domestic letters sent from that city. The tax helped pay for Talca's bicentenary celebration. Value 15 cents.

Nos. 326 and 347 Surcharged

Eº 0,10
Art. 77
LEY
17272

1970 **Unwmk.** **Litho.** ***Perf. 14x13***

RA1 A159 10c on 2c ultra 20 15

Perf. 14x14½

RA2 A170 10c on 6c rose lil 20 15
Set value 16

Chilean Arms — PT1

Perf. 14½x14

1970, Apr. 23 **Litho.** **Unwmk.**

RA3 PT1 10c blue 15 15

See No. RA6.

No. RA3 Surcharged in Red

Eº0,15 a

Eº0,15 b

1971-72

RA4 PT1 (a) 15c on 10c bl 15 15
RA5 PT1 (b) 15c on 10c bl ('72) 15 15
Set value 16

Type of 1970

1972, July **Litho.** ***Perf. 14½x14***

RA6 PT1 15c rose red 20 15

No. RA6 Surcharged in Ultramarine

Eº0,20

1972-73

RA7 PT1 20c on 15c rose red 15 15
RA8 PT1 50c on 15c rose red ('73) 15 15
Set value 16

No. RA8 has 9 bars instead of 8.
The surtax on Nos. RA1-RA8 was for modernization of postal system. Compulsory on all inland mail.

PARCEL POST POSTAL TAX STAMP

Pres. J. J. Prieto V. — PPT1

Unwmk.

1957, Apr. 8 **Litho.** ***Perf. 14***

QRA1 PPT1 15p green 25 25

The surtax aided the Prieto Foundation. No. QRA1 was required on parcel post entering or leaving Chile.

CHINA

LOCATION — Eastern Asia
GOVT. — Republic
AREA — 2,903,475 sq. mi.
POP. — 462,798,093 (1948)

10 Candareen = 1 Mace
10 Mace = 1 Tael
100 Cents = 1 Dollar (Yuan) (1897)

Watermarks

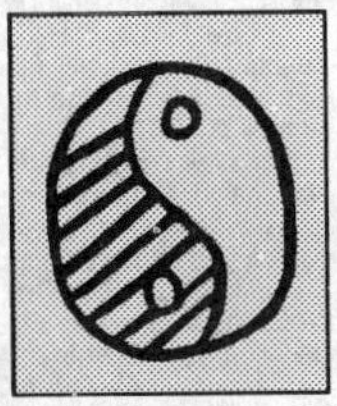

Wmk. 103- Yin-Yang Symbol

Wmk. 261- Character Yu (Post) Multiple

Issues of the Imperial Maritime Customs Post

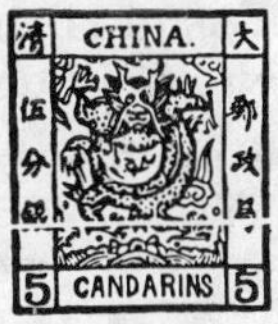

Imperial Dragon — A1

1878 **Unwmk.** **Typo.** ***Perf. 12½***
Thin Paper
Stamps printed 2½-3¼mm apart

1 A1 1c green 150.00 85.00
2 A1 3c brown red 250.00 45.00
3 A1 5c orange 300.00 50.00

Imperforate essays of Nos. 1-3 have an extra circle near the dragon's lower left foot. Copies with the circle completely or mostly removed are proofs or unfinished stamps.

1882

Thin or Pelure Paper
Stamps printed 4½mm apart

4 A1 1c green 250.00 100.00
5 A1 3c brown red 425.00 60.00
6 A1 5c orange yellow 10,000. 500.00

Value for No. 6 is for faulty copies.

1883 ***Rough to smooth Perf. 12½***
Medium to Thick Opaque Paper
Stamps printed 2½ to 3¼mm apart

7 A1 1c green 150.00 80.00
a. Vert. pair, imperf. between 15,000.
8 A1 3c brown red 250.00 50.00
a. Vert. pair, imperf. between 15,000.
9 A1 5c yellow 550.00 55.00

Nos. 1-9 were printed from plates of 25, 20 or 15 individual copper dies, but only No. 5 exists in the 15-die setting. Many different printings and plate settings exist. All values occur in a wide variety of shades and papers. The effect of climate on certain papers has produced the varieties on so-called toned papers in Nos. 1-15.
Value for No. 8a is for a damaged copy.
Counterfeits, frequently with forged cancellations, occur in all early Chinese issues.

Imperial Dragon — A2

1885 **Wmk. 103** ***Perf. 12½***

10 A2 1c green 30.00 8.50
a. Vert. pair, imperf. btwn. 7,000.
b. Horiz. pair, imperf. btwn.
11 A2 3c lilac 60.00 9.00
c. Horiz. pair, imperf. btwn. 9,000.
b. Vert. pair, imperf. btwn. 10,000.
12 A2 5c grnsh yel 75.00 12.00
a. 5c bister brown 80.00 14.00
b. Vert. pair, imperf. btwn. 10,000.
c. Horiz. pair, imperf. btwn. 10,000.
Nos. 10-12 (3) 165.00 29.50

1888 ***Perf. 11½-12***

13 A2 1c green 12.00 9.00
14 A2 3c lilac 40.00 5.00
b. Double impression
15 A2 5c grnsh yellow 60.00 15.00
b. Horiz. pair, imperf. vert. 4,500.
c. Double impression 350.00 350.00
Nos. 13-15 (3) 112.00 29.00

Nos. 10-15 were printed from plates made of 40 individual copper dies, arranged in two panes of 20 each. Several different settings exist of all values.
Imperforates of Nos. 13-15 are considered proofs by most authorities.
Stamps overprinted "Formosa" in English or Chinese are proofs.
For surcharges see Nos. 25-27, 75-77.

"Shou" and "Wu Fu" — A3

Dragon and Hydrangea Leaves — A4

"Pa Kua" Signs in Corners — A5

Dragon and Peony — A6

Carp, the Messenger Fish — A7

Dragon, "Pa Kua" and Immortelle — A8

Dragons and "Shou" — A9

Dragons and Giant Peony — A10

Junk on the Yangtse — A11

1894 **Lithographed in Shanghai**

16	A3	1c orange red	5.25	8.00
a.		Vert. pair, imperf. btwn.	1,800.	1,500.
b.		Horiz. pair, imperf. btwn.	2,500.	1,800.
c.		Vert. pair, imperf. horiz.	1,500.	1,500.
17	A4	2c green	8.00	4.00
a.		Horiz. pair, imperf. btwn.	275.00	
18	A5	3c orange yel	5.50	3.00
a.		Vert. pair, imperf. btwn.	1,500.	1,500.
b.		Horiz. pair, imperf. btwn.	1,800.	1,500.
19	A6	4c rose pink	35.00	22.50
a.		Horiz. pair, imperf. btwn.	1,800.	
20	A7	5c dull orange	60.00	47.50
a.		Horiz. pair, imperf. btwn.	2,000.	
21	A8	6c brown	12.00	6.00
a.		Vert. pair, imperf. btwn.	*4,500.*	
b.		Horiz. pair, imperf. btwn.	*4,500.*	
22	A9	9c dull green	45.00	10.00
a.		Imperf., pair	600.00	
b.		Imperf. vert., pair	2,000.	
c.		Imperf. horiz., pair	2,000.	
d.		Vert. pair, imperf. btwn.	2,500.	
e.		Tete beche pair	625.00	500.00
f.		Tete beche pair, imperf. horiz.	3,000.	
g.		Tete beche pair, imperf. vert.	3,000.	
h.		Vert. strip of 3, imperf. btwn.	3,000.	
23	A10	12c orange	85.00	22.50
24	A11	24c carmine	140.00	30.00
a.		Vert. pair, imperf. btwn.	*5,000.*	

60th birthday of Tsz'e Hsi, the Empress Dowager. All values exist in several distinct shades.

On Mar. 20, 1896, the Customs Post was changed, by Imperial Edict, effective Jan. 1, 1897, to a National Post and the dollar was adopted as the unit of currency.

Time was required to work out details of the Imperial Post and design new stamps. As a provisional measure, stocks of Nos. 16-24 were ordered surcharged with new values in dollars and cents. It is believed that only the Shanghai office stock of Nos. 16-24 (plus any reserve stock at the printers) was surcharged with small figures of value. Other post offices throughout China were instructed to return all unoverprinted stocks on receipt of the new surcharges.

Early in the year it was apparent that all stamps would be exhausted before the new issues were ready (Nos. 86-97), and since the stones from which Nos. 16-24 had been printed no longer existed, new stones were made from the original transfers. A printing from the new stones was made early in 1897 and surcharged with large figures of value spaced 2 1/2mm below the Chinese characters. During the surcharging, sheets from the 1894 (original) printing were received from outlying post offices and surcharged as they arrived. A small quantity of the 1897 printing reached the public without surcharge (Nos. 16n-24n).

Additional stamps were still required and another printing was made from the new stones and surcharged with large figures, but in a new setting with 1 1/2mm between the Chinese characters and the value. Additional sheets of the 1894 printing were received from the most distant post offices and were also surcharged with the 1 1/2mm setting. Thus there are four different sets of the large-figure surcharges. All these stamps were regularly issued but no attempt was made by the post office to separate printings. Some values are difficult to distinguish as to printing, particularly in used condition.

See No. 73. For surcharges see Nos. 28-72, 74.

1897 **Lithographed in Shanghai**

16n	A3	1c red orange	*275.*
17n	A4	2c yellow green	*400.*
18n	A5	3c chrome yellow	*300.*
p.		3c yellow buff	*600.*
19n	A6	4c pale rose	*325.*
20n	A7	5c yellow	*300.*
21n	A8	6c red brown	*450.*
22n	A9	9c yellowish green	*1,000.*
23n	A10	12c pale orange yellow	*1,000.*
24n	A11	24c rose red	*800.*

The colors of the 1897 printings are pale or dull; the gum is thin and white. The 1894 printing has a thicker, yellowish gum.

The set of 9 values on thick unwatermarked paper is a special printing ordered by P. G. von Mollendorf, a Customs official, for presentation purposes. Value, set, $900.

For surcharges see Nos. 47-55, 65-72.

Issues of the Chinese Government Post

Preceding Issues Surcharged in Black

貳洋暫
分銀作
2
cents.

Small Numerals
Surcharged on Nos. 13-15

1897, Jan. 2 ***Perf. 11 1/2-12***

25	A2	1c on 1c	13.00	12.50
26	A2	2c on 3c	60.00	25.00
27	A2	5c on 5c	35.00	10.00

Surcharged on Nos. 16-24

28	A5	1/2c on 3c	7.00	5.75
a.		"1" instead of "1/2"	150.00	150.00
b.		Horiz. pair, imperf. btwn.	1,600.	
c.		Vert. pair, imperf. horiz.	1,600.	1,500.
d.		Double surcharge	*8,500.*	
e.		Vert. pair, imperf. between	1,600.	
29	A3	1c on 1c	6.00	6.00
a.		Inverted surcharge	1,800.	1,800.
30	A4	2c on 2c	6.00	3.50
a.		Horiz. pair, imperf. vert.	1,100.	
b.		Vert. pair, imperf. btwn.	1,500.	
c.		Double surcharge	*5,000.*	
d.		Inverted surcharge		10,000.
e.		Horiz. pair, imperf. btwn.	1,400.	
31	A6	4c on 4c	4.00	3.50
a.		Double surcharge	*8,000.*	*8,000.*
b.		Vert. pair, imperf. btwn.	1,500.	1,500.
c.		Horiz. pair, imperf. btwn.	1,500.	1,500.
32	A7	5c on 5c	6.00	3.50
a.		Vert. pair, imperf. btwn.	1,600.	
33	A8	8c on 6c	8.00	5.00
a.		Vert. pair, imperf. btwn.	1,000.	1,000.
b.		Vert. strip of 3, imperf. btwn.	1,100.	1,100.
c.		Horiz. pair, imperf. btwn.	1,200.	1,200.
34	A8	10c on 6c	20.00	30.00
b.		Vert. pair, imperf. btwn.	1,000.	1,000.
c.		Horiz. pair, imperf. vert.	1,200.	
35	A9	10c on 9c	140.00	35.00
a.		Double surcharge	*6,000.*	*6,000.*
b.		Inverted surcharge	*10,000.*	*10,000.*
36	A10	10c on 12c	90.00	50.00
a.		Vert. pair, imperf. horiz.	850.00	
37	A11	30c on 24c	165.00	65.00
a.		Vert. pair, imperf. between	4,000.	

Preceding Issues Surcharged in Black

貳洋暫
分銀作
2
cents.

Large Numerals
Numerals 2 1/2mm below Chinese characters

1897, Mar.

Surcharged on Nos. 16-24

38	A5	1/2c on 3c	1,400.	400.
b.		Inverted surcharge		2,750.
39	A3	1c on 1c	85.	85.
40	A4	2c on 2c	190.	110.
41	A6	4c on 4c	190.	125.
b.		Horiz. pair, imperf. btwn.		
42	A7	5c on 5c	90.	90.
43	A8	8c on 6c	900.	900.
44	A9	10c on 9c	300.	200.
45	A10	10c on 12c	4,500.	600.
46	A11	30c on 24c	525.	500.
b.		2mm spacing between "30" and "cents."	*12,000.*	

Same Surcharge on Nos. 16n-24n

47	A5	1/2c on 3c	5.00	11.00
a.		"cen" for "cent"	425.00	400.00
b.		Vert. pair, imperf. btwn.	950.00	950.00
c.		Vert. pair, imperf. horiz.	300.00	425.00
d.		As "a" and "c"	6,000.	6,000.
48	A3	1c on 1c	5.00	6.00
a.		Horiz. pair, imperf. btwn.		1,000.
49	A4	2c on 2c	5.00	3.00
50	A6	4c on 4c	6.00	5.00
a.		Horiz. pair, imperf. btwn.	1,500.	1,500.
51	A7	5c on 5c	10.00	3.50
52	A8	8c on 6c	140.00	75.00
53	A9	10c on 9c	45.00	15.00
a.		10c on 9c emerald	65.00	26.00
54	A10	10c on 12c	60.00	15.00
55	A11	30c on 24c	140.00	50.00
a.		2mm spacing btwn "30" and "cents"	*1,000.*	325.00
b.		Vert. pair, imperf. btwn.	*3,750.*	

Numerals 1 1/2mm below Chinese characters

1897, May

Surcharged on Nos. 16-24

56	A5	1/2c on 3c org yel	*1,500.*	*125.*
57	A3	1c on 1c	110.	75.
58	A4	2c on 2c		300.
59	A6	4c on 4c	100.	100.
60	A7	5c on 5c	60.	60.
61	A8	8c on 6c	575.	375.
62	A9	10c on 9c	125.	75.
63	A10	10c on 12c	550.	450.
64	A11	30c on 24c	*6,500.*	

Same Surcharge on Nos. 16n-24n

65	A5	1/2c on 3c	3.75	2.00
a.		Inverted surcharge	1,100.	400.00
b.		1/2mm spacing	1,500.	1,200.
66	A3	1c on 1c	5.50	3.50
67	A4	2c on 2c	6.50	4.50
a.		Inverted surcharge	3,000.	
68	A6	4c on 4c	75.00	55.00
a.		Inverted surcharge	450.00	450.00
69	A7	5c on 5c	77.50	45.00
70	A9	10c on 9c	50.00	20.00
a.		Inverted surcharge	400.00	400.00
71	A10	10c on 12c	100.00	27.50
72	A11	30c on 24c	10,000.	1,500.

Same Surcharge (1 1/2mm Spacing) on Type A12, and

A12

A12a

Redrawn Designs
Printed from New Stones

1897

73	A12	1/2c on 3c yel	110.00	70.00
a.		1/2mm spacing	750.00	750.00
74	A12a	2c on 2c yel grn	25.00	10.00
a.		Horiz. pair, imperf. btwn.	*6,000.*	

Nos. 73 and 74 were surcharged on stamps printed from new stones, which differ slightly from the originals. On No. 73 the numeral "3" and symbols in the four corner panels have been enlarged and strengthened. On No. 74, the numeral "2" has a thick, flat base.

Surcharged on Nos. 13-15

75	A2	1c on 1c green	190.00
76	A2	2c on 3c lilac	450.00
77	A2	5c on 5c grnsh yel	80.00

Type A13 Surcharged in Black:

A13

政郵清大
分壹當
one cent
a

b

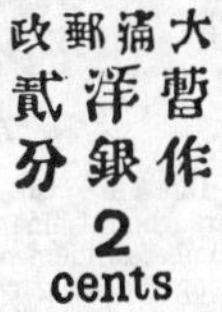
c

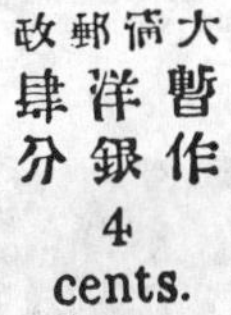
d

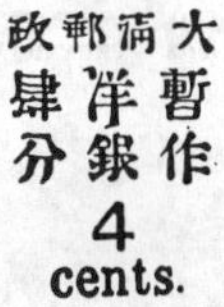
e

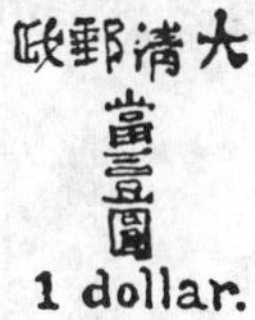
f

g

1897 Unwmk. *Perf. 12 to 15*

78	A13 (a) 1c on 3c red	60.00	45.00
a.	No period after "cent"	90.00	37.50
b.	Central character with large "box"	90.00	87.50
79	A13 (b) 2c on 3c red	125.00	70.00
a.	Inverted surcharge	4,250.	2,000.
b.	Inverted "S" in "CENTS"	150.00	150.00
c.	No period after "CENTS"	140.00	140.00
d.	Comma after "CENTS"	140.00	140.00
e.	Double surcharge	*10,000.*	
f.	Dbl. surch., both inverted		
g.	Double surch. (blk & grn)	*10,000.*	
80	A13 (c) 2c on 3c red	90.00	40.00
81	A13 (d) 4c on 3c red	*7,000.*	*3,250.*
a.	Double surcharge (blk & vio)	*12,000.*	*6,500.*
82	A13 (e) 4c on 3c red	125.00	60.00
83	A13 (f) $1 on 3c red	*225,000.*	
a.	No period after "r"		
84	A13 (g) $1 on 3c red	825.00	400.00
85	A13 (g) $5 on 3c red	7,500.	7,000.
a.	Inverted surcharge	*15,000.*	*10,000.*

A few copies of the 3c red exist without surcharge; one canceled. No. 79 with green surcharge is a trial printing.

Dragon
A14

Carp
A15

Wild Goose — A16

"Imperial Chinese Post"
Lithographed in Japan
Perf. 11, 11½, 12

1897, Aug. 16 Wmk. 103

86	A14 ½c purple brn	1.75	1.10
a.	Horiz. pair, imperf. btwn.	225.00	
87	A14 1c yellow	2.00	1.25
88	A14 2c orange	1.75	1.00
a.	Vert. pair, imperf. horiz.	250.00	
89	A14 4c brown	3.00	1.25
a.	Horiz. pair, imperf. btwn.	400.00	
90	A14 5c rose red	4.00	1.25
91	A14 10c dk green	10.00	1.25
92	A15 20c maroon	19.00	5.00
93	A15 30c red	27.50	12.50
94	A15 50c yellow grn	30.00	15.00
a.	50c black green	275.00	
b.	50c blue green	600.00	
95	A16 $1 car & rose	100.00	70.00
a.	Horiz. pair, imperf. vert.	1,500.	
96	A16 $2 orange & yel	600.00	625.00
a.	Horiz. pair, imperf. vert.	1,600.	
97	A16 $5 yel grn & pink	350.00	350.00

The inner circular frames and outer frames of Nos. 86-91 differ for each denomination.

No. 97 imperforate was not regularly issued. **Copies have been privately perforated and offered as No. 97.** Shades occur in most values of this issue.

A17

A18

A19

"Chinese Imperial Post"
Engraved in London

1898 Wmk. 103 *Perf. 12 to 16*

98	A17 ½c chocolate	1.00	50
a.	Vert. pair, imperf. btwn.		200.00
99	A17 1c ocher	1.25	50
a.	Vert. pair, imperf. btwn.	90.00	90.00
b.	Horiz. pair, imperf. btwn.	140.00	140.00
100	A17 2c scarlet	1.50	35
a.	Vert. pair, imperf. btwn.	80.00	80.00
b.	Horiz. pair, imperf. vert.		
101	A17 4c orange brn	1.65	45
a.	Vert. pair, imperf. btwn.	150.00	
b.	Horiz. pair, imperf. vert.	100.00	100.00
c.	Horiz. pair, imperf. btwn.	225.00	225.00
d.	Horiz. strip of 3, imperf. btwn.	350.00	350.00
102	A17 5c salmon	3.00	85
a.	Vert. pair, imperf. btwn.	120.00	120.00
b.	Horiz. pair, imperf. btwn.	165.00	165.00
103	A17 10c dk blue grn	3.00	40
a.	Vert. or horiz. pair, imperf. btwn	150.00	150.00
104	A18 20c claret	17.50	3.00
a.	Horiz. pair, imperf. btwn.	250.00	
b.	Vert. pair, imperf. horiz.	250.00	250.00
105	A18 30c dull rose	14.00	1.25
a.	Horiz. pair, imperf. btwn.	250.00	
b.	Vert. pair, imperf. horiz.	250.00	
106	A18 50c lt green	22.50	4.00
a.	Vert. pair, imperf. btwn.	375.00	
107	A19 $1 red & pale rose	100.00	7.75
108	A19 $2 brn, red & yel	190.00	32.50
109	A19 $5 dp green & sal	325.00	90.00
a.	Horiz. pair, imperf. btwn.	*5,000.*	
b.	Vert. pair, imperf. btwn.	*5,250.*	
	Nos. 98-109 (12)	680.40	141.55

No. 98 surcharged "B. R. A.-5-Five Cents" in three lines in black or green, was surcharged by British military authorities shortly after the Boxer riots for use from military posts in an occupied area along the Peking-Mukden railway. Usually canceled in violet.

See note following No. 122.

1900(?)-06 Unwmk. *Perf. 12 to 16*

110	A17 ½c brown	60	30
a.	Horiz. or vert. pair, imperf. btwn.	175.00	175.00
111	A17 1c ocher	60	30
a.	Horiz. pair, imperf. btwn.	125.00	125.00
b.	Vert. pair, imperf. btwn.	110.00	110.00
c.	Vert. pair, imperf. horiz.	110.00	110.00
112	A17 2c scarlet	1.25	30
a.	Horiz. or vert. pair, imperf. btwn	65.00	65.00
c.	Vert. pair, imperf. horiz.	65.00	65.00
d.	Horiz. pair, imperf. vert.	65.00	65.00
e.	Vert. strip of 3, imperf. btwn.	85.00	85.00
113	A17 4c orange brn	1.25	25
a.	Horiz. or vert. pair, imperf. btwn	175.00	175.00
114	A17 5c rose red	10.00	1.25
a.	Vert. pair, imperf. btwn.	120.00	
b.	Vert. pair, imperf. horiz.	100.00	
115	A17 5c orange	8.00	1.25
a.	5c yellow	100.00	12.00
b.	Vert. pair, imperf. btwn.	150.00	
c.	Horiz. pair, imperf. btwn.	150.00	
116	A17 10c green	8.00	25
a.	Vert. pair, imperf. btwn.	125.00	
b.	Horiz. pair, imperf. btwn.	125.00	
c.	Vert. pair, imperf. horiz.	125.00	
d.	Vert. strip of 3, imperf. btwn.	190.00	
117	A18 20c red brown	5.75	25
a.	Horiz. pair, imperf. btwn.	150.00	
b.	Vert. pair, imperf. btwn.	125.00	
118	A18 30c dull red	9.00	50
a.	Vert. pair, imperf. btwn.	300.00	
119	A18 50c yellow grn	18.00	1.00
120	A19 $1 red & pale rose ('06)	57.50	5.00
121	A19 $2 brn red & yel ('06)	125.00	13.00
122	A19 $5 dp green & sal	225.00	75.00
	Nos. 110-122 (13)	469.95	98.65

See #124-130. For surcharges and overprints see #123, 134-177, J1-J6, Offices in Tibet 1-11.

Diagonal Half of No. 112 Surcharged on Stamp and Envelope

Postage
1 Cent
Paid

1903

123	A17	1c on half of 2c scarlet, on cover	500.00	

Excellent forgeries of No. 123 are plentiful, particularly on pieces of cover.

1905-10

124	A17	2c green ('08)	50	30
a.		Horiz. pair, imperf. btwn.	150.00	150.00
b.		Vert. pair, imperf. btwn.	150.00	150.00
c.		Horiz. pair, imperf. vert.	150.00	
d.		Horiz. strip of 4, imperf. btwn.	200.00	
125	A17	3c slate grn ('10)	1.50	30
a.		Horiz. or vert. pair, imperf. btwn	95.00	
126	A17	4c ver ('09)	1.50	30
127	A17	5c violet	2.00	30
a.		5c lilac	2.00	30
b.		Horiz. or vert. pair, imperf. btwn	175.00	
d.		Vert. pair, imperf. horiz.	75.00	
128	A17	7c maroon ('10)	6.00	3.25
129	A17	10c ultra ('08)	4.50	25
a.		Horiz. or vert. pair, imperf. btwn	125.00	
c.		Vert. pair, imperf. horiz.	100.00	100.00
130	A18	16c olive grn ('07)	19.00	6.00
		Nos. 124-130 (7)	35.00	10.70

Temple of Heaven, Peking — A20

1909 *Perf. 14*

131	A20	2c orange & green	4.00	2.25
132	A20	3c orange & blue	4.00	2.25
133	A20	7c orange & brn vio	4.00	2.25
		Nos. 131-133 (3)	12.00	6.75

1st year of the reign of Hsuan T'ung, who later became Henry Pu-yi and then Emperor Kang Teh of Manchukuo.

Stamps of 1902-10 Overprinted with Chinese Characters

Foochow Issue

Overprinted in Red or Black 立中時臨

1912 *Perf. 12 to 16*

134	A17	3c slate grn (R)	95.	55.
135	A19	$1 red & pale rose	1,200.	1,000.
136	A19	$2 brn red & yel	1,600.	1,050.
137	A19	$5 dp grn & sal	2,500.	1,100.

The overprint "Ling Shih Chung Li" or "Provisional Neutrality," signified that the P.O. was conducted neutrally by agreement between the Manchu and opposing forces.

Nanking Issue

Overprinted in Red or Black

中華
立中時臨
民國

138	A17	1c ocher (R)	65.	50.
139	A17	3c slate grn (R)	50.	45.
140	A17	7c maroon	200.	150.
141	A18	16c olive grn (R)	800.	600.
142	A18	50c yellow grn (R)	1,300.	900.
143	A19	$1 red & pale rose	1,200.	825.
144	A19	$2 brown red & yel	2,250.	2,250.
145	A19	$5 dp green & sal	4,000.	4,000.

Vertical overprint reads: "Chung Hwa Min Kuo" (Republic of China).

Stamps of this issue were also used in Shanghai and Hankow.

Additional values were overprinted but not issued. Excellent forgeries of the overprints of Nos. 134-145 exist.

Issues of the Republic

Overprinted in Black or Red 中華民國

Overprinted by the Maritime Customs Statistical Department, Shanghai

146	A17	1/2c brown	55	15
a.		Inverted overprint	17.50	16.00
b.		Double overprint	50.00	
147	A17	1c ocher (R)	80	15
a.		Vert. pair, imperf. horiz.	90.00	90.00
b.		Inverted overprint	80.00	50.00
c.		Double overprint	90.00	75.00
d.		Horiz. pair, imperf. btwn.	140.00	75.00
e.		Horiz. pair, imperf. vert.	70.00	
f.		Pair, one without overprint	70.00	
148	A17	2c green (R)	80	15
a.		Vert. pair, imperf. btwn.	90.00	90.00
149	A17	3c slate grn (R)	1.00	15
a.		Inverted overprint	55.00	30.00
b.		Horiz. or vert. pair, imperf. btwn	140.00	90.00
d.		Horiz. pair, imperf. vert.	60.00	
150	A17	4c vermilion	1.90	25
a.		Vert. pair, imperf. btwn.	400.00	
151	A17	5c violet (R)	2.25	15
a.		Horiz. pair, imperf. btwn.		
152	A17	7c maroon	3.25	75
153	A17	10c ultra (R)	3.50	40
a.		Double overprint	90.00	
b.		Pair, one without overprint	350.00	
c.		Brownish red overprint	9.00	5.00
d.		Inverted overprint	125.00	125.00
154	A18	16c olive grn (R)	6.50	3.00
155	A18	20c red brown	6.50	1.65
156	A18	30c rose red	8.00	1.65
157	A18	50c yel grn (R)	14.00	1.65
158	A19	$1 red & pale rose	100.00	6.00
a.		Inverted overprint		*5,500.*
159	A19	$2 brn red & yel	80.00	17.00
a.		Inverted overprint	150.00	150.00
160	A19	$5 dp grn & sal	225.00	175.00
		Nos. 146-160 (15)	454.05	208.10

Stamps with blue overprint similar to the preceding were not an official issue but were privately made by a printer in Tientsin.

Overprinted in Red 中華民國

Overprinted by the Commercial Press, Shanghai

This type differs in that the top character is shifted slightly to right and the bottom character is larger and has small "legs".

161	A17	1c ocher	2.25	40
a.		Inverted overprint	72.50	72.50
b.		Vert. pair, imperf. btwn.	125.00	
c.		Double overprint	80.00	
162	A17	2c green	16.00	1.00
a.		Inverted overprint	650.00	500.00
b.		Vert. pair, imperf. btwn.	150.00	
c.		Horiz. pair, imperf. btwn.	175.00	
d.		Horiz. strip of 3, imperf. btwn.	275.00	

Overprinted in Blue, Carmine or Black 中華民國

Overprinted by Waterlow & Sons, London

163	A17	1/2c brown (Bl)	60	32
a.		Vert. pair, imperf. btwn.	600.00	600.00
164	A17	1c ocher (C)	60	32
a.		Horiz. pair, imperf. btwn.	100.00	
165	A17	2c green (C)	1.00	40
166	A17	3c slate grn (C)	1.25	50
a.		Inverted overprint		900.00
167	A17	4c vermilion (Bk)	1.65	65
168	A17	5c violet (C)	2.50	60
169	A17	7c maroon (Bk)	11.00	9.00
170	A17	10c ultra (C)	5.00	1.00
a.		Vert. pair, imperf. btwn.	300.00	300.00
171	A18	16c olive grn (R)	15.00	4.50
172	A18	20c red brn (Bk)	9.00	1.65
173	A18	30c dull red (Bk)	20.00	2.50
174	A18	50c yellow grn (R)	37.50	4.00
175	A19	$1 red & pale rose (Bk)	50.00	5.00
176	A19	$2 brn red & yel (Bk)	165.00	75.00
177	A19	$5 dp grn & sal (C)	225.00	175.00
		Nos. 163-177 (15)	545.10	280.44

Due to instructions issued to postmasters throughout China at the time of the Revolution, a number of them prepared unauthorized overprints using the same characters as the overprints prepared by the government. While many were made in good faith, some, like the blue overprints from Tientsin, were bogus, and the status of certain others is extremely dubious.

Dr. Sun Yat-sen — A21

1912, Dec. 14 *Perf. 14 1/2*

178	A21	1c orange	1.50	1.50
179	A21	2c yellow grn	1.50	1.25
180	A21	3c slate grn	1.50	1.40
181	A21	5c rose lilac	3.00	1.50
182	A21	8c dp brown	3.00	2.50
183	A21	10c dull blue	3.00	2.50
184	A21	16c olive grn	7.00	4.50
185	A21	20c maroon	10.00	3.50
186	A21	50c dk green	22.50	20.00
187	A21	$1 brown red	82.50	32.50
188	A21	$2 yellow brn	175.00	175.00
189	A21	$5 gray	92.50	90.00
		Nos. 178-189 (12)	403.00	336.15

Honoring the leader of the Revolution.

President Yuan Shih-kai — A22

1912, Dec. 14

190	A22	1c orange	1.10	1.00
191	A22	2c yellow green	1.10	1.00
192	A22	3c slate green	1.10	80
193	A22	5c rose lilac	1.10	1.00
194	A22	8c deep brown	3.00	1.25
195	A22	10c dull blue	1.25	1.10
196	A22	16c olive green	3.75	5.25
197	A22	20c maroon	2.75	4.00
198	A22	50c dark green	15.00	11.00
199	A22	$1 brown red	47.50	25.00
200	A22	$2 yellow brown	65.00	22.50
201	A22	$5 gray	150.00	150.00
		Nos. 190-201 (12)	292.65	223.90

Honoring the 1st pres. of the Republic.

Junk — A24

Reaping Rice — A25

Gateway, Hall of Classics, Peking — A26

DESIGN A24

London Printing: Vertical shading lines under top panel fine, junk with clear diagonal shading lines on sails, right pennant of junk usually long, lines in water weak except directly under junk.

Peking Printing: Vertical shading lines under top panel and inner vertical frame line much heavier, water and sails of junk more evenly and strongly colored, white wave over "H" of "CHINA" pointed upward, touching the junk.

DESIGN A25

London: Front hat brim thick and nearly straight, left foot touches shadow.

Peking: Front hat brim thin and strongly upturned, left foot and sickle clearly outlined in white, shadow of middle tree lighter than those of the right and left trees.

DESIGN A26

London: Light colored walk clearly defined almost to the doorway, figure in right doorway "T" shaped with strong horizontal cross-bar, white panel in base of central tower rectangular, vertical stroke in top left character uniformly thick at its base, tree to right of doorway ends in minute dots.

Peking: Walk more heavily shaded near doorway, especially at right; figure in right doorway more like a "Y", white panel at base of central tower is a long oval, right vertical stroke in top left character incurved near its base, tree at right has five prominent dots at top.

London Printing: By Waterlow & Sons, London, perf. 14 to 15.

Peking Printing: By the Chinese Bureau of Engraving and Printing, Peking, perf. 14.

London Printing

1913, May 5 *Perf. 14-15*

202 A24 ½c black brn 40 15
a. Horiz. or vert. pair, imperf. btwn. 100.00
203 A24 1c orange 40 15
a. Horiz. pair, imperf. btwn. 150.00
b. Vert. pair, imperf. btwn. 80.00
c. Horiz. strip of 5, imperf. btwn 400.00
204 A24 2c yellow grn 1.25 15
a. Horiz. pair, imperf. btwn. 225.00
205 A24 3c blue grn 1.75 15
a. Horiz. pair, imperf. btwn. 100.00
b. Vert. pair, imperf. btwn. 250.00
206 A24 4c scarlet 4.50 35
207 A24 5c rose lilac 9.00 35
208 A24 6c gray 2.00 50
209 A24 7c violet 9.00 3.25
210 A24 8c brown org 12.00 1.00
211 A24 10c dk blue 10.00 50
a. Horiz. pair, imperf. btwn. 200.00 200.00
b. Vert. pair, imperf. btwn. 225.00 150.00
212 A25 15c brown 13.00 3.00
213 A25 16c olive grn 7.00 1.00
214 A25 20c brown red 9.50 80
215 A25 30c brown vio 12.00 1.00
a. Horiz. pair, imperf. btwn. 225.00 175.00
216 A25 50c green 18.00 80
217 A26 $1 ocher & blk 57.50 1.75
218 A26 $2 blue & blk 80.00 6.50
219 A26 $5 scarlet & blk 150.00 45.00
220 A26 $10 yel grn & blk 550.00 500.00
Nos. 202-220 (19) 947.30 566.40

First Peking Printing

1915 *Perf. 14*

221 A24 ½c black brn 40 15
222 A24 1c orange 40 15
223 A24 2c yellow grn 75 15
224 A24 3c blue grn 75 15
225 A24 4c scarlet 6.00 15
226 A24 5c rose lilac 2.50 15
a. Booklet pane of 4 100.00
227 A24 6c gray 5.00 20
228 A24 7c violet 5.00 2.25
229 A24 8c brown org 2.50 20
230 A24 10c dk blue 2.50 40
a. Booklet pane of 4 100.00
231 A25 15c brown 14.00 2.50
232 A25 16c olive grn 4.50 40
233 A25 20c brown red 4.00 40
234 A25 30c brown vio 5.00 40
235 A25 50c green 7.00 40
236 A26 $1 ocher & blk 35.00 50
237 A26 $2 blue & blk 70.00 1.65
a. Center inverted 20,000.
238 A26 $5 scarlet & blk 200.00 16.00
239 A26 $10 yel grn & blk 300.00 100.00
Nos. 221-239 (19) 665.30 126.20

1919

240 A24 1½c violet 1.40 35
241 A25 13c brown 3.50 40
242 A26 $20 yellow & blk 1,400. 1,600.

Nos. 226 and 230 overprinted in red with five characters in vertical column were for postal savings use.

The higher values of the 1913-19 issues are often overprinted with Chinese characters, which are the names of various postal districts. Stamps were frequently stolen while in transit to post offices. The overprints served to protect them, since the stamps could only be used in the districts for which they were overprinted.

For surcharges and overprints see Nos. 288, B1-B3, Sinkiang 1-38.

Yeh Kung-cho, Hsu Shi-chang and Chin Yun-peng — A27

1921, Oct. 10

243 A27 1c orange 3.75 90
244 A27 3c blue green 3.75 90
245 A27 6c gray 3.75 90
246 A27 10c blue 3.75 90
Nos. 243-246 (4) 15.00 3.60

National Post Office, 25th anniversary.
For overprints see Sinkiang Nos. 39-42.

A28

1923 **Red Surcharge**

247 A28 2c on 3c blue grn 1.40 35
a. Inverted surcharge *19,000.*

Second Peking Printing

A29

A30

A31

Types of 1913-19 Issues
Re-engraved

Type A29: Most of the whitecaps in front of the junk have been removed and the water made darker. The shading lines have been removed from the arabesques and pearls above the top inscription. The inner shadings at the top and sides of the picture have been cut away.

Type A30: The heads of rice in the side panels have a background of crossed lines instead of horizontal lines. The Temple of Heaven is strongly shaded and has a door. There are rows of pearls below the Chinese characters in the upper corners. The arabesques above the top inscription have been altered and are without shading lines.

Type A31: The curved line under the inscription at top is single instead of double. There are four vertical lines, instead of eight, at each side of the picture. The trees at the sides of the temple had foliage in the 1913-19 issues, but now the branches are bare. There are numerous other alterations in the design.

1923 *Perf. 14*

248 A29 ½c black brown 60 15
a. Horiz. pair, imperf. btwn. 150.00 150.00
b. Horiz. pair, imperf. vert. 125.00 125.00
249 A29 1c orange 40 15
a. Imperf., pair 75.00
b. Horiz. pair, imperf. vert. 75.00
c. Booklet pane of 6 80.00
d. Booklet pane of 4 40.00
250 A29 1½c violet 80 60
251 A29 2c yellow grn 65 15
252 A29 3c blue green 1.00 15
a. Booklet pane of 6 65.00
253 A29 4c gray 8.00 48
254 A29 5c claret 1.00 28
a. Booklet pane of 4 80.00
255 A29 6c scarlet 2.00 28
256 A29 7c violet 2.50 28
257 A29 8c orange 4.00 28
258 A29 10c blue 2.50 20
a. Booklet pane of 6 100.00
b. Booklet pane of 2 125.00
259 A30 13c brown 8.75 38
260 A30 15c dp blue 3.00 38
261 A30 16c olive grn 4.00 38
262 A30 20c brown red 3.00 24
263 A30 30c purple 9.00 24
264 A30 50c dp green 15.00 38
265 A31 $1 org brn & sep 15.00 38
266 A31 $2 blue & red brn 26.00 48
267 A31 $5 red & slate 40.00 1.90
268 A31 $10 green & claret 165.00 25.00
269 A31 $20 plum & blue 350.00 57.50
Nos. 248-269 (22) 662.20 90.26

Nos. 249 and 275 exist with webbing watermark from experimental printing.

To prevent speculation and theft, the dollar denominations were overprinted with single characters in red for use in Kwangsi ($1-$20) and Kweichow ($1-$5).

See Nos. 275, 324. For surcharges and overprints see Nos. 274, 289, 311, 325, 330, 339-340, Szechwan 1-3, Yunnan 1-20, Manchuria 1-20, Sinkiang 47-69, 114, C1-C4.

Temple of Heaven, Peking — A32

1923, Oct. 17 *Perf. 14*

270 A32 1c orange 2.75 75
271 A32 3c blue green 2.75 1.50
272 A32 4c red 5.75 1.50
273 A32 10c blue 9.00 1.65
Nos. 270-273 (4) 20.25 5.40

Adoption of Constitution, October, 1923.
For overprints see Sinkiang Nos. 43-46.

No. 253 Surcharged in Red

3 叁分 暫作 Cts.

1925

274 A29 3c on 4c gray 1.50 15
a. Inverted surcharge *22,500. 10,000.*
b. Vert. pair, imperf. btwn.

Junk Type of 1923

1926

275 A29 4c olive green 1.00 15
a. Horiz. pair, imperf. vert. 150.00
b. Horiz. pair, imperf. btwn. 150.00
c. Horiz. strip of 3, imperf. btwn. 200.00

Marshal Chang Tso-lin — A34

President Chiang Kai-shek — A35

1928, Mar. 1 *Perf. 14*

276 A34 1c brown orange 1.00 1.00
277 A34 4c olive green 2.50 1.50
278 A34 10c dull blue 6.00 2.50
279 A34 $1 red 32.50 35.00
Nos. 276-279 (4) 42.00 39.50

Assumption of office by Marshal Chang Tso-lin. The stamps of this issue were only available for postage in the Provinces of Chihli and Shantung and at the Offices in Manchuria and Sinkiang.

For overprints see Manchuria Nos. 21-24, Sinkiang 70-73.

1929, May

280 A35 1c brown orange 1.25 40
281 A35 4c olive green 1.65 80
282 A35 10c dark blue 12.00 1.65
283 A35 $1 dark red 60.00 60.00
Nos. 280-283 (4) 74.90 62.85

Unification of China.
For overprints see Yunnan Nos. 21-24, Manchuria 25-28, Sinkiang 74-77.

Sun Yat-sen Mausoleum, Nanking — A36

1929, May 30 *Perf. 14*

284 A36 1c brown orange 80 65
285 A36 4c olive green 90 65
286 A36 10c dark blue 5.50 2.00
287 A36 $1 dark red 52.50 30.00
Nos. 284-287 (4) 59.70 33.30

The transfer of Dr. Sun Yat-sen's remains from Peiping to the mausoleum at Nanking.

For overprints see Yunnan Nos. 25-28, Manchuria 29-32, Sinkiang 78-81.

Nos. 224 and 252 Surcharged in Red

1 壹分 暫作 Ct.

1930

288 A24 1c on 3c blue green 1.00 1.65
289 A29 1c on 3c blue green 50 30
a. No period after "Ct" 15.00 15.00

See Nos. 311, 325, 330.

Dr. Sun Yat-sen — A37

Type I - Double-lined circle in the sun.
Type II - Heavy, single-lined circle in the sun.

Printed by De la Rue & Co., Ltd., London

Perf. 11½x12½, 12½x13, 12½, 13½

1931 **Engr.**

Type I

290 A37 1c orange 35 15
291 A37 2c olive green 35 15
292 A37 4c green 75 15
293 A37 20c ultra 75 15
294 A37 $1 org brn & dk brn 6.00 25
295 A37 $2 blue & org brn 15.00 80
296 A37 $5 dull red & blk 22.50 1.50
Nos. 290-296 (7) 45.70 3.15

Stamps issued prior to 1933 were printed by a wet-paper process, and owing to shrinkage such stamps are 1-1½mm narrower than the later dry-printed stamps. Early printings are perf. 12½x13. Nos. 304, 305 and 306 were later perf. 11½x12½.

1931-37

Type II

297 A37 2c olive grn 30 15
298 A37 4c green 30 15
299 A37 5c green ('33) 30 15
300 A37 15c dk green 3.25 50
301 A37 15c scarlet ('34) 35 15
302 A37 20c ultra ('37) 35 15
303 A37 25c ultra 35 35
304 A37 $1 org brn & dk brn 6.50 20
305 A37 $2 blue & org brn 12.00 45
306 A37 $5 dull red & blk 24.00 1.40
Nos. 297-306 (10) 47.70 3.65

See #631-635. For surcharges and overprints see #341, 343, 678, 682, 684-685, 689-691, 768, 843, 1N1, 2N1-2N5, 2N57-2N59, 2N83-2N84, 2N101-2N106, 2N116, 2N124-2N126, 3N1-3N5, 4N1-4N5, 5N1-5N4, 6N1-6N5, 7N1-7N4, 7N54, 8N2-8N3, 8N43-8N44, 8N54, 8N57, 8N69-8N71, 8N85, 9N1-9N5, Taiwan 19, 21-22, Northeastern

Provinces 44, Szechwan 4-11, Yunnan 29-44, Sinkiang 82-97.

"Nomads in the Desert" — A38

1932 Unwmk. *Perf. 14*

307	A38	1c deep orange	20.00	15.00
308	A38	4c olive green	20.00	15.00
309	A38	5c claret	20.00	15.00
310	A38	10c deep blue	20.00	15.00
		Nos. 307-310 (4)	80.00	60.00

Northwest Scientific Expedition of Sven Hedin. A small quantity of this issue was sold at face at Peking and several other cities. The bulk of the issue was furnished to Hedin and sold at $5 (Chinese) a set for funds to finance the expedition.

#252 Surcharged in Black Like #288

1932

311	A29	1c on 3c blue green	2.00	1.00

Martyrs Issue

Teng Keng — A39

Ch'en Ying-shih — A40

Chu Chih-hsin — A45

Sung Chiao-jen — A46

Huang Hsing — A47

Liao Chung-kai — A48

1932-34 *Perf. 14*

312	A39	½c black brown	15	15
313	A40	1c orange ('34)	15	15
314	A39	2½c rose lilac ('33)	15	15
315	A48	3c dp brown ('33)	15	15
316	A45	8c brown orange	20	15
317	A46	10c dull violet	18	15
318	A45	13c blue green	25	15
319	A46	17c brown olive	20	15
320	A47	20c brown red	42	15
321	A48	30c brown violet	70	15
322	A47	40c orange	60	25
323	A40	50c green ('34)	2.00	25
		Nos. 312-323 (12)	5.15	
		Set value		75

Perfs. 12 to 13 and compound and with secret marks are listed as Nos. 402-439. No. 316 re-drawn is No. 485.

For overprints and surcharge see Nos. 342, 472, 474, 478-479, 486-487, 490, 531-536, 539-541, 544-549, 616, 619, 622-624, 647-659, 662-663, 665, 669, 672, 698, 704, 711, 713-715, 720-721, 831, 846-847, 867, 870, 872, 881-882, J120-J121, 1N14-1N15, 1N59, 2N6-2N9, 2N32-2N56, 2N60, 2N76-2N82, 2N85, 2N87-2N90, 2N107-2N115, 2N118, 2N121-2N123, 3N6-3N10, 3N34-3N55, 3N59, 4N6-4N9, 4N39-4N64, 4N69, 5N5-5N8, 5N34-5N60, 5N65, 6N6-6N8, 6N35-6N61, 6N66, 7N5-7N7, 7N30-7N53, 7N55, 7N59, 8N1, 8N4, 8N28-8N42, 8N45, 8N47-8N50, 8N60-8N61, 8N68, 8N73, 8N76-8N79, 8N89, 8N97, 8N99-8N100, 8N103-8N104, 9N72-9N77, Taiwan 14-17, 20, 28A, 74, Northeastern Provinces 6-8, 11, Szechwan 12-23, Yunnan 49-60, Sinkiang 102-113, 140-161, 197.

Junk Type of 1923 Issue

1933 *Perf. 14*

324	A29	6c brown	16.00	1.00

#275 Surcharged in Red Like #288

1933

325	A29	1c on 4c olive green	1.25	25
a.		No period after "Ct"	15.00	15.00

Tan Yuan-chang — A49

1933, Jan. 9

326	A49	2c olive green	2.00	25
327	A49	5c green	2.00	25
328	A49	25c ultra	6.00	85
329	A49	$1 red	45.00	10.00
		Nos. 326-329 (4)	55.00	11.35

Tan Yuan-chang, more commonly known as Tan Yen-kai, a prominent statesman in China since the revolution of 1912 and Pres. of the Executive Dept. of the Natl. Government. Placed on sale Jan. 9, 1933, the date of the ceremony in celebration of the completion of the Tan Yuan-chang Memorial Hall and Tomb at Mukden.

For overprints see Yunnan Nos. 45-48, Sinkiang 98-101.

#251 Surcharged in Red Like #288

1935 *Perf. 14*

330	A29	1c on 2c yellow grn	2.00	15

Emblem of New Life Movement A50

Four Virtues of New Life A51

Lighthouse — A52

1936, Jan. 1

331	A50	2c olive green	50	15
332	A50	5c green	80	15
333	A51	20c dark blue	4.25	60
334	A52	$1 rose red	19.00	2.50
		Nos. 331-334 (4)	24.55	3.40

"New Life" movement.

Methods of Mail Transportation A53

Maritime Scene — A54

Shanghai General Post Office — A55

Ministry of Communications, Nanking — A56

1936, Oct. 10

335	A53	2c orange	35	15
336	A54	5c green	45	15
337	A55	25c blue	3.00	55
338	A56	$1 dk carmine	19.00	2.25
		Nos. 335-338 (4)	22.80	3.10

Founding of the Chinese PO, 40th anniv.

Nos. 260 and 261 Surcharged in Red

1936, Oct. 11

339	A30	5c on 15c dp blue	80	30
340	A30	5c on 16c olive grn	1.65	75

No. 298 Surcharged in Red

1937

341	A37	1c on 4c green, type II	50	20
a.		Upper left character missing		

Nos. 322 and 303 Surcharged in Black or Red

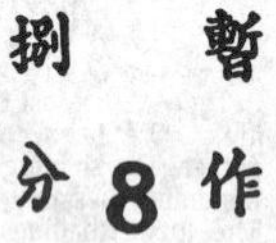

1938 *Perf. 12½, 14*

342	A47	8c on 40c orange (Bk)	90	40
343	A37	10c on 25c ultra (R)	50	20

Dr. Sun Yat-sen — A57

Type I - Coat button half circle. Six lines of shading above head. Top frame partially shaded with vertical lines.

Type II - Coat button complete circle. Nine lines of shading above head. Top frame partially shaded with vertical lines.

Type III - Coat button complete circle. Nine lines of shading above head. Top frame line fully shaded with vertical lines.

Printed by the Chung Hwa Book Co.

1938 Unwmk. Engr. *Perf. 12½*

Type I

344	A57	$1 henna & dk brn	60.00	5.75
345	A57	$2 dp blue & org brn	12.00	2.75
346	A57	$5 red & grnsh blk	75.00	10.00
		Nos. 344-346 (3)	147.00	18.50

1939

Type II

347	A57	$1 henna & dk brn	12.00	60
348	A57	$2 dp blue & org brn	15.00	2.50

1939-43

Type III

349	A57	2c olive green	15	15
350	A57	3c dull claret	15	15
351	A57	5c green	15	15
352	A57	5c olive green	15	15
353	A57	8c olive green	15	15
354	A57	10c green	15	15
355	A57	15c scarlet	85	50
356	A57	15c dk vio brn ('43)	11.00	*20.00*
357	A57	16c olive gray	1.00	35
358	A57	25c dk blue	25	40
359	A57	$1 henna & dk brn	1.25	40
360	A57	$2 dp blue & org brn	2.50	40
a.		Imperf., pair	250.00	
361	A57	$5 red & grnsh blk	1.65	40
362	A57	$10 dk green & dull pur	10.00	1.50
363	A57	$20 rose lake & dk blue	21.00	20.00
		Nos. 349-363 (15)	50.40	*44.85*

Several values exist imperforate, but these were not regularly issued. No. 361 imperforate is printer's waste.

See Nos. 368-401, 506-524. For surcharges and overprints see Nos. 440-448, 473, 475-477, 480-481, 482-484, 489, 537-538, 615, 618, 620, 660-661, 664, 666-668, 673-676, 680-681, 686, 688, 699-703, 707-709, 717, 719, 830, J67-J68, M2, M11-M12, 1N2-1N13, 1N23-1N42, 1N57-1N58, 2N10-2N31, 2N61-2N75, 2N86, 2N91-2N93, 2N117, 2N119-2N120, 3N11-3N33, 3N56-3N58, 3N60-3N61, 4N10-4N38, 4N65-4N68, 4N70-4N71, 5N9-5N33, 5N61-5N64, 5N66-5N68, 6N9-6N34, 6N62-6N65, 6N67-6N69, 7N8-7N29, 7N56-7N58, 7N60-7N61, 8N5-8N27, 8N46, 8N51-8N53, 8N55-8N56, 8N58-8N59, 8N62-8N67, 8N72, 8N74-8N75, 8N80-8N84, 8N86-8N88, 8N90, 8N95-8N96, 8N98, 8N101-8N102, 8N105-8N106, 9N6-9N71, 9N97, 9N99, Taiwan 78, 84, Northeastern Provinces 9-10, Sinkiang 115-139, 174-188, 196, 198.

Chinese and American Flags and Map of China — A58

Printed by American Bank Note Co.

Frame Engr., Center Litho.

1939, July 4 Unwmk. *Perf. 12*

Flag in Deep Rose and Ultramarine

364	A58	5c dark green	1.00	38
365	A58	25c deep blue	1.00	55
366	A58	50c brown	2.75	75
367	A58	$1 rose carmine	4.25	1.50
		Nos. 364-367 (4)	9.00	3.18

150th anniv. of the US Constitution.

Type of 1939-41 Issue
Re-engraved

2c, 1939-41

Re-engraved

8c, 1939-41

Re-engraved

1940 *Perf. 12½*

368	A57	2c olive green	15	15
369	A57	8c olive green	15	15
		Set value	20	20

Type of 1938-41 Issue

1940 Unwmk. *Perf. 14*

Type III

370	A57	2c olive green	1.90	65
371	A57	5c green	3.00	1.75
372	A57	$1 henna & dk brn	67.50	12.50
373	A57	$2 dp blue & org brn	14.00	3.50
374	A57	$5 red & grnsh blk	14.00	5.00
375	A57	$10 dk grn & dull pur	37.50	5.75
		Nos. 370-375 (6)	137.90	29.15

See surcharge note following No. 363.

Type of 1939-41

1940 Wmk. 261 *Perf. 12½*

Type III

376	A57	$1 henna & dk brn	3.00	*7.50*
377	A57	$2 dp blue & org brn	3.00	*7.50*
378	A57	$5 red & grnsh blk	8.00	*15.00*
379	A57	$10 dk green & dull pur	12.00	*25.00*
380	A57	$20 rose lake & dp blue	16.00	*25.00*
		Nos. 376-380 (5)	42.00	*80.00*

See surcharge note following No. 363.

Printed by the Dah Tung Book Co.
Type III with Secret Marks
Five Cent

Type III- Characters joined

Secret Mark- Characters not joined

Eight Cent

Type III- Characters not joined

Secret Mark- Characters joined

Ten Cent

Type III- Characters sharp and well shaped

Secret Mark- Characters coarse and varying in thickness

Dollar Values

Type III

Secret Mark

1940 Unwmk. *Perf. 14*

381	A57	5c green	15	15
382	A57	5c olive green	15	15
383	A57	8c olive green	35	15
a.		Without "star" in uniform button	1.00	1.00
384	A57	10c green	15	15
385	A57	30c scarlet	22	15
386	A57	50c dk blue	35	15
387	A57	$1 org brn & sepia	70	15
388	A57	$2 dp blue & yel brn	70	30
389	A57	$5 red & slate grn	70	40
390	A57	$10 dk grn & dull pur	2.50	1.00
391	A57	$20 rose lake & dk blue	5.00	2.50
		Nos. 381-391 (11)	10.97	5.25

Type III with Secret Marks

1940 Wmk. 261 *Perf. 14*

392	A57	5c green	15	15
393	A57	5c olive green	15	15
394	A57	10c green	25	15
395	A57	30c scarlet	15	15
396	A57	50c dk blue	42	15
397	A57	$1 org brn & sepia	3.25	2.00
398	A57	$2 dp blue & yel brn	2.75	*4.00*
399	A57	$5 red & slate grn	3.25	*6.00*
400	A57	$10 dk grn & dull pur	10.00	*13.00*
401	A57	$20 rose lake & dk blue	16.00	14.00
		Nos. 392-401 (10)	36.37	*39.75*

Nos. 383, 384, 385, 397, 400 and 401 exist perf. 12½, but were not issued with this perforation.

See surcharge note following No. 363.

Types of 1932-34
Martyrs Issue with Secret Mark

1932-34 Issue. In the left Chinese character in bottom row, the two parts are not joined.

Secret Mark, 1940-41 Issue. The two parts are joined.

Perf. 12½, 13 and Compound

1940-41 Wmk. 261

402	A39	½c olive blk	25	15
403	A40	1c orange	25	15
404	A46	2c dp blue ('41)	25	15
405	A39	2½c rose lilac	25	15
406	A48	3c dp yellow brn	25	15
407	A39	4c pale vio ('41)	25	15
408	A48	5c dull red org ('41)	25	15
409	A45	8c dp orange	25	15
410	A46	10c dull violet	25	15
411	A45	13c dp yellow grn	25	15
412	A48	15c brown car	25	15
413	A46	17c brown olive	25	15
414	A47	20c lt blue	25	15
415	A45	21c olive brn ('41)	25	15
416	A40	25c red vio ('41)	25	15
417	A46	28c olive ('41)	25	15
418	A48	30c brown car	25	15
a.		Vert. pair, imperf. btwn.	125.00	
419	A47	40c orange	25	15
420	A40	50c green	25	15

Unwmk.

421	A39	½c olive black	15	15
422	A40	1c orange	15	15
a.		Without secret mark	1.50	1.50
b.		Horiz. pair, imperf. vert.	57.50	
423	A46	2c dp blue	15	15
a.		Vert. pair, imperf. horiz.	42.50	
b.		Horiz. pair, imperf. between	150.00	
424	A39	2½c rose lilac	15	15
425	A48	3c dp yel brn	15	15
426	A39	4c pale violet	15	15
427	A48	5c dull red org	15	15
428	A45	8c dp orange	15	15
429	A46	10c dull violet	2.25	15
430	A45	13c dp yel grn	15	15
431	A48	15c brown car	15	15
432	A46	17c brn olive	15	15
433	A47	20c lt blue	15	15
a.		Vert. pair, imperf. horiz.	110.00	
b.		Horiz. pair, imperf. vert.	110.00	
434	A45	21c olive brn	15	15
435	A40	25c rose vio	15	15
436	A46	28c olive	15	15
437	A48	30c brown car	2.00	75
438	A47	40c orange	15	15
439	A40	50c green	15	15
		Nos. 402-439 (38)	11.55	
		Set value		5.00

Several values exist imperforate, but they were not regularly issued.

Used values are for favor cancels. Postally used copies sell for more.

See surcharge note following No. 323.

Regional Surcharges.

The regional surcharges, Nos. 440 to 448, 482 to 484, 486 to 491 and 525 to 549, have been listed according to the basic stamps, with black or red surcharges. The surcharges of the individual provinces, plus Hong Kong and Shanghai, are noted in small type. The numeral following each letter is the surcharge denomination. These surcharges are identified by the following letters:

a- Hong Kong	i- Kwangsi
b- Shanghai	j- Kwangtung
bx- Anhwei	k- Western Szechwan
c- Hunan	l- Yunnan
d- Kansu	m- Honan
e- Kiangsi	n- Shensi
f- Eastern Szechwan	o- Kweichow
g- Chekiang	p- Hupeh
h- Fukien	

Regional Surcharges on Stamps of 1939-40:

Hong Kong a4

Shanghai b3

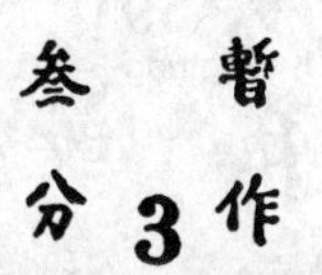

Hunan — c3

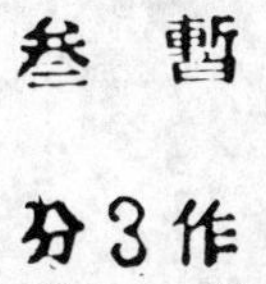

Kansu — d3

Kiangsi — e3

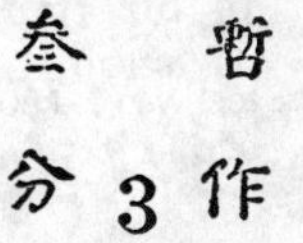

Eastern Szechwan — f3

Chekiang — g3

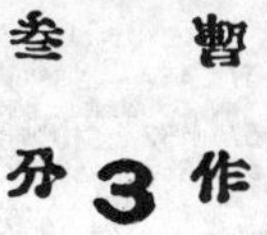

1940-41 Unwmk. *Perf. 12½, 14*

Carmine Surcharge

440	A57	4c on 5c ol grn (#382)	50	50
r.		Lower right character duplicated at left	20.00	30.00

Black Surcharge

441	A57	3c on 5c grn (#351) (b3)	80	1.00
442	A57	3c on 5c ol grn (#352) (c3, d3)	50	1.25
443	A57	3c on 5c grn (#381) (b3)	50	1.00
444	A57	3c on 5c ol grn (#382) (e3)	60	75
r.		Lower left character duplicated at right (Kiangsi)	37.50	37.50
		(b3) Shanghai	60	1.25
		(f3) Eastern Szechwan	60	1.50

The Kansu surcharges of #442 are of 6 types. Differences include formation of top part of fen character (at left of "3"), fen with low right hook, height of "3" (5-4mm), space between upper and lower characters (6-9mm), etc.

1940-41 Wmk. 261 *Perf. 14*

445	A57	3c on 5c grn (#392) (e3)	50	1.00
r.		Lower left character duplicated at right (Kiangsi)	30.00	30.00
		(b3, c3) Shanghai, Hunan	50	1.25
446	A57	3c on 5c ol grn (#393) (b3)	50	1.50
		(f3) Eastern Szechwan	60	1.25
r.		Lower left character duplicated at right (f3)	55.00	60.00

Red Surcharge

447	A57	3c on 5c grn (#392) (g3)	1.00	75
448	A57	3c on 5c ol grn (#393) (g3)	2.00	2.75

Dr. Sun Yat-sen — A59

Printed by American Bank Note Co.

1941 Unwmk. Engr. *Perf. 12*

449	A59	½c sepia	15	15
450	A59	1c orange	15	15
451	A59	2c brt ultra	15	15
452	A59	5c green	15	15
453	A59	8c red orange	15	15
454	A59	8c turq green	15	15
455	A59	10c brt green	15	15
456	A59	17c olive	2.25	3.00
457	A59	25c rose violet	15	30
458	A59	30c scarlet	15	15
459	A59	50c dk blue	15	15
460	A59	$1 brown & blk	22	15
461	A59	$2 blue & blk	22	15
a.		Center inverted	*12,500.*	
462	A59	$5 scarlet & blk	38	15
463	A59	$10 green & blk	1.50	1.00
464	A59	$20 rose vio & blk	1.50	1.25
		Set value	7.00	

For surcharges see Nos. 488, 491, 542-543, 617, 621, 670, 677, 687, 705-706, 712, 716, 718, M1, M3-M4, 1N16-1N22, 1N43-1N56, 9N78-9N96, 9N98, 9N100.

Industry and Agriculture — A60

1941, June 21 *Perf. 12½*

465	A60	8c green	15	20
466	A60	21c red brown	15	20
467	A60	28c dk olive grn	15	20
468	A60	33c vermilion	35	1.25
469	A60	50c dp ultra	90	60
470	A60	$1 dk violet	1.25	60
		Nos. 465-470 (6)	2.95	3.05

Souvenir Sheet

Imperf

Typo.

471		Sheet of 6	30.00	30.00
a.	A60	8c dull green	2.00	2.00
b.	A60	21c dark orange brown	2.00	2.00
c.	A60	28c dull yellow green	2.00	2.00
d.	A60	33c red	2.00	2.00
e.	A60	50c dull blue	2.00	2.00
f.	A60	$1 dark violet	2.00	2.00

The Thrift Movement and its aim to "Save for Reconstruction."

Issued in sheets measuring 155x171mm, without gum.

This sheet exists with additional blue marginal overprints in Russia, French and Chinese reading "Souvenir of the Exhibition of the Russian Philatelic Society in China, Shanghai, China, Feb. 28, 1943."

The overprinting was applied by the society, and when so overprinted this sheet had no franking power.

Stamps of 1939-41 Overprinted in Carmine or Blue

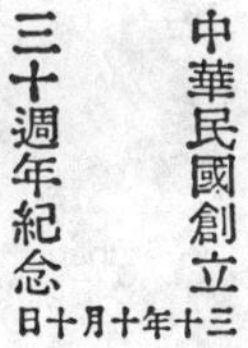

1941, Oct. 10 *Perf. 12½, 14, 13*

472	A40	1c dull orange	15	*35*
473	A57	2c olive grn (C)	15	*35*
474	A39	4c pale violet (C)	15	*35*
475	A57	8c ol grn (#369) (C)	15	*35*
476	A57	10c green (#354) (C)	15	*35*
477	A57	16c ol gray (#357) (C)	15	*35*
478	A45	21c olive brn (C)	15	*35*
479	A46	28c olive (C)	20	*1.10*
480	A57	30c scarlet	45	*2.25*
481	A57	$1 hn & dk brn (#359)	2.25	2.25
		Nos. 472-481 (10)	3.95	*8.05*

Chinese Republic, 30th anniversary.

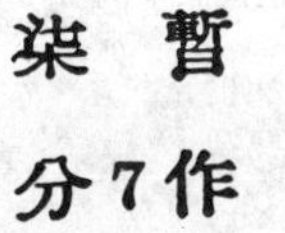

Kiangsi e7

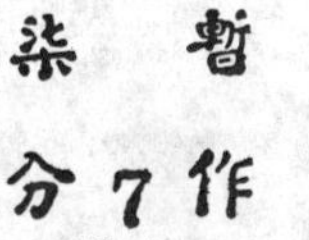

Eastern Szechwan f7

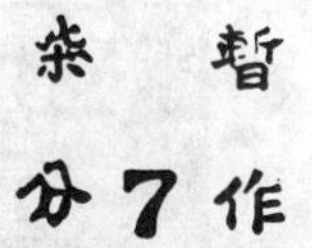

Chekiang — g7

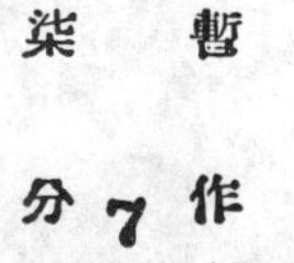

Fukien — h7

1941 Unwmk. *Perf. 12½, 14*

482	A57	7c on 8c (#353) (g7, h7)	50	50
483	A57	7c on 8c (#369) (f7)	40	50
484	A57	7c on 8c (#383) (h7)	50	80
		(e7) Kiangsi	60	80
		(g7) Chekiang	60	1.00
r.		Without "star" in uniform button	60.00	

Type of 1932-34 Re-engraved

1941 Unwmk. *Perf. 14*

485	A45	8c deep orange	10.00	50.00

The original stamps are 19½mm wide, the re-engraved 21mm.

Eleven other values of the Martyrs Issue and types A37 and A57 exist re-engraved, but were not issued.

Hunan — c1

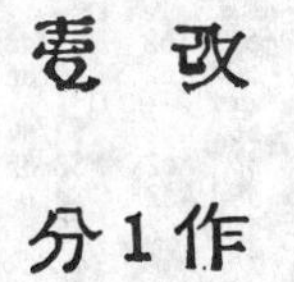

Kiangsi — e1

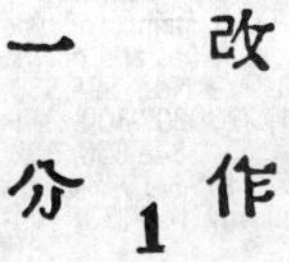

Fukien — h1

Kwangsi — i1

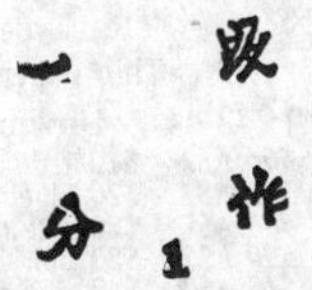

Kwangtung — j1

1942

Red Surcharge

486	A39	1c on ½c blk brn (#312) (c1, i1)	75	50
		(c1) Hunan	1.50	*2.50*
487	A39	1c on ½c ol blk (#421) (e1)	40	1.50
		(c1) Hunan	50	*1.00*
		(i1) Kwangsi	75	*2.25*
		(h1) Fukien	2.50	*6.00*
488	A59	1c on ½c sepia (#449) (j1)	60	*1.50*
		(c1) Hunan	1.00	*2.25*

Hunan c40 · Eastern Szechwan f40 · Western Szechwan k40 · Yunnan l40

Red Surcharge

489	A57	40c on 50c dk bl (#386) (f40)	60	75
		(k40) Western Szechwan	3.50	*4.50*
		(l40) Yunnan	3.00	*3.00*
	r.	Inverted surcharge (Yunnan)	85.00	

Wmk. 261

490	A40	40c on 50c grn (#420) (c40)	1.50	*4.50*

Unwmk.

491	A59	40c on 50c dk bl (#459) (c40)	1.25	*5.50*

Dr. Sun Yat-sen — A62

Central Trust Printing

Perf. 10½-11, 11½-12½, 13 and Compounds

1942-43 **Typo.**

Without Gum

492	A62	10c dp green ('43)	15	25
493	A62	16c dull ol brn	7.75	*25.00*
	a.	Perf 10½	175.00	125.00
494	A62	20c dk ol grn ('43)	15	15
	a.	Perf. 11	5.00	5.00
495	A62	25c brown vio	15	15
496	A62	30c dull ver	15	15
	a.	Perf. 11	2.25	2.25
497	A62	40c dk red brn ('43)	16	25
	a.	Perf. 11x13	70.00	
	b.	Perf. 11	10.00	10.00
498	A62	50c sage green	15	15
	a.	Perf. 11	1.75	2.00
499	A62	$1 rose lake	22	15
	a.	Perf. 11	30.00	30.00
500	A62	$1 dull grn ('43)	22	15
501	A62	$1.50 dp blue ('43)	22	15
	a.	Perf. 11	200.00	200.00
502	A62	$2 dk blue grn	22	15
503	A62	$3 dk yellow ('43)	22	15
504	A62	$4 red brown	22	15
505	A62	$5 cerise ('43)	22	15
		Nos. 492-505 (14)	10.20	27.15

Many shades and part-perforate varieties exist.

See Nos. 550 to 563 for other stamps of type A62 with secret mark and new values and colors. For surcharges and overprints see Nos. 525-530, 671, 683, 692-694, 696, 771, 773, 807-809, 811-820, 824-827, 832, 834-834A, 836, 848-850, 852-854, 857, 860-863, 876, 879, M5-M10, Taiwan 55, 86, 99, Kwangsi 6-7, Sinkiang 162-173, 194-195.

Type of 1938

Thin Paper Without Gum

1942-44 **Unwmk.** **Engr.** ***Imperf.***

506	A57	$10 red brown	28	15
507	A57	$20 blue grn	28	22
508	A57	$20 rose red ('44)	3.75	1.10
509	A57	$30 dull vio ('43)	28	30
510	A57	$40 rose red ('43)	28	25
511	A57	$50 blue	65	40
512	A57	$100 org brn ('43)	1.40	1.00

Rouletted

513	A57	$5 lilac gray ('44)	3.75	4.00
	a.	Rouletted x perf. 12½	20.00	22.50
514	A57	$10 red brown	2.25	2.00
515	A57	$50 blue	2.25	2.00
	a.	Rouletted x imperf.		
		Nos. 506-515 (10)	15.17	11.42

1942-45 ***Perf. 12½ to 15***

516	A57	$4 dp blue ('43)	18	18
517	A57	$5 lilac gray ('43)	28	22
518	A57	$10 red brown	28	22
519	A57	$20 blue grn ('43)	22	22
520	A57	$20 rose red ('45)	40.00	50.00
521	A57	$30 dull vio ('43)	35	25
522	A57	$40 rose ('43)	40	32
523	A57	$50 blue	40	35
524	A57	$100 org brn ('45)	40.00	50.00
		Nos. 516-524 (9)	82.11	101.76

See surcharge note following No. 363.

No. 493 Overprinted in Black or Red

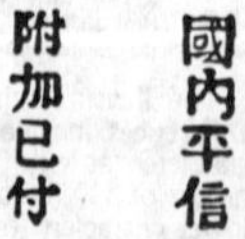

1942

525	A62	(i) 16c (Bk)	35.00	70.00
		(c) Hunan	275.00	
		(k) Western Szechwan	65.00	75.00
		(m) Honan	500.00	525.00
	r.	Perf. 10½ (Kwangsi)	325.00	
		(n) Shensi	100.00	125.00
	s.	Inverted ovpt. (Shensi)	150.00	
526	A62	(d) 16c (R)	8.00	15.00
		(bx) Anhwei	300.00	300.00
		(e) Kiangsi	18.00	35.00
		(f) Eastern Szechwan	35.00	40.00
	r.	Perf. 10½ (E. Szechwan)	400.00	
		(h) Fukien	110.00	100.00
		(j) Kwangtung	350.00	350.00
		(l) Yunnan	18.00	30.00
	s.	Horiz. pair, imperf. btwn (Yunnan)	200.00	
		(o) Kweichow	85.00	50.00
		(p) Hupeh, perf. 10½	600.00	500.00
	t.	Perf. 13 (Hupeh)	1,200.	900.00

This overprint means "Domestic Ordinary Letter Surcharge Paid." It was applied in various sizes and types by 14 districts, 9 using red ink, 5 using black. (The Anhwei overprint comes in two types.) These overprinted stamps were briefly sold for $1.16 before the government ordered their sale suspended. The vertical bars and 50c surcharge of Nos. 527-528 were then applied.

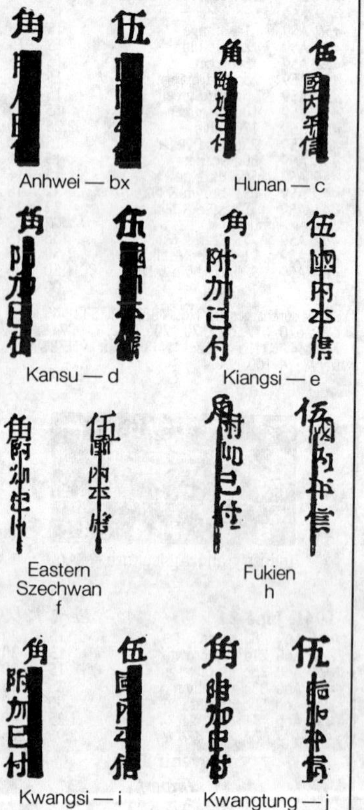

Anhwei — bx · Hunan — c · Kansu — d · Kiangsi — e · Eastern Szechwan f · Fukien h · Kwangsi — i · Kwangtung — j

Western Szechwan — k · Yunnan — l · Honan — m · Shensi — n · Kweichow — o · Hupeh — p

Nos. 525-526 Surcharged "50 cents" and 2 Vertical Bars in Black or Red

1942 **Unwmk.**

527	A62	50c on 16c (Bk) (c,f)	1.75	2.00
		(i) Kwangsi	3.00	4.00
		(k) Western Szechwan	5.00	5.00
	r.	Inverted surch. (W. Szech.)	90.00	
	s.	"k" surcharge on #493	90.00	
		(m) Honan	4.50	5.50
		(n) Shensi	2.50	3.00
528	A62	50c on 16c (R) (d)	2.50	2.50
		(bx) Anhwei	15.00	30.00
		(e) Kiangsi	4.00	5.00
		(h) Fukien	4.50	5.00
		(j) Kwangtung	4.50	3.00
		(l) Yunnan	4.50	6.00
		(o) Kweichow	2.50	4.50
	r.	Inverted surch. (Kweichow)	75.00	
		(p) Hupeh	2.50	3.50
	s.	"p" surch. on #526(f)	75.00	75.00

Many varieties of Nos. 527-528 exist, including narrow or wide spacing between the two top characters, or between the vertical bars, or both.

Surcharges on stamps perf. 10½ (basic No. 493a) usually sell at much higher prices.

General Issue · Hunan — c50 · Eastern Szechwan — f50 · Chekiang — g50 · Kwangsi — i50 · Kwangtung — j50 · Western Szechwan — k50 · Honan — m50 · Shensi — n50 · Kweichow — o50

No. 493 Surcharged in Black, Red or Carmine

1943 **Unwmk.**

529	A62	50c on 16c (Bk) (m50)	3.00	3.75
		(n50) Shensi	5.50	4.00
	r.	Perf. 11x13 (Shensi)	65.00	
530	A62	50c on 16c (C)	75	1.00
		(c50) Hunan	2.00	4.00
	r.	Inverted surch. (Hunan)	35.00	
		(f50) Eastern Szechwan	1.50	2.00
		(g50) Chekiang	12.00	15.00
		(i50) Kwangsi	4.50	5.50
		(j50) Kwangtung	3.50	5.50
		(k50) Western Szechwan	3.50	4.50
		(m50) Honan	6.00	9.00
		(o50) Kweichow	6.00	9.50
	s.	"05" instead of "50" (Kweichow)	250.00	

Many varieties of Nos. 529-530 exist, such as narrow or wide spacing horizontally or vertically between the overprinted Chinese characters.

Surcharges on No. 493a (perf. 10½) usually sell at much higher pricess.

The General Issue type, No. 530, was distributed to all head offices, which in turn supplied the post offices under their direction. It is surcharged in carmine; the other stamps listed under No. 530 are surcharged in red or carmine.

Hunan — c20 · Kansu — d20 · Kiangsi e20 · Eastern Szechwan f20 · Fukien h20 · Kwangsi i20 · Kwangtung j20 · Western Szechwan k20 · Yunnan — l20 · Honan — m20 · Shensi n20 · Kweichow o20 · Hupeh — p20

1943 **Wmk. 261, Unwmkd.**

On No. 318

531	A45	20c on 13c (k20)	60	*1.00*
		(d20) Kansu	1.00	*2.00*
		(n20) Shensi	80	*1.50*
532	A45	20c on 13c (i20;R)	60	1.00
		(c20) Hunan	500.00	
		(e20) Kiangsi	125.00	
		(j20) Kwangtung	37.50	40.00

(p20) Hupeh 75 1.00

On No. 411

533 A45 20c on 13c (n20) 45 1.50
(d20) Kansu 1.00 2.50
(k20) Western Szechwan 80 1.75
(l20) Yunnan 4.00 1.25
(m20) Honan 200.00
534 A45 20c on 13c (f20, p20;R) 70 65
(c20) Hunan 1.25 75
(e20) Kiangsi 1.00 90
(h20) Fukien 2.50 4.50
(i20) Kwangsi 75 1.00
(j20) Kwangtung 8.00 9.00
(o20) Kweichow 1.00 1.50

On No. 430

535 A45 20c on 13c (l20) 70 1.50
(d20) Kansu 1.00 1.10
(k20) Western Szechwan 14.00 22.50
(m20) Honan 1.25 3.00
(n20) Shensi 1.00 2.00
536 A45 20c on 13c (f20;i20;R) 60 1.25
(c20) Hunan 5.00 5.50
(e20) Kiangsi 2.00 2.00
(j20) Kwangtung 1.00 1.00
(o20) Kweichow 1.00 4.00
(p20) Hupeh 1.00 1.50

On No. 357

537 A57 20c on 16c (k20, n20) 80 1.50
(c20) Hunan 1.25 2.00
(d20) Kansu 1.00 1.00
(m20) Honan 2.00 1.00
538 A57 20c on 16c (e20, i20, o20;R) 1.00 1.50
(c20) Hunan 3.00 5.00
(j20) Kwangtung 15.00 27.50

On No. 413

539 A46 20c on 17c (c20;R) 80 1.50
(i20) Kwangsi 1.00 1.00
(j20) Kwangtung 18.00 20.00

On No. 432

540 A46 20c on 17c (k20) 1.00 2.00
(d20) Kansu 2.00 2.25
(m20) Honan 15.00 20.00
541 A46 20c on 17c (e20;R) 1.00 2.00
(j20) Kwangtung 1.40 4.00
(o20) Kweichow 1.25 2.50

On No. 456

542 A59 20c on 17c (m20) 120.00 125.00
543 A59 20c on 17c (c20;R) 12.00 14.00

On No. 415

544 A45 20c on 21c (e20;R) 6.00 7.00

On No. 434

545 A45 20c on 21c (c20, k20) 90 1.50
(d20) Kansu 1.25 2.50
(l20) Yunnan 1.00 1.50
(m20) Honan 1.25 3.00
546 A45 20c on 21c (f20;R) 50 1.50
(e20) Kiangsi 80 2.00
(h20) Fukien 1.00 1.75
(i20) Kwangsi 1.25 1.50
(j20) Kwangtung 1.25 2.50
(o20) Kweichow 1.25 1.00
(p20) Hupeh 80 2.00

On No. 417

547 A46 20c on 28c (e20;R) 300.00 350.00

On No. 436

548 A46 20c on 28c (l20) 1.00 2.50
(d20) Kansu 9.00 11.00
(k20) Western Szechwan 20.00 22.50
(m20) Honan 16.00 20.00
549 A46 20c on 28c (i20, e20;R) 70 1.75
(c20) Hunan 1.00 1.75
(h20) Fukien 1.00 2.00
(j20) Kwangtung 1.00 2.50
(o20) Kweichow 2.25 2.00

Many varieties of Nos. 531-549 exist, such as narrow or wide spacing between the overprinted Chinese characters, and "20" higher or lower than illustrated.

Type of 1942-43
Pacheng Printing

1944-46 Unwmk. *Perf. 12*
Without Gum

550 A62 30c chocolate 26 8.00
551 A62 $1 green 1.75 1.50
552 A62 $2 dk vio brn 15 15
a. Imperf., pair 10.00 10.00
553 A62 $2 dk bl grn 15 15
a. Perf. 10½ 27.50 22.50
554 A62 $2 deep blue 90 60
555 A62 $3 lt yellow 22 15
556 A62 $4 violet brn 15 15
a. Imperf., pair 50.00
557 A62 $5 car ('46) 15 15
a. Perf. 10½ 37.50 32.50
558 A62 $6 gray vio ('45) 15 15
559 A62 $10 red brn ('45) 15 15
a. Imperf., pair 50.00
560 A62 $20 dp ultra ('46) 15 15
561 A62 $50 dk green ('46) 90 15
562 A62 $70 lilac ('46) 18 15
563 A62 $100 lt brown ('46) 15 15
Set value 5.00 10.80

In the Pacheng printing of the Central Trust type stamps, the secret mark "C" has been added below the lower left foliate ornament beneath the sun emblem. On the $3, it is below the right ornament. New values also include a "P" at right of sun emblem on the $6 and $10, and at right of necktie on the $20. Some values of Pacheng printing exist on paper with elephant watermark in sheet.

See surcharge note following No. 505.

Dr. Sun Yat-sen
A63

Allegory of Savings
A64

1944-46 Unwmk. Typo. *Perf. 12½*
Without Gum

565 A63 40c brown red 20 20
566 A63 $2 gray brown 20 20
567 A63 $3 red 20 20
a. $3 orange red 1.75 1.75
568 A63 $3 lt red brown ('45) 30 30
569 A63 $6 pale lilac gray ('45) 20 20
570 A63 $10 dull lake ('45) 20 20
571 A63 $20 rose ('45) 20 20
a. Perf. 15½ 125.00 125.00
572 A63 $50 lt brown ('46) 35 35
573 A63 $70 rose violet ('46) 35 35
Nos. 565-573 (9) 2.20 2.20

For surcharges see Nos. 772, 774, 828, 833, 835, 836A, 839, 842, 851, 864, 868, 873-875, 877, 880. Taiwan 81, 98, Sinkiang 200-201.

1944-45 Engr. *Perf. 13*
Without Gum

574 A64 $40 indigo ('45) 15 15
575 A64 $50 yellow grn ('45) 15 15
576 A64 $100 yellow brn 15 15
577 A64 $200 dk green ('45) 15 15
Nos. 574-577 (4) 60 60

All four values were printed on thick paper; the first three were also printed on thin paper.

For surcharges see Szechwan Nos. F1, F3.

Dr. Sun Yat-sen
A65 A66

1944, Dec. 25 Litho.
Without Gum

578 A65 $2 deep green 25 25
579 A65 $5 fawn 25 50
580 A65 $6 dull rose vio 50 75
581 A65 $10 violet blue 1.00 1.25
582 A65 $20 carmine 2.00 2.25
Nos. 578-582 (5) 4.00 5.00

50th anniversary of the Kuomintang.

1945, Mar. 12
Without Gum

583 A66 $2 gray green 15 16
584 A66 $5 red brown 30 24
585 A66 $6 dk vio blue 38 30
586 A66 $10 lt blue 60 50
587 A66 $20 rose 80 65
588 A66 $30 buff 1.25 1.00
Nos. 583-588 (6) 3.48 2.85

Death of Dr. Sun Yat-sen, 20th anniv.

Dr. Sun Yat-sen — A67

1945-46 Without Gum *Perf. 12½*

589 A67 $2 green 20 30
590 A67 $5 dull green 20 30
591 A67 $10 dk blue 20 30
a. Imperf., pair 60.00
592 A67 $20 carmine ('46) 20 30
a. Imperf., pair 60.00
Nos. 589-592 (4) 80 1.20

For surcharges see Nos. 695, 697, 837, 855, Taiwan 58, 82, 87-88.

Statue of Liberty, Map of China, Flags of Great Britain, China and United States, and Chiang Kai-shek
A68

1945, July 7 Unwmk. Engr. *Perf. 12*
Flags in Dark Blue and Red

593 A68 $1 dp blue 15 15
594 A68 $2 dull green 28 35
595 A68 $5 olive gray 28 35
596 A68 $6 brown 65 80
597 A68 $10 rose lilac 2.75 4.50
598 A68 $20 car rose 1.90 5.50
Nos. 593-598 (6) 6.01 11.65

Signing of a Treaty in 1943 between Great Britain, the US and China.

Pres. Lin Sen (1864-1943)
A69

Pres. Chiang Kai-shek
A70

1945, Aug. Unwmk. *Perf. 12*

599 A69 $1 dp ultra & blk 15 15
600 A69 $2 myrtle grn & blk 15 15
601 A69 $5 red & blk 15 15
602 A69 $6 purple & blk 90 70
603 A69 $10 choc & blk 1.40 2.00
604 A69 $20 olive grn & blk 2.00 2.50
Nos. 599-604 (6) 4.75 5.65

1945, Oct. 10
Flag in Rose Red and Violet Blue

605 A70 $2 green 45 70
606 A70 $4 dk blue 45 70
607 A70 $5 olive gray 45 70
608 A70 $6 bister brown 1.10 1.65
609 A70 $10 gray 1.50 2.00
610 A70 $20 red violet 2.50 3.75
Nos. 605-610 (6) 6.45 9.50

Inauguration of Chiang Kai-shek as president, Oct. 10, 1943.

President Chiang Kai-shek — A71

1945, Oct. 10 Typo. *Perf. 13*
Without Gum
Flag in Carmine and Blue

611 A71 $20 green & blue 24 16
612 A71 $50 bister brn & bl 42 28
613 A71 $100 blue 40 30
614 A71 $300 rose red & blue 40 30
Nos. 611-614 (4) 1.46 1.04

Victory of the Allied Nations over Japan.

C. N. C. Surcharges

The green surcharges on Nos. 615 to 621, and the surcharges on Nos. 647 to 721, and 768 to 774 represent Chinese National Currency and were applied at Shanghai.

Stamps of 1938-41 Surcharged in Black with Chinese Characters and New Value in Checkered Rectangle at Bottom, Resurcharged in Green

壹 國
角 幣

1945 *Perf. 12, 12½*

615 A57 10c on $20 on 3c (#350) 15 15
616 A46 15c on $30 on 2c (#423) 15 15
a. Horiz. pair, imperf. between 90.00
b. Vert. pair, imperf. between 85.00
617 A59 25c on $50 on 1c (#450) 15 15
618 A57 50c on $100 on 3c (#350) 15 15
619 A40 $1 on $200 on 1c (#422) 15 15
a. Horiz. pair, imperf. between 90.00
620 A57 $2 on $400 on 3c (#350) 15 15
621 A59 $5 on $1000 on 1c (#450) 15 15
Set value 30 45

The black (first) surcharges on Nos. 615 to 621 represent Nanking puppet government currency.

In the green surcharge, the characters at the left express the new value and are either two or four in number.

Types of 1932-34, Re-engraved, and Surcharged in Green with Horizontal Bar and Four or Five Chinese Characters and Overprinted in Black:

北 華

Perf. 14

622 A47 $10 on 20c brown red 3.25 4.50
623 A47 $20 on 40c orange 18.00 20.00
a. Green surcharge inverted 50.00
624 A48 $50 on 30c violet brn 10.00 12.00
Nos. 622-624 (3) 31.25 36.50

These provisional surcharges were applied in Honan in National currency to stamps of the Hwa Pei (North China) government. The black overprint reads: "Hwa Pei."

The two-character "Hwa Pei" overprint was applied to various stamps in 1941-43 by the North China puppet government. See Nos. 8N1-8N53, 8N60-8N84.

Dr. Sun Yat-sen
A72 A73

1945, Dec. Typo. *Perf. 12*
Without Gum

625 A72 $20 dp carmine 15 16
626 A72 $30 dp blue 15 16
627 A72 $40 orange 15 16
628 A72 $50 green 15 16
629 A72 $100 dk brown 15 16
630 A72 $200 brown violet 15 16
Set value 75

For surcharges see Nos. 810, 829, 838, 865, J110-J119, Taiwan 75, Kwangsi F2, Szechwan F2, F4, Yunnan 66-67, 71.

Type of 1931-37
Perf. 12½, 13x12½, 13½

1946 Unwmk.

631 A37 $1 dk violet 18 15
632 A37 $2 olive grn 18 15
633 A37 $20 brt yel grn 20 15
634 A37 $30 chocolate 20 15
635 A37 $50 red orange 25 15
Nos. 631-635 (5) 1.01 75

For surcharges see Nos. 678, 684, 689-690, 768, 843.

1946-47 Engr. *Perf. 14*
Without Gum

636 A73 $20 carmine 65 15
637 A73 $30 dk blue ('47) 15 15
638 A73 $50 purple 15 15
639 A73 $70 red org ('47) 12.50 1.10
640 A73 $100 dk carmine 15 15
641 A73 $200 olive grn ('47) 15 15
642 A73 $500 brt bl grn ('47) 15 15
643 A73 $700 red brown ('47) 15 15
644 A73 $1000 rose lake 30 15
645 A73 $3000 blue 80 20
646 A73 $5000 dp green & ver 85 20
Nos. 636-646 (11) 16.00
Set value 2.00

For surcharges see Nos. 679, 769, 775, 823, 837A, 844-845, 856, 866, 875A, 878, Taiwan 18, 23-28, 54, 76-77, 100, Northeastern Provinces 41-43, Fukien 5-6, Hunan 1, E1, F1, Kwangsi 11, F2, Szechwan F5-F8, Sinkiang 202-204, People's Republic of China 3L53, 3L67-3L68, 6L28.

Stamps of 1932-41 Surcharged in Black

Perf. 12½, 13, 13x12, 14

Wmk. 261

647	A45	$20 on 8c (#409)	15	60
648	A39	$30 on ½c (#402)	850.00	
649	A45	$50 on 21c (#415)	15	15
650	A45	$70 on 13c (#411)	15	20
651	A46	$100 on 28c (#417)	15	60

Unwmk.

652	A39	$3 on 2½c (#424)	2.50	3.50
653	A48	$10 on 15c (#431)	20	20
654	A45	$20 on 8c (#428)	20	20
655	A47	$20 on 20c (#433)	30	30
656	A39	$30 on ½c (#421)	20	20
657	A45	$50 on 21c (#434)	30	40
657A	A45	$70 on 13c (#318)	85.00	60.00
658	A45	$70 on 13c (#430)	30	40
659	A46	$100 on 28c (#436)	30	30

Stamps and Types of 1931-1946 Surcharged in Black or Carmine

Perf. 12½, 13, 14

1946-47 Wmk. 261

660	A57	$50 on 5c green (#392)	30	50
661	A57	$50 on 5c ol grn (#393)	20.00	16.00
662	A48	$50 on 5c dl red org (#408)	15	1.00
663	A40	$100 on 1c org (#403)	15	1.00

Perf. 12, 12½, 12½x13, 13, 14

1946-47 Unwmk.

664	A57	$20 on 3c (#350)	15	30
665	A45	$20 on 8c (#428)	15	20
666	A57	$50 on 3c (#350)	15	15
667	A57	$50 on 5c (#352)	15	20
668	A57	$50 on 5c (#382)	75	1.50
669	A48	$50 on 5c (#427)	15	15
670	A59	$50 on 5c (#452)	20	20
671	A62	$50 on $1 (#500)	15	15
672	A40	$100 on 1c (#422)	15	15
a.		Without secret mark (#422a)	60.00	60.00
673	A57	$100 on 3c (#350)	15	15
674	A57	$100 on 8c (#353)	9.50	9.50
675	A57	$100 on 8c (#369)	50	30
676	A57	$100 on 8c (#383)	30	30
a.		Without "star" in uniform button (No. 383a)	17.50	15.00
677	A59	$100 on 8c (#454)	15	15
678	A37	$100 on $1 (#631)	20	20
679	A73	$100 on $20 (#636)	30	30
680	A57	$200 on 10c (#354)	25	25
681	A57	$200 on 10c (#384)	25	60
682	A37	$200 on $4 dl bl	15	15
a.		Double surcharge	15.00	
683	A62	$250 on $1.50 (#501)	20	20
a.		Perf. 11	350.00	350.00
684	A37	$250 on $2 (#632)	20	20
685	A37	$250 on $5 car	15	15
686	A57	$300 on 10c (#354)	15	15
687	A59	$300 on 10c (#455)	15	15
688	A57	$500 on 3c (#350)	15	15
689	A37	$500 on $20 (#633)	15	15
690	A37	$800 on $30 (#634)	15	15
691	A37	$1000 on 2c (#297)	50	20
692	A62	$1000 on $2 (#552)	15	15
a.		Imperf., pair	15.00	15.00
693	A62	$1000 on $2 (#553)	15	25
694	A62	$1000 on $2 (#554)	20	20
695	A67	$1000 on $2 (#589)	15	15
696	A62	$2000 on $5 (#557)	15	15
697	A67	$2000 on $5 dl grn (C) (#590)	15	15
		Nos. 664-697 (34)	16.50	17.45

Nos. 682 and 685 were not issued without surcharge. No. 682 is perf. 13x13½; No. 685, perf. 12x12½.

The characters at the left express the new value and vary in number.

Stamps of 1938-41 Surcharged in Black

Perf. 12, 12½, 13, 14

1946 Wmk. 261

698	A45	$20 on 8c (#409)	90.00	90.00
699	A57	$50 on 5c (#392)	15	30
700	A57	$50 on 5c (#393)	15	1.00

1946-48 Unwmk.

700A	A57	$20 on 5c (#381)	500.00	
701	A57	$20 on 8c (#353)	15	15
702	A57	$20 on 8c (#369)	30	30
703	A57	$20 on 8c (#383)	15	15
a.		Without "star" in uniform button (No. 383a)	4.00	4.00
b.		Inverted surcharge	17.50	
c.		Dbl. surch., one on back	30.00	30.00
d.		Double surcharge	30.00	
704	A45	$20 on 8c (#428)	15	15
a.		Double surcharge	20.00	
705	A59	$20 on 8c (#453)	15	15
706	A59	$20 on 8c (#454)	15	15
a.		Inverted surcharge	12.00	
b.		Double surcharge	12.00	
707	A57	$50 on 5c (#351)	6.00	5.50
708	A57	$50 on 5c (#352)	15	15
a.		Inverted surcharge	25.00	
709	A57	$50 on 5c (#381)	60	60
710	A57	$50 on 5c (#382)	15	25
711	A48	$50 on 5c (#427)	15	15
a.		Inverted surcharge	25.00	
712	A59	$50 on 5c (#452)	15	15
a.		Double surcharge	15.00	

Stamps of 1939-41 Surcharged in Blue or Red

1946 Wmk. 261 *Perf. 12½*

713	A40	$10 on 1c org (#403)	15	15
a.		Inverted surcharge	35.00	
714	A48	$20 on 3c dp yel brn (#406)	400.00	375.00

1946 Unwmk. *Perf. 12, 12½, 13*

715	A40	$10 on 1c org (#422)	15	15
a.		Without secret mark (#422a)	8.00	10.00
b.		Inverted surcharge	7.00	9.00
716	A59	$10 on 1c org (#450)	15	15
a.		Double surcharge	25.00	
717	A57	$20 on 2c ol grn (R) (#368)	15	15
718	A59	$20 on 2c brt ultra (R) (#451)	15	15
a.		Inverted surcharge	17.50	
b.		Double surcharge	15.00	
719	A57	$20 on 3c dl cl (#350)	15	15
a.		Double surcharge	20.00	
720	A48	$20 on 3c dp yel brn (#425)	15	15
721	A39	$30 on 4c pale vio (R) (#426)	15	25
a.		Inverted surcharge	8.00	
		Set value	56	83

President Chiang Kai-shek — A74

Perf. 10½-11½

1946, Oct. 31 Engr. Unwmk.

722	A74	$20 carmine	32	40
723	A74	$30 green	32	40
724	A74	$50 vermilion	32	40
725	A74	$100 yellow grn	32	40
726	A74	$200 yellow org	32	40
727	A74	$300 magenta	32	40
		Nos. 722-727 (6)	1.92	2.40

60th birthday of Chiang Kai-shek.

Printed by Dah Yeh Printing Co.; the earlier ones are gumless, the later ones gummed.

See Taiwan Nos. 29-34, Northeastern Provinces 30-35.

Printed by Dah Tung Book Co.

Without Gum

Perf. 14

722a	A74	$20 carmine	1.00	1.25
723a	A74	$30 green	1.00	1.25
724a	A74	$50 vermilion	1.00	1.25
725a	A74	$100 yellow green	1.00	1.25
726a	A74	$200 yellow orange	1.00	1.25
727a	A74	$300 magenta	1.00	1.25
		Nos. 722a-727a (6)	6.00	7.50

Assembly House, Nanking — A75

1946, Nov. 15 Litho. *Perf. 14*

Without Gum

728	A75	$20 green	38	25
729	A75	$30 blue	38	25
730	A75	$50 dk brown	38	25
a.		Horiz. pair, imperf. between	50.00	60.00
731	A75	$100 carmine	38	25
		Nos. 728-731 (4)	1.52	1.00

Convening of National Assembly.

For surcharges see Taiwan Nos. 10-13, Northeastern Provinces 26-29.

Entrance to Dr. Sun Yat-sen Mausoleum — A76

Dr. Sun Yat-sen — A77

1947, May 5 Engr.

732	A76	$100 dp green	15	20
733	A76	$200 deep blue	15	20
734	A76	$250 carmine	15	20
735	A76	$350 lt brown	15	20
736	A76	$400 dp claret	15	20
		Nos. 732-736 (5)	75	1.00

First anniversary of return of Chinese National Government to Nanking.

See Taiwan Nos. 35-39, Northeastern Provinces 36-40.

1947 *Perf. 12½, 11½x12½*

737	A77	$500 olive grn	15	15
738	A77	$1000 green & car	15	15
739	A77	$2000 dp blue & red brn	15	15
740	A77	$5000 org red & blk	15	15
		Nos. 737-740 (4)	60	60

For surcharge see Szechwan No. 50.

Confucius A78

Confucius' Lecturing School A79

Tomb of Confucius — A80

Temple of Confucius — A81

1947, Aug. 27 Litho. *Perf. 14*

Without Gum

741	A78	$500 carmine rose	35	25

Engr.

742	A79	$800 yellow brown	35	25
743	A80	$1250 blue green	35	25
744	A81	$1800 blue	35	25
		Nos. 741-744 (4)	1.40	1.00

Sun Yat-sen and Plum Blossoms A82

Chinese Flag and Map of Taiwan A83

1947-48 Engr. *Perf. 14*

Without Gum

745	A82	$150 dk blue	15	18
746	A82	$250 dp lilac	20	15
747	A82	$500 blue grn	15	15
748	A82	$1000 red	15	15
749	A82	$2000 vermilion	16	15
750	A82	$3000 blue	15	15
751	A82	$4000 gray ('48)	16	15
752	A82	$5000 dk brown	15	15
753	A82	$6000 rose lilac ('48)	16	15
754	A82	$7000 lt red brn ('48)	16	15
755	A82	$10,000 dp blue & car	50	15
756	A82	$20,000 car & yel grn	22	15
757	A82	$50,000 grn & dk bl	50	15
758	A82	$100,000 dl yel & ol grn ('48)	75	15
759	A82	$200,000 vio brn & dp bl ('48)	1.00	30
760	A82	$300,000 sep & org brn ('48)	1.00	30
761	A82	$500,000 dk Prus grn & sep ('48)	1.25	30
		Nos. 745-761 (17)	6.81	
		Set value		1.75

See Nos. 788-799. For similar type see Formosa A1. For surcharges see Nos. 770, 804-806, 821-822, 840-841, 858-859, 869, 871, 880A-880B, 885A-885E, 1025-1036, Taiwan 56-57, 59, 89, Fukien 1-4, 7-12, 19-23, Hunan 2-5, C1, Kiangsi 1-3, C1, E1, F1-F2, Kwangsi 8-10, 12-17, Shensi 1-2, C1, E1, Szechwan 24-49, Yunnan 61-62, 69, 205-207, People's Republic of China 3L69-3L70, 3L76, 4L63-4L64, 6L22, 6L27, 6L29, 6L32.

1947, Oct. 25

With Gum

762	A83	$500 carmine	25	22
763	A83	$1250 deep green	25	22

Restoration of Taiwan to China, 2nd anniv.

Mobile Post Office — A84

Street-Corner Branch Post Office — A85

1947, Nov. 5

764	A84	$500 carmine	22	15
765	A85	$1000 lilac	22	15
766	A85	$1250 green	22	15
767	A84	$1800 deep blue	22	15
		Nos. 764-767 (4)	88	
		Set value		50

Stamps and Type of 1943-47 Surcharged in Black or Green

1947-48 Unwmk. *Perf. 12½, 13, 14*

768	A37	$500 on $20 brt yel grn (#633)	15	15
769	A73	$1250 on $70 red org (#639)	15	15
770	A82	$1800 on $350 yel org	15	15
771	A62	$2000 on $3 dk yel ('48) (#503)	15	15
772	A63	$2000 on $3 red (#567)	15	15
a.		On #567a	3.00	2.00
773	A62	$3000 on $3 lt yel ('48) (#555)	15	15
774	A63	$3000 on $3 lt red brn (G) ('48) (#568)	15	15
		Set value	35	60

The characters at the left express the new value and vary in number.

No. 640 Surcharged

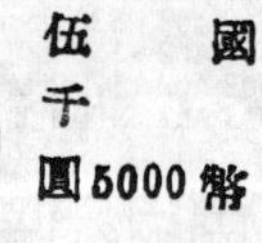

1948, Aug. *Perf. 14*

775	A73	$5000 on $100 dk car	3.50	25.00

No. 775 received its surcharge in Kwangsi for use in that province.

Map of China and Mail-carrying Vehicles — A86

Rural Mail Delivery — A87

Early and Modern Mail Transportation A88

1947, Dec. 16 **Engr.** ***Perf. 12***

776 A86 $100 violet	15	15
777 A87 $200 brt green	15	15
778 A87 $300 red brown	15	15
779 A88 $400 scarlet	15	15
780 A88 $500 brt vio blue	15	15
Nos. 776-780 (5)	75	
Set value		65

Chinese Postal Administration, 50th anniv.

National Assembly Building and New Constitution A89

1947, Dec. 25 ***Perf. 14***

Without Gum

781 A89 $2000 brt red	20	16
782 A89 $3000 blue	20	16
783 A89 $5000 deep green	20	16
Nos. 781-783 (3)	60	48

1st anniv. of the adoption of China's new constitution, Dec. 25, 1946.

Chinese Stamps of 1947 and 1912 — A90

Perf. 14, Imperf.

1948, Mar. 20 **Litho.**

Without Gum

784 A90 $5000 dk car rose	30	1.00
a. Vert. pair, imperf. btwn	30.00	
785 A90 $5000 dk green	30	1.00
a. Vert. pair, imperf. btwn	20.00	

Stamp exhibitions at Nanking, Mar. 20 (No. 784), and at Shanghai, May 19 (No. 785).

Sun Yat-sen Memorial Hall, Taipei — A91

1948, Apr. 28 **Engr.** ***Perf. 14***

786 A91 $5000 violet	15	15
787 A91 $10000 red	15	15
Set value	20	

Restoration of Formosa to China, 3rd anniv.

Sun Yat-sen Type of 1947-48

1948

Without Gum

788 A82 $20000 rose pink	30	15
789 A82 $30000 chocolate	20	15
790 A82 $40000 green	20	15
791 A82 $50000 dp blue	20	15
792 A82 $100000 dull grn	20	15
793 A82 $200000 brn vio	50	15
794 A82 $300000 yel grn	75	15
795 A82 $500000 lil rose	75	15
796 A82 $1000000 claret	50	15
797 A82 $2000000 vermilion	1.00	15
798 A82 $3000000 ol bis	1.75	22
799 A82 $5000000 ultra	3.00	45
Nos. 788-799 (12)	9.35	
Set value		1.40

Zeros for "cents" omitted.

For surcharges see Nos. 841, 871, 880A-880B, 885A-885E, 1025-1028, 1031-1036.

Early Ship and Modern Hai Tien — A92

Passenger Ship Kiang Ya — A93

1948, Aug. 16

Without Gum

800 A92 $20000 blue	15	15
801 A92 $30000 rose lilac	15	15
802 A93 $40000 yel brown	15	15
803 A93 $60000 vermilion	15	15
Set value	20	

75th anniversary of the China Merchants' Steam Navigation Company.

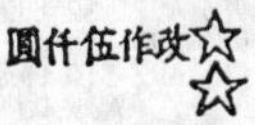

Type of 1947-48 Surcharged in Black

1948 **Unwmk.** ***Perf. 14***

804 A82 $4000 on $100 car	15	60
805 A82 $5000 on $100 car	15	15
806 A82 $8000 on $700 red brn	15	15
Set value	18	70

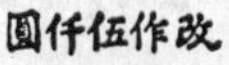

Stamps of 1942-46 Surcharged in Black or Red

1948 ***Perf. 12½, 13***

807 A62 $5000 on $1 (#500)	16	16
808 A62 $5000 on $1 (#551)	8.50	11.00
809 A62 $5000 on $2 (#502)	16	20
810 A72 $10000 on $20 (#625)	16	20
811 A62 $20000 on 10c (#492)	16	20
812 A62 $20000 on 50c (#498;R)	16	20
813 A62 $30000 on 30c (#496)	16	20
a. Perf. 10½	15.00	15.00
Nos. 807-813 (7)	9.46	12.16

Nos. 492, 556 and 558 Surcharged in Black or Carmine

1948

814 A62 $15,000 on 10c dp grn	15	15
815 A62 $15,000 on $4 vio brn	15	15
816 A62 $15,000 on $6 gray vio (C)	15	15
Set value	25	35

No. 498, 494 and 504 Surcharged in Black

1948 **Unwmk.** ***Perf. 11½, 13***

817 A62 $15,000 on 50c, perf. 13	15	15
a. Perf. 11½	7.00	
818 A62 $40,000 on 20c dk ol grn	15	15
a. Perf. 11	6.50	5.00
819 A62 $60,000 on $4 red brn	15	15
Set value	25	35

Gold Yuan Surcharges

(Nos. 820-885E)

Stamps of 1942-47 Surcharged in Black, Carmine or Red

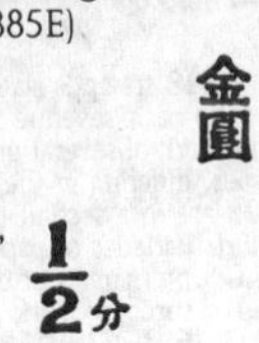

1948 ***Perf. 14, 13, 11***

820 A62 ½c on 30c (#496)	15	15
821 A82 ½c on $500 (Bk) (#747)	15	15
822 A82 ½c on $500 (C) (#747)	15	15
823 A73 1c on $20 (#636)	15	15
824 A62 2c on $1.50 (R) (#501)	15	15
825 A62 3c on $5 (#505)	15	15
826 A62 4c on $1 (#499)	15	15
827 A62 5c on 50c (#498)	15	15
a. Perf. 11	3.75	3.75
Set value	50	50

On No. 820-827, the position of the surcharged denomination and "Gold Yuan" characters varies, the aim being to obliterate the original denomination.

Stamps of 1940-48 Surcharged in Black, Violet, Carmine, Blue or Green

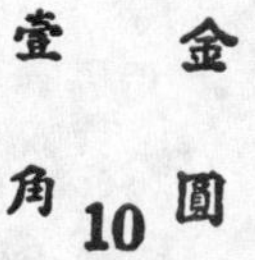

Perf. 12, 12½, 13, 14, 12½x13

1948-49

828 A63 5c on $20 (#571)	15	15
829 A72 5c on $30 (C) (#626)	15	15
a. Double surcharge	15.00	
830 A57 10c on 2c (#368)	15	15
831 A39 10c on 2½c (#424)	15	15
832 A62 10c on 25c (V) (#495)	15	15
833 A63 10c on 40c (#565)	15	15
834 A62 10c on $1 (#500)	15	15
834A A62 10c on $1 (#551)	125.00	125.00
835 A63 10c on $2 (#566)	15	15
836 A62 10c on $20 (C) (#560)	15	15
836A A63 10c on $20 (#571)	80.00	75.00
837 A67 10c on $20 (#592)	15	15
837A A73 10c on $20 (#636)	60	75
838 A72 10c on $30 (C) (#626)	15	*25*
839 A63 10c on $70 (#573)	15	15
a. Double surcharge	12.00	
840 A82 10c on $7000 (#754)	15	15
841 A82 10c on $20,000 (#788)	15	15
842 A63 20c on $6 (#569)	15	15
843 A37 20c on $30 (#634)	15	15
844 A73 20c on $30 (C) (#637)	15	15
845 A73 20c on $100 (#640)	15	15
a. Inverted surcharge	17.00	
b. Double surcharge	12.50	
846 A39 50c on ½c (#312)	30.00	30.00
847 A39 50c on ½c (#421)	15	15
a. Inverted surcharge	25.00	
848 A62 50c on 20c (#494)	15	15
849 A62 50c on 30c (Bl) (#496)	15	15
850 A62 50c on 40c (V) (#497)	15	15
a. Perf. 11	6.00	6.75
851 A63 50c on 40c (V) (#565)	15	15
852 A62 50c on $4 (#556)	15	15
853 A62 50c on $4 (Bl) (#556)	15	15
854 A62 50c on $20 (C) (#560)	15	15
855 A67 50c on $20 (V) (#592)	15	*20*
856 A73 50c on $20 (#636)	15	15
857 A62 50c on $70 (C) (#562)	15	15
858 A82 50c on $6000 (#753)	15	15
859 A82 50c on $6000 (Bl) (#753)	15	15
860 A62 $1 on 30c (#550)	15	15
a. Perf. 11	10.00	13.00
861 A62 $1 on 40c (#497)	15	15
a. Perf. 11	1.50	1.25
862 A62 $1 on $1 (#499)	15	15
863 A62 $1 on $5 (#557)	15	15
864 A63 $2 on $2 (R) (#566)	15	15
865 A72 $2 on $20 (#625)	15	15
866 A73 $2 on $100 (#640)	15	15
867 A46 $5 on 17c (#432)	15	15
868 A63 $5 on $2 (#566)	15	15
869 A82 $5 on $3000 (C) (#750)	15	15
870 A47 $8 on 20c (#433)	15	15
871 A82 $8 on $30,000 (C) (#789)	15	15
872 A47 $10 on 40c (#438)	15	15
873 A63 $10 on $2 (G) (#566)	15	15
874 A63 $10 on $2 (C) (#566)	15	15
875 A63 $20 on $2 (C) (#566)	15	15
875A A73 $20 on $20 (#636)	1.25	1.45
876 A62 $50 on 30c (#496)	15	15
877 A63 $50 on $2 (Bl) (#566)	15	15
878 A73 $80 on $20 (#636)	15	15
879 A62 $100 on $1 (#551)	15	15
a. Perf. 11	*35.00*	*35.00*
880 A63 $100 on $2 (C) (#566)	15	15
880A A82 $50,000 on $20,000 (#788)	50	30
880B A82 $100,000 on $30,000 (V) (#789)	1.25	60

Wmk. 261

881 A39 10c on 2½c (#405)	15	*50*
882 A39 50c on ½c (#402)	15	*50*
Nos. 828-882 (61)	246.70	242.05

Characters at left express the new value. Style of characters and numerals varies.

Nos. Q7 to Q9 Surcharged in Black or Carmine

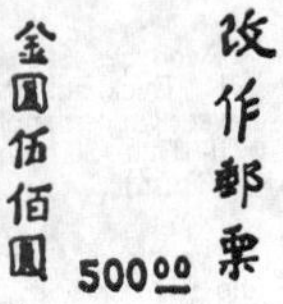

1948 **Unwmk.** ***Perf. 12½***

883 PP2 $200 on $3000 red org	15	15
884 PP2 $500 on $5000 dk bl (C)	15	15
885 PP2 $1000 on $10,000 vio	15	15
Set value	20	20

Nos. 788-791 Surcharged in Gold Yuan in Red (Nos. 885A, 885D-885E) or Black (Nos. 885B-885C) at Foochow

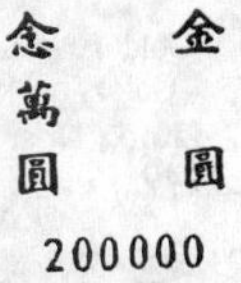

1949, Apr. 30 **Unwmk.** ***Perf. 14***

885A $20,000 on $40,000	9.00	12.00
885B $50,000 on $30,000	9.00	12.00
885C $100,000 on $20,000	9.00	12.00
885D $200,000 on $40,000	9.00	12.00
885E $200,000 on $50,000	9.00	12.00
Nos. 885A-885E (5)	45.00	60.00

Issued in Fukien Postal District.

Dr. Sun Yat-sen — A94

1949 **Unwmk.** **Engr.** ***Perf. 14***

Without Gum

886 A94 $1 orange	15	15
887 A94 $10 green	15	15
888 A94 $20 vio brown	15	15
889 A94 $50 dk Prus grn	15	15
890 A94 $100 org brn	15	15
891 A94 $200 red org	15	15
892 A94 $500 rose lilac	15	15
893 A94 $800 car rose	15	*40*
894 A94 $1000 blue	15	15

Redrawn

Engr.

Perf. 12½

895 A94 $10 green	15	*2.00*
a. Perf. 14	2.25	*3.00*
896 A94 $20 violet brn	15	15
a. Perf. 14	45	*1.25*
Set value	35	*3.25*

Small "T" at left of necktie on #895-896a.

Redrawn

1949 **Litho.** ***Perf. 12½***

Without Gum

897 A94 $50 grnsh gray	15	*1.25*
898 A94 $100 dk org brn	15	*18*
899 A94 $200 orange red	15	*1.25*
900 A94 $500 rose lil	15	15

901	A94	$1000 deep blue	15	24
902	A94	$2000 violet	15	15
903	A94	$5000 light blue	15	15
904	A94	$10,000 sepia	15	15
905	A94	$20,000 apple grn	15	25
906	A94	$50,000 rose pink	15	20
907	A94	$80,000 brn red	40	60
908	A94	$100,000 bl grn	20	20
		Set value	1.35	

Diagonal lines have been added to the background of the redrawn design.

Zeros for "cents" omitted on No. 908.

See Nos. 973-981. For surcharges see Nos. 991-1006, 1057-1060, Fukien 13-17, Szechwan 51, Tsingtau 1-4, Yunnan 63-65, 68, 70, People's Republic of China 4L34-4L44, 4L48-4L60, 5L43-5L50, 5L54-5L59, 5L91-5L95, 6L1-6L16, 6L23-6L26, 6L30-6L31, 7L6-7L8, 7L13-7L16, 8L12-8L13, 8L48-8L51.

Plane, Train and Ship — A95

Two types, 50c on $20:

I- Thick numerals in "20." Vertical stroke in lower right corner of vignette. (Dah Tung Book Co.)

II- Thin "20." No vertical stroke in corner. (Central Trust.)

Two types, $2 on $50, $10 on $30, $100 on $50 and $300 on $50:

III- "Y" in lower right corner of vignette. (Dah Yeh Printing Co.)

IV- No "Y" in corner. (Dah Tung, Central Trust or Chung Ming.)

Two types, $50 on $300 and $1000 on $100:

V- Projection on left frame column below foliate ornament. (Dah Yeh Printing Co.)

VI- No projection. (Dah Tung Book Co.)

Gold Yuan Surcharge in Black or Other Colors on Revenue Stamps Type A95

Litho.; Nos. 923, 933, 935-936 Engr.

1949 ***Perf. 12½, 13, 14***

Without Gum

913	50c on $20 red brn, I	15	15
a.	50c on $20 brown, II	15	15
914	$1 on $15 red org	15	15
915	$2 on $50 dk bl, IV (C)	15	15
a.	Type III	25	25
916	$3 on $50 dk bl (Bl)	15	15
917	$3 on $50 dk bl	15	15
918	$5 on $500 brn	15	15
919	$10 on $30 dk vio, III (Bl)	15	15
a.	Type IV	40	40
b.	Double surcharge, IV		
920	$15 on $20 org brn (Bl)	15	15
921	$25 on $20 org brn (G)	15	15
922	$50 on $50 dk bl (R O)	15	15
923	$50 on $300 grn, VI (C)	15	15
a.	$50 on $300 yel grn, V (C)	15	15
924	$80 on $50 dk bl (Dk Br)	15	15
925	$100 on $50 dk bl, IV	15	15
a.	Type III	2.00	6.75
926	$200 on $50 dk bl	15	15
927	$200 on $500 brn (Bl)	15	15
928	$300 on $50 dk bl, III (C)	15	15
a.	Type IV	60	1.00
929	$300 on $50 dk bl (Br)	55	55
930	$500 on $15 red org (Bl)	22	22
931	$500 on $30 dk vio	22	22
932	$1000 on $50 dk bl (C)	28	28
933	$1000 on $100 ol grn, V	28	28
a.	Type VI	2.50	4.50
934	$1500 on $50 dk bl (Bl)	1.40	1.40
935	$2000 on $300 grn (Bl)	28	28
a.	Horiz. pair, imperf. between		
936	$5000 on $100 ol grn (C)	250.00	
	Set value, #913-935	4.75	4.85

No. 936 was officially authorized, but never issued.

Key pattern of overprinted border inverted and in 2 or 3 detached sections at top and bottom in Blue, Black or Green

1949 **Hankow Prints** **Litho.**

Without Gum

Type A95

937	$50 on $10 (Bk)	5.50	4.50
938	$100 on $10	6.50	6.00
939	$500 on $10 (Bk)	4.00	4.00
940	$1000 on $10	4.00	4.00
941	$5000 on $20	8.75	7.50
942	$10,000 on $20 (Bk)	8.75	6.00
943	$50,000 on $20	10.00	7.00
944	$100,000 on $20 (Bk)	13.00	8.00
945	$500,000 on $20	200.00	100.00
946	$2,000,000 on $20 (G)	500.00	150.00
947	$5,000,000 on $20	900.00	300.00
	Nos. 937-944 (8)	60.50	47.00

The $10 stamp is slate green, the $20 red brown.

The basic revenue stamps of Nos. 915-947 were the work of several printers. There are three main types, differing in the bottom label. Nos. 922 and 925 are in a second type: Nos. 923 and 930 in a third. Varieties of paper, color and overprint exist.

Counterfeits exist of Nos. 945-947.

For surcharges and overprints see Nos. 960-970, C63, E13, F3, J122-J126, Hopeh 1-2, People's Republic of China 5L51-5L53, 6L17-6L21.

Redrawn Coarse Impression

1949 **Litho.**

Without Gum

Size: 18¼x20¾mm

951	A94	$50 green	30	20.00
952	A94	$1000 dp blue	25	25
953	A94	$5000 carmine	25	25
954	A94	$10,000 brown	30	70
955	A94	$20,000 orange	50	50
956	A94	$50,000 blue	1.00	1.00
957	A94	$200,000 violet	1.75	80
958	A94	$500,000 vio brn	1.75	60
		Nos. 951-958 (8)	6.10	24.10

Zeros for "cents" omitted on Nos. 957-958.

See surcharge note following No. 900.

Locomotive and Ship — A96

1949, May 1 **Litho.** ***Perf. 12½***

Without Gum

959	A96	orange	1.50	1.00
a.		Rouletted	8.00	3.50

Nos. 959, C62, E12 and F2 were printed without denomination and sold at the daily rate of the yuan. This was necessitated by the gold yuan inflation.

For surcharges and overprints see Nos. 1130, 1213, Taiwan 97, Fukien 18, Kansu 1, People's Republic of China 24-29, 101-104, 4L31-4L33, 4L45-4L47, 4L61-4L62, 7L9-7L12, 8L52-8L54.

Revenue Stamps Overprinted in Black

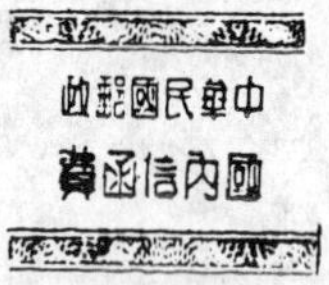

1949, May ***Perf. 12½, 13, 14***

Without Gum

960	A95	$30 dark violet	65.00	45.00

Engr.

961	A95	$200 violet brown	8.00	5.00
962	A95	$500 dark green	11.00	6.00
		Nos. 960-962 (3)	84.00	56.00

A similar overprint appears on #C63, E13, F3, differing in 2nd and 3rd characters of bottom row.

Silver Yuan Surcharge in Black o Other Colors

1949 **Litho.**

963	A95	1c on $5000 brn (G)	3.75	2.00
964	A95	4c on $100 ol grn (Bl)	1.50	80
965	A95	4c on $3000 org)	1.50	50
966	A95	10c on $50 dk bl (RV)	1.50	60
967	A95	10c on $1000 car	3.00	80
a.		Inverted surcharge	55.00	
968	A95	20c on $1000 red (V)	3.00	1.00
b.		Inverted surcharge	24.00	
968A	A95	50c on $30 dk vio (C)	20.00	2.00
969	A95	50c on $50 dk bl (C)	3.75	80
970	A95	$1 on $50 dk bl	3.00	2.00
		Nos. 963-970 (9)	41.00	10.50

Nos. 963-965 and 967 are engraved.

Sun Type of 1949 Redrawn Coarse Impression

1949 ***Perf. 12½, 13 or Compound***

973	A94	1c apple green	14.00	1.65
974	A94	2c orange	2.75	1.65
975	A94	4c blue green	15	15
976	A94	10c deep lilac	15	20
977	A94	16c orange red	40	2.00
978	A94	20c blue	25	25
979	A94	50c dk brown	1.25	4.00
980	A94	100c deep blue	150.00	150.00
981	A94	500c scarlet	175.00	175.00
		Nos. 973-981 (9)	343.95	334.90

For surcharges see Nos. 1057-1060.

Flying Geese Over Globe — A97

Pigeons, Globe and Wreath — A98

1949, May **Litho.** ***Perf. 12½***

Without Gum

984	A97	$1 brown org	5.50	5.50
985	A97	$2 blue	22.50	8.00
986	A97	$5 car rose	27.50	10.00
987	A97	$10 blue grn	32.50	22.50
		Nos. 984-987 (4)	88.00	46.00

Five other denominations - 10c, 16c, 50c, $20 and $50 - were also printed at Shanghai, but were not issued.

For surcharges see Nos. 1007-1011, 1042-1045, 1061-1063, People's Republic of China 49-56, 5LQ17-5LQ26, 7L17-7L18, 8L14-8L16.

Engraved and Typographed

1949, Aug. 1 **Without Gum** ***Imperf.***

988	A98	$1 org red & blk	5.00	6.50

75th anniv. of the UPU.

Exists with black denomination omitted.

Summer Palace, Peiping — A99

Bronze Bull and Kunming Lake — A100

Engraved and Typographed

1949, Aug. ***Rouletted***

Without Gum

989	A99	15c org brn & grn	2.25	3.50
990	A100	40c dl grn & car	2.50	3.50
a.		2nd and 3rd characters at top transposed	60.00	75.00

Silver Yuan Surcharge in Black on 1949 Sun Yat-sen Issues

1

分壹

1949 ***Perf. 12½, 14***

991	A94	1c on $100 org brn (890)	7.50	4.00
992	A94	1c on $100 dk org brn (898)	7.50	4.00
993	A94	2½c on $500 rose lil (892)	10.00	4.50
a.		Inverted surcharge	32.50	
994	A94	2½c on $500 rose lil (900)	10.00	5.00
995	A94	15c on $10 grn (887)	16.00	17.50
a.		Inverted surcharge	37.50	
996	A94	15c on $20 vio brn (896)	22.50	27.50
		Nos. 991-996 (6)	73.50	62.50

Silver Yuan Surcharge in Black or Carmine

5 伍 分

997	A94	2½c on $50 grn (951)	1.00	1.50
998	A94	2½c on $50,000 bl (956)	3.00	1.50
999	A94	5c on $1000 dp bl (952) (C)	3.00	1.25
1000	A94	5c on $20,000 org (955)	2.00	1.25
1001	A94	5c on $200,000 vio (957) (C)	2.00	1.25
1002	A94	5c on $500,000 vio brn (958)	2.00	1.25
1003	A94	10c on $5000 car (953)	4.00	3.00
1004	A94	10c on $10,000 brn (954)	4.00	3.00
1005	A94	15c on $200 red org (891)	6.00	5.00
1006	A94	25c on $100 dk org brn (896)	12.00	12.00
		Nos. 997-1006 (10)	39.00	31.00

REPUBLIC OF CHINA

(Taiwan)

LOCATION — Taiwan (Formosa) (since 1949)

GOVT. — Republic

AREA — 13,892 sq. mi.

POP. — 16,700,000 (est. 1978)

CAPITAL — Taipei

Stamps issued and used in Taiwan after Communist forces occupied the Chinese mainland include Taiwan Nos. 91-96, 101-103, J10-J17.

Catalogue values for unused stamps in this country are for Never Hinged items, beginning with Scott 1124 in the regular postage section, Scott C69 in the airpost section, and Scott J142 in the postage due section.

Watermarks

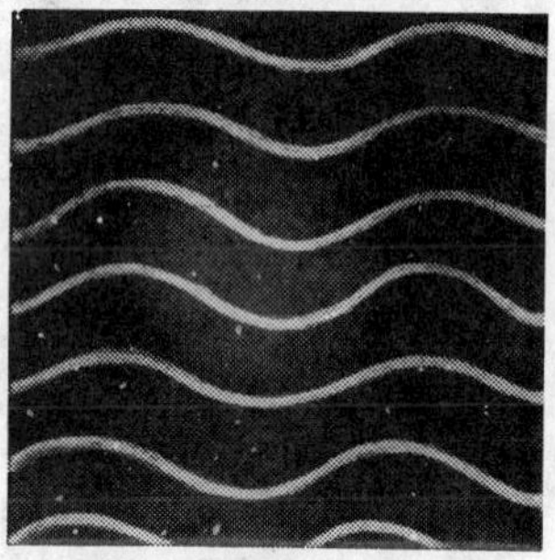

Wmk. 281- Wavy Lines

Wmk. 323- Seal Character (found with "Yu" in various arrangements)

Wmk. 368- JEZ Multiple

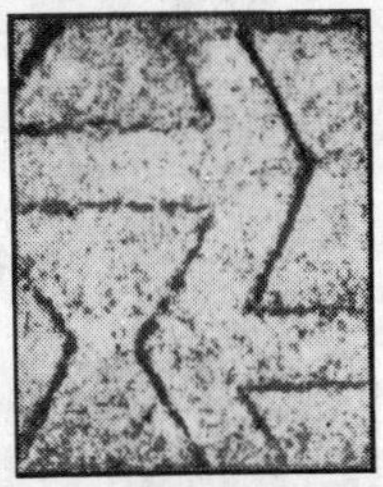

Wmk. 370-Geometrical Design

Type of 1949 with Value Omitted Surcharged in Various Colors

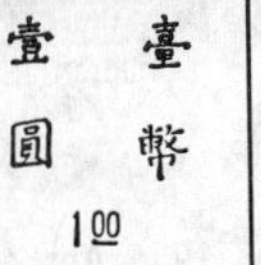

1950, Jan. 1 Unwmk. *Perf. 12½*

1007	A97	$1 green (Bk)	110.00	4.00
1008	A97	$2 green (C)	110.00	10.00
1009	A97	$5 green (V)	1,100.	42.50
1010	A97	$10 green (Br)	950.00	65.00
1011	A97	$20 green (Dk Bl)	2,100.	475.00
		Nos. 1007-1011 (5)	4,370.	596.50

Two printings of the $1 and $2 show minor differences.

Cheng Ch'eng-kung (Koxinga) — A101

1950, June 26 Typo. *Rouletted*

Without Gum

1012	A101	3c dk gray grn	70	1.00
1013	A101	10c orange brn	70	15
1014	A101	15c orange yel	12.00	2.75
1015	A101	20c emerald	1.90	15
1016	A101	30c claret	25.00	15.00
1017	A101	40c red orange	3.00	15
1018	A101	50c chocolate	6.25	65
1019	A101	80c carmine	6.25	2.75
1020	A101	$1 ultra	6.50	1.00
1021	A101	$1.50 green	19.00	2.50
1022	A101	$1.60 blue	25.00	2.50
1023	A101	$2 red violet	32.50	3.00
1024	A101	$5 aqua	100.00	10.00
		Nos. 1012-1024 (13)	238.80	41.60

Part perf pairs exist of the 10c, 20c, 80c.
For surcharges see Nos. 1070-1072, 1105-1108, 1118-1119.

Nos. 751, 753, 788-791, 793, 795-799 Surcharged in Carmine or Black

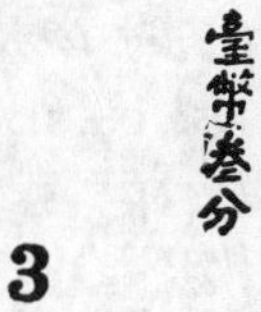

1950, Mar. 25 Engr. *Perf. 14*

1025	A82	3c on $30,000	3.75	2.25
1026	A82	3c on $40,000 (C)	3.75	2.25
1027	A82	3c on $50,000 (C)	4.75	3.00
1028	A82	5c on $200,000	4.75	2.25
1029	A82	10c on $4000	9.25	4.50
1030	A82	10c on $6000	15.00	4.50
1031	A82	10c on $20,000	15.00	4.50
1032	A82	10c on $2,000,000	15.00	4.50
1033	A82	20c on $500,000	35.00	4.50
1034	A82	20c on $1,000,000	45.00	8.00
1035	A82	30c on $3,000,000	52.50	10.00
1036	A82	50c on $5,000,000 (C)	95.00	10.00
		Nos. 1025-1036 (12)	298.75	60.25

Inverted Surcharge

1029a	A82	10c on $4000	110.00
1030a	A82	10c on $6000	250.00
1032a	A82	10c on $2,000,000	150.00
1033a	A82	20c on $500,000	200.00
1034a	A82	20c on $1,000,000	200.00

No. 1031 exists with inverted surcharge.

Allegory of Election — A102

Perf. 12x12½, Imperf.

1951, Mar. 20 Engr. Unwmk.

Without Gum

1037	A102	40c carmine	11.00	65
a.		Horiz. pair, imperf. btwn.	90.00	
1038	A102	$1 dp blue	22.50	1.75
1039	A102	$1.60 purple	32.50	3.00
1040	A102	$2 brown	52.50	5.00
		Nos. 1037-1040 (4)	118.50	10.40

Souvenir Sheet

Imperf

1041	A102	$2 dp bl grn	*400.00*	*400.00*

Adoption of local self-government in Taiwan.

Type A97 Surcharged A103

Farmer and Scroll Announcing Tax Reduction A104

Surcharge in Various Colors

1951, July 19 *Perf. 12½*

Without Gum

1042	A103	$5 green (R Br)	30.00	9.00
1043	A103	$10 green (Bk)	82.50	9.00
1044	A103	$20 green (R)	375.00	22.50
1045	A103	$50 green (P)	675.00	80.00
		Nos. 1042-1045 (4)	1,162.	120.50

1952, Jan. 1 *Perf. 14*

Without Gum

1046	A104	20c red orange	6.25	2.00
1047	A104	40c dk green	12.50	2.75
1048	A104	$1 brown	16.00	6.75
1049	A104	$1.40 dp blue	26.00	5.75
1050	A104	$2 dk gray	47.50	20.00
1051	A104	$5 brown car	62.50	11.00
		Nos. 1046-1051 (6)	170.75	48.25

Land tax reduction of 37.5% in Taiwan.
Value, imperf. set, $500.

Pres. Chiang Kai-shek, Flag and Followers A105

1952, Mar. 1 Unwmk. *Perf. 14*

Without Gum

Flag in Violet Blue and Carmine

1052	A105	40c rose car	7.25	1.25
a.		Vert. pair, imperf. btwn.	72.50	
1053	A105	$1 dp green	13.00	3.75
1054	A105	$1.60 brown org	27.50	3.00
a.		Horiz. pair, imperf. btwn.	150.00	
1055	A105	$2 brt blue	45.00	13.00
1056	A105	$5 violet brn	40.00	6.25
		Nos. 1052-1056 (5)	145.25	27.25

2nd anniv. of Chiang Kai-shek's return to the presidency.
Value, imperf. set, $225.
See Nos. 1064-1069.

Nos. 975-976, 978-979 Surcharged in Black

1952 *Perf. 12½*

1057	A94	3c on 4c bl grn	4.50	4.00
1058	A94	3c on 10c dp lil	4.50	4.00
a.		Inverted surcharge		
1059	A94	3c on 20c blue	4.50	4.00
1060	A94	3c on 50c dk brn	4.50	4.00
		Nos. 1057-1060 (4)	18.00	16.00

Geese Type of 1949 with Value Omitted Surcharged

1952, Dec. 8

1061	A97	$10 green (P)	55.00	9.00
1062	A97	$20 green (R)	200.00	20.00
1063	A97	$50 green (Bk)	1,200.	675.00

Chiang Type of 1952 Redrawn

Perf. 12½

1953, Mar. 1 Engr. Unwmk.

Without Gum

Flag in Dark Blue & Carmine

1064	A105	10c red org	6.00	1.75
1065	A105	20c green	6.00	1.75
1066	A105	40c rose pink	11.00	2.50
1067	A105	$1.40 blue	20.00	3.50
1068	A105	$2 brown	27.50	6.75
1069	A105	$5 rose vio	55.00	10.50
		Nos. 1064-1069 (6)	125.50	26.75

Chiang Kai-shek's return to presidency, 3rd anniv.
Many differences in redrawn design. Value, imperf. set, $275.

Nos. 1020, 1014, 1016 and 1022 Surcharged in Various Colors

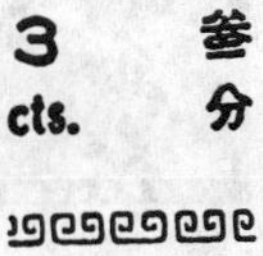

1953-54 *Rouletted*

1070	A101	3c on $1 ultra (C)	1.25	80
1070A	A101	10c on 15c org yel (G) ('54)	11.00	1.40
1071	A101	10c on 30c cl (Bl)	1.25	70
1072	A101	20c on $1.60 bl (Bk)	1.25	70
		Nos. 1070-1072 (4)	14.75	3.60

Chinese characters and ornamental device at bottom differ on each value.

Nurse and Patients — A106

1953, July 1 Litho. *Perf. 12½*

Without Gum

Cross in Red, Burelage Color in Italics

1073	A106	40c brown, *buff*	12.00	1.65
1074	A106	$1.60 blue, *bl*	17.00	1.40
1075	A106	$2 green, *yel*	42.50	2.25
1076	A106	$5 red org, *org*	55.00	7.75
		Nos. 1073-1076 (4)	126.50	13.05

Chinese Anti-Tuberculosis Association.

Pres. Chiang Kai-shek — A107

1953, Oct. 31 Engr.

Without Gum

1077	A107	10c dk brown	1.50	15
1078	A107	20c lilac	4.50	15
1079	A107	40c dp green	4.50	15

1080 A107 50c dp pink 4.50 24
1081 A107 80c brown bis 24.00 3.25
1082 A107 $1 dp ol grn 11.00 20
1083 A107 $1.40 dp blue 20.00 42
1084 A107 $1.60 dp car 24.00 32
1085 A107 $1.70 apple grn 15.00 3.00
1086 A107 $2 brown 16.00 20
1087 A107 $3 dk blue 87.50 7.50
1088 A107 $4 aqua 35.00 65
1089 A107 $5 red org 17.50 85
1090 A107 $10 dk green 32.50 1.40
1091 A107 $20 dk brn lake 87.50 3.25
a. Souvenir folder 350.00
Nos. 1077-1091 (15) 385.00 21.73

67th birthday of Pres. Chiang Kai-shek.
No. 1091a contains Nos. 1077-1091 imperf., arranged in 3 sheets of 5 stamps each.

Silo Highway Bridge
A108

Forest of Evergreens
A109

Design: $1.60 and $5, Silo bridge, side view.

1954, Jan. 28 Unwmk. *Perf. 12½*
Without Gum
Various Frames

1092 A108 40c vermilion 5.75 1.10
1093 A108 $1.60 blue vio 85.00 2.25
1094 A108 $3.60 sepia 27.50 4.75
1095 A108 $5 magenta 100.00 6.75
a. Souvenir folder 700.00
Nos. 1092-1095 (4) 218.25 14.85

Opening of Silo bridge, 1st anniversary.
No. 1095a contains one sheet of 4 containing Nos. 1092-1095 imperforate.

1954, Mar. 12 *Perf. 12x12½*
Without Gum

1096 A109 40c shown 27.50 85
1097 A109 $10 Nursery 82.50 5.50

Issued to publicize forest conservation.

Runner — A110

Globe, Bridge and Ship — A111

1954, Mar. 29
Without Gum

1098 A110 40c dp ultra 24.00 1.75
1099 A110 $5 carmine 62.50 7.25

11th Youth Day, Mar. 29, 1954.

1954, Oct. 21 *Perf. 12*
Without Gum

1100 A111 40c red orange 13.00 55
1101 A111 $5 deep blue 11.00 2.50

2nd Overseas Chinese Day, Oct. 21, 1954.

Ex-Prisoner with Broken Chains — A112

Designs: $1, Ex-prisoner with torch and flag, UN emblem. $1.60, Torch and date.

1955, Jan. 23

1102 A112 40c blue green 1.75 80
a. Vert. pair, imperf. btwn. 150.00
1103 A112 $1 sepia 12.50 5.00
1104 A112 $1.60 lake 16.00 4.25
Nos. 1102-1104 (3) 30.25 10.05

Honoring Chinese who fought on the side of the North Korean army, who, when released January 23, 1955, chose to return to the Republic of China.

Nos. 1019-1021, 1017 Surcharged in Brown, Blue or Green:

分 叁 角 壹

a

0.10 b

角 貳

c

0.20

1955 *Rouletted*

1105 A101(a) 3c on $1 (Br) 3.50 75
1106 A101(b) 10c on 80c (Bl) 3.50 75
1107 A101(b) 10c on $1.50 (Bl) 3.50 75
1108 A101(c) 20c on 40c (G) 3.50 75
Nos. 1105-1108 (4) 14.00 3.00

Hand Planting Evergreen Tree — A113

Chiang Kai-shek, Flags, Building — A114

Design: $50, Seedling and map of Taiwan.

1955, Apr. 1 *Perf. 12*
Without Gum

1109 A113 $20 dp carmine 26.00 1.75
1110 A113 $50 blue 62.50 4.25

Issued to publicize forest conservation.

1955, May 20 Engr. *Perf. 12*
Without Gum

1111 A114 20c olive 3.50 15
1112 A114 40c blue green 3.25 15
1113 A114 $2 carmine rose 8.25 85
1114 A114 $7 dp ultra 12.50 2.00
a. Souv. sheet of 4, #1111-1114, imperf. 250.00 250.00
Nos. 1111-1114 (4) 27.50 3.15

First anniversary of Pres. Chiang Kai-shek's re-election.
No. 1114a is perf. 12 at right edge of sheet. Value is for sheet with right selvage.

Armed Forces Emblem — A115

1955, Sept. 3
Without Gum

1115 A115 40c dk blue 1.25 32
1116 A115 $2 orange ver 15.00 75
1117 A115 $7 blue green 15.00 3.00
a. Sheet of 3, #1115-1117, imperf. 500.00 500.00
Nos. 1115-1117 (3) 31.25 4.07

Armed Forces Day, Sept. 3.
No. 1117a is perf. 12 at right edge of sheet. Value is for sheet with right selvage.

Nos. 1017, 1018 and C64 Surcharged in Magenta

角 貳

0.20

1955 Typo. *Rouletted*

1118 A101 20c on 40c red orange 4.50 45
1119 A101 20c on 50c chocolate 4.50 45
1120 AP6 20c on 60c dp blue 4.50 45
Nos. 1118-1120 (3) 13.50 1.35

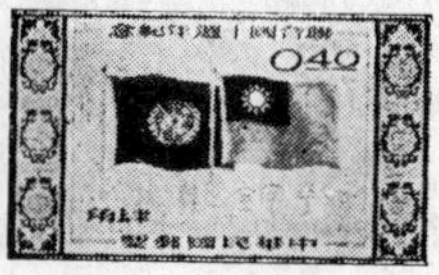
Flags of UN and China
A116

1955, Oct. 24 Engr. *Perf. 11½*
Without Gum

1121 A116 40c dk blue 2.00 15
1122 A116 $2 dk car rose 5.75 1.00
1123 A116 $7 slate green 7.25 2.25
Nos. 1121-1123 (3) 15.00 3.40

10th anniv. of the UN, Oct. 24, 1955.

Catalogue values for unused stamps in this section, from this point to the end of the section, are for Never Hinged items.

Pres. Chiang Kai-shek
A117

Birthplace of Sun Yat-sen
A118

1955, Oct. 31 Photo. *Perf. 13½*

1124 A117 40c dk bl, red & brn 3.50 15
1125 A117 $2 grn, red & dk bl 10.50 1.10
1126 A117 $7 brn, red & grn 14.00 2.25
a. Souv. sheet of 3, #1124-1126, imperf. 200.00 200.00
Nos. 1124-1126 (3) 28.00 3.50

69th birthday of Pres. Chiang Kai-shek.
No. 1126a is perf. 12 at right edge of sheet. Value is for sheet with right selvage.

1955, Nov. 12 Engr. *Perf. 12*
Without Gum

1127 A118 40c blue 3.25 45
1128 A118 $2 red brown 7.50 1.40
1129 A118 $7 rose lake 13.00 2.50
Nos. 1127-1129 (3) 23.75 4.35

90th anniversary, birth of Sun Yat-sen.

No. 959a Surcharged in Bright Green

角 貳

0.20

1956 Litho. *Rouletted*

1130 A96 20c on orange 30 15

See No. 1213.

China Map and Transportation Methods — A119

Wmk. 281
1956, Mar. 20 Engr. *Perf. 12*
Without Gum

1131 A119 40c dk carmine 1.25 15
1132 A119 $1 intense blk 2.50 75
1133 A119 $1.60 chocolate 4.75 30
1134 A119 $2 dk green 6.50 75
Nos. 1131-1134 (4) 15.00 1.95

60th anniv. of the founding of the modern Chinese postal system.

Souvenir Sheets
Imperf

1135 A119 $2 magenta 50.00 20.00
1136 A119 $2 red 50.00 20.00

Exhib. for the 60th anniv. of the modern Chinese postal system, Mar. 20, 1956.

Children at Play
A120

Early and Modern Locomotives
A121

1956, Apr. 4 Unwmk. *Perf. 12*
Without Gum

1137 A120 40c emerald 1.25 15
1138 A120 $1.60 dk blue 3.50 22
1139 A120 $2 dk carmine 4.00 1.10
Nos. 1137-1139 (3) 8.75 1.47

Children's Day, Apr. 4, 1956.

1956, June 9 Wmk. 281 Vert.
Without Gum

1140 A121 40c rose car 2.50 22
1141 A121 $2 blue 3.25 35
1142 A121 $8 green 9.25 1.75
Nos. 1140-1142 (3) 15.00 2.32

75th anniversary of Chinese Railroads.

Pres. Chiang Kai-shek
A122 A123

A124

Various Portraits of Chiang
Perf. 14½x13½, 14½ (A123), 13½x14½

1956, Oct. 31 Photo. Unwmk.

1143 A122 20c red orange 2.25 15
1144 A122 40c car rose 3.75 15
1145 A123 $1 brt ultra 4.50 20
1146 A123 $1.60 red lilac 5.50 20
1147 A124 $2 red brown 11.00 25
1148 A124 $8 brt grnsh bl 27.50 1.10
Nos. 1143-1148 (6) 54.50 2.05

70th birthday of Pres. Chiang Kai-shek.

Types of Special Delivery, Air Post and Registration Stamps of 1949 Surcharged in Black or Maroon

分叁 分叁 角壹

3 3 0.10
a b c

1956 Unwmk. Litho. *Rouletted*
Without Gum

1150 SD2(a) 3c red violet 1.00 25
a. Perf. 12½ 3.00 40
1151 AP5(b) 3c blue green (M) 1.00 25
1152 R2(c) 10c brt red 1.00 25
Nos. 1150-1152 (3) 3.00 75

Telecommunications Emblem and Radio Tower — A125

Wmk. 281

1956, Dec. 28 Engr. *Perf. 12*

Without Gum

1153	A125	40c	dp ultra	52	16
1154	A125	$1.40	carmine	1.00	16
1155	A125	$1.60	dk green	1.25	16
1156	A125	$2	chocolate	7.25	50
			Nos. 1153-1156 (4)	10.02	98

Chinese telegraph service, 75th anniv.

Map of China — A126

Mother Instructing Mencius — A127

Pin Perf., Perf. 12x12½

1957 Litho. Wmk. 281

Without Gum

1157	A126	3c	brt blue	95	15
1158	A126	10c	violet	95	15
1159	A126	20c	red orange	95	15
1160	A126	40c	rose red	95	15

Unwmk.

1161	A126	$1	orange brown	1.65	15
1162	A126	$1.60	green	2.25	15
			Nos. 1157-1162 (6)	7.70	
			Set value		65

Map inscription reads: "Recovery of Mainland." See Nos. 1177-1182.

Unwmk.

1957, May 12 Engr. *Perf. 12*

Design: $3, Mother tattooing Yueh Fei.

Without Gum

1163	A127	40c	green	85	25
1164	A127	$3	redsh brown	2.25	50

Issued to honor Mother's Day, 1957.

Badge of Chinese Boy Scouts A128

1957, Aug. 11

Without Gum

1165	A128	40c	lilac	60	20
1166	A128	$1	green	1.00	30
1167	A128	$1.60	dk blue	1.40	40
			Nos. 1165-1167 (3)	3.00	90

Cent. of the birth of Lord Baden-Powell and to publicize the World Scout Jubilee Jamboree, England, Aug. 1-12.

Globe, Radio Tower and Microphone A129

1957, Sept. 16

Without Gum

1168	A129	40c	vermilion	38	20
1169	A129	50c	brt rose lil	75	35
1170	A129	$3.50	dk blue	1.90	60
			Nos. 1168-1170 (3)	3.03	1.15

30th anniv. of Chinese broadcasting.

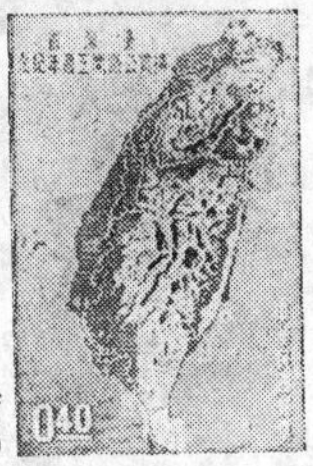

Map of Taiwan — A130

1957, Oct. 26

Without Gum

1171	A130	40c	blue green	1.75	28
1172	A130	$1.40	lt ultra	4.50	1.10
1173	A130	$2	gray	5.75	1.65
			Nos. 1171-1173 (3)	12.00	3.03

Start of construction on the Cross Island Highway, Taiwan.

Freighter "Hai Min" and River Boat "Kiang Foo" A131

1957, Dec. 16 Engr. *Perf. 12*

Without Gum

1174	A131	40c	dp ultra	30	16
1175	A131	80c	rose lake	75	28
1176	A131	$2.80	vermilion	1.90	90
			Nos. 1174-1176 (3)	2.95	1.34

85th anniv. of the establishment of the China Merchants Steam Navigation Co.

Type of 1957

Pin Perf., Perf. 12x12½

1957, Dec. 25 Typo. Unwmk.

Without Gum

Dark Blue Frames

1177	A126	3c	brt blue	70	15
1178	A126	10c	violet	70	15
1179	A126	20c	brick red	70	15
1180	A126	40c	rose red	1.75	15
1181	A126	$1	dp org brn	1.75	15
1182	A126	$1.60	dp green	2.50	15
			Nos. 1177-1182 (6)	8.10	
			Set value		62

Butterfly A132

Mme. Chiang Kai-shek Orchid A133

Perf. 13½

1958, Mar. 20 Unwmk. Photo.

Various Insects in Natural Colors

1183	A132	10c	pale grn, grn & blk	1.65	22
1184	A132	40c	lem, pink, grn & blk	1.65	38
1185	A132	$1	yel grn & mar	2.00	38
1186	A132	$1.40	yel, org & blk	2.75	52
1187	A132	$1.60	pale brn & dk pur	3.00	52
1188	A132	$2	brt yel, org & blk	4.00	75
			Nos. 1183-1188 (6)	15.05	2.77

1958, Mar. 20

Orchids: 20c, Formosan Wilson, horiz. $1.40, Klotzsch. $3, Fitzgerald, horiz.

Orchids in Natural Colors

1189	A133	20c	chocolate	1.75	20
1190	A133	40c	purple	1.75	20
1191	A133	$1.40	dk vio brn	3.50	35
1192	A133	$3	dark blue	5.25	75
			Nos. 1189-1192 (4)	12.25	1.50

World Health Organization Emblem A134

1958, May 28 Engr. *Perf. 12*

Without Gum

1193	A134	40c	dark blue	35	15
1194	A134	$1.60	brick red	35	15
1195	A134	$2	deep red lilac	50	50
			Nos. 1193-1195 (3)	1.20	80

10th anniv. of the WHO.

President's Mansion, Taipei — A135

Wmk. 323

1958, Sept. 20 Engr. *Perf. 12*

Without Gum

1196	A135	$10	blue green	9.50	15
a.			Granite paper ('63)	7.25	15
1197	A135	$20	car rose	15.00	32
a.			Granite paper ('63)	11.00	15
1198	A135	$50	red brown	47.50	1.90
1199	A135	$100	dk blue	85.00	3.50
			Nos. 1196-1199 (4)	157.00	5.87

See #1349-1351. For surcharge see #J131.

Taiwan Farm Scene A136

1958, Oct. 1 Unwmk.

Without Gum

1200	A136	20c	emerald	35	25
1201	A136	40c	black	35	25
1202	A136	$1.40	brt magenta	1.40	25
1203	A136	$3	ultra	3.75	50
			Nos. 1200-1203 (4)	5.85	1.25

10th anniversary of the Joint Commission on Rural Reconstruction.

Pres. Chiang Kai-shek — A137

1958, Oct. 31 Photo. *Perf. 13½*

1204	A137	40c	multicolored	65	25

Pres. Chiang Kai-shek on his 72nd birthday.

UNESCO Building, Paris A138

1958, Nov. 3 Engr. *Perf. 12*

Without Gum

1205	A138	20c	dark blue	15	15
1206	A138	40c	green	18	15
1207	A138	$1.40	orange ver	65	45
1208	A138	$3	red lilac	95	65
			Nos. 1205-1208 (4)	1.93	1.40

UNESCO Headquarters in Paris opening, Nov. 3.

Flame from Liberty Torch Encircling Globe — A139

1958, Dec. 10 Unwmk.

Without Gum

1209	A139	40c	green	15	16
1210	A139	60c	gray brown	20	16
1211	A139	$1	carmine	52	16
1212	A139	$3	ultra	1.00	40
			Nos. 1209-1212 (4)	1.87	88

10th anniversary of the signing of the Universal Declaration of Human Rights.

0.20

No. 959a Surcharged in Bright Green

角貳

Rouletted

1958, Dec. 11 Litho. Unwmk.

Without Gum

1213	A96	20c	on orange	25	15

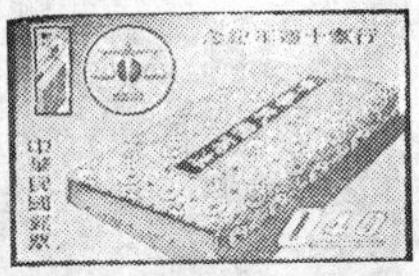

Ballot Box, Scales and Constitution A140

1958, Dec. 25 Engr. *Perf. 12*

Without Gum

1214	A140	40c	green	40	24
1215	A140	50c	dull pur	55	24
1216	A140	$1.40	car rose	1.75	30
1217	A140	$3.50	dk blue	3.00	90
			Nos. 1214-1217 (4)	5.70	1.68

Adoption of the constitution, 10th anniv.

Chu Kwang Tower, Quemoy — A141

1959-60 Wmk. 323 Litho. *Perf. 12*

Without Gum

1218	A141	3c	orange	16	15
1218A	A141	5c	lt yel grn ('60)	16	15
1219	A141	10c	lilac	16	15
1220	A141	20c	ultra	16	15
1221	A141	40c	brown	32	15
1222	A141	50c	bluish grn	55	15
1223	A141	$1	rose red	1.00	15
1224	A141	$1.40	yel grn	1.25	15
1225	A141	$2	gray grn	1.25	15
1226	A141	$2.80	rose pink	2.75	15
1227	A141	$3	slate blue	2.75	15
			Nos. 1218-1227 (11)	10.51	1.65

See Nos. 1270-1283.

ILO Emblem and Headquarters, Geneva A142

1959, June 15 Engr. *Perf. 12*
Without Gum

1228	A142	40c	blue	15	15
1229	A142	$1.60	dk brown	26	15
1230	A142	$3	brt blue grn	52	24
1231	A142	$5	orange ver	1.50	60
	Nos. 1228-1231 (4)			2.43	1.14

40th anniversary of the ILO.

Bugler and Tents A143

1959, July 8 Unwmk.
Without Gum

1232	A143	40c	carmine	38	25
1233	A143	50c	dark blue	1.10	25
1234	A143	$5	green	3.00	95
	Nos. 1232-1234 (3)			4.48	1.45

10th World Boy Scout Jamboree, Makiling National Park, Philippines, July 17-26.

Inscribed Stone, Mt. Tai-wu, Quemoy — A144

Map of Taiwan Straits A145

1959, Sept. 3 Engr. *Perf. 12*
Without Gum

1235	A144	40c	brown	32	15
1236	A145	$1.40	ultra	80	15
1237	A145	$2	green	1.75	15
1238	A144	$3	dk blue	2.25	32
	Nos. 1235-1238 (4)			5.12	
	Set value				70

Defense of Quemoy and Matsu islands.
For overprints see Nos. 1258-1259.

Pigeons Circling Globe A146

1959, Oct. 4
Without Gum

1239	A146	40c	blue	22	16
1240	A146	$1	rose carmine	42	25
1241	A146	$2	gray brown	70	16
1242	A146	$3.50	red orange	1.65	60
	Nos. 1239-1242 (4)			2.99	1.17

Intl. Letter Writing Week, Oct. 4-10.

National Taiwan Science Hall, Taipei — A147

1959, Nov. 12 Photo. *Perf. 13x13½*

1243	A147	40c	shown	1.00	25
1244	A147	$3	Front view	2.00	75

Emblem A148

1959, Dec. 7 Engr. *Perf. 12*
Without Gum

1245	A148	40c	blue green	25	20
1246	A148	$1.60	red lilac	70	32
1247	A148	$3	orange	1.10	60
	Nos. 1245-1247 (3)			2.05	1.12

Intl. Confederation of Free Trade Unions, 10th anniv.

Sun Yat-sen, Lincoln and Flags A149

Perf. 13½, 12
1959, Dec. 25 Photo. Unwmk.

1248	A149	40c	multicolored	60	35
1249	A149	$3	multicolored	90	65

Issued to honor Sun Yat-sen and Abraham Lincoln as "Leaders of Democracy."

Mailman on Motorcycle Delivering Night Mail — A150

Postal Launch A151

1960, Mar. 20 Engr. *Perf. 11½*
Without Gum

1250	A150	$1.40	dk violet brn	75	18
1251	A151	$1.60	ultra	1.10	52

Issued to publicize the Prompt Delivery Service.

WRY Uprooted Oak Emblem — A152

1960, Apr. 7 Photo. *Perf. 13*

1252	A152	40c	blk, red brn & emer	32	15
1253	A152	$3	blk, red org & grn	70	38

Issued to publicize World Refugee Year, July 1, 1959-June 30, 1960.

Cross Island Highway, Taiwan A153

Design: $1, $2, Road through tunnel, vert.

Perf. 11½
1960, May 9 Engr. Unwmk.
Without Gum

1254	A153	40c	green	55	15
1255	A153	$1	dk blue	1.90	38
1256	A153	$2	brown vio	75	18
1257	A153	$3	brown	2.75	24
a.	Souv. sheet of 2, #1255, 1257, wmk. 323			*250.00*	*75.00*
	Nos. 1254-1257 (4)			5.95	95

Opening of the Cross Island Highway, Taiwan.

Red Overprint on Nos. 1237-1238 Chinese and English: "Welcome U.S. President Dwight D. Eisenhower 1960"

1960, June 18 Unwmk. *Perf. 12*

1258	A145	$2	green	1.25	30
a.	Inverted overprint			200.00	200.00
1259	A144	$3	dk blue	2.50	50

Eisenhower's visit to China, June 18, 1960.

Phonopost — A154

1960, June 27
Without Gum

1260	A154	$2	red orange	1.10	35

Phonopost Service of the Chinese armed forces.

Two Horses and Groom, by Han Kan — A155

Paintings from Palace Museum, Taichung: $1, Two Riders, by Wei Yen. $1.60, Flowers and Birds by Hsiao Yung, vert. $2, Pair of Mandarin Ducks by Monk Hui Ch'ung.

1960, Aug. 4 Photo. *Perf. 13*

1261	A155	$1	ol gray, blk & brn	4.50	1.50
1262	A155	$1.40	bis brn, blk & fawn	5.75	1.50
1263	A155	$1.60	multicolored	7.00	1.50
1264	A155	$2	beige, blk & gray grn	13.00	1.90
	Nos. 1261-1264 (4)			30.25	6.40

Chinese paintings, 7th-11th centuries.
For other painting types with large straight numerals in the upper corners and large Chinese characters on the side see A186, A241 and A285.

Youth Corps Flag and Summer Activities A156

Reforestation A157

Design: $3, similar to 50c, horiz.

1960, Aug. 20 Engr. *Perf. 12*
Without Gum

1265	A156	50c	slate green	30	15
1266	A156	$3	copper brown	1.10	55

Summer activities of China Youth Corps.

1960, Aug. 29 Photo. *Perf. 13½x13*

Designs: $2, Protection of forest. $3, Timber industry.

1267	A157	$1	multicolored	1.50	16
1268	A157	$2	multicolored	3.75	65
1269	A157	$3	multicolored	3.75	65
a.	Souvenir sheet of 3			24.00	16.00
	Nos. 1267-1269 (3)			9.00	1.46

Fifth World Forestry Congress, Seattle, Washington, Aug. 29-Sept. 10.
No. 1269a contains Nos. 1267-1269 assembled as a triptych, 65½x40mm and imperf., but with simulated black perforations.

Chu Kwang Tower, Quemoy — A158

Sports — A159

1960-61 Wmk. 323 Litho. *Perf. 12*
Without Gum

1270	A158	3c	lt red brown	15	15
1271	A158	40c	pale violet	15	15
1272	A158	50c	orange ('61)	15	15
1273	A158	60c	rose lilac	15	15
1274	A158	80c	pale green	28	15
1275	A158	$1	gray green ('61)	2.00	15
1276	A158	$1.20	gray olive	95	15
1277	A158	$1.50	ultra	95	15
1278	A158	$2	car rose ('61)	2.25	15
1279	A158	$2.50	pale blue	2.25	15
1280	A158	$3	bluish green	2.00	15
1281	A158	$3.20	lt red brown	3.50	15
1282	A158	$3.60	vio blue ('61)	3.00	35
1283	A158	$4.50	vermilion	5.75	50
	Nos. 1270-1283 (14)			23.53	
	Set value				2.00

1962-64

Granite Paper
Without Gum

1270a	A158	3c	light red brown	1.25	15
1270B	A158	10c	emerald ('63)	3.00	15
1271a	A158	40c	pale violet	1.25	15
1274a	A158	80c	pale green	2.25	15
1275a	A158	$1	gray green ('63)	8.50	15
1278a	A158	$2	carmine rose	9.25	15
1281a	A158	$3.20	red brown ('64)	9.25	15
1282A	A158	$4	brt blue grn	20.00	26
1283a	A158	$4.50	vermilion	9.25	38
	Nos. 1270a-1283a (9)			64.00	
	Set value				1.25

Two types of No. 1271a: I. Seven lines in "0" of "40." II. Eight lines in "0."

Perf. 12½
1960, Oct. 25 Photo. Unwmk.

1284	A159	50c	Diving	65	15
1285	A159	80c	Discus thrower	65	18
1286	A159	$2	Basketball	1.00	28
1287	A159	$2.50	Soccer	1.65	35
1288	A159	$3	Hurdling	1.90	55
1289	A159	$3.20	Runner	3.25	70
	Nos. 1284-1289 (6)			9.10	2.21

Bronze Wine Container, 1751-1111 B.C. — A160

Flat Bowl, 1111-771 B.C. — A161

Ancient Chinese Art Treasures: $1, Cauldron, 1111-771 B.C. $1.20, Porcelain vase, 960-1126 A.D. $1.50, Perforated tube, 1111-771 B.C. $2, Jug in shape of monk's cap, 1368-1661 A.D. $2.50, Jade flower vase, 1368-1661, A.D.

1961 Photo. *Perf. 13*

1290	A160	80c lt ol, blk & dk vio	3.00	30
1291	A160	$1 sal, bl & blk	3.00	38
1292	A160	$1.20 yel, brn & ultra	4.00	75
1293	A160	$1.50 lil, bl & sep	4.00	1.00
1294	A160	$2 pale grn, dk grn & red brn	5.25	75
1295	A160	$2.50 grnsh bl & dk vio	6.00	85
		Nos. 1290-1295 (6)	25.25	4.03

Issue dates: Nos. 1290, 1292, 1295, Feb. 1. Nos. 1291, 1293-1294, May 1.

1961

Designs: 80c, Palace perfumer, 1662-1911. $1, Corn vase, 770-221 B.C. $2, Jade tankard, 960-1126 A.D. $4, Glazed washer, 1127-1279 A.D. $4.50, Jade chimera, 8 B.C.-206 A.D.

1296	A160	80c pink, brn, bl & yel	1.75	30
1297	A160	$1 cit, blk & brn	5.25	30
1298	A161	$1.50 sal & ind	5.25	1.50
1299	A160	$2 bl, blk & rose	5.25	1.10
1300	A161	$4 red, blk & bluish gray	17.50	1.10
1301	A161	$4.50 grnsh bl, blk & brn	15.00	3.00
		Nos. 1296-1301 (6)	50.00	7.30

Issue dates: Nos. 1296-1298, Aug. 15. Nos. 1299-1301, Sept. 15.

1962

Designs: 80c, Topaz twin wine vessels, 1662-1911 A.D. $1, Squat pouring vase, 1751-1111 B.C. $2.40, Vase, 1368-1661 A.D. $3, Wine vase, 1751-1111 B.C. $3.20, Covered porcelain jar, 1662-1911 A.D. $3.60, Perforated disc, 206 B.C.-8 A.D.

1302	A160	80c crim, blk & ocher	2.00	15
1303	A160	$1 blue & vio blk	3.25	15
1304	A160	$2.40 hn brn, blk & bl	7.75	50
1305	A160	$3 blue, blk & pink	19.00	1.50
1306	A160	$3.20 ultra, lt grn & red	22.50	15
1307	A160	$3.60 yel, blk & brn	19.00	1.00
		Nos. 1302-1307 (6)	73.50	3.45

Issue dates: Nos. 1303-1304, 1307, Jan. 15. Nos. 1302, 1305-1306, Feb. 15.

Farmer with Mechanized Plow — A162

Madame Chiang Kai-shek and League Emblem — A163

1961, Feb. 4 Engr. *Perf. 12*

Without Gum

1308	A162	80c rose violet	60	16
1309	A162	$2 green	2.00	60
1310	A162	$3.20 vermilion	2.00	25
		Nos. 1308-1310 (3)	4.60	1.01

1961 agricultural census.

Unwmk.

1961, Mar. 8 Photo. *Perf. 13*

Portrait in Black

1311	A163	80c lt grn & car rose	1.25	30
1312	A163	$1 yel grn & car rose	2.75	60
1313	A163	$2 org brn & car rose	2.75	60
1314	A163	$3.20 lil & car rose	6.50	1.25
		Nos. 1311-1314 (4)	13.25	2.75

10th anniversary of the Chinese Women's Anti-Aggression League.

Spiny Lobster and Mail Order Service Emblem — A164

Jeme Tien-yow and Pataling Tunnel — A165

1961, Mar. 20 Engr. *Perf. 11½*

Without Gum

1315	A164	$3 slate green	2.50	35

Issued to publicize the mail order service for consumer goods.

1961, Apr. 26 *Perf. 11½*

Without Gum

Design: $2, Jeme Tien-yow and 1909 locomotive, horiz.

1316	A165	80c lilac	55	15
1317	A165	$2 black	2.50	60

Centenary of the birth of Jeme Tien-yow, builder of the Peking-Kalgan railroad.

Map of China inscribed: "Recovery of the Mainland" — A166

Pres. Chiang Kai-shek — A167

1961, May 20 Photo. *Perf. 13½*

1318	A166	80c multicolored	1.50	25
1319	A167	$2 multicolored	5.25	1.25
a.		Souvenir sheet of 2	18.00	20.00

1st anniversary of Pres. Chiang Kai-shek's 3rd term inauguration.

No. 1319a contains one each of Nos. 1318-1319, imperf. with simulated perforations. Without gum.

Convair 880-M, Biplane of 1921 and Flag — A168

1961, July 1 *Perf. 13x12½*

1320	A168	$10 multicolored	3.75	1.50

40th anniversary of civil air service.

Sun Yat-sen and Chiang Kai-shek — A169

Flag and Map of China — A170

Perf. 13½

1961, Oct. 10 Unwmk. Photo.

1321	A169	80c gray, lt brn & sl	1.00	16
1322	A170	$5 gray, ultra, red & beige	4.00	1.75
a.		Souvenir sheet of 2	15.00	10.00

50th anniv. of the Republic of China. No. 1322a contains one each of Nos. 1321-1322, imperf. with simulated perforations. No gum.

Green Lake — A171

Oil Refinery — A173

Lotus Pond A172

Taiwan Scenery: $2, Sun-Moon Lake. $3.20, Wulai waterfalls.

Perf. 13½x14, 14x13½

1961, Oct. 31 Unwmk.

1323	A171	80c multicolored	2.75	18
1324	A172	$1 multicolored	7.75	75
1325	A172	$2 multicolored	7.75	75
1326	A171	$3.20 multicolored	17.50	1.10
		Nos. 1323-1326 (4)	35.75	2.78

1961, Nov. 14 *Perf. 11½*

Designs: $1.50, Steel works. $2.50, Aluminum plant. $3.20, Fertilizer plant, horiz.

1327	A173	80c multicolored	1.25	15
1328	A173	$1.50 multicolored	3.75	75
1329	A173	$2.50 multicolored	3.75	75
1330	A173	$3.20 multicolored	7.25	65
		Nos. 1327-1330 (4)	16.00	2.30

Chinese industrial development and the Golden Jubilee Convention of the Chinese Institute of Engineers, Nov. 13-16.

Atomic Reactor, Tsing-Hwa University A174

Atomic Reactor in Operation A175

Design: $3.20, Atomic symbol and laboratory, Tsing-Hwa, horiz.

1961-62 Photo. *Perf. 12½*

1331	A174	80c multicolored	1.25	15
1332	A175	$2 multi ('62)	2.75	1.65
1333	A175	$3.20 multi ('62)	4.50	1.10
		Nos. 1331-1333 (3)	8.50	2.90

Inauguration on Apr. 13, 1961, of the 1st Chinese atomic reactor at the National Tsing-Hwa University Institute of Nuclear Science.

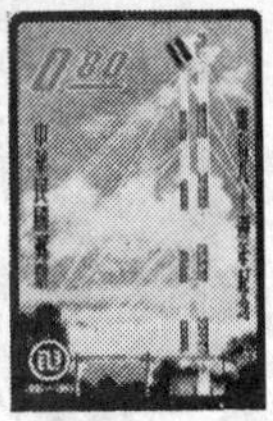

Microwave Reflector and Telegraph Wires — A176

Design: $3.20, Microwave parabolic antenna and mountains, horiz.

1961, Dec. 28 *Perf. 12½*

1334	A176	80c multicolored	45	16
1335	A176	$3.20 multicolored	2.50	1.00

80th anniv. of Chinese telecommunications.

Mechanical Postal Equipment and Twine Tying Machine A176a

Perf. 11½

1962, Mar. 20 Engr. Wmk. 323

Without Gum

1336	A176a	80c chocolate	1.00	35

Yu Shan Observatory A177

Observation Balloon, Earth and Cumulus Clouds A178

Design: $1, Map showing route of typhoon Pamela, Sept. 1961, horiz.

1962

Without Gum

1337	A177	80c brown	38	15
1338	A178	$1 bluish black	2.75	45
1339	A178	$2 green	1.65	90
		Nos. 1337-1339 (3)	4.78	1.50

Issue dates: 80c, $2, Mar. 23; $1, May 7. World Meteorological Day, Mar. 23.

Child Receiving Milk, UN Emblem A179

1962, Apr. 4

Without Gum

1340	A179	80c rose red	26	15
1341	A179	$3.20 green	1.75	55
a.		Souvenir sheet of 2	18.00	4.00

15th anniv. of UNICEF. No. 1341a contains one each of Nos. 1340-1341 imperf. with simulated perforations.

Malaria Eradication Emblem — A180

Perf. 12½

1962, Apr. 7 Unwmk. Photo.

1342 A180 80c dk bl, red & lt grn 65 22
1343 A180 $3.60 brn, pink & grn 1.40 1.10

WHO drive to eradicate malaria.

Yu Yu-jen — A181

Cheng Ch'eng-kung (Koxinga) — A182

1962, Apr. 24 *Perf. 13*

1344 A181 80c gray, blk & pink 1.65 25

Issued to honor Yu Yu-jen, newspaper reporter, revolutionary leader and co-worker of Sun Yat-sen, on his 84th birthday.

1962, Apr. 29

1345 A182 80c dp claret 1.65 32
1346 A182 $2 dk green 4.25 75

300th anniversary (in 1961) of the recovery of Taiwan from the Dutch by Koxinga.

Emblem of Intl. Cooperative Alliance — A183

Clasped Hands Across Globe — A184

Wmk. 323
1962, July 7 Engr. *Perf. 12*
Without Gum

1347 A183 80c brown 55 15
1348 A184 $2 violet 1.50 52

Intl. Cooperative Movement and 40th Intl. Cooperative Day, July 7, 1962.

Mansion Type of 1958

1962, July 20
Without Gum

1349 A135 $5 gray green 2.25 15
1350 A135 $5.60 violet 2.50 15
1351 A135 $6 orange 2.75 15
Nos. 1349-1351 (3) 7.50 45

1963
Granite Paper

1349a A135 $5 gray green 2.00 15
1350a A135 $5.60 violet 3.25 15
1351a A135 $6 orange 3.50 15
Nos. 1349a-1351a (3) 8.75 45

"Art and Science" — A185

Designs: $2, "Education," book and UNESCO emblem, horiz. $3.20, "Communications," globes, horiz.

1962, Aug. 28 Wmk. 323 *Perf. 12*
Without Gum

1352 A185 80c lilac rose 32 15
1353 A185 $2 rose claret 1.90 50
1354 A185 $3.20 yellow green 1.75 35
Nos. 1352-1354 (3) 3.97 1.00

UNESCO activities in China.

Emperor T'ai Tsung, T'ang Dynasty, 627-649
A186

Emperors: $2, T'ai Tsu, Sung dynasty, 960-975. $3.20, T'ai Tsu, Yuan dynasty (Genghis Khan), 1206-27. $4, T'ai Tsu, Ming dynasty, 1368-98.

1962, Sept. 20 Photo. Unwmk.

1355 A186 80c multicolored *8.25 1.75*
1356 A186 $2 multicolored *42.50 9.25*
1357 A186 $3.20 multicolored *47.50 10.00*
1358 A186 $4 multicolored *42.50 9.25*
Nos. 1355-1358 (4) *140.75 30.25*

Lions International Emblem — A187

1962, Oct. 8 *Perf. 13*

1359 A187 80c multicolored 65 18
1360 A187 $3.60 multicolored 3.00 1.00
a. Souvenir sheet of 2 30.00 8.00

45th anniv. of Lions Intl. No. 1360a contains one each of Nos. 1359-1360, imperf. with simulated perforations.

Pole Vaulting — A188

Shooting A189

1962, Oct. 25 Unwmk. *Perf. 13*

1361 A188 80c multicolored 1.10 20
1362 A189 $3.20 multicolored 2.25 45

Sports meet.

Young Farmers and 4-H Emblem A190

Flag, Liner of China Merchants' Steam Navigation Co. A191

Design: $3.20, 4-H emblem and rice.

Wmk. 323
1962, Dec. 7 Engr. *Perf. 12*
Without Gum

1363 A190 80c carmine 50 18
1364 A190 $3.20 green 1.50 55
a. Souvenir sheet of 2 24.00 10.00

10th anniv. of the 4-H Club in China. No. 1364a contains one each of Nos. 1363-1364, imperf. with simulated perforations.

Perf. 13½

1962, Dec. 16 Unwmk. Photo.

Design: $3.60, Company's Pacific navigation chart and freighter, horiz.

1365 A191 80c multicolored 1.25 18
1366 A191 $3.60 multicolored 3.75 1.00

90th anniversary of the China Merchants' Steam Navigation Co., Ltd.

Farm Woman, Tractor and Plane Dropping Food over Mainland — A192

Perf. 12½

1963, Mar. 21 Unwmk. Photo.

1367 A192 $10 multicolored 4.00 90

FAO "Freedom from Hunger" campaign.

Torch, Young Couple and Martyrs' Monument, Canton A193

Perf. 11½

1963, Mar. 29 Wmk. 323 Engr.
Without Gum

1368 A193 80c purple 32 15
1369 A193 $3.20 green 1.65 45

Issued for the 20th Youth Day.

Swallows, Pagoda and AOPU Emblem — A194

Designs: $2, Northern gannet, horiz. $6, Japanese crane and pine.

Unwmk.
1963, Apr. 1 Photo. *Perf. 13*

1370 A194 80c multicolored 3.00 22
1371 A194 $2 multicolored 3.00 22
1372 A194 $6 multicolored 10.50 3.25
Nos. 1370-1372 (3) 16.50 3.69

1st anniversary of the formation of the Asian-Oceanic Postal Union, AOPU.

Refugee Girl (Li Ying) and Map of China — A195

Refugees Fleeing Mainland A196

Perf. 11½

1963, June 27 Wmk. 323 Engr.
Without Gum

1373 A195 80c bluish black 90 24
1374 A196 $3.20 dp claret 2.00 35

1st anniv. of the evacuation of Chinese mainland refugees from Hong Kong to Taiwan. Designs from photographs of refugees.

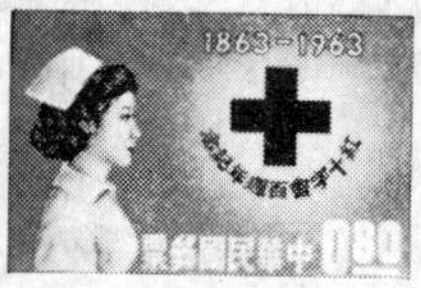

Nurse and Red Cross — A197

Design: $10, Globe and Red Cross.

Perf. 12½

1963, Sept. 1 Unwmk. Photo.

1375 A197 80c black & carmine 2.50 24
1376 A197 $10 slate, gray & car 7.50 2.50

Centenary of International Red Cross.

Basketball Player, Stadium and Asian Cup — A198

Design: $2, Hands reaching for ball and Asian cup.

Wmk. 323
1963, Nov. 20 Engr. *Perf. 12*
Without Gum

1377 A198 80c lilac rose 38 15
1378 A198 $2 violet 2.00 75

The 2nd Asian Basketball Championship, Taipei, Nov. 20.

UN Emblem, Torch and Men — A199

Scales and Men of Various Races — A200

1963, Dec. 10 Wmk. 323 *Perf. 11½*
Without Gum

1379 A199 80c brt green 52 25
1380 A200 $3.20 maroon 1.40 40

Universal Declaration of Human Rights, 15th anniversary.

Village and Orchids A201

"Kindle the Fire of Conscience" A202

Perf. 13½x13

1963, Dec. 17 Photo. Unwmk.

1381 A201 40c multicolored 2.00 42
1382 A202 $4.50 multicolored 7.00 2.00

Contribution of the Good-People-Good-Deeds campaign to improve ethical standards.

Sun Yat-sen and Book, "Three Principles of the People" A203

1963, Dec. 25 *Perf. 13*

1383	A203	$5 blue & multi	11.00	1.25

"Land-to-the-Tillers" program, 10th anniv. An 80c was prepared but not issued.

Torch A204

Hands Unchained A205

Perf. 11½
1964, Jan. 23 Wmk. 323 Engr.
Without Gum

1384	A204	80c red orange	35	20
1385	A205	$3.20 indigo	2.25	40

Liberty Day, 10th anniversary.

Broadleaf Cactus A206

Wu Chih-hwei A207

Designs: $1, Crab cactus. $3.20, Nopalxochia. $5, Grizzly bear cactus.

Perf. 12½
1964, Feb. 27 Unwmk. Photo.
Plants in Original Colors

1386	A206	80c dp plum & fawn	1.90	20
1387	A206	$1 dk blue & car	5.25	1.00
1388	A206	$3.20 green	7.75	20
1389	A206	$5 lilac & yellow	10.50	1.00
		Nos. 1386-1389 (4)	25.40	2.40

Perf. 11½
1964, Mar. 25 Engr. Wmk. 323
Without Gum

1390	A207	80c black brown	1.50	15

Centenary of the birth of Wu Chih-hwei (1865-1953), politician and leader of the Kuomintang.

Chu Kwang Tower, Quemoy — A208

Perf. 13x12½
1964-66 Wmk. 323 Litho.
Granite Paper; Without Gum

1391	A208	3c sepia	35	15
1392	A208	5c brt yel grn ('65)	35	15
1393	A208	10c yellow grn	35	15
1394	A208	20c slate grn ('65)	35	15
1395	A208	40c rose red	35	15
1396	A208	50c brown	35	15
1397	A208	80c orange ('65)	85	15
1398	A208	$1 violet ('65)	1.10	15
1399	A208	$1.50 brt lilac ('66)	1.50	24
1400	A208	$2 lilac rose	1.50	15
1401	A208	$2.50 ultra ('65)	1.50	15
1402	A208	$3 slate	2.75	15
1403	A208	$3.20 brt blue	3.50	15
1404	A208	$4 brt green	4.25	15
		Nos. 1391-1404 (14)	19.05	
		Set value		1.50

Nurses Holding Candles — A209

Florence Nightingale and Student Nurse — A210

1964, May 12 Engr. *Perf. 11½*
Without Gum

1406	A209	80c violet blue	95	28
1407	A210	$4 red	3.00	55

Issued for Nurses Day.

Shihmen Reservoir A211

Designs: $1, Irrigation system. $3.20, Main dam and power plant. $5, Spillway.

Perf. 12½
1964, June 14 Unwmk. Photo.

1408	A211	80c multicolored	2.25	20
1409	A211	$1 multicolored	2.25	20
1410	A211	$3.20 multicolored	4.00	50
1411	A211	$5 multicolored	11.00	2.00
		Nos. 1408-1411 (4)	19.50	2.90

Completion of Shihmen Reservoir.

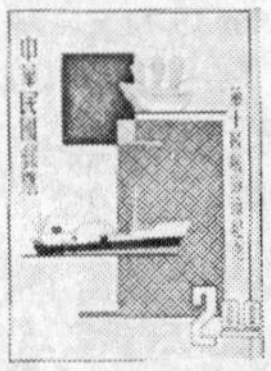
15th Century Ship, Modern Liner — A212

Perf. 11½
1964, July 11 Engr. Wmk. 323
Without Gum

1412	A212	$2 orange	52	32
1413	A212	$3.60 brt green	1.00	48

China's 10th Navigation Day.

Bananas A213

Unwmk.
1964, July 25 Photo. *Perf. 14*

1414	A213	80c shown	*9.50*	45
1415	A213	$1 Oranges	*16.00*	1.40
1416	A213	$3.20 Pineapple	*21.00*	85
1417	A213	$4 Watermelon	*35.00*	2.25
		Nos. 1414-1417 (4)	*81.50*	4.95

Artillery, Warships, Jet Fighters — A214

Perf. 11½
1964, Sept. 3 Wmk. 323 Engr.
Without Gum

1418	A214	80c dk blue	60	15
1419	A214	$6 violet brown	3.25	60

Issued for the 10th Armed Forces Day.

Unisphere, Flags of China and US — A215

Chinese Pavilion, NY World's Fair — A216

1964, Sept. 10 Photo. Unwmk.

1420	A215	80c violet & multi	55	24
1421	A216	$5 blue & multi	4.50	1.00

NY World's Fair, 1964-65. See #1450-1451.

Cowboy Carrying Calf, and Ranch A217

Bicycling A218

Perf. 11½
1964, Sept. 24 Wmk. 323 Engr.
Without Gum

1422	A217	$2 brown lake	1.75	22
1423	A217	$4 dk vio blue	4.25	75

Animal Protection Week, Sept. 24-30.

1964, Oct. 10 Without Gum

Sports: $1, Runner. $3.20, Gymnast on rings. $10, High jump.

1424	A218	80c vio blue	60	15
1425	A218	$1 rose red	1.00	20
1426	A218	$3.20 dull blue grn	2.25	20
1427	A218	$10 lilac	6.25	1.90
		Nos. 1424-1427 (4)	10.10	2.45

18th Olympic Games, Tokyo, Oct. 10-25.

Hsü Kuang-chi A219

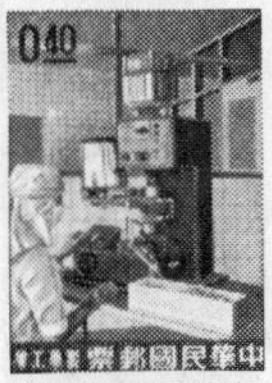
Pharmaceutical Industry A220

Textile Industry — A221

1964, Nov. 8 Engr. *Perf. 11½*
Without Gum

1428	A219	80c indigo	2.00	15

Issued to honor Hsü Kuang-chi (1562-1633), scholar and statesman.

1964, Nov. 11 Photo. Unwmk.

Designs: $2, Chemical industry. $3.60, Cement industry.

1429	A220	40c multi	1.50	40
1430	A221	$1.50 multi	4.00	1.25
1431	A220	$2 multi	4.50	52
1432	A221	$3.60 multi	8.75	1.00
		Nos. 1429-1432 (4)	18.75	3.17

Dr. Sun Yat-sen — A222

Eleanor Roosevelt and Scales of Justice — A223

1964, Nov. 24 Engr. Wmk. 323
Without Gum

1433	A222	80c green	2.25	28
1434	A222	$3.60 purple	3.50	52

Founding of the Kuomintang by Sun Yat-sen, 70th anniversary.

Unwmk.
1964, Dec. 10 Photo. *Perf. 13*

1435	A223	$10 violet & brown	1.40	50

Issued to honor Eleanor Roosevelt (1884-1962) on the 16th anniversary of the Universal Declaration of Human Rights.

Scales, Code Book and Plum Blossom A224

Rotary Emblem and Mainspring A225

Perf. 11½
1965, Jan. 11 Wmk. 323 Engr.
Without Gum

1436	A224	80c carmine rose	65	28
1437	A224	$3.20 dull slate grn	60	42

The 20th Judicial Day.

1965, Feb. 23 Wmk. 323 *Perf. 11½*
Without Gum

1438	A225	$1.50 vermilion	40	16
1439	A225	$2 emerald	1.10	25
1440	A225	$2.50 blue	1.50	32
		Nos. 1438-1440 (3)	3.00	73

Rotary International, 60th anniversary.

Double Carp Design — A226

Madame Chiang Kai-shek — A227

Perf. 11½
1965, Mar. 29 Wmk. 323 Engr.
Granite Paper; Without Gum

1441	A226	$5 purple	14.00	32
1442	A226	$5.60 dp blue	8.00	4.00
1443	A226	$6 brown	7.00	1.00
1444	A226	$10 lilac rose	16.00	25
1445	A226	$20 rose car	18.00	75
1446	A226	$50 green	35.00	2.75
1447	A226	$100 crimson rose	80.00	4.75
		Nos. 1441-1447 (7)	178.00	13.82

1965, Apr. 17 Photo. Unwmk.

1448 A227 $2 multicolored 11.00 32
1449 A227 $6 salmon & multi 27.50 3.50

Chinese Women's Anti-Aggression League, 15th anniversary.

Unisphere and Chinese Pavilion — A228

"100 Birds Paying Homage to Queen Phoenix" and Unisphere — A229

1965, May 8

1450 A228 $2 blue & multi 7.50 35
1451 A229 $10 red, ocher & bis 27.50 2.00

New York World's Fair, 1964-65.

ITU Emblem, Old and New Communication Equipment A230

Design: $5, similar to 80c, vert.

Perf. 13½x13, 13x13½

1965, May 17 Photo. Unwmk.

1452 A230 80c multicolored 50 16
1453 A230 $5 multicolored 2.50 65

Centenary of the ITU.

Red Sea Bream A231

Fish: 80c, White pomfret. $2, Skipjack, vert. $4, Moonfish.

1965, July 1 ***Perf. 13***

1454 A231 40c multicolored 2.25 60
1455 A231 80c multicolored 4.50 60
1456 A231 $2 multicolored 5.75 75
1457 A231 $4 multicolored 14.00 1.65
Nos. 1454-1457 (4) 26.50 3.60

Issued for Fishermen's Day.

Confucius A232

ICY Emblem A233

Portraits: $2.50, Yueh Fei. $3.50, Wen Tien-hsiang. $3.60, Mencius.

Perf. 11½

1965-66 Wmk. 323 Engr.

Without Gum

1458 A232 $1 dp carmine 2.00 32
1459 A232 $2.50 black brn 2.00 45
1460 A232 $3.50 dk red 4.25 55
1461 A232 $3.60 dk blue 5.50 65
Nos. 1458-1461 (4) 13.75 1.97

Issue dates: Nos. 1458, 1461, Sept. 28, 1965. Nos. 1459-1460, Sept. 3, 1966.
The $2.50 and $3.50 have colored background.

See Nos. 1507-1508.

Unwmk.

1965, Oct. 24 Photo. ***Perf. 13***

Design: $6, ICY emblem, horiz.

1462 A233 $2 brn, blk & gold 95 15
1463 A233 $6 brt grn, red & gold 4.75 1.10

International Cooperation Year, 1965.

Street Crossing, Traffic Light A234

Sun Yat-sen A235

Perf. 11½

1965, Nov. 1 Wmk. 323 Engr.

Without Gum

1464 A234 $1 brown violet 1.40 45
1465 A234 $4 crimson rose 2.50 1.10

Issued to publicize traffic safety.

Perf. 13½

1965, Nov. 12 Unwmk. Photo.

Designs: $4, Dr. Sun Yat-sen, portrait at right. $5, Sun Yat-sen and flags, horiz.

1466 A235 $1 multicolored 1.90 15
1467 A235 $4 multicolored 5.75 42
1468 A235 $5 multicolored 10.50 1.90
Nos. 1466-1468 (3) 18.15 2.47

Children with New Year's Firecrackers A236

Dragon Dance, "Dragon Playing Ball" A237

1965, Dec. 1 Photo. ***Perf. 13***

1469 A236 $1 multi 4.50 32
1470 A237 $4.50 multi 5.50 1.25

Lien Po from "Marshal and Prime Minister Reconciled" — A238

Facial Paintings for Chinese Operas: $3, Kuan Yü from "Reunion at Ku City." $4, Gen. Chang Fei from "The Battle of Chang Pan Hill." $6, Buddha from "The Flower-Scattering Angel."

1966, Feb. 15 Unwmk. ***Perf. 11½***

1471 A238 $1 olive & multi 16.00 42
1472 A238 $3 multicolored 15.00 32
1473 A238 $4 multicolored 16.00 42
1474 A238 $6 ver & multi 27.50 2.75
Nos. 1471-1474 (4) 74.50 3.91

Postal Service Emblem Held by Carrier Pigeon — A239

Stone, Mt. Tai-wu, Quemoy, and Mailman A240

Designs (postal service emblem and): $3, Postal Museum. $4, Mailman climbing symbolic slope.

1966, Mar. 20 Photo. ***Perf. 12½***

1475 A239 $1 green & multi 2.00 24
1476 A240 $2 multicolored 2.00 24
1477 A240 $3 multicolored 3.25 30
1478 A239 $4 multicolored 5.75 95
Nos. 1475-1478 (4) 13.00 1.73

China postal service, 70th anniversary.

Fishing on a Snowy Day, "Five Dynasties" (907-960) A241

Paintings from Palace Museum: $3.50, Calves on the Plain, Sung artist (960-1126). $4.50, Winter landscape, Sung artist (960-1126). $5, Magpies, by Lin Ch'un, Southern Sung dynasty (1127-1279).

1966, May 20 Photo. ***Perf. 13***

1479 A241 $2.50 blk, brn & red 9.50 42
1480 A241 $3.50 bis brn, blk & gray 7.75 52
1481 A241 $4.50 blk, buff & sl 7.75 1.25
1482 A241 $5 multicolored 21.00 1.65
Nos. 1479-1482 (4) 46.00 3.84

Inauguration of Pres. Chiang Kai-shek for a 4th term.

Dragon Boat Race — A242

Lion Dance — A243

Design: $4, Lady Chang O flying to the Moon.

1966 Unwmk.

1483 A242 $2.50 multi 9.50 38
1484 A242 $4 multi 5.50 38
1485 A243 $6 multi 5.25 75
Nos. 1483-1485 (3) 20.25 1.51

Issued for the Dragon Boat, Mid-Autumn and Lunar New Year Festivals. Issue dates: $2.50, June 23; $4, Sept. 29; $6, Nov. 26.

Flags of China and Argentina A244

1966, July 9 Photo. ***Perf. 13***

1486 A244 $10 multicolored 3.00 60

150th anniversary of Argentina's Independence.

Lin Sen — A245

Flying Geese — A246

Perf. 11½

1966, Aug. 1 Wmk. 323 Engr.

Without Gum

1487 A245 $1 dk brown 1.50 15

Centenary of the birth of Lin Sen (1867-1943), Chairman of the Nationalist Government of China (1931-43).

1966-67 ***Perf. 11½ Rough***

Granite Paper; Without Gum

1496 A246 $3.50 brown 52 15
1497 A246 $4 vermilion 65 15
1498 A246 $4.50 brt green 85 26
1499 A246 $5 rose lilac 85 15
1500 A246 $5.50 yel grn ('67) 85 26
1501 A246 $6 brt blue 2.50 65
1502 A246 $6.50 violet 1.65 40
1503 A246 $7 black 1.40 15
1504 A246 $8 car rose ('67) 1.65 26
Nos. 1496-1504 (9) 10.92 2.43

The $4.50, $5, $6, $7 and $8 were reissued with gum in 1970-71.

Pres. Chiang Kai-shek in Chung San Robe — A247

Design: $5, Chiang Kai-shek in marshal's uniform.

Unwmk.

1966, Oct. 31 Photo. ***Perf. 13***

1505 A247 $1 multicolored 1.00 28
1506 A247 $5 multicolored 5.00 1.40

Chiang Kai-shek's inauguration for a fourth term as president, May 20, 1966.

Famous Men Type of 1965-66 with Frame Line

Portraits: No. 1507, Tsai Yuan-pei (1868-1940), educator. No. 1508, Chiu Ching (1875-1907), woman educator and revolutionist.

1967 Wmk. 323 Engr. ***Perf. 11½***

Without Gum

1507 A232 $1 violet blue 1.65 25
1508 A232 $1 black 1.65 25

Issue dates: #1507, Jan. 11. #1508, July 15. No. 1507 is on granite paper.

Motorized Mailman and Microwave Station — A248

"Transportation" and Radar Weather Station — A249

Unwmk.

1967, Mar. 15 Photo. *Perf. 13*

1511	A248	$1	multicolored	1.10	25
1512	A249	$5	multicolored	1.90	75

Issued to publicize the progress in communication and transportation services.

Pres. Chiang Kai-shek and Chinese Flag — A250

Chu Yuan, 332-295 B.C. — A251

Design: $4, Different frame.

1967, May 20 Litho. *Perf. 13*

1513	A250	$1	multicolored	1.65	48
1514	A250	$4	multicolored	3.50	60

First anniversary of President Chiang Kai-shek's 4th-term inauguration.

Perf. 11½

1967, June 12 Wmk. 323 Engr.

Portraits: $2, Li Po (705-760). $2.50, Tu Fu (712-770). $3, Po Chu-i (772-846).

Granite Paper; Without Gum

1515	A251	$1	black	1.90	15
1516	A251	$2	brown	3.25	25
1517	A251	$2.50	brown blk	3.75	38
1518	A251	$3	grnsh black	3.75	32
	Nos. 1515-1518 (4)			12.65	1.10

Issued for Poets' Day.

Hotei, Wood Carving — A252

World Map — A253

Handicrafts: $2.50, Vase and plate. $3, Dolls. $5, Palace lanterns.

Perf. 11½

1967, Aug. 12 Unwmk. Photo.

1519	A252	$1	gray & multi	1.40	55
1520	A252	$2.50	multi	2.75	55
1521	A252	$3	multi	3.75	65
1522	A252	$5	multi	5.50	2.50
	Nos. 1519-1522 (4)			13.40	4.25

Taiwan handicraft industry.

Perf. 11½

1967, Sept. 25 Wmk. 323 Engr.

Granite Paper; Without Gum

1523	A253	$1	vermilion	16	15
1524	A253	$5	blue	85	45

1st Conference of the World Anti-Communist League, WACL, Taipei, Sept. 25-29.

Players on Stilts: "The Fisherman and the Woodcutter" A254

Unwmk.

1967, Oct. 10 Photo. *Perf. 13*

1525	A254	$4.50	multi	1.25	30

Issued for the 56th National Day.

Maroon Oriole A255

Formosan Birds: $1, Formosan barbet, vert. $2.50, Formosan green pigeon. $3, Formosan blue magpie. $5, Crested serpent eagle, vert. $8, Mikado pheasants.

1967, Nov. 25 Photo. *Perf. 11*

Granite Paper

1526	A255	$1	multi	1.65	22
1527	A255	$2	multi	3.75	22
1528	A255	$2.50	multi	3.75	28
1529	A255	$3	multi	4.00	28
1530	A255	$5	multi	10.50	40
1531	A255	$8	multi	15.00	1.00
	Nos. 1526-1531 (6)			38.65	2.40

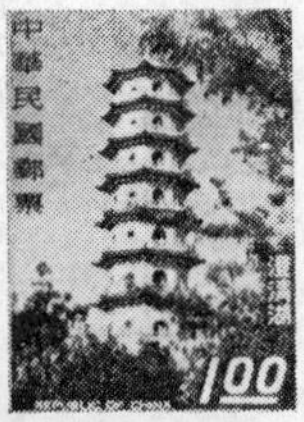

Chung Hsing Pagoda — A256

Buddha, Changhua A257

Designs: $2.50, Seashore, Yeh Liu Park. $5, National Palace Museum, Taipei.

Unwmk.

1967, Dec. 10 Photo. *Perf. 13*

1532	A256	$1	multi	90	15
1533	A257	$2.50	multi	2.75	50
1534	A257	$4	multi	3.75	32
1535	A257	$5	multi	5.75	85
	Nos. 1532-1535 (4)			13.15	1.82

Issued for International Tourist Year 1967.

China Park, Manila, and Flags — A258

1967, Dec. 30 *Perf. 13½*

1536	A258	$1	multicolored	48	18
1537	A258	$5	multicolored	1.50	45

Sino-Philippine Friendship Year 1966-67.

Sun Yat-sen Building, Yangmingshan

A259 A259a

Perf. 13x12½

1968-75 Litho. Wmk. 323

Granite Paper

1538	A259	5c	lt brown	25	15
1539	A259	10c	grnsh blk	25	15
1540	A259	50c	brt rose lil	25	15
1541	A259	$1	vermilion	60	15
1542	A259	$1.50	emerald	1.25	22
1543	A259	$2	plum	1.25	15
1544	A259	$2.50	blue	1.25	15
1545	A259	$3	grnsh blue	2.50	22
	Nos. 1538-1545 (8)			7.60	
	Set value				1.00

For overprints see Nos. 1723-1725.

Coil Stamps

Perf. 13 Horiz.

Photo. Unwmk.

1546	A259a	$1	carmine rose	26	26
1547	A259a	$1	vermilion	24	24

Issued dates: 50c, $1, $2.50, Jan. 23, 1968; No. 1546, Mar. 20, 1970; No. 1547, Jan. 28, 1975; others July 11, 1968.

Inscription on No. 1546 is in color with white background. On No. 1547 it is white with colored background.

Harvesting Sugar Cane A260

Jade Cabbage, 1662-1911 A261

Unwmk.

1968, Mar. 1 Photo. *Perf. 13*

1548	A260	$1	olive & multi	1.25	15
1549	A260	$4	multicolored	1.75	45

1968, Mar. 29 Unwmk. *Perf. 13*

Ancient Art Treasures: $1.50, Jade battle axe. $2, Porcelain flower bowl, 960-1126 A.D., horiz. $2.50, Cloisonné enamel vase, 1723-1736 A.D. $4, Agate flower holder in shape of finger citrus, 1662-1911 A.D., horiz. $5, Sacrificial kettle, 1111-771 B.C.

1550	A261	$1	rose & multi	1.25	22
1551	A261	$1.50	blue & multi	2.50	45
1552	A261	$2	blue & multi	3.50	18
1553	A261	$2.50	dull rose & multi	3.50	45
1554	A261	$4	pink & multi	3.75	52
1555	A261	$5	blue & multi	5.25	70
	Nos. 1550-1555 (6)			19.75	2.52

For similar artifact designs inscribed "Republic of China," with single-color denominations in slanted numerals and the cents underlined, see types A276, A291, A323, A336, A372, A384, A395, A411.

Artifact designs with denominations in outlined numerals begin with type A439.

View of City in Cathay (1) — A262

Views: No. 1557, City and wall of Forbidden City (2). No. 1558, Wall at right, bridge at left (3). No. 1559, Queen's ship landing at left (4). No. 1560, Palace (5). $5, City wall and gate. $8, Suburb around Great Bridge. Design from scroll "A City in Cathay," painted 1736.

1968, June 18 Photo. *Perf. 13½*

Size: 50x29mm

1556	A262	$1	multicolored	1.25	20
1557	A262	$1	multicolored	1.25	20
1558	A262	$1	multicolored	1.25	20
1559	A262	$1	multicolored	1.25	20
1560	A262	$1	multicolored	1.25	20
a.	Strip of 5, #1556-1560			6.75	6.75

Size: 60x31mm

Perf. 13x13½

1561	A262	$5	multicolored	9.25	1.75
1562	A262	$8	multicolored	14.00	2.00
	Nos. 1556-1562 (7)			29.50	

Nos. 1556-1560 printed se-tenant in sheet of 50 with horizontal strips of five containing one of each.

See Nos. 1610-1614. For similar designs see types A281, A299, A326, A343.

Entrance Gate, Taroko Gorge — A263

Design: $8, Sun Yat-sen Building, Yangmingshan.

1968, Feb. 12 Photo. *Perf. 13*

1563	A263	$5	multicolored	2.50	28
1564	A263	$8	multicolored	2.50	28

The 17th Annual Conference of the Pacific Area Travel Association.

Vice President Chen Cheng — A264

Flying Geese — A265

1968, Mar. 5

1565	A264	$1	brown & multi	1.00	20

Vice President Chen Cheng (1898-1965).

Wmk. 323

1968, Mar. 20 Litho. *Perf. 12*

Granite Paper

1566	A265	$1	vermilion	1.00	20

Souvenir Sheet

Imperf

1567	A265	$3	green	10.00	1.50

90th anniv. of Chinese postage stamps. No. 1567 contains one stamp with simulated perforations.

WHO Emblem and "20" — A266

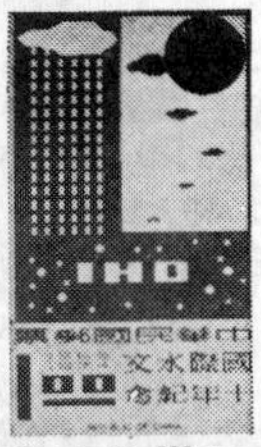

Symbolic Water Cycle — A267

1968, Apr. 7 Engr. *Perf. 12*

Granite Paper

1568	A266	$1	green	30	15
1569	A266	$5	scarlet	70	38

20th anniv. of WHO.

Perf. 11½

1968, June 6 Wmk. 323 Litho.

Granite Paper

1570	A267	$1	green & org	30	20
1571	A267	$4	brt blue & org	70	20

Hydrological Decade (UNESCO) 1965-74.

Broadcasting to Mainland China A268

Dual Carriers for FM Broadcasting A269

Wmk. 323

1968, Aug. 1 Litho. *Perf. 12*

Granite Paper

1572	A268	$1	bl, vio bl & gray	30	20
1573	A269	$4	lt ultra & ver	70	20

40th anniv. of the Broadcasting Corp. of China, and the inauguration of frequency modulation broadcasting.

Human Rights Flame — A270

Crop Improvement and Extension Work — A271

1968, Sept. 3

Granite Paper

1574	A270	$1	multicolored	35	20
1575	A270	$5	multicolored	90	20

International Human Rights Year 1968.

Wmk. 323

1968, Sept. 30 Litho. *Perf. 12*

Granite Paper

1576	A271	$1	yel, bister & dk brn	30	15
1577	A271	$5	yel, emer & dk grn	70	40

Joint Commission on Rural Reconstruction, 20th anniversary.

Javelin — A272

Designs: $2.50, Weight lifting. $5, Pole vault, horiz. $8, Woman hurdling, horiz.

Unwmk.

1968, Oct. 12 Photo. *Perf. 13*

1578	A272	$1	multi	35	15
1579	A272	$2.50	multi	52	22
1580	A272	$5	multi	85	15
1581	A272	$8	pink & multi	1.25	45
			Nos. 1578-1581 (4)	2.97	97

19th Olympic Games, Mexico City, Oct. 12-27.

Pres. Chiang Kai-shek and Whampoa Military Academy A273

Designs: $2, Pres. Chiang Kai-shek reviewing forces of the Northern Expedition. $2.50, Suppression of bandits, reconstruction work and New Life Movement emblem. $3.50, Marco Polo Bridge near Peking and victory parade, Nanking. $4, Original copy of Constitution of Republic of China. $5, Nationalist Chinese flag flying over mainland China.

1968, Oct. 31 *Perf. 11½x12*

1582	A273	$1	multi	80	22
1583	A273	$2	multi	1.25	32
1584	A273	$2.50	multi	1.25	32
1585	A273	$3.50	multi	1.50	32
1586	A273	$4	multi	2.00	65
1587	A273	$5	multi	2.25	65
			Nos. 1582-1587 (6)	9.05	2.48

Chiang Kai-shek's achievements for China.

Cock — A274

Flag — A275

1968, Nov. 12 Litho. *Perf. 12*

Granite Paper

1588	A274	$1	pink & multi	32.50	32
1589	A274	$4.50	lilac & multi	32.50	5.25

Issued for use on New Year's greetings.

1968, Dec. 25 Wmk. 323 *Perf. 12½*

Granite Paper

1590	A275	$1	multicolored	42	20
1591	A275	$5	lt blue & multi	90	40

Constitution of the Republic of China, 20th anniversary.

Jade Belt Buckle, 1662-1911 A276

Ancient Art Treasures: $1.50, Yellow jade vase, 960-1126 A.D., vert. $2, Cloisonne enamel square teapot, 1662-1911 A.D. $2.50, Kuei, sacrificial bronze vessel, 722-481 B.C. $4, Heavenly ball vase, 1368-1661 A.D., vert. $5, Gourd-shaped vase, 1662-1911 A.D., vert.

Unwmk.

1969, Jan. 15 Photo. *Perf. 13*

1592	A276	$1	dl rose & multi	1.00	15
1593	A276	$1.50	rose & multi	1.25	28
1594	A276	$2	brt rose & multi	1.25	20
1595	A276	$2.50	lt blue & multi	2.25	32
1596	A276	$4	tan & multi	2.75	32
1597	A276	$5	pale blue & multi	3.75	70
			Nos. 1592-1597 (6)	12.25	1.97

Servicemen and Savings Emblem — A277

Wmk. 323

1969, Feb. 1 Engr. *Perf. 12*

Granite Paper

1598	A277	$1	dull red brn	28	22
1599	A277	$4	dp blue	75	28

Military Savings Program, 10th anniv.

Ti (Flute) A278

Musical Instruments: $2.50, Sheng (13 bamboo pipes connected at the base). $4, P'i p'a (lute). $5, Cheng (zither).

Unwmk.

1969, Mar. 16 Photo. *Perf. 13*

1600	A278	$1	buff & multi	45	15
1601	A278	$2.50	lt ap grn & multi	90	15
1602	A278	$4	pink & multi	1.90	48
1603	A278	$5	lt grnsh bl & multi	1.90	28
			Nos. 1600-1603 (4)	5.15	1.06

Sun Yat-sen Building and Kuomintang Emblem A279

Double Carp Design A280

1969, Mar. 29 Litho. *Perf. 13½*

1604	A279	$1	multicolored	50	20

10th Natl. Cong. of the Chinese Nationalist Party (Kuomintang), Mar. 29. A $2.50 stamp portraying Sun Yat-sen and Chiang Kai-shek was prepared but not issued.

Perf. 13½x12½

1974 Engr. Wmk. 323

Granite Paper

1606	A280	$10	dark blue	1.50	15
1607	A280	$20	dark brown	3.00	15
1608	A280	$50	green	7.50	38
1609	A280	$100	bright red	12.00	1.00
			Nos. 1606-1609 (4)	24.00	1.68

1969

Perf. 11½

1606a	A280	$10		2.00	15
1607a	A280	$20		2.75	15
1608a	A280	$50		7.50	25
1609a	A280	$100		11.50	65
			Nos. 1606a-1609a (4)	23.75	1.20

The 1969 issue is 27mm high; 1974, 28mm. See No. 1980.

Bridal Procession — A281

Designs: No. 1610, Musicians and standard bearer from bridal procession. $2.50, Emigrant farm family in oxcart. $5, Art gallery. $8, Roadside food stands. Designs from scroll "A City in Cathay," painted in 1736.

Perf. 13½

1969, May 20 Unwmk. Photo.

1610	A281	$1	multi	1.00	15
1611	A281	$1	multi	1.00	15
a.			Pair, #1610-1611	2.25	22
1612	A281	$2.50	multi	3.00	45
1613	A281	$5	multi	3.25	55
1614	A281	$8	multi	5.50	90
			Nos. 1610-1614 (5)	13.75	2.20

ILO Emblem — A282

Perf. 11½

1969, June 15 Engr. Wmk. 323

Granite Paper

1615	A282	$1	dark blue	35	15
1616	A282	$8	dark carmine	1.10	40

ILO, 50th anniversary.

Family at Dinner Table and Dressing — A283

Pupils in Laboratory and Playing — A284

Designs: $2.50, Housecleaning and obeying traffic rules. $4, Recreation (music, fishing, basketball) and education.

Perf. 11½

1969, July 15 Engr. Wmk. 323

1617	A283	$1	brick red	16	15
1618	A283	$2.50	blue	52	28
1619	A283	$4	green	52	22
			Nos. 1617-1619 (3)	1.20	65

Model Citizen's Life Movement.

1969, Sept. 1 Wmk. 323 *Perf. 11½*

Design: $1, $5, Pupils with book and various school activities, horiz.

Granite Paper

1620	A284	$1	brt red	40	18
1621	A284	$2.50	brt green	65	18
1622	A284	$4	dk blue	80	22
1623	A284	$5	brown	1.10	32
			Nos. 1620-1623 (4)	2.95	90

Free 9-year education system, 1st anniv.

Wild Flowers and Pheasants, by Lu Chih (Ming) — A285

Paintings: $2.50, Bamboo and birds, Sung dynasty. $5, Flowers and Birds, Sung dynasty. $8, Cranes and Flowers, by G. Castiglione, S.J. (1688-1766).

1969, Oct. 9 Photo. *Perf. 13½*

1624	A285	$1	multi	1.25	18
1625	A285	$2.50	multi	2.50	35
1626	A285	$5	multi	5.00	55
1627	A285	$8	multi	9.25	90
			Nos. 1624-1627 (4)	18.00	1.98

Golden Scepter Rose — A286

Rocket and Radar Station — A287

Roses: $1, "Charles Mollerin," called black rose. $5, Peace. $8, Josephine Bruce.

1969, Oct. 31 Litho. *Perf. 14*

1628	A286	$1	lt vio & multi	80	15
1629	A286	$2.50	lt bl & multi	1.90	18
1630	A286	$5	dl org & multi	3.50	45
1631	A286	$8	ap grn & multi	4.00	35
			Nos. 1628-1631 (4)	10.20	1.13

Perf. 11½

1969, Nov. 21 Wmk. 323 Engr.

1632	A287	$1	rose claret	80	15

The 30th Air Defense Day.

Symbol of International Cooperation A288

Pekingese A289

1969, Nov. 25

1633 A288	$1 rose claret		26	16
1634 A288	$5 green		75	24

5th General Assembly of the Asian Parliamentary Union, Taipei, Nov. 24-28.

1969, Dec. 1 **Litho.** ***Perf. 12***

Granite Paper

1635 A289	50c	red & multi	1.25	32
1636 A289	$4.50	green & multi	8.75	1.65

Issued for use on New Year's greetings.

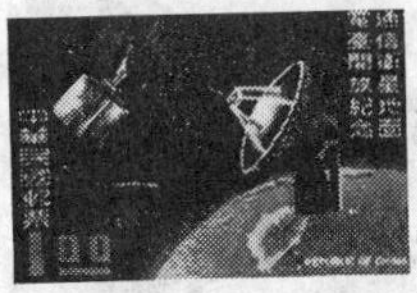

Satellite, Earth Station and Map of Taiwan A290

Unwmk.

1969, Dec. 28 **Photo.** ***Perf. 13***

1637 A290	$1	brown & multi	55	15
1638 A290	$5	vio blue & multi	1.65	32
1639 A290	$8	purple & multi	1.75	55
		Nos. 1637-1639 (3)	3.95	1.02

Inauguration of the Communication Satellite Earth Station at Chin-Shan-Li, Dec. 28.

Agate Grinding Stone, 1662-1911 A291

Ancient Art Treasures: $1, Carved lacquer ware vase, 1662-1911, vert. $2, White jade Chin-li-chih melons, 1662-1911. $2.50, Black jade shepherd and ram, 206 B.C.-220 A.D. $4, Chien-lung twin porcelain vase, 1736-1796, vert. $5, Ju porcelain vase with 3 bulls, 960-1126, vert.

1970, Jan. 23

1640 A291	$1	lt grnsh bl & multi	65	24
1641 A291	$1.50	pale bl & multi	1.10	30
1642 A291	$2	grn & multi	1.10	30
1643 A291	$2.50	pink & multi	2.00	30
1644 A291	$4	ol bis & multi	3.25	30
1645 A291	$5	ultra & multi	4.00	60
		Nos. 1640-1645 (6)	12.10	2.04

Hsuan Chuang A292

Chu Hsi A293

Design: $2.50, Hua To.

Perf. 11½

1970, Feb. 20 **Wmk. 323** **Engr.**

Granite Paper

1646 A292	$1	car rose	80	18
1647 A293	$2.50	blue grn	1.25	25
1648 A293	$4	blue	1.75	32
		Nos. 1646-1648 (3)	3.80	75

Issued in memory of Hsuan Chuang (602-664), who propagated Buddhism in China; Chu Hsi (1130-1200), who developed Neo-Confucianism, and Hua To (3rd century A.D.) physician and surgeon.

EXPO '70 Pavilion, Emblem and Flags of Participants A294

Design: $5, Chinese pavilion, EXPO '70 emblem, exhibition and Chinese flags.

Unwmk.

1970, Mar. 13 **Photo.** ***Perf. 13***

1649 A294	$5	org red & multi	65	30
1650 A294	$8	lt blue & multi	1.10	45

EXPO '70 International Exhibition, Osaka, Japan, Mar. 15-Sept. 13.

Nimbus III and WMO Emblem — A295

Design: $1, Agricultural meteorological station and tropical landscape, vert.

Perf. 14x13½, 13½x14

1970, Mar. 23 **Litho.** **Wmk. 323**

Granite Paper

1651 A295	$1	green & multi	30	15
1652 A295	$8	blue & multi	95	45

10th Annual World Meteorological Day.

Martyrs' Shrine, Taipei — A296

Shrine's Gate — A297

Unwmk.

1970, Mar. 29 **Photo.** ***Perf. 13***

1653 A296	$1	multicolored	55	15
1654 A297	$8	multicolored	1.75	48

Completion of the Martyrs' Shrine in Northern Taipei, dedicated to the memory of 72 young revolutionaries who died Mar. 29, 1911.

Yueh Fei Fighting for Lost Territories A298

Characters from Chinese Operas: $2.50, Emperor Shun and stepmother. $5, The Lady Warrior Chin Liang-yu. $8, Kuan Yu and groom.

1970, May 4 **Unwmk.** ***Perf. 13½***

1655 A298	$1	multi	1.00	18
1656 A298	$2.50	multi	1.75	40
1657 A298	$5	multi	2.50	55
1658 A298	$8	multi	5.50	85
		Nos. 1655-1658 (4)	10.75	1.98

"One Hundred Horses" (Detail) by Lang Shih-ning — A299

Three Horses Playing — A300

Designs (Horses): No. 1660, Trees in left background. No. 1661, Tree trunk in lower left corner. No. 1662, Group of trees at right. No. 1663, Barren tree at right. $8, Groom roping horses. Designs from scroll "One Hundred Horses" by Lang Shih-ning (Giuseppe Castiglione, 1688-1766).

Perf. 13½

1970, June 18 **Unwmk.** **Photo.**

1659 A299	$1	multi	1.00	18
1660 A299	$1	multi	1.00	18
1661 A299	$1	multi	1.00	18
1662 A299	$1	multi	1.00	18
1663 A299	$1	multi	1.00	18
a.		Strip of 5, #1659-1663	5.00	
1664 A300	$5	bister & multi	4.75	90
1665 A300	$8	dl yel & multi	6.25	1.10
		Nos. 1659-1665 (7)	16.00	2.90

Lai-tsu Amusing his Old Parents — A301

Chinese Fairy Tales: No. 1667, Man disguised as deer, and hunters. No. 1668, Boy cooling his father's bed. No. 1669, Boy fishing through ice. No. 1670, Son reunited with old mother. No. 1671, Emperor tasting mother's medicine. No. 1672, Boy saving oranges for mother. No. 1673, Boy saving father from tiger.

Perf. 13½

1970, July 10 **Wmk. 323** **Litho.**

Granite Paper

1666 A301	10c	red & multi	15	15
1667 A301	10c	car rose & multi	15	15
1668 A301	10c	lt vio & multi	15	15
1669 A301	10c	gray & multi	15	15
1670 A301	10c	emerald & multi	15	15
1671 A301	50c	bister & multi	20	15
1672 A301	$1	sky blue & multi	50	18
1673 A301	$1	dp blue & multi	50	18
		Nos. 1666-1673 (8)	1.95	
		Set value		70

See Nos. 1726-1733.

Man's First Step onto Moon — A302

Designs: $1, Pres. Chiang Kai-shek's message brought to the moon. $5, Neil A. Armstrong, Michael Collins, Edwin E. Aldrin, Jr., and moon, horiz.

Perf. 13½x13, 13x13½

1970, July 21 **Photo.** **Unwmk.**

1674 A302	$1	yellow & multi	65	15
1675 A302	$5	lt yel grn & multi	1.10	30
1676 A302	$8	blue & multi	1.65	65
		Nos. 1674-1676 (3)	3.40	1.10

1st anniv. of man's 1st landing on the moon.

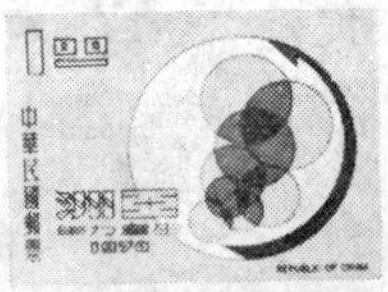

Asian Productivity Year Symbol — A303

Perf. 13½

1970, Aug. 18 **Wmk. 323** **Litho.**

Granite Paper

1677 A303	$1	emerald & multi	42	15
1678 A303	$5	blue & multi	90	38

Issued to publicize Asian Productivity Year.

Flags of China and UN — A304

1970, Sept. 19 **Wmk. 323** ***Perf. 12***

Granite Paper

1679 A304	$5	blue, car & blk	1.40	50

25th anniversary of the United Nations.

Postal Zone Map — A305

Postal Code Emblem — A306

1970, Oct. 8 **Litho.**

1680 A305	$1	lt blue & multi	40	20
1681 A306	$2.50	green & multi	1.00	35

Issued to publicize the postal code system.

Eleventh Month Scroll — A307

Designs: A scroll series, "Activities of the 12 Months," painted on silk by a group of painters of the Ch'ien Lung court (1736-1796). Chinese number in parenthesis at right of denomination tells month.

Jan., Feb., Mar.

(一) (二) (三)

Perf. 13½x13

1970-71 Photo. Unwmk.

1682	A307	$1	multi	95	52
1683	A307	$2.50	multi	2.25	70
1684	A307	$5	multi	3.75	1.10

Apr., May, June

(四) (五) (六)

1685	A307	$1	multi	95	42
1686	A307	$2.50	multi	2.25	80
1687	A307	$5	multi	3.75	80

July, Aug., Sept.

(七) (八) (九)

1688	A307	$1	multi	95	28
1689	A307	$2.50	multi	2.25	42
1690	A307	$5	multi	3.75	70

Oct., Nov., Dec.

(十) (一十) (二十)

1691	A307	$1	multi	5.75	28
1692	A307	$2.50	multi	7.50	42
1693	A307	$5	multi	13.00	70
			Nos. 1682-1693 (12)	47.10	7.14

Issue dates: Nos. 1691-1693, Oct. 21, 1970. Nos. 1682-1684, Jan. 14, 1971. Nos. 1685-1687, Apr. 26, 1971. Nos. 1688-1690, Aug. 27, 1971.

Family at Home — A308

Piggy Bank — A309

Design: $4, Family of 5 going on an excursion, vert.

Perf. 13½x14, 14x13½

1970, Nov. 11 Litho. Wmk. 323

Granite Paper

1694	A308	$1	multicolored	50	20
1695	A308	$4	yel grn & multi	1.50	30

Issued to publicize family planning.

1970, Dec. 1 *Perf. 12½x12*

Granite Paper

1696	A309	50c	multi	1.10	35
1697	A309	$4.50	bl & multi	5.25	65

Issued for use on New Year's greetings.

Tibia Fusus Shells — A310

Rare Taiwan Shells: $2.50, Harpeola kurodai. $5, Conus stupa kuroda. $8, Entemnotrochus rumphii.

1971, Feb. 25 *Perf. 13x13½*

1698	A310	$1	vio & multi	42	16
1699	A310	$2.50	multi	65	28
1700	A310	$5	org & multi	1.65	50
1701	A310	$8	grn & multi	2.75	30
			Nos. 1698-1701 (4)	5.47	1.24

The Scott Catalogue value is a retail value; that is, what you could expect to pay for the stamp in a grade of Fine-Very Fine. The value listed reflects recent actual dealer selling prices.

Sun Yat-sen Building, Yangmingshan A311

Passbook and Postal Savings Certificate A312

Perf. 13½x12½

1971 Litho. Wmk. 323

Granite Paper

1702	A311	5c	brown	15	15
1703	A311	10c	dk gray	15	15
1704	A311	50c	brt rose lil	22	15
1705	A311	$1	vermilion	22	15
1706	A311	$1.50	ultra	1.50	15
1707	A311	$2	plum	1.50	15
1708	A311	$2.50	emerald	3.00	15
1709	A311	$3	aqua	3.00	15
			Nos. 1702-1709 (8)	9.74	
			Set value		75

Perf. 13½x14

1971, Mar. 20 Litho. Wmk. 323

Design: $4, People and hand dropping coin into bank.

1712	A312	$1	yel grn & multi	15	15
1713	A312	$4	ver & multi	1.10	30

Publicizing Chinese Postal Savings Service.

Cooperation Emblem, Farmers A313

Rock Monkey A314

Design: $8, Chinese teaching rice farming to Africans, horiz.

Unwmk.

1971, May 20 Photo. *Perf. 13*

1714	A313	$1	multicolored	24	15
1715	A313	$8	multicolored	1.10	38

Sino-African Technical Cooperation Committee, 10th anniversary.

1971, June 25 *Perf. 11½*

Taiwan Animals: $2, White-face flying squirrel. $3, Chinese pangolin. $5, Formosan sika deer. $2, $3, $5 are horiz.

1716	A314	$1	gold & multi	65	20
1717	A314	$2	gold & multi	65	20
1718	A314	$3	gold & multi	1.75	55
1719	A314	$5	gold & multi	1.75	55
			Nos. 1716-1719 (4)	4.80	1.50

Pitcher — A315

Designs: $2.50, Players at base, horiz. $4, Batter and catcher.

1971, July 29 Photo. *Perf. 13*

1720	A315	$1	multi	25	15
1721	A315	$2.50	multi	35	22
1722	A315	$4	multi	65	22
			Nos. 1720-1722 (3)	1.25	59

Pacific Regional competition for the 1971 Little League World Series.

Nos. 1541, 1544-1545 Overprinted in Magenta or Red

Perf. 13x12½

1971, Sept. 9 Litho. Wmk. 323

Granite Paper

1723	A259	$1	ver (M)	20	15
1724	A259	$2.50	blue (R)	55	20
1725	A259	$3	grnsh blue (R)	40	28
			Nos. 1723-1725 (3)	1.15	63

Chinese victory in 1971 Little League World Series, Williamsport, Pa., Aug. 24.

Fairy Tale Type of 1970

Chinese Fairy Tales (Filial Piety): No. 1726, Birds and elephant helping in rice field. No. 1727, Son gathering mulberries for mother. No. 1728, Son gathering firewood. No. 1729, Son, mother and bandits. No. 1730, Son carrying heavy burden. 50c, Son digging for bamboo shoots in winter. No. 1732, Man and wife working as slaves. No. 1733, Father, son and carriage.

1971, Sept. 22 *Perf. 13½*

Granite Paper

1726	A301	10c	dp org & multi	20	15
1727	A301	10c	lilac & multi	20	15
1728	A301	10c	ocher & multi	20	15
1729	A301	10c	dp car & multi	20	15
1730	A301	10c	lt ultra & multi	20	15
1731	A301	50c	multicolored	20	15
1732	A301	$1	emerald & multi	50	15
1733	A301	$1	lt red brn & multi	50	15
			Nos. 1726-1733 (8)	2.20	
			Set value		75

Flag of China, "Double Ten" and Anniversary Emblems A316

Designs (Flag of China and): $2.50, National anthem. $5, Gen. Chiang Kai-shek. $8, Sun Yat-sen.

1971, Oct. 10 Photo. *Perf. 13*

1734	A316	$1	orange & multi	32	15
1735	A316	$2.50	multi	48	15
1736	A316	$5	green & multi	1.00	35
1737	A316	$8	olive & multi	1.40	35
			Nos. 1734-1737 (4)	3.20	1.00

60th National Day.

Bird in Flight (AOPU Emblem) A317

Perf. 13½x14

1971, Nov. 8 Litho. Wmk. 323

1738	A317	$2.50	yellow & multi	50	20
1739	A317	$5	orange & multi	50	20

Asian-Oceanic Postal Union Executive Committee Session, Taipei, Nov. 8-15.

"White Frost Hawk," by Lang Shih-ning A318

Dog Series I

Designs: $2, "Star-Glancing Wolf." $2.50, "Golden-Winged Face." $5, "Young Black Dragon." $8, "Young Gray Dragon."

Designs from painting series "Ten Prized Dogs," by Lang Shih-ning (Giuseppe Castiglione, 1688-1766).

Perf. 13½x13

1971, Nov. 16 Litho. Unwmk.

1740	A318	$1	Facing left	95	20
1741	A318	$2	Lying down	1.40	28
1742	A318	$2.50	Scratching	1.50	52
1743	A318	$5	Facing right	2.75	80
1744	A318	$8	Looking back	5.50	1.65
			Nos. 1740-1744 (5)	12.10	3.45

Dog Series II

Designs: $1, "Black with Snow-white Paws." $2, "Yellow Leopard." $2.50, "Flying Magpie." $5, "Heavenly Lion." $8, "Mottled Tiger."

1972, Jan. 12

1745	A318	$1	Facing right	3.25	20
1746	A318	$2	Walking	3.75	25
1747	A318	$2.50	Sleeping	4.75	45
1748	A318	$5	Facing left	8.50	1.00
1749	A318	$8	Sitting	20.00	1.65
			Nos. 1745-1749 (5)	40.25	3.55

Squirrels A319

Perf. 13½x12½

1971, Dec. 1 Wmk. 323

1750	A319	Block of 4	4.50	22
a.		50c in UL corner	75	15
b.		50c in UR corner	75	15
c.		50c in LL corner	75	15
d.		50c in LR corner	75	15
1751	A319	Block of 4	19.00	2.50
a.		$4.50 in UL corner	4.50	60
b.		$4.50 in UR corner	4.50	60
c.		$4.50 in LL corner	4.50	60
d.		$4.50 in LR corner	4.50	60

New Year 1972.

Flags of China and Jordan — A320

1971, Dec. 16 *Perf. 13½*

Granite Paper

1752	A320	$5	multicolored	1.00	25

50th anniversary of the founding of the Hashemite Kingdom of Jordan.

Cargo Ship "Hai King" — A321

Design: $7, Ocean liner and map of Pacific Ocean, vert.

1971, Dec. 16 *Perf. 12½*

1753	A321	$4	grn, dk bl & red	45	45
1754	A321	$7	ocher & multi	75	50

Centenary of China Merchants Steam Navigation Co.

Downhill Skiing, Olympic Rings — A322

Designs: $5, Cross-country skiing. $8, Giant slalom.

1972, Feb. 3 *Perf. 13½*

1755	A322	$1 org, blk & bl	16	15
1756	A322	$5 yel grn, dp org & blk	45	20
1757	A322	$8 red, gray & blk	60	20
		Nos. 1755-1757 (3)	1.21	55

11th Winter Olympic Games, Sapporo, Japan, Feb. 3-13.

Vase, 18th Century — A323

Porcelain Series I

Porcelain Masterworks of Ching Dynasty: $2, Covered jar. $2.50, Pitcher. $5, Vase with 5 openings and dragon design. $8, Covered jar with children design.

Perf. 11½

1972, Mar. 20 Photo. Unwmk.

1758	A323	$1 vio & multi	1.10	18
1759	A323	$2 plum & blue	1.10	22
1760	A323	$2.50 org ver & bl	1.10	22
1761	A323	$5 bis brn & bl	2.50	32
1762	A323	$8 sl grn & multi	3.25	55
		Nos. 1758-1762 (5)	9.05	1.49

See Nos. 1812-1821, 1864-1868.

Nine Flying Doves — A324

Perf. 13½x14

1972, Apr. 1 Litho. Wmk. 323

1763	A324	$1 lt bl & blk	30	20
1764	A324	$5 lt vio & blk	90	35

Asian-Oceanic Postal Union, 10th anniv.

"Dignity with Self-reliance" — A325

Perf. 13½x12½

1972-75 Litho. Wmk. 323

1765	A325	5c brown & yel	15	15
1766	A325	10c blue & org	15	15
1767	A325	20c cl & yel grn ('75)	15	15
1768	A325	50c lil & lil rose	15	15
1769	A325	$1 red & brt bl	15	15
1770	A325	$1.50 yel & dk bl	35	15
1771	A325	$2 mar & org	35	15
1772	A325	$2.50 emer & ver	35	15
1773	A325	$3 red & lt grn	50	15
		Set value	2.00	75

Souvenir Sheet

Imperf

1775	A325	Sheet of 2	5.00	2.00

No. 1775 commemorates ROCPEX '72 Philatelic Exhibition, Taipei, Oct. 24-Nov. 2. It contains 2 stamps similar to Nos. 1771 and 1773 with simulated perforations.

Issue dates: $1, $1.50, $2, $3, May 20, 1972; 5c, 10c, 50c, $2.50, No. 1775, Oct. 24, 1972; 20c, 1975.

For overprints see Nos. 1787-1790.

Emperor Shih-tsung's Procession — A326

Messengers on Horseback — A327

Designs from scrolls depicting Emperor Shih-tsung's (reigned 1522-1566) journey to and from tombs at Cheng-tien. No. 1776 shows land journey departure and is designed from right to left. No. 1779 shows return trip by boat and is designed from left to right. The 5 stamps of Nos. 1776 and 1780 are numbered 1 to 5 in Chinese (see illustrations with Nos. 1682-1686 for numerals).

1972 Photo. Unwmk. *Perf. 13½*

1776		Strip of 5	3.75	60
a.		A326 $1 shown (1)	75	15
b.		A326 $1 Seven carriages (2)	75	15
c.		A326 $1 Carriage drawn by 23 horses (3)	75	15
d.		A326 $1 Procession (4)	75	15
e.		A326 $1 Emperor under 2 canopies (5)	75	15
1777	A327	$2.50 shown	2.00	16
1778	A327	$5 Guards with flags, fans & spears	3.00	22
1779	A327	$8 Sedan chair carried by 28 men	5.25	45
1780		Strip of 5	3.75	60
a.		A326 $1 Three barges (1)	75	15
b.		A326 $1 Procession, sedan chairs (2)	75	15
c.		A326 $1 Two barges with trunks (3)	75	15
d.		A326 $1 Procession on land (4)	75	15
e.		A326 $1 Procession, 2 sedan chairs (5)	75	15
1781	A327	$2.50 Courtiers at city welcoming Emperor	2.00	16
1782	A327	$5 Orchestra on horseback	3.00	22
1783	A327	$8 Barges	3.00	45
		Nos. 1776-1783 (8)	25.75	2.86

Issue dates: No. 1776-1779, June 14; Nos. 1780-1783, July 12.

First Day Covers A328

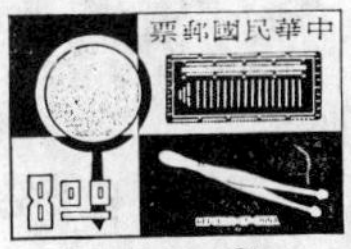

Magnifying Glass, Tongs, Gauge A329

Design: $2.50, Sun Yat-sen stamp of 1971 (type A311) under magnifying glass.

Wmk. 323

1972, Aug. 9 Engr. *Perf. 12*

1784	A328	$1 dk vio blue	18	15
1785	A328	$2.50 brt green	22	16
1786	A329	$8 scarlet	65	25
		Nos. 1784-1786 (3)	1.05	56

Promotion of philately. Printed in sheets of 40. Each sheet contains 4 blocks of 10 stamps surrounded by margins with inscriptions.

Nos. 1768-1770, 1772 Overprinted in Dark Blue or Red

Perf. 13½x12½

1972, Sept. 9 Litho. Wmk. 323

1787	A325	$1 red & brt bl (DB)	15	15
1788	A325	$1.50 yel & dk bl (R)	28	30
1789	A325	$2 maroon & org (R)	28	15
1790	A325	$3 red & lt grn (DB)	28	18
		Nos. 1787-1790 (4)	99	78

China's championship victories in the Little League World Series, Gary, Ind., and in the Senior League World Series, Williamsport, Pa., Aug. 1972.

Emperor Yao (2357-2258 B.C.) — A330

Mountain Climbing — A331

Rulers: $4, Emperor Shun (ruled 2255-2208 B.C.). $4.50, Yu, the Great (ruled 2205-2198 B.C.). $5, King T'ang (ruled 1783-1754 B.C.). $5.50, King Wen (ruled 1171-1122 B.C.). $6, King Wu (ruled 1121-1114 B.C.). $7, Chou Kung (died 1105 B.C.). $8, Confucius (551-479 B.C.).

1972-73 Engr. *Perf. 12*

Granite Paper

1791	A330	$3.50 dk blue	60	24
1792	A330	$4 rose red	60	24
1793	A330	$4.50 bluish lil	70	24
1794	A330	$5 brt green	85	24
1795	A330	$5.50 dp org ('73)	1.25	24
1796	A330	$6 dp claret ('73)	1.25	28
a.		Perf. 13½x12½ ('76)	1.25	28
1797	A330	$7 sepia ('73)	1.25	28
a.		Perf. 13½x12½ ('76)	1.25	28
1798	A330	$8 indigo ('73)	1.25	38
a.		gray, perf. 13½x12½ ('76)	1.75	38
		Nos. 1791-1798 (8)	7.75	2.14

In the first printing, Nos. 1791-1794, 1796-1798 measure 32mm high. In a 1974 reissue they are 33mm.

Unwmk.

1972, Oct. 31 Photo. *Perf. 12*

Designs (China Youth Corps emblem and): $2.50, Skiing (skiers forming circle). $4, Diving. $8, Parachute jumping.

1800	A331	$1 green & multi	15	15
1801	A331	$2.50 blue & multi	38	15
1802	A331	$4 orange & multi	48	15
1803	A331	$8 multicolored	1.10	32
		Nos. 1800-1803 (4)	2.11	77

China Youth Corps, 20th anniversary.

JCI Emblem — A332

1972, Nov. 12 Litho. Wmk. 323

1804	A332	$1 multicolored	16	15
1805	A332	$5 orange & multi	40	20
1806	A332	$8 multicolored	65	50
		Nos. 1804-1806 (3)	1.21	85

27th Junior Chamber International (JCI) World Congress, Taipei, Nov. 12-19.

Electronic Mail Sorter A333

Plane, Ship and Pier A334

Progress of Communications System on Taiwan: $5, Highway overpass over railroad.

Perf. 11½

1972, Nov. 12 Wmk. 323 Engr.

1807	A333	$1 red	16	15
1808	A334	$2.50 blue	32	24
1809	A334	$5 dk vio brn	75	45
		Nos. 1807-1809 (3)	1.23	84

Cow and Calf (Parental Love) — A335

1972, Dec. 1 Litho. *Perf. 12*

1810	A335	50c red & blk	1.90	42
1811	A335	$4.50 yel, red & brn	5.00	1.10

New Year 1973. Printed in sheets of 80, divided into 4 panes of 20, separated by vertical and horizontal gutters 2 rows wide. 20 red chops meaning "Happy New Year" are printed in the gutters.

Porcelain Type of 1972 and

Stem Bowl with Dragons A336

Porcelain Series II

Porcelain Masterworks of Ming Dynasty: $1, Covered vase with fruits and flowers. $2, Vase with ornamental and floral design. $2.50, Vase imitating ancient bronze. $5, Flask with flowers of 4 seasons. $8, Garlic head vase.

1973 Photo. *Perf. 11½*

1812	A323	$1 gray & multi	50	15
1813	A323	$2 lt brn & multi	75	28
1814	A323	$2.50 brt grn & multi	1.90	28
1815	A323	$5 ultra & multi	3.50	52
1816	A323	$8 olive & multi	5.25	85
		Nos. 1812-1816 (5)	11.90	2.08

Porcelain Series III

Ming Porcelain: $2, Refuse container with dragons. $2.50, Covered jar with lotus. $5, Covered jar with horses. $8, Bowl with figures of immortals.

1817	A336	$1 gray & multi	26	18
1818	A336	$2 lt vio & multi	42	32
1819	A336	$2.50 dk red & multi	1.25	32
1820	A336	$5 blue & multi	1.25	48
1821	A336	$8 dp org & multi	2.75	80
		Nos. 1817-1821 (5)	5.93	2.10

Issue dates: Nos. 1812-1816, Jan. 10; Nos. 1817-1821, Mar. 24.

See Nos. 1865-1868.

Oyster Fairy and Fisherman's Dance — A337

1973, Feb. 7 Photo. *Perf. 11½*

Granite Paper

1822	A337	$1 Kicking shuttlecock, vert.	65	15
1823	A337	$4 Shown	1.25	20
1824	A337	$5 Rowing boat over land	1.25	25
1825	A337	$8 Old man carrying young lady, vert.	1.75	40
		Nos. 1822-1825 (4)	4.90	1.00

Chinese folklore popular entertainment.

Bamboo Boat — A338

Taiwanese Handicrafts: $2.50, Painted marble vase, vert. $5, Painted glass plate. $8, Doll, bride-groom carrying bride on back, vert.

Perf. 13½x14½, 14½x13½

1973, Mar. 9 Photo.

1826 A338 $1 multi 22 15
1827 A338 $2.50 multi 50 24
1828 A338 $5 multi 80 28
1829 A338 $8 multi 85 48
Nos. 1826-1829 (4) 2.37 1.15

Federation Emblem, Cargo Hook, Crane — A339

Emblem, Tractor, New Buildings — A340

Perf. 12½

1973, Apr. 2 Litho. Wmk. 323

1830 A339 $1 salmon & multi 15 15
1831 A340 $5 blue & blk 65 35

12th convention of International Federation of Asian and Western Pacific Contractors Association, Taipei, Apr. 2-10.

Pres. Chiang Kai-shek, Flag of China — A341

Lin Tse-hsü — A342

Design: $4, like $1 with different border.

Unwmk.

1973, May 20 Photo. *Perf. 12*

1832 A341 $1 yellow & multi 35 28
1833 A341 $4 dk grn & multi 90 60

First anniversary of Pres. Chiang Kai-shek's inauguration for a fifth term.

Wmk. 323

1973, June 3 Engr. *Perf. 12*

1834 A342 $1 sepia 40 25

Lin Tse-hsü (1785-1850), Governor of Hunan and Kwantung, who destroyed large quantity of opium at Humen, Kwantung, June 3, 1839.

Willows and Palace Gate in the Morning — A343

Lady Watering Peonies, Stone Ornament A344

Design from scroll "Spring Morning in the Han Palace," by Chiu Ying. The five stamps of No. 1835 are numbered 1 to 5 and the five stamps of No. 1838 are numbered 6-10 in Chinese (see illustrations with Nos. 1682-1691 for numerals). The stamps are numbered and listed from right to left.

1973 Photo. Unwmk. *Perf. 11½*

Granite Paper

1835 Strip of 5 4.00 1.25
a. A343 $1 shown (1) 26 15
b. A343 $1 Ladies feeding peacocks (2) 26 15
c. A343 $1 Lady watering peonies (3) 26 15
d. A343 $1 Pear tree in bloom (4) 26 15
e. A343 $1 Lady musicians (5) 26 15
1836 A344 $5 shown 3.50 60
1837 A344 $8 Lady musicians 4.50 1.00
1838 Strip of 5 4.00 1.25
a. A343 $1 Ladies playing go (6) 26 15
b. A343 $1 Various games (7) 26 15
c. A343 $1 Talking and playing music (8) 26 15
d. A343 $1 Artist painting portrait (9) 26 15
e. A343 $1 Sentries guarding wall (10) 26 15
1839 A344 $5 Ladies playing go 3.50 60
1840 A344 $8 Girl chasing butterfly 4.50 1.00
Nos. 1835-1840 (6) 24.00 5.70

Issue dates: Nos. 1835-1837, June 20; Nos. 1838-1840, July 18.

Fan, Bamboo Design, by Hsiang Te-hsin — A345

Designs: Painted fans, Ming dynasty.

Perf. 12½x13

1973, Aug. 15 Photo. Wmk. 368

1841 A345 $1 bis & multi 22 18
1842 A345 $2.50 bis & multi 52 24
1843 A345 $5 bis & multi 90 35
1844 A345 $8 bis & multi 1.40 60
Nos. 1841-1844 (4) 3.04 1.37

See Nos. 1934-1937.

Little League Emblem A346

INTERPOL Emblem A347

Perf. 13½

1973, Sept. 9 Litho. Wmk. 370

1845 A346 $1 yel, car & dk bl 35 20
1846 A346 $4 yel, grn & dk bl 1.50 40

Chinese victory in Little League Twin Championships, Gary, Ind., and Williamsport, Pa.

Wmk. 370

1973, Sept. 11 Litho. *Perf. 12*

1847 A347 $1 blue & org 15 15
1848 A347 $5 green & org 38 30
1849 A347 $8 magenta & org 60 50
Nos. 1847-1849 (3) 1.13 95

50th anniversary of International Criminal Police Organization.

Ch'iu Feng-chia — A348

Perf. 11½

1973, Oct. 5 Wmk. 323 Engr.

1850 A348 $1 violet black 50 30

2nd meeting of overseas Hakkas, Taipei, Oct. 5-7, and to honor Ch'iu Feng-chia (1864-1912), Hakka scholar, poet and revolutionist.

Tsengwen Reservoir A349

Tsengwen Dam — A350

Perf. 13½

1973, Oct. 31 Photo. Unwmk.

1851 Strip of 3 75 50
a. A349 $1 Upper shore 24 15
b. A349 $1 shown 24 15
c. A349 $1 Lower shore 24 15

Perf. 12x11½

1852 A350 $5 shown 90 42
1853 A350 $8 Spillway 1.40 70
Nos. 1851-1853 (3) 3.05 1.62

Inauguration of Tsengwen Reservoir. No. 1851 printed se-tenant in sheets of 15.

Tiger — A351

Perf. 12½

1973, Dec. 1 Litho. Wmk. 370

1854 A351 50c multi 50 30
1855 A351 $4.50 multi 1.65 60

New Year 1974.

"Snow-dotted Eagle," by Lang Shih-ning — A352

Designs: No. 1857, "Comfortable Ride." No. 1858, "Red Flower Eagle." No. 1859, "Cloud-running Steed." No. 1860, "Sky-running steed." $2.50, "Red Jade Seat." $5, "Thunderclap Steed." $8, "Arabian Champion." Designs from painting series "Ten Prized Horses," by Lang Shih-ning (Giuseppe Castiglione, 1688-1766).

1973 Litho. Unwmk. *Perf. 13*

Without Gum

1856 A352 50c shown 24 20
1857 A352 $1 Pinto, blk tail 90 20
1858 A352 $1 Facing left 90 20
1859 A352 $1 Facing right 90 20
1860 A352 $1 Pinto, white tail 90 20
a. Block of 4, #1857-1860 3.75 3.00
1861 A352 $2.50 Palomino 2.00 40
1862 A352 $5 Grazing 3.00 60
a. Souvenir sheet of 4 24.00 7.50
1863 A352 $8 Brown stallion 5.00 75
Nos. 1856-1863 (8) 13.84 2.75

No. 1862a contains 4 stamps with simulated perforations similar to Nos. 1856-1857, 1861-1862.

Issued: 50c, $2.50, $5, Nov. 21; others Dec. 21.

Porcelain Types of 1972-73

Porcelain Series IV

Porcelain Masterworks of Sung Dynasty: $1, Vase. $2, Three-tiered vase. $2.50, Lotus-shaped bowl. $5, Incense burner. $8, Incense burner on stand.

1974, Jan. 16 Photo. *Perf. 11½*

1864 A323 $1 ultra & multi 28 15
1865 A336 $2 multicolored 60 22
1866 A336 $2.50 red & multi 75 22
1867 A336 $5 lilac & multi 1.25 32
1868 A336 $8 green & multi 1.75 55
Nos. 1864-1868 (5) 4.63 1.46

Juggler — A353

Taroko Gorge, Hualien — A354

Design: $8, Magician producing dishes from his robe, horiz.

1974, Feb. 6 Photo. *Perf. 11½*

1869 A353 $1 yellow & multi 22 15
1870 A353 $8 yellow & multi 1.40 15
Set value 15

1974, Mar. 22 Photo. *Perf. 12*

Designs: $2.50, Luce Chapel, Tunghai University. $5, Tzu En Pagoda, Sun Moon Lake. $8, Goddess of Mercy, Keelung.

1871 A354 $1 multi 32 15
1872 A354 $2.50 multi 85 15
1873 A354 $5 multi 1.25 18
1874 A354 $8 multi 2.00 25
Nos. 1871-1874 (4) 4.42 73

Taiwan landmarks.

Fighting Cocks (Brass) A355

Designs: $2.50, Grapes and bowl with fruit (imitation jade). $5, Fisherman (wood carving), vert. $8, Basket with plastic roses, vert.

Perf. 13½x14½, 14½x13½

1974, Apr. 10

1875 A355 $1 blue grn & multi 15 15
1876 A355 $2.50 brown & multi 50 25
1877 A355 $5 crimson & multi 80 32
1878 A355 $8 multicolored 1.25 48
Nos. 1875-1878 (4) 2.70 1.20

Taiwanese handicraft products.

Sun Yat-sen Memorial Hall — A356

Taiwan landmarks: $2.50, Reaching-moon Tower, Cheng Ching Lake. $5, Orchid Island (boats). $8, Penghu Interisland Bridge.

1974, May 15 Photo. *Perf. 11½*

Granite Paper

1879 A356 $1 blue & multi 18 15
1880 A356 $2.50 blue & multi 52 15
1881 A356 $5 blue & multi 80 15
1882 A356 $8 blue & multi 1.50 22
Nos. 1879-1882 (4) 3.00
Set value 55

Pres. Chiang and Gate of Whampoa Military Academy — A357

Marching Cadets and Entrance Gate — A358

Perf. 11½

1974, June 16 Engr. Wmk. 323

1883 A357	$1	carmine rose	16	15
1884 A358	$14	violet blue	65	50

50th anniversary of the founding of the Whampoa Military Academy.

Long-distance Runner and Olympic Rings — A359

The Boy Wang Ch'i Fighting Invaders — A360

Design: $8, Women's relay race and Olympic rings.

1974, June 23 Litho. *Perf. 12½*

1885 A359	$1	blue, blk & red	15	15
1886 A359	$8	pink, blk & red	80	45

80th anniv. of Intl. Olympic Committee.

1974, July 15 Wmk. 370 *Perf. 13½*

Folk Tales: No. 1888, T'i Ying pleading for her father before the Emperor. No. 1889, Wen Yen-po flushing out ball caught in tree. No. 1890, Boy Wang Hua returning gold piece he found. No. 1891, Pu Shih, a rich sheep raiser and benefactor. No. 1892, K'ung Yung as a child choosing smallest pear. No. 1893, Tung Yu studying. No. 1894, Szu Ma-kuang saving playmate from drowning in water jar.

1887 A360	50c	olive & multi	15	15
1888 A360	50c	ultra & multi	15	15
1889 A360	50c	ocher & multi	15	15
1890 A360	50c	red brn & multi	15	15
a.		Block of 4, #1887-1890	60	60
1891 A360	$1	green & multi	35	35
1892 A360	$1	lilac & multi	35	35
1893 A360	$1	blue & multi	35	35
1894 A360	$1	car & multi	35	35
a.		Block of 4, #1891-1894	1.50	1.50
		Nos. 1887-1894 (8)	2.00	2.00

For similar designs see types A380, A427, A456, A495.

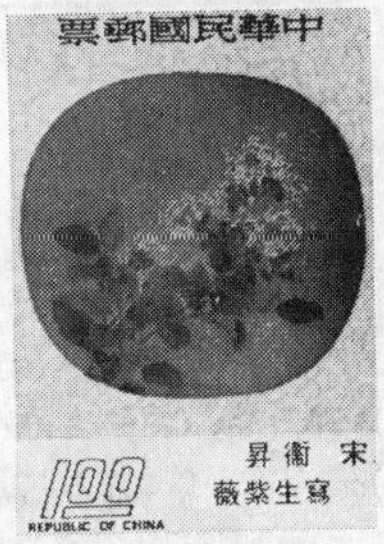
Myrtle, by Wei Sheng — A361

Silk Fan Paintings, Sung Dynasty (960-1279 A.D.): $2.50, Cabbage and Insects, by Hsu Ti. $5, Hibiscus, Cat and Dog, by Li Ti. $8, Pomegranate and Birds, by Wu Ping. Fans from National Palace Museum.

Perf. 13x12½

1974, Aug. 14 Photo. Wmk. 368

1895 A361	$1	multi	18	15
1896 A361	$2.50	multi	52	25
1897 A361	$5	multi	1.00	32
1898 A361	$8	multi	1.25	48
		Nos. 1895-1898 (4)	2.95	1.20

See Nos. 1950-1953.

Battle at Marco Polo Bridge, July 7, 1937 A362

Perf. 13½

1974, Sept. 3 Litho. Wmk. 370

1899 A362	$1	multicolored	15	15

Souvenir Sheet

Wmk. 323

Without Gum; Granite Paper

1900	Sheet of 8	9.00	9.00
a.	A362 $1, single stamp	75	75

20th Armed Forces Day. No. 1900 commemorates Armed Forces Stamp Exhibition, Sun Yat-sen Memorial Hall, Sept. 3-9.

Chrysanthemum A363

Designs: Various chrysanthemums.

Unwmk.

1974, Sept. 30 Photo. *Perf. 12*

Granite Paper

1901 A363	$1	lilac & multi	15	15
1902 A363	$2.50	multi	65	22
1903 A363	$5	orange & multi	95	30
1904 A363	$8	multi	1.50	45
		Nos. 1901-1904 (4)	3.25	1.12

Rep. of China Pavilion, EXPO Emblem A364

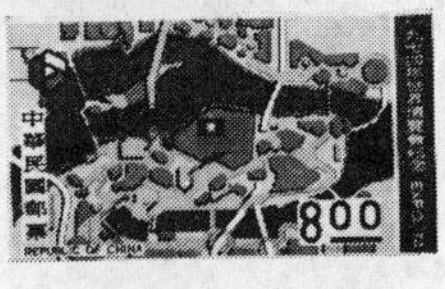
Map of Fair Grounds, Chinese Flag A364a

Wmk. 370

1974, Oct. 10 Litho. *Perf. 13*

1905 A364	$1	multi	15	15
1906 A364a	$8	multi	50	50

EXPO '74, Spokane, Wash., May 4-Nov. 4. Theme, "Preserve the Environment."

Steel Mill, Kaohsiung A365

Taichung Harbor A366

Designs: $1, Taiwan North Link Railroad and map. $2, Oil refinery. $2.50, Electric train. $3.50, Taoyuan International Airport. $4, Taiwan North-South Highway and map. $4.50, Kaohsiung shipyard. $5, Su-ao Port.

Perf. 13x12½, 12½x13

1974, Oct. 31 Wmk. 323

1907 A365	50c	lilac, yel & brn	15	15
1908 A365	$1	green & org	15	15
1909 A365	$2	blue & yel	15	15
1910 A365	$2.50	emer & org	15	15
1911 A366	$3	ocher & ultra	15	15
1912 A366	$3.50	sl grn & yel	16	15
1913 A366	$4	brown & yel	18	15
1914 A366	$4.50	ver & bl	18	15
1915 A366	$5	sepia & dk bl	25	15
		Set value	1.10	75

Major construction projects.

See Nos. 2009-2017, 2068-2076. For overprints see Nos. 2064-2065, 2112-2113.

Agaricus Bisporus — A367

Edible Mushrooms: $2.50, Pleurotus ostreatus. $5, Dictyophora indusiata. $8, Flammulina velutipes.

Perf. 11½

1974, Nov. 15 Unwmk. Photo.

1916 A367	$1	multi	15	15
1917 A367	$2.50	multi	38	20
1918 A367	$5	multi	70	25
1919 A367	$8	multi	80	38
		Nos. 1916-1919 (4)	2.03	98

9th Intl. Scientific Congress on the Cultivation of Edible Fungi, Taipei, Nov. 1974.

Batters and World Map — A368

Pitcher and Championship Banners — A369

Perf. 13½

1974, Nov. 24 Wmk. 323 Litho.

1920 A368	$1	multicolored	15	15
1921 A369	$8	multicolored	50	38

China's victory in 1974 Little League Baseball World Series Triple Championships.

Rabbit — A370

Acrobat with Iron Rod — A371

Perf. 12½

1974, Dec. 10 Photo. Wmk. 323

1922 A370	50c	orange & multi	26	18
1923 A370	$4.50	brown & multi	1.10	38

New Year 1975.

1975, Jan. 15 Unwmk. *Perf. 11½*

Design: $5, Two acrobats spinning tops, horiz.

Granite Paper

1924 A371	$4	yellow & multi	50	48
1925 A371	$5	yellow & multi	90	55

Children Watching Puppet Show — A372

Ceremonial New Year Greetings — A373

Designs from scroll "Festivals for the New Year," by Ting Kuan-p'eng. Nos. 1926a-1926e are numbered 1-5 in Chinese.

1975, Feb. 25 Photo. *Perf. 11½*

Granite Paper

1926	Strip of 5	2.00	55
a.	A372 $1 Ceremonial New Year Greetings (1)	28	15
b.	A372 $1 Man with trained monkey (2)	28	15
c.	A372 $1 Crowd and musicians (3)	28	15
d.	A372 $1 Picnic under a tree (4)	28	15
e.	A372 $1 shown (5)	28	15
1927 A373	$2.50 shown	1.25	28
1928 A373	$5 Children buying firecrackers	2.00	60
1929 A373	$8 Children and man with trained monkey	4.75	95
	Nos. 1926-1929 (4)	10.00	2.38

Sun Yat-sen Memorial Hall, Taipei A374

Sun Yat-sen's Handwriting A375

Sun Yat-sen, Bronze Statue in Memorial Hall — A376

Sun Yat-sen Memorial Hall, St. John's University, NY — A377

Perf. 13½x14, 14x13½

1975, Mar. 12 Litho.

1930 A374	$1	green & multi	15	15
1931 A375	$4	yel grn & multi	35	20
1932 A376	$5	yellow & multi	45	25
1933 A377	$8	gray & multi	75	40
		Nos. 1930-1933 (4)	1.70	1.00

Dr. Sun Yat-sen (1866-1925), statesman and revolutionary leader.

Fan Type of 1973 Inscribed "Landscape" (1st Character, 2nd Row)

山水

Designs: Painted fans, Ming Dynasty. Second row of inscription gives design description.

Perf. 12¹/₂x13

1975, Apr. 16 Photo. Wmk. 368

1934	A345	$1 bister & multi	22	15
1935	A345	$2.50 bister & multi	70	22
1936	A345	$5 bister & multi	1.00	42
1937	A345	$8 bister & multi	1.10	65
		Nos. 1934-1937 (4)	3.02	1.44

Yuan-chin coin, 1122-221 B.C. — A378

Ancient Chinese Coins: $4, Pan-liang, 221-207 B.C. $5, Five chu, 206 B.C.-220 A.D. $8, Five chu, 502-557 A.D.

Wmk. 323

1975, May 20 Litho. ***Perf. 13***

1938	A378	$1 salmon & multi	20	15
1939	A378	$4 yellow & multi	70	18
1940	A378	$5 dl yel & multi	90	22
1941	A378	$8 lt vio & multi	1.75	35
		Nos. 1938-1941 (4)	3.55	90

The Cloth-bag Monk, by Chang Hung (1577-1668) A379

Chinese Paintings: $4, Lao-tzu Riding Buffalo, by Chao Pu-chih (1053-1110). $5, Portrait of Shih-te, by Wang Wen (1497-1576). $8, Splashed-ink Immortal, by Liang K'ai (early 13th century).

Perf. 11¹/₂

1975, June 18 Photo. Unwmk.

Granite Paper

1942	A379	$2 blk, buff & ver	65	16
1943	A379	$4 blk, gray & red	1.40	30
1944	A379	$5 blk, yel & ver	1.75	42
1945	A379	$8 tan, red & blk	3.25	60
		Nos. 1942-1945 (4)	7.05	1.48

Chu Yin Reading by the Light of Fireflies — A380

Folk Tales: No. 1947, Hua Mu-lan going to war for her father. No. 1948, King Kou Chien tasting gall. $5, Chou Ch'u killing tiger.

Perf. 14x13¹/₂

1975, July 16 Litho. Wmk. 368

1946	A380	$1 olive & multi	15	15
1947	A380	$2 bis brn & multi	25	25
1948	A380	$2 lt grn & multi	25	25
1949	A380	$5 blue & multi	75	38
		Nos. 1946-1949 (4)	1.40	1.03

See Nos. 2108-2111.

Cherry-Apple Blossoms, by Lin Ch'un — A381

Silk Fan Paintings, Sung Dynasty: $2, Spring Blossoms and Butterfly, by Ma K'uei. $5, Monkeys and Deer, by I Yüan-chih. $8, Tame Sparrow among Bamboo.

Perf. 13x12¹/₂

1975, Aug. 15 Litho. Wmk. 323

1950	A381	$1 multicolored	22	15
1951	A381	$2 multicolored	70	20
1952	A381	$5 multicolored	1.40	28
1953	A381	$8 multicolored	1.65	60
		Nos. 1950-1953 (4)	3.97	1.23

See Nos. 2001-2004.

Gen. Chang Tzu-chung (1891-1940) — A382

Portraits: No. 1955, Maj. Gen. Kao Chih-hong (1908-37). No. 1956, Capt. Sha Shih-chiun (1896-1938). No. 1957, Maj. Gen. Hsieh Chin-yuan (1905-41). No. 1958, Lt. Yen Hai-wen (1916-37). No. 1959, Lt. Gen. Tai An-lan (1905-42).

Wmk. 323

1975, Sept. 3 Engr. ***Perf. 12***

1954	A382	$2 carmine	16	16
1955	A382	$2 sepia	16	16
1956	A382	$2 dull green	16	16
1957	A382	$5 violet blk	35	35
1958	A382	$5 vio blue	35	35
1959	A382	$5 dk blue	35	35
		Nos. 1954-1959 (6)	1.53	1.53

Martyrs of the resistance fight against Japan.

Lotus Pond with Willows, by Madame Chiang — A383

Paintings by Madame Chiang Kai-shek: $5, Sun Breaks through Mountain Clouds. $8, A Pair of Pine Trees. $10, Fishing and Farming.

Perf. 13¹/₂

1975, Oct. 31 Litho. Unwmk.

1960	A383	$2 multi	80	18
1961	A383	$5 multi	2.00	38
1962	A383	$8 multi	2.75	60
1963	A383	$10 multi	3.50	85
		Nos. 1960-1963 (4)	9.05	2.01

For similar design see type A404.

Cauldron with Phoenix Handles, 481-221 B.C. — A384

Ancient Bronzes: $2, Rectangular cauldron, 1122-722 B.C., vert. $8, Flat jar, 481-221 B.C. $10, 3-legged wine vessel, 1766-1122 B.C., vert.

1975, Nov. 12 Photo. ***Perf. 12***

1964	A384	$2 pink & multi	20	15
1965	A384	$5 lt blue & multi	60	18
1966	A384	$8 yellow & multi	95	28
1967	A384	$10 lilac & multi	1.25	35
		Nos. 1964-1967 (4)	3.00	96

For similar design see type A395. No. 1964 has 7 Chinese characters at left, No. 2005 has 4. No. 1967 has 4 characters at left, No. 2008 has 5.

Dragon, Nine-Dragon Wall, Peihai — A385

Techi Dam — A386

Perf. 12¹/₂

1975, Dec. 1 Litho. Wmk. 323

1968	A385	$1 orange & multi	26	18
1969	A385	$5 green & multi	1.25	75

New Year 1976.

1975, Dec. 17 Unwmk. ***Perf. 13¹/₂***

Design: $10, Panoramic view of Techi Dam.

1970	A386	$2 green & multi	15	15
1971	A386	$10 blue & multi	55	55

Completion of Techi Dam, Tachia River.

Biathlon and Olympic Rings — A387

Designs (Olympic Rings and): $5, Luge. $8, Skiing.

1976, Jan. 15 Litho. ***Perf. 13¹/₂***

1972	A387	$2 blue & multi	16	16
1973	A387	$5 blue & multi	32	22
1974	A387	$8 blue & multi	50	32
		Nos. 1972-1974 (3)	98	70

12th Winter Olympic Games, Innsbruck, Austria, Feb. 4-15.

Chin, Oldest Chinese Instrument A388

Musical Instruments: $5, Se, c. 2900 B.C. $8, Standing kong-ho (harp). $10, Sleeping kong-ho.

1976, Feb. 11 Unwmk. ***Perf. 14***

1975	A388	$2 yellow & multi	20	15
1976	A388	$5 org & multi	40	18
1977	A388	$8 grnsh bl & multi	60	25
1978	A388	$10 multicolored	80	35
		Nos. 1975-1978 (4)	2.00	93

For similar design see Type A407.

Double Carp Type of 1969

Perf. 13¹/₂x12¹/₂

1976, Dec. 15 Engr. Unwmk.

1980	A280	$14 car rose	80	50

Mail Collecting A389

Mail Sorting — A390

Postal Service, 80th Anniv.: $8, Mail transport. $10, Mail delivery.

Perf. 13¹/₂

1976, Mar. 20 Litho. Wmk. 323

1984	A389	$2 yellow & multi	16	15
1985	A390	$5 green & multi	32	15
1986	A390	$8 blue & multi	48	22
1987	A389	$10 orange & multi	60	28
a.		Souv. sheet of 4, #1984-1987	10.00	7.00
		Nos. 1984-1987 (4)	1.56	80

Pres. Chiang Kai-shek A391

People Paying Homage — A392

Designs: No. 1990, Pres. Chiang lying in state. No. 1991, Hearse leaving funeral chapel. $5, People along funeral route. $8, Spirit tablet in Tzuhu Guest House. $10, Tzuhu Guest House, Pres. Chiang's burial place.

1976, Apr. 4

1988	A391	$2 gray & multi	15	15
1989	A392	$2 gray & multi	15	15
1990	A392	$2 gray & multi	15	15
1991	A392	$2 gray & multi	18	15
1992	A392	$5 gray & multi	35	20
1993	A392	$8 gray & multi	55	30
1994	A392	$10 gray & multi	65	38
		Nos. 1988-1994 (7)	2.18	1.48

Pres. Chiang Kai-shek (1887-1975), first death anniversary.

Flags of China and US — A393

Perf. 13¹/₂

1976, May 29 Litho. Wmk. 323

1995	A393	$2 multicolored	15	15
1996	A393	$10 yellow & multi	48	40

American Bicentennial.

Coin, 12th Century B.C. — A394

Cauldron, Shang Dynasty — A395

Bronze Shovel Coins (pu): $5, Pointed-feet coin, 481-221 B.C. $8, Round-feet coin, 722-481 B.C. $10, Square-feet coin, 3rd-2nd centuries B.C.

1976, June 16

1997 A394 $2 salmon & multi 15 15
1998 A394 $5 lt blue & multi 42 18
1999 A394 $8 gray & multi 60 25
2000 A394 $10 multicolored 85 35
Nos. 1997-2000 (4) 2.02 93

Fan Painting Type of 1975

Silk Fan Paintings, Sung Dynasty: $2, Hibiscus, by Li Tung. $5, Lilies, by Lin Ch'un. $8, Deer and Pine, by Mou Chung-fu. $10, Quail and Wild Flowers, by Li An-chung.

Perf. 13x12½

1976, July 14 Litho. Wmk. 323

2001 A381 $2 multicolored 32 16
2002 A381 $5 multicolored 85 26
2003 A381 $8 multicolored 1.25 35
2004 A381 $10 multicolored 1.50 40
Nos. 2001-2004 (4) 3.92 1.17

1976, Aug. 25 Photo. *Perf. 11½*
Granite Paper

Ancient Bronzes: $5, 3-legged cauldron, Chou Dynasty (1122-722 B.C.). $8, Wine container, Chou Dynasty. $10, Wine vessel with spout, Shang Dynasty (1766-1122 B.C.).

2005 A395 $2 rose & multi 25 15
2006 A395 $5 lt blue & multi 75 18
2007 A395 $8 yellow & multi 1.00 25
2008 A395 $10 lilac & multi 1.40 35
Nos. 2005-2008 (4) 3.40 93

Construction Types of 1974

Designs: $1, Taiwan North Link railroad and map. $2, Railroad electrification. $3, Taichung Harbor. $4, Taiwan North-South Highway and map. $5, Steel Mill, Kaohsiung. $6, Taoyuan International Airport. $7, Kao-hsiung shipyard. $8, Oil refinery. $9, Su-ao Port.

Perf. 13½x12½, 12½x13½

1976 Litho. Wmk. 323

2009 A365 $1 carmine & grn 15 15
2010 A365 $2 orange & multi 16 15
2011 A366 $3 violet & multi 18 15
2012 A366 $4 carmine & multi 25 15
2013 A365 $5 green & brn 32 15
2014 A366 $6 brown & multi 35 15
2015 A366 $7 brown & multi 38 15
2016 A365 $8 carmine & grn 50 18
2017 A366 $9 olive & blue 50 18
Nos. 2009-2017 (9) 2.79
Set value 90

Chiang Kai-shek and Mother — A396

Sun Yat-sen and Chiang Kai-shek at Canton Station — A397

Design: $5, Chiang Kai-shek, portrait.

1976, Oct. 31 Litho. *Perf. 13½*

2023 A396 $2 multicolored 20 16
2024 A396 $5 multicolored 40 22
2025 A397 $10 multicolored 75 50
Nos. 2023-2025 (3) 1.35 88

Pres. Chiang Kai-shek, 90th anniv. of birth.

Flags of Kuomintang and China — A398

Sun Yat-sen and Chiang Kai-shek A399

1976, Nov. 12 *Perf. 13½x14*

2026 A398 $2 multicolored 15 15
2027 A399 $10 multicolored 48 35
a. Souv. sheet of 2, #2026-2027 4.50 4.50

11th National Kuomintang Cong., Taipei.

Brazen Serpent — A400

1976, Dec. 15 Wmk. 323 *Perf. 12½*

2028 A400 $1 red, lilac & gold 24 15
2029 A400 $5 plum, yel & gold 1.25 32

New Year 1977.

Bird and Plum Blossoms, by Ch'en Hung-shou A401

Chinese Paintings: $8, "Wintry Days" (pine), by Yang Wei-chen. $10, Rock and Bamboo, by Hsia Ch'ang.

Perf. 11½

1977, Jan. 12 Photo. Unwmk.
Granite Paper

2030 A401 $2 multicolored 75 16
2031 A401 $8 multicolored 2.25 42
2032 A401 $10 multicolored 3.00 45
Nos. 2030-2032 (3) 6.00 1.03

Black-naped Orioles — A402

Birds of Taiwan: $8, Common Kingfisher. $10, Chinese pheasant-tailed jacana.

1977, Feb. 16 Litho.

2033 A402 $2 multicolored 32 15
2034 A402 $8 multicolored 75 30
2035 A402 $10 multicolored 1.25 45
Nos. 2033-2035 (3) 2.32 90

See Nos. 2163-2165.

Census Emblem, Industry and Commerce A403

Perf. 13½

1977, Mar. 16 Litho. Unwmk.

2036 A403 $2 red & multi 15 15
2037 A403 $10 purple & multi 50 50

Industry and Commerce Census.

Green Mountains Rising into Clouds, by Madame Chiang — A404

Landscapes, by Madame Chiang Kai-shek: $5, Boat in the Beauty of Spring. $8, Scholar beside Waterfall. $10, Water Rises to Meet the Bridge.

Perf. 11½

1977, Mar. 31 Unwmk. Photo.
Granite Paper

2038 A404 $2 multi 60 15
2039 A404 $5 multi 1.25 35
2040 A404 $8 multi 1.90 55
2041 A404 $10 multi 2.25 70
Nos. 2038-2041 (4) 6.00 1.75

League Emblem A405

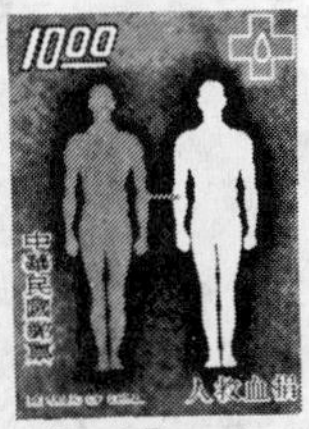

Blood Donation A406

1977, Apr. 18 Litho. *Perf. 12½*

2042 A405 $2 carmine & multi 18 15
2043 A405 $10 green & multi 55 50

10th World Anti-Communist League Conference.

1977, May 5 Wmk. 323 *Perf. 13½*

Design: $2, Donating blood, horiz.

2044 A406 $2 red & blk 15 15
2045 A406 $10 red & blk 48 48

Blood donation movement.

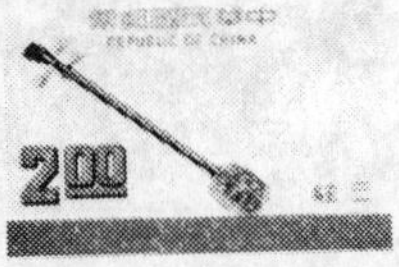

San-hsien A407

Musical Instruments: $5, Tung-hsiao (bamboo flute). $8, Yang-chin (butterfly harpsichord). $10, Pai-hsiao (pipes). Background shows musician playing instrument.

Unwmk.

1977, June 21 Photo. *Perf. 14*

2046 A407 $2 multi 16 15
2047 A407 $5 multi 32 20
2048 A407 $8 multi 45 28
2049 A407 $10 multi 55 32
Nos. 2046-2049 (4) 1.48 95

Idea Leuconoe — A408

Protected Butterflies: $4, Hebomoia glaucippe formosana. $6, Stichophthalma howqua formosana. $10, Atrophaneura horishana.

1977, July 20 Litho. *Perf. 13½*

2050 A408 $2 ver & multi 38 18
2051 A408 $4 lt grn & multi 75 25
2052 A408 $6 lt bl & multi 1.10 38
2053 A408 $10 yellow & multi 1.40 52
Nos. 2050-2053 (4) 3.63 1.33

National Palace Museum A409

Temple — A410

Children's Drawings: $2, Sea Goddess Festival. $4, Boats on Shore of Lan-yu.

Perf. 13½

1977, Aug. 27 Litho. Wmk. 323

2054 A409 $1 multicolored 15 15
2055 A409 $2 multicolored 20 15
2056 A409 $4 multicolored 32 24
2057 A410 $5 multicolored 40 28
Nos. 2054-2057 (4) 1.07
Set value 60

8th Exhib. of World School Children's Art.

Carved Lacquer Plate, Wan-li Ware — A411

Ancient Carved Lacquer Ware: $5, Bowl, Ching dynasty. $8, Round box, Ming dynasty. $10, Four-tiered box, Ching dynasty.

Perf. 13x14

1977, Sept. 28 Photo. Wmk. 368

2058 A411 $2 multicolored 28 15
2059 A411 $5 multicolored 60 20
2060 A411 $8 multicolored 95 28
2061 A411 $10 multicolored 1.25 32
Nos. 2058-2061 (4) 3.08 95

Lions International, Emblem and Activities — A412

Unwmk.

1977, Oct. 8 Litho. *Perf. 13*

2062 A412 $2 multicolored 15 15
2063 A412 $10 multicolored 50 45

Intl. Association of Lions Clubs, 60th anniv.

Nos. 2069 and 2075 Overprinted in Claret

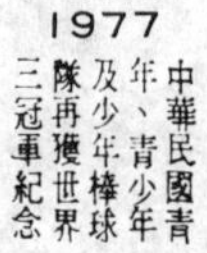

Perf. 13½x12½

1977, Sept. 9 Litho. Unwmk.

2064 A365 $2 orange & multi 15 15
2065 A365 $8 carmine & grn 45 35

Little League baseball championship.

Chinese Quality Mark — A413

Perf. 13x12½

1977, Oct. 14 Litho. Unwmk.

2066 A413 $2 red & multi 15 15
2067 A413 $10 blue & multi 60 35

International Standardization Day.

Construction Types of 1974
Redrawn: Numerals Outlined

Designs as 1976 Issue.

Perf. 13½x12½, 12½x13½

1977 Litho. Unwmk.

Granite Paper

2068 A365 $1 car & dp grn 15 15
2069 A365 $2 ver & multi 16 15
2070 A366 $3 violet & multi 24 15
2071 A366 $4 carmine & multi 28 15
2072 A365 $5 green & multi 38 15
2073 A366 $6 sepia & multi 40 15
2074 A366 $7 sepia & multi 42 20
2075 A365 $8 red lil & multi 52 20
2076 A366 $9 olive & multi 52 22
Nos. 2068-2076 (9) 3.07
Set value 1.35

Numerals are in solid color on #1907-1915, 2009-2017; in outline on #2068-2076.
For overprints see #2064-2065, 2112-2113.

Man and Heart — A414

White Stallion — A415

Perf. 13½x12½

1977, Nov. 12 Litho. Wmk. 323

2077 A414 $2 multicolored 15 15
2078 A414 $10 multicolored 48 48

Physical health, cardiac care.

Perf. 12½

1977, Dec. 1 Unwmk. Litho.

New Year 1978: $5, Two horses, horiz. Designs from painting "100 Horses," by Lang Shih-ning.

2079 A415 $1 red & multi 24 15
2080 A415 $5 emerald & multi 1.25 35

First Page of Constitution — A416

Pres. Chiang Accepting Constitution, 1946 — A417

1977, Dec. 25 Litho. *Perf. 13½*

2081 A416 $2 multicolored 15 15
2082 A417 $10 multicolored 55 40

30th anniversary of the Constitution.

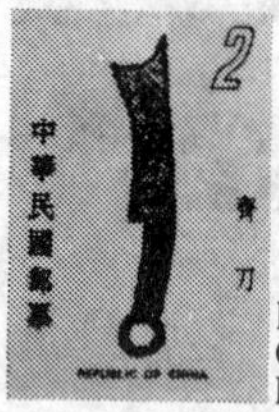

Knife Coin with 3 Characters, 403-221 B.C. — A418

Designs: Ancient knife coins.

1978, Jan. 18 Wmk. 323 *Perf. 13½*

2083 A418 $2 salmon & multi 32 15
2084 A418 $5 lt blue & blk 70 15
2085 A418 $8 lt gray & multi 1.00 26
2086 A418 $10 tan & multi 1.40 28
Nos. 2083-2086 (4) 3.42 84

China No. 1 and Flag of China — A419

Designs: $5, No. 464 (Sun Yat-sen). $10, No. 1204 (Chiang Kai-shek).

1978, Feb. 21 Litho. *Perf. 13½*

2087 A419 $2 brown & multi 16 15
2088 A419 $5 blue & multi 32 24
2089 A419 $10 orange & multi 60 48
a. Souv. sheet of 3, #2087-2089 10.50 4.00
Nos. 2087-2089 (3) 1.08 87

Centenary of Chinese postage stamps.

Sun Yat-Sen Memorial Hall — A420

China Nos. 2079 and 2 — A421

Perf. 14x12½, 12½x14

1978, Mar. 20 Wmk. 323

2090 A420 $2 multicolored 18 15
2091 A421 $10 multicolored 48 40

ROCPEX '78 Phil. Exhib., Taipei, Mar. 20-29.

Chiang Kai-shek with Revolutionary Army — A422

Pres. Chiang Kai-shek (1887-1975); $2, as young man, 1912, vert. $8, Making speech at Mt. Lu, July 17, 1937. $10, Reviewing Armed Forces on National Day, 1956, and Chinese flags, vert.

1978, Apr. 5 Wmk. 323 *Perf. 13½*

2092 A422 $2 violet & multi 15 16
2093 A422 $5 green & multi 40 25
2094 A422 $8 blue & multi 55 48
2095 A422 $10 vio blue & multi 70 52
Nos. 2092-2095 (4) 1.80 1.41

Nuclear Reactor and Plant — A423

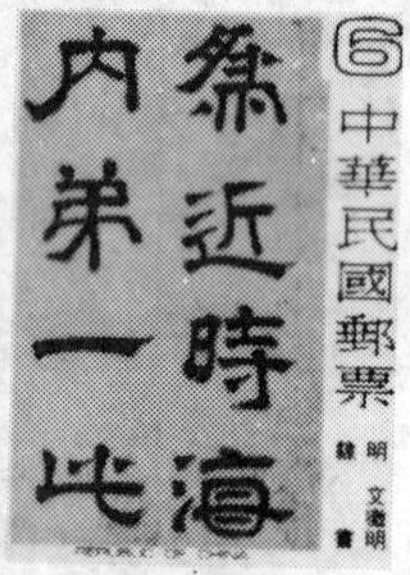

Poem by Wen Cheng-ming (1470-1559) — A424

Perf. 13½x12½

1978, Apr. 28 Unwmk.

2096 A423 $10 multicolored 65 25

First nuclear power plant on Taiwan.

Perf. 13½

1978, May 20 Wmk. 323 Litho.

Chinese Calligraphy: $2, Letter by Wang Hsi-chih (307-365). $4, Eulogy by Chu Sui-liang (596-658). $8, From Autobiography of Huai-su, Tang Dynasty. $10, Poem by Ch'ang Piao, Sung Dynasty.

2097 A424 $2 multicolored *65* 15
2098 A424 $4 multicolored *1.10* 28
2099 A424 $6 multicolored *1.65* 42
2100 A424 $8 multicolored *2.25* 55
2101 A424 $10 multicolored *3.25* 70
Nos. 2097-2101 (5) *8.90* 2.10

Head and Dao Cancer Fund Emblem — A425

Carved Lacquer Vase, Ming Dynasty — A426

1978, June 15 Litho. *Perf. 13½*

2102 A425 $2 red, org & ol 15 15
2103 A425 $10 dk & lt bl & grn 55 38

Cancer prevention.

1978, July 12

Ancient Carved Lacquer Ware: $2, Box with dragon and cloud design, Ch'ing dynasty, horiz. $5, Double box on legs, Ch'ing dynasty, horiz. $8, Round box with peonies, Ming dynasty, horiz.

2104 A426 $2 gray olive & multi 22 15
2105 A426 $5 gray olive & multi 35 18
2106 A426 $8 gray olive & multi 60 28
2107 A426 $10 gray olive & multi 80 32
Nos. 2104-2107 (4) 1.97 93

Tsu Ti Practicing with his Sword — A427

Folk Tales: No. 2109, Pan Ch'ao, diplomat and governor. No. 2110, Tien Tan's "Fire Bull Battle." $5, Liang Hung-yu, a general's wife, who served as drummer in battle.

Perf. 13½

1978, Aug. 16 Litho. Wmk. 323

2108 A427 $1 multicolored 20 15
2109 A427 $2 bis & multi 42 18
2110 A427 $2 gray & multi 42 18
2111 A427 $5 multicolored 80 38
Nos. 2108-2111 (4) 1.84 89

For similar designs see types A456, A495.

Nos. 2071 and 2073 Overprinted in Red

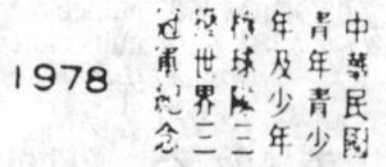

1978, Sept. 9 *Perf. 12½x13*

2112 A366 $4 multicolored 20 20
2113 A366 $6 multicolored 35 35

Triple championships won by Chinese teams in Little League World Series. "1978" overprint on $4 at left, on $6 at right.

Ixias Pyrene — A428

Protected Butterflies: $4, Euploea sylvestor swinhoei. $6, Cyrestis thyodamas formosana. $10, Byasa polyeuctes termessus.

1978, Sept. 20

2114 A428 $2 multicolored 52 20
2115 A428 $4 multicolored 80 25
2116 A428 $6 multicolored 1.10 38
2117 A428 $10 multicolored 2.00 60
Nos. 2114-2117 (4) 4.42 1.43

Scout Symbols — A429

Tropical Tomatoes — A430

1978, Oct. 5 Litho. *Perf. 13½*

2118 A429 $2 multicolored 22 22
2119 A429 $10 multicolored 32 32

5th Chinese Boy Scout Jamboree, Cheng Ching Lake, Oct. 5-12.

1978, Oct. 23 Wmk. 323

Design: $10, Tropical tomatoes, horiz.

2120 A430 $2 multicolored 25 15
2121 A430 $10 multicolored 1.25 45

International Symposium on Tropical Tomatoes, Taiwan, Oct. 23-28.

Sino-Saudi Bridge A431

Design: $6, Buttresses of bridge, flags of Taiwan and Saudi Arabia, horiz.

1978, Oct. 31

2122	A431	$2 multicolored	35	20
2123	A431	$6 multicolored	1.10	40

Completion of Sino-Saudi Bridge over Cho-Shui River.

National Flag — A432

1978-80 *Perf. 13½*

2124	A432	$1 red & dk bl, I	15	15
a.		Bklt. pane of 16 ($5, $6, $8, $10, 3 $1, 9 $2)	10.00	
b.		Type II	15	15
2125	A432	$2 red & dk bl, I	15	15
a.		Bklt. pane of 15 + label	14.00	
b.		Type II	15	15
2126	A432	$3 yel grn & multi ('80)	45	15
2127	A432	$4 bis & multi ('80)	52	15
2128	A432	$5 dk grn & multi, I	38	15
a.		Type II	38	15
2129	A432	$6 brn org & multi	45	15
2130	A432	$7 dk brn & multi ('80)	52	15
2131	A432	$8 dk grn & multi, I	65	20
a.		Type II	65	20
2132	A432	$10 brt bl & multi ('79)	90	22
2133	A432	$12 brt rose lil & multi ('80)	90	24
		Nos. 2124-2133 (10)	5.07	
		Set value		1.50

Two types exist: I. Second line (red) below flag is same width as blue line. II. Second line is a hairline, notably thinner. The $3, $4, $7 and $12 were issued only in type II; $6, $10, Nos. 2134, 2124a, only in type I.

Nos. 2129-2133 have colorless inscriptions and denomination in a panel of solid color.

Nos. 2124a, 2125a have selvage inscribed in blue. 1980 printings are in green or red.

Coil Stamp

1980, Jan. 15 *Perf. 12 Horiz.*

2134	A432	$2 multicolored	25	18

See Nos. 2288-2300. For overprints see Nos. 2540-2541.

Three Rams, by Emperor Hsuan-tsung A433

Taoyuan International Airport A434

Perf. 12½

1978, Dec. 1 Litho. Wmk. 323

2135	A433	$1 multicolored	18	15
2136	A433	$5 multicolored	1.00	45

New Year 1979.

1978, Dec. 31 *Perf. 13½*

Design: $10, Passenger terminal and control tower, horiz.

2137	A434	$2 multicolored	16	15
2138	A434	$10 multicolored	65	45

Completion of Taoyuan Intl. Airport.

Oracle Bones and Inscription, 1766-1123 B.C. — A435

Antiquities and Inscriptions: $5, Lehchi cauldron, 722-481 B.C. $8, Small seal (turtle), 206 B.C.-8 A.D. $10, Inscribed stone tablet, 175-183 A.D.

1979, Jan. 17

2139	A435	$2 multicolored	35	15
2140	A435	$5 multicolored	1.00	35
2141	A435	$8 multicolored	2.00	55
2142	A435	$10 multicolored	2.50	75
		Nos. 2139-2142 (4)	5.85	1.80

Origin and development of Chinese characters.

Chihkan Tower, 1653 — A436

Taiwan Scenery: $5, Shrine of Confucius, 1665. $8, Shrine of Koxinga, 1661. $10, Eternal Castle and moat.

1979, Feb. 11 Litho. *Perf. 13½*

2143	A436	$2 multicolored	20	15
2144	A436	$5 multicolored	40	18
2145	A436	$8 multicolored	75	28
2146	A436	$10 multicolored	1.00	35
		Nos. 2143-2146 (4)	2.35	96

Children Playing on Winter Day, Sung Dynasty A437

1979, Mar. 8

2147	A437	Block of 4	10.50	2.00
a.		$5 in UL corner	2.50	45
b.		$5 in UR corner	2.50	45
c.		$5 in LL corner	2.50	45
d.		$5 in LR corner	2.50	45
e.		Souvenir sheet of 4, #2147	20.00	5.00

Lu Hao-tung — A438

Yellow Jade Brush Holder — A439

Perf. 13x12½

1979, Mar. 29 Engr. Wmk. 323

2148	A438	$2 blue	35	20

Lu Hao-tung (1868-1895), revolutionist.

Unwmk.

1979, Apr. 12 Photo. *Perf. 12*

Ancient Brush Washers: $5, White jade, Ming Dynasty. $8, Dark green jade, Ch'ing Dynasty. $10, Bluish jade, Ch'ing Dynasty. All horiz.

Granite Paper

2149	A439	$2 multicolored	18	18
2150	A439	$5 multicolored	60	35
2151	A439	$8 multicolored	1.00	60
2152	A439	$10 multicolored	1.25	75
		Nos. 2149-2152 (4)	3.03	1.88

For similar artifacts designs with single-color background and denominations in outlined numerals with the cents, see types A453, A469, A489, A523, A547, A582.

Plum Blossoms, Natl. Flower A440 A440a

Perf. 13½x12½

1979-92 Engr. Wmk. 323

Granite Paper

2153	A440	$10 dk blue	45	15
a.		Plain paper ('88)	80	30
2154	A440	$20 brown	70	15
b.		Plain paper ('87)	1.60	60
2154A	A440	$40 brt car, plain paper ('85)	1.40	15
2155	A440	$50 dull grn	1.75	15
a.		Plain paper ('87)	1.90	65
2156	A440	$100 vermilion	4.75	1.25
e.		Plain paper ('92)	4.75	4.75

Perf. 14x13½

2156A	A440a	$300 pur & red org ('83)	21.00	4.25
c.		Plain paper ('91)	25.00	4.25
2156B	A440a	$500 ver & brn ('82)	35.00	7.50
d.		Plain paper ('91)	40.00	7.50
		Nos. 2153-2156B (7)	65.05	13.60

Issued: #2156c-2156d, May 1. #2156e, Jan. 7

City Houses and Garden — A441

Design: $10, Rural landscape, horiz.

Perf. 13x12½, 12½x13

1979, June 5 Litho.

2157	A441	$2 multicolored	16	15
2158	A441	$10 multicolored	85	42

Protection of the Environment.

Bankbook and Computer Department A442

Designs: $2, Children at counter, vert. $5, People standing in line, vert. $10, Hand putting coin in savings bank, symbolic tree.

1979, July 1 Wmk. 323 *Perf. 13½*

2159	A442	$2 multicolored	15	15
2160	A442	$5 multicolored	32	15
2161	A442	$8 multicolored	48	18
2162	A442	$10 multicolored	55	32
		Nos. 2159-2162 (4)	1.50	80

Postal savings, 60th anniversary.

Bird Type of 1977

Birds of Taiwan: $2, Swinoe's pheasant. $8, Steere's babbler. $10, Formosan yuhina.

1979, Aug. 8 *Perf. 11½*

2163	A402	$2 multicolored	32	15
2164	A402	$8 multicolored	1.25	32
2165	A402	$10 multicolored	1.40	35
		Nos. 2163-2165 (3)	2.97	82

Rowland Hill, Penny Black A443

Perf. 13½x13

1979, Aug. 27 Litho. Wmk. 323

2166	A443	$10 multicolored	80	30

Sir Rowland Hill (1795-1879), originator of penny postage.

Jar with Rope Design, Shang Dynasty — A444

Ancient Chinese Pottery: $5, Two-handled jar, Shang dynasty. $8, Red jar with "ears," Han dynasty. $10, Green glazed jar, Han dynasty.

1979, Sept. 12 *Perf. 13½*

2167	A444	$2 multicolored	32	15
2168	A444	$5 multicolored	1.00	16
2169	A444	$8 multicolored	1.65	28
2170	A444	$10 multicolored	2.00	35
		Nos. 2167-2170 (4)	4.97	94

Children and IYC Emblem — A445

1979, Sept. 28 Litho. *Perf. 13½*

2171	A445	$2 multicolored	15	15
2172	A445	$10 multicolored	50	40

International Year of the Child.

Trade Symbols, Competition Emblem A446

1979, Nov. 11 Litho. *Perf. 13½*

2173	A446	$2 blue & multi	15	15
2174	A446	$10 green & multi	50	40

10th National Vocational Training Competition, Taichung, Nov. 11.

Trees on a Winter Plain, by Li Ch'eng — A447

Paintings: $5, Bamboo, Wen T'ung. $8, Old tree, bamboo and rock, by Chao Meng-fu. $10, Twin Pines, by Li K'an.

1979, Nov. 21

2175 A447 $2 multicolored		35	18
2176 A447 $5 multicolored		1.25	28
2177 A447 $8 multicolored		2.25	45
2178 A447 $10 multicolored		2.75	55
	Nos. 2175-2178 (4)	6.60	1.46

Monkey — A448

1979, Dec. 1 ***Perf. 12½***

2179 A448 $1 yellow & multi	45	15
2180 A448 $6 tan & multi	2.50	60

New Year 1980.

Rotary Emblem and "75" — A449

Rotary Intl., 75th Anniv.: $12, Anniv. emblem.

1980, Feb. 23 **Litho.** ***Perf. 13½***

2181 A449 $2 multicolored	15	15
2182 A449 $12 multi, vert.	85	45

Mt. Hohuan A450

Taiwan Landscapes (East-West Cross-Island Highway): $2, Tunnel of Nine Turns, vert. $12, Bridge, Tien Hsiang, vert.

1980, Mar. 1 **Wmk. 323**

2183 A450 $2 multicolored		15	15
2184 A450 $8 multicolored		75	22
2185 A450 $12 multicolored		1.10	45
	Nos. 2183-2185 (3)	2.00	82

A451

A452

Perf. 13½x12½

1980, Mar. 29 **Engr.**

Granite Paper

2186 A451 $2 red brown	20	15

Shih Chien-Ju (1879-1900), revolutionist.

1980, Apr. 4 **Litho.** ***Perf. 13½***

2187 A452 $2 Chung-cheng Memorial Hall		15	15
2188 A452 $8 Quotation		40	30
2189 A452 $12 Bronze statue		55	55
	Nos. 2187-2189 (3)	1.10	1.00

Chiang Kai-shek (1887-1975), 5th anniv. of death.

Melon-shaped Jade Brush Washer, Ming Dynasty A453

Jade Pottery: $2, Jar with dragons, Sung dynasty, vert. $8, Monk's alms bowl, Ch'ing dynasty. $10, Yellow jade brush washer, Ch'ing dynasty.

1980, May 20 **Photo.** ***Perf. 12***

Granite Paper

2190 A453 $2 multicolored		22	15
2191 A453 $5 multicolored		65	18
2192 A453 $8 multicolored		1.10	28
2193 A453 $10 multicolored		1.50	35
	Nos. 2190-2193 (4)	3.47	96

Energy Conservation — A454

1980, July 15 **Litho.** ***Perf. 13½***

2194 A454 $2 multicolored	15	15
2195 A454 $12 multicolored	60	45

A455

A456

T'ang Dynasty pottery.

1980, Aug. 18 **Litho.** ***Perf. 13½***

2196 A455 $2 Soldier		26	15
2197 A455 $5 Roosters		85	18
2198 A455 $8 Horse		1.50	28
2199 A455 $10 Camel		1.90	35
	Nos. 2196-2199 (4)	4.51	96

Perf. 14x13½

1980, Sept. 23 **Litho.** **Wmk. 323**

Folk Tales: $1, Grinding mortar into a needle. No. 2201, Confucius Returning Lost Article (shown). No. 2202, Wen Tien-hsiang in jail. $5, Sending coal in snow.

2200 A456 $1 multicolored		15	15
2201 A456 $2 multicolored		25	15
2202 A456 $2 multicolored		25	20
2203 A456 $5 multicolored		85	35
	Nos. 2200-2203 (4)	1.50	
	Set value		60

Railroad Electrification A457

1980, Oct. 10 ***Perf. 13½x14***

2204 A457 $2 shown	35	20
2205 A457 $2 Taichung Harbor	35	20
2206 A457 $2 Chiang Kai-shek Airport	35	20
2207 A457 $2 Steel Mill	35	20
2208 A457 $2 Sun Yat-sen Freeway	35	20
2209 A457 $2 Nuclear power plant	35	20
2210 A457 $2 Petrochemical plants	35	20
2211 A457 $2 Su-ao Harbor	35	20
2212 A457 $2 Kaohsiung shipyard	35	20
2213 A457 $2 North link railroad	35	20
a. Souv. sheet of 10, #2204-2213	10.50	10.50
b. Block of 10, #2204-2213	3.50	3.50
Nos. 2204-2213 (10)	3.50	2.00

Completion of major construction projects.

10th National Savings Day — A458

Perf. 13½

1980, Oct. 25 **Litho.** **Wmk. 323**

2214 A458 $2 Ancient coin and coin banks	15	15
2215 A458 $12 shown	85	45

Landscape, by Ch'iu Ying, Ming Dynasty A459

1980, Nov. 12 **Litho.** ***Perf. 13½***

2216 A459 Block of 4	9.50	2.25
a. $5 in UL corner	2.25	52
b. $5 in UR corner	2.25	52
c. $5 in LL corner	2.25	52
d. $5 in LR corner	2.25	52
e. Souvenir sheet	20.00	20.00

Cock — A460

Faces, Flag, Census Form — A461

1980, Dec. 1 ***Perf. 12½***

2217 A460 $1 multicolored	38	15
2218 A460 $6 multicolored	2.50	45
a. Souv. sheet, 2 each #2217-2218	10.00	10.00

New Year 1981.

1980, Dec. 13 ***Perf. 13½***

2219 A461 $2 shown	15	15
2220 A461 $12 Buildings, horiz.	70	42

1980 population and housing census.

TIROS-N Satellite — A462

Design: $10, Central weather bureau, horiz.

1981, Jan. 28 **Litho.** ***Perf. 13½***

2221 A462 $2 multicolored	15	15
2222 A462 $10 multicolored	65	42

Completion of meteorological satellite ground station, Taipei.

"Happiness" A463

New Year 1981 (Calligraphy): No. 2224, Wealth. No. 2225, Longevity. No. 2226, Joy.

1981, Feb. 3 ***Perf. 13½x12½***

2223 A463 $5 multi, 5 at B	1.10	15
2224 A463 $5 multi, 5 at R	1.10	15
2225 A463 $5 multi, 5 at L	1.10	15
2226 A463 $5 multi, 5 at T	1.10	15
a. Block of 4, #2223-2226	5.00	2.00

International Year of the Disabled A464

1981, Feb. 19 **Litho.** ***Perf. 13½***

2227 A464 $2 multicolored	15	15
2228 A464 $12 multicolored	52	25
Set value		30

Mt. Ali A465

1981, Mar. 1

2229 A465 $2 shown		15	15
2230 A465 $7 Oluanpi Beach		75	32
2231 A465 $12 Sun Moon Lake		1.40	35
	Nos. 2229-2231 (3)	2.30	82

A $2 multicolored stamp for the 12th National Kuomintang Congress at Taipei was prepared for release Mar. 29, 1981, but not issued. It showed Sun Yat-sen, Chiang Kai-shek, flags of China and the Kuomintang and a map of China.

Children in Forest A467

Children's Day: Drawings.

1981, Apr. 4

2233 A467 $1 multicolored	15	15
2234 A467 $2 multicolored	15	15
2235 A467 $5 multicolored	18	18
2236 A467 $7 multicolored	25	25
Set value	50	50

Chiang Kai-shek Memorial Hall — A468

1981, Apr. 5 ***Perf. 12½x13½***

2237 A468 20c bluish lilac	15	15
a. Photo. ('87)	15	15
2238 A468 40c crim rose	15	15
a. Photo. ('87)	15	15
2239 A468 50c dull red brn	15	15
a. Photo. ('88)	15	15
Set value	35	25

Chiang Kai-shek (1887-1975).

See Nos. 2601-2603.

Cloisonne Enamel Brush Washer, 15th Cent. — A469

Cloisonne Enamel: $5, Ritual vessel, 15th cent., vert. $8, Plate, 17th cent. $10, Vase, Ming Dynasty, vert.

1981, May 20 Photo. *Perf. 12*
Granite Paper

2240	A469	$2	multicolored	22	15
2241	A469	$5	multicolored	60	18
2242	A469	$8	multicolored	90	28
2243	A469	$10	multicolored	1.25	35
			Nos. 2240-2243 (4)	2.97	96

For similar enamelware stamps see Nos. 2318-2321, 2348-2351, 2410-2413.

Early & Modern Locomotives — A470

Linnaeus Crab — A471

Perf. 12½
1981, June 9 Litho. Wmk. 323

2244	A470	$2	shown	15	15
2245	A470	$14	Trains, horiz.	90	50

Railroad service centenary.

1981, June 14 *Perf. 13½*

2246	A471	$2	De Haan crab, horiz.	15	15
2247	A471	$5	shown	38	22
2248	A471	$8	Miers crab, horiz.	65	28
2249	A471	$14	Rathbun crab	1.10	45
			Nos. 2246-2249 (4)	2.28	1.10

Central Weather Bureau, 40th Anniv. — A472

1981, July 1 Litho. *Perf. 13½*

2250	A472	$2	multicolored	15	15
2251	A472	$14	multicolored	90	50

Scene from The Cowherd and the Weaving Maid — A473

Designs: Scenes from the Cowherd and the Weaving Maid.

1981, Aug. 6 Litho. *Perf. 13½x14*

2252	A473	$2	multicolored	22	15
2253	A473	$4	multicolored	42	20
2254	A473	$8	multicolored	1.10	35
2255	A473	$14	multicolored	2.25	65
			Nos. 2252-2255 (4)	3.99	1.35

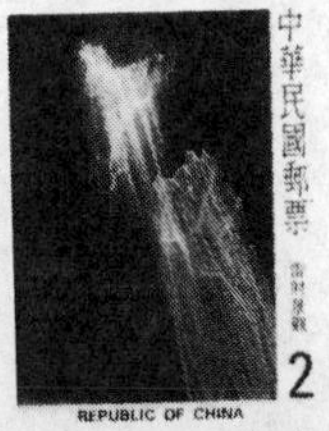

First Lasography Exhibition — A474

Lasography Designs.

1981, Aug. 15 *Perf. 13½*

2256	A474	$2	multicolored	15	15
2257	A474	$5	multicolored	32	28
2258	A474	$8	multicolored	55	45
2259	A474	$14	multicolored	1.00	75
			Nos. 2256-2259 (4)	2.02	1.63

Soccer Players
A475 A476

1981, Sept. 9 Litho. *Perf. 13½*

2260	A475	$5	multicolored	50	15
2261	A476	$5	multicolored	50	15
a.			Pair, #2260-2261	1.00	60
			Set value		20

Sports Day.

A477

70th Anniv. of Republic: No. 2263, Eastward Expedition (soldiers on Hill). No. 2264, Northward Expedition (Chiang on horse). No. 2265, Resistance War with Japan (Chiang, fist raised). No. 2266, Suppression of Communist Rebels (Battle scene). No. 2267, Counter-offensive and unification. $8, Chiang Kai-shek. $14, Sun Yat-sen.

1981, Oct. 10 *Perf. 13½*

2262	A477	$2	multicolored	15	15
2263	A477	$2	multicolored	15	15
2264	A477	$2	multicolored	15	15
2265	A477	$2	multicolored	15	15
2266	A477	$3	multicolored	22	20
2267	A477	$3	multicolored	22	20
2268	A477	$8	multicolored	60	30
2269	A477	$14	multicolored	1.25	45
a.			Souv. sheet of 8, #2262-2269	9.00	3.00
			Nos. 2262-2269 (8)	2.89	
			Set value		1.35

No. 2269a issued Oct. 25.

ROCPEX TAIPEI '81 Intl. Philatelic Exhibition, Taipei, Oct. 25-Nov. 2 — A478

1981, Oct. 25

2270	A478	$2	multicolored	15	15
2271	A478	$14	multicolored	55	40

Boys Playing Games (#2272a) A479

Designs: a.-j. "One Hundred Boys," Sung Dynasty scroll (each stamp is numbered from 1 to 10 in Chinese. See illustrations with Nos. 1682-1691 for numerals.) Two strips of 5 each in continuous design.

1981, Nov. 12

2272		Block of 10	15.00	3.50
a.-e.	A479	$2 single (top row)	1.40	25
f.-j.	A479	$2 single (bottom row)	1.40	25

New Year 1982 (Year of the Dog) — A480

Information Week, Dec. 6-12 — A481

Perf. 12½
1981, Dec. 1 Litho. Wmk. 323

2273	A480	$1	multicolored	24	15
2274	A480	$10	multicolored	2.25	48
a.			Souv. sheet, 2 each #2273-2274	10.00	1.25

1981, Dec. 7 *Perf. 14x13½*

2275	A481	$2	multi	20	15

Telecommunications Centenary — A482

Perf. 14x13½, 13½x14
1981, Dec. 28

2276	A482	$2	Telephone, vert.	15	15
2277	A482	$3	Old, new phones	15	15
2278	A482	$8	Submarine cable	40	22
2279	A482	$18	Computers, vert.	95	50
			Nos. 2276-2279 (4)	1.65	1.02

Floral Arrangement — A483

Designs: Various floral arrangements in Ming vases.

Perf. 13½
1982, Jan. 23 Litho. Wmk. 323

2280	A483	$2	multicolored	15	15
2281	A483	$3	multicolored	16	15
2282	A483	$8	multicolored	52	25
2283	A483	$18	multicolored	1.25	55
			Nos. 2280-2283 (4)	2.08	1.10

Compare with designs A559, A584.

The Ku Cheng Reunion — A484

Designs: Opera scenes.

Perf. 13½
1982, Feb. 15 Litho. Wmk. 323

2284	A484	$2	multicolored	42	16
2285	A484	$3	multicolored	52	22
2286	A484	$4	multicolored	1.25	25
2287	A484	$18	multicolored	4.75	85
			Nos. 2284-2287 (4)	6.94	1.48

Flag Type of 1978
Value Colorless in Colored Panel

1981 Litho. *Perf. 13½*
Panel Color

2288	A432	$1	dk blue	15	15
2289	A432	$1.50	lt olive	15	15
2290	A432	$2	dk olive bis	15	15
2291	A432	$3	red	16	15
2292	A432	$4	blue	32	15
2293	A432	$5	sepia	38	16
2294	A432	$6	orange	45	18
2295	A432	$7	green	50	18
2296	A432	$8	magenta	60	20
2297	A432	$9	olive grn	65	22
2298	A432	$10	dk purple	70	24
2299	A432	$12	lilac	90	32
2300	A432	$14	dk green	1.00	35
			Nos. 2288-2300 (13)	6.11	
			Set value		2.10

Second line (red) below flag is a hairline, notably thinner.

For overprints see Nos. 2540-2541.

Tubercle Bacillus Centenary A485

Cheng Shih-liang, Revolutionary A486

Perf. 13½
1982, Mar. 24 Litho. Wmk. 323

2309	A485	$2	multicolored	15	15

Perf. 13½x12½
1982, Mar. 29 Engr.
Granite Paper

2310	A486	$2	carmine rose	15	15

Children's Day — A487

Designs: Various children's drawings.

1982, Apr. 4 Litho.

2311	A487	$2	multi, vert.	16	15
2312	A487	$3	multicolored	24	15
2313	A487	$5	multicolored	60	16
2314	A487	$8	multicolored	1.00	22
			Nos. 2311-2314 (4)	2.00	68

Dentists' Day — A488

1982, May 4 Litho. *Perf. 13½*

2315	A488	$2	Tooth, boy	22	15
2316	A488	$3	Flossing, brushing	30	15
2317	A488	$10	Examination	1.40	42
			Nos. 2315-2317 (3)	1.92	
			Set value		60

Champleve Enamel Cup and Saucer, 18th Cent. A489

Painted Enamelware: $5, Cloisonne gold-plated duck Ch'ien-lung period (1736-1795), vert. $8, Incense burner, K'ang-hsi period (1662-1722). $12, Cloisonne pitcher, Ch'ien-lung period, vert.

1982, May 20 Photo. *Perf. 12*
Granite Paper

2318	A489	$2	multicolored	42	15
2319	A489	$5	multicolored	1.00	15
2320	A489	$8	multicolored	1.75	15
2321	A489	$12	multicolored	2.75	25
			Nos. 2318-2321 (4)	5.92	
			Set value		56

See Nos. 2348-2351.

Poets' Day — A490

Tang Dynasty Poetry Illustrations (618-906): $2, Spring Dawn, by Meng Hao-Jan. $3, On Looking for a Hermit and Not Finding Him, by Chia Tao. $5, Summer Dying, by Liu Yu-Hsi. $18, Looking at the Snow Drifts on South Mountain, by Tsu Yung. Chinese characters are to the left of the denominations on Nos. 2322-2325, Nos. 2396-2399 have no characters to the left of the denominations.

Perf. 13½

1982, June 25 Litho. Wmk. 323

2322 A490 $2 multicolored *1.00* 18
2323 A490 $3 multicolored *1.65* 22
2324 A490 $5 multicolored *4.00* 45
2325 A490 $18 multicolored *13.00* 1.25
Nos. 2322-2325 (4) *19.65*
Set value 68

See Nos. 2352-2355.

5th World Women's Softball Championship, Taipei, July 1-12 — A491

1982, July 2

2326 A491 $2 lt grn & multi 15 15
2327 A491 $18 tan & multi 1.10 52

Scouting Year A492

1982, July 18

2328 A492 $2 Crossing bridge, Baden-Powell 15 15
2329 A492 $18 Emblem, camp 90 52

Stamp in Tongs — A493

1982, Aug. 9

2330 A493 $2 shown 15 15
2331 A493 $18 Album stamps magnified 90 52

Carved Lion, Tsu Shih Temple — A494

Hsun Kuan Saving Hsiang-cheng City — A495

Tsu Shih Temple of Sanhsia Architecture: $3, Lion brackets, horiz. $5, Sub-lintels. $18, Tiled roof, horiz.

1982, Sept. 1 Litho. *Perf. 13½*

2332 A494 $2 multicolored 16 15
2333 A494 $3 multicolored 32 15
2334 A494 $5 multicolored 48 15
2335 A494 $18 multicolored 1.65 55
Nos. 2332-2335 (4) 2.61 1.00

1982, Oct. 15 *Perf. 14x13½*

Designs: Scenes from The Thirty-Six Examples of Filial Piety, Folk Tale collection by Wu Yen-huan.

2336 A495 $1 multicolored 16 15
2337 A495 $2 multicolored 32 15
2338 A495 $3 multicolored 45 22
2339 A495 $5 multicolored 1.25 24
Nos. 2336-2339 (4) 2.18
Set value 60

30th Anniv. of China Youth Corps A496

1982, Oct. 31

2340 A496 $2 Riding 15 15
2341 A496 $3 Raising flag, vert. 15 15
2342 A496 $18 Mountain climbing 85 60
Nos. 2340-2342 (3) 1.15
Set value 75

Seated Lohan (Buddhist Saint) — A497

New Year 1983 (Year of the Boar) — A498

Paintings of Lohan, Hanging Scrolls by Liu Sung-nien, 13th cent.

Perf. 13x12½

1982, Nov. 12 Litho. Wmk. 323

2343 A497 $2 multicolored 65 15
2344 A497 $3 multicolored 95 18
2345 A497 $18 multicolored 8.25 1.10
a. Souv. sheet of 3, #2343-2345 *21.00* 10.00
Nos. 2343-2345 (3) 9.85 1.43

No. 2345a comes overprinted in red in the sheet margins.

1982, Dec. 1 *Perf. 12½*

2346 A498 $1 multicolored 45 15
2347 A498 $10 multicolored 4.50 60
a. Souv. sheet, 2 each #2346-2347 *15.00* 2.50
Set value 65

Enamelware Type of 1982

Designs: $2, Square basin, Ch'ing Dynasty (1644-1911). $3, Vase, Ch'ien-lung period (1736-1795), vert. $4, Tea pot, Ch'ien-lung period. $18, Elephant vase, Ch'ing Dynasty, vert.

1983, Jan. 5 Photo. *Perf. 12*
Granite Paper

2348 A489 $2 multicolored 22 15
2349 A489 $3 multicolored 28 15
2350 A489 $4 multicolored 50 20
2351 A489 $18 multicolored 2.50 60
Nos. 2348-2351 (4) 3.50
Set value 90

Poetry Illustration Type of 1982

Sung Dynasty Poetry: $2, Seeing the Flowers Fade Away. $3, River. $5, Freckled with Clouds is the Azure Sky. $11, Yielding Fine Fragrance in the Snow. Nos. 2352-2355 vert.

Perf. 13½

1983, Feb. 10 Litho. Wmk. 323

2352 A490 $2 multicolored *1.90* 32
2353 A490 $3 multicolored *2.25* 42
2354 A490 $5 multicolored *5.75* 55
2355 A490 $11 multicolored *12.50* 1.00
Nos. 2352-2355 (4) *22.40* 2.29

Mt. Jade, Taiwan — A499

1983, Mar. 1

2356 A499 $2 Wawa Valley, vert. 22 15
2357 A499 $3 University Pond, vert. 30 15
2358 A499 $18 shown 2.50 75
Nos. 2356-2358 (3) 3.02 1.05

400th Anniv. of Arrival of Matteo Ricci (1552-1610), Italian Missionary — A500

Perf. 14x13½

1983, Apr. 3 Litho. Wmk. 323

2359 A500 $2 Globe 18 15
2360 A500 $18 Great Wall 1.50 52

Mandarin Phonetic Symbols, 70th Anniv. — A501

Scenes from Lady White Snake Fairytale — A502

Perf. 13½

1983, May 22 Litho. Wmk. 323

2361 A501 $2 Wu Ching-heng, inventor 15 15
2362 A501 $18 Children writing 1.10 52

1983, June 15 *Perf. 14x13½*

2363 A502 $2 multicolored 26 15
2364 A502 $3 lt blue & multi 32 15
2365 A502 $3 orange & multi 32 15
2366 A502 $18 multicolored 3.00 70
Nos. 2363-2366 (4) 3.90 1.15

A503

A504

Various bamboo carved objects. Nos. 2367-2369 Ch'ing dynasty.

Perf. 13½

1983, July 14 Litho. Wmk. 323

2367 A503 $2 Bamboo jug 26 15
2368 A503 $3 Tao-t'ieh motif vase 38 15
2369 A503 $4 Landscape sculpture 55 20
2370 A503 $18 Brush holder, Ming dynasty 3.75 55
Nos. 2367-2370 (4) 4.94 1.05

Perf. 13½

1983, Aug. 5 Litho. Wmk. 323

2371 A504 $2 Globe 15 15
2372 A504 $18 Emblem 90 52

World Communications Year.

Fishing Industry (Local Fish) A505

1983, Aug. 20

2373 A505 $2 Epinephelus tauvina 15 15
2374 A505 $18 Saurida undosquamis 1.00 52

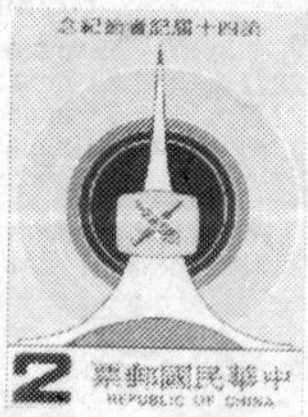

40th Journalists' Day — A506

1983, Sept. 1

2375 A506 $2 multicolored 20 15

Views of Mongolia and Tibet — A507

1983, Sept. 15

2376 A507 $2 Village 18 15
2377 A507 $3 Potala Palace 25 16
2378 A507 $5 Sheep grazing 60 25
2379 A507 $11 Camel caravan 1.40 52
Nos. 2376-2379 (4) 2.43 1.08

2nd East Asian Bird Protection Conference, Oct. — A508

1983, Oct. 8 Litho. *Perf. 13½*

2380 A508 $2 Lanius cristatus, vert. 18 15
2381 A508 $18 Butastur indicus 1.90 52

A509

A510

Plum Blossoms, Photography by Hu Ch'ung-hsien.

1983, Oct. 31 Litho. *Perf. 14x13½*

2382 A509 $2 multicolored 16 15
2383 A509 $3 multi, diff. 20 15
2384 A509 $5 multi, diff. 50 20
2385 A509 $11 multi, diff. 1.10 42
Nos. 2382-2385 (4) 1.96 92

1983, Nov. 6 *Perf. 13x13½, 13½x13*

2386 A510 $2 JCI and Congress emblems 15 15
2387 A510 $18 Globe and emblems, horiz 90 52

Jaycees Intl., 38th World Congress, Taipei.

8th Asian-Pacific Cardiology Congress — A511

1983, Nov. 27 Litho. *Perf. 13½*

2388 A511 $2 shown 15 15
2389 A511 $18 Electrocardiogram 1.10 52

New Year 1984 (Year of the Rat) — A512

1983, Dec. 1 Litho. *Perf. 12½*

2390 A512 $1 multicolored 55 15
2391 A512 $10 multicolored 7.00 65
a. Souv. sheet, 2 each #2390-2391 *30.00* 7.50

Literacy Week A513

1983, Dec. 17 Litho. *Perf. 13½*

2392 A513 $2 shown 15 15
2393 A513 $18 Modern family, vert. 90 52

World Freedom Day — A514

1984, Jan. 23 Litho. *Perf. 13½*

2394 A514 $2 Korean War Patriots 15 15
2395 A514 $18 Intl. support 1.10 52

Drama Day — A515

Yuan Dynasty Poetry Illustrations by Tien-shih Lin (Poems by): $2, Kuan Yun-shih. $3, Po Pu. $5, Chang Ko-chiu. $18, Shang Cheng-shu. (See note with Nos. 2322-2325.)

1984, Feb. 15 Litho. *Perf. 13½*

2396 A515 $2 multicolored *1.00* 20
2397 A515 $3 multicolored *1.65* 24
2398 A515 $5 multicolored *3.50* 32
2399 A515 $18 multicolored *14.00* 1.25
Nos. 2396-2399 (4) *20.15* 2.01

A516

A517

A518

Arbor Day — A519

1984, Mar. 12 Litho. *Perf. 13½x14*

2400 A516 $2 multicolored 1.00 15
2401 A517 $2 multicolored 1.00 15
2402 A518 $2 multicolored 1.00 15
2403 A519 $2 multicolored 1.00 15
a. Block of 4, #2400-2403 4.00 1.00
Set value 24

Lin Chueh-min — A520

Central News Agency, 60th Anniv. — A521

1984, Mar. 29 Engr. *Perf. 13x12½*
Granite Paper

2404 A520 $2 dk green 20 15

Perf. 14x13½
1984, Apr. 1 Litho. Wmk.

2405 A521 $2 Emblem 15 15
2406 A521 $10 Emblem, satellite, dish antenna 52 35

God of Longevity A522

Ch'ing Dynasty Enamelware A523

Paintings by Chang Ta-chien (1899-1983): $2, Five Auspicious Tokens. $18, Lotus Blossoms in Ink Splash.

Perf. 11½
1984, Apr. 20 Litho. Wmk. 323

2407 A522 $2 multicolored 70 15
2408 A522 $5 multicolored 2.00 15
2409 A522 $18 multicolored 7.25 60
Nos. 2407-2409 (3) 9.95 90

1984, May 20 Photo. *Perf. 12*
Granite Paper

2410 A523 $2 Cup, pot, plate, horiz. 18 15
2411 A523 $3 Wine jug 28 15
2412 A523 $4 Teapot 50 15
2413 A523 $18 Candle holder 2.25 60
Nos. 2410-2413 (4) 3.21 1.05

China Airlines World-wide Service Inauguration A524

1984, May 31 Litho. *Perf. 13½x14*

2414 A524 $2 Jet circling globe 16 15
2415 A524 $7 Globe, jet 45 22
2416 A524 $11 New York City 70 38
2417 A524 $18 Amsterdam 1.10 52
Nos. 2414-2417 (4) 2.41 1.27

30th Navigation Day — A525

Perf. 13½x13
1984, July 11 Litho. Wmk. 323

2418 A525 $2 Container ship 25 15
2419 A525 $18 Oil tanker 3.50 52

1984 Summer Olympics — A526

Alpine Plants — A527

Perf. 13½x14, 14x13½
1984, July 28

2420 A526 $2 Judo, horiz. 15 15
2421 A526 $5 Archery 32 16
2422 A526 $18 Swimming, horiz. 1.25 65
Nos. 2420-2422 (3) 1.72 96

1984, Aug. 8 *Perf. 13*

2423 A527 $2 Gentiana arisanensis 32 15
2424 A527 $3 Epilobium nankotaizanense 42 15
2425 A527 $5 Adenophora uehatae 85 15
2426 A527 $18 Aconitum fukutomei 3.50 85
Nos. 2423-2426 (4) 5.09
Set value 1.05

The Eighteen Scholars, Sung Dynasty Hanging Scroll — A528

Details.

Wmk. 323
1984, Aug. 20 Litho. *Perf. 13*

2427 A528 $2 Playing instruments *1.40* 15
2428 A528 $3 Playing chess *2.00* 16
2429 A528 $5 Practicing calligraphy *4.25* 22
2430 A528 $18 Painting *17.50* 95
Nos. 2427-2430 (4) *25.15* 1.48

Athletics Day

A529 A530

1984, Sept. 9

2431 A529 $5 Two players 50 15
2432 A530 $5 One player 50 15
a. Pair, #2431-2432 1.00 60
Set value 20

A531

A532

1984, Sept. 9

2433 A531 $10 "20," map of Asia 50 25

Asian-Pacific Parliamentarians' Union, 20th anniv.

1984, Oct. 10 Litho. *Perf. 12½*

2434 A532 $2 No. 1458 15 15
2435 A532 $5 No. 296 26 16
2436 A532 $18 Museum 1.00 65
a. Souv. sheet of 3, #2434-2436 9.00 2.00
Nos. 2434-2436 (3) 1.41 96

Postal Museum opening.

Flag, Alliance Emblem — A533

Veteran's Assistance — A534

1984, Oct. 16 *Perf. 13½*

2437 A533 $2 multicolored 25 15

Grand Alliance for China's Reunification Under the Three Principles of the People Convention, Taipei, Oct. 16-17.

1984, Nov. 1 Litho. *Perf. 13½*

2438 A534 $2 Vignettes 25 15

Pine Tree A535

Bamboo A535a

Plum Tree — A535b

Market value for a particular scarce stamp may remain relatively low if few collectors want it.

1984-88

2439 A535 $2 multicolored 15 15
2440 A535a $8 multicolored 45 15
2441 A535b $10 grayish tan background 52 15
a. Pale yellow bister background 35 15
Nos. 2439-2441 (3) 1.12
Set value 30

Issue dates: Nos. 2439-2441, Nov. 12. No. 2441a, Jan. 12, 1988. See Nos. 2495-2503.

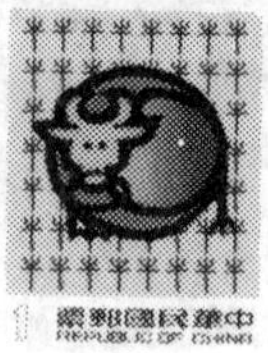

A536

A537

1984, Dec. 1 ***Perf. 12x12½***

2442 A536 $1 multicolored 35 15
2443 A536 $10 multicolored 3.50 38
a. Min. sheet, 2 each #2442-2443 *8.00* 2.50
Set value 45

New Year 1985 (Year of the Ox).

1985, Jan. 11 Litho. ***Perf. 13½***

2444 A537 $5 Scales, legal codes 30 15

Judicial Day 1985.

Quemoy and Matsu Scenes — A538

1985, Jan. 23 Litho. ***Perf. 13½x14***

2445 A538 $2 Ku-kang Lake, Quemoy 20 15
2446 A538 $5 Kuang-hai Stone, Quemoy 60 18
2447 A538 $8 Sheng-li Reservoir, Matsu 1.00 28
2448 A538 $10 Tung-chu Lighthouse, Matsu 1.10 32
Nos. 2445-2448 (4) 2.90 93

Sir Robert Hart (1835-1911) — A539

1985, Feb. 15 Litho. ***Perf. 14x13½***

2449 A539 $2 No. 1 30 15

Inspector General of Chinese Customs, 1863-1908, and founder of the Chinese Postal Service.

Lo Fu-hsing (1886-1914) A540

Tsou Jung (1882-1905) A541

1985, Feb. 24 ***Perf. 13x13½***

2450 A540 $2 multicolored 30 15

Perf. 13½x12½

1985, Mar. 29 Engr.

Granite Paper

2451 A541 $3 green 30 15

Chung-cheng Memorial Hall Main Gate — A542

1985, Apr. 5 Litho. ***Perf. 13***

2452 A542 $2 shown 15 15
2453 A542 $8 Tzuhu Memorial 70 24
2454 A542 $10 Chiang Kai-shek, vert. 95 30
Nos. 2452-2454 (3) 1.80 69

Tenth death anniv. of Chiang Kai-shek.

A543

A544

1985, May 8 Litho. ***Perf. 13½***

2455 A543 $2 Carnation 70 15
2456 A543 $2 Day lily 70 15
a. Pair, #2455-2456 1.50 15

Mother's Day.

1985, May 18

2457 A544 $5 Tunnel to Chi-chin Island 35 25

Kaohsiung Cross-Harbor Tunnel, 1st anniv.

Girl Scouts, 75th Anniv. — A545

Perf. 13½

1985, June 1 Litho. Wmk. 323

2458 A545 $2 multicolored 15 15
2459 A545 $18 multicolored 1.10 48

The Book of Odes, Confucius A545a

1985, June 22 Litho. Wmk. 323

2460 A545a $2 Spring *95* 15
2461 A545a $5 Summer *3.00* 30
2462 A545a $8 Fall *4.75* 48
2463 A545a $10 Winter *5.25* 60
Nos. 2460-2463 (4) *13.95* 1.53

Fruit — A546

Perf. 13½x14

1985, July 5 Litho. Wmk. 323

2464 A546 $2 Wax Jambo 40 15
2465 A546 $3 Guava 52 15
2466 A546 $5 Carambola 1.10 18
2467 A546 $8 Litchi nut 2.25 28
Nos. 2464-2467 (4) 4.27 76

Ch'ing Dynasty (1644-1911) Ivory Carvings A547

1985, July 18 Wmk. 323 ***Perf. 13½***

2468 A547 $2 Dragon Boat 16 15
2469 A547 $3 Landscape 24 15
2470 A547 $5 Melon, water container 60 15
2471 A547 $18 Brush holder, vert. 2.50 52
Nos. 2468-2471 (4) 3.50 97

T'ang Dynasty (618-907) Aristocrat — A548

Designs: $5, Sung Dynasty (960-1280) palace woman. $8, Yuan Dynasty (1280-1368) aristocrat. $11, Ming Dynasty (1368-1644) aristocrat.

1985, Aug. 1 Wmk. 323 ***Perf. 13½***

2472 A548 $2 multicolored 45 15
2473 A548 $5 multicolored 1.50 16
2474 A548 $8 multicolored 2.75 25
2475 A548 $11 multicolored 3.25 35
Nos. 2472-2475 (4) 7.95 91

4th Asian Conf. on Costume, Aug. 3.

See #2549-2552, 2605-2608, 2660-2663. In the 2 rows of Chinese characters above the denomination, the right row has 3 characters and a dot on #2472-2475, 4 characters and a dot on #2549-2552. #2605-2608, 2660-2663 have solid black numerals.

Social Welfare Program A549

Perf. 13½x14

1985, Aug. 1 Wmk. 323

2476 A549 $2 Heart, bird feeding young 25 15

Historic Sites A550

Perf. 13½

1985, Sept. 3 Litho. Wmk. 323

2477 A550 $2 Taipei North Gate 18 15
2478 A550 $5 San Domingo Fort, Tamsui 52 15
2479 A550 $8 Lung Shun Temple, Lukang 85 22
2480 A550 $10 Confucius Temple, Changhua 1.10 28
Nos. 2477-2480 (4) 2.65 80

Bonsai — A551

Trade Shows — A552

Perf. 13½x14

1985, Sept. 22 Wmk. 323

2481 A551 $2 Oak 15 15
2482 A551 $5 Five-leaf pine 32 16
2483 A551 $8 Lohan pine 55 25
2484 A551 $18 Banyan 1.25 60
Nos. 2481-2484 (4) 2.27 1.16

1985, Oct. 5 ***Perf. 13½***

Taipei World Trade Center and show emblems: a, Sporting goods. b, Toys and gifts. c, Electronics. d, Machinery. Se-tenant in continuous design.

2485 Strip of 4 2.75 45
a.-d. A552 $2 any single 65 15

Scenes of Modern Taiwan, Map, Flag — A553

1985, Oct. 25

2486 A553 $2 shown 20 15
2487 A553 $18 Chiang Kai-shek, Triumphal Arch 1.75 52

Defeat of Japanese army, end of World War II, and return of Taiwan to control of the Republic, 40th anniv.

7th Asian Conference on Mental Retardation A554

Sun Yat-sen and Birthplace A555

1985, Nov. 8 ***Perf. 14x13½***

2488 A554 $2 multicolored 15 15
2489 A554 $11 multicolored 90 32
Set value 40

1985, Nov. 12 ***Perf. 13½***

2490 A555 $2 multicolored 15 15
2491 A555 $18 multicolored 1.40 52

Postal Life Insurance, 50th Anniv. — A556

New Year 1986 (Year of the Tiger) — A557

1985, Dec. 1

2492 A556 $2 multicolored 30 15

1985, Dec. 1 *Perf. 12½*

2493 A557 $1 multicolored 18 15
2494 A557 $10 multicolored 1.75 38
a. Min. sheet, 2 each #2493-2494 *12.00* 3.50
Set value 45

Flora Types of 1984

1986, Jan. 10 Litho. *Perf. 13½*

2495 A535 $1 multicolored 15 15
2496 A535a $11 multicolored 65 15
2497 A535b $18 multicolored 1.00 15

1988, Feb. 12

2498 A535 $1.50 multicolored 15 15
2499 A535a $7.50 multicolored 60 16
2500 A535b $16 multicolored 1.40 35

No. 2500 has value expressed in dollars and cents.

1989, Feb. 24

2501 A535 $3 multicolored 24 15
2502 A535a $16.50 multicolored 1.40 35
2503 A535b $21 multicolored 1.75 42
Nos. 2495-2503 (9) 7.34 2.03

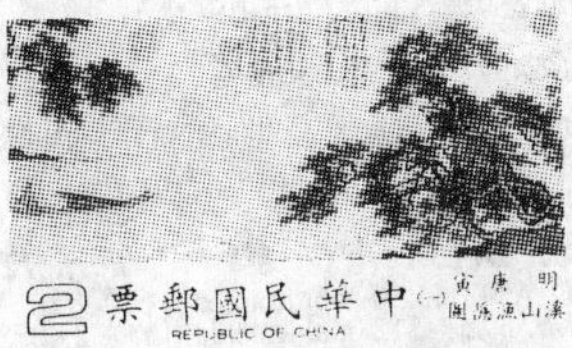

Cultural Renaissance Movement — A558

Painting: Hermit Anglers on a Mountain Stream, Ming Dynasty, 1386-1644. Se-tenant in a continuous design. (Each stamp is numbered from 1 to 5 in Chinese. See illustrations with Nos. 1682-1691 for numerals.)

1986, Jan. 28 Litho. *Perf. 13½*

2507 Strip of 5 *7.50* 30
a.-e. A558 $2 any single *1.50* 15

See No. 2604.

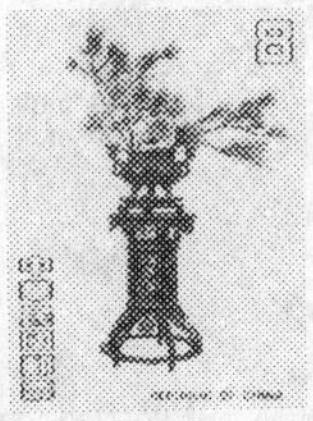

Floral Arrangements A559

Perf. 13½

1986, Feb. 20 Litho. Wmk. 323

2517 A559 $2 denom. UL 15 15
2518 A559 $5 denom. UR 40 15
2519 A559 $8 shown 65 24
2520 A559 $10 denom. UL 80 30
Nos. 2517-2520 (4) 2.00 84

Compare with designs A483, A584.

Natl. Postal Service, 90th Anniv. A560

Designs: $2, Unloading express mail at airport. $5, Motorcycle delivery, vert. $8, Technological innovations, vert. $10, Electronic sorting machine.

1986, Mar. 20

2521 A560 $2 multicolored 15 15
2522 A560 $5 multicolored 30 15
2523 A560 $8 multicolored 48 25
2524 A560 $10 multicolored 60 30
a. Souv. sheet of 4, #2521-2524 5.50 2.00
Nos. 2521-2524 (4) 1.53 85

Chen Tien-hua (1875-1905), Revolutionary — A561

Perf. 13½x12½

1986, Mar. 29 Engr.

Granite Paper

2525 A561 $2 violet 15 15

Yushan Natl. Park — A562

1986, Apr. 10 Litho. *Perf. 13½*

2526 A562 $2 multicolored 38 15
2527 A562 $5 multi, diff. 1.10 15
2528 A562 $8 multi, diff. 1.90 28
2529 A562 $10 multi, diff. 2.25 35
Nos. 2526-2529 (4) 5.63 93

Power Plants — A563

1986, Apr. 29

2530 A563 $2 Hydro-electric 15 15
2531 A563 $8 Thermo-electric 50 22
2532 A563 $10 Nuclear 60 28
Nos. 2530-2532 (3) 1.25 65

Economic prosperity through energy development.

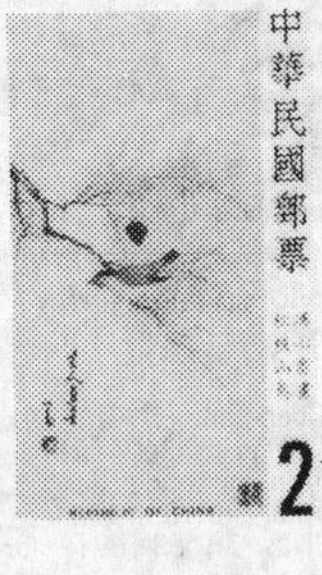

Paintings by P'u Hsin-yu (1896-1963) — A564

1986, May 22 *Perf. 11½*

2533 A564 $2 Bird 80 15
2534 A564 $8 Landscape 3.75 35
2535 A564 $10 Woman in forest 5.00 42
Nos. 2533-2535 (3) 9.55 92

Asian Productivity Org., 25th Anniv. A565

1986, June 3 *Perf. 13x13½*

2536 A565 $2 multicolored 16 15
2537 A565 $11 multicolored 80 32
Set value 40

Natl. Productivity Center, 30th anniv.

Coral-reef Fish — A566

Designs: a, Chrysiptera starcki. b, Chelmon rostratus. c, Chaetodon xanthurus. d, Chaetodon quadrimaculatus. e, Chaetodon meyeri. f, Genicanthus semifasciatus. g, Genicanthus semifasciatus. h, Pomacanthus annularis. i, Lienardella fasciata. j, Balistapus undulatus.

1986, June 3 *Perf. 13½*

2538 Block of 10 4.00 1.25
a.-j. A566 $2 any single 40 15

Protection of Intellectual Property Rights — A567

1986, June 12

2539 A567 $2 Macaw 50 15

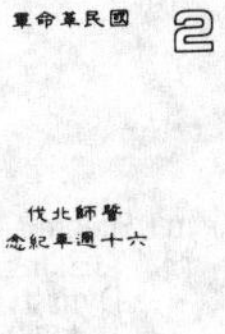

Nos. 2294, 2297 Surcharged

1986, July 9 Litho. *Perf. 13½*

2540 A432 $2 on $6 multi 15 15
2541 A432 $8 on $9 multi 48 30

60th Anniv. of northward expedition by the national revolutionary army.

Bridges A568

1986, July 30

2542 A568 $2 Tzu Mu, 1965 35 15
2543 A568 $5 Chang Hung, 1968 85 15
2544 A568 $8 Kuan Fu, 1977 1.40 24
2545 A568 $10 Kuan Tu, 1983 2.00 30
Nos. 2542-2545 (4) 4.60 84

Love between Liang Shanpo and Chu Yingtai, Folk Tale — A569

Cartoons by Huang Mu-ts'un: a, Yingtai disguised to go to school. b, Yingtai and Shanpo meet in class. c, The friends at pond. d, Yingtai summoned home for arranged marriage. e, Yingtai and Shanpo ascend to heaven as butterflies (each stamp is numbered from 1 to 5 in Chinese. See illustrations with Nos. 1682-1691 for numerals.)

1986, Aug. 12 *Perf. 12½*

2546 Strip of 5 4.75 75
a.-e. A569 $5 any single 90 15

Social Awareness Campaign A570

1986, Sept. 12 Litho. *Perf. 13½*

2547 A570 $2 Rainbow, children 15 15
2548 A570 $8 Children, adults 60 30

Folk Costumes — A571

Designs: $2, Shang Dynasty (1766-1122 B.C.) aristocrat. $5, Warring States (403-221 B.C.) aristocrat. $8, Later Han Dynasty (A.D. 25-221) empress. $10, Flying ribbons gown, Wei and Tsin Dynasties (A.D. 221-420) aristocrat.

1986, Sept. 23 Litho. *Perf. 13½*

2549 A571 $2 multicolored 60 15
2550 A571 $5 multicolored 1.40 18
2551 A571 $8 multicolored 2.25 30
2552 A571 $10 multicolored 3.00 35
Nos. 2549-2552 (4) 7.25 98

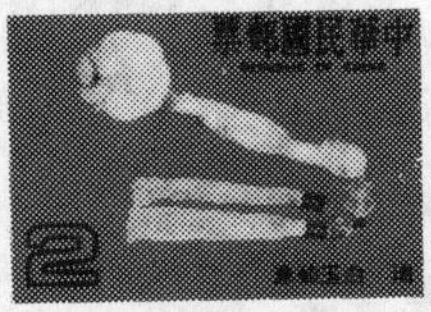

Ch'ing Dynasty Ju-i Scepters A572

1986, Oct. 10 Photo. *Perf. 14½x15*

2553 A572 $2 White jade 22 15
2554 A572 $3 Red coral 32 15
2555 A572 $4 Redwood and gems 45 15
2556 A572 $18 Gilded wood 2.00 60
Nos. 2553-2556 (4) 2.99 1.05

See Nos. 2582-2585.

Chiang Kai-shek A573

Portrait and: $5, Map and flag. $8, Emblem. $10, Flags on globe.

1986, Oct. 31 Litho. *Perf. 13½*

2557 A573 $2 multicolored 24 15
2558 A573 $5 multicolored 55 15
2559 A573 $8 multicolored 95 24
2560 A573 $10 multicolored 1.10 30
a. Souv. sheet of 4, #2557-2560 9.00 3.00
Nos. 2557-2560 (4) 2.84 84

Cultural Heritage A574

Architecture: $2, Chin-Kuang Fu land development and defense fund building, 1826. $5, Erh-shawan Gun Emplacement, Keelung, 1841, restored 1979. $8, Fort Hsi T'ai, 1886. $10, Matsu Temple, Peng-hu, renovated 1563-1624.

1986, Nov. 14 Litho. *Perf. 13½*

2561 A574 $2 multicolored 18 15
2562 A574 $5 multicolored 42 18
2563 A574 $8 multicolored 70 28
2564 A574 $10 multicolored 90 35
Nos. 2561-2564 (4) 2.20 96

New Year 1987 (Year of the Hare) — A575

1986, Dec. 1 *Perf. 12½*

2565 A575 $1 dl pink & multi 18 15
2566 A575 $10 pale grn & multi 1.75 40
a. Souv. sheet, 2 each #2565-2566 *15.00* 2.50

Kenting, 1st Natl. Park — A576

1987, Jan. 8 **Litho.** *Perf. 13½*

2567 A576 $2 Garden 35 15
2568 A576 $5 Shore rocks 70 20
2569 A576 $8 Shore and hill 1.10 32
2570 A576 $10 Shore and rocks, diff. 1.50 40
Nos. 2567-2570 (4) 3.65 1.07

Folk Art — A577

Puppets: $2, Hand puppet. $5, Marionette. $18, Shadow puppet.

1987, Feb. 12 **Litho.** *Perf. 14x13½*

2571 A577 $2 multicolored 32 15
2572 A577 $5 multicolored 48 15
2573 A577 $18 multicolored 2.25 60
Nos. 2571-2573 (3) 3.05
Set value 75

Speedpost A578

Wu Yueh (1878-1905), Revolutionary A579

1987, Mar. 20 **Litho.** *Perf. 14x13½*

2574 A578 $2 multicolored 15 15
2575 A578 $18 multicolored 90 55
Set value 60

Stamp Day.

Perf. 13½x12½

1987, Mar. 29 **Engr.**

2576 A579 $2 orange 70 15

Landscapes Painted by Madame Chiang Kai-shek — A580

Designs: $2, Singing Creek with Bamboo Orchestra. $5, Mountains Draped in Clouds. $8, Vista of Tranquility. $10, Mountains after a Snowfall.

1987, Apr. 10 **Litho.** *Perf. 13½*

2577 A580 $2 blk, buff & ver 55 15
2578 A580 $5 blk, buff & ver 1.50 25
2579 A580 $8 blk, buff & ver 2.25 38
2580 A580 $10 blk, buff & ver 2.75 48
Nos. 2577-2580 (4) 7.05 1.26

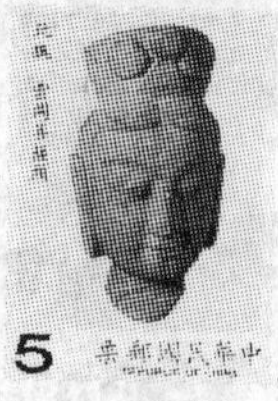

Stone Sculptures — A581

Designs: a, Head of a Bodhisattva, sandstone, Norther Wei Dynasty (386-534). b, Standing Buddha, limestone, Northern Ch'i Dynasty (550-577). c, Head of a Bodhisattva, sandstone, T'ang Dynasty (618-907). d, Seated Buddha, alabaster, T'ang Dynasty.

1987, Apr. 23

2581 Strip of 4 3.00 1.40
a.-d. A581 $5 any single 65 35

No. 2581a shows seven Chinese characters at left; No. 2581c shows five.

Ju-i Scepters, Ch'ing Dynasty A582

1987, May 7 **Photo.** *Perf. 14½x15*

2582 A582 $2 Silver and gems 55 15
2583 A582 $3 Gold and gems 80 15
2584 A582 $4 Gilded, jade and inlaid gems 1.10 15
2585 A582 $18 Gilded, inlaid malachite 4.50 65
Nos. 2582-2585 (4) 6.95
Set value 90

Feitsui Reservoir Inauguration A583

1987, June 6 **Litho.** *Perf. 13½x14*

2586 A583 $2 Reservoir 16 15
2587 A583 $18 Hsintien Stream, reservoir 1.65 65

Flower Arrangements by Huang Yung-ch'uan A584

Lions Club Intl. 70th Annual Convention, Taipei A585

1987, June 19 *Perf. 13½*

2588 A584 $2 denom. LL 20 15
2589 A584 $5 denom. LL 48 20
2590 A584 $8 Flowers in brown vase 75 28
2591 A584 $10 denom. UR 95 35
Nos. 2588-2591 (4) 2.38 98

Compare with designs A483, A559.

1987, July 1

2592 A585 $2 multicolored 15 15
2593 A585 $18 multicolored 1.10 65

Sino-Japanese War, 50th Anniv. A586

Wang Yun-wu (1888-1979), Lexicographer A587

1987, July 7 *Perf. 14x13½*

2594 A586 $1 Battle front 15 15
2595 A586 $2 Chiang Kai-shek giving speech 15 15
2596 A586 $5 Public donating funds 35 16
2597 A586 $6 Troops marching 42 18
2598 A586 $8 Signing of peace treaty 58 25
2599 A586 $18 Parade 1.25 52
Nos. 2594-2599 (6) 2.90 1.41

1987, Aug. 14 *Perf. 13½*

2600 A587 $2 gray black 20 15

Memorial Hall Type of 1981

Perf. 12½x13½

1987, Sept. 24 **Photo.**

2601 A468 10c lake 15 15
2602 A468 30c brt green 15 15
2603 A468 60c brt blue 30 15
Set value 50 25

A588

Cultural Renaissance Movement — A589

Scroll, 1543, by Weng Chen-ming (1470-1559), a copy of Chao Po-su's *Red Cliff.* Nos. 2604a-2604e and 2604f-2604j are printed in continuous designs. (Each stamp is numbered from 1 to 10 in Chinese. See illustrations with Nos. 1682-1691 for numerals.)

1987, Sept. 22 **Engr.** *Perf. 13½*

2604 Block of 10 10.00 3.50
a.-e. A588 $3 any single 75 32
f.-j. A589 $3 any single 75 32

Folk Costumes — A590

Designs: $1.50, Han woman, early Ch'ing Dynasty (1644-1911). $3, Wife of a Ch'ing Dynasty Manchu Bannerman. $7.50, Urban woman wearing Manchu ch'i-p'ao dress, c. 1912. $18, Short jacket over long skirt, c. 1920.

1987, Oct. 2 **Litho.**

2605 A590 $1.50 multicolored *35* 15
2606 A590 $3 multicolored *75* 15
2607 A590 $7.50 multicolored *1.75* 26
2608 A590 $18 multicolored *4.50* 65
Nos. 2605-2608 (4) *7.35* 1.21

Nos. 2605-2608 have 3 groups of 2 smaller Chinese characters above denomination. Nos. 2660-2663 have 2 groups of 2 and 4 characters.

A591

A592

1987, Nov. 12 *Perf. 13½x14*

2609 A591 $3 Ta Chen Tian temple, Taichung 24 15
2610 A591 $18 Confucius 1.40 65

Intl. Symposium on Confucianism, Taipei, Nov. 12-17.

1987, Dec. 1 *Perf. 12½*

2611 A592 $1.50 multicolored 30 15
2612 A592 $12 multicolored 2.00 40
a. Souv. sheet, 2 each #2611-2612 13.00 3.00
Set value 45

New Year 1988 (Year of the Dragon).

Constitution, 40th Anniv. A593

1987, Dec. 25 **Litho.** *Perf. 13½*

2613 A593 $3 multicolored 16 15
2614 A593 $16 multi, diff. 85 65

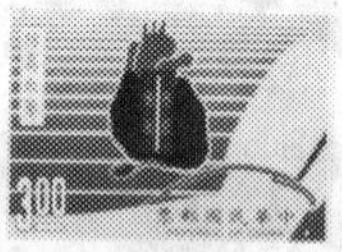

Prevent Hypertension Campaign — A594

1988, Jan. 8 *Perf. 12½x13½*

2615 A594 $3 multicolored 25 15

Fruit Tree Blossoms — A595

Perf. 13½

1988, Feb. 4 **Litho.** **Wmk. 323**

2616 A595 $3 Prunus mume 70 16
2617 A595 $7.50 Prunus armeniaca 1.65 45
2618 A595 $12 Prunus persica 2.50 68
a. Min. sheet of 3, #2616-2618 *27.50* *27.50*

Perf. 13½

1988, May 5 **Litho.** **Wmk. 323**

2619 A595 $3 Paeonia suffruticosa 70 18
2620 A595 $7.50 Punica granatum 1.65 45
2621 A595 $12 Nelumbo nucifera 2.50 72
a. Min. sheet of 3, #2619-2621 *16.00* *16.00*

Perf. 13½

1988, Aug. 9 **Litho.** **Wmk. 323**

2622 A595 $3 Impatiens balsamina 70 18
2623 A595 $7.50 Osmanthus fragrans 1.65 45

2624 A595 $12 Chrysanthemum morifolium 2.50 72
a. Min. sheet of 3, #2622-2624 *13.00* *13.00*

Perf. 13½

1988, Nov. 7 Litho. Wmk. 323

2625 A595 $3 Hibiscus mutabilis 60 18
2626 A595 $7.50 Camellia japonica 1.40 45
2627 A595 $12 Narcissus tazetta 2.00 72
a. Min. sheet of 3, #2625-2627 *14.00* *14.00*
Nos. 2616-2627 (12) 18.55 5.34

Tourism Day — A596

Folk art: $3, Modeled dough figurines. $7.50, Blown sweet-malt sugar candy. $16, Sugar paintings.

Perf. 13½x14

1988, Mar. 2 Litho. Wmk. 323

2628 A596 $3 multicolored 50 16
2629 A596 $7.50 multicolored 1.00 45
2630 A596 $16 multicolored 2.50 90
Nos. 2628-2630 (3) 4.00 1.51

A597

A598

Perf. 13½x12½

1988, Mar. 29 Engr. Wmk. 323

2631 A597 $3 brown 30 18

Hsu Hsi-lin (1873-1907), hero of the revolution.

1988 Litho. *Perf. 13½*

2632 A598 $1.50 Biotechnology 15 15
2633 A598 $3 Energy resources 18 16
2634 A598 $7 Immunization 42 35
2635 A598 $7.50 Automation 45 38
2636 A598 $10 Telecommunications 60 50
2637 A598 $12 Laser technology 70 60
2638 A598 $16 Micro-optics 95 80
2639 A598 $16.50 Agricultural research 95 85
Nos. 2632-2639 (8) 4.40 3.79

Industrialization by technological development. Issued: $3, $7.50, $10, $16, Apr. 22; other, May 9.

Police Day — A599

Perf. 13½

1988, June 15 Litho. Wmk. 323

2640 A599 $3 Traffic control 20 18
2641 A599 $12 Rescue operations 80 72

Amphibians A600

1988, July 8 *Perf. 13½x14*

2642 A600 $1.50 Microhyla butleri *48* 15
2643 A600 $3 Rana taipehensis *95* 18
2644 A600 $7.50 Microhyla inornata *2.50* 45
2645 A600 $16 Rhacophorus smaragdinus *5.00* 1.00
Nos. 2642-2645 (4) *8.93* 1.78

China Broadcasting Corp. (BBC), 60th Anniv. A601

Perf. 13½

1988, Aug. 1 Litho. Wmk. 323

2646 A601 $3 multicolored 25 18

Victory at the Battle of Kinmen, 30th Anniv. A602

Designs: $1.50, Chiang Kai-shek and artillery commander. $3, With troops. $7.50, Cannon. $12, Tanks.

1988, Aug. 23

2647 A602 $1.50 multicolored 15 15
2648 A602 $3 multicolored 18 18
2649 A602 $7.50 multicolored 48 45
2650 A602 $12 multicolored 75 62
Nos. 2647-2650 (4) 1.56 1.40

Sports Promotion — A603

Designs: Nos. 2651-2652, Basketball. Nos. 2653-2654, Baseball.

1988, Sept. 9

2651 A603 $5 Players 85 30
2652 A603 $5 Players 85 30
a. Pair, #2651-2652 1.75 1.20
2653 A603 $5 Batter 85 30
2654 A603 $5 Catcher 85 30
a. Pair, #2653-2654 1.75 1.20
Nos. 2651-2654 (4) 3.40 1.20

#2652a, 2654a have continuous designs.

Yangmingshan Natl. Park — A604

1988, Sept. 16

2655 A604 $1.50 Volcanic crater *16* 15
2656 A604 $3 Lake *32* 15
2657 A604 $7.50 Tatun Volcanic Range *85* 30
2658 A604 $16 Dormant volcano *1.65* 65
Nos. 2655-2658 (4) *2.98* 1.25

Lofty Mount Lu, a Hanging Scroll, 1467, By Shen Chou (1427-1509) — A605

Painting details: a, UL. b, UR. c, LL. d, LR.

Perf. 11½

1988, Oct. 9 Litho. Wmk. 323

2659 A605 Block of 4 *6.00* 1.20
a.-d. $5 any single *1.50* 30

Folk Costumes — A606

Designs: $2, Shang Dynasty (1766-1122 B.C.) nobleman. $3, Warring States (403-221) B.C.) ruler. $7.50, Wei-Chin Period (221-420) official. $12, Northern Dynasties (502-581) official.

Perf. 13½x14

1988, Mar. 2 Litho. Wmk. 323

2660 A606 $2 multicolored *40* 15
2661 A606 $3 multicolored *60* 18
2662 A606 $7.50 multicolored *1.50* 45
2663 A606 $12 multicolored *2.50* 72
Nos. 2660-2663 (4) *5.00* 1.50

Nos. 2721-2724 have groups of 2 and 6 Chinese characters above denomination; Nos. 2660-2663 groups of 2 and 4; #2794-2797 groups of 1 and 5.

A607

A608

1988, Dec. 1 *Perf. 12½*

2664 A607 $2 multicolored *80* 15
2665 A607 $13 multicolored *5.25* 78
a. Souv. sheet, 2 each #2664-2665 *15.00* 15.00

New Year 1989 (Year of the Snake).

Perf. 13½

1989, Jan. 4 Litho. Wmk. 323

2666 A608 $3 black 45 18

Tai Ch'uan-hsien (1890-1949), party leader.

Pres. Chiang Ching-kuo (1910-88) A609

1989, Jan. 13

2667 A609 $3 shown 16 15
2668 A609 $6 Suffrage 32 28
2669 A609 $7.50 Industry 40 35
2670 A609 $16 Children 90 75
Nos. 2667-2670 (4) 1.78 1.53

Ni Ying-tien (1884-1910), Revolution Leader — A610

Perf. 13½x12½

1989, Mar. 28 Engr. Wmk. 323

2671 A610 $3 black 25 20

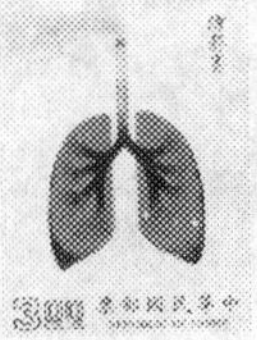

Stop Smoking — A611

Lighthouses — A612

Perf. 13½x12½

1989, Apr. 7 Litho. Wmk. 323

2672 A611 $3 multicolored 25 20

1989-91 *Perf. 13½*

2673 A612 75c Mu Tou Yu 15 15
2674 A612 $2 Lu Tao 18 15
2675 A612 $2.25 Pen Chia Yu 24 15
2676 A612 $3 Pitou Chiao 26 15
2677 A612 $4.50 Tungyin Tao 38 16
2678 A612 $6 Chilai Pi 55 32
2679 A612 $7 Fukwei Chiao 65 42
2680 A612 $7.50 Hua Yu 70 39
2681 A612 $9 Oluan Pi 80 32
2682 A612 $10 Kaohsiung 90 52
2683 A612 $10.50 Yuweng Tao 95 40
2683A A612 $12 Tungchu Tao 1.10 62
2683B A612 $13 Yeh Liu 1.25 48
2683C A612 $15 Tungchi Yu 1.40 90
2684 A612 $16.50 Chimei Yu 1.50 85
Nos. 2673-2684 (15) 11.01 5.98

Issue dates: $7, $15, May 19, 1990. $6, $12, Jan. 9, 1991. $2, $3, $7.50, $10, $16.50, May 20, 1991. Others, 1989.

See Nos. 2811-2823.

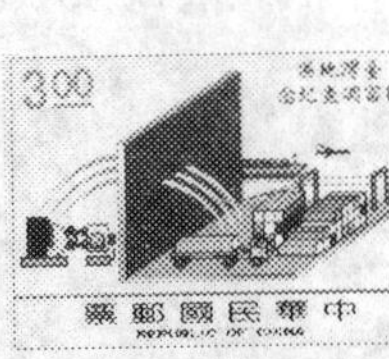

1st Natl. Wealth Survey A613

1989, May 18 Litho. *Perf. 13½*

2685 A613 $3 multicolored 45 20

Ch'u Ts'u Collection of Poems, 722-481 B.C. — A614

Excerpts: $3, "I once tended nine fields of orchids; Also I had planted a hundred rods of melilotus" (Li Sao). $7.50, "No grief is greater than parting of the living; No joy is more than making new friends" (Chiu Ko, shao ssu ming). $12, "Since my heart is straight and good, Why should I be chagrined at living remote and neglected?" (Chiu Chang, she chiang). $16, "The steed will not gallop itself into servitude; The phoenix has no appetite for slave food." (Chiu Pien).

Perf. 11½x12

1989, June 7 Photo. Granite Paper

2686 A614	$3	Man overlooking fields	45	20
2687 A614	$7.50	Map, woman on path	1.10	50
2688 A614	$12	Man holding staff	1.90	80
2689 A614	$16	Man, stallion, stone gate	2.50	1.10
		Nos. 2686-2689 (4)	5.95	2.60

Compare with types A629, A663. Nos. 2686-2689 have two Chinese characters near denomination. Nos. 2725-2728 have groups of 3 and 4 characters.

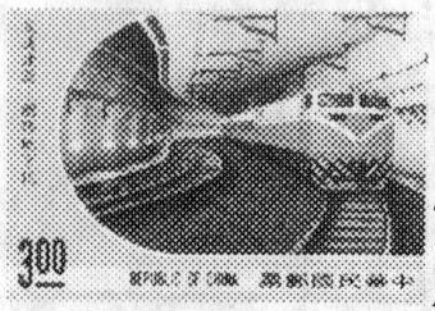

Taipei Subway Inauguration A615

1989, June 27 Litho. *Perf. 13½*

2690 A615	$3	Subway tunnel	25	20
2691 A615	$16	Entering underground	1.25	1.10

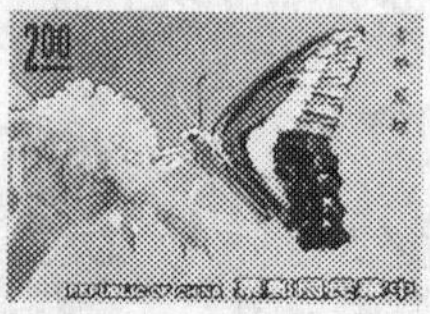

Butterflies A616

Designs: $2, *Graphium sarpedon connectens.* $3, *Papilio memnon heronus.* $7.50, *Princeps demoleus libanius.* $9, *Pachliopa aristolochiae interpositas.*

Perf. 13½

1989, July 14 Litho. Wmk. 323

2692 A616	$2	multicolored	50	15
2693 A616	$3	multicolored	85	16
2694 A616	$7.50	multicolored	2.00	42
2695 A616	$9	multicolored	2.50	50
		Nos. 2692-2695 (4)	5.85	1.23

Compare with design A627.

Ch'ing Dynasty Teapots from I-Hsing of Kiangsu, 1644-1911 A617

1989, July 28 *Perf. 13½x14*

2696 A617	$2	multicolored	28	15
2697 A617	$3	multi, diff.	45	16
2698 A617	$12	multi, diff.	1.75	65
2699 A617	$16	multi, diff.	2.40	90
		Nos. 2696-2699 (4)	4.88	1.86

For stamps with teapot designs and solid black denominations see Nos. 2760-2764.

Intl. Seminar on Fan Chung-yen (989-1052), Military Leader and Civil Service Reformer — A618

Perf. 14x13½

1989, Sept. 1 Litho. Wmk. 323

2700 A618 $12	multicolored	90	65

Autumn Colors on the Ch'iao and Hua Mountains, 14th Cent., by Ch'iao Meng-fu A619

Designs: a, Right side of mountain, trees. b, Trees, left side of mountain. c, House, trees. d, shown.

Perf. 13½

1989, Oct. 5 Litho. Wmk. 323

2701	Strip of 4	11.00	3.00
a.-d.	A619 $7.50 any single	2.75	75

Social Welfare A619a

1989, Nov. 3 Litho. *Perf. 13½*

2701E A619a $3	multicolored	25	16

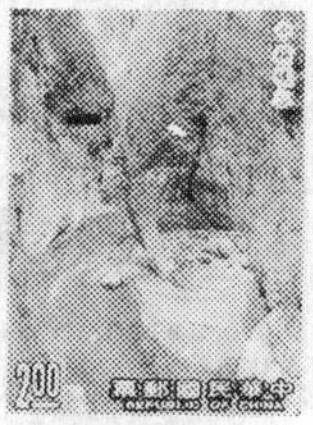

Taroko Natl. Park — A620

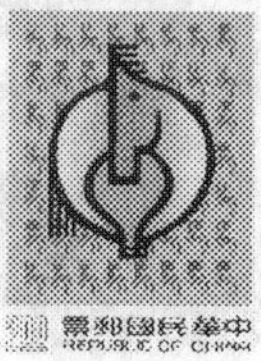

New Year 1990 (Year of the Horse) — A621

Designs: $2, Marble gorge, Liwu River. $3, Hohuan Mountain. $12, Waterfall, Cirque of Nanhu. $16, Chingshui Cliff.

Perf. 13½

1989, Nov. 28 Litho. Wmk. 323

2702 A620	$2	multicolored	15	15
2703 A620	$3	multicolored	16	16
2704 A620	$12	multicolored	65	65
2705 A620	$16	multicolored	90	90
		Nos. 2702-2705 (4)	1.86	1.86

1989, Dec. 1 *Perf. 12½*

2706 A621	$2	multicolored	22	15
2707 A621	$13	multicolored	1.65	75
a.		Souv. sheet, 2 each #2706-2707	7.50	3.00

Yu Lu — A622

Men Shen, "guardian spirits" (likenesses of legendary beings placed on residence doors at the new year): No. 2708, Yu Lu. No. 2709, Shen Shu. No. 2710, Wei-ch'ih Ching-te. No. 2711, Ch'in Shu-pao.

Perf. 13½

1990, Jan. 19 Litho. Wmk. 323

2708 A622	$3	shown	1.75	22
2709 A622	$3	"$3" at LR	1.75	22
a.		Pair, #2708-2709	3.50	3.50
2710 A622	$7.50	"$7.50" at LL	3.75	55
2711 A622	$7.50	"$7.50" at LR	3.75	55
a.		Pair, #2710-2711	7.50	7.50
		Nos. 2708-2711 (4)	11.00	1.54

Nos. 2709a, 2711a have continuous designs.

A623

Scenery — A624

Designs: $2, Lishan House, Pear Mountain. $18, Tayu Pass, Tayuling, vert.

Perf. 13½

1990, Feb. 10 Litho. Wmk. 323

2712 A623	$2	multicolored	20	15
2713 A624	$18	multicolored	1.75	1.10

Labor Insurance System, 40th Anniv. — A625

1990, Mar. 1

2714 A625 $3	multicolored	50	18

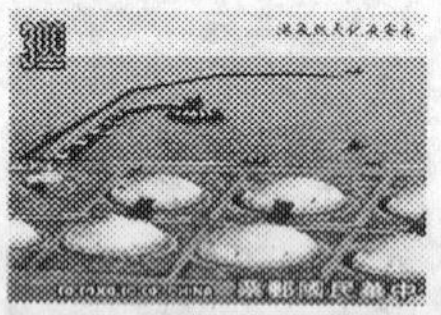

Liquefied Natural Gas — A626

Designs: $3, Terminal, Yung-an Hsiang of Kaohsiung. $16, Container ship, map, refinery, vert.

1990, Mar. 31 Litho. *Perf. 13½*

2715 A626	$3	multicolored	24	18
2716 A626	$16	multicolored	1.25	92

Butterflies A627

1990, Apr. 20

2717 A627	$2	*Salatura genutia*	18	15
2718 A627	$3	*Hypolimnas misippus*	28	18
2719 A627	$7.50	*Pieris canidia*	75	42
2720 A627	$9	*Precis almana*	80	52
		Nos. 2717-2720 (4)	2.01	1.27

Compare with design A616.

Folk Costumes — A628

Designs: $2, Official, Sui and T'ang Dynasties (589-907). $3, Official, T'ang and Sung Dynasties (618-1280). $7.50, Royal guardsman, Chin and Yuan Dynasties (1115-1368). $12, Highest ranking civil official, Ming Dynasty (1368-1644).

1990, May 10 Litho. *Perf. 13½*

2721 A628	$2	multicolored	32	15
2722 A628	$3	multicolored	55	18
2723 A628	$7.50	multicolored	1.25	42
2724 A628	$12	multicolored	2.25	70
		Nos. 2721-2724 (4)	4.37	1.45

See note after No. 2663.

Yueh Fu Classical Poetry — A629

Lyrics from Tzu-yeh folk songs, Six Dynasties (222-589): $3, Spring Song at Midnight. $7.50, Summer Song at Midnight. $12, Autumn Song at Midnight. $16, Winter Song at Midnight.

Perf. 11½

1990, June 27 Litho. Wmk. 323

Granite Paper

2725 A629	$3	shown	60	20
2726 A629	$7.50	Couple, river	1.50	50
2727 A629	$12	Washing clothes, river	2.50	80
2728 A629	$16	River in winter	3.50	1.10
		Nos. 2725-2728 (4)	8.10	2.60

Bonsai A630

Designs: $3, *Pinus thunbergii parl.* $6.50, *Ehretia microphylla lamk.* $12, *Buxus harlandii hance.* $16, *Celtis sinensis pers.*

1990, July 20 *Perf. 13½*

2729 A630	$3	multicolored	22	20
2730 A630	$6.50	multicolored	48	42
2731 A630	$12	multicolored	85	80
2732 A630	$16	multicolored	1.10	1.00
		Nos. 2729-2732 (4)	2.65	2.42

Snuff Bottles — A631

1990, Aug. 9

2733 A631	$3	Bamboo stem shaped	24	20
2734 A631	$6	Peony motif	48	40
2735 A631	$9	Amber	70	58
2736 A631	$16	White jade	1.25	1.00
		Nos. 2733-2736 (4)	2.67	2.18

Formosan Firecrest
A632

1990, Aug. 20 Litho. *Perf. 13½*

2737 A632 $2 shown 18 15
2738 A632 $3 Laughing thrush 28 15
2739 A632 $7.50 White-eared sibia 65 38
2740 A632 $16 Yellow tit 1.40 80
Nos. 2737-2740 (4) 2.51 1.48

Sports — A633

1990, Sept. 8 Litho. *Perf. 13½*

2741 A633 $2 Sprint 15 15
2742 A633 $3 Long jump 22 15
2743 A633 $7 Pole vault 52 42
2744 A633 $16 High hurdle 1.15 80
Nos. 2741-2744 (4) 2.04 1.52

Flying Tigers, 50th Anniv.
A634

1990, Sept. 26 Litho. *Perf. 13½*

2745 A634 $3 multicolored 45 15

Children's Drawings
A635

1990, Oct. 9

2746 A635 $2 Cat 16 15
2747 A635 $3 Peacocks 24 15
2748 A635 $7.50 Chickens 60 38
2749 A635 $12 Cattle 1.00 65
Nos. 2746-2749 (4) 2.00 1.33

National Theater
A636

Photo. & Engr.

1990, Oct. 30 *Perf. 13½*

2750 A636 $3 shown 28 15
2751 A636 $12 Natl. concert hall 1.10 65

A637

A638

Ancient money.

1990, Nov. 5 Litho. *Perf. 13x13½*

2752 A637 $2 Shell 15 15
2753 A637 $3 Oyster 16 15
2754 A637 $6.50 Bone 35 35
2755 A637 $7.50 Jade 40 39
2756 A637 $9 Bronze 50 50
Nos. 2752-2756 (5) 1.56 1.54

1990, Dec. 1 *Perf. 12½*

2757 A638 $2 multicolored 50 15
2758 A638 $13 multicolored 1.75 65
a. Souv. sheet, 2 each #2757-2758 10.50 2.50

New Year 1991 (Year of the Sheep).

Hu Shih (1891-1962), Educator — A639

Perf. 13½

1990, Dec. 17 Engr. Wmk. 323

2759 A639 $3 purple 22 15

Teapots, Natl. Palace Museum
A640

Teapots: $2, Blue phoenix, Ming Dynasty. $3, Dragon handle and spout, Ming Dynasty. $9, Blue landscape, flowered top, Ch'ing Dynasty. $12, Rectangular, passion flower motif, Ch'ing Dynasty. $16, Rectangular, flower motif, Ch'ing Dynasty.

1991, Jan. 18 Photo. *Perf. 12*

Granite Paper

2760 A640 $2 yel, blk & blue 15 15
2761 A640 $3 brt yel grn & blk 22 15
2762 A640 $9 pink & multi 66 45
2763 A640 $12 vio & multi 88 60
2764 A640 $16 lt bl & multi 1.25 95
Nos. 2760-2764 (5) 3.16 2.30

God of Happiness — A641

God of Joy — A642

1991, Feb. 7 Litho. *Perf. 13½*

2765 A641 $3 shown 45 15
2766 A641 $3 God of Wealth 45 15
2767 A642 $7.50 shown 1.10 39
2768 A642 $7.50 God of Longevity 1.10 39
Nos. 2765-2768 (4) 3.10 1.08

1991 *Perf. 13½ Vert.*

2765a A641 $3 1.00 15
2766a A641 $3 1.00 15
2767a A642 $7.50 1.00 15
2768a A642 $7.50 1.00 15
b. Bklt. pane of 8, 2 each #2765a-2768a + label 12.00

Native Plants
A643

Designs: $2, Petasites formosanus. $3, Heloniopsis acutifolia. $7.50, Disporum shimadai. $9, Viola nagasawai.

1991, Mar. 12 Litho. *Perf. 13½*

2769 A643 $2 multicolored 15 15
2770 A643 $3 multicolored 22 15
2771 A643 $7.50 multicolored 55 39
2772 A643 $9 multicolored 66 45

1991, June 12

Designs: $2, Gaultheria itoana. $3, Lysionotus montanus. $7.50, Leontopodium microphyllum. $9, Gentiana flavo-maculata.

2773 A643 $2 multicolored 15 15
2774 A643 $3 multicolored 22 15
2775 A643 $7.50 multicolored 55 40
2776 A643 $9 multicolored 65 45

1991, Sept. 12

Designs: $3.50, Rosa transmorrisonensis. $5, Impatiens devolii. $9, Impatiens uniflora. $12, Impatiens tayemonii.

2777 A643 $3.50 multicolored 25 18
2778 A643 $5 multicolored 38 25
2779 A643 $9 multicolored 65 45
2780 A643 $12 multicolored 88 62

1991, Dec. 12

Designs: $3.50, Kalanchoe garambiensis. $5, Pieris taiwanensis. $9, Pleione formosana. $12, Elaeagnus oldhamii.

2781 A643 $3.50 multicolored 25 15
2782 A643 $5 multicolored 38 25
2783 A643 $9 multicolored 70 48
2784 A643 $12 multicolored 90 60
Nos. 2769-2784 (16) 7.54 5.27

Hsiung Cheng-Chi (1887-1910), Revolutionary — A644

Perf. 13½x12½

1991, Mar. 28 Engr.

2785 A644 $3 blue 22 15

Republic of China, 80th Anniv.
A645

1991, Mar. 28 Litho. *Perf. 13½*

2786 A645 $3 Agriculture 22 15
2787 A645 $7.50 Science & technology 55 39
2788 A645 $12 Cultural activities 88 60
2789 A645 $16 Transportation 1.20 80
Nos. 2786-2789 (4) 2.85 1.94

Children's Toys — A646

Folk Costumes — A647

1991, Apr. 20 Litho. *Perf. 13½*

2790 A646 $3 Bamboo pony 22 15
2791 A646 $3 Woven-grass grasshopper 22 15
2792 A646 $3 Top 22 15
2793 A646 $3 Pinwheels 22 15
a. Souv. sheet of 4, #2790-2793 5.00 2.00
Nos. 2790-2793 (4) 88 60

See Nos. 2840-2843. Compare with design A616.

1991 *Perf. 13½ Vert.*

2790a A646 $3 1.25 15
2791a A646 $3 1.25 15
2792a A646 $3 1.25 15
2793b A646 $3 1.25 15
c. Bklt. pane, 2 each #2790a-2793b + label 11.00
Nos. 2790a-2793b (4) 5.00 60

1991, June 29 Litho. *Perf. 13½*

Ch'ing Dynasty (1644-1911): $2, Winter court hat, Mang robe. $3, Summer court hat, surcoat. $7.50, Winter overcoat. $12, Common hat, traveling robe.

2794 A647 $2 multicolored 30 15
2795 A647 $3 multicolored 45 15
2796 A647 $7.50 multicolored 1.10 40
2797 A647 $12 multicolored 1.75 62
Nos. 2794-2797 (4) 3.60 1.32

See note after No. 2724.

Nos. 2794-2797 have groups of one and five Chinese characters.

Traffic Safety Year — A648

1991, July 17 Litho. *Perf. 13½*

2798 A648 $3 shown 30 15
2799 A648 $7.50 Don't drink & drive 75 40

Cloisonne Enamel Lions, Ch'ing Dynasty (1644-1911)
A649 A649a

1991, July 20 Litho. *Perf. 12½*

2800 A649 yel grn & multi
2801 A649a violet & multi
Set value 1.90

#2800 paid basic domestic rate, #2801 paid basic express mail rate on date of issue.

Fruits — A650

Birds — A651

1991, Aug. 10 Litho. *Perf. 14x13½*

2802 A650 $3 Strawberry 22 15
2803 A650 $7.50 Grapes 55 40
2804 A650 $9 Mango 65 48
2805 A650 $16 Sugar apple 1.20 85
Nos. 2802-2805 (4) 2.62 1.88

1991, Aug. 24 *Perf. 13½*

Designs: a, Myiophoneus insularis. b, Cinclus pallasii. c, Aix galericulata. d, Nycticorax nycticorax. e, Egretta garzetta. f, Rhyacornis fuliginosus. g, Enicurus scouleri. h, Motacilla cinerea. i, Alcedo atthis. j, Motacilla alba.

2806 Block of 10 3.80 2.80
a.-j. A651 $5 any single 38 28

Outdoor Activities
A652

Perf. 13½

1991, Sept. 27 Litho. Wmk. 323

2807 A652 $2 Rock climbing 15 15
2808 A652 $3 Fishing 22 15
2809 A652 $7.50 Bird watching 55 40
2810 A652 $10 Playing in water 75 60
Nos. 2807-2810 (4) 1.67 1.30

Intl. Federation of Camping and Caravaning, 1991 Rally.

Lighthouse Type of 1989
Inscription Panel in Blue

1991, Oct. 2 *Perf. 13½*

2811 A612 50c like #2683C 15 15
2811A A612 $1 like #2683 15 15
2812 A612 $3.50 like #2678 25 18
2813 A612 $5 like #2679 38 25
a. Booklet pane of 10 4.00
2814 A612 $12 like #2683A 90 60
a. $12 Booklet pane of 5 + label 4.75
2816 A612 $19 like #2684A 1.45 98
2817 A612 $20 like #2678 1.50 1.00
2818 A612 $26 like #2683 2.00 1.35
2819 A612 $28 like #2684 2.10 1.40

1992

2820 A612 $7 like #2676 52 35
2821 A612 $9 like #2681 68 45
2822 A612 $10 like #2682 75 50
2823 A612 $13 like #2675 95 65
Nos. 2811-2823 (13) 11.78 8.01

Issue dates: 50c, $3.50, $5, $12, Oct. 2; No. 2814a, Sept. 26, 1992; $1, $19, $20, Mar. 2, 1992; $26, $28, May 20, 1992; $7, $9, $10, $13, Aug. 21, 1992.

This is an expanding set. Numbers will change.

Peacocks by Lan Shih-ning (Giuseppe Castiglione, 1688-1768)
A653

Design: $20, Peacock spreading tail feathers.

Perf. 12x11½

1991, Oct. 30 Photo. Unwmk.

Granite Paper

2826 A653 $5 multicolored 38 25
2827 A653 $20 multicolored 1.50 1.20
a. Souvenir sheet of 1 3.00 2.00

New Year 1992 (Year of the Monkey) — A654

Perf. 12½

1991, Nov. 30 Litho. Wmk. 323

2828 A654 $3.50 org & multi 25 18
2829 A654 $13 tan & multi 95 70
a. Souv. sheet, 2 each #2828-2829 3.00 2.00

Chinese Books
A655

Perf. 13½

1992, Jan. 17 Litho. Wmk. 323

2830 A655 $3.50 Scroll 25 18
2831 A655 $5 Fold bindings 38 25
2832 A655 $9 Butterfly bindings 70 48
2833 A655 $15 String bindings 1.10 85
Nos. 2830-2833 (4) 2.43 1.76

Good Fortune and Satisfaction
A656

Five Blessings Upon the House
A657

Nienhwa paintings: No. 2835, Peace in the Wake of Firecrackers. No. 2837, An Abundance for Every Year.

1992, Jan. 27 Litho. *Perf. 13½*

2834 A656 $5 multicolored 38 25
2835 A656 $5 multicolored 38 25
2836 A657 $12 multicolored 90 60
2837 A657 $12 multicolored 90 60
a. Bklt. pane, 2 each #2834-2837 + label 5.20
Nos. 2834-2837 (4) 2.56 1.70

Lunar New Year.

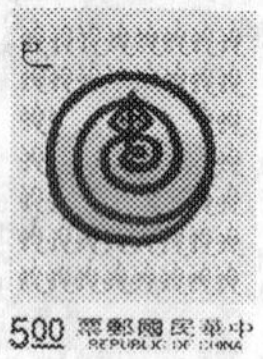

A658

A659

Lunar New Year: a, like #2664. b, like #2611. c, like #2565. d, like #2493. e, like #2442. f, like #2390. g, like #2346. h, like #2273. i, like #2217. j, like #2828. k, like #2757. l, like #2706.

Perf. 12½

1992, Feb. 18 Litho. Wmk. 323

2838 A658 $5 Block of 12, #a.-l., ver & multi 4.60 3.05
m. Sheet of 12, #2838a-2838l 4.60 3.05

1992, Mar. 12 *Perf. 13½*

Trees: a, Chamaecyparis formosensis. b, Chamaecyparis taiwanensis. c, Calocedrus formosana. d, Cunninghamia konishii. e. Taiwania cryptomerioides.

2839 A659 $5 Strip of 5, #a.-e. 1.90 65

Children's Toys Type of 1991

1992, Apr. 29 Litho. *Perf. 13½*

2840 A646 $5 Walking on iron pots 38 25
2841 A646 $5 Chopstick gun 38 25
2842 A646 $5 Hoop rolling 38 25
2843 A646 $5 Grass fighting 38 25
a. Sheet of 4, #2840-2843 *5.00 5.00*
b. As "a," imperf. (simulated perfs), red inscription in sheet margin *17.50 17.50*
c. Bklt. pane, 2 ea #2840-2843 + label 3.25
Nos. 2840-2843 (4) 1.52 1.00

Issue date: No. 2843b, May 15.

A660

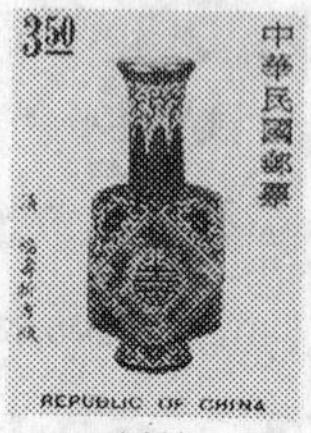

A661

Mother and son in: $3.50, Spring. $5, Summer. $9, Autumn. $10, Winter.

Perf. 13½

1992, May 9 Litho. Wmk. 323

2844 A660 $3.50 multicolored 25 18
2845 A660 $5 multicolored 38 25
2846 A660 $9 multicolored 70 48
2847 A660 $10 multicolored 75 50
Nos. 2844-2847 (4) 2.08 1.41

Parent-child relationships.

Perf. 13½

1992, June 25 Litho. Wmk. 323

Glassware Decorated with Enamel - Vases: $3.50, Faceted, decorated with bats and longevity characters. $5, Double-lobed, with children at play. $7, Flowered. $17, Tutoring scene.

Background colors

2848 A661 $3.50 pink 25 18
2849 A661 $5 green 38 25
2850 A661 $7 bister 55 42
2851 A661 $17 blue 1.30 1.00
Nos. 2848-2851 (4) 2.48 1.85

Stone Lion of Lugouqiao
A662

Various stone lions.

Perf. 13½

1992, July 7 Engr. Wmk. 323

2852 A662 $5 olive green & purple 38 25
2853 A662 $5 blue & brown 38 25
2854 A662 $12 orange & olive green 90 60
2855 A662 $12 purple & black 90 60
Nos. 2852-2855 (4) 2.56 1.70

Ku Shih Classical Poetry — A663

Excerpts: $3.50, "Flesh and body are as closely linked as leaves to a tree." $5, "Once a man and woman get married, conjugal love will last forever without doubt." $9, "Man takes pains to uphold virtue." $15, "Tartar horses lean toward the northern wind."

1992, Aug. 8 Litho.

2856 A663 $3.50 Children playing near tree 25 18
2857 A663 $5 Man & woman 38 25
2858 A663 $9 Couple near stream 68 45
2859 A663 $15 Horse, tree 1.10 72
Nos. 2856-2859 (4) 2.41 1.60

Life in the Countryside
A664

Scenes of temple fair: a, Two women, man beating drum, crowd. b, Vendor with basket. c, People playing musical instruments. d, Man with food cart. e, Women with umbrella, basket.

Perf. 11½

1992, Sept. 22 Litho. Wmk. 323

2860 A664 $5 Strip of 5, #a.-e. 1.85 60

Silk Tapestries
A665

Ming Dynasty Silk Tapestry Drawing on Life: $5, Two Birds Perched on a Red Camellia Branch. $12, Two Birds Playing on a Peach Branch.

1992, Oct. 9 Litho. *Perf. 11½*

Granite Paper

2861 A665 $5 multicolored 38 25
2862 A665 $12 multicolored 90 60
a. Sheet of 2, #2861-2862 1.30 85

Chinese Opera — A666

Actors, props: $3.50, Nin Hsiang-ju's carting to a party from "The General and Premier." $5, Hsao En rowing a boat from "The Lucky Pearl." $9, Wang Chao-chun making peace with the frontier from "Chao-chun Serves as an Envoy." $12, Scene with red sedan chair from "Escort to the Wedding."

Perf. 13½

1992, Oct. 21 Litho. Wmk. 323

2863 A666 $3.50 multicolored 25 18
2864 A666 $5 multicolored 38 25
2865 A666 $9 multicolored 68 45
2866 A666 $12 multicolored 90 60
Nos. 2863-2866 (4) 2.21 1.48

Alishan Forest Railway — A667

1992, Nov. 5 *Perf. 11½*

2867 A667 $5 Steam engine 38 25
2868 A667 $15 Diesel engine 1.15 75

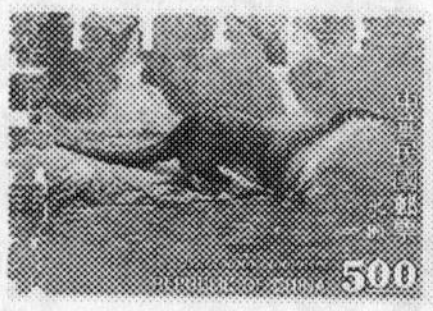

Endangered Mammals of Taiwan
A668

Designs: a, Lutra lutra chinensis. b, Pteropus dasymallus formosus. c, Neofelis nebulosa brachyurus. d, Selenarctos thibetanus formosanus.

Perf. 11½x12

1992, Nov. 25 Photo. Unwmk.

Granite Paper

2869 A668 $5 Block of 4, #a.-d. 1.55 1.00

New Year 1993 (Year of the Rooster) — A669

Design: $13, Rooster facing left.

Perf. 12½

1992, Dec. 1 Litho. Wmk. 323

2870 A669 $3.50 red & multi 26 18
a. Perf. 13½ vert. 28 20
2871 A669 $13 pur & multi 95 62
a. Souv. sheet, 2 each #2870-2871 2.45 2.45
b. As "a" with added inscription in border 2.45 2.45
c. Bklt. pane, 5 ea #2870-2871 6.25
d. Perf. 13½ vert. 1.05 68
e. Booklet pane, 6 each #2870a, 2871d + label 8.10

Inscription on No. 2871b reads "Philippine Stamp Exhibition 1992-Taipei" in English and Chinese.

Johann Adam Schall von Bell (1592-1666), Astronomer and Missionary A670

1992 Dec. 10 *Perf. 11½*

2872 A670 $5 multicolored 38 25

Traditional Nienhwas of Window Frames — A671

Perf. 11½

1993, Jan. 7 Litho. Wmk. 323

Background Color

2873 A671 $5 brt green 40 25
2874 A671 $5 red lilac 40 25
2875 A671 $12 yellow 95 60
2876 A671 $12 red 95 60
a. Bklt. pane, 2 each #2873-2876 5.50
Nos. 2873-2876 (4) 2.70 1.70

Lunar New Year.

Perf. 13½ Vert.

2873a A671 $5 40 25
2874a A671 $5 40 25
2875a A671 $12 95 60
2876b A671 $12 95 60
c. Booklet pane, 2 each #2873a-2875a, 2876b + label 5.50

Nos. 2873a-2875a, 2876b are 29x43mm.

Traditional Crafts A672

1993, Jan. 16

2877 A672 $3.50 Clip & paste moldings 28 18
2878 A672 $5 Lanterns 40 25
2879 A672 $9 Pottery jars 70 45
2880 A672 $15 Oil paper umbrella 1.20 75
Nos. 2877-2880 (4) 2.58 1.63

Chinese Creation Story — A673

Designs: $3.50, Pan Gu's creation of the universe, vert. $5, Pan Gu transmitted himself into all creatures. $9, Nu Wa created human beings with pestled earth. $19, Nu Wa mended sky with smelted stone, vert.

1993, Feb. 6 ***Perf. 12x11½, 11½x12***

2881 A673 $3.50 multicolored 28 18
2882 A673 $5 multicolored 40 25
2883 A673 $9 multicolored 70 45
2884 A673 $19 multicolored 1.50 1.00
Nos. 2881-2884 (4) 2.88 1.88

Lucky Animals — A674

Water Plants — A675

Perf. 13½

1993, Mar. 2 Litho. Wmk. 323

2885 A674 $3.50 Mandarin duck 28 18
2886 A674 $5 Chinese unicorn 40 25
2887 A674 $10 Deer 80 52
2888 A674 $15 Crane 1.20 78
Nos. 2885-2888 (4) 2.68 1.73

See Nos. 2920-2923.

1993, Mar. 12 *Perf. 11½*

2889 A675 $5 Nymphaea x hybrida 40 25
2890 A675 $9 Nuphar shimadai 70 45
2891 A675 $12 Eichhornia crassipes 95 60
Nos. 2889-2891 (3) 2.05 1.30

A676

1993 Litho. Wmk. 323 *Perf. 11½*

2892 A676 $5 Sandbag tossing 38 25
2893 A676 $5 Bamboo dragonfly twisting 38 25
2894 A676 $5 Rubber band skipping 38 25
2895 A676 $5 Waist-strength dueling 38 25
a. Souvenir sheet of 4, #2892-2895 1.55 1.55
b. As "a," with green & black inscriptions in border 1.55 1.55
c. As "a," with red inscription in border 1.55 1.55
Nos. 2892-2895 (4) 1.52 1.00

Inscriptions on No. 2895b read "AUSTRALIAN STAMP EXHIBITION 1993-TAIPEI" in Chinese and English.

Inscription on No. 2895c reads "Chinese Stamp Exhibition-Thailand" in Chinese.

Nos. 2895b-2895c each have perforations extending into the margin at top (#2895c) or bottom (#2895b).

Issue dates: Nos. 2892-2895, 2895a, Apr. 20. No. 2895b, Apr. 23. No. 2895c, Apr. 30.

Perf. 13½ Vert.

2892a A676 $5 38 25
2893a A676 $5 38 25
2894a A676 $5 38 25
2895d A676 $5 38 25
e. Bklt. pane, 2 each #2892a-2894a, 2895d + label 3.25

A677

Yangtze River A678

Designs: No. 2896, Source on Ching-Kang-Chang Plateau. No. 2897, Abrupt bend, Chinsha River. No. 2898, Narrow waterway, Roaring Tiger Gorge, Chinsha River. No. 2899, Sheer cliffs, Chuntang Gorge. $9, Three Small Gorges (Dragon Gate, Pawu, and Titsui).

Perf. 13x13½

1993, May 15 Litho. Wmk. 323

2896 A677 $3.50 shown 28 18
2897 A677 $3.50 multicolored 28 18
2898 A678 $5 shown 38 25
2899 A677 $5 multicolored 38 25
2900 A677 $9 multicolored 68 45
Nos. 2896-2900 (5) 2.00 1.31

Environmental Protection
A679 A680

Children's paintings: $5, No More Noise Pollution, by Yen Chao-min. $17, Clothing My Hometown with Green, by Hu Hui-chun.

Perf. 12½x13½, 13½x12½

1993, June 5

2901 A679 $5 multicolored 38 25
2902 A680 $17 multicolored 1.30 1.00

Ch'eng-hua Porcelain, Natl. Palace Museum A681

Cups decorated in tou-ts'ai: $3.50, Human figures. $5, Chickens. $7, Flowers and fruits. $9, Dragon.

1993, June 30 *Perf. 12*

2903 A681 $3.50 multicolored 28 20
2904 A681 $5 multicolored 38 25
2905 A681 $7 multicolored 55 40
2906 A681 $9 multicolored 68 50
Nos. 2903-2906 (4) 1.89 1.35

Vocational Training A682

Perf. 12½

1993, July 24 Litho. Wmk. 323

2907 A682 $3.50 Graphic artist 28 20
2908 A682 $5 Computer operator 38 25
2909 A682 $9 Carpenter 68 50
2910 A682 $12 Welder 90 68
Nos. 2907-2910 (4) 2.24 1.63

Parent-Child Relationship A683

Silhouettes: $3.50, Adult carrying child on shoulders. $5, Father playing flute for daughter. $9, Father teaching daughter. $10, Father, adult son enjoying wildlife.

Perf. 11½

1993, Aug. 4 Litho. Wmk. 323

Background Color

2911 A683 $3.50 tan 28 22
2912 A683 $5 green 38 28
2913 A683 $9 lilac 68 52
2914 A683 $10 red brown 75 58
Nos. 2911-2914 (4) 2.09 1.60

Souvenir Sheet

Taipei '93, Asian Intl. Philatelic Exhibition — A684

Enjoying Antiques, by Tu Chin, 15th cent: a, Man carrying stick. b, Man selecting antiques from table. c, Man seated in chair. d, Two people at table.

Perf. 12x11½

1993, Aug. 14 Photo. Unwmk.

Granite Paper

2915 A684 $5 Sheet of 4, #a.-d. 1.50 1.15

Persimmon A685

Loquat A686

1993, Sept. 10 Litho. *Perf. 12½*

2916 A685 $5 shown 38 28
2917 A685 $5 Peach 38 28
2918 A686 $12 shown 90 68
2919 A686 $12 Papaya 90 68
Nos. 2916-2919 (4) 2.56 1.92

Lucky Animals Type of 1993

Perf. 13½

1993, Sept. 29 Litho. Wmk. 323

2920 A674 $1 Blue dragon 15 15
2921 A674 $2.50 White tiger 18 15
2922 A674 $9 Linnet 65 42
2923 A674 $19 Black tortoise 1.40 90
Nos. 2920-2923 (4) 2.38 1.62

Taiwan Area Games, Taoyuan A687

Stone Lions A688

Designs: a, Taekwondo. b, Pommel horse.

Perf. 12½

1993, Oct. 20 Litho. Wmk. 323

2924 A687 $5 Pair, #a.-b. 75 75

1993, Oct. 30

Stone lions from: $3.50, Taipei New Park. $5, Hsinchu City Council. $9, Hsinchu City God Temple. $12, Fort Providentia, Tainan.

2925 A688 $3.50 multicolored 25 16
2926 A688 $5 multicolored 38 25
2927 A688 $9 multicolored 65 45
2928 A688 $12 multicolored 90 60
Nos. 2925-2928 (4) 2.18 1.46

Syrmaticus Mikado A689

Designs: a, Hatchling. b, Mother with chicks. c, Immature female, male. d, Adult female, male (profile, showing plumage).

Perf. 11½

1993, Nov. 17 Photo. Unwmk.
Granite Paper

2929 A689 $5 Strip of 4, #a.-d. 1.50 1.50

New Year 1994 (Year of the Dog) — A690

Design: $13, Dog facing left.

Perf. 12½

1993, Dec. 1 Litho. Wmk. 323

2930 A690 $3.50 red & multi 25 16
a. Perf. 13½ vert. 25 16
b. As "a," bklt. pane of 12 + label 3.00
2931 A690 $13 green & multi 1.00 65
a. Souvenir sheet, 2 each #2930-2931 1.25 85
b. As "a," overprinted in red 1.25 85

No. 2931b is inscribed in Chinese for Kaohsiung Kuo-kuang Stamp Exhibition-1993, and has additional perforations extending into top and bottom margins.

Asian Vegetable Research and Development Center, 20th Anniv. — A691

1993, Dec. 7

2932 A691 $5 shown 38 25
2933 A691 $13 Researchers in field 1.00 65

Formation of Constitutional Court — A692

Perf. 12½

1994, Jan. 11 Litho. Wmk. 323

2934 A692 $5 multicolored 38 25

Paper Making — A693

Flowers — A694

Designs: No. 2935, Cutting bamboo. No. 2936, Cooking bamboo. No. 2937, Pouring syrup into wooden panel. No. 2938, Stacking panel. No. 2939, Drying paper.

1994, Jan. 24 *Perf. 12x12½*

2935 A693 $3.50 multicolored 28 18
2936 A693 $3.50 multicolored 28 18
2937 A693 $5 multicolored 38 25
2938 A693 $5 multicolored 38 25
2939 A693 $12 multicolored 90 60
Nos. 2935-2939 (5) 2.22 1.46

1994, Feb. 17 *Perf. 12½*

2940 A694 $5 Clivia miniata 38 25
2941 A694 $12 Cymbidium sinense 90 60
2942 A694 $19 Primula malacoides 1.40 95
Nos. 2940-2942 (3) 2.68 1.80

Kinmen Wind Lion Lords — A695

Various Wind Lion Lords.

1994, Mar. 18 Litho. *Perf. 12½*

2943 A695 $5 green & multi 38 25
2944 A695 $9 yellow & multi 70 45
2945 A695 $12 orange yellow & multi 90 60
2946 A695 $17 blue & multi 1.25 80
Nos. 2943-2946 (4) 3.23 2.10

Children at Play — A696

Designs: No. 2947, Playing with paper boat. No. 2948, Fighting with water gun. No. 2949, Throwing paper airplane. No. 2950, Playing "train" with rope.

Perf. 12½

1994, Apr. 2 Litho. Wmk. 323

2947 A696 $5 multicolored 38 25
2948 A696 $5 multicolored 38 25
2949 A696 $5 multicolored 38 25
2950 A696 $5 multicolored 38 25
a. Souvenir sheet of 4, #2947-2950 1.50 1.00
Nos. 2947-2950 (4) 1.52 1.00

Perf. 13½ Vert.

2947a A696 $5 38 25
2948a A696 $5 38 25
2949a A696 $5 38 25
2950b A696 $5 38 25
c. Booklet pane, 2 each #2947a-2949a, 2950b + label 3.25

A697

A698

Life in the countryside: $5, Playing chess. $10, Playing musical instruments. $12, Telling stories. $19, Drinking tea.

Perf. 12½

1994, Apr. 25 Litho. Wmk. 323

2951 A697 $5 multicolored 38 25
2952 A697 $10 multicolored 75 48
2953 A697 $12 multicolored 90 60
2954 A697 $19 multicolored 1.40 95
Nos. 2951-2954 (4) 3.43 2.28

1994, May 7

Mother, baby birds: $5, Malay bittern. $7, Little tern, horiz. $10, Common noddy, horiz. $12, Muller's barbet.

2955 A698 $5 multicolored 38 25
2956 A698 $7 multicolored 52 35
2957 A698 $10 multicolored 75 48
2958 A698 $12 multicolored 90 55
Nos. 2955-2958 (4) 2.55 1.63

A699

A700

Protection of Intellectual Property Rights: $5, Palm-shaped book. $15, Human head, computer disk.

Perf. 12½

1994, May 28 Litho. Wmk. 323

2959 A699 $5 multicolored 38 25
2960 A699 $15 multicolored 1.10 70

1994, June 11

Designs: $5, Care for Lost Children. $15, Care for the aged.

2961 A700 $5 multicolored 38 25
2962 A700 $17 multicolored 1.25 85

Intl. Olympic Committee, Cent. — A701

1994, June 23

2963 A701 $5 shown 38 25
2964 A701 $15 Sporting events 1.10 70

A702

A703

Shei-pa Natl. Park: $5, Tapachienshan. $7, Sheisan Landslide Scar. $10, Holy Ridge. $17, Shiahtsuei Lake.

Perf. 12½

1994, July 1 Litho. Wmk. 323

2965 A702 $5 multicolored 38 25
2966 A702 $7 multicolored 52 35
2967 A702 $10 multicolored 75 48
2968 A702 $17 multicolored 1.25 85
Nos. 2965-2968 (4) 2.90 1.93

1994, July 30 *Perf. 11½x12*

Design: $5, Portrait of Chien Mu (b. 1895), educator.

2969 A703 $5 multicolored 38 25

Intl. Year of the Family A704

Designs: $5, Rainbow, window. $15, Globe, house.

1994, Aug. 25 *Perf. 11½*

2970 A704 $5 multicolored 38 25
2971 A704 $15 yel & multi 1.10 70

Invention Myths — A705

Designs: $5, Sueirenjy digging wood to obtain fire. $10, Fushijy drawing Pa-Kua. $12, Shennungjy making agricultural tools. $15, Tsang-jier creating written characters.

1994, Sept. 17 Photo. *Perf. 11½*
Granite Paper

2972 A705 $5 multicolored 38 25
2973 A705 $10 multicolored 75 48
2974 A705 $12 multicolored 90 60
2975 A705 $15 multicolored 1.10 70
Nos. 2972-2975 (4) 3.13 2.03

A706

A707

Design: $5, Dr. Lin Yutang, linguist, writer, 100th birthday.

Perf. 12½

1994, Oct. 8 Litho. Wmk. 323

2976 A706 $5 multicolored 38 25

1994, Oct. 17

Designs: $5, Cheng Ho's ship. $17, Chart, ship, Cheng Ho.

2977 A707 $5 multicolored 38 25
2978 A707 $17 multicolored 1.25 85

World Trade Week.

Sun Yat-sen, Founding of Kuomintang, Cent. — A708

Design: $19, Democratic elections, factories, economic development.

Perf. 12½

1994, Nov. 24 Litho. Wmk. 323

2979 A708 $5 multicolored 38 25
2980 A708 $19 multicolored 1.40 95

A709

A710

1994, Nov. 29

2981 A709 $3.50 Facing right 28 18
a. Perf. 13½ vert. 28 18
b. As "a," booklet pane of 6 1.75
Complete booklet, 2 #2981b + label 3.50
2982 A709 $13 Facing left 1.00 65
a. Souvenir sheet, 2 each #2981-2982 2.50 1.65

New Year 1995 (Year of the Boar).

1994, Dec. 24 Litho. *Perf. 12½*

2983 A710	$5 Portrait	38	25
2984 A710	$15 Greeting farm family	1.10	70

Pres. Yen Chia-kan, 1st death anniv.

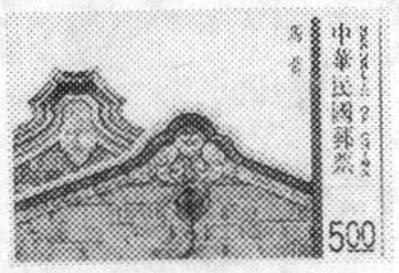

Traditional Architecture A711

Roof lines: No. 2985, Horse's back (illustrated). No. 2986, Swallow's tail. $12, Talisman (stove and bowl). $19, Cylinder-shaped brick.

Perf. 12½x12

1995, Jan. 10 Litho. Wmk. 323

2985 A711	$5 multicolored	38	25
2986 A711	$5 multicolored	38	25
2987 A711	$12 multicolored	90	60
2988 A711	$19 multicolored	1.40	95
	Nos. 2985-2988 (4)	3.06	2.05

Ancient Chinese Engravings — A712

Various floral designs.

1995, Jan. 24 *Perf. 13½*

2989 A712	$3.50 multicolored	28	18
2990 A712	$5 multicolored	38	25
2991 A712	$19 multicolored	1.40	95
2992 A712	$26 multicolored	2.00	1.40
	Nos. 2989-2992 (4)	4.06	2.78

SEMI-POSTAL STAMPS

SP1

Red or Blue Surcharge

1920, Dec. 1 Unwmk. *Perf. 14, 15*

B1 SP1	1c on 2c green	4.00	1.25
B2 SP1	3c on 4c scar (B)	5.50	2.25
B3 SP1	5c on 6c gray	8.00	2.75
	Nos. B1-B3 (3)	17.50	6.25

The surcharge represents the actual franking value. The extra cent helped victims of the 1919 Yellow River flood.

War Refugees SP2

Black Surcharge

1944, Oct. 10 Engr. *Perf. 12*

B4 SP2	$2 +$2 on 50c + 50c	20	25
B5 SP2	$4 +$4 on 8c + 8c	20	25
B6 SP2	$5 +$5 on 21c + 21c	55	75
B7 SP2	$6 +$6 on 28c + 28c	85	1.00
B8 SP2	$10 +$10 on 33c + 33c	1.40	1.75
B9 SP2	$20 +$20 on $1 + $1	2.75	3.50
a.	Sheet of 6, #B4-B9	32.50	20.00
	Nos. B4-B9 (6)	5.95	7.50

The borders of each stamp differ slightly in design. The surtax was for war refugees.

Nos. B4-B8 exist without surcharge, but were not regularly issued.

Great Wall of China — SP4

Chinese Refugee Family — SP5

1948, July 5 Litho. *Perf. 14, Imperf.*

Without Gum

Cross in Carmine

B11 SP4	$5000 + $2000 vio	15	15
B12 SP4	$10,000 + $2000 brn	15	15
B13 SP4	$15,000 + $2000 gray	15	15
a.	Cross omitted		
	Set value	36	36

The surtax was for anti-tuberculosis work.

Republic of China (Taiwan)

1954, Oct. 1 Engr. *Perf. 12*

Without Gum

B14 SP5	40c + 10c dp bl	16.00	2.50
B15 SP5	$1.60 + 40c lil rose	40.00	20.00
B16 SP5	$5 + $1 red	95.00	100.00
	Nos. B14-B16 (3)	151.00	122.50

The surtax was used to aid in the evacuation of Chinese from North Viet Nam.

AIR POST STAMPS

Curtiss "Jenny" over Great Wall (Bars of Republic flag on tail) — AP1

1921, July 1 Unwmk. Engr. *Perf. 14*

C1 AP1	15c bl grn & blk	18.00	18.00
C2 AP1	30c scar & blk	18.00	20.00
C3 AP1	45c dull vio & blk	18.00	16.00
C4 AP1	60c dk blue & blk	22.50	20.00
C5 AP1	90c ol grn & blk	32.50	32.50
	Nos. C1-C5 (5)	109.00	106.50

(Nationalist sun emblem on tail) — AP2

1929, July 5

C6 AP2	15c blue grn & blk	2.25	42
C7 AP2	30c dk red & blk	3.50	1.65
C8 AP2	45c dk vio & blk	7.75	5.00
C9 AP2	60c dk blue & blk	7.75	6.25
C10 AP2	90c ol grn & blk	8.75	11.00
	Nos. C6-C10 (5)	30.00	24.32

Junkers F-13 over Great Wall — AP3

1932-37

C11 AP3	15c gray grn	35	35
C12 AP3	25c orange ('33)	35	35
C13 AP3	30c red	35	35
C14 AP3	45c brown vio	35	35
C15 AP3	50c dk brown ('33)	35	35
C16 AP3	60c dk blue	35	35
C17 AP3	90c olive grn	35	35
C18 AP3	$1 yellow grn ('33)	35	35
C19 AP3	$2 brown ('37)	90	35
C20 AP3	$5 brown car ('37)	2.25	2.75
	Nos. C11-C20 (10)	5.95	5.90

See #C21-C40. For surcharges and overprints see #C41-C52, C54-C60, 9N111-9N114, 9NC1-9NC7, Szechwan C1, C3-C6, Sinkiang C5-C19.

Type of 1932-37, with secret mark

1932-37 Issue. Lower part of left character joined

Secret Mark, 1940-41 Issue. Separated.

Perf. 12, 12½, 12½x13, 13

1940-41 Wmk. 261

C21 AP3	15c gray green	40	40
C22 AP3	25c yellow org	40	40
C23 AP3	30c red	40	40
a.	Vert. pair, imperf. between	175.00	
C24 AP3	45c dull rose vio ('41)	40	40
C25 AP3	50c brown	40	40
C26 AP3	60c dp blue ('41)	40	40
C27 AP3	90c olive ('41)	40	40
C28 AP3	$1 apple grn ('41)	40	40
C29 AP3	$2 lt brown ('41)	40	40
C30 AP3	$5 lake	60	1.00
	Nos. C21-C30 (10)	4.20	4.60

Unwmk.

Perf. 12½, 13, 13½

C31 AP3	15c gray green ('41)	15	15
C32 AP3	25c lt orange ('41)	15	15
C33 AP3	30c lt red ('41)	15	15
C34 AP3	45c dl rose vio ('41)	15	15
C35 AP3	50c brown	15	15
C36 AP3	60c blue ('41)	15	15
C37 AP3	90c lt olive ('41)	15	15
C38 AP3	$1 apple grn ('41)	42	48
C39 AP3	$2 lt brown ('41)	65	75
C40 AP3	$5 lake ('41)	50	55
	Set value	2.20	2.50

For surcharges see note following No. C20.

Nos. C11 and C12 Surcharged

圓叁拾伍幣國

5300

1946, May 2 Unwmk. *Perf. 14*

C41 AP3	$53 on 15c	35	*75*
C42 AP3	$73 on 25c	600.00	625.00

Forgeries of No. C42 exist.

On Nos. C23, C21, C22, C29 and C30

Perf. 13, 13x12, 12½

Wmk. 261

C43 AP3	$23 on 30c red	15	*30*
C44 AP3	$53 on 15c gray grn	12.00	*14.00*
C45 AP3	$73 on 25c yel org	15	*30*
C46 AP3	$100 on $2 lt brown	15	*15*
C47 AP3	$200 on $5 lake	15	*15*
	Nos. C43-C47 (5)	12.60	14.90

On Nos. C33, C31, C32, C39 and C40

Perf. 13, 13x12, 13x12½, 12½

Unwmk.

C48 AP3	$23 on 30c lt red	15	25
a.	Inverted surcharge	85.00	
b.	"2300" omitted	42.50	
c.	Last character (kuo) of surch. omitted	55.00	
C49 AP3	$53 on 15c gray grn	15	25
a.	Horiz. pair, imperf. btwn.		575.00
C50 AP3	$73 on 25c lt orange	15	25
a.	Inverted surcharge	450.00	
C51 AP3	$100 on $2 lt brown	15	15
C52 AP3	$200 on $5 lake	15	15
a.	Inverted surcharge	67.50	
	Set value, #C48-C52	25	

The surcharges on #C41-C52 represent Chinese natl. currency and were applied at Shanghai.

Douglas DC-4 over Sun Yat-sen Mausoleum, Nanking AP4

1946, Sept. 10 Litho. *Perf. 14*

Without Gum

C53 AP4	$27 blue	15	30

For surcharges see Nos. C61, Szechwan C2.

No. C23 Surcharged in Black

圓萬壹作改

10000 00

1948, May 18 Wmk. 261 *Perf. 13x12*

C54 AP3	$10,000 on 30c red	15	*30*

Same, in Black or Carmine, on Nos. C33, C32, C37, C36, C18 and C38

Perf. 12½, 13x12½, 14

Unwmk.

C55 AP3	$10,000 on 30c lt red	15	*15*
C56 AP3	$20,000 on 25c lt org	15	*15*
C57 AP3	$30,000 on 90c lt ol (C)	15	*15*
C58 AP3	$50,000 on 60c blue (C)	15	*20*
C59 AP3	$50,000 on $1 yel grn (C)	60.00	60.00
C60 AP3	$50,000 on $1 ap grn (C)	15	*20*

改作壹萬圓

10000 00

Perf. 14

C61 AP4	$10,000 on $27 bl	15	*50*
	Nos. C54-C61 (8)	61.05	61.65

Douglas DC-4 and Arrow — AP5

Perf. 12½

1949, May 2 Unwmk. Litho.

Without Gum

C62 AP5	blue green	3.00	3.50
a.	Rouletted	4.00	5.00

See note after No. 959.

For overprints see Taiwan #C1, Fukien #C1, Kansu #C1, PRC #102.

Revenue Stamp Overprinted in Blue

中華民國郵政
國內航空費

1949, May Engr. *Perf. 14*

C63 A95	$100 olive green	25.00	25.00

See note after No. 962.

Republic of China (Taiwan)

Cheng Ch'eng-kung (Koxinga) — AP6

Rouletted

1950, Sept. 26 Unwmk. Typo.

Without Gum

C64 AP6	60c deep blue	11.00	5.00

For surcharge see No. 1120.

Plane over City Gate, Taipei — AP7

Jet Planes above Chung Shan Bridge — AP8

Two Doves Near Koxinga Shrine — AP9

1954 Engr. *Perf. 11½*
Without Gum

C65 AP7	$1 dk brown	15.00	75
a.	Vert. pair, imperf. btwn.	225.00	
C66 AP8	$1.60 olive blk	10.50	65
a.	Vert. pair, imperf. btwn.	150.00	
b.	Horiz. pair, imperf. btwn.	110.00	130.00
C67 AP9	$5 grnsh blue	13.00	75
	Nos. C65-C67 (3)	38.50	2.15

No. C67 Surcharged in Red

1958, Dec. 11
Without Gum

C68 AP9	$3.50 on $5 grnsh bl	2.50	1.50

Catalogue values for unused stamps in this section, from this point to the end of the section, are for Never Hinged items.

Sea Gull — AP10

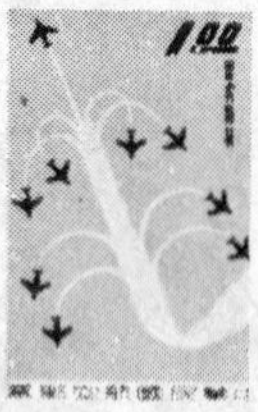

Sabre Jets in Bomb Burst Formation — AP11

1959, Mar. 20 Photo. *Perf. 13*

C69 AP10	$8 bl, gray & blk	4.00	40

1960, Feb. 29 Unwmk. *Perf. 13*

Plane Formations: $2, Loop, horiz. $5, Diamond formation passing over grounded plane, horiz.

C70 AP11	$1 multicolored	4.00	45
C71 AP11	$2 multicolored	4.00	28
C72 AP11	$5 multicolored	8.00	55
	Nos. C70-C72 (3)	16.00	1.28

Issued to honor the Chinese Air Force and the "Thunder Tiger" aerobatic team.

Jet Airliner over Pitan Bridge — AP12

Designs: $6, Jet over Tropic of Cancer monument, Kiai, vert. $10, Jet over Lion Head mountain, Sinchu, vert.

1963, Aug. 14 Photo. *Perf. 13*

C73 AP12	$2.50 multi	4.00	15
C74 AP12	$6 multi	7.50	15
C75 AP12	$10 multi	14.00	85
	Nos. C73-C75 (3)	25.50	1.15

Boeing 727 over Chilin Pavilion, Grand Hotel — AP13

Wild Geese Flying over Mountains — AP14

Design: $8, Boeing 727 over National Palace Museum, Taipei.

1967, Apr. 1 Unwmk. *Perf. 13*

C76 AP13	$5 multicolored	2.75	15
C77 AP13	$8 multicolored	3.75	52

1969, Aug. 14 Photo. *Perf. 13*

Wild Geese flying over: $5, The sea. $8, The land, horiz.

C78 AP14	$2.50 multicolored	1.75	16
C79 AP14	$5 multicolored	3.00	32
C80 AP14	$8 multicolored	4.00	50
	Nos. C78-C80 (3)	8.75	98

Presidential Palace and Tzu-Ch'iang Squadron AP15

1980, June 18 Litho. *Perf. 13½*

C81 AP15	$5 shown	25	18
C82 AP15	$7 China Airlines jet	42	30
C83 AP15	$12 China flag, jet	72	52
	Nos. C81-C83 (3)	1.39	1.00

Civil Aeronautics Administration, 37th Anniv. — AP16

Jet Airliners over: $7, Chiang Kai-shek Intl. Airport, vert. $11, Chung Cheng Memorial Hall. $18, Sun Yat-sen Memorial Hall.

Perf. 14x13½, 13½x14
1984, Jan. 20 Litho.

C84 AP16	$7 multicolored	42	15
C85 AP16	$11 multicolored	65	20
C86 AP16	$18 multicolored	1.10	40
	Nos. C84-C86 (3)	2.17	75

Airplane AP17

1987, Aug. 4 Litho. *Perf. 13½*

C87 AP17	$9 multicolored	52	32
C88 AP17	$14 multicolored	85	52
C89 AP17	$18 multicolored	1.10	65
	Nos. C87-C89 (3)	2.47	1.49

SPECIAL DELIVERY STAMPS

Design: Dragon in irregular oval.

Stamp 8x2½ inches, divided into four parts by perforation or serrate rouletting.

Values of Nos. E1-E8 are for used mailer's receipts. Complete unused strips of four are exceptionally scarce because the first section (#1) was to remain in the P.O. booklet.

The mailer received the righthand section (#4), usually canceled, as a receipt. The middle two sections were canceled and attached to the letter. Upon arrival at the destination P.O. they were canceled again, usually on the back, with the righthand copy (#3) retained by that P.O. The lefthand copy (#2) was signed by the recipient and returned to the original P.O. as evidence of delivery. Sections 2 and 3 usually are thin or badly damaged.

Unused strips of three (#2-4) can be found of Nos. E3-E8.

"Chinese Imperial Post Office" in lines, repeated to form the background which is usually lighter in color than the rest of the design.

Dragon's head facing downward
Background with period after "POSTOFFICE."
No Date

1905 Unwmk. *Perf. 11*

E1	10c grass green	350.00

Serrate Roulette in Black

E2	10c deep green	250.00

1907-10

Dragon's head facing forward
Background with no period after "POSTOFFICE"
No Date

E3	10c light bluish green	150.00

1909-11

Background with date at bottom

E4	10c green (Feby 1909)	100.00
E5	10c bl grn (Jan. 1911)	100.00

1912

"Imperial Post Office" in serifed letters repeated to form the background.
No Date, No Border
Background of 30 or 28 lines

E6	10c green (30 lines)	50.00
a.	28 lines	100.00

Background of 35 lines of sans-serif letters
Colored Border

E8	10c green	100.00

On No. E8 the medallion in the third section has Chinese characters in the background instead of the usual English inscriptions. E6 and E8 occur with many types of four-character overprints reading "Republic of China," applied locally but unofficially at various post offices.

1913

Design: Wild Goose. Stamp 7½x2¾ inches, divided into five parts.
"Chinese Post Office" in sans-serif letters, repeated to form the background of 28 lines. With border.
Serrate Roulette in Black

E9	10c green	300.00	20.00

Unused values for Nos. E9-E10 are for complete strips of five parts. Used values are for single parts.

1914

"Chinese Post Office" in antique letters, forming a background of 29 or 30 lines. No border.
Serrate Roulette in Green

E10	10c green	75.00	2.50

On No. E9 the background is in sans-serif capitals, the Chinese and English inscriptions are on white tablets and the serial numbers are in black.

On No. E10 the background is in antique capitals and extends under the inscriptions. The serial numbers are in green.

NOTE:

In February, 1916, the Special Delivery Stamps were demonetized and became merely receipts without franking value. To mark this, four of the five sections of the stamp had the letters A, B, C, D either handstamped or printed on them.

SD1

1941 Unwmk. Typo. *Rouletted*
Without Gum

E11 SD1	($2) car & yel	20.00	20.00

Motorcycle Messenger — SD2

1949, July Litho. *Perf. 12½*
Without Gum

E12 SD2	red violet	4.25	*10.00*
a.	Rouletted	5.50	*10.00*

See note after No. 959.

For surcharge and overprints see Nos. 1150, Taiwan E1, Fukien E1.

Revenue Stamp Overprinted in Purple Brown

1949

Without Gum

E13 A95	$10 grnsh gray	12.00	9.00

See note after No. 962.

REGISTRATION STAMPS

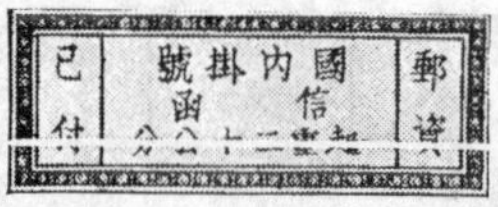

R1

1941 Unwmk. Typo. *Rouletted*
Without Gum

F1 R1	($1.50) green & buff	15.00	10.00

Mountain Scene — R2

1949, July Litho. *Perf. 12½*
Without Gum

F2 R2	carmine	4.50	*6.00*
a.	Rouletted	5.50	*10.00*

See note after No. 959.

For surcharge and overprints see Nos. 1152, Taiwan F1, Fukien F1, PRC 103.

Revenue Stamp Overprinted in Carmine

1949

F3 A95	$50 dark blue	11.00	8.00

See note after No. 962.

POSTAGE DUE STAMPS

Regular Issue of 1902-03 Overprinted in Black

1904 Unwmk. *Perf. 14 to 15*

J1	A17	½c chocolate	4.50	1.40
J2	A17	1c ocher	5.00	1.75
J3	A17	2c scarlet	6.00	2.25
J4	A17	4c red brn	6.50	3.25
J5	A17	5c salmon	12.00	5.50
J6	A17	10c dk blue grn	16.00	8.00
a.		Vert. pair, imperf. btwn.	350.00	
		Nos. J1-J6 (6)	50.00	22.15

D1

1904 — Engr.

No.	Type	Description	Unused	Used
J7	D1	½c blue	1.75	35
a.		Horiz. pair, imperf. btwn.	200.00	200.00
J8	D1	1c blue	3.00	35
J9	D1	2c blue	2.50	35
a.		Horiz. pair, imperf. btwn.	225.00	200.00
J10	D1	4c blue	4.50	45
J11	D1	5c blue	4.25	60
J12	D1	10c blue	4.25	1.10
J13	D1	20c blue	15.00	2.25
J14	D1	30c blue	19.00	15.00
		Nos. J7-J14 (8)	54.25	20.45

Arabic numeral of value at left on #J12-J14.

1911

No.	Type	Description	Unused	Used
J15	D1	1c brown	5.00	1.25
J16	D1	2c brown	10.00	10.00

The ½c, 4c, 5c and 20c in brown exist but were not issued as they arrived in China after the downfall of the Ching dynasty.

Issue of 1904 Overprinted in Red 臨時中立

1912

No.	Type	Description	Unused	Used
J19	D1	½c blue	350.	275.
J20	D1	4c blue	400.	325.
J21	D1	5c blue	450.	425.
J22	D1	10c blue	700.	550.
J23	D1	20c blue	1,500.	1,300.
J24	D1	30c blue	1,500.	1,300.

Nos. J15-J16 exist with this overprint, but were not regularly issued.

中華民國
Nos. J25-J33

中華
民國
Nos. J34-J42

1912

Overprinted in Red

No.	Type	Description	Unused	Used
J25	D1	½c blue	15	15
J26	D1	1c brown	25	25
a.		Horiz. pair, imperf. btwn.	375.00	
b.		Inverted overprint	150.00	
J27	D1	2c brown	30	25
J28	D1	4c blue	2.00	1.00
J29	D1	5c blue	60.00	65.00
J30	D1	5c brown	1.00	65
a.		Inverted overprint	125.00	100.00
J31	D1	10c blue	4.00	60
J32	D1	20c blue	5.50	2.00
J33	D1	30c blue	9.50	5.75
		Nos. J25-J33 (9)	82.70	75.65

1912

Overprinted in Black

No.	Type	Description	Unused	Used
J34	D1	½c blue	4.75	1.25
J35	D1	½c brown	60	25
J36	D1	1c brown	52	50
a.		Inverted overprint	150.00	125.00
J37	D1	2c brown	1.90	65
J38	D1	4c blue	3.75	1.50
J39	D1	5c brown	5.75	1.75
a.		Horiz. pair, imperf. btwn.	500.00	
J40	D1	10c blue	9.00	4.00
J41	D1	20c brown	21.00	12.00
J42	D1	30c blue	37.50	30.00
		Nos. J34-J42 (9)	84.77	51.90

D4 D5 D6

Printed by Waterlow & Sons

1913, May — *Perf. 14, 15*

No.	Type	Description	Unused	Used
J43	D4	½c blue	50	18
a.		Horiz. pair, imperf. btwn.	175.00	
J44	D4	1c blue	1.00	18
J45	D4	2c blue	2.00	1.25
J46	D4	4c blue	1.50	15
J47	D4	5c blue	2.50	15
J48	D4	10c blue	5.00	85
J49	D4	20c blue	9.50	4.75
J50	D4	30c blue	12.00	2.50
		Nos. J43-J50 (8)	34.00	10.01

Printed by the Chinese Bureau of Engraving & Printing

1915 — **Re-engraved** — *Perf. 14*

No.	Type	Description	Unused	Used
J51	D4	½c blue	40	15
J52	D4	1c blue	1.00	15
J53	D4	2c blue	1.00	15
J54	D4	4c blue	1.00	15
J55	D4	5c blue	2.00	40
J56	D4	10c blue	2.50	60
J57	D4	20c blue	6.50	1.00
J58	D4	30c blue	26.00	2.50
		Nos. J51-J58 (8)	40.40	5.10

In the upper part of the stamps of type D4 there is an ornament of five marks like the letter "V". Below this is a curved label with an inscription in Chinese characters. On the 1913 stamps there are two complete background lines between the ornament and the label. The 1915 stamps show only one unbroken line at this place. There are other minute differences in the engraving of the stamps of the two issues.

1932 — *Perf. 14*

No.	Type	Description	Unused	Used
J59	D5	½c orange	15	15
J60	D5	1c orange	15	15
J61	D5	2c orange	15	15
J62	D5	4c orange	35	20
J63	D5	5c orange	35	20
J64	D5	10c orange	70	40
J65	D5	20c orange	1.00	50
J66	D5	30c orange	1.25	50
		Nos. J59-J66 (8)	4.10	2.25

See Nos. J69-J79. For surcharges see Nos. 1NJ1, 9NJ1-9NJ4.

Regular Stamps of 1939 Overprinted in Black or Red

暫作
欠資

1940

No.	Type	Description	Unused	Used
J67	A57	$1 henna & dk brn (Bk)	1.25	3.00
J68	A57	$2 dl bl & org brn (R)	1.50	4.00

Type of 1932
Printed by The Commercial Press, Ltd.

Perf. 12½, 12½x13, 13

1940-41 — **Engr.**

No.	Type	Description	Unused	Used
J69	D5	½c yellow orange	15	24
J70	D5	1c yellow orange	15	24
J71	D5	2c yellow orange ('41)	15	24
J72	D5	4c yellow orange	15	24
J73	D5	5c yellow orange ('41)	50	24
J74	D5	10c yellow orange ('41)	15	24
J75	D5	20c yellow orange ('41)	15	24
J76	D5	30c yellow orange	15	24
J77	D5	50c yellow orange	15	28
J78	D5	$1 yellow orange	15	28
J79	D5	$2 yellow orange	30	48
		Set value	1.70	

For surcharge see No. 1NJ1.

Thin Paper Without Gum

1944 — **Typo.** — *Perf. 13*

No.	Type	Description	Unused	Used
J80	D6	10c bluish green	15	15
J81	D6	20c light chalky blue	15	15
J82	D6	40c dull rose	15	15
J83	D6	50c bluish green	15	15
J84	D6	60c dull blue	15	15
J85	D6	$1 dull rose	15	20
J86	D6	$2 lilac brown	15	24
		Set value	47	84

D7

D8

1945 — **Without Gum** — **Unwmk.**

No.	Type	Description	Unused	Used
J87	D7	$2 rose carmine	15	70
J88	D7	$5 rose carmine	15	70
J89	D7	$8 rose carmine	15	70
J90	D7	$10 rose carmine	15	95
J91	D7	$20 rose carmine	15	95
J92	D7	$30 rose carmine	15	95
		Set value	33	

For surcharges see Nos. J102-J109.

Thin Paper Without Gum

1947 — **Litho.** — *Perf. 14*

No.	Type	Description	Unused	Used
J93	D8	$50 plum	15	32
J94	D8	$80 plum	15	32
J95	D8	$100 plum	15	32
J96	D8	$160 plum	15	32
J97	D8	$200 plum	15	32
J98	D8	$400 violet brown	15	32
J99	D8	$500 violet brown	15	32
a.		Vert. pair, imperf. between	20.00	
J100	D8	$800 violet brown	15	32
J101	D8	$2000 violet brown	15	32
		Set value	72	

Type of 1945, Redrawn
Surcharged with New Value in Black

1948 — **Engr.** — *Perf. 13½x14*

Without Gum

No.	Type	Description	Unused	Used
J102	D7	$1000 on $20 dp claret	15	45
J103	D7	$2000 on $30 dp claret	15	45
J104	D7	$3000 on $50 dp claret	15	45
J105	D7	$4000 on $100 dp claret	15	45
J106	D7	$5000 on $200 dp claret	15	45
J107	D7	$10,000 on $300 dp claret	15	52
J108	D7	$20,000 on $500 dp claret	15	52
J109	D7	$30,000 on $1000 deep cl	15	65
		Set value	89	

There are many differences in the redrawn design.

No. 627 Surcharged in Black

改作欠資
金圓
壹分
1

1949 — *Perf. 12*

No.	Type	Description	Unused	Used
J110	A72	1 (c) on $40 orange	15	32
J111	A72	2 (c) on $40 orange	15	32
J112	A72	5 (c) on $40 orange	15	32
J113	A72	10 (c) on $40 orange	15	32
J114	A72	20 (c) on $40 orange	15	32
J115	A72	50 (c) on $40 orange	15	40
J116	A72	$1 on $40 orange	15	40
J117	A72	$2 on $40 orange	15	40
J118	A72	$5 on $40 orange	15	65
J119	A72	$10 on $40 orange	20	40
		Set value	1.18	

Republic of China (Taiwan)

No. 438 Surcharged in Green or Black

臺幣
肆角
欠資
40 40

1951 — **Unwmk.** — *Perf. 12½*

No.	Type	Description	Unused	Used
J120	A47	40c on 40c org (G)	15.00	20.00
J121	A47	80c on 40c org (Bk)	15.00	20.00

Revenue Stamps Surcharged in Various Colors

中華民國郵政
欠資台幣壹角
10

1953 — **Unwmk.** — *Perf. 12½, 14*

Without Gum

No.	Type	Description	Unused	Used
J122	A95	10c on $50 dk bl (O)	18.00	3.75
J123	A95	20c on $100 ol grn (Dk Br)	18.00	3.75
J124	A95	40c on $20 org brn	18.00	1.10
J125	A95	80c on $500 sl grn (Dk Bl)	26.00	2.25
J126	A95	$1 on $30 dk vio (G)	26.00	7.50
		Nos. J122-J126 (5)	106.00	18.35

D9 D10 D11

1956 — **Unwmk.** — **Litho.** — *Perf. 12½*

Without Gum

No.	Type	Description	Unused	Used
J127	D9	20c rose car, & lt bl	90	20
J128	D9	40c green & buff	1.75	20
J129	D9	80c brown & gray	3.75	20
J130	D9	$1 ultra & pink	3.75	20
		Nos. J127-J130 (4)	10.15	80

No. 1197 Surcharged in Dark Violet

500
欠資
伍
圓

Wmk. 323

1961, Dec. 28 — **Engr.** — *Perf. 12*

Without Gum

No.	Type	Description	Unused	Used
J131	A135	$5 on $20 car rose	2.00	65

Nos. 1274, 1282-1283 Surcharged in Black, Carmine Rose or Blue

010
欠資
壹角

1964-65 — **Litho.**

No.	Type	Description	Unused	Used
J132	A158	10c on 80c pale grn	18	15
J133	A158	20c on $3.60 vio bl (CR) ('65)	28	15
J134	A158	40c on $4.50 ver (B) ('65)	55	15
		Nos. J132-J134 (3)	1.01	
		Set value		30

1966-76 — **Wmk. 323** — *Perf. 12½*

Granite Paper; Without Gum

No.	Type	Description	Unused	Used
J135	D10	10c dk brn & lil	26	15
J136	D10	20c blue & yel	38	15
J137	D10	50c vio bl & lt bl ('70)	65	15
J138	D10	$1 purple & sal	50	15
J139	D10	$2 grn & lt bl	65	15
J140	D10	$5 red & sal	1.25	30
a.		$5 org red & pale yel	1.25	30
J141	D10	$10 lil rose & pink ('76)	20.00	60
		Nos. J135-J141 (7)	23.69	
		Set value		1.30

The 50c, $10 and No. J140a are gummed. The $1 and $2 were reissued with gum in 1968 and 1973 respectively. No. J140a and the $10 are on ordinary paper.

Catalogue values for unused stamps in this section, from this point to the end of the section, are for Never Hinged items.

1984-88 — **Litho.** — *Perf. 12½*

No.	Type	Description	Unused	Used
J142	D11	$1 rose & violet	15	15
J143	D11	$2 yellow & blue	15	15
J143A	D11	$3 pale grn & brt rose lil	24	18
J144	D11	$5 blue & yellow	25	16
J144B	D11	$5.50 rose lil & brt blue	45	35
J144C	D11	$7.50 bister yel & dp violet	60	45
J145	D11	$10 yel & lil rose	50	32
J155	D11	$20 sky blue & citron	1.60	1.20
		Nos. J142-J155 (8)	3.94	2.96

Issued: $3, $5.50, $7.50, $20, Apr. 1, 1988. Others, Mar. 15, 1984.

PARCEL POST STAMPS

PP1 PP2 PP3

1945-48 Unwmk. Engr. *Perf. 13*
Without Gum

Q1	PP1	$500 green	1.75	15
Q2	PP1	$1000 blue	1.75	15
Q3	PP1	$3000 rose red	6.00	15
Q4	PP1	$5000 brown	90.00	3.00
Q5	PP1	$10,000 lil gray	150.00	3.75
Q6	PP1	$20,000 red org	*1,500.*	
		Nos. Q1-Q5 (5)	249.50	7.20

No. Q6 was prepared but not issued.
For surcharges see People's Republic of China Nos. 5LQ1-5LQ2, 5LQ27-5LQ28.

Perf. 12½

Q7	PP2	$3000 red org	16.00	20
Q8	PP2	$5000 dk blue	24.00	20
Q9	PP2	$10,000 violet	24.00	30
Q10	PP2	$20,000 dk red	24.00	30

Perf. 13½

Q11	PP3	$1000 org yel	4.50	75
Q12	PP3	$3000 bl grn	5.00	75
Q13	PP3	$5000 org red	5.00	75
Q14	PP3	$7000 dl blue	5.00	75
Q15	PP3	$10,000 car rose	5.75	75
Q16	PP3	$30,000 olive	5.75	75
Q17	PP3	$50,000 indigo	5.75	75
Q18	PP3	$70,000 org brn	8.00	75
Q19	PP3	$100,000 dp plum	8.00	75

Denomination Tablet Without Inner Frame

Q20	PP3	$200,000 dk grn	11.00	1.00
Q21	PP3	$300,000 pink	11.00	1.00
Q22	PP3	$500,000 vio brn	11.00	1.25
Q23	PP3	$3,000,000 sl blue	12.00	1.75
Q24	PP3	$5,000,000 lilac	12.00	1.75
Q25	PP3	$6,000,000 ol gray	13.00	2.00
Q26	PP3	$8,000,000 scarlet	13.00	2.25
Q27	PP3	$10,000,000 sage grn	16.00	3.00
		Nos. Q11-Q27 (17)	151.75	20.75

Zeros for "cents" omitted on Nos. Q23-Q27.
See Taiwan Nos. Q1-Q5. For surcharges see Nos. 883-885, Northeastern Provinces Q1, Szechwan Q1, People's Republic of China 3LQ1-3LQ9, 5LQ3-5LQ16, 5LQ29-5LQ30.

圓拾圓金
10
圓拾圓金

Nos. Q11-Q15, Q23-Q24 Surcharged in Black or Carmine

1949 Unwmk. *Perf. 13½*

Q32	PP3	$10 on $3000	4.00	15
Q33	PP3	$20 on $5000	4.00	15
Q34	PP3	$50 on $10,000	4.00	15
Q35	PP3	$100 on $3,000,000 (C)	5.00	15
Q36	PP3	$200 on $5,000,000	9.00	15
Q37	PP3	$500 on $1000	18.00	15
Q38	PP3	$1000 on $7000	18.00	25
		Nos. Q32-Q38 (7)	62.00	
		Set value		81

5 characters in each line on Nos. Q33-Q38.

MILITARY STAMPS

No. 454 Overprinted in Dull Red 郵 軍

1943-44 Unwmk. *Perf. 12*

M1	A59	8c turquoise green	2.00	3.00

Nos. 383, 453-454 Overprinted in Red or Black 郵 軍

6mm between characters
Perf. 14, 12½

M2	A57	8c olive green	2.00	3.00
a.		8mm between characters	2.50	3.75
M3	A59	8c red orange (B)	225.00	
M4	A59	8c turquoise green	5.00	4.50

No. 493 Overprinted in Red 郵 軍

Perf. 13

M5	A62	16c dull olive brn	3.00	3.00
a.		Perf. 10½-11	100.00	

No. M5 overprinted in black is a proof.

Stamps of 1942-44 Overprinted in Carmine or Black 郵 軍

M6	A62	50c sage green (C)	1.75	2.75
M7	A62	$1 rose lake	2.50	3.75
M8	A62	$1 dull green	2.50	3.75
M9	A62	$2 dk blue grn (C)	4.00	6.00
M10	A62	$2 dk vio brn ('44)	50.00	50.00
		Nos. M6-M10 (5)	60.75	66.25

Nos. 383 and 357 Overprinted in Red 郵 軍

1944 *Perf. 12, 14*

M11	A57	8c olive green	2.50	3.75
a.		Right character inverted	150.00	
M12	A57	16c olive gray	30.00	30.00

Anti-Aircraft Guns — M1

1945, Jan. 1 Typo. *Perf. 12½*
Thin Paper Without Gum

M13	M1	rose	50	*3.00*

For overprints see Northeastern Provinces Nos. M2-M3.

TAIWAN

(Formosa)
100 Sen = 1 Yen
100 Cents = 1 Dollar

Stamps and Types of Japan (Taiwan) Overprinted in Black

中華民國
臺灣省

Values in Sen and Yen
Black Overprint

1945 Unwmk. Litho. *Imperf.*
Stamps Divided by Lines of Colored Dashes

1	A1	3s carmine	55	75
2	A1	5s blue grn	65	60
3	A1	10s pale blue	75	60
a.		Inverted overprint	40.00	
b.		Double overprint	50.00	
4	A1	30s dk blue	2.75	2.25
5	A1	40s violet	2.25	2.25
6	A1	50s gray brn	2.75	2.25
7	A1	1y olive grn	3.75	3.00

Same Overprint on Types of Japan

8	A99	5y gray grn	14.00	9.00
9	A100	10y brown vio	18.00	10.50
a.		Inverted overprint	135.00	
		Nos. 1-9 (9)	45.45	31.20

The basic stamps of this issue were prepared by Japanese authorities for Taiwan use before the end of World War II when the island reverted to Chinese control. They are printed on crude buff or white wove paper. The overprint translates: "For Use in Taiwan, Chinese Republic."
A second overprinting of Nos. 2-3 was made with a different font.

China, Nos. 728-731, Surcharged in Black

限臺灣省貼用
70 錢拾柒

1946 *Perf. 14*
Without Gum

10	A75	70s on $20 green	1.25	*2.75*
a.		Inverted surcharge	135.00	
11	A75	1y on $30 blue	1.75	*3.50*
12	A75	2y on $50 dk brn	1.25	*3.50*
13	A75	3y on $100 car	1.75	*3.50*
		Nos. 10-13 (4)	6.00	*13.25*

Convening of the Chinese Natl. Assembly.

China Issues and Types of 1940-1946 Surcharged in Black

用貼灣臺限

錢 拾
a

Perf. 12½, 12½x13, 13, 13x12½, 14
1946-47

14	A46	2s on 2c dp bl	15	38
15	A48	5s on 5c dl red org	15	22
16	A39	10s on 4c pale vio	15	28
17	A48	30s on 15c brn car	15	22
18	A73	50s on $20 car	24	18
19	A37	65s on $20 brt yel grn	28	38
20	A47	1y on 20c lt bl	15	18
a.		Inverted surcharge	65.00	
21	A37	1y on $30 choc	18	28
22	A37	2y on $50 red org	32	38
23	A73	3y on $100 dk car	15	18
24	A73	5y on $200 ol grn	15	18
25	A73	10y on $500 brt bl grn	18	28
26	A73	20y on $700 red brn	60	45
27	A73	50y on $1000 rose lake	95	70
28	A73	100y on $3000 blue	1.10	70
		Nos. 14-28 (15)	4.90	4.99

The bottom line of the surcharge expresses the new value and consists of 2, 3 or 4 characters.
Nos. 14, 18-19, 21-28 issued in 1947.

Same Surcharge on China No. 412

1947 Wmk. 261 *Perf. 13*

28A	A48	30s on 15c brn car	40.00	75.00

Type of China, 1946, Inscribed:

貼 臺
用 灣

1947 Unwmk. Engr. *Perf. 11, 11½*

29	A74	70c carmine	1.25	*2.00*
30	A74	$1 green	1.25	*2.00*
31	A74	$2 vermilion	1.25	*2.00*
32	A74	$3 yel grn	1.25	*2.00*
33	A74	$7 yel org	1.25	*2.00*
34	A74	$10 magenta	1.25	*2.00*
		Nos. 29-34 (6)	7.50	*12.00*

60th birthday of Chiang Kai-shek.

Type of China, 1947, Inscribed:

用貼灣臺

1947 *Perf. 14*

35	A76	50c deep green	1.50	2.50
36	A76	$3 deep blue	1.50	2.50
37	A76	$7.50 carmine	1.50	2.50
38	A76	$10 light brown	1.50	2.50
39	A76	$20 deep claret	1.50	2.50
		Nos. 35-39 (5)	7.50	12.50

First anniversary of return of Chinese National Government to Nanking.

Dr. Sun Yat-sen — A1

1947, July 10
Without Gum

40	A1	$1 dk brown	70	22
41	A1	$2 org brn	45	22
42	A1	$3 blue grn	45	22
43	A1	$5 vermilion	45	22
44	A1	$9 deep blue	45	22
45	A1	$10 brt rose car	45	22
46	A1	$20 deep green	45	26
47	A1	$50 rose lilac	45	22
48	A1	$100 blue	45	32
49	A1	$200 dark red	45	35
		Nos. 40-49 (10)	4.75	2.47

The 30c gray and $7.50 orange were not regularly issued without surcharge.
See #63-68. For overprint and surcharges see #51-53, 69-73, 101-103, J10-J17.

Type of 1947 Surcharged in Black

改作伍佰圓
500.00
b

1948 Unwmk. *Perf. 14*

51	A1	$25 on $100 blue	1.00	1.00
52	A1	$500 on $7.50 org	1.00	50
53	A1	$1000 on 30c gray	4.00	2.00
		Nos. 51-53 (3)	6.00	3.50

Stamps of China, 1943-48, Surcharged Type "a" in Black or Carmine

1948-49 *Perf. 12½, 14*

54	A73	$5 on $70 red org	32	*2.00*
55	A62	$10 on $3 dk yel	1.25	2.00
56	A82	$10 on $150 dk bl (C)	32	50
57	A82	$20 on $250 dp lil (C)	32	50
58	A67	$100 on $20 car	525.00	525.00
59	A82	$1000 on $20,000 rose pink ('49)	1.50	1.50
		Nos. 54-59 (6)	528.71	531.50

The bottom line of the surcharge expresses the new value and consists of 2 or 3 characters.

Type of 1947

1949 Engr. *Perf. 14*

63	A1	$25 olive grn	50	25
64	A1	$5000 ocher	5.00	40
65	A1	$10,000 apple grn	5.00	3.00
66	A1	$20,000 ol bister	5.00	3.00
67	A1	$30,000 indigo	5.00	60
68	A1	$40,000 violet brn	4.00	50
		Nos. 63-68 (6)	24.50	7.75

For overprint and surcharges see #101, 103, J12.

No. 42 and Type of 1947 Surcharged Type "b" in Black, Carmine Violet or Red Violet

1949

69	A1	$300 on $3 bl grn	55	18
70	A1	$1000 on $3 bl grn (C)	95	35
71	A1	$2000 on $3 bl grn (V)	85	26
72	A1	$3000 on $3 bl grn (RV)	3.25	75
73	A1	$3000 on $7.50 org	45.00	1.50
		Nos. 69-73 (5)	50.60	3.04

For overprints see Nos. J10-J11.

Stamps of China, 1940-47, Surcharged Type "a" in Black or Carmine
Perf. 12½, 13x13½, 14

74	A39	$2 on 2½c rose lil (#424)	35	35
75	A72	$5 on $40 org (#627)	42	*1.00*
76	A73	$5 on $50 pur (C) (#638)	42	25
77	A73	$5 on $100 dk car (#640)	42	40
78	A57	$20 on 2c ol grn (#368)	42	50
81	A63	$100 on $20 rose (#571)	70	40
82	A67	$200 on $10 dk bl (C) (#591)	1.10	90
84	A57	$500 on $30 dl vio (#521)	3.50	1.75
86	A62	$800 on $4 red brn (#504)	3.00	*3.00*
87	A67	$5000 on $10 dk bl (#591)	3.50	2.50
88	A67	$10,000 on $20 car (#592)	5.00	2.75
89	A82	$200,000 on $3000 bl (C) (#750)	300.00	20.00
		Nos. 74-89 (12)	318.83	33.80

Northeastern Provinces No. 47, Surcharged in Green, Red Violet, Black or Blue

貳分 臺幣
2 ★★★ 2

1949-50

91	A2	2c on $44 (G)	16.00	3.00
92	A2	5c on $44 (RV) ('50)	17.50	3.00
a.		Violet surcharge	20.00	6.00
93	A2	10c on $44 (RV) ('50)	20.00	3.00
94	A2	20c on $44 (Bk) ('50)	27.50	6.00
a.		Double surcharge	47.50	

95 A2 30c on $44 (Bl) ('50) 30.00 8.00
96 A2 50c on $44 (Bl) ('50) 40.00 14.00
Nos. 91-96 (6) 151.00 37.00

China 959a, Overprinted in Black 用貼灣臺限

Overprint 15mm Wide

1949 Unwmk. *Rouletted 9½*
97 A96 orange 38 20

China Nos. 567, 498 and 640 Surcharged Type "a" in Black

1948-49 Unwmk. *Perf. 12½, 13, 14*
98 A63 $20 on $3 red 2.00 1.25
99 A62 $50 on 50c sage grn 1.50 1.00
a. Perf. 11 10.00 12.00
100 A73 $600 on $100 dk car 7.00 2.50
Nos. 98-100 (3) 10.50 4.75

Botton line of surcharge consists of 3 characters.
No. 99 has two settings of surcharge: I. Spacing 10mm between rows of characters. II. Spacing 12mm.

Nos. 67, 47 and 68 Surcharged in Violet or Black 臺幣壹角 10

1949 *Perf. 14*
101 A1 2c on $30,000 ind (V) 20.00 7.00
102 A1 10c on $50 rose lil 15.00 4.00
103 A1 10c on $40,000 vio brn 40.00 10.00
Nos. 101-103 (3) 75.00 21.00

Numerals slightly larger on Nos. 101-103.
For similar surcharges on China type A82 see China Nos. 1025-1036.

AIR POST STAMP

China No. C62a, Overprinted in Black 用貼灣臺限

Overprint 15mm Wide

1949 Unwmk. *Rouletted 9½*
C1 AP5 blue green 3.00 1.00

SPECIAL DELIVERY STAMP

China No. E12a, Overprinted in Black 用貼灣臺限

Overprint 12½mm Wide

1950 Unwmk. *Rouletted 9½*
E1 SD2 red violet 1.00 *2.00*

REGISTRATION STAMP

China No. F2a Overprinted in Black 用貼灣臺限

Overprint 12mm Wide

1950 Unwmk. *Rouletted 9½*
F1 R2 carmine 1.00 1.00

TAIWAN POSTAGE DUE STAMPS

D1

Unwmk.
1948, Feb. 10 Litho. *Perf. 14*
Without Gum
J1 D1 $1 blue 90 *1.25*
J2 D1 $3 blue 90 *2.00*
J3 D1 $5 blue 90 *2.25*
J4 D1 $10 blue 90 *1.75*
J5 D1 $20 blue 90 *1.50*
Nos. J1-J5 (5) 4.50 *8.75*

Nos. J1-J4 Surcharged in Carmine 改作伍拾圓 5000

1948, Dec. 4
J6 D1 $50 on $1 blue 6.75 6.75
J7 D1 $100 on $3 blue 6.75 6.75
J8 D1 $300 on $5 blue 6.75 6.75
J9 D1 $500 on $10 blue 6.75 6.75
Nos. J6-J9 (4) 27.00 27.00

Nos. 70, 72 and 64 Handstamped in Violet 欠資

1949, Aug. 5
J10 A1 $1000 on $3 bl grn 12.00 12.00
J11 A1 $3000 on $3 bl grn 15.00 15.00
J12 A1 $5000 ocher 25.00 25.00
Nos. J10-J12 (3) 52.00 52.00

No. 48 Surcharged in Various Colors 欠資 臺幣肆分 4

1950
J13 A1 4c on $100 bl (Br) 15.00 8.00
J14 A1 10c on $100 bl (RV) 20.00 22.50
J15 A1 20c on $100 bl (Bk) 10.00 *18.00*
J16 A1 40c on $100 bl (C) 45.00 *75.00*
J17 A1 $1 on $100 bl (Bl) 30.00 *40.00*
Nos. J13-J17 (5) 120.00 163.50

TAIWAN PARCEL POST STAMPS

Type of China, Parcel Post Stamps of 1945-48 With Added Inscription:

1949 Unwmk. Engr. *Perf. 14*
Q1 PP3 $100 bluish grn *125.00* 15
Q2 PP3 $300 rose car *125.00* 15
Q3 PP3 $500 olive green *125.00* 15
Q4 PP3 $1000 slate *125.00* 15
Q5 PP3 $3000 deep plum *125.00* 15
Nos. Q1-Q5 (5) 625.00
Set value 50

Chinese characters in lower corners have colorless background; denomination tablet in color.

OCCUPATION STAMPS

Issued Under Japanese Occupation

Canceled Stamps
Postally used stamps of the Japanese occupation generally have heavy, smudgy cancels.

Kwangtung

China No. 297 Overprinted in Black 用貼省粵

1942 Unwmk. *Perf. 12½*
1N1 A37 2c olive green 3.50 3.50
a. Inverted overprint 60.00

Same Overprint in Red or Black on Stamps of China, 1939-41
Perf. 12½, 14
1N2 A57 3c dl cl (#350) 2.00 1.75
1N3 A57 8c ol grn (#383) 2.00 1.50
1N4 A57 10c grn (#354) (R) 2.00 1.75
1N5 A57 10c grn (#384) (R) 2.00 2.00
1N6 A57 16c ol gray (#357) 3.00 2.50
1N7 A57 30c scar (#385) 2.50 2.00
1N8 A57 50c dk bl (#386) (R) 2.50 2.00
1N9 A57 $1 org brn & sep (#387) 5.00 3.00
1N10 A57 $2 dp bl & yel brn (#388) 4.00 2.50
1N11 A57 $5 red & sl grn (#389) 6.00 3.50
1N12 A57 $10 dk grn & dl pur (#390) 11.00 6.00
1N13 A57 $20 rose lake & dk bl (#391) 5.75 3.25

Same Overprint on China Nos. 422 and 433
Perf. 12½
1N14 A40 1c orange 1.50 1.75
a. Inverted overprint 60.00 60.00
1N15 A47 20c lt blue 1.75 2.00

Same Overprint on Stamps of China, 1941
Perf. 12
1N16 A59 1c orange 1.50 1.75
1N17 A59 5c green 1.50 1.50
1N18 A59 8c turq grn 1.50 1.65
1N19 A59 10c brt green 2.50 2.50
1N20 A59 17c olive 2.00 2.50
1N21 A59 30c scarlet 2.50 2.50
1N22 A59 50c dk blue 2.00 2.25
Nos. 1N1-1N22 (22) 68.00 53.65

Stamps of China, 1939-41 Overprinted in Black 粵省貼用

1942 *Perf. 12½, 14*
1N23 A57 2c olive grn (#368) 50 50
1N24 A57 3c dl claret (#350) 50 50
1N25 A57 5c olive grn (#352) 50 50
1N26 A57 8c olive grn (#353) 175.00
1N27 A57 8c olive grn (#369) 60 60
1N28 A57 10c green (#354) 90 90
1N29 A57 16c ol gray (#357) 90 90
1N30 A57 25c dk bl (#358) 90 90
1N31 A57 30c scarlet (#385) 60 60
1N32 A57 50c dk blue (#386) 2.00 1.50
1N33 A57 $1 org brn & sep (#387) 5.00 5.00
1N34 A57 $2 dp bl & yel brn (#388) 6.50 6.50
1N35 A57 $5 red & sl grn (#389) 8.25 8.25
1N36 A57 $10 dk grn & dl pur (#390) 12.50 12.50
1N37 A57 $20 rose lake & dk bl (#391) 12.00 15.00
Nos. 1N23-1N25,1N27-1N37 (14) 51.65 54.15

No. 1N26 is valued in fine condition.

Same Overprint on China Nos. 397-401

1942 Wmk. 261 *Perf. 14*
1N38 A57 $1 org brn & sep 5.00 6.00
1N39 A57 $2 dp bl & yel brn 5.00 6.50
1N40 A57 $5 red & sl grn 8.00 10.00
1N41 A57 $10 dk grn & dl pur 10.00 14.00
1N42 A57 $20 rose lake & dk bl 10.00 12.00
Nos. 1N38-1N42 (5) 38.00 48.50

Same Overprint on Stamps of China, 1941

1942 Unwmk. *Perf. 12*
1N43 A59 2c brt ultra 25 35
1N44 A59 5c green 25 35
1N45 A59 8c red org 30 35
1N46 A59 8c turq grn 30 35
1N47 A59 10c brt green 45 50
1N48 A59 17c olive 50 75
1N49 A59 25c rose vio 50 75
1N50 A59 30c scarlet 50 80
1N51 A59 50c dk blue 50 80
1N52 A59 $1 brn & blk 3.75 3.75
1N53 A59 $2 bl & blk 4.50 4.50
1N54 A59 $5 scar & blk 3.75 3.75
1N55 A59 $10 grn & blk 6.50 6.50
1N56 A59 $20 rose vio & blk 7.75 7.75
Nos. 1N43-1N56 (14) 29.80 31.25

China Nos. 354 and 369 Surcharged in Black 粵省貼用 $200 暫售貳佰圓

1945 Unwmk. *Perf. 12½*
1N57 A57 $200 on 10c grn 80.00 50.00
1N58 A57 $400 on 8c ol grn 80.00 50.00

China No. 422 Surcharged in Black 暫售肆佰圓 400

1945
1N59 A40 $400 on 1c org 450.00 400.00

OCCUPATION POSTAGE DUE STAMPS

China, No. J79 Surcharged Diagonally with New Value Between Parallel Lines in Black

1945 Unwmk. *Perf. 12½*
1NJ1 D5 $100 on $2 yel org 500.00 550.00
a. Inverted surcharge 750.00

MENG CHIANG (Inner Mongolia)

Nos. 297-298, 301-303 Overprinted

疆蒙 疆蒙

Characters 4mm High — I Characters 5mm High — II

1941 Engr. Unwmk.
2N1 A37 2c #297, I 75 1.00
a. Type II 1.20 1.50
2N2 A37 4c #298, II 35.00 35.00
a. Type I 35.00 35.00
2N3 A37 15c #301, I 3.00 4.00
a. Type II 2.50 4.00
2N4 A37 20c #302, I 8.00 10.00
a. Type II 6.00 6.00
2N5 A37 25c #303, II 3.25 4.00
a. Type I 35.00 35.00

For surcharge see No. 2N116.

On Nos. 312, 314, 318, 321

1941 *Perf. 14*
2N6 A39 ½c #312, I 7.00 7.00
a. Type II 12.00 12.00
2N7 A39 2½c #314, II 75 40
a. Type I 3.50 3.50
2N8 A45 13c #318, II 75 40
a. Type I 80.00 85.00
2N9 A48 30c #321, II 50.00 50.00

On Stamps of 1939-41

1941 *Perf. 12½*
2N10 A57 2c #368, II 1.00 1.00
2N11 A57 3c #350, I 1.00 1.00
a. Type II 50 50
2N12 A57 5c #352, I 1.00 1.00
a. Type II 1.50 1.50
2N13 A57 8c #353, I 50 25
a. Type II 1.25 1.25
2N14 A57 8c #369, II 3.50 3.00
2N15 A57 10c #354, II 1.50 1.25
2N16 A57 16c #357, II 2.00 2.00
2N17 A57 $1 #359, II 7.00 7.00
a. Type I 250.00 250.00
b. #347, I 60.00 60.00
2N18 A57 $5 #361, II 50.00 50.00

For surcharges see Nos. 2N117, 2N119.

On Stamps of 1940 with Secret Marks

1941 Unwmk. *Perf. 14*
2N19 A57 5c #382, II 75 75
2N20 A57 8c #383, I 2.00 1.50
a. Type II 35.00 35.00
2N21 A57 10c #384, I 1.50 75
a. Type II 1.50 1.00
2N22 A57 30c #385, I 3.00 2.75
a. Type II 1.50 1.50
2N23 A57 50c #386, I 4.00 4.00
a. Type II 4.00 4.00
2N24 A57 $1 #387, I 7.00 7.50
a. Type II 13.00 10.00
2N25 A57 $2 #388, I 7.00 7.50
a. Type II 20.00 20.00
2N26 A57 $5 #389, I 35.00 35.00
a. Type II 50.00 50.00
2N27 A57 $10 #390, II 40.00 40.00
a. Type I 45.00 45.00
2N28 A57 $20 #391, II 60.00 60.00
a. Type I 65.00 65.00

For surcharge see No. 2N120.

On Stamps of 1940 with Secret Marks

1941 Wmk. 261 *Perf. 14*

2N29 A57 10c #394, II 2.00 1.75
2N30 A57 30c #395, II 3.00 3.50
a. Type I 45.00 45.00
2N31 A57 50c #396, II 2.75 2.75
Nos. 2N29-2N31 (3) 7.75 8.00

On Stamps of 1940-41 (Martyrs) with Secret Marks

Perf. 12½, 13 & Compound

1941 Wmk. 261

2N32 A39 ½c #402, II 7.00 8.00
2N33 A40 1c #403, I 2.50 1.50
a. Type II .50 .50
2N34 A39 2½c #405, II 60.00 60.00
a. Type I 45.00 45.00
2N35 A48 3c #406, II 1.50 1.50
2N36 A46 10c #410, I 10.00 10.00
a. Type II 7.50 7.50
2N37 A46 17c #413, II 30.00 30.00
a. Type I 60.00 60.00
2N38 A40 25c #416, II 2.00 2.00
2N39 A48 30c #418, II 40.00 40.00
a. Type I 50.00 50.00
2N40 A47 40c #419, II 3.00 3.00
a. Type I 6.00 6.00
2N41 A40 50c #420, I 6.00 6.00
a. Type II 35.00 35.00

Unwmk.

2N42 A39 ½c #421, I 1.50 1.75
a. Type II .75 .55
2N43 A40 1c #422, I 1.00 .75
a. Type II 2.00 2.00
2N44 A46 2c #423, I 3.00 2.00
2N45 A48 3c #425, I 2.00 2.00
a. Type II 1.75 1.00
2N46 A39 4c #426, II 1.25 1.00
2N47 A45 8c #428, II 12.00 12.00
a. Type I 60.00 60.00
2N48 A46 10c #429, I 12.00 12.00
a. Type II 40.00 40.00
2N49 A45 13c #430, I 4.00 4.00
a. Type II 12.00 12.00
2N50 A48 15c #431, II 2.00 2.00
2N51 A46 17c #432, I 2.00 2.00
a. Type II 2.00 2.00
2N52 A47 20c #433, II 1.75 2.00
a. Type I 3.00 3.00
2N53 A45 21c #434, II 2.50 2.50
2N54 A40 25c #435, I 3.50 3.00
2N55 A46 28c #436, II 2.50 2.50
2N56 A40 50c #439, II 4.50 4.50
a. Type I 8.00 8.00

For surcharges see Nos. 2N114-2N115, 2N118, 2N121-2N122.

China Nos. 297-298, 302 Surcharged in Black

疆 蒙

分 壹

1942 Unwmk. *Perf. 12½, 13*

2N57 A37 1c on 2c ol grn 6.00 6.00
2N58 A37 2c on 4c grn 4.50 3.50
2N59 A37 10c on 20c ultra 15.00 15.00
Nos. 2N57-2N59 (3) 25.50 24.50

Same, on China No. 313

Perf. 14

2N60 A40 ½c on 1c org 12.00 12.00

Same, on Stamps of China, 1938-41

Perf. 12½

2N61 A57 1c on 2c (#368) 1.25 1.00
2N62 A57 4c on 8c (#353) 4.00 3.50
a. Inverted surcharge 50.00 50.00
2N63 A57 4c on 8c (#369) 1.00 1.00
2N64 A57 5c on 10c (#354) .75 .50
2N65 A57 8c on 16c (#357) 3.00 1.00
2N66 A57 50c on $1 (#359) 7.00 7.00
a. On No. 347 40.00 40.00
b. On No. 344 300.00 300.00
2N67 A57 $1 on $2 (#360) 40.00 40.00
Nos. 2N61-2N67 (7) 57.00 54.00

No. 2N66b was issued without gum.

Same, on Stamps of China, 1940

Perf. 14

2N68 A57 4c on 8c (#383) .30 .30
2N69 A57 15c on 30c (#385) 3.50 3.00
a. Inverted surcharge 50.00 50.00
2N70 A57 25c on 50c (#386) 4.00 4.00
2N71 A57 50c on $1 (#387) 3.00 2.50
2N72 A57 $1 on $2 (#388) 6.50 6.50
2N73 A57 $5 on $10 (#390) 30.00 30.00
2N74 A57 $10 on $20 (#391) 45.00 45.00
Nos. 2N68-2N74 (7) 92.30 91.30

Same, on China No. 395

1942 Wmk. 261 *Perf. 14*

2N75 A57 15c on 30c scar 45.00 45.00

Same, on China Nos. 418 and 419

Perf. 12½, 13

2N76 A48 15c on 30c brn car 30.00 30.00
2N77 A47 20c on 40c org 5.50 5.50

Same, on Stamps of China, 1940-41

1942 Unwmk.

2N78 A40 ½c on 1c org .20 .20
2N79 A39 2c on 4c pale vio 2.50 2.50
2N80 A47 10c on 20c lt bl 4.50 4.50
2N81 A47 20c on 40c org 10.00 10.00
2N82 A40 25c on 50c grn 15.00 15.00
Nos. 2N78-2N82 (5) 32.20 32.20

Same Surcharge on "New Peking" Prints

Perf. 14

2N83 A37 1c on 2c ol grn 3.00 3.00
2N84 A37 2c on 4c dl grn .45 .45
2N85 A46 5c on 10c dl vio 3.00 3.75
2N86 A57 8c on 16c ol gray .75 .30
2N87 A47 10c on 20c red brn 3.00 3.00
2N88 A48 15c on 30c brn car 1.00 1.50
2N89 A47 20c on 40c org 5.00 5.50
2N90 A40 25c on 50c grn 1.50 2.50
2N91 A57 50c on $1 org brn & sep 6.00 6.00
2N92 A57 $1 on $2 dp bl & org brn 15.00 14.00
2N93 A57 $5 on $10 dk grn & dl pur 30.00 30.00
Nos. 2N83-2N93 (11) 68.70 70.00

The "New Peking" printings were made by the Chinese Bureau of Engraving and Printing for use in Japanese controlled areas of North China. They are on thin, poor quality paper, with dull gum or without gum and there are slight alterations in the designs.

Dragon-Carved Pillar and Doves — A1

Mining Coal — A2

Wmk. Characters in Circle in Sheet

1943 Engr. *Perf. 12xPin-perf. 12*

2N94 A1 4f deep orange .20 *.60*
2N95 A1 8f dark blue .25 *.75*

5th anniv. of the Inner Mongolia post and telegraph service.

The watermark, which is 40mm in diameter and covers four stamps, occurs three times in the sheet.

1943 Unwmk. Photo. *Perf. 12*

2N96 A2 8f Prus green .20 *.75*
2N97 A2 4f brown red .25 *.90*

2nd anniv. of the "Greater East Asia War."

Flying Horse — A3

Yun Wang — A4

1944 *Perf. 12½x12, 12x12½*

2N98 A3 4f rose .15 *.75*
2N99 A4 8f dull blue .25 *.75*

5th anniv. of the founding of the Federal Autonomous Government of Mongolia, Sept. 1, 1939.

Industrial Plant — A5

1944, Dec. 8 Photo. *Perf. 12x12½*

2N100 A5 8f red brown .20 *1.25*

3rd anniv. of the "Greater East Asia War" and to encourage production increase.

New Peking Printings of 1942 Overprinted in Black

疆 蒙

1945 Unwmk. Engr. *Perf. 14*

Without Gum

2N101 A37 2c olive grn 7.00 7.00
2N102 A37 4c dull grn 10.00 10.00
2N103 A37 5c green 6.00 6.00
2N104 A57 $1 org brn & sep 2.00 2.00
2N105 A57 $2 dp bl & org brn 8.00 8.00
2N106 A57 $5 red & grnsh blk 17.50 17.50

Same Overprint on New Peking Printings of Martyrs Issue

2N107 A40 1c orange .60 .60
2N108 A45 8c dp orange .20 .20
2N109 A46 10c dl violet .18 .18
2N110 A47 20c red brown 1.00 1.00
2N111 A48 30c brown car .20 .30
2N112 A47 40c orange .20 .20
2N113 A40 50c green 5.00 5.00
Nos. 2N101-2N113 (13) 57.88 57.98

For surcharges see Nos. 2N123-2N127.

Stamps of Meng Chiang, 1941, Surcharged in Red or Black

角 伍

50c

角 壹 圓 壹

10c $1

1945

2N114 A39 10c on ½c ol blk (#2N42) (R) 3.00 2.50
a. 10c on ½c ol bk (#2N42a) 1.00 1.25
2N115 A40 10c on 1c org (#2N43a) (R) .50 .75
a. Without secret mark (China #313) 30.00 30.00
b. On #2N43 1.50 2.00
2N116 A37 50c on 2c ol grn (#2N1a) (Bk) 14.00 14.00
b. On #2N1 15.00 15.00
2N117 A57 50c on 2c ol grn (#2N10) (Bk) .45 .60
2N118 A39 50c on 4c pale vio (#2N46) (R) .45 .45
2N119 A57 50c on 5c ol grn (#2N12a) (R) .30 .40
a. On #2N12 6.50 6.50
2N120 A57 50c on 5c ol grn (#2N19) (R) .50 .60
Nos. 2N114-2N120 (7) 19.20 19.30

Same Surcharge on #2N32, 2N33a

1945 Wmk. 261

2N121 A39 10c on ½c ol blk (R) 12.50 12.50
2N122 A40 10c on 1c orange (R) .75 1.00
a. On #2N33 37.50 10.00

Same Surcharge on Nos. 2N107, 2N101-2N103 and 2N108

1945 Unwmk.

2N123 A40 10c on 1c org (R) .20 .20
2N124 A37 50c on 2c ol grn (Bk) 2.00 2.00
2N125 A37 50c on 4c dl grn (R) 3.00 3.00
2N126 A37 50c on 5c green .35 .35
2N127 A45 $1 on 8c dp org (R) .50 .50
Nos. 2N123-2N127 (5) 6.05 6.05

NORTH CHINA

Honan

Nos. 297-298, 301-303 Overprinted

南 河 南 河

I II

1941 Engr. Unwmk.

3N1 A37 2c #297, II 4.00 3.00
a. Type I 5.00 5.00
3N2 A37 4c #298, I 4.75 4.25
a. Type II 15.00 15.00
3N3 A37 15c #301, II 2.00 1.00
a. Type I 1.25 1.25
3N4 A37 20c #302, I 4.00 4.00
3N5 A37 25c #303, II 10.00 10.00

1941 *Perf. 14*

3N6 A39 ½c #312, I 1.00 1.00
a. Type II 15.00 15.00
3N7 A39 2½c #314, II 1.00 1.00
a. Type I .75 .75
3N8 A45 13c #318, II .90 .90
a. Type I 60.00 60.00
3N9 A48 30c #321, II 8.00 8.00
3N10 A47 40c #322, II 65.00 65.00

On Stamps of 1939-41

1941 *Perf. 12½*

3N11 A57 2c #368, II .40 .40
3N12 A57 3c #350, II .75 .30
a. Type I .45 .40
3N13 A57 5c #352, II .60 .30
a. Type I .75 .75
3N14 A57 8c #353, II 1.00 .50
a. Type I .90 .65
3N15 A57 10c #354, II .50 .40
3N16 A57 16c #357, II .50 .40
3N17 A57 $1 #359, II 8.00 8.00
a. Type I 200.00 200.00
b. On #347, I 40.00 40.00
3N18 A57 $5 #361, II 50.00 50.00

For overprints see Nos. 3N56, 3N58, 3N61.

On Stamps of 1940 with Secret Marks

1941 Unwmk. *Perf. 14*

3N20 A57 5c #382, II 1.25 .25
3N21 A57 8c #383, II .35 .25
3N22 A57 10c #384, II .60 .40
3N23 A57 30c #385, I 5.00 5.00
a. Type II 5.00 5.00
3N24 A57 50c #386, I 2.00 2.00
a. Type II 8.00 8.00
3N25 A57 $1 #387, I 4.00 1.75
a. Type II 40.00 30.00
3N26 A57 $2 #388, I 7.00 6.00
a. Type II 12.00 8.00
3N27 A57 $5 #389, I 20.00 20.00
a. Type II 45.00 45.00
3N28 A57 $10 #390, II 30.00 30.00
a. Type I 77.50 77.50
3N29 A57 $20 #391, II 60.00 50.00
a. Type I 70.00 65.00

On Stamps of 1940 with Secret Marks

1941 Wmk. 261 *Perf. 14*

3N30 A57 5c #392, II 12.00 5.00
3N31 A57 5c #393, II 6.00 3.00
3N32 A57 30c #395, II 25.00 25.00
a. Type I 12.00 12.00
3N33 A57 50c #396, II 12.00 12.00

On Stamps of 1940-41 (Martyrs) with Secret Marks

Perf. 12½, 13 & Compound

1941 Wmk. 261

3N34 A39 ½c #402, II 1.50 1.50
3N35 A40 1c #403, II .50 .35
a. Type I 1.00 1.00
3N36 A39 2½c #405, II 8.00 8.00
3N37 A46 10c #410, I 20.00 4.50
a. Type II 8.00 8.00
3N38 A45 13c #411, II 2.75 2.75
3N39 A46 17c #413, II 2.50 2.50
a. Type I 6.50 6.00
3N40 A40 25c #416, II 2.00 2.00
3N41 A47 40c #419, II 3.00 3.00
a. Type I 9.00 9.00

Unwmk.

3N42 A39 ½c #421, II .75 .75
a. Type I 1.50 .75
3N43 A40 1c #422, I 1.25 1.00
a. Type II 2.00 1.50
3N44 A46 2c #423, I 6.00 5.00
3N45 A48 3c #425, I 1.00 1.00
3N46 A39 4c #426, II .50 .30
3N47 A46 10c #429, I 20.00 20.00
3N48 A45 13c #430, II 2.00 2.00
a. Type I 10.00 10.00
3N49 A48 15c #431, II 1.00 1.50
3N50 A46 17c #432, II 2.00 2.00
a. Type I 8.00 8.00
3N51 A47 20c #433, II 1.25 1.25
a. Type I 30.00 20.00
3N52 A45 21c #434, II 2.00 2.00
3N53 A40 25c #435, I 2.50 2.50
3N54 A46 28c #436, II 2.00 2.00

For overprints see Nos. 3N55, 3N59.

Overprinted in Red

坡 嘉 新
念紀落陷

1942

3N55 A39 4c #3N46 1.50 1.50
3N56 A57 8c #3N14 15.00 20.00
3N57 A57 8c #369, II 3.50 4.50
Nos. 3N55-3N57 (3) 20.00 26.00

The fall of Singapore.

Overprinted in Red

國建國洲滿
念紀年週十

1942

3N58 A57 2c #3N11 6.00 7.00
3N59 A39 4c #3N46 10.00 15.00
3N60 A57 8c #369, II 25.00 30.00
3N61 A57 8c #3N14 20.00 25.00
Nos. 3N58-3N61 (4) 61.00 77.00

Formation of Manchukuo, 10th anniv.

Hopei

Nos. 297-298, 301-303 Overprinted

北 河 北 河
I II

1941 **Engr.** **Unwmk.**
4N1 A37 2c #297, II 80 80
a. Type I 2.00 2.00
4N2 A37 4c #298, I 2.00 1.50
a. Type II 50.00 50.00
4N3 A37 15c #301, II 2.00 1.25
a. Type I 3.25 2.50
4N4 A37 20c #302, II 1.00 1.00
4N5 A37 25c #303, II 4.75 4.75
a. Type I 70.00 60.00

On Nos. 312, 314, 318, 321

1941 *Perf. 14*
4N6 A39 ½c #312, II 30 50
a. Type I 70 70
4N7 A39 2½c #314, II 40 40
a. Type I 40 50
4N8 A45 13c #318, II 1.00 1.00
a. Type I 1.75 1.75
4N9 A48 30c #321, II 3.00 3.00

On Stamps of 1939-41

1941 *Perf. 12½*
4N10 A57 2c #368, II 30 25
4N11 A57 2c #349, II 40 40
4N12 A57 3c #350, II 25 25
a. Type I 1.25 1.25
4N13 A57 5c #352, II 35 25
a. Type I 1.10 75
4N14 A57 8c #353, II 25 25
a. Type I 1.10 75
4N15 A57 8c #369, II 2.00 1.00
4N16 A57 10c #354, II 30 30
4N17 A57 16c #357, II 1.50 60
4N18 A57 $1 #359, II 5.00 5.00
a. On #347, I 160.00 160.00
4N19 A57 $2 #360, II 7.00 7.00
a. Type I 30.00 25.00
4N20 A57 $5 #361, II 25.00 25.00
a. Type I 25.00 30.00
4N21 A57 $10 #362, II 125.00 125.00
4N22 A57 $20 #363, II 250.00 250.00

For overprints see Nos. 4N66-4N68, 4N70.

On Stamps of 1940 with Secret Marks

1941 **Unwmk.** *Perf. 14*

Type II

4N24 A57 5c #382 35 30
4N25 A57 8c #383 1.00 75
4N26 A57 10c #384 30 30
4N27 A57 30c #385 75 60
4N28 A57 50c #386 1.50 1.50
4N29 A57 $1 #387 3.00 2.75
4N30 A57 $2 #388 7.00 6.00
4N31 A57 $5 #389 30.00 30.00
4N32 A57 $10 #390 25.00 20.00
4N33 A57 $20 #391 40.00 30.00
Nos. 4N24-4N33 (10) 108.90 92.20

For overprints see Nos. 4N65, 4N71.

Type I

4N24a A57 5c 75 30
4N25a A57 8c 35.00 35.00
4N26a A57 10c 75 75
4N28a A57 50c 1.25 1.00
4N29a A57 $1 4.00 2.75
4N30a A57 $2 17.00 12.00
4N31a A57 $5 35.00 30.00
4N32a A57 $10 45.00 30.00
4N33a A57 $20 65.00 60.00
Nos. 4N24a-4N33a (9) 203.75 171.80

On Stamps of 1940 with Secret Marks

1941 **Wmk. 261** *Perf. 14*
4N34 A57 5c #392, II 30 30
4N35 A57 5c #393, II 75 30
4N36 A57 10c #394, II 35 25
4N37 A57 30c #395, II 2.25 2.00
a. Type I 3.00 2.50
4N38 A57 50c #396, II 1.25 1.00
Nos. 4N34-4N38 (5) 4.90 3.85

On Stamps of 1940-41 (Martyrs) with Secret Marks

Perf. 12½, 13 & Compound

1941 **Wmk. 261**

Type II

4N39 A39 ½c #402 75 50
4N40 A40 1c #403 1.00 35
4N41 A46 2c #404 60 60
4N42 A39 2½c #405 75 75
4N43 A48 3c #406 1.25 1.00
4N44 A46 10c #410 1.50 1.50
4N45 A45 13c #411 1.50 1.50
4N46 A46 17c #413 2.00 2.00
4N47 A40 25c #416 1.75 1.75
4N48 A48 30c #418 8.00 8.00
4N49 A47 40c #419 2.00 1.50
Nos. 4N39-4N49 (11) 21.10 19.45

Type I

4N40a A40 1c 60 35
4N44a A46 10c 1.00 1.00
4N46a A46 17c 2.00 2.00
4N48a A48 30c 17.00 17.00
4N49a A47 40c 3.00 2.50
Nos. 4N40a-4N49a (5) 23.60 22.85

Unwmk.

Type II

4N50 A39 ½c #421 75 35
4N51 A40 1c #422 1.50 25
4N53 A48 3c #425 1.50 1.50
4N54 A39 4c #426 75 50
4N55 A45 8c #428 1.00 1.00
4N56 A46 10c #429 1.50 1.50
4N57 A45 13c #430 2.25 2.00
4N58 A48 15c #431 2.50 1.50
4N59 A46 17c #432 2.00 1.50
4N60 A47 20c #433 2.00 60
4N61 A45 21c #434 3.00 1.50
4N62 A40 25c #435 2.00 2.00
4N63 A46 28c #436 1.50 75
Nos. 4N50-4N63 (13) 22.25 14.95

Type I

4N50a A39 ½c 1.00 1.00
4N51a A40 1c 1.50 25
4N52 A46 2c #423 30 15
4N53a A48 3c 75 75
4N55a A45 8c 2.25 1.50
4N57a A45 13c 2.00 1.50
4N59a A46 17c 3.50 3.50
4N60a A47 20c 2.50 2.00
4N62a A40 25c 3.00 3.00
Nos. 4N50a-4N62a (9) 16.80 13.65

For overprints see Nos. 4N64, 4N69.

Honan Singapore Overprint in Red

1942
4N64 A39 4c #4N54 75 2.00
4N65 A57 8c #4N25 2.50 2.75
4N66 A57 8c #4N14 1.75 2.00
4N67 A57 8c #4N15 6.00 8.00
Nos. 4N64-4N67 (4) 11.00 14.75

Honan Anniv. of Manchukuo Overprint in Red

1942
4N68 A57 2c #4N10 4.50 5.00
4N69 A39 4c #4N54 4.25 5.00
4N70 A57 8c #4N14 45.00 50.00
4N71 A57 8c #4N25 6.00 6.50
Nos. 4N68-4N71 (4) 59.75 66.50

Shansi

Nos. 297-298, 301, 303 Overprinted

西 山 西 山
I II

1941 **Engr.** **Unwmk.**
5N1 A37 2c #297, II 2.50 2.50
a. Type I 2.50 2.50
5N2 A37 4c #298, I 40.00 40.00
a. Type II 80.00 80.00
5N3 A37 15c #301, I 3.00 3.00
a. Type II 1.50 2.00
5N4 A37 25c #303, II 4.00 4.00
a. Type I 35.00 35.00

On Nos. 312, 314, 318, 321

1941 *Perf. 14*
5N5 A39 ½c #312, II 55 55
a. Type I 1.25 1.25
5N6 A39 2½c #314, II 75 75
a. Type I 1.50 95
5N7 A45 13c #318, II 1.00 1.25
a. Type I 100.00 100.00
5N8 A48 30c #321, II 6.00 6.00
Nos. 5N5-5N8 (4) 8.30 8.55

On Stamps of 1939-41

1941 *Perf. 12½*
5N9 A57 2c #368, II 50 50
5N10 A57 3c #350, II 75 50
a. Type I 7.50 7.50
5N11 A57 5c #352, II 1.50 1.00
a. Type I 2.00 2.00
5N12 A57 8c #353, II 75 75
a. Type I 1.50 1.00
5N13 A57 8c #369, II 25.00 15.00
5N14 A57 10c #354, II 1.25 1.00
5N15 A57 16c #357, II 3.00 3.00
5N16 A57 $1 #359, II 7.00 7.00
5N17 A57 $2 #360, II 30.00 30.00
5N18 A57 $5 #361, II 35.00 35.00
Nos. 5N9-5N18 (10) 104.75 93.75

For overprints see Nos. 5N62-5N64, 5N66-5N67.

On Stamps of 1940 with Secret Marks

1941 **Unwmk.** *Perf. 14*
5N19 A57 5c #382, II 30 25
5N20 A57 8c #383, II 75 50
5N21 A57 10c #384, II 1.25 75
a. Type I 75 75
5N22 A57 30c #385, I 1.75 1.50
a. Type II 1.25 1.00
5N23 A57 50c #386, I 2.25 2.00
a. Type II 3.50 3.50
5N24 A57 $1 #387, I 7.00 5.00
a. Type II 20.00 10.00
5N25 A57 $2 #388, I 12.00 5.00
a. Type II 10.00 8.00
5N26 A57 $5 #389, II 25.00 20.00
a. Type I 60.00 60.00
5N27 A57 $10 #390, II 40.00 40.00
a. Type I 45.00 45.00
5N28 A57 $20 #391, II 50.00 45.00
a. Type I 60.00 60.00

For overprints see Nos. 5N61, 5N68.

On Stamps of 1940 with Secret Marks

1941 **Wmk. 261** *Perf. 14*
5N29 A57 5c #392, II 90 90
5N30 A57 5c #393, II 40 40
5N31 A57 10c #394, II 75 75
5N32 A57 30c #395, I 45.00 45.00
5N33 A57 50c #396, I 4.00 3.50
Nos. 5N29-5N33 (5) 51.05 50.55

On Stamps of 1940-41 (Martyrs) with Secret Marks

Perf. 12½, 13 & Compound

1941 **Wmk. 261**
5N34 A39 ½c #402, II 75 75
5N35 A40 1c #403, II 60 50
a. Type I 75 50
5N36 A46 2c #404, II 1.50 1.50
5N37 A39 2½c #405, I 5.00 5.00
5N38 A46 10c #410, I 4.50 3.50
5N39 A45 13c #411, II 2.00 2.00
5N40 A46 17c #413, I 15.00 15.00
5N41 A40 25c #416, II 2.00 2.00
5N42 A48 30c #418, II 70.00 70.00
a. Type I 80.00 75.00
5N43 A47 40c #419, II 2.75 3.00
a. Type I 15.00 15.00
5N44 A40 50c #420, II 3.00 3.00
a. Type I 20.00 20.00

Unwmk.

5N45 A39 ½c #421, II 50 75
a. Type I 1.75 1.75
5N46 A40 1c #422, II 75 75
a. Type I 1.50 1.00
5N47 A46 2c #423, II 45 45
5N48 A48 3c #425, I 5.00 5.00
5N49 A39 4c #426, II 75 35
5N50 A45 8c #428, I 8.00 8.00
a. Type II 10.00 10.00
5N51 A46 10c #429, I 25.00 25.00
a. Type II 30.00 30.00
5N52 A45 13c #430, I 12.00 12.00
a. Type II 10.00 10.00
5N53 A48 15c #431, II 2.00 2.00
5N54 A46 17c #432, II 2.00 2.00
a. Type I 2.75 2.75
5N55 A47 20c #433, II 2.00 2.00
a. Type I 2.00 2.00
5N56 A45 21c #434, II 2.00 2.00
5N57 A40 25c #435, I 2.00 2.00
5N58 A46 28c #436, II 2.00 2.00
5N59 A40 50c #439, II 7.00 7.00

For overprints see Nos. 5N60, 5N65.

Honan Singapore Overprint in Red

1942
5N60 A39 4c #5N49 1.60 2.25
5N61 A57 8c #5N20 3.00 3.00
5N62 A57 8c #5N12 4.25 5.75
5N63 A57 8c #5N13 6.00 8.00
Nos. 5N60-5N63 (4) 14.85 19.00

Honan Anniv. of Manchukuo Overprint in Red

1942
5N64 A57 2c #5N9 5.00 6.00
5N65 A39 4c #5N49 7.50 10.00
5N66 A57 8c #5N12 25.00 30.00
5N67 A57 8c #5N13 40.00 45.00
5N68 A57 8c #5N20 25.00 25.00
Nos. 5N64-5N68 (5) 102.50 116.00

Shantung

Nos. 297-298, 301-303 Overprinted

東 山 東 山
I II

1941 **Engr.** **Unwmk.**
6N1 A37 2c #297, II 80 75
a. Type I 1.50 1.50
6N2 A37 4c #298, I 5.00 4.00
a. Type II 3.00 3.00
6N3 A37 15c #301, II 1.00 1.00
a. Type I 1.50 1.50
6N4 A37 20c #302, II 2.00 1.75
6N5 A37 25c #303, II 3.25 2.75
a. Type I 135.00 135.00

On Nos. 312, 314, 318

1941 *Perf. 14*
6N6 A39 ½c #312, II 50 50
a. Type I 75 70
6N7 A39 2½c #314, II 75 50
a. Type I 60 50
6N8 A45 13c #318, II 85 75
a. Type I 14.00 14.00
Nos. 6N6-6N8 (3) 2.10 1.75

On Stamps of 1939-41

1941 *Perf. 12½*
6N9 A57 2c #349, II 40 30
6N10 A57 2c #368, II 75 30
6N11 A57 3c #350, II 30 25
a. Type I 75 75
6N12 A57 5c #352, II 50 30
a. Type I 50 30
6N13 A57 8c #353, II 30 25
a. Type I 30 30
6N14 A57 8c #369, II 30 30
6N15 A57 10c #354, II 30 25
6N16 A57 16c #357, II 2.00 2.00
6N17 A57 $1 #359, II 6.00 6.00
a. Type I 175.00 175.00
b. On No. 347, I 40.00 40.00
6N18 A57 $5 #361, II 30.00 30.00
Nos. 6N9-6N18 (10) 40.85 39.95

For overprints see Nos. 6N62, 6N64-6N65, 6N67-6N68.

On Stamps of 1940 with Secret Marks

1941 **Unwmk.** *Perf. 14*
6N20 A57 5c #382, II 75 40
6N21 A57 8c #383, I 70 60
a. Type II 25 25
6N22 A57 10c #384, II 40 30
6N23 A57 30c #385, II 1.00 75
a. Type I 3.50 3.50
6N24 A57 50c #386, II 4.50 4.00
a. Type I 4.00 3.00
6N25 A57 $1 #387, II 4.00 3.00
a. Type I 7.50 7.50
6N26 A57 $2 #388, II 7.00 6.00
a. Type I 10.00 10.00
6N27 A57 $5 #389, II 20.00 15.00
a. Type I 30.00 25.00
6N28 A57 $10 #390, II 40.00 30.00
a. Type I 50.00 50.00
6N29 A57 $20 #391, II 55.00 50.00
a. Type I 55.00 50.00

For overprints see Nos. 6N63, 6N69.

On Stamps of 1940 with Secret Marks

1941 **Wmk. 261** *Perf. 14*
6N30 A57 5c #392, II 40 40
6N31 A57 5c #393, II 40 30
6N32 A57 10c #394, II 3.00 2.00
6N33 A57 30c #395, II 3.00 2.50
a. Type I 12.00 10.00
6N34 A57 50c #396, II 2.00 2.00
a. Type I 5.50 5.50
Nos. 6N30-6N34 (5) 8.80 7.20

On Stamps of 1940-41 (Martyrs) with Secret Marks

Perf. 12½, 13 & Compound

1941 **Wmk. 261**
6N35 A39 ½c #402, II 1.25 1.25
6N36 A40 1c #403, II 1.25 75
a. Type I 1.00 75
6N37 A39 2½c #405, II 4.00 4.00
6N38 A46 10c #410, I 1.75 1.25
6N39 A45 13c #411, II 2.00 1.00
6N40 A46 17c #413, II 2.25 2.25
a. Type I 5.00 5.00
6N41 A40 25c #416, II 2.00 2.00
6N42 A48 30c #418, I 16.00 20.00
6N43 A47 40c #419, II 2.00 2.00
a. Type I 16.00 16.00
6N44 A40 50c #420, II 4.00 4.00
Nos. 6N35-6N44 (10) 36.50 38.50

Unwmk.

6N45 A39 ½c #421, II 75 35
a. Type I 1.50 1.00
6N46 A40 1c #422, II 75 25
a. Type I 1.50 1.00
b. On No. 422a, II 50.00 50.00
6N48 A46 2c #423, II 75 50
6N49 A48 3c #425, I 1.50 1.50
a. Type II 2.00 2.75
6N50 A39 4c #426, II 40 25
6N51 A45 8c #428, II 1.50 1.50
a. Type I 16.00 15.00
6N52 A46 10c #429, I 4.50 4.00
6N53 A45 13c #430, II 2.00 2.00
a. Type I 1.50 1.50
6N54 A48 15c #431, II 1.00 1.00
6N55 A46 17c #432, II 1.50 1.50
a. Type I 2.00 2.00
6N56 A47 20c #433, II 2.00 1.50
a. Type I 3.50 2.50
6N57 A45 21c #434, II 2.00 1.50
6N58 A40 25c #435, I 2.75 1.50
6N59 A46 28c #436, II 2.00 1.00
6N60 A40 50c #439, II 6.00 6.00

For overprints see Nos. 6N61, 6N66.

Honan Singapore Overprint in Red

1942
6N61 A39 4c #6N50 1.00 1.50
6N62 A57 8c #6N13 10.00 12.00
6N63 A57 8c #6N21a 12.50 12.50
6N64 A57 8c #6N14 2.50 3.00
Nos. 6N61-6N64 (4) 26.00 29.00

Honan Anniv. of Manchukuo Overprint in Red

1942

6N65 A57	2c #6N10	2.00	2.50
6N66 A39	4c #6N50	2.25	2.75
6N67 A57	8c #6N13	12.00	15.00
6N68 A57	8c #6N14	30.00	35.00
6N69 A57	8c #6N21a	2.00	2.50
	Nos. 6N65-6N69 (5)	48.25	57.75

Supeh

Nos. 297-298, 301-302 Overprinted

北 蘇 北 蘇

I II

1941 Engr. Unwmk.

7N1 A37	2c #297, I	5.00	4.25
a.	Type II	10.00	10.00
7N2 A37	4c #298, I	22.50	22.50
a.	Type II	55.00	
7N3 A37	15c #301, I	1.75	1.75
a.	Type II	1.50	1.50
7N4 A37	20c #302, II	1.75	1.75

On Nos. 312, 314, 318

1941 ***Perf. 14***

7N5 A39	½c #312, I	2.00	2.00
7N6 A39	2½c #314, II	75	75
a.	Type I	75	75
7N7 A45	13c #318, II	75	85
a.	Type I	70.00	70.00

On Stamps of 1939-41

1941 ***Perf. 12½***

7N8 A57	2c #368, II	75	75
7N9 A57	3c #350, II	75	75
a.	Type I	12.00	10.00
7N10 A57	5c #352, II	75	75
a.	Type I	1.50	1.00
7N11 A57	8c #353, I	1.00	1.25
a.	Type II	1.75	1.75
7N12 A57	8c #369, II	20.00	16.50
7N13 A57	10c #354, II	1.00	75
7N14 A57	16c #357, II	75	75
7N15 A57	$1 #359, II	9.00	9.00
a.	On No. 347, I	125.00	125.00
	Nos. 7N8-7N15 (8)	34.00	30.50

For overprints see Nos. 7N56-7N58, 7N60-7N61.

On Stamps of 1940 with Secret Marks

1941 Unwmk. ***Perf. 14***

7N17 A57	5c #382, II	75	50
7N18 A57	8c #383, II	40	40
7N19 A57	10c #384, I	1.75	1.00
a.	Type II	1.50	40
7N20 A57	30c #385, II	4.00	2.50
a.	Type I	1.25	1.00
7N21 A57	50c #386, II	2.25	2.25
a.	Type I	2.00	2.00
7N22 A57	$1 #387, I	12.00	10.00
a.	Type II	25.00	20.00
7N23 A57	$2 #388, I	17.00	17.00
a.	Type II	12.00	10.00
7N24 A57	$5 #389, I	25.00	25.00
a.	Type II	55.00	45.00
7N25 A57	$10 #390, II	50.00	50.00
a.	Type I	45.00	30.00
7N26 A57	$20 #391, II	60.00	60.00
a.	Type I	65.00	50.00

On Stamps of 1940 with Secret Marks

1941 Wmk. 261 ***Perf. 14***

7N27 A57	10c #394, II	2.25	2.25
7N28 A57	30c #395, I	7.00	7.00
7N29 A57	50c #396, I	9.00	9.00
	Nos. 7N27-7N29 (3)	18.25	18.25

On Stamps of 1940-41 (Martyrs) with Secret Marks

Perf. 12½, 13 & Compound

1941 Wmk. 261

7N30 A39	½c #402, II	1.50	1.50
7N31 A40	1c #403, II	1.00	1.00
a.	Type I	75	75
7N32 A46	2c #404, II	75	75
7N33 A39	2½c #405, I	17.00	15.00
7N34 A46	10c #410, I	10.00	10.00
7N35 A45	13c #411, II	3.00	2.50
7N36 A46	17c #413, II	2.75	2.75
a.	Type I	60.00	60.00
7N37 A40	25c #416, II	2.00	2.00
7N38 A48	30c #418, I	6.00	6.00
7N39 A47	40c #419, II	2.75	2.75
a.	Type I	4.50	4.00
7N40 A40	50c #420, I	60.00	60.00
	Nos. 7N30-7N40 (11)	106.75	104.25

Unwmk.

7N41 A39	½c #421, II	1.50	1.50
a.	Type I	1.50	1.50
7N42 A40	1c #422, II	75	50
7N43 A46	2c #423, I	6.00	6.00
7N44 A48	3c #425, I	2.00	2.00
7N45 A39	4c #426, II	50	50
7N46 A46	10c #429, I	25.00	25.00
7N47 A45	13c #430, I	3.00	3.00
7N48 A48	15c #431, II	2.00	2.00
7N49 A46	17c #432, II	2.00	2.00
a.	Type I	2.75	2.75
7N50 A47	20c #433, II	2.00	2.00
a.	Type I	3.00	3.00
7N51 A45	21c #434, II	2.00	2.00
7N52 A40	25c #435, I	2.50	2.00
a.	Type II	8.00	8.00
7N53 A46	28c #436, II	2.00	2.00
	Nos. 7N41-7N53 (13)	51.25	50.50

For overprints see Nos. 7N55, 7N59.

Honan Singapore Overprint in Red

1942

7N54 A37	4c #298, II	32.50	32.50
7N55 A39	4c #7N45	3.75	4.00
7N56 A57	8c #7N11a	9.00	12.00
7N57 A57	8c #7N12	8.00	10.00
	Nos. 7N54-7N57 (4)	53.25	58.50

Honan Anniv. of Manchukuo Overprint in Red

1942

7N58 A57	2c #7N8	8.00	10.00
7N59 A39	4c #7N45	7.50	10.00
7N60 A57	8c #7N11a	45.00	50.00
7N61 A57	8c #7N12	50.00	55.00
	Nos. 7N58-7N61 (4)	110.50	125.00

North China

For use in Honan, Hopei, Shansi, Shantung and Supeh (Northern Kiangsu)

Stamps of China, 1931-37 Surcharged North China (Hwa Pei) and Half of Original Value

北 華

分 壹

1942 Unwmk. ***Perf. 14, 12½***

8N1 A40	½c on 1c (#313)	45	45
8N2 A37	1c on 2c (#297)	50	30
8N3 A37	2c on 4c (#298)	1.00	75
8N4 A45	4c on 8c (#316)	110.00	

Same Surcharge on Stamps of 1938-41

Perf. 12½

8N5 A57	1c on 2c (#349)	2.25	2.25
8N6 A57	1c on 2c (#368)	30	15
8N7 A57	4c on 8c (#353)	1.00	55
8N8 A57	4c on 8c (#369)	35	20
8N9 A57	5c on 10c grn	45	20
8N10 A57	8c on 16c ol gray	1.25	45
8N11 A57	50c on $1 (#359)	5.00	5.00
8N12 A57	50c on $1 (#344)	425.00	425.00
8N13 A57	50c on $1 (#347)	70.00	70.00
8N14 A57	$1 on $2 (#360)	7.00	7.00
8N15 A57	$1 on $2 (#345)	20.00	20.00
8N16 A57	$1 on $2 (#348)	95.00	95.00

No. 8N12 was issued without gum.
For overprint see No. 8N58.

Same Surcharge on China Nos. 383-388, 390-391

Perf. 14

8N17 A57	4c on 8c ol grn	50	50
8N18 A57	5c on 10c grn	60	60
8N19 A57	15c on 30c scar	1.00	65
a.	Inverted surcharge	60.00	60.00
8N20 A57	25c on 50c dk bl	1.00	75
8N21 A57	50c on $1 org brn & sep	2.25	2.00
8N22 A57	$1 on $2 dp bl & yel brn	3.75	3.75
8N23 A57	$5 on $10 dk grn & dl pur	30.00	30.00
8N24 A57	$10 on $20 rose lake & dk bl	30.00	30.00
	Nos. 8N17-8N24 (8)	69.10	68.25

For overprint see No. 8N55.

Same Surcharge on China Nos. 394-396

Wmk. 261

8N25 A57	5c on 10c grn	45	45
8N26 A57	15c on 30c scarlet	2.00	2.50
8N27 A57	25c on 50c dk bl	85	85
	Nos. 8N25-8N27 (3)	3.30	3.80

Same Surcharge on Stamps of 1940-41

1942 Wmk. 261 ***Perf. 12½, 13***

8N28 A40	½c on 1c org	20	15
8N29 A46	1c on 2c dp bl	1.25	1.25
8N30 A45	4c on 8c dp org	12.00	12.00
8N31 A46	5c on 10c dl vio	1.50	1.50
8N32 A48	15c on 30c brn car	6.00	6.00
8N33 A47	20c on 40c org	3.50	1.25
8N34 A40	25c on 50c grn	3.00	3.00
	Nos. 8N28-8N34 (7)	27.45	25.15

Unwmk.

8N35 A40	½c on 1c org (#422)	20	15
a.	½c on 1c org (#422a)	8.00	8.00
8N36 A46	1c on 2c dp bl	75	75
8N37 A39	2c on 4c pale vio	60	25
8N38 A45	4c on 8c dp org	75	75
8N39 A46	5c on 10c dl vio	1.50	1.50
8N40 A47	10c on 20c lt bl	1.00	30
8N41 A47	20c on 40c org	2.50	50
8N42 A40	25c on 50c grn	2.00	2.00
	Nos. 8N35-8N42 (8)	9.30	6.20

Same Surcharge on "New Peking" Prints

Perf. 14

8N43 A37	1c on 2c ol grn	25	15
8N44 A37	2c on 4c dl grn	40	15
a.	Inverted surcharge	30.00	
8N45 A45	4c on 8c dp org	25	15
8N46 A57	8c on 16c ol gray	25	15
8N47 A47	10c on 20c red brn	1.25	75
8N48 A48	15c on 30c brn car	50	50
8N49 A47	20c on 40c org	1.00	20
a.	Inverted surcharge	35.00	
8N50 A40	25c on 50c grn	1.00	50
8N51 A57	50c on $1 org brn & sep	2.00	2.00
8N52 A57	$1 on $2 dp bl & org brn	2.50	2.00
8N53 A57	$5 on $10 dk grn & dl pur	12.00	12.00
	Nos. 8N43-8N53 (11)	21.40	18.55

See note after No. 2N93.
For overprints see #8N54, 8N56-8N57, 8N59.

Nos. 8N44, 8N17 and 8N46 with Additional Overprint in Red

邦友
界租 還交
念紀

1943 Unwmk. ***Perf. 14***

8N54 A37	2c on 4c dl grn	20	40
8N55 A57	4c on 8c ol grn	75	1.00
8N56 A57	8c on 16c ol gray	75	1.00
	Nos. 8N54-8N56 (3)	1.70	2.40

Return of the Foreign Concessions to China.

Nos. 8N44, 8N8 and 8N46 with Additional Overprint in Red

局總 政郵
立成
念紀年週五

1943, Aug. 15 ***Perf. 14, 12½***

8N57 A37	2c on 4c dl grn	25	35
8N58 A57	4c on 8c ol grn	25	35
8N59 A57	8c on 16c ol gray	30	50
	Nos. 8N57-8N59 (3)	80	1.20

North China Postal Service, 5th anniv.

Stamps of China, 1934-41, Overprinted in Black

北 華

1943, Nov. 1

8N60 A40	1c org (#313)	50	50
8N61 A40	1c org (#422)	60	50
8N62 A57	10c grn (#354)	30	30
8N63 A57	$2 dp bl & yel brn (#388)	16.00	10.00
8N64 A57	$5 red & grnsh blk (#361)	10.00	10.00
8N65 A57	$5 red & sl grn (#389)	7.00	6.00
8N66 A57	$10 dk grn & dl pur (#390)	10.00	7.00
8N67 A57	$20 rose lake & dk bl (#391)	50.00	50.00
	Nos. 8N60-8N67 (8)	94.40	84.30

Same Overprint on "New Peking" Prints

8N68 A40	1c orange	20	15
8N69 A37	2c olive grn	20	30
8N70 A37	4c dull green	20	30
8N71 A37	5c green	20	25
8N72 A57	9c olive grn	20	30
8N73 A46	10c dl violet	20	15
8N74 A57	16c olive gray	20	30
8N75 A57	18c olive gray	20	30
8N76 A47	20c henna	30	30
8N77 A48	30c brown car	20	15
8N78 A47	40c brt orange	20	20
a.	Inverted overprint	30.00	30.00
8N79 A40	50c green	1.50	1.50
8N80 A57	$1 org brn & sep	2.50	50
8N81 A57	$2 bl & org brn	1.50	1.25
8N82 A57	$5 red & sl grn	3.00	4.00
8N83 A57	$10 dk grn & dl pur	3.75	4.25
8N84 A57	$20 rose lake & dk bl	6.00	6.00
	Nos. 8N68-8N84 (17)	20.55	20.20

See note after No. 2N93.

For overprints see Nos. 8N85-8N90, 8N95-8N106.

Nos. 8N70 and 8N62 with Additional Overprint in Red

戰 參
念紀年週一

1944, Jan. 9

8N85 A37	4c dull green	25	25
8N86 A57	10c green	25	30

1st anniv. of the declaration of war against the Allies by North China.

Nos. 8N72, 8N75, 8N79 and 8N80 with Additional Overprint in Red

會員委務政
念紀年週四

1944, Mar. 30

8N87 A57	9c olive green	35	45
8N88 A57	18c olive gray	35	45
8N89 A40	50c green	1.75	2.00
8N90 A57	$1 org brn & sepia	1.50	2.00
a.	Red overprint inverted	25.00	25.00
	Nos. 8N87-8N90 (4)	3.95	4.90

4th anniv. of the North China Political Council.

Shanghai-Nanking Nos. 9N101-9N104 Surcharged North China (Hwa Pei) and New Value in Red or Black

華北玖分 (a)
華北壹角捌分 (b)
華北叁角陸分 (c)
華北玖角 (d)

1944 ***Perf. 12½x12, 12x12½***

8N91 OS1 (a)	9c on 50c org	50	35
8N92 OS1 (b)	18c on $1 grn (R)	50	35
a.	Double surcharge	25.00	25.00
8N93 OS2 (c)	36c on $2 dp bl (R)	75	1.00
8N94 OS2 (d)	90c on $5 car rose	75	1.25
	Nos. 8N91-8N94 (4)	2.50	2.95

Nos. 8N72, 8N75, 8N79 and 8N80 Overprinted in Red or Blue

立成局總政郵
念紀年週六

1944, Aug. 15

8N95 A57	9c olive grn	50	75
8N96 A57	18c olive gray	50	75
8N97 A40	50c green	1.00	1.25
8N98 A57	$1 org brn & sep (Bl)	2.00	2.25
	Nos. 8N95-8N98 (4)	4.00	5.00

6th anniv. of the General P.O. Dept. of North China.

North China Nos. 8N76, 8N79-8N81 Overprinted in Blue or Black

席 主 汪
念 紀 典 葬

1944, Dec. 5

8N99 A47	20c henna (Bl)	1.50	1.75
8N100 A40	50c green (Bl)	1.50	1.75
8N101 A57	$1 org brn & sep (Bl)	3.50	4.00
8N102 A57	$2 bl & org brn	1.00	1.25
	Nos. 8N99-8N102 (4)	7.50	8.75

Death of Wang Ching-wei, puppet ruler of China.

North China Nos. 8N76, 8N79-8N81 Overprinted in Red or Black

年週二戰參
念 紀

1945

8N103 A47	20c henna	1.25	1.40
8N104 A40	50c green (R)	2.50	2.50
8N105 A57	$1 org brn & sep	1.50	1.75
8N106 A57	$2 bl & org brn	1.25	1.50
	Nos. 8N103-8N106 (4)	6.50	7.15

2nd anniv. of the declaration of war.

Shanghai-Nanking Nos. 9N105-9N106 Surcharged in Red

華北伍角

1945 ***Perf. 12x12½***

8N107	OS3	50c on $3 lt org	35	50
8N108	OS3	$1 on $6 blue	35	50

Return of the foreign concessions in Shanghai.

Dragon Pillar — OS1

Dr. Sun Yat-sen — OS2

Designs: $2, Long Bridge and White Pagoda. $5, Tower in Imperial City. $10, Marble Boat, Summer Palace.

1945 Unwmk. Litho. ***Perf. 14***

Various Papers

8N109	OS1	$1 dull yellow	1.00	1.00
8N110	OS1	$2 deep blue	20	35
8N111	OS1	$5 carmine	60	40
8N112	OS1	$10 dull green	30	35
		Nos. 8N109-8N112 (4)	2.10	2.10

North China Political Council, 5th anniv.

1945

Without Gum; Various Papers

8N113	OS2	$1 bister	20	20
8N114	OS2	$2 dark blue	75	75
8N115	OS2	$5 fawn	1.50	1.50
8N116	OS2	$10 sage green	1.50	1.25
8N117	OS2	$20 dull violet	1.25	1.00
8N118	OS2	$50 brown	15.00	15.00
		Nos. 8N113-8N118 (6)	20.20	19.70

Nos. 8N113-8N118 without "Hwa Pei" overprint are proofs.

Wutai Mountain, Shansi — OS3

Designs: $10, Kaifeng Iron Pagoda. $20, International Bridge, Tientsin. $30, Taishan Mountain, Shantung. $50, General Post Office, Peking.

1945, Aug. 15

Without Gum; Various Papers

8N119	OS3	$5 gray green	20	50
8N120	OS3	$10 dull brown	35	50
8N121	OS3	$20 dull purple	35	50
8N122	OS3	$30 slate blue	75	1.00
8N123	OS3	$50 carmine	1.50	1.50
		Nos. 8N119-8N123 (5)	3.30	4.00

North China Postal Directorate, 7th anniv.

Shanghai and Nanking

China Nos. 299-303 Surcharged

貳角伍分 暫售 25

a

暫售 陸圓 6.00

b

Overprinted Type "b"

1942-45 Unwmk. ***Perf. 12½, 13½***

9N1	A37	$6 on 5c green	75	1.00
9N2	A37	$20 on 15c scar	25	40
9N3	A37	$500 on 15c dk grn	75	1.25
9N4	A37	$1000 on 20c ultra	75	1.00
9N5	A37	$1000 on 25c ultra	1.50	2.00
		Nos. 9N1-9N5 (5)	4.00	5.65

A $1000 on 20c ultramarine, No. 293, exists.

Surcharged Type "a" (Nos. 9N6-9N10) or Type "b" (Nos. 9N11-9N40) on Type A57 Stamps of 1939-41

Perf. 12½

9N6	25c on 5c (#352)	20	25
9N7	30c on 2c (#368)	20	25
9N8	50c on 3c (#350)	20	25
9N9	50c on 5c (#352)	20	20
9N10	50c on 8c (#353)	20	20
9N11	$1 on 8c (#353)	20	15
9N12	$1 on 8c (#369)	10.00	10.00
9N13	$1 on 15c (#356)	20	15
9N14	$1.30 on 16c (#357)	20	30
9N15	$1.50 on 3c (#350)	20	20
9N16	$2 on 5c (#352)	20	20
9N17	$2 on 10c (#354)	20	25
9N18	$3 on 15c (#356)	20	25
9N19	$4 on 16c (#357)	35	20
9N20	$5 on 15c (#356)	20	20
9N21	$6 on 5c (#351)	30	30
a.	Perf. 14 (#371)	20.00	20.00
9N22	$6 on 5c (#352)	20	25
9N23	$6 on 8c (#353)	30	30
9N24	$6 on 8c (#369)	500.00	500.00
9N25	$6 on 10c (#354)	20	20
9N26	$10 on 10c (#354)	20	20
9N27	$10 on 16c (#357)	35	20
9N28	$20 on 3c (#350)	20	20
9N29	$20 on 15c (#355)	35	55
9N30	$20 on 15c (#356)	30	30
9N31	$20 on $2 (#360)	1.00	1.50
9N32	$100 on 3c (#350)	35	30
9N33	$500 on 8c (#353)	1.00	1.25
9N34	$500 on 8c (#369)	18.00	20.00
9N35	$500 on 10c (#354)	75	75
9N36	$500 on 15c (#355)	50	50
9N37	$500 on 15c (#356)	75	75
9N38	$500 on 16c (#357)	1.00	1.00
9N39	$1000 on 25c (#358)	75	75
9N40	$2000 on $5 (#361)	1.00	1.00
	Nos. 9N1-9N23,9N25-9N40 (39)	44.45	49.00

Nos. 381-391 (Type A57) Surcharged with Type "b"

Perf. 14

9N41	$1 on 8c ol grn	20	25
9N42	$1.70 on 30c scar	25	35
a.	Perf. 12½	2.50	2.50
9N43	$2 on 5c ol grn	30	40
9N44	$2 on $1 org brn & sep	75	1.25
9N45	$3 on 8c ol grn	45	40
a.	$3 on 8c olive green (#383a)	25.00	25.00
b.	"3" with flat top	30	30
9N46	$6 on 5c grn	30	30
9N47	$6 on 5c ol grn	30	30
9N48	$6 on 8c ol grn	30	30
9N49	$10 on 10c grn	30	30
a.	Perf. 12½	75	1.00
9N50	$20 on $2 dp bl & yel brn	50	50
9N51	$50 on 30c scar	45	50
9N52	$50 on 50c dk bl	50	50
9N53	$50 on $5 red & sl grn	50	50
9N54	$50 on $20 rose lake & dk bl	1.75	2.00
9N55	$100 on $10 dk grn & dl pur	90	90
9N56	$200 on $20 rose lake & dk bl	50	50
9N57	$500 on 8c ol grn	8.00	9.00
a.	$500 on 8c ol grn (#383a)	15.00	18.00
9N58	$500 on 10c grn	1.50	1.75
9N59	$1000 on 30c scar	75	1.00
9N60	$1000 on 50c dk bl	50	65
9N61	$1000 on $2 dp bl & yel brn	1.25	1.65
9N62	$2000 on $5 red & sl grn	70	70

China Nos. 392-395 and 399-401 (Type A57) Surcharged with Type "b"

1942-45 Wmk. 261 ***Perf. 14***

9N63	$2 on $1 org brn & sep, perf. 12½	60	80
9N64	$6 on 5c grn	30	30
9N65	$6 on 5c ol grn	75	75
9N66	$50 on $5 red & sl grn	35	40
a.	Numeral tablet violet	60	60
9N67	$100 on $10 dk grn & dl pur	35	40
9N68	$200 on $20 rose lake & dk bl	40	40
9N69	$500 on 10c grn	50	50
9N70	$1000 on 30c scar	2.00	2.50
9N71	$5000 on $10 dk grn & dl pur, perf. 12½	5.50	5.50
a.	Perf. 14	45.00	30.00
	Nos. 9N41-9N71 (31)	31.70	35.55

Nos. 9N63 and 9N71 were not issued without surcharge. A $50 on 30c scarlet exists.

Same Surch. on Stamps of 1940-41

Perf. 12½, 13

Wmk. 261

9N72	A46	$30 on 2c dp bl	60.00	60.00

A $7.50 on ½c and a $15 on 1c are known.

Unwmk.

9N73	A39	$7.50 on ½c ol blk	50	75
9N74	A40	$15 on 1c org	25	40
a.		Without secret mark	30.00	30.00
9N75	A46	$30 on 2c dp bl	75	1.00
9N76	A40	$200 on 1c org	30	40
9N77	A45	$200 on 8c dp org	40	50
		Nos. 9N73-9N77 (5)	2.20	3.05

Surcharged Type "a" (Nos. 9N78-9N81) or Type "b" (Nos. 9N82-9N96) on Type A59 Stamps of 1941

Perf. 12

9N78	5c on ½c sepia	20	20
9N79	10c on 1c orange	20	20
9N80	20c on 1c orange	20	20
9N81	40c on 5c green	20	20
9N82	$5 on 5c green	20	20
9N83	$10 on 10c brt grn	20	20
9N84	$50 on ½c sepia	20	20
9N85	$50 on 1c orange	25	30
9N86	$50 on 17c olive	25	40
9N87	$200 on 5c green	25	30
9N88	$200 on 8c turq grn	20	20
9N89	$200 on 8c red org	25	45
9N90	$500 on $5 scar & blk	25	30
9N91	$1000 on 1c orange	25	40
9N92	$1000 on 25c rose vio	30	40
9N93	$1000 on 30c scarlet	75	40
9N94	$1000 on $2 bl & blk	65	70
9N95	$1000 on $10 grn & blk	30	40
9N96	$2000 on $5 scar & blk	75	75
	Nos. 9N78-9N96 (19)	5.85	6.40

Stamps of China 1939-41 Surcharged in Red or Blue

收回租界紀念
三十二年
八月一日
貳角伍分

1943 Unwmk. ***Perf. 12, 12½***

9N97	A57	25c on 5c grn	15	*35*
9N98	A59	50c on 8c red org (Bl)	15	*35*
9N99	A57	$1 on 16c ol gray	15	*35*
9N100	A59	$2 on 50c dk bl	15	*35*
		Set value	30	

Issued to commemorate the return of the foreign concessions in Shanghai.

Wheat and Cotton — OS1

Purple Mountain, Nanking OS2

Perf. 12½x12, 12x12½

1944 Engr. Unwmk.

9N101	OS1	50c orange	15	*25*
9N102	OS1	$1 green	15	*25*
9N103	OS2	$2 dp bl	15	*30*
9N104	OS2	$5 car rose	15	*30*
		Set value	25	

4th anniv. of the puppet government at Nanking.
For surcharges see Nos. 8N91-8N94, 9N107-9N110.

Map of Foreign Concessions in Shanghai — OS3

1944 ***Perf. 12x12½***

9N105	OS3	$3 lt org	15	*25*
9N106	OS3	$6 blue	15	*25*
		Set value	15	

1st anniversary of the return of the foreign concessions in Shanghai.
For surcharges see Nos. 8N107-8N108.

Nos. 9N101-9N104 Surcharged in Black with Type "b"

1945, Mar. 30

9N107	OS1	$15 on 50c org	15	*25*
9N108	OS1	$30 on $1 grn	15	*25*
9N109	OS2	$60 on $2 dp bl	15	*30*
9N110	OS2	$200 on $5 car rose	15	*30*
		Set value	25	

China Nos. C31, C32, C36 and C38 Surcharged in Red, Green, Orange or Carmine

防空 1000

暫售 壹仟圓

1945 ***Perf. 12½, 13***

9N111	AP3	$150 on 15c (R)	15	*15*
9N112	AP3	$250 on 25c (G)	15	*25*
9N113	AP3	$600 on 60c (O)	15	*25*
9N114	AP3	$1,000 on $1 (C)	15	*25*
		Set value	35	

Issue as air raid precaution propaganda.

SHANGHAI AND NANKING AIR POST STAMPS

China Nos. C35 and C38 Surcharged in Black

10

國內明片之航空費已付

The surcharges on Nos. 9NC1-9NC7 were in Japanese currency because all air mail then was carried by Japanese planes.

The surcharges translate: (10c) "Airmail fee for postcard within the nation has been paid." (20c) "Airmail fee for letter within the nation has been paid."

1941 Unwmk. ***Perf. 12½***

9NC1	AP3	10(s) on 50c brown	15	*25*
9NC2	AP3	20(s) on $1 apple grn	15	*25*
		Set value	20	

Two types of surcharge exist on No. 9NC1.

Similar Surcharge on No. C28

1941 Wmk. 261 ***Perf. 13***

9NC3	AP3	20(s) on $1 ap grn	10.00	12.50

Nos. C37 and C39 Surcharged

35

寄日本信函航空費已付

The surcharges translate: (18c and 25c) "Airmail fee for postcard to Japan has been paid." (35c) "Airmail fee for letter to Japan has been paid."

1941 Unwmk. ***Perf. 12½, 13***

9NC4	AP3	18(s) on 90c lt olive	15	*40*
9NC5	AP3	25(s) on 90c lt olive	15	*30*
9NC6	AP3	35(s) on $2 lt brn	15	*30*
		Set value	30	

No. 9NC6 with Additional Surcharge in Red

Perf. 12½

9NC7	AP3	60(s) on 35(s) on $2	15	*25*

SHANGHAI AND NANKING POSTAGE DUE STAMPS

Postage Due Stamps of China 1932 Surcharged in Black

改作 壹圓 1.00

1945		Unwmk.	Perf. 14	
9NJ1	D5	$1 on 2c org	15	30
9NJ2	D5	$2 on 5c org	15	30
9NJ3	D5	$5 on 10c org	15	30
9NJ4	D5	$10 on 20c org	15	30
		Set value	40	

Northeastern Provinces

民 中

國 華

With the end of World War II and the collapse of Manchukuo, the Northeastern Provinces reverted to China. In many Manchurian towns and cities, the Manchukuo stamps were locally handstamped in ideograms: "Republic of China," "China Postal Service" or "Temporary Use for China." A typical example is shown above.

Dr. Sun Yat-sen
A1 A2

Black Surcharge

1946, Feb.		Unwmk. Typo.	Perf. 14	
1	A1	50c on $5 red	15	45
2	A1	50c on $10 grn	40	65
3	A1	$1 on $10 grn	15	32
4	A1	$2 on $20 brn vio	15	45
5	A1	$4 on $50 brn	15	32
		Set value	70	

The two characters at left express the new value.

Stamps of China, 1938-41 Overprinted 用貼北東限

1946, Apr.		Perf. 12½, 13, 13½, 14		
6	A40	1c org (#422)	15	25
7	A48	3c dp yel brn (#425)	15	25
8	A48	5c dl red org (#427)	15	25
9	A57	10c grn (#354)	15	25
10	A57	10c grn (#384)	15	25
11	A47	20c lt bl (#433)	15	25
a.		Horiz. pair, imperf. btwn	45.00	
		Nos. 6-11 (6)	90	1.50

1946, July		Engr. Without Gum	Perf. 14	
12	A2	5c lake	15	52
13	A2	10c orange	15	52
14	A2	20c yel grn	15	52
15	A2	25c blk brn	15	70
16	A2	50c red org	15	35
17	A2	$1 blue	15	35
18	A2	$2 dk vio	15	35
19	A2	$2.50 indigo	15	52
20	A2	$3 brown	15	35
21	A2	$4 org brn	15	52
22	A2	$5 dk grn	15	35
23	A2	$10 crimson	15	35
24	A2	$20 olive	15	35
25	A2	$50 blue vio	15	35
		Set value	1.80	

Two types of $4, $10, $20 and $50: I- Character *kuo* directly left of sun emblem is open at upper and lower left corners of "box." Diagonal stroke from top center to lower right has no hook at bottom. II- Character is closed at left corners. Diagonal stroke has hook at bottom.

See Nos. 47-52, 61-63. For surcharges see Nos. M1, Taiwan 91-96, People's Republic of China 35-48, 3L37-3L52, 3L55-3L66, 3L71-3L75.

China Nos. 728-731 Surcharged in Black

限東北貼用

2⁰⁰ 圓貳

1946				
26	A75	$2 on $20 green	15	70
27	A75	$3 on $30 blue	15	1.10
28	A75	$5 on $50 dark brown	15	45
29	A75	$10 on $100 carmine	15	70
		Nos. 26-29 (4)	60	

Convening of Chinese National Assembly.

Type of China, 1946, Inscribed: 貼 東 / 用 北

1947		Engr.	Perf. 11, 11½	
30	A74	$2 carmine	26	75
31	A74	$3 green	35	75
32	A74	$5 vermilion	35	75
33	A74	$10 yel grn	45	75
34	A74	$20 yel org	52	75
35	A74	$30 magenta	52	75
		Nos. 30-35 (6)	2.45	4.50

60th birthday of Chiang Kai-shek.

Type of China, 1947, Inscribed: 用貼北東

1947		Unwmk. Engr.	Perf. 14	
36	A76	$2 deep green	20	40
37	A76	$4 deep blue	20	40
38	A76	$6 carmine	20	40
39	A76	$10 lt brown	20	40
40	A76	$20 deep claret	20	40
		Nos. 36-40 (5)	1.00	2.00

First anniversary of return of Chinese National Government to Nanking.

China Nos. 644 to 646 and 634 Surcharged in Black

用貼北東限

叁 改

佰

圓 300⁰⁰ 作

1947			Perf. 12½, 14	
41	A73	$100 on $1000 rose lake	18	65
42	A73	$300 on $3000 bl	18	65
43	A73	$500 on $5000 dp grn & ver	18	1.00
44	A37	$500 on $30 choc	75	65
		Nos. 41-44 (4)	1.29	

Type of 1946

1947		Engr. Without Gum	Perf. 14	
47	A2	$44 dk car rose	17.50	25.00
48	A2	$100 dp grn	15	25
49	A2	$200 rose brn	15	42
50	A2	$300 bluish grn	18	85
51	A2	$500 rose car	18	25
52	A2	$1000 dp orange	25	25
		Nos. 47-52 (6)	18.41	27.02

For surcharges see note following No. 25.

Stamps and Types of 1946-47 Surcharged in Black or Red

壹仟伍佰圓 改

1500 作

1948		Unwmk.	Perf. 14	
53	A2	$1500 on 20c yel grn	26	1.65
54	A2	$3000 on $1 blue	18	42
55	A2	$4000 on 25c blk brn (R)	18	42
56	A2	$8000 on 50c red org	18	42
57	A2	$10,000 on 10c org	22	42
58	A2	$50,000 on $109 dk grn (R)	40	1.65
59	A2	$100,000 on $65 dl grn	40	1.65
60	A2	$500,000 on $22 gray (R)	60	1.40
		Nos. 53-60 (8)	2.42	8.03

Type of 1946

1947, Nov. 5		Without Gum		
61	A2	$22 gray	25.00	
62	A2	$65 dull green	30.00	
63	A2	$109 dark green	37.50	
		Nos. 61-63 (3)	92.50	

For surcharges see note following No. 25.

POSTAGE DUE STAMPS

D1

1947		Unwmk. Engr. Without Gum	Perf. 14	
J1	D1	10c dark blue	15	1.50
J2	D1	20c dark blue	15	2.00
J3	D1	50c dark blue	15	1.25
J4	D1	$1 dark blue	15	75
J5	D1	$2 dark blue	15	1.00
J6	D1	$5 dark blue	15	75
		Set value	50	

Nos. J1 to J3 Surcharged in Red

拾改

圓作

1948				
J7	D1	$10 on 10c dark blue	15	1.75
J8	D1	$20 on 20c dark blue	15	1.50
J9	D1	$50 on 50c dark blue	15	2.00
		Set value	35	

The surcharge reads "Changed to . . . dollars." Characters at the left express the new value and vary on each denomination.

MILITARY STAMPS

No. 16 Surcharged in Black

郵軍

作暫

圓肆拾肆

1947		Unwmk.	Perf. 14	
M1	A2	$44 on 50c red org	3.00	6.00

The surcharge reads: "Army Post. Temporarily for 44 dollars."

China No. M13 Overprinted in Black 用貼北東限

Thin Paper Without Gum

Perf. 12½

M2	M1	rose	75	3.00

China No. M13 Overprinted in Black 用貼北東限

M3	M1	rose	20.00	12.00

PARCEL POST STAMP

China No. Q25 Surcharged in Black

用貼北東限

伍 改

拾

萬

圓 作

1948		Unwmk. Engr. Without Gum	Perf. 13½	
Q1	PP3	$500,000 on $5,000,000 lilac	75.00	

The use of this handstamp from Anhwei has not been verified.

Fukien Province

壹 郵

Stamps of China, 1945-49, Surcharged

分 資

1

1949		Engr. Without Gum	Perf. 14	
1	A82	1c on $500 bl grn	5.00	5.50
2	A82	1c on $7000 lt red brn	12.00	14.00
3	A82	2c on $2,000,000 ver	3.00	3.00
4	A82	2½c on $50,000 dp bl	12.00	10.00
5	A73	4c on $100 dk car	2.50	2.50
6	A73	10c on $200 ol grn	3.50	3.50
7	A82	10c on $3000 bl	2.00	2.00
8	A82	10c on $4000 gray	3.00	3.00
9	A82	10c on $6000 rose lil	3.00	3.00
10	A82	10c on $100,000 dl grn	3.00	3.00
11	A82	10c on $1,000,000 cl	3.00	3.00
12	A82	40c on $200,000 brn vio	4.50	4.50
		Nos. 1-12 (12)	56.50	57.00

The surcharge on No. 2 is handstamped and in slightly larger characters.

Issue dates: No. 2, May 10; others, June.

China Nos. 973, 975-978 Overprinted 州 福

1949, June		Litho.	Perf. 12½, 13	
13	A94	1c apple grn	7.50	5.00
14	A94	4c blue green	4.75	1.00
15	A94	10c deep lilac	27.50	13.00
16	A94	16c orange red	5.75	10.00
17	A94	20c blue	14.00	10.00
		Nos. 13-17 (5)	59.50	39.00

Same Overprint on China No. 959

1949, July		Litho.	Perf. 12½	
18	A96	orange	35.00	30.00

Same Overprint on Fukien Nos. 1, 3-4, 8, 11 in Black or Red

1949, June		Engr.	Perf. 14	
19	A82	1c on $500 bl grn	72.50	72.50
20	A82	2c on $2,000,000 ver	24.00	24.00
21	A82	2½c on $50,000 dp bl	40.00	40.00
22	A82	10c on $4000 gray	19.00	19.00
23	A82	10c on $1,000,000 claret	65.00	25.00
		Nos. 19-23 (5)	220.50	180.50

AIR POST STAMP

China No. C62 Overprinted as Nos. 13-17

1949, July		Litho.	Perf. 12½	
C1	AP5	blue green	30.00	15.00

SPECIAL DELIVERY STAMP

China No. E12 Overprinted as Nos. 13-17

1949, July		Litho.	Perf. 12½	
E1	SD2	red violet	21.00	10.00

REGISTRATION STAMPS

China No. F2 Overprinted as Nos. 13-17

1949, July		Litho.	Perf. 12½	
F1	R2	carmine	21.00	10.00

Demand, as well as supply, determine a stamp's market value.

Hunan Province

China No. 640 Surcharged

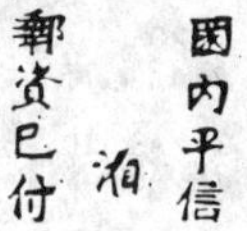

1949, May		Engr.		Perf. 14
1	A73	on $100 dk car	7.50	4.50

The first printing of surcharge on No. 1 is in smaller characters.

China Nos. 797, 788, 750, 747 Surcharged

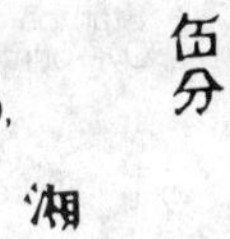

1949, May		Engr.		Perf. 14
2	A82	1c on $2,000,000 ver	14.00	14.00
3	A82	2c on $20,000 rose pink	14.00	14.00
4	A82	5c on $3000 blue	14.00	14.00
5	A82	10c on $500 blue grn	14.00	14.00
		Nos. 2-5 (4)	56.00	56.00

AIR POST STAMP

China No. 790 Surcharged

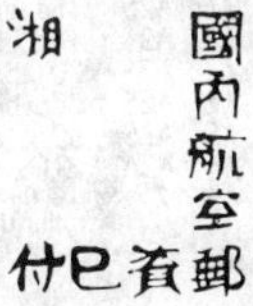

1949, May		Engr.		Perf. 14
C1	A82	On $40,000 green	12.00	12.00

SPECIAL DELIVERY STAMP

China No. 637 Surcharged as No. F1 in Red

1949, May		Engr.		Perf. 14
E1	A73	On $30 dark blue	12.00	12.00

REGISTRATION STAMP

China No. 754 Surcharged

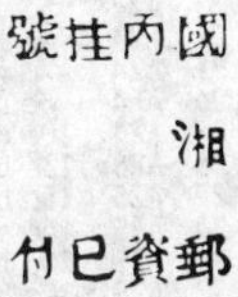

1949, May		Engr.		Perf. 14
F1	A73	On $7000 lt red brn	15.00	15.00

Hupeh Province

China Type A95 Surcharged

1949, May				Litho.
1	A95	1c on $20 red brn	32.50	30.00
2	A95	10c on $20 red brn	32.50	30.00

Kansu Province

China No. 959 Handstamped in Purple

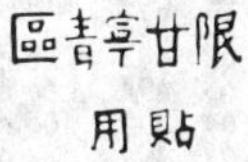

1949, Aug.		Litho.	Perf. 12½
1	A96	orange	450.00

AIR POST STAMP

Same Handstamp Overprinted on China No. C62 in Red

1949, Aug.		Litho.	Perf. 12½
C1	AP5	blue green	450.00

Counterfeits exist.

Kiangsi Province

China Nos. 789-791 Surcharged

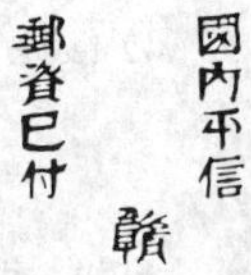

1949		Engr.		Perf. 14
1	A82	On $30,000 choc	25.00	20.00
2	A82	On $40,000 green	25.00	20.00
3	A82	On $50,000 dp bl	25.00	20.00
		Nos. 1-3 (3)	75.00	60.00

AIR POST STAMP

Similar Surcharge on China No. 754

1949		Engr.		Perf. 14
C1	A82	On $7000 lt red brn	30.00	30.00

Third and fourth characters in right column of surcharge read "Air Mail" in Chinese on No. C1, "Registered" on Nos. F1-F2.

SPECIAL DELIVERY STAMP

Similar Surcharge on China No. 750

1949		Engr.		Perf. 14
E1	A82	On $3000 blue	30.00	20.00

See note below No. C1.

REGISTRATION STAMPS

Similar Surcharge on China Nos. 747 and 754

1949		Engr.		Perf. 14
F1	A82	On $500 bl grn	30.00	20.00
F2	A82	On $7000 lt red brn	30.00	20.00

Kwangsi Province

China Nos. 811 and 818 Also Surcharged in Red

1949, May 21				Typo.
6	A62	5c on $20,000 on 10c dp grn	12.50	12.50
7	A62	5c on $40,000 on 20c dk ol grn	27.50	27.50

China Stamps of 1946-48 Surcharged in Black or Red

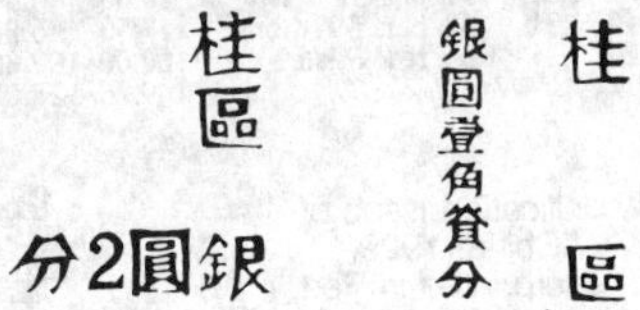

a b

1949		Engr.		Perf. 14
		Type "a" Surcharge		
8	A82	½c on $500,000 lil rose	19.00	12.00
9	A82	1c on $200,000 brn vio	7.50	4.00
10	A82	2c on $300,000 yel grn	37.50	20.00
11	A73	5c on $3000 blue	8.00	5.00
12	A82	5c on $3000 blue	7.50	4.50
13	A82	5c on $40,000 grn	7.50	5.00
		Type "b" Surcharge		
14	A82	13c on $50,000 dp bl (R)	9.25	6.00
15	A82	13c on $50,000 dp bl	22.50	12.00
16	A82	17c on $7000 lt red brn	11.00	7.50
17	A82	21c on $100,000 dl grn	13.00	8.00
		Nos. 8-17 (10)	142.75	84.00

Shensi Province

China Nos. 747, 750 Surcharged

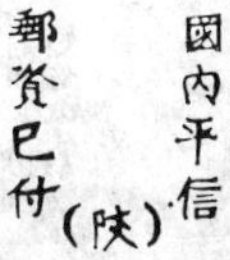

1949, May		Engr.		Perf. 14
1	A82	On $500 bl grn	19.00	19.00
2	A82	On $3000 blue	19.00	19.00

AIR POST STAMP

Similar Surcharge on China No. 754

1949, May		Engr.		Perf. 14
C1	A82	On $7000 lt red brn	30.00	30.00

SPECIAL DELIVERY STAMP

Similar Surcharge on China No. 746 in Red

1949, May		Engr.		Perf. 14
E1	A82	On $250 dp lil	30.00	30.00

REGISTRATION STAMPS

Similar Surcharge on China Nos. 626, 637 in Red

1949, May		Typo.		Perf. 12
F1	A72	on $30 dp bl	35.00	35.00
F2	A73	on $30 dk bl	25.00	25.00

Szechwan Province

Re-engraved Issue of China, 1923, Overprinted

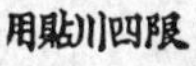

1933		Unwmk.		Perf. 14
1	A29	1c orange	5.00	50
2	A29	5c claret	5.00	65
3	A30	50c deep green	15.00	3.00
		Nos. 1-3 (3)	25.00	4.15

The overprint reads "For use in Szechwan Province exclusively".

Same on Sun Yat-sen Issue of 1931-37 Type II

1933-34				Perf. 12½
4	A37	2c olive grn	42	28
5	A37	5c green	8.50	70
6	A37	15c dk green	1.40	85
7	A37	15c scar ('34)	2.75	3.50
8	A37	25c ultra	2.25	55
9	A37	$1 org brn & dk brn	4.25	1.10
10	A37	$2 bl & org brn	13.00	1.65
11	A37	$5 dl red & blk	37.50	6.75
		Nos. 4-11 (8)	70.07	15.38

Same on Martyrs Issue of 1932-34

1933				Perf. 14
12	A39	½c black brn	20	15
13	A40	1c orange	18	15
14	A39	2½c rose lilac	1.00	80
15	A48	3c deep brown	85	70
16	A45	8c brown org	70	20
17	A46	10c dull violet	1.50	15
18	A45	13c blue green	1.50	28
19	A46	17c brown olive	1.75	40
20	A47	20c brown red	1.90	28
21	A48	30c brown violet	1.75	28
22	A47	40c orange	4.25	28
23	A40	50c green	10.50	40
		Nos. 12-23 (12)	26.08	4.07

Stamps of China, 1947-48, Surcharged

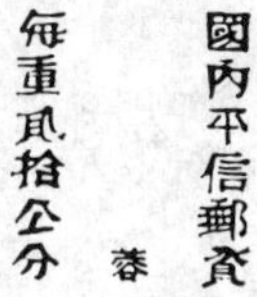

1949		Engr.		Perf. 14
24	A82	on $150 dk bl	20.00	20.00
25	A82	on $250 dp lil	20.00	20.00
26	A82	on $500 bl grn	4.00	4.00
27	A82	on $1000 red	12.00	12.00
28	A82	on $2000 ver	4.00	4.00
29	A82	on $3000 bl	4.00	4.00
30	A82	on $4000 gray	4.00	4.00
31	A82	on $5000 dk brn	20.00	20.00
32	A82	on $6000 rose lil	4.00	4.00
33	A82	on $7000 lt red brn	20.00	20.00
34	A82	on $10,000 dk bl & car	4.00	4.00
35	A82	on $20,000 rose pink	8.00	8.00
36	A82	on $30,000 choc	4.00	4.00
37	A82	on $50,000 grn & dk bl	4.00	4.00
38	A82	on $50,000 dp bl	6.00	6.00
39	A82	on $100,000 dl yel & ol	7.00	7.00
40	A82	on $100,000 dl grn	8.00	8.00
41	A82	on $200,000 vio brn & dp bl	8.00	8.00
42	A82	on $200,000 brn vio	8.00	8.00
43	A82	on $300,000 sep & org brn	12.50	12.50
44	A82	on $300,000 yel grn	15.00	15.00
45	A82	on $500,000 dk Prus grn & sep	4.00	4.00
46	A82	on $1,000,000 cl	13.00	13.00
47	A82	on $2,000,000 ver	8.00	8.00
48	A82	on $3,000,000 ol bis	8.00	8.00
49	A82	on $5,000,000 ultra	30.00	30.00
		Nos. 24-49 (26)	259.50	259.50

Several of Nos. 24-49 exist with inverted surcharge and a few with bottom character of left row repeated in right row, same position.

Counterfeits exist.

China No. 737 Surcharged in Purple

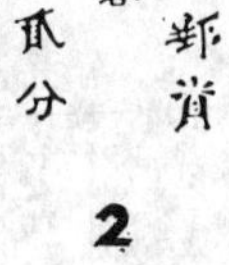

1949				Perf. 12½
50	A77	2c on $500 ol grn	18.00	25.00

China No. 975 Handstamp Surcharged in Purple

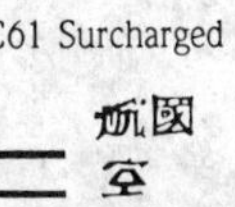

1949				Litho.
51	A94	2½c on 4c bl grn	16.00	20.00

SZECHWAN AIR POST STAMPS

China Nos. C55-C58, C60-C61 Surcharged

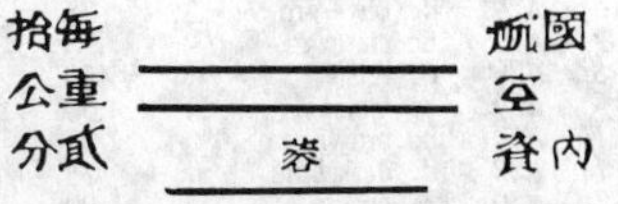

Perf. 12½, 13x12½, 14

1949, July **Unwmk.**

C1	AP3	On $10,000 on 30c	3.00	3.00
a.		On #CS4		425.00
C2	AP4	On $10,000 on $27	5.00	7.00
a.		Second surch. invtd.	190.00	
b.		On #CS3	110.00	
C3	AP3	On $20,000 on 25c	5.00	6.00
C4	AP3	On $30,000 on 90c	6.75	8.00
C5	AP3	On $50,000 on 60c	45.00	55.00
C6	AP3	On $50,000 on $1	8.00	11.00
		Nos. C1-C6 (6)	72.75	90.00

On No. C2 characters of overprint are arranged in two horizontal rows, and two of four lines are vertical.

SZECHWAN REGISTRATION STAMPS

Stamps of China, 1944-47, Surcharged 掛號郵資 國內信函 貳

Engraved; Typographed (A72)

1949 *Perf. 12, 13, 14*

F1	A64	On $100 yel brn	35.00
F2	A72	On $100 dk brn	50.00
F3	A64	On $200 dk grn	15.00
F4	A72	On $200 brn vio	15.00
F5	A73	On $200 ol grn	80.00
F6	A73	On $500 brt bl grn	80.00
F7	A73	On $700 red brn	100.00
F8	A73	On $5000 dp grn & ver	65.00
		Nos. F1-F8 (8)	440.00

PARCEL POST STAMP

China No. Q10 Surcharged 壹分 貳

1949 **Engr.** *Perf. 12½*

Q1	PP2	1c on $20,000 dk red	150.00

No. Q1 is also found with surcharged value repeated in 5 characters at top of stamp.

Tsingtau

China Nos. 890, 903, 945, 894 Handstamp Surcharged in Purple Blue or Red 壹分 銀圓 (島青)

Engraved; Lithographed

1949, May *Perf. 14, 12½*

1	A94	1c on $100 org brn (P)	30.00	18.00
2	A94	4c on $5000 lt bl (P)	30.00	24.00
3	A94	6c on $500 rose lil (B)	30.00	24.00
4	A94	10c on $1000 bl (R)	30.00	18.00
		Nos. 1-4 (4)	120.00	84.00

Yunnan Province

Stamps of China, 1923-26, Overprinted 用貼省滇限

The overprint reads "For exclusive use in the Province of Yunnan". It was applied to prevent stamps being purchased in the depreciated currency of Yunnan and used elsewhere.

1926 **Unwmk.** *Perf. 14*

1	A29	½c blk brn	1.00	20
2	A29	1c orange	1.00	15
3	A29	1½c violet	2.00	2.00
4	A29	2c yellow grn	1.00	25
5	A29	3c blue green	75	20
6	A29	4c olive grn	75	25
7	A29	5c claret	75	25
8	A29	6c red	1.50	60
9	A29	7c violet	1.50	1.00
10	A29	8c brown org	1.25	65
11	A29	10c dark blue	75	15
12	A30	13c brown	1.00	1.00
13	A30	15c dark blue	1.00	85
14	A30	16c olive grn	1.00	1.00
15	A30	20c brown red	2.00	1.50
16	A30	30c brown vio	2.50	2.50
17	A30	50c deep green	2.50	2.50
18	A31	$1 org brn & sep	10.00	6.50
19	A31	$2 blue & red brn	17.50	6.50
20	A31	$5 red & slate	100.00	100.00
		Nos. 1-20 (20)	149.75	128.05

Unification Issue of China, 1929, Overprinted in Red 貼用 滇省

1929 *Perf. 14*

21	A35	1c brown org	95	95
22	A35	4c olive grn	1.90	1.90
23	A35	10c dark blue	3.75	3.75
24	A35	$1 dark red	47.50	47.50
		Nos. 21-24 (4)	54.10	54.10

Similar Overprint in Black on Sun Yat-sen Mausoleum Issue
Characters 15½-16mm apart

25	A36	1c brown orange	70	70
26	A36	4c olive green	95	95
27	A36	10c dark blue	2.50	2.50
28	A36	$1 dark red	32.50	32.50
		Nos. 25-28 (4)	36.65	36.65

London Print Issue of China, 1931-37, Overprinted 用貼省滇限

1932-34 **Unwmk.** *Perf. 12½*

Type I (double circle)

29	A37	1c orange	1.50	1.50
30	A37	2c olive grn	1.75	2.75
31	A37	4c green	1.75	2.75
32	A37	20c ultra	1.50	1.50
33	A37	$1 org brn & dk brn	19.00	14.00
34	A37	$2 bl & org brn	37.50	37.50
35	A37	$5 dl red & blk	110.00	92.50
		Nos. 29-35 (7)	173.00	152.50

Type II (single circle)

36	A37	2c olive grn	3.50	3.50
37	A37	4c green	1.50	1.50
38	A37	5c green	5.00	5.00
39	A37	15c dk green	3.50	3.50
40	A37	15c scar ('34)	3.50	4.00
41	A37	25c ultra	3.50	4.00
42	A37	$1 org brn & dk brn	24.00	18.00
43	A37	$2 bl & org brn	47.50	22.50
44	A37	$5 dl red & blk	95.00	90.00
		Nos. 36-44 (9)	187.00	152.00

Nos. 36-39, 41-44 were overprinted in London as well as in Peking. The overprints differ in minor details. Value of London overprints (8), $350.

Tan Yuan-chang Issue of China, 1933, Overprinted 貼用 滇省

1933 *Perf. 14*

45	A49	2c olive green	95	70
46	A49	5c green	1.10	70
47	A49	25c ultra	2.50	1.65
48	A49	$1 red	32.50	19.00
		Nos. 45-48 (4)	37.05	22.05

Martyrs Issue of China, 1932-34, Overprinted 用貼省滇限

1933

49	A39	½c blk brown	42	32
50	A40	1c orange	60	48
51	A39	2½c rose lilac	1.25	1.25
52	A48	3c deep brown	1.25	80
53	A45	8c brown org	85	40
54	A46	10c dull vio	1.25	1.25
55	A45	13c blue grn	85	40
56	A46	17c brn olive	1.65	1.65
57	A47	20c brown red	1.00	80
58	A48	30c brown vio	3.00	2.25
59	A47	40c orange	13.00	13.00
60	A40	50c green	15.00	13.00
		Nos. 49-60 (12)	40.12	35.60

China No. 324 was overprinted with characters arranged vertically, like Sinkiang No. 114, but was not issued.

China Stamps of 1945-49 Surcharged in Black or Blue 壹 角10 滇省貼用

Engraved; Lithographed; Typographed

1949 *Perf. 12, 12½, 14*

61	A82	1c on $200,000 brn vio	5.00	4.25
62	A82	1.2c on $40,000 grn	5.00	4.25
63	A94	6c on $200 red org	5.00	4.25
64	A94	10c on $20,000 org	5.00	4.25
65	A94	12c on $50 dk Prus grn (Bl)	5.00	4.25
66	A72	12c on $50 grnsh gray (Bl)	5.00	4.25
67	A72	12c on $200 brn vio (Bl)	5.00	4.25
68	A94	30c on $20 vio brn	5.00	4.25
69	A82	$1.20 on $100,000 dl grn	10.00	8.50
		Nos. 61-69 (9)	50.00	42.50

China No. 888 and 630 Surcharged 4 肆分 郵資 滇

1949 **Engr.** *Perf. 14*

70	A94	4c on $20 vio brn	90.00

Typo. *Perf. 12*

71	A72	12c on $200 brn vio	150.00

Manchuria

Kirin and Heilungkiang Issue

Stamps of China, 1923-26, Overprinted

用貼黑吉限

The overprint reads: "For use in Ki-Hei District" the two names being abbreviated.

The intention of the overprint was to prevent the purchase of stamps in Manchuria, where the currency was depreciated, and their resale elsewhere.

1927 **Unwmk.** *Perf. 14*

1	A29	½c black brn	1.00	18
2	A29	1c orange	1.00	15
3	A29	1½c violet	65	55
4	A29	2c yellow grn	1.00	18
5	A29	3c blue grn	40	38
6	A29	4c olive grn	25	15
7	A29	5c claret	40	18
8	A29	6c red	50	28
9	A29	7c violet	1.00	95
10	A29	8c brown org	1.00	95
11	A29	10c dk blue	1.00	22
12	A30	13c brown	1.50	1.40
13	A30	15c dk blue	2.00	1.40
14	A30	16c olive grn	2.00	1.25
15	A30	20c brown red	3.00	1.40
16	A30	30c brown vio	4.00	1.65
17	A30	50c dp green	5.00	1.90
18	A31	$1 org brn & sep	12.00	3.75
19	A31	$2 bl & red brn	30.00	9.50
20	A31	$5 red & slate	140.00	110.00
		Nos. 1-20 (20)	207.70	136.42

Several values of this issue exist with inverted overprint, double overprint and in pairs with one overprint omitted. These "errors" were not regularly issued. Forgeries also exist.

Chang Tso-lin Stamps of 1928 Overprinted in Red or Blue 貼用 吉黑

1928 *Perf. 14*

21	A34	1c brown org (R)	95	95
22	A34	4c olive grn (R)	95	95
23	A34	10c dull blue (R)	1.90	1.90
24	A34	$1 red (Bl)	24.00	24.00
		Nos. 21-24 (4)	27.80	27.80

Unification Issue of China, 1929, Overprinted in Red as in 1928

1929

25	A35	1c brown orange	70	70
26	A35	14c olive green	1.90	70
27	A35	10c dark blue	6.00	6.00
28	A35	$1 dark red	42.50	42.50
		Nos. 25-28 (4)	51.10	49.90

Similar Overprint in Black on Sun Yat-sen Mausoleum Issue of China
Characters 15-16mm apart

1929 *Perf. 14*

29	A36	1c brown orange	1.25	1.40
30	A36	4c olive green	1.65	1.65
31	A36	10c dark blue	3.75	2.75
32	A36	$1 dark red	42.50	42.50
		Nos. 29-32 (4)	49.15	48.30

Sinkiang

Stamps of China, 1913-19, Overprinted in Black or Red 限新省貼用

The first character of overprint is ½mm out of alignment, to the left, and the overprint measures 16mm.

1915 **Unwmk.** *Perf. 14, 15*

1	A24	½c black brn	50	38
2	A24	1c orange	50	30
3	A24	2c yellow grn	60	52
4	A24	3c slate grn	60	26
5	A24	4c scarlet	90	45
6	A24	5c rose lilac	90	38
7	A24	6c gray	1.25	1.10
8	A24	7c violet	1.75	1.50
9	A24	8c brown orange	1.25	75
10	A24	10c dark blue	1.75	1.10
11	A25	15c brown	1.75	1.40
12	A25	16c olive grn	4.50	3.00
13	A25	20c brown red	4.50	3.00
14	A25	30c brown violet	6.00	3.00
15	A25	50c deep green	15.00	6.50
16	A26	$1 ocher & blk (R)	75.00	27.50
a.		Second & third characters of overprint transposed	*7,500.*	
		Nos. 1-16 (16)	116.75	51.14

Stamps of China, 1913-19, Overprinted in Black or Red 限新省貼用

The five characters of overprint are correctly aligned and measure 15½mm.

1916-19

17	A24	½c black brn	35	25
18	A24	1c orange	35	25
19	A24	1½c violet	80	75
20	A24	2c yellow grn	35	25
21	A24	3c slate grn	80	32
22	A24	4c scarlet	80	50
23	A24	5c rose lilac	80	35
24	A24	6c gray	1.10	50
25	A24	7c violet	2.75	2.00
26	A24	8c brown org	2.00	1.25
27	A24	10c dark blue	1.50	50
28	A25	13c brown	2.50	2.25
29	A25	15c brown	2.75	2.25
30	A25	16c olive grn	2.25	1.90
31	A25	20c brown red	2.00	1.25
32	A25	30c brown vio	3.25	2.50
33	A25	50c deep green	4.00	2.25
34	A26	$1 ocher & blk (R)	9.00	4.50
35	A26	$2 dk bl & blk (R)	14.00	5.00
36	A26	$5 scar & blk (R)	32.50	16.00
37	A26	$10 yel grn & blk (R)	125.00	90.00
38	A26	$20 yel & blk (R)	350.00	275.00
		Nos. 17-38 (22)	558.85	409.82

For overprint see No. C4.

China Nos. 243-246 Overprinted 用貼省新限

1921 *Perf. 14*

39	A27	1c orange	95	95
40	A27	3c blue green	1.90	1.90
41	A27	6c gray	4.75	4.75
42	A27	10c blue	37.50	37.50
		Nos. 39-42 (4)	45.10	45.10

Constitution Issue of China, 1923, Overprinted 貼用 新疆省

1923

No.	Type	Description	Unused	Used
43	A32	1c orange	2.75	2.75
44	A32	3c blue green	3.25	3.25
45	A32	4c red	4.75	4.75
46	A32	10c blue	14.00	14.00
		Nos. 43-46 (4)	24.75	24.75

Stamps of China, 1923-26, Overprinted as in 1916-19, in Black or Red

1924

Re-engraved

No.	Type	Description	Unused	Used
47	A29	½c black brn	50	50
48	A29	1c orange	50	50
49	A29	1½c violet	1.00	90
50	A29	2c yellow grn	50	50
51	A29	3c blue grn	50	50
52	A29	4c gray	1.65	1.10
53	A29	5c claret	50	45
54	A29	6c red	2.50	1.10
55	A29	7c violet	1.65	1.75
56	A29	8c org brn	*4.25*	*1.75*
57	A29	10c dark blue	85	35
58	A30	13c red brown	1.90	2.00
59	A30	15c deep blue	3.00	2.50
60	A30	16c olive grn	3.00	2.50
61	A30	20c brown red	3.75	2.25
62	A30	30c brown vio	3.75	2.25
63	A30	50c deep green	4.25	2.25
64	A31	$1 org brn & sep (R)	8.00	2.50
65	A31	$2 bl & red brn (R)	16.00	5.00
66	A31	$5 red & sl (R)	32.50	12.00
67	A31	$10 grn & cl (R)	125.00	65.00
68	A31	$20 plum & bl (R)	190.00	125.00
		Nos. 47-68 (22)	405.55	232.65

See #69, 114. For overprints see #C1-C3.

Same Overprint on China No. 275

1926

No.	Type	Description	Unused	Used
69	A29	4c olive green	2.00	2.00

Chang Tso-lin Stamps of China, 1928, Overprinted in Red or Blue 貼 新 用 疆

1928 *Perf. 14*

No.	Type	Description	Unused	Used
70	A34	1c brn org (R)	90	90
71	A34	4c ol grn (R)	1.40	1.40
72	A34	10c dull bl (R)	3.25	3.25
73	A34	$1 red (Bl)	27.50	27.50
		Nos. 70-73 (4)	33.05	33.05

Unification Issue of China, 1929, Overprinted in Red as in 1928

1929

No.	Type	Description	Unused	Used
74	A35	1c brown org	1.40	1.40
75	A35	4c olive grn	2.25	2.25
76	A35	10c dk blue	5.50	5.50
77	A35	$1 dk red	40.00	40.00
		Nos. 74-77 (4)	49.15	49.15

Similar Overprint in Black on Sun Yat-sen Mausoleum Issue of China Characters 15mm apart

1929 *Perf. 14*

No.	Type	Description	Unused	Used
78	A36	1c brown org	95	95
79	A36	4c olive grn	1.40	1.40
80	A36	10c dark blue	3.25	3.25
81	A36	$1 dark red	37.50	37.50
		Nos. 78-81 (4)	43.10	43.10

Stamps of Sun Yat-sen Issue of 1931-37 Overprinted 用貼省新限

1932 **Type I** *Perf. 12½*

No.	Type	Description	Unused	Used
82	A37	1c orange	70	1.00
83	A37	2c olive grn	1.40	2.00
84	A37	4c green	1.25	2.25
85	A37	20c ultra	1.90	2.00
86	A37	$1 org brn & dk brn	4.25	4.00
87	A37	$2 bl & org brn	8.50	8.00
88	A37	$5 dl red & blk	17.00	16.00
		Nos. 82-88 (7)	35.00	35.25

No. 83 was overprinted in Shanghai in 1938. The overprint differs in minor details.

1932-38

Type II

No.	Type	Description	Unused	Used
89	A37	2c olive grn	22	40
90	A37	4c green	52	60
91	A37	5c green	35	50
92	A37	15c dk green	42	1.00
93	A37	15c scar ('34)	42	60
93A	A37	20c ultra ('38)	35	40
94	A37	25c ultra	52	60
95	A37	$1 org brn & dk brn	2.50	2.50
96	A37	$2 bl & org brn	6.50	6.25
97	A37	$5 dl red & blk	18.00	17.00
		Nos. 89-97 (10)	29.80	29.85

Nos. 89, 90 and 94 were overprinted in London, Peking and Shanghai. Nos. 92, 95-97 exist with London and Peking overprints. Nos. 91 and 93 exist with Peking and Shanghai overprints. No. 93A is a Shanghai overprint. The overprints differ in minor details.

Tan Yuan-chang Issue of China, 1933, Overprinted as in 1928

1933 *Perf. 14*

No.	Type	Description	Unused	Used
98	A49	2c olive grn	1.40	1.40
99	A49	5c green	1.90	1.90
100	A49	25c ultra	6.00	6.00
101	A49	$1 red	37.50	37.50
		Nos. 98-101 (4)	46.80	46.80

Stamps of China Martyrs Issue of 1932-34 Overprinted 用貼省新限

1933-34

No.	Type	Description	Unused	Used
102	A39	½c black brown	15	38
103	A40	1c orange	75	1.10
104	A39	2½c rose lilac	18	38
105	A48	3c deep brown	18	38
106	A45	8c brown orange	45	75
107	A46	10c dull violet	15	38
108	A45	13c blue green	18	55
109	A46	17c brown olive	18	38
110	A47	20c brown red	75	1.25
111	A48	30c brown violet	25	45
112	A47	40c orange	38	55
113	A40	50c green	45	45
		Nos. 102-113 (12)	4.05	7.00

Nos. 102-113 were originally overprinted in Peking. In 1938, Nos. 103-105, 108-112 were overprinted in Shanghai. The two overprints differ in minor details. No. 105, Shanghai overprint, is scarce. Value $35.

China No. 324 Overprinted as in 1916-19

1936 *Perf. 14*

No.	Type	Description	Unused	Used
114	A29	6c brown	9.00	10.00

Stamps of China, 1939-40 Overprinted in Black

1940-45 **Unwmk.** *Perf. 12½*

Type III

No.	Type	Description	Unused	Used
115	A57	2c olive green	75	90
116	A57	3c dull claret ('41)	15	25
117	A57	5c green	15	25
118	A57	5c olive green	15	35
119	A57	8c olive green ('41)	20	35
120	A57	10c green ('41)	15	35
121	A57	15c scarlet	30	65
122	A57	16c olive gray ('41)	30	90
123	A57	25c dark blue	45	90
124	A57	$1 hn & dk brn (type II)	4.00	5.50
125	A57	$2 dp bl & org brn (type I)	4.00	5.75
126	A57	$5 red & grnsh blk	15.00	16.00
		Nos. 115-126 (12)	25.60	32.15

Perf. 14

With Secret Marks

No.	Type	Description	Unused	Used
127	A57	8c ol grn (#383a)	30	65
a.		On #383	6.50	8.50
128	A57	10c green ('41)	1.40	3.75
129	A57	30c scarlet ('45)	15	65
130	A57	50c dk blue ('45)	30	65
131	A57	$1 org brn & sep	30	85
132	A57	$2 dp bl & org brn	30	1.00
133	A57	$5 red & sl grn	1.10	1.65
134	A57	$10 dk grn & dl pur	85	2.50
135	A57	$20 rose lake & dk bl	2.75	4.25
		Nos. 127-135 (9)	7.45	15.95

Wmk. Character Yu (Post) (261)

Perf. 14

No.	Type	Description	Unused	Used
136	A57	5c olive green	15	38
137	A57	10c green	18	45
138	A57	30c scarlet	18	52
139	A57	50c dark blue	22	60
		Nos. 136-139 (4)	73	1.95

Martyrs Issue, 1940-41, Overprinted in Black 用貼省新限

Perf. 12, 12½, 13, 13x12, 13½x13

1941-45 **Wmk. 261**

No.	Type	Description	Unused	Used
140	A40	1c orange	16	*30*
141	A39	2½c rose lilac	16	*75*
142	A45	8c dp org ('45)	1.50	*1.75*
143	A46	10c dull vio	22	*55*
144	A45	13c dp yel grn	42	*90*
145	A46	17c brown olive	42	*1.10*
146	A40	25c red vio ('45)	85	*1.25*
147	A47	40c orange ('45)	1.25	*1.25*
		Nos. 140-147 (8)	4.98	*7.85*

Unwmk.

No.	Type	Description	Unused	Used
148	A39	½c olive blk	16	*38*
149	A40	1c orange ('45)	16	*30*
150	A46	2c dp blue ('45)	20	*45*
151	A48	3c dp yel brn	15	*70*
152	A39	4c pale vio ('45)	15	*60*
153	A45	8c dp orange	16	*75*
154	A45	13c dp yel grn ('45)	24	*55*
155	A48	15c brn car ('45)	15	*55*
156	A46	17c brn ol ('45)	40	*60*
157	A47	20c lt blue ('45)	16	*38*
158	A45	21c ol brn ('45)	24	*60*
159	A46	28c olive ('45)	28	*75*
160	A47	40c orange ('45)	1.25	*2.25*
161	A40	50c green ('45)	40	*58*
		Nos. 148-161 (14)	4.10	*9.44*

Stamps of China, 1942-43 Overprinted in Carmine, Black or Red 用貼省新限

1944 *Perf. 12½, 13*

Without Gum

No.	Type	Description	Unused	Used
162	A62	10c dp grn (C)	45	*2.25*
163	A62	20c dk ol grn (C)	1.10	*2.25*
164	A62	25c violet brn	15	*2.50*
165	A62	30c dk orange	30	*2.75*
166	A62	40c red brown	15	*2.50*
167	A62	50c sage green	15	*1.50*
a.		Perf. 11	6.00	7.00
168	A62	$1 rose lake	90	*1.50*
169	A62	$1 dull green	15	*2.50*
170	A62	$1.50 dp bl (C)	15	*2.75*
171	A62	$2 dk bl grn (R)	60	*2.00*
172	A62	$3 yellow	15	*3.50*
173	A62	$5 cerise	60	*3.25*
		Nos. 162-173 (12)	4.85	*29.25*

For surcharges see Nos. 194-195.

Same Overprint on Stamps of China, 1942-43, in Black

1944-46 *Imperf.*

No.	Type	Description	Unused	Used
174	A57	$10 red brown	30.00	35.00
175	A57	$20 rose red	1.00	*4.50*
176	A57	$30 dull vio	1.00	*4.50*
177	A57	$40 rose red	1.50	*4.75*
178	A57	$50 blue ('46)	450.00	500.00
179	A57	$100 orange brn	2.00	*5.25*

Perf. 13½

No.	Type	Description	Unused	Used
180	A57	$4 dp blue	15	*3.00*
181	A57	$5 lilac gray	25	*2.50*
182	A57	$10 red brn	25	*2.50*
183	A57	$20 blue grn	75	*2.75*
184	A57	$20 rose red	40.00	45.00
185	A57	$30 dull vio	1.00	*3.50*
186	A57	$40 rose	1.00	*3.50*
187	A57	$50 blue	1.25	*3.00*
188	A57	$100 orange brn	45.00	45.00
		Nos. 174-177,179-188 (14)	125.15	*164.75*

Nos. 162 and 164 Surcharged in Black 改作壹 角貳分

1944, Aug. 1

No.	Type	Description	Unused	Used
194	A62	12c on 10c dp grn	60	*1.50*
195	A62	24c on 25c brn vio	60	*1.50*

Stamps of China, 1940-41, Overprinted in Black at Chengtu, Szechwan 用貼省新限

1943

No.	Type	Description	Unused	Used
196	A57	10c green (#354)	4.00	6.25
197	A47	20c lt blue (#433)	3.50	5.75

Wmk. 261 *Perf. 14*

No.	Type	Description	Unused	Used
198	A57	50c dk blue (#396)	4.50	7.00

China Nos. 565 and 567 Overprinted in Black 用貼省新限

1945 **Unwmk.** *Perf. 12½*

No.	Type	Description	Unused	Used
200	A63	40c brown red	20	65
201	A63	$3 red	20	65

China Nos. 640-642, 788, 751, 753 Surcharged in Black or Red 改作 伍分 用貼新疆省

1949 **Engr.** *Perf. 14*

No.	Type	Description	Unused	Used
202	A73	1c on $100 dk car	9.00	11.00
203	A73	3c on $200 ol grn (R)	9.00	11.00
204	A73	5c on $500 brt bl grn (R)	9.00	11.00
205	A82	10c on $20,000 rose pink	9.00	11.00
206	A82	50c on $4000 gray (R)	32.50	*32.50*
207	A82	$1 on $6000 rose lil	40.00	*40.00*
		Nos. 202-207 (6)	108.50	116.50

AIR POST STAMPS

Sinkiang Nos. 53, 57, 59, 32 Overprinted in Red 空航

1932-33 **Unwmk.** *Perf. 14*

No.	Type	Description	Unused	Used
C1	A29	5c claret ('33)	125.	75.
C2	A29	10c dk blue ('33)	125.	60.
C3	A30	15c deep blue	1,000.	250.
C4	A25	30c brown vio	375.	275.

Counterfeits exist of Nos. C1-C19.

Air Post Stamps of China, 1932-37 Handstamped in Dull Red

用貼省新限

1942

No.	Type	Description	Unused	Used
C5	AP3	15c gray green	2.50	3.00
C6	AP3	25c orange	160.00	125.00
C7	AP3	30c red	6.50	12.00
C8	AP3	45c brown vio	4.25	7.50
C9	AP3	50c dk brown	19.00	22.50
C10	AP3	60c dk blue	4.00	8.25
C11	AP3	90c olive grn	22.50	30.00
C12	AP3	$1 yellow grn	5.00	9.00
		Nos. C5-C12 (8)	223.75	217.25

Same Handstamped Overprint on Air Post Stamps of China, 1940-41 in Dull Red

Perf. 12½, 13, 13½

1942 **Wmk. 261**

No.	Type	Description	Unused	Used
C13	AP3	15c gray green	2.25	3.00
C14	AP3	25c yellow org	2.25	3.00

1942 **Unwmk.**

No.	Type	Description	Unused	Used
C15	AP3	25c lt orange	1.75	2.00
C16	AP3	30c lt red	2.75	3.00
C17	AP3	50c brown	3.75	3.75
C18	AP3	$2 lt brown	19.00	20.00
C19	AP3	$5 lake	19.00	20.00
		Nos. C15-C19 (5)	46.25	48.75

Twelve values exist with this overprint in black. Their status has not been determined. Inverted overprints exist in both red and black.

Official Perforated Characters

For use on official mail, various Sinkiang stamps were perforated with an arrangement of four Chinese characters ("For Official Business Only"). These include Nos. 1-38, 47-69, 114.

OFFICES IN TIBET

12 Pies = 1 Anna
16 Annas = 1 Rupee

Stamps of China, Issues of 1902-10, Surcharged

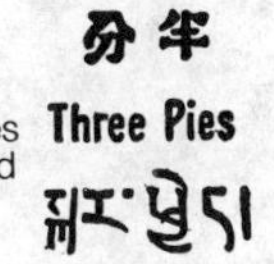

1911 **Unwmk.** *Perf. 12 to 16*

No.	Type	Description	Unused	Used
1	A17	3p on 1c ocher	4.00	5.00
a.		Inverted surcharge	400.00	
2	A17	½a on 2c grn	4.00	5.00
3	A17	1a on 4c ver	4.00	5.00
4	A17	2a on 7c mar	6.00	7.50
5	A17	2½a on 10c ultra	8.00	10.00
6	A18	3a on 16c ol grn	15.00	20.00
a.		Large "S" in "Annas"	500.00	
7	A18	4a on 20c red brn	15.00	20.00
8	A18	6a on 30c rose red	25.00	30.00
9	A18	12a on 50c yel grn	92.50	92.50
10	A19	1r on $1 red & pale rose	225.00	225.00
11	A19	2r on $2 red & yel	450.00	450.00
		Nos. 1-11 (11)	848.50	870.00

CHINA, PEOPLE'S REPUBLIC OF

LOCATION — Eastern Asia
GOVT. — Communist Republic
POP. — 1,015,400,000 (est. 1983)
CAPITAL — Beijing (Peking)

The communists completed their conquest of all mainland China in 1949. They established the Central Government and General Postal Administration in Peking. They ordered all but two regions to stop selling regional issues by June 30, 1950, extending validity one year from that date. The Northeast and Port Arthur-Dairen regions were exempted because their currency had a different value. These two regions stopped using separate issues at the end of 1950. Thereafter unified issues were used throughout mainland China.

After currency revaluation Mar. 1, 1955, reprints were prepared and put on sale by the Philatelic Agency in order to supply stocks of exhausted issues for collectors. Minor differences in design or paper distinguish the reprints. They are of commemorative and special issues up to the gymnastics set of 1952. Reprints are less expensive. Values are for original issues. Reprint distinctions are footnoted.

Most used stamps before 1970 exist primarily canceled to order. Postally used copies generally sell for ½ the unused value.

Commemorative issues, beginning in 1949, and special issues, beginning in 1951, bear 4 numbers in lower margin: 1. Issue number. 2. Total of stamps in set. 3. Position of stamp in set. 4. Cumulative number of stamp (usually in parenthesis). A fifth number, the year of issue, was added in 1952.

The numbering system varies at times, with all numbers omitted on Nos. 938-1046.

In certain sets listings include parenthetically the position-in-set number. During some periods these parentheses in listings hold the stamp's cumulative number. Issue numbers are noted when one or more designs are not illustrated.

All stamps to the beginning of 1960 were issued without gum, except as noted. After that date, most stamps have gum, which is translucent and almost invisible. All issues are unwatermarked, unless otherwise noted.

100 fen = 1 yuan ($)

Catalogue values for unused stamps in this country are for Never Hinged items, beginning with Scott 487 in the regular postage section, Scott B1 in the semi-postal section.

Lantern and Gate of Heavenly Peace — A1

Globe and Hand Holding Hammer — A2

1949, Oct. 8 **Litho.** ***Perf. 12½***

1	A1	$30 blue		1.25	1.50
2	A1	$50 rose red		1.25	1.50
3	A1	$100 green		1.25	1.50
4	A1	$200 maroon		1.25	1.50
		Nos. 1-4 (4)		5.00	6.00

1st session of Chinese People's Consultative Political Conference. See #1L121-1L124.

Original

Reprint

Reprints have altered ornament on lantern base. On originals, it is a full oval; in reprints, only a partial circle. Value, set, $1.

1949, Nov. 16

5	A2	$100 carmine	2.25	4.50
6	A2	$300 slate green	2.25	4.50
7	A2	$500 dark blue	2.25	4.50
		Nos. 5-7 (3)	6.75	13.50

Asiatic and Australasian Congress of the World Federation of Trade Unions, Peking.
The $100, imperf., is of dubious status.
See Nos. 1L133-1L135.

Original

Reprint

Reprints show heavier shading on index finger and thumb. Value, set $1.

Conference Hall, Peking — A3

Mao Tse-tung on Rostrum — A4

1950, Feb. 1 **Engr.** ***Perf. 14***

8	A3	$50 red	1.75	2.25
9	A3	$100 blue	1.75	2.25
10	A4	$300 red brown	1.75	2.00
11	A4	$500 green	1.75	2.00
		Nos. 8-11 (4)	7.00	8.50

Chinese People's Consultative Political Conference. See Nos. 1L136-1L139.

Original

Reprint

Nos. 8-9: First character in top inscription shows a square, reprints an oblong.
Nos. 10-11: Originals have heavy crosshatching and lines which touch back of head and top of rostrum. Reprints have lighter lines which do not touch head or top of rostrum. Reprints, value set $4.

Gate of Heavenly Peace (same size) — A5

First Issue: Top line of shading broken at right.

1950, Feb. 10 **Litho.** ***Perf. 12½***

12	A5	$200 green	4.00	1.00
13	A5	$300 brn red	15	20
14	A5	$500 red	15	15
15	A5	$800 orange	37.50	18
16	A5	$1000 dull violet	1.00	15
17	A5	$2000 olive	6.00	38
18	A5	$5000 brt pink	15	65
19	A5	$8000 blue	15	2.00
20	A5	$10,000 brown	50	1.00
		Nos. 12-20 (9)	49.60	5.71

1950, June 9 **Typo.**

Second Issue: Top line of shading extends to frame line at right.

21	A5	$1000 dull violet	30	15
22	A5	$3000 red brown	30	15
23	A5	$10,000 brown	30	15
		Nos. 21-23 (3)	90	
		Set value		30

Other Gate of Heavenly Peace issues are illustrated where they are listed. See A10, A13, A14 and A42 for similar designs.

For similar types with Chinese characters in upper right corner see Northeast China A28, A29, Port Arthur & Darien A11, North China A8.

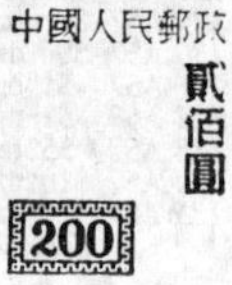

China Nos. 959, C62, E12, F2 Surcharged in Blue, Black, Green or Red

Rouletted, Perf. 12½ (#27, 29)

1950, Mar. **Litho.**

24	SD2	$100 on red vio (Bl)	16	48
a.		Perf. 12½	4.00	2.50
25	R2	$200 on red (Bk)	1.65	40
a.		Perf. 12½	12.50	1.60
26	AP5	$300 on bl grn (Bk)	18	60
a.		Perf. 12½	15	70
27	A96	$500 on orange (Bk)	15	24
a.		Perf. 14	80.00	47.50
28	A96	$800 on orange (R)	1.65	16
a.		Perf. 12½	7.75	60
b.		Perf. 14	80.00	55.00
29	A96	$1000 on orange (Bk)	15	20
a.		Perf. 14	15	16
		Nos. 24-29 (6)	3.94	2.08

No. 27 exists with green surcharge.

Harvesters with Ox — A6

1950, May

30	A6	$20,000 on $10,000 red	325.00	21.00

No. 30 is surcharged on an unissued stamp of East China.

Flag, Mao Tse-tung, Gate of Heavenly Peace — A7

1950, July 1 ***Perf. 14***

Yellow Stars

31	A7	$800 green & red	13.00	2.50
32	A7	$1000 brown & red	13.00	5.00
33	A7	$2000 dk brown & red	13.00	6.00
34	A7	$3000 dk blue & red	13.00	7.00
		Nos. 31-34 (4)	52.00	20.50

Inauguration of the People's Republic, Oct. 1, 1949. See Nos. 1L150-1L153.

Original

Reprint

Originals have a single curved line in jacket button, reprints have an extra dot in button. Value, set $3.

Sun Yat-sen Stamps of Northeastern Provinces Surcharged in Red, Black or Blue

1950, July 1 **Engr.**

35	A2	$50 on 20c yel grn	1.50	4.00
36	A2	$50 on 25c blk brn	2.75	1.75
37	A2	$50 on 50c red org (Bk)	20	50
38	A2	$100 on $2.50 ind	75	50
39	A2	$100 on $3 brn (Bk)	9.00	50
40	A2	$100 on $4 org brn, Type II (Bl)	7.00	2.75
a.		Type I	*150.00*	125.00
41	A2	$100 on $5 dk grn (Bk)	9.00	50
42	A2	$100 on $10 crim, Type II (Bl)	11.00	4.00
a.		Type I	*300.00*	
43	A2	$400 on $20 ol, Type II (Bl)	11.00	4.00
a.		Type I	*150.00*	100.00
44	A2	$400 on $44 dk car rose (Bl)	45	2.50
45	A2	$400 on $65 dl grn	45.00	8.00
46	A2	$400 on $100 dp grn	10.00	2.50
47	A2	$400 on $200 rose brn (Bk)	50.00	3.50
48	A2	$400 on $300 bluish grn	50.00	3.50
		Nos. 35-48 (14)	207.65	38.50

Flying Geese Type of China Surcharged in Red, Blue, Green, Brown or Black

1950, Aug. 1 *Perf. 12½, Imperf.*

49	A97	$50 on 10c dk bl (R)	15	25
50	A97	$100 on 16c ol, imperf. (Bl)	15	25
51	A97	$100 on 50c dl grn, imperf. (Bl)	15	15
52	A97	$200 on $1 org (G)	15	15
53	A97	$200 on $2 bl (Br)	6.00	50
54	A97	$400 on $5 car rose (Bk)	15	25
55	A97	$400 on $10 bl grn (Bk)	15	80
56	A97	$400 on $20 pur (Bk)	20	1.00
		Nos. 49-56 (8)	7.10	3.35

Dove of Peace, by Picasso — A8

Chinese Flag and "1" — A9

1950, Aug. 1 **Engr.** *Perf. 14*

57	A8	$400 brown	4.00	1.00
58	A8	$800 green	4.00	1.00
59	A8	$2000 blue	4.00	1.00
		Nos. 57-59 (3)	12.00	3.00

World Peace Campaign. See Nos. 1L154-1L156.

Paper of originals appears bright under ultraviolet lamp. That of reprints looks dull. Value, set $4.

1950 **Engr. & Litho.**

Flag in Red & Yellow

60	A9	$100 purple	12.00	3.25
61	A9	$400 red brown	12.00	5.50
62	A9	$800 green	12.00	3.25
63	A9	$1000 lt olive	12.00	3.50
64	A9	$2000 blue	12.00	5.50
		Nos. 60-64 (5)	60.00	21.00

First anniversary of the Chinese People's Republic. Size of $800: 38x46mm; others 26x32mm.

Issue dates: No. 62, Oct. 1; others Oct. 31. See Nos. 1L157-1L161.

$800

Original

Reprint

Reprints are a brighter red, leaves beside "1" are gray brown instead of reddish brown. On the $800 the arrangement of dots in background differs in relationship to large star. Value, set $6.50.

Gate of Heavenly Peace (same size) — A10

"Communication" and Map of China — A11

Third Issue: Cloud almost touches character at upper left. Cloud breaks inner frame line at top.

1950 **Litho.**

65	A10	$100 lt grnsh bl	37.50	*7.00*
66	A10	$200 green	165.00	*8.75*
67	A10	$300 dk car	1.50	*3.00*
68	A10	$400 grnsh gray	60	*3.00*
69	A10	$500 carmine	40	*3.25*
70	A10	$800 orange	3.00	24
71	A10	$2000 gray olive	80	40
		Nos. 65-71 (7)	208.80	*25.64*

Issue dates: $800, Oct. 8; $500, $2000, Dec. 1; others, Oct. 6.

1950, Nov. 1 **Litho.**

72	A11	$400 grn & brn	3.50	3.50
73	A11	$800 car & grn	3.50	3.50

First All-China Postal Conference, Peking. See Nos. 1L162-1L163.

Original

Reprint

Originals have 3 lines below horizontal bar below the 2nd character; reprints have four. Value, set $1.25.

Stalin and Mao Tse-tung — A12

1950, Dec. 1 **Engr.** *Perf. 14*

74	A12	$400 red	4.75	4.00
75	A12	$800 dp green	4.75	3.00
76	A12	$2000 dk blue	4.75	4.00
		Nos. 74-76 (3)	14.25	11.00

Signing of Sino-Soviet Treaty of Friendship, Alliance and Mutual Assistance. See Nos. 1L176-1L178.

Paper of originals appears bright under ultraviolet lamp. That of reprints looks dull. Value, set $3.50.

East China Issue of 1949 Surcharged in Red, Black, Brown or Blue

Train and Postal Runner — A12a

1950, Dec. **Litho.** *Perf. 12½*

77	A12a	$50 on $10 dp ultra (R)	15	15
78	A12a	$100 on $15 org ver (Bk)	15	15
a.		$100 on $15 red (Bk), perf. 14	15	15
79	A12a	$300 on $50 car (Bk)	15	15
80	A12a	$400 on $1600 vio bl (Br)	85	15
81	A12a	$400 on $2000 brn vio (Bl)	40	15
		Nos. 77-81 (5)	1.70	
		Set value		49

East China Issue of 1949 Surcharged in Red or Black

Chairman Mao — A12b

1950, Dec.

82	A12b	$50 on $10 ultra (R)	16	15
83	A12b	$400 on $15 ver (Bk)	16	15
84	A12b	$400 on $2000 grn (Bk)	1.25	15
		Nos. 82-84 (3)	1.57	
		Set value		30

(same size) — A13

(same size) — A14

Fourth Issue: Similar to 3rd issue, but large cloud does not break inner frame line at top.

1950-51 **Litho.**

85	A13	$100 lt blue	1.65	50
86	A13	$200 dull green	1.90	50
87	A13	$300 dull lilac	38	*3.50*
88	A13	$400 gray grn	38	50
89	A13	$500 carmine	15	*75*
90	A13	$800 orange	65.00	1.00
a.		Imperf., pair	*2,000.*	
91	A13	$1000 violet	52	50
92	A13	$2000 olive	225.00	2.00
93	A13	$3000 brown	15	*4.00*
94	A13	$5000 pink	15	*4.00*
		Nos. 85-94 (10)	295.28	*17.25*

Issue dates: $200, $300, $500, $800, $2000, $5000, Dec. 22, 1950; others June 8, 1951.

1951, Jan. 18 **Engr.** *Perf. 14*

Fifth Issue: Colored network on surface in salmon.

95	A14	$10,000 brown	1.50	*6.75*
96	A14	$20,000 olive	1.50	*5.50*
97	A14	$30,000 green	20.00	*22.50*
98	A14	$50,000 violet	60.00	11.00
99	A14	$100,000 scarlet	1,750.	110.00
100	A14	$200,000 blue	1,750.	110.00
		Nos. 95-100 (6)	3,583.	265.75

Unit Issue of China Surcharged

中國人民郵政
伍
圓
5

1951, May 2 **Litho.** *Perf. 12½*

101	SD2	$5 on rose lilac	2.25	25
102	AP5	$10 on brt grn	16	15
103	R2	$15 on red	15	15
104	A96	$25 on orange	48	15
		Nos. 101-104 (4)	3.04	
		Set value		49

Issued for use in Northeast China, but available for use throughout China. Nos. 101-104 rouletted were sold for philatelic purposes only. Value, set $1.25.

Chairman Mao Tse-tung — A15

1951, July 1 **Engr.** *Perf. 14*

105	A15	$400 chestnut	3.50	1.25
106	A15	$500 deep green	3.50	1.25
107	A15	$800 crimson	3.50	1.25
		Nos. 105-107 (3)	10.50	3.75

Chinese Communist Party, 30th anniv.

Reprints are on whiter, thinner and harder paper. Value, set $2.50.

Picasso Dove — A16

1951, Aug. 15 *Perf. 12½*

108	A16	$400 orange brn	6.00	1.50
109	A16	$800 blue grn	6.00	90
110	A16	$1000 dull vio	6.00	1.50
		Nos. 108-110 (3)	18.00	3.90

Reprints are perf 14. Value, set $4.50.

Remittance Stamp of China Surcharged in Carmine or Black

(same size) — A17

Engraved, Commercial Press

1951, Sept. *Perf. 12½*

111	A17	$50 on $2 bl grn (C)	20	*75*

Typo., Kang Hwa Printing Co.
Rouletted 9½

112 A17	$50 on $2 gray bl (C)	45	75
113 A17	$50 on $5 red org (Bk)	15	*75*
114 A17	$50 on $50 gray (C)	4.50	75

Lithographed, Central Trust Co.
Perf. 13

115 A17	$50 on $50 gray blk (C)	15	*75*

Lithographed, Chung Hwa Book Co.
Perf. 11½

116 A17	$50 on $50 gray (C)	1.65	75
	Nos. 111-116 (6)	7.10	4.50

National Emblem — A18

Engraved; Background Network Lithographed in Yellow

1951, Oct. 1 ***Perf. 14***

117 A18	$100 Prus bl	5.00	1.65
118 A18	$200 brown	5.00	1.25
119 A18	$400 orange	5.00	1.65
120 A18	$500 green	5.00	1.25
121 A18	$800 carmine	5.00	1.25
	Nos. 117-121 (5)	25.00	7.05

Reprints exist but difficult to distinguish; paper whiter, and colors slightly brighter. Value, set $2.

Rough Perfs

Rough perforations are normal on many early issues. These include Nos. 122-123, 136-140, 155-176, 239-240, 299-300, 453-456, 467-482, 629-634, 684-707, 737-745 and probably others.

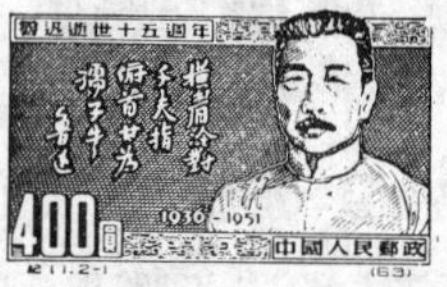

Lu Hsun and Quotation A19

1951, Oct. 19 **Litho.** ***Perf. 12½***

122 A19	$400 lilac	3.50	2.25
123 A19	$800 green	3.50	2.25

15th anniversary of the death of Lu Hsun (1881-1936), writer.

Original

Reprint

Reprints have dot in triangle at lower right; no dot in original. Value, set, 75 cents.

Peasant Uprising, Chintien — A20

Design: Nos. 126-127, Coin of Taiping Regime and decrees of peasant government.

1951, Dec. 15 **Engr.** ***Perf. 14***

124 A20	$400 green	5.25	1.65
125 A20	$800 scarlet	5.25	1.65
126 A20	$800 orange	5.25	1.65
127 A20	$1000 dp blue	5.25	2.50
	Nos. 124-127 (4)	21.00	7.45

Centenary of Taiping Peasant Rebellion.

Original

Reprint

Reprints of Nos. 124-125 have additional short stroke at upper left.

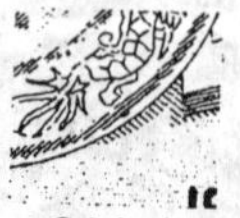

Original

Reprint

Reprints of Nos. 126-127 have two short strokes on scale near tail of right dragon on coin. Value, Nos. 124-127, $1.50.

Old and New Methods of Agriculture A21

1952, Jan. 1

128 A21	$100 scarlet	3.00	2.50
129 A21	$200 bright blue	3.00	2.50
130 A21	$400 deep brown	3.00	1.65
131 A21	$800 green	3.00	1.65
	Nos. 128-131 (4)	12.00	8.30

Agrarian reform.

Original

Reprint

One short horizontal line between legs of plower; 2 lines in reprints. Value, set $1.25.

Potala Monastery, Lhasa — A22

Designs: Nos. 134-135, Farmer plowing with yaks.

1952, Mar. 15 ***Perf. 12½***

132 A22	$400 vermilion	4.00	2.50
133 A22	$800 claret	4.00	2.50
134 A22	$800 bl grn	4.00	1.65
135 A22	$1000 dl vio	4.00	1.65
	Nos. 132-135 (4)	16.00	8.30

Liberation of Tibet.

Reprints, perf 14, have a small Chinese character at lower left of the vignette which is missing in the original. Value, set $1.50.

Children of Four Races — A23

Hammer and Sickle on Numeral 1 — A24

1952, Apr. 12 **Litho.**

136 A23	$400 dull grn	24	15
137 A23	$800 vio blue	24	15
	Set value		15

Intl. Child Protection Conf., Vienna.

1952, May 1

Labor Day: No. 139, Dove rising from worker's hand. No. 140, Dove, hammer, wheat and chimneys.

138 A24	$800 scarlet	15	15
139 A24	$800 blue grn	15	15
140 A24	$800 orange brn	35	15
	Nos. 138-140 (3)	65	
	Set value		15

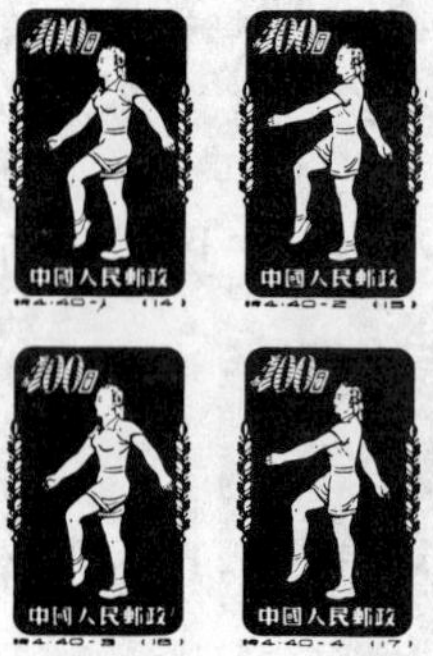

Physical Exercises — A25

Stamps printed in blocks of four for each color, each block representing a specific setting-up exercise; exercises coincided with a national radio program. Where exercise positions are identical within the block, the serial number (in parenthesis) is the only means of differentiation.

1952, June 20

141 A25	Block of 4	22.50	22.50
a.	$400 vermilion (1)	3.00	1.00
b.	$400 vermilion (2)	3.00	1.00
c.	$400 vermilion (3)	3.00	1.00
d.	$400 vermilion (4)	3.00	1.00
142 A25	Block of 4	22.50	22.50
a.	$400 blue (5)	3.00	1.00
b.	$400 blue (6)	3.00	1.00
c.	$400 blue (7)	3.00	1.00
d.	$400 blue (8)	3.00	1.00
143 A25	Block of 4	22.50	22.50
a.	$400 brown red (9)	3.00	1.00
b.	$400 brown red (10)	3.00	1.00
c.	$400 brown red (11)	3.00	1.00
d.	$400 brown red (12)	3.00	1.00
144 A25	Block of 4	22.50	22.50
a.	$400 yellow green (13)	3.00	1.00
b.	$400 yellow green (14)	3.00	1.00
c.	$400 yellow green (15)	3.00	1.00
d.	$400 yellow green (16)	3.00	1.00
145 A25	Block of 4	22.50	22.50
a.	$400 red orange (17)	3.00	1.00
b.	$400 red orange (18)	3.00	1.00
c.	$400 red orange (19)	3.00	1.00
d.	$400 red orange (20)	3.00	1.00
146 A25	Block of 4	22.50	22.50
a.	$400 dull blue (21)	3.00	1.00
b.	$400 dull blue (22)	3.00	1.00
c.	$400 dull blue (23)	3.00	1.00
d.	$400 dull blue (24)	3.00	1.00
147 A25	Block of 4	22.50	22.50
a.	$400 orange (25)	3.00	1.00
b.	$400 orange (26)	3.00	1.00
c.	$400 orange (27)	3.00	1.00
d.	$400 orange (28)	3.00	1.00
148 A25	Block of 4	22.50	22.50
a.	$400 dull purple (29)	3.00	1.00
b.	$400 dull purple (30)	3.00	1.00
c.	$400 dull purple (31)	3.00	1.00
d.	$400 dull purple (32)	3.00	1.00
149 A25	Block of 4	22.50	22.50
a.	$400 yellow bister (33)	3.00	1.00
b.	$400 yellow bister (34)	3.00	1.00
c.	$400 yellow bister (35)	3.00	1.00
d.	$400 yellow bister (36)	3.00	1.00
150 A25	Block of 4	22.50	22.50
a.	$400 sky blue (37)	3.00	1.00
b.	$400 sky blue (38)	3.00	1.00
c.	$400 sky blue (39)	3.00	1.00
d.	$400 sky blue (40)	3.00	1.00
	Nos. 141-150 (10)	225.00	225.00

Originals are on thin gray paper, colors darker. Reprints on thicker white paper, colors brighter. Value, set $13.

Hunting, Wei Dynasty, A.D. 386-580 A26

Designs from Murals in Cave Temples at Tunhuang, Kansu Province: No. 152, Lady attendants, Sui Dynasty, 581-617 A.D. No. 153, Gandharvas (mythology), Tang Dynasty, 618-906. No. 154, Dragon, Tang Dynasty.

1952, July 1 **Engr.**

151 A26	$800 slate green (1)	28	25
152 A26	$800 chocolate (2)	28	25
153 A26	$800 indigo (3)	28	25
154 A26	$800 dk vio (4)	28	25
	Nos. 151-154 (4)	1.12	1.00

"Glorious Mother Country," 1st series.

Marco Polo Bridge, near Peking A27

Designs: No. 156, Cavalry passing through Great Wall. No. 157, Departure of New Fourth Army. No. 158, Mao Tse-tung and Gen. Chu Teh planning counter-attack.

1952, July 7 **Litho.** ***Perf. 14***

155 A27	$800 brt blue	25	22
156 A27	$800 blue grn	50	45
157 A27	$800 plum	25	22
158 A27	$800 scarlet	15	15
	Nos. 155-158 (4)	1.15	1.04

15th anniversary of war against Japan.

Soldier and Tanks — A28

Designs: No. 159, Soldier, sailor and airman, vert. No. 161, Sailor and warships. No. 162, Airman and planes.

1952, Aug. 1 **Engr.** ***Perf. 12½***

159 A28	$800 carmine	26	18
160 A28	$800 deep green	52	35
161 A28	$800 purple	26	18
162 A28	$800 orange brown	26	18
	Nos. 159-162 (4)	1.30	89

25th anniv. of People's Liberation Army.

Huai River Sluice Dam A29

Designs: No. 164, Train on the Chengtu-Chungking Railway. No. 165, Oil refinery and derricks in the Northwest. No. 166, Mechanized state farm.

1952, Oct. 1 ***Perf. 14***

163 A29	$800 dk violet	26	15
164 A29	$800 red	26	15
165 A29	$800 dk vio brn	26	15
166 A29	$800 dp green	26	15
	Nos. 163-166 (4)	1.04	60

"Glorious Mother Country," 2nd series.

Doves and Globe A30

Designs: Nos. 167-168, Picasso dove over Pacific, vert. $2500, as No. 169.

1952, Oct. 2 *Perf. 14*

167	A30	$400	maroon	24	24
168	A30	$800	red	24	24
169	A30	$800	brown orange	24	24
170	A30	$2500	deep green	48	48
			Nos. 167-170 (4)	1.20	1.20

Peace Conf. of the Asian and Pacific Regions.

Volunteers on the March A31

Designs: No. 172, Chinese peasants loading supplies. No. 173, Volunteers attacking across river. No. 174, Meeting of Chinese and Korean troops.

1952, Oct. 25

171	A31	$800	blue green (1)	20	15
172	A31	$800	vermilion (2)	20	15
173	A31	$800	violet (3)	30	20
174	A31	$800	lake brown (4)	38	25
			Nos. 171-174 (4)	1.08	75

2nd anniv. of Chinese Volunteers in Korea.

Woman Textile Worker A32

Design: No. 176, Farm woman with sickle.

1953, Mar. 10

175	A32	$800	carmine	22	16
176	A32	$800	emerald	26	18

International Women's Day.

Textile Worker — A33

Karl Marx — A34

Designs: $200, Shepherdess. $250, Stone lion. $800, Lathe operator. $1600, Coal miners. $2000, Corner tower of Forbidden City, Peking.

1953 Litho. *Perf. 14, 12½ ($250)*

177	A33	$50	magenta	35	18
178	A33	$200	emerald	18	15
179	A33	$250	ultra	2.50	1.10
180	A33	$800	blue grn	15	15
181	A33	$1600	gray	35	18
182	A33	$2000	red org	15	15
			Nos. 177-182 (6)	3.68	1.91

Issue dates: Nos. 177-181, Mar. 25; No. 182, May 23.

1953, May 20 Engr. *Perf. 14*

183	A34	$400	dk brown	28	15
184	A34	$800	slate grn	48	26

135th anniv. of the birth of Karl Marx.

Workers and Banners — A35

1953, June 25

185	A35	$400	Prus blue	35	15
186	A35	$800	carmine	24	15

7th All-China Trade Union Congress.

Picasso Dove — A36

1953, July 25

187	A36	$250	blue grn	40	15
188	A36	$400	org brn	20	15
189	A36	$800	purple	30	15
			Nos. 187-189 (3)	90	45

World Peace.

Groom, Wei Dynasty, 386-580 A37

Scenes from Tunhuang Murals: No. 191, Court Players, Wei Dynasty. No. 192, Battle Scene, Sui Dynasty, 581-617. No. 193, Ox-drawn palanquin, Tang Dynasty, 618-906.

1953, Sept. 1

190	A37	$800	dp green (1)	65	15
191	A37	$800	red org (2)	15	15
192	A37	$800	Prus blue (3)	32	15
193	A37	$800	car (4)	15	15
			Nos. 190-193 (4)	1.27	60

"Glorious Mother Country," 3rd series.

Stalin and Mao on Kremlin Terrace A38

Statue of Stalin at Volga-Don Canal — A39

Designs: No. 195, Lenin proclaiming Soviet power. No. 197, Stalin as orator.

1953, Oct. 5

194	A38	$800	green (1)	75	30
195	A38	$800	carmine (2)	32	15
196	A39	$800	brt blue (3)	30	15
197	A39	$800	org brn (4)	24	15
			Nos. 194-197 (4)	1.61	75

35th anniversary of the Russian October Revolution.

Stamps in same designs with two additional characters meaning "Soviet" in the single-line Chinese inscription, and in different colors, were unofficially released at several small post offices in Hunan, Fukien and Canton areas in February, 1953, but were withdrawn after only a small number had been sold. Value, set $3,500 unused, $2,000 canceled.

Compass, 3rd Century B.C. — A40

Designs: No. 199, Seismoscope, later Han Dynasty. No. 200, Drum cart to measure distance, Chin Dynasty. No. 201, Armillary sphere, Ming Dynasty.

1953, Dec. 1

198	A40	$800	indigo (1)	45	15
199	A40	$800	dk green (2)	15	15
200	A40	$800	dk blue (3)	26	15
201	A40	$800	choc (4)	26	15
			Nos. 198-201 (4)	1.12	60

Major inventions by ancient and medieval Chinese scientists.
"Glorious Mother Country," 4th series.

Francois Rabelais — A41

(same size) Gate of Heavenly Peace — A42

Designs: $400, Jose Marti, Cuban revolutionary. $800, Chu Yuan (350-275 B.C.), philosopher. $2200, Nicolaus Copernicus, astronomer.

1953, Dec. 30

202	A41	$250	slate grn (3)	25	20
203	A41	$400	brown blk (4)	25	20
204	A41	$800	indigo (1)	25	20
205	A41	$2200	choc (2)	25	20
			Nos. 202-205 (4)	1.00	80

1954, Apr. 16 **Litho.**

Sixth Issue: Inscription at upper right.

206	A42	$50	carmine	15	15
207	A42	$100	lt blue	15	15
208	A42	$200	green	15	15
209	A42	$250	ultra	1.25	15
210	A42	$400	gray grn	15	15
211	A42	$800	orange	15	15
212	A42	$1600	gray	15	*65*
213	A42	$2000	olive	15	*32*
			Set value	2.00	

Textile Plant, Harbin — A43

Lenin — A44

Designs: $200, Tangku Harbor. $250, Tienshui-Lanchow railroad bridge, Kansu Province. $400, Heavy machine-building plant, Taiyuan, Shansi. No. 218, Automatic blast, furnace, Anshan, Manchuria. No. 219, Fushun open-cut coal mine. $2000, Automatic power plant, Northeast. $3200, Prospecting in Tayeh district, Hupeh.

1954, May 1 **Engr.**

214	A43	$100	brown olive	26	15
215	A43	$200	blue green	26	15
216	A43	$250	violet	15	15
217	A43	$400	black	26	15
218	A43	$800	claret	15	15
219	A43	$800	indigo	15	15
220	A43	$2000	red	15	15
221	A43	$3200	dark brown	40	40
			Nos. 214-221 (8)	1.78	
			Set value		1.30

Economic progress.

1954, June 30 **Engr.**

Designs: $400, Lenin and Stalin Monument, Gorki, horiz. $2000, Lenin proclaiming Soviet power.

222	A44	$400	deep green	22	20
223	A44	$800	dark brown	15	15
224	A44	$2000	deep carmine	85	30
			Nos. 222-224 (3)	1.22	65

30th anniversary of the death of Lenin.

Pottery Vessels, Neolithic Period, 2000 B. C. — A45

Archeological Treasures: No. 226, Stone clime, Shang Dynasty, c. 1200 B.C. No. 227, Kuo Chi Tsu-pai bronze basin, Middle Chou Dynasty, 816 B.C. No. 228, Lacquered box and wine cup, Warring States Period, 403-221 B.C.

1954, Aug. 25

225	A45	$800	brown	26	16
226	A45	$800	indigo	26	16
227	A45	$800	Prus bl	26	16
228	A45	$800	dk car	26	16
			Nos. 225-228 (4)	1.04	64

"Glorious Mother Country," 5th series.

Pipe Production, Anshan Steel Mill — A46

Stalin Statue, by Tomsky — A47

Design: $800, Rolling mill, Anshan.

1954, Oct. 1

229	A46	$400	Prus green	52	20
230	A46	$800	vio brown	52	20

1954, Oct. 15

Designs: $800, Stalin portrait. $2000, Stalin viewing hydroelectric plant.

Size: 21x45mm

231	A47	$400	black	95	30

Size: 26x37mm

232	A47	$800	black brn	22	15

Size: 42x26mm

233	A47	$2000	dp red	22	15
			Nos. 231-233 (3)	1.39	60

First anniversary of the death of Stalin.

Exhibition Building, Peking — A48

1954, Nov. 7

234	A48	$800 brown, *cream*	7.00	3.00
a.		Size: 53½x24mm	10.00	3.00

Russian Economic and Cultural Exhibition, Peking. No. 234 measures 52½x24½mm.

Apprentices and Lathe — A49

Progress in Technology: $800, Heavy machinery and workers.

1954, Dec. 15

235	A49	$400	dk olive grn	24	15
236	A49	$800	brt red	16	15

Woman Worker Voting — A50

People Celebrating Opening of Congress — A51

1954, Dec. 30

237	A50	$400 deep claret	15	15
238	A51	$800 bright red	38	22
		Set value	48	30

First National Congress.

Flags, Worker and Woman Holding Constitution — A52

1954, Dec. 30

239	A52	$400 brown, *buff*	20	15
240	A52	$800 brt red, *yel*	20	15

Adoption of Constitution.

High-tension Pylon — A53

1955, Feb. 25

241	A53	$800 dk Prus bl	50	18

Development of electric power.

Factory Health Workers and Red Cross — A54

1955, June 25 **Engr.; Cross Typo.**

242	A54	8f dp grn & red	7.00	1.00

50th anniversary of Chinese Red Cross.

Stalin and Mao in Kremlin A55

Soviet Specialist and Chinese Worker — A56

1955, July 25 **Engr.**

243	A55	8f brown red	6.00	42
244	A56	20f olive blk	6.00	1.50

5th anniv. of Sino-Soviet Friendship Treaty.

Chang Heng (78-139), Astronomer — A57

Portraits of Scientists: No. 246, Tsu Chung-chih (429-500), mathematician. No. 247, Chang Sui (683-727), astronomer. No. 248, Li Shih-chen (1518-1593), physician and pharmacologist.

1955, Aug. 25 ***Perf. 14***

245	A57	8f sepia, *buff*	1.10	26
a.		Min. sheet, sepia, *white*	12.50	2.75
246	A57	8f dp grn, *buff*	1.10	26
a.		Min. sheet, deep green, *white*	12.50	2.75
247	A57	8f black, *buff*	1.10	26
a.		Min. sheet, blk, *white*	12.50	2.75
248	A57	8f claret, *buff*	1.10	26
a.		Min. sheet, claret, *white*	12.50	2.75
		Nos. 245-248 (4)	4.40	1.04

Miniature sheets contain one imperf. stamp.

Steel Pouring Ladle A58

1955-56 **Litho.**

Position-in-set number in ( )

249	A58	8f shown (1)	38	15
250	A58	8f High tension line (2)	38	15
251	A58	8f Mechanized coal mining (3)	38	15
252	A58	8f Tank cars and derricks (4)	38	15
253	A58	8f Heavy machine shop (5)	38	15
254	A58	8f Soldier on guard (6)	38	15
255	A58	8f Spinning machine (7)	38	15
256	A58	8f Workers discussing 5-year plan (8)	38	15
257	A58	8f Combine harvester (9)	38	15
258	A58	8f Milk production (10)	38	15
259	A58	8f Dam (11)	38	15
260	A58	8f Pottery industry (12) ('56)	38	15
261	A58	8f Truck (13)	38	15
262	A58	8f Ship at dock (14)	38	15
263	A58	8f Geological survey (15)	38	15
264	A58	8f Higher education (16)	38	15
265	A58	8f Family (17)	38	15
266	A58	8f Workers' rest home (18) ('56)	38	15
		Nos. 249-266 (18)	6.84	
		Set value		2.25

1st 5 Year Plan. Issued: #249-257, Oct. 1; #258-259, 261-265, Dec. 15; #260, 266, Feb. 24, 1956.

Lenin — A59

Engels — A60

1955, Dec. 15 **Engr.** ***Perf. 14***

267	A59	8f dk blue grn	5.50	25
268	A59	20f dk rose car	5.50	2.25

85th anniversary of the birth of Lenin.

1955, Dec. 15

269	A60	8f deep orange	5.50	25
270	A60	20f brown	5.50	2.25

135th anniversary of the birth of Friedrich Engels (1820-1895), German socialist.

Storming Lu Ting Bridge A61

Crossing Great Snow Mountains — A62

1955, Dec. 30

271	A61	8f dark red	4.75	38
272	A62	8f dark blue	4.75	1.65

Long March of Chinese Communist army, 20th anniversary.

Miner A63

Gate of Heavenly Peace A64

Designs: 1f, Machinist. 2f, Airman. 2½f, Nurse. 4f, Soldier. 8f, Steel worker. 10f, Scientist. 20f, Farm woman. 50f, Sailor.

1955-56 **Litho.** ***Perf. 14***

273	A63	½f orange brn	4.50	25
274	A63	1f purple	4.50	26
275	A63	2f green	4.50	15
276	A63	2½f blue ('56)	4.50	15
277	A63	4f gray olive	4.50	26
278	A63	8f red org (Peking printing)	4.50	95
a.		Perf. 12½ (Shanghai printing)	140.00	8.00
279	A63	10f claret ('56)	35.00	15
280	A63	20f dp blue	7.00	15
281	A63	50f gray	7.00	15
		Nos. 273-281 (9)	76.00	2.47

Engr.

282	A64	$1 claret ('56)	1.00	26
283	A64	$2 sepia ('55)	1.75	26
284	A64	$5 indigo ('56)	3.00	42
285	A64	$10 dp org ('56)	9.00	4.25
286	A64	$20 gray vio ('56)	15.00	17.00
		Nos. 282-286 (5)	29.75	22.19

Nos. 282-286 are the 7th Gate Issue.

Trucks, Mountains, Highway Map — A65

Suspension Bridge over Tatu River — A66

Design: No. 289, First truck arriving in Lhasa, and the Potala.

1956, Mar. 10 **Engr.**

287	A65	4f dp blue	50	16
288	A66	8f dk brown	50	16
289	A65	8f carmine	50	16
		Nos. 287-289 (3)	1.50	48

Completion of Sikang-Tibet and Chinghai-Tibet Highways.

Summer Palace and Marble Boat — A67

Famous Views of Imperial Peking: No. 291, Peihai Park with Jade Belt Marble Bridge. No. 292, Gate of Heavenly Peace. No. 293, Temple of Heaven. No. 294, Great Throne Hall, Forbidden City.

1956-57

290	A67	4f car rose (1)	1.00	22
291	A67	4f bl grn (2)	1.00	22
292	A67	8f red org (3) ('57)	1.00	22
293	A67	8f Prus bl (4)	1.00	22
294	A67	8f yel brn (5)	1.00	22
		Nos. 290-294 (5)	5.00	1.10

Issue dates: No. 292, Feb. 20, 1957; others, June 15, 1956.

No. 292 exists with sun rays in background.

Salt Making A68

Designs: No. 296, Dwelling of the Eastern Han period. No. 297, Duck hunting and harvesting. No. 298, Carriage crossing bridge.

1956, Oct. 1

295	A68	4f gray olive	25	15
296	A68	4f slate blue	25	15
297	A68	8f gray brown	25	15
298	A68	8f sepia	25	15
		Nos. 295-298 (4)	1.00	
		Set value		50

Murals, Tung Han Dynasty, 250 B.C.-220 A.D., found near Chengtu.

Ancient Coins and "Save" — A69

1956, Oct. 1

299	A69	4f yellow brown	5.00	70
300	A69	8f rose red	5.00	70

Promotion of saving.

Gate of Heavenly Peace — A70

Sun Yat-sen — A71

1956, Nov. 10

301 A70	4f dk green	3.00	50
302 A70	8f brt red	3.00	50
303 A70	16f dk carmine	3.00	1.00
	Nos. 301-303 (3)	9.00	2.00

8th National Congress of the Communist Party of China.

1956, Nov. 12

304 A71	4f brown, *cream*	6.00	15
305 A71	8f dp blue, *cream*	6.00	1.40

90th anniversary of birth of Sun Yat-sen.

Weight Lifting — A72

1957, Mar. 20 Litho. *Perf. 12½*

Hibiscus red and green; inscription brown

306 A72	4f Shot put (2)	70	18
307 A72	4f shown (5)	70	18
308 A72	8f Track (1)	70	18
309 A72	8f Soccer (3)	70	18
310 A72	8f Bicycling (4)	70	18
	Nos. 306-310 (5)	3.50	90

First National Workers' Sports Meeting.

Truck Factory No. 1, Changchun — A73

China's truck industry: 8f, Trucks rolling off assembly line.

1957, May 1 Engr. *Perf. 14*

311 A73	4f light brown	25	20
312 A73	8f slate green	25	20

Nanchang Uprising — A74

Designs: No. 314, Mao and Chu Teh at Chingkanshan. No. 315, Crossing Yellow River. No. 316, Liberation of Nanking, Apr. 23, 1949.

1957

313 A74	4f blk vio (1)	3.25	90
314 A74	4f slate grn (2)	3.25	1.50
315 A74	8f red brn (3)	3.25	60
316 A74	8f dp blue (4)	3.25	60
	Nos. 313-316 (4)	13.00	3.60

30th anniversary of People's Liberation Army. Issue dates: Nos. 313, 315, Aug. 10; No. 314, Aug. 30; No. 316, Dec. 30.

Congress Emblem — A75

1957, Sept. 30

317 A75	8f chocolate	3.50	42
318 A75	22f indigo	3.50	75

4th International Trade Union Congress, Leipzig, Oct. 4-15.

Yangtze River Bridge A76

Design: 20f, Road leading to and over bridge.

1957, Oct. 1

319 A76	8f scarlet	50	26
320 A76	20f slate blue	50	15

Completion of Yangtze River Bridge at Wuhan.

Fireworks over Kremlin — A77

Designs: 8f, Hammer and sickle over globe and broken chain. 20f, Stylized dove and olive branch. 22f, Hands of three races holding book with Marx and Lenin. 32f, Star and pylon.

1957, Nov. 7

321 A77	4f brt red	4.00	40
322 A77	8f chocolate	4.00	40
323 A77	20f dp green	4.00	40
324 A77	22f red brown	4.00	40
325 A77	32f dp blue	4.00	2.50
	Nos. 321-325 (5)	20.00	4.10

40th anniv. of Russian October Revolution.

Map of Yellow River Basin A78

Designs: No. 327, Sanmen Gorge dam and powerhouse. No. 328, Ocean liner on Yellow River. No. 329, Dam, irrigation canals and tree-bordered fields.

1957, Dec. 30

326 A78	4f deep orange (1)	3.75	1.50
327 A78	4f deep blue (2)	3.75	1.90
328 A78	8f deep lake (3)	3.75	75
329 A78	8f blue green (4)	3.75	75
	Nos. 326-329 (4)	15.00	4.90

Yellow River control plan.

Old Man and Young Drummer A79

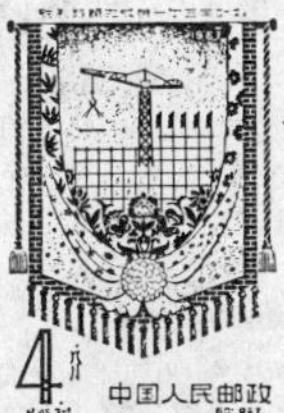

Crane, Dove and Flowers A80

1957, Dec. 30 Litho.

330 A79	8f shown (1)	38	22
331 A79	8f Plowman (2)	38	15
332 A79	8f Woman planting tree (3)	38	15
333 A79	8f Harvest (4)	38	15
	Nos. 330-333 (4)	1.52	
	Set value		55

Agricultural cooperation.

1958, Jan. 30 Engr.

Designs (Congratulatory Banner and): 8f, Crane with hot ingots, cotton bolls and wheat. 16f, Train on bridge, ship and plane.

334 A80	4f emer, *cream*	25	15
335 A80	8f red, *cream*	25	22
336 A80	16f ultra, *cream*	25	15
	Nos. 334-336 (3)	75	
	Set value		45

Fulfillment of First Five-Year Plan.

Sungyu Pagoda, Honan — A81

Trilobite, Kaoli — A82

Ancient Pagodas: No. 338, Chienhsun Pagoda, Yunnan. No. 339, Sakyamuni Pagoda, Shansi. No. 340, Flying Rainbow Pagoda, Shansi.

1958, Mar. 15 Engr.

337 A81	8f sepia (1)	50	15
338 A81	8f Prus blue (2)	50	15
339 A81	8f maroon (3)	50	15
340 A81	8f dp green (4)	50	28
	Nos. 337-340 (4)	2.00	73

1958, Apr. 15

Designs: 8f, Lufeng dinosaur. 16f, Choukoutien sino-megaceros.

341 A82	4f black	26	16
342 A82	8f sepia	26	24
343 A82	16f slate green	26	16
	Nos. 341-343 (3)	78	56

Prehistoric animals of China.

Heroes Monument A83

1958, May 1

344 A83	8f scarlet	8.00	1.40
a.	Souvenir sheet, imperf.	57.50	30.00

Unveiling of People's Heroes Monument, Peking. No. 344a issued May 30.

Karl Marx — A84

Cogwheels and Factories — A85

Design: 22f, Marx Speaking to German Workers' Educational Association, London, painting by Zhukow.

1958, May 5

345 A84	8f chocolate	6.00	1.00
346 A84	22f dk green	6.00	2.00

140th anniversary of the birth of Karl Marx (1818-1883).

1958, May 25

347 A85	4f brt grnsh bl	5.00	*3.25*
348 A85	8f red lilac	5.00	75

8th All-China Trade Union Cong., Peking.

Dove over Globe — A86

Mother and Child — A87

1958, June 1

349 A86	8f vio blue	5.00	24
350 A86	20f blue grn	5.00	3.00

4th Congress of the Intl. Democratic Women's Federation, Vienna, June 1958.

1958, June 1 Litho.

Children's Day: No. 352, Watering sunflowers. No. 353, Playing hide-and-seek. No. 354, Sailing toy boat.

351 A87	8f green & multi (1)	4.50	1.00
352 A87	8f green & multi (2)	4.50	1.00
353 A87	8f green & multi (3)	4.50	1.00
354 A87	8f green & multi (4)	4.50	1.00
	Nos. 351-354 (4)	18.00	4.00

Kuan Han-ching — A88

Designs (Operas): 4f, "Dream of Butterflies." 20f, "The Riverside Pavilion."

1958, June 20 Engr.

355 A88	4f indigo, *cr*	9.25	*2.25*
356 A88	8f brown, *cr*	9.25	42
357 A88	20f black, *cr*	9.25	60
a.	Souvenir sheet of 3, *ivory*	125.00	70.00
	Nos. 355-357 (3)	27.75	*3.27*

700th anniversary of publication of works of Kuan Han-ching (1210-1280), dramatist. No. 357a contains 3 imperf. stamps similar to Nos. 355-357. Size: 130x100mm. Issued June 28.

Planetarium A89

Design: 20f, Telescope and stars over Peking.

1958, June 25

358 A89	8f dk green	5.00	90
359 A89	20fr indigo	5.00	2.00

First Chinese planetarium, Peking.

Marx and Engels — A90

Wild Goose and Broadcasting Tower — A91

Design: 8f, Cover of first edition of the Communist Manifesto.

1958, July 1

360	A90	4f dk red vio	6.50	2.25
361	A90	8f Prus blue	6.50	20

110th anniversary of publication of the Communist Manifesto.

1958, July 10

362	A91	4f ultra	4.50	32
363	A91	8f dp green	4.50	1.10

1st Conference of the Ministers of Posts and Telecommunications of Socialist Countries, Moscow, Dec. 3-17, 1957.

Peony and Doves — A92

Bronze Weather Vane — A93

Designs: 8f, Olive branch with ribbon and clouds. 22f, Atomic energy symbol over factories.

1958, July 20

364	A92	4f red	7.00	1.00
365	A92	8f green	7.00	7.00
366	A92	22f red brown	7.00	3.00
		Nos. 364-366 (3)	21.00	11.00

Congress for Disarmament and International Cooperation, Stockholm, July 17-22.

1958, Aug. 25

Designs: No. 368, Weather balloon. No. 369, Typhoon tower and weather map of Asia.

367	A93	8f yel bis & blk (1)	30	16
368	A93	8f blue & blk (2)	30	16
369	A93	8f brt grn & blk (3)	30	16
		Nos. 367-369 (3)	90	48

Meteorological services in ancient and modern China.

"5" Encircling IUS Emblem — A94

1958, Sept. 4

370	A94	8f rose lilac	5.50	42
371	A94	22f dp blue grn	5.50	1.00

5th Congress of the International Union of Students, Peking, Sept. 4-13.

Telegraph Building, Peking — A95

1958, Sept. 29

372	A95	4f greenish black	1.00	18
373	A95	8f rose red	1.00	18

Opening of Telegraph Building, Peking.

Exhibition Emblem and Exhortation — A96

Designs: No. 375, Dragon over clouds signifying "aiming high." No. 376, Flying horses, signifying "great leap forward" in production.

1958, Oct. 1

374	A96	8f slate grn (1)	4.50	22
375	A96	8f rose car (2)	4.50	22
376	A96	8f red brown (3)	4.50	1.00
		Nos. 374-376 (3)	13.50	1.44

National Exhibition of Industry and Communications, Peking.

Worker and Excavator A97

Design: 8f, Completed dam and pylon.

1958, Oct. 25

377	A97	4f dk brown	20	15
378	A97	8f dp Prus blue	22	15

13 Ming Tombs Reservoir completion.

Sputnik over Armillary Sphere — A98

Designs: 8f, Sputnik 3 in orbit. 10f, Trajectories of 3 Sputniks over earth.

1958, Oct. 30

379	A98	4f scarlet	2.50	35
380	A98	8f dp vio bl	2.50	35
381	A98	10f dp grn	2.50	2.00
		Nos. 379-381 (3)	7.50	2.70

Anniversary of first earth satellite launched by the USSR.

Chinese and North Korean Soldiers A99

Designs: No. 383, Chinese soldier embracing Korean woman. No. 384, Chinese girl presenting flowers to returning soldier.

1958, Nov. 20

382	A99	8f brt purple (1)	40	28
383	A99	8f chestnut (2)	40	15
384	A99	8f rose car (3)	40	15
		Nos. 382-384 (3)	1.20	
		Set value		50

Return of the Chinese Volunteers from Korea.

Forest and Mountains A100

Peony A101

Afforestation: No. 386, Mounted forest patrol. No. 387, Mechanized lumbering, horiz. No. 388, Tree-planting: "Turning the Country Green," horiz.

1958, Dec. 15

385	A100	8f dp blue grn (1)	1.25	55
386	A100	8f slate grn (2)	1.25	18
387	A100	8f dk purple (3)	1.25	18
388	A100	8f indigo (4)	1.25	38
		Nos. 385-388 (4)	5.00	1.29

1958, Sept. 25 **Litho.**

Designs: 3f, Lotus. 5f, Chrysanthemums.

389	A101	1½f lilac rose	4.00	28
390	A101	3f blue grn	4.00	90
391	A101	5f dp orange	4.00	15
		Nos. 389-391 (3)	12.00	1.33

Atomic Reactor A102

1958, Dec. 30 **Engr.**

392	A102	8f shown	4.50	*3.00*
393	A102	20f Cyclotron	4.50	48

Inauguration of China's first atomic reactor and cyclotron, Peking.

Children Launching Model Planes — A103

Camel Carrying Load — A104

Designs: 8f, Gliders over trees. 10f, Parachutists descending. 20f, Small monoplanes in mid-air.

1958, Dec. 30

394	A103	4f carmine	45	22
395	A103	8f dp slate grn	45	15
396	A103	10f dk brown	45	15
397	A103	20f Prus blue	45	15
		Nos. 394-397 (4)	1.80	
		Set value		55

Sports-aviation publicity.

1959, Jan. 1

Designs: No. 399, Pomegranates. No. 400, Rooster. No. 401, Theatrical figure.

398	A104	8f vio & blk (1)	3.50	15
399	A104	8f dp bl grn & blk (2)	3.50	60
400	A104	8f red & blk (3)	3.50	60
401	A104	8f dp bl & blk (4)	3.50	1.65
		Nos. 398-401 (4)	14.00	3.00

Paper cut-outs (folk art).

Red Flag, Mao and Workers — A105

Women Workers and Atomic Model — A106

Designs: 8f, Traditional and modern blast furnaces. 10f, Steel works and workers.

1959

402	A105	4f brt red	4.50	42
403	A105	8f lake	4.50	42
404	A105	10f deep red	4.50	42
		Nos. 402-404 (3)	13.50	1.26

"Great Leap Forward" in steel production. Issue dates: 4f, 8f, Feb. 19; 10f, May 25.

1959, Mar. 8

Design: 22f, Chinese and Soviet women holding banners dated "3.8".

405	A106	8f emerald, *cr*	45	30
406	A106	22f magenta, *cr*	45	15

International Women's Day.

Natural History Museum — A107

1959, Apr. 1

407	A107	4f greenish blue	30	15
408	A107	8f olive brown	30	15
		Set value		25

Opening of Museum of Natural History, Peking.

Wheat — A108

Designs on Chinese Flag: No. 410, Rice. No. 411, Cotton bolls. No. 412, Soybeans, rapeseed and peanuts.

1959, Apr. 25

409	A108	8f red (1)	1.00	20
410	A108	8f red (2)	1.00	20
411	A108	8f red (3)	1.00	20
412	A108	8f red (4)	1.00	20
a.		Block of 4, #409-412	5.50	2.00

Successful harvest, 1958.

A109

A110

Designs: 4f, Marx, Lenin and workers. 8f, Black, yellow and white fists holding banner. 22f, Steel workers parading with banners dated "5.1."

1959, May 1

413	A109	4f ultra	6.00	50
414	A109	8f red	6.00	50
415	A109	22f emerald	6.00	50
		Nos. 413-415 (3)	18.00	1.50

International Labor Day.

1959, June 20

Design: 8f, Peking airport. 10f, Plane loading on runway.

416	A110	8f lilac & blk	6.25	90
417	A110	10f ol gray & blk	6.25	90

Opening of new Peking Airport.

Students with Marx-Lenin Banners A111

Design: 8f, Workers with banners of Mao.

1959, July 1 **Photo.** ***Perf. 11x11½***

418	A111	4f gray, red & dk brn	9.00	2.75
419	A111	8f bis, red & dk brn	9.00	2.75

40th anniv. of the May 4th students' uprising.

Frederick Joliot-Curie — A112

Design: 22f, Three races, dove and olive branch.

1959, July 25 Engr. *Perf. 11½*

420	A112	8f violet brn	6.00	*3.50*
421	A112	22f dk violet	6.00	15

10th anniv. of the World Peace Movement.

Stamp Printing Plant, Peking
A113

1959, Aug. 15 *Perf. 11x11½*

422	A113	8f dp blue grn	7.75	2.50

Sino-Czechoslovak cooperation in stamp production.

Table Tennis — A114

1959, Aug. 30 Litho. *Perf. 14*

423	A114	4f black & blue	1.65	35
424	A114	8f black & red	1.65	24

25th World Table Tennis Championships, Dortmund, German Democratic Republic.

Soviet Space Rocket
A115

Backyard Steel Production
A116

1959, Sept. 10 Photo. *Perf. 11½*

425	A115	8f Prus bl, red & blk	10.00	3.00

Launching of first Russian space rocket, Jan. 2, 1959.

1959, Sept. 25 Engr.

Designs: #426, Sun rising over "industry and agriculture." #428, Farming. #429, Trade. #430, Education. #431, Militia. #432, Communal dining. #433, Nursery. #434, Care for the aged. #435, Health services. #436, Flutist; culture and sports. #437, Flower symbolizing unity of industry, agriculture, trade, education and armed forces.

Position-in-set number in ( ).

426	A116	8f rose (1)	42	15
427	A116	8f violet brn (2)	42	15
428	A116	8f dp orange (3)	42	15
429	A116	8f slate grn (4)	42	15
430	A116	8f dp blue (5)	42	15
431	A116	8f olive (6)	42	15
432	A116	8f indigo (7)	42	15
433	A116	8f lilac rose (8)	42	15
434	A116	8f gray blk (9)	42	15
435	A116	8f emerald (10)	42	15
436	A116	8f dk violet (11)	42	15
437	A116	8f red (12)	42	15
		Nos. 426-437 (12)	5.04	1.80

First anniversary of Peoples' Communes.

Mao and Gate of Heavenly Peace — A117

National Emblem — A118

Blast Furnaces — A119

Celebration at Gate of Heavenly Peace — A120

Mao Proclaiming Republic — A121

1959, Sept. 28 Photo. *Perf. 11½x11*

Designs: 8f, Marx, Lenin and Kremlin. 22f, Dove over globe.

With Gum

438	A117	8f lt brown & red	10.00	5.50
439	A117	8f dull blue & red	10.00	1.75
440	A117	22f blue grn & red	10.00	1.00
		Nos. 438-440 (3)	30.00	8.25

1959, Oct. 1 Litho. *Perf. 14*

441	A118	4f pale grn, red & gold	4.75	4.25
442	A118	8f gray, red & gold	4.75	42
443	A118	10f lt blue, red & gold	4.75	42
444	A118	20f pale brn, red & gold	4.75	2.50
		Nos. 441-444 (4)	19.00	7.59

Engraved and Photogravure

1959, Oct. 1 *Perf. 11½x11*

Designs: No. 446, Large coal mine. No. 447, Planer, Wuhan heavy machinery plant. No. 448, Wuhan Yangtze River Bridge. No. 449, Combine harvester. No. 450, Hsinankiang hydroelectric station. No. 451, Spinning machine. No. 452, Kirin chemical fertilizer plant.

With Gum

445	A119	8f brown & rose red (1)	65	20
446	A119	8f brown & gray (2)	65	20
447	A119	8f brown & yel brn (3)	65	20
448	A119	8f brown & stl bl (4)	65	20
449	A119	8f brown & org (5)	65	20
450	A119	8f brown & ol (6)	65	20
451	A119	8f brown & bl grn (7)	65	20
452	A119	8f brown & vio (8)	65	20
		Nos. 445-452 (8)	5.20	1.60

Designs: 10f, Workers and factory, vert. No. 455, People rejoicing, vert.

1959, Oct. 1 Litho. *Perf. 14*

Inscribed: 1949-1959

453	A120	8f cream & multi	2.25	75
454	A120	10f cream & multi	2.25	75
455	A120	20f cream & multi	2.25	75

Engr.

456	A121	20f deep carmine	15.00	9.00
		Nos. 453-456 (4)	21.75	11.25

Nos. 438-456 commemorate 10th anniversary of the Proclamation of the People's Republic of China.

A122

A123

Designs: No. 457, Pioneers' emblem. No. 458, Pioneer Bugler. No. 459, Schoolgirl. No. 460, Girl using rain gauge. No. 461, Boy planting tree. No. 462, Girl figure skater.

1959, Nov. 10 Photo. *Perf. 11½*

457	A122	4f red yel & blk (1)	2.50	28
458	A122	4f Prus bl & red (2)	2.50	28
459	A122	8f brn & red (3)	2.50	28
460	A122	8f dk bl & red (4)	2.50	28
461	A122	8f red & grn (5)	2.50	28
462	A122	8f mag & red (6)	2.50	28
		Nos. 457-462 (6)	15.00	1.68

10th anniversary of the Young Pioneers. Black inscription on No. 457 engraved.

1959, Dec. 1 Engr.

Designs: 4f, Exhibition emblem, communications symbols. 8f, Exhibition emblem and chimneys.

463	A123	4f dark blue	40	15
464	A123	8f red	40	15
		Set value		25

Exhibition of Industry and Communications, Peking.

Palace of Nationalities
A124

Engraved, Frame Lithographed

1959, Dec. 10 *Perf. 14*

465	A124	4f red & blk	2.25	65
466	A124	8f brt grn & blk	2.25	95

Inauguration of the Cultural Palace of Nationalities, Peking.

Athletes' Monument and Track — A125

Designs: No. 468, Parachuting. No. 469, Marksmanship. No. 470, Diving. No. 471, Table tennis. No. 472, Weight lifting. No. 473, High jump. No. 474, Rowing. No. 475, Track. No. 476, Basketball. No. 477, Traditional Chinese fencing. No. 478, Motorcycling. No. 479, Gymnastics. No. 480, Bicycling. No. 481, Horsemanship. No. 482, Soccer.

1959, Dec. 28 Litho.

467	A125	8f bis, blk & gray (1)	95	18
468	A125	8f dl bl, blk & gray (2)	95	28
469	A125	8f red brn & blk (3)	95	18
470	A125	8f grn, blk & brn (4)	95	18
471	A125	8f brt grn, blk, brn & gray (5)	95	18
472	A125	8f gray, blk & brn (6)	95	18
473	A125	8f dl bl, blk & brn (7)	95	18
474	A125	8f Prus grn, blk & brn (8)	95	18
475	A125	8f org, blk & brn (9)	95	18
476	A125	8f dl vio, blk & brn (10)	95	18
477	A125	8f lt ol, blk & brn (11)	95	18
478	A125	8f bl, blk & gray (12)	95	18
479	A125	8f gray bl, blk, grn, & bl (13)	95	18
480	A125	8f gray, blk, brn, & vio (14)	95	18
481	A125	8f red org, blk, brn, & gray (15)	95	18
482	A125	8f lt gray, blk, brn, & red (16)	95	18
		Nos. 467-482 (16)	15.20	2.98

First National Sports Meeting, Peking.

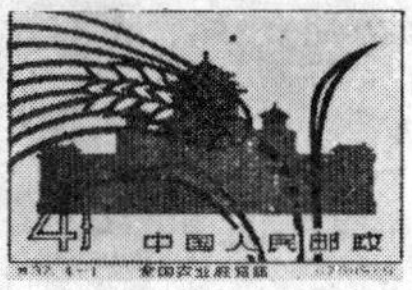

Wheat and Main Pavilion
A126

Designs (Pavilion and): 8f, Meteorological symbols. 10f, Domestic animals. 20f, Fish.

1960, Jan. 20 Engr. & Litho.

Cream Background

483	A126	4f black & org	45	15
484	A126	8f black & dull bl	45	15
485	A126	10f black & org brn	45	15
486	A126	20f black & grnsh bl	45	28
		Nos. 483-486 (4)	1.80	73

Opening of the National Agricultural Exhibition Halls, Peking.

With Gum

From No. 487 onward all stamps were issued with gum except as noted.

Catalogue values for unused stamps in this section, from this point to the end of the section, are for Never Hinged items.

Conference Hall, Tsunyi
A127

Designs: 8f, Mao addressing conference. 10f, Crossing Chinsha River.

Engraved (4f, 10f); Photogravure (8f)

1960, Jan. 25 *Perf. 11x11½*

487	A127	4f violet & blue	7.75	70
488	A127	8f red & multi	7.75	*4.00*
489	A127	10f slate green	7.75	1.40
		Nos. 487-489 (3)	23.25	*6.10*

25th anniversary of the Communist Party Conference at Tsunyi.

Clara Zetkin (1857-1933)
A128

Chinese and Russian Workers
A129

Designs: 8f, Mother, child and dove. 10f, Woman tractor driver. 22f, Women of three races.

1960, Mar. 8 Photo. *Perf. 11½x11*

490	A128	4f black & multi	1.25	52
491	A128	8f black & multi	1.25	52
492	A128	10f black & multi	1.25	52
493	A128	22f black & multi	1.25	52
		Nos. 490-493 (4)	5.00	2.08

50th anniv. of International Women's Day.

1960, Mar. 10

Designs: 8f, Chinese and Russian flags. 10f, Chinese and Russian soldiers.

494	A129	4f dk brown	8.75	1.50
495	A129	8f red, yel & blk	8.75	1.50
496	A129	10f dp blue	8.75	6.00
		Nos. 494-496 (3)	26.25	9.00

10th anniv. of Sino-Soviet Treaty of Friendship. Black inscription engraved on No. 495.

Flags of Hungary and China
A130

Design: 8f, Parliament Building, Budapest.

1960, Apr. 4 *Perf. 11x11½*

497 A130 8f yel, blk, red & grn 7.25 1.50
498 A130 8f blue, red & blk 7.25 5.50

15th anniv. of the liberation of Hungary.

Lenin Speaking — A131

Lunik 2, Earth and Russian Arms — A132

Designs: 8f, Portrait of Lenin. 20f, Lenin talking with Smolny Palace guard.

Engraved (4f, 20f); Engraved and Photogravure (8f)

1960, Apr. 22 *Perf. 11½x11*

499 A131 4f violet brn 9.00 1.40
500 A131 8f org red & blk 9.00 5.25
501 A131 20f dk brown 9.00 1.40
Nos. 499-501 (3) 27.00 8.05

90th anniversary of the birth of Lenin.

1960, Apr. 30 **Engr.** *Perf. 11½*

Design: 10f, Lunik 3 over earth.

502 A132 8f red 3.25 1.00
503 A132 10f green 3.25 1.00

Russian space flights.

Pioneers and Flags of Czechoslovakia and China — A133

View of Prague with Charles Bridge
A134

Perf. 11½x11; 11x11½

1960, May 9 **Photo.**

504 A133 8f yellow & multi 6.50 3.00
505 A134 8f dp green 6.50 3.00

Liberation of Czechoslovakia, 15th anniv.

Nostril Bouquet
A135

Designs: Various goldfish.

1960, June 1 *Perf. 11x11½*

506 A135 4f shown (1) 15.00 85
507 A135 4f Black-back dragon eye (2) 15.00 85
508 A135 4f Bubble eye (3) 15.00 85
509 A135 4f Red tiger head (4) 15.00 85
510 A135 8f Pearl scale (5) 15.00 85
511 A135 8f Blue dragon eye (6) 15.00 85
512 A135 8f Skyward eye (7) 15.00 85
513 A135 8f Red cap (8) 15.00 85
514 A135 8f Purple cap (9) 15.00 6.00
515 A135 8f Red head (10) 15.00 6.00
516 A135 8f Red and white dragon eye (11) 15.00 6.00
517 A135 8f Red dragon eye (12) 15.00 6.00
Nos. 506-517 (12) 180.00 30.80

Sow with Litter
A136

Designs: No. 519, Pig being inoculated. No. 520, Pigs. No. 521, Pig and mechanized feeding. No. 522, Pig and bales.

1960, June 15

518 A136 8f red & blk (1) 9.00 1.00
519 A136 8f dp grn & blk (2) 9.00 1.00
520 A136 8f lil rose & blk (3) 9.00 1.00
521 A136 8f lt yel grn & blk (4) 9.00 1.00
522 A136 8f org & blk (5) 9.00 6.00
Nos. 518-522 (5) 45.00 10.00

Flag Inscribed "Serving the Workers" — A137

Flowers, Flags of North Korea and China — A138

Design: 8f, Inscribed stone seal.

1960, July 30 **Photo.** *Perf. 11½x11*

523 A137 4f lt grn, red, pink & brn 7.00 2.00

Photogravure & Engraved

524 A137 8f pale bl, red & bis 7.00 2.00

3rd National Congress for Literature and Arts, Peking.

1960, Aug. 15 **Photo.**

Design: 8f, Flying horse of Korea.

525 A138 8f red & multi 9.00 2.75
526 A138 8f ultra, red & ind 9.00 2.75

15th anniversary of the liberation of Korea.

Railroad Station, Peking — A139

Design: 10f, Train arriving at station.

1960, Aug. 30 *Perf. 11½*

527 A139 8f blue, cr & brn 8.00 3.00
528 A139 10f bluish grn, cr & ind 8.00 3.00

Opening of new Peking Railroad Station.

Girls and Flags of North Viet Nam and China
A140

Lake of the Returning Sword, Hanoi
A141

Worker and Fresh-air Installation
A142

Perf. 11x11½, 11½x11

1960, Sept. 2

529 A140 8f red & multi 3.25 1.90
530 A141 8f red, gray grn & gray 3.25 1.10

15th anniversary of the Democratic Republic of North Viet Nam.

1960, Sept. 10 *Perf. 11½*

Designs: No. 532, Exterminator. No. 533, Window cleaning. No. 534, Medical examination of child. No. 535, Physical exercise.

531 A142 8f black & org (1) 1.10 15
532 A142 8f indigo & sl (2) 1.10 22
533 A142 8f brown & bl (3) 1.10 30
534 A142 8f maroon & ocher (4) 1.10 42
535 A142 8f indigo & brt grn (5) 1.10 35
Nos. 531-535 (5) 5.50 1.44

National health campaign.

Great Hall of the People — A143

Design: 10f, Inside view.

1960, Oct. 1

536 A143 8f yellow & multi 8.00 3.75
537 A143 10f brown & multi 8.00 3.75

Completion of the Great Hall of the People, Peking.

Dr. Norman Bethune — A144

Engels Addressing Congress at The Hague — A145

Design: No. 539, Dr. Bethune operating on a soldier.

Photo. (No. 538); Engr. (No. 539)

1960, Nov. 20 *Perf. 11½x11*

538 A144 8f red & multi 2.25 48
539 A144 8f sepia 2.25 48

Dr. Norman Bethune (1890-1939), Canadian surgeon with 8th Army.

Engr. (8f); Photo. (10f)

1960, Nov. 28

Designs: 10f, Portrait of Engels.

540 A145 8f brown 8.00 3.00
541 A145 10f blue & multi 8.00 3.00

140th anniversary of the birth of Friedrich Engels (1820-1895), German Socialist.

"Hwang Shi Ba"
A146

Freighter
A147

1960-61 **Photo.**

Various Chrysanthemums in Natural Colors

542 A146 4f bl gray (1) 10.00 2.25
543 A146 4f pink (2) 10.00 2.25
544 A146 8f dk gray (3) 10.00 2.25
545 A146 8f dp blue (4) 10.00 2.25
546 A146 8f green (5) 10.00 2.25
547 A146 8f magenta (6) 10.00 2.25
548 A146 8f olive (7) 10.00 2.25
549 A146 8f grnsh bl (8) 10.00 2.25
550 A146 10f gray (9) 10.00 2.25
551 A146 10f choc (10) 10.00 2.25
552 A146 20f dp blue (11) 10.00 2.25
553 A146 20f brt red (12) 10.00 2.25
554 A146 22f olive bis (13) 10.00 2.25
555 A146 22f carmine (14) 10.00 2.25
556 A146 30f grnsh gray (15) 10.00 2.25
557 A146 30f brt pink (16) 10.00 2.25
558 A146 35f dp green (17) 10.00 2.25
559 A146 52f brt lilac rose (18) 10.00 2.25
Nos. 542-559 (18) 180.00 40.50

Issue dates: Nos. 548-550, 557-559, Dec. 10, 1960; Nos. 545-547, 554-556, Jan. 18, 1961; Nos. 542-544, Feb. 24, 1961.

1960, Dec. 15 *Perf. 11½*

Without Gum

560 A147 8f deep blue 4.75 2.00

Launching of first 10,000-ton Chinese-built freighter.

Pantheon, Paris — A148

Design: 8f, Proclamation of the Commune.

Engraved and Photogravure

1961, Mar. 18 *Perf. 11½x11*

561 A148 8f gray blk & red 5.50 1.10
562 A148 8f brown & red 5.50 1.10

90th anniversary of the Paris Commune.

Championship Symbol and Jasmine — A149

Designs: 10f, Table tennis racket and ball; Temple of Heaven. 20f, Table tennis match. 22f, Peking workers' gymnasium.

1961, Apr. 5 **Photo.** *Perf. 11*

563 A149 8f multicolored 1.10 15
564 A149 10f multicolored 1.10 15
565 A149 20f multicolored 1.10 15
566 A149 22f multicolored 1.10 25
a. Souvenir sheet of 4, #563-566 *325.00 200.00*
Nos. 563-566 (4) 4.40 70

26th World Table Tennis Championships, Peking.

Jeme Tien-yow — A150

Design: 10f, Train and tunnel, Peking-Changchow Railroad.

1961, June 20 *Perf. 11½x11*

567 A150	8f ol grn & blk		2.25	42
568 A150	10f org brn & brn		2.25	42

Centenary of the birth of Jeme Tien-yow, railroad construction engineer.

Congress Building, Shanghai — A151

Designs: 8f, August 1st Building, Nanchang. 10f, Provisional Central Government Office, Juikin. 20f, Pagoda Hill, Yenan. 30f, Gate of Heavenly Peace, Peking.

1961, July 1 *Perf. 11½*

569 A151	4f gold, red & cl	9.00	95
570 A151	8f gold, red & bl grn	9.00	95
571 A151	10f gold, red & yel brn	9.00	2.00
572 A151	20f gold, red & ultra	9.00	95
573 A151	30f gold, red & org red	9.00	1.10
	Nos. 569-573 (5)	45.00	5.95

40th anniv. of the Chinese Communist Party.

August 1 Building, Nanchang — A152

Designs: 3f, 4f, 5f, Trees and Sha Cho Pa Building, Juikin. 8f, 10f, 20f, Pagoda Hill, Yenan. 22f, 30f, 50f, Gate of Heavenly Peace, Peking.

1961-62 **Engr.** *Perf. 11*

Without Gum

Size: 24x16mm

574 A152	1f vio blue	4.75	1.25
575 A152	1½f maroon	4.75	25
576 A152	2f indigo	4.75	1.25
577 A152	3f dull vio	4.75	25
578 A152	4f green	4.75	25
579 A152	5f gray	4.75	1.25
580 A152	8f sepia	4.75	25
581 A152	10f brt lil rose	4.75	25
582 A152	20f grnsh bl	4.75	25
583 A152	22f brown	4.75	25
584 A152	30f blue	4.75	25
585 A152	50f vermilion	4.75	25
	Nos. 574-585 (12)	57.00	6.00

Issue dates: 1f, 1½f, 5f, July 20, 1962; others July 20, 1961.

See Nos. 647-654, 1059-1064.

Flowers, Flags of Mongolia and China A153

Design: 10f, Parliament, Ulan Bator, and statue of Sukhe Bator.

1961, July 11 **Photo.** *Perf. 11x11½*

586 A153	8f crimson, ultra & yel	9.50	90
587 A153	10f orange, blk & yel	9.50	4.75

40th anniv. of the Mongolian People's Republic.

Military Museum — A154

Photo. & Engr.

1961, Aug. 1 *Perf. 11½*

588 A154	8f gray bl, brn & grn	12.00	2.75
589 A154	10f gray, blk & grn	12.00	30

Opening of the People's Revolutionary Military Museum.

Uprising at Wuchang A155

Sun Yat-sen — A156

Perf. 11x11½, 11½x11

1961, Oct. 10 **Photo.**

590 A155	8f gray & blk	8.00	*3.25*
591 A156	10f tan & black	8.00	35

50th anniversary of the 1911 Revolution.

Donkey — A157

Rejoicing Tibetans — A158

Designs: 8f, 10f, 20f, 22f, Horses; 30f, 50f, Camels. Ceramic statuettes from Tang Dynasty (618-906) graves.

1961, Nov. 10 *Perf. 11½x11*

Statuettes in Original Colors

592 A157	4f dull blue	5.75	1.10
593 A157	8f gray green	5.75	1.10
594 A157	8f dp purple	5.75	1.10
595 A157	10f dp blue	5.75	1.00
596 A157	20f olive	5.75	1.10
597 A157	22f blue grn	5.75	45
598 A157	30f red brown	5.75	1.10
599 A157	50f slate	5.75	1.10
	Nos. 592-599 (8)	46.00	8.05

1961, Nov. 25

Designs: 8f, Woman sower. 10f, Celebration of bumper crop. 20f, People's representatives. 30f, Tibetan children.

600 A158	4f brn & ocher	12.00	15
601 A158	8f brn & lt bl grn	12.00	52
602 A158	10f brn & yel	12.00	15
603 A158	20f brn & rose	12.00	5.00
604 A158	30f brn & bluish gray	12.00	5.00
	Nos. 600-604 (5)	60.00	10.82

Rebirth of the Tibetan people.

Lu Hsun — A159

1962, Feb. 26

605 A159	8f red brown & blk	60	25

80th anniv. of the birth of Lu Hsun, writer.

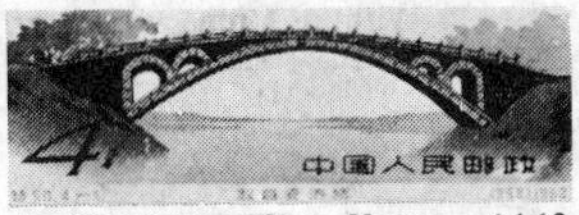

An Chi Bridge, Chao Hsien — A160

Bridges of Ancient China: 8f, Pao Tai, Soochow. 10f, Chu Pu, Kwan Hsien. 20f, Chen Yang, San Kiang.

1962, May 15 *Perf. 11*

606 A160	4f dk gray blue	1.25	24
607 A160	8f dp green	1.25	24
608 A160	10f brown	1.25	15
609 A160	20f grnsh blue	1.25	1.25
	Nos. 606-609 (4)	5.00	1.88

Tu Fu — A161

Cranes and Bamboo — A162

Design: 4f, Tu Fu memorial pavilion, Chengtu.

1962, May 25 *Perf. 11½x11*

610 A161	4f ol bis & blk	9.50	30
611 A161	8f grnsh bl & blk	9.50	60

Poet Tu Fu, 1,250th anniversary of birth.

1962, June 10

Designs: 10f, Two cranes in flight. 20f, Crane on rock.

612 A162	8f tan & multi	13.00	2.25
613 A162	10f blue & multi	13.00	1.40
614 A162	20f bister & multi	13.00	1.40
	Nos. 612-614 (3)	39.00	5.05

"The Sacred Crane," from paintings by Chen Chi-fo.

Cuban Soldier and Flag — A163

Designs: 10f, Sugar cane worker. 22f, Militiaman and woman.

1962, July 10 *Perf. 11x11½*

615 A163	8f car, rose & blk	25.00	1.50
616 A163	10f green & blk	25.00	50
617 A163	22f ultra & blk	25.00	9.00
	Nos. 615-617 (3)	75.00	11.00

Support of Cuba.

Torch and Map of Algeria — A164

Mei Lan-fang — A165

Design: 22f, Algerian soldiers and flag.

1962, July 10 *Perf. 11½x11*

618 A164	8f dp brown & red org	60	20
619 A164	22f ocher & dp brn	60	30

Support of Algeria.

1962 *Perf. 11½x11, 11x11½*

Designs (Mei Lan-fang in Women's Roles): No. 621, Beating drum. No. 622, With fan. 10f, Lady Yu with swords. 20f, With bag. 22f, Heavenly Maiden, horiz. 30f, With spinning wheel, horiz. 50f, Kneeling, horiz. $3, Scene from opera "Drunken Beauty."

620 A165	4f tan & multi	32.50	3.25
621 A165	8f tan & multi	32.50	3.25
622 A165	8f gray & multi	32.50	32
623 A165	10f gray & multi	32.50	3.25
624 A165	20f lt green & multi	32.50	1.65
625 A165	22f cream & multi	32.50	12.50
626 A165	30f lt blue & multi	32.50	16.00
627 A165	50f buff & multi	32.50	19.00
	Nos. 620-627 (8)	260.00	59.22

Souvenir Sheet

Perf. 11

628 A165	$3 brown & multi	*1,300.*	*600.00*

Stage art of Mei Lan-fang, actor.

Issue dates: 4f, 8f, 10f, Aug. 8; $3, Sept. 15; others Sept. 1. Nos. 620-627 exist imperf. Value, set $1,300.

No. 628 contains one 48x58mm stamp and almost always has some faults.

Flower Drum Dance, Han — A166

Folk Dances: 8f, Ordos, Mongolia. 10f, Catching shrimp, Chuang. 20f, Friend, Yi. 30f, Fiddle dance, Tibet. 50f, Tambourine dance, Uighur.

Cumulative numbers 246-251 at lower right.

1962, Oct. 15 **Litho.** *Perf. 12½*

Without Gum

629 A166	4f cream & multi	65	15
630 A166	8f cream & multi	65	15
631 A166	10f cream & multi	65	18
632 A166	20f cream & multi	65	50
633 A166	30f cream & multi	65	42
634 A166	50f cream & multi	65	55
	Nos. 629-634 (6)	3.90	1.95

See Nos. 696-707.

Soldiers Storming Winter Palace — A167

Design: 8f, Lenin leading soldiers, vert.

1962, Nov. 7 **Photo.** *Perf. 11½*

635 A167	8f black & red	11.00	80
636 A167	20f slate grn & red	11.00	2.75

45th anniversary of the Russian Revolution.

Monument and Map of Albania
A168

Tsai Lun, Inventor of Papermaking
A169

Design: 10f, Albanian flag and Girl Pioneer.

1962, Nov. 28 ***Perf. 11½x11***

637	A168	8f Prus blue & sepia	1.25	30
638	A168	10f red, yel, & blk	1.25	30

50th anniversary of Albanian independence.

1962, Dec. 1 ***Perf. 11½x11***

Designs: No. 640, Paper making. No. 641, Sun Szu-miao, physician. No. 642, Writing medical treatise. No. 643, Shen Ko, geologist. No. 644, Making field notes. No. 645, Kuo Shou-chin, astronomer. No. 646, Astronomical instrument.
Cumulative numbers 297-304 at lower right.

639	A169	4f multicolored	3.25	38
640	A169	4f multicolored	3.25	20
641	A169	8f multicolored	3.25	20
642	A169	8f multicolored	3.25	38
643	A169	10f multicolored	3.25	20
644	A169	10f multicolored	3.25	42
645	A169	20f multicolored	3.25	42
646	A169	20f multicolored	3.25	42
		Nos. 639-646 (8)	26.00	2.62

Scientists of ancient China.

Building Type of 1961

Designs: 1f, 2f, Building, Nanchang. 3f, 4f, Trees and Sha Cho Pa Building. 8f, 10f, 20f, Pagoda Hill, Yenan. 30f, Gate of Heavenly Peace, Peking.

1962, Jan. Litho. ***Rough Perf. 12½***
Size: 21x16mm
Without Gum

647	A152	1f ultra	55	15
648	A152	2f greenish gray	55	15
649	A152	3f violet gray	55	15
650	A152	4f green	55	15
651	A152	8f dk olive, perf. 14	55	15
b.		Perf. 11x11½	5.00	
652	A152	10f brt rose lilac	55	15
653	A152	20f slate blue	55	15
654	A152	30f dull blue	55	15
		Nos. 647-654 (8)	4.40	1.20

Tank Monument, Havana
A170

Crowd in Havana — A171

Designs: No. 656, Cuban revolutionaries. No. 658, Crowd in Peking. No. 659, Cuban soldier. No. 660, Castro and Cuban flag.

Perf. 11½, 11x11½

1963, Jan. 1 **Photo.**

655	A170	4f red & blk brn	15.00	15
656	A170	4f green & blk	15.00	15
657	A171	8f dull red & brn	15.00	1.10
658	A171	8f dull red & brn	15.00	22
659	A170	10f ocher & blk	15.00	4.50
660	A170	10f red, blue & blk	15.00	*15.00*
		Nos. 655-660 (6)	90.00	*21.12*

4th anniversary of the Cuban revolution.

Green Dragontail
A172

Karl Marx
A173

1963 **Without Gum** ***Perf. 11***

661	A172	4f Tibetan clouded yellow (1)	6.00	65
662	A172	4f Tritailed glory (2)	6.00	65
663	A172	4f Neumogeni jungle queen (3)	6.00	65
664	A172	4f Washan swordtail (4)	6.00	1.50
665	A172	4f Striped ringlet (5)	6.00	65
666	A172	8f shown (6)	6.00	38
667	A172	8f Dilunulated peacock (7)	6.00	65
668	A172	8f Yamfly (8)	6.00	28
669	A172	8f Golden kaiser-i-hind (9)	6.00	28
670	A172	8f Mushaell hairstreak (10)	6.00	28
671	A172	10f Yellow orange-tip (11)	6.00	28
672	A172	10f Great jay (12)	6.00	38
673	A172	10f Striped punch (13)	6.00	28
674	A172	10f Hainan violet-beak (14)	6.00	28
675	A172	10f Omeiskipper (15)	6.00	28
676	A172	20f Philippines birdwing (16)	6.00	65
677	A172	20f Richtofenis red apollo (17)	6.00	65
678	A172	22f Blue-banded king crow (18)	6.00	85
679	A172	30f Solskyi copper (19)	6.00	2.00
680	A172	50f Yunnan clipper (20)	6.00	5.00
		Nos. 661-680 (20)	120.00	16.62

Issue dates: Nos. 666-675, July 15; others Apr. 5.

1963, May 5 ***Perf. 11½***

Designs: No. 682, "Workers of the World, Unite" on cover of first edition of Communist Manifesto. No. 683, Marx and Engels.

Without Gum

681	A173	8f black, gold & sal (1)	7.50	2.25
682	A173	8f gold & red (2)	7.50	2.25
683	A173	8f gold & choc (3)	7.50	2.25
		Nos. 681-683 (3)	22.50	6.75

145th anniversary of birth of Karl Marx (1818-1883), German political philosopher.

Child with Top — A174

Designs (Child): No. 685, eating berries. No. 686, as traffic policeman. No. 687, with windmill. No. 688, listening to caged cricket. No. 689, with sword. No. 690, embroidering. No. 691, with umbrella. No. 692, playing with sand. No. 693, playing table tennis. No. 694, learning to add. No. 695, with kite.

1963, June 1 **Litho.** ***Perf. 12½***
Without Gum
Multicolored Designs

684	A174	4f grnsh gray (1)	85	15
685	A174	4f tan (2)	85	15
686	A174	4f gray (3)	85	15
687	A174	8f blue (4)	85	15
688	A174	8f tan (5)	85	15
689	A174	8f dp gray (6)	85	15
690	A174	8f citron (7)	85	15
691	A174	8f gray (8)	85	15
692	A174	10f green (9)	85	18
693	A174	10f violet (10)	85	18
694	A174	20f bister (11)	85	52
695	A174	20f green (12)	85	52
		Nos. 684-695 (12)	10.20	
		Set value		2.00

Children's Day. Value, imperf set $65.

Dance Type of 1962

Folk Dances: 4f, Weavers' dance, Puyi. 8f, Kazakh. 10f, Olunchun. 20f, Labor dance, Kaochan. 30f, Reed pipe dance, Miao. 50f, Fan dance, Korea.
Cumulative numbers 261-266 at lower right.

1963, June 15 ***Perf. 12½***
Without Gum

696	A166	4f cream & multi	90	15
697	A166	8f cream & multi	90	15
698	A166	10f cream & multi	90	18
699	A166	20f cream & multi	90	40
700	A166	30f cream & multi	90	45
701	A166	50f cream & multi	90	75
		Nos. 696-701 (6)	5.40	2.08

1963, June 30 **Without Gum**

Folk Dances: 4f, "Wedding Ceremony," Yu. 8f, "Encircling Mountain Forest," Pai. 10f, Long drum dance, Yao. 20f, Third day of the third month dance, Li. 30f, Knife dance, Kawa. 50f, Peacock dance, Thai.
Cumulative numbers 279-284 at lower right.

702	A166	4f cream & multi	90	15
703	A166	8f cream & multi	90	15
704	A166	10f cream & multi	90	16
705	A166	20f cream & multi	90	48
706	A166	30f cream & multi	90	48
707	A166	50f cream & multi	90	65
		Nos. 702-707 (6)	5.40	2.07

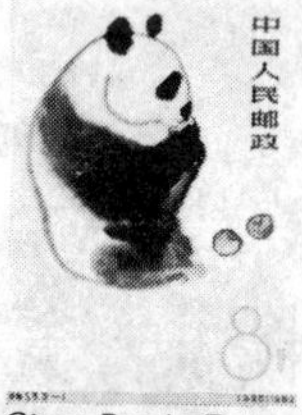

Giant Panda Eating Apples — A175

Table Tennis Player — A176

Designs: No. 709, Giant panda eating bamboo shoots. 10f, Two pandas, horiz.

1963, Aug. 5 **Photo.** ***Perf. 11½x11***
Size: 28x38mm

708	A175	8f pale blue & blk	21.00	42
709	A175	8f pale blue & blk	21.00	3.75

Size: 50x29mm
Perf. 11½

710	A175	10f olive & blk	21.00	42
		Nos. 708-710 (3)	63.00	4.59

Value, imperf set $125.

1963, Sept. 10 **Engr.** ***Perf. 11½***

Design: No. 712, Trophies won by Chinese team.

711	A176	8f dk olive grn	9.50	3.25
712	A176	8f brown	9.50	26

27th World Table Tennis Championships.

Snub-nosed Langur — A177

Jade-green Screen Mountain — A178

Designs: 10f, Two monkeys playing. 22f, Two monkeys grooming.

1963, Sept. 23 **Photo.** ***Perf. 11½x11***

713	A177	8f gray & multi	6.00	22
714	A177	10f gray & multi	6.00	22
715	A177	22f gray & multi	6.00	3.75
		Nos. 713-715 (3)	18.00	4.19

Value, imperf set $80.

Engraved and Photogravure
1963, Oct. 15 ***Perf. 11½***

Hwang Shan Landscapes (Yellow Mountains), Anhwei Province. #724-731 horiz.

716	A178	4f shown (1)	11.00	1.50
717	A178	4f "Guests Welcoming Pines" (2)	11.00	1.50
718	A178	4f Pines and Rock Behind the Sea (3)	11.00	1.50
719	A178	4f Terrace of Keeping Cool (4)	11.00	1.50
720	A178	8f Mount of Heavenly Capital (5)	11.00	1.50
721	A178	8f Mount of Scissors (6)	11.00	1.50
722	A178	8f Forest of Ten Thousand Pines (7)	11.00	1.50
723	A178	8f "Brush Blooming in Dream" (8)	11.00	1.50
724	A178	10f Mount of Lotus Flower (9)	11.00	1.50
725	A178	10f Cumulus Cloud over West Sea (10)	11.00	1.50
726	A178	10f Old Pines of Hwang Shan (11)	11.00	1.50
727	A178	10f "Watching the Clouds over West Sea" (12)	11.00	1.50
728	A178	20f Mount of Stalagmites (13)	11.00	1.50
729	A178	22f "Stone Monkey Watching the Sea" (14)	11.00	1.50
730	A178	30f Forest of Lions (15)	11.00	*7.75*
731	A178	50f Three Fairy Tales of Pen Lai (16)	11.00	1.50
		Nos. 716-731 (16)	176.00	*30.25*

Soccer Player — A179

Athletes and Banners — A180

Designs: No. 733, Discus, women's. No. 734, Diving, men's. No. 735, Gymnastics, women's.

Engraved and Photogravure
1963, Nov. 17 ***Perf. 11***

732	A179	8f gray, red & blk (1)	9.00	80
733	A179	8f gray, ultra & blk (2)	9.00	80
734	A179	8f lt grn, brn & blk (3)	9.00	80
735	A179	8f gray, lil rose & blk (4)	9.00	80

Photo. ***Perf. 11½***

736	A180	10f red & multi (5)	9.00	1.75
		Nos. 732-736 (5)	45.00	4.95

Games of the Newly Emerging Forces, Djakarta.

Clay Rooster and Goat — A181

Chinese Folk Toys: No. 738, Cloth camel. No. 739, Cloth tigers. No. 740, Clay ox and rider. No. 741, Cloth rabbit, wooden doll, clay roosters. No. 742, Straw rooster. No. 743, Cloth donkey and bird. No. 744, Clay lion. No. 745, Cloth tiger and tumbler doll.

1963, Dec. 10 Litho. *Perf. 11½*
Toys Multicolored; Without Gum

737 A181	4f bister (1)		32	15
738 A181	4f gray (4)		32	15
739 A181	4f lt blue (7)		32	15
740 A181	8f bister (2)		32	15
741 A181	8f gray (5)		32	15
742 A181	8f lt blue (8)		32	15
743 A181	10f bister (3)		32	15
744 A181	10f gray (6)		32	15
745 A181	10f lt blue (9)		32	15
	Nos. 737-745 (9)		2.88	1.35

Armed Vietnamese Family — A182

Flags of Cuba and China — A183

Liberation of South Viet Nam: No. 747, Militia with Vietnamese flag.

1963, Dec. 20 Photo. *Perf. 11½x11*

746 A182	8f tan, blk & red	2.25	1.25
747 A182	8f red & multi	2.25	1.75

1964, Jan. 1

Design: No. 749, Boy waving Cuban flag.

748 A183	8f red, yel, bl & ind	8.50	65
749 A183	8f multicolored	8.50	3.25

5th anniversary of the liberation of Cuba.

Woman Driving Tractor — A184

Woman of the People's Commune: No. 751, harvesting. No. 752, picking cotton. No. 753, picking fruit. No. 754, reading book. No. 755, on guard duty.

1964, Mar. 8

750 A184	8f ol, pink & brn (1)	75	24
751 A184	8f brn yel & org (2)	75	24
752 A184	8f gray & multi (3)	75	24
753 A184	8f black, org & bl (4)	75	24
754 A184	8f green & multi (5)	75	24
755 A184	8f lilac & multi (6)	75	24
	Nos. 750-755 (6)	4.50	1.44

Chinese and African Men — A185

Design: No. 757, African drummer.

1964, Apr. 12 Photo. *Perf. 11*

756 A185	8f red & multi	85	25
757 A185	8f black & dk brn	85	25

African Freedom Day.

Marx, Engels, Lenin and Stalin — A186

Design: No. 759, Banners and workers.

1964, May 1 *Perf. 11½*

758 A186	8f gold, red & blk	11.00	*4.50*
759 A186	8f gold, red & blk	11.00	*4.50*

Labor Day.

Orchard, Yenan — A187

Yenan, Shrine of the Chinese Revolution: No. 761, Central Auditorium, Yang Chia Ling. No. 762, Mao's office and residence. No. 763, Auditorium, Wang Chia Ping. No. 764, Border Region Assembly Hall. No. 765, Pagoda Hill and Bridge.

1964, July 1 Photo. *Perf. 11x11½*

760 A187	8f multicolored (1)	4.25	55
761 A187	8f multicolored (2)	4.25	55
762 A187	8f multicolored (3)	4.25	55
763 A187	8f multicolored (4)	4.25	55
764 A187	8f multicolored (5)	4.25	55
765 A187	52f multicolored (6)	4.25	2.25
	Nos. 760-765 (6)	25.50	5.00

Map and Flag of Viet Nam — A188

Alchemist's Glowing Crucible — A189

1964, July 20 *Perf. 11½*

766 A188	8f multicolored	15.00	3.00

Victory in South Viet Nam.

1964, Aug. 5 *Perf. 11½x11*

767 A189	4f shown (1)	6.75	24
768 A189	4f Night-shining jade (2)	6.75	24
769 A189	8f Purple Kuo's cap (3)	6.75	15
770 A189	8f Chao pink (4)	6.75	15
771 A189	8f Yao yellow (5)	6.75	24
772 A189	8f Twin beauty (6)	6.75	15
773 A189	8f Ice-veiled ruby (7)	6.75	15
774 A189	10f Gold-sprinkled Chinese ink (8)	6.75	16
775 A189	10f Cinnabar jar (9)	6.75	16
776 A189	10f Lan Tien jade (10)	6.75	15
777 A189	10f Imperial robe yellow (11)	6.75	16
778 A189	10f Hu red (12)	6.75	16
779 A189	20f Pea green (13)	6.75	6.00
780 A189	43f Wei purple (14)	6.75	6.00
781 A189	52f Intoxicated celestial peach (15)	6.75	6.00
	Nos. 767-781 (15)	101.25	20.11

Souvenir Sheet
Perf. 11½
Without Gum

782 A189	$2 Glorious crimson & great gold pink	*525.00*	*250.00*

No. 782 contains one 48x59mm stamp.

Wine Cup — A190

Grain Harvest — A191

Designs: Sacrificial bronze vessels of Yin dynasty, prior to 1050 B.C.

Engraved and Photogravure
1964, Aug. 25 *Perf. 11½x11*

783 A190	4f shown (1)	3.75	1.10
784 A190	4f Ku beaker (2)	3.75	1.10
785 A190	8f Kuang wine urn (3)	3.75	16
786 A190	8f Chia wine cup (4)	3.75	16
787 A190	10f Tsun wine vessel (5)	3.75	20
788 A190	10f Yu wine urn (6)	3.75	20
789 A190	20f Tsun wine vessel (7)	3.75	35
790 A190	20f Ceremonial cauldron (8)	3.75	35
	Nos. 783-790 (8)	30.00	3.62

1964, Sept. 26 Photo.

Designs: #792, Students planting trees. #793, Study period. #794, Scientific experimentation.

791 A191	8f multicolored (1)	75	25
792 A191	8f multicolored (2)	75	25
793 A191	8f multicolored (3)	75	25
794 A191	8f multicolored (4)	75	25
	Nos. 791-794 (4)	3.00	1.00

Youth helping in agriculture.

Marx, Engels, Trafalgar Square, London — A192

People with Banners — A193

1964, Sept. 28 *Perf. 11½*

795 A192	8f red, gold & red brn	25.00	18.00

Centenary of the First International.

1964, Oct. 1

Designs: No. 797, Gate of Heavenly Peace and Chinese flag. No. 798, People with banners, facing left.

796 A193	8f cream & multi (1)	16.00	55
797 A193	8f cream & multi (2)	16.00	55
798 A193	8f cream & multi (3)	16.00	55
a.	Souvenir sheet of 3	*1,000.*	*350.00*
b.	Strip of 3, #796-798	72.50	9.00
	Nos. 796-798 (3)	48.00	1.65

15th anniv. of the People's Republic.

No. 798a contains No. 798b in continuous design without separating perfs. No. 798a almost always has some faults.

Oil Derricks — A194

Oil industry: 4f, Geological surveyors and truck, horiz. 8f, "Christmas tree" and extraction accessories. 10f, Oil refinery. 20f, Tank cars, horiz.

1964, Oct. 1

799 A194	4f lt blue & multi	18.00	15
800 A194	8f lt blue & multi	18.00	15
801 A194	8f lilac & multi	18.00	20
802 A194	10f slate & multi	18.00	15
803 A194	20f brown & multi	18.00	*14.00*
	Nos. 799-803 (5)	90.00	*14.65*

Albanian and Chinese Flags — A195

Design: 10f, Enver Hoxha and Albanian coat of arms.

1964, Nov. 29 *Perf. 11x11½*

804 A195	8f red & multi	12.50	*95*
805 A195	10f red, yel & blk	12.50	10.00

20th anniv. of the liberation of Albania.

Power Dam Construction A196

Designs: No. 807, Installation of turbogenerator rotor. No. 808, Main dam. 20f, Pylon.

1964, Dec. 15 *Perf. 11½*

806 A196	4f multicolored	21.00	16
807 A196	8f multicolored	21.00	16
808 A196	8f multicolored	21.00	15
809 A196	20f multicolored	21.00	12.00
	Nos. 806-809 (4)	84.00	12.47

Hsin An Kiang Dam and hydroelectric power station.

Fertilizer Industry — A197

Designs (Chemical Industry): No. 811, Plastics. No. 812, Medicines. No. 813, Rubber. No. 814, Insecticides. No. 815, Industrial acids. No. 816, Industrial alkalies. No. 817, Synthetic fibers.

1964, Dec. 30 Photo. & Engr.

810 A197	8f red & blk (1)	1.00	26
811 A197	8f yel grn & blk (2)	1.00	18
812 A197	8f brown & blk (3)	1.00	18
813 A197	8f lilac rose & blk (4)	1.00	18
814 A197	8f blue & blk (5)	1.00	18
815 A197	8f orange & blk (6)	1.00	35
816 A197	8f violet & blk (7)	1.00	35
817 A197	8f brt green & blk (8)	1.00	35
	Nos. 810-817 (8)	8.00	2.03

Mao Studying Map — A198

Mao Tse-tung — A199

Design: No. 819, Victory at Lushan Pass.

1965, Jan. 31 Photo. *Perf. 11*

818	A198	8f red & multi	20.00	5.00
819	A198	8f red & multi	20.00	5.00

Perf. 11½x11

820	A199	8f gold & multi	20.00	5.00
		Nos. 818-820 (3)	60.00	15.00

Tsunyi Conference, 30th anniversary.

Conference Hall, Bandung — A200

Lenin — A201

Design: No. 822, Asians and Africans applauding.

1965, Apr. 18 *Perf. 11½x11*

821	A200	8f cream & multi	50	18
822	A200	8f cream & multi	50	18

10th anniversary of the Bandung, Indonesia, Conference, Apr. 1955.

1965, Apr. 25 *Perf. 11½*

823	A201	8f red, choc & sal	14.00	7.25

95th anniversary of the birth of Lenin.

Chinese Player — A202

1965, Apr. 25 *Perf. 11½*

824	A202	8f shown (1)	45	15
825	A202	8f European woman (2)	45	15
826	A202	8f Chinese woman (3)	45	15
827	A202	8f European man (4)	45	15
a.		Block of 4, #824-827	1.90	60
		Set value		38

28th World Table Tennis Championships, Ljubljana, Yugoslavia, Apr. 15-25.

Climbers on Mt. Minya Konka — A203

Marx and Lenin — A204

Mountain Climbers: No. 829, on Muztagh Ata. No. 830, on Mt. Jolmo Lungma (Mt. Everest). No. 831, Women camping on Kongur Tiubie Tagh. No. 832, on Shisha Pangma.

1965, May 25 Photo. & Engr.

828	A203	8f blue, blk & ol (1)	3.00	50
829	A203	8f blue, blk & ol (2)	3.00	50
830	A203	8f ultra, blk & gray (3)	3.00	50
831	A203	8f lt bl, blk & yel gray (4)	3.00	50
832	A203	8f ultra, blk & gray (5)	3.00	50
		Nos. 828-832 (5)	15.00	2.50

Chinese mountaineering achievements, 1957-64.

1965, June 21 Photo. *Perf. 11½x11*

833	A204	8f red, yel & blk	13.00	7.25

Postal Ministers' Congress, Peking.

Tseping Valley A205

Chingkang Mountains, Cradle of the Chinese Revolution.

1965, July 1 *Perf. 11x11½*

834	A205	4f shown (1)	8.00	15
835	A205	8f San Wan Tsun (2)	8.00	15
836	A205	8f Octagon Bldg., Mao Ping (3)	8.00	15
837	A205	8f River and Bridge at Lung Shih (4)	8.00	85
838	A205	8f Ta Ching Tsun (5)	8.00	15
839	A205	10f Bridge across the Lung Yuan (6)	8.00	15
840	A205	10f Hwang Yang Moun-tain (7)	8.00	2.00
841	A205	52f Chingkang peaks (8)	8.00	2.00
		Nos. 834-841 (8)	64.00	5.60

Soldiers with Books — A206

1965, Aug. 1 *Perf. 11½*

Without Gum

842	A206	8f shown (1)	8.00	2.75
843	A206	8f Soldiers reading Little Red Books (2)	8.00	2.75
844	A206	8f With shell and artil-lery (3)	8.00	35
845	A206	8f Rifle instruction (4)	8.00	35
846	A206	8f Sewing jacket (5)	8.00	35
847	A206	8f Bayonet charge (6)	8.00	4.00
848	A206	8f With Banner (7)	8.00	4.00
849	A206	8f Military band (8)	8.00	4.00
		Nos. 842-849 (8)	64.00	18.55

People's Liberation Army. Nos. 846-849 vertical.

"Welcome to Peking" — A207

Designs: No. 851, Chinese and Japanese young men. No. 852, Chinese and Japanese girls. No. 853, Musical entertainment. No. 854, Emblem of meeting.

1965, Aug. 25 *Perf. 11½x11*

850	A207	4f yellow & multi	70	20
851	A207	8f pink & multi	70	24
852	A207	8f multicolored	70	24
853	A207	10f multicolored	70	24
854	A207	22f lt blue & multi	70	52
		Nos. 850-854 (5)	3.50	1.44

Chinese-Japanese Youth Meeting, Peking.

North Vietnamese Soldier — A208

Peoples of the World — A209

Designs: No. 856, Soldier with guns. No. 857, Soldier giving victory salute.

1965, Sept. 2 *Perf. 11½x11*

855	A208	8f red & red brn (1)	1.10	15
856	A208	8f red & blk (2)	1.10	15
857	A208	8f red & vio brn (3)	1.10	15

Perf. 11½

858	A209	8f black & red (4)	1.10	15
		Nos. 855-858 (4)	4.40	60

Struggle of the people of Viet Nam.

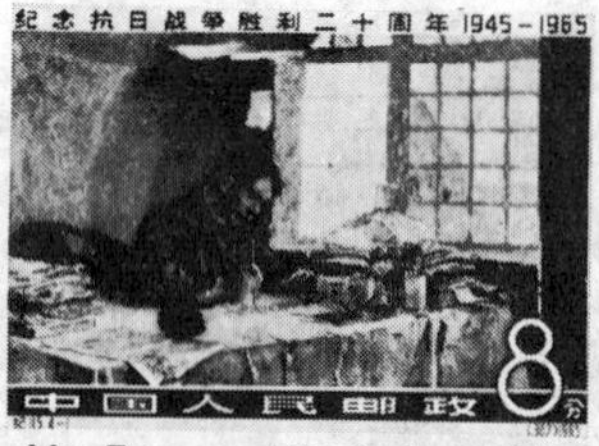

Mao Tse-tung at His Desk — A210

Crossing Yellow River — A211

Victory Monument — A212

Design: No. 862, Recruits in cart.

1965, Sept. 3 *Perf. 11*

859	A210	8f red & multi (1)	8.00	2.25

Perf. 11x11½, 11½x11

860	A211	8f red & dk grn (2)	8.00	6.75
861	A212	8f red & dk brn (3)	8.00	55
862	A211	8f red & dk grn (4)	8.00	55
		Nos. 859-862 (4)	32.00	10.10

20th anniversary of victory over Japan.

2nd National Games — A213

National Games Opening Ceremonies — A214

Perf. 11½x11, 11 (A214)

1965, Sept. 28

863	A213	4f Soccer (1)	9.50	35
864	A213	4f Archery (2)	9.50	35
865	A213	8f Javelin (3)	9.50	35
866	A213	8f Gymnastics (4)	9.50	35
867	A213	8f Volleyball (5)	9.50	35
868	A214	10f shown (6)	9.50	35
869	A213	10f Bicyling (7)	9.50	35
870	A213	20f Diving (8)	9.50	85
871	A213	22f Hurdles (9)	9.50	1.10
872	A213	30f Weight lifting (10)	9.50	1.90
873	A213	43f Basketball (11)	9.50	3.75
		Nos. 863-873 (11)	104.50	10.05

Government Building A215

Textile Workers A216

Designs: 1½f, 5f, 22f, Gate of Heavenly Peace. 2f, 8f, 30f, People's Hall. 3f, 10f, 50f, Military Museum.

1965-66 *Perf. 11½x11*

Without Gum

874	A215	1f brown	15	15
875	A215	1½f red lil	15	30
876	A215	2f green	15	15
877	A215	3f bl grn	15	15
878	A215	4f brt bl	15	15
879	A215	5f vio brn ('66)	16	15
880	A215	8f rose red	16	15
881	A215	10f gray ol	16	15
882	A215	20f violet	16	15
883	A215	22f orange	80	15
884	A215	30f yel grn	80	15
885	A215	50f dp bl ('66)	80	75
		Nos. 874-885 (12)	3.79	
		Set value		1.55

1965, Nov. 30

886	A216	8f shown (1)	9.50	15
887	A216	8f Machine shop (2)	9.50	15
888	A216	8f Welder (3)	9.50	15
889	A216	8f Students (4)	9.50	2.75
890	A216	8f Militia (5)	9.50	2.75
		Nos. 886-890 (5)	47.50	5.95

Women workers.

Soccer — A217

Children's Sports: No. 892, Racing. No. 893, Tobogganing and skating. No. 894, Gymnastics. No. 895, Swimming. No. 896, Rifle practice. No. 897, Jumping rope. No. 898, Table tennis.

1966, Feb. 25 *Perf. 11*

891	A217	4f emerald & multi (1)	15	15
892	A217	4f yel brown & multi (2)	15	15
893	A217	8f blue & multi (3)	24	20
894	A217	8f yellow & multi (4)	24	20
895	A217	8f grnsh bl & multi (5)	24	20
896	A217	8f green & multi (6)	24	20
897	A217	10f orange & multi (7)	35	25
898	A217	52f grnsh gray & multi (8)	2.00	1.25
		Nos. 891-898 (8)	3.61	2.60

Mobile Transformer A218

New Industrial Machinery: No. 900, Electron microscope, vert. No. 901, Lathe. No. 902, Vertical boring and turning machine, vert. No. 903, Gear-grinding machine. No. 904, Hydraulic press. No. 905, Milling machine. No. 906, Electron accelerator, vert.

Perf. 11x11½, 11½x11

1966, Mar. 30 Photo. & Engr.

899 A218 4f yellow & blk (1) 7.00 28
900 A218 8f blk & lt ultra (2) 7.00 28
901 A218 8f sal pink & blk (3) 7.00 28
902 A218 8f olive & blk (4) 7.00 28
903 A218 8f rose lil & blk (5) 7.00 28
904 A218 10f gray & blk (6) 7.00 1.90
905 A218 10f bl grn & blk (7) 7.00 1.90
906 A218 22f lilac & blk (8) 7.00 1.90
Nos. 899-906 (8) 56.00 7.10

Military and Civilian Workers A219

Women in Various Occupations: No. 908, Train conductor. No. 909, Red Cross worker. No. 910, Kindergarten teacher. No. 911, Road sweeper. No. 912, Hairdresser. No. 913, Bus conductor. No. 914, Traveling saleswoman. No. 915, Canteen worker. No. 916, Rural mail carrier.

1966, May 10 *Perf. 11x11½*

907 A219 8f red & multi (1) 35 20
908 A219 8f pale grn & multi (2) 35 20
909 A219 8f yellow & multi (3) 35 20
910 A219 8f green & multi (4) 35 20
911 A219 8f salmon & multi (5) 35 20
912 A219 8f pale bl & bl (6) 35 20
913 A219 8f yellow & multi (7) 35 20
914 A219 8f tan & multi (8) 35 20
915 A219 8f yel grn & multi (9) 35 20
916 A219 8f green & multi (10) 35 20
Nos. 907-916 (10) 3.50 2.00

Statue "Thunderstorm" — A220

Design: 22f, Open book and association emblem.

1966, June 27 *Perf. 11*

917 A220 8f red & black 1.65 32
918 A220 22f red, gold & yel 2.75 65

Afro-Asian Writers' Assoc. Conf., Peking.

Sun Yat-sen — A221

1966, Nov. 12 *Perf. 11½x11*

919 A221 8f sepia & lt buff 18.00 6.00

Birth centenary of Sun Yat-sen.

Athletes Holding Portrait of Mao — A222

Two Women Athletes with Little Red Book — A223

Designs: No. 921, Athletes holding Little Red Books. No. 923, Athletes reading Mao texts.

1966, Dec. 31 *Perf. 11*

920 A222 8f red & multi (1) 10.00 3.50
921 A222 8f red & multi (2) 10.00 3.50

Perf. 11x11½

922 A223 8f blue & multi (3) 10.00 3.50
923 A223 8f blue & multi (4) 10.00 3.50
Nos. 920-923 (4) 40.00 14.00

1st Athletic Games of the New Emerging Nations.

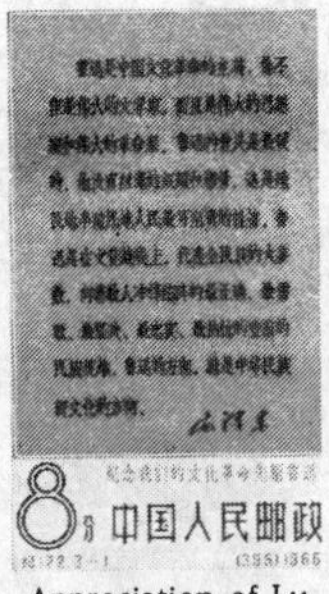

Appreciation of Lu Hsun by Mao — A224

"Be Resolute ...," by Mao Tse-tung — A225

Designs: No. 925, Portrait of Lu Hsun. No. 926, Lu Hsun's handwriting (3 vert. rows).

Engr. & Photo.; Photo. (#925)

1966, Dec. 31 *Perf. 11½*

924 A224 8f red & black (1) 15.00 4.25
925 A224 8f red & multi (2) 15.00 4.25
926 A224 8f red & black (3) 15.00 4.25
Nos. 924-926 (3) 45.00 12.75

Lu Hsun, Revolutionary writer (1881-1936).

Perf. 11½x11, 11½ (No. 928)

1967, Mar. 10 Photo.

Designs: No. 928, Drilling crew fighting natural gas fire, horiz. No. 929, Attempt to close fire-engulfed valve.

Sizes: Nos. 927, 929, 26x38mm; No. 928, 49x29mm

927 A225 8f red, gold & blk 11.00 3.00
928 A225 8f brick red & blk 11.00 3.00
929 A225 8f brick red & blk 11.00 3.00
Nos. 927-929 (3) 33.00 9.00

Heroic oil well firefighters.

Liu Ying-chun — A226

1967, Mar. 25 *Perf. 11½x11*

930 A226 8f shown (1) 8.25 1.90
931 A226 8f With book by Mao (2) 8.25 1.90
932 A226 8f Holding bridle of horse (3) 8.25 1.90
933 A226 8f With film slide (4) 8.25 1.90
934 A226 8f Lecturing (5) 8.25 1.90
935 A226 8f Fatal attempt to stop runaway horse (6) 8.25 1.90
Nos. 930-935 (6) 49.50 11.40

In memory of soldier Liu Ying-chun, hero.

Industrial Growth — A227

Design: No. 937, Banners and people facing left: agricultural growth.

1967, Apr. 15 *Perf. 11*

936 A227 8f red & multi 16.00 2.50
937 A227 8f red & multi 16.00 2.50

Third Five-Year Plan.

Mao Tse-tung — A228

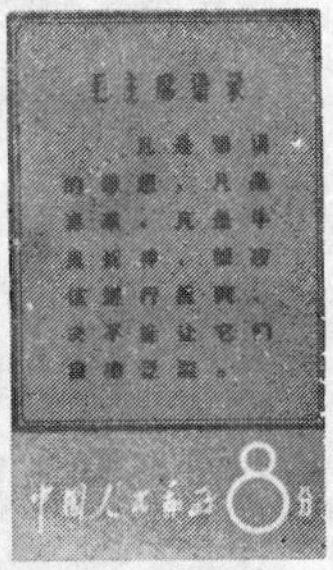

Thoughts of Mao — A229

1967, Apr. 20 *Perf. 11½*

938 A228 8f red & multi 24.00 7.00

Red & Gold

939 A229 8f 39 characters 24.00 7.00
940 A229 8f 50 characters 24.00 7.00
941 A229 8f 39 characters in 6 lines 24.00 7.00
942 A229 8f 53 characters 24.00 7.00
943 A229 8f 46 characters 24.00 7.00
a. Strip of 5, #939-943 175.00 62.50

Gold & Red

944 A229 8f 41 characters 24.00 7.00
945 A229 8f 49 characters 24.00 7.00
946 A229 8f 35 characters 24.00 7.00
947 A229 8f 22 characters 24.00 7.00
948 A229 8f 29 characters 24.00 7.00
a. Strip of 5, #944-948 175.00 62.50
Nos. 938-948 (11) 264.00 77.00

Thoughts of Mao Tse-tung.

No numbers appear below design on Nos. 938-1046.

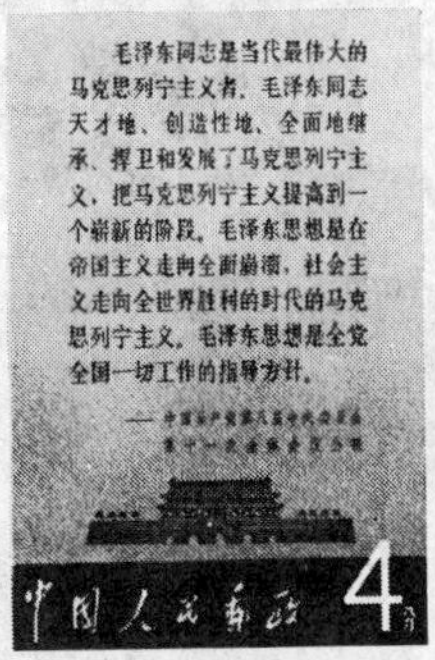

Gate of Heavenly Peace and Text from C. C. P. Communique Praising Mao — A230

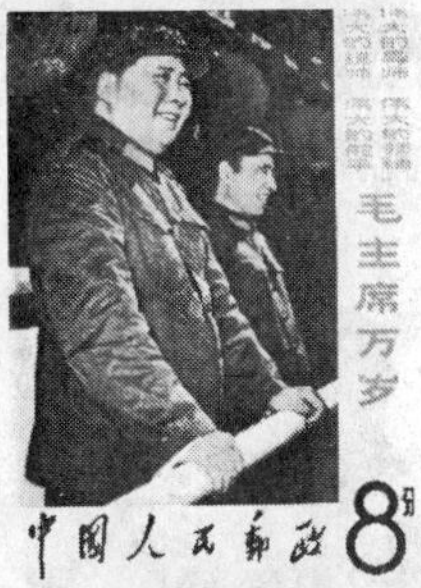

Mao and Lin Piao — A231

Designs: No. 950, Mao and poem. No. 951, Mao among people of various races. No. 952, Mao facing left and Red Guards with books. No. 953, Mao with upraised right hand. No. 954, Mao leaning on rail, horiz. 10f, Mao and Lin Piao in discussion, horiz.

Engraved and Photogravure

1967 *Perf. 11x11½*

Size: 36x56mm

949 A230 4f yel, red & mar 17.00 2.75

Photo.

950 A230 8f yel, brn, & red 17.00 2.75
951 A230 8f yel, red & multi 17.00 2.75
952 A230 8f yel, red & multi 17.00 2.75

Size: 36x50mm, 50x36mm

Perf. 11

953 A231 8f black & multi 17.00 2.75
954 A231 8f black & multi 90.00 25.00
955 A231 8f lt blue & multi 32.50 25.00
956 A231 10f black & multi 67.50 25.00
Nos. 949-956 (8) 275.00 88.75

"Mao Tse-tung Our Great Teacher."

Issue dates: Nos. 949-953, May 1; Nos. 954-956, Sept. 20.

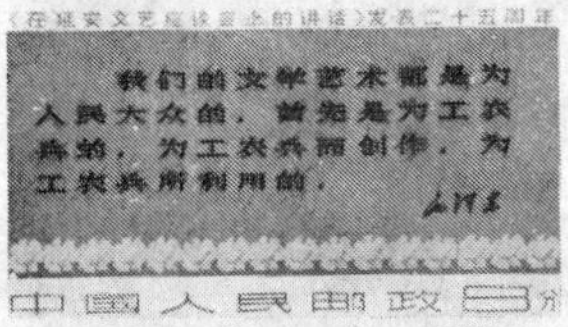

Mao Text (4 lines) — A232

Parade of Supporters — A233

Design: No. 958, Mao text (5 lines).

Engraved and Photogravure

1967, May 23 *Perf. 11½*

957 A232 8f black, red & yel 50.00 5.25
958 A232 8f black, red & yel 50.00 5.25

Photo. *Perf. 11*

959 A233 8f multicolored 50.00 5.25
Nos. 957-959 (3) 150.00 15.75

25th anniversary of Mao Tse-tung's "Talks on Literature and Art" in Yenan.

Mao Tse-tung — A234

1967 Engr. *Perf. 11*

960 A234 4f brown 21.00 8.50
961 A234 8f carmine 21.00 8.50
962 A234 35f dk brown 21.00 8.50

963	A234 43f vermilion	21.00	8.50
964	A234 52f carmine	21.00	8.50
	Nos. 960-964 (5)	105.00	42.50

46th anniv. of Chinese Communist Party. Issue dates: 8f, July 1, others Sept.

Mao, "Sun of the Revolution" — A235

Design: No. 966, Mao and people of various races.

1967, Oct. 1 ***Perf. 11½x11***

965	A235 8f multicolored	18.00	9.00
966	A235 8f multicolored	18.00	9.00

People's Republic of China, 18th anniv.

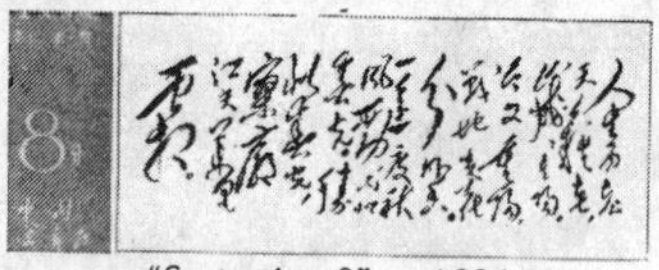
"September 9" — A236

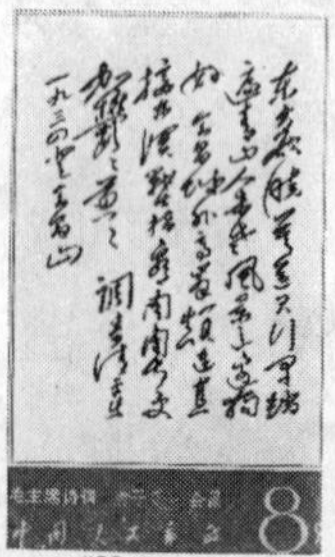
"Huichang" A237

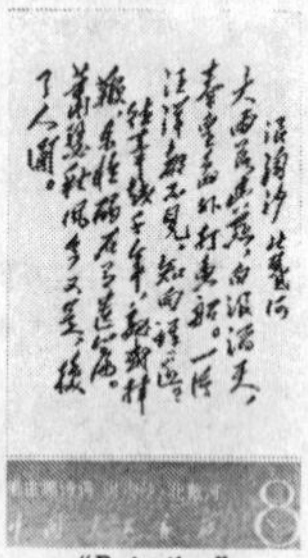
"Peitaiho" A238

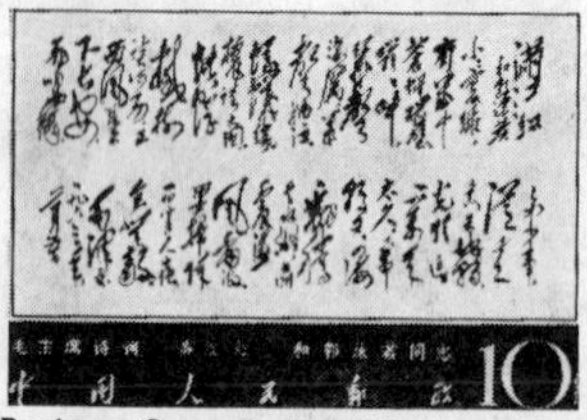
Reply to Comrade Kuo Mo-jo — A239

Mao Tse-tung Writing Poems — A240

Designs (Poems by Mao): No. 967, "The Long March." No. 968, "Liupanshan." No. 969, shown. No. 970, "The Cave of the Fairies." No. 971, "Snow." No. 972, "Lushan Pass." No. 975, "Conquest of Nanking." No. 976, "The Yellow Crane Pavilion." No. 977, "Swimming." No. 979, "Changsha."

1967-68 **Photo.** ***Perf. 11***

Size: 79x18½mm

967	A236 4f 9 characters, UL panel ('68)	32.50	7.00
968	A236 4f 11 characters, UL panel ('68)	32.50	7.00

Size: 60x24mm

Perf. 11½

969	A236 8f shown, 10 characters in UL panel	21.00	2.75
970	A236 8f 21 characters in UL panel	21.00	2.75
971	A236 8f 11 characters in UL panel	32.50	7.00
972	A236 8f 9 characters in UL panel	32.50	7.00

Size: 29x50mm

973	A237 8f shown	21.00	2.75
974	A238 8f shown	32.50	7.00
975	A238 8f 3 rows in bottom panel	21.00	2.75
976	A238 8f 2 rows in bottom panel	32.50	7.00

Size: 52x38mm

Perf. 11

977	A239 8f 3 short vert. rows, at left of poem	32.50	7.00
978	A239 10f shown	32.50	7.00
979	A239 10f undivided text	21.00	2.75
980	A240 10f red, yel & multi	26.00	7.00
	Nos. 967-980 (14)	391.00	76.75

Poems by Mao Tse-tung. Issue dates: Nos. 969-970, 980, Oct. 1, 1967; Nos. 973-974, 977, May 20, 1968; others July 20, 1968.

Lin Piao's Epigram on Mao Tse-tung A241

1967, Dec. 26 **Photo.** ***Perf. 11x11½***

981	A241 8f red & gold	22.50	5.00

Mao and Parade of Artists — A242

"Raid on White Tiger Regiment" — A243

"Red Detachment of Women" — A244

1968 ***Perf. 11½x11; 11 (983, 990)***

982	A242 8f shown (56x36mm)	11.00	2.00
983	A242 8f "The Red Lantern," vert.	11.00	2.00
984	A243 8f shown	11.00	2.00
985	A243 8f "Shachiapang" (women & soldier)	11.00	2.00
986	A243 8f "On the Dock"	11.00	2.00
987	A243 8f "Taking Bandits' Fort"	11.00	2.00
988	A244 8f shown	22.50	6.00
989	A244 8f "The White-haired Girl"	22.50	6.00
990	A242 8f Mao with Orchestra & Chorus (50x36mm)	16.00	6.00
	Nos. 982-990 (9)	127.00	30.00

Mao's direction for revolutionary literature and art. Issue dates: Nos. 982-987, Jan. 30; Nos. 988-990, May 1.

"Unite still more closely . . ." — A245

1968, May 31 **Photo.** ***Perf. 11***

991	A245 8f red, gold & red brn	26.00	7.25

Mao Tse-tung's statement of support of Afro-Americans.

Statement about Cultural Revolution — A246

Directives of Chairman Mao: No. 993, Experiences of Revolutionary Committee. No. 994, Leadership role of Revolutionary Committee. No. 995, Basic principle of reform. No. 996, Purpose of Cultural Revolution.

1968, July 20 **Photo.** ***Perf. 11½***

No. of Lines Over Signature

992	A246 8f shown	32.50	10.00
993	A246 8f 5	32.50	10.00
994	A246 8f 4½	32.50	10.00
995	A246 8f 4	32.50	10.00
996	A246 8f 8	32.50	10.00
a.	Strip of 5, #992-996	*550.00*	*125.00*
	Nos. 992-996 (5)	162.50	50.00

Lin Piao's Statement, July 26, 1965 — A247

1968, Aug. 1 **Engr. & Photo.**

997	A247 8f red, gold & blk	8.50	6.00

Chinese People's Liberation Army, 41st anniv.

Mao Tse-tung Going to An Yuan, 1921 — A248

1968, Aug. 1 ***Perf. 11x11½***

998	A248 8f multicolored	22.50	4.00

Shade varieties include varying amount of red in clouds.

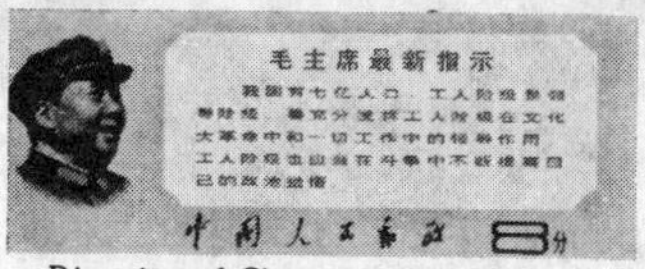

Directive of Chairman Mao — A249

1968, Nov. 30 ***Perf. 11½***

999	A249 8f red & blk brn	25.00	8.75

China Map, Worker, Farmer and Soldier — A249a

1968, Nov. **Photo.** ***Perf. 11½x11***

999A	A249a 8f red, bl & bis	*5,750.*	*3,000.*

Map inscribed: "The entire nation is red." Issued in Canton and quickly withdrawn because Taiwan appears white instead of red.

Woman, Miner and Soldier Holding Little Red Book — A250

1968, Dec. 26 ***Perf. 11x11½***

1000	A250 8f multicolored	11.00	3.50

Canceled-to-order
From about this point on stamps are valued postally used.

Yangtze Bridge, Nanking A251

Road across Bridge — A252

Designs: No. 1003, Side view. 10f, Aerial view.

Lithographed, *Perf. 11½x11 (A251)*; Photogravure, *Perf. 11½ (A252)*

1969

Without Gum

1001	A251 4f multicolored	5.00	2.25
1002	A252 8f multicolored	5.00	4.25
1003	A252 8f multicolored	5.00	2.25
1004	A251 10f multicolored	5.00	2.25
	Nos. 1001-1004 (4)	20.00	11.00

Inauguration of Yangtze Bridge at Nanking on Dec. 29, 1968.

Singer and Pianist A253

Designs (Piano Music from the Opera, "The Red Lantern"): No. 1006, Woman singer and pianist.

1969, Aug. Photo. *Perf. 11x11½*
Without Gum

1005	A253	8f multicolored	12.50	2.25
1006	A253	8f multicolored	12.50	2.25

Harvest A254

1969, Oct.

1007	A254	4f shown	5.00	2.50
a.		Brown omitted	50.00	40.00
1008	A254	8f Two harvesters	5.00	2.50
1009	A254	8f Harvesters with Little Red Books	10.00	3.75
1010	A254	10f Red Cross worker examining baby	5.00	1.25
		Nos. 1007-1010 (4)	25.00	10.00

Agriculture students.

Armed Forces and Slogan — A255

Guarding the Coast — A256

Designs: No. 1013, 43f, Snow patrol, vert.

1969, Oct. *Perf. 11½*

1011	A255	8f red & multi	4.00	*2.75*
a.		Bayonets omitted	80.00	40.00
1012	A256	8f blue & multi	4.00	*2.75*
1013	A256	8f blue & multi	4.00	*2.75*
1014	A256	35f black & multi	4.00	*4.25*
1015	A256	43f black & multi	4.00	*4.25*
		Nos. 1011-1015 (5)	20.00	*16.75*

Defense of Chen Pao-tao (Damansky Islands) in Ussuri River.

Farm Woman — A257

Designs: 8f, Foundry worker. 10f, Soldier.

1969, Dec. *Perf. 10; 11½ (#1017)*
Without Gum

1016	A257	4f ver & dk pur	55	1.25
1017	A257	8f ver & dk brn	55	1.25
1018	A257	10f ver & blk	55	1.25
		Nos. 1016-1018 (3)	1.65	3.75

Perforation

Nos. 1016-1018 and some succeeding issues bear two kinds of perforation: clean (Peking) and rough (Shanghai).

Building — A258

Communist Party Building, Shanghai — A259

Agriculture Building, Canton — A260

Foundry Worker — A261

Two types of 8f Gate of Heavenly Peace:
I- Strong, definite halo around sun.
II- Halo missing, white shades gradually into red.

1969-72 Photo. *Perf. 10, 11½*
Without Gum

1019	A258	1f shown	15	*18*
1020	A259	1½f shown	95	70
a.		Perf. 11½	5.50	5.00
1021	A260	2f shown	15	*15*
1022	A260	3f 1929 Party Day House, Pu Tien	15	15
1023	A260	4f Mao's Home and Office, Yunnan	15	*15*
1024	A261	5f Woman Tractor Driver	1.25	75
1025	A260	8f Gate of Heavenly Peace, type II	1.25	35
a.		Type I	2.00	60
1026	A259	8f Heroes Monument	1.25	70
a.		Perf. 11½	4.00	3.00
1027	A260	8f Pagoda Hill, Yenan	1.25	*3.50*
1028	A260	8f Gate of Heavenly Peace (no sun)	16	15
1029	A260	10f Monument, Tsu Ping	20	22
1030	A259	20f Conference Hall, Tsunyi	1.25	1.40
a.		Perf. 11½	5.50	4.00
1031	A260	20f Highway ('72)	25	22
1032	A260	22f Shao Shan Village, Birthplace of Mao	30	35
1033	A260	35f Conference Hall	40	35
1034	A260	43f Chingkang Peaks	50	35
1035	A259	50f as 4f, different view	2.75	1.40
1036	A260	52f People's Hall, Peking	65	35
1037	A261	$1 shown ('70)	2.75	2.75
		Nos. 1019-1037 (19)	15.76	14.17

Kin Hsün-hua — A262

Mounted Patrol — A263

1970, Jan. Without Gum *Perf. 11½*

1045	A262	8f red & black	10.50	*10.50*
a.		8f red & gray brown	12.00	12.00

Death of Kin Hsün-hua in Kirin border flood.

1970, Aug. 1
Without Gum

1046	A263	8f yel grn & multi	4.50	4.50

People's Liberation Army, 43rd anniv.

Beginning with No. 1047 commemorative stamps carry a cumulative number in parenthesis at lower left and the year at lower right. Where such numbers help to identify, they are quoted in parenthesis.

Cpl. Yang Tse-jung — A264

Ensemble — A265

1970, Aug. 1 *Perf. 11½x11, 11x11½*

1047	A264	8f shown (1)	4.00	4.00
1048	A264	8f Armed guards (2)	4.00	4.00
1049	A264	8f Yang leaping through forest (3)	4.00	4.00
1050	A265	8f shown (4)	4.00	4.00
1051	A265	8f Yang in folk costume (5)	4.00	4.00
1052	A265	8f Four actors (6)	4.00	4.00
		Nos. 1047-1052 (6)	24.00	24.00

Scenes from opera "Taking Tiger Mountain by Strategy." Nos. 1048, 1052, horizontal.

Frontier Guard A266

1971, Jan. Litho. *Perf. 10*
Without Gum

1053	A266	4f multicolored	1.00	1.00
a.		Perf. 11½	2.00	75
b.		Perf. 11½x10	4.00	
c.		Perf. 10x11½	5.00	

Banner of the Commune — A267

Street Battle, Paris, 1871 — A268

Designs: 10f, Proclamation of the Commune. 22f, Rally.

Perf. 11½x11, 11x11½
1971, Mar. 18 Litho. & Engr.

1054	A267	4f salmon & multi	8.00	8.00
1055	A268	8f ver, pink & brn	8.00	8.00
1056	A267	10f ver, pink & dk brn	8.00	8.00
1057	A268	22f ver, pink & dk brn	8.00	8.00
		Nos. 1054-1057 (4)	32.00	32.00

Centenary of the Paris Commune.

Redrawn Building Type of 1961

Designs: 2f, 3f, August 1 building, Nanchang. 4f, 52f, Gate of Heavenly Peace, Peking. 10f, 20f, Pagoda Hill, Yenan.

1971 Litho. *Perf. 11x11½*
Size: 21x16mm
Without Gum

1059	A152	2f slate green	2.00	2.00
1060	A152	3f sepia	2.00	2.00
1061	A152	4f brt pink	2.00	2.00
1062	A152	10f brt rose lil	2.00	2.00
1063	A152	20f dk blue grn	2.00	2.00
1064	A152	52f orange	2.00	2.00
		Nos. 1059-1064 (6)	12.00	12.00

Paper of Nos. 1059-1064 is white. That of Nos. 647-654 is toned.

Communist Party Building, Shanghai — A269

People and Factories — A270

Designs: No. 1068, Peasant Movement Training Institute. No. 1069, Ching Kang Peaks. No. 1070, Conference Building, Tsunyi. No. 1071, Pagoda Hill, Yenan. No. 1073, People and People's Hall, Peking. No. 1074, People and Pagoda Hill, Yenan. 22f, Gate of Heavenly Peace, Peking.

1971, July 1 Photo. *Perf. 11½*
Red and Gold Frame

1067	A269	4f vermilion (12)	2.25	2.25
1068	A269	4f brt grn (13)	2.25	2.25
1069	A269	8f grnsh bl & red (14)	2.25	2.25
1070	A269	8f ol blk (15)	2.25	2.25
1071	A269	8f bis, grn & red (16)	2.25	2.25
1072	A270	8f yel, red & multi (18)	2.25	2.25
1073	A270	8f yel, red & multi (19)	2.25	2.25
1074	A270	8f yel, red & multi (20)	2.25	2.25
a.		Strip of 3, #1072-1074	7.50	7.50
1075	A269	22f red, gold & brn (17)	2.25	2.25
		Nos. 1067-1075 (9)	20.25	20.25

50th anniv. of the Chinese Communist Party. No. 1074a has a continuous design.

Welcome — A271

Hoxha — A272

Designs: No. 1077, Chinese and African players. No. 1078, Chinese and African girl players. 43f, Games' emblem.

1971, Nov. 3 Litho. *Perf. 11½*

1076	A271	8f lilac rose & multi	65	65
1077	A271	8f lt yellow & multi	65	65
1078	A271	8f dk green & multi	65	65
1079	A271	43f grn, gold & org	3.50	3.50
		Nos. 1076-1079 (4)	5.45	5.45

Afro-Asian Table Tennis Games, Peking.

1971, Nov. 3 Photo. *Perf. 11*

Designs: No. 1081, Party's birthplace. No. 1082, Albanian flag. 52f, Albanian partisans, horiz.

1080	A272	8f Prus blue & multi	2.25	2.25
1081	A272	8f buff & multi	2.25	2.25
1082	A272	8f red, yel & multi	2.25	2.25
1083	A272	52f lt blue & multi	2.25	2.25
		Nos. 1080-1083 (4)	9.00	9.00

30th anniversary of the founding of Albanian Communist Party.

Yenan Pagoda and 1942 Meeting House A273

1972, May 23 Photo. *Perf. 11*

1084 A273 8f shown (33)	2.75	2.75
1085 A273 8f Uniformed choir (34)	2.75	2.75
1086 A273 8f "Brother & Sister" (35)	2.75	2.75
1087 A273 8f Outdoor performance (36)	2.75	2.75
1088 A273 8f "The Red Signal Lantern" (37)	2.75	2.75
1089 A273 8f Dancer from "The Red Company of Women" (38)	2.75	2.75
Nos. 1084-1089 (6)	16.50	16.50

30th anniversary of the publication of the Discussions on Literature and Art at the Yenan Forum.

Various Ball Games — A274

Workers' Gymnastics — A275

1972, June 10

1090 A274 8f shown (39)	1.00	1.00
1091 A275 8f shown (40)	1.00	1.00
1092 A275 8f Tug of war (41)	1.00	1.00
1093 A275 8f Mountain climbers and tents (42)	1.00	1.00
1094 A275 8f Children diving & swimming (43)	1.00	1.00
Nos. 1090-1094 (5)	5.00	5.00

10th anniversary of Mao Tse-tung's edict on physical culture.

Ocean Freighter Fenglei — A276

1972, July 10 Photo. *Perf. 11½*

1095 A276 8f shown (29)	2.00	2.00
1096 A276 8f Tanker Taching No. 30 (30)	2.00	2.00
1097 A276 8f Cargo-passenger ship Changzeng (31)	2.00	2.00
1098 A276 8f Dredger Xienfeng (32)	2.00	2.00
Nos. 1095-1098 (4)	8.00	8.00

Table Tennis Players' Welcome A277

Perf. 11½x11, 11x11½

1972, Sept. 2

1099 A277 8f Championship emblem, vert (45)	70	15
1100 A277 8f shown (46)	70	15
1101 A277 8f Table tennis (47)	70	15
1102 A277 22f Women from different countries, vert. (48)	3.00	65
Nos. 1099-1102 (4)	5.10	1.10

First Asian table tennis championships.

Wang Chin-hsi — A278

Workers on Cliffs along Canal — A279

Engraved and Photogravure

1972, Dec. 25 *Perf. 11½x11*

1103 A278 8f multicolored (44)	2.00	2.00

Wang Chin-hsi, the Iron Man, fighter for the working class.

1972, Dec. 30

Designs: No. 1105, Canal flowing through tunnel. No. 1106, Bridge. No. 1107, Canal along cliffs.

1104 A279 8f multicolored (49)	60	60
1105 A279 8f multicolored (50)	60	60
1106 A279 8f multicolored (51)	60	60
1107 A279 8f multicolored (52)	60	60
Nos. 1104-1107 (4)	2.40	2.40

Construction of Red Flag Canal, Linhsien county, Honan.

Giant Panda — A280

Woman Coal Miner — A281

Designs: Pandas in various positions. The 8f stamps are horizontal.

Perf. 11½x11, 11x11½

1973, Jan. 15 Photo.

Designs in Black and Red

1108 A280 4f lt yel grn (61)	7.50	7.50
1109 A280 8f buff (59)	7.50	7.50
1110 A280 8f lt tan (60)	7.50	7.50
1111 A280 10f pale green (58)	7.50	7.50
1112 A280 20f pale bl gray (57)	7.50	7.50
1113 A280 43f pale lilac (62)	7.50	7.50
Nos. 1108-1113 (6)	45.00	45.00

1973, Mar. 8 Photo. *Perf. 11½x11*

1114 A281 8f shown (63)	90	90
1115 A281 8f Committee member (64)	90	90
1116 A281 8f Telephone line worker (65)	90	90
Nos. 1114-1116 (3)	2.70	2.70

Intl. Working Women's Day. Designs are after paintings from an exhib. for 30th anniv. of the Yenan Forum on Literature and Art.

Dancing Girl — A282

Tournament Emblem — A283

1973, June 1 Photo. *Perf. 11*

1117 A282 8f shown (86)	52	52
1118 A282 8f Musician, boy (87)	52	52
1119 A282 8f Girl with scarf (88)	52	52
1120 A282 8f Boy with tambourine (89)	52	52
1121 A282 8f Girl with drum (90)	52	52
a. Strip of 5, #1117-1121	3.00	3.00
Nos. 1117-1121 (5)	2.60	2.60

1973, Aug. 25 Photo. *Perf. 11½*

Designs: No. 1123, Visitors from Asia, Africa and Latin America arriving by plane. No. 1124, Woman player. 22f, African, Asian and Latin American women.

1122 A283 8f multicolored (91)	1.00	1.00
1123 A283 8f multicolored (92)	1.00	1.00
1124 A283 8f multicolored (93)	1.00	1.00
1125 A283 22f multicolored (94)	1.00	1.00
Nos. 1122-1125 (4)	4.00	4.00

Asian, African and Latin American Table Tennis Friendship Invitational Tournament.

The White-haired Girl — A284

Designs: Scenes from the ballet "The White-haired Girl." Nos. 1126, 1129 vert.

1973, Sept. 25 Photo. *Perf. 11½*

1126 A284 8f multicolored (53)	1.50	1.50
1127 A284 8f multicolored (54)	1.50	1.50
1128 A284 8f multicolored (55)	1.50	1.50
1129 A284 8f multicolored (56)	1.50	1.50
Nos. 1126-1129 (4)	6.00	6.00

Fair Building, Canton — A285

1973, Oct. 15 Photo. *Perf. 11*

1130 A285 8f multicolored (95)	2.00	2.00

Export Commodities Fall Fair, Canton.

Teapot with Blue Phoenix Design — A286

Excavated Works of Art: No. 1132, Silver pot with horse design. No. 1133, Black pottery horse. No. 1134, Woman, clay figurine. No. 1135, Carved stone pillar base. No. 1136, Galloping bronze horse. No. 1137, Bronze inkwell (toad). No. 1138, Bronze lamp, Chang Hsin Palace. No. 1139, Bronze tripod. No. 1140, Square bronze pot. 20f, Bronze wine vessel. 52f, Painted red clay tripod.

1973, Nov. 20 *Perf. 11½*

1131 A286 4f ol bis & multi (66)	42	42
1132 A286 4f ver & multi (67)	42	42
1133 A286 8f yel grn & multi (68)	42	42
1134 A286 8f brt rose & multi (69)	42	42
1135 A286 8f lt vio & multi (70)	42	42
1136 A286 8f yel bis & multi (71)	42	42
1137 A286 8f lt bl & multi (72)	42	42
1138 A286 8f gray & multi (73)	42	42
1139 A286 10f yel bis & multi (74)	42	42
1140 A286 10f dp org & multi (75)	42	42
1141 A286 20f lil & multi (76)	1.00	1.00
1142 A286 52f grn & multi (77)	2.75	2.75
Nos. 1131-1142 (12)	7.95	7.95

Marginal Markings

Marginal inscriptions on stamps of 1974-91 start at lower left with "J" for commemoratives and "T" for "special issues," followed by three numbers indicating (a) set sequence for the year, (b) total of stamps in set, and (c) number of stamp within set. At right appears the year date. Listings include the "c" number parenthetically. The "a" number is included only when it will help identify stamps not illustrated.

Example: T26 (6-3), the 3rd stamp of 6 from the 26th special set. Set numbers and or positions will be shown only when they help identify a stamp. An illustrated single stamp set will not have these numbers in the listings.

Woman Gymnast — A287

Designs: No. 1144, Gymnast on rings. No. 1145, Aerial split over balance beam, woman. No. 1146, Gymnast on parallel bars. No. 1147, Uneven bars, woman. No. 1148, Gymnast on horse. T.1.

1974, Jan. 1 Photo. *Perf. 11½x11*

1143 A287 8f lt grn & multi (1)	3.25	3.25
1144 A287 8f lt vio & multi (2)	3.25	3.25
1145 A287 8f lt blue & multi (3)	3.25	3.25
1146 A287 8f sal & multi (4)	3.25	3.25
1147 A287 8f yel & multi (5)	3.25	3.25
1148 A287 8f lil rose & multi (6)	3.25	3.25
Nos. 1143-1148 (6)	19.50	19.50

Girls Twirling Bamboo Diabolos — A288

Designs: No. 1149, Lion Dance, vert. No. 1150, Handstand on chairs, vert. No. 1152, Men balancing jar. No. 1153, Plate spinning, vert. No. 1154, Twirling umbrella, vert. T.2.

1974, Jan. 21 *Perf. 11*

1149 A288 8f brown & multi (1)	3.25	3.25
1150 A288 8f Prus bl & multi (2)	3.25	3.25
1151 A288 8f lilac & multi (3)	3.25	3.25
1152 A288 8f dull bl & multi (4)	3.25	3.25
1153 A288 8f ol grn & multi (5)	3.25	3.25
1154 A288 8f gray & multi (6)	3.25	3.25
Nos. 1149-1154 (6)	19.50	19.50

Traditional acrobatics.

Shao Shan — A289

Transportation by Railroad A290

Designs: 1½f, Site of 1st National Communist Party Congress. 2f, Peasant Movement Institute, Kwangchow. 3f, Headquarters of Nanchang Uprising. 4f, Great Hall of the People, Peking. 5f, View of Wen Chia Shih. 8f, Tien An Men. 10f, Tzeping in Chingkang Mountains. 20f, Site of Kutien Meeting. 22f, Tsunyi Conference site. 35f, Yenan (bridge). 43f, Hsi Pai Ho, Communist Party meeting site. 50f, Fairy Cave, Lushan. 52f, Monument to People's Heroes. $2, Trucks on mountain road.

1974 Litho. *Perf. 11*

Without Gum

1163	A289	1f sl grn & pale grn	15	15
1164	A289	1½f car & buff	15	45
1165	A289	2f dk blue & pale grn	15	15
1166	A289	3f dk ol & yel	15	15
1167	A289	4f red & yel	15	15
1168	A289	5f brn & lt yel	15	15
1169	A289	8f dull mag & buff	15	15
a.		Perf. 11½x12	4.00	
1170	A289	10f blue & pink	15	15
1171	A289	20f dk red & buff	20	20
1172	A289	22f vio & lt yel	24	24
1173	A289	35f mar & lt yel	32	32
1174	A289	43f red brn & buff	45	*85*
1175	A289	50f dk blue & pink	*2.75*	*52*
1176	A289	52f sepia & buff	52	52

Photogravure & Engraved

1177	A290	$1 multicolored	1.00	42
1178	A290	$2 multicolored	2.00	65
		Nos. 1163-1178 (16)	8.68	5.22

Capital Stadium — A290a

Design: 8f, Hotel Peking.

1974, Dec. 1 Photo. *Perf. 11*

Without Gum

1179	A290a	4f black & yel grn	18	15
1180	A290a	8f black & ultra	32	15
		Set value		20

"Veteran Secretary" — A291

Well Diggers — A292

Designs: Nos. 1183-1186 horizontal. T.3.

1974, Apr. 20 Photo. *Perf. 11*

1181	A291	8f shown (1)	1.65	1.65
1182	A292	8f shown (2)	1.65	1.65
1183	A291	8f Spring hoeing (3)	1.65	1.65
1184	A291	8f Farmers (4)	1.65	1.65
1185	A292	8f Farm (5)	1.65	1.65
1186	A291	8f Bumper crops (6)	1.65	1.65
		Nos. 1181-1186 (6)	9.90	9.90

Paintings by farmers of Huhsien County, shown at exhibition in Peking.

Mailman on Motorcycle — A293

1974, May 15 Photo. *Perf. 11*

1187	A293	8f shown (1)	4.00	4.00
1188	A293	8f People of the world (2)	4.00	4.00
1189	A293	8f Great Wall (3)	4.00	4.00
		Nos. 1187-1189 (3)	12.00	12.00

Centenary of the UPU. J.1.

Barefoot Doctor Inoculating Children A294

Designs (Barefoot Doctors): No. 1191, Crossing stream at night to reach patient, vert. No. 1192, Gathering herbs, vert. No. 1193, Acupuncture treatment for farmer in the field.

Perf. 11x11½, 11½x11

1974, June 26 Photo.

1190	A294	8f multicolored (82)	75	75
1191	A294	8f multicolored (83)	75	75
1192	A294	8f multicolored (84)	75	75
1193	A294	8f multicolored (85)	75	75
		Nos. 1190-1193 (4)	3.00	3.00

Steel Worker Wang Chin-hsi — A295

Designs: No. 1195, Workers studying Mao's writings around campfire. No. 1196, Drilling for oil in winter. No. 1197, Scientific industrial management. No. 1198, Oil derricks and farms. T.4.

1974, Sept. 30 Photo. *Perf. 11*

1194	A295	8f multicolored (5-1)	1.25	1.25
1195	A295	8f multicolored (5-2)	1.25	1.25
1196	A295	8f multicolored (5-3)	1.25	1.25
1197	A295	8f multicolored (5-4)	1.25	1.25
1198	A295	8f multicolored (5-5)	1.25	1.25
		Nos. 1194-1198 (5)	6.25	6.25

The workers of Taching as examples of achievement.

Members of Tachai Commune — A296

Designs: No. 1200, Farmers leveling mountains and fields in winter. No. 1201, Scientific farming. No. 1202, Trucks carrying surplus harvest. No. 1203, Young workers with banner. T.5.

1974, Sept. 30

1199	A296	8f multi (5-1)	90	90
1200	A296	8f multi (5-2)	90	90
1201	A296	8f multi (5-3)	90	90
1202	A296	8f multi (5-4)	90	90
1203	A296	8f multi (5-5)	90	90
		Nos. 1199-1203 (5)	4.50	4.50

The farmers of Tachai as examples of achievement.

Arms of Republic and Members of Ethnic Groups — A297

Taching Steel Worker — A298

Designs: No. 1206, Tachai farm woman. No. 1207, Soldier, planes and ships. J.3.

1974, Oct. 1

1204	A297	8f multi (1-1)	4.25	4.25
1205	A298	8f multi (3-1)	1.25	1.25
1206	A298	8f multi (3-2)	1.25	1.25
1207	A298	8f multi (3-3)	1.25	1.25
a.		Strip of 3, #1205-1207	4.00	4.00
		Nos. 1204-1207 (4)	8.00	8.00

People's Republic of China, 25th anniv.

Export Commodities Fair Building, Canton — A299

1974, Oct. 15

1208	A299	8f multicolored	2.00	2.00

Chinese Export Commodities Fair, Canton.

Guerrillas' Monument, Permet, Albania — A300

Albanian Patriots and Coat of Arms — A301

1974, Nov. 29 Photo. *Perf. 11½x11*

1209	A300	8f multicolored	2.25	2.25
1210	A301	8f multicolored	2.25	2.25

Albania's liberation, 30th anniversary.

Water-cooled Generator — A302

Industrial Products: No. 1212, Motorized rice sprouts transplanter. No. 1213, Universal cylindrical grinding machine. No. 1214, Open-air rock drill, vert. All dated 1973.

Photogravure and Engraved

1974, Dec. 23 *Perf. 11*

1211	A302	8f violet & multi (78)	2.25	2.25
1212	A302	8f yel grn & multi (79)	2.25	2.25
1213	A302	8f ver & multi (80)	2.25	2.25
1214	A302	8f blue & multi (81)	2.25	2.25
		Nos. 1211-1214 (4)	9.00	9.00

Congress Delegates — A303

Designs: No. 1216, Red flags, constitution and flowers. No. 1217, Worker, farmer and soldier, agriculture and industry. J.5.

1975, Jan. 25 Photo. *Perf. 11½*

1215	A303	8f gold & multi (3-1)	2.50	2.50
1216	A303	8f gold & multi (3-2)	2.50	2.50
1217	A303	8f gold & multi (3-3)	2.50	2.50
		Nos. 1215-1217 (3)	7.50	7.50

Fourth National People's Congress, Peking.

Teacher Studying Revolutionary Works A304

Designs: No. 1219, Teacher, children and horse. No. 1220, Outdoors class. No. 1221, Class held in boat. T.9.

1975, Mar. 8 Photo. *Perf. 11*

1218	A304	8f multi (4-1)	3.00	3.00
1219	A304	8f multi (4-2)	3.00	3.00
1220	A304	8f multi (4-3)	3.00	3.00
1221	A304	8f multi (4-4)	3.00	3.00
		Nos. 1218-1221 (4)	12.00	12.00

Rural women teachers and for International Working Women's Day.

"Broadsword," Encounter Position — A305

Designs: No. 1223, Exercise with 2 swords (woman). No. 1224, Graceful boxing (woman). No. 1225, Man leaping with spear. No. 1226, Woman holding cudgel. 43f, Two women with spears against man with cudgel.

1975, June 10 Photo. *Perf. 11x11½*

Size: 39x29mm

1222	A305	8f (6-1)	2.50	2.50
1223	A305	8f (6-2)	2.50	2.50
1224	A305	8f (6-3)	2.50	2.50
1225	A305	8f (6-4)	2.50	2.50
1226	A305	8f (6-5)	2.50	2.50

Size: 59x29mm

1227	A305	43f red & multi (6-6)	5.00	5.00
		Nos. 1222-1227 (6)	17.50	17.50

Wushu ("Kung Fu"), self-defense exercises. Tête bêche in sheets of 50 (5x10).

Mass Judgment and Criticisms — A306

Designs: No. 1229, Brigade leader writing wall newspaper. No. 1230, Study and criticism on battlefield, horiz. No. 1231, Former "slave" led into battle by criticism of Lin Piao and Confucius, horiz. T.8.

Perf. 11½x11, 11x11½

1975, Aug. 20 Photo.

1228	A306	8f red & multi (4-1)	3.00	3.00
1229	A306	8f red & multi (4-2)	3.00	3.00
1230	A306	8f red & multi (4-3)	3.00	3.00
1231	A306	8f red & multi (4-4)	3.00	3.00
		Nos. 1228-1231 (4)	12.00	12.00

Campaign to encourage criticism of Lin Piao and Confucius.

Athletes Studying Theory of Dictatorship of Proletariat — A307

3rd National Sports Meet: No. 1232, Women athletes leading parade, vert. No. 1234, Women volleyball players. No. 1235, Runner, soldier, farmer and worker, vert. No. 1236, Young athlete and various sports. No. 1237, Athletes of various races and horse race. 35f, Children and diving tower, vert. J.6.

1975, Sept. 12 Photo. *Perf. 11½*

1232 A307 8f multi (7-1) 60 60
1233 A307 8f multi (7-2) 60 60
1234 A307 8f multi (7-3) 60 60
1235 A307 8f multi (7-4) 60 60
1236 A307 8f multi (7-5) 60 60
1237 A307 8f multi (7-6) 60 60
1238 A307 35f multi (7-7) 2.50 2.50
Nos. 1232-1238 (7) 6.10 6.10

Mountaineers A308

Mt. Everest A309

Design: No. 1240, Mountaineers raising Chinese flag on summit, horiz. T.15.

1975 Photo. *Perf. 11½x11, 11x11½*

1239 A308 8f multi (3-2) 35 35
1240 A308 8f multi (3-3) 35 35
1241 A309 43f multi (3-1) 1.25 1.25
Nos. 1239-1241 (3) 1.95 1.95

Chinese Mt. Everest expedition.

Agricultural Workers with Book — A310

Designs: No. 1243, Workers carrying load. No. 1244, Woman driving harvester combine. J.7.

1975, Oct. 1 *Perf. 11½*

1242 A310 8f multi (3-1) 1.65 1.65
1243 A310 8f multi (3-2) 1.65 1.65
1244 A310 8f multi (3-3) 1.65 1.65
Nos. 1242-1244 (3) 4.95 4.95

National Conference to promote learning from Tachai's achievements in agriculture.

Girl Giving Boy Red Scarf — A311

Designs (Children): No. 1246, Putting up wall posters criticizing Lin Piao and Confucius. No. 1247, Studying. No. 1248, Harvesting. 52f, Physical training. T.14.

1975, Dec. 1 Photo. *Perf. 11½*

1245 A311 8f multi (5-1) 52 52
1246 A311 8f multi (5-2) 52 52
1247 A311 8f multi (5-3) 52 52
1248 A311 8f multi (5-4) 52 52
1249 A311 52f multi (5-5) 4.00 4.00
Nos. 1245-1249 (5) 6.08 6.08

Moral, intellectual and physical progress of Chinese children.

Woman Plowing Rice Field — A312

Designs: No. 1251, Mechanized rice planting. No. 1252, Drainage and irrigation. No. 1253, Woman spraying insecticide over cotton field. No. 1254, Combine. T.13.

1975, Dec. 15 *Perf. 11*

1250 A312 8f multi (5-1) 1.40 1.40
1251 A312 8f multi (5-2) 1.40 1.40
1252 A312 8f multi (5-3) 1.40 1.40
1253 A312 8f multi (5-4) 1.40 1.40
1254 A312 8f multi (5-5) 1.40 1.40
Nos. 1250-1254 (5) 7.00 7.00

Priority program of farm mechanization.

Farmland and Irrigation Canal — A313

Designs of Nos. 1255-1270 numbered J.8.

1976, Feb. 20 Photo. *Perf. 11½*

1255 A313 8f shown (16-1) 1.65 1.65
1256 A313 8f Irrigation canal (16-2) 1.65 1.65
1257 A313 8f Fertilizer plant (16-3) 1.65 1.65
1258 A313 8f Textile plant (16-4) 1.65 1.65
1259 A313 8f Anshan Iron and Steel Co. (16-5) 1.65 1.65

Nos. 1255-1270 commemorate fulfillment of 4th Five-year Plan.

1976, Apr. 9

1260 A313 8f Coal freight trains (16-6) 1.65 1.65
1261 A313 8f Hydroelectric station (16-7) 1.65 1.65
1262 A313 8f Ship building (16-8) 1.65 1.65
1263 A313 8f Oil industry (16-9) 1.65 1.65
1264 A313 8f Pipe line and port (16-10) 1.65 1.65

1976, June 12

1265 A313 8f Train on viaduct (16-11) 1.65 1.65
1266 A313 8f Scientific research (16-12) 1.65 1.65
1267 A313 8f Classroom (16-13) 1.65 1.65
1268 A313 8f Health Center (16-14) 1.65 1.65
1269 A313 8f Apartment houses (16-15) 1.65 1.65
1270 A313 8f Department store (16-16) 1.65 1.65
Nos. 1255-1270 (16) 26.40 26.40

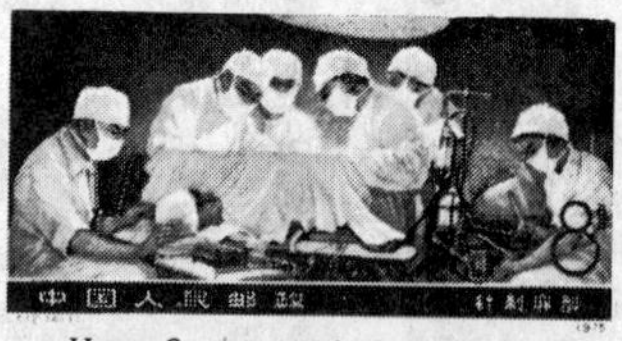

Heart Surgery with Acupuncture Anesthesia — A314

Designs (Operating Room and): No. 1272, Man driving tractor with severed arm restored. No. 1273, Man exercising broken arm in cast. No. 1274, Patient threading needle after cataract operation. T.12.

1976, Apr. 9 Photo. *Perf. 11½*

1271 A314 8f brn & multi (4-1) 1.75 1.75
1272 A314 8f yel grn & multi (4-2) 1.75 1.75
1273 A314 8f bl grn & multi (4-3) 1.75 1.75
1274 A314 8f vio bl & multi (4-4) 1.75 1.75
Nos. 1271-1274 (4) 7.00 7.00

Achievements in medical and health services.

Students in May 7 School — A315

Designs: No. 1276, Students as farm workers. No. 1277, Production brigade. J.9.

1976, May 7 Photo. *Perf. 11½*

1275 A315 8f multi (3-1) 1.40 1.40
1276 A315 8f multi (3-2) 1.40 1.40
1277 A315 8f multi (3-3) 1.40 1.40
Nos. 1275-1277 (3) 4.20 4.20

Chairman Mao's May 7 Directive, 10th anniv.

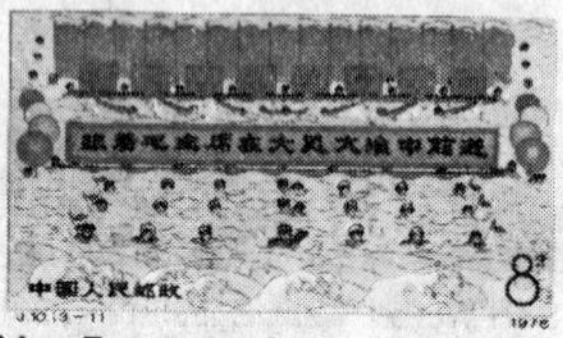

Mass Training in Swimming — A316

Designs: No. 1279, Swimmers crossing Yangtze River. No. 1280, Swimmers walking into the surf. J.10.

1976, July 16 Photo. *Perf. 11½*

Size: 47x27mm

1278 A316 8f multi (3-1) 1.40 1.40

Size: 35x27mm

1279 A316 8f multi (3-2) 1.40 1.40
1280 A316 8f multi (3-3) 1.40 1.40
Nos. 1278-1280 (3) 4.20 4.20

Chairman Mao's swim in Yangtze River, 10th anniversary.

Workers, Peasants and Soldiers Going to College — A317

Designs: No. 1282, Classroom. No. 1283, Instruction on construction site. No. 1284, Computer room. No. 1285, Graduates returning home. T.18.

1976, Sept. 6 Photo. *Perf. 11½*

1281 A317 8f multi (5-1) 1.50 1.50
1282 A317 8f multi (5-2) 1.50 1.50
1283 A317 8f multi (5-3) 1.50 1.50
1284 A317 8f multi (5-4) 1.50 1.50
1285 A317 8f multi (5-5) 1.50 1.50
Nos. 1281-1285 (5) 7.50 7.50

Success of proletarian education system.

Power Line Repair by Woman — A318

Designs: No. 1287, Insulator repair. No. 1288, Cherry picker. No. 1289, Transformer repair. T.16.

1976, Sept. 15

1286 A318 8f multi (4-1) 1.25 1.25
1287 A318 8f multi (4-2) 1.25 1.25
1288 A318 8f multi (4-3) 1.25 1.25
1289 A318 8f multi (4-4) 1.25 1.25
Nos. 1286-1289 (4) 5.00 5.00

Maintenance of high power lines.

Lu Hsun — A319

Designs: No. 1291, Lu Hsun sick, writing in bed. No. 1292, Lu Hsun with worker, soldier and peasant. J.11.

Photo. & Engr.

1976, Oct. 19 *Perf. 11x11½*

1290 A319 8f multi (3-1) 2.50 2.50

Photo.

1291 A319 8f multi (3-2) 2.50 2.50
1292 A319 8f multi (3-3) 2.50 2.50
Nos. 1290-1292 (3) 7.50 7.50

Lu Hsun (1881-1936), writer and revolutionary leader.

Old Farmer Tying Towel on Student's Head — A320

Designs: No. 1294, Student teaching farm woman, horiz. No. 1295, Students climbing mountain for new water resources. No. 1296, Student testing wheat, horiz. 10f, Student feeding lamb. 20f, Frontier guards, horiz. T.17.

1976, Dec. 22 Photo. *Perf. 11½*

1293 A320 4f multi (6-1) 75 75
1294 A320 8f multi (6-2) 75 75
1295 A320 8f multi (6-3) 75 75
1296 A320 8f multi (6-4) 75 75
1297 A320 10f multi (6-5) 75 75
1298 A320 20f multi (6-6) 3.25 3.25
Nos. 1293-1298 (6) 7.00 7.00

Students' efforts to help poor country people.

Mao's Home, Shaoshan — A321

Shaoshan, Mao's birthplace: No. 1300, School building. No. 1301, Farmers' Association building. 10f, Railroad station. T.11.

1976, Dec. 26 *Perf. 11*

1299 A321 4f multi (4-1) 1.40 1.40
1300 A321 8f multi (4-2) 1.40 1.40
1301 A321 8f multi (4-3) 1.40 1.40
1302 A321 10f multi (4-4) 1.40 1.40
Nos. 1299-1302 (4) 5.60 5.60

Chou En-lai — A322

Designs: No. 1304, Chou giving report at 10th Party Congress. No. 1305, Chou with Wang Chinhsi, famous oil worker, horiz. No. 1306, Chou with people of Tachai, 1973, horiz. J.13.

1977, Jan. 8 Photo. *Perf. 11½*

1303 A322 8f multi (4-1) 75 75
1304 A322 8f multi (4-2) 75 75
1305 A322 8f multi (4-3) 75 75
1306 A322 8f multi (4-4) 75 75
Nos. 1303-1306 (4) 3.00 3.00

Premier Chou En-lai (1898-1976), a founder of Chinese Communist Party, 1st death anniversary.

Liu Hu-lan, an Inspiration — A323

Liu Hu-lan, Chinese heroine: No. 1307, Liu Hu-lan monument. No. 1308, Mao Tse-tung quotation: "A great life-a glorious death." J.12.

1977, Jan. 31

1307 A323 8f multi (3-1) 2.00 2.00
1308 A323 8f multi (3-2) 2.00 2.00
1309 A323 8f multi (3-3) 2.00 2.00
Nos. 1307-1309 (3) 6.00 6.00

Uprising in Taiwan A324

Design: 10f, Gate of Heavenly Peace, Peking; Sun Moon Lake, Taiwan, Taiwanese people holding PRC flag. J.14.

1977, Feb. 28 Photo. *Perf. 11*

1310 A324 8f multi (2-1) 1.65 1.65
1311 A324 10f multi (2-2) 1.65 1.65

Uprising of the people of Taiwan, Feb. 28, 1947.

Sharpshooters — A325

Militia Women: No. 1313, Women horseback riders. No. 1314, Underground defense tunnel. T.10.

1977, Mar. 8 *Perf. 11½*

1312 A325 8f multi (3-1) 2.25 2.25
1313 A325 8f multi (3-2) 2.25 2.25
1314 A325 8f multi (3-3) 2.25 2.25
Nos. 1312-1314 (3) 6.75 6.75

Forestry — A326

Designs: 1f, Coal mining. 1½f, Sheepherding. 2f, Export (loading railroad car onto ship). 4f, Hydroelectric station. 5f, Fishery. 8f, Combine in field. 10f, Radio tower and mail truck. 20f, Steel production. 30f, Trucks on mountain road. 40f, Textiles. 50f, Tractor assembly line. 60f, Offshore oil rigs and birds, setting sun. 70f, Railroad bridge, Yangtze Gorge. No numbers.

1977 Photo. *Perf. 11½*

1315 A326 1f yel grn, red & blk 15 15
1316 A326 1½f bl grn, yel grn & brn 15 *40*
1317 A326 2f org, bl & blk 15 15
1318 A326 3f ol & dk grn 15 15
1319 A326 4f lil, org & blk 15 15
1320 A326 5f lt ol & ultra 15 15
1321 A326 8f red & yel 15 15
1322 A326 10f lt grn, org & bl 15 15
1323 A326 20f org, yel & brn 28 15
1324 A326 30f bl, lt grn & blk 32 15
1325 A326 40f multicolored 35 32
1326 A326 50f cit, red & blk 40 18
1327 A326 60f pur, yel & org 55 24
1328 A326 70f blue & multi 65 40
Nos. 1315-1328 (14) 3.75
Set value 2.10

Address by Party Committee A327

Designs: No. 1330, Planting new rice fields. No. 1331, Farmers reading wall newspaper. No. 1332, Land reclamation. T.22.

1977, Apr. 9 *Perf. 11x11½*

1329 A327 8f multi (4-1) 75 75
1330 A327 8f multi (4-2) 75 75
1331 A327 8f multi (4-3) 75 75
1332 A327 8f multi (4-4) 75 75
Nos. 1329-1332 (4) 3.00 3.00

Building Tachai-type communities throughout China.

Worker at Microphone — A328

Designs: No. 1334, Drilling for oil during snowstorm. No. 1335, Crowd advancing under Red banner. No. 1336, Workers, industrial complex, rocket blast-off. J.15.

1977, Apr. 25 *Perf. 11*

1333 A328 8f multi (4-1) 95 95
1334 A328 8f multi (4-2) 95 95
1335 A328 8f multi (4-3) 95 95
1336 A328 8f multi (4-4) 95 95
Nos. 1333-1336 (4) 3.80 3.80

Conference on learning from Taching workers in industry.

Mongolians Hailing Anniversary A329

Designs: 10f, Iron and steel complex, iron ore train. 20f, Cattle grazing in improved pasture. J.16.

1977, May 1 *Perf. 11x11½*

1337 A329 8f multi (3-1) 65 65
1338 A329 10f multi (3-2) 65 65
1339 A329 20f multi (3-3) 1.25 1.25
Nos. 1337-1339 (3) 2.55 2.55

30th anniversary of Inner Mongolian Autonomous Region.

1877 Flag of Romania and Oak Leaves — A330

Mihai Viteazu Memorial (16th Century Hero) — A331

Design: 10f, Battle of Smirdan, by N. Grigorescu. J.17.

1977, May 9 Photo. *Perf. 11*

1340 A330 8f multi (3-1) 95 95
1341 A331 10f multi (3-2) 95 95
1342 A331 20f multi (3-3) 2.00 2.00
Nos. 1340-1342 (3) 3.90 3.90

Centenary of Romanian independence.

Yenan "Let 100 Flowers Bloom" A332

Design: No. 1344, Hammer, sickle, gun and flowers; "Proletarian revolutionary literature will prosper." J.18.

1977, May, 23

1343 A332 8f grn, red & gold 60 60
1344 A332 8f lt brn, red & gold 60 60

Yenan Forum on Literature and Art, 35th anniversary.

Chu Teh — A333

Designs: No. 1346, Chu Teh, last address to Congress. No. 1347, Chu Teh at his desk, horiz. No. 1348, Chu Teh on horseback as commander of Red Army. J.19.

1977, July 6 Photo. *Perf. 11½*

1345 A333 8f multi (4-1) 38 38
1346 A333 8f multi (4-2) 38 38
1347 A333 8f multi (4-3) 38 38
1348 A333 8f multi (4-4) 38 38
Nos. 1345-1348 (4) 1.52 1.52

Chu Teh (1886-1976), Commander of Red Army, Chairman of National People's Congress.

Military under Mao's Banner — A334

Designs: No. 1350, Red Flag, Soldiers, Chingkang Mountains. No. 1351, Guerrilla fighters returning to base. No. 1352, Guerrillas crossing Yangtze. No. 1353, National defense. J.20.

1977, Aug. 1

1349 A334 8f multi (5-1) 80 80
1350 A334 8f multi (5-2) 80 80
1351 A334 8f multi (5-3) 80 80
1352 A334 8f multi (5-4) 80 80
1353 A334 8f multi (5-5) 80 80
Nos. 1349-1353 (5) 4.00 4.00

Liberation Army Day, 50th anniversary of People's Army.

Gate of Heavenly Peace, People and Red Flags — A335

Designs: No. 1355, People marching under Red Flag with Mao's portrait. No. 1356, People marching under Red Flag with hammer and sickle. J.23.

1977, Aug. 22 Photo. *Perf. 11½x11*

1354 A335 8f multi (3-1) 1.65 1.65
1355 A335 8f multi (3-2) 1.65 1.65
1356 A335 8f multi (3-3) 1.65 1.65
Nos. 1354-1356 (3) 4.95 4.95

11th National Congress of the Communist Party of China.

Chairman Mao — A336

Designs (Mao Portraits): No. 1358, as young man in Shansi. No. 1359, addressing Communist Party in Plenary Session. No. 1360, Proclaiming People's Republic at Gate of Heavenly Peace. No. 1361, at airport with Chou En-lai and Chu Teh, horiz. No. 1362, Reviewing Army as old man. J.21.

1977, Sept. 9 Photo. *Perf. 11½*

1357 A336 8f multi (6-1) 32 32
1358 A336 8f multi (6-2) 32 32
1359 A336 8f multi (6-3) 32 32
1360 A336 8f multi (6-4) 32 32
1361 A336 8f multi (6-5) 32 32
1362 A336 8f multi (6-6) 32 32
Nos. 1357-1362 (6) 1.92 1.92

Mao-Tse-tung (1893-1976), first death anniversary.

Mao Memorial Hall — A337

Completion of Mao Memorial Hall: No. 1364, Chairman Hua's inscription. J.22.

1977, Sept. 9

1363 A337 8f lt ultra & multi 1.75 1.75
1364 A337 8f lt grn, tan & gold 1.75 1.75

Tractors Moving Drilling Tower — A338

Designs: No. 1366, Shui Pow Tsi oil well and women workers. No. 1367, Construction of oil pipe line, Taching, and silos. No. 1368, Tung Fang Hung oil refinery, Peking. No. 1369, Taching oil loaded into tanker in harbor. 20f, Off-shore drilling platform "Pohai No. 1." T.19.

1978, Jan. 31 Photo. *Perf. 11*

1365 A338 8f multi (6-1) 52 52
1366 A338 8f multi (6-2) 52 52
1367 A338 8f multi (6-3) 52 52

1368 A338 8f multi (6-4)		52	52
1369 A338 8f multi (6-5)		52	52
1370 A338 20f multi (6-6)		1.00	1.00
	Nos. 1365-1370 (6)	3.60	3.60

Development of Chinese oil industry.

"Army Teaching Militia" — A339

Design: No. 1372, "Army helping with rice planting." T.23.

1978, Feb. 5 Photo. *Perf. 11*

1371 A339 8f multi (2-1)	75	75
1372 A339 8f multi (2-2)	75	75

Army and people working as a family.

Red Flags, Mao Tse-tung — A340

Constitution and Red Flags — A341

Design: No. 1375, Atom symbol over symbols of agriculture and industry. All designs include Great Hall of the People, Peking, and flowers. J.24.

1978, Feb. 26

1373 A340 8f multi (3-1)		60	60
1374 A341 8f multi (3-2)		60	60
1375 A340 8f multi (3-3)		60	60
	Nos. 1373-1375 (3)	1.80	1.80

5th National People's Congress.

Mao's Eulogy for Lei Feng — A342

Lei Feng, Studying Mao's Works — A343

Design: No. 1377, Chairman Hua's thoughts (5 lines). J.26.

1978, Mar. 5

1376 A342 8f gold & red (3-1)		65	65
1377 A342 8f gold & red (3-2)		65	65
1378 A343 8f multicolored (3-3)		65	65
	Nos. 1376-1378 (3)	1.95	1.95

Lei Feng (1940-1962), communist fighter; 15th anniversary of Chairman Mao's eulogy "Learn from Comrade Lei Feng."

Hsiang Ching-yu — A344

Yang Kai-hui — A345

1978, Mar. 8

1379 A344 8f multi (2-1)	50	50
1380 A345 8f multi (2-2)	50	50

Hsiang Ching-yu, pioneer of Women's Movement, executed 1928; Yang Kai-hui, communist fighter, executed 1930. J.27.

Conference Emblem — A346

Designs: No. 1382, Banners symbolizing industry, agriculture, defense and science. No. 1383, Red flag, atom symbol and globe. J.25.

1978, Mar. 18 Litho. *Perf. 11½x11*

1381 A346 8f gold & red (3-1)		40	40
1382 A346 8f multi (3-2)		40	40
1383 A346 8f multi (3-3)		40	40
a. Souvenir sheet of 3	*110.00*		
	Nos. 1381-1383 (3)	1.20	1.20

Natl. Science Conf. No. 1383a contains Nos. 1381-1383 with simulated perforations. Sold for 50 fen.

Release of Weather Balloon A347

Weather Observations: No. 1385, Radar station, typhoon watch. No. 1386, Computer, weather maps. No. 1387, Local weather observers. No. 1388, Rockets intercepting hail clouds. T.24.

1978, Apr. 25 Photo. *Perf. 11x11½*

1384 A347 8f multi (5-1)		30	30
1385 A347 8f multi (5-2)		30	30
1386 A347 8f multi (5-3)		30	30
1387 A347 8f multi (5-4)		25	25
1388 A347 8f multi (5-5)		25	25
	Nos. 1384-1388 (5)	1.40	1.40

Galloping Horse — A348

Children Playing Soccer — A349

Designs: Galloping Horses, by Hsu Peihung (1895-1953). 40f, 50f, 60f, 70f, $5, horiz. T.28.

1978, May 5 *Perf. 11½x11, 11x11½*

1389 A348 4f multi (10-1)		26	26
1390 A348 8f multi (10-2)		26	26
1391 A348 8f multi (10-3)		26	26
1392 A348 10f multi (10-4)		26	26
1393 A348 20f multi (10-5)		75	75
1394 A348 30f multi (10-6)		95	95
1395 A348 40f multi (10-7)		1.40	1.40
1396 A348 50f multi (10-8)		1.50	1.50
1397 A348 60f multi (10-9)		2.00	2.00
1398 A348 70f multi (10-10)		2.25	2.25
	Nos. 1389-1398 (10)	9.89	9.89

Souvenir Sheet

1399 A348 $5 multicolored	*95.00*

No. 1399 contains one stamp showing 4 horses, size: 89x39mm.

1978, June 1 *Perf. 11½*

Designs: No. 1401, Children on the beach. No. 1402, Little girls dancing. No. 1403, Children taking long walks. 20f, Children exercising for good health. T.21.

Size: 22x27mm

1400 A349 8f multi (5-2)	30	30
1401 A349 8f multi (5-3)	30	30
1402 A349 8f multi (5-4)	30	30
1403 A349 8f multi (5-5)	30	30

Size: 48x28mm

1404 A349 20f multi (5-1)		30	30
	Nos. 1400-1404 (5)	1.50	1.50

Build up your health while young.

Synthetic Fiber Feeder A350

Designs: No. 1406, Drawing out threads. No. 1407, Weaving. No. 1408, Dyeing and printing. No. 1409, Finished products. T.25.

1978, June 15 Photo. *Perf. 11½*

1405 A350 8f multi (5-1)		40	40
1406 A350 8f multi (5-2)		40	40
1407 A350 8f multi (5-3)		40	40
1408 A350 8f multi (5-4)		40	40
1409 A350 8f multi (5-5)		40	40
a. Strip of 5, #1405-1409		2.00	2.00
	Nos. 1405-1409 (5)	2.00	2.00

Chemical fiber industry. No. 1409a has continuous design.

Conference Emblem A351

"Develop Economy and Ensure Supplies" A352

1978, June 20 *Perf. 13*

1410 A351 8f multi (2-1)	45	45
1411 A352 8f multi (2-2)	45	45

Natl. Conf. on Learning from Taching and Tachai in Finance and Trade. J.28.

New Pastures, Mongolia — A353

Designs: No. 1413, Kazakh shepherds selecting sheep for breeding. No. 1414, Mechanized shearing of sheep, Tibet, T.27.

1978, June 30 Photo. *Perf. 11½*

1412 A353 8f multi (3-1)		65	65
1413 A353 8f multi (3-2)		65	65
1414 A353 8f multi (3-3)		65	65
	Nos. 1412-1414 (3)	1.95	1.95

Learning from Tachai in developing animal husbandry and new pastoral areas.

Coke Oven — A354

Iron and Steel Industry: No. 1416, Iron furnace. No. 1417, Pouring steel. No. 1418, Steel rolling. No. 1419, Finished iron and steel products. T.26.

1978, July 22

1415 A354 8f multi (5-1)		48	48
1416 A354 8f multi (5-2)		48	48
1417 A354 8f multi (5-3)		48	48
1418 A354 8f multi (5-4)		48	48
1419 A354 8f multi (5-5)		48	48
	Nos. 1415-1419 (5)	2.40	2.40

Iron Fist to Prevent Revisionism A355

Jug in Shape of Sheep A356

Designs: No. 1421, "Carrying forward revolutionary tradition." No. 1422, "Strenuous training in military skills to wipe out enemy." T.32.

1978, Aug. 1 Photo. *Perf. 11½*

1420 A355 8f multi (3-1)		70	70
1421 A355 8f multi (3-2)		70	70
1422 A355 8f multi (3-3)		70	70
	Nos. 1420-1422 (3)	2.10	2.10

"Learn from Hard-boned 6th Company." (A military unit since 1939).

Souvenir Sheets
Booklet Panes

Heavy speculation in stamps in China is centered around the souvenir sheets and booklet panes. These generally are trading by the 100 and being held off the normal philatelic market. Values are not being assigned until true market values can be established.

1978, Aug. 26

Arts and Crafts: 4f, Giant lion (toy; horiz.). No. 1425, Rhinoceros (lacquer ware; horiz). 10f, Cat (embroidery). 20f, Bag (weaving; horiz.). 30f, Teapot in shape of peacock (cloisonné). 40f, Plate with lotus, and swan-shaped box (lacquer ware; horiz.). 50f, Dragon flying in sky (ivory). 60f, Sun rising (jade; horiz.). 70f, Flight to human world (ivory). $3, Flying fairies (arts and crafts; horiz.). T.29.

1423 A356 4f multi (10-1)		16	16
1424 A356 8f multi (10-2)		16	16
1425 A356 8f multi (10-3)		16	16
1426 A356 10f multi (10-4)		16	16
1427 A356 20f multi (10-5)		38	38
1428 A356 30f multi (10-6)		45	45
1429 A356 40f multi (10-7)		60	60
1430 A356 50f multi (10-8)		80	80
1431 A356 60f multi (10-9)		1.00	1.00
1432 A356 70f multi (10-10)		1.25	1.25
	Nos. 1423-1432 (10)	5.12	5.12

Souvenir Sheet

1433 A356 $3 multi

No. 1433 contains one 85x36mm stamp.

Women, Atom Symbol, Rocket and Wheat A357

1978, Sept. 8 Photo. *Perf. 11*

1434 A357 8f multicolored	1.00	25

4th National Women's Congress.

Ginseng — A358

Flag, Wheat, Cogwheel, Plane, Atom Symbols — A359

Medicinal Plants: No. 1436, Horn of plenty. No. 1437, Blackberry lily. No. 1438, Balloonflower. 55f, Rhododendron dauricum. T.30.

1978, Sept. 15

1435	A358	8f multi (5-1)	25	25
1436	A358	8f multi (5-2)	25	25
1437	A358	8f multi (5-3)	25	25
1438	A358	8f multi (5-4)	25	25
1439	A358	55f multi (5-5)	2.00	2.00
		Nos. 1435-1439 (5)	3.00	3.00

1978, Oct. 11 Photo. *Perf. 11*

1440	A359	8f multicolored	1.00	1.00

9th National Trade Union Congress.

Youth League Emblem A360

1978, Oct. 16

1441	A360	8f multicolored	1.25	1.25

10th Natl. Communist Youth League Cong.

Chinese and Japanese Girls Exchanging Gifts — A361

Great Wall and Mt. Fuji — A362

1978, Oct. 22

1442	A361	8f multicolored	25	25
1443	A362	55f multicolored	1.50	1.50

Signing of Sino-Japanese Peace and Friendship Treaty.

Moslem, Chinese and Mongolian People — A363

Chinsha River Bridge, West Szechuan — A364

Designs: No. 1445, Loading coal at Holan Mountain. 10f, Irrigated rice fields and boxthorn. J.29.

1978, Oct. 25

1444	A363	8f multi (3-1)	48	48
1445	A363	8f multi (3-2)	48	48
1446	A363	10f multi (3-3)	48	48
		Nos. 1444-1446 (3)	1.44	1.44

20th anniversary of founding of Ningsia Moslem Autonomous Region.

1978, Nov. 1 Photo. *Perf. 11½x11*

Highway Bridges: No. 1448, Hsinhong bridge, Wuhsi. No. 1449, Chiuhsikou bridge, Fengdu. No. 1450, Chinsha River bridge, West Szechuan. 60f, Shangyeh bridge, Sanmen. $2, Hsiang-kiang River bridge. T.31.

1447	A364	8f multi (5-1)	25	25
1448	A364	8f multi (5-2)	25	25
1449	A364	8f multi (5-3)	25	25
1450	A364	8f multi (5-4)	25	25
1451	A364	60f multi (5-5)	2.50	2.50
		Nos. 1447-1451 (5)	3.50	3.50

Souvenir Sheet

1452	A364	$2 multi		

No. 1452 contains one 86x37mm stamp.

Mechanical Transplanting of Rice Seedlings — A365

Paintings: No. 1454, Spraying fields. No. 1455, Seed selection. No. 1456, Trade. No. 1457, Delivery of public grain in city. T.34.

1978, Nov. 30 *Perf. 11½*

1453	A365	8f multi (5-1)	1.50	1.50
1454	A365	8f multi (5-2)	1.50	1.50
1455	A365	8f multi (5-3)	1.50	1.50
1456	A365	8f multi (5-4)	1.50	1.50
1457	A365	8f multi (5-5)	1.50	1.50
a.		Strip of 5, #1453-1457	8.00	8.00

Agricultural progress. No. 1457a has a continuous design.

Dancers and Fireworks — A366

Designs: No. 1459, Industry, vert. 10f, Agriculture, vert. J.33.

1978, Dec. 11 Photo. *Perf. 11*

1458	A366	8f multi (3-1)	90	90
1459	A366	8f multi (3-2)	90	90
1460	A366	10f multi (3-3)	90	90
		Nos. 1458-1460 (3)	2.70	2.70

20th anniversary of Kwangsi Chuang Autonomous Region.

Miners with Pneumatic Drill — A367

Mine Development: 4f, Old Tibetan peasant reporting to surveyor. 10f, Open-cut mining with power shovel. 20f, Loaded electric train in pit. T.20.

1978, Dec. 29 Photo. & Engr.

1461	A367	4f multi (4-1)	16	16
1462	A367	8f multi (4-2)	32	32
1463	A367	10f multi (4-3)	42	42
1464	A367	20f multi (4-4)	65	65
		Nos. 1461-1464 (4)	1.55	1.55

A368

A369

Golden Pheasants: 4f, Roosting on rock. 8f, In flight. 45f, Seeking food. T.35.

1979, Jan. 25 Photo. *Perf. 11½*

1465	A368	4f multi (3-1)	60	60
1466	A368	8f multi (3-2)	60	60
1467	A368	45f multi (3-3)	2.50	2.50
		Nos. 1465-1467 (3)	3.70	3.70

1979, Mar. 14 Photo. *Perf. 11½x11*

1468	A369	8f Albert Einstein, equation	1.00	75

Phoenix Battling Monster, Praying Woman A370

Design: 60f, Man riding dragon to heaven. Designs from silk paintings found in Changsha tomb, Warring States Period (475-221 B.C.). T.33.

1979, Mar. 29 *Perf. 11*

1469	A370	8f multi (2-1)	55	42
1470	A370	60f multi (2-2)	2.75	2.00

Summer Palace — A371

Photo., Photo. & Engr. ($5)

1979-80 *Perf. 13*

1471	A371	$1 Pagoda ('80)	65	25
1472	A371	$2 Shown	1.25	55
1473	A371	$5 Temple, Beihai Park ('80)	4.50	1.25
		Nos. 1471-1473 (3)	6.40	2.05

Hammer and Sickle "51" and Bars from "International" — A372

1979, May 1 Photo. *Perf. 11*

1474	A372	8f multicolored	60	50

International Labor Day, 90th anniv.

"Tradition of May 4th Movement" A373

Young Woman, Rocket, Antenna, Nuclear Reactor A374

1979, May 4

1475	A373	8f multicolored	50	38
1476	A374	8f multicolored	50	38

60th anniversary of May 4th Movement.

IYC Emblem, Children Holding Balloons — A375

Children of Three Races, IYC Emblem — A376

1979, May 25 *Perf. 11½*

1477	A375	8f multicolored	65	65
1478	A376	60f multicolored	4.50	4.50

International Year of the Child.

Great Wall in Spring A377

Designs (The Great Wall): No. 1480, in summer. No. 1481, in autumn. 60f, in winter. $2, Guard tower. T.38.

1979, June 25 Photo. *Perf. 11*

1479	A377	8f multi (4-1)	75	75
1480	A377	8f multi (4-2)	75	75
1481	A377	8f multi (4-3)	75	75
1482	A377	60f multi (4-4)	4.25	4.25
		Nos. 1479-1482 (4)	6.50	6.50

Souvenir Sheet

1483	A377	$2 multi		

For overprint see No. 1492.

Roaring Tiger — A379

Manchurian Tiger: 8f, Two young tigers. 60f, Tiger at rest. T.40.

1979, July 20 *Perf. 11½x11*

1484	A379	4f multi (3-1)	30	30
1485	A379	8f multi (3-2)	30	30
1486	A379	60f multi (3-3)	1.75	1.75
		Nos. 1484-1486 (3)	2.35	2.35

Mechanical Harvesting — A380

Work of the Communes: No. 1488, Forestry. No. 1489, Raising ducks. No. 1490, Women weaving baskets. 10f, Fishing. T.39.

1979, Aug. 10 *Perf. 11½*

1487 A380 4f multi (5-1)	65	65
1488 A380 8f multi (5-2)	65	65
1489 A380 8f multi (5-3)	65	65
1490 A380 8f multi (5-4)	65	65
1491 A380 10f multi (5-5)	65	65
Nos. 1487-1491 (5)	3.25	3.25

No. 1483 Overprinted with Gold Inscription and "1979"
Souvenir Sheet

1979, Aug. 25 **Photo.** *Perf. 11*

1492 A377 $2 multicolored

31st International Stamp Exhibition, Riccione, Italy. J41 (1-1).
Forged overprints exist.

Games Emblem, Sports — A381

Emblem and: No. 1494, Soccer, badminton, high jump, speed skating. No. 1495, Fencing, skiing, gymnastics, diving. No. 1496, Motorcycling, table tennis, basketball, archery. No. 1497, Emblem only, vert. J.43.

1979, Sept. 15 *Perf. 11½x11*

1493 A381 8f multi (4-1)	35	35
1494 A381 8f multi (4-2)	35	35
1495 A381 8f multi (4-3)	35	35
1496 A381 8f multi (4-4)	35	35
a. Block of 4, #1493-1496	1.50	1.50

Souvenir Sheet
Perf. 11½

1497 A381 $2 multi

4th National Games. Size of stamp in No. 1497: 22x26mm.

Flag and Rainbow — A382

Design: No. 1499, Flag and mountains.

1979, Oct. 1 **Photo.** *Perf. 11½*

1498 A382 8f multicolored	1.00	1.00
1499 A382 8f multicolored	1.00	1.00

National Emblem — A383

Dancers — A384

1979, Oct. 1 **Photo.** *Perf. 11½*

1500 A383 8f multicolored 1.25 1.25

Souvenir Sheet

1501 A383 $1 multicolored *21.00*

1979, Oct. 1 **Photo.** *Perf. 11½*

Designs: #1503-1505, various dances. J.47.

1502 A384 8f multi (4-1)	35	15
1503 A384 8f multi (4-2)	35	15
1504 A384 8f multi (4-3)	35	15
1505 A384 8f multi (4-4)	35	15
a. Block of 4, #1502-1505	1.50	75

Tractor, Aerial Crop Spraying, Irrigation — A385

Designs: No. 1507, Gear, computers. No. 1508, Rocket, submarine, jets. No. 1509, Atom symbol. J.48.

1979, Oct. 1 **Photo.** *Perf. 11½*

1506 A385 8f multi (4-1)	35	35
1507 A385 8f multi (4-2)	35	35
1508 A385 8f multi (4-3)	35	35
1509 A385 8f multi (4-4)	35	35
Nos. 1506-1509 (4)	1.40	1.40

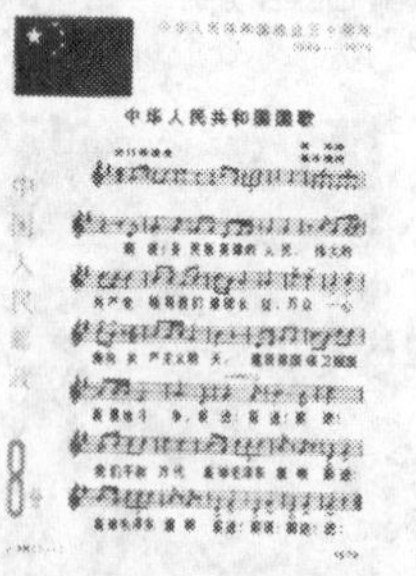

National Anthem A386

1979, Oct. 1 **Engr.** *Perf. 11*

1510 A386 8f multicolored 1.00 1.00

Exhibition Emblem — A387

Children Flying Model Planes — A388

1979, Oct. 3

1511 A387 8f multicolored 75 30

Junior National Scientific and Technological Exhibition.

1979, Oct. 3

Designs: No. 1513, Girls and microscope. No. 1514, Children and telescope. No. 1515, Boy catching butterflies. No. 1516, Girl taking meteorological readings. No. 1517, Boys sailing model boat. No. 1518, Girl with book. T.41.

1512 A388 8f multi (6-1)	26	26
1513 A388 8f multi (6-2)	26	26
1514 A388 8f multi (6-3)	26	26
1515 A388 8f multi (6-4)	26	26
1516 A388 8f multi (6-5)	26	26
1517 A388 60f multi (6-6)	1.10	1.10
Nos. 1512-1517 (6)	2.40	2.40

Souvenir Sheet
Perf. 11

1518 A388 $2 multi

Study Science from Childhood. No. 1518 contains one stamp, size: 90x40mm.

Yu Shan Mountain A389

Taiwan Landscapes: No. 1520, Sun and Moon Lake. No. 1521, Chihkan Tower. No. 1522, Suao-Hualien Highway. 55f, Tian Xiang Falls. 60f, Banping Mountain. T.42.

1979, Oct. 20 **Photo.** *Perf. 11x11½*

1519 A389 8f multi (6-1)	52	52
1520 A389 8f multi (6-2)	52	52
1521 A389 8f multi (6-3)	52	52
1522 A389 8f multi (6-4)	52	52
1523 A389 55f multi (6-5)	2.50	2.50
1524 A389 60f multi (6-6)	2.50	2.50
Nos. 1519-1524 (6)	7.08	7.08

Arts Symbols A390

Design: 8f, Seals and modernization symbols. J.39.

1979, Oct. 30

1525 A390 4f multicolored	40	28
1526 A390 8f multicolored	70	45

4th Natl. Cong. of Literary and Art Workers.

Train in Tunnel A391

Railroads: No. 1528, Mountain bridge. No. 1529, Freight train. T.36.

1979, Oct. 30 **Photo. & Engr.**

1527 A391 8f multi (3-1)	50	50
1528 A391 8f multi (3-2)	50	50
1529 A391 8f multi (3-3)	50	50
Nos. 1527-1529 (3)	1.50	1.50

Chrysanthemum Petal — A392

Camellias: No. 1531, Lion head. No. 1532, Camellia chryantha. 10f, Small osmanthus leaf. 20f, Baby face. 30f, Cornelian. 40f, Peony camellia. 50f, Purple gown. 60f, Dwarf rose. 70f, Willow leaf spinel pink. $2, Red jewelry. T.37.

1979, Nov. 10 **Photo.** *Perf. 11x11½*

1530 A392 4f multi (10-1)	40	40
1531 A392 8f multi (10-2)	40	40
1532 A392 8f multi (10-3)	40	40
1533 A392 10f multi (10-4)	40	40
1534 A392 20f multi (10-5)	70	70
1535 A392 30f multi (10-6)	85	85
1536 A392 40f multi (10-7)	1.50	1.50
1537 A392 50f multi (10-8)	1.50	1.50
1538 A392 60f multi (10-9)	1.75	1.75
1539 A392 70f multi (10-10)	2.00	2.00
Nos. 1530-1539 (10)	9.90	9.90

Souvenir Sheet
Perf. 11½x11

1540 A392 $2 multi

No. 1540 contains one 86x36mm stamp.

No. 1540 Overprinted and Numbered in Gold in Margin
Souvenir Sheet

1979, Nov. 10

1541 A392 $2 multicolored

People's Republic of China Phil. Exhib., Hong Kong, 1979. J.42 (1-1).
Forged overprints exist.

Norman Bethune Treating Soldier — A393

Design: 70f, Bethune statue.

1979, Nov. 12

1542 A393 8f multi (2-2)	32	32
1543 A393 70f multi (2-1)	2.50	2.50

Dr. Norman Bethune, 40th death anniv. J.50.

Central Archives Hall — A394

Intl. Archives Weeks: No. 1545, Gold archive cabinet, vert. 60f, Pavilion. J.51.

Perf. 11x11½, 11½x11

1979, Nov. 26 **Photo.**

1544 A394 8f multi (3-1)	60	60
1545 A394 8f multi (3-2)	60	60
1546 A394 60f multi (3-3)	2.50	2.50
Nos. 1544-1546 (3)	3.70	3.70

Monkey King in Waterfall Cave — A395

Monkey King, Scenes from Pilgrimage to the West (Novel): No. 1548, Fighting Necha, son of Prince Li. No. 1549, In Mother Queen's peach orchard. No. 1550, In the alchemy furnace. 10f, Subduing the white bone demon. 20f, With palm leaf fan. 60f, In cobweb cave. 70f, Walking on scripture-seeking route. T.43.

1979, Dec. 1 *Perf. 11½x11*

1547 A395 8f multi (8-1)	75	75
1548 A395 8f multi (8-2)	75	75
1549 A395 8f multi (8-3)	75	75
1550 A395 8f multi (8-4)	75	75
1551 A395 10f multi (8-5)	75	75
1552 A395 20f multi (8-6)	1.25	1.25
1553 A395 60f multi (8-7)	4.25	4.25
1554 A395 70f multi (8-8)	4.75	4.75
Nos. 1547-1554 (8)	14.00	14.00

Stalin Delivering Speech A396

Joseph Stalin (1879-1953): No. 1555, Portrait of Stalin, vert. J.49.

Perf. 11x11½, 11½x11

1979, Dec. 21 **Engr.**

1555 A396 8f brown (2-1)	55	55
1556 A396 8f black (2-2)	55	55

A397

A398

1980 Photo. *Perf. 11½*

1557 A397 4f Peony (16-1) 38 38
1558 A397 4f Squirrels and grapes (16-2) 38 38
1559 A397 8f Crabs candle and wine (16-3) 38 38
1560 A397 8f Tadpoles in mountain spring (16-4) 38 38
1561 A397 8f Chicks (16-5) 38 38
1562 A397 8f Lotus (16-6) 38 38
1563 A397 8f Red plum (16-7) 38 38
1564 A397 8f Kingfisher (16-8) 38 38
1565 A397 10f Bottle gourd (16-9) 38 38
1566 A397 20f Voice of autumn (16-10) 55 55
1567 A397 30f Wisteria (16-11) 80 80
1568 A397 40f Chrysanthemums (16-12) 1.10 1.10
1569 A397 50f Shrimp (16-13) 1.25 1.25
1570 A397 55f Litchi (16-14) 1.40 1.40
1571 A397 60f Cabbages, mushrooms (16-15) 1.65 1.65
1572 A397 70f Peaches (16-16) 1.75 1.75
Nos. 1557-1572 (16) 11.92 11.92

Souvenir Sheet

1573 A397 $2 Evergreen

Qi Baishi paintings. Issue dates: Nos. 1557-1560, 1569-1572, Jan. 15; others, May 20. No. 1573 contains one 37½x61mm stamp. T. 44.

1980, Jan. 25 *Perf. 11½x11*

Opera Masks: No. 1574, Meng Liang Mask from Hongyang Cave Opera. No. 1575, Li Kui, from Black Whirlwind. No. 1576, Huang Gai, from Meeting of Heroes. No. 1577, 10f, Lu Zhishen, from Wild Boar Forest. 20f, Lian Po, from Reconciliation between the General and Minister. 60f, Zhang Fei, from Reed Marsh. 70f, Dou Erdun, from Stealing the Emperor's Horse, T. 45.

1574 A398 4f multi (8-1) 55 55
1575 A398 4f multi (8-2) 55 55
1576 A398 8f multi (8-3) 55 55
1577 A398 8f multi (8-4) 55 55
1578 A398 10f multi (8-5) 55 55
1579 A398 20f multi (8-6) 1.10 1.10
1580 A398 60f multi (8-7) 4.00 4.00
1581 A398 70f multi (8-8) 4.00 4.00
Nos. 1574-1581 (8) 11.85 11.85

Speed Skating, Olympic Rings — A399

Monkey, New Year — A400

Olympic Rings and: No. 1582, Chinese flag. No. 1584, Figure skating. 60f, Downhill skiing. J.54.

1980, Feb. 13

1582 A399 8f multi (4-1) 25 25
1583 A399 8f multi (4-2) 25 25
1584 A399 8f multi (4-3) 25 25
1585 A399 60f multi (4-4) 1.25 1.25
Nos. 1582-1585 (4) 2.00 2.00

13th Winter Olympic Games, Lake Placid, NY, Feb. 12-24.

Engraved and Photogravure

1980, Feb. 15 *Perf. 11½*

1586 A400 8f multicolored *52.50 20.00*

Clara Zetkin — A401

Photogravure & Engraved

1980, Mar. 8 *Perf. 11½x11*

1587 A401 8f black & yel 1.00 1.00

International Working Women's Day, 70th anniv., founded by Clara Zetkin (1857-1933).

Orchard A402

Afforestation: 8f, Trees lining highway. 10f, Aerial seeding. 20f, Trees surrounding factory. T.48.

1980, Mar. 12 *Perf. 11x11½*

1588 A402 4f multi (4-1) 15 15
1589 A402 8f multi (4-2) 20 20
1590 A402 10f multi (4-3) 28 28
1591 A402 20f multi (4-4) 60 60
Nos. 1588-1591 (4) 1.23 1.23

Apsaras, Symbols of Modernization — A403

1980, Mar. 15 Photo. *Perf. 11½*

1592 A403 8f multicolored 1.00 1.00

2nd National Conference of the Scientific and Technical Association of China.

Mail Transport (T.49) — A404

1980, Mar. 20 *Perf. 11x11½*

1593 A404 2f Ship (4-1) 30 30
1594 A404 4f Bus (4-2) 35 35
1595 A404 8f Train (4-3) 2.50 2.50
1596 A404 10f Jet (4-4) 2.50 2.50
Nos. 1593-1596 (4) 5.65 5.65

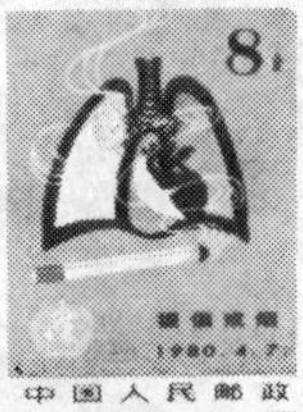
Lungs, Heart, Cigarette, WHO Emblem — A405

Statue of Chien Chen (688-763) — A406

1980, Apr. 7 *Perf. 11½x11*

1597 A405 8f shown (2-1) 42 42
1598 A405 60f Faces (2-2) 3.00 3.00

Fight against cigarette smoking. J.56.

Perf. 11x11½, 11½x11

1980, Apr. 13

Loan to China by Japan of statue of Chien Chen (Jian Zhen), Buddhist missionary to Japan (754-763): No. 1600, Chien Chen Memorial Hall, Yangchou, horiz. 60f, Chien Chen's ship, horiz. His name in Japan is Ganjin. J.55.

1599 A406 8f multi (3-1) 1.10 1.10
1600 A406 8f multi (3-2) 1.10 1.10
1601 A406 60f multi (3-3) 6.75 6.75
Nos. 1599-1601 (3) 8.95 8.95

Lenin's 110th Birthday — A407

Swallow Chick Kite — A408

Photogravure and Engraved

1980, Apr. 22 *Perf. 11½x11*

1602 A407 8f multicolored 1.10 1.10

1980, May 10 Photo. *Perf. 11½*

Designs: Kites. T.50.

1603 A408 8f shown (4-1) 75 75
1604 A408 8f Slender-swallow (4-2) 75 75
1605 A408 8f Semi-slender swallow (4-3) 75 75
1606 A408 70f Dual swallows (4-4) 4.75 4.75
Nos. 1603-1606 (4) 7.00 7.00

Hare Running from Fallen Papaya — A409

1980, June 1 Photo. *Perf. 11x11½*

1607 Strip of 4 + label 3.50 3.50
a. A409 8f shown (4-1) 75 75
b. A409 8f Hare fox, monkey running away (4-2) 75 75
c. A409 8f Lion instructing animals (4-3) 75 75
d. A409 8f Discovery of fallen papaya (4-4) 75 75

Gu Dong fairy tale. T.51.

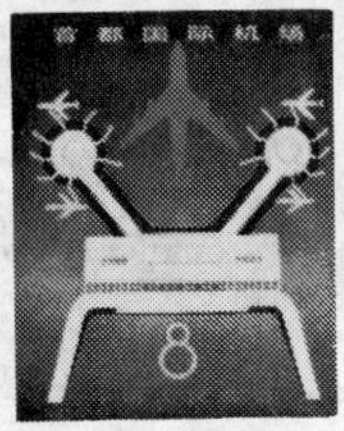
Terminal Building, Jets — A410

1980, June 20 *Perf. 11½*

1608 A410 8f Shown (2-1) 55 55
1609 A410 10f Runways, jets (2-2) 65 65

Peking Intl. Airport opening. T.47.

Sika Stag — A411

White Lotus — A412

1980, July 18 Photo. *Perf. 11½*

1610 A411 4f Shown (3-1) 22 22
1611 A411 8f Doe and fawn (3-2) 40 40
1612 A411 60f Herd (3-3) 3.00 3.00
Nos. 1610-1612 (3) 3.62 3.62

T.52.

1980, Aug. 4

1613 A412 8f Shown (4-1) 90 90
1614 A412 8f Rose-tipped snow (4-2) 90 90
1615 A412 8f Buddha's seat (4-3) 90 90
1616 A412 70f Variable charming face (4-4) 8.00 8.00
Nos. 1613-1616 (4) 10.70 10.70

Souvenir Sheet

1617 A412 $1 Fresh lotus on rippling water

#1617 contains one 48x88mm stamp. T.54.

Pearl Cave, Sword-cut Stone Sculptures — A413

Guilin Landscapes: No. 1619, Three mountains, distant views. No. 1620, Nine-horse fresco hill. No. 1621, Egrets around aged banyan. No. 1622, Western hills at sunset, vert. No. 1623, Moonlight on Lijiang River, vert. 60f, Springhead, ancient ferry, vert. 70f, Scenic path, Yangshue, vert. T.53.

1980, Aug. 30 Photo. *Perf. 11½*

1618 A413 8f multi (8-1) 65 65
1619 A413 8f multi (8-2) 65 65
1620 A413 8f multi (8-3) 65 65
1621 A413 8f multi (8-4) 65 65
1622 A413 8f multi (8-5) 65 65
1623 A413 8f multi (8-6) 65 65
1624 A413 60f multi (8-7) 4.25 4.25
1625 A413 70f multi (8-8) 4.75 4.75
Nos. 1618-1625 (8) 12.90 12.90

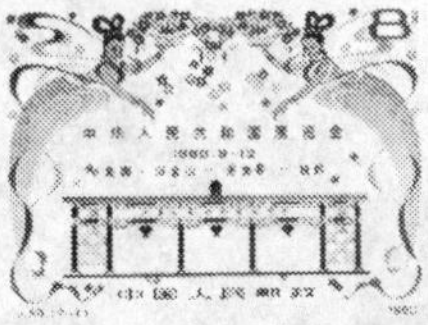
Entrance Gate and Good Fairies A414

Great Wall, Symbols of Chicago, San Francisco and New York — A415

1980, Sept. 13 Photo. *Perf. 11x11½*

1626 A414 8f multicolored 35 35
1627 A415 70f multicolored 3.25 3.25

Exhibitions of the People's Republic of China in San Francisco, Chicago and New York, Sept.-Dec. Sheets of 12 were sold only at US exhibitions at varying prices.

Romanian Flag, Warrior and Scroll — A416

1980, Sept. 20 Photo. *Perf. 11½x11*

1628 A416 8f multicolored 80 80

2050th anniversary of Dacia, first independent Romanian state.

UNESCO Exhibition of Drawings and Paintings (J.60) — A417

1980, Oct. 8 *Perf. 11½*

1629 A417 8f Sea of Clouds, by Liu Haisu (3-1) 80 80
1630 A417 8f Oriole and Magnolia, by Yu Feian, vert., (3-2) 80 80
1631 A417 8f Camels, by Wu Zuoren (3-3) 80 80
Nos. 1629-1631 (3) 2.40 2.40

Scenes from Tarrying Garden (T.56) — A418

1980, Oct. 25 **Photo.** *Perf. 11½*

1632 A418 8f Quxi Tower (4-1) 2.00 2.00
1633 A418 8f Yuancui Pavilion (4-2) 2.00 2.00
1634 A418 10f Hanbi Shanfang (4-3) 2.50 2.50
1635 A418 60f Guanyun Peak (4-4) 14.00 14.00
Nos. 1632-1635 (4) 20.50 20.50

Xu Guangpi (1562-1633), Agronomist A419

Shooting, Olympic Rings A420

Scientists of Ancient China: No. 1637, Li Bing, hydraulic engineer, 3rd century B.C. No. 1638, Jia Sixie, agronomist, 5th century. 60f, Huang Daopo, textile expert, 13th century. J.58.

Photogravure and Engraved

1980, Nov. 20 *Perf. 11½x11*

1636 A419 8f multi (4-1) 65 65
1637 A419 8f multi (4-2) 65 65
1638 A419 8f multi (4-3) 65 65
1639 A419 60f multi (4-4) 4.50 4.50
Nos. 1636-1639 (4) 6.45 6.45

1980, Nov. 26 **Photo.**

1640 A420 4f shown (5-1) 15 15
1641 A420 8f Gymnastics (5-2) 22 22
1642 A420 8f Diving (5-3) 22 22
1643 A420 10f Volleyball (5-4) 32 32
1644 A420 60f Archery (5-5) 2.00 2.00
Nos. 1640-1644 (5) 2.91 2.91

Return to International Olympic Committee, 1st anniversary. J.62.

Chinese River Dolphin A421

Photogravure & Engraved

1980, Dec. 25 *Perf. 11x11½*

1645 A421 8f shown (2-1) 35 35
a. Booklet pane of 6 2.50
1646 A421 60f Dolphins (2-2) 2.25 2.25
a. Booklet pane of 1 2.50

Cock — A422

Photogravure & Engraved

1981, Jan. 5 *Perf. 11½*

1647 A422 8f multicolored 3.00 1.00
a. Booklet pane of 12 16.00

New Year 1981.

Early Morning in Xishuang Bana (T.55) — A423

Perf. 11x11½, 11½x11

1981, Jan. 20 **Photo.**

1648 A423 4f shown (6-1) 24 24
1649 A423 4f Dai mountain village (6-2) 24 24
1650 A423 8f Rainbow over Lanchang River (6-3) 48 48
1651 A423 8f Ancient temple vert. (6-4) 48 48
1652 A423 8f Moonlit night, vert. (6-5) 48 48
1653 A423 60f Phoenix tree, vert. (6-6) 4.25 4.25
Nos. 1648-1653 (6) 6.17 6.17

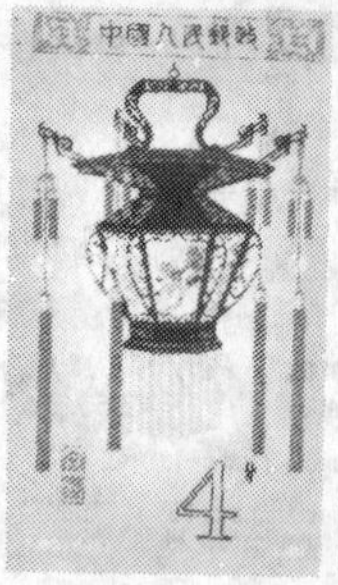

Flower Basket Palace Lantern — A424

Designs: Palace lanterns. T.60.

1981, Feb. 19 **Photo.** *Perf. 11½*

1654 A424 4f multi (6-1) 25 25
1655 A424 8f multi (6-2) 55 55
1656 A424 8f multi (6-3) 55 55
1657 A424 8f multi (6-4) 55 55
1658 A424 20f multi (6-5) 1.10 1.10
1659 A424 60f multi (6-6) 4.00 4.00
Nos. 1654-1659 (6) 7.00 7.00

Crossing River, Scene from Marking the Gunwale A425

Designs: Scenes from Marking the Gunwale fable. T.59.

1981, Mar. 10 **Photo.** *Perf. 11x11½*

1660 A425 8f Text (5-1) 50 35
1661 A425 8f shown (5-2) 50 35
1662 A425 8f Dropping sword in water (5-3) 50 35
1663 A425 8f Marking gunwale (5-4) 50 35
1664 A425 8f Searching for sword (5-5) 50 35
a. Bklt. pane, 2 each #1660-1664 5.00
b. Strip of 5, #1660-1664 2.50 1.75

Chinese Juniper A426

Designs: Miniature landscapes. T.61.

1981, Mar. 31 *Perf. 11½*

1665 A426 4f Chinese elm, vert. (6-1) 24 24
1666 A426 8f Juniper, vert. (6-2) 45 45
1667 A426 8f Maidenhair tree, vert. (6-3) 45 45
1668 A426 10f shown (6-4) 55 55
1669 A426 20f Persimmon (6-5) 1.25 1.25
1670 A426 60f Juniper (6-6) 3.50 3.50
Nos. 1665-1670 (6) 6.44 6.44

Vase with Tiger-shaped Handles A427

Cizhou Kiln Ceramic Pottery: 4f, Vase with two tigers, Song Dynasty, vert. No. 1672, Black glazed jar, Jin Dynasty. No. 1673, Amphora, vert. No. 1674, Jar with two phoenixes (Yuan Dynasty). 10f, Flat flask, Yuan Dynasty. T.62.

1981, Apr. 15 **Photo.** *Perf. 11½x11*

1671 A427 4f multi (6-1) 20 20
1672 A427 8f multi (6-2) 38 38
1673 A427 8f multi (6-3) 38 38
1674 A427 8f multi (6-4) 38 38
1675 A427 10f multi (6-5) 45 45
1676 A427 60f multi (6-6) 2.75 2.75
Nos. 1671-1676 (6) 4.54 4.54

Panda and Colored Stamps — A428

1981, Apr. 29 **Photo.** *Perf. 11½x11*

1677 A428 8f shown (2-1) 18 15
1678 A428 60f Boat, bird (2-2) 1.25 85
a. Booklet pane (8 #1677, souv. sheet with 1677-1678 3.50

Qinchuan Steer — A429

Cattle Breeds: No. 1680, Binhu buffalo. No. 1681, Yak. No. 1682, Black and white dairy cows. 10f, Pasture red cow. 55f, Simmental cross-breed. T.63.

1981, May 5 *Perf. 11x11½*

1679 A429 4f multi (6-1) 16 16
1680 A429 8f multi (6-2) 28 28
1681 A429 8f multi (6-3) 28 28
1682 A429 8f multi (6-4) 28 28
1683 A429 10f multi (6-5) 35 35
1684 A429 55f multi (6-6) 1.90 1.90
Nos. 1679-1684 (6) 3.25 3.25

Mail Delivery Slogan — A430

13th World Telecommunications Day — A431

1981, May 9 *Perf. 11*

1685 A430 8f multicolored 80 20

1981, May 17 *Perf. 11½x11*

1686 A431 8f multicolored 80 20

Construction Worker — A432

Telephone Building, Peking — A433

1981, May 20 *Perf. 11½*

1687 A432 8f shown (4-1) 25 20
1688 A432 8f Miner (4-2) 25 20
1689 A432 8f Children crossing street (4-3) 25 20
1690 A432 8f Farm worker (4-4) 25 20
Nos. 1687-1690 (4) 1.00 80

National Safety Month. J.65.

1981, June 5 **Engr.** *Perf. 11½x11*

1691 A433 8f violet brown 25 25

Swaythling Cup, Men's Team Table Tennis — A434

36th World Table Tennis Championships Victory: No. 1692a, St. Bride Vase, men's singles (7-3). No. 1692b, Iran Cup, men's doubles (7-4). No. 1692c, G. Geist Prize, women's singles (7-5). No. 1692d, W.J. Pope Trophy, women's doubles (7-6). No. 1692e, Heydusek Prize, mixed doubles (7-7). No. 1694, Marcel Corbillon Cup, women's team. Nos. 1693-1694 printed in sheets of 16 (8 each) with 2 labels. J.71.

1981, June 30 **Photo.** *Perf. 11½x11*

1692 Strip of 5 1.00 1.00
a.-e. A434 20f multi 20 20
1693 A434 20f multi (7-1) 50 50
1694 A434 20f multi (7-2) 50 50

Chinese Communist Party, 60th Anniv. A435

1981, July 1 **Photo.** *Perf. 11x11½*

1695 A435 8f multi 60 30

Hanpo Pass, Lushan Mountains (T.67) A436

Photogravure & Engraved

1981, July 20 *Perf. 12½x12*
1696 A436 8f Five-veteran Peak, vert. (7-1) 40 40
1697 A436 8f shown (7-2) 40 40
1698 A436 8f Yellow Dragon Pool, vert. (7-3) 40 40
1699 A436 8f Sunlit Peak (7-4) 40 40
1700 A436 8f Three-layer Spring, vert. (7-5) 40 40
1701 A436 8f Stone and pines (7-6) 40 40
1702 A436 60f Dragon-head Cliff, vert. (7-7) 5.50 5.50
Nos. 1696-1702 (7) 7.90 7.90

Tremella Fuciformis — A437

Designs: Edible mushrooms. T.66.

1981, Aug. 6 **Photo.** *Perf. 11½*
1703 A437 4f shown (6-1) 18 18
1704 A437 8f Dictyophora indusiata (6-2) 30 30
1705 A437 8f Hericium erinaceus (6-3) 30 30
1706 A437 8f Russula rubra (6-4) 30 30
1707 A437 10f Lentinus edodes (6-5) 35 35
1708 A437 70f Agaricus bisporus (6-6) 2.50 2.50
Nos. 1703-1708 (6) 3.93 3.93

Quality Month (J.66) — A438

Lunan Stone Forest, Yunn — A439

1981, Sept. 1 **Photo.** *Perf. 11½x11*
1709 A438 8f Silver medal (2-1) 25 25
1710 A438 8f Gold medal (2-2) 25 25

1981, Sept. 18 *Perf. 11½*

Designs: Views of limestone formations, Lunan Stone Forest. #1711-1713 horiz. T.64.

1711 A439 8f multi (5-1) 28 28
1712 A439 8f multi (5-2) 28 28
1713 A439 8f multi (5-3) 28 28
1714 A439 10f multi (5-4) 35 35
1715 A439 70f multi (5-5) 3.25 3.25
Nos. 1711-1715 (5) 4.44 4.44

Lu Xun, Writer, Birth Centenary (J.67) — A440

1981, Sept. 25
1716 A440 8f shown (2-1) 20 15
1717 A440 20f Portrait (diff.) (2-2) 45 35

Sun Yat-sen and Text — A441

70th Anniv. of 1911 Revolution: No. 1719, 72 Martyrs Grave, Huang Hua Gang. No. 1720, Hubei Provincial Government Headquarters, 1911. J.68.

1981, Oct. 10 **Photo.** *Perf. 11x11½*
1718 A441 8f multi (3-1) 40 40
1719 A441 8f multi (3-2) 40 40
1720 A441 8f multi (3-3) 40 40
Nos. 1718-1720 (3) 1.20 1.20

Asian Conference of Parliamentarians on Population and Development, Peking, Oct. 27 (J.73) — A442

Perf. 11½x11, 11x11½

1981, Oct. 27
1721 A442 8f Tree, vert. (2-1) 15 15
1722 A442 70f shown (2-2) 90 90

Huang Guo Shu Falls — A443

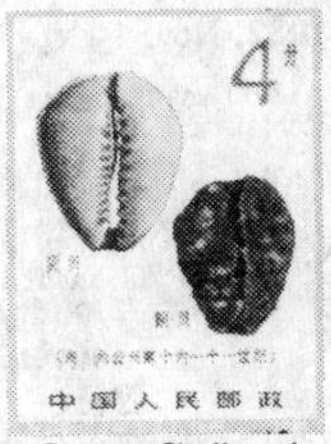

Cowrie Shell and Shell-shaped Coin — A444

1981-83 **Engr.** *Perf. 13x13½*
1723 A443 1f Xishuang Banna 15 15
1724 A443 1½f Mt. Hua 15 15
1725 A443 2f Mt. Tai 15 15
1726 A443 3f shown 15 15
1727 A443 4f Hainan Isld. 15 15
1728 A443 5f Tiger Hill, Suzhou 15 15
1729 A443 8f Great Wall 15 15
1730 A443 10f Immense Forest 15 15
1731 A443 20f Mt. Tian 15 15
1732 A443 30f Grassland, Inner Mongolia 22 20
1733 A443 40f Stone Forest 28 25
1734 A443 50f Banping Mountain 35 30
1735 A443 70f Mt. Qomolangma 52 45
1736 A443 80f Seven-Star Crag 60 55
1737 A443 $1 Three Gorges, Changjiang River 70 60
1738 A443 $2 Guilin landscape 1.40 1.25
1739 A443 $5 Mt. Huangshan 3.50 3.00
Nos. 1723-1739 (17) 8.92 7.95

Issue dates: Nos. 1737-1739, Oct. 9, 1982; Nos. 1732, 1734-1736 Apr. 1, 1983.

Photo. *Perf. 11½*
1726a A443 3f 15 15
1727a A443 4f 15 15
1729a A443 8f 20 20
1730a A443 10f 24 24
1731a A443 20f 52 52
Nos. 1726a-1731a (5) 1.26 1.26

Nos. 1727a, 1729a, 1730a exist tagged. Values 10-15% higher.

Photogravure and Engraved

1981, Oct. 29 *Perf. 11½x11*

Ancient Coins. T.65.

1740 A444 4f shown (8-1) 15 15
1741 A444 4f Shovel (8-2) 15 15
1742 A444 8f Shovel, diff. (8-3) 18 18
1743 A444 8f Shovel, diff. (8-4) 18 18
1744 A444 8f Knife (8-5) 18 18
1745 A444 8f Knife (8-6) 18 18
1746 A444 60f Knife, diff. (8-7) 1.90 1.90
1747 A444 70f Gong (8-8) 2.00 2.00
Nos. 1740-1747 (8) 4.92 4.92

See Nos. 1765-1772.

A445

A446

1981, Nov. 10 **Photo.** *Perf. 11½x11*
1748 A445 8f multicolored 32 32

Intl. Year of the Disabled.

1981-82 **Photo.** *Perf. 11*

Twelve Beauties, from The Dream of Red Mansions, by Cao Xueqin.

1749 A446 4f Daiyu (12-1) 20 20
1750 A446 4f Baochai (12-2) 20 20
1751 A446 8f Yuanchun (12-3) 40 40
1752 A446 8f Yingchun (12-4) 40 40
1753 A446 8f Tanchun (12-5) 40 40
1754 A446 8f Xichun (12-6) 40 40
1755 A446 8f Xiangyuh (12-7) 40 40
1756 A446 10f Liwan (12-8) 55 55
1757 A446 20f Xifeng (12-9) 1.00 1.00
1758 A446 30f Sister Qiao (12-10) 1.65 1.65
1759 A446 40f Keqing (12-11) 2.00 2.00
1760 A446 80f Miaoyu (12-12) 4.25 4.25
Nos. 1749-1760 (12) 11.85 11.85

Souvenir Sheet

1761 A446 $2 Baoyu, Daiyu *22.50*

No. 1761 contains one 59x39mm stamp. Issue dates: Nos. 1749, 1751, 1753, 1755, 1757, 1759, 1761, Nov. 20, 1981; others, Apr. 24, 1982. T.69.

A447

A448

1981, Dec. 21 **Photo.**
1762 A447 8f Girl playing (2-1) 32 25
1763 A447 20f Girl holding trophy (2-2) 65 55

Women's team victory in 3rd World Cup Volleyball Championship (J.76).

Photogravure & Engraved

1982, Jan. 5 *Perf. 11½*
1764 A448 8f multicolored 1.00 1.00
a. Booklet pane of 10 + label *6.00*

New Year 1982 (Year of the Dog).

Coin Type of 1981

1982, Feb. 12
1765 A444 4f Guilian mask (8-1) 15 15
1766 A444 4f Shu shovel (8-2) 15 15
1767 A444 8f Xia zhuan shovel (8-3) 16 16
1768 A444 8f Han Dan shovel (8-4) 16 16
1769 A444 8f Knife (8-5) 16 16
1770 A444 8f Ming knife (8-6) 16 16
1771 A444 70f Jin hua knife (8-7) 1.50 1.50
1772 A444 80f Yi Liu Hua coin (8-8) 1.75 1.75
Nos. 1765-1772 (8) 4.19 4.19

T.71.

Nie Er (1912-1935), Natl. Anthem Composer A449

1982, Feb. 15 *Perf. 11x11½*
1773 A449 8f multicolored 30 30

Intl. Drinking Water and Sanitation Decade, 1981-1990 — A450

1982, Mar. 1 *Perf. 11½x11*
1774 A450 8f multicolored 30 30

TB Bacillus Centenary A451

1982, Mar. 24 *Perf. 11x11½*
1775 A451 8f multicolored 30 20

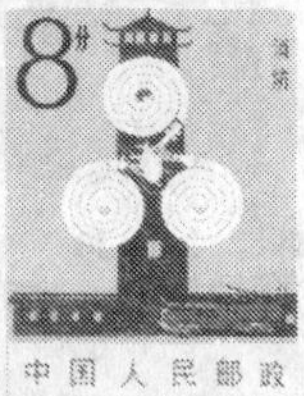

Fire Control (T.76) — A452

1982, May 8 **Photo.** *Perf. 11½x11*
1776 A452 8f Water hoses (2-1) 25 25
1777 A452 8f Chemical extinguisher (2-2) 25 25

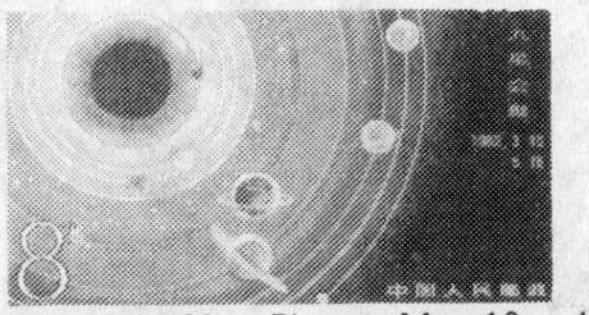

Syzygy of the Nine Planets, Mar. 10 and May 16 — A453

1982, May 16 *Perf. 11½*
1778 A453 8f multicolored 40 40

Medicinal Herbs — A454

Soong Ching Ling (1893-1981), Sun Yat-sen's Widow — A455

1982, May 20 *Perf. 11½x11*
1779 A454 4f Hemerocallis flava (6-1) 15 15
1780 A454 8f Fritillaria unibracteata (6-2) 15 15
1781 A454 8f Aconitum carmichaeli (6-3) 15 15
1782 A454 10f Lilium brownii (6-4) 20 20
1783 A454 20f Arisaema (6-5) 32 32
1784 A454 70f Paeonia lactiflora (6-6) 1.40 1.40
Nos. 1779-1784 (6) 2.37 2.37

Souvenir Sheet

1785 A454 $2 Iris tectorum maxim *7.00*

No. 1785 contains one 89x39mm stamp. Nos. 1779-1784 numbered T.72.

1982, May 29 *Perf. 11½*
1786 A455 8f Addressing Consultative Conf. (2-1) 20 20
1787 A455 20f Portrait (2-2) 60 60

J.82.

Sable (T.68) A456

1982, June 20 Photo. *Perf. 11½*
1788 A456 8f shown (2-1) 32 32
1789 A456 80f Sable, diff. (2-2) 1.65 1.65
a. Bklt. pane of 8, 6 8f plus sheetlet of 2 (8f, 80f) 3.50

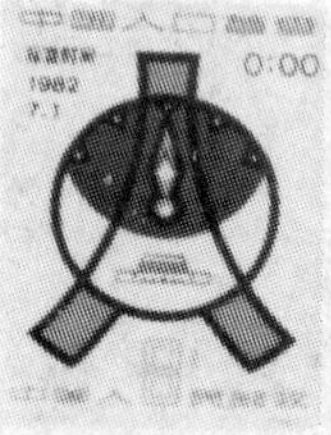
A457

A458

1982, June 30 *Perf. 11½x11*
1790 A457 8f multicolored 16 16

Natl. census, July 1.

1982, July 25 Photo. *Perf. 11½x11*
1791 A458 8f multicolored 16 15

2nd UN Conference on Peaceful Uses of Outer Space, Vienna, Aug. 9-21.

Strolling in Autumn Woods, by Shen Zhou, Ming Dynasty — A459

Fan Paintings (Ming or Qing Dynasty): No. 1793, Jackdaw on Withered Tree, by Tang Yin. No. 1794 Bamboo and Sparrows, by Zhou Zhimian. 10f, Writing Poem under Pine, by Chen Hongshou and Bai Han. 20f, Chrysanthemums, by Yun Shouping, Qing. 70f, Birds, Crape Myrtle and Chinese Parasol, by Wang Wu, Qing. T.77.

1982, July 31 *Perf. 11½*
1792 A459 4f multi (6-1) 18 18
1793 A459 8f multi (6-2) 18 18
1794 A459 8f multi (6-3) 18 18
1795 A459 10f multi (6-4) 26 26
1796 A459 20f multi (6-5) 60 60
1797 A459 70f multi (6-6) 2.00 2.00
Nos. 1792-1797 (6) 3.40 3.40

A460

A461

1982, Aug. 25 *Perf. 11½x11*
1798 A460 8f multicolored 16 16

60th anniv. of Chinese Geological Society.

1982, Aug. 25 Photo. *Perf. 11½x11*
1799 A461 4f Orpiment (4-1) 15 15
1800 A461 8f Stibnite (4-2) 15 15
1801 A461 10f Cinnabar (4-3) 20 20
1802 A461 20f Wolframite (4-4) 40 40
Nos. 1799-1802 (4) 90 90

T.73.

Souvenir Sheet

Messenger, Tomb Mural, Jiayu Pass, Wei-Jin Period — A462

1982, Aug. 25
1803 A462 $1 multicolored *6.00*

All-China Philatelic Federation, 1st Cong.

12th Natl. Communist Party Congress — A463

Hoopoe — A464

1982, Sept. 1 *Perf. 11½*
1804 A463 8f multicolored 18 18

1982, Sept. 10 *Perf. 11½x11*
1805 A464 8f shown (5-1) 20 16
1806 A464 8f Swallows (5-2) 20 16
1807 A464 8f Oriole (5-3) 20 16
1808 A464 20f Swifts (5-4) 55 45
1809 A464 70f Woodpecker (5-5) 2.50 2.00
Nos. 1805-1809 (5) 3.65 2.93

Souvenir Sheet

1810 A464 $2 Cuckoos *9.00*

#1810 contains one 56x36mm stamp. T.79.

Japan-China Relations Normalization, 10th Anniv. — A465

World Food Day — A466

Flower Paintings: 8f, Plum blossoms, by Guan Shanyue. 70f, Hibiscus, by Xiao Shufang. J.84.

1982, Sept. 29 *Perf. 11*
1811 A465 8f multi (2-1) 15 15
1812 A465 70f multi (2-2) 1.10 1.10

1982, Oct. 16 *Perf. 11½*
1813 A466 8f multicolored 25 25

Guo Morou (1892-1978), Acad. of Sciences Pres. — A467

Bodhisattva, 11th Cent. Sculpture — A468

Designs: Portraits. J.87.

1982, Nov. 16 Photo. *Perf. 11½x11*
1814 A467 8f multi (2-1) 15 15
1815 A467 20f multi (2-2) 25 25

1982, Nov. 19 *Perf. 11*

Liao Dynasty Buddha Sculptures, Lower Huayan Monastery. T.74.

1816 A468 8f multi (4-1) 25 25
1817 A468 8f multi (4-2) 25 25
1818 A468 8f multi (4-3) 25 25
1819 A468 70f multi (4-4) 2.25 2.25
Nos. 1816-1819 (4) 3.00 3.00

Souvenir Sheet

Perf. 11x11½

1820 A468 $2 multicolored *10.00*

No. 1820 contains one 36x55mm stamp.

Dr. D.S. Kotnis, Indian Physician in 8th Army (J.83) A469

Perf. 11½x11, 11x11½

1982, Dec. 9 **Photo.**
1821 A469 8f Portrait, vert. (2-1) 15 15
1822 A469 70f Riding horse (2-2) 90 90

11th Communist Youth League Natl. Congress A470

1982, Dec. 20 *Perf. 11x11½*
1823 A470 8f multicolored 20 20

Bronze Wine Container — A471

Western Zhou Dynasty Bronze (1200-771 B.C.): No. 1825, Three-legged cooking pot. No. 1826, Food bowl. No. 1827, Three-legged cooking pot (diff.). No. 1828, Animal-shaped wine container. 10f, Wine container with lid. 20f, Round food bowl. 70f, Square wine container. T.75.

Photogravure & Engraved

1982, Dec. 25 *Perf. 11*
1824 A471 4f multi (8-1) 16 16
1825 A471 4f multi (8-2) 16 16
1826 A471 8f multi (8-3) 28 28
1827 A471 8f multi (8-4) 28 28
1828 A471 8f multi (8-5) 28 28
1829 A471 10f multi (8-6) 42 42
1830 A471 20f multi (8-7) 70 70
1831 A471 70f multi (8-8) 3.00 3.00
Nos. 1824-1831 (8) 5.28 5.28

New Year 1983 (Year of the Pig) — A472

1983, Jan. 5 *Perf. 11½*
1832 A472 8f multicolored *1.10 1.10*
a. Booklet pane of 12

Stringed Instruments (T.81) A473

Perf. 11½x11, 11x11½

1983, Jan. 20
1833 A473 4f Konghou (5-1) 20 20
1834 A473 8f Ruan (5-2) 45 45
1835 A473 8f Qin, horiz. (5-3) 45 45
1836 A473 10f Piba (5-4) 60 60
1837 A473 70f Sanxian (5-5) 4.00 4.00
Nos. 1833-1837 (5) 5.70 5.70

60th Anniv. of Peking-Hankow Railroad Workers' Strike (J.89) — A474

1983, Feb. 7 Photo. *Perf. 11½x11*
1838 A474 8f Memorial Tower, Zhengzhou (2-1) 22 22
1839 A474 8f Monument, Jiangan (2-2) 22 22

The Western Chamber, Traditional Opera, by Wang Shifu (1271-1368) A475

Scenes from the opera.

1983, Feb. 21 Photo. *Perf. 11x11½*
1840 A475 8f multi (4-1) 52 52
1841 A475 8f multi (4-2) 52 52
1842 A475 10f multi (4-3) 70 70
1843 A475 80f multi (4-4) 6.75 6.75
Nos. 1840-1843 (4) 8.49 8.49

Souvenir Sheet

Photogravure and Engraved

Perf. 12

1844 A475 $2 multicolored *20.00*

#1844 contains one 27x48mm stamp. T.82.

Karl Marx (1818-1883) (J.90) — A476

Photogravure & Engraved

1983, Mar. 14 ***Perf. 11½x11***

1845 A476 8f Portrait (2-1) 18 18
1846 A476 20f Making speech (2-2) 38 38

Tomb of the Yellow Emperor (T.84) — A477

Photogravure & Engraved

1983, Apr. 5 ***Perf. 11½***

1847 A477 8f Tomb, vert. (3-1) 18 18
1848 A477 10f Hall of Founder of Chinese Culture (3-2) 22 22
1849 A477 20f Cypress tree, vert. (3-3) 45 45
Nos. 1847-1849 (3) 85 85

World Communications Year — A478

1983, Apr. 28 **Photo.** ***Perf. 11½***

1850 A478 8f multicolored 50 50

Male Chinese Alligator (T.85) — A479

Photogravure & Engraved

1983, May 24 ***Perf. 11***

1851 A479 8f shown (2-1) 24 24
1852 A479 20f Female, hatching eggs (2-2) 55 55

Kitten, by Tan Arxi — A480

Various children's drawings. T.86.

1983, June 1 ***Perf. 11½x11***

1853 A480 8f multi (4-1) 20 20
1854 A480 8f multi (4-2) 20 20
1855 A480 8f multi (4-3) 20 20
1856 A480 8f multi (4-4) 20 20
Nos. 1853-1856 (4) 80 80

6th Natl. People's Congress (J.94) A481

1983, June 6 ***Perf. 11x11½***

1857 A481 8f Hall (2-1) 16 16
1858 A481 20f Natl. anthem score (2-2) 35 35

Terra Cotta Figures, Qin Dynasty (221-207 BC) — A482

1983, June 30

1859 A482 8f Soldiers (4-1) 24 24
1860 A482 8f Heads (4-2) 24 24
1861 A482 10f Soldiers, horses (4-3) 35 35
1862 A482 70f Excavation site (4-4) 2.50 2.50
a. Bklt. pane of 8 (#1859, 3 #1860, 3 #1861, #1862)
Nos. 1859-1862 (4) 3.33 3.33

Souvenir Sheet

1863 A482 $2 Soldier leading horse *12.00*
a. Booklet pane

#1863 contains one 59x39mm stamp. T.88.

A483

A484

Female roles in Peking opera (T.87).

1983, July 20 **Photo.** ***Perf. 11***

1864 A483 4f Sun Yujiao (8-1) 16 16
1865 A483 8f Chen Miaochang (8-2) 30 30
1866 A483 8f Bai Suzhen (8-3) 30 30
1867 A483 8f Sister Thirteen (8-4) 30 30
1868 A483 10f Qin Xianglian (8-5) 35 35
1869 A483 20f Yang Yuhuan (8-6) 75 75
1870 A483 50f Cui Yingying (8-7) 1.75 1.75
1871 A483 80f Mu Guiying (8-8) 3.00 3.00
Nos. 1864-1871 (8) 6.91 6.91

1983, Aug. 10 **Photo.** ***Perf. 11½***

Paintings by Liu Lingcang.

1872 A484 8f Li Bai (4-1) 20 20
1873 A484 8f Du Fu (4-2) 20 20
1874 A484 8f Han Yu (4-3) 20 20
1875 A484 70f Liu Zongyuan (4-4) 2.50 2.50
Nos. 1872-1875 (4) 3.10 3.10

Poets and philosophers of ancient China (J.92).

5th Natl. Women's Congress — A485

1983, Sept. 1 **Photo.** ***Perf. 11½***

1876 A485 8f multicolored 18 18

5th National Games (J.93) — A486

1983, Sept. 16 **Photo.** ***Perf. 11½***

1877 A486 4f Emblem (6-1) 15 15
1878 A486 8f Gymnast (6-2) 15 15
1879 A486 8f Badminton (6-3) 15 15
1880 A486 8f Diving (6-4) 15 15
1881 A486 20f High jump (6-5) 40 40
1882 A486 70f Wind surfing (6-6) 1.65 1.65
Nos. 1877-1882 (6) 2.65 2.65

Family Planning (T.91) A487

1983, Sept. 19 ***Perf. 11x11½***

1883 A487 8f One child (2-1) 20 20
1884 A487 8f Cultivated land (2-2) 20 20

10th Intl. Trade Union Congress — A488

1983, Oct. 18 **Litho.** ***Perf. 11½***

1885 A488 8f multicolored 18 18

Swans (T.83) — A489

Perf. 11x11½ on 3 sides

1983, Nov. 18 **Photo.**

1886 A489 8f (4-1) 20 20
1887 A489 8f (4-2) 20 20
1888 A489 10f (4-3) 22 22
1889 A489 80f (4-4) 1.65 1.65
a. Booklet pane, 7 #1886, 1 each #1887-1889 *4.00*
Nos. 1886-1889 (4) 2.27 2.27

A490

A491

Various photos. J.96.

1983, Nov. 24 **Photo.** ***Perf. 11½***

1890 A490 8f multi (4-1) 15 15
1891 A490 8f multi (4-2) 15 15
1892 A490 8f multi (4-3) 15 15
1893 A490 8f multi (4-4) 15 15
Nos. 1890-1893 (4) 60 60

85th birth anniv. of Liu Shaoqi, political leader.

1983, Nov. 29 **Photo.** ***Perf. 11½***

1894 A491 8f No. 117 (2-1) 22 22
1895 A491 20f No. 4L1 (2-2) 48 48

CHINAPEX '83 Natl. Philatelic Exhibition (J.99).

A492

A493

Various portraits. J.97.

1983, Dec. 26 **Photo.** ***Perf. 11½***

1896 A492 8f 1925 (4-1) 15 15
1897 A492 8f 1945 (4-2) 15 15
1898 A492 10f 1952 (4-3) 16 16
1899 A492 20f 1961 (4-4) 40 40
Nos. 1896-1899 (4) 86 86

90th birth anniv. of Mao Tse-tung.

Photogravure and Engraved

1984, Jan. 5 ***Perf. 11½***

1900 A493 8f multicolored 1.10 50
a. Booklet pane of 12 5.25

New Year 1984 (Year of the Rat).

Souvenir Sheets
Booklet Panes

Heavy speculation in stamps in China is centered around the souvenir sheets and booklet panes. These generally are trading by the 100 and being held off the normal philatelic market. Values are not being assigned until true market values can be established.

Beauties Wearing Flowers — A494

Portions of painting by Zhou Fang (Tang Dynasty). T.89.

1984, Mar. 24 **Photo.** ***Perf. 11***

1901 A494 8f multi (3-1) 24 24
1902 A494 10f multi (3-2) 35 35
1903 A494 70f multi (3-3) 3.00 3.00
Nos. 1901-1903 (3) 3.59 3.59

Souvenir Sheet

1904 A494 $2 Entire painting *21.00*

No. 1904 contains one 162x40mm stamp.

Chinese Roses (T.93) — A495

Ren Bishi (1904-50), Statesman — A496

1984, Apr. 20 **Photo.** ***Perf. 11½***

1905 A495 4f Spring of Shanghai (6-1) 15 15
1906 A495 8f Rosy Dawn of Pujiang River (6-2) 16 16
1907 A495 8f Pearl (6-3) 16 16
1908 A495 10f Black whirlwind (6-4) 22 22

1909 A495 20f Yellow flower in battlefield (6-5) 40 40
1910 A495 70f Blue Phoenix (6-6) 1.50 1.50
Nos. 1905-1910 (6) 2.59 2.59

1984, Apr. 30 ***Perf. 11½x11***
1911 A496 8f multicolored 16 16

Crested Ibis (T.94) A497

1984, May 15 Photo. ***Perf. 11x11½***
1912 A497 8f Flying (3-1) 15 15
1913 A497 8f Wading (3-2) 15 15
1914 A497 80f Perching (3-3) 90 90
Nos. 1912-1914 (3) 1.20 1.20

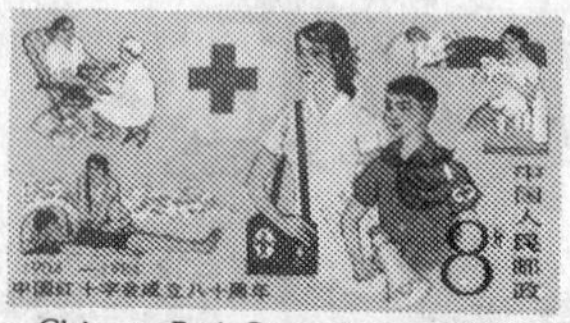

Chinese Red Cross Society, 80th Anniv. — A498

1984, May 29 ***Perf. 11½***
1915 A498 8f multicolored 16 16

Gezhou Dam, Yangtze River (T.95) — A499

1984, June 15 **Photo.**
1916 A499 8f Dam (3-1) 16 16
1917 A499 10f Bridge, vert. (3-2) 20 20
1918 A499 20f Lock Gate #2 (3-3) 45 45
Nos. 1916-1918 (3) 81 81

Zhuo Zheng Garden, Suzhou (T.96) — A500

Photogravure & Engraved
1984, June 30 ***Perf. 11½x11***
1919 A500 8f Inverted Image Tower (4-1) 15 15
1920 A500 8f Loquat Garden (4-2) 15 15
1921 A500 10f Water Court, Xiao Cang Lang (4-3) 16 15
1922 A500 70f Yuanxiang Hall, Yiyu Study (4-4) 1.25 70
Nos. 1919-1922 (4) 1.71
Set value 90

1984 Summer Olympics A501

1984, July 28 Photo. ***Perf. 11½***
1923 A501 4f Shooting (6-1) 15 15
1924 A501 8f High jump (6-2) 15 15
1925 A501 8f Weight lifting (6-3) 15 15
1926 A501 10f Gymnastics (6-4) 15 15
1927 A501 20f Volleyball (6-5) 22 22
1928 A501 80f Diving (6-6) 95 95
Nos. 1923-1928 (6) 1.77 1.77

Souvenir Sheet
1929 A501 $2 Athletes, rings *3.00*

#1929 contains one 61x38mm stamp. J.103.

Calligraphy A502

Luanhe River Water Diversion Project (T.97) A503

Artworks by Wu Changshuo. T.98.

1984, Aug. 27 Photo. ***Perf. 11½***
1930 A502 4f shown (8-1) 15 15
1931 A502 4f A Pair of Peaches (8-2) 15 15
1932 A502 8f Lotus (8-3) 16 16
1933 A502 8f Wistaria (8-4) 16 16
1934 A502 8f Peony (8-5) 16 16
1935 A502 10f Chrysanthemum (8-6) 20 20
1936 A502 20f Plum Blossom (8-7) 38 38
1937 A502 70f Seal Cutting (8-8) 1.40 1.40
Nos. 1930-1937 (8) 2.76 2.76

Perf. 11½x11, 11 (#1939)
1984, Sept. 11 **Photo.**
1938 A503 8f multi (3-1) 15 15
1939 A503 10f multi, horiz. (3-2) 15 15
1940 A503 20f multi (3-3) 28 28
Set value 50 50

Chinese-Japanese Youth (J.104) — A504

1984, Sept. 24 Photo. ***Perf. 11½***
1941 A504 8f Neighbors (3-1) 15 15
1942 A504 20f Planting tree (3-2) 20 20
1943 A504 80f Dancing (3-3) 90 90
Nos. 1941-1943 (3) 1.25 1.25

People's Republic, 35th Anniv. (J.105) — A505

1984, Oct. 1 Photo. ***Perf. 11½x11***
Size: 26x35mm
1944 A505 8f Engineer (5-1) 15 15
1945 A505 8f Farm woman (5-2) 15 15
1946 A505 8f Scientist (5-4) 15 15
1947 A505 8f Soldier (5-5) 15 15

Size: 36x48mm
Perf. 11
1948 A505 20f Birds (5-3) 22 22
Set value 55 55

110th Birth Anniv. of Chen Jiageng (J.106) A506

1984, Oct. 21 Photo. ***Perf. 12½x12***
1949 A506 8f Chen Jiageng (2-1) 15 15
1950 A506 80f Jimei School (2-2) 80 80

The Maiden's Study — A507

Scenes from The Peony Pavilion, by Tang Xianzu. T.99.

Photogravure & Engraved
1984, Oct. 30 ***Perf. 11***
1951 A507 8f shown (4-1) 15 15
1952 A507 8f In the dreamland (4-2) 15 15
1953 A507 20f Du Liniang drawing self-portrait (4-3) 32 32
1954 A507 70f Married to Liu Mengmai (4-4) 1.40 1.40
Nos. 1951-1954 (4) 2.02 2.02

Souvenir Sheet
Perf. 11½
1955 A507 $2 Playing in the garden *7.00*

No. 1955 contains one 90x60mm stamp.

Emei Shan Mountain Scenery (T.100) — A508

1984, Nov. 16 ***Perf. 11***
1956 A508 4f Baoguo Temple (6-1) 15 15
1957 A508 8f Leiyin Temple (6-2) 15 15
1958 A508 8f Hongchun Lawn (6-3) 15 15
1959 A508 10f Elephant bath (6-4) 18 18
1960 A508 20f Woyun Temple (6-5) 35 35
1961 A508 80f Shining Cloud Sea at Jinding (6-6) 1.65 1.65
Nos. 1956-1961 (6) 2.63 2.63

A509

A510

Portraits.

1984, Dec. 15 Photo. ***Perf. 11½x11***
1962 A509 8f During the Long March (3-1) 15 15
1963 A509 10f At 7th Natl. Party Congress (3-2) 15 15
1964 A509 20f In motorcade (3-3) 28 20
Set value 50 38

Former party secretary Ren Bishi (1904-50).

1984, Dec. 25 ***Perf. 11***
1965 A510 8f Flower arrangement 20 20

Chinese insurance industry.

New Year 1985 (Year of the Ox) — A511

Photogravure & Engraved
1985, Jan. 5 ***Perf. 11½***
1966 A511 8f T.102 50 50
a. Bklt. pane of 4 + 8 plus label *5.00*

Zunyi Meeting, 50th Anniv. — A512

Paintings: 8f, The Zunyi Meeting, by Liu Xiangping. 20f, The Red Army Successfully Arrived in Northern Shaanxi, by Zhao Yu. J.107.

1985, Jan. 15 Photo. ***Perf. 11x11½***
1967 A512 8f multi (2-1) 15 15
1968 A512 20f multi (2-2) 24 24
Set value 30 30

A513

A514

Lantern Folk Festival: No. 1969, Lotus of Good Luck. No. 1970, Auspicious dragon and phoenix. No. 1971, A hundred flowers blossoming. 70f, Prosperity and affluence. T.104.

1985, Feb. 28 ***Perf. 11½***
1969 A513 8f multi (4-1) 16 16
1970 A513 8f multi (4-2) 16 16
1971 A513 8f multi (4-3) 16 16
1972 A513 70f multi (4-4) 1.25 1.25
Nos. 1969-1972 (4) 1.73 1.73

1985, Mar. 8
1973 A514 20f multicolored 20 15

UN Decade for Women (1976-85).

Mei (Prunus mume) (T.103) — A515

1985, Apr. 5 ***Perf. 11***
1974 A515 8f Green calyx (6-1) 15 15
1975 A515 8f Pendant mei (6-2) 15 15
1976 A515 8f Contorted dragon (6-3) 15 15
1977 A515 10f Cinnabar (6-4) 15 15
1978 A515 20f Versicolor mei (6-5) 26 15
1979 A515 80f Apricot mei (6-6) 1.10 55
Nos. 1974-1979 (6) 1.96
Set value 90

Souvenir Sheet

Perf. 11½

1980 A515 $2 Duplicate and condensed fragrance mei 5.00

No. 1980 contains one 93x52mm stamp.

A516

A518

A517

1985, May 1 **Photo.** ***Perf. 11***

1981 A516 8f Huizo Guild Hall, Guangzhou 15 15

All-China Fed. of Trade Unions.

1985, May 4 **Photo.**

1982 A517 20f multicolored 20 15

Intl. Youth Year.

1985, May 24 ***Perf. 11½***

Paintings of giant pandas: 8f, 20f, 50f, 80f, by Han Meilin; $3, by Wu Zuoren. T.106.

1983 A518 8f multi (4-1), vert. 15 15
1984 A518 20f multi (4-2) 15 15
1985 A518 50f multi (4-3), vert. 40 40
1986 A518 80f multi (4-4) 60 60
Nos. 1983-1986 (4) 1.30 1.30

Souvenir Sheet

Perf. 11x11½

1987 A518 $3 multi, vert. 2.00

No. 1987 contains one 39x59mm stamp.

Xian Xinghai (1905-1945), Composer — A519

Agnes Smedley, 1892-1950 (3-1) — A520

Design: Bust, by Cao Chongen and music from The Yellow River Cantata.

1985, June 13 **Photo.** ***Perf. 11½x11***

1988 A519 8f multicolored 15 15

1985, June 25

American journalists: 20f, Anna Louise Strong, 1885-1970 (3-2). 80f, Edgar Snow, 1905-1972 (3-3). J.112.

1989 A520 8f multicolored 15 15
1990 A520 20f multicolored 20 18
1991 A520 80f multicolored 80 75
Nos. 1989-1991 (3) 1.15 1.08

Zheng He's West Seas Expedition, 580th Anniv. — A521

Designs: No. 1992, Portrait of the navigator (4-1). No. 1993, Peace envoy (4-2). 20f, Trade, cultural exchange (4-3). 80f, Honored for navigational feats (4-4). J.113.

1985, July 11 ***Perf. 11½***

1992 A521 8f multicolored 15 15
1993 A521 8f multicolored 15 15
1994 A521 20f multicolored 22 22
1995 A521 80f multicolored 85 85
Nos. 1992-1995 (4) 1.37 1.37

Xu Beihong, 1895-1953, Painter (J.114) A522

Perf. 11½x11, 11x11½

1985, July 19

1996 A522 8f Self-portrait (2-1), vert. 24 24
1997 A522 20f shown (2-2) 75 75

A523

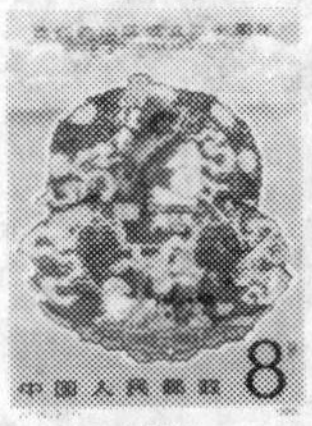
A524

Designs: 8f, Lin Zexu, 1785-1850, statesman, patriot. 80f, Burning opium at Humen, bas-relief.

1985, Aug. 30 ***Perf. 11***

1998 A523 8f multi (2-1) 15 15

Size: 51x22mm

1999 A523 80f multi (2-2) 45 45

Lin Zexu's ban of the opium trade catalyzed the Anglo-Chinese Opium Wars. J.115.

1985, Sept. 1 ***Perf. 11½x11***

2000 A524 8f Prosperity (3-1) 15 15
2001 A524 10f Celebration (3-2) 22 22
2002 A524 20f Abundant Harvest (3-3) 50 50
Nos. 2000-2002 (3) 87 87

Tibet Autonomous Region, 20th anniv. (J.116).

End of World War II, 40th Anniv. A525

Woodcuts by Wu Biduan: 8f, The Chinese Army Rose Against the Japanese Agressors at Logouqiao (2-1). 80f, The Eighth Route Army and Militia Fought Around the Great Wall (2-2). J.117.

1985, Sept. 3 ***Perf. 11***

2003 A525 8f multi 15 15
2004 A525 80f multi 45 40
Set value 50 45

2nd Natl. Worker's Games, Sept. 8-15, Beijing A526

Competitors from various events and: 8f, Men's bicycling (2-1). 20f, Women hurdlers (2-2). J.118.

1985, Sept. 8 ***Perf. 11x11½***

2005 A526 8f multi 15 15
2006 A526 20f multi 24 24
Set value 28 28

Xinjiang Uygur Autonomous Region, 30th Anniv. (J.119) — A527

1985, Oct. 1 **Photo.** ***Perf. 11½***

2007 A527 8f Oasis in the Gobi, woman (3-1) 15 15
2008 A527 10f Oil field, Lake Tianchi (3-2) 15 15
2009 A527 20f Tianshan pasture, woman (3-3) 22 22
Set value 40 40

Size of No. 2008, 60x30mm.

1st Natl. Youth Games, Oct. 6-15, Zhengzhou (J.121) — A528

1985, Oct. 6 ***Perf. 11½x11***

2010 A528 8f Girls' track & field (2-1) 15 15
2011 A528 20f Boys' basketball (2-2) 38 38

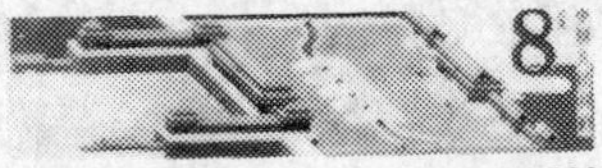
Forbidden City Main Buildings — A529

1985, Oct. 10 ***Perf. 11½***

2012 A529 8f multi (4-1) 15 15
2013 A529 8f multi (4-2) 15 15
2014 A529 20f multi (4-3) 16 16
2015 A529 80f multi (4-4) 70 70
a. Vert. strip of 4, #2012-2057 1.25 1.25

Palace Museum, 60th anniv. J.120.

Zou Taofen (1895-1935), Journalist (J.122) — A530

1985, Nov. 5 ***Perf. 11½x11***

2016 A530 8f Portrait (2-1) 15 15
2017 A530 20f Epitaph by Zhou Enlai (2-2) 22 22
a. Pair, #2016-2017 30 30

December 9th Revolution, 50th Anniv. — A531

1985, Dec. 9 ***Perf. 11½***

2018 A531 8f Memorial Pavilion 15 15

New Year 1986 — A532

Natl. Space Industry — A533

Photogravure & Engraved

1986, Jan. 5 ***Perf. 11½***

2019 A532 8f multicolored 50 30
a. Bklt. pane of 4 + 8 with label btwn 3.00

1986, Feb. 1 **Photo.**

Designs: 4f, 1st experimental satellite. No. 2021, Recoverable satellite. No. 2022, Underwater rocket launch. 10f, Rocket launch. 20f, Earth satellite receiver. 70f, Satellite trajectory diagram. T.108.

2020 A533 4f multi (6-1) 15 15
2021 A533 8f multi (6-2) 15 15
2022 A533 8f multi (6-3) 15 15
2023 A533 10f multi (6-4) 15 15
2024 A533 20f multi (6-5) 16 15
2025 A533 70f multi (6-6) 60 45
Nos. 2021-2025 (5) 1.21
Set value 65

Dong Biwu (1886-1975), Party Founder (J.123) — A534

Lin Boqu (1886-1960), Party Leader (J.124) — A535

Photogravure and Engraved

1986, Mar. 5 ***Perf. 11½x11***

2026 A534 8f 1975 (2-1) 15 15
2027 A534 20f 1945 (2-2) 24 24
Set value 32 32

1986, Mar. 20

2028 A535 8f shown (2-1) 15 15
2029 A535 20f Boqu standing (2-2) 24 24
Set value 32 32

Marshal He Long (1896-1969), Revolution Leader (J.126) A536

1986, Mar. 22 ***Perf. 11x11½***

2030 A536 8f shown (2-1) 15 15
2031 A536 20f Long on horseback (2-2) 24 24
Set value 32 32

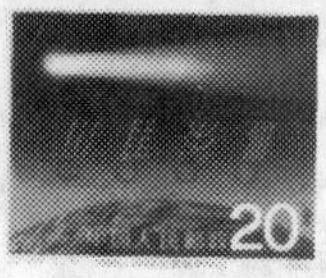
Halley's Comet — A537

1986, Apr. 11 Photo. *Perf. 11½*
2032 A537 20f dk bl & gray 30 25

White Crane (T.110) A538

Perf. 11x11½, 11½x11
1986, May 22
2033 A538 8f Two cranes (3-1) 15 15
2034 A538 10f One flying (3-2), vert. 15 15
2035 A538 70f Four cranes (3-3), vert. 90 45
Nos. 2033-2035 (3) 1.20
Set value 55

Souvenir Sheet
2036 A538 $2 Flock *2.50*

No. 2036 contains one 116x25mm stamp.

Li Weihan (1896-1984), Party Leader (J.127) A539

1986, June 2 *Perf. 11x11½*
2037 A539 8f Portrait (2-1) 15 15
2038 A539 20f Writing (2-2) 28 28
Set value 35 35

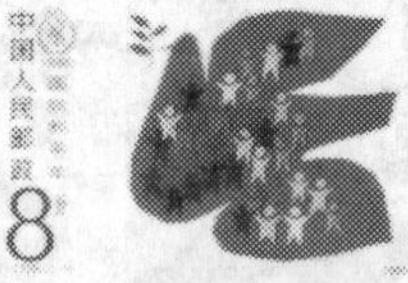
Intl. Peace Year — A540

1986, June 16 *Perf. 11*
2039 A540 8f multi 15 15

Mao Dun (1896-1981), Writer (J.129) A541

1986, July 4 *Perf. 11x11½*
2040 A541 8f Portrait (2-1) 15 15
2041 A541 20f Portrait, diff. (2-2) 28 28
Set value 35 35

Wang Jiaxiang (1906-1974), Party Leader (J.130) A542

1986, Aug. 15
2042 A542 8f Portrait (2-1) 15 15
2043 A542 20f Portrait, diff. (2-2) 28 28
Set value 35 35

Teacher's Day — A543

1986, Sept. 10 *Perf. 11*
2044 A543 8f multi 15 15

Magnolia Liliflora (T.111) A544

1986, Sept. 23 *Perf. 11x11½*
2045 A544 8f Blossom (3-1) 15 15
2046 A544 8f Two blossoms (3-2) 15 15
2047 A544 70f Blossom, diff. (3-3) 80 80
Nos. 2045-2047 (3) 1.10 1.10

Souvenir Sheet
2048 A544 $2 Three blossoms *4.00*

No. 2048 contains one 132x70mm stamp.

Folk Houses — A545

Perf. 13x13½, 11x11½, (1½f, 3f, #2057-2062)
1986, Apr. 1 Photo.
2049 A545 1f Inner Mongolia 15 15
2050 A545 1½f Tibet 15 15
2051 A545 2f Northeastern China 15 15
2052 A545 3f Hunan 15 15
2053 A545 4f So. Yangtze River 15 15
2054 A545 8f Beijing 15 15
2055 A545 10f Yunnan 15 15
2056 A545 20f Shanghai 16 16
2057 A545 30f Anhui 25 25
2058 A545 40f No. Shaanxi 32 32
2059 A545 50f Sichuan 42 42
2060 A545 90f Taiwan 75 75
2061 A545 $1 Fujian 85 85
2062 A545 $1.10 Zhejiang 95 95
Set value 4.00 4.00

Issue dates: 3f, Dec. 25. 4f, $1, Oct. 15. 20f, 50f, Sept. 10. 40f, Nov. 15. Others, Apr. 1.
Postal forgeries of No. 2056 exist.
See Nos. 2198-2207.

1989-90 Photo.
2055a Perf. 11x11½ ('89) 15 15
2056a Perf. 11x11½ ('89) 25 15
2057a Perf. 13x13½ ('90) 45 25
2058a Perf. 13x13½ 60 32
2059a Perf. 13x13½ ('89) 75 40
2061a Perf. 13x13½ ('90) 1.50 80

Souvenir Sheet

All-China Philatelic Federation, 2nd Congress — A546

1986, Oct. 17 Litho. *Perf. 11½*
2063 A546 $2 Jade lion *4.00*

Leaders of the 1911 Revolution (J.132) A547

1986, Oct. 10 Photo. *Perf. 11x11½*
2064 A547 8f Sun Yat-sen (3-1) 15
2065 A547 10f Huang Xing (3-2) 15
2066 A547 40f Zhang Taiyan (3-3) 80
Nos. 2064-2066 (3) 1.10

Souvenir Sheet

Sun Yat-sen (1866-1925) — A548

1986, Nov. 12 *Perf. 11½*
2067 A548 $2 multicolored *3.50*

Marshal Zhu De (1886-1976) (J.134) — A549

Designs: 20f, Orating.

1986, Dec. 1 Engr. *Perf. 11½x11*
2068 A549 8f sepia (2-1) 15 15
2069 A549 20f myrtle grn (2-2) 28 20
Set value 35 27

Sports of Ancient China — A550

Stone carvings. T.113.

Perf. 11½x11, 11x11½
1986, Dec. 20 Photo.
2070 A550 8f Archery (4-1), vert. 15
2071 A550 8f Weiqi (4-2) 15
2072 A550 10f Golf (4-3) 15
2073 A550 50f Soccer (4-4), vert. 1.10
Nos. 2070-2073 (4) 1.55

A551

A552

Photogravure & Engraved
1987, Jan. 5 *Perf. 11½*
2074 A551 8f blk, dk pink & yel grn 45
a. Bklt. pane of 4 + 8 + label *3.50*

New Year 1987 (Year of the Hare).

1987, Feb. 20 Photo. *Perf. 11½*
2075 A552 8f Traveling (3-1) 15
2076 A552 20f Writing in cave (3-2) 50
2077 A552 40f Mountain climbing (3-3) 1.00
Nos. 2075-2077 (3) 1.65

Xu Xiake (1587-1621), Ming Dynasty geographer (J.136).

Birds of Prey (T.114) — A553

1987, Mar. 20
2078 A553 8f Kite (4-1) 15 15
2079 A553 8f Sea eagle (4-2), vert. 15 15
2080 A553 10f Vulture (4-3), vert. 15 15
2081 A553 90f Buzzard (4-4) 1.25 1.25
Nos. 2078-2081 (4) 1.70 1.70

Liao Zhongkai (1877-1925), National Party Leader (J.137) — A554

1987, Apr. 23 *Perf. 11½x11*
2082 A554 8f shown (2-1) 15
2083 A554 20f Liao, He Xiangning (2-2) 28
Set value 35

Kites (T.115) — A555

A556

1987, Apr. 1
2084 A555 8f Hawk (4-1) 15
2085 A555 8f Dragon (4-2) 15
a. Pair, #2084-2085 26
2086 A555 30f Symbolic octagon (4-3) 75
2087 A555 30f Phoenix (4-4) 75
a. Pair, #2086-2087 1.50
Nos. 2084-2087 (4) 1.80

Nos. 2085a, 2087a have continuous designs.

1987, Apr. 28

Portraits of Ye Jianying (1897-1986), central committee vice chairman (J.138).

2088 A556 8f multi (3-3) 15
2089 A556 10f multi (3-2) 15
2090 A556 30f multi (3-1) 55
Nos. 2088-2090 (3) 85

Caves of the Thousand Buddhas, Dunhuang, Gansu Province — A557

Petroglyphs: 8f, Worshipping Bodhisattvas, Northern Liang Dynasty. 10f, Deer King Jatka, Northern Wei Dynasty. 20f, Heavenly Musicians, Northern Wei Dynasty. 40f, Flying Devata, Northern Wei Dynasty. $2, Mahasattva Jataka. T.116.

1987, May 20 *Perf. 11½*

2091 A557 8f multi (4-1) 16
2092 A557 10f multi (4-2) 18
2093 A557 20f multi (4-3) 40
2094 A557 40f multi (4-4) 85
Nos. 2091-2094 (4) 1.59

Souvenir Sheet

2095 A557 $2 multi *4.50*

No. 2095 contains one 92x73mm stamp.
See Nos. 2149-2152, 2283-2286, 2407-2411, 2505-2508.

Children's Day Festival A558

Children's drawings: No. 2096, Happy Holiday, by Yan Qinghui, age 7. No. 2097, Peace and Happiness, by Liu Yuan, age 7. T.117.

1987, June 1 *Perf. 12½x12*

2096 A558 8f shown (2-1) 15
2097 A558 8f multi, vert. (2-2) 15
Set value 20

Rural Development A559

Postal Savings Bank Inauguration A560

1987, June 25 *Perf. 11½*

2098 A559 8f Village, southeast China (4-1) 15
2099 A559 8f Market (4-2) 15
2100 A559 10f Dairy industry (4-3) 16
2101 A559 20f Theater (4-4) 30
Nos. 2098-2101 (4) 76

Nos. 2099-2100 horiz. T.118.

1987, July 1

2102 A560 8f multicolored 15

Esperanto Language Movement, Cent. — A561

1987, July 26

2103 A561 8f lt olive grn, blk & brt blue 15

People's Liberation Army, 60th Anniv. (J.140) A562

1987, Aug. 1 *Perf. 11*

2104 A562 8f Flag, Great Wall (4-1) 15
2105 A562 8f Rocket launch, soldier, village (4-2) 15
2106 A562 10f Submarine, sailor (4-3) 15
2107 A562 30f Aircraft, pilot (4-4) 38
Nos. 2104-2107 (4) 83

Intl. Year of Shelter for the Homeless A563

1987, Aug. 20 *Perf. 11*

2108 A563 8f gray, dk car rose & blk 15

Chinese Art Festival, Sept. 5-25, Beijing — A564

Fairy Tales — A565

1987, Sept. 5 *Perf. 11*

2109 A564 8f brt red, gold & blk 15

1987, Sept. 25 *Perf. 11½*

Designs: 4f, Pan Gu inventing the universe. No. 2111, Nu Wa creating man. No. 2112, Yi shooting nine suns. 10f, Chang'e flying to the moon. 20f, Kua Fu pursuing the sun. 90f, Jing Wei filling the sea. T.120.

2110 A565 4f multi (6-1) 15
2111 A565 8f multi (6-2) 15
2112 A565 8f multi (6-3) 15
2113 A565 10f multi (6-4) 15
2114 A565 20f multi (6-5) 18
2115 A565 90f multi (6-6) 75
Set value 1.20

Communist Party of China, 13th Natl. Congress A566

1987, Oct. 25 *Perf. 11*

2116 A566 8f multicolored 15

Yellow Crane Tower (T.121) A567

1987, Oct. 30

2117 A567 8f shown (4-1) 15
2118 A567 8f Yue Yang Tower (4-2) 15
2119 A567 10f Teng Wang Pavilion (4-3) 18
2120 A567 90f Peng Lai Pavilion (4-4) 1.50
a. Min. sheet of 4, #2117-2120 *4.75*
Nos. 2117-2120 (4) 1.98

No. 2120a sold for $1.50.

6th Natl. Games (J.144) — A568

1987, Nov. 20 *Perf. 11½x11*

2121 A568 8f Pole vault (4-1) 15
2122 A568 8f Softball (4-2) 15
2123 A568 30f Weight lifting (4-3) 20
2124 A568 50f Diving (4-4) 32
Set value 65

Souvenir Sheet

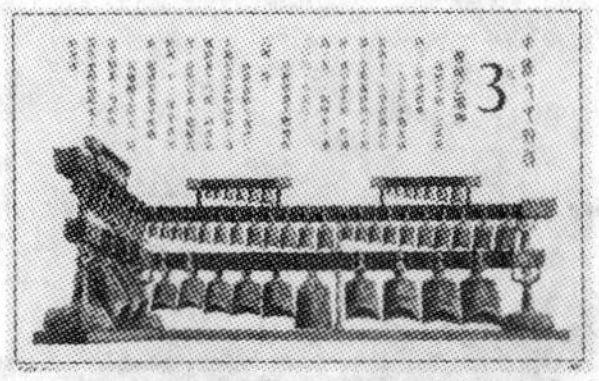

Bronze Bells from the Tomb of Marquis Yi of the Zeng State (c. 433 B.C.), Hubei Province — A569

1987, Dec. 10 **Litho.** ***Imperf.***

2125 A569 $3 multicolored *3.50*

Classic Literature — A570

Outlaws of the Marsh: 8f, Shi Jin practicing martial arts. 10f, Sagacious Lu, the "Tattooed Monk," uprooting a willow tree. 30f, Lin Chong seeking shelter from snow storm at the Mountain Spirit Temple. 50f, Song Jiang helps Ward Chief Chao Gai flee. $2, Outlaws of the Marsh capture treasures. T.123.

1987, Dec. 20 **Photo.** *Perf. 11*

2126 A570 8f multi (4-1) 16
2127 A570 10f multi (4-2) 20
2128 A570 30f multi (4-3) 60
2129 A570 50f multi (4-4) 1.00
Nos. 2126-2129 (4) 1.96

Souvenir Sheet

Perf. 11½x11

2130 A570 $2 multi *5.75*

No. 2130 contains one 90x60mm stamp.
See Nos. 2216-2219, 2373-2377, 2449-2452.

New Year 1988 (Year of the Dragon) — A571

Cai Yuanpei (1868-1940), Education Reformer ((J.145) — A572

Photo. & Engr.

1988, Jan. 5 *Perf. 11½*

2131 A571 8f multicolored *45*
a. Bklt. pane of 4 + 8 with label between 2.25

1988, Jan. 11 **Photo.** *Perf. 11½x11*

2132 A572 8f shown (2-1) 15
2133 A572 20f Seated (2-2) 15
Set value 20

Tao Zhu (1908-1969), Party Leader (J.146) A573

1988, Jan. 16 *Perf. 11x11½*

2134 A573 8f shown (2-1) 15
2135 A573 20f Zhu, diff. (2-2) 15
Set value 20

Folklore (T.125) A574

1988, Feb. 10

2136 A574 8f shown (4-1) 15
2137 A574 10f multi, diff. (4-2) 15
2138 A574 20f multi, diff. (4-3) 15
2139 A574 30f multi, diff. (4-4) 24
Set value 50

A575

A576

1988, Mar. 25 **Photo.** *Perf. 11½*

2140 A575 8f multicolored 15

7th Natl. People's Congress.

1988, Apr. 20 **Photo.** *Perf. 11½*

2141 A576 8f Wuzhi Mountain (4-1) 15
2142 A576 10f Wanquan River (4-2) 15
2143 A576 30f "End of the Earth" (4-3) 18
2144 A576 $1.10 "Deer Turning Its Head" (4-4) 70
Nos. 2141-2144 (4) 1.18

Establishment of Hainan Province (J.148).

Modern Scientists A577

Designs: 8f, Li Siguang, geologist. 10f, Zhu Kezhen, meteorologist and geographer. 20f, Wu Youxun, physicist. 30f, Hua Luogeng, mathematician. J.149.

1988, Apr. 28 *Perf. 11x11½*

2145 A577 8f multi (4-1) 15
2146 A577 10f multi (4-2) 15
2147 A577 20f multi (4-3) 16
2148 A577 30f multi (4-4) 26
Set value 55

Dunhuang Petroglyphs Type of 1987

Petroglyphs from the Caves of the Thousand Buddhas, Dunhuang, Gansu Province: No. 2149, Hunting, Western Wei Dynasty. No. 2150, Fishing, Western Wei Dynasty. 10f, Farming, Northern Zhou Dynasty. 90f, Building a Pagoda, Northern Zhou Dynasty. T.126.

1988, May 25 *Perf. 11½x11*

2149	A557	8f multi (4-1)	*15*
2150	A557	8f multi (4-2)	*15*
2151	A557	10f multi (4-3)	*15*
2152	A557	90f multi (4-4)	*1.10*
		Nos. 2149-2152 (4)	*1.55*

Environmental Protection — A578

1988, June 5 **Photo.** ***Perf. 11***

2153	A578	8f Soil (4-1)	15
2154	A578	8f Air (4-2)	15
2155	A578	8f Water (4-3)	15
2156	A578	8f Prevent noise pollution (4-4)	15
a.		Block of 4, #2153-2156	40

Souvenir Sheet

China Nos. 1-3 — A579

1988, July 2 **Photo. & Engr.** ***Perf. 13***

2157	A579	$3 multicolored	*2.50*

Postage stamps of China, 110th anniv.

11th Asian Games (in 1990), Beijing (J.151) A580

1988, July 20 **Photo.** ***Perf. 11x11½***

2158	A580	8f Emblem (2-1)	15
2159	A580	30f Character trademark (2-2)	28
		Set value	35

See No. 2300a.

Signing of the Sino-Japanese Peace Treaty, 10th Anniv. (J.152) — A581

1988, Aug. 12 **Photo.** ***Perf. 11***

2160	A581	8f Peony (2-1)	15
2161	A581	$1.60 Sakura (2-2)	75
a.		Pair, #2160-2161	80

Achievements in Construction A582

Designs: 8f, Coal-loading wharf, Ch'in-huang-tao Port. 10f, Ethylene refinery, Qilu. 20f, Pao-shan steel plant, Shanghai. 30f, Central Television Broadcasting Station. T.128.

1988, Sept. 2 **Photo.** ***Perf. 11***

2162	A582	8f multi (4-1)	15
2163	A582	10f multi (4-2)	15
2164	A582	20f multi (4-3)	15
2165	A582	30f multi (4-4)	16
		Set value	40

See Nos. 2221-2224, 2279-2282, 2354-2357.

Mt. T'ai Shan, Shantung Province (T.130) — A583

1988, Sept. 14 **Photo. & Engr.**

2166	A583	8f T'ai Shan Temple (4-1)	16
2167	A583	10f Ladder to Heaven (4-2)	22
2168	A583	20f Daguang peak (4-3)	42
2169	A583	90f Sun-watching peak (4-4)	1.90
		Nos. 2166-2169 (4)	2.70

Liao Chengzhi (1908-1983), Party Leader (J.153) — A584

1988, Sept. 25 **Photo.** ***Perf. 11½x11***

2170	A584	8f shown (2-1)	15
2171	A584	20f Writing (2-2)	15
		Set value	20

Marshal Peng Dehuai (1898-1974), Party Leader (J.155) A585

1988, Oct. 24 **Photo.** ***Perf. 11x11½***

2172	A585	8f shown (2-1)	15
2173	A585	20f Peng in uniform (2-2)	15
		Set value	20

1st Natl. Farmers' Games (J.154) A586

1988, Oct. 9 **Photo.** ***Perf. 11½***

2174	A586	8f Cycling (2-1)	15
2175	A586	20f Javelin (2-2)	15
		Set value	25

Literary Masterpieces — A587

The Romance of the Three Kingdoms, by Luo Guanzhong, 14th cent.: No. 2176, Three heroes' sworn brotherhood (4-1). No. 2177, Battle between Lu Bu and the heroes, vert. (4-2). No. 2178, Struggle between man and woman at Fengyi Pavilion (4-3). No. 2179, Two noblemen, vert. (4-4). No. 2180, Guan Yu's battle through five passes. T.131.

Perf. 11½x11, 11x11½

1988, Nov. 25 **Photo.**

2176	A587	8f multicolored	15
2177	A587	8f multicolored	15
2178	A587	30f multicolored	50
2179	A587	50f multicolored	80
		Nos. 2176-2179 (4)	1.60

Souvenir Sheet

Perf. 11

2180	A587	$3 multicolored	*8.00*

See Nos. 2310-2313, 2403-2406, 2539-2543.

A588

A589

1988, Dec. 5 **Photo.** ***Perf. 11***

2181	A588	20f multi	15

Intl Volunteers' Day.

1988, Dec. 20 **Photo.** ***Perf. 11½x11***

Milu, *Elaphurus davidianus* (T.132).

2182	A589	8f Buck (2-1)	15
2183	A589	40f Herd (2-2)	65

Exist imperf. Value, each $2.

Orchids (T.129) — A590

1988, Dec. 25 ***Perf. 12***

2184	A590	8f Da yi pin (4-1)	15
2185	A590	10f Dragon (4-2)	18
2186	A590	20f Large phoenix tail (4-3)	35
2187	A590	50f Silver-edged black (4-4)	90
		Nos. 2184-2187 (4)	1.58

Souvenir Sheet

Perf. 11½x11

2188	A590	$2 Red lotus petal	*4.00*

No. 2188 contains one 55x37mm stamp.

A591

A592

Grotto Statuary: $2, Buddha. $5, Warrior, Longmen Grotto, Henan. $10, Goddess. $20, Woman and birds.

Perf. 11½x11

1988-89 **Photo & Engr.**

2189	A591	$2 buff & reddish blk	55	28
2190	A591	$5 buff & grnh blk	1.25	65
2191	A591	$10 buff & brn blk	2.75	1.40
a.		Souv. sheet of 1, buff & sepia		
2192	A591	$20 buff & indigo	5.50	2.75
		Nos. 2189-2192 (4)	10.05	5.08

Issue dates: $2, Nov. 30; $5, Aug. 10; $10, Oct. 15; $20, Oct. 20.

No. 2191a released on Oct. 12, 1989, for the China Natl. Philatelic Exhibition and the 40th anniv. of the People's Republic.

Nos. 2189-2192, 2191a are almost always found with small ink spots on the stamps. Values are for stamps in this condition.

Photo. & Engr.

1989, Jan. 5 ***Perf. 11½***

2193	A592	8f multicolored	50
a.		Bklt. pane of 4+8 with label between	2.00

New Year 1989 (Year of the Snake).

Qu Qiubai (1899-1935), Party Leader (J.157) A593

1989, Jan. 29 **Photo.** ***Perf. 11x11½***

2194	A593	8f multi (2-1)	15
2195	A593	20f multi, diff. (2-2)	15
		Set value	20

Brown-eared Pheasant, *Crossoptilon mantchuricum* (T.134) — A594

1989, Feb. 21 ***Perf. 11½***

2196	A594	8f multi (2-1)	15
2197	A594	50f multi, diff. (2-2)	42

Folk Houses Type of 1986

1989-91 **Photo.** ***Perf. 13x13½***

2198	A545	5f Shandong	15	15
2199	A545	15f Guangxi	15	15
2200	A545	25f Ningxia	15	15
2201	A545	80f Shanxi	42	26
2204	A545	$1.30 Qinghai	52	42
2206	A545	$1.60 Guizhou	65	52
2207	A545	$2 Jiangxi	52	65
		Nos. 2198-2207 (7)	2.56	

Issue dates: 5f, June 10, 1991. 15f, Nov. 25, 1990. 25f, Nov. 10, 1990. 80f, Sept. 20, 1990. $1.30, $1.60, Mar. 10, 1989. $2, Apr. 25, 1991.

This is an expanding set. Numbers will change again if necessary.

Silk Painting Excavated from Han Tomb No. 1 at Mawangdui, Changsha (T.135) — A595

1989, Mar. 25 Photo. *Perf. 11½*

2208 A595 8f In the Heavens (3-1) 15
2209 A595 20f On the Earth, vert. (3-2) 15
2210 A595 30f In the Netherworld, vert. (3-3) 18
Set value 35

Textured Paper, Without Gum
Size: 90x165mm
Imperf

2211 A595 $5 Entire painting *2.50*

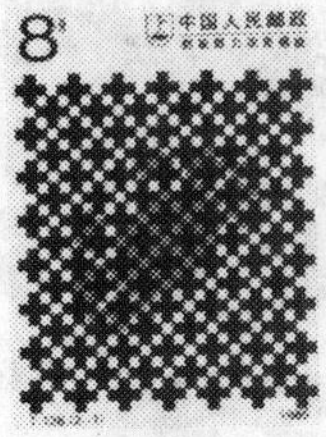

Prevention and Resistance of Cancer (T.136) — A596

1989, Apr. 7 Litho. *Perf. 12*

2212 A596 8f shown (2-1) 15
2213 A596 20f Woman's thermogram (2-2) 15
Set value 20

May Fourth Movement, 70th Anniv. (J.158) A597

1989, May 4 Photo. *Perf. 11*

2214 A597 8f Bas-relief 15

Interparliamentary Union, Cent. — A598

1989, June 29 Photo. *Perf. 11x11½*

2215 A598 20f multi 15

Literature Type of 1987

Outlaws of the Marsh: 8f, Wu Song slaying a tiger on Jingyang Ridge. 10f, Qin Ming dodging arrows. 20f, Hua Rong shooting a wild goose on Mt. Liangshan. $1.30, Li Kui fighting Zhang Shun from a junk. T.138.

1989, July 25 Photo. *Perf. 11*

2216 A570 8f multi (4-1) 15
2217 A570 10f multi (4-2) 15
2218 A570 20f multi (4-3) 28
2219 A570 $1.30 multi (4-4) 1.65
Nos. 2216-2219 (4) 2.23

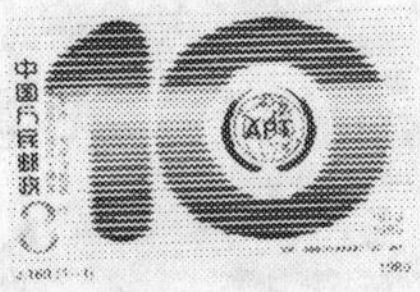

Asia-Pacific Telecommunity, 10th Anniv. — A599

1989, Aug. 4 Litho. *Perf. 12*

2220 A599 8f multi 15

Type of 1988

Achievements in Engineering and Construction: 8f, Beijing Intl. Telecommunications Building, vert. 10f, Xi Qu Coal Mine, Gu Jiao, Shanxi Province. 20f, Long Yang Gorge Hydroelectric Power Station, Qinghai Province. 30f, Da Yao Shan Tunnel of the Guangzhou-Heng Yang Railway. T.139.

1989, Aug. 10 Photo. *Perf. 11*

2221 A582 8f multi (4-1) 15
2222 A582 10f multi (4-2) 15
2223 A582 20f multi (4-3) 15
2224 A582 30f multi (4-4) 16
Set value 35

Mt. Huashan — A601

Designs: 8f, Five prominent peaks. 10f, View from atop Huashan. 20f, 1000-foot precipice. 90f, Blue Dragon Ridge. T.140.

1989, Aug. 25 Photo. & Engr.

2225 A601 8f multi (4-1) 15
2226 A601 10f multi (4-2) 15
2227 A601 20f multi (4-3) 20
2228 A601 90f multi (4-4) 85
Nos. 2225-2228 (4) 1.35

Modern Art — A602

Paintings: 8f, *The Fable of the White Snake,* by Ye Qianyu. 20f, *Lijiang River in Fine Rain,* by Li Keran. 50f, *Marching Together,* by Wu Zuoren. T.141

1989, Sept. 1 Photo.

2229 A602 8f multi (3-1) 15
2230 A602 20f multi (3-2) 22
2231 A602 50f multi (3-3) 50
Nos. 2229-2231 (3) 87

People's Political Conference — A603

1989, Sept. 21 *Perf. 12*

2232 A603 8f No. 2 15

A604

Confucius (551-479 B.C.) — A605

Designs: 8f, The lecture in the Apricot Temple, Qufu. $1.60, Confucius riding in an ox cart. J.162.

1989, Sept. 28 Photo. *Perf. 11*

2233 A604 8f shown (2-1) 15
2234 A604 $1.60 multi (2-2) 90

Souvenir Sheet
Litho.
Imperf
Without Gum

2235 A605 $3 multi *2.50*

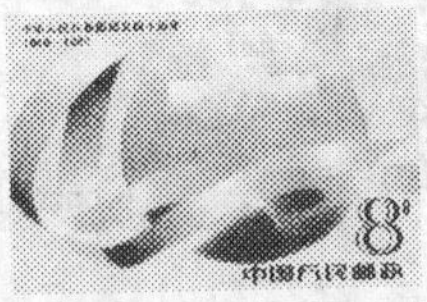

A606

Gate of Heavenly Peace — A607

1989, Oct. 1 Photo. *Perf. 11x11½*

2236 A606 8f shown (4-1) 15
2237 A606 10f Flowers (4-2) 15
2238 A606 20f Five stars (4-3) 15
2239 A606 40f Construction (4-4) 26
Set value 50

Souvenir Sheet
Litho.
Imperf
Without Gum

2240 A607 $3 shown *2.50*

PRC, 40th anniv. J.163.

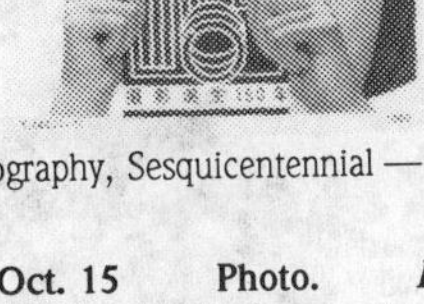

Photography, Sesquicentennial — A608

1989, Oct. 15 Photo. *Perf. 11*

2241 A608 8f multicolored 15

Li Dazhao (1889-1927), Party Leader (J.164) — A609

1989, Oct. 29 Photo. *Perf. 11½*

2242 A609 8f Dazhao, soldiers (2-1) 15
2243 A609 20f Dazhao, text (2-2) 15
Set value 15

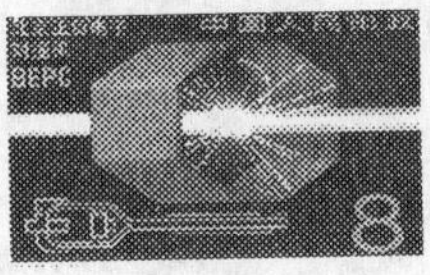

Positron Collider Produced in Beijing A610

1989, Nov. 1 *Perf. 11*

2244 A610 8f multicolored 15

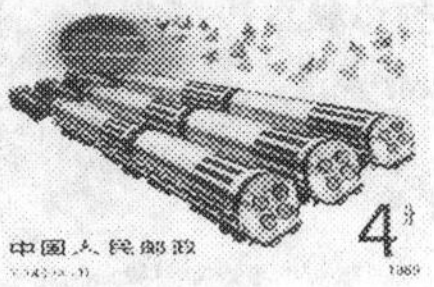

Rocket Defense A611

Designs: 4f, Transporting 3 rockets. 8f, Disassembled rocket on transport. 10f, Launch, vert. 20f, Stage separation in space. T.143.

1989, Nov. 15 Litho. *Perf. 12*

2245 A611 4f multicolored (4-1) 15
2246 A611 8f multicolored (4-2) 15
2247 A611 10f multicolored (4-3) 15
2248 A611 20f multicolored (4-4) 15
Set value 30

A612

Views of West Lake (T.144) — A613

1989, Nov. 25 Photo. *Perf. 11x11½*

2249 A612 8f multi (4-1) 15
2250 A612 10f multi, diff. (4-2) 15
2251 A612 30f multi, diff. (4-3) 28
2252 A612 40f multi, diff. (4-4) 35
Set value 80

Souvenir Sheet
Perf. 11½x11

2253 A613 $5 multicolored *3.00*

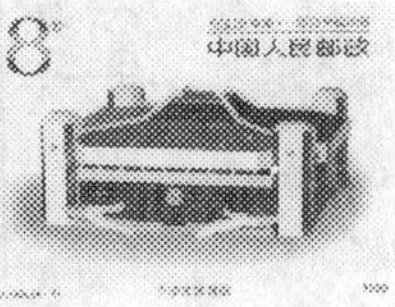

11th Asian Games A614

Various stadiums. J.165.

1989, Dec. 15 — *Perf. 11x11½*

2254 A614 8f multi (4-1) 15
2255 A614 10f multi (4-2) 15
2256 A614 30f multi (4-3) 15
2257 A614 $1.60 multi (4-4) 70
Set value 90

See Nos. 2295-2300.

A615

Narcissus (T.147) — A616

Photo & Engr.

1990, Jan. 5 — *Perf. 11½*

2258 A615 8f multicolored 45 20
a. Bklt. pane of 12 + 4 labels 2.00

New Year 1990 (Year of the Horse).

1990, Feb. 10 Photo. — *Perf. 11x11½*

2259 A616 8f multi (4-1) 15
2260 A616 20f multi, diff. (4-2) 15
2261 A616 30f multi, diff. (4-3) 15
2262 A616 $1.60 multi, diff. (4-4) 75
Set value 1.00

Norman Bethune (1890-1939), Surgeon (J.166) A617

Perf. 11x11½

1990, Mar. 3 — **Litho. & Engr.**

2263 A617 8f In Canada (2-2) 15
2264 A617 $1.60 In China (2-1) 65
a. Pair, #2263-2264 70

See Canada #1264-1265.

Intl. Women's Day — A618

1990, Mar. 8 Photo. — *Perf. 11½x11*

2265 A618 20f multicolored 15

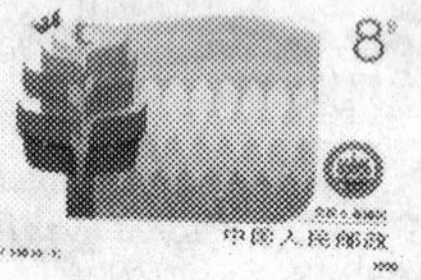

Afforestation (T.148) A619

1990, Mar. 12 — *Perf. 11*

2266 A619 8f Bird, flora (4-1) 15
2267 A619 10f Buildings (4-2) 15
2268 A619 20f Great Wall, forest, (4-3) 15
2269 A619 30f Bushes, evergreens (4-4) 15
Set value 35

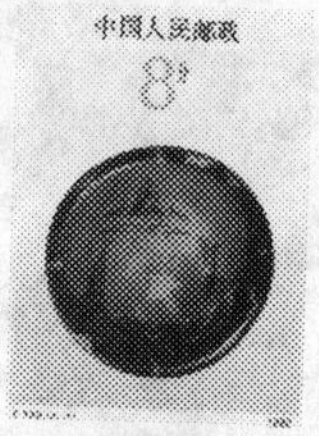

Pottery (T.149) — A620

1990, Apr. 10 Litho. — *Perf. 12*

2270 A620 8f multi (4-1) 15
2271 A620 20f multi (4-2) 15
2272 A620 30f multi (4-3) 15
2273 A620 50f multi (4-4) 22
Set value 50

Li Fuchun (1900-1975), Party Leader (J.168) A621

1990, May 22 Photo. — *Perf. 11x11½*

2274 A621 8f shown 15
2275 A621 20f In uniform (2-2) 15
Set value 20

Bronze Head — A622

Bronze treasures from Emperor Qin Shi Huang Mausoleum: 50f, Horse head. $5, Chariots. T.151.

1990, June 20 Photo. — *Perf. 11½x11*

2276 A622 8f shown (2-1) 15
2277 A622 50f multicolored (2-2) 25
Set value 30

Miniature Sheet

Size: 141x79mm

2278 A622 $5 multicolored 2.25

Achievements Type of 1988

Designs: 8f, 2nd automobile factory. 10f, Yizheng Joint Corporation of Chemical Fiber Industry. 20f, Shengli Oil Field. 30f, Qinshan Nuclear Power Station. T.152.

1990, June 30 Litho. — *Perf. 12*

2279 A582 8f shown (4-1) 15
2280 A582 10f multicolored (4-2) 15
2281 A582 20f multicolored (4-3) 15
2282 A582 30f multicolored (4-4) 20
Set value 45

Type of Dunhuang Petroglyphs of 1987

Murals: 8f, Flying Devatas. 10f, Worshipping Bodhisatva. 30f, Savior Avolokitesvara. 50f, Indra. T.150.

1990, July 10 — *Perf. 11½x11*

2283 A557 8f multi (4-1) 15
2284 A557 10f multi, vert. (4-2) 16
2285 A557 30f multi, vert. (4-3) 45
2286 A557 50f multi (4-4) 75
Nos. 2283-2286 (4) 1.51

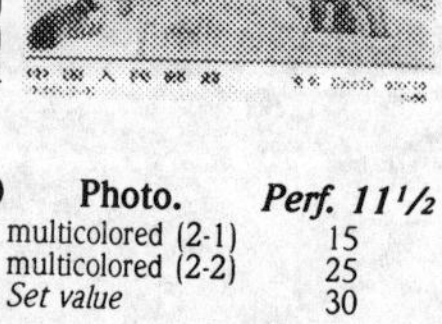

Snow Leopard (Uncia Uncia) (T.153) A624

1990, July 20 Photo. — *Perf. 11½*

2287 A624 8f multicolored (2-1) 15
2288 A624 50f multicolored (2-2) 25
Set value 30

Chinese Soviet Post Stamp of 1931 A625

Design: 20f, Chinese Red Post issue of West Fukien, 1929. J.169.

1990, Aug. 1 Litho. — *Perf. 12*

2289 A625 8f multi (2-1) 15
2290 A625 20f multi, diff. (2-2) 15
Set value 20

Zhang Wentian (1900-1990) (J.170) A626

1990, Aug. 30 — *Perf. 11x11½*

2291 A626 8f shown (2-1) 15
2292 A626 20f multi, diff. (2-2) 15
Set value 20

Intl. Literacy Year — A627

Chinese Films — A628

1990, Sept. 8 — *Perf. 11½x11*

2293 A627 20f multicolored 15

1990, Sept. 21 Litho. — *Perf. 11*

2294 A628 20f multicolored 15

11th Asian Games, Beijing (J.172) — A629

1990, Sept. 22 — *Perf. 11x11½*

2295 A629 4f Running (6-1) 15
2296 A629 8f Gymnastics (6-2) 15
2297 A629 10f Karate (6-3) 15
2298 A629 20f Volleyball (6-4) 15
2299 A629 30f Swimming (6-5) 18
2300 A629 $1.60 Shooting (6-6) 95
a. Souv. sheet of 12, #2158-2159, 2254-2257, 2295-2300 4.75
Set value 1.40

Souvenir Sheet

Sportphilex '90, Beijing — A629a

1990, Sept. 21 Litho. — *Perf. 11½*

2300B A629a $10 multicolored

Modern Scientists A630

Designs: 8f, Lin Qiaozhi, obstetrician. 10f, Zhang Yuzhe, astronomer. 20f, Hou Debang, chemist. 30f, Ding Ying, agronomist. J.173.

1990, Oct. 10 Litho. — *Perf. 12*

2301 A630 8f multicolored (4-1) 15
2302 A630 10f multicolored (4-2) 15
2303 A630 20f multicolored (4-3) 18
2304 A630 30f multicolored (4-4) 26
Set value 60

Mt. Hengshan — A631

Designs: 8f, Towering Temple. 10f, South Sacred Mountain. 20f, Forested mountainside. 50f, Imposing Zhurong Peak. T.155.

1990, Nov. 5 Photo. & Engr. — *Perf. 11*

2305 A631 8f multicolored (4-1) 15
2306 A631 10f multicolored (4-2) 15
2307 A631 20f multicolored (4-3) 22
2308 A631 50f multicolored (4-4) 55
Nos. 2305-2308 (4) 1.07

See Nos. 2342-2345.

Souvenir Sheet

China Philatelic Federation, 3rd Congress — A632

1990, Nov. 28 *Perf. 11½x11*
2309 A632 $2 multicolored *2.50*

Two types of No. 2309 exist. Either two or three of the horizontal bars in seventh character from top right are connected at left side.

Literature Type of 1988

Romance of the Three Kingdoms by Luo Guanzhong: No. 2310, Night Attack on Wuchao. No. 2311, Making Three Calls at the Thatched Cottage. 30f, Rescuing the Master Single-handedly. 50f, Turning the Changban Bridge Upside Down. T.157.

1990, Dec. 10 Photo. *Perf. 11½x11*
2310 A587 20f multicolored (4-1) 16
2311 A587 20f multi, vert. (4-2) 16
2312 A587 30f multicolored (4-3) 25
2313 A587 50f multi, vert. (4-4) 42
Nos. 2310-2313 (4) 99

Han Xizai's Night Revels by Gu Hongzhong — A633

Designs: a, Guests enjoying food, music (5-1). b, Music and dance (5-2). c, Hand washing (5-3). d, Musicians (5-4). e, Guests departing (5-5). T.158. (Illustration reduced).

1990, Dec. 20 Litho. *Perf. 12*
2314 Strip of 5 2.50
a.-e. A633 50f any single 50

New Year 1991 (Year of the Sheep) — A634

Photo. & Engr.

1991, Jan. 5 *Perf. 11½*
2315 A634 20f multicolored 45
a. Bklt. pane of 12 + label 2.00

Dujiangyan Irrigation Project — A635

Designs: 20f, Yuzui, flood control. 50f, Feishayan, drainage. 80f, Baopingkou, water volume control. T.156.

1991, Feb. 20 Photo. *Perf. 11½x11*
2316 A635 20f multicolored 15
2317 A635 50f multicolored 32
2318 A635 80f multicolored 52
Nos. 2316-2318 (3) 99

A636

A637

1991, Mar. 18
2319 A636 20f multicolored 15

Paris Commune, 120th anniv.

1991, Apr. 20 Photo. *Perf. 10*
2320 A637 20f multi (2-1) 15
a. Perf. 11½x11 40

Perf. 11½x11
2321 A637 50f Child & adult hands (2-2) 20

Family planning (T.160).

Horned Animals (T.161) A638

1991, May 10 *Perf. 11x11½*
2322 A638 20f Saiga tatarica (4-1) 15
2323 A638 20f Budorcas taxicolor (4-2) 15
2324 A638 50f Ovis ammon (4-3) 18
2325 A638 $2 Capra ibex (4-4) 75
Nos. 2322-2325 (4) 1.23

A639

A640

1991, May 23 Photo. *Perf. 11*
2326 A639 25f Song and dance (2-1) 15
2327 A639 50f Golden bridge (2-2) 22

Souvenir Sheet
2328 A639 $2 No. 132, cranes 3.00

Occupation of Tibet, 40th anniv. (J.176).

1991, June 22 *Perf. 11½x11*
2329 A640 20f multicolored 15

Antarctic Treaty, 30th anniv.

Rhododendrons — A641

Varieties of rhododendrons. T.162.

1991, June 25 Litho. *Perf. 12*
2330 A641 10f Delavayi (8-1) 15
2331 A641 15f Molle (8-2) 15
2332 A641 20f Simsii (8-3) 15
2333 A641 20f Fictolacteum (8-4) 15
2334 A641 50f Agglutinatum, vert. (8-5) 22
2335 A641 80f Fortunei, vert. (8-6) 35
2336 A641 90f Giganteum, vert. (8-7) 40
2337 A641 $1.60 Rex, vert. (8-8) 70
Nos. 2330-2337 (8) 2.27

Souvenir Sheet

Perf. 11½
2338 A641 $5 Wardii *4.00*

No. 2338 contains one 80x40mm stamp.

Chinese Communist Party, 70th Anniv. (J.178) A642

1991, July 1 Photo. *Perf. 11x11½*
2339 A642 20f shown (2-1) 15
2340 A642 50f Hammer and sickle (2-2) 25

Peasant Uprising, 209B.C. A643

1991, July 7
2341 A643 20f brown 15

Mt. Hengshan Type of 1990

Designs: No. 2342, Monastery on mountainside. No. 2343, Snow-covered mountain top. 55f, Inscription carved into mountainside. 80f, Hidden monastery. T.163.

1991, July 20 Photo. & Engr. *Perf. 11*
2342 A631 20f multi (4-1) 18
2343 A631 20f multi (4-2) 18
2344 A631 55f multi (4-3) 48
2345 A631 80f multi (4-4) 65
Nos. 2342-2345 (4) 1.49

Intl. Union for Quaternary Research, 13th Conf. — A644

1991, Aug. 2 Photo. *Perf. 11x11½*
2346 A644 20f multicolored 15

Chengde Mountain Resort — A645

Ch'ing Dynasty Royal Gardens: 15f, Pine valleys. 20f, Mid-lake pavilion. 90f, Islet, maple trees. $2, Chengde Royal Summer Resort. T.164.

1991 *Perf. 11½x11*
2347 A645 15f multi (3-1) 15
2348 A645 20f multi (3-2) 16
2349 A645 90f multi (3-3) 70
Nos. 2347-2349 (3) 1.01

Souvenir Sheet
2350 A645 $2 multicolored *2.50*

No. 2350 contains one 90x40mm stamp. Issue dates: $2, Aug. 19. Others, Aug. 10.

A646

A647

Chen Yi, (b. 1901), party leader (J.181).

1991, Aug. 26 Photo. *Perf. 11½x11*
2351 A646 20f shown (2-1) 15
2352 A646 50f Verse (2-2) 25

1991, Sept. 14
2353 A647 80f Disaster relief 30

Achievements Type of 1988

Designs: 20f, Luoyang glassworks. 25f, Urumchi chemical fertilizer project. 55f, Dalian expressway, Shenyang. 80f, Xichang satellite launching center. T.165.

1991, Sept. 20 Litho. *Perf. 12*
2354 A582 20f multi (4-1) 15
2355 A582 25f multi (4-2) 15
2356 A582 55f multi (4-3) 20
2357 A582 80f multi (4-4) 30
Nos. 2354-2357 (4) 80

Revolutionary Heroes A648

Designs: No. 2358, Xu Xilin (1873-1907). No. 2359, Qiu Jin (1879-1907). No. 2360, Song Jiaoren (1882-1913). J.182.

1991, Oct. 10 Photo. *Perf. 11x11½*
2358 A648 20f multi (3-1) 15
a. Perf. 10 50

Perf. 10
2359 A648 20f multi (3-2) 15
2360 A648 20f multi (3-3) 15

Jingdezhen Chinaware A649

Designs: 15f, Glazed wine pot and warming bowl, Song Dynasty, vert. No. 2362, Porcelain vase, Yuan Dynasty, vert. No. 2363, Jar, Ming Dynasty. 25f, Porcelain vase, Ch'ing Dynasty, vert. 50f, Modern underglazed plate, vert. $2, Modern octagonal eggshell bowl, T.166.

Perf. 11½, 11½x11 (#2362), 11x11½ (#2363)

1991, Oct. 11 Photo.
2361 A649 15f multi (6-1) 15
2362 A649 20f multi (6-2) 15
2363 A649 20f multi (6-3) 15
2364 A649 25f multi (6-4) 15
2365 A649 50f multi (6-5) 18
2366 A649 $2 multi (6-6) 75
Set value 1.20

1991
2361a Perf. 11½x11 15
2362a Perf. 11x11½ 15
2363a Perf. 11½ 15
2364a Perf. 11½x11 18
2365a Perf. 11½x11 35
2366a Perf. 11x11½ 1.40

Tao Xingzhi, Educator, Birth Cent. (J.183) — A650

1991, Oct. 18 Litho. *Perf. 12*
2367 A650 20f shown (2-1) 15
2368 A650 50f Wearing robe (2-2) 22
Set value 30

Xu Xiangqian, Revolutionary Leader, 90th Birth Anniv. (J.184) A651

1991, Nov. 8 *Perf. 11x11½*
2369 A651 20f shown (2-1) 15
2370 A651 50f In uniform (2-2) 22
Set value 30

1st Women's Soccer World Championships, Guangdong Province (J.185) — A652

Designs: 50f, Woman kicking soccer ball.

1991, Nov. 16 *Perf. 11½x11*
2371 A652 20f red & multi (2-1) 15
2372 A652 50f grn & multi (2-2) 22
Set value 30

Literature Type of 1987

Outlaws of the Marsh: 20f, Dai Zong sends a false letter from Liangshan Marsh. No. 2374, Ten feet of steel alone captures Stumpy Tiger Wang. No. 2375, Mistress Gu breaks open the jail in Dengzhou to rescue the Xie Brothers. 90f, Sun Li offers a plan to attack Zhu Family manor. $3, Mount Liangshan gallants raid the execution grounds. T.167.

1991, Nov. 19 *Perf. 11*
2373 A570 20f multi (4-1) 15
2374 A570 25f multi (4-2) 15
2375 A570 25f multi (4-3) 15
2376 A570 90f multi (4-4) 45
Nos. 2373-2376 (4) 90

Souvenir Sheet
Perf. 11x11½
2377 A570 $3 multicolored *3.00*

No. 2377 contains one 60x90mm stamp.

Beginning with No. 2378 stamps are inscribed "CHINA" and are numbered chronologically with the year followed by the number of the set. Additional numbers in parentheses indicate the number and position of each stamp in a set. We will note these only when helpful in identifying stamps.

New Year 1992, Year of the Monkey
A653 A654

Photo. & Engr.
1992, Jan. 25 *Perf. 11½*
2378 A653 20f Monkey, peach 15
2379 A654 50f Magpies, plum branches 22

Storks — A655

Conifers — A656

1992, Feb. 20 **Photo.** *Perf. 11x11½*
2380 A655 20f Ciconia nigra 15
2381 A655 $1.60 Ciconia ciconia 75

1992, Mar. 10 **Litho.** *Perf. 12½*

Designs: 20f, Metasequoia glyptostroboides. 30f, Cathaya argyrophylla. 50f, Taiwania flousiana. 80f, Abies beshanzuensis.

2382 A656 20f multicolored 15
2383 A656 30f multicolored 15
2384 A656 50f multicolored 22
2385 A656 80f multicolored 38
Nos. 2382-2385 (4) 90

Marine Life — A660

1992, Apr. 15 **Photo.** *Perf. 11*
2386 A660 20f Pagrosomus major 15
2387 A660 25f Penaeus chinesis 15
2388 A660 50f Chlamys farreri 18
2389 A660 80f Laminaria japonica 28
Set value 62

Publication of "Discussions on Literature and Art at the Yenan Forum," 50th Anniv. — A661

1992, May 23 **Photo.** *Perf. 11½x11*
2390 A661 20f orange, black & red 15

A662

A663

1992, June 5 **Litho.** *Perf. 12*
2392 A662 20f multicolored 15

UN Conf. on Human Development, 20th anniv.

1992, June 28

Insects: 20f, Coccinella septempunctata. 30f, Sympetrum croceolum. 50f, Chrysopa septempunctata. $2, Tenodera aridifolia sinensis.

2393 A663 20f multicolored 15
2394 A663 30f multicolored 15
2395 A663 50f multicolored 22
2396 A663 $2 multicolored 90
Nos. 2393-2396 (4) 1.42

1992 Summer Olympics, Barcelona A664

1992, July 25 **Photo.** *Perf. 11*
2397 A664 20f Basketball, vert. 15
2398 A664 25f Women's gymnastics 15
2399 A664 50f Women's diving 18
2400 A664 80f Weight lifting, vert. 28
Nos. 2397-2400 (4) 76

Souvenir Sheet
2401 A664 $5 Runners *2.00*

No. 2401 contains one 54x40mm stamp.

Intl. Space Year — A665

1992, Aug. 18 **Litho.** *Perf. 12*
2402 A665 20f multicolored 15

Literature Type of 1988

Romance of the Three Kingdoms by Luo Guanzhong: 20f, Verbal battle with scholars. 50f, Goading Sun Quan with sarcasm, vert. 30f, Jiang Gan stealing the letter. $1.60, Gathering arrows with straw-covered boats, vert.

Perf. 11½x11, 11x11½
1992, Aug. 25 **Photo.**
2403 A587 20f multi (4-1) 15
2404 A587 30f multi (4-2) 15
2405 A587 50f multi (4-3) 18
2406 A587 $1.60 multi (4-4) 60
Nos. 2403-2406 (4) 1.08

Dunhuang Petroglyphs Type of 1987

Murals: 20f, Bodhisattva, vert. 25f, Musical performance, vert. 55f, Flight of a dragon. 80f, Envoy to the western regions. $5, Avalokitesvara-Bodhisattva, vert.

1992, Sept. 15 *Perf. 11*
2407 A557 20f multi (4-1) 15
2408 A557 25f multi (4-2) 15
2409 A557 55f multi (4-3) 20
2410 A557 80f multi (4-4) 28
Nos. 2407-2410 (4) 78

Souvenir Sheet
Perf. 11½
2411 A557 $5 multicolored *2.00*

No. 2411 contains one 52x70mm stamp.

Normalization of Diplomatic Relations Between China and Japan, 20th Anniv. A666

Designs: 20f, Cranes, Great Wall of China, Mt. Fuji. $2, Japanese, Chinese children, dove.

1992, Sept. 29 **Photo.** *Perf. 11x11½*
2412 A666 20f multi (2-1) 15
2413 A666 $2 multi (2-2) 72

A667

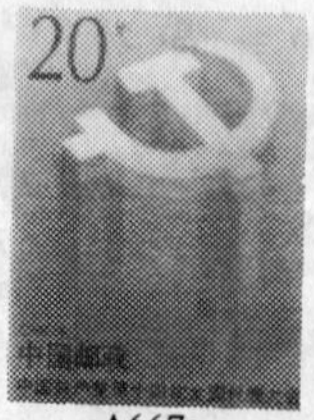
A667a

Statue of Mazu, Chinese Goddess of the Sea.

1992, Oct. 4 **Litho.** *Perf. 12*
2414 A667 20f multicolored 15

1992, Oct. 12 **Photo.** *Perf. 11½x11*
2414A A667a 20f multicolored 15

14th Chinese Communist Party Congress.

Jiao Yulu (1922-1964), Communist Party Leader — A668

1992, Oct. 28 **Litho.** *Perf. 12*
2415 A668 20f multicolored 15

Famous Men — A669

Designs: 20f, Xiong Qinglai, mathematician. 30f, Tang Feifan, microbiologist. 50f, Zhang Xiaoqian, physician. $1, Liang Sicheng, architect.

1992, Nov. 20
2416 A669 20f multi (4-1) 15
2417 A669 30f multi (4-2) 15
2418 A669 50f multi (4-3) 18
2419 A669 $1 multi (4-4) 36
Set value 72

Luo Ronghuan, Leader of People's Army, 90th Anniv. of Birth — A670

1992, Nov. 26 **Photo.** *Perf. 11x11½*
2420 A670 20f In dress uniform (2-1) 15
2421 A670 50f In field uniform (2-2) 18
Set value 26

Constitution of the People's Republic of China, 10th Anniv. — A671

1992, Dec. 4 *Perf. 11½x11*
2422 A671 20f multicolored 15

Liu Bocheng, Leader of People's Army, Birth Cent. — A672

Designs: 20f, In dress uniform. 50f, During period of Long March, vert.

1992, Dec. 4 *Perf. 11x11½, 11½x11*
2423 A672 20f multi (2-1) 15
2424 A672 50f multi (2-2) 18
Set value 26

Quingtian Stone Carvings — A673

1992, Dec. 15 Litho. *Perf. 12*

2425 A673 10f Spring (4-1) 15
2426 A673 20f Chinese sorghum (4-2) 15
2427 A673 40f Harvest (4-3) 15
2428 A673 $2 Blooming flowers, full moon (4-4) 75
Set value 1.03

New Year 1993 (Year of the Rooster)
A674 A675

Photo. & Engr.

1993, Jan. 5 *Perf. 11½*

2429 A674 20f red & black (2-1) 15
2430 A675 50f red, white & blk (2-2) 18
Set value 26

Madam Song Quingling, Chinese Communist Leader, Birth Cent. — A676

1993, Jan. 20 Photo. *Perf. 11x11½*

2431 A676 20f Portrait (2-1) 15
2432 A676 $1 With children (2-2) 38
Set value 46

Camelus Bactrianus Ferus A677

1993, Feb. 20 Litho. *Perf. 12*

2433 A677 20f shown (2-1) 15
2434 A677 $1.60 Adult, young (2-2) 55
Set value 62

8th Natl. People's Congress A678

1993, Mar. 15 Litho. *Perf. 12*

2435 A678 20f multicolored 15

A679 A680

Game of Weiqi (Go): 20f, Painting of players of ancient times. $1.60, Game board showing Chinese-style position.

1993, Apr. 30 Litho. *Perf. 12*

2436 A679 20f multi (2-1) 15
2437 A679 $1.60 multi (2-2) 55

1993, May 15 Litho. *Perf. 12*

20th Cent. Revolutionaries: 20f, Li Jishen (1885-1959), horiz. 30f, Zhang Lan (1872-1955). 50f, Shen Junru (1875-1963). $1, Huang Yanpei (1878-1965), horiz.

2438 A680 20f multi (4-1) 15
2439 A680 30f multi (4-2) 15
2440 A680 50f multi (4-3) 18
2441 A680 $1 multi (4-4) 38
Nos. 2438-2441 (4) 86

See Nos. 2483-2486.

First East Asian Games — A681

1993, May 9 Photo. *Perf. 12*

2442 A681 50f Runner (2-1) 18
2443 A681 50f Mascot (2-2) 18
a. Pair, #2442-2443 36

No. 2443a printed in continuous design.

Bamboo — A682

Designs: 20f, Phyllostachys nigra. 30f, Phyllostachys aureosulcata spectabilis. 40f, Bambusa ventricosa. $1, Pseudosasa amabilis. $5, Phyllostachys heterocycla pubescens, horiz.

1993, June 15 Litho. *Perf. 12½*

2444 A682 20f multi (4-1) 15
2445 A682 30f multi (4-2) 15
2446 A682 40f multi (4-3) 15
2447 A682 $1 multi (4-4) 38
Nos. 2444-2447 (4) 83

Souvenir Sheet

Photo.

Perf. 11

2448 A682 $5 multicolored 1.90

No. 2448 contains one 54x40mm stamp.

Literature Type of 1987

Outlaws of the Marsh: 20f, Chai Jin is trapped in Gaotang. 30f, Shi Qian steals armor. 50f, Xu Ning teaches how to use barbed lance. $2, Shi Xiu leaps from building to rescue condemned man from execution.

1993, Aug. 20 Photo. *Perf. 11*

2449 A570 20f multi (4-1) 15
2450 A570 30f multi (4-2) 15
2451 A570 50f multi (4-3) 16
2452 A570 $2 multi (4-4) 65
Set value 98

Changbai Mountains — A683

1993, Sept. 3 *Perf. 11½x11*

2453 A683 20f Tianchi (4-1) 15
2454 A683 30f Alpine tundra (4-2) 15
2455 A683 50f Waterfall (4-3) 16
2456 A683 $1 Mixed forest (4-4) 32
Set value 65

Seventh Natl. Games — A684 Longmen Grottoes — A685

1993, Sept. 4

2457 A684 20f multicolored 15

1993, Sept. 5 Litho. *Perf. 12*

Designs: 20f, Rocana, Ancestor Worshipping Temple. 30f, Sakyamuni, Middle Binyang Cave, Northern Wei. 50f, Maharaja, devas treading on Yaksha. $1, Bodhisattva at the left side of Rocana, Guyang Cave, Northern Wei. $5, Ancestor Worshipping Temple.

2458 A685 20f multi (4-1) 15
2459 A685 30f multi (4-2) 15
2460 A685 50f multi (4-3) 16
2461 A685 $1 multi (4-4) 32
Set value 65

Souvenir Sheet

2462 A685 $5 multicolored *1.90*

No. 2462 contains one 120x40mm stamp.

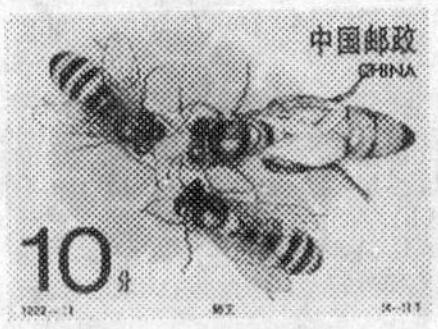

Honey Bees — A686

1993, Sept. 21 Photo. *Perf. 11½*

2463 A686 10f Queen and two bees (4-1) 15
2464 A686 15f Extracting nectar (4-2) 15
2465 A686 20f Two Zhonghua bees (4-3) 15
2466 A686 $2 Two bees in flight (4-4) 65
Set value 1.00

Lacquerware — A687

1993, Oct. 20 Photo. *Perf. 12*

2467 A687 20f Bowl (4-1) 15
2468 A687 30f Duck (4-2) 15
2469 A687 50f Round tray (4-3) 16
2470 A687 $1 Lidded box (4-4) 32
Set value 65

Paintings, by Zheng Banqiao — A688

Designs: 10f, Bamboo, rock on fan. No. 2472, Orchard. No. 2473, Orchard, bamboo, rock on scroll, vert. 30f, Bamboo, rock on scroll, vert. 50f, Vase and chrysanthemums. $1.60, Chinese calligraphy on fan.

1993, Nov. 22 Litho. *Perf. 12½*

2471 A688 10f multi (6-1) 15
2472 A688 20f multi (6-2) 15
2473 A688 20f multi (6-3) 15
2474 A688 30f multi (6-4) 15
2475 A688 50f multi (6-5) 16
2476 A688 $1.60 multi (6-6) 52
Set value 94

A689 A690

1993, Nov. 26 *Perf. 12*

2477 A689 20f multicolored 15

Yang Hucheng, birth cent.

1993 Photo. *Perf. 11½*

Mao Tse-tung (1893-1976).

2478 A690 20f shown (2-1) 15
2479 A690 $1 Portrait, seated (2-2) 38

Souvenir Sheet

2480 A690 $5 Standing by Great Wall *1.90*

Issue dates: $5, Nov. 16. 20f, $1, Dec. 26. No. 2480 contains one 48x58mm stamp.

New Year 1994 (Year of the Dog)
A691 A692

1994, Jan. 5 Photo. *Perf. 11½*

2481 A691 20f multi (2-1) 15
2482 A692 50f yel, red & blk (2-2) 18
Set value 25

20th Cent. Revolutionaries Type

Designs: No. 2483, Chen Qiyou, horiz. No. 2484, Chen Shutong. No. 2485, Ma Xulun. No. 2486, Xu Deheng, horiz.

1994, Feb. 25 Litho. *Perf. 12*

2483 A680 20f blk & brn (4-1) 15
2484 A680 20f blk & brn (4-2) 15
2485 A680 50f blk & brn (4-3) 18
2486 A680 50f blk & brn (4-4) 18
Set value 45

Sturgeon — A693

Designs: 20f, Huso dauricus. 40f, Acipenser sinensis. 50f, Psephurus gladius. $1, Acipenser dabryanus.

1994, Mar. 18 Litho. *Perf. 12½*

2487 A693 20f multi (4-1) 15
2488 A693 40f multi (4-2) 15
2489 A693 50f multi (4-3) 15
2490 A693 $1 multi (4-3) 25
Set value 50

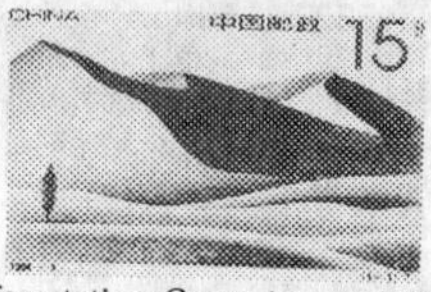

Afforestation Campaign — A694

Designs: 15f, Sand dunes. 20f, Flowers on sand dune. 40f, Forest of poplars. 50f, Oasis.

1994, Apr. 21 Litho. *Perf. 12*

2491 A694 15f multi (4-1)	15	
2492 A694 20f multi (4-2)	15	
2493 A694 40f multi (4-3)	15	
2494 A694 50f multi (4-4)	15	
Set value	32	

Teapots — A695

Style of teapot: 20f, Round, three-legged. 30f, Square, four-legged. 50f, Eight diagrams. $1, Round-eared.

1994, May 5 Litho. *Perf. 12*

2495 A695 20f multi (4-1)	15	
2496 A695 30f multi (4-2)	15	
2497 A695 50f multi (4-3)	15	
2498 A695 $1 multi (4-4)	25	
Set value	48	

Huangpu Military School, 70th Anniv. A696

1994, June 16 Litho. *Perf. 12*

2499 A696 20f multicolored 15

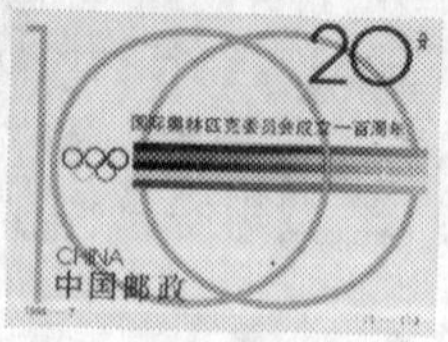

Intl. Olympic Committee, Cent. — A697

1994, June 23

2500 A697 20f multicolored 15

Ancient Chinese Writers — A698

Designs: 20f, Tao Yuanming holding basket of flowers. 30f, Cao Zhi holding sword at side. 50f, Si Maqian writing on scroll. $1, Qu Yuan walking away with sword under arm.

1994, June 25

2501 A698 20f multi (4-1)	15	
2502 A698 30f multi (4-2)	15	
2503 A698 50f multi (4-3)	15	
2504 A698 $1 multi (4-4)	25	
Set value	48	

Dunhuang Petroglyphs Type of 1987

Frescos: 10f, Flying Devata. 20f, Vimalakirti. 50f, Z. Yichao on the march. $1.60, Sorceresses.

1994, July 16 Photo. *Perf. 11*

2505 A557 10f multi (4-1)	15	
2506 A557 20f multi (4-2)	15	
2507 A557 50f multi (4-3)	15	
2508 A557 $1.60 multi (4-4)	38	
Set value	60	

Zhaojun's Marriage to Xiongnu — A699

1994, Aug. 25 Photo. *Perf. 11½x11*

2509 A699 20f Zhaojun (2-1)	15	15
2510 A699 50f Leaving home (2-2)	15	15

Souvenir Sheet

Perf. 11½

2511 A699 $3 Wedding 75 75

No. 2511 contains one 85x46mm stamp.

Sixth Far East and South Pacific Games for the Disabled, Beijing — A700

1994, Sept. 4 Litho. *Perf. 12*

2512 A700 20f multicolored 15 15

Wulingyuan State Forest Park — A701

Designs: 20f, South Gate to Heaven, vert. 30f, Shentangwan, vert. 50f, No. One Bridge. $1, Writing-brush Peak. $3, Picturesque corridor.

1994, Sept. 25 Litho. *Perf. 12*

2513 A701 20f multi (4-1)	15	
2514 A701 30f multi (4-2)	15	
2515 A701 50f multi (4-3)	15	
2516 A701 $1 multi (4-4)	25	
Set value	50	

Souvenir Sheet

Perf. 11½x12

2517 A701 $3 multicolored 75

No. 2517 contains one 50x36mm stamp.

Wuyi Mountains — A702

Designs: a, Jade-girl Peak (4-1). b, Nine-bend Brook (4-2). c, Guadun Village (4-3). d, Alpine Grassland (4-4).

1994, Sept. 30 *Perf. 12*

2518 Strip of 4	60	
a.-d. A702 50f any single	15	

Listening to the Rapids, by Fu Baoshi (1904-65) A703

Paintings: No. 2520, Appreciating a Painting. No. 2521, Dadi's Thatched Hut. 40f, Playing the Ruan. 50f, At Hupao. $1, The Road to Shanyin.

1994, Oct. 5

2519 A703 10f multi (6-1)	15	
2520 A703 20f multi (6-2)	15	
2521 A703 20f multi (6-3)	15	
2522 A703 40f multi (6-4)	15	
2523 A703 50f multi (6-5)	15	
2524 A703 $1 multi (6-6)	25	
Set value	55	

Nos. 2525-2527 are not assigned.

Cranes — A704

Photo. & Engr.

1994, Oct. 9 *Perf. 11x11½*

2528 A704 20f Whooping crane (2-1)	15	15
2529 A704 $2 Black-necked crane (2-2)	50	50

See US Nos. 2867-2868.

Souvenir Sheet

UPU, 120th Anniv. — A705

Illustration reduced.

1994, Oct. 9 Litho. *Perf. 12*

2530 A705 $3 multicolored 75

Gorges of Yangtze River — A706

Designs: 10f, Baidicheng. No. 2532, Qutang Gorge. No. 2533, Wuxia Gorge. 30f, Goddess Peak. 50f, Xiling Gorge. $1, Qu Yuan Memorial Temple. $5, The Three Gorges.

1994, Nov. 4 Photo. *Perf. 12*

2531 A706 10f multi (6-1)	15	
2532 A706 20f multi (6-2)	15	
2533 A706 20f multi (6-3)	15	
2534 A706 30f multi (6-4)	15	
2535 A706 50f multi (6-5)	15	
2536 A706 $1 multi (6-6)	22	
Set value	53	

Souvenir Sheet

Perf. 11½x11

2537 A706 $5 multicolored 1.25

No. 2537 contains one 116x35mm stamp.

Souvenir Sheet

All-China Philatelic Federation, 4th Congress — A707

Illustration reduced.

1994, Nov. 17 Litho. *Perf. 11*

2538 A707 $3 multicolored 70

Literature Type of 1988

Romance of the Three Kingdoms by Luo Guanzhong: 20f, Composing a poem with a lance in hands. 30f, Liu Bei's marriage, vert. 50f, Overwhelming Xiaoyaojin with prowess. $1, Campsites burned, vert.

$5, Fierce battle at Chibi.

Perf. 11½x11, 11x11½

1994, Nov. 24 Photo.

2539 A587 20f multi (4-1)	15	
2540 A587 30f multi (4-2)	15	
2541 A587 50f multi (4-3)	15	
2542 A587 $1 multi (4-4)	22	
Set value	46	

Souvenir Sheet
Perf. 11

2543 A587 $5 multicolored 1.25

No. 2543 contains one 158x36mm stamp.

Special Economic Zones A708

Designs: a, Shenzhen (5-1). b, Zhuhai (5-2). c, Shantou (5-3). d, Xiamen (5-4). e, Hainan (5-4).

1994, Dec. 10 Litho. *Perf. 12*

2544 A708 50f Strip of 5, #a.-e. 60

Pagodas of Ancient China — A709

Designs: No. 2545, Dayan Pagoda, Cien Temple. No. 2546, Zhenguo Pagoda, Kaiyuan Temple. 50f, Liuhe Pagoda, Kaihua Temple. $2, Youguo Temple.

Photo. & Engr.

1994, Dec. 15 *Perf. 11½x11*

2545	A709	20f tan, brn & blk (4-1)	15
2546	A709	20f tan, brn & blk (4-2)	15
2547	A709	50f tan, brn & blk (4-3)	15
2548	A709	$2 tan, brn & blk (4-4)	48
		Set value	65

New Year 1995 (Year of the Boar)
A711 A712

Photo. & Engr.

1995, Jan. 5 *Perf. 11½*

2550	A711	20f multi (2-1)	15
2551	A712	50f multi (2-2)	15
		Set value	16

Winter Scenes A713

Designs: 20f, Snow willows, Cold River. 50f, Ice & snow on jade trees, vert.

1995, Jan. 12 Litho. *Perf. 12*

2552	A713	20f multicolored	15
2553	A713	50f multicolored	15
		Set value	16

SEMI-POSTAL STAMPS

Catalogue values for unused stamps in this section are for Never Hinged items.

Girl Holding Ball — SP1

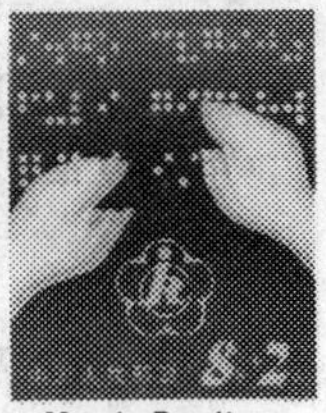

Hands Reading Braille — SP2

1984, Feb. 16 Photo. *Perf. 11½*

B1	SP1 8f + 2f shown (2-1)	15	20
B2	SP1 8f + 2f Boy, panda (2-2)	15	20

Surtax for China Children's Fund. T.92.

1985, Mar. 15 Photo. *Perf. 11½*

B3	SP2 8f + 2f shown (4-1)	15	15
B4	SP2 8f + 2f Sign language, lip reading (4-2)	15	15
B5	SP2 8f + 2f Artificial limb (4-3)	15	15
B6	SP2 8f + 2f Handicapped person in wheelchair (4-4)	15	15
	Nos. B3-B6 (4)	60	60

Surtax for China Welfare Fund. T.105.

Children (T.137) SP3

1989, June 1 Litho. *Perf. 12*

B7	SP3 8f +4f Friends (4-1)	15	15
B8	SP3 8f +4f Penguins (4-2)	15	15
B9	SP3 8f +4f Bird, Moon, Sun (4-3)	15	15
B10	SP3 8f +4f Girl, boy playing ball (4-4)	15	15
a.	Strip of 4, #B7-B10	35	50
	Set value	35	35

Intl Children's Day, 40th anniv., and 10th Intl. Year of the Child. Surtax for China Children's Fund.

AIR POST STAMPS

Mail Plane and Temple of Heaven — AP1

1951, May 1 Engr. *Perf. 12½*
Without Gum

C1	AP1	$1000 carmine	15	15
C2	AP1	$3000 green	18	15
C3	AP1	$5000 orange	15	15
C4	AP1	$10,000 vio brn & grn	15	25
C5	AP1	$30,000 dk bl & brn	4.50	75
		Nos. C1-C5 (5)	5.13	1.45

Planes at Airport — AP2

Designs: 28f, Plane over winding mountain highway. 35f, Plane over railroad yard. 52f, Plane over ship.

1957-58 *Perf. 14*

C6	AP2	16f indigo	7.50	15
C7	AP2	28f olive black	7.50	15
C8	AP2	35f slate	7.50	4.00
C9	AP2	52f Prus blue ('58)	7.50	50
		Nos. C6-C9 (4)	30.00	4.80

POSTAGE DUE STAMPS

Grain and Cogwheel — D1

D2

1950, Sept. 1 Typo. *Perf. 12½*
Without Gum

J1	D1	$100 steel blue	15	15
J2	D1	$200 steel blue	15	15
J3	D1	$500 steel blue	15	15
J4	D1	$800 steel blue	18.00	15
J5	D1	$1000 steel blue	28	40
J6	D1	$2000 steel blue	28	40
J7	D1	$5000 steel blue	20	60
J8	D1	$8000 steel blue	20	1.00
J9	D1	$10,000 steel blue	38	2.00
		Nos. J1-J9 (9)	19.79	5.00

1954, Aug. 18 Litho. *Perf. 14*

J10	D2	$100 red	1.65	15
J11	D2	$200 red	52	15
J12	D2	$500 red	1.65	15
J13	D2	$800 red	15	15
J14	D2	$1600 red	15	15
		Nos. J10-J14 (5)	4.12	
		Set value		47

MILITARY STAMP

Red Star, 8-1 in Center — M1

1953, Aug. 1 Litho. *Perf. 14*
Without Gum

M1 M1 $800 yel, orange & red (Army) 15.00 15.00

This stamp was printed in deep purple, orange & red for the Air Force, and blue, orange & red for the Navy. These were not issued.

NORTHEAST CHINA

The Northeast Liberation Area included the provinces of Liaoning, Kirin, Jehol and Heilungkiang, the area generally known as Manchuria under the Japanese. The first post war issues were local overprints on stamps of Manchukuo. In early 1946, a Ministry of Posts and Telegraphs served the areas already liberated, and in August, 1946, a Communications Committee of the Political Council was established. In June, 1947, these postal services were subordinated to the Harbin General Post Office, and this was extended to Changchun on Oct. 22, 1948, and to Mukden on Nov. 4, 1948. It was rapidly extended to cover all Manchuria.

Rough Perfs
Rough perforations are normal on most regional issues.

All Stamps Issued without Gum

Mao Tse-tung
A1 A2

1946, Feb. Unwmk. Litho. *Perf. 11*

1L1	A1	$1 violet	12.00	9.00
1L2	A2	$2 vermilion	75	1.00
1L3	A2	$5 orange	75	1.00
a.		Booklet pane of 6	150.00	
1L4	A2	$10 blue	75	1.00
a.		Booklet pane of 6	150.00	
		Nos. 1L1-1L4 (4)	14.25	12.00

Value, imperf set $90.
For surcharges see Nos. 1L20-1L23, 1L49-1L50, 1L89, 1L91, 1L93.

Map of China, Lion, Hyena and Chiang Kai-shek — A3

1946, Dec. 12 *Perf. 10½*

1L5	A3	$1 violet	1.50	1.50
1L6	A3	$2 orange	1.50	1.50
1L7	A3	$5 org brn	7.00	7.00
1L8	A3	$10 lt grn	10.00	10.00
a.		Imperf., pair	40.00	
		Nos. 1L5-1L8 (4)	20.00	20.00

10th anniversary of the capture of Chiang Kai-shek at Sian.

Railroad Workers, Chengchow — A4

1947, Feb. 7 *Perf. 10½*

1L9	A4	$1 pink	35	*1.00*
1L10	A4	$2 dull grn	70	*1.00*
1L11	A4	$5 pink	1.40	1.40
1L12	A4	$10 dull grn	3.50	3.50
		Nos. 1L9-1L12 (4)	5.95	6.90

24th anniversary of the Chengchow railroad workers' strike and massacre.

Women (Worker, Soldier and Farmer) — A5

Wmk. Chinese Characters in Sheet

1947, Mar. 8 *Perf. 10½x11*

1L13	A5	$5 brick red	60	60
1L14	A5	$10 brown	60	60

International Women's Day, March 8.
Exists imperf.

郵 東

Same Overprinted in Green ("Northeast Postal Service")

政 北

1947, Mar. 18

1L15	A5	$5 brick red	2.75	3.25
1L16	A5	$10 brown	2.75	3.25

Exists imperf.

Children Carrying Banner — A6

1947, Apr. 4 *Perf. 11x10½*

Granite Paper

1L17	A6	$5 rose red	2.00	2.25
1L18	A6	$10 lt green	2.00	3.00
1L19	A6	$30 orange	2.00	4.00
		Nos. 1L17-1L19 (3)	6.00	9.25

Children's Day.

Nos. 1L1-1L2 Surcharged in Red, Brown, Black, Blue or Green

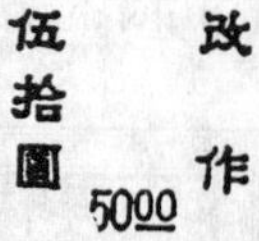

1947, Apr. **Unwmk.** *Perf. 11*

1L20	A1	$50 on $1 vio (R)	19.00	19.00
a.		Brown surcharge	19.00	19.00
1L21	A2	$50 on $2 ver	19.00	19.00
a.		Brown surcharge	19.00	19.00
1L22	A1	$100 on $1 vio	19.00	19.00
a.		Green surcharge	19.00	19.00
1L23	A2	$100 on $2 ver (Bl)	19.00	19.00
a.		Green surcharge	19.00	19.00
		Nos. 1L20-1L23 (4)	76.00	76.00

Farmer and Worker — A7

Ax Severing Chain — A8

Wmk. Chinese Characters in Sheet

1947, May 1 *Perf. 10½x11*

Granite Paper

1L24	A7	$10 orange red	1.25	1.25
1L25	A7	$30 ultra	1.75	1.75
1L26	A7	$50 gray green	3.00	3.00
		Nos. 1L24-1L26 (3)	6.00	6.00

Labor Day. Value, imperf. pairs, set $300.

1947, May 4 *Perf. 11*

1L27	A8	$10 brt green	2.50	2.50
1L28	A8	$30 brown	2.50	2.50
1L29	A8	$50 violet	3.00	3.00
		Nos. 1L27-1L29 (3)	8.00	8.00

28th anniversary of the students' revolt at Peking University against the 1918 peace treaty. Value, imperf. pairs, set $350.

Workers with Banner: "Oppose Imperialist Aggression" A9

1947, May 30 *Perf. 10½x11*

Banner in Red

1L30	A9	$2 brt lilac	2.50	2.50
1L31	A9	$5 brt green	2.50	2.50
1L32	A9	$10 yellow	2.50	2.50
1L33	A9	$20 violet	2.50	2.50
1L34	A9	$30 red brn	2.50	2.50
1L35	A9	$50 dk blue	2.50	2.50
1L36	A9	$100 brown	2.50	2.50
a.		Souvenir sheet of 7	60.00	
		Nos. 1L30-1L36 (7)	17.50	17.50

22nd anniversary of the Shanghai-Nanking Road incident. No. 1L36a is on granite paper and contains 7 imperf. stamps similar to Nos. 1L30-1L36. Size: 215x158mm. Value, imperf. pairs, ordinary paper, set $500.

Mao and Communist Flag — A10

1947, July 1 *Perf. 10½x11*

1L37	A10	$10 red	4.00	4.00
1L38	A10	$30 brt lilac	4.00	4.00
1L39	A10	$50 rose brn	11.00	11.00
1L40	A10	$100 vermilion	13.00	13.00
		Nos. 1L37-1L40 (4)	32.00	32.00

26th anniversary of the founding of the Chinese Communist Party.

Hand Holding Rifle — A11

1947, July 7 *Perf. 10½*

1L41	A11	$10 orange	4.50	4.50
1L42	A11	$30 green	4.50	4.50
1L43	A11	$50 dull blue	4.50	4.50
1L44	A11	$100 brown	4.50	4.50
a.		Souvenir sheet of 4	80.00	50.00
		Nos. 1L41-1L44 (4)	18.00	18.00

10th anniversary of the start of Sino-Japanese War. No. 1L44a contains 4 imperf. stamps similar to Nos. 1L41-1L44. Size: 149x107mm. Exist imperf. Value, set of pairs $800.

White Mountain and Black Water, Northeast China — A12

Wmk. Zigzag Lines (141)

1947, Aug. 15 *Perf. 10½*

1L45	A12	$10 brown org	12.00	10.00
1L46	A12	$30 lt ol grn	1.40	10.00
1L47	A12	$50 blue grn	1.40	10.00
1L48	A12	$100 sepia	12.00	10.00
		Nos. 1L45-1L48 (4)	26.80	40.00

2nd anniversary of the reoccupation of Northeast China and the surrender of Japan.

Nos. 1L1-1L2 Surcharged in Black, Red, Green or Blue

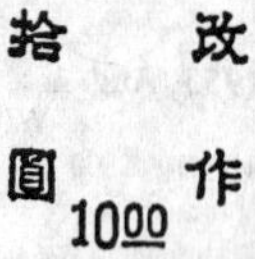

1947, Aug. 29 **Unwmk.** *Perf. 11*

1L49	A1	$5 on $1 vio	20.00	20.00
a.		Red surcharge	20.00	20.00
b.		Green surcharge	20.00	20.00
1L50	A2	$10 on $2 ver	20.00	20.00
a.		Blue surcharge	20.00	20.00
b.		Green surcharge	20.00	20.00

Map of Manchuria — A13

1947, Sept. 18 **Unwmk.**

White Paper

1L51	A13	$10 gray grn	8.00	8.00
1L52	A13	$20 rose lil	8.00	8.00
1L53	A13	$30 blk brn	8.00	8.00
1L54	A13	$50 carmine	8.00	8.00
		Nos. 1L51-1L54 (4)	32.00	32.00

16th anniversary of Japanese attack on Mukden, Sept. 18, 1931.

Northeast Political Council Offices — A14

Mao Tse-tung (Value figures repeated) — A15

1947, Oct. 10 *Perf. 10½*

1L55	A14	$10 yel org	21.00	21.00
1L56	A14	$20 rose red	21.00	21.00
1L57	A14	$100 brown	60.00	60.00
		Nos. 1L55-1L57 (3)	102.00	102.00

35th anniversary of the founding of the Chinese Republic.

1947, Oct. 10 **White Paper** *Perf. 11*

1L58	A15	$1 brown	20	1.50
1L59	A15	$5 gray grn	4.00	1.50
1L60	A15	$10 brt grn	12.00	8.00
1L61	A15	$15 bluish lil	12.00	8.00
1L62	A15	$20 brt rose	15	1.50
1L63	A15	$30 green	15	2.00
1L64	A15	$50 blk brn	15.00	10.00
1L65	A15	$90 blue	4.00	4.00
		Nos. 1L58-1L65 (8)	47.50	36.50

Newsprint

1L66	A15	$100 red	15	
a.		White paper	2.00	2.00
1L67	A15	$500 red org	16.00	16.00
a.		White paper	25.00	25.00

Type A22 resembles A15, but has "YUAN" at upper right.

The $1, $90 were also printed on newsprint.

See footnote following No. 1L72.

See Nos. 1L68-1L72. For surcharges see Nos. 1L84-1L88, 1L90, 1L92, 1L94.

1947, Nov. **Redrawn**

White Paper

1L68	A15	$50 lt grn	75	1.50
1L69	A15	$150 red org, wmkd. Chinese characters	1.00	1.50
a.		Unwatermarked	2.50	
1L70	A15	$250 bluish lil	25	1.50
a.		Wmkd. Chinese characters	75	1.50

Nos. 1L69 and 1L69a exist in same sheet.

1947, Dec. **Unwmk.**

Newsprint

1L71	A15	$300 green	40.00	25.00
1L72	A15	$1000 yellow	1.00	1.00
a.		White paper	1.00	1.00
		Nos. 1L68-1L72 (5)	43.00	30.50

Panel below portrait 8½x3mm on Nos. 1L68-1L70; 7x3mm on No. 1L58-1L67. Nos. 1L68-1L70 have different ornamental border. Nos. 1L71-1L72 without zeros for cents.

For surcharges see Nos. 1L90, 1L92, 1L94.

Hand Holding Torch — A16

1947, Dec. 12 **Unwmk.** *Perf. 11*

White Paper

1L73	A16	$30 rose red	7.00	7.00
1L74	A16	$90 dk bl	7.00	7.00
1L75	A16	$150 green	7.00	7.00
		Nos. 1L73-1L75 (3)	21.00	21.00

11th anniversary of the capture of Chiang Kai-shek at Sian.

Tomb of Gen. Li Chao-lin — A17

Globe and Banner — A18

1948, Mar. 9 **Unwmk.** *Perf. 10½x11*

1L76	A17	$30 green	10.00	10.00
a.		Granite paper, wmkd.	9.00	9.00
1L77	A17	$150 vio gray	10.00	10.00
a.		Granite paper, wmkd.	9.00	9.00

2nd anniversary of the assassination of Gen. Li Chao-lin, Commander of 3rd Army.

Wmk. Chinese Characters in Sheet

1948, May 1 *Perf. 11x10½*

1L78	A18	$50 red	6.00	10.00
1L79	A18	$150 green	75	15.00
1L80	A18	$250 lilac	75	30.00
		Nos. 1L78-1L80 (3)	7.50	55.00

Labor Day.

Student, Torch and Banner — A19

1948, May 4 **Unwmk.** *Perf. 10½x11*

Granite paper

1L81	A19	$50 green	9.00	9.00
1L82	A19	$150 brown	9.00	9.00
1L83	A19	$250 red	9.00	9.00
		Nos. 1L81-1L83 (3)	27.00	27.00

Youth Day, May 4.

Nos. 1L58, 1L61, 1L59, 1L63, 1L65, 1L2-1L4, 1L68-1L69, 1L71 Surcharged in Black, Blue, Red or Green

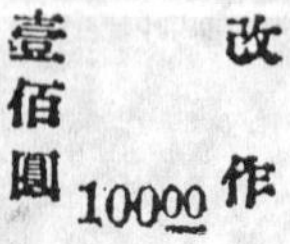

1948-49 *Perf. 11*

1L84	A15	$100 on $1	60.00	45.00
a.		Blue surcharge	50.00	50.00
1L85	A15	$100 on $15	17.50	17.50
a.		Blue surcharge	50.00	50.00
1L86	A15	$300 on $5 (R)	55.00	25.00
1L87	A15	$300 on $30 (R)	8.50	10.00
1L88	A15	$300 on $90 (R)	8.50	10.00
1L89	A2	$500 on $2	5.00	5.00
1L90	A15	$500 on $50 (R, '49)	27.50	20.00
1L91	A2	$1500 on $5 (Bl)	5.00	5.00
1L92	A15	$1500 on $150 (G; '49)	6.00	6.00
1L93	A2	$2500 on $10 (R)	5.00	5.00
1L94	A15	$2500 on $300 ('49)	5.00	5.00
		Nos. 1L84-1L94 (11)	203.00	153.50

Crane Operator — A20

Wmk. Chinese Characters in Sheet

1948, May *Perf. 11*

1L95	A20	$100 red & pink	40	40
1L96	A20	$300 vio brn & yel	1.40	1.40
1L97	A20	$500 bl & grn	1.40	1.40
		Nos. 1L95-1L97 (3)	3.20	3.20

6th All-China Labor Conference, Harbin.

Farmer, Worker and Soldier Saluting — A21

Mao Tse-tung ("YUAN" at upper right) — A22

1948, Dec. 3 **Unwmk.** *Perf. 11x10½*

White paper

1L98	A21	$500 vermilion	3.50	3.50
1L99	A21	$1500 brt grn	7.00	7.00
1L100	A21	$2500 brown	11.00	11.00
		Nos. 1L98-1L100 (3)	21.50	21.50

Liberation of Northeast China.

1949, Feb. *Perf. 11*

1L101	A22	$300 olive	35	60
1L102	A22	$500 orange	90	1.00
1L103	A22	$1500 bl grn	35	60
1L104	A22	$4500 brown	35	60
1L105	A22	$6500 dk bl	35	70
		Nos. 1L101-1L105 (5)	2.30	3.50

See type A15. For surcharges see Nos. 1L126-1L129, 1L131-1L132.

Workers, Globe and Flag — A23

Fields and Factories — A24

1949, May 1 *Perf. 11½*

1L106 A23	$1000 red & dl bl	15	25
1L107 A23	$1500 red & pale bl	15	25
1L108 A23	$4500 rose & ol brn	15	35
1L109 A23	$6500 dl org & grn	50	42
1L110 A23	$10,000 mar & ultra	50	50
	Nos. 1L106-1L110 (5)	1.45	1.77

Labor Day.

1949 *Perf. 10, 11*

1L111 A24	$5000 Prus bl	4.25	1.00
1L112 A24	$10,000 org brn	52	50
1L113 A24	$50,000 green	15	*2.00*
1L114 A24	$100,000 violet	15	*8.00*
	Nos. 1L111-1L114 (4)	5.07	*11.50*

Production in agriculture and industry.

Workers with Flags — A25

Heroes' Monument, Harbin — A26

1949, July 1 *Perf. 11*

1L115 A25	$1500 vio, lt bl & red	15	25
1L116 A25	$4500 dk brn, lt bl & ver	90	30
1L117 A25	$6500 gray, lt bl & rose red	15	50
	Nos. 1L115-1L117 (3)	1.20	1.05

28th anniversary of the founding of the Chinese Communist Party.

1949, Aug. 15 *Perf. 11½x11*

1L118 A26	$1500 brick red	15	50
1L119 A26	$4500 yel grn	22	50
1L120 A26	$6500 lt blue	1.10	50
	Nos. 1L118-1L120 (3)	1.47	1.50

4th anniversary of the Reoccupation, and the surrender of Japan.

東北貼用

(Enlarged)

"Northeast Postal Service"

The following commemorative issues are similar to those of the People's Republic of China, with the 4 characters shown added in different sizes and various arrangements. Reprints were also issued similar to those of the PRC.

Chinese Lantern Type of PRC, 1949

1949, Sept. 12 **Litho.** *Perf. 12½*

1L121 A1	$1000 dp blue	3.75	4.25
1L122 A1	$1500 scarlet	3.75	4.25
1L123 A1	$3000 green	3.75	4.25
1L124 A1	$4500 maroon	3.75	4.25
	Nos. 1L121-1L124 (4)	15.00	17.00

Reprints exist. Value, set $2.

Factory — A27

1949, Oct. *Perf. 11x10½*

1L125 A27	$1500 orange	25	40

For surcharge see No. 1L130.

Nos. 1L101, 1L103-1L105, 1L125 Surcharged in Black or Green

1949, Nov. 20

1L126 A22	$2000 on $300	32.50	2.50
1L127 A22	$2000 on $4500 (G)	18.00	15.00
1L128 A22	$2500 on $1500	65	3.00
1L129 A22	$2500 on $6500	18.00	10.00
1L130 A27	$5000 on $1500	45	70
1L131 A22	$20,000 on $4500	28	3.00
1L132 A22	$35,000 on $300	40	4.00
	Nos. 1L126-1L132 (7)	70.28	38.20

Globe and Hammer Type of PRC

1949, Nov. 15 *Perf. 12½*

1L133 A2	$5000 crimson	60.00	60.00
1L134 A2	$20,000 dp green	60.00	60.00
1L135 A2	$35,000 vio blue	60.00	60.00
	Nos. 1L133-1L135 (3)	180.00	180.00

Reprints, Value, set $32.50.

Mao and Conference Hall Types of PRC

1950, Feb. 1 *Perf. 14*

1L136 A3	$1000 vermilion	7.50	7.50
1L137 A3	$1500 dp blue	7.50	7.50
1L138 A4	$5000 dk vio brn	7.50	7.50
1L139 A4	$20,000 green	7.50	7.50
	Nos. 1L136-1L139 (4)	30.00	30.00

Reprints exist. Value, set $1.75.

Gate of Heavenly Peace (same size) — A28

1950 *Perf. 10½*

Narrow horizontal shading

1L140 A28	$500 olive	50	50
1L141 A28	$1000 orange	50	50
1L142 A28	$1000 lil rose	2.00	50
1L143 A28	$2000 gray grn	15	15
1L144 A28	$2500 yellow	1.00	15
1L145 A28	$5000 dp org	21.00	20
1L146 A28	$10,000 brn org	1.00	50
1L147 A28	$20,000 vio brn	15	20
1L148 A28	$35,000 dp blue	15	35
1L149 A28	$50,000 brt grn	50	70
	Nos. 1L140-1L149 (10)	26.95	3.75

See A29.

Flag and Mao Type of PRC

1950, July 1 *Perf. 14*

Yellow Stars

1L150 A7	$5000 grn & red	11.00	11.00
1L151 A7	$10,000 brn & red	11.00	11.00
1L152 A7	$20,000 dk brn & red	11.00	11.00
1L153 A7	$30,000 dk vio bl & red	12.00	12.00
	Nos. 1L150-1L153 (4)	45.00	45.00

Reprints exist. Value, set $3.

Picasso Dove Type of PRC

1950, Aug. 1 **Engr.** *Perf. 14*

1L154 A8	$2500 brown	8.00	8.00
1L155 A8	$5000 green	8.00	8.00
1L156 A8	$20,000 blue	8.00	8.00
	Nos. 1L154-1L156 (3)	24.00	24.00

Reprints exist. Value, set $4.

Flag Type of PRC

1950, Oct. 1 **Engr. & Litho.**

Flag in Red & Yellow

1L157 A9	$1000 purple	11.00	11.00
1L158 A9	$2500 org brn	11.00	11.00
1L159 A9	$5000 dp grn	11.00	11.00
1L160 A9	$10,000 olive	11.00	11.00
1L161 A9	$20,000 blue	11.00	11.00
	Nos. 1L157-1L161 (5)	55.00	55.00

Size of #1L159: 38x47mm, others 26x33mm.
Reprints exist. Value, set $5.

Postal Conference Type of PRC

1950, Nov. 1 **Litho.**

1L162 A11	$2500 grn & dp org	4.75	4.75
1L163 A11	$5000 car & grn	4.75	4.75

Reprints exist. Value, set, $2.

Gate of Heavenly Peace (same size) — A29

1950-51 *Perf. 10½*

Wide horizontal shading

1L164 A29	$5000 orange	2.25	1.25
1L165 A29	$30,000 scarlet	42	*3.00*
1L166 A29	$100,000 violet	4.75	3.25

Wmk. Zigzag Lines (141)

1L167 A29	$250 brown	35	30
1L168 A29	$500 olive	35	30
1L169 A29	$1000 lil rose	42	50
1L170 A29	$2000 dl grn ('51)	15	50
1L171 A29	$2500 yellow	15	50
1L172 A29	$5000 orange	35	50
1L173 A29	$10,000 brn org ('51)	50	50
1L174 A29	$12,500 maroon	15	50
1L175 A29	$20,000 dp brn ('51)	50	1.00
	Nos. 1L164-1L175 (12)	10.34	12.10

A $50,000 green was prepared, but not issued, Value $7.50.

Stalin and Mao Tse-tung Type of PRC

Unwmk.

1950, Dec. 1 **Engr.** *Perf. 14*

1L176 A12	$2500 red	6.75	6.75
1L177 A12	$5000 dp green	6.75	6.75
1L178 A12	$20,000 dk blue	6.75	6.75
	Nos. 1L176-1L178 (3)	20.25	20.25

Reprints exist. Value, set $6.

NORTHEAST CHINA PARCEL POST STAMPS

Locomotive — PP1

1951 **Litho.** *Perf. 10½*

1LQ1	$100,000 purple	40.00

Imperf

1LQ2	$300,000 brown	165.00
1LQ3	$500,000 grnsh bl	250.00
1LQ4	$1,000,000 ver	400.00

Value, Nos. 1LQ2-1LQ4 perf. 10½, $1,000.
For similar type see North China PP1.

PORT ARTHUR AND DAIREN

The Liaoning Postal Administration was established on April 1, 1946, in accordance with the Sino-Soviet Treaty, but was renamed one week later the Port Arthur and Dairen Postal Administration. On Apr. 3, 1947, it was combined with telecommunications and renamed the Kwantung Post and Telegraph General Administration. On May 1, 1949, the name was again changed to Port Arthur and Dairen Post and Telegraph Administration. Postal tariffs were based on local currency and both Manchukuo and Japanese stamps were overprinted for use.

Manchukuo Nos. 162 and 94 Handstamp Surcharged in Violet ("Liaoning Post")

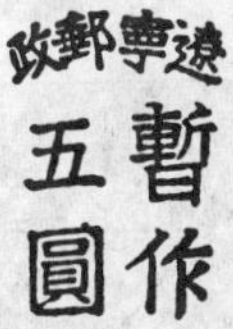

1946, Mar. 15

With Gum

2L1 A19	20f on 30f buff	60.00	60.00
2L2 A18	1y on 12f org	35.00	35.00

Same Surcharge on Japan Nos. 260, 337, 195, 244, 263, 342 in Violet, Red or Black

1946, Apr. 1

2L3 A85	20f on 3s grn (V)	12.50	12.50
2L4 A151	1y on 17s gray vio (R)	10.50	10.50
2L5 A57	5y on 6s car	27.50	27.50
2L6 A57	5y on 6s crim	27.50	27.50
2L7 A88	5y on 6s org	20.00	20.00
2L8 A154	15y on 40s dk vio	77.50	77.50
	Nos. 2L1-2L8 (8)	270.50	270.50

Surcharge sideways on Nos. 2L5-2L6.

Japan Nos. 260 and 263 Surcharged

1946, Apr.

2L9 A85	1y on 3s grn	*350.00*
2L10 A88	5y on 6s org	*230.00*

Sha Ho Kow (suburb of Dairen) issue. The status of this issue is in question.

Manchukuo Nos. 84, 88 and 98 Handstamp Surcharged in Green, Red or Black

1946, May 1

2L11 A16	1y on 1f red brn (G)	17.00	17.00
2L12 A18	5y on 4f lt ol grn (R)	22.50	22.50
2L13 A19	15y on 30f chnt brn	45.00	45.00
	Nos. 2L11-2L13 (3)	84.50	84.50

Transfer of postal administration and Labor Day.

Manchukuo Nos. 159, 86 and 94 Surcharged in Green, Red or Black

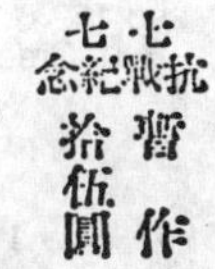

1946, July 7

2L14 A17	1y on 6f crim rose (G)	15.00	15.00
2L15 A17	5y on 2f lt grn (R)	65.00	65.00
2L16 A18	15y on 12f dp org	90.00	90.00
	Nos. 2L14-2L16 (3)	170.00	170.00

Outbreak of war with Japan, 9th anniv.

Manchukuo Nos. 94, 84 and 158 Surcharged in Black, Green or Red

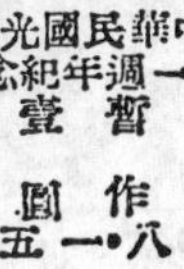

1946, Aug. 15

2L17 A18	1y on 12f dp org	27.50	27.50
2L18 A16	5y on 1f red brn (G)	50.00	50.00
2L19 A10	15y on 5f gray blk (R)	100.00	100.00
	Nos. 2L17-2L19 (3)	177.50	177.50

Surrender of Japan, first anniversary.

Manchukuo Nos. 159, 94 and 86 Surcharged in Green, Black or Red

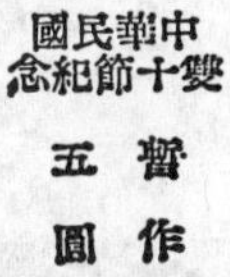

1946, Oct. 10

2L20 A17	1y on 6f crim rose (G)	27.50	27.50
2L21 A18	5y on 12f dp org	50.00	50.00
2L22 A17	15y on 2f lt grn (R)	100.00	100.00
	Nos. 2L20-2L22 (3)	177.50	177.50

35th anniversary of Chinese revolution.

Manchukuo Nos. 84, 159 and 94 Surcharged in Black, Green or Blue

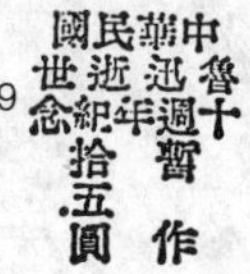

1946, Oct. 19

2L23 A16	1y on 1f red brn	45.00	45.00
2L24 A17	5y on 6f crim rose (G)	70.00	70.00
2L25 A18	15y on 12f dp org (Bl)	110.00	110.00
	Nos. 2L23-2L25 (3)	225.00	225.00

10th anniversary of the death of Lu Hsun (1881-1936), writer.

Manchukuo Nos. 86, 159 and 95 Surcharged in Red, Green or Black

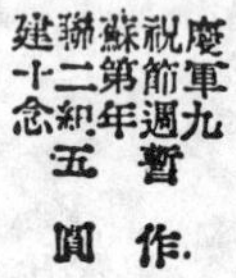

1947, Feb. 20

2L26 A17	1y on 2f lt grn (R)	45.00	45.00
2L27 A17	5y on 6f crim rose (G)	85.00	85.00
2L28 A18	15y on 13f dk red brn	190.00	190.00
	Nos. 2L26-2L28 (3)	320.00	320.00

29th anniversary of the Red (USSR) Army.

Manchukuo Nos. 86, 159 and 162 Surcharged in Red, Green or Black

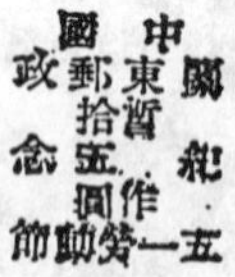

1947, May 1

2L29 A17	1y on 2f lt grn (R)	22.50	22.50
2L30 A17	5y on 6f crim rose (G)	65.00	65.00
2L31 A19	15y on 30f buff	100.00	100.00
	Nos. 2L29-2L31 (3)	187.50	187.50

Labor Day.

Manchukuo Nos. 86, 88, 98 and 162 Surcharged ("Kwantung Postal Service, China")

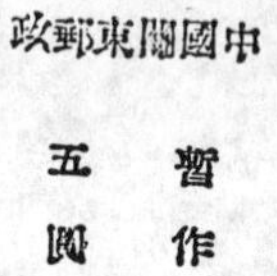

1947, Sept. 15

2L32 A17	5y on 2f lt grn	30.00	25.00
2L33 A18	15y on 4f lt ol grn	50.00	40.00
2L34 A19	20y on 30f red brn	75.00	60.00
2L35 A19	20y on 30f buff	80.00	75.00
	Nos. 2L32-2L35 (4)	235.00	200.00

Manchukuo Nos. 86 and 159 Surcharged in Red and Green

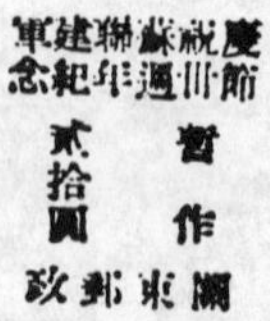

Sacred Golden Kite (same size) — A1

1948, Feb. 20

2L36 A17	10y on 2f lt grn (R)	100.00	100.00
2L37 A17	20y on 6f crim rose (G)	120.00	120.00
2L38 A1	100y on bl & red brn	500.00	500.00

30th anniversary of the Red (USSR) Army. No. 2L38 is on an ungummed label for the 2600th anniv. of the Japanese Empire.

Japan No. 260 and Manchukuo Nos. 84, 86 and 88 Surcharged in Red, Blue or Black

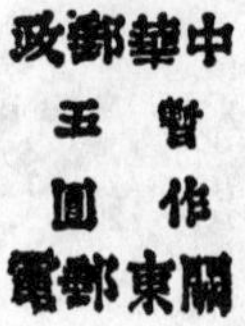

1948, July

2L39 A85	5y on 3s grn (R)	80.00	80.00
2L40 A16	10y on 1f red brn (Bl)	145.00	145.00
2L41 A17	50y on 2f lt grn	325.00	325.00
2L42 A18	100y on 4f lt ol grn (R)	600.00	600.00

Smaller Characters on Bottom Line

2L43 A17	10y on 2f lt grn (R)	200.00	145.00
2L44 A16	50y on 1f red brn	250.00	200.00

Stamps of Manchukuo Nos. 84, 86 and 88 Surcharged in Blue, Red or Black

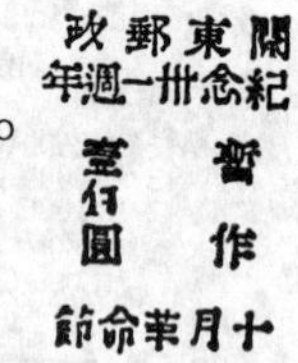

1948, Nov. 1

2L45 A16	10y on 1f red brn (Bl)	500.00	500.00
2L46 A17	50y on 2f lt grn (R)	500.00	500.00
2L47 A18	100y on 4f lt ol grn	525.00	525.00

31st anniversary of the Russian Revolution.

Manchukuo Nos. 86 and 161 Surcharged in Red or Green

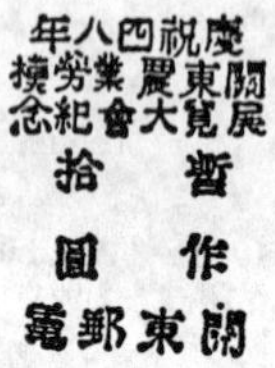

1948, Nov. 15

2L48 A17	10y on 2f lt grn	700.00	400.00
2L49 A17	50y on 20f brn (G)	800.00	800.00

Kwantung Agricultural and Industrial Exhibition.

Manchukuo Nos. 86, 88 and 161 Surcharged in Red, Black or Green

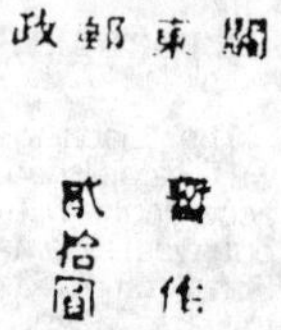

1949, Jan.

2L50 A17	20y on 2f lt grn (R)	500.00
2L51 A18	50y on 4f lt ol grn	700.00
2L52 A17	100y on 20f brn (G)	700.00

Without Gum

From No. 2L56 onward all stamps were issued without gum except as noted.

Farmer and Worker — A2

Train and Ship — A3

Ship at Dock (No. 2L55) — A4

(No. 2L56)

1949 Litho. *Perf. 11, 11½*

2L53 A2	5y pale grn	1.50	2.50
2L54 A3	10y orange	10.00	7.00
2L55 A4	50y vermilion	15.00	10.00
2L56 A4	50y red (redrawn)	20.00	15.00
	Nos. 2L53-2L56 (4)	46.50	34.50

Issue dates: #2L56, July 7; others Apr. 1.

For surcharges see Nos. 2L62-2L66.

Worker, Flag and Means of Transport — A5

1949, May 1 *Perf. 11*

2L57 A5	10y rose pink	10.00	10.00
a.	10y vermilion	75.00	75.00

Labor Day. #2L57a is from a worn plate.

Mao Tse-tung and Red Flag — A6

Heroes Monument, Dairen — A7

1949, July 1

2L59 A6	50y red	20.00	20.00

28th anniversary of the founding of the Chinese Communist Party.

1949, Sept.

2L60 A7	10y red, bl & ol	13.00	13.00
a.	10y red, bl & pale bl	100.00	85.00

4th anniversary of victory over Japan and opening of the Dairen Industrial Fair.

Nos. 2L53-2L54 Surcharged in Red or Black

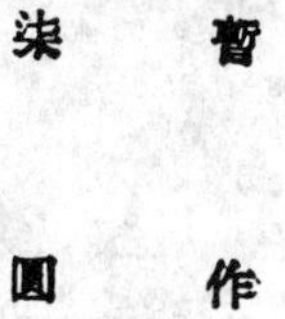

a

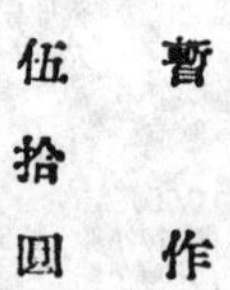

b

c

1949, Sept. With Gum

2L62 A2(a)	7y on 5y (R)	30.00	25.00
2L63 A2(a)	7y on 5y	30.00	25.00
2L64 A2(b)	50y on 5y (R)	85.00	70.00
2L65 A3(b)	100y on 10y	450.00	350.00
2L66 A3(c)	500y on 10y (R)	600.00	400.00
	Nos. 2L62-2L66 (5)	1,195.	870.00

Size of surcharge on No. 2L63: 16x19mm.

A 500y on 5y, red surcharge "c," and a 500y on 10y orange, surcharge "b" were prepared but not issued.

Stalin and Lenin — A8

1949, Nov. 7 *Perf. 11x11½*

2L68 A8	10y dl bl grn (shades)	10.00	10.00

32nd anniversary of the Russian Revolution.

Workers Saluting Mao, Star and Flag — A9

1949, Nov. 16 *Perf. 11*

2L69 A9	35y dk bl, red, & yel	12.00	12.00

Founding of the People's Republic of China.

Stalin — A10

(same size) Gate of Heavenly Peace — A11

1949, Dec. 20 *Perf. 11½*

2L70 A10	20y dl mag	21.00	21.00
2L71 A10	35y rose red	21.00	21.00

70th birthday of Stalin.

1950, Mar. 10 Typo. *Perf. 10½*

2L72 A11	10y Prus blue	7.00	*3.25*
2L73 A11	20y dull grn	30.00	20.00
2L74 A11	35y red	1.25	*3.00*
2L75 A11	50y deep pur	3.00	*4.00*
2L76 A11	100y lilac rose	1.00	*7.00*
	Nos. 2L72-2L76 (5)	42.25	*37.25*

NORTH CHINA

The North China Liberation Area included the provinces of Hopeh, Chahar, Shansi and Suiyuan. The original postal service, begun in the Shansi-Hopeh-Chahar Border Area in December, 1937, became the North China Postal and Telegraph Administration in May, 1949.

All Stamps Issued without Gum

Large Victory Issue

Cavalry Man Holding Nationalist Flag — A1

Wmk. Wavy Lines

1946, Mar. *Perf. 10½*

Granite Paper

Size: 34½x42mm

3L1 A1	$1 red brown	1.00	90
a.	Newsprint	11.00	11.00
3L2 A1	$2 gray grn	1.00	90
3L3 A1	$4 vermilion	1.10	90
3L4 A1	$5 vio brn	1.10	90
3L5 A1	$8 vio bl	1.10	90

3L6 A1 $10 dp car 1.10 90
3L7 A1 $12 yellow 3.75 3.75
3L8 A1 $20 lt green 6.75 6.75
Nos. 3L1-3L8 (8) 16.90 15.90

Defeat of Japan.

Small Victory Issue

Perf. 10½x10, 9½ rough

1946, May Unwmk.

Granite paper

Size: 20x21mm

3L9 A1 $1 red org 1.00 1.00
3L10 A1 $2 green 1.50 1.00
3L11 A1 $3 lt lilac 3.00 4.00
3L12 A1 $5 dull pur 4.00 15
3L13 A1 $8 dk blue 6.00 8.00
3L14 A1 $10 rose red 1.50 2.00
3L15 A1 $15 purple 30.00 20.00
3L16 A1 $20 green 3.00 3.00
3L17 A1 $30 brt grnsh bl 2.50 3.50
3L18 A1 $40 brt rose lilac 3.00 3.00
3L19 A1 $50 brown 20.00 25
3L20 A1 $60 myrtle green 30.00 75

Wmk. Wavy Lines

3L21 A1 $100 orange 1.00 2.00
3L22 A1 $200 dull blue 1.00 2.00
3L23 A1 $500 rose 10.00 25.00
Nos. 3L9-3L23 (15) 117.50 75.65

North China Postal and Telegraph Administration

Charging Infantrymen A2

Agriculture and Industry A3

1949, Jan. Unwmk. *Imperf.*

White Paper

3L24 A2 50c brown lake 90 30
3L25 A2 $1 Prussian blue 90 30

Newsprint

3L26 A2 $2 apple green 90 30
3L27 A2 $3 dull violet 90 30
3L28 A2 $5 brown 90 30
3L29 A3 $6 deep rose 90 80
a. White paper 90 80
3L30 A2 $10 blue grn 15 80
3L31 A2 $12 dp car 90 30
Nos. 3L24-3L31 (8) 6.45 3.40

No. 3L29 issued in Peking, others in Tientsin.

Remittance Stamps of China Surcharged

A4

壹
$1

叁
$3

1949, Jan. Engr. *Perf. 13*

Small Central Characters

3L32 A4 50c on $50 brn blk 3.25 1.00
3L33 A4 $1 on $50 gray blk 2.50 1.00
3L34 A4 $3 on $50 gray 2.50 1.50

Large Central Characters

3L35 A4 50c on $50 blk 1.50 1.50
3L36 A4 $6 on $20 dk vio brn 1.50 1.50
Nos. 3L32-3L36 (5) 11.25 6.50

Issued in Tientsin.

For surcharges see Nos. 3LQ10-3LQ21.

Sun Yat-sen Type A2 of Northeastern Provinces and China No. 640 Surcharged in Black, Red, Green or Blue

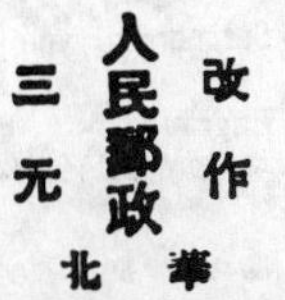

#3L37-3L45, 3L47-3L50, 3L52

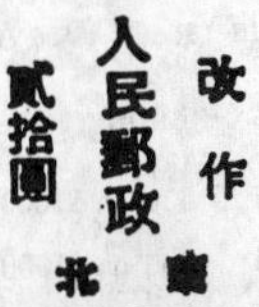

#3L46, 3L51, 3L53

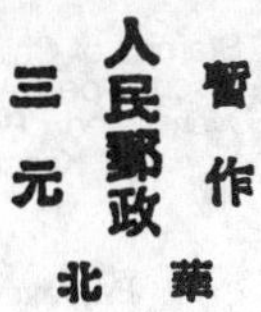

c

Type "b," bottom character of left vertical row (yuan) differs. Type "c," top character of right vertical row differs.

1949, Mar. 7 *Perf. 14*

3L37 A2 50c on 5c lake 22 1.25
3L38 A2 $1 on 10c org 22 1.00
3L39 A2 $2 on 20c yel grn 37.50 12.00
3L40 A2 $3 on 50c red org 22 75
3L41 A2 $4 on $5 dk grn 3.75 1.00
3L42 A2 $6 on $10 crim 90 1.00
3L43 A2 $10 on $300 bluish grn 1.10 2.00
3L44 A2 $12 on $1 bl 1.10 1.50
3L45 A2 $18 on $3 brn 1.10 75
3L46 A2 $20 on 50c red org (Bl) 1.10 50
3L47 A2 $20 on $20 ol, II 1.10 2.00
a. Type I 9.00 9.00
3L48 A2 $30 on $2.50 ind (R) 1.10 2.00
3L49 A2 $40 on 25c blk brn (R) 3.75 3.00
3L50 A2 $50 on $109 dk grn (R) 8.00 4.00
3L51 A2 $80 on $1 bl (R) 13.00 1.50
3L52 A2 $100 on $65 dl grn (R) 16.00 4.00
3L53 A73 $100 on $100 dk car, surch. 16mm wide (Bl) 22.50 1.50
a. Surcharge 14mm wide 24.00 10.00

1949, Apr.

3L55 A2 (c) $2 on 20c yel grn 1.10 1.50
3L56 A2 (c) $3 on 50c red org 18 1.00
3L57 A2 (c) $4 on 25c blk grn 8.00 2.00
3L58 A2 (c) $6 on $10 crim, II 3.75 2.00
a. Type I 8.00 10.00
3L59 A2 (c) $12 on $1 blue 65 65

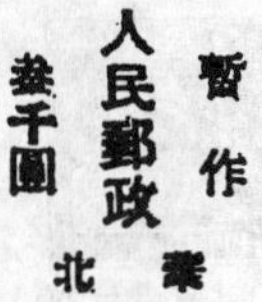

d

e

1949, Apr.

Type "d"

3L60 A2 $1 on 25c blk grn (G) 15 60
3L61 A2 $10 on $300 bluish grn (R) 8.00 2.75
3L62 A2 $20 on 50c red org (G) 11.00 12.00
3L63 A2 $20 on $20 ol (R) 5.50 2.00
3L64 A2 $40 on 25c blk brn (R) 5.50 2.25
3L65 A2 $50 on $109 dk grn, surch. 15mm wide (R) 8.00 6.00
a. Surcharge 13mm wide 27.50 8.00
3L66 A2 $80 on $1 bl (R) 5.50 3.00

Type "d" On Stamps on China

3L67 A73 $100 on $100 dk car (G) 45.00 15.00
3L68 A73 $300 on $700 red brn (Bl) 9.00 6.00
3L69 A82 $500 on $500 bl grn (R) 6.75 2.00
3L70 A82 $3000 on $3000 bl (R) 9.00 2.00

Type "e" On Stamps of Northeastern Provinces

1949, Aug.

3L71 A2 $10 on $10 crim, II (Bl) 5.50 1.50
a. Type I 11.00 11.00
3L72 A2 $30 on 20c yel grn (R) 5.50 1.00
3L73 A2 $50 on $44 dk car rose (Bl) 5.50 55
3L74 A2 $100 on $3 brn (Bl) 9.00 3.00
3L75 A2 $200 on $4 org brn, II (Bl) 16.00 10.00
a. Type I 300.00 150.00

On China No. 754 in Blue

3L76 A82 $10 on $7000 lt red brn 9.00 4.00
Nos. 3L37-3L76 (39) 290.24 120.55

Overprints on Nos. 3L71 and 3L76 have 2 characters in center row.

Farmer and Worker on Globe — A5

1949, May 1 Engr. *Perf. 14*

3L77 A5 $20 crimson 1.65 65
3L78 A5 $40 dark blue 1.65 80
3L79 A5 $60 brown org 1.65 65
3L80 A5 $80 dk green 1.65 1.00
3L81 A5 $100 purple 1.65 1.00
Nos. 3L77-3L81 (5) 8.25 4.10

Labor day. Exists imperf. Value, set $10. Also issued in blocks of 4, imperf between.

Mao Tse-tung (Chinese Numeral) — A6

Mao Tse-tung (Arabic Numeral) — A7

1949, July 1 *Perf. 14*

3L82 A6 $10 red 42 60
3L83 A7 $20 dk blue 42 60
3L84 A6 $50 orange 2.50 60
3L85 A7 $80 dk green 52 1.00
3L86 A6 $100 purple 2.50 1.00
3L87 A7 $120 olive 35 1.00
3L88 A6 $140 vio brn 2.50 1.00
Nos. 3L82-3L88 (7) 9.21 5.80

28th anniv. of the founding of the Chinese Communist Party. Value, imperf, set $35.

(same size) Gate of Heavenly Peace — A8

Farmers and Factory — A9

1949, Nov. 26 Litho. *Perf. 12½*

3L89 A8 $50 orange 20 2.75
3L90 A8 $100 crimson 15 35
3L91 A8 $200 green 50 45
3L92 A8 $300 rose brn 8.00 90
3L93 A8 $400 blue 8.00 90
3L94 A8 $500 brown 8.00 55
3L95 A8 $700 violet 2.75 2.75
Nos. 3L89-3L95 (7) 27.60 8.65

1949, Dec. Engr. *Perf. 14*

3L96 A9 $1000 orange 2.00 50
3L97 A9 $3000 dark blue 15 40
3L98 A9 $5000 crimson 15 75
3L99 A9 $10,000 red brown 15 1.50
Nos. 3L96-3L99 (4) 2.45 3.15

NORTH CHINA PARCEL POST STAMPS

Parcel Post Stamps of China Nos. Q23-Q27 (Type PP3) Surcharged in Red, Black or Blue

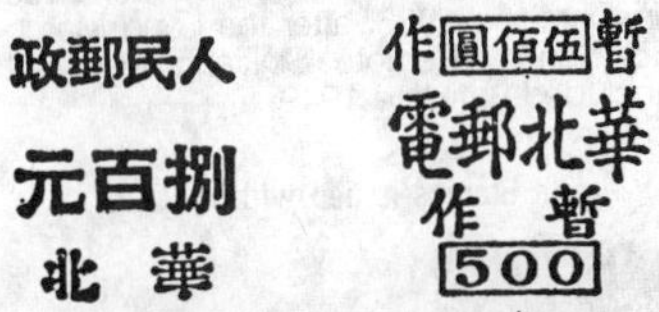

a b

1949, June

Surcharged Type "a"

3LQ1 $300 on $6,000,000 (R) 30.00
3LQ2 $400 on $8,000,000 (Bl) 30.00
3LQ3 $500 on $10,000,000 (R) 30.00
3LQ4 $800 on $5,000,000 (R) 30.00
3LQ5 $1000 on $3,000,000 (R) 40.00

Surcharged Type "b"

3LQ6 $500 on $3,000,000 40.00
3LQ7 $1000 on $5,000,000 50.00
3LQ8 $3000 on $8,000,000 125.00
3LQ9 $5000 on $10,000,000 165.00
Nos. 3LQ1-3LQ9 (9) 540.00

Nos. 3LQ8-3LQ9 have large numerals unboxed.

Remittance Stamps of China (like North China Type A4) Surcharged in Black or Red

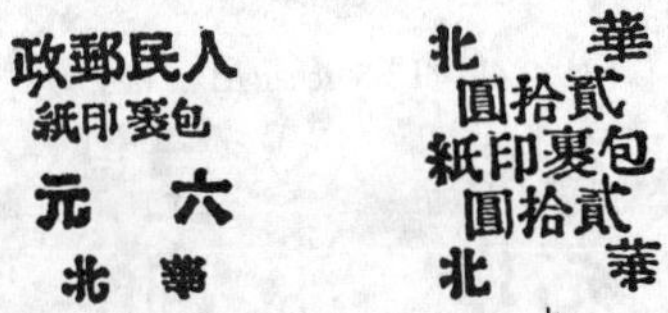

a b

Peking Surcharge "a"

1949, June Litho. *Perf. 13*

3LQ10 $6 on $5 ver 3.25
3LQ11 $20 on $50 gray 3.25
3LQ12 $50 on $20 dk vio brn 3.25
3LQ13 $100 on $10 ol grn 6.50

Tientsin Surcharge "b"

Engr. *Perf. 14*

3LQ14 $20 on $1 brn org 12.00 5.00
a. Perf. 12½ 20.00 6.00
3LQ15 $30 on $2 dk grn 12.00 3.50
a. Red surcharge 20.00 6.00
3LQ16 $30 on $10 ol grn 90.00 37.50
3LQ17 $100 on $10 gray grn (R) 12.00 5.00

Litho.

Perf. 13

3LQ18 $50 on $5 red 12.00 5.00

Engr.

Perf. 14

3LQ19 $20 on $1 org brn 35.00 15.00

Perf. 12½

3LQ20 $100 on $10 yel grn (R) 60.00 27.50

Typo.

Roulette 9½

3LQ21 $30 on $2 bl grn (R) 45.00 19.00

The surcharge on No. 3LQ19 is without first and last lines.

Locomotive — PP1

1949, Nov. Engr. *Perf. 14*

3LQ22 PP1 $500 crimson 5.00 5.00
3LQ23 PP1 $1000 deep blue 8.50
3LQ24 PP1 $2000 green 12.50
3LQ25 PP1 $5000 dp olive 27.50
3LQ26 PP1 $10,000 orange 50.00
3LQ27 PP1 $20,000 red brn 130.00
3LQ28 PP1 $50,000 brn pur 250.00
Nos. 3LQ22-3LQ28 (7) 483.50

NORTHWEST CHINA

The Northwest China Liberation Area consisted of the provinces of Sinkiang, Tsinghai, Ningsia and the western part of Shensi. The area was first established as the Shensi-Kansu-Ningsia Border Area in October, 1936, after the Long March to Yenan. Remote Sinkiang was not included until late 1949.

All Stamps Issued without Gum

Pagoda on Yenan Hill — A1

1945, Mar. Litho. *Imperf.*
4L1 A1 $1 green 15.00
4L2 A1 $5 dk blue 100.00
4L3 A1 $10 rose red 14.00
4L4 A1 $50 dull pur 11.00
4L5 A1 $100 yel org 14.00
Nos. 4L1-4L5 (5) 154.00

Rouletted 9
4L1a A1 $1 80.00
4L2a A1 $5 115.00
4L3a A1 $10 80.00

First issue; denomination in Chinese and Arabic. Heavy shading at top of vignette. Columns at sides.
See types A2, A3 and A4. For surcharges see Nos. 4L6-4L10, 4L23.

Nos. 4L1-4L2 Surcharged in Red:

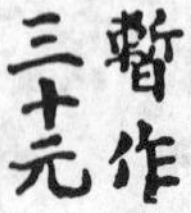

a

b

c

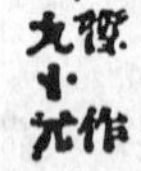
d

1946, Nov.
4L6 A1 (a) $30 on $1 grn 20.00
4L7 A1 (b) $30 on $1 grn *100.00*
a. Rectangular lower left character *675.00*
4L8 A1 (c) $30 on $1 grn 15.00
4L9 A1 (b) $60 on $1 grn
4L10 A1 (d) $90 on $5 dk bl 20.00

Surcharges on Nos. 4L7a and 4L9 are type "b" as illustrated. Surcharge on No. 4L7 differs from "b," having lower left character as in type "a."

Pagoda on Yenan Hill (same size)
A2 A3

1948, June
4L11 A2 $100 buff 140.00
4L12 A2 $300 rose pink 1.00
4L13 A2 $500 red 3.50
4L14 A2 $1000 blue 3.50
4L15 A2 $2000 yel grn 24.00
4L16 A2 $5000 dull pur 10.00
Nos. 4L11-4L16 (6) 182.00

Second issue; denominations in Chinese only. Many shades and proofs exist.
For surcharge see No. 4L24.

1948, Dec.
4L17 A3 10c yel org 1.50
4L18 A3 20c lemon 1.50
4L19 A3 $1 dk blue 1.50
4L20 A3 $2 vermilion 1.50
4L21 A3 $5 pale bl grn 9.00
4L22 A3 $10 violet 13.50
Nos. 4L17-4L22 (6) 28.50

Third issue; ornamental border at sides. Many shades exist.

Nos. 4L2 and 4L13 Surcharged in Red or Black

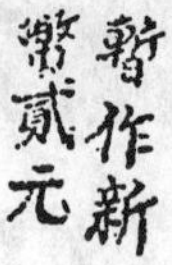

1949, Jan.
4L23 A1 $1 on $5 dk bl 45.00
4L24 A2 $2 on $500 red 20.00

Pagoda on Yenan Hill — A4

1949, May 1
4L25 A4 50c yel to olive 15 20
4L26 A4 $1 dl bl to indigo 15 20
4L27 A4 $3 ol yel to org yel 15 20
4L28 A4 $5 blue green 80 20
4L29 A4 $10 vio to dp vio 3.00 3.00
4L30 A4 $20 pink to rose red 4.00 4.00
Nos. 4L25-4L30 (6) 8.25 7.80

Fourth issue; light shading at top of vignette, columns without ornaments at sides. Many shades exist.

China Nos. 959, F2 and E12 Overprinted ("People's Post, Shensi")

1949, June 13 Engr. *Perf. 12½*
4L31 A96 orange 15.00 15.00
4L32 R2 carmine 27.50 27.50
4L33 SD2 red vio 27.50 27.50
Nos. 4L31-4L33 (3) 70.00 70.00

Stamps of China, Sun Yat-sen Type A94 of 1949, Overprinted in Black or Red ("People's Post, Shensi")

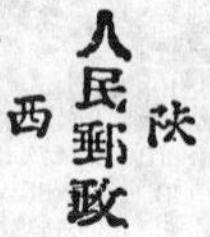

Lithographed; Engraved
1949, July 1 *Perf. 14, 12½*
4L34 $10 green (887) 1.10 1.00
4L35 $20 vio brn (888) 2.25 2.00
4L36 $20 vio brn (896) 1.10 1.00
4L37 $50 dk Prus grn (889; R) 5.75 5.00
4L38 $50 grn (951) 5.75 5.00
4L39 $100 org brn (890) 14.00 6.00
4L40 $500 ros lil (892) 20.00 6.00
4L41 $1000 dp bl (952; R) 27.50 8.00
4L42 $2000 vio (902;R) 27.50 8.00
4L43 $5000 car (953) 40.00 15.00
4L44 $10,000 brn (954) 75.00 32.00
Nos. 4L34-4L44 (11) 219.95 89.00

Kansu-Ningsia-Tsinghai Area, Lanchow Overprints

China Nos. 959a, F2 and E12 Overprinted ("People's Post, Kansu")

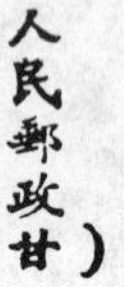

1949, Oct. Engr. *Rouletted*
4L45 A96 orange 18.00 18.00

Perf. 12½
4L46 R2 carmine 25.00 25.00
4L47 SD2 red vio 25.00 25.00
Nos. 4L45-4L47 (3) 68.00 68.00

Stamps of China, Sun Yat-sen Type A94 of 1949, Overprinted ("People's Post, Kansu")

Engraved; Lithographed
1949, Oct. *Perf. 14, 12½*
4L48 $10 grn (887) 3.25 1.50
4L49 $20 vio brn (888) 3.25 3.00
4L50 $50 dk Prus grn (889) 9.00 8.00
4L51 $100 org brn (890) 3.25 3.00
4L52 $100 dk org brn (898) 5.00 4.00
4L53 $200 red org (891) 6.50 5.00
4L54 $500 rose lil (892) 6.50 5.00
4L55 $1000 blue (894) 3.25 3.00
4L56 $1000 dp bl (901) 6.50 5.00
4L57 $2000 vio (902) 11.00 9.00
4L58 $5000 lt bl (903) 22.00 18.00
4L59 $10,000 sepia (904) 30.00 25.00
4L60 $20,000 ap grn (905) 60.00 50.00
Nos. 4L48-4L60 (13) 169.50 139.50

No. 4L54-4L60 exist with wider spaced overprints.

China Nos. 959, F2 and 791-792 Surcharged in Black or Red ("People's Post, Sinkiang")

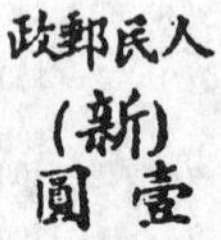

1949, Oct.
4L61 A96 $1 on org 25.00 25.00
4L62 R2 $3 on car 25.00 25.00
4L63 A82 10c on $50,000 dp bl (R) 25.00 25.00
4L64 A82 $1.50 on $100,000 dl grn (R) 25.00 30.00
Nos. 4L61-4L64 (4) 100.00 105.00

Northwest People's Post

Mao Tse-tung — A5 Great Wall — A6

1949, Oct. 15 Litho. *Imperf.*
4L65 A5 $50 rose 2.00 1.50
a. $200 cliche in $50 plate 120.00
4L66 A6 $100 dark blue 15 15
4L67 A5 $200 orange 15 75
4L68 A6 $400 sepia 2.00 95
Nos. 4L65-4L68 (4) 4.30 3.35

EAST CHINA

The East China Liberation Area included the provinces of Shantung, Kiangsu, Chekiang, Anhwei and Fukien. The original postal service established in Shantung in 1941, became the East China Posts and Telegraph General Office in July, 1948.

All Stamps Issued without Gum

Mao Tse-tung — A1 Transportation and Tower — A2

1948, Mar. Litho. *Perf. 10½*
5L1 A1 $50 yel org 1.40 1.00
5L2 A1 $100 dp rose 4.50 3.50
5L3 A1 $200 drk vio bl 4.50 3.50
5L4 A1 $300 brt grn 4.50 3.50
5L5 A1 $500 dp blue 1.75 1.50
5L6 A1 $800 vermilion 4.50 4.00
5L7 A1 $1000 dk blue 9.00 8.00
5L8 A1 $5000 rose 18.00 15.00
5L9 A1 $10,000 dp car 32.50 25.00
Nos. 5L1-5L9 (9) 80.65 65.00

Many varieties, including unissued imperforates exist.

Perf. 9 to 11 and compound
1949, Apr. Litho.
5L10 A2 $1 yel grn 15 15
5L11 A2 $2 blue grn 15 15
5L12 A2 $3 dull red 15 15
5L13 A2 $5 pale brn (ovpt. 4x4mm) 15 15
a. Without overprint 60.00 60.00
b. Overprint 3x3mm 1.00 1.00
5L14 A2 $10 ultra 15 15
5L15 A2 $13 brt vio 15 15
5L16 A2 $18 brt blue 15 15
5L17 A2 $21 vermilion 20 20
5L18 A2 $30 gray 20 20
5L19 A2 $50 crimson 25 *35*
5L20 A2 $100 olive 10.50 9.00
Nos. 5L10-5L20 (11) 12.20 10.80

Seventh anniv. of Shantung Communist Postal Administration. The overprint on the $5, character "yu" meaning "Posts," obliterates Japanese flag on tower, erroneously included in design. Value, imperfs. of Nos. 5L10-5L12, 5L13a, 5L14-5L20 on different paper, set $75.

Train and Postal Runner (1949.2.7) A3 Mao, Soldiers, Map A4

1949, Apr. Litho. *Perf. 8 to 11*
5L21 A3 $1 brt emer 15 15
5L22 A3 $2 blue grn 15 15
5L23 A3 $3 dk red 15 15
5L24 A3 $5 brown 15 15
5L25 A3 $10 ultra 30 15
5L26 A3 $13 brt vio 15 15
5L27 A3 $18 brt blue 15 15
5L28 A3 $21 vermilion 15 15
5L29 A3 $30 slate 15 18
5L30 A3 $50 crimson 18 18
5L31 A3 $100 olive 38 38
Set value 1.45 1.55

7th anniv. of Shantung P. O., Feb. 7. Imperf. sets were sold by the Philatelic Dept., Tientsin P.O. Value $25. See Nos. 5L69-5L76. For surcharges see People's Republic of China Nos. 77-81.

1949, Apr. *Perf. 9½ to 11 and comp.*
5L32 A4 $1 brt emer 15 15
5L33 A4 $2 blue grn 15 15
5L34 A4 $3 dull red 15 15
5L35 A4 $5 brown 15 15
5L36 A4 $10 ultra 15 15
5L37 A4 $13 brt vio 15 15
5L38 A4 $18 brt blue 15 15
5L39 A4 $21 vermilion 15 15
5L40 A4 $30 gray 15 15
5L41 A4 $50 crimson 15 15
5L42 A4 $100 olive 1.40 1.40
Set value 2.10 2.10

Victory of Hwai-Hai (Hwaiying and Haichow). Imperf. sets were sold by the Philatelic Dept., Tientsin P.O. Value, set $60.

Stamps of China, Sun Yat-sen Type of 1949, Surcharged in Red or Black

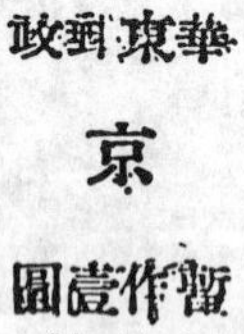

(Nanking)
a

(Wuhu)
b

1949, May 4 Engr. *Perf. 12½*
5L43 A94 (a) $1 on $10 grn (895, R) 50 50
a. Perf. 13 3.00 3.00
5L44 A94 (a) $3 on $20 vio brn (896) 50 50
a. Perf. 13 75 2.00
b. Perf. 14 5.50 5.50
c. Surcharge inverted 200.00

Sun Yat-sen Type A94 Surcharged Type "b"

Lithographed, Engraved
1949, May *Perf. 12½, 14*
5L45 $30 on $1000 dp bl (901 7.50 5.00
5L46 $30 on $1000 bl (894) 7.50 5.00
5L47 $50 on $200 org red (899) 7.50 5.00

5L48 $100 on $5000 lt bl (903, R) 16.00 13.00
5L49 $300 on $10,000 sep (904, R) 50.00 40.00
5L50 $500 on $200 org red (899) 75.00 60.00
Nos. 5L45-5L50 (6) 163.50 128.00

Many varieties exist.

China Nos. 913a and 913 Surcharged in Blue, Green, Black or Red

(East China)

1949, May Litho. *Perf. 12½*

5L51 A95 $5 on 50c on $20 brn, II (B) 14.00 10.00
a. Green surcharge 100.00 50.00
5L52 A95 $10 on 50c on $20 brn, II 14.00 10.00
5L53 A95 $20 on 50c on $20 red brn, II (R) 14.00 10.00
a. Type I (R) 20.00 20.00
Nos. 5L51-5L53 (3) 42.00 30.00

Stamps of China, Sun Yat-sen Type of 1949, Surcharged in Black or Red

(Hangchow)

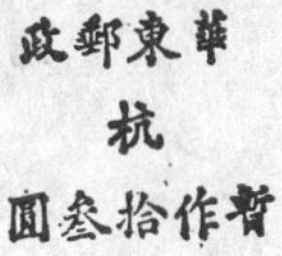

Engr., Litho. (No. 5L57)
1949, June 25 *Perf. 14, 12½*

5L54 A94 $1 on $1 org (886) 1.40 1.25
5L55 A94 $3 on $20 vio brn (896, R) 75 70
5L56 A94 $5 on $100 org brn (890) 3.75 1.65
5L57 A94 $5 on $100 dk org brn (898) 1.75 50
5L58 A94 $10 on $50 dk Prus grn (889, R) 13.00 10.50
5L59 A94 $13 on $10 grn (895) 28 60
Nos. 5L54-5L59 (6) 20.93 15.20

East China Liberation Area

Maps of Shanghai and Nanking — A5

1949, May 30 Litho. *Perf. 8½ to 11*

5L60 A5 $1 org ver 15 20
5L61 A5 $2 blue grn 15 20
5L62 A5 $3 brt vio 15 15
5L63 A5 $5 vio brn 15 15
5L64 A5 $10 ultra 15 15
5L65 A5 $30 slate 15 20
5L66 A5 $50 carmine 15 40
5L67 A5 $100 olive 15 20
5L68 A5 $500 orange 1.25 1.50
Set value 2.00

Liberation of Shanghai and Nanking. Many shades, paper and perforation varieties and imperfs. exist.

Train and Postal Runner Type Dated "1949"

1949, July-1950, Feb. *Perf. 12½, 14*

5L69 A3 $10 dp ultra 15 15
5L70 A3 $15 org ver 15 40
a. $15 red, perf. 14 25 15
5L71 A3 $30 slate grn 15 15
a. Perf. 12½ 15 15
5L72 A3 $50 carmine 15 40
5L73 A3 $60 bl grn, perf. 14 15 1.00
5L74 A3 $100 ol, perf. 14 2.25 40
5L75 A3 $1600 vio bl ('50) 55 3.00
5L76 A3 $2000 brn vio ('50) 70 3.00
Nos. 5L69-5L76 (8) 4.25 8.50

Chu Teh, Mao, Troops with Flags
A7

Mao Tse-tung
A8

1949, Aug. 17 *Perf. 12½*

5L77 A7 $70 orange 15 15
5L78 A7 $270 crimson 15 15
5L79 A7 $370 emerald 30 30
5L80 A7 $470 vio brn 50 40
5L81 A7 $570 blue 15 30
Nos. 5L77-5L81 (5) 1.25 1.30

22nd anniv. of the People's Liberation Army. For similar type see Southwest China A1.

1949, Oct.

5L82 A8 $10 dk blue 1.50 5.00
5L83 A8 $15 vermilion 1.90 2.50
5L84 A8 $70 brown 15 15
5L85 A8 $100 vio brn 15 15
5L86 A8 $150 orange 15 15
5L87 A8 $200 grnsh gray 15 15
5L88 A8 $500 gray bl 15 15
5L89 A8 $1000 rose 15 15
5L90 A8 $2000 emerald 15 15
Nos. 5L82-5L90 (9) 4.45 8.55

For surcharges see People's Republic of China Nos. 82-84.

Stamps of China, Sun Yat-sen Type of 1949 Surcharged in Black or Red

1949, Nov. Litho. *Perf. 12½*

5L91 A94 $400 on $200 org red (899) 24.00 65
5L92 A94 $1000 on $50 grnsh gray (897, R) 2.00 65
5L93 A94 $1200 on $100 dk org brn (898) 15 1.50
5L94 A94 $1600 on $20,000 ap grn (905) 15 65
5L95 A94 $2000 on $1000 dp bl (952,R) 15 65
a. Perf. 14 90.00 25.00
Nos. 5L91-5L95 (5) 26.45 4.10

EAST CHINA PARCEL POST STAMPS

Parcel Post Stamps of China 1945-48 Surcharged

(Shantung)

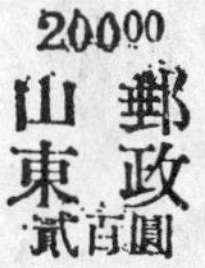

1949, Aug. 1 Engr. *Perf. 13*

5LQ1 PP1 $200 on $500 grn 8.00 8.00
5LQ2 PP1 $500 on $1000 bl 8.00 8.00

Type PP3 *Perf. 13½*

5LQ3 $200 on $200,000 dk grn 40.00 30.00
5LQ4 $200 on $10,000,000 sage grn 8.00 8.00
5LQ5 $500 on $7000 dl bl 90.00 60.00
5LQ6 $500 on $50,000 indigo 8.00 8.00
5LQ7 $1000 on $10,000 car rose 8.00 8.00
5LQ8 $1000 on $100,000 dk rose brn 8.00 8.00
5LQ9 $1000 on $300,000 pink 6.00 6.00
5LQ10 $1000 on $500,000 vio brn 50.00 45.00
5LQ11 $1000 on $8,000,000 org ver 8.00 8.00
5LQ12 $2000 on $5,000,000 dl vio 12.00 12.00
5LQ13 $2000 on $6,000,000 brn blk 12.00 12.00
5LQ14 $3000 on $30,000 ol 20.00 17.50
5LQ15 $3000 on $70,000 org brn 20.00 17.50
5LQ16 $5000 on $3,000,000 dl bl 25.00 22.50
Nos. 5LQ1-5LQ16 (16) 331.00 278.50

China Type A97, No. 987 Surcharged

$200 $500
$1000 $2000
$5000 $10,000

1949, Sept. 7 Litho. *Perf. 12½*

5LQ17 $200 on $10 32.50 15.00
5LQ18 $500 on $10 32.50 15.00
5LQ19 $1000 on $10 32.50 15.00
5LQ20 $2000 on $10 32.50 15.00
5LQ21 $5000 on $10 32.50 15.00
5LQ22 $10,000 on $10 32.50 15.00
Nos. 5LQ17-5LQ22 (6) 195.00 90.00

Flying Geese Type of China, 1949, and China Nos. 984-986 Surcharged in Red or Black

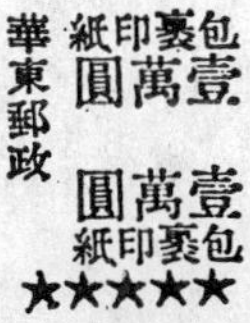

1950, Jan. 28

5LQ23 A97 $5000 on 10c bl vio (R) 97.50 50.00
5LQ24 A97 $10,000 on $1 brn org 97.50 50.00
5LQ25 A97 $20,000 on $2 bl 97.50 50.00
5LQ26 A97 $50,000 on $5 car rose 97.50 50.00
Nos. 5L23-5L26 (4) 390.00 200.00

Parcel Post Stamps of China Type PP3, Nos. Q1-Q2, Q12-Q13 Surcharged in Red or Black

1950, Jan. 28 Engr. *Perf. 13, 13½*

5LQ27 $5000 on $500 grn (R) 20 50.00
5LQ28 $10,000 on $1000 bl (R) 120.00 50.00
5LQ29 $20,000 on $3000 bl grn 120.00 80.00
5LQ30 $50,000 on $5000 org red 12.00 50.00
Nos. 5L27-5L30 (4) 252.20 230.00

CENTRAL CHINA

The Central Chinese Liberation Area included the provinces of Honan, Hupeh, Hunan and Kiangsi. The area was established between August and September, 1949, following the liberation of Hankow.

All Stamps Issued without Gum

Hupeh Postal and Telegraph Administration

Stamps of China, Sun Yat-sen Type A94 of 1949, Surcharged ("Chinese P.O., Temporary Use")

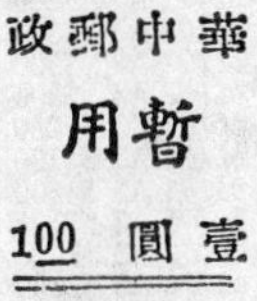

Engraved; Lithographed
1949, June 4 *Perf. 14, 12½*

Thin parallel lines

6L1 $1 on $200 red org (891) 75 75
6L2 $6 on $10,000 sep (904) 75 75
6L3 $15 on $1 org (886) 75 75
6L4 $30 on $100 org brn (890) 3.50 3.50
6L5 $30 on $100 dk org brn (898) 75 75
6L6 $50 on $20 vio brn (896) 12.00 12.00
6L7 $80 on $1000 dp bl (901) 2.25 2.25

Thick parallel lines

6L8 $1 on $200 red org (891) 3.50 3.50
6L9 $3 on $5000 lt bl (903) 50 50
6L10 $10 on $500 rose lil (892) 50 50
6L11 $10 on $500 rose lil (900) 3.50 3.50
6L12 $50 on $20 vio brn (888) 3.50 3.50
6L13 $50 on $20 vio brn (896) 1.00 1.00
6L14 $80 on $1000 bl (894) 3.50 3.50
6L15 $80 on $1000 dp bl (901) 12.00 12.00
6L16 $100 on $50 dk Prus grn (903) 1.50 1.50
Nos. 6L1-6L16 (16) 50.25 50.25

Kiangsi Postal and Telegraph Administration.

Central Trust Revenue Stamps of China Surcharged ("People's Post, Kiangsi")

(same size) — A1

$30

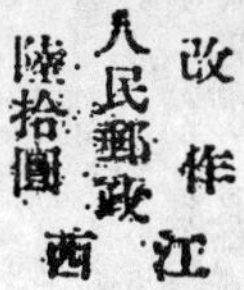

$60

1949, June 20 Engr. *Perf. 12½*

6L17 A1 $3 on $30 pur 1.00 1.00
6L18 A1 $15 on $15 red org 1.00 1.00
6L19 A1 $30 on $50 dk bl 1.00 1.00
6L20 A1 $60 on $50 dk bl 1.00 1.00
6L21 A1 $130 on $15 red org 1.00 1.00

The $15 surcharge has 3 characters in left vertical row, the $130 surcharge has 5.

Same Surcharge on Sun Yat-sen Issues of China, 1945-49

Engraved, Lithographed
Perf. 14, 12½

6L22 A82 $1 on $250 dp lil (746) 3.00 3.00
6L23 A94 $5 on $1000 dp bl (901) 3.00 3.00
6L24 A94 $5 on $2000 vio (902) 3.00 3.00
6L25 A94 $5 on $5000 lt bl (903) 1.00 1.00
6L26 A94 $10 on $1000 bl (894) 3.00 3.00
6L27 A82 $20 on $4000 gray 1.00 1.00
6L28 A73 $30 on $100 dk car 3.00 3.00
6L29 A82 $30 on $20,000 rose pink 1.00 1.00
6L30 A94 $80 on $500 rose lil (900) 1.00 1.00
6L31 A94 $100 on $1000 dp bl (901) 1.00 1.00
6L32 A82 $200 on $250 dp lil 2.00 2.00
Nos. 6L17-6L32 (16) 27.00 27.00

Central China Posts and Telegraph Administration

Farmer, Soldier and Worker
A2 A3

I- Top white line of square character (yuan) at upper left does not touch left vertical stroke. No gap in shading between soldier's feet.
II- Top line connects with left vertical stroke. Gap in shading between feet.

Perf. 10 to 11½ & Comp.
1949 Litho.

6L33 A2 $1 orange 7.25 7.25
6L34 A2 $3 brn org 2.50 2.50
6L35 A2 $6 emerald 2.50 2.50
6L36 A3 $7 yel brn 40 40
6L37 A2 $10 bl grn 15 24
6L38 A3 $14 org brn 14.00 7.25
6L39 A2 $15 ultra 32 15
6L40 A2 $30 grn, type I 15 15
a. Type II 15 15
6L41 A3 $35 gray bl 9.50 7.25
6L42 A2 $50 rose vio 8.00 4.75
6L43 A3 $70 dp grn 15 15
6L44 A2 $80 pink 40 40
6L45 A3 $100 bl grn 24 24
6L46 A3 $220 rose red 3.25 3.25
Nos. 6L33-6L46 (14) 48.81 36.48

For surcharges and overprints see Nos. 6L63-6L65, 6L66-6L73, 6L75, 6L90-6L98, 6L100-6L108.

Star Enclosing Map of Hankow Area — A4

Two types of $500:
I- Thick numerals of "500." No period after "500."
II- Thin numerals and period.

Two types of $1000:
I- No period after "1000."
II- Period after "1000."

1949, July

6L48	A4	$110 org brn	25	25
6L49	A4	$130 violet	3.75	25
6L50	A4	$200 dp org	15	25
6L51	A4	$290 brown	1.50	75
6L52	A4	$370 dk bl	1.50	50
6L53	A4	$500 lt bl, I	3.75	1.00
a.		$500 blue, II	18.00	6.00
6L54	A4	$1000 dk red, I	25.00	2.50
a.		$1000 dull red, II	18.00	4.50
6L55	A4	$5000 brown	75	2.00
6L56	A4	$10,000 brt pink	1.50	3.00
		Nos. 6L48-6L56 (9)	38.15	10.50

For surcharges and overprints see Nos. 6L74, 6L76-6L81, 6L99, 6L109.

Hankow River Customs Building A5

River Wall, Wuchang — A6

Design: $290, $370, River scene, Hanyang.

1949, Aug. 16 *Perf. 11, Imperf.*

6L57	A5	$70 green	1.00	80
6L58	A5	$220 crimson	1.00	80
6L59	A5	$290 brown	1.00	80
6L60	A5	$370 brt blue	1.00	80
6L61	A6	$500 purple	1.00	*1.00*
6L62	A6	$1000 vermilion	1.00	*1.50*
		Nos. 6L57-6L62 (6)	6.00	*5.70*

Liberation of Hankow, Wuchang and Hanyang.
For overprints see Nos. 6L82-6L87.

Nos. 6L35, 6L39 and 6L40 Surcharged in Red ("Honan Renminbi Currency")

柒拾圓 人民幣
省南河

1949, July

6L63	A2	$7 on $6 emer	6.50	6.50
6L64	A2	$14 on $15 ultra	7.50	7.50
6L65	A2	$70 on $30 grn	11.00	11.00
		Nos. 6L63-6L65 (3)	25.00	25.00

Surcharge shown is for $70. The $7 has 5 characters in left column and no bottom line.

Issues of 1949 Overprinted ("Honan Renminbi Currency")

人民幣 河南省

1949, Aug.

6L66	A2	$3 brn org	85	85
6L67	A3	$7 yel brn	85	85
6L68	A2	$10 bl grn	1.75	1.75
6L69	A3	$14 org brn	1.75	1.75
6L70	A2	$30 yel grn (6L40a)	1.75	1.75
6L71	A3	$35 gray bl	85	85
6L72	A2	$50 rose vio	6.25	6.25
6L73	A3	$70 dp grn	1.75	1.75
6L74	A4	$110 org brn	12.00	12.00
6L75	A3	$220 rose red	3.50	3.50
6L76	A4	$290 brown	12.00	12.00
6L77	A4	$370 blue	14.00	14.00
6L78	A4	$500 bl, II	20.00	20.00
6L79	A4	$1000 dk red, I	30.00	30.00
6L80	A4	$5000 brown	77.50	77.50
6L81	A4	$10,000 brt pink	165.00	165.00
		Nos. 6L66-6L81 (16)	349.80	349.80

Width of the overprint varies slightly.

Nos. 6L57-6L62 Overprinted ("Honan Renminbi Currency")

人民幣 河南省

1949, Aug. *Perf. 11, Imperf.*

6L82	A5	$70 green	4.50	4.50
6L83	A5	$220 crimson	4.50	4.50
6L84	A5	$290 brown	4.50	4.50
6L85	A5	$370 brt bl	4.50	4.50
6L86	A6	$500 purple	4.50	4.50
6L87	A6	$1000 vermilion	4.50	4.50
		Nos. 6L82-6L87 (6)	27.00	27.00

Width of overprint on Nos. 6L82-6L85, 7mm; on Nos. 6L86-6L87, 12mm.

Changchow Issue Surcharged in Red ("Honan Renminbi Currency")

(same size) Mao Tse-tung — A7

1949, Sept. *Perf. 10*

6L88	A7	$290 on $30 yel grn	45.00	30.00
6L89	A7	$370 on $30 yel grn	60.00	40.00

Issues of 1949 Surcharged

作 改
圓 佰 貳
200.00

1950, Jan.

6L90	A2	$200 on $1	45	2.00
6L91	A2	$200 on $3	2.75	2.00
6L92	A2	$200 on $6	45	2.00
6L93	A3	$200 on $7	2.75	2.00
6L94	A3	$200 on $14	2.75	2.00
6L95	A3	$200 on $35	2.75	2.00
6L96	A3	$200 on $70	2.75	2.00
6L97	A2	$200 on $80	2.75	2.00
6L98	A3	$200 on $220	2.75	2.00
6L99	A4	$200 on $370	45	2.00
6L100	A3	$300 on $70	45	2.00
6L101	A2	$300 on $80	45	2.00
6L102	A3	$300 on $220	15	2.00
6L103	A2	$1200 on $3	27.50	15.00
6L104	A3	$1200 on $7	5.50	3.00
6L105	A3	$1500 on $14	8.00	2.00
6L106	A2	$2100 on $1	37.50	15.00
6L107	A2	$2100 on $6	37.50	15.00
6L108	A3	$2100 on $35	11.50	2.50
6L109	A4	$5000 on $370	4.50	3.00
		Nos. 6L90-6L109 (20)	153.65	81.50

Two types of surcharge exist, differing in spacing of characters in top row.

CENTRAL CHINA PARCEL POST STAMPS

Star and Map of Hankow — PP1

1949, Nov. **Litho.** *Perf. 11, 11½*

6LQ1	PP1	$5000 brown	85	2.00
6LQ2	PP1	$10,000 scarlet	6.00	4.00
6LQ3	PP1	$20,000 dk sl grn	2.25	6.00
6LQ4	PP1	$50,000 vermilion	85	20.00
		Nos. 6LQ1-6LQ4 (4)	9.95	32.00

SOUTH CHINA

The South China Liberation Area included the provinces of Kwangtung and Kwangsi and Hainan Island. The South China Postal and Telegraph Administration was organized on or about Nov. 4, 1949.

All Stamps Issued without Gum

Pearl River Bridge, Canton — A1

1949, Nov. 4 **Litho.** *Imperf.*

7L1	A1	$10 green	15	15
7L2	A1	$20 sepia	15	15
7L3	A1	$30 violet	15	15
7L4	A1	$50 carmine	15	15
7L5	A1	$100 ultramarine	20	15
		Set value	45	35

For surcharges see Nos. 7L19-7L23.

China Nos. 993-995 With Additional Overprint in Red ("Liberation of Swatow")

暫 解
用 放

1949, Nov. 9

7L6	A94	2½c on $500 rose lil (993)	12.50	12.50
a.		Handstamped	30.00	30.00
7L7	A94	2½c on $500 rose lil (994)	20.00	20.00
a.		Handstamped	30.00	30.00
7L8	A94	15c on $10 grn (995)	15.00	15.00
a.		Handstamped	40.00	40.00

On Unit Issues of China, 1949

7L9	A96	org (959)	15.00	12.00
7L10	AP5	bl grn (C62)	15.00	12.00
7L11	SD2	red vio (E12)	15.00	12.00
7L12	R2	car (F2)	15.00	12.00

On Sun Yat-sen and Flying Geese Issues of China

7L13	A94	2c org (974)	30.00	30.00
7L14	A94	4c bl grn (975)	350.00	250.00
7L15	A94	10c dp lil (976)	18.00	14.00
7L16	A94	20c bl (978)	18.00	14.00
7L17	A97	$1 brn org (984)	18.00	14.00
7L18	A97	$10 bl grn (987)	230.00	190.00
		Nos. 7L6-7L18 (13)	771.50	607.50

Nos. 7L1-7L3 Surcharged in Red or Green

300

圓佰叁作改

1950, Jan.

7L19	A1	$300 on $30 vio (R)	3.50	1.00
7L20	A1	$500 on $20 brn (R)	3.50	1.00
7L21	A1	$800 on $30 vio (G)	3.50	1.25
7L22	A1	$1000 on $10 gray grn (R)	3.50	1.00
7L23	A1	$1000 on $20 brn (R)	3.50	1.00
		Nos. 7L19-7L23 (5)	17.50	5.25

SOUTHWEST CHINA

The Southwest China Liberation Area included the provinces of Kweichow, Szechwan, Yunnan, Sikang and Tibet. The Southwest Postal and Telegraph Administration was organized on or about Nov. 15, 1949 after the liberation of Kweiyang, capital of Kweichow Province.

All Stamps Issued without Gum

Chu Teh, Mao and Troops — A1

1949, Dec. **Litho.** *Perf. 12½*

8L1	A1	$10 deep blue	1.50	1.00
8L2	A1	$20 rose claret	15	1.00
8L3	A1	$30 dp org	15	50
8L4	A1	$50 gray grn	35	50
8L5	A1	$100 carmine	15	50
8L6	A1	$200 blue	50	60
8L7	A1	$300 bl vio	75	1.00
8L8	A1	$500 dk gray	1.90	1.90
8L9	A1	$1000 pale pur	3.75	3.75
8L10	A1	$2000 green	11.00	11.00
8L11	A1	$5000 orange	30.00	30.00
		Nos. 8L1-8L11 (11)	50.20	51.75

For surcharges and overprints see Nos. 8L21-8L29, 8L40-8L47, 8L55.

China Nos. 974-975, 984, 986-987 Surcharged ("Kweichow People's Post")

貳拾圓 人民郵政 改作
區 20.00 黔

1949, Dec. 1 *Perf. 12½*

8L12	A94	$20 on 2c org	4.50	4.50
8L13	A94	$50 on 4c bl grn	4.50	4.50
8L14	A97	$100 on $1 brn org	7.25	7.25
8L15	A97	$400 on $5 car rose	22.50	22.50
8L16	A97	$2000 on $10 bl grn	55.00	55.00
		Nos. 8L12-8L16 (5)	93.75	93.75

Map of China, Flag Planted in Southwest — A2

1950, Jan. **Litho.** *Perf. 9 to 11½*

8L17	A2	$20 dark blue	15	40
8L18	A2	$30 green	50	40
8L19	A2	$50 red	20	60
8L20	A2	$100 brown	20	60
		Nos. 8L17-8L20 (4)	1.05	2.00

Liberation of the Southwest.
For surcharges see #8L30-8L39, 8L56-8L59.

Nos. 8L5-8L6 Surcharged

圓仟貳作改

Perf. 12½

8L21	A1	$300 on $100 car	10.50	3.50
8L22	A1	$500 on $100 car	15	1.00
8L23	A1	$1200 on $100 car	70	2.00
8L24	A1	$1500 on $200 bl	70	2.00
8L25	A1	$2000 on $200 bl	17.50	10.50
		Nos. 8L21-8L25 (5)	29.55	19.00

Nos. 8L5-8L6 Overprinted ("East Szechwan")

（川東）

1950, Jan.

8L26	A1	$100 carmine	4.00	4.00
8L27	A1	$200 blue	4.00	4.00

Nos. 8L5-8L6 Handstamp Surcharged

壹仟伍百 改作

1950, Jan.

8L28	A1	$1200 on $100 car	15.00	15.00
8L29	A1	$1500 on $200 bl	60.00	15.00

Many varieties, including wide and narrow settings, exist.

Nos. 8L17-8L20 Surcharged in Black or Red

叁仟圓 改作 伍仟圓
$3000 $5000

壹萬圓 貳萬圓 伍萬圓
$10,000 $20,000 $50,000

陸拾圓 $60
叁佰圓 $300

1950 *Perf. 9 to 11½*

8L30	A2	$60 on $30	20.00	6.00
8L31	A2	$150 on $30	20.00	6.00
8L32	A2	$300 on $20 (R)	2.00	2.50
8L33	A2	$300 on $100	20.00	6.00
8L34	A2	$1500 on $100	24.00	15.00
8L35	A2	$3000 on $50	6.00	10.00
8L36	A2	$5000 on $50	5.00	12.00
8L37	A2	$10,000 on $50	50.00	25.00
8L38	A2	$20,000 on $50	3.00	20.00
8L39	A2	$50,000 on $50	5.00	30.00
		Nos. 8L30-8L39 (10)	155.00	132.50

Nos. 8L5-8L7 Overprinted ("West Szechwan") 川 西

1950, Jan. *Perf. 12½*

8L40	A1	$100 carmine	20.00	20.00
8L41	A1	$200 pale blue	20.00	20.00
8L42	A1	$300 blue violet	20.00	20.00
		Nos. 8L40-8L42 (3)	60.00	60.00

Nos. 8L4-8L7 Surcharged

蓉
圓百伍作改

蓉
圓仟貳作改
$2000

1950, Jan.

8L43	A1	$500 on $100	8.00	6.00
a.		Narrow spacing	70.00	60.00
8L44	A1	$800 on $100	8.00	6.00
8L45	A1	$1000 on $50	10.00	8.00
8L46	A1	$2000 on $200	17.50	15.00
8L47	A1	$3000 on $300	32.50	27.50
		Nos. 8L43-8L47 (5)	76.00	62.50

Two lines of surcharge 7mm apart on No. 8L43, 4mm on No. 8L43a.

China Nos. 975 and 977 Surcharged

政郵民人 政郵民人

蓉 圓百貳 $200
蓉 圓仟壹 $1000

Perf. 12½, 13 or Compound

1950, Jan.

8L48	A94	$100 on 4c	8.00	8.00
8L49	A94	$200 on 4c	15.00	15.00
8L50	A94	$800 on 16c	47.50	47.50
8L51	A94	$1000 on 16c	135.00	135.00
		Nos. 8L48-8L51 (4)	205.50	205.50

Unit Issue of China Overprinted ("Southwest People's Post") 人民郵政 西南

1950, Jan. **Engr.** *Perf. 12½*

8L52	A96	orange	125.00	100.00
a.		Rouletted	125.00	120.00
8L53	SD2	red violet	125.00	120.00
8L54	R2	carmine	125.00	120.00
		Nos. 8L52-8L54 (3)	375.00	340.00

On No. 8L54, space between overprint columns is 3mm and right column is raised to height of left.

Nos. 8L3, 8L17-8L20 Surcharged in Black or Red

改作 捌百元

1950, Mar. *Perf. 12½, 9 to 11½*

8L55	A1	$800 on $30	42.00	35.00
8L56	A2	$1000 on $50	9.00	7.50
8L57	A2	$2000 on $100	12.00	9.00
8L58	A2	$4000 on $20 (R)	35.00	25.00
8L59	A2	$5000 on $30	55.00	45.00
		Nos. 8L55-8L59 (5)	153.00	121.50

CILICIA

LOCATION — A territory of Turkey, in Southeastern Asia Minor
GOVT. — Former French occupation
AREA — 6,238 sq. mi.
POP. — 383,645
CAPITAL — Adana

British and French forces occupied Cilicia in 1918 and in 1919 its control was transferred to the French. Eventually part of Cilicia was assigned to the French Mandated Territory of Syria but by the Lausanne Treaty of 1923 which fixed the boundary between Syria and Turkey, Cilicia reverted to Turkey.

40 Paras = 1 Piaster

Issued under French Occupation

The overprint on Nos. 2-93 is often found inverted, double, etc.

Numbers in parentheses are those of basic Turkish stamps.

Turkish Stamps of 1913-19 Handstamped CILICIE

Perf. 11½, 12, 12½, 13½

1919 **Unwmk.**

On Pictorial Issue of 1913

2	A24	2pa red lil (254)	45	45
3	A25	4pa dk brn (255)	45	45
4	A27	6pa dk bl (257)	3.50	2.25
5	A32	1¾pi sl & red brn (262)	75	50

On Issue of 1915

6	A17	1pi bl (300)	40	40
7	A21	20pa car rose (318)	45	45
9	A22	20pa car rose (330)	55	55

On Commemorative Issue of 1916

10	A41	20pa ultra (347)	40	40
11	A41	1pi vio & blk (348)	65	65
12	A41	5pi yel brn & blk (349)	40	40

On Issue of 1916-18

13	A44	10pa grn (424)	40	40
14	A47	50pa ultra (428)	6.00	2.00
15	A51	25pi car, *straw* (434)	60	60
16	A52	50pi car (437)	75	75
17	A52	50pi ind (438)	8.00	8.00

On Issue of 1917

18	A53	5pi on 2pa Prus bl (547)	2.00	1.65

On Issue of 1919

19	A47	50pa ultra (555)	5.00	1.50
20	A48	2pi org brn & ind (556)	5.00	1.50
21	A49	5pi pale bl & blk (557)	3.75	90

On Newspaper Stamp of 1916

22	N3	5pa on 10pa gray grn (P137)	45	45

On Semi-Postal Stamps of 1916

23	A17	1pi bl (B19)	40	40
24	A21	20pa car rose (B28)	30	30
25	A21	1pi ultra (B29)	75	75
		Nos. 2-25 (23)	41.40	25.70

Turkish Stamps of 1913-18 Handstamped CILICIE

1919

On Pictorial Issue of 1913

31	A24	2pa red lil (254)	40	40
32	A25	4pa dk brn (255)	40	40

On Issue of 1915

33	A17	1pi bl (300)	50	50
34	A22	20pa car rose (330)	40	40

On Commemorative Issue of 1916

35	A41	20pa ultra (347)	1.00	1.00
36	A41	1pi vio & blk (348)	25	25

On Issue of 1917

40	A53	5pi on 2pa Prus bl (547)	1.25	1.25

On Newspaper Stamp of 1916

41	N3	5pa on 10pa gray grn (P137)	1.00	1.00

On Semi-Postal Stamps of 1916

42	A17	1pi blue (B19)	50	50
43	A21	20pa car rose (B28)	40	40
		Nos. 31-43 (10)	6.10	6.10

Turkish Stamps of 1913-19 Handstamped *Cilicie*

1919

On Pictorial Issue of 1913

51	A24	2pa red lil (254)	40	40
52	A25	4pa dk brn (255)	40	40

On Issue of 1915

53	A17	1pi blue (300)	25	25
55	A22	5pa ocher (328)	2.50	1.40
56	A22	20pa car rose (330)	25	25

On Commemorative Issue of 1916

57	A41	20pa ultra (347)	40	40
58	A41	1pi vio & blk (348)	40	40
59	A41	5pi yel brn & blk (349)	50	50

On Issue of 1916

59A	A17	1pi blue (372)	27.50	27.50

On Issue of 1916-18

60	A43	5pa org (421)	3.50	3.50
61	A46	1pi dl vio (426)	2.00	1.40
63	A52	50pi grn, *straw* (439)	15.00	5.00

On Issue of 1917

64	A53	5pi on 2pa Prus bl (547)	5.50	2.50

On Newspaper Stamp of 1916

65	N3	5pa on 10pa gray grn (P137)	40	40

On Semi-Postal Stamps of 1916

66	A17	1pi blue (B19)	2.50	1.00
67	A19	20pa car (B26)	7.50	3.00
68	A21	20pa car rose (B28)	57.50	22.50
69	A21	20pa car rose (B31)	1.50	1.50
		Nos. 51-69 (18)	128.00	72.30

Turkey No. 424 Handstamped *T.E.O. Cilicie*

1919

71	A44	10pa green	40 40

"T.E.O." stands for "Territoires Ennemis Occupés."

Turkish Stamps of 1913-19 Overprinted in Black, Red or Blue — T. E. O. Cilicie

In this setting there are various broken and wrong font letters and the letter "i" is sometimes replaced by a "t."

1919 **On Pictorial Issue of 1913**

75	A30	1pi blue (R) (260)	20	15

On Issue of 1915

76	A21	20pa car rose (318)	2.00	2.00

On Commemorative Issue of 1916

77	A41	20pa ultra (347)	20	20
78	A41	1pi vio & blk (348)	40	25

On Issue of 1916-18

79	A43	5pa org (Bl) (421)	15	15
80	A44	10pa grn (424)	20	20
81	A45	20pa dp rose (Bk) (425)	5.00	5.00
82	A45	20pa dp rose (Bl) (425)	15	15
83	A48	2pi org brn & ind (429)	25	25
83C	A49	5pi pale bl & blk (R) (430)	30	25
84	A51	25pi car, *straw* (434)	5.00	3.50
85	A52	50pi grn, *straw* (439)	32.50	25.00

On Issue of 1917

85A	A53	5pi on 2pa Prus bl (547)		
86	A53	5pi on 2pa Prus bl (548)	1.75	1.75

On Newspaper Stamps of 1916-19

87	N3	5pa on 10p gray grn (P137)	1.00	1.00
88	N4	5pa on 2pa ol grn (P173)	15	15

On Semi-Postal Stamps of 1915-17

90	A21	20pa car rose (B28)	1.10	1.10
91	A41	10pa car (B42)	15	15
92	A11	10pa on 20pa vio brn (B38)	15	15
93	SP1	10pa red vio (B46)	25	25

It is understood that the newspaper and semi-postal stamps overprinted "Cilicie" were used as ordinary postage stamps.

A1

1920 **Blue Surcharge** *Perf. 11½*

98	A1	70pa on 5pa red	50	50
99	A1	3½pi on 5pa red	1.10	1.10

Nos. 98-99 exist with surcharge double, inverted, double with one inverted, "OCCUPTTION," etc. Value, $1 to $2 each.

French Offices in Turkey No. 26 Surcharged — T. E. O 20 PARAS

1920 *Perf. 14x13½*

100	A3	20pa on 10c rose red	30	30
a.		"PARAS" omitted	9.00	9.00
b.		Surcharged on back	1.65	1.65

Three types of "20" exist on No. 100.

Stamps of France, 1900-17, Surcharged — O. M. F. Cilicie 5 PARAS

1920

101	A16	5pa on 2c vio brn	25	25
102	A22	10pa on 5c grn	30	30
103	A22	20pa on 10c red	40	40
104	A22	1pi on 25c bl	50	50
105	A20	2pi on 15c gray grn	4.00	4.00
106	A18	5pi on 40c red & gray bl	6.00	6.00
107	A18	10pi on 50c bis brn & lav	5.50	5.50
108	A18	50pi on 1fr cl & ol grn	37.50	37.50
109	A18	100pi on 5fr dk bl & buff	425.00	425.00
		Nos. 101-109 (9)	479.45	479.45

Nos. 106 to 109 surcharged in four lines.

"O.M.F." stands for "Occupation Militaire Francaise."

Stamps of France, 1917, Surcharged — O. M. F. Cilicie SAND. EST 20 PARAS

1920

110	A16	5pa on 2c vio brn	2.50
111	A22	10pa on 5c grn	2.50
112	A22	20pa on 10c red	1.25
113	A22	1pi on 25c blue	1.25
114	A20	2pi on 15c gray grn	6.00

115 A18 5pi on 40c red & gray bl 37.50
116 A18 20pi on 1fr cl & ol grn 52.50
Nos. 110-116 (7) 103.50

On Nos. 115 and 116 "SAND. EST" is placed vertically. "Sand. Est" is an abbreviation of Sandjak de l'Est (Eastern County).

Nos. 110-116 were prepared for use, but never issued.

Stamps of France, 1900-17, Surcharged

O. M. F.
Cilicie
10
PARAS

1920

117	A16	5pa on 2c vio brn	15	15
a.		Inverted surcharge	5.00	4.75
b.		Double surcharge	6.00	
c.		"Cillilie"	4.75	4.75
d.		Surcharge 5pi (error)	10.00	10.00
119	A22	10pa on 5c grn	15	15
a.		Inverted surcharge	5.00	4.50
b.		Surch. 5pa (error), invtd.	10.00	10.00
121	A22	20pa on 10c red	15	15
a.		Inverted surcharge	5.00	4.50
b.		Surch. 10pa (error), invtd.	11.00	11.00
122	A22	1pi on 25c bl	15	15
a.		Double surcharge	8.00	
b.		Inverted surcharge	5.00	4.50
123	A20	2pi on 15c gray grn	25	25
a.		Double surcharge	8.00	
b.		Inverted surcharge	5.00	4.50
124	A18	5pi on 40c red & gray bl	55	55
a.		Double surcharge	12.00	
b.		Inverted surcharge	7.00	6.50
c.		"PIASRTES"	10.00	10.00
125	A18	10pi on 50c bis brn & lavender	1.00	1.00
a.		"PIASRTES"	10.00	10.00
126	A18	50pi on 1fr claret & ol grn	3.00	3.00
a.		"PIASRTES"	12.50	12.50
b.		Inverted surcharge	14.00	12.00
127	A18	100pi on 5fr dk bl & buff	7.50	7.50
a.		"PIASRTES"	25.00	25.00
		Nos. 117-127 (9)	12.90	12.90

This surcharge has "O.M.F." in thicker letters than the preceding issues.

There were two printings of this surcharge which may be distinguished by the space of 1 or 2mm between "Cilicie" and the numeral.

For overprints see Nos. C1-C2.

AIR POST STAMPS

Nos. 123 and 124 Handstamped

POSTE PAR AVION

Perf. 14x13½

1920, July 15 **Unwmk.**

C1 A20 2pi on 15c gray grn
C2 A18 5pi on 40c red & gray bl
a. "PIASRTES"

A very limited number of Nos. C1 and C2 were used on two air mail flights between Adana and Aleppo. At a later date impressions from a new handstamp were struck "to oblige" on stamps of the regular issue of 1920 (Nos. 123, 124, 125 and 126) that were in stock at the Adana Post Office.

Counterfeits exist.

POSTAGE DUE STAMPS

Turkish Postage Due Stamps of 1914 Handstamped

Handstamped **CILICIE**

1919 **Unwmk.** ***Perf. 12***

J1	D1	5pa claret	1.75	1.75
J2	D2	20pa red	1.75	1.75
J3	D3	1pi dark blue	3.25	3.25
J4	D4	2pi slate	3.25	3.25
		Nos. J1-J4 (4)	10.00	10.00

Handstamped **CILICIE**

J5	D1	5pa claret	1.50	1.50
J6	D2	20pa red	1.50	1.50
J7	D3	1pi dark blue	4.00	4.00
J8	D4	2pi slate	3.25	3.25
		Nos. J5-J8 (4)	10.25	10.25

Handstamped *Cilicie*

J9	D1	5pa claret	1.65	1.65
J10	D2	20pa red	1.65	1.65
J11	D3	1pi dark blue	3.25	3.25
J12	D4	2pi slate	4.00	4.00
		Nos. J9-J12 (4)	10.55	10.55

Postage Due Stamps of France Surcharged

O. M. F.
Cilicie
2
PIASTRES

1921

J13	D2	1pi on 10c choc	3.25	3.25
J14	D2	2pi on 20c olive grn	3.50	3.50
J15	D2	3pi on 30c red	4.00	4.00
J16	D2	4pi on 50c vio brn	3.25	3.25
		Nos. J13-J16 (4)	14.00	14.00

COCHIN CHINA

LOCATION — The southernmost state of French Indo-China in the Cambodian Peninsula.
GOVT. — French Colony
AREA — 26,476 sq. mi.
POP. — 4,615,968
CAPITAL — Saigon

100 Centimes = 1 Franc

Surcharged in Black on Stamps of French Colonies:

5 a **5 C. CH.** b **5** c

1886-87 **Unwmk.** ***Perf. 14x13½***

1	A9(a)	5c on 25c yel, *straw*	90.00	60.00
2	A9(b)	5c on 2c brn, *buff*	6.00	6.00
3	A9(b)	5c on 25c yel, *straw*	7.00	7.00
4	A9(c)	5c on 25c blk, *rose* ('87)	18.00	17.00
a.		Double surch., one of type b	*1,750.*	*900.00*
b.		Triple surch., two of type b		
c.		Inverted surcharge		
		Nos. 1-4 (4)	121.00	90.00

15 / 15

1888

5 A9 15c on half of 30c brn, *bis* 16.00

No. 5 was prepared but not issued.

The so-called Postage Due stamps were never issued.

Stamps of Cochin China were superseded by those of Indo-China in 1892.

COLOMBIA

LOCATION — On the northwest coast of South America, bordering on the Caribbean Sea and the Pacific Ocean
GOVT. — Republic
AREA — 456,535 sq. mi.
POP. — 28,240,000 (est. 1984)
CAPITAL — Bogota

In 1810 the Spanish Viceroyalty of New Granada gained its independence and with Venezuela and Ecuador formed the State of Greater Colombia. In 1832 this state split into three independent units as Venezuela, Ecuador and the Republic of New Granada. The name of the country has been, successively, Granadine Confederation (1858-61), United States of New Granada (1861), United States of Colombia (1861-65), and the Republic of Colombia (1885 to date).

100 Centavos = 1 Peso

Catalogue values for unused stamps in this country are for Never Hinged items, beginning with Scott 594 in the regular postage section, Scott B1 in the semi-postal section, Scott C200 in the airpost section, Scott CE1 in the airpost special delivery section, Scott E2 in the special delivery section, and Scott RA33 in the postal tax section.

Values of early Colombia stamps vary according to condition. Quotations for Nos. 1-34 are for fine copies. Very fine to superb specimens sell at much higher prices, and inferior or poor copies sell at reduced prices, depending on the condition of the individual specimen.

In the earlier days many towns did not have handstamps for canceling and stamps were canceled with pen and ink. Pen cancellations, therefore, do not indicate fiscal use. (Postage stamps were not used for revenue purposes.) Values of Nos. 1-128 are for pen-canceled specimens. Those with handstamped cancellations sell for considerably more.

Fractions of many Colombian stamps of both early and late issues are found canceled, their use to pay postage having been tolerated even though forbidden by the postal laws and regulations. Many are known to have been made for philatelic purposes.

Watermarks

Wmk. 116- Crosses and Circles

Wmk. 127- Quatrefoils

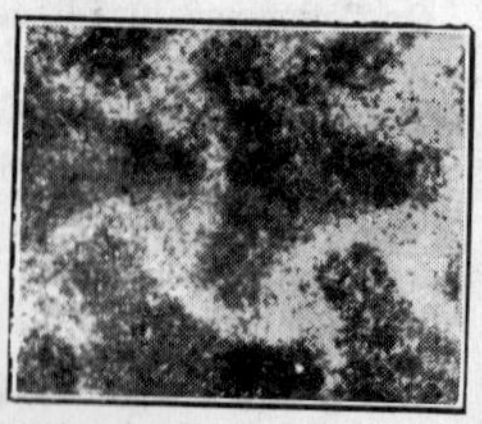
Wmk. 194- Multiple Curvilinear Triangles

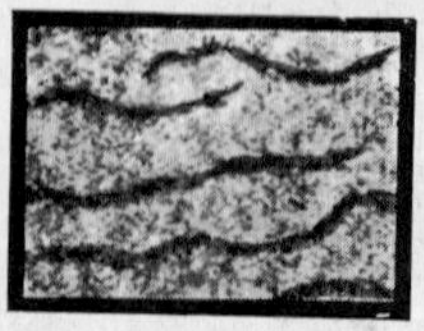
Wmk. 229- Wavy Lines

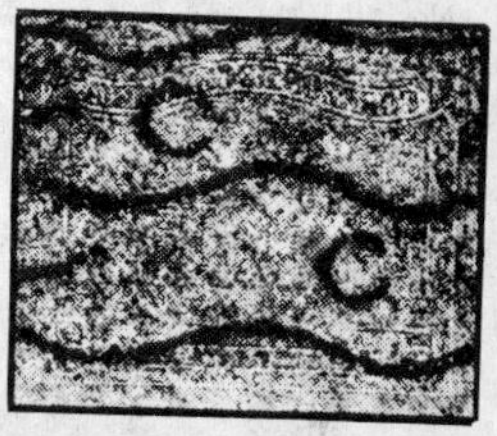
Wmk. 255- Wavy Lines and C Multiple

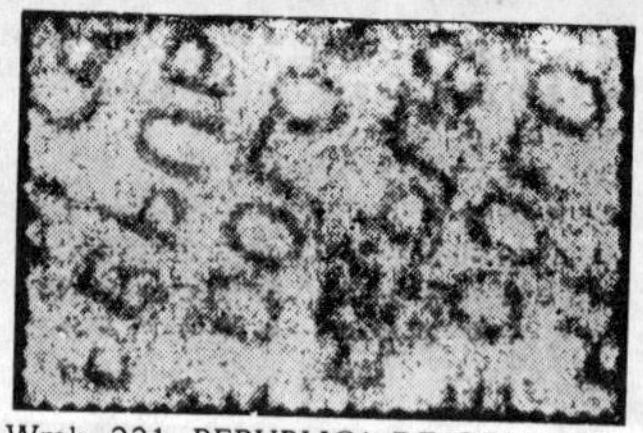
Wmk. 331- REPUBLICA DE COLOMBIA

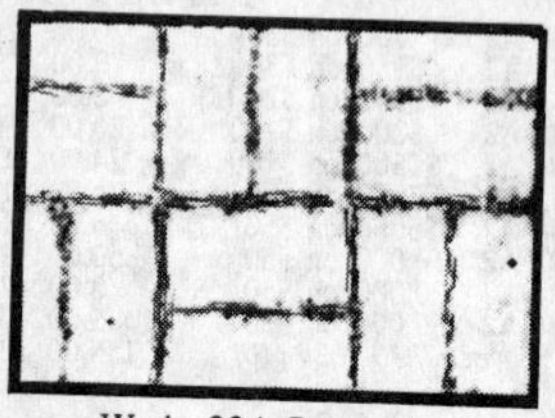
Wmk. 334- Rectangles

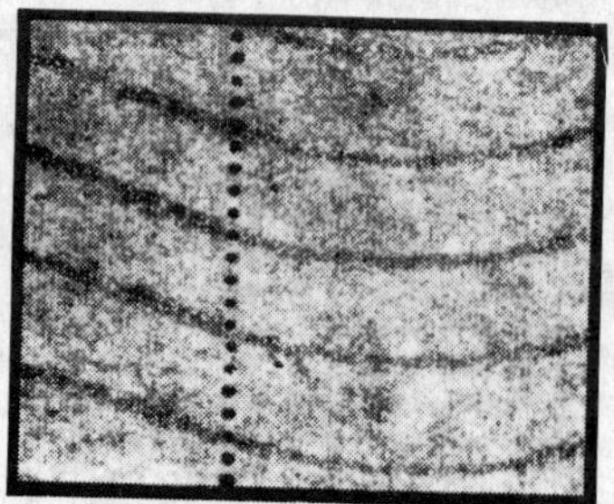
Wmk. 346- Parallel Curved Lines

Granadine Confederation

Coat of Arms
A1 A2

Type A1- Asterisks in frame. Wavy lines in background.

Type A2- Diamond-shaped ornaments in frame. Straight lines in background. Numerals larger.

1859 **Unwmk.** **Litho.** ***Imperf.***

Wove Paper

1	A1	2½c green	70.00	77.50
a.		2½c yellow green	70.00	77.50
2	A1	5c blue	95.00	62.50
a.		Tête bêche pair	*2,750.*	*5,750.*
3	A1	5c violet	175.00	80.00
b.		"50" instead of "5"		
4	A1	10c red brn	80.00	57.50
a.		10c buff	80.00	57.50
6	A1	20c blue	80.00	50.00
a.		20c gray blue	80.00	50.00
b.		Se-tenant with 5c		
c.		Tête bêche pair	*25,000.*	*25,000.*
7	A1	1p carmine	50.00	85.00
a.		1p rose	50.00	85.00
8	A1	1p rose, *bluish*	250.00	

The 10c green is an essay.

Reprints of No. 7 are in brown rose or brown red. Wavy lines of background are much broken; no dividing lines between stamps.

1860

Laid Paper

9 A2 5c lilac 200.00 150.00

Wove Paper

10	A2	5c gray lilac	55.00	45.00
a.		5c lilac	55.00	45.00
11	A2	10c yel buff	50.00	40.00
a.		Tête bêche pair	*5,500.*	
12	A2	20c blue	125.00	100.00

United States of New Granada

Arms of New Granada — A3

1861

13 A3	2½c black	875.00	250.00
14 A3	5c yellow	250.00	125.00
a.	5c buff	250.00	125.00
16 A3	10c blue	750.00	125.00
17 A3	20c red	350.00	175.00
18 A3	1p pink	750.00	275.00

There are 54 varieties of the 5c, 20c, and 1 peso.
Forgeries exist of Nos. 13-18.

United States of Colombia

Coat of Arms
A4 A5 A6

1862

19 A4	10c blue	150.	85.
20 A4	20c red	*2,750.*	500.
21 A4	50c green	150.	110.
22 A4	1p red lilac	400.	110.
23 A4	1p red lil, *bluish*	*3,250.*	*1,300.*

No. 23 is on a thinner, coarser wove paper than Nos. 19-22.

1863

24 A5	5c orange	60.00	45.00
a.	Star after "Cent"	70.00	52.50
25 A5	10c blue	140.00	17.50
a.	Period after "10"	150.00	20.00
26 A5	20c red	140.00	55.00
a.	Star after "Cent"	150.00	60.00
b.	Transfer of 50c in stone of 20c	*14,000.*	*4,500.*

Bluish Paper

28 A5	10c blue	100.00	25.00
a.	Period after "10"	110.00	26.00
29 A5	50c green	125.00	55.00
a.	Star after "Cent"	130.00	60.00

Ten varieties of each.

1864

Wove Paper

30 A6	5c orange	45.00	27.50
a.	Tête bêche pair	350.00	325.00
31 A6	10c blue	35.00	11.00
a.	Period after 10	35.00	11.00
32 A6	20c scarlet	60.00	40.00
33 A6	50c green	50.00	40.00
34 A6	1p red violet	225.00	125.00

Two varieties of each.

Arms of Colombia
A7 A9

A8

1865

35 A7	1c rose	7.50	7.50
a.	bluish pelure paper	17.50	15.00
36 A8	2½c black, *lilac*	14.00	9.00
37 A9	5c yellow	27.50	14.00
a.	5c orange	27.50	14.00
38 A9	10c violet	40.00	3.00
39 A9	20c blue	40.00	14.00
40 A9	50c green	70.00	37.50
41 A9	50c grn (small figures)	70.00	37.50
42 A9	1p vermilion	77.50	12.50
a.	1p rose red	77.50	12.50
b.	Period after "PESO"	85.00	14.00

Ten varieties of each of the 5c, 10c, 20c, and 50c, and six varieties of the 1 peso. No. 36 was used as a carrier stamp.

A10

A11

A12

A13

A14

A15

A16

1866

White Wove Paper

45 A10	5c orange	42.50	20.00
46 A11	10c lilac	10.00	3.50
a.	Pelure paper	14.00	9.00
47 A12	20c light blue	25.00	15.50
a.	Pelure paper	40.00	32.50
48 A13	50c green	10.50	9.00
49 A14	1p rose red, *bluish*	57.50	22.50
a.	1p vermilion	57.50	22.50
51 A15	5p blk, *green*	300.00	150.00
52 A16	10p blk, *vermilion*	225.00	140.00

There are several varieties of the 1 peso having the letters "U," "N," "S" and "O" smaller.

A17

A18

A19

A20

A21

TEN CENTAVOS:
Type I- "B" of "COLOMBIA" over "V" of "CENTAVOS".
Type II- "B" of "COLOMBIA" over "VO" of "CENTAVOS."
ONE PESO:
Type I- Long thin spear heads. Diagonal lines in lower part of shield.
Type II- Short thick spear heads. Horizontal and a few diagonal lines in lower part of shield.
Type III- Short thick spear heads. Crossed lines in lower part of shield. Ornaments at each side of circle are broken. (See No. 97.)

1868

53 A17	5c orange	42.50	37.50
54 A18	10c lil (I)	2.50	75
a.	10c red violet (I)	2.50	75
b.	10c lilac (II)	2.50	75
c.	10c red violet (II)	2.50	75
d.	Printed on both sides	5.00	1.75
55 A19	20c blue	1.75	85
56 A20	50c yel grn	2.00	1.40
57 A21	1p ver (II)	2.50	1.50
a.	Tête bêche pair	100.00	85.00
b.	1p rose red (I)	35.00	20.00
c.	1p rose red (II)	2.50	1.50
	Nos. 53-57 (5)	51.25	42.00

See Nos. 83-84, 96-97.
Counterfeits or reprints.
10c- There is a large white dot at the upper left between the circle enclosing the "X" and the ornament below.
50c- There is a shading of dots instead of dashes below the ribbon with motto. There are crossed lines in the lowest section of the shield instead of diagonal or horizontal ones.
1p- The ornaments in the lettered circle are broken. There are crossed lines in the lowest section of the shield. These counterfeits, or reprints, are on white paper, wove and laid, on colored wove paper and in fancy colors.

A22

Two varieties

1869-70

Wove Paper

59 A22	2½c black, *violet*	2.75	1.75
a.	Laid paper ('70)	190.00	190.00
b.	Laid batonné paper ('70)	17.50	17.50

Nos. 59, 59a and 59b were used as carrier stamps.
Counterfeits, or reprints, are on magenta paper wove or ribbed.

A23

A24

1870

Wove Paper

62 A23	5c orange	1.25	1.00
a.	5c yellow	1.25	1.00
63 A24	25c black, *blue*	10.00	9.50

See No. 89.
In the counterfeits, or reprints, of No. 63, the top of the "2" of "25" does not touch the down stroke. The counterfeits are on paper of various colors.

A25

A26

5 pesos. The ornament at the left of the "C" of "Cinco" cuts into the "C," and the shading of the flag is formed of diagonal lines.
10 pesos. The stars have extra rays between the points, and the central part of the shield has some horizontal lines of shading at each end.

1870

Surface Colored, Chalky Paper

64 A25	5p blk, *green*	60.00	47.50
65 A26	10p blk, *vermilion*	70.00	47.50

See Nos. 77-79, 125-126.

A27

A28

A29

TEN CENTAVOS:
Type I- "S" of "CORREOS" 2½mm high. First "N" of "NACIONALES" small.
Type II- "S" of "CORREOS" 2mm high. First "N" of "NACIONALES" wide.

1871-74

Thin Porous Paper

66 A27	1c green ('72)	2.25	2.25
67 A27	1c rose ('73)	2.25	2.25
a.	1c carmine ('73)	2.25	2.25
68 A28	2c brown	1.00	1.00
a.	2c red brown	1.00	1.00
69 A29	10c vio (I) ('74)	1.50	1.25
a.	10c lilac (I) ('74)	1.50	1.25
b.	10c violet (II) ('74)	1.50	1.25
c.	10c lilac (II) ('74)	1.50	1.25
d.	Laid paper, as #69 ('72)	85.00	85.00
e.	Laid paper, as "b" ('72)	85.00	85.00
	Nos. 66-69 (4)	7.00	6.75

Counterfeits or reprints.
1c- The outer frame of the shield is broken near the upper left corner and the "A" of "Colombia" has no cross-bar.
2c- There are scratches across "DOS" and many white marks around the letters on the large "2." The counterfeits, or reprints, are on white wove and bluish white laid paper.

Condor — A30

Liberty Head
A31 A32

5 pesos, redrawn- The ornament at the left of the "C" only touches the "C," and the shading of the flag is formed of vertical and diagonal lines.
10 pesos, redrawn- The stars are distinctly five pointed, and there is no shading in the central part of the shield.

1877

Wove Paper

73 A30	5c purple	4.25	1.50
a.	5c lilac	4.25	1.50

74 A31 10c bis brn 2.00 60
a. 10c red brown 2.00 60
b. 10c violet brown 2.00 60
75 A32 20c blue 2.50 90
a. 20c violet blue 5.25 2.50
77 A26 10p blk, *rose* 70.00 50.00
78 A25 5p blk, *lt grn*, redrawn 25.00 25.00
79 A26 10p blk, *rose*, redrawn 10.00 2.00
a. 10p blk, *dark rose*, redrawn 10.00 2.00
Nos. 73-79 (6) 113.75 80.00

Stamps of the issues of 1871-77 are known with private perforations of various gauges, also with sewing machine perforation.

In the counterfeits, or reprints, of the 5 pesos the ornament at the left of the "C" of "Cinco" is separated from the "C" by a black line.

In the counterfeits, or reprints, of the 10 pesos the outer line of the double circle containing "10" is broken at the top, below "OS" of "Unidos," and the vertical lines of shading contained in the double circle are very indistinct. There is a colorless dash below the loop of the "P" of "Pesos."

1876-79

Laid Paper

80 A30 5c lilac 50.00 50.00
81 A31 10c brown 27.50 20.00
82 A32 20c blue 60.00 50.00
83 A20 50c green ('79) 62.50 47.50
84 A21 1p pale red (II) ('79) 40.00 11.00
Nos. 80-84 (5) 240.00 178.50

1879

Wove Paper

89 A24 25c green 24.00 25.00

1881

Blue Wove Paper

93 A30 5c violet 12.00 8.50
a. 5c lilac 12.00 8.50
94 A31 10c brown 7.00 1.90
95 A32 20c blue 7.00 2.75
96 A20 50c yel grn 7.75 5.50
97 A21 1p ver (III) 10.50 5.50
Nos. 93-97 (5) 44.25 24.15

For types of 1p, see note over No. 53.

Reprints of the 10c and 20c are much worn. On the 10c the letters "TAVOS" of "CENTAVOS" often touch. On the 20c the letters "NT" of "VEINTE" touch and the left arm of the "T" is too long. Reprints of the 25c, 50c and 1p have the characteristics previously described. The reprints are on white wove or laid paper, on colored papers, and in fancy colors. Stamps on green paper exist only as reprints.

A34

A35

A36

1 centavo- The period before "UNION" is round and there are rays between the stars and the condors.

2 centavos- The "2's" and "C's" in the corners are placed upright.

5 centavos- The last star at the right almost touches the frame.

10 centavos- The letters of the inscription are thin; there are rays between the stars and the condor.

1881 ***Imperf.***

White Wove Paper

103 A34 1c green 3.00 3.00
104 A35 2c vermilion 1.25 1.10
a. 2c rose 1.50 1.10
106 A34 5c blue 3.50 1.25
a. Printed on both sides
107 A36 10c violet 2.50 85
108 A34 20c black 2.75 1.40
Nos. 103-108 (5) 13.00 7.60

The stamps of this issue are found with perforations of various gauges, also sewing machine perforation, all of which are unofficial.

See Nos. 112, 114-115.

Liberty Head — A37

A37a

1881 ***Imperf.***

109 A37 1c blk, *green* 2.00 3.50
110 A37 2c blk, *lilac rose* 2.00 3.50
111 A37 5c blk, *lilac* 5.00 1.25
Nos. 109-111 (3) 9.00 8.25

Nos. 109 to 111 are found with regular or sewing machine perforation, unofficial.

Reprints:

1c- The top line of the stamp and the top frame extend to the left. 2c. There is a curved line over the scroll below the "AV" of "CENTAVOS."

5c- There are scratches across the "5" in the upper left corner. All three values were reprinted on the three colors of paper of the originals.

Redrawn

1 centavo- The period before "UNION" is square and the rays between the stars and the condor have been wholly or partly erased.

2 centavos- The "2's" and "C's" in the corners are placed diagonally.

5 centavos- The last star at the right touches the wing of the condor.

10 centavos- The letters of the inscription are thick; there are no rays under the stars; the last star at the right touches the wing of the condor and this wing touches the frame.

1883 ***Imperf.***

112 A34 1c green 3.75 3.75
113 A37a 2c rose 1.25 1.25
114 A34 5c blue 3.00 85
a. 5c ultramarine 3.00 85
b. Printed on both sides, reverse ultra 20.00 17.50
115 A36 10c violet 4.00 1.25
Nos. 112-115 (4) 12.00 7.10

The stamps of this issue are found with regular or sewing machine perforation, privately applied.

A38

A39

1883 ***Perf. 10½, 12, 13½***

116 A38 1c gray grn, *grn* 70 70
a. Imperf., pair 3.50 3.50
117 A39 2c red, *rose* 70 1.00
a. 2c org red, *rose* 70 1.00
b. 2c red, *buff* 5.00 5.00
c. Imperf., pair (#117 or 117a) 3.50 3.50
d. "DE LOS" in very small caps 10.00 10.00
118 A38 5c blue, *bluish* 1.75 1.25
a. 5c dk bl, *bluish* 1.75 85
b. 5c blue 2.50 1.75
c. Imperf., pair (#118 or 118a) 6.00 6.00
d. As "b," imperf., pair 8.50 8.50
119 A39 10c org, *yel* 85 1.10
a. "DE LOS" in large caps 45.00 20.00
b. Imperf., pair 5.25 5.25
120 A39 20c vio, *lilac* 1.00 1.10
a. Imperf., pair 3.50 3.50
122 A38 50c brn, *buff* 2.00 2.50
a. Perf. 12 2.00 2.50
123 A38 1p claret, *bluish* 3.75 1.50
a. Imperf., pair 12.50 12.50
Nos. 116-123 (7) 10.75 9.15

Redrawn Types of 1877

1883 (?) ***Perf. 10½, 12***

125 A25 5p orange brown 7.50 4.00
126 A26 10p black, *gray* 7.50 4.00

1886 ***Perf. 10½, 11½, 12***

127 A38 5p brown, *straw* 5.50 5.50
a. Imperf., pair 25.00 25.00
128 A38 10p black, *rose* 6.75 6.75
a. Imperf., pair 25.00 25.00

Republic of Colombia

A40

Simón Bolívar — A41

Pres. Rafael Núñez — A42

1886 ***Perf. 10½ and 13½***

129 A40 1c grn, *grn* 1.25 60
a. Imperf., pair 5.00 5.00
130 A41 5c blue, *bl* 1.25 35
a. 5c ultra, *blue* 1.25 35
b. Imperf., pair (#130) 5.00 5.00
131 A42 10c orange 2.75 60
a. Imperf., pair 7.00 7.00
b. Pelure paper 3.50 85
Nos. 129-131 (3) 5.25 1.55

Gen. Antonio Jose de Sucre y Alcala — A43

Gen. Antonio Nariño — A44

1887

133 A43 2c org red, *rose* 1.75 85
a. 2c orange red, *yellowish* 4.50 4.50
b. 2c orange red 5.25 5.25
c. Imperf., pair (#133) 7.75 7.75
134 A44 20c pur, *grysh* 2.25 85
a. Imperf., pair 6.25 6.25
b. Pelure paper 2.75 1.75

Impressions of No. 134 on white, blue or greenish blue paper were not regularly issued.

Stamps inscribed "Colombia" that show the Panama Canal area were used in Panama and can be found in Vol. 4.

Arms — A45

Nariño — A46

1888

135 A45 50c brn, *buff* 1.25 1.40
a. Imperf., pair 4.50 4.50
136 A45 1p claret, *bluish* 6.00 1.75
137 A45 1p claret 2.50 1.25
138 A45 5p org brn 6.25 4.25
139 A45 5p black 11.00 7.00
140 A45 10p black, *rose* 13.00 5.25
Nos. 135-140 (6) 40.00 20.90

See Nos. 154, 156-157.

1889

141 A46 20c pur, *grayish* 1.40 1.00
a. Imperf., pair 6.75 6.75

Impressions on white, blue or greenish blue paper were not regularly issued.

A47

A48

A49

A50

A51

1890-91 ***Perf. 10½, 13½, 11***

142 A47 1c grn, *grn* 1.40 1.25
143 A48 2c org red, *rose* 60 70
144 A49 5c bl, *grnsh bl* 1.00 35
a. 5c deep blue, *blue* 1.00 35
b. Imperf., pair 4.00 4.00
146 A50 10c brn, *yel* 60 35
a. 10c brown, *buff* 60 35
147 A51 20c vio, pelure paper 2.75 3.50
Nos. 142-147 (5) 6.35 6.15

A52

A52a

A53

A53a

A54

Perf. 10½, 12, 13½, 14 to 15½

1892-99

Ordinary Paper

148 A47 1c red, *yel* 55 28
149 A52 2c red, *rose* 27.50 27.50
150 A52 2c green 35 22
a. 2c yellow green 35 22
151 A49 5c blk, *buff* 5.00 28
152 A52a 5c org brn, *pale buff* 75 20
a. 5c red brown, *salmon* ('97) 75 20
153 A50 10c bis brn, *rose* 52 28
a. 10c brown, *brownish* 52 28
154 A53 20c brn, *bl* 52 30
a. 20c red brown, *blue* 52 30
b. 20c yel brn, *grnsh bl* ('97) 3.50 9.00
c. 20c brown, *buff* ('97) 12.50 9.00
155 A45 50c vio, *vio* 85 52
156 A53a 50c red vio, *vio* ('99) 1.10
157 A54 1p bl, *grnsh* 1.40 35
a. 1p blue, *buff* 1.40 35
158 A45 5p red, *pale rose* 5.50 2.25
159 A45 10p blue 10.50 2.50
a. Thin, pale rose paper 20.00 5.50
Nos. 148-159 (12) 54.54 34.68

Type A53a is a redrawing of type A45. The letters of the inscriptions are slightly larger and the numerals "50" slightly smaller than in type A45.

The 20c brown on white paper is believed to be a chemical changeling.

Nos. 148, 150-152a, 153-155, 157, 159 exist imperf. Value per pair, $5-$7.50.

A56

1899

162 A56 1c red, *yellow* 50 30
163 A56 5c red brn, *sal* 50 30
164 A56 10c brn, *lil rose* 1.50 75
165 A56 50c blue, *lilac* 1.00 95
Nos. 162-165 (4) 3.50 2.30

Cartagena Issues

A57

1899 **Blue Overprint** ***Imperf.***

167 A57 5c red, *buff* 24.00 24.00
a. Sewing machine perf. 24.00 24.00
168 A57 10c ultra, *buff* 24.00 24.00
a. Sewing machine perf. 24.00 24.00

Nos. 168 and 168a differ slightly from the illustration.

Bolivar No. 55 Overprinted with 7 Parallel Wavy Lines and:

A58

A59

A60

A61

Perf. 14 (#169), Sewing Machine Perf.

1899 **Purple Overprint**

169	A18 1c black	50.00	50.00
170	A58 1c brn, *buff*	17.00	17.00
a.	Altered from 10c	25.00	25.00
171	A59 2c blk, *buff*	17.00	17.00
a.	Altered from 10c	25.00	25.00
172	A60 5c mar, *grnsh bl*	14.00	14.00
a.	Perf. 12	14.00	14.00
b.	Without overprint	8.75	8.75
173	A61 10c red, *sal*	14.00	14.00
a.	Perf. 12	14.00	14.00
	Nos. 169-173 (5)	112.00	112.00

Types A58 and A59 illustrate Nos. 170a and 171a, which were made from altered plates of the 10c (No. 168). Nos. 170 and 171 were made from altered plate of the 5c denomination (No. 167), show part of the top flag of the "5" and differ slightly from the illustrations.

Nos. 170-173 exist imperf. Values about same as perf.

A62

1900 ***Imperf.***

Purple Overprint

174	A62 5c red	20.00	20.00
a.	Perf. 12	27.50	27.00

A63

A64

"Gobierno Provisorio" at Top

1900 **Litho.** ***Perf. 12 Vertically***

175	A63 1c (ctvo) blk, *bl grn*	35.00	6.00
a.	"cvo."	90.00	12.00
b.	"cvos."	35.00	6.00
c.	"centavo"	42.50	6.00
176	A63 2c black	25.00	3.50
177	A63 5c blk, *pink*	25.00	3.50
a.	Name at side (V)	50.00	6.50
178	A63 10c blk, *pink*	25.00	4.00
a.	Name at side (V)	50.00	7.50
179	A63 20c blk, *yellow*	35.00	6.00
a.	Name at side (G)	70.00	10.00
	Nos. 175-179 (5)	145.00	23.00

"Gobierno Provisional" at Top

Name at Side in Black or Green

180	A64 1c (ctvo.) blk, *bl grn*	35.00	5.00
a.	"centavo"	100.00	15.00
181	A64 2c blk, *bl grn*	20.00	4.00
182	A64 5c blk (G)	20.00	4.00
a.	"ctvos." smaller	40.00	6.00
183	A64 10c blk, *pink*	20.00	4.00
184	A64 20c blk, *yel* (G)	35.00	6.00
	Nos. 180-184 (5)	130.00	23.00

Issues of the rebel provisional government in Cucuta.

A65

A66

1901 ***Sewing Machine Perf.***

Purple Overprint

185	A65 1c black	85	85
a.	Without overprint	1.90	1.90
b.	Double overprint	2.00	2.00
c.	Imperf., pair	2.00	2.00
d.	Inverted overprint	1.00	1.00
186	A66 2c blk, *rose*	85	85
a.	Imperf., pair	2.00	2.00
b.	Without overprint	1.90	1.90
c.	Double overprint	2.00	2.00

A67

A68

1901

Rose Overprint

187	A67 1c blue	85	85
a.	Imperf., pair	3.00	3.00
188	A68 2c brown	85	85
a.	Imperf., pair	3.00	3.00
b.	Without overprint	85	85

A69

A70

Sewing Machine or Regular Perf. 12, 12½

1902

Magenta Overprint

189	A69 5c violet	1.75	1.75
a.	Without overprint	1.75	1.75
b.	Double overprint	1.75	1.75
c.	Imperf., pair	3.75	3.75
190	A70 10c yel brn	1.75	1.75
a.	Double overprint	1.75	1.75
b.	Imperf., pair	3.75	3.75
c.	Without overprint	1.75	1.75
d.	Printed on both sides	2.50	2.50

A71

A72

1902

Magenta Overprint

191	A71 5c yel brn	1.75	1.75
a.	Without overprint	1.65	1.65
b.	Imperf., pair	5.00	5.00
192	A71 10c black	1.25	1.25
a.	Without overprint	1.00	1.00
b.	Imperf., pair	7.50	7.50
193	A72 20c maroon	4.00	2.50
b.	Imperf., pair	12.50	12.50
	Nos. 191-193 (3)	7.00	5.50

Nos. 191-193 exist tête bêche. Value of 10c and 20c, each $12.50.

Washed copies of Nos. 167-174, 185-193 are offered as "without overprint."

Barranquilla Issues

Magdalena River — A75

Iron Quay at Sabanilla — A76

La Popa Hill — A77

1902-03 ***Imperf.***

194	A75 2c green	1.25	1.25
195	A75 2c dk bl	1.25	1.25
196	A75 2c rose	17.50	17.50
197	A76 10c scarlet	85	70
198	A76 10c orange	10.00	10.00
199	A76 10c rose	85	70
200	A76 10c maroon	1.40	1.40
201	A76 10c claret	1.40	1.40
202	A77 20c violet	2.75	2.75
a.	Laid paper		
203	A77 20c dl bl	7.50	7.50
204	A77 20c dl bl, *pink*	110.00	110.00
205	A77 20c car rose	16.00	16.00
	Nos. 194-205 (12)	170.75	170.45

Sewing Machine Perf. and Perf. 12

194a	A75 2c green	7.50	7.50
195a	A75 2c dark blue	7.50	7.50
196a	A75 2c carmine	35.00	35.00
197a	A76 10c scarlet	3.50	3.50
198a	A76 10c orange	27.50	27.50
199a	A76 10c rose	5.50	5.50
200a	A76 10c maroon	5.50	5.50
201a	A76 10c claret	5.50	5.50
202b	A77 20c purple	55	55
c.	20c lilac	55	55
203a	A77 20c dull blue	7.50	7.50
204a	A77 20c dull blue, *rose*	140.00	140.00
205b	A77 20c carmine rose	55.00	55.00
	Nos. 194a-205b (12)	300.55	300.55

See Nos. 240-245.

Cruiser "Cartagena" — A78

Bolívar — A79

General Próspero Pinzón — A80

A81

A82

1903-04 ***Imperf.***

209	A78 5c blue	2.00	2.00
210	A78 5c bister	2.75	2.75
211	A79 50c yellow	3.00	3.00
212	A79 50c green	3.50	3.50
213	A79 50c scarlet	3.50	3.50
214	A79 50c carmine	3.50	3.50
a.	50c rose	3.50	3.50
215	A79 50c pale brn	3.50	3.50
216	A80 1p yel brn	1.40	1.40
217	A80 1p rose	2.00	2.00
218	A80 1p blue	2.00	2.00
219	A80 1p violet	20.00	20.00
220	A81 5p claret	4.25	4.25
221	A81 5p pale brn	6.50	6.50
222	A81 5p bl grn	6.00	6.00
223	A82 10p pale grn	6.25	6.25
224	A82 10p claret	20.00	20.00
	Nos. 209-224 (16)	90.15	90.15

Nos. 216 and 217 measure 20½x26½mm and No. 218, 18x24mm. Stamps of this issue exist with forged perforations.

Perf. 12

209a	A78 5c blue	7.00	7.00
210a	A78 5c bister	7.50	7.50
211a	A79 50c yellow	12.50	12.50
b.	50c orange	12.50	12.50
212a	A79 50c green	20.00	20.00
213a	A79 50c scarlet	9.00	9.00
214b	A79 50c rose	9.00	9.00
215a	A79 50c pale brown	9.00	9.00
216a	A80 1p yellow brown	4.00	4.00
217a	A80 1p rose	6.00	6.00
218a	A80 1p blue	6.00	6.00
219a	A80 1p violet	50.00	50.00
220a	A81 5p claret	16.00	16.00
221a	A81 5p pale brown	18.00	18.00
222a	A81 5p blue green	15.00	15.00
223a	A82 10p pale green	25.00	25.00
224a	A82 10p claret	60.00	60.00
	Nos. 209a-224a (16)	274.00	274.00

Laid Paper

240	A76 10c dk bl, *lil*	5.00	5.00
241	A76 10c dk bl, *bluish*	3.00	3.00
242	A76 10c dk bl, *brn*	3.00	3.00
243	A76 10c dk bl, *sal*	7.00	7.00
244	A76 10c dk bl, *grnsh bl*	4.00	4.00
245	A76 10c dk bl, *dp rose*	3.00	3.00
	Nos. 240-245 (6)	25.00	25.00

Perf. 12

240a	A76 10c dk bl, *lilac*	10.50	10.50
241a	A76 10c dk bl, *bluish*	7.50	7.50
242a	A76 10c dk bl, *brn*	7.50	7.50
243a	A76 10c dk bl, *salmon*	55.00	55.00
244a	A76 10c dk bl, *grnsh bl*	16.00	16.00
245a	A76 10c dk bl, *deep rose*	7.50	7.50
	Nos. 240a-245a (6)	104.00	104.00

A82a

Imperf., Sewing Machine Perf.

1902 **Typeset**

255	A82a 10c black, *rose*	3.50	3.50
256	A82a 20c blk, *orange*	2.50	2.50

This issue was printed in either Cali or Popayan.

Medellin Issue

A83

1902

257	A83 1c grn, *straw*	22	42
258	A83 2c salmon, *rose*	22	42
259	A83 5c dp bl, *grnsh*	22	42
260	A83 10c pale brn, *straw*	22	42
261	A83 20c pur, *rose*	35	42
262	A83 50c dl rose, *grnsh*	1.75	2.50
263	A83 1p blk, *yellow*	3.50	5.25
264	A83 5p slate, *blue*	27.50	27.50
265	A83 10p dk brn, *rose*	17.50	17.50
	Nos. 257-265 (9)	51.48	54.85

For overprint see No. L8.

Imperf., Pairs

257a	A83 1c	8.50	8.50
258a	A83 2c	8.50	8.50
259a	A83 5c	8.50	8.50
260a	A83 10c	8.50	8.50
261a	A83 20c	8.50	8.50
262a	A83 50c	8.50	8.50
263a	A83 1p	22.50	22.50
264a	A83 5p	62.50	62.50
265a	A83 10p	50.00	50.00

Regular Issue

A84

A85

A86

A87

A88

A89

A90

A91

A92

1902 *Imperf.*

266	A84	2c blk, *rose*	16	16
267	A85	4c red, *grn*	18	18
268	A86	5c grn, *bl*	18	18
269	A87	10c blk, *pink*	18	18
c.		10c blk, *rose*	75	50
270	A88	20c brn, *buff*	18	18
271	A89	50c dk grn, *rose*	1.00	1.00
272	A90	1p pur, *buff*	42	42
273	A91	5p grn, *bl*	3.25	3.25
274	A92	10p grn, *pale grn*	10.00	5.00
		Nos. 266-274 (9)	15.55	10.55

For overprint see No. H13.

Sewing Machine Perf.

266a	A84	2c blk, *rose*	1.40	1.40
267a	A85	4c red, *grn*	1.25	1.25
268a	A86	5c grn, *blue*	1.50	1.50
269a	A87	10c blk, *pink*	1.50	1.50
270a	A88	20c brn, *buff*	2.50	2.00
271a	A89	50c dk grn, *rose*	5.00	4.00
272a	A90	1p pur, *buff*	6.00	5.00
273a	A91	5p grn, *blue*	27.50	27.50
274a	A92	10p grn, *pale grn*	50.00	50.00
		Nos. 266a-274a (9)	96.65	94.15

1903 *Perf. 12*

266b	A84	2c blk, *rose*	1.10	1.10
269b	A87	10c blk, *pink*	1.25	1.25
270b	A88	20c brn, *buff*	1.25	1.25
272b	A90	1p pur, *buff*	2.50	2.50
273b	A91	5p grn, *blue*	22.50	22.50
274b	A92	10p grn, *pale grn*	40.00	35.00
		Nos. 266b-274b (6)	68.60	63.60

1903 *Imperf.*

284	A85	4c blue, *grn*	22	22
285	A86	5c blue, *blue*	22	22
286	A88	20c blue, *buff*	22	22
288	A89	50c blue, *rose*	1.40	1.40
		Nos. 284-288 (4)	2.06	2.06

Sewing Machine Perf.

284a	A85	4c blue, *grn*	1.75	1.40
285a	A86	5c blue, *blue*	1.75	1.40
286a	A88	20c blue, *buff*	2.50	2.00
288a	A89	50c blue, *rose*	5.00	4.50
		Nos. 284a-288a (4)	11.00	9.30

Perf. 12

284b	A85	4c blue, *grn*	2.00	2.00
285b	A86	5c blue, *blue*	2.00	2.00
286b	A88	20c blue, *buff*	2.75	2.75
288b	A89	50c blue, *rose*	7.50	7.50
		Nos. 284b-288b (4)	14.25	14.25

A93

1904 **Pelure Paper** *Imperf.*

303	A93	½c yellow brn	1.00	1.00
304	A90	1c blue green	1.00	1.00
a.		1c yellow green	1.00	1.00
306	A84	2c blue	90	60
307	A86	5c carmine	1.00	1.00
308	A87	10c violet	1.00	90
		Nos. 303-308 (5)	4.90	4.50

For overprint see No. H13.

1904 *Perf. 13*

303a	A93	½c yellow brown	3.00	3.00
304b	A90	1c blue green	4.00	3.50
c.		1c yellow green	5.00	4.50
306a	A84	2c blue	2.50	2.50

Perf. 12

307a	A86	5c carmine	2.25	2.25
308a	A87	10c violet	2.25	2.25
		Nos. 303a-308a (5)	14.00	13.50

A94

A95

Pres. José Manuel Marroquín — A96

Imprint: "Lit. J.L.Arango Medellin. Col."

1904 **Wove Paper** *Perf. 12*

314	A94	½c yellow	65	15
315	A94	1c green	65	15
316	A94	2c rose	65	15
317	A94	5c blue	1.00	15
318	A94	10c violet	1.40	15
319	A94	20c black	1.40	22
320	A95	1p brown	15.00	2.50
321	A96	5p red & blk, *yel*	45.00	45.00
322	A96	10p bl & blk, *grnsh*	45.00	45.00
		Nos. 314-322 (9)	110.75	93.47

Redrawn

314a	A94	½c	65	15
315a	A94	1c	65	15
316a	A94	2c	65	15
317a	A94	5c	1.00	15
319a	A94	20c	1.40	22
		Nos. 314a-319a (5)	4.35	82

Imperf., Pairs

314b	A94	½c	2.50	2.50
315b	A94	1c	2.00	2.00
316b	A94	2c	2.50	2.50
317b	A94	5c	2.50	2.50
318a	A94	10c	3.25	3.25
319b	A94	20c	6.00	6.00
320a	A95	1p	50.00	50.00

On the redrawn types, the imprint is close to the base of the design instead of being spaced from it. On the redrawn 2c and 5c, the lower end of the vertical white line below "OR" of "CORREOS" forms a hook which turns to the right instead of to the left as in the originals.

See Nos. 325-330. For surcharges see Nos. 351-354, L1-L7, L9-L13, L15-L25.

A97

100p has different frame.

1903 *Imperf.*

323	A97	50p org yel, *pale pink*	70.00	70.00
324	A97	100p dk bl, *dk rose*	60.00	60.00

Imprint: "Lit. Nacional"

Perf. 10, 13, 13½ and Compound

1908

325	A94	½c orange	60	15
a.		½c yellow	60	15
b.		Imperf., pair	2.00	1.50
c.		Without imprint	4.00	4.00
326	A94	1c yel grn	60	15
a.		Without imprint	60	15
d.		Imperf., pair	3.00	2.50
327	A94	2c red	60	15
a.		2c carmine	60	15
b.		Imperf., pair	3.00	2.50
328	A94	5c blue	52	15
a.		Imperf., pair	5.00	4.00
329	A94	10c violet	*40.00*	70
330	A94	20c gray blk	*40.00*	50
		Nos. 325-330 (6)	*82.32*	
		Set value		1.45

The above stamps may be easily distinguished from those of 1904 by the perforation, by the height of the design, 24mm instead of 23mm, and by the "Lit. Nacional" imprint.

Camilo Torres A99

Policarpa Salavarrieta A100

Bolívar Demanding Liberation of Slaves — A105

Designs: 2c, Nariño. 5c, Bolívar. 10c, Francisco José de Caldas. 20c, Francisco de Paula Santander. 10p, Bolívar Resigning.

1910, Aug. **Engr.** *Perf. 12*

331	A99	½c violet & blk	48	38
a.		Center inverted	425.00	425.00
332	A100	1c deep green	38	38
333	A100	2c scarlet	32	25
334	A100	5c deep blue	1.25	45
335	A100	10c plum	10.00	5.00
336	A100	20c black brn	15.00	5.50
337	A105	1p dk violet	50.00	18.00
338	A105	10p claret	200.00	140.00
		Nos. 331-338 (8)	277.43	169.96

Colombian independence centenary.

Caldas A107

Monument to Battle of Boyacá A113

View of Cartagena — A114

Coat of Arms — A118

Designs: 1c, Torres. 2c, Narino. 4c, Santander. 5c, Bolivar. 10c, Jose Maria Cordoba. 1p, Sucre. 2p, Rufino Cuervo. 5p, Antonio Ricaurte y Lozano.

1917 **Engr.** *Perf. 14*

339	A107	½c bister	35	15
340	A107	1c green	30	15
341	A107	2c car rose	30	15
342	A107	4c violet	90	30
343	A107	5c dull blue	1.40	16
344	A107	10c gray	1.25	16
345	A113	20c red	3.00	18
346	A114	50c carmine	1.50	18
347	A107	1p brt blue	11.00	40
348	A107	2p orange	10.00	45
349	A107	5p gray	17.50	6.00
350	A118	10p dk brown	32.50	12.00
		Nos. 339-350 (12)	80.00	20.28

The 1c, 5c, 10c, 50c, 2p, 5p and 10p also exist perf. 11½ and 11½ compounded with 14.

Litho. varieties of Nos. 343, 345 and 346 are counterfeits made to defraud the government.

Imperforate copies of Nos. 339-350 are not known to have been regularly issued.

See Nos. 373-374, 400-405. For overprints and surcharges see Nos. 369-370, 377, 409-410, 440, C1, O3, O5-O9.

Nos. 318-319, 329-330 Surcharged in Red

Especie
Provisional
$ 0.00½

1918

On Issue of 1904

351	A94	½c on 20c black	1.00	25
352	A94	3c on 10c violet	2.50	70

On Issue of 1908

353	A94	½c on 20c gray blk	8.00	5.00
354	A94	3c on 10c violet	12.00	4.25
		Nos. 351-354 (4)	23.50	10.20

Nos. 351-354 inclusive exist with surcharge reading up or down. On one stamp in each sheet the letter "S" in "Especie" is omitted. All denominations exist with a small zero before the decimal in the surcharge.

A119

A120

1918 **Litho.** *Perf. 13½*

358	A119	3c red	50	15
a.		Imperf., pair	4.00	4.00

1920 **Engr.** *Perf. 14*

359	A120	3c red, *org*	30	15
a.		Imperf., pair	3.00	3.00

See Nos. 371-372. For surcharge see No. 453.

A121

A122

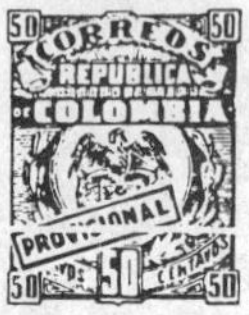
A123

Perf. 10, 13½ and Compound

1920-21 **Litho.**

360	A121	½c yellow	52	22
361	A121	1c green	85	15
362	A121	2c red	65	15
363	A122	3c green	65	15
a.		3c yellow green	65	15
364	A121	5c blue	95	22
365	A121	10c violet	3.00	1.50
366	A121	20c deep green	8.00	3.50
367	A123	50c dark red	8.00	3.50
		Nos. 360-367 (8)	22.62	9.39

The tablet with "PROVISIONAL" was added separately to each design on the various lithographic stones and its position varies slightly on different stamps in the sheet. For some values there were two or more stones, on which the tablet was placed at various angles.

Nos. 360-366 exist imperf.

See No. 375.

No. 342 Surcharged in Red

PROVICIONAL
$ 003
a

PROVISIONAL
$0.03
(15mm wide) — b

1921

369	A107 (a)	3c on 4c violet	80	25
a.		Double surcharge	13.00	
370	A107 (b)	3c on 4c violet	3.50	2.00

See No. 377.

Types of 1917-21

1923-24 **Engr.** *Perf. 13½*

371	A120	1½c chocolate	1.00	50
372	A120	3c blue	50	15
373	A107	5c claret ('24)	2.00	18
374	A107	10c blue	7.50	40

Litho.

375	A121	10c dark blue	10.00	6.00
		Nos. 371-375 (5)	21.00	7.23

No. 342 Surcharged in Red

PROVISIONAL
$003
(18mm wide)

1924

377 A107	3c on 4c vio	3.00	1.25
a.	Double surcharge	12.00	
b.	Double surch., one invtd.	12.00	
c.	With added surch. "3cs." in red		

A124

1924-25 Litho. *Perf. 10, 10x13½*

379 A124	1c red	70	18
380 A124	3c dp blue ('25)	70	18

Exist imperf. Value, each pair $5.

A125

A126

Black, Red or Green Surch. & Ovpt.

Imprint of Waterlow & Sons

1925 *Perf. 14, 14½*

382 A125	1c on 3c bis brn	30	15
383 A126	4c violet (R)	38	20
a.	Inverted surcharge	7.00	7.00

Imprint of American Bank Note Co.

Perf. 12

384 A125	1c on 3c bis brn	6.00	5.00
a.	Inverted surcharge	15.00	15.00
385 A126	4c violet (G)	40	30
a.	Inverted overprint	7.50	7.50
	Nos. 382-385 (4)	7.08	5.65

Correos

Provisional

Revenue stamps of basic types A125 and A126 were handstamped as above in violet or blue by the Cali post office in 1925, but were not authorized by the government. Denominations so overprinted are 1c, 2c, 3c, 4c and 5c.

A127

A128

Perf. 10, 13½x10

1926 Litho. Wmk. 194

395 A127	1c gray green	35	15
396 A128	4c deep blue	35	15

Exist imperf. Value, each pair $4.

Types of 1917 and

Sabana Station — A129

1926-29 Unwmk. Engr. *Perf. 14*

400 A107	4c deep blue	40	15
401 A118	8c dark blue	50	15
402 A107	30c olive bister	4.75	60
403 A129	40c brn & yel brn	7.50	1.00
404 A107	5p violet	7.50	70
a.	Perf. 11 ('29)	12.00	1.00
405 A118	10p green	12.00	2.00
a.	Perf. 11 ('29)	25.00	4.00
	Nos. 400-405 (6)	32.65	4.60

For surcharges and overprint see #09-410, O4.

Death of Bolívar A130

1930, Dec. 17 *Perf. 12½*

408 A130	4c dk blue & blk	28	24

Cent. of the death of Simón Bolívar. See Nos. C80-C82.

Nos. 400 and 402 Surcharged in Red or Dark Blue

1
CENTAVO

1932, Jan. 20 *Perf. 14*

409 A107	1c on 4c dp bl (R)	30	15
a.	Inverted surcharge	5.25	5.25
410 A107	20c on 30c ol bis	8.00	70
a.	Inverted surcharge	17.50	
b.	Double surcharge	17.50	

Emerald Mine — A131

Oil Wells — A132

Coffee Cultivation — A133

Platinum Mine — A134

Gold Mining A135

Christopher Columbus A136

Imprint: "Waterlow & Sons Ltd. Londres"

1932 Wmk. 229 *Perf. 12½*

411 A131	1c green	50	15
412 A132	2c red	50	15
413 A133	5c brown	55	15
414 A134	8c blue blk	3.50	48
415 A135	10c yellow	2.75	15
416 A136	20c dk blue	8.00	35
	Nos. 411-416 (6)	15.80	
	Set value		1.05

See #441-442, 464-466a, 517. For surcharges see #455, 527, O1, O10-O11, O13, RA30.

Pedro de Heredia — A137

Coffee Picking — A138

Perf. 11½

1934, Jan. 10 Unwmk. Litho.

417 A137	1c dark green	2.00	60
418 A137	5c chocolate	2.75	50
419 A137	8c dark blue	2.00	60
	Nos. 417-419 (3)	6.75	1.70

400th anniv. of Cartagena. See Nos. C111-C114.

1934, Dec. Engr. *Perf. 12*

420 A138	5c brown	2.25	15

Discus Thrower — A139

Post and Telegraph Building — A145

Allegory of Olympic Games at Barranquilla A140

Foot Race — A141

Tennis A142

Pier at Puerto Colombia A143

View of the Bay — A144

Designs: 2c, Soccer. 10c, Hurdling. 15c, Athlete in stadium. 18c, Baseball. 24c, Swimming. 50c, View of Barranquilla. 2p, Monument to Flag. 5p, Coat of Arms. 10p, Condor.

1935, Jan. 26 Litho. *Perf. 11½*

421 A139	2c bluish grn & buff	1.00	40
422 A139	4c deep green	1.00	40
423 A140	5c dk brn & yel	1.00	40
a.	Horiz. pair, imperf. btwn.	200.00	
424 A141	7c dk carmine	1.65	1.50
425 A142	8c blk & pink	1.90	1.50
426 A141	10c brown & bl	2.25	1.25
427 A143	12c indigo	2.50	2.00
428 A141	15c bl & red brn	4.50	3.50
429 A141	18c dk vio & buff	5.25	5.25
430 A144	20c purple & grn	5.25	4.50
431 A144	24c bluish grn & ultra	5.25	5.25
432 A144	50c ultra & buff	8.00	7.00
433 A145	1p drab & blue	72.50	40.00
434 A145	2p dull grn & gray	100.00	72.50
435 A145	5p pur blk & bl	325.00	250.00
436 A145	10p black & gray	400.00	350.00
	Nos. 421-436 (16)	937.05	745.45

3rd Natl. Olympic Games, Barranquilla. Counterfeits of 10p exist.

Oil Wells — A155

Gold Mining — A157

Imprint: "American Bank Note Co."

1935, Mar. Unwmk. Engr. *Perf. 12*

437 A155	2c carmine rose	32	15
439 A157	10c deep orange	18.00	15
	Set value		15

See Nos. 468, 470, 498, 516. For surcharge and overprints see Nos. 496, 596, O2.

No. 347 Surcharged in Black

12
CENTAVOS

1935, Aug. *Perf. 14*

440 A107	12c on 1p brt bl	3.00	1.40

Types of 1932

Imprint: "Lit. Nacional Bogotá"

1935-36 Litho. *Perf. 11, 11½, 12½*

441 A131	1c lt green	15	15
a.	Imperf., pair	3.50	
442 A133	5c brown ('36)	55	15
a.	Imperf., pair	4.00	4.00
	Set value		15

For surcharge see No. 527.

Bolívar A159

Tequendama Falls A160

Wmk. Wavy Lines. (229)

1937 Engr. *Perf. 12½*

443 A159	1c deep green	16	15
a.	Perf. 14		
444 A160	12c deep blue	2.50	95

See No. 570. For surcharges and overprints see Nos. 454, 456, C231, C326, O12.

Soccer Player — A161

Runner — A163

Discus Thrower — A162

1937, Jan. 4 Photo. Unwmk.

445 A161	3c lt green	1.25	85
446 A162	10c carmine rose	2.25	1.75
447 A163	1p black	24.00	24.00
	Nos. 445-447 (3)	27.50	26.60

National Olympic Games, Manizales. For surcharge see No. 452.

Exposition Palace A164

Stadium at Barranquilla A165

Monument to the Colors — A166

1937, Jan. 4

448 A164 5c violet brown 42 30
449 A165 15c blue 3.50 3.50
450 A166 50c orange brn 9.25 7.50
Nos. 448-450 (3) 13.17 11.30

Barranquilla National Exposition.

Stamps of 1926-37 Surcharged in Black

1
CENTAVO

1937-38 Unwmk. *Perf. 12½*

452 A161 1c on 3c lt grn 75 75
a. Inverted surcharge 1.75 1.75
453 A118 5c on 8c dk bl 38 35
a. Inverted surcharge 1.75 1.75

Wmk. 229

454 A160 2c on 12c dp bl 38 35
455 A134 5c on 8c bl blk 42 55
a. Invtd. surcharge 1.50 1.50
456 A160 10c on 12c dp bl ('38) 4.25 85
a. Dbl. surcharge 8.50 8.50
Nos. 452-456 (5) 6.18 2.85

Calle del Arco — A168

Entrance to Church of the Rosary — A169

Arms of Bogotá — A170

Gonzálo Jiménez de Quesada — A171

Bochica A172

Santo Domingo Convent A173

Mass of the Conquistadors — A174

1938, July 27 Unwmk. *Perf. 12½*

457 A168 1c yellow green 15 15
458 A169 2c scarlet 15 15
459 A170 5c brown blk 16 15
460 A171 10c brown 45 22
461 A172 15c brt blue 1.75 1.10
462 A173 20c brt red vio 1.75 1.10
463 A174 1p red brown 26.00 20.00
Nos. 457-463 (7) 30.41 22.87

Bogotá, 400th anniversary.

Types of 1932
Imprint: "Litografia Nacional Bogotá"

1938, Dec. 5 Litho. *Perf. 10½, 11*

464 A132 2c rose 80 28
465 A135 10c yellow 2.00 30
466 A136 20c dull blue 7.50 1.00
a. 20c dk bl, perf. 12½ ('44) 50.00 5.00
Nos. 464-466 (3) 10.30 1.58

Types of 1935 and

Bolívar A175

Coffee Picking A176

Arms of Colombia A177

Christopher Columbus A178

Caldas A179

Sabana Station A180

Imprint: "American Bank Note Co."

Wmk. 255

1939, Mar. 3 Engr. *Perf. 12*

467 A175 1c green 15 15
468 A155 2c car rose 16 15
469 A176 5c dull brown 16 15
470 A157 10c deep orange 85 15
471 A177 15c dull blue 2.50 15
472 A178 20c violet blk 6.00 20
473 A179 30c olive bister 3.50 30
474 A180 40c bister brn 10.00 2.75
Nos. 467-474 (8) 23.32 4.00

See Nos. 497-499, 515, 518, 574. For surcharges and overprints see Nos. 506-507, 520-522, 596, RA26, RA47.

Gen. Santander A181

Allegory A182

Gen. Santander A183

Statue at Cúcuta A184

Birthplace of Santander A185

Church at Rosario A186

Paya — A187

Bridge at Boyacá — A188

Death of General Santander — A189

Invasion of the Liberators — A190

Perf. 13x13½, 13½x13

1940, May 6 Engr. Wmk. 229

475 A181 1c olive green 20 16
476 A182 2c dk carmine 40 30
477 A183 5c sepia 20 15
478 A184 8c carmine 1.50 1.50
479 A185 10c orange yel 65 50
480 A186 15c dark blue 1.75 1.10
481 A187 20c green 2.25 1.75
482 A188 50c violet 5.25 5.00
483 A189 1p deep rose 17.00 17.00
484 A190 2p orange 52.50 52.50
Nos. 475-484 (10) 81.70 79.96

Centenary of the death of General Francisco Santander.

Tobacco Plant — A194

Gen. Santander — A195

Garcia Rovira A196

R. Galan A197

Antonio Sucre — A198

Arms of Palmira — A199

1940-43 Engr. Wmk. 255 *Perf. 12*

488 A194 8c rose car & grn 1.00 55
489 A195 15c dp blue ('43) 1.10 22
490 A196 20c gray blk ('41) 2.75 35
491 A197 40c brown bis ('41) 1.90 35
492 A198 1p black 6.75 52
Nos. 488-492 (5) 13.50 1.99

See #500, 554. For overprint see #RA28.

Unwmk.

1942, July 4 Litho. *Perf. 11*

493 A199 30c claret 1.70 60

8th Natl. Agricultural Exposition, held at Palmira.

Paradise of Isaacs, Palmira — A200

Signing Treaty of the Wisconsin — A201

1942, July 4

494 A200 50c lt blue grn 2.25 85

Issued in honor of the writer, Jorge Isaacs.

1942, Nov. 21 *Perf. 10½*

495 A201 10c dull orange 1.10 50
a. "2. XI.1902" instead of "21. XI. 1902" 14.00 15.00
b. Perf. 12 3.00 3.00

40th anniv. of the signing of the Treaty of the Wisconsin, Nov. 21, 1902.

No. 470 Surcharged in Black

5
Centavos

1944 Wmk. 255 *Perf. 12*

496 A157 5c on 10c dp org 15 15

Counterfeits exist of No. 496 with inverted or double surcharge.

Types of 1935-41 and

National Shrine — A202

San Pedro Alejandrino — A203

Imprint: "Columbian Bank Note Co."

1944-45 Unwmk. Engr. *Perf. 11*

497 A175 1c green 15 15
498 A155 2c rose 15 15
499 A176 5c dull brown 15 15
500 A196 20c gray black 2.50 75
501 A202 30c dl ol grn ('45) 1.40 95
502 A203 50c rose 1.75 95
Nos. 497-502 (6) 6.10 3.10

No. 499 Surcharged in Black

1
CENTAVO

1944, Oct.

506 A176 1c on 5c dull brn 15 15
507 A176 2c on 5c dull brn 15 15
Set value 16 16

Nos. 506 and 507 exist with inverted or double surcharge, created by favor.

Flag — A204

Arms — A205

Murillo Toro — A206

Hospital of St. John of God — A207

Virrey Solis — A208

1944, Oct. 10 Litho.

508 A204 2c ultra & bis 20 20
a. Sheet of 18 10.00
b. Imperf., pair 10.00
509 A205 5c ultra & bis 20 20
a. Sheet of 22 12.00
b. Imperf., pair 10.00
510 A206 20c blk & bluish grn 80 80
a. Sheet of 8 10.00
b. Imperf., pair 15.00
511 A207 40c blk & red 3.75 3.75
a. Sheet of 4 13.00
512 A208 1p blk & red 8.00 8.00
a. Sheet of 2 17.00
Nos. 508-512 (5) 12.95 12.95

Souvenir Sheet

Perf. 11x11½ All Around, Stamps Imperf.

513 Sheet of 5, #508-512 12.00 12.00

75th anniv. of Gen. Benevolent Assoc. of Cundinamarca.

Nos. 508-513 were printed in composite sheets containing one each of Nos. 508a, 509a, 510a, 511a and 512a, and two of 513. Fifty of these were presented to government officials.

Murillo Toro A210

San Pedro Alejandrino A211

1944, Nov. 10 ***Perf. 11***
514 A210 5c lt brown 28 15

Types of 1932-39 and A211
Imprint: "Litografia Nacional Bogota"

1944 Litho. ***Perf. 12½***
515 A175 1c dp green 35 15
a. 1c olive green 35 15
b. Imperf., pair 1.75 1.75
516 A155 2c dk carmine 35 15
a. Imperf., pair 1.75 1.75
517 A135 10c yellow org 2.75 45
518 A179 30c gray olive 7.50 3.50
a. Imperf., pair 27.50
519 A211 50c rose 8.00 3.75
Nos. 515-519 (5) 18.95 8.00

No. 469 Overprinted in Green, Blue or Red

Wmk. 255

1945, July 19 Engr. ***Perf. 12***
520 A176 5c dull brn (G) 16 15
521 A176 5c dull brn (R) 16 15
522 A176 5c dull brn (Bl) 16 15
Nos. 520-522 (3) 48
Set value 24

Portraits are Joseph Stalin, Franklin D. Roosevelt and Winston Churchill.

Clock Tower, Cartagena — A212

1945, Nov. 15
523 A212 50c olive black 3.75 1.25

For overprints see Nos. 543-544.

Sierra Nevada of Santa Marta — A213

Designs: 30c, Seaplane Tolima. 50c, San Sebastian Fort, Cartagena.

Unwmk.

1945, Dec. 14 Litho. ***Perf. 11***
524 A213 20c light green 1.50 1.00
525 A213 30c pale blue 1.50 1.00
526 A213 50c salmon pink 1.50 1.00
Nos. 524-526 (3) 4.50 3.00

25th anniv. of the 1st airmail service in America, according to the inscription, but earlier services are known to have existed.

No. 442 Surcharged in Black

1
UN CENTAVO

1946, Mar. 8 ***Perf. 11x11½, 12½***
527 A133 1c on 5c brown 15 15
a. Inverted surcharge 90

Gen. Antonio Jose de Sucre — A216

Wmk. 255

1946, Apr. 16 Engr. ***Perf. 12***

Size: 19x26½mm
528 A216 1c brn & turq grn 15 15
529 A216 2c vio & rose car 15 15

Size: 23x31mm
530 A216 5c sepia & blue 15 15
531 A216 9c dk grn & red 55 55
532 A216 10c ultra & org 40 35
533 A216 20c blk & dp org 40 22
534 A216 30c brn red & grn 65 22
535 A216 40c ol blk & red vio 65 30
536 A216 50c dp brn & vio 65 30
Nos. 528-536 (9) 3.75 2.39

Map of South America A217

National Observatory A218

Unwmk.

1946, June 7 Litho. ***Perf. 11***
537 A217 15c ultra 50 30
a. Imperf., pair 4.00

1946, Aug.
538 A218 5c fawn 32 15
a. Imperf., pair 4.00

See No. 565.

Andrés Bello — A219

Joaquín de Cayzedo y Cuero — A220

Wmk. 255

1946, Sept. 3 Engr. ***Perf. 12***
539 A219 3c sepia 15 15
540 A219 10c orange 52 32
541 A219 15c slate black 60 32
Nos. 539-541 (3) 1.27 79

80th anniv. of the death of Andrés Bello (1781-1865), poet and educator. See No. C145.

1946, Sept. 20 Wmk. 229 ***Perf. 12½***
542 A220 2p bluish green 4.50 1.25

See No. 568. For surcharge see No. 613.

Type of 1945, Overprinted in Black or Green

V JUEGOS C.
A. Y DEL C.
1946

1946, Dec. 6 Wmk. 255 ***Perf. 12***
543 A212 50c red (Bk) 2.50 1.40
a. Double overprint 25.00
544 A212 50c red (G) 2.50 1.40
a. Double overprint 25.00

5th Central American and Caribbean Championship Games.

Coffee — A221

Engraved and Lithographed

1947, Jan. 10 Wmk. 229 ***Perf. 12½***
545 A221 5c multicolored 40 15

Colombian Orchid: Masdevallia Nycterina — A222

Designs (Orchids): 2c, Miltonia vexillaria. No. 548, Cattleya chocoensis. No. 549, Odontoglossum crispum. No. 550, Cattleya dowiana aurea. 10c, Cattleya labiata trianae.

1947, Feb. 7 Wmk. 255 ***Perf. 12***
546 A222 1c multicolored 32 15
547 A222 2c multicolored 32 15
548 A222 5c multicolored 75 15
549 A222 5c multicolored 75 15
550 A222 5c multicolored 75 15
551 A222 10c multicolored 1.25 32
Nos. 546-551 (6) 4.14 1.07

Antonio Nariño — A228

Alberto Urdaneta y Urdaneta — A229

Perf. 12½

1947, May 9 Litho. Unwmk.
552 A228 5c blue, *grnsh* 26 15
553 A229 10c red brn, *grnsh* 32 15
Nos. 552-553,C146-C147 (4) 1.43 95

4th Pan-American Press Congress, 1946.

Sucre Type of 1940

1947 Wmk. 255 Engr. ***Perf. 12***
554 A198 1p violet 2.50 1.00

José Celestino Mutis and José Jerónimo Triana — A230

Miguel A. Caro and Rufino J. Cuervo — A231

1947 Wmk. 229 ***Perf. 12½***
555 A230 25c olive green 65 24
556 A231 3p dark purple 4.00 3.25

See Nos. 567, 569. For surcharge see No. 610.

Metropolitan Cathedral, Plaza Bolívar, Bogotá A232

National Capitol A233

Ministry of Foreign Affairs A234

A235

1948, Apr. 2
557 A232 5c black brown 15 15
558 A233 10c orange 55 55
559 A234 15c dark blue 55 55
Nos. 557-559,C148-C149 (5) 2.30 2.30

Miniature Sheet

Imperf
560 A235 50c slate 1.50 1.50

9th Pan-American Conf., Bogotá.

No. RA5A Overprinted in Black

C

1948 Unwmk. ***Perf. 12½***

Without Gum
561 PT3 1c yellow orange 15 15

The letter "C" is the initial of "CORREOS."

Nos. RA33, RA24 and RA25 Overprinted in Black

CORREOS

1948 Wmk. 255 ***Perf. 12.***
562 PT6 1c olive 15 15
563 PT6 2c green 15 15
564 PT6 20c brown 16 15
Set value 26 15

Nos. 561-564 exist with inverted and double overprints.

Observatory Type of 1946

Unwmk.

1948, June 30 Litho. ***Perf. 11***
565 A218 5c blue 20 15

Simón Bolívar — A236

Carlos Martinez Silva — A237

Wmk. 255

1948, May 29 **Engr.** ***Perf. 12***
566 A236 15c green 40 18

Types of 1946-47

1948 **Unwmk.** ***Perf. 12½***
567 A230 25c green 30 15
568 A220 2p dp green 55 15
569 A231 3p dp red violet 70 15
Nos. 567-569 (3) 1.55
Set value 35

Falls Type of 1937

1948 **Wmk. 229**
570 A160 10c red 15 15

For overprints see Nos. C231, C326.

Perf. 13½

1948, Dec. 21 **Unwmk.** **Litho.**
571 A237 40c carmine 40 25

Juan de Dios Carrasquilla A238

1949, May 20 **Wmk. 229** ***Perf. 12½***
572 A238 5c bister 15 15

75th anniv. of the foundation of the Colombian Soc. of Agriculture.

Julio Garavito Armero A239

Arms of Colombia A240

Wmk. 229

1949, Apr. 24 **Engr.** ***Perf. 12***
573 A239 4c green 32 15

Issued to honor Julio Garavito Armero (1865-1920), mathematician.

Coffee Type of 1939.
Imprint: "American Bank Note Co."

1949, Aug. 4 **Wmk. 255**
574 A176 5c blue 15 15

1949, Oct. 7 **Unwmk.** ***Perf. 13***
575 A240 15c blue 18 15

Issued to honor the new Constitution. See Nos. C164-C165.

Shield and Tree A241

Francisco Javier Cisneros A242

1949, Oct. 13 **Wmk. 229** ***Perf. 12½***
576 A241 5c olive 15 15

4th anniv. of Colombia's 1st Forestry Cong. and propaganda for the government's reforestation program.

1949, Dec. 15 **Photo.** **Unwmk.**
577 A242 50c red vio & yel 1.00 60
578 A242 50c green & vio 1.00 60
579 A242 50c brown & lt bl 1.00 60
Nos. 577-579 (3) 3.00 1.80

50th anniv. (in 1948) of the death of Francisco Javier Cisneros.

Masdevallia Chimaera — A243

Odontoglossum Crispum — A244

Eastern Hemisphere — A245

Designs: 3c, Cattleya labiata trianae. 4c, Masdevallia nycterina. 5c, Cattleya dowiana aurea. 11c, Miltonia vexillaria. 18c, Santo Domingo post office.

1950, Aug. 22 **Photo.** ***Perf. 13***
580 A243 1c brown 15 15
581 A244 2c violet 15 15
582 A243 3c rose lilac 16 15
583 A243 4c emerald 24 15
584 A243 5c red orange 65 15
585 A244 11c red 1.50 1.50
586 A244 18c ultra 1.25 55
Nos. 580-586 (7) 4.10 2.80

Miniature Sheet
Imperf

587 A245 50c orange yel 1.25 1.25

75th anniv. (in 1949) of the UPU. See No. C199. For surcharge see No. C232.

Antonio Baraya — A246

Perf. 12½

1950, Nov. 27 **Unwmk.** **Engr.**
588 A246 2c red 15 15

Colombian Farm A247

1950, Dec. 28 **Photo.** ***Perf. 11½***
589 A247 5c dp car & buff 20 15
590 A247 5c bl grn & gray 20 15
591 A247 5c vio bl & gray 20 15
Nos. 589-591 (3) 60
Set value 21

Issued to publicize rural life.

Arms of Bogotá A248

Arms of Colombia A249

Perf. 12x12½

1950, Dec. 28 **Engr.** **Wmk. 255**
592 A248 5p deep green 2.50 38
593 A249 10p red orange 7.50 65

Catalogue values for unused stamps in this section, from this point to the end of the section, are for Never Hinged items.

Map and Badge A250

Guillermo Valencia A251

Perf. 12½x13

1951, Jan. 30 **Photo.** **Unwmk.**
594 A250 20c red, yel & bl 40 15

60th anniversary (in 1947) of the formation of the Colombian Society of Engineers.

1951, Oct. 20 **Engr.** ***Perf. 13x13½***
595 A251 25c black 90 20

Issued to honor Guillermo Valencia (1873-1943), newspaper founder, governor of Cauca, presidential candidate, author.

No. 468 Overprinted in Black

REVERSION
CONCESION MARES
25 Agosto 1951

1951, Dec. 11 **Wmk. 255** ***Perf. 12***
596 A155 2c carmine rose 15 15

Issued to publicize the reversion of the Mares oil concession to Colombia.

Nicolas Osorio — A252

Portraits: No. 598, Pompilio Martinez. No. 599, Ezequiel Uriocoechea. No. 600, Jose M. Lombana.

Perf. 11½

1952, Aug. 6 **Unwmk.** **Engr.**
Various Frames
597 A252 1c deep blue 15 15
598 A252 1c deep blue 15 15
599 A252 1c deep blue 15 15
600 A252 1c deep blue 15 15
Set value 28 20

Nos. 597-600 were printed in a single sheet containing four panes of twenty-five each, separated by double rows of ornamental tabs. Although inscribed "sobretasa," the stamps were for ordinary postage.

Footnotes near stamp listings often refer to other stamps of the same design.

Types of Postal Tax Stamps of 1945-50 and

Communications Building
A253 A253a

1952 ***Perf. 12***
601 A253 5c ultra 25 15

Wmk. 255

602 PT10 20c brown 7.50 16
603 PT6 25c dk gray 7.50 3.50
604 PT10 25c blue green 75 15
605 A253a 50c orange yel 20.00 10.00
606 A253a 1p rose carmine 2.00 32
607 A253a 2p lilac rose 20.00 8.00
608 A253a 2p violet 2.25 50
Nos. 601-608 (8) 60.25 22.78

Although inscribed "sobretasa," Nos. 601-608 were issued for ordinary postage.
For surcharges see Nos. 612, RA48.

Cathedral of Manizales — A254

Perf. 11½

1952, Oct. 10 **Photo.** **Unwmk.**
609 A254 23c blue & gray blk 35 20

Centenary of city of Manizales.
For surcharge see No. 619.

No. 555 Surcharged in Blue

1ª CONFERENCIA 1952 SIDERURGICA LATINO-AMERICANA. 15

1952, Oct. 30 **Wmk. 229** ***Perf. 12½***
610 A230 15c on 25c olive green 40 20

Latin American Siderurgical Conf., 1952. See No. C226.

Queen Isabella I and Monument — A255

Perf. 12½

1953, Mar. 10 **Unwmk.** **Engr.**
611 A255 23c blue & black 60 50

5th centenary of the birth of Queen Isabella I of Spain.
For surcharge see No. 693.

Nos. 606 and 568 Surcharged with New Values in Dark Blue

1953, Oct. 19 **Wmk. 255**
612 A253a 40c on 1p rose car 1.25 15
613 A220 50c on 2p dp green 1.25 15

Manuel Ancizar — A256

Portraits: 23c, José Jeronimo Triana. 30c, Manuel Ponce de Leon. 1p, Agustin Codazzi.

Perf. 12½x13

1953, Nov. Engr. Unwmk.

Frames in Black

614 A256	14c rose red	50	50
615 A256	23c ultra	40	20
616 A256	30c chocolate	35	15
617 A256	1p emerald	35	15
	Nos. 614-617 (4)	1.60	1.00

Cent. (in 1950) of the establishment of the Chorographic Commission. See Nos. 687, 690, 692. For surcharges and overprint see Nos. 620, 687, 690, 692, C284.

Murillo Toro and Map — A257

Engraved and Lithographed

1953, Dec. 12 Wmk. 255 *Perf. 12*

Black Surcharge

618 A257 5c on 5p multi 25 15

2nd Natl. Phil. Exhib., Bogotá, Dec. 1953. See No. C237.

Nos. 609 and 614 Surcharged with New Value or New Value and Ornaments

1953 Unwmk. *Perf. 11½, 12½x13*

619 A254	5c on 23c (C)	35	20
620 A256	5c on 14c (Bk)	35	25

No. 614 surcharged "CINCO" in blue is listed as No. 687.

Symbolical of St. Francis Receiving Christ's Wounds — A258

1954, Apr. 23 Photo. *Perf. 11½*

621 A258 5c sepia & green 25 15

400th anniversary of the establishment of Colombia's first Franciscan community.

Soldier, Map and Arms A259

1954, June 13 Engr. *Perf. 13*

622 A259 5c dull blue 18 15

1st anniv. of the assumption of the presidency by Gen. Gustavo Rojas Pinilla. See Nos. C255, 637a.

Sports Emblem — A260

Design: 10c, Stadium and athlete holding arms of Colombia.

1954, July 18 Unwmk.

623 A260	5c deep blue	40	15
624 A260	10c red	60	15
	Nos. 623-624,C256-C257 (4)	2.55	80

7th Natl. Athletic Games, Cali, July 1954.

History Academy Seal — A261

1954, July 24

625 A261 5c ultra & green 20 15

50th anniversary (in 1952) of the Colombian Academy of History.

Convent and Cell of St. Peter Claver — A262

1954, Sept. 9

627 A262	5c dark green	15	15
a.	Souvenir sheet	2.25	2.25

300th anniversary of the death of St. Peter Claver.

No. 627a contains one stamp similar to No. 627, but printed in greenish black. Sheet size: 121x129½mm. See Nos. C258-C258a.

Mercury — A263

1954, Oct. 29

628 A263	5c orange	28	15
	Nos. 557-559,C148-C149 (5)	2.30	
	Set value		25

1st Intl. Fair and Exhibition, Bogota, 1954.

Tapestry Madonna A264

College Cloister A265

Designs: 10c, Brother Cristobal de Torres. 20c, College chapel and arms.

Perf. 12½x11½, 11½x12½

1954, Dec. 6

629 A264	5c orange & blk	24	15
630 A264	10c blue	24	15
631 A265	15c violet brn	28	15
632 A265	20c black & brn	55	35
a.	Souvenir sheet	3.75	3.75
	Nos. 629-632,C263-C266 (8)	3.48	
	Set value		1.55

300th anniv. (in 1953) of the founding of the Senior College of Our Lady of the Rosary, Bogota.

No. 632a contains four stamps similar to Nos. 629-632, but printed in different colors: 5c yellow and black, 10c green, 15c dull violet, 20c black and light-blue.

Steel Mill — A266

José Marti — A267

1954, Dec. 12 *Perf. 12½x13*

633 A266 5c ultra & blk 20 15

Issued to mark the opening of the Paz del Rio steel mill, October 1954. See No. C267.

1955, Jan. 28 *Perf. 13½x13*

634 A267 5c deep carmine 15 15

Centenary of the birth of José Marti (1853-1895), Cuban patriot. See No. C268.

Arms, Flags and Soldiers Building Bridge A268

1955, Mar. 23 *Perf. 12½*

635 A268 10c claret 20 15

Issued to honor Colombian soldiers who served in Korea, 1951-53. See Nos. 637a, C269.

Fleet Emblem — A269

M. S. City of Manizales and New York Skyline A270

1955, Apr. 12 Unwmk.

636 A269	15c deep green	20	15
637 A270	20c violet	20	15
a.	Souvenir sheet	4.00	4.25
	Nos. 636-637,C270-C271 (4)	1.23	
	Set value		20

Grand-Colombian Merchant Fleet.

No. 637a contains four stamps similar to Nos. 622, 635-637, but printed in different colors: 5c blue, 10c dark carmine, 15c green, 20c purple.

Hotel Tequendama and Church of San Diego — A271

1955, May 16 Photo. *Perf. 11½x12*

638 A271 5c blue 15 15

See No. C273.

Bolivar's Country Estate, Bogotá A272

1955, Sept. 28 Engr. *Perf. 12½*

639 A272 5c deep ultra 15 15

50th anniv. of Rotrary Intl. See No. C274.

Belalcazar, Jiménez de Quesada and Balboa A273

Caravels and Columbus A274

Design: 5c, San Martin, Bolivar and Washington.

Engraved and Photogravure

1955, Oct. 29 *Perf. 13x12½*

640 A273	2c yel grn & brn	15	15
641 A273	5c brt bl & brn	15	15
642 A274	23c lt ultra & blk	25	15
a.	Souvenir sheet	8.00	5.00
	Nos. 640-642,C275-C280 (9)	11.10	10.05

7th Cong. of the Postal Union of the Americas and Spain, Bogota, Oct. 12-Nov. 9, 1955.

No. 642a contains one each of Nos. 640-642, printed in slightly different shades.

José Eusebio Caro — A275

1955, Nov. 29 Engr. *Perf. 13½x13*

643 A275 5c brown 15 15

José Eusebio Caro (1817-53), poet. See #C281.

Departmental Issue

Map — A276

View of San Andres Harbor — A277

Cattle at Waterhole A278

Designs: 2c, Docks, Atlantico. 3c, "Industry," Antioquia. 4c, Cartagena Harbor, Bolivar. No. 647, Steel Mill, Boyaca. No. 648, Cattle, Cordoba. No. 649, Map. No. 650, San Andres Harbor. No. 651, Cacao picker, Cauca. 10c, Coffee picker, Caldas. 15c, Salt Mine Chapel, Zipaquira, Cundinamarca. 20c, Tropical plants and map, Choco. 23c, Harvester, Huila. 25c, Banana Plantation, Magdalena. 30c, Gold mining, Nariño. 40c, Tobacco plantation, Santander. 50c, Oil wells, North Santander. 60c, Cotton plantation, Tolima. 1p, Sugar industry, Cauca. 3p, Amazon river at Leticia, Amazonas. 5p, Windmills and panoramic view, La Guajira. 10p, Rubber plantation, Vaupes.

Perf. 13½x13, 13x13½, 13
Engr.; Engr. & Litho.

1956 **Unwmk.**

Various Frames

644 A277	2c car & grn	15	15
645 A276	3c brn vio & blk	15	15
646 A277	4c grn & blk	15	15
647 A276	5c dk brn & bl	15	15
648 A277	5c ol & dk vio brn	25	15
649 A276	5c bl & blk	22	15
650 A277	5c car & grnsh bl	18	15
651 A277	5c ol grn & red brn	18	15
652 A276	10c org & blk	18	15
653 A276	15c ultra & blk	22	15
654 A276	20c dk brn & bl	18	15
655 A277	23c ultra & ver	30	18
656 A277	25c ol grn & blk	30	18
657 A277	30c ultra & brn	18	15
658 A277	40c dl pur & red brn	18	15
659 A277	50c dk grn & blk	18	15
660 A277	60c pale brn & grn	18	15
661 A278	1p mag & grnsh bl	1.40	18
662 A278	2p grn & red brn	1.75	22
663 A278	3p car & blk	2.25	50
664 A278	5p brn & lt ultra	4.00	1.25
665 A276	10p red brn & grn	10.00	6.50
	Nos. 644-665 (22)	22.73	
	Set value		9.75

Nos. 645, 647, 649, 652-654 measure 27x32mm, No. 665 27x37mm. See Nos. 681-684, 685, 688-689. For surcharges and overprints see Nos. 685, 688-689, C289, C312.

Columbus and Proposed Lighthouse A279

1956, Oct. 12 **Photo.** ***Perf. 12***
666 A279 3c gray black 15 15

Issued in honor of Christopher Columbus. See Nos. C285, C306.

Altar of St. Elizabeth and Tomb of Jimenez de Quesada — A280

1956, Nov. 19 **Unwmk.**
667 A280 5c red lilac 15 15

7th cent. of St. Elizabeth of Hungary, patron saint of Sante Fé de Bogotá. See No. C286.

St. Ignatius of Loyola — A281

Javier Pereira — A282

1956, Nov. 26 **Engr.** ***Perf. 12½x13***
668 A281 5c blue 18 15

400th anniv. of the death of St. Ignatius of Loyola. See No. C287. For overprint see No. C324.

1956, Dec. 28 **Unwmk.** ***Perf. 12***
669 A282 5c blue 15 15

Issued to honor 167-year-old Javier Pereira. See No. C288.

Emblem and Dairy Farm — A283

Designs: 2c, Emblem and tractor. 5c, Emblem, coffee and corn.

1957, Mar. 5 **Photo.** ***Perf. 14x13½***

670 A283	1c lt ol grn	15	15
671 A283	2c lt brn	15	15
672 A283	5c lt bl	15	15
	Set value, #670-672, C292-C296	1.30	85

Agrarian Savings Bank of Colombia, 25th anniv. For overprint see No. C322.

Arms of Military Academy and Gen. Rafael Reyes A284

Design: 10c, Arms and Academy.

1957, July 20 **Engr.** ***Perf. 12½***

673 A284	5c blue	15	15
674 A284	10c orange	15	15
a.	Souv. sheet of 2	10.50	10.50
	Set value, #673-674, C299-C300	55	25

50th anniv. of the Colombian Military Academy.
No. 674a contains one each of Nos. 673-674 in slightly different shades.
For overprints see Nos. C328, C312.

Statue of José Matias Delgado — A285

1957, Sept. 16 **Photo.** ***Perf. 12***
675 A285 2c rose brn 15 15

Issued in honor of Jose Matias Delgado, liberator of El Salvador. See No. C301.

Santo Michelena, Marcos V. Crespo, P. Alcantara Herran and UPU Monument A286

1957, Oct. 10 **Unwmk.**

676 A286	5c green	15	15
677 A286	10c gray	15	15
	Set value, #676-677, C302-C303	48	30

Intl. Letter Writing Week and 14th UPU Cong.

St. Vincent de Paul and Children — A287

1957, Oct. 18
678 A287 1c dark olive green 15 15

Colombian Society of St. Vincent de Paul, cent. See No. C304. For overprint see No. C323.

Fencer A288

1957, Nov. 22 **Photo.** ***Perf. 12***
679 A288 4c lilac 15 15

3rd South American Fencing Championship. See No. C305. For overprint see No. C332.

Francisco José de Caldas and Hypsometer A289

1958, May 12 **Unwmk.** ***Perf. 12***

680 A289	10c black	25	15
	Nos. 680,C309-C310 (3)	1.05	
	Set value		30

International Geophysical Year, 1957-58.

Departmental Issue
Type of 1956

Designs as before.

1958 **Engr.** ***Perf. 13***

681 A276	3c ultra & brn	15	15
682 A276	3c ol grn & pur	15	15
683 A276	10c grn & brn	15	15
684 A276	10c dk bl & brn	15	15
	Set value	36	20

Nos. 646, C291, 614, 653, 655, 616, C308, 615 and 611 Surcharged with New Value, and Old Value Obliterated, or Overprinted in Dark Blue or Green

Perf. 12½, 12½x13, 13

1958-59 **Unwmk.**

685 A277	2c on 4c grn & blk	15	15
686 AP48	5c dp plum & multi ('59)	15	15
687 A256	5c on 14c blk & rose red ("CINCO") ('59)	30	30
688 A276	5c on 15c ultra & blk	15	15
689 A277	5c on 23c ultra & ver (G)	24	16
690 A256	5c on 30c blk & choc	15	15
691 AP40	10c on 25c rose vio	15	15
692 A256	20c on 23c blk & ultra (G) ('59)	24	18
693 A255	20c on 23c bl & blk ('59)	24	18
	Set value	1.50	1.10

On No. 686 the words "Correo Extra Rapido" are obliterated in dark blue.

Father Rafael Almanza and Church of San Diego, Bogota — A290

1958, Oct. 23 **Photo.** ***Perf. 14x13***

695 A290	10c purple	15	15
	Nos. 695,C313-C314 (3)	55	
	Set value		20

For overprint see #C336.

Msgr. R. M. Carrasquilla and Church — A291

1959, Jan. 22 ***Perf. 14x13***

696 A291	10c dk red brn	15	15
	Nos. 696,C315-C316 (3)	95	
	Set value		26

Cent. of the birth of Msgr. R. M. Carrasquilla (1857-1930), rector of Our Lady of the Rosary Seminary, Bogotá. For overprints see #C335, C341.

Miss Universe 1959 — A292

Jorge Eliecer Gaitan — A293

1959, June 26 **Photo.** ***Perf. 11½***

697 A292	10c multi	15	15
	Nos. 697,C317-C318 (3)	34.05	33.75

Luz Marina Zuluaga, Miss Universe, 1959. For overprint see No. C342.

1959, July 28 **Engr.** ***Perf. 12x13½***

698 A293	10c on 3c gray bl (Bl)	15	15
699 A293	30c rose vio	40	20
	Nos. 698-699,C319-C320 (4)	3.35	2.85

Issued in honor of Jorge Eliecer Gaitan (1898-1948), lawyer and politician.
No. 698 exists without blue surcharge.

Gen. Francisco de Paula Santander — A294

Designs: Nos. 701, 703, Simon Bolivar.

1959 **Litho.** **Wmk. 331** ***Perf. 12½***

700 A294	5c brown & yel	15	15
701 A294	5c ultra & bl	15	15
702 A294	10c gray & grn	15	15
703 A294	10c gray & red	15	15
	Nos. 700-703,C389 (5)	3.60	
	Set value		80

Capitol, Bogota A295

1959

704 A295	2c dk bl & red brn	15	15
705 A295	3c blk brn & lil	15	15
	Set value	20	18

Stamp of 1859 and Mail Transport by Mule — A296

Two-Toed Sloth — A297

Designs (various stamps of 1859 and): 10c, Mail boat on the Magdalena river. 25c, Train.

Unwmk.

1959, Dec. 1 Photo. *Perf. 12*

709 A296 5c org & grn	15	15
710 A296 10c rose cl & bl	15	15
711 A296 15c car rose & grn	32	32
712 A296 25c bl & red brn	42	32
Nos. 709-712,C351-C354 (8)	4.69	2.93

Centenary of Colombian postage stamps.

1960, Feb. 12 *Perf. 12*

Designs: 10c, Alexander von Humboldt. 20c, Spider monkey.

713 A297 5c grnsh bl & brn	25	15
714 A297 10c blk & dp car	25	15
715 A297 20c cit & gray brn	25	15
Nos. 713-715,C357-C359 (6)	4.75	3.25

Cent. of the death of Alexander von Humboldt (1769-1859), German naturalist and geographer.
For overprint and surcharge see #C411, C413.

Anthurium Andreanum A298

Lincoln Statue, Washington A299

Flower: 20c, Espeletia grandiflora.

1960, May 10

716 A298 5c multi	15	15
717 A298 20c brn, yel & gray ol	15	15
Nos. 716-717,C360-C370 (13)	12.90	14.80

See #C420-C425. For overprint see #C412.

Perf. 10½

1960, June 10 Litho. Wmk. 331

718 A299 20c rose lil & blk	18	20
Nos. 718,C375-C376 (3)	1.28	95

Floredo House, Cradle of the Republic A300

Arms of Santa Cruz de Mompox — A301

Design: 5c, First coins of Republic.

Unwmk.

1960, July 19 Photo. *Perf. 12*

719 A301 5c grn & ocher	15	15
720 A300 20c ol bis & mar	15	15
721 A301 20c multi	15	18
Nos. 719-721,C377-C385 (12)	5.80	4.58

Colombia's independence, 150th anniv.

St. Isidore and Farm Animals — A302

Design: 20c, Nativity by Gregorio de Arce Vasquez y Ceballos.

1960, Sept. 26 *Perf. 12*

722 A302 10c multi	15	15
723 A302 20c multi	15	15
Nos. 722-723,C387 (3)	46	
Set value		35

St. Isidore the Farmer, patron saint of the rural people.
See Nos. 747, C388, C439-C440.

UN Headquarters and Emblem — A303

Wmk. 331

1960, Oct. 24 Litho. *Perf. 11*

724 A303 20c blk & pink 15 15

Souvenir Sheet

Imperf

725 A303 50c dk brn, brt grn & blk 2.50 2.50

15th anniversary of the United Nations.

Pan-American Highway through Colombia — A304

Alfonso Lopez — A305

1961, Mar. 7 Unwmk. *Perf. 10½x11*

726 A304 20c brn & grnsh bl	60	60
Nos. 726,C390-C393 (5)	2.60	3.20

8th Pan-American Highway Congress, Bogota, May 20-29, 1960.

1961, Mar. 22 Photo. *Perf. 12½*

727 A305 10c brt rose & brn	16	15
728 A305 20c vio & brn	16	15
Nos. 727-728,C394-C395 (4)	1.00	
Set value		38

Alfonso Lopez (1886-1959), President of Colombia. See No. C396.

Cauca River Bridge, Cali A306

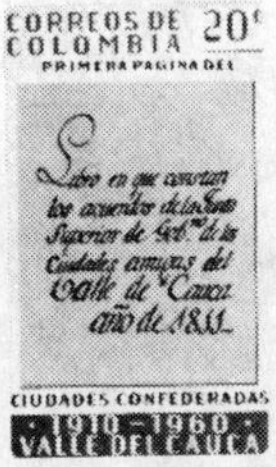

Page from Resolutions of Confederated Cities — A307

1961-62 *Perf. 12½x13, 13½x13*

729 A306 10c red brn, bl, grn & red ('62)	15	15
730 A307 20c pale brn & blk	15	15
Nos. 729-730,C397-C401 (7)	2.75	
Set value		1.30

50th anniversary (in 1960) of the Department of Valle del Cauca.

View of Cucuta and Arms A308

Design: No. 732, Arms of Ocana and Pamplona.

1961, Aug. 29 *Perf. 13x13½*

731 A308 20c bl, blk, yel & red	15	15
732 A308 20c ocher, ultra & red	15	15
Nos. 731-732,C402-C403 (4)	1.05	
Set value		25

50th anniv. (in 1960) of the Department of North Santander.

Arms of Popayan A309

Basketball A310

Designs: No. 734, Arms of Barranquilla. No. 735, Arms of Bucaramanga.

Perf. 12½x13

1961, Oct. 10 Unwmk.

Arms in Multicolor

733 A309 10c blue & silver	15	15
734 A309 20c blue & yellow	15	15
735 A309 20c blue & gold	15	15
Nos. 733-735,C404-C408 (8)	2.40	
Set value		60

Issued to honor Atlantico Department.

1961, Dec. 16 Litho. *Perf. 13½x14*

736 A310 20c shown	15	15
737 A310 20c Runners	15	15
738 A310 20c Boxers	24	15
739 A310 25c Soccer	15	15
Nos. 736-739,C414-C418 (9)	3.04	
Set value		1.00

4th Bolivarian Games, Barranquilla, 1961.

Colombian Anti-Malaria Emblem — A311

Engineers Society Emblem — A312

Design: 50c, Malaria eradication emblem and mosquito in swamp.

1962, Apr. 12 Unwmk. *Perf. 12*

740 A311 20c lt bis & red	15	15
741 A311 50c bis & ultra	16	15
Nos. 740-741,C426-C428 (5)	4.45	4.37

1962, June 12 Photo. *Perf. 11½x12*

742 A312 10c multi	25	22
Nos. 742,C429-C432 (5)	2.30	2.18

Colombian Society of Engineers, 75th anniv.

Flags of American Nations — A313

Woman Casting Ballot and Statue of Policarpa Salavarrieta — A314

1962, June 28 *Perf. 13*

Flags in National Colors

743 A313 25c blk & org ver 15 15

Souvenir Sheet

744 A313 2.50p blk & yel 3.00 3.00

70th anniv. of the founding of the Organization of American States.
See No. C433.

Perf. 12x12½

1962, July 20 Litho. Wmk. 229

745 A314 10c lt bl, gray & blk 15 15

Issued to publicize women's political rights. See Nos. 752, C434, C448-C450.

Scouts at Campfire and Tents A315

Railroad Map of Colombia A316

Perf. 11½x12

1962, July 28 Photo. Unwmk.

746 A315 10c brt grnsh bl & brn	32	32
Nos. 746,C435-C438 (5)	5.41	4.74

Colombian Boy Scouts, 30th anniv.

St. Isidore Type of 1960 Redrawn

1962, Aug. 28 *Perf. 12*

747 A302 10c pink & multi	15	15
Nos. 747,C439-C440 (3)	3.80	3.80

The frame on No. 747 is solid color with white inscription similar to type AP82.

1962, Sept. 28 *Perf. 12½*

748 A316 10c blk, gray, grn & red	15	15
Nos. 748,C441-C444 (5)	5.60	4.35

Progress of Colombian railroads and the completion of the Atlantic Line from Santa Marta to Bogota.

Post Horn — A317

Perf. 13½x14

1962, Oct. 18 Litho. Wmk. 346

749 A317 20c gold, dl gray vio & blk	15	15
Nos. 749,C445-C446 (3)	65	
Set value		20

50th anniv. of the founding of the Postal Union of the Americas and Spain, UPAE.

"Virgin of the Rock" — A318

Red Cross Centenary Emblem — A319

1963, Mar. 11 **Wmk. 346**
750 A318 60c multi 15 15

Vatican II, the 21st Ecumenical Council of the Roman Catholic Church. See No. C447.

1963, May 1 ***Perf. 12x12½***
751 A319 5c olive bister & red 15 15

Centenary of International Red Cross.

Women's Rights Type of 1962

1963, July 11 **Wmk. 346**
752 A314 5c org, gray & blk 15 15
Nos. 752,C448-C450 (4) 94
Set value 20

Manuel Mejia J. and Flag of National Coffee Growers Assn. A320

Perf. 12½x13

1965, Feb. 10 **Engr.** **Unwmk.**
753 A320 25c rose & blk 15 15
Nos. 753,C464-C466 (4) 4.30 85

Manuel Mejia J. (1887-1958), banker and manager of the National Coffee Growers Association.

Julio Arboleda (1817-62), Writer, Soldier and Statesman A321

1966, Mar. 9 **Litho.** ***Perf. 14x13½***
754 A321 5c lt brn, lt yel grn & blk 15 15

Spanish Galleon, 16th Century A322

History of Maritime Mail: 15c, Rio Hacha brigantine, 1850. 20c, Uraba canoe. 40c, Magdalena River steamship and barge, 1900. 50c, Modern motor ship and sea gull.

1966, June 16 **Photo.** **Unwmk.**
755 A322 5c org & multi 15 15
756 A322 15c car rose, blk & brn 15 15
757 A322 20c brt grn, org & blk 15 15
758 A322 40c dp bl & multi 20 15
759 A322 50c pale bl & multi 50 22
Nos. 755-759 (5) 1.15
Set value 44

Plumed Hogfish A323

Design: 10p, Bat ray and brittle starfish.

1966, Aug. 25 **Photo.** ***Perf. 12½x13***
760 A323 80c multi 16 15
761 A323 10p multi 5.00 6.00
Nos. 760-761,C481-C483 (5) 15.26 16.05

Arms of Venezuela, Colombia and Chile — A324

1966, Oct. 11 **Litho.** ***Perf. 14x13½***
762 A324 40c yel & multi 15 15
Nos. 762,C484-C485 (3) 59
Set value 20

Visits of Eduardo Frei and Raul Leoni, presidents of Chile and Venezuela.

Camilo Torres, 1766-1816, Lawyer — A325

Portraits: 60c, Jorge Tadeo Lozano (1771-1816), naturalist. 1p, Francisco Antonio Zea (1776-1822), naturalist and politician.

Perf. 13½x14

1967, Jan. 18 **Litho.** **Unwmk.**
763 A325 25c vio & bis 15 15
764 A325 60c dk red brn & bis 15 15
765 A325 1p grn & bis 30 15
Set value, #763-765, C486-C487 75 42

Issued to honor famous men of Colombia.

Map of South America and Arms — A326

1967, Feb. 2 **Litho.** ***Perf. 14x13½***
766 A326 40c multi 15 15
767 A326 60c multi 15 15
Nos. 766-767,C488 (3) 65
Set value 30

Declaration of Bogota for cooperation and world peace, signed by Colombia, Chile, Ecuador, Peru and Venezuela.

Monochaetum Orchid and Bee — A327

Orchid: 2p, Passiflora vitifolia and butterfly.

1967, May 23 **Litho.** ***Perf. 14***
768 A327 25c multi 15 15
769 A327 2p multi 1.00 1.00
Nos. 768-769,C489-C491 (5) 2.94 1.75

1st Natl. Orchid Exhib. and the Topical Phil. Flora and Fauna Exhib., Medellin, Apr. 1967.

Lions Emblem — A328

SENA Emblem — A329

1967, July 12 **Litho.** ***Perf. 13½x14***
770 A328 10p multi 3.00 2.00

50th anniv. of Lions Intl. See No. C492.

Lithographed and Embossed

1967, Sept. 20 **Unwmk.**
771 A329 5p gold, brt grn & blk 1.10 25

10th anniv. of Natl. Apprenticeship Service, SENA. See No. C494.

Gold Diadem in Calima Style — A330

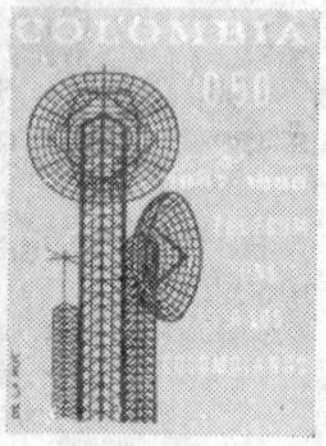

Radar Installation — A331

Pre-Columbian Art: 3p, Gold statuette, ornamental globe and bird, horiz.

Perf. 13½x14, 14x13½

1967, Oct. 13 **Photo.**
772 A330 1.60p brt rose lil, gold & brn 50 15
773 A330 3p dk bl, gold & brn 70 28
Nos. 772-773,C495-C497 (5) 11.25 9.15

Meeting of the UPU Committee of Postal Studies, Bogota, Oct., 1967.

1968, May 14 **Litho.** ***Perf. 13½x14***

Design: 1p, Map of communications network.

774 A331 50c brt yel grn, blk & org brn 15 15
775 A331 1p multi 20 15
Nos. 774-775,C498-C499 (4) 66
Set value 25

20th anniv. of the National Telecommunications Service (TELECOM).

The Eucharist — A332

St. Augustin, by Gregorio Vasquez — A333

1968, June 6 **Litho.** ***Perf. 13½x14***
776 A332 60c multi 15 15
Nos. 776,C500-C501 (3) 60
Set value 20

39th Eucharistic Congress, Bogotá, Aug. 18-25.

1968, Aug. 13 **Photo.** ***Perf. 13***

Designs: 60c, The Gathering of Manna, by Gregorio Vasquez. 1p, The Marriage of the Virgin, by Baltazar de Figueroa. 5p, Jeweled monstrance, c. 1700. 10p, Pope Paul VI, painting by Roman Franciscan nuns.

777 A333 25c multicolored 15 15
778 A333 60c multicolored 15 15
779 A333 1p multicolored 15 15
780 A333 5p multicolored 52 15
781 A333 10p multicolored 1.10 45
a. Souvenir sheet of 2 1.90 95
Nos. 777-781,C502-C506 (10) 7.50
Set value 2.90

39th Eucharistic Congress. Bogotá, Aug. 18-25. No. 781a contains two imperf. stamps similar to Nos. 780-781.

Pope Paul VI — A334

Arms of National University — A335

1968, Aug. 22 **Litho.** ***Perf. 13½x14***
782 A334 25c multi 15 15
Nos. 782,C507-C509 (4) 80
Set value 30

Visit of Pope Paul VI to Colombia, Aug. 22-24.

1968, Oct. 29 **Litho.** ***Perf. 13½x14***
783 A335 80c multi 15 15

Centenary of the founding of the National University. See No. C510.

Stamp of Antioquia, 1868 — A336

Institute Emblem — A337

1968, Nov. 20 **Litho.** ***Perf. 12x12½***
784 A336 30c emer & bl 15 15

Souvenir Sheet

785 A336 5p lt olive & blue 2.50 2.50

Cent. of the 1st postage stamps of Antioquia and the 7th Natl. Phil. Exhib., Medellin, Nov. 20-29.

1969, Mar. 5 **Litho.** ***Perf. 13½x14***
786 A337 20c multi 15 15

25th anniv. (in 1967) of the Inter-American Agricultural Sciences Institute. See No. C511.

Battle of Boyaca (Detail), by José Maria Espinosa — A338

Design: 30c, Army of liberation crossing Pisba Pass, by Francisco Antonio Caro.

1969, July 24 **Litho.** ***Perf. 13½x14***
787 A338 20c gold & multi 15 15
788 A338 30c gold & multi 15 15
Nos. 787-788,C517 (3) 78
Set value 30

Sesquicentennial of the fight for independence.

"Poverty"
A339

1970, Mar. 1 Litho. *Perf. 14*
789 A339 30c bl & multi 15 15

Colombian Institute for Family Welfare and 10th anniv. of the Children's Rights Law.

Greek Mask and Pre-Columbian Symbol of Literary Contest — A340

1970, Sept. 12 Litho. *Perf. 14x13½*
790 A340 30c dk brn, red org & ocher 15 15

3rd Latin American Theatrical Festival of the Universities, Manizales, Sept. 12-20.

Colombian Stamps, Envelope and Emblem
A341

1970, Sept. 24 Litho. *Perf. 14x13½*
791 A341 2p brt bl & multi 30 15

Issued to publicize Philatelic Week.

Arms of Ibague and Discobolus
A342

1970, Oct. 13
792 A342 80c buff, emer & sepia 20 15

9th National Games in Ibague.

St. Theresa, by Baltazar de Figueroa — A343

1970, Oct. 28 Litho. *Perf. 13½x14*
793 A343 2p multi 40 15

Elevation of St. Theresa (1515-1582), to Doctor of the Church. See No. C568. For overprint see No. C568.

Casa Cural
A344

1971, May 20 Litho. *Perf. 14x13½*
794 A344 1.10p multi 26 15

Fourth centenary (in 1970) of the founding of Guacari, Valle. See No. 809.

Dancers and Music, Currulao — A345

Design: 1p, Chicha Maya dancers and music.

1971 Litho. *Perf. 13½x14*

795 A345	1p pink & multi	30	15
796 A345	1.10p lt bl & multi	30	15
	Set value		16

Souvenir Sheets

Imperf

797	Sheet of 3	3.25	3.00
a.	A345 2.50p Napanga	35	35
b.	A345 2.50p Joropo	35	35
c.	A345 5p Guabina	70	70
798	Sheet of 3	3.25	3.00
a.	A345 4p Bambuco	55	55
b.	A345 4p Cumbia	55	55
c.	A345 4p Currulao	55	55

Issue dates: No. 795, Dec. 20; No. 796, Aug. 5; Nos. 797-798, Aug. 10.

Constitutional Assembly, by Delgado — A346

1971, Oct. 2 *Perf. 14*
801 A346 80c multi 20 15

Sequicentennial of Gran Colombian Constitutional Assembly in Rosario del Cucuta. See No. C589. For overprint see No. C589.

Arrows Emblem — A347

1972, Feb. 24 *Perf. 13½x14*
802 A347 60c blk & gray 28 15

Inter-Governmental Committee on European Migration, 20th anniversary.

Student and World Map — A348

1972, Mar. 15 *Perf. 14x13½*
803 A348 1.10p lt grn & brn 20 15

20th anniv. of ICETEX, an organization which furnishes financial help for educational purposes and for technical studies abroad.

UN Emblem, Soldier and Frigate
A349

1972, Apr. 7
804 A349 1.20p lt bl & multi 20 15

20th anniv. of the Colombian Battalion in Korea.

Mother Francisca Josefa del Castillo — A350

Handicraft — A351

1972, Apr. 6 *Perf. 13½x14*
805 A350 1.20p brn & multi 20 15

Tercentenary (in 1971) of the birth of Mother Francisca Josefa del Castillo, Poor Clare abbess and writer.

1972, Apr. 11

806 A351	1.10p multi	35	15
	Nos. 806,C569-C571 (4)	1.55	70

Colombian artisans.

Maxillaria Triloris — A352

Emeralds — A353

1972, Apr. 20
807 A352 20p green & multi 3.75 1.25

10th Natl. Phil. Exhib., Medellin.

1972, June 16 Litho. *Perf. 13½x14*
808 A353 1.10p multi 50 15

Type of 1971

Design: Antonio Nariño House.

1972, June 17 *Perf. 14x13½*
809 A344 1.10p multi 50 15

4th centenary, town of Leyva.

San Andres and Providencia Islands — A354

1972, June 24 *Perf. 13½x14*
810 A354 60c bl & multi 20 15

Sesquicentennial of annexation by Colombia of San Andres and Providencia Islands.

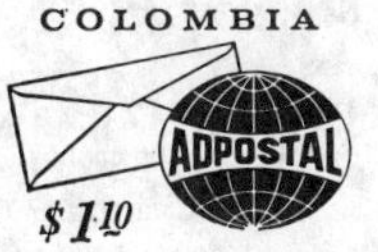

Postal Service Emblem — A355

1972, Nov. 15 Litho. *Perf. 12½x12*
811 A355 1.10p emerald 15 15

Family — A356

1972, Nov. 23
812 A356 60c orange 15 15

Social progress.

Radio League Emblem
A357

Human Figure, Tamalameque
A358

1973, Apr. 6 Litho. *Perf. 12x12½*
813 A357 60c lt bl, ultra & red 20 15

40th anniversary of the Colombian Radio Amateurs' League.

1973, June 15 Litho. *Perf. 13½x14*

Excavated Ceramic Artifacts: 1p, Winged urn, Tairona. 1.10p, Jug, Muisca.

814 A358	60c lt bl & multi	24	15
815 A358	1p org & multi	45	15
816 A358	1.10p vio bl & multi	30	15
	Nos. 814-816,C583-C586 (7)	4.14	
	Set value		1.75

Antonio Nariño, by José M. Espinosa — A359

Child — A360

1973, Dec. 13 Litho. *Perf. 13½x14*

817	A359	60c multi	15	15

Sesquicentennial of the death of General Antonio Nariño (1765-1823).

1973, Dec. 17

818	A360	1.10p multi	20	15

National Campaign for Children's Welfare.

Symbols of Financial Controls A361

1973, Dec. 20 Litho. *Perf. 14x13½*

819	A361	80c ultra, ocher & blk	15	15

50th anniv. of Comptroller-general's Office.

Mother Laura Montoya — A362

1974, June 18 Litho. *Perf. 13½x14*

820	A362	1p multi	20	15

Mother Laura Montoya (1874-1949), founder and Mother Superior of the Missionaries of Mary Immaculata and St. Catherine of Siena.

Runner and Games' Emblem A363

1974, July 18 Litho. *Perf. 14x13½*

821	A363	2p ver, yel & brn	25	15

10th National Games, Pereira.

José Rivera A364

1974, Aug. 3 Litho. *Perf. 14x13½*

822	A364	10p grn & multi	1.10	15

50th anniv. of the publication of "La Voragine" (The Whirlpool) by José Eustasio Rivera.

Abstract Pattern — A365

Train Emerging from Tunnel — A366

1974, Oct. 24 Litho. *Perf. 13½x14*

823	A365	1.10p multi	25	15

Cent. of Natl. Insurance Co. See No. C610.

1974, Nov. 27 Litho. *Perf. 13½x14*

824	A366	1.10p multi	20	15

Centenary of the Antioquia railroad.

Boy, Puppy and Soccer Ball — A367

Christmas: 1p, Girl with racket and kitten.

1974, Dec. 9

825	A367	80c multi	20	15
826	A367	1p multi	20	15
		Set value		15

A368

1975, Apr. 11 Litho. *Perf. 14x13½*

827	A368	80c Gold Animal	20	15
828	A368	1.10p Gold necklace	20	15
		Nos. 827-828,C621-C622 (4)	3.10	
		Set value		85

Pre-Columbian Sinu culture artifacts. For surcharge see No. 840.

Guglielmo Marconi — A369

Santa Marta Cathedral — A370

1975, June 2 Litho. *Perf. 13½x14*

829	A369	3p multi	16	15

Birth centenary of Guglielmo Marconi (1874-1937), Italian electrical engineer and inventor.

1975, July 26

830	A370	80c multi	15	15

400th anniv. of Santa Marta City. See #C623.

Rafael Nuñez — A371

Arms of Medellin — A372

1975, Sept. 28 Litho. *Perf. 13½x14*

831	A371	1.10p multi	15	15

Rafael Nunez (1825-1894), philosopher, poet, political leader, birth sesquicentenary.

For surcharge see No. 848.

1975-79 *Perf. 13½x14, 12 (1.20p)*

832	A372	1p shown	30	15
833	A372	1.20p Ibagué	15	15
834	A372	1.20p Tunja	15	15
835	A372	1.50p Cucuta	30	15
836	A372	1.50p Cartagena	15	15
836A	A372	4p Sogamoso	50	15
837	A372	5p Popayan	30	15
838	A372	5p Barranquilla	28	15
839	A372	10p San Gil	50	15
839A	A372	10p Socorro	50	15
		Nos. 832-839A (10)	3.13	
		Set value		75

1p for the tercentenary of Medellin; No. 835, the cent. of Cucuta's reconstruction.

Issued: 1975- 1p, Nov. 4; No. 835, Nov. 29; 1976- No. 836, Feb. 10; No. 833, July 30; No. 834, Dec. 20; 1977- No. 837, Aug. 30; No. 838, Sept. 20; 1979- 10p, Aug. 9; 4p, Sept. 14.

See #905-913, C818. For surcharge see #849.

No. 827 Surcharged **$ 1.20**

1975 *Perf. 14x13½*

840	A368	1.20p on 80c multi	15	15

Purace Indians, Cauca — A373

1976, Nov. 10 Litho. *Perf. 13½x14*

841	A373	1.50p multi	15	15

Callicore A374

Designs: 5p, Morpho (butterfly). 20p, Anthurium.

1976, Nov. 17 *Perf. 12*

842	A374	3p multi	50	15
843	A374	5p multi	75	20
844	A374	20p multi	2.25	75
		Nos. 842-844 (3)	3.50	1.10

Rotary Emblem — A375

1976, Dec. 3 Litho. *Perf. 12*

845	A375	1p multi	15	15

Rotary Club of Colombia, 50th anniversary.

Declaration of Independence, by John Trumbull — A376

1976, Dec. 21 Litho. *Perf. 12*

846	A376	Strip of 3	9.00	10.50
a.-c.		30p any single	2.75	2.00

American Bicentennial. No. 846 printed in sheets of 4 triptychs.

Policeman with Dog — A377

1976, Dec. 29 *Perf. 13½x14*

847	A377	1.50p multi	20	15

Honoring the National Police.

For surcharge see No. 850.

Nos. 831, 834, 847 Surcharged in Light Brown

1977, June Litho. *Perf. 13½x14, 12*

848	A371	2p on 1.10p multi	20	15
849	A372	2p on 1.20p multi	15	15
850	A377	2p on 1.50p multi	25	15
		Nos. 848-850 (3)	60	
		Set value		25

Souvenir Sheet

Postal Museum, Bogota — A378

1977, July 27 Litho. *Perf. 14*

855	A378	25p multi	2.50	2.50

Postal Museum, Bogotá.

Mother and Child — A379

1977-78 Litho. *Perf. 12*

856	A379	2p multi	15	15
857	A379	2.50p multi ('78)	90	15
		Set value		15

National good nutrition plan. Issue dates: 2p, Aug. 30. 2.50p, Jan. 26.

Jacana and Eichhornia
A380

Fidel Cano, by Francisco Cano
A381

Design: 20p, Mayan cotinga and pyrostegia venusta.

1977, Sept. 6 **Litho.** ***Perf. 14***
858 A380 10p multi 1.00 25
859 A380 20p multi 1.50 40
Nos. 858-859,C644-C647 (6) 4.30 1.25

1977, Sept. 16 ***Perf. 14***
860 A381 4p multi 20 15

90th anniversary of El Espectador, newspaper founded by Fidel Cano.

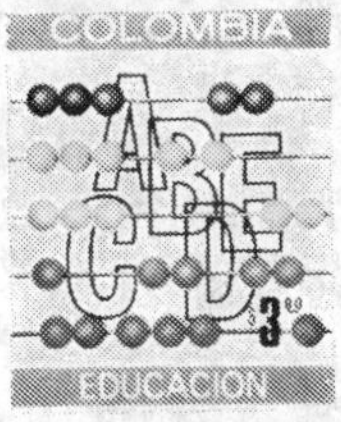

Abacus and Alphabet
A382

Cattleya Triannae
A383

1977, Sept. 16 ***Perf. 13½x14***
861 A382 3p multi 15 15

Popular education.

1978-79 **Litho.** ***Perf. 12***
862 A383 2.50p multi 15 15
863 A383 3p multi ('79) 16 15
Set value 15

Issue dates: 2.50p, Apr. 18. 3p, May 10.

Sprinting and Games Emblem
A384

Sports: a, sprinting. b, basketball. c, baseball. d, boxing. e. bicycling. f, fencing. g, soccer. h, gymnastics. i, judo. j, weight lifting. k, wrestling. l, swimming. m, tennis. n, target shooting. o, volleyball. p, water polo.

1978, June 27 **Litho.** ***Perf. 14***
868 Sheet of 16 15.00 3.50
a.-p. A384 10p, any single 90 20

13th Central American and Caribbean Games, Medellin.

"Sigma 2" by Alvaro Herrán
A385

1978, June 30
869 A385 8p multi 40 16

Chamber of Commerce, Bogota, centenary.

Gen. Tomás Cipriano de Mosquera (1778-1878), Statesman
A386

1978, Oct. 6 **Litho.** ***Perf. 12***
870 A386 6p multi 42 15

Anthurium Narinenses — A387

1979, July 23 ***Perf. 12***
871 A387 3p red & multi 16 15
872 A387 3p pur & multi 16 15
873 A387 3p rose & pur 16 15
874 A387 3p white & multi 16 15
a. Block of 4, #871-874 65 25

Gen. Rafael Uribe, by Acevedo Bernal — A388

1979, Oct. 31 **Litho.** ***Perf. 12***
875 A388 8p multi 40 15

Gen. Rafael Uribe, statesman, 60th death anniversary.

Village, by Leonor Alarcon — A389

1979, Nov. 22 ***Perf. 14***
876 A389 15p multi 1.00 35

Community Work Boards, 20th anniversary.

Introduction of Color Television
A390

1980, Mar. 4 **Litho.** ***Perf. 14***
877 A390 5p multi 35 15

Bullfight, Arms of Cali — A391

1980, Mar. 25
878 A391 5p multi 50 15

Cali Tourist Festival, Dec. 25, 1979-Jan. 2, 1980.

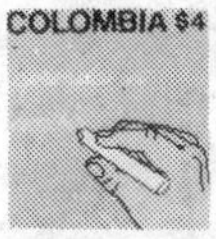

"Learn to Write" — A392

1980, Apr. 25 **Litho.** ***Perf. 12½***
879 Block of 30 10.00 10.00
a. A392 4p, any single 20 15

Each stamp shows letter of alphabet and corresponding animal or subject. Issued in sheets of 90 (30x3).

Villavicencio Festival — A393

Design: 9p, Vallenato festival.

1980 **Litho.** ***Perf. 14***
880 A393 5p multi 30 15
881 A393 9p multi 30 15

Issue dates: 5p, July 15; 9p, June 17.

Gustavo Uribe Ramirez and Tree
A394

1980, Aug. 5 **Litho.** ***Perf. 12***
882 A394 10p multi 30 15

Gustavo Uribe Ramirez (1893-1968), ecologist.

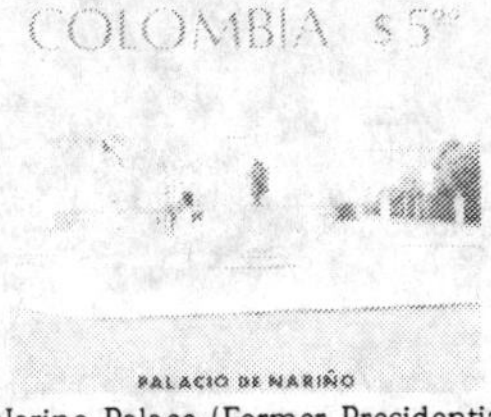

Narino Palace (Former Presidential Residence) — A395

1980, Sept. 19 **Litho.** ***Perf. 14***
883 A395 5p multi 45 15

Monument to First Pioneers of 1819, Armenia
A396

1980, Oct. 14
884 A396 5p multi 40 15

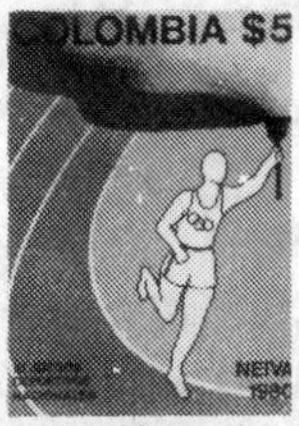

11th National Games, Neiva — A397

Fight against Cancer — A398

1980, Nov. 28 ***Perf. 13½x14***
885 A397 5p multi 45 15

1980, Dec. 9
886 A398 10p multi 30 15

Xavier Universary Law Faculty, 50th Anniversary
A399

1980, Dec. 16 **Litho.** ***Perf. 14½***
887 A399 20p multi 55 15

Death of Bolivar — A400

1980, Dec. 17 ***Perf. 12***
888 A400 25p multi 1.00 60

Simon Bolivar, death sesquicentennial. See No. C696.

José Maria Obando, President of Colombia A401

115th Anniv. of Constitution (Former Presidents): b, Jose Hilario Lopez. c, Manuel Murillo Toro. d, Santiago Perez. e, Rafael Reyes. f, Carlos E. Restrepo. g, Jose Vicente Concha. h, Miguel Abadia Mendez. i, Eduardo Santos. j, Mariano Ospina Perez.

1981, June 9 Litho. *Perf. 12*

889	Strip of 10	1.50	
a.-j.	A401 5p multi	15	15

1981, Sept. 23 Litho. *Perf. 12*

Designs: a, Rafael Nunez (1825-94). b, Marco Fidel Suarez (1855-1927). c, Pedro Nel Ospina (1858-1927). d, Enrique Olaya Herrera (1880-1937). e, Alfonso Lopez Pumarejo (1886-1959). f, Aquileo Parra (1825-1900). g, Santos Gutierrez (1820-72). h, Tomas Cipriano de Mosquera (1789-1878). i, Mariano Ospina Rodriguez. j, Pedro Alcantara Herran (1800-72).

890	Strip of 10	17.50	
a.-j.	A401 7p multi	1.75	35

1981, Aug. 11 Litho. *Perf. 12*

Designs like No. 889.

891	Strip of 10	27.50	
a.-j.	A401 7p multi	2.75	75

1981, Nov. 11 Litho. *Perf. 12*

Designs: a, Manuel Maria Mallarino. b, Santos Acosta. c, Eustorgio Salgar. d, Julian Trujillo. e, Francisco Javier Zaldua. f, Guillermo Leon Valencia. g, Laureano Gomez. h, Manuel A. Sanclemente. i, Miguel Antonio Caro. j, Jose Eusebio Otalora.

892	Strip of 10	11.00	
a.-j.	A401 7p multi	1.10	25

1981, Dec. 15 Litho. *Perf. 12*

Designs: a, Ruben Piedrahita Arango. b, Jorge Holguin. c, Ramon Gonzalez Valencia. d, Jose Manuel Marroquin. e, Carlos Holguin. f, Bartolome Calvo. g, Sergio Camargo. h, Jose Maria Rojas Garrido. i, J.M. Campo Serrano. j, Eliseo Payan.

893	Strip of 10	8.50	
a.-j.	A401 7p multi	80	20

1982, May 3 *Perf. 12*

Designs: a, Simon Bolivar. b, Francisco de Paula Santander. c, Joaquin Mosquera. d, Domingo Caicedo. e, Jose Ignacio de Marquez. f, Roberto Urdaneta Arbelaez. g, Carlos Lozano y Lozano. h, Guillermo Quintero Calderon. i, Jose de Obaldia. j, Juan de Dios Aranzazu.

894	Strip of 10	7.75	
a.-j.	A401 7p multi	75	20

Jose Maria Villa and West Bridge over Cauca River — A404

1981, Nov. 25 Litho. *Perf. 14x13½*

895	A404 60p multi	1.00	25

Agrarian, Mineral and Industrial Credit Bank, 50th Anniv. — A405

Los Nevados Park — A406

1981, Dec. 9 Litho. *Perf. 14*

896	A405 15p multi	35	15

1981, Dec. 10 Litho. *Perf. 13½x14*

897	A406 20p multi	60	15

Girl Sitting on Fence — A407

1982, Feb. 22 Litho. *Perf. 12½x12*

898	Strip of 3	2.00	1.10
a.	A407 30p shown	60	25
b.	A407 30p Girl, basket	60	25
c.	A407 30p Boy, wheelbarrow	60	25

Floral Bouquet — A408

Hipotecario Bank, 50th Anniv. — A409

Designs: Various floral arrangements.

1982, July 28

900	Strip of 10	3.50	3.50
a.	A408 7p, any single	30	15

1982, July 29 *Perf. 14*

901	A409 9p blk & grn	20	15

St. Thomas Aquinas (1225-1274) — A410

Paintings by Zurbaran.

1982 Litho. *Perf. 12*

902	A410 5p multi	15	15
903	A410 5p St. Teresa of Avila	15	15
904	A410 5p St. Francis of Assisi	15	15
	Nos. 902-904 (3)	45	
	Set value		15

Issued: #902, Aug. 6; #903, Sept. 28; #904, Oct. 4.

Arms Type of 1975

1982-90 Litho. *Perf. 14, 12 (50p)*

905	A372 10p shown	24	15
905A	A372 10p San Juan de Pasto	24	15
906	A372 16p Rionegro	45	20
907	A372 20p Santa Fe de Bogota	42	20
907A	A372 20p Santiago de Cali	24	15
908	A372 23p Honda	55	25
911	A372 50p Cartago	30	15
913	A372 55p Antioquia ('86)	60	25
	Nos. 905-913 (8)	3.04	1.50

Issue dates: 16p, 23p, No. 905, Dec. 7; No. 907, Mar. 1, 1983; No. 905A, Apr. 12, 1983; No. 907A, July 25, 1986; 55p, Aug. 5, 1986; 50p, May 30, 1990.

See No. C818.

This is an expanding set. Numbers will change if necessary.

Gabriel Marquez, 1982 Nobel Prize, Literature — A412

1982, Dec. 10 *Perf. 13½x14*

917	A412 7p gray & grn	20	15

See No. C731-C732.

Public Education Bicentenary (Society of Mary for Education) A413

1983, May 6

918	A413 9p gold & blk	35	20

José Maria Espinosa Prieto, Painter — A414

250th Anniv. of City of Cucuta — A415

1983, June 3 *Perf. 12*

919	A414 9p Self-portrait, 1860	16	15

1983, June 23 Litho. *Perf. 12*

920	A415 9p multi	16	15

Porfirio Barba-Jacob (1883-1942), Poet — A416

1983, July 29 Litho. *Perf. 13½x14*

921	A416 9p Portrait	16	15

Simon Bolivar, 200th Birth Anniv. A417

1983, July 24 *Perf. 12*

922	A417 9p multi	20	15

See Nos. C736-C737.

Royal Spanish Botanical Exhibition, 200th Anniv. — A418

1983, Aug. 18 *Perf. 14*

923	A418 9p Cinchona lancefolia	20	15
924	A418 9p Passiflora laurifolia	20	15
925	A418 60p Cinchona cordiflora	1.10	50
	Nos. 923-925,C738-C740 (6)	3.10	
	Set value		1.08

Dawn in the Andes, by Alejandro Obregon A420

1983, Oct. 5 Litho. *Perf. 12*

928	A420 20p multi	40	15

See No. C741.

Francisco de Paula Santander (1792-1840), General — A421

1984, Mar. 6 Litho. *Perf. 14½x14*

929	A421 12p light olive green	20	15
930	A421 12p pale carmine	20	15
931	A421 12p light ultra	20	15
	Nos. 929-931 (3)	60	
	Set value		21

Admiral Jose Prudencio Padilla (1784-1831) A423

1984, May 17 Litho. *Perf. 12*

933	A423 10p multi	16	15

Luis Antonio Calvo (1882-1945) Composer A424

1984, July 26

934	A424 18p multi	30	15

Diego Fallon (1834-1905), Educator, Musician, Poet — A425

1984, Aug. 31 *Perf. 12*
935 A425 20p multi 30 15

Candelario Obeso (1849-1884), Writer A426

1984, Sept. 4 *Perf. 14x13½*
936 A426 20p multi 30 15

Site of Marandua, Future City — A427

1984, Sept. 28 *Perf. 12*
937 A427 15p multi 22 15

See No. C744.

Christmas 1984 — A428

Nativity and Children Playing, by Jose Uriel Sierra, Age 7.

1984, Dec. 14
938 A428 12p multi 20 15

See No. C746.

Dr. Luis Eduardo Lopez, Education Minister A429

1984, Dec. 21
939 A429 22p multi 35 15

Maria Concepcion Loperena de Fernandez de Castro, Independence War Heroine — A430

1985, Jan. 6
940 A430 12p multi 22 15

Gonzalo Mejia (1885-1956) A431

1985, Feb. 25
941 A431 12p Portrait, biplane, camera 20 15

Aviation, motion picture and meat exporting industrialist.

Self-portrait with Wife — A432

1985, Feb. 25
942 A432 37p multi 62 30

Pedro Nel Gomez (1899-1984), painter. See No. C748.

Fauna — A433

1985 *Perf. 14*
943 A433 12p Hydrochaeris hydrochaeris 16 15

Perf. 13

944 A433 15p Felis pardalis 20 15
945 A433 15p Tremarctos ornatus, vert. 20 15
946 A433 20p Tapirus pinchaque 28 15
Nos. 943-946,C758 (5) 1.49
Set value 57

Carlos Gardel (1890-1935), Entertainer A434

Camina Literacy Program A435

1985, June 23 *Perf. 14*
947 A434 15p Portrait, Fokker F-31 Tri-motor 20 15

1985, Nov. 25 *Perf. 13½x14*
948 A435 15p Tree, alphabet 20 15

Christmas 1985 — A436

1985, Dec. 4 **Litho.** *Perf. 13*
949 A436 15p multi 20 15

Rafael Pombo Children's Foundation. See No. C755.

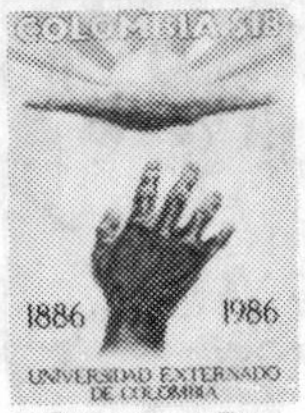

Eduardo Carranza (b. 1913), Poet — A437

Colombian Free University, Cent. — A438

1986, Feb. 13
950 A437 18p multi 24 15

1986, Feb. 14
951 A438 18p multi 24 15

Gen. Antonio Ricaurte (b. 1786), Liberator A439

1986, May 7 **Litho.** *Perf. 13*
952 A439 18p Leiva birthplace 24 15

Jose Asuncion Silva (1865-1896), Poet, and Scene from Nocturno A440

1986, May 30 **Litho.** *Perf. 12*
953 A440 18p multi 22 15

Fernando Gomez Martinez (1897-1985), Journalist — A441

1986, June 19
954 A441 24p multi 30 15

Santiago de Cali, 450th Anniv. A442

1986, July 25 **Litho.** *Perf. 13*
955 A442 25p La Merced 30 15

A443

A444

Monsignor Jose Vicente Castro Silva (1885-1968), rector of the Mayor del Rosario School: portrait by Ricardo Gomez.

1986, Aug. 4 **Litho.** *Perf. 12*
956 A443 20p multi 22 15

1986, Oct. 14 **Litho.** *Perf. 12*
957 A444 40p Natl. University 45 15

Faculties: Fine Arts, cent., and Architecture, 50th anniv.

Rafael Maya (1897-1980), Poet, and Salamanca University Entrance A445

1986, Oct. 15
958 A445 25p multi 28 15

See No. C772.

Condor in Flight — A446

Deroptius Accipritrinus — A446a

Designs: No. 962, Inia goefrenis. No. 963, Procyon cancrivorus. No. 964, Monachus tropicalis. No. 965, Pteronura brasiliensis. No. 966, Trichechus manatus. No. 967, Odocoileus virginianus. No. 968, Trogon personatos personatos. Nos. 962-968 horiz.

1986-89 **Litho.** *Perf. 12*
959 A446 20p ultra 22 15
960 A446 25p ultra ('87) 30 15

Perf. 14½x14, 14x14½

961 A446a 30p grn ('87) 35 15
962 A446a 30p dull vio ('87) 35 15

Engr.
Wmk. 334

963 A446a 35p chest brn ('88) 35 15
964 A446a 35p dark grn ('88) 35 15
965 A446a 40p deep org ('88) 40 15
966 A446a 40p gray ('88) 28 15
967 A446a 40p tan ('89) 28 15
968 A446a 45p dark vio ('88) 32 15
Nos. 959-968 (10) 3.20
Set value 1.08

Issue dates: 20p, Nov. 6. 25p, May 25. No. 961, June 8. No. 962, Dec. 24. No. 963, Aug. 6. No. 964, Sept. 20. No. 965, Sept. 20. No. 966, Nov. 29. No. 967, Apr. 29. No. 968, Dec. 16.
See Nos. 996, 1000, C778-C781.

A447

A448

1987, Jan. 29 **Unwmk.** *Perf. 12*
969 A447 25p multi 45 15

Pedro Uribe Mejia (1886-1972), pioneer of Colombian coffee industry.

1987, May 3 *Perf. 13½x13*
970 A448 500p Santa Barbara Church 4.75 1.60

Mompox, 450th anniv.

Writers
A449

Portraits and scenes from works: 70p, Jorge Isaacs (1837-1895), novelist, and scene from *Maria.* 90p, Aurelio Martinez Mutis (1884-1954), poet, and scene from *La Epopeya del Condor.*

1987 ***Perf. 12***

971 A449 70p multi		75	25
972 A449 90p multi		1.00	32

Issue dates: 70p, July 28. 90p, Sept. 2.

A450

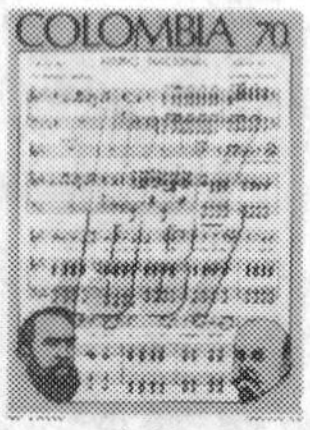

A451

1987 **Litho.** ***Perf. 13½x13***

Social Security & Communications.

973 A450 35p multi 38 15

1988, May 25 **Litho.** ***Perf. 12***

Natl. Anthem, Cent.: Score, lyricist Rafael Nunez and composer Oreste Sindici. Dated 1987.

974 A451 70p multi 65 22

Human Rights — A452

Perf. 14½x14, 14x14½

1988-89 **Engr.**

975 A452 30p Life	28	15
976 A452 35p Suffrage	32	15
977 A452 40p Association, horiz.	38	15
978 A452 45p Culture, horiz.	30	15
Nos. 975-978 (4)	1.28	
Set value		42

Issue dates: 30p, 35p, May 12. 40p, July 1. 45p, Oct. 27, 1989.

See Nos. C797, C807.

Pasto, 450th Anniv.
A453

1988, May 20 **Litho.** ***Perf. 12***

979 A453 60p Cathedral, Pasto 60 20

Dated 1987.

Values quoted in this catalogue are for stamps graded Fine-Very Fine and with no faults. An illustrated guide to grade is provided in the "Catalogue Information" section of the Introduction.

Bogota Aqueduct and Sewage System, Cent. — A454

1988, May 20

980 A454 100p Waterfall 95 32

Maria Currea de Aya (1888-1985), Women's Rights Activist
A455

1988, May 27

981 A455 80p multi 75 25

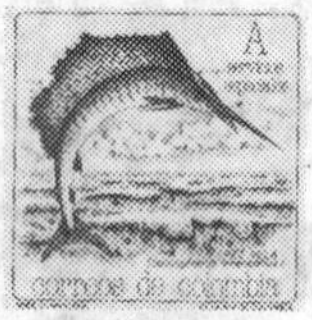

A456

A457

Sailfish, *Istiaophorus Americanus.*

Perf. 14x13½

1988, July 19 **Engr.** **Wmk. 334**

982 A456 (A) dark blue	3.75	2.00
983 A456 (B) Prus blue	95	32

At the time of issue, No. 982 was sold for 400p and No. 983 for 100p. See type A486.

Unwmk.

1988, Aug. 10 **Litho.** ***Perf. 12***

984 A457 120p multi 1.05 35

San Bartolome College, founded in 1604.

Jorge Alvarez Lleras (1885-1952), Engineer and Director of the Natl. Astronomical Observatory
A458

1988, Aug. 17

985 A458 90p multi 80 20

Pres. Eduardo Santos (1888-1974) — A459

1988, Aug. 30

986 A459 80p multi 70 18

Andres Bello Seminary
A460

Unwmk.

1988, Dec. 27 **Litho.** ***Perf. 12***

987 A460 115p multi 82 28

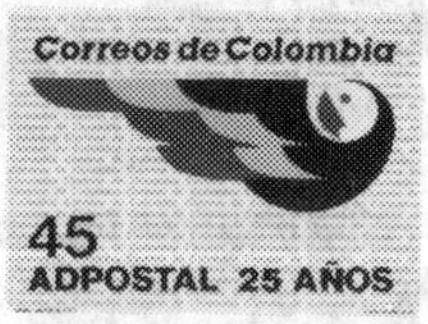

Adpostal, 25th Anniv.
A461

1989, May 3

988 A461 45p multi 32 15

Military Leaders — A462

Bolivar and Santander at the Los Llanos Campaign — A463

1989 **Litho.** ***Perf. 12***

989 A462 40p Santander	28	15
990 A462 40p Bolivar	28	15
991 A463 45p multi	38	15
Nos. 989-991 (3)	94	
Set value		30

Liberation campaign, 170th anniv.

Issued: #989, Aug. 25; #990, July 25; 45p, Aug. 7.

From Boyaca to Santa Fe
A464 A465

1989, Aug. 7 **Litho.** ***Perf. 12***

992 A464 45p multi	38	15
993 A465 45p multi	38	15
a. Pair, #992-993	80	30

Liberation campaign, 170th anniv.

Liberation Campaign Triptych — A466

Designs: a, Gen. Santander, liberation force. b, Simon Bolivar riding mount. c, Insurgent cavalry.

Unwmk.

1989, Aug. 7 **Litho.** ***Perf. 13***

994 A466 Strip of 3	90	30
a.-c. 45p any single	30	15

Liberation Campaign, 170th anniv.

Tunja, 450th Anniv.
A467

1989, Aug. 8 ***Perf. 12***

995 A467 45p multicolored 30 15

Fauna Type of 1988

Designs: No. 996, Harpia harpyja, horiz. No. 997, Urocyon cinereoargenteus. No. 998, Dendrobates histrionicus. No. 1000, Phenacosaurus indenenae. No. 1001, Cebuella pygmaea. No. 1002, Eurypyga helias, horiz.

Perf. 14½x14, 14x14½

1989-90 **Engr.** **Wmk. 334**

996 A446a 45p black	30	15
997 A446a 50p blue gray	30	15
998 A446a 50p deep claret	30	15
1000 A446a 55p red brown	38	15
1001 A446a 60p brown	35	15
1002 A446a 60p org brown	35	15
Nos. 996-1002 (6)	1.98	
Set value		66

Issue dates: 45p, Sept. 7; Nos. 997, 1001, Mar. 1, 1990; No. 998, Apr. 25; 55p, Aug. 18; No. 1002, Aug. 6.

This is an expanding set. Numbers will change if necessary.

A468

A469

1989, Aug. 30 **Unwmk.** ***Perf. 12***

1011 A468 135p multicolored 90 30

City of Armenia, cent.

1990, Mar. 28 **Litho.** ***Perf. 12***

1012 A469 60p Espeletia hartwegiana 35 15

Gen. Francisco De Paula Santander (1792-1840)
A470

1990, May 6 ***Perf. 14x13½***

1013 A470 50p multicolored	30	15
Nos. 1013,C823-C827 (6)	3.40	
Set value		45

See Nos. 1046-1047.

General Santander Police Academy, 50th Anniv. — A471

1990, May 16 *Perf. 12*
1014 A471 60p multicolored 35 15

Department of La Guajira A473

1990, July 1 *Perf. 12*
1016 A473 60p multicolored 35 15

Ceiba Pentandra A474

1990, July 15 Litho. *Perf. 12*
1017 A474 60p multicolored 35 15

A475 A476

1990, Aug. 8 Litho. *Perf. 12*
1018 A475 70p Tibouchina lepidota 65 23

Unwmk.
1990, Aug. 28 Litho. *Perf. 14*
1019 A476 70p Ceroxylon quindiuense 38 15

A477 A478

1990, Sept. 28 *Perf. 12*
1020 A477 60p St. John Bosco 35 15

Salesian Order in Colombia, cent.

1991, Mar. 28 Litho. *Perf. 12*
1021 A478 70p multicolored 38 15

Miraculous Christ, Pilgrimage Church of Buga.

Moths and Butterflies A479

1991, Apr. 18 Litho. *Perf. 14*
1022 A479 70p Callithea philotima 32 15
1023 A479 70p Anaea syene, vert. 32 15
1024 A479 80p Thecla coronata, vert. 38 15
1025 A479 80p Agrias amydon 38 15
1026 A479 170p Morpho rhetenor 78 28
1027 A479 190p Heliconius longarenus 90 30
Nos. 1022-1027 (6) 3.08 1.18

Nos. 1025-1027 are airmail.

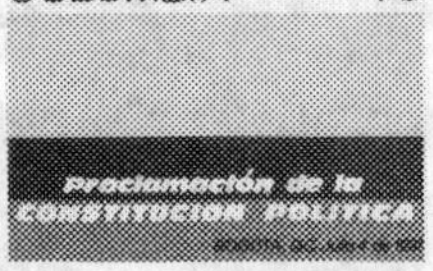

New Constitution A480

1991, July 4 Litho. *Perf. 14*
1028 A480 70p multicolored 35 15

A481 A482

1991, July 19 *Perf. 12*
1029 A481 80p multicolored 38 15

Pres. Dario Echandia Olaya (1897-1989). See No. 1042.

1991, Aug. 7
1030 A482 70p multicolored 35 15

Col. Antanasio Girardot (1791-1813).

A483 A484

1991, Aug. 15 Litho. *Perf. 14*
1031 A483 80p multicolored 38 15

Luis Carlos Galan Sarmiento (1943-1989), political reformer.

1991, Aug. 24 *Perf. 12*

Pre-Columbian Artifacts: 80p, Statue of cat god. No. 1033, Pitcher from tomb of high official. No. 1034, Statue with two heads. 210p, Flying fish, horiz.

1032 A484 80p multicolored 38 15
1033 A484 90p multicolored 40 15
1034 A484 90p multicolored 40 15
1035 A484 210p multicolored 95 30
Nos. 1032-1035 (4) 2.13 75

Nos. 1034-1035 are airmail.

Colonial Architecture A485

Designs: 80p, Cloister of St. Augustine, Tunja. No. 1037, Community Bridge, Chia. No. 1038, Roadside Chapel, Pamplona, vert. 190p, Church of Immaculate Conception, Bogota, vert.

1991 Litho. *Perf. 12*
1036 A485 80p multicolored 38 15
1037 A485 90p multicolored 48 15
1038 A485 90p multicolored 40 15
1039 A485 190p multicolored 85 25
Nos. 1036-1039 (4) 2.11
Set value 60

Issue dates: No. 1037, Sept. 9. Others, Sept. 27. Nos. 1038-1039 are airmail.

Istiaphorus Americanus A486

1991, Sept. 3 *Perf. 14*
1040 A486 830p multicolored 4.25 1.40

Colombian Police Force, Cent. — A487

1991, Oct. 12 *Perf. 12*
1041 A487 80p multicolored 42 15

President Type of 1991

Pres. Alberto Lleras Camargo (1906-1990)

1991, Nov. 5
1042 A481 80p multicolored 42 15

A489 A490

1991, Dec. 17 Litho. *Perf. 12*
1043 A489 80p Sogamoso City Hall 42 15

1992 Litho. *Perf. 14*

Designs: No. 1044, Diana Turbay Quintero (1950-91), journalist. No. 1045, Indalecio Lievano Aguirre (1917-82), diplomat.

1044 A490 80p multicolored 42 15
1045 A490 80p multicolored 38 15

Issued: #1044, Jan. 24; #1045, Apr. 21.

Santander Type of 1990 and

Battle of Boyaca — A491a

1992, Apr. 2 *Perf. 14*

Size: 26x37mm

1046 A470 80p Monument 38 15
1047 A470 190p Portrait 85 25

Souvenir Sheet

Perf. 13½x14

1047A A491a 950p multicolored 4.00 4.00

Nos. 1047-1047A are airmail. Gen. Francisco de Paula Santander, bicent. of birth.

A492 A493

Ministers of Justice: 100p, Enrique Low Murtra (1939-1991). 110p, Rodrigo Lara Bonilla (1946-1984).

1992, Apr. 30 Litho. *Perf. 12*
1048 A492 100p multicolored 42 15
1049 A492 110p multicolored 48 15
Set value 15

1992, May 18 *Perf. 14*
1050 A493 110p multicolored 48 32

15th natl. games, Barranquilla

Wildlife — A494

1992, Apr. 14 Litho. *Perf. 12*
1051 A494 (B) Oroaetus icidori 70 48
1052 A494 (A) Tremarctos ornatus 3.50 2.25

Nos. 1051-1052 had face values of 200p and 950p respectively on date of issue.

Endangered Species A495

1992, Aug. 4
1053 A495 100p Crocodylus acatus 45 30
1054 A495 100p Vultur gryphus, vert. 45 30

A496

A497

1992, Aug. 24 Litho. *Perf. 14*
1055 A496 100p multicolored 40 28
1056 A496 110p multicolored 45 30

Maria Lopez de Escobar, founder of the House of the Mother and Child. No. 1056 is airmail.

1992, Sept. 23 Litho. *Perf. 12*
1057 A497 100p multicolored 42 30

Conference of First Ladies of the Americas and Caribbean, Cartagena.

Recycling — A498

1992, Oct. 9 Litho. *Perf. 12*
1058 A498 100p multicolored 42 30

Discovery of America, 500th Anniv. — A499

Paintings: 100p, Zenaida, by Ana Mercedes Hoyos. No. 1060, Estudio Para 1/500, by Beatriz Gonzalez. No. 1061, Blue Eagle, by Alejandro Obregon. 230p, Cantileo, by Luis Luna. 260p, Corn, by Antonio Caro. 400p, Grand Curtain, by Luis Caballero. 440p, Homage to Guatavita, by Alejandro Obregon.

1992, Oct. 5 Litho. *Perf. 13½x14*
1059 A499 100p multicolored 42 30
1060 A499 110p multicolored 45 32
1061 A499 110p multicolored 45 32
1062 A499 230p multicolored 95 68
1063 A499 260p multicolored 1.10 78
Nos. 1059-1063 (5) 3.37 2.40

Souvenir Sheets
Perf. 12
1064 A499 400p multicolored 1.65 1.65
1065 A499 440p multicolored 1.80 1.80

Nos. 1061-1063 are airmail.

World Post Day — A500

1992, Oct. 19 Litho. *Perf. 12*
1066 A500 (B) multicolored 95 65

No. 1066 had face value of 200p on day of issue.

Christmas — A501

Children's paintings of: 100p, Nativity scene. 110p, Adoration of the Magi.

1992, Nov. 20 Litho. *Perf. 12*
1067 A501 100p multicolored 40 28
1068 A501 110p multicolored 45 32

No. 1068 is airmail.

Three Musicians, by Fernando Botero A502

1993, Feb. 5 Litho. *Perf. 12*
1069 A502 (B) multicolored 95 65

No. 1069 had a face value of 250p on day of issue.

Lions Intl. Campaign Against Amblyopia A503

1993, Mar. 26 *Perf. 14*
1070 A503 100p multicolored 38 28

Holy Week in Popayan A504

1993, Apr. 5 *Perf. 14x13½*
1071 A504 (B) multicolored 95 65

No. 1071 had a face value of 250p on day of issue.

A505

A506

1993, Apr. 7 *Perf. 12*
1072 A505 (B) multicolored 95 65

Pan American Health Organization, 90th anniv.
No. 1072 had a face value of 250p on day of issue.

1993, Apr. 14
1073 A506 (B) multicolored 95 65

Franciscans of Mary Immaculate, cent. No. 1073 had a face value of 250p on day of issue.

A507

A508

1993, Apr. 22 Litho. *Perf. 14*
1074 A507 (B) multicolored 90 60

EXFILBO '93, 18th Natl. Philatelic Exhibition. No. 1074 had a face value of 250p on day issue.

1993, July 2 Litho. *Perf. 12*
1075 A508 250p Guillermo Cano, writer 95 65

Human Rights A509

Designs: a, 150p, Rights of prisoners. b, 150p, Rights of the elderly. c, 200p, Rights of the infirm. d, 200p, Children's rights. e, 220p, Women's rights. f, 220p, Rights of the poor. g, 460p, Right to clean environment. h, 520p, Rights of indigenous people.

Painting: 800p, Peace, Rights, and Freedom, by Alfredo Vivero, vert.

1993, June 10 *Perf. 14*
1076 A509 Block of 8, #a.-h. 8.00 5.60

Souvenir Sheet
1077 A509 800p multicolored 3.00 2.00

Nos. 1076e-1076h are airmail.

Amazon Region of Colombia — A510

Designs: No. 1078a, Parrot. No. 1078b, Anaconda. No. 1079a, Victoria regia. No. 1079b, Flor ipecacuana. 880p, Map, native, horiz.

1993 Litho. *Perf. 12*
1078 A510 150p Pair, #a.-b. 1.10 75
1079 A510 220p Pair, #a.-b. 1.65 1.00

Souvenir Sheet
1080 A510 880p multicolored 3.00 2.00

Nos. 1079-1080 are airmail.

Famous People — A511

Designs: a, 150p, Alberto Pumarejo (1893-1970). b, 150p, Lorencita Villegas de Santos (1892-1960). c, 200p, Meliton Rodriguez (1875-1942). d, 200p, Tomas Carrasquilla (1858-1940).

1993 Litho. *Perf. 14x13½*
1081 A511 Block of 4, #a.-d. 2.50 1.65

Christmas — A512

1993, Nov. 30 *Perf. 12*
1082 A512 200p Holy Family 70 48
1083 A512 220p Shepherd 1.50 1.00

No. 1083 is airmail.

Tourism A513

Designs: No. 1084a, San Andres Providence. b, Cocuy Natl. Park. c, Lake Cocha. d, Waterfalls, Serrania de la Macarena. 250p, Lake Otun. No. 1086a, Chicamocha River. b, Sierra Nevada de Santa Marta mountains. 520p, Penol Reservoir.

1993, Dec. 1 Litho. *Perf. 12*
1084 A513 220p Block of 4, #a.-d. 3.00 2.00
1085 A513 250p multicolored 85 55
1086 A513 460p Pair, #a.-b. 3.00 2.00
1087 A513 520p multicolored 1.75 1.10
Nos. 1084-1087 (4) 8.60 5.65

Nos. 1084, 1086-87 are airmail.

A514

A515

1993, Dec. 21	Litho.	*Perf. 14*	
1088 A514 150p multicolored		52	35

Natl. Museum, 170th anniv.

1994, Jan. 25	Litho.	*Perf. 14*	
1089 A515 300p Marie Poussepin		1.10	70

A516

A517

Birds: 180p, Ognorhynchus icterotis. 240p, Rallus semiplumbeus. 270p, Semnornis ramphastinus, horiz. 560p, Anas cyanoptera, horiz.

1994, Mar. 4			
1090 A516 180p multicolored		65	42
1091 A516 240p multicolored		85	55
1092 A516 270p multicolored		1.00	65
1093 A516 560p multicolored		2.00	1.25
Nos. 1090-1093 (4)		4.50	2.87

Nos. 1092-1093 are airmail.

1994, Apr. 11	Litho.	*Perf. 14*	
1094 A517 300p multicolored		95	60

Air Force, 75th anniv.

Latin American Presidential Summit, Cartagena — A518

1994, June 14	Litho.	*Perf. 14*	
1095 A518 300p shown		95	60
1096 A518 630p Flags		2.00	1.40

No. 1096 is airmail.

1994 World Cup Soccer Championships, US — A519

World Cup Trophy and: 180p, Soccer player, Colombian flag. 270p, Two players with ball. 560p, Soccer ball, Colombian flag, vert.

1110p, Soccer player offering hand to another.

1994, May 26		*Perf. 12*	
1097 A519 180p multicolored		60	38
1098 A519 270p multicolored		90	55
1099 A519 560p multicolored		1.90	1.25
Nos. 1097-1099 (3)		3.40	2.18

Souvenir Sheet

1100 A519 1110p multicolored	3.75	2.50

Nos. 1098-1099 are airmail.

Ricardo Rendon (1894-1931), Artist — A520

1993 Census — A521

1994, June 30	Litho.	*Perf. 12*	
1101 A520 240p black		70	45

1994		*Perf. 14*	
1102 A521 240p multicolored		70	45

Ministry of Communications Inravision, 30th Anniv. — A522

1994		
1103 A522 180p multicolored	52	32

Intl. Year of the Family A523

1994	Litho.	*Perf. 14*	
1104 A523 300p multicolored		1.00	65

America Issue — A524

Methods of mail delivery: 270p, Horse, bicycle. 300p, Men holding stamps showing truck, ship, plane.

1994	Litho.	*Perf. 13*	
1105 A524 270p multicolored		90	60
1106 A524 300p multicolored		1.00	65

No. 1105 is airmail.

Colombian Society of Engineers, Cent. A525

1994	Litho.	*Perf. 12*	
1107 A525 180p multicolored		60	40

SEMI-POSTAL STAMP

Catalogue values for unused stamps in this section are for Never Hinged items.

Girl Giving First Aid — SP1

Perf. 13½x14

1966, Apr. 26	Litho.	Unwmk.	
B1 SP1 5c + 5c multicolored		15	15

Issued for the Red Cross.

AIR POST STAMPS

No. 341 Overprinted

1er.
Servicio
Postal
Aereo
6.-18-19

1919	Unwmk.	*Perf. 14*	
C1 A107 2c car rose		2,750.	1,200.
a. Numerals "1" with serifs		*5,500.*	*3,250.*

Used for the first experimental flight from Barranquilla to Puerto Colombia, June 18, 1919.

Values are for faulty copies.

Issued by Compania Colombiana de Navegacion Aerea

From 1920 to 1932 the internal airmail service of Colombia was handled by the Compania Colombiana de Navegacion Aerea (1920) and the Sociedad Colombo-Alemana de Transportes Aéreos, known familiarly as "SCADTA" (1920-1932). These organizations under government contracts operated and maintained their own post offices, and issued stamps which were the only legal franking for airmail service during this period, both in the internal and international mails. All letters had to bear government stamps as well.

Woman and Boy Watching Plane — AP1

Designs: No. C3, Clouds and small biplane at top. No. C4, Tilted plane viewed close-up from above. No. C5, Flier in plane watching biplane. No. C6, Lighthouse. No. C7, Fuselage and tail of biplane. No. C8, Condor on cliff. No. C9, Plane at rest; pilot foreground. No. C10, Ocean liner.

1920, Feb.	Unwmk.	Litho.	*Imperf.*
Without Gum			
C2 AP1	10c multi	2,000.	1,500.
C3 AP1	10c multi	2,400.	1,500.
C4 AP1	10c multi	3,000.	1,500.
C5 AP1	10c multi	2,750.	1,500.
C6 AP1	10c multi	2,400.	1,500.
C7 AP1	10c multi	6,750.	3,000.
C8 AP1	10c multi	3,000.	2,400.
a.	Without overprint		
C9 AP1	10c multi	2,250.	1,500.
C10 AP1	10c multi	3,000.	2,100.

Flier in Plane Watching Biplane — AP2

1920, Mar.			
C11 AP2 10c green		42.50	*70.00*

Four other 10c stamps, similar to No. C11, have two designs showing plane, mountains and water. They are printed in deep green or light brown red. Some authorities state that these four were not used regularly.

Issued by Sociedad Colombo-Alemana de Transportes Aereos (SCADTA)

Seaplane over Magdalena River — AP3

1920-21	Litho.	*Perf. 12*	
C12 AP3 10c yel ('21)		32.50	25.00
C13 AP3 15c blue ('21)		32.50	27.50
C14 AP3 30c blk, *rose*		14.00	10.00
C15 AP3 30c rose ('21)		32.50	24.00
C16 AP3 50c pale grn		32.50	27.50
Nos. C12-C16 (5)		144.00	114.00

For surcharges see Nos. C17-C24, C36-C37.

No. C16 Handstamp Surcharged in Violet or Black:

(Illustrations of types "a" to "e" are reduced in size.)

VALOR 10 CENTAVOS
a

VALOR 10 CENTAVOS
b

Valor 10 Céntavos
c

VALOR 30 Ctvos
S.C.A.T.A
d

30¢ 30¢
e

$030
f

$030¢
g

1921				
C17 AP3 (a)	10c on 50c		450.	450.
C18 AP3 (b)	10c on 50c		450.	450.
C19 AP3 (c)	10c on 50c		*875.*	*700.*
C20 AP3 (b)	30c on 50c		450.	450.
C21 AP3 (d)	30c on 50c		550.	550.
C22 AP3 (e)	30c on 50c		1,000.	1,000.
C23 AP3 (f)	30c on 50c		775.	675.
C24 AP3 (g)	30c on 50c		775.	675.

Plane over Magdalena River — AP4

Plane over Bogota Cathedral — AP5

1921 *Perf. 11½*

C25 AP4 5c org yel 3.25 3.50
C26 AP4 10c slate grn 1.10 80
C27 AP4 15c org brn 1.10 90
C28 AP4 20c red brn 1.75 1.25
a. Horiz. pair, imperf. vert. 140.00
C29 AP4 30c green 1.40 40
C30 AP4 50c blue 1.75 65
C31 AP4 60c vermilion 9.00 7.00
C32 AP5 1p gray black 10.00 7.00
C33 AP5 2p rose 20.00 14.00
C34 AP5 3p violet 45.00 40.50
C35 AP5 5p olive grn 300.00 250.00
Nos. C25-C35 (11) 394.35 326.00

Exist imperf.
For surcharge see No. C52.

Nos. C16 and C12 Handstamp Surcharged

(Illustration of type "h" is reduced in size.)

VALOR 20 Ctvs.
h

30 cent.
i

1921-22 *Perf. 12*

C36 AP3 (h) 20c on 50c 1,200. 850.00
C37 AP3 (i) 30c on 10c 500.00 325.00

Seaplane over Magdalena River — AP6

Plane over Bogota Cathedral — AP7

1923-28 **Wmk. 116** *Perf. 14x14½*

C38 AP6 5c org yel 85 20
C39 AP6 10c green 85 18
C40 AP6 15c carmine 85 18
C41 AP6 20c gray 85 15
C42 AP6 30c blue 85 15
C43 AP6 40c pur ('28) 7.00 5.00
C44 AP6 50c green 1.25 20
C45 AP6 60c brown 1.90 20
C46 AP6 80c ol grn ('28) 20.00 19.00
C47 AP7 1p black 8.50 2.00
C48 AP7 2p red org 13.00 4.00
C49 AP7 3p violet 27.50 17.50
C50 AP7 5p olive grn 45.00 24.00
Nos. C38-C50 (13) 128.40 72.76

For surcharges and overprints see Nos. C51, C53-C54, CF1.

Nos. C41 and C31 Surcharged in Carmine and Dark Blue:

30 30 Provisional 30 30
No. C51 No. C52

1923

C51 AP6 30c on 20c gray (C) 60.00 35.00
C52 AP4 30c on 60c ver 50.00 27.50

Nos. C41-C42 Overprinted in Black

1928 **Wmk. 116** *Perf. 14x14½*

C53 AP6 20c gray 50.00 50.00
C54 AP6 30c blue 50.00 50.00

Goodwill flight of Lt. Benjamin Mendez from New York to Bogota.

Magdalena River and Tolíma Volcano AP8

Columbus' Ship and Plane AP9

1929, June 1 **Wmk. 127** *Perf. 14*

C55 AP8 5c yel org 75 35
C56 AP8 10c red brn 75 28
C57 AP8 15c dp grn 75 35
C58 AP8 20c carmine 75 15
C59 AP8 30c gray bl 75 28
C60 AP8 40c dl vio 90 28
C61 AP8 50c dk ol grn 1.75 40
C62 AP8 60c org brn 1.75 40
C63 AP8 80c green 6.00 4.00
C64 AP9 1p blue 7.00 2.50
C65 AP9 2p brn org 11.00 4.00
C66 AP9 3p pale rose vio 22.50 20.00
C67 AP9 5p olive grn 52.50 40.00
Nos. C55-C67 (13) 107.15 72.99

For surcharges and overprints see Nos. C80-C95, CF2, CF4.

For International Airmail

AP10

AP11

1929, June 1 **Wmk. 127** *Perf. 14*

C68 AP10 5c yel org 4.00 5.00
C69 AP10 10c red brn 75 2.00
C70 AP10 15c dp grn 75 2.00
C71 AP10 20c carmine 75 2.50
C72 AP10 25c vio bl 75 45
C73 AP10 30c gray bl 75 65
C74 AP10 50c dk ol grn 75 1.25
C75 AP10 60c brown 1.75 2.00
C76 AP11 1p blue 3.50 5.00
C77 AP11 2p red org 5.00 7.00
C78 AP11 3p violet 65.00 62.50
C79 AP11 5p olive grn 80.00 90.00
Nos. C68-79 (12) 163.75 180.35

This issue was sold abroad for use on correspondence to be flown from coastal to interior points of Colombia. Cancellations are those of the country of origin rather than Colombia.
For overprint see No. CF3.

Nos. C63, C66 and C64 Surcharged in Black:

SIMON BOLIVAR
10 — 10
1830 — 1930
m

1830 1930
SIMON BOLIVAR
30 — 30
cts. cts.
n

1930, Dec. 15

C80 AP8(m) 10c on 80c 4.25 4.50
C81 AP9(n) 20c on 3p 8.25 9.00
C82 AP9(n) 30c on 1p 9.00 9.00
Nos. C80-C82 (3) 21.50 22.50

Simon Bolivar (1783-1830).

Colombian Government Issues

Nos. C55-C67 Overprinted in Black:

CORREO AEREO
o

CORREO AEREO
p

Wmk. 127

1932, Jan. 1 **Typo.** *Perf. 14*

C83 AP8(o) 5c yel org 8.00 8.00
C84 AP8(o) 10c red brn 1.75 50
C85 AP8(o) 15c dp grn 3.00 3.00
C86 AP8(o) 20c carmine 1.50 30
C87 AP8(o) 30c gray bl 1.50 50
C88 AP8(o) 40c dl vio 2.00 1.00
C89 AP8(o) 50c dk ol grn 4.00 3.00
C90 AP8(o) 60c org brn 3.25 3.00
C91 AP8(o) 80c green 14.00 14.00
C92 AP9(p) 1p blue 11.00 9.00
C93 AP9(p) 2p brn org 30.00 27.50
C94 AP9(p) 3p pale rose vio 60.00 52.50
C95 AP9(p) 5p ol grn 100.00 110.00
Nos. C83-C95 (13) 240.00 232.30

Coffee AP12

Gold AP16

Designs: 10c, 50c, Cattle. 15c, 60c, Petroleum. 20c, 40c, Bananas. 3p, 5p, Emerald.

1932-39 **Wmk. 127** **Photo.** *Perf. 14*

C96 AP12 5c org & blk brn 90 26
C97 AP12 10c lake & blk 1.00 22
C98 AP12 15c bl grn & vio blk 45 16
C99 AP12 15c ver & vio blk ('39) 2.50 15
C100 AP12 20c car & ol blk 70 15
C101 AP12 20c turq grn & ol blk ('39) 3.50 32
C102 AP12 30c dk bl & blk brn 1.65 16
C103 AP12 40c dk vio & ol bis 85 15
C104 AP12 50c dk grn & brnsh blk 3.50 1.25
C105 AP12 60c dk brn & blk vio 1.10 26
C106 AP12 80c grn & blk brn 5.50 2.00
C107 AP16 1p dk bl & ol bis 9.00 1.25
C108 AP16 2p org brn & ol bis 10.00 2.25
C109 AP16 3p dk vio & emer 17.00 6.25
C110 AP16 5p gray blk & emer 47.50 20.00
Nos. C96-C110 (15) 105.15 34.83

For overprint see No. CF5.

Nos. C104, C106-C108 Surcharged:

1533
CARTAGENA
1933
10 10
a

1533 1933
CARTAGENA
20 centavos 20
b

1934, Jan. 5

C111 AP12(a) 10c on 50c 3.50 3.50
C112 AP12(a) 15c on 80c 4.75 4.75
C113 AP16(b) 20c on 1p 5.25 5.25
C114 AP16(b) 30c on 2p 5.75 5.75
Nos. C111-C114 (4) 19.25 19.25

400th anniversary of Cartagena.

Nos. C100 and C103 Surcharged in Black or Carmine:

5 cts 15

1939, Jan. 15

C115 AP12 5c on 20c (Bk) 35 35
C116 AP12 5c on 40c (C) 35 25
C117 AP12 15c on 20c (Bk) 1.50 50
a. Double surcharge 12.00
b. Pair, one with dbl. surch. 14.00
c. Inverted surcharge 12.00 12.00

No. CF5 Surcharged in Black

C118 AP12 5c on 20c 70 70
Nos. C115-C118 (4) 2.90 1.80

Nos. C102-C103 Surcharged in Black or Red

15 cts

1940, Oct. 20

C119 AP12 15c on 30c 1.25 50
a. Inverted surcharge 12.00
C120 AP12 15c on 40c (R) 2.50 85
a. Double surcharge 12.00

Pre-Columbian Monument — AP18

Proclamation of Independence AP22

Designs: 10c, 40c, Symbol of Legend of El Dorado. 15c, 50c, Spanish Fortifications, Cartagena. 20c, 60c, Colonial Bogotá. 2p, 5p, National Library, Bogota.

Unwmk.

1941, Jan. 28 **Engr.** *Perf. 12*

C121 AP18 5c gray blk 15 15
C122 AP18 10c yel org 15 15
C123 AP18 15c car rose 16 15
C124 AP18 20c yel grn 35 15
a. Horiz. pair, imperf. vert. 87.50
C125 AP18 30c deep blue 35 15
C126 AP18 40c rose lake 70 15
C127 AP18 50c turq grn 70 15
C128 AP18 60c sepia 70 15
C129 AP18 80c olive blk 1.90 50
C130 AP22 1p bl & blk 3.25 50
C131 AP22 2p red org & blk 5.25 2.00
C132 AP22 3p vio & blk 14.00 5.00
C133 AP22 5p lt grn & blk 27.50 17.50
Nos. C121-C133 (13) 55.16 26.70

See #C151-C163, C217-C225. For overprints see #C175-C198, C200-C216, C226, C290.

Bay of Santa Maria — AP24

National Capitol, Bogotá — AP27

Designs: 5c, 20c, 50c, San Sebastian Fort, Cartagena. 10c, 30c, 60c, Tequendama Waterfall.

Unwmk.

1945, Nov. 3 **Litho.** *Perf. 11*

C134 AP24 5c bl gray 15 15
C135 AP24 10c yel org 15 15
C136 AP24 15c rose 15 15
C137 AP24 20c lt yel grn 30 15
C138 AP24 30c ultra 30 15
C139 AP24 40c claret 52 15
C140 AP24 50c bluish grn 55 16
C141 AP24 60c lt vio brn 2.25 80
C142 AP24 80c dk sl grn 3.50 80
C143 AP27 1p dk bl 5.00 75
C144 AP27 2p red org 7.00 2.50
Nos. C134-C144 (11) 19.87 5.91

Part-perforate varieties exist for all denominations except 80c.

Imperf., Pairs

C134a AP24 5c 8.50
C135a AP24 10c 8.50
C136a AP24 15c 8.50
C137a AP24 20c 8.50
C138a AP24 30c 8.50
C139a AP24 40c 8.50
C140a AP24 50c 8.50
C141a AP24 60c 8.50
C142a AP24 80c 10.50
C143a AP27 1p 17.50
C144a AP27 2p 60.00

Bello Type of Regular Issue, 1946

Wmk. 255

1946, Sept. 3 **Engr.** *Perf. 12*

C145 A219 5c deep blue 16 15

Francisco José de Caldas — AP29

Manuel del Socorro Rodriguez — AP30

Perf. 12½

1947, May 9	Litho.	Unwmk.	
C146 AP29	5c dp bl, *grnsh*	35	20
C147 AP30	10c red org, *grnsh*	50	45

4th Pan-American Press Congress (1946).

Chancellery Patio AP31

Capitol, Patio Rafael Nunez AP32

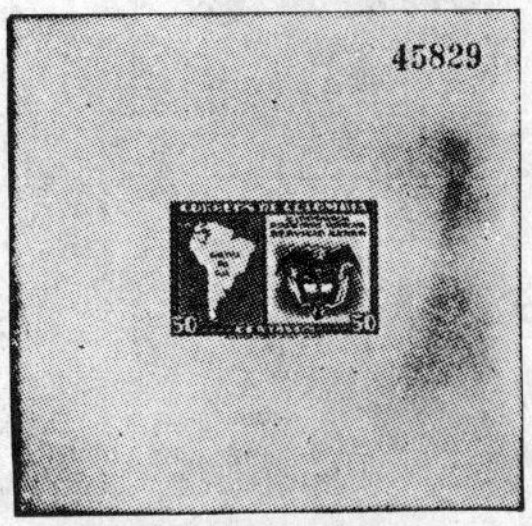

AP33

1948, Apr. 2	Engr.	Wmk. 229	
C148 AP31	5c dk brn	15	15
C149 AP32	15c deep blue	90	90

Miniature Sheet

Imperf

C150 AP33	50c brown	1.40	1.40

9th Pan-American Conference, Bogotá.

Types of 1941

1948, July 21	Unwmk.	*Perf. 12*	
C151 AP18	5c org yel	15	15
C152 AP18	10c scarlet	15	15
C153 AP18	15c dp bl	15	15
C154 AP18	20c violet	15	15
C155 AP18	30c yel grn	35	15
C156 AP18	40c gray	40	15
C157 AP18	50c rose lake	42	15
C158 AP18	60c ol gray	70	15
C159 AP18	80c red brn	85	16
C160 AP22	1p ol grn & vio brn	1.40	32
C161 AP22	2p dp grn & brt bl	2.50	65
C162 AP22	3p rose car & blk	5.50	3.75
C163 AP22	5p lt brn & turq grn	14.00	7.00
	Nos. C151-C163 (13)	26.72	13.08

"Air Week" 5c Blue

The War and Air Department issued a 5c blue stamp in May, 1949, to publicize Air Week (Semana de Aviacion). The design shows a coat-of-arms, inscribed "FAC," superimposed upon an outline map of Colombia. This stamp had no franking value and its use was optional during May 16-23.

Justice and Liberty AP34

Wing AP35

Design: 10c, Liberty holding tablet of laws.

1949, Oct. 7	Unwmk.	*Perf. 13*	
C164 AP34	5c bl grn	15	15
C165 AP34	10c orange	15	15
	Set value	20	15

Issued to honor the new Constitution.

For Domestic Postage

1950, June 22	Litho.	*Perf. 12*	
C166 AP35	5c org yel	25	25
C167 AP35	10c brn red	35	35
C168 AP35	15c lt bl	40	30
C169 AP35	20c lt grn	60	75
C170 AP35	30c lilac gray	1.50	2.00
C171 AP35	60c chocolate	1.90	2.50

With Network as in Parenthesis

C172 AP35	1p gray (buff)	14.00	16.00
C173 AP35	2p bl (pale grn)	14.00	16.00
C174 AP35	5p red brn (red brn)	40.00	45.00
	Nos. C166-C174 (9)	73.00	83.15

No. C172 was issued both with and without network.

Nos. C151-C157 and C160-C163 Overprinted in Black

L

1950, July 18			
C175 AP18	5c org yel	15	15
C176 AP18	10c scarlet	15	15
C177 AP18	15c dp bl	15	15
C178 AP18	20c violet	20	15
C179 AP18	30c yel grn	32	20
C180 AP18	40c gray	80	32
C181 AP18	50c rose lake	42	26
C182 AP22	1p ol grn & vio brn	2.50	2.25
C183 AP22	2p dp grn & brt bl	3.75	3.25
C184 AP22	3p rose car & blk	11.00	11.00
C185 AP22	5p lt brn & turq grn	24.00	24.00
	Nos. C175-C185 (11)	43.44	41.88

Nos. C151-C163 Overprinted in Black

A

1950, July 12			
C186 AP18	5c org yel	15	15
C187 AP18	10c scarlet	15	15
C188 AP18	15c dp bl	15	15
C189 AP18	20c violet	18	15
C190 AP18	30c yel grn	18	15
C191 AP18	40c gray	42	15
C192 AP18	50c rose lake	42	15
C193 AP18	60c ol gray	70	16
C194 AP18	80c red brn	1.00	40
C195 AP22	1p ol grn & vio brn	1.10	50
C196 AP22	2p dp grn & brt bl	3.00	1.40
C197 AP22	3p rose car & blk	7.25	6.50
C198 AP22	5p lt brn & turq grn	16.00	14.00
	Nos. C186-C198 (13)	30.70	24.01

On Nos. C175-C198, "L" stands for LANSA, "A" for AVIANCA.

UPU Type
Miniature Sheet
Unwmk.

1950, Aug. 22	Photo.	*Imperf.*	
C199 A245	50c gray	1.00	1.00

75th anniv. (in 1949) of the UPU.

Catalogue values for unused stamps in this section, from this point to the end of the section, are for Never Hinged items.

Types of 1941 Overprinted at Lower Right in Black

L

Unwmk.

1951, Sept. 15	Engr.	*Perf. 12*	
C200 AP18	40c org yel	1.50	1.25
C201 AP18	50c ultra	1.50	1.25
C202 AP18	60c gray	1.50	1.25
C203 AP18	80c car rose	1.10	95
C204 AP22	1p red org & red brn	3.75	3.00
C205 AP22	2p rose car & bl	4.00	3.00
C206 AP22	3p choc & emer	10.00	8.00
C207 AP22	5p org & gray	30.00	30.00
	Nos. C200-C207 (8)	53.35	48.70

Types of 1941 Overprinted at Lower Right in Black

A

1951-54			
C208 AP18	40c org yel	3.25	55
C209 AP18	50c ultra	4.00	60
C210 AP18	60c gray	3.00	45
a.	Overprint centered	1.65	52
C211 AP18	80c car rose	85	30
C212 AP22	1p red org & red brn	3.25	50
C213 AP22	1p ol grn & vio brn ('54)	4.00	75
C214 AP22	2p rose car & bl	3.25	52
C215 AP22	3p choc & emer	5.00	1.40
C216 AP22	5p org & gray	10.00	1.90
	Nos. C208-C216 (9)	36.60	6.97

All values except the 2p and 3p exist without overprint.

Types of 1941

1952, May 10		Engr.	
C217 AP18	5c ultra	30	15
C218 AP18	10c ultra	30	16
C219 AP18	15c ultra	30	16
C220 AP18	20c ultra	70	25
C221 AP18	30c ultra	1.75	55

Color Change

C222 AP18	5c car rose	30	15
C223 AP18	10c car rose	30	16
C224 AP18	20c car rose	70	18
C225 AP18	30c car rose	1.40	28
	Nos. C217-C225 (9)	6.05	2.04

Type of 1941 Surcharged in Blue

1º CONFERENCIA
1952
LATINO AMERICANA
70 Ctvos.
SIDERURGICA

1952, Oct. 30			
C226 AP18	70c on 80c car rose	1.50	70

Latin American Siderurgical Conf., 1952.

Type of Postal Tax Stamps, 1948-50, Nos. 602 and 604 Surcharged or Overprinted in Black

CORREO
5
AEREO

1953	Wmk. 255	*Perf. 12*	
C227 PT10	5c on 8c blue	15	15
C228 PT10	15c on 20c brn	24	15
C229 PT10	15c on 25c bl grn	1.00	15
C230 PT10	25c blue green	35	15
	Nos. C227-C230 (4)	1.74	
	Set value		24

Many varieties of overprint or surcharge exist on Nos. C227-C231.

No. 570 Overprinted "AEREO" in Blue

1953, Aug.	Wmk. 229	*Perf. 12½*	
C231 A160	10c red	15	15

"Extra Rapido"

Stamps inscribed "Extra Rapido" are for use on domestic airmail carried by airlines other than AVIANCA.

No. 585 Surcharged and Overprinted "Extra Rapido" in Dark Blue

CORREO
5
EXTRA
RAPIDO
5

1953	Unwmk.	*Perf. 13*	
C232 A244	5c on 11c red	35	35

Capitol and Arms — AP37

Revenue Stamps Overprinted "Correo Extra-Rapido"
Gray Security Paper

1953	Wmk. 255	Engr.	*Perf. 12*	
C233 AP37	1c on 2c green		15	15
C234 AP37	50c red orange		16	15
	Set value			15

AP38

Real Estate Tax Stamps Ovptd. "Correo Extra-Rapido" in Black or Carmine

1953			
C235 AP38	5c red org	20	15
C236 AP38	20c brn (C)	25	15
	Set value		15

On 20c, overprint is at bottom of stamp and two lines of ornaments cover real estate tax inscription at top.

Castillo y Rada and Map — AP39

Real Estate Tax Stamp Surcharged "Correo Aereo, II Exposicion Filatelica Nacional, Bogota Dicbre 1953, 15 Centavos"

1953, Dec. 12		Engr. & Litho.	
C237 AP39	15c on 10p multi	35	16

2nd Natl. Philatelic Exhib., Bogota, Dec. 1953.

No. RA45 Overprinted in Black

CORREO
EXTRA-RAPIDO

1953			
C238 PT10	10c purple	15	15

Galeras Volcano — AP40

Retreat of San Diego — AP41

Designs: No. C241, Las Lajas Shrine, Narino. No. C242, 50c, Bolivar monument. 20c, 80c, Ruiz mountain, Manizales. 40c, George Isaacs monument, Cali. 60c, Monkey Fountain, Tunja. 1p, Stadium, Medellin. 2p, Pastelillo Fort, Cartagena. 3p, Santo Domingo University gate. 5p, Las Lajas Shrine. 10p, Map of Colombia.

Perf. 13½x13, 13

1954, Jan. 15 Engr. Unwmk.

C239 AP40 5c dp red vio 15 15
C240 AP41 10c black 15 15
C241 AP40 15c red org 18 15
C242 AP40 15c car rose 18 15
C243 AP40 20c brown 18 15
C244 AP40 30c brn org 18 15
C245 AP40 40c blue 18 15
C246 AP40 50c dk vio brn 22 15
C247 AP40 60c dk brn 30 15
C248 AP40 80c red brn 65 15

Size: 37x27mm

Center in Black

C249 AP41 1p dp bl 2.25 32
C250 AP41 2p dk grn 3.50 30
C251 AP41 3p car rose 8.00 1.00

Size: 38x32mm, 32x38mm

C252 AP41 5p dk grn & red brn 8.75 2.50
C253 AP40 10p gray grn & red org 11.00 6.00
Nos. C239-C253 (15) 35.87 11.62

See Nos. C307-C308. For surcharges and overprints see Nos. 691, C321, C325, C330, C333-C334, C343-C346.

Condor Carrying Shield — AP42

Inscribed: "Correo Extra-Rapido"

1954, Apr. 23 Litho. ***Perf. 12½***

C254 AP42 5c lilac rose 60 28

For overprint see No. RA53.

Soldier-Map-Arms Type of Regular Issue, 1954

1954, June 13 Engr. ***Perf. 13***

C255 A259 15c carmine 28 15

See No. C271a.

Games Type of Regular Issue, 1954

Design: 20c, Stadium and Athlete holding arms of Colombia.

1954, July 18

C256 A260 15c chocolate 55 15
C257 A260 20c dp bl grn 1.00 35

Church of St. Peter Claver, Cartagena — AP45

1954, Sept. 9

C258 AP45 15c brown 24 15
a. Souvenir sheet 2.25 2.25

St. Peter Claver, 300th death anniv.
No. C258a contains one stamp similar to No. C258, but printed in red brown.

Mercury Type of Regular Issue, 1954.

1954, Oct. 29

C259 A263 15c dp bl 30 15

Inscribed "Extra Rapido"

C260 A263 50c scarlet 28 15
Set value 15

Archbishop Manuel José Mosquera, Death Cent. — AP47

Inscribed: "Correo Extra Rapido"

1954, Nov. 17

C261 AP47 2c yellow green 15 15

Virgin of Chiquinquira AP48

Inscribed: "Correo Extra Rapido"

1954, Dec. 4 Engr. & Litho.

C262 AP48 5c org brn & multi 15 15

See No. C291. For overprint see No. 686.

College Types of Regular Issue, 1954.

Designs: 20c, Brother Cristobal de Torres. 50c, College chapel and arms.

Perf. 12½x11½, 11½x12½

1954, Dec. 6 Engr. Unwmk.

C263 A264 15c org & blk 24 15
C264 A264 20c ultra 35 15
C265 A265 25c dk brn 48 15
C266 A265 50c blk & car 1.10 60
a. Souvenir sheet 4.00 4.00
Nos. C263-C266 (4) 2.17 1.05

No. C266a contains four stamps similar to Nos. C263-C266, but printed in different colors: 15c red and black, 20c pale purple, 25c brown, 50c black and olive green.

Steel Mill Type of Regular Issue

1954, Dec. 12 ***Perf. 12½x13***

C267 A266 20c grn & blk 1.00 60

Marti Type of Regular Issue, 1955

1955, Jan. 28 ***Perf. 13½x13***

C268 A267 15c dp grn 28 15

Korean Veterans Type of Regular Issue, 1955

1955, Mar. 23 ***Perf. 12½***

C269 A268 20c dk grn 50 16

Merchant Fleet Types of Regular Issue, 1955

1955, Apr. 12 ***Perf. 12½***

C270 A269 25c black 28 15
C271 A270 50c dk grn 55 32
a. Souvenir sheet 4.00 4.00

No. C271a contains four stamps similar to Nos. C255, C269-C271, but printed in different colors; 15c lilac red, 20c olive, 25c bluish black, 50c bluish green.

Marco Fidel Suarez (1855-1927), Pres. 1918-21 — AP56

Inscribed: "Correo Extra Rapido"

1955, April 23 ***Perf. 13***

C272 AP56 10c deep blue 15 15

Hotel-Church Type of Regular Issue, 1955

1955, May 16 Photo. ***Perf. 11½x12***

C273 A271 15c rose brown 25 15

Rotary Type of Regular Issue, 1955

Unwmk.

1955, Oct. 17 Engr. ***Perf. 13***

C274 A272 15c dk car rose 25 15

O'Higgins, Santander and Sucre AP59

Ferdinand the Catholic and Queen Isabella I AP60

Designs: 2c, Atahualpa, Tisquesuza and Montezuma. 20c, Marti, Hidalgo and Petion. 1p, Artigas, Solano Lopez and Murillo. 2p, Abdon Calderon, Baron de Rio Branco and José de La Mar.

1955, Oct. 12 Engr. & Photo.

Inscribed: "Extra Rapido"

C275 AP59 2c dl brn & blk 15 15
C276 AP60 5c dk brn & yel 15 15

Regular Air Post

C277 AP59 15c rose car & blk 20 15
C278 AP59 20c pale brn & blk 30 15
a. Souvenir sheet of 2 10.00 6.50

Inscribed: "Extra Rapido"

C279 AP60 1p ol gray & brn 5.75 5.00
C280 AP60 2p vio & blk 4.00 4.00
Nos. C275-C280 (6) 10.55 9.60

7th Cong. of the Postal Union of the Americas and Spain, Bogota, Oct. 12-Nov. 9, 1955.
No. C278a contains one each of Nos. C277-C278 printed in different shades.

Caro Type of Regular Issue, 1955

1955, Nov. 29 Engr. ***Perf. 13½x13***

C281 A275 15c gray green 24 15

University of Salamanca AP62

Inscribed: "Extra Rapido"

1955, Nov. 29 Unwmk. ***Perf. 13***

C282 AP62 20c dk brn 15 15

University of Salamanca, 7th centenary.

Type of Postal Tax Stamp of 1948-50 Surcharged

CORREO
2
EXTRA-RAPIDO

1956 Wmk. 255 Engr. ***Perf. 12***

C283 PT10 2c on 8c blue 15 15

No. 617 Overprinted in Black **EXTRA-RAPIDO**

1956 Unwmk. ***Perf. 12½x13***

C284 A256 1p blk & emer 25 15

Columbus Type of Regular Issue

1956, Oct. 11 Photo. ***Perf. 12***

C285 A279 15c intense blue 50 15

See No. C306.

St. Elizabeth Type of Regular Issue

1956, Nov. 19

C286 A280 15c red brn 28 18

St. Ignatius Type of Regular Issue

1956, Nov. 26 Engr. ***Perf. 12½x13***

C287 A281 5c brown 18 15

Javier Pereira — AP63

1956, Dec. 28 Unwmk. ***Perf. 12***

C288 AP63 20c rose carmine 15 15

Issued to honor 167-year-old Javier Pereira.

No. 649 and Type of 1941 Overprinted in Red "EXTRA RAPIDO"

1957 ***Perf. 13½x13***

C289 A276 5c bl & blk 6.50 2.50

Perf. 12

C290 AP22 5p org & gray 5.75 5.75

The overprint measures 14mm.

Virgin Type of 1954

Engraved and Lithographed

1957, May 23 Unwmk. ***Perf. 13***

C291 AP48 5c dp plum & multi 15 15

Bank Type of Regular Issue, 1957.

Designs: C292, 20c, Emblem and dairy farm. 10c, Emblem and tractor. 15c, Emblem, coffee and corn. C293, Emblem, cow, horse and herd.

1957 Photo. ***Perf. 14x13½***

C292 A283 5c chocolate 15 15
C293 A283 5c orange 15 15
C294 A283 10c green 48 38
C295 A283 15c black 26 15
C296 A283 20c dl red 16 18
Nos. C292-C296 (5) 1.20
Set value 72

No. C292 is inscribed "Extra Rapido."
No. C292 issued Mar. 5, others May 23.

Cyclist AP64

1957, July 6 Unwmk. ***Perf. 12***

C297 AP64 2c brown 15 15
C298 AP64 5c ultra 16 16
Set value 28 28

Seventh Bicycle Tour of Colombia.

Academy Type of Regular Issue

Designs: 15c, Coat of arms and Gen. Rafael Reyes. 20c, Coat of arms and Academy.

1957, July 20 Engr. ***Perf. 12½***

C299 A284 15c rose car 15 15
C300 A284 20c brown 26 15
Set value 15

Delgado Type of Regular Issue, 1957

1957, Sept. 15 Photo. ***Perf. 12***

C301 A285 10c slate blue 16 15

UPU Type of Regular Issue, 1957

1957, Oct. 10

C302 A286 15c dk red brn 16 15
C303 A286 25c dk bl 16 15
Set value 16

St. Vincent de Paul Type of Regular Issue, 1957

1957, Oct. 18

C304 A287 5c rose brn 16 15

Fencing Type of Regular Issue, 1957

1957, Nov. 23 ***Perf. 12***

C305 A288 20c dk red brn 24 16

Columbus Type of Regular Issue, 1956, Inscribed "Extra Rapido"

1958, Jan. 8 Unwmk. *Perf. 12*

C306 A279 3c dark green 15 15

Scenic Type of 1954

Design: 25c, Las Lajas Shrine.

1958, June 20 Engr. *Perf. 13*

C307 AP40 25c dk bl 28 15
C308 AP40 25c rose vio 28 15
Set value 15

IGY Type of Regular Issue, 1958

1958, May 12 Photo. *Perf. 12*

C309 A289 25c green 48 15

Inscribed "Extra Rapido"

C310 A289 1p purple 32 15
Set value 20

No. 659 Overprinted "AEREO" in Carmine

1958, Oct. 16 Engr. *Perf. 13*

C312 A277 50c dk grn & blk 40 15

Almanza Type of Regular Issue, 1958

1958, Oct. 23 Photo. *Perf. 14x13*

C313 A290 25c dk gray 25 15

Inscribed "Extra Rapido"

C314 A290 10c ol grn 15 15
Set value 15

Carrasquilla Type of Regular Issue

1959, Jan. 22 Photo. *Perf. 14x13*

C315 A291 25c car rose 20 15
C316 A291 1p dk bl 60 16
Set value 21

Miss Universe Type of Regular Issue

1959, June 26 Unwmk. *Perf. 11½*

C317 A292 1.20p multi 1.40 1.10
C318 A292 5p multi 32.50 32.50

Gaitan Type of Regular Issue, 1959, Inscribed "Extra Rapido" and Surcharged in Black or Blue

1959, July 28 Engr. *Perf. 12x13½*

C319 A293 2p on 1p blk 1.40 1.25
C320 A293 2p on 1p blk (Bl) 1.40 1.25

The 1p black, type A293, exists without surcharge.

No. C247 Surcharged with New Value in Dark Blue; Old Value Obliterated

1959, Aug. 24 Unwmk. *Perf. 13*

C321 AP40 50c on 60c dk brn 1.25 40

Regular and Air Post Issues of 1948-59 Overprinted in Black or Red

1959-60

C322 A283 5c orange 25 25
C323 A287 5c rose brn ('60) 40 50
C324 A281 5c brn (R) 30 30
C325 AP41 10c black 15 15
a. Double overprint 2.50 2.50
C326 A160 10c red, #C231 28 15
a. Double overprint 1.40 1.40
C328 A284 15c rose car 20 15
a. Inverted overprint 3.00 3.00
C330 AP40 20c brown 15 15
a. Double overprint 1.40 1.40
C331 A284 20c brown 16 16
C332 A288 20c dk red brn ('60) 15 20
C333 AP40 25c rose vio ('60) 15 15
C334 AP40 25c dk bl 15 15
C335 A291 25c car rose 16 15
C336 A290 25c dk gray 15 15
C338 AP40 30c brn org 15 15
C340 AP40 50c on 60c dk brn 28 15
C341 A291 1p dk bl 65 15
a. Double overprint 2.50 2.50
C342 A292 1.20p brn, ultra, car & ol 1.00 80
C343 AP41 2p dk grn & blk 1.40 20
C344 AP41 3p car rose & blk 3.75 48
a. Double overprint 8.50 8.50
C345 AP41 5p dk grn & red brn 5.25 1.10
a. Double overprint 8.50 8.50
b. Inverted overprint 8.50 8.50
C346 AP40 10p gray grn & red org 6.50 2.25
Nos. C322-C346 (21) 21.63
Set value 6.95

Issued following agreement between the Colombian government and AVIANCA to unify the air postage used on all mail carried by AVIANCA.
Vertical overprint on Nos. C342 and C346.

Airmail Stamp of 1919 and Planes AP66

Designs: 60c, No. C349a, C350a, Planes of 1919 and 1959. C349b, C350b, Stamp of 1919 and Planes.

Unwmk.

1959, Dec. 5 Photo. *Perf. 12*

C347 AP66 35c lt bl, blk & red 60 15
C348 AP66 60c yel grn & gray 40 15
Set value 15

Souvenir Sheets

C349 Sheet of 2 4.50 4.50
a. AP66 1p orange & gray 65 65
b. AP66 1p lilac, gray & red 65 65

Inscribed "Extra Rapido"

1960, May 17

C350 Sheet of 2 4.50 4.50
a. AP66 1.50p red orange & gray 85 85
b. AP66 1.50p olive, gray & rose 85 85

Nos. C347-C350 for the 40th anniv. of air post service and of the AVIANCA company.

Type of Regular Issue, 1959 and

1859 Stamp and Seaplane AP67

Tête Bêche 5c Stamps of 1859 — AP68

Designs (various stamps of 1859 and): 10c, Map of Colombia. 25c, Pres. Mariano Ospina. 1.20p, Plane over mountains.

1959, Dec. 1 Photo. *Perf. 12*

C351 A296 25c choc & red 50 24
C352 AP67 50c ver & ultra 1.00 50
C353 AP67 1.20p yel grn & car 2.00 1.10

Inscribed "Extra Rapido"

C354 A296 10c lemon & vio 15 15
Nos. C351-C354 (4) 3.65 1.99

Souvenir Sheet

Wmk. 331

1959, Dec. 23 Litho. *Imperf.*

C355 AP68 5p blue, *pink* 11.00 11.00

Cent. of Colombian postage stamps.
No. C355 exists with inscription "VALOR $5.10" instead of "VALOR $5."

Eldorado Airport, Bogota — AP69

1960, Jan. 5 Wmk. 331 *Perf. 12½*

C356 AP69 35c blk & ocher 50 25
C356A AP69 60c ver & gray 65 42

Inscribed "Extra Rapido"

C356B AP69 1p Prus bl & gray 85 60
Nos. C356-C356B (3) 2.00 1.27

Ant Bear — AP70

Designs: 1.30p, Armadillo. 1.45p, Parrot fish.

Unwmk.

1960, Feb. 12 Photo. *Perf. 12*

C357 AP70 35c sepia 85 15
C358 AP70 1.30p rose car & dk brn 1.75 1.40
C359 AP70 1.45p lt bl, bl & yel 1.40 1.25
Nos. C357-C359 (3) 4.00 2.80

Alexander von Humboldt, German naturalist and geographer (1769-1859).

Flower Type of Regular Issue, 1960

Flowers: Nos. C360, C362, C366, Passiflora mollissima. Nos. C361, C364, C367, Odontoglossum luteo purpureum. Nos. C363, C369, Anthurium andreanum. Nos. C365, C370, Stanhopea tigrina. No. C368, Espeletia grandiflora.

1960, May 10 Photo. *Perf. 12*

Flowers in Natural Colors

C360 A298 5c dk bl 15 15
C361 A298 35c maroon 40 15
C362 A298 60c dk bl 75 55
C363 A298 1.45p dk brn 1.00 85

Inscribed "Extra Rapido"

C364 A298 5c maroon 15 15
C365 A298 10c brown 15 15
C366 A298 1p dk bl 2.00 2.50
C367 A298 1p maroon 2.00 2.50
C368 A298 1p brown 2.00 2.50
C369 A298 1p brown 2.00 2.50
C370 A298 1p brown 2.00 2.50
Nos. C360-C370 (11) 12.60 14.50

See Nos. C420-C425.

Fleeing Family and Uprooted Oak Emblem — AP71

Perf. 10, 11

1960, May 24 Litho. Wmk. 331

C371 AP71 60c bl grn & gray 30 20

World Refugee Year, July 1, 1959-June 30, 1960.

Souvenir Sheet

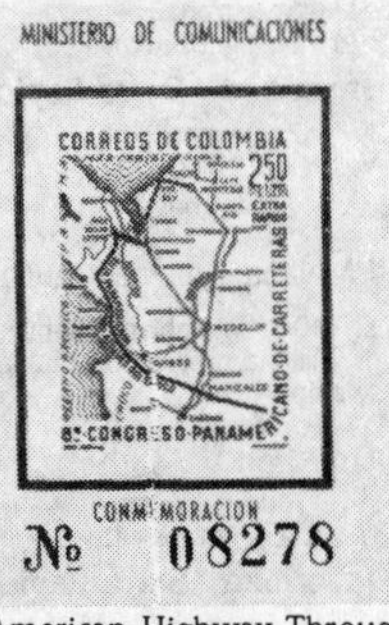

Pan-American Highway Through Colombia — AP72

1960, May 28 Litho. *Imperf.*

C372 AP72 2.50p brn & aqua 5.00 5.00

Issued to commemorate the 8th Pan-American Highway Congress, Bogota, May 20-29.

Lincoln Type of Regular Issue

1960, June 6 *Perf. 10½*

C375 A299 40c dl red brn & blk 85 60
C376 A299 60c rose red & blk 25 15

Type of Regular Issue and

Joaquin Camacho, Jorge Tadeo Lozano and Jose Miguel Pey — AP73

Flag, Coins and Arms of Mompox and Cartagena — AP74

Designs: No. C378, Arms of Cartagena. 35c, 1.45p, Colombian flag. 60c, Andres Rosillo, Antonio Villavicencio and Joaquin Caicedo. 1p, Manuel de Bernardo Alvarez and Joaquin Gutierrez. 1.20p, Jose Antonio Galan statue. 1.30p, Front page of newspaper La Bagatela, 1811. 1.65p, Antonia Santos, Jose Acevedo y Gomez and Liborio Mejia.

Unwmk.

1960, July 20 Photo. *Perf. 12*

C377 AP73 5c lil & brn 15 15
C378 A301 5c dp bl grn & multi 15 15
C379 AP73 35c multi 15 15
C380 AP73 60c red brn & grn 40 15
C381 AP73 1p ver & sl grn 85 60
C382 A301 1.20p ultra & ind 85 60
C383 AP73 1.30p org & blk 85 60
C384 AP73 1.45p multi 1.10 85
C385 AP73 1.65p grn & brn 85 85
Nos. C377-C385 (9) 5.35 4.10

Souvenir Sheet

Stamps Inscribed "Extra Rapido"

C386 AP74 Sheet of 4 3.75 3.75
a. 50c deep claret & multi 60 60
b. 50c green & multi 60 60
c. 1p brown olive, yel, blue & car 60 60
d. 1p lilac & gray 60 60

150th anniv. of Colombia's independence.

St. Isidore Type of Regular Issue, 1960

Designs: 35c, No. C388a, St. Isidore and farm animals. No. C388b, Nativity.

Unwmk.

1960, Sept. 26 Photo. *Perf. 12*

C387 A302 35c multi 16 15

Souvenir Sheet

Stamps Inscribed "Extra Rapido"

C388 A302 Sheet of 2 6.00 6.00
a. 1.50p multi 2.00 2.00
b. 1.50p multi 2.00 2.00

See Nos. C439-C440.

Type of Regular Issue, 1959

Perf. 12½

1960, Nov. 23 Litho. Wmk. 331

C389 A294 35c Bolivar 3.00 40

Pan-American Highway Type of Regular Issue, 1961

1961, Mar. 7 Unwmk. *Perf. 10½x11*

C390 A304 10c rose lil & emer 50 65
C391 A304 20c ver & lt bl 50 65
C392 A304 30c blk & emer 50 65

Inscribed "Extra Rapido"

C393 A304 10c dk bl & emer 50 65
Nos. C390-C393 (4) 2.00 2.60

8th Pan-American Highway Congress, Bogota, May 20-29, 1960.

Lopez Type of Regular Issue, 1961

1961, Mar. 22 Photo. *Perf. 12½*

C394 A305 35c bl & brn 52 15

Inscribed "Extra Rapido"

C395 A305 10c emer & brn 16 15
Set value 17

Souvenir Sheet

C396 A305 1p lil & brn 3.50 3.50

Brother Damian and San Francisco Church, Cali AP75

Designs: 10c, View of Cali, vert. No. 398, Emblem of University del Valle, vert. 1.30p, Fine Arts School, Cali. 1.45p, Agricultural College, Palmira.

Perf. 13x13½, 13½x13

1961, Aug. 17 Photo. Unwmk.

C397 AP75 35c vio brn & ol 30 15
C398 AP75 35c ol & grn 30 15
C399 AP75 1.30p sep & pink 85 45
C400 AP75 1.45p multi 85 60

Inscribed: "Extra Rapido"

C401 AP75 10c brn & yel grn 15 15
Nos. C397-C401 (5) 2.45
Set value 1.20

50th anniv. (in 1960) of the department of Valle del Cauca.

View of Cucuta AP76

Design: 10c, Church of the Rosary, Cucuta (vert.).

1961, Aug. 29

C402 AP76 35c brn ol & grn 60 15

Inscribed: "Extra Rapido"

C403 AP76 10c dk brn & gray grn 15 15
Set value 15

50th anniv. (in 1960) of the department of North Santander.

Old and New Ships of Barranquilla AP77

Arms and View of San Gil — AP78

Hotel, Popayan AP79

Statue of Christ in Procession AP80

Design: 1.45p, View of Velez.

Perf. 12½x13, 13x12½

1961, Oct. 10 Photo. Unwmk.

C404 AP77 35c gold & bl 45 15
C405 AP78 35c bl grn, yel & red 45 15
C406 AP79 35c car & brn 45 15
C407 AP78 1.45p brn & grn 45 20

Inscribed: "Extra Rapido"

C408 AP80 10c brn & yel 15 15
Nos. C404-C408 (5) 1.95
Set value 46

Souvenir Sheets
Types of Regular and Air Post Issues

Designs, No. C409: 35c, Barranquilla arms. 40c, Popayan arms. c, Arms and view of San Gil. d, Holy Week in Popayan. No. C410: a, Old and new ships at Barranquilla. b, Hotel, Popayan. c, Bucaramanga arms. d, Holy Week in Popayan.

C409 Sheet of 4 5.00 5.50
a. A309 35c gold & multi 45 45
b. A309 40c gold & multi 45 45
c. AP78 1p blue, yellow & red 90 90
d. AP80 1p carmine rose & yellow 90 90

Stamps Inscribed: "Extra Rapido"

C410 Sheet of 4 5.00 5.50
a. AP77 50c gold & carmine rose 70 70
b. AP79 50c gold & blue 70 70
c. A309 50c pink & multi 70 70
d. AP80 50c blue & yellow 70 70

Nos. C404-C408 are in honor of the Atlantico Department. Nos. C409-C410 are in honor of the Departments of Atlantico, Cauca and Santander.

Nos. 713, 716 and 715 Overprinted and Surcharged

1961, Sept. *Perf. 12*

C411 A297 5c grnsh bl & brn 15 15
C412 A298 5c multi 15 15
C413 A297 10c on 20c cit & gray brn 15 15
Set value 30 19

"Aereo" in script on No. C412.
See Nos. C420-C425.

Sports Type of Regular Issue, 1961

Designs: No. C414, Women divers. No. C415, Tennis, mixed doubles. 1.45p, No. C419b, Baseball. No. C417, Torch bearer. Nos. C418, C419a, Bolivar statue and flags of six participating nations. No. C419c, Soccer. No. C419d, Basketball.

1961, Dec. 16 Litho. *Perf. 13½x14*

C414 A310 35c ultra, yel & brn 60 15
C415 A310 35c car, yel & brn 60 15
C416 A310 1.45p Prus grn, yel & brn 85 55

Inscribed: "Extra Rapido"

C417 A310 10c car lake, yel & brn 15 15
C418 A310 10c ol, yel, bl & red 15 15
Nos. C414-C418 (5) 2.35
Set value 75

Souvenir Sheet
Stamps Inscribed: "Extra Rapido"
Imperf

C419 Sheet of 4 5.00 5.00
a. A310 50c multi 42 42
b. A310 50c multi 42 42
c. A310 1p multi 85 85
d. A310 1p multi 85 85

Flower Type of 1960

Flowers: 5c, Passiflora mollissima. 10c, Espeletia grandiflora. 20c, 2p, Odontoglossum luteo purpureum. 25c, Stanhopea tigrina. 60c, Anthurium Andreanum.

Unwmk.
1962, Jan. 30 Photo. *Perf. 12*
Flowers in Natural Colors

C420 A298 5c gray 15 15
C421 A298 10c gray blue 15 15
C422 A298 20c rose lilac 15 15
C423 A298 25c citron 25 15
C424 A298 60c light brown 25 25

Inscribed "Extra Rapido"

C425 A298 2p salmon pink 2.00 1.75
Nos. C420-C425 (6) 2.95
Set value 1.92

Anti-Malaria Type of Regular Issue.

Designs: 40c, Colombian anti-malaria emblem. 1p, 1.45p, Malaria eradication emblem and mosquito in swamp.

1962, Apr. 12 Litho. *Perf. 12*

C426 A311 40c yel & red 16 15
C427 A311 1.45p gray & ultra 48 42

Inscribed "Extra Rapido"

C428 A311 1p yel grn & ultra 3.50 3.50
Nos. C426-C428 (3) 4.14 4.07

WHO drive to eradicate malaria.

Type of Regular Issue, 1962 and

Abelardo Ramos and Engineering School, Cauca — AP81

Designs: 10c, Miguel Triana, Andres A. Arroyo and Monserrate shrine with cable cars. 15c, Diodoro Sanchez and first meeting place of Engineers Society. 2p, Engineers Society emblem.

1962, June 12 Photo. *Perf. 11½x12*

C429 AP81 5c bl & dp rose 15 15
C430 AP81 10c grn & sepia 15 15
C431 AP81 15c lilac & sepia 25 16

Inscribed: "Extra Rapido"

C432 A312 2p blk, yel, red & bl 1.50 1.50
Nos. C429-C432 (4) 2.05 1.96

75th anniv. of the founding of the Colombian Soc. of Engineers and 6th Natl. Cong. of Engineers.

American States Type of 1962

1962, June 28 Photo. *Perf. 13*
Flags in National Colors

C433 A313 35c blk & bl 35 15

Women's Rights Type of 1962

Perf. 12x12½
1962, July 20 Litho. Wmk. 229

C434 A314 35c ocher, gray & blk 20 15

See Nos. C448-C450.

Scout Type of 1962

Designs: 15c, No. C438, Scouts at campfire and tents. 40c and No. C437, Girl Scouts.

Perf. 11½x12

1962, July 26 Photo. Unwmk.

C435 A315 15c brn & rose 20 15
C436 A315 40c dp claret & pink 24 20
C437 A315 1p bl & buff 90 32

Inscribed "Extra Rapido"

C438 A315 1p pur & yel 3.75 3.75
Nos. C435-C438 (4) 5.09 4.42

Nos. C435 and C438 for 30th anniv. of the Colombian Boy Scouts. Nos. C436 and C437 for the 25th anniv. of the Girl Scouts.

Nativity by Gregorio Vasquez — AP82

Design: 2p, St. Isidore, similar to type A302.

Inscribed "Extra Rapido"

Unwmk.
1962, Aug. 28 Photo. *Perf. 12*

C439 AP82 10c gray & multi 15 15
C440 AP82 2p gray & multi 3.50 3.50

See Nos. C387-C388.

Type of Regular Issue, 1962 and

Pres. Aquileo Parra and Magdalena River Bridge AP83

Design: 5c, Locomotives of 1854 and 1961. 10c, Railroad map of Colombia.

1962, Sept. 28 Photo. *Perf. 12½*

C441 AP83 5c sep & slate grn 15 15
C442 A316 10c multi 15 15

Engr.

C443 AP83 1p dl pur & brn 1.40 15

Inscribed: "Extra Rapido."

C444 AP83 5p bl, brn & dl grn 3.75 3.75
Nos. C441-C444 (4) 5.45 4.20

Progress of Colombian railroads and completion of the Atlantic Line from Santa Maria to Bogota.

UPAE Type of Regular Issue

Designs: 50c, Map of Americas and carrier pigeon. 60c, Post horn.

Perf. 13½x14

1962, Oct. 18 Litho. Wmk. 346

C445 A317 50c sl grn & gold 28 15
C446 A317 60c gold & plum 22 15
Set value 15

Pope John XXIII — AP84

1963, Mar. 11

C447 AP84 60c gold, red brn, buff & red 20 15

Vatican II, the 21st Ecumenical Council of the Roman Catholic Church.

Women's Rights Type of 1962

1963-64 *Perf. 12x12½*

C448 A314 5c sal, gray & blk ('64) 15 15
C449 A314 45c pale grn, gray & blk 32 15
C450 A314 45c brt pink, gray & blk 32 15
Nos. C448-C450 (3) 79
Set value 15

Games Emblem — AP85

1963, Aug. 12 *Perf. 13x14*

C451 AP85 20c gray & multi 15 15
C452 AP85 80c buff & multi 15 15
Set value 15

South American Athletic Championships (22nd for men, 12th for women), Cali, June 30-July 7.

Bolivar Statue by Arenas-Betancourt — AP86

Perf. 14x13½

1963, Aug. 30 Unwmk.

C453 AP86 1.90p ol bis & bl 20 15

Centenary of the city of Pereira.
For surcharge see No. C574.

Tennis Player — AP87

1963, Oct. 11 *Perf. 13½x14*

C454 AP87 55c multi 15 15

30th South American Tennis Championships, Medellin, Oct. 3-13.

Pres. John F. Kennedy and Alliance for Progress Emblem AP88

1963, Dec. 17 Litho. *Perf. 14x13½*

C455 AP88	10c multi	15	15

President John F. Kennedy (1917-1963).

Church of the True Cross, National Pantheon, Bogota — AP89

Design: 2p, Christ of the Martyrs, bell and tomb.

Perf. 13½x14

1964, Mar. 10 Photo. Unwmk.

C459 AP89	1p multi	25	15
C460 AP89	2p multi	32	18
Set value			25

View of Cartagena AP90

1964, Mar. 18 Litho. *Perf. 14x13½*

C461 AP90	3p vio, bl, ocher & brn	1.40	60

Cartagena's independence in 1811, Simon Bolivar's visit in 1812 and the siege of 1815.

Eleanor Roosevelt — AP91

1964, Nov. 10 Photo. *Perf. 12*

C462 AP91	20c ol & dl red brn	15	15

Eleanor Roosevelt (1884-1962).

Alberto Castilla and Score of "El Bunde" — AP92

1964, Nov. 10 Unwmk.

C463 AP92	30c ol bis & Prus grn	15	15

Department of Tolima and Maestro Alberto Castilla (1878-1937) who in 1906 founded the Tolima Conservatory of Music in Ibague.

Mejia Type of Regular Issue

Designs (Mejia portrait and): 45c, Women picking coffee. 5p, Mules carrying coffee bags. 10p, Loading coffee on freighter "Manuel Mejia."

1965, Feb. 10 Engr. *Perf. 12½x13*

C464 A320	45c brn & blk	15	15
C465 A320	5p gray grn & blk	1.75	30
C466 A320	10p ultra & blk	2.25	25
Nos. C464-C466 (3)		4.15	70

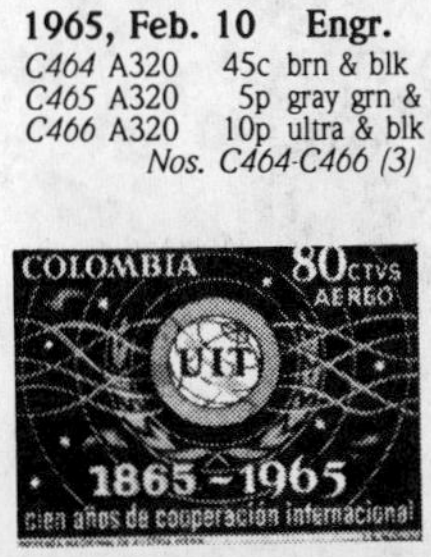

ITU Emblem AP93

1965, Oct. 25 Photo. *Perf. 12*

C467 AP93	80c Prus bl, lt bl & red	15	15

Cent. of the ITU.

Cattleya Truanae — AP94

Cent. of the Telegraph in Colombia — AP95

1965, Oct. 3 Litho. *Perf. 13½x14*

C468 AP94	20c yel & multi	15	15

Fifth Philatelic Exhibition.

1965, Nov. 1 *Perf. 13½x14, 14x13½*

Design: No. C469, Pres. Manuel Murillo Toro statue, telegraph and orbits. No. C470, Telegraph and satellites over South America, horiz.

C469 AP95	60c multi	15	15
C470 AP95	60c multi	15	15
Set value			15

Junkers F-13 Seaplane, 1920 AP96

History of Colombian Aviation: 10c, Dornier Wal, 1924. 20c, Dornier Mercur, 1926. 50c, Trimotor Ford, 1932. 60c, De Havilland biplane, 1930. 1p, Douglas DC-4, 1947. 1.40p, Douglas DC-3, 1944. 2.80p, Superconstellation 1049, 1951. 3p, Boeing 720B jet, 1961.

Perf. 14x13½

1965-66 Photo. Unwmk.

C471 AP96	5c multi	15	15
C472 AP96	10c multi	15	15
C473 AP96	20c multi	15	15
C474 AP96	50c multi	15	15
C475 AP96	60c multi	30	15
C476 AP96	1p multi	60	15
C477 AP96	1.40p multi	80	15
C478 AP96	2.80p multi	1.50	60
C479 AP96	3p multi	2.00	85
Nos. C471-C479 (9)		5.80	
Set value			1.90

Issue dates: 5c, 60c, 3p, Dec. 13, 1965; 10c, 1p, 1.40p, July 15, 1966; 20c, 50c, 2.80p, Dec. 14, 1966.

Automobile Club Emblem and Car on Road — AP97

1966, Feb. 16 Litho. *Perf. 14x13½*

C480 AP97	20c multi	15	15

25th anniv. (in 1965) of the Automobile Club of Colombia.

Fish Type of Regular Issue

Fish: 2p, Flying fish. 2.80p, Queen angelfish. 20p, King mackerel.

1966, Aug. 25 Photo. *Perf. 12½x13*

C481 A323	2p multi	35	15
C482 A323	2.80p multi	1.00	1.00
C483 A323	20p multi	8.75	8.75
Nos. C481-C483 (3)		10.10	9.90

Coat of Arms Type of Regular Issue

1966, Oct. 11 Litho. *Perf. 14x13½*

C484 A324	1p ultra & multi	24	15
C485 A324	1.40p red & multi	20	15
Set value			15

Portrait Type of Regular Issue

Portraits: 80c, Father Felix Restrepo Mejia, S.J. (1887-1965), theologian and scholar. 1.70p, José Joaquin Casas (1866-1951), educator and diplomat.

Perf. 13½x14

1967, Jan. 18 Litho. Unwmk.

C486 A325	80c dk bl & bis	15	15
C487 A325	1.70p blk & bis	24	15
Set value			17

Declaration of Bogota Type

1967, Feb. 2 Litho. *Perf. 14x13½*

C488 A326	3p multi	35	16

See note after No. 767.

Orchid Type of Regular Issue

Orchids: 1p, Cattleya dowiana aurea, vert. 1.20p, Masdevallia coccinea, vert. 5p, Catasetum macrocarpum and bee.

1967, May 23 Litho. *Perf. 14*

C489 A327	1p multi	32	15
C490 A327	1.20p multi	22	15
C491 A327	5p multi	1.25	30
a.	Souv. sheet of 3, #C489-C491	2.00	2.00
Nos. C489-C491 (3)		1.79	
Set value			48

Lions Type of Regular Issue

1967, July 12 Litho. *Perf. 13½x14*

C492 A328	25c multi	15	15

"First Caesarean Section" by Grau — AP98

Perf. 14x13½

1967, Sept. 7 Litho. Unwmk.

C493 AP98	80c multi	15	15

Issued to publicize the 6th Congress of Colombian Surgeons, Bogota, Sept. 25.

SENA Type of Regular Issue

Lithographed and Embossed

1967, Sept. 20 *Perf. 13½x14*

C494 A329	2p gold, ver & blk	48	15

Pre-Columbian Art Type

Designs: 30c, Bird pectoral. 5p Ornamental pectoral. 20p, Pitcher.

1967, Oct. 13 Photo. *Perf. 13½x14*

C495 A330	30c ver, gold & brn	15	15
C496 A330	5p red, gold & brn	1.65	32
a.	Souvenir sheet of 2	2.00	1.65
C497 A330	20p vio, gold & brn	8.25	8.25
Nos. C495-C497 (3)		10.05	8.72

No. C496a also commemorates the 6th Natl. Phil. Exhib. No. C496a contains 2 imperf. stamps in changed colors similar to Nos. C495-C496 (30c has green background and 5p maroon background).

Telecommunications Type

Designs: 50c, Signal lights. 1p, Early Bird satellite, Southern Cross and radar.

Perf. 13½x14

1968, May 14 Litho. Unwmk.

C498 A331	50c blk, ver & emer	15	15
C499 A331	1p ultra, yel & gray	16	15
Set value			15

Eucharist Type of Regular Issue

1968, June 6 Litho. *Perf. 13½x14*

C500 A332	80c rose lil, red, yel & blk	15	15
C501 A332	3p bl, red, yel & blk	30	15
Set value			15

Eucharistic Congress Type

Designs: 80c, The Last Supper, by Gregorio Vasquez, horiz. 1p, St. Francis Xavier Preaching, by Gregorio Vasquez. 2p, The Dream of the Prophet Elias, by Gregorio Vasquez. 3p, Monstrance, c. 1700. 20p, Pope Paul VI, painting by Roman Franciscan nuns.

1968, Aug. 13 Photo. *Perf. 13*

C502 A333	80c multi	18	15
C503 A333	1p multi	25	15
C504 A333	2p multi	35	15
C505 A333	3p lil & multi	65	15
C506 A333	20p gold & multi	4.00	2.00
Nos. C502-C506 (5)		5.43	
Set value			2.20

Shrine of the Eucharist, Bogotá AP99

Designs: 1.20p, Pope Paul VI giving blessing and Papal arms, vert. 1.80p, Cathedral of Bogotá, vert.

Perf. 14x13½, 13½x14

1968, Aug. 22 Litho.

C507 AP99	80c multi	15	15
C508 AP99	1.20p multi	20	15
C509 AP99	1.80p multi	30	15
Nos. C507-C509 (3)		65	
Set value			26

Visit of Pope Paul VI to Colombia.

Computer Symbols — AP100

1968, Oct. 29 Litho. *Perf. 13½x14*

C510 AP100	20c buff, car & grn	15	15

Cent. of the Natl. University and the 1st Data Processing Cong. in 1967 at the University.

Agriculture Institute Type of Regular Issue

1968, Mar. 5 Litho. *Perf. 13½x14*

C511 A337	1p gray & multi	18	15

Microscope and Pen — AP101

1969, Mar. 24 Litho. *Perf. 14*

C512 AP101	5p blk, yel, ver & pur	1.10	15

20th anniv. (in 1968) of the University of the Andes.

Alexander von Humboldt and Andes AP102

1969, May 3 Litho. *Perf. 14x13½*

C513 AP102	1p grn & brn	15	15

Alexander von Humboldt (1769-1859), German naturalist and traveler.

Map of Colombia, Amphibian Plane and Letter AP103

Design: 1.50p, No. C516b, Globe, letter, and jet of Avianca airlines.

1969, June 18 Litho. *Perf. 14x13½*

C514	AP103	1p multi		16	15
C515	AP103	1.50p multi		24	15
		Set value			15

Souvenir Sheet

Imperf

C516	Sheet of 2		3.50	3.50
a.	AP103 5p green & multi		70	70
b.	AP103 5p violet & multi		70	70

50th anniv. of the 1st air post flight in Colombia. No. C516 also for 8th Natl. Philatelic Exhibition, EXFILBA 69, Barranquilla, June 18-22. No. C516 contains 2 stamps in the designs of the 1p and 1.50p.

Independence Type of Regular Issue

Design: 2.30p, Simon Bolivar, José Antonio Anzoategui, Francisco de Paula Santander and victorious army entering Bogotá, Sept. 18, 1819; painting by Ignacio Castillo Cervantes.

1969, July 24 Litho. *Perf. 13½x14*

C517	A338	2.30p gold & multi	48	16

Social Security Emblem — AP104

Neurosurgeons' Congress Emblem — AP105

1969, Oct. 29 Litho. *Perf. 13½x14*

C518	AP104	20c emer & blk	15	15

20th anniv. of the Colombian Institute of Social Security.

1969, Oct. 29

C519	AP105	70c vio, red & yel	25	15

Issued to publicize the 13th Congress of Latin-American Neurosurgeons, Bogotá.

Junkers F-13 AP106

Designs: No. C521, C522b, Globe with airlines from Bogota and Boeing jet. No. C522a, like No. C520.

1969, Nov. 28 Litho. *Perf. 14x13½*

C520	AP106	2p grn & multi	32	15
C521	AP106	3.50p ultra & multi	48	28

Souvenir Sheet

Imperf

C522	Sheet of 2	3.50	3.50
a.	AP106 3.50p light green & multi	52	52
b.	AP106 5p ultra & multi	75	75

50th anniv. of AVIANCA; No. C522 also publicizes the 1st Interamerican Phil. Exhib., Bogota, Nov. 28-Dec. 7.

No. C522 contains 2 imperf. stamps.

Child Mailing Letter — AP107

Christmas: 1.50p, Praying child and gifts.

1969, Dec. 16 Litho. *Perf. 13½x14*

C523	AP107	60c ocher & multi	42	18
C524	AP107	1p multi	42	15
C525	AP107	1.50p multi	48	18
		Nos. C523-C525 (3)	1.32	51

Radar Station and Pre-Columbian Head — AP108

1970, Mar. 25 Litho. *Perf. 14x13½*

C526	AP108	1p dl grn, blk & brick red	28	15

Issued to publicize the opening of the communications satellite earth station at Chocontá in Cundinamarca Province.

Emblem of Colombian Youth Sports Institute — AP109

Art Exhibition Emblem — AP110

Design: 2.30p, Games' emblem (dove and 3 rings).

1970, Apr. 6 Litho. *Perf. 13½x14*

C527	AP109	1.50p dk ol grn, yel & blk	28	16
C528	AP109	2.30p red & multi	42	16

9th Natl. Youth Games, Ibague, July 10-20.

1970, Apr. 30 Litho. *Perf. 13½x14*

C529	AP110	30c multi	15	15

2nd Biennial Art Exhib., Medellin, May 1-June 14.

Eduardo Santos, Rural and Urban Buildings AP111

1970, June 18 Litho. *Perf. 14x13½*

C530	AP111	1p grn, yel & blk	16	15

Issued to commemorate the founding (in 1939) of the Territorial Credit Institute.

UN Emblem, Scales and Dove — AP112

EXFILCA Emblem — AP113

1970, June 26 *Perf. 13½x14*

C531	AP112	1.50p dk bl, lt bl & yel	16	15

25th anniversary of United Nations.

1970, Nov. Litho. *Perf. 13½x14*

C532	AP113	10p bl, gold & blk	3.50	26

EXFILCA 70, 2nd Interamerican Philatelic Exhib., Caracas, Venezuela, Nov. 27-Dec. 6.

Mother Juana Ruperta in Napanga Costume and Music by Efrain Orozco — AP114

Designs: 1p, Dancers from Eastern Plains and music by Alejandro Wills. No. C535, Guabina man, woman and folk song. No. C536, Bambuco man and woman, and music. No. C537, Man and woman dancing the Cumbia, and music.

1970-71 Litho. *Perf. 13½x14*

C533	AP114	60c dp lil rose & multi	48	25
C534	AP114	1p ultra & multi	32	15
C535	AP114	1.30p bl & multi	42	15
C536	AP114	1.30p emer & multi ('71)	42	15
C537	AP114	1.30p lil & multi ('71)	32	15
		Nos. C533-C537 (5)	1.96	
		Set value		52

Athlete and Games Emblem — AP115

Design: 2p, Games emblem.

1971, Mar. 11

C542	AP115	1.50p multi	90	90
C543	AP115	2p blk, org & grn	80	55

6th Pan-American Games, Cali, July 30-Aug. 13.

Gilberto Alzate Avendano AP116

1971, Apr. 29 Litho. *Perf. 14x13½*

C544	AP116	1p bl & multi	40	26

Avendano (1910-60), journalist and popular leader.

Commemorative Medal — AP117

Lithographed and Embossed

1971, June 21 *Perf. 14x13½*

C545	AP117	1p sl grn & gold	50	28

Centenary (in 1970) of the Bank of Bogota.

Olympic Center — AP118

Soccer — AP119

Designs (Games Emblem and): #C546-C546C, Olympic Center. #547, Soccer. #C548, Wrestling. #C549, Bicycling. #C550, Volleyball. #C551, Diving (women). #C552, Fencing. #C553, Sailing. #C554, Equestrian. #C555, Jumping. #C556, Rowing. #C557, Cali emblem. #C558, Basketball (women). #C559, Stadium. #C560, Baseball. #C561, Hockey. #C562, Weight lifting. #C563, Medals. #C564, Boxing. #C565, Gymnastics (women). #C566, Sharpshooting.

1971, July 16 Litho. *Perf. 13½x14*

Multicolored and Emblem Color:

C546	AP118	1.30p	yellow	1.25	28
C546A	AP118	1.30p	green	1.25	28
C546B	AP118	1.30p	blue	1.25	28
C546C	AP118	1.30p	carmine	1.25	28
C547	AP119	1.30p	emerald	1.25	28
C548	AP119	1.30p	lilac	1.25	28
C549	AP119	1.30p	blue	1.25	28
C550	AP119	1.30p	carmine	1.25	28
C551	AP119	1.30p	blue	1.25	28
C552	AP119	1.30p	carmine	1.25	28
C553	AP119	1.30p	blue	1.25	28
C554	AP119	1.30p	gray	1.25	28
C555	AP119	1.30p	green	1.25	28
C556	AP119	1.30p	blue	1.25	28
C557	AP118	1.30p	orange	1.25	28
C558	AP119	1.30p	carmine	1.25	28
C559	AP118	1.30p	light blue	1.25	28
C560	AP119	1.30p	plum	1.25	28
C561	AP119	1.30p	yel grn	1.25	28
C562	AP119	1.30p	pink	1.25	28
C563	AP118	1.30p	deep org	1.25	28
C564	AP119	1.30p	plum	1.25	28
C565	AP119	1.30p	lilac rose	1.25	28
C566	AP119	1.30p	green	1.25	28
a.	Sheet of 25, #C546-C566			32.50	7.00

6th Pan American Athletic Games, Cali. No. C546B appears twice in sheet.

Battle of Carabobo, by Martin Tovar y Tovar — AP120

1971, Nov. 25 Litho. *Perf. 13½x14*

C567	AP120	1.50p multi	1.00	16

Sesquicentennial of the Battle of Carabobo.

St. Theresa Type of Regular Issue Overprinted "AEREO"

1972 Litho. *Perf. 13½x14*

C568	A343	2p multi	30	15

See note after No. 793.

Vendor — AP121

Designs: 50c, Woman wearing shawl, and woven shawl. 3p, Fruit vendor (puppet).

1971, Apr. 11 Litho. *Perf. 13½x14*

C569	AP121	50c multi	35	16
C570	AP121	1p multi	35	15
C571	AP121	3p multi	50	24
		Nos. C569-C571 (3)	1.20	55

Colombian artisans.

Mormodes Rolfeanum AP122

1972, Apr. 20 *Perf. 14x13½*

C572	AP122	1.30p multi	45	15

7th World Orchidology Congress, Medellin.

Congo Grande Dancer — AP123

Laureano Gomez, by Ridriguez Cubillos — AP124

1972, June 21 Litho. *Perf. 13½x14*
C573 AP123 1.30p multi 50 15

International Carnival of Barranquilla.

No. C453 Surcharged in Brown **$ 1.30** ▬

1972, Oct. 5 Litho. *Perf. 14x13½*
C574 AP86 1.30p on 1.90p 55 16

1972 *Perf. 13½x14*

Design: 1.30p, Guillermo Leòn Valencia Muñoz.

C575 AP124 1.30p multi 15 15
C576 AP124 1.30p multi 18 15
Set value 15

Laureano Gomez (1898-1966), Guillermo Leon Valencia Munoz (1909-71), Presidents of Colombia.
Issue dates: No. C575, Oct. 17. No. C576, Nov. 28.

Benito Juarez — AP125

Rebecca Fountain — AP126

1972, Dec. 12 *Perf. 13½x14*
C577 AP125 1.50p multi 20 15

Centenary of the death of Benito Juarez (1806-1872), revolutionary leader and president of Mexico.

1972, Dec. 19 Litho.
C578 AP126 80c multi 45 45
C579 AP126 1p multi 40 15

"Bucaramanga" — AP127

1972, Dec. 22 *Perf. 14x13½*
C580 AP127 5p multi 85 15

350th anniversary of the founding of Bucaramanga.

Xavier University AP128

1973, May 8 Litho. *Perf. 14x13½*
C581 AP128 1.30p lt grn & sep 25 15
C582 AP128 1.50p lt bl & sep 25 15
Set value 15

350th anniversary of the founding of Xavier University in Bogotá.

Ceramic Type of Regular Issue

Excavated Ceramic Artifacts: 1p, Winged urn, Tairona. 1.30p, Woman and child, Sinu. 1.70p, Two-headed figure, Quimbaya. 3.50p, Man, Tumaco.

1973 Litho. *Perf. 13½x14*
C583 A358 1p multi 1.00 1.00
C584 A358 1.30p multi 50 15
C585 A358 1.70p multi 55 24
C586 A358 3.50p multi 1.10 28
Nos. C583-C586 (4) 3.15 1.67

Issue dates: 1p, Oct. 11; others, June 15.

Battle of Maracaibo, by Manuel F. Rincon AP129

1973, July 24 Litho. *Perf. 14x13½*
C587 AP129 10p bl & multi 2.00 16

Battle of Maracaibo, sesquicentennial.

Bank Emblem AP130

1973, Oct. 1 Litho. *Perf. 14x13½*
C588 AP130 2p multi 20 15

50th anniv. of the Bank of the Republic.

No. 801 Overprinted "AEREO"

1973, Oct. 11 *Perf. 14*
C589 A346 80c multi 28 15

Pres. Pedro Nel Ospina, by Coroleano Leudo — AP131

Arms of Toro — AP132

1973, Nov. 9 *Perf. 13½x14*
C590 AP131 1.50p multi 25 15

50th anniversary of the Ministry of Communications founded under Pres. Ospina.

1973, Dec. 1
C591 AP132 1p multi 15 15

4th centenary of the founding of Toro, Valle del Cauca.

Bolivar, Battle of Bombona AP133

1973, Dec. 7 Litho. *Perf. 14x13½*
C592 AP133 1.30p multi 15 15

Sesquicentennial (in 1972) of the Battle of Bombona.

Nicolaus Copernicus AP134

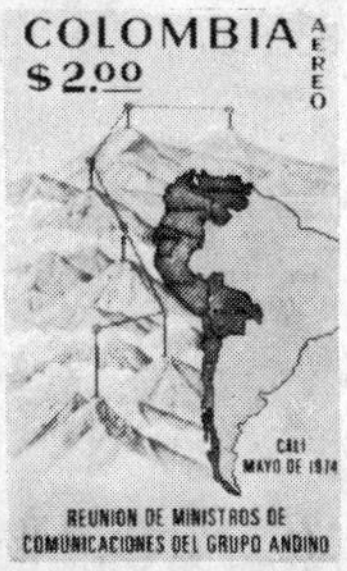

Andes, Map of South America AP135

1974, Feb. 19 Litho. *Perf. 13½x14*
C593 AP134 2.50p multi 50 16

500th anniversary of the birth of Nicolaus Copernicus (1473-1543), Polish astronomer.

1974, May 11 Litho. *Perf. 14*
C594 AP135 2p multi 35 15

Meeting of Communications Ministers of Members of the Andean Group, Cali, May 7-11, 1974.

Television Set — AP136

1974, July 16 Litho. *Perf. 14x13½*
C595 AP136 1.30p org, blk & brn 16 15

20th anniversary of Colombian television and 10th anniversary of INRAVISION, the National Institute of Radio and Television.

Championship Emblem AP137

1974, Aug. 5 Litho. *Perf. 14x13½*
C596 AP137 4.50p multi 30 15

2nd World Swimming Championships, Cali.

Condor — AP138

1974, Aug. 28 *Perf. 14*
C597 AP138 1.50p multi 25 15

Bank of Colombia centenary.

UPU Envelope AP139

1974, Sept. 9 Litho. *Perf. 14*
C598 AP139 20p multi 2.50 28

Centenary of Universal Postal Union.

Symbol of Flight — AP140

1974, Sept. *Perf. 12x12½*
C599 AP140 20c olive 15 15

Gen. José Maria Cordoba — AP141

White-tailed Trogon, Letter — AP142

1974, Oct. 14 Litho. *Perf. 13½x14*
C609 AP141 1.30p multi 20 15

Sesquicentennial of the Battles of Junin and Ayacucho.

Insurance Type of 1974

Design: 3p, Abstract pattern.

1974, Oct. 24 Litho. *Perf. 13½x14*
C610 A365 3p multi 28 15

Perf. 13½x14, 14x13½
1974, Nov. 14

Designs (UPU Letter and): 1.30p, Keelbilled Toucan, horiz. 2p, Peruvian cock-of-the-rock, horiz. 2.50p, Scarlet macaw.

C611 AP142 1p multi 16 15
C612 AP142 1.30p multi 20 15
C613 AP142 2p multi 28 15
C614 AP142 2.50p multi 30 15
Nos. C611-C614 (4) 94
Set value 28

Centenary of Universal Postal Union.
For surcharge see No. C656.

Forest No. 1, by Roman Roncancio — AP143

Boy with Thorn in Finger, by Gregorio Vazquez AP144

Paintings: 3p, Women Fruit Vendors, by Miguel Diaz Vargas (1886-1956). 5p, Annunciation, Santafereña School, 17th-18th cent.

Perf. 13½x14, 14x13½
1975, Mar. 12 Litho.
C615 AP143 2p multi 60 15
C616 AP144 3p multi 40 15
C617 AP144 4p multi 50 16
C618 AP144 5p multi 1.00 25
Nos. C615-C618 (4) 2.50
Set value 55

Modern and Colonial Colombian paintings.

Trees and Lake AP145

Design: 6p, Victoria regia, Amazon River.

1975, Mar. 12 *Perf. 14x13½*

C619 AP145 1p yel & multi 15 15
C620 AP145 6p yel & multi 60 15
Set value 15

Nature conservation of trees and Amazon Region.

Gold Treasure Type of 1975

Designs: 2p, Nose pendant. 10p, Alligator-shaped staff ornament.

1975, Apr. 11 Litho. *Perf. 14x13½*

C621 A368 2p grn, gold & brn 45 15
C622 A368 10p multi 2.25 60

El Rodadero, Santa Maria AP146

1975, July 26 Litho. *Perf. 14x13½*

C623 AP146 2p multi 15 15

400th anniversary of Santa Maria City.

AP147

AP148

1975, Aug. 31 Litho. *Perf. 13½x14*

C624 AP147 4p multi 20 15

Intl. Women's Year 1975. Maria de Jesus Paramo de Collazos founded 1st normal school for women in Bucaramanga in 1875.

1976, Mar. 12 Litho. *Perf. 13½x14*

C625 AP148 5p "Sugar Cane" 85 30

4th Congress of Latin-American and Caribbean sugar-exporting countries, Cali, Mar. 8-12.

View of Bogota — AP149

1976, July 2 Litho. *Perf. 12*

C626 AP149 10p shown 1.25 90
C627 AP149 10p Barranquilla 1.25 90
C628 AP149 10p Cali 1.25 90
C629 AP149 10p Medellin 1.25 90
a. Block of 4, #C626-C629 5.00 4.00

Habitat, UN Conf. on Human Settlements, Vancouver, Canada, May 31-June 11.

University Emblem and "90" — AP150

1976, Aug. 6 Litho. *Perf. 13½x14*

C630 AP150 5p lt bl & multi 52 15

University of Colombia, 90th anniversary.

Miguel Samper — AP151

Telephone, 1895 — AP152

1976, Oct. 29 Litho. *Perf. 13½x14*

C631 AP151 2p multicolored 20 15

Samper (1825-99), economist and writer.

1976, Nov. 2

C632 AP152 3p multicolored 16 15

Centenary of first telephone call by Alexander Graham Bell, Mar. 10, 1876.

747 Jumbo Jet — AP153

1976, Dec. 3 Litho. *Perf. 12*

C633 AP153 2p multicolored 15 15

Inauguration of 747 jumbo jet service by Avianca. For surcharge see No. C636.

Convent, Church and Plaza de San Francisco — AP154

1976, Dec. 29 Litho. *Perf. 14*

C634 AP154 6p multicolored 50 15

150th anniv. of the Congress of Panama.

Souvenir Sheet

Bank of the Republic Emblem — AP155

1977, June 6 Litho. *Perf. 14*

C635 AP155 25p multicolored 5.50 5.50

Opening of Philatelic Museum of Medellin under auspices of Banco de la Republica.

No. C633 Surcharged in Light Brown

1977, June Litho. *Perf. 12*

C636 AP153 3p on 2p multi 15 15

Coffee AP156

Coffee Grower, Pack Mule AP157

1977-78 Litho. *Perf. 12½*

C640 AP156 3p multicolored 15 15
C641 AP156 3.50p multicolored ('78) 16 15
Set value 15

Colombian coffee.

1977, Aug. 9 Litho. *Perf. 13½x14*

C642 AP157 10p multicolored 50 15

National Federation of Coffee Growers, 50th anniversary.

Beethoven and 9th Symphony AP158

Games' Emblem AP159

1977, Aug. 17

C643 AP158 8p multicolored 50 15

Sesquicentennial of the death of Ludwig van Beethoven (1770-1827).

Bird Type of 1977

Tropical Birds and Plants: No. C644, Woodpecker and meriania. C645, Purple gallinule and water lilies. No. C646, Xipholaena punicea and cochlospermum orinocense. No. C647, Crowned flycatcher and jacaranda copaia.

1977, Sept. 6 Litho. *Perf. 14*

C644 A380 5p multicolored 40 15
C645 A380 5p multicolored 40 15
C646 A380 10p multicolored 50 15
C647 A380 10p multicolored 50 15
Nos. C644-C647 (4) 1.80 60

1977, Sept. 9 *Perf. 12x12½*

C648 AP159 6p multicolored 24 15

13th Central American and Caribbean Games, Medellin, 1978.

La Cayetana, by Enrique Grau AP160

Design: No. C650, Water Nymphs, by Beatriz Gonzalez.

1977, Sept. 13 *Perf. 14x13½*

C649 AP160 8p multicolored 45 15
C650 AP160 8p multicolored 45 15

Women's suffrage, 20th anniversary.

Judge Francisco Antonio Moreno, by Joaquin Gutierrez AP161

Design: 25p, Viceroy Manuel de Guirior.

1977, Sept. 13 *Perf. 12*

C651 AP161 20p multicolored 1.25 75
C652 AP161 25p multicolored 1.75 1.10

Bicentenary of National Library.

Federico Lleras Acosta — AP162

Cauca University Arms — AP163

1977, Sept. 27 Litho. *Perf. 14*

C653 AP162 5p multicolored 26 15

Dr. Federico Lleras Acosta, veterinarian and bacteriologist; birth centenary.

1977, Oct. 14

C654 AP163 5p multicolored 28 15

Sesquicentennial of the University of Cauca.

CUDECOM Building, Bogota AP164

1977, Oct. 14

C655 AP164 1.50p multicolored 15 15

Colombian Society of Engineers, 90th anniversary.

No. C612 Surcharged with New Value and Bars in Brown

1977, Dec. 3 Litho. *Perf. 14x13½*

C656 AP142 2p on 1.30p multi 28 15

Lost City, Tayrona Culture AP165

Creator of Energy, by Arenas Betancourt AP166

1978, Apr. 18 **Litho.** ***Perf. 12½***
C657 AP165 3.50p multicolored 20 15

1978, Apr. 25 ***Perf. 12***
C658 AP166 4p bl & multi 24 15

Sesquicentennial of Antioquia University Law School.

Column of the Slaves — AP167

Statue of Catalina, Cartagena — AP168

1978, May 9
C659 AP167 2.50p multicolored 24 15

Sesquicentennial of Ocana Convention (meeting of various political groups).

1978, May 30 **Litho.** ***Perf. 12***
C660 AP168 4p blk & lt bl 24 15

Sesquicentennial of University of Cartagena.

Gold Pendant, Tolima — AP169

1978, July 11 **Litho.** ***Perf. 12x12½***
C661 AP169 3.50p multicolored 20 15

Apotheosis of Spanish Language, by Luis Alberto Acuña — AP170

1978, Aug. 9 ***Perf. 14***
C662 AP170 Strip of 3 4.75 4.75
a.-c. 11p, any single 1.10 1.10

Millennium of Spanish language.

Presidential Guard — AP171

Figure, Muisca Culture — AP172

1978, Aug. 16 ***Perf. 13½x14***
C663 AP171 9p multicolored 45 45

Presidential Guard Battalion, 50th anniv.

1978, Sept. 12 **Litho.** ***Perf. 12½***
C664 AP172 3.50p multicolored 20 15

Apse of Carmelite Church — AP173

1978, Oct. 12 ***Perf. 13***
C665 AP173 30p multicolored 2.50 40

Souvenir Sheet

Perf. 13½x14

C666 AP173 50p multicolored 3.25 3.25

ESPAMER '78 Philatelic Exhibition, Bogota, Oct. 12-21.

Owl, Gold Ornament, Calima AP174

Virgin and Child, by Gregorio Vasquez AP175

Designs: No. C669, Gold frog, Quimbaya culture. No. C670, Gold nose pendant, Tairona, horiz.

1978-80 **Litho.** ***Perf. 12½***
C667 AP174 3.50p multicolored 20 15
C668 AP174 4p multi ('79) 20 15
C669 AP174 4p multi ('79) 20 15
C670 AP174 5p multi ('80) 20 15
Nos. C667-C670 (4) 80
Set value 21

1978, Nov. 28 ***Perf. 13½x14***
C671 AP175 2.50p multicolored 15 15

Christmas 1978.

Bull Ring, Cathedral, Manizales AP176

1979, Jan. 6 **Litho.** ***Perf. 14***
C672 AP176 7p multicolored 60 20

Manizales Fair.

Children Playing Hopscotch, and IYC Emblem — AP177

Designs: No. C674, Child at blackboard and UNESCO emblem, horiz. No. C675, The Paper Collector, by Omar Gordillo, and UN emblem.

Perf. 13½x14, 14x13½

1979, July 19
C673 AP177 8p multicolored 30 30
C674 AP177 12p multicolored 45 45
C675 AP177 12p multicolored 45 45
Nos. C673-C675 (3) 1.20 1.20

International Year of the Child.

Rio Prado Hydroelectric Station — AP178

1979, Aug. 24 ***Perf. 13½x14***
C676 AP178 5p multicolored 48 15

Tomb, 6th Century — AP179

1979, Sept. 25 **Litho.** ***Perf. 14***
C677 AP179 8p multicolored 55 35

San Augustin Archaeological Park.

Gonzalo Jimenez de Quesada, by C. Leudo — AP180

1979, Oct. 11 ***Perf. 12***
C678 AP180 20p multicolored 1.50 48

Gonzalo Jimenez de Quesada (1500-1579), Spanish conquistador.

Hill, Penny Black, Colombia No. 1 — AP181

1979, Oct. 23 ***Perf. 13½x14***
C679 AP181 15p multicolored 60 20

Sir Rowland Hill (1795-1879), originator of penny postage.

Amazon Region — AP182

Tourism: 14p, San Fernando Fortress.

1979 **Litho.** ***Perf. 13½x14***
C680 AP182 7p multicolored 35 15
C681 AP182 14p multicolored 90 60

Issue dates: 7p, Nov. 16; 14p, Nov. 9.
See Nos. C717-C719.

Nativity — AP183

Creche Sculptures: No. C682, Three Kings and soldiers. No. C684, Shepherds.

1979, Nov. 30 ***Perf. 12***
C682 AP183 3p multicolored 35 35
C683 AP183 3p multicolored 35 35
C684 AP183 3p multicolored 35 35
a. Strip of 3, #C682-C684 1.15 1.00

Christmas 1979.

AP184

AP185

Magdalena Bridge, Avianca emblem.

1979, Dec. 5 ***Perf. 14***
C685 AP184 15p multicolored 60 16

Barranquilla, 350th anniversary; Avianca National Airline, 60th anniversary.

1980, Feb. 15 ***Perf. 13½x14***

Boy Playing Flute, by Judith Leyster.

C686 AP185 6p multicolored 45 20

2nd International Music Competition, Ibague, Dec. 1979.

Gen. Antonio José de Sucre, 150th Death Anniversary
AP186

1980, Feb. 15 Litho. *Perf. 12½x12*

C687	AP186 12p multicolored		45	16

The Watchman, by Edgar Negret
AP187

1980, Feb. 26 *Perf. 12x12½*

C688	AP187 25p multicolored		1.65	80

Virgin Mary, by Real del Sarte, 1929 — AP188

1980, May 23 Litho. *Perf. 14x13½*

C689	AP188 12p multicolored		30	15

Apparition of the Virgin Mary to Sister Catalina Labouri Gontard, 150th anniv.

San Gil Produce Market, by Luis Roncancio — AP189

1980, May 27 *Perf. 13½x14*

C690	AP189 12p multicolored		50	25

Pres. Enrique Olaya Herrera, by Miguel Diaz Vargas — AP190

1980, Oct. 28 Litho. *Perf. 12*

C691	AP190 20p multicolored		1.00	40

Enrique Olaya Herrera (1880-1936), president, 1930-1934.

The Boy Fishing in a Bucket
AP191

Christmas 1980 (Christmas Stories by Rafael Pombo): No. C693, The Frog and the Mouse. No. C694, The Seven Lives of the Cat.

1980, Nov. 21 Litho. *Perf. 14½*

C692	AP191 4p multicolored		20	16
C693	AP191 4p multicolored		20	16
C694	AP191 4p multicolored		20	16
	Nos. C692-C694 (3)		60	48

28th World Golf Cup, Cajica — AP192

1980, Dec. 9 Litho. *Perf. 13½x14*

C695	AP192 30p multicolored		1.40	40

Bolivar Type of 1980

Simon Bolivar Death Sesquicentennial: 6p, Portrait, last words to Colombia, vert.

1980, Dec. 17 *Perf. 12*

C696	A400 6p multicolored		60	45

St. Peter Claver Holding Cross — AP193

1981, Jan. 13 *Perf. 14½*

C697	AP193 15p multicolored		48	16

St. Peter Claver (1580-1654), helped American Indians.

Sculptured Bird, San Augustin — AP194

Archaeological Finds: No. C699, Funeral chamber, Tierradentro. No. C700, Chamber hallway, Tierradentro. No. C701, Statue of man, San Augustin.

1981, May 12 Litho. *Perf. 14*

C698	AP194 7p multicolored		35	15
C699	AP194 7p multicolored		35	15
C700	AP194 7p multicolored		35	15
C701	AP194 7p multicolored		35	15
a.	Block of 4, #C698-C701		1.40	75

See Nos. C707-C710D.

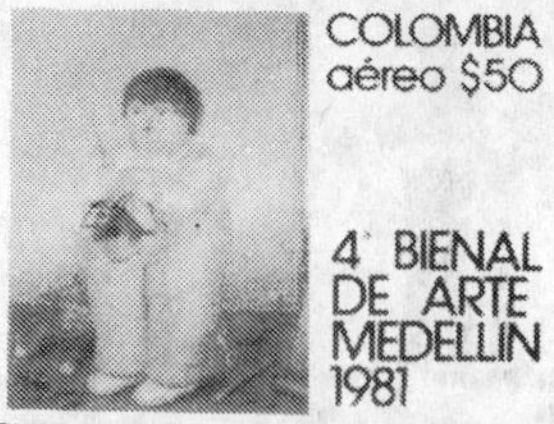

Child with Hobby Horse, by Fernando Botero — AP195

4th Biennial Arts show, Medellin: 20p, Square Abstract, by Omar Rayo. 25p, Flowers, by Alejandro Obregon.

1981, May 15 *Perf. 12*

C702	AP195 20p multicolored		85	16
C703	AP195 25p multicolored		1.00	28
C704	AP195 50p multicolored		1.75	75
	Nos. C702-C704 (3)		3.60	1.19

8th South American Swimming Championships, Medellin — AP196

1981, June 5

C705	AP196 15p multicolored		50	25

Santamaria Bull Ring, 50th Anniv. — AP197

1981, June 9 Litho. *Perf. 12*

C706	AP197 30p multicolored		2.00	1.25

AP197a AP197b

AP197c AP197d
Quimbaya Culture

1981, Sept. 23 Litho. *Perf. 14*

Yellow Background

C707	AP197a 9p Man		45	15
C708	AP197b 9p Seated man		45	15
C709	AP197c 9p Seal, print		45	15
C710	AP197d 9p Jug		45	15
e.	Block of 4, #C707-C710		1.80	75

AP197e AP197f

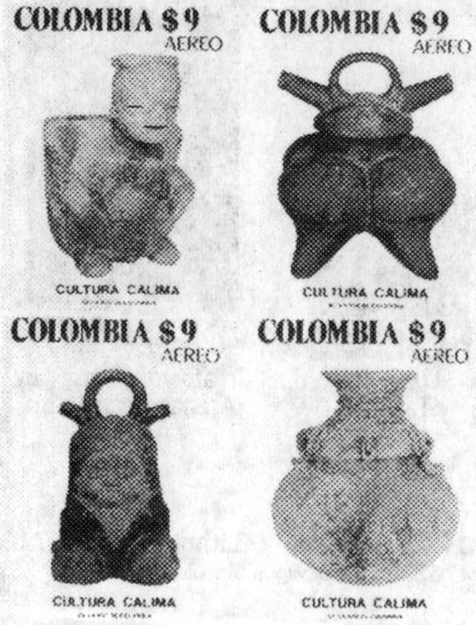

AP197g AP197h
Calima Culture

1981, Dec. 17

White Background

C710A	AP197e 9p Anthropomorphic container		45	15
C710B	AP197f 9p Jar		45	15
C710C	AP197g 9p Anthropomorphic jar		45	15
C710D	AP197h 9p Urn		45	15
f.	Block of 4, #C710A-C710D		1.80	75

Fruit
AP198

1981, Nov. 3 Litho. *Perf. 14*

C711	Block of 6		8.50	6.25
a.-f.	AP198 25p, any single		1.25	55

Revolt of the Comuneros, 200th Anniv. — AP199

1981, Nov. 21 Litho. *Perf. 12*

C712	AP199 20p multicolored		55	28

Jose Manuel Restrepo, Historian, 1775?-1860?
AP200

Andres Bello, 1780?-1865
AP201

1981, Dec. 1 Litho. *Perf. 12*

C713	AP200 35p multicolored		90	35

1981, Dec. 11 Litho. *Perf. 12*

C714	AP201 18p multicolored		48	15

Colombia's Admission to UPU, 100th Anniv. AP202

Designs: 30p, No. 103. 50p, Hemispheres, Nos. 104-108.

1981 **Litho.** *Perf. 12*

C715 AP202 30p multicolored	70	35

Size: 100x70mm

Imperf

C716 AP202 50p multicolored	1.40	1.25

Dates of issue: #C715, Dec. 18. #C716, Dec. 28.

Tourism Type of 1979

1982 **Litho.** *Perf. 12*

C717 AP182 20p Solano Bay	48	20
C718 AP182 20p Tota Lake, Boyaca	48	20
C719 AP182 20p Corrales, Boyaca	48	20
Nos. C717-C719 (3)	1.44	60

Issue dates: #C717, June 2; others, June 16.

1982 World Cup — AP202a

Designs: Players and team emblems.

1982, June 21 *Perf. 14*

C720 Sheet of 15	5.00	3.00
a. AP202a 9p, any single	30	15

Bogota Gun Club Centenary AP202b

1982, July 16 *Perf. 12*

C721 AP202b 20p multicolored	50	15

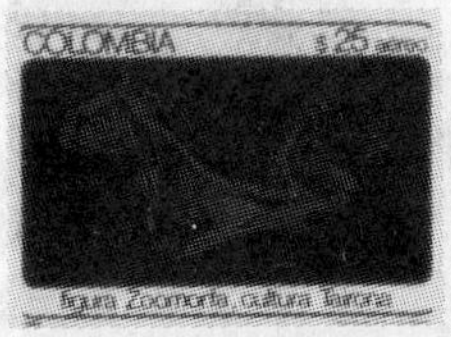

Gold Crocodile Figure, Tairona Culture AP202c

Tairona Culture Exhibit, Gold Museum: Various figures. Nos. C723-C727 vert.

1982, July 28

Gold, Black and:

C722 AP202c 25p light brn	70	40
C723 AP202c 25p brt pink	70	40
C724 AP202c 25p green	70	40
C725 AP202c 25p dark blue	70	40
C726 AP202c 25p violet	70	40
C727 AP202c 25p red	70	40
Nos. C722-C727 (6)	4.20	2.40

Government Buildings, Pereira — AP203

1982, Aug. 4 **Litho.** *Perf. 12*

C728 AP203 35p multicolored	85	40

Biplane in Flight, by Edgar Antonio Bustos AP204

1982, Aug. 5 *Perf. 14*

C729 AP204 18p multicolored	50	20

American Air Forces Cooperation System.

Magdalena River AP205

1982, Oct. 21 **Litho.** *Perf. 12*

C730 AP205 30p multicolored	70	35

Marquez Type of 1982

1982, Dec. 10 *Perf. 13½x14*

C731 A412 25p gray & bl	60	16
C732 A412 30p gray & brn	85	20

San Andres Archipelago — AP206

1983, Apr. 9 **Litho.** *Perf. 12*

C733 AP206 25p Liberty Fort	48	15

Opening of Las Gaviotas (The Seagulls) Ecological Center, Bogota — AP207

1983, June 1 **Litho.**

C734 AP207 12p multicolored	30	15

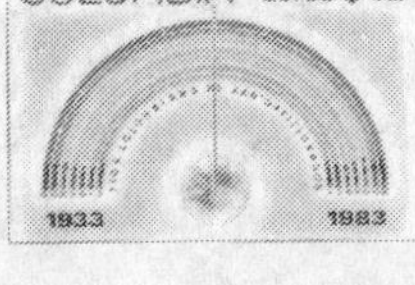

50th Anniv. of Radio Amateurs League AP208

1983, June 11 *Perf. 14x13½*

C735 AP208 12p multicolored	30	15

Bolivar Type of 1983

1983, July 24 *Perf. 12*

C736 A417 30p multicolored	60	20
C737 A417 100p multicolored	2.00	1.50

Botanical Exhibition Type of 1983

1983, Aug. 18 *Perf. 14*

C738 A418 12p Begonia guaduensis	30	15
C739 A418 12p Chinchona ovaliflora	30	15
C740 A418 40p Begonia urticae	1.00	40
Nos. C738-C740 (3)	1.60	70

Cartagena, 450th Anniv. — AP208a

1983, Sept. 9 **Litho.** *Perf. 12*

C740A AP208a 12p Customs Square	24	15
C740B AP208a 35p Historic sites, Cartagena	70	30

Painting Type of 1983

1983, Oct. 5 **Litho.** *Perf. 12*

C741 A420 30p multicolored	50	15

Scouting Year — AP209

Coffee Beans — AP210

1983, Oct. 24

C742 AP209 12p multicolored	20	15

1984, Mar. 28 **Litho.** *Perf. 14½x14*

C743 AP210 14p multicolored	20	15

Marandua City Type of 1984

1984, Sept. 28 *Perf. 12*

C744 A427 30p multicolored	48	15

AP211

AP212

1984, Nov. 2

C745 AP211 45p multicolored	70	22

45th Congress of Americanists, Bogota, 1985.

Christmas Type of 1984

1984, Dec. 14

C746 A428 14p multicolored	22	15

1985, Feb. 15

Design: Dove, map and flags of Colombia, Mexico, Costa Rica and Venezuela.

C747 AP212 40p multicolored	68	32

Contadora Group of Latin American countries.

Gomez Type of 1985

1985, Feb. 25

C748 A432 40p multicolored	68	32

Birds — AP213

AP214

1985

C749 AP213 14p Dryocopus lineatus nuperus	20	15
C750 AP213 20p Xiphorhynchus picus	28	15
C751 AP213 50p Eriocnemis cupreoventris	70	22
C752 AP213 55p Momotus momota	78	25
Nos. C749-C752 (4)	1.96	77

Issue dates: 14p, Apr. 12. 20p, 50p, Aug. 6. 55p, Aug. 29.

1985, July 15

C753 AP214 20p multicolored	28	15

Almirante Padilla Naval School, 50th anniv.

1985 Census AP215

1985, Oct. 15 *Perf. 12*

C754 AP215 20p multicolored	28	15

Christmas Type of 1985

1985, Dec. 4 **Litho.** *Perf. 13*

C755 A436 20p Girl, Christmas tree	28	15

Alfonso Lopez Pumarejo (1886-1959), President, 1934-38, 1942-45 — AP216

1986, Jan. 31

C756 AP216 24p multicolored	30	15

Coffee Berries, Natl. Cycling Team AP217

1986, Feb. 4

C757 AP217 60p multicolored	75	25

Natl. Coffee Producers Assoc. sponsorship of natl. cycling team, 25th anniv.

Fauna Type of 1985

1986, Feb. 18

C758 A433 50p Pudu mephistophiles	65	22

Set Values

A 15-cent minimum now applies to individual stamps and sets. Where the 15-cent minimum per stamp would increase the value of a set beyond retail, there is a "Set Value" notation giving the retail value of the set.

World Communications Day — AP218

Intl. Peace Year — AP219

1986, May 17 **Litho.** ***Perf. 13***
C759 AP218 50p multicolored 65 22

1986, June 13 **Litho.** ***Perf. 13***
C760 AP219 55p multicolored 65 22

AP220

AP221

1986, July 1 **Litho.** ***Perf. 13***
C761 AP220 24p Portrait, papal arms 32 15
C762 AP220 55p Portrait, Medellin cathedral, horiz. 65 22
C763 AP220 60p Blessing crowd, horiz. 70 24
Nos. C761-C763 (3) 1.67 61

Souvenir Sheet

C764 AP220 200p Praying, Madonna of Bogota 1.40 1.40

Visit of Pope John Paul II.
Nos. C762-C763 each printed in sheets of 20 with se-tenant labels picturing religious symbols.

1986, July 15 ***Perf. 12***
C765 AP221 25p multicolored 30 15

Enrique Santos Montejo (1886-1971), journalist.

Bach, Handel and Schutz, Composers AP222

1986, July 17 ***Perf. 13***
C766 AP222 70p Bach 82 40
C767 AP222 100p Text, music 1.15 55

Salesian Order Education in Colombia, Cent. AP223

1986, July 23 ***Perf. 12***
C768 AP223 25p De La Salle, founder 30 15

Completion of Coal Mining Complex, El Cerrejon AP224

1986, July 29 **Litho.** ***Perf. 12***
C769 AP224 55p multi 62 20

AP225

Natl. Constitution, Cent. — AP226

Designs: 25p, The Five Signators, by R. Vasquez, detail, and Bogota Cathedral. 200p, Pres. Nunez and Miguel Antonio Caro, Natl. Council of Delegates chairman, and Presidential Palace, constitution.

1986, Aug. 5 **Litho.** ***Perf. 14***
C770 AP225 25p multi 28 15

Souvenir Sheet
Perf. 12

C771 AP226 200p multi 2.25 75

Poet Type of 1986

Design: Federico Garcia Lorca (1898-1936), poet, and birthplace, Fuentevaqueros, Granada, Spain.

1986, Sept. 26 **Litho.** ***Perf. 12***
C772 A445 60p multi 68 24

Gratitude for Intl. Aid after the Armero Mudslide Disaster AP227

1986, Nov. 13
C773 AP227 50p multi 55 18

Christmas — AP228

Wood sculpture: Virgin Mestiza, Nerina.

1986, Dec. 19 **Litho.** ***Perf. 12***
C774 AP228 25p multi 28 15

The Apotheosis of Popayan, by Ephrain Martinez Zambrano (1898-1956) — AP229

1987, Jan. 13
C775 AP229 100p Popayan riding horse 1.10 50
C776 AP229 100p Onlookers 1.10 50
a. Pair, #C775-C776 2.25 2.25

No. C776a has a continuous design.

AP230

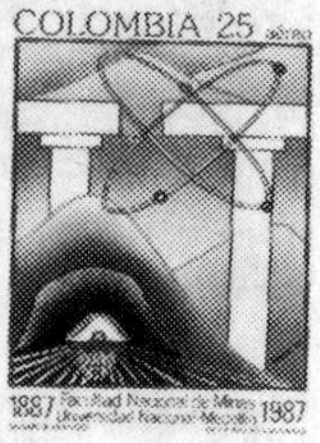

AP231

1987, Mar. 16 **Litho.** ***Perf. 12***
C777 AP230 30p multi 32 15

The Conversion of St. Augustine of Hippo, 1600th anniv.

Type of 1987

Designs: 30p, Phoenicopterus ruber. 35p, Pseudemys scripta, horiz. No. C780, Crax alberti. No. C781, Symphysodon aequifasciatum, horiz.

Perf. 14½x14, 14x14½

1987-89 **Wmk. 334**
C778 A446a 30p lake 35 15
C779 A446a 35p dark red brn 40 15
C780 A446a 45p dark blue gray 32 15
C781 A446a 45p blue 32 15
Nos. C778-C781 (4) 1.39
Set value 49

Issue dates: 30p, June 8. 35p, Dec. 24. No. C780, Dec. 6, 1988. No. C781, June 23, 1989.
This is an expanding set. Numbers will change if necessary.

Perf. 13½x13

1987, Apr. 10 **Unwmk.**
C783 AP231 25p multi 30 15

Natl. University School of Mining, Medellin, cent.

Purebred Horses AP232

1987, June 17 ***Perf. 12***
C784 AP232 60p White horse 70 22
C785 AP232 70p Black horse 85 28

El Espectador Newspaper, Cent. — AP233

Design: Frontispieces from 1887, 1915, 1948, 1974 and portraits of founder Don Fidel Cano, editors Don Luis Cano, Luis Gabriel Cano Isaza and Alfonso Cano Isaza.

1987, July 24 ***Perf. 12½x12***
C786 AP233 60p multi 70 22

Intl. Year of Shelter for the Homeless — AP234

1987, Sept. 21 ***Perf. 14***
C787 AP234 60p multi 65 22

Flags AP235

1987, Nov. 27 **Litho.** ***Perf. 13x13½***
C788 AP235 80p multi 82 28

ist Meeting of the eight Latin-American Presidents, Acapulco, Nov.

Christmas — AP236

1987, Dec. 8 **Litho.** ***Perf. 14***
C789 AP236 30p multi 30 15

Rural Telephone System AP237

1988, Feb. 4 **Litho.** ***Perf. 14***
C790 AP237 70p multi 80 28

Founding of Bogota, 450th Anniv. — AP238

1988, Apr. 11 **Litho.** ***Perf. 12***
C791 AP238 70p multi 65 22

Bogota, 450th Anniv. AP238a

Unwmk.

1988, July 1 **Litho.** ***Perf. 12***
C792 AP238a 80p Modern district, vert. 75 25
C793 AP238a 90p Colonial district 85 28

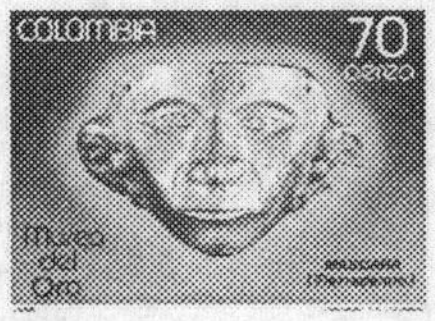

Gold Artifacts
AP239

Artifacts in the Gold Museum: 70p, Mask. 80p, Two-headed human figure inside a circle, Muisca tribe. 90p, Ritual figure of the Quimbaya.

1988 ***Perf. 12***
C794 AP239 70p multi 65 30
C795 AP239 80p multi 65 22
C796 AP239 90p multi 72 35
Nos. C794-C796 (3) 2.02 87

Issue dates: 70p, May 13, 80p, 90p, Oct. 7.

Human Rights Type of 1988

Perf. 14x14½

1988, July 1 Engr. Wmk. 334
C797 A452 40p Communication, horiz. 38 15

AP240

Christmas — AP241

1988, Sept. 28 Litho. ***Perf. 12***
C798 AP240 80p multi 70 18

Zipa Tisquesusa (d. 1538), Chibcha Indian leader during revolt against Spanish Conquistadors.

1988, Nov. 23 Litho. ***Perf. 12***
C799 AP241 40p multi 35 15

Agustin Nieto Caballero (1889-1975), Educator
AP242

Unwmk.

1989, Mar. 18 Litho. ***Perf. 12***
C800 AP242 100p multi 72 25

Pres. Laureano Gomez (1889-1965)
AP243

1989, Mar. 29
C801 AP243 45p multi 32 15

Intl. Coffee Organization
AP244

1989, Apr. 3
C802 AP244 110p multi 82 28

12th Session of the UN Commission on Human Rights — AP245

1989, Apr. 28
C803 AP245 100p multi 72 25

French Revolution, Bicent.
AP246

1989, June 29 Litho. ***Perf. 12***
C804 AP246 100p multi 70 24

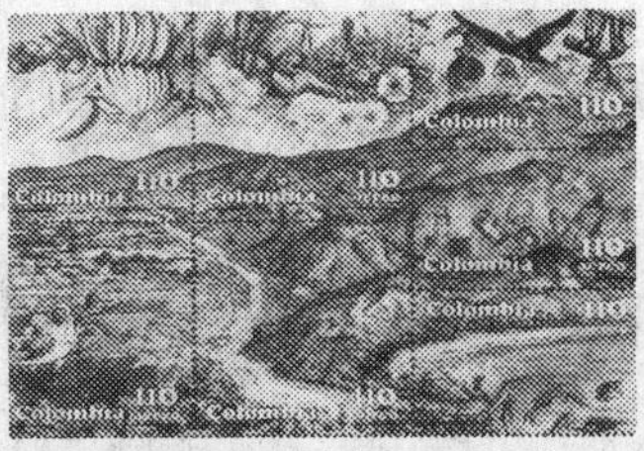
PHILEXFRANCE '89 — AP247

Designs: a, Bananas, tropical fruits. b, Fruits, flowers. c, Birds, animals. d, Precious gems, metals and mineral resources. e, View of fields, Colombian carrying produce basket. f, Waterfall. g, Fish, coast. (Illustration reduced.)

1989 Litho. ***Perf. 14***
C805 AP247 Pane of 7 5.25 2.00
a.-g. 110p any single 75 25

No. C805 printed in sheets containing panes of 7, rouletted between.

Souvenir Sheet

Los Lanceros, by R. Arenas Betancur — AP248

1989 Litho. ***Perf. 12***
C806 AP248 250p multicolored 1.65 55

Human Rights Type of 1988

Perf. 14½x14

1989, Aug. 18 Engr. Wmk. 334
C807 A452 55p Family 38 15

Natl. Anti-Drugs Campaign — AP249

Unwmk.

1989, Aug. 23 Litho. ***Perf. 12***
C808 AP249 115p multicolored 75 25

America Issue
AP250

UPAE emblem and artifacts or customs of pre-Columbian peoples: 115p, Quimbaya, Calima or Tolima gold smiths. 130p, Potter and Sinu ceramic figurine.

1989 ***Perf. 12***
C809 AP250 115p multicolored 75 25
C810 AP250 130p multicolored 88 28

Issue dates: 115p, Oct. 12; 130p, Aug. 23.

Joaquin Quijano Mantilla (1878-1944), Journalist
AP251

1989, Sept. 29 ***Perf. 12***
C811 AP251 170p multicolored 1.15 38

Arts and Crafts in Barro-Raquira
AP252

1989 Litho. ***Perf. 12***
C812 AP252 55p multicolored 38 15

Christmas.

Boeing 767
AP253

1989, Dec. 5 Litho. ***Perf. 12***
C813 AP253 130p multicolored 90 30

Bolivar Installed at the Congress of Angostura, by Tito Salas — AP254

1989, Dec. 12
C814 AP254 130p multicolored 90 30

Creation of the Republic, 1819.

Fathers of the Nation Leaving the Constitutional Convention
AP255

1989, Dec. 12
C815 AP255 130p shown 90 30
C816 AP255 130p Arms 90 30
C817 AP255 130p Temple of the Rosary 90 30
Nos. C815-C817 (3) 2.70 90

Constitution of the Republic, 1821.

Arms Type of Regular Issue, 1982

1990, Mar. 1 Litho. ***Perf. 12***
C818 A372 60p Velez 30 15

Presidential Summit, Cartagena
AP256

1990, Feb. 15 Litho. ***Perf. 12***
C819 AP256 130p Plaza de la Aduana 55 18

Colombian National Radio, 50th Anniv. — AP257

1990, Feb. 16 Litho. ***Perf. 12***
C820 AP257 150p multicolored 65 20

Teresa Cuervo Borda (1889-1976), Art Historian
AP258

1990, Mar. 28 Litho. ***Perf. 12***
C821 AP258 60p multicolored 35 15

Second Latin American Theater Festival, Bogota — AP259

1990, Apr. 10
C822 AP259 150p buff, tan & gold 78 26

Santander Type of 1990

Designs: No. C823, Santander holding the Constitution. No. C824, Central Cemetery, Bogata and National Pantheon. No. C825, Santander, as organizer of public education. No. C826, "Postman of New Granada" (Man and burro) by Joseph Brown and Jose Maria del Castillo, horiz. 500p, Santander on death bed.

1990, May 6 *Perf. 14x13½*

C823 A470	60p multicolored	25	15
C824 A470	60p multicolored	25	15
C825 A470	70p multicolored	30	15
C826 A470	70p multicolored	30	15
	Nos. C823-C826 (4)	1.10	
	Set value		36

Souvenir Sheet

Perf. 12

C827 A470 500p multi	2.00	66

No. C827 contains one 54x40mm stamp.

First Postage Stamp, 150th Anniv. AP260

1990, May 6 *Perf. 14*

C828 AP260 150p multicolored 65 22

Trans-Caribbean Fiber Optic Cable — AP261

1990, May 19 *Perf. 12*

C829 AP261 150p multicolored 65 22

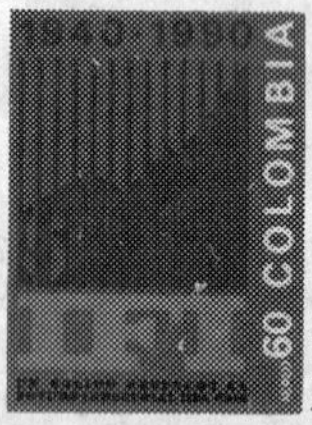

Institute of Industrial Development, 25th Anniv. — AP262

1990, May 22

C830 AP262 60p multicolored 35 15

Souvenir Sheet

World Cup Soccer Championships, Italy — AP263

1990, June 8

C831 AP263 500p multicolored 2.00 66

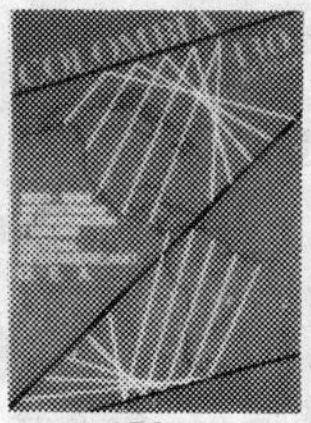
AP264

AP265

1990, June 27

C832 AP264 130p multicolored 55 18

Organization of American States, cent.

1990, July 26

C833 AP265 170p multicolored 72 24

Museum of Gold, 50th Anniv.

Dolphins, Marine Birds AP266

1990, Oct. 12 **Litho.** *Perf. 12*

C834 AP266 150p shown	58	20
C835 AP266 170p Jungle fauna, vert.	65	22

AP267

AP268

1990, Nov. 16 **Litho.** *Perf. 12*

C836 AP267 70p multicolored 38 15

Monastery of Our Lady of Las Lajas..

1991, Feb. 8 **Litho.** *Perf. 12*

C837 AP268 170p multicolored 80 30

Newspaper Publishing, 200th Anniv.

AP269

AP270

1990, Nov. 1 **Litho.** *Perf. 12*

C838 AP269 70p multicolored 38 15

Christmas.

1991, May 31 **Litho.** *Perf. 14*

Whales and Dolphins: 80p, Megaptera novaeangliae, breaching. 170p, Megaptera novaeangliae, diving. 190p, Inia geoffrensis, Sotalia fluviatilis, horiz.

C839 AP270 80p multicolored	35	15
C840 AP270 170p multicolored	75	30
C841 AP270 190p multicoloed	85	32
Nos. C839-C841 (3)	1.95	77

America Issue AP271

1991, Oct. 11 **Litho.** *Perf. 14*

C842 AP271 90p shown	45	15
C843 AP271 190p Ship arriving in New World	85	25

Adoration of the Magi — AP272

1991, Dec. 20 **Litho.** *Perf. 14*

C844 AP272 90p multicolored 45 15

Christmas.

AP273

AP274

1991, Dec. 2

C845 AP273 190p Country flags 85 25

Fifth summit of Latin American presidents.

1992, Feb. 8 **Litho.** *Perf. 12*

C846 AP274 210p multicolored 95 28

8th UNCTAD Conference, Cartagena.

Proclamation of New Constitution, July 4, 1991 AP275

1991, Nov. 27 **Litho.** *Perf. 14*

C847 AP275 90p multicolored 40 15

Export Products — AP276

Copyright Protection — AP277

1992, Mar. 11 *Perf. 12*

C848 AP276 90p Flowers	40	15
C849 AP276 210p Fruits, vegetables, horiz.	95	28

1992, Apr. 13 **Litho.** *Perf. 12*

C850 AP277 190p multicolored 85 25

1992 Summer Olympics — AP278

1992, June 4 **Litho.** *Perf. 14*

C851 AP278 110p multicolored 48 32

Earth Summit '92 — AP279

Designs: a, Tree, mountain landscape. b, Birds in tree.

1992, June 2 **Litho.** *Perf. 14*

C852 A279 230p Pair, #a.-b. 2.10 1.40

America Issue — AP280

Paintings: 230p, Discovery of America by Christopher Columbus, by Salvador Dali. 260p, Magical America, Myth and Legend, by Alfredo Vivero.

1992, July 22 *Perf. 14x13½*

C853 AP280 230p multicolored	1.00	70
C854 AP280 260p multicolored	1.15	75

McDonnell Douglas MD83 AP281

1992, Sept. 22 **Litho.** *Perf. 12*

C855 AP281 110p multicolored 45 30

Curtain of Colon Theatre AP282

1992, Oct. 12 **Litho.** *Perf. 12*

C856 AP282 230p multicolored 95 65

AP283

AP284

1992, Nov. 27 Litho. *Perf. 12*
C857 AP283 230p Gloria Lara, 1938-82 95 65

1993, June 7 Litho. *Perf. 12*
C858 AP284 220p multicolored 85 60

1993 American Soccer Cup, Ecuador.

Intl. Year of Indigenous People — AP285

1993, July 1 *Perf. 14*
C859 AP285 460p multicolored 1.75 1.25

South American Eliminations for 1994 World Cup Soccer Championships, US — AP286

1993, July 31 Litho. *Perf. 12*
C860 AP286 220p multicolored 80 52

AP287

AP288

America Issue (Endangered species): a, 220p, Saguinus oedipus. b, 220p, Porphyrula martinica. c, 460p, Rupicola peruviana. d, 520p, Trichecus manatus.

1993, Oct. 19 Litho. *Perf. 12*
C861 AP287 Block of 4, #a.-d. 4.75 3.25

1994, Mar. 21 Litho. *Perf. 12*
C862 AP288 630p multicolored 2.25 1.40

Intl. Decade for Natural Disaster Reduction.

Beatification of Josemaria Escriva de Balaguer — AP289

1994, May 17 Litho. *Perf. 13½x14*
C863 AP289 560p multicolored 1.90 1.25

First Airmail Delivery, 75th Anniv. AP290

Design: 270p, William Knox Martin, airplane over Port Colombia, 1919.

1994, July 29 Litho. *Perf. 14*
C864 AP290 270p multicolored 90 55

AIR POST SPECIAL DELIVERY STAMPS

Catalogue values for unused stamps in this section are for Never Hinged items.

Post Horn and Wings APSD1

Unwmk.
1958, May 19 Litho. *Perf. 12*
CE1 APSD1 25c dk bl & red 35 15

Same Overprinted Vertically in Red

1959
CE2 APSD1 25c dk bl & red 30 15

Jet Plane and Envelope — APSD2

1963, Oct. 4 *Perf. 14*
CE3 APSD2 50c red & blk 20 15

Aviation Type of Air Post Issue

History of Colombian Aviation: 80c, Boeing 727 jet, 1966.

Perf. 14x13½
1966, Dec. 14 Photo. Unwmk.
CE4 AP96 80c crim & multi 35 15

AIR POST REGISTRATION STAMPS

Issued by Sociedad Colombo-Alemana de Transportes Aereos (SCADTA)

No. C41 Overprinted in Red **R**

1923 Wmk. 116 *Perf. 14x14½*
CF1 AP6 20c gray 2.50 1.10

No. C58 Overprinted in Black **R**

1929 Wmk. 127 *Perf. 14*
CF2 AP8 20c carmine 4.00 1.10

Same Overprint on No. C71
CF3 AP10 20c carmine 6.50 6.00

Colombian Government Issues
Same Overprint on No. C86

1932
CF4 AP8 20c carmine 6.50 6.00

No. C100 Overprinted **R**

CF5 AP12 20c car & ol blk 4.50 1.25

SPECIAL DELIVERY STAMPS

Special Delivery Messenger — SD1

1917 Unwmk. Engr. *Perf. 14*
E1 SD1 5c gray green 1.00 1.50

Catalogue values for unused stamps in this section, from this point to the end of the section, are for Never Hinged items.

SD2

1987, July 31 Litho. *Perf. 14*
E2 SD2 25p emerald & ver 30 30
E3 SD2 30p emerald & ver 35 35

REGISTRATION STAMPS

R1

R2

1865 Unwmk. Litho. *Imperf.*
F1 R1 5c black 70.00 37.50
F2 R2 5c black 60.00 37.50

R3

R4

1870

White Paper

Vertical Lines in Background
F3 R3 5c black 1.75 1.75
F4 R4 5c black 1.75 1.75

Horizontal Lines in Background
F5 R3 5c black 6.00 6.00
F6 R4 5c black 1.75 1.75
Nos. F3-F6 (4) 11.25 11.25

Reprints of Nos. F3 to F6 show either crossed lines or traces of lines in background.

R5

R6

1881 *Imperf.*
F7 R5 10c violet 37.50 40.00
a. Sewing machine perf. 42.50 47.50
b. Perf. 11 47.50 50.00

1883 *Perf. 12, 13½*
F8 R6 10c red, *orange* 1.40 1.75

R7

1889-95 *Perf. 12, 13½*
F9 R7 10c red, *grysh* 5.25 2.50
F10 R7 10c red, *yelsh* 5.25 2.50
F11 R7 10c dp brn, *rose buff* ('95) 1.40 1.10
F12 R7 10c yel brn, *lt buff* ('92) 1.40 1.10
Nos. F9-F12 (4) 13.30 7.20

Nos. F9-F12 exist imperf. Values same as for perf.

R9

1902 *Imperf.*
F13 R9 20c red brown, *blue* 1.40 1.40
a. Sewing machine perf. 3.75 3.75
b. Perf. 12 3.75 3.75

Medellin Issue

R10

1902 *Perf. 12*

Laid Paper
F16 R10 10c blk vio 12.50 12.50
a. Wove paper 17.50 17.50

Regular Issue

1903 *Imperf.*
F17 R9 20c blue, *blue* 1.40 1.40
a. Sewing machine perf. 4.00 4.00
b. Perf. 12 4.00 4.00

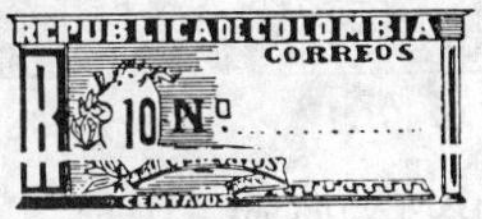
R11

1904 Pelure Paper *Imperf.*
F19 R11 10c purple 3.00 3.00
a. Sewing machine perf. 4.00 3.00
b. Perf. 12 5.00 4.00

R12

Imprint: "J. L. Arango"

1904 *Perf. 12*

Wove Paper
F20 R12 10c purple 2.00 50
a. Imperf., pair 6.25 6.25

Imprint: "Lit. Nacional"

1909 *Perf. 10, 14, 10x14, 14x10*

F21 R12 10c purple	2.25	70
a. Imperf., pair	5.00	5.00

For overprints see Nos. LF1-LF4.

Execution at Cartagena in 1816 R13

1910, July 20 **Engr.** *Perf. 12*

F22 R13 10c red & black	17.50	*75.00*

Centenary of National Independence.

Pier at Puerto Colombia R14

Tequendama Falls — R15

Perf. 11, 11½, 14, 11½x14

1917, Aug. 25

F23 R14 4c green & ultra	50	*2.50*
a. Center inverted	575.00	575.00
F24 R15 10c deep blue	1.90	60

R16

1925 **Litho.** *Perf. 10x13½*

F25 R16 (10c) blue	3.50	1.50
a. Imperf., pair	12.00	10.00
b. Perf. 13½x10	6.00	4.00

ACKNOWLEDGMENT OF RECEIPT STAMPS

AR1

AR2

1893 **Unwmk.** **Litho.** *Perf. 13½*

H1 AR1 5c ver, *blue*	4.25	4.25

1894 *Perf. 12*

H2 AR1 5c vermilion	3.50	4.00

1902-03 *Imperf.*

H3 AR2 10c blue, *blue*	2.75	2.75
a. 10c, blue, *greenish blue*	2.75	2.75
b. Sewing machine perf.	2.75	2.75
c. Perf. 12	2.75	2.75

The handstamp "AR" in circle is believed to be a postmark.

AR2a

Purple Handstamp

1903 *Imperf.*

H4 AR2a 10c black, *pink*	20.00	20.00

AR3

AR4

1904 **Pelure Paper** *Imperf.*

H12 AR3 5c pale blue	10.50	10.50
a. Perf. 12	10.50	10.50

No. 307 Overprinted in Black, Green or Violet **A R**

H13 A86 5c carmine	17.50	17.50

1904 *Perf. 12*

H16 AR4 5c blue	3.25	2.75
a. Imperf., pair	8.75	8.75

For overprints see Nos. LH1-LH2.

General José Acevedo y Gómez — AR5

1910, July 20 **Engr.**

H17 AR5 5c orange & green	5.75	*16.00*

Centenary of National Independence.

Sabana Station AR6

Map of Colombia AR7

1917 *Perf. 14*

H18 AR6 4c bister brown	1.75	2.00
H19 AR7 5c orange brown	1.50	1.75
a. Imperf., pair	11.00	

LATE FEE STAMPS

LF1

LF2

1886 **Unwmk.** **Litho.** *Perf. 10½*

I1 LF1 2½c blk, *lilac*	3.25	2.50
a. Imperf., pair	12.00	12.00

1892 *Perf. 12, 13½*

I2 LF2 2½c dk bl, *rose*	2.75	2.00
a. Imperf., pair	12.00	
I3 LF2 2½c ultra, *pink*	2.75	2.00

LF3

LF4

1902 *Imperf.*

I4 LF3 5c purple, *rose*	85	85
a. Perf. 12	1.75	1.75

1914 *Perf. 10, 13½*

I6 LF4 2c vio brown	4.00	4.00
I7 LF4 5c blue green	4.00	3.25

Retardo

Refardo 1921

Overprints illustrated above are unauthorized and of private origin.

POSTAGE DUE STAMPS

These are not, strictly speaking, postage due stamps but were issued to cover an additional fee, "Sobreporte," charged on mail to foreign countries with which Colombia had no postal conventions.

D1

D2

D3

1866 **Unwmk.** **Litho.** *Imperf.*

J1 D1 25c black, *blue*	35.00	35.00
J2 D2 50c black, *yellow*	35.00	35.00
J3 D3 1p black, *rose*	95.00	80.00
Nos. J1-J3 (3)	165.00	150.00

DEPARTMENT STAMPS

These stamps are said to be for interior postage, to supersede the separate issues for the various departments.

Regular Issues Handstamped in Black, Violet, Blue or Green — a

Correos Departa- mentales

On Stamps of 1904

1909 **Unwmk.** *Perf. 12*

L1 A94 ½c yellow	2.00	2.00
a. Imperf., pair	6.00	6.00
L2 A94 1c yel grn	3.00	2.00
L3 A94 2c red	4.50	3.00
a. Imperf., pair	12.50	12.50
L4 A94 5c blue	5.00	3.25
L5 A94 10c violet	7.00	7.00
L6 A94 20c black	11.00	10.00
L7 A95 1p brown	18.00	17.00

On Stamp of 1902

L8 A83 10p dk brn, *rose*	20.00	20.00
Nos. L1-L8 (8)	70.50	64.25

On Stamps of 1908

Perf. 10, 13, 13½ and Compound

L9 A94 ½c orange	2.00	2.00
a. Imperf., pair	6.00	6.00
L10 A94 1c green	4.00	3.25
a. Without imprint	5.00	5.00
L11 A94 2c red	4.50	3.25
a. Imperf., pair		
L12 A94 5c blue	4.50	3.25
a. Imperf., pair	12.50	12.50
L13 A94 10c violet	6.00	6.00

On Tolima Stamp of 1888

Perf. 10½

L14 A23 1p red brn	12.50	12.50
Nos. L9-L14 (6)	33.50	30.25

Regular Issues Handstamped — b

Correos Depmentales

On Stamps of 1904

Perf. 12

L15 A94 ½c yellow	2.00	2.00
L16 A94 1c yel grn	3.50	3.00
L17 A94 2c red	6.00	5.00
L18 A94 5c blue	6.00	5.00
L19 A94 10c violet	8.00	6.00
L20 A94 20c black	11.00	11.00
L21 A94 1p brown	20.00	20.00
Nos. L15-L21 (7)	56.50	52.00

On Stamps of 1908

Perf. 10, 13, 13½

L22 A94 ½c orange	2.25	2.25
L23 A94 1c yel grn	6.25	6.25
L24 A94 2c red	5.00	5.00
a. Imperf., pair	12.50	12.50
L25 A94 5c light blue	6.00	5.00
Nos. L22-L25 (4)	19.50	18.50

The handstamps on Nos. L1-L25 are, as usual, found inverted and double.

DEPARTMENT REGISTRATION STAMPS

Registration Stamps Handstamped like Nos. L1-L25

On Registration Stamp of 1904

1909 **Unwmk.** *Perf. 12*

LF1 R12 (a) 10c purple	25.00	25.00
LF2 R12 (b) 10c purple	25.00	25.00

On Registration Stamp of 1909

Perf. 10, 13

LF3 R12 (a) 10c purple	25.00	25.00
LF4 R12 (b) 10c purple	25.00	25.00
Nos. LF1-LF4 (4)	100.00	100.00

Nos. LF1-LF4 exist imperf. Value per pair, $100.

DEPARTMENT ACKNOWLEDGMENT OF RECEIPT STAMPS

Acknowledgment of Receipt Stamp of 1904 Handstamped like Nos. L1-L25

1909 **Unwmk.** *Perf. 12*

LH1 AR4 (a) 5c blue	25.00	25.00
a. Imperf., pair	100.00	
LH2 AR4 (b) 5c blue	25.00	25.00
a. Imperf., pair	100.00	

LOCAL STAMPS FOR THE CITY OF BOGOTA

A1

Pelure Paper

1889 **Unwmk.** **Litho.** *Perf. 12*

LX1 A1 ½c black	95	95
a. Imperf., pair	6.00	6.00

Impressions on bright blue and blue-gray paper were not regularly issued.

A2

A3

White Wove Paper

1896 *Perf. 12, 13½*

LX2 A2 ½c black	95	95

1903 *Imperf.*
LX3 A3 10c black, *pink* 1.25 1.25
a. Perf. 12 5.00 5.00

OFFICIAL STAMPS

Stamps of 1917-1937 Overprinted in Black or Red:

OFICIAL
a

OFICIAL
b

1937 Unwmk. *Perf. 11, 12, 13½*

O1	A131 (a)	1c green	15	15
O2	A157 (a)	10c dp org	15	15
O3	A107 (b)	30c olive bis	1.75	1.00
O4	A129 (b)	40c brn & yel brn	1.50	80
O5	A114 (b)	50c car	1.00	50
O6	A107 (b)	1p lt bl	5.00	4.00
O7	A107 (b)	2p org	10.00	6.50
O8	A107 (b)	5p gray	37.50	27.50
O9	A118 (b)	10p dk brn	110.00	100.00

Wmk. 229
Perf. 12½

O10	A132 (a)	2c red	15	15
O11	A133 (a)	5c brn	15	15
O12	A160 (a)	12c dp bl (R)	1.00	50
O13	A136 (b)	20c dk bl (R)	1.65	60
		Nos. O1-O13 (13)	170.00	142.00

Tall, wrong font "I's" in OFICIAL exist on all stamps with "a" overprint.

POSTAL TAX STAMPS

"Greatest Mother" PT1

Perf. 11½
1935, May 27 Unwmk. Litho.
RA1 PT1 5c olive blk & scar 2.00 75

Required on all mail during Red Cross Week in 1935 (May 27-June 3) and in 1936.

Mother and Child — PT2

Perf. 10½, 10½x11
1937, May 24 Unwmk.
RA2 PT2 5c red 70 28

Required on all mail during Red Cross Week. The tax was for the Red Cross.

Ministry of Posts and Telegraphs Building
PT3 PT4

1939-45 Litho. *Perf. 10½, 12½*

RA3	PT3	¼c dp bl	15	15
RA3A	PT3	¼c dk vio brn ('45)	15	15
RA4	PT3	½c pink	15	15
RA5	PT3	1c violet	30	15
RA5A	PT3	1c yel org ('45)	1.50	60
RA6	PT3	2c pck grn	40	15
RA7	PT3	20c lt brn	3.50	1.25
		Nos. RA3-RA7 (7)	6.15	
		Set value		1.65

Obligatory on all mail. The tax was for the construction of the new Communications Building.
The 25c of type PT3 and PT4 were not usable on postal matter.

For overprint see No. 561.

Perf. 12½x13
1940, Jan. 20 Engr. Wmk. 229

RA8	PT4	¼c ultra	15	15
RA9	PT4	½c carmine	15	15
RA10	PT4	1c violet	15	15
RA11	PT4	2c bl grn	24	15
RA12	PT4	20c brown	1.00	24
		Set value	1.35	44

See note after No. RA7. See No. RA18.

"Protection" — PT5

1940, Apr. 25 Wmk. 255 *Perf. 12*
RA13 PT5 5c rose carmine 24 15

See No. RA17.

Postal Tax Stamps of 1939 Surcharged in Black

$ 0,0½
MEDIO CENTAVO

1943 Unwmk. *Perf. 10½*

RA14	PT3	½c on 1c violet	15	15
a.		Inverted surcharge	1.50	
RA15	PT3	½c on 2c pck grn	15	15
RA16	PT3	½c on 20c lt brn	15	15
		Set value	20	20

Types of 1940
Imprint: "Litografia Colombia Bogota S.A."

1944 Litho. *Perf. 11*
RA17 PT5 5c dark rose 30 15

Imprint: "Lito-Colombia Bogota-Colombia"

RA18 PT4 ¼c ultra 15 15
Set value 36 20

Ministry of Posts and Telegraphs Building — PT6

1945-48 Wmk. 255 Engr. *Perf. 12*

RA19	PT6	¼c ultra	15	15
RA20	PT6	¼c sepia ('46)	15	15
RA21	PT6	½c car rose	15	15
RA22	PT6	½c dp mag ('46)	15	15
RA23	PT6	1c vio ('46)	15	15
RA23A	PT6	1c red org ('46)	15	15
RA24	PT6	2c grn ('46)	15	15
RA25	PT6	20c brn ('46)	90	22
a.		20c red brown ('48)	60	15
		Set value	1.25	55

These stamps were obligatory on all mail. The surtax was for the construction of the new Communications Building. See Nos. 603, RA33. For overprints see Nos. 562-564.

No. 469 Overprinted in Carmine

1946, May 25
RA26 A176 5c dull brown 35 15

The surtax was for the Red Cross.

Ministry of Posts and Telegraphs Building — PT7

1946 Unwmk. Litho. *Perf. 11*
RA27 PT7 3c blue 15 15

No. 490 Overprinted in Carmine SOBRETASA

1947 Wmk. 255 *Perf. 12*
RA28 A196 20c gray black 3.00 1.25

Arms of Colombia and Red Cross — PT8

PT9

Perf. 12½
1947, Sept. Unwmk. Engr.
RA29 PT8 5c car lake 15 15

The surtax of Nos. RA29 and RA40 was for the Red Cross. See No. RA40.

No. 466 Overprinted Like No. RA28 in Carmine

RA30 A136 20c dark blue 10.00 7.00

Catalogue values for unused stamps in this section, from this point to the end of the section, are for Never Hinged items.

Type of 1945

1947 Wmk. 255 Engr. *Perf. 12*
RA33 PT6 1c olive bister 15 15

Black Surcharge

1948 Unwmk. Litho. *Perf. 11*

RA36	PT9	1c on 5c lt brn	15	15
RA37	PT9	1c on 10c lt vio	15	15
RA38	PT9	1c on 25c red	15	15
RA39	PT9	1c on 50c ultra	15	15
		Set value	24	20

Type of 1947

1948 *Perf. 10½*
RA40 PT8 5c vermilion 15 15

Ministry of Posts and Telegraphs Building — PT10

Mother and Child — PT11

1948-50 Wmk. 255 Engr. *Perf. 12*

RA41	PT10	1c rose car ('49)	15	15
RA42	PT10	2c green ('50)	15	15
RA43	PT10	3c blue	15	15
RA44	PT10	5c gray	15	15
RA45	PT10	10c purple	22	15
		Set value	47	25

A 25c stamp of type PT10 was for use on telegrams, later for regular postage. See Nos. 602, 604. For overprints and surcharge see Nos. C227-C230, C238, C283, RA51.

Unwmk.
1950, May 25 Litho. *Perf. 11*
Dark Blue Surcharge

RA46	PT11	5c on 2c gray, red, blk & yel	75	30
a.		"195" instead of "1950"	1.40	1.40
b.		Top bar and "19" of "1950" omitted	1.40	1.40

Marginal perforations omitted, creating 26 straight-edged copies in each sheet of 44. Surtax for Red Cross.

No. 574 Overprinted in Black SOBRETASA

1950, May 26 Wmk. 255 *Perf. 12*
RA47 A176 5c blue 15 15
a. Inverted overprint 90

Telegraph Stamp Surcharged in Black

RA48 A253a 8c on 50c org yel 15 15
Set value 15

Fiscal stamps of type A253a were available for postal use after May 9, 1952. See Nos. 605-608.

Arms and Cross — PT12

Bartolome de Las Casas Aiding Youth — PT13

Perf. 12½
1951, May Unwmk. Engr.

RA49	PT12	5c red	22	15
RA50	PT13	5c carmine	22	15
		Set value		15

The surtax was for the Red Cross.

No. RA43 Surcharged with New Value in Black

1951 Wmk. 255 *Perf. 12*
RA51 PT10 1c on 3c blue 15 15

Type of 1951
Engraved; Cross Lithographed

1953 Unwmk. *Perf. 12½*
RA52 PT13 5c grn & car 22 15

Surtax of Nos. RA52-RA60 for the Red Cross.

No. C254 Overprinted with Cross and Bar in Carmine

1954
RA53 AP42 5c lilac rose 60 50

St. Peter Claver Offering Gifts to Slaves — PT14

Engraved; Cross Typographed
1955, May 2 Unwmk. *Perf. 13*
RA54 PT14 5c dp plum & red 22 15

Death of St. Peter Claver, 300th anniv.

Jean Henri Dunant and Santiago Samper Brush PT15

Photo.; Red Cross & "Cruz Roja" Engr.
1956, June 1 Unwmk. *Perf. 13*
RA55 PT15 5c brown & red 22 15

Nurses and Ambulances — PT16

1958, June 2 Photo. *Perf. 12*
RA56 PT16 5c gray & red 15 15

St. Louisa de Marillac and Church
PT17

Design: No. RA58, Henri Dunant and battle scene.

1960, Sept. 1 **Litho.** ***Perf. 11***

RA57 PT17 5c brown & rose 22 15
RA58 PT17 5c vio blue & rose 22 15
Set value 16

No. RA57 for 3rd cent. of the Sisters of Charity. No. RA58 for cent. (in 1959) of the Red Cross idea.

Manuelita de la Cruz — PT18

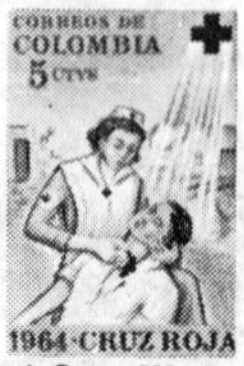

Red Cross Worker, Patient — PT19

1961, Nov. 2 **Engr.** ***Perf. 13***

RA59 PT18 5c dull pur & red 15 15
RA60 PT18 5c brown & red 15 15
Set value 15

Issued in memory of Red Cross Nurse Manuelita de la Cruz, who died in the line of duty during the floods of 1955. Obligatory on domestic mail for a month.

1965, Apr. 30 **Photo.** ***Perf. 12***

RA61 PT19 5c blue gray & red 15 15

Obligatory on domestic mail during May.

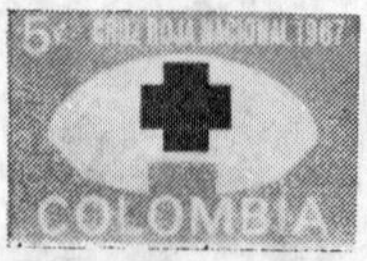

Nurse's Cap — PT20

Red Cross — PT21

1967, June 1 **Litho.** ***Perf. 12***

RA62 PT20 5c brt bl & red 15 15

1969, July 1 **Litho.** ***Perf. 12x12½***

RA63 PT21 5c vio bl & red 15 15

Child Care — PT22

1970, July 1 **Litho.** ***Perf. 12½x12***

RA64 PT22 5c light bl & red 15 15

ANTIOQUIA

Originally a State, now a Department of the Republic of Colombia. Until the revolution of 1885, the separate states making up the United States of Colombia were sovereign governments in their own right. On August 4, 1886, the National Council of Bogotá, composed of two delegates from each state, adopted a new constitution which abolished the sovereign rights of states, which then became departments with governors appointed by the President of the Republic. The nine original states represented at the Bogotá Convention retained some of their previous rights, as management of their own finances, and all issued postage stamps until as late as 1904. For Panama's issues, see Panama Nos. 1-30.

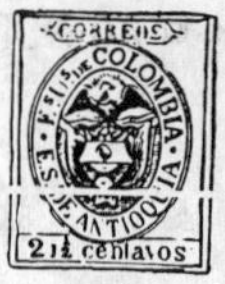

Coat of Arms
A1 A2

A3

A4

Wove Paper

1868 **Unwmk.** **Litho.** ***Imperf.***

1 A1 2½c blue 600. 400.
2 A2 5c green 450. 300.
3 A3 10c lilac 1,350. 550.
4 A4 1p red 350. 275.

Reprints of Nos. 1, 3 and 4 are on a bluish white paper and all but No. 3 have scratches across the design.

A5

A6

A7

A8

A9

A10

1869

5 A5 2½c blue 2.50 2.50
6 A6 5c green 4.00 4.00
7 A7 5c green 4.00 4.00
8 A8 10c lilac 5.00 3.00
9 A9 20c brown 5.00 3.00
10 A10 1p rose red 10.00 10.00
a. 1p vermilion 20.00 20.00
Nos. 5-10 (6) 30.50 26.50

Reprints of Nos. 7, 8 and 10 are on a bluish white paper; reprints of Nos. 5 and 10a on white paper. The 10c blue is believed to be a reprint.

A11

A12

A13

A14

A15

A16

A17

A18

1873

12 A11 1c yel grn 3.50 3.25
a. 1c green 3.50 3.25
13 A12 5c green 6.00 5.00
14 A13 10c lilac 17.50 17.50
15 A14 20c yel brn 6.00 6.00
a. 20c dark brown 6.00 6.00
16 A15 50c blue 1.40 1.40
17 A16 1p vermilion 2.50 2.50
18 A17 2p blk, *yellow* 6.25 6.25
19 A18 5p blk, *rose* 55.00 47.50

A19

A20

Liberty Head
A21 A22

Pedro Justo Berrio — A23

1875-85

20 A19 1c blk, *grn*, unglazed ('76) 1.25 1.25
a. Glazed paper 1.75 1.75
b. 1c blk, *lt grn*, laid paper ('85) 3.00 3.00
21 A19 1c blk ('76) 90 90
a. Laid paper 110.00 90.00
22 A19 1c bl grn ('85) 1.75 1.75
23 A19 1c red lil, laid paper ('85) 1.75 1.75
24 A20 2½c blue 1.75 1.75
a. Pelure paper ('78) *1,350.* *1,100.*
25 A21 5c green 12.00 11.00
a. Laid paper 110.00 72.50
26 A22 5c green 12.00 11.00
a. Laid paper 110.00 72.50
27 A23 10c lilac 18.00 17.00
a. Laid paper 110.00 100.00
28 A20 10c vio, pelure paper ('78) *750.00* 600.00

Arms — A24

Liberty — A25

A26

A27

1878-85

29 A24 2½c blue, pelure paper 2.00 2.00
30 A24 2½c grn ('83) 1.75 1.75
a. Laid paper ('83) 55.00 42.50
31 A24 2½c blk, *buff* ('85) 5.00 5.00
32 A25 5c grn ('83) 3.00 3.00
a. Pelure paper 22.50 22.50
b. Laid paper ('82) 30.00 10.00
33 A25 5c vio ('83) 7.00 6.00
a. 5c blue violet ('83) 7.00 6.00
34 A26 10c vio, laid paper ('82) 125.00 50.00
35 A26 10c scar ('83) 1.75 1.75
a. Tete beche pair 40.00 40.00
36 A27 20c brn ('83) 3.00 3.00
a. Laid paper ('82) 4.00 4.00

A28

A29

Liberty — A30

Coat of Arms — A31

1883-85

37 A28 5c brown 3.50 2.75
a. Laid paper 150.00 67.50
38 A28 5c grn ('85) 100.00 35.00
a. Laid paper ('85) 110.00 60.00
39 A28 5c yel, laid paper ('85) 4.00 3.50
40 A29 10c bl grn, laid paper 4.00 4.00
41 A29 10c bl, *bl* ('85) 4.00 3.50
42 A29 10c lil, laid paper ('85) 7.50 5.75
a. Wove paper ('85) 82.50 35.00
43 A30 20c bl, laid paper ('85) 3.50 3.50

1886

Wove Paper

55 A31 1c grn, *pink* 45 45
56 A31 2½c blk, *orange* 45 45
57 A31 5c ultra, *buff* 1.40 1.40
a. 5c blue, *buff* 2.50 2.50
58 A31 10c rose, *buff* 1.25 1.25
a. Transfer of 50c in stone of 10c 60.00 60.00
59 A31 20c dk vio, *buff* 1.25 1.25
61 A31 50c yel brn, *buff* 2.25 2.25
62 A31 1p yel, *grn* 3.50 3.50
63 A31 2p green, *vio* 3.50 3.50
Nos. 55-63 (8) 14.05 14.05

1887-88

64 A31 1c red, *vio* 35 35
65 A31 2½c lil, *pale lil* 35 52
66 A31 5c car, *buff* 50 50
67 A31 5c red, *grn* 2.50 1.50
68 A31 10c brn, *grn* 52 75
Nos. 64-68 (5) 4.22 3.62

Medellin Issue

A32

A33

A34

A35

1888 **Typeset**

69 A32 2½c blk, *yellow* 11.00 11.00
70 A33 5c blk, *yellow* 6.00 6.00
71 A34 5c red, *yellow* 3.50 3.50
Nos. 69-71 (3) 20.50 20.50

Two varieties of No. 69, six of No. 70 and ten of No. 71.

1889

72 A35 2½c red 5.50 5.50

Ten varieties including "eentavos."

Regular Issue

Coat of Arms
A36 A37

A38

A39

A40

A41

1889		**Litho.**	***Perf. 13½***	
73	A36	1c blk, *rose*	24	24
74	A36	2½c blk, *blue*	24	24
75	A36	5c blk, *yellow*	30	30
76	A36	10c blk, *green*	30	30
		Nos. 73-76 (4)	1.08	1.08

1890				
78	A37	20c blue	1.25	1.25
79	A38	50c vio brn	2.50	2.50
a.		Transfer of 20c in stone of 50c	82.50	82.50
80	A38	50c green	2.00	2.00
81	A39	1p red	1.75	1.75
82	A40	2p blk, *mag*	12.00	12.00
83	A41	5p blk, *org red*	20.00	20.00
		Nos. 78-83 (6)	39.50	39.50

Nos. 73-76, 82-83 exist imperf.

The so-called "errors" of Nos. 73 to 76, printed on paper of wrong colors, are essays or, possibly, reprints. They exist perforated and imperforate.

See No. 96.

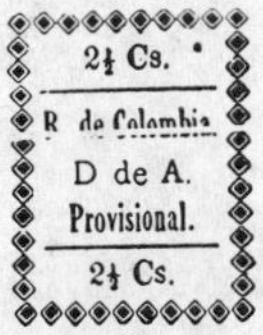

A42

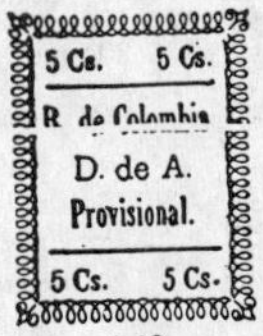

A43

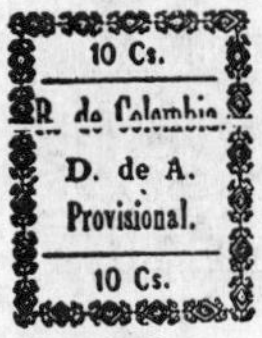

A44

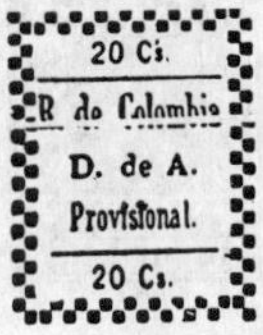

A45

1890		**Typeset**	***Perf. 14***	
84	A42	2½c blk, *buff*	1.75	1.75
85	A43	5c blk, *orange*	1.75	1.75
86	A44	10c blk, *buff*	6.00	6.00
87	A44	10c blk, *rose*	7.50	7.50
88	A45	20c blk, *orange*	7.50	7.50
		Nos. 84-88 (5)	24.50	24.50

20 varieties of the 5c, 10 each of the other values.

A46

A47

1892		**Litho.**	***Perf. 13½***	
89	A46	1c brn, *brnsh*	35	35
90	A46	2½c pur, *lil*	35	35
92	A46	5c blk, *gray*	1.00	50
a.		Transfer of 2½c in stone of 5c	150.00	
		Nos. 89-92 (3)	1.70	1.20

1893				
93	A46	1c blue	24	24
94	A46	2½c green	35	35
95	A46	5c vermilion	24	24
96	A36	10c pale brn	24	24
		Nos. 93-96 (4)	1.07	1.07

1896			***Perf. 14***	
97	A47	2c gray	24	24
98	A47	2c lil rose	24	24
99	A47	2½c brown	24	24
100	A47	2½c steel blue	24	24
101	A47	3c orange	24	24
102	A47	3c olive grn	24	24
103	A47	5c green	24	24
104	A47	5c yel buff	24	24
105	A47	10c brn vio	48	48
106	A47	10c violet	48	48
107	A47	20c brn org	1.00	1.00
108	A47	20c blue	1.00	1.00
109	A47	50c gray brn	1.00	1.00
110	A47	50c rose	85	85
111	A47	1p bl & blk	15.00	15.50
112	A47	1p rose red & blk	15.00	15.00
113	A47	2p org & blk	47.50	47.50
114	A47	2p dk grn & blk	47.50	47.50
115	A47	5p red vio & blk	80.00	80.00
116	A47	5p pur & blk	80.00	80.00
		Nos. 97-116 (20)	291.73	292.23

#115-116 with centers omitted are proofs.

General José María Córdoba — A48

1899			***Perf. 11***	
117	A48	½c grnsh bl	15	15
118	A48	1c slate blue	15	15
119	A48	2c slate brown	15	15
120	A48	3c red	15	15
121	A48	4c bister brown	15	15
122	A48	5c green	15	15
123	A48	10c scarlet	15	15
124	A48	20c gray violet	15	15
125	A48	50c olive bister	15	15
126	A48	1p greenish blk	15	15
127	A48	2p olive gray	15	15
		Set value	66	1.10

Numerous part-perf. and imperf. varieties of Nos. 117-127 exist.

A49

A50

A50a

1901		**Typeset**	***Perf. 12***	
128	A49	1c red	24	24
129	A50	1c ultra	60	60
130	A50	1c bister	60	60
130A	A50a	1c dull red	60	60
130B	A50a	1c ultra	4.00	4.00
		Nos. 128-130B (5)	6.04	6.04

Eight varieties of No. 128, four varieties of Nos. 129-130B.

A51

A52

Atanasio Girardot
A53

Dr. José Félix Restrepo
A54

1902		**Litho.**	**Wove Paper**	
131	A51	1c brt rose	18	15
a.		Laid paper	60	60
b.		Imperf., pair	2.50	
132	A51	2c blue	15	15
a.		Transfer of 3c in stone of 2c	5.00	5.00
133	A51	3c green	15	15
a.		Imperf., pair	4.00	
134	A51	4c dull vio	15	15
135	A52	5c rose red	18	18
136	A53	10c rose lilac	15	15
a.		Small head	5.00	5.00
b.		10c rose	15	15
137	A53	20c gray grn	18	18
138	A53	30c brt rose	18	18
139	A53	40c blue	18	18
140	A53	50c brn, *yel*	18	18
		Laid Paper		
141	A54	1p pur & blk	70	70
142	A54	2p rose & blk	70	70
143	A54	5p sl bl & blk	1.25	1.25
		Nos. 131-143 (13)	4.33	4.30

1903		**Wove Paper**		
143A	A51	1c blue	15	15
144	A51	2c violet	15	15
a.		Imperf.	2.50	

A55 A56 A57

Designs: 1p, Francisco Antonio Zea. 2p, Custodio Garcia Rovira. 3p, La Pola (Policarpa Salavarrieta). 4p, J. M. Restrepo. 5p, José Fernández Madrid. 10p, Juan del Corral.

1903-04				
145	A55	4c yellow brn	20	20
146	A55	5c blue	20	20
147	A56	10c yellow	20	20
148	A56	20c purple	20	20
149	A56	30c brown	60	60
150	A56	40c green	60	60
151	A56	50c rose	20	20
152	A57	1p olive gray	60	60
153	A57	2p purple	60	60
154	A57	3p dk blue	60	60
155	A57	4p dull red	1.00	1.00
156	A57	5p red brown	3.00	1.50
157	A57	10p scarlet	6.50	3.50
		Nos. 145-157 (13)	14.50	10.00

Nos. 145-146, 151, 153-157 exist imperf. Value of pairs, $3 to $4.

Manizales Issue

Stamps of these designs are local private post issues.

OFFICIAL STAMPS Stamps of 1903-04 with overprint "OFICIAL" were never issued.

REGISTRATION STAMPS

R1

1896		**Unwmk.**	**Litho.**	***Perf. 14***	
F1	R1	2½c rose		1.10	1.10
F2	R1	2½c dull blue		1.10	1.10

Córdoba
R2

R3

R4

1899			***Perf. 11***	
F3	R2	2½c dull blue	24	24
F4	R3	10c red lilac	24	24

1902			***Perf. 12***	
F5	R4	10c purple, *blue*	30	30
a.		Imperf.		

ACKNOWLEDGMENT OF RECEIPT STAMPS

AR1

1902-03		**Unwmk.**	**Litho.**	***Perf. 12***	
H1	AR1	5c black, *rose*		90	90
H2	AR1	5c slate ('03)		30	30

LATE FEE STAMPS

Córdoba — LF1

1899		**Unwmk.**	**Litho.**	***Perf. 11***	
I1	LF1	2½c dark green		24	24
a.		Imperf., pair		2.75	

LF2

LF3

1901		**Typeset**	***Perf. 12***	
I2	LF2	2½c red violet	52	52
a.		2½c purple	52	52

1902			**Litho.**	
I3	LF3	2½c violet	18	18

City of Medellin

Stamps of the designs shown were not issued by any governmental agency but by the Sociedad de Mejoras Publicas.

BOLIVAR

Originally a State, now a Department of the Republic of Colombia. (See Antioquia.)

A1

1863-66 Unwmk. Litho. *Imperf.*

1	A1	10c green	*850.00*	*500.00*
a.		Five stars below shield	*1,850.*	*2,000.*
2	A1	10c red ('66)	24.00	24.00
a.		Diagonal half used as 5c on cover		50.00
b.		Five stars below shield	60.00	60.00
3	A1	1p red	5.00	6.50

Fourteen varieties of each. Counterfeits of Nos. 1 and 1a exist.

Coat of Arms
A2 A3

A4

A5

1873

4	A2	5c blue	5.50	5.50
5	A3	10c violet	5.50	5.50
6	A4	20c yel grn	22.50	22.50
7	A5	80c vermilion	47.50	47.50
		Nos. 4-7 (4)	81.00	81.00

A6

A7

A8

Bolívar — A9

1874-78

8	A6	5c blue	20.00	10.00
9	A7	5c blue ('78)	6.25	6.25
10	A8	10c vio ('77)	3.00	3.00
		Nos. 8-10 (3)	29.25	19.25

Dated "1879"

1879 White Wove Paper *Perf. 12½*

11	A9	5c blue	24	24
a.		Imperf., pair	80	
12	A9	10c violet	18	18
13	A9	20c red	24	24
a.		20c green (error)	10.00	10.00

Bluish Laid Paper

15	A9	5c blue	24	24
a.		Imperf., pair	2.00	
16	A9	10c violet	1.65	1.65
a.		Imperf., pair	4.00	
17	A9	20c red	32	32
a.		Imperf., pair	1.75	
		Nos. 11-17 (6)	2.87	2.87

Stamps of 80c and 1p on white wove paper and 1p on bluish laid paper were prepared but not placed in use.

Dated "1880"

1880 White Wove Paper *Perf. 12½*

19	A9	5c blue	24	24
a.		Imperf., pair	1.65	
20	A9	10c violet	32	32
a.		Imperf., pair	1.65	
21	A9	20c red	32	32
a.		20c green (error)	13.00	13.00
23	A9	80c green	2.25	2.25
24	A9	1p orange	2.50	2.50
a.		Imperf., pair	5.50	
		Nos. 19-24 (5)	5.63	5.63

Bluish Laid Paper

25	A9	5c blue	24	24
a.		Imperf., pair	1.25	
26	A9	10c violet	2.25	2.25
27	A9	20c red	32	32
a.		Imperf., pair	2.75	
28	A9	1p orange	400.00	
a.		Imperf.	*450.00*	

A11

A12

A13

A15

A16

Dated "1882"
White Wove Paper

1882 *Perf. 12, 16x12*

29	A11	5c blue	32	32
30	A12	10c lilac	24	24
31	A13	20c red	32	32
33	A15	80c green	65	65
34	A16	1p orange	65	65
		Nos. 29-34 (5)	2.18	2.18

Nos. 29, 30 and 34 are known imperforate. They are printer's waste and were not issued through post offices.

A17

A18

1882 Engr. *Perf. 12*

35	A17	5p bl & rose red	60	60
a.		Imperf., pair	4.75	
b.		Perf. 16	7.50	6.25
c.		Perf. 14	6.25	6.25
36	A17	10p brn & bl	1.65	1.65
a.		Imperf., pair	8.00	
b.		Perf. 16	7.00	5.50
c.		Rouletted	8.00	8.00

Dated "1883"

1883 Litho. *Perf. 12, 16x12*

37	A11	5c blue	18	18
a.		Imperf., pair	80	
b.		Perf. 12	3.00	1.00
38	A12	10c lilac	24	24
39	A13	20c red	24	24
41	A15	80c green	32	32
42	A16	1p orange	60	60
a.		Perf. 16x12	2.00	2.00
		Nos. 37-42 (5)	1.58	1.58

Dated "1884"

1884

43	A11	5c blue	32	32
a.		Perf. 12	10.00	9.25
44	A12	10c lilac	18	18
45	A13	20c red	18	18
a.		Perf. 12	4.25	4.25
47	A15	80c green	24	24
a.		Perf. 12	2.00	2.00
48	A16	1p orange	32	32
		Nos. 43-48 (5)	1.24	1.24

Dated "1885"

1885

49	A11	5c blue	15	15
50	A12	10c lilac	15	15
51	A13	20c red	15	15
53	A15	80c green	24	24
54	A16	1p orange	32	32
		Nos. 49-54 (5)	1.01	1.01

The note after No. 34 will also apply to imperforate stamps of the 1884-85 issues.

1891 *Perf. 14*

55	A18	1c black	32	32
56	A18	5c orange	32	32
a.		Imperf., pair	80	
57	A18	10c carmine	32	32
58	A18	20c blue	60	60
59	A18	50c green	90	90
60	A18	1p purple	90	90
		Nos. 55-60 (6)	3.36	3.36

For overprint see Colombia No. 169.

Bolívar
A19

José Fernández Madrid
A20

Manuel
Rodriguez
Torices
A21

José María
García de
Toledo
A22

1903 Laid Paper *Imperf.*

62	A19	50c dk bl, *pink*	60	60
a.		Bluish paper	60	60
63	A19	50c sl grn, *pink*	60	60
a.		Rose paper	2.00	2.00
b.		Greenish blue paper	3.00	3.00
c.		Yellow paper	4.00	4.00
d.		Brown paper	4.00	4.00
e.		Salmon paper	7.50	7.50
64	A19	50c pur, *pink*	2.00	2.00
a.		White paper	4.00	4.00
b.		Brown paper	4.00	4.00
c.		Greenish blue paper	4.00	4.00
d.		Lilac paper	4.00	4.00
e.		Rose paper	3.50	3.50
f.		Yellow paper	4.00	4.00
g.		Salmon paper	6.00	6.00
h.		As "a," wove paper	9.00	9.00
65	A20	1p org, *sal*	60	60
a.		Yellow paper	4.50	4.50
b.		Greenish blue paper	15.00	15.00
66	A20	1p gray grn, *lil*	1.40	1.40
a.		Yellow paper	6.50	6.50
b.		Salmon paper	7.50	7.50
c.		Green paper	7.50	7.50
d.		White wove paper	10.00	
67	A21	5p car rose, *lil*	60	60
a.		Brown paper	1.10	1.10
b.		Yellow paper	1.10	1.10
c.		Greenish blue paper	4.50	4.50
d.		Bluish paper	6.00	6.00
e.		Salmon paper	7.50	7.50
f.		Rose paper	9.00	9.00
68	A22	10p dk bl, *bluish*	1.25	1.25
a.		Greenish blue paper	1.25	1.25
b.		Rose paper	7.50	7.50
c.		Salmon paper	7.50	7.50
d.		Yellow paper	7.50	7.50
e.		Brown paper	8.50	8.50
f.		Lilac paper	10.00	10.00
g.		White paper	9.00	9.00
69	A22	10p pur, *grnsh bl*	3.50	3.50
a.		Bluish paper	7.50	7.50
b.		Rose paper	6.75	6.75
c.		Yellow paper	7.50	7.50
d.		Brown paper	7.50	7.50
		Nos. 62-69 (8)	10.55	10.55

Sewing Machine Perf.

Laid Paper

70	A19	50c dk bl, *pink*	1.00	1.00
a.		Bluish paper	1.00	1.00
71	A19	50c sl grn, *pink*	2.00	2.00
72	A19	50c pur, *grnsh bl*	4.00	4.00
a.		White paper	4.00	4.00
b.		White wove paper	7.50	
73	A20	1p org, *sal*	2.00	2.00
74	A20	1p gray grn, *lil*	9.00	9.00
a.		Yellow paper	9.00	9.00
75	A21	5p car rose, *yel*	1.65	1.65
a.		Lilac paper	4.00	4.00
b.		Brown paper	4.00	4.00
c.		Bluish paper	5.50	5.50
d.		White wove paper	9.00	
76	A22	10p dk bl, *grnsh bl*	4.50	4.50
a.		Bluish paper	7.00	7.00
b.		Yellow paper	9.00	9.00
c.		As "b," wove paper	10.00	
77	A22	10p pur, *grnsh bl*	7.00	7.00
a.		Bluish paper	11.00	11.00
b.		Rose paper	8.00	8.00
c.		Yellow paper	11.00	11.00
		Nos. 70-77 (8)	31.15	31.15

José María del
Castillo y
Rada — A23

Manuel
Anguiano — A24

Pantaleón C.
Ribón — A25

1904 *Sewing Machine Perf.*

89	A23	5c black	24	24
90	A24	10c brown	24	24
91	A25	20c red	30	30
92	A25	20c red brown	60	60
		Nos. 89-92 (4)	1.38	1.38

Imperf., pairs

89a	A23	5c black	3.50	3.50
90a	A24	10c brown	2.75	2.75
91a	A25	20c red	6.50	6.50
92a	A25	20c red brown	6.50	6.50

A26

A27

A28

1904 *Imperf.*

93	A26	½c black	60	60
a.		Tête bêche pair	3.50	3.50
94	A27	1c blue	1.10	1.10
95	A28	2c purple	1.25	1.25
		Nos. 93-95 (3)	2.95	2.95

REGISTRATION STAMPS

Simón Bolívar
R1 R2

White Wove Paper
Perf. 12½, 16x12

1879 Unwmk. Litho.
F1 R1 40c brown 70 70

Bluish Laid Paper
F2 R1 40c brown 70 70
a. Imperf., pair 3.25

Dated "1880"

1880

White Wove Paper
F3 R1 40c brown 32 32

Bluish Laid Paper
F4 R1 40c brown 65 65
a. Imperf., pair 3.50

Dated "1882" to "1885"
White Wove Paper

1882-85 ***Perf. 16x12***
F5 R2 40c brown (1882) 32 32
F6 R2 40c brown (1883) 24 24
F7 R2 40c brown (1884) 24 24
F8 R2 40c brown (1885) 32 32
Nos. F5-F8 (4) 1.12 1.12

Perf. 12
F5a R2 40c 18.00
F6a R2 40c 9.25
F7a R2 40c 9.50
F8a R2 40c 2.50
Nos. F5a-F8a (4) 39.25

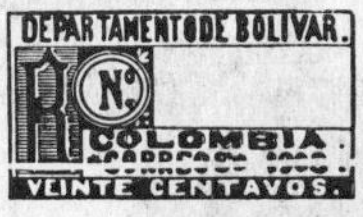

R3

Laid Paper

1903 ***Imperf.***
F9 R3 20c orange, *rose* 60 60
a. Salmon paper 1.10 1.10
b. Greenish blue paper 6.00 6.00

Sewing Machine Perf.
F10 R3 20c orange, *rose* 2.50 2.50
a. Salmon paper 2.50 2.50
b. Greenish blue paper 6.00 6.00

R4

1904

Wove Paper
F11 R4 5c black 3.25 3.25

ACKNOWLEDGMENT OF RECEIPT STAMPS

AR1 AR2

1903 Unwmk. Litho. ***Imperf.***

Laid Paper
H1 AR1 20c org, *rose* 2.50 2.50
a. Yellow paper 1.25 1.25
b. Greenish blue paper 5.00 5.00
H2 AR1 20c dk bl, *yel* 2.00 2.00
a. Brown paper 3.50 3.50
b. Rose paper 2.50 2.50
c. Salmon paper 7.00 7.00
d. Greenish blue paper 7.00 7.00

Sewing Machine Perf.
H3 AR1 20c org, *grnsh bl* 6.25 6.25
a. Yellow paper 7.25 7.25
H4 AR1 20c dk bl, *yel* 7.25 7.25
a. Lilac paper 7.25 7.25
Nos. H1-H4 (4) 18.00 18.00

1904

Wove Paper
H5 AR2 2c red 1.10 1.10

LATE FEE STAMPS

LF1

1903 Unwmk. Litho. ***Imperf.***

Laid Paper
I1 LF1 20c car rose, *bluish* 60 60
I2 LF1 20c pur, *bluish* 55 55
a. Rose paper 2.00 2.00
b. Brown paper 2.00 2.00
c. Lilac paper 2.00 2.00
d. Yellow paper 6.25 6.25

Sewing Machine Perf.
I3 LF1 20c car rose, *bluish* 3.50 3.50
I4 LF1 20c pur, *bluish* 3.50 3.50
a. Rose paper 6.00 6.00
b. Lilac paper 6.00 6.00
c. Yellow paper 10.00 10.00
Nos. I1-I4 (4) 8.15 8.15

BOYACA

Originally a State, now a Department of the Republic of Colombia. (See Antioquia.)

Diego Mendoza Pérez — A1

1902 Unwmk. Litho. ***Perf. 13½***

Wove Paper
1 A1 5c blue green 70 70
a. Bluish paper 90.00 90.00
b. Imperf., pair 12.50

Laid Paper
Perf. 12
2 A1 5c green 100.00 100.00

Coat of Arms
A2 A3

Gen. Próspero Pinzón — A4

A5

Monument of Battle of Boyacá — A6

President José Manuel Marroquin — A7

1903 Litho. ***Imperf.***
4 A2 10c dark gray 24 24
5 A3 20c red brown 32 32
6 A5 1p red 3.00 3.00
a. 1p claret 3.50 3.50
8 A6 5p black, *rose* 1.10 1.10
a. 5p black, *buff* 11.00 11.00
9 A7 10p black, *buff* 1.10 1.10
a. 10p black, *rose* 11.00 11.00
b. Tête bêche pair 15.00
Nos. 4-9 (5) 5.76 5.76

Perf. 12
10 A2 10c dark gray 30 30
11 A3 20c red brown 35 35
12 A4 50c green 32 32
13 A4 50c dull blue 2.00 2.00
14 A5 1p red 32 32
a. 1p claret 3.00 3.00
16 A6 5p black, *rose* 11.00 11.00
a. 5p black, *buff* 9.50 9.50
17 A7 10p black, *buff* 1.10 1.10
a. 10p black, *rose* 11.00 11.00
b. Tête bêche pair 12.00 12.00
Nos. 10-17 (7) 15.39 15.39

Statue of Bolívar — A8

1904
18 A8 10c orange 24 24
a. Imperf., pair 3.50 3.50

CAUCA

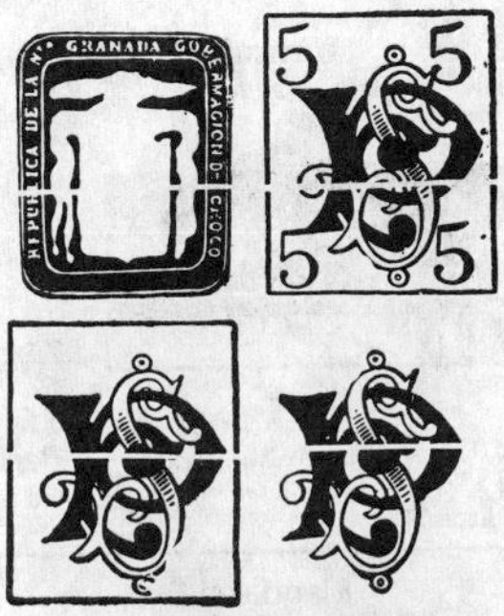

Stamps of these designs were issued by a provincial post between 1879 (?) and 1890.

Stamps of this design are believed to be of private origin and without official sanction.

Items inscribed "No hay estampillas" (No stamps available) and others inscribed "Manuel E. Jiménez" are considered by specialists to be receipt labels, not postage stamps.

CUNDINAMARCA

Originally a State, now a Department of the Republic of Colombia.

Coat of Arms
A1 A2

1870 Unwmk. Litho. ***Imperf.***
1 A1 5c blue 3.75 3.75
2 A2 10c red 12.00 12.00

The counterfeits, or reprints, show traces of the cuts made to deface the dies.

A3 A4

A5 A6

1877-82
3 A3 10c red ('82) 2.50 2.50
a. Laid paper ('77) 3.50 3.50
4 A4 20c green ('82) 5.50 5.50
a. Laid paper ('77) 9.00 9.00
7 A5 50c purple ('82) 6.25 6.25
8 A6 1p brown ('82) 8.75 8.75
Nos. 3-8 (4) 23.00 23.00

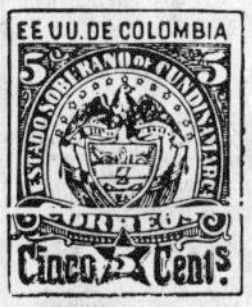

A7

1884
10 A7 5c blue 60 60
11 A7 5c blue (redrawn) 60 60
a. Tête bêche pair 60.00 60.00

The redrawn stamp has no period after "COLOMBIA."

A8

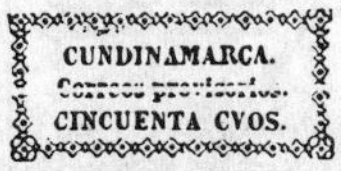

A9

A10

Foreign postal stationery (stamped envelopes, postal cards and air letter sheets) is beyond the scope of this catalogue.

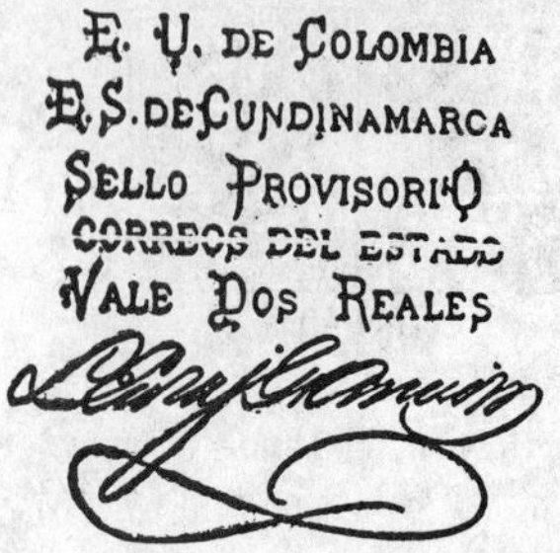

A11

1883 — **Typeset**

13	A8	10c blk, *yellow*	10.00	10.00
14	A9	50c blk, *rose*	10.00	10.00
15	A10	1p blk, *brown*	27.50	27.50
16	A11	2r blk, *green*	*1,600.*	

Typeset varieties exist: 4 of the 10c, 2 each of 50c and 1p.

Some experts doubt that No. 16 was issued. The variety without signature and watermarked "flowers" is believed to be a proof. Forgeries exist.

A12

1886 — **Litho.**

17	A12	5c blue	60	60
18	A12	10c red	3.50	3.50
19	A12	10c red, *lilac*	1.90	1.90
20	A12	20c green	3.00	3.00
a.		20c yellow green	3.50	3.50
21	A12	50c purple	4.00	4.00
22	A12	1p orange brown	4.25	4.25
		Nos. 17-22 (6)	17.25	17.25

Nos. 17 to 22 have been reprinted. The colors are aniline and differ from those of the original stamps. The impression is coarse and blurred.

A13

A14

A15

A16

A17

A18

A19

A20

A21

1904 — ***Perf. 10½, 12***

23	A13	1c orange	24	24
24	A14	2c gray blue	24	24
25	A15	3c rose	35	35
26	A15	5c olive grn	35	35
27	A16	10c pale brn	35	35
28	A17	15c pink	35	35
29	A18	20c blue, *grn*	35	35
30	A18	20c blue	60	60
31	A19	40c blue	60	60
32	A19	40c blue, *buff*	17.50	17.50
33	A20	50c red vio	60	60
34	A21	1p gray grn	48	48
		Nos. 23-34 (12)	22.01	22.01

Imperf

23a	A13	1c orange	70	70
24a	A14	2c blue	70	70
b.		2c slate	6.00	6.00
25a	A15	3c rose	80	80
26a	A15	5c olive green	1.50	1.50
27a	A16	10c pale brown	2.00	2.00
28a	A17	15c pink	50	50
29a	A18	20c blue, *green*	2.00	2.00
30a	A18	20c blue	2.00	2.00
31a	A19	40c blue	60	60
32a	A19	40c blue, *buff*	17.50	17.50
33a	A20	50c red violet	60	60
34a	A21	1p gray green	60	60
		Nos. 23a-34a (12)	29.50	29.50

REGISTRATION STAMPS

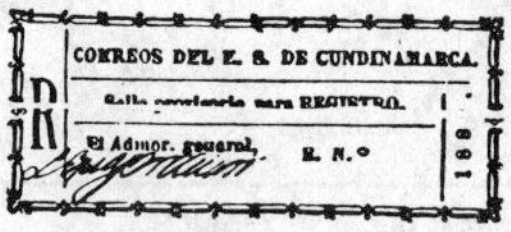

R1

1883 — **Unwmk.** — ***Imperf.***

F1	R1	black, *orange*	12.00	13.00

R2

1904 — ***Perf. 12***

F2	R2	10c bister	80	80
a.		Imperf.	3.50	3.50

Magdalena

Items inscribed "No hay estampillas" (No stamps available) are considered by specialists to be not postage stamps but receipt labels.

Panama

Issues of Panama as a state and later Department of Colombia are listed with the Republic of Panama issues (Nos. 1-30).

SANTANDER

Originally a State, now a Department of the Republic of Colombia.

Coat of Arms

A1 A2

1884 — **Unwmk.** — **Litho.** — ***Imperf.***

1	A1	1c blue	24	24
a.		1c gray blue	40	40
2	A2	5c red	40	40
3	A2	10c bluish purple	1.40	1.40
a.		Tête bêche pair		
		Nos. 1-3 (3)	2.04	2.04

No. 2 exists unofficially perforated 14.

A3

A4

1886 — ***Imperf.***

4	A3	1c blue	70	70
5	A3	5c red	24	24
6	A3	10c red violet	40	40
a.		10c deep violet	40	40
b.		Inscribed "CINCO CENTAVOS"	20.00	20.00
		Nos. 4-6 (3)	1.34	1.34

The numerals in the upper corners are omitted on No. 5, while on No. 6 there are no numerals in the side panels. No. 6 exists unofficially perforated 12.

1887

7	A4	1c blue	18	18
a.		1c ultramarine	1.25	1.25
8	A4	5c red	1.25	1.25
9	A4	10c violet	4.00	4.00
		Nos. 7-9 (3)	5.43	5.43

A5

A6

A7

1889 — ***Perf. 11½ and 13½***

10	A5	1c blue	24	24
11	A6	5c red	1.25	1.25
12	A7	10c purple	40	40
a.		Imperf., pair	16.00	
		Nos. 10-12 (3)	1.89	1.89

A8

A9

1892 — ***Perf. 13½***

13	A8	5c red, *rose buff*	1.00	1.00

1895-96

14	A9	5c brown	70	70
15	A9	5c yel grn ('96)	70	70

A10

A11

A12

1899 — ***Perf. 10***

16	A10	1c black, *green*	32	32
17	A11	5c black, *pink*	32	32

Perf. 13½

18	A12	10c blue	70	70
a.		Perf. 12	1.00	1.00
		Nos. 16-18 (3)	1.34	1.34

A13

1903 — ***Imperf.***

19	A13	50c red	52	52
a.		50c rose	52	52
b.		"SANTENDER"	2.50	2.50
c.		"Corrcos"	2.50	2.50
d.		"Corceos"	2.50	2.50
e.		Tête bêche pair	4.75	4.75
f.		Pair, one without overprint	2.75	2.75

The overprint "Correos de Departmento Bucaramanga" on the 50c red revenue stamp has been proved to be a cancellation.

A14

A15

Arms
A16

Locomotive
A17

A18

A19

A20

1904 — ***Imperf.***

22	A14	5c dark green	24	24
a.		5c yellow green	40	40
24	A15	10c rose	15	15
25	A16	20c brown violet	15	15
26	A17	50c yellow	16	16
27	A18	1p black	16	16
28	A19	5p dark blue	32	32
29	A20	10p carmine	40	40
		Nos. 22-29 (7)	1.58	1.58

1905

30	A14	5c pale blue	40	40
31	A15	10c red brown	40	40
32	A16	20c yellow green	40	40
33	A17	50c red violet	60	60
34	A18	1p dark blue	60	60
35	A19	5p pink	60	60
36	A20	10p red	1.65	1.65
		Nos. 30-36 (7)	4.65	4.65

A21

1907 — ***Imperf.***

37	A21	½c on 50c rose	52	52

City of Cucuta

Stamps of these and similar designs on white and yellow paper, with and without surcharges of ½c, 1c or 2c, are believed to have been produced without government authorization.

TOLIMA

Originally a State, now a Department of the Republic of Colombia.

A1

1870 Unwmk. Typeset *Imperf.*

White Wove Paper

1	A1	5c black	47.50	27.50
2	A1	10c black	47.50	27.50

Printed from two settings. Setting I, ten types of 5c. Setting II, six types of 5c and four types of 10c.

Blue Laid Batonné Paper

3	A1	5c black	*750.00*	

Buff Laid Batonné Paper

4	A1	5c black	110.00	72.50

Blue Wove Paper

5	A1	5c black	60.00	40.00

Blue Vertically Laid Paper

6	A1	5c black	90.00	62.50
a.		Paper with ruled blue vertical lines		

Blue Horizontally Laid Paper

7	A1	5c black	90.00	62.50

Blue Quadrille Paper

8	A1	5c black	90.00	80.00

Ten varieties each of Nos. 3-5 and 7; 20 varieties each of Nos. 6 and 8.

Official imitations were made in 1886 from new settings of the type. There are only 2 varieties of each value. They are printed on blue and white paper, wove, batonné, laid, etc.

A2

A3

A4

A5

Yellowish White Wove Paper

1871 Litho. *Imperf.*

9	A2	5c deep brown	1.75	1.75
a.		5c red brown	1.75	1.75
b.		Value reads "CINGO"	30.00	30.00
10	A3	10c blue	4.75	4.75
11	A4	50c green	6.25	6.25
12	A5	1p carmine	9.50	9.50
		Nos. 9-12 (4)	22.25	22.25

The 5p stamps, type A2, are bogus varieties made from an altered die of the 5c.

The 10c, 50c and 1 peso stamps have been reprinted on bluish white wove paper. They are from new plates and most copies show traces of fine lines with which the dies had been defaced. Reprints of the 5c have a large cross at the top. The 10c on laid batonné paper is known only as a reprint.

A6

A7

A8

A9

1879

Grayish or White Wove Paper

14	A6	5c yellow brown	35	35
a.		5c purple brown	35	35
15	A7	10c blue	40	40
16	A8	50c green, *bluish*	40	40
a.		White paper	1.25	1.25
17	A9	1p vermilion	1.75	1.75
a.		1p carmine rose	7.25	7.25
		Nos. 14-17 (4)	2.90	2.90

A10

Coat of Arms — A12

1883 *Imperf.*

18	A6	5c orange	35	35
19	A7	10c vermilion	70	70
20	A10	20c violet	1.10	1.10
		Nos. 18-20 (3)	2.15	2.15

1884 *Imperf.*

23	A12	1c gray	15	15
24	A12	2c rose lilac	15	15
a.		2c slate	15	15
25	A12	2½c dull orange	15	15
26	A12	5c brown	15	15
27	A12	10c blue	30	30
a.		10c slate	18	18
28	A12	20c lemon	30	30
a.		Laid paper	4.00	4.00
29	A12	25c black	24	24
30	A12	50c green	24	24
31	A12	1p vermilion	32	32
32	A12	2p violet	48	48
a.		Value omitted	22.50	22.50
33	A12	5p yellow	32	32
34	A12	10p lilac rose	90	90
a.		Laid paper	22.50	22.50
b.		10p gray	*125.00*	
		Nos. 23-34 (12)	3.70	3.70

A13

A14

Condor with Long Wings Touching Flagstaffs

A15 A16

1886 Litho. *Perf. 10½, 11*

White Paper

36	A13	5c brown	1.25	1.25
a.		5c yellow brown	1.25	1.25
b.		Imperf., pair	16.00	
37	A14	10c blue	3.50	3.50
a.		Imperf., pair	16.00	
38	A15	50c green	3.00	3.00
a.		Imperf., pair	16.00	
39	A16	1p vermilion	2.50	2.50
a.		Imperf., pair	24.00	
		Nos. 36-39 (4)	10.25	10.25

No. 38 has been reprinted in pale gray green, perforated 10½, and No. 39 in bright vermilion, perforated 11½. The impressions show many signs of wear.

Lilac Tinted Paper

36c	A13	5c orange brown	12.00	12.00
37b	A14	10c blue	12.00	12.00
38b	A15	50c green	9.00	9.00
39b	A16	1p vermilion	8.00	8.00
		Nos. 36c-39b (4)	41.00	41.00

Items similar to A15 and A16 but with condor with long wings and upper flagstaffs omitted are forgeries.

A17

A18

Condor with Short Wings

A19 A20

1886 White Paper *Perf. 12*

44	A19	1c gray	6.25	6.25
45	A17	2c rose lilac	6.50	6.50
46	A18	2½c dull org	19.00	19.00
47	A19	5c brown	8.00	8.00
48	A20	10c blue	8.00	8.00
49	A20	20c lemon	6.50	6.50
a.		Tête bêche pair	225.00	225.00
50	A20	25c black	6.25	6.25
51	A20	50c green	3.50	3.00
52	A20	1p vermilion	5.00	4.25
53	A20	2p violet	7.25	7.25
b.		Tête bêche pair	175.00	175.00
54	A20	5p orange	13.00	13.00
55	A20	10p lilac rose	7.25	7.25
		Nos. 44-55 (12)	96.50	95.25

Imperf., Pairs

44a	A19	1c	16.00
47a	A19	5c	27.50
48a	A20	10c	27.50
52a	A20	1p	20.00
53a	A20	2p	25.00
54a	A20	5p	32.50
55a	A20	10p	16.00

A23

1888 *Perf. 10½*

62	A23	5c red	15	15
63	A23	10c green	30	30
64	A23	50c blue	80	80
65	A23	1p red brown	1.75	1.75
		Nos. 62-65 (4)	3.00	3.00

For overprint see Colombia No. L14.

1895 *Perf. 12, 13½*

66	A23	1c blue, *rose*	24	24
67	A23	2c grn, *lt grn*	24	24
68	A23	5c red	15	15
69	A23	10c green	50	50
70	A23	20c blue, *yellow*	30	30
71	A23	1p brown	2.00	2.00
		Nos. 66-71 (6)	3.43	3.43

Imperf., Pairs

62a	A23	5c	2.75	
63a	A23	10c	3.25	
64a	A23	50c	4.75	4.75
65a	A23	1p	7.25	
66a	A23	1c	7.25	
67a	A23	2c	7.25	
70a	A23	20c	8.00	

"No Hay Estampillas"

Items inscribed "No hay estampillas" (No stamps available) are considered by specialists to be not postage stamps but receipt labels.

"Honda Issue"

This item seems to be of private origin.

Regular Issue

A24

A25

A26

A27

A28

A29

A30

A31

Sewing Machine or Regular Perf. 12

1903-04 Litho.

79	A24	4c black, *green*	24	24
80	A25	10c dull blue	24	24
81	A26	20c orange	48	48
82	A27	50c black, *rose*	25	25
a.		50c black, *buff*	18	18
84	A28	1p brown	18	18
85	A29	2p gray	18	18
86	A30	5p red	18	18
a.		Tête bêche pair	5.00	5.00
87	A31	10p black, *blue*	25	25
a.		10p black, *light green*	25	25
b.		10p black, *grn, glazed*	3.50	3.50
		Nos. 79-87 (8)	2.00	2.00

Imperf

79a	A24	4c black, *green*	24	24
80a	A25	10c dull blue	18	18
81a	A26	20c orange	1.10	1.10
82b	A27	50c black, *rose*	1.50	1.50
c.		50c black, *buff*	1.50	1.50
84a	A28	1p brown	18	18
85a	A29	2p gray	25	25
86b	A30	5p red	25	25
c.		Tête bêche pair	5.00	5.00
87c	A31	10p black, *blue*	2.25	2.25
d.		Tête bêche pair		
e.		10p black, *light green*	3.50	3.50
f.		10p black, *green, glazed*	18.00	18.00
		Nos. 79a-87c (8)	5.95	5.95

COMORO ISLANDS

LOCATION — In Mozambique Channel between Madagascar and Mozambique

GOVT. — Republic

AREA — 838 sq. mi.

POP. — 385,000 (est. 1983)

CAPITAL — Moroni

The Comoro Archipelago consists of the islands of Mayotte, Anjouan, Grand Comoro (Grande Comore) and Moheli, which issued their own stamps as French protectorates or colonies from 1887-1914. The archipelago was attached to Madagascar from 1914 to 1946, when it became a separate French territory. In July 1975, Anjouan, Grand

Comoro and Moheli united to declare independence as the State of Comoro. Mayotte remained French.

100 Centimes = 1 Franc

Catalogue values for all unused stamps in this country are for Never Hinged items.

Anjouan Bay — A2

Comoro Woman Grinding Grain — A3

Moroni Mosque on Grand Comoro — A4

1950 Unwmk. Engr. *Perf. 13*
30 A2 10c blue 15 15
31 A2 50c green 15 15
32 A2 1fr dk ol brn 15 15
33 A3 2fr brt grn 20 20
34 A3 5fr purple 20 20
35 A3 6fr vio brn 28 28
36 A4 7fr red 28 28
37 A4 10fr dk grn 35 35
38 A4 11fr dp ultra 42 42
Nos. 30-38 (9) 2.18 2.18

Imperforates
Most Comoro Islands stamps exist imperforate in issued and trial colors, and also in small presentation sheets in issued colors.

Military Medal Issue.
Common Design Type
1952 Engraved and Typographed
39 CD101 15fr multi 21.00 21.00

Mosque of Ouani, Anjouan — A5

Coelacanth A6

1952-54 Engr.
40 A5 15fr dark brown 45 45
41 A5 20fr red brown 60 60
42 A6 40fr aqua & indigo ('54) 8.00 6.25
Nos. 40-42 (3) 9.05 7.30

FIDES Issue
Common Design Type
1956 Unwmk. *Perf. 13x12½*
43 CD103 9fr dp vio 50 40

Human Rights Issue
Common Design Type
1958 Engr. *Perf. 13*
44 CD105 20fr ol grn & dk bl 3.00 3.00

Flower Issue
Common Design Type
1959 Photo. *Perf. 12½x12*
45 CD104 10fr Colvillea 1.50 1.00

View of Dzaoudzi and Radio Symbol — A8

Comoro radio station: 25fr, Radio tower and radio waves over Islands.

1960, Dec. 23 Engr. *Perf. 13*
46 A8 20fr maroon, vio bl & grn 45 40
47 A8 25fr ultra, brn & grn 60 60

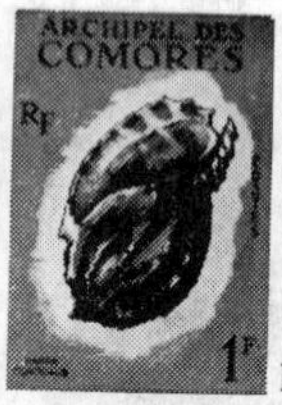

Harpa Conoidalis — A9

Sea Shells: 50c, Cypraecassis rufa. 2fr, Murex ramosus. 5fr, Turbo marmoratus. 20fr, Pterocera scorpio. 25fr, Charonia tritonis.

1962, Jan. 13 Photo.
Shells in Natural Colors
48 A9 50c lilac & brn 20 20
49 A9 1fr yel & red 20 20
50 A9 2fr pale grn & pink 25 25
51 A9 5fr yel & grn 55 55
52 A9 20fr salmon & brn 1.25 1.25
53 A9 25fr bister & pink 1.60 1.60
Nos. 48-53,C5-C6 (8) 14.05 13.55

Wheat Emblem and Globe — A10

1963, Mar. 21 Engr. *Perf. 13*
54 A10 20fr choc & dk grn 1.50 1.40

FAO "Freedom from Hunger" campaign.

Red Cross Centenary Issue
Common Design Type
1963, Sept. 2 Unwmk. *Perf. 13*
55 CD113 50fr emer, gray & car 2.50 2.25

Human Rights Issue
Common Design Type
1963, Dec. 10 Engr.
56 CD117 15fr dk red & yel grn 2.25 2.00

Tobacco Pouch — A13

Grand Comoro Canoe — A14

Designs: 4fr, Censer. 10fr, Carved lamp.

1963, Dec. 27 *Perf. 13*
Size: 22x36mm
57 A13 3fr multi 15 15
58 A13 4fr org, dp cl & sl grn 16 16
59 A13 10fr org brn, dk red brn & grn 35 35
Nos. 57-59,C8-C9 (5) 3.66 2.51

Common Design Types pictured in section at front of book.

Philatec Issue
Common Design Type
1964, Mar. 31
60 CD118 50fr dk bl, red & grn 1.10 1.10

1964, Aug. 7 Photo. *Perf. 13x12½*
Design: 30fr, Boutre felucca.
Size: 22x37mm
61 A14 15fr multi 40 40
62 A14 30fr lt grn & multi 65 65

See Nos. C10-C11.

Spiny Lobster — A15

Designs: 12fr, Hammerhead shark, horiz. 20fr, Turtle, horiz. 25fr, Merou fish.

1965, Dec. 20 Engr. *Perf. 13*
63 A15 1fr grn, lil & ocher 15 15
64 A15 12fr org red, slate & gray 35 25
65 A15 20fr org, red & bl grn 40 35
66 A15 25fr bl grn, dk brn & red 45 40
Nos. 63-66 (4) 1.35 1.15

Hotel Itsandra, Moroni — A16

Design: 15fr, Lake Salé, Grand Comoro.

1966, Dec. 19 Photo. *Perf. 12½x13*
67 A16 15fr multi 25 20
68 A16 25fr multi 35 20

See Nos. C18-C19.

Comoro Sunbird A17

Birds: 10fr, Malachite kingfisher. 15fr, Rothschild's fody. 30fr, Cuckoo-roller.

1967, June 20 Photo. *Perf. 12½x13*
Size: 36x23mm
69 A17 2fr ocher & multi 40 40
70 A17 10fr lil & multi 55 55
71 A17 15fr yel grn & multi 65 65
72 A17 30fr pink & multi 1.10 1.10
Nos. 69-72,C20-C21 (6) 5.00 3.62

For surcharge see No. 133.

WHO Anniversary Issue
Common Design Type
1968, May 4 Engr. *Perf. 13*
73 CD126 40fr grn, vio & dp car 55 45

Surgeonfish A19

Design: 25fr, Imperial angelfish.

1968, Aug. 1 Engr. *Perf. 13*
Size: 36x22mm
74 A19 20fr vio bl, yel & red brn 25 25
75 A19 25fr Prus bl, dk bl & org 35 35

See Nos. C23-C24. For surcharge and overprint see Nos. C52, C74.

Human Rights Year Issue
Common Design Type
1968, Aug. 10 Engr. *Perf. 13*
76 CD127 60fr brn, grn & org 60 60

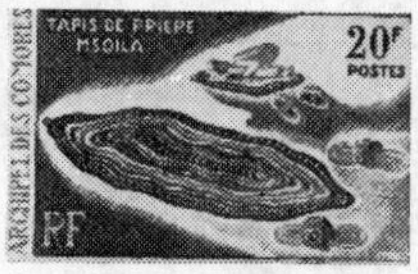

Msoila Prayer Rug and Praying Man — A20

Designs: Each stamp shows a different prayer position.

1969, Feb. 27 Engr. *Perf. 13*
77 A20 20fr bl grn, rose red & pur 20 16
78 A20 30fr pur, rose red & bl grn 25 22
79 A20 45fr rose red, pur & bl grn 40 35
Nos. 77-79 (3) 85 73

Vanilla Flower A21

Design: 15fr, Flower of ylang-ylang tree. 25fr, Poinsettia (country name in upper right corner).

1969-70 Photo. *Perf. 12½x13*
Size: 36x23mm
80 A21 10fr multi 16 15
81 A21 15fr multi 22 18
82 A21 25fr multi ('70) 35 22
Nos. 80-82,C26-C28 (6) 4.13 2.95

Issue dates: #80-81, Mar. 20. #82, Mar. 5.

ILO Issue
Common Design Type
1969, Nov. 24 Engr. *Perf. 13*
83 CD131 5fr org, emer & gray 16 15

UPU Headquarters Issue
Common Design Type
1970, May 20 Engr. *Perf. 13*
84 CD133 65fr pur, bl grn & red brn 80 55

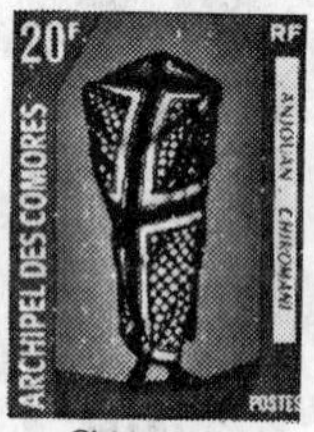

Chiromani Costume, Anjouan — A22

Friday Mosque — A23

Design: 25fr, Bouiboui costume, Grand Comoro.

1970, Oct. 30 Photo. *Perf. 12½x13*
85 A22 20fr grn, yel & red 25 22
86 A22 25fr brn, yel & dk bl 35 25

1970, Dec. 18 Engr. *Perf. 13*
87 A23 5fr rose car, grn & grnsh bl 16 15
88 A23 10fr dp lil, grn & vio 22 16
89 A23 40fr cop red, grn & dp brn 38 30
Nos. 87-89 (3) 76 61

Great White Egret — A24

Pyrostegia Venusta — A25

Birds: 10fr, Comoro pigeon. 15fr, Green-backed heron. 25fr, Comoro blue pigeon. 35fr, Humbolt's flycatcher. 40fr, Allen's gallinule.

1971, Mar. 12 Photo. *Perf. 12½x13*

90	A24	5fr multi	15	15
91	A24	10fr yel & multi	18	15
92	A24	15fr bl & multi	20	15
93	A24	25fr org & multi	30	22
94	A24	35fr yel grn & multi	55	40
95	A24	40fr gray & multi	65	55
		Nos. 90-95 (6)	2.03	1.62

For overprint see No. 145.

1971, July 19 Photo. *Perf. 13*

Flowers: 3fr, Dogbane, horiz. 20fr, Frangipani.

Size: 22x36mm, 36x22mm

96	A25	1fr ver & grn	15	15
97	A25	3fr yel, grn & red	16	15
98	A25	20fr ver & grn	45	30
		Nos. 96-98,C37-C38 (5)	2.11	1.35

For surcharges see Nos. 131-132, C75, C83.

Lithograph Cone — A26

Sea Shells: 10fr, Pacific lettered cone. 20fr, Aulicus cone. 35fr, Polita nerita. 60fr, Snake-head cowrie.

1971, Oct. 4

99	A26	5fr lt ultra & multi	15	15
100	A26	10fr multi	16	15
101	A26	20fr vio & multi	22	20
102	A26	35fr lt bl & multi	40	30
103	A26	60fr lt vio & multi	55	55
		Nos. 99-103 (5)	1.48	1.35

For surcharge see No. 150.

De Gaulle Issue

Common Design Type

Designs: 20fr, Gen. de Gaulle, 1940. 35fr, Pres. de Gaulle, 1970.

1971, Nov. 9 Engr. *Perf. 13*

104	CD134	20fr dk car & blk	35	16
105	CD134	35fr dk car & blk	45	38

Louis Pasteur, Slides, Microscope A27

1972, Aug. 2

106	A27	65fr indigo, org, & ol brn	65	50

Sesquicentennial of the birth of Louis Pasteur (1822-1895), chemist.

Type of Air Post Issue 1971

Designs: 10fr, View of Goulaivoini. 20fr, Bay, Mitsamiouli. 35fr, Gate and fountain, Foumbouni. 50fr, View of Moroni.

1973, June 28 Photo. *Perf. 13*

107	AP10	10fr bl & multi	16	15
108	AP10	20fr grn & multi	25	22
109	AP10	35fr bl & multi	45	42
110	AP10	50fr bl & multi	55	50
		Nos. 107-110,C53 (5)	2.66	2.09

For overprint see No. 143.

Bank of Madagascar and Comoros A28

Buildings in Moroni: 15fr, Post and Telecommunications Administration. 20fr, Prefecture.

1973, July 10 Photo. *Perf. 13x12½*

111	A28	5fr multi	15	15
112	A28	15fr multi	15	15
113	A28	20fr multi	25	22
		Nos. 111-113 (3)	55	52

For surcharge see No. 134.

Salimata Hamissi Mosque A29

Design: 20fr, Zaouiyat Chaduli Mosque, vert.

Perf. 12½x13, 13x12½

1973, Oct. 20 Photo.

114	A29	20fr multi	22	20
115	A29	35fr multi	42	40

For surcharges see Nos. 135, 138.

Cheikh Mausoleum A30

Design: 50fr, Mausoleum of President Said Mohamed Cheikh (different view).

1974, Mar. 16 Engr. *Perf. 13*

116	A30	35fr grn, ol brn & blk	38	30
117	A30	50fr grn, ol brn & blk	50	42

For surcharge see No. 140.

Koran Stand, Anjouan A31

Designs: 15fr, Carved combs, vert. 20fr, 3-legged table, vert. 75fr, Sugar press.

1974, May 10 Photo. *Perf. 12½x13*

118	A31	15fr emer & multi	16	15
119	A31	20fr grn & multi	22	16
120	A31	35fr multi	35	25
121	A31	75fr multi	60	55
		Nos. 118-121 (4)	1.33	1.11

For overprints and surcharge see #137, 141, 149.

UPU Emblem, Symbolic Postmark A32

1974, Oct. 9 Engr. *Perf. 13x12½*

122	A32	30fr multi	25	22

Centenary of Universal Postal Union.
For surcharge see No. 155.

Bracelet A33

1975, Feb. 28 Engr. *Perf. 13*

123	A33	20fr shown	22	20
124	A33	35fr Diadem	38	35
125	A33	120fr Saber	1.10	1.00
126	A33	135fr Dagger	1.20	1.10
		Nos. 123-126 (4)	2.90	2.65

For surcharges see Nos. 136, 142, 151, 154.

Mohani Village, Moheli — A34

Designs: 50fr, Djoezi Village, Moheli. 55fr, Chirazi tombs.

1975, May 26 Photo. *Perf. 13*

127	A34	30fr vio bl & multi	20	15
128	A34	50fr Prus bl & multi	38	25
129	A34	55fr grn & multi	40	42
		Nos. 127-129 (3)	98	82

For overprints and surcharge see #139, 146, 148.

Skin Diver Photographing Coelacanth — A35

1975, June 27 Engr. *Perf. 13*

130	A35	50fr multi	55	40

1975 coelacanth expedition.
For overprint see No. 147.

STATE OF COMORO

In 1978 the islands' name became the Federal and Islamic Republic of the Comoros.

Issues of 1971-75 Surcharged and Overprinted with Bars and: "ETAT COMORIEN" in Black, Silver or Red.

Tambourine Player — A36

Design: No. 153, Women dancers and tambourine players.

Printing & Perforations as Before, Photogravure (A36)

1975 *Perf. 13 (A36)*

131	A25	5fr on 1fr	15	15
132	A25	5fr on 3fr	15	15
133	A17	10fr on 2fr	30	30
134	A28	15fr on 20fr (R)	15	15
135	A29	15fr on 20fr (S)	15	15
136	A33	15fr on 20fr	15	15
137	A31	20fr	18	15
138	A29	25fr on 35fr	22	20
139	A34	30fr	25	22
140	A30	30fr on 35fr	25	22
141	A31	30fr on 35fr	25	22
142	A33	30fr on 35fr	25	22
143	AP10	35fr	30	25
144	SP2	35fr on 35fr + 10fr	30	25
145	A24	40fr	38	30
146	A34	50fr	45	40
147	A35	50fr	45	40
148	A34	50fr on 55fr (S)	45	40
149	A31	75fr	75	60
150	A26	75fr on 60fr (S)	75	60
151	A33	100fr on 120fr	90	80
152	A36	100fr bl & multi	90	80
153	A36	100fr on 150fr (S)	90	80
154	A33	200fr on 135fr	1.75	1.50
155	A32	500fr on 30fr	4.50	4.00
		Nos. 131-155 (25)	15.23	13.38

Nos. 152-153 exist without overprint or surcharge. No. 155 exists with red surcharge.

Litho. & Embossed "Gold Foil" Stamps
These stamps generally are of a different design format than the rest of the issue. Since there is a commemorative inscription tying them to the issue a separate illustration is not being shown.

Apollo-Soyuz — A37

Spacecraft and astronauts: 10fr, Soyuz lift-off, Alexei A. Leonov and Valeri N. Kubasov, vert. 30fr, Apollo lift-off, Thomas P. Stafford, Vance D. Brand, Donald K. Slayton, vert. 50fr, Meeting in space, vert. 100fr, Chairman Brezhnev, President Ford talking with astronauts and cosmonauts. 200fr, Spacecraft preparing to dock. 400f, Return to Earth. 500fr, Spacecraft, mission emblems. 1500fr, Apollo-Soyuz crew. No. 164, Preparing to dock, diff.

1975, Dec. 15 Litho. *Perf. 13½*

156	A37	10fr	multicolored
157	A37	30fr	multicolored
158	A37	50fr	multicolored
159	A37	100fr	multicolored
160	A37	200fr	multicolored
161	A37	400fr	multicolored

Litho. & Embossed

Size: 45x45mm

162	A37	1500fr	gold & multi

Souvenir Sheets

Litho.

163	A37	500fr	multicolored

Litho. & Embossed

164	A37	1500fr	gold & multi

Nos. 159-164 are airmail. No. 163 contains one 64x44mm stamp. No. 164 contains one 45x45mm stamp.
For overprints see Nos. 477-478.

A38

American Revolution, Bicent. — A39

Designs: 15fr, Lewis and Clark, Blackfoot Indian. 25fr, John C. Fremont, Kit Carson, Indian dancer. 35fr, Daniel Boone, Buffalo Bill Cody, wagon train. 40fr, Richard E. Egan, Johnny Frey, Pony Express. 75fr, Henry Wells, William G. Fargo, stagecoach. 400fr, Frontiersman, Indian. 500fr, Leland Stanford, Thomas C. Dunant, transcontinental railroad. 1000fr, George Washington, winter at Valley Forge. 1500fr, John Paul Jones, ship.

1976, Jan. 15 Litho.

165	A38	15fr	multicolored
166	A38	25fr	multicolored
167	A38	35fr	multicolored
168	A38	40fr	multicolored
169	A38	75fr	multicolored
170	A38	500fr	multicolored

Litho. & Embossed

171	A39	1000fr	gold & multi

Souvenir Sheets

Litho.

172 A38 400fr multicolored

Litho. & Embossed

173 A39 1500fr gold & multi

Nos. 170-173 are airmail. See Nos. 230, 232 and note after No. 479.

1976 Winter Olympics, Innsbruck — A40

1976, Mar. 30 **Litho.**

174 A40 5fr Women's figure skating
175 A40 30fr Slalom skiing
176 A40 35fr Speed skating
177 A40 50fr Downhill skiing
178 A40 200fr Ski jumping
179 A40 400fr Cross country skiing

Litho. & Embossed

Size: 56x35mm

180 A40 1000fr Downhill skier, hockey

Souvenir Sheets

Litho.

181 A40 500fr Hockey

Litho. & Embossed

182 A40 1000fr Olympic Rings

Nos. 178-182 are airmail. Nos. 181-182 contain one 58x35mm stamp. For overprint see No. 471.

1976 Summer Olympics, Montreal — A41

1976, Mar. 30 **Litho.**

183 A41 20fr Runner, Athens, 1896
184 A41 25fr Sprints
185 A41 40fr High jump, Paris, 1900
186 A41 75fr High jump
187 A41 100fr Women stretching, St. Louis, 1904
188 A41 500fr Uneven parallel bars

Souvenir Sheet

189 A41 400fr Olympic Stadium, Montreal

Nos. 187-189 are airmail.
For overprint see No. 476.

Fairy Tales — A42

1976, June 28

190 A42 15fr Hansel & Gretel
191 A42 30fr Alice in Wonderland
192 A42 35fr Pinocchio
193 A42 40fr Good Little Henry
194 A42 50fr Peter and the Wolf
195 A42 400fr Thousand and One Nights

No. 195 is airmail. Nos. 190-191, 193, 195 are vert.

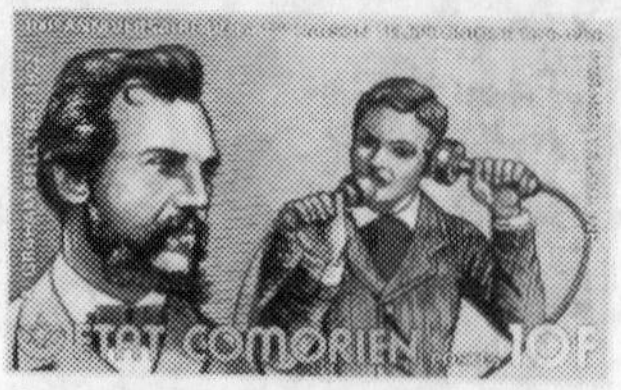

Invention of Telephone, Cent. — A43

Designs: 10fr, A. G. Bell, 1st telephone. 25fr, Charles Bourseul, Paris-London phone service, 1891. 75fr, Philipp Reis, telephone operators. 100fr, Earth to Moon to Earth communications. 200fr, Satellite. 400fr, Ship-to-Satellite communications. No. 201, Satellite in orbit, antenna. No. 203, Global communications.

1976, July 1

196 A43 10fr multicolored
197 A43 25fr multicolored
198 A43 75fr multicolored
199 A43 100fr multicolored
200 A43 200fr multicolored
201 A43 500fr multicolored

Souvenir Sheets

202 A43 400fr multicolored
203 A43 500fr multicolored

Nos. 199-203 are airmail. Nos. 202-203 contain a 73x44mm stamp. For overprint see No. 472.

Comoro Flag, Map and Government Buildings A44

1976, Nov. 18 **Litho.** ***Perf. 13½***

204 A44 30fr multi 16 15
205 A44 50fr multi 25 16

1st anniversary of independence.
For overprints and surcharges see Nos. 353-356 and footnote after No. 356.

Viking Probe to Mars — A45

Designs: 5fr, Nicolaus Copernicus, rocket launch. 10fr, Albert Einstein, Carl Sagan, Thomas Young, horiz. 25fr, Viking probe orbiting Mars. 35fr, Discovery of America by Vikings, horiz. 100fr, Flag, Viking landing on Mars. 500fr, Viking emblem, surface of Mars, horiz. 400fr, Viking probe. No. 212, Wagon train, frontiersman, rocket launch. No. 214, Viking on Martian surface, robotic shovel.

1976, Nov. 23

206 A45 5fr multicolored
207 A45 10fr multicolored
208 A45 25fr multicolored
209 A45 35fr multicolored
210 A45 100fr multicolored
211 A45 500fr multicolored

Litho. & Embossed

Size: 57x39mm

212 A45 1500fr gold & multi

Souvenir Sheets

Litho.

213 A45 400fr multicolored

Litho. & Embossed

214 A45 1500fr gold & multi

American Revolution, bicentennial. Nos. 211-214 are airmail. No. 213 contains one 60x42mm stamp.

UN Postal Administration, 25th Anniv. — A46

Designs: 15fr, UN #24, irrigating field. 30fr, UN #43, doctor, nurse. 50fr, UN #162, mother holding child. 75fr, UN #42, communications satellite in orbit. 200fr, UN #32, Concorde, Zeppelin. 400fr, UN #18, cargo plane. 500fr, People passing letters around globe.

1976, Nov. 25 **Litho.**

215 A46 15fr multicolored
216 A46 30fr multicolored
217 A46 50fr multicolored
218 A46 75fr multicolored
219 A46 200fr multicolored
220 A46 400fr multicolored

Souvenir Sheet

221 A46 500fr multicolored

Nos. 219-221 are airmail. No. 221 contains one 57x40mm stamp. For overprints see Nos. 282-284, 473.

Comoro Flag, UN Headquarters and Emblem A47

1976, Nov. 25

222 A47 40fr multi 20 15
223 A47 50fr multi 25 16

1st anniv. of UN membership.

Type of 1976 and

US Bicentennial — A48

Civil War Battles: 10fr, Fort Sumter, Lincoln. 30fr, Bull Run, Gen. P.G.T. Beauregard, vert. 50fr, Antietam, Gen. Joseph E. Johnston. 100fr, Gettysburg, Gen. Meade. 200fr, Chattanooga, Gen. Sherman, vert. 400fr, Appomattox, Gen. Pickett. 500fr, Surrender at Appomattox, Generals Lee and Grant. 1000fr, Lincoln, battlefield. No. 230, Pres. Kennedy, lunar lander.

1976, Dec. 30 **Litho.**

224 A48 10fr multicolored
225 A48 30fr multicolored
226 A48 50fr multicolored
227 A48 100fr multicolored
228 A48 200fr multicolored
229 A48 400fr multicolored

Litho. & Embossed

Size: 61x51mm

230 A39 1500fr gold & multi

Souvenir Sheets

Litho.

231 A48 500fr multicolored

Litho. & Embossed

232 A39 1000fr gold & multi

American Revolution bicentennial. Nos. 227-232 are airmail. No. 231 contains one 60x42mm stamp.

Endangered Species — A49

1976, Dec. 30 **Litho.**

233 A49 15fr Andean condor, vert.
234 A49 20fr Australian tiger cat
235 A49 35fr Leopard, vert.
236 A49 40fr White rhinoceros
237 A49 75fr Nyala, vert.
238 A49 400fr Orangutan

Souvenir Sheet

239 A49 500fr Lemur, vert.

Nos. 238-239 airmail. No. 239 contains one 40x58mm stamp.
See note after No. 479.

Endangered Species A50

1977, Apr. 14

240 A50 10fr Wolf
241 A50 30fr Aye-aye
242 A50 40fr Cephalopus zebra
243 A50 50fr Giant tortoise
244 A50 200fr Ocelot
245 A50 400fr Penguin

Souvenir Sheet

246 A50 500fr Sumatran tiger

Nos. 244-246 airmail. No. 246 contains one 58x40mm stamp.

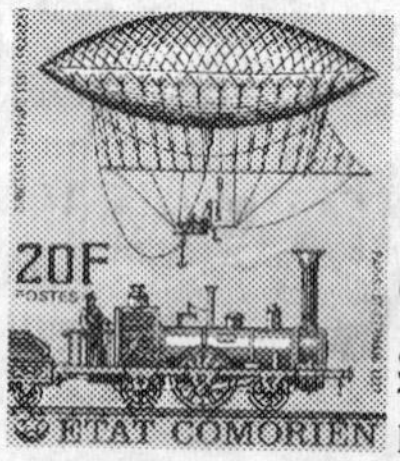

Giffard Airship, 1851 and Paris-St. Germain Train, 1837, France — A51

Airships & Locomotives: 25fr, Santos-Dumont's airship, 1906, Brazilian Tander 120FIN, Brazil. 50fr, Astra, 1914, Trans-Siberian Express, 1905, Russia. 75fr, R.34, 1919, Southern Belle, 1910, Great Britain. 200fr, Navy airship, Pacific Class locomotive, 1930, US. No. 252, Hindenburg, Rheingold Express, 1933, Germany. No. 253, Graf-Zeppelin, 1928, Nord-Express Type 231, 1925, Germany.

1977, Apr. 14

247 A51 20fr multicolored
248 A51 25fr multicolored
249 A51 50fr multicolored
250 A51 75fr multicolored
251 A51 200fr multicolored
252 A51 500fr multicolored

Souvenir Sheet

253 A51 500fr multi, horiz.

Nos. 251-253 are airmail. No. 253 contains one 58x39mm stamp.

Nobel Prize, 75th Anniv. — A52

Nobel Prize winners: 30fr, Medicine. 40fr, Physics. 50fr, Literature. 100fr, Physics. 200fr, Chemistry. 400fr, Peace.

1977, July 7

254 A52 30fr multicolored
255 A52 40fr multicolored
256 A52 50fr multicolored
257 A52 100fr multicolored
258 A52 200fr multicolored
259 A52 400fr multicolored

Souvenir Sheet

260 A52 500fr Nobel medal

Nos. 258-260 are airmail.
See note after No. 479.

Peter Paul Rubens, 400th Birth Anniv. — A53

Portraits: 20fr, Portrait of the Artist's Daughter, Clara. 25fr, Suzanne Fourment. 50fr, Toilet of Venus, (detail). 75fr, Ceres (detail). 200fr, Young Woman with Blonde Braided Hair. No. 266, Helene Fourment in her Wedding Dress. No. 267, Self-portrait.

1977, July 7

261 A53 20fr multicolored
262 A53 25fr multicolored
263 A53 50fr multicolored
264 A53 75fr multicolored
265 A53 200fr multicolored
266 A53 500fr multicolored

Souvenir Sheet

267 A53 500fr multicolored

Nos. 265-267 are airmail.
See note after No. 479.

Fish A54

1977, Nov. 21

268 A54 30fr Swordfish
269 A54 40fr Gaterin
270 A54 50fr Sea scorpion
271 A54 100fr Chaetodon lunula
272 A54 200fr Amphiprion
273 A54 400fr Tetrodon

Souvenir Sheet

274 A54 500fr Coelacanth

Nos. 272-274 airmail. No. 274 contains one 52x47mm stamp.

Space Exploration — A55

1977, Nov. 21

275 A55 30fr Jupiter lander
276 A55 50fr Voyager probe, Uranus, vert.
277 A55 75fr Pioneer probe, Venus
278 A55 100fr Space shuttle, vert.
279 A55 200fr Viking III, Mars
280 A55 400fr Apollo-Soyuz, vert.

Souvenir Sheet

281 A55 500fr Allegory of the Sun

Nos. 279-281 airmail. No. 281 contains one 52x42mm stamp.

No. 219 Overprinted in One Line in Gold, Silver or Red
"Paris-New-York - 22 nov. 1977"

1977, Nov. 22

282 A46 200fr multicolored
283 A46 200fr multicolored (S)
284 A46 200fr multicolored (R)

Birds — A56

1978, Feb. 6

285 A56 15fr Porphyrula alleni
286 A56 20fr Merops supercimosus
287 A56 35fr Alcedo vintsioides johannae
288 A56 40fr Terpsiphone
289 A56 75fr Nectarinia comorensis
290 A56 400fr Egretta alba

Souvenir Sheet

291 A56 500fr Foudia eminentissima, horiz.

Nos. 290-291 are airmail. For overprint and surcharges see Nos. 444-448.

World Cup Soccer Championships, Argentina — A57

Designs: 30fr, Greece, 5th. cent. B.C. 50fr, Brittany, 19th cent. 75fr, London, 14th cent. 100fr, Italy, 18th cent. 200fr, England, 19th cent. 400fr, English Cup match, 1891. 500fr, English Cup final, 1962. No. 298, Player, satellite. No. 300, Players.

1978, Feb. 6

292 A57 30fr multicolored
293 A57 50fr multicolored
294 A57 75fr multicolored
295 A57 100fr multicolored
296 A57 200fr multicolored
297 A57 400fr multicolored

Litho. & Embossed

Size: 60x42mm

298 A57 1000fr gold & multi

Souvenir Sheets

Litho.

299 A57 500fr multicolored

Litho. & Embossed

300 A57 1000fr gold & multi

Nos. 296-300 are airmail. No. 300 contains one 60x42mm stamp. For overprints and surcharges see Nos. 402-408, 449-453.

Composers — A58

1978, Apr. 5 **Litho.**

301 A58 30fr J.S. Bach
302 A58 40fr W.A. Mozart
303 A58 50fr Berlioz
304 A58 100fr Verdi
305 A58 200fr Tchaikovsky
306 A58 400fr George Gershwin

Souvenir Sheet

307 A58 500fr Beethoven

Nos. 305-307 are airmail. For overprints and surcharges see Nos. 454-458.

Albrecht Durer, 450th Death Anniv. A59

Portraits: 20fr, Oswolt Krel. 25fr, Elspeth Tucher. 50fr, Hieronymus Holzschuher. 75fr, Young Woman. 200fr, Emperor Maximilian I. No. 313, Young Woman, (detail). No. 314, Self-portrait.

1978, Apr. 5

308 A59 20fr multicolored
309 A59 25fr multicolored
310 A59 50fr multicolored
311 A59 75fr multicolored
312 A59 200fr multicolored
313 A59 500fr multicolored

Souvenir Sheet

314 A59 500fr multicolored

Nos. 312-314 airmail. No. 314 contains one 42x52mm stamp. See note after No. 479.

Issues Not Valid for Postage

The government changed in May, 1978. A number of sets that had not been issued seem to have been invalid for postage until they were overprinted with the new country name. These are a set of 9 for the 25th anniv. of Elizabeth's coronation, a set of 7 for butterflies, a set of 6 for the 10th Intl. Communications Year, a set of 7 for the history of aviation, a set of 9 for Rubens, and a set of 9 for Durer.

These unoverprinted sets are no scarcer than the previous listed issues. See note after No. 479.

Islamic Republic

Nos. 204-205 Surcharged and Overprinted with 3 Lines and: "République / Fédérale / et Islamique / des Comores"

1978, July 24 **Litho.** ***Perf. 13½***

353 A44 30fr multi
354 A44 40fr on 30fr multi
355 A44 50fr multi
356 A44 100fr on 50fr multi

Nos. 353 and 355 were also overprinted to commemorate Queen Elizabeth II coronation anniversary; Capt. James Cook; World Cup Soccer winner; Albrecht Dürer; First powered flight; Railroad anniversary; Voyager I and II; Intl. Year of the Child; 1980 Olympic Games; World Cup Soccer, Espana '82.

Europe-Africa A66

Various satellites or spacecraft.

1978, Dec. 16

386 A66 10fr multicolored
387 A66 25fr multicolored
388 A66 35fr multicolored
389 A66 50fr multicolored
390 A66 100fr multicolored
391 A66 500fr multicolored

Souvenir Sheet

392 A66 500fr multicolored

Nos. 390-392 airmail. No. 392 contains one 61x40mm stamp.

Sir Rowland Hill — A67

1978, Dec. 16

393 A67 20fr Saxony #1
394 A67 30fr Netherlands #1
395 A67 40fr Great Britain #2
396 A67 75fr US #2
397 A67 200fr France #33
398 A67 400fr Basel #3L1

Litho. & Embossed

Size: 39x58mm

399 A67 1500fr British Guiana #13

Souvenir Sheets

Litho.

400 A67 500fr Moheli, Mayotte, Anjouan, Grand Comoro #1

Litho. & Embossed

401 A67 1500fr Hill, Mauritius #3

Nos. 397-401 are airmail. No. 400 contains one 57x49mm stamp. No. 401 contains one 58x39mm stamp.

Nos. 292-297 Ovptd. with New Country Name in Black on Silver and
1 ARGENTINE
2 HOLLANDE
3 BRESIL

1978, Dec. 16

402 A57 30fr multicolored
403 A57 50fr multicolored
404 A57 75fr multicolored
405 A57 100fr multicolored
406 A57 200fr multicolored
407 A57 400fr multicolored

Nos. 406-407 are airmail. No. 408 is the souvenir sheet.
Exists with Country name in red on silver.

Galileo and Voyager I — A68

Exploration of Solar System: 30fr, Kepler and Voyager II. 40fr, Copernicus and Voyager I, 100fr, Huygens and Voyager II. 200fr, William Herschel and Voyager II. 400fr, Urbain Leverrier and Voyager II. 500fr, Voyagers I and II, symbolic solar system.

1979, Feb. 19 **Litho.** ***Perf. 13***

409 A68 20fr multi	15	15
410 A68 30fr multi	15	15
411 A68 40fr multi	22	15
412 A68 100fr multi	45	22
413 A68 200fr multi	90	40
414 A68 400fr multi	2.00	80
Nos. 409-414 (6)	3.87	1.87

Souvenir Sheet

415 A68 500fr multi	2.75	1.10

Nos. 413-415 airmail.

Philidor, Anderssen, Steinitz and King — A69

Design: 100fr, Chess pieces and board, Venetian chess player. 500fr, Chess Grand Masters Alekhine, Spassky, Fischer, and bishop.

1979, Feb. 19

416 A69	40fr multi	18	15
417 A69	100fr multi	45	16
418 A69	500fr multi	2.25	90
	Nos. 416-418 (3)	2.88	1.21

Chess Grand Masters. No. 418 airmail.

Nos. 419-425 are reserved for Summer Olympics set of 6 with one souvenir sheet, released Mar. 28, 1979.

Charaxes Defulvata — A71

Birds: 50fr, Leptosomus discolor. 75fr, Bee eater.

1979, Apr. 10 Litho. *Perf. 12½*

426 A71	30fr multi	20	15
427 A71	50fr multi	35	15
428 A71	75fr multi	55	22
	Nos. 426-428 (3)	1.10	52

Otto Lilienthal and Glider — A72

History of Aviation: No. 430, Wright brothers and Flyer A. No. 431, Louis Bleriot and Bleriot XI. 100fr, Claude Dornier and Dornier-Wal hydrofoil. 200fr, Charles Lindbergh and Spirit of St. Louis.

1979, May 2 *Perf. 13*
Black Overprint and Surcharge

429 A72	30fr multi	20	20
430 A72	50fr multi	65	65
431 A72	50fr on 75fr multi	70	1.70
432 A72	100fr multi	1.40	1.40
433 A72	200fr multi	1.10	1.10
	Nos. 429-433 (5)	4.05	5.05

No. 433 airmail.
For unoverprinted stamps see note after No. 314.

Papilio Dardanus Cenea A73

Butterflies: 15fr, Papilio dardanus. 30fr, Chrysiridia croesus. 50fr, Precis octavia. 75fr, Bunaea alcinoe.

1979, May 2
Black Overprint and Surcharge

434 A73	5fr on 20fr multi	15	15
435 A73	15fr multi	15	15
436 A73	30fr multi	25	25
437 A73	50fr multi	50	50
438 A73	75fr multi	80	80
	Nos. 434-438 (5)	1.85	1.85

For unoverprinted stamps see note after No. 314.

Man Reading Proclamation — A74

1979, May 2 Litho. *Perf. 13½*
Black Surcharge and Overprint

439 A74	5fr on 25fr coronation coach	
440 A74	10fr Drummer	
441 A74	50fr on 40fr with crown, orb, scepter	
442 A74	50fr on 200fr shown	
443 A74	100fr St. Edward's Crown	

No. 442 is airmail.
For unoverprinted stamps see note after No. 314.

Nos. 285-289 Overprinted or Surcharged like A72-A74

1979, May 2 Litho. *Perf. 13*

444 A56	15fr multi	15	15
445 A56	30fr on 35fr multi	25	25
446 A56	50fr on 20fr multi	55	55
447 A56	50fr on 40fr multi	55	55
448 A56	200fr on 75fr multi	1.40	1.40
	Nos. 444-448 (5)	2.90	2.90

Nos. 292-296 Overprinted or Surcharged like A72-A74

1979, May 2 Litho. *Perf. 13*

449 A57	1fr on 100fr multi	15	15
450 A57	2fr on 75fr multi	15	15
451 A57	3fr on 30fr multi	15	15
452 A57	50fr multi	40	40
453 A57	200fr multi	1.40	1.40
	Nos. 449-453 (5)	2.25	2.25

No. 453 airmail.

Nos. 301-305 Overprinted or Surcharged like A72-A74

1979, May 2 *Perf. 13½*

454 A58	5fr on 100fr multi	15	15
455 A58	30fr multi	20	20
456 A58	40fr multi	22	22
457 A58	50fr multi	38	38
458 A58	50fr on 200fr multi	40	40
	Nos. 454-458 (5)	1.35	1.35

No. 458 airmail.

Nos. 459-465 are reserved for Intl. Year of the Child set of 6 with one souvenir sheet, released May 30, 1979.

Litchi Nuts — A76

Basketball Players — A77

1979, June 15 Litho. *Perf. 12½*

466 A76	60fr shown	40	20
467 A76	70fr Papayas	45	22
468 A76	100fr Avocados	65	30
469 A76	125fr Bananas	80	50
	Nos. 466-469 (4)	2.30	1.22

For surcharges see Nos. 515, 533.

1979, Aug. 28 Litho. *Perf. 13*

470 A77	200fr multi	1.10	80

Indian Ocean Olympics.

Nos. 176, 198, 218, 187, 159-160 and Type A78 Overprinted in Black

Mariner — A78

Designs: No. 475, Apollo-Soyuz. No. 479, Molniya.

Printing & Perfs. as Before, Litho. (A78)

1979, Sept. 15 *Perf. 13 (A78)*

471 A40	35fr multi	22
472 A43	75fr multi	50
473 A46	75fr multi	50
474 A78	75fr multi	50
475 A78	100fr multi	65
476 A41	100fr multi	70
477 A37	100fr multi	65
478 A37	200fr multi	1.40
479 A78	200fr multi	1.40
	Nos. 471-479 (9)	6.52

Nos. 476-479 airmail.
For type A78 see note after No. 314.

Nos. 166-167, 169, 235-236, 257, 262, 309, 311, the unissued Rubens set (4 values) and Durer set (5 values) exist with this overprint, supposedly also issued Sept. 15.

Dugout on Beach — A80

Anjouan Puppet — A81

1980, Jan. 4 Litho. *Perf. 13*

498 A80	60fr multi	25	15
499 A81	100fr multi	40	20

For surcharge see No. 534.

Sultan Said Ali — A82

1980, Feb. 20 *Perf. 12½x13*

500 A82	40fr shown	15	15
501 A82	60fr Sultan Ahmed	25	15

Sherlock Holmes, Doyle — A83

1980, Feb. 25 *Perf. 12½*

502 A83	200fr multi	1.40	75

Sir Arthur Conan Doyle (1859-1930), writer.
For surcharge see No. 513.

Grand Mosque, Holy Ka'aba, Mecca — A84

1980, Mar. 12 *Perf. 13x12½*

503 A84	75fr multi	30	20

Hegira, 1500th anniv.
For surcharge see No. 514.

Year of the Holy City of Jerusalem A85

1980, Mar. 12 *Perf. 13x13½*

504 A85	60fr multi	25	15

Kepler, Copernicus and Pluto — A86

1980, Apr. 30 Litho. *Perf. 12½*

505 A86	400fr multi	2.00	1.50

Discovery of Pluto, 50th anniversary.
For surcharge see No. 531.

Muscle System, Avicenna — A87

1980, Apr. 30 Engr. *Perf. 13*

506 A87	60fr multi	25	20

Avicenna, Arab physician, birth millennium.

Soccer Players — A88

World Cup Soccer 1982; Various soccer scenes. 60fr, 150fr, 500fr, vert.

1981, Feb. 20 Litho. *Perf. 12½*

507 A88 60fr multi 30 15
508 A88 75fr multi 35 15
509 A88 90fr multi 42 20
510 A88 100fr multi 55 25
511 A88 150fr multi 80 28
Nos. 507-511 (5) 2.42 1.03

Souvenir Sheet

512 A88 500fr multi 2.50 1.00

For overprints and surcharge see Nos. 532, 555-560.

Nos. 502-503, 469 Surcharged and

Merops Superciliosus — A89

Perf. 12½, 13x12½ (No. 514)
1981, Feb. Litho.
Red, Black or Blue Surcharge

513 A83 15fr on 200fr multi 15 15
514 A84 20fr on 75fr multi 15 15
515 A76 40fr on 125fr multi (Bk) 25 25
516 A89 60fr on 75fr multi (Bl) 40 40
Nos. 513-516 (4) 95 95

A90

Space Exploration: 50fr, Apollo program, vert. 75fr, 100fr, 500fr, Columbia space shuttle.

1981, July 13 Litho. *Perf. 14*

517 A90 50fr multi 22 15
518 A90 75fr multi 30 15
519 A90 100fr multi 42 25
520 A90 450fr multi 2.00 1.00
Nos. 517-520 (4) 2.94 1.55

Souvenir Sheet

521 A90 500fr multi 2.50 1.00

For overprint see No. 599.

Prince Charles and Lady Diana, Buckingham Palace — A91

1981, Sept. 1 Litho. *Perf. 14½*

522 A91 125fr shown 50 20
523 A91 200fr Highwood House 1.00 40
524 A91 450fr Carnarvon Castle 2.00 90
a. Souvenir sheet of 3 3.50 1.50
Nos. 522-524 (3) 3.50 1.50

Royal wedding. No. 524a contains Nos. 522-524 in changed colors.
For overprints see Nos. 551-553.

Flag Type of 1979

1981, Oct. Litho. *Perf. 13*

526 O1 5fr multi 15 15
527 O1 15fr multi 15 15
528 O1 25fr multi 15 15
529 O1 35fr multi 15 15
530 O1 75fr multi 30 20
Set value 65 43

Nos. 505, 509, 468, 499 Surcharged

1981, Nov. Litho. *Perf. 12½*

531 A86 5fr on 400fr multi 15 15
532 A88 20fr on 90fr multi 15 15
533 A76 45fr on 100fr multi 20 15
534 A81 45fr on 100fr multi 20 15
Set value 50 26

75th Anniv. of Grand Prix — A92

Designs: Winners and their Cars.

1981, Dec. 28 Litho. *Perf. 12½*

535 A92 20fr Mercedes, 1914 15 15
536 A92 50fr Delage, 1925 22 15
537 A92 75fr Rudi Caracciola, 1926 38 15
538 A92 90fr Stirling Moss, 1955 40 20
539 A92 150fr Maserati, 1957 65 30
Nos. 535-539 (5) 1.80 95

Souvenir Sheet
Perf. 13

540 A92 500fr Changing wheels, vert. 2.25 1.00

For overprint see No. 600.

Scouting Year — A93

1982, Jan. 5 *Perf. 12½*

541 A93 50fr Climbing rocks 22 15
542 A93 75fr Boating 35 15
543 A93 250fr Sailing 1.10 50
544 A93 350fr Sailing, diff. 1.60 75
Nos. 541-544 (4) 3.27 1.55

Souvenir Sheet
Perf. 13

545 A93 500fr Baden-Powell 2.50 1.10

For overprint see No. 601.

21st Birthday of Princess of Wales — A94

Designs: Various portraits of Princess Diana.

1982, July 1 Litho. *Perf. 14*

546 A94 200fr multi 80 40
547 A94 300fr multi 1.10 60

Souvenir Sheet

548 A94 500fr multi 2.00 1.00

Johannes von Goethe (1749-1832) A95

1982, July

549 A95 75fr multi 30 15
550 A95 350fr multi 1.40 65

Nos. 522-524a Overprinted in Blue: "NAISSANCE ROYALE 1982"

1982, July 31 *Perf. 14½*

551 A91 125fr multi 50 40
552 A91 200fr multi 75 60
553 A91 450fr multi 1.75 1.50
a. Souvenir sheet of 3 2.50 3.50
Nos. 551-553 (3) 3.00 2.50

Birth of Prince William of Wales, June 21.

Nos. 507-512 Overprinted with Finalists and Score in Red

1982, Sept. 20 Litho. *Perf. 12½*

555 A88 60fr multi 25 18
556 A88 75fr multi 30 22
557 A88 90fr multi 35 25
558 A88 100fr multi 40 30
559 A88 150fr multi 55 40
Nos. 555-559 (5) 1.85 1.35

Souvenir Sheet

560 A88 500fr multi 2.00 2.00

Italy's victory in 1982 World Cup.

Paintings by Norman Rockwell A96

1982, Oct. 11 Litho. *Perf. 14*

561 A96 60fr 1931 30 15
562 A96 75fr 1925 38 15
563 A96 100fr 1922 45 20
564 A96 150fr 1919 75 30
565 A96 200fr 1924 1.00 35
566 A96 300fr 1918 1.50 60
Nos. 561-566 (6) 4.38 1.75

Sultans of Anjouan — A97

1982, Dec. *Perf. 12½x13, 13x12½*

567 A97 30fr Said Mohamed Sidi, vert. 15 15
568 A97 60fr Ahmed Abdallah, vert. 25 15
569 A97 75fr Salim 30 20
570 A97 300fr Sidi, Abdallah 1.10 80
Nos. 567-570 (4) 1.80 1.30

Landscapes — A98

1983, Sept. 30 Litho. *Perf. 13*

571 A98 60fr D'Ziani Lake 25 15
572 A98 100fr Sunset 40 25
573 A98 175fr Anjouan, vert. 75 40
574 A98 360fr Itsandra 1.40 80
575 A98 400fr Anjouan, diff. 1.60 1.10
Nos. 571-575 (5) 4.40 2.70

Woman from Moheli A99

1983, Oct. 17 Litho. *Perf. 12½x13*

576 A99 30fr shown 15 15
577 A99 45fr Woman, diff. 20 15
578 A99 50fr Man from Mayotte 22 15
Nos. 576-578 (3) 57
Set value 34

Horses — A100

1983, Nov. 30 Litho. *Perf. 13*

579 A100 75fr Arabian 30 15
580 A100 100fr Anglo-Arabian 40 18
581 A100 125fr Lippizaner 50 20
582 A100 150fr Tennessee 60 25
583 A100 200fr Appaloosa 80 35
584 A100 300fr Pure English 1.10 55
585 A100 400fr Clydesdale 1.60 65
586 A100 500fr Andalusian 2.00 1.00
Nos. 579-586 (8) 7.30 3.33

Double Portrait, by Raphael A101

1983, Dec. 30 Litho. *Perf. 13*

587 A101 100fr shown 40 20
588 A101 200fr Girl, fresco detail 80 30
589 A101 300fr St. George Killing Dragon 1.10 60
590 A101 400fr Balthazar Castiglione 1.60 75
Nos. 587-590 (4) 3.90 1.85

For surcharge see No. 703.

Ships and Automobiles — A102

1984, Oct. 9 Litho. *Perf. 12½*

591 A102 100fr William Fawcett 28
592 A102 100fr De Dion, 1885 28
593 A102 150fr Lightning 40
594 A102 150fr Benz Victoria, 1893 40
595 A102 200fr Rapido 60
596 A102 200fr Columbia Electric, 1901 60

597 A102 350fr Sindia 80
598 A102 350fr Fiat, 1902 80
Nos. 591-598 (8) 4.16

Souvenir Sheets

Nos. 521, 540, 545, C126, C131 Ovptd. with Exhibition in Black, Blue, Red or Gold

1985, Mar. 11 ***Perf. 14, 13***

599 A90 500fr '85 / HAMBOURG (Bk) 1.50
600 A92 500fr TSUKUBA EXPO '85 (Bl) 1.50
601 A93 500fr ARGENTINA '85/BUENOS AIRES (R) 1.50
602 AP31 500fr Rome, ITALIA '85 emblem (R) 1.50
603 AP32 500fr OLYM - PHILEX/ '85 / LAUSANNE (G) 1.50
Nos. 599-603 (5) 7.50

Nos. 602-603 airmail.

Victor Hugo (1802-1885), Author, Pantheon, Paris — A103

Anniversaries and events: 200fr, IYY, Jules Verne (1828-1905), author. 300fr, IYY, Mark Twain (1835-1910), author. 450fr, Queen Mother, 85th birthday, vert. 500fr, Statue of Liberty, cent., vert.

1985, May 27 **Litho.** ***Perf. 13***

604 A103 100fr multi 25
605 A103 200fr multi 55
606 A103 300fr multi 75
607 A103 450fr multi 1.10
608 A103 500fr multi 1.40
Nos. 604-608 (5) 4.05

For surcharge see No. 704.

Sea Shells A104

1985, Oct. 23 ***Perf. 14***

609 A104 75fr Lambis chiragra 20
610 A104 125fr Strombe lentifinosum 35
611 A104 200fr Tonna gala 55
612 A104 300fr Cymbium glans 75
613 A104 450fr Lambis crocata 1.10
Nos. 609-613 (5) 2.95

Comoros Admission to UN, 10th Anniv. — A105

1985, Nov. 12 **Litho.** ***Perf. 13x12½***

614 A105 5fr multi 15 15
615 A105 30fr multi 15 15
616 A105 75fr multi 25 15
617 A105 125fr multi 42 22
618 A105 400fr multi 1.40 65
Nos. 614-618 (5) 2.37
Set value 1.10

Moroni Rotary Club, 20th Anniv. — A106

1985, Nov. 30 ***Perf. 13***

619 A106 25fr multi 15 15
620 A106 75fr multi 25 15
621 A106 125fr multi 42 22
622 A106 500fr multi 1.75 1.00
Nos. 619-622 (4) 2.57 1.52

Mushrooms — A107

1985, Dec. 24 ***Perf. 13½***

623 A107 75fr Boletus edulis 25 15
624 A107 125fr Sarcoscypha coccinea 42 22
625 A107 200fr Hypholoma fasciculare 70 38
626 A107 350fr Astraeus hygrometricus 1.25 60
627 A107 500fr Armillariella mellea 2.00 1.00
Nos. 623-627 (5) 4.62 2.35

Health Year — A108

1986, Oct. 2 **Litho.** ***Perf. 15x14½***

628 A108 25fr Pediatric examination 15 15
629 A108 100fr Weighing child 65 32
630 A108 200fr Immunization 1.40 70
Nos. 628-630 (3) 2.20 1.17

For surcharge see No. 705.

Musical Instruments A109

1986, Dec. 24 **Litho.** ***Perf. 13***

631 A109 75fr Ndzoumara 40 20
632 A109 125fr Ndzedze 70 35
633 A109 210fr Gaboussi 1.15 58
634 A109 500fr Ngoma 2.75 1.40
Nos. 631-634 (4) 5.00 2.53

Role of Women in National Development — A110

1987, Mar. 7 **Litho.** ***Perf. 13***

635 A110 75fr Working fields 40 20
636 A110 125fr Harvesting crops, vert. 68 35
637 A110 1000fr Basketweaving 5.25 2.65
Nos. 635-637 (3) 6.33 3.20

Service Organizations A111

Emblems and activities: 75fr, Nos. 642, Kiwanis or 643c, Rotary Intl. for child survival. 125fr, Nos. 641, Kiwanis or 643b, Lions Intl. for aid to the handicapped. 210fr, No. 643a, Kiwanis helping poor and homeless children.

1988 **Litho.** ***Perf. 13½***

638 A111 75fr dk bl, lt bl & multi 52 25
639 A111 125fr dk brn, lt brn & multi 90 45
640 A111 210fr org, yel & multi 1.50 75
641 A111 425fr red, pink & multi 3.00 1.50
642 A111 500fr bl, yel & multi 3.60 1.80
643 Strip of 3 8.10 4.05
a. A111 210fr grn, lt grn & multi 1.50 75
b. A111 425fr pur, pink & multi 3.00 1.50
c. A111 500fr red, org & multi 3.60 1.80
Nos. 638-643 (6) 17.62 8.80

For surcharges see Nos. 654-656.

A112

1988 Olympics, Calgary and Seoul — A113

1988 **Litho.** ***Perf. 13½***

644 A112 75fr Women's figure skating 52 25
645 A112 100fr Running 70 35
646 A112 125fr Women's speed skating 88 45
647 A112 150fr Equestrian 1.05 52
648 A112 350fr Two-man luge 2.50 1.25
649 A112 400fr Biathlon 2.80 1.40
650 A112 500fr Pole vault 3.50 1.75
651 A112 600fr Soccer 4.25 2.10
Nos. 644-651 (8) 16.20 8.07

Souvenir Sheets

652 A113 750fr Women's downhill skiing, satellite 5.25 5.25
653 A113 750fr Track, satellite 5.25 5.25

Nos. 649 and 651-653 are airmail.

No. 643 and Service Organization Types Surcharged

Designs: No. 655, like #643b. No. 656, like #643c.

1988, July 18 **Litho.** ***Perf. 13½***

654 Strip of 3 3.75 1.90
a. A111 75fr on 210fr #643a 48 25
b. A111 200fr on 425fr #643b 1.30 65
c. A111 300fr on 500fr #643c 1.95 1.00
655 A111 125fr on 425fr pur, lt pur & multi, blk letters 80 40
656 A111 400fr on 500fr car, pink & multi 2.60 1.30
Nos. 654-656 (3) 7.15 3.60

Nos. 655-656 not issued without surcharge.

Discovery of America, 500th Anniv. (in 1992) — A114

Designs: 75fr, Christopher Columbus, *Santa Maria*. 125fr, Martin Alonzo Pinzon (c. 1441-1493), *Pinta*. 150fr, Vicente Yanez Pinzon (c. 1460-1523), *Nina*. 250fr, Search for Cipango, legendary rich islands off the coast of Asia. 375fr, *Santa Maria* shipwrecked. 450fr, Preparing for 4th voyage. 750fr, Samana Cay landing.

1988, Apr. 18 **Litho.** ***Perf. 13½***

657 A114 75fr multi 50 25
658 A114 125fr multi 82 40
659 A114 150fr multi 98 50
660 A114 250fr multi 1.65 82
661 A114 375fr multi 2.45 1.20
662 A114 450fr multi 3.00 1.50
Nos. 657-662 (6) 9.40 4.67

Souvenir Sheet

663 A114 750fr multi, horiz. 5.00 5.00

Nos. 661-663 airmail. No. 663 contains one 42x30mm stamp.

For surcharge see No. 702.

1992 Summer Olympics, Barcelona A115

1988, Apr. 18

664 A115 75fr Discus, vert. 50 25
665 A115 100fr shown 65 32
666 A115 125fr Cycling 82 40
667 A115 150fr Wrestling 98 50
668 A115 375fr Basketball, vert. 2.45 1.20
669 A115 600fr Tennis, vert. 3.90 1.95
Nos. 664-669 (6) 9.30 4.62

Souvenir Sheet

670 A115 750fr Marathon, vert. 5.00 5.00

Nos. 668-670 are airmail.

Famous Men — A116

Rotary Intl. — A117

Design: 150fr, Yuri Gagarin (1934-1968), USSR, cosmonaut. 300fr, Jean-Henri Dunant, Red Cross founder. 400fr, Roger Clemens, baseball player. 500fr, Gary Kasparov, USSR, 1985 world chess champion. 600fr, Paul Harris, US, Rotary founder. 750fr, Neil Armstrong walking on the Moon, John F. Kennedy. No. 678, The Thinker by Rodin, Rotary Intl. emblem.

1988, Dec. 6 **Litho.** ***Perf. 13½***

671 A116 150fr multi 1.05 52
672 A116 300fr multi 2.10 1.05
673 A116 400fr multi 2.70 1.35
674 A116 500fr multi 3.50 1.75

675	A116	600fr multi	4.25	2.15
a.		Souv. sheet of 5, #671-675 + label		
		Nos. 665-669 (5)	8.80	4.37

Litho. & Embossed

676 A117 1500fr gold & multi

Souvenir Sheets

Litho.

677	A116	750fr multi	5.25	5.25

Litho. & Embossed

678 A117 1500fr gold & multi

Intl. Red Cross, 125th anniv. (300fr), Rotary Intl. (600fr, Nos. 676, 678). Nos. 674-678 are airmail.

Inventors and Sportsmen A118

Portraits and modes of transportation: Designs: 75fr, Alain Prost, F-1 MacLaren-Honda. 125fr, George Stephenson and locomotive *Borsig of 1935.* 500fr, Ettore Bugatti (1881-1947), 1939 Bugatti Aravis Type 57. 600fr, Rudolf Diesel (1858-1913) and V200 BB diesel-electric locomotive. 750fr, Dennis Conner, captain of the *Stars and Stripes,* winner of the 1987 America's Cup. No. 684, Michael Fay, patron of the *New Zealand,* an entry in the America's Cup. No. 685, Enzo Ferrari and 1989 Ferrari Formula 1, horiz.

1988, Dec. 27 Litho. *Perf. 13½*

679	A118	75fr multi	52	25
680	A118	125fr multi	82	40
681	A118	500fr multi	3.50	1.75
682	A118	600fr multi	3.90	1.95
683	A118	750fr multi	4.75	2.35
684	A118	1000fr multi	6.50	3.25
		Nos. 679-684 (6)	19.99	9.95

Souvenir Sheet

685	A118	1000fr multi	6.50	6.50

Nos. 683-685 are airmail.

Scouts, Butterflies and Birds — A119

Scouts involved in various activities and species: 50fr, Gathering specimens, *Papilio nireus aristophontes oberthur* female. 75fr, Studying specimen and male. 150fr, Cooking out, *Charaxes fulvescens separanus poulton.* 375fr, Picking mushrooms, *Lonchura cucullatus.* 450fr, Examining specimen, *Charaxes castor comoranus rothschild.* 500fr, Identifying specimen, *Zosterops maderaspatana.* 750fr, Studying specimens, *Foudia omissa* and *Charaxes paradoxa lathy* female. No. 692, Photographing specimen, Junonia rhadama. No. 694, Examining specimen, Agapornis cana cana.

1989 Litho.

686	A119	50fr multi	32	16
687	A119	75fr multi	48	25
688	A119	150fr multi	98	50
689	A119	375fr multi	2.45	1.20
690	A119	450fr multi	2.90	1.45
691	A119	500fr multi	3.25	1.60
		Nos. 686-691 (6)	10.38	5.16

Litho. & Embossed

692 A119 1500fr gold & multi

Souvenir Sheets

Litho.

693	A119	750fr multi	4.75	4.75

Litho. & Embossed

694 A119 1500fr gold & multi

Nos. 690-694 are airmail. Issue dates: Nos. 692, 694, May 15, others, Mar. 15.

Gold Medalists of the 1988 Summer Olympics A120

Communication satellites, various equestrians and their mounts: 75fr, Nicole Uphoff, West Germany, individual dressage, and Aussat K3. 150fr, Pierre Durand, France, individual jumping, and Brazilsat. 375fr, Janos Martinek, Hungary, individual modern pentathlon, and ECS 4. 600fr, Mark Todd, New Zealand, individual three-day event, and Olympus. 750fr, Team jumping, West Germany, and satellite. No. 699, Pierre Durand, France, individual show jumping. No. 701, Nicole Uphoff, West Germany, individual dressage.

1989, Apr. 10 Litho. *Perf. 13½*

695	A120	75fr multi	48	25
696	A120	150fr multi	95	48
697	A120	375fr multi	2.40	1.20
698	A120	600fr multi	3.75	1.90
		Nos. 695-698 (4)	7.58	3.83

Litho. & Embossed

699 A120 1500fr gold & multi

Souvenir Sheets

Litho.

700	A120	750fr multi	4.75	4.75

Litho. & Embossed

701 A120 1500fr gold & multi

No. 701 contains one 39x38mm stamp. Nos. 698-701 are airmail.

Nos. 660, 588, 605 and 630 Surcharged

1989 Litho. *Perfs. as Before*

702	A114	25fr on 250fr #660	18	15
703	A101	150fr on 200fr #588	1.05	52
704	A103	150fr on 200fr #605	1.05	52
705	A108	150fr on 200fr #630	1.05	52
		Nos. 702-705 (4)	3.33	1.71

1992 Summer Olympics, Barcelona — A121

1989, Apr. 26 Litho. *Perf. 13½*

706	A121	75fr Running	50	25
707	A121	150fr Soccer	1.00	50
708	A121	300fr Tennis	2.00	1.00
709	A121	375fr Baseball	2.50	1.25
710	A121	500fr Pommel horse	3.25	1.60
711	A121	600fr Table tennis	4.00	2.00
		Nos. 706-711 (6)	13.25	6.60

Souvenir Sheet

712	A121	750fr Equestrian	5.00	5.00

Nos. 710-712 are airmail.

Dr. Joseph-Ignace Guillotin (1738-1814) — A122

French Revolution, Bicentennial: 150fr, French artillery, Gen. Francois-Christophe Kellerman (1735-1820). 375fr, Royalist insurgents and leader, Jean Cotterau (1757-1794). 600fr, King Louis XVI (1774-1792), troops. 1000fr, Storming of the Bastille and Jacques Necker, statesman (1732-1804). No. 717, Lafayette, Mounier, Sieyes and Declaration of the Rights of Man and Citizen. No. 719, Robespierre and St. Just before the Convention on 9 Thermidor.

1989, Oct. 25 Litho. *Perf. 13½*

713	A122	75fr multicolored	60	30
714	A122	150fr multicolored	1.10	55
715	A122	375fr multicolored	2.80	1.40
716	A122	600fr multicolored	4.50	2.25
		Nos. 713-716 (4)	9.00	4.50

Litho. & Embossed

717 A122 1500fr gold & multi

Souvenir Sheets

Litho.

718	A122	1000fr multicolored	7.50	3.75

Litho. & Embossed

719 A122 1500fr gold & multi

Philexfrance 1989. No. 716-719 are airmail. No. 714 incorrectly inscribed "Francois-Etienne." Nos. 713-717 exist in souvenir sheets of 1.

Airport Pavilion A124

Designs: 10fr, 25fr, Airport pavilion. 50fr, 75fr, 150fr, Federal Assembly.

1990, Apr. 1 Litho. *Perf. 13*

722	A124	5fr brn, org & brt red	15	15
723	A124	10fr brn, org & brt bl	15	15
724	A124	25fr brn, org & brt grn	20	15
725	A124	50fr blk & brt red	40	20
726	A124	75fr blk & brt bl	60	30
727	A124	150fr blk & grn	1.20	60
		Nos. 722-727 (6)	2.70	
		Set value		1.30

World Cup Soccer Championships, Italy — A125

Players from: 50fr, Brazil. 75fr, England. 100fr, Federal Republic of Germany. 150fr, Belgium. 375fr, Italy. 600fr, Argentina. 750fr, Argentina and Italy.

1990 Litho. *Perf. 13½*

728	A125	50fr multicolored	40	20
729	A125	75fr multicolored	60	30
730	A125	100fr multicolored	75	38
731	A125	150fr multicolored	1.10	55
732	A125	375fr multicolored	2.80	1.40
733	A125	600fr multicolored	4.50	2.25
		Nos. 728-733 (6)	10.15	5.08

Litho. & Embossed

734 A125 1500fr gold & multi

Souvenir Sheets

Litho.

735	A125	750fr multicolored	5.00	5.00

Litho. & Embossed

736 A125 1500fr gold & multi

Nos. 732-736 are airmail.

Telecom '91 A125a

1990, Oct. 29 Litho. *Perf. 13½*

736A	A125a	75fr Emblem, vert.	1.25	60
736B	A125a	150fr shown	2.50	1.25

Nos. 736A-736B exist imperf.

A126

Designs: 75fr, Hubble Space Telescope placed in orbit. 150fr, Pope John Paul II, Pres. Gorbachev meet Dec. 3, 1989. 200fr, Kevin Mitchell, San Francisco Giants, Natl. League Most Valuable Player, 1989. 250fr, De Gaulle, France, and Adenauer, West Germany, meet in Sept. 1962. 300fr, Cassini probe to Titan, 2002. 375fr, Bullet train and Concorde, France. 450fr, Gary Kasparov, World Chess Champion. 500fr, Paul Harris (1868-1947), founder of Rotary Intl.

1990, Nov. 26 Litho. *Perf. 13½*

737	A126	75fr sil & multi	70	35
738	A126	150fr sil & multi	1.40	70
739	A126	200fr sil & multi	1.90	95
740	A126	250fr sil & multi	2.35	1.15
741	A126	300fr sil & multi	2.80	1.40
742	A126	375fr sil & multi	3.50	1.75
743	A126	450fr sil & multi	4.20	2.10
744	A126	500fr sil & multi	4.70	2.35
		Nos. 737-744 (8)	21.55	10.75

Nos. 743-744 are airmail.

A127

A128

Winter Olympics participants: 75fr, Edi Reinalter, Switzerland, slalom, 1948. 100fr, Canadian hockey team, 1924. 375fr, Gratia Van der Oye, women's slalom, Holland, 1936. 600fr, Heikki Hasu, Finland, combined cross country and ski jumping, 1948. 750fr, Helene Engelman & Alfred Berger, Austria, pairs figure skating, 1924. No. 751, Speed skater, horiz. No. 751A, Luge, horiz.

1990, Dec. 10

746	A127	75fr multicolored	70	35
747	A127	100fr multicolored	95	48
748	A127	375fr multicolored	3.50	1.75
749	A127	600fr multicolored	5.60	2.80
		Nos. 746-749 (4)	10.75	5.38

Souvenir Sheet

750	A127	750fr multicolored	7.00	3.50

Litho. & Embossed

751 A127 1500fr gold & multi

Souvenir Sheet

751A A127 1500fr gold & multi

1992 Winter Olympics, Albertville. Nos. 748-751A are airmail. No. 750 contains one 36x41mm stamp.

1991, May 17 Litho. *Perf. 13½*

Ground station, Moroni Volo-Volo.

752	A128	75fr multicolored	55	28
753	A128	150fr multicolored	1.15	58
754	A128	225fr multicolored	1.70	85
755	A128	300fr multicolored	2.30	1.15
756	A128	500fr multicolored	3.80	1.90
		Nos. 752-756 (5)	9.50	4.76

Indian Ocean Conference A129

1991, June 17

757	A129	75fr multicolored	60	30
758	A129	150fr multicolored	1.15	60
759	A129	225fr multicolored	1.70	85
		Nos. 757-759 (3)	3.45	1.75

World War II, 50th Anniv. A130

Actors, Films: 150fr, Errol Flynn, Objective Burma. 300fr, Henry Fonda, The Longest Day. 450fr, Humphrey Bogart, Sahara.

1991, Aug. 5

760 A130 150fr sil & multi	1.15	58
761 A130 300fr sil & multi	2.30	1.15
762 A130 450fr sil & multi	3.45	1.75
Nos. 760-762 (3)	6.90	3.48

No. 762 is airmail. Nos. 760-762 exist in souvenir sheets of 1.

A131

Charles de Gaulle A132

De Gaulle and: 125fr, Battle of Koufra. 375fr, Battle of Britain. 500fr, Battle of Monte Cassino. 1000fr, Airplanes. 1500fr, De Gaulle at podium.

1991, Aug. 5 Litho. *Perf. 13½*

763 A131 125fr multi	95	48
764 A131 375fr multi	2.85	1.45
765 A131 500fr multi	3.80	1.90
Nos. 763-765 (3)	7.60	3.83

Souvenir Sheet

766 A131 1000fr multi	7.60	3.80

Litho. & Embossed

767 A132 1500fr gold & multi		

Nos. 765-767 are airmail. No. 767 exists in souvenir sheet of 1.

Anniversaries and Events — A133

Designs: 100fr, Satellite Columbus in polar orbit. 150fr, Gandhi. 250fr, Jean-Henri Dunant. 300fr, Wolfgang Amadeus Mozart. 375fr, Brandenburg Gate. 400fr, Konrad Adenauer. 450fr, Elvis Presley. 500fr, Ferdinand von Zeppelin.

1991, Nov. 18 Litho. *Perf. 13½*

768 A133 100fr multicolored	1.65	85
769 A133 150fr multicolored	2.50	1.25
770 A133 250fr multicolored	4.25	2.00
771 A133 300fr multicolored	5.00	2.50
772 A133 375fr multicolored	6.25	3.00
773 A133 400fr multicolored	6.50	3.25
774 A133 450fr multicolored	7.50	3.75
a. Souv. sheet, 1 each #771, #774	12.50	6.25
775 A133 500fr multicolored	8.50	4.25
a. Souv. sheet, 1 each #772-773, 775	21.50	
Nos. 768-775 (8)	42.15	20.85

Nobel Peace Prize, 90th anniv. (#770). Mozart, bicent. of death (#771). Brandenburg Gate, bicent. (#772). Konrad Adenauer, 25th anniv. of death (#773). Elvis Presley, 15th anniv. of death (in 1992) (#774). Count Zeppelin, 75th anniv. of death (in 1992) (#775).

Nos. 774-775 are airmail. Nos. 768-775 exist in souvenir sheets of 1.

Mushrooms A134

1992, Mar. 23 Litho. *Perf. 13½*

776 A134 75fr Cepe comestible	58	30
777 A134 150fr Geastre en etoile	1.10	58
778 A134 600fr Pezize ecarlate	4.75	2.50
Nos. 776-778 (3)	6.43	3.38

No. 778 is airmail. Nos. 776-778 exist imperf. and in souvenir sheets of one.

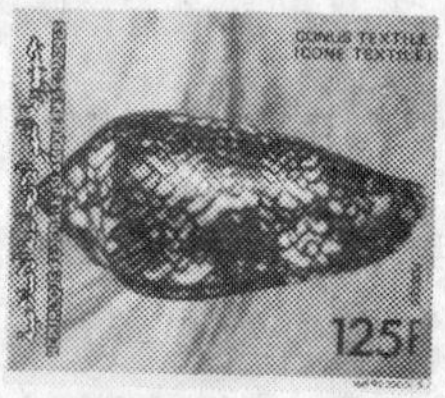

Shells A135

1992, Mar. 23

779 A135 125fr Conus textile	1.00	50
780 A135 150fr Cypraecassis rufa	1.10	58
781 A135 500fr Leporicypraea mappa	4.00	2.00
Nos. 779-781 (3)	6.10	3.08

Souvenir Sheet

782 A135 750fr Nautilus pompilius	6.00	3.00

Nos. 781-782 are airmail. Nos. 779-781 exist imperf. and in souvenir sheets of one. No. 782 exists imperf.

Space Programs A136

Designs: 75fr, Mercury rocket, chimpanzee Ham, US. 125fr, Mars Observer, US. No. 785, Veronica rocket, cat Felix, France. No. 786, Mars rover, US, Mars car, USSR. 500fr, Phobos project, USSR. 600fr, Sputnik II, dog Laika, USSR. 1000fr, Viking, US, vert.

1992, Mar. 30 Litho. *Perf. 13½*

783 A136 75fr multicolored	60	30
784 A136 125fr multicolored	1.00	50
785 A136 150fr multicolored	1.20	60
786 A136 150fr multicolored	1.20	60
787 A136 500fr multicolored	4.00	2.00
a. Souv. sheet of 3, #784, 786-787	*11.50*	*5.75*
788 A136 600fr multicolored	4.80	2.40
a. Souv. sheet of 3, #783, 785, 788	*11.50*	*5.75*
Nos. 783-788 (6)	12.80	6.40

Souvenir Sheet

789 A136 1000fr multicolored	8.00	4.00

Nos. 787-789 are airmail. Nos. 783-788 exist imperf. and in souvenir sheets of one. No. 789 contains one 30x42mm stamp.

Voyages of Discovery A137

Designs: 75fr, Space shuttle Endeavour, sailing ship Endeavour, Capt. Cook. 100fr, Satellite, sailing ship Golden Hinde, Sir Francis Drake. 150fr, ISO observation satellite, sailing ship Susan Constant, John Smith. 225fr, Probe B, sailing ship Discovery, Robert F. Scott. 375fr, Magellan probe over Venus, sailing ship, Ferdinand Magellan. 500fr, Newton probe, sailing ship Sao Gabriel, Vasco da Gama.

1992, May 28 Litho. *Perf. 13½*

790 A137 75fr multicolored	70	35
791 A137 100fr multicolored	95	48
792 A137 150fr multicolored	1.50	70
793 A137 225fr multicolored	2.25	1.10
794 A137 375fr multicolored	3.50	1.75
795 A137 500fr multicolored	4.75	2.50
Nos. 790-795 (6)	13.65	6.88

Nos. 794-795 are airmail. Nos. 790-795 exist imperf. in souvenir sheets of one. A number has been reserved for a 1000fr souvenir sheet issued with this set.

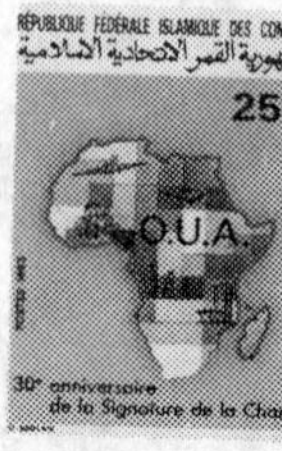

Organization of African Unity, 30th Anniv. — A138

1993, Feb. 15 Litho. *Perf. 13½x13*

797 A138 25fr blue & multi	20	15
798 A138 50fr pink & multi	40	20

Perf. 12

799 A138 75fr green & multi	60	30
800 A138 150fr vermilion & multi	1.20	60
Nos. 797-800 (4)	2.40	1.25

1994 World Cup Soccer Championships, US — A139

Intl. Telecommunications Day — A140

1993, May 12 Litho. *Perf. 13x12½*

801 A139 25fr red & multi	20	15
802 A139 75fr brown & multi	60	30
803 A139 100fr blue & multi	80	40
804 A139 150fr green & multi	1.20	60
Nos. 801-804 (4)	2.80	1.45

1993, May 17

805 A140 50fr red & multi	40	20
806 A140 75fr blue & multi	60	30
807 A140 100fr green & multi	80	40
808 A140 150fr black & multi	1.20	60
Nos. 805-808 (4)	3.00	1.50

Miniature Sheet

Prehistoric Animals A141

Designs: a, 75fr, Edaphosaurus. b, 75fr, Moschops. c, 75fr, Sauroctonus. d, 75fr, Ornitholestes. e, 75fr, Kentrosaurus. f, 75fr, Compsognathus. g, 75fr, Styracosaurus. h, 75fr, Acanthopholis. i, 150fr, Edmontonia. j, 150fr, Struthiomimus. k, 450fr, Dromiceiomimus. l, 450fr, Iguanodon. m, 150fr, Diatryma. n, 150fr, Uintatherium. o, 525fr, Synthetoceras. p, 525fr, Euryapteryx.

1200fr, Tyrannosaurus rex.

1994, Apr. 5 Litho. *Perf. 13½*

809 A141 Sheet of 16, #a.-p.	18.00	9.00

Souvenir Sheet

810 A141 1200fr multicolored	6.75	3.50

No. 810 is airmail and contains one 42x60mm stamp.

Miniature Sheet

Flora A142

Orchids: No. 811a, 75fr, Hibiscus syriacus. 150fr, Pyrostegia venusta. 525fr, Allamanda cathartica.

Vegetables: No. 811b, 75fr, Anacardier. 150fr, Manioc. 525fr, Cacao.

Mushrooms: No. 811c, 75fr, Suillus lutens. 150fr, Lycogala epidendron. 525fr, Clathrus ruber.

Butterflies, insects: No. 812a, 75fr, Colotis zoe. b, 150fr, Acherontia atropos. c, 450fr, Danaus chrysippus. d, 75fr, Charaxes comoranus. e, 150fr, Euchloron megaera. f, 450fr, Papilio phorbanta. g, 75fr, Hypurgus ova. h, 150fr, Onthophagus catta. i, 450fr, Echinosoma bolivari.

1994 Litho. *Perf. 13½*

811 A142 Sheet of 3	12.00	6.00
a. Strip of 3	*4.00*	*2.00*
b. Strip of 3	*4.00*	*2.00*
c. Strip of 3	*4.00*	*2.00*
d. Souvenir sheet, #811a	*12.00*	*6.00*
e. Souvenir sheet, #811b	*12.00*	*6.00*
f. Souvenir sheet, #811c	*12.00*	*6.00*

Miniature Sheet

812 A142 Sheet of 9, #a.-i.	11.00	5.50
j. Souvenir sheet, #812a-812c	*12.00*	*6.00*
k. Souvenir sheet, #812d-812f	*12.00*	*6.00*
l. Souvenir sheet, #812g-812i	*12.00*	*6.00*

SEMI-POSTAL STAMPS

Anti-Malaria Issue

Common Design Type

Perf. 12½x12

1962, Apr. 7 Engr. Unwmk.

B1 CD108 25fr + 5fr brt pink	1.10	1.10

WHO drive to eradicate malaria.

Nurse Feeding Infant — SP1

Mother and Child — SP2

1967, July 3 **Engr.** ***Perf. 13***
B2 SP1 25fr + 5fr multi 75 75

For the Red Cross.

1974, Aug. 10 **Engr.** ***Perf. 13***
B3 SP2 35fr + 10fr red & dk brn 55 55

For the Red Cross.
For surcharge see No. 144.

Miniature Sheet

Space Achievements — SP3

World Philatelic Programs emblems (stamp collecting or Halley's Comet) and astronomer or satellite: a, Galileo. b, Copernicus. c, Kepler. d, Halley. e, *Planet A*, Japan, and 3 stars. f, *ICE*, US. g, *Planet A*, 5 stars. h, *Vega*, USSR.

1988 **Litho.** ***Perf. 13½***
B4 Sheet of 8 11.25 11.25
a.-h. SP3 200fr +10fr multi 1.40 1.40

See No. C193.

AIR POST STAMPS

Comoro Village — AP1

Comoro Men and Moroni Mosque — AP2

Design: 200fr, Mosque of Ouani, Anjouan.

1950-54 **Unwmk.** **Engr.** ***Perf. 13***
C1 AP1 50fr grn & red brn 1.40 65
C2 AP2 100fr dk brn & red 2.00 65
C3 AP1 200fr dk grn, rose brn & pur ('54) 8.00 4.00
Nos. C1-C3 (3) 11.40 5.30

Liberation Issue
Common Design Type

1954, June 6
C4 CD102 15fr sep & red 11.00 8.00

Madrepora Fructicosa — AP3

Design: 100fr, Coral, shells and sea anemones.

1962, Jan. 13 **Photo.** ***Perf. 12½x13***
C5 AP3 100fr multi 2.00 2.00
C6 AP3 500fr multi 8.00 7.50

Telstar Issue
Common Design Type

1962, Dec. 5 **Engr.** ***Perf. 13***
C7 CD111 25fr dp vio, dl pur & red lil 1.50 80

Type of Regular Issue, 1963
Unwmk.

1963, Dec. 27 **Engr.** ***Perf. 13***
Size: 26½x48mm
C8 A13 65fr Baskets 1.00 60
C9 A13 200fr Pendant 2.00 1.25

Boat Type of Regular Issue

1964, Aug. 7 **Photo.** ***Perf. 13***
Size: 27x48mm
C10 A14 50fr Mayotte pirogue 75 30
C11 A14 85fr Schooner 1.10 65

Olympic Torch and Boxers — AP4

Order of Star of Grand Comoro — AP5

1964, Oct. 10 **Engr.** ***Perf. 13***
C12 AP4 100fr red brn, dk brn & gray grn 1.25 1.25

18th Olympic Games, Tokyo, Oct. 10-25.

1964, Dec. 10 **Photo.** ***Perf. 13***
C13 AP5 500fr multi 5.50 3.25

ITU Issue
Common Design Type

1965, May 17 **Engr.** ***Perf. 13***
C14 CD120 50fr gray, grnsh bl & ol 4.25 3.75

French Satellite A-1 Issue
Common Design Type

Designs: 25fr, Diamant rocket and launching installations. 30fr, A-1 satellite.

1966, Jan. 17 **Engr.** ***Perf. 13***
C15 CD121 25fr dk pur & ultra 80 80
C16 CD121 30fr dk pur & ultra 1.25 1.25
a. Strip of 2, #C15-C16 + label 2.50 2.50

French Satellite D-1 Issue
Common Design Type

1966, May 16 **Engr.** ***Perf. 13***
C17 CD122 30fr dk grn, org & brn 90 60

Old Gun Battery, Dzaoudzi — AP6

Design: 200fr, Ksar Castle, Mutsamudu, vert.

1966, Dec. 19 **Photo.** ***Perf. 13***
C18 AP6 50fr multi 50 42
C19 AP6 200fr multi 1.75 1.00

Bird Type of Regular Issue

Birds: 75fr, Madagascar paradise flycatchers. 100fr, Blue-cheeked bee eaters.

1967, June 20 **Photo.** ***Perf. 13***
Size: 27x48mm
C20 A17 75fr yel grn & multi 90 32
C21 A17 100fr lt bl & multi 1.40 60

Woman Skier — AP7

1968, Apr. 29 **Engr.** ***Perf. 13***
C22 AP7 70fr brt grn, lt bl & choc 80 50

10th Winter Olympic Games, Grenoble, France, Feb. 6-18, 1968.

Fish Type of Regular Issue

Designs: 50fr, Moorish idol. 90fr, Diagramma lineatus.

1968, Aug. 1 **Engr.** ***Perf. 13***
Size: 47½x27mm
C23 A19 50fr plum blk & yel 65 60
C24 A19 90fr brt grn, yel & gray grn 1.10 90

For surcharge and overprint see Nos. C52, C74.

Swimmer, Butterfly Stroke — AP8

1969, Jan. 27 **Photo.** ***Perf. 12½***
C25 AP8 65fr ver, grnsh bl & blk 90 65

Issued to commemorate the 19th Olympic Games, Mexico City, Oct. 12-27.

Flower Type of Regular Issue, 1969.

Designs: 50fr, Heliconia sp., vert. 85fr, Tuberose, vert. 200fr, Orchid (angraecum eburneum), vert.

1969, Mar. 20 **Photo.** ***Perf. 13***
Size: 27x48mm
C26 A21 50fr gray & multi 65 50
C27 A21 85fr multi 1.00 65
C28 A21 200fr dk red & multi 1.75 1.25
Nos. C26-C28 (3) 3.40 2.40

Concorde Issue
Common Design Type

1969, Apr. 17 **Engr.**
C29 CD129 100fr pur & brn org 3.75 3.00

View of EXPO, Globe and Moon — AP9

Design: 90fr, Geisha, map of Japan and EXPO emblem.

1970, Sept. 13 **Photo.** ***Perf. 13***
C30 AP9 60fr slate & multi 60 40
C31 AP9 90fr multi 60 40

EXPO '70 International Exposition, Osaka, Japan, Mar. 15-Sept. 13.

Sunset over Mutsamudu — AP10

Map of Archipelago — AP11

Designs: 20fr, Sada Village, Mayotte. 65fr, Old Iconi Palace, Grand Comoro. 85fr, Nioumatchoua Island, Moheli.

1971, May 3 **Photo.** ***Perf. 13***
C32 AP10 15fr dk bl & multi 15 15
C33 AP10 20fr multi 22 15
C34 AP10 65fr grn & multi 45 22
C35 AP10 85fr bl & multi 55 30

Engr.

C36 AP11 100fr brn red, grn & vio bl 1.00 50
Nos. C32-C36 (5) 2.37 1.32

See Nos. 107-110, C45-C49, C53, C62-C64. For overprints and surcharges see Nos. 143, C69, C71, C73, C76-C77, C79-C80, C82, C84.

Flower Type of Regular Issue

Flowers: 60fr, Hibiscus schizopetalus. 85fr, Acalypha sanderii.

1971, July 19 **Photo.** ***Perf. 13***
Size: 27x48mm
C37 A25 60fr grn, ver & yel 60 30
C38 A25 85fr grn, red & yel 75 45

For surcharge see No. C75.

Mural, Moroni Airport — AP12

Designs: 85fr, Mural in Arrival Hall, Moroni Airport. 100fr, View of Moroni Airport.

1972, Mar. 30 **Photo.** ***Perf. 13***
C39 AP12 65fr gray & multi 32 28
C40 AP12 85fr gray & multi 48 28

Engr.

C41 AP12 100fr brn, bl & slate grn 80 40
Nos. C39-C41 (3) 1.60 96

New airport in Moroni.

Eiffel Tower and Moroni Telephone Exchange — AP13

Design: 75fr, Frenchman and Comoro Islander talking on telephone, radio tower and beacons.

1972, Apr. 24

C42	AP13 35fr dl red & gray	18	15
C43	AP13 75fr dk car, vio & bl	35	18

First radio-telephone connection between France and Comoro Islands.

Underwater Spear-fishing — AP14

1972, July 5 Engr. *Perf. 13*

C44	AP14 70fr vio bl, brt grn & mar	55	40

For surcharge see No. C78.

Types of 1971

1972, Nov. 15 Photo.

Designs: 20fr, Cape Sima. 35fr, Bambao Palace. 40fr, Domoni Palace. 60fr, Gomajou Peninsula. 100fr, Map of Anjouan Island.

C45	AP10 20fr brn & multi	15	15
C46	AP10 35fr dk grn & multi	22	18
C47	AP10 40fr bl & multi	28	20
C48	AP10 60fr grnsh blk & multi	38	30
	Engr.		
C49	AP11 100fr mar, bl & sl grn	75	50
	Nos. C45-C49 (5)	1.78	1.33

Pres. Said Mohamed Cheikh (1904-70) — AP15

1973, Mar. 16 Photo. *Perf. 13*

C50	AP15 20fr multi	15	15
C51	AP15 35fr multi	25	15

For overprints see Nos. C70, C72.

No. C24 Surcharged

120F

Mission Internationale pour l'étude du Cœlacanthe

1973, Apr. 30 Engr. *Perf. 13*

C52	A19 120fr on 90fr multi	85	65

Intl. Commission for Coelacanth Studies.

Map of Grand Comoro AP16

1973, June 28 Engr. *Perf. 13*

C53	AP16 135fr vio, bl & dk brn	1.25	80

See Nos. C65, C68. For surcharges see Nos. C90-C92.

Karthala Volcano AP17

1973, July 16 Photo. *Perf. 13x12½*

C54	AP17 120fr multi	85	65

Eruption of Karthala, Sept. 1972.
For surcharge see No. C89.

Armauer G. Hansen — AP18

Design: 150fr, Nicolaus Copernicus (1473-1543), Polish astronomer.

1973, Sept. 5 Engr. *Perf. 13*

C55	AP18 100fr brn, dk bl & sl grn	85	65
C56	AP18 150fr grnsh bl, vio bl & choc	1.25	75

Cent. of the discovery of the Hansen bacillus, the cause of leprosy.
For overprint and surcharge see Nos. C81, C93.

Pablo Picasso (1881-1973) AP19

1983, Sept. 30 Photo.

C57	AP19 200fr blk & multi	1.40	1.00

Souvenir Sheet

C58	AP19 100fr blk & multi	90	90

For overprint see No. C87.

Order of the Star of Anjouan — AP20

Said Omar ben Soumeth — AP21

1974, Jan. 7 Photo. *Perf. 13*

C59	AP20 500fr brn, bl & gold	3.00	2.50

For overprint see No. C95.

Perf. 13x13½, 13½x13

1974, Jan. 31

Design: 135fr, Grand Mufti Said Omar, horiz.

C60	AP21 135fr blk & multi	80	65
C61	AP21 200fr blk & multi	1.40	1.00

For overprint and surcharge see Nos. C85, C88.

Types of 1971-73

Designs (Views on Mayotte): 20fr, Moya Beach. 35fr, Chiconi. 90fr, Port Mamutzu. 120fr, Map of Mayotte.

1974, Aug. 31 Photo. *Perf. 13*

C62	AP10 20fr bl & multi	15	15
C63	AP10 35fr grn & multi	25	20
C64	AP10 90fr multi	60	50
	Engr.		
C65	AP16 120fr ultra & grn	75	60
	Nos. C62-C65 (4)	1.75	1.45

Jet Take-off — AP22

1975, Jan. 10 Engr. *Perf. 13*

C66	AP22 135fr multi	90	65

First direct route Moroni-Hahaya-Paris.
For surcharge see No. C86.

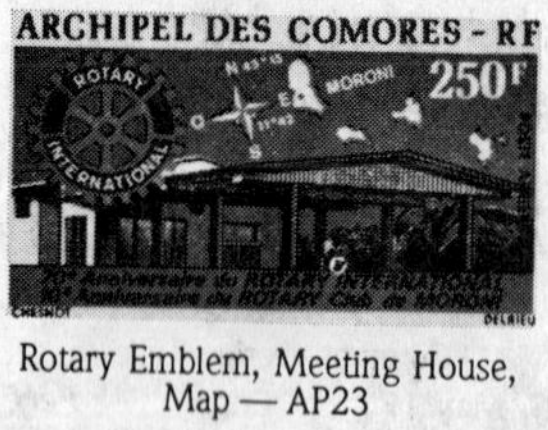

Rotary Emblem, Meeting House, Map — AP23

1975, Feb. 23 Photo. *Perf. 13*

C67	AP23 250fr multi	1.65	1.25

Rotary Intl., 70th anniv., Moroni Rotary Club, 10th anniv.
For surcharge see No. C94.

Map Type of 1973

Design: 230fr, Map of Moheli, horiz.

1975, May 26 Engr. *Perf. 13*

C68	AP16 230fr ocher, ol grn & bl	1.65	1.25

STATE OF COMORO

Issues of 1968-75 Surcharged and Overprinted with Bars and: "ETAT COMORIEN" in Black, Silver, Red or Orange

1975 Printing & Perfs. as Before

C69	AP10 10fr on 20fr #C62	15	15
C70	AP15 20fr (S)	20	15
C71	AP10 30fr on 35fr (R) #C63	25	20
C72	AP15 35fr (S)	30	22
C73	AP10 40fr (O)	38	25
C74	A19 50fr	45	30
C75	A25 75fr on 60fr	70	45
C76	AP10 75fr on 60fr	70	45
C77	AP10 75fr on 65fr (O)	70	45
C78	AP14 75fr on 70fr	70	45
C79	AP11 100fr #C36	90	60
C80	AP11 100fr #C49	90	60
C81	AP18 100fr	90	60
C82	AP10 100fr on 85fr (O)	90	60
C83	A25 100fr on 85fr	90	60
C84	AP10 100fr on 90fr	90	60
C85	AP21 100fr on 135fr (S)	90	60
C86	AP22 100fr on 135fr	90	60
C87	AP19 200fr (S)	1.75	1.25
C88	AP21 200fr (S)	1.75	1.25
C89	AP17 200fr on 120fr	1.75	1.25
C90	AP16 200fr on 120fr	1.75	1.25
C91	AP16 200fr on 135fr	1.75	1.25
C92	AP16 200fr on 230fr	1.75	1.25
C93	AP18 400fr on 150fr	4.00	2.50
C94	AP23 400fr on 250fr	4.00	2.50
C95	AP20 500fr	4.50	3.25
	Nos. C69-C95 (27)	34.73	23.62

See postage section for airmail stamps that are part of joint postage/airmail sets.

Rotary Emblem, Landscape AP26

1979, July 31 Litho. *Perf. 13x12½*

C107	AP26 400fr multi	3.00	1.65

Rotary International.

IYC Emblem, Mother and Child — AP27

1979, July 31 *Perf. 13x13½*

C108	AP27 250fr multi	1.65	1.25

Intl. Year of the Child. See No. CB1. For surcharges see Nos. C121, C202.

Dimadjou Dispensary, Map of Southern Africa, Emblem AP28

1980, Feb. 23 Litho. *Perf. 12½*

C109	AP28 100fr shown	50	30
C110	AP28 260fr Globe, Concorde, emblem	1.40	65

Rotary International, 75th anniv. and Moroni Rotary Club, 15th anniv. (100fr).
For surcharges see Nos. C119-C120.

First Transatlantic Flight, 50th Anniversary — AP29

1980, May 30 Litho. *Perf. 13*

C111	AP29 200fr multi	1.00	70

No. C111 Surcharged in Blue

1981, Feb. Litho. *Perf. 13*

C112	AP29	30fr on 200fr multi	20	20

The Dove and the Rainbow, by Picasso — AP30

Picasso Birth Centenary: 70fr, Still Life on a Sideboard. 150fr, Studio with Plaster Head. 250fr, Bowl and Pot, vert. 500fr, The Red Tablecloth.

1981, June 30 Litho. *Perf. 12½*

C113	AP30	40fr multi	16	15
C114	AP30	70fr multi	25	15
C115	AP30	150fr multi	65	35
C116	AP30	250fr multi	1.10	55
C117	AP30	500fr multi	2.00	1.10
		Nos. C113-C117 (5)	4.16	2.30

For surcharge see No. C118.

#C114, C109-C110, CB1 Surchd.

1981, Nov. Litho. *Perf. 12½, 13*

C118	AP30	10fr on 70fr multi	15	15
C119	AP28	10fr on 100fr multi	15	15
C120	AP28	50fr on 260fr multi	20	15
C121	AP27	50fr on 200fr+30fr multi	20	15
		Set value	54	32

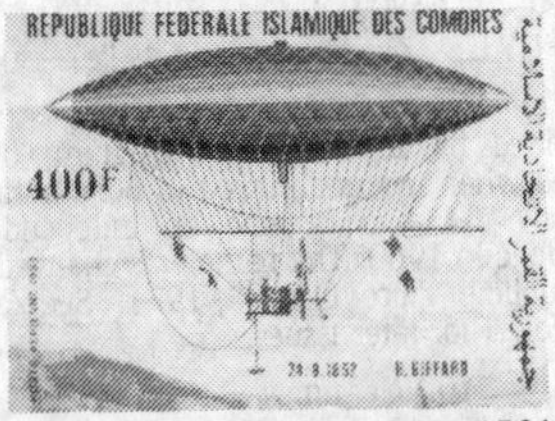

Manned Flight Bicentenary — AP31

Balloons. 100fr, 200fr, 300fr, 500fr vert.

1983, Apr. 20 Litho. *Perf. 13*

C122	AP31	100fr Montgolfiere, 1783	40	20
C123	AP31	200fr Lunardi, 1784	80	40
C124	AP31	300fr Blanchard and Jeffries, 1785	1.10	60
C125	AP31	400fr Giffard, 1852	1.60	80
		Nos. C122-C125 (4)	3.90	2.00

Souvenir Sheet

C126	AP31	500fr Paris Siege, 1870	2.00	1.00

For overprint see No. 602.

Pre-Olympic Year Sailing — AP32

1983, June 30 Litho. *Perf. 13*

C127	AP32	150fr Type 470	60	30
C128	AP32	200fr Flying Dutchman	80	40
C129	AP32	300fr Type 470, diff.	1.10	60
C130	AP32	400fr Finn	1.60	75
		Nos. C127-C130 (4)	4.10	1.85

Souvenir Sheet

C131	AP32	500fr Solding	2.25	1.10

For overprint and surcharge see Nos. 603, C206.

1984 Summer Olympics — AP33

1984, July 10 Litho. *Perf. 13*

C132	AP33	60fr Basketball	25	15
C133	AP33	100fr Basketball, diff.	40	20
C134	AP33	165fr Basketball, diff.	65	35
C135	AP33	175fr Baseball, horiz.	70	35
C136	AP33	200fr Baseball, horiz.	80	40
		Nos. C132-C136 (5)	2.80	1.45

Souvenir Sheet

C137	AP33	500fr Basketball, diff.	2.00	1.00

Nos. C132-C134 vert.

Development Conference — AP34

1984, July 2 Litho. *Perf. 13*

C138	AP34	475fr Tools for development	1.60	

Audubon Bicentenary — AP35

1985, Jan. 15 Litho. *Perf. 13*

C139	AP35	100fr Hirundo rustica, vert.	28	
C140	AP35	125fr Icterus galbula, vert.	35	
C141	AP35	150fr Buteo lineatus	40	
C142	AP35	500fr Sphyropicus varius	1.40	
		Nos. C139-C142 (4)	2.43	

Moroni Port Missile Defense — AP36

Design: No. C146, Ngome Ntsoudjini Scout troop.

1985, May 20 Litho. *Perf. 13x12½*

C145	AP36	200fr multi	55	
C146	AP36	200fr multi	55	

PHILEXAFRICA '85, Lome. Nos. C145-C146 printed se-tenant with center labels picturing map of Africa or UAPT emblem.

For surcharges see Nos. C207-C208.

Natl. Flag, Sun, Outline Map of Islands — AP37

1985, July 6

C147	AP37	10fr multi	15	
C148	AP37	15fr multi	15	
C149	AP37	125fr multi	35	
C150	AP37	300fr multi	75	
		Nos. C147-C150 (4)	1.40	

Natl. independence, 10th anniv.

Runners — AP38

1985, Nov. 12

C151	AP38	250fr shown	65	
C152	AP38	250fr Mining	65	

PHILEXAFRICA '85, Lome, Togo, Nov. 16-24. Nos. C151-C152 printed se-tenant with center label picturing map of Africa or UAPT emblem.

For surcharges see Nos. C204-C205.

Air Transport Union, UTA, 50th Anniv. — AP39

1985, Dec. 30 Litho. *Perf. 13*

C153	AP39	25fr F-AOUL seaplane	15	15
C154	AP39	75fr Camel driver, DC-9	20	15
C155	AP39	100fr Noratlas and Heron DC-4s	35	16
a.		Souv. sheet of 3, #C153-C155, perf. 12½	55	55
C156	AP39	125fr UTA cargo plane	42	22

Size: 40x52mm

Perf. 12½x13

C157	AP39	1000fr Aircraft, 1935-1985	3.75	1.75
a.		Souv. sheet of 2, #C156-C157, perf. 12½	3.25	3.25
		Nos. C153-C157 (5)	4.87	2.43

Halley's Comet — AP40

Comets, astronomers and probes.

1986, Mar. 7 *Perf. 13*

C158	AP40	125fr Edmond Halley, Giotto probe	65	32
C159	AP40	150fr Giacobini-Zinner, 1959	80	40
C160	AP40	225fr Encke, 1961	1.25	60
C161	AP40	300fr Bradfield, 1980	1.65	80
C162	AP40	450fr Planet A probe	2.50	1.25
		Nos. C158-C162 (5)	6.85	3.37

1986 World Cup Soccer Championships, Mexico — AP41

Various soccer plays.

1986, June 11 Litho. *Perf. 13*

C163	AP41	125fr multi	70	35
C164	AP41	210fr multi	1.25	60
C165	AP41	500fr multi	2.75	1.40
C166	AP41	600fr multi	3.50	1.10
		Nos. C163-C166 (4)	8.20	3.45

Tennis at the 1988 Summer Olympics — AP42

Various players.

1987, Jan. 28 Litho. *Perf. 13½*

C167	AP42	150fr multi	82	40
C168	AP42	250fr multi	1.40	70
C169	AP42	500fr multi	2.75	1.40
C170	AP42	600fr multi	3.25	1.65
		Nos. C167-C170 (4)	8.22	4.15

For overprints and surcharge see Nos. C183-C186, C203.

World Wildlife Fund — AP43

Various pictures of the mongoose lemur.

1987, Feb. 18 *Perf. 13*

C171	AP43	75fr multi, vert.	40	20
C172	AP43	100fr multi	55	28
C173	AP43	125fr multi	70	35
C174	AP43	150fr multi	82	40
		Nos. C171-C174 (4)	2.47	1.23

1988 Winter Olympics, Calgary AP44

1987, Apr. 10 Litho. *Perf. 13½*

C175	AP44	150fr Slalom	82	40
C176	AP44	225fr Ski jumping	1.25	62
C177	AP44	500fr Women's giant slalom	2.75	1.40
C178	AP44	600fr Luge	3.25	1.65
		Nos. C175-C178 (4)	8.07	4.07

AP45

Aviation History AP46

Designs: 200fr, Inventors Didier Daurat and Raymond Vanier with 1935 Air Blue F-ANR1. 300fr, Farman biplane, 1st scheduled airmail delivery, Paris-LeMans-St. Nazaire, Aug. 17, 1918. 500fr, Bleriot aircraft, 1st scheduled airmail delivery, Vilacoublay-Vendome-Poitiers-Pauillac, Oct. 15, 1913. 1000fr, Henri Pequet and his aircraft, Feb. 18, 1911.

1987, Dec. 29 Litho. *Perf. 13*

C179	AP45	200fr multi	1.30	65
C180	AP45	300fr multi	1.95	1.00
C181	AP45	500fr multi	3.25	1.65

Perf. 12½x13

C182	AP46	1000fr multi	6.50	3.25
		Nos. C179-C182 (4)	13.00	6.55

Airmail history exposition, Allahabad.

Nos. C167-C170 Ovptd. in Red for 1988 Olympic Tennis Champions

Overprint includes name of athlete and "Medaille d'or / Seoul" or "Medaille / d'argent / Seoul."

1988, Nov. Litho. *Perf. 13½*

C183	AP42	150fr	"Miloslav Mecir / (Tchec.)"	95	48
C184	AP42	250fr	"Tim Mayotte / (U.S.A.)"	1.60	80
C185	AP42	500fr	"Steffi Graf / (R.F.A.)"	3.25	1.60
C186	AP42	600fr	"Gabriela Sabatini / (Argentine)"	3.85	1.95
			Nos. C183-C186 (4)	9.65	4.83

Early Aviators and Aircraft — AP47

Designs: 100fr, Alberto Santos-Dumont (1873-1932), and *Bagatelle*, 1st documented power flight in Europe, Oct. 23, 1906. 150fr, Wright Brothers and *Flyer A*. 200fr, Louis Bleriot (1872-1936) and *Bleriot XI*, 1st crossing of the English Channel in a heavier-than-air craft, July 25, 1909. 300fr, Henri Farman (1874-1958) and Voisin biplane, 1st fixed-route 1-kilometer circular flight, Jan. 13, 1908. 500fr, Gabriel (1880-1973) and Charles (1882-1912) Voisin, established 1st biplane factory (1908), and Voisin biplane. 800fr, Roland Garros (1888-1918), 1st trans-Mediterranean flight, Sept. 23, 1913.

1988, Dec. 7 Litho. *Perf. 13*

C187	AP47	100fr pur	65	32
C188	AP47	150fr brt lil rose	95	48
C189	AP47	200fr blk	1.30	65
C190	AP47	300fr dark yel org	1.90	95
C191	AP47	500fr dark blue	3.20	1.60
C192	AP47	800fr lt olive grn	5.10	2.55
		Nos. C187-C192 (6)	13.10	6.55

For surcharge see No. C209.

Souvenir Sheet

Space Achievements — AP48

Design: World Philatelic Programs stamp collecting emblem, Soviet satellite and Edmond Halley.

1988 Litho. *Perf. 13½*

C193	AP48	750fr multi	5.00	5.00

Nos. C108, C168, C151-C152, C128, C145-C146 and C189 Surcharged

1989 Litho. *Perfs. as Before*

C202	AP27	5fr on 250fr	#C108	15	15
C203	AP42	25fr on 250fr	#C168	18	15
C204	AP38	50fr on 250fr	#C151	35	18
C205	AP38	50fr on 250fr	#C152	35	18
C206	AP32	150fr on 200fr	#C128	1.05	52
C207	AP36	150fr on 200fr	#C145	1.05	52
C208	AP36	150fr on 200fr	#C146	1.05	52
C209	AP47	150fr on 200fr	#C189	1.05	52
		Nos. C202-C209 (8)		5.23	2.74

Nos. C204-C205 and C207-C208 printed se-tenant with labels between.

World Cup Soccer, Championships, Italy — AP50

Various soccer plays and map of Italy.

1990, June Litho. *Perf. 13*

C210	AP50	75fr multicolored	60	30
C211	AP50	150fr multicolored	1.20	60
C212	AP50	500fr multicolored	3.75	1.90
C213	AP50	1000fr multicolored	8.00	4.00
		Nos. C210-C213 (4)	13.55	6.80

Souvenir Sheet

Garry Kasparov, Anatoly Karpov, Russian Chess Champions — AP51

Litho. & Embossed

1991, Aug. 5 *Perf. 13½*

C214	AP51	1500fr gold & multi		

World Chess Championships.

1992 Summer Olympics, Barcelona AP52

Litho. & Embossed

1992, July 28 *Perf. 13½*

C215	AP52	1500fr gold & multi	24.00	12.00

AIR POST SEMI-POSTAL STAMP

Type of Air Post 1979

Design: IYC emblem, mother and son.

1979, July 31 Litho. *Perf. 13½x13*

CB1	AP27	200fr + 30fr multi	1.10	1.10

International Year of the Child.
For surcharge see No. C121.

POSTAGE DUE STAMPS

Anjouan Mosque D1

Coelacanth D2

1950 Unwmk. Engr. *Perf. 14x13*

J1	D1	50c deep green	20	20
J2	D1	1fr black brown	20	20

1954

J3	D2	5fr dk brown & green	28	28
J4	D2	10fr gray & red brown	38	38
J5	D2	20fr indigo & blue	60	60
		Nos. J3-J5 (3)	1.26	1.26

Hibiscus — D3

Designs: 2fr, 15fr, 40fr, 50fr, vertical.

1977, Nov. 19 Litho. *Perf. 13½*

J6	D3	1fr shown	15	15
J7	D3	2fr Pineapple	15	15
J8	D3	5fr White butterfly	15	15
J9	D3	10fr Chameleon	15	15
J10	D3	15fr Blooming banana	15	15
J11	D3	20fr Orchids	15	15
J12	D3	30fr Allamanda cathartica	15	15
J13	D3	40fr Cashews	15	15
J14	D3	50fr Custard apple	16	15
J15	D3	100fr Breadfruit	35	16
J16	D3	200fr Vanilla	65	35
J17	D3	500fr Ylang ylang	1.60	80
		Set value	3.35	1.80

OFFICIAL STAMPS

Comoro Flag — O1

Perf. 13x12½

1979-85 Litho. Unwmk.

O1	O1	5fr multi	15	15
O2	O1	10fr multi	15	15
O3	O1	20fr multi	15	15
O4	O1	30fr multi	18	15
O5	O1	40fr multi	25	16
O6	O1	60fr multi ('80)	22	16
O7	O1	75fr multi ('85)	20	15
O8	O1	100fr multi	50	35
		Nos. O1-O8 (8)	1.80	
		Set value		1.00

See Nos. 526-530.

Pres. Said Mohamed Cheikh (1904-1970) — O2

1980-85

O9	O2	100fr multi	35	25
O10	O2	125fr multi ('85)	35	22
O11	O2	400fr multi	1.40	1.00
		Nos. O9-O11 (3)	2.10	1.47

CONGO DEMOCRATIC REPUBLIC

LOCATION — Central Africa
GOVT. — Republic
AREA — 895,348 sq. mi. (estimated)
POP. — 22,480,000 (est. 1971)
CAPITAL — Kinshasa (Leopoldville)

Congo was an independent state, founded by Leopold II of Belgium, until 1908 when it was annexed to Belgium as a colony. Congo became an independent republic in 1960. The name was changed to Republic of Zaire, Oct. 28, 1971. See Zaire in Vol. 5 for later issues.

100 Centimes = 1 Franc
100 Sengi = 1 Li-Kuta,
100 Ma-Kuta = 1 Zaire (1967)

Catalogue values for all unused stamps in this country are for Never Hinged items.

Belgian Congo Flower Issue of 1952-53 Overprinted or Surcharged **CONGO**

Perf. 11½

1960, June 6 Photo. Unwmk.

Flowers in Natural Colors

Size: 21x25½mm

Granite Paper

323	A86	10c dp plum & ocher	15	15
324	A86	10c on 15c red & yel grn	15	15
325	A86	20c grn & gray	15	15
326	A86	40c grn & sal	15	15
327	A86	50c on 60c bl grn & pink	15	15
328	A86	50c on 75c dp plum & gray	15	15
329	A86	1fr car & yel	15	15
330	A86	1.50fr vio & ap grn	15	15
331	A86	2fr ol grn & buff	15	15
332	A86	3fr ol grn & pink	15	15
333	A86	4fr choc & lil	15	15
334	A86	5fr dp plum & lt bl grn	15	15
335	A86	6.50fr dk car & lil	22	15
336	A86	8fr grn & lt yel	32	15
337	A86	10fr dp plum & pale ol	45	15
338	A86	20fr vio bl & dl sal	90	35

Overprinted **CONGO**

Size: 22x32mm

339	A86	50fr dp plum & gray bl	4.75	2.25
340	A86	100fr grn & buff	8.25	4.00
		Nos. 323-340 (18)	16.69	8.85

Nos. 324, 327-328 exist without "CONGO" overprint but with surcharge.

Belgian Congo Animal Issue, Nos. 306-317, Overprinted or Surcharged in Red, Blue, Black or Brown

CONGO

341	A92	10c	bl & brn (R)	15	15
342	A93	20c	red org & sl (Bl)	15	15
343	A92	40c	brn & bl (Bk)	15	15
344	A93	50c	brt ultra, red & sep (R)	15	15
345	A92	1fr	brn, grn & blk (Br)	15	15
346	A93	1.50fr	blk & org yel (R)	15	15
347	A92	2fr	crim, blk & brn (Bl)	15	15
348	A93	3.50fr	on 3fr blk, gray & lil rose (Bk)	15	15
349	A92	5fr	brn, dk brn & brt grn (Br)	15	15
350	A93	6.50fr	bl, brn & org yel (R)	18	15
a.			Black overprint	32	15
351	A92	8fr	org brn, ol bis & lil (Br)	20	15
352	A93	10fr	multi (R)	30	15
			Set value	1.40	90

Same Overprint on Belgian Congo No. 318

1960

353	A94	50c	gldn brn, ocher & red brn	40	40

Same Overprint and Surcharge of New Value on Belgian Congo Nos. 321-322

Inscription in French

354	A95	3.50fr	on 3fr gray & red	40	32

Inscription in Flemish

355	A95	3.50fr	on 3fr gray & red	40	32
			Nos. 353-355 (3)	1.20	1.04

Map of Congo A93a

1960 Photo. *Perf. 11½*

356	A93a	20c	brown	15	15
357	A93a	50c	rose red	15	15
358	A93a	1fr	green	15	15
359	A93a	1.50fr	red brn	15	15
360	A93a	2fr	rose car	15	15
361	A93a	3.50fr	lilac	15	15
362	A93a	5fr	brt bl	15	15
363	A93a	6.50fr	gray	20	15
364	A93a	10fr	orange	32	15
365	A93a	20fr	ultra	50	24
			Set value	1.70	90

Congo's Independence.
For overprints see Nos. 371-380.

Flag, People and Broken Chain — A94

1961 Unwmk. *Perf. 11½*

Flag in Blue and Yellow

366	A94	2fr	rose vio	15	15
367	A94	3.50fr	vermilion	15	15
368	A94	6.50fr	yel brn	15	15
369	A94	10fr	brt grn	24	15
370	A94	20fr	car rose	42	30
			Nos. 366-370 (5)	1.11	
			Set value		62

Signing of the Independence Agreement by Belgium, Jan. 4, 1959.

Nos. 356-365 Overprinted in Blue, Black or Red: "Conference Coquilhatville Avril Mai 1961"

1961

371	A93a	20c	brn (Bl)	40	40
372	A93a	50c	rose red (Bk)	40	40
373	A93a	1fr	grn (R)	40	40
374	A93a	1.50fr	red brn (Bl)	40	40
375	A93a	2fr	rose car (Bk)	40	40
376	A93a	3.50fr	lil (Bl)	40	40
377	A93a	5fr	brt bl (R)	40	40
378	A93a	6.50fr	gray (R)	40	40
379	A93a	10fr	org (Bk)	40	40
380	A93a	20fr	ultra (R)	40	40
			Nos. 371-380 (10)	4.00	4.00

Coquilhatville Conf., Apr.-May, 1961.

Pres. Joseph Kasavubu A95

Kasavubu and Map of Congo A96

Design: 10fr, 20fr, 50fr, 100fr, Kasavubu in uniform and map.

Perf. 11½

1961, June 30 Unwmk. Photo.

Portrait and Inscription in Dark Brown

381	A95	10c	yellow	15	15
382	A95	20c	dp rose	15	15
383	A95	40c	bl grn	15	15
384	A95	50c	salmon	15	15
385	A95	1fr	lilac	15	15
386	A95	1.50fr	lt brn	15	15
387	A95	2fr	brt grn	15	15
388	A96	3.50fr	rose pink	15	15
389	A96	5fr	gray	1.10	15
390	A96	6.50fr	ultra	30	15
391	A96	8fr	olive	52	15
392	A95	10fr	lt vio	70	15
393	A95	20fr	orange	70	15
394	A95	50fr	lt bl	1.10	30
395	A95	100fr	ap grn	1.65	50
			Nos. 381-395 (15)	7.27	
			Set value		1.96

First anniversary of independence.

Nos. 381-387, 389 and 392 Overprinted: "REOUVERTURE du PARLEMENT JUILLET 1961"

1961

Portrait and Inscription in Dark Brown

396	A95	10c	yellow	15	15
397	A95	20c	dp rose	15	15
398	A95	40c	bl grn	15	15
399	A95	50c	salmon	28	20
400	A95	1fr	lilac	28	20
401	A95	1.50fr	lt brn	70	60
402	A95	2fr	brt grn	70	60
403	A96	5fr	gray	70	60
404	A95	10fr	lt vio	85	70
			Nos. 396-404 (9)	3.96	3.35

Congolese parliament re-opening, July, 1961.

Dag Hammarskjold and Map of Africa with Congo — A97

Malaria Eradication Emblem and Mosquito — A98

1962, Jan. 20 Photo. *Perf. 11½*

Gray Background

405	A97	10c	dk brn	15	15
406	A97	20c	Prus bl	15	15
407	A97	30c	brown	15	15
408	A97	40c	dk bl	15	15
409	A97	50c	brn red	15	15
410	A97	3fr	ol grn	1.65	1.10
411	A97	6.50fr	dk vio	55	35
412	A97	8fr	red brn	65	45
			Nos. 405-412 (8)	3.60	
			Set value		2.20

Souvenir Sheets

Imperf

413	A97	25fr	blk brn	2.75	2.75
a.			Overprint in green	1.00	1.00

Nos. 405-413 issued in memory of Dag Hammarskjold, Secretary General of the United Nations, 1953-61.

No 413a is overprinted "30 Juin 1962" on stamp and "2eme Anniversaire de l'Independance" on sheet margin. Issued June 30, 1962.

For overprints see Nos. 417-424.

1962, June 15

Granite Paper

414	A98	1.50fr	yel, blk & dk red	15	15
415	A98	2fr	yel grn, brn & bl grn	28	15
416	A98	6.50fr	ultra, blk & mar	15	15
			Set value	48	30

WHO drive to eradicate malaria.

Nos. 405-412 Overprinted in Blue, Purple, Black or Carmine

"Paix, Travail, Austerite ..
C. ADOULA
11 juillet 1962

1962, Oct. 15

Gray Background

417	A97	10c	dk brn (Bl)	15	15
418	A97	20c	Prus bl (P)	15	15
419	A97	30c	brn (Bk)	15	15
420	A97	40c	dk bl (C)	15	15
421	A97	50c	brn red (Bl)	1.10	50
422	A97	3fr	ol grn (P)	15	15
423	A97	6.50fr	dk vio (Bk)	20	15
424	A97	8fr	red brn (C)	28	15
			Set value	2.00	95

Reorganization of Adoula administration.

Canceled to Order

Starting in 1963, values in the used column are for "canceled to order" stamps. Postally used copies sell for much more.

A99

1963, Jan. 28 Engr. *Perf. 10½x13*

425	A99	2fr	dull purple	90	1.00
426	A99	4fr	red	15	15
427	A99	7fr	dark blue	15	15
428	A99	20fr	slate green	20	15
			Nos. 425-428 (4)	1.40	1.45

Congo's 1st participation at the UPU Cong., New Delhi, Mar. 1963.

For overprints see Nos. 468-471.

Shoebill — A100

Birds: 10c, Pelicans. 20c, Crested guinea fowl, horiz. 30c, Openbill. 40c, White-bellied storks, horiz. 2fr, Marabou. 3fr, Greater flamingos, horiz. 4fr, Congolese peacock. 5fr, Hartlaub ducks, horiz. 6fr, Secretary bird. 7fr, Black-casqued hornbill, horiz. 8fr, Sacred ibis and nest. 10fr, Crowned crane, horiz. 20fr, Saddle-bill stork, horiz.

1963 Unwmk. Photo. *Perf. 11½*

429	A100	10c	pink, ultra & ocher	15	15
430	A100	20c	rose red, bl & blk	15	15
431	A100	30c	grn, ocher & blk	15	15
432	A100	40c	gray, org & blk	15	15
433	A100	1fr	brn, emer & gray	15	15
434	A100	2fr	gray, red & ind	1.10	32
435	A100	3fr	ol grn, blk & rose	15	15
436	A100	4fr	car rose, vio bl & grn	15	15
437	A100	5fr	lake, lt bl & blk	15	15
438	A100	6fr	pur, yel & blk	1.10	32
439	A100	7fr	bl grn, blk & ind	15	15
440	A100	8fr	yel, org & blk	15	15
441	A100	10fr	bl, blk & rose	15	15
442	A100	20fr	cit, red & blk	15	15
			Set value	3.35	1.30

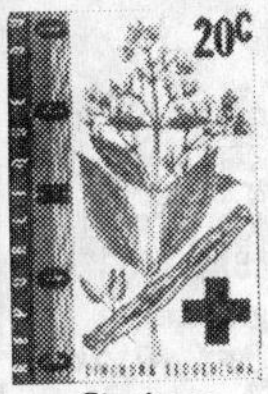

Cinchona Ledgeriana A101

Red Cross Nurse A102

Designs: 10c, 30c, 5fr, Strophanthus sarmentosus.

Perf. 12½x13½, 13½x12½

1963, May 25 Engr. Unwmk.

Cross in Red

443	A101	10c	vio & dl grn	15	15
444	A101	20c	magenta & bl	15	15
445	A101	30c	grn & org	15	15
446	A101	40c	bl & vio	15	15
447	A101	5fr	ol & rose claret	15	15
448	A101	7fr	org & blk	15	15
449	A102	9fr	gray olive & red	15	15
450	A102	20fr	purple & red	1.10	65
			Set value	1.55	1.00

International Red Cross centenary.

A souvenir sheet of three contains imperf. 58fr, 7fr, and 20fr stamps similar to Nos. 447, 448 and 450, but in changed colors. Size: 109x75mm. Value $10.

Men Joining Hands and Map of Congo — A103

1963, June 29 Photo. *Perf. 11½*

451	A103	4fr	multi	85	30
452	A103	5fr	multi	15	15
453	A103	9fr	multi	15	15
454	A103	12fr	multi	18	15
			Nos. 451-454 (4)	1.33	
			Set value		50

Issued to celebrate national reconciliation.

Bulldozer and Kabambare Sewer, Leopoldville — A104

Designs: 30c, 5fr, 12fr, Excavator and blueprint. 50c, 9fr, Building Ituri road.

1963, July 1 Engr. Unwmk.

455	A104	20c	multi	15	15
456	A104	30c	multi	15	15
457	A104	50c	multi	15	15
458	A104	3fr	multi	85	32
459	A104	5fr	multi	15	15
460	A104	9fr	multi	15	15
461	A104	12fr	multi	15	15
			Set value	1.35	72

Issued to publicize aid to Congo by the European Economic Community.

Leopoldville Airport N'Djili A105

Design: 5fr, 7fr, 50fr, Tail assembly and airport.

1963, Nov. 30 Photo. *Perf. 11½*

462	A105	2fr	gray, yel & red brn	15	15
463	A105	5fr	mag, vio & yel	15	15
464	A105	6fr	bl, yel & dk brn	85	35
465	A105	7fr	multi	22	15
466	A105	30fr	lil, yel & ol	35	24
467	A105	50fr	multi	40	25
			Nos. 462-467 (6)	2.12	1.29

Issued to publicize Air Congo.

For surcharge see No. 606.

Nos. 425-428 Overprinted with Silver Frame on Three Sides and Black Inscription: "15e anniversaire / 10 DECEMBRE 1948 / DROITS DE L'HOMME / 10 DECEMBRE 1963"

Engraved and Typographed

1963, Dec. 10 *Perf. 10½x13*

468 A99 2fr dull purple 15 15
469 A99 4fr red 15 15
470 A99 7fr dark blue 18 18
471 A99 20fr slate green 20 20
Set value 52 52

15th anniversary of Universal Declaration of Human Rights.

Nos. 468-471 exist with side date panels transposed ("1963" at left, "1948" at right). Value, each $3.50.

Laboratory Technician and Atomic Emblem — A106

Designs: 1.50fr, 60fr, University. 8fr, 75fr, First African nuclear reactor. 25fr, 100fr, University and crest.

1964, Feb. 1 Photo. *Perf. 14x12½*

472 A106 50c multi 15 15
473 A106 1.50fr multi 15 15
474 A106 8fr multi 1.65 1.50
475 A106 25fr multi 15 15
476 A106 30fr multi 20 15
477 A106 60fr multi 35 30
478 A106 75fr multi 50 50
479 A106 100fr multi 65 55
a. Souv. sheet of 3 2.25 2.25
Nos. 472-479 (8) 3.80 3.45

10th anniversary of Lovanium University, Leopoldville.

No. 479a contains 3 imperf. multicolored stamps: 20fr, design as 50c; 30fr, as 8fr; 100fr.

Belgian Congo Issues of 1952-59 Overprinted "REPUBLIQUE DU CONGO" and Surcharged in Black on Overprinted Metallic Panels

1964 *Perf. 11½*

480 A93 1fr on 20c red org & sl (#307) 15 15
481 A86 2fr on 1.50fr (#273) 1.40 90
482 A93 5fr on 6.50fr (#315) 22 15
483 A86 8fr on 6.50fr (#278) 25 15

Republic Issues of 1960-61 Surcharged in Black of Overprinted Metallic Rectangles or Ovals

484 A86 1fr on 6.50fr (#335) 15 15
485 A93 1fr on 20c (#342) 15 15
486 A86 2fr on 1.50fr (#330) 15 15
487 A95 3fr on 20c (#382) 15 15
488 A95 4fr on 40c (#383) 15 15
489 A93 5fr on 6.50fr ("Congo" red) (#350) 22 15
a. "Congo" black 22 15
490 A93a 6fr on 6.50fr (#363) 22 15
491 A93a 7fr on 20c (#356) 32 18
Nos. 480-491 (12) 3.53
Set value 2.15

Pole Vault A107

Sports: 7fr, 20fr, Javelin, vert. 8fr, 100fr, Hurdling.

Perf. 11½

1964, July 13 Unwmk. Photo.

Granite Paper

492 A107 5fr gray, dk brn & car 15 15
493 A107 7fr rose, vio & emer 85 35
494 A107 8fr org, yel, red brn & vio bl 15 15
495 A107 10fr bl, vio brn & mag 15 15
496 A107 20fr gray grn, red brn & ver 15 15
497 A107 100fr lil, dk brn & grn 85 20
a. Souv. sheet of 3 3.50 3.50
Nos. 492-497 (6) 2.30
Set value 80

18th Olympic Games, Tokyo, Oct. 10-25. No. 497a contains 3 imperf. stamps (20fr orange & dark brown, pole vault; 30fr citron and dark brown, hurdling; 100fr dull green and dark brown, javelin). Sheet issued Sept. 10.

National Palace, Leopoldville A108

1964, Sept. 15

Granite Paper

498 A108 50c lil rose & bl 15 15
499 A108 1fr bl & lil rose 15 15
500 A108 2fr brn red & vio 15 15
501 A108 3fr emer & red 15 15
502 A108 4fr org & vio bl 15 15
503 A108 5fr gray vio & emer 15 15
504 A108 6fr sep & org 15 15
505 A108 7fr gray ol & red brn 15 15
506 A108 8fr rose red & vio bl 1.45 32
507 A108 9fr vio bl & rose red 15 15
508 A108 10fr brn ol & grn 15 15
509 A108 20fr bl & brn org 15 15
510 A108 30fr dk car rose & grn 15 15
511 A108 40fr ultra & dk car rose 22 15
512 A108 50fr brn org & grn 30 15
513 A108 100fr slate & ver 55 15
Set value 3.35 1.15

For overprints and surcharges see Nos. 574-577, 593-598, 609-615, 670-671, 673-674, 676-677, 680, 684-687.

Pres. John F. Kennedy (1917-63) A109

1964, Dec. 8 Photo. *Perf. 13½*

514 A109 5fr dk bl & blk 15 15
515 A109 6fr rose cl & blk 15 15
516 A109 9fr brn & blk 15 15
517 A109 30fr pur & blk 28 15
518 A109 40fr dl grn & blk 1.65 50
519 A109 60fr red brn & blk 45 20
Nos. 514-519 (6) 2.83
Set value 90

Souvenir Sheet

520 A109 150fr blk & mar 2.00 2.00

Rocket and Unisphere A110

Basketball A111

Engraved and Typographed

1965, Mar. 1 Unwmk. *Perf. 12*

521 A110 50c lil & blk 15 15
522 A110 1.50fr bl & lil 15 15
523 A110 2fr red brn & brt grn 15 15
524 A110 10fr brt grn & dk red 65 40
525 A110 18fr vio bl & brn 15 15
526 A110 27fr rose red & grn 22 15
527 A110 40fr gray & org 32 15
Set value 1.40 80

New York World's Fair, 1964-65.

1965, Apr. Photo. *Perf. 13½*

Designs: 6fr, 40fr, Soccer, horiz. 15fr, 60fr, Volleyball.

528 A111 5fr blk, grnsh bl & ocher 15 15
529 A111 6fr blk, bl gray & crim 15 15
530 A111 15fr blk, org & yel grn 15 15
531 A111 24fr blk, rose lil & brt grn 20 15
532 A111 40fr blk, brt grn & ultra 1.10 40
533 A111 60fr blk, bl & red lil 35 15
Nos. 528-533 (6) 2.10
Set value 80

First African Games, Leopoldville, Mar. 31-Apr. 7, 1965.

For surcharges see Nos. 604-605.

Earth and Satellites A112

Designs: 9fr, 15fr, 20fr, 40fr, Satellites at left, globe at right.

Perf. 14x14½

1965, June 28 Photo. Unwmk.

534 A112 6fr blk, sal & vio 15 15
535 A112 9fr blk, lt grn & gray 15 15
536 A112 12fr org, gray & blk 15 15
537 A112 15fr grn, ultra & blk 15 15
538 A112 18fr blk, lt grn & gray 1.00 28
539 A112 20fr blk, sal & vio 15 15
540 A112 30fr grn, ultra & blk 22 15
541 A112 40fr org, gray & blk 30 15
Nos. 534-541 (8) 2.27
Set value 80

Cent. of the ITU.

Congolese Paratrooper and Parachutes A113

1965, July 5 *Perf. 13x14*

542 A113 5fr brt bl & brn 15 15
543 A113 6fr org & brn 15 15
544 A113 7fr br grn & brn 40 18
545 A113 9fr brt pink & brn 15 15
546 A113 18fr lem & brn 15 15
Set value 72 46

Fifth anniversary of independence.

Matadi Harbor and ICY Emblem — A114

Designs (ICY Emblem and): 8fr, 25fr, Katanga mines. 9fr, 60fr, Tshopo Dam, Stanleyville.

1965, Oct. 25 Photo. *Perf. 13x14*

547 A114 6fr ultra, blk & yel 15 15
548 A114 8fr org red, blk & bl 15 15
549 A114 9fr bl grn, blk & brn org 15 15
550 A114 12fr car rose, blk & gray 75 30
551 A114 25fr ol, blk & rose red 18 15
552 A114 60fr gray, blk & org 35 15
Nos. 547-552 (6) 1.73
Set value 62

International Cooperation Year, 1965.

For overprints and surcharges see Nos. 559-560, 607-608.

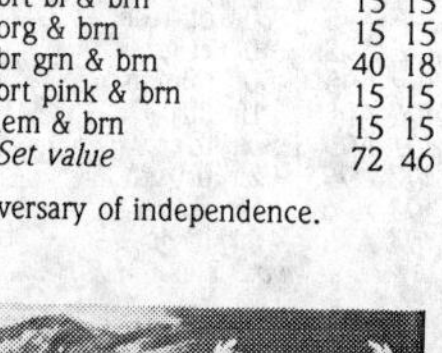

Soldiers Giving First Aid — A115

The Army Serving the Country: 7fr, Bridge building. 9fr, Feeding child. 19fr, Maintenance of telegraph lines. 20fr, House building. 30fr, Soldier and flag. (19fr, 20fr, 30fr, vert.)

Perf. 12½x13, 13x12½

1965, Nov. 17

553 A115 5fr sal, brn & red 15 15
554 A115 7fr yel & grn 15 15
555 A115 9fr ol & brn 15 15
556 A115 19fr brt grn & brn 60 35
557 A115 20fr lt bl & brn 15 15
558 A115 30fr multi 22 15
Nos. 553-558 (6) 1.42
Set value 68

See Nos. 582-586. For surcharges see Nos. 602, 678-679, 683.

Nos. 551-552 Overprinted with UN Emblem and "6e Journée Météorologique Mondiale / 23.3.66." on Metallic Strip

1966, Mar. 23 Photo. *Perf. 13x14*

559 A114 25fr ol & blk 70 35
560 A114 60fr gray & blk 70 52

6th World Meteorological Day.

Woman's Head and Goat — A116

Designs: 10fr, Sculptured heads. 12fr, Sitting figure and two heads, vert. 53fr, Figure with earrings and kneeling woman with bowl, vert.

Perf. 11½x13, 13x11½

1966, Apr. 23 Litho. Unwmk.

561 A116 10fr red, blk & gray 15 15
562 A116 12fr grn, blk & bl 15 15
563 A116 15fr dp bl, blk & lil 15 15
564 A116 53fr dp rose, blk & vio bl 1.00 85
Nos. 561-564 (4) 1.45 1.30

Intl. Negro Arts Festival, Dakar, Senegal, Apr. 1-24.

Pres. Joseph Desiré Mobutu and Fishing Industry A117

Pres. Mobutu and: 4fr, Pyrethrum harvest. 6fr, Building industry. 8fr, Winnowing rice. 10fr, Cotton harvest. 12fr, Banana harvest. 15fr, Cacao harvest. 24fr, Pineapple harvest. No. 573a, Pres. Mobutu without cap, and men rolling up sleeves.

1966, May 1 Photo. *Perf. 11½*

565 A117 2fr dk brn & dk bl 15 15
566 A117 4fr dk brn & org 15 15
567 A117 6fr dk brn & ol 65 55
568 A117 8fr dk brn & brt grnsh bl 15 15
569 A117 10fr dk brn & brn red 15 15
570 A117 12fr dk brn & vio 15 15
571 A117 15fr dk brn & lt ol grn 15 15
572 A117 24fr dk brn & lil rose 20 15
Set value 1.25 1.05

Souvenir Sheet

Perf. 11x11½

573 Sheet of 4 70 70
a. A117 15fr red, black & ultra 15 15

Lt. Gen. Joseph Desiré Mobutu, Pres. of Congo, and publicizing the "Back to Work" campaign.

For surcharges see Nos. 601, 603, 616, 619-624, 672, 675, 681-682.

Nos. 510-513 Overprinted

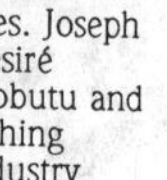

1966, June 13 *Perf. 11½*

574 A108 30fr dk car rose & grn 65 65
575 A108 40fr ultra & dk car rose 65 65
576 A108 50fr brn org & grn 70 70
577 A108 100fr slate & ver 70 70
Nos. 574-577 (4) 2.70 2.70

Inauguration of WHO Headquarters, Geneva.

The Scott Catalogue value is a retail value; that is, what you could expect to pay for the stamp in a grade of Fine-Very Fine. The value listed reflects recent actual dealer selling prices.

Soccer Player — A118

Designs: 30fr, Two soccer players. 50fr, Three soccer players. 60fr, Jules Rimet Cup, soccer ball and globe.

1966, July 25 Photo. *Perf. 14*

578 A118 10fr ocher, vio & brt grn 15 15
579 A118 30fr brt rose lil, vio & ap grn 22 15
580 A118 50fr ap grn, Prus bl & tan 85 85
581 A118 60fr brt grn, dk brn & gold 42 35
Nos. 578-581 (4) 1.64 1.50

World Cup Soccer Championship, Wembley, England, July 11-30.
For overprints see Nos. 587-590.

Army Type of 1965

The Army Serving the Country: 2fr, Soldiers giving first aid. 6fr, Feeding child. 10fr, House building, vert. 18fr, Bridge building. 24fr, Soldier and flag, vert.

1966, Aug. 8 *Perf. 12½x13, 13x12½*

582 A115 2fr ver, ind & red 15 15
583 A115 6fr ultra red brn 15 15
584 A115 10fr yel grn & red brn 40 35
585 A115 18fr car rose & vio 15 15
586 A115 24fr multi 15 15
Set value 78 66

Nos. 578-581 Overprinted in Black, Carmine or Green: "FINALE / ANGLETERRE-ALLEMAGNE / 4-2"

1966, Nov. 14 Photo. *Perf. 14*

587 A118 10fr pair, B and C 28 28
588 A118 30fr pair, B and G 90 80
589 A118 50fr pair, B and C 1.40 1.25
590 A118 60fr pair, B and C 1.70 1.50
Nos. 587-590 (4) 4.28 3.83

England's victory in the World Soccer Cup Championship. The two colors of the overprint alternate in the sheets.

Souvenir Sheets

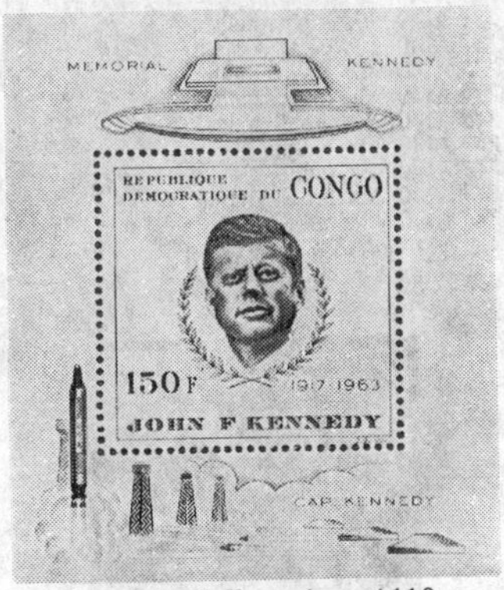

Pres. John F. Kennedy — A119

1966, Dec. 28 Engr. *Perf. 13*

591 A119 150fr brown 2.75 2.75
592 A119 150fr slate 2.75 2.75

Issued in memory of Pres. John F. Kennedy. No. 591 has slate green, No. 592 deep orange marginal design. Two imperf. sheets exist: 150fr brown with violet blue margin and 150fr slate with lilac margin. Size: 65x76mm. Value $4.25 each.

Nos. 498-503 Surcharged in Black, Red or Maroon

5 K

4e Sommet OUA
KINSHASA
du 11 au 14 - 9 - 67

1967, Sept. 11 Photo. *Perf. 11½*

593 A108 1k on 2fr 15 15
a. Inverted overprint 6.00
594 A108 3k on 5fr 15 15
595 A108 5k on 4fr 15 15
596 A108 6.60k on 1fr (R) 22 15
a. Inverted overprint 4.75
597 A108 9.60k on 50c 35 25
a. Inverted overprint 4.75
598 A108 9.80k on 3fr (M) 50 35
Nos. 593-598 (6) 1.52
Set value 1.00

Souvenir Sheet

Map of Africa, Torch — A120

599 A120 50k grnsh bl, blk & red 1.50 1.50

4th meeting of the Org. for African Unity, Kinshasa (Leopoldville), Sept. 9-11.
No. 599 in other colors was not a postal issue.

Souvenir Sheet

Horn Blower and EXPO Emblem — A121

1967, Sept. 28 Engr. *Perf. 11½*

600 A121 50k dk brn 1.65 1.65

EXPO '67, International Exhibition, Montreal, Apr. 28-Oct. 27, 1967.

Nos. 565-566 and 582 Overprinted: "NOUVELLE CONSTITUTION 1967" and Surcharged with New Value on Metallic Panel in Magenta or Brown

Perf. 11½, 12½x13

1967, Oct. 9 Photo.

601 A117 4k on 2fr (M) 15 15
602 A115 5k on 2fr (B) 20 15
603 A117 21k on 4fr (M) 85 65
Nos. 601-603 (3) 1.20 95

Promulgation of the Constitution, June 4, 1967.

Nos. 528 and 530 Surcharged with New Value and Overprinted: "1ere Jeux Congolais / 25/6 au 2/7/1967 / Kinshasa"

1967, Oct. 16 Photo. *Perf. 13½*

604 A111 1k on 5fr multi 15 15
605 A111 9.60k on 15fr multi 50 50

First Congolese Games, Kinshasa, June 25-July 2, 1967.

No. 465 Surcharged with New Value and Overprinted: "1er VOL BAC / ONE ELEVEN / 14/5/67"

1967, Oct. 16 *Perf. 11½*

606 A105 9.60k on 7fr multi 65 15

1st flight of the BAC 111 in the service of Air Congo, May 14, 1967.

Nos. 547 and 549 Surcharged in Red or Black: "JOURNEE MONDIALE / DE L'ENFANCE / 8-10-67"

1968, Feb. 10 Photo. *Perf. 13x14*

607 A114 1k on 6fr (R) 15 15
608 A114 9k on 9fr (B) 50 50

Intl. Children's Day. The surcharge is on a rectangle printed in metallic ink.

Nos. 498, 504 and 501 Surcharged in Blue or Red: "Année Internationale / du Tourisme 24-10-1967"

1968, Feb. 10 *Perf. 11½*

609 A108 5k on 50c lil rose & bl (Bl) 18 18
610 A108 10k on 6fr sepia & org (R) 40 40
611 A108 15k on 3fr emer & red (R) 55 55
Nos. 609-611 (3) 1.13 1.13

International Tourist Year. The surcharge is on a rectangle printed in metallic ink.

Nos. 500, 498 and 502 Surcharged in Black, Violet Blue or Gold

1968, July Photo. *Perf. 11½*

612 A108 1k on 2fr 15 15
613 A108 2k on 50c (VBl) 15 15
614 A108 2k on 50c (G) 15 15
615 A108 9.60k on 4fr 40 40
Set value 67 67

The surcharge on No. 612 consists of a black rectangle and new denomination in upper right corner; the surcharge on No. 613 has a violet blue rectangle with denomination printed in white on it; on No. 614 the rectangle is gold and the denomination black; on No. 615 the rectangle is black and the denomination white.

No. 565 Surcharged in White on Black Rectangle

1968, Oct. Photo. *Perf. 11½*

616 A117 10k on 2fr dk brn & dk bl 40 15

Leopard A122

1968, Nov. 5 Litho. *Perf. 10½*

617 A122 2k brt grnsh bl & blk 15 15
618 A122 9.60k red & blk 40 15
Set value 15

Mobutu Type of 1966 Surcharged 1K

1968, Dec. 20 Photo. *Perf. 11½*

619 A117 15s on 2fr sep & brt bl 15 15
620 A117 1k on 6fr sep & brn 15 15
621 A117 3k on 10fr sep & emer 15 15
622 A117 5k on 12fr sep & org 15 15
623 A117 20k on 15fr sep & brt grn 60 42
624 A117 50k on 24fr sep & brt lil 1.65 1.10
Nos. 619-624 (6) 2.85
Set value 1.80

Human Rights Flame — A123

1968, Dec. 30 *Perf. 12½x13*

625 A123 2k lt ultra & brt grn 15 15
626 A123 9.60k grn & dp car 35 22
627 A123 10k brt lil & brn 35 22
628 A123 40k org brn & pur 1.40 1.00
Nos. 625-628 (4) 2.25 1.59

International Human Rights Year.

Type of 1968 Overprinted in Gold

1969, Jan. 27 Photo. *Perf. 12½x13*

629 A123 2k ap grn & red brn 15 15
630 A123 9.60k rose & emer 35 22
631 A123 10k gray & ultra 35 22
632 A123 40k grnsh bl & pur 1.40 1.00
Nos. 629-632 (4) 2.25 1.59

4th summit meeting of OCAM (Organisation Communitee Afrique et Malgache), Kinshasa, Jan. 27.

Kinshasa Fair Emblem and Cotton Boll — A124

Designs (Fair Emblem and): 6k, Copper. 9.60k, Coffee. 9.80k, Diamond. 11.60k, Oil palm fruits.

1969, May 2 Photo. *Perf. 12½x13*

633 A124 2k brt pur, gold & red lil 15 15
634 A124 6k grn, gold & bl grn 22 22
635 A124 9.60k brn, gold & lt brn 35 15
636 A124 9.80k ultra & gold 35 32
637 A124 11.60k hn brn, gold & brn 45 45
Nos. 633-637 (5) 1.52 1.29

Kinshasa Fair, Limete, June 30-July 21.

Fair Entrance, Emblem — A125

Designs (Fair Emblem and): 3k, Gecomin Mining Co. Pavilion. 10k, Administration Building. 25k, Pavilion of the Organization for African Unity.

1969, June 30 Photo. *Perf. 11½*

Granite Paper

638 A125 2k brt rose lil & gold 15 15
639 A125 3k blue & gold 15 15
640 A125 10k lt ol grn & gold 32 25
641 A125 25k copper red & gold 75 65
Nos. 638-641 (4) 1.37 1.20

Kinshasa Fair, Limete, June 30-July 21.

Congo Arms — A126

Pres. Mobutu — A127

1969, July-Sept. Litho. *Perf. 14*

642 A126 10s org & blk 15 15
643 A126 15s ultra & blk 15 15
644 A126 30s brt grn & blk 15 15
645 A126 60s brt rose lil & blk 15 15
646 A126 90s dp bis & blk 15 15

Perf. 13

647 A127	1k	sky bl & multi	15	15
648 A127	2k	org & multi	15	15
649 A127	3k	multi	15	15
650 A127	5k	brt rose & multi	15	15
651 A127	6k	ultra & multi	15	15
652 A127	9.60k	multi	22	15
653 A127	10k	lt lil & multi	32	15
654 A127	20k	yel & multi	65	32
655 A127	50k	multi	1.65	70
656 A127	100k	fawn & multi	3.00	1.25
		Set value	6.50	3.10

Well Driller, by Oscar Bonnevalle — A128

Paintings: 4k, Preparation of cocoa, by Jean Van Noten. 8k, Dock workers, by Constantin Meunier. 10k, Poultry shop, by Henri Evenepoel. 15k, Steel industry, by Constantin Meunier.

Perf. 13x14, 14x13 (8k)

1969, Dec. 15 **Litho.**

Size: 41x41mm

657 A128	3k	multi	15	15
658 A128	4k	multi	15	15

Size: 28x41mm

659 A128	8k	multi	25	22

Size: 41x41mm

660 A128	10k	multi	42	32
661 A128	15k	multi	85	50
		Nos. 657-661 (5)	1.82	1.34

50th anniv. of the ILO.

Souvenir Sheet

Adoration of the Kings, by Rubens — A129

1969, Dec. **Engr.** ***Perf. 13***

662 A129	50k	red lilac	1.50	1.50

Issued for Christmas 1969.

Pres. Mobutu, Map and Flag of Congo A130

1970, June 30 **Litho.** ***Perf. 13½x13***

663 A130	10s	multi	15	15
664 A130	90s	pur & multi	15	15
665 A130	1k	brn & multi	15	15
666 A130	2k	multi	15	15
667 A130	7k	multi	24	15
668 A130	10k	multi	35	22
669 A130	20k	multi	70	50
		Set value	1.50	1.05

10th anniversary of independence.

Issues of 1964-1966 Surcharged

=
0,20 K

Perf. 11½, 12½x13, 13x12½

1970, Sept. 24 **Photo.**

670 A108	10s	on 1fr (#499)	15	15
671 A108	20s	on 2fr (#500)	15	15
672 A117	20s	on 2fr (#565)	15	15
673 A108	30s	on 3fr (#501)	15	15
674 A108	40s	on 4fr (#502)	15	15
675 A117	40s	on 4fr (#566)	15	15
676 A108	60s	on 7fr (#505)	70	52
677 A108	90s	on 9fr (#507)	70	52
678 A115	90s	on 9fr (#555)	15	15
679 A115	1k	on 7fr (#554)	15	15
680 A108	1k	on 6fr (#504)	15	15
681 A117	1k	on 12fr (#570)	70	52
682 A117	2k	on 24fr (#572)	15	15
683 A115	2k	on 24fr (#586)	15	15
684 A108	3k	on 30fr (#510)	70	52
685 A108	4k	on 40fr (#511)	15	15
686 A108	5k	on 50fr (#512)	1.65	1.10
687 A108	10k	on 100fr (#513)	70	50
		Set value	6.30	4.60

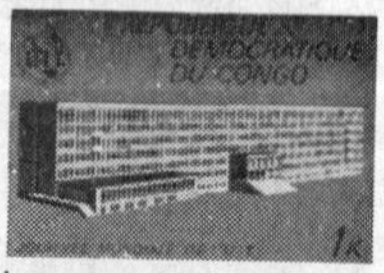

Telecommunications Building, Geneva — A131

Designs: 2k, 6.60k, UPU Headquarters, Bern. 9.80k, 10k, 11k, UN Headquarters, NY.

1970, Oct. 24 **Photo.** ***Perf. 11½***

688 A131	1k	pink & grn	15	15
689 A131	2k	org & grn	15	15
690 A131	6.60k	grnsh bl & rose car	22	15
691 A131	9.60k	yel & vio bl	30	15
692 A131	9.80k	lt ultra & brn	30	15
693 A131	10k	lt pur & brn	30	18
694 A131	11k	rose & brn	35	22
		Nos. 688-694 (7)	1.77	
		Set value		90

ITU; new UPU Headquarters, Bern; 25th anniv. of the UN.

Pres. Mobutu, Congolese Flag and Arch — A132

1970, Nov. 24 **Litho.** ***Perf. 13***

695 A132	2k	yel & multi	15	15
696 A132	10k	bl & multi	40	25
697 A132	20k	red & multi	85	55
		Nos. 695-697 (3)	1.40	95

Fifth anniversary of new government.

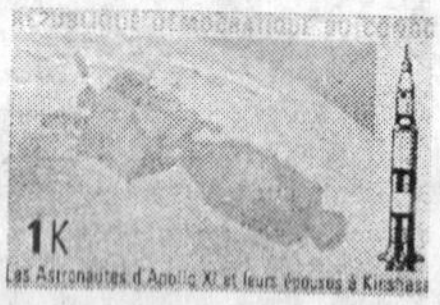

Apollo 11 in Flight A133

Designs: 2k, Astronaut and spacecraft on moon. 7k, Pres. Mobutu decorating astronauts' wives. 10k, Pres. Mobutu with Neil A. Armstrong, Col. Edwin E. Aldrin, Jr. and Lt. Col. Michael Collins. 30k, Armstrong, Aldrin and Collins in space suits.

1970, Dec. 24 ***Perf. 13x13½***

698 A133	1k	bl & blk	15	15
699 A133	2k	brt pur & blk	15	15
700 A133	7k	dl org & blk	30	20
701 A133	10k	rose red & blk	32	25
702 A133	30k	grn & blk	1.00	70
		Nos. 698-702 (5)	1.92	1.45

Visit of US Apollo 11 astronauts and their wives to Kinshasa.

Metopodontus Savagei — A134

Designs: Various insects of Congo.

1971, Jan. 25 **Photo.** ***Perf. 11½***

703 A134	10s	dl rose & multi	15	15
704 A134	50s	gray & multi	15	15
705 A134	90s	multi	15	15
706 A134	1k	citron & multi	15	15
707 A134	2k	gray grn & multi	15	15
708 A134	3k	lt vio & multi	15	15
709 A134	5k	bl & multi	40	25
710 A134	10k	multi	65	42
711 A134	30k	grn & multi	1.65	1.00
712 A134	40k	ocher & multi	2.00	1.25
		Nos. 703-712 (10)	5.60	
		Set value		3.25

Colotis Protomedia — A135

Designs: Various butterflies and moths of Congo.

1971, Feb. 24

713 A135	10s	lt ultra & multi	15	15
714 A135	20s	choc & multi	15	15
715 A135	70s	dp org & multi	15	15
716 A135	1k	vio bl & multi	15	15
717 A135	3k	multi	15	15
718 A135	5k	dk grn & multi	32	20
719 A135	10k	multi	52	32
720 A135	15k	emer & multi	85	50
721 A135	25k	yel & multi	1.10	70
722 A135	40k	multi	2.00	1.25
		Nos. 713-722 (10)	5.54	3.72

UN Emblem, Racial Unity — A136

1971, Mar. 21 **Photo.** ***Perf. 11½***

723 A136	1k	lt grn & multi	15	15
724 A136	4k	gray & multi	15	15
725 A136	5k	lt lil & multi	15	15
726 A136	10k	lt bl & multi	32	20
		Set value	60	42

Intl. year against racial discrimination.

Hypericum Bequaertii A137

Flowers: 4k, Dissotis brazzae. 20k, Begonia wollastonii. 25k, Cassia alata.

1971, May 24 **Litho.** ***Perf. 14***

727 A137	1k	multi	15	15
728 A137	4k	multi	20	15
729 A137	20k	multi	85	32
730 A137	25k	multi	1.10	65
		Nos. 727-730 (4)	2.30	1.27

Obelisk at N'sele, Pres. Mobutu — A138

1971, May 20 **Photo.** ***Perf. 11½***

731 A138	4k	gold & multi	15	15

4th anniversary of the People's Revolutionary Movement.

Radar Station A139

Designs: 1k, Waves. 6k, Map of Africa with telecommunications network.

1971, June 25 **Photo.** ***Perf. 11½***

732 A139	1k	rose & multi	15	15
733 A139	3k	yel & multi	15	15
734 A139	6k	lt bl & multi	25	15
		Set value	42	27

3rd World Telecommunications Day, May 17 (1k); opening of satellite telecommunications ground station, Kinshasa, June 30 (3k); Pan-African telecommunication system (6k).

Grass Monkeys A140

Designs: 20s, Moustached monkeys, vert. 70s, De Brazza's monkeys. 1k, Yellow baboons. 3k, Pygmy chimpanzee, vert. 5k, Mangabeys, vert. 10k, Owlfaced monkeys. 15k, Diana monkeys. 25k, Black-and-white colobus, vert. 40k, L'Hoest's monkeys, vert.

1971, Aug.

735 A140	10s	vio & multi	15	15
736 A140	20s	lt bl & multi	15	15
737 A140	70s	ocher & multi	15	15
738 A140	1k	gray & multi	15	15
739 A140	3k	rose & multi	22	15
740 A140	5k	brn & multi	52	15
741 A140	10k	multi	90	22
742 A140	15k	multi	1.65	48
743 A140	25k	brt bl & multi	2.75	75
744 A140	40k	red & multi	3.75	95
		Nos. 735-744 (10)	10.39	
		Set value		2.80

Hotel Inter-Continental, Kinshasa — A141

1971, Oct. 2 **Photo.** ***Perf. 13***

745 A141	2k	silver & multi	15	15
746 A141	12k	gold & multi	42	15
		Set value		20

Man Reading — A142

Designs: 2.50k, Open book and abacus. 7k, Five letters surrounding symbolic head.

1971, Oct. 24

747	A142	50s multi	15	15
748	A142	2.50k multi	15	15
749	A142	7k multi	42	15
		Set value	57	26

Fight against illiteracy.

Succeeding issues are listed in Vol. 5 under Zaire.

SEMI-POSTAL STAMPS

Women Carrying Food, Wheat Emblem, and Tractor SP22

1963, Mar. 21 Photo. *Perf. 14x13*

B48	SP22	5fr + 2fr multi	15	15
B49	SP22	9fr + 4fr multi	30	15
B50	SP22	12fr + 6fr multi	32	22
B51	SP22	20fr + 10fr multi	1.65	1.50
		Nos. B48-B51 (4)	2.42	2.02

FAO "Freedom from Hunger" campaign.

CONGO PEOPLE'S REPUBLIC

(ex-French)

LOCATION — West Africa at equator
GOVT. — Republic
AREA — 132,046 sq. mi.
POP. — 1,740,000 (est. 1984)
CAPITAL — Brazzaville

The former French colony of Middle Congo became a member state of the French Community on November 28, 1958, and achieved independence on August 15, 1960. For some years before 1958, the colony was joined with three other French territories to form French Equatorial Africa. Issues of Middle Congo (1907-1933) are listed under that heading.

100 Centimes = 1 Franc

Catalogue values for all unused stamps in this country are for Never Hinged items.

Allegory of New Republic A7

1959 Unwmk. Engr. *Perf. 13*

89	A7	25fr brn, dp claret, org & ol	30	15

1st anniv. of the proclamation of the Republic.

Imperforates
Most stamps of the Republic of the Congo exist imperforate in issued and trial colors, and also in small presentation sheets in issued colors.

C.C.T.A. Issue
Common Design Type

1960 Unwmk. *Perf. 13*

90	CD106	50fr dl grn & plum	60	55

President Fulbert Youlou — A8

Flag, Map and UN Emblem — A9

1960

91	A8	15fr grn, blk & car	16	15
92	A8	85fr indigo & car	70	35

1961, Mar. 11 *Perf. 13*
Flag in Green, Yellow & Red

93	A9	5fr vio brn & dk bl	15	15
94	A9	20fr org & dk bl	20	15
95	A9	100fr grn & dk bl	1.00	90
		Nos. 93-95 (3)	1.35	1.20

Congo's admission to United Nations.

Rainbow Runner A10

Designs (fish): 50c, 3fr, Rainbow runner. 1fr, 2fr, Sloan's viperfish. 5fr, Hatchet fish. 10fr, A deep-sea fish.

1961, Nov. 28 Engr.

96	A10	50c brn, ol grn & salmon	15	15
97	A10	1fr bl grn & sepia	15	15
98	A10	2fr ultra, sep & dk grn	15	15
99	A10	3fr dk bl, grn & salmon	15	15
100	A10	5fr red brn, grn & blk	20	15
101	A10	10fr blue & red brn	20	15
		Set value	68	55

Brazzaville Market — A11

1962, Mar. 23 Unwmk. *Perf. 13*

102	A11	20fr blk, red & grn	16	15

Abidjan Games Issue
Common Design Type

Designs: 20fr, Boxing. 50fr, Running, finish line.

1962, July 21 Photo. *Perf. 12½x12*

103	CD109	20fr car, brt pink, brn & blk	18	15
104	CD109	50fr car, brt pink, brn & blk	40	30
		Nos. 103-104,C7 (3)	1.48	1.07

Common Design Types pictured in section at front of book.

African-Malgache Union Issue
Common Design Type

1962, Sept. 8

105	CD110	30fr multi	38	38

Waves Around Globe — A11a

Design: 100fr, Orbit patterns around globe.

1963, Sept. 19 *Perf. 12½*

106	A11a	25fr org, grn & ultra	25	20
107	A11a	100fr lt red brn, bl & plum	90	70

Issued to publicize space communications.

King Makoko's Collar — A12

Unwmk.
1963, Oct. 21 Engr. *Perf. 13*

108	A12	10fr showm	15	15
109	A12	15fr Kebekebe mask	16	15
		Set value		15

UNESCO Emblem, Scales and Tree — A12a

1963, Dec. 10 Unwmk. *Perf. 13*

110	A12a	25fr grn, dk bl & brn	22	16

15th anniv. of the Universal Declaration of Human Rights.

Barograph and WMO Emblem A12b

1964, Mar. 23 Engr.

111	A12b	50fr grn, red brn & ultra	42	42

Fourth World Meteorological Day.

Mechanic with Machine — A13

1964, Apr. 8

112	A13	20fr grnsh bl, mag & dk brn	22	15

Training of technicians.

Corn and Tools — A14

1964, Apr. 24 Unwmk. *Perf. 13*

113	A14	80fr brn, grn & brn car	65	35

Importance of manual labor.

Diaboua Ballet — A15

Kébékébé Dance — A16

Carved Figure — A17

1964, May 8 Engr.

114	A15	30fr multi	35	20
115	A16	60fr multi	60	40

1964, May 22

116	A17	50fr brn red & sepia	42	35

Classroom A18

1964, May 26

117	A18	25fr dk brn, red & blue	22	15

Issued to publicize education.

Type of Air Post Issue, 1963, Inscribed: "1er ANNIVERSAIRE DE LA REVOLUTION/FETE NATIONALE/15 AOUT 1964"

1964, Aug. 15 Photo. *Perf. 13x12*

118	AP5	20fr lt bl, red, ocher, dk brn & grn	18	15

1st anniv. of the revolution and Natl. Feast Day, Aug. 15.

Fire Squid — A19

Design: 15fr, Johnson's deep-sea angler (fish).

1964, Oct. 20 Engr. *Perf. 13*

119	A19	2fr ver, lt grn & brn	15	15
120	A19	15fr vio, lt ol grn & dp cl	22	15
		Set value		19

Cooperation Issue
Common Design Type

1964, Nov. 7 Unwmk. *Perf. 13*

121	CD119	25fr car, brt grn & dk brn	22	16

The lack of a value for a listed item does not necessarily indicate rarity.

Communications Emblems — A20

1965, Jan. 1 Litho. *Perf. 12½x13*
122 A20 25fr ol, red brn & blk 25 16

Issued to commemorate the establishment of the national postal administration.

Sitatunga
A21

Dancer on Stilts
A22

Design: 20fr, Elephant, horiz.

1965, Mar. 15 Engr. *Perf. 13*
123 A21 15fr redsh brn, dl grn & bl 20 15
124 A21 20fr blk, dp bl & sl grn 20 15
125 A22 85fr lil & multi 70 60
Nos. 123-125 (3) 1.10 90

Pres. Alphonse Massamba-Debat — A23

1965-66 Photo. *Perf. 12x12½*
126 A23 20fr dk brn, grn & yel 16 15
127 A23 25fr brn, bl grn, emer & blk ('66) 22 15
128 A23 30fr brn, bl grn, org & blk ('66) 25 15
Nos. 126-128 (3) 63
Set value 34

Soccer Player — A24

Designs: 25fr, Games' emblem (map of Africa and runners). 50fr, Field ball player. 85fr, Runner. 100fr, Bicyclist.

1965, July 17 Photo. *Perf. 12½*

Size: 28x28mm

129 A24 25fr blk, red, yel & grn 16 15

Size: 34x34mm

130 A24 40fr yel grn & multi 30 20
131 A24 50fr red & multi 32 20
132 A24 85fr blk & multi 55 35
133 A24 100fr yel & multi 65 42
a. Min. sheet of 5, #129-133 3.00 3.00
Nos. 129-133 (5) 1.98 1.32

1st African Games, Brazzaville, July 18-25.

Arms of Congo — A25

1965, Nov. 15 Litho. *Perf. 12½x13*
134 A25 20fr multi 20 15

Cooperative Village A26

Design: 30fr, Gymnastic drill team with streamers.

1966, Feb. 18 *Perf. 12½x13*
135 A26 25fr multi 20 15
136 A26 30fr multi 25 16

Sculptured Mask — A27

Designs: 30fr, Weaver, painting. 85fr, String instrument, painting, horiz.

Perf. 13x12½, 12½x13
1966, Apr. 9 Photo.
137 A27 30fr multi 25 15
138 A27 85fr multi 70 42
139 A27 90fr multi 80 45
Nos. 137-139 (3) 1.75 1.02

Issued to publicize the International Negro Arts Festival, Dakar, Senegal, Apr. 1-24.

Men and Clocks — A28

1966, Apr. 15 *Perf. 12½x12*
140 A28 70fr pale brn, ocher & dk brn 75 30

Issued to publicize the introduction of the shorter work day (less lunch time, earlier quitting time).

WHO Headquarters, Geneva A29

1966, May 3 Photo. *Perf. 12½x13*
141 A29 50fr org yel, vio & bl 25 16

Inauguration of the WHO Headquarters, Geneva.

Church of St. Peter Claver A30

Women's Basketball A31

1966, June 15 Photo. *Perf. 13x12½*
142 A30 70fr multi 70 30

1966, July 15 Engr. *Perf. 13*

Sport: 1fr, Women's volleyball, horiz. 3fr, Women's field ball, horiz. 5fr, Athletes of various races. 10fr, Torch bearer. 15fr, Soccer and gold medal of First African Games.

143 A31 1fr ultra, choc & ol 15 15
144 A31 2fr choc, grn & bl 15 15
145 A31 3fr dk grn, dk car & choc 15 15
146 A31 5fr sl, emer & choc 15 15
147 A31 10fr dl bl, dk grn & vio 16 15
148 A31 15fr vio, car & choc 20 15
Set value 61 42

Jules Rimet Cup and Globe — A32

1966, July 15 Photo. *Perf. 12½x12*
149 A32 30fr brt red, gold, blk & bl 35 18

8th World Soccer Cup Championship, Wembley, England, July 11-30.

Savorgnan de Brazza School A33

1966, Sept. 15 Photo. *Perf. 12½x12*
150 A33 30fr dk pur, grn, yel & blk 25 15

Pointe-Noire Railroad Station — A34

1966, Oct. 15 Engr. *Perf. 13*
151 A34 60fr grn, red & brn 60 22

Student with Microscope A35

Balumbu Mask A36

1966, Nov. 28 Engr. *Perf. 13*
152 A35 90fr brn, grn & ind 80 50

20th anniv. of UNESCO.

1966, Dec. 12 Engr. *Perf. 13*

Masks: 10fr, Kuyu. 15fr, Bakwélé. 20fr, Batéké.

153 A36 5fr car rose & dk brn 15 15
154 A36 10fr Prus bl & brn 15 15
155 A36 15fr sep, dl org & dk bl 16 15
156 A36 20fr dp bl & multi 20 15
Nos. 153-156 (4) 66
Set value 32

Order of the Revolution and Map — A37

Learning the Alphabet A38

Design: 45fr, Harvesting and loading sugar cane, and sugar mill.

Perf. 12x12½, 12½x12
1967, Mar. 15 Photo.
157 A37 20fr org & multi 20 15
158 A38 25fr blk, ocher & dk car 20 15
159 A38 45fr blk, yel grn & lt bl 40 20
Nos. 157-159 (3) 80 50

Issued to honor the members of the Order of the Revolution (20fr); to publicize the literacy campaign (25fr); to publicize, sugar production (45fr).

Mahatma Gandhi — A39

Fruit Vendor — A40

1967, Apr. 21 Engr. *Perf. 13*
160 A39 90fr bl & blk 70 40

Issued in memory of Mohandas K. Gandhi (1869-1948), Hindu nationalist leader.

1967, June Photo. *Perf. 13x12½*

Dolls: 5fr, "Elegant Lady." 25fr, Woman pounding saka-saka. 30fr, Mother and child.

161 A40 5fr gold & multi 15 15
162 A40 10fr yel grn & multi 15 15
163 A40 25fr lt ultra & multi 20 15
164 A40 30fr multi 25 16
Nos. 161-164 (4) 75
Set value 48

ITY Emblem, Village and Waterfall A41

1967, July 5 Engr. *Perf. 13*
165 A41 60fr rose cl, org & ol grn 55 35

Issued for International Tourist Year, 1967.

Symbols of Cooperation A42

Arms of Brazzaville A43

Europafrica Issue, 1967

1967, July 20 Photo. *Perf. 12x12½*

166 A42 50fr multi	42	20

1967, Aug. 15 Litho. *Perf. 12½x13*

167 A43 30fr yel & multi	30	15

Fourth anniversary of the revolution.

UN Emblem, Dove and People — A44

Boy and UNICEF Emblem — A45

1967, Oct. 24 Photo. *Perf. 13x12½*

168 A44 90fr bl, dk brn, red brn & yel	90	50

Issued for United Nations Day, Oct. 24.

1967, Dec. 11 Engr. *Perf. 13*

169 A45 90fr mar, blk & ultra	80	42

21st anniv. of UNICEF.

Albert Luthuli, Dove and Globe — A46

1968, Jan. 29 Engr. *Perf. 13*

170 A46 30fr brt grn & ol bis	25	16

Albert Luthuli (1899-1967) of South Africa, winner of 1960 Nobel Peace Prize.

Arms of Pointe Noire — A47

1968, Feb. 20 Litho. *Perf. 12½x13*

171 A47 10fr brt pink & multi	15	15

Motherhood A48

Mayombe Viaduct A49

1968, May 25 Engr. *Perf. 13*

172 A48 15fr dk car rose, sky bl & blk	16	15

Issued for Mother's Day.

1968, June 24

173 A49 45fr maroon, slate grn & bl	35	16

A50

1968, July 29 Photo. *Perf. 13x12½*

174 A50 5fr Daimler, 1889	15	15
175 A50 20fr Berliet, 1897	20	16
176 A50 60fr Peugeot, 1898	55	30
177 A50 80fr Renault, 1900	75	40
178 A50 85fr Fiat, 1902	80	45
Nos. 174-178,C67-C68 (7)	5.45	3.01
Nos. 174-178 (5)	2.45	1.46

Tanker, Refinery and Map of Area Served — A50a

1968, July 30 *Perf. 12½*

179 A50a 30fr multi	25	15

Issued to commemorate the opening of the Port Gentil (Gabon) Refinery, June 12, 1968.

UN Emblem and Tree of Life — A51

1968, Nov. 28 Engr. *Perf. 13*

180 A51 25fr dk grn, red & dp lil	25	15

20th anniv. of WHO.

Development Bank Issue

Common Design Type

1969, Sept. 10 Engr. *Perf. 13*

181 CD130 25fr car rose, grn & ocher	22	15
182 CD130 30fr bl, grn & ocher	25	15
Set value		20

Bicycle A52

Designs (Bicycles and Motorcycles): 75fr, Hirondelle. 80fr, Folding bicycle. 85fr, Peugeot. 100fr, Excelsior Manxman. 150fr, Norton. 200fr, Brough Superior "Old Bill." 300fr, Matchless and N.L.G.-J.A.P.S.

1969, Oct. 6 Engr. *Perf. 13*

183 A52 50fr multi	40	20
184 A52 75fr multi	60	28
185 A52 80fr multi	65	30
186 A52 85fr multi	70	35
187 A52 100fr multi	85	42
188 A52 150fr multi	1.10	60
189 A52 200fr multi	2.00	75
190 A52 300fr multi	2.75	1.25
Nos. 183-190 (8)	9.05	4.15

Mayombe Train and Tourist Year Emblem A53

Design: 40fr, Train and Mbamba Tunnel, vert.

Perf. 13x12½, 12½x13

1969, Oct. 20 Photo.

191 A53 40fr multi	38	18
192 A53 60fr multi	45	20

Issued for African Tourist Year.

Loutete Cement Works — A54

Loutete Cement Works: 15fr, Mixing tower, vert. 25fr, Cable transport, vert. 30fr, General view of plant.

1969, Dec. 10 Engr. *Perf. 13*

193 A54 10fr dk gray, rose cl & dk ol	15	15
194 A54 15fr Prus bl, red brn & pur	15	15
195 A54 25fr mar, brn & Prus bl	20	15
196 A54 30fr vio brn, ultra & blk	22	15
a. Min. sheet of 4, #193-196	80	80
Nos. 193-196 (4)	72	
Set value		40

ASECNA Issue

Common Design Type

1969, Dec. 12

197 CD132 100fr dull brown	90	42

Pineapple Harvest and ILO Emblem A55

Design: 30fr, Worker at lathe and ILO emblem.

1969, Dec. 20 Engr. *Perf. 13*

198 A55 25fr bl, olive & brn	20	15
199 A55 30fr rose red, choc & slate	22	15

50th anniv. of the ILO.

SOTEXCO Textile Plant, Kinsoundi A56

Designs: 20fr, Women in spinnery. 25fr, Hand-printing textiles. 30fr, Checking woven cloth.

1970, Jan. 20

200 A56 15fr grn, blk & lil	15	15
201 A56 20fr plum, car & sl grn	15	15
202 A56 25fr bl, sl & brn	20	15
203 A56 30fr gray, car rose & brn	25	15
Nos. 200-203 (4)	75	
Set value		42

Hotel Cosmos, Brazzaville A57

1970, Jan. 30

204 A57 90fr sl grn, bl & red brn	65	30

The status of the three sets for Kennedy, etc., Summer Olympics, and Baroque paintings is not certain.

Linzolo Church — A58

Diosso Gorge — A59

Design: 90fr, Foulakari waterfall.

1970 Engr. *Perf. 13*

205 A58 25fr multi	16	15
206 A59 70fr multi	40	18
207 A59 90fr multi	55	22
Nos. 205-207 (3)	1.11	55

Issue dates: 25fr, Feb. 10; others, Feb. 25.

Volvaria Esculenta — A60

Mushrooms: 10fr, Termitomyces entolomoides. 15fr, Termitomyces microcarpus. 25fr, Termitomyces aurantiacus. 30fr, Termitomyces mammiformis. 50fr, Tremella fuciformis.

1970, Mar. 31 Photo. *Perf. 13*

208 A60 5fr multi	15	15
209 A60 10fr multi	15	15
210 A60 15fr multi	16	15
211 A60 25fr multi	30	15
212 A60 30fr multi	35	18
213 A60 50fr multi	45	30
Nos. 208-213 (6)	1.56	
Set value		88

Laying Coaxial Cable — A61

Design: 30fr, Full view of rail car; 3 cable layers on railway roadbed.

1970, Apr. 30 Engr. *Perf. 13*

214 A61 25fr dk brn & multi	22	15
215 A61 30fr brn & multi	25	15

Issued to publicize the laying of the coaxial cable linking Brazzaville and Pointe Noire.

For surcharges see Nos. 263-264.

UPU Headquarters Issue

Common Design Type

1970, May 20

216 CD133 30fr dk pur, gray & mag	30	15

Mother Feeding Child — A62

Dag Hammarskjold, UN Emblem — A63

Design: 90fr, Mother nursing infant.

1970, May 30 **Photo.**

217 A62	85fr vio bl & multi	65	38
218 A62	90fr lil & multi	70	40

Issued for Mother's Day.

1970, June 20 **Engr.** ***Perf. 13***

UN Emblem and: No. 220, Trygve Lie, horiz. No. 221, U Thant, horiz.

219 A63	100fr scar, dk red & dk pur	80	50
220 A63	100fr dk red, ultra & ind	80	50
221 A63	100fr grn, emer & dk red	80	50
a.	Souv. sheet of 3, #219-221	3.00	3.00
	Nos. 219-221 (3)	2.40	1.50

25th anniv. of the UN and to honor its Secretaries General.

Brillantaisia Vogeliana A64

Sternotomis Variabilis — A65

Designs (Plants and Beetles): 2fr, Plectranthus decurrens. 3fr, Myrianthemum mirabile. 5fr, Connarus griffonianus. 15fr, Chelorrhina polyphemus. 20fr, Metopodontus savagei.

Perf. 12¹/₂x12, 12x12¹/₂

1970, June 30 **Photo.**

222 A64	1fr dk grn & multi	15	15
223 A64	2fr multi	15	15
224 A64	3fr indigo & multi	15	15
225 A64	5fr lemon & multi	15	15
226 A65	10fr lilac & multi	15	15
227 A65	15fr orange & multi	15	15
228 A65	20fr multi	18	15
	Set value	68	50

For surcharge see No. 288.

Stegosaurus A66

Prehistoric Fauna: 20fr, Dinotherium, vert. 60fr, Brachiosaurus, vert. 80fr, Arsinoitherium.

1970, July 20

229 A66	15fr dl grn, ocher & red brn	16	15
230 A66	20fr lt bl & multi	20	15
231 A66	60fr lt bl & multi	50	18
232 A66	80fr lt bl & multi	75	35
	Nos. 229-232 (4)	1.61	83

Mikado 141, 1932 — A67

Locomotives: 60fr, Steam locomotive 130+032, 1947. 75fr, Alsthom BB 1100, 1962. 85fr, Diesel BB BB 302, 1969.

1970, Aug. 20 **Engr.** ***Perf. 13***

233 A67	40fr mag, bl grn & blk	40	20
234 A67	60fr blk, bl & grn	55	25
235 A67	75fr red, bl & blk	65	30
236 A67	85fr car, sl grn & ocher	80	38
	Nos. 233-236 (4)	2.40	1.13

Cogniauxia Padolaena — A68

Green Night Adder — A69

Tropical Flowers: 2fr, Celosia cristata. 5fr, Plumeria acutifolia. 10fr, Bauhinia variegata. 15fr, Poinsettia. 20fr, Thunbergia grandiflora.

1971, Feb. 10 **Photo.** ***Perf. 12x12¹/₂***

237 A68	1fr lil & multi	15	15
238 A68	2fr yel & multi	15	15
239 A68	5fr ultra & multi	15	15
240 A68	10fr yel & multi	15	15
241 A68	15fr multi	22	15
242 A68	20fr dk red & multi	25	15
	Set value	78	48

Perf. 12x12¹/₂, 12¹/₂x12

1971, June 26 **Photo.**

Reptiles: 10fr, African Egg-eating snake, horiz. 15fr, Flap-necked chameleon. 20fr, Nile crocodile, horiz. 25fr, Rock python, horiz. 30fr, Gaboon viper. 40fr, Brown house snake, horiz. 45fr, Jameson's mamba.

243 A69	5fr multi	15	15
244 A69	10fr multi	15	15
245 A69	15fr multi	16	15
246 A69	20fr red & multi	20	16
247 A69	25fr grn & multi	25	20
248 A69	30fr multi	35	25
249 A69	40fr bis & multi	35	30
250 A69	45fr multi	42	35
	Nos. 243-250 (8)	2.03	1.71

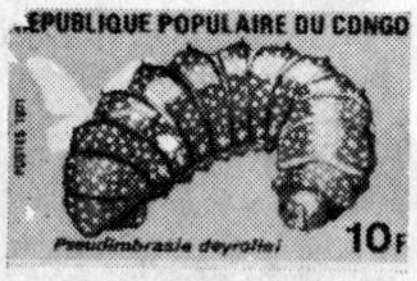

Pseudimbrasia Deyrollei A70

Caterpillars: 15fr, Bunaea alcinoe, vert. 20fr, Epiphora vacuna ploetzi. 25fr, Imbrasia eblis. 30fr, Imbrasia dione, vert. 40fr, Holocera angulata.

1971, July 3 ***Perf. 13***

251 A70	10fr ver, blk & grn	15	15
252 A70	15fr multi	16	15
253 A70	20fr yel grn, blk & ocher	22	18
254 A70	25fr multi	25	20
255 A70	30fr red, blk & yel	35	25
256 A70	40fr bl, blk & org	50	38
	Nos. 251-256 (6)	1.63	1.31

Boy Scout — A70a

Scouts, Lord Baden-Powell — A70b

Designs: c, Scout facing left. d, Scout facing forward. e, Lord Baden-Powell.

Embossed on Metallic Foil

1971, July 14 ***Die Cut Perf. 10¹/₂***

256A A70a	90fr Block of 4, #b.-e, silver	
256F A70b	1000fr gold	

No. 256F is airmail.

Cymothoe Sangaris A71

Butterflies and Moths: 40fr, Papilio dardanus, vert. 75fr, Iolaus timon. 90fr, Papilio phorcas, vert. 100fr, Euchloron megaera.

Perf. 12¹/₂x12, 12x12¹/₂

1971, Oct. 15

257 A71	30fr yel & multi	35	20
258 A71	40fr grn & multi	42	30
259 A71	75fr multi	70	42
260 A71	90fr multi	90	60
261 A71	100fr ultra & multi	1.10	80
	Nos. 257-261 (5)	3.47	2.32

Black and White Men Working Together — A72

1971, Oct. 30 ***Perf. 13x12¹/₂***

262 A72	50fr org & multi	35	16

Intl. Year Against Racial Discrimination.

Nos. 214-215 Surcharged

REPUBLIQUE POPULAIRE
DU CONGO
30F
INAUGURATION
DE LA LIAISON COAXIALE
18-11-71

1971, Nov. 18 **Engr.** ***Perf. 13***

263 A61	30fr on 25fr multi	25	16
264 A61	40fr on 30fr multi	35	20

Inauguration of cable service between Brazzaville and Pointe Noire. Words of surcharge arranged differently on No. 264.

Map of Congo — A73

1971, Dec. 31 **Photo.** ***Perf. 12¹/₂x13***

265 A73	30fr bl & multi	22	16
266 A73	40fr yel grn & multi	25	15
267 A73	100fr gray & multi	70	38
	Nos. 265-267 (3)	1.17	69

"Labor, Democracy, Peace."

Lion — A74

Animals: 2fr, African elephants. 3fr, Leopard. 4fr, Hippopotamus. 5fr, Gorilla, vert. 20fr, Potto. 30fr, De Brazza's monkey. 40fr, Pygmy chimpanzee, vert.

1972, Jan. 31 **Engr.** ***Perf. 13***

268 A74	1fr grn & multi	15	15
269 A74	2fr dk red & multi	15	15
270 A74	3fr red brn & multi	15	15
271 A74	4fr vio & multi	15	15
272 A74	5fr brn & multi	15	15
273 A74	20fr org & multi	20	16
274 A74	30fr ocher & multi	35	18
275 A74	40fr Prus bl & multi	42	30
	Set value	1.25	90

WHO, 25th Anniv. — A75

Perf. 12¹/₂x13, 13x12¹/₂

1973, June 30 **Typo.**

276 A75	40fr WHO Emblem	20	15
277 A75	50fr WHO emblem, horiz.	25	15
	Set value		24

Kronenbourg Brewery A76

Designs (Brewery Trademark and): 40fr, Laboratory. 75fr, Vats and controls. 85fr, Automatic control room. 100fr, Pressure room. 250fr, Bottling plant.

1973, July 15 **Engr.** ***Perf. 13***

278 A76	30fr red & multi	16	15
279 A76	40fr red & multi	20	15
280 A76	75fr red & multi	38	20
281 A76	85fr red & multi	55	25
282 A76	100fr red & multi	70	40
283 A76	250fr red & multi	1.50	70
	Nos. 278-283 (6)	3.49	1.85

Kronenbourg Brewery, Brazzaville.

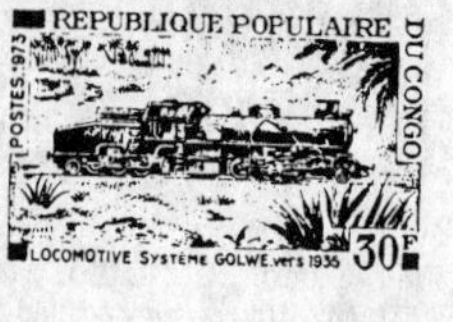

Golwe Locomotive, 1935 — A77

Locomotives: 40fr, Diesel, 1935. 75fr, Diesel Whithcomb, 1946. 85fr, Diesel CC200.

1973, Aug. 1 **Engr.** ***Perf. 13***

284 A77	30fr indigo & multi	25	16
285 A77	40fr vio bl & multi	35	16
286 A77	75fr multi	60	25
287 A77	85fr multi	65	35
	Nos. 284-287 (4)	1.85	92

No. 225 Surcharged with New Value, 2 Bars, and Overprinted in Ultramarine: "SECHERESSE SOLIDARITE AFRICAINE"

1973, Aug. 16 **Photo.** ***Perf. 12¹/₂x12***

288 A64	100fr on 5fr multi	55	38

African solidarity in drought emergency.

African Postal Union Issue
Common Design Type

1973, Sept. 12 **Engr.** *Perf. 13*

289 CD137 100fr bl grn, vio & brn 50 25

Bees, Beehive, Honeycomb A78

1973, Dec. 10 **Engr.** *Perf. 13*

290 A78 30fr sl grn, dk red & bl 18 15
291 A78 40fr sl bl, sl grn & lt grn 22 15

"Work and economy."

Family, UN and FAO Emblems A79

Designs: 40fr, Grain, emblems. 100fr, Grain, emblems, vert.

1973, Dec. 10

292 A79 30fr dk car & dk brn 18 15
293 A79 40fr dk grn, yel & ind 22 15
294 A79 100fr grn, brn & org 55 35
Nos. 292-294 (3) 95
Set value 52

World Food Program, 10th anniversary.

Amilcar Cabral, Cattle and Child — A80

1974, July 15 **Engr.** *Perf. 13*

295 A80 100fr multi 50 35

First death anniversary of Amilcar Cabral (1924-1973), leader of anti-Portuguese guerrilla activity in Portuguese Guinea.

Félix Eboué, Cross of Lorraine A81

1974, Aug. 31 **Litho.** *Perf. 13*

296 A81 30fr bl & multi 16 15
297 A81 40fr brt pink & multi 22 15
Set value 24

Félix A. Eboué (1884-1944), Governor of Chad, first colonial governor to join Free French in WWII, 30th death anniversary.

Pineapples A82

1974, Nov. 12

298 A82 30fr shown 16 15
299 A82 30fr Bananas 16 15
300 A82 30fr Safous 16 15
301 A82 40fr Avocados 22 15
302 A82 40fr Mangos 22 15
303 A82 40fr Papaya 22 15
304 A82 40fr Orange 22 15
Nos. 298-304 (7) 1.36
Set value 86

Charles de Gaulle and Conference Building — A83

1974, Nov. 25 **Engr.** *Perf. 13*

305 A83 100fr multi 50 35

Brazzaville Conference, 25th anniversary.

George Stephenson and Various Locomotives — A84

1974, Dec. 15

306 A84 75fr slate green & olive 38 22

George Stephenson (1781-1848), English inventor and railroad founder.

UDEAC Issue

Presidents and Flags of Cameroun, CAR, Congo, Gabon and Meeting Center — A84a

1974, Dec. 8 **Photo.** *Perf. 13*

307 A84a 40fr gold & multi 22 15

See note after Cameroun No. 595.
See No. C195.

Irish Setter — A85

Designs: Dogs.

1974, Dec. 15 **Photo.** *Perf. 13x13½*

308 A85 30fr shown 22 15
309 A85 40fr Borzoi 30 15
310 A85 75fr Pointer 50 22
311 A85 100fr Great Dane 65 38
Nos. 308-311 (4) 1.67 90

1974, Dec. 15

Designs: Cats.

312 A85 30fr Havana chestnut 22 15
313 A85 40fr Red Persian 30 15
314 A85 75fr Blue British 50 22
315 A85 100fr African serval 65 38
Nos. 312-315 (4) 1.67 90

Labor Party Flags and People — A86

Design: 40fr, Hands holding flowers and tools.

1974, Dec. 31 **Engr.** *Perf. 13x12½*

316 A86 30fr red & multi 16 15
317 A86 40fr red & multi 22 15
Set value 20

5th anniversary of Congolese Labor Party and of introduction of red flag.

Symbols of Development — A87

U Thant and UN Headquarters — A88

Paul G. Hoffman and UN Emblem A89

Perf. 13x12½, 12½x13

1975, Feb. 28 **Litho.**

318 A87 40fr multi 20 15
319 A88 50fr light blue & multi 22 15
320 A89 50fr yellow & multi 22 15
Nos. 318-320 (3) 64 45

National economic development.

Map of China and Mao Tse-tung — A90

1975, Mar. 9 **Engr.** *Perf. 13*

321 A90 75fr multi 40 25

25th anniv. of the PRC.

Woman Breaking Bonds, Women's Activities, Map of Congo — A91

1975, June 20 **Litho.** *Perf. 12½*

322 A91 40fr gold & multi 25 15

Revolutionary Union of Congolese Women, URFC, 10th anniversary.

CARA Soccer Team — A92

Design: 40fr, Team captain and manager receiving trophy, vert.

1975, July 15 **Litho.** *Perf. 12½*

323 A92 30fr multi 18 15
324 A92 40fr multi 22 15

CARA team, winners of African Soccer Cup 1974.

Citroen, 1935 — A93

Designs: Early autombiles.

1975, July 17 *Perf. 12*

325 A93 30fr shown 16 15
326 A93 40fr Alfa Romeo, 1911 22 15
327 A93 50fr Rolls Royce, 1926 25 20
328 A93 75fr Duryea, 1893 40 30
Nos. 325-328 (4) 1.03 80

Tipoye Transport — A94

1975, Aug. 5

329 A94 30fr shown 15 15
330 A94 40fr Dugout canoe 20 15
Set value 21

Traditional means of transportation.

Raising Red Flag — A95

1975, Aug. 15

331 A95 30fr shown 16 15
332 A95 40fr National Conference 22 15

2nd anniv. of installation of popular power (30fr) and 3rd anniv. of Natl. Conf. (40fr).

Line Fishing — A96

Woman Pounding "Foufou" — A97

Traditional Fishing: 30fr, Trap fishing, horiz. 60fr, Spear fishing. 90fr, Net fishing, horiz.

1975, Aug. 31 Litho. *Perf. 12*

333 A96 30fr multi 16 15
334 A96 40fr multi 22 15
335 A96 60fr multi 35 20
336 A96 90fr multi 45 35
Nos. 333-336 (4) 1.18 85

1975, Sept. 5

Household Tasks: No. 338, Woman chopping wood. 40fr, Woman preparing manioc, horiz.

337 A97 30fr multi 16 15
338 A97 30fr multi 16 15
339 A97 40fr multi 22 15
Nos. 337-339 (3) 54
Set value 34

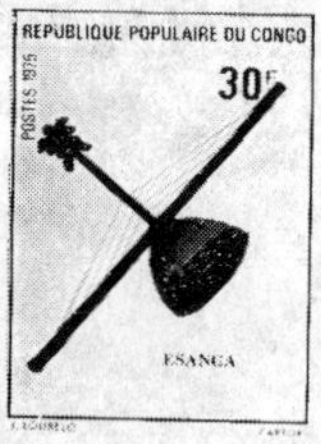

Musical Instruments — A98

1975, Sept. 20 *Perf. 12½*

340 A98 30fr Esanga 16 15
341 A98 40fr Kalakwa 22 15
342 A98 60fr Likembe 35 22
343 A98 75fr Ngongui 40 25
Nos. 340-343 (4) 1.13 77

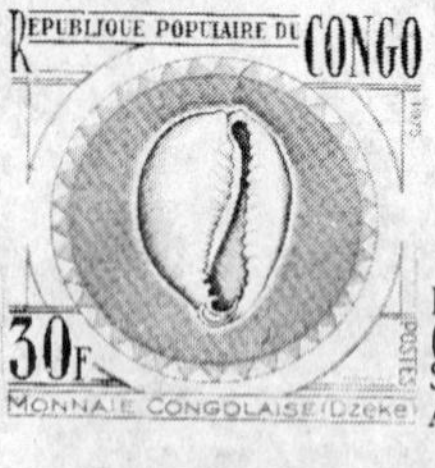

Dzeke (Congolese) Shell Money A99

Ancient Money: No. 346, like No. 344. Nos. 345, 347, Okengo, Congolese, iron bar. 40fr, Gallic coin, c. 60 B.C. 50fr, Roman denarius, 37 B.C. 60fr, Danubian coin, 2nd cent. B.C. 85fr, Greek stater, 4th cent. B.C.

1975-76 Engr. *Perf. 13*

344 A99 30fr red & multi 16 15
345 A99 30fr vio & multi 16 15
346 A99 35fr ol & multi 20 15
347 A99 35fr dk car rose & multi 20 15
348 A99 40fr Prus bl & brn 22 15
349 A99 50fr Prus bl & ol 25 16
350 A99 60fr dk grn & brn 35 22
351 A99 85fr mag & sl grn 42 25
Nos. 344-351 (8) 1.96 1.38

Nos. 346-347 inscribed "1976" and issued Mar. 1976; others issued Oct. 5, 1975.

Moschops — A100

Pre-historic Animals: 70fr, Tyrannosaurus. 95fr, Cryptocleidus. 100fr, Stegosaurus.

1975, Oct. 15 Litho. *Perf. 13*

352 A100 55fr multi 30 20
353 A100 75fr multi 40 22
354 A100 95fr multi 50 35
355 A100 100fr multi 55 38
Nos. 352-355 (4) 1.75 1.15

Albert Schweitzer (1875-1965), Medical Missionary — A101

1975, Oct. 15 Engr.

356 A101 75fr ol, brn & red 40 25

Alexander Fleming A102

Designs: No. 358, André Marie Ampère. No. 359, Clement Ader.

1975, Nov. 15 Engr. *Perf. 13*

357 A102 60fr brn, grn & blk 35 20
358 A102 95fr blk, red & grn 50 38
359 A102 95fr red, blue & indigo 50 38
Nos. 357-359 (3) 1.35 96

Fleming (1881-1955), developer of penicillin; Ampère (1775-1836), physicist; Ader (1841-1925), aviation pioneer.

UN Emblem "ONU" and "30" — A103

1975, Dec. 20 Engr. *Perf. 13*

360 A103 95fr car, ultra & grn 50 38

United Nations, 30th anniversary.

Women's Broken Chain — A104

Design: 60fr, Equality between man and woman, globe, IWY emblem.

1975, Dec. 20 Litho. *Perf. 12½*

361 A104 35fr mag, ocher & gray 20 15
362 A104 60fr ultra, brn & blk 35 22

International Women's Year, 1975.

Pres. Marien Ngouabi, Flag and Workers — A105

Echo of the P.C.T. A106

Perf. 12½x12, 13x12½

1975, Dec. 31

363 A105 30fr multi 16 15
364 A106 35fr multi 20 15
Set value 20

6th anniversary of the Congolese Labor Party (P.C.T.). See No. C215.

A.G. Bell and 1876 Telephone A107

1976, Apr. 25 Litho. *Perf. 12½x13*

365 A107 35fr yel, brn & org brn 20 15

Cent. of 1st telephone call by Alexander Graham Bell, Mar. 10, 1876. See No. C229.

Women Selling Fruit and Vegetables A108

1976, Sept. 19 Litho. *Perf. 12½x13*

366 A108 35fr shown 20 15
367 A108 60fr Market scene 35 20

Congolese Coiffure — A109

Designs: Various women's hair styles.

1976, Oct. 10 Litho. *Perf. 13*

368 A109 35fr multi 20 15
369 A109 60fr multi 35 22
370 A109 95fr multi 50 35
371 A109 100fr multi 55 38
Nos. 368-371 (4) 1.60 1.10

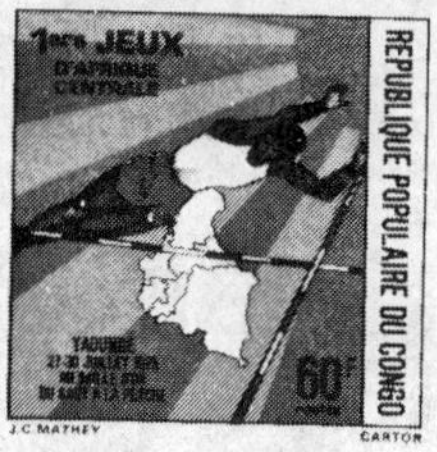

Pole Vault, Map of Central Africa A110

Design: 95fr, Long jump and map of Central Africa.

1976, Oct. 25 *Perf. 12½*

372 A110 60fr yel & multi 25 18
373 A110 95fr yel & multi 38 28

Gold medalists, 1st Central African Games, Yaoundé, July 27-30, 1975. See Nos. C230-C231.

Antelope A111

1976, Oct. 27 Litho. *Perf. 12½*

Size: 36x36mm

374 A111 5fr shown 15 15
375 A111 10fr Buffalos 15 15
376 A111 15fr Hippopotamus 15 15
377 A111 20fr Wart hog 15 15
378 A111 25fr Elephants 15 15
Set value 43 31

1976, Dec. 8

Designs: Birds.

Size: 26x36mm

379 A111 5fr Saddle-bill storks 15 15

Size: 36x36mm

380 A111 10fr Malachite kingfisher 15 15
381 A111 20fr Crowned cranes 15 15
Set value 22 18

Bicycling, Map of Participants A112

Heliotrope A113

1976, Dec. 21 Photo. *Perf. 12½x13*

382 A112 35fr shown 20 15
383 A112 60fr Fieldball 35 22
384 A112 80fr Running 42 35
385 A112 95fr Soccer 50 38
Nos. 382-385 (4) 1.47 1.10

First Central African Games, Libreville, Gabon, June-July 1976.

1976, Dec. 23 Photo. *Perf. 12½x13*

Flowers: 5fr, Water lilies. 15fr, Bird-of-paradise flower.

386 A113 5fr multi 15 15
387 A113 10fr multi 15 15
388 A113 15fr multi 20 15
Set value 39 17

Torch and Olive Branches A114

1976, Dec. 25 Litho. *Perf. 12½x13*

389 A114 35fr multi 15 20

National Pioneer Movement.

The Spirit of '76 A115

Designs: 125fr, Pulling down George III statue. 150fr, Battle of Princeton. 175fr, Generals of Revolutionary War. 200fr, Burgoyne's surrender at Saratoga. 500fr, Battle of Lexington.

1976, Dec. 29 Litho. *Perf. 14*

390 A115 100fr multi	65	25
391 A115 125fr multi	80	35
392 A115 150fr multi	90	38
393 A115 175fr multi	1.10	50
394 A115 200fr multi	1.25	55
Nos. 390-394 (5)	4.70	2.03

Souvenir Sheet

395 A115 500fr multi 3.25 1.40

American Bicentennial.

Dugout Canoe Race — A116

Design: 60fr, 2-man dugout canoes.

1977, Mar. 27 Litho. *Perf. 13x13½*

396 A116 35fr multi	22	15
397 A116 60fr multi	38	22

Dugout canoe races on Congo River.

Lilan Goua — A117

Fresh-water Fish: 15fr, Liko ko. 25fr, Liyan ga. 35fr, Mbessi. 60fr, Mongandza.

1977, June 15 Litho. *Perf. 12½*

398 A117 10fr multi	15	15
399 A117 15fr multi	15	15
400 A117 25fr multi	16	15
401 A117 35fr multi	22	15
402 A117 60fr multi	38	22
Nos. 398-402 (5)	1.06	
Set value		58

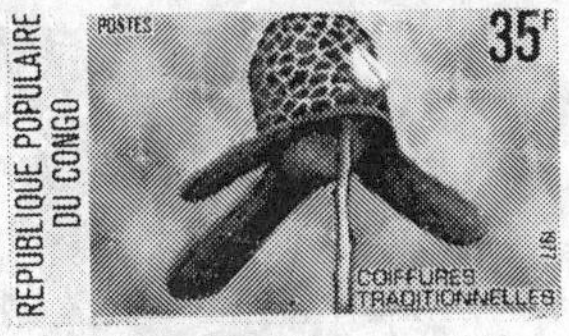

Traditional Headdress — A118

1977, June 30 Litho. *Perf. 12½*

403 A118 35fr shown	20	15
404 A118 60fr Leopard cap	35	22

See Nos. C234-C235.

Bondjo Wrestling — A119

Designs: 40fr, 50fr, Bondjo wrestling (different). 40fr, horiz.

1977, July 15

405 A119 25fr multi	15	15
406 A119 40fr multi	20	16
407 A119 50fr multi	25	20
Nos. 405-407 (3)	60	51

"Schwaben" LZ 10, 1911 — A120

Zeppelins: 60fr, "Viktoria Luise." LZ 11, 1913. 100fr, LZ 120. 200fr, LZ 127. 300fr, "Graf Zeppelin II" LZ 130.

1977, Aug. 5 Litho. *Perf. 11*

408 A120 40fr multi	22	15
409 A120 60fr multi	40	20
410 A120 100fr multi	65	22
411 A120 200fr multi	1.25	55
412 A120 300fr multi	2.00	80
Nos. 408-412 (5)	4.52	1.92

History of the Zeppelin. Exist imperf. See No. C236.

Coat of Arms and Rising Sun — A121

1977, Aug. 15

413 A121 40fr multi 20 16

14th anniversary of the revolution.

Victor Hugo and The Hunchback of Notre Dame — A122

Designs (Hugo and): 60fr, Les Miserables. 100fr, Les Travailleurs de la Mer (octopus).

1977, Aug. 20 Engr. *Perf. 13*

414 A122 35fr multi	20	15
415 A122 60fr multi	35	22
416 A122 100fr multi	55	40
Nos. 414-416 (3)	1.10	77

Victor Hugo (1802-1885), French novelist.

Mao Tse-tung A123

Lithographed; Gold Embossed

1977, Sept. 9 *Perf. 12x12½*

417 A123 400fr red & gold 2.25 1.60

Chairman Mao Tse-tung (1893-1976), Chinese Communist leader, 1st death anniv.

Peter Paul Rubens A124

1977, Sept. 20 Gold Embossed

418 A124 600fr gold & lt bl 3.25 2.50

Peter Paul Rubens (1577-1640), painter.

Child Leading Blind Woman Across Street A125

1977, Oct. 22 Litho. *Perf. 12½x13*

419 A125 35fr multi 20 15

World Health Day: To see is life.

15-Cent Minimum Value

The minimum value for a single stamp is 15 cents. This value reflects the costs of handling inexpensive stamps.

Paul Kamba and Records A126

1977, Oct. 29

420 A126 100fr multi 55 25

Paul Kamba (1912-1950), musician.

Trajan Vuia and Flying Machine — A127

Designs: 75fr, Louis Bleriot and plane. 100fr, Roland Garros and plane. 200fr, Charles Lindbergh and Spirit of St. Louis. 300fr, Tupolev Tu-144. 500fr, Lindbergh and Spirit of St. Louis over ship in Atlantic.

1977, Nov. 18 Litho. *Perf. 14*

421 A127 60fr multi	30	18
422 A127 75fr multi	35	22
423 A127 100fr multi	50	22
424 A127 200fr multi	2.00	50
425 A127 300fr multi	1.50	70
Nos. 421-425 (5)	4.65	1.82

Souvenir Sheet

426 A127 500fr multi 2.75 1.25

History of aviation.

Elizabeth II and Prince Philip A128

Design: 300fr, Elizabeth II wearing Crown.

1977, Dec. 21

427 A128 250fr multi	1.20	65
428 A128 300fr multi	1.50	70

25th anniv. of the reign of Queen Elizabeth II. See #C239. For overprints see #468-469, C244.

King Baudouin A129

Design: No. 430, Charles de Gaulle.

1977, Dec. 21

429 A129 200fr multi 1.25 65
430 A129 200fr multi 1.25 65

King Baudouin of Belgium and Charles de Gaulle, president of France.

Ambete Sculpture — A130

Congolese art: 85fr, Babembe sculpture.

1978, Feb. 18 Engr. *Perf. 13*

431 A130 35fr lt brn & multi 20 15
432 A130 85fr lt grn & multi 45 35

St. Simon, by Rubens A131

Rubens Paintings: 140fr, Duke of Lerma. 200fr, Madonna and Saints. 300fr, Rubens and his Wife Helena Fourment. 500fr, Farm at Laeken.

1978, Mar. 7 Litho. *Perf. 13½x14*

433 A131 60fr gold & multi 40 16
434 A131 140fr gold & multi 90 30
435 A131 200fr gold & multi 1.25 45
436 A131 300fr gold & multi 2.00 65
Nos. 433-436 (4) 4.55 1.56

Souvenir Sheet

437 A131 500fr gold & multi 3.25 1.40

Peter Paul Rubens, 400th birth anniv.

Pres. Ngouabi and Microphones A132

Designs: 60fr, Ngouabi at his desk, horiz. 100fr, Portrait.

Perf. 12½x13, 13x12½

1978, Mar. 18 Litho.

438 A132 35fr multi 20 15
439 A132 60fr multi 35 22
440 A132 100fr multi 55 40
Nos. 438-440 (3) 1.10 77

Pres. Marien Ngouabi, 1st death anniv.

Ferenc Puskas and Argentina '78 Emblem — A133

Players and Emblem: 75fr, Giacinto Facchetti. 100fr, Bobby Moore. 200fr, Raymond Kopa. 300fr, Pele. 500fr, Franz Beckenbauer.

1978, Apr. 4 *Perf. 14x13½*

441 A133 60fr multi 35 20
442 A133 75fr multi 40 22
443 A133 100fr multi 50 25
444 A133 200fr multi 1.25 60
445 A133 300fr multi 1.50 75
Nos. 441-445 (5) 4.00 2.02

Souvenir Sheet

446 A133 500fr multi 2.50 1.00

11th World Cup Soccer Championship, Argentina, June 1-25.

For overprints see Nos. 481-486.

Pearl S. Buck and Chinese Women — A134

Nobel Prize winners: 75fr, Fridtjof Nansen, refugees and Nansen passport. 100fr, Henri Bergson, book and flame. 200fr, Alexander Fleming and Petri dish. 300fr, Gerhart Hauptmann and book. 500fr, Henri Dunant and Red Cross Station.

1978, Apr. 29

447 A134 60fr multi 40 22
448 A134 75fr multi 45 25
449 A134 100fr multi 60 30
450 A134 200fr multi 1.40 65
451 A134 300fr multi 1.75 90
Nos. 447-451 (5) 4.60 2.32

Souvenir Sheet

452 A134 500fr multi 3.25 1.40

African Buffalos A135

Endangered animals and Wildlife Fund Emblem: 35fr, Okapi, vert. 85fr, Rhinoceros. 150fr, Chimpanzee, vert. 200fr, Hippopotamus. 300fr, Buffon's kob, vert.

1978 *Perf. 14½*

453 A135 35fr multi 22 16
454 A135 60fr multi 40 20
455 A135 85fr multi 55 28
456 A135 150fr multi 90 40
457 A135 200fr multi 1.40 60
458 A135 300fr multi 1.90 80
Nos. 453-458 (6) 5.37 2.44

Issue dates: 35fr, Aug. 11. Others, July 11.

Emblem, Young People, Gun and Fist — A136

1978, July 28 *Perf. 12½*

459 A136 35fr multi 20 15

11th World Youth Festival, Havana, July 28-Aug. 5.

Pyramids and Camels — A137

Seven Wonders of the Ancient World: 50fr, Hanging Gardens of Babylon. 60fr, Statue of Zeus, Olympia. 95fr, Colossus of Rhodes. 125fr, Mausoleum of Halicarnassus. 150fr, Temple of Artemis, Ephesus. 200fr, Lighthouse, Alexandria. 300fr, Map of Eastern Mediterranean showing locations. (50fr, 60fr, 95fr, 125fr, 200fr, vertical.)

1978, Aug. 12 Litho. *Perf. 14*

460 A137 35fr multi 22 15
461 A137 50fr multi 35 16
462 A137 60fr multi 40 20
463 A137 95fr multi 60 30
464 A137 125fr multi 80 38
465 A137 150fr multi 1.00 45
466 A137 200fr multi 1.25 55
467 A137 300fr multi 2.00 80
Nos. 460-467 (8) 6.62 2.99

Nos. 427-428 Overprinted in Silver: "ANNIVERSAIRE DU COURONNEMENT 1953-1978"

1978, Sept. Litho. *Perf. 14*

468 A128 250fr multi 1.40 50
469 A128 300fr multi 1.60 65

25th anniversary of corporation of Queen Elizabeth II. See No. C244.

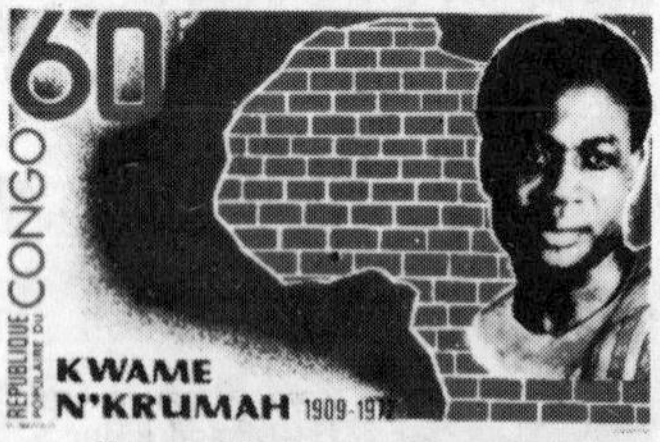

Kwame Nkrumah and Map of Africa — A138

1978, Sept. 23 Litho. *Perf. 13x12½*

470 A138 60fr multi 35 16

Nkrumah (1909-72), pres. of Ghana.

Wild Boar Hunt — A139

Local hunting and fishing: 50fr, Fish smoking. 60fr, Hunter with spears and dog, vert.

1978 Litho. *Perf. 12*

471 A139 35fr multi 22 16
472 A139 50fr multi 35 22
473 A139 60fr multi 40 25
Nos. 471-473 (3) 97 63

Issue dates: 35fr, 60fr, Oct. 5; 50fr, Oct. 10.

View of Kalchreut, by Dürer — A140

Paintings by Dürer: 150fr, Elspeth Tucher, vert. 250fr, "The Great Piece of Turf," vert. 350fr, Self-portrait, vert.

1978, Nov. 23 Litho. *Perf. 14*

474 A140 65fr multi 42 28
475 A140 150fr multi 1.00 70
476 A140 250fr multi 1.60 1.10
477 A140 350fr multi 2.25 1.50
Nos. 474-477 (4) 5.27 3.58

Albrecht Dürer (1471-1528), German painter.

Basketmaker — A141

Productive Labor: 90fr, Woodcarver. 140fr, Women hoeing field.

1978, Nov. 18 Litho. *Perf. 12½*

Size: 25x36mm

478 A141 85fr multi 60 40
479 A141 90fr multi 60 40

Size: 27x48mm

Perf. 12

480 A141 140fr multi 90 65
Nos. 478-480 (3) 2.10 1.45

Nos. 441-446 Overprinted in Silver:
a. "1962 VAINQUEUR: BRESIL"
b. "1966 VAINQUEUR: / GRANDE BRETAGNE"
c. "1970 VAINQUEUR: / BRESIL"
d. "1974 VAINQUEUR: / ALLEMAGNE (RFA)"
e. "1978 VAINQUEUR: / ARGENTINE"
f. "ARGENTINE-PAYS BAS 3-1/25 juin 1978"

1978, Nov. *Perf. 14x13½*

481 A133 (a) 60fr multi 40 25
482 A133 (b) 75fr multi 50 35
483 A133 (c) 100fr multi 65 45
484 A133 (d) 200fr multi 1.40 90
485 A133 (e) 300fr multi 2.00 1.40
Nos. 481-485 (5) 4.95 3.35

Souvenir Sheet

486 A133 (f) 500fr multi 3.50

Winners, World Soccer Cup Championships 1962-1978.

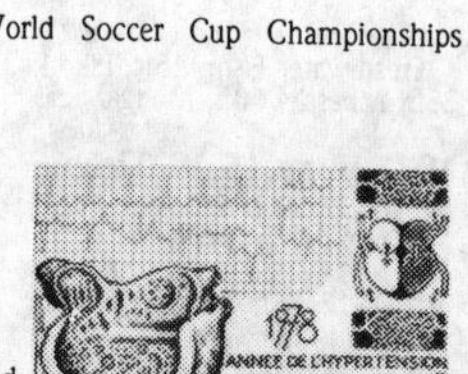

Heart and Charts A142

1978, Dec. 16 Engr. *Perf. 13*

487 A142 100fr multi 65 45

Fight against hypertension.

Party Emblem and Road — A143

1978, Dec. 31 Litho. ***Perf. 12½x12***

488 A143 60fr multi 40 25

Congolese Labor Party, 9th anniversary.

Capt. Cook, Polynesians and House — A144

Capt. James Cook (1728-1779): 150fr, Island scene. 250fr, Polynesian longboats. 350fr, Capt. Cook's ships off Hawaii.

1979, Jan. 16 ***Perf. 14½***

489 A144 65fr multi		38	28
490 A144 150fr multi		1.00	70
491 A144 250fr multi		1.60	1.10
492 A144 350fr multi		2.25	1.50
	Nos. 489-492 (4)	5.23	3.58

Pres. Marien Ngouabi — A145

1979, Mar. 18 Litho. ***Perf. 12***

493 A145 35fr multi 22 15
494 A145 60fr multi 40 25

Assassination of President Ngouabi, 2nd anniv.

"1979," IYC Emblem, Child A146

A146a

1979 Litho. ***Perf. 12½x13***

495 A146 45fr multi 30 20
496 A146 75fr multi 50 35

Souvenir Sheet

Perf. 14½

496A A153a 250fr multi

International Year of the Child.
Issued: 45fr, 75fr, Apr. 30. 250fr, Sept. 5.

Pottery Vases and Solanum — A147

Design: 150fr, Mail runner, Concorde, train, UPU emblem, envelope.

1979, June 8 Litho. ***Perf. 13***

497 A147 60fr multi 40 22

Engr.

498 A147 150fr multi 1.00 60

Philexafrique II, Libreville, Gabon, June 8-17. Nos. 497, 498 each printed in sheets of 10 with 5 labels showing exhibition emblem.

Rowland Hill, Diesel Locomotive, Germany No. 78 — A148

Designs (Rowland Hill and): 100fr, Old steam locomotive and France No. B10. 200fr, Diesel locomotive and US No. 245. 300fr, Steam locomotive and England-Australia First Aerialpost vignette, 1919. 500fr, Electric train, Concorde and Middle Congo No. 75.

1979, June ***Perf. 14***

499 A148 65fr multi		42	28
500 A148 100fr multi		65	45
501 A148 200fr multi		1.40	90
502 A148 300fr multi		2.00	1.25
	Nos. 499-502 (4)	4.47	2.88

Souvenir Sheet

503 A148 500fr multi 3.50

Sir Rowland Hill (1795-1879), originator of penny postage.

Salvador Allende, Flags, Demonstrators — A149

1979, July 21 Litho. ***Perf. 12½***

504 A149 100fr multi 65 45

Salvador Allende, president of Chile.

Old Man Telling Stories — A150

1979, July 28

505 A150 45fr multi 30 20

Story telling as education.

Handball Players A151

Designs: 75fr, Players and ball (vert.). 250fr, Pres. Ngouabi, cup on map of Africa, player.

1979, July 31 Litho. ***Perf. 12½***

Size: 40x30mm, 30x40mm

506 A151 45fr multi 30 20
507 A151 75fr multi 50 35

Size: 22x40mm

Perf. 12x12½

508 A151 250fr multi 1.60 1.25

Marien Ngouabi Handball Cup.

Map and Flag of Congo A152

1979, Aug. 15

509 A152 50fr multi 35 22

16th anniversary of revolution.

Souvenir Sheet

Virgin and Child, by Dürer A153

1979, Aug. 13 ***Perf. 13½***

510 A153 500fr red brn & lt grn 3.50

Albrecht Dürer (1471-1528), German engraver and painter.

Bach and Contemporary Instruments — A155

Design: No. 512, Albert Einstein, astronauts on moon.

1979, Sept. 10 ***Perf. 13½***

511 A155 200fr multi 1.40 90
512 A155 200fr multi 1.40 90

Yoro Fishing Port — A156

1979, Sept. 26 Litho. ***Perf. 12½***

513 A156 45fr shown 30 20
514 A156 75fr Port at night 50 35

Mukukulu Dam — A157

1979, Oct. 5 ***Perf. 12½x12***

515 A157 20fr multi 15 15
516 A157 45fr multi 30 20

Emblem, Control Tower, Jets — A158

1979, Dec. 12 Litho. ***Perf. 12½***

517 A158 100fr multi 65 50

ASECNA (Air Safety Board), 20th anniv.

Congolese Labor Party, 10th Anniversary A159

1979, Dec. 31

518 A159 45fr multi 30 15

A160

A161

1980, Mar. 30 Litho. ***Perf. 12½***

519 A160 45fr multi 30 25
520 A160 95fr multi 60 45

Post Office, 15th Anniversary.

1980, May 5

521 A161 100fr multi 55 25

Visit of Pope John Paul II.

Rotary International, 75th Anniversary — A162

1980, May 10 Litho. ***Perf. 12½***

522 A162 150fr multi 1.00 50

Pointe Noire Foundry A163

1980, June 18 Litho. ***Perf. 12½***

523 A163 30fr shown		16	15
524 A163 35fr Different view		18	15
	Set value		18

Claude Chappe, Tower A164

1980, June 21 Litho. *Perf. 12½*
525 A164 200fr multi 1.10 55

Claude Chappe (1763-1805), French engineer.

Mossaka Harbor — A165

1980, June 23
532 A165 45fr shown 25 15
533 A165 90fr Different view 50 22

Papilio Dardanus (Front and Back) — A167

Human Rights Emblem, People — A169

July 31st Hospital — A168

1980, July 12 Litho. *Perf. 12½*
534 A167 5fr shown 15 15
535 A167 15fr Kalima aethiops 15 15
536 A167 20fr Papilio demodocus 16 15
537 A167 60fr Euphaedra 42 16
538 A167 90fr Hypolimnas misippus 65 25
Nos. 534-538 (5) 1.53
Set value 56

Souvenir Sheet

539 A167 300fr Charaxes smaragdalis 2.25

1980, July 31
540 A168 45fr multi 25 15

1980, Aug. 2
541 A169 350fr shown 2.00 1.00
542 A169 500fr Man breaking chain 2.50 2.50

Human Rights Convention, 32nd anniv.

Citizens and Congolese Arms — A170

1980, Aug. 15 *Perf. 12½*
543 A170 75fr shown 40 20
544 A170 95fr Dove on flag, fists, vert. 50 25
545 A170 150fr Dove holding Congolese arms 80 40
Nos. 543-545 (3) 1.70 85

August 13-15th Revolution, 17th anniv.

Coffee and Cocoa Trees on Map of Congo — A171

Coffee and Cocoa Day: 95fr, Branches, map of Congo.

1980, Aug. 18 *Perf. 13½x13*
546 A171 45fr multi 22 15
547 A171 95fr multi 50 25

Logging A172

1980, Aug. 28
548 A172 70fr shown 40 20
549 A172 75fr Wood transport 40 20

Pres. Neto of Angola, 1st Death Anniv. — A173

Lark — A174

1980, Sept. 11
550 A173 100fr multi 55 25

1980, Sept. 17

Designs: Birds.

551 A174 45fr multi, horiz. 30 15
552 A174 75fr multi, horiz. 55 25
553 A174 90fr multi, horiz. 60 30
554 A174 150fr multi 1.00 50
555 A174 200fr multi 1.40 65
556 A174 250fr multi 1.60 80
a Souv. sheet of 6, #551-556 7.00
Nos. 551-556 (6) 5.45 2.65

World Tourism Conference, Manila, Sept. 27 — A175

1980, Sept. 27 Litho. *Perf. 13½x13*
557 A175 100fr multi 55 25

First Day of School Term — A176

1980, Oct. 2 Photo. *Perf. 13*
558 A176 50fr multi 25 15

First House in Brazzaville — A177

Brazzaville Centenary: 65fr, First native village. 75fr, Old Town Hall, 1912. 150fr, View from bank of Bacongo, 1912. 200fr, Meeting of explorer Savorgnan de Brazza and chief Makoko, 1880.

1980, Oct. 3 Litho. *Perf. 12½*
559 A177 45fr multi 25 15
560 A177 65fr multi 35 18
561 A177 75fr multi 40 20
562 A177 150fr multi 80 40
563 A177 200fr multi 1.10 55
Nos. 559-563 (5) 2.90 1.48

Boys on Bank of Congo River — A178

1980, Oct. 30
564 A178 80fr shown 42 20
565 A178 150fr Djoue Bridge 80 40

Revolutionary Stadium and Athletes — A179

1980, Nov. 20 *Perf. 13x12½*
566 A179 60fr multi 35 16

Rebuilt Railroad Bridge over Congo River A180

1980, Nov. 29 *Perf. 13x13½*
567 A180 75fr multi 40 20

Mangoes, Loudima Fruit Packing Station A181

1980, Dec. 2 *Perf. 13*
568 A181 10fr shown 15 15
569 A181 25fr Oranges 15 15
570 A181 40fr Citrons 20 15
571 A181 85fr Mandarins 45 22
Nos. 568-571 (4) 95
Set value 44

African Postal Union, 5th Anniversary — A182

1980, Dec. 24 *Perf. 13½*
572 A182 100fr multi 55 25

Moungouni Earth Satellite Station A183

1980, Dec. 30 *Perf. 12½*
573 A183 75fr multi 40 20

Hertzian Wave Communication, Brazzaville — A184

1980, Dec. 30 *Perf. 12½x12*
574 A184 150fr multi 80 40

1980 African Handball Champion Team — A185

Perf. 12½x13, 13x12½

1981, Jan. 26 Litho.
575 A185 100fr Receiving cup, vert. 55 25
576 A185 150fr shown 80 40

Pres. Denis Sassou-Nguesso — A186

1981, Feb. 5 Litho. *Perf. 12½*
577 A186 45fr multi 25 15
578 A186 75fr multi 40 20
579 A186 100fr multi 55 25
Nos. 577-579 (3) 1.20 60

Columbia Space Shuttle Orbiting Earth A187

Space Conquest: 100fr, Luna 17, 1970. 200fr, 300fr, 500fr, Columbia space shuttle, 1981.

1981, May 4 Litho. *Perf. 14x13½*
580 A187 100fr multi 55 25
581 A187 150fr multi 80 40
582 A187 200fr multi 1.10 55
583 A187 300fr multi 1.60 80
Nos. 580-583 (4) 4.05 2.00

Souvenir Sheet

584 A187 500fr multi 2.50 1.40

For overprint see No. 725.

Fight Against Apartheid — A188

Twin Palm Tree of Louingui — A189

1981, May 5 Litho. *Perf. 12½*
585 A188 100fr deep blue 55 25

1981, May 22 *Perf. 12x12½*
586 A189 75fr multi 40 20

13th World Telecommunications Day — A190

1981, June 6 *Perf. 12½*
587 A190 120fr multi 60 30

Rubber Extraction — A191

1981, June 27 *Perf. 13*
588 A191 50fr shown 25 15
589 A191 70fr Sap draining 40 16

Intl. Year of the Disabled A192

1981, June 29 Engr.
590 A192 45fr multi 25 15

See No. B7.

Bird Trap — A194

Designs: Animal traps. 10fr vert.

1981, July
596 A194 5fr multi 15 15
597 A194 10fr multi 15 15
598 A194 15fr multi 15 15
599 A194 20fr multi 15 15
600 A194 30fr multi 15 15
601 A194 35fr multi 20 15
Set value 69 38

Mausoleum of King Maloango — A195

1981, July 4 Litho. *Perf. 12½*
602 A195 75fr shown 40 20
603 A195 150fr Mausoleum, portrait 80 40

Prince Charles and Lady Diana, Coach A196

Royal wedding: Couple and coaches.

1981, Sept. 1 Litho. *Perf. 14½*
604 A196 100fr multi 55 25
605 A196 200fr multi 1.10 55
606 A196 300fr multi 1.60 80
Nos. 604-606 (3) 3.25 1.60

Souvenir Sheet

607 A196 400fr multi 2.25 1.10

World Food Day — A197

1981, Oct. 16 Litho. *Perf. 13½x13*
608 A197 150fr multi 80 55

12th World UPU Day — A198

1981, Oct. 24 Engr. *Perf. 13x12½*
609 A198 90fr multi 50 22

Royal Guard A199

1981, Oct. 31 Litho. *Perf. 12½x13*
610 A199 45fr multi 22 15

Eradication of Manioc Beetle — A200

Natl. Red Cross — A201

1981, Nov. 18 Litho. *Perf. 12½*
611 A200 75fr multi 40 20

1981, Nov. 18 *Perf. 13*
612 A201 10fr Bandaging patient 15 15
613 A201 35fr Treating child 15 15
614 A201 60fr Drawing well water 35 16
Nos. 612-614 (3) 65
Set value 31

Giant Baobab ("Tree of Savorgnan de Brazza") A202

1981, Dec. 19 Litho. *Perf. 13*
615 A202 45fr multi 22 15
616 A202 75fr multi 40 20

Fetish Figure — A203

Designs: Various carved figures.

1981, Dec. 19 *Perf. 13x12½*
617 A203 15fr multi 15 15
618 A203 25fr multi 15 15
619 A203 45fr multi 22 15
620 A203 50fr multi 25 15
621 A203 60fr multi 35 16
Nos. 617-621 (5) 1.12
Set value 54

Caves of Bangou A204

1981, Dec. 29 *Perf. 13x13½*
622 A204 20fr multi 15 15
623 A204 25fr multi 15 15
Set value 24 15

King Makoko and His Queen, Ivory Sculptures by R. Engongodzo A205

Perf. 13½x13, 13x13½

1982, Feb. 27 Litho.
624 A205 25fr Woman, vert. 15 15
625 A205 35fr Woman, diff., vert. 15 15
626 A205 100fr shown 55 25
Nos. 624-626 (3) 85
Set value 42

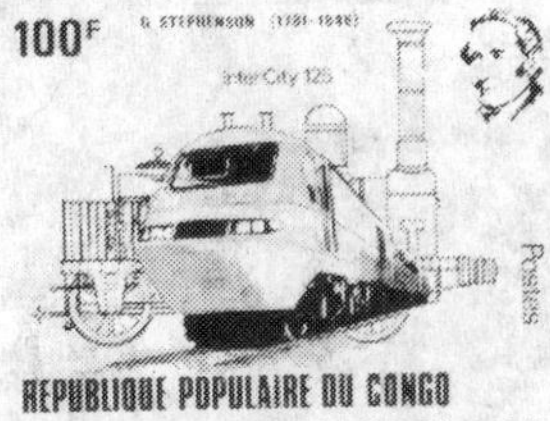

George Stephenson (1781-1848) and Inter City 125, Gt. Britain — A206

Locomotives: 150fr, Sinkansen Bullet Train, Japan. 200fr, Advanced Passenger Train, Gt. Britain. 300fr, TGV-001, France.

1982, Mar. 2 Litho. *Perf. 12½*
627 A206 100fr multi 55 25
628 A206 150fr multi 80 40
629 A206 200fr multi 1.10 55
630 A206 300fr multi 1.60 80
Nos. 627-630 (4) 4.05 2.00

Scouting Year A207

1982, Apr. 13 Litho. *Perf. 13*
631 A207 100fr Looking through binoculars 55 25
632 A207 150fr Reading map 80 40
633 A207 200fr Helping woman 1.10 55
634 A207 300fr Crossing rope bridge 1.60 80
Nos. 631-634 (4) 4.05 2.00

Souvenir Sheet

635 A207 500fr Hiking, horiz. 3.00 1.75

For overprint see No. 726.

Franklin Roosevelt A208

1982, June 12 Litho. *Perf. 13*
636 A208 150fr shown 80 40
637 A208 250fr Washington 1.40 65
638 A208 350fr Goethe 2.00 90
Nos. 636-638 (3) 4.20 1.95

21st Birthday of Princess Diana, July 1 — A209

1982, June 12 *Perf. 14*

639 A209 200fr Candles 1.10 55
640 A209 300fr "21" 1.60 80

Souvenir Sheet

641 A209 500fr Diana 2.50 1.40

5-Year Plan, 1982-1986 — A210

Perf. 13x12½, 12½x13

1982, June 19

642 A210 60fr Road construction 25 15
643 A210 100fr Communications, vert. 40 20
644 A210 125fr Operating room equipment, vert. 50 22
645 A210 150fr Hydroelectric power, vert. 65 30
Nos. 642-645 (4) 1.80 87

ITU Plenipotentiary Conference, Nairobi — A211

1982, June 26 *Perf. 13*

646 A211 300fr multi 1.60 80

Nos. 604-607 Overprinted in Blue: "NAISSANCE ROYALE 1982"

1982, July 30 *Perf. 14½*

647 A196 100fr multi 55 25
648 A196 200fr multi 1.10 55
649 A196 300fr multi 1.60 80
Nos. 647-649 (3) 3.25 1.60

Souvenir Sheet

650 A196 400fr multi 2.25 1.10

Birth of Prince William of Wales, June 21.

Nutrition Campaign — A212

1982, July 24 **Litho.** *Perf. 12½*

651 A212 100fr multicolored 55 25

WHO African Headquarters, Brazzaville — A213

1982, July 24 **Litho.** *Perf. 12½*

652 A213 125fr multicolored 65 35

TB Bacillus Centenary — A214

1982, Aug. 7 *Perf. 12½x12*

653 A214 250fr Koch, bacillus 1.40 65

Pres. Sassou-Nguesso and 1980 Simba Prize — A215

1982, Oct. 20 **Litho.** *Perf. 13*

654 A215 100fr multi 55 25

Turtles — A216

Various turtles and tortoises.

1982, Dec. 1

655 A216 30fr multi 16 15
656 A216 45fr multi 22 15
657 A216 55fr multi 30 15
Nos. 655-657 (3) 68
Set value 35

Boy Gathering Coconuts — A217

Nest in Tree Trunk — A218

1982, Dec. 11

658 A217 100fr multi 55 25

1982, Dec. 29 *Perf. 12½*

659 A218 40fr shown 20 15
660 A218 75fr Nests in palm tree 40 20
661 A218 100fr Woven nest on thorn branch 55 25
Nos. 659-661 (3) 1.15 60

Hertzian Wave Communication Network — A219

1982, Dec. 30 *Perf. 13x12½*

662 A219 45fr multi 22 15
663 A219 60fr multi 35 16
664 A219 95fr multi 50 25
Nos. 662-664 (3) 1.07 56

30th Anniv. of Customs Cooperation Council — A220

1983, Jan. 26 **Litho.** *Perf. 12½x13*

665 A220 100fr Headquarters 55 25

Mausoleum of Pres. Marien Ngouabi — A221

1983, Feb. 8 *Perf. 13*

666 A221 60fr multi 35 16
667 A221 80fr multi 42 20

Ironsmiths — A222

1983 *Perf. 12½*

668 A222 45fr shown 22 15
669 A222 150fr Weaver, vert. 80 40

Issue dates: 45fr, Mar. 5; 150fr, Feb. 24.

Carved Chess Pieces, by R. Engongonzo — A223

Various pieces.

1983, Feb. 26 *Perf. 13*

670 A223 40fr multi 22 15
671 A223 60fr multi 35 16
672 A223 95fr multi 50 25
Nos. 670-672 (3) 1.07 56

Easter 1983 — A224

Raphael drawings. 200fr, 400fr vert.

1983, Apr. 20 **Litho.** *Perf. 13*

673 A224 200fr Transfiguration study 1.10 55
674 A224 300fr Deposition from Cross 1.60 80
675 A224 400fr Christ in Glory 2.00 1.10
Nos. 673-675 (3) 4.70 2.45

Seashells — A225

1983 **Litho.** *Perf. 15x14*

675A A225 25fr multi
676 A225 35fr multi 15 15
677 A225 65fr multi 16 15

Dated 1982.

A226

A227

Various traditional combs.

1983, May *Perf. 14*

678 A226 30fr multi 15 15
679 A226 70fr multi 18 15
680 A226 85fr multi 22 15
Nos. 678-680 (3) 55
Set value 27

Perf. 12½x13

1983, Aug. 10 **Litho & Engr.**

681 A227 60fr multi 16 15
682 A227 100fr multi 25 15
Set value 22

20th anniv. of revolution.

Centenary of the Arrival of Christian Missionaries — A228

Churches and Clergymen: 150fr, A. Carrie, Church of the Sacred Heart, Loango, vert. 250fr, Msgr. Augouard; St. Louis, Liranga; St. Joseph, Linzolo.

1983, Aug. 23 *Perf. 12½*

683 A228 150fr multi 40 20
684 A228 250fr multi 65 35

Local Flowers — A229

1984, Jan. 20 Litho. ***Perf. 12½***

685 A229	5fr	Liana thunderaie, vert.	15	15
686 A229	15fr	Bougainvillea	15	15
687 A229	20fr	Anthurium, vert.	15	15
688 A229	45fr	Allamanda	15	15
689 A229	75fr	Hibiscus, vert.	20	15
		Set value	47	32

35th Anniv. of World Peace Council A230

1984, Mar. 31 Litho. ***Perf. 13x12½***

690 A230	50fr	multi	15	15
691 A230	100fr	multi	30	15
		Set value		22

Anti-Nuclear Arms Campaign — A231

1984, May 31 Litho. ***Perf. 12x12½***

692 A231	200fr	Explosion, victims	60	30

Agriculture Day — A232

Perf. 13x13½, 13½x13

1984, June 30 Litho.

693 A232	10fr	Rice	15	15
694 A232	15fr	Pineapples	15	15
695 A232	60fr	Manioc, vert.	16	15
696 A232	100fr	Palm tree, map, vert.	32	16
		Set value	58	34

Congress Palace — A233

1984, July 27 ***Perf. 13***

697 A233	60fr	multi	16	15
698 A233	100fr	multi	30	15
		Set value		23

Chinese-Congolese cooperation.

CFCO-Congo Railways, 50th Anniv. A234

1984, July 30 ***Perf. 13½***

699 A234	10fr	Loulombo Station	15	15
700 A234	25fr	Les Bandas Chinese Labor Camp	15	15
701 A234	125fr	"50"	40	20
702 A234	200fr	Admin. bldg.	60	30
		Nos. 699-702 (4)	1.30	
		Set value		60

Locomotives — A235

Ships on the Congo River — A236

1984, Aug. 24 ***Perf. 12½***

703 A235	100fr	CC 203	30	15
704 A236	100fr	Tugboat	30	15
705 A235	150fr	BB 103	45	22
706 A236	150fr	Pusher tugboat	45	22
707 A235	300fr	BB-BB 301	90	45
708 A236	300fr	Dredger	90	45
709 A235	500fr	BB 420 L'Eclair	1.50	75
710 A236	500fr	Cargo ship	1.50	75
		Nos. 703-710 (8)	6.30	3.14

World Fisheries Year — A237

1984, Oct. 16 ***Perf. 13½***

711 A237	5fr	Basket of fish	15	15
712 A237	20fr	Net fishermen in boat	15	15
713 A237	25fr	School of fish	15	15
714 A237	40fr	Net fisherman	15	15
715 A237	55fr	Trawler	15	15
		Set value	42	28

Anti-polio Campaign — A238

M'Bamou Palace Hotel, Brazzaville — A239

1984, Oct. 30

716 A238	250fr	Disabled men, hand	65	35
717 A238	300fr	Target, disabled women, horiz.	80	42

1984, Dec. 15 ***Perf. 14½***

718 A239	60fr	multi	16	15
719 A239	100fr	multi	25	15
		Set value		22

Fauna A240

1984, Dec. ***Perf. 15x14½***

720 A240	30fr	Pangolin	15	15
721 A240	70fr	Bat	20	15
722 A240	85fr	Civet cat	22	15
		Nos. 720-722 (3)	57	
		Set value		27

Congo River Logging A241

1984, Dec. ***Perf. 13½x13***

723 A241	60fr	Log raft, crew hut	16	15
724 A241	100fr	Tugboat pushing logs	25	15
		Set value		22

Souvenir Sheets

Nos. 584, 635 Ovptd. with Exhibition in Black or Green

1985, Mar. 8 ***Perf. 14x13½, 13***

725 A187	500fr	TSUKUBA EXPO '85	1.40	65
726 A207	500fr	ITALIA '85 emblem, ROME (G)	1.40	65

See Nos. C336-C337.

Zonocerus Variegatus — A242

1985, Mar. 15 ***Perf. 13***

727 A242	125fr	multi	35	16

Burial of a Teke Chief — A243

1985, Apr. 30 ***Perf. 12½***

728 A243	225fr	multi	65	32

Edible Fruit — A244

1985, June 15 ***Perf. 13½***

729 A244	5fr	Trichoscypha acuminata, vert.	15	15
730 A244	10fr	Aframomum africanum	15	15
731 A244	125fr	Gambeya lacuurtiana	35	16
732 A244	150fr	Landolphia jumelei	40	20
		Set value	85	46

Sizes: #729, 22x36mm, #731, 36x22mm.

Lions Club Intl., 30th Anniv. — A245

1985, June 25 ***Perf. 12½***

733 A245	250fr	Flag, District 403B	65	35

Russian Soldier, Kremlin, Fall of Berlin A246

1985, July 27 ***Perf. 12***

734 A246	60fr	multi	16	15

Defeat of Nazi Germany, end of World War II, 40th anniv.

Lady Olave Baden-Powell, Girl Guides Founder — A247

Anniversaries and events: 150fr, Girl Guides, 75th anniv. 250fr, Jacob Grimm, fabulist; Sleeping Beauty. 350fr, Johann Sebastian Bach, composer; European Music Year, St. Thomas Church organ, Leipzig. 450fr, Queen Mother, 85th birthday, vert. 500fr, Statue of Liberty, cent., vert.

1985, Aug. 26 ***Perf. 13***

735 A247	150fr	multi	45	22
736 A247	250fr	multi	80	40
737 A247	350fr	multi	1.10	55
738 A247	450fr	multi	1.25	60
739 A247	500fr	multi	1.50	70
		Nos. 735-739 (5)	5.10	2.47

PHILEXAFRICA '85, Lome, Togo, Nov. 16-24 — A248

1985, Oct. 10 ***Perf. 13x12½***

740 A248	250fr	shown	90	45
741 A248	250fr	Airport, postal van	90	45

Nos. 740-741 printed se-tenant with center label picturing map of Africa or UAPT emblem.

Mushrooms — A249

1985, Dec. 14 Litho. ***Perf. 13***

742 A249	100fr	Coprinus, vert.	38	20
743 A249	150fr	Cortinarius	55	25
744 A249	200fr	Armillariella mellea	75	38
745 A249	300fr	Dictyophora	1.10	55
746 A249	400fr	Crucibulum vulgare	1.50	70
		Nos. 742-746 (5)	4.28	2.08

Arbor Day — A250

Children's Hoop Races — A251

1986, Mar. 6 *Perf. 13½*
747 A250 60fr Planting sapling 32 16
748 A250 200fr Map, lifecycle diagram 1.10 55

1986, Apr. 30 *Perf. 12½*
749 A251 5fr Two boys 15 15
750 A251 10fr One boy 15 15
751 A251 60fr Three boys, horiz. 32 16
a. Souvenir sheet of 3, Nos. 749-751 45 28
Set value 43 26

A252

A253

1986, June 5 **Litho.** *Perf. 13½*
752 A252 60fr Garbage disposal 32 16
753 A252 125fr Dumping garbage 75 38

Intl. Environment Day.

1986, July 15 **Litho.** *Perf. 13x12½*

Traditional Modes of Transporting Goods: 5fr, Basket on head, child in sling carrier. 10fr, Child in carrier on hip, large basket strapped to forehead. 60fr, Man carrying load on shoulder.

754 A253 5fr multi 15 15
755 A253 10fr multi 15 15
756 A253 60fr multi 32 16
Set value 43 26

Mission of the Sisters of St. Joseph of Cluny, Cent. — A254

1986, Aug. 19 **Litho.** *Perf. 12½x13*
757 A254 230fr multi 1.40 70

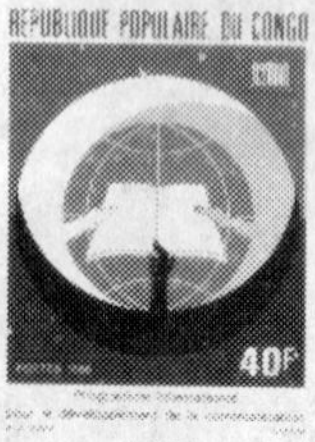

A255

A256

1986, Aug. 30 **Litho.** *Perf. 13½*
758 A255 40fr multi 22 15
759 A255 60fr multi 35 18
760 A255 100fr multi 60 30
Nos. 758-760 (3) 1.17 63

UNESCO intl. communications development program.

1986, Sept. 15 **Litho.** *Perf. 13½*
761 A256 100fr multi 60 30

Intl. Peace Year.

World Food Day — A257

1986, Oct. 16
762 A257 75fr Food staples 40 20
763 A257 120fr Mother feeding child 80 40

UN Child Survival Campaign A258

Mothers, children and pinwheels in various designs.

1986, Oct. 27
764 A258 15fr multi, vert. 15 15
765 A258 30fr multi 16 15
766 A258 70fr multi, vert. 38 20
Nos. 764-766 (3) 69
Set value 33

A258a

A259

1986, Dec. 5 **Litho.** *Perf. 12x12½*
766A A258a 100fr multi 65 32

27th Soviet Communist Party congress.

1987, Feb. 10 **Litho.** *Perf. 13½*
767 A259 30fr multi 16 15
768 A259 45fr multi 25 15
769 A259 75fr multi 40 20
770 A259 120fr multi 65 32
Nos. 767-770 (4) 1.46 82

Election of President Sassou-Nguesso, head of the Organization of African States.

Traditional Wedding A260

1987, Feb. 18 **Litho.** *Perf. 12½x13*
771 A260 5fr multi 15 15
772 A260 15fr multi 15 15
773 A260 20fr multi 15 15
Set value 25 16

The Blue Lake — A261

1987, July 16 *Perf. 12½*
774 A261 5fr multi 15 15
775 A261 15fr multi 15 15
776 A261 75fr multi 42 22
777 A261 120fr multi 68 35
Nos. 774-777 (4) 1.40
Set value 66

Pres. Marien Ngouabi A262

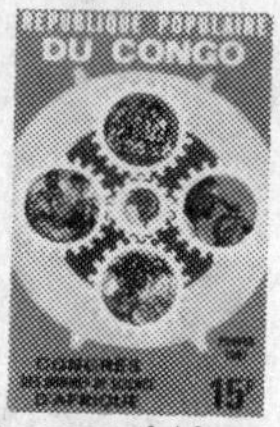

Congress of African Scientists A263

1987, July 16 *Perf. 13*
778 A262 75fr multi 42 22
779 A262 120fr multi 68 35

Tenth death anniv.

1987, Sept. 10 *Perf. 13x12½*
780 A263 15fr multi 15 15
781 A263 90fr multi 60 30
782 A263 230fr multi 1.55 78
Nos. 780-782 (3) 2.30 1.23

4th African Games, Nairobi — A264

1987, Oct. 30 *Perf. 12½*
783 A264 75fr multi 55 28
784 A264 120fr multi 88 45

Raoul Follereau (1903-1977), Philanthropist A265

1987, Oct. 20 *Perf. 13½*
785 A265 120fr multi 88 45

Cure leprosy.

FAO, 40th Anniv. — A266

1987, Nov. 17 *Perf. 12½*
786 A266 300fr multi 2.15 1.10

Anti-Apartheid Campaign — A267

Nelson Mandela — A268

Perf. 13½x15, 14½x15
1987, Sept. 21 **Litho.**
787 A267 60fr multi 42 20
788 A268 240fr multi 1.75 88

Natl. UNICEF Vaccination Campaign A269

Africa Fund A270

Perf. 13½x14½, 14½x13½
1987, Sept. 28
789 A269 30fr Inoculating adults, horiz. 22 15
790 A269 45fr shown 32 16
791 A269 500fr Inoculating children, horiz. 3.50 1.75
Nos. 789-791 (3) 4.04 2.06

No. 791 is airmail.

1987, Sept. 28 *Perf. 13½x15*
792 A270 25fr multi 18 15
793 A270 50fr multi 36 18
794 A270 70fr multi 50 25
Nos. 792-794 (3) 1.04 58

Self-sufficiency in Food Production by the Year 2000 — A271

1987, Nov. 20 **Litho.** *Perf. 13½*
795 A271 20fr multi 15 15
796 A271 55fr multi 40 20
797 A271 100fr multi 72 35
Nos. 795-797 (3) 1.27 70

Simon Kimbangu (b. 1887), Founder of the Church of Christ on Earth — A272

1987, Nov. 28 *Perf. 12½*
798 A272 75fr Kimbangu, vert. 55 28
799 A272 120fr Kimbangu, parrot, vert. 85 42
800 A272 240fr Kimbanguist Church, Nkamba 1.70 85
a. Souvenir sheet of 3, #798-800 3.10 1.55
Nos. 798-800 (3) 3.10
Set value 52

October Revolution, Russia, 70th Anniv. A273

Design: Lenin inspecting revolutionary troops, Red Square, from an unspecified painting.

1988, Feb. 19 **Litho.** *Perf. 12½x12*
801 A273 75fr multi 50 25
802 A273 120fr multi 80 40

African Writers Opposing Apartheid — A274

Intl. Fund for Agricultural Development (IFAD), 10th Anniv. — A275

1988, Apr. 6 Litho. *Perf. 13½*

803 A274 15fr multi	15	15
804 A274 60fr multi	45	22
805 A274 75fr multi	52	25
Nos. 803-805 (3)	1.12	62

1988, Apr. 30

806 A275 240fr multi	1.70	85

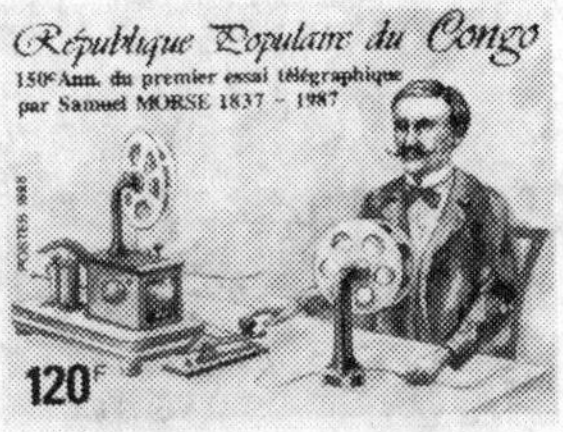
Invention of the Telegraph by Samuel Morse, 150th Anniv. (in 1987) — A276

1988, Apr. 28

807 A276 90fr Morse, vert.	65	32
808 A276 120fr shown	85	42

A277

A278

1988, Sept. 20 Litho. *Perf. 13½*

809 A277 5fr Eucalyptus trees, Brazzaville	15	15
810 A277 10fr Stop cutting down trees	15	15
Set value	15	15

Fight against desertification.

1988, Aug. 12 Litho. *Perf. 13½*

Campaigns: No. 812, Return to the Land Campaign (farming). 120fr, Self-sufficiency in food production.

811 A278 75fr shown	52	25
812 A278 75fr multi	52	25
813 A278 120fr multi	82	40
Nos. 811-813 (3)	1.86	90

Congo Revolution, 25th anniv.

Yoro Fishing Village A279

1988, Sept. 1

814 A279 35fr shown	24	15
815 A279 40fr Liberty Place	28	15

Intl. Day for the Fight Against AIDS — A280

1988, Dec. 1 Litho. *Perf. 13½*

816 A280 60fr shown	38	20
817 A280 75fr Emblem	48	25
818 A280 180fr Modified UN emblem, campaign emblem	1.15	58
Nos. 816-818 (3)	2.01	1.03

Natl. Committee for the Fight Against AIDS and Evangelical Anglican Church of Congo anti-AIDS campaign.

February 5 Movement, 10th Anniv. A281

1989, Apr. 21 Litho. *Perf. 13½*

819 A281 75fr Rally	45	22
820 A281 120fr Pres. Sassou-Nguesso, natl. achievements	72	35

UN Declaration of Human Rights, 40th Anniv. (in 1988) A282

1989, May 19 *Perf. 13*

821 A282 120fr multi	78	40
822 A282 350fr multi	2.25	1.15

Marien Nguabi, Founder of Congo Labor Party A282a

1989, July 31 Litho. *Perf. 12½x13*

822A A282a 240fr red & yellow	1.70	85

Red Cross and Red Crescent Societies, 125th Annivs. A283

Designs: 120fr, Dunant, emblem, Congo Red Cross.

1989, Sept. 19 Litho. *Perf. 13*

823 A283 75fr shown	48	25
824 A283 120fr multicolored	78	40

No. 824 is airmail.

Organization of African Unity, 25th Anniv. — A284

1989, Oct. 19 Litho. *Perf. 12½*

825 A284 120fr multicolored	78	40

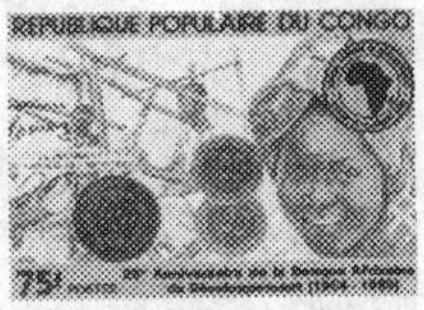
African Development Bank, 25th Anniv. A285

1989, Dec. 22 Litho. *Perf. 12½x13*

826 A285 75fr multicolored	55	28
827 A285 120fr multicolored	85	42

WHO, 40th Anniv. (in 1988) A286

1989, Dec. 28 Litho. *Perf. 12½*

828 A286 60fr shown	42	20
829 A286 75fr Blood donation, vert.	55	28

See Nos. 846-847 for overprints.

Congo Labor Party (PCT), 20th Anniv. — A287

1989, Dec. 22 Litho. *Perf. 13x12½*

830 A287 75fr multicolored	55	28
831 A287 120fr multicolored	85	42

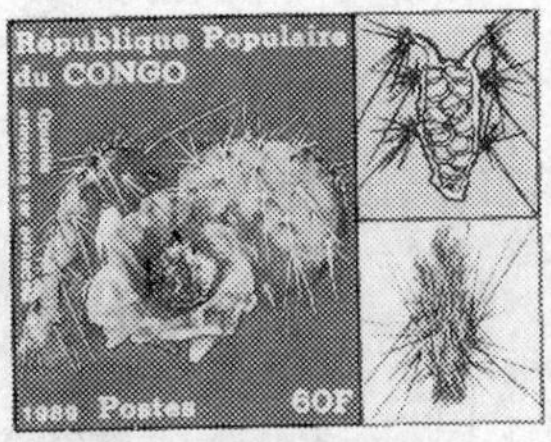
Cacti A288

Perf. 12½x13, 13x12½

1989, Nov. 22

832 A288 35fr *Opuntia phaeacantha discata*	25	15
833 A288 40fr *Opuntia ficus indica*	28	15
834 A288 60fr *Opuntia erinacea*	42	22
835 A288 75fr *Opuntia rufida*	55	28
836 A288 120fr *Opuntia leptocaulis*	85	42
Nos. 832-836 (5)	2.35	1.22

Souvenir Sheet

Perf. 12½

837 A288 220fr *Opuntia compresa*	1.60	80

Nos. 832-833, 835 and 837 vert. No. 837 contains one 32x40mm stamp.

1992 Winter Olympics, Albertville A289

1989, Dec. 22 *Perf. 12½*

838 A289 75fr Ice dancing	52	26
839 A289 80fr Nordic skiing	55	28
840 A289 100fr Speed skating	70	35
841 A289 120fr Luge	85	42
842 A289 200fr Alpine skiing	1.40	70
843 A289 240fr Ice hockey	1.70	85
844 A289 400fr Ski jumping	2.80	1.40
Nos. 838-844 (7)	8.52	4.26

Souvenir Sheet

Perf. 13

845 A289 500fr Bobsled	3.50	1.75

No. 845 contains one 32x40mm stamp.

Nos. 828-829 Ovptd. "NOTRE PLANETE, NOTRE SANTE PENSER GLOBALEMENT AGIR LOCALEMENT" in 3 or 5 Lines

1990 *Perf. 12½*

846 A286 60fr multicolored	42	20
847 A286 75fr multicolored	55	28

Health care for everyone.

Intl. Literacy Year — A290

1990, June 26 Litho. *Perf. 13½*

848 A290 75fr bl, blk & yel	55	28

Birds — A291

Designs: 25fr, Tourterelle des bois. 50fr, Fauvette pitchou, vert. 70fr, Faucon crecerelle, vert. 150fr, Perroquet gris, vert.

1990, July 10

849 A291 25fr multicolored	18	15
850 A291 50fr multicolored	36	18
851 A291 70fr multicolored	50	25
852 A291 150fr multicolored	1.10	55
Nos. 849-852 (4)	2.14	1.13

Dance Masks — A292

Flowering Plants — A293

1990, July 24 *Perf. 13*

853 A292	120fr Mondo		85	42
854 A292	360fr Bapunu		2.60	1.30
855 A292	400fr Kwele		2.90	1.45
	Nos. 853-855 (3)		6.35	3.17

1990, Sept. 15 **Litho.** *Perf. 12½*

856 A293	30fr Tournesol (sunflower)	25	15
857 A293	45fr Cassia alata, horiz.	35	18
858 A293	75fr Oeillette (opium poppy)	60	30
859 A293	90fr Acalypha sanderil	70	35
	Nos. 856-859 (4)	1.90	98

1992 Summer Olympics, Barcelona — A294

1990, June 28 **Litho.** *Perf. 13½*

860 A294	100fr Street scene, vert.	80	40
861 A294	150fr shown	1.20	60
862 A294	200fr Sailing, diff.	1.60	80
863 A294	240fr Marketplace	1.90	95
864 A294	350fr Harbor	2.80	1.40
865 A294	500fr Monument, vert.	4.00	2.00
	Nos. 860-865 (6)	12.30	6.15

Souvenir Sheet

866 A294	750fr Cathedral, vert.	6.00	3.00

Nos. 864-865 airmail. Nos. 860-865 exist in miniature sheets of 1.

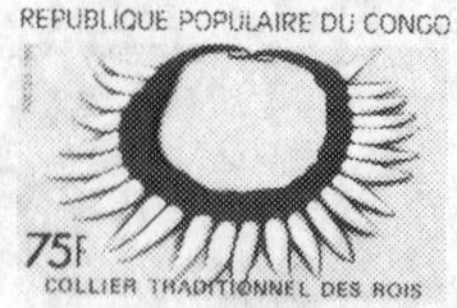

Royal Necklaces A295

1990, Aug. 18 **Litho.** *Perf. 13½*

867 A295	75fr shown	65	32
868 A295	100fr Necklace, diff.	85	42

Boy Scouts Observing Nature — A296

Scout: 35fr, Photographing butterfly, Euphaedra eusimoides. 40fr, Picking mushrooms, Armillaria mellea. 75fr, Drawing butterfly, Palla decius. 80fr, Using magnifying glass, Kallima ansorgei. 500fr, Using microscope, Cortinarius speciocissimus. 600fr, Feeding butterfly, Graphium illyris. 750fr, Photographing mushrooms, Volvariella bombycina.

1991, June 8 **Litho.** *Perf. 13½*

869 A296	35fr multicolored	30	15
870 A296	40fr multicolored	35	18
871 A296	75fr multicolored	65	32
872 A296	80fr multicolored	70	35
873 A296	500fr multicolored	4.15	2.10
874 A296	600fr multicolored	4.85	2.45
a.	Min. sheet of 4, #869, 871-872, 874	11.00	5.50
	Nos. 869-874 (6)	11.00	5.55

Souvenir Sheet

875 A296	750fr multicolored	6.20	3.10

Nos. 869-874 exist in souvenir sheets of 1. Nos. 873-875 are airmail.

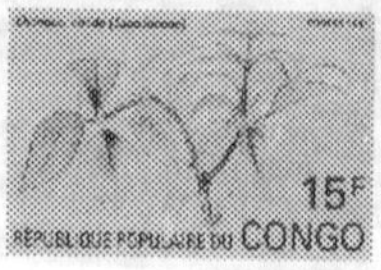

Medicinal Plants — A297

Designs: 15fr, Ocimum viride. 20fr, Kalanchoe pinnata, vert. 30fr, Euphorbia hirta. 60fr, Catharanthus roseus, vert. 75fr, Bidens pilosa, vert. 100fr, Brillantaisia patula, vert. 120fr, Cassia occidentalis, vert.

1991, Jan. 30 **Litho.** *Perf. 11½*

876 A297	15fr multicolored	15	15
877 A297	20fr multicolored	15	15
878 A297	30fr multicolored	22	15
879 A297	60fr multicolored	45	22
880 A297	75fr multicolored	55	28
881 A297	100fr multicolored	75	38
882 A297	120fr multicolored	90	45
	Nos. 876-882 (7)	3.17	1.78

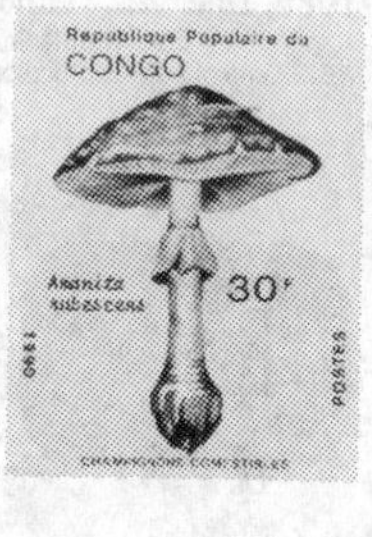

Mushrooms A298

1991, Mar. 25 **Litho.** *Perf. 13*

883 A298	30fr Amanita rubescens	24	15
883A A298	45fr Catathelasma imperiale	38	18
883B A298	75fr Amanita caesarea	60	30
883C A298	90fr Boletus regius	75	38
883D A298	120fr Pluteus cervinus	1.00	50
883E A298	150fr Boletus chrysenteron	1.20	60
883F A298	200fr Agaricus arvensis	1.60	80
	Nos. 883-883F (7)	5.77	2.91

A number has been reserved for a souvenir sheet with this set.

African Tourism Year — A299

1991, Apr. 15 **Litho.** *Perf. 13½*

884 A299	75fr shown	55	30
885 A299	120fr Zebra, map	90	45

Allegory of New Republic — A300

1991, May 13 **Litho.** *Perf. 13*

888 A300	15fr blue	15	15
890 A300	30fr brt grn	22	15
893 A300	60fr org yel	42	22
894 A300	75fr brt pink	52	28
898 A300	120fr dk brown	85	42
	Nos. 888-898 (5)	2.16	1.22

This is an expanding set. Numbers will change if necessary.

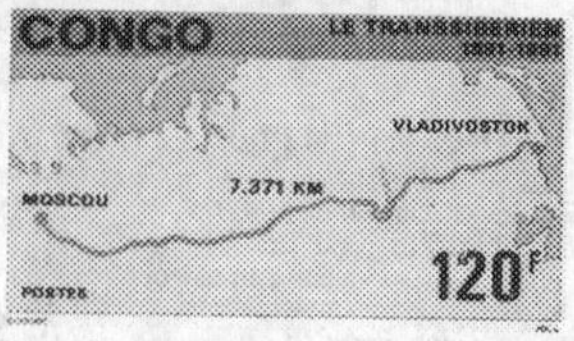

Trans-Siberian Railroad, Cent. — A301

1991, June 6 **Litho.** *Perf. 13*

899 A301	120fr Map	90	45
900 A301	240fr Map, train	1.80	90

Telecom 91 — A302

1991, June 29 **Litho.** *Perf. 13*

901 A302	75fr multi	55	30
902 A302	120fr multi, vert.	90	45

6th World Forum and Exposition on Telecommunications, Geneva, Switzerland.

Insects — A303

A304

1991, July 2 *Perf. 12½*

903 A303	75fr Peanut beetle	55	30
904 A303	120fr Centaur, horiz.	90	45
905 A303	200fr Coffee beetle	1.50	75
906 A303	300fr Goliath beetle	2.20	1.10
	Nos. 903-906 (4)	5.15	2.60

1991, July 16 **Litho.** *Perf. 12½*

907 A304	75fr Water conservation	55	28

Amnesty Intl., 30th Anniv. A305

Designs: 40fr, Candle, sun, vert. 75fr, "30," broken chains, vert.

1991, Aug. 13 *Perf. 13½*

908 A305	40fr multicolored	30	15
909 A305	75fr multicolored	55	28
910 A305	80fr multicolored	60	30
	Nos. 908-910 (3)	1.45	73

Congo Postage Stamps, Cent. — A306

Designs: 75fr, Similar to French Congo #1. 120fr, Similar to Congo Republic #89. 240fr, Similar to Congo Republic #89. 500fr, Similar to French Congo #1, 35 and Congo Republic #89.

Perf. 13x13½

1991, Aug. **Litho. & Engr.**

911 A306	75fr beige & dk grn	55	28
912 A306	120fr beige, dk grn & brn	90	45
913 A306	240fr multicolored	1.75	90
914 A306	500fr multicolored	3.70	1.85
a.	Strip of 4, #911-914	6.90	3.45

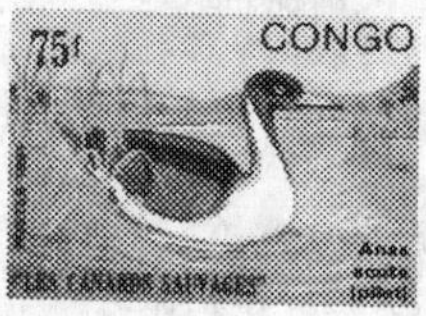

Ducks A307

1991, Aug. 8 **Litho.** *Perf. 12½*

915 A307	75fr Anas acuta	55	28
916 A307	120fr Somateria mollissima, vert.	90	45
917 A307	200fr Anas clypeata, vert.	1.50	75
918 A307	240fr Anas platyrhynchos	1.80	90
	Nos. 915-918 (4)	4.75	2.38

Automobiles and Space — A308

Designs: 35fr, Ferrari 512S by Pininfarina. 40fr, Vincenzo Lancia, Lancia Stratos by Bertone. 75fr, Maybach Zeppelin type 12, Wilhelm Maybach. 80fr, Mars Observer, 1992. 500fr, Magellan probe surveying Venus. 600fr, Magnification of Sun, Ulysses probe. 750fr, Crew of Apollo 11.

1991, Aug. 23 **Litho.** *Perf. 13½*

919 A308	35fr multicolored	28	15
920 A308	40fr multicolored	32	16
921 A308	75fr multicolored	60	30
922 A308	80fr multicolored	65	32
923 A308	500fr multicolored	4.00	2.00
924 A308	600fr multicolored	4.75	2.35
	Nos. 919-924 (6)	10.60	5.28

Souvenir Sheet

925 A308	750fr multicolored	5.90	2.95

Nos. 923-925 are airmail. No. 925 contains one 60x42mm stamp.

Butterflies — A309

1991, Aug. 31 *Perf. 11½*

926 A309	75fr Petit bleu	60	30
927 A309	120fr Charaxe	95	48
928 A309	240fr Papillon feuille, vert.	1.90	95
929 A309	300fr Papillon de l'oranger, vert.	2.40	1.20
	Nos. 926-929 (4)	5.85	2.93

Celebrities and Organizations — A310

Designs: 100fr, Bo Jackson, baseball and football player. 150fr, Nick Faldo, golfer. 200fr, Rickey Henderson, Barry Bonds, baseball players. 240fr, Gary Kasparov, World Chess Champion. 300fr, Starving child, Lions and Rotary Clubs emblems. 350fr, Wolfgang Amadeus Mozart. 400fr, De Gaulle, Churchill. 500fr, Jean-Henri Dunant, founder of Red Cross. 750fr, De Gaulle, vert.

1991, Sept. 2 *Perf. 13½*

930	A310	100fr multicolored	80	40
931	A310	150fr multicolored	1.20	60
932	A310	200fr multicolored	1.60	80
933	A310	240fr multicolored	1.90	95
934	A310	300fr multicolored	2.40	1.20
935	A310	350fr multicolored	2.75	1.40
936	A310	400fr multicolored	3.20	1.60
937	A310	500fr multicolored	4.00	2.00
		Nos. 930-937 (8)	17.85	8.95

Souvenir Sheet

938	A310	750fr multicolored	5.90	2.95

Nos. 936-938 are airmail. No. 938 contains one 35x50mm stamp.

Gen. Charles de Gaulle in Africa — A311

Designs: 120fr, De Gaulle, Free French flag, vert. 240fr, De Gaulle, Appeal of Brazzaville, 1940.

Perf. 13½x13, 13x13½

1991, Sept. 2

939	A311	75fr multicolored	60	30
940	A311	120fr multicolored	95	45
941	A311	240fr multicolored	1.90	95
		Nos. 939-941 (3)	3.45	1.70

A312

Paintings — A313

1991, Oct. 12 *Perf. 11½*

942	A312	75fr multicolored	60	30
943	A313	120fr multicolored	95	45

Discovery of America, 500th Anniv. (in 1992) — A314

Designs: 20fr, Portrait of Christopher Columbus by Sebastian Del Pombo. 35fr, Portrait of Columbus. 40fr, Portrait of Columbus facing right. 55fr, Santa Maria. 75fr, Nina. 150fr, Pinta. 200fr, Arms and signature of Columbus.

1991, May 30 *Perf. 13*

944	A314	20fr multicolored	15	15
945	A314	35fr multicolored	28	15
946	A314	40fr multicolored	30	15
947	A314	55fr multicolored	45	22
948	A314	75fr multicolored	60	30
949	A314	150fr multicolored	1.20	60
950	A314	200fr multicolored	1.60	80
		Nos. 944-950 (7)	4.58	2.37

Primates A315

1991, Dec. 13 **Litho.** *Perf. 13*

951	A315	30fr Cercopithecus diana	24	15
952	A315	45fr Pan troglodytes	38	18
953	A315	60fr Theropithecus gelada	48	24
954	A315	75fr Papio hamadryas	60	30
955	A315	90fr Macaca nemestrina	75	38
956	A315	120fr Gorilla gorilla	1.00	50
957	A315	240fr Mandrillus sphinx	1.95	1.00
		Nos. 951-957 (7)	5.40	2.75

Nos. 953-957 are vert. A number has been reserved for a souvenir sheet with this set.

Anniversaries and Events A316

Designs: 50fr, Launching of Sputnik II with dog, Laika, 1957. 75fr, Mahatma Gandhi and Martin Luther King, Jr. 1964. 120fr, Launching of Meteosat and ERS-1 over Europe and Africa. 240fr, Maybach Zeppelin automobile and Ferdinand von Zeppelin, 75th death anniversary. 300fr, Konrad Adenauer, 25th death anniversary and opening of the Brandenburg Gate, 1989. 500fr, Pope John Paul II's visit to Africa. 600fr, Elvis Presley, American entertainer.

1992, Feb. 4 **Litho.** *Perf. 13½*

959	A316	50fr multicolored	38	20
960	A316	75fr multicolored	58	30
961	A316	120fr multicolored	95	48
962	A316	240fr multicolored	1.90	95
963	A316	300fr multicolored	2.35	1.15
964	A316	500fr multicolored	3.90	2.00
a.		Souvenir sheet of 3, #960, 963-964	11.50	5.75
		Nos. 959-964 (6)	10.06	5.08

Souvenir Sheet

965	A316	600fr multicolored	4.70	2.35

Nos. 959-964 exist in souvenir sheets of 1. Nos. 962, 964-965 are airmail.

Explorers — A317

Birds — A318

Genoa '92: 75fr, Juan de la Cosa, nautical chart. 95fr, Martin Alonso Pinzon, astrolabe. 120fr, Alonso de Ojeda, hour glass. 200fr, Vicente Yanez Pinzon, sun dial. 250fr, Bartholomew Columbus, quadrant.

1992, Oct. 21 **Litho.** *Perf. 13*

966	A317	75fr multicolored	60	30
967	A317	95fr multicolored	75	38
968	A317	120fr multicolored	1.00	50
969	A317	200fr multicolored	1.60	80
970	A317	250fr multicolored	2.00	1.00
		Nos. 966-970 (5)	5.95	2.98

A number has been reserved for a souvenir sheet with this set.

1992, Oct. 21

Designs: 60fr, Sagittarius serpentarius. 75fr, Ephippiorhynchus senegalensis. 120fr, Bugeranus carunculatus. 200fr, Ardea melanocephala. 250fr, Phoenicopterus ruber roseus.

972	A318	60fr multicolored	48	24
973	A318	75fr multicolored	60	30
974	A318	120fr multicolored	1.00	50
975	A318	200fr multicolored	1.60	80
976	A318	250fr multicolored	2.00	1.00
		Nos. 972-976 (5)	5.68	2.84

A number has been reserved for a souvenir sheet with this set.

1992 Winter Olympics, Albertville — A320

1992 Summer Olympics, Barcelona — A321

Gold medalists: 150fr, N. Mishkutyonok, A. Dmitriev, pairs figure skating, Unified team. 200fr, I. Appelt, H. Winkler, G. Haldacher, T. Schroll, 4-man bobsled, Austria. 500fr, Gunda Niemann, speed skating, Germany. 600fr, Bjorn Daehlie, cross-country skiing, Norway. 750fr, Alberto Tomba, giant slalom, Italy.

1992 **Litho.** *Perf. 13½*

984	A320	150fr multicolored	1.20	1.20
985	A320	200fr multicolored	1.60	1.60
986	A320	500fr multicolored	4.00	4.00
987	A320	600fr multicolored	4.75	4.75
		Nos. 984-987 (4)	11.55	11.55

Souvenir Sheet

988	A320	750fr multicolored	6.00	6.00

Nos. 986-988 are airmail. No. 988 contains one 35x50mm stamp. Name on No. 987 spelled incorrectly.

1992

Barcelona landmarks, Olympic event: 75fr, Steeple of La Sagrada Familia, baseball. 100fr, The Muse, Palace of Music, running. 150fr, Cupola interior, long jump. 200fr, St. Paul Hospital, pole vault. 400fr, Sculpture, by Miro, shot put. 500fr, Galley, Maritime Museum, table tennis. 750fr, La Sagrada Familia, tennis.

989	A321	75fr multicolored	60	30
990	A321	100fr multicolored	80	40
991	A321	150fr multicolored	1.20	60
992	A321	200fr multicolored	1.60	80
993	A321	400fr multicolored	3.20	3.20
994	A321	500fr multicolored	4.00	4.00
		Nos. 989-994 (6)	11.40	9.30

Souvenir Sheet

995	A321	750fr multicolored	6.00	6.00

Nos. 993-995 are airmail.

Christmas — A321a

Paintings: 95fr, The Madonna of the Grand Duke, by Raphael. 200fr, The Madonna with a Book, by Botticelli. 250fr, The Madonna Carondelet, by Fra Bartolommeo. 400fr, Madonna and Child, by Raphael.

1992 **Litho.** *Perf. 12½*

995A	A321	95fr multicolored	70	35
995B	A321	200fr multicolored	1.50	75
995C	A321	250fr multicolored	1.90	95
		Nos. 995A-995C (3)	4.10	2.05

Souvenir Sheet

995D	A321	400fr multicolored	3.00	1.50

Nos. 995A-995D were not available until late 1993.

Birds of Prey — A322

A323

1993, Jan. 15 **Litho.** *Perf. 12½x13*

996	A322	45fr Charognard	38	20
997	A322	75fr Vulture	65	32
998	A322	120fr Eagle	1.00	50
		Nos. 996-998 (3)	2.03	1.02

1993 **Litho.** *Perf. 13½*

Traditional ceramics.

999	A323	45fr Liloko	35	18
1000	A323	75fr Mbeya	60	30
1001	A323	120fr Jug with ladles, Mbeya	1.00	50
		Nos. 999-1001 (3)	1.95	98

Wild Flowers — A326

Designs: 75fr, Hibiscus schizopetalus. 95fr, Pentas lanceolata. 120fr, Ricinus communis. 200fr, Delonix regia. 250fr, Stapelia gigantea.

1993, May 20 **Litho.** *Perf. 12½*

1016	A326	75fr multicolored	*1.65*	*80*
1017	A326	95fr multicolored	*2.00*	*1.00*
1018	A326	120fr multicolored	*2.50*	*1.25*
1019	A326	200fr multicolored	*4.25*	*2.00*
1020	A326	250fr multicolored	*5.50*	*2.75*
		Nos. 1016-1020 (5)	*15.90*	*7.80*

Deep Sea Submersibles A327

1993, June 25

1021	A327	75fr Transport PC-1202	*1.65*	*80*
1022	A327	95fr J. Sea Link 1	*2.00*	*1.00*
1023	A327	120fr Nemo	*2.50*	*1.25*
1024	A327	200fr Robot	*4.25*	*2.25*
1025	A327	250fr Alvin	*5.50*	*2.75*
		Nos. 1021-1025 (5)	*15.90*	*8.05*

A number has been reserved for a souvenir sheet with this set.

SEMI-POSTAL STAMPS

Anti-Malaria Issue

Common Design Type

1962, Apr. 7 **Engr.** *Perf. 12½x12*

B3	CD108	25fr + 5fr bister	42	42

Freedom from Hunger Issue

Common Design Type

1963, Mar. 21 **Unwmk.** *Perf. 13*

B4	CD112	25fr + 5fr vio bl, bl grn & brn	40	40

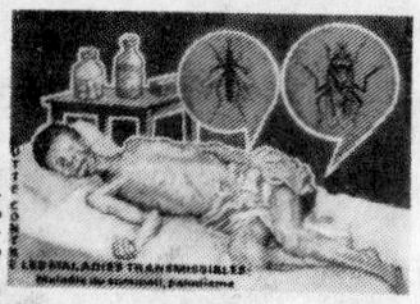

Boy Suffering from Sleeping Sickness — SP1

Fight Against Communicable Diseases; 40fr+5fr, Examination, treatment, vert.

1981, June 6	**Litho.**	***Perf. 13***	
B5 SP1 40fr + 5fr multi		25	15
B6 SP1 65fr + 10fr multi		40	20

IYD Type of 1981

1981, June 29	***Perf. 12½***		
B7 A192 75fr + 5fr multi		42	20

AIR POST STAMPS

Olympic Games Issue

French Equatorial Africa No. C37 Surcharged in Red Like Chad No. C1

1960 **Unwmk.** **Engr.**	***Perf. 13***		
C1 AP8 250fr on 500fr grnsh blk, blk & sl		3.50	3.50

17th Olympic Games, Rome, Aug. 25-Sept. 11.

Helicrysum Mechowiam — AP1

Flowers: 200fr, Cogniauxia podolaena. 500fr, Thesium tencio.

1961, Sept. 28 **Engr.**	***Perf. 13***		
C2 AP1 100fr grn, lil & yel		90	60
C3 AP1 200fr bl grn, yel & brn		1.75	80
C4 AP1 500fr brn red, yel & sl grn		4.00	1.75
Nos. C2-C4 (3)		6.65	3.15

Air Afrique Issue

Common Design Type

1961, Nov. 25 **Unwmk.**	***Perf. 13***		
C5 CD107 50fr lil rose, sl grn & grn		40	35

Loading Timber, Pointe-Noire Harbor — AP2

1962, June 8 **Photo.**	***Perf. 12½x12***		
C6 AP2 50fr multi		40	35

Opening of the Intl. Fair and Exhib., Pointe-Noire, June 8-11.

Abidjan Games — AP3

Costus Spectabilis — AP4

1962, July 21	***Perf. 12x12½***		
C7 AP3 100fr Basketball		90	62

1963 **Unwmk.**	***Perf. 13***		

Design: 250fr, Mountain acanthus.

C8 AP4 100fr multi		90	55
C9 AP4 250fr multi		2.25	1.25

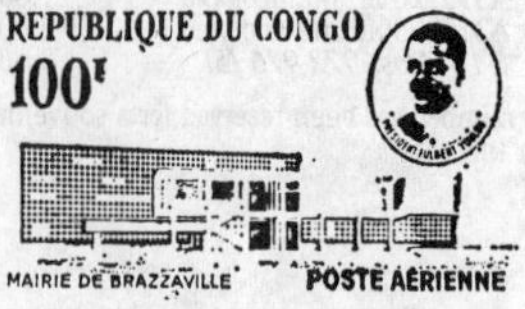

Brazzaville City Hall and Pres. Fulbert Youlou — AP4a

1963, Aug. **Photo.**	***Perf. 13x12***		
C10 AP4a 100fr multi		37.50	37.50

African Postal Union Issue

Common Design Type

1963, Sept. 8	***Perf. 12½***		
C13 CD114 85fr pur, ocher & red		60	42

Air Afrique Issue, 1963

Common Design Type

Perf. 13x12

1963, Nov. 19 **Unwmk.**	**Photo.**		
C14 CD115 50fr multi		42	35

Liberty Place, Brazzaville — AP5

1963, Nov. 28			
C15 AP5 25fr multi		22	16

See No. 118.

Europafrica Issue

Common Design Type

1963, Nov. 30	***Perf. 12x13***		
C16 CD116 50fr gray, yel & dk brn		55	38

Timber Industry — AP6

1964, May 12 **Engr.**	***Perf. 13***		
C17 AP6 100fr grn, brn red & blk		80	45

Chiefs of State Issue

Map and Presidents of Chad, Congo, Gabon and CAR — AP6a

1964, June 23 **Photo.**	***Perf. 12½***		
C18 AP6a 100fr multi		80	45

See note after Central African Republic No. C19.

Europafrica Issue, 1964

Sunburst, Wheat, Cogwheel and Globe — AP7

1964, July 20	***Perf. 12x13***		
C19 AP7 50fr yel, Prus bl & mar		42	25

See note after Cameroun No. 402.

Hammer Thrower, Olympic Flame and Stadium — AP8

50fr, 100fr, vert.

1964, July 30 **Engr.**	***Perf. 13***		
C20 AP8 25fr shown		22	15
C21 AP8 50fr Weight lifter		42	30
C22 AP8 100fr Volleyball		80	65
C23 AP8 200fr High jump		1.60	1.25
a. Min. sheet of 4, #C20-C23		4.00	4.00
Nos. C20-C23 (4)		3.04	2.35

Issued for the 18th Olympic Games, Tokyo, Oct. 10-25, 1964.

Communications Symbols — AP8a

1964, Nov. 2 **Litho.**	***Perf. 12½x13***		
C24 AP8a 25fr dl rose & dk brn		25	20

See note after Chad No. C19.

Town Hall, Brazzaville — AP9

1965, Jan. 30 **Photo.**	***Perf. 12½***		
C25 AP9 100fr multi		80	42

Coupling Hooks — AP10

1965, Feb. 27 **Photo.**	***Perf. 13x12***		
C26 AP10 50fr multi		42	25

Economic Europe-Africa Association.

Breguet Dial Telegraph, ITU Emblem and Telstar — AP11

1965, May 17 **Engr.**	***Perf. 13***		
C27 AP11 100fr dk bl, ocher & brn		90	55

Cent. of the ITU.

Pope John XXIII (1881-1963), St. Peter's Cathedral AP12

Perf. 12½x13

1965, June 26 **Photo.**	**Unwmk.**		
C28 AP12 100fr gldn brn & multi		80	60

Pres. John F. Kennedy — AP13

Log Rolling — AP14

Portraits: 25fr on 50fr, Patrice Lumumba, premier of Congo Republic (ex-Belgian). 50fr, Sir Winston Churchill. 80fr, Barthélémy Boganda, premier of Central African Republic.

1965, June	***Perf. 12½***		
C29 AP13 25fr on 50fr dk brn & red		25	25
a. Surcharge omitted		15.00	15.00
C30 AP13 50fr dk brn & yel grn		60	60
C31 AP13 80fr dk brn & bl		80	80
C32 AP13 100fr dk brn & org yel		1.00	1.00
a. Min. sheet of 4, #C29-C32		3.50	3.50
Nos. C29-C32 (4)		2.65	2.65

A second miniature sheet contains one each of Nos. C29a, C30-C32. Value, $30.

Issue dates: 25fr, 80fr, June 25, 50fr, 100fr, No. C32a, June 26.

1965, Aug. 14 **Engr.**	***Perf. 13***		
C33 AP14 50fr grn, brn & red brn		50	25

Issued to publicize national unity.

World Map and Symbols of Agriculture and Industry — AP15

1965, Oct. 18 Engr. *Perf. 13*

C34 AP15 50fr dk bl, blk, brn & org 50 35

International Cooperation Year, 1965.

Abraham Lincoln — AP16

1965, Dec. 15 Photo. *Perf. 13*

C35 AP16 90fr pink & multi 70 42

Centenary of death of Abraham Lincoln.

Charles de Gaulle, Torch and Map of Africa — AP17

1966, Feb. 28 Engr. *Perf. 13*

C36 AP17 500fr dk red, dk grn & dk red brn 9.00 7.50

22nd anniv. of the Brazzaville Conf.

D-1 Satellite over Brazzaville Space Tracking Station — AP18

Grain, Atom Symbol and Map of Africa and Europe — AP19

1966, May 15 Engr. *Perf. 13*

C37 AP18 150fr blk, dl red & bl grn 1.25 60

1966, July 20 Photo. *Perf. 12x13*

C38 AP19 50fr multi 55 35

See note after Gabon No. C46.

Pres. Massamba-Debat and President's Palace — AP20

3rd anniv. of the Revolution: 30fr, Robespierre and storming of the Bastille. 50fr, Lenin and storming of the Winter Palace.

1966, Aug. 15 Photo. *Perf. 12x12½*

C39 AP20 25fr multi	20	15
C40 AP20 30fr multi	22	15
C41 AP20 50fr multi	40	20
a. Souv. sheet of 3, #C39-C41	1.00	1.00
Nos. C39-C41 (3)	82	
Set value		40

Air Afrique Issue, 1966

Common Design Type

1966, Aug. 31 Photo. *Perf. 13*

C42 CD123 30fr lil, lem & blk 30 15

Dr. Albert Schweitzer — AP21

1966, Sept. 4 Photo. *Perf. 12½*

C43 AP21 100fr red, blk, bl & lil 80 55

Issued to honor Dr. Albert Schweitzer (1875-1965), medical missionary.

AP22

AP23

1966, Dec. 26 Photo. *Perf. 13*

C44 AP22 100fr Crab, microscope and pagoda 80 42

9th Intl. Anticancer Cong., Tokyo. Oct. 23-29.

1967 Photo. *Perf. 13*

Birds: 50fr, Social Weaver. 75fr, European Bee-eater. 100fr, Lilac-breasted roller. 150fr, Regal sunbird. 200fr, Crowned cranes. 250fr, Secretary bird. 300fr, Knysna touraco.

C45 AP23 50fr multi	65	25
C46 AP23 75fr multi	90	38
C47 AP23 100fr multi	1.10	55
C48 AP23 150fr multi	1.40	75
C49 AP23 200fr multi	1.90	90
C50 AP23 250fr multi	2.25	1.25
C51 AP23 300fr multi	2.75	1.50
Nos. C45-C51 (7)	10.95	5.58

Issue dates: Nos. C45-C47, Feb. 13. Others, June 20.

Shackled Hands AP24

1967, May 24 Photo. *Perf. 12½x13*

C52 AP24 500fr multi 4.50 2.00

Issued for African Liberation Day.

Sputnik 1, Explorer 6 and Earth — AP25

Space Craft: 75fr, Ranger 6, Lunik 2 and moon. 100fr, Mars 1, Mariner 4 and Mars. 200fr, Gemini, Vostok and earth.

1967, Aug. 1 Engr. *Perf. 13*

C53 AP25 50fr multi	40	22
C54 AP25 75fr multi	60	35
C55 AP25 100fr multi	80	55
C56 AP25 200fr multi	1.60	1.10
Nos. C53-C56 (4)	3.40	2.22

Space explorations.

African Postal Union Issue, 1967

Common Design Type

1967, Sept. 9 Engr. *Perf. 13*

C57 CD124 100fr ver, ol & emer 80 45

Boy Scouts, Tents and Jamboree Emblem — AP26

Design: 70c, Borah Peak, Idaho; tents, Scout sign and Jamboree emblem.

1967, Sept. 29

C58 AP26 50fr multi	38	20
C59 AP26 70fr multi	55	25

12th Boy Scout World Jamboree, Farragut State Park, ID, Aug. 1-9.

Sikorsky S-43 and Map of Africa — AP27

1967, Oct. 2 Photo. *Perf. 13*

C60 AP27 30fr multi 30 16

30th anniv. of the 1st airmail connection by Aeromaritime Lines from Casablanca to Pointe-Noire.

Men of Four Races Dancing on Globe — AP28

1968, Feb 8 Engr. *Perf. 13*

C61 AP28 70fr dk brn, ultra & emer 60 35

Friendship among peoples.

The Oath of the Horatii, by Jacques Louis David — AP29

Paintings: 25fr, On the Barricades, by Delacroix. No. C63, Grandfather and Grandson, by Ghirlandajo, vert. No. C64, The Demolition of the Bastille, by Hubert Robert. 200fr, Negro Woman Arranging Peonies, by Jean F. Bazille.

1968 Photo. *Perf. 12x12½, 12½x12*

C62 AP29 25fr multi	20	15
C63 AP29 30fr multi	35	20
C64 AP29 30fr multi	22	15
C65 AP29 100fr multi	90	55
C66 AP29 200fr multi	2.00	1.25
Nos. C62-C66 (5)	3.67	2.30

Issue dates: Nos. C62, C64, Aug. 15. Nos. C63, C65-C66, Mar. 20.

See Nos. C78-C81, C111-C115.

Early Automobile Type

1968, July 29 Photo. *Perf. 13x12½*

C67 A50 150fr Ford, 1915	1.40	65
C68 A50 200fr Citroen, 1922	1.60	90

Europafrica Issue

Square Knot — AP30

1968, July 20 Photo. *Perf. 13*

C69 AP30 50fr multi 38 16

5th anniv. of the economic agreement between the European Economic Community and the African and Malgache Union.

Martin Luther King, Jr. — AP31

Robert F. Kennedy — AP32

1968, Aug. 5 *Perf. 12½*

C70 AP31 50fr lt grn, Prus grn & blk 38 16

1968, Sept. 30 Photo. *Perf. 13x12½*

C71 AP32 50fr dp car, ap grn & blk 42 20

Running — AP33

Olympic Rings and: 20fr, Soccer, vert. 60fr, Boxing, vert. 85fr, High jump.

1968, Dec. 27 Engr. *Perf. 13*

C72 AP33	5fr emer, brt bl & choc	15	15
C73 AP33	20fr dk bl, brn & dk grn	16	15
C74 AP33	60fr mar, brt grn & choc	50	25
C75 AP33	85fr blk, car rose & choc	65	35
	Nos. C72-C75 (4)	1.46	
	Set value		73

Issued to commemorate the 19th Olympic Games, Mexico City, Oct. 12-27.

PHILEXAFRIQUE Issue

G. De Gueidan, by Nicolas de Largillière AP34

1968, Dec. 30 Photo. *Perf. 12½*

C76 AP34 100fr pink & multi 90 70

Issued to publicize PHILEXAFRIQUE, Philatelic Exhibition, in Abidjan, Feb. 14-23. Printed with alternating pink label.

See Nos. C89-C93.

2nd PHILEXAFRIQUE Issue

Common Design Type

Design: 50fr, Middle Congo No. 72 and Pointe-Noire harbor.

1969, Feb. 14 Engr. *Perf. 13*

C77 CD128 50fr car rose, sl grn & bis brn 50 42

Painting Type of 1968.

Paintings: 25fr, Battle of Rivoli, by Carle Vernet. 50fr, Battle of Marengo, by Jacques Augustin Pajou. 75fr, Battle of Friedland, by Horace Vernet. 100fr, Battle of Jena, by Charles Thevenin.

1969, May 20 Photo. *Perf. 12x12½*

C78 AP29	25fr vio bl & multi	25	16
C79 AP29	50fr cop red & multi	50	35
C80 AP29	75fr grn & multi	70	35
C81 AP29	100fr brn & multi	1.10	50
	Nos. C78-C81 (4)	2.55	1.36

Bicentenary of birth of Napoleon I.

Ernesto Ché Guevara — AP35

1969, June 10 Photo. *Perf. 12½*

C82 AP35 90fr brn, org & blk 70 38

Issued in memory of Ernesto Ché Guevara (1928-1967), Cuban revolutionist.

Doll, Train and Space Toy — AP36

1969, June 20 Engr. *Perf. 13*

C83 AP36 100fr mag, org & gray 80 42

Issued to publicize the International Toy Fair, Nuremberg, Germany.

Europafrica Issue, 1969

Ribbon Tied Around Bar — AP37

1969, Aug. 5 Photo. *Perf. 13x12*

C84 AP37 50fr bl grn, lil & blk 35 20

See note after Chad No. C11.

Armstrong, Aldrin and Collins — AP38

Painter, Poto-Poto School — AP39

Souvenir Sheet

Design: No. C85b, Blast-off from Moon.

Embossed on Gold Foil

1969, Sept. 15 *Imperf.*

C85 Sheet of 2 14.00 14.00

See note after Algeria No. 427. No. C85 contains one each of Nos. C85a and C85b with simulated perforations. Size: 65x52mm.

1970, Feb. 20 Engr. *Perf. 13*

Designs: 150fr, Sculpture lesson (man, infant and sculpture). 200fr, Potter working on vase.

C86 AP39	100fr multi	55	25
C87 AP39	150fr multi	80	40
C88 AP39	200fr multi	90	65
	Nos. C86-C88 (3)	2.25	1.30

Painting Type (Philexafrique) of 1968

Paintings: 150fr, Child with Cherries, by John Russell. 200fr, Erasmus, by Hans Holbein the Younger. 250fr, "Silence" (head), by Bernardino Luini. 300fr, Scene from the Massacre of Scio, by Delacroix. 500fr, The Capture of Constantinople by the Crusaders, by Delacroix.

1970 Photo. *Perf. 12½*

C89 AP34	150fr lil & multi	1.40	60
C90 AP34	200fr multi	1.60	80
C91 AP34	250fr brn & multi	1.90	1.00
C92 AP34	300fr multi	2.50	1.10
C93 AP34	500fr brn & multi	3.50	1.90
	Nos. C89-C93 (5)	10.90	5.40

Aurichalcite — AP40

1970, Mar. 20

C94 AP40	100fr shown	75	38
C95 AP40	150fr Dioptase	1.25	55

Lenin — AP41

Karl Marx — AP42

1970, June 25 Photo. *Perf. 12½*

C96 AP41	45fr shown	35	15
C97 AP41	75fr Lenin, seated	50	22

Centenary of the birth of Lenin (1870-1924), Russian communist leader.

1970, July 10 Engr. *Perf. 13*

Design: No. C99, Friedrich Engels.

C98 AP42	50fr emer, dk brn & dk red	38	20
C99 AP42	50fr ultra, dk brn & dk red	38	20

Issued in memory of Karl Marx (1818-1883) and Friedrich Engels (1820-1895), German socialist writers.

Otto Lilienthal's Glider, 1891 — AP43

Designs: 50fr, "Spirit of St. Louis," Lindbergh's first transatlantic solo flight, 1927. 70fr, Sputnik 1, first satellite in space. 90fr, First man on the moon, Apollo 11, 1969.

1970, Sept. 5 Engr. *Perf. 13*

C100 AP43	45fr dp car, bl & ol bis	38	20
C101 AP43	50fr emer, sl grn & brn	38	20
C102 AP43	70fr brt bl, ol bis & dp car	55	25
C103 AP43	90fr brn, bl & ol gray	75	38
	Nos. C100-C103 (4)	2.06	1.03

Forerunners of space exploration.

Saint on Horseback — AP44

Marilyn Monroe and NYC — AP45

Designs from Stained Glass Windows, Brazzaville Cathedral: 150fr, Saint with staff. 250fr, The Elevation of the Host, from rose window.

1970, Dec. 10 Photo. *Perf. 12½*

C104 AP44	100fr multi	50	28
C105 AP44	150fr multi	90	45
C106 AP44	250fr multi	1.50	80
a.	Souv. sheet of 3, #C104-C106	3.00	3.00
	Nos. C104-C106 (3)	2.90	1.53

Christmas 1970.

1971, Mar. 16 Engr. *Perf. 13*

Portraits: 150fr, Martine Carol and Paris. 200fr, Erich von Stroheim and Vienna. 250fr, Sergei Eisenstein and Moscow.

C107 AP45	100fr brt grn, red brn & ultra	65	25
C108 AP45	150fr brn, brt lil & ultra	1.10	40
C109 AP45	200fr choc & ultra	1.40	60
C110 AP45	250fr brt grn, brn vio & ultra	1.60	65
	Nos. C107-C110 (4)	4.75	1.90

History of motion pictures.

Painting Type of 1968

Paintings: 100fr, Christ Carrying Cross, by Paolo Veronese. 150fr, Christ on the Cross, Burgundian School, 1500, vert. 200fr, Descent from the Cross, by Rogier van der Weyden. 250fr, Christ Laid in the Tomb, Flemish School, 1500, vert. 500fr, Resurrection, by Hans Memling, vert.

1971, Apr. 26 Photo. *Perf. 13*

C111 AP29	100fr grn & multi	60	30
C112 AP29	150fr grn & multi	90	40
C113 AP29	200fr grn & multi	1.25	60
C114 AP29	250fr grn & multi	1.50	75
C115 AP29	500fr grn & multi	3.25	1.65
	Nos. C111-C115 (5)	7.50	3.70

Easter 1971.

Map of Africa and Telecommunications System — AP46

1971, June 18 Photo. *Perf. 12½*

C116 AP46	70fr bl, gray & dk brn	42	20
C117 AP46	85fr bl, lil rose & dk brn	50	25
C118 AP46	90fr grn, yel & dk brn	55	30
	Nos. C116-C118 (3)	1.47	75

Pan-African telecommunications system.

Globe and Waves AP47

1971, June 19

C119 AP47 65fr lt bl & multi 40 18

3rd World Telecommunications Day.

Japanese Mask and Play — AP48

Olympic Torch and Rings — AP49

Design: 150fr, Japanese and African women, symbolic leaves.

1971, June 28 Engr. *Perf. 13*

C120 AP48	75fr lil, blk & mag	55	25
C121 AP48	150fr dk brn, brn red & red lil	1.00	55

PHILATOKYO '71 International Stamp Exhibition, Tokyo, Apr. 20-30.

13th World Boy Scout Jamboree, Japan, gold foil 1000fr airmail and silver foil souv. sheet of four 90fr, issued July 14. Nos. 71C01-71C02.

1971, July 20 Engr. *Perf. 13*

Design: 350fr, Olympic rings and various sports, horiz.

C122 AP49 150fr brt rose lil, org & sl grn 1.10 60
C123 AP49 350fr bis, brt grn & vio 2.50 1.10

Pre-Olympic Year, 1971.

Scout Emblem, Japanese Dragon and African Carved Canoe — AP50

Designs (Boy Scout Emblem and): 90fr, Japanese mask and African boy, vert. 100fr, Japanese woman and African drummer, vert. 250fr, Congolese mask.

1971, Aug. 25

C124 AP50 85fr multi 65 30
C125 AP50 90fr multi 70 35
C126 AP50 100fr multi 80 40
C127 AP50 250fr multi 2.00 90
Nos. C124-C127 (4) 4.15 1.95

13th Boy Scout World Jamboree, Asagiri Plain, Japan, Aug. 2-10.

Olympic Rings and Running — AP51

Designs (Olympic Rings and): 85fr, Hurdles. 90fr, Weight lifting, boxing, discus, running, javelin. 100fr, Wrestling. 150fr, Boxing.

1971, Sept. 30

C128 AP51 75fr plum, bl & dk brn 45 20
C129 AP51 85fr scar, sl & dk brn 50 22
C130 AP51 90fr vio bl & dk brn 60 30
C131 AP51 100fr brn & sl 65 35
C132 AP51 150fr grn, red & dk brn 1.10 55
Nos. C128-C132 (5) 3.30 1.62

75th anniversary of the first modern Olympic Games.

Congo No. C36 and de Gaulle — AP52

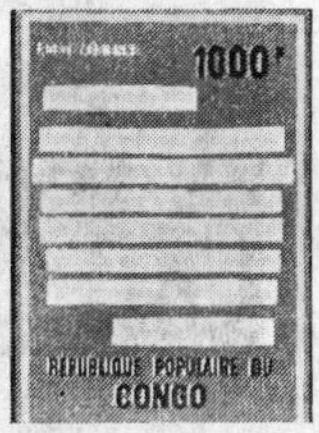

Pres. Marien Ngouabi's Tribute to de Gaulle — AP53

Design: No. C135, Charles de Gaulle.

1971, Nov. 9

C133 AP52 500fr sl grn & multi 3.25 3.25

Lithographed; Gold Embossed
Perf. 12½

C134 AP53 1000fr gold, grn & red 8.50 8.50
C135 AP53 1000fr gold, grn & red 8.50 8.50
a. Pair, #C134-C135 17.50 17.50

Charles de Gaulle (1890-1970), president of France.

African Postal Union Issue, 1971
Common Design Type

Design: 100fr, Allegory of Congo Republic (woman) and UAMPT Building, Brazzaville.

1971, Nov. 13 Photo. *Perf. 13x13½*

C136 CD135 100fr bl & multi 70 38

Flag of Congo Republic and "Revolution" — AP54

1971, Nov. 30

C137 AP54 100fr red & multi 65 35

8th anniversary of revolution.

Workers and Flag — AP55

Design: 40fr, Flag of Congo Republic and sun.

1971, Dec. 31 Photo. *Perf. 13x12½*

C138 AP55 30fr multi 16 15
C139 AP55 40fr red & multi 22 15
Set value 22

2nd anniv. of founding of Congolese Labor Party (#C138), and adoption of red flag (#C139).

Book Year Emblem — AP56

1972, June 3 Litho. *Perf. 12½*

C140 AP56 50fr red, grn & yel 25 15

International Book Year 1972.

Congolese Soccer Team — AP57

Design: No. C142, Captain of winning team and cup, vert.

1973, Feb. 22 Photo. *Perf. 13*

C141 AP57 100fr ultra, red & blk 65 42
C142 AP57 100fr red, yel & blk 65 42

Girl Holding Bird, Environment Emblem — AP58

1973, Mar. 5 Engr.

C143 AP58 85fr org, sl grn & bl 42 25

UN Conference on Human Environment, Stockholm, Sweden, June 5-16, 1972.

Miles Davis — AP59

Designs: 140fr, Ella Fitzgerald. 160fr, Count Basie. 175fr, John Coltrane.

1973, Mar. 5 Photo. *Perf. 13x13½*

C144 AP59 125fr multi 65 35
C145 AP59 140fr multi 70 38
C146 AP59 160fr multi 90 42
C147 AP59 175fr multi 1.00 50
Nos. C144-C147 (4) 3.25 1.65

Black American jazz musicians.

Olympic Rings, Hurdling — AP60

Designs (Olympic Rings and): 150fr, Pole vault, vert. 250fr, Wrestling.

1973, Mar. 15 Engr. *Perf. 13*

C148 AP60 100fr lil rose & vio 65 35
C149 AP60 150fr emer & vio 1.00 50
C150 AP60 250fr bl & mag 1.60 90
Nos. C148-C150 (3) 3.25 1.75

20th Olympic Games, Munich, Aug. 26-Sept. 11, 1972.

Refinery and Storage Tanks, Djéno — AP61

Designs: 230fr, Off-shore drilling platform, vert. 240fr, Workers assembling drill, vert. 260fr, Off-shore drilling installation.

1973, Mar. 20

C151 AP61 180fr red, bl & ind 1.10 55
C152 AP61 230fr red, bl & blk 1.40 65
C153 AP61 240fr red, ind & brn 1.50 80
C154 AP61 260fr red, bl & blk 1.75 90
Nos. C151-C154 (4) 5.75 2.90

Oil installations, Pointe-Noire.

Astronauts, Landing Module and Lunar Rover on Moon — AP62

1973, Mar. 31

C155 AP62 250fr multi 1.60 1.00

Apollo 17 US moon mission, Dec. 7-19, 1972.

ITU Emblem, Symbols of Communications AP63

1973, May 24 Engr. *Perf. 13*

C156 AP63 120fr multi 55 25

5th International Telecommunications Day.

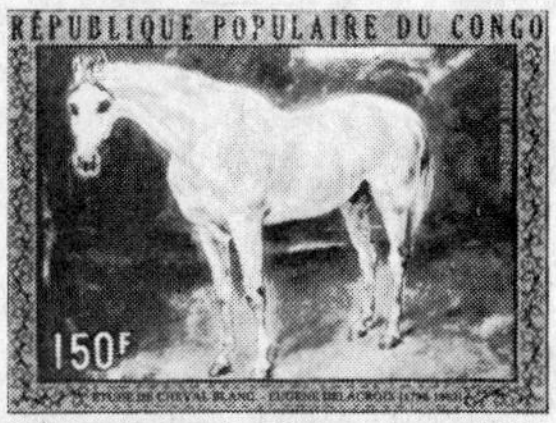

White Horse, by Delacroix — AP64

Designs: Paintings by Eugene Delacroix.

1973, June 30 Photo. *Perf. 13*

C157 AP64 150fr shown 90 90
C158 AP64 250fr Lion sleeping 1.50 1.25
C159 AP64 300fr Lion and tiger 1.75 1.50
Nos. C157-C159 (3) 4.15 3.65

See Nos. C169-C171.

Copernicus and Heliocentric System — AP65

1973, June 30 Engr.

C160 AP65 50fr multi 30 22

500th anniversary of the birth of Nicolaus Copernicus (1473-1543), Polish astronomer.

Plane, Ship, Rocket, Village, Sun and Clouds — AP66

1973, July

C161 AP66 50fr red & multi 25 20

Cent. of intl. meteorological cooperation.

Pres. Marien Ngouabi — AP67

1973, Aug. 12 **Photo.** ***Perf. 13***

C162 AP67 30fr multi	16	15
C163 AP67 40fr aqua & multi	20	15
C164 AP67 75fr red & multi	42	20
Nos. C162-C164 (3)	78	
Set value		37

10th anniversary of independence.

Stamps, Album, African Woman AP68

Designs: 40fr, No. C167, Stamps in shape of map of Congo, album, globe. No. C168, Like 30fr.

1973, Aug. 12

C165 AP68 30fr pur & multi	16	15
C166 AP68 40fr multi	20	15
C167 AP68 100fr dk brn & multi	50	38
C168 AP68 100fr ocher & multi	50	38
Nos. C165-C168 (4)	1.36	1.06

Nos. C165, C168 for the 10th anniv. of the revolution, Nos. C166-C167 the Intl. Philatelic Exhib., Brazzaville.

Painting Type of 1973 Inscribed "EUROPAFRIQUE"

Designs: Details from "Earth and Paradise," by Jan Brueghel, the Elder.

1973, Oct. 10 **Photo.** ***Perf. 13***

C169 AP64 100fr Spotted hyena	65	50
C170 AP64 100fr Leopard and lion	65	50
C171 AP64 100fr Elephant and creatures	65	50
Nos. C169-C171 (3)	1.95	1.50

US and Russian Spacecraft Docking — AP69

Design: 80fr, US and USSR spacecraft docked in space and emblems of 1975 joint space mission.

1973, Oct. 15 **Engr.** ***Perf. 13***

C172 AP69 40fr bl, red & brn	22	15
C173 AP69 80fr red, grn & bl	42	25

Planned joint US and Soviet space missions.
For overprint see No. C251.

UPU Monument, Satellites, Big Dipper — AP70

1973, Nov. 20 **Engr.** ***Perf. 13***

C174 AP70 80fr vio bl & lt bl	42	22

Universal Postal Union Day.

Astronauts Working in Space — AP71

Design: 40fr, Spacecraft and Skylab docking in space.

1973, Nov. 30

C175 AP71 30fr ultra, sl grn & choc	16	15
C176 AP71 40fr mag, org & sl grn	22	16

Skylab, first space laboratory.

Goalkeeper, Soccer — AP72

Design: 100fr, Soccer player kicking ball.

1973, Dec. 20

C177 AP72 40fr sl grn, sepia & brn	20	16
C178 AP72 100fr pur, red & slate grn	65	38

World Soccer Cup, Munich, 1974.

John F. Kennedy (1917-1963) AP73

1973, Dec. 20 **Photo.** ***Perf. 12½***

C179 AP73 150fr ultra, gold & blk	80	50

Runners — AP74

Flag over Map of Congo — AP75

1973, Dec. 20 **Engr.** ***Perf. 13***

C180 AP74 40fr sl grn, red & brn	22	16
C181 AP74 100fr red, sl grn, & brn	65	38

2nd African Games, Lagos, Nigeria.

1973, Dec. 31 **Photo.**

C182 AP75 40fr dp grn & multi	20	15

4th anniversary of Congolese Labor Party and of the Congo Red Flag.

Soccer and Games Emblem — AP76

1974, June 20 **Photo.** ***Perf. 13***

C183 AP76 250fr multi	1.40	90

World Cup Soccer Championship, Munich, June 13-July 7.

Astronauts Yuri A. Gagarin and Alan B. Shepard — AP77

Designs: 30fr, Space, globe, Russian and American flags with names of astronauts who perished in space. 100fr, Alexei Leonov and Neil A. Armstrong in space and on moon.

1974, June 30 **Engr.** ***Perf. 13***

C184 AP77 30fr red, ultra & brn	16	15
C185 AP77 40fr red, bl & brn	22	15
C186 AP77 100fr car, grn & brn	65	40
Nos. C184-C186 (3)	1.03	70

For overprint see No. C254.

Soccer Game Superimposed on Ball — AP78

Link-up Emblem, Stages of Link-up — AP79

1974, July 31 **Photo.** ***Perf. 13***

C187 AP78 250fr multi	1.40	90

Germany's victory in World Cup Soccer Championship.

1974, Aug. 8 **Engr.** ***Perf. 13***

Design: 300fr, Spacecraft docking over globe, horiz.

C188 AP79 200fr pur, bl & red	1.10	80
C189 AP79 300fr multi	1.60	1.10

Russo-American space cooperation.
For overprint see No. C255.

Symbols of Communications, UPU Emblem — AP80

1974, Aug. 10

C190 AP80 500fr blk & red	2.00	1.50

Centenary of Universal Postal Union.
For surcharge see No. C194.

Lenin and Pendulum Trace Pattern — AP81

1974, Sept. 16 **Engr.** ***Perf. 13***

C191 AP81 150fr multi	80	55

Lenin (1870-1924).

Churchill and Order of the Garter AP82

Marconi and Wireless Telegraph AP83

1974, Oct. 1 **Litho.** ***Perf. 13***

C192 AP82 200fr lt grn & multi	1.10	65
C193 AP83 200fr lt ultra & multi	1.10	65

Birth centenaries of Sir Winston Churchill (1874-1965), statesman; and of Guglielmo Marconi (1874-1937), Italian electrical engineer and inventor.

No. C190 Surcharged in Violet Blue with New Value, 2 Bars and: "9 OCTOBER 1974"

1974, Oct. 9

C194 AP80 300fr on 500fr multi	1.60	1.10

Universal Postal Union Day.

UDEAC Issue

Presidents and Flags of Cameroun, CAR, Gabon and Congo — AP83a

1974, Dec. 8 **Photo.** ***Perf. 13***

C195 AP83a 100fr gold & multi	55	40

See note after Cameroun No. 595.

Regatta at Argenteuil, by Monet — AP84

Impressionist Paintings: 40fr, Seated Dancer, by Degas. 50fr, Girl on Swing, by Renoir. 75fr, Girl with Straw Hat, by Renoir. All vertical.

1974, Dec. 15

C196 AP84 30fr gold & multi	22	16
C197 AP84 40fr gold & multi	25	20
C198 AP84 50fr gold & multi	42	35
C199 AP84 75fr gold & multi	45	38
Nos. C196-C199 (4)	1.34	1.09

National Fair — AP85

1974, Dec. 20

C200 AP85 30fr multi	16	15

National Fair, Aug. 24-Sept. 8.

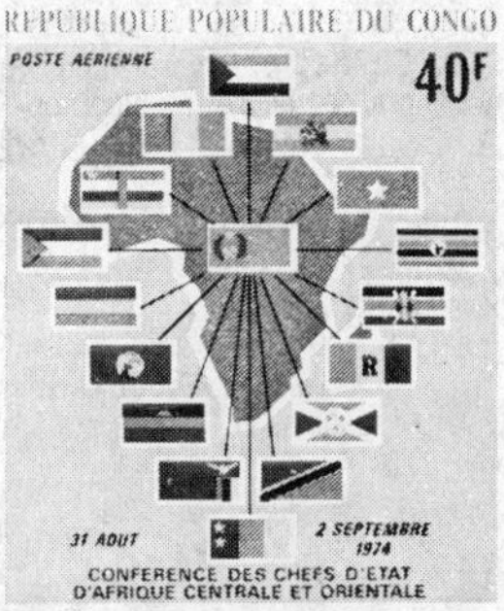

Flags of Participating Nations, Map of Africa — AP86

1974, Dec. 20 *Perf. 13*

C201 AP86 40fr ultra & multi	25	16

Conference of Chiefs of State of Central and East Africa, Brazzaville, Aug. 31-Sept. 2.

"Five Weeks in a Balloon," by Jules Verne AP87

Design: 50fr, "Around the World in 80 Days," by Jules Verne.

1975, June 30 **Litho.** *Perf. 12½*

C202 AP87 40fr multi	22	15
C203 AP87 50fr multi	25	16

Jules Verne (1828-1905), French science fiction writer, 70th death anniversary.

Paris-Brussels Train, 1890 — AP88

Design: 75fr, Santa Fe, 1880.

1975, June 30

C204 AP88 50fr ocher & multi	25	16
C205 AP88 75fr lt bl & multi	40	22

Soyuz and Apollo-Soyuz Emblem AP89

Design: 100fr, Apollo and emblem.

1975, July 20 **Litho.** *Perf. 12½*

C206 AP89 95fr org, blk & mag	50	35
C207 AP89 100fr vio, bl & blk	55	40

Apollo Soyuz space test project (Russo-American space cooperation), launching July 15; link-up, July 17.

For overprints see Nos. C252-C253.

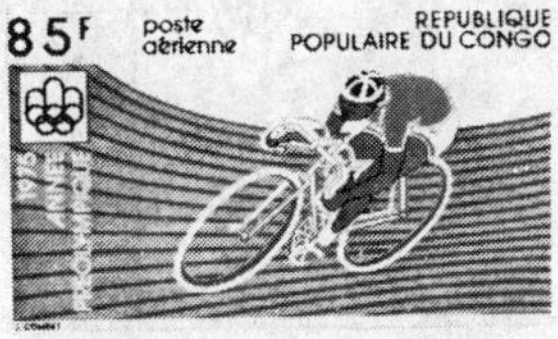

Bicycling and Montreal Olympic Emblem — AP90

Designs (Montreal Olympic Emblem and): 40fr, Boxing, vert. 50fr, Basketball, vert. 95fr, High jump. 100fr, Javelin. 150fr, Running.

Perf. 12½x13, 13x12½

1975, Oct. 30 **Photo.**

C208 AP90 40fr multi	22	15
C209 AP90 50fr red & multi	25	16
C210 AP90 85fr bl & multi	45	35
C211 AP90 95fr org & multi	50	38
C212 AP90 100fr multi	55	40
C213 AP90 150fr multi	80	60
Nos. C208-C213 (6)	2.77	2.04

Pre-Olympic Year 1975.

Map of Africa, Sports and Flags — AP91

Workers and Flag — AP92

1975, Dec. 20 **Litho.** *Perf. 12½*

C214 AP91 30fr multi	15	15

10th anniversary of first African Games, Brazzaville.

1975, Dec. 31 **Litho.** *Perf. 12½*

C215 AP92 60fr multi	35	20

Congolese Labor Party (P.C.T.), 6th anniv.

Alphonse Fondere — AP93

Historic Ships: 5fr, like 30fr. 40fr, Hamburg, 1839. 15fr, 50fr, Gomer, 1831. 20fr, 60fr, Great Eastern, 1858. 95fr, J.M. White II, 1878.

1976 **Engr.** *Perf. 13*

C216 AP93 5fr multi	15	15
C217 AP93 10fr multi	15	15
C218 AP93 15fr multi	15	15
C219 AP93 20fr multi	15	15
C220 AP93 30fr multi	16	15
C221 AP93 40fr multi	20	16
C222 AP93 50fr multi	25	20
C223 AP93 60fr multi	35	22
C224 AP93 95fr multi	50	38
Set value	1.75	1.25

Issued: #C216-C219, May; #C220-C224, Mar. 7.

Europafrica Issue 1976

Peasant Family, by Louis Le Nain — AP94

Paintings: 80fr, Boy with Top, by Jean B. Chardin. 95fr, Venus and Aeneas, by Nicolas Poussin. 100fr, The Rape of the Sabine Women, by Jacques Louis David.

1976, Mar. 20 **Litho.** *Perf. 12½*

C225 AP94 60fr gold & multi	35	20
C226 AP94 80fr gold & multi	42	30
C227 AP94 95fr gold & multi	50	38
C228 AP94 100fr gold & multi	55	40
Nos. C225-C228 (4)	1.82	1.28

Nos. C225-C228 printed in sheets of 8 stamps and horizontal gutter with commemorative inscription.

Telephone Type of 1976

1976, Apr. 25 **Litho.** *Perf. 12½x13*

C229 A107 60fr pink, maroon & crim	35	22

Sports Type of 1976

Designs: 150fr, Runner and map of Central Africa. 200fr, Discus and map.

1976, Oct. 25 *Perf. 12½*

C230 A110 150fr multi	60	45
C231 A110 200fr multi	80	55

Map of Africa, Flag and OAU Headquarters — AP95

1976, Dec. 16 **Typo.** *Perf. 13x14*

C232 AP95 60fr multi	35	22

13th anniversary of the Organization for African Unity.

Europafrica Issue

Map of Europe and Africa — AP96

1977, June 28 **Litho.** *Perf. 13*

C233 AP96 75fr multi	40	35

Headdress Type of 1977

1977, June 30 *Perf. 12½*

Designs: 250fr, Two straw caps. 300fr, Beaded cap.

C234 A118 250fr multi	1.40	1.00
C235 A118 300fr multi	1.60	1.25

Zeppelin Type of 1977
Souvenir Sheet

Design: 500fr, LZ 127 over US Capitol.

1977, Aug. 5 **Litho.** *Perf. 11*

C236 A120 500fr multi	2.50	1.00

No. C236 exists imperf.

Checkerboard AP97

1977, Aug. 20 **Engr.** *Perf. 13*

C237 AP97 60fr red & blk	35	22

Lomé Convention on General Agreement on Tariffs and Trade (GATT).

Newton, Intelsat Satellite and Classical "Planets" — AP98

1977, Aug. 25

C238 AP98 140fr multi	75	60

Isaac Newton (1642-1727), natural philosopher and mathematician.

Elizabeth II Type of 1977
Souvenir Sheet

Design: 500fr, Royal family on balcony.

1977, Dec. 21 **Litho.** *Perf. 14*

C239 A128 500fr multi	2.50	1.00

For overprint see No. C244.

Mallard AP99

Birds: 75fr, Purple heron, vert. 150fr, Reed warbler, vert. 240fr, Hoopoe, vert.

Perf. 13x12½, 12½x13

1978, May 22

C240 AP99 65fr multi	35	22
C241 AP99 75fr multi	40	20
C242 AP99 150fr multi	80	42
C243 AP99 240fr multi	1.25	65
Nos. C240-C243 (4)	2.80	1.49

Souvenir Sheet
No. C239 Overprinted in Silver:
"ANNIVERSAIRE DU / COURONNEMENT / 1953-1978"

1978, Sept. **Litho.** *Perf. 14*

C244 A128 500fr multi	2.75	1.10

25th anniv. of coronation of Elizabeth II.

Philexafrique II-Essen Issue
Common Design Types

Designs: No. C245, Leopard and Congo No. C243. No. C246, Eagle and Wurttemberg No. 1.

1978, Nov. 1 **Litho.** ***Perf. 12½***

C245 CD138 100fr multi		65	40
C246 CD139 100fr multi		65	40
a. Pair, #C245-C246		1.30	1.00

Map of Africa, Satellites — AP100

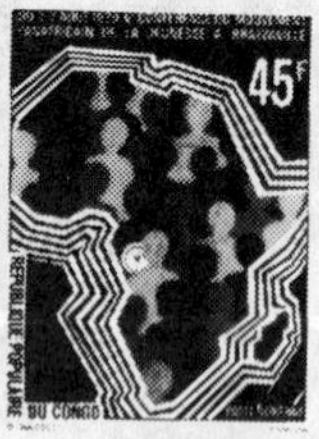

Map of Africa and People — AP101

1978, Nov. 25 **Engr.** ***Perf. 13***

C247 AP100 100fr multi 65 40

Pan-African Telecommunications Network, PANAFEL.

1979, Aug. 2 **Litho.** ***Perf. 12½***

C248 AP101 45fr multi	30	20
C249 AP101 75fr multi	50	35

5th Conference of Panafrican Youth Movement, Brazzaville, Aug. 2-7.

Abala Peasant Woman AP102

1979, Aug. 20

C250 AP102 150fr multi 1.00 60

Nos. C173, C206-C207, C186, C189 Overprinted "ALUNISSAGE APOLLO XI / JUILLET 1969" and Emblem

Perf. 13, 12½

1979, Nov. 5 **Engr., Litho.**

C251 AP69 80fr multi	55	35
C252 AP89 95fr multi	60	40
C253 AP89 100fr multi	65	42
C254 AP77 100fr multi	65	42
C255 AP79 300fr multi	2.00	1.40
Nos. C251-C255 (5)	4.45	2.99

Apollo 11 moon landing, 10th anniversary.

Runner, Olympic Rings — AP103

Pre-Olympic Year: 100fr, Boxing. 200fr, Fencing, vert. 300fr, Soccer. 500fr, Moscow '80 emblem, vert.

1979 **Litho.** ***Perf. 13½***

C256 AP103 65fr multi	40	20
C257 AP103 100fr multi	60	30
C258 AP103 200fr multi	1.10	60
C259 AP103 300fr multi	2.00	90
C260 AP103 500fr multi	3.00	1.50
Nos. C256-C260 (5)	7.10	3.50

Cross-Country Skiing — AP104

Lake Placid '80 Emblem and: 60fr, Slalom. 200fr, Ski jump, 350fr, Downhill skiing, horiz. 500fr, Woman skier.

1979, Dec ***Perf. 14½***

Size: 24x42mm, 42x24mm

C261 AP104 40fr multi	25	18
C262 AP104 60fr multi	40	28
C263 AP104 200fr multi	1.40	90
C264 AP104 350fr multi	2.25	1.50

Size: 31½x46½mm

Perf. 14

C265 AP104 500fr multi	3.50	2.25
Nos. C261-C265 (5)	7.80	5.11

13th Winter Olympic Games, Lake Placid, NY, Feb. 12-24, 1980.

Overprinted with Names of Winners

1980, Apr. 28

C266 AP104 40fr Zimiatov	20	15
C267 AP104 60fr Moser-Proell	32	16
C268 AP104 200fr Tomanen	1.10	55
C269 AP104 350fr Stock	1.75	90
C270 AP104 500fr Stenmark-Wenzel	2.50	1.40
Nos. C266-C270 (5)	5.87	3.16

Long Jump, Olympic Rings AP105

Olympic rings and long jump scenes. Nos. C266, C268-C269 vert.

1980, May 2 **Litho.** ***Perf. 14½***

C271 AP105 75fr multi	40	20
C272 AP105 150fr multi	80	40
C273 AP105 250fr multi	1.40	65
C274 AP105 350fr multi	1.90	90
Nos. C271-C274 (4)	4.50	2.15

Souvenir Sheet

C275 AP105 500fr multi 2.75 1.40

22nd Summer Olympic Games, Moscow, July 19-Aug. 3.
For overprints see Nos. C292-C296.

Stadium, Mascot, Madrid Club Emblem — AP106

Stadium, Mascot and Club Emblem: 75fr, Zaragoza. 100fr, Madrid Athletic Club. 150fr, Valencia. 175fr, Spain. 250fr, Barcelona.

1980, June 23 **Litho.** ***Perf. 14x13½***

C276 AP106 60fr multi	35	16
C277 AP106 75fr multi	42	20
C278 AP106 100fr multi	30	30
C279 AP106 150fr multi	90	45
C280 AP106 175fr multi	1.00	80
Nos. C276-C280 (5)	2.97	1.91

Souvenir Sheet

C281 AP106 250fr multi 1.50 80

World Soccer Cup 1982.
For overprints see Nos. C298-C303.

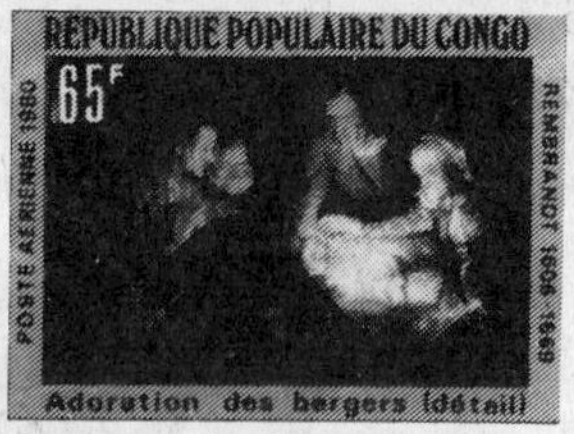

Adoration of the Shepherds — AP107

Rembrandt Paintings: 100fr, The Burial. 200fr, Christ at Emmaus. 300fr, Annunciation, vert. 500fr, Crucifixion, vert.

1980, July 4 ***Perf. 12½***

C282 AP107 65fr multi	35	20
C283 AP107 100fr multi	55	25
C284 AP107 200fr multi	1.10	55
C285 AP107 300fr multi	1.60	80
C286 AP107 500fr multi	2.75	1.25
Nos. C282-C286 (5)	6.35	3.05

Albert Camus (1913-1960), Writer — AP108

Design: 150fr, Jacques Offenbach (1819-1880), composer, vert.

1980, July 5 **Engr.** ***Perf. 13***

C287 AP108 100fr multi	60	30
C288 AP108 150fr multi	90	45

Raffia Dancing Skirts AP109

Traditional Dancing Costumes: 300fr, Tam-tam dancers, vert. 350fr, Masks.

1980, Aug. 6 **Litho.** ***Perf. 13½***

C289 AP109 250fr multi	1.40	65
C290 AP109 300fr multi	1.60	80
C291 AP109 350fr multi	1.90	90
Nos. C289-C291 (3)	4.90	2.35

Nos. C271-C275 Overprinted with Winner and Country

1980, Nov. 14 **Litho.** ***Perf. 14½***

C292 AP105 75fr multi	40	20
C293 AP105 150fr multi	80	40
C294 AP105 250fr multi	1.40	65
C295 AP105 350fr multi	2.00	90
Nos. C292-C295 (4)	4.60	2.15

Souvenir Sheet

C296 AP105 500fr multi 2.75 1.40

The Studio by Picasso AP109a

1981, July 4 ***Perf. 12½***

C296A AP109a 100fr shown	55	25
C296B AP109a 150fr Landscape	80	40
C296C AP109a 200fr Cannes Studio	1.10	55
C296D AP109a 300fr Still Life	1.60	80
C296E AP109a 500fr Still Life, diff.	2.75	1.25
Nos. C296A-C296E (5)	6.80	3.25

1st Seminar on Petroleum, Gas and Energy Alternatives, Brazzaville AP109b

1981 **Litho.** ***Perf. 12½***

C296F AP109b 75fr multicolored

Numbers have been reserved for two additional values in this set. The editors would like to see the 100fr and 150fr stamps.

1350th Anniv. of Mohamed's Death at Medina — AP110

1982, July 17 **Litho.** ***Perf. 13***

C297 AP110 400fr Medina Mosque minaret 2.25 1.10

Nos. C276-C281 Overprinted with Finalists and/or Scores in Black on Silver

1982, Oct. 7 **Litho.** ***Perf. 14x13½***

C298 AP106 60fr multi	35	16
C299 AP106 75fr multi	40	20
C300 AP106 100fr multi	55	25
C301 AP106 150fr multi	80	40
C302 AP106 175fr multi	90	45
Nos. C298-C302 (5)	3.00	1.46

Souvenir Sheet

C303 AP106 250fr multi 1.40 65

30th Anniv. of Amelia Earhart's Transatlantic Flight — AP111

1982, Dec. 4 **Engr.** ***Perf. 13***

C304 AP111 150fr multi 80 40

Wind Surfing AP112

Various wind surfing scenes, 1984 Olympic Games, 100fr, 300fr, 400fr vert.

1983, June 4 **Litho.** ***Perf. 13***

C305 AP112 100fr multi	45	22
C306 AP112 200fr multi	1.00	50
C307 AP112 300fr multi	1.50	70
C308 AP112 400fr multi	2.00	1.00
Nos. C305-C308 (4)	4.95	2.42

Souvenir Sheet

C309 AP112 500fr multi 7.50 1.40

For overprint see No. C336.

Manned Flight Bicentenary AP113

Various balloons.

1983, June 7

C310 AP113	100fr	Montgolfiere, 1783	40	20
C311 AP113	200fr	Flesselles, 1784	80	40
C312 AP113	300fr	Auguste Piccard, 1931	1.25	60
C313 AP113	400fr	Don Piccard	1.65	90
		Nos. C310-C313 (4)	4.10	2.10

Souvenir Sheet

C314 AP113	500fr	Mail transport balloon, 1870	2.50	1.40

For overprint see No. C337.

Christmas 1983 AP114

Various Virgin and Child Paintings by Botticelli.

1984, Jan. 21 **Litho.** ***Perf. 13***

C315 AP114	150fr	multi	45	22
C316 AP114	350fr	multi	1.10	60
C317 AP114	500fr	multi	1.60	80
		Nos. C315-C317 (3)	3.15	1.62

Vase of Flowers, by Manet (1832-83) AP115

Paintings: 200fr, Small Holy Family, by Raphael. 300fr, La Belle Jardiniere, by Raphael. 400fr, Virgin of Loretto, by Raphael. 500fr, Portrait of Richard Wagner (1813-83), by Giuseppe Tivoli.

1984, Feb. 24 **Litho.** ***Perf. 13***

C318 AP115	100fr	multi	30	15
C319 AP115	200fr	multi	60	30
C320 AP115	300fr	multi	80	40
C321 AP115	400fr	multi	1.25	60
C322 AP115	500fr	multi	1.59	70
		Nos. C318-C322 (5)	4.54	2.15

1984 Summer Olympics — AP116

1984, Mar. 31 ***Perf. 13***

C323 AP116	45fr	Judo, vert.	15	15
C324 AP116	75fr	Judo, diff.	20	15
C325 AP116	150fr	Wrestling	45	22
C326 AP116	175fr	Fencing	55	25
C327 AP116	350fr	Fencing, diff.	1.10	55
		Nos. C323-C327 (5)	2.45	1.32

Souvenir Sheet

C328 AP116	500fr	Boxing	1.50	70

1984 Summer Olympic Gold Medalists — AP117

Sailing/yachting: 100fr, Stephan Van Den Berg, Netherlands, Windglider Class, vert. 150fr, US, Soling Class. 200fr, Spain, 470 Class. 500fr, US, Flying Dutchman Class, vert.

1984, Dec. 18 **Litho.** ***Perf. 13***

C329 AP117	100fr	multi	38	20
C330 AP117	150fr	multi	60	28
C331 AP117	200fr	multi	70	38
C332 AP117	500fr	multi	2.00	90
		Nos. C329-C332 (4)	3.68	1.76

Virgin and Child, by Giovanni Bellini (c. 1430-1516) — AP118

Religious paintings: 100fr, Holy Family, by Andrea del Sarto (1486-1530), vert. 400fr, Virgin with Angels, by Cimabue (c. 1240-1302), vert.

1985, Feb. 12 **Litho.** ***Perf. 13***

C333 AP118	100fr	multi	25	15
C334 AP118	200fr	multi	55	25
C335 AP118	400fr	multi	1.00	50
		Nos. C333-C335 (3)	1.80	90

Christmas 1984.

Souvenir Sheets

Nos. C309, C314 Ovptd. with Exhibition in Blue or Green

1985, Mar. 8 ***Perf. 13***

C336 AP112	500fr	OLYMPHILEX '85 / LAUSANNE (B)	1.40	65
C337 AP113	500fr	MOPHILA '85 / HAM - BURG (G)	1.40	65

Audubon Birth Bicentenary — AP119

Illustrations of North American bird species by Audubon. Nos. C338-C339 vert.

1985, Apr. 11 ***Perf. 13½***

C338 AP119	100fr	Passiformes fringillidae	25	15
C339 AP119	150fr	Eudocimus ruber	40	20
C340 AP119	200fr	Buteo jamaicensis	55	25
C341 AP119	350fr	Camptorhynchus labradorius	90	45
		Nos. C338-C341 (4)	2.10	1.05

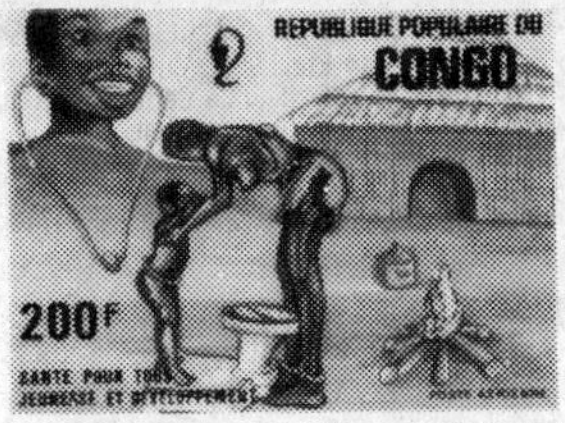

PHILEXAFRICA '85, Lome — AP120

Youths in public service activities.

1985, May 20 ***Perf. 13***

C342 AP120	200fr	Community health care	55	25
C343 AP120	200fr	Agriculture	55	25
a.		Pair, #C342-C343 + label	1.10	75

Admission to UN, 25th Anniv. — AP121

1985, Aug. 13

C344 AP121	190fr	multi	60	28

UN, 40th Anniv. — AP122

1985, Oct. 25 ***Perf. 12½***

C345 AP122	180fr	Rainbow, emblem	60	30

Christmas — AP123

Paintings: 100fr, The Virgin and the Infant Jesus, by David. 200fr, Adoration of the Magi, by Hieronymus Bosch (1450-1516). 400fr, Virgin and Child, by Van Dyck.

1985, Dec. 20 **Litho.** ***Perf. 13***

C346 AP123	100fr	multi	40	18
C347 AP123	200fr	multi	70	38
C348 AP123	400fr	multi	1.50	75
		Nos. C346-C348 (3)	2.60	1.31

Nos. C346-C347 vert.

Halley's Comet — AP124

1986, Feb. 17

C349 AP124	125fr	Halley, comet	68	35
C350 AP124	150fr	West's Comet, 1976	82	40
C351 AP124	225fr	Ikeya Seki's Comet, 1965	1.25	62
C352 AP124	300fr	Trajectory diagram	1.65	82
C353 AP124	350fr	Comet, Vega probe	2.00	1.00
		Nos. C349-C353 (5)	6.40	3.19

Nos. C350-C351 vert.

Cosmos-Frantel Hotel — AP125

1986, May 1 ***Perf. 13½***

C354 AP125	250fr	multi	1.40	70

1986 World Cup Soccer Championships, Mexico — AP126

Various soccer plays.

1986, July 22 **Litho.** ***Perf. 13***

C355 AP126	150fr	multi	90	45
C356 AP126	250fr	multi	1.50	75
C357 AP126	440fr	multi	2.75	1.40
C358 AP126	600fr	multi	3.75	1.10
		Nos. C355-C358 (4)	8.90	3.70

Air Africa, 25th Anniv. — AP127

1986, Nov. 29 **Litho.** ***Perf. 13½***

C359 AP127	200fr	multi	1.10	55

1988 Winter Pre-Olympics, Calgary — AP128

1986, Dec. 15 ***Perf. 13***

C360 AP128	150fr	Downhill skiing	80	40
C361 AP128	250fr	Bobsled	1.35	68
C362 AP128	440fr	Women's cross-country skiing	2.40	1.20
C363 AP128	600fr	Ski jumping	3.25	1.60
		Nos. C360-C363 (4)	7.80	3.88

Nos. C361-C362 vert.

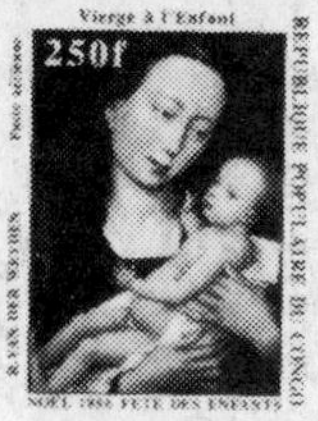

Christmas — AP129

Paintings by Rogier van der Weyden (c.1399-1464): 250fr, Virgin and Child. 440fr, The Nativity. 500fr, Virgin with Carnation.

1986, Dec. 23 *Perf. 13½*

C364 AP129 250fr multi 1.35 68
C365 AP129 440fr multi 2.40 1.20
C366 AP129 500fr multi 2.75 1.35
Nos. C364-C366 (3) 6.50 3.23

Crocodiles, World Wildlife Fund — AP130

1987, Jan. 22 *Perf. 13*

C367 AP130 75fr Osteolaemus tetraspis 40 20
C368 AP130 100fr Crocodylus cataphractus 55 28
C369 AP130 125fr Osteolaemus tetraspis, diff. 68 35
C370 AP130 150fr Crocodylus cataphractus, diff. 80 40
Nos. C367-C370 (4) 2.43 1.23

1988 Summer Olympics, Seoul — AP131

1987, July 11 **Litho.** *Perf. 13*

C371 AP131 100fr Backstroke 70 35
C372 AP131 200fr Freestyle 1.50 75
C373 AP131 300fr Breaststroke 2.25 1.10
C374 AP131 400fr Butterfly 2.75 1.40
Nos. C371-C374 (4) 7.20 3.60

Souvenir Sheet

C375 AP131 750fr Start of event 5.25 2.75

Launch of Sputnik, First Artificial Satellite, 30th Anniv. — AP132

1987, June 5 *Perf. 12½x12*

C376 AP132 60fr multi 42 20
C377 AP132 240fr multi 1.75 85

Butterflies — AP133

1987, Sept. 4 *Perf. 12½*

C378 AP133 75fr Precis epicleli 50 25
C379 AP133 120fr Deilephila nerii 80 40
C380 AP133 450fr Euryphene senegalensis 3.00 1.50
C381 AP133 550fr Precis almanta 3.75 1.10
Nos. C378-C381 (4) 8.05 3.25

Coubertin, Eternal Flame and Greece No. 125 — AP134

Cameo portrait, athletes and stamps: 120fr, Runners, France No. 198. 350fr, Congo Republic No. C22, hurdler. 600fr, High jump, Congo Republic No. C75.

1987, Nov. 4

C382 AP134 75fr shown 55 28
C383 AP134 120fr multi 88 45
C384 AP134 350fr multi 2.50 1.25
C385 AP134 600fr multi 4.25 2.15
Nos. C382-C385 (4) 8.18 4.13

Pierre de Coubertin (1863-1937), promulgator of the modern Olympics.

Arrival of Schweitzer in Lambarene, 75th Anniv. — AP135

1988, Apr. 17 **Litho.** *Perf. 12½*

C386 AP135 240fr multi 1.70 85

Dr. Albert Schweitzer (1875-1965), Nobel Peace Prize winner of 1952, founded Lambarene Hospital, Gabon, in 1913.

1988 Summer Olympics, Seoul — AP136

Pentathlon: 75fr, Swimming. 170fr, Cross-country running, vert. 200fr, Shooting. 600fr, Equestrian. 700fr, Fencing.

1988, June 10 **Litho.** *Perf. 13*

C387 AP136 75fr multi 50 25
C388 AP136 170fr multi 1.15 58
C389 AP136 200fr multi 1.35 68
C390 AP136 600fr multi 4.00 2.00
Nos. C387-C390 (4) 7.00 3.51

Souvenir Sheet

C391 AP136 750fr multi 5.00 2.50

Elimination Matches, 1990 World Cup Soccer Championships — AP137

Various athletes and cities in Italy.

1989, June 15 **Litho.** *Perf. 13*

C392 AP137 75fr Bari 45 22
C393 AP137 120fr Rome 72 35
C394 AP137 500fr Florence 3.00 1.50
C395 AP137 550fr Naples 3.25 1.65
Nos. C392-C395 (4) 7.42 3.72

PHILEXFRANCE '89 — AP138

Paintings: 300fr, Storming of the Bastille, July 14, 1789, from a gouache by J.P. Houel. 400fr, Eiffel Tower, by G. Seurat.

1989, June 22

C396 AP138 300fr multi 1.80 90
C397 AP138 400fr multi 2.40 1.20

French revolution, bicent. (300fr); Eiffel Tower, cent. (400fr).

First Moon Landing, 20th Anniv. AP139

Man's first step on the Moon: No. C398, Astronaut on ladder. No. C399, Conducting experiments on the Moon's surface.

1989, June 22

C398 AP139 400fr multi 2.50 1.25
C399 AP139 400fr multi 2.50 1.25

World Cup Soccer Championships, Italy — AP140

Various soccer plays and architecture.

1990, June 8 **Litho.** *Perf. 13*

C400 AP140 120fr multicolored 95 48
C401 AP140 240fr multicolored 1.85 95
C402 AP140 500fr multicolored 3.85 1.95
C403 AP140 600fr multicolored 4.65 2.35
Nos. C400-C403 (4) 11.30 5.73

Pan African Postal Union, 10th Anniv. — AP141

1991, Jan. 10 **Litho.** *Perf. 13½*

C404 AP141 60fr shown 48 24
C405 AP141 120fr Emblem 95 48

1992 Winter Olympics, Albertville AP142

1991, June 8 **Litho.** *Perf. 13½*

C406 AP142 120fr Ice hockey 1.15 58
C407 AP142 300fr Speed skating 2.90 1.45

Litho. & Embossed

C408 AP142 1500fr Slalom skiing

Numbers have been reserved for souvenir sheets in this set.

1992 Summer Olympics, Barcelona AP143

Designs: No. C411, Equestrian. No. C412, Long jump.

1992 **Litho. & Embossed** *Perf. 13½*

C411 AP143 1500fr gold & multi

Souvenir Sheet

C412 AP143 1500fr gold & multi

AIR POST SEMI-POSTAL STAMPS

Hathor Pillar — SPAP1

Unwmk.

1964, Mar. 9 Engr. *Perf. 13*

CB1	SPAP1	10fr + 5fr vio & chnt	18	15
CB2	SPAP1	25fr + 5fr org brn & slate grn	30	22
CB3	SPAP1	50fr + 5fr slate grn & brn red	55	45
		Nos. CB1-CB3 (3)	1.03	82

UNESCO world campaign to save historic monuments in Nubia.

POSTAGE DUE STAMPS

Messenger — D6

MH. 1521 Broussard Plane — D7

Early Transportation: 1fr, Litter. 2fr, Canoe. 5fr, Bicyclist. 10fr, Steam locomotive. 25fr, Seaplane.

Unwmk.

1961, Dec. 4 Engr. *Perf. 11*

J34	D6	50c ultra, ol bis & red	15	15
J35	D6	1fr red brn, red & grn	15	15
J36	D6	2fr grn, ultra & brn	15	15
J37	D6	5fr pur & gray brn	15	15
J38	D6	10fr bl, grn & chocolate	25	25
J39	D6	25fr bl, dk grn & dk brn	55	55

Modern transportation: 1fr, Land Rover. 2fr, River boat transporting barge. 5fr, Trailer-truck. 10fr, Diesel locomotive. 25fr, Boeing 707 jet plane.

J40	D7	50c ultra, olive bis & red	15	15
J41	D7	1fr red & grn	15	15
J42	D7	2fr ultra, grn & brn	15	15
J43	D7	5fr pur & gray brn	15	15
J44	D7	10fr dk grn & chocolate	25	25
J45	D7	25fr bl, dk grn & sepia	55	55
		Set value	2.00	2.00

The two types of each value in Nos. J34-J45 (early and modern transportation) were printed tête bêche, se-tenant at the base.

Flowers — D8

Flowers: 2fr, Phaeomeria magnifica. 5fr, Millettia laurentii. 10fr, Tuberose. 15fr, Pyrostegia venusta. 20fr, Hibiscus.

1971, Mar. 25 Photo. *Perf. 12x12½*

J46	D8	1fr multi	15	15
J47	D8	2fr multi	15	15
J48	D8	5fr pink & multi	15	15
J49	D8	10fr dk grn & multi	15	15
J50	D8	15fr multi	16	16
J51	D8	20fr multi	25	25
		Set value	66	66

Flowers and Fruit — D9

1986, June 5 Litho. *Perf. 13*

J52	D9	5fr Passiflora quadrangulares	15	15
J53	D9	10fr Cannaceae, vert.	15	15
J54	D9	15fr Ananas comosus, vert.	15	15
		Set value	21	15

OFFICIAL STAMPS

Coat of Arms — O1

1968-70 Unwmk. Typo. *Perf. 14x13*

O1	O1	1fr multi ('70)	15	15
O2	O1	2fr multi ('70)	15	15
O3	O1	5fr multi ('70)	15	15
O4	O1	10fr multi ('70)	20	15
O5	O1	25fr emer & multi	16	15
O6	O1	30fr red & multi	20	15
O7	O1	50fr multi ('70)	60	30
O8	O1	85fr multi ('70)	1.10	60
O9	O1	100fr multi ('70)	1.40	70
O10	O1	200fr multi ('70)	2.00	1.50
		Nos. O1-O10 (10)	6.11	4.00

CORFU

LOCATION — An island in the Ionian Sea opposite the Greek-Albanian border
GOVT. — A department of Greece
AREA — 245 sq. mi.
POP. — 114,620 (1938)
CAPITAL — Corfu

In 1923 Italy occupied Corfu (Kerkyra) during a controversy with Greece over the assassination of an Italian official in Epirus. Italy again occupied Corfu in 1941-43.

100 Centesimi = 1 Lira
100 Lepta = 1 Drachma

ISSUED UNDER ITALIAN OCCUPATION

Watermark

Wmk. 140- Crown

Italian Stamps of 1901-23 Overprinted **CORFÙ**

1923, Sept. 20 Wmk. 140 *Perf. 14*

N1	A48	5c green	2.00	2.00
N2	A48	10c claret	2.00	2.00
N3	A48	15c slate	2.00	2.00
N4	A50	20c brown orange	2.00	2.00
N5	A49	30c orange brown	2.00	2.00
N6	A49	50c violet	2.00	2.00
N7	A49	60c blue	2.00	2.00
N8	A46	1 l brown & green	2.00	2.00
		Nos. N1-N8 (8)	16.00	16.00

Italian Stamps of 1901-23 Surcharged **CORFÙ Lepta 25**

1923, Sept. 24

N9	A48	25 l on 10c claret	8.00	5.00
N10	A49	60 l on 25c blue	4.00	
N11	A49	70 l on 30c org brn	4.00	
N12	A49	1.20d on 50c violet	6.00	5.00
N13	A46	2.40d on 1 l brn & grn	6.00	5.00
N14	A46	4.75d on 2 l grn & org	4.00	
		Nos. N9-N14 (6)	32.00	

Nos. N10, N11, N14 were not placed in use.

Issue for Corfu and Paxos

Nos. N15-N34, NC1-NC12, NJ1-NJ11 and NRA1-NRA3 have been extensively counterfeited, some with forged cancellations.

Stamps of Greece, 1937-38, Overprinted in Black **CORFU**

Perf. 12x13½, 12½x12, 13½x12

1941, June 5 Wmk. 252

N15	A69	5 l brn red & blue	4.00	3.00
N16	A70	10 l bl & brn red (On 397)	1.50	1.25
N17	A70	10 l bl & brn red (On 413)	50.00	50.00
N18	A71	20 l black & grn	1.00	1.00
N19	A72	40 l green & blk	1.50	1.50
N20	A73	50 l brown & blk	2.00	2.00
N21	A74	80 l ind & yel brn	2.00	2.00
N22	A67	1d green	2.50	2.00
N23	A84	1.50d green	6.50	6.00
N24	A75	2d ultra	1.65	1.25
N25	A67	3d red brown	2.25	2.00
N26	A76	5d red	3.00	2.00
N27	A77	6d olive brown	3.00	3.00
N28	A78	7d dark brown	3.00	2.50
N29	A67	8d deep blue	2.75	2.00
N30	A79	10d red brown	40.00	32.50
N31	A80	15d green	5.00	4.50
N32	A81	25d dark blue	4.50	4.00
N33	A84	30d orange brown	14.00	11.00
N34	A67	100d carmine lake	25.00	22.50
		Nos. N15-N34 (20)	175.15	156.00

AIR POST STAMPS

Greece Nos. C37 and C26-C35, Overprinted Like Nos. N15-N34

Perf. 12½x13, 13x12½, 13½x12½

1941, June 5 Unwmk.

NC1	D3	50 l dk brown	2.50	2.50
NC2	AP16	1d red	52.50	37.50
NC3	AP17	2d gray blue	3.00	3.00
NC4	AP18	5d violet	3.00	3.00
NC5	AP19	7d deep ultra	3.00	3.00
NC6	AP20	10d bister brn (On C26)	75.00	50.00
NC7	AP20	10d brown org (On C35)	10.50	11.50
NC8	AP21	25d rose	18.00	19.00
NC9	AP22	30d dark green	16.00	19.00
NC10	AP23	50d violet	21.00	22.50
a.		Double overprint		*150.00*
NC11	AP24	100d brown	*375.00*	*250.00*

On No. C36

Serrate Roulette 13½

NC12	D3	50 l violet brown	12.50	10.00
a.		On No. C36a		

POSTAGE DUE STAMPS

Postage Due Stamps of Greece, 1913-35 Overprinted Like Nos. N15-N34

1941, June 5 Unwmk.

Serrate Roulette 13½

NJ1	D3	10 l carmine	1.00	1.00
NJ2	D3	25 l ultra	1.00	1.00
NJ3	D3	80 l lilac brown	75.00	60.00

Perf. 12½x13, 13½x12½

NJ4	D3	1d lt bl (On J80)	*200.00*	*137.50*
NJ5	D3	2d light red	1.50	1.10
NJ6	D3	5d gray	5.00	4.50
NJ7	D3	10d gray green	3.00	3.00
NJ8	D3	15d red brown	3.00	3.00
NJ9	D3	25d light red	3.00	3.00
NJ10	D3	50d orange	4.00	4.00
NJ11	D3	100d slate green	95.00	60.00

POSTAL TAX STAMPS

Greece Nos. RA61-RA63, Overprinted Like Nos. N15-N34

1941, June 5 Unwmk. *Perf. 13½x12*

NRA1	PT7	10 l brt rose, *pale rose*	75	75
NRA2	PT7	50 l gray grn, *pale grn*	75	50
NRA3	PT7	1d dull blue, *lt bl*	4.00	3.50
		Nos. NRA1-NRA3 (3)	5.50	4.75

Stamps overprinted "CORFU" were replaced by Italian stamps overprinted "Isole Jonie." (See Ionian Islands.)

COSTA RICA

LOCATION — Central America between Nicaragua and Panama
GOVT. — Republic
AREA — 19,344 sq. mi.
POP. — 2,450,226 (1984)
CAPITAL — San Jose

8 Reales= 100 Centavos= 1 Peso
100 Centimos= 1 Colon (1900)

Catalogue values for unused stamps in this country are for Never Hinged items, beginning with Scott 238 in the regular postage section, Scott C117 in the air post section, Scott CE1 in the air post special delivery section, Scott E1 in the special delivery section, and Scott RA1 in the postal tax section.

Watermarks

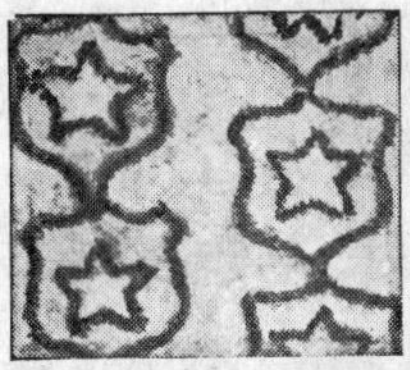

Wmk. 215- Small Star in Shield, Multiple

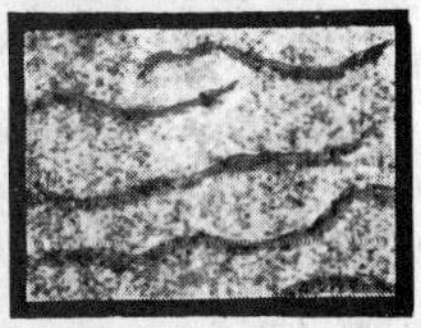

Wmk. 229- Wavy Lines

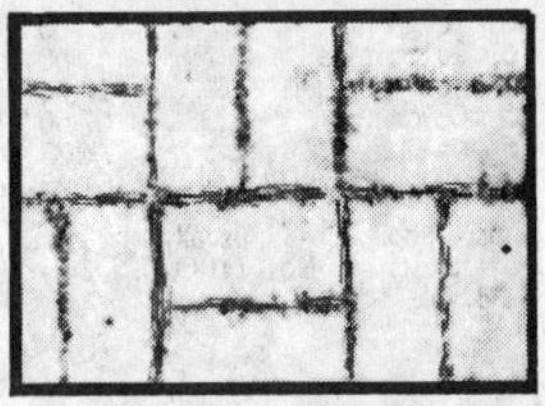

Wmk. 334- Rectangles

Values for Nos. 1-15 are for stamps in fine condition.

Coat of Arms — A1

1863 Unwmk. Engr. *Perf. 12*

1	A1	½r blue	45	60
a.		½r light blue	45	90
b.		Pair, imperf. between	150.00	
2	A1	2r scarlet	90	1.40
3	A1	4r green	10.00	10.00
4	A1	1p orange	20.00	20.00
		Nos. 1-4 (4)	31.35	32.00

The ½r was printed from two plates. The second is in light blue with little or no sky over the mountains.

Imperforate copies of Nos. 1-2 are corner copies from poorly perforated sheets.

Nos. 1-3 Surcharged in Red or Black:

1 cto. (a) **1** *cto.* (b) **2** cts. (c)

5 cts. U.P.U.	20 CTS U.P.U.
d	e

1881-82

Red or Black Surcharge

7	A1(a)	1c on ½r ('82)	1.75	
a.		On No. 1a	10.00	
8	A1(b)	1c on ½r ('82)	10.00	
9	A1(c)	2c on ½r, #1a	1.50	
a.		On No. 1	6.00	
12	A1(c)	5c on ½r	4.50	
13	A1(d)	5c on ½r ('82)	50.00	
14	A1(d)	10c on 2r (Bk) ('82)	60.00	
15	A1(e)	20c on 4r ('82)	225.00	

Overprints with different fonts and "Oficial" were never placed in use, and are said to have been surcharged to a dealer's order. The ½r surcharged "DOS CTS" is not a postage stamp.

Postally used copies of Nos. 7-15 are rare. Fake cancellations exist.

Counterfeits exist of surcharges on #7-15.

Gen. Prospero Fernández
A6

President Bernardo Soto Alfaro
A7

1883, Jan. 1

16	A6 1c green		60	35
17	A6 2c carmine		60	45
18	A6 5c blue violet		12.00	35
19	A6 10c orange		67.50	4.50
20	A6 40c blue		75	75
		Nos. 16-20 (5)	81.45	6.40

Unused copies of 40c usually lack gum.

For overprints see Nos. O1-O20, O24, Guanacaste 1-38, 44.

1887

21	A7 5c blue violet	5.25	40
22	A7 10c orange	1.50	55

Unused copies of 5c usually lack gum.

For overprints see Nos. O22-O23, Guanacaste 42-43, 45.

A8

A9

1889

Black Overprint

23	A8 1c rose	2.50	70
24	A9 5c brown	2.50	70

Vertical and inverted overprints are fakes.

For overprints see Guanacaste Nos. 47-54.

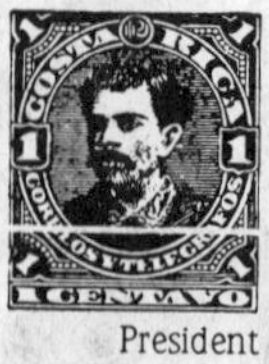

President Soto Alfaro
A10 A11

A12

A13

A14

A15

A16

A17

A18

A19

1889 *Perf. 14-16 & Compound*

25	A10 1c brown	24	30
a.	Horiz. pair, imperf. vert	60.00	
b.	Imperf. pair	75.00	
c.	Horiz. or vert. pair, imperf. btwn.	70.00	
26	A11 2c dark green	18	30
a.	Imperf., pair	30.00	
b.	Vert. pair, imperf. horiz.	40.00	
c.	Horiz. pair, imperf. btwn.	40.00	
27	A12 5c orange	35	18
a.	Imperf., pair	85.00	
b.	Horiz. pair, imperf. btwn.	70.00	
28	A13 10c red brown	30	24
a.	Vert. or horiz. pair, imperf. btwn.	70.00	
29	A14 20c yellow green	20	18
a.	Vert. pair, imperf. horiz.	60.00	
b.	Horizontal pair, imperf. btwn.	60.00	
30	A15 50c rose red	75	
	Telegram cancel		40
31	A16 1p blue	1.10	
	Telegram cancel		55
32	A17 2p dull violet	6.00	
a.	2p slate	6.00	
	Telegram cancel		4.00
33	A18 5p olive green	20.00	
	Telegram cancel		10.00
34	A19 10p black	85.00	
	Telegram cancel		52.50
	Nos. 25-34 (10)	114.12	

Nos. 30-34 normally were used on telegrams and most copies were peeled off of the forms and sold by the government.

For overprints see Nos. O25-O30, Guanacaste 55-67.

Arms of Costa Rica
A20 A21

A22

A23

A24

A25

A26

A27

A28

A29

1892 *Perf. 12-15 & Compound*

35	A20 1c grnsh blue	20	28
36	A21 2c yellow	20	28
37	A22 5c red lilac	20	15
a.	5c violet	45.00	28
38	A23 10c lt green	65	22
a.	Horiz. pair, imperf. btwn.	52.50	
39	A24 20c scarlet	10.00	22
a.	Horiz. pair, imperf. btwn.		37.50
40	A25 50c gray blue	4.75	3.25
41	A26 1p green, *yel*	90	60
42	A27 2p brown red, *lilac*	2.50	80
a.	2p rose red, *pale lil*	10.00	80
43	A28 5p dk blue, *blue*	2.00	80
44	A29 10p brown, *pale buff*	25.00	4.00
a.	10p brown, *yellow*	7.00	
	Nos. 35-44 (10)	46.40	10.60

Imperfs. of Nos. 35-44 are proofs.

For overprints see Nos. O31-O36.

Statue of Juan Santamaría
A30

Juan Mora Fernández
A31

View of Port Limón — A32

Braulio Carillo ("Branlio" on stamp) — A33

National Theater — A34

José M. Castro — A35

Birris Bridge — A36

Juan Rafael Mora — A37

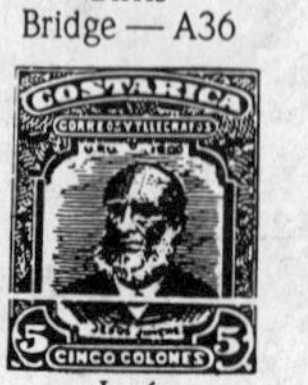

Jesús Jiménez — A38

Coat of Arms — A39

1901, Jan. *Perf. 12-15½*

45	A30 1c green & blk	35	15
a.	Horiz. pair, imperf. btwn.		
46	A31 2c vermilion & blk	45	15
47	A32 5c gray blue & blk	60	15
a.	Vert. pair, imperf. btwn.	110.00	
48	A33 10c ocher & blk	1.50	15
49	A34 20c lake & blk	10.00	22
a.	Vert. pair, imperf. btwn.	110.00	
50	A35 50c dull lil & dk bl	4.00	1.10
51	A36 1col ol bis & blk	50.00	2.75
52	A37 2col car rose & dk grn	11.00	2.75
53	A38 5col brown & blk	50.00	2.75
54	A39 10col yel grn & brn red	22.50	2.25
	Nos. 45-54 (10)	150.40	12.42

The 2c exists with center inverted.

Nos. 45-57 in other colors are private reprints made in 1948. They have little value.

For surcharge and overprints see Nos. 58, 78, O37-O44.

Remainders

In 1914 the government sold a large quantity of stamps at very much less than face value. The lot included most regular issues from 1901 to 1911 inclusive, postage due stamps of 1903 and official stamps of 1901-03. These stamps were canceled with groups of thin parallel bars. The higher valued used stamps, such as Nos. 64, 65-68a, sell for much less than the values quoted which are for stamps with regular postal cancellations. A few sell for much higher prices.

José M. Cañas — A40

Julián Volio — A41

Eusebio Figueroa Oreamuno — A42

1903 *Perf. 13½, 14, 15*

55	A40 4c red vio & blk	1.75	80
56	A41 6c olive grn & blk	7.00	2.25
57	A42 25c gray lil & brn	15.00	28
	Nos. 55-57 (3)	23.75	3.33

For overprints see Nos. 81, O45-O47.

No. 49 Surcharged in Black:

UN CENTIMO

1905

58	A34 1c on 20c lake & blk	60	55
a.	Inverted surcharge	10.00	4.75
b.	Diagonal surcharge	60	55

Specimens surcharged in other colors are proofs.

Statue of Juan Santamaria
A43

Juan Mora Fernández
A44

José M. Cañas
A45

Mauro
Fernández
A46

Braulio
Carrillo — A47

Julián
Volio — A48

Eusebio Figueroa
Oreamuno — A49

José M.
Castro — A50

Jesús
Jiménez — A51

Juan Rafael
Mora — A52

Perf. 11x14, 14 (1c, 5c, 25c)

1907 **Unwmk.**

59	A43	1c red brn & ind	45	15
a.		Perf. 11x14	10.00	1.00
60	A44	2c yel grn & blk	75	15
a.		Perf. 14	75	15
61	A45	4c car & indigo	6.00	1.10
a.		Perf. 14	250.00	32.50
62	A46	5c yel & dull bl	55	15
a.		Perf. 11x14	40.00	1.00
63	A47	10c blue & blk	20.00	16
a.		Perf. 14	90	42
64	A48	20c olive grn & blk	10.00	4.00
a.		Perf. 14	10.00	4.00
65	A49	25c gray lil & blk	2.00	55
a.		Perf. 11x14	50.00	9.00
66	A50	50c red lil & blue	30.00	25.00
a.		Perf. 14	50.00	30.00
67	A51	1col brown & blk	20.00	19.00
a.		Perf. 14	20.00	18.00
68	A52	2col claret & grn	75.00	60.00
a.		Perf. 14	125.00	90.00
		Nos. 59-68 (10)	164.75	110.26
		Nos. 59a-68a (10)	556.65	186.07

Imperforate copies of the above set are either proofs or from unfinished sheets, which were placed on the market in London. A few were postally used. The 1c, 2c, 5c, 20c, 50c, 1 col and 2 col exist with center inverted.

Nos. 59-68 exist with papermaker's watermark.

For overprints see Nos. 77, 79-80, 82-84, O48-O55, O60-O64.

Statue of Juan
Santamaria
A53

Juan Mora
Fernández
A54

José M.
Cañas — A55

Mauro
Fernández — A56

Braulio Carrillo — A57

Julián
Volio — A58

Eusebio Figueroa
Oreamuno
A59

Jesús Jiménez
A60

1910 *Perf. 12*

69	A53	1c brown	15	15
70	A54	2c dp green	18	15
71	A55	4c scarlet	18	15
72	A56	5c orange	75	15
73	A57	10c deep blue	15	15
74	A58	20c olive grn	18	15
75	A59	25c dp violet	8.00	55
76	A60	1col dk brown	35	40
		Nos. 69-76 (8)	9.94	
		Set value		1.42

For overprints and surcharge see Nos. 111C-111J, B1, C2, O56-O59.

No. 60a Overprinted in Red *19¹¹*

1911 *Perf. 14*

77	A44	2c yel grn & blk	1.25	80
a.		Inverted overprint	5.00	5.00
b.		Double overprint, both inverted	42.50	

Stamps of 1901-07 Overprinted in Red or Black * 1911 *

78	A30	1c grn & blk (R)	60	28
a.		Black overprint	32.50	18.00
b.		Inverted overprint		
79	A43	1c red brn & ind (Bk)	55	28
a.		Inverted overprint	4.25	3.50
b.		Double overprint	5.00	5.00
80	A44	2c yel grn & blk (Bk)	55	28
a.		Inverted overprint	3.50	3.50
b.		Dbl. ovpt., one as on No. 77	25.00	25.00
c.		Double overprint, one inverted	13.00	13.00
d.		Pair, one stamp No. 77	25.00	18.00
e.		Perf. 11x14	1.25	35

No. 55 Overprinted in Black

Habilitado
1911

81	A40	4c red vio & blk	90	55

Stamps of 1907 Overprinted in Blue, Black or Rose

Habilitado
1911

Perf. 14, 11x14 (#83, 84)

82	A46	5c yel & bl (Bl)	55	15
a.		"Habilitada"	3.25	2.50
b.		"2911"	5.50	3.25
c.		Roman "I" in "1911"	3.00	2.00
d.		Double overprint	5.00	5.00
e.		Inverted overprint	5.50	3.75
f.		Black overprint	7.75	2.00
g.		Triple overprint	5.50	
h.		Vert. pair, imperf. horiz.	37.50	
83	A47	10c bl & blk (Bk)	1.25	70
a.		As "83," Roman "I" in "1911"	7.00	5.00
c.		As "83," double overprint	19.00	11.50
d.		Perf. 14	1.65	1.10
84	A47	10c bl & blk (R)	4.75	4.50
a.		Roman "I" in "1911"	15.00	14.00
c.		Perf. 14	19.00	11.50
		Nos. 77-84 (8)	10.40	7.54

Many counterfeits of overprint exist.

A61

A62

A63

Telegraph Stamps Surcharged in Rose, Blue or Black

1911 *Perf. 12, 14, 14x11*

86	A61	1c on 10c bl (R)	18	15
a.		"Coereos"	7.75	5.50
b.		Inverted surcharge		
87	A61	1c on 10c bl (Bk)	*175.00*	*100.00*
88	A61	1c on 25c vio (Bk)	18	15
a.		"Coereos"	7.75	5.50
b.		Pair, one without surcharge	19.00	
c.		Double surcharge	7.75	
e.		Double surch., one inverted	11.50	
89	A61	1c on 50c red brn (Bl)	35	35
a.		Inverted surcharge	5.00	5.00
b.		Double surcharge	4.25	
90	A61	1c on 1col brn (R)	35	35
91	A61	1c on 5col red (Bl)	65	50
92	A61	1c on 10col dk brn (R)	80	65
93	A62	2c on 5c brn org (Bk)	2.75	1.90
a.		Inverted surcharge	*7.75*	*3.75*
b.		"Correos" inverted	*15.00*	
c.		Double surcharge	7.75	
94	A62	2c on 10c bl (R)	100.00	
a.		Perf. 14	*300.00*	
b.		"Correos" inverted		
c.		As "b," perf. 14		
95	A62	2c on 50c cl (Bk)	35	45
a.		Inverted surcharge	3.75	3.25
b.		Double surcharge	11.50	
c.		Perf. 14	50.00	20.00
96	A62	2c on 1col brn (Bk)	65	65
a.		Inverted surcharge	11.50	
b.		Double surcharge	15.00	
97	A62	2c on 2col car (Bk)	50	50
a.		Inverted surcharge	7.00	5.00
b.		"Correos" inverted	7.75	5.50
c.		Double surcharge		
d.		Perf. 14	20.00	15.00
98	A62	2c on 5col grn (Bk)	65	65
a.		Inverted surcharge	9.00	7.00
b.		"Correos" inverted	*15.00*	*4.25*
c.		Perf. 14	3.00	2.00
99	A62	2c on 10col mar (Bk)	80	65
a.		"Correos" inverted		
b.		Perf. 14	3.00	3.00
100	A63	5c on 5c org (Bl)	35	15
a.		Double surcharge	7.00	7.00
b.		Inverted surcharge	7.00	5.00
c.		Pair, one without surcharge	16.00	

Counterfeits exist of Nos. 87, 94 and all minor varieties. Used copies of No. 94 with target cancels are counterfeits.

Nos. 93-99 exist with papermaker's watermark.

Coffee
Plantation
A64

1921, June 17 **Litho.** *Perf. 11½*

103	A64	5c bl & blk	1.50	1.50
a.		Tête bêche pair	3.00	3.00
b.		Imperf., pair	10.50	
c.		As "a," imperf.	27.50	

Centenary of coffee raising in Costa Rica.

Liberty with Torch of
Freedom — A65

1921 **Typo.** *Perf. 11*

104	A65	5c violet	50	30
a.		Imperf.	50.00	

Cent. of Central American independence.

For overprint see No. 111.

Juan
Mora
and
Julio
Acosta
A66

1921, Sept. 15 *Perf. 11½*

105	A66	2c orange & blk	85	80
106	A66	3c green & blk	85	80
107	A66	6c scarlet & blk	1.10	90
108	A66	15c dk blue & blk	2.75	2.75
109	A66	30c orange brn & blk	4.50	4.50
		Nos. 105-109 (5)	10.05	9.75

Centenary of Central American independence. Issue requested by Costa Rican Philatelic Society. Authorized by decree calling for 2,000 of 30c and 5,000 each of other values. Many more were printed illegally including imperforates, color changes and inverted centers.

Each sheet of 20 (4x5) contains 5 tête-bêche pairs.

Simón Bolívar — A67

1921 **Engr.** *Perf. 12*

110	A67	15c deep violet	25	15

For overprint No. 110a see set following No. 111. For surcharge see No. 148

No. 104 Overprinted

CORREOS
1922

1922 *Perf. 11*

111	A65	5c violet	40	25
a.		Inverted overprint	10.00	
b.		Double overprint	15.00	

Stamps of 1910-1921 Overprinted in Blue, Red, Black or Gold

1922 *Perf. 12*

111C	A53	1c brown (Bl)	15	15
111D	A54	2c deep green (R)	20	15
111E	A55	4c scarlet	15	15
111F	A56	5c orange	40	30
111G	A57	10c deep blue (R)	40	25
111H	A67	15c deep violet (G)	2.00	1.50
		Nos. 111C-111H (6)	3.30	2.50

Inverted overprints occur on all values. Counterfeits exist.

No. 72 Overprinted

1923

111J	A56	5c orange	50	50
k.		"VD." for "UD."	*60.00*	*60.00*

Jesús Jiménez — A68

1923, June 18 Litho. *Perf. 11½*

112	A68	2c brown	15	15
113	A68	4c green	15	15
114	A68	5c blue	30	15
115	A68	20c carmine	18	20
116	A68	1col violet	30	32
		Nos. 112-116 (5)	1.08	97

Pres. Jesús Jiménez (1823-98).

Nos. 112-116, imperf, were not regularly issued. Value, set $2.

For overprints see Nos. O65-O69.

National Monument A70

Harvesting Coffee — A71

Banana Growing — A73

General Post Office — A74

Columbus Soliciting Aid of Isabella — A75

Christopher Columbus A76

Columbus at Cariari — A77

Map of Costa Rica — A78

Manuel M. Gutiérrez — A79

1923-26 Engr. *Perf. 12*

117	A70	1c violet	15	15
118	A71	2c yellow	26	15
119	A73	4c deep green	52	30
120	A74	5c light blue	90	15
121	A74	5c yellow grn ('26)	26	15
122	A75	10c red brn	1.65	15
123	A75	10c car rose ('26)	35	15
124	A76	12c carmine rose	5.25	1.75
125	A77	20c deep blue	7.00	60
126	A78	40c orange	6.75	1.50
127	A79	1col olive green	1.90	60
		Nos. 117-127 (11)	24.99	5.65

See Nos. 151-156. For surcharges and overprints see Nos. 136-140, 147, 189, 218, C2.

Rodrigo Arias Maldonado — A80

1924 *Perf. 12½*

128	A80	2c dark green	15	15
a.		Perf. 14	15	15

See No. 162.

Map of Guanacaste A81

Mission at Nicoya — A82

1924 Litho. *Perf. 12*

129	A81	1c carmine rose	30	20
130	A81	2c violet	30	20
131	A81	5c green	30	20
132	A81	10c orange	2.00	50
133	A82	15c light blue	65	42
134	A82	20c gray black	1.10	70
135	A82	25c light brown	1.50	1.25
		Nos. 129-135 (7)	6.15	3.47

Centenary of annexation of Province of Guanacaste to Costa Rica.

Exist imperf. Value, set, $35.

Stamps of 1923 Surcharged:

a

b

1925

136	A74(a)	3c on 5c lt blue	20	15
137	A75(a)	6c on 10c red brn	28	25
138	A78(a)	30c on 40c orange	52	40
139	A79(b)	45c on 1col ol grn	90	50
a.		Double surcharge		
		Nos. 136-139 (4)	1.90	1.30

No. 124 Surcharged

=10 10=

1926

140	A76	10c on 12c car rose	1.00	30

College of San Luis, Cartago — A83

Chapui Asylum, San José — A84

Normal School, Heredia — A85

Ruins of Ujarrás — A86

1926 Unwmk. Engr. *Perf. 12½*

143	A83	3c ultra	15	15
144	A84	6c dark brown	32	20
145	A85	30c deep orange	75	25
146	A86	45c black violet	2.00	85
		Nos. 143-146 (4)	3.22	1.45

For surcharges see Nos. 190-190D, 217.

No. 124 Surcharged in Black:

1928, Jan. 7 *Perf. 12*

147	A76	10c on 12c car rose	4.00	4.00

Issued in honor of Col. Charles A. Lindbergh during his Good Will Tour of Central America.

The surcharge has been privately reprinted using an original die. They can be distinguished by distict dots under the "10s." All errors and inverted surcharges are reprints.

No. 110 Surcharged **5 5**

1928

148	A67	5(c) on 15c dp violet	15	15
a.		Inverted surcharge	25.00	

Type I — A88

CORREOS	**CORREOS**
5	**5**
CENTIMOS	**CENTIMOS**
Type II	Type III
CORREOS	**CORREOS**
5	**5**
CENTIMOS	**CENTIMOS**
Type IV	Type V

Surcharge Typo. (I-V) & Litho. (V)

1929 *Perf. 12½*

149	A88	5c on 2col car (I)	28	18
a.-d.		Types II-V	28	18

Telegraph Stamp Surcharged for Postage as in 1929, Surcharge Lithographed

1929

150	A88	13c on 40c deep grn	15	15
a.		Inverted surcharge	85	70

Excellent counterfeits exist of No. 150a.

Types of 1923-26 Issues Dated "1929"

Imprint of Waterlow & Sons

1930 Size: 26x21½mm *Perf. 12½*

151	A70	1c dark violet	15	15
155	A74	5c green	15	15
156	A75	10c carmine rose	35	15
		Nos. 151-156 (3)	65	
		Set value		24

Juan Rafael Mora — A89

1931

157	A89	13c carmine rose	20	15

For surcharge see No. 209.

Seal of Costa Rica Philatelic Society ("Octubre 12 de 1932") A90

1932, Oct. 12 *Perf. 12*

158	A90	3c orange	22	15
159	A90	5c dark green	35	22
160	A90	10c carmine rose	40	25
161	A90	20c dark blue	50	32
		Nos. 158-161 (4)	1.47	94

Phil. Exhib., Oct. 12, 1932. See #179-183.

Maldonado Type of 1924

1934 *Perf. 12½*

162	A80	3c dark green	15	15

Red Cross Nurse — A91

1935, May 31 *Perf. 12*

163	A91	10c rose carmine	32	15

50th anniv. of the founding of the Costa Rican Red Cross Society.

Air View of Cartago — A92

Miraculous Statuette and View of Cathedral A93

Vision of 1635 — A94

1935, Aug. *Perf. 12½*

164	A92	5c green	15	15
165	A93	10c carmine	30	15
166	A92	30c orange	45	20
167	A94	45c dark violet	1.10	35
168	A93	50c blue black	1.75	75
		Nos. 164-168 (5)	3.75	1.60

Tercentenary of the Patron Saint, Our Lady of the Angels, of Costa Rica.

Map of Cocos Island — A95

1936, Jan. 29 *Perf. 14, 11½ (25c)*

169	A95	4c ocher	20	15
170	A95	8c dark violet	28	15
171	A95	25c orange	30	15
172	A95	35c brown vio	45	15
173	A95	40c brown	60	20
174	A95	50c yellow	60	50
175	A95	2col yellow grn	8.00	6.00
176	A95	5col green	20.00	12.00
		Nos. 169-176 (8)	30.43	19.30

Exist imperf. Value, set, $40.
For surcharges see Nos. 196-200, C55-C56.

Map of Cocos Island and Ships of Columbus
A96

1936, Dec. 5 *Perf. 12*

177	A96	5c green	15	15
178	A96	10c carmine rose	15	15
		Set value	24	15

For overprints see Nos. 247, O80-O81.

Seal of Costa Rica Philatelic Society ("Diciembre 1937") — A97

1937

179	A97	2c dark brown	15	15
180	A97	3c black	15	15
181	A97	5c green	15	15
182	A97	10c orange red	18	15
		Nos. 179-182 (4)	63	60

Souvenir Sheet

Imperf

183		Sheet of 4	45	45
a.	A97	2c dark brown	15	15
b.	A97	3c black	15	15
c.	A97	5c green	15	15
d.	A97	10c orange red	15	15

Phil. Exhib., Dec. 1937.

Purple Guaria Orchid, National Flower — A98

Tuna
A99

Native with Donkey Carrying Bananas
A101

Designs: 3c, Cacao pod. 10c, Coffee harvesting.

1937-38 **Wmk. 229** *Perf. 12½*

184	A98	1c green & vio ('38)	28	15
185	A98	3c chocolate ('38)	15	15

Unwmk. *Perf. 12*

186	A99	2c olive gray	18	15
187	A101	5c dark green	20	15
188	A101	10c carmine rose	28	18
		Nos. 184-188 (5)	1.09	
		Set value		54

National Exposition.

No. 125 Overprinted in Black **1938**

1938 **Unwmk.** *Perf. 12*

189	A77	20c deep blue	32	15

No. 146 Surcharged in Red:

a

b

c

d

e **15 Cts.**

1940 *Perf. 12½*

190	A86(a)	15c on 45c black vio	40	20
190A	A86(b)	15c on 45c black vio	40	20
190B	A86(c)	15c on 45c black vio	40	20
190C	A86(d)	15c on 45c black vio	52	25
190D	A86(e)	15c on 45c black vio	40	15
		Nos. 190-190D (5)	2.12	1.00

No. 190D exists with inverted surcharge. Value, $5.

Allegory
A103

Overprinted "Dia Panamericano de la Salud / 2 Diciembre 1940" and Arc

1940, Dec. 2 **Engr.** *Perf. 12*

191	A103	5c green	20	15
192	A103	10c rose carmine	22	15
193	A103	20c deep blue	55	18
194	A103	40c brown	1.10	80
195	A103	55c orange yellow	2.25	95
		Nos. 191-195 (5)	4.32	2.23

Pan-American Health Day. See #C46-C54.
Exist without overprint.

Stamps of 1936 Surcharged in Black:

15
CENTIMOS
15

1941 *Perf. 14, 11½*

196	A95	15c on 25c orange	22	20
197	A95	15c on 35c brn vio	22	20
198	A95	15c on 40c brown	22	20
199	A95	15c on 2col yel grn	22	20
200	A95	15c on 5col green	40	35
		Nos. 196-200 (5)	1.28	1.15

Nos. 196-200 exist with surcharge inverted. Value, $5 a set.

National Stadium
A104

Engr.; Flags Typo. in Natl. Colors

1941, May 8 *Perf. 12½*

201	A104	5c green	75	20
a.		Flags omitted	60.00	
202	A104	10c orange	60	20
203	A104	15c car rose	90	30
204	A104	25c dk blue	1.00	42
205	A104	40c chestnut	4.00	1.25
206	A104	50c purple	5.00	1.50
207	A104	75c red orange	8.00	3.00
208	A104	1col dk carmine	15.00	6.00
		Nos. 201-208 (8)	35.25	12.87

Caribbean and Central American Soccer Championship. See #C57-C66, C121-C123.

No. 157 Surcharged in Black **5 Céntimos 5**

1941 *Perf. 12*

209	A89	5c on 13c car rose	15	15

Cleto González Viquez — A105

Design: 5c, José Rodriguez.

1941-45 **Engr.** *Perf. 12½*

210	A105	3c dp orange	16	15
210A	A105	3c dp plum ('43)	16	15
210B	A105	3c carmine ('45)	16	15
211	A105	5c dp violet	20	15
211A	A105	5c brown blk ('43)	20	15
		Nos. 210-211A (5)	88	
		Set value		54

See No. 256.

Old University of Costa Rica — A106

New National University
A107

1941, Aug. 26 *Perf. 12*

212	A106	5c green	35	15
213	A107	10c yellow org	38	15
214	A106	15c lilac rose	50	15
215	A107	25c dull blue	75	20
216	A106	50c fawn	3.00	1.25
		Nos. 212-216 (5)	4.98	1.90

National University, founded in 1940. See Nos. C74-C80.

Nos. 144, 189 Surcharged in Black or Red

15 CENTIMOS 15

1942 *Perf. 12½, 12*

217	A84	5c on 6c dk brn	18	15
218	A77	15c on 20c dp bl (R)	24	15

Nos. 217-218 exist with inverted surcharge. Value, each $5.

Torch of Freedom, "Victory" and Flags of American Nations
A108

Juan Mora Fernández
A109

1942, Sept. 25 *Perf. 12*

219	A108	5c rose	20	15
220	A108	5c yellow grn	20	15
221	A108	5c purple	20	15
222	A108	5c dp blue	20	15
223	A108	5c red orange	20	15
		Nos. 219-223 (5)	1.00	
		Set value		50

For overprints see Nos. 238-241.

1943-47 **Engr.**

Designs: 2c, Bruno Carranza. 3c, Tomas Guardia. 5c, Manuel Aguilar. 15c, Francisco Morazan. 25c, Jose M. Alfaro. 50c, Francisco M. Oreamuno. 1col, Jose M. Castro. 2col, Juan Rafael Mora.

224	A109	1c red lilac	15	15
225	A109	2c black	15	15
226	A109	3c deep blue	15	15
227	A109	5c brt blue grn	15	15
a.		5c bright green ('47)	15	15
228	A109	15c scarlet	20	15
229	A109	25c brt ultra	1.00	15
230	A109	50c dp violet	2.00	45
231	A109	1col black brown	3.00	1.50
232	A109	2col deep orange	4.00	2.00
		Nos. 224-232 (9)	10.80	4.85

See Nos. 344-368, C81-C91A, C124-C127, C154-C158, C179-C181, C768-C772, C790-C794, C854-C858. For surcharges see Nos. C154-C158, C182, C184-C185.

View of San Ramón
A118

1944, Jan. 19

233	A118	5c dark green	15	15
234	A118	10c orange	15	15
235	A118	15c rose pink	24	15
236	A118	40c gray black	90	45
237	A118	50c deep blue	1.50	75
		Nos. 233-237 (5)	2.94	
		Set value		1.40

100th anniv. of the founding of the City of San Ramón. See Nos. C94-C102.

Catalogue values for unused stamps in this section, from this point to the end of the section, are for Never Hinged items.

Nos. 220-223 Overprinted in Red or Black

La entrevista
de los
Presidentes
De la Guardia
y Picado
contribuirá a
afianzar la
unidad
Continental.
18 setiembre
1944

1944, Sept. 18

238	A108	5c yel green	15	15
239	A108	5c purple (R)	15	15
240	A108	5c dp blue (R)	15	15
241	A108	5c red orange	15	15
		Set value	48	40

Amicable settlement of a boundary dispute with Panama. This overprint also exists on No. 219.

Mauro Fernández (1844-1905), Statesman — A119

Unwmk.

1945, July 21 **Engr.** ***Perf. 14***
242 A119 20c deep green 25 15

For surcharge see No. 246.

Coffee Harvesting A120

1945, Oct. 9 ***Perf. 12***
243 A120 5c dk green & blk 15 15
244 A120 10c orange & blk 18 15
245 A120 20c car rose & blk 22 20
Nos. 243-245 (3) 55
Set value 40

No. 242 Surcharged in Red Brown

1946 **Unwmk.** ***Perf. 14***
246 A119 15c on 20c dp green 20 15

Exists with inverted surcharge. Value, $5.

No. O80 Overprinted in Red

CORREOS
1947

1947, Mar. 19 ***Perf. 12***
247 A96 5c green 15 15

Exist with inverted overprint. Value, $5.

Cervantes — A121

Wmk. 215

1947, Nov. 10 **Engr.** ***Perf. 14***
249 A121 30c deep blue 20 15
250 A121 55c deep carmine 35 30

400th anniv. of the birth of Miguel de Cervantes Saavedra, novelist, playwright and poet.

Franklin D. Roosevelt — A122

1947, Aug. 26 **Unwmk.** ***Perf. 12***
251 A122 5c brt green 15 15
252 A122 10c car rose 15 15
253 A122 15c ultra 20 18
254 A122 25c orange red 25 25
255 A122 50c lilac 50 35
Nos. 251-255,C160-C167 (13) 6.59 5.65

For surcharges see Nos. C224-C226.

Small Portrait Type of 1941

Design: 3c, Bishop Bernardo A. Theil.

1948 ***Perf. 12½***
256 A105 3c deep ultra 15 15

Old University of Costa Rica — A123

1953, June 25 **Litho.** ***Perf. 12***
Black Surcharge
257 A123 5c on 10c green 15 15

Revenue Stamp Surcharged in Red or Blue — A124

1955-56 **Unwmk.** **Engr.** ***Perf. 12***
258 A124 5c on 2c emerald 15 15
259 A124 15c on 2c emer (Bl) 18 15
260 A124 15c on 2c emer ('56) 18 15
Nos. 258-260,C341-C344 (7) 1.54
Set value 1.00

For surcharges see #C341-C344, C431-C433.

Justo A. Facio A125

Anglo-Costa Rican Bank A126

1960, Apr. 20 **Photo.** ***Perf. 13½***
261 A125 10c brown red 15 15

Centenary of the birth (in 1859) of Prof. Justo A. Facio. Exists imperf.

Nos. RA12-RA15 Surcharged in Red

1963
10
CENTIMOS

1963, Mar.
262 PT3 10c on 5c dk car 16 15
263 PT3 10c on 5c sepia 16 15
264 PT3 10c on 5c dull grn 16 16
265 PT3 10c on 5c blue 16 15
Nos. 262-265 (4) 64 61

1963 **Unwmk.** ***Perf. 13½***
266 A126 10c gray 15 15

Centenary of the Anglo-Costa Rican Bank.

Arms of San José — A127

Alberto M. Brenes Mora — A128

Coats of Arms: 35c, Cartago. 50c, Heredia. 55c, Alajuela. 65c, Guanacaste. 1col, Puntarenas. 2col, Limon.

1969, Sept. 14 **Litho.** ***Perf. 14x13½***
267 A127 15c multicolored 15 15
268 A127 35c multicolored 15 15
269 A127 50c gray & multi 15 15
270 A127 55c buff & multi 16 20
271 A127 65c multicolored 24 25
272 A127 1col pink & multi 1.00 25
273 A127 2col multicolored 1.00 50
Nos. 267-273 (7) 2.85 1.65

1976, Mar. 1 **Litho.** ***Perf. 10½***
274 A128 1col violet blue 25 20
Nos. 274,C653-C657 (6) 2.80 2.25

Prof. Alberto Manuel Brenes Mora, botanist, birth centenary.

Map of Costa Rica, Reader with Book — A129

1978, July 17 **Litho.** ***Perf. 13½***
275 A129 50c multicolored 15 15

National five-year literacy plan.

A130

A131

1983, May 17 **Litho.** ***Perf. 13x13½***
276 A130 10c multicolored 15 15
277 A130 50c multicolored 15 15
278 A130 10col multicolored 70 25
Set value 80 35

World Communications Year.

1983, May 30 **Litho.** ***Perf. 10½***
279 A131 20col black 1.40 50

First World Congress of Human Rights, 1982.

UPU Membership Centenary — A132

1983, June 30 **Litho.** ***Perf. 16***
280 A132 3col #17, monument 75 15
281 A132 10col #20, headquarters 1.50 28

French Alliance Centenary — A133

1983, July 21 **Litho.** ***Perf. 11***
282 A133 12col Scene in San Jose, by Christina Fournier 85 28

Christmas 1983 — A134

Nativity tableau in continuous design. Illustration reduced.

1983, Dec. 5 **Litho.** ***Perf. 13½***
283 A134 1.50col multi 15 15
284 A134 1.50col multi 15 15
285 A134 1.50col multi 15 15
Set value 30 15

Costa Rican Gardens Association.

Fishery Development Administration — A135

1983, Dec. 19 **Litho.** ***Perf. 13½***
286 A135 8.50col multi 56 18

Local Birds — A136

1984, Jan. 9 **Litho.** ***Perf. 13½***
287 A136 10c Quetzal 20 15
288 A136 50c Cyanerpes cyaneus 20 15
289 A136 1col Turdus grayi 20 15
290 A136 1.50col Momotus momota 20 15
291 A136 3col Colibri thalassinus 50 15
292 A136 10col Notiochelindon cyanoleuca 1.50 15
Nos. 287-292 (6) 2.80
Set value 35

Dated 1983. 10c, 1.50col, 3col vert.

José Joaquin Mora, Hero of 1856 Independence Campaign A137

Paintings, Juan Santamaria Museum, San José: 1.50col, Pancha Carrasco. 3 col, Death of Juan Santamaria, horiz. 8.50col, Juan Rafael Mora Porras.

1984, Apr. 10 **Litho.** ***Perf. 10½***
293 A137 50c multi 15 15
294 A137 1.50col multi 15 15
295 A137 3col multi 15 15
296 A137 8.50col multi 18 15
Set value 34 20

For surcharge see No. 440.

Jesus Bonilla Chavarria, Composer — A138

Musicians and Composers: 5col, Benjamin Gutierrez (b. 1937). 12col, Pilar Jimenez (1835-1922). 13col, Jose Daniel Zuniga Zeledon (1889-1981).

1984, May 30 **Litho.** ***Perf. 13½***
297 A138 3.50col blk & lil 15 15
298 A138 5col blk & pink 15 15
299 A138 12col blk & grn 24 15
300 A138 13col blk & yel 26 15
Set value 68 22

Figurines, Jade Museum — A139

1984 Summer Olympics — A140

1984, June 27 Litho. *Perf. 13½*

301 A139 4col Man (pendant) 15 15
302 A139 7col Seated man 15 15
303 A139 10col Dish, horiz. 20 15
Nos. 301-303 (3) 50
Set value 15

1984, July 27

304 A140 1col Basketball 15 15
305 A140 8col Swimming 15 15
306 A140 11col Bicycling 22 15
307 A140 14col Running 28 15
308 A140 20col Boxing 40 15
309 A140 30col Soccer 60 16
Nos. 304-309 (6) 1.80
Set value 50

Public Street Lighting Centenary — A141

1984, Aug. 9 Litho. *Perf. 10½*

310 A141 6col Street scene by Luis Chacon 15 15

10th Natl. Stamp Exhibition, Sept. 10-16 A142

1984, Sept. 10 Litho. *Perf. 10½*

311 A142 10col Natl. monument 20 15
312 A142 10col Juan Mora Fernandez monument 20 15
a. Min. sheet, 2 each #311-312 1.50
Set value 15

Natl. Arms — A143

1984, Oct. 29 Engr. *Perf. 14x13½*

313 A143 100col dk green 4.00 3.00
314 A143 100col yel org 4.00 3.00

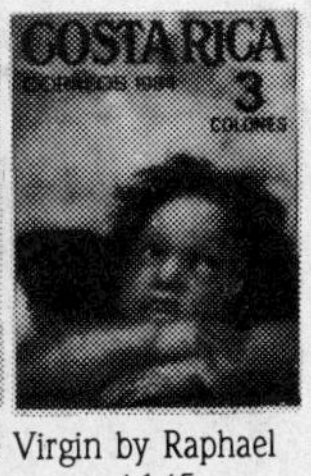

Detail from Sistine Virgin by Raphael
A144 A145

1984, Dec. 7 Litho. *Perf. 10½*

315 A144 3col multi 15 15
316 A145 3col multi 15 15
a. Pair, #315-316 15 15

20th Intl. Bicycle Race, Costa Rica — A146

1984, Dec. 19 Litho. *Perf. 13½*

317 A146 6col multi 28 28

Intl. Youth Year A147

1985, Jan. 31 *Perf. 10½*

322 A147 11col IYY emblem, No. C476 45 45

Scouting Movement, 75th anniv.

Labor Monument, San Jose — A148

Natl. values: 11col, Freedom of speech- wooden hand printing press. 13col, Neutrality- dove, natl. flag, outline map.

1985, Feb. 28

323 A148 6col shown 28 28
324 A148 11col bl, blk & yel 44 44
325 A148 13col multi 52 52

Size: 68x38mm

326 A148 30col Nos. 323-325 1.15 1.15
Nos. 323-326 (4) 2.39 2.39

Natl. Red Cross Cent., UN 40th Anniv. A149

1985, May 3 *Perf. 10½*

327 A149 3col No. 163 15 15
328 A149 5col No. C120, vert. 25 25

Club Emblem A150

1st Club Pres., Ricardo Saprissa Ayma — A151

Design: No. 330, Hands holding soccer ball.

1985, July 16 *Perf. 10½*

329 A150 3col multi 15 15
330 A150 3col multi 15 15
a. Pair, #329-330 30 30
331 A151 6col multi 28 28
Nos. 329-331 (3) 58 58

Saprissa Soccer Club, 50th Anniv.

Orchids — A152

1985, Dec. 3

332 A152 6col Brassia arcuigera 42 42
333 A152 6col Encyclia peraltensis 42 42
334 A152 6col Maxillaria especie 42 42
a. Strip of 3, #332-334 90 90
335 A152 13col Oncidium turialbae 90 90
336 A152 13col Trichopilia marginata 90 90
337 A152 13col Stanhopea ecornuta 90 90
a. Strip of 3, #335-337 1.80 1.80
Nos. 332-337 (6) 3.96 3.96

11th Natl. Philatelic Exposition A153

1985, Dec. 3 Litho. *Perf. 13½*

338 A153 20col No. C41 80 20

Christmas 1985 — A153a

1985, Dec. 12 Litho. *Perf. 10½*

338A A153a 3col multi 15 15

Compulsory Education, Cent. — A154

Designs: 3col, Primary school, horiz. 30col, Mauro Fernandez Acuna, founder.

1986, Feb. 28 *Perf. 13½*

339 A154 3col pale yel & brn 15 15
340 A154 30col pale pink & brn 1.20 30
Set value 35

Agriculture Students — A155

1986, Mar. 21 *Perf. 10½*

341 A155 10col shown 40 15
342 A155 10col IDB emblem 40 15
343 A155 10col Capo Bianco fisherman 40 15
a. Strip of 3, #341-343 1.20 1.20
Set value 30

Inter-American Development Bank Annual Governors' Assembly, San Jose.

Presidents Type of 1943

Designs: Nos. 344, 349, 354, 359, 364, Francisco J. Orlich Bolmarcich, 1962-66.

Nos. 345, 350, 355, 360, 365, Jose Joaquin Trejos Fernandez, 1966-70.

Nos. 346, 351, 356, 361, 366, Daniel Oduber Quiros, 1974-78.

Nos. 347, 352, 357, 362, 367, Rodrigo Carazo Oido, 1978-82.

Nos. 348, 353, 358, 363, 368, Luis Alberto Monge Alvarez, 1982-86.

1986, May 12 Litho. *Perf. 10½*

344 A109 3col turq blue 18 15
345 A109 3col turq blue 18 15
346 A109 3col turq blue 18 15
347 A109 3col turq blue 18 15
348 A109 3col turq blue 18 15
a. Strip of 5, #344-348 90 25
349 A109 6col yel brn 35 15
350 A109 6col yel brn 35 15
351 A109 6col yel brn 35 15
352 A109 6col yel brn 35 15
353 A109 6col yel brn 35 15
a. Strip of 5, #349-353 1.75 30
354 A109 10col brn org 60 15
355 A109 10col brn org 60 15
356 A109 10col brn org 60 15
357 A109 10col brn org 60 15
358 A109 10col brn org 60 15
a. Strip of 5, #354-358 3.00 50
359 A109 11col slate gray 65 15
360 A109 11col slate gray 65 15
361 A109 11col slate gray 65 15
362 A109 11col slate gray 65 15
363 A109 11col slate gray 65 15
a. Strip of 5, #359-363 3.25 60
364 A109 13col olive 75 15
365 A109 13col olive 75 15
366 A109 13col olive 75 15
367 A109 13col olive 75 15
368 A109 13col olive 75 15
a. Strip of 5, #364-368 3.75 70
Nos. 344-368 (25) 12.65
Set value 2.35

1986 World Cup Soccer Championships, Mexico — A156

1986, May 30 Litho. *Perf. 13½*

369 A156 1col Players 15 15
370 A156 1col Character trademark, vert. 15 15
371 A156 4col as No. 370 16 15
372 A156 6col as No. 369 24 15
373 A156 11col Players, diff. 45 15
Nos. 369-373 (5) 1.15
Set value 33

Intl. Peace Year — A157

Gold Museum, Central Bank of Costa Rica — A158

Peace in many languages: a, "Hoa binh," etc. b, "Vrede," etc. c, "Pace," etc.

1986, July 31 Litho. *Perf. 10½*

374 Strip of 3 55 15
a.-c. A157 5col, any single 18 15

1986, Sept. 19 *Perf. 13½*

Designs: Various undescribed works of Pre-Columbian art.

375 Strip of 5 1.10 30
a.-e. A158 6col any single 22 15
376 Strip of 5 2.25 60
a.-e. A158 13col any single 45 15

A159

Fauna and Flora — A160

1986, Dec. 16 Litho. *Perf. 13x13½*

377 A159 2col Centurio senex	15	15
378 A159 3col Glossophaga soricina	15	15
379 A159 4col Ectophylla alba	15	15
380 A159 5col Ectophylla alba, diff.	18	15
381 A159 6col Agalychnis callidryas	22	15
382 A159 10col Dendrobates pumilio	38	15
383 A159 11col Hyla ebraccata	40	15
384 A159 20col Phyllobates lugubris	75	18
Nos. 377-384 (8)	2.38	
Set value		64

Souvenir Sheet

Perf. 12½x12

385 A160 50col Agalychnis callidryas, diff.	*25.00*	*7.00*

Natl. Science and Technology Day — A161

Mural (detail), by Francisco Amighetti, Clorito Picado Social Security Clinic.

1987, July 31 Litho. *Perf. 10½*

386 A161 8col multi	32	15

Natl. Museum, Cent. — A162

Artifacts: No. 387a, Dowel-shaped figure of a man. No. 387b, Ape-like carved stone figurine. No. 387c, Polished stone ritual figure. No. 387d, Carved granite capital. No. 387e, Two-legged pot. No. 388a, Bowl. No. 388b, Sculpture. No. 388c, Water jar.

1987, Aug. 7

387 Strip of 5	1.60	40
a.-e. A162 8col any single	32	15
388 Strip of 3	1.80	45
a.-c. A162 15col any single	60	15
Nos. 387-388 (2)	3.40	85

Horse-drawn Wagon — A163

1987, Oct. 26

389 A163 20col shown	78	20
390 A163 20col Street in old San Jose	78	20
391 A163 20col Provincial coat of arms	78	20
Nos. 389-391 (3)	2.34	60

City of San Jose, 250th anniv. Rotary Club, 60th anniv.

Columbus Day — A164

1987, Oct. 26 *Perf. 10½*

392 A164 30col Map, 16th cent.	1.15	30

Day of the Race; 495th anniv. of Columbus's departure from Palos, Spain, on first journey to the New World.

Discovery of America, 500th Anniv. (in 1992) — A165

Pres. Oscar Arias, 1987 Nobel Peace Prize Winner — A166

Maps of Honduras, Nicaragua, Costa Rica and Panama, believed to be Asia by Columbus: No. 393, Costa Rica, 16th cent. No. 394, Map of "Asia" by Bartholomeu Columbus (1461-1514).

1987, Nov. 20 Litho. *Perf. 13½*

393 A165 4col yel & dk red brn	16	15
394 A165 4col yel & dk red brn	16	15
a. Pair, #393-394	32	15

1987, Dec. 2 *Perf. 10½*

395 A166 10col multi	30	15

Two Houses, a Watercolor by Fausto Pacheco (1899-1966) — A167

1987, Dec. 22 Litho. *Perf. 10½*

396 A167 1col multi	15	15

Intl. Year of Shelter for the Homeless.

17th General Conference for the Preservation of Natural Resources — A168

1988, Feb. 1 Litho. *Perf. 13½*

397 A168 5col Green turtle	20	15
398 A168 5col Emblem, golden toad	20	15
399 A168 5col Blue butterfly	20	15
Nos. 397-399 (3)	60	
Set value		15

Intl. Red Cross and Red Crescent Organizations, 125th Annivs. — A169

1988, Apr. 18 Litho. *Perf. 10½*

400 A169 30col lt blue & dark red	1.00	25

North and South Campaign A170

1988, June 6 Photo. *Perf. 11½*

Granite Paper

401 A170 18col Adult education	60	15
402 A170 20col Cultural radio programs	68	18

Cultural cooperation with Liechtenstein. See Liechtenstein Nos. 886-887. For overprint see No. C921.

A171

A172

1988, June 27 Litho. *Perf. 10½*

403 A171 3col dk blue, dark red & yel	15	15

Anglo-Costa Rican Bank, 125th anniv.

1988, Sept. 16 Litho. *Perf. 13½*

404 A172 25col Character trademark	68	18
405 A172 25col Games emblem	68	18
a. Pair, #404-405	1.40	40

1988 Summer Olympics, Seoul.

Girls' High School, Cent. — A173

1988, Oct. 17 Litho. *Perf. 10½*

406 A173 10col Student, courtyard	28	15

A174

A175

1988, Nov. 18

407 A174 10col gray, greenish bl & red brn	25	15

Educator Omar Dengo (1888-1928) and the Teachers' College, Heredia.

1988, Nov. 28 *Perf. 13½*

Design: Indian glass-bead and lion-tooth necklace.

408 A175 4col multi	15	15

Discovery of America, 500th anniv. (in 1992).

A176

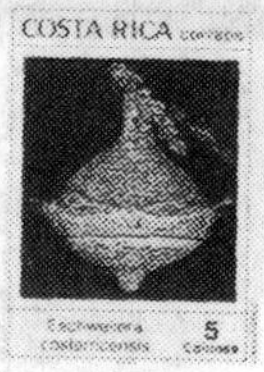

A177

1988, Dec. 26 Litho. *Perf. 10½*

409 A176 2col Observation tower	15	15

Natl. Meteorological Institute, cent. For surcharge see No. 439.

1989, Feb. 28

Designs: Indigenous flora.

410 A177 5col *Eschweilera costaricensis*	15	15
411 A177 10col *Heliconia wagneriana*	25	15
412 A177 15col *Heliconia lophocarpa*	38	15
413 A177 20col *Aechmea magdalenae*	50	15
414 A177 25col *Psammisia ramiflora*	62	16
415 A177 30col *Passiflora vitifolia*	75	20
Nos. 410-415 (6)	2.65	
Set value		68

A178

A179

1989, July 1 Litho. *Perf. 10½*

416 A178 30col Nation at Arms	75	20

French Revolution, bicent.

1989, Aug. 28 Litho. *Perf. 13½*

417 A179 10col Sugar mill	25	15

Grecia County, 151st anniv.
For overprints see Nos. RA106-RA109.

America Issue — A180

UPAE emblem and pre-Columbian stone carvings: 50col, Three-footed bench for grinding corn. 100col, Sphere.

Perf. 12½x12

Litho. & Engr.

1989, Oct. 12 Wmk. 334

418 A180 50col multi	1.20	30
419 A180 100col multi	2.45	62

For overprint see No. C916.

A181

A182

Perf. 10½

1989, Oct. 23 Litho. Unwmk.

420 A181 10col Orchid 25 15

"100 Years of Democracy" summit of Presidents.

Perf. 13½

1989, Nov. 27 Litho. Unwmk.

421 A182 18col Map, H.F. Pittier, emblem 42 15

Natl. Geographic Institute, cent.
For surcharge see No. 452.

America Issue — A183

Pre-Columbian gold frog figurine and facing portraits of Ferdinand V and Isabella I on gold coin struck by Spain from 1476 to 1516.

1989, Dec. 4 ***Perf. 10½***

422 A183 4col multicolored 15 15

Discovery of America, 500th anniv. (in 1992).

Natl. Theater, Cent. A184

Perf. 10½

1990, Feb. 27 Litho. Unwmk.

423 A184 5col *Coffee Allegory* 15 15

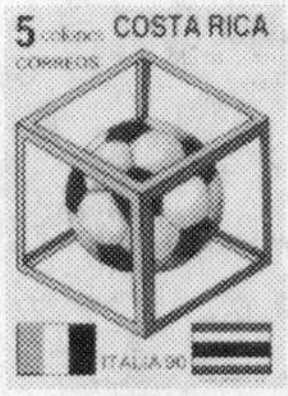

World Cup Soccer Championships, Italy — A185

1990, June 1 Litho. ***Perf. 10½***

424 A185 5col multicolored 22 15

Univ. of Costa Rica, 50th Anniv. A187

1990, Aug. 24 Litho. ***Perf. 10½***

426 A187 18col multicolored 40 15

Education, Democracy, Peace — A188

Litho. & Engr.

1990, Oct. 31 ***Perf. 12½***

427 A188 100col shown	2.25	55
428 A188 200col Flag as map	4.50	1.10
429 A188 500col National arms	11.00	2.75
Nos. 427-429 (3)	17.75	4.40

For overprints see Nos. 448, C920.

Hospitals — A190

America Issue — A191

Designs: No. 431, St. Vincent de Paul Hospital, Heredia. No. 432, Natl. Psychiatric hospital.

1990, Dec. 18 Engr. ***Perf. 13x12½***

431 A190 50col multicolored	1.10	28
432 A190 100col multicolored	2.25	55

1990, Dec. 21 Litho. ***Perf. 10½***

433 A191 18col Ara macao	36	15
434 A191 18col Ara ambigua	36	15
a. Pair, #433-434	75	20
435 A191 24col Cassia grandis	48	15
436 A191 24col Tabebuia ochracea	48	15
a. Pair, #435-436	1.00	25
Nos. 433-436 (4)	1.68	
Set value		48

Costa Rica-Panama Border Treaty, 50th Anniv. — A192

Designs: a, Flags, national arms. b, Presidents. c, Map.

1991, May 24 Litho. ***Perf. 10½***

437 A192 10col Strip of 3, #a.-c. 70 18

Discovery of America, 500th Anniv. (in 1992) — A193

1991, Oct. 11 Litho. ***Perf. 13½***

438 A193 4col multicolored 15 15

Nos. 409, 296 Surcharged

3.00
COLONES

1
Colón

1991, Oct. 21 Litho. ***Perf. 10½***

439 A176 1col on 2col #409	15	15
440 A137 3col on 8.50col #296	15	15
Set value	15	15

Former Presidents, Supreme Court of Justice — A194

Designs: a, Benito Serrano Jimenez. b, Luis Davila Solera. c, Fernando Baudrit Solera. d, Alejandro Alvarado Garcia.

Perf. 14½x13½

1992, Feb. 28 Litho.

441 A194 5col Strip of 4, #a.-d. 1.40 35

DINADECO, Natl. Directorate of Community Development, 25th Anniv. — A195

1992, Apr. 28 Litho. ***Perf. 10½***

442 A195 15col multicolored 1.05 28

Compare with No. C505.

A196

A197

1992, May 26 Litho. ***Perf. 13½***

443 A196 15col lake & black 1.05 28

Dr. Solon Nunez Frutos, public health pioneer.

1992, July 17 Litho. ***Perf. 13***

Solar Eclipse: a, Total eclipse. b, Post Office Bldg. during eclipse. c, Partial eclipse.

444 A197 45col Strip of 3, #a.-c. 3.25 80

A198

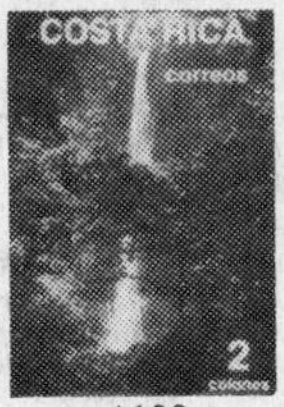

A199

1992, Aug. 14 Litho. ***Perf. 13½***

445 A198 35col multicolored 85 22

Interamerican Institute for Agricultural Cooperation, 50th anniv.

1992, Nov. 5 Litho. ***Perf. 10½***

446 A199 2col Waterfall	15	15
447 A199 15col Coastline	22	15
Set value	27	15

Cocos Island, 450th anniv. of discovery.

No. 427 Ovptd. "CENTENARIO / DE LIMON"

Litho. & Engr.

1992, Nov. 27 ***Perf. 12½***

448 A188 100col black & blue 1.45 35

America Issue — A200

1992, Dec. 15 Litho. ***Perf. 10½***

449 A200 15col Anolis townsendi	22	15
450 A200 35col Pinaroloxias inornata	85	22
Set value		28

Natl. Theater A201

Detail from painting "Allegory of Fine Arts," by Roberto Fontana.

1993, Jan. 29 Litho. ***Perf. 10½***

451 A201 20col multicolored 28 15

5
colones

No. 421 Surcharged

1993, Mar. 26 Litho. ***Perf. 13½***

452 A182 5col on 18col multi 16 15

Protection of the Dolphin A202

1993, May 17 Litho. ***Perf. 10½***

453 A202 10col Delphinus delphis	15	15
454 A202 20col Stenella coeruleoalbus	28	15
Set value		21

Costa Rican Civil Service, 40th Anniv. — A203

1993, May 28 Litho. ***Perf. 13½***

455 A203 5col multicolored 15 15

Costa Rican Chamber of Industries, 50th Anniv. A204

1993, July 15 ***Perf. 10½***

456 A204 45col multicolored 65 32

School of Communication Sciences, University of Costa Rica, 25th Anniv. — A205

1993, Aug. 19 **Litho.** ***Perf. 13½***

457 A205 20col black, blue & red	28	15

Protection of the Tropical Rain Forest — A206

1993, Aug. 27 ***Perf. 10½***

458 A206 2col Passiflora vitifolia	15	15
459 A206 35col Gurania megistantha	50	25
Set value	53	26

Social Guarantees and Labor Code, 50th Anniv. A207

1993, Sept. 14 **Litho.** ***Perf. 10½***

460 A207 20col multicolored	42	22

A208

A209

1993, Oct. 25 **Litho.** ***Perf. 13½***

461 A208 45col multicolored	90	45

Intl. Assoc. of Professional Custom-House Agents, 15th Congress.

1993, Nov. 26 ***Perf. 10½***

462 A209 20col multicolored	42	22

Miguel Angel Castro Carazo (1893-1960), educator and humanitarian.

A211

A212

1993, Dec. 23 **Litho.** ***Perf. 10½***

464 A211 20col multicolored	40	20

Law School of Costa Rica, 150th anniv.

1994, Mar. 8 **Litho.** ***Perf. 13***

465 A212 20col Natl. Theater	40	20

Marine Life — A213

Designs: 5col, Cyphoma gibbosum. 10col, Ophioderma rubicundum. 15col, Myripristis jacobus. 20col, Holocanthus passer. 35col, Paranthias furcifer. 45col, Tubastraea coccinea. 50col, Acanthaster planci. 55col, Ocypode. 70col, Arothron meleagris. 100col, Thalassoma lucasanum.

Litho. & Embossed

1994, Apr. 29 ***Perf. 12½x12***

466 A213 5col multicolored	15	15
467 A213 10col multicolored	20	15
468 A213 15col multicolored	28	15
469 A213 20col multicolored	38	20
470 A213 35col multicolored	65	32
471 A213 45col multicolored	85	42
472 A213 50col multicolored	95	48
473 A213 55col multicolored	1.10	55
474 A213 70col multicolored	1.40	70
Nos. 466-474 (9)	5.96	3.12

Souvenir Sheet

Perf. 13

475 A213 100col multicolored	2.00	2.00

SEMI-POSTAL STAMPS

No. 72 Surcharged in Red

+ 5c

1922 **Unwmk.** ***Perf. 12***

B1 A56 5c + 5c orange	50	20

Issued for the benefit of the Costa Rican Red Cross Society. In 1928, owing to a temporary shortage of the ordinary 5c stamp, No. B1 was placed on sale as a regular 5c stamp, the surtax being disregarded.

Discus Thrower — SP1

Trophy — SP2

Parthenon SP3

1924 **Litho.** ***Imperf.***

B2 SP1 5c dark green	1.50	2.00
B3 SP2 10c carmine	1.50	2.00
B4 SP3 20c dark blue	3.50	3.00
a. Tête bêche pair	14.00	16.00

Perf. 12

B5 SP1 5c dark green	1.50	2.00
B6 SP2 10c carmine	1.50	2.00
B7 SP3 20c dark blue	3.00	3.50
a. Tête bêche pair	14.00	16.00
Nos. B2-B7 (6)	12.50	14.50

These stamps were sold at a premium of 10c each, to help defray the expenses of athletic games held at San José in Dec. 1924.

AIR POST STAMPS

Airplane — AP1

Perf. 12½

1926, June 4 **Unwmk.** **Engr.**

C1 AP1 20c ultramarine	2.00	35

No. 123 Overprinted

CORREO AEREO

1930, Mar. 14 ***Perf. 12***

C2 A75 10c carmine rose	1.00	15

The existance of genuine inverted or double overprints is in doubt.

AP3

1930-32 ***Perf. 12½***

C3 AP3 5c on 10c dk brn ('32)	15	15
C4 AP3 20c on 50c ultra	15	15
C5 AP3 40c on 50c ultra	30	15
Nos. C3-C5 (3)	60	
Set value		30

The existance of genuine inverted or double surcharges of Nos. C3-C5 is in doubt.

Telegraph Stamp Overprinted

Correo Aereo

1930, Mar. 19

C6 AP3 1col orange	1.50	30

No. O79 Surcharged in Red

1930, Mar. 11

C7 O7 8c on 1col lilac & blk	45	35
C8 O7 20c on 1col lilac & blk	60	45
C9 O7 40c on 1col lilac & blk	1.25	90
C10 O7 1col on 1col lilac & blk	1.75	1.25
Nos. C7-C10 (4)	4.05	2.95

AP6

AP7

Red Surcharge on Revenue Stamps

1931-32 ***Perf. 12***

C11 AP6 2col on 2col gray grn	20.00	20.00
C12 AP6 3col on 5col lil brn	20.00	20.00
C13 AP6 5col on 10col gray blk	20.00	20.00
Nos. C11-C13 (3)	60.00	60.00

There were two printings of this issue which were practically identical in the colors of the stamps and the surcharges.

Nos. C11 and C13 have the date "1929" on the stamp, No. C12 has "1930."

Black Overprint on Telegraph Stamp

1932, Mar. 8 ***Perf. 12½***

C14 AP7 40c green	1.50	30
a. Inverted overprint	18.00	

Mail Plane about to Land — AP8

Allegory of Flight — AP9

1934, Mar. 14 ***Perf. 12***

C15 AP8 5c green	15	15
C16 AP8 10c car rose	15	15
C17 AP8 15c chocolate	35	15
C18 AP8 20c dp blue	40	15
C19 AP8 25c dp orange	50	15
C20 AP8 40c olive blk	90	15
C21 AP8 50c gray blk	60	15
C22 AP8 60c org yel	1.25	18
C23 AP8 75c dull vio	1.75	45
C24 AP9 1col dp rose	1.40	15
C25 AP9 2col lt blue	1.50	60
C26 AP9 5col black	4.00	4.00
C27 AP9 10col red brn	6.50	6.50
Nos. C15-C27 (13)	19.45	12.93

Stamps Nos. C15 to C27 with holes punched through were for use of government officials.

See Nos. C216-C219. For overprints see Nos. C67-C73, C92-C93, C103-C116, CO1-CO13.

Airplane over Poás Volcano — AP10

1937, Feb. 10

C28 AP10 1c black	15	15
C29 AP10 2c brown	15	15
C30 AP10 3c dk violet	15	15
Set value	36	30

First Fair of Costa Rica.

Puntarenas AP11

National Bank — AP12

Perf. 12, 12½

1937, Dec. 15 **Unwmk.**

C31 AP11 2c black gray	15	15
C32 AP11 5c green	15	15
C33 AP11 20c deep blue	28	22
C34 AP11 1.40col olive brn	2.75	2.75
Nos. C31-C34 (4)	3.33	3.27

1938, Jan. 11 **Wmk. 229** ***Perf. 12½***

C35 AP12 1c purple	15	15
C36 AP12 3c red org	15	15
C37 AP12 10c car rose	15	15
C38 AP12 75c brown	1.50	1.50
Set value	1.74	1.70

Nos. C31-C38 commemorate the Natl. Products Exposition held at San José, Dec. 1937.

Airport Administration Building, La Sabana AP13

1940, May 2 **Engr.** **Unwmk.**

C39 AP13 5c green	15	15
C40 AP13 10c rose pink	15	15
C41 AP13 25c lt blue	15	15
C42 AP13 35c red brown	22	22
C43 AP13 60c red org	35	35
C44 AP13 85c violet	1.00	85
C45 AP13 2.35col turq grn	5.50	5.50
Nos. C39-C45 (7)	7.52	7.37

Opening of the Intl. Airport at La Sabana.

Duran Sanatorium AP14

Overprinted "Dia Panamericano de la Salud / 2 Diciembre 1940" and Bar in Black

1940, Dec. 2 *Perf. 12*

C46 AP14	10c scarlet	15	15
C47 AP14	15c purple	15	15
C48 AP14	25c lt blue	28	24
C49 AP14	35c bister brn	45	40
C50 AP14	60c pck green	55	55
C51 AP14	75c olive	1.25	1.40
C52 AP14	1.35col red org	5.50	5.50
C53 AP14	5col sepia	24.00	24.00
C54 AP14	10col red lilac	75.00	75.00
	Nos. C46-C54 (9)	107.33	107.39

Pan-American Health Day. Exist without overprint. Few copies of C53-C54 were sold for postal purposes, nearly all having been obtained by philatelic speculators.

No. 174 Surcharged in Black or Blue

AEREO

Aviación Panamericana

Dic. 17 1940

15 CENTIMOS 15

1940, Dec. 17 *Perf. 14*

C55 A95	15c on 50c yel (Bk)	50	45
C56 A95	30c on 50c yel (Bl)	50	45

Pan-American Aviation Day, proclaimed by President F. D. Roosevelt.

The 15c surch. exists on #171, value $30.

International Soccer Game at National Stadium — AP15

1941, May 8 *Perf. 12*

C57 AP15	15c red	70	15
C58 AP15	30c dp ultra	80	22
C59 AP15	40c red brown	80	32
C60 AP15	50c purple	1.10	70
C61 AP15	60c brt green	1.40	80
C62 AP15	75c yel org	2.25	1.25
C63 AP15	1col dull vio	4.00	4.00
C64 AP15	1.40col rose	8.25	8.25
C65 AP15	2col blue grn	16.00	16.00
C66 AP15	5col black	35.00	35.00
	Nos. C57-C66 (10)	70.30	66.69

Caribbean and Central American Soccer Championship. See Nos. C121-C123. For surcharges see Nos. C145-C147.

Air Post Stamps of 1934 Overprinted or Surcharged in Black with New Values and Bars

Mayo 1941

Tratado Limítrofe
Costa Rica - Panamá

1941, June 2

C67 AP8	5c on 20c dp bl	18	15
C68 AP8	15c on 20c dp bl	22	18
C69 AP8	40c on 75c dl vio	32	22
C70 AP9	65c on 1col dp rose	60	50
C71 AP9	1.40col on 2col lt bl	3.00	3.00
C72 AP9	5col black	11.00	11.00
C73 AP9	10col red brn	12.50	12.50
	Nos. C67-C73 (7)	27.82	27.55

Issued in commemoration of the settlement of the Costa Rica-Panama border dispute.

Nos. C67-C73 are found with hyphen omitted in overprint. Nos. C67-C69 with inverted overprint.

University Types of 1941

1941, Aug. 26 *Perf. 12*

C74 A107	15c salmon	22	15
C75 A106	30c lt blue	32	15
C76 A107	40c orange	38	28
C77 A106	60c turq green	48	40
C78 A107	1col violet	1.90	1.90
C79 A106	2col black	4.75	4.75
C80 A107	5col sepia	15.00	15.00
	Nos. C74-C80 (7)	23.05	22.63

Portrait Type of 1943-47

Designs: 40c, Manuel Aguilar. No. C83, Francisco Morazan. No. C83A, Jose R. De Gallegos. 50c, Jose M. Alfaro. 60c, Francisco M. Oreamuno. 65c, Jose M. Castro. 85c, Juan Rafael Mora. 1col, Jose M. Montealegre. 1.05col, Braulio Carrillo. 1.15col, Jesus Jimenez. 1.40col, Bruno Carranza. 2col, Tomas Guardia.

1943-45 **Engr.**

C81	A109	10c rose pink	15	15
C82	A109	40c blue	20	15
C82A	A109	40c car rose	20	15
C83	A109	45c magenta	30	22
C83A	A109	45c black	18	15
C84	A109	50c turq grn	1.50	18
C84A	A109	50c red org	28	18
C85	A109	60c brt ultra	40	15
C85A	A109	60c brt grn	18	15
C86	A109	65c scarlet	75	22
C86A	A109	65c brt ultra	20	18
C87	A109	85c dp org	90	30
C87A	A109	85c dull pur	1.10	38
C88	A109	1col black	1.10	40
C88A	A109	1col scarlet	45	18
C88B	A109	1.05col bis brn	60	40
C89	A109	1.15col red brn	1.50	1.40
C89A	A109	1.15col green	2.00	1.10
C90	A109	1.40col dp vio	2.25	1.90
C90A	A109	1.40col org yel	1.40	1.25
C91	A109	2col black	3.50	1.10
C91A	A109	2col ol grn	1.10	28
		Nos. C81-C91A (22)	20.24	10.57

Issue date: Nos. C82A, C83A, C84A, C85A, C86A, C87A, C88A, C88B, C89A, C90A, C91A, 1945. See Nos. C124-C127, C179-C181. For surcharges see Nos. C154-C158, C182, C184-C185.

Nos. C26-C27 Overprinted in Red or Blue

Legislacion Social
15 Setiembre 1943

1943, Sept. 16

C92 AP9	5col black (R)	3.00	2.25
C93 AP9	10col red brown (Bl)	6.00	4.00

Mercury and Plane — AP31

1944, Jan. 19

C94	AP31	10c red org	15	15
C95	AP31	15c dk car	18	15
C96	AP31	40c brt ultra	30	22
C97	AP31	45c dp red lil	35	28
C98	AP31	60c turq grn	48	40
C99	AP31	1col dk red brn	1.10	80
C100	AP31	1.40col gray blk	6.00	5.00
C101	AP31	5col violet	16.00	15.00
C102	AP31	10col black	45.00	40.00
		Nos. C94-C102 (9)	69.56	62.00

City of San Ramón founding, 100th anniv.

Very few copies of the 5col or 10col stamps were sold for postal purposes, nearly all having been obtained by philatelic speculators.

No. CO10 With Additional Overprint in Black **1944**

1944, Nov. 22

C103 AP9	1col deep rose	70	35
a.	Blue overprint	55.00	

Nos. CO1-CO13 Overprinted in Carmine or Black **1945**

1945, Jan. 12 **Unwmk.** *Perf. 12*

C104 AP8	5c green	60	55
C105 AP8	10c car rose (Bk)	60	55
C106 AP8	15c chocolate	60	55
C107 AP8	20c deep blue	35	32
C108 AP8	25c dp org (Bk)	60	60
C109 AP8	40c ol blk	35	32
C110 AP8	50c gray blk	60	60
C111 AP8	60c org yel (Bk)	90	32
C112 AP8	75c dull violet	75	60
C113 AP9	1col dp rose (Bk)	75	32
C114 AP9	2col light blue	4.75	4.50
C115 AP9	5col black	6.00	5.50
C116 AP9	10col red brn (Bk)	9.00	8.25
	Nos. C104-C116 (13)	25.85	22.98

No. C104 exists inverted and overprinted in black.

Catalogue values for unused stamps in this section, from this point to the end of the section, are for Never Hinged items.

AP32

Telegraph Stamps Overprinted in Black or Carmine

1945, Feb. 28 **Unwmk.** *Perf. 12½*

C117 AP32	40c green (C)	25	15
C118 AP32	50c ultra (C)	30	15
C119 AP32	1col orange (Bk)	65	40
	Nos. C117-C119 (3)	1.20	70

#C117 exists with inverted overprint. Value, $5.

Florence Nightingale and Edith Cavell AP33

1945 **Engr.**

C120 AP33	1col black & car	75	50

60th anniv. of the Costa Rican Red Cross Soc. For surcharge see No. C183.

Soccer Type of 1941
Inscribed: "Febrero 1946"

1946, May 13 *Perf. 12*

C121 AP15	25c green	75	60
C122 AP15	30c dull yellow	75	60
C123 AP15	55c deep blue	90	60
	Nos. C121-C123 (3)	2.40	1.80

Portrait Type of 1943-47

Designs: 25c, Aniceto Esquivel. 30c, Vicente Herrera. 55c, Prospero Fernandez. 75c, Bernardo Soto.

1946, May 12

C124 A109	25c blue	20	15
C125 A109	30c red brown	25	20
C126 A109	55c plum	40	30
C127 A109	75c blue green	60	40
	Nos. C124-C127 (4)	1.45	1.05

Hospital of St. John of God — AP38

1946, June 24 **Unwmk.** *Perf. 12½*
Center in Black

C128 AP38	5c yel grn	15	15
C129 AP38	10c dk brown	15	15
C130 AP38	15c carmine	15	15
C131 AP38	25c dk blue	16	16
C132 AP38	30c dp org	32	24
C133 AP38	40c olive grn	16	16
C134 AP38	50c violet	28	28
C135 AP38	60c dk sl grn	60	55
C136 AP38	75c brown	48	40
a.	Horiz. pair, imperf. btwn.	100.00	
C137 AP38	1col blue	60	32
C138 AP38	2col brn org	90	70
C139 AP38	3col dk vio brn	1.75	1.75
C140 AP38	5col yellow	2.25	2.25
	Nos. C128-C140 (13)	7.95	7.26

Rafael Iglesias — AP39

Designs: 3col, Ascensión Esquivel. 5col, Cleto González Viquez. 10col, Ricardo Jiménez Oreamuno.

1947, Jan. 15 **Wmk. 215** *Perf. 14*
Center in Black

C141 AP39	2col blue	1.10	80
C142 AP39	3col dp car	1.65	1.10
C143 AP39	5col dk green	2.50	1.65
C144 AP39	10col orange	4.75	3.00
	Nos. C141-C144 (4)	10.00	6.55

Nos. C121-C123 Surcharged in Black

Habilitado para

₡ 0.15

Decreto Nº 16 de
28 de abril de 1947

1947, May 5 **Unwmk.** *Perf. 12*

C145 AP15	15c on 25c green	90	75
C146 AP15	15c on 30c dull yel	90	75
C147 AP15	15c on 55c dp blue	90	75
	Nos. C145-C147 (3)	2.70	2.25

Exist with inverted surcharge.

Columbus in Cariari AP43

1947, May 19 **Engr.** *Perf. 12½*
Center in Black

C148 AP43	25c green	24	15
C149 AP43	30c dp ultra	24	15
C150 AP43	40c red orange	35	15
C151 AP43	45c violet	45	24
C152 AP43	50c brt carmine	50	20
C153 AP43	65c brown org	1.40	70
	Nos. C148-C153 (6)	3.18	1.59

For surcharges see Nos. C178, C220-C223.

Nos. C84A, C85A, C127, C88A, and C88B Surcharged with New Value in Black or Red

1947, June 3 *Perf. 12*

C154 A109	15c on 50c red org	25	15
C155 A109	15c on 60c brt grn (R)	25	15
C156 A109	15c on 75c bl grn (R)	25	15
C157 A109	15c on 1col scar	30	15
C158 A109	15c on 1.05col bis brn	25	15
	Nos. C154-C158 (5)	1.30	
	Set value		63

#C155 is known with black surcharge. Value, $10. #C156 with inverted surcharge. Value, $10.

Early Steam Locomotive AP44

1947, Nov. 10 *Perf. 12½*

C159 AP44	35c bl grn & blk	1.00	25

Electric railroad to the Pacific coast, 50th anniv.

Roosevelt Type of Regular Issue

1947, Aug. 26 *Perf. 12*

C160 A122	15c green	15	15
C161 A122	30c car rose	15	15
C162 A122	45c red brown	22	20
C163 A122	65c org yel	25	22
C164 A122	75c blue	32	22
C165 A122	1col ol grn	50	38
C166 A122	2col black	1.25	1.00
C167 A122	5col scarlet	2.50	2.25
	Nos. C160-C167 (8)	5.34	4.57

For surcharges see Nos. C224-C226.

National Theater AP46

Rafael Iglesias AP47

1948, Jan. 26 *Perf. 12½*

Center in Black

C168 AP46	15c brt ultra	15	15
C169 AP46	20c red	18	15
C170 AP47	35c dk green	25	22
C171 AP46	45c purple	35	25
C172 AP46	50c carmine	35	25
C173 AP46	75c red vio	75	75
C174 AP46	1col olive	1.40	1.10
C175 AP46	2col red brn	2.25	1.50
C176 AP47	5col org yel	3.50	3.25
C177 AP47	10col brt bl	8.00	6.00
	Nos. C168-C177 (10)	17.18	13.62

50th anniversary of National Theater.

No. C150 Surcharged in Carmine

HABILITADO
PARA
₡ 0.35

1948, Apr. 21

C178 AP43	35c on 40c	35	35

Exists with surcharge inverted.

Portrait Type of 1943-47

Designs: 5c, Salvador Lara. 15c, Carlos Duran.

1948 **Engr.** *Perf. 12*

C179 A109	5c sepia	32	15
C180 A109	10c olive brown	32	15
C181 A109	15c violet	32	15
	Nos. C179-C181 (3)	96	
	Set value		26

Nos. C88B, C120, C89A and C90A Surcharged in Carmine or Black

1824-1949
125 Aniversario
de la Anexión
Guanacaste
₡ 0.55

Perf. 12½, 12

1949, Aug. 28 **Unwmk.**

C182 A109	35c on 1.05col bis brn	18	15
C183 AP33	50c on 1col blk & car	30	25
a.	2nd & 3rd lines both read "125 Aniversario"	6.75	6.75
C184 A109	55c on 1.15col grn	48	40
C185 A109	55c on 1.40col org yel (Bk)	48	38
	Nos. C182-C185 (4)	1.44	1.18

125th anniv. of the annexation of the province of Guanacaste.

Overprint differs on No. C183, with "Guanacaste" in capitals, and lower case "a" in "Anexión."

The variety "l" for "i" in "Anexion" is found on Nos. C182, C184 and C185.

Symbols of UPU — AP48

1950, Jan. 11 **Photo.** *Perf. 11½*

C186 AP48	15c lilac rose	15	15
C187 AP48	25c chalky blue	15	15
C188 AP48	1col gray green	32	15
	Nos. C186-C188 (3)	62	
	Set value		20

75th anniv. of the UPU.

Battle of El Tejar, Cartago AP49

Occupation of Limón — AP50

Bull (Cattle Raising) — AP51

Designs: 25c, Lucha ranch. 35c, Trenches of San Isidro Battalion. 55c and 75c, Observation post. 80c and 1col, Dr. Carlos Luis Valverde.

Inscribed: "Guerra de Liberacion Nacional 1948"

Engraved; Center Photogravure

1950, July 20 *Perf. 12½*

Center in Black

C189 AP49	15c brt car	15	15
C190 AP50	20c dull green	20	15
C191 AP49	25c dull blue	24	15
C192 AP49	35c chestnut	28	15
C193 AP49	55c lilac	55	20
C194 AP49	75c red org	90	32
C195 AP50	80c gray	90	50
C196 AP50	1col org yel	1.25	55
	Nos. C189-C196 (8)	4.47	2.17

2nd anniv. of the War for Natl. Liberation.

Inscribed: "Feria Nacional Agricola Ganadera e Industrial Cartago 1950"

1950, July 27

Designs: 1c, 10c, 2col, Bull. 2c, 30c and 3col, Tuna fishing. 3c and 65c, Pineapple. 5c, 50c and 5col, Bananas. 45c, 80c and 10col, Coffee picker.

Center in Black

C197 AP51	1c brt green	15	15
C198 AP51	2c brt blue	15	15
C199 AP51	3c chocolate	15	15
C200 AP51	5c dp ultra	15	15
C201 AP51	10c green	15	15
C202 AP51	30c purple	20	15
C203 AP51	45c vermilion	22	15
C204 AP51	50c blue gray	35	15
C205 AP51	65c dk blue	40	20
C206 AP51	80c dp rose	85	55
C207 AP51	2col org yel	2.25	1.65
C208 AP51	3col blue	5.00	4.00
C209 AP51	5col carmine	7.25	6.00
C210 AP51	10col dp claret	7.25	6.00
	Nos. C197-C210 (14)	24.52	19.60

National Agricultural, Livestock and Industrial Fair, Cartago, 1950.

For surcharge see No. RA1.

Queen Isabella I and Caravels of Columbus AP52

Unwmk.

1952, Mar. 4 **Engr.** *Perf. 13*

C211 AP52	15c carmine	15	15
C212 AP52	20c orange	22	15
C213 AP52	25c ultra	32	15
C214 AP52	55c dp green	1.00	24
C215 AP52	2col violet	2.00	45
	Nos. C211-C215 (5)	3.69	1.14

500th anniversary of the birth of Queen Isabella I of Spain.

Mail Plane Type of 1934

1952-53 *Perf. 12*

C216 AP8	5c blue	32	15
C217 AP8	10c green	32	15
C218 AP8	15c car rose ('53)	38	15
C219 AP8	35c purple	1.00	20
	Nos. C216-C219 (4)	2.02	
	Set value		50

Nos. C149-C151, C153 Surcharged in Red: "HABILITADO PARA CINCO CENTIMOS 1953"

1953, Apr. 24 *Perf. 12½*

Center in Black

C220 AP43	5c on 30c dp ultra	1.00	85
C221 AP43	5c on 40c red org	15	15
C222 AP43	5c on 45c vio	15	15
C223 AP43	5c on 65c brn org	20	15
	Nos. C220-C223 (4)	1.50	1.30

Nos. C161-C163 Surcharged in Black

15 —o— 15

1953, Apr. 11 *Perf. 12*

C224 A122	15c on 30c car rose	15	15
C225 A122	15c on 45c red brn	15	15
C226 A122	15c on 65c org yel	15	15
	Nos. C224-C226 (3)	45	
	Set value		32

Refinery of Vegetable Oils and Fats — AP53

Industries: 10c, Pottery. 15c, Sugar. 20c, Soap. 25c, Lumber. 30c, Matches. 35c, Textiles. 40c, Leather. 45c, Tobacco. 50c, Preserving. 55c, Canning. 60c, General. 65c, Metals. 75c, Pharmaceuticals. 80c, Pharmaceuticals. 1col, Paper. 2col, Rubber. 3col, Airplane maintenance. 5col, Marble. 10col, Beer.

Engraved; Center Photogravure

1954-59 **Unwmk.** *Perf. 13x12½*

Center in Black

C227	AP53	5c red	15	15
C228	AP53	10c dk blue	15	15
C229	AP53	15c green	15	15
C230	AP53	20c violet	15	15
C231	AP53	25c magenta	15	15
C232	AP53	30c purple	30	18
C233	AP53	35c red vio	15	15
C234	AP53	40c black	25	15
C235	AP53	45c dk green	50	20
C236	AP53	50c vio brown	32	15
C237	AP53	55c yellow	22	15
C238	AP53	60c brown	60	30
C239	AP53	65c carmine	70	45
C240	AP53	75c violet	1.10	40
C240A	AP53	80c pur & gray	52	45
C241	AP53	1col blue	32	18
a.		Imperf., pair	80.00	
C242	AP53	2col rose pink	1.00	55
C243	AP53	3col ol grn	1.50	90
C244	AP53	5col black	2.25	75
C245	AP53	10col yellow	6.50	5.00
		Nos. C227-C245 (20)	16.98	10.71

Issue dates: 30c, 35c, 60c, 65c, 75c, 2col, 3col, Oct. 20. 80c, Oct. 2, 1959. Others, Sept. 1.

See Nos. C252-C255. For surcharges and overprint see Nos. C314-C315, C334-C336, RA2, RA11.

Globe, Rotary Emblem — AP54

Map of Costa Rica — AP55

Designs: 25c, Hand protecting boy. 40c, 2col, Hospital. 45c, Globe and palm leaves. 60c, Lighthouse.

1956, Feb. 7 **Engr.** *Perf. 12*

C246 AP54	10c green	15	15
C247 AP54	25c dk blue	15	15
C248 AP54	40c dk brown	35	28
C249 AP54	45c brt red	24	20
C250 AP54	60c dk red vio	28	24
C251 AP54	2col yel org	70	50
	Nos. C246-C251 (6)	1.87	1.52

50th anniv. of Rotary Intl. (in 1955).

Industries Type of 1954

Designs as in 1954.

Engraved; Center Photogravure

1956, Feb. 17 *Perf. 12*

Center in Black

C252 AP53	5c ultra	15	15
C253 AP53	10c vio blue	15	15
C254 AP53	15c org yel	15	15
C255 AP53	75c red org	30	16
	Nos. C252-C255 (4)	75	
	Set value		34

1957, June 21 **Engr.** *Perf. 13½x13*

Designs: 10c, Map of Guanacaste. 15c, Inn. 20c, House of Santa Rosa. 25c, Gen. Jose Manuel Quiros. 30c, Old Presidential Palace. 35c, Joaquin Bernardo Calvo. 40c, Luis Molina. 45c, Gen. Jose Joaquin Mora. 50c, Gen. Jose Maria Canas. 55c, Juan Santamaria monument. 60c, National monument. 65c, Antonio Vallerriestra. 70c, Ramon Castilla y Marquesado. 75c, San Carlos fortress. 80c, Francisco Maria Oreamuno. 1col, Pres. Juan Rafael Mora.

C256 AP55	5c lt blue	15	15
C257 AP55	10c green	15	15
C258 AP55	15c dp orange	15	15
C259 AP55	20c lt brown	24	15
C260 AP55	25c vio blue	24	15
C261 AP55	30c violet	35	15
C262 AP55	35c car rose	35	15
C263 AP55	40c slate	35	15
C264 AP55	45c rose red	40	16
C265 AP55	50c ultra	40	16
C266 AP55	55c ocher	70	16
C267 AP55	60c brt car	55	24
C268 AP55	65c carmine	60	24
C269 AP55	70c orange yel	75	30
C270 AP55	75c emerald	70	28
C271 AP55	80c dk brown	80	35
C272 AP55	1col black	85	35
	Nos. C256-C272 (17)	7.73	3.44

Centenary of War of 1856-57.

Cleto Gonzalez Viquez AP56

Highway and Gonzalez Viquez AP57

Designs: 10c, Ricardo Jimenez Oreamuno. 20c, Puntarenas wharf and Jimenez. 35c, Post and Telegraph Bldg. and Jimenez. 55c, Pipeline and Gonzalez Viquez. 80c, National Library and Gonzalez Viquez. 1col, Electric train and Jimenez. 2col, Gonzales and Jimenez.

1959, Nov. 23 **Engr.** *Perf. 13½*

C274 AP56	5c car & ultra	15	15
C275 AP56	10c red & gray	15	15

Perf. 13½x13

C276 AP57	15c dk bl grn & blk	15	15
C277 AP57	20c car & brn	15	15
C278 AP57	35c rose lil & bl	15	15
C279 AP57	55c olive & vio	25	18
C280 AP57	80c ultra	40	30
C281 AP57	1col orange & mar	40	28
C282 AP57	2col gray & mar	1.00	75
	Nos. C274-C282 (9)	2.80	
	Set value		1.84

For surcharge and overprint see #C337, C339.

Soccer — AP58

Designs: Various soccer scenes.

Perf. 13½

1960, Mar. 7 **Unwmk.** **Photo.**

C283 AP58	10c black	15	15
C284 AP58	25c ultra	15	15
C285 AP58	35c red orange	15	15
C286 AP58	50c red brown	20	15

C287 AP58 85c Prus green 65 50
C288 AP58 5col dp claret 2.00 2.00
Nos. C283-C288 (6) 3.30 3.10

Souvenir Sheet

Imperf

C289 AP58 2col blue 1.00 1.00

3rd Pan-American Soccer Games, San José, Mar. 1960.
Nos. C283-C288 exist imperf.

WRY Uprooted Oak Emblem — AP59

1960, Apr. 7 Unwmk. *Perf. 11½*

Granite Paper

C290 AP59 35c vio bl, blk & yel 20 15
C291 AP59 85c black & brt pink 40 32

Refugee Year, July 1, 1959-June 30, 1960.

Banner and "OEA" AP60

Designs: 35c, "OEA" in oval. 55c, Clasped hands. 2col, "OEA" and map of Americas. 5col, Flags forming bird. 10col, Map of Costa Rica, flags and "OEA."

1960, Aug. 15 Litho. *Perf. 10*

C292 AP60 25c black & multi 15 15
a. Multi, impression sideways 45.00
C293 AP60 35c multicolored 32 30
a. Pair, imperf. between 30.00
C294 AP60 55c multicolored 50 40
C295 AP60 5col multicolored 3.00 2.75
C296 AP60 10col black & multi 5.00 4.00
Nos. C292-C296 (5) 8.97 7.60

Souvenir Sheet

Imperf

C297 AP60 2col multicolored 2.25 2.25

Pan-American Conf., San Jose, Aug. 15.

St. Louisa de Marillac and Orphanage AP61

St. Vincent de Paul — AP62

Designs: 25c, St. Vincent and old seminary. 50c, St. Louisa and sickroom. 1col, St. Vincent and new seminary.

1960, Oct. 26 Engr. *Perf. 14x13½*

C298 AP61 10c green 15 15
C299 AP61 25c carmine 15 15
C300 AP61 50c dk blue 22 15
C301 AP61 1col brown org 40 32
C302 AP62 5col brown 2.00 1.65
Nos. C298-C302 (5) 2.92 2.42

300th anniv. of the deaths of St. Vincent (1581?-1660) and St. Louisa (1591-1660). Exist imperf.

Runner AP63

Sports: 2c, Woman swimmer. 3c, Bicyclist. 4c, Weight lifter. 5c, Woman tennis player. 10c, Boxers. 25c, Soccer player. 85c, Basketball player. 1col, Baseball batter. 5col, Romulus and Remus statue. 10col, Pistol marksman.

Perf. 13½x14

1960, Dec. 14 Photo. Unwmk.

Designs in Black

C303 AP63 1c brt yel 15 15
C304 AP63 2c lt ultra 15 15
C305 AP63 3c dp rose 15 15
C306 AP63 4c yellow 15 15
C307 AP63 5c brt yel grn 15 15
C308 AP63 10c pink 15 15
C309 AP63 25c lt bl grn 15 15
C310 AP63 85c lilac 90 75
C311 AP63 1col gray 1.10 90
C312 AP63 10col lt vio 9.00 7.25
Nos. C303-C312 (10) 12.05 9.95

Souvenir Sheets

Perf. 14x13½, Imperf.

C313 AP63 5col multi 3.50 3.50

17th Olympic Games, Rome, Aug. 25-Sept. 11.
Nos. C303-C312 exist imperf.

No. C255 Surcharged and Overprinted in Blue or Ultramarine: "XV Campeonato Mundial de Beisbol de Aficionados"

Engraved and Photogravure

1961, Apr. 21 *Perf. 12*

Center in Black

C314 AP53 25c on 75c red org (Bl) 20 15
C315 AP53 75c red orange (U) 55 22

15th Amateur Baseball Championships.

Alberto Brenes C. AP64

Miguel Obregon AP65

Portraits: No. C317, Manuel Aguilar. No. C318, Agustin Gutierrez L. No. C319, Vicente Herrera.

1961, June 12 Photo. *Perf. 12*

C316 AP64 10c deep claret 15 15
C317 AP64 10c blue 15 15
C318 AP64 25c bright violet 15 15
C319 AP64 25c gray 15 15
Set value 38 34

First Continental Congress of Lawyers, San José, June 11-15. Exist imperf.
See Nos. C330-C333.

1961, July 19 Litho. *Perf. 13½*

C320 AP65 10c Prussian green 15 15

Birth centenary of Prof. Miguel Obregon L. Exists imperf.

UN Food and Agriculture Organization AP66

UN day (UN Organizations): 20c, WHO. 25c, ILO. 30, ITU. 35c, World Meteorological Organization. 45c, UNESCO. 85c, ICAO. 5col, "United Nations" holding the world. 10col, Int. Bank for Reconstruction and Development.

Perf. 11½

1961, Oct. 24 Unwmk. Engr.

C321 AP66 10c lt grn 15 15
C322 AP66 20c orange 15 15
C323 AP66 25c Prus grn 18 15
C324 AP66 30c dk bl 18 15
C325 AP66 35c car rose 85 20
C326 AP66 45c violet 30 18
C327 AP66 85c blue 65 50
C328 AP66 10col dk sl grn 4.75 4.00
Nos. C321-C328 (8) 7.21 5.48

Souvenir Sheet

Imperf

C329 AP66 5col ultra 2.75 2.75

For overprint see No. C338.

Portrait Type of 1961

Portraits: No. C330, Dr. José Maria Soto Alfaro. No. C331, Dr. Elias Rojas Roman. No. C332, Dr. Andres Saenz Llorente. No. C333, Dr. Juan José Ulloa Giralt.

1961 Photo. *Perf. 13½*

C330 AP64 10c bl grn 15 15
C331 AP64 10c violet 15 15
C332 AP64 25c dk gray 20 15
C333 AP64 25c dp claret 20 15
Set value 58 40

9th Congress of Physicians of Central America and Panama.

Nos. C229, C236 and C280 Surcharged in Black, Orange or Red

Engraved; Center Photogravure

1962 *Perf. 13x12½, 13½x13*

C334 AP53 10c ("10") on 15c 15 15
C334A AP53 10c ("c0.10") on 15c (R) 15 15
C335 AP53 25c on 15c 16 15
C336 AP53 35c on 50c (O) 25 16

Engr.

C337 AP57 85c on 80c (R) 70 55
Nos. C334-C337 (5) 1.41 1.16

Nos. C324 and C282 Overprinted in Red: "II CONVENCION FILATELICA CENTROAMERICANA SETIEMBRE 1962"

1962, Sept. 12 *Perf. 11½, 13½x13*

C338 AP66 30c dark blue 48 38
C339 AP57 2col gray & mar 1.50 1.10

2nd Central American Phil. Convention.

Revenue Stamp Surcharged with New Values and "CORREO AEREO" in Red

1962 Engr. *Perf. 12*

C341 A124 25c on 2c emer 15 15
C342 A124 35c on 2c emer 15 15
C343 A124 45c on 2c emer 25 22
C344 A124 85c on 2c emer 48 40
Nos. C341-C344 (4) 1.03 92

Arms and Malaria Eradication Emblem — AP67

1963, Feb. 14 Photo. *Perf. 11½*

C345 AP67 25c brt rose 15 15
C346 AP67 35c brn org 16 15
C347 AP67 45c ultra 28 20
C348 AP67 85c bl grn 45 38
C349 AP67 1col dk bl 60 50
Nos. C345-C349 (5) 1.64 1.38

WHO drive to eradicate malaria.

Central American Tapir AP68

Designs: 5c, Paca. 25c, Jaguar. 30c, Ocelot. 35c, Whitetail deer. 40c, Manatee. 85c, White-throated capuchin monkey. 5col, White-lipped peccary.

Perf. 13½

1963, May Unwmk. Photo.

C354 AP68 5c yel ol & brn 15 15
C355 AP68 10c orange & sl 15 15
C356 AP68 25c blue & yel 18 15
C357 AP68 30c lt yel grn & brn 32 20
C358 AP68 35c bis & red brn 45 15
C359 AP68 40c emer & sl bl 55 25
C360 AP68 85c green & blk 85 40
C361 AP68 5col gray grn & choc 4.75 2.75
Nos. C354-C361 (8) 7.40 4.20

Stamp of 1863 and Packet "William Le Lacheur" AP69

Issue of 1863 and: 2col, Recaredo Bonilla Carrillo, Postmaster, 1862-63. 3col, Burros, overland mail transport, 1839. 10col, Burro railway car.

1963, June 26 Litho.

C362 AP69 25c dl rose & chlky bl 15 15
C363 AP69 2col gray bl & org 1.25 75
C364 AP69 3col bister & emer 2.50 1.40
C365 AP69 10col dl grn & ocher 7.00 4.25
Nos. C362-C365 (4) 10.90 6.55

Centenary of Costa Rica's stamps.

Souvenir Sheets

Stamps of 1863 and San José Postmark — AP70

Perf. 13½, Imperf.

1963, June 26 Unwmk.

C366 AP70 5col bl, red, grn & org 3.50 3.50

Cent. of Costa Rica's stamps.
In 1968 copies of No. C366 were overprinted "2-4 Agosto 1968" and "III Exposicion Filatelica Nacional / 'Costa Rica 68'." Value $6.

Animal Type of 1963 Surcharged in Red

Designs: 10c on 1c, Little anteater. 25c on 2c, Gray fox. 35c on 3c, Armadillo. 85c on 4c, Great anteater.

1963, Sept. 14 Photo. *Perf. 13½*

C367 AP68 10c on 1c brt grn & org brn 20 15
C368 AP68 25c on 2c org yel & ol grn 20 15
C369 AP68 35c on 3c bluish grn & brn 28 15
C370 AP68 85c on 4c dp rose & dk brn 52 22
Nos. C367-C370 (4) 1.20
Set value 48

Many copies of #C370 exist without surcharge.

Pres. Kennedy — AP71

Ancestral Figure — AP72

Portraits- Presidents: 25c, Francisco J. Orlich, Costa Rica. 30c, Julio A. Rivera, El Salvador. 35c, Miguel Ydigoras F., Guatemala. 85c, Dr. Ramon Villeda M., Honduras. 1col, Luis A. Somoza, Nicaragua. 3col, Roberto F. Chiari, Panama.

1963, Dec. 7 Unwmk. *Perf. 14*

Portraits in Black Brown

C371	AP71	25c vio brn	15	15
C372	AP71	30c brt lil rose	15	15
C373	AP71	35c ocher	15	15
C374	AP71	85c gray bl	32	22
C375	AP71	1col org brn	32	25
C376	AP71	3col lt ol grn	1.65	1.10
C377	AP71	5col gray	2.25	1.65
		Nos. C371-C377 (7)	4.99	3.67

Meeting of Central American Presidents with Pres. John F. Kennedy, San José, Mar. 18-20, 1963.

1963-64 Photo. *Perf. 12*

Ancient Art: 5c, Dog, horiz. 10c, Ornamental stool, horiz. 25c, Male figure. 30c, Ceremonial dancer. 35c, Ceramic vase. 50c, Frog. 55c, Bell. 75c, Six-limbed figure. 85c, Seated man. 90c, Bird-shaped jug. 1col, Twin human beaker, horiz. 2col, Alligator, horiz. 3col, Twin-tailed lizard. 5col, Figure under arch. 10col, Polished stone figure.

C378	AP72	5c lt yel grn & Prus grn	15	15
C379	AP72	10c buff & dk grn	15	15
C380	AP72	25c rose & dk brn	15	15
C381	AP72	30c ocher & Prus grn ('64)	16	15
C382	AP72	35c sal & sl grn	18	15
C383	AP72	45c lt bl & dk brn	18	15
C384	AP72	50c dl bl & dk brn	24	15
C385	AP72	55c yel grn & dk brn	32	15
C386	AP72	75c ocher & dk red brn	32	15
C387	AP72	85c yel & red brn	85	35
C388	AP72	90c cit & red brn	1.10	35
C389	AP72	1col lt bl & dk brn	65	22
C390	AP72	2col buff & dk grn	1.00	42
C391	AP72	3col yel grn & dk brn	1.75	70
C392	AP72	5col cit & sep	3.25	1.25
C393	AP72	10col rose lil & sl grn	5.25	3.00
		Nos. C378-C393 (16)	15.70	7.64

For surcharges and overprint see Nos. C395, C397-C378, C400, C426-C428.

Flags of Central American States — AP73

Alfredo Gonzalez F. — AP74

1964 *Perf. 14*

C394	AP73	30c bl, gray, red & blk	32	25

Central American Independence issue. For surcharge see No. C396.

Nos. C381, C394 and C387 Surcharged **₡ 0.05**

1964, Oct. *Perf. 12, 14*

C395	AP72	5c on 30c	15	15
C396	AP73	15c on 30c	15	15
C397	AP72	15c on 85c	15	15
		Set value	22	18

No. C388 Surcharged: "C 0.15 / CONFERENCIA POSTAL / DE PARIS - 1864"

1964 *Perf. 12*

C398	AP72	15c on 90c cit & red brn	15	15

Paris Postal Conference.

1965, June Photo. *Perf. 12*

C399	AP74	35c dk blue green	30	15

50th anniv. of the National Bank and honoring Alfredo Gonzalez F., 1st governor of the bank.

No. C390 Overprinted: "75 ANIVERSARIO / ASILO CHAPUI / 1890-1965"

1965, Aug. 14 Unwmk. *Perf. 12*

C400	AP72	2col buff & dk grn	1.00	60

75th anniv. of Chapui Asylum, San José.

Girl, FAO Emblem and Hands Holding Grain — AP75

Church of Nicoya — AP76

Designs (FAO Emblem and): 15c, Map of Costa Rica and silos, horiz. 50c, World population chart and children. 1 col, Plane over map of Costa Rica, horiz.

1965 Litho. *Perf. 14*

C401	AP75	15c lt brn & blk	15	15
C402	AP75	35c blk & yel	15	15
C403	AP75	50c ultra & dk grn	20	15
C404	AP75	1col grn, blk & sil	38	20
		Nos. C401-C404 (4)	88	
		Set value		53

FAO "Freedom from Hunger" campaign.

1965, Dec. 20 *Perf. 13½x14*

Designs: 5c, Leonidas Briceno B. 15c, Scroll dated "25 de Julio de 1964." 35c, Map of Guanacaste and Nicoya peninsula. 50c, Dancing couple. 1col, Map showing local products.

C405	AP76	5c red brn & blk	15	15
C406	AP76	10c bl & gray	15	15
C407	AP76	15c bis & slate	15	15
C408	AP76	35c blue & slate	15	15
C409	AP76	50c gray & vio bl	22	15
C410	AP76	1col buff & slate	50	35
		Set value	1.00	72

Acquisition of the Nicoya territory.

Runner and Olympic Rings AP77

Pres. Kennedy Speaking in San José Cathedral AP78

Olympic Rings and Emblem: 10c, Bicyclists. 40c, Judo. 65c, Basketball. 80c, Soccer. 1col, Hands holding torches, and Mt. Fuji.

1965, Dec. 23 *Perf. 13x13½*

C411	AP77	5c bis & multi	15	15
C412	AP77	10c lt lil & multi	15	15
C413	AP77	40c multi	15	15
C414	AP77	65c lem & multi	24	15
C415	AP77	80c tan & multi	35	20
C416	AP77	1col multi	48	28
a.		Souv. sheet of 2	3.00	3.00
		Nos. C411-C416 (6)	1.52	
		Set value		84

18th Olympic Games, Tokyo, Oct. 10-25, 1964. No. C416a contains two 1col stamps, one like No. C416, the other with gray background replacing yellow orange. Sheet also exists imperf, same value.

Perf. 13½x13, 13x13½

1965, Dec. 23 Litho. Unwmk.

Designs: 45c, Friendship 7 capsule circling globe, and Kennedy, horiz. 85c, Kennedy and John, Jr. 1col, Curtis-Lee Mansion and flame from Kennedy grave, Arlington, Va.

C417	AP78	45c brt bl & lil	18	15
C418	AP78	55c org & brt bl	25	18
C419	AP78	85c gray, dk brn & red brn	40	25
C420	AP78	1col multi	48	30
a.		Souv. sheet of 2	1.10	1.10
		Nos. C417-C420 (4)	1.31	88

President John F. Kennedy (1917-63). No. C420a contains two 1col stamps, one like No. C420, the other with green background replacing dark blue. Sheet also exists imperf, same value.

For surcharges see Nos. C429-C430.

Firemen with Hoses — AP79

Designs: 5c, Fire engine "Knox," horiz. 10c, 1866 fire pump. 35c, Fireman's badge. 50c, Emblem and flags of Confederation of Central American Fire Brigades.

1966, Mar. 12 Litho. *Perf. 11*

C421	AP79	5c black & red	28	15
C422	AP79	10c bister & red	35	15
C423	AP79	15c blk, red brn & red	52	18
C424	AP79	35c black & yel	90	24
C425	AP79	50c dk blue & red	1.90	35
		Nos. C421-C425 (5)	3.95	1.07

Centenary of San José Fire Brigade.

Nos. C381, C383, C386 and C418-C419 Surcharged

C0.15 a **C 0.50** b

1966 Photo. *Perf. 12*

C426	AP72(a)	15c on 30c	15	15
C427	AP72(a)	15c on 45c	15	15
C428	AP72(a)	35c on 75c	20	15

Litho. *Perf. 13x13½*

C429	AP78(a)	35c on 55c	20	15
C430	AP78(b)	50c on 85c	35	20
		Nos. C426-C430 (5)	1.05	
		Set value		60

Revenue Stamps (Basic Type of A124) Surcharged

1966, Dec. Engr. *Perf. 12*

C431	A124	15c on 5c blue	15	15
C432	A124	35c on 10c claret	16	15
C433	A124	50c on 20c rose red	25	15
		Nos. C431-C433 (3)	56	
		Set value		30

Central Bank of Costa Rica — AP80

1967, Mar. Litho. *Perf. 11*

C434	AP80	5c brt grn	15	15
C435	AP80	15c brown	15	15
C436	AP80	35c scarlet	20	15
		Set value	37	23

Power Lines — AP81

Telecommunications Building, San Pedro — AP82

Electrification Program: 15c, Telephone Central. 25c, La Garita Dam. 35c, Rio Mache Reservoir. 50c, Cachi Dam.

1967, Apr. 24 Litho. *Perf. 11*

C437	AP81	5c dk gray	15	15
C438	AP82	10c brt rose	15	15
C439	AP81	15c brn org	15	15
C440	AP82	25c brt ultra	15	15
C441	AP82	35c brt grn	18	15
C442	AP82	50c red brn	32	18
		Set value	84	52

Chondrorhyncha Aromatica AP83

Institute Emblem AP84

Orchids: 10c, Miltonia endresii. 15c, Stanhopea cirrhata. 25c, Trichopilia suavis. 35c, Odontoglossum schlieperianum. 50c, Cattleya skinneri. 1col, Cattleya dowiana. 2col, Odontoglossum chiriquense.

1967, June 15 Engr. *Perf. 13x13½*

Orchids in Natural Colors

C443	AP83	5c multicolored	15	15
C444	AP83	10c olive & multi	18	15
C445	AP83	15c multicolored	18	15
C446	AP83	25c multicolored	38	15
C447	AP83	35c dull vio & multi	38	15
C448	AP83	50c brown & multi	48	15
C449	AP83	1col vio & multi	1.25	32
C450	AP83	2col dk ol bis & multi	2.00	65
		Nos. C443-C450 (8)	5.00	
		Set value		1.54

Issued for the University Library.

1967, Oct. 6 Litho. *Perf. 13x13½*

C451	AP84	50c vio bl, lt bl & bl	20	18

Inter-American Agriculture Institute, 25th anniv.

Church of Solitude — AP85

LACSA Emblem — AP86

Costa Rican Churches: 10c, Basilica of Santo Domingo, Heredia. 15c, Cathedral of Tilaran. 25c, Cathedral of Alajuela. 30c, Mercy Church. 35c, Basilica of Our Lady of Angels. 40c, Church of St. Raphael, Heredia. 45c, Ujarras ruins. 50c, Ruins of parish church, Cartago. 55c, Cathedral of San José. 65c, Parish church, Puntarenas. 75c, Church of Orosi. 80c, Cathedral of St. Isidro, the General. 85c, St. Ramon Church. 90c, Church of the Abandoned. 1col, Coronado Church. 2col, Church of St. Teresita. 3col, Parish Church, Heredia. 5col, Carmelite Church. 10col, Limon Cathedral.

1967, Dec. 15 Engr. *Perf. 12½*

C452	AP85	5c green	15	15
C453	AP85	10c blue	15	15
C454	AP85	15c lilac	15	15
C455	AP85	25c dl yel	15	15
C456	AP85	30c org brn	15	15
C457	AP85	35c lt bl	15	15
C458	AP85	40c dp org	15	15
C459	AP85	45c dl bl grn	15	15
C460	AP85	50c olive	18	15
C461	AP85	55c brown	18	15
C462	AP85	65c car rose	32	22
C463	AP85	75c sepia	35	25
C464	AP85	80c yellow	65	35
C465	AP85	85c vio blk	75	35
C466	AP85	90c emerald	75	45
C467	AP85	1col slate	60	25
C468	AP85	2col brt grn	2.75	1.40
C469	AP85	3col orange	4.00	2.25
C470	AP85	5col vio blue	4.00	2.25
C471	AP85	10col carmine	4.75	3.25
		Nos. C452-C471 (20)	20.48	12.52

See Nos. C561-C576.

Perf. 13x13½, 13½x13

1967, Dec. 12 **Litho. & Engr.**

Design: 45c, LACSA emblem and jet, horiz. 50c, Decorated wheel and anniversary emblem.

C472	AP86	40c ultra, grnsh bl & gold	15	15
C473	AP86	45c blk, pale grn, ultra & gold	18	15
C474	AP86	50c blue & multi	20	18
		Nos. C472-C474 (3)	53	48

20th anniv. (in 1966) of Lineas Aereas Costaricenses, LACSA, Costa Rican Airlines.

Scout Directing Traffic AP87

Runner AP88

Designs: 25c, Campfire under palm tree. 35c, Flag of Costa Rica, Scout flag and emblem. 50c, Encampment, horiz. 65c, Photograph of first Scout troop, horiz.

1968, Mar. 15 *Perf. 13*

C475	AP87	15c lt bl, blk & lt brn	15	15
C476	AP87	25c lt ultra, vio bl & org	16	15
C477	AP87	35c blue & multi	24	15
C478	AP87	50c multicolored	28	20
C479	AP87	65c sal, dk bl & brn	40	24
		Nos. C475-C479 (5)	1.23	
		Set value		72

Costa Rican Boy Scouts, 50th anniversary.

1968, Jan. 17 **Litho.** *Perf. 10x11*

Sports: 40c, Women's running. 55c, Boxing. 65c, Bicycling. 75c, Weight lifting. 1col, High diving. 3col, Rifle shooting.

C481	AP88	30c multi	15	15
C482	AP88	40c multi	16	15
C483	AP88	55c multi	24	16
C484	AP88	65c lil & multi	30	16
C485	AP88	75c multi	30	16
C486	AP88	1col multi	35	24
C487	AP88	3col multi	1.50	90
		Nos. C481-C487 (7)	3.00	1.92

19th Olympic Games, Mexico City, Oct. 12-27.

Philatelic Exhibition Emblem — AP89

1969, June 5 **Litho.** *Perf. 11x10*

C488	AP89	35c multicolored	15	15
C489	AP89	40c pink & multi	15	15
C490	AP89	50c lt blue & multi	18	15
C491	AP89	2col multicolored	65	48
		Nos. C488-C491 (4)	1.13	
		Set value		78

4th Natl. Philatelic Exhib., San José, June 5-8.

ILO Emblem AP90

1969, Oct. 29 **Litho.** *Perf. 10*

C492	AP90	35c bl grn & blk	18	15
C493	AP90	50c scarlet & blk	27	15
		Set value		25

50th anniv. of the ILO.

Soccer — AP91

Stylized Crab — AP92

Designs: 65c, Soccer ball, map of North and Central America. 85c, Soccer player. 1col, Two players in action.

1969, Nov. 23 **Litho.** *Perf. 11x10*

C494	AP91	65c gray & multi	24	16
C495	AP91	75c multicolored	24	16
C496	AP91	85c multicolored	30	20
C497	AP91	1col pink & multi	35	24
		Nos. C494-C497 (4)	1.13	76

Issued to publicize the 4th Soccer Championships (CONCACAF), Nov. 23-Dec. 7.

1970, May 14 **Litho.** *Perf. 12½*

C498	AP92	10c blk & lil rose	15	15
C499	AP92	15c blk & yel	15	15
C500	AP92	50c blk & brn org	20	15
C501	AP92	1.10col blk & emer	50	20
		Set value	80	40

10th Inter-American Cancer Cong., May 22-29.

Costa Rica No. 124, Magnifying Glass and Stamps — AP93

Design: 2col, Father and son with stamps and album.

1970, Sept. 14 **Litho.** *Perf. 11*

C502	AP93	1col ultra, brn & car rose	95	20
C503	AP93	2col blk, pink & ultra	1.10	50

The 5th National Philatelic Exhibition.

EXPO Emblem and Costa Rican Cart — AP94

Designs (EXPO Emblem and): 10c, Japanese floral arrangement, vert. 35c, Pavilion and Tower of the Sun. 40c, Japanese tea ceremony. 45c, Woman picking coffee, vert. 55c, Earth seen from moon, vert.

1970, Oct. 22 **Litho.** *Perf. 13x13½*

C504	AP94	10c multi	15	15
C505	AP94	15c grn & multi	15	15
C506	AP94	35c bl & multi	15	15
C507	AP94	40c gray & multi	20	15
C508	AP94	45c multi	20	15
C509	AP94	55c blk & multi	20	15
		Nos. C504-C509 (6)	1.05	
		Set value		62

EXPO '70 International Exhibition, Osaka, Japan, Mar. 15-Sept. 13.

Escazu Valley, by Margarita Bertheau — AP95

Paintings: 25c, "Irazu," by Rafael A. Garcia, vert. 80c, Shore landscape, by Teodorico Quiros. 1col, "The Other Face," by Cesar Valverde. 2.50col, Mother and Child, by Luis Daell, vert.

1970, Nov. 4 **Litho.** *Perf. 12½*

C510	AP95	25c multi	65	32
C511	AP95	45c multi	65	32
C512	AP95	80c multi	1.00	52
C513	AP95	1col multi	1.00	60
C514	AP95	2.50col multi	2.00	1.00
		Nos. C510-C514 (5)	5.30	2.76

Arms of Costa Rica, 1964 — AP96

National Theater — AP97

Various Coats of Arms, dated: 10c, Nov. 27, 1906. 15c, Sept. 29, 1848. 25c, Apr. 21, 1840. 35c, Nov. 22, 1824. 50c, Nov. 2, 1824. 1col, Mar. 6, 1824. 2col, May 10, 1823.

1971, Feb. 10 **Litho.** *Perf. 14x13½*

C515	AP96	5c buff & multi	20	15
C516	AP96	10c multi	20	15
C517	AP96	15c yel & multi	24	15
C518	AP96	25c pink & multi	28	15
C519	AP96	35c multi	32	16
C520	AP96	50c rose & multi	35	16
C521	AP96	1col beige & multi	40	20
C522	AP96	2col multi	80	40
		Nos. C515-C522 (8)	2.79	
		Set value		1.30

1971, Apr. 14 **Litho.** *Perf. 11*

C523	AP97	2col plum	38	30

Organization of American States meeting.

José Matias Delgado, Manuel José Arce AP98

Flag of Costa Rica — AP99

Independence Leaders: 10c, Miguel Larreinaga and Manuel Antonio de la Cerda, Nicaragua. 15c, José Cecilio del Valle, Dionisio de Herrera, Honduras. 35c, Pablo Alvarado and Florencio del Castillo, Costa Rica. 50c, Antonio Larrazabal and Pedro Molina, Guatemala. 2col, Costa Rica coat of arms.

1971, Sept. 14 *Perf. 13*

C524	AP98	5c multi	15	15
C525	AP98	10c multi	15	15
C526	AP98	15c gray, brn & blk	15	15
C527	AP98	35c multi	15	15
C528	AP98	50c multi	15	15
C529	AP99	1col multi	20	15
C530	AP99	2col multi	40	32
		Set value	1.00	78

Central American independence, sesqui.

Soccer Federation Emblem AP100

Children of the World AP101

1971, Dec. 6

C531	AP100	50c multi	15	15
C532	AP100	60c multi	15	15
		Set value		20

50th anniv. of Soccer Federation of Costa Rica.

1972, Jan. 11 *Perf. 12½*

C533	AP101	50c multi	15	15
C534	AP101	1.10col red & multi	30	25

25th anniv. (in 1971) of UNICEF.

Tree of Guanacaste AP102

Designs: 40c, Hermitage, Liberia. 55c, Petroglyphs, Rincón Brujo. 60c, Painted head, sculpture from Curubandé, vert.

1972, Feb. 28 *Perf. 11*

C535	AP102	20c brn, ol & brt grn	15	15
C536	AP102	40c brn & ol	15	15
C537	AP102	55c blk & brn	15	15
C538	AP102	60c blk, buff & ver	20	15
		Nos. C535-C538 (4)	65	
		Set value		44

Bicentenary of the founding of the city of Liberia, Guanacaste.

Farm and Family AP103

Inter-American Exhibitions AP104

Designs: 45c, Cattle, dairy products and meat, horiz. 50c, Kneeling figure with plant. 10col, Farmer and map of Americas.

1972, June 30 **Litho.** *Perf. 12½*

C539	AP103	20c multi	15	15
C540	AP103	45c multi	15	15
C541	AP103	50c dp yel, grn & blk	15	15
C542	AP103	10col brn, org & blk	1.75	1.00
		Nos. C539-C542 (4)	2.20	
		Set value		1.20

30th anniversary of the Inter-American Institute of Agricultural Sciences.

1972, Aug. 26 **Litho.** *Perf. 13*

C543	AP104	50c org & brn	15	15
C544	AP104	2col bl & vio	38	30

4th Interamerican Philatelic Exhibition, EXFILBRA, Rio de Janeiro, Aug. 26-Sept. 2.

First Book Printed in Costa Rica — AP105

Intl. Book Year: 50c, 5col, National Library, horiz.

1972, Dec. 7 Litho. *Perf. 12½*

C545 AP105	20c brt bl	15	15
C546 AP105	50c gold & multi	15	15
C547 AP105	75c multi	15	15
C548 AP105	5col multi	95	75
	Nos. C545-C548 (4)	1.40	
	Set value		1.00

Road to Irazú Volcano AP106

1972-73 *Perf. 11x11½, 11½x11*

C549 AP106	5c like 20c	15	15
C550 AP106	15c Coco-Culebra Bay	15	15
C551 AP106	20c shown	15	15
C552 AP106	25c like 15c	15	15
C553 AP106	40c Manuel Antonio Beach	15	15
C554 AP106	45c Tourist Office emblem	15	15
C555 AP106	50c Lindora Lake	15	15
C556 AP106	60c San Jose P.O., vert.	18	15
C557 AP106	80c like 40c	22	18
C558 AP106	90c like 45c	22	18
C559 AP106	1col like 50c	22	18
C560 AP106	2col like 60c	45	35
	Set value	1.95	1.50

Tourism year of the Americas.

Issue dates: 20c, 25c, 80c, 90c, 1col and 2col, Dec. 26, 1972. Others, Mar. 21, 1973.

No. C555 exists eith inverted center, used only.

Church Type of 1967

Designs as before.

1973, July 16 Engr. *Perf. 12½*

C561 AP85	5c sl grn	15	15
C562 AP85	10c olive	15	15
C563 AP85	15c orange	15	15
C564 AP85	25c brown	15	15
C565 AP85	30c rose claret	15	15
C566 AP85	35c violet	15	15
C567 AP85	40c brt grn	15	15
C568 AP85	45c dull yel	18	15
C569 AP85	50c rose mag	18	15
C570 AP85	55c blue	18	15
C571 AP85	65c black	24	18
C572 AP85	75c rose red	24	18
C573 AP85	80c yel grn	24	18
C574 AP85	85c lilac	28	24
C575 AP85	90c brt pink	28	24
C576 AP85	1col dk blue	28	24
	Nos. C561-C576 (16)	3.15	
	Set value		2.20

Human Rights Flame AP107

OAS Emblem AP108

1973, Dec. 10 Photo. *Perf. 10½*

C577 AP107	50c black & red	15	15

25th anniversary of the Universal Declaration of Human Rights.

1973, Dec. 17 Litho. *Perf. 10½*

C578 AP108	20c dk bl & dp car	15	15

25th anniv. of the OAS.

Values quoted in this catalogue are for stamps graded Fine-Very Fine and with no faults. An illustrated guide to grade is provided in the "Catalogue Information" section of the Introduction.

Joaquin Vargas Calvo — AP109

AP110

1974, Jan. 14

C579 AP109	20c shown	15	15
C580 AP109	20c Alejandro Monestel	15	15
C581 AP109	20c Julio Mata	15	15
C582 AP109	60c Julio Fonseca	18	15
C583 AP109	2col Rafael A. Chaves	45	32
C584 AP109	5col Manuel M. Gutierrez	1.10	90
	Nos. C579-C584 (6)	2.18	
	Set value		1.50

Costa Rican composers honored by the National Symphony Orchestra.

Revenue Stamps Overprinted "Habilitado para Correo Aereo"

1974, Apr. 5 Engr. *Perf. 12*

C585 AP110	50c brown	15	15
C586 AP110	1col violet	22	15
C587 AP110	2col orange	42	25
C588 AP110	5col olive	1.65	1.25
	Nos. C585-C588 (4)	2.44	1.80

Telephone Building, San Pedro — AP111

EXFILMEX 74 Emblem — AP112

Designs: 65c, Rio Macho Control, horiz. 85c, Turbines, Rio Macho Center. 1.25col, Cachi Dam and reservoir, horiz. 2col, I.C.E. Headquarters.

1974, July 30 Litho. *Perf. 10½*

C589 AP111	50c gold & multi	15	15
C590 AP111	65c gold & multi	20	15
C591 AP111	85c gold & multi	25	15
C592 AP111	1.25col gold & multi	30	20
C593 AP111	2col gold & multi	50	30
	Nos. C589-C593 (5)	1.40	95

25th anniversary of Costa Rican Electrical Institute (I.C.E.).

1974, Aug. 22 *Perf. 13*

C594 AP112	65c green	16	15
C595 AP112	3col lilac rose	60	42

5th Inter-American Philatelic Exhibition, EXFILMEX-74 UPU, Mexico City, Oct. 26-Nov. 3.

Map of Costa Rica, 4-S Emblem AP113

Design: 50c, Young harvesters and 4-S emblem.

1974, Oct. 7 Litho. *Perf. 12x11*

C596 AP113	20c brt grn	15	15
C597 AP113	50c multi	15	15
	Set value	25	15

25th anniversary of 4-S Clubs of Costa Rica (similar to US 4-H Clubs).

Roberto Brenes Mesen AP114

"Life Insurance" AP115

Designs: 85c, "Love and Death," manuscript, horiz. 5col, Hands of writer.

1974, Oct. 14 Litho. *Perf. 10½*

C598 AP114	20c blk & brn	15	15
C599 AP114	85c blk & red	22	16
C600 AP114	5col blk & red brn	1.10	85
	Nos. C598-C600 (3)	1.47	1.16

Birth centenary of Roberto Brenes Mesen, educator and writer.

1974, Oct. 30 *Perf. 14*

Designs: 20c, Ricardo Jiménez Oreamuno and Tomás Soley Güell, horiz. 50c, Harvest Insurance (hand holding shovel; horiz.). 85c, Maritime insurance (hand holding paper boat). 1.25col, INS emblem. 2col, Workers rehabilitation (arm with crutch). 2.50col, Workers' Compensation (hand holding wrench). 20col, Fire insurance (hands protecting house).

C601 AP115	20c multi	15	15
C602 AP115	50c multi	15	15
C603 AP115	65c multi	15	15
C604 AP115	85c multi	16	15
C605 AP115	1.25col multi	25	16
C606 AP115	2col multi	42	25
C607 AP115	2.50col multi	55	42
C608 AP115	20col multi	4.25	4.25
	Nos. C601-C608 (8)	6.08	5.68

Costa Rican Insurance Institute (Instituto Nacional de Seguros, INS), 50th anniversary.

For surcharges see Nos. C721-C722.

WPY Emblem — AP116

Oscar J. Pinto F. — AP117

1974, Nov. 13 Litho. *Perf. 11x11½*

C609 AP116	2col vio bl & red	42	25

World Population Year.

1974, Dec. 2 *Perf. 13*

Designs: 50c, Alberto Montes de Oca D., champion sharpshooter. 1col, Eduardo Garnier, sports promoter. O. J. Pinto, introducer of soccer.

C610 AP117	20c gray & dk bl	15	15
C611 AP117	50c gray & dk bl	15	15
C612 AP117	1col gray & dk bl	25	15
	Nos. C610-C612 (3)	55	
	Set value		30

First Central American Olympic Games, held in Guatemala, 1973.

Mormodes Buccinator AP118

Masdevallia Ephippium AP119

Designs: Orchids.

Perf. 10½, 13½

1975, Mar. 7 Litho.

C613 AP118	25c *shown*	40	15
C614 AP118	25c *Gongora clavi-odora*	40	15
C615 AP119	25c *shown*	40	15
C616 AP119	25c *Encyclia spondiadum*	40	15
a.	Block of 4, #C613-C616	1.60	1.00
C617 AP118	65c *Lycaste skinneri alba*	60	18
C618 AP118	65c *Peristeria elata*	60	18
C619 AP119	65c *Miltonia roezelii*	60	18
C620 AP119	65c *Brassavola digbyana*	60	18
a.	Block of 4, #C617-C620, 10½	2.50	2.00
b.	Block of 4, #C617-C620, 13½	20.00	
C621 AP118	80c *Epidendrum mirabile*	80	27
C622 AP118	80c *Barkeria lindleyana*	80	27
C623 AP119	80c *Cattleya skinneri*	80	27
C624 AP119	80c *Sobralia macrantha*	80	27
a.	Block of 4, #C621-C624	3.50	2.50
C625 AP118	1.40col *Lycaste cruenta*	1.00	32
C626 AP118	1.40col *Oncidium obry- zatum*	1.00	32
C627 AP119	1.40col *Gongora armeniaca*	1.00	32
C628 AP119	1.40col *Sievekingia suavis*	1.00	32
a.	Block of 4, #C625-C628	4.50	4.00
	Perf. 13½		
C629 AP118	1.75col *Hexisea imbricata*	1.00	35
C630 AP118	2.15col *Warcewiczella discolor*	1.00	35
C631 AP119	2.50col *Oncidium kramerianum*	1.50	55
C632 AP119	3.25col *Cattleya dowiana*	2.00	65
a.	Block of 4, #C629-C632	9.00	7.50
	Nos. C613-C632 (20)	16.70	5.58

5th National Flower Exhibition.

Nos. C613-C628 were printed in both perforations on two different papers: dull finish and shiny. Nos. C629-C632 were printed on shiny paper.

Most copies of Nos. 617-620, perf 13½ were surcharged.

For overprints and surcharges see Nos. C715-C720, C723-C728.

Radio Club Emblem AP120

Members' Flags and Emblem AP121

Design: 2col, Federation emblem.

1975, Apr. 16 Litho. *Perf. 13½*

C633 AP120	1col blk & red lil	45	15
C634 AP121	1.10col multi	55	18
C635 AP120	2col blk & bl	90	27
	Nos. C633-C635 (3)	1.90	60

16th Central American Radio Amateurs' Convention, San José, May 2-4.

Nicoya Beach — AP122

Designs: 75c, Driving cattle. 1col, Colonial Church, Nicoya. 3col, Savannah riders, vert.

1975, Aug. 1 Litho. *Perf. 13½*

C636	AP122	25c gray & multi	15	15
C637	AP122	75c gray & multi	25	15
C638	AP122	1col gray & multi	30	18
C639	AP122	3col gray & multi	90	75
		Nos. C636-C639 (4)	1.60	1.23

Sesqui. of annexation of Nicoya District.

Costa Rica #158 AP123

Designs (Type A90 of 1932): No. C641, #159. No. C642, #160. No. C643, #161.

1975, Aug. 14 Litho. *Perf. 12*

C640	AP123	2.20col blk & org	42	35
C641	AP123	2.20col blk & dk grn	42	35
C642	AP123	2.20col blk & car rose	42	35
C643	AP123	2.20col blk & dk bl	42	35
a.		Block of 4, #C640-C643	1.75	1.75

6th Natl. Phil. Exhib., San José, Aug. 14-17.
For surcharges see Nos. C885-C892.

IWY Emblem — AP124

1975, Oct. 9 Litho. *Perf. 10½*

C644	AP124	40c vio bl & red	15	15
C645	AP124	1.25col blk & ultra	20	15
		Set value		22

International Women's Year 1975.

UN Emblem — AP125

UN, 30th Anniv.: 60c, UN General Assembly, horiz. 1.20col, UN Headquarters, NY.

1975, Oct. 24 *Perf. 12*

C646	AP125	10c bl & blk	15	15
C647	AP125	60c multi	15	15
C648	AP125	1.20col multi	20	15
		Set value	40	31

The Visitation, by Jorge Gallardo AP126

"20-30" Club Emblem AP127

Paintings by Jorge Gallardo: 1col, Nativity and Star. 5col, St. Joseph in his Workshop, Virgin and Child.

1975, Nov. 3 *Perf. 10½*

C649	AP126	50c multi	16	15
C650	AP126	1col multi	28	15
C651	AP126	5col multi	1.00	70
		Nos. C649-C651 (3)	1.44	1.00

Christmas 1975.

1976, Jan. 16 Litho. *Perf. 12*

C652	AP127	1col multi	15	15

"20-30" Club of Costa Rica, 20th anniv.

Quercus Brenessi Trel AP128

"Literary Development" AP129

Plants: 30c, Maxillaria albertii schecht. 55c, Calathea brenesii standl. 2col, Brenesia costaricensis schlecht. 10col, Philodendron brenesii standl.

1976, Mar. 1 *Perf. 10½*

C653	AP128	5c multi	15	15
C654	AP128	30c multi	15	15
C655	AP128	55c multi	15	15
C656	AP128	2col tan & multi	35	20
C657	AP128	10col multi	1.75	1.40
		Nos. C653-C657 (5)	2.55	2.05

Prof. Alberto Manuel Brenes Mora, botanist, birth centenary.

1976, Apr. 9 Litho. *Perf. 16*

Designs: 1.10col, Man holding book, stylized. 5col, Costa Rican flag emanating from book, horiz.

C658	AP129	15c multi	15	15
C659	AP129	1.10col multi	15	15
C660	AP129	5col multi	90	70
		Nos. C658-C660 (3)	1.20	1.00

Publishing in Costa Rica.

Postrider, 1839 AP130

Costa Rica No. 13, Post Office AP131

Designs: 65c, Costa Rica No. 14 and Post Office. 85c, Costa Rica No. 15 and Post Office. 2col, UPU Monument, Bern, vert.

1976, May 24 *Perf. 10½*

C661	AP130	20c ap grn & blk	15	15
C662	AP131	50c bis & multi	15	15
C663	AP131	65c multi	15	15
C664	AP131	85c multi	16	15
C665	AP130	2col blk & lt bl	35	28
		Nos. C661-C665 (5)	96	
		Set value		64

Cent. of UPU (in 1974).
Nos. C662-C664 exist without the surcharges on reproductions of Nos. 13-15.

Telephones, 1876 and 1976 — AP132

Designs: 2col, Wall telephone. 5col, Alexander Graham Bell.

1976, June 28

C666	AP132	1.60col lt bl & blk	28	20
C667	AP132	2col multi	35	20
C668	AP132	5col yel & blk	90	70
		Nos. C666-C668 (3)	1.53	1.10

Centenary of first telephone call by Alexander Graham Bell, Mar. 10, 1876.

Inverted Center Stamp of 1901 and Association Emblems AP133

Design: 5col, 1901 stamp between Costa Rican Philatelic Society and Interamerican Philatelic Federation emblems.

1976, Nov. 11 Litho. *Perf. 10½*

C669	AP133	50c multi	15	15
C670	AP133	1col multi	16	15
C671	AP133	2col multi	35	20
		Nos. C669-C671 (3)	66	
		Set value		37

Souvenir Sheet

Perf. 12, Imperf.

C672	AP133	5col multi	90	90

7th Natl. Phil. Exhib. and 9th Plenary Assembly of the Interamerican Phil. Fed. (FIAF), San José, Nov. 1976.
No. C670 exists in colors of No. C671.

"Seeing Eye" and Map of Costa Rica — AP134

Amadeo Quiros Blanco — AP135

1976, Nov. 22 *Perf. 16*

C673	AP134	35c blk & bl	15	15
C674	AP135	2col multi	35	20
		Set value		28

General Audit Office, 25th anniversary.

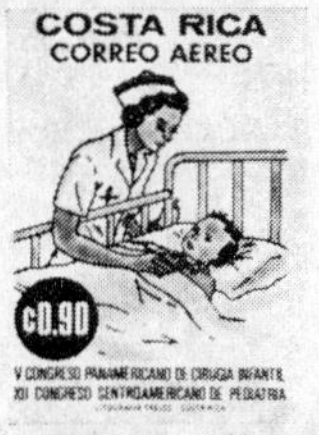

Nurse Attending Child — AP136

LACSA Circling Globe — AP137

Design: 1.10col, National Children's Hospital, horiz.

1976, Nov. 29

C675	AP136	90c multi	16	15
C676	AP136	1.10col multi	20	16

5th Panamerican Congress of Pediatric Surgery and 12th Congress of Pediatrics.

1976, Dec. 1 *Perf. 10½*

Designs: 1.20col, Route map. 3col, LACSA emblem and Costa Rican flag.

C677	AP137	1col multi	16	15
C678	AP137	1.20col multi	20	15
C679	AP137	3col multi	52	30
		Nos. C677-C679 (3)	88	60

Costa Rican Air Lines (LACSA), 30th anniversary.

Boston Tea Party AP138

US Bicent.: 5col, Declaration of Independence. 10col, Ringing Liberty Bell to announce Independence, vert.

1976, Dec. 24

C680	AP138	2.20col multi	38	28
C681	AP138	5col multi	90	70
C682	AP138	10col multi	1.75	1.40
		Nos. C680-C682 (3)	3.03	2.38

Tree of Guanacaste AP139

Felipe J. Alvarado AP140

Designs (Rotary Emblem and): 60c, Dr. Paul Blanco Cervantes Hospital, horiz. 3col, Map of Costa Rica, horiz. 10col, Paul Harris.

1977, Mar. 31 Litho. *Perf. 16*

C683	AP139	40c multi	15	15
C684	AP140	50c multi	15	15
C685	AP139	60c multi	15	15
C686	AP139	3col multi	70	42
C687	AP140	10col multi	2.00	1.40
		Nos. C683-C687 (5)	3.15	2.27

Rotary Club of San José, 50th anniversary.

Boruca Cloth AP141

Design: 1.50col, Painted wood ornament.

1977, Feb. 22

C688	AP141	75c multi	15	15
C689	AP141	1.50col multi	28	15
		Set value		24

Natl. Artisan & Small Industry Program.

Juana Pereira AP142

Alonso de Anguciana de Gamboa AP143

Designs: 1col, First Church of Our Lady of the Angels, horiz. 1.10col, Our Lady of the Angels (gold sculpture). 1.25col, Crown of Our Lady of the Angels.

1977, June 6 Litho. *Perf. 10½*

C690 AP142	50c multi	15	15
C691 AP142	1col multi	16	15
C692 AP142	1.10col multi	20	15
C693 AP142	1.25col multi	24	16
	Nos. C690-C693 (4)	75	
	Set value		47

50th anniv. of the coronation of Our Lady of the Angels, patron saint of Costa Rica.

1977, July 4 Litho. *Perf. 10½*

Designs: 75c, Church of Esparza. 1col, Statue of Our Lady of Candlemas. 2col, Statue of Diego de Artieda y Chirino.

C694 AP143	35c multi	15	15
C695 AP143	75c multi	15	15
C696 AP143	1col multi	16	15
C697 AP143	2col multi	35	28
	Nos. C694-C697 (4)	81	
	Set value		56

400th anniv. of the founding of Esparza.
For surcharge see No. C883.

CARE Emblem and Child — AP144

Design: 1col, CARE emblem and soybeans, horiz.

1977, Sept. 14 Litho. *Perf. 16*

C698 AP144	80c multi	15	15
C699 AP144	1col multi	16	15
	Set value		20

20th anniversary of CARE (relief organization) in Costa Rica.

Institute's Emblem — AP145

First Map of Americas, 1540 AP146

1977, Oct. 21 Litho. *Perf. 16*

C700 AP145	50c blk & multi	15	15
C701 AP146	1.40col blk & multi	24	20
	Set value		27

Hispanic Cultural Institute of Costa Rica, 25th anniversary.

Mercy Church, by Ricardo Ulloa B. — AP147

Health Ministry Emblem — AP148

Paintings: 1col, Christ, by Floria Pinto de Herrero. 5col, St. Francis and the Birds, by Louisa Gonzalez Y Saenz.

1977, Nov. 9 Litho. *Perf. 10½*

C702 AP147	50c multi	15	15
C703 AP147	1col multi	16	15
C704 AP147	5col multi	90	70
	Nos. C702-C704 (3)	1.21	1.00

1977, Nov. 16 *Perf. 16*

C705 AP148	1.40col multi	24	20

Creation of Ministry of Health.

Picnic — AP149

San Martin — AP150

Designs: 50c, Weaver. 2col, Beach scene. 5col, Fruit and vegetable market. 10col, Swans on lake.

1978, Mar. 21 Litho. *Perf. 10½*

C706 AP149	50c blk & multi	15	15
C707 AP149	1col blk & multi	16	15
C708 AP149	2col blk & multi	35	20
C709 AP149	5col blk & multi	90	70
C710 AP149	10col blk & multi	1.90	1.40
	Nos. C706-C710 (5)	3.46	2.60

Conf. of Latin American Tourist Organizations.

1978, Aug. 7 Litho. *Perf. 10½*

C711 AP150	5col multi	1.00	65

Gen. José de San Martin (1778-1850), soldier and statesman, fought for South American independence.

Geographical Institute Emblem — AP151

University Federation Emblem — AP152

1978, Aug. 28 Litho. *Perf. 12½*

C712 AP151	5col multi	85	60

Pan-American Geography and History Institute, 50th anniversary. Exists imperf.

1978, Sept. 18 *Perf. 11*

C713 AP152	80c ultra	15	15

Central American University Federation, 30th anniversary.

Emblems AP153

1978, Oct. 24 *Perf. 16*

C714 AP153	2col aqua, blk & gold	32	24

6th Interamerican Philatelic Exhibition, Argentina 78, Buenos Aires, Oct. 1978.

Nos. C629-C631 Overprinted: "50 Aniversario del / primer vuelo de PAN AM / en Costa Rica / 1928-1978"

1978, Nov. 1 Litho. *Perf. 13½*

C715 AP118	1.75col multi	30	20
C716 AP118	2.15col multi	35	25
C717 AP119	2.50col multi	42	30
	Nos. C715-C717 (3)	1.07	75

1st Pan Am flight in Costa Rica, 50th anniv.

Nos. C629-C631 Overprinted: "50 Aniversario de la / visita de Lindbergh a / Costa Rica 1928-1978"

1978, Nov. 1

C718 AP118	1.75col multi	30	20
C719 AP118	2.15col multi	35	25
C720 AP119	2.50col multi	45	30
	Nos. C718-C720 (3)	1.10	75

50th anniversary of Lindbergh's visit.

Nos. C603 and C607 Surcharged with New Value, 4 Bars and: "Centenario del / Asilo Carlos / Maria Ulloa / 1878-1978"

1978, Nov. 8 *Perf. 14*

C721 AP115	50c on 65c multi	15	15
C722 AP115	2col on 2.50col multi	32	24

Asilo Carlos Maria Ulloa, birth centenary.

No. C617-C620, C630-C631 Surcharged with New Value and 4 Bars

Perf. 10½, 13½

1978, Nov. 13 Litho.

C723 AP118	50c on 65c	15	15
C724 AP118	50c on 65c	15	15
C725 AP119	50c on 65c	15	15
C726 AP119	50c on 65c	15	15
a.	Block of 4, #C723-C726	60	40
C727 AP118	1.20col on 2.15col	35	15
C728 AP119	2col on 2.50col	52	24
	Nos. C723-C728 (6)	1.47	
	Set value		66

#C723-C726, perf. 13½, value $20, unused, $10, used, each. #C726a, unused, $150.

Star over Map of Costa Rica AP154

"Flying Men," Chorotega AP155

1978, Nov. 13 *Perf. 10½*

C729 AP154	50c blue & blk	15	15
C730 AP154	1col rose lil & blk	15	15
C731 AP154	5col orange & blk	90	60
a.	Strip of 3, #C729-C731	1.25	

Christmas 1978. #C729-C731 printed in sheets of 100 and se-tenant in sheet of 15 (3x5).

1978, Nov. 20 *Perf. 11½*

Designs: 1.20col, Oviedo giving his History of Indies to Duke of Calabria, horiz. 10col, Lord of Oviedo's coat of arms.

C732 AP155	85c multi	15	15
C733 AP155	1.20col blk & lt bl	20	15
C734 AP155	10col multi	1.90	1.25
	Nos. C732-C734 (3)	2.25	1.55

500th birth anniv. of Gonzalo Fernandez de Oviedo, 1st chronicler of Spanish Indies.

Msgr. Domingo Rivas AP156

San José Cathedral AP157

1978, Dec. 6 *Perf. 16, 13½ (20col)*

C735 AP156	1col black & indigo	15	15
C736 AP157	20col multicolored	3.50	3.25

Centenary of the Cathedral of San José.

View of Coco Island — AP158

Designs: 2.10, 3, 5 col, various views of Coco Island. 10col, Installation of memorial plaque, people and flag. 5, 10col vert.

1979, Apr. 30 Litho. *Perf. 10½*

C737 AP158	90c multi	22	15
C738 AP158	2.10col multi	50	24
C739 AP158	3col multi	70	38
C740 AP158	5col multi	1.25	60
C741 AP158	10col multi	2.25	1.25
a.	Souv. sheet of 5, #C737-C741	5.00	4.00
	Nos. C737-C741 (5)	4.92	2.62

Visit of Pres. Rodrigo Carazo Odio to Coco Island, June 24, 1978, in the interest of national defense.

Shrimp AP159

Designs: 85c, Mahogany snapper. 1.80col, Corvina. 3col, Crayfish. 10col, Tuna.

1979, May 14 Litho. *Perf. 13½*

C742 AP159	60c multi	15	15
C743 AP159	85c multi	15	15
C744 AP159	1.80col multi	35	22
C745 AP159	3col multi	52	40
C746 AP159	10col multi	1.75	1.25
	Nos. C742-C746 (5)	2.92	2.17

Marine life protection.

Hungry Nestlings, IYC Emblem — AP160

Microwave Transmitters, Mt. Irazu — AP161

1979, May 24 *Perf. 11*

C747 AP160	1col multi	38	18
C748 AP160	2col multi	75	38
C749 AP160	20col multi	7.50	5.00
	Nos. C747-C749 (3)	8.63	5.56

International Year of the Child.

1979, June 28 Litho. *Perf. 14*

Design: 1col, Arenal Dam, horiz.

C750 AP161	1col multi	20	15
C751 AP161	5col multi	1.00	70

Costa Rican Electricity Institute, 30th anniversary.

Costa Rica No. 1 and Rowland Hill AP162

Design: 10col, Penny Black and Hill.

1979, July 16 *Perf. 13*

C752 AP162	5col lil rose & bl gray	1.00	70
C753 AP162	10col dl bl & blk	1.75	1.25

Sir Rowland Hill (1795-1879), originator of penny postage.

Poverty, by Juan Ramon Bonilla — AP163

National Sculpture Contest: 60c, Hope, by Hernan Gonzalez. 2.10col, Cattle, by Victor M. Bermudez, horiz. 5col, Bust of Clorito Picado, by Juan Rafael Chacon. 20col, Mother and Child, by Francisco Zuniga.

1979, July 16 Litho. *Perf. 12*

C754	AP163	60c	multi	15	15
C755	AP163	1col	multi	22	15
C756	AP163	2.10col	multi	38	28
C757	AP163	5col	multi	1.10	75
C758	AP163	20col	multi	4.25	3.50
	Nos. C754-C758 (5)			6.10	4.83

Danaus Plexippus — AP164

Butterflies: 1col, Phoebis philea. 1.80col, Rothschildia. 2.10col, Prepona omphale. 2.60col, Marpesia marcella. 4.05col, Morpho cypris.

1979, Aug. 31 Litho. *Perf. 13½*

C759	AP164	60c	multi	*1.25*	30
C760	AP164	1col	multi	*2.50*	30
C761	AP164	1.80col	multi	*3.75*	50
C762	AP164	2.10col	multi	*5.00*	50
C763	AP164	2.60col	multi	*5.00*	1.00
C764	AP164	4.05col	multi	*7.50*	1.50
	Nos. C759-C764 (6)			*25.00*	4.10

SOS Emblem, Houses AP165

Children's Drawings: 5col, 5.50col, Landscapes, diff.

1979, Sept. 18

C765	AP165	2.50col	multi	50	35
C766	AP165	5col	multi	1.00	70
C767	AP165	5.50col	multi	1.10	80
	Nos. C765-C767 (3)			2.60	1.85

SOS Children's Villages, 30th anniversary.

President Type of 1943

Presidents of Costa Rica: 60c, Rafael Iglesias C. 85c, Ascension Esquivel Ibarra. 1col, Cleto Gonzalez Viquez. 2col, Ricardo Jimenez Oreamuno.

1979, Oct. 8 Litho. *Perf. 13½*

C768	A109	10c	dk blue	15	15
C769	A109	60c	dull pur	15	15
C770	A109	85c	red org	16	15
C771	A109	1col	red org	20	15
C772	A109	2col	brown	40	28
a.	Strip of 5, #C768-C772			1.10	75
	Nos. C768-C772 (5)			1.06	
	Set value				68

Printed in sheets of 100 and se-tenant in sheets of 25 (5x5).

See Nos. C790-C794.

Holy Family, Creche AP167

Reforestation AP168

1979, Nov. 16 Litho. *Perf. 12½*

C773	AP167	1col	multi	20	15
C774	AP167	1.60col	multi	35	24

Christmas 1979.

1980, Jan. 14 Litho. *Perf. 11*

C775	AP168	1col	multi	16	15
C776	AP168	3.40col	multi	55	40

Anatomy Lesson, by Rembrandt AP169

1980, Feb. 7 Litho. *Perf. 10½*

C777	AP169	10col	multi	2.50	1.25

Legal medicine teaching in Costa Rica, 50th anniversary.

Rotary Intl., 75th Anniv. — AP170

Gulf of Nicoya, Satellite Photo — AP171

1980, Feb. 26 *Perf. 16*

C778	AP170	2.10col	multi	32	24
C779	AP170	5col	multi	80	60

1980, Mar. 10 Litho. *Perf. 12½*

C780	AP171	2.10col	Puerto Limon	32	24
C781	AP171	5col	shown	80	60

14th Intl. Symposium on Remote Sensing of the Environment, San José, Apr. 23-30. Exist imperf.

Soccer, Moscow '80 Emblem — AP172

Poas Volcano — AP173

1980, Apr. 16 Litho. *Perf. 10½*

C782	AP172	1col	shown	*16*	15
C783	AP172	3col	Bicycling	*3.00*	50
C784	AP172	4.05col	Baseball	*6.00*	75
C785	AP172	20col	Swimming	*15.00*	3.25
	Nos. C782-C785 (4)			*24.16*	4.65

22nd Summer Olympic Games, Moscow, July 19-Aug. 3.

1980, May 14 Litho. *Perf. 10½*

C786	AP173	1col	shown	16	15
C787	AP173	2.50col	Cahuita Beach	40	28

National Parks Service, 10th anniversary.

José Maria Zeledon Brenes, Score — AP174

Design: 10col, Manuel Maria Gutierrez.

1980, June 25 Litho. *Perf. 12½*

C788	AP174	1col	multi	16	15
C789	AP174	10col	multi	1.50	1.25

National anthem composed by Brenes (words) and Gutierrez (music). Exist imperf.

President Type of 1943

Presidents of Costa Rica: 1col, Alfredo Gonzalez F. 1.60col, Federico Tinoco G. 1.80col, Francisco Aguilar B. 2.10col, Julio Acosta G. 3col, Leon Cortes C.

1980, Aug. 14 Litho. *Perf. 11*

C790	A109	1col	dk red	16	15
C791	A109	1.60col	slate bl	24	16
C792	A109	1.80col	brown	28	20
C793	A109	2.10col	dl grn	32	24
C794	A109	3col	dk pur	48	32
	Nos. C790-C794 (5)			1.48	1.07

8th Natl. Phil. Exhib. — AP175

Fruits — AP176

1980, Sept. 11 *Perf. 13½*

C795	AP175	5col	multi	80	60
C796	AP175	20col	multi	3.25	2.75

1980, Sept. 24 *Perf. 10½*

C797	AP176	10c	shown	15	15
C798	AP176	60c	Cacao	15	22
C799	AP176	1col	Coffee	16	15
C800	AP176	2.10col	Bananas	32	24
C801	AP176	3.40col	Flowers	55	40
C802	AP176	5col	Sugar cane	80	20
	Nos. C797-C802 (6)			2.13	1.36

Giant Tree, by Jorge Carvajal AP177

Virgin and Child, by Raphael AP178

Paintings: 2.10col, Secret Look, by Rolando Cubero. 2.45col, Consuelo, by Fernando Carballo. 3col, Volcano, by Lola Fernandez. 4.05col, attending Mass, by Francisco Amighetti.

1980, Oct. 22 Litho. *Perf. 10½*

C803	AP177	1col	multi	16	15
C804	AP177	2.10col	multi	32	24

Size: 28x30mm

C805	AP177	2.45col	multi	40	32

Size: 22x36mm

C806	AP177	3col	multi	48	35
C807	AP177	4.05col	multi	65	48
	Nos. C803-C807 (5)			2.01	1.54

1980, Nov. 11 *Perf. 13½*

Christmas 1980: 10col, Virgin and Child and St. John, by Raphael.

C808	AP178	1col	multi	16	15
C809	AP178	10col	multi	1.50	1.50

Juan Santamaria International Airport — AP179

1980, Dec. 11 Litho. *Perf. 10½*

Sizes: 30x30mm, 31x25mm (1.30col), 25x32mm (2.60col)

C810	AP179	1col	Caldera Harbor	16	15
C811	AP179	1.30col	shown	20	16
C812	AP179	2.10col	Rio Frio Railroad Bridge	32	24
C813	AP179	2.60col	Highway to Colon	40	32
C814	AP179	5col	Huetar post office	80	60
	Nos. C810-C814 (5)			1.88	1.47

Paying your taxes means progress.

For surcharge see No. C884.

Repertorio Americano Cover, J. Garcia Monge and Signature AP180

1981, Jan. 2 Litho. *Perf. 10½*

C815	AP180	1.60col	multi	24	16
C816	AP180	3col	multi	48	32

Birth centenary of J. Garcia Monge, founder of Repertorio Americano journal.

Arms of Aserri (Site of Cornea Bank) AP181

Harpia Harpyja AP182

1981, Jan. 28 Litho. *Perf. 13½*

C817	AP181	1col	shown	16	15
C818	AP181	1.80col	Eye	28	20
C819	AP181	5col	Rojas	80	60
	Nos. C817-C819 (3)			1.24	95

Establishment of human cornea bank, founded by Abelardo Rojas.

1980, Dec. 23 *Perf. 11*

C820	AP182	2.10col	shown	75	24
C821	AP182	2.50col	Ara macao	1.00	32
C822	AP182	3col	Felis concolor	1.25	35
C823	AP182	5.50col	Ateles geoffrovi	2.50	65
	Nos. C820-C823 (4)			5.50	1.56

Medical and Surgical Clinic — AP183

1981, Apr. 8 Litho. *Perf. 10½*

C824	AP183	5c	shown	15	15
C825	AP183	10c	Physiology class	15	15
C826	AP183	50c	Medical school, A. Chavarria (1st dean)	15	15
C827	AP183	1.30col	Music school	15	15
C828	AP183	3.40col	Carlos Monge Alfaro Library	20	16
C829	AP183	4.05col	R.F. Brenes, rector (1952-1961), vert.	24	20
	Set value			67	57

University of Costa Rica, 40th anniversary.

Mail Transport by Horse AP184

1981, May 6 Litho. Perf. 10½

C830 AP184 1col shown 16 15
C831 AP184 2.10col Train, 1857 32 24
C832 AP184 10col Mail carriers, 1858 1.50 1.25
Nos. C830-C832 (3) 1.98 1.64

Heinrich von Stephan (1831-97), UPU founder.

13th World Telecommunications Day — AP185

1981, May 18 Perf. 11

C833 AP185 5col multi 80 60
C834 AP185 25col multi 4.00 2.75

Bishop Bernardo Thiel AP186

Juan Santamaria AP187

1981, June 8 Litho. Perf. 10½

C835 Strip of 5, stained glass windows 50 40
a. AP186 1col Sts. Peter & Paul 15 15
b. AP186 1col St. Vincent de Paul 15 15
c. AP186 1col Death of St. Joseph 15 15
d. AP186 1col Archangel Michael 15 15
e. AP186 1col Holy Family 15 15
C836 AP186 2col shown 20 15

Consecration of Bernardo Augusto Thiel as Bishop of San Jose.

1981, June 26 Perf. 13½

C837 AP187 1col shown 15 15
C838 AP187 2.45col Alajuela Cathedral, horiz. 25 15
Set value 21

Alajuela province.

Potters — AP188

1981, July 10 Litho. Perf. 10½

C839 AP188 15c shown 15 15
C840 AP188 1.60col Bricklayers 15 15
C841 AP188 1.80col Farmers 15 15
C842 AP188 2.50col Fishermen 16 15
C843 AP188 3col Nurse, patient 20 16
C844 AP188 5col Children, traffic policeman 40 24
Nos. C839-C844 (6) 1.21
Set value 72

Model of New Natl. Archives AP189

Natl. Archives Centenary: 1.40col, Leon Fernandez Bonilla, founder, vert. 2col, Arms, vert. 3col, St. Thomas University, former headquarters.

1981, Aug. 24 Litho. Perf. 13½

C845 AP189 1.40col multi 15 15
C846 AP189 2col multi 16 15
C847 AP189 3col multi 20 16
C848 AP189 3.50col multi 24 20
Nos. C845-C848 (4) 75
Set value 54

Men Reaching for Sun, Map AP190

1981, Sept. 9 Litho. Perf. 11

C849 AP190 1col Man in wheelchair, stairs, vert. 15 15
C850 AP190 2.60col Man reaching for scale, vert. 20 15
C851 AP190 10col shown 70 52
Nos. C849-C851 (3) 1.05
Set value 70

Intl. Year of the Disabled.

World Food Day — AP191

1981, Oct. 16 Litho. Perf. 10½

C852 AP191 5col multi 40 24
C853 AP191 10col multi 70 52

President Type of 1943

President of Costa Rica: 1col, Rafael A. Calderon Guardia, 1940. 2col, Teodoro Picado Michalski, 1944. 3col, José Figueres Ferrer, 1953. 5col, Otilio Ulate Blanco, 1949. 10col, Mario Echandi Jimenez, 1958.

1981, Dec. 7 Litho. Perf. 13½

C854 A109 1col pink 15 15
C855 A109 2col orange 16 15
C856 A109 3col green 20 16
C857 A109 5col dk bl 35 24
C858 A109 10col blue 70 52
Nos. C854-C858 (5) 1.56 1.22

Bar Assoc. of Costa Rica Centenary (1981) — AP192

1982, Mar. 22 Litho. Perf. 13½

C859 AP192 1col Emblem, horiz. 15 15
C860 AP192 2col E. Figueroa, 1st pres. 15 15
C861 AP192 20col Bar building, horiz. 1.25 60
Nos. C859-C861 (3) 1.55
Set value 72

National Progress AP193

1982 Perf. 10½

C862 AP193 95c Housing 15 15
C863 AP193 1.15col Agricultural fair 15 15
C864 AP193 1.45col Education 15 15
C865 AP193 1.65col Drinkable water 15 15
C866 AP193 1.80col Rural medical care 15 15
C867 AP193 2.10col Recreational areas 15 15
C868 AP193 2.35col Natl. Theater Square 15 15
C869 AP193 2.60col Communications 15 15
C870 AP193 3col Electric railroad 15 15
C871 AP193 4.05col Irrigation 16 15
Set value 1.15 88

Issue dates: 1.80col, 2.10col, 2.60col, 3col, 4.05col, May 5; others, June 16.

City of Alajuela Bicentenary AP194

Perez Zeledon County, 50th Anniv. (1981) AP195

Designs: 5col, Central Park Fountain. 10col, Juan Santamaria Historical and Cultural Museum, horiz. 15col, Church of Christ of Esquipulas. 20col, Monsignor Esteban Lorenzo de Tristan, 25col, Father Juan Manuel Lopez del Corral.

1982, Aug. 9

C872 AP194 5col multi 28 16
C873 AP194 10col multi 55 28
C874 AP194 15col multi 80 60
C875 AP194 20col multi 1.10 60
C876 AP194 25col multi 1.40 80
Nos. C872-C876 (5) 4.13 2.44

1982, Aug. 30

Designs: 10c, Saint's Stone. 50c, Monument to Mothers. 1col, Pedro Perz Zeledon. 1.25col, St. Isidore Labrador Church. 3.50col, Municipal Building, horiz. 4.25col, Arms.

C877 AP195 10c multi 15 15
C878 AP195 50c multi 15 15
C879 AP195 1col multi 15 15
C880 AP195 1.25col multi 15 15
C881 AP195 3.50col multi 20 15
C882 AP195 4.25col multi 24 16
Set value 72 50

Nos. C695 and C813 Surcharged

1982, Oct. 28 Litho. Perf. 10½

C883 AP143 3col on 75c multi 20 15
C884 AP179 5col on 2.60col multi 32 16

Nos. C640-C643 Surcharged and Overprinted: "IX EXPOSICION FILATELICA - 1982"

1982, Oct. 28 Perf. 12

C885 AP123 8.40col on #C640 48 40
C886 AP123 8.40col on #C641 48 40
C887 AP123 8.40col on #C642 48 40
C888 AP123 8.40col on #C643 48 40
C889 AP123 9.70col on #C640 60 48
C890 AP123 9.70col on #C641 60 48
C891 AP123 9.70col on #C642 60 48
C892 AP123 9.70col on #C643 60 48
Nos. C885-C892 (8) 4.32 3.52

9th Natl. Stamp Exhibition.

TB Bacillus Centenary — AP196

Pan-American Blood Donors' Society, 7th Cong. — AP197

1982, Nov. 19 Perf. 13½

C893 AP196 1.50col Koch 15 15
C894 AP196 3col Koch, slide 16 15
C895 AP196 3.30col Health Ministry 20 15
Nos. C893-C895 (3) 51
Set value 28

1982, Nov. 25 Perf. 11

C896 AP197 30col Natl. Blood Assoc. emblem 1.50 1.00
C897 AP197 50col Cong. emblem 2.50 1.50

AP198

AP199

1982, Dec. 13 Litho. Perf. 10½

C898 AP198 8.40col Emblem, horiz. 40 20
C899 AP198 9.70col Emblem, diff. 48 24
C900 AP198 11.70col Handshake, horiz. 60 28
C901 AP198 13.05col Emblem, diff., horiz. 65 32
Nos. C898-C901 (4) 2.13 1.04

Inter-Governmental Migration Committee, 30th anniv.

1983, Jan. 3 Perf. 16

Designs: 4.80col, St. Francis of Assisi, (1182-1226), by El Greco. 7.40col, Portrait, diff.

C902 AP199 4.80col multi 24 15
C903 AP199 7.40col multi 35 15
Set value 20

For surcharges see Nos. C908-C911.

Visit of Pope John Paul II — AP200

Bolivar, by Francisco Zuniga Chavarria — AP201

1983, Mar. 1 Litho. Perf. 10½

C904 AP200 5col multi 1.00 15
C905 AP200 10col multi 1.00 40
C906 AP200 15col multi 2.50 60
Nos. C904-C906 (3) 4.50 1.15

1983, July 22 Litho. Perf. 16

C907 AP201 10col multi 55 20

Nos. C902-C903 Surcharged

1983, Sept. 23 Litho. Perf. 16

C908 AP199 10c on 4.80col 15 15
C909 AP199 50c on 4.80col 15 15
C910 AP199 1.50col on 7.40col 15 15
C911 AP199 3col on 7.40col 15 15
Set value 45 20

LACSA Costa Rica Airlines, 40th Anniv. — AP202

Various childrens' drawings.

1986, Dec. 12 Litho. Perf. 13½

C912 AP202 1col Adriana E. Hidalgo 15 15
C913 AP202 7col Osvaldo A.G. Vega 28 15
C914 AP202 16col David V. Rodriguez 65 18
Nos. C912-C914 (3) 1.08
Set value 30

Roman Macaya Lahmann, Aviation Pioneer AP203

1988, Sept. 26 Litho. Perf. 10½

C915 AP203 10col multi 28 15

No. 418 Ovptd. **LEY 7097 CORREO AEREO**

1990, Nov. 5
C916 A180 50col multicolored 1.10 28

Bagging Coffee Beans — AP204

Perf. 10½
1990, Nov. 16 Litho. Unwmk.
C917 AP204 50col multicolored 1.10 28

AP205

AP206

1990, Dec. 6
C918 AP205 50col blue & black 1.10 28

First postage stamps, 150th anniv.

1991, Mar. 25 Litho. *Perf. 10½*

Design: Banana Picker, 1897, by Alleardo Villa.

C919 AP206 30col multicolored 65 16

National Theater.

No. 428 Overprinted **Aéreo EXFILCORI '91**

Litho. & Engr.
1991, Sept. 13 ***Perf. 12½***
C920 A188 200col on #428 4.50 1.10

12th Natl. Philatelic Exposition.

No. 402 Overprinted CENTENARIO DEL BALONCESTO CORREO AEREO

1991, Oct. 11 Litho. *Perf. 11½*
Granite Paper
C921 A170 20col multicolored 1.40 35

Basketball, cent.

Social Security Administration, 50th Anniv. — AP207

1991, Nov. 1 Litho. *Perf. 13½*
C922 AP207 15col multicolored 1.05 28

La Poesia by Vespaciano Bignami — AP208

1992, Jan. 24 Litho. *Perf. 10½*
C923 AP208 35col multicolored 2.50 65

National Theater.

Discovery of America, 500th Anniv. — AP209

Columbus' ships: a, Nina. b, Santa Maria. c, Pinta.

1992, Oct. 8 Litho. *Perf. 13½*
C924 AP209 45col Strip of 3, #a.-c. 2.00 50

Intl. Arts Festival — AP210

1993, Mar. 15 Litho. *Perf. 13½*
C925 AP210 45col multicolored 65 16

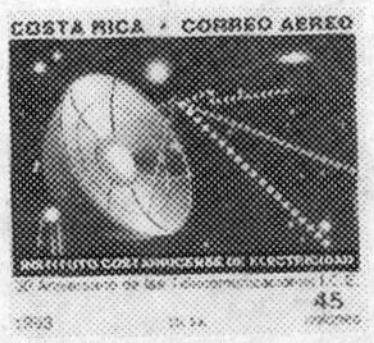

Telecommunications Institute, 30th Anniv. — AP211

1993, Nov. 25 Litho. *Perf. 13½*
C926 AP211 45col multicolored 90 45

Ministry of the Interior, 150th Anniv. AP212

1994, Mar. 8 Litho. *Perf. 10½*
C927 AP212 45col multicolored 90 45

Intl. Year of the Family — AP213

1994, May 5 Litho. *Perf. 10½*
C928 AP213 45col multicolored 90 45

AIR POST SPECIAL DELIVERY STAMPS

Catalogue values for unused stamps in this section are for Never Hinged items.

UPU Headquarters and Monument, Bern — APSD1

Perf. 10x11
1970, May 20 Litho. Unwmk.
CE1 APSD1 35c multi 20 15
CE2 APSD1 60c multi 30 15

Opening of the UPU Headquarters in Bern. The red and black label attached to the 60c is inscribed "EXPRES." Values are for stamps with label attached.

Stamps with labels removed were used for regular airmail.

AIR POST OFFICIAL STAMPS

Air Post Stamps of 1934 Overprinted in Red **OFICIAL**

1934 Unwmk. *Perf. 12*

CO1	AP8	5c	green	20	20
CO2	AP8	10c	car rose	20	20
CO3	AP8	15c	chocolate	35	35
CO4	AP8	20c	deep blue	55	55
CO5	AP8	25c	deep org	55	55
CO6	AP8	40c	olive blk	60	60
CO7	AP8	50c	gray blk	60	60
CO8	AP8	60c	org yel	75	75
CO9	AP8	75c	dull vio	75	75
CO10	AP9	1col	deep rose	1.10	1.10
CO11	AP9	2col	light blue	3.50	3.50
CO12	AP9	5col	black	6.50	6.50
CO13	AP9	10col	red brown	7.75	7.75
			Nos. CO1-CO13 (13)	23.40	23.40

For overprints see Nos. C103-C116.

SPECIAL DELIVERY STAMPS

Catalogue values for unused stamps in this section are for Never Hinged items.

Winged Letter SD1

Unwmk.
1972, Mar. 20 Litho. *Perf. 11*
E1 SD1 75c brown & red 18 15
E2 SD1 1.50col blue & red 38 25

1973 ***Perf. 11x12***
E3 SD1 75c green & red 18 15

1973, Nov. 5 Litho.
E4 SD1 75c lilac & orange 95 55

Concorde SD2

1976, May 17 Litho. *Perf. 16*
E5 SD2 1col vermilion & multi 18 15

SD3

SD4

1979, June 15 Litho. *Perf. 12½*
E6 SD3 2col multi 38 25

1980, Dec. 18 Litho. *Perf. 12½*
E7 SD4 2col multi 38 25

1982, Dec. 20 Litho. *Perf. 11*
E8 SD4 4col multi 38 25

POSTAGE DUE STAMPS

D1

D2

1903 Unwmk. Engr. *Perf. 14*
Numerals in Black

J1	D1	5c	slate blue	5.00	90
J2	D1	10c	brown orange	5.00	65
J3	D1	15c	yellow green	2.00	1.75
J4	D1	20c	carmine	2.25	1.65
J5	D1	25c	slate gray	3.00	1.75
J6	D1	30c	brown	4.50	2.50
J7	D1	40c	olive bister	4.50	2.50
J8	D1	50c	red violet	4.50	2.00
			Nos. J1-J8 (8)	30.75	13.70

1915 Litho. *Perf. 12*

J9	D2	2c	orange	15	15
J10	D2	4c	dark blue	15	15
J11	D2	8c	gray green	40	40
J12	D2	10c	violet	16	16
J13	D2	20c	brown	20	20
			Nos. J9-J13 (5)	1.06	1.06

OFFICIAL STAMPS

Official stamps, to about 1915, normally were not canceled when affixed to official mail in the 19th century. Occasionally they were canceled in a foreign country of destination. Used values are for favor-canceled specimens or for stamps without gum.

Regular Issues Overprinted

Overprinted in Red, Black, Blue or Green **Oficial**

1883-85 Unwmk. *Perf. 12*

O1	A6	1c	green (R)	1.25	1.00
O2	A6	1c	green (Bk)	1.25	1.00
O3	A6	2c	carmine (Bk)	1.50	1.25
O4	A6	2c	carmine (Bl)	1.65	1.40
O5	A6	5c	blue vio (R)	3.25	2.75
O6	A6	10c	orange (G)	4.25	3.50
O7	A6	40c	blue (R)	4.25	3.50
			Nos. O1-O7 (7)	17.40	14.40

Overprinted **OFICIAL**

1886

O8 A6	1c green (Bk)		1.00	1.00
O9 A6	2c carmine (Bk)		1.50	1.50
O10 A6	5c blue vio (R)		15.00	10.00
O11 A6	10c orange (Bk)		15.00	10.00
	Nos. O8-O11 (4)		32.50	22.50

Overprinted **OFICIAL**

O12 A6	1c green (Bk)	90	90
O13 A6	2c carmine (Bk)	1.25	1.25
O14 A6	5c blue vio (R)	15.00	10.00
O15 A6	10c orange (Bk)	15.00	10.00
	Nos. O12-O15 (4)	32.15	22.15

Nos. O8-O11 and O12-O15 exist setenant in vertical pairs.

Overprinted in Black **Oficial**

O16 A6	5c blue vio	35.00	25.00
O17 A6	10c orange	175.00	150.00

Overprinted **OFICIAL.**

1887

O18 A6	1c green	50	50
O19 A6	2c carmine	45	45
O21 A6	10c orange	20.00	12.00
c.	Double overprint	30.00	
O22 A7	5c blue vio	5.00	2.25
O23 A7	10c orange	45	45
c.	Double overprint	25.00	
O24 A6	40c blue	45	45
	Nos. O18-O24 (6)	26.85	16.10

Overprinted "OFICAL"

O18a A6	1c green		
O19a A6	2c carmine	*10.00*	*10.00*
O22a A7	5c blue violet	*10.00*	
O23a A7	10c orange	*10.00*	*2.75*
O24a A6	40c blue	*12.00*	*12.00*
	Nos. O18a-O24a (4)	*42.00*	

Dangerous counterfeits exist of Nos. O18a-O24a.

Without Period

O18b A6	1c green	65	65
O19b A6	2c carmine	65	65
O22b A7	5c blue violet	2.50	2.50
O23b A7	10c orange	95	
	Nos. O18b-O23b (4)	4.75	

Nos. O18b-O23b are from a separate plate. No. O21 exists without period (position 32). These must be collected in pairs.

Issues of 1889-1901 Overprinted **OFICIAL**

1889 *Perf. 14, 15*

O25 A10	1c brown	20	20
O26 A11	2c dk green	20	20
O27 A12	5c orange	20	20
O28 A13	10c red brown	20	20
O29 A14	20c yellow grn	20	20
O30 A15	50c rose red	1.00	1.00
	Nos. O25-O30 (6)	2.00	2.00

1892

O31 A20	1c grnsh blue	24	24
O32 A21	2c yellow	24	24
O33 A22	5c violet	24	24
O34 A23	10c lt green	1.00	1.00
O35 A24	20c scarlet	16	15
O36 A25	50c gray blue	50	50
	Nos. O31-O36 (6)	2.38	2.37

1901-02

O37 A30	1c green & blk	35	35
O38 A31	2c ver & blk	35	35
O39 A32	5c gray bl & blk	35	35
O40 A33	10c ocher & blk	60	60
O41 A34	20c lake & blk	85	85
O42 A35	50c lilac & dk bl	2.75	2.75
O43 A36	1col ol bis & blk	8.00	8.00
	Nos. O37-O43 (7)	13.25	13.25

No. 46 Overprinted in Green **PROVISORIO** **OFICIAL**

1903

O44 A31	2c ver & blk	2.25	2.25
b.	"PROVISIORO"	6.00	6.00
d.	Inverted overprint	6.00	4.00
f.	As "b," inverted	10.00	8.00

Counterfeit overprints exist.

Regular Issue of 1903 Overprinted Like Nos. O25-O43

1903 *Perf. 14, 12½x14*

O45 A40	4c red vio & blk	1.10	1.10
O46 A41	6c ol grn & blk	1.25	1.25
O47 A42	25c gray lil & brn	8.00	4.50
	Nos. O45-O47 (3)	10.35	6.85

Counterfeit overprints exist.

Regular Issue of 1907 Overprinted **OFICIAL**

1908 *Perf. 14, 11x14*

O48 A43	1c red brn & ind	15	15
O49 A44	2c yel grn & blk	15	15
O50 A45	4c car & ind	15	15
O51 A46	5c yel & dull bl	15	15
O52 A47	10c blue & blk	90	90
O53 A49	25c gray lil & blk	16	16
O54 A50	50c red lil & bl	28	28
O55 A51	1col brown & blk	70	70
	Nos. O48-O55 (8)	2.64	2.64

Various varieties of the overprint and basic stamps exist.

Imperf examples of Nos. O48, O49, O53 were found in 1970.

Regular Issue of 1910 Overprinted in Black **OFICIAL** **15 VI · 1917**

1917

O56 A56	5c orange	22	22
a.	Inverted overprint	3.00	2.50
O57 A57	10c deep blue	18	18
a.	Inverted overprint		

OFICIAL
✱15✱
CENTIMOS

O2

1920 **Red Surcharge** *Perf. 12*

O58 O2	15c on 20c olive grn	50	50

A56

A45

A43

OFICIAL

1921 **Black Surcharge** *Perf. 12, 14*

O59 A56	10c on 5c org	30	24
a.	"10 CTS." inverted	16.00	
O60 A45	4c car & indigo	28	28
a.	"1291" for "1921"	11.00	
O61 A43	6c on 1c red brn & indigo	40	40
O62 A49	20c on 25c gray lil & blk	40	40

Overprinted like No. O60

O63 A50	50c red lil & bl	1.50	1.50
O64 A51	1col brn & blk	2.75	2.75
	Nos. O59-O64 (6)	5.63	5.57

Nos. O60 to O64 exist with date and new values inverted. These may be printer's waste but probably were deliberately made.

Regular Issue of 1923 Overprinted **OFICIAL**

1923 *Perf. 11½*

O65 A68	2c brown	22	22
O66 A68	4c green	15	15
O67 A68	5c blue	22	22
O68 A68	20c carmine	15	15
O69 A68	1col violet	30	30
	Nos. O65-O69 (5)	1.04	1.04

Nos. O65 to O69 exist imperforate but were not regularly issued in that condition.

O7

1926 **Unwmk.** **Engr.** *Perf. 12½*

O70 O7	2c ultra & blk	15	15
O71 O7	3c mag & blk	15	15
O72 O7	4c lt bl & blk	15	15
O73 O7	5c grn & blk	15	15
O74 O7	6c ocher & blk	15	15
O75 O7	10c rose red & blk	15	15
O76 O7	20c ol grn & blk	15	15
O77 O7	30c red org & blk	15	15
O78 O7	45c brown & blk	18	18
O79 O7	1col lilac & blk	28	28
	Set value	1.10	1.10

See #O82-O94. For surcharges see #C7-C10.

Regular Issue of 1936 Overprinted in Black **OFICIAL**

1936 **Unwmk.** *Perf. 12*

O80 A96	5c green	15	15
O81 A96	10c carmine rose	15	15
	Set value	16	16

Type of 1926

1937 *Perf. 12½*

O82 O7	2c vio & blk	15	15
O83 O7	3c bis brn & blk	15	15
O84 O7	4c rose car & blk	15	15
O85 O7	5c ol grn & blk	15	
O86 O7	8c blk brn & blk	15	
O87 O7	10c rose lake & blk	15	
O88 O7	20c ind & blk	15	15
O89 O7	40c red org & blk	20	20
O90 O7	55c dk vio & blk	28	
O91 O7	1col brn vio & blk	24	24
O92 O7	2col gray bl & blk	48	48
O93 O7	5col dl yel & blk	2.50	2.50
O94 O7	10col blue & blk	16.00	16.00
	Nos. O82-O94 (13)	20.75	

Nine stamps of this series exist with perforated star (2c, 3c, 4c, 20c, 40c, 1col, 2col, 5col, 10col). These were issued to officials for postal purposes. Unpunched copies were sold to collectors but had no franking power. Values for unused are for unpunched.

POSTAL TAX STAMPS

Catalogue values for unused stamps in this section are for Never Hinged items.

Most postal tax issues were to benefit the Children's Village and were obligatory on all mail during Dec.

No. C198 Surcharged in Red: "Sello de Navidad Pro-Ciudad de Los Niños 5 5"

Engraved; Center Photogravure

1958 **Unwmk.** *Perf. 12½*

RA1 AP51	5c on 2c brt bl & blk	15	15

Similar Surcharge in Green on Type of 1954

Design: Like No. C228, pottery.

RA2 AP53	5c on 10c dk bl & blk	35	15
a.	Inverted surcharge	7.50	

Father Edward J. Flanagan — PT1

Father Peralta — PT2

Paintings: No. RA4, Boy by El Greco. No. RA5, Boy by Jose Ribera. No. RA6, Girl by Amadeo Modigliani.

Perf. 13½

1959, Nov. 25 **Unwmk.** **Photo.**

RA3 PT1	5c green	25	20
RA4 PT1	5c dl gray vio	25	20
RA5 PT1	5c olive	25	20
RA6 PT1	5c lilac rose	25	20
	Nos. RA3-RA6 (4)	1.00	80

Exist imperf.

1960 **Litho.** *Perf. 14*

Designs: No. RA8, Girl by Renoir. No. RA9, Boys with cups by Velazquez. No. RA10, Singing children, sculpture by F. Zuñiga.

RA7 PT2	5c chocolate	25	20
RA8 PT2	5c dp org	25	20
RA9 PT2	5c plum	25	20
RA10 PT2	5c grysh bl	25	20
	Nos. RA7-RA10 (4)	1.00	80

Exist imperf.

#C229 Surcharged Like #RA1-RA2

Engraved; Center Photogravure

1961 *Perf. 13x12½*

RA11 AP53	5c on 15c grn & blk	22	15

Nicolas, Son of Rubens — PT3

Boys in Workshop — PT4

Designs: No. RA13, Madonna by Bellini. RA14, Angel playing stringed instrument by Melozzo. RA15, Msgr. Rubén Odio H.

1962 **Photo.** *Perf. 13½*

RA12 PT3	5c dark carmine	25	20
RA13 PT3	5c sepia	25	20
RA14 PT3	5c dull green	25	20
RA15 PT3	5c blue	25	20
	Nos. RA12-RA15 (4)	1.00	80

For surcharges see Nos. 262-265.

Type of 1962, Inscribed "1963"
Designs as before

1963 **Photo.** *Perf. 13½*

RA16 PT3	5c sepia (RA12)	25	15
RA17 PT3	5c ultra (RA13)	25	15
RA18 PT3	5c dk car (RA14)	25	15
RA19 PT3	5c black (RA15)	25	15
	Nos. RA16-RA19 (4)	1.00	60

1964 **Litho.** *Perf. 12½*

Designs: No. RA21, Two playing boys. No. RA22, Teacher and children. No. RA23, Priest with boys.

RA20 PT4	5c bright green	25	15
RA21 PT4	5c rose lilac	25	15
RA22 PT4	5c blue	25	15
RA23 PT4	5c brown	25	15
	Nos. RA20-RA23 (4)	1.00	60

Brother Casiano de Madrid PT5

Christmas Ornaments PT6

Designs: No. RA25, National Children's Hospital. No. RA26, Poinsettia. No. RA27, Santa Claus with children (diamond).

1965, Dec. 10 Litho. *Perf. 10*

RA24	PT5	5c	red brn	18	15
RA25	PT5	5c	green	18	15
RA26	PT5	5c	red	18	15
RA27	PT5	5c	ultra	18	15
			Nos. RA24-RA27 (4)	72	60

1966 Litho. *Perf. 11*

RA28	PT6	5c	shown	18	15
RA29	PT6	5c	Angel	18	15
RA30	PT6	5c	Church	18	15
RA31	PT6	5c	Reindeer	18	15
			Nos. RA28-RA31 (4)	72	
			Set value		32

General Post Office, San José — PT7

1967, Mar. Litho. *Perf. 11*

RA32	PT7	10c	blue	15	15

No. RA32 was issued as a postal tax stamp to be used by organizations normally allowed free postage. On Dec. 15, 1972, it was authorized for use as an ordinary postage stamp.

Madonna and Child — PT8

Star of Bethlehem, Mother and Child — PT9

1967 Litho. *Perf. 11*

RA33	PT8	5c	ol grn	15	15
RA34	PT8	5c	dp lil rose	15	15
RA35	PT8	5c	brt bl	15	15
RA36	PT8	5c	grnsh bl	15	15
			Set value	48	40

1968, Dec. Litho. *Perf. 12½*

RA37	PT9	5c	gray	15	15
RA38	PT9	5c	rose red	15	15
RA39	PT9	5c	dk rose brn	15	15
RA40	PT9	5c	bis brn	15	15
			Set value	48	40

Madonna and Child — PT10

Christ Child, Star — PT11

1969, Dec. Litho. *Perf. 12½*

RA41	PT10	5c	dk bl	15	15
RA42	PT10	5c	orange	15	15
RA43	PT10	5c	brn red	15	15
RA44	PT10	5c	bl grn	15	15
			Set value	20	20

1970, Dec. Litho. *Perf. 12½*

RA45	PT11	5c	brt pur	15	15
RA46	PT11	5c	lil rose	15	15
RA47	PT11	5c	olive	15	15
RA48	PT11	5c	ocher	15	15
			Set value	20	20

Christ Child and "PAX" — PT12

Madonna and Child — PT13

1971, Nov. 29

RA49	PT12	10c	dk bl	15	15
RA50	PT12	10c	orange	15	15
RA51	PT12	10c	brown	15	15
RA52	PT12	10c	green	15	15
			Set value	28	20

1972, Nov. 30 *Perf. 11x11½*

RA53	PT13	10c	dk bl	15	15
RA54	PT13	10c	brt red	15	15
RA55	PT13	10c	lilac	15	15
RA56	PT13	10c	green	15	15
			Set value	28	20

Madonna and Child — PT14

Boys Eating Cake, by Murillo — PT15

1973, Nov. 30 Litho. *Perf. 12½*

RA57	PT14	10c	purple	15	15
RA58	PT14	10c	car rose	15	15
RA59	PT14	10c	gray	15	15
RA60	PT14	10c	org brn	15	15
			Set value	28	20

1974, Nov. 25 *Perf. 13*

Paintings: No. RA62, Virgin and Child, with St. John, by Raphael. No. RA63, Maternity, by Juan R. Bonilla. No. RA64, Praying Child, by Reynolds.

RA61	PT15	10c	brt pink	15	15
RA62	PT15	10c	rose lil	15	15
RA63	PT15	10c	dk gray	15	15
RA64	PT15	10c	vio bl	15	15
			Set value	24	20

See No. RA110.

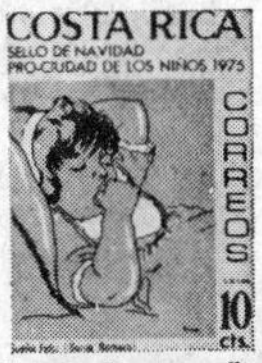

"Happy Dreams," by Sonia Romero — PT16

Virgin and Child, by Hans Memling — PT17

Paintings: No. RA66, Virgin with Carnation, by Leonardo da Vinci. No. RA67, Children with Tortoise, by Francisco Amighetti. No. RA68, Boy with Pigeon, by Picasso.

1975, Nov. 25 Litho. *Perf. 10½*

RA65	PT16	10c	gray	15	15
RA66	PT16	10c	red lil	15	15
RA67	PT16	10c	org brn	15	15
RA68	PT16	10c	brt bl	15	15
			Set value	20	20

1976, Nov. 24 Litho. *Perf. 10½*

Paintings: No. RA70, Boy with Sombrero, by Auguste Renoir. No. RA71, Meditation (Boy), by Floria Pinto de Herrero. No. RA72, Gaston de Mezerville (boy), by Lolita Zeller de Peralta.

RA69	PT17	10c	rose lil	15	15
RA70	PT17	10c	rose car	15	15
RA71	PT17	10c	gray	15	15
RA72	PT17	10c	vio bl	15	15
			Set value	20	20

Boy's Head, by Amparo Cruz — PT18

Boy with Kite — PT19

Paintings: No. RA74, Girl's head, by Rubens. No. RA75, Girl and infant, by Cristina Fournier. No. RA76, Mariano Goya, by Goya.

1977, Nov. Litho. *Perf. 10½*

RA73	PT18	10c	gray ol	15	15
RA74	PT18	10c	rose red	15	15
RA75	PT18	10c	brt ultra	15	15
RA76	PT18	10c	brt rose lil	15	15
			Set value	20	20

1978, Nov. 20 Litho. *Perf. 12½*

Designs: Nos. RA78-RA79, Girl flying kite.

RA77	PT19	10c	magenta	15	15
RA78	PT19	10c	slate	15	15
RA79	PT19	10c	lilac	15	15
RA80	PT19	10c	vio bl	15	15
			Set value	20	20

Boy Leaning on Tree — PT20

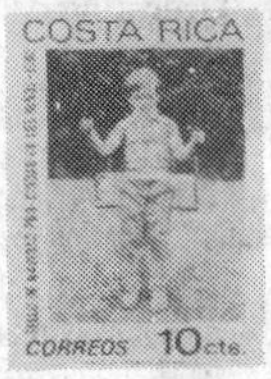

Boy on Swing — PT21

1979, Nov. 19 Litho. *Perf. 12½*

RA81	PT20	10c	blue	15	15
RA82	PT20	10c	orange	15	15
RA83	PT20	10c	magenta	15	15
RA84	PT20	10c	green	15	15
			Set value	20	20

1980, Nov. 18 Litho. *Perf. 12½*

RA85	PT21	10c	brt bl	15	15
RA86	PT21	10c	brt yel	15	15
RA87	PT21	10c	crim rose	15	15
RA88	PT21	10c	brt grn	15	15
			Set value	20	20

Boy Riding Toy Car — PT22

Youth Running Machine — PT23

1981, Nov. 19 Litho. *Perf. 11*

RA89	PT22	10c	blue	15	15
RA90	PT22	10c	green	15	15
RA91	PT22	10c	red	15	15
RA92	PT22	10c	orange	15	15
			Set value	20	20

1982, Nov. 19 Litho. *Perf. 10½*

RA93	PT23	10c	red	15	15
RA94	PT23	10c	gray	15	15
RA95	PT23	10c	purple	15	15
RA96	PT23	10c	grnsh bl	15	15
			Set value	20	20

Youths Working on Wheelchair — PT24

Girl on Bicycle — PT25

1983, Nov. 24 Litho. *Perf. 16*

RA97	PT24	10c	red	15	15
RA98	PT24	10c	orange	15	15
RA99	PT24	10c	ultra	15	15
RA100	PT24	10c	green	15	15
			Set value	20	20

Christmas 1983.

1984, Nov. 20 Litho. *Perf. 10½*

RA101	PT25	10c	violet	15	15

Christmas 1984.

Taking a Child in Out of the Cold — PT26

Depressed Child — PT27

1985, Dec. 1 Litho. *Perf. 13*

RA102	PT26	10c	dull brn	20	15

Christmas 1985.

1986, Dec. 1 Litho. *Perf. 10½*

RA103	PT27	10c	lemon	15	15

Christmas stamps, 25th anniv.; Christmas 1986.

Christmas — PT28

Teaching Children — PT29

1987, Dec. 1 Litho. *Perf. 10½*

RA104	PT28	10c	dk ol bis & brt bl	15	15

No postal tax stamp was issued for 1988.

1989, Dec. 1 Litho. *Perf. 13½*

RA105	PT29	1col	blue, blk & brt ap-ple grn	15	15

Christmas 1989.

No. 417 Ovptd. in Red, Blue, Green, or Orange

LEY 7157 PRO-CIUDAD DE LOS NIÑOS 1990

1990, Nov. 16 Litho. *Perf. 13½*

RA106	A179	10col	multi (R)	25	15
RA107	A179	10col	multi (Bl)	25	15
RA108	A179	10col	multi (G)	25	15
RA109	A179	10col	multi (O)	25	15
			Nos. RA106-RA109 (4)	1.00	
			Set value		24

Art Type of 1974

Design: 10col, Praying Child, by Reynolds.

1991, Nov. 18 Litho. *Perf. 10½*

RA110	PT15	10col	dark ultra	70	18

Boy in Workshop — PT30

Children's Village — PT31

1992, Dec. 1 Litho. *Perf. 10½*

RA111	PT30	10col	red	15	15

Christmas.

1993, Nov. 17

RA112	PT31	10col	multicolored	22	15

Christmas.

Christmas — PT32

1994, Nov. 23 Litho. *Perf. 10½*

RA113	PT32	11col lilac & slate	15	15

GUANACASTE

(A province of Costa Rica)

LOCATION — Northwestern coast of Central America
AREA — 4,000 sq. mi. (approx.)
POP. — 69,531 (estimated)
CAPITAL — Liberia

Residents of Guanacaste were allowed to buy Costa Rican stamps, overprinted "Guanacaste," at a discount from face value because of the province's isolation and climate, which makes it difficult to keep mint stamps. Use was restricted to the province.

Counterfeits of most Guanacaste overprints are plentiful.

On Issue of 1883
Overprinted Horizontally in Black

16mm **Guanacaste**

1885 Unwmk. *Perf. 12*

1	A6	1c green	3.00	3.00
2	A6	2c carmine	3.00	3.00
a.		"Gnanacaste"	50.00	
3	A6	10c orange	12.00	11.00
a.		"Gnanacaste"	65.00	

Same Overprint in Red

4	A6	1c green	3.00	3.00
a.		"Gnanacaste"	40.00	
b.		Overprinted in black & red	110.00	
5	A6	5c blue violet	15.00	3.00
a.		"Gnanacaste"	65.00	
6	A6	40c blue	15.00	15.00

Overprinted Horizontally in Black

17½mm **Guanacaste**

7	A6	1c green	5.00	5.00
8	A6	2c carmine	5.00	5.00
9	A6	5c blue violet	15.00	4.00
10	A6	10c orange	15.00	10.00
11	A6	40c blue	37.50	37.50

Same Overprint in Red

12	A6	5c blue violet	32.50	13.00
13	A6	40c blue	*1,500.*	

Overprinted Horizontally in Black

18½mm- c **Guanacaste**

14	A6	2c carmine	5.25	5.25
15	A6	10c orange	35.00	30.00

Same Overprint in Red

16	A6	1c green	4.50	4.50
a.		Double ovpt., one in blk	125.00	
17	A6	5c blue violet	25.00	7.00
18	A6	40c blue	37.50	37.50

Same Overprint, Vertically in Black

19	A6	1c green	*2,250.*	*1,600.*
20	A6	2c carmine	*1,500.*	*900.00*
21	A6	5c blue violet	225.00	100.00
22	A6	10c orange	45.00	40.00

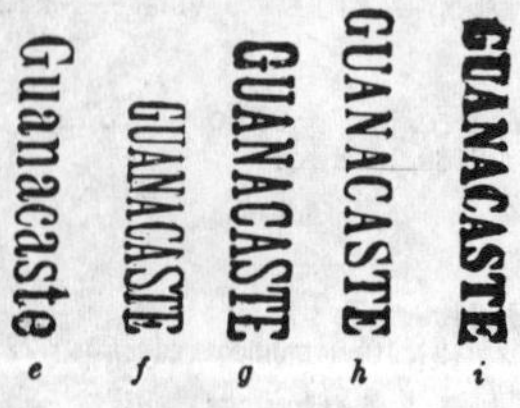

e f g h i

Overprinted Type e, Vertically

23	A6	1c green	175.00	75.00
24	A6	2c carmine	125.00	70.00
25	A6	5c blue violet	125.00	45.00
26	A6	10c orange	60.00	45.00

Overprinted Type f, Vertically

27	A6	1c green	450.00	175.00
28	A6	2c carmine	175.00	125.00
29	A6	5c blue violet	250.00	100.00
30	A6	10c orange	70.00	60.00

Overprinted Type g, Vertically

31	A6	1c green	600.00	225.00
32	A6	2c carmine	400.00	225.00
33	A6	5c blue violet	375.00	125.00
34	A6	10c orange	150.00	125.00

Overprinted Type h, Vertically

35	A6	1c green	250.00	100.00
36	A6	2c carmine	125.00	80.00
37	A6	5c blue violet	175.00	75.00
38	A6	10c orange	35.00	25.00

The authenticity of Costa Rica Nos. 16-19 with overprint "i" has not been established.

On Issues of 1883-87

Overprinted Horizontally in Black **Guanacaste**

1888-89

42	A7	5c blue violet	13.00	2.00

Overprinted Horizontally in Black **Guanacaste**

43	A7	5c blue violet	13.00	2.00

Overprinted Horizontally in Black **Guanacaste**

44	A6	2c carmine	2.00	
45	A7	10c orange	2.00	
a.		Inverted overprint		

On Issue of 1889
Overprinted Like Nos. 7-13, Horizontally

1889

47	A8	2c blue	20.00

Vertically

48	A8	2c blue (c)	175.00
49	A8	2c blue (e)	75.00
51	A8	2c blue (f)	75.00
52	A8	2c blue (g)	225.00
54	A8	2c blue (h)	100.00

Nos. 47-54 are overprinted "Correos." Copies without "Correos" are known postally used, and are valued the same as Nos. 47-54, unused.

Dangerous counterfeits exist of Nos. 1-54.

On Nos. 25-33

Overprinted Horizontally in Black **GUANACASTE**

1889 *Perf. 14 and 15*

55	A10	1c brown	4.00	2.75
56	A11	2c dk grn	2.75	1.65
57	A12	5c orange	4.00	1.65
58	A13	10c red brn	4.00	2.00
59	A14	20c yel grn	1.00	1.00
60	A15	50c rose red	1.65	1.65
61	A16	1p blue	2.25	2.25
62	A17	2p violet	4.50	4.50
63	A18	5p ol grn	30.00	25.00
		Nos. 55-63 (9)	54.15	42.45

Overprinted "GUAGACASTE"

60a	A15	50c rose red	80.00	
61a	A16	1p blue	80.00	80.00
62a	A17	2p violet	80.00	80.00
63a	A18	5p olive green	80.00	80.00

Overprinted Horizontally in Black **GUANACASTE**

64	A10	1c brown	2.00	1.10
a.		Vert. pair, imperf. between		
65	A11	2c dark green	2.00	1.10
66	A12	5c orange	2.00	1.10
67	A13	10c red brown	2.00	1.10
		Nos. 64-67 (4)	8.00	4.40

CRETE

LOCATION — An island in the Mediterranean Sea south of Greece
GOVT. — A department of Greece
AREA — 3,235 sq. mi.
POP. — 336,150 (1913)
CAPITAL — Canea

Formerly Crete was a province of Turkey. After an extended period of civil wars, France, Great Britain, Italy and Russia intervened and declaring Crete an autonomy, placed it under the administration of Prince George of Greece as High Commissioner. In October, 1908, the Cretan Assembly voted for union with Greece and in 1913 the union was formally effected.

40 Paras = 1 Piaster
4 Metallik = 1 Grosion (1899)
100 Lepta = 1 Drachma (1900)

Issued Under Joint Administration of France, Great Britain, Italy and Russia

British Sphere of Administration
District of Heraklion (Candia)

A1

A2

Handstamped
1898 Unwmk. *Imperf.*

1	A1	20pa violet	400.00	200.00

1898 Litho. *Perf. 11½*

2	A2	10pa blue	8.00	1.65
a.		Horiz. pair, imperf. btwn.		
b.		Imperf., pair	250.00	
3	A2	20pa green	8.00	1.65
a.		Imperf., pair	250.00	

1899

4	A2	10pa brown	8.00	1.65
a.		Horiz. pair, imperf. btwn.		
b.		Imperf., pair	250.00	
5	A2	20pa rose	8.00	1.65
a.		Imperf., pair	250.00	

Used values for Nos. 2-5 are for CTO's (single-line Heraklion cancel.)

Counterfeits exist of Nos. 1-5.

Reprints exist of Nos. 2-5.

Russian Sphere of Administration
District of Rethymnon

Coat of Arms
A3 A4

1899 Handstamped *Imperf.*

10	A3	1m green	6.00	3.50
11	A3	2m black	6.00	3.50
12	A3	2m rose	250.00	200.00
13	A4	1m blue	70.00	16.00

Nos. 10-13 exist on both wove and laid papers. Counterfeits exist.

Poseidon's Trident
A5 A5a

1899 Litho. *Perf. 11½*
With Control Mark Overprinted in Violet
Without Stars at Sides

14	A5	1m orange	75.	55.
15	A5	2m orange	75.	55.
16	A5	1gr orange	75.	55.
17	A5	1m green	75.	55.
18	A5	2m green	75.	55.
19	A5	1gr green	75.	55.
20	A5	1m yellow	75.	55.
21	A5	2m yellow	75.	55.
22	A5	1gr yellow	75.	55.
23	A5	1m rose	75.	55.
24	A5	2m rose	75.	55.
25	A5	1gr rose	75.	55.
26	A5	1m violet	75.	55.
27	A5	2m violet	75.	55.
28	A5	1gr violet	75.	55.
29	A5	1m blue	75.	55.
30	A5	2m blue	75.	55.
31	A5	1gr blue	75.	55.
32	A5	1m black	1,250.	1,050.
33	A5	2m black	1,200.	1,050.
34	A5	1gr black	1,200.	1,050.

With Stars at Sides

35	A5a	1m blue	24.00	11.00
36	A5a	2m blue	6.50	4.75
37	A5a	1gr blue	4.00	3.00
38	A5a	1m rose	45.00	37.50
39	A5a	2m rose	6.50	4.75
40	A5a	1gr rose	4.00	3.00
41	A5a	1m green	20.00	11.00
42	A5a	2m green	6.50	4.75
43	A5a	1gr green	4.00	3.00
44	A5a	1m violet	20.00	11.00
45	A5a	2m violet	6.50	4.75
46	A5a	1gr violet	4.00	3.50
		Nos. 35-46 (12)	151.00	102.00

Nearly all of Nos. 14 to 46 may be found without control mark, with double control marks and in various colors.

Counterfeits exist of Nos. 14-46.

Issued by the Cretan Government

Hermes — A6

Hera — A7

Prince George of Greece — A8

Talos — A9

Minos — A10

St. George and the Dragon — A11

1900, Mar. 1 Engr. *Perf. 14*

50	A6	1 l violet brown	20	20
51	A7	5 l green	1.10	20
52	A8	10 l red	1.50	20
53	A7	20 l carmine rose	4.50	60
		Nos. 50-53 (4)	7.30	1.20

See #64-71. For overprints and surcharges see #54-63, 72-73, 85, 88, 93, 97-99, 108, 111.

Overprinted **ΠΡΟΣΩΡΙΝΟΝ**

Red Overprint

54	A8	25 l blue	1.90	60
55	A6	50 l lilac	2.00	1.00
56	A9	1d gray violet	9.00	7.50
57	A10	2d brown	22.50	20.00
58	A11	5d green & blk	75.00	75.00
		Nos. 54-58 (5)	110.40	104.10

Black Overprint

59	A8	25 l blue	1.90	65
60	A6	50 l lilac	1.90	1.10
61	A9	1d gray violet	9.00	3.50
a.		Inverted overprint	500.00	500.00
62	A10	2d brown	18.00	12.50
63	A11	5d green & blk	40.00	40.00
		Nos. 59-63 (5)	70.80	57.75

1901

Without Overprint

64	A6	1 l bister		70
65	A7	20 l orange	4.00	70
66	A8	25 l blue	7.50	30
67	A6	50 l lilac	25.00	20.00
68	A6	50 l ultra	12.00	10.00
69	A9	1d gray violet	25.00	20.00
70	A10	2d brown	8.00	7.00
71	A11	5d green & blk	8.00	7.00
		Nos. 64-71		65.70
		Nos. 65-71	89.50	

No. 64 is a revenue stamp that was used for postage for a short time. Unused, it can only be considered as a revenue.

Types A6 to A8 in olive yellow, and types A9 to A11 in olive yellow and black are revenue stamps.

See note following No. 53.

Surcharges with the year "1922" on designs A6, A8, A9, A11, A13, A15-A23 and D1 are listed under Greece.

No. 66 Overprinted in Black **ΠΡΟΣΩΡΙΝΟΝ**

1901

72	A8	25 l blue	27.50	65
a.		First letter of ovpt. invtd.	150.00	150.00

No. 65 Surcharged in Black **5 5**

1904, Dec.

73	A7	5 l on 20 l orange	3.75	65
a.		Without "5" at right	100.00	50.00

Mycenaean Seal — A12

Britomartis (Cortyna Coin) — A13

Prince George — A14

Kydon and Dog (Cydonia Coin) — A15

Triton (Itanos Coin) — A16

Ariadne (Knossos Coin) — A17

Zeus as Bull Abducting Europa Cortyna Coin) — A18

Palace of Minos Ruins, Knossos A19

Arkadi Monastery and Mt. Ida — A20

1905, Feb. 15

74	A12	2 l dull violet	1.90	40
75	A13	5 l yellow grn	4.00	40
76	A14	10 l red	4.00	40
77	A15	20 l blue grn	4.00	75
78	A16	25 l ultra	5.50	75
79	A17	50 l yellow brn	6.50	4.50
80	A18	1d rose car & dp brn	45.00	45.00
81	A19	3d orange & blk	32.50	32.50
82	A20	5d ol grn & blk	13.00	12.00
		Nos. 74-82 (9)	116.40	96.70

For overprints see Nos.86-87, 89, 91-92, 94-95, 104, 106, 109-110, 112-113, 115-120.

The so-called revolutionary stamps of 1905 were issued for sale to collectors and, so far as can be ascertained, were of no postal value whatever.

A. T. A. Zaimis — A21

Prince George Landing at Suda A22

1907, Aug. 28

83	A21	25 l blue & blk	30.00	80
84	A22	1d green & blk	7.50	8.00

Administration under a High Commissioner.

For overprints see Nos. 90, 105, 107.

Stamps of 1900-1907 Overprinted in Black **ΕΛΛΑΣ**

1908, Sept. 21

85	A6	1 l violet brn	50	45
86	A12	2 l dull violet	50	45
87	A13	5 l yellow grn	60	45
88	A8	10 l red	90	45
89	A15	20 l blue grn	3.50	70
90	A21	25 l blue & blk	6.25	70
91	A17	50 l yellow brn	8.00	2.25
92	A18	1d rose car & dp brn	50.00	50.00
93	A10	2d brown	7.50	6.00
94	A19	3d orange & blk	26.00	26.00
95	A20	5d ol grn & blk	22.50	22.50
		Nos. 85-95 (11)	126.25	109.95

This overprint exists inverted and double, as well as with incorrect, reversed, misplaced and omitted letters. Similar errors are found on the Postage Due and Official stamps with this overprint.

Hermes by Praxiteles — A23

1908

96	A23	10 l brown red	2.00	80
a.		Pair, one without overprint	8.00	
b.		Inverted overprint	15.00	
c.		Double overprint	15.00	

Nos. 96 and 114 were not regularly issued without overprint.

For overprints see Nos. 103, 114.

No. 53 Surcharged **ΕΛΛΑΣ ΠΡΟΣΟΡΙΝΟΝ 5 5**

1909

97	A7	5 l on 20 l car rose	90.00	90.00

Forgeries exist of No. 97.

On No. 65

98	A7	5 l on 20 l orange	1.75	1.25
a.		Inverted surcharge		

Overprinted on Nos. 64, J1 **ΕΛΛΑΣ ΠΡΟΣΟΡΙΝΟΝ**

99	A6	1 l bister	1.25	1.25
100	D1	1 l red	1.25	1.25

No. J4 Surcharged **ΕΛΛΑΣ 2 ΠΡΟΣΩΡΙΝΟΝ**

101	D1	2 l on 20 l red	1.25	1.25
b.		Inverted surcharge	10.00	
c.		Second letter of surcharge "D" instead of "P"	30.00	30.00

No. J4 Surcharged **ΕΛΛΑΣ 2 ΠΡΟΣΩΡΙΝΟΝ**

102	D1	2 l on 20 l red	1.25	1.00

Overprinted in Black:

ΕΛΛΑΣ a **ΕΛΛΑΣ** b

ΕΛΛΑΣ c

103	A23(a)	10 l brown red	4.00	60
a.		Inverted overprint	40.00	
104	A15(a)	20 l blue grn	4.75	80
105	A21(c)	25 l blue & blk	5.00	1.50
106	A17(a)	50 l yellow brn	9.00	4.00
107	A22(b)	1d green & blk	8.00	7.50
108	A10(a)	2d brown	8.00	7.50
109	A19(b)	3d orange & blk	70.00	65.00
110	A20(b)	5d ol grn & blk	22.50	22.50
		Nos. 103-110 (8)	131.25	109.40

Stamps of 1900-08 Overprinted in Red or Black **ΕΛΛΑΣ**

1909-10

111	A6	1 l violet brown	30	20
112	A12	2 l dull violet	30	20
113	A13	5 l yellow green	30	20
114	A23	10 l brown red (Bk)	75	20
115	A15	20 l blue green	2.75	60
116	A16	25 l ultra	3.25	60
117	A17	50 l yellow brn	8.00	4.75
118	A18	1d rose car & dp brn (Bk)	47.50	47.50
119	A19	3d orange & blk	40.00	40.00
120	A20	5d ol grn & blk	27.50	27.50
		Nos. 111-120 (10)	130.65	121.75

POSTAGE DUE STAMPS

D1

1901 Unwmk. Litho. *Perf. 14*

J1	D1	1 l red	20	20
J2	D1	5 l red	60	40
J3	D1	10 l red	1.00	40
J4	D1	20 l red	1.25	1.00
J5	D1	40 l red	12.00	15.00
J6	D1	50 l red	12.00	15.00
J7	D1	1d red	12.00	15.00
J8	D1	2d red	12.00	12.00
		Nos. J1-J8 (8)	51.05	59.00

For overprints and surcharges see Nos. 100-102, J9-J26.

Surcharged in Black **I ΔΡΑΧΜΗ**

1901

J9	D1	1d on 1d red	9.00	9.00

Overprinted **ΕΛΛΑΣ**

1908

J10	D1	1 l red	40	40
J11	D1	5 l red	80	70
J12	D1	10 l red	80	70
J13	D1	20 l red	2.00	2.00
J14	D1	40 l red	8.00	8.00
J15	D1	50 l red	8.00	8.00
J16	D1	1d red	85.00	85.00
J17	D1	1d on 1d red	8.00	8.00
J18	D1	2d red	12.00	12.00
		Nos. J10-J18 (9)	125.00	124.80

Nos. J10-J18 exist with inverted overprint.

Counterfeits of No. J16 exist.

Overprinted **ΕΛΛΑΣ**

1910

J19	D1	1 l red	35	20
J20	D1	5 l red	1.25	20
J21	D1	10 l red	80	40
J22	D1	20 l red	3.25	1.25
J23	D1	40 l red	8.00	8.00
J24	D1	50 l red	10.50	10.00
J25	D1	1d red	20.00	20.00
J26	D1	2d red	20.00	20.00
		Nos. J19-J26 (8)	64.15	60.05

OFFICIAL STAMPS

O1

O2

Unwmk.

1908, Jan. 14 Litho. *Perf. 14*

O1	O1	10 l dull claret	12.50	2.00
O2	O2	30 l blue	32.50	2.00

Nos. O1-O2 exist imperf.

Overprinted **ΕΛΛΑΣ**

O3	O1	10 l dull claret	14.00	2.00
a.		Inverted overprint	55.00	
O4	O2	30 l blue	32.50	2.00
a.		Inverted overprint	60.00	

Overprinted **ΕΛΛΑΣ**

1910

O5	O1	10 l dull claret		2.00	2.00
O6	O2	30 l blue		2.00	2.00

Nos. O5-O6 remained in use until 1922, nine years after union with Greece.

CROATIA

LOCATION — Southeastern Europe
GOVT. — Independent state
AREA — 44,453 sq. mi.
POP. — 7,000,000 (approx.)
CAPITAL — Zagreb

The Independent Croatian State of 1941-45 became part of the Yugoslav Federation in 1945.

Croatia declared its independence in 1991.

100 Paras = 1 Dinar
100 Banica = 1 Kuna
100 Paras = 1 Dinar (1991)
1 Kuna = 100 Lipa (1994)

Catalogue values for unused stamps in this country are for Never Hinged items, beginning with Scott 100 in the regular postage section, Scott B100 in the semi-postal section, Scott C1 in the airmail section and Scott RA20 in the postal tax section.

Watermark

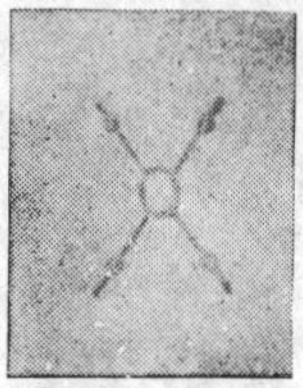

Wmk. 278- Network Connecting Circles

Yugoslavia Nos. 143 to 148B Overprinted in Black

NEZAVISNA DRŽAVA HRVATSKA
IIIIII

Perf. 12½

1941, Apr. 12 Unwmk. Typo.

1	A16	50p orange		90	*2.25*
2	A16	1d yel grn		90	*2.55*
3	A16	1.50d red		90	*1.25*
4	A16	2d dp magenta		90	*1.75*
5	A16	3d dl red brn		1.75	*4.50*
6	A16	4d ultra		1.75	*5.00*
7	A16	5d dk bl		2.50	*5.50*
8	A16	5.50d dk vio brn		2.50	*6.00*
			Nos. 1-8 (8)	12.10	*28.80*

The overprint exists inverted on Nos. 1-6; double on Nos. 2, 3 and 5.

Yugoslavia Nos. 142 to 154 Overprinted in Black

1941, Apr. 21

9	A16	25p black	15	*30*
10	A16	50p orange	15	*30*
11	A16	1d yel grn	15	*30*
12	A16	1.50d red	15	*30*
13	A16	2d dp magenta	15	*60*
14	A16	3d dl red brn	15	*90*
15	A16	4d ultra	28	*1.00*
16	A16	5d dk bl	45	*1.00*
17	A16	5.50d dk vio brn	45	*1.25*
18	A16	6d slate bl	55	*1.75*
19	A16	8d sepia	90	*1.75*
20	A16	12d brt vio	1.10	*2.50*
21	A16	16d dl vio	1.25	*3.00*
22	A16	20d blue	1.50	*3.50*
23	A16	30d bright pink	2.25	*5.50*
		Nos. 9-23 (15)	9.63	*23.95*

The overprint exists inverted on Nos. 9-11, 17 and 20; double on Nos. 9, 12 and 17.

Yugoslavia Nos. 147, 148 Surcharged in Black

1941, May 16

24	A16	1d on 3d dl red brn	18	*30*
25	A16	2d on 4d ultra	18	*30*

The overprint exists inverted and double on Nos. 24-25.

Postage Due Stamps of Yugoslavia, Nos. J28, J30 to J32, Overprinted in Black

1941, May 17

26	D4	50p violet	15	*22*
27	D4	2d dp bl	28	*50*
28	D4	5d orange	28	*50*
29	D4	10d chocolate	40	*70*
		Nos. 26-29 (4)	1.11	*1.92*

Counterfeit overprints on Nos. 1-29 are plentiful.

Imperforates
Nearly all Croatian stamps, from No. 30 through 80, B3 through B76, J6 through J25, O1 through O24 and RA1 through RA7 exist imperforate.

Ozalj Castle — A1

Designs: 50b, City of Jajce. 75b, Old Warasdin. 1k, Velebit Mountains. 1.50k, Zelanjak. 2k, Zagreb Cathedral. 3k, Osjek Cathedral. 4k, Drina River. No. 38, Konjica. No. 39, Zemun. 6k, Dubrovnik. 7k, Save River. 8k, Sarajevo. 10k, Plitvice. 12k, Klis Fortress, Split. 20k, Hvar. 30k, Syrmia. 50k, Senj. 100k, Banjaluka (without "F.I.").

1941-43 Unwmk. Photo. *Perf. 11.*
Ordinary Paper

30	A1	25b henna	15	15
31	A1	50b slate blue	15	15
32	A1	75b dk ol grn	15	15
33	A1	1k Prussian grn	15	15
34	A1	1.50k deep green	15	15
35	A1	2k car lake	15	15
36	A1	3k brn red	15	15
37	A1	4k dp ultra	15	15
38	A1	5k black	50	45
39	A1	5k blue	15	15
40	A1	6k lt ol brn	15	15
41	A1	7k org red	15	15
42	A1	8k chestnut	15	15
43	A1	10k dark plum	25	15
44	A1	12k olive brn	32	25
45	A1	20k gldn brn	25	15
46	A1	30k blk brn	32	18
47	A1	50k dk slate grn	55	25
48	A1	100k violet	80	*1.50*
		Set value	3.70	*3.60*

Nos. 31, 35 and 43 exist on thin to pelure paper. Shades of all values exist.

For overprints and surcharge see #49-51, 53.

Tête bêche Pairs

30a	A1	25b	15	*30*
31a	A1	50b	15	*30*
33a	A1	1k	30	*52*
34a	A1	1.50k	30	*35*
35a	A1	2k	20	*30*
37a	A1	4k	20	*35*
38a	A1	5k	1.65	*3.00*
40a	A1	6k	20	*35*
41a	A1	7k	20	*35*
42a	A1	8k	60	*90*
43a	A1	10k	1.10	*1.25*
45a	A1	20k	1.10	*1.50*
46a	A1	30k	90	*1.50*
47a	A1	50k	4.50	*8.75*
		Nos. 30a-47a (14)	11.55	*19.72*

Types of 1941 Overprinted in Brown or Green

1942, Apr. 9

49	A1	2k dk brn	15	*22*
50	A1	5k dk car	22	*35*
51	A1	10k dk bl grn (G)	30	*60*
		Nos. 49-51 (3)	67	*1.17*

First anniversary of Croatian independence.

Banjaluka ("F.I." at upper right) — A20

1942, June 13

52	A20	100k violet	1.50	*2.50*

Banjaluka Philatelic Exhibition.

No. 35 Surcharged in Red Brown with New Value and Bar

1942, June 23

53	A1	25b on 2k carmine lake	15	*22*
a.		Tête bêche pair	30	*60*

Trakoscan Castle — A21

Catherine Zrinski — A23

Design: 12.50k, Citadel of Veliki Tabor.

1943

Pelure Paper

54	A21	3.50k brn car	30	30
55	A21	12.50k vio blk	30	30

No. 54 exists on ordinary paper.

1943, June 7 Engr. *Perf. 12½*

Designs: 2k, Fran Krsto Frankopan. 3.50k, Peter Zrinski.

Various Frames

56	A23	1k dark blue	15	*15*
57	A23	2k dk olive grn	15	*15*
58	A23	3.50k dark red	15	*22*
		Set value	30	

Rugjer Boscovich A26

Ante Pavelich A27

1943, Dec. 13 *Perf. 11*

59	A26	3.50k copper red	15	*24*
60	A26	12.50k dk vio brn	22	*35*

Rugjer Boscovich (1711-1787). Serbo-Croat mathematician and physicist.

1943-44 Litho. *Perf. 12½, 14*

61	A27	25b org ver	15	*15*
62	A27	50b Prus bl	15	*15*
63	A27	75b olive grn	15	*15*
64	A27	1k lt grn	15	*15*
65	A27	1.50k dl gray vio	15	*15*
66	A27	2k rose lake	15	*15*
67	A27	3k rose brn	15	*15*
68	A27	3.50k brt bl	15	*15*
a.		3.50k dark blue, perf. 11½	1.10	*2.00*
69	A27	4k brt red vio	15	*15*
70	A27	5k ultra	15	*15*
71	A27	8k org brn	15	*15*
72	A27	9k rose pink	15	*15*
73	A27	10k vio brn	15	*15*
74	A27	12k dk ol bis	15	*15*
75	A27	12.50k gray blk	15	*15*
76	A27	18k dull brn	15	*15*
77	A27	32k dark brn	15	*15*
78	A27	50k grnsh bl	15	*15*
79	A27	70k orange	22	*30*
80	A27	100k violet	45	*50*
		Set value	2.00	*3.00*

Nos. 61 and 63 measure 20½x26mm. Nos. 62 and 64-80 measure 22x27½mm.

Issue dates: 2k, 1943; No. 68a, June 13, 1943, Pavelich's birthday; others, 1944.

"Labor Day 1945" — A28

1945 Photo. *Perf. 11½*

81	A28	3.50k red brown	15	*90*

Catalogue values for unused stamps in this section, from this point to the end of the section, are for Never Hinged items.

Nos. RA20, RA20a Surcharged in Black and Gold

1991, Nov. 21 Litho. *Perf. 14*

100	PT10 4d on 1.20d #RA20		*45*
a.	Perf. 11x10½		*45*

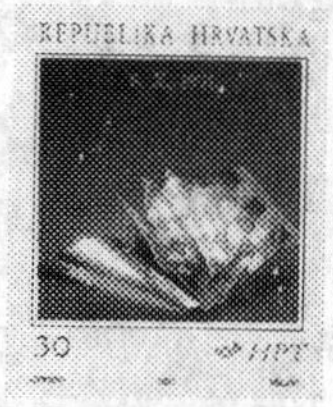

Declaration of Independence, Oct. 8, 1991 — A35

Christmas — A36

1991, Dec. 10 *Perf. 12*

101	A35 30d multicolored		*2.00*

1991, Dec. 11 *Perf. 12*

Creche figures of the Holy Family from Kosljun Monastery, Krk.

102	A36 4d multicolored		*75*

No. RA21 Surcharged in Black and Gold

1992, Jan. 3 *Perf. 10½x11*

103	PT11 20d on 1.70d #RA21		*52*

Croatian Arms — A37

1992, Jan. 15 *Perf. 11x10½*

104	A37 10d multicolored		*22*
a.	Perf. 14		*22*

See No. RA22.

1992 Winter Olympics, Albertville — A38

1992, Feb. 4 *Perf. 11x10½*

105 A38 30d multicolored 2.00

Croatian Cities and Landmarks A39

A39a

A39b

Designs: 6d, Knin. 7d, Eltz Castle, Vukovar. 20d, Church, Ilok. 30d, Starcevic Street, Gospic. 45d, Rector's Palace, Dubrovnik. 50d, St. Jakov's Cathedral, Sibenik. 100d, Vinkovci. 200d, Pazin, vert. No. 118, Beli Monastery. No. 119, Krapina. 500d, Slavonski Brod. 1000d, Varazdin. 2000d, Karlovac. 5000d, Zadar, vert. 10,000d, Vis.

1992-94 *Perf. 14*

107	A39	6d	multicolored	*15*
108	A39	7d	multicolored	*24*
112	A39	20d	multicolored	*24*
a.		Perf. 11x10½		*1.05*
113	A39	30d	multicolored	*75*
114	A39	45d	multicolored	*1.50*
115	A39	50d	multicolored	*1.65*
116	A39a	100d	multicolored	*42*
117	A39a	200d	multicolored	*32*
118	A39	300d	multicolored	*4.00*
119	A39b	300d	multicolored	*95*
122	A39a	500d	multicolored	*1.25*
123	A39a	1000d	multicolored	*1.90*
123A	A39a	2000d	multicolored	*2.25*
123B	A39a	5000d	multicolored	*2.50*
123C	A39a	10,000d	multicolored	*4.50*
	Nos. 107-123C (15)			*22.62*

Issue dates: 6d, Apr. 18. 7d, Apr. 8. No. 112, Feb. 28. No. 112a, Sept. 9. 30d, May 21. 45d, Apr. 14. 50d, Apr. 28. No. 118, June 26. 100d, Dec. 14, 1992. No. 119, 500d, Feb. 9, 1993. 1000d, Mar. 16, 1993. 200d, Apr. 22, 1993. 2000d, May 20, 1993. 5000d, Sept. 24, 1993. 10,000d, 2/22/94.

This is an expanding set. Numbers may change.

Statue of King Tomislav — A40

1992, May 5 Engr. *Perf. 12½ Horiz.*

Coil Stamp

124 A40 10d dark green 25

Railroad Station, Zagreb, Cent. — A41

1992, June 30 Litho. *Perf. 14*

125 A41 30d multicolored *75*

Matica, Society of Knowledge and Literacy, 150th Anniv. — A42

1992, July 8

126 A42 20d red, gold & black *35*

Bishop Josip Juraj Strossmayer, Founder A43

1992, July 9

127 A43 30d multicolored *45*

Croatian Academy of Arts and Sciences, 125th anniv., in 1991.

1992 Summer Olympics, Barcelona — A44

Design: 105d, Abstract design.

1992, July 25

128 A44 40d shown *48*
129 A44 105d multicolored *1.25*

Flowers — A45

Designs: 30d, Edraianthus pumilio. 85d, Degenia velebitica, vert.

1992, July 28

130 A45 30d multicolored *38*
131 A45 85d multicolored *1.05*

Wildlife — A46

Designs: 40d, Monticola solitarius. 75d, Elaphe situla.

1992, July 31

132 A46 40d multicolored *48*
133 A46 75d multicolored *90*

Discovery of America, 500th Anniv. — A47

Europa: 30d, 60d, Sailing ship. 75d, 130d, Indian in Chicago, by Ivan Mestrovic (1883-1962).

1992 Litho. *Perf. 14*

134 A47 30d multicolored *36*
135 A47 60d multicolored *75*
136 A47 75d red & black *90*
137 A47 130d red, blk & gold *1.60*
Nos. 134-137 (4) *3.61*

Issue dates: 30d, 75d, July 31; others, Sept. 4.

A48

A49

1992, Oct. 2

138 A48 40d multicolored *35*
139 A48 130d multi, diff. *1.05*

Declaration of Croatian Literary Language, 25th Anniv. (#133). Spelling reform by Dr. Ivan Broz, cent. (#134).

1992, Oct. 16

140 A49 90d multicolored *58*

City of Samobor, 750th Anniv.

Gift of the St. Juraj Church by Archbishop Mucimir, 1100th Anniv. — A50

1992, Oct. 30

141 A50 60d multicolored *38*

Reign of King Bela IV, 750th Anniv. — A51

1992, Nov. 16 Litho. *Perf. 14*

142 A51 180d multicolored *95*

Christmas — A52

1992, Dec. 7

143 A52 80d multicolored *38*

Blaz Lorkovic (1839-1892), Scientist — A53

Kolo Literature Review, 150th Anniv. — A54

1992, Dec. 21

144 A53 250d multicolored *85*

1992, Dec. 22

145 A54 300d multicolored *1.15*

Ivan Bunic-Vucic (1592-1658) — A55

1992, Dec. 29

146 A55 350d multicolored *1.30*

Nikola Tesla (1856-1943), Physicist — A56

1993, Jan. 30

147 A56 250d multicolored *70*

Self-Portrait, by Ferdo Quiquerez (1845-1893) A57

1993, Feb. 10

148 A57 100d multicolored *25*

Wildlife — A58

1993, Feb. 23 Litho. *Perf. 14*

149 A58 500d Cervus elaphus *1.15*
150 A58 550d Haliaeetus albicilla *1.30*

Self-Portrait, by Zlatko Sulentic (1893-1971) A59

1993, Mar. 17

151 A59 350d multicolored *65*

Lipik Health and Convalescent Home, Cent. — A60

1993, Apr. 22 Litho. *Perf. 14*

152 A60 400d multicolored *75*

Ivan Goran Kovacic (1913-1943), Author — A61

1993, Apr. 24
153 A61 200d multicolored *35*

59th PEN Congress, Dubrovnik A62

1993, Apr. 24
154 A62 800d multicolored *1.25*

Ivan Kukuljevic (1816-89), Politician, Historian, Writer — A63

1993, May 2 **Litho.** ***Perf. 14***
155 A63 500d multicolored *75*

Croatian Natl. Theatre, Split, Cent. — A64

Pag, 500th Anniv. — A65

1993, May 6 **Litho.** ***Perf. 14***
156 A64 600d multicolored *85*

1993, May 18
157 A65 800d multicolored *95*

Croatian Membership in United Nations, 1st Anniv. — A66

1993, May 22
158 A66 500d multicolored *58*

Europa A67

Contemporary paintings by: 700d, Ivo Dulcic (1916-75). 1000d, Miljenko Stancic (1926-77). 1100d, Ljubo Ivancic (b. 1925).

1993, June 5
159 A67 700d multicolored *75*
160 A67 1000d multicolored *1.00*
161 A67 1100d multicolored *1.10*
a. Miniature sheet, 2 each #159-161 *5.75*
Nos. 159-161 (3) *2.85*

Intl. Art Biennial, Venice — A68

Works of art by: 250d, Milivoj Bijelic. 600d, Ivo Dekovic. 1000d, Zeljko Kipke.

1993, June 10 **Litho.** ***Perf. 14***
162 A68 250d multicolored *25*
a. Souvenir sheet of 4 *1.00*
163 A68 600d multicolored *75*
a. Souvenir sheet of 4 *3.00*
164 A68 1000d multicolored *1.00*
a. Souvenir sheet of 4 *4.00*
Nos. 162-164 (3) *2.00*

1993 Mediterranean Games — A69

1993, June 15 **Litho.** ***Perf. 14***
165 A69 700d multicolored *75*

Adolf Waldinger (1843-1904), Painter — A70

1993, June 16
166 A70 300d multicolored *32*

Famous Croatian Battles A71

1993, July 6 **Litho.** ***Perf. 14***
167 A71 800d Krbavskom, 1493 *65*
168 A71 1300d Sisak, 1593 *1.05*

Miroslav Krleza (1893-1981), Writer — A72

1993, July 7
169 A72 400d multicolored *35*

Croatian Membership in UPU, 1st Anniv. — A73

1993, July 20 **Litho.** ***Perf. 14***
170 A73 1800d multicolored *1.40*

Vlaho Paljetak (1893-1944), Composer — A74

1993, Aug. 7
171 A74 500d multicolored *35*

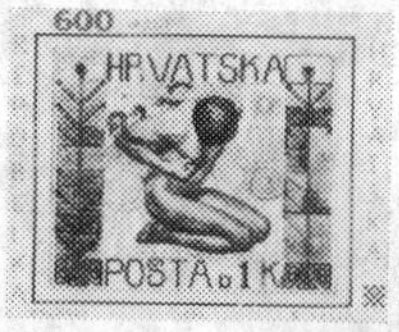

Stamp Day — A75

1993, Sept. 9 **Litho.** ***Perf. 14***
172 A75 600d multicolored *35*

Map of Istria, 1620 — A76

1993, Sept. 20
173 A76 2200d multicolored *1.10*

Incorporation of Istria, Rijeka and Zadar into Croatia, 50th anniv.

Tadija Smiciklas (1843-1914), Historian — A77

1993, Oct. 1
174 A77 800d black, gold & red *42*

Archaelogical Museum, Split, Cent. — A78

1993, Oct. 27
175 A78 1000d multicolored *45*

A79

A80

1993, Nov. 17 **Litho.** ***Perf. 14***
176 A79 3000d multicolored *1.40*

Uprising of 13th Pioneer Battalion, Villefranche-de-Rouergue, France, 50th anniv.

1993, Nov. 18

Design: 900d, Josip Eugen Tomic (1843-1906), writer.

177 A80 900d multicolored *42*

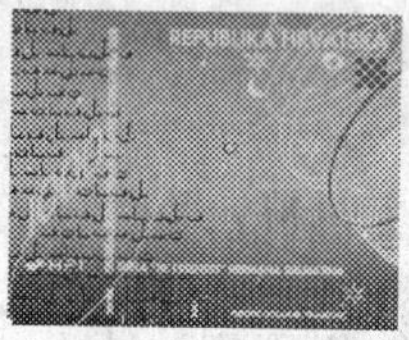

Publication of De Esscentiis, by Hermana Dalmatin, 850th Anniv. — A81

1993, Nov. 30
178 A81 1000d multicolored *45*

Christmas — A82

Paintings: 1000d, Christmas at the Front, by Miroslav Sutej. 4000d, Birth of Christ, 15th cent. fresco, Marienkirch of Dvigrad.

1993, Dec. 3
179 A82 1000d multicolored *42*
180 A82 4000d multicolored *1.75*

Organized Skiing in Croatia, Cent. — A83

1993, Dec. 15
181 A83 1000d multicolored *42*

Croatian Natl. Guard, 125th Anniv. — A84

1993, Dec. 22

182 A84 1100d multicolored *45*

Printers of Senj, 500th Anniv. — A85

1994, Jan. 29

183 A85 2200d multicolored *95*

1994 Winter Olympics, Lillehammer A86

1994, Feb. 12

184 A86 4000d multicolored *1.75*

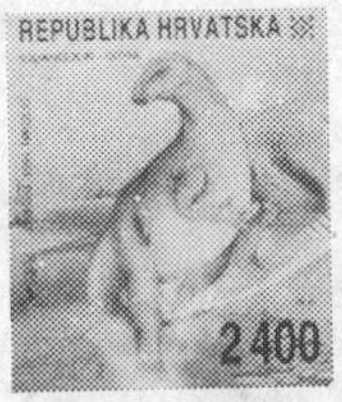

Dinosaurs from Western Istria — A87

Designs: a, 2400d, Iguanodons. b, 4000d, Map, skeleton.

1994, Mar. 7

185 A87 Pair, #a.-b. *2.75*

Nos. 185a-185b are a continuous design.

Zora Dalmatinska Magazine, 150th Anniv. — A88

1994, Mar. 15

186 A88 800d multicolored *38*

Croatian University, Zagreb, 325th Anniv. — A89

Design: 2200d, University building, Emperor Leopold I's seal, vice-chancellor's chain.

1994, Apr. 19 Litho. *Perf. 14*

187 A89 2200d multicolored *1.00*

Protect the Environment A90

ILO, 75th Anniv. A91

1994, Apr. 22 Litho. *Perf. 14*

188 A90 3800d Canis lupus *1.75*

1994, May 2

189 A91 1000d multicolored *48*

A92

Europa A93

European inventions, discoveries: 3800d, Faust Vrancic (1551-1617), parachute. 4000d, Slavoljub Penkala (1871-1922), fountain pen.

1994, May 16

190 A92 3800d multicolored *1.75*
191 A93 4000d multicolored *1.90*

A94

A95

1994, June 3

192 A94 2.40k Iris croatica *1.10*
193 A94 4k Colchicum visianii *1.90*

1994, June 7

Design: 1d, Drazen Petrovic (1964-93), basketball player.

194 A95 1d multicolored *48*

Tourism in Croatia, 150th Anniv. — A96

Designs: 80 l, Plitvice Lakes Natl. Park. 1k, Waterfalls, Krka River. 1.10k, Kornati Islands Natl. Park. 2.20k, Kopacki Trscak nature reserve. 2.40k Sailboats, Opatijska Riviera resort. 3.80k, Brijuni islands. 4k, Trakoscan castle, Zagorje.

1994, June 15 Litho. *Perf. 14*

196 A96 80 l multicolored *38*
197 A96 1k multicolored *45*
198 A96 1.10k multicolored *50*
200 A96 2.20k multicolored *1.00*
201 A96 2.40k multicolored *1.10*
206 A96 3.80k multicolored *1.75*
207 A96 4k multicolored *1.90*
a. Min. sheet of 7, #196-198, 200-201, 206-207 + 2 labels *7.25*
Nos. 196-207 (7) *7.08*

Issued: 80 l, 1k, 1.10k, 2.20k, 2.40k, 3.80k, 4k, 6/15/94. This is an expanding set. Numbers may change.

Croatian Musicians A97

Designs: 1k, Kresimir Baranovic (1894-1975), composer, vert. 2.20k, Vatroslav Lisinski (1819-54), composer, vert. 2.40k, Pauline Liederbuch (b.1644), harpist.

1994, June 20

211 A97 1k multicolored *45*
212 A97 2.20k multicolored *1.00*
213 A97 2.40k multicolored *1.10*
Nos. 211-213 (3) *2.55*

Croatian Fraternal Union, Cent. — A98

1994, Aug. 15 Litho. *Perf. 14*

214 A98 2.20k multicolored *1.10*

Intl. Year of the Family — A99

1994, Aug. 31

215 A99 80 l multicolored *40*

Intl. Olympic Committee, Cent. — A100

1994, Sept. 10

216 A100 1k multicolored *50*

Visit of Pope John Paul II — A101

1994, Sept. 10

217 A101 1k multicolored *50*

No. 217 printed with se-tenant label.

Antoine de Saint-Exupery (1900-44), Aviator, Author A102

1994, Sept. 20

218 A102 3.80k multicolored *1.90*

13th Intl. Congress on Early Christian Archeology A103

1994, Sept. 23

219 A103 4k multicolored *2.00*

No. 219 printed with se-tenant label.

Modern Croation Paintings A104

Designs: 2.40k, Still Life with Fruits and Basket, by Marino Tartaglia, 1926. 3.80k, In the Park, by Milan Steiner, c. 1918. 4k, Self-portrait, by Vilko Gecan, 1929.

1994, Oct. 12

220 A104 2.40k multicolored *1.25*
221 A104 3.80k multicolored *1.90*
222 A104 4k multicolored *2.00*
Nos. 220-222 (3) *5.15*

Ivan Belostenec (1594-1675), Writer & Lexicographer A105

1994, Nov. 9

223 A105 2.20k multicolored *1.10*

City of Zagreb, Zagreb Bishopric, 900th Anniv. A106

Designs: No. 224a, 1k, Zagreb exchange building, designed by V. Kovacic, S. Penkala's airplane, Cibona office tower, designed by Hrzic, Pitesa and Serbetic. b, 1k, Maxi Cat, by Zlatko Grgic, Zagreb School of Animated Film. c, 1k, St. Mark's Church, Gradec; photo of gas lantern, by Toso Dabac. d, 4k, Late Gothic bishop's staff, Valvasor's view of Zagreb.

13.50k, Zagreb street scene, Penkala's airplane, vert.

1994, Nov. 16

224 A106 Strip of 4, #a.-d. *3.50*

Souvenir Sheet

225 A106 13.50k multicolored *6.75*

No. 224 is a continuous design. No. 225 contains one 24x48mm stamp.

Christmas A107

Design: 1k, Epiphany, by unknown sculptor.

1994, Dec. 1 **Litho.** ***Perf. 14***
226 A107 1k multicolored *50*

Virgin Mary's Sanctuary, Loreto, 700th Anniv. A108

Design: 4k, The Moving of the Holy House, by Giovanni Battista Tiepolo.

1994, Dec. 10
227 A108 4k multicolored *1.90*

SEMI-POSTAL STAMPS

Types of Yugoslavia, 1941, Overprinted in Gold "NEZAVISNA / DRZAVA / HRVATSKA"

Perf. 11½

1941, May 10 **Unwmk.** **Engr.**
B1 SP80 1.50d + 1.50d bl blk 7.25 *13.00*
B2 SP81 4d + 3d choc 7.25 *13.00*

Five thousand sets of Yugoslavia Nos. 142-154 were overprinted "NEZAVISNA DRZAVA HRVATSKA 10. IV. 1941" and small shield in red or blue, in 1941. Sold for double face value. Value, set, $225.

Costume of Sinj, Dalmatia — SP1

Soldiers with Arms of the Axis States — SP4

Designs (Costumes): 2k+2k, Travnik, Bosnia. 4k+4k, Turopolje, Croatia.

1941, Oct. 12 **Photo.** ***Perf. 10½x10***
B3 SP1 1.50k + 1.50k Prus bl & red 18 *35*
B4 SP1 2k + 2k ol brn & red 28 *45*
B5 SP1 4k + 4k brn lake & red 45 *1.10*
Nos. B3-B5 (3) 91 *1.90*

The surtax aided the Croatian Red Cross. Sheets of 20 stamps and 5 labels.

1941, Dec. 3 ***Perf. 11***
B6 SP4 4k + 2k blue 90 *2.00*

The surtax was used for Croatian Volunteers in the East.

Model Plane — SP5

Model Plane — SP6

Designs: 3k+3k, Boy with model plane. 4k+4k, Model seaplane in flight.

1942, Mar. 25
B7 SP5 2k + 2k sepia 22 *35*
B8 SP6 2.50k + 2.50k dl grn 28 *60*
B9 SP5 3k + 3k brn car 32 *70*
B10 SP6 4k + 4k dp bl 50 *1.00*
Nos. B7-B10 (4) 1.32 *2.65*

Nos. B7-B10 were issued in sheets of 25 and in sheets of 24 plus label.

Souvenir Sheets
Perf. 11

B11 Sheet of 2 14.00 *22.50*
a. SP5 2k+8k brown carmine 5.25 *9.00*
b. SP5 3k+12k deep blue 5.25 *9.00*

Imperf

B12 Sheet of 2 14.00 *22.50*
a. SP5 2k+8k deep blue 5.25 *9.00*
b. SP5 3k+12k brown carmine 5.25 *9.00*

The sheets measure 125x110mm.
Aviation Exposition of Zagreb. The surtax aided society of Croatian Wings (Hrvatska Krila).
Nos. B11-B12 exist with colors of stamps and inscriptions transposed.

Boy Trumpeters SP10

Triumphal Arch SP11

Mother and Child — SP12

1942, July 5 ***Perf. 11½***
B13 SP10 3k + 1k lake 35 *60*
B14 SP11 4k + 2k dk brn 38 *75*
B15 SP12 5k + 5k dp bl grn 50 *90*
Nos. B13-B15 (3) 1.23 *2.25*

The surtax was for national welfare.

Matthew Gubec SP13

Ante Starcevich SP14

SP15

1942, Nov. 22 ***Perf. 14½***
B16 SP13 3k + 6k dark red 15 *30*
B17 SP14 4k + 7k sepia 15 *30*

Souvenir Sheets
Perf. 12, Imperf.

B18 SP15 5k + 20k dull blue 7.25 *8.25*

Heroes of Senj, May 9, 1937. Nos. B16-B17 were printed in sheets of 16 + 9 labels, each bearing a hero's name. The surtax aided the Natl. Youth Soc.

Sestine Peasant — SP16

Croatian Labor Corpsman — SP20

Designs: 3k+1k, Slavonian peasant. 4k+2k, Bosnian peasant. 10k+5k, Dalmatian peasant. 13k+6k, Sestine peasant.

1942, Oct. 4 ***Perf. 11½***
B20 SP16 1.50k + 50b org brn & red 40 *75*
B21 SP16 3k + 1k dl pur & red 40 *75*
B22 SP16 4k + 2k dp bl & red 50 *1.00*
B23 SP16 10k + 5k dk ol bis & red 70 *1.50*
B24 SP16 13k + 6k rose lake & red 1.50 *3.00*
Nos. B20-B24 (5) 3.50 *7.00*

The surtax aided the Croatian Red Cross.
Issued in sheets of 24 stamps plus label.

1943, Jan. 17 **Wmk. 278** ***Perf. 11***

Designs: 3k+3k, Corpsman with wheelbarrow. 7k+4k, Corpsman plowing.

B25 SP20 2k + 1k ol gray & sepia 95 *1.90*
B26 SP20 3k + 3k brn & sepia 95 *1.90*
B27 SP20 7k + 4k gray bl & sepia 95 *1.90*
Nos. B25-B27 (3) 2.85 *5.70*

The surtax aided the State Labor Service (Drzavna Radna Sluzba). Issued in sheets of 9.

Arms of Zagreb and "Golden Bull" — SP23

1943, Mar. 23 **Unwmk.**
B28 SP23 3.50k (+ 6.50k) bril ultra 60 *1.65*

700th anniversary of Zagreb's "Golden Bull," a Magna Carta of civic rights and privileges granted to the city in 1242 by King Bela because the Croats annihilated Tartar hordes at Grobnik.
Issued in sheets of 8 with marginal inscriptions.

Ante Pavelich — SP24

Sailor at Sea of Azov — SP26

1943, Apr. 10 ***Perf. 14***
B29 SP24 5k + 3k copper red 15 *30*
B30 SP24 7k + 5k dark green 15 *30*

Surtax aided the National Youth Society.
Issued in sheets of 100, and in miniature sheets of 16 stamps + 9 labels.

Souvenir Sheets

1943, May 17 ***Perf. 12, Imperf.***
B31 SP24 12k + 8k dp ultra 4.50 *7.25*

1943, July 1 ***Perf. 11***

Designs: 2k+1k, Flier at Sevastopol and Rzhev. 3.50k+1.50k, Infantrymen at Stalingrad. 9k+4.50k, Panzer Division at Don River.

B33 SP26 1k + 50b grn 15 *15*
B34 SP26 2k + 1k dk red 15 *15*
B35 SP26 3.50k + 1.50k dk bl 15 *15*
B36 SP26 9k + 4.50k chestnut 15 *15*
Set value 32

Souvenir Sheets
Perf. 11, Imperf.

B37 Sheet of 4 90 *2.50*
a. SP26 1k+50b dark blue 18 *30*
b. SP26 2k+1k green 18 *30*
c. SP26 3.50k+1.50k dk red brown 18 *30*
d. SP26 9k+4.50k bluish black 18 *30*

Issued to honor the Croatian Legion which fought with the Germans in Russia.
The surtax aided the Croatian Legion.

St. Mary's Church and Cistercian Cloister, Zagreb, in 1650 SP31

1943, Sept. 12 **Engr.** ***Perf. 14½***
B39 SP31 18k + 9k dl gray vio 80 *1.65*

Souvenir Sheet
Perf. 12½

B40 SP31 18k + 9k blk brn 3.50 *6.00*

Croatian Phil. Soc. Exhibition at Zagreb.

No. B39 Overprinted in Red **HRVATSKO MORE 8. IX. 1943.**

1943, Sept. 12
B41 SP31 18k + 9k dl gray vio 3.00 *5.00*

Return to Croatia of the Dalmatian and Croatian coasts.

Mother and Children SP33

Nurse and Patient SP34

1943, Oct. 3 **Litho.** ***Perf. 11***
Cross in Red

B42 SP33 1k + 50b bl grn 15 *22*
B43 SP33 2k + 1k bril car 15 *22*
B44 SP33 3.50k + 1.50k brt bl 15 *22*
B45 SP34 8k + 3k red brn 15 *22*
B46 SP34 9k + 4k yel grn 18 *30*
B47 SP33 10k + 5k dp vio 22 *35*
B48 SP34 12k + 6k brt ultra 28 *45*
B49 SP33 12.50k + 6k dk brn 40 *70*
B50 SP34 18k + 8k brn org 55 *90*
B51 SP34 32k + 12k dk gray 90 *1.50*
Nos. B42-B51 (10) 3.13 *5.08*

The surtax aided the Croatian Red Cross.

Post Horn and Arms — SP35

Carrier Pigeon and Plane — SP36

Mercury
SP37

Winged Wheel
SP38

1944, Feb. 3

B52	SP35	7k + 3.50k ol bis & red	15	*15*
B53	SP36	16k + 8k bl & dk bl	15	*18*
B54	SP37	24k + 12k red & rose red	15	*28*
B55	SP38	32k + 16k gray & red	28	*55*
		Set value	60	

The surtax benefited communications and railway employees. Sheets of 9.

St. Sebastian
SP39

War Invalids
SP40

Statue of Ancient Croatian King — SP41

Death of King Peter Svacic, 1097 — SP42

1944, Feb. 15

B56	SP39	7k + 3.50k org red & rose car	15	*18*
B57	SP40	16k + 8k yel grn & dk grn	15	*30*
B58	SP41	24k + 12k yel brn & red	15	*30*
B59	SP42	32k + 16k bl & dk bl	30	*60*
		Nos. B56-B59 (4)	75	*1.38*

The surtax aided wounded war victims.

Issued in sheets of eight stamps, with marginal inscriptions and a central label picturing St. Sebastian.

Black Legion in Combat — SP43

Guarding the Drina — SP44

Jure Francetich — SP45

1944, May 22 Photo. *Imperf.*

B60	SP43	3.50k + 1.50k brn red	15	15
B61	SP44	12.50k + 6.50k slate bl	15	15
B62	SP45	18k + 9k olive brn	15	15
		Set value	24	24

Third anniversary of Croatian independence.

The surtax aided the National Youth Society. Sheets of 20.

Perf. 14½

B63	SP45	12.50k + 287.50k int blk	1.75	*9.00*

Issued to commemorate Jure Francetich.

Labor Corpsmen Marching — SP46

Corpsman Digging — SP47

Designs: 18k+9k, Officer instructing corpsman. 32k+16k, Pavelich reviewing Labor Corps. Sheets of 8 plus label.

Perf. 11, 12½, 14½

1944, Aug. 20 Engr.

B65	SP46	3.50k + 1k dk red	15	15
B66	SP47	12.50k + 6k sepia	15	15
B67	SP47	18k + 9k dk bl	15	18
B68	SP47	32k + 16k gray grn	15	18
		Set value	30	

Souvenir Sheet

Perf. 12½

B69	SP47	32k + 16k dk brn, *cr*	1.25	2.50

The surtax aided the State Labor Service (Drzavna Radna Sluzba).

Palm Leaf — SP51

1944, Nov. 12 Litho. *Perf. 11*

B70	SP51	2k + 1k dl grn & red	15	15
B71	SP51	3.50k + 1.50k car lake & red	15	15
B72	SP51	12.50k + 6k ind & red	15	20
		Set value	23	

The surtax aided the Croatian Red Cross. Sheets of 16.

Men of Storm Division SP52

Designs: 70k+70k, Soldiers of Storm Division in action. 100k+100k, Storm Division emblem.

1944 Unwmk. Litho. *Perf. 11*

B73	SP52	50k + 50k brick red	35.00	*75.00*
B74	SP52	70k + 70k sepia	35.00	*75.00*
B75	SP52	100k + 100k chlky bl, pale bl & dp bl	35.00	*75.00*
		Nos. B73-B75 (3)	105.00	*225.00*

Souvenir Sheet

B76		Sheet of 3	650.00	*1,000.*
a.		SP52 50k + 50k brick red		
b.		SP52 70k + 70k sepia		
c.		SP52 100k + 100k chalky, pale & deep blue		

Nos. B76a to B76c are inscribed "O. A." in brick red at right below design. The sheet measures 216x132mm. The surtax aided the First Croatian Storm Division. Counterfeits are plentiful.

Postman
SP55

Telephone Line Repairman
SP56

Designs; 24k+12k, Switchboard operator. 50k+25k, 100k+50k, Postman delivering parcel. Sheets of 8.

1945 Photo.

B77	SP55	3.50k + 1.50k sl gray	15	*15*
B78	SP56	12.50k + 6k brn car	15	*15*
B79	SP56	24k + 12k dk grn	15	*20*
B80	SP56	50k + 25k brn vio	15	*30*
		Set value	38	

Souvenir Sheet

B81	SP56	100k + 50k dp brn	1.75	*3.50*

The surtax on Nos. B77-B81 aided employees of the P.T.T.

Catalogue values for unused stamps in this section, from this point to the end of the section, are for Never Hinged items.

Famous Croatians — SP60

Designs: No. B100, Ban Josip Jelacic (1801-59). No. B101, Dr. Ante Starcevic (1823-96). 7d + 3d, Stjepan Radic (1871-1928).

1992 Litho. *Perf. 11x10½*

B100	SP60	4d +2d multi	*48*	
B101	SP60	4d +2d multi	*48*	

Perf. 14

B102	SP60	7d +3d multi	*38*	
		Nos. B100-B102 (3)	*1.34*	

Issue dates: No. B100, Feb. 1. No. B101, Mar. 4. No. B102, Apr. 2. This is an expanding set. Numbers may change.

The surcharge on Nos. B100-B102 was initially an obligatory tax on all internal and overseas mail. From May 15, 1992, these stamps were valid for postage at their 6d or 10d face values.

AIR POST STAMPS

Catalogue values for unused stamps in this section are for Never Hinged items.

Airplane, Zagreb Cathedral and Port of Dubrovnik — AP1

Designs: No. C2, Airplane over ruins of Diocletian's Palace, Split. No. C3, Coat of arms, aiplane, Zagreb Cathedral and Pula amphitheatre. No. C4, Paper Airplane Made from Picture of Osijek Cathedral.

1991-92 Litho. *Perf. 11x10½*

C1	AP1	1d multicolored	*15*	
a.		Perf. 14	*15*	
C2	AP1	2d multicolored	*25*	
a.		Perf. 14	*25*	
C3	AP1	3d multicolored	*38*	
C4	AP1	4d multicolored	*30*	
		Nos. C1-C4 (4)	*1.08*	

Issue dates: No. C1, Sept. 9. No. C1a, June 24, 1992. No. C2, Oct. 9. No. C2a, 1992. No. C3, Nov. 20. No. C4, Feb. 14, 1992.

POSTAGE DUE STAMPS

Yugoslavia Nos. J28-J32 Overprinted in Black

1941, Apr. 26 Unwmk. *Perf. 12½*

J1	D4	50p violet	18	*30*
a.		50p rose violet	4.00	*6.00*
J2	D4	1d deep magenta	18	*30*
J3	D4	2d deep blue	5.25	*9.00*
J4	D4	5d orange	52	*90*
J5	D4	10d chocolate	2.75	*4.50*
		Nos. J1-J5 (5)	8.88	*15.00*

The overprint on the 50p exists inverted. Counterfeit overprints exist.

D1

D2

1941, Sept. 12 Litho. *Perf. 11*

J6	D1	50b carmine lake	15	*20*
J7	D1	1k carmine lake	15	*20*
J8	D1	2k carmine lake	15	*38*
J9	D1	5k carmine lake	22	*45*
J10	D1	10k carmine lake	35	*60*
		Nos. J6-J10 (5)	1.02	*1.83*

1943 *Perf. 11½, 12x12½, 12½*

Size: 24x24mm

J11	D2	50b lt blue & gray	15	15
J12	D2	1k lt blue & gray	15	15
J13	D2	2k lt blue & gray	15	*15*
J14	D2	4k lt blue & gray	15	*20*
J15	D2	5k lt blue & gray	15	*22*
J16	D2	6k lt blue & gray	15	*20*
J17	D2	10k blue & indigo	15	*28*
J18	D2	15k blue & indigo	15	*28*
J19	D2	20k blue & indigo	50	*80*
		Set value	1.35	

1942, July 30 *Perf. 10½, 11½*

Size: 25x24¼mm

J20	D2	50b lt blue & gray	15	*15*
J21	D2	1k lt blue & gray	15	*15*
J22	D2	2k lt blue & gray	18	*28*
J23	D2	5k lt blue & gray	15	*25*
J24	D2	10k lt blue & blue	32	*52*
J25	D2	20k lt blue & blue	55	*90*
		Nos. J20-J25 (6)	1.50	*2.25*

OFFICIAL STAMPS

Croatian Coat of Arms
O1 O2

Perf. 10½, 11½

1942-43 Unwmk. Litho.

Ordinary Paper

O1	O1	25b rose lake	15	15
O2	O1	50b slate blk	15	15
O3	O1	75b gray grn	15	15
O4	O1	1k org brn	15	15
O5	O1	2k turq bl	15	*15*
O6	O1	3k vermilion	15	15
O7	O1	4k brn vio	15	15
O8	O1	5k ultra	18	*35*
a.		Thin paper	4.50	*2.00*
O9	O1	6k brt vio	15	15
O10	O1	10k lt grn	15	15
O11	O1	12k brn rose	15	*15*
O12	O1	20k dark blue	15	*15*
O13	O2	30k brn vio & gray	15	*15*
O14	O2	40k vio blk & gray	15	*15*
O15	O2	50k brn lake & gray	32	*35*
O16	O2	100k blk & pink	32	*35*
		Set value	1.70	*2.35*

1943-44 Thin Paper *Perf. 11½*

O17	O1	25b claret	15	15
O18	O1	50b gray	15	15
O19	O1	75b dull green	15	15
O20	O1	1k org brn	15	15
O21	O1	2k slate blue	15	15
O22	O1	3.50k car rose	15	15
a.		Ordinary paper	4.50	*8.50*
O23	O1	6k brt red vio	15	15
O24	O1	12.50k deep orange	15	15
a.		Ordinary paper	3.00	*5.50*
		Set value	40	64

POSTAL TAX STAMPS

Nurse and Soldier — PT1

Wounded Soldier — PT2

Unwmk.

1942, Oct. 4 Litho. *Perf. 11*

RA1 PT1 1k olive grn & red 20 *30*

The tax aided the Croatian Red Cross. Issued in sheets of 24 plus label.

1943, Oct. 3

RA2 PT2 2k blue & red 15 *20*

The tax aided the Croatian Red Cross.

Ruins — PT3

Wounded Soldier — PT4

1944, Jan. 1 Photo. *Perf. 12*

RA3 PT3	1k dk slate green	15	*15*
RA4 PT4	2k carmine lake	15	*15*
RA5 PT4	5k black	15	*15*
RA6 PT4	10k deep blue	15	*22*
RA7 PT4	20k brown	28	*45*
	Set value	61	

Catalogue values for unused stamps in this section, from this point to the end of the section, are for Never Hinged items.

Interior of Zagreb Cathedral — PT10

1991, Apr. 1 Litho. *Perf. 14*

RA20 PT10 1.20d black & gold *38*
- *a.* Perf. 11x10½ *38*
- *b.* Perf. 11 *38*

Worker's Fund. No. RA20 was required on mail during April 1991.

For surcharges see Nos. 100, 100a.

15-Cent Minimum Value

The minimum catalogue value is 15 cents. Separating se-tenant pieces into individual stamps does not increase the value of the stamps since demand for the separated stamps may be small.

Shrine of the Virgin, 700th Anniv. — PT11

1991, May 16 *Perf. 10½x11*

RA21 PT11 1.70d multicolored *55*

Workers' Fund. No. RA21 was required on mail May 16-31, 1991.

Croatian Arms Type of 1992

1991, July 1 *Perf. 11x10½*

RA22 A37 2.20d multicolored *1.15*

No. RA22 was required on mail during July 1991.

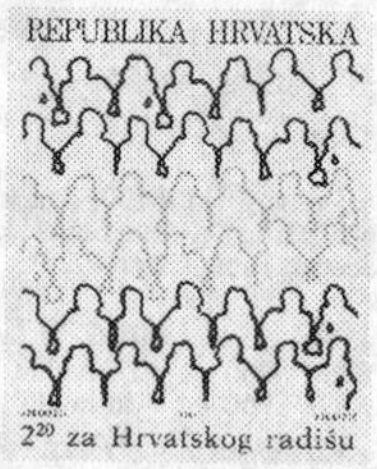

Members of Parliament PT12

1991, Aug. 1 *Perf. 11x10½*

RA23 PT12 2.20d multicolored *1.15*

Worker's Fund. No. RA23 was required on mail during Aug. 1991.

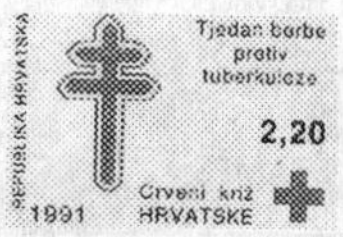

Red Cross and Tuberculosis PT13

1991, Sept 14 *Perf. 11*

RA24 PT13 2.20d blue & red *70*

Required on mail Sept. 14-21, 1991.

Re-erection of Ban Josip Jelacic Equestrian Statue, Zagreb — PT14

1991, Nov. 1 *Perf. 11x10½*

RA25 PT14 2.20d multicolored *38*
- *a.* Imperf. *70*

Worker's Fund. No. RA25 was required on mail during Nov. 1991.

"VUKOVAR" with Barbed Wire — PT16

1992, Jan. 1 Litho. *Perf. 11x10½*

RA32 PT16 2.20d black & brown *30*
- *a.* Imperf. *55*

Vukovar Refugee's Fund. No. RA32 was required on mail during Jan. 1992.

Red Cross PT17

Red Cross and Solidarity PT18

1992 *Perf. 11*

RA33 PT17 3d red & black *15*

RA34 PT18 3d red & black *15*

Issue dates: No. RA33, May 8. No. RA34, June 1.

No. RA33 was required on mail May 8-15, 1992; No. RA34, June 1-7, 1992.

Madonna of Bistrica — PT19

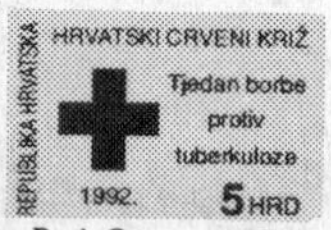

Red Cross — PT20

1992, Aug. 1 Litho. *Perf. 14*

RA35 PT19 5d blue & gold *15*

No. RA35 was required on mail, Aug. 1-8, 1992.

1992, Sept. 21 Litho. *Perf. 11*

RA36 PT20 5d black & red *25*

Required on mail Sept. 21-28, 1992.

St. George Slaying Dragon — PT21

1992, Nov. 4 *Perf. 14*

RA37 PT21 15d multicolored *15*

Cancer Research League. No. RA37 was required on mail Nov. 4-11, 1992.

See No. RA43.

Red Cross — PT22

1993, May 8 Litho. *Rough Perf. 11*

RA38 PT22 80d black & red *18*

No. RA38 was required on mail May 8-15, 1993.

Red Cross and Solidarity PT23

1993, June 1

RA39 PT23 100d black & red *1.10*

No. RA39 was required on mail June 1-7, 1993.

Cardinal Stepinac (1898-1960) — PT24

1993, July 15 Litho. *Perf. 14*

RA40 PT24 150d multicolored *18*

Required on mail July 15-22, 1993.

Zrinski-Frankopan Foundation — PT25

Design: 200d, Gen. Peter Zrinski (1621-1671), Politician and Fran Krsto Frankopan, Count of Tersat (1643-1671), Poet.

1993, Aug. 12 Litho. *Perf. 14*

RA41 PT25 200d gray & blue *18*

Required on mail Aug. 12-19, 1993.

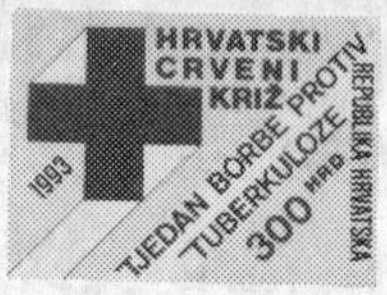

Red Cross Campaign Against Tuberculosis PT26

1993, Sept. 14 Litho. *Perf. 11*

RA42 PT26 300d gray, red & black *20*

Required on mail Sept. 14-21, 1993.

St. George Slaying Dragon Type of 1992

1993, Oct. 11 Litho. *Perf. 14*

RA43 PT21 400d multicolored *25*

Cancer Research League. Required on mail Oct. 11-31, 1993.

Save the Children of Croatia — PT27

1993, Nov. 1 *Perf. 13½x14*

RA44 PT27 400d multicolored *22*

Required on mail Nov. 1-30, 1993.

Croatian Red Cross — PT28

1994, May 5 Litho. *Perf. 11*

RA45 PT28 500d multicolored *25*

Required on mail May 8-15, 1994.

Red Cross Solidarity
PT29

Ludberg Church
PT30

1994, May 5	**Litho.**			***Perf. 11***
RA46	PT29	50 l multicolored	25	

Required on mail June 1-7, 1994.

1994, July 15				***Perf. 14***
RA47	PT30	50 l multicolored	25	

Required on mail July 15-22, 1994.

Save the Children of Croatia — PT31

St. George Slaying Dragon — PT32

1994, Aug. 16	**Litho.**			***Perf. 14***
RA48	PT31	50 l multicolored	22	

Required on mail Aug. 16-29, 1994.

1994, Sept. 1			
RA49	PT32	50 l multicolored	25

Cancer Research League. Required on mail Sept. 1-8, 1994.

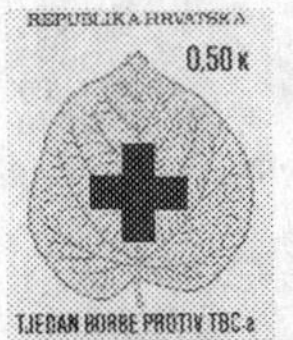

PT33

PT34

1994, Sept. 14				***Perf. 11***
RA50	PT33	50 l black, green & red	40	

Red Cross Campaign against Tuberculosis. Required on mail Sept. 14-21, 1994.

1994, Oct. 15	**Litho.**			***Perf. 14***
RA51	PT34	50 l multicolored	28	

Town of Slavonski Brod, 750th anniv.

CUBA

LOCATION — The largest island of the West Indies; south of Florida
GOVT. — Former Spanish possession
AREA — 44,206 sq. mi.
POP. — 6,743,000 (est. 1960)
CAPITAL — Havana

Formerly a Spanish possession, Cuba made several unsuccessful attempts to gain her freedom, which finally led to the intervention of the US in 1898. In that year under the Treaty of Paris, Spain relinquished the island to the US in trust for its inhabitants. In 1902 a republic was established and the Cuban Congress took over the government from the military authorities.

8 Reales Plata = 1 Peso
100 Centesimos = 1 Escudo or Peseta (1867)
1000 Milesimas = 100 Centavos = 1 Peso

Catalogue values for unused stamps in this country are for Never Hinged items, beginning with Scott 402 in the regular postage section, Scott B3 in the semi-postal section, Scott C38 in the airpost section, Scott CB1 in the airpost semi-postal section, Scott E15 in the special delivery section, and Scott RA1 in the postal tax section.

Pen cancellations are common on the earlier stamps of Cuba. Stamps so canceled sell for very much less than those with postmark cancellations.

Watermarks

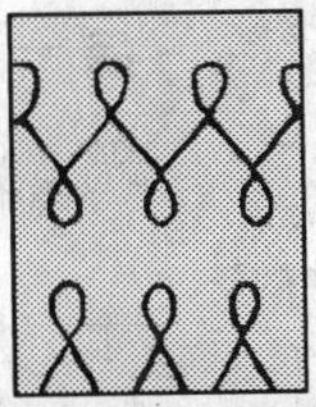

Wmk. 104- Loops

Wmk. 105- Crossed Lines

Wmk. 106- Star

Wmk. 229- Wavy Lines

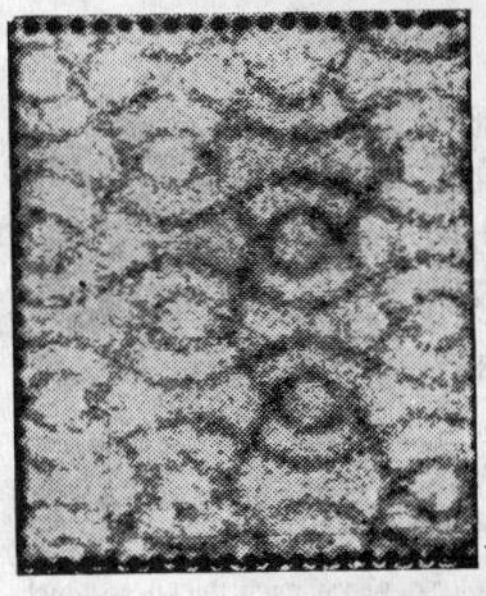

Wmk. 320

Wmk. 321- "R de C"

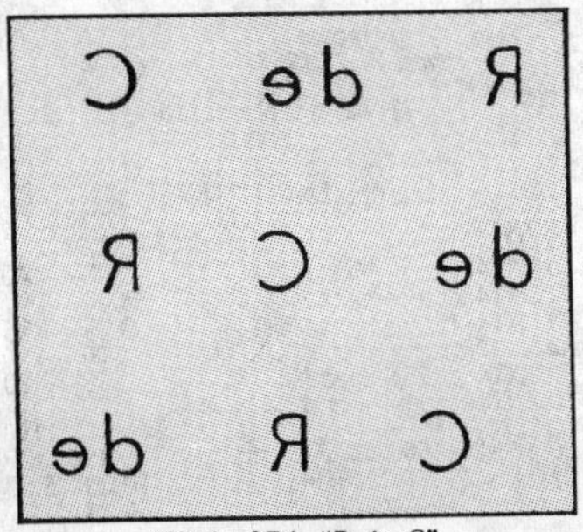

Wmk. 376- "R de C"

Issued under Spanish Dominion

Used also in Puerto Rico: Nos. 1-3, 9-14, 17-21, 32-34, 35A-37, 39-41, 43-45, 47-49, 51-53, 55-57.

Queen Isabella II — A1

Blue Paper

1855	**Typo.**	**Wmk. 104**		***Imperf.***
1	A1	½r p blue green	32.50	2.00
2	A1	1r p gray green	32.50	2.75
3	A1	2r p carmine	150.00	10.00
4	A1	2r p orange red	165.00	11.00
		Nos. 1-4 (4)	380.00	25.75

Nos. 2-3 also used in Philippines.
See Nos. 9-14. For surcharges see Nos. 5-8, 15.

Counterfeit surcharges are plentiful.

Nos. 3-4 Surcharged **Y ¼**

1855-56				
5	A1	¼r p on 2r p carmine	675.00	180.00
6	A1	¼r p on 2r p org red		275.00

Surcharged **Y ¼**

7	A1	¼r p on 2r p carmine	500.00	90.00
a.		Without fraction bar		325.00
8	A1	¼r p on 2r p org red	675.00	175.00
a.		Without fraction bar		450.00

The "Y ¼" surcharge met the "Ynterior" rate for delivery within the city of Havana.

Rough Yellowish Paper

1856				**Wmk. 105**
9	A1	½r p grnsh blue	7.50	1.25
10	A1	1r p green	350.00	10.50
a.		1r p emerald	400.00	13.00
11	A1	2r p orange red	225.00	14.00

White Smooth Paper

1857				**Unwmk.**
12	A1	½r p blue	4.00	60
13	A1	1r p gray green	3.75	60
a.		1r p pale yellow green	6.00	1.40
14	A1	2r p dull rose	15.00	2.75
		Nos. 12-14 (3)	22.75	3.95

Surcharged **Y ¼**

1860				
15	A1	¼r p on 2r p dl rose	175.00	60.00
a.		1 of ¼ inverted	210.00	125.00

Queen Isabella II
A2 A3

1862-64				***Imperf.***
16	A2	¼r p black	21.00	10.00
17	A3	¼r p blk, *buff* ('64)	21.00	10.00
18	A3	½r p green ('64)	4.75	70
19	A3	½r p grn, *pale rose* ('64)	11.00	3.00
20	A3	1r p bl, *sal* ('64)	4.75	1.00
a.		Diagonal half used as ½r p on cover		100.00
21	A3	2r p ver, *buff* ('64)	27.50	7.75
		Nos. 16-21 (6)	90.00	32.45

No. 17 Overprinted in Black **66**

1866				
22	A3	¼r p black, *buff*	65.00	22.50

Exists with handstamped "1866."

A5

A6

1866				
23	A5	5c dull violet	47.50	22.50
24	A5	10c blue	1.75	1.00
25	A5	20c green	1.65	1.00
26	A5	40c rose	11.00	9.00
		Nos. 23-26 (4)	61.90	33.50

Stamps Dated "1867"

1867				***Perf. 14***
27	A5	5c dull violet	35.00	13.00
28	A5	10c blue	6.00	1.00
a.		Imperf., pair	18.00	6.00
29	A5	20c green	6.00	1.00
a.		Imperf., pair	40.00	65.00
30	A5	40c rose	12.50	7.50
		Nos. 27-30 (4)	59.50	22.50

Stamps Dated "1868"

1868				
31	A6	5c dull violet	20.00	8.25
32	A6	10c blue	3.75	1.75
a.		Diagonal half used as 5c on cover		100.00
33	A6	20c green	7.50	3.50
a.		Diagonal half used as 10c on cover		125.00
34	A6	40c rose	14.00	8.00
		Nos. 31-34 (4)	45.25	21.50

Nos. 31-34 Overprinted in Black **HABILITADO POR LA NACION.**

1868				
35	A6	5c dull violet	55.00	25.00
35A	A6	10c blue	55.00	25.00
36	A6	20c green	55.00	25.00
37	A6	40c rose	55.00	25.00
		Nos. 35-37 (4)	220.00	100.00

1869				**Stamps Dated "1869"**
38	A6	5c rose	45.00	12.00
39	A6	10c red brown	4.25	1.75
a.		Diagonal half used as 5c on cover		75.00
40	A6	20c orange	8.50	2.75
41	A6	40c dull violet	35.00	8.25
		Nos. 38-41 (4)	92.75	24.75

Nos. 38-41 Ovptd. Like Nos. 35-37

42	A6	5c rose	140.00	32.50
43	A6	10c red brown	52.50	20.00
44	A6	20c orange	42.50	27.50
45	A6	40c dull violet	65.00	27.50
		Nos. 42-45 (4)	300.00	107.50

"Espana"
A8 A9

1870 *Perf. 14*

46 A8 5c blue 110.00 45.00
47 A8 10c green 3.00 90
a. Diagonal half used as 5c on cover 90.00
48 A8 20c red brown 3.00 90
a. Diagonal half used as 10c on cover 90.00
49 A8 40c rose 150.00 25.00

1871

50 A9 12c red lilac 19.00 8.00
a. Imperf., pair 55.00 55.00
51 A9 25c ultra 2.50 80
a. Imperf., pair 27.50 27.50
b. Diagonal half used as 12c on cover 125.00
52 A9 50c gray green 2.50 80
a. Imperf., pair 42.50 30.00
b. Diagonal half used as 25c on cover 125.00
53 A9 1p pale brown 25.00 8.00
a. Imperf., pair 42.50 42.50
Nos. 50-53 (4) 49.00 17.60

King Amadeo — A10

1873 *Perf. 14*

54 A10 12½c dark green 35.00 12.50
55 A10 25c gray 2.50 1.00
a. Diagonal half used as 12½c on cover 75.00
56 A10 50c brown 1.40 1.25
a. Imperf., pair 37.50 37.50
b. Half used as 25c on cover 75.00
57 A10 1p red brown 200.00 40.00
a. Diagonal half used as 50c on cover 200.00

"España" A11

Coat of Arms A12

1874

58 A11 12½c brown 13.00 6.00
59 A11 25c ultra 1.00 1.00
a. Diagonal half used as 12½c on cover 75.00
60 A11 50c dp violet 1.75 1.00
61 A11 50c gray 1.75 1.00
a. Diagonal half used as 25c on cover 75.00
62 A11 1p carmine 75.00 30.00
a. Imperf., pair 175.00 175.00
Nos. 58-62 (5) 92.50 39.00

1875

63 A12 12½c lt violet 1.10 60
a. Imperf., pair 35.00
64 A12 25c ultra 55 48
a. Imperf., pair 35.00
b. Diagonal half used as 12½c on cover 75.00
65 A12 50c blue green 55 48
a. Imperf., pair 35.00
b. Diagonal half used as 25c on cover 45.00
66 A12 1p brown 7.75 4.75
a. 1p dk brown 7.75 4.75
b. Half used as 50c on cover 85.00
Nos. 63-66 (4) 9.95 6.31

King Alfonso XII
A13 A14

1876

67 A13 12½c green 2.00 50
68 A13 25c gray 70 32
a. Diagonal half used as 12½c on cover 75.00
69 A13 50c ultra 70 40
a. Imperf., pair 11.50
70 A13 1p black 8.00 3.50
a. Imperf., pair 27.50
Nos. 67-70 (4) 11.40 4.72

1877

71 A14 10c lt green 32.50
72 A14 12½c gray 7.00 1.25
a. Imperf., pair 20.00
73 A14 25c dk green 52 40
a. Imperf., pair 20.00
74 A14 50c black 52 40
a. Imperf., pair 20.00
b. Half used as 25c on cover 75.00
75 A14 1p brown 22.50 15.00
Nos. 71-75 (5) 63.04

No. 71 was not placed in use.

Stamps Dated "1878"

1878

76 A14 5c blue 48 40
77 A14 10c black 55.00
78 A14 12½c brown bis 3.25 1.25
a. 12½c gray bister 2.00 1.00
79 A14 25c dp green 35 20
b. Diagonal half used as 12½c on cover 60.00
80 A14 50c dk blue grn 35 20
81 A14 1p carmine 10.00 5.50
Nos. 76-81 (6) 69.43

No. 77 was not placed in use.

Imperf., Pairs

76a A14 5c blue 20.00
77a A14 10c black 150.00
78b A14 12½c brown bister 20.00
79a A14 25c deep green 20.00
80a A14 50c dk blue green 20.00
81a A14 1p carmine 40.00

Stamps Dated "1879"

82 A14 5c slate black 70 35
83 A14 10c orange 125.00 65.00
84 A14 12½c rose 70 35
85 A14 25c ultra 50 35
a. Diagonal half used as 12½c on cover 75.00
b. Imperf., pair 40.00 30.00
86 A14 50c gray 45 30
a. Diagonal half used as 25c on cover 75.00
87 A14 1p olive bister 21.00 12.00
Nos. 82-87 (6) 148.35 78.35

A15

A16

A17

1880

88 A15 5c green 38 15
89 A15 10c lake 60.00
90 A15 12½c gray 38 15
91 A15 25c gray blue 38 15
a. Diagonal half used as 12½c on cover 75.00
92 A15 50c brown 38 15
a. Half used as 25c on cover 75.00
93 A15 1p yellow brn 7.00 3.00
Nos. 88-93 (6) 68.52

No. 89 was not placed in use.

1881

94 A16 1c green 38 15
95 A16 2c lake 32.50
96 A16 2½c olive bister 65 30
97 A16 5c gray blue 38 15
98 A16 10c yellow brown 38 15
99 A16 20c dark brown 7.00 5.00
Nos. 94-99 (6) 41.29

No. 95 was not placed in use.

1882

100 A17 1c green 45 32
101 A17 2c lake 2.75 32
102 A17 2½c dk brown 6.00 2.00
103 A17 5c gray blue 2.75 70
a. Diagonal half used as 2½c on cover 75.00
104 A17 10c olive bister 45 15
105 A17 20c red brown 77.50 32.50
Nos. 100-105 (6) 89.90 35.99

See #121-131. For surcharges see #106-120.

Issue of 1882 Surcharged or Overprinted in Black, Blue or Red:

a

b

c

d

e

1883

Type "a"

106 A17 5 on 5c (R) 1.75 90
a. Triple surcharge
b. Double surcharge 3.25 3.25
c. Inverted surcharge 2.50 2.50
d. Without "5" in surcharge 7.25 7.25
e. Dbl. surch., types "a" & "d"
107 A17 10 on 10c (Bl) 1.75 90
a. Inverted surcharge
b. Double surcharge 2.75
108 A17 20 on 20c 22.50 19.00
a. "10" instead of "20" 50.00 50.00
b. Double surcharge

Type "b"

109 A17 5 on 5c (R) 1.75 90
a. Inverted surcharge 2.50 2.50
b. Double surcharge 3.50
110 A17 10 on 10c (Bl) 2.75 1.50
a. Inverted surcharge 3.50 3.50
b. Double surcharge
111 A17 20 on 20c 25.00 18.00
a. Double surcharge
b. Dbl. surch., types "b" & "c"

Type "c"

112 A17 5 on 5c (R) 1.75 1.10
a. Inverted surcharge
b. Dbl. surch., types "c" & "d" 4.25
113 A17 10 on 10c (Bl) 4.25 1.75
a. Inverted surcharge
b. Double surcharge
114 A17 20 on 20c 35.00 18.00
a. "10" instead of "20" 90.00 90.00
b. Double surcharge
c. Dbl. surch., types "a" & "c"

Type "d"

115 A17 5 on 5c (R) 1.75 1.10
a. Inverted surcharge 2.50 2.50
b. Double surcharge
116 A17 10 on 10c (Bl) 4.25 1.75
a. Inverted surcharge
b. Double surcharge
117 A17 20 on 20c 60.00 25.00
a. Dbl. surch., types "a" & "d"

Type "e"

118 A17 5c gray blue (R) 2.75 1.65
a. Double overprint 4.50
119 A17 10c olive bis (Bl) 4.25 3.50
a. Double overprint
120 A17 20c red brown 72.50 32.50
a. Double overprint
Nos. 106-120 (15) 242.00 127.55

Handstamped overprints and surcharges are counterfeits.

Type of 1882

Original

1st retouch

2d retouch

The differences between the stamps of 1882 and the various retouches are as follows:

Original state: The medallion is surrounded by a heavy line of color of nearly even thickness, touching the horizontal line below the word "Cuba" (or "Filipinas," "Puerto Rico", as the case may be); the opening in the hair above the temple is narrow and pointed.

1st retouch: The line around the medallion is thin, except at the upper right, and does not touch the horizontal line above it; the opening in the hair is slightly wider and a trifle rounded; the lock of hair above the forehead is shaped like a broad "V" and ends in a point; there is a faint white line below it, which is not found on the stamps in the original state. Owing to wear of the plate the shape of the lock of hair and the width of the white line below it vary.

2nd retouch: The opening in the hair forms a semi-circle; the lock above the forehead is nearly straight, having only a slight wave, and the white line is much broader than before.

1883-86

121 A17 1c grn, 2nd retouch 1.25 15
122 A17 2½c olive bister 32 15
124 A17 2½c violet 32 15
a. 2½c red lilac ('85) 40 15
b. 2½c ultramarine 110.00 42.50
125 A17 5c gray bl, 1st retouch 1.25 15
126 A17 5c gray bl, 2nd retouch 4.00 1.00
a. Diagonal half used as 2½c on cover 30.00
127 A17 10c brn, 1st retouch 1.65 50
a. Diagonal half used as 5c on cover 30.00
128 A17 20c olive bister 11.50 2.75
Nos. 121-128 (7) 20.29 4.85

1888

129 A17 2½c red brown 2.25 1.25
130 A17 10c blue 1.25 80
a. Diagonal half used as 5c on cover
131 A17 20c brnsh gray 11.00 4.75
Nos. 129-131 (3) 14.50 6.80

King Alfonso XIII
A18 A19

1890-97

132 A18 1c gray brn 11.00 4.25
133 A18 1c ol gray ('91) 7.00 90
134 A18 1c ultra ('94) 2.00 35
135 A18 1c dk vio ('96) 1.00 16
136 A18 2c slate blue 4.25 1.00
137 A18 2c lil brn ('91) 1.00 35
138 A18 2c rose ('94) 17.50 2.50
139 A18 2c claret ('96) 6.00 60
140 A18 2½c emerald 7.00 1.75
141 A18 2½c salmon ('91) 21.00 4.25
142 A18 2½c lilac ('94) 1.75 24
143 A18 2½c rose ('96) 70 15
144 A18 5c olive gray 70 52
145 A18 5c emer ('91) 90 45
146 A18 5c sl blue ('96) 35 15
147 A18 10c brn vio 1.75 60
148 A18 10c claret ('91) 1.25 45
149 A18 10c emer ('96) 2.00 16
150 A18 20c dk vio 80 52
151 A18 20c ultra ('91) 11.00 4.25
152 A18 20c red brn ('94) 17.50 4.25
153 A18 20c vio ('96) 17.50 5.25
154 A18 40c org brn ('97) 35.00 10.50
155 A18 80c lil brn ('97) 45.00 14.00
Nos. 132-155 (24) 213.95 57.60

Imperf., Pairs

134a A18 1c ultramarine 150.00
138a A18 2c rose 150.00
142a A18 2½c lilac 150.00
145a A18 5c emerald 150.00
148a A18 10c claret 150.00
152a A18 20c red brown 200.00

1898

156 A19 1m orange brn 15 15
157 A19 2m orange brn 15 15
158 A19 3m orange brn 15 15
159 A19 4m orange brn 3.25 1.40
160 A19 5m orange brn 15 15
161 A19 1c black vio 15 15
162 A19 2c dk blue grn 15 15
163 A19 3c dk brown 15 15
164 A19 4c orange 9.75 3.50
165 A19 5c car rose 70 16
a. Imperf., pair 100.00
166 A19 6c dk blue 15 15
a. Imperf., pair 100.00
167 A19 8c gray brown 70 35
168 A19 10c vermilion 70 35
169 A19 15c slate green 3.25 35
170 A19 20c maroon 40 16
171 A19 40c dark lilac 1.65 35
172 A19 60c black 1.65 35
173 A19 80c red brown 11.00 7.00
174 A19 1p yel green 11.00 7.00
175 A19 2p slate blue 16.00 7.00
Nos. 156-175 (20) 61.25 29.17

Nos. 156-160 were issued for use on newspapers.
For surcharges see Nos. 176-189C, 196-200.

Issued under Administration of the United States
Puerto Principe Issue

Issues of Cuba of 1898 and 1896 Surcharged:

HABILITADO
1
cent.
a

HABILITADO
1
cents.
b

HABILITADO
2
cents.
c

HABILITADO
2
cents.
d

HABILITADO
3
cents.
e

HABILITADO
3
cents.
f

HABILITADO
5
cents.
g

HABILITADO
5
cents.
h

HABILITADO
5
cents.
i

HABILITADO
5
cents.
j

HABILITADO
3
cents.
k

HABILITADO
3
cents.
l

HABILITADO
10
cents.
m

Types a, c, d, e, f, g and h are 17 1/2mm high, the others are 19 1/2mm high.

Black Surcharge On Nos. 156, 157, 158 and 160

1898-99

176 (a) 1c on 1m org brn 45.00 30.00
177 (b) 1c on 1m org brn 45.00 35.00
a. Broken figure "1" 75.00 65.00
b. Inverted surcharge 200.00
d. As "a," inverted *250.00*
178 (c) 2c on 2m org brn 22.50 18.00
a. Inverted surcharge 250.00 50.00
179 (d) 2c on 2m org brn 40.00 35.00
a. Inverted surcharge 350.00 100.00
179B (k) 3c on 1m org brn 300.00 175.00
c. Double surcharge 1,500. 750.00
179D (l) 3c on 1m org brn *1,500.* *675.00*
e. Double surcharge
179F (e) 3c on 2m org brn *1,500.*

Value is for copy with minor faults.

179G (f) 3c on 2m org brn *2,000.*

Value is for copy with minor faults.

180 (e) 3c on 3m org brn 27.50 30.00
a. Inverted surcharge *100.00*
181 (f) 3c on 3m org brn 75.00 75.00
a. Inverted surcharge *200.00*
182 (g) 5c on 1m org brn 700.00 200.00
a. Inverted surcharge *500.00*
183 (h) 5c on 1m org brn *1,300.* *500.00*
a. Inverted surcharge *700.00*
184 (g) 5c on 2m org brn 750.00 250.00
185 (h) 5c on 2m org brn 1,500. 500.00
186 (g) 5c on 3m org brn 165.00
a. Inverted surcharge 700.00
187 (h) 5c on 3m org brn 400.00
a. Inverted surcharge 1,000.
188 (g) 5c on 5m org brn 70.00 60.00
a. Inverted surcharge 400.00 200.00
b. Double surcharge
189 (h) 5c on 5m org brn 350.00 250.00
a. Inverted surcharge 400.00
b. Double surcharge

The 2nd printing of Nos. 188-189 has shiny ink. Values are for the 1st printing.

189C (i) 5c on 5m org brn *7,500.*

Black Surcharge on No. P25

190 (g) 5c on 1/2m bl grn 250.00 75.00
a. Inverted surcharge 500.00 150.00
b. Pair, right stamp without surcharge 500.00

Value for No. 190b is for pair with unsurcharged copy at right. Exists with unsurcharged stamp at left.

191 (h) 5c on 1/2m bl grn 300.00 90.00
a. Inverted surcharge 200.00
192 (i) 5c on 1/2m bl grn 550.00 200.00
a. Dbl. surch., one diagonal *8,500.*
193 (j) 5c on 1/2m bl grn 700.00 300.00

Red Surcharge on No. 161

196 (k) 3c on 1c blk vio 60.00 35.00
a. Inverted surcharge 300.00
197 (l) 3c on 1c blk vio 125.00 55.00
a. Inverted surcharge 300.00
198 (i) 5c on 1c blk vio 20.00 25.00
a. Inverted surcharge 125.00
b. Surcharge vert. up *3,500.*
c. Double surcharge *400.00* *600.00*
d. Dbl. invtd. surch.

No. 198b exists reading down.

199 (j) 5c on 1c blk vio 50.00 50.00
a. Inverted surcharge 250.00
b. Vertical surcharge *2,000.*
c. Double surcharge 1,000. 600.00
200 (m) 10c on 1c blk vio 20.00 *50.00*
a. Broken figure "1" 40.00 *100.00*

Black Surcharge on Nos. P26-P30

201 (k) 3c on 1m bl grn 350. 350.
a. Inverted surcharge 450.
b. "EENTS" 550. 450.
c. As "b," inverted 850.
202 (l) 3c on 1m bl grn 500. 400.
a. Inverted surcharge 850.
203 (k) 3c on 2m bl grn 850. 350.
a. "EENTS" 1,250. 450.
b. Inverted surcharge 850.
c. As "a," inverted 950.
204 (l) 3c on 2m bl grn 1,250. 600.
a. Inverted surcharge 750.
205 (k) 3c on 3m bl grn 900. 350.
a. Inverted surcharge 500.
b. "EENTS" 1,250. 450.
c. As "b," inverted 700.
206 (l) 3c on 3m bl grn 1,200. 550.
a. Inverted surcharge 700.
211 (i) 5c on 1m bl grn 1,800.
a. "EENTS" 2,500.
212 (j) 5c on 1m bl grn 2,500.
213 (i) 5c on 2m bl grn 1,800.
a. "EENTS" 1,900.
214 (j) 5c on 2m bl grn 1,900.
(i) 5c on 3m bl grn 500.
a. "EENTS" 1,000.
216 (j) 5c on 3m bl grn 1,000.
217 (i) 5c on 4m bl grn *2,500.* 900.
a. "EENTS" *3,000.* 1,500.
b. Inverted surcharge *2,000.*
c. As "a," inverted 2,000.
218 (j) 5c on 4m bl grn *1,500.*
a. Inverted surcharge *2,000.*
219 (i) 5c on 8m bl grn *2,500.* 1,250.
a. Inverted surcharge 1,500.
b. "EENTS" 1,800.
c. As "b," inverted 2,500.
220 (j) 5c on 8m bl grn 2,000.
a. Inverted surcharge 2,500.

CUBA

United States Nos. 279, 267, 279B, 268, 281, 282C and 283 Surcharged in Black

1 c.
de PESO.

1899 Wmk. 191 *Perf. 12*

221 A87 1c on 1c yel grn 4.50 30
222 A88 2c on 2c car 5.00 35
a. 2c on 2c red 5.50 25
c. Inverted surcharge *3,500.* *3,500.*
223 A88 2 1/2c on 2c carmine 3.00 40
a. 2 1/2c on 2c red 3.50 1.40
224 A89 3c on 3c pur 8.50 1.50
a. Period btwn. "B" and "A" 25.00 25.00
225 A91 5c on 5c bl 8.50 1.75
226 A94 10c on 10c brn, type I 16.00 5.50
b. "CUBA" omitted *4,000.* *4,000.*
226A A94 10c on 10c brn, type II *5,000.*
Nos. 221-226 (6) 45.50 9.80

The 2 1/2c was sold and used as a 2c stamp.

Excellent counterfeits of this and the preceding issue exist, especially inverted and double surcharges.

Issues of the Republic under US Military Rule

Statue of Columbus
A20

Royal Palms
A21

"Cuba"
A22

Ocean Liner
A23

Cane Field — A24

1899 Engr. Wmk. 191C *Perf. 12*

227 A20 1c yel grn 3.50 15
228 A21 2c carmine 3.50 15
a. 2c scarlet 3.50 15
b. Booklet pane of 6 ('02) *2,000.*
229 A22 3c purple 3.50 16
230 A23 5c blue 3.50 20
231 A24 10c brown 11.00 50
Nos. 227-231 (5) 25.00 1.16

No. 228b was issued by the Republic.

Issues of the Republic

No. 229 Surcharged in Carmine

HABILITADO
UN CENTAVO 1 OCTUBRE 1902

1902, Sept. 30

232 A22 1c on 3c purple 1.00 50
a. Inverted surcharge 150.00 150.00
b. Surcharge sideways (numeral horizontal)
c. Double surcharge 200.00 200.00

Counterfeits of the errors are plentiful.

Re-engraved

The re-engraved stamps of 1905-07 may be distinguished from the issue of 1899 as follows:

ORIGINAL RE-ENGRAVED

1c- The ends of the label inscribed "Centavo" are rounded instead of square.

2c- The foliate ornaments, inside the oval disks bearing the numerals of value, have been removed.

5c- Two lines forming a right angle have been added in the upper corners of the label bearing the word "Cuba."

10c- A small ball has been added to each of the square ends of the label bearing the word "Cuba."

1905 Unwmk. *Perf. 12*

233 A20 1c green 1.65 15
234 A21 2c rose 1.10 15
a. Booklet pane of 6 135.00
236 A23 5c blue 32.50 1.00
237 A24 10c brown 3.00 45
Nos. 233-237 (4) 38.25 1.75

Maj. Gen. Antonio Maceo — A26

1907

238 A26 50c gray bl & blk 1.00 75

Bartolomé Masó
A27

Máximo Gómez
A28

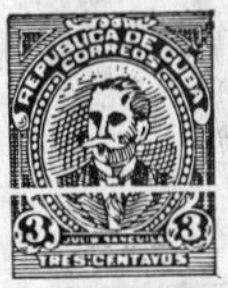
Julio Sanguily
A29

Ignacio Agramonte
A30

Calixto García
A31

José M. Rodriquez y Rodriquez (Mayia)
A32

Carlos Roloff — A33

1910, Feb. 1

239 A27 1c grn & vio 75 15
a. Center inverted 150.00 *150.00*
240 A28 2c car & grn 1.50 15
a. Center inverted 500.00 *500.00*
241 A29 3c vio & bl 1.00 20
242 A30 5c bl & grn 14.00 80
243 A31 8c ol & vio 1.00 32
244 A32 10c brn & bl 6.25 65
a. Center inverted 750.00
245 A26 50c vio & blk 1.50 48
246 A33 1p slate & blk 7.00 4.00
Nos. 239-246 (8) 33.00 6.75

1911-13

247 A27 1c green 45 15
248 A28 2c car rose 60 15
a. Booklet pane of 6 ('13) 75.00
250 A30 5c ultra 1.50 15
251 A31 8c ol grn & blk 90 60
252 A33 1p black 4.25 2.00
Nos. 247-252 (5) 7.70 3.05

Map of Cuba — A34

1914-15

253 A34 1c green 42 15
a. Booklet pane of 6 80.00
254 A34 2c car rose 60 15
a. Booklet pane of 6 80.00
255 A34 2c red ('15) 1.25 15
a. Booklet pane of 6 80.00
256 A34 3c violet 4.00 30
257 A34 5c blue 5.75 15
258 A34 8c ol grn 4.50 60
259 A34 10c brown 8.50 30
260 A34 10c ol grn ('15) 10.00 45
261 A34 50c orange 65.00 8.75
262 A34 1p gray 90.00 20.00
Nos. 253-262 (10) 190.02 31.00

Imperf. pairs, value each $100 to $500.

Gertrudis Gómez de Avellaneda, Cuban Poetess (1814-73)
A34a

1914

263	A34a	5c blue	10.50	5.00

José Martí
A35

Máximo Gómez
A36

José de la Luz Caballero — A37

Calixto García — A38

Ignacio Agramonte
A39

Tomás Estrada Palma
A40

José A. Saco
A41

Antonio Maceo
A42

Carlos Manuel de Céspedes — A43

1917-18 Unwmk. *Perf. 12*

264	A35	1c bl grn	80	15
a.		Booklet pane of 6	37.50	
b.		Booklet pane of 30	250.00	
265	A36	2c rose	60	15
a.		Booklet pane of 6	50.00	
b.		Booklet pane of 30	210.00	
266	A36	2c lt red ('18)	60	15
a.		Booklet pane of 6	50.00	
267	A37	3c violet	1.00	15
a.		Imperf. pair	275.00	
b.		Booklet pane of 6	50.00	
268	A38	5c dp bl	2.00	15
269	A39	8c red brn	4.75	15
270	A40	10c yel brn	2.50	15
271	A41	20c gray grn	9.50	1.00
272	A42	50c dl rose	11.00	1.00
273	A43	1p black	11.00	1.00
		Nos. 264-273 (10)	43.75	
		Set value		3.50

1925-28 Wmk. 106 *Perf. 12*

274	A35	1c bl grn	1.25	15
a.		Booklet pane of 30	325.00	
275	A36	2c brt rose	1.10	15
a.		Booklet pane of 6	70.00	
b.		Booklet pane of 30	325.00	
276	A38	5c dp bl	2.25	15
277	A39	8c red brn ('28)	4.50	50
278	A40	10c yel brn ('27)	5.25	60
279	A41	20c olive grn	8.25	1.00
		Nos. 274-279 (6)	22.60	2.55

1926 *Imperf.*

280	A35	1c blue green	1.10	95
281	A36	2c brt rose	1.00	80
282	A38	5c deep blue	1.65	1.65
		Nos. 280-282 (3)	3.75	3.40

See Nos. 304-310. For overprint and surcharge see Nos. 317-318, 644.

Arms of Republic
A44

1927, May 20 Unwmk. *Perf. 12*

283	A44	25c violet	7.25	3.00

25th anniversary of the Republic.
For surcharges see Nos. 355, C3.

Tomás Estrada Palma — A45

Designs: 2c, Gen. Gerardo Machado. 5c, Morro Castle. 8c, Havana Railway Station. 10c, Presidential Palace. 13c, Tobacco Plantation. 20c, Treasury Building. 30c, Sugar Mill. 50c, Havana Cathedral. 1p, Galician Clubhouse, Havana.

1928, Jan. 2 Wmk. 106

284	A45	1c deep green	32	20
285	A45	2c brt rose	32	20
286	A45	5c deep blue	95	30
287	A45	8c lt red brn	1.50	75
288	A45	10c bister brn	80	50
289	A45	13c orange	1.25	50
290	A45	20c olive grn	1.50	65
291	A45	30c dk violet	2.75	50
292	A45	50c carmine rose	4.50	1.75
293	A45	1p gray black	9.00	4.00
		Nos. 284-293 (10)	22.89	9.35

Sixth Pan-American Conference.

Capitol, Havana
A55

1929, May 18

294	A55	1c green	25	40
295	A55	2c carmine rose	25	35
296	A55	5c blue	38	50
297	A55	10c bister brn	75	60
298	A55	20c violet	2.50	2.50
		Nos. 294-298 (5)	4.13	4.35

Opening of the Capitol, Havana.

Hurdler — A56

1930, Mar. 15 Engr.

299	A56	1c green	40	25
300	A56	2c carmine	40	25
301	A56	5c deep blue	60	25
302	A56	10c bister brn	90	80
303	A56	20c violet	4.00	2.50
		Nos. 299-303 (5)	6.30	4.05

2nd Central American Athletic Games.

Types of 1917 Portrait Issue
Flat Plate Printing

1930-45 Wmk. 106 Engr. *Perf. 10*

304	A35	1c blue green	85	25
a.		Booklet pane of 6	50.00	
b.		Booklet pane of 30		
305	A36	2c brt rose	160.00	75.00
a.		Booklet pane of 6	1,200.	
305B	A37	3c dk rose vio ('42)	2.25	30
c.		Booklet pane of 6	42.50	
306	A38	5c dk blue	2.75	20
306A	A39	8c red brn ('45)	2.75	25
307	A40	10c brown	2.75	25
a.		10c yellow brown ('35)	3.50	75
307B	A41	20c olive grn ('41)	4.75	75
		Nos. 304-307B (7)	176.10	77.00

Nos. 305 and 305B were printed for booklet panes and all copies have straight edges.
For surcharge see No. 644.

Rotary Press Printing

308	A35	1c blue grn	1.10	15
309	A36	2c brt rose	1.10	15
a.		Booklet pane of 50		
310	A37	3c violet	1.50	15
a.		3c dull violet ('38)	1.10	15
b.		3c rose violet ('41)	1.10	15
c.		Booklet pane of 50		
		Set value		30

Flat plate stamps measure 18½x21½mm; rotary press, 19x22mm.

The Mangos of Baragua — A57

War Memorial — A61

Battle of Mal Tiempo
A58

Battle of Coliseo
A59

Maceo, Gómez and Zayas — A60

Perf. 12½

1933, Apr. 23 Photo. Wmk. 229

312	A57	3c dk brown	55	15
313	A58	5c dk blue	55	25
314	A59	10c emerald	1.65	25
315	A60	13c red	1.65	65
316	A61	20c black	3.25	2.00
		Nos. 312-316 (5)	7.65	3.30

War of Independence and dedication of the "Soldado Invasor" monument.

Types of 1917 Issues with Carmine or Black Overprint Reading Up or Down

GOBIERNO REVOLUCIONARIO 4-9-1933

Rotary Press Printing
Wmk. 106

1933, Dec. 23 Engr. *Perf. 10*

317	A35	1c blue green (C)	30	15

With Additional Surcharge of New Value and Bars

318	A37	2c on 3c vio (Bk)	30	15

Establishment of a revolutionary junta.

Dr. Carlos J. Finlay — A62

1934, Dec. 3 Engr. *Perf. 10*

319	A62	2c dark carmine	45	15
320	A62	5c dark blue	1.00	35

Cent. of the birth of Dr. Carlos J. Finlay (1833-1915), physician-biologist who found that a mosquito transmitted yellow fever.

Pres. José Miguel Gómez — A63

Gómez Monument — A64

1936, May *Perf. 10*

322	A63	1c green	28	15
323	A64	2c carmine	65	15

Unveiling of a monument to Gen. José Miguel Gómez, ex-president.

Matanzas Issue

Map of Cuba
A65

Designs: 2c, Map of Free Zone. 4c, S. S. "Rex" in Matanzas Bay. 5c, Ships in Matanzas Bay. 8c, Caves of Bellamar. 10c, Valley of Yumuri. 20c, Yumuri River. 50c, Ships Leaving Port.

Perf. 12½

1936, May 5 Photo. Wmk. 229

324	A65	1c blue green	20	15
325	A65	2c red	30	15
326	A65	4c claret	65	20
327	A65	5c ultra	55	20
328	A65	8c orange brn	1.25	50
329	A65	10c emerald	1.00	50
330	A65	20c brown	2.50	1.75
331	A65	50c slate	4.00	2.50
		Nos. 324-331,C18-C21,CE1,E8 (14)	24.08	13.58

Exist imperf. Value 20% more.

"Peace and Work"
A73

Máximo Gómez Monument — A74

Torch — A75

"Independence" — A76

"Messenger of Peace" — A77

1936, Nov. 18 *Perf. 12½*

332	A73	1c emerald	20	15
333	A74	2c crimson	24	15
334	A75	4c maroon	30	15
335	A76	5c ultra	1.00	40
336	A77	8c dk green	1.65	80
		Nos. 332-336,C22-C23,E9 (8)	7.64	3.32

Maj. Gen. Máximo Gómez, birth centenary.

Sugar Cane — A78

Primitive Sugar Mill — A79

Modern Sugar Mill — A80

Wmk. 106

1937, Oct. 2	**Engr.**	***Perf. 10***	
337 A78 1c yellow green		35	22
338 A79 2c red		25	15
339 A80 5c bright blue		35	28
Nos. 337-339 (3)		95	65

Cuban sugar cane industry, 400th anniv.

Argentine Emblem — A81

Mountain Scene (Bolivia) — A82

Arms of Brazil — A83

Canadian Scene — A84

Camilo Henriquez (Chile) — A85

Gen. Francisco de Paula Santander (Colombia) — A86

Natl. Monument (Costa Rica) — A87

Autograph of José Marti (Cuba) — A88

Columbus Lighthouse (Dominican Rep.) A89

Juan Montalvo (Ecuador) A90

Abraham Lincoln (US) A91

Quetzal and Scroll (Guatemala) A92

Arms of Haiti — A93

Francisco Morazán (Honduras) — A94

Fleet of Columbus — A95

Wmk. 106

1937, Oct. 13	**Engr.**	***Perf. 10***	
340 A81 1c dp green		35	42
341 A82 1c green		35	42
342 A83 2c carmine		35	42
343 A84 2c carmine		35	42
344 A85 3c violet		1.00	1.25
345 A86 3c violet		1.00	1.25
346 A87 4c bister brn		1.10	1.50
347 A88 4c bister brn		2.00	2.50
348 A89 5c blue		1.00	1.25
349 A90 5c blue		1.00	1.25
350 A91 8c citron		7.00	8.50
351 A92 8c citron		1.75	2.00
352 A93 10c maroon		1.75	2.00
353 A94 10c maroon		1.75	2.00
354 A95 25c rose lilac		17.50	21.00
Nos. 340-354,C24-C29,E10-E11 (23)		76.25	85.68

Nos. 340-354 were sold by the Cuban PO for 3 days, Oct. 13-15, during which no other stamps were sold. They were postally valid for the full face value. Proceeds from their three-day sale above 30,000 pesos were paid by the Cuban POD to the Assoc. of American Writers and Artists. Remainders were overprinted "SVP" (Without Postal Value).

No. 283 Surcharged in Green

1937, Nov. 19	**Unwmk.**	***Perf. 12***	
355 A44 10c on 25c violet		6.75	1.40

Centenary of Cuban railroads.

Ciboney Indian and Cigar — A96

Cigar and Globe — A97

Tobacco Plant and Cigars — A98

1939, Aug. 28	**Wmk. 106**	***Perf. 10***	
356 A96 1c yellow green		15	15
357 A97 2c red		30	15
358 A98 5c brt ultra		60	15
Nos. 356-358 (3)		1.05	
Set value			20

General Calixto García
A99 A100

1939, Nov. 6	***Perf. 10, Imperf.***		
359 A99 2c dark red		30	15
360 A100 5c deep blue		60	28

Birth centenary of General Garcia.

Gonzalo de Quesada — A101

1940, Apr. 30	**Engr.**	***Perf. 10***	
361 A101 2c rose red		38	22

Pan American Union, 50th anniversary.

Rotary Club Emblem, Cuban Flag and Tobacco Plant — A102

Lions Emblem, Cuban Flag and Royal Palms — A103

1940, May 18	**Wmk. 106**	***Perf. 10***	
362 A102 2c rose red		65	48

Rotary Intl. Convention held at Havana.

1940, July 23			
363 A103 2c orange vermilion		95	48

Lions International Convention, Havana.

Dr. Nicolás J. Gutiérrez A104

1940, Oct. 28		
364 A104 2c orange ver	40	25
365 A104 5c blue	50	30
a. Sheet of four, imperf., unwmkd.	2.50	2.50
b. As "a," black overprint ('51)	3.00	3.00

100th anniv. of the publication of the 1st Cuban Medical Review, "El Repertorio Medico Habanero."

No. 365a contains 2 each of Nos. 364-365 imperf. and sold for 25c.

For overprint see No. C43A.

In 1951 No. 365a was overprinted in black: "50 Aniversario Descubrimiento Agente Transmisor de la Flebre Amarilla por el Dr. Carlos J. Finlay Honor a los Martires de la Ciencia 1901 1951." The overprint is illustrated over No. C43A, but does not include the plane and "Correo Aereo."

Major General Guillermo Moncada — A105

Moncada Riding into Battle A106

1941, June 25		
366 A105 3c dk brown, *buff*	70	18
367 A106 5c bright blue	70	35

Maj. Gen. Guillermo Moncada (1841-96).

Globe Showing Western Hemisphere — A107

"Labor: Wealth of America" — A109

Maceo, Bolívar, Juárez, Lincoln and Arms of Cuba A108

Tree of Fraternity, Havana — A110

Statue of Liberty — A111

Perf. 10, Imperf.

1942, Feb. 23	**Wmk. 106**	
368 A107 1c emerald	16	15
369 A108 3c orange brown	20	15
370 A109 5c blue	35	15
371 A110 10c red violet	80	38
372 A111 13c red	1.00	65
Nos. 368-372 (5)	2.51	1.48

Issued to publicize the spirit of Democracy in the Americas.

The imperforate varieties are without gum.

Ignacio Agramonte Loynaz — A112

Rescue of Sanguily by Agramonte A113

1942, Apr. 10	***Perf. 10***	
373 A112 3c bister brn	45	22
374 A113 5c brt blue, *bluish*	85	32

100th anniv. of the birth of Ignacio Agramonte Loynaz, patriot.

"Unmask the Fifth Columnists" — A114

"Be Careful, The Fifth Column is Spying on You" — A115

"Destroy it. The Fifth Column is like a Serpent" — A116

"Fulfill your Patriotic Duty by Destroying the Fifth Column" — A117

"Don't be Afraid of the Fifth Column. Attack it" — A118

1943, July 5

375 A114	1c dk blue grn	22	15
376 A115	3c red	32	15
377 A116	5c brt blue	38	15
378 A117	10c dull brown	95	32
379 A118	13c dull rose vio	1.90	95
	Nos. 375-379 (5)	3.77	1.72

General Eloy Alfaro and Flags of Cuba and Ecuador A119

1943, Sept. 20

380 A119 3c green 70 15

100th anniv. of the birth of General Eloy Alfaro of Ecuador.

Retirement Security A120

1943, Nov. 8 Wmk. 106 *Perf. 10*

381 A120	1c yellow green	30	15
382 A120	3c vermilion	35	15
383 A120	5c bright blue	40	22

1944, Mar. 18

384 A120	1c bright yel grn	75	30
385 A120	3c salmon	90	30
386 A120	5c light blue	1.50	75
	Nos. 381-386 (6)	4.20	1.87

Half the proceeds from the sale of Nos. 381-386 were used for the Communications Ministry Employees' Retirement Fund.

Portrait of Columbus — A121

Bartolomé De Las Casas — A122

First Statue of Columbus at Cárdenas — A123

Discovery of Tobacco A124

Columbus Sights Land A125

1944, May 19

387 A121	1c dk yel grn	18	18
388 A122	3c brown	30	18
389 A123	5c brt blue	40	18
390 A124	10c dk violet	1.00	60
391 A125	13c dk red	2.00	1.00
	Nos. 387-391,C36-C37 (7)	4.83	2.49

450th anniv. of the discovery of America.

Major General Carlos Roloff — A126

Americas Map and 1st Brazilian Postage Stamps — A127

1944, Aug. 21

392 A126 3c violet 28 18

100th anniv. of the birth of Maj. Gen. Carlos Roloff.

1944, Dec. 20 Engr.

393 A127 3c brown orange 85 32

Cent. of the 1st postage stamps of the Americas, issued by Brazil in 1843.

Seal of the Society — A128

Luis de las Casas and Luis Maria Penalyer A129

1945, Oct. 5 Wmk. 106 *Perf. 10*

394 A128	1c yellow green	15	15
395 A129	2c scarlet	22	15
	Set value		18

Sesquicentenary of the founding of the Economic Society of Friends of the Country.

Aged Couple A130

1945, Dec. 27

396 A130	1c dk yellow grn	25	15
397 A130	2c scarlet	40	15
398 A130	5c cobalt blue	75	18

1946, Mar. 26

399 A130	1c brt yellow grn	50	15
400 A130	2c salmon pink	40	15
401 A130	5c light blue	60	25
	Nos. 396-401 (6)	2.90	
	Set value		79

See note after No. 386.

Catalogue values for unused stamps in this section, from this point to the end of the section, are for Never Hinged items.

Gabriel de la Concepcion Valdés Plácido A131

1946, Feb. 5

402 A131 2c scarlet 90 18

Cent. of the death of the poet Gabriel de la Concepcion Valdés.

Manuel Marquez Sterling — A132

Globe and Cross — A133

1946, Apr. 30

403 A132 2c scarlet 90 18

Founding of the Manuel Marquez Sterling Professional School of Journalism, 3th anniv.

1946, July 4 Engr.

404 A133 2c scarlet, *pink* 85 18

80th anniv. of the Intl. Red Cross.

Cow and Milkmaid — A134

Franklin D. Roosevelt — A135

1947, Feb. 20 Wmk. 106 *Perf. 10*

405 A134 2c scarlet 75 15

1947 National Livestock Exposition.

1947, Apr. 12

406 A135 2c vermilion 28 15

2nd anniv. of the death of Franklin D. Roosevelt.

Antonio Oms Sarret and Aged Couple A136

1947, Oct. 20

407 A136	1c dp yellow grn	15	15
408 A136	2c scarlet	20	15
409 A136	5c lt blue	45	40
	Nos. 407-409 (3)	80	70

See note after No. 386.

Marta Abreu Arenabio de Estevez A137

"Charity" A138

Marta Abreu Monument, Santa Clara A139

"Patriotism" A140

1947, Nov. 29

410 A137	1c dp yellow grn	20	15
411 A138	2c scarlet	30	15
412 A139	5c brt blue	50	25
413 A140	10c dk violet	1.00	50
	Nos. 410-413 (4)	2.00	1.05

Birth cent. of Marta Abreu Arenabio de Estevez, philanthropist and humanitarian.

Armauer Hansen A141

1948, Apr. 9

414 A141 2c rose carmine 75 15

International Leprosy Congress, Havana.

Mother and Child — A142

1948, Oct. 15 **Engr.**

415 A142 1c yellow grn 32 15
416 A142 2c scarlet 45 15
417 A142 5c brt blue 95 20
Nos. 415-417 (3) 1.72
Set value 40

See note after No. 386.

Death of José Martí — A143

Martí Rowing to Shore — A144

1948, Nov. 10 **Wmk. 106** ***Perf. 10***

418 A143 2c scarlet 35 15
419 A144 5c brt blue 80 18

50th anniversary of the death of José Martí, patriot (in 1945).

Tobacco Picking — A145

Liberty Carrying Flag and Cigars — A146

Cigar and Arms of Cuba — A147

1948, Dec. 6
Size: 22½x26mm

420 A145 1c green 15 15
421 A146 2c rose car 25 15
422 A147 5c brt blue 35 15
Nos. 420-422 (3) 75
Set value 18

Cuba's tobacco industry. See Nos. 445-447. For overprints and surcharge see Nos. 448-451, 512.

Equestrian Statue of Gen. Antonio Maceo — A148

Sword Salute to Maceo — A149

Designs: 2c, Portrait of Maceo. 5c, Mausoleum, El Cacahual. 10c, East to West invasion. 20c, Battle of Peralejo. 50c, Declaration of Baragua. 1p, Death of Maceo at San Pedro.

1948, Dec. 15 **Wmk. 229** ***Perf. 12½***

423 A148 1c blue green 18 18
424 A148 2c red 18 18
425 A148 5c blue 32 18
426 A149 8c black & brown 45 30
427 A149 10c brown & bl grn 45 20
428 A149 20c blue & car 1.90 90
429 A149 50c car & ultra 3.00 2.00
430 A149 1p black & violet 6.25 2.75
Nos. 423-430 (8) 12.73 6.69

Birth cent. (in 1945) of Maceo.

Symbol of Pharmacy A150

Morro Lighthouse A151

1948, Dec. 28 ***Perf. 10***

431 A150 2c rose carmine 75 15

1st Pan-American Congress of Pharmacy, Havana, Dec. 1948.

1949, Jan. 17 **Wmk. 229** ***Perf. 12½***

432 A151 2c carmine 75 15

Centenary (in 1944) of the erection of the Morro Lighthouse.

Jagua Castle, Cienfuegos A152

1949, Jan. 27 **Wmk. 106** ***Perf. 10***

433 A152 1c yellow green 40 15
434 A152 2c rose red 80 20

200th anniv. of the construction of Jagua Castle and the cent. of the publication of the 1st newspaper in Cienfuegos.

Manuel Sanguily y Garritt — A153

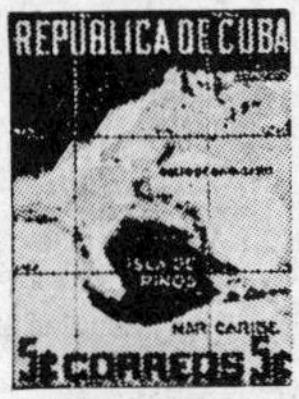

Map of Isle of Pines — A154

1949, Mar. 31

435 A153 2c rose red 35 15
436 A153 5c blue 75 22

Manuel Sanguily y Garritt (1848-1925), cabinet member, editor, author.

1949, Apr. 26

437 A154 5c blue 90 70

20th anniv. of the recognition of Cuban ownership of the Isle of Pines.

Ismael Cespedes — A155

1949, Sept. 28

438 A155 1c yellow green 40 15
439 A155 2c scarlet 40 15
440 A155 5c brt blue 90 20
Nos. 438-440 (3) 1.70
Set value 40

See note after No. 386.

Gen. Enrique Collazo — A156

Enrique José Varona — A157

1950, Feb. 28 **Engr.** ***Perf. 10***

441 A156 2c scarlet 50 15
442 A156 5c brt blue 1.00 20

Centenary (in 1948) of the birth of General Enrique Collazo.

1950, Feb. 28

443 A157 2c scarlet 40 15
444 A157 5c brt blue 80 20

Centenary of the birth of Enrique José Varona, writer and patriot.

Tobacco Types of 1948

1950, June 20 **Re-engraved**
Size: 21x25mm

445 A145 1c green 40 15
446 A146 2c rose red 40 15
447 A147 5c blue 60 16
Nos. 445-447 (3) 1.40
Set value 32

The re-engraved stamps show slight differences in many minor details.

For overprints and surcharge see #448-451, 512.

No. 446 Overprinted in Black

BANCO NACIONAL DE CUBA INAUGURACION 27 ABRIL 1950

1950, Apr. 27

448 A146 2c rose red 75 20

Natl. Bank of Cuba opening, Apr. 27, 1950.

Re-engraved Tobacco Types of 1950 Overprinted in Carmine

U.P.U 1874 1949

1950, May 18

449 A145 1c yellow green 15 15
450 A146 2c lilac rose 20 15
451 A147 5c light blue 38 15
Nos. 449-451 (3) 73
Set value 30

75th anniv. (in 1949) of the UPU.
No. 451 exists with surcharge inverted.

Manuel Balanzategui, Antonio L. Pausa and Train Wreck A158

Fernando Figueredo A159

1950, Sept. 21 **Engr.**

452 A158 1c yellow grn 35 15
453 A158 2c scarlet 35 15
454 A158 5c brt blue 75 20
Nos. 452-454 (3) 1.45
Set value 40

1951, Mar. 17 **Wmk. 106** ***Perf. 10***

455 A159 1c green 40 15
456 A159 2c scarlet 40 15
457 A159 5c brt blue 75 15
Nos. 455-457 (3) 1.55
Set value 31

Three-fourths of the proceeds from the sale of these stamps were used for the Communication Ministry Employees' Retirement Fund.

See Nos. 474, C51-C56, E15. For surcharges see Nos. 474, C51-C56, E15.

Miguel Teurbe Tolón and Flag — A160

Narciso Lopez — A161

Emilia Teurbe Tolón Sewing Flag — A162

Cuban Flag — A163

Engraved and Lithographed

1951, July 3 **Wmk. 229** ***Perf. 13***

458 A160 1c Prus grn, ultra & red 24 15
459 A161 2c red & gray blk 35 15
460 A162 5c ultra & red 75 28
461 A163 10c rose vio, bl & red 1.25 40
Nos. 458-461,C41-C43,E13 (8) 9.89 3.18

Centenary of adoption of Cuba's flag.

Clara Louise Maass and Hospitals — A164

Hospitals: Lutheran Memorial, Newark, N.J. and Las Animas, Havana.

Wmk. 106

1951, Aug. 24 **Engr.** ***Perf. 10***

462 A164 2c scarlet 90 20

75th anniv. of the birth of Clara Louise Maass, (1876-1901), American nurse and martyr in yellow fever fight.

Airmail Type and

José Raul Capablanca A165

Capablanca Club, Havana A166

Design: 2c, Capablanca making "The Exact Play."

Wmk. 229

1951, Nov. 1 **Photo.** ***Perf. 13***

463 A165 1c blue grn & org 2.25 38
464 AP27 2c rose car & dk brn 2.75 75
465 A166 5c black & dp ultra 5.25 1.25
Nos. 463-465,C44-C46,E14 (7) 39.75 7.38

Jose Raul Capablanca, World Chess titlist (1921). Value imperf., set of 7 pairs, $1,500.

Antonio Guiteras Holmes — A167

Guiteras Preparing Social Legislation A168

Fort of the Morrillo A169

Wmk. 106

1951, Oct. 22 Engr. *Perf. 10*

466 A167	1c yellow green	22	15
467 A168	2c rose carmine	40	15
468 A169	5c deep blue	65	15
Nos. 466-468,C47-C49 (6)		4.62	1.50

16th anniv. of the Action of the Morrillo and to honor Antonio Guiteras Holmes, who was killed there.

Souvenir sheets containing stamps similar to Nos. 466-468, but in different colors, are listed as Nos. C49a-C49b.

Poinsettia A170

Maj. Gen. José Maceo A171

1951, Dec. 1 Engr. and Typo.

469 A170	1c green & car	1.75	25
470 A170	2c rose car & grn	2.00	38

See Nos. 498-499.

1952, Feb. 6 Engr.

471 A171	2c yellow brown	40	15
472 A171	5c indigo	90	15

Birth centenary of Maceo.
See note after No. C49.

Isabella I — A172

Receipt of Autonomy — A173

1952, Feb. 22

473 A172	2c bright red	60	15

500th anniv. of the birth of Queen Isabella I of Spain.

Souvenir sheets containing 2c stamps of type A172 are listed as Nos. C50a-C50b.

Type of 1951 Surcharged in Green

1952, Mar. 18

474 A159	10c on 2c yel brn	1.25	25

Perf. 12½

1952, May 27 Wmk. 106 Engr.

Designs: 2c, Tomas Estrada Palma and Luis Estevez Romero. 5c, Barnet, Finlay, Guiteras and Nuñez. 8c, Capitol. 20c, Map, Central Highway. 50c, Sugar Mill.

Centers in Black

475 A173	1c dk green	22	15
476 A173	2c dk carmine	28	15
477 A173	5c dk blue	32	15
478 A173	8c dk brown car	55	15
479 A173	20c dk olive grn	1.40	40
480 A173	50c dp orange	2.75	80
Nos. 475-480,C57-C60,E16 (11)		12.27	4.05

50th anniv. of the Republic of Cuba.

Hands Holding Coffee Beans A174

Designs: 2c, Map and man picking coffee beans. 5c, Farmer with pan of beans.

1952, Aug. 22 Wmk. 229 *Perf. 13½*

481 A174	1c green	40	15
482 A174	2c rose red	75	15
483 A174	5c dk vio bl & aqua	1.00	20
Nos. 481-483 (3)		2.15	50

Bicentenary of coffee cultivation.

Col. Charles Hernandes y Sandrino A175

Alonso Alvarez de la Campa A176

1952, Oct. 7 Wmk. 106 *Perf. 10*

484 A175	1c yellow grn	20	15
485 A175	2c scarlet	35	15
486 A175	5c blue	40	15
487 A175	8c black	1.10	30
488 A175	10c brown red	1.10	30
489 A175	20c brown	4.00	2.50
Nos. 484-489,C63-C72,E17 (17)		30.95	16.10

See note after No. 457.

Frame Engraved; Center in Black

1952, Nov. 27

Portraits: 2c, Carlos A. Latorre. 3c, Anacleto Bermudez. 5c, Eladio G. Toledo. 8c, Angel Laborde. 10c, Jose M. Medina. 13c, Pascual Rodriguez. 20c, Carlos Verdugo.

490 A176	1c green	25	15
491 A176	2c carmine	50	15
492 A176	3c purple	60	15
493 A176	5c blue	60	15
494 A176	8c bister brn	1.25	32
495 A176	10c orange brn	1.00	28
496 A176	13c lilac rose	2.00	40
497 A176	20c olive grn	3.00	70
Nos. 490-497,C73-C74 (10)		12.85	3.90

81st anniv. of the execution of 8 medical students.

Christmas Type of 1951
Dated "1952-1953"

Frame Engr.; Center Typo.

1952, Dec. 1

Centers: Tree.

498 A170	1c yel grn & car	4.00	1.00
499 A170	3c vio & dk grn	4.00	1.00

Birthplace of José Martí — A177

Marti at St. Lazarus Quarry — A178

Designs: No. 501, Court martial. No. 502, artiano house, Havana. No. 504, El Abra ranch, Isle of Pines. No. 505, Symbols, "Marti the Poet." No. 506, Marti and Bolivar statue, Caracas. No. 507, At desk in New York. No. 508, House where revolutionary party was formed. No. 509, First issue of "Patria."

1953 Engr. *Perf. 10*

500 A177	1c dk grn & red brn	15	15
501 A177	1c dk grn & red brn	15	15
502 A177	3c purple & brn	25	15
503 A178	3c purple & brn	25	15
504 A177	5c dp bl & dk brn	40	18
505 A178	5c ultra & brn	40	18
506 A178	10c red brn & blk	1.00	38
507 A178	10c dk brn & blk	1.00	38
508 A178	13c dk ol grn & dk brn	1.65	80
509 A177	13c dk ol grn & brn	1.65	1.00
Nos. 500-509,C79-C89 (21)		25.50	11.98

Centenary of birth of José Martí.

Rafael Montoro Valdez — A179

Francisco Carrera Justiz — A180

1953, Mar. 5

510 A179	3c dark violet	35	15

Cent. of the birth of Rafael Montoro Valdez, statesman.

1953, Mar. 9

511 A180	3c rose red	25	15

Issued to honor Francisco Carrera Justiz, educator and statesman.

No. 446 Surcharged with New Value

1953, June 16

512 A146	3c on 2c rose red	60	15

Board of Accounts Bldg., Havana — A181

1953, Nov. 3 Engr.

513 A181	3c blue	20	15
Nos. 513,C90-C91 (3)		2.85	1.27

1st Intl. Cong. of Boards of Accounts, Havana, Nov. 2-9.

Miguel Coyula Llaguno — A182

Communications Assoc. Flag — A183

Designs: 3c, 8c, Enrique Calleja Hensell. 10c, Antonio Ginard Rojas.

1954 Dated 1953

514 A182	1c green	22	15
515 A182	3c rose red	22	15
516 A183	5c blue	90	15
517 A182	8c brn car	1.40	32
518 A182	10c brown	2.25	50
Nos. 514-518,C92-C95,E19 (10)		15.81	8.92

Nos. 515 and 517 show the same portrait, but inscriptions are arranged differently.
See note after No. 457.

José Martí — A184

Maximo Gomez — A184a

Portraits: 3c, José de la Luz Caballero. 4c, Miguel Aldama. 5c, Calixto Garcia. 8c, Ignacio Agramont. 10c, Tomas Estrada Palma. 13c, Carlos J. Finlay. 14c, Serafin Sanchez. 20c, José Antonio Saco. 50c, Antonio Maceo. 1p, Carlos Manuel de Cespedes.

1954-56 Wmk. 106 *Perf. 10*

519 A184	1c green	25	15
520 A184a	2c rose car	25	15
521 A184	3c violet	25	15
521A A184	4c red lil ('56)	30	15
522 A184a	5c slate bl	35	15
523 A184a	8c car lake	50	15
524 A184	10c sepia	50	15
525 A184	13c org red	75	15
525A A184a	14c gray ('56)	1.00	15
526 A184	20c olive	1.50	15
527 A184a	50c org yel	2.50	25
528 A184a	1p orange	5.00	38
Nos. 519-528 (12)		13.15	
Set value			1.35

See Nos. 674-680. For surcharges see Nos. 636, 641-643.

Maj. Gen. José M. Rodriguez — A185

Design: 5c, Gen. Rodriguez on horseback.

1954, June 8 Engr. *Perf. 12½*

Center in Dark Brown

529 A185	2c dark carmine	65	15
530 A185	5c deep blue	1.40	20

Cent. of the birth of Maj. Gen. José Maria Rodriguez (in 1851).

Gen. Batísta Sanatorium A186

1954, Sept. 21 Wmk. 106 *Perf. 10*

531 A186	3c deep blue	30	15

See No. C107.

Santa Claus — A187

Maria Luisa Dolz — A188

1954, Dec. 15

532 A187	2c dk grn & car	4.00	38
533 A187	4c car & dk grn	3.50	38

Christmas 1954.

1954, Dec. 23

534 A188	4c deep blue4	25	15

Cent. of the birth of Maria Luisa Dolz, educator and defender of women's rights. See No. C108.

Cuban Flag and Scouts Saluting — A189

1954, Dec. 27 *Perf. 12½*

535 A189	4c dark green	75	15

Issued to publicize the national patrol encampment of the Boy Scouts of Cuba.

Rotary Emblem and Paul P. Harris — A190

1955, Feb. 23 Engr. Wmk. 106

536 A190 4c blue	75	15

Rotary International, 50th anniversary. See No. C109.

Maj. Gen. Francisco Carrillo — A191

Portrait: 5c, Gen. Carrillo standing.

1955, Mar. 8 ***Perf. 10***

537 A191 2c brt red & dk bl	40	15
538 A191 5c dk bl & dk brn	75	15
Set value		20

Cent. of the birth of Maj. Gen. Francisco Carrillo (1851-1926).

Stamp of 1885 and Convent of San Francisco A192

Designs (including 1855 stamp): 4c, Volanta carriage. 10c, Havana, 19th century. 14c, Captain general's residence.

1955, Apr. ***Perf. 12½***

539 A192 2c lil rose & dk grnsh bl	75	16
540 A192 4c ocher & dk grn	1.00	16
541 A192 10c ultra & dk red	2.25	90
542 A192 14c grn & dp org	5.50	1.00
Nos. 539-542,C110-C113 (8)	17.75	6.07

Cent. of Cuba's 1st postage stamps.

Maj. Gen. Mario G. Menocal — A193

Gen. Emilio Nuñez — A194

Portraits: 10c, J. G. O. Gomez. 14c, A. Sanchez de Bustamente.

1955, June 22

543 A193 2c dark green	50	15
544 A194 4c lilac rose	60	15
545 A193 10c deep blue	1.00	24
546 A194 14c gray violet	2.00	35
Nos. 543-546,C114-C116,E20 (8)	14.35	6.39

See note after No. 457.

Turkey A195

Gen. Emilio Nuñez A196

1955, Dec. 15 Engr.

547 A195 2c slate grn & dk car	3.75	38
548 A195 4c rose lake & brt grn	3.75	30

Christmas 1955.

1955, Dec. 27

549 A196 4c claret	50	15
Nos. 549,C127-C128 (3)	3.00	1.05

Cent. of the birth of Gen. Emilio Nunez, Cuban revolutionary hero.

Francisco Cagigal de la Vega (1695-1777) A197

Julian del Casal A198

1956, Mar. 27 ***Perf. 12½***

552 A197 4c rose brn & slate bl	50	15

Cuban post bicent. See No. C129.

1956, May 2

Portraits: 4c, Luisa Perez de Zambrana. 10c, Juan Clemente Zenea. 14c, José Joaquin Palma.

Portraits in Black

553 A198 2c green	24	15
554 A198 4c rose lilac	30	15
555 A198 10c blue	60	15
556 A198 14c violet	75	18
Nos. 553-556,C131-C133,E21 (8)	8.64	3.28

See note after No. 457.

Victor Muñoz — A199

Masonic Temple, Havana — A200

1956, May 13

557 A199 4c brn & grn	25	15

Issued in honor of Victor Munoz (1873-1922), founder of Mother's Day in Cuba. See No. C134.

1956, June 5

558 A200 4c blue	50	15

See No. C135.

Virgin of Charity, El Cobre — A201

"The Cry of Yara" — A202

1956, Sept. 8 ***Perf. 12½***

559 A201 4c brt bl & yel	40	15

Issued in honor of Our Lady of Charity of Cobre, patroness of Cuba. See No. C149.

1956, Oct. 10

560 A202 4c dk grn & brn	25	15

Cuba's independence from Spain.

Raimundo G. Menocal — A203

The Three Wise Men — A204

1956, Dec. 3 Wmk. 106 ***Perf. 12½***

561 A203 4c dk brn	25	15

Cent. of the birth of Prof. Raimundo G. Menocal, physician.

1956, Dec. 1

562 A204 2c red & slate grn	2.00	60
563 A204 4c slate grn & red	2.00	40

Christmas 1956.

Martin Morua Delgado A205

Boy Scouts at Campfire A206

1957, Jan. 30

564 A205 4c dark green	25	15

Delgado, patriot, birth cent.

1957, Feb. 22 Wmk. 106 ***Perf. 12½***

565 A206 4c slate grn & red	45	18

Cent. of the birth of Lord Baden-Powell, founder of the Boy Scouts. See No. C152.

"The Blind," by M. Vega — A207

Paintings: 4c, "The Art Critics" by M. Melero. 10c, "Volanta in Storm" by A. Menocal. 14c, "The Convalescent" by L. Romañach.

1957, Mar. Engr. ***Perf. 12½***

Side and Lower Inscriptions in Dark Brown

566 A207 2c olive green	22	15
567 A207 4c orange red	28	15
568 A207 10c olive green	40	25
569 A207 14c ultra	55	25
Nos. 566-569,C153-C155,E22 (8)	8.65	3.10

See note after No. 457.

Emblem of Philatelic Club of Cuba A208

Juan F. Steegers A209

1957, Apr. 24

570 A208 4c ocher, blue & red	30	15

Issued for Stamp Day, Apr. 24, and the National Philatelic Exhibition. See No. C156.

1957, Apr. 30

571 A209 4c blue	25	15

Juan Francisco Steegers y Perera (1856-1921), dactyloscopy pioneer. See No. C157.

Victoria Bru Sanchez A210

Joaquin de Aguero in Battle of Jucaral A211

1957, June 3 Wmk. 106 ***Perf. 12½***

572 A210 4c indigo	25	15

1957, July 4

573 A211 4c dk grn	25	15

Issued to honor Joaquin de Aguero, Cuban freedom fighter and patriot. See No. C162.

Boy, Dogs and Cat — A212

Col. Rafael Manduley del Rio — A213

1957, July 17

574 A212 4c Prus grn	1.00	30

Mrs. Jeanette Ryder, founder of the Humane Society of Cuba. See Nos. C163-C163a.

1957, July 31

575 A213 4c Prus grn	25	15

Issued to honor Col. Manduley del Rio, patriot, on the cent. of his birth (in 1856).

Palace of Justice A214

1957, Sept. 2 Engr. ***Perf. 12½***

576 A214 4c blue gray	25	15

Opening of the new Palace of Justice in Havana. See No. C165.

Generals of the Liberation A215

1957, Sept. 26

577 A215 4c dl grn & red brn	50	15
578 A215 4c dl bl & red brn	50	15
579 A215 4c rose & brn	50	15
580 A215 4c org yel & brn	50	15
581 A215 4c lt vio & brn	50	15
Nos. 577-581 (5)	2.50	
Set value		50

Generals of the army of liberation.

1st Publication Printed in Cuba — A216

Patio — A217

1957, Oct. 18 Wmk. 106 *Perf. 12½*

582 A216 4c slate blue		25	15
	Nos. 582,C167-C168 (3)	1.75	65

José Marti National Library.

1957, Nov. 19

583 A217 4c red brn & grn		25	15
	Nos. 583,C173-C174 (3)	2.35	95

Cent. of the 1st Cuban Normal School.

Trinidad, Founded 1514 — A218

Fortifications, Havana, 1611 — A219

Views: 10c, Padre Pico street, Santiago de Cuba. 14c, Church of Our Lady, Camaguey.

1957, Dec. 17 Engr. *Perf. 12½*

584 A218 2c brn & ind		18	15
585 A219 4c sl grn & brn		25	15
586 A219 10c sep & red		75	20
587 A219 14c grn & dk red		65	15
	Nos. 584-587,C175-C177,E23 (8)	7.33	2.91

See note after No. 457.

Nativity — A220

1957, Dec. 20

588 A220 2c multi	1.75	50
589 A220 4c multi	1.75	38

Christmas 1957.

Dayton Hedges and Ariguanabo Textile Factory A221

1958, Jan. 30 Wmk. 106 *Perf. 12½*

590 A221 4c blue	25	15

Issued to honor Dayton Hedges, founder of Cuba's textile industry. See No. C178.

Dr. Francisco Dominguez Roldan — A222

José Ignacio Rivero y Alonso — A223

1958, Feb. 21

591 A222 4c green	25	15

Roldan (1864-1942), who introduced radiotherapy and physiotherapy to Cuba.

1958, Apr. 1

592 A223 4c light olive grn	25	15

José Ignacio Rivero y Alonso, editor of Diario de la Marina, 1919-44. See No. C179.

Map of Cuba and Mail Route, 1756 A224

1958, Apr. 24 *Perf. 12½*

593 A224 4c dk grn, aqua & buff	30	15

Issued for Stamp Day, Apr. 24 and the National Philatelic Exhibition. See No. C180.

Maj. Gen. José Miguel Gomez A225

Nicolas Ruiz Espadero A226

1958, June 6 Wmk. 106 *Perf. 12½*

594 A225 4c slate	25	15

Maj. Gen. José Miguel Gomez, President of Cuba, 1909-13. See No. C181.

1958, June 27 *Perf. 12½*

Musicians: 4c, Ignacio Cervantes. 10c, José White. 14c, Brindis de Salas.

Indigo Emblem

595 A226 2c brown	28	15
596 A226 4c dk gray	28	15
597 A226 10c ol grn	40	15
598 A226 14c red	55	20

Physicians: 2c, Tomas Romay Chacon. 4c, Angel Arturo Aballi. 10c, Fernando Gonzalez del Valle. 14c, Vicente Antonio de Castro.

Green Emblem

599 A226 2c brown	32	15
600 A226 4c gray	55	20
601 A226 10c dk car	40	18
602 A226 14c dk bl	55	22

Lawyers: 2c, Jose Maria Garcia Montes. 4c, Jose A. Gonzalez Lanuza. 10c, Juan B. Hernandez Barreiro. 14c, Pedro Gonzalez Llorente.

Red Emblem

603 A226 2c sepia		28	15
604 A226 4c gray		40	20
605 A226 10c olive grn		48	15
606 A226 14c slate blue		55	20
	Nos. 595-606 (12)	5.04	
	Set value		1.78

For surcharges see Nos. 629-631.

Carlos de la Torre — A227

1958, Aug. 29 Engr. Wmk. 321

607 A227 4c violet blue		30	15
	Nos. 607,C182-C184 (4)	7.80	4.55

Dr. Carlos de la Torre y Huerta (1858-1950), naturalist. For surcharge see No. 632.

Poey's "Memorias" Title Page — A228

Felipe Poey — A229

1958, Sept. 26 Wmk. 106

608 A228 2c blk & lt vio		35	15
609 A229 4c brn blk		45	15
	Nos. 608-609,C185-C191,E26-E27 (11)	47.30	18.05

Felipe Poey (1799-1891), naturalist.

Theodore Roosevelt — A230

Cattleyopsis Lindenii Orchid — A231

1958, Oct. 27 *Perf. 12½*

610 A230 4c gray grn	30	15

Theodore Roosevelt, birth cent. See #C192.

Engraved and Photogravure

1958, Dec. 16 Wmk. 321 *Perf. 12½*

Christmas: 4c, Oncidium Guibertianum Orchid.

611 A231 2c multi	1.75	50
612 A231 4c multi	2.00	50

For surcharge see No. 633.

Flag and Revolutionary A232

Gen. Adolfo Flor Crombet (1848-95) A233

Engr. & Typo.

1959, Jan. 28 Wmk. 321

613 A232 2c car rose & gray	15	15

Day of Liberation, Jan. 1, 1959.

1959, Mar. 18 Engr. Wmk. 106

614 A233 4c slate green	30	15

For surcharge see No. 634.

Maria Teresa Garcia Montes A234

Carlos Manuel de Cespedes A235

1959, Nov. 11 *Perf. 12½*

615 A234 4c brown	20	15

Issued to honor Maria Teresa Garcia Montes (1880-1930), founder of the Musical Arts Society. See No. C198. For surcharge see No. 635.

1959, Oct. 10 Wmk. 106 *Perf. 12½*

Presidents: No. 617, Salvador Cisneros Betancourt. No. 618, Manuel de Jesus Calvar. No. 619, Bartolomé Maso. No. 620, Juan B. Spotorno. No. 621, Tomas Estrada Palma. No. 622, Francisco Javier de Céspedes. No. 623, Vicente Garcia.

616 A235 2c slate blue		32	15
617 A235 2c green		32	15
618 A235 2c dp vio		32	15
619 A235 2c org brn		32	15
620 A235 4c dk car		40	20
621 A235 4c dp brn		40	20
622 A235 4c dk gray		40	20
623 A235 4c dk vio		40	20
	Nos. 616-623 (8)	2.88	1.40

Issued to honor former Cuban presidents.

No. B3 Surcharged in Red: "HABILITADO PARA / 2¢"

1960

624 SP2 2c on 2c + 1c car & ultra	50	15

See No. C199.

Rebel Attack on Moncada Barracks A236

Designs: 2c, Rebels disembarking from "Granma." 10c, Battle of the Uvero. 12c, Map of Cuba and rebel ("The Invasion").

1960, Jan. 28 Wmk. 320

625 A236 1c gray ol, bl & ver		16	15
626 A236 2c bl, gray ol & brn		22	15
627 A236 10c bl, gray ol & red		42	15
628 A236 12c brt bl, brn & grn		60	15
	Nos. 625-628,C200-C202 (7)	6.40	2.60

First anniversary of revolution.

Stamps of 1956-59 Surcharged with New Value in Carmine or Silver

1960, Feb. 3

629 A226 1c on 4c dk gray & ind		35	15
630 A226 1c on 4c gray & grn		55	25
631 A226 1c on 4c gray & red		35	15
632 A227 1c on 4c vio bl		35	15
633 A231 1c on 4c multi (S)		90	50
634 A233 1c on 4c slate grn		32	15
635 A234 1c on 4c brown		35	15
636 A184a 2c on 14c gray		45	15
	Nos. 629-636,C203-C204 (10)	5.12	2.25

Tomas Estrada Palma Statue, Havana A237

17th Olympic Games, Rome, Aug. 25-Sept. 11 A238

Statues: 2c, Mambi Victorioso (Battle of San Juan Hill), Santiago de Cuba. 10c, Marta Abreo de Estevez. 12c, Ignacio Agramonte, Camaguey.

Perf. 12½

1960, Mar. 28 — Wmk. 321 — Engr.

637	A237	1c brn & dk bl	20	15
638	A237	2c grn & red	30	15
639	A237	10c choc & red	75	15
640	A237	12c gray ol & vio	1.00	20
		Nos. 637-640,C206-C208 (7)	6.10	2.15

See note after No. 386

Nos. 521A, 522 and 525 Surcharged "HABILITADO / PARA / 2¢" in Violet Blue, Red or Black

1960 — Wmk. 106 — *Perf. 10*

641	A184	2c on 4c red lil (VB)	50	15
642	A184a	2c on 5c sl bl (R)	60	15
643	A184	2c on 13c org red	75	22

No. 307B Surcharged "HABILITADO / 10¢"

644	A41	10c on 20c ol grn	50	15
		Nos. 641-644 (4)	2.35	
		Set value		54

Perf. 12½

1960, Sept. 22 — Engr. — Wmk. 321

645	A238	1c Sailboats	15	15
646	A238	2c Marksman	25	15

For souvenir sheet see No. C213a.

Camilo Cienfuegos and View of Escolar A239

1960, Oct. 27 — Litho. — Unwmk.

647	A239	2c brn, bl, grn & red	15	15

1st anniv. of the death of Camilo Cienfuegos, revolutionary hero.

Morning Glory A240

Tobacco and Christmas Hymn A241

1960 — Litho. — *Perf. 12½*

648	A240	1c red	55	50
649	A241	1c Tobacco	75	75
650	A241	1c Mariposa	75	75
651	A241	1c Guaiacum	75	75
652	A241	1c Coffee	75	75
a.		Block of 4, #649-652	4.50	
653	A240	2c ultra	75	75
654	A241	2c Tobacco	2.00	2.00
655	A241	2c Mariposa	2.00	2.00
656	A241	2c Guaiacum	2.00	2.00
657	A241	2c Coffee	2.00	2.00
a.		Block of 4, #654-657	12.00	
658	A240	10c ocher	2.25	2.00
659	A241	10c Tobacco	5.50	5.00
660	A241	10c Mariposa	5.50	5.00
661	A241	10c Guaiacum	5.50	5.00
662	A241	10c Coffee	5.50	5.00
a.		Block of 4, #659-662	35.00	
		Nos. 648-662 (15)	36.55	34.25

Issued for Christmas 1960.

Nos. 648-662 were printed in three sheets of 25. Nine stamps of type A240 form a center cross, stamps of type A241 form a block of four in each corner with the musical bars joined in an oval around the floral designs.

"Public Capital for Economic Benefit" — A242

Designs: 2c, Chart and symbols of agriculture and industry. 6c, Cogwheels.

Perf. 11½

1961, Jan. 10 — Unwmk. — Photo.

663	A242	1c yel, blk & org	20	15
664	A242	2c bl, blk & red	20	15
665	A242	6c yel, red org & blk	50	25
		Nos. 663-665,C215-C218 (7)	4.40	2.45

Issued to publicize the conference of underdeveloped countries, Havana.

Jesus Menéndez and Sugar Cane — A243

1961, Jan. 22 — Litho. — *Perf. 12½*

666	A243	2c dk grn & brn	20	15

Jesus Menéndez, leader in sugar industry.

Same Overprinted in Red: "PRIMERO DE MAYO 1961 ESTAMOS VENCIENDO"

1961, May 2

667	A243	2c dk grn & brn	30	25

Issued for May Day, 1961.

Dove and UN Emblem A244

1961, Apr. 12 — Litho. — *Perf. 12½*

668	A244	2c red brn & yel grn	30	15
669	A244	10c emer & rose lil	50	20
a.		Souv. sheet, #668-669, imperf.	1.00	
		Nos. 668-669,C222-C223 (4)	1.70	80

15th anniv. (in 1960) of the UN.

Maceo Stamp of 1907 and 1902 Simulated Cancel A245

Stamp Day: 1c, Revolutionary 10c stamp of 1874 and 1868 "cancel." 10c, No. 613 and "cancel."

1961, Apr. 24 — Unwmk.

670	A245	1c dull rose & dk grn	18	15
671	A245	2c salmon & dk grn	18	15
672	A245	10c pale grn, car rose & blk	38	22
		Nos. 670-672 (3)	74	52

For overprint see No. 681.

Hand Releasing Dove — A246

1961, July 26 — *Perf. 12½*

673	A246	2c blk, red, yel & gray	30	15

26th of July (1953) movement, Castro's revolt against Fulgencio Batista.

Burelage on back consisting of wavy lines and diagonal rows of "CUBA CORREOS" in pale salmon.

Portrait Type of 1954

Designs: Same as before. On the 2c, "1833" is replaced by "?".

Wmk. 321 (Nos. 674, 676); Unwmkd.
Perf. 12½ (Nos. 674, 676); Rouletted

1961-69 — Engr.

674	A184	1c brown red	
675	A184	1c lt blue ('69)	
676	A184a	2c slate green	
677	A184a	2c yel grn ('69)	
678	A184	3c org ('64)	
679	A184	13c brn ('64)	
680	A184	20c lilac ('69)	

Issue dates: Nos. 674, 676, Aug. 1, 1961. Nos. 678-679, Dec. 7, 1964. Others, Sept. 1969.

For Nos. 675, 677-680, see embargo note following No. 702.

No. 672 Ovptd. in Red — primera exposición filatélica oficial oct. 7-17. 1961

Perf. 12½

1961, Oct. 7 — Litho. — Unwmk.

681	A245	10c pale grn, car rose & blk	

1st Official Phil. Exhib., Havana, Oct. 7-17.

Education Year — A247

Designs: One letter (per stamp) of "CUBA," book and various quotations by Jose Marti about the virtues of literacy.

1961, Nov. 22

682	A247	1c pale grn, red & blk	
683	A247	2c blue, red & blk	
684	A247	10c vio, red & blk	
685	A247	12c org, red & blk	

A248

Christmas A249

Designs: 1c, Snails. 2c, Birds, vert. 10c, Butterflies.

1961, Dec. 1

686	A248	1c Polymita flammulata	
687	A249	1c Polymita fulminata	
688	A249	1c Polymita nigrofasciata	
689	A249	1c Polymita fuscolimbata	
690	A249	1c Polymita roseolimbata	
a.		Block of 5 + label, Nos. 686-690	
691	A248	2c Cuban grassquit	
692	A249	2c Cuban macaw	
693	A249	2c Cuban trogon	
694	A249	2c Bee hummingbird	
695	A249	2c Ivory-billed woodpecker	
a.		Block of 5 + label, Nos. 691-695	
696	A248	10c Othreis toddi	
697	A249	10c Uranidia boisduvalii	
698	A249	10c Phoebis avellaneda	
699	A249	10c Phaloe cubana	
700	A249	10c Papilio gundlachianus	
a.		Block of 5 + label, Nos. 696-700	

Stamps of the same denomination printed se-tenant in sheets of 20 stamps plus 5 labels picturing bells and star. Stamps of Type A249 are arranged in blocks of 4; Type A248 stamps and labels form a cross in sheet.

See Nos. 760-774, 912-926, 1025-1039, 1179-1193, 1303-1317, 1464-1478 and 1572-1586.

3rd Anniv. of the Revolution — A250

1962, Jan. 3

701	A250	1c multi	
702	A250	2c multi	

See Nos. C226-C228.

Importation Prohibited

Cuban stamps issued after No. 673 have not been valued because the embargo on trade with Cuba, proclaimed Feb. 7, 1962, by President Kennedy, prohibits the importation from any country of stamps of Cuban origin, used or unused.

Natl. Militia A251

Silhouettes of militiamen and women and their peace-time occupations: 1c, Farmer. 2c, Welder. 3c, Seamstress.

1962, Feb. 26

703	A251	1c blue grn & blk	
704	A251	2c deep blue & blk	
705	A251	10c brt org & blk	

Bay of Pigs Invasion, 1st Anniv. — A252

1962, Apr. 17

706	A252	2c multi	
707	A252	3c multi	
708	A252	10c multi	

1st West Indies Packet A253

1962, Apr. 24

709	A253	10c red & gray	

Stamp Day. See No. E32.

Intl. Labor Day — A254

1962, May 1

710	A254	2c ocher & blk	
711	A254	3c ver & blk	
712	A254	10c greenish blue & blk	

Natl. Sports Institute (INDER) Emblem and Athletes
A255

1962, July 25 **Wmk. 321**

713 A255 1c Judo
714 A255 1c Discus
715 A255 1c Gymnastics
716 A255 1c Wrestling
717 A255 1c Weight lifting
718 A255 2c Roller skating
719 A255 2c Equestrian
720 A255 2c Archery
721 A255 2c Bicycling
722 A255 2c Bowling
723 A255 3c Power boating
724 A255 3c One-man kayak
725 A255 3c Swimming
726 A255 3c Sculling
727 A255 3c Yachting
728 A255 9c Soccer
729 A255 9c Volleyball
730 A255 9c Baseball
731 A255 9c Basketball
732 A255 9c Tennis
733 A255 10c Boxing
734 A255 10c Underwater fishing
735 A255 10c Model-plane flying
736 A255 10c Pistol shooting
737 A255 10c Water polo
738 A255 13c Paddleball
739 A255 13c Fencing
740 A255 13c Sports Palace
741 A255 13c Chess
742 A255 13c Jai alai

Stamps of the same denomination printed se-tenant in sheets of 25. Various combinations possible.

9th Anniv. of the Revolution
A256

Attack on Moncada Barracks: Abel Santamaria and: 2c, Barracks under siege. 3c, Children at Moncada School.

1962, July 26

743 A256 2c brn car & dark ultra
744 A256 3c dark ultra & brn car

8th World Youth Festival for Peace and Friendship, Helsinki, July 28-Aug. 6 — A257

1962, July 28

745 A257 2c Dove, emblem
746 A257 3c Hand grip, emblem
a. Min. sheet of 2, Nos. 745-746, imperf.

9th Central American and Caribbean Games, Kingston, Jamaica, Aug. 11 - 25 — A258

1962, Aug. 27

747 A258 1c Boxing
748 A258 2c Tennis
749 A258 3c Baseball
750 A258 13c Fencing

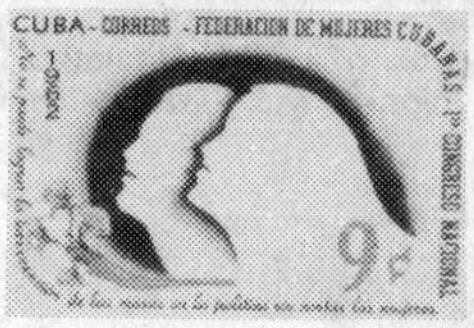

A259

First Natl. Congress of the Federation of Cuban Women — A260

1962, Oct. 1

751 A259 9c rose, blk & grn
752 A260 13c blk, grn & lt blue

Latin American University Games — A261

1962, Oct. 13 **Wmk. 106**

753 A261 1c Running
754 A261 2c Baseball
755 A261 3c Basketball
756 A261 13c World map

World Health Organization Campaign to Eradicate Malaria — A262

Designs: 1c, Magnified specimen of the parasitic protozoa, microscope. 2c, Swamp and mosquito. 3c, Chemist's structural formulas for quinine, cinchona plant.

1962, Dec. 14

757 A262 1c multi
758 A262 2c multi
759 A262 3c multi

Christmas Type of 1961

Designs: 2c, Reptiles. 3c, Insects, vert. 10c, Rodents.

1962, Dec. 21 **Unwmk.**

760 A248 2c Epicrates angulifer
761 A249 2c Cricosaurus typica
762 A249 2c Anolis equestris
763 A249 2c Tropidophis wrighti
764 A249 2c Cyclura macleayi
a. Block of 5 + label, Nos. 760-764
765 A248 3c Cubispa turquino
766 A249 3c Chrysis superba
767 A249 3c Essostruta roberto
768 A249 3c Hortensia conciliata
769 A249 3c Lachnopus argus
a. Block of 5 + label, Nos. 765-769
770 A248 10c Monophyllus cubanus
771 A249 10c Capromys pilorides
772 A249 10c Capromys pre-hensilis
773 A249 10c Atopogale cubana
774 A249 10c Capromys prehensilis
a. Block of 5 + label, Nos. 770-774

Christmas 1962. See note after No. 700.

Soviet Space Flights — A263

Spacecraft and cosmonauts: 1c, Vostok 1, Yuri A. Gagarin, Apr. 12, 1961. 2c, Vostok 2, Gherman S. Titov, Aug. 6-7, 1961. 3c, Vostok 3, Andrian G. Nikolaev, Aug. 11-15, 1962, and Vostok 4, Pavel R. Popovich, Aug. 12-15, 1962. 9c, Vostok 5, Valery F. Bykovsky, June 14-19, 1963. 13c, Vostok 6, Valentina V. Tereshkova, June 16-19, 1963.

1963-64 **Wmk. 321**

775 A263 1c ultra, red & yel
776 A263 2c grn, yel & rose lake
777 A263 3c yel, vio & ver
778 A263 9c red, dark vio & yel
779 A263 13c dark blue green, dull red brown & yel

Issue dates: 1c, 2c, 3c, Feb. 26. Others, Aug. 15, 1964.

Attack of the Presidential Palace, 6th Anniv.
A264

Designs: 9c, Guerillas attacking palace. 13c, Four student leaders. 30c, Jose A. Echeverria, Menelad Mora.

1963, Mar. 13

780 A264 9c dark red & blk
781 A264 13c chalky blue & sep
782 A264 30c org & grn

4th Pan American Games, Sao Paulo, Brazil, Apr. 20-May 5 — A265

1963, Apr. 20

783 A265 1c Baseball
784 A265 13c Boxing

Stamp Day
A266

Design: 3c, Mask mailbox, 19th cent. 10c, Mask mailbox at the Plaza de la Catedral, Havana.

1963, Apr. 25

785 A266 3c black & dark org
786 A266 10c black & pur

See Nos. 828-829, 956-957 and 1102-1103.

Labor Day — A267

1963, May 1

787 A267 3c shown
788 A267 13c Four workers

Intl. Children's Week, June 1-7
A268

1963, June 1

789 A268 3c blue blk & bister brn
790 A268 30c blue blk & red

Ritual Effigy — A269

Broken Chains at Moncada — A270

Taino Civilization artifacts: 3c, Wood-carved throne, horiz. 9c, Stone-carved figurine.

1963, June 29

791 A269 2c org & red brn
792 A269 3c ultra & red brn
793 A269 9c rose & gray

Montane Anthropology Museum, 60th anniv.

1963, July 26

Designs: 2c, Attack on the Presidential Palace. 3c, The insurrection. 7c, Strike of April 9. 9c, Triumph of the revolution. 10c, Agricultural reform and nationalization of industry. 13c, Bay of Pigs victory.

794 A270 1c pink & blk
795 A270 2c lt blue & vio brn
796 A270 3c lt vio & brn
797 A270 7c apple green & rose
798 A270 9c olive bister & rose vio
799 A270 10c beige & sage grn
800 A270 13c pale org & slate blue

Indigenous Fruit — A271

1963, Aug. 19

801 A271 1c Star apple
802 A271 2c Cherimoya
803 A271 3c Cashew nut
804 A271 10c Custard apple
805 A271 13c Mangoes

Geometric Shapes — A272

View of a Town — A273

Designs: No. 806, Circle, triangle, square, vert. No. 807, Roof, window, vert. No. 808, View of a town. No. 809, View of a town in blue. No. 810, View of a town in olive bister and red. No. 811, Circle, triangle, vert. No. 812, House, roof and doorway, vert. No. 813, House, girders.

1963, Sept. 29 **Unwmk.**

806 A272 3c multi
807 A272 3c multi
808 A273 3c multi
809 A273 3c multi
810 A273 13c multi
811 A272 13c multi
812 A272 13c multi
813 A272 13c multi

7th Intl. Congress of the Intl. Union of Architects.

Ernest Hemingway (1899-1961), American Author — A274

Hemingway and: 3c, The Old Man and the Sea. 9c, For Whom the Bell Tolls. 13c, Hemingway Museum (former residence), San Francisco de Paula, near Havana.

1963, Dec. 5 **Wmk. 321**

814 A274 3c brn & lt blue
815 A274 9c sage grn & pink
816 A274 13c blk & yel grn

Natl. Museum, 50th Anniv. A275

Works of art: 2c, El Zapateo (Dance), by Victor P. Landaluze. 3c, Abduction of the Mulatto Women, by Carlos Enriquez, vert. 9c, Greek Panathean amphora, vert. 13c, My Beloved (bust of a young woman), by Jean Antoine Houdon, vert.

1964, Mar. 19 **Unwmk.**

817 A275 2c multi
818 A275 3c multi
819 A275 9c multi
820 A275 13c multi

General Strike on Apr. 9, 6th Anniv. — A276

Rebel leaders: 2c, Bernardo Juan Borrell. 3c, Marcelo Salado. 10c, Oscar Lucero. 13c, Sergio Gonzalez.

1964, Apr. 9

821 A276 2c blk, yel grn & dull org
822 A276 3c blk, red & dull org
823 A276 10c blk, pur & beige
824 A276 13c blk, brt blue & beige

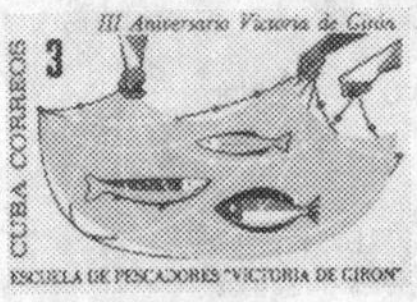

Bay of Pigs Invasion, 3rd Anniv. — A277

Designs: 3c, Fish in net. 10c, Victory Monument. 13c, Fallen eagle, vert.

1964, Apr. 17

825 A277 3c multi
826 A277 10c multi
827 A277 13c multi

Stamp Day Type of 1963

Stamp Day 1964: 3c, Vicente Mora Pera, 1st postal director. 13c, Unissued provisional stamp, 1871.

1964, Apr. 24

828 A266 3c ocher & dull lil
829 A266 13c dull vio & lt olive grn

Labor Day — A278

Diplomatic Relations with China — A279

1964, May 1

830 A278 3c Industry
831 A278 13c Agriculture

1964, May 15

Designs: 1c, China Monument, Havana. 2c, Cuban and Chinese farmers. 3c, Natl. flags.

832 A279 1c multi
833 A279 2c org brn, blk & apple grn
834 A279 3c multi

15th UPU Congress, Vienna, May-June A280

1964, May 29

835 A280 13c Hemispheres on world map
836 A280 30c Heinrich von Stephan
837 A280 50c UPU Monument, Bern

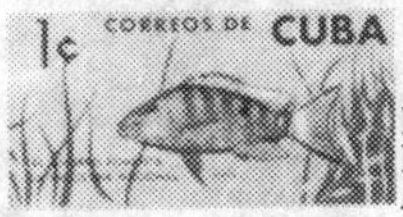

Development of Natl. Industry A281

1964, June 16

838 A281 1c Fish
839 A281 2c Cow
840 A281 13c Chickens

Merchant Fleet — A282

1964, June 30

841 A282 1c Rio Jibacoa
842 A282 2c Camilo Cienfuegos
843 A282 3c Sierra Maestra
844 A282 9c Bahia de Siguanea
845 A282 10c Oriente

Unification of Viet Nam — A283

Designs: 2c, Vietnamese guerrilla, American soldier. 3c, Northerner and southerner shaking hands over map of united Viet Nam. 10c, Ox-drawn plow, machinised harvester. 13c, Natl. flags and profiles of Cuban and Vietnamese farmers.

1964, July 20

846 A283 2c multi
847 A283 3c multi
848 A283 10c multi
849 A283 13c multi

11th Anniv. of the Revolution A284

1964 Summer Olympics, Tokyo, Oct. 10-25 A285

Designs: 3c, Raul Gomez Garcia and poem. 13c, Cover of La Historia Me Absolvera, by Fidel Castro.

1964, July 25

850 A284 3c red, tan & blk
851 A284 13c multi

1964, Oct. 10 **Wmk. 376** ***Perf. 10***

852 A285 1c Gymnastics
853 A285 2c Rowing
854 A285 3c Boxing
855 A285 7c Running, horiz.
856 A285 10c Fencing, horiz.
857 A285 13c Foil, cleats, oar, boxing glove, sun, horiz.

Satellite and Globe A286

Satellite and Partial Globe A287

No. C31 and Partial Globe A288

Various satellites and rockets.

1964, Oct. 15

858 A286 1c shown
859 A287 1c shown
860 A287 1c Globe LL
861 A287 1c Globe UR
862 A287 1c Globe UL
a. Block of 5 + label, Nos. 858-862
863 A286 2c Spacecraft and globe
864 A287 2c Globe LR
865 A287 2c Globe LL
866 A287 2c Globe UR
867 A287 2c Globe UL
a. Block of 5 + label, Nos. 863-867
868 A286 3c Satellite and globe
869 A287 3c Globe LR
870 A287 3c Globe LL
871 A287 3c Globe UR
872 A287 3c Globe UL
a. Block of 5 + label, Nos. 868-872
873 A286 9c Satellite and globe, diff
874 A287 9c Globe LR
875 A287 9c Globe LL
876 A287 9c Globe UR
877 A287 9c Globe UL
a. Block of 5 + label, Nos. 873-877
878 A286 13c Satellite and globe, diff.
879 A287 13c Globe LR
880 A287 13c Globe LL
881 A287 13c Globe UR
882 A287 13c Globe UR
a. Block of 5 + label, Nos. 878-882
883 A288 50c blk & lt grn
a. Souvenir sheet of one, Wmk. 321

Experimental Cuban postal rocket flight, 25th anniv. Stamps of the same denomination printed se-tenant in sheets of 20 stamps and 5 inscribed labels. Stamps of Type A287 arranged in blocks of 4 with a complete globe in center of block; Type A286 stamps and labels form a cross in center of sheet. Inscribed "1939-Cohete Postal Cubano-1964." No. 883a contains one 46x28mm stamp.

Type of A288 Ovptd. in Silver

1964, Oct. 17 **Unwmk.**

884 A288 50c dark red brown & lt grn

No. 884 not issued without overprint.

40th Death Anniv. of Lenin — A289

Havana Zoo — A290

Designs: 13c, Lenin Mausoleum, horiz. 30c, Lenin, star, hammer and sickle.

1964, Nov. 7 **Wmk. 376**

885 A289 3c org & blk
886 A289 13c pur, pink & blk
887 A289 30c blue & blk

1964, Nov. 25

888 A290 1c Leopard, horiz.
889 A290 2c Elephant
890 A290 3c Fallow deer
891 A290 4c Kangaroo, horiz.
892 A290 5c Lions, horiz.
893 A290 6c Eland, horiz.
894 A290 7c Zebra, horiz.
895 A290 8c Hyena, horiz.
896 A290 9c Tiger, horiz.
897 A290 10c Guanaco, horiz.
898 A290 13c Chimpanzees, horiz.
899 A290 20c Peccary, horiz.
900 A290 30c Raccoon
901 A290 40c Hippopotamus, horiz.
902 A290 50c Tapir, horiz.
903 A290 60c Dromedary
904 A290 70c Bison, horiz.
905 A290 80c Black bear
906 A290 90c Water buffalo, horiz.

Size: 47x32mm

907 A290 1p Deer in nature park, horiz.

Heroes of the 1895 War of Independence — A291

1964, Dec. 7

908 A291 1c Jose Marti
909 A291 2c Antonio Maceo
910 A291 3c Maximo Gomez
911 A291 13c Calixto Garcia

Christmas Type of 1961

Designs: 2c, Coral. 3c, Jellyfish. 10c, Starfish and sea-urchins.

1964, Dec. 18

912 A248 2c Dwarf cup coral
913 A249 2c Eusmilia fastigiata
914 A249 2c Acropora palmata
915 A249 2c Acropora profilera
916 A249 2c Diploria labyrinthiformis
a. Block of 5 + label, Nos. 912-916
917 A248 3c Condylactis gigantea
918 A249 3c Physalia physalis
919 A249 3c Aurelia aurita
920 A249 3c Linuche unguiculata

921 A249 3c Cassiopea frondosa
a. Block of 5 + label, Nos. 917-921
922 A248 10c Neocrinus blakei
923 A249 10c Eucidaris tribuloidas
924 A249 10c Tripneutes
925 A249 10c Ophiocoma echinata
926 A249 10c Oreaster celiculatus
a. Block of 5 + label, Nos. 922-926

Christmas 1964. See note after No. 700.

Dr. Tomas Romay (1764-1849), Physician and Scientist — A292

Romay Monument — A293

Designs: 2c, First vaccination against smallpox. 3c, Portrait and treatise on vaccination.

1964, Dec. 21

927 A292 1c blk & olive brn
928 A292 2c blk & tan
929 A293 3c olive & dark red brown
930 A293 10c bister & blk

Second Declaration of Havana — A294

Map of Latin America and ripples or map of Cuba and peasant breaking shackles under text from the Declaration of Havana: No. 931a, 932a "Visperas de su muerte..." No. 931b, 932b, "Un continente, que juntos suponen representos..." No. 931c, 932c, "Y no se ocultaran ni el gobierna..." No. 931d, 932d, "Millones de mulatos latinamericanos que saben..." No. 931e, "A labran la tierra en condiciones..."

1964, Dec. 23

931 Strip of 5
a.-e. A294 3c any single
932 Strip of 5
a.-e. A294 13c any single

Nos. 931-932 printed in sheets of 25 (5x5).

Dioramas in New Cuban Postal Museum — A295

1965, Jan. 4

Yellow & Black Border

933 A295 13c Maritime Post
934 A295 30c Insurrection Post

Souvenir Sheet

Imperf

935 Sheet of 2
a. A295 13c like #933, blue & blk border
b. A295 30c like #934, blue & blk border

Stamps in #935 have simulated perforations; buff margin is inscribed "PRECIO 50c" LR.

Fishing Fleet A296

1965, May 1

936 A296 1c Schooner
937 A296 2c Omicron
938 A296 3c Victoria
939 A296 9c Cardenas
940 A296 10c Sigma
941 A296 13c Lambda

Intl. Women's Day — A297

1965, Mar. 8

942 A297 3c Lidia Doce
943 A297 13c Clara Zetkin

Technical Revolution A298

Designs: 3c, Jose Antonio Echeverria University School. 13c, Stylized symbols of science and research, molecular structure and satellite dish.

1965, Mar. 31

944 A298 3c tan, blk & dark red brn
945 A298 13c multi

Cosmonauts, Rocket — A299

Designs: 30c, Cosmonauts Pavel I. Balyayev, Aleksei A. Leonov taking first space walk.

1965, Apr. 2

946 A299 30c dark blue, blk & brn
947 A299 50c brt pink & blue blk

Flight of Voskhod 2, the first man to walk in space, Mar. 17.

Abstract Wood Carving by Eugenio Rodriguez — A300

Abraham Lincoln — A301

Paintings in the Natl. Museum, Havana: 3c, Garden with Sunflowers, by Victor Manuel. 10c, Abstract, by Wilfredo Lam, horiz. 13c, Children, by Enrique Ponce, horiz.

1965, Apr. 12

948 A300 2c multi

Size: 35x46mm

949 A300 3c multi

Size: 46x35mm

950 A300 10c multi

Size: 43x37mm

951 A300 13c multi

1965, Apr. 15

Designs: 1c, Log cabin, birth site, horiz. 2c, Memorial, Washington, DC, horiz. 3c, Monument, Washington, DC. 13c, Portrait, quote.

952 A301 1c yel bister, red brn & gray
953 A301 2c lt blue & dark blue
954 A301 3c red org, blk & blue blk
955 A301 13c org, blk & blue blk

Stamp Day Type of 1963

Stamp Day 1965: 3c, 18th Cent. postmarks and packet. 13c, No. C16 and airplanes over capital.

1965, Apr. 24

956 A266 3c sep & dark org
957 A266 13c brt blue, sal rose & blk

Intl. Quiet Sun Year — A302

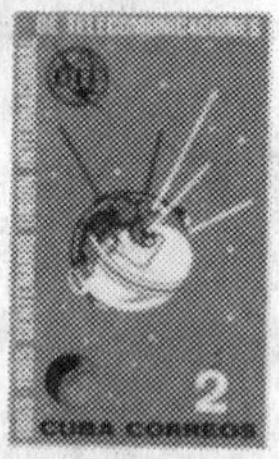

Intl. Telecommunications Union, Cent. — A303

1965, May 10

958 A302 1c Sun, Earth's magnetic pole, horiz.
959 A302 2c Sun Year emblem
960 A302 3c Earth's magnetic field, horiz.
961 A302 6c Atmospheric currents, horiz.
962 A302 30c Solar rays on planet surface
963 A302 50c Effect on satellite orbits, horiz.
a. Souv. sheet of one, imperf.
b. As "a," changed colors

Stamps in Nos. 963a-963b have simulated perforations.

Stamp in No. 963b is blue blk, Prus blue, org yel & red. Issued Oct. 10 for the Philatelic Space Exhibition, Havana, Oct. 10-17.

1965, May 17

964 A303 1c Station, horiz.
965 A303 2c Satellite
966 A303 3c Telstar, horiz.
967 A303 10c Telstar, receiving station
968 A303 30c ITU emblem, horiz.

9th Communist World Youth and Students Congress — A304

1965, June 10

969 A304 13c Flags of Cuba and Algeria, emblem
970 A304 30c Flags, guerrillas

Matias Perez, Cuban Aeronautics Pioneer A305

1965, June 23

971 A305 3c pink & blk
972 A305 13c dull vio & blk, diff.

Flowers and Maps of Their Locations — A306

1965, July 20

973 A306 1c Rosa canina, Europe
974 A306 2c Chrysanthemum hortorum, Asia
975 A306 3c Strelitzia reginae, Africa
976 A306 4c Dahlia pinnata, No. America
977 A306 5c Cattleya labiata, So. America
978 A306 13c Grevillea banksii, Oceania
979 A306 30c Brunfelsia nitida, Cuba

1st Natl. Games A307

1965, July 25

980 A307 1c Swimming
981 A307 2c Basketball
982 A307 3c Gymnastics
983 A307 30c Hurdling

Revolution Museum Opening A308

1965, July 26

984 A308 1c Anti-tank guns
985 A308 2c Tanks
986 A308 3c Bazookas
987 A308 10c Uniform, guerillas
988 A308 13c Compass, yacht Granma

A309

1965, Aug. 20

989 A309 1c Finlay's signature
990 A309 2c Anopheles mosquito
991 A309 3c Portrait
992 A309 7c Microscope
993 A309 9c Portrait, diff.
994 A309 10c Monument
995 A309 13c Discussing theory with doctors

Carlos J. Finlay (1833-1915), discovered transmission of yellow fever via anopheles mosquito. Nos. 990-995 vert.

Butterflies A310

1965, Sept. 22 **Unwmk.**

996 A310 2c Dismorphia cubana
997 A310 2c Anetia numidia briarea
998 A310 2c Carathis gortynoides
999 A310 2c Hymenitis cubana
1000 A310 2c Eubaphe heros
a. Strip of 5, Nos. 996-1000

1001 A310 3c Lycorea ceres demeter
1002 A310 3c Eubaphe disparitis
1003 A310 3c Siderone nemesis
1004 A310 3c Syntomidopsis variegata
1005 A310 3c Ctenuchidia virgo
a. Strip of 5, Nos. 1001-1005
1006 A310 13c Prepona antimache crossina
1007 A310 13c Sylepta reginalis
1008 A310 13c Chlosyne perezi perezi
1009 A310 13c Anaea clytemnestra iphigenia
1010 A310 13c Anetia cubana
a. Strip of 5, Nos. 1006-1010

Cuban Mint, 50th Anniv. A311

Coins (obverse and reverse).

1965, Oct. 13
1011 A311 1c 20 centavos, 1962
1012 A311 2c 1 peso, 1934
1013 A311 3c 40 centavos, 1962
1014 A311 8c 1 peso, 1915
1015 A311 10c Marti peso, 1953
1016 A311 13c 20 pesos, 1915

Tropical Fruit — A312

1965, Nov. 15 *Perf. 12½*
1017 A312 1c Oranges
1018 A312 2c Custard apples
1019 A312 3c Papayas
1020 A312 4c Bananas
1021 A312 10c Avocado
1022 A312 13c Pineapple
1023 A312 20c Guavas
1024 A312 50c Marmalade plums

Christmas Type of 1961

Birds.

1965, Dec. 1
1025 A248 3c Icterus galbula
1026 A249 3c Passerina ciris
1027 A249 3c Setophaga ruticillar
1028 A249 3c Dendroica tusca
1029 A249 3c Pheucticus ludovicianus
a. Block of 5 + label, Nos. 1025-1029
1030 A248 5c Pyranga olivacea
1031 A249 5c Dendroica dominica
1032 A249 5c Vermivora pinus
1033 A249 5c Protonotaria citrea
1034 A249 5c Wilsonia citrina
a. Block of 5 + label, Nos. 1030-1034
1035 A248 13c Passerina cyanea
1036 A249 13c Anas discors
1037 A249 13c Aix sponsa
1038 A249 13c Spatula clypeata
1039 A249 13c Nycticorax hoactli
a. Block of 5 + label, Nos. 1035-1039

Christmas 1965. See note after No. 700.

Intl. Athletic Competition, Havana, 7th Anniv. — A313

1965, Dec. 11 **Wmk. 376** *Perf. 10*
1040 A313 1c Hurdling
1041 A313 2c Discus
1042 A313 3c Shot put
1043 A313 7c Javelin
1044 A313 9c High jump
1045 A313 10c Hammer throw
1046 A313 13c Running

Fish in the Natl. Aquarium A314

1965, Dec. 5 **Unwmk.** *Perf. 12½*
1047 A314 1c Echeneis naucrates
1048 A314 2c Katsuwonus pelamis
1049 A314 3c Abudefduf saxatilis
1050 A314 4c Istiophorus
1051 A314 5c Epinephelus striatus
1052 A314 10c Lutianus analis
1053 A314 13c Ocyurus chrysurus
1054 A314 30c Holocentrus ascensionis

Andre Voisin (d. 1964), French Naturalist A315

1965, Dec. 21 **Wmk. 376**
1055 A315 3c shown
1056 A315 13c Portrait, flags, microscope, plant

Transportation — A316

1965, Dec. 30
1057 A316 1c Skoda bus, Czechoslovakia
1058 A316 2c Ikarus bus, Hungary
1059 A316 3c Leyland bus, G.B.
1060 A316 4c TEM-4 locomotive, USSR
1061 A316 7c BB-69.000 locomotive, France
1062 A316 10c Remolcador tugboat, DDR
1063 A316 13c 15 de Marzo freighter, Spain
1064 A316 20c Ilyushin 18 jet, USSR

A317

7th Anniv. of the Revolution A318

1966, Jan. 2
1065 A317 1c Guerrillas
1066 A317 2c Commander and tank
1067 A317 3c Sailor, patrol boat
1068 A318 10c Jet aircraft
1069 A318 13c Rocket

Conference of Asian, African and South American Countries, Havana A319

1966, Jan. 3
1070 A319 2c Emblem at R
1071 A319 3c Emblem at L
1072 A319 13c Emblem at center

Guardalabarca Beach — A320

1966, Feb. 10
1073 A320 1c shown
1074 A320 2c Gran Piedra mountain
1075 A320 3c Guama Village
1076 A320 13c Soroa waterfall, vert.

11th Medical and 7th Natl. Dental Congresses A321

1966, Feb. 28 **Wmk. 376**
1077 A321 3c multi
1078 A321 13c multi, diff.

Folk Art A322

1966, Feb. 28 **Unwmk.**
1079 A322 1c Afro-cuban ritual puppet
1080 A322 2c Sombreros
1081 A322 3c Ceramic vase
1082 A322 7c Lanterns, lamp
1083 A322 9c Table lamp
1084 A322 10c Shark, wood sculpture
1085 A322 13c Snail-shell necklace, earrings

Nos. 1079-1083 vert.

Chelsea College, by Canaletto A323

Ceramics and paintings in the National Museum: 1c, Ming vase. 3c, Portrait of a Lady, by Goya. 13c, Portrait of Fayum, bas-relief. Nos. 1086, 1088-1089 vert.

1966, Mar. 31 **Wmk. 376**
1086 A323 1c multi
1087 A323 2c multi
1088 A323 3c multi
1089 A323 13c multi

First Man in Space, 5th Anniv. A324

Designs: 1c, Konstantin Eduardovich Tsiolkovsky (1857-1935), Soviet rocket and space sciences pioneer. 2c, Cosmonauts in training, vert. 3c, Yuri Gagarin, rocket, Earth. 7c, Cosmonauts Nikolaev and Popovich, vert. 9c, Tereshkova and Bykovsky. 10c, Komarov, Feoktistov and Yegarov. 13c, Leonov taking first space walk.

1966, Apr. 12
1090 A324 1c multi
1091 A324 2c multi
1092 A324 3c multi
1093 A324 7c multi
1094 A324 9c multi
1095 A324 10c multi
1096 A324 13c multi

Bay of Pigs Invasion, 5th Anniv. A325

1966, Apr. 17
1097 A325 2c Tank
1098 A325 3c Burning ship, plane crash
1099 A325 9c Tank in ditch
1100 A325 10c Soldier, gunners
1101 A325 13c Operations map

Stamp Day Type of 1963

Designs: 3c, Cuban Postal Museum interior. 13c, No. 613 and stamp collector.

1966, Apr. 24
1102 A266 3c sage grn & sal rose
1103 A266 13c brn, sal rose & blk

Stamp Day 1966. 1st Anniv. of the Cuban Postal Museum (No. 1102); 1st anniv. of the Cuban Philatelic Federation (No. 1103).

Flowers and Symbols of Industry — A326

1966, May 1
1104 A326 2c Anvil
1105 A326 3c Machete
1106 A326 10c Hammer
1107 A326 13c Hemisphere, gearwheel

Labor Day.

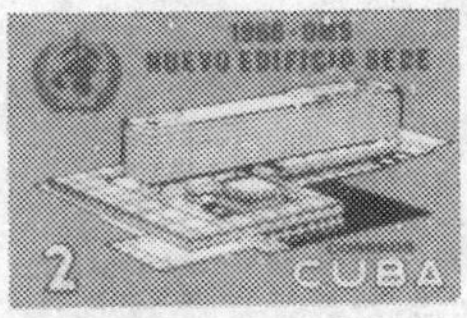

Opening of the World Health Organization Headquarters, Geneva — A327

Views of WHO headquarters and emblem or emblem on flag.

1966, May 3
1108 A327 2c blk & yel org
1109 A327 3c blk, lt blue & yel org
1110 A327 13c blk, lt blue & yel org

10th Central American and Caribbean Games, Puerto Rico, June 11-25
A328

1966, June 11

1111 A328 1c Running, vert.
1112 A328 2c Rifle shooting
1113 A328 3c Baseball, vert.
1114 A328 7c Volleyball, vert.
1115 A328 9c Soccer, vert.
1116 A328 10c Boxing, vert.
1117 A328 13c Basketball, vert.

Progress in Education
A329

Designs: 1c, Makarenko School, Playa de Tarara. 2c, Natl. Literacy Campaign Museum. 3c, Lantern, literacy campaign emblem for 1961. 10c, Frank Pais education team in the mountains. 13c, Farmer, factory worker.

1966, June 15

1118 A329 1c grn & blk
1119 A329 2c yel, olive bister & blk
1120 A329 3c brt blue, lt blue & blk
1121 A329 10c golden brn, brn & blk
1122 A329 13c multi

1st Graduating class of Makarenko School (1c), 5th anniv. of the Natl. Literacy Campaign (3c), 4th anniv. of agricultural and industrial trade education (13c).

12th Congress of the Cuban Labor Organization — A330

1966, Aug. 12

1123 A330 3c multi

Sea Shells — A331

1966, Aug. 25 **Unwmk.**

1124 A331 1c Liguus flammellus
1125 A331 2c Cypraea zebra
1126 A331 3c Strombus pugilis
1127 A331 7c Aequipecten muscosu
1128 A331 9c Liguus fasciatus crenatus
1129 A331 10c Charonia variegata
1130 A331 13c Liguus fasciatus archeri

Breeding Messenger Pigeons
A332

1966, Sept. 18 **Wmk. 376**

1131 A332 1c shown
1132 A332 2c Timer
1133 A332 3c Coops
1134 A332 7c Breeder tending coops
1135 A332 9c Pigeons in yard
1136 A332 10c Two men, message

Size: 47x32mm

1137 A332 13c Baracoa to Havana championship flight, July 26, 1959

Provincial and Natl. Coats of Arms, Map of Cuba — A333

17th World Chess Olympiad, Havana — A334

1966, Oct. 10

1138 A333 1c Pinar del Rio
1139 A333 2c Havana
1140 A333 3c Matanzas
1141 A333 4c Las Villas
1142 A333 5c Camaguey
1143 A333 9c Oriente

Size: 30x48mm

1144 A333 13c National arms

1966, Oct. 18

1145 A334 1c Pawn
1146 A334 2c Rook
1147 A334 3c Knight
1148 A334 9c Bishop
1149 A334 10c Queen, games, horiz.
1150 A334 13c King and emblem, horiz.

Souvenir Sheet

Imperf

1151 A334 30c Capablanca Vs. Lasker, 1914, horiz.

No. 1151 contains one 49½x31mm stamp.

Cuban-Soviet Diplomatic Relations — A335

1966, Nov. 7

1152 A335 2c Lenin Hospital
1153 A335 3c Oil tanker, world map
1154 A335 10c Workers, gearwheels
1155 A335 13c Agriculture

2nd Song Festival
A336

Cuban composers and their compositions.

1966, Nov. 18

1156 A336 1c Amadeo Roldan
1157 A336 2c Eduardo Sanchez de Fuentes
1158 A336 3c Moises Simons
1159 A336 7c Jorge Anckermann
1160 A336 9c Alejandro G. Caturla
1161 A336 10c Eliseo Grenet
1162 A336 13c Ernesto Lecuona

Viet Nam War — A337

Flag of Viet Nam and: 2c, US aircraft discharging bombs, dead cattle. 3c, Gas mask and victims. 13c, US bombs, women and children.

1966, Nov. 23

1163 A337 2c multi
1164 A337 3c multi
1165 A337 13c multi

10th Anniv. of Successful Revolution Campaigns — A338

Revolution leaders and scenes of the insurrection.

1966, Nov. 30

1166 A338 1c Antonio Fernandez
1167 A338 2c Candido Gonzalez
1168 A338 3c Jose Tey
1169 A338 7c Tony Aloma
1170 A338 9c Otto Paralleda
1171 A338 10c Juan Manuel Marquez
1172 A338 13c Frank Pais

Intl. Leisure Time and Recreation Seminar
A339

1966, Dec. 2

1173 A339 3c shown
1174 A339 9c World map, stopwatch, eye
1175 A339 13c Earth, clock, emblem

1st Natl. Telecommunications Forum — A340

1966, Dec. 12

1176 A340 3c shown
1177 A340 10c Satellite in orbit
1178 A340 13c Shell, satellite
 a. Souv. sheet of 3, #1176-1178, imperf.

No. 1178a sold for 30c.

Christmas Type of 1961

1966, Dec. 20 **Unwmk.**

1179 A248 1c Cypripedium eurylochus
1180 A249 1c Cattleya speciosissima
1181 A249 1c Cattleya mendelii majestica
1182 A249 1c Cattleya trianae amesiana
1183 A249 1c Cattleya labiata macfarlanei
 a. Block of 5 + label, Nos. 1179-1183
1184 A248 3c Cypripedium morganiae burfordense
1185 A249 3c Cattleya Countess of Derby
1186 A249 3c Cypripedium hookerae volunteanum
1187 A249 3c Cattleya warscewiczii reginae burfordense
1188 A249 3c Cypripedium stonei cannartae
 a. Block of 5 + label, Nos. 1184-1188
1189 A248 13c Cattleya mendelii Duchess of Montrose
1190 A249 13c Oncidium macranthum
1191 A249 13c Cypripedium stonei platytoenium
1192 A249 13c Cattleya dowiana aurea
1193 A249 13c Laelia anceps
 a. Block of 5 + label, Nos. 1189-1193

Christmas 1966. See note after No. 700.

8th Anniv. of the Revolution — A341

1967, Jan. 2

1194 A341 3c Liberation, 1959
1195 A341 3c Agrarian Reform, 1960
1196 A341 3c Education, 1961
1197 A341 3c Agriculture, 1965
 a. Strip of 4, Nos. 1194-1197
1198 A341 13c Rodin's Thinker, Planning, 1962
1199 A341 13c Organization, 1963
1200 A341 13c Economy, 1964
1201 A341 13c Solidarity, 1966
 a. Strip of 4, Nos. 1198-1201

Nos. 1198-1201 vert.

Spring, by Jorge Arche — A342

Paintings in the Natl. Museum: 1c, Coffee Machine, by Angel Acosta Leon, vert. 2c, Country People, by Eduardo Abela, vert. 13c, Still-life, by Amelia Pelaez, vert. 30c, Landscape, by Gonzalo Escalante.

1967, Feb. 27

1202 A342 1c multi
1203 A342 2c multi
1204 A342 3c multi
1205 A342 13c multi
1206 A342 30c multi

Natl. Events, Mar. 13, 1957
A343

1967, Mar. 13 **Wmk. 376**

1207 A343 3c Attack on Presidential Palace

Size: 41x28mm

1208 A343 13c Landing of Corynthia
1209 A343 30c Cienfuego revolt

Evolution of Man — A344

Prehistoric men: 2c, Australopithecus. 3c, Pithecanthropus erectus. 4c, Sinanthropus pekinensis. 5c, Neanderthal man. 13c, Cro-magnon man carving tusk. 20c, Cro-magnon man painting petroglyph.

1967, Mar. 31 **Unwmk.**

1210 A344 1c multi
1211 A344 2c multi
1212 A344 3c multi
1213 A344 4c multi
1214 A344 5c multi
1215 A344 13c multi
1216 A344 20c multi

Stamp Day A345

Carriages.

1967, Apr. 24

1217 A345 3c Victoria
1218 A345 9c Volante
1219 A345 13c Quitrin

EXPO '67, Montreal, Apr. 28-Oct. 27 A346

1967, Apr. 28

1220 A346 1c Cuban pavilion
1221 A346 2c Space exploration
1222 A346 3c Petroglyph, hieroglyph
1223 A346 13c Agriculture, computer technology
1224 A346 20c Athletes

Botanical Gardens, Sequicentennial A347

Flowering plants.

1967, May 30

1225 A347 1c Eugenia malaccencis
1226 A347 2c Jacaranda filicifolia
1227 A347 3c Coroupita guianensis
1228 A347 4c Spathodea campanulata
1229 A347 5c Cassia fistula
1230 A347 13c Plumieria alba
1231 A347 20c Erythrina poeppigiana

Natl. Ballet — A348

1967, June 15

1232 A348 1c Giselle
1233 A348 2c Swan Lake
1234 A348 3c Don Quixote
1235 A348 4c Calaucan
1236 A348 13c Swan Lake
1237 A348 20c Nutcracker

Intl. Ballet Festival, Havana.

5th Pan American Games, Winnipeg, Canada, July 22-Aug. 7 — A349

1st Conference of Latin American Solidarity Organization (OLAS) — A350

1967, July 22

1238 A349 1c Baseball, horiz.
1239 A349 2c Swimming, horiz.
1240 A349 3c Basketball
1241 A349 4c Gymnastic rings
1242 A349 5c Water polo
1243 A349 13c Weight lifting, horiz.
1244 A349 20c Javelin

1967, July 28 **Wmk. 376**

Portrait of representative, map of South American homeland: No. 1245, Camilo Torres, Colombia. No. 1246, Luis de la Puente Uceda, Peru. No. 1247, Luis A. Turcios Lima, Guatemala. No. 1248, Fabricio Ojeda, Venezuela.

1245 A350 13c pale grn, blk & red
1246 A350 13c lil, blk & red
1247 A350 13c dark chalky blue, blk & red
1248 A350 13c golden brn, blk & red

Portrait of Sonny Rollins, by Alan Davie A351

Bathers, by Gustave Singier A352

Modern Art: No. 1250, Twelve Selenities, by Felix Labisse. No. 1251, Night of the Drinker, by Friedensreich Hundertwasser. No. 1252, Figure, by Mariano. No. 1253, All-Souls, by Wilfredo Lam. No. 1254, Darkness and Cracks, by Antonio Tapies. No. 1256, Torso of a Muse, by Jean Arp. No. 1257, Figure, by M.W. Svanberg. No. 1258, Oppenheimer's Information, by Erro. No. 1259, Where Cardinals Are Born, by Max Ernst. No. 1260, Havana Landscape, by Portocarrero. No. 1261, EG 12, by Victor Vasarely. No. 1262, Frisco, by Alexander Calder. No. 1263, The Man with the Pipe, by Picasso. No. 1264, Abstract Composition, by Sergei Poliakoff. No. 1265, Painting, by Bram van Velde. No. 1266, Sower of Fires, by R. Matta. No. 1267, The Art of Living, by Rene Magritte. No. 1268, Poem, by Joan Miro. No. 1269, Young Tigers, by Jean Messagier. No. 1270, Painting, by M. Vieira da Silva. No. 1271, Live Cobra, by Pierre Alechinsky. No. 1272, Stalingrad, by Asger Jorn. 30c, Warriors, by Edouard Pignon. 50c, Cloister, a mural at the exhibition representing the Salon de Mayo pictures.

1967, July 29 **Unwmk.**

1249 A351 1c shown
1250 A351 1c multi
1251 A351 1c multi
1252 A351 1c multi
1253 A351 1c multi
a. Strip of 5, Nos. 1249-1253

Sizes: 36½x54mm, 36½x53mm, 36½x45mm, 36½x41mm

1254 A352 2c multi
1255 A352 2c shown
1256 A352 2c multi
1257 A352 2c multi
1258 A352 2c multi
a. Strip of 5, Nos. 1254-1258

Sizes: 36½x54mm, 36½x40mm, 36½x42mm, 36½x49mm

1259 A352 3c multi
1260 A352 3c multi
1261 A352 3c multi
1262 A352 3c multi
1263 A352 3c multi
a. Strip of 5, Nos. 1259-1263

Sizes: 35x15mm, 35x67mm, 35x46½mm, 35x55mm

1264 A352 4c multi
1265 A352 4c multi
1266 A352 4c multi
1267 A352 4c multi
1268 A352 4c multi
a. Strip of 5, Nos. 1264-1268

Sizes: 49x32mm, 49x35mm, 49x46mm

1269 A351 13c multi
1270 A351 13c multi
1271 A351 13c multi
1272 A351 13c multi
a. Strip of 4, Nos. 1269-1272

Size: 54x32mm

1273 A351 30c multi

Souvenir Sheet

Imperf

1274 A351 50c multi

Salon de Mayo Art Exhibition, Havana. No. 1274 contains one 88x45mm stamp with simulated perforations. Issued Oct. 7.

World Underwater Fishing Championships — A353

1967, Sept. 5

1275 A353 1c Green moray
1276 A353 2c Octopus
1277 A353 3c Great barracuda
1278 A353 4c Blue shark
1279 A353 5c Spotted jewfish
1280 A353 13c Sting ray
1281 A353 20c Green turtle

Soviet Space Program — A354

1967, Oct. 4 **Wmk. 376**

1282 A354 1c Sputnik 1
1283 A354 2c Lunik 3
1284 A354 3c Venusik
1285 A354 4c Cosmos
1286 A354 5c Mars 1
1287 A354 9c Electron 1 & 2
1288 A354 10c Luna 9
1289 A354 13c Luna 10
a. Souv. sheet of 8, #1282-1289, imperf.

Stamps in #1289a have simulated perfs.

50th Anniv. of the October Revolution, Russia — A355

Paintings: 1c, Storming the Winter Palace, by Sokolov, Skalia and Miasnikov. 2c, Lenin Addressing Congress, by W.A. Serov. 3c, Lenin, by H.D. Nalbandian. 4c, Lenin Explaining Electrification Map, by L.A. Schmatko. 5c, Dawn of the Five-Year Plan, by J.D. Romas. 13c, Kusnetzkroi Steel Furnace No. 1, by P. Kotov. 30c, Victory, by A. Krivonogov.

1967, Nov. 7 **Unwmk.**

1290 A355 1c 64x36mm
1291 A355 2c 48x36mm
1292 A355 3c
1293 A355 4c 48x36mm
1294 A355 5c 50x36mm
1295 A355 13c 36x50mm
1296 A355 30c 50x36mm

Castle of the Royal Forces, Havana A356

Historic architecture: 2c, Iznaga Tower, Trinidad, vert. 3c, Castle of Our Lady of the Angels, Cienfuegos. 4c, St. Francis de Paula Church, Havana. 13c, St. Francis Convent, Havana. 30c, Castle del Morro, Santiago de Cuba.

1967, Nov. 7 **Wmk. 376**

Sizes: 26x47mm (1c), 41x29mm (3c, 4c), 38½x31mm (13c)

1297 A356 1c multi
1298 A356 2c multi
1299 A356 3c multi
1300 A356 4c multi
1301 A356 13c multi
1302 A356 30c multi

Christmas Type of 1961

Birds.

1967, Dec. 20

1303 A248 1c Struthia camelus australis
1304 A249 1c Chysolophus pictus
1305 A249 1c Ciconia ciconia ciconia
1306 A249 1c Balearica pavonina
1307 A249 1c Dromiceius novaehollandiae
a. Block of 5 + label, Nos. 1303-1307
1308 A248 3c Anodorhynchus hyacinthus
1309 A249 3c Psittacus erithacus
1310 A249 3c Domicella garrula
1311 A249 3c Ramphastos sulfuratus
1312 A249 3c Kakatoe galerita galerita
a. Block of 5 + label, Nos. 1308-1312
1313 A248 13c Phoenicopterus ruber
1314 A249 13c Pelecanus erythrorhynchos
1315 A249 13c Alopochen aegyptiacus
1316 A249 13c Dendronessa galericulata
1317 A249 13c Chenopsis atrata
a. Block of 5 + label, Nos. 1313-1317

Christmas 1967. See note after No. 700.

Ernesto "Che" Guevara (1928-1967), Revolution Leader A356a

1968, Jan. 3

1318 A356a 13c blk, dark red & buff

Cultural Congress, Havana A357

Abstract designs: No. 1319, Independence fostering culture. No. 1320, Integral formation of man. No. 1321, Responsibility of intellectuals. No. 1322, Relationship between culture and the mass media. No. 1323, The arts versus science and technology. Nos. 1319-1322 vert.

1968, Jan. 4

1319 A357 3c multi
1320 A357 3c multi
1321 A357 13c multi
1322 A357 13c multi
1323 A357 30c multi

Canaries and Breeding Cycles — A358

1968, Apr. 13

1324 A358 1c F.C.C. 4016
1325 A358 2c A.C.C. 774
1326 A358 3c A.C.C. 122
1327 A358 4c F.C.C. 4477
1328 A358 5c A.C.C 117
1329 A358 13c A.N.R. 1175
1330 A358 20c A.C.C. 777

Stamp Day — A359

Paintings: 13c, The Village Postman, by J. Harris. 30c, The Philatelist, by G. Sciltian.

1968, Apr. 24 **Unwmk.**

1331 A359 13c multi
1332 A359 30c multi

World Health Organization, 20th Anniv. A360

1968, May 10 **Wmk. 376**

1333 A360 13c Nurse, mother, child
1334 A360 30c Surgeons

Intl. Children's Day — A361

1968, June 1

1335 A361 3c multi

Seville Camaguey Flight, 35th Anniv. — A362

1968, June 20

1336 A362 13c Plane Four Winds
1337 A362 30c Capt. Berberan, Lt. Collar, pilots

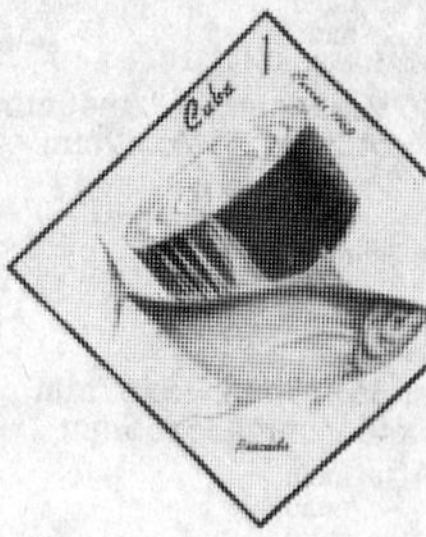

Natl. Food Production — A363

1968, June 29

1338 A363 1c Yellow tuna, can
1339 A363 2c Cow, dairy products
1340 A363 3c Rooster, eggs
1341 A363 13c Rum, sugar cane
1342 A363 20c Crayfish, box

Attack of Moncada Barracks, 15th Anniv. A364

1968, July 26

Size: 43x29mm (13c)

1343 A364 3c Siboney farmhouse
1344 A364 13c Assault route, Santiago de Cuba
1345 A364 30c Students, school

Committee for the Defense of the Revolution, 8th Anniv. — A365

1968, Sept. 28

1346 A365 3c multi

Guerilla Day A366

Che Guevara and: 1c, Rifleman and "En Cualquier Lugar..." 3c, Machine gunners and "Crear tres muchos Viet Nam." 9c, Silhouette of battalion and "Este Tipo De Lucha..." 10c, Guerillas cheering and "Hoy aquilatamos..." 13c, Map of Caribbean, So. America and "Hasta La Victoria Siempre."

1968, Oct. 8

1347 A366 1c gold, brt blue grn & blk
1348 A366 3c gold, org brn blk
1349 A366 9c multi
1350 A366 10c gold, lt olive grn & blk
1351 A366 13c gold, red org & blk

Cuban War of Independence, Cent. — A367

Independence fighters and scenes.

1968, Oct. 10 **Unwmk.**

1352 A367 1c C.M. de Cespedes, broken wheel
1353 A367 1c E. Betances, horsemen, flag
1354 A367 1c I. Agramonte, Clavellinas Monument
1355 A367 1c A. Maceo, Baragua Protest
1356 A367 1c J. Marti, horsemen
a. Strip of 5, Nos. 1352-1356
1357 A367 3c M. Gomez, The Invasion
1358 A367 3c J.A. Mella, declaration
1359 A367 3c A. Guiteras, El Morrillo monument
1360 A367 3c A. Santamaria, attack on Moncada Barracks
1361 A367 3c F. Paiz memorial
a. Strip of 5, Nos. 1357-1361
1362 A367 9c J. Echeverria, student protest
1363 A367 13c C. Cienfuegos, insurrection
1364 A367 30c Che Guevara, 1st Declaration of Havana

Souvenir Sheet

The Burning of Bayamo, by J.E. Hernandez Giro — A368

1968, Oct. 18 ***Imperf.***

1365 A368 50c multi

Natl. Philatelic Exhibition, independence cent. Stamp in No. 1365 has simulated perforations.

19th Summer Olympics, Mexico City, Oct. 12-27 — A369

1968, Oct. 21 ***Perf. 12½***

1366 A369 1c Parade of athletes
1367 A369 2c Women's basketball, vert.
1368 A369 3c Hammer throw, vert.
1369 A369 4c Boxing
1370 A369 5c Water polo
1371 A369 13c Pistol shooting

Size: 32x50mm

1372 A369 30c Mexican flag, calendar stone

Souvenir Sheet

Imperf

1373 A369 50c Running

Stamp in #173 has simulated perforations.

Civilian Activities of the Armed Forces A370

1968, Dec. 2 **Wmk. 376** ***Perf. 12½***

1374 A370 3c Crop dusting
1375 A370 9c Che Guevara's Brigade
1376 A370 10c Road building
1377 A370 13c Plowing, harvesting

San Alejandro School of Painting, Sesquicentennial — A371

Paintings: 1c, Manrique de Lara's Family, by Jean Baptiste Vermay, vert. 2c, Seascape, by Leopoldo Romanach. 3c, Wild Cane, by Antonio Rodriguez, vert. 4c, Self-portrait, by Miguel Melero, vert. 5c, The Lottery List, by Jose Joaquin Tejada. 13c, Portrait of Nina, by Armando B. Menocal, vert. 30c, Landscape, by Esteban B. Chartrand. 50c, Siesta, by Guillermo Collazo.

1968, Dec. 30 **Unwmk.**

Sizes: 38x48mm (1c, 3c), 39x50mm (4c, 13c), 53x36mm (30c)

1378 A371 1c multi
1379 A371 2c multi
1380 A371 3c multi
1381 A371 4c multi
1382 A371 5c multi
1383 A371 13c multi
1384 A371 30c multi

Souvenir Sheet

Imperf

1385 A371 50c multi

No. 1385 contains one 52x41½mm stamp that has simulated perforations.

10th Anniv. of the Revolution A372

1969, Jan. 3 **Wmk. 376** ***Perf. 12½***

1386 A372 13c multi

Villaclarenos Rebellion, Cent. — A373

1969, Feb. 6

1387 A373 3c Gutierrez and Sanchez

Women's Day — A374

Design: Mariana Grajales, rose and statue.

1969, Mar. 8

1388 A374 3c multi

Cuban Pioneers and Young Communists Unions — A375

1969, Apr. 4

1389 A375 3c Pioneers
1390 A375 13c Young Communists

Guaimaro Assembly, Cent.
A376

1969, Apr. 10
1391 A376 3c dark brn

The Postman, by Jean C. Cazin
A377

Paintings: 30c, Portrait of a Young Man, by George Romney.

1969, Apr. 24 **Unwmk.**
1392 A377 13c multi

Size: 35½x43½mm

1393 A377 30c multi

Stamp Day.

Agrarian Reform, 10th Anniv.
A378

1969, May 17 **Wmk. 376**
1394 A378 13c multi

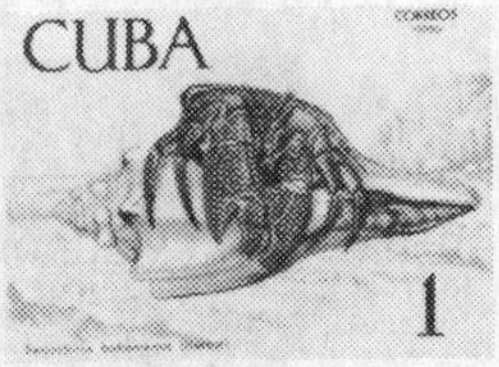

Marine Life
A379

1969, May 20 **Unwmk.**
1395 A379 1c Petrochirus bahamensis
1396 A379 2c Stenopus hispidus
1397 A379 3c Panulirus argus
1398 A379 4c Callinectes sapidus
1399 A379 5c Gecarcinus ruricola
1400 A379 13c Macrobrachium carcinus
1401 A379 30c Carpilius coralinus

Intl. Labor Organization, 50th Anniv. — A380

1969, June 6 **Wmk. 376**
1402 A380 3c shown
1403 A380 13c Blacksmith breaking chains

Paintings in the Natl. Museum — A381

Designs: 1c, Flowers, by Raul Milian, vert. 2c, Annunciation, by Antonia Eiriz. 3c, Factory, by Marcelo Pogolotti, vert. 4c, Territorial Waters, by Luis Martinez Pedro, vert. 5c, Miss Sarah Gale, by John Hoppner, vert. 13c, Two Women Wearing Mantilla, by Ignacio Zuloaga. 30c, Virgin and Child, by Francisco de Zurburan.

1969, June 15 **Unwmk.**
1404 A381 1c 39x59mm
1405 A381 2c
1406 A381 3c 39½x49mm
1407 A381 4c 39½x43mm
1408 A381 5c 39½x45½mm
1409 A381 13c 38x41½mm
1410 A381 30c 39x45mm

Broadcasting Institute — A382

1969, July 5 **Wmk. 376**
1411 A382 3c shown
1412 A382 13c Hemispheres, tower
1413 A382 1p Waves on graph

Fish
A383

1969, July 20 **Unwmk.**
1414 A383 1c Apogon maculatus
1415 A383 2c Bodianus rufus
1416 A383 3c Microspathodon chrysurus
1417 A383 4c Gramma loreto
1418 A383 5c Chromis marginatus
1419 A383 13c Myripristis jacobus
1420 A383 30c Nomeus gronovii, vert.

Natl. Film Industry, 10th Anniv. — A384

1969, Aug. 5 **Wmk. 376**
1421 A384 1c Poster
1422 A384 3c Documentaries
1423 A384 13c Cartoons
1424 A384 30c Entertainers

Napoleon in Milan, by Andrea Appiani — A385

Paintings in the Napoleon Museum, Havana: 2c, Hortensia de Beauharnais, by Francois Gerard. 3c, Napoleon as First Consul, by J.B. Regnault. 4c, Elisa Bonaparte, by Robert Lefevre. 5c, Napoleon Planning Coronation Ceremony, by J.G. Vibert, horiz. 13c, Napoleon as Cuirassier Corporal, by Jean Meissonier. 30c, Napoleon Bonaparte, by LeFevre.

1969, Aug. 20 **Unwmk.**
1425 A385 1c
1426 A385 2c 41½x55mm
1427 A385 3c 45½x56mm
1428 A385 4c 43x62½mm
1429 A385 5c 63x47½mm
1430 A385 13c 43x62½mm
1431 A385 30c 45x59½mm

See Nos. 2448-2453.

Cuba's Victory at the 17th World Amateur Baseball Championships, Santo Domingo — A386

1969, Sept. 11
1432 A386 13c multi

No. 1432 printed se-tenant with inscribed label listing finalists.

Alexander von Humboldt (1769-1859), German Naturalist — A387

1969, Sept. 14
1433 A387 3c Surinam eel
1434 A387 13c Night ape
1435 A387 30c Condors

World Fencing Championships, Havana — A388

Designs: 1c, Ancient Egyptians in combat. 2c, Roman gladiators. 2c, Viking and Norman. 4c, Medieval tournament. 5c, French musketeers. 13c, Japanese samurai. 30c, Mounted Cubans, War of Independence. 50c, Modern fencers.

1969, Oct. 2
1436 A388 1c multi
1437 A388 2c multi
1438 A388 3c multi
1439 A388 4c multi
1440 A388 5c multi
1441 A388 13c multi
1442 A388 30c multi

Souvenir Sheet

Imperf

1443 A388 50c multi

Stamp in No. 1443 has simulated perforations.

Natl. Revolutionary Militia, 10th Anniv. — A389

1969, Oct. 26 **Wmk. 376**
1444 A389 3c multi

Disappearance of Maj. Camilo Cienfuegos, 10th Anniv. — A390

1969, Oct. 28
1445 A390 13c multi

Agriculture — A391

1969, Nov. 2 **Unwmk.**
1446 A391 1c Strawberries, grapes
1447 A391 1c Onions, asparagus
1448 A391 1c Rice
1449 A391 1c Banana
1450 A391 3c Pineapple, vert.
1451 A391 3c Tobacco, vert.
1452 A391 3c Citrus fruits, vert.
1453 A391 3c Coffee, vert.
1454 A391 3c Rabbits, vert.
1455 A391 10c Pigs, vert.
1456 A391 13c Sugar cane
1457 A391 30c Bull

Stamps of the same denomination printed se-tenant in strips.

Sporting Events — A392

1969, Nov. 15
1458 A392 1c 2nd Natl. Games
1459 A392 2c 11th Anniv. Games
1460 A392 3c Barrientos Commemorative, vert.
1461 A392 10c 2nd Olympic Trials, vert.
1462 A392 13c 6th Socialist Bicycle Race, vert.
1463 A392 30c 6th Capablanca Memorial Chess Championships, vert.

Christmas Type of 1961

Flowering plants.

1969, Dec. 1

1464 A248 1c Plumbago capensis
1465 A249 1c Petrea volubilis
1466 A249 1c Clitoria ternatea
1467 A249 1c Duranta repens
1468 A249 1c Ruellia tuberosa
a. Block of 5 + label, Nos. 1464-1468
1469 A248 3c Turnera ulmifolia
1470 A249 3c Thevetia peruviana
1471 A249 3c Hibiscus elatus
1472 A249 3c Allamanda cathartica
1473 A249 3c Cosmos sulphureus
a. Block of 5 + label, Nos. 1469-1473
1474 A248 13c Delonix regia
1475 A249 13c Neriun oleander
1476 A249 13c Cordia sebestena
1477 A249 13c Lochnera rosea
1478 A249 13c Jatropha integerrima
a. Block of 5 + label, Nos. 1474-1478

Christmas 1969. See note after No. 700.

Zapata Swamp Fauna
A393

1969, Dec. 15

1479 A393 1c Trelanorhynus variabilis
1480 A393 2c Hyla insulsa
1481 A393 3c Atractosteus tristoechus
1482 A393 4c Capromys nana
1483 A393 5c Crocodylus rhombifer
1484 A393 13c Amazona leucocephala
1485 A393 30c Agelaius phoeniceus assimilis

Nos. 1482, 1484-1485 vert.

Tourism — A394

1970, Jan. 25 **Wmk. 376**

1486 A394 1c Jibacoa Beach
1487 A394 3c Trinidad City
1488 A394 13c Santiago de Cuba
1489 A394 30c Vinales Valley

Medicinal Plants — A395

1970, Feb. 10 **Unwmk.**

1490 A395 1c Guarea guara
1491 A395 3c Ocimum sanctum
1492 A395 10c Canella winterana
1493 A395 13c Bidens pilosa
1494 A395 30c Turnera ulmifolia
1495 A395 50c Picramnia pentandra

The Scott editorial staff regrettably cannot accept requests to identify, authenticate, or appraise stamps and postal markings.

11th Central American and Caribbean Games, Panama, Feb. 28-Mar. 14 — A396

1970, Feb. 28 **Wmk. 376**

1496 A396 1c Weight lifting
1497 A396 3c Boxing
1498 A396 10c Gymnastics
1499 A396 13c Running
1500 A396 30c Fencing

Souvenir Sheet

Imperf

1501 A396 50c Baseball

No. 1501 contains one 50x37mm stamp that has simulated perforations.

EXPO '70, Osaka, Japan, Mar. 15-Sept. 13 — A397

1970, Mar. 15

1502 A397 1c Enjoying life
1503 A397 2c Improving on nature, vert.
1504 A397 3c Better living standard
1505 A397 13c Intl. cooperation, vert.
1506 A397 30c Cuban pavilion

Speleological Soc., 30th Anniv. — A398

Petroglyphs in Cuban caves: 1c, Ambrosio Cave, Varadero Matanzas. 2c, Cave No. 1, Punta del Este, Isle of Pines. 3c, Pichardo Cave, Cubitas Camaguey Mountains. 4c, Ambrosio Cave, diff. 5c, Cave No. 1, diff. 13c, Garcia Ribiou Cave, Havana. 30c, Cave No. 2, Punta del Este.

1970, Mar. 28 **Unwmk.**

Sizes: 29x45mm (1c, 3c, 4c, 13c)

1507 A398 1c multi
1508 A398 2c shown
1509 A398 3c multi
1510 A398 4c multi
1511 A398 5c multi
1512 A398 13c multi
1513 A398 30c multi

Aviation Pioneers
A399

1970, Apr. 10

1514 A399 3c Jose D. Blino
1515 A399 13c Adolfo Teodore

Lenin Birth Centenary — A400

Paintings and quotes: 1c, Lenin in Kazan, by O. Vishniakov. 2c, Young Lenin, by V. Prager. 3c, Second Socialist Party Congress, by Y. Vinagradov. 4c, First Manifesto, by F. Golubkov. 5c, First Day of Soviet Power, by N. Babasiuk. 13c, Lenin in Smolny, by M. Sokolov. 30c, Autumn in Gorky, by A. Varlamov. 50c, Lenin at Gorky, by N. Bashkakov.

1970, Apr. 22

Sizes: 67½x46mm (1c, 4c, 5c)

1516 A400 1c multi
1517 A400 2c shown
1518 A400 3c multi
1519 A400 4c multi
1520 A400 5c multi
1521 A400 13c multi
1522 A400 30c multi

Souvenir Sheet

Imperf

1523 A400 50c multi

No. 1523 contains one 48x46mm stamp that has simulated perforations.

Stamp Day — A401

1970, Apr. 24

1524 A401 13c The Letter, by J. Arche

Size: 30x44mm

1525 A401 30c Portrait of A Cadet, Anonymous

Da Vinci's Anatomical Drawing, Earth, Moon — A402

1970, May 17 **Wmk. 376**

1526 A402 30c multi

World Telecommunications Day.

Ho Chi Minh (1890-1969), President of North Viet Nam — A403

1970, May 19 **Unwmk.**

1527 A403 1c Vietnamese fisherman

Size: 32x44mm

1528 A403 3c Two women
1529 A403 3c Plowing field

Size: 33x45mm

1530 A403 3c Teacher, students in air-raid shelter
1531 A403 3c Nine women in paddy

Size: 34x41½mm

1532 A403 3c Camouflaged machine shop

Size: 34x39mm

1533 A403 13c shown

Cuban Cigar Industry
A404

1970, July 5

1534 A404 3c Plantation, Eden cigar band
1535 A404 13c Factory, El Mambi band
1536 A404 30c Packing cigars, Lopez Hermanos band

Projected Sugar Production: Over 10 Million Tons — A405

1970, July 26

1537 A405 1c Cane-crushing
1538 A405 2c Sowing and crop dusting
1539 A405 3c Cutting sugar cane
1540 A405 10c Transporting cane
1541 A405 13c Modern cutting machine
1542 A405 30c Intl. Brigade, cane cutters, vert.
1543 A405 1p Sugar warehouse

Pedro Figueredo (d. 1870), Composer
A406

Versions of the Natl. Anthem.

1970, Aug. 17

1544 A406 3c 1868 Version
1545 A406 20c 1898 Version

Women's Federation, 10th Anniv. — A407

1970, Aug. 23

1546 A407 3c multi

Militia, by Servando C. Moreno — A408

Paintings in the Natl. Museum: 2c, Washerwomen, by Aristides Fernandez. 3c, Puerta del Sol, Madrid, by L. Paret Y Alcazar. 4c, Fishermen's Wives, by Joaquin Sorolla. 5c, Portrait of a Woman, by Thomas de Keyser. 13c, Mrs. Edward Foster, by Sir Thomas Lawrence. 30c, Tropical Gypsy, by Victor M. Garcia.

1970, Aug. 31

1547 A408 1c shown

Size: 45x41mm

1548 A408 2c multi
1549 A408 3c multi

Size: 40x41mm

1550 A408 4c multi

Size: 38x45½mm

1551 A408 5c multi
1552 A408 13c multi
1553 A408 30c multi

See Nos. 1640-1646, 1669-1675, 1773-1779.

Havana Declaration, 10th Anniv. — A409

1970, Sept. 2

1554 A409 3c Jose Marti Square

Committee for the Defense of the Revolution, 10th Anniv. A410

1970, Sept. 28

1555 A410 3c multi

39th Sugar Technician's Assoc. (ATAC) Conference — A411

1970, Oct. 11

1556 A411 30c multi

Wildlife A412

1970, Oct. 20

1557 A412 1c Numida meleagris galeata
1558 A412 2c Dendrocygna arborea
1559 A412 3c Phasianus colchicus torquatus
1560 A412 4c Zenaida macroura macroura
1561 A412 5c Colinus virginianus cubanensis
1562 A412 13c Sus scrofa
1563 A412 30c Odocoileus virginianus

Black-magic Feast, by M. Puente — A413

Afro-Cuban folk paintings: 3c, Hat Dance, by V.P. Landaluze. 10c, Los Hoyos Conga Dance, by Domingo Ravenet. 13c, Climax of the Rumba, by Eduardo Abela.

1970, Nov. 5

Sizes: 36x48½mm (3c, 13c), 44½x44mm (10c)

1564 A413 1c shown
1565 A413 3c multi
1566 A413 10c multi
1567 A413 13c multi

Road Safety Week A414

1970, Nov. 15

1568 A414 3c Zebra, road signs
1569 A414 9c Prudence the Bear

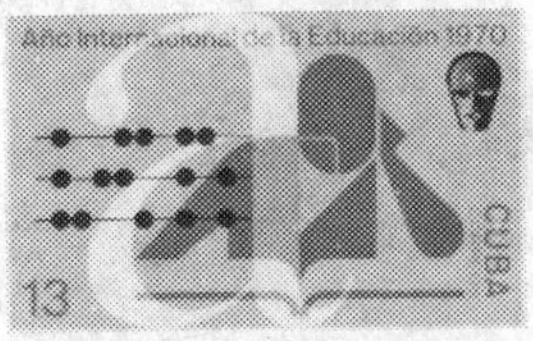

Intl. Education Year — A415

1970, Nov. 20

1570 A415 13c Abacus, "a"
1571 A415 30c Cow, microscope

Christmas Type of 1961

Birds.

1970, Dec. 1

1572 A248 1c Dives atroviolaceus
1573 A249 1c Glaucidium siju siju
1574 A249 1c Todus multicolor
1575 A249 1c Xiphidiopicus percussus percussus
1576 A249 1c Ferminia cerverai
a. Block of 5 + label, Nos. 1572-1576
1577 A248 3c Teretistris fornsi
1578 A249 3c Myadestes elisabeth elisabeth
1579 A249 3c Polioptila lembeyei
1580 A249 3c Vireo gundlachii gundlachii
1581 A249 3c Teretistris fernandinae
a. Block of 5 + label, Nos. 1577-1581
1582 A248 13c Torreornis inexpectata inexpectata
1583 A249 13c Chondrohierax wilsonii
1584 A249 13c Accipiter gundlachi
1585 A249 13c Starnoenas cyanocephala
1586 A249 13c Aratinga euops
a. Block of 5 + label, Nos. 1582-1586

Christmas 1970. See note after No. 700.

Camilo Cienfuegos Military Academy A416

1970, Dec. 2

1587 A416 3c multi

7th Congress of the Intl. Organization of Journalists A417

1971, Jan. 4

1588 A417 13c multi

World Meteorology Day — A418

1971, Feb. 16

Size: 39½x35½mm (3c)

1589 A418 1c Class, weather chart, computer, vert.
1590 A418 3c Weather map
1591 A418 8c Equipment, vert.
1592 A418 30c shown

6th Pan American Games, Cali, Colombia — A419

1971, Feb. 20

1593 A419 1c Emblem, vert.
1594 A419 2c Women's running, vert.
1595 A419 3c Rifle shooting
1596 A419 4c Gymnastics, vert.
1597 A419 5c Boxing, vert.
1598 A419 13c Water polo
1599 A419 30c Baseball

Porcelain and Mosaics in the Metropolitan Museum, Havana — A420

Designs: 1c, Parisian vase, 19th cent. 3c, Mexican bowl, 17th cent. 10c, Parisian vase, diff. 13c, Colosseum, Italian mosaic, 19th cent. 20c, Mexican bowl, 17th cent. 30c, St. Peter's Square, Italian mosaic, 19th cent.

1971, Mar. 11

Sizes: 34½x53mm (1c, 10c), 46x53mm (3c), 42x48mm (20c)

1600 A420 1c multi
1601 A420 3c multi
1602 A420 10c multi
1603 A420 13c shown
1604 A420 20c multi
1605 A420 30c multi

See Nos. 1699-1705.

Natl. Child Centers, 10th Anniv. — A421

1971, Apr. 10

1606 A421 3c multi

Manned Space Flight 10th Anniv. — A422

Cosmonauts in training.

1971, Apr. 12

1607 A422 1c multi
1608 A422 2c multi, diff.
1609 A422 3c multi, diff.
1610 A422 4c multi, diff.
1611 A422 5c multi, diff.
1612 A422 13c multi, diff.
1613 A422 30c multi, diff.

Souvenir Sheet

Imperf

1614 A422 50c multi

Stamp in #1614 has simulated perf.

Bay of Pigs Invasion, 10th Anniv. A423

1971, Apr. 17

1615 A423 13c multi

Stamp Day — A424

Packets: 13c, Jeune Richard attacking the Windsor Castle, 1807. 30c, Orinoco.

1971, Apr. 24

1616 A424 13c multi
1617 A424 30c multi

Cuban Intl. Broadcast Service, 10th Anniv. — A425

1971, May 1 **Wmk. 376**

1618 A425 3c multi
1619 A425 50c multi

Orchids A426

1971, May 15

1620 A426 1c Cattleya skinnerii
1621 A426 2c Vanda hibrida
1622 A426 3c Cypripedium collossum
1623 A426 4c Cypripedium gloucophyllum
1624 A426 5c Vanda tricolor
1625 A426 13c Cypripedium mowgh
1626 A426 30c Cypripedium solum

See Nos. 1677-1683 and 1780-1786.

Enrique Loynaz del Castillo (b. 1861), Composer — A427

1971, June 5 **Wmk. 376**

1627 A427 3c Portrait, Invasion Hymn

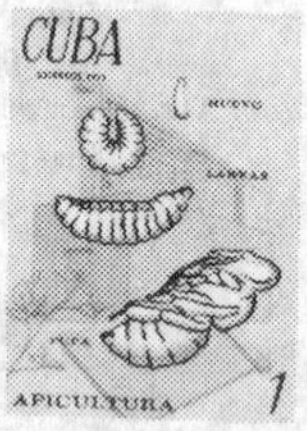

Bee Keeping — A428

1971, June 20 **Unwmk.**

1628 A428 1c Egg, larvae, pupa
1629 A428 3c Worker
1630 A428 9c Drone
1631 A428 13c Defense of hive
1632 A428 30c Queen

Children's Drawings — A429

1971, Aug. 30

Size: 45x39mm

1633 A429 1c Sailboat
1634 A429 3c The Little Train

Sizes: 45½x35½mm (9c, 13c), 47x37½mm (10c)

1635 A429 9c Sugar Cane Cutter
1636 A429 10c Return of the Fishermen
1637 A429 13c The Zoo

Size: 47x42mm

1638 A429 20c House and Garden

Size: 31½x50mm

1639 A429 30c Landscape

Art Type of 1970

Paintings in the Natl. Museum: 1c, St. Catherine of Alexandria, by F. Zurburan. 2c, The Cart, by Federico Americo. 3c, St. Christopher and Child, by J. Bassano. 4c, Little Devil, by Rene Portocarrero. 5c, Portrait of a Woman, by Nicolas Maes. 13c, Phoenix, by Raul Martinez. 30c, Sir William Pitt, by Thomas Gainsborough.

1971, Sept. 20

1640 A408 1c 31x55mm
1641 A408 2c 48x37mm
1642 A408 3c 31x55mm
1643 A408 4c 37x48mm
1644 A408 5c 37x48mm
1645 A408 13c 39x48½mm
1646 A408 30c 39x48½mm

Sport Fishing — A431

1971, Oct. 30

1647 A431 1c Albula vulpes
1648 A431 2c Seriola species
1649 A431 3c Micropterus salmoides
1650 A431 4c Coryphaena hippurus
1651 A431 5c Megalops atlantica
1652 A431 13c Acanthocybium solandri
1653 A431 30c Makaira ampla

19th World Amateur Baseball Championships — A432

1971, Nov. 22 **Wmk. 376**

1654 A432 3c shown
1655 A432 1p Globe as baseball

Execution of Medical Students, Cent. A433

Paintings: 3c, Dr. Fermin Valdez Dominguez, anonymous. 13c, Execution of the Medical Students, by M. Mesa. 30c, Capt. Federico Capdevila, anonymous.

1971, Nov. 27 **Unwmk.**

Size: 61½x46mm (13c)

1656 A433 3c multi
1657 A433 13c multi
1658 A433 30c multi

Spindalis Zena Pretrei A434

Birds: 1c, Falco sparverius sparverioides vigors. 2c, Glaucidium siju siju. 3c, Priotelus temnurus temnurus. 4c, Saurothera merlini merlini. 5c, Nesoceleus fernandinae. 30c, Mimocichla plumbea rubripes. 50c, Chlorostilbon ricordii ricordii and Archilochus colubris. Nos. 1659-1663 vert.

1971, Dec. 10

1659 A434 1c multi
1660 A434 2c multi
1661 A434 3c multi
1662 A434 4c multi
1663 A434 5c multi
1664 A434 13c shown
1665 A434 30c multi

Size: 55½x29mm

1666 A434 50c multi

Death centenary of Ramon de la Sagra, naturalist.

Cuba's Victory at the World Amateur Baseball Championships — A435

1971, Dec. 8 **Wmk. 376**

1667 A435 13c multi

UNICEF, 25th Anniv. — A436

1971, Dec. 11

1668 A436 13c multi

Art Type of 1970

Paintings in the Natl. Museum: 1c, Arrival of an Ambassador, by Vittore Carpaccio. 2c, Senora Malpica, by G. Collazo. 3c, La Chorrera Tower, by Esteban Chartrand. 4c, Creole Landscape, by Carlos Enriquez. 5c, Sir William Lemon, by George Romney. 13c, Landscape, by Henry Cleenewerk. 30c, Valencia Beach, by Joaquin Sorolla y Bastida.

1972, Jan. 25 **Unwmk.**

1669 A408 1c 50x33mm
1670 A408 2c 27½x52mm
1671 A408 3c 50x33mm
1672 A408 4c 35x43mm
1673 A408 5c 35x43mm
1674 A408 13c 43x33mm
1675 A408 30c 43x33mm

Academy of Sciences, 10th Anniv. — A437

1972, Feb. 20 **Wmk. 376**

1676 A437 13c Capitol Type of 1929

Orchid Type of 1971

1972, Feb. 25 **Unwmk.**

1677 A426 1c Brasso cattleya sindorossiana
1678 A426 2c Cypripedium doraeus
1679 A426 3c Cypripedium exul
1680 A426 4c Cypripedium rosy dawn
1681 A426 5c Cypripedium champolliom
1682 A426 13c Cypripedium bucolique
1683 A426 30c Cypripedium sullanum

Eduardo Agramonte (1849-1872), Physicist A438

1972, Mar. 8

1684 A438 3c Portrait by F. Martinez

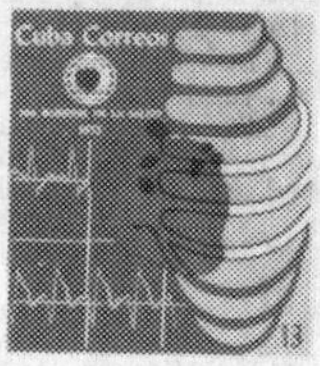

World Health Day — A439

1972, Apr. 7 **Wmk. 376**

1685 A439 13c multi

Soviet Space Program — A440

1972, Apr. 12 **Unwmk.**

1686 A440 1c Sputnik 1
1687 A440 2c Vostok 1
1688 A440 3c Valentina Tereshkova
1689 A440 4c Alexei Leonov
1690 A440 5c Lunokhod 1, moon vehicle
1691 A440 13c Linking Soyuz capsules
1692 A440 30c Victims of Soyuz 11 accident

Stamp Day — A441

Designs: 13c, Postmaster-Gen. Vicente Mora Pera, by Ramon Loy. 30c, Soldier's Letter, Cuba to Venezuela, 1897.

1972, Apr. 24

1693 A441 13c shown

Size: 48x39mm

1694 A441 30c multi

Labor Day — A442

Jose Marti, Ho Chi Minh — A443

3rd Conference Against War in Indo-China, May 19 — A444

1972, May 1 **Wmk. 376**

1695 A442 3c multi

1972, May 19

1696 A443 3c shown
1697 A444 13c shown
1698 A443 30c Roses, conference emblem

Metropolitan Museum Type of 1971

Portraits: 1c, Salvador del Muro, by J. Del Rio. 2c, Luis de las Casas, by Del Rio. 3c, Cristopher Columbus, anonymous. 4c, Tomas Gamba, by V. Escobar. 5c, Maria Galarraga, by Escobar. 13c, Isabel II, by Federico Madrazo. 30c, Carlos II, by Miguel Melero.

1972, May 25 **Unwmk.**

Size: 34x43½mm

1699 A420 1c multi
1700 A420 2c multi
1701 A420 3c multi
1702 A420 4c multi
1703 A420 5c multi

Size: 34x51½mm

1704 A420 13c multi
1705 A420 30c multi

Children's Songs Competition, Natl. Library A445

1972, June 5 **Wmk. 376**

1706 A445 3c multi

Thoroughbred Horses — A446

1972, June 30 **Unwmk.**

1707 A446 1c Tarpan
1708 A446 2c Kertag
1709 A446 3c Creole
1710 A446 4c Andalusian
1711 A446 5c Arabian
1712 A446 13c Quarter horse
1713 A446 30c Pursang

Frank Pais (d. 1957), Educator, Revolutionary — A447

1972, July 26 **Wmk. 376**

1714 A447 13c blk & red

1972 Summer Olympics, Munich, Aug. 26-Sept. 10 — A448

1972, Aug. 26 **Unwmk.**

1715 A448 1c Athlete, emblems, vert.
1716 A448 2c "M," boxing
1717 A448 3c "U," weight lifting
1718 A448 4c "N," fencing
1719 A448 5c "I," rifle shooting
1720 A448 13c "C," running
1721 A448 30c "H," basketball

Souvenir Sheet

Imperf

1722 A448 50c Gymnastics

Stamp in No. 1722 has simulated perforations.

Intl. Hydrological Decade — A449

Landscapes: 1c, Tree Trunks, by Domingo Ramos. 3c, Cyclone, by Tiburcio Lorenzo. 8c, Vinales, by Ramos. 30c, Forest and Brook, by Antonio R. Morey, vert.

1972, Sept. 20

1723 A449 1c multi
1724 A449 3c multi
1725 A449 8c multi
1726 A449 30c multi

Butterflies from the Gundlach Collection — A450

1972, Sept. 25

1727 A450 1c Papilio thoas oviedo
1728 A450 2c Papilio devilliers
1729 A450 3c Papilio polixenes polixenes
1730 A450 4c Papilio androgeus epidaurus
1731 A450 5c Papilio cayguanabus
1732 A450 13c Papilio andraemon hernandezi
1733 A450 30c Papilio celadon

A451

Miguel de Cervantes Saavedra (1547-1616), Spanish Author — A452

Paintings by A. Fernandez: 3c, In La Mancha, vert. 13c, Battle with Wine Skins. 30c, Don Quixote de La Mancha, vert. 50c, Scene from Don Quixote, by Jose Moreno Carbonero.

1972, Sept. 29

Size: 34½x46mm (3c, 30c)

1734 A451 3c multi
1735 A451 13c shown
1736 A451 30c multi

Souvenir Sheet

Perf. 12½ on 3 Sides

1737 A452 50c shown

Guerrilla Day, 5th Anniv. A453

1972, Oct. 8

1738 A453 3c Ernesto "Che" Guevara
1739 A453 13c Tamara "Tania" Bunke
1740 A453 30c Guido "Inti" Peredo

Traditional Musical Instruments A454

1972, Oct. 25

1741 A454 3c Abwe (rattles)
1742 A454 13c Bonko enchemiya (drum)
1743 A454 30c Iya (drum)

MATEX '72, 3rd Natl. Philatelic Exhibition, Matanzas — A455

1972, Nov. 18 **Wmk. 376**

1744 A455 13c No. 467
1745 A455 30c No. C49

Nos. 1744-1745 printed se-tenant with insribed labels picturing Type A232, emblem of the Cuban Philatelic Federation.

Historic Ships A456

1972, Nov. 30 **Unwmk.**

1746 A456 1c Viking long boat, 6th-9th cent.
1747 A456 2c Caravel, 15th cent., vert.
1748 A456 3c Galleass, 16th cent.
1749 A456 4c Galleon, 17th cent., vert.
1750 A456 5c Clipper, 19th cent.
1751 A456 13c Steam packet, 19th cent.

Size: 52½x29mm.

1752 A456 30c Atomic icebreaker Lenin, 20th cent.

UNESCO Save Venice Campaign — A457

1972, Dec. 8

1753 A457 3c Lion of St. Mark
1754 A457 13c Bridge of Sighs, vert.
1755 A457 30c St. Mark's Cathedral

Cuba, World Amateur Baseball Champion in 1972 — A458

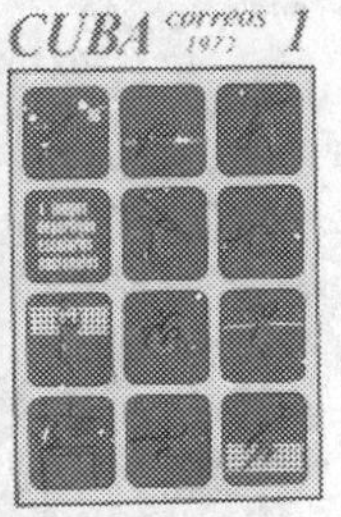

Sport Events, 1972 — A459

1972, Dec. 15

1756 A458 3c Umpire

1972, Dec. 22

1757 A459 1c shown
1758 A458 2c Pole vault
1759 A458 3c like No. 1756
1760 A458 4c Wrestling
1761 A458 5c Fencing
1762 A458 13c Boxing
1763 A458 30c Marlin

Barrientos Memorial Athletics Championships, 11th Amateur Baseball Championships, Cerro Pelado Intl. Tournament, Central American and Caribbean Fencing Tournament, Giraldo Cordova Tournament, Ernest Hemingway Natl. Fishing Contest.

No. 1759 inscribed "XI serie nacional de beisbol aficionado."

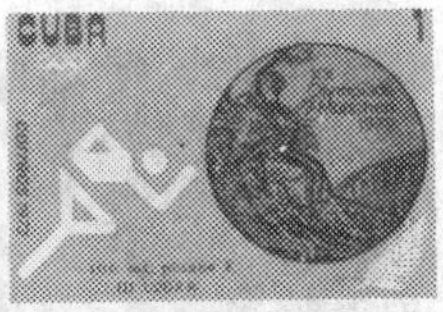

Medals Won by Cubans at the 1972 Summer Olympics, Munich A460

Designs: 1c, Bronze medal, Women's 100-meter. 2c, Bronze, women's relay. 3c, Gold, 54kg boxing. 4c, Silver, 81kg boxing. 5c, Bronze, 51kg boxing. 13c, Gold, 87kg boxing. 30c, Gold, silver cup, heavyweight boxing. 50c, Bronze medal, basketball.

1973, Jan. 28

1764 A460 1c multi
1765 A460 2c multi
1766 A460 3c multi
1767 A460 4c multi
1768 A460 5c multi
1769 A460 13c multi
1770 A460 30c multi

Souvenir Sheet

Imperf

1771 A460 50c multi

Stamp in No. 1771 has simulated perforations.

A461

A462

Portrait by A.M. Esquivel.

1973, Feb. 10

1772 A461 13c multi

Gertrudis Gomez de Avellaneda (1814-1873), poet.

Art Type of 1970

Paintings in the Natl. Museum: 1c, Bathers in the Lagoon, by C. Enriquez. 2c, Still-life, by W.C. Heda. 3c, Gallantry, by P. Landaluze. 4c, Return in the Late Afternoon, by C. Troyon. 5c, Elizabetta Mascagni, by F.X. Fabre. 13c, The Picador, by De Lucas Padilla, horiz. 30c, In the Garden, by Arburu Morell.

1973, Feb. 28
Sizes: 36x46mm, 46x36mm

1773 A408 1c multi
1774 A408 2c multi
1775 A408 3c multi
1776 A408 4c multi
1777 A408 5c multi
1778 A408 13c multi
1779 A408 30c multi

Orchid Type of 1971

1973, Mar. 26

1780 A426 1c Dendrobium hybrid
1781 A426 2c Cypripedium exul
1782 A426 3c Vanda miss. joaquin rose marie
1783 A426 4c Phalaenopsis schilleriana
1784 A426 5c Vanda gilbert tribulet
1785 A426 13c Dendrobium hybrid, diff.
1786 A426 30c Arachnis catherine

1973, Apr. 7 **Wmk. 376**

1787 A462 10c multi, *buff*

World Health Day. World Health Organization, 25th anniv.

Anti-Polio Campaign — A463

1973, Apr. 9 **Unwmk.**

1788 A463 3c multi

Soviet Space Program A464

1973, Apr. 12

1789 A464 1c Soyuz rocket launch, vert.
1790 A464 2c Luna 1, Moon
1791 A464 3c Luna 16 taking-off from Moon, vert.
1792 A464 4c Venus 7
1793 A464 5c Molnia 1, vert.
1794 A464 13c Mars 3
1795 A464 30c Radar observation ship, Yuri Gagarin

Stamp Day A465

Postmarks: 13c, Santiago de Cuba, 1760. 30c, Havana, 1760.

1973, Apr. 24

1796 A465 13c multi
1797 A465 30c multi

See Nos. 1888-1891.

Portrait by A. Espinosa — A466

1973, May 11

1798 A466 13c multi

Maj.-Gen. Ignacio Agramonte (1841-1873).

Birthplace, Torun, and Inventions — A467

Copernicus Monument, Warsaw — A468

1973, May 25

1799 A467 3c shown
1800 A467 13c Copernicus, spacecraft
1801 A467 30c Manuscript, Frombork Tower

Souvenir Sheet
Perf. 12½ on 3 Sides

1802 A468 50c shown

500th anniversary of the birth of Nicolaus Copernicus (1473-1543), Polish astronomer.

Improvement of School Education — A469

1973, June 12 **Wmk. 376**

1803 A469 13c multi

Cattle — A470

1973, June 28 **Unwmk.**

1804 A470 1c Jersey
1805 A470 2c Charolaise
1806 A470 3c Creole
1807 A470 4c Swiss
1808 A470 5c Holstein
1809 A470 13c Santa gertrudis
1810 A470 30c Brahman

A471

A472

1973, July 10 **Wmk. 376**

1811 A471 13c multi

10th Communist Festival of Youths and Students, East Berlin.

1973, July 26 **Unwmk.**

1812 A472 3c Siboney Farm, Santiago de Cuba
1813 A472 13c Moncada Barracks
1814 A472 30c Revolution Plaza, Havana

20th anniv. of the Revolution.

10th Anniv. of the Revolutionary Navy A473

1973, Aug. 3 **Wmk. 376**

1815 A473 3c Midshipman, missile frigate

Interior, by Manuel Vicens A474

Paintings in the Natl. Museum: 1c, Amalia of Saxony, by J.K. Rossler. 3c, Margarita of Austria, by J. Pantoja de la Cruz. 4c, City Hall Official, anonymous. 5c, View of Santiago de Cuba, by Hernandez Giro. 12c, The Catalan, by J.J. Tejada. 30c, Alley in Guayo, by Tejada.

1973, Aug. 30 **Unwmk.**
Sizes: 26½x41mm (1c, 3c), 28½x39mm (4c, 13c, 30c)

1816 A474 1c multi
1817 A474 2c multi
1818 A474 3c multi
1819 A474 4c multi
1820 A474 5c multi
1821 A474 13c multi
1822 A474 30c multi

WMO Emblem, Paintings by J. Madrazo A475

1973, Sept. 4

1823 A475 8c Spring
1824 A475 8c Summer
1825 A475 8c Fall
1826 A475 8c Winter

World Meteorogogical Organization, cent. Nos. 1823-1826 printed se-tenant in strips of 4; frame reversed on 2nd and 4th stamp in strip.

A476

A477

27th World and 1st Pan American Weight Lifting Championships: Various weightlifting positions.

1973, Sept. 12

1827 A476 1c shown
1828 A476 2c multi, diff.
1829 A476 3c multi, diff.
1830 A476 4c multi, diff.
1831 A476 5c multi, diff.
1832 A476 13c multi, diff.
1833 A476 30c multi, diff.

1973, Sept. 28

Flowering plants.

1834 A477 1c Erythrina standleyana
1835 A477 2c Lantana camara
1836 A477 3c Canavalia maritima
1837 A477 4c Dichromena colorata
1838 A477 5c Borrichia arborescens
1839 A477 13c Anguria pedata
1840 A477 30c Cordia sebestena

8th World Trade Union Congress, Varna, Bulgaria A478

1973, Oct. 5 **Wmk. 376**

1841 A478 13c multi

Cuban Natl. Ballet, 25th Anniv. — A479

Sea Shells — A480

1973, Oct. 28 **Unwmk.**

1842 A479 13c gold & brt ultra

1973, Oct. 29

1843 A480 1c Liguus fasciatus fasciatus
1844 A480 2c Liguus fasciatus guitarti
1845 A480 3c Liguus fasciatus whartoni
1846 A480 4c Liguus fasciatus angelae
1847 A480 5c Liguus fasciatus trinidadense
1848 A480 13c Liguus blainianus
1849 A480 30c Liguus vittatus

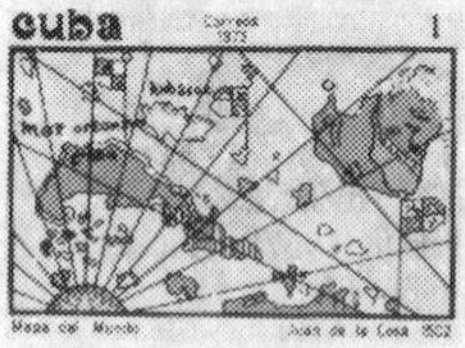

Maps of Cuba A481

1973, Oct. 29

1850 A481 1c Juan de la Cosa, 1502
1851 A481 3c Ortelius, 1572
1852 A481 13c Bellini, 1762
1853 A481 40c 1973

15th Anniversary of the Revolution — A482

1974, Jan. 2

1854 A482 1c No. 625
1855 A482 3c No. 626
1856 A482 13c No. C200
1857 A482 40c No. C201

Woman, by F. Ponce de Leon — A483

Amilcar Cabral — A484

Portraits in the Camaguey Museum: 3c, Mexican Girls, by J. Arche. 8c, Young Woman, by A. Menocal. 10c, Mulatto Woman Drinking from Coconut, by L. Romanach. 13c, Head of an Old Man, by J. Arburu.

1974, Jan. 10

1858 A483 1c multi
1859 A483 3c multi
1860 A483 8c multi
1861 A483 10c multi
1862 A483 13c multi

1974, Jan. 20

1863 A484 13c multi

Amilcar Cabral, Guinea-Bissau freedom fighter, 1st death anniv.

Lenin, by I.V. Kosmin — A485

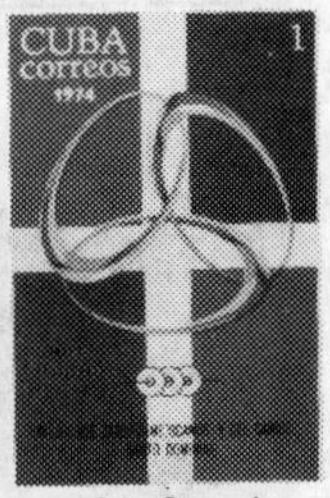

12th Central American and Caribbean Games, Santo Domingo — A486

1974, Jan. 21

1864 A485 30c multi

50th death anniv. of Lenin.

1974, Feb. 8

1865 A486 1c Emblem
1866 A486 2c Javelin
1867 A486 3c Boxing
1868 A486 4c Baseball, horiz.
1869 A486 13c Basketball, horiz.
1870 A486 30c Volleyball, horiz.

Portrait by F. Martinez — A487

Portrait of a Man, by J.B. Vermay — A488

1974, Feb. 27

1871 A487 13c multi

Carlos M. de Cespedes (d. 1874), patriot.

1974, Mar. 7

Paintings in the Natl. Museum: 2c, The Wet Nurse, by C.A. Van Loo. 3c, Cattle in River, by R. Morey. 4c, Village, by Morey. 13c, Faun and Bacchus, by Rubens. 30c, Young Woman Playing Cards, by R. Madrazo.

1872 A488 1c shown
1873 A488 2c multi
1874 A488 3c multi
1875 A488 4c multi
1876 A488 13c multi
1877 A488 30c multi

Council for Mutual Economic Assistance (COMECON), 25th Anniv. — A489

1974, Mar. 15

1878 A489 30c Comecon building, Moscow

Visit of Leonid I. Brezhnev to Cuba, Jan. 28-Feb. 3 — A490

1974, Mar. 28

1879 A490 13c Jose Marti, Lenin, flags
1880 A490 30c Brezhnev, Fidel Castro

Science Fiction A491

Paintings by A. Sokolov.

1974, Apr. 12

1881 A491 1c Martian Crater
1882 A491 2c Fiery Labyrinth
1883 A491 3c Amber Wave
1884 A491 4c Flight Through Space
1885 A491 13c Planet in Nebula
1886 A491 30c World of Two Suns

Cosmonauts Day.

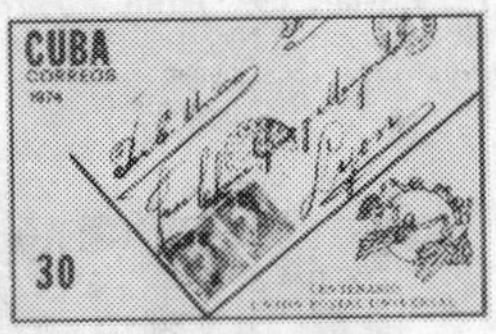

UPU, Cent. A492

1974, Apr. 15

1887 A492 30c Letter, 1874

Stamp Day Type of 1973

Postmarks.

1974, Apr. 24

1888 A465 1c Havana
1889 A465 3c Matanzas
1890 A465 13c Trinidad
1891 A465 20c Guana Vacoa

COMITE DEPORTIVO DE LOS EJERCITOS AMIGOS 18th Sports Congress of Friendly Armies — A493

1974, May 5 **Wmk. 376**

1892 A493 3c multi

Felipe Poey (1799-1891), Naturalist — A494

Designs: 1c, 4c, Butterflies. 2c, 13c, Sea shells. 3c, 30c, 50c, Fish.

1974, May 26 ***Perf. 12½x12***

1893 A494 1c Eumaeus atala atala
1894 A494 2c Pineria terebra
1895 A494 3c Chaetodon sedentarius
1896 A494 4c Eurema dina dina
1897 A494 13c Hemitrochus fuscolabiata
1898 A494 30c Eupomacentrus partitus

Souvenir Sheet

Imperf

1899 A494 50c Apogon binotatus

Stamp in #1899 has simulated perforations.

Havana Philharmonic Orchestra, 50th Anniv. — A495

Designs: 1c, Antonio Mompo and cello. 3c, Cesar Perez Sentenat and piano. 5c, Pedro Mercado and trumpet. 10c, Pedro Sanjuan and Havana Philharmonic emblem. 13c, Roberto Ondina and flute.

1974, June 8 ***Perf. 12½***

1900 A495 1c multi
1901 A495 3c multi
1902 A495 5c multi
1903 A495 10c multi
1904 A495 13c multi

Garden Flowers — A496

1974, June 12

1905 A496 1c Heliconia humilis
1906 A496 2c Anthurium andraeanum
1907 A496 3c Canna generalis
1908 A496 4c Alpinia purpurata
1909 A496 13c Gladiolus grandiflorus
1910 A496 30c Amomum capitatum

A497

A498

World Amateur Boxing Championships: Emblem and various boxers.

Perf. 12x12½

1974, Aug. 24 **Litho.** **Unwmk.**

1911 A497 1c multi
1912 A497 3c multi
1913 A497 13c multi

1974, Aug. 28 ***Perf. 13***

Extinct birds.

1914 A498 1c Dodo
1915 A498 3c Ara de Cuba (parrot)
1916 A498 8c Passenger pigeon
1917 A498 10c Moa
1918 A498 13c Great auk

Pres. Salvador Allende of Chile (d. 1973) A499

1974, Sept. 11

1919 A499 13c multi

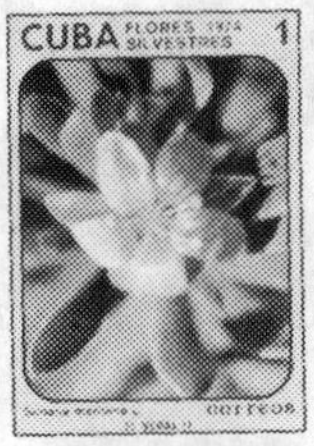

Wildflowers A500

Model Aircraft A501

1974, Sept. 14 ***Perf. 13x12½***

1920 A500 1c Suriana maritima
1921 A500 3c Cassia ligustrina
1922 A500 8c Flaveria linearis
1923 A500 10c Stachytarpheta jamaicensis
1924 A500 13c Bacopa monnieri

1974, Sept. 22 ***Perf. 12½***

1925 A501 1c shown
1926 A501 3c Sky diving
1927 A501 8c Glider
1928 A501 10c Crop dusting
1929 A501 13c Commercial aviation

Civil Aeronautic Institute, 10th anniv. Nos. 1927-1929 horiz.

History of Cuban Baseball A502

1974, Oct. 3 ***Perf. 13***

1930 A502 1c Indians playing ball
1931 A502 3c 1st Official game, 1874
1932 A502 8c Emilio Sabourin
1933 A502 10c Umpire, players, 1974
1934 A502 13c Latin-American Stadium, Havana

Nos. 1930-1932 vert.

Mambi 10c Stamp (Revolutionary Junta Issue), Cent. — A503

1974, Oct. 10

1935 A503 13c multi

16th Conference of Customs Organizations of Socialist Countries — A504

1974, Oct. 15
1936 A504 30c Comecon Building, Moscow

Disappearance of Major Camilo Cienfuegos, 15th Anniv. — A505

Wmk. 376
1974, Oct. 28 Litho. ***Perf. 13***
1937 A505 3c multi

8th World Mining Conference — A506

1974, Nov. 3
1938 A506 13c multi

Petroleum Institute, 15th Anniv. A507

1974, Nov. 20
1939 A507 3c multi

Intersputnik Earth Station Opening — A508

1974, Nov. 30 **Unwmk.**
1940 A508 3c shown
1941 A508 13c Satellite, satellite dish
1942 A508 1p Satellite, flags

Philatelic Federation, 10th Anniv. A509

1974, Nov. 30 ***Perf. 12½x13***
1943 A509 30c multi

Souvenir Sheet

Mercury — A510

1974, Dec. 6 ***Imperf.***
1944 A510 50c multi

4th Natl. Phil. Exhib., Havana.

1st World Peace Congress, 25th Anniv. — A511

1974, Dec. 16 Wmk. 376 ***Perf. 13***
1945 A511 30c *F. Joliot-Curie*, by Picasso

Ruben Martinez Villena (b. 1899), Revolutionary — A512

1974, Dec. 20 **Unwmk.**
1946 A512 3c red org & yel

Souvenir Sheet

Cuban Victories, 1st Amateur Boxing Championships — A513

1975, Jan. 6 Litho. ***Imperf.***
1947 A513 50c Trophy

The World, by Marcelo Pogolotti A514

Paintings in the Natl. Museum: 2c, *The Silk-Cotton Tree*, by Henry Cleenewerk. 3c, *Landscape*, by Guillermo Collazo. 5c, *Still-life*, by Francisco Peralta. 13c, *Maria Wilson*, by Federico Martinez, vert. 30c, *The Couple*, by Mariano Fortuny.

1975, Jan. 20 ***Perf. 13***
1948 A514 1c multi
1949 A514 2c multi
1950 A514 3c multi
1951 A514 5c multi
1952 A514 13c multi
1953 A514 30c multi

Intl. Women's Year A515

1975, Feb. 6
1954 A515 13c multi

Fishing Industry — A516

Various fish and fishing vessels.

1975, Feb. 22
1955 A516 1c Long-finned tuna
1956 A516 2c Tuna
1957 A516 3c Mediterranean grouper
1958 A516 8c Hake
1959 A516 13c Prawn
1960 A516 30c Lobster

Minerals — A517

1975, Mar. 15 Litho. ***Perf. 13x12½***
1961 A517 3c Nickel
1962 A517 13c Copper
1963 A517 30c Chromium

Cosmonaut's Day — A518

Perf. 13x12½, 12½x13
1975, Apr. 12
1964 A518 1c Cosmodrome
1965 A518 2c Probe, vert.
1966 A518 3c Eclipse
1967 A518 5c Threshold to Space
1968 A518 13c Mean Moon of Mars
1969 A518 30c Cosmonaut's view of Earth

The future of space.

Stamp Day A519

Various covers.

1975, Apr. 24 ***Perf. 13***
1970 A519 3c multi
1971 A519 13c multi
1972 A519 30c multi

Victory Over Fascism, 30th Anniv. A520

Design: Raising red flag over Reichstag, Berlin.

1975, May 9 ***Perf. 13x12½***
1973 A520 30c multi

A521

Works in the Decorative Art Museum — A522

Designs: 1c, Sevres porcelain vase, vert. 2c, Meissen porcelain statue *Shepherdess and Dancers*, vert. 3c, Chinese porcelain dish *Lady with Parasol*. 5c, Chinese screen detail *The Phoenix*, vert. 13c, *Allegory of Music*, by Francois Boucher (1703-70), vert. 30c, *Portrait of a Lady*, by L. Tocque, vert. 50c, *The Swing*, by Hubert Robert (1733-1808).

Perf. 12½x13, 13x12½
1975, May 10
1974 A521 1c multi
1975 A521 2c multi
1976 A521 3c shown
1977 A521 5c multi
1978 A521 13c multi
1979 A521 30c multi

Souvenir Sheet
Perf. 13x12½ on 3 Sides
1980 A522 50c shown

No. 1980 contains one 25x39mm stamp.

Intl. Children's Day A523

Wmk. 376

1975, May 31 **Litho.** ***Perf. 13***
1981 A523 3c multi

Indigenous Birds — A524

1975, June 18 **Unwmk.**
1982 A524 1c *Vireo gundlachi*
1983 A524 2c *Gymnoglaux lawrenci*
1984 A524 3c *Aratingo eoups*
1985 A524 5c *Staroenas cyanocephala*
1986 A524 13c *Chondrohierax wilsoni*
1987 A524 30c *Cyanolimnas cerverai*

See #2121-2125, 2180-2182, C276-C276.

Scientific Investigation Center, 10th Anniv. — A525

1975, July 1 ***Perf. 12½***
1988 A525 13c multi

Irrigation and Drainage Commission, 25th Anniv. — A526

1975, Aug. 2 ***Perf. 13***
1989 A526 13c multi

Afforestation A527

1975, Aug. 20
1990 A527 1c *Cedrela mexicana*
1991 A527 3c *Swietenia mahagoni*
1992 A527 5c *Calophyllum brasiliense*
1993 A527 13c *Hibiscus tiliaceus*
1994 A527 30c *Pinus caribaea*

Cuban Women's Federation, 15th Anniv. — A528

1975, Aug. 23
1995 A528 3c multi

Intl. Conference on the Independence of Puerto Rico — A529

1975, Sept. 5 **Litho.**
1996 A529 13c multi

A530

A531

7th Pan American Games, Mexico: Aztec calendar stone and various athletes.

1975, Sept. 20 ***Perf. 12½x13***
1997 A530 1c Baseball
1998 A530 3c Boxing
1999 A530 5c Basketball
2000 A530 13c High jump
2001 A530 30c Weight lifting

Souvenir Sheet

Imperf

2002 A530 50c Stone, emblem

1975, Sept. 28 ***Perf. 12½x13***
2003 A531 3c multi

Revolutionary Defense Committees (CDR), 15th anniv.

Friendship Among the Peoples Institute, 15th Anniv. A532

1975, Oct. 8 ***Perf. 12½x13***
2004 A532 3c multi

Natl. Bank, 25th Anniv. A533

Designs: 1-peso coins and banknotes identified by serial numbers.

1975, Oct. 13 ***Perf. 13x12½***
2005 A533 13c Coin, 1915
2006 A533 13c C882736A, 1934
2007 A533 13c A000387A, 1946
2008 A533 13c 933906, 1964
2009 A533 13c K000000, 1976
a. Strip of 5, Nos. 2005-2009

Locomotives — A534

1975, Oct. 28 **Unwmk.** ***Perf. 12½***
2010 A534 1c *La Junta*, 1837
2011 A534 3c Steam engine 2-8-0 *No. 12*
2012 A534 5c Diesel TEM 4 *No. 51010*
2013 A534 13c Diesel DVM 9 *I-7 55*
2014 A534 30c Diesel M 62K *No. 61601*

Railway history.

Development of the Textile Industry — A535

1975, Nov. 10 ***Perf. 13x12½***
2015 A535 13c Bobbins, flag, loom operator

Veterinary Medicine A536

Parasites and host species.

1975, Nov. 25 **Litho.** ***Perf. 13***
2016 A536 1c *Haemonchus*, lamb
2017 A536 2c *Ancylostoma caninum*, dog
2018 A536 3c *Dispharynx nasuta*, rooster
2019 A536 5c *Gasterophilus intestinalis*, horse
2020 A536 13c *Ascaris lumbricoides*, pig
2021 A536 30c *Boophilus microplus*, bull

Manuel Ascunce Domenech Educational Detachment A537

1975, Nov. 27 **Litho.**
2022 A537 3c multi

Development of Agriculture and Animal Husbandry — A538

1975, Dec. 15 **Litho.** ***Perf. 13x12½***
2023 A538 13c Irrigation

1st Communist Party Congress — A539

Perf. 12½x13, 13x12½

1975, Dec. 17
2024 A539 3c "1," revolutionaries, vert.
2025 A539 13c shown
2026 A539 30c Party leaders

8th Latin-American Obstetrics and Gynecology Congress — A540

1976, Jan. 24 ***Perf. 13***
2027 A540 3c multi

Paintings in Natl. Museums A541

Designs: 1c, *Seated Woman*, by Victor Manuel, vert. 2c, *Garden*, by Santiago Rusinol. 3c, *Guadalquivir River*, by Manuel Barron y Carrillo. 5c, *Self-portrait*, by Jan Havicksz Steen, vert. 13c, *Portrait of a Woman*, by Louis Michel Van Loo, vert. 30c, *La Chula*, by Jose Arburu Morell, vert.

1976, Jan. 30 ***Perf. 13, 12½ (3c, 30c)***
Sizes: 29x40mm (1c, 5c, 13c), 40x29mm (2c), 44x27mm (3c), 27x44mm (30c)
2028 A541 1c multi
2029 A541 2c multi
2030 A541 3c multi
2031 A541 5c multi
2032 A541 13c multi
2033 A541 30c multi

10th Cong. of Ministers from Socialist Communications Organizations, Feb. 12, Havana — A542

1976, Feb. 12 **Litho.** ***Perf. 13***
2034 A542 13c multi

Hunting Dogs A543

1976, Feb. 20

2035 A543 1c American foxhound
2036 A543 2c Labrador retriever
2037 A543 3c Borzoi
2038 A543 5c Irish setter
2039 A543 13c Pointer
2040 A543 30c Cocker spaniel

Socialist Constitution — A544

1976, Feb. 24 *Perf. 12½*

2041 A544 13c Natl. flag, arms, anthem

Chess Champions — A545

Designs: 1c, Ruy Lopez Segura and chessboard. 2c, Francois Philidor and frontispiece of his book, *Analysis of the Game of Chess.* 3c, Wilhelm Steinitz and knight. 13c, Emanuel Lasker and king. 30c, Jose Raul Capablanca learning to play chess as a small boy.

1976, Mar. 15 *Perf. 13x12½*

2042 A545 1c multi
2043 A545 2c multi
2044 A545 3c multi
2045 A545 13c multi
2046 A545 30c multi

Havana Radio Intl. Broadcasts, 15th Anniv. — A546

1976, Mar. 26

2047 A546 50c multi

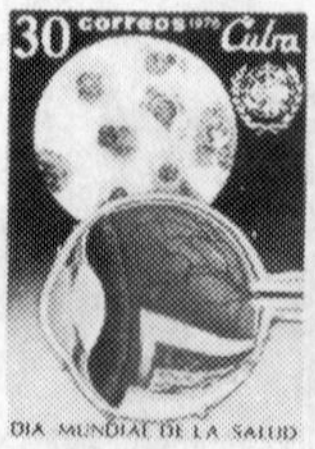

World Health Day — A547

Child Care Centers, 15th Anniv. — A548

1976, Apr. 7

2048 A547 30c multi

1976, Apr. 10 *Perf. 12½x13*

2049 A548 3c multi

1st Manned Space Flight, 15th Anniv. A549

1976, Apr. 12 *Perf. 13*

2050 A549 1c Gagarin, lift-off
2051 A549 2c V. Tesreshkova, rockets
2052 A549 3c A. Leonov's space walk, vert.
2053 A549 5c Spacecraft, vert.
2054 A549 13c Spacecraft, diff., vert.
2055 A549 30c Space link-up

Bay of Pigs Invasion, 15th Anniv. A550

Perf. 13x12½, 12½x13

1976, Apr. 17

2056 A550 3c shown
2057 A550 13c Bomber, pilot
2058 A550 30c Soldiers exulting, vert.

Natl. Militia, 17th anniv. (3c); Air Force, 15th anniv. (13c); proclamation of the socialist revolution, 15th anniv. (30c).

Nat. Assoc. of Small Farmers (ANAP), 15th Anniv. A551

1976, May 17 *Perf. 13x12½*

2059 A551 3c multi

1976 Summer Olympics, Montreal — A552

1976, May 25 *Perf. 12½x13*

2060 A552 1c Volleyball
2061 A552 2c Basketball
2062 A552 3c Long jump
2063 A552 4c Boxing
2064 A552 5c Weight lifting
2065 A552 13c Judo
2066 A552 30c Swimming

Souvenir Sheet

Imperf

2067 A552 50c Character trademark (otter)

See Nos. 2106, 2112.

Modern Secondary Schools A553

1976, June 12 **Litho.** *Perf. 13*

2068 A553 3c red, pale grn & blk

Indigenous Birds — A554

1976, June 15 *Perf. 13x12½*

2069 A554 1c *Teretistris fornsi*
2070 A554 2c *Glaucidium siju*
2071 A554 3c *Nesoceleus fernandinae*
2072 A554 5c *Todus multicolor*
2073 A554 13c *Accipiter gundlachi*
2074 A554 30c *Priotelus temnurus*

EXPO '76, USSR A555

1976, July 5 *Perf. 12½x13, 13x12½*

2075 A555 1c Anatomical scanning device
2076 A555 3c Child, doe
2077 A555 10c Cosmonauts
2078 A555 30c Tupolev supersonic jet

Public health and industrial safety (1c), environmental protection (3c), space exploration (10c) and modern transportation (30c). Nos. 2075-2077 vert.

Death Cent. of "El Inglesito" — A556

1976, Aug. 4 *Perf. 13*

2079 A556 13c Henry M. Reeve

Portrait of J. Dabour, by G. Collazo — A557

Paintings by Collazo: 2c, *The Art Lovers*, horiz. 3c, *The Patio.* 5c, *Coconut Tree.* 13c, *New York Studio*, horiz. 30c, *R. Emelina Collazo.*

Perf. 13, 12½x13 (5c, 30c), 13x12½ (13c)

1976, Sept. 2

Sizes: 33x44mm, 44x33mm (2c), 31x46mm (5c, 30c), 46x31mm (13c)

2080 A557 1c multi
2081 A557 2c multi
2082 A557 3c multi
2083 A557 5c multi
2084 A557 13c multi
2085 A557 30c multi

Camilo Cienfuegos Military Schools, 10th Anniv. A558

1976, Sept. 23 *Perf. 13*

2086 A558 3c multi

Development of the Merchant Marine — A559

Various cargo and passenger ships.

1976, Oct. 2 *Perf. 12½*

2087 A559 1c multi
2088 A559 2c multi
2089 A559 3c multi
2090 A559 5c multi
2091 A559 13c multi
2092 A559 30c multi

8th Intl. Health Film Festival of Socialist Countries, Havana — A560

1976, Oct. 4 *Perf. 13x12½*

2093 A560 3c multi

5th Intl. Ballet Festival, Havana A561

Scenes from ballets. 2c, 5c, 13c, 30c vert.

1976, Nov. 6 *Perf. 13*

2094 A561 1c *Apollo*
2095 A561 2c *The River and the Forest*
2096 A561 3c *Giselle*
2097 A561 5c *Oedipus Rex*
2098 A561 13c *Carmen*
2099 A561 30c *Vital Song*

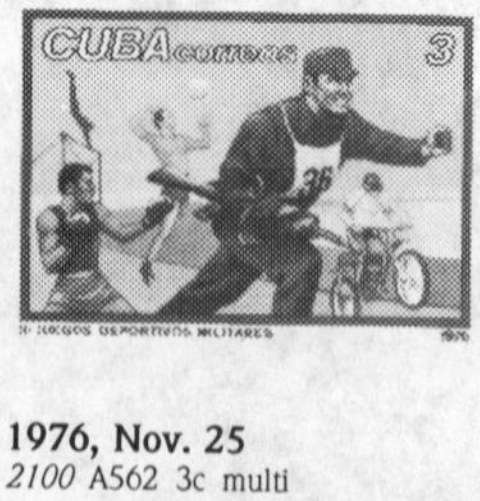

3rd Military Games A562

1976, Nov. 25 *Perf. 13*

2100 A562 3c multi

Granma Landings, 20th Anniv. A563

1976, Dec. 2 *Perf. 13x12½*

2101 A563 1c Landing craft
2102 A563 3c Landing force
2103 A563 13c Castro, soldiers
2104 A563 30c Globe, rifles

Souvenir Sheet

Cuban Landscape, by F. Cadava — A564

1976, Dec. 8 *Perf. 13x13½*

2105 A564 50c multi

CIENFUEGOS '76, 5th natl. phil. exhib.

Summer Olympics Type of 1976 and

Victory of Cuban Athletes at the Montreal Games — A565

1976, Dec. 10 *Perf. 12½x13*

2106 A565 1c Volleyball
2107 A565 2c Hurdles
2108 A565 3c Running (starting blocks)
2109 A565 8c Boxing
2110 A565 13c Running (finish line)
2111 A565 30c Judo

Souvenir Sheet

Imperf

2112 A552 50c like No. 2063

Paintings in the Natl. Museum A566

Designs: 1c, *Golden Cross Inn,* by S. Scott. 3c, *Portrait of a Man,* by J.C. Verspronck, vert. 5c, *Venetian Landscape,* by Francesco Guardi. 10c, *Valley Corner,* by H. Cleenewerck, vert. 13c, *F. Xaviera Paula,* anonymous, vert. 30c, *F. de Medici,* by C. Allori, vert.

Perf. 13, 12½x13 (3c, 10c, 30c), 12½ (13c)

1977, Jan. 18

Sizes: 40x29mm, 27x42mm (3c, 10c, 30c), 27x43½mm (13c)

2113 A566 1c multi
2114 A566 3c multi
2115 A566 5c multi
2116 A566 10c multi
2117 A566 13c multi
2118 A566 30c multi

Rural Transport A567

1977, Feb. 15 *Perf. 13*

2119 A567 3c multi

Constitution of Popular Government — A568

1976, Dec. 1 *Perf. 13x12½*

2120 A568 13c multi

Bird Type of 1975

1977, Feb. 25 *Perf. 13*

2121 A524 1c *Xiphidiopicus percussus*
2122 A524 4c *Tiaris canora*
2123 A524 10c *Dives atroviolaceus*
2124 A524 13c *Ferminia cerverai*
2125 A524 30c *Mellisuga helenae*

Lenin Park Aquarium, Havana A569

1977, Mar. 15

2126 A569 1c *Chichlasoma meeki*
2127 A569 3c *Barbus tetrazona tetrazona*
2128 A569 5c *Cyprinus carpio*
2129 A569 10c *Betta splendens*
2130 A569 13c *Pterophyllum scalare,* vert.
2131 A569 30c *Hemigrammus caudovittatus*

Sputnik (1st Artificial Satellite), 20th Anniv. — A570

Designs: 1c, DDR No. 370, *Sputnik.* 3c, Hungary No. 1216, *Luna 16.* 5c, North Korean Intl. Geophysical Year 10-won stamp of 1958, *Cosmos.* 10c, Poland No. 822, *Sputnik 3.* 13c, Yugoslavia No. 870, Earth, Moon. 30c, Cuba No. 866, Earth, Moon. 50c, Russia No. 2021, *Sputnik.*

1977, Apr. 12 *Perf. 13x12½*

2132 A570 1c multi
2133 A570 3c multi
2134 A570 5c multi
2135 A570 10c multi
2136 A570 13c multi
2137 A570 30c multi

Souvenir Sheet

Imperf

2138 A570 50c multi

No. 2138 has simulated perfs.

Antonio Maria Romeu (1876-1955), Composer — A571

1977, May 10 **Litho.** *Perf. 13*

2139 A571 3c multi

See No. C251.

Flowering Plants — A572

1977, May 31

2140 A572 1c *Hibiscus rosa sinensis*
2141 A572 2c *Nerium oleander*
2142 A572 5c *Allamanda cathartica*
2143 A572 10c *Pelargonium zonale*

Dr. Juan Tomas Roig (b. 1877), botanist. See Nos. C252-C254.

Fire Prevention Week A573

1977, June 20

2144 A573 1c shown
2145 A573 2c Horse-drawn fire pump, diff.
2146 A573 6c Early motorized vehicle
2147 A573 10c Modern truck
2148 A573 13c Turntable-ladder truck
2149 A573 30c Crane vehicle

Natl. Decorations (Ribbons and Medals of Honor) — A574

1977, July 26 *Perf. 12x12½*

2150 A574 1c shown
2151 A574 3c multi, diff.

See Nos. C255-C256.

Paintings by Jorge Arche A575

Perf. 13x12½, 12½x13 (10c), 13 (5c)

1977, Aug. 25

Sizes: 26x38mm, 29x40mm (5c), 38x26mm (10c)

2152 A575 1c *Portrait of Mary*
2153 A575 3c *Jose Marti*
2154 A575 5c *Portrait of Aristides*
2155 A575 10c *Bathers*

Nos. 2152-2154 vert. See Nos. C257-C259.

4th Military Spartakiad (Summer Sports) — A576

1977, Sept. 10 *Perf. 13*

2156 A576 1c Boxing
2157 A576 3c Volleyball
2158 A576 5c Parachuting
2159 A576 10c Running

See Nos. C260-C261.

Intl. Airmail Service, 50th Anniv. A577

Designs: 1c, Biplane and No. C62. 2c, Three-engine plane and Cuba-Key West 1st flight cancel, Oct. 28, 1927. 5c, Flying boat and intl. airmail service 1st flight cachet. 10c, Jet aircraft and Havana-Madrid cachet, Apr. 26, 1948.

1977, Oct. 27 **Litho.** *Perf. 12x12½*

2160 A577 1c multi
2161 A577 2c multi
2162 A577 5c multi
2163 A577 10c multi

See Nos. C263-C264.

October Revolution, Russia, 60th Anniv. — A578

1977, Nov. 7 *Perf. 13x12½*

2164 A578 3c Cruiser *Aurora*
2165 A578 13c Lenin, Flags
2166 A578 30c Hammer, sickle, symbols of agriculture, technology

Felines, Havana Zoo — A579

1977, Nov. 24 **Litho.** *Perf. 13*

2167 A579 1c Cat
2168 A579 2c Black panther
2169 A579 8c Puma
2170 A579 10c Leopard

See Nos. C266-C267.

Martyrs of the Revolution, 20th Death Annivs. — A580

1977, Dec. 2 *Perf. 12½x12*

2171 A580 3c Cienfuegos Uprising
2172 A580 20c Siege on the Presidential Palace

See No. C268.

Intl. Measurement System — A581

1977, Dec. 9

2173 A581 3c multi

Havana University, 250th Anniv. — A582

1978, Jan. 5 *Perf. 13x12½*

2174 A582 3c multi

See Nos. C270-C271.

Landscape with Figures, by J. Pilliment A583

Paintings in the Natl. Museum of Art: 1c, *Seated Woman*, by R. Mandrazo, vert. 4c, *Girl*, by J. Sorolla, vert. 10c, *The Cow*, by E. Abela.

Perf. 12x12½, 13 (4c, 6c, 10c)

1978, Feb. 20

Sizes: 27x42mm, 29x40mm (4c), 40x29mm (6c, 10c)

2175 A583 1c multi
2176 A583 4c multi
2177 A583 6c shown
2178 A583 10c multi

See Nos. C273-C274.

Frontier Troops, 15th Anniv. — A584

1978, Mar. 5 *Perf. 13*

2179 A584 13c multi

Bird Type of 1975

Perf. 13, 12½x12 (4c)

1978, Mar. 10 **Size: 42x27mm**

2180 A524 1c *Myadestes elisabeth*
2181 A524 4c *Polioptila lembeyei*
2182 A524 10c *Teretistris fernandinae*

Name of bird inscribed below vignette. See Nos. C275-C276.

Cosmonaut's Day — A585

1978, Apr. 12 *Perf. 13*

2183 A585 1c Intercosmos, vert.
2184 A585 2c Luna 24
2185 A585 5c Venus 9, vert.
2186 A585 10c Cosmos

See Nos. C278-C279.

9th World Trade Unions Congress, Prague A586

1978, Apr. 16

2187 A586 30c ver, deep brn & blk

Cactus Flowers — A587

1978, May 15 *Perf. 12½x13 (1c), 13*

2188 A587 1c *Melocactus guitarti*
2189 A587 4c *Leptocereus wrightii*
2190 A587 6c *Opuntia militaris*
2191 A587 10c *Cylindropuntia hystrix*

Natl. Botanical Gardens. See #C281-C282.

Lenin Park Aquarium, Havana A588

1978, June 15 *Perf. 13*

2192 A588 1c *Barbus arulios*
2193 A588 4c *Hiphessobrycon flammeus*
2194 A588 6c *Poecilia reticulata*
2195 A588 10c *Colis lalia*

See Nos. C286-C287.

MEDELLIN '78, 13th Central American and Caribbean Games — A589

1978, July 1

2196 A589 1c Basketball, vert.
2197 A589 3c Boxing, vert.
2198 A589 5c Weight lifting, vert.
2199 A589 10c Fencing

See Nos. C288-C289.

Attack on Moncada Barracks, 25th Anniv. — A590

1978, July 26

2200 A590 3c multi

See Nos. C290-C291.

World Youth and Students Festival, Havana A591

Natl. flags and views of host cities.

1978, July 28

2201 A591 3c Prague, 1947
2202 A591 3c Budapest, 1949
2203 A591 3c Berlin, 1951
2204 A591 3c Bucharest, 1953
2205 A591 3c Warsaw, 1955
a. Strip of 5, Nos. 2201-2205

See Nos. C292-C297.

Young Workers' Army, 5th Anniv. — A592

1978, Aug. 3

2206 A592 3c multi

Tuna Industry A593

1978, Aug. 30 *Perf. 12½x12*

2207 A593 1c Tuna boat
2208 A593 2c Processing ship
2209 A593 5c Shrimp boat
2210 A593 10c Inshore stern trawler

See Nos. C298-C299.

Paintings by Amelia Pelaez del Casal (1896-1968) — A594

Perf. 13x12½, 13 (3c, 6c), 12½x13

1978, Sept. 15

2211 A594 1c *The White Mantle*
2212 A594 3c *Still-life with Flowers*, vert.
2213 A594 6c *Women*, vert.
2214 A594 10c *Fish*, vert.

See Nos. C301-C303.

African Fauna, Havana Zoo A595

1978, Oct. 20 *Perf. 13*

2215 A595 1c Rhinoceros
2216 A595 4c Okapi, vert.
2217 A595 6c Mandrill
2218 A595 10c Giraffe, vert.

See Nos. C307-C308.

Natl. Ballet, 30th Anniv. A596

1978, Oct. 28 *Perf. 13x12½*

2219 A596 3c *Grande Pas de Quatre*

See Nos. C309-C310.

A597 A598

Flowers of the Pacific: Various species.

1978, Nov. 30 **Litho.** *Perf. 13*

2220 A597 1c multi
2221 A597 4c multi
2222 A597 6c multi
2223 A597 10c multi

See Nos. C311-C312.

1979, Jan. 1 *Perf. 12½x13 (3c), 13*

2224 A598 3c Castro, soldier
2225 A598 13c Industry
2226 A598 1p Flag, globe, flame

Triumph of the Revolution, 20th anniv.

Doves and Pigeons — A599

1979, Jan. 30 ***Perf. 13***

2227 A599 1c *Starnoenas cyanocephala*
2228 A599 3c *Geotrygon chysia*
2229 A599 7c *Geotrygon caniceps*
2230 A599 8c *Geotrygon montana*
2231 A599 13c *Columba leucocephala*
2232 A599 30c *Columba inornata*

Paintings in the Natl. Museum of Art — A600

Designs: 1c, *Genre Scene*, by David Teniers. 3c, *Arrival of Spanish Troops*, by J. Louis Meissonier. 6c, *A Joyful Gathering*, by Sir David Wilkie. 10c, *A Robbery*, by E. De Lucas Padilla. 13c, *Tea Time*, by R. Madrazo, vert. 30c, *Peasants in Front of a Tavern*, by Adriaen van Ostade.

1979, Feb. 20

2233 A600 1c multi
2234 A600 3c multi
2235 A600 6c multi
2236 A600 10c multi
2237 A600 13c multi
2238 A600 30c multi

See Nos. 2262-2267, C317.

Marine Flora — A601

1979, Mar. 20

2239 A601 3c *Nymphaea capensis*
2240 A601 10c *Nymphaea ampla*
2241 A601 13c *Nymphaea coerulea*
2242 A601 30c *Nymphaea rubra*

All are incorrectly inscribed "Nymphaca."

A602

A603

1979, Mar. 24

2243 A602 3c multi

Cuban film industry, 20th anniv.

1979, Apr. 12

2244 A603 1c Rocket launch
2245 A603 4c Soyuz
2246 A603 6c Salyut
2247 A603 10c Link-up
2248 A603 13c Soyuz, Salyut
2249 A603 30c Parachute landing

Cosmonaut's Day. See No. C315.

6th Summit Meeting of Non-Aligned Countries — A604

1979, Apr. 17

2250 A604 3c Understanding, cooperation
2251 A604 13c Fight colonialism
2252 A604 30c New world economic order

House of the Americas Museum, 20th Anniv. — A605

1979, Apr. 28 ***Perf. 13x12½***

2253 A605 13c Cuna Indian tapestry

Agrarian Reform, 20th Anniv. — A606

1979, May 17 ***Perf. 12½x12***

2254 A606 3c multi

Souvenir Sheet

The Party, by Jules Pascin — A607

1979, May 18 ***Perf. 13***

2255 A607 50c multi

PHILASERDICA '79 phil. exhib., Sofia.

Nocturnal Butterflies A608

1979, May 25

2256 A608 1c *Eulepidotis rectimargo*
2257 A608 4c *Othreis materna*
2258 A608 6c *Noropsis hieroglyphica*
2259 A608 10c *Heterochroma*
2260 A608 13c *Melanchroia regnatrix*
2261 A608 30c *Attera gemmata*

Art Type of 1979

Paintings by Victor Emmanuel Garcia (d. 1969): 1c, *Main Avenue, Paris*. 3c, *Portrait of Enmita*. 6c, *San Juan River, Matanzas*. 10c, *Woman Carrying Hay*. 13c, *Still-life with Vase*. 30c, *Street at Night*. Nos. 2262-2267 vert.

1979, June 15

2262 A600 1c multi
2263 A600 3c multi
2264 A600 6c multi
2265 A600 10c multi
2266 A600 13c multi
2267 A600 30c multi

See No. C317.

World Peace Council, 30th Anniv. A609

1979, June 29 ***Perf. 12½x13***

2268 A609 30c multi

1980 Summer Olympics, Moscow — A610

1979, July 30 ***Perf. 13x12½***

2269 A610 1c Wrestling
2270 A610 4c Boxing
2271 A610 6c Women's volleyball
2272 A610 10c Shooting
2273 A610 13c Weight lifting
2274 A610 30c High jump

Roses — A611

A612

1979, Aug. 20 ***Perf. 13***

2275 A611 1c *Rosa eglanteria*
2276 A611 2c *Rosa centifolia anemonoides*
2277 A611 3c *Rosa indica vulgaris*
2278 A611 5c *Rosa eglanteria punicea*
2279 A611 10c *Rosa sulfurea*
2280 A611 13c *Rosa muscosa alba*
2281 A611 20c *Rosa gallica purpurea velutina*

1979, Aug. 30

2282 A612 13c multi

Council for Mutual Economic Assistance, 30th anniv.

Cubana Airlines, 50th Anniv. A613

Various aircraft.

1979, Oct. 8

2283 A613 1c Ford trimotor
2284 A613 2c Sikorsky S-38
2285 A613 3c Douglas DC-3
2286 A613 4c Douglas DC-6
2287 A613 13c Ilyushin IL-14
2288 A613 40c Tupolev TU-104

Disappearance of Camilo Cienfuegos, 20th Anniv. — A614

1979, Oct. 28

2289 A614 3c multi

Reinoso, Sugar Cane and Blossom A615

1979, Nov. 12

2290 A615 13c multi

Sugar Cane Research Institute, 15th anniv., and sesquicentennial of the birth of Alvaro Reinoso.

Zoo Animals A616

1979, Nov. 15

2291 A616 1c Chimpanzees
2292 A616 2c Leopards
2293 A616 3c Deer
2294 A616 4c Lion cubs
2295 A616 5c Bear cubs
2296 A616 13c Squirrels
2297 A616 30c Pandas
2298 A616 50c Tiger cubs

Insects A617

1980, Jan. 25

2299 A617 1c *Rhina oblita*
2300 A617 5c *Odontocera josemartii*, vert.
2301 A617 6c *Pinthocoelium columbinum*
2302 A617 10c *Calasoma splendida*, vert.
2303 A617 13c *Homophileurus cubanus*, vert.
2304 A617 30c *Heterops dimidiata*, vert.

1980 Summer Olympics, Moscow — A618

1980, Feb. 20 *Perf. 12½*
2305 A618 1c Weight lifting
2306 A618 2c Shooting
2307 A618 5c Javelin
2308 A618 6c Wrestling
2309 A618 8c Judo
2310 A618 10c Running
2311 A618 13c Boxing
2312 A618 30c Women's volleyball

Souvenir Sheet

Imperf

2313 A618 50c Mischa character

No. 2313 contains one 32x40mm stamp.

Paintings in the Natl. Museum A619

Designs: 1c, *The Oak Trees,* by Henry Joseph Harpignies, vert. 4c, *Family Reunion,* by Willem van Mieris. 6c, *Domestic Fowl,* by Melchior De Hondecoeter, vert. 9c, *Innocence,* by William A. Bougereau, vert. 13c, *Venetial Scene II,* by Michele Marieschi. 30c, *Spanish Peasant Woman,* by Joaquin Dominguez Bequer, vert.

Perf. 12½, 13 (9c, 30c), 12½x13 (13c)

1980, Mar. 11

Sizes: 29x40mm, 40x29mm (4c), 28x42mm (9c, 30c), 38x26mm (13c)

2314 A619 1c multi
2315 A619 4c multi
2316 A619 6c multi
2317 A619 9c multi
2318 A619 15c multi
2319 A619 30c multi

Souvenir Sheet

LONDON '80 — A620

1980, Apr. 1 *Perf. 13*
2320 A620 50c *Malvern Hall,* by John Constable

Intercosmos Program — A621

1980, Apr. 12
2321 A621 1c Emblem, flags
2322 A621 4c Astrophysics
2323 A621 6c Satellite communications
2324 A621 10c Meteorology
2325 A621 13c Biology and medicine
2326 A621 30c Surveying satellite

Cuban Postage Stamps, 125th Anniv. — A622

1980, Apr. 24 *Perf. 12½*
2327 A622 30c Nos. 1, 7 and 613

Orchids — A623

1980, May 20 *Perf. 13*
2328 A623 1c *Bletia purpurea*
2329 A623 4c *Oncidium leiboldii*
2330 A623 6c *Epidendrum cochieatum*
2331 A623 10c *Cattleyopsis lindenii*
2332 A623 13c *Encyclia fucata*
2333 A623 30c *Encyclia phoenicea*

Marine Mammals A624

1980, June 20
2334 A624 1c *Tursiops truncatus*
2335 A624 3c *Megaptera novaeangliae,* vert.
2336 A624 13c *Ziphius cavirostris*
2337 A624 30c *Monachus tropicalis*

Urban Reform Campaign, 20th Anniv. — A625

Nationalization of Foreign Industry, 20th Anniv. — A626

Perf. 13x12½, 12½x13

1980, July 26
2338 A625 3c multi
2339 A626 13c multi

Moncada Program.

Colonial Copperware A627

Perf. 12½, 12½x13 (13c)

1980, July 29

Sizes: 27x43½mm, 38x26mm (13c)

2340 A627 3c Wine pitcher, 19th cent.
2341 A627 13c Oil jar, 18th cent.
2342 A627 30c Lidded pitcher, 19th cent.

Cuban Women's Federation, 20th Anniv. — A628

1980, Aug. 23 *Perf. 13*
2343 A628 3c multi

Souvenir Sheet

ESPAMER '80, Madrid — A629

Design: *Clotilde Passing Through the Country Garden,* by Joaquin Sorolla y Bastida.

1980, Aug. 29
2344 A629 50c multi

Postage stamps of Spain, 130th anniv.

1st Havana Declaration, 20th Anniv. — A630

1980, Sept. 2
2345 A630 13c multi

Construction of Naval Vessels in Cuba, 360th Anniv. — A631

Ships under construction: 1c, *Our Lady of Atocha,* galleon, 1620. 3c, *El Rayo,* warship, 1749. 7c, *Santisima Trinidad,* 1769. 10c, *Santisima Trinidad,* diff., 1805, vert. 13c, Steamships *Congreso* and *Colon,* 1851. 30c, Cardenas and Chullima shipyards.

1980, Sept. 15
2346 A631 1c multi
2347 A631 3c multi
2348 A631 7c multi
2349 A631 10c multi
2350 A631 13c multi
2351 A631 30c multi

A633

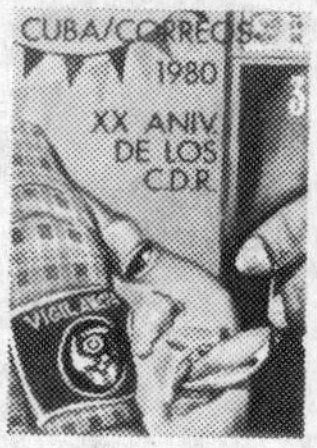

A634

1980, Sept. 26 *Perf. 13*
2354 A633 13c multi

Fidel Castro's 1st speech before the UN General Assembly, 20th anniv.

1980, Sept. 28 *Perf. 13x12½*
2355 A634 3c multi

Revolutionary defense committees, 20th anniv.

Souvenir Sheet

ESSEN '80, 49th Intl. Philatelic Federation Congress — A635

Painting: *Portrait of a Lady,* by Ludger Tom Ring The Younger.

1980, Oct. 2 **Litho.** *Perf. 13*
2356 A635 50c multi

Early Locomotives — A636

1980, Oct. 15
2357 A636 1c Josefa
2358 A636 2c Chaparra Sugar Co. No. 22
2359 A636 7c Steam storage locomotive
2360 A636 10c 2-4-2 locomotive
2361 A636 13c 2-4-0 locomotive
2362 A636 30c Oil combustion engine, 1909

Lighthouses A637

1980, Oct. 30
2363 A637 3c Roncali, San Antonio
2364 A637 13c Jagua, Cienfuegos
2365 A637 30c Maisi Point, Guantanamo

See Nos. 2440-2442, 2553-2555, 2614-2616.

Victory of Cuban Athletes at the 1980 Summer Olympics, Moscow — A638

1980, Nov. 10 **Litho.** *Perf. 12½x12*

2366 A638 13c Bronze medals
2367 A638 30c Silver medals
2368 A638 50c Gold medals

Nos. 2366-2368 each printed se-tenant with label containing statistical data.

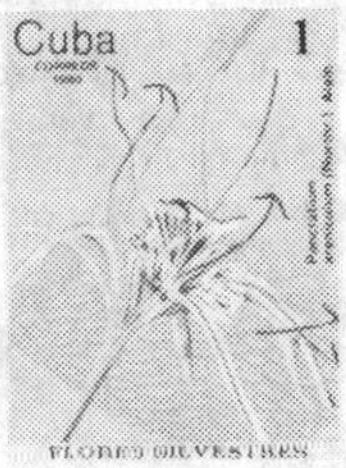

Wildflowers A639

1980, Nov. 20 *Perf. 13*

2369 A639 1c *Pancratium arenicolum*
2370 A639 4c *Urechites lutea*
2371 A639 6c *Solanum elaegnifolium*
2372 A639 10c *Hamelia patens*
2373 A639 13c *Morinda royoc*
2374 A639 30c *Centrosema virginianum*

Souvenir Sheet

7th Natl. Stamp Exhibition — A640

1980, Nov. 22

2375 A640 50c Mail train

2nd Communist Party Congress — A641

1980, Dec. 17

2376 A641 3c shown
2377 A641 13c Industry, communication
2378 A641 30c Athletics, elderly, education

Paintings in the Natl. Museum of Art — A642

Designs: 1c, *Lady Mayo*, by Anton Van Dyck, vert. 6c, *The Spinner*, by Giovanni Battista Piazzeta, vert. 10c, *Daniel Collyer*, by Francis Cotes, vert. 13c, *Palm Gardens, Mallorca*, by Santiago Rusinol Prats. 20c, *Landscape with Roadway and Houses*, by Frederick Waters Watts. 50c, *Landscape with Sheep*, by Jean-Francois Millet.

1981, Jan. 20

2379 A642 1c multi
2380 A642 6c multi
2381 A642 10c multi
2382 A642 13c multi
2383 A642 20c multi
2384 A642 50c multi

See Nos. 2510-2515.

Pelagic Fish A643

1981, Feb. 25

2385 A643 1c *Isurus oxyrhynchus*
2386 A643 3c *Lampris regius*
2387 A643 10c *Istiophorus platypterus*
2388 A643 13c *Mola mola*, vert.
2389 A643 30c *Coruphaena hippurus*
2390 A643 50c *Tetrapturus albidus*

1982 World Cup Soccer Championships, Spain — A644

Globe and various soccer players.

1981, Mar. 20 *Perf. 12½*

2391 A644 1c multi
2392 A644 2c multi
2393 A644 3c multi
2394 A644 10c multi, vert.
2395 A644 13c multi, vert.
2396 A644 50c multi

Souvenir Sheet

Perf. 13

2397 A644 1p Soccer ball, flag

No. 2397 contains one 40x32mm stamp.

Opening of the 1st Kindergarten, 20th Anniv. — A645

1981, Apr. 10 *Perf. 13*

2398 A645 3c multi

1st Man in Space, 20th Anniv. A646

Designs: 1c, Jules Verne, Russian scientist Konstantin E. Tsiolkovski, and Sergei P. Korolev, designer of the 1st Soviet spacecraft, vert. 2c, Yuri Gagarin, 1st man in space. 3c, Valentina Tereshkova, 1st woman in space, and *Vostok 6*. 5c, Aleksei A. Leonov, 1st man to walk in space. 13c, Konstantin Feoktistov, Boris Yegorov and Vladimir Komarov, *Voskhod 1* crew, 1st 3-man orbital flight. 30c, Valeri Ryumen and Leonid Popov, set a space endurance record. 50c, Arnaldo Tamayo, 1st Cuban cosmonaut, and Soviet cosmonaut Yuri Romanenko on joint space flight, vert.

1981, Apr. 12 *Perf. 12½*

2399 A646 1c multi
2400 A646 2c multi
2401 A646 3c multi
2402 A646 5c multi
2403 A646 13c multi
2404 A646 30c multi
2405 A646 50c multi

A647

1981, Apr. 19 **Litho.** *Perf. 13*

2406 A647 3c multi, vert.
2407 A647 13c multi, vert.
2408 A647 30c multi

Creation of armed forces (DAAFAR) (3c), Bay of Pigs Invasion, 20th Anniv. (13c), Proclamation of the socialist revolution (30c).

Attack on Goicuria Barracks, 25th Anniv. A648

1981, Apr. 29

2409 A648 3c multi

Natl. Assoc. of Small Farmers (ANAP), 20th Anniv. A649

1981, May 17

2410 A649 3c multi

Souvenir Sheet

WIPA '81 — A650

1981, May 22 **Litho.**

2411 A650 50c Austria No. 643

Fighting Cocks — A651

Perf. 12½x13, 13x12½

1981, May 25

2412 A651 1c Canelo, vert.
2413 A651 3c Cenizo
2414 A651 7c Blanco, vert.
2415 A651 13c Pinto, vert.
2416 A651 30c Giro
2417 A651 50c Jabao, vert.

Ministry of the Interior, 20th Anniv. — A652

1981, June 6 *Perf. 13*

2418 A652 13c multi

Souvenir Sheet

Mother and Child, by Zlatka Dabova — A653

1981, June 14

2419 A653 50c gold, sil & blk

Bulgaria, 1300th anniv. BULGARIA '81 phil. exhib.

Horse-drawn Carriages — A654

1981, June 25

2420 A654 1c Streetcar
2421 A654 4c Bus
2422 A654 9c Breake
2423 A654 13c Landau
2424 A654 30c Phaeton
2425 A654 50c Funeral coach

House in the Country, by Mario Caridad — A655

1981, July 15 *Perf. 12½*

2426 A655 30c multi

Intl. Year of the Disabled.

Sandinistas, 25th Anniv. — A656

1981, July 23 *Perf. 13*
2427 A656 13c multi

State Institutions, 20th Annivs. — A657

1981, July 26 *Perf. 12½*
2428 A657 3c multi
2429 A657 13c multi, diff.
2430 A657 30c multi, diff.

Institute for Sports, Physical Education and Recreation (3c); Radio Havana (13c); and Ministry of Foreign Trade (MINCEX) (30c).

Carlos J. Finlay and Cent. of His Theory of Biological Vectors — A658

1981, Aug. 14 *Perf. 13*
2431 A658 13c multi

Nonaligned Countries Movement, 20th Anniv. — A659

1981, Sept. 1
2432 A659 50c multi

Horses — A660

Illustration reduced. Nos. 2433-2437 vert.

1981, Sept. 15 *Perf. 13*
Size: 29x40mm
2433 A660 1c multi
2434 A660 3c multi, diff.
2435 A660 8c multi, diff.
2436 A660 13c multi, diff.
2437 A660 30c multi, diff.
Size: 68x27mm
Perf. 12½
2438 A660 50c Herd

Souvenir Sheet

Idyll in a Tea House, by Kitagawa Utamaro — A661

1981, Oct. 9 *Perf. 13*
2439 A661 50c multi

PHILATOKYO '81.

Lighthouse Type of 1980

1981, Oct. 15 **Litho.**
2440 A637 3c North Rock
2441 A637 13c Lucrecia Point
2442 A637 40c East Guano

Jose Marti Natl. Library, 80th Anniv. — A662

Sugar mills, lithographs from *Los Ingenios*, by Eduardo Laplante (b. 1818): 3c, Flor de Cuba, 1838. 13c, El Progreso, 1845. 30c, Santa Teresa, 1847.

1981, Oct. 18 *Perf. 12½x12*
2443 A662 3c multi
2444 A662 13c multi
2445 A662 30c multi

Pablo Picasso (b. 1881) and No. 1263 A663

1981, Oct. 25 *Perf. 12½x13*
2446 A663 30c multi

Souvenir Sheet

ESPAMER '81, Buenos Aires — A664

1981, Nov. 13 *Perf. 13*
2447 A664 1p Packet

Art Type of 1969

Paintings in the Napoleon Museum: 1c, *Napoleon in Coronation Costume*, anonymous. 3c, *Napoleon with Landscape in the Background*, by Jean Horace Vernet. 10c, *Bonaparte in Egypt*, by Edouard Detaille. 13c, *Napoleon on Horseback*, by Hippolyte Bellange. 30c, *Napoleon in Normandy*, by Bellange. 50c, *Death of Napoleon*, anonymous.

1981, Dec. 1 *Perf. 12½*
Sizes: 42x58mm, 58x42mm (3c, 13c, 30c, 50c)
2448 A385 1c multi
2449 A385 3c multi, horiz.
2450 A385 10c multi
2451 A385 13c multi, horiz.
2452 A385 30c multi, horiz.
2453 A385 50c multi, horiz.

Napoleon Museum, 20th anniv.

25th Annivs. A665

1981, Dec. 2 *Perf. 13*
2454 A665 3c Revolutionaries, vert.
2455 A665 20c Marksman
2456 A665 1p Yacht *Granma*

November 30th insurrection (3c); creation of the revolutionary armed forces (20c); and disembarking of revolutionary forces (1p).

Fauna — A666

1981, Dec. 14 **Litho.** *Perf. 12½x12*
2457 A666 1c Hummingbird
2458 A666 2c Parakeet
2459 A666 5c Hutia
2460 A666 20c Almiqui
2461 A666 35c Manatee
2462 A666 40c Crocodile

Fernando Ortiz, Folklorist, Birth Cent. A667

1981, Dec. 20 *Perf. 12½x13*
2463 A667 3c Portrait by Jorge Arche y Silva
2464 A667 10c Hanging idol
2465 A667 30c Arara drum
2466 A667 50c Chango statue

Literacy Campaign, 20th Anniv. — A668

1981, Dec. 25 *Perf. 12½x12*
2467 A668 5c Conrado Benitez
2468 A668 5c Manuel Asunce

Printed se-tenant.

A669

1982 World Cup Soccer Championships, Spain — A670

Various athletes.

1982, Jan. 15 *Perf. 13*
2469 A669 1c multi, vert.
2470 A669 2c multi, vert.
2471 A669 5c multi, vert.
2472 A669 10c multi, vert.
2473 A669 20c shown
2474 A669 40c multi
2475 A669 50c multi, vert.

Souvenir Sheet

2476 A670 1p shown

No. 2476 contains one 32x40mm stamp.

10th World Trade Unions Congress, Havana — A671

1982, Feb. 10 **Litho.**
2477 A671 30c Lazaro Pena, delegate

Butterflies — A672

1982, Feb. 25 *Perf. 12½*
2478 A672 1c *Euptoieta hegesia*
2479 A672 4c *Metamorpha stelenes insularis*
2480 A672 5c *Heliconius charithonius ramsdeni*
2481 A672 20c *Phoebis avellaneda*
2482 A672 30c *Hamadryas ferox diasia*
2483 A672 50c *Marpesia eleuchea*

Exports — A673

Designs: 3c, Sugar (processing plant). 4c, Lobster (fishing boat). 6c, Canned fruits. 7c, Agricultural machinery. 8c, Nickel (passenger jet, industrial complex, car). 9c, Rum. 10c, Coffee. 30c, Fresh fruit. 50c, Tobacco. 1p, Cement. Nos. 2489-2493 vert.

Perf. 12x12½, 12½x12

1982, Feb. 26
2484 A673 3c lt grn
2485 A673 4c car rose
2486 A673 6c dull blue
2487 A673 7c brt org
2488 A673 8c brt vio
2489 A673 9c slate
2490 A673 10c dull red brn
2491 A673 30c bister
2492 A673 50c orange
2493 A673 1p olive bister

Tulips
A674

1982, Mar. 30 *Perf. 12$^1/_2$x13*

2494 A674 1c Greenland
2495 A674 3c Mariette
2496 A674 8c Ringo
2497 A674 20c La Tulipe Noire
2498 A674 30c Jewel of Spring
2499 A674 50c Orange Parrot

Communist Youth Organization, 20th Anniv. — A675

1982, Apr. 4 *Perf. 13*

2500 A675 5c multi

2nd UN-Pacific Congress on the Peaceful Use of Outer Space A676

1982, Apr. 12

2501 A676 1c *Mars*
2502 A676 3c *Venera*
2503 A676 6c *Salyut-Soyuz* link-up
2504 A676 20c *Lunokhod* moon vehicle
2505 A676 30c *Venera* with heat shield
2506 A676 50c *Cosmos*

Cover
A677

1982, Apr. 24 *Perf. 12$^1/_2$x12*

2507 A677 20c Havana-Veracruz
2508 A677 30c Havana-Tampico

Stamp Day. English post office, 1842-1877 (20c); and French post office, 1862-1877 (30c).

Broadcasting and Television Institute (ICRT), 20th Anniv. — A678

1982, May 24 *Perf. 12x12$^1/_2$*

2509 A678 30c multi

Art Type of 1981
With Larger Type

Paintings in the Natl. Museum of Art: 1c, *Portrait of a Youth* (girl), by Jean B. Greuze, vert. 3c, *Procession in Brittany*, by Jules Breton. 9c, *Landscape*, by Jean Piliment. 20c, *Late Afternoon*, by William A. Bourgueran, vert. 30c, *Tiger*, by Ferdinand V.E. Delacroix. 40c, *The Chair*, by Wilfredo Lam, vert.

Perf. 13, 13x12$^1/_2$ (3c), 12x12$^1/_2$ (20c, 40c), 12$^1/_2$x12 (30c)

1982, May 31 **Litho.**

2510 A642 1c 29x40mm
2511 A642 3c 46x36mm
2512 A642 9c 40x29mm
2513 A642 20c 27x42mm
2514 A642 30c 42x27mm
2515 A642 40c 27x42mm

Souvenir Sheet

PHILEXFRANCE '82 — A679

1982, June 7 *Perf. 13*

2516 A679 1p Steamship *Louisiana* at St. Nazaire

DEPORFILEX '82 — A680

1982, June 10 *Perf. 13x12$^1/_2$*

2517 A680 20c Hurdler, No. 300

Reptiles
A681

1982, June 15 *Perf. 13*

2518 A681 1c *Pseudemys decussata*
2519 A681 2c *Tropidophis pardalis*
2520 A681 3c *Crocodylus rhombifer*
2521 A681 20c *Cyclura nubila*
2522 A681 30c *Anolis allisonis*
2523 A681 50c *Alsophis canthergerus*

George Dimitrov (1882-1949), Bulgarian Prime Minister — A682

1982, June 18

2524 A682 30c multi

Koch, Bacillus
A683

1982, July 18

2525 A683 20c multi

Discovery of the tubercle bacillus by Dr. Robert Koch, cent.

14th Central American and Caribbean Games — A684

1982, Aug. 1

2526 A684 1c Baseball
2527 A684 2c Boxing
2528 A684 10c Water polo
2529 A684 20c Javelin
2530 A684 35c Weight lifting
2531 A684 50c Volleyball

Hydraulic Development Plan, 20th Anniv. — A685

Designs: 5c, Fruit, *Eichornia crassipes*, ship. 20c, Arid soil, *Nymphaea alba*, irrigation and reservoir systems.

1982, Aug. 9

2532 A685 5c multi
2533 A685 20c multi

Souvenir Sheet

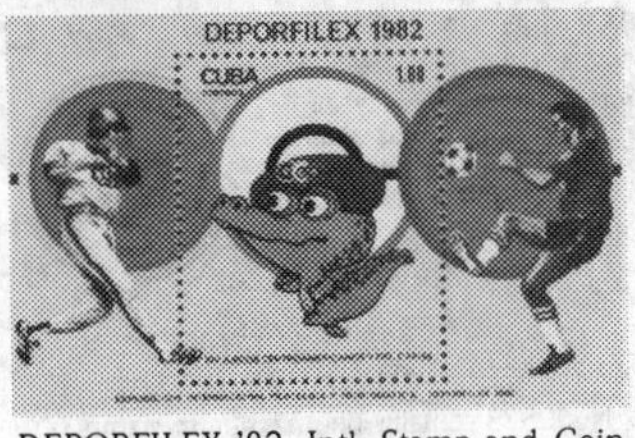

DEPORFILEX '82, Intl. Stamp and Coin Exhibition — A686

1982, Aug. 10 **Litho.**

2534 A686 1p Cuco, character trademark

14th Central American and Caribbean Games.

Namibia Day
A687

1982, Aug. 26

2535 A687 50c multi

1982 World Cup Soccer Championships, Spain — A688

Various athletes.

1982, Aug. 30

2536 A688 5c multi
2537 A688 20c multi
2538 A688 30c multi
2539 A688 50c multi

Also exist in miniature sheets of 16 + 9 labels containing 4 each Nos. 2536-2539 in blocks of 4.

Natl. Folklore Ensemble, 20th Anniv.
A689

Paintings by V.P. Landaluze.

1982, Sept. 10

2540 A689 20c *Little Devil*, vert.
2541 A689 30c *Day of Kings*

Prehistoric Fauna
A690

1982, Sept. 15 **Litho.**

2542 A690 1c *Ornimegalonyx oteroi*, vert.
2543 A690 5c *Crocodylus rhombifer*
2544 A690 7c *Aquila borrasi*, vert.
2545 A690 20c *Geocapromys colombianus*
2546 A690 35c *Megalocnus rodens*, vert.
2547 A690 50c *Nesophontes micrus*

15th Death Anniv. of Che Guevara — A691

1982, Oct. 8 *Perf. 13x12$^1/_2$*

2548 A691 20c multi

Discovery of America, 490th Anniv. — A692

1982, Oct. 12 *Perf. 13*
2549 A692 5c shown
2550 A692 20c *Santa Maria*, vert.
2551 A692 35c *Pinta*, vert.
2552 A692 50c *Nina*, vert.

Lighthouse Type of 1980

1982, Oct. 25
2553 A637 5c Jutias Caye
2554 A637 20c Paredon Grande Caye
2555 A637 30c Morro Santiago de Cuba

George Washington, 250th Birth Anniv. — A693

Designs: Quotations and anonymous oil paintings, 18th-19th cent.

1982, Oct. 29 *Perf. 12x12½*
2556 A693 5c multi
2557 A693 20c multi, diff.

Souvenir Sheet

8th Natl. Philatelic Exposition, Ciego de Avila — A694

1982, Nov. 13
2558 A694 1p Paddle steamer *Almendares*

8th Congress of the Cuban Philatelic Federation, Nov. 13-22.

Lenin Natl. Park, 10th Anniv. A695

1982, Dec. 28
2559 A695 5c multi

Chess Champion Jose Raul Capablanca and King — A696

1982, Dec. 29
2560 A696 5c shown
2561 A696 20c Rook
2562 A696 30c Knight
2563 A696 50c Queen
a. Bklt. pane of 4, Nos. 2560-2563

Exist in sheets of 4+2 labels picturing chessmen.

USSR, 60th Anniv. A697

1982, Dec. 30 *Perf. 13x12½*
2564 A697 30c multi

World Communications Year — A698

1983, Jan. 24 **Litho.** *Perf. 13*
2565 A698 20c multi

No. 507 and Birthplace — A699

1983, Jan. 28 *Perf. 13x12½*
2566 A699 5c multi

Jose Marti (b. 1853), writer, revolution leader.

1984 Summer Olympics, Los Angeles — A700

1983, Jan. 31 *Perf. 13*
2567 A700 1c Javelin
2568 A700 5c Volleyball
2569 A700 6c Basketball
2570 A700 20c Weight lifting
2571 A700 30c Wrestling
2572 A700 50c Boxing

Souvenir Sheet

Perf. 13½x13

2573 A700 1p Judo

No. 2573 contains one 32x40mm stamp.

Radio Rebelde, 25th Anniv. — A701

1983, Feb. 24 *Perf. 13*
2574 A701 20c multi

Karl Marx, Death Cent. A702

1983, Mar. 14
2575 A702 30c multi

1st Manned Balloon Flight, Bicent. — A703

Various balloons.

1983, Mar. 30
2576 A703 1c multi
2577 A703 3c multi
2578 A703 5c multi
2579 A703 7c multi
2580 A703 30c multi
2581 A703 50c multi

Souvenir Sheet

2582 A703 1p Jose D. Blino

No. 2582 contains one 32x40mm stamp.

Cosmonauts' Day — A704

1983, Apr. 12 **Litho.**
2583 A704 1c *Vostok 1*
2584 A704 4c Satellite *Frances D1*
2585 A704 5c *Mars 2*
2586 A704 20c *Soyuz*
2587 A704 30c Meteorological satellite
2588 A704 50c Intercosmos satellite

Stamp Day A705

1983, Apr. 24
2589 A705 20c Havana-Key West cover
2590 A705 30c Spain-Havana cover

1st Intl. airmail services.

Souvenir Sheet

TEMBAL '83, Basel — A706

1983, May 21 *Perf. 13½x13*
2591 A706 1p Weasel

Simon Bolivar, Liberator of South America A707

1983, July 24 *Perf. 12½x13*
2592 A707 5c Jose Rafael de las Heras
2593 A707 20c Bolivar

Attack of Moncada Barracks, 30th Anniv. A708

Designs: 5c, Jose Marti, Moncada barracks. 20c, Abel Santamaria, Jose Luis Tasende and Boris Luis Santa Coloma, martyrs, vert. 30c, *History Will Absolve Me*, declaration of Fidel Castro, vert.

1983, July 26 *Perf. 13*
2594 A708 5c multi
2595 A708 20c multi
2596 A708 30c multi

Souvenir Sheet

Alberto Santos-Dumont (1873-1932) — A709

1983, July 29 *Perf. 13x13½*
2597 A709 1p Dumont's aircraft

BRASILIANA '83, Rio; 140th anniv. of 1st stamp issued in the Americas.

9th Pan American Games, Caracas — A710

1983, Aug. 14 *Perf. 13x12½*

2598 A710 1c Weight lifting
2599 A710 2c Volleyball
2600 A710 3c Baseball
2601 A710 20c High jump
2602 A710 30c Basketball
2603 A710 50c Boxing

Port, by Claude Joseph Vernet — A711

1983, Sept. 5

2604 A711 30c multi

French alliance, cent.

Pres. Salvador Allende of Chile (d. 1973) — A712

1983, Sept. 12

2605 A712 20c multi

1st Congress of Farmers at Arms, 25th Anniv. — A713

1983, Sept. 21 *Perf. 12½x12*

2606 A713 5c multi

Raphael, 500th Birth Anniv. — A714

1983, Sept. 30 **Litho.** *Perf. 13*

2607 A714 1c *Girl with Veil*
2608 A714 2c *The Cardinal*
2609 A714 5c *Francesco M. Della Rovere*
2610 A714 20c *Portrait of a Youth*
2611 A714 30c *Magdalena Doni*
2612 A714 50c *La Fornarina*

State Quality Seal A715

1983, Oct. 14

2613 A715 5c multi

Lighthouse Type of 1980

1983, Oct. 20

2614 A637 5c Carapachibey
2615 A637 20c Cadiz Bay
2616 A637 30c Gobernadora Point

Turtles A716

1983, Nov. 15

2617 A716 1c *Eretmochelys imbricata*
2618 A716 2c *Lepidochelys kempi*
2619 A716 5c *Chrysemys decussata*
2620 A716 20c *Caretta caretta*
2621 A716 30c *Chelonia mydas*
2622 A716 50c *Dermochelys coriacea*

World Communications Year — A717

1983, Nov. 23

2623 A717 1c Bell's Gallow Frame, telephone
2624 A717 5c Telegram, airmail
2625 A717 10c Satellite, satellite dish
2626 A717 20c Television, radio
2627 A717 30c 24th Communications conf.

Nos. 319 and 990 A718

1983, Dec. 3 *Perf. 13x12½*

2628 A718 20c multi

See note after No. 320.

Flowers, Birds — A719

Flowers — A720

1983, Dec. 20 *Perf. 13*

2629 A719 5c *Opuntia dillenii*
2630 A719 5c *Euphorbia podocarpifolia*
2631 A719 5c *Dinema cubincola*
2632 A719 5c *Guaiacum officinale*
2633 A719 5c *Magnolia cubensis*
a. Strip of 5, Nos. 2629-2633
2634 A719 5c *Jatropha angustifolia*
2635 A719 5c *Cochlospermum vitifolium*
2636 A719 5c *Tabebuia lepidota*
2637 A719 5c *Kalmiella ericoides*
2638 A719 5c *Jatropha integerrima*
2639 A719 5c *Melocactus actinacanthus*
2640 A719 5c *Cordia sebestana*
2641 A719 5c *Tabernae - montana apoda*
2642 A719 5c *Lantana camara*
2643 A719 5c *Cordia gerascanthus*
a. Block of 10, Nos. 2634-2643
2644 A719 5c *Tiaris canora*
2645 A719 5c *Phaethon lepturus*
2646 A719 5c *Myadestes elisabeth*
2647 A719 5c *Saurothera merlini*
2648 A719 5c *Polioptila lembeyei*
a. Strip of 5, Nos. 2644-2648
2649 A719 5c *Mellisuga helenae*
2650 A719 5c *Mimus polyglottos*
2651 A719 5c *Todus multicolor*
2652 A719 5c *Amazona leucocephala*
2653 A719 5c *Ferminia cerverai*
2654 A719 5c *Pelecanus occidentalis*
2655 A719 5c *Melanerpes superciliaris*
2656 A719 5c *Mimocichla plumbea*
2657 A719 5c *Aratinga euops*
2658 A719 5c *Sturnella magna*
a. Block of 10, Nos. 2649-2658

Souvenir Sheets

2658B A719 100c *Hedychium coronarium*
2658C A719 100c *Priotelus temnurus*

1983, Dec. 30 *Perf. 12½*

2659 A720 60c Tobacco
2660 A720 70c Lily
2661 A720 80c Mariposa
2662 A720 90c Orchid

25th Anniv. of the Revolution — A721

1983, Dec. 31 **Litho.** *Perf. 13*

2663 A721 5c shown
2664 A721 20c Flags, Santa Clara Rlwy. tracks

25th Anniv. of the Revolution — A722

1984, Jan. 8

2665 A722 20c Guevara, Castro
2666 A722 20c Star
2667 A722 20c PCC emblem, workers

Printed se-tenant.

Lenin, 60th Death Anniv. A723

1984, Jan. 21 *Perf. 12½x12*

2668 A723 30p Spasski Tower, Russia Nos. 295, 265

Cuban Labor Union, 45th Anniv. A724

1984, Jan. 28 *Perf. 13*

2669 A724 5c multi

Butterflies — A725

1984, Jan. 31 *Perf. 13x12½*

2670 A725 1c *Ixias balice*
2671 A725 2c *Phoebis avellaneda*
2672 A725 3c *Anthocaris sara*
2673 A725 5c *Victorina*
2674 A725 20c *Heliconius cydno cydnides*
2675 A725 30c *Parides gundlachianus calzadillae*
2676 A725 50c *Catagramma sorana*

Marine Mammals — A726

Perf. 12x12½, 12½x12

1984, Feb. 15

2677 A726 1c *Grampus griseus,* vert.
2678 A726 2c *Delphinus delphis,* vert.
2679 A726 5c *Physeter catodon*
2680 A726 6c *Stenella plagiodon,* vert.
2681 A726 10c *Pseudorca crassidens*
2682 A726 30c *Tursiops truncatus,* vert.
2683 A726 50c *Megaptera novaeangliae*

Augusto C. Sandino (1893-1934), Nicaraguan Revolutionary — A727

1984, Feb. 21 *Perf. 13*

2684 A727 20c multi

Red Cross in Cuba, 75th Anniv. — A728

1984, Mar. 10

2685 A728 30c Flag, No. 404

Cuban Film Industry, 25th Anniv. A729

1984, Mar. 24

2686 A729 20c multi

Caribbean Flowers — A730

1984, Mar. 29
2687 A730 1c *Brownea grandiceps*
2688 A730 2c *Couroupita guianensis*
2689 A730 5c *Triplaris surinamensis*
2690 A730 20c *Amherstia nobilis*
2691 A730 30c *Plumieria alba*
2692 A730 50c *Delonix regia*

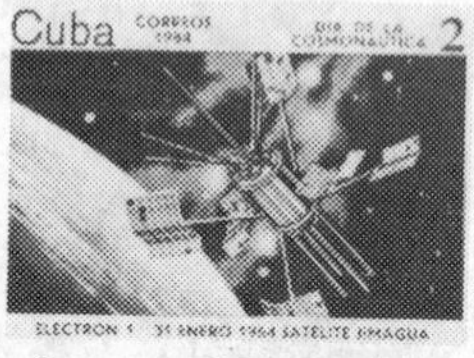

Cosmonauts' Day — A731

1984, Apr. 12
2693 A731 2c *Electron 1,* 1964
2694 A731 3c *Electron 2,* 1964
2695 A731 5c *Intercosmos 1,* 1969
2696 A731 10c *Mars 5,* 1974
2697 A731 30c *Soyuz,* 1969
2698 A731 50c USSR-Bulgaria space flight, 1979

Souvenir Sheet

Perf. 12½

2699 A731 1p *Luna 1,* 1959

No. 2699 contains one 32x40mm stamp.

Mothers' Day — A732

1984, Apr. 19 ***Perf. 13***
2700 A732 20c Red roses
2701 A732 20c Pink roses

Stamp Day — A733

Designs: Mural, by R. Rodriguez Radillo (details).

1984, Apr. 24 ***Perf. 13x12½***
2702 A733 20c Mexican runner
2703 A733 30c Egyptian boatman

See Nos. 2787-2788, 2860-2861, 3025-3026, 3122-3123, 3213-3214.

Souvenir Sheet

ESPANA '84, Madrid — A734

1984, Apr. 27 ***Perf. 13x13½***
2704 A734 1p Clipper ship

Women's Basketball, 1984 Summer Olympics A735

1984, May 5 ***Perf. 13***
2705 A735 20c multi

Agrarian Reform Act, 25th Anniv. A736

1984, May 17 ***Perf. 13½x13***
2706 A736 5c multi

Banco Popular de Ahorro, 1st Anniv. — A737

1984, May 18 ***Perf. 13***
2707 A737 5c multi

Antiguan Locomotives — A738

1984, June 11 ***Perf. 12½x12***
2708 A738 1c multi
2709 A738 4c multi, diff.
2710 A738 5c multi, diff.
2711 A738 10c multi, diff.
2712 A738 30c multi, diff.
2713 A738 50c multi, diff.

Souvenir Sheet

19th UPU Congress, HAMBURG '84 — A739

1984, June 19 ***Perf. 13x13½***
2714 A739 1p Nos. 73, 232

Intl. Olympic Committee, 90th Anniv. — A740

1984, June 23 ***Perf. 13***
2715 A740 30c Coubertin, torch-bearer

Children's Day A741

1984, July 15 ***Perf. 12½x13***
2716 A741 5c multi

1984 Summer Olympics, Los Angeles — A742

1984, July 28 ***Perf. 13***
2717 A742 1c Wrestling
2718 A742 3c Discus
2719 A742 5c Volleyball
2720 A742 20c Boxing
2721 A742 30c Basketball
2722 A742 50c Weight lifting

Souvenir Sheet

Perf. 12½

2723 A742 1p Baseball

No. 2723 contains one 32x40mm stamp.

Emilio Roig de Leuchsenring (1889-1964), Historian — A743

1984, Aug. 8 ***Perf. 13***
2724 A743 5c multi

Friendship Games, Aug. 18-26, Havana A744

1984, Aug. 18
2725 A744 3c Volleyball
2726 A744 5c Women's volleyball
2727 A744 8c Water polo
2728 A744 30c Boxing

Cattle Breeding A745

1984, Sept. 20
2729 A745 2c Artificial pastures
2730 A745 3c Cuban carib
2731 A745 5c Charolaise, vert.
2732 A745 30c Cuban cebu, vert.
2733 A745 50c White-udder

Souvenir Sheet

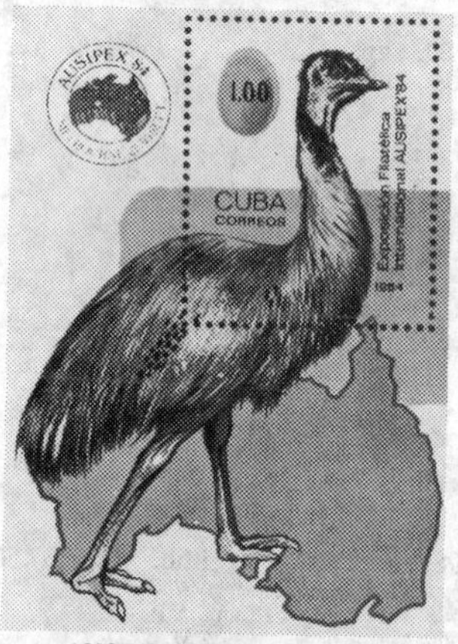

AUSIPEX '84, Sept. 21-30, Melbourne — A746

1984, Sept. 21 ***Perf. 12½***
2734 A746 1p Emu

Fauna — A747

1984, Oct. 10 *Perf. 13*

2735 A747 1c *Polymita*
2736 A747 2c *Solenodon cubanus*
2737 A747 3c *Alsophis canther-igerus*
2738 A747 4c *Osteopilus septen-trionalis*
2739 A747 5c *Mellisuga helenae*
2740 A747 10c *Capromys melanurus*
2741 A747 30c *Todus multicolor*
2742 A747 50c Parrots (cotorra)

Souvenir Sheet

ESPAMER '85, Havana — A748

1984, Oct. 12

2743 Sheet of 4+2 labels
a. A748 5c Ferdinand, Isabella
b. A748 20c Departure from Palos
c. A748 30c *Nina, Pinta, Santa Maria*
d. A748 50c Landing in America

Columbus Day.

Souvenir Sheet

9th Natl. Phil. Exhibition, Oct. 20-28, Santiago de Cuba — A749

1984, Oct. 20 *Perf. 12½*

2744 A749 1p multicolored

Natl. Revolutionary Militia, 25th Anniv. A750

1984, Oct. 26 *Perf. 12½x13*

2745 A750 5c multi

Disappearance of Camilo Cienfuegos, 25th Anniv. — A751

1984, Oct. 28 *Perf. 13x12½*

2746 A751 5c multi

UN Child Survival Campaign A752

1984, Nov. 11 *Perf. 13*

2747 A752 5c Breast-feeding

Classic Automobiles — A753

1984, Nov. 25

2748 A753 1c 1909 Morgan
2749 A753 2c 1922 Austin
2750 A753 5c 1903 De Dion-Bouton
2751 A753 20c 1908 Ford Model T
2752 A753 30c 1885 Benz
2753 A753 50c 1910 Benz

Postal Museum, 20th Anniv. — A754

1985, Jan. 2 *Perf. 13x12½*

2754 A754 20c multi

Portrait of Celia Sanchez, by E. Escobedo — A755

1985, Jan. 11 *Perf. 13*

2755 A755 5c multi

Celia Sanchez (1920-1980), party leader.

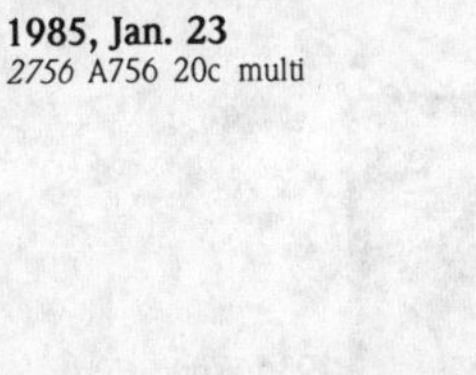

PORTO '85, Intl. Pigeon Exhibition A756

1985, Jan. 23

2756 A756 20c multi

1986 World Cup Soccer Championships, Mexico — A757

Athletes and Flags of previous host nations.

1985, Jan. 25

2757 A757 1c Chile, 1962
2758 A757 2c Great Britain, 1966
2759 A757 3c Mexico, 1970
2760 A757 4c Federal Republic of Germany, 1974
2761 A757 5c Argentina, 1978
2762 A757 30c Spain, 1982
2763 A757 50c Sweden, 1958

Souvenir Sheet

Perf. 12½

2764 A757 1p Mexico, 1986

No. 2764 contains one 40x32mm stamp.

Bacanao Natl. Park — A758

Dinosaurs.

1985, Feb. 14 *Perf. 13x12½*

2765 A758 1c Pteranodon
2766 A758 2c Brontosaurus
2767 A758 4c Iguanodontus
2768 A758 5c Estegosaurus
2769 A758 8c Monoclonius
2770 A758 30c Corythosaurus
2771 A758 50c Tyrannosaurus

13th Congress of the Postal Unions of the Americas, Havana — A759

Design: Uruguay #196, congress emblem and Brazil #287. Illustration reduced.

1985, Mar. 11 *Perf. 12½x12*

2772 A759 20c multi

ESPAMER '85 A760

Indian activities: 1c, Playing ball. 2c, Medicine man preparing calumet and other ritual items. 5c, Net and spear fishing. 20c, Potter. 30c, Hunting. 50c, Hollowing-out canoe, decorating paddle. 1p, Cooking.

1985, Mar. 19 *Perf. 12½x13*

2773 A760 1c multi
2774 A760 2c multi
2775 A760 5c multi
2776 A760 20c multi
2777 A760 30c multi
2778 A760 50c multi

Souvenir Sheet

Perf. 12½

2779 A760 1p multi

No. 2779 contains one 32x40mm stamp.

An imperf. souvenir sheet exists containing Nos. 2773-2779.

Cosmonauts' Day — A761

Designs: 2c, Spacecraft orbiting Moon. 3c, Two spacecraft. 10c, Space walkers linked. 13c, Space walkers welding. 20c, *Vostok 2.* 50c, *Lunayod 1* moon vehicle.

1985, Apr. 12 *Perf. 13x12½*

2780 A761 2c multi
2781 A761 3c multi
2782 A761 10c multi
2783 A761 13c multi
2784 A761 20c multi
2785 A761 50c multi

12th Youth and Students Festival, Moscow — A762

1985, Apr. 19 *Perf. 13*

2786 A762 30c Lenin Mausoleum

Stamp Day Type of 1984

Mural, by R. Rodriguez Radillo (1967), details: 20c, Roman charioteer (courier of *Cursus Publicus*). 35c, Medieval nobleman, monks (monastic messenger mail).

1985, Apr. 24 *Perf. 13x12½*

2787 A733 20c multi
2788 A733 35c multi

Mothers' Day — A763

1985, May 2 *Perf. 13*

2789 A763 1c Peonies
2790 A763 4c Carnations
2791 A763 5c Dahlias
2792 A763 13c Roses
2793 A763 20c Roses, diff.
2794 A763 50c Tulips

50th Death Anniv. of Antonio Guiteras and Carlos Aponte, Revolutionaries — A764

1985, May 9 *Perf. 12¹/₂x12*
2795 A764 5c multi

End of WWII, 40th Anniv. A765

1985, May 10
2796 A765 5c shown
2797 A765 20c Soviet memorial, Berlin-Treptow
2798 A765 30c Dove

Souvenir Sheet

ARGENTINA '85, Buenos Aires — A766

1985, June 5 *Perf. 13¹/₂x13*
2799 A766 1p *Vulture gryphus*

Motorcycle, Cent. — A767

1985, June 28 *Perf. 13*
2800 A767 2c 1885 Daimler
2801 A767 5c 1910 Kaiser Tricycle
2802 A767 10c 1925 Fanomobile
2803 A767 30c 1926 Mars A20
2804 A767 50c 1936 Simson BSW

Development of Health Care Since the Revolution — A768

1985, July 18 *Perf. 12¹/₂x12*
2805 A768 5c Hospitals

Federation of Cuban Women (FMC), 25th Anniv. — A769

1985, Aug. 23
2806 A769 5c multi

No. 2807 printed se-tenant with label picturing federation emblem.

Universiade Games, Japan — A770

1985, Aug. 27 *Perf. 13*
2807 A770 50c multi

1st Havana Declaration, 25th Anniv. — A771

1985, Sept. 2
2808 A771 5c Jose Marti statue, revolutionaries

Souvenir Sheet

ITALIA '85 — A772

1985, Sept. 25 *Perf. 12¹/₂*
2809 A772 1p Roman galley

Revolutionary Defense Committees (CDR), 25th Anniv. — A773

1985, Sept. 28 *Perf. 13*
2810 A773 5c multi

Aquarium Fish A774

1985, Sept. 30 **Litho.**
2811 A774 1c *Centropyge argi*
2812 A774 3c *Holacanthus tricolor*
2813 A774 5c *Chaetodon capistratus*
2814 A774 10c *Chaetodon sedentarius*
2815 A774 20c *Chaetodon ocellatus*
2816 A774 50c *Holacanthus ciliaris*

Communist Party Central Committee, 20th Anniv. — A775

1985, Oct. 1
2817 A775 5c multi

Souvenir Sheet

EXFILNA '85 — A776

1985, Oct. 18
2818 A776 1p Spain No. C45, Cuba No. 387

UN, 40th Anniv. — A777

1985, Oct. 24
2819 A777 20c multi

Sites on the UNESCO World Heritage List A778

Designs: 2c, Plaza Vieja, 16th cent. 5c, Royal Army Castle, c. 1558. 20c, Havana Cathedral, c. 1748. 30c, Captains-General Palace (Havana City Museum), 1776. 50c, The Temple, 1827.

1985, Nov. 25
2820 A778 2c multi
2821 A778 5c multi
2822 A778 20c multi
2823 A778 30c multi
2824 A778 50c multi

1986 World Cup Soccer Championships, Mexico — A779

Various athletes.

1986, Jan. 20
2825 A779 1c multi
2826 A779 4c multi
2827 A779 5c multi
2828 A779 10c multi
2829 A779 30c multi
2830 A779 50c multi

Souvenir Sheet

Perf. 13¹/₂x13

2831 A779 1p multi

No. 2831 contains one 32x40mm stamp.

3rd Communist Party Congress, Havana — A780

1986, Feb. 4 *Perf. 13*
2832 A780 5c shown
2833 A780 20c Party and natl. flags, emblem

Natl. Sports Institute (INDER), 25th Anniv. A781

1986, Feb. 23
2834 A781 5c multi

A782

A783

1986, Feb. 23
2835 A782 5c multi

Ministry of Domestic Trade, 25th anniv.

1986, Feb. 25 *Perf. 12¹/₂x12*

Exotic flowers in the Botanical Gardens.

2836 A783 1c *Tecomaria capensis*
2837 A783 3c *Michelia champaca*
2838 A783 5c *Thunbergia grandiflora*
2839 A783 8c *Dendrobium phalaenopsis*
2840 A783 30c *Allamanda violacea*
2841 A783 50c *Rhodactus bleo*

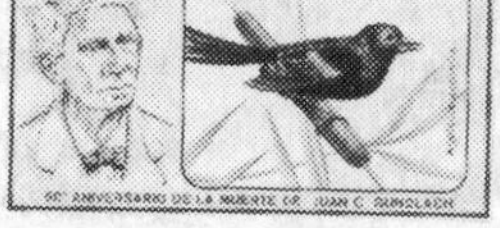

Gundlach and Birds A784

1986, Mar. 14 **Litho.** *Perf. 13¹/₂x13*
2842 A784 1c *Agelaius assimilis*
2843 A784 3c *Dendroica pityophila*
2844 A784 7c *Myiarchus sagrae*
2845 A784 9c *Dendroica petechia gundlachi*
2846 A784 30c *Geotrygon caniceps*
2847 A784 50c *Colaptes auratus chrysocaulosus*

Juan Cristobal Gundlach (d. 1896), ornithologist.

Pioneers Youth Organization, Founded by Jose Marti, 25th Anniv. — A785

1986, Apr. 3 *Perf. 13*
2848 A785 5c Induction

150th Birth Anniv. of Maximo Gomez — A786

1986, Apr. 4
2849 A786 20c multi

A787 A788

1986, Apr. 10 *Perf. 12½*
2850 A787 5c multi

Kindergartens, 25th anniv.

1986, Apr. 12 *Perf. 13x13½*

1st Man in Space, 25th Anniv.: 1c, *Vostok* and rocket designer Sergei Korolev. 2c, Yuri Gagarin, *Vostok 1.* 5c, Valentina Tereshkova, *Vostok 6.* 20c, *Salyut-Soyuz* space link. 30c, Capsule landing. 50c, *Soyuz* rocket launch. 1p, Konstantin Tsiolkovski (1857-1935), rocket scientist.

2851 A788 1c multi
2852 A788 2c multi
2853 A788 5c multi
2854 A788 20c multi
2855 A788 30c multi
2856 A788 50c multi

Souvenir Sheet

Perf. 12½

2857 A788 1p multi

No. 2857 contains one 32x40mm stamp.

Natl. Flag and No. 2407 — A789

1986, Apr. 19 *Perf. 13*
2858 A789 5c shown
2859 A789 20c Banners, natl. crest

Bay of Pigs invasion, 25th anniv. (5c); Proclamation of Socialist Revolution, 25th anniv. (20c).

Stamp Day Type of 1984

Mural, by R. Rodriguez Radillo (1967), details.

1986, Apr. 24 *Perf. 13x12½*
2860 A733 20c Mail coach, 18th-19th cent.
2861 A733 30c Pony Express

Radio Havana, 25th Anniv. — A790

1986, May 1
2862 A790 5c multi

EXPO '86, Vancouver — A791

Locomotives: 1c, *Stourbridge Lion,* 1829, US. 4c, Stephenson's *Rocket,* 1829, GB. 5c, 1st Russian locomotive, 1845. 8c, Seguin's locomotive, 1830, France. 30c, 1st Canadian locomotive, 1836. 50c, Urban locomotive, Belgian Grand Central Rlwy., 1872. 1p, US locomotive pulling Cuban sugar train, 1837.

1986, May 2 **Litho.** *Perf. 12½x12*
2863 A791 1c multi
2864 A791 4c multi
2865 A791 5c multi
2866 A791 8c multi
2867 A791 30c multi
2868 A791 50c multi

Souvenir Sheet

Perf. 13x13½

2869 A791 1p multi

No. 2869 contains one 40x32mm stamp.

Assoc. of Small Farmers, (ANAP), 25th Anniv. A792

1986, May 17 *Perf. 13*
2870 A792 5c multi

Intl. Peace Year A793

1986, June 2
2871 A793 30c multi

Ministry of the Interior (MININT), 25th Anniv. — A794

1986, June 6
2872 A794 5c multi

Martin Luther King, Jr. A795

1986, June 27 *Perf. 13½x13*
2873 A795 20c multi

Bonifacio Byrne (d. 1936), Poet A796

1986, July 5 *Perf. 13*
2874 A796 5c multi

Cuban Union of Writers and Artists (UNEAC), 25th Anniv. — A797

Sandanista Movement in Nicaragua (FSLN), 25th Anniv. — A798

1986, July 10 *Perf. 13x12½*
2875 A797 5c multi

1986, July 23 *Perf. 13x12*

Design: Augusto Cesar Sandino and Carlos Fonseca.

2876 A798 20c multi

Ministry of Transportation, 25th Anniv. — A799

1986, Aug. 1 *Perf. 13*
2877 A799 5c multi

7th University Games of Central America and the Caribbean — A800

1986, Aug. 9
2878 A800 20c multi

Souvenir Sheet

STOCKHOLMIA '86 — A801

Designs: a, 2c Mambi Revolutionary stamp of 1897. b, Sweden Type A7, cancellation.

1986, Aug. 28 *Perf. 12½*
2879 A801 Sheet of 2
a.-b. 50c multi

Nonaligned Countries Movement, 25th Anniv. — A802

1986, Sept. 1 *Perf. 13½x13*
2880 A802 50c multi

Orchids — A803

1986, Sept. 15 *Perf. 12½*
2881 A803 1c *Cattleya hardyana*
2882 A803 4c *Brassolaelio cattleya*
2883 A803 5c *Phalaenopsis marget moses*
2884 A803 10c *Laelio cattleya prism palette*
2885 A803 30c *Phalaenopsis violacea*
2886 A803 50c *Disa uniflora*

Latin American History A804

Pre-Columbian artifacts: No. 2887, Mayan dwelling and votive jade sculpture. No. 2888, Inca vase and Tiahuanacu sun gate (Bolivia). No. 2889, Spain No. C47, discovery of America 500th anniv. emblem, scroll. No. 2890, Diaguitan duck-shaped pitcher and Pucara de Quitor ruins (Chile). No. 2891, San Agustin Archaeological Park megaliths and Quimbayan sculpture (Colombia). No. 2892, Moler grinding stone and Chorotega ceramic figurine. No. 2893, Tabaco idol and Indian dwelling (Cuba). No. 2894, Spain No. C38. No. 2895, Taino dwelling and chair (Dominica). No. 2896, Tolita statue and Ingapirca Castle ruins. No. 2897, Maya vase and Tikal Temple (Guatemala). No. 2898, Copan ruins and Maya idol. No. 2899, Spain No. C37. No. 2900, Chichen Itza Temple and Zapotecan urn (Mexico). No. 2901, Punta de Zapote megaliths and Ometepe ceramic figurine. No. 2902, Tonosi lidded ceramic bowl and Barriles monoliths. No. 2903, Ruins at Machu-Picchu and Inca statue (Peru). No. 2904, Spain No. C49. No. 2905, Teepees and triangular sculpture (Puerto Rico). No. 2906, Fertility statue from Santa Ana and Santo Domingo Cave.

1986, Oct. 12 *Perf. 13*
2887 A804 1c multi
2888 A804 1c multi
2889 A804 1c multi
2890 A804 1c multi

2891 A804 1c multi
a. Strip of 5, Nos. 2887-2891
2892 A804 5c multi
2893 A804 5c multi
2894 A804 5c multi
2895 A804 5c multi
2896 A804 5c multi
a. Strip of 5, Nos. 2892-2896
2897 A804 10c multi
2898 A804 10c multi
2899 A804 10c multi
2900 A804 10c multi
2901 A804 10c multi
a. Strip of 5, Nos. 2897-2901
2902 A804 20c multi
2903 A804 20c multi
2904 A804 20c multi
2905 A804 20c multi
2906 A804 20c multi
a. Strip of 5, Nos. 2902-2906

Discovery of America, 500th anniv. (in 1992). See Nos. 2966-2985, 3065-3084, 3253-3272, 3463-3466.

Intl. Brigades, Spain, 50th Anniv. — A805

1986, Oct. 14 *Perf. 12½x12*
2907 A805 30c multi

Paintings in the Natl. Museum A806

Designs: 2c, *Two Children*, by Gutierrez de la Vega, vert. 4c, *Sed*, by Jean-Georges Vibert. 6c, *Virgin and Child*, by Niccolo Abbate, vert. 10c, *Bullfight*, by Eugenio de Lucas Velazquez. 30c, *The Five Senses*, anonymous. 50c, *Arrival at Thomops Castle*, by Jean Louis Ernest.

1986, Nov. 5 *Perf. 13*
2908 A806 2c multi
2909 A806 4c multi
2910 A806 6c multi
2911 A806 10c multi
2912 A806 30c multi
2913 A806 50c multi

Anniversaries A807

1986, Dec. 2 **Litho.** *Perf. 12½*
2914 A807 5c *Granma*

Size: 26x38mm

2915 A807 20c Soldier, rifle, flag

Granma Landings, 30th anniv. (5c); Revolutionary Armed Forces, 30th anniv. (20c).

Scholarship Program, 25th Anniv. A808

1986, Dec. 22 *Perf. 13*
2916 A808 5c Guevara, students

Natl. Literacy Campaign, 25th Anniv. — A809

1986, Dec. 25 *Perf. 13x12½*
2917 A809 5c Marti, man learning to write

Siege of La Plata, 30th Anniv. A810

1987, Jan. 17 *Perf. 12½x12*
2918 A810 5c Map, revolutionaries

Paintings in the Natl. Museum A811

Designs: 3c, *Gypsy*, by Joaquin Sorolla, vert. 5c, *Sir Walter Scott*, by Sir John W. Gordon, vert. 10c, *Farm Meadows*, by Alfred de Breanski. 20c, *Still-life*, by Isaac van Duynen. 30c, *Landscape with Figures*, by Francesco Zuccarelli. 40c, *The Failure* (defeated bullfighter), by Ignacio Zuloaga, vert.

1987, Feb. 5 *Perf. 13*
2919 A811 3c multi
2920 A811 5c multi
2921 A811 10c multi
2922 A811 20c multi
2923 A811 30c multi
2924 A811 40c multi

Siege of the Presidential Palace, 30th Anniv. — A812

1987, Mar. 13 *Perf. 12½x12*
2925 A812 5c Palace, van, Echeverra

Lazarus Ludwig Zamenhof and Russia Type A77 — A813

1987, Mar. 16 *Perf. 13½x13*
2926 A813 30c multi

Esperanto, cent.

Souvenir Sheet

EXFILNA '87, 10th Natl. Stamp Exposition, Holguin — A814

1987, Mar. 28 *Perf. 13x13½*
2927 A814 1p Nos. 552, C129

25th Anniv. and 5th Cong. of the Youth Communist League (U.J.C.) — A815

1987, Apr. 4 *Perf. 13*
2928 A815 5c multi

Intercosmos, 20th Anniv. — A816

1987, Apr. 12 **Litho.** *Perf. 12½x12*
2929 A816 3c *Intercosmos 1*
2930 A816 5c *Intercosmos 2*
2931 A816 10c *TD*
2932 A816 20c *Cosmos 93*
2933 A816 30c *Molniya*
2934 A816 50c *Vostok 3*

Souvenir Sheet
Perf. 13½x13

2935 A816 1p Rocket, *Vostok 3*

No. 2935 contains one 32x40mm stamp.

Stamp Day A817

Stamped covers and canceled stamps.

1987, Apr. 24 *Perf. 13*
2936 A817 30c Havana, 1890
2937 A817 50c Santiago de Cuba, 1869

Mothers' Day — A818

Various dahlias and roses.

1987, May 2
2938 A818 3c multi
2939 A818 5c multi
2940 A818 10c multi
2941 A818 13c multi
2942 A818 30c multi
2943 A818 50c multi

Bone-lengthening Procedure (Femur in Frame) — A819

1987, May 4
2944 A819 5c multi

ORTOPEDIA '87, medical congress for orthopedists from Spanish and Portuguese-speaking countries, Havana.

Cuban Broadcasting and Television Institute, 25th Anniv. — A820

1987, May 24 *Perf. 13*
2945 A820 5c multi

Battle of Uvero, 30th Anniv. A821

1987, May 28 *Perf. 13½x13*
2946 A821 5c Views of monument, Sierra Maestra Mts.

CAPEX '87 — A822

Natl. flags, stamps and 19th cent. mail carriers pictured on cigarette cards: 3c, Messenger, llamas and Bolivia Type A9. 5c, Early p.o., automobile and France Type A17. 10c, Messengers riding elephants and Thailand Type A2. 20c, Messenger riding camel and stamp of Egypt, 1879. 30c, Mail troika and stamp of Russia. 50c, Post rider and stamp of Indo-China. 1p, Post rider and Mambi Revolutionary stamp.

1987, June 15 *Perf. 12½x13*
2947 A822 3c multi
2948 A822 5c multi
2949 A822 10c multi
2950 A822 20c multi
2951 A822 30c multi
2952 A822 50c multi

Souvenir Sheet

Perf. 13½x13

2953 A822 1p multi

No. 2953 contains one 32x40mm stamp.

Dinosaur Exhibits, Bacanao Natl. Park A823

1987, June 25 ***Perf. 13***

2954 A823 3c multi
2955 A823 5c multi
2956 A823 10c multi
2957 A823 20c multi
2958 A823 35c multi
2959 A823 40c multi

Frank Pais (d. 1957), Teacher and Student Leader A824

1987, July 30 ***Perf. 12½x12***

2960 A824 5c Pais, Rafael Maria Mendive University

10th Pan American Games, Indianapolis — A825

1987, Aug. 8

2961 A825 50c multi

Printed se-tenant with inscribed label picturing the 1991 Havana Games character trademark.

Siege of Cienfuegos, 30th Anniv. — A826

1987, Sept. 5 ***Perf. 13***

2962 A826 5c Memorial

Souvenir Sheet

HAFNIA '87, Denmark — A827

1987, Sept. 16 ***Perf. 13½x13***

2963 A827 1p Danish mailman, 1887, Type A6

Souvenir Sheet

ESPAMER '87, La Coruna, Oct. 2-12 — A828

1987, Oct. 2

2964 A828 1p La Coruna Port, 1525

20th Heroic Guerrillas Day — A829

1987, Oct. 8 ***Perf. 12½x12***

2965 A829 50c Coins, #1364

Latin American History Type of 1986

Indians and birds: No. 2966, Tehuelche Indian of Argentina and *Habia rubica.* No. 2967, *Ramphastos cuvieri* and Tibirica Indian of Brazil. No. 2968, Spain No. C31 and discovery of America 500th anniv. emblem. No. 2969, *Vulture gryphus* and Lautaro Indian of Chile. No. 2970, Calarca Indian of Colombia and *Opisthocomus hoazin.* No. 2971, *Priotelus temnurus* and Hatuey Indian of Cuba. No. 2972, *Columbigallina passerina* and Enriquillo Indian of the Dominican Republic. No. 2973, Spain No. 427. No. 2974, *Semnornis ramphastinus* and Ruminahui Indian of Ecuador. No. 2975, *Pharomachrus mocinno* and Tecum Uman Indian of Guatemala. No. 2976, Anacaona Indian of Haiti and *Aramas guarauna.* No. 2977, Lempira Indian of Honduras and *Diglossa baritula.* No. 2978, Spain No. C42. No. 2979, *Onychorhinchus mexicanus* and Cuauhtemoc Indian of Mexico. No. 2980, *Setofaga picta* and Nicarao Indian of Nicaragua. No. 2981, *Rupicola peruviana* and Atahualpa Indian of Peru. No. 2982, Atlacatl Indian of El Salvador and *Bluteo jamaicensis.* No. 2983, Spain No. 432. No. 2984, Abayuba Indian of Uruguay and *Phytotoma rutila.* No. 2985, Guaycaypuro Indian of Venezuela and *Ara arauna.*

1987, Oct. 12 ***Perf. 13***

2966 A804 1c multi
2967 A804 1c multi
2968 A804 1c multi
2969 A804 1c multi
2970 A804 1c multi
a. Strip of 5, Nos. 2966-2970
2971 A804 5c multi
2972 A804 5c multi
2973 A804 5c multi
2974 A804 5c multi
2975 A804 5c multi
a. Strip of 5, Nos. 2971-2975
2976 A804 10c multi
2977 A804 10c multi
2978 A804 10c multi
2979 A804 10c multi
2980 A804 10c multi
a. Strip of 5, Nos. 2976-2980
2981 A804 20c multi
2982 A804 20c multi
2983 A804 20c multi
2984 A804 20c multi
2985 A804 20c multi
a. Strip of 5, Nos. 2981-2985

Discovery of America, 500th anniv. (in 1992). *Vultur* is spelled incorrectly on No. 2969.

October Revolution, Russia, 70th Anniv. — A830

1987, Nov. 7 ***Perf. 12½x12***

2986 A830 30c Soviet spacecraft, Russia No. 379

Cuban Railway, 150th Anniv. — A831

Stamps on stamps.

1987, Nov. 19 ***Perf. 13x12½***

2987 A831 3c No. 453
2988 A831 5c No. 1061
2989 A831 10c No. 2010
2990 A831 20c No. 2011
2991 A831 35c No. 2360
2992 A831 40c No. 2361

Souvenir Sheet

Perf. 13x13½

2993 A831 1p No. 355

No. 2993 contains 40x32mm one stamp.

An imperf. sheet containing Nos. 2987-2992 exists, inscribed to promote the 17th Pan American Railway Congress.

San Alejandro Art School, 170th Anniv. — A832

Paintings: 1c, *Landscape,* by Domingo Ramos. 2c, *Portrait of Rodriguez Morey,* by Eugenio Gonzalez Olivera. 5c, *Wagons,* by Eduardo Morales. 10c, *Portrait of Elena Herrera,* by Armando Menocal, vert. 30c, *Rape of Dejanira,* by Miguel Melero, vert. 50c, *The Card Player,* by Leopoldo Romanach.

Perf. 13x12½, 12½x13

1988, Jan. 12

2994 A832 1c multi
2995 A832 2c multi
2996 A832 5c multi
2997 A832 10c multi
2998 A832 30c multi
2999 A832 50c multi

Poisonous Mushrooms A833

1988, Feb. 15 ***Perf. 13***

3000 A833 1c *Boletus satanas*
3001 A833 2c *Amanita citrina*
3002 A833 3c *Tylopilus felleus*
3003 A833 5c *Paxillus involutus*
3004 A833 10c *Inocybe patouillardii*
3005 A833 30c *Amanita muscaria*
3006 A833 50c *Hypholoma fasciculare*

Radio Rebelde, 30th Anniv. — A834

1988, Feb. 24 ***Perf. 12½x12***

3007 A834 5c multi

Monuments A835

1988 **Litho.** ***Perf. 13***

3008 A835 5c Mario Munoz, Santiago de Cuba
3009 A835 5c Frank Pais Memorial, eternal flame

Battle fronts, 30th annivs. Issue dates: No. 3008, Mar. 5. No. 3009, Mar. 11.

Mothers' Day — A836

1988, Mar. 30

3010 A836 1c Red roses
3011 A836 2c Pale pink roses
3012 A836 3c Daisies
3013 A836 5c Dahlias
3014 A836 13c White roses
3015 A836 35c Carnations
3016 A836 40c Pink roses

Cosmonauts' Day — A837

1988, Apr. 12

3017 A837 2c *Gorizont*
3018 A837 3c *Mir-Kvant* space link
3019 A837 4c *Signo 3*
3020 A837 5c Mars, space probe
3021 A837 10c *Phobos*
3022 A837 30c *Vega*
3023 A837 50c Spacecraft

Souvenir Sheet

Perf. 13½x13

3024 A837 1p Spacecraft, diff.

No. 3024 contains one 32x40mm stamp.

Stamp Day Type of 1984

Mural, by R. Rodriguez Radillo (1967) details: 30c, Mail coach, telegraph operator. 50c, Passenger pigeon.

1988, Apr. 24 ***Perf. 13x12½***

3025 A733 30c multi
3026 A733 50c multi

Institute for Research on Sugar Cane and Byproducts (ICIDCA), 25th Anniv. — A838

1988, May 23 ***Perf. 12½x12***

3027 A838 5c multi

Cubana Airlines Transatlantic Flights — A839

1988, May 25

3028 A839 2c Madrid, 1948
3029 A839 4c Prague, 1961
3030 A839 5c Berlin, 1972
3031 A839 10c Luanda, 1975
3032 A839 30c Paris, 1983
3033 A839 50c Moscow, 1987

Souvenir Sheet

FINLANDIA '88 — A840

1988, June 1 *Perf. 12½*

3034 A840 1p Steam packet *Furst Menschikoff*

Postal Union of the Americas and Spain (UPAE) Conference on Stamps of the Americas, Havana — A841

Illustration reduced.

1988, June 20 *Perf. 12½x12*

3035 A841 20c multi

Beetles A842

1988, June 30 *Perf. 13*

3036 A842 1c *Megasoma elephas fabricus*
3037 A842 3c *Platycoelia flavoscutellata ohaus,* vert.
3038 A842 4c *Plusiotis argenteola bates*
3039 A842 5c *Heterosternus oberthuri ohaus*
3040 A842 10c *Odontotaenius zodiacus truqui*
3041 A842 35c *Chrysophora chrysochlora latreille,* vert.
3042 A842 40c *Phanaeus leander waterhouse*

Jose Raul Capablanca (1888-1942), Chess Champion — A843

Perf. 12½x13, 13x12½

1988, July 15

3043 A843 30c Chessmen, vert.
3044 A843 40c J. Corza, Capablanca
3045 A843 50c Lasker, Capablanca
3046 A843 1p Winning configuration, 1921, vert.
3047 A843 3p Portrait by E. Valderrama, vert.
3048 A843 5p Chessmen, Capablanca

Souvenir Sheets

3049 Sheet of 2
  a. A843 30c No. 464, vert.
  b. like No. 3043, size: 32x40mm
3050 Sheet of 2
  a. A843 40c No. 465
  b. like No. 3044, size: 40x32mm
3051 Sheet of 2
  a. A843 50c No. C44
  b. like No. 3045, size: 40x32mm
3052 Sheet of 2
  a. A843 1p No. 464, vert.
  b. like No. 3046, size: 32x40mm
3053 Sheet of 2
  a. A843 3p No. C46, vert.
  b. like No. 3047, size: 32x40mm
3054 Sheet of 2
  a. A843 5p No. C45, vert.
  b. like No. 3048, size: 32x40mm

Attack on Moncada Barracks, 35th Anniv. A844

1988, July 26 *Perf. 13*

3055 A844 5c blk, yel ocher & red

Souvenir Sheet

PRAGA '88 — A845

1988, Aug. 26 *Perf. 12½*

3056 A845 1p Czechoslovakia No. 45

Czechoslovakian postage stamps, 70th anniv.

Revolutionary Invasion Force, 30th Anniv. — A846

1988, Aug. 31 *Perf. 12½x12*

3057 A846 5c multi

World Marxist Review, 30th Anniv. A847

1988, Sept. 1 *Perf. 13*

3058 A847 30c multi

Locomotives A848

1988, Sept. 19 *Perf. 12½x13*

3059 A848 20c Stephenson's *Rocket,* 1837
3060 A848 30c Miller, US, 1839
3061 A848 50c *La Junta*
3062 A848 1p J.G. Brill trolley, US, 1922
3063 A848 2p TEM 4K, USSR, c. 1960
3064 A848 5p CAP 9 electric, c. 1988

Latin American History Type of 1986

Natl. arms and patriots: No. 3065, San Martin, Argentina. No. 3066, M.A. Padilla, Bolivia. No. 3067, No. 390 and discovery of America 500th anniv. emblem. No. 3068, Tiradentes, Brazil. No. 3069, O'Higgins, Chile. No. 3070, A. Narino, Colombia. No. 3071, Marti, Cuba. No. 3072, No. 391 and emblem. No. 3073, Duarte, Dominican Republic. No. 3074, Sucre, Ecuador. No. 3075, M.J. Arce, El Salvador. No. 3076, Dessalines, Haiti. No. 3077, No. C36 and emblem. No. 3078, Hidalgo, Mexico. No. 3079, J.D. Estrada, Nicaragua. No. 3080, Diaz, Paraguay. No. 3081, F. Bolognesi, Peru. No. 3082, No. C37 and emblem. No. 3083, Artigas, Uruguay. No. 3084, Bolivar, Venezuela.

1988, Oct. 12 *Perf. 13*

3065 A804 1c multi
3066 A804 1c multi
3067 A804 1c multi
3068 A804 1c multi
3069 A804 1c multi
  a. Strip of 5, Nos. 3065-3069
3070 A804 5c multi
3071 A804 5c multi
3072 A804 5c multi
3073 A804 5c multi
3074 A804 5c multi
  a. Strip of 5, Nos. 3070-3074
3075 A804 10c multi
3076 A804 10c multi
3077 A804 10c multi
3078 A804 10c multi
3079 A804 10c multi
  a. Strip of 5, Nos. 3075-3079
3080 A804 20c multi
3081 A804 20c multi
3082 A804 20c multi
3083 A804 20c multi
3084 A804 20c multi
  a. Strip of 5, Nos. 3080-3084

Discovery of America, 500th anniv. (in 1992).

Havana Museum, 20th Anniv. — A849

Design: Captain-General's Palace and Maces of Municipal Havana.

1988, Oct. 16 Litho. *Perf. 12½x12*

3085 A849 5c multi

Anniversaries — A850

1988, Oct. 28 *Perf. 13*

3086 A850 5c *Swan Lake*
3087 A850 5c Theater in 1838 and 1988
  a. Pair, Nos. 3086-3087

Natl. Ballet, 40th anniv. (No. 3086); Grand Theater of Havana, 150th anniv. (No. 3087).

Intl. Literacy Year A851

1988, Dec. 5

3088 A851 5c multi

UN Declaration of Human Rights, 40th Anniv. — A851a

1988, Dec. 10

3088A A851a 30c multi

Battle of Santa Clara, 30th Anniv. A852

1988, Dec. 28 *Perf. 13x12½*

3089 A852 30c Monument, Che Guevara Plaza

30th Anniv. of the Revolution — A853

1989, Jan. 1 *Perf. 13*

3090 A853 5c multi
3091 A853 20c multi
3092 A853 30c multi
3093 A853 50c multi

Edible Mushrooms — A854

1989, Jan. 10

3094 A854 2c *Pleurotus levis*
3095 A854 3c *Pleurotus floridanus*
3096 A854 5c *Amanita caesarea*
3097 A854 10c *Lentinus cubensis*
3098 A854 40c *Pleurotus ostreatus* (brown)
3099 A854 50c *Pleurotus ostreatus* (yellow)

2c, 3c, 5c, 40c, 50c, vert.

Souvenir Sheet

INDIA '89 — A855

1989, Jan. 20
3100 A855 1p Indian River Post, 1858

Central Organization of Cuban Trade Unions (CTC), 50th Anniv. — A856

1989, Jan. 28 ***Perf. 12½***
3101 A856 5c No. 2477, CTC emblem

Butterflies A857

1989, Feb. 15
3102 A857 1c *Metamorpho dido*
3103 A857 3c *Callithea saphhira*
3104 A857 5c *Papilio zagreus*
3105 A857 10c *Mynes sestia*
3106 A857 30c *Papilio dardanus*
3107 A857 50c *Catagranma sorana*

1990 World Cup Soccer Championships, Italy — A858

Various athletes.

1989, Mar. 15 ***Perf. 13***
3108 A858 1c multi
3109 A858 3c multi, diff.
3110 A858 5c multi, diff.
3111 A858 10c multi, diff.
3112 A858 30c multi, diff.
3113 A858 50c multi, diff.

Souvenir Sheet
Perf. 12½
3114 A858 1p multi, diff., horiz.

No. 3114 contains one 40x32mm stamp.

Natl. Revolutionary Police (PNR), 30th Anniv. — A859

1989, Mar. 23 ***Perf. 13***
3115 A859 5c multi

Cosmonauts' Day — A860

Spacecraft and rocket mail covers: 1c, *Zodiac* and cover, Australia 1934. 3c, Lighthouse and cover, India, 1934. 5c, Cover, England, 1934. 10c, *Icarus* and cover, The Netherlands, 1935. 40c, *La Douce France* and cover, France, 1935. 50c, Rocket mail cover, Cuba, 1939.

1989, Apr. 12
3116 A860 1c multi
3117 A860 3c multi
3118 A860 5c multi
3119 A860 10c multi
3120 A860 40c multi
3121 A860 50c multi

Stamp Day Type of 1984

Details of mural by R. Rodriguez Radillo (1967): 30c, Mail coach, satellite dish. 50c, Galleon, longboats, train, passenger pigeon, horses.

1989, Apr. 24 Litho. ***Perf. 13x12½***
3122 A733 30c multi
3123 A733 50c multi

Casa de Las Americas, 30th Anniv. A861

1989, Apr. 28 ***Perf. 12½x13***
3124 A861 5c multi

BULGARIA '89 — A862

1989, May 1 ***Perf. 12½***
3125 A862 1p Bulgaria No. 346

58th FIP Congress and 101st anniv. of Bulgarian Railways.

Cuban Postal Code A863

1989, May 5 ***Perf. 13***
3126 A863 5c multi

Mothers' Day — A864

Perfume bottles and flowers.

1989, May 10
3127 A864 1c Habano, tobacco
3128 A864 3c Violeta, violets
3129 A864 5c Mariposa, mariposa
3130 A864 13c Coral Negro, roses
3131 A864 30c Ala Alonso, jasmine
3132 A864 50c D'Man, lemon blossoms

Agrarian Reform Law, 30th Anniv. — A865

1989, May 17 ***Perf. 12x12½***
3133 A865 5c multi

Council for Mutual Economic Assistance (CAME), 40th Anniv. A866

1989, June 1 Litho. ***Perf. 12½x13***
3134 A866 30c multi

13th World Communist Youth and Student Festival, Pyongyang — A867

1989, July 1 Litho. ***Perf. 12½***
3135 A867 30c multi

Souvenir Sheet

Rouget de Lisle Singing La Marseillaise, by Pils — A868

1989, July 7 ***Perf. 13***
3136 A868 1p multi

PHILEXFRANCE '89, French revolution bicent. and Cuban revolution 30th anniv.

BRASILIANA '89 — A869

Exotic birds. (Illustration reduced.)

1989, July 28 Litho. ***Perf. 12½***
3137 A869 1c *Ramphastos toco*
3138 A869 3c *Agamia agami*
3139 A869 5c *Eudocimus ruber*
3140 A869 10c *Psophia leucoptera*
3141 A869 35c *Harpia harpyja*
3142 A869 50c *Cephatopterus ornatus*

Warships A870

1989, Sept. 29 Litho. ***Perf. 12½***
3143 A870 1c *El Fenix*
3144 A870 3c *Triunfo*
3145 A870 5c *El Rayo*
3146 A870 10c *San Carlos*
3147 A870 30c *San Jose*
3148 A870 50c *San Genaro*

America Issue — A871

UPAE emblem and pre-Columbian art: 5p, Stone carving, Indians in dugout canoe. 20p, Petroglyph, Indian drawing on stone wall.

1989, Oct. 12 ***Perf. 12½x12***
3149 A871 5c multi
3150 A871 20c multi

Latin American History
A872

Writers and orchids: No. 3151, Domingo Sarmiento (1811-1888), Argentine educator, and *Govenia utriculata.* No. 3152, Joaquim Maria Machado de Assis (1839-1908), Brazilian novelist, and *Laelia grandis.* No. 3153, Salvador No. 69 and discovery of America anniv. emblem. No. 3154, Jorge Isaacs (1837-1895), Colombian novelist, and *Cattleya trianae.* No. 3155, Alejo Carpentier, Cuban writer, and *Cochleanthes discolor.* No. 3156, Pablo Neruda (1904-1973), Chilean poet, and *Oxalis adenophylla.* No. 3157, Pedro Urena, Dominican writer, and *Epidendrum fragrans.* No. 3158, Salvador No. 86 and anniv. emblem. No. 3159, Juan Montalvo (1832-1889), Ecuadorian satirist, and *Miltonia vexillaria.* No. 3160, Miguel Asturias (1899-1974), Guatemalan writer awarded the 1966 Lenin Peace Prize and 1967 Nobel Prize for literature, and *Odontoglossum rossii.* No. 3161, Jose C. del Valle, Honduran writer, and *Laelia anceps.* No. 3162, Alfonso Reyes (1889-1959), Mexican poet, and *Laelia anceps alba.* No. 3163, Salvador No. 87 and anniv. emblem. No. 3164, Ruben Dario (1867-1917), Nicaraguan poet, and *Brassavola acaulis.* No. 3165, Belisario Porras (1856-1942), president of Panama, and *Pescatorea celina.* No. 3166, Ricardo Palma (1833-1919), Peruvian writer, and *Coryanthes leucocorys.* No. 3167, Eugenio Maria de Hostos (1839-1903), Puerto Rican writer, and *Guzmania berteroniana.* No. 3168, Salvador No. 88 and anniv. emblem. No. 3169, Jose E. Rodo (1872-1917), Uruguayan philosopher, essayist, and *Cypella hebertii.* No. 3170, Romulo Gallegos, Venezuelan writer, and *Cattleya mossiae.*

1989, Oct. 27 **Litho.** ***Perf. 13***

3151 A872 1c multicolored
3152 A872 1c multicolored
3153 A872 1c multicolored
3154 A872 1c multicolored
3155 A872 1c multicolored
a. Strip of 5, Nos. 3151-3155
3156 A872 5c multicolored
3157 A872 5c multicolored
3158 A872 5c multicolored
3159 A872 5c multicolored
3160 A872 5c multicolored
a. Strip of 5, Nos. 3156-3160
3161 A872 10c multicolored
3162 A872 10c multicolored
3163 A872 10c multicolored
3164 A872 10c multicolored
3165 A872 10c multicolored
a. Strip of 5, Nos. 3161-3165
3166 A872 20c multicolored
3167 A872 20c multicolored
3168 A872 20c multicolored
3169 A872 20c multicolored
3170 A872 20c multicolored
a. Strip of 5, Nos. 3166-3170

Discovery of America 500th anniv. (in 1992).

Disappearance of Camilo Cienfuegos, 30th Anniv. — A873

1989, Oct. 28

3171 A873 5c multicolored

Founding of the City of Trinidad, 475th Anniv.
A874

1989, Nov. 6 ***Perf. 12½x13***

3172 A874 5c multicolored

Paintings in the Natl. Museum
A875

Designs: 1p, *Familiar Scene,* by Antoine Faivre. 2p, *Flowers,* by Emile Jean Horace Vernet (1789-1863). 5p, *The Judgement of Paris,* by Charles Le Brun (1619-1690). 20p, *Outskirts of Nice,* by Eugene Louis Boudin (1824-1898). 30p, *Portrait of Sarah Bernhardt,* by G.J.V. Clairin. 50p, *Fishermen in Port,* by C.J. Vernet.

Perf. 12½, 12½x13 (30p)

1989, Nov. 20 **Litho.**

Size of 30p: 36x46mm

3173 A875 1c multicolored
3174 A875 2c multicolored
3175 A875 5c multicolored
3176 A875 20c multicolored
3177 A875 30c multicolored
3178 A875 50c multicolored

11th Pan-American Games, Havana, 1991 — A876

1989, Dec. 15 **Litho.** ***Perf. 12½***

3179 A876 5c Cycling
3180 A876 5c Fencing
3181 A876 5c Water polo
3182 A876 5c Shooting
3183 A876 5c Archery
3184 A876 20c Tennis, vert.
3185 A876 30c Swimming, vert.
3186 A876 35c Diving, vert.
3187 A876 40c Field hockey
3188 A876 50c Basketball, vert.

Jose Marti's *Golden Age,* Cent. — A877

1989, Dec. 20 ***Perf. 13***

3189 A877 5c scar, light blue & blk

Cuban Postal Museum, 25th Anniv. — A878

1990, Jan. 2 ***Perf. 13x12½***

3190 A878 5c *Almendares*
3191 A878 30c Mail train

Speleological Soc., 50th Anniv. — A879

(Illustration reduced).

1990, Jan. 15 ***Perf. 12½***

3192 A879 30c multicolored

1990 World Cup Soccer Championships, Italy — A880

Various Italian architecture and athletes: No. 3193a, Dribbling (in red and blue). No. 3193b, Heading (in red and green). No. 3193c, Kicking (in green). 10c, Goalie catching ball. 30c, Dribbling, diff. 50c, Kicking, diff. 1p, Goalie catching ball, diff.

1990, Jan. 30 **Litho.** ***Perf. 12½***

3193 Strip of 3
a.-c. A880 5c any single
3194 A880 10c multicolored
3195 A880 30c multicolored
3196 A880 50c multicolored

Souvenir Sheet

3197 A880 1p multicolored

No. 3193 has a continuous design picturing The Colosseum.

1992 Summer Olympics, Barcelona — A881

1990, Feb. 20 **Litho.** ***Perf. 12½***

3198 A881 1c Baseball
3199 A881 4c Running
3200 A881 5c Basketball
3201 A881 10c Women's volleyball
3202 A881 30c Wrestling
3203 A881 50c Boxing

Souvenir Sheet

3204 A881 1p High jump

Nos. 3198-3201 and 3203 are vert.
No. 3204 contains one 40x32mm stamp.

75th Universal Esperanto Congress — A882

1990, Mar. 7

3205 A882 30c Tower of Babel

No. 3205 printed se-tenant with inscribed label publicizing the congress.

Souvenir Sheet

1992 Winter Olympics, Albertville — A883

1990, Mar. 30 **Litho.** ***Perf. 13***

3206 A883 1p multicolored

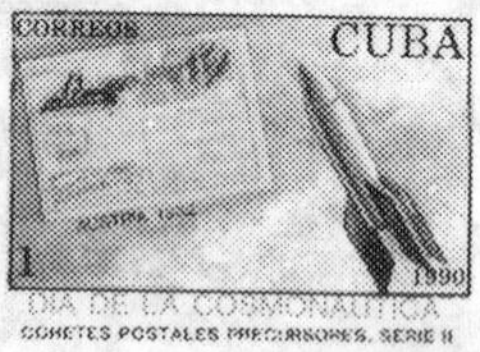

Cosmonauts' Day — A884

Spacecraft and rocket mail covers: 1c, Austria, 1932. 2c, Germany, 1933. 3c, Netherlands, 1934. 10c, Belgium, 1935. 30c, Yugoslavia, 1935. 50c, United States, 1936.

1990, Apr. 12 ***Perf. 12½***

3207 A884 1c multicolored
3208 A884 2c multicolored
3209 A884 3c multicolored
3210 A884 10c multicolored
3211 A884 30c multicolored
3212 A884 50c multicolored

Stamp Day Type of 1984

Details of mural by R. Rodriguez Radillo (1967): 30c, Train station. 50c, Jet aircraft in flight.

1990, Apr. 24 ***Perf. 13x12½***

3213 A733 30c multicolored
3214 A733 50c multicolored

Labor Day, Cent.
A885

1990, Apr. 30 ***Perf. 13***

3215 A885 5c multicolored

Souvenir Sheet

Great Britain No. 1 on Cover — A886

1990, May 3
3216 A886 1p multicolored

Stamp World London '90, Penny Black 150th anniv.

Penny Black, 150th Anniv. A887

Portraits of Sir Rowland Hill and stamps of Great Britain.

1990, May 6 Litho. *Perf. 12½x12*
3217 A887 2c No. 1
3218 A887 3c No. 2
3219 A887 5c Type A5
3220 A887 10c No. 5
3221 A887 30c First day postmark
3222 A887 50c 5 #1 on Mulready envelope

Celia Sanchez Manduley (1920-1980) A888

1990, May 9 *Perf. 12½x13*
3223 A888 5c multicolored

Ho Chi Minh (1890-1969), Vietnamese Communist Party Leader — A889

1990, May 19 *Perf. 12½*
3224 A889 50c multicolored

Oceanography Institute, 25th Anniv. — A890

Designs: 5c, Specimen analysis and *Lachnolaimus maximus.* 30c, Research ship, fish, coral reef. 50c, Specimen collection and *Panullrus argus.*

1990, June 18 Litho. *Perf. 12½*
3225 A890 5c multicolored
3226 A890 30c multicolored
3227 A890 50c multicolored

5th Latin American Botanical Conference A891

1990, June 25 Litho. *Perf. 12½*
3228 A891 3c Banara minutiflora
3229 A891 5c Oplonia nannophylla
3230 A891 10c Jacquinia brunnescens
3231 A891 30c Rondeletia brachycarpa
3232 A891 50c Rondeletia odorata

Tourism A892

1990, June 30
3233 A892 5c Wind surfing
3234 A892 10c Spear fishing
3235 A892 30c Deep sea fishing
3236 A892 40c Hunting

Nos. 3233, 3236 vert.

Art Treasures A893

Designs: 5c, "La Flauta Del Dios Pan." 20c, "Un Pastor." 50c, "Ganimedes." 1p, "Venus Anadiomena."

1990, July 20
3237 A893 5c multicolored
3238 A893 20c multicolored
3239 A893 50c multicolored
3240 A893 1p multicolored

Birds A894

1990, Aug. 24 Litho. *Perf. 13*
3241 A894 2c Podiceps cristatus
3242 A894 3c Gallirallus australis
3243 A894 5c Nestor notabilis
3244 A894 10c Xenicus longipes
3245 A894 30c Cracticus torquatus
3246 A894 50c Prostemadera novaeseelandiae

Souvenir Sheet

3247 A894 1p Kiwi

New Zealand '90. No. 3247 contains one 39x31mm stamp.

8th UN Congress on Crime Prevention — A895

1990, Aug. 27 Litho. *Perf. 12½*
3248 A895 50c blue, silver & red

Discovery of America, 500th Anniv. (in 1992) — A896

1990, Oct. 12 Litho. *Perf. 12½*
3249 A896 5c Ship, shore
3250 A896 20c Columbus, village

Cuban Television, 40th Anniv. A897

1990, Oct. 12 Litho. *Perf. 13*
3251 A897 5c multicolored

Nationalization of Railroads, 30th Anniv. — A898

1990, Oct. 13 *Perf. 13x12½*
3252 A898 50c multicolored

Latin American History Type of 1986

Latin American stamps or flags and costumes: No. 3253, Argentina. No. 3254, Bolivia. No. 3255, Argentina No. 91. No. 3256, Colombia. No. 3257, Costa Rica. No. 3258, Cuba. No. 3259, Chile. No. 3260, Dominican Republic No. 110. No. 3261, Ecuador. No. 3262, El Salvador. No. 3263, Guatemala. No. 3264, Mexico. No. 3265, Puerto Rico No. 133. No. 3266, Nicaragua. No. 3267, Panama. No. 3268, Paraguay. No. 3269, Peru. No. 3270, El Salvador No. 103. No. 3271, Puerto Rico. No. 3272, Venezuela.

1990, Oct. 27 *Perf. 12½*
3253 A804 1c multicolored
3254 A804 1c multicolored
3255 A804 1c multicolored
3256 A804 1c multicolored
3257 A804 1c multicolored
a. Strip of 5, Nos. 3253-3257
3258 A804 5c multicolored
3259 A804 5c multicolored
3260 A804 5c multicolored
3261 A804 5c multicolored
3262 A804 5c multicolored
a. Strip of 5, Nos. 3258-3262
3263 A804 10c multicolored
3264 A804 10c multicolored
3265 A804 10c multicolored
3266 A804 10c multicolored
3267 A804 10c multicolored
a. Strip of 5, Nos. 3263-3267
3268 A804 20c multicolored
3269 A804 20c multicolored
3270 A804 20c multicolored
3271 A804 20c multicolored
3272 A804 20c multicolored
a. Strip of 5, Nos. 3268-3272

Discovery of America, 500th anniv. (in 1992).

11th Jai Alai World Championships A899

1990, Nov. 14 Litho. *Perf. 12½*
3273 A899 30c multicolored

No. 3273 printed with se-tenant label.

11th Pan American Games, Havana — A900

1990, Nov. 15 Litho. *Perf. 12½*
3274 A900 5c Judo
3275 A900 5c Sailing
3276 A900 5c Kayak
3277 A900 5c Rowing
3278 A900 5c Equestrian
3279 A900 10c Table tennis
3280 A900 20c Men's gymnastics, vert.
3281 A900 30c Baseball, vert.
3282 A900 35c Team handball, vert.
3283 A900 50c Soccer, vert.

See Nos. 3311-3320.

A901

Butterflies — A902

1990, Nov. 20 Litho. *Perf. 13*
3284 A901 5c Boxing
3285 A901 30c Baseball
3286 A901 50c Volleyball

16th Central American and Caribbean Games, Mexico.

1991, Jan. 25 Litho. *Perf. 12½*
3287 A902 2c Chioides marmorosa
3288 A902 3c Composia fidelissima
3289 A902 5c Danaus plexippus
3290 A902 10c Hypolimnas misippus
3291 A902 30c Hypna iphigenia
3292 A902 50c Hemiargus ammon

Jose Luis Guerra Aguiar (1914-1990), Director of Postal Museum — A903

1991, Feb. 17 Litho. *Perf. 12½*
3293 A903 5c multicolored

A904

A905

1991, Feb. 20

3294 A904 1c Long jump
3295 A904 2c Javelin
3296 A904 3c Field hockey
3297 A904 5c Weight lifting
3298 A904 40c Cycling
3299 A904 50c Gymnastics

Souvenir Sheet

3300 A904 1p Torchbearer

1992 Summer Olympics, Barcelona.

1991, Apr. 12 Litho. *Perf. 13*

1st Man in Space, 30th anniv.: 5c, Yuri Gagarin. No. 3302, Cosmonaut Y. Romanenko. No. 3303, Cosmonaut A. Tamayo. No. 3304, Mir space station. No. 3305, Mir space station, docked Soyuz, earth. 50c, Soviet space shuttle Buran.

3301 A905 5c multicolored
3302 A905 10c multicolored
3303 A905 10c multicolored
a. Pair, #3302-3303
3304 A905 30c multicolored
3305 A905 30c multicolored
a. Pair, #3304-3305
3306 A905 50c multicolored

Proclamation of the Socialist Revolution, 30th Anniv. — A906

Design: 50c, Ship, jet on fire.

1991, Apr. 19 *Perf. 12½*

3307 A906 5c multicolored
3308 A906 50c multicolored

Bay of Pigs invasion, 30th anniv., No. 3308.

Stamp Day — A907

Details from mural by R. Rodriguez Radillo: 30c, Rocket lift-off. 50c, Dish antenna, horiz.

Perf. 12½x13, 13x12½

1991, Apr. 24

3309 A907 30c multicolored
3310 A907 50c multicolored

11th Pan American Games Type of 1990

1991, May 15 Litho. *Perf. 12½*

3311 A900 5c Volleyball
3312 A900 5c Rhythmic gymnastics
3313 A900 5c Synchronized swimming
3314 A900 5c Weight lifting
3315 A900 5c Baseball
3316 A900 10c Bowling
3317 A900 20c Boxing
3318 A900 30c Running
3319 A900 35c Wrestling
3320 A900 50c Karate

Nos. 3311-3315 & 3317 are vert.

Airships A908

Designs: 5c, First ellipsoidal, 1784, J.B.M. Meusnier. 10c, First with steam engine, 1852, H. Giffard. 20c, First with gas engine, 1872, P. Haenlein. 30c, First with gasoline engine, 1896, H. Wolfert. 50c, First rigid aluminum, 1897, D. Schwarz. 1p, LZ-129 Hindenburg, 1936, F. von Zeppelin.

1991, July 1 Litho. *Perf. 13*

3321 A908 5c multicolored
3322 A908 10c multicolored
3323 A908 20c multicolored
3324 A908 30c multicolored
3325 A908 50c multicolored
3326 A908 1p multicolored

Espamer '91, Buenos Aires, Argentina.

Simon Bolivar A909

1991, June 22 Litho. *Perf. 12½x13*

3327 A909 50c multicolored

Amphictyonic Cong. of Panama, 165th anniv.

Birds A910

Designs: 45c, Melanerpes superciliaris. 50c, Myadestes elisabeth. 2p, Priotelus temnurus. 4p, Tiaris canora. 5p, Campephilus principalis. 10p, Amazona leucocephala, horiz. 16.45p, Mellisuga helenae, horiz.

Perf. 12½x13, 13x12½

1991, July 15

3328 A910 45c multicolored
3329 A910 50c multicolored
3330 A910 2p multicolored
3331 A910 4p multicolored
3332 A910 5p multicolored
3333 A910 10p multicolored
3334 A910 16.45p multicolored

Tourism — A911

Designs: No. 3335, Varadero Beach, vert. No. 3336, Cayo Largo, vert. No. 3337, Artillerymen at fortress San Carlos de la Cabana. No. 3338, Tres Reyes del Morro Castle.

1991, July 30

3335 A911 20c multicolored
3336 A911 20c multicolored
3337 A911 30c multicolored
3338 A911 30c multicolored

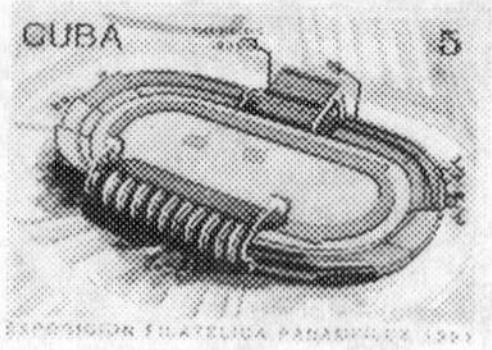

Panamfilex '91 A912

11th Pan American Games venues: 5c, Pan American Stadium. 20c, Swimming venue. 30c, Multisports center. 50c, Velodrome. 1p, Havana City Coliseum and Sports Center.

1991, Aug. 4 Litho. *Perf. 12½*

3339 A912 5c multicolored
3340 A912 20c multicolored
3341 A912 30c multicolored
3342 A912 50c multicolored

Souvenir Sheet

3343 A912 1p multicolored

No. 3343 contains one 40x32mm stamp.

Paintings A913

Designs: 5c, Kataoka Dengoemon Takafusa, by Utagawa Kuniyoshi. 10c, Evening Walk, by Hosoda Eishi. 20c, Courtesans, by Torii Kiyonaga. 30c, Conversation, by Utamaro. 50c, Bridge at Inaribashi, by Hiroshige. 1p, On the Terrace, by Kiyonaga.

1991, Sept. 9 Litho. *Perf. 12½x13*

3344 A913 5c multicolored
3345 A913 10c multicolored
3346 A913 20c multicolored
3347 A913 30c multicolored
3348 A913 50c multicolored
3349 A913 1p multicolored

Phila Nippon '91, Tokyo.

Souvenir Sheet

1992 Winter Olympics, Albertville — A914

1991, Sept. 25 Litho. *Perf. 12½*

3350 A914 1p multicolored

Cuban Communist Party, 4th Congress — A915

1991, Oct. 10

3351 A915 5c shown
3352 A915 50c Congress symbol

Discovery of America, 500th Anniv. (in 1992) — A916

Designs: 5c, Columbus, Vicente and Martin Pinzon. 20c, Santa Maria, Nina and Pinta.

1991, Oct. 12

3353 A916 5c multicolored
3354 A916 20c multicolored

Jose Marti A917

1991, Oct. 15 *Perf. 13x12½*

3355 A917 50c multicolored

Publication of "Simple Verses," cent.

Latin American History A918

Stamps or musicians and instruments: No. 3356, Julian Aguirre, Argentina, charango. No. 3357, Eduardo Caba, Bolivia, antara. No. 3358, Chile #2. No. 3359, Heitor Villalobos, Brazil, resonator trumpet. No. 3360, Guillermo Uribe-Holguin, Colombia, drum. No. 3361, Miguel Failde, Cuba, claves. No. 3362, Enrique Soro, Chile, drum. No. 3363, Chile #57. No. 3364, Segundo L. Moreno, Ecuador, xylophone. No. 3365, Ricardo Castillo, Guatemala, marimba. No. 3366, Carlos Chavez, Mexico, guitar. No. 3367, Luis A. Delgadillo, Nicaragua, maracas. No. 3368, Chile #69. No. 3369, Alfredo De Saint-Malo, Panama, mejorana. No. 3370, Jose Asuncion Flores, Paraguay, harp. No. 3371, Daniel Alomia, Peru, flute. No. 3372, Juan Morell y Campos, Puerto Rico, cuatro. No. 3373, Chile #72. No. 3374, Eduardo Farini, Uruguay, drums. No. 3375, Juan V. Lecuna, Venezuela, cuatro, diff.

1991, Oct. 27 *Perf. 13*

3356 A918 1c multicolored
3357 A918 1c multicolored
3358 A918 1c multicolored
3359 A918 1c multicolored
3360 A918 1c multicolored
a. Strip of 5, #3356-3360
3361 A918 5c multicolored
3362 A918 5c multicolored
3363 A918 5c multicolored
3364 A918 5c multicolored
3365 A918 5c multicolored
a. Strip of 5, #3361-3365
3366 A918 10c multicolored
3367 A918 10c multicolored
3368 A918 10c multicolored
3369 A918 10c multicolored
3370 A918 10c multicolored
a. Strip of 5, #3366-3370

3371 A918 20c multicolored
3372 A918 20c multicolored
3373 A918 20c multicolored
3374 A918 20c multicolored
3375 A918 20c multicolored
a. Strip of 5, #3371-3375

Discovery of America, 500th anniv. in 1992 (Nos. 3358, 3363, 3368, 3373).

Jose Marti Pioneers Organization, 1st Congress — A919

1991, Oct. 29
3376 A919 5c multicolored

Toussaint L'Ouverture (1743-1803) A920

1991, Nov. 20 *Perf. 12½x13*
3377 A920 50c multicolored

Haitian Revolution, Bicent.

Cuban Revolutionary Armed Forces, 35th Anniv. — A921

Design: 50c, Landing of the Granma expedition, 35th anniv., vert.

Perf. 12½x12, 12x12½
1991, Dec. 2 **Litho.**
3378 A921 5c multicolored
3379 A921 50c multicolored

Gen. Ignacio Agramonte (1841-1873), Revolutionary Hero A922

1991, Dec. 23 **Litho.** *Perf. 12½x13*
3380 A922 5c multicolored

Souvenir Sheet

1992 Winter Olympics, Albertville — A923

1992, Jan. 15 *Perf. 13*
3381 A923 1p multicolored

1992 Summer Olympics, Barcelona A924

1992, Jan. 20 **Litho.** *Perf. 13x12½*
3382 A924 3c Table tennis
3383 A924 5c Handball
3384 A924 10c Shooting
3385 A924 20c Long jump, vert.
3386 A924 35c Judo
3387 A924 50c Fencing

Souvenir Sheet
Perf. 12½
3388 A924 100c Rhythmic gymnastics, vert.

No. 3388 contains one 32x40mm stamp.

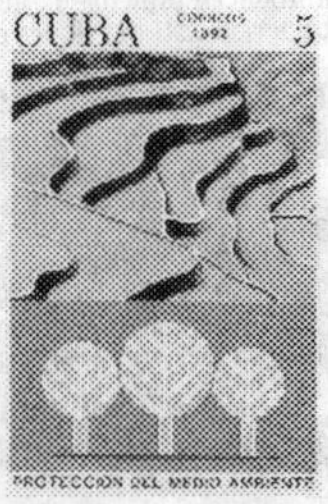

Environmental Protection — A925

1992, Feb. 10 *Perf. 13*
3389 A925 5c Terraced hillsides
3390 A925 20c Save the whales
3391 A925 35c Ozone hole over Antarctica
3392 A925 40c Nuclear disarmament

Dogs A926

1992, Mar. 10 **Litho.** *Perf. 13x12½*
3393 A926 5c Boxer
3394 A926 10c Great dane
3395 A926 20c German shepherd
3396 A926 30c Various breeds
3397 A926 35c Doberman pinscher
3398 A926 40c Fox terrier
3399 A926 50c Poodle

Souvenir Sheet
Perf. 12½
3400 A926 1p Bichon frise, vert.

No. 3400 contains one 32x40mm stamp.
Nos. 3401-3404 will not be assigned.

Union of Young Communists, 30th Anniv. — A928

1992, Apr. 4 **Litho.** *Perf. 13*
3405 A928 5c multicolored

Cuban Revolutionary Party, Cent. — A929

1992, Apr. 10 *Perf. 13x12½*
3406 A929 5c multicolored
3407 A929 50c multicolored

Discovery of America, 500th Anniv. — A930

1992, Apr. 14 *Perf. 12½*
3408 A930 5c Landing at Bariay
3409 A930 20c Landing at San Salvador

Granada '92 Philatelic Exhibition A931

Views of the Alhambra, Granada: 5c, With Sierra Nevada mountains beyond. 10c, Arches at sunset. 20c, Interior architecture. 30c, Patio, fountain of lions. 35c, Bedroom. 50c, View of Albaicin.

1992, Apr. 17 *Perf. 13*
3410 A931 5c multicolored
3411 A931 10c multicolored
3412 A931 20c multicolored
3413 A931 30c multicolored
3414 A931 35c multicolored
3415 A931 50c multicolored

La Bodeguita Del Medio Restaurant, 50th Anniv. A932

1992, Apr. 26
3416 A932 50c multicolored

Fish A933

1992, May 15 **Litho.** *Perf. 12½*
3417 A933 5c Holacanthus isabelita
3418 A933 10c Equetus lanceolatus
3419 A933 20c Acanthurus coeruleus
3420 A933 30c Abudefduf saxatilis
3421 A933 50c Micropathodon chrysurus

Orchids — A934

1992, June 20 **Litho.** *Perf. 12½*
3422 A934 3c Cattleya hibrida
3423 A934 5c Phalaenopsis
3424 A934 10c Cattleyopsis lindenii
3425 A934 30c Bletia purpurea
3426 A934 35c Oncidium luridum
3427 A934 40c Vanda hibrida

Soroa Orchid Garden, 40th anniv.

Mellisuga Helenae A935

1992, July 7 *Perf. 13*
3428 A935 5c Sitting on nest
3429 A935 10c Wings extended
3430 A935 20c Sitting on branch
3431 A935 30c In flight

World Wildlife Fund.

Tourism A936

1992, July 15 **Litho.** *Perf. 12½*
3432 A936 10c Guardalavaca Beach
3433 A936 20c Bucanero Hotel
3434 A936 30c Sailing ship, Havana
3435 A936 50c Varadero Beach

Souvenir Sheet

Expo '92, Seville — A937

1992, July 27 **Litho.** *Perf. 13*
3436 A937 1.50p multicolored

1992 Summer Olympics, Barcelona
A938

Athlete, sport: 5c, Eligio (Kid Chocolate) Sardinas, boxing. 35c, Ramon Fonst, fencing. 40c, Sergio Martinez, cycling. 50c, Martin Dihigo, baseball.

1992, July 20 Litho. ***Perf. 12¹/₂x13***
3437 A938 5c multicolored
3438 A938 35c multicolored
3439 A938 40c multicolored
3440 A938 50c multicolored

Olymphilex '92.

Discovery of America, 500th Anniv.
A939

Designs: 5c, Alvarez Cabral. 10c, Alonso Pinzon. 20c, Alonso de Ojeda. 30c, Amerigo Vespucci. 35c, Prince Henry the Navigator. 40c, Bartolomeu Dias. 0p, Columbus' fleet, vert.

1992, Sept. 18 Litho. ***Perf. 12¹/₂***
3441 A939 5c multicolored
3442 A939 10c multicolored
3443 A939 20c multicolored
3444 A939 30c multicolored
3445 A939 35c multicolored
3446 A939 40c multicolored

Souvenir Sheet

Perf. 13

3447 A939 1p multicolored

Genoa '92. No. 3447 contains one 32x40mm stamp.

1992 Summer Olympics Medal Winners, Barcelona
A940

Medals and participants in events: No. 3448, Bronze, 4x100-meter relay, women's high jump, and women's 800-meter. No. 3449, Gold, high jump, women's discus. No. 3450, Silver, 4x400-meter relay, bronze, discus. No. 3451, Gold and silver, boxing. No. 3452, Gold, baseball. No. 3453, Gold, women's volleyball. No. 3454, Gold, silver, and bronze, judo. No. 3455, Gold and bronze, Greco-Roman and freestyle wrestling. No. 3456, Silver and bronze, fencing, silver, weight lifting.

1992, Sept. 24 Litho. ***Perf. 13***
3448 A940 5c multicolored
3449 A940 5c multicolored
3450 A940 5c multicolored
3451 A940 20c multicolored
3452 A940 20c multicolored
3453 A940 20c multicolored
3454 A940 50c multicolored
3455 A940 50c multicolored
3456 A940 50c multicolored

6th World Track and Field Cup, Havana
A941

1992, Sept. 24 Litho. ***Perf. 13***
3457 A941 5c High jump
3458 A941 20c Javelin
3459 A941 30c Hammer throw
3460 A941 40c Long jump, vert.
3461 A941 50c Hurdles, vert.

Souvenir Sheet

3462 A941 1p Women's relay

No. 3462 contains one 40x32mm stamp.

Latin American History Type of 1986

Discovery of America: No. 3463a, Columbus, Queen Isabella. b, Columbus at Rabida Monastery. c, Columbus, pointing up, outlining his plan. d, Columbus, with scroll, before Salamanca Council. e, Departure of Columbus' fleet from Palos.

No. 3464a, Three ships stopping at Canary Islands. b, Columbus speaking to crew. c, Land sighted, Oct. 12, 1492. d, Columbus landing in New World. e, Meeting natives.

No. 3465a, Grounding of Santa Maria at Hispanola. b, Arrival of Nina at Palos. c, Columbus welcomed in Barcelona. d, Columbus describes his voyage to Ferdinand and Isabella. e, Departure of fleet from Cadiz on second voyage.

No. 3466a, King and Queen welcome Columbus. b, Fleet on Columbus' third voyage. c, Columbus deported from Hispanola to Spain as prisoner. d, Columbus on ship, fourth voyage. e, Death of Columbus, May 20, 1506 in Valladolid.

1992, Oct. 3 ***Perf. 13***
3463 A804 1c Strip of 5, #a.-e.
3464 A804 5c Strip of 5, #a.-e.
3465 A804 10c Strip of 5, #a.-e.
3466 A804 20c Strip of 5, #a.-e.

Jose Maria Chacon y Calvo (1892-1969), Historian — A942

1992, Oct. 29 ***Perf. 13***
3467 A942 30c multicolored

Churches — A943

Designs: 5c, Basilica of Nuestra Senora de la Caridad del Cobre. 20c, Santa Maria del Rosario Church. 30c, Espiritu Santo Church. 50c, Santo Angel Custodio Church.

1992, Nov. 10 Litho. ***Perf. 12¹/₂***
3468 A943 5c multicolored
3469 A943 20c multicolored
3470 A943 30c multicolored
3471 A943 50c multicolored

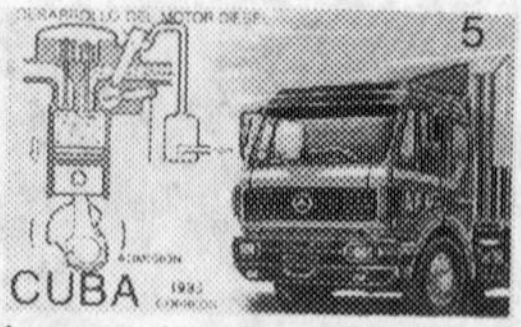

Development of the Diesel Engine — A944

1993, Jan. 20 Litho. ***Perf. 12¹/₂***
3472 A944 5c Truck
3473 A944 10c Automobile
3474 A944 30c Tugboat
3475 A944 40c Locomotive
3476 A944 50c Tractor

Souvenir Sheet

3477 A944 1p Rudolf Diesel

No. 3477 contains one 40x32mm stamp. Rudolf Diesel, 80th anniv. of death (#3477).

Davis Cup Tennis Competition — A945

Various tennis players in action.

Perf. 12x12¹/₂, 12¹/₂x12

1993, Feb. 10 Litho.
3478 A945 5c multi, vert.
3479 A945 20c multi, vert.
3480 A945 30c multi, vert.
3481 A945 35c multicolored
3482 A945 40c multicolored

Souvenir Sheet

Perf. 12¹/₂

3483 A945 1p multicolored

No. 3483 contains one 40x32mm stamp.

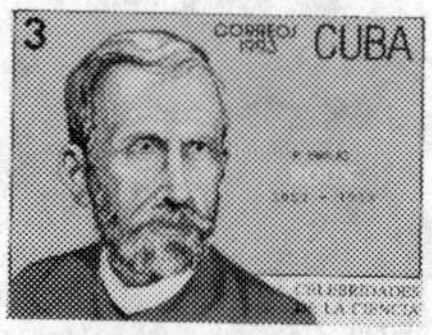

Scientists
A946

Designs: 3c, Pierre-Paul-Emile Roux (1853-1933), bacteriologist. 5c, Carlos J. Finlay (1833-1915), suggested mosquito as carrier of yellow fever. 10c, Ivan Petrovich Pavlov (1849-1936), physiologist, investigated conditioned reflexes. 20c, Louis Pasteur, chemist, developer of pasteurization. 30c, Santiago Ramon y Cajal (1852-1934), histologist, isolated the neuron. 35c, Sigmund Freud, psychoanalyst. 40c, Wilhelm Conrad Roentgen, physicist, discoverer of x-ray. 50c, Joseph Lister, surgeon, introduced principle of antisepsis. 1p, Robert Koch, bacteriologist, developer of tuberculin, vert.

1993, Mar. 3 Litho. ***Perf. 12¹/₂***
3484 A946 3c multicolored
3485 A946 5c multicolored
3486 A946 10c multicolored
3487 A946 20c multicolored
3488 A946 30c multicolored
3489 A946 35c multicolored
3490 A946 40c multicolored
3491 A946 50c multicolored

Souvenir Sheet

3492 A946 1p multicolored

Bicycles
A947

Bicycles designed by: 3c, Leonardo da Vinci, 15th cent. 5c, Karl Von Drais de Sauerbrun, 1813. 10c, Ernest Michaux, 1856. 20c, James Starley, 1869. 30c, Harry Lawson, 1879. 35c, Guaso (Cuba), 1992.

1993, Apr. 14 ***Perf. 13***
3493 A947 3c multicolored
3494 A947 5c multicolored
3495 A947 10c multicolored
3496 A947 20c multicolored
3497 A947 30c multicolored
3498 A947 35c multicolored

Cuban Natl. Museum, 80th Anniv.
A948

Paintings by Joaquin Sorolla y Bastida (1863-1923): 3c, Child Eating Watermelon, 1920, vert. 5c, Valencian Fisherwomen, 1909. 10c, Regattas. 20c, Contadina, 1889. 40c, Summer, 1904. 50c, Boats on the Ocean, 1908.

1993, May 29 Litho. ***Perf. 13x12¹/₂***
3499 A948 3c multicolored

Perf. 12¹/₂x13

3500 A948 5c multicolored
3501 A948 10c multicolored
3502 A948 20c multicolored
3503 A948 40c multicolored
3504 A948 50c multicolored

Water Birds
A949

Perf. 12¹/₂, 13x12¹/₂ (5, 30c)

1993, June 15
3505 A949 3c Jacana spinosa
3506 A949 5c Ardea herodias, vert.
3507 A949 10c Himantopus mexicanus
3508 A949 20c Nycticorax nycticorax
3509 A949 30c Grus canadensis, vert.
3510 A949 50c Aramus guarauna

Brasiliana '93. Nos. 3506, 3510 are 27x44mm.

Anniversaries — A950

Designs: No. 3511, Jose Marti, Moncada Barracks. No. 3512, "History Will Absolve Me," declaration of Fidel Castro, Marti. No. 3513, Jose Marti, Rafael M. Mendive, vert. No. 3514, Carlos Manuel de Cespedes, gear wheels.

1993, July 26 Litho. ***Perf. 13***
3511 A950 5c multicolored
3512 A950 5c multicolored
3513 A950 5c multicolored
3514 A950 5c multicolored

Attack on Moncada Barracks, 40th anniv. (#3511). Declaration of Fidel Castro, 40th anniv. (#3512). Birth of Jose Marti, 140th anniv. (#3513). Declaration of the Ten Years' War, 125th anniv. (#3514).

Flowers from Cienfuegos Botanical Gardens — A951

1993, Aug. 20
3515 A951 3c Sedum allantoides
3516 A951 5c Heliconia caribaea
3517 A951 10c Anthurium andraeanum
3518 A951 20c Pseudobombax ellipticum
3519 A951 35c Ixora coccinea
3520 A951 50c Callistemon specious

Bangkok '93, Intl. Philatelic Exhibition — A952

Butterflies: 3c, Battus devillievs. 5c, Anteos maerula. 20c, Ascia monuste evonima. 30c, Junonia coenia. 35c, Anartia jatrophae guantanamo. 50c, Hypolimnas misippus.

1993, Sept. 10 Litho. *Perf. 13*
3521 A952 3c multicolored
3522 A952 5c multicolored
3523 A952 20c multicolored
3524 A952 30c multicolored
3525 A952 35c multicolored
3526 A952 50c multicolored

Endangered Species — A953

1993, Oct. 12 Litho. *Perf. 13*
3527 A953 5c Phoenicopterus ruber
3528 A953 50c Ajaia ajaja

Latin American Revolutionaries A954

Flags, map and: No. 3529, Simon Bolivar. No. 3530, Jose Marti. No. 3531, Benito Juarez, Mexican President. No. 3532, Ernesto "Che" Guevara.

1993, Oct. 27 Litho. *Perf. 13*
3529 A954 50c multicolored
3530 A954 50c multicolored
3531 A954 50c multicolored
3532 A954 50c multicolored
a. Block of 4, #3529-3532

17th Central American and Caribbean Games, Ponce, Puerto Rico — A955

1993, Nov. 10 Litho. *Perf. 12½*
3533 A955 5c Swimming
3534 A955 10c Pole vault
3535 A955 20c Boxing
3536 A955 35c Gymnastics, vert.
3537 A955 50c Baseball, vert.

Souvenir Sheet

3538 A955 1p Basketball

No. 3538 contains one 40x32mm stamp.

Mariana Grajales (1808-93), Patriot — A956

Peter I. Tchaikovsky (1840-93), Composer — A957

1993, Nov. 27 *Perf. 13*
3539 A956 5p multicolored

1993, Nov. 30
3540 A957 5c Portrait
3541 A957 20c Swan Lake Ballet
3542 A957 30c Statue
3543 A957 50c Museum, horiz.

A958

A959

1994, Jan. 20 Litho. *Perf. 13*
3544 A958 5c multicolored

35th anniv. of the Revolution.

1994, Jan. 1

Various soccer players.

3545 A959 5c multicolored
3546 A959 20c multicolored
3547 A959 30c multicolored
3548 A959 35c multicolored
3549 A959 40c multicolored
3550 A959 50c multicolored

Souvenir Sheet

3551 A959 1p multicolored

1994 World Cup Soccer Championships, US. No. 3551 contains one 40x31mm stamp.

Cats A960

1994, Feb. 15 Litho. *Perf. 12½*
3552 A960 5c Blue Persian
3553 A960 10c Havana
3554 A960 20c Maine coon
3555 A960 30c Blue British shorthair
3556 A960 35c Bicolor Persian
3557 A960 50c Gold chinchilla

Souvenir Sheet

Perf. 13

3558 A960 1p Abyssinian, vert.

No. 3558 contains one 30x38mm stamp.

Medicinal Plants — A961

Designs: 5c, Salvia officinalis. 10c, Aloe barbadensis. 20c, Helianthus annuus. 30c, Matricaria chamomilla. 40c, Calendula officinalis. 50c, Tilia platyphyllos.

1994, Mar. 30 Litho. *Perf. 12½*
3559 A961 5c multicolored
3560 A961 10c multicolored
3561 A961 20c multicolored
3562 A961 30c multicolored
3563 A961 40c multicolored
3564 A961 50c multicolored

Carriages — A962

Designs: 5c, Public coach, 1860. 10c, Coach of Ferdinand VII, Maria Louisa. 30c, Louis XV-style coach. 35c, Elizabeth II gala day's coach. 40c, Catalina II's summer coach. 50c, Volanta habanera.

1994, Apr. 20 *Perf. 12½x12*
3565 A962 5c multicolored
3566 A962 10c multicolored
3567 A962 30c multicolored
3568 A962 35c multicolored
3569 A962 40c multicolored
3570 A962 50c multicolored

No. 3570 is 68x37mm.

Aquaculture — A963

Designs: 5c, Crassostrea rhizophorae. 20c, Cardisoma guanhumi. 30c, Tilapia melanopleura. 35c, Hippospongia lachne. 40c, Panulirus argus. 50c, Cyprinus carpio.

1994, May 10 Litho. *Perf. 12½*
3571 A963 5c multicolored
3572 A963 20c multicolored
3573 A963 30c multicolored
3574 A963 35c multicolored
3575 A963 40c multicolored
3576 A963 50c multicolored

Intl. Olympic Committee, Cent. — A964

1994, June 23 Litho. *Perf. 12½*
3577 A964 5c Flag, runners
3578 A964 30c Flag, world map
3579 A964 50c Flag, Olympic flame

Scientists A965

Designs: 5c, Michael Faraday (1791-1867), physicist. 10c, Marie Curie (1867-1934), physical chemist. 20c, Pierre Curie (1859-1906), chemist. 30c, Albert Einstein (1879-1955), physicist, mathematician. 40c, Max Planck (1858-1947), theoretical physicist. 50c, Otto Hahn (1879-1968), physical chemist.

1994, July 20 Litho. *Perf. 12½*
3580 A965 5c multicolored
3581 A965 10c multicolored
3582 A965 20c multicolored
3583 A965 30c multicolored
3584 A965 40c multicolored
3585 A965 50c multicolored

Cactus Flowers A966

Designs: 5c, Opuntia dillenii. 10c, Opuntia millspaughii, vert. 30c, Leptocereus santamarinae. 35c, Pereskia marcanoi. 40c, Dendrocereus nudiflorus, vert. 50c, Pilocereus robinii.

1994, Aug. 15 Litho. *Perf. 12½*
3586 A966 5c multicolored
3587 A966 10c multicolored
3588 A966 30c multicolored
3589 A966 35c multicolored
3590 A966 40c multicolored
3591 A966 50c multicolored

Souvenir Sheet

2nd Spanish-Cuban Philatelic Exhibition, Havana — A967

Design: 1p, Cuban postal rocket, #C31.

1994, Sept. 18
3592 A967 1p multicolored

Experimental postal rocket flight, 55th anniv.

Dogs A968

1994, Sept. 20
3593 A968 5c Rough collie
3594 A968 20c American cocker spaniel
3595 A968 30c Dalmatian
3596 A968 40c Afghan hound
3597 A968 50c English cocker spaniel

Cayo Largo Island A969

Fauna: 15c, Carpilius corallinus. 65c, Cyclura nubila, vert. 75c, Pelecanus occidentalis. 4p, Chelonia mydas.

1994, Sept. 30 Litho. *Perf. 12½*
3598 A969 15c multicolored
3599 A969 65c multicolored
3600 A969 75c multicolored
3601 A969 1p multicolored

A970

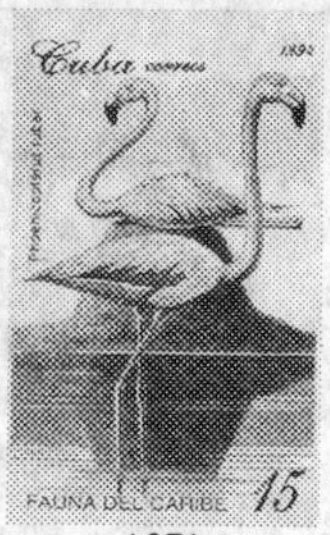

A971

1994, Oct. 28
3602 A970 15c multicolored

Camilo Cienfuegos Gorriaran, revolutionary, 35th anniv. of disappearance.

1994, Oct. 30

Fauna of the Caribbean: 10c, Epinephelus flavolimbatus, horiz. No. 3604, Phoenicopterus ruber. No. 3605, Aetobatus narinari. No. 3606, Istiophorus platypterus, horiz. No. 3607, Tursiops truncatus, horiz. No. 3608, Pelecanus occidentalis.

3603 A971 10c multicolored
3604 A971 15c multicolored
3605 A971 15c multicolored
3606 A971 15c multicolored
3607 A971 65c multicolored
3608 A971 65c multicolored

ICAO, 50th Anniv. A972

1994, Nov. 9
3609 A972 65c multicolored

Zoological Garden, Havana, 55th Anniv. — A973

1994, Nov. 14 **Litho.** *Perf. 13*
3610 A973 15c Bronze monument
3611 A973 65c Ara chloroptera
3612 A973 75c Carduelis carduelis

Cuban Philatelic Federation, 30th Anniv. A974

1994, Nov. 20
3613 A974 15c multicolored

America Issue A975

Postal transportation: 15c, 18th Cent. Spanish galleon, maritime postal service, vert. 65c, 19th Cent. postal rider, insurgent postal service.

1994, Dec. 12
3614 A975 15c multicolored
3615 A975 65c multicolored

Postal Museum, 30th Anniv. — A976

1995, Jan. 2
3616 A976 15c multicolored

SEMI-POSTAL STAMPS

Pierre and Marie Curie — SP1

Wmk. 106
1938, Nov. 23 **Engr.** *Perf. 10*
B1 SP1 2c + 1c salmon 2.25 90
B2 SP1 5c + 1c deep ultra 2.25 1.10

40th anniv. of the discovery of radium by Pierre and Marie Curie. Surtax for the benefit of the Intl. Union for the Control of Cancer.

Catalogue values for unused stamps in this section, from this point to the end of the section, are for Never Hinged items.

"Agriculture" Supporting "Industry" SP2

Engr., Center Typo.
1959, May 7 **Wmk. 321** *Perf. 12½*
B3 SP2 2c + 1c car & ultra 35 15

Agricultural reforms. See No. CB1. For surcharges see Nos. 624, C199.

Nurse SP3

Perf. 12½, Imperf.
1959, Sept. 22 **Photo.** **Wmk. 229**
B4 SP3 2c + 1c crimson rose 30 15

AIR POST STAMPS

Seaplane over Havana Harbor AP1

Wmk. 106
1927, Nov. 1 **Engr.** *Perf. 12*
C1 AP1 5c dark blue 2.25 20

For overprint see No. C30.

Type of 1927 Issue Overprinted

LINDBERGH
FEBRERO 1928

1928, Feb. 8
C2 AP1 5c carmine rose 1.25 1.25

No. 283 Surcharged in Red

CORREO AEREO NACIONAL

10¢ 10¢

1930, Oct. 27 **Unwmk.**
C3 A44 10c on 25c violet 1.25 1.25

Airplane and Coast of Cuba — AP3

For Foreign Postage

1931, Feb. 26 **Wmk. 106** *Perf. 10*
C4 AP3 5c green 38 15
C5 AP3 10c dk blue 38 15
C6 AP3 15c rose 75 28
C7 AP3 20c brown 75 15
C8 AP3 30c dk violet 1.10 18
C9 AP3 40c dp orange 2.50 35
C10 AP3 50c olive grn 3.00 35
C11 AP3 1p black 4.50 90
Nos. C4-C11 (8) 13.36 2.51

See No. C40. For surcharges see Nos. C16-C17, C203, C225.

Airplane AP4

For Domestic Postage

1931-46
C12 AP4 5c rose vio ('32) 30 15
a. 5c brown violet ('36) 30 15
C13 AP4 10c gray blk 30 15
C14 AP4 20c car rose 2.25 75
C14A AP4 20c rose pink ('46) 95 18
C15 AP4 50c dark blue 3.75 75
Nos. C12-C15 (5) 7.55 1.98

See #C130. For overprints see #C31, E29-E30.

Type of 1931 Surcharged in Black

PRIMER TREN AEREO
INTERNACIONAL. 1935
O'Meara y du Pont +10 cts.

1935, Apr. 24 *Perf. 10*
C16 AP3 10c + 10c red 7.25 6.00
a. Double surcharge 110.00

Imperf
C17 AP3 10c + 10c red 18.00 19.00

Matanzas Issue

Air View of Matanzas AP5

Designs: 10c, Airship "Macon." 20c, Airplane "The Four Winds." 50c, Air View of Fort San Severino.

Perf. 12½
1936, May 5 **Photo.** **Wmk. 229**
C18 AP5 5c violet 38 25
C19 AP5 10c yel org 75 38
C20 AP5 20c green 2.50 1.50
C21 AP5 50c greenish slate 4.50 3.00
Nos. C18-C21 (4) 8.13 5.13

Exist imperf. Value 20% more.

"Lightning" AP9

Allegory of Flight AP10

1936, Nov. 18
C22 AP9 5c violet 1.00 22
C23 AP10 10c org brn 1.25 35

Major Gen. Maximo Gomez, birth cent.

Flat Arch (Panama) — AP11

Carlos Antonio López (Paraguay) — AP12

Inca Gate, Cuzco (Peru) AP13

Atlacatl (Salvador) AP14

José Enrique Rodó (Uruguay) — AP15

Simón Bolívar (Venezuela) — AP16

Wmk. 106
1937, Oct. 13 **Engr.** *Perf. 10*
C24 AP11 5c red 4.25 4.25
C25 AP12 5c red 4.25 4.25
C26 AP13 10c blue 5.00 5.00
C27 AP14 10c blue 5.00 5.00
C28 AP15 20c green 5.50 6.25
C29 AP16 20c green 5.50 6.25
Nos. C24-C29 (6) 29.50 31.00

For the benefit of the Assoc. of American Writers and Artists. See note after No. 354.

Type of 1927 Overprinted in Black

1913 1938
ROSILLO
Key West-Habana

1938, May **Wmk. 106**
C30 AP1 5c dk org 2.00 1.10

1st airplane flight from Key West to Havana, made by Domingo Rosillo, 1913.

Type of 1931-32 Overprinted

EXPERIMENTO DEL COHETE Postal AÑO DE 1939

1939, Oct. 15

C31 AP4 10c emerald		14.00	5.00

Issued in connection with an experimental postal rocket flight held at Havana.

Sir Rowland Hill, Map of Cuba and First Stamps of Britain, Spanish Cuba and Republic of Cuba — AP17

1940, Nov. 28 Engr. Wmk. 106

C32 AP17 10c brown	2.00	1.25

Souvenir Sheet

Unwmk. *Imperf.*

C33 Sheet of 4	10.00	10.00
a. AP17 10c light brown	2.50	1.00

Cent. of the 1st postage stamp.

Sheet sold for 60c.

No. C33 exists with each of the four stamps overprinted in black: "Exposicion de la ACNU/24 de Octubre de 1951/Dia de las Naciones" and "Historia de la Aviacion" in lower margin. Value, $60.

For overprints see Nos. C39, C211.

Poet José Heredia and Palms — AP18

Heredia and Niagara Falls — AP19

1940, Dec. 30 Wmk. 106

C34 AP18 5c emerald	1.00	90
C35 AP19 10c greenish slate	2.00	1.25

Death cent. of José Maria Heredia y Campuzano (1803-39), poet and patriot.

First Cuban Land Sighted by Columbus AP20

Columbus Lighthouse AP21

1944, May 19

C36 AP20 5c olive green	30	15
C37 AP21 10c slate black	65	20
Set value		27

450th anniv. of the discovery of America.

Catalogue values for unused stamps in this section, from this point to the end of the section, are for Never Hinged items.

Conference of La Mejorana (Meceo, Gomez and Marti) AP22

1948, May 21 Wmk. 229 *Perf. 12½*

C38 AP22 8c org yel & blk	1.40	60

50th anniv. of the start of the War of 1895.

Souvenir Sheet
No. C33 Overprinted in Ultramarine

CONVENCION
MAYO 21-22-23 1948
AMERICAN AIR MAIL SOCIETY

1948, May 21 Unwmk. *Imperf.*

C39 AP17 Sheet of 4	7.50	7.00

The overprint is applied in the center of the four 10c stamps, so that a portion falls on each.

American Air Mail Soc. Convention, Havana, May 21 to 23, 1948. The sheets sold for 60c each.

Type of 1931

1948, June 15 Wmk. 106 *Perf. 10*

C40 AP3 8c orange brown	1.25	20

Narciso Lopez Landing at Cárdenas — AP23

Flag on Cuban Fort — AP24

Flag on Morro Castle, Havana — AP25

Engraved and Lithographed

1951, July 3 Wmk. 229 *Perf. 13*

C41 AP23 5c ol grn, ultra & red	90	20
C42 AP24 8c red brn, bl & red	1.40	20
C43 AP25 25c gray blk, bl & red	2.00	1.25
Nos. C41-C43 (3)	4.30	1.65

Centenary of adoption of Cuba's flag.

Souvenir Sheet
No. 365a Overprinted in Green

CORREO AEREO

50 ANIVERSARIO DESCUBRIMIENTO AGENTE TRANSMISOR DE LA FIEBRE AMARILLA POR EL DR. CARLOS J. FINLAY

HONOR A LOS MARTIRES DE LA CIENCIA

1901 1951

Illustration reduced.

1951, Aug. 24 Unwmk. *Imperf.*

C43A Sheet of 4	6.00	5.00

50th anniv. of the discovery of the cause of yellow fever by Dr. Carlos J. Finlay, and to honor the martyrs of science.

Resignation Play of Dr. Lasker AP26

Capablanca Making "The Exact Play" — AP27

Wmk. 229

1951, Nov. 1 Photo. *Perf. 13*

C44 AP26 5c shown	3.00	50
C45 AP27 8c shown	5.00	75
C46 A165 25c Capablanca	9.00	2.00
Nos. C44-C46 (3)	17.00	3.25

30th anniv. of the winning of the World Chess title by José Raul Capablanca.

Morrillo Types of Regular Issue

Wmk. 106

1951, Nov. 22 Engr. *Perf. 10*

C47 A167 5c violet	70	15
C48 A168 8c dp grn	90	15
C49 A169 25c dk brn	1.75	75
a. Souv. sheet of 6, black brown, perf. 13	30.00	30.00
b. Souv. sheet of 6, grn, imperf.	125.00	125.00
Nos. C47-C49 (3)	3.35	1.05

Nos. C49a and C49b contain one each of the 1c, 2c and 5c of types A167-A169 and of the 5c, 8c and 25c airmail stamps of types A167-A169. Sheets are unwatermarked and measure 124x133mm.

Isabella Type of Regular Issue, 1952

1952, Feb. 22

C50 A172 25c purple	2.00	80
a. Souv. sheet of 2, perf. 11	12.50	12.50
b. Souv. sheet of 2, imperf.	15.00	15.00

Nos. C50a and C50b contain one each of a 2c of type A172 and a 25c air-mail stamp of type A172. In No. C50a, the 2c and marginal inscriptions are brown carmine; the 25c, dark blue. In No. C50b, the 2c and marginal inscriptions are dark blue; the 25c, brown carmine. Sheets measure 108x18mm.

Type of Regular Issue of 1951 Surcharged in Various Colors

5¢

AEREO

1952, Mar. 18

Color: Yellow Brown

C51 A159 5c on 2c	50	15
C52 A159 8c on 2c (C)	1.00	15
C53 A159 10c on 2c (Bl)	1.00	15
C54 A159 25c on 2c (V)	1.50	1.00
C55 A159 50c on 2c (C)	5.00	2.00
C56 A159 1p on 2c (Bl)	12.50	7.50
Nos. C51-C56 (6)	21.50	10.95

Country School AP32

Entrance, University of Havana AP33

Designs: 10c, Presidential Mansion, 25c, Banknote.

Perf. 12½

1952, May 27 Wmk. 106 Engr.

Centers Various Shades of Green

C57 AP32 5c dk pur	40	15
C58 AP33 8c dk red	60	15
C59 AP32 10c dp blue	1.25	20
C60 AP32 25c dk vio brn	2.00	1.00
Nos. C57-C60 (4)	4.25	1.50

Foundation of the Republic of Cuba, 50th anniv.

Plane and Map — AP34

Agustín Parlá — AP35

1952, July 22 Engr. *Perf. 10*

C61 AP34 8c black	90	55
a. Souv. sheet, 8c deep blue	10.00	10.00
b. Souv. sheet, 8c deep green	10.00	10.00
C62 AP35 25c ultra	2.50	1.65
a. Souv. sheet, 25c deep blue	10.00	10.00
b. Souv. sheet, 25c deep green	10.00	10.00

30th anniv. of the Key West-Mariel flight of Agustin Parla.

The four souvenir sheets are perf. 11.

Col. Charles Hernandes y Sandrino — AP36

1952, Oct. 7

C63 AP36 5c orange	50	15
C64 AP36 8c brt yel grn	50	15
C65 AP36 10c dk brown	65	15
C66 AP36 15c dk Prus grn	1.25	50
C67 AP36 20c aqua	1.65	65
C68 AP36 25c crimson	1.25	65
C69 AP36 30c dk vio bl	3.25	1.65
C70 AP36 45c rose lilac	3.25	2.25
C71 AP36 50c indigo	2.00	1.65
C72 AP36 1p bister	6.50	3.25
Nos. C63-C72 (10)	20.80	11.05

Three-fourths of the proceeds from the sale were used for the Communications Ministry Employees' Retirement Fund.

Entrance, University of Havana — AP37

F. V. Dominguez, M. Estebanez and F. Capdevila — AP38

1952, Nov. 27 Engr.; Center Typo.

C73 AP37 5c ind & dk blue	90	35
C74 AP38 25c org & dk grn	2.75	1.25

81st anniv. of the execution of 8 medical students.

AP39

Lockheed Constellation Airliners AP40

1953, May 22 — **Engr.**

C75	AP39	8c orange brn	42	15
C76	AP39	15c scarlet	1.65	24

Typographed and Engraved

C77	AP40	2p dp green & dk brn	27.50	10.00
C78	AP40	5p blue & dk brn	35.00	16.00
		Nos. C75-C78 (4)	64.57	26.39

See #C120-C121. For surcharge see #C224.

Page of Manifesto of Montecristi AP42

House of Maximo Gomez AP43

Designs: No. C79, Marti in Kingston, Jamaica. No. C80, With Workers in Tampa, Florida. No. C83, Marti addressing liberating army. No. C84, Portrait. No. C85, Dos Rios obelisk. No. C86, Marti's first tomb. No. C87, Present tomb. No. C88, Monument in Havana. No. C89, Martian forge.

1953 — **Engr.** — ***Perf. 10***

C79	AP42	5c dk car & blk	30	15
C80	AP43	5c dk car & blk	30	15
C81	AP43	8c dk green & blk	75	18
C82	AP42	8c dk green & blk	75	18
C83	AP43	10c dk blue & dk car	1.50	50
C84	AP42	10c dk blue & dk car	1.50	50
C85	AP43	15c violet & gray	1.25	90
C86	AP42	15c violet & gray	1.25	90
C87	AP42	25c brown & car	3.00	1.25
C88	AP42	25c brown & car	3.00	1.25
C89	AP43	50c yellow & bl	5.00	2.50
		Nos. C79-C89 (11)	18.60	8.46

Cent. of the birth of José Marti.

Board of Accounts Building — AP44

Design: 25c, Plane above Board of Accounts Bldg.

1953, Nov. 3

C90	AP44	8c rose carmine	90	22
C91	AP44	25c dk gray grn	1.75	90

1st Intl. Cong. of Boards of Account, Havana, Nov. 2-9, 1953.

Miguel Coyula Llaguno — AP45

Antonio Ginard Rojas — AP46

Designs: 10c, Gregorio Hernandez Saez. 1p, Communications Association Flag.

1954

C92	AP45	5c dark blue	32	15
C93	AP46	8c red violet	40	25
C94	AP46	10c orange	85	35
C95	AP45	1p black	6.00	6.00
		Nos. C92-C95 (4)	7.57	6.75

See note after No. C72.

Four-engine Plane and Cane Field — AP47

Plane and Harvesters Cutting Cane — AP48

Designs in Lower Triangle: 10c, Tractor pulling loaded wagons. 15c, Train of sugar cane. 20c, Modern mill. 25c, Evaporators. 30, Sacks of sugar. 40c, Loading sugar on ship. 45c, Ox cart. 50c, Primitive sugar mill. 1p, Alvaro Reinoso.

1954, Apr. 27 — **Engr.**

C96	AP47	5c yellow green	40	15
C97	AP48	8c brown	90	15
C98	AP48	10c dark green	1.00	18
C99	AP48	15c henna brn	50	40
C100	AP48	20c blue	70	65
C101	AP48	25c scarlet	1.00	65
C102	AP48	30c lilac rose	1.75	95
C103	AP48	40c deep blue	2.00	1.25
C104	AP48	45c violet	4.00	2.50
C105	AP48	50c brt blue	3.00	1.65
C106	AP47	1p dk gray blue	5.50	3.25
		Nos. C96-C106 (11)	20.75	11.78

For surcharges see Nos. C204.

Sanatorium Type of Regular Issue

1954, Sept. 21 — **Wmk. 106** — ***Perf. 10***

C107	A186	9c deep green	1.00	50

Dolz Type of Regular Issue, 1954

1954, Dec. 23

C108	A188	12c carmine	1.00	50

Rotary Type of Regular Issue, 1955

1955, Feb. 23

C109	A190	12c carmine	1.00	50

Stamps of 1855 and 1905, Palace of Fine Arts AP52

Designs (including 2 stamps): 12c, Plaza de la Fraternidad. 24c, View of Havana. 30c, Plaza de la Republica.

1955, Apr. 24 — ***Perf. 12½***

C110	AP52	8c dk grnsh bl & grn	1.25	50
C111	AP52	12c dk ol grn & red	1.50	35
C112	AP52	24c dk red & ultra	1.75	1.00
C113	AP52	30c dp org & brn	3.75	2.00
		Nos. C110-C113 (4)	8.25	3.85

Cent. of Cuba's 1st postage stamps.

Mariel Bay — AP53

Views: 12c, Varadero beach. 1p, Vinales valley.

1955, June 22 — **Wmk. 106**

C114	AP53	8c dk car & dk grn	75	30
C115	AP53	12c dk ocher & brt bl	1.00	25
C116	AP53	1p dk grn & ocher	6.00	4.00
		Nos. C114-C116 (3)	7.75	4.55

See note after No. C72.

Map of Crocier's 1914 Flight — AP54

Design: 30c, Crocier in plane.

1955, July 4 — ***Perf. 10***

C117	AP54	12c red & dk grn	60	20
C118	AP54	30c dk grn & mag	2.25	60

35th anniv. of the death of Jaime Gonzalez Crocier, aviation pioneer.

Cuban Museum, Tampa, Fla. — AP55

1955, July 1 — **Engr.** — ***Perf. 12½***

C119	AP55	12c red & dk brn	1.25	35

Cent. of Tampa's incorporation as a town.

Lockheed Type of 1953

Typographed and Engraved

1955, Sept. 21 — **Wmk. 106**

C120	AP40	2p bl & ol grn	17.50	8.50
C121	AP40	5p dp rose & ol grn	37.50	16.50

Wright Brothers' Plane and Stamps AP56

Designs: 12c, Spirit of St. Louis. 24c, Graf Zeppelin. 30c, Constellation passenger plane. 50c, Convair jet fighter.

Engraved and Photogravure

1955, Nov. 12 — **Wmk. 106** — ***Perf. 12½***

Inscription and Plane in Black

C122	AP56	8c car & bl	1.00	35
C123	AP56	12c yel grn & car	2.25	70
C124	AP56	24c vio & car	7.00	2.50
C125	AP56	30c bl & red org	6.00	3.25
C126	AP56	50c ol grn & red org	8.00	4.00
a.		Souvenir sheet of 5	27.50	27.50
		Nos. C122-C126 (5)	24.25	10.80

International Centenary Philatelic Exhibition in Havana, Nov. 12-19, 1955.

No. C126a is printed on thick paper and measures 140x178mm. It contains one each of Nos. C122-C126 with the background of each stamp printed in a different color from the perforated stamps.

"Three Friends" and Gen. Emilio Nunez AP57

Design: 12c, Landing on the Cuban Coast.

1955, Dec. 27 — **Engr.** — **Unwmk.**

C127	AP57	8c ultra & dk car	1.00	40
C128	AP57	12c grn & dk red brn	1.50	50

Gen. Emilio Nunez, Cuban revolutionary hero, birth cent.

Post Type of Regular Issue, 1956

Design: 12c, Bishop P. A. Morell de Santa Cruz (1694-1768).

1956, Mar. 27 — **Wmk. 106**

C129	A197	12c dk brn & grn	90	30

Plane Type of 1931-46

1956 — **Engr.** — ***Perf. 10***

C130	AP4	50c greenish blue	2.00	1.00

Portrait Type of Regular Issue, 1956.

1956, May 2 — ***Perf. 12½***

Portraits: 8c, Gen. Julio Sanguily. 12c, Gen. José Maria Aguirre. 30c, Col. Ernesto Ponts Sterling.

Portraits in Black

C131	A198	8c brown	75	20
C132	A198	12c dull yellow	1.25	20
C133	A198	30c indigo	2.25	1.50
		Nos. C131-C133 (3)	4.25	1.90

See note after No. C72.

Mother and Child — AP60

Masonic Temple Havana — AP61

1956, May 13 — **Wmk. 106** — ***Perf. 12½***

C134	AP60	12c ultra & red	1.00	25

Issued in honor of Mother's Day 1956.

1956, June 5

C135	AP61	12c olive green	60	20

Pigeon — AP62

Gundlach Hawk — AP63

Birds: 8c, Wood duck. 19c, Herring gulls. 24c, White pelicans. 29c, Common merganser. 30c, Quail. 50c, Herons (great white, great blue and Wurdemann's). 1p, Northern caracara. 2p, Middle American jacana. 5p, Ivory-billed woodpecker.

1956

C136	AP62	8c blue	40	18
C137	AP62	12c gray blue	5.50	15
C138	AP63	14c green	1.10	25
C139	AP63	19c redsh brn	80	55
C140	AP63	24c lilac rose	95	55
C141	AP62	29c green	1.25	55
C142	AP62	30c dk ol bis	1.50	80
C143	AP63	50c slate blk	3.00	1.10
C144	AP63	1p dk car rose	4.75	2.25
C145	AP62	2p rose violet	10.50	4.25
C146	AP63	5p brt red	24.00	8.75
		Nos. C136-C146 (11)	53.75	19.38

See Nos. C205, C235-C237. For surcharges and overprints see Nos. C147, C151, C197, C209-C210.

Inauguración
Edificio Club
Filatélico de la
República de Cuba
Julio 13 de 1956.

8¢

Type of 1956 Surcharged

Design: 24c, White pelicans.

1956, July 13

C147	AP63	8c on 24c deep org	75	35

Opening of the new building of the Cuba Philatelic Club, Havana, July 14, 1956.

Hubert de Blanck — AP64

Church of Our Lady of Charity — AP65

1956, July 6
C148 AP64 12c ultra 70 25

Hubert de Blanck (1856-1932), composer.

1956, Sept. 8
C149 AP65 12c green & car 90 40
a. Souvenir sheet of 2, imperf. 8.00 7.00

Issued in honor of Our Lady of Charity of Cobre, patroness of Cuba.
No. C149a contains one each of Nos. 559 and C149. No. C149a exists with yellow of No. 559 omitted.

Benjamin Franklin AP66

1956, Oct. 5 Engr. *Perf. 12½*
C150 AP66 12c red brn 1.00 40

Type of 1956 Surcharged in Blue

Design: 2p, Middle American jacana.

1956, Oct. 26 Wmk. 106
C151 AP62 12c on 2p dk gray 1.00 75

Issued in honor of the 12th Inter-American Press Association Conference, Havana.

Lord Baden-Powell — AP67

1957, Feb. 22
C152 AP67 12c slate 1.50 35

Centenary of the birth of Lord Baden-Powell, founder of the Boy Scouts.

Hanabanilla Waterfall AP68

Designs: 12c, Sierra de Cubitas. 30c, Puerto Boniato.

1957, Mar. 29
C153 AP68 8c blue & red 75 20
C154 AP68 12c green & red 1.20 25
C155 AP68 30c ol grn & dk pur 2.00 1.00
Nos. C153-C155 (3) 3.95 1.45

See note after No. 457.

Philatelic Club, Havana AP69

Fingerprint AP70

1957, Apr. 24 Wmk. 106 *Perf. 12½*
C156 AP69 12c yel, grn & brn 1.00 25

Stamp Day, and the Natl. Phil. Exhib.

1957, Apr. 30
C157 AP70 12c claret brown 1.00 20

Birth cent. (in 1856) of Juan Francisco Steegers y Perera, dactyloscopy pioneer.

Baseball Player — AP71

1957, May 17 Wmk. 106 *Perf. 12½*
C158 AP71 8c shown 1.00 35
C159 AP71 12c Ballerina 1.75 40
C160 AP71 24c Girl diver 2.50 1.00
C161 AP71 30c Boxers 3.50 1.50
Nos. C158-C161 (4) 8.75 3.25

Issued to honor young Cuban athletes.

Joaquin de Aguero AP72

Jeanette Ryder AP73

1957, July 4
C162 AP72 12c indigo 1.00 25

Issued to honor Joaquin de Aguero, Cuban freedom fighter and patriot.

1957, July 17
C163 AP73 12c dk red brn 1.00 35
a. Pair, #574, C163 2.00 1.00

Mrs. Jeanette Ryder, founder of the Humane Society of Cuba.

José M. de Heredia y Girard — AP74

John Robert Gregg — AP75

1957, Aug. 16 Engr. Wmk. 106
C164 AP74 8c dk blue vio 50 25

José Maria de Heredia y Girard (1842-1905), Cuban born French poet.

Justice Type of Regular Issue, 1957

1957, Sept. 2 *Perf. 12½*
C165 A214 12c green 1.00 50

1957, Oct. 1
C166 AP75 12c dark green 95 35

90th anniv. of the birth of John Robert Gregg, inventor of the Gregg shorthand system.

D. Figarola Caneda — AP76

José Marti National Library — AP77

1957, Oct. 18 Wmk. 106 *Perf. 12½*
C167 AP76 8c ultra 55 25
C168 AP77 12c chocolate 95 25

José Marti National Library.

Map of Cuba and UN Emblem — AP78

1957, Oct. 24
C169 AP78 8c dk green & brn 60 20
C170 AP78 12c car rose & grn 85 40
C171 AP78 30c ind & brt pink 2.00 90

Issued for United Nations Day, 1957.

Map of Cuba and Florida — AP79

1957, Oct. 28
C172 AP79 12c dk red brn & bl 85 40

30th anniv. of airmail service from Key West to Havana.

Type of Regular Issue, 1957 and

Stairway and Bell Tower — AP80

Design: 12c, Facade of Normal School.

1957, Nov. 19 Engr. *Perf. 12½*
C173 A217 12c indigo & ocher 85 20
C174 AP80 30c dk car & gray 1.25 60

View Types of Regular Issue, 1957

Views: 8c, El Viso Fort, El Caney. 12c, Sancti Spiritus Church. 30c, Concordia Bridge, Matanzas.

1957, Dec. 17 *Perf. 12½*
C175 A218 8c dk gray & red 75 28
C176 A219 12c brown & gray 1.00 28
C177 A218 30c red brn & bl gray 1.50 95
Nos. C175-C177 (3) 3.25 1.51

See note after No. C72.

Hedges Types of Regular Issue, 1958

Design: 8c, Dayton Hedges and Matanzas rayon factory.

1958, Jan. 30 Wmk. 106 *Perf. 12½*
C178 A221 8c green 1.00 40

Diario de la Marina Building — AP81

1958, Apr. 1
C179 AP81 29c black 3.50 2.00

Jose Ignacio Rivero y Alonso, editor of the newspaper, Diario de la Marina.

Map Showing Sea Mail Route, 1765 AP82

1958, Apr. 24 Wmk. 106 *Perf. 12½*
C180 AP82 29c dk bl aqua & buff 2.50 1.25

Issued for Stamp Day, Apr. 24, and the National Philatelic Exhibition.

Gen. Gomez in Battle — AP83

Snail (Polymita Picta) — AP84

1958, June 6 Engr.
C181 AP83 12c slate green 80 25

Issued in honor of Maj. Gen. José Miguel Gomez, President of Cuba, 1909-13.

1958, Aug. 29 Wmk. 321 *Perf. 12½*

Fossils: 12c, Megalocnus Rodens. 30c, Ammonite.

C182 AP84 8c gray, red & yel 1.50 90
C183 AP84 12c brn, *yel grn* 2.50 1.50
C184 AP84 30c grn, *pink* 3.50 2.00
Nos. C182-C184 (3) 7.50 4.40

Centenary of the birth of Dr. Carlos de la Torre, naturalist.

Papilio Caiguanabus AP85

Cuban Sea Bass AP86

Designs: 12c, Teria gundlachia. 14c, Teria ebriola. 19c, Nathalis felicia. 29c, Butter Hamlet. 30c, Tattler.

1958, Sept. 26 Wmk. 106 *Perf. 12½*
C185 AP85 8c multicolored 1.75 50
C186 AP85 12c emer, blk & org 2.00 50
C187 AP85 14c multicolored 3.00 75
C188 AP85 19c bl, blk & yel 3.75 1.00
C189 AP86 24c multicolored 4.50 1.00
C190 AP86 29c blk, brn & ultra 7.00 1.25
C191 AP86 30c blk, yel grn & sep 8.00 1.75
Nos. C185-C191 (7) 30.00 6.75

Felipe Poey (1799-1891), naturalist.

Battle of San Juan Hill, 1898 — AP87

Perf. 12½

1958, Oct. 27 Wmk. 106 Engr.

C192 AP87 12c black brown 1.00 30

Birth centenary of Theodore Roosevelt.

UNESCO Building, Paris — AP88

Design: 30c, "UNESCO" and map of Cuba.

1958, Nov. 7

C193 AP88 12c dk slate grn 1.00 40
C194 AP88 30c dp ultra 2.25 1.35

UNESCO Headquarters in Paris opening, Nov. 3.

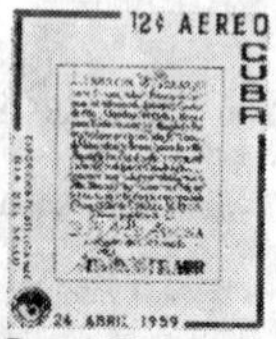

Postal Notice of 1765 — AP89

Musical Arts Building — AP90

Design: 30c, Administrative postal book of St. Cristobal, Havana, 1765.

1959, Apr. 24 Wmk. 321 *Perf. 12½*

C195 AP88 12c Prus blue & sep 65 25
C196 AP89 30c sepia & Prus bl 1.25 85

Issued for Stamp Day, Apr. 24, and the National Philatelic Exhibition.

Type of 1956 Surcharged with New Value, Bar and "ASTA" Emblem in Dark Blue

1959, Oct. 17 Wmk. 321 *Perf. 12½*

C197 AP63 12c on 1p emer 1.00 40

Issued to publicize the meeting of the American Soc. of Travel Agents, Oct. 17-23.

Perf. 12½

1959, Nov. 11 Wmk. 106 Engr.

C198 AP90 12c yellow green 1.00 25

40th anniversary of the Musical Arts Society.

No. CB1 Surcharged in Red: "HABILITADO PARA / 12c"

Engr. & Typo.

1960 Wmk. 321 *Perf. 12½*

C199 SPAP1 12c on 12 + 3c car & grn 1.50 75

Type of Regular Issue, 1960.

Designs: 8c, Battle of Santa Clara. 12c, Rebel forces entering Havana. 29c, Bank-note changing hands ("Clandestine activities in the cities").

Perf. 12½

1960, Jan. 28 Wmk. 320 Engr.

C200 A236 8c bl, gray ol & sal 1.00 25
C201 A236 12c gray ol & ocher 1.50 25
C202 A236 29c gray & car 2.50 1.50
Nos. C200-C202 (3) 5.00 2.00

Nos. C9 and C104 Surcharged "12c" in Red

1960, Feb. 3 Wmk. 106

C203 AP3 12c on 40c dp org 75 30
C204 AP48 12c on 45c vio 75 30

Pigeon Type of 1956

1960, Feb. 12 Wmk. 321

C205 AP62 12c brt blue grn 50 15

Statue Type of Regular Issue, 1960.

Statues: 8c, José Marti, Matanzas. 12c, Heroes of the Cacarajicara, Pinar del Rio. 30c, Cosme de la Torriente, Isle of Pines, horiz.

1960, Mar. 28 *Perf. 12½*

C206 A237 8c gray & car 60 25
C207 A237 12c blue & car 1.00 25
C208 A237 30c violet & brn 2.25 1.00
Nos. C206-C208 (3) 3.85 1.50

See note after No. 386.

Type of 1956 and No. C33 Overprinted in Dark Blue

1960, Apr. 24 Wmk. 321 *Perf. 12½*

C209 AP62 8c orange yel 30 20
C210 AP62 12c cerise 50 20

Souvenir Sheet

C211 AP17 Sheet of 4 20.00 20.00

Stamp Day, Apr. 24, 1960, and Natl. Phil. Exhib. No. C211 has added marginal inscription in dark blue for cent. of the ¼r on 2r (No. 15).

Type of Olympic Games Issue, 1960

Perf. 12½

1960, Sept. 22 Wmk. 321 Engr.

C212 A238 8c Boxer 40 20
C213 A238 12c Runner 60 40
a. Souvenir sheet of 4 3.00

17th Olympic Games, Rome, Aug. 25-Sept. 11. No. C213a contains one each imperf. of types of Nos. 645-646 and Nos. C212-C213 in dark blue.

No. C3 and Flight Symbols of 1930, 1960 AP91

1960, Oct. 30 Litho. Unwmk.

C214 AP91 8c multicolored 2.00 1.50

30th anniv. of national air mail service.

Sword of Sheaf of Wheat — AP92

Designs: 12c, Two workers, horiz. 30c, Three maps, horiz. 50c, Hand inscribed "Peace" in 5 languages.

1961, Jan. 10 Photo. *Perf. 11½*

Granite Paper

C215 AP92 8c multicolored 30 20
C216 AP92 12c multicolored 45 20
C217 AP92 30c black & red 1.25 50
C218 AP92 50c blk, bl & red 1.50 1.00
Nos. C215-C218 (4) 3.50 1.90

Conf. of Underdeveloped Countries, Havana.

José Marti and "Declaration of Havana" AP93

Background in Spanish, English or French.

1961, Jan. 28 Litho. *Perf. 12½*

C219 AP93 8c pale grn, blk & red 1.00 60
C220 AP93 12c org yel, blk & pale vio 1.50 1.00
C221 AP93 30c pale bl, blk & pale brn 2.50 1.50
a. Souvenir sheet of 3 6.50 6.50
Nos. C219-C221 (9) 15.00 9.30

Declaration of Havana, Sept. 1, 1960.

Sheets of 25 are imprinted in margin "E" for Spanish, "I" for English or "F" for French.

No. C221a contains one each of Nos. C219-C221, imperf. The 8c has background in Spanish, the 12c in English and the 30e in French.

UN Type of 1961

1961, Apr. 12 Unwmk. *Perf. 12½*

C222 A244 8c dp car & yel 30 15
C223 A244 12c brt ultra & org 60 30
a. Souv. sheet of 2, #C222-C223, imperf. 2.00

Nos. C76 and C7 Surcharged

HABILITADO PARA 8 cts.

Wmk. 106

1961, Oct. 1 Engr. *Perf. 10*

C224 AP39 8c on 15c No. C76
C225 AP3 8c on 20c No. C7

Revolution Anniv. Type of 1962

Perf. 12½

1962, Jan. 3 Litho. Unwmk.

C226 A250 8c multi
C227 A250 12c multi
C228 A250 30c multi

1st Sugarcane Harvest in Socialist Cuba, 1st Anniv. — AP94

1962, Jan. 16

C229 AP94 8c salmon pink & dark brn
C230 AP94 12c bluish lil & blk

Importation Prohibited

Cuban stamps issued after No. C230 have not been valued because the embargo on trade with Cuba, proclaimed Feb. 7, 1962, by President Kennedy, prohibits the importation from any country of stamps of Cuban origin, used or unused.

Intl. Radio Service AP95

1962, Mar. 26 Wmk. 321

C231 AP95 8c multi
C232 AP95 12c multi
C233 AP95 30c multi
C234 AP95 1p multi

Bird Type of 1956

1962, July 20 Engr. Wmk. 321

C235 AP63 1p like #C144, royal blue
C236 AP62 2p like #C145, dark red
C237 AP63 5p like #C146, rose lake

PRAGA '62 — AP96

1962, Aug. 18 Litho.

C238 AP96 31c Czechoslovakia No. 1080

Souvenir Sheet

Imperf

C239 AP96 31c like No. C238

No. C239 contains one 60x35½mm stamp.

Achievements of the Revolution — AP97

1966, July 26 Wmk. 376 *Perf. 12½*

C240 AP97 1c Agrarian reform
C241 AP97 2c Industrialization
C242 AP97 3c Urban reform
C243 AP97 7c Eradication of unemployment
C244 AP97 9c Education
C245 AP97 10c Public health
C246 AP97 13c Excerpt from *La Historia Me Absolvera,* by Castro

Camaguey-Seville Flight, 35th Anniv. — AP98

1971, Jan. 12 Unwmk.

C247 AP98 13c Aircraft
C248 AP98 30c Map, Lieut. Menendez Palaez

Havana-Santiago de Chile Direct Air Service, 1st Anniv. — AP99

1972, June 26 Wmk. 376

C249 AP99 25c multi

6th Congress of Latin American and Caribbean Exporters of Sugar, Havana — AP100

Perf. 12½x12

1977, Feb. 28 Unwmk.

C250 AP100 13c multi

Composer Type of 1977

1977, May 10 *Perf. 13*

C251 A571 13c Jorge Ankerman and score

Flower Type of 1977

1977, May 31

C252 A572 13c *Caesalpinia pulcherrima*
C253 A572 30c *Catharanthus roseus*

Souvenir Sheet

Perf. 13½x13

C254 A572 50c Juan Tomas Roig

No. C254 contains one 32x40mm stamp.

Natl. Decorations Type of 1977

1977, July 26 *Perf. 12x12½*

C255 A574 13c multi, diff.
C256 A574 30c multi, diff.

Art Type of 1977

Paintings by Jorge Arche: 13c, *My Wife and I*, vert. 30c, *Domino Players*. 50c, *Self-portrait*, vert.

1977, Aug. 25 ***Perf. 13x12½***

Size: 26x38mm

C257 A575 13c multi

Size: 40x29mm

Perf. 13

C258 A575 30c multi

Souvenir Sheet

Perf. 13½x13

C259 A575 50c multi

No. C259 contains one 32x40mm stamp.

Spartakiad Type of 1977

1977, Sept. 10 ***Perf. 13***

C260 A576 13c Grenade-throwing
C261 A576 30c Rifle-shooting, horiz.

10th Heroic Guerrilla's Day AP101

1977, Oct. 8 ***Perf. 12½x13***

C262 AP101 13c Guerrilla fighters

Airmail Service Type of 1977

1977, Oct. 27 ***Perf. 12x12½***

C263 A577 13c Havana-Mexico cachet
C264 A577 30c Havana-Prague cachet

Souvenir Sheet

Adoration of the Magi, by Rubens — AP102

1977, Nov. 18 ***Perf. 13***

C265 AP102 50c multi

Ruben's 400th birth anniv.

Havana Zoo Type of 1977

1977, Nov. 24

C266 A579 13c Tiger
C267 A579 30c Lion

Revolution Martyrs Type of 1977

1977, Dec. 2 ***Perf. 12½x12***

C268 A580 13c *Corynthia* landing

Pan American Health Organization (OPS), 75th Anniv. — AP103

1977, Dec. 2

C269 AP103 13c multi

Havana University Type of 1978

1978, Jan. 5 ***Perf. 13x12½***

C270 A582 13c Crossed sabres, university
C271 A582 30c University, statue, crowd

Portrait of Jose Marti (b. 1853), by A. Menocal — AP104

1978, Jan. 28

C272 AP104 13c multi

Art Type of 1978

Paintings in the Nat. Museum of Art: 13c, *El Guadalquivir*, by M. Barrow. 30c, *Portrait of H.E. Ridley*, by J.J. Masqueries, vert.

1978, Feb. 20 ***Perf. 12½x12, 13***

Sizes: 42x27mm, 29x40mm

C273 A583 13c multi
C274 A583 30c multi

Bird Type of 1975

1978, Mar. 10 ***Perf. 12½x12, 13***

Size: 42x27mm, 27x42mm

C275 A524 13c *Torreornis inexpectata*, horiz.
C276 A524 30c *Ara tricolor*

Baragua Protest, Cent. — AP105

1978, Mar. 15 ***Perf. 13x13½***

C277 AP105 13c *Antonio Maceo*, by A. Melero

Cosmonaut's Day Type of 1978

1978, Apr. 12 ***Perf. 13***

C278 A585 13c *Venus 10*

Size: 36x46mm

Perf. 12½x13

C279 A585 30c *Lunokhod 2*, vert.

SOCFILEX '78, Budapest — AP106

1978, May 7 ***Perf. 13x12½***

C280 AP106 30c Parliament, Hungary No. 217

Cactus Type of 1978

1978, May 15 ***Perf. 13***

C281 A587 13c *Rhodocactus cubensis*
C282 A587 30c *Harrisia taetra*

World Telecommunications Day — AP107

1978, May 17

C283 AP107 30c multi

Organization of African Unity, 15th Anniv. — AP108

1978, May 25 ***Perf. 13x12½***

C284 AP108 30c multi

Souvenir Sheet

CAPEX '78, Toronto — AP109

1978, June 9 ***Perf. 13x13½***

C285 AP109 50c *Niven, Wales*, by G.H. Russell

Aquarium Type of 1978

1978, June 15 ***Perf. 13***

C286 A588 13c *Carassias auratus*, vert.
C287 A588 30c *Symphysodon aequifasciata axelrodi*

MEDELLIN Games Type of 1978

1978, July 1

C288 A589 13c Volleyball
C289 A589 30c Running

Attack on Moncada Type of 1978

1978, July 26

C290 A590 13c Soldiers bearing rifles
C291 A590 30c Stylized dove, banners

Youth Festival Type of 1978

Natl. flags and views of host cities.

1978, July 28

C292 A591 13c Moscow, 1957
C293 A591 13c Vienna, 1959
C294 A591 13c Helsinki, 1962
C295 A591 13c Sofia, 1968
C296 A591 13c Berlin, 1973
a. Strip of 5, Nos. C292-C296

Size: 46x36mm

Perf. 13x12½

C297 A591 30c Havana, 1978

Tuna Industry Type of 1978

1978, Aug. 30 ***Perf. 12½x12***

C298 A593 13c Stern trawler
C299 A593 30c Refrigerator ship

Souvenir Sheet

PRAGA '78 — AP110

1978, Sept. 8 ***Perf. 13***

C300 AP110 50c *Marina*, by A. Brandeis

Art Type of 1978

Paintings by Amelia Pelaez del Casal (1896-1968).

1978, Sept. 15 ***Perf. 12x12½, 13***

C301 A594 13c *Yellow Flowers*, vert.
C302 A594 30c *Still-life in Blue*, vert.

Souvenir Sheet

Perf. 13½x13

C303 A594 50c *Portrait of Amelia*, by L. Romanach, vert.

No. C303 contains one 32x40mm stamp.

Socialist Communication Organizations Congress (OSS), 20th Anniv. — AP111

1978, Sept. 25 ***Perf. 13***

C304 AP111 30c multi

Souvenir Sheet

EXFILNA '78, 6th Natl. Philatelic Exposition — AP112

1978, Oct. 10 ***Imperf.***

C305 AP112 50c 1st Postal Card, issued in 1878

No. C305 has simulated perfs.

Intl. Anti-Apartheid Year — AP113

1978, Oct. 16 *Perf. 12½*
C306 AP113 13c multi

Zoo Type of 1978

1978, Oct. 20 *Perf. 13*
C307 A595 13c *Acinonyx jubatos*
C308 A595 30c *Loxodonta africana,* vert.

Natl. Ballet Type of 1978

1978, Oct. 28 *Perf. 12½x13*
C309 A596 13c *Giselle,* vert.
C310 A596 30c *Genesis,* vert.

Pacific Flora Type of 1978

1978, Nov. 30 *Perf. 13*
C311 A597 13c multi, diff.
C312 A597 30c multi, diff.

25th Death Anniv. of Julius and Ethel Rosenberg, American Communists Executed for Espionage — AP114

1978, Dec. 20
C313 AP114 13c multi

Julio A. Mella (d. 1929) AP115

1979, Jan. 10
C314 AP115 13c multi

Cosmonaut's Day Type of 1979
Souvenir Sheet

1979, Apr. 12 *Perf. 13½x13*
C315 A603 50c Orbital complex

No. C315 contains one 32x40mm stamp.

Intl. Year of the Child — AP116

1979, June 1 *Perf. 13x12½*
C316 AP116 13c multi

Art Type of 1979

1979, June 15 *Perf. 13½x13*
C317 A600 50c *Portrait of Victor Emmanuel Garcia,* by J. Arche, vert.

No. C317 contains one 32x40mm stamp.

CARIFESTA '79, Festival of Caribbean Peoples, Havana AP117

1979, July 16 *Perf. 12½x13*
C318 AP117 13c multi

10th World Universiade Games, Mexico City — AP118

1979, Sept. 1 *Perf. 13x12½*
C319 AP118 13c grn, pale grn & gold

6th Conference of Nonaligned Countries — AP119

1979, Sept. 3
C320 AP119 50c Convention Palace

Sir Rowland Hill (d. 1879), Originator of Penny Postage — AP120

1979, Sept. 4 *Perf. 13½x13*
C321 AP120 30c Hill, casket

SOCFILEX '79, Bucharest — AP121

Illustration reduced.

1979, Oct. 25 *Perf. 12½*
C322 AP121 30c Romania No. 683, flags

Intl. Radio Consultative Committee (CCIR), 50th Anniv. — AP122

1979, Nov. 30 *Perf. 12½x12*
C323 AP122 30c Ground receiving station

1st Soviet-Cuban Joint Space Flight — AP123

1980, Sept. 23 *Perf. 12½*
C324 AP123 13c multi
C325 AP123 30c multi

Capt. Mariano Barberan, Lt. Joaquin Collar, and Their Airplane Cuatro Vientos. AP124

1993, June 11 **Litho.** *Perf. 13*
C326 AP124 30c multicolored

First Flight Between Seville and Camaguey, 60th anniv.

AIR POST SEMI-POSTAL STAMP

> Catalogue values for unused stamps in this section are for Never Hinged items.

Farm Couple and Factory SPAP1

Engr. & Typo.

1959, May 7 **Wmk. 321** *Perf. 12½*
CB1 SPAP1 12c + 3c car & grn 1.25 50

Agricultural reforms. See No. C199.

AIR POST SPECIAL DELIVERY STAMPS

Matanzas Issue

Matanzas Harbor APSD1

Perf. 12½

1936, May 5 **Photo.** **Wmk. 229**
CE1 APSD1 15c light blue 2.50 1.25

Exists imperf. Value $5 unused, $2.50 used.

SPECIAL DELIVERY STAMPS

Issued under US Administration

US No. E5 Surcharged in Red

CUBA.
10c.
de PESO

1899 **Wmk. 191** *Perf. 12*
E1 SD3 10c on 10c blue 110.00 75.00
a. No period after "CUBA" 350.00 300.00

Issues of the Republic under US Military Rule

Special Delivery Messenger SD2

Inscribed: "Immediata"

1899 **Wmk. U S-C (191C)** **Engr.**
E2 SD2 10c orange 42.50 12.50

Issues of the Republic

Inscribed: "Inmediata"

1902 *Perf. 12*
E3 SD2 10c orange 1.00 75

J. B. Zayas — SD3

1910 **Unwmk.**
E4 SD3 10c orange & blue 11.00 3.25
a. Center inverted 725.00

Airplane and Morro Castle — SD4

1914, Feb. 24 *Perf. 12*
E5 SD4 10c dark blue 15.00 1.25

1927 **Wmk. Star (106)**
E6 SD4 10c deep blue 12.00 50

1935 *Perf. 10*
E7 SD4 10c blue 12.00 40

Matanzas Issue

Mercury SD5

Wmk. Wavy Lines (229)

1936, May 5 **Photo.** *Perf. 12½*
E8 SD5 10c deep claret 3.00 1.25

Exists imperf. Value $6 unused, $2.50 used.

"Triumph of the Revolution" SD6

1936, Nov. 18
E9 SD6 10c red orange 2.00 1.10

Maj. Gen. Máximo Gómez (1836-1905).

Temple of Quetzalcoatl (Mexico) SD7

Ruben Dario (Nicaragua) SD8

Wmk. 106
1937, Oct. 13 Engr. *Perf. 10*
E10 SD7 10c dp org 4.25 4.25
E11 SD8 10c dp org 4.25 4.25

Issued for the benefit of the Association of American Writers and Artists. See note after No. 354.

Letter and Symbols of Transportation SD9

1945, Oct. 30
E12 SD9 10c olive brown 2.00 20

Governor's Building, Cárdenas SD10

Engraved and Lithographed
1951, July 3 Wmk. 229 *Perf. 13*
E13 SD10 10c hn brn, ultra & red 3.00 55

Cent. of the adoption of Cuba's flag.

Chess Type of Regular Issue, 1951
1951, Nov. 1 Photo.
E14 A166 10c dk grn & rose brn 12.50 1.75

Catalogue values for unused stamps in this section, from this point to the end of the section, are for Never Hinged items.

10¢

Type of Regular Issue of 1951 Surcharged in Red Violet

E. ESPECIAL

Wmk. 106
1952, Mar. 18 Engr. *Perf. 10*
E15 A159 10c on 2c yel brn 3.00 95

Arms and Bars from National Hymn — SD12

Roseate Tern — SD13

1952, May 27 *Perf. 12½*
E16 SD12 10c dp org & bl 2.50 75

Issued to commemorate the 50th anniversary of the founding of the Republic of Cuba.

Type of Air Post Stamps of 1952 Inscribed: "Entrega Especial"
1952, Oct. 7 *Perf. 10*
E17 AP36 10c pale olive grn 3.00 1.50

Three-fourths of the proceeds from the sale of No. E17 were used for the Communications Ministry Employees' Retirement Fund.

1953, July 28
E18 SD13 10c blue 2.75 75

Gregorio Hernandez Saez SD14

Felix Varela SD15

1954, Feb. 23
E19 SD14 10c olive green 3.25 90

1955, June 22 *Perf. 12½*
E20 SD15 10c brn car 2.50 95

See note after No. E17.

Portrait Type of Regular Issue, 1956 Inscribed: "Entrega Especial"

Portrait: 10c, Jose Jacinto Milanes.

1956, May 2 Wmk. 106
E21 A198 10c dk car rose & blk 2.50 75

See note after No. E17.

Painting Type of Regular Issue, 1957, Inscribed: "Entrega Especial"

Painting: 10c, "Yesterday" by E. Garcia Cabrera.

1957, Mar. 15 Engr. *Perf. 12½*
E22 A207 10c dk brn & turq bl 3.25 85

See note after No. E17.

View Type of Regular Issue, 1957, Inscribed: "Entrega Especial."

View: 10c, Independence square, Pino del Rio.

1957, Dec. 17
E23 A218 10c dk pur & brn 2.25 75

See note after No. E17.

View in Havana and Messenger SD16

1958, Jan. 10 Engr.
E24 SD16 10c blue 1.50 55
E25 SD16 20c green 2.00 65

See Nos. E28, E31.

Fish Type of Air Post Issue, 1958, Inscribed "Entrega Especial."

Fish: 10c, Blackfish snapper. 20c, Mosquitofish.

1958, Sept. 26 Wmk. 106 *Perf. 12½*
E26 AP86 10c blk, bl, pink & yel 4.00 2.00
E27 AP86 20c blk, ultra & pink 12.50 9.00

See note after No. C191.

Messenger Type of 1958
1960 Wmk. 321 *Perf. 12½*
E28 SD16 10c brt vio 1.75 50

Plane Type of Air Post Issue, of 1931-46, Surcharged in Black or Red: "HABILITADO ENTREGA ESPECIAL 10¢"
1960 Wmk. 106 *Perf. 10*
E29 AP4 10c on 20c car rose 1.40 50
E30 AP4 10c on 50c grnsh bl (R) 1.10 50

Messenger Type of 1958
1961, June 28 Wmk. 321 *Perf. 12½*
E31 SD16 10c orange 1.75 65

West Indies Packet Type of 1962
Perf. 12½
1962, Apr. 24 Litho. Unwmk.
E32 A253 10c buff, dull ultra & brn

POSTAGE DUE STAMPS

Issued under Administration of the United States

Postage Due Stamps of the US Nos. J38, J39, J41 and J42 Surcharged in Black like Nos. 221-226A

1899 Wmk. 191 *Perf. 12*
J1 D2 1c on 1c dp claret 30.00 3.50
J2 D2 2c on 2c dp claret 27.50 3.50
a. Inverted surcharge 2,000.
J3 D2 5c on 5c dp claret 30.00 3.50
J4 D2 10c on 10c dp claret 24.00 1.50
Nos. J1-J4 (4) 111.50 12.00

Issues of the Republic

D1

1914 Unwmk. Engr. *Perf. 12*
J5 D1 1c carmine rose 6.50 1.00
J6 D1 2c carmine rose 8.00 1.00
J7 D1 5c carmine rose 12.00 2.00
Nos. J5-J7 (3) 26.50 4.00

1927-28
J8 D1 1c rose red 3.50 70
J9 D1 2c rose red 5.50 70
J10 D1 5c rose red 6.50 1.00
Nos. J8-J10 (3) 15.50 2.40

NEWSPAPER STAMPS

Issued under Spanish Dominion

N1

N2

1888 Unwmk. Typo. *Perf. 14*
P1 N1 ½m black 16 25
P2 N1 1m black 20 30
P3 N1 2m black 20 30
P4 N1 3m black 1.50 1.00
P5 N1 4m black 1.75 1.90
P6 N1 8m black 7.00 8.25
Nos. P1-P6 (6) 10.81 12.00

1890
P7 N2 ½m red brown 45 60
P8 N2 1m red brown 45 60
P9 N2 2m red brown 75 85
P10 N2 3m red brown 90 1.00
P11 N2 4m red brown 7.00 5.00
P12 N2 8m red brown 7.00 5.00
Nos. P7-P12 (6) 16.55 13.05

1892
P13 N2 ½m violet 15 28
P14 N2 1m violet 15 28
P15 N2 2m violet 15 28
P16 N2 3m violet 90 28
P17 N2 4m violet 3.50 1.65
P18 N2 8m violet 7.25 2.75
Nos. P13-P18 (6) 12.10 5.52

1894
P19 N2 ½m rose 15 30
a. Imperf. pair 22.50
P20 N2 1m rose 40 30
P21 N2 2m rose 40 30
P22 N2 3m rose 1.65 1.25
P23 N2 4m rose 2.75 1.50
P24 N2 8m rose 5.00 3.50
Nos. P19-P24 (6) 10.35 7.15

1896
P25 N2 ½m blue green 15 28
P26 N2 1m blue green 15 28
P27 N2 2m blue green 15 28
P28 N2 3m blue green 2.25 1.40
P29 N2 4m blue green 5.00 6.50
P30 N2 8m blue green 9.00 9.50
Nos. P25-P30 (6) 16.70 18.24

For surcharges see Nos. 190-193, 201-220.

POSTAL TAX STAMPS

Catalogue values for unused stamps in this section are for Never Hinged items.

Mother and Child — PT1

Nurse with Child — PT2

Wmk. Star. (106)
1938, Dec. 1 Engr. *Perf. 10*
RA1 PT1 1c bright green 1.25 16

The tax benefited the National Council of Tuberculosis fund for children's hospitals. Obligatory on all mail during December and January. This note applies also to Nos. RA2-RA4, RA7-RA10, RA12-RA15, RA17-RA21.

1939, Dec. 1
RA2 PT2 1c orange vermilion 75 16

"Health" Protecting Children — PT3

1940, Dec. 1
RA3 PT3 1c deep blue 75 16

Mother and Child — PT4

Victory — PT5

1941, Dec. 1
RA4 PT4 1c olive bister 75 16

1942-44
RA5 PT5 ½c orange 32 15
RA6 PT5 ½c gray ('44) 42 15

Issue dates: No. RA5, July 1, 1942. No. RA6, Oct. 3, 1944.

Type of 1941 Overprinted "1942" in Black
1942, Dec. 1
RA7 PT4 1c salmon 80 25
a. Inverted overprint 60.00 50.00

As PT3 — PT6

As PT4 — PT7

1943, Dec. 1
RA8 PT6 1c brown 75 16

1949, Dec. 9
RA9 PT7 1c blue 50 16

Type of 1949 Inscribed: "1950"

1950, Dec. 1 **Engr.**
RA10 PT7 1c rose red 50 15

Proposed Communications Building
PT8 PT10

Woman Holding Child Aloft — PT9

Child — PT11

1951, June 5 **Wmk. 106** ***Perf. 10***
RA11 PT8 1c violet 75 15

The tax was to help build a new Communications Building. This note applies also to Nos. RA16, RA34, RA43.

1951, Dec. 1
RA12 PT9 1c violet blue 42 15
RA13 PT9 1c brown carmine 42 15
RA14 PT9 1c olive bister 42 15
RA15 PT9 1c deep green 42 15
Nos. RA12-RA15 (4) 1.68
Set value 20

1952, Feb. 8
RA16 PT10 1c dark blue 30 15

See Nos. RA34, RA43.

1952, Dec. 1
RA17 PT11 1c rose carmine 75 15
RA18 PT11 1c yellow green 75 15
RA19 PT11 1c blue 75 15
RA20 PT11 1c orange 75 15
Nos. RA17-RA20 (4) 3.00
Set value 50

Hands Reaching for Lorraine Cross — PT12

Child's Head, Lorraine Cross — PT13

1953, Dec. 1 ***Perf. 9½***
RA21 PT12 1c rose carmine 50 15

1954, Nov. 1 ***Perf. 9½x10***
RA22 PT13 1c rose red 75 18
RA23 PT13 1c violet 75 18
RA24 PT13 1c bright blue 75 18
RA25 PT13 1c emerald 75 18
Nos. RA22-RA25 (4) 3.00 72

The tax benefited the Natl. Council of Tuberculosis fund for children's hospitals. Obligatory on all mail during Nov., Dec., Jan. & Feb. This note applies also to #RA26-RA33, RA35-RA42.

Rose and Watering Can — PT14

Child and Protective Hands — PT15

1955, Nov. 1
RA26 PT14 1c red orange 75 15
RA27 PT14 1c red lilac 75 15
RA28 PT14 1c bright blue 75 15
RA29 PT14 1c orange yellow 75 15
Nos. RA26-RA29 (4) 3.00
Set value 50

1956, Nov. 1
RA30 PT15 1c rose red 75 15
RA31 PT15 1c yellow brown 75 15
RA32 PT15 1c bright blue 75 15
RA33 PT15 1c emerald 75 15
Nos. RA30-RA33 (4) 3.00
Set value 50

Building Type of 1952

1957, Jan. 18 ***Perf. 10***
RA34 PT10 1c rose red 30 15

Mother and Child by Silvia Arrojo Fernandez PT16

National Council of Tuberculosis PT17

Wmk. 321

1957, Nov. 1 **Engr.** ***Perf. 10***
RA35 PT16 1c dull rose 65 15
RA36 PT16 1c bright blue 65 15
RA37 PT16 1c gray 65 15
RA38 PT16 1c emerald 65 15
Nos. RA35-RA38 (4) 2.60
Set value 50

1958
RA39 PT17 1c rose red 35 15
RA40 PT17 1c red brown 35 15
RA41 PT17 1c gray 35 15
RA42 PT17 1c emerald 35 15
Nos. RA39-RA42 (4) 1.40
Set value 50

Building Type of 1952

1958 **Wmk. 321**
RA43 PT10 1c rose red 30 15

CYRENAICA

LOCATION — In northern Africa bordering on the Mediterranean Sea
GOVT. — Former Italian colony
AREA — 75,340 sq. mi.
POP. — 225,000 (approx. 1934)
CAPITAL — Bengasi (Benghazi)

Cyrenaica was incorporated in the kingdom of Libya in 1951.

100 Centesimi = 1 Lira
1000 Milliemes = 1 Pound (1950)

Catalogue values for unused stamps in this country are for Never Hinged items, beginning with Scott 65 in the regular postage section, Scott J1 in the postage due section.

Used values in italics are for postaly used stamps. CTO's or stamps with fake cancels sell for about the same as unused, hinged stamps.

Watermarks

Wmk. 140- Crown

Propaganda of the Faith Issue

Italy Nos. 143-146 Overprinted **CIRENAICA**

1923, Oct. 24 **Wmk. 140** ***Perf. 14***
1 A68 20c ol grn & brn org 1.10 *5.50*
2 A68 30c claret & brn org 1.10 *5.50*
3 A68 50c vio & brn org 85 *4.50*
4 A68 1 l bl & brn org 85 *4.50*
Nos. 1-4 (4) 3.90 *20.00*

Fascisti Issue

Italy Nos. 159-164 Overprinted in Red or Black **CIRENAICA**

1923, Oct. 29 **Unwmk.** ***Perf. 14***
5 A69 10c dk grn (R) 1.00 *4.50*
6 A69 30c dk vio (R) 1.00 *4.50*
7 A69 50c brn car 1.00 *4.50*

Wmk. 140
8 A70 1 l blue 1.00 *4.50*
9 A70 2 l brown 1.00 *4.50*
10 A71 5 l blk & bl (R) 1.00 *7.25*
Nos. 5-10 (6) 6.00 *29.75*

Manzoni Issue

Italy Nos. 165-170 Overprinted in Red **CIRENAICA**

1924, Apr. 1 ***Perf. 14***
11 A72 10c brn red & blk 65 *5.00*
12 A72 15c bl grn & blk 65 *5.00*
13 A72 30c blk & slate 65 *5.00*
14 A72 50c org brn & blk 65 *5.00*
15 A72 1 l bl & blk 5.00 *32.50*
a. Double overprint 110.00 *275.00*
16 A72 5 l vio & blk 130.00 *575.00*
Nos. 11-16 (6) 137.60 *627.50*

Vertical overprints on Nos. 11-14 are essays. On Nos. 15-16 the overprint is vertical at the left.

Victor Emmanuel Issue

Italy Nos. 175-177 Overprinted **CIRENAICA**

1925-26 **Unwmk.** ***Perf. 11***
17 A78 60c brn car 18 *2.00*
18 A78 1 l dark blue 18 *2.00*
19 A78 1.25 l dk bl ('26) 65 *6.00*
a. Perf. 13½ 55.00 *150.00*
Nos. 17-19 (3) 1.01 *10.00*

Issue dates: Nov. 1925, July 1926.

Saint Francis of Assisi Issue

Italian Stamps of 1926 Overprinted **CIRENAICA**

1926, Apr. 12 **Wmk. 140** ***Perf. 14***
20 A79 20c gray grn 85 *3.00*
21 A80 40c dk vio 85 *3.00*
22 A81 60c red brn 85 *3.00*

Overprinted in Red **Cirenaica**

Unwmk.
23 A82 1.25 l dk bl, perf. 11 85 *3.00*
24 A83 5 l + 2.50 l ol grn 2.25 *5.50*
Nos. 20-24 (5) 5.65 *17.50*

Volta Issue

Type of Italy 1927, Overprinted **Cirenaica**

1927, Oct. 10 **Wmk. 140** ***Perf. 14***
25 A84 20c purple 2.00 *7.25*
26 A84 50c dp org 2.50 *5.00*
27 A84 1.25 l brt bl 3.00 *7.25*
Nos. 25-27 (3) 7.50 *19.50*

#25 exists with overprint omitted. See Italy.

Monte Cassino Issue

Types of 1929 Issue of Italy, Overprinted in Red or Blue **CIRENAICA**

1929, Oct. 14
28 A96 20c dk grn (R) 1.10 *5.00*
29 A96 25c red org (Bl) 1.10 *5.00*
30 A98 50c + 10c crim (Bl) 1.10 *7.25*
31 A98 75c + 15c ol brn (R) 1.10 *7.25*
32 A96 1.25 l + 25c dk vio (R) 2.00 *7.25*
33 A98 5 l + 1 l saph (R) 2.00 *7.25*

Overprinted in Red **Cirenaica**

Unwmk.
34 A100 10 l + 2 l gray brn 2.00 *10.00*
Nos. 28-34 (7) 10.40 *49.00*

Royal Wedding Issue

Type of Italian Stamps of 1930 Overprinted **CIRENAICA**

1930, Mar. 17 **Wmk. 140**
35 A101 20c yel grn 45 *2.00*
36 A101 50c + 10c dp org 32 *2.50*
37 A101 1.25 l + 25c rose red 32 *3.00*
Nos. 35-37 (3) 1.09 *7.50*

#35 exists with overprint omitted. See Italy.

Ferrucci Issue

Types of Italian Stamps of 1930, Overprinted in Red or Blue **Cirenaica**

1930, July 26
38 A102 20c violet (R) 45 *1.50*
39 A103 25c dk grn (R) 45 *1.50*
40 A103 50c black (R) 45 *1.50*
41 A103 1.25 l dp bl (R) 45 *1.50*
42 A104 5 l + 2 l dp car 1.90 *3.00*
Nos. 38-42 (5) 3.70 *9.00*

Virgil Issue

Types of Italian Stamps of 1930 Overprinted in Red or Blue

CIRENAICA

1930, Dec. 4
43 A106 15c vio blk 30 *1.50*
44 A106 20c org brn (Bl) 30 *1.50*
45 A106 25c dk grn 30 *1.25*
46 A106 30c lt brn (Bl) 30 *1.50*
47 A106 50c dl vio 30 *1.25*
48 A106 75c rose red (Bl) 30 *1.50*
49 A106 1.25 l gray bl 30 *1.50*

Unwmk.
50 A106 5 l + 1.50 l dk vio 1.65 *6.00*
51 A106 10 l + 2.50 l ol brn (Bl) 1.65 *6.00*
Nos. 43-51 (9) 5.40 *22.00*

Saint Anthony of Padua Issue

Types of Italian Stamps of 1931 Overprinted in Blue or Red

CIRENAICA

1931, May 7 **Wmk. 140**
52 A116 20c brown (Bl) 55 *2.00*
53 A116 25c green (R) 55 *2.00*
54 A118 30c gray brn (Bl) 55 *2.00*
55 A118 55c dl vio (Bl) 55 *2.00*
56 A120 1.25 l slate bl (R) 55 *2.00*

Overprinted like Nos. 23-24 in Red or Black

Unwmk.
57 A121 75c black (R) 55 *2.00*
58 A122 5 l + 2.50 l dk brn 1.65 *7.25*
Nos. 52-58 (7) 4.95 *19.25*

Carabineer A1

1934, Oct. 16 Photo. Wmk. 140

59	A1	5c dk ol grn & brn	1.25	*4.00*
60	A1	10c brn & blk	1.25	*4.00*
61	A1	20c scar & indigo	1.25	*4.00*
62	A1	50c pur & brn	1.25	*4.00*
63	A1	60c org brn & ind	1.25	*4.00*
64	A1	1.25 l dk bl & grn	1.25	*4.00*
		Nos. 59-64 (6)	7.50	*24.00*

2nd Colonial Art Exhibition held at Naples. See Nos. C24-C29.

Catalogue values for unused stamps in this section, from this point to the end of the section, are for Never Hinged items.

Autonomous State

Senussi Warrior
A2 A3

Perf. 12½

1950, Jan. 16 Unwmk. Engr.

65	A2	1m dark brown	15	15
66	A2	2m rose car	15	15
67	A2	3m orange	15	15
68	A2	4m dark green	55	60
69	A2	5m gray	15	15
70	A2	8m red orange	15	30
71	A2	10m purple	18	30
72	A2	12m red	18	35
73	A2	20m deep blue	18	30
74	A3	50m choc & ultra	1.40	*3.00*
75	A3	100m bl blk & car rose	4.00	*8.50*
76	A3	200m vio & pur	5.25	*12.00*
77	A3	500m dk grn & org	17.00	*30.00*
		Nos. 65-77 (13)	29.49	*55.95*

SEMI-POSTAL STAMPS

Many issues of Italy and Italian Colonies include one or more semipostal denominations. To avoid splitting sets, these issues are generally listed as regular postage unless all values carry a surtax.

Holy Year Issue

Italian Semi-Postal Stamps of 1924 Overprinted in Black or Red

CIRENAICA

1925, June 1 Wmk. 140 *Perf. 12*

B1	SP4	20c + 10c dk grn & brn	95	*3.00*
B2	SP4	30c + 15c dk brn & brn	95	*3.00*
B3	SP4	50c + 25c vio & brn	95	*3.00*
B4	SP4	60c + 30c dp rose & brn	95	*3.00*
B5	SP8	1 l + 50c dp bl & vio (R)	95	*3.00*
B6	SP8	5 l + 2.50 l org brn & vio (R)	95	*3.00*
		Nos. B1-B6 (6)	5.70	*18.00*

Colonial Institute Issue

"Peace" Substituting Spade for Sword — SP1

1926, June 1 Typo. *Perf. 14*

B7	SP1	5c + 5c brown	20	*1.50*
B8	SP1	10c + 5c olive grn	20	*1.50*
B9	SP1	20c + 5c blue grn	20	*1.50*
B10	SP1	40c + 5c brown red	20	*1.50*
B11	SP1	60c + 5c orange	20	*1.50*
B12	SP1	1 l + 5c blue	20	*1.50*
		Nos. B7-B12 (6)	1.20	*9.00*

Surtax for Italian Colonial Institute.

Types of Italian Semi-Postal Stamps of 1926 Overprinted like Nos. 17-19

1927, Apr. 21 Unwmk. *Perf. 11*

B13	SP10	40c + 20c dk brn & blk	80	*3.50*
B14	SP10	60c + 30c brn red & ol brn	80	*3.50*
B15	SP10	1.25 l + 60c dp bl & blk	80	*3.50*
B16	SP10	5 l + 2.50 l dk grn & blk	1.25	*4.50*
		Nos. B13-B16 (4)	3.65	*15.00*

The surtax on these stamps was for the charitable work of the Voluntary Militia for Italian National Defense.

Allegory of Fascism and Victory — SP2

1928, Oct. 15 Wmk. 140 *Perf. 14*

B17	SP2	20c + 5c bl grn	50	*2.50*
B18	SP2	30c + 5c red	50	*2.50*
B19	SP2	50c + 10c purple	50	*2.50*
B20	SP2	1.25 l + 20c dk bl	50	*2.50*
		Nos. B17-B20 (4)	2.00	*10.00*

46th anniv. of the Societa Africana d'Italia. The surtax aided that society.

Types of Italian Semi-Postal Stamps of 1926 Overprinted in Red or Black like Nos. 52-56

1929, Mar. 4 Unwmk. *Perf. 11*

B21	SP10	30c + 10c red & blk	85	*3.50*
B22	SP10	50c + 20c vio & blk	85	*3.50*
B23	SP10	1.25 l + 50c brn & bl	1.00	*5.00*
B24	SP10	5 l + 2 l ol grn & blk (Bk)	1.00	*5.00*
		Nos. B21-B24 (4)	3.70	*17.00*

Surtax for the charitable work of the Voluntary Militia for Italian Natl. Defense.

Types of Italian Semi-Postal Stamps of 1926 Overprinted in Black or Red like Nos. 52-56

1930, Oct. 20 *Perf. 14*

B25	SP10	30c + 10c dk grn & bl grn (Bk)	3.75	*10.00*
B26	SP10	50c + 10c dk grn & vio	3.75	*10.00*
B27	SP10	1.25 l + 30c ol brn & red brn	3.75	*10.00*
B28	SP10	5 l + 1.50 l ind & grn	11.00	*32.50*
		Nos. B25-B28 (4)	22.25	*62.50*

Surtax for the charitable work of the Voluntary Militia for Italian Natl. Defense.

Sower — SP3

1930, Nov. 27 Photo. Wmk. 140

B29	SP3	50c + 20c ol brn	75	*4.00*
B30	SP3	1.25 l + 20c dp bl	75	*4.00*
B31	SP3	1.75 l + 20c green	75	*4.00*
B32	SP3	2.55 l + 50c purple	1.25	*4.00*
B33	SP3	5 l + 1 l dp car	1.25	*4.00*
		Nos. B29-B33 (5)	4.75	*20.00*

25th anniv. of the Italian Colonial Agricultural Institute. The surtax was for the aid of that institution.

AIR POST STAMPS

Air Post Stamps of Tripolitania, 1931, Overprinted in Blue like Nos. 38-42

1932, Jan. 7 Wmk. 140 *Perf. 14*

C1	AP1	50c rose car	35	15
C2	AP1	60c dp org	1.50	*7.25*
C3	AP1	80c dl vio	1.50	*7.25*
		Nos. C1-C3 (3)	3.35	*14.65*

Air Post Stamps of Tripolitania, 1931, Overprinted in Blue

CIRENAICA

1932, May 12

C4	AP1	50c rose car	45	24
C5	AP1	80c dull violet	2.00	*10.00*

This overprint was also applied to the 60c, Tripolitania No. C9. The overprinted stamp was never used in Cyrenaica, but was sold at Rome in 1943 by the Postmaster General for the Italian Colonies. Value $4.

Arab on Camel — AP2

Airplane in Flight AP3

1932, Aug. 8 Photo.

C6	AP2	50c purple	70	15
C7	AP2	75c brn rose	1.65	2.75
C8	AP2	80c deep blue	1.65	2.75
C9	AP3	1 l black	24	15
C10	AP3	2 l green	50	*1.50*
C11	AP3	5 l deep car	1.00	*4.50*
		Nos. C6-C11 (6)	5.74	*11.80*

For surcharges and overprint see #C20-C23.

Graf Zeppelin Issue

Zeppelin and Clouds forming Pegasus AP4

Zeppelin and Ancient Galley — AP5

Zeppelin and Giant Bowman AP6

1933, Apr. 15

C12	AP4	3 l dk brn	4.00	*35.00*
C13	AP5	5 l purple	4.00	*35.00*
C14	AP6	10 l dp grn	4.00	*60.50*
C15	AP5	12 l deep blue	4.00	*85.00*
C16	AP4	15 l carmine	4.00	*72.50*
C17	AP6	20 l black	4.00	*100.00*
		Nos. C12-C17 (6)	24.00	*388.00*

North Atlantic Cruise Issue

Airplane Squadron and Constellations AP7

1933, June 1

C18	AP7	19.75 l grn & dp bl	10.00	*250.00*
C19	AP7	44.75 l red & indigo	10.00	*250.00*

Type of 1932 Overprinted and Surcharged

1934, Jan. 20

C20	AP3	2 l on 5 l org brn	1.40	*27.50*
C21	AP3	3 l on 5 l yel grn	1.40	*27.50*
C22	AP3	5 l ocher	1.40	*27.50*
C23	AP3	10 l on 5 l rose	1.40	*27.50*
		Nos. C20-C23 (4)	5.60	*110.00*

For use on mail to be carried on a special flight from Rome to Buenos Aires.

Transport Plane — AP8

Venus of Cyrene — AP9

1934, Oct. 9

C24	AP8	25c sl bl & org red	1.10	*4.00*
C25	AP8	50c dk grn & ind	1.10	*4.00*
C26	AP8	75c dk brn & org red	1.10	*4.00*
a.		Imperf.	185.00	
C27	AP9	80c org brn & ol grn	1.10	*4.00*
C28	AP9	1 l scar & ol grn	1.10	*4.00*
C29	AP9	2 l dk bl & brn	1.10	*4.00*
		Nos. C24-C29 (6)	6.60	*24.00*

2nd Colonial Arts Exhib. held at Naples.

AIR POST SEMI-POSTAL STAMPS

King Victor Emmanuel III — SPAP1

Wmk. 104

1934, Nov. 5 Photo. *Perf. 14*

CB1	SPAP1	25c + 10c gray grn	1.25	*5.00*
CB2	SPAP1	50c + 10c brn	1.25	*5.00*
CB3	SPAP1	75c + 15c rose red	1.25	*5.00*
CB4	SPAP1	80c + 15c brn blk	1.25	*5.00*
CB5	SPAP1	1 l + 20c red brn	1.25	*5.00*
CB6	SPAP1	2 l + 20c brt bl	1.25	*5.00*
CB7	SPAP1	3 l + 25c pur	10.50	*40.00*
CB8	SPAP1	5 l + 25c org	10.50	*40.00*
CB9	SPAP1	10 l + 30c dp vio	10.50	*40.00*
CB10	SPAP1	25 l + 2 l dp grn	10.50	*40.00*
		Nos. CB1-CB10 (10)	49.50	*190.00*

65th birthday of King Victor Emmanuel III and the non-stop flight, Rome-Mogadiscio.

AIR POST SEMI-POSTAL OFFICIAL STAMP

Type of Air Post Semi-Postal Stamps, 1934, Overprinted Crown and "SERVIZIO DI STATO" in Black

1934, Nov. 5 Wmk. 140 *Perf. 14*

CBO1	SPAP1	25 l + 2 l cop red		*1,150.*

POSTAGE DUE STAMPS

Catalogue values for unused stamps in this section are for Never Hinged items.

D1

Perf. 12½

1950, July 1 Unwmk. Engr.

J1	D1	2m dark brown	10.00	*25.00*
J2	D1	4m deep green	10.00	*25.00*
J3	D1	8m scarlet	10.00	*25.00*
J4	D1	10m vermilion	10.00	*25.00*
J5	D1	20m orange yel	10.00	*25.00*
J6	D1	40m deep blue	10.00	*25.00*
J7	D1	100m dark gray	10.00	*25.00*
		Nos. J1-J7 (7)	70.00	*175.00*

CZECHOSLOVAKIA

LOCATION — Central Europe
GOVT. — Republic
AREA — 49,355 sq. mi.
POP. — 15,395,970 (1983)
CAPITAL — Prague

The Czechoslovakian Republic consists of Bohemia, Moravia and Silesia, Slovakia and Ruthenia (Carpatho-Ukraine). In March 1939, a German protectorate was established over Bohemia and Moravia, as well as over Slovakia which had meanwhile declared its independence. Ruthenia was incorporated in the territory of Hungary. These territories were returned to the Czechoslovak Republic in 1945, except for Ruthenia, which was ceded to Russia. Czechoslovakia became a federal state on Jan. 2, 1969.

On Jan. 1, 1993 Czechoslovakia separated into Slovakia and the Czech Republic.

See Volume 5 for the stamps of Slovakia.

100 Haleru = 1 Koruna

Catalogue values for unused stamps in this country are for Never Hinged items, beginning with Scott 142 in the regular postage section, Scott B144 in the semi-postal section, Scott C19 in the air post section, Scott EX1 in the personal delivery section, Scott J58 in the postage due section, Scott O1 in the officials section, and Scott P14 in the newspaper section.

Watermarks

Wmk. 107- Linden Leaves (Vertical)

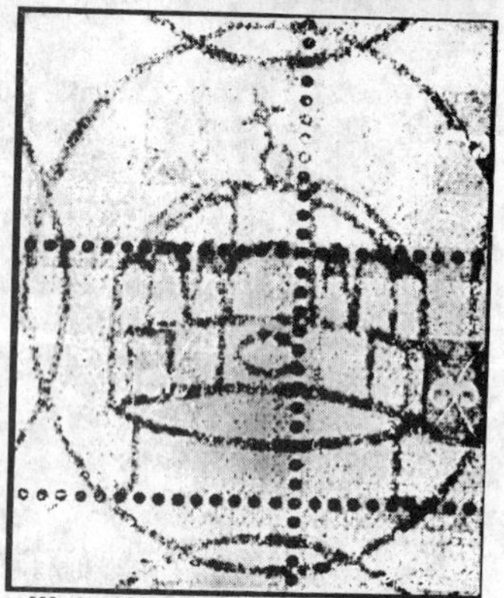
Wmk. 135- Crown in Oval or Circle, Sideways

Wmk. 136

Wmk. 136a

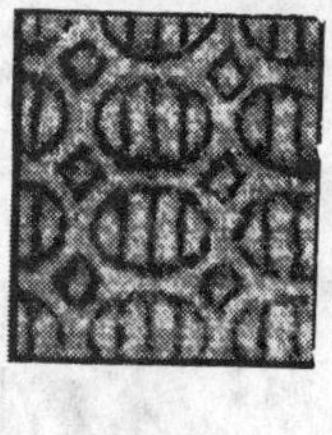
Wmk. 341- Striped Ovals

Stamps of Austria overprinted "Ceskoslovenska Republika," lion and "Cesko Slovensky Stat," "Provisorni Ceskoslovenska Vlada" and Arms, and "Ceskoslovenska Statni Posta" and Arms were made privately. A few of them were passed through the post but all have been pronounced unofficial and unauthorized by the Postmaster General.

During the occupation of part of Northern Hungary by the Czechoslovak forces, stamps of Hungary were overprinted "Cesko Slovenska Posta," "Ceskoslovenska Statni Posta" and Arms, and "Slovenska Posta" and Arms. These stamps were never officially issued though copies have passed the post.

Hradcany at Prague — A1

1918-19 Unwmk. Typo. *Imperf.*

1	A1	3h red violet	15	15
2	A1	5h yellow green	15	15
3	A1	10h rose	15	15
4	A1	20h bluish green	15	15
5	A1	25h deep blue	16	15
6	A1	30h bister	26	15
7	A1	40h red orange	26	15
8	A1	100h brown	85	15
9	A1	200h ultra	1.40	15
10	A1	400h purple	1.65	15

On the 3h-40h "Posta Ceskoslovenska" is in white on a colored background; on the higher values the words are in color on a white background.

The 25h in ultramarine was not valid for postage.

Nos. 1-6 exist as tete-beche gutter pairs.

See #368, 1554, 1600. For surcharges see #B130, C1, C4, J15, J19-J20, J22-J23, J30.

Perf. 11½, 13½

13	A1	5h yellow green	32	16
a.		Perf. 11½x10½	1.10	30
14	A1	10h rose	24	15
15	A1	20h bluish green	24	15
a.		Perf. 11½	50	25
16	A1	25h deep blue	26	15
a.		Perf. 11½	1.40	60
20	A1	200h ultra	2.75	15
		Nos. 1-10,13-16,20 (15)	8.99	
		Set value		1.00

All values of this issue exist with various private perforations and copies have been used on letters.

The 3, 30, 40, 100 and 400h formerly listed are now known to have been privately perforated.

A2

Type II- Sun behind cathedral. Colorless foliage in foreground.

Type III- Without sun. Shaded foliage in foreground.

Type IV- No foliage in foreground. Positions of buildings changed. Letters redrawn.

1919 *Imperf.*

23	A2	1h dark brown (II)	15	15
25	A2	5h blue green (IV)	18	15
27	A2	15h red (IV)	26	26
29	A2	25h dull violet (IV)	18	15
30	A2	50h dull violet (II)	18	15
31	A2	50h dark blue (IV)	18	15
32	A2	60h orange (III)	65	26
33	A2	75h slate (IV)	52	15
34	A2	80h olive grn (III)	65	26
36	A2	120h gray black (IV)	1.00	26
38	A2	300h dark green (III)	4.00	26
39	A2	500h red brown (IV)	2.00	26
40	A2	1000h violet (III)	8.50	1.40
a.		1000h bluish violet	19.00	3.00
		Nos. 23-40 (13)	18.45	
		Set value		3.30

Perf. 11½, 13½, 13½x11½

1919-20

41	A2	1h dk brown (II)	15	15
42	A2	5h blue grn (IV), perf. 13½	15	15
a.		Perf. 11½	20.00	7.50
43	A2	10h yellow grn (IV)	25	15
a.		Imperf.	19.00	17.50
b.		Perf. 11½	15.00	1.25
44	A2	15h red (IV)	15	15
a.		Perf. 11½x10½	15.00	5.00
b.		Perf. 11½x13½	35.00	10.00
c.		Perf. 13½x10½	77.50	20.00
45	A2	20h rose (IV)	28	15
a.		Imperf.	55.00	40.00
46	A2	25h dull vio (IV), perf. 11½	50	18
a.		Perf. 11½x10½	20.00	60
b.		Perf. 13½x10½	25.00	14.00
47	A2	30h red violet (IV)	20	15
a.		Imperf.	95.00	77.50
b.		Perf. 14x13½	300.00	50.00
c.		30h deep violet	20	15
d.		As "c," perf. 14x13½	300.00	50.00
e.		As "c," imperf.	200.00	150.00
50	A2	60h orange (III)	40	15
a.		Perf. 14x13½	20.00	10.00
53	A2	120h gray black (IV)	5.75	3.00
		Nos. 41-53 (9)	7.83	
		Set value		3.60

Nos. 43a, 45a and 47a were imperforate by accident and not issued in quantities as were Nos. 23 to 40.

Rouletted stamps of the preceding issues are said to have been made by a postmaster in a branch post office at Prague, or by private firms, but without authority from the Post Office Department.

The 50, 75, 80, 300, 500 and 1000h have been privately perforated.

Unlisted color varieties of types A1 and A2 were not officially released, and some are printer's waste.

For surcharges see Nos. B131, C2-C3, C5-C6, J16-J18, J21, J24-J29, J31, J42-J43.

Pres. Thomas Garrigue Masaryk — A4

1920 *Perf. 13½*

61	A4	125h gray blue	90	15
a.		125h ultramarine	40.00	25.00
62	A4	500h slate, *grysh*	4.00	1.90
a.		Imperf.	25.00	
63	A4	1000h blk brn, *brnsh*	7.00	3.50
		Nos. 61-63 (3)	11.90	5.55

Nos. 61, 61a, 63 imperf. were not regularly issued.

For surcharge see No. B131.

Carrier Pigeon with Letter — A5

Czechoslovakia Breaking Chains to Freedom — A6

Hussite Priest — A7

Agriculture and Science — A8

1920 *Perf. 14*

65	A5	5h dark blue	15	15
a.		Perf. 13½	65.00	17.50
66	A5	10h blue green	15	15
a.		Perf. 13½	50.00	21.00
67	A5	15h red brown	15	15
68	A6	20h rose	15	15
69	A6	25h lilac brown	15	15
70	A6	30h red violet	15	15
71	A6	40h red brown	15	15
a.		Tête bêche pair	2.75	1.75
b.		Perf. 13½	45	15
72	A6	50h carmine	26	15
73	A6	60h dark blue	32	15
a.		Tête bêche pair	6.25	4.00
b.		Perf. 13½	2.75	32

Photo.

74	A7	80h purple	32	16
75	A7	90h black brown	50	32

Typo.

76	A8	100h dark green	50	15
77	A8	200h violet	1.00	15
78	A8	300h vermilion	2.25	15
a.		Perf. 14x13½	6.00	50
79	A8	400h brown	6.50	85
80	A8	500h deep green	7.75	85
a.		Perf. 14x13½	67.50	8.00
81	A8	600h deep violet	10.00	85
a.		Perf. 14x13½	250.00	10.00
		Nos. 65-81 (17)	30.45	
		Set value		3.60

No. 69 has background of horizontal lines.

Imperfs. were not regularly issued.

Nos. 71 and 73 exist as tete-beche gutter pairs.

For surcharges and overprint see Nos. C7-C9, J44-J56.

1920-25 *Perf. 14*

82	A5	5h violet	15	15
a.		Tête bêche pair	2.00	1.40
b.		Perf. 13½	1.00	60
83	A5	10h olive bister	15	15
a.		Tête bêche pair	3.75	2.50
b.		Perf. 13½	35	15
84	A5	20h deep orange	15	15
a.		Tête bêche pair	30.00	10.50
b.		Perf. 13½	6.00	90
85	A5	25h blue green	15	15
86	A5	30h deep violet ('25)	2.00	15
87	A6	50h yellow green	30	15
a.		Tête bêche pair	32.50	27.50
b.		Perf. 13½	16.00	2.75
88	A6	100h dark brown	48	15
a.		Perf. 13½	25.00	28
89	A6	150h rose	3.25	75
a.		Perf. 13½	62.50	1.40
90	A6	185h orange	1.25	15
91	A6	250h dark green	3.25	30
		Nos. 82-91 (10)	11.13	
		Set value		1.50

Imperfs. were not regularly issued.

Nos. 82-84, 87 exist as tete-beche gutter pairs.

Type of 1920 Issue Redrawn

Type I- Rib of leaf below "O" of POSTA is straight and extends to tip. White triangle above book is entirely at left of twig. "P" has a stubby, abnormal appendage.

Type II- Rib is extremely bent; does not reach tip. Triangle extends at right of twig. "P" like Type I.

Type III- Rib of top left leaf is broken in two. Triangle like Type II. "P" has no appendage.

1923 *Perf. 14, 14x13½*

92 A8 100h red, *yellow*, III, perf. 14x13½ 1.25 15
a. Type I, perf. 14 2.25 15
b. Type I, perf. 14x13½ 2.75 15
c. Type II, perf. 14 2.25 15
d. Type II, perf. 14x13½ 2.75 15
e. Type III, perf. 14 14.00 15
93 A8 200h blue, *yellow*, II, perf. 14 6.00 15
a. Type II, perf. 14x13½ 12.50 25
b. Type III, perf. 14 9.50 28
c. Type III, perf. 14x13½ 52.50 52
94 A8 300h violet, *yellow*, I, perf. 14 5.25 15
a. Type II, perf. 14 42.50 40
b. Type II, perf. 14x13½ 87.50 55
c. Type III, perf. 14x13½ 10.50 15
d. Type III, perf. 14 24.00 35
Nos. 92-94 (3) 12.50
Set value 25

President Masaryk
A9 A10

Perf. 14x13½, 13½

1925 **Photo.** **Wmk. 107**

Size: 19½x23mm

95 A9 40h brown orange 1.00 15
96 A9 50h olive green 1.90 15
97 A9 60h red violet 2.25 15
Nos. 95-97 (3) 5.15
Set value 32

Distinctive Marks of the Engravings.

I, II, III- Background of horizontal lines in top and bottom tablets. Inscriptions in Roman letters with serifs.

IV- Crossed horizontal and vertical lines in the tablets. Inscriptions in Antique letters without serifs.

I, II, IV- Shading of crossed diagonal lines on the shoulder at the right.

III- Shading of single lines only.

I- "T" of "Posta" over middle of "V" of "Ceskoslovenska." Two short horizontal lines in lower part of "A" of "Ceskoslovenska."

II- "T" over right arm of "V." One short line in "A."

III- "T" as in II. Blank space in lower part of "A."

IV- "T" over left arm of "V."

Wmk. Horizontally (107)
Engr.
I. First Engraving
Size: 19¾x22½mm

98 A10 1k carmine 1.25 15
99 A10 2k deep blue 3.00 26
100 A10 3k brown 5.75 65
101 A10 5k blue green 1.90 45
Nos. 98-101 (4) 11.90 1.51

Wmk. Vertically (107)
Size: 19¼x23mm

101A A10 1k carmine 140.00 5.25
101B A10 2k deep blue 175.00 17.50
101C A10 3k brown 525.00 17.50
101D A10 5k blue green 5.00 2.00

II. Second Engraving
Wmk. Horizontally (107)
Size: 19x21½mm

102 A10 1k carmine 57.50 50
103 A10 2k deep blue 4.75 25
104 A10 3k brown 5.75 50
Nos. 102-104 (3) 68.00 1.25

III. Third Engraving
Size: 19-19½x21½-22mm
Perf. 10

105 A10 1k carmine rose 1.75 15
a. Perf. 14 17.50 15

IV. Fourth Engraving
Size: 19x22mm

1926 *Perf. 10*

106 A10 1k carmine rose 1.25 15

Perf. 14

108 A10 3k brown 7.00 15
Set value 20

There is a 2nd type of No. 106: with long mustache. Same values. See No. 130.

Karlstein Castle — A11

1926, June 1 **Engr.** ***Perf. 10***

109 A11 1.20k red violet 48 40
110 A11 1.50k car rose 32 15
111 A11 2.50k dark blue 4.00 35
Nos. 109-111 (3) 4.80 90

See Nos. 133, 135.

Karlstein Castle — A12

Pernstein Castle — A13

Orava Castle A14

Masaryk A15

Strahov Monastery A16

Hradcany at Prague A17

Great Tatra — A18

1926-27 **Engr.** **Wmk. 107**

114 A13 30h gray green 1.25 15
115 A14 40h red brown 50 15
116 A15 50h deep green 50 15
117 A15 60h red vio, *lil* 85 15
118 A16 1.20k red violet 4.00 1.50

Perf. 13½

119 A17 2k blue 90 15
a. 2k ultramarine 3.00 50
120 A17 3k deep red 1.75 15
121 A18 4k brown vio ('27) 4.00 50
122 A18 5k dk green ('27) 17.00 3.00
Nos. 114-122 (9) 30.75 5.90

No. 116 exists in two types. The one with short, straight mustache at left sells for several times as much as that with longer wavy mustache.

See Nos. 137-140.

Coil Stamps
Perf. 10 Vertically

123 A12 20h brick red 75 40
a. Vert. pair, imperf. horiz. 100.00
124 A13 30h gray green 50 15
a. Vert. pair, imperf. horiz. 100.00
125 A15 50h deep green 25 15
Nos. 123-125 (3) 1.50 70

See No. 141.

1927-31 **Unwmk.** ***Perf. 10***

126 A13 30h gray green 24 15
127 A14 40h deep brown 65 15
128 A15 50h deep green 20 15
129 A15 60h red violet 65 15
130 A10 1k carmine rose 1.10 15
131 A15 1k deep red 75 15
132 A16 1.20k red violet 40 15
133 A11 1.50k carmine ('29) 55 15
134 A13 2k deep green ('29) 45 15
135 A11 2.50k dark blue 5.50 30
136 A14 3k red brown ('31) 55 15
Nos. 126-136 (11) 11.04
Set value 90

No. 130 exists in two types. The one with longer mustache at left sells for several times as much as that with the short mustache.

1927-28 ***Perf. 13½***

137 A17 2k ultra 85 15
138 A17 3k deep red ('28) 1.90 65
139 A18 4k brown violet ('28) 6.00 1.00
140 A18 5k dark green ('28) 6.25 50
Nos. 137-140 (4) 15.00 2.30

Coil Stamp

1927 ***Perf. 10 Vertically***

141 A12 20h brick red 50 15

Catalogue values for unused stamps in this section, from this point to the end of the section, are for Never Hinged items.

Hradec Castle — A19

Brno Cathedral — A25

Masaryk — A27

10th anniv. of Czech. independence: 40h, Town Hall, Levoca. 50h, Telephone exchange, Prague. 60h, Town of Jasina. 1k, Hluboka Castle. 1.20k, Pilgrims' House, Velehrad. 2.50k, Great Tatra. 5k, Old City Square, Prague.

1928, Oct. 22 ***Perf. 13½***

142 A19 30h black 15 15
143 A19 40h red brown 20 15
144 A19 50h dark brown 22 15
145 A19 60h orange red 22 15
146 A19 1k carmine 30 18
147 A19 1.20k brown vio 70 48
148 A25 2k ultra 80 48
149 A19 2.50k dark blue 2.00 1.25
150 A27 3k dark brown 1.75 75
151 A25 5k deep violet 2.50 1.90
Nos. 142-151 (10) 8.84 5.64

From one to three sheets each of Nos. 142-148, perf 12½, appeared on the market in the early 1950's.

Coat of Arms — A29

1929-37 ***Perf. 10***

152 A29 5h dark ultra ('31) 15 15
153 A29 10h bister brn ('31) 15 15
154 A29 20h red 15 15
155 A29 25h green 15 15
156 A29 30h red violet 15 15
157 A29 40h dk brown ('37) 22 15
a. 40h red brown ('37) 1.00 15

Coil Stamp
Perf. 10 Vertically

158 A29 20h red 20 15
Set value 75 45

For overprints see Bohemia and Moravia Nos. 1-5, Slovakia 2-6.

St. Wenceslas A30

Founding St. Vitus' Cathedral A31

Design: 3k, 5k, St. Wenceslas martyred.

1929, May 14 ***Perf. 13½***

159 A30 50h gray green 42 15
160 A30 60h slate violet 70 15
161 A31 2k dull blue 1.50 45
162 A30 3k brown 1.75 22
163 A30 5k brown violet 8.75 2.75
Nos. 159-163 (5) 13.12 3.72

Millenary of the death of St. Wenceslas.

Statue of St. Wenceslas and National Museum, Prague — A33

1929 ***Perf. 10***

164 A33 2.50k deep blue 65 15

Brno Cathedral A34

Tatra Mountain Scene A35

Design: 5k, Old City Square, Prague.

1929, Oct. 15 ***Perf. 13½***

165 A34 3k red brown 2.50 15
166 A35 4k indigo 4.50 60
167 A35 5k gray green 6.00 35
Nos. 165-167 (3) 13.00 1.10

See No. 183.

A37

Type I 

Type II 

Two types of 50h:
I- A white space exists across the bottom of the vignette between the coat, shirt and tie and the "HALERU" frame panel.
II- An extra frame line has been added just above the "HALERU" panel which finishes off the coat and tie shading evenly.

1930, Jan. 2 *Perf. 10*

168 A37 50h myrtle green (II)	15	15
a. Type I	90	15
169 A37 60h brown violet	60	15
170 A37 1k brown red	26	15
Nos. 168-170 (3)	1.01	
Set value		15

See No. 234.

Coil Stamp

1931 *Perf. 10 Vertically*

171 A37 1k brown red 1.50 75

President Masaryk — A38

St. Nicholas' Church, Prague — A39

1930, Mar. 1 *Perf. 13½*

175 A38 2k gray green	85	30
176 A38 3k red brown	1.50	30
177 A38 5k slate blue	4.50	2.00
178 A38 10k gray black	9.00	4.00
Nos. 175-178 (4)	15.85	6.60

Eightieth birthday of President Masaryk.

1931, May 15

183 A39 10k black violet 10.50 2.50

Krivoklat Castle — A40

Krumlov Castle — A42

Design: 4k, Orlik Castle.

1932, Jan. 2 *Perf. 10*

184 A40 3.50k violet	2.25	90
185 A40 4k deep blue	2.75	40
186 A42 5k gray green	3.00	40
Nos. 184-186 (3)	8.00	1.70

A43

A44

Miroslav Tyrs — A45

1932, Mar. 16

187 A43 50h yellow green	45	15
188 A43 1k brown carmine	85	15
189 A44 2k dark blue	8.00	45
190 A44 3k red brown	14.00	45
Nos. 187-190 (4)	23.30	1.20

1933, Feb. 1

191 A45 60h dull violet 28 15

Miroslav Tyrs (1832-84), founder of the Sokol movement; and the 9th Sokol Congress (#187-190).

First Christian Church at Nitra
A46 A47

1933, June 20

192 A46 50h yellow green	45	15
193 A47 1k carmine rose	4.50	25
Set value		33

Prince Pribina who introduced Christianity into Slovakia and founded there the 1st Christian church in A.D. 833.
All gutter pairs are vertical.

Bedrich Smetana, Czech Composer and Pianist, 50th Death Anniv. — A48

1934, Mar. 26 **Engr.** *Perf. 10*

194 A48 50h yellow green 40 15

Consecration of Legion Colors at Kiev, Sept. 21, 1914 — A49

Ensign Heyduk with Colors A51

Legionnaires A52

Design: 1k, Legion receiving battle flag at Bayonne.

1934, Aug. 15 *Perf. 10*

195 A49 50h green	32	15
196 A49 1k rose lake	50	15
197 A51 2k deep blue	2.25	25
198 A52 3k red brown	3.50	25
Nos. 195-198 (4)	6.57	
Set value		60

20th anniv. of the Czechoslovakian Legion which fought in WWI.

Antonin Dvorak, (1841-1904), Composer — A53

1934, Nov. 22

199 A53 50h green 30 15

Pastoral Scene — A54

1934, Dec. 17 *Perf. 10*

200 A54 1k claret	48	15
a. Souv. sheet of 15, perf. 13½	175.00	175.00
b. As "a," single stamp	6.00	5.00
201 A54 2k blue	1.75	35
a. Souv. sheet of 15, perf. 13½	600.00	525.00
b. As "a," single stamp	22.50	22.50

Centenary of the National Anthem.
Nos. 200a & 201a have thick paper, darker shades, no gum. Forgeries exist.

President Masaryk
A55 A56

1935, Mar. 1

202 A55 50h green, *buff*	28	15
203 A55 1k claret, *buff*	52	15
204 A56 2k gray blue, *buff*	1.40	30
205 A56 3k brown, *buff*	2.75	30
Nos. 202-205 (4)	4.95	
Set value		76

85th birthday of President Masaryk. See No. 235.

Monument to Czech Heroes at Arras, France — A57

1935, May 4

206 A57 1k rose	55	15
207 A57 2k dull blue	1.50	18
Set value		38

20th anniversary of the Battle of Arras.

Gen. Milan Stefánik — A58

Sts. Cyril and Methodius — A59

1935, May 18

208 A58 50h green 20 15

1935, June 22

209 A59 50h green	15	15
210 A59 1k claret	32	15
211 A59 2k deep blue	1.25	28
Nos. 209-211 (3)	1.72	
Set value		38

Millenary of the arrival in Moravia of the Apostles Cyril and Methodius.

Masaryk A60

Statue of Macha, Prague A61

1935, Oct. 20 *Perf. 12½*

212 A60 1k rose lake 15 15

No. 212 exists imperforate. See No. 256. For overprints see Bohemia and Moravia Nos. 9-10, Slovakia 12.

1936, Apr. 30

213 A61 50h deep green	15	15
214 A61 1k rose lake	30	15
Set value		15

Karel Hynek Macha (1810-1836), Bohemian poet.

Jan Amos Komensky (Comenius) — A61a

Pres. Eduard Benes — A62

Gen. Milan Stefánik — A63

1936

215 A61a 40h dark blue	15	15
216 A62 50h dull green	15	15
217 A63 60h dull violet	15	15
Set value	35	15

See #252, 255. For overprints see Bohemia and Moravia #6, 8, Slovakia 7, 9-11.

Castle Palanok near Mukacevo — A64

Town of Banska Bystrica — A65

Castle at Zvikov — A66

Ruins of Castle at Strecno — A67

Castle at Cesky Raj — A68

Palace at Slavkov (Austerlitz) — A69

Statue of King George of Podebrad — A70

Town Square at Olomouc — A71

Castle Ruins at Bratislava — A72

1936, Aug. 1

218 A64 1.20k rose lilac	15	15
219 A65 1.50k carmine	15	15
220 A66 2k dark blue green	15	15
221 A67 2.50k dark blue	28	15
222 A68 3k brown	32	15
223 A69 3.50k dark violet	1.40	35
224 A70 4k dark violet	60	15
225 A71 5k green	55	15
226 A72 10k blue	1.50	35
Nos. 218-226 (9)	5.10	
Set value		1.15

For overprints and surcharge see Nos. 237-238, 254A, Bohemia and Moravia 11-12, 14-19, Slovakia 13-14, 16-23.

President Benes — A73

Soldiers of the Czech Legion — A74

1937, Apr. 26 Unwmk. *Perf. 12½*
227 A73 50h deep green 15 15

For overprints see Nos. 236, Slovakia 8.

1937, June 15
228 A74 50h deep green 15 15
229 A74 1k rose lake 26 15
Set value 15

20th anniv. of the Battle of Zborov.

Cathedral at Prague — A75

Jan Evangelista Purkyne — A76

1937, July 1
230 A75 2k green 60 15
231 A75 2.50k blue 90 30

16th anniv. of the founding of the "Little Entente."

1937, Sept. 2
232 A76 50h slate green 16 15
233 A76 1k dull rose 18 15
Set value 15

150th anniv. of the birth of Purkyne, Czech physiologist.

Masaryk Types of 1930-35

1937, Sept. *Perf. 12½*
234 A37 50h black 15 15

With date "14.IX. 1937" in design
235 A56 2k black 35 15
Set value 15

Death of former President Thomas G. Masaryk on Sept. 14, 1937.

International Labor Bureau Issue

Stamps of 1936-37 Overprinted in Violet or Black **B.I.T.1937**

1937, Oct. 6 *Perf. 12½*
236 A73 50h dp green (Bk) 28 30
237 A65 1.50k carmine (V) 38 40
238 A66 2k dp green (V) 60 65
Nos. 236-238 (3) 1.26 1.35

Bratislava Philatelic Exhibition Issue
Souvenir Sheet

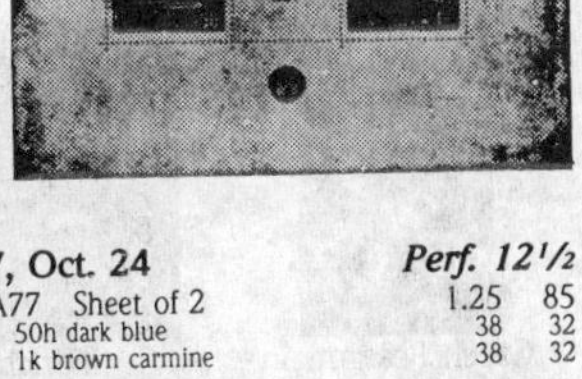
A77

1937, Oct. 24 *Perf. 12½*
239 A77 Sheet of 2 1.25 85
a. 50h dark blue 38 32
b. 1k brown carmine 38 32

The stamps show a view of Poprad Lake (50h) and the tomb of General Milan Stefanik (1k).
No. 239 overprinted "Liberation de la Tchechoslovaquie, 28-X-1945" etc., was sold at a philatelic exhibition in Brussels, Belgium.

St. Barbara's Church, Kutna Hora — A79

Peregrine Falcon, Sokol Emblem — A80

1937, Dec. 4
240 A79 1.60k olive green 15 15

For overprints see Bohemia and Moravia Nos. 13, Slovakia 15.

1938, Jan. 21
241 A80 50h deep green 25 15
242 A80 1k rose lake 35 15
Set value 15

10th Intl. Sokol Games. Imperf. copies of No. 242 are essays. Nos. 241-242 se-tenant with labels sell slightly higher.

Legionnaires
A81 A82

Legionnaire — A83

1938
243 A81 50h deep green 15 15
244 A82 50h deep green 15 15
245 A83 50h deep green 15 15
Set value 30 15

20th anniv. of the Battle of Bachmac, Vouziers and Doss Alto. #243-245 se-tenant with label sell slightly higher.

Jindrich Fügner, Co-Founder of Sokol Movement — A84

1938, June 18 *Perf. 12½*
246 A84 50h deep green 15 15
247 A84 1k rose lake 15 15
248 A84 2k slate blue 42 15
Set value 60 15

10th Sokol Summer Games. Nos. 246-248 se-tenant with labels sell slightly higher.

View of Pilsen — A85

Cathedral of Kosice — A86

1938, June 24
249 A85 50h deep green 15 15

Provincial Economic Council meeting, Pilsen.

For overprint see Bohemia & Moravia #7.

1938, July 15 *Perf. 12½*
250 A86 50h deep green 15 15

Kosice Cultural Exhibition.

Prague Philatelic Exhibition Issue
Souvenir Sheet

Vysehrad Castle - Hradcany A87

1938, June 26 *Perf. 12½*
251 A87 Sheet of 2 4.00 3.00
a. 50h dark blue 1.50 1.50
b. 1k deep carmine 1.50 1.50

Stefánik Type of 1936

1938, Nov. 21
252 A63 50h deep green 20 15

Allegory of the Republic — A89

1938, Dec. 19 Unwmk.
253 A89 2k lt ultra 28 15
254 A89 3k pale brown 32 15

20th anniv. of Independence. See No. B153.

"Wir sind frei!"
Stamps of Czechoslovakia, 1918-37, overprinted with a swastika in black or red and "Wir sind frei!" were issued locally and unofficially in 1938 as Czech authorities were evacuating and German authorities arriving. They appeared in the towns of Asch, Karlsbad, Reichenberg-Maffersdorf, Rumburg, etc.
The overprint, sometimes including a surcharge or the town name (as in Karlsbad), exists on many values of postage, air post, semi-postal, postage due and newspaper stamps.

No. 226 Surcharged in Orange Red

1939, Jan. 18 Unwmk. *Perf. 12½*
254A A72 300h on 10k blue 75 *3.50*

Opening of the Slovakian Parliament.

View of Jasina — A89a

Perf. 12½
1939, Mar. 15 Engr. Unwmk.
254B A89a 3k ultra 12.50 *25.00*

Inauguration of the Carpatho-Ukraine Diet, Mar. 2, 1939.
Printed for use in the province of Carpatho-Ukraine but issued in Prague at the same time.
Used value is for red commemorative cancel.

Stefánik Type of 1936

1939 Engr. *Perf. 12½*
255 A63 60h dark blue 17.50 *25.00*

Used exclusively in Slovakia.

Masaryk Type of 1935 with hyphen in Cesko-Slovensko

1939, Apr. 23
256 A60 1k rose lake 15 15

Linden Leaves and Buds — A90

1945 Photo. *Perf. 14*
256A A90 10h black 15 15
257 A90 30h yellow brown 15 15
258 A90 50h dark green 15 15
258A A90 60h dark blue 15 15

Engr.
(Buds Open)
Perf. 12½
259 A90 60h blue 15 15
259A A90 80h orange ver 15 15
260 A90 1.20k rose 15 15
261 A90 3k violet brown 15 15
262 A90 5k green 15 15
Set value 45 45

Thomas G. Masaryk — A91

Coat of Arms — A92

1945-46 Photo. *Perf. 12*
262A A91 5h dull violet ('46) 15 15
262B A91 10h orange yel ('46) 15 15
262C A91 20h dk brown ('46) 15 15
263 A91 50h brt green 15 15
264 A91 1k orange red 15 15
265 A91 2k chalky blue 25 25
Set value 60 53

1945 *Imperf.*
266 A92 50h olive gray 15 15
267 A92 1k brt red vio 15 15
268 A92 1.50k dk carmine 15 15
269 A92 2k deep blue 15 15
269A A92 2.40k henna brn 30 20
270 A92 3k brown 15 15
270A A92 4k dk slate grn 15 15
271 A92 6k violet blue 25 15
271A A92 10k sepia 38 20
Set value 1.25 75

Nos. 266-217A exist in 2 printings. Stamps of the 1st printing are on thin, hard paper in sheets of 100; those of the 2nd printing on thick, soft wove paper in sheets of 200.

Staff Capt. Ridky (British Army) — A93

Dr. Miroslav Novak (French Army) — A94

Capt. Otakar Jaros (Russian Army) — A95

Staff Capt. Stanislav Zimprich (Foreign Legion) — A96

2nd Lt. Jiri Kral (French Air Force) — A97

Josef Gabcik (Parachutist) — A98

Staff Capt. Alois Vasatko (Royal Air Force) — A99

Private Frantisek Adamek (British Colonial Service) — A100

Perf. 11½x12½

1945, Aug. 18 **Engr.**

272	A93	5h	intense blue	15	15
273	A94	10h	dark brown	15	15
274	A95	20h	brick red	15	15
275	A96	25h	rose red	15	15
276	A97	30h	purple	15	15
277	A98	40h	sepia	15	15
278	A99	50h	dark olive	15	15
279	A100	60h	violet	15	15
280	A93	1k	carmine	15	15
281	A94	1.50k	lake	15	15
282	A95	2k	ultra	15	15
283	A96	2.50k	deep violet	15	15
284	A97	3k	sepia	15	15
285	A98	4k	rose lilac	15	15
286	A99	5k	myrtle green	20	15
287	A100	10k	brt ultra	65	16
			Set value	1.80	90

Flags of Russia, Great Britain, US and Czechoslovakia A101

View of Banská Bystrica A102

Patriot Welcoming Russian Soldier, Turciansky A103

Ruins of Castle at Sklabina A104

Czech Patriot, Strecno — A105

1945, Aug. 29 **Photo.** ***Perf. 10***

288	A101	1.50k	brt carmine	15	15
289	A102	2k	brt blue	15	15
290	A103	4k	dark brown	30	30
291	A104	4.50k	purple	30	30
292	A105	5k	deep green	75	75
			Nos. 288-292 (5)	1.65	1.65

National uprising against the Germans.

A card contains one each of Nos. 288-292 on thin cardboard, ungummed. Size: 148x210mm. Sold for 50k.

Stefánik - Benes - Masaryk
A106 A107 A108

1945-47 **Engr.** ***Perf. 12, 12½***

293	A106	30h	rose violet	15	15
294	A107	60h	blue	15	15
294A	A106	1k	red org ('47)	15	15
295	A108	1.20k	car rose	15	15
295A	A108	1.20(k)	rose lil ('46)	15	15
296	A106	2.40(k)	rose	15	15
297	A107	3k	red violet	16	15
297A	A108	4k	dark blue ('46)	15	15
298	A108	5k	Prus green	16	15
299	A107	7k	gray	18	15
300	A106	10k	gray blue	45	15
300A	A106	20k	sepia ('46)	90	18
			Set value	2.30	72

1945 **Photo.** ***Perf. 14***

301	A108	50h	brown	15	15
302	A106	80h	dark green	15	15
303	A107	1.60(k)	olive green	15	15
304	A108	15k	red violet	55	15
			Set value	73	25

Statue of Kozina and Chod Castle, Domazlice — A109

Red Army Soldier — A110

1945, Nov. 28 **Engr.** ***Perf. 12½***

305	A109	2.40k	rose carmine	15	15
306	A109	4k	blue	20	15

250th anniv. of the death of Jan Sladky Kozina, peasant leader.

1945, Mar. 26 **Litho.** ***Imperf.***

307	A110	2k	crimson rose	38	35
308	A110	5k	slate black	1.75	1.50
309	A110	6k	ultramarine	45	42
			Nos. 307-309 (3)	2.58	2.27

Souvenir Sheet

1945, July 16

Gray Burelage

310	Sheet of 3	3.00	2.50
a.	A110 2k crimson rose	40	30
b.	A110 5k slate black	40	30
c.	A110 6k ultramarine	40	30

Return of Pres. Benes, Apr., 1945.

Clasped Hands A112

Karel Havlícek Borovsky A113

1945 ***Rouletted 12½***

311	A112	1.50k	brown red	2.50	2.50
312	A112	9k	red orange	55	60
313	A112	13k	orange brown	75	75
314	A112	20k	blue	2.00	2.00
			Nos. 311-314 (4)	5.80	5.85

1946, July 5 **Engr.** ***Perf. 12½***

315	A113	1.20k	gray black	18	18

Borovsky (1821-56), editor and writer.

Old Town Hall, Brno — A114

Hodonin Square — A115

Perf. 12½x12, 12x12½

1946, Aug. 3 **Engr.** **Unwmk.**

316	A114	2.40k	deep rose	18	15
317	A115	7.40k	dull violet	32	15
			Set value		21

See No. B159.

President Eduard Benes — A116

1946, Oct. 28

318	A116	60h	indigo	15	15
319	A116	1.60k	dull green	15	15
320	A116	3k	red lilac	15	15
321	A116	8k	sepia	22	15
			Set value	44	20

Flag, Symbols A117

Saint Adalbert A118

1947, Jan. 1 ***Perf. 12½***

322	A117	1.20k	Prus green	15	15
323	A117	2.40k	deep rose	15	15
324	A117	4k	deep blue	32	15
			Nos. 322-324 (3)	62	
			Set value		20

Czechoslovakia's two-year reconstruction and rehabilitation program.

1947, Apr. 23

326	A118	1.60k	gray	48	28
327	A118	2.40k	rose carmine	80	65
328	A118	5k	blue green	1.00	42
			Nos. 326-328 (3)	2.28	1.35

950th anniv. of the death of Saint Adalbert, Bishop of Prague.

Grief — A119

Allegorical Figure — A120

1947, June 10 **Engr.**

329	A119	1.20k	black	30	25
330	A119	1.60k	slate black	38	38
331	A120	2.40k	brown violet	48	48
			Nos. 329-331 (3)	1.16	1.11

Destruction of Lidice, 5th anniversary.

World Federation of Youth Symbol — A121

Thomas G. Masaryk — A122

1947, July 20

332	A121	1.20k	violet brown	30	15
333	A121	4k	slate	35	15

World Youth Festival held in Prague, July 20-Aug. 17.

1947, Sept. 14

334	A122	1.20k	gray blk, *buff*	16	15
335	A122	4k	blue blk, *cream*	40	15
			Set value		25

Death of Masaryk, 10th anniv.

Msgr. Stefan Moyses — A123

1947, Oct. 19

336	A123	1.20k	rose violet	16	15
337	A123	4k	deep blue	35	18
			Set value		28

150th anniversary of the birth of Stefan Moyses, first Slovakian chairman of the Slavic movement.

"Freedom from Social Oppression" A124

1947, Oct. 26 **Photo.** ***Perf. 14***

338	A124	2.40k	brt carmine	20	20
339	A124	4k	brt ultra	35	15

30th anniversary of the Russian revolution of October, 1917.

Benes A125

"Czechoslovakia" Greeting Sokol Marchers A126

1948, Feb. 15 **Photo.**

Size: 17½x21½mm

340	A125	1.50k	brown	15	15

Size: 19x23mm

341	A125	2k	deep plum	15	15
342	A125	5k	brt ultra	15	15
			Set value	26	15

1948, Mar. 7 **Engr.** ***Perf. 12½***

343	A126	1.50k	brown	15	15
344	A126	3k	rose carmine	15	15
345	A126	5k	blue	30	15
			Set value	50	20

The 11th Sokol Congress.

King Charles IV — A127

St. Wenceslas, King Charles IV — A128

1948, Apr. 7

346	A127	1.50k	black brown	15	15
347	A128	2k	dark brown	15	15
348	A128	3k	brown red	18	15
349	A127	5k	dark blue	38	15
			Nos. 346-349 (4)	86	
			Set value		33

600th anniv. of the foundation of Charles University, Prague.

Czech Peasants in Revolt — A129

Jindrich Vanicek — A130

Unwmk.

1948, May 14 Photo. *Perf. 14*

350 A129 1.50k dk olive brown	15	15

Centenary of abolition of serfdom.

1948, June 10 Engr. *Perf. 12½*

Designs: 1.50k, 2k, Josef Scheiner.

351 A130 1k dark green	15	15
352 A130 1.50k sepia	15	15
353 A130 2k gray blue	18	15
354 A130 3k claret	26	15
Set value	60	35

11th Sokol Congress, Prague, 1948.

Frantisek Palacky & F. L. Rieger — A131

Miloslav Josef Hurban — A132

1948, June 20 Unwmk.

355 A131 1.50k gray	15	15
356 A131 3k brown carmine	18	15
Set value		16

Constituent Assembly at Kromeriz, cent.

1948, Aug. 27 *Perf. 12½*

Designs: 3k, Ludovit Stur. 5k, Michael M. Hodza.

357 A132 1.50k dark brown	15	15
358 A132 3k carmine lake	15	15
359 A132 5k indigo	25	15
Nos. 357-359 (3)	55	
Set value		26

Cent. of 1848 insurrection against Hungary.

Eduard Benes A133

Czechoslovak Family A134

1948, Sept. 28

360 A133 8k black	20	15

President Eduard Benes, 1884-1948.

1948, Oct. 28 *Perf. 12½x12*

361 A134 1.50k deep blue	15	15
362 A134 3k rose carmine	20	16
Set value	28	23

Czechoslovakia's Independence, 30th anniv.

Pres. Klement Gottwald — A135

1948-49 *Perf. 12½*

Size: 18½x23½mm

363 A135 1.50k dk brown	15	15
364 A135 3k car rose	25	15
a. 3k rose brown	40	15
365 A135 5k gray blue	22	15

Size: 23½x29mm

366 A135 20k purple	1.10	15
Nos. 363-366 (4)	1.72	
Set value		27

See Nos. 373, 564, 600-604.

Souvenir Sheet

1948, Nov. 23 Unwmk. *Imperf.*

367 A135 30k rose brown	3.50	2.75

52nd birthday of Pres. Klement Gottwald (1896-1953).

Hradcany Castle Type of 1918
Souvenir Sheet

1948, Dec. 18

368 A1 10k dk blue violet	1.25	90

1st Czechoslovak postage stamp, 30th anniv.

Czechoslovak and Russian Workmen Shaking Hands — A138

Lenin — A139

1948, Dec. 12 *Perf. 12½*

369 A138 3k rose carmine	20	15

5th anniv. of the treaty of alliance between Czechoslovakia and Russia.

1949, Jan. 21 Engr. *Perf. 12½*

370 A139 1.50k violet brown	25	15
371 A139 5k deep blue	25	20

25th anniversary of the death of Lenin.

Gottwald Type of 1948 Inscribed: "UNOR 1948" and

Gottwald Addressing Meeting — A140

1949, Feb. 25 Photo. *Perf. 14*

372 A140 3k red brown	15	15

Perf. 12½

Engr.

Size: 23½x29mm

373 A135 10k deep green	60	25
Set value		30

1st anniv. of Gottwald's speech announcing the appointment of a new government. No. 372 exists in a souvenir sheet of 1. It was not sold to the public.

A141

A142

Designs (Writers): 50h, P. O. Hviezdoslav. 80h, V. Vancura. 1k, J. Sverma. 2k, Julius Fucik. 4k, Jiri Wolker. 8k, Alois Jirasek.

1949 Photo. *Perf. 14*

374 A141 50h violet brown	15	15
375 A141 80h scarlet	15	15
376 A141 1k dk olive green	15	15
377 A141 2k brt blue	38	15

Perf. 12½

Engr.

378 A141 4k violet brown	38	15
379 A141 8k brown black	48	15
Nos. 374-379 (6)	1.69	
Set value		30

1949, May 20

Designs: 3k, Stagecoach and Train. 5k, Postrider and post bus. 13k, Sailing ship and plane.

380 A142 3k brown carmine	1.40	1.40
381 A142 5k deep blue	70	40
382 A142 13k deep green	1.40	75
Nos. 380-382 (3)	3.50	2.55

75th anniv. of the UPU.

Reaping — A143

Communist Emblem and Workers — A144

Workman, Symbol of Industry — A145

Perf. 12½x12, 12x12½

1949, May 24 Unwmk.

383 A143 1.50k deep green	60	60
384 A144 3k brown carmine	30	30
385 A145 5k deep blue	60	60
Nos. 383-385 (3)	1.50	1.50

No. 384 for the ninth meeting of the Communist Party of Czechoslovakia, May 25, 1949.

Bedrich Smetana and Natl. Theater, Prague — A146

Aleksander Pushkin — A147

1949, June 4 *Perf. 12½x12*

386 A146 1.50k dull green	20	15
387 A146 5k deep blue	55	20
Set value		28

125th anniv. of the birth of Bedrich Smetana, composer.

1949, June 6 *Perf. 12x12½*

388 A147 2k olive gray	32	25

150th anniversary of the birth of Aleksander S. Pushkin.

Frederic Chopin and Conservatory, Warsaw — A148

1949, June 24 *Perf. 12½x12*

389 A148 3k dark red	35	20
390 A148 8k violet brown	90	50

Cent. of the death of Frederic F. Chopin.

Globe and Ribbon — A149

Zvolen Castle — A150

1949, Aug. 20 *Perf. 12½x12*

391 A149 1.50k violet brown	25	20
392 A149 5k ultra	60	40

50th Prague Sample Fair, Sept. 11-18, 1949.

Starting in 1949, commemorative stamps which are valued in italics were issued in smaller quantities than those in the balance of the set and sold at prices higher than face value.

1949, Aug. 28 *Perf. 12½*

393 A150 10k rose lake	80	15

Early Miners — A151

Miner of Today — A152

Design: 5k, Mining Machine.

1949, Sept. 11 *Perf. 12½*

394 A151 1.50k sepia	90	55
395 A152 3k carmine rose	*4.25*	*1.50*
396 A151 5k deep blue	*3.50*	*1.50*
Nos. 394-396 (3)	*8.65*	*3.55*

700th anniv. of the Czechoslovak mining industry; 150th anniv. of the miner's laws.

Construction Workers — A153

Joseph V. Stalin — A154

1949, Dec. 11 *Perf. 12½*

397 A153 1k shown	2.50	75
398 A153 2k Machinist	1.50	38

2nd Trade Union Congress, Prague, 1949.

1949, Dec. 21 Unwmk.

Design: 3k, Stalin facing left.

Cream Paper

399 A154 1.50k greenish gray	*1.25*	*60*
400 A154 3k claret	*3.50*	*1.40*

70th birthday of Joseph V. Stalin.

Skier — A155

Efficiency Badge — A156

Engr., Photo. (3k)

1950, Feb. 15 *Perf. 12½, 13½*

401 A155 1.50k gray blue	*2.00*	*75*
402 A156 3k vio brn, *cr*	2.00	1.25
403 A155 5k ultramarine	*2.50*	*1.50*
Nos. 401-403 (3)	*6.50*	*3.50*

51st Ski Championship for the Tatra cup, Feb. 15-26, 1950.

Vladimir V. Mayakovsky, Poet, 20th Death Anniv. — A157

1950, Apr. 14 Engr. *Perf. 12½*

404 A157	1.50k dark brown		*2.25*	*1.10*
405 A157	3k brown red		2.25	85

See Nos. 414-417, 422-423, 432-433, 464-465, 477-478.

Soviet Tank Soldier and Hradcany A158

Designs: 2k, Hero of Labor medal. 3k, Two workers (militiamen) and Town Hall, Prague. 5k, Text of government program and heraldic lion.

1950, May 5

406 A158	1.50k gray green	42	20
407 A158	2k dark brown	*90*	*70*
408 A158	3k brown red	32	20
409 A158	5k dark blue	52	16
	Nos. 406-409 (4)	*2.16*	*1.26*

5th anniv. of the Czechoslovak People's Democratic Republic.

Factory and Young Couple with Tools A159

Designs: 2k, Steam shovel. 3k, Farmer and farm scene. 5k, Three workers leaving factory.

1950, May 9 Engr.

410 A159	1.50k dark green	90	75
411 A159	2k dark brown	*1.00*	*75*
412 A159	3k rose red	45	35
413 A159	5k deep blue	45	35
	Nos. 410-413 (4)	*2.80*	*2.20*

Canceled to Order

The government philatelic department started about 1950 to sell canceled sets of new issues. Values in the second ("used") column are for these canceled-to-order stamps. Postally used copies are worth more.

Portrait Type of 1950

Design: S. K. Neumann.

1950, June 5 Unwmk. *Perf. 12½*

414 A157	1.50k deep blue	15	15
415 A157	3k violet brown	*95*	*75*

Stanislav Kostka Neumann (1875-1947), journalist and poet.

1950, June 21

Design: Bozena Nemcova.

416 A157	1.50k deep blue	*1.25*	*75*
417 A157	7k dark brown	30	20

Bozena Nemcova (1820-1862), writer.

Liberation of Colonies — A160

Designs: 2k, Allegory, Fight for Peace. 3k, Group of Students. 5k, Marching Students with flags.

1950, Aug. 14

418 A160	1.50k dark green	15	15
419 A160	2k sepia	*85*	*55*
420 A160	3k rose carmine	16	15
421 A160	5k ultra	40	35
	Nos. 418-421 (4)	*1.56*	*1.20*

2nd International Students World Congress, Prague, Aug. 12-24, 1950.

Portrait Type of 1950

Design: Zdenek Fibich.

1950, Oct. 15

422 A157	3k rose brown	*90*	*55*
423 A157	8k gray green	35	20

Centenary of the birth of Zdenek Fibich, musician.

Miner, Soldier and Farmer A161

Czech and Soviet Soldiers A162

1950, Oct. 6

424 A161	1.50k slate	*60*	*60*
425 A162	3k carmine rose	30	30

Issued to publicize Czech Army Day.

Prague Castle, 16th Century A163

Prague, 1493 — A164

Designs: 3k, Prague, 1606. 5k, Prague, 1794.

1950, Oct. 21 *Perf. 14*

426 A163	1.50k black	3.25	3.00
427 A164	2k chocolate	3.25	3.00
428 A164	3k brown carmine	3.25	3.00
429 A164	5k gray	3.25	3.00
a.	Block of 4, #426-429	17.50	16.00

See Nos. 434-435.

Communications Symbols — A165

1950, Oct. 25 *Perf. 12½*

430 A165	1.50k chocolate	15	15
431 A165	3k brown carmine	*85*	*30*
	Set value		*35*

1st anniv. of the foundation of the Intl. League of P.T.T. Employees.

Portrait Type of 1950

Design: J. Gregor Tajovsky.

1950, Oct. 26

432 A157	1.50k brown	*1.00*	*60*
433 A157	5k deep blue	*65*	30

10th anniversary of the death of J. Gregor Tajovsky (1874-1940), Slovakian writer.

Scenic Type of 1950

Design: Prague, 1950.

1950, Oct. 28

434 A164	1.50k indigo	35	15
a.	Souvenir sheet of 4, imperf.	12.50	10.00
435 A164	3k brown carmine	*65*	*50*

Czech and Soviet Steel Workers A166

1950, Nov. 4 Unwmk.

436 A166	1.50k chocolate	30	20
437 A166	5k deep blue	*65*	*48*

Issued to publicize the 2nd meeting of the Union of Czechoslovak-Soviet Friendship.

Dove by Picasso — A167

1951, Jan. 20 Photo. *Perf. 14*

438 A167	2k deep blue	*4.00*	*2.75*
439 A167	3k rose brown	2.50	1.75

1st Czechoslovak Congress of Fighters for Peace, held in Prague.

Julius Fucik — A168

1951, Feb. 17 Engr. *Perf. 12½*

440 A168	1.50k gray	42	30
441 A168	5k gray blue	*1.10*	*75*

Drop Hammer — A169

Installing Gear — A170

1951, Feb. 24

442 A169	1.50k gray blk	15	15
443 A170	3k violet brn	15	15
444 A169	4k gray blue	*65*	*48*
	Nos. 442-444 (3)	*95*	
	Set value		*60*

Women Machinists A171

Apprentice Miners A172

Designs: 3k, Woman tractor operator. 5k, Women of different races.

1951, Mar. 8 Photo. *Perf. 14*

445 A171	1.50k olive brown	22	15
446 A171	3k brown car	*90*	*52*
447 A171	5k blue	40	15
	Nos. 445-447 (3)	*1.52*	*82*

International Women's Day, Mar. 8.

1951, Apr. 12 Engr. *Perf. 12½*

448 A172	1.50k gray	*45*	*24*
449 A172	3k red brown	15	15
	Set value		*31*

Plowing — A173

Collective Cattle Breeding — A174

1951, Apr. 28 Photo. *Perf. 14*

450 A173	1.50k brown	50	50
451 A174	2k dk green	*75*	*65*

Tatra Mountain Recreation Center A175

Mountain Recreation Centers: 2k, Beskydy (Beskids). 3k, Krkonose (Carpathians).

1951, May 5 Engr. *Perf. 12½*

452 A175	1.50k deep green	20	15
453 A175	2k dark brown	*75*	*50*
454 A175	3k rose brown	30	15
	Nos. 452-454 (3)	*1.25*	*80*

Issued to publicize the summer opening of trade union recreation centers.

Klement Gottwald and Joseph Stalin A176

Factory Militiaman A177

Red Army Soldier and Partisan A178

Marx, Engels, Lenin and Stalin A179

1951 Unwmk. *Perf. 12½*

455 A176	1.50k olive gray	65	25
456 A177	2k red brown	22	15
457 A178	3k rose brown	22	15
458 A176	5k deep blue	*2.00*	*1.40*
459 A179	8k gray	60	25
	Nos. 455-459 (5)	*3.69*	*2.20*

30th anniv. of the founding of the Czechoslovak Communist Party.

A180

A181

Design: 1k, 2k, Antonin Dvorák. 1.50k, 3k, Bedrich Smetana.

1951, May 30

460 A180	1k redsh brown	25	15
461 A180	1.50k olive gray	*70*	*32*
462 A180	2k dk redsh brn	*85*	*70*
463 A180	3k rose brown	25	15
	Nos. 460-463 (4)	*2.05*	*1.32*

International Music Festival, Prague.

Portrait Type of 1950

1951, June 21

Portrait: Bohumir Smeral (facing right).

464 A157 1.50k dark gray 45 35
465 A157 3k rose brown 40 15

10th anniv. of the death of Bohumir Smeral, political leader.

1951, June 21

466 A181 1k shown 65 28
467 A181 1.50k Discus 45 28
468 A181 3k Soccer 1.10 28
469 A181 5k Skier 2.25 1.25
Nos. 466-469 (4) 4.45 2.09

Issued to honor the 9th Congress of the Czechoslovak Sokol Federation.

Scene from "Fall of Berlin" A182

Scene from "The Great Citizen" A183

1951, July 14

470 A182 80h rose brown 30 20
471 A183 1.50k dark gray 30 20
472 A182 4k gray blue 1.25 75
Nos. 470-472 (3) 1.85 1.15

International Film Festival, Karlovy Vary, July 14-29, 1951.

Alois Jirásek — A184

"Fables and Fate" A185

Design: 4k, Scene from "Reign of Tabor."

1951, Aug. 23 Engr. *Perf. 12½*

473 A184 1.50k gray 35 15
474 A184 5k dark blue 1.65 1.25

Photo.

Perf. 14

475 A185 3k dark red 35 15
476 A185 4k dark brown 35 18
Nos. 473-476 (4) 2.70 1.73

Cent. of the birth of Alois Jirásek, author.

Portrait Type of 1950

Design: Josef Hybes (1850-1921), co-founder of Czech Communist Party.

1951, July 21 Engr.

477 A157 1.50k chocolate 15 15
478 A157 2k rose brn 55 35
Set value 45

"Ostrava Region" — A186

Mining Iron Ore — A187

1951, Sept. 9

479 A186 1.50k dk brown 15 15
480 A187 3k rose brown 15 15
481 A186 5k deep blue 1.10 90
Nos. 479-481 (3) 1.40
Set value 1.02

Miner's Day, Sept. 9, 1951.

Soldiers on Parade — A188

Designs: 1k, Gunner and field gun. 1.50k, Klement Gottwald. 3k, Tankman and tank. 5k, Aviators.

Perf. 14 (80h, 5k), 12½

Photo. (80h, 5k), Engr.

1951, Oct. 6

Inscribed: "Den CS Armady 1951"

482 A188 80h olive brown 25 22
483 A188 1k dk olive grn 25 22
484 A188 1.50k sepia 40 22
485 A188 3k claret 50 22
486 A188 5k blue 1.10 75
Nos. 482-486 (5) 2.50 1.63

Issued to publicize Army Day, Oct. 6, 1951.

Stalin and Gottwald A189

Lenin, Stalin and Soldiers A190

1951, Nov. 3 Engr. *Perf. 12½*

487 A189 1.50k sepia 15 15
488 A190 3k red brown 16 15
489 A189 4k deep blue 1.10 40
Nos. 487-489 (3) 1.41
Set value 50

Issued to publicize the month of Czechoslovak-Soviet friendship, 1951.

Peter Jilemnicky A191

Ladislav Zapotocky A192

1951, Dec. 5 Unwmk.

491 A191 1.50k redsh brown 24 15
492 A191 2k dull blue 48 35

Peter Jilemnicky (1901-1949), writer.

1952, Jan. 12 *Perf. 11½*

493 A192 1.50k brown red 15 15
494 A192 4k gray 45 45

Centenary of the birth of Ladislav Zapotocky, Bohemian socialist pioneer.

Jan Kollar — A193

Lenin and Lenin Hall — A194

1952, Jan. 30 Unwmk. *Perf. 11½*

495 A193 3k dark carmine 15 15
496 A193 5k violet blue 65 50
Set value 55

Jan Kollar (1793-1852), poet.

1952, Jan. 30 *Perf. 12½*

497 A194 1.50k rose carmine 15 15
498 A194 5k deep blue 65 35
Set value 43

6th All-Russian Party Conf., 40th anniv.

Emil Holub and African — A195

Gottwald Metallurgical Plant — A196

1952, Feb. 21 *Perf. 11½*

499 A195 3k red brown 50 30
500 A195 5k gray 1.75 1.10

Death of Emil Holub, explorer, 50th anniv.

1952, Feb. 25 Photo. *Perf. 14*

Designs: 2k, Foundry. 3k, Chemical plant.

501 A196 1.50k sepia 25 15
502 A196 2k red brown 1.00 60
503 A196 3k scarlet 15 15
Nos. 501-503 (3) 1.40
Set value 75

Student, Soldier and Worker — A197

Youths of Three Races — A198

1952, Mar. 21 Unwmk. *Perf. 14*

504 A197 1.50k blue 15 15
505 A198 2k olive black 22 15
506 A197 3k lake 85 50
Nos. 504-506 (3) 1.22
Set value 65

International Youth Day, Mar. 25, 1952.

Similar to Type of 1951

Portrait: Otakar Sevcik.

1952, Mar. 22 Engr. *Perf. 12½*

507 A184 2k choc, *cr* 50 40
508 A184 3k rose brn, *cr* 15 15

Otakar Sevcik, violinist, birth cent.

Jan A. Komensky A199

Industrial and Farm Women A200

1952, Mar. 28

509 A199 1.50k dk brown, *cr* 1.25 60
510 A199 11k dk blue, *cr* 25 15

360th anniv. of the birth of Jan Amos Komensky (Comenius), teacher and philosopher.

1952, Mar. 8

511 A200 1.50k dp blue, *cr* 1.00 50

International Women's Day Mar. 8, 1952.

Woman and Children A201

Antifascist A202

1952, Apr. 12

512 A201 2k chocolate, *cr* 75 40
513 A201 3k dp claret, *cr* 16 15
Set value 46

Intl. Conf. for the Protection of Children, Vienna, Apr. 12-16, 1952.

1952, Apr. 11 Photo. *Perf. 14*

514 A202 1.50k red brown 15 15
515 A202 2k ultra 60 45
Set value 50

Day of International Solidarity of Fighters against Fascism, Apr. 11, 1952.

Harvester — A203

Design: 3k, Tractor and Seeders.

1952, Apr. 30

516 A203 1.50k deep blue 90 65
517 A203 2k brown 20 15
518 A203 3k brown red 20 15
Nos. 516-518 (3) 1.30 95

Youths Carrying Flags A204

1952, May 1

519 A204 3k brown red 55 40
520 A204 4k dk red brown 70 60

Issued to publicize Labor Day, May 1, 1952.

Crowd Cheering Soviet Soldiers A205

1952, May 9

521 A205 1.50k dark red 60 50
522 A205 5k deep blue 1.25 1.00

Liberation of Czechoslovakia from German occupation, 7th anniversary.

Czechoslovakia stamps can be mounted in the Scott Czechoslovakia album.

Children
A206

J. V. Myslbek
A207

Design: 3k, "Pioneer" teaching children.

1952, May 31 Engr. *Perf. 12½*

523 A206	1.50k dk brn, *cr*	15	15
524 A206	2k Prus grn, *cr*	*90*	*45*
525 A206	3k rose brn, *cr*	15	15
	Nos. 523-525 (3)	*1.20*	
	Set value		*55*

International Children's Day May 31, 1952.

1952, June 2

Design: 8k, Allegory, "Music."

526 A207	1.50k red brown	20	15
527 A207	2k dark brown	*95*	*95*
528 A207	8k gray green	15	15
	Nos. 526-528 (3)	*1.30*	*1.25*

Joseph V. Myslbek (1848-1922), sculptor.

Beethoven
A208

House of Artists
A209

1952, June 7 Unwmk. *Perf. 11½*

529 A208	1.50k sepia	35	25
530 A209	3k red brown	35	25
531 A208	5k indigo	*1.25*	*75*
	Nos. 529-531 (3)	*1.95*	*1.25*

International Music Festival, Prague, 1952.

Lidice, Symbol of a New Life — A210

1952, June 10 *Perf. 12½*

532 A210	1.50k dk violet brn	15	15
533 A210	5k dark blue	*75*	*50*
	Set value		*55*

Destruction of Lidice, 10th anniversary.

Jan Hus — A211

Bethlehem Chapel — A212

1952, July 5

534 A211	1.50k brown	15	15
535 A212	3k red brown	15	15
536 A211	5k black	*85*	*65*
	Nos. 534-536 (3)	*1.15*	*95*

550th anniv. of the installation of Jan Hus as pastor of Bethlehem Chapel, Prague.

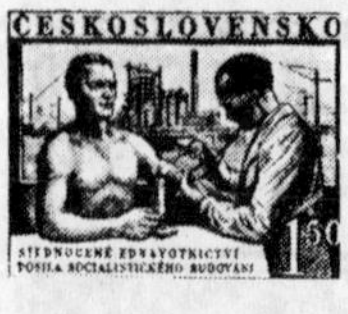
Doctor Examining Patient — A213

Design: 2k, Doctor, Nurse, Mother and child.

1952, July 31

537 A213	1.50k dark brown	*70*	*50*
538 A213	2k blue violet	16	15
539 A213	3k rose brown	16	15
	Nos. 537-539 (3)	*1.02*	
	Set value		*60*

Czechoslovakia's Unified Health Service.

Relay Race — A214

1952, Aug. 2 *Perf. 11½*

540 A214	1.50k shown	65	35
541 A214	2k Canoeing	*1.75*	*75*
542 A214	3k Cycling	35	35
543 A214	4k Hockey	*2.25*	*2.00*
	Nos. 540-543 (4)	*5.00*	*3.45*

Issued to publicize Czechoslovakia's Unified Physical Education program.

F. L. Celakovski
A215

Mikulas Ales
A216

1952, Aug. 5 *Perf. 12½*

544 A215	1.50k dark brown	15	15
545 A215	2k dark green	*75*	*50*
	Set value		*55*

Centenary of the death of Frantisek L. Celakovski, poet and writer.

Perf. 11x11½

1952, Aug. 30 Engr. Unwmk.

546 A216	1.50k dk gray grn	35	25
547 A216	6k red brown	*2.00*	*1.50*

Birth centenary of Mikulas Ales, painter.

17th Century Mining Towers — A217

Jan Zizka — A218

Designs: 1.50k, Coal Excavator. 2k, Peter Bezruc mine. 3k, Automatic coaling crane.

1952, Sept. 14 *Perf. 12½*

548 A217	1k sepia	*85*	*50*
549 A217	1.50k dark blue	15	15
550 A217	2k olive gray	15	15
551 A217	3k violet brown	18	15
	Nos. 548-551 (4)	*1.33*	
	Set value		*67*

Miners' Day, Sept. 14, 1952. No. 550 also for the 85th anniv. of the birth of Peter Bezruc (Vladimir Vasek), poet.

1952, Oct. 5 Engr. *Perf. 11½*
Inscribed: ". . . . Armady 1952,"

Designs: 2k, Fraternization with Russians. 3k, Marching with flag.

552 A218	1.50k rose lake	15	15
553 A218	2k olive bister	15	15
554 A218	3k dk car rose	15	15
555 A218	4k gray	*1.10*	*85*
	Nos. 552-555 (4)	*1.55*	
	Set value		*1.00*

Issued to publicize Army Day, Oct. 5, 1952.

Souvenir Sheet

Statues to Bulgarian Partisans and to Soviet Army — A219

1952, Oct. 18 Unwmk. *Perf. 12½*

556 A219	Sheet of 2	65.00	17.50
a.	2k deep carmine	20.00	5.75
b.	3k ultramarine	20.00	5.75

National Philatelic Exhibition, Bratislava, Oct. 18-Nov. 2, 1952.

Danube River, Bratislava — A220

1952, Oct. 18

557 A220	1.50k dark brown	15	15

National Philatelic Exhibition, Bratislava.

Conference with Lenin and Stalin — A221

Worker and Nurse Holding Dove and Olive Branch — A222

1952, Nov. 7

558 A221	2k brown black	*1.00*	*75*
559 A221	3k carmine	15	15

35th anniv. of the Russian Revolution and to publicize Czechoslovak-Soviet friendship.

1952, Nov. 15 Photo. *Perf. 14*

560 A222	2k brown	*85*	*50*
561 A222	3k red	15	15

Issued to publicize the first State Congress of the Czechoslovak Red Cross.

Matej Louda, Hussite Leader, Painted by Mikulas Ales
A223

Design: 3k, Dragon-killer Trutnov, painted by Ales.

1952, Nov. 18 Engr. *Perf. 11½*

562 A223	2k red brown	20	15
563 A223	3k grnsh gray	*30*	*15*
	Set value		*16*

Mikulas Ales, painter, birth cent.

Gottwald Type of 1948-49

1952, June 2 Unwmk. *Perf. 12½*
Size: 19x24mm

564 A135	1k dark green	15	15

"Peace" Flags — A224

Dove by Picasso — A225

1952, Dec. 12 Photo. *Perf. 14*

565 A224	3k red brown	25	15
566 A224	4k deep blue	*80*	*50*
	Set value		*55*

Issued to publicize the Congress of Nations for Peace, Vienna, Dec. 12-19, 1952.

1953, Jan. 17

Design: 4k, Czech Family.

567 A225	1.50k dark brown	15	15
568 A225	4k slate blue	*60*	*30*
	Set value		*35*

2nd Czechoslovak Peace Congress.

Smetana Museum — A226

Design: 4k, Jirásek Museum.

1953, Feb. 10 Engr. *Perf. 11½*

569 A226	1.50k dk violet brn	15	15
570 A226	4k dark gray	*1.00*	*65*
	Set value		*70*

Prof. Zdenek Nejedly, 75th birth anniv.

Martin Kukucin
A227

Jaroslav Vrchlicky
A228

Designs: 2k, Karel Jaromir Erben. 3k, Vaclav Matej Kramerius. 5k, Josef Dobrovsky.

1953, Feb. 28

571 A227	1k gray	15	15
572 A228	1.50k olive	15	15
573 A228	2k rose lake	15	15
574 A228	3k lt brown	20	15
575 A228	5k slate blue	*1.10*	*1.10*
	Set value	*1.50*	*1.40*

Issued to honor Czech writers and poets: 1k, 25th anniv. of death of Kukucin. 1.50k, birth cent. of Vrchlicky. 2k, cent. of completion of "Kytice" by Erben. 3k, birth bicent. of Kramerius. 5k, birth bicent. of Dobrovsky.

Militia
A229

Gottwald
A230

Design: 8k, Portraits of Stalin and Gottwald and Peoples Assembly.

Perf. 13½x14

1953, Feb. 25 Photo. Unwmk.

576 A229 1.50k deep blue	15	15
577 A230 3k red	15	15
578 A229 8k dark brown	*1.10*	*75*
Nos. 576-578 (3)	*1.40*	
Set value		*88*

5th anniv. of the defeat of the attempt to reinstate capitalism.

Book and Torch — A231

Design: 3k, Bedrich Vaclavek.

1953, Mar. 5 Engr. *Perf. 11½*

579 A231 1k sepia	*70*	*50*
580 A231 3k orange brown	15	15

Bedrich Vaclavek (1897-1943), socialist writer.

Stalin Type of 1949

Inscribed "21 XII 1879-5 III 1953"

1953, Mar. 12

581 A154 1.50k black	25	15

Death of Joseph Stalin, Mar. 5, 1953.

Mother and Child — A232

Girl Revolutionist — A233

1953, Mar. 8

582 A232 1.50k ultra	15	15
583 A233 2k brown red	*75*	*35*
Set value		*40*

International Women's Day.

Klement Gottwald — A234

1953, Mar. 19

584 A234 1.50k black	15	15
585 A234 3k black	15	15
Set value		15

Souvenir Sheet

Imperf

586 A234 5k black	2.25	1.75

Death of Pres. Klement Gottwald, Mar. 14, 1953.

Josef Pecka, Ladislav Zapotocky and Josef Hybes A236

1953, Apr. 7 Unwmk. *Perf. 11½*

587 A236 2k lt violet brn	15	15

75th anniversary of the first congress of the Czech Social Democratic Party.

Cyclists — A237

1953, Apr. 29

588 A237 3k deep blue	45	25

6th International Peace Bicycle Race, Prague-Berlin-Warsaw.

Medal of "May 1, 1890" A238

Designs: 1.50k, Lenin and Stalin. 3k, May Day Parade. 8k, Marx and Engels.

Engraved and Photogravure

1953, Apr. 30 *Perf. 11½x11, 14*

589 A238 1k chocolate	*1.00*	*70*
590 A238 1.50k dark gray	15	15
591 A238 3k carmine lake	15	15
592 A238 8k dk gray green	25	15
Nos. 589-592 (4)	*1.55*	
Set value		*95*

Issued to publicize Labor Day, May 1, 1953.

Sowing Grain — A239

1953, May 8 Photo. *Perf. 14*

593 A239 1.50k shown	30	15
594 A239 7k Reaper	*95*	*75*

Socialization of the village.

Dam — A240

Welder — A241

Design: 3k, Iron works.

1953, May 8 *Perf. 11½*

595 A240 1.50k gray	*52*	*45*
596 A241 2k blue gray	15	15
597 A240 3k red brown	15	15
Nos. 595-597 (3)	*82*	
Set value		*55*

Josef Slavik — A242

Leos Janacek — A243

1953, June 19

598 A242 75h dp gray blue	*42*	*15*
599 A243 1.60k dark brown	85	15
Set value		*22*

Issued on the occasion of the International Music Festival, Prague, 1953.

Gottwald Type of 1948-49

Perf. 12½ (15h, 1k), 11½ (20h, 3k)

1953

600 A135 15h yellow green	15	15
601 A135 20h dk violet brn	20	15
602 A135 1k purple	60	15
603 A135 3k brown car	15	15
604 A135 3k gray	65	15
Nos. 600-604 (5)	1.75	
Set value		25

Nos. 600-604 vary slightly in size.

Pres. Antonin Zapotocky — A244

1953, June 19 Photo. *Perf. 14*

605 A244 30h violet blue	45	15
606 A244 60h cerise	25	15
Set value		15

Julius Fucik A245

Book and Carnation A246

1953, Sept. 8 Engr. *Perf. 12½*

607 A245 40h dk violet brn	22	15
608 A246 60h pink	*40*	*25*
Set value		*30*

10th anniv. of the death of Julius Fucik, Communist leader executed by the Nazis.

Miner and Flag — A247

Design: 60h, Oil field and workers.

1953, Sept. 10 *Perf. 11½*

609 A247 30h gray	20	15
610 A247 60h brown vio	*75*	*50*
Set value		*55*

Miner's Day, Sept. 10, 1953.

Volleyball Game — A248

Motorcyclist — A249

Design: 60h, Woman throwing javelin.

1953, Sept. 15

611 A248 30h brown red	*1.50*	*1.50*
612 A249 40h dk violet brn	3.00	85
613 A248 60h rose violet	3.00	85
Nos. 611-613 (3)	7.50	*3.20*

Hussite Warrior — A250

Pres. Antonin Zapotocky — A251

Designs: 60h, Soldier presenting arms. 1k, Red army soldiers.

1953, Oct. 8

614 A250 30h brown	28	15
615 A250 60h rose lake	65	15
616 A250 1k brown red	*1.25*	*70*
Nos. 614-616 (3)	*2.18*	*1.00*

Issued to publicize Army Day, Oct. 3, 1953.

1953 Unwmk. *Perf. 11½, 12½*

617 A251 30h violet blue	26	15
618 A251 60h carmine rose	50	15
Set value		15

No. 617 is perf. 11½ and measures 19x23mm, No. 618 perf. 12½ and 18½x23½mm.

See No. 780.

Charles Bridge and Prague Castle — A252

Korean and Czech Girls — A253

1953, Aug. 15 Engr. *Perf. 11½*

619 A252 5k gray	2.25	15

1953, Oct. 11 *Perf. 11x11½*

620 A253 30h dark brown	3.00	1.50

Czechoslovakia's friendship with Korea.

Flags, Hradcany Castle and Kremlin — A254

Designs: 60h, Lomonosov University, Moscow. 1.20k, Lenin Ship Canal.

1953, Nov. 7

621 A254 30h dark gray	*1.10*	*75*
622 A254 60h dark brown	1.25	85
623 A254 1.20k ultra	2.25	1.50
Nos. 621-623 (3)	*4.60*	*3.10*

Czechoslovak-Soviet friendship month.

Emmy Destinn, Opera Singer — A255

National Theater, Prague — A256

Portrait: 2k, Eduard Vojan, actor.

1953, Nov. 18 *Perf. 14*

624 A255 30h blue black	85	40
625 A256 60h brown	25	15
626 A255 2k sepia	*2.25*	*65*
Nos. 624-626 (3)	*3.35*	*1.20*

Natl. Theater founding, 70th anniv.

Josef Manes — A257

Vaclav Hollar — A258

1953, Nov. 28 *Perf. 11x11½*
627 A257 60h brown carmine 35 15
628 A257 1.20k deep blue *1.10 52*

Issued to honor Josef Manes, painter.

1953, Dec. 5

Design: 1.20k, Head framed, facing right.

629 A258 30h brown black 20 15
630 A258 1.20k dark brown *80 45*

Vaclav Hollar, artist and etcher.

Leo N. Tolstoi — A259

1953, Dec. 29 **Unwmk.**
631 A259 60h dark green 20 15
632 A259 1k chocolate *1.10 65*

Leo N. Tolstoi, 125th birth anniv.

Locomotive A260

Design: 1k, Plane loading mail.

Engraved, Center Photogravure

1953, Dec. 29 *Perf. 11½x11*
633 A260 60h brn org & gray vio 45 25
634 A260 1k org brn & brt bl *1.25 75*

Lenin — A261

Lenin Museum, Prague — A262

1954, Jan. 21 **Engr.** *Perf. 11½*
635 A261 30h dark brown 45 15
636 A262 1.40k chocolate *1.00 90*

30th anniversary of the death of Lenin.

Klement Gottwald — A263

Design: 2.40k, Revolutionist with flag.

Perf. 11x11½, 14x13½

1954, Feb. 18
637 A263 60h dark brown 30 15
638 A263 2.40k rose lake *4.25 1.50*

25th anniversary of the fifth congress of the Communist Party in Czechoslovakia.

Gottwald Mausoleum, Prague — A264

Gottwald and Stalin A265

Design: 1.20k, Lenin & Stalin mausoleum, Moscow.

1954, Mar. 5 *Perf. 11½, 14x13½*
639 A264 30h olive brown 20 15
640 A265 60h deep ultra 26 15
641 A264 1.20k rose brown *1.25 85*
Nos. 639-641 (3) *1.71 1.15*

1st anniv. of the deaths of Stalin and Gottwald.

Two Runners — A266

Group of Hikers — A267

Design: 1k, Woman swimmer.

1954, Apr. 24 *Perf. 11½*
642 A266 30h dark brown 1.75 75
643 A267 80h dark green *5.75 3.50*
644 A266 1k dk violet blue 1.10 70
Nos. 642-644 (3) *8.60 4.95*

Nurse — A268

Designs: 15h, Construction worker. 40h, Postwoman. 45h, Ironworker. 50h, Soldier. 75h, Lathe operator. 80h, Textile worker. 1k, Farm woman. 1.20k, Scientist and microscope. 1.60k, Miner. 2k, Physician and baby. 2.40k, Engineer. 3k, Chemist.

1954 *Perf. 12½x12, 11½x11*
645 A268 15h dark green 22 15
646 A268 20h lt violet 28 15
647 A268 40h dark brown 40 15
648 A268 45h dk gray blue 15 15
649 A268 50h dk gray green 28 15
650 A268 75h deep blue 28 15
651 A268 80h violet brown 28 15
652 A268 1k green 55 15
653 A268 1.20k dk violet blue 28 15
654 A268 1.60k brown blk 95 15
655 A268 2k orange brown 1.25 15
656 A268 2.40k violet blue 1.00 15
657 A268 3k carmine 1.40 15
Nos. 645-657 (13) 7.32
Set value 75

Antonin Dvorák — A269

Prokop Divis — A270

Portraits: 40h, Leos Janacek. 60h, Bedrich Smetana.

1954, May 22 *Perf. 11x11½*
658 A269 30h violet brown 85 20
659 A269 40h brick red *1.40 20*
660 A269 60h dark blue 90 16
Nos. 658-660 (3) *3.15 56*

"Year of Czech Music," 1954.

1954, June 15
661 A270 30h gray 15 15
662 A270 75h violet brown *65 50*

200th anniv. of the invention of a lightning conductor by Prokop Divis.

Slovak Insurrectionist A271

Anton P. Chekhov A272

Design: 1.20k, Partisan woman.

1954, Aug. 28 *Perf. 11½*
663 A271 30h brown orange 18 15
664 A271 1.20k dark blue *80 75*

Slovak national uprising, 10th anniv.

1954, Sept. 24
665 A272 30h dull gray grn 15 15
666 A272 45h dull gray brn *90 65*

50th anniv. of the death of Chekhov, writer.

Soviet Representative Giving Agricultural Instruction A273

Designs: 60h, Soviet industrial instruction. 2k, Dancers (cultural collaboration).

1954, Nov. 6 *Perf. 11½x11*
667 A273 30h yellow brown 15 15
668 A273 60h dark blue 20 15
669 A273 2k vermilion *1.25 1.25*
Nos. 667-669 (3) *1.60 1.55*

Czechoslovak-Soviet friendship month.

Jan Neruda — A274

Portraits: 60h, Janko Jesensky. 1.60k, Jiri Wolker.

1954, Nov. 25 *Perf. 11x11½*
670 A274 30h dark blue 85 15
671 A274 60h dull red *1.40 50*
672 A274 1.60k sepia 35 18
Nos. 670-672 (3) *2.60 83*

Issued to honor Czechoslovak poets.

View of Telc — A275

Views: 60h, Levoca. 3k, Ceske Budejovice.

1954, Dec. 10 **Engr. & Photo.**
673 A275 30h black & bis 35 15
674 A275 60h brown & bis 35 15
675 A275 3k black & bis *2.00 1.50*
Nos. 673-675 (3) *2.70 1.80*

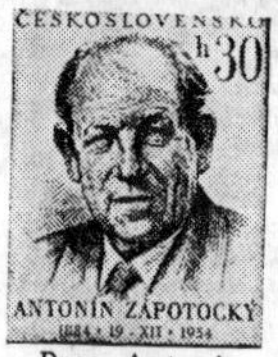

Pres. Antonin Zapotocky A276

Attacking Soldiers A278

1954, Dec. 18 **Engr.** *Perf. 11½*
676 A276 30h black brown 45 15
677 A276 60h dark blue 25 15

Souvenir Sheet

Imperf

678 A276 2k deep claret 5.00 3.00

70th birthday of Pres. Antonin Zapotocky. See Nos. 829-831.

1954, Oct. 3 *Perf. 11½*

Design: 2k, Soldier holding child.

679 A278 60h dark green 32 15
680 A278 2k dark brown *1.00 95*

Army Day, Oct. 6, 1954.

Woman Holding Torch — A279

Comenius University Building — A280

Design: 45h, Ski jumper.

1955, Jan. 20 **Engr.**
681 A279 30h red 1.90 25

Engraved and Photogravure

682 A279 45h black & blue 2.50 16

First National Spartacist Games, 1955.

1955, Jan. 28 **Engr.** *Perf. 11½*

Design: 75h, Jan A. Komensky medal.

683 A280 60h deep green 20 15
684 A280 75h chocolate *90 45*

35th anniversary of the founding of Comenius University, Bratislava.

Czechoslovak Automobile A281

Designs: 60h, Textile worker. 75h, Lathe operator.

1955, Mar. 15 **Unwmk.**
685 A281 45h dull green *65 45*
686 A281 60h dk violet blue 15 15
687 A281 75h sepia 35 15
Nos. 685-687 (3) *1.15*
Set value *55*

Woman Decorating Soviet Soldier — A282

Stalin Memorial, Prague — A283

Designs: 35h, Tankman with flowers. 60h, Children greeting soldier.

1955, May 5 Engr. *Perf. 11½*

688 A282	30h blue		25	15
689 A282	35h dark brown		*75*	*50*
690 A282	60h cerise		25	15

Photo.

691 A283	60h sepia		40	15
	Nos. 688-691 (4)		*1.65*	
	Set value			*65*

10th anniv. of Czechoslovakia's liberation.

Music and Spring — A284

Foundry Worker — A285

Design: 1k, Woman with lyre.

1955, May 12 Engr. & Photo.

692 A284	30h black & pale blue	35	25
693 A284	1k black & pale rose	*1.10*	*1.00*

International Music Festival, Prague, 1955.

1955, May 12 Engr.

Design: 45h, Farm workers.

694 A285	30h violet	15	15
695 A285	45h green	*60*	*45*
	Set value		*50*

Issued to publicize the third congress of the Trade Union Revolutionary Movement.

Woman Athlete — A286

Jakub Arbes — A287

Designs: 60h, Dancing couple. 1.60k, Athlete.

1955, June 21

696 A286	20h	violet blue	*65*	*35*
697 A286	60h	green	25	15
698 A286	1.60k	red	65	24
	Nos. 696-698 (3)		*1.55*	*74*

Issued to publicize the first National Spartacist Games, Prague, June-July, 1955.

1955

Portraits: 30h, Jan Stursa. 40h, Elena Marothy-Soltesova. 60h, Josef Vaclav Sladek. 75h, Alexander Stepanovic Popov. 1.40k, Jan Holly. 1.60k, Pavel Josef Safarik.

699 A287	20h	brown	25	15
700 A287	30h	black	25	15
701 A287	40h	gray green	75	15
702 A287	60h	black	50	15
703 A287	75h	claret	*1.10*	*70*
704 A287	1.40k	black, *cr*	50	18
705 A287	1.60k	dark blue	50	15
	Nos. 699-705 (7)		*3.85*	
	Set value			*1.20*

Various anniversaries of prominent Slavs.

Girl and Boy of Two Races — A288

Costume of Ocova, Slovakia — A289

1955, July 20

706 A288	60h violet blue	30	15

5th World Festival of Youth in Warsaw, July 31-Aug. 14.

1955, July 25

Regional Costumes: 75h, Detva man, Slovakia. 1.60k, Chodsko man, Bohemia. 2k, Hana woman, Moravia.

Frame and Outlines in Brown

707 A289	60h	orange & rose	*8.25*	*5.75*
708 A289	75h	orange & lilac	*4.75*	*3.00*
709 A289	1.60k	blue & orange	*8.25*	*4.75*
710 A289	2k	yellow & rose	*9.00*	*6.50*
	Nos. 707-710 (4)		*30.25*	*20.00*

Carp A290

Designs: 30h, Beetle. 35h, Gray Partridge. 1.40k, Butterfly. 1.50k, Hare.

1955, Aug. 8 Engr. & Photo.

711 A290	20h	sepia & lt bl	1.10	15
712 A290	30h	sepia & pink	65	15
713 A290	35h	sepia & buff	65	15
714 A290	1.40k	sepia & cream	*2.75*	*2.00*
715 A290	1.50k	sepia & lt grn	65	25
	Nos. 711-715 (5)		*5.80*	*2.70*

Tabor A291

Designs: 45h, Prachatice. 60h, Jindrichuv Hradec.

1955, Aug. 26 Engr.

716 A291	30h violet brown	20	15
717 A291	45h rose carmine	*75*	*60*
718 A291	60h sage green	20	15
	Nos. 716-718 (3)	*1.15*	
	Set value		*70*

Issued to publicize the architectural beauty of the towns of Southern Bohemia.

Souvenir Sheet

Various Views of Prague — A292

1955, Sept. 10 Engr. *Perf. 14x13½*

719 A292	Sheet of 5	22.50	20.00
a.	30h gray black	3.75	3.50
b.	45h gray black	3.75	3.50
c.	60h rose lake	3.75	3.50
d.	75h rose lake	3.75	3.50
e.	1.60k gray black	3.75	3.50

International Philatelic Exhibition, Prague, Sept. 10-25, 1955. Size: 145x110mm. Exists imperf., value $40.

Motorcyclists A293

Workers, Soldier and Pioneer A294

1955, Aug. 28

720 A293	60h violet brown	2.25	50

30th International Motorcycle Races at Gottwaldov, Sept. 13-18, 1955.

1955, Oct. 6 Unwmk. *Perf. 11½*

Army Day: 60h, Tanks and planes.

721 A294	30h violet brown	25	15
722 A294	60h slate	*1.25*	*1.25*

Hans Christian Andersen — A295

Portraits: 40h, Friedrich von Schiller. 60h, Adam Mickiewicz. 75h, Walt Whitman.

1955, Oct. 27

723 A295	30h brown red	15	15
724 A295	40h dark blue	*95*	*65*
725 A295	60h deep claret	15	15
726 A295	75h greenish black	30	15
	Nos. 723-726 (4)	*1.55*	
	Set value		*85*

Issued in honor of these four poets and to mark the 100th anniversary of the publication of Walt Whitman's "Leaves of Grass."

Railroad Bridge A296

Designs: 30h, Train crossing bridge. 60h, Train approaching tunnel. 1.60k, Miners' housing project.

Inscribed: "Stavba Socialismu"

1955, Dec. 15

727 A296	20h	dull green	25	20
728 A296	30h	violet brown	25	15
729 A296	60h	slate	25	15
730 A296	1.60k	carmine rose	50	15
	Nos. 727-730 (4)		1.25	
	Set value			35

Issued to publicize socialist public works.

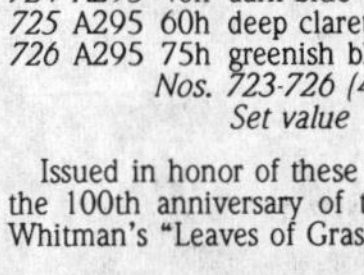
Hydroelectric Plant — A297

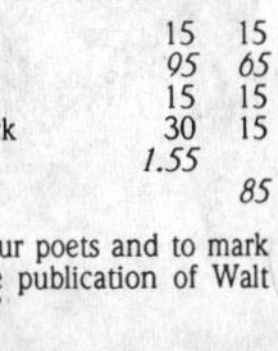
Jewelry — A298

2nd Five Year Plan: 10h, Miner with drill. 25h, Building construction. 30h, Harvester. 60h, Metallurgical plant.

Inscribed: "Druhy Petilety Plan 1956-1960."

1956, Feb. 20 *Perf. 11½x11*

731 A297	5h violet brown	20	15
732 A297	10h gray black	20	15
733 A297	25h dk car rose	20	15
734 A297	30h green	20	15
735 A297	60h violet blue	20	15
	Nos. 731-735 (5)	1.00	
	Set value		25

1956, Mar. 17 *Perf. 11x11½*

736 A298	30h shown	22	15
737 A298	45h Glassware	*3.75*	*2.00*
738 A298	60h Ceramics	65	15
739 A298	75h Textiles	22	15
	Nos. 736-739 (4)	*4.84*	*2.45*

Products of Czechoslovakian industries.

Karlovy Vary (Karlsbad) A299

"We Serve our People" A300

Various Spas: 45h, Marianske Lazne (Marienbad). 75h, Piestany. 1.20k, Tatry Vysne Ruzbachy (Tatra Mountains).

1956, Mar. 17

740 A299	30h	olive green	1.10	25
741 A299	45h	brown	85	20
742 A299	75h	claret	*6.00*	*4.00*
743 A299	1.20k	ultra	42	15
	Nos. 740-743 (4)		*8.37*	*4.60*

Issued to publicize Czechoslovakian spas.

1956, Apr. 9 Photo. *Perf. 11x11½*

Designs: 60h, Russian War Memorial, Berlin. 1k, Tank crewman with standard.

744 A300	30h olive brown	28	15
745 A300	60h carmine rose	28	15
746 A300	1k ultra	*4.75*	*3.00*
	Nos. 744-746 (3)	*5.31*	*3.30*

Exhibition: "The Construction and Defense of our Country," Prague, Apr., 1956.

Cyclists — A301

Girl Basketball Players — A302

Athletes and Olympic Rings — A303

Engraved and Photogravure

1956, Apr. 25 Unwmk. *Perf. 11½*

747 A301	30h green & lt blue	*2.50*	*20*
748 A302	45h dk blue & car	1.00	20
749 A303	75h brown & lemon	1.00	20
	Nos. 747-749 (3)	*4.50*	*60*

9th Intl. Peace Cycling Race, Warsaw-Berlin-Prague, May 1-15, 1956 (No. 747). 5th European Womens' Basketball Championship (No. 748). Summer Olympics, Melbourne, Nov. 22-Dec. 8, 1956 (No. 749).

Mozart — A304

Home Guard — A305

Designs: 45h, Josef Myslivecek. 60h, Jiri Benda. 1k, Bertramka House, Prague. 1.40k, Xaver Dusek (1731-1799) and wife Josepha. 1.60k, Nostic Theater, Prague.

1956, May 12 Engr.

Design in Gray Black

750	A304	30h bister		60	50
751	A304	45h gray green		*11.00*	*8.50*
752	A304	60h pale rose lilac		40	15
753	A304	1k salmon		1.00	30
754	A304	1.40k lt blue		2.25	25
755	A304	1.60k lemon		60	15
		Nos. 750-755 (6)		*15.85*	*9.85*

200th anniv. of the birth of Wolfgang Amadeus Mozart and to publicize the International Music Festival in Prague.

1956, May 25

756	A305	60h violet blue	60	15

Issued to commemorate the first meeting of the Home Guard, Prague, May 25-27, 1956.

Josef Kajetan Tyl — A306

River Patrol — A307

Portraits: 20h, Ludovit Stur. 30h, Frana Sramek. 1.40k, Karel Havlicek Borovsky.

1956, June 23

757	A306	20h dull purple	55	15
758	A306	30h blue	30	15
759	A306	60h black	30	15
760	A306	1.40k claret	*2.75*	*1.40*
		Nos. 757-760 (4)	*3.90*	*1.85*

Issued to honor various Czechoslovakian writers. See Nos. 781-784, 873-876.

1956, July 8 ***Perf. 11x11½***

Design: 60h, Guard and dog.

761	A307	30h ultra	*85*	*26*
762	A307	60h green	16	15
		Set value		*31*

Issued to honor men of Frontier Guard.

Type of 1956 and

Steeplechase — A308

1956, Sept. 8 Unwmk. ***Perf. 11½***

763	A308	60h indigo & bister	*1.75*	*40*
764	A308	80h brown vio & vio	1.00	15
765	A303	1.20k slate & orange	75	20
		Nos. 763-765 (3)	*3.50*	*75*

Steeplechase, Pardubice, 1956 (No. 763). Marathon race, Kosice, 1956 (No. 764). Olympic Games, Melbourne, Nov. 22-Dec. 8 (No. 765).

Woman Gathering Grapes — A309

Fishermen A310

Designs: 35h, Women gathering hops. 95h, Logging.

1956, Sept. 20 Engr.

766	A309	30h brown lake	25	15
767	A309	35h gray green	25	20
768	A310	80h dark blue	45	15
769	A310	95h chocolate	*1.50*	*1.40*
		Nos. 766-769 (4)	*2.45*	*1.90*

Issued to publicize natural resources.

European Timetable Conf., Prague, Nov. 9-13 — A311

A312

Locomotives: 10h, 1846. 30h, 1855. 40h, 1945. 45h, 1952. 60h, 1955. 1k, 1954.

1956, Nov. 9 Unwmk. ***Perf. 11½***

770	A311	10h brown	1.25	15
771	A312	30h gray	50	15
772	A312	40h green	3.00	15
773	A312	45h brown car	*14.00*	*9.50*
774	A312	60h indigo	50	15
775	A312	1k ultra	1.00	15
		Nos. 770-775 (6)	*20.25*	*10.25*

Costume of Moravia — A313

Regional Costumes (women): 1.20k, Blata, Bohemia. 1.40k, Cicmany, Slovakia. 1.60k, Novohradsko, Slovakia.

1956, Dec. 15 ***Perf. 13½***

776	A313	30h brn, ultra & car	1.90	60
777	A313	1.20k brn, car & ultra	1.50	15
778	A313	1.40k brn, ocher & ver	*3.75*	*1.75*
779	A313	1.60k brn, car & grn	1.90	40
		Nos. 776-779 (4)	*9.05*	*2.90*

See Nos. 832-835.

Zapotocky Type of 1953

1956, Oct. 7 Unwmk. ***Perf. 12½***

780	A251	30h blue	30	15

Portrait Type of 1956

Portraits: 15h, Ivan Olbracht. 20h, Karel Toman. 30h, F. X. Salda. 1.60k, Terezia Vansova.

1957, Jan. 18 Engr. ***Perf. 11½***

781	A306	15h dk red brn, *cr*	20	15
782	A306	20h dk green, *cr*	20	15
783	A306	30h dk brown, *cr*	20	15
784	A306	1.60k dk blue, *cr*	38	15
		Nos. 781-784 (4)	98	
		Set value		26

Issued in honor of Czechoslovakian writers.

Kolin Cathedral A315

Views: No. 786, Banska Stiavnica. No. 787, Uherske Hradiste. No. 788, Karlstein. No. 789, Charles Bridge, Prague. 1.25k, Moravska Trebova.

1957, Feb. 23

785	A315	30h dk blue gray	15	15
786	A315	30h rose violet	15	15
787	A315	60h deep rose	35	15
788	A315	60h gray green	35	15
789	A315	60h brown	26	15
790	A315	1.25k gray	*1.25*	*1.25*
		Nos. 785-790 (6)	*2.51*	
		Set value		*1.50*

Issued to commemorate anniversaries of various towns and landmarks.

Komensky Mausoleum, Naarden — A316

Jan A. Komensky — A317

Farm Woman — A318

Old Prints: 40h, Komensky teaching. 1k, Sun, moon, stars and earth.

Perf. 11½x11, 14 (A317)

1957, Mar. 28 Engr. Unwmk.

791	A316	30h pale brown	24	15
792	A316	40h dark green	24	15
793	A317	60h chocolate	*1.25*	*75*
794	A316	1k carmine rose	45	15
		Nos. 791-794 (4)	*2.18*	
		Set value		*1.00*

300th anniv. of the publication of "Didactica Opera Omnia" by J. A. Komensky (Comenius). No. 793 issued in sheets of four.

1957, Mar. 22 ***Perf. 11½***

795	A318	30h lt blue green	35	15

3rd Cong. of Agricultural Cooperatives.

Cyclists A319

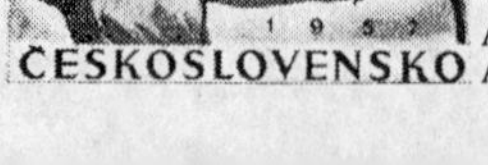

Woman Archer A320

Boxers — A321

Rescue Team A322

Perf. 11½x11, 11x11½

1957, Apr. 30

796	A319	30h sepia & ultra	25	15
797	A319	60h dull grn & bis	*1.50*	*1.25*
798	A320	60h gray & emer	25	15
799	A321	60h sepia & org	25	15
800	A322	60h violet & choc	25	15
		Nos. 796-800 (5)	*2.50*	
		Set value		*1.50*

10th Intl. Peace Cycling Race, Prague-Berlin-Warsaw (#796-797). Intl. Archery Championships (#798). European Boxing Championships, Prague (#799). Mountain Climbing Rescue Service (#800).

Jan V. Stamic — A323

Musicians: No. 802, Ferdinand Laub. No. 803, Frantisek Ondricek. No. 804, Josef B. Foerster. No. 805, Vitezslav Novak. No. 806, Josef Suk.

1957, May 12 ***Perf. 11½***

801	A323	60h purple	25	15
802	A323	60h black	25	15
803	A323	60h slate blue	25	15
804	A323	60h brown	25	15
805	A323	60h dull red brn	60	15
806	A323	60h blue green	25	15
		Nos. 801-806 (6)	1.85	
		Set value		45

Spring Music Festival, Prague.

Josef Bozek — A324

School of Engineering — A325

Portraits: 60h, F. J. Gerstner. 1k, R. Skuhersky.

1957, May 25

807	A324	30h bluish black	15	15
808	A324	60h gray brown	25	15
809	A324	1k rose lake	25	15
810	A325	1.40k blue violet	55	15
		Nos. 807-810 (4)	1.20	
		Set value		30

School of Engineering in Prague, 250th anniv.

Pioneer and Philatelic Symbols — A326

Design: 60h, Girl and carrier pigeon.

Engraved and Photogravure

1957, June 8 *Perf. 11½*

811	A326	30h	olive grn & org	50	15

Engr. *Perf. 13½*

812	A326	60h	brn & vio bl	*1.25*	*1.00*

Youth Philatelic Exhibition, Pardubice.

"Grief" A327

Motorcyclists A328

Design: 60h, Rose, symbol of new life.

1957, June 10

813	A327	30h	black	25	15
814	A327	60h	blk & rose red	*55*	*22*
			Set value		32

Destruction of Lidice, 15th anniversary.

1957, July 5 *Perf. 11½*

815	A328	60h	dk gray & blue	60	15

32nd International Motorcycle Race.

Karel Klic — A329

Josef Ressel — A330

1957, July 5

816	A329	30h	gray black	15	15
817	A330	60h	violet blue	24	15
			Set value		15

Klic, inventor of photogravure, and Ressel, inventor of the ship screw.

Chamois — A331

Gentian A332

Designs: 30h, Brown bear. 60h, Edelweiss. 1.25k, Tatra Mountains.

1957, Aug. 28 **Engr.** *Perf. 11½*

818	A331	20h	emer & brnsh gray	60	35
819	A331	30h	lt blue & brn	50	15
820	A332	40h	gldn brn & vio bl	75	15
821	A332	60h	yellow & grn	35	15

Size: 48x28½mm

822	A332	1.25k	ol grn & bis	*1.50*	*1.25*
			Nos. 818-822 (5)	*3.70*	
			Set value		*1.80*

Tatra Mountains National Park.

"Marycka Magdonova" A333

Man Holding Banner of Trade Union Cong. A334

Engraved and Photogravure

1957, Sept. 15 **Unwmk.** *Perf. 11½*

823	A333	60h	black & dull red	30	15

90th birthday of Petr Bezruc, poet and author of "Marycka Magdonova."

1957, Sept. 28 **Engr.**

824	A334	75h	rose red	38	15

4th Intl. Trade Union Cong., Leipzig, Oct. 4-15.

Television Transmitter and Antennas — A335

Design: 60h, Family watching television.

1957, Oct. 19 **Engr.** *Perf. 11½*

825	A335	40h	dk blue & car	20	15
826	A335	60h	redsh brown & emer	24	15
			Set value		15

Issued to publicize the television industry.

Worker, Globe and Lenin A336

Design: 60h, Worker, factory, hammer and sickle.

1957, Nov. 7 *Perf. 12x11½*

827	A336	30h	claret	20	15
828	A336	60h	gray blue	24	15
			Set value		15

Russian Revolution, 40th anniversary.

Zapotocky Type of 1954 dated: 19 XII 1884-13 XI 1957

1957, Nov. 18 **Unwmk.** *Perf. 11½*

829	A276	30h	black	15	15
830	A276	60h	black	22	15
			Set value		15

Souvenir Sheet

Imperf

831	A276	2k	black	1.00	75

Death of Pres. Antonin Zapotocky.

Costume Type of 1956

Regional Costumes: 45h, Pilsen woman, Bohemia. 75h, Slovacko man, Moravia. 1.25k, Hana woman, Moravia. 1.95k, Teshinsko woman, Silesia.

1957, Dec. 18 **Engr.** *Perf. 13½*

832	A313	45h	brn, bl & dk red	2.50	1.00
833	A313	75h	dk brn, red & grn	1.75	80
834	A313	1.25k	dk brn, scar & ocher	2.50	75
835	A313	1.95k	sepia, bl & ver	*3.00*	*2.00*
			Nos. 832-835 (4)	*9.75*	*4.55*

A337

A338

Designs: 30h, Radio telescope and observatory. 45h, Meteorological station in High Tatra. 75h, Sputnik 2 over Earth.

1957, Dec. 20 *Perf. 11½*

836	A337	30h	violet brn & yel	1.75	70
837	A338	45h	sepia & lt bl	45	35
838	A337	75h	claret & blue	2.50	1.00
			Nos. 836-838 (3)	4.70	2.05

IGY, 1957-58. No. 838 also for the launching of Sputnik 2, Nov. 3, 1957.

Girl Skater — A339

Litomysl Castle — A340

Designs: 40h, Canoeing. 60h, Volleyball. 80h, Parachutist. 1.60k, Soccer.

1958, Jan. 25 **Engr.** *Perf. 11½x12*

839	A339	30h	rose violet	1.25	25
840	A339	40h	blue	25	15
841	A339	60h	redsh brown	25	15
842	A339	80h	violet blue	*1.50*	*50*
843	A339	1.60k	brt green	45	15
			Nos. 839-843 (5)	*3.70*	*1.20*

Issued to publicize various sports championship events in 1958.

1958, Feb. 10 *Perf. 11½*

Design: 60h, Bethlehem Chapel.

844	A340	30h	green	20	15
845	A340	60h	redsh brown	20	15
			Set value		15

80th anniversary of the birth of Zdenek Nejedly, restorer of Bethlehem Chapel.

Giant Excavator — A341

Jewelry — A342

Peace Dove and: 60h, Soldiers, flame and banner, horiz. 1.60k, Harvester and rainbow, horiz.

1958, Feb. 25

846	A341	30h	gray violet & yel	20	15
847	A341	60h	gray brown & car	25	15
848	A341	1.60k	green & dull yel	50	15
			Nos. 846-848 (3)	95	
			Set value		21

10th anniv. of the "Victorious February."

Engraved and Photogravure

1958 **Unwmk.** *Perf. 11½*

Designs: 45h, Dolls. 60h, Textiles. 75h, Kaplan turbine. 1.20k, Glass.

849	A342	30h	rose car & blue	15	15
850	A342	45h	rose red & pale lil	20	15
851	A342	60h	violet & aqua	15	15
852	A342	75h	ultra & salmon	*1.10*	*75*
853	A342	1.20k	blue grn & pink	28	15
			Nos. 849-853 (5)	*1.88*	
			Set value		*1.00*

Issued for the Universal and International Exposition at Brussels.

King George of Podebrad A343

Design: 60h, View of Prague, 1628.

1958, May 19 **Engr.**

854	A343	30h	carmine rose	35	15
855	A343	60h	violet blue	30	15
			Set value		15

Issued to publicize the National Archives Exhibition, Prague, May 15-Aug. 15.

"Towards the Stars" — A344

Women of Three Races — A345

Boy, Girl and Globes A346

1958, May 26

856	A344	30h	carmine rose	*75*	*35*
857	A345	45h	rose violet	20	15
858	A346	60h	blue	18	15
			Nos. 856-858 (3)	*1.13*	*65*

The Soc. for Dissemination of Political and Cultural Knowledge (#856). 4th Cong. of the Intl. Democratic Women's Fed. (#857). 1st World Trade Union Conf. of Working Youths, Prague, July 14-20 (#858).

Grain, Hammer and Sickle A347

Atomic Reactor A348

Design: 45h, Map of Czechoslovakia, hammer and sickle.

1958, May 26

859	A347	30h	dull red	16	15
860	A347	45h	green	16	15
861	A348	60h	dark blue	20	15
			Nos. 859-861 (3)	52	
			Set value		17

11th Congress of the Czech Communist Party and the 15th anniv. of the Russo-Czechoslovakian Treaty.

Karlovy Vary
A349

Various Spas: 40h, Podebrady. 60h, Marianske Lazne. 80h, Luhacovice. 1.20k, Strbske Pleso. 1.60k, Trencianske Teplice.

1958, June 25

862	A349	30h rose claret	15	15
863	A349	40h redsh brown	15	15
864	A349	60h gray green	15	15
865	A349	80h sepia	20	15
866	A349	1.20k violet blue	32	15
867	A349	1.60k lt violet	*1.10*	*80*
		Nos. 862-867 (6)	*2.07*	
		Set value		*1.15*

Telephone Operator
A350

Pres. Novotny
A351

Design: 45h, Radio transmitter.

1958, June 20

868	A350	30h black & brn org	25	15
869	A350	45h black & lt grn	35	20
		Set value		28

Conference of Postal Ministers of Communist Countries, Prague, June 30-July 9.

1958-59 ***Perf. 12½***

870	A351	30h brt violet blue	20	15
b.		Perf. 11½	20	20
870A	A351	30h lt violet ('59)	*80*	*50*
871	A351	60h carmine rose	22	15

Perf. 11½

Redrawn

871A	A351	60h rose red	20	15
		Nos. 870-871A (4)	*1.42*	
		Set value		*70*

On No. 871 the top of the "6" turns down; on No. 871A it is open.

Czechoslovak Pavilion, Brussels — A352

1958, July 15 **Engr. & Photo.**

872	A352	1.95k lt blue & bis brn	90	15

Czechoslovakia Week at the Universal and International Exhibition at Brussels.

Portrait Type of 1956

Portraits: 30h, Julius Fucik. 45h, G. K. Zechenter 60h, Karel Capek. 1.40k, Svatopluk Cech.

1958, Aug. 20 **Engr.** ***Perf. 11½***

873	A306	30h rose red	25	15
874	A306	45h violet	*1.25*	*50*
875	A306	60h dk blue gray	15	15
876	A306	1.40k gray	50	15
		Nos. 873-876 (4)	*2.15*	
		Set value		*75*

Death anniversaries of four famous Czechs.

The Artist and the Muse — A353

1958, Aug. 20 ***Perf. 14***

877	A353	1.60k black	2.75	1.25

85th birthday of Max Svabinsky, artist and engraver.

Children's Hospital, Brno
A354

Designs: 60h, New Town Hall, Brno. 1k, St. Thomas Church. 1.60k, View of Brno.

1958, Sept. 6 **Unwmk.** ***Perf. 11½***

Size: 40x23mm

878	A354	30h violet	15	15
879	A354	60h rose red	20	15
880	A354	1k brown	45	15

Perf. 14

Size: 50x28mm

881	A354	1.60k dk slate grn	*1.90*	*1.75*
		Nos. 878-881 (4)	*2.70*	*2.20*

Natl. Phil. Exhib., Brno, Sept. 9.

No. 881 sold for 3.10k, including entrance ticket to exhibition. Issued in sheets of four.

Lepiota Procera — A355

Children on Beach — A356

Mushrooms: 40h, Boletus edulis. 60h, Krombholzia rufescens. 1.40k, Amanita muscaria L. 1.60k, Armillariella mellea.

1958, Oct. 6 ***Perf. 14***

882	A355	30h dk brn, grn & buff	25	15
883	A355	40h vio brn & brn org	25	15
884	A355	60h black, red & buff	25	15
885	A355	1.40k brown, scar & grn	75	25
886	A355	1.60k blk, red brn & ol	*2.75*	*1.10*
		Nos. 882-886 (5)	*4.25*	*1.80*

1958, Oct. 24 **Unwmk.** ***Perf. 14***

Designs: 45h, Mother, child and bird. 60h, Skier.

887	A356	30h blue, yel & red	15	15
888	A356	45h ultra & carmine	24	15
889	A356	60h brown, blue & yel	35	15
		Nos. 887-889 (3)	74	
		Set value		30

UNESCO Headquarters in Paris opening, Nov. 3.

Bozek's Steam Car of 1815
A357

Designs: 45h, "Präsident" car of 1897. 60h, "Skoda" sports car. 80h, "Tatra" sedan. 1k, "Autocar Skoda" bus. 1.25k, Trucks.

Engraved and Photogravure

1958, Dec. 1 ***Perf. 11½x11***

890	A357	30h vio blk & buff	50	15
891	A357	45h ol & lt ol grn	38	15
892	A357	60h ol gray & sal	55	15
893	A357	80h claret & bl grn	38	15
894	A357	1k brn & lt yel grn	38	15
895	A357	1.25k green & buff	*2.00*	*60*
		Nos. 890-895 (6)	*4.19*	
		Set value		*1.05*

Issued to honor the automobile industry.

Stamp of 1918 and Allegory — A358

1958, Dec. 18 **Engr.** ***Perf. 11x11½***

896	A358	60h dark blue gray	28	15

40th anniv. of the 1st Czechoslovakian postage stamp.

Ice Hockey
A359

Sports: 30h, Girl throwing javelin. 60h, Ice hockey. 1k, Hurdling. 1.60k, Rowing. 2k, High jump.

1959, Feb. 14 ***Perf. 11½x11***

897	A359	20h dk brown & gray	26	15
898	A359	30h red brn & org brn	26	15
899	A359	60h dk bl & pale grn	20	15
900	A359	1k maroon & citron	38	15
901	A359	1.60k dull vio & lt bl	55	15
902	A359	2k red brn & lt bl	*1.75*	*1.00*
		Nos. 897-902 (6)	*3.40*	
		Set value		*1.30*

Congress Emblem — A360

"Equality of All Races" — A361

Design: 60h, Industrial and agricultural workers and emblem.

1959, Feb. 27 ***Perf. 11½***

903	A360	30h maroon & lt blue	15	15
904	A360	60h dk blue & yellow	16	15
		Set value		15

4th Agricultural Cooperative Cong. in Prague.

1959, Mar. 23

Designs: 1k, "Peace." 2k, Mother and Child: "Freedom for Colonial People."

905	A361	60h gray green	18	15
906	A361	1k gray	25	15
907	A361	2k dk gray blue	*1.25*	*50*
		Nos. 905-907 (3)	*1.68*	
		Set value		*64*

10th anniversary of the signing of the Universal Declaration of Human Rights.

Girl Holding Doll — A362

Frederic Joliot Curie — A363

Designs: 40h, Pioneer studying map. 60h, Pioneer with radio. 80h, Girl pioneer planting tree.

1959, Mar. 28 **Engr. & Photo.**

908	A362	30h violet bl & yel	20	15
909	A362	40h indigo & ultra	20	15
910	A362	60h black & lilac	15	15
911	A362	80h brown & lt green	30	15
		Nos. 908-911 (4)	85	
		Set value		45

10th anniv. of the Pioneer organization.

1959, Apr. 17 **Engr.**

912	A363	60h sepia	75	25

Frederic Joliot Curie and the 10th anniversary of the World Peace Movement.

"Reaching for the Moon" — A364

Town Hall Pilsen — A365

1959, Apr. 17

913	A364	30h violet blue	95	25

2nd Cong. of the Czechoslovak Assoc. for the Propagation of Political and Cultural knowledge.

1959, May 2

Designs: 60h, Part of steam condenser turbine. 1k, St. Bartholomew's Church, Pilsen. 1.60k, Part of lathe.

914	A365	30h lt brown	15	15
915	A365	60h violet & lt grn	20	15
916	A365	1k violet blue	30	15
917	A365	1.60k black & yellow	*1.25*	*85*
		Nos. 914-917 (4)	*1.90*	
		Set value		*1.05*

2nd Pilsen Stamp Exhib. in connection with the centenary of the Skoda (Lenin) armament works.

Factory and Emblem
A366

Inscribed: "IV Vseodborovy sjezd, 1959"

1959, May 13

918	A366	30h shown	15	15
919	A366	60h Dam	20	15
		Set value		15

4th Trade Union Congress.

Zvolen Castle A367

1959, June 13

920	A367	60h	gray olive & yel	30	15

Regional Stamp Exhibition, Zvolen, 1959.

Frantisek Benda — A368

Aurel Stodola — A369

Portraits: 30h, Vaclav Kliment Klicpera. 60h, Karel V. Rais. 80h, Antonin Slavicek. 1k, Peter Bezruc.

1959, June 22 *Perf. 11½x11*

921	A368	15h	violet blue	15	15
922	A368	30h	orange brown	15	15
923	A369	40h	dull green	15	15
924	A369	60h	dull red brn	25	15
925	A369	80h	dull violet	25	15
926	A368	1k	dark brown	25	15
			Nos. 921-926 (6)	1.20	
			Set value		35

View of the Fair Grounds A370

Designs: 60h, Fair emblem and world map. 1.60k, Pavilion "Z."

Inscribed: "Mezinarodni Veletrh Brne 6.-20.IX. 1959"

Engraved and Photogravure

1959, July 20 **Unwmk.** *Perf. 11½*

927	A370	30h	lilac & yellow	15	15
928	A370	60h	dull blue	25	15
929	A370	1.60k	dk blue & bister	40	15
			Nos. 927-929 (3)	80	
			Set value		20

International Fair at Brno, Sept. 6-20.

Revolutionist and Flag — A371

Slovakian Fighter — A372

Design: 1.60k, Linden leaves, sun and factory.

Perf. 11½

1959, Aug. 29 **Unwmk.** **Engr.**

930	A371	30h	black & rose	16	15
931	A372	60h	carmine rose	25	15
932	A371	1.60k	dk blue & yel	45	15
			Nos. 930-932 (3)	86	
			Set value		20

Natl. Slovakian revolution, 15th anniv. and Slovakian Soviet Republic, 40th anniv.

Alpine Marmots A373

1959, Sept. 25 **Engr. & Photo.**

933	A373	30h	shown	35	15
934	A373	40h	Bison	50	15
935	A373	60h	Lynx, vert.	1.00	15
936	A373	1k	Wolf	*1.75*	*80*
937	A373	1.60k	Red deer	75	15
			Nos. 933-937 (5)	*4.35*	*1.40*

Tatra National Park, 10th anniv.

Lunik 2 Hitting Moon and Russian Flag A374

1959, Sept. 23 *Perf. 11½*

938	A374	60h	dk red & lt ultra	85	25

Issued to commemorate the landing of the Soviet rocket on the moon, Sept. 13, 1959.

Stamp Printing Works, Peking A375

1959, Oct. 1

939	A375	30h	pale green & red	20	15

10 years of Czechoslovakian-Chinese friendship.

Haydn — A376

Great Spotted Woodpecker — A377

Design: 3k, Charles Darwin.

1959, Oct. 16 **Engr.** *Perf. 11½*

940	A376	60h	violet black	45	15
941	A376	3k	dark red brown	*1.10*	*52*

150th death anniv. of Franz Joseph Haydn, Austrian composer, and 150th birth anniv. of Charles Darwin, English naturalist.

1959, Nov. 16 *Perf. 14*

Birds: 30h, Blue tits. 40h, Nuthatch. 60th, Golden oriole. 80h, Goldfinch. 1k, Bullfinch. 1.20k, European kingfisher.

942	A377	20h	multicolored	42	15
943	A377	30h	multicolored	42	15
944	A377	40h	multicolored	*1.65*	*1.00*
945	A377	60h	multicolored	42	15
946	A377	80h	multicolored	42	20
947	A377	1k	multicolored	42	15
948	A377	1.20k	multicolored	85	50
			Nos. 942-948 (7)	*4.60*	*2.30*

Nikola Tesla A378

Designs: 30h, Alexander S. Popov. 35h, Edouard Branly. 60h, Guglielmo Marconi. 1k, Heinrich Hertz. 2k, Edwin Howard Armstrong and research tower, Alpine, N. J.

Engraved and Photogravure

1959, Dec. 7 *Perf. 11½*

949	A378	25h	black & pink	*50*	*15*
950	A378	30h	black & orange	15	15
951	A378	35h	black & lt vio	16	15
952	A378	60h	black & blue	20	15
953	A378	1k	black & lt grn	25	15
954	A378	2k	black & bister	*1.50*	*42*
			Nos. 949-954 (6)	*2.76*	
			Set value		*75*

Issued to honor inventors in the fields of telegraphy and radio.

Gymnast — A379

2nd Winter Spartacist Games: 60h, Skier. 1.60k, Basketball players.

1960, Jan. 20 *Perf. 11½*

955	A379	30h	salmon pink & brn	50	15
956	A379	60h	lt blue & blk	20	15
957	A379	1.60k	bister & brn	30	25
			Nos. 955-957 (3)	1.00	
			Set value		45

1960, June 15 **Unwmk.**

Designs: 30h, Two girls in "Red Ball" drill. 60h, Gymnast with stick. 1k, Three girls with hoops.

958	A379	30h	lt grn & rose claret	15	15
959	A379	60h	pink & black	25	15
960	A379	1k	ocher & vio bl	45	15
			Nos. 958-960 (3)	85	
			Set value		32

2nd Summer Spartacist Games, Prague, June 23-July 3.

River Dredge Boat A380

Ships: 60h, River tug. 1k, Tourist steamer. 1.20k, Cargo ship "Lidice."

1960, Feb. 22 *Perf. 11½*

961	A380	30h	slate grn & sal	45	15
962	A380	60h	maroon & pale bl	15	15
963	A380	1k	dk violet & yel	45	15
964	A380	1.20k	lilac & pale grn	*60*	*90*
			Nos. 961-964 (4)	*1.65*	*1.35*

Ice Hockey Players — A381

Design: 1.80k, Figure skaters.

1960, Feb. 27

965	A381	60h	sepia & lt blue	30	25
966	A381	1.80k	black & lt green	*3.25*	*2.50*

8th Olympic Winter Games, Squaw Valley, Calif., Feb. 18-29, 1960.

1960, June 15 **Unwmk.**

Designs: 1k, Running. 1.80k, Women's gymnastics. 2k, Rowing.

967	A381	1k	black & orange	42	16
968	A381	1.80k	black & sal pink	1.00	25
969	A381	2k	black & blue	*1.65*	*95*
			Nos. 967-969 (3)	*3.07*	*1.36*

17th Olympic Games, Rome, Aug. 25-Sept. 11.

Trencin Castle — A382

Castles: 10h, Bezdez. 20h, Kost. 30h, Pernstein. 40h, Kremnica. 50h, Krivoklát castle. 60h, Karlstein. 1k, Smolenice. 1.60k, Kokorin.

1960-63 **Engr.** *Perf. 11½*

970	A382	5h	gray violet	15	15
971	A382	10h	black	15	15
972	A382	20h	brown org	25	15
973	A382	30h	green	16	15
974	A382	40h	brown	16	15
974A	A382	50h	black ('63)	16	15
975	A382	60h	rose red	25	15
976	A382	1k	lilac	30	15
977	A382	1.60k	dark blue	60	15
			Nos. 970-977 (9)	2.18	
			Set value		45

1961, Oct. **Wmk. 341**

977A	A382	30h	green	1.50	15

Lenin — A383

Soldier Holding Child — A384

1960, Apr. 22 **Unwmk.**

978	A383	60h	gray olive	40	20

90th anniversary of the birth of Lenin.

1960, May 5 **Engr. & Photo.**

Designs: No. 980, Child eating pie. No. 981, Soldier helping concentration camp victim. No. 982, Welder and factory, horiz. No. 983, Tractor driver and farm, horiz.

979	A384	30h	maroon & lt blue	25	15
980	A384	30h	dull red	20	15
981	A384	30h	green & dull blue	20	15
982	A384	60h	dk blue & buff	35	15
983	A384	60h	redsh brn & yel grn	35	15
			Nos. 979-983 (5)	1.35	
			Set value		35

15th anniversary of liberation.

Steelworker — A385

Design: 60h, Farm woman and child.

1960, May 24

984	A385	30h	maroon & gray	16	15
985	A385	60h	green & pale blue	28	15
			Set value		15

1960 parliamentary elections.

Red Cross Nurse Holding Dove A386

Fire Fighters A387

1960, May 26 **Unwmk.**

986	A386	30h brown car & bl	16	15
987	A387	60h dk blue & pink	28	15
		Set value		15

3rd Congress of the Czechoslovakian Red Cross (No. 986), and the 2nd Fire Fighters' Congress (No. 987).

Hand of Philatelist with Tongs and Two Stamps A388

Design: 1k, Globe and 1937 Bratislava stamp (shown in miniature on 60h).

1960, July 11 ***Perf. 11½***

988	A388	60h black & dull yel	40	15
989	A388	1k black & blue	60	15
		Set value		18

Issued to publicize the National Stamp Exhibition, Bratislava, Sept. 24-Oct. 9.
See Nos. C49-C50.

Stalin Mine, Ostrava-Hermanovice A390

Viktorin Cornelius, Lawyer A391

Designs: 20h, Power station, Hodonin. 30h, Gottwald iron works, Kuncice. 40h, Harvester. 60h, Oil refinery.

1960, July 25

992	A390	10h black & pale grn	16	15
993	A390	20h maroon & lt bl	16	15
994	A390	30h indigo & pink	16	15
995	A390	40h green & pale lilac	16	15
996	A390	60h dk blue & yel	20	15
		Nos. 992-996 (5)	84	
		Set value		30

Issued to publicize the new five-year plan.

1960, Aug. 23 **Engr.**

Portraits: 20h, Karel Matej Capek-Chod, writer. 30h, Hana Kvapilova, actress. 40h, Oskar Nedbal, composer. 60h, Otakar Ostrcil, composer.

997	A391	10h black	20	15
998	A391	20h red brown	20	15
999	A391	30h rose red	25	15
1000	A391	40h dull green	35	15
1001	A391	60h gray violet	25	15
		Nos. 997-1001 (5)	1.25	
		Set value		45

See Nos. 1037-1041.

Skoda Sports Plane Flying Upside Down A392

1960, Aug. 28 **Engr. & Photo.**

1002	A392	60h violet blue & blue	75	15

1st aerobatic world championships, Bratislava.

Constitution and "Czechoslovakia" — A393

1960, Sept. 18

1003	A393	30h violet bl & pink	20	15

Proclamation of the new socialist constitution.

Workers Reading Newspaper A394

Man Holding Newspaper — A395

1960, Sept. 18

1004	A394	30h slate & ver	15	15
1005	A395	60h black & rose	22	15
		Set value		15

Day of the Czechoslovak Press, Sept. 21, 1960, and 40th anniv. of the Rudé Právo paper.

Globes and Laurel A396

1960, Sept. 18 **Engr.**

1006	A396	30h dk blue & bister	25	15

World Federation of Trade Unions, 15th anniv.

Black-crowned Night Heron — A397

Doronicum Clusii (Thistle) — A398

Birds: 30h, Great crested grebe. 40h, Lapwing. 60h, Gray heron. 1k, Graylag goose, horiz. 1.60k, Mallard, horiz.

Engraved and Photogravure

1960, Oct. 24 **Unwmk.** ***Perf. 11½***

Designs in Black

1007	A397	25h pale vio blue	15	15
1008	A397	30h pale citron	50	15
1009	A397	40h pale blue	25	15
1010	A397	60h pink	35	15
1011	A397	1k pale yellow	50	15
1012	A397	1.60k lt violet	*2.00*	*1.00*
		Nos. 1007-1012 (6)	*3.75*	
		Set value		*1.45*

1960, Nov. 21 **Engr.** ***Perf. 14***

Flowers: 30h, Cyclamen. 40h, Primrose. 60h, Hen-and-chickens. 1k, Gentian. 2k, Pasqueflower.

1013	A398	20h black, yel & grn	25	15
1014	A398	30h black, car rose & grn	32	15
1015	A398	40h black, yel & grn	32	15
1016	A398	60h black, pink & grn	32	15
1017	A398	1k black, bl, vio & grn	55	15
1018	A398	2k black, lil, yel & grn	*2.25*	*1.00*
		Nos. 1013-1018 (6)	*4.01*	
		Set value		*1.50*

Alfons Mucha — A399

1960, Dec. 18 **Engr.** ***Perf. 11½x12***

1019	A399	60h dk blue gray	30	15

Day of the Czechoslovak Postage Stamp and birth cent. of Alfons Mucha, designer of the 1st Czechoslovakian stamp (Type A1).

Rolling-mill Control Bridge — A400

Athletes with Flags — A401

Designs: 30h, Turbo generator. 60h, Ditch-digging machine.

1961, Jan. 20 **Unwmk.** ***Perf. 11½***

1020	A400	20h blue	15	15
1021	A400	30h rose	15	15
1022	A400	60h brt green	22	15
		Nos. 1020-1022 (3)	52	
		Set value		15

Third Five-Year Plan.

Perf. 11x11½, 11½x11

1961, Feb. 20 **Engr. & Photo.**

Designs: No. 1024, Motorcycle race, horiz. 40h, Sculling, horiz. 60h, Ice skater. 1k, Rugby. 1.20k, Soccer. 1.60k, Long-distance runners.

1023	A401	30h rose red & bl	20	15
1024	A401	30h dk blue & car	20	15
1025	A401	40h dk gray & car	35	15
1026	A401	60h lilac & blue	30	15
1027	A401	1k ultra & yel	30	15
1028	A401	1.20k green & buff	50	15
1029	A401	1.60k sepia & salmon	*2.00*	*1.00*
		Nos. 1023-1029 (7)	*3.85*	
		Set value		*1.45*

Various sports events.

Exhibition Emblem A402

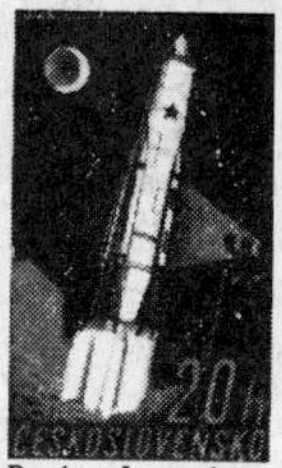

Rocket Launching A403

1961, Mar. 6 **Engr.** ***Perf. 11½***

1030	A402	2k dk blue & red	1.25	15

"Praga 1962" International Stamp Exhibition, Prague, Sept. 1962.

1961, Mar. 6 **Engr. & Photo.**

Designs: 30h, Sputnik III, horiz. 40h, As 20h, but inscribed "Start Kosmicke Rakety k Venusi - 12.II.1961". 60h, Sputnik I, horiz. 1.60k, Interplanetary station, horiz. 2k, Similar to type A404, without commemorative inscription.

1031	A403	20h violet & pink	35	15
1032	A403	30h dk green & buff	50	15
1033	A403	40h dk red & yel grn	35	15
1034	A403	60h violet & buff	25	15
1035	A403	1.60k dk bl & pale grn	35	15
1036	A403	2k mar & pale bl	*1.90*	*1.10*
		Nos. 1031-1036 (6)	*3.70*	
		Set value		*1.55*

Issued to publicize Soviet space research.

Portrait Type of 1960

Portraits: No. 1037, Jindrich Mosna. No. 1038, Pavol Orszagh Hviezdoslav. No. 1039, Alois Mrstik. No. 1040, Joza Uprka. No. 1041, Josef Hora.

1961, Mar. 27 ***Perf. 11½***

1037	A391	60h green	20	15
1038	A391	60h dark blue	20	15
a.		"ORSZACH" instead of "ORSZAGH"	*30.00*	*15.00*
1039	A391	60h dull claret	20	15
1040	A391	60h gray	20	15
1041	A391	60h sepia	20	15
		Nos. 1037-1041 (5)	1.00	
		Set value		25

Man Flying into Space A404

1961, Apr. 13

1042	A404	60h car & pale bl	35	15
1043	A404	3k ultra & yel	*2.00*	*60*
		Set value		*65*

1st man in space, Yuri A. Gagarin, Apr. 12, 1961. See No. 1036.

Flute Player — A405

Blast Furnace and Mine, Kladno — A406

1961, Apr. 24 **Engr.**

1044	A405	30h shown	25	15
1045	A405	30h Dancer	38	15
1046	A405	60h Lyre player	25	15
		Nos. 1044-1046 (3)	88	
		Set value		35

Prague Conservatory of Music, 150th anniv.

1961, Apr. 24

1047	A406	3k dull red	75	15

Marching Workers — A407

Woman with Hammer and Sickle — A408

Klement Gottwald Museum A409

Designs: No. 1050, Lenin Museum. No. 1051, Crowd with flags. No. 1053, Man saluting Red Star.

1961, May 10

1048 A407	30h	dull violet	15	15
1049 A409	30h	dark blue	15	15
1050 A409	30h	redsh brown	15	15
1051 A407	60h	vermilion	20	15
1052 A408	60h	dark green	20	15
1053 A408	60h	carmine	20	15
		Nos. 1048-1053 (6)	1.05	
		Set value		30

Czech Communist Party, 40th anniversary.

Puppet — A410

Designs: Various Puppets.

Engraved and Photogravure

1961, June 20 Unwmk. *Perf. 11½*

1054 A410	30h	ver & yel	15	15
1055 A410	40h	sepia & bluish grn	20	15
1056 A410	60h	vio bl & sal	20	15
1057 A410	1k	green & lt blue	20	15
1058 A410	1.60k	mar & pale vio	*1.25*	*35*
		Nos. 1054-1058 (5)	2.00	
		Set value		*55*

Woman, Map of Africa and Flag of Czechoslovakia — A411

1961, June 26

1059 A411	60h	red & blue	25	15

Issued to publicize the friendship between the people of Africa and Czechoslovakia.

Map of Europe and Fair Emblem A412

Designs (Fair emblem and): 60h Horizontal boring machine, vert. 1k, Scientists' meeting and nuclear physics emblem.

1961, Aug. 14 *Perf. 11½*

1060 A412	30h	dk bl & pale grn	15	15
1061 A412	60h	green & pink	25	15
1062 A412	1k	vio brn & lt bl	35	15
		Nos. 1060-1062 (3)	75	
		Set value		20

International Trade Fair, Brno, Sept. 10-24.

Sugar Beet, Cup of Coffee and Bags of Sugar A413

Charles Bridge, St. Nicholas Church and Hradcany A414

1961, Sept. 18 Unwmk. *Perf. 11½*

1063 A413	20h	shown	15	15
1064 A413	30h	Clover	15	15
1065 A413	40h	Wheat	15	15
1066 A413	60h	Hops	20	15
1067 A413	1.40k	Corn	35	15
1068 A413	2k	Potatoes	*1.25*	*55*
		Nos. 1063-1068 (6)	2.25	
		Set value		*85*

1961, Sept. 25

1069 A414	60h	violet bl & car	70	15

26th session of the Governor's Council of the Red Cross Societies League, Prague.

Orlik Dam and Kaplan Turbine A415

Designs: 30h, View of Prague, flags and stamps. 40h, Hluboká Castle, river and fish. 60h, Karlovy Vary and cup. 1k, Pilsen and beer bottle. 1.20k, North Bohemia landscape and vase. 1.60k, Tatra mountains, boots, ice pick and rope. 2k, Ironworks, Ostrava Kuncice and pulley. 3k, Brno and ball bearing. 4k, Bratislava and grapes. 5k, Prague and flags.

1961 Unwmk. *Perf. 11½*

Size: 41x23mm

1070 A415	20h	gray & blue	*25*	*22*
1071 A415	30h	vio blue & red	18	15
1072 A415	40h	dk blue & lt grn	*40*	*25*
1073 A415	60h	dk blue & yel	*30*	*18*
1074 A415	1k	maroon & green	55	45
1075 A415	1.20k	green & pink	*55*	*35*
1076 A415	1.60k	brown & vio bl	90	52
1077 A415	2k	black & ocher	1.10	85
1078 A415	3k	ultra & yel	*1.50*	*65*
1079 A415	4k	purple & sal	*2.00*	*1.10*

Perf. 13½

Engr.

Size: 50x29mm

1080 A415	5k	multicolored	*20.00*	*16.00*
		Nos. 1070-1080 (11)	*27.73*	*20.72*

"PRAGA 1962 World Exhib. of Postage Stamps," Aug. 18-Sept. 2, 1962. No. 1080 was printed in sheet of 4.

Globe A416

Engraved and Photogravure

1961, Nov. 27 *Perf. 11½*

1081 A416	60h	red & ultra	28	15

Issued to publicize the Fifth World Congress of Trade Unions, Moscow, Dec. 4-16.

Orange Tip Butterfly — A417

Bicyclists — A418

Designs (butterflies): 20h, Zerynthia hypsipyle Sch. 30h, Apollo. 40h, Swallowtail. 60h, Peacock. 80h, Mourning cloak (Camberwell beauty). 1k, Underwing (moth). 1.60k, Red admiral. 2k, Brimstone (sulphur).

1961, Nov. 27 Engr.

1082 A417	15h	multicolored	35	15
1083 A417	20h	multicolored	50	15
1084 A417	30h	multicolored	75	15
1085 A417	40h	multicolored	75	18
1086 A417	60h	multicolored	75	25
1087 A417	80h	multicolored	1.00	25
1088 A417	1k	multicolored	1.00	25
1089 A417	1.60k	multicolored	1.40	35
1090 A417	2k	multicolored	*3.50*	*1.25*
		Nos. 1082-1090 (9)	10.00	2.98

Printed in sheets of ten.

Engraved and Photogravure

1962, Feb. 5 Unwmk. *Perf. 11½*

Sports: 40h, Woman gymnast. 60h, Figure skaters. 1k, Woman bowler. 1.20k, Goalkeeper, soccer. 1.60k, Discus thrower.

1091 A418	30h	black & vio bl	18	15
1092 A418	40h	black & yel	18	15
1093 A418	60h	slate & grnsh bl	25	15
1094 A418	1k	black & pink	25	15
1095 A418	1.20k	black & green	25	15
1096 A418	1.60k	blk & dull grn	*1.40*	*60*
		Nos. 1091-1096 (6)	*2.51*	
		Set value		*90*

Various 1962 sports events.

No. 1095 does not have the commemorative inscription.

Karel Kovarovic — A419

Frantisek Zaviska and Karel Petr A420

Designs: 20h, Frantisek Skroup. 30h, Bozena Nemcova. 60h, View of Prague and staff of Aesculapius. 1.60k, Ladislav Celakovsky. 1.80k, Miloslav Valouch and Juraj Hronec.

1962, Feb. 26 Engr.

1097 A419	10h	red brown	15	15
1098 A419	20h	violet blue	15	15
1099 A419	30h	brown	15	15
1100 A420	40h	claret	15	15
1101 A419	60h	black	20	15
1102 A419	1.60k	slate green	52	15
1103 A420	1.80k	dark blue	60	15
		Set value	1.50	40

Various cultural personalities and events.

Miner and Flag A421

1962, Mar. 19 Engr. & Photo.

1104 A421	60h	indigo & rose	25	15

30th anniv. of the miners' strike at Most.

"Man Conquering Space" — A422

Soviet Spaceship Vostok 2 — A423

Designs: 40h, Launching of Soviet space rocket. 80h, Multi-stage automatic rocket. 1k, Automatic station on moon. 1.60k, Television satellite.

1962, Mar. 26

1105 A422	30h	dk red & lt blue	25	15
1106 A422	40h	dk blue & sal	25	15
1107 A423	60h	dk blue & pink	25	15
1108 A423	80h	rose vio & lt grn	60	15
1109 A422	1k	indigo & citron	35	15
1110 A423	1.60k	green & buff	*1.75*	*75*
		Nos. 1105-1110 (6)	*3.45*	
		Set value		*1.15*

Issued to publicize space research.

Polar Bear — A424

Zoo Animals: 30h, Chimpanzee. 60h, Camel. 1k, African and Indian elephants, horiz. 1.40k, Leopard, horiz. 1.60k, Przewalski horse, horiz.

1962, Apr. 24 Unwmk. *Perf. 11½*

Design and Inscriptions in Black

1111 A424	20h	grnsh blue	25	15
1112 A424	30h	violet	25	15
1113 A424	60h	orange	25	15
1114 A424	1k	green	50	15
1115 A424	1.40k	carmine rose	50	20
1116 A424	1.60k	lt brown	*1.75*	*90*
		Nos. 1111-1116 (6)	*3.50*	
		Set value		*1.40*

Child and Grieving Mother — A425

Klary's Fountain, Teplice — A426

Design: 60h, Flowers growing from ruins of Lezáky.

1962, June 9 Engr. & Photo.

1118 A425	30h	black & red	30	15
1119 A425	60h	black & dull bl	35	15
		Set value		15

20th anniversary of the destruction of Lidice and Lezáky by the Nazis.

1962, June 9

1120 A426	60h	dull grn & yel	35	15

1,200th anniversary of the discovery of the medicinal springs of Teplice.

Malaria Eradication Emblem, Cross and Dove
A427

Soccer Goalkeeper
A428

Design: 3k, Dove and malaria eradication emblem.

1962, June 18

1121 A427 60h black & crimson 16 15
1122 A427 3k dk blue & yel *1.25 60*

WHO drive to eradicate malaria.

1962, June 20 Unwmk. *Perf. 11½*

1123 A428 1.60k green & yellow 1.10 15

Czechoslovakia's participation in the World Cup Soccer Championship, Chile, May 30-June 17. See No. 1095.

Soldier in Swimming Relay Race
A429

"Agriculture"
A430

Designs: 40h, Soldier hurdling. 60h, Soccer player. 1k, Soldier with rifle in relay race.

1962, July 20

1124 A429 30h green & lt ultra 15 15
1125 A429 40h dk purple & yel 15 15
1126 A429 60h brown & green 20 15
1127 A429 1k dk blue & sal pink 35 15
Nos. 1124-1127 (4) 85
Set value 25

2nd Summer Spartacist Games of Friendly Armies, Prague, Sept., 1962.

1962 Engr. *Perf. 13½*

Designs: 60h, Astronaut in capsule. 80h, Boy with flute, horiz. 1k, Workers of three races, horiz. 1.40k, Children dancing around tree. 1.60k, Flying bird, horiz. 5k, View of Prague, horiz.

1128 A430 30h multicolored 1.50 90
1129 A430 60h multicolored 65 55
a. Miniature sheet of 8 *15.00 12.50*
1130 A430 80h multicolored 2.25 1.25
1131 A430 1k multicolored 3.25 2.25
1132 A430 1.40k multicolored 3.25 2.25
1133 A430 1.60k multicolored *4.25 3.50*
Nos. 1128-1133 (6) *15.15 10.70*

Souvenir Sheet

1134 A430 5k multicolored *12.00 10.00*
a. Imperf. *35.00 30.00*

"PRAGA 1962 World Exhib. of Postage Stamps," Aug. 18-Sept. 2, 1962. No. 1133 also for FIP Day, Sept. 1. Printed in sheets of 10.

No. 1129a contains 4 each of Nos. 1128-1129 and 2 labels arranged in 2 rows of 2 se-tenant pairs of Nos. 1128-1129 with label between. Sold for 5k, only with ticket.

No. 1134 contains one 51x30mm stamp. Sold only with ticket.

Children in Day Nursery and Factory
A431

Sailboat and Trade Union Rest Home, Zinkovy — A432

Engraved and Photogravure

1962, Oct. 29 Unwmk. *Perf. 11½*

1135 A431 30h black & lt blue 20 15
1136 A432 60h brown & yellow 20 15
Set value 15

Cruiser "Aurora" — A433

1962, Nov. 7

1137 A433 30h black & gray bl 15 15
1138 A433 60h black & pink 20 15
Set value 15

Russian October revolution, 45th anniv.

Cosmonaut and Worker — A434

Lenin — A435

1962, Nov. 7

1139 A434 30h dark red & blue 15 15
1140 A435 60h black & dp rose 20 15
Set value 15

40th anniversary of the USSR.

Symbolic Crane — A436

Designs: 40h, Agricultural products, vert. 60h, Factories.

1962, Dec. 4

1141 A436 30h dk red & yel 15 15
1142 A436 40h gray blue & yel 20 15
1143 A436 60h black & dp rose 30 15
Nos. 1141-1143 (3) 65
Set value 25

Communist Party of Czechoslovakia, 12th cong.

Ground Beetle — A437

Table Tennis — A438

Beetles: 30h, Cardinal beetle. 60h, Stag beetle, vert. 1k, Great water beetle. 1.60k, Alpine longicorn, vert. 2k, Ground beetle, vert.

1962, Dec. 15 Engr. *Perf. 14*

1144 A437 20h multicolored 22 15
1145 A437 30h multicolored 22 15
1146 A437 60h multicolored 22 15
1147 A437 1k multicolored 65 16
1148 A437 1.60k multicolored 1.00 30
1149 A437 2k multicolored *2.25 1.25*
Nos. 1144-1149 (6) *4.56*
Set value *1.90*

Engraved and Photogravure

1963, Jan. *Perf. 11½*

Sports: 60h, Bicyclist. 80h, Skier. 1k, Motorcyclist. 1.20k, Weight lifter. 1.60k, Hurdler.

1150 A438 30h black & dp grn 18 15
1151 A438 60h black & orange 18 15
1152 A438 80h black & ultra 18 15
1153 A438 1k black & violet 25 15
1154 A438 1.20k black & pale brn 30 20
1155 A438 1.60k black & carmine 40 20
Nos. 1150-1155 (6) 1.49
Set value 68

Various 1963 sports events.

Industrial Plant, Laurel and Star — A439

Symbol of Child Welfare Home — A440

Industrial Plant and Symbol of Growth — A441

1963, Feb. 25 Unwmk. *Perf. 11½*

1156 A439 30h carmine & lt bl 15 15
1157 A440 60h black & car 20 15
1158 A441 60h black & red 20 15
Nos. 1156-1158 (3) 55
Set value 15

15th anniv. of the "Victorious February" and 5th Trade Union Cong.

Artists' Guild Emblem — A442

Juraj Jánosik — A443

Eduard Urx — A444

National Theater, Prague — A445

Designs: No. 1163, Woman reading to children. No. 1164, Juraj Pálkovic. 1.60k, Max Svabinsky.

Engr. & Photo.; Engr. (A444)

1963, Mar. 25 Unwmk. *Perf. 11½*

1159 A442 20h black & Prus bl 15 15
1160 A443 30h car & lt bl 15 15
1161 A444 30h carmine 15 15
1162 A445 60h dl red brn & lt bl 15 15
1163 A444 60h green 15 15
1164 A444 60h black 25 15
1165 A444 1.60k brown 52 15
Set value 1.25 35

Various cultural personalities and events.

Boy and Girl with Flag
A446

Television Transmitter
A447

Engraved and Photogravure

1963, Apr. 18 *Perf. 11½*

1166 A446 30h slate & rose red 20 15

The 4th Congress of Czechoslovak Youth.

1963, Apr. 25

Design: 40h, Television camera, mast and set, horiz.

1167 A447 40h buff & slate 20 15
1168 A447 60h dk red & lt blue 25 15
Set value 15

Czechoslovak television, 10th anniversary.

Rocket to the Sun
A448

Designs: 50h, Rockets and Sputniks leaving Earth. 60h, Spacecraft to and from Moon. 1k, 3k, Interplanetary station and Mars 1. 1.60k, Atomic rocket and Jupiter. 2k, Rocket returning from Saturn.

1963, Apr. 25

1169 A448 30h red brn & buff 15 15
1170 A448 50h slate & bluish grn 20 15
1171 A448 60h dk green & yel 25 15
1172 A448 1k dk gray & sal 45 15
1173 A448 1.60k gray brn & lt grn 75 20
1174 A448 2k dk purple & yel *2.50 75*
Nos. 1169-1174 (6) *4.30*
Set value *1.20*

Souvenir Sheet

Imperf

1175 A448 3k Prus grn & org red *3.00 2.50*

No. 1175 issued for 1st Space Research Exhib., Prague, Apr. 1963.

Studio and Radio
A449

Design: 1k, Globe inscribed "Peace" and aerial mast, vert.

1963, May 18 Unwmk. *Perf. 11½*

1176 A449 30h choc & pale grn 15 15
1177 A449 1k bluish grn & lilac 30 15
Set value 15

40th anniversary of Czechoslovak radio.

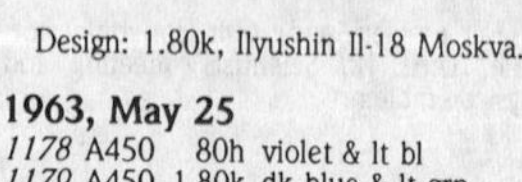
Tupolev Tu-104B Turbojet
A450

Design: 1.80k, Ilyushin Il-18 Moskva.

1963, May 25

1178 A450 80h violet & lt bl 35 15
1179 A450 1.80k dk blue & lt grn 75 15
Set value 15

40th anniversary of Czechoslovak airlines.

9th Cent. Ring, Map of Moravian Settlements — A451

Woman Singing — A452

Design: 1.60k, Falconer, 9th cent. silver disk.

1963, May 25

1180 A451 30h lt green & blk 18 15
1181 A451 1.60k dull yel & blk 45 15
Set value 15

1100th anniversary of Moravian empire.

1963, May 25 **Engr.**

1182 A452 30h bright red 40 15

60th anniversary of the founding of the Moravian Teachers' Singing Club.

Kromeriz Castle and Barley — A453

Centenary Emblem, Nurse and Playing Child — A454

Engraved and Photogravure

1963, June 20 Unwmk. ***Perf. 11½***

1183 A453 30h slate grn & yel 30 15

Natl. Agricultural Exhib. and 700th anniv. of Kromeriz.

1963, June 20

1184 A454 30h dk gray & car 40 15

Centenary of the International Red Cross.

Bee, Honeycomb and Emblem — A455

Liberec Fair Emblem — A456

1963, June 20

1185 A455 1k brown & yellow 40 15

19th Intl. Beekeepers Cong., Apimondia, 1963.

1963, July 13

1186 A456 30h black & dp rose 35 15

Liberec Consumer Goods Fair.

Town Hall, Brno — A457

Cave, Moravian Karst — A458

Design: 60h, Town Hall tower, Brno.

1963, July 29

1187 A457 30h lt blue & maroon 18 15
1188 A457 60h pink & dk blue 25 15
Set value 15

International Trade Fair, Brno.

1963, July 29

Designs: No. 1190, Trout, Hornad Valley. 60h, Great Hawk Gorge. 80h, Macocha mountains.

1189 A458 30h brown & lt bl 20 15
1190 A458 30h dk bl & dull grn 20 15
1191 A458 60h green & blue 20 15
1192 A458 80h sepia & pink 22 15
Nos. 1189-1192 (4) 82
Set value 30

Blast Furnace — A459

1963, Aug. 15 Unwmk. ***Perf. 11½***

1193 A459 60h blk & bluish grn 25 15

30th Intl. Cong. of Iron Founders, Prague.

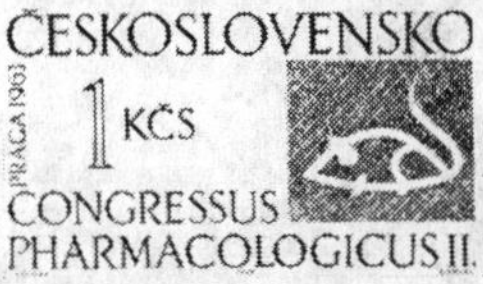

White Mouse A460

1963, Aug. 15

1194 A460 1k black & carmine 40 15

2nd Intl. Pharmacological Cong., Prague.

Farm Machinery for Underfed Nations — A461

Wooden Toys — A462

1963, Aug. 15 **Engr.**

1195 A461 1.60k black 40 15

FAO "Freedom from Hunger" campaign.

1963, Sept. 2 Engr. ***Perf. 13½***

Folk Art (Inscribed "UNESCO"): 80h, Cock and flowers. 1k, Flowers in vase. 1.20k, Janosik, Slovak hero. 1.60k, Stag. 2k, Postilion.

1196 A462 60h red & vio bl 25 15
1197 A462 80h multi 35 20
1198 A462 1k multi 45 25
1199 A462 1.20k multi 45 18
1200 A462 1.60k multi 45 18
1201 A462 2k multi 2.50 1.00
Nos. 1196-1201 (6) 4.45 1.96

Sheets of 10.

Canoeing — A463

Tree and Star — A464

Sports: 40h, Volleyball. 60h, Wrestling. 80h, Basketball. 1k, Boxing. 1.60k, Gymnastics.

Engraved and Photogravure

1963, Oct. 26 ***Perf. 11½***

1202 A463 30h indigo & grn 25 15
1203 A463 40h red brn & lt bl 25 15
1204 A463 60h brn red & yel 25 15
1205 A463 80h dk pur & dp org 25 15
1206 A463 1k ultra & dp rose 25 15
1207 A463 1.60k vio bl & ultra *2.00 1.00*
Nos. 1202-1207 (6) *3.25 1.75*

1964 Olympic Games, Tokyo.

1963, Dec. 11 Unwmk. ***Perf. 11½***

Design: 60h, Star, hammer and sickle.

1208 A464 30h bis brn & lt bl 15 15
1209 A464 60h carmine & gray 20 15
Set value 15

Russo-Czechoslovakian Treaty, 20th anniv.

Atom Diagrams Surrounding Head — A465

Chamois — A466

1963, Dec. 12 **Engr.**

1210 A465 60h dark purple 40 15

3rd Congress of the Association for the Propagation of Scientific Knowledge.

1963, Dec. 14 ***Perf. 14***

Animals: 40h, Alpine ibex. 60h, Mouflon. 1.20k, Roe deer. 1.60k, Fallow deer. 2k, Red deer.

1211 A466 30h multi 50 25
1212 A466 40h multi 55 35
1213 A466 60h brown, yel & grn 70 30
1214 A466 1.20k multi 75 25
1215 A466 1.60k multi 1.25 35
1216 A466 2k multi *4.00 2.00*
Nos. 1211-1216 (6) *7.75 3.50*

Figure Skating — A467

Ice Hockey — A468

Designs: 80h, Skiing, horiz. 1k, Field ball player.

Engraved and Photogravure

1964, Jan. 20 Unwmk. ***Perf. 11½***

1217 A467 30h violet bl & yel 15 15
1218 A467 80h dk blue & org 15 15
1219 A467 1k brown & lilac 35 15
Nos. 1217-1219 (3) 65
Set value 25

Intl. University Games (30h, 80h) and the World Field Ball Championships (1k).

1964, Jan. 20

1220 A468 1k shown 85 35
1221 A468 1.80k Toboggan 1.00 60
1222 A468 2k Ski jump *2.50 2.25*
Nos. 1220-1222 (3) *4.35 3.20*

9th Winter Olympic Games, Innsbruck, Jan. 29-Feb. 9, 1964.

Magura Rest Home, High Tatra — A469

Design: 80h, Slovak National Insurrection Rest Home, Low Tatra.

1964, Feb. 19 Unwmk. ***Perf. 11½***

1223 A469 60h green & yellow 20 15
1224 A469 80h violet bl & pink 20 15
Set value 15

Skiers and Ski Lift A470

Designs: 60h, Automobile camp, Telc. 1k, Fishing, Spis Castle. 1.80k, Lake and boats, Cesky Krumlov.

1964, Feb. 19 **Engr. & Photo.**

1225 A470 30h dk vio brn & bl 15 15
1226 A470 60h slate & car 25 15
1227 A470 1k brown & olive 40 15
1228 A470 1.80k slate grn & org 65 25
Nos. 1225-1228 (4) 1.45
Set value 45

Moses, Day and Night by Michelangelo — A471

Designs: 60th, "A Midsummer Night's Dream," by Shakespeare. 1k, Man, telescope and heaven, vert. 1.60k, King George of Podebrad (1420-71).

1964, Mar. 20

1229 A471 40h black & yel grn 20 15
1230 A471 60h slate & car 20 15
1231 A471 1k black & lt blue 35 15
1232 A471 1.60k black & yellow 45 15
a. Souvenir sheet of 4 ('88) 2.00 2.00
Nos. 1229-1232 (4) 1.20
Set value 35

400th anniv. of the death of Michelangelo (40h); 400th anniv. of the birth of Shakespeare (60h); 400th anniv. of the birth of Galileo (1k); 500th anniv. of the pacifist efforts of King George of Podebrad (1.60k).

No. 1232a for PRAGA '88.

Yuri A. Gagarin — A472

Astronauts: 60h, Gherman Titov. 80h, John H. Glenn, Jr. 1k, Scott M. Carpenter, vert. 1.20k, Pavel R. Popovich and Andrian G. Nikolayev. 1.40k, Walter M. Schirra, vert. 1.60k, Gordon L. Cooper, vert. 2k, Valentina Tereshkova and Valeri Bykovski, vert.

1964, Apr. 27 Unwmk. ***Perf. 11½***

Yellow Paper

1233 A472 30h black & vio bl 50 25
1234 A472 60h dk grn & dk car 25 15
1235 A472 80h dk car & vio 50 20
1236 A472 1k ultra & rose vio 25 25
1237 A472 1.20k ver & ol gray 50 35
1238 A472 1.40k black & dl grn 1.25 50
1239 A472 1.60k pale pur & Prus grn *3.00 1.50*
1240 A472 2k dk blue & red 1.00 40
Nos. 1233-1240 (8) *7.25 3.60*

World's first 10 astronauts.

Creeping Bellflower A473

Film "Flower" and Karlovy Vary Colonnade A474

Flowers: 80h, Musk thistle. 1k, Chicory. 1.20k, Yellow iris. 1.60k, Gentian. 2k, Corn poppy.

1964, June 15 Engr. *Perf. 14*

1241 A473	60h	dk grn, lil & org	1.25	25
1242 A473	80h	blk, grn & red lil	1.25	25
1243 A473	1k	vio bl, grn & pink	1.25	45
1244 A473	1.20k	black, yel & grn	1.25	30
1245 A473	1.60k	violet & grn	1.25	40
1246 A473	2k	vio, red & grn	*4.50*	*2.00*
		Nos. 1241-1246 (6)	*10.75*	*3.65*

Engraved and Photogravure

1964, June 20 Unwmk. *Perf. 13½*

1247 A474 60h black, blue & car 1.25 15

14th Intl. Film Festival at Karlovy Vary, July 4-19.

Silesian Coat of Arms — A475

Young Miner of 1764 — A476

1964, June 20 *Perf. 11½*

1248 A475 30h black & yel 25 15

150th anniv. of the Silesian Museum, Opava.

1964, June 20

1249 A476 60h sepia & lt grn 25 15

Mining School at Banska Stiavnica, bicent.

Skoda Fire Engine A477

1964, June 20

1250 A477 60h car rose & lt bl 35 15

Voluntary fire brigades in Bohemia, cent.

ČESKOSLOVENSKO
Gulls, Hradcany Castle, Red Cross — A478

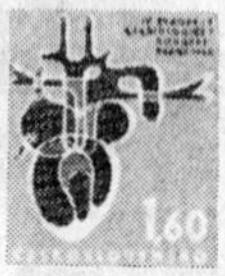

Human Heart — A479

1964, July 10

1251 A478 60h car & bluish gray 35 15

4th Czechoslovak Red Cross Congress at Prague.

1964, July 10

1252 A479 1.60k ultra & car 60 15

4th European Cardiological Cong. at Prague.

Partisans, Girl and Factories — A480

Battle Scene, 1944 — A481

Design: 60h, Partisans and flame.

Engraved and Photogravure

1964, Aug. 17 Unwmk. *Perf. 11½*

1253 A480	30h	brown & red	15	15
1254 A480	60h	dk blue & red	20	15
1255 A481	60h	black & red	20	15
		Nos. 1253-1255 (3)	55	
		Set value		15

20th anniv. of the Slovak Natl. Uprising; No. 1255, 20th anniv. of the Battles of Dukla Pass.

Hradcany at Prague — A482

Discus Thrower and Pole Vaulter — A483

Design: 5k, Charles Bridge and Hradcany.

1964, Aug. 30 *Perf. 11½x12*

1256 A482 60h black & red 48 15

Souvenir Sheet

Engr. *Imperf.*

1257 A482 5k deep claret 1.90 1.50

Millenium of the Hradcany, Prague. No. 1257 stamp size: 30x50mm.

Engraved and Photogravure

1964, Sept. 2 *Perf. 13½*

Designs: 60h, Bicycling, horiz. 1k, Soccer. 1.20k, Rowing. 1.60k, Swimming, horiz. 2.80k, Weight lifting, horiz.

1258 A483	60h	multi	35	25
1259 A483	80h	multi	50	25
1260 A483	1k	multi	50	25
1261 A483	1.20k	multi	60	30
1262 A483	1.60k	multi	75	35
1263 A483	2.80k	multi	*4.00*	*2.00*
		Nos. 1258-1263 (6)	*6.70*	*3.40*

Issued to commemorate the 18th Olympic Games, Tokyo, Oct. 10-25. Sheets of 10.

Miniature Sheet

Space Ship Voskhod I, Astronauts and Globe — A484

1964, Nov. 12 Unwmk. *Perf. 11½*

1264 A484 3k dk bl & dl lil, *buff* 4.50 3.50

Russian 3-man space flight of Vladimir M. Komarov, Boris B. Yegorov and Konstantin Feoktistov, Oct. 12-13.

Steam Engine and Atomic Power Plant — A485

Diesel Engine "CKD Praha" — A486

1964, Nov. 16 Engr.

1265 A485 30h dull red brown 15 15

Engraved and Photogravure

1266 A486	60h	green & salmon	20	15
		Set value	25	15

Traditions and development of engineering; No. 1265 for 150th anniv. of the First Brno Engineering Works, No. 1266 for the engineering concern CKD Praha.

European Redstart — A487

Birds: 60h, Green woodpecker. 80h, Hawfinch. 1k, Black woodpecker. 1.20k, European robin. 1.60k, European roller.

1964, Nov. 16 Litho. *Perf. 10½*

1267 A487	30h	multicolored	15	15
1268 A487	60h	black & multi	25	15
1269 A487	80h	multicolored	50	15
1270 A487	1k	multicolored	50	25
1271 A487	1.20k	lt vio bl & blk	35	25
1272 A487	1.60k	yellow & blk	1.25	60
		Nos. 1267-1272 (6)	3.00	
		Set value		1.30

Dancer A488

"In the Sun" Preschool Children A489

Designs: 60h, "Over the Obstacles," teenagers. 1k, "Movement and Beauty," woman flag twirler. 1.60k, Runners at start.

Engraved and Photogravure

1965 Unwmk. *Perf. 11½*

1273 A488 30h red & lt blue 15 15

Perf. 11½x12

1274 A489	30h	vio bl & car	15	15
1275 A489	60h	brown & ultra	20	15
1276 A489	1k	black & yellow	25	15
1277 A489	1.60k	maroon & gray	60	24
		Nos. 1273-1277 (5)	1.35	
		Set value		50

3rd Natl. Spartacist Games. Issue dates: No. 1273, Jan. 3. Nos. 1274-1277, May 24.

Mountain Rescue Service — A490

Arms and View, Beroun — A491

Designs: No. 1279, Woman gymnast. No. 1280, Bicyclists. No. 1281, Women hurdlers.

1965, Jan. 15 Unwmk. *Perf. 11½*

1278 A490	60h	violet & blue	22	15
1279 A490	60h	maroon & ocher	22	15
1280 A490	60h	black & carmine	22	15
1281 A490	60h	green & yellow	22	15
		Nos. 1278-1281 (4)	88	
		Set value		20

Mountain Rescue Service (#1278); 1st World Championship in Artistic Gymnastics, Prague, Dec. 1965 (#1279); World Championship in Indoor Bicycling, Prague, Oct. 1965 (#1280); "Universiada 1965," Brno (#1281).

1965, Feb. 15

Designs: No. 1283, Town Square, Domazlice. No. 1284, Old and new buildings, Frydek-Mystek. No. 1285, Arms and view, Lipnik. No. 1286, Fortified wall, City Hall and Arms, Policka. No. 1287, View and hops, Zatek. No. 1288, Small fortress and rose, Terezin.

1282 A491	30h	vio bl & lt bl	15	15
1283 A491	30h	dull pur & yel	15	15
1284 A491	30h	slate & gray	15	15
1285 A491	30h	green & bis	15	15
1286 A491	30h	brown & tan	15	15
1287 A491	30h	dk blue & cit	15	15
1288 A491	30h	black & rose	15	15
		Nos. 1282-1288 (7)	1.05	
		Set value		35

Nos. 1282-1287 for 700th anniv. of the founding of various Bohemian towns; No. 1288 the 20th anniv. of the liberation of the Theresienstadt (Terezin) concentration camp.

Sun's Corona A492

Space Research: 30h, Sun. 60h, Exploration of the Moon. 1k, Twin space craft, vert. 1.40k, Space station. 1.60k, Exploration of Mars, vert. 2k, USSR and US Meteorological collaboration.

Perf. 12x11½, 11½x12

1965, Mar. 15

1289 A492	20h	rose & red lilac	25	15
1290 A492	30h	rose red & yel	25	15
1291 A492	60h	bluish blk & yel	25	15
1292 A492	1k	purple & pale blue	50	15
1293 A492	1.40k	black & salmon	50	20
1294 A492	1.60k	black & pink	50	20
1295 A492	2k	bluish blk & lt bl	*1.50*	*1.00*
		Nos. 1289-1295 (7)	*3.75*	
		Set value		*1.75*

Space research; Nos. 1289-1290 also for the Intl. Quiet Sun Year, 1964-65.

Frantisek Ventura, Equestrian; Amsterdam, 1928 — A493

Czechoslovakian Olympic Victories: 30h, Discus, Paris, 1900. 60h, Running, Helsinki, 1952. 1k, Weight lifting, Los Angeles, 1932. 1.40k, Gymnastics, Berlin, 1936. 1.60k, Double sculling, Rome, 1960. 2k, Women's gymnastics, Tokyo, 1964.

1965, Apr. 16 *Perf. 11½x12*

1296	A493	20h	choc & gold	22	15
1297	A493	30h	indigo & emer	22	15
1298	A493	60h	ultra & gold	22	15
1299	A493	1k	red brn & gold	35	22
1300	A493	1.40k	dk sl grn & gold	75	60
1301	A493	1.60k	black & gold	80	60
1302	A493	2k	maroon & gold	1.10	45
			Nos. 1296-1302 (7)	3.66	2.32

Astronauts Virgil Grissom and John Young — A494

Designs: No. 1304, Alexei Leonov floating in space. No. 1305, Launching pad at Cape Kennedy. No. 1306, Leonov leaving space ship.

1965, Apr. 17 *Perf. 11x11½*

1303	A494	60h	slate bl & lil rose	25	15
1304	A494	60h	vio blk & blue	25	15
1305	A494	3k	slate bl & lil rose	1.50	1.00
1306	A494	3k	vio blk & blue	1.50	1.00
			Nos. 1303-1306 (4)	3.50	2.30

Issued to honor American and Soviet astronauts. Printed in sheets of 25; one sheet contains 20 No. 1303 and 5 No. 1305, the other sheet contains 20 No. 1304 and 5 No. 1306.

Russian Soldier, View of Prague and Guerrilla Fighters A495

Designs: No. 1308, Blast furnace, workers and tank. 60h, Worker and factory. 1k, Worker and new constructions. 1.60k, Woman farmer, new farm buildings and machinery.

1965, May 5 **Engr.** *Perf. 13½*

1307	A495	30h	dk red, blk & ol	15	15
1308	A495	30h	multicolored	15	15
1309	A495	60h	vio bl, red & blk	24	15
1310	A495	1k	dp org, blk & brn	38	15
1311	A495	1.60k	yellow, red & blk	70	20
			Nos. 1307-1311 (5)	1.62	
			Set value		46

20th anniv. of liberation from the Nazis.

Slovakian Kopov Dog A496

Dogs: 40h, German shepherd. 60h, Czech hunting dog with pheasant. 1k, Poodle. 1.60k, Czech terrier. 2k, Afghan hound.

1965, June 10 *Perf. 12x11½*

1312	A496	30h	black & red org	35	15
1313	A496	40h	black & yellow	35	15
1314	A496	60h	black & ver	25	15
1315	A496	1k	black & dk car rose	80	15
1316	A496	1.60k	black & orange	50	25
1317	A496	2k	black & orange	1.50	65
			Nos. 1312-1317 (6)	3.75	
			Set value		1.25

World Dog Show at Brno and the International Dog Breeders Congress, Prague.

UN Headquarters Building, NY — A497

Designs: 60h, UN Emblem and inscription. 1.60k, ICY emblem.

1965, June 24 *Perf. 12x11½*

1318	A497	60h	dk red brn & yel	18	15
1319	A497	1k	ultra & lt blue	35	15
1320	A497	1.60k	gold & dk red	50	35
			Nos. 1318-1320 (3)	1.03	
			Set value		45

20th anniv. of the UN and the ICY, 1965.

Trade Union Emblem A498

1965, June 24 **Engr.**

1321	A498	60h	dk red & ultra	25	15

20th anniv. of the Intl. Trade Union Federation.

Women and Globe — A499

1965, June 24 *Perf. 11½x12*

1322	A499	60h	violet blue	25	15

20th anniv. of the Intl. Women's Federation.

Children's House (Burgraves' Palace), Hradcany — A500

Matthias Tower — A501

1965, June 25 *Perf. 11½*

1323	A500	30h	slate green	20	15
1324	A501	60h	dark brown	25	15
			Set value		15

Issued to publicize the Hradcany, Prague.

Marx and Lenin — A502

1965, July 1 **Engr. & Photo.**

1325	A502	60h	car rose & gold	20	15

6th conf. of Postal Ministers of Communist Countries, Peking, June 21-July 15.

Joseph Navratil — A503

Jan Hus — A504

Gregor Johann Mendel A505

Costume Jewelry A506

Bohuslav Martinu A507

Seated Woman and University of Bratislava A508

ITU Emblem and Communication Symbols — A509

Macromolecular Symposium Emblem — A510

Design: No. 1327, Ludovit Stur (diff. frame).

1965 **Unwmk.** *Perf. 11½*

1326	A503	30h	black & fawn	15	15
1327	A503	30h	black & dull grn	15	15
1328	A504	60h	black & crimson	20	15
1329	A505	60h	vio bl & red	20	15
1330	A506	60h	purple & gold	20	15
1331	A507	60h	black & orange	20	15
1332	A508	60h	brn, *yel*	20	15
1333	A509	1k	orange & blue	35	15
1334	A510	1k	black & dp org	35	15
			Nos. 1326-1334 (9)	2.00	
			Set value		45

No. 1326, Navratil (1798-1865), painter; No. 1327, Stur (1815-56), Slovak author and historian; No. 1328, the 550th anniv. of the death of Hus, religious reformer;

No. 1329, cent. of publication of Mendel's laws of inheritance; No. 1330 publicizes the "Jablonec 1965" costume jewelry exhib.; No. 1331, Martinu (1890-1959), composer; No. 1332, 500th anniv. of the founding of the University of Bratislava as Academia Istropolitana; No. 1333, cent. of the ITU; No. 1334, Intl. Symposium on Macromolecular Chemistry, Prague, Sept. 1-8.

"Young Woman at her Toilette," by Titian — A512

Help for Flood Victims — A513

Rescue of Flood Victims A514

Miniature Sheet

1965, Aug. 12

1336	A512	5k	multicolored	3.75	2.00

Hradcany Art Gallery. #1336 contains one stamp.

1965, Sept. 6 **Engr.**

1337	A513	30h	violet blue	15	15

Engraved and Photogravure

1338	A514	2k	dk ol grn & ol	65	45

Help for Danube flood victims in Slovakia.

Dotterel A515

Mountain Birds: 60h, Wall creeper, vert. 1.20k, Lesser redpoll. 1.40k, Golden eagle, vert. 1.60k, Ring ouzel. 2k, Eurasian nutcracker, vert.

1965, Sept. 20 **Litho.** *Perf. 11*

1339	A515	30h	multi	24	15
1340	A515	60h	multi	24	15
1341	A515	1.20k	multi	32	15
1342	A515	1.40k	multi	75	25
1343	A515	1.60k	multi	60	30
1344	A515	2k	multi	1.40	1.25
			Nos. 1339-1344 (6)	3.55	2.25

Levoca — A516

Medicinal Plants — A517

Views of Towns: 10h, Jindrichuv Hradec. 20h, Nitra. 30h, Kosice. 40h, Hradec Králové. 50h, Telc. 60h, Ostrava. 1k, Olomouc. 1.20k, Ceske Budejovice. 1.60k, Cheb. 2k, Brno. 3k, Bratislava. 5k, Prague.

Engraved and Photogravure

1965-66 *Perf. 11½x12*

Size: 23x19mm

1345	A516	5h	black & yel	15	15
1346	A516	10h	ultra & ol bis	15	15
1347	A516	20h	black & lt bl	15	15
1348	A516	30h	vio bl & lt grn	15	15
1348A	A516	40h	dk brn & lt bl ('66)	15	15
1348B	A516	50h	black & ocher ('66)	16	15
1348C	A516	60h	red & gray ('66)	22	15
1348D	A516	1k	pur & pale grn ('66)	30	15

Perf. 11½x11

Size: 30x23mm

1349	A516	1.20k	slate & lt bl	35	15
1350	A516	1.60k	indigo & yel	45	15
1351	A516	2k	sl grn & pale yel	55	15
1352	A516	3k	brown & yellow	75	15
1353	A516	5k	black & pink	1.25	15
			Nos. 1345-1353 (13)	4.78	
			Set value		82

1965, Dec. 3 **Engr.** *Perf. 14*

1354	A517	30h	Coltsfoot	20	15
1355	A517	60h	Meadow saffron	25	15
1356	A517	80h	Corn poppy	35	15
1357	A517	1k	Foxglove	60	20
1358	A517	1.20k	Arnica	50	25
1359	A517	1.60k	Cornflower	75	40
1360	A517	2k	Dog rose	*3.75*	*1.50*
			Nos. 1354-1360 (7)	*6.40*	*2.80*

Strip of "Stamps" — A518

Engraved and Photogravure

1965, Dec. 18 *Perf. 11½*

1361	A518	1k	dark red & gold	2.75	2.25

Issued for Stamp Day, 1965.

Romain Rolland (1866-1944), French Writer — A519

Symbolic Musical Instruments & Names of Composers — A520

Portraits: No. 1362, Stanislav Sucharda (1866-1916), sculptor. No. 1363, Ignac Josef Pesina (1766-1808), veterinarian. No. 1365, Donatello (1386-1466), Italian sculptor.

1966, Feb. 14 Engr. *Perf. 11½*

1362 A519	30h	deep green	15	15
1363 A519	30h	violet blue	15	15
1364 A519	60h	rose lake	20	15
1365 A519	60h	brown	20	15
		Nos. 1362-1365 (4)	70	
		Set value		20

1966, Jan. 15 Engr. & Photo.

1366 A520 30h black & gold 30 20

Czech Philharmonic Orchestra, 70th anniv.

Figure Skating Pair A521

Designs: No. 1368, Man skater. No. 1369, Volleyball player, spiking, vert. 1k, Volleyball player, saving, vert. 1.60k, Woman skater. 2k, Figure skating pair.

1966, Feb. 17

1367 A521	30h	dk car rose	15	15
1368 A521	60h	green	20	15
1369 A521	60h	carmine & buff	20	15
1370 A521	1k	vio & lt bl	30	15
1371 A521	1.60k	brown & yellow	40	15
1372 A521	2k	blue & grnsh bl	*2.00*	*40*
		Nos. 1367-1372 (6)	*3.25*	
		Set value		*75*

#1367-1368, 1371-1372 for the European Figure Skating Championships, Bratislava; #1369-1370 for the World Volleyball Championships.

Souvenir Sheet

Girl Dancing — A522

1966, Mar. 21 Engr. *Imperf.*

1373 A522 3k slate bl, red & bl 1.75 1.50

Cent. of the opera "The Bartered Bride" by Bedrich Smetana.

"Ajax" 1841 A523

Locomotives: 30h, "Karlstejn" 1865. 60h, Steam engine, 1946. 1k, Steam engine with tender, 1946. 1.60k, Electric locomotive, 1964. 2k, Diesel locomotive, 1964.

1966, Mar. 21 *Perf. 11½x11*

Buff Paper

1374 A523	20h	sepia	30	15
1375 A523	30h	dull violet	30	15
1376 A523	60h	dull purple	30	15
1377 A523	1k	dark blue	50	15
1378 A523	1.60k	dk blue grn	60	20
1379 A523	2k	dark red	*3.00*	*90*
		Nos. 1374-1379 (6)	*5.00*	
		Set value		*1.45*

European Perch A524

Fish: 30h, Brown trout, vert. 1k, Carp. 1.20k, Northern pike. 1.40k, Grayling. 1.60k, Eel.

Perf. 13x13½, 13½x13

1966, Apr. 22 Litho. Unwmk.

1380 A524	30h	multi	25	15
1381 A524	60h	multi	35	15
1382 A524	1k	multi	50	15
1383 A524	1.20k	multi	50	20
1384 A524	1.40k	multi	85	25
1385 A524	1.60k	multi	*2.75*	*1.10*
		Nos. 1380-1385 (6)	*5.20*	*2.00*

Intl. Fishing Championships, Svit, Sept. 3-5.

WHO Headquarters, Geneva — A525

Engraved and Photogravure

1966, Apr. 25 *Perf. 12x11½*

1386 A525 1k dk blue & lt blue 40 15

Opening of the WHO Headquarters, Geneva.

Symbolic Handshake and UNESCO Emblem — A526

1966, Apr. 25 *Perf. 11½*

1387 A526 60h bister & olive gray 15 15

20th anniv. of UNESCO.

Prague Castle Issue

Belvedere Palace and St. Vitus' Cathedral — A527

Crown of St. Wenceslas, 1346 — A528

Design: 60h, Madonna, altarpiece from St. George's Church.

1966, May 9 Engr. *Perf. 11½*

1388 A527 30h dark blue 20 15

Engraved and Photogravure

1389 A527 60h blk & yel bis 50 15
Set value 25

Souvenir Sheet

Engr.

1390 A528 5k multi 2.75 2.50

See Nos. 1537-1539.

Tiger Swallowtail A529

Butterflies and Moths: 60h, Clouded sulphur. 80h, European purple emperor. 1k, Apollo. 1.20k, Burnet moth. 2k, Tiger moth.

1966, May 23 Engr. *Perf. 14*

1391 A529	30h	multi	22	15
1392 A529	60h	multi	45	15
1393 A529	80h	multi	45	15
1394 A529	1k	multi	45	20
1395 A529	1.20k	multi	90	25
1396 A529	2k	multi	*2.25*	*1.25*
		Nos. 1391-1396 (6)	*4.72*	*2.15*

Sheets of ten.

Flags of Russia and Czechoslovakia — A530

Designs: 60h, Rays surrounding hammer and sickle "sun." 1.60k, Girl's head and stars.

Engraved and Photogravure

1966, May 31 *Perf. 11½*

1397 A530	30h	dk bl & crim	15	15
1398 A530	60h	dk bl & red	20	15
1399 A530	1.60k	red & dk bl	50	15
		Nos. 1397-1399 (3)	85	
		Set value		18

13th Congress of the Communist Party of Czechoslovakia.

Dakota Chief — A531

Designs: 20h, Indians, canoe and tepee, horiz. 30h, Tomahawk. 40h, Haida totem poles. 60h, Kachina, good spirit of the Hopis. 1k, Indian on horseback hunting buffalo, horiz. 1.20k, Calumet, Dakota peace pipe.

1966, June 20

Size: 23x40mm

1400 A531	20h	vio bl & dp org	18	15
1401 A531	30h	blk & dl org	18	15
1402 A531	40h	blk & lt bl	18	15
1403 A531	60h	grn & yel	22	15
1404 A531	1k	pur & emer	22	15
1405 A531	1.20k	vio bl & rose lil	35	28

Perf. 14

Engr.

Size: 23x37mm

1406 A531	1.40k	multi	*1.65*	*90*
		Nos. 1400-1406 (7)	*2.98*	
		Set value		*1.50*

Cent. of the Náprstek Ethnographic Museum, Prague, and "The Indians of North America" exhibition.

Model of Molecule — A532

Engraved and Photogravure

1966, July 4 Unwmk. *Perf. 11½*

1407 A532 60h blk & lt bl 20 15

Czechoslovak Chemical Society, cent.

"Guernica" by Pablo Picasso — A533

1966, July 5

Size: 75x30mm

1408 A533 60h blk & pale bl 1.25 1.25

30th anniversary of International Brigade in Spanish Civil War.

Sheets of 15 stamps and 5 labels inscribed "Picasso-Guernica 1937."

Pantheon, Bratislava — A534

Atom Symbol and Sun — A535

Designs: No. 1410, Devin Castle and Ludovit Stur. No. 1411, View of Nachod. No. 1412, State Science Library, Olomouc.

1966, July 25 Engr.

1409 A534	30h	dl pur	16	15
1410 A534	60h	dk bl	22	15
1411 A534	60h	green	22	15
1412 A534	60h	sepia	22	15
		Nos. 1409-1412 (4)	82	
		Set value		20

No. 1409, Russian War Memorial, Bratislava; No. 1410, the 9th cent. Devin Castle as symbol of Slovak nationalism; No. 1411, 700th anniv. of the founding of Nachod; No. 1412, the 400th anniv. of the State Science Library, Olomouc.

Engraved and Photogravure

1966, Aug. 29 *Perf. 11½*

1413 A535 60h blk & red 20 15

Issued to publicize Jachymov (Joachimsthal), where pitchblende was first discovered, "cradle of the atomic age."

Brno Fair Emblem — A536

Olympia Coin and Olympic Rings — A537

1966, Aug. 29

1414	A536	60h blk & red	20	15

8th International Trade Fair, Brno.

1966, Aug. 29

Design: 1k, Olympic flame, Czechoslovak flag and Olympic rings.

1415	A537	60h blk & gold	18	15
1416	A537	1k dk bl & red	50	30
		Set value		35

70th anniv. of the Olympic Committee.

Missile Carrier, Tank and Jet Plane A538

1966, Aug. 31

1417	A538	60h blk & apple grn	30	15

Issued to commemorate the maneuvers of the armies of the Warsaw Pact countries.

Mercury A539

Designs: 30h, Moravian silver thaler, 1620, reverse and obverse, vert. 1.60k, Old and new buildings of Brno State Theater. 5k, International Trade Fair Administration Tower and postmark, vert.

1966, Sept. 10

1418	A539	30h dk red & blk	25	15
1419	A539	60h org & blk	25	15
1420	A539	1.60k blk & brt grn	75	25
		Nos. 1418-1420 (3)	1.25	
		Set value		38

Souvenir Sheet

1421	A539	5k multi	2.50	2.50

Brno Philatelic Exhibition, Sept. 11-25. No. 1421 contains one 30x40mm stamp.

First Meeting in Orbit — A540

Designs: 30h, Photograph of far side of Moon and Russian satellite. 60h, Photograph of Mars and Mariner 4. 80th, Soft landing on Moon. 1k, Satellite, laser beam and binary code. 1.20k, Telstar over Earth and receiving station.

1966, Sept. 26 *Perf. 11½*

1422	A540	20h vio & lt grn	15	15
1423	A540	30h blk & sal pink	15	15
1424	A540	60h slate & lilac	25	15
1425	A540	80h dk pur & lt bl	25	15
1426	A540	1k blk & vio	30	15
1427	A540	1.20k red & bl	*1.65*	*45*
		Nos. 1422-1427 (6)	*2.75*	
		Set value		*95*

Issued to publicize American and Russian achievements in space research.

Badger A541

Game Animals: 40h, Red deer, vert. 60h, Lynx. 80h, Hare. 1k, Red fox. 1.20k, Brown bear, vert. 2k, Wild boar.

1966, Nov. 28 **Litho.** *Perf. 13½*

1428	A541	30h multi	18	15
1429	A541	40h multi	20	15
1430	A541	60h multi	25	15
1431	A541	80h multi *(europaens)*	35	15
a.		80h multi *(europaeus)*	4.75	3.50
1432	A541	1k multi	45	20
1433	A541	1.20k multi	45	25
1434	A541	2k multi	*2.75*	*1.50*
		Nos. 1428-1434 (7)	*4.63*	*2.55*

The sheet of 50 of the 80h contains 40 with misspelling "europaens" and 10 with "europaeus."

"Spring" by Vaclav Hollar, 1607-77 A542

Paintings: No. 1436, Portrait of Mrs. F. Wussin, by Jan Kupecky (1667-1740). No. 1437, Snow Owl by Karel Purkyne (1834-1868). No. 1438, Tulips by Vaclav Spála (1885-1964). No. 1439, Recruit by Ludovít Fulla (1902-1980).

1966, Dec. 8 **Engr.** *Perf. 14*

1435	A542	1k black	4.50	4.25
1436	A542	1k multicolored	2.75	2.25
1437	A542	1k multicolored	2.75	2.25
1438	A542	1k multicolored	2.75	2.25
1439	A542	1k multicolored	*22.50*	*19.00*
		Nos. 1435-1439 (5)	*35.25*	*30.00*

Printed in sheets of 4 stamps and 2 labels. The labels in sheet of No. 1435 are inscribed "Vaclav Hollar 1607-1677" in fancy frame. Other labels are blank.

See No. 1484.

Symbolic Bird — A543

Engraved and Photogravure

1966, Dec. 17 *Perf. 11½*

1440	A543	1k dp blue & yel	65	65

Issued for Stamp Day.

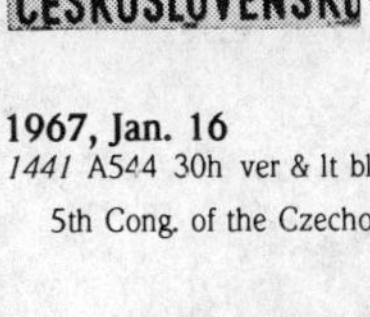

Youth — A544

1967, Jan. 16 *Perf. 11½*

1441	A544	30h ver & lt bl	18	15

5th Cong. of the Czechoslovak Youth Org.

Symbolic Flower and Machinery A545

1967, Jan. 16

1442	A545	30h carmine & yel	18	15

6th Trade Union Congress, Prague.

Parents with Dead Child — A545a

1967, Jan. 16 *Perf. 11½*

1442A	A545a	60h black & salmon	25	15

"Peace and Freedom in Viet Nam."

View of Jihlava and Tourist Year Emblem A546

Views and Tourist Year Emblem: 40h, Spielberg Castle and churches, Brno. 1.20k, Danube, castle and churches, Bratislava. 1.60k, Vlatava River bridges, Hradcany and churches, Prague.

1967, Feb. 13 **Engr.** *Perf. 11½*

Size: 40x23mm

1443	A546	30h brown violet	15	15
1444	A546	40h maroon	15	15

Size: 75x30mm

1445	A546	1.20k violet blue	40	16
1446	A546	1.60k black	*1.10*	*50*
		Nos. 1443-1446 (4)	1.80	
		Set value		*76*

International Tourist Year, 1967.

Black-tailed Godwit — A547

Birds: 40h, Shoveler, horiz. 60h, Purple heron. 80h, Penduline tit. 1k, Avocet. 1.40k, Black stork. 1.60k, Tufted duck, horiz.

1967, Feb. 20 **Litho.** *Perf. 13½*

1447	A547	30h multi	15	15
1448	A547	40h multi	24	15
1449	A547	60h multi	24	15
1450	A547	80h multi	50	15
1451	A547	1k multi	50	20
1452	A547	1.40k multi	32	20
1453	A547	1.60k multi	*2.50*	*1.00*
		Nos. 1447-1453 (7)	*4.45*	
		Set value		*1.80*

Solar Research and Satellite — A548

Space Research: 40h, Space craft, rocket and construction of station. 60h, Man on moon and orientation system. 1k, Exploration of solar system and rocket. 1.20k, Lunar satellites and moon photograph. 1.60k, Planned lunar architecture and moon landing.

Engraved and Photogravure

1967, Mar. 24 *Perf. 11½*

1454	A548	30h yel & dk red	15	15
1455	A548	40h vio bl & blk	15	15
1456	A548	60h lilac & grn	15	15
1457	A548	1k brt pink & sl	18	15
1458	A548	1.20k lt violet & blk	30	18
1459	A548	1.60k brn lake & blk	*1.10*	*60*
		Nos. 1454-1459 (6)	*2.03*	
		Set value		*1.00*

Gothic Painting, by Master Theodoric A549

Designs: 40h, "Burning of Master Hus," from Litomerice Hymnal. 60h, Modern glass sculpture. 80h, "The Shepherdess and the Chimney Sweep," Andersen fairy tale, painting by J. Trnka. 1k, Section of pressure vessel from atomic power station. 1.20k, Three ceramic figurines, by P. Rada. 3k, Montreal skyline and EXPO '67 emblem.

1967, Apr. 10 **Engr.** *Perf. 14*

Size: 37x23mm

1460	A549	30h multi	15	15
1461	A549	40h multi	15	15
1462	A549	60h multi	16	15
1463	A549	80h multi	22	15
1464	A549	1k multi	25	22
1465	A549	1.20k multi	*1.10*	*60*
		Nos. 1460-1465 (6)	*2.03*	*1.42*

Souvenir Sheet

Perf. 11½

Size: 40x30mm

1466	A549	3k multi	1.75	1.50

EXPO '67, International Exhibition, Montreal, Apr. 28-Oct. 27, 1967.

Canoe Race A550

Women Playing Basketball — A551

Designs: No. 1468, Wheels, dove and emblems of Warsaw, Berlin, Prague. 1.60k, Canoe slalom.

Perf. 12x11½, 11½x12

1967, Apr. 17 **Engr. & Photo.**

1467	A550	60h black & brt bl	20	15
1468	A550	60h black & salmon	20	15
1469	A551	60h black & grnsh bl	20	15
1470	A551	1.60k black & brt vio	*1.25*	*50*
		Nos. 1467-1470 (4)	*1.85*	
		Set value		*68*

No. 1467, 5th Intl. Wild-Water Canoeing Championships; No. 1468, 20th Warsaw-Berlin-Prague Bicycle Race: No. 1469, Women's Basketball Championships; No. 1470, 10th Intl. Water Slalom Championships.

The index in each volume of the Scott Catalogue contains many listings that help identify stamps.

"Golden Street" — A552

Designs: 60h, Interior of Hall of King Wenceslas. 5k, St. Matthew, from illuminated manuscript, 11th century.

1967, May 9 ***Perf. 11½x11***

1471 A552	30h	rose claret	20	15
1472 A552	60h	bluish black	45	15
		Set value		20

Souvenir Sheet

Perf. 11½

1473 A552	5k	multicolored	2.75	2.50

Issued to publicize the Castle of Prague.

Stylized Lyre with Flowers — A553

Old-New Synagogue, Prague — A554

1967, May 10 ***Perf. 11½***

1474 A553	60h	dull pur & brt grn	28	15

Prague Music Festival.

1967, May 22 ***Perf. 11½***

Designs: 30h, Detail from Torah curtain, 1593. 60h, Prague Printer's emblem, 1530. 1k, Mikulov jug, 1804. 1.40k, Memorial for Concentration Camp Victims 1939-45, Pincas Synagogue (menorah and tablet). 1.60k, Tombstone of David Gans, 1613.

1475 A554	30h	dull red & lt bl	15	15
1476 A554	60h	blk & lt grn	20	15
1477 A554	1k	dk bl & rose lil	25	15
1478 A554	1.20k	dk brn & mar	40	15
1479 A554	1.40k	black & yellow	40	15
1480 A554	1.60k	green & yel	*5.00*	*2.75*
		Nos. 1475-1480 (6)	*6.40*	*3.50*

Issued to show Jewish relics. The items shown on the 30h, 60h and 1k are from the State Jewish Museum, Prague.

"Lidice" A555

Prague Architecture A556

1967, June 9 **Unwmk.** ***Perf. 11½***

1481 A555	30h	black & brt rose	20	15

25th anniversary of the destruction of Lidice by the Nazis.

1967, June 10 **Engr. & Photo.**

1482 A556	1k	black & gold	45	20

Issued to publicize the 9th Congress of the International Union of Architects, Prague.

Peter Bezruc A557

1967, June 21

1483 A557	60h	dull rose & blk	25	15

Centenary of the birth of Peter Bezruc, poet and writer.

Painting Type of 1966

Design: 2k, Henri Rousseau (1844-1910), self-portrait.

1967, June 22 **Engr.** ***Perf. 11½***

1484 A542	2k	multicolored	1.75	1.25

Praga 68, World Stamp Exhibition, Prague, June 22-July 7, 1968. Printed in sheets of 4 stamps (2x2), separated by horizontal gutter with inscription and picture of Natl. Gallery, site of Praga 68.

View of Skalitz — A558

Designs: No. 1486, Mining tower and church steeple, Pribram. No. 1487, Hands holding book and view of Presov.

1967, Aug. 21 **Engr.** ***Perf. 11½***

1485 A558	30h	violet blue	15	15
1486 A558	30h	slate green	15	15
1487 A558	30h	claret	15	15
		Set value	25	15

Issued to commemorate anniversaries of the towns of Skalitz, Pribram and Presov.

Colonnade and Spring, Karlovy Vary and Communications Emblem — A559

1967, Aug. 21 **Engr. & Photo.**

1488 A559	30h	violet bl & gold	28	15

Issued to commemorate the 5th Sports and Cultural Festival of the Employees of the Ministry of Communications, Karlovy Vary.

Ondrejov Observatory and Galaxy — A560

1967, Aug. 22 **Engr.**

1489 A560	60h	vio bl, rose lil & sil	75	25

13th Cong. of the Intl. Astronomical Union.

Orchid — A561

Flowers from the Botanical Gardens: 30h, Cobaea scandens. 40h, Lycaste deppei. 60h, Glottiphyllum davisii. 1k, Anthurium. 1.20k, Rhodocactus. 1.40k, Moth orchid.

1967, Aug. 30 **Litho.** ***Perf. 12½***

1490 A561	20h	multicolored	15	15
1491 A561	30h	pink & multi	15	15
1492 A561	40h	multicolored	25	15
1493 A561	60h	lt blue & multi	30	15
1494 A561	1k	multicolored	50	18
1495 A561	1.20k	lt yellow & multi	60	30
1496 A561	1.40k	multicolored	*1.75*	*45*
		Nos. 1490-1496 (7)	*3.70*	
		Set value		*1.25*

Red Squirrel A562

Animals from the Tatra National Park: 60h, Wild cat. 1k, Ermine. 1.20k, Dormouse. 1.40k, Hedgehog. 1.60k, Pine marten.

Engraved and Photogravure

1967, Sept. 25 ***Perf. 11½***

1497 A562	30h	black, yel & org	25	15
1498 A562	60h	black & buff	25	15
1499 A562	1k	black & lt blue	32	15
1500 A562	1.20k	brn, pale grn & yel	50	15
1501 A562	1.40k	black, pink & yel	60	18
1502 A562	1.60k	black, org & yel	*2.50*	*1.00*
		Nos. 1497-1502 (6)	*4.42*	
		Set value		*1.55*

Rockets and Weapons — A563

1967, Oct. 6 **Engr.** ***Perf. 11½***

1503 A563	30h	slate green	30	15

Day of the Czechoslovak People's Army.

Cruiser "Aurora" Firing at Winter Palace A564

Designs: 60h, Hammer and sickle emblems and Red Star, vert. 1k, Hands reaching for hammer and sickle, vert.

1967, Nov. 7 **Engr. & Photo.**

1504 A564	30h	black & dk car	15	15
1505 A564	60h	black & dk car	15	15
1506 A564	1k	black & dk car	20	15
		Set value	38	18

Russian October Revolution, 50th anniv.

The Conjurer, by Frantisek Tichy A565

Paintings: 80h, Don Quixote, by Cyprian Majernik. 1k, Promenade in the Park, by Norbert Grund. 1.20k, Self-portrait, by Peter J. Brandl. 1.60k, Saints from Jan of Jeren Epitaph, by Czech Master of 1395.

1967, Nov. 13 **Engr.** ***Perf. 11½***

1507 A565	60h	multi	25	20
1508 A565	80h	multi	25	20
1509 A565	1k	multi	50	40
1510 A565	1.20k	multi	50	40
1511 A565	1.60k	multi	*4.50*	*3.75*
		Nos. 1507-1511 (5)	*6.00*	*4.95*

Sheets of 4. See Nos. 1589-1593, 1658-1662, 1711-1715, 1779-1783, 1847-1851, 1908-1913, 2043-2047, 2090-2093, 2147-2151, 2265-2269, 2335-2339, 2386-2390, 2437-2441, 2534-2538, 2586-2590, 2634-2638, 2810-2813, 2843-2847, 2872-2874, 2908-2910, 2936-2938.

Pres. Antonin Novotny — A566

1967, Dec. 9 **Engr.** ***Perf. 11½***

1512 A566	2k	blue gray	90	15
1513 A566	3k	brown	1.40	15
		Set value		15

Czechoslovakia Nos. 65, 71 and 81 of 1920 — A567

1967, Dec. 18

1514 A567	1k	maroon & silver	95	75

Issued for Stamp Day.

Symbolic Flag and Dates — A568

1968, Jan. 15 **Engr.** ***Perf. 11½***

1515 A568	30h	red, dk bl & ultra	25	15

50th anniversary of Czechoslovakia.

Figure Skating and Olympic Rings — A569

Designs (Olympic Rings and): 1k, Ski course. 1.60k, Toboggan chute. 2k, Ice hockey.

1968, Jan. 29 **Engr. & Photo.**

1516 A569	60h blk, yel & ocher	18	15
1517 A569	1k ol grn, lt bl & lem	24	15
1518 A569	1.60k blk, lil & bl grn	42	18
1519 A569	2k blk, ap grn & lt bl	*1.25*	55
	Nos. 1516-1519 (4)	*2.09*	*1.03*

10th Winter Olympic Games, Grenoble, France, Feb. 6-18.

Factories and Rising Sun — A570

Design: 60h, Workers and banner.

1968, Feb. 25 ***Perf. 11½x12***

1520 A570	30h car & dk bl	15	15
1521 A570	60h car & dk bl	18	15
	Set value		15

20th anniversary of February Revolution.

Map of Battle of Sokolow — A571

Human Rights Flame — A572

1968, Mar. 8 ***Perf. 11½***

1522 A571	30h blk, brt bl & car	25	15

Engr.

1523 A572	1k rose carmine	65	30
	Set value		35

25th anniv. of the Battle of Sokolow, Mar. 8, 1943, against the German Army, No. 1522; Intl. Human Rights Year, No. 1523.

Janko Kral and Liptovsky Mikulas — A573

Karl Marx — A574

Girl's Head — A575

Arms and Allegory — A576

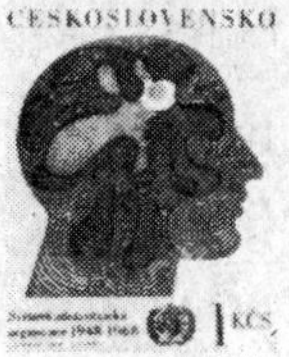

Head — A577

1968, Mar. 25 **Engr.**

1524 A573	30h green	15	15
1525 A574	30h claret	15	15

Engraved and Photogravure

1526 A575	30h dk red & gold	15	15
1527 A576	30h dk blue & dp org	15	15
1528 A577	1k multicolored	50	20
	Nos. 1524-1528 (5)	1.10	
	Set value		40

The writer Janko Kral and the Slovak town Liptovsky Mikulas (No. 1524); 150th anniv. of the birth of Karl Marx (No. 1525); cent. of the cornerstone laying of the Prague Natl. Theater (No. 1526); 150th anniv. of the Prague Natl. Museum (No. 1527); 20th anniv. of WHO (1k).

Symbolic Radio Waves A578

Design: No. 1530, Symbolic television screens.

1968, Apr. 29 ***Perf. 11½***

1529 A578	30h blk, car & vio bl	15	15
1530 A578	30h blk, car & vio bl	15	15
	Set value		15

45th anniv. of Czechoslovak broadcasting (#1529), 15th anniv. of television (#1530).

Olympic Rings, Mexican Sculpture and Diver — A579

Olympic Rings and: 40h, Runner and "The Sanctification of Quetzalcoatl." 60h, Volleyball and Mexican ornaments. 1k, Czechoslovak and Mexican Olympic emblems and carved altar. 1.60k, Soccer and ornaments. 2k, View of Hradcany, weather vane and key.

1968, Apr. 30

1531 A579	30h black, bl & car	15	15
1532 A579	40h multi	16	15
1533 A579	60h multi	25	15
1534 A579	1k multi	35	15
1535 A579	1.60k multi	50	20
1536 A579	2k black & multi	*2.00*	*55*
	Nos. 1531-1536 (6)	*3.41*	
	Set value		*1.05*

Issued to publicize the 19th Olympic Games, Mexico City, Oct. 12-27.

Prague Castle Types of 1966

Designs: 30h, Tombstone of Bretislav I. 60h, Romanesque door knocker, St. Wenceslas Chapel. 5k, Head of St. Peter, mosaic from Golden Gate of St. Vitus Cathedral.

1968, May 9 ***Perf. 11½***

1537 A527	30h multicolored	15	15
1538 A527	60h black, red & cit	20	15
	Set value		15

Souvenir Sheet

Engr.

1539 A528	5k multicolored	2.50	2.50

Pres. Ludvik Svoboda — A580

1968-70 **Engr.** ***Perf. 11½***

1540 A580	30h ultramarine	15	15
1540A A580	50h green ('70)	15	15
1541 A580	60h maroon	15	15
1541A A580	1k rose car ('70)	30	15
	Nos. 1540-1541A (4)	75	
	Set value		20

Shades exist of No. 1541A.

"Business," Sculpture by Otto Gutfreund — A581

Cabaret Performer, by Frantisek Kupka A582

Designs (The New Prague): 40h, Broadcasting Corporation Building. 60h, New Parliament. 1.40k, Tapestry by Jan Bauch "Prague 1787." 3k, Presidential standard.

Engr. & Photo.; Engr. (2k)

1968, June 5

1542 A581	30h black & multi	18	15
1543 A581	40h black & multi	18	15
1544 A581	60h dk brown & multi	24	15
1545 A581	1.40k dk brown & multi	60	15
1546 A582	2k indigo & multi	*1.75*	*1.75*
1547 A581	3k black & multi	75	50
	Nos. 1542-1547 (6)	*3.70*	*2.85*

1968, June 21 ***Perf. 11½***

Designs (The Old Prague): 30h, St. George's Basilica. 60h, Renaissance fountain. 1k, Villa America-Dvorak Museum, 18th cent. building. 1.60k, Emblem from the House of Three Violins, 18th cent. 2k, Josefina, by Josef Manes. 3k, Emblem of Prague, 1475.

1548 A581	30h green, gray & yel	20	15
1549 A581	60h dk vio, ap grn & gold	20	15
1550 A581	1k black, lt bl & pink	30	15
1551 A581	1.60k slate grn & multi	55	20
1552 A582	2k brown & multi	*1.25*	*1.25*
1553 A581	3k blk, yel, bl & pink	1.25	30
	Nos. 1548-1553 (6)	*3.75*	*2.20*

Nos. 1542-1553 publicized the Praga 68 Philatelic Exhibition. Nos. 1542-1545, 1547-1551, 1553 issued in sheets of 15 + 15 labels with Praga 68 emblem and inscription. Nos. 1546, 1552 issued in sheets of 4 (2x2) with one horizontal label between top and bottom rows showing Praga 68 emblem.

Souvenir Sheet

View of Prague and Emblems — A583

Engraved and Photogravure

1968, June 22 ***Imperf.***

1554 A583	10k multicolored	3.75	3.50

Praga 68 and 50th anniv. of Czechoslovak postage stamps. Sold only together with a 5k admission ticket to the Praga 68 philatelic Exhibition.

Madonna with the Rose Garlands, by Dürer A584

1968, July 6 ***Perf. 11½***

1555 A584	5k multicolored	3.75	2.25

FIP Day, July 6. Issued in sheets of 4 (2x2) with one horizontal label between, showing Praga 68 emblem.

Stagecoach on Rails A585

Design: 1k, Steam and electric locomotives.

1968, Aug. 6

1556 A585	60h multicolored	32	15
1557 A585	1k multicolored	45	18

No. 1556: 140th anniv. of the horse-drawn railroad Ceské Budejovice to Linz; No. 1557: cent. of the Ceské Budejovice to Plzen railroad.

6th Intl. Slavonic Cong. in Prague — A586

1968, Aug. 7 ***Perf. 11½***

1558 A586	30h vio blue & car	50	15

Ardspach Rocks and Ammonite — A587

Designs: 60h, Basalt formation and frog skeleton fossil. 80h, Rocks, basalt veins and polished agate. 1k, Pelecypoda (fossil shell) and Belanske Tatra mountains. 1.60k, Trilobite and Barrande rock formation.

1968, Aug. 8

1559	A587	30h black & citron	15	15
1560	A587	60h black & rose cl	16	15
1561	A587	80h black, lt vio & pink	20	15
1562	A587	1k black & lt blue	25	15
1563	A587	1.60k black & bister	*1.40*	*65*
		Nos. 1559-1563 (5)	*2.16*	
		Set value		*1.00*

Issued to publicize the 23rd International Geological Congress, Prague, Aug. 8-Sept. 3.

Raising Slovak Flag A588

Design: 60h, Slovak partisans, and mountain.

1968, Sept. 9 Engr. *Perf. 11½*

1564	A588	30h ultra	15	15
1565	A588	60h red	20	15
		Set value		15

No. 1564 for the Slovak Natl. Council, No. 1565 the 120th anniv. of the Slovak national uprising.

Flowerpot, by Jiri Schlessinger (age 10) — A589

Drawings by Children in Terezin Concentration Camp: 30h, Jew and Guard, by Jiri Beutler (age 10). 60h, Butterflies, by Kitty Brunnerova (age 11).

Engraved and Photogravure

1968, Sept. 30 *Perf. 11½*

Size: 30x23mm

1566	A589	30h blk, buff & rose lil	15	15
1567	A589	60h black & multi	18	15

Perf. 12x11½

Size: 41x23mm

1568	A589	1k black & multi	30	15
		Nos. 1566-1568 (3)	63	
		Set value		25

30th anniversary of Munich Pact.

Arms of Regional Capitals — A590

Arms of Prague — A591

1968, Oct. 21 *Perf. 11½*

1569	A590	60h Banská Bystrica	15	15
1570	A590	60h Bratislava	15	15
1571	A590	60h Brno	15	15
1572	A590	60h Ceské Budejovice	15	15
1573	A590	60h Hradec Králové	15	15
1574	A590	60h Kosice	15	15
1575	A590	60h Ostrava (horse)	15	15
1576	A590	60h Plzen	15	15
1577	A590	60h Ustí nad Labem	15	15

Perf. 11½x16

1578	A591	1k shown	75	25
		Nos. 1569-1578 (10)	2.10	
		Set value		80

#1578 issued in sheets of 10. See #1652-1657, 1742-1747, 1886-1888, 2000-2001.

Flag and Linden Leaves A592

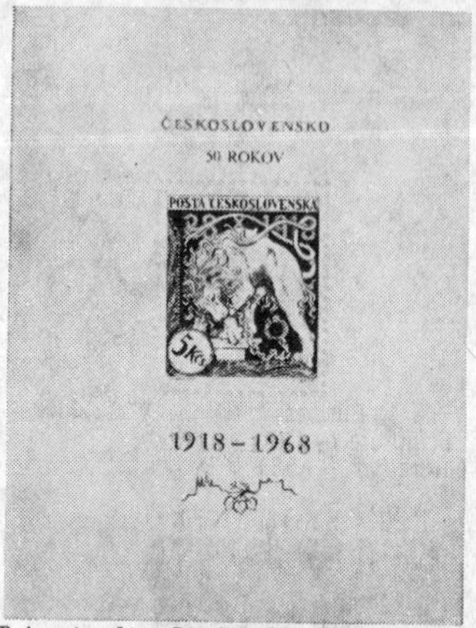

Bohemian Lion Breaking Chains (Type SP1 of 1919) — A593

Design: 60h, Map of Czechoslovakia, linden leaves, Hradcany in Prague and Castle in Bratislava.

1968, Oct. 28 *Perf. 12x11½*

1579	A592	30h dp blue & magenta	20	15
1580	A592	60h blk, gold, red & ultra	20	15
		Set value		15

Souvenir Sheet

Engr.

Perf. 11½x12

1581	A593	5k red	2.50	2.25

Founding of Czechoslovakia, 50th anniv.

Ernest Hemingway A594

Cinderlad A595

Caricatures: 30h, Karel Capek (1890-1938), writer. 40h, George Bernard Shaw. 60h, Maxim Gorki. 1k, Pablo Picasso. 1.20k, Taikan Yokoyama (1868-1958), painter. 1.40k, Charlie Chaplin.

Engraved and Photogravure

1968, Nov. 18 *Perf. 11½x12*

1582	A594	20h black, org & red	15	15
1583	A594	30h black & multi	15	15
1584	A594	40h black, lilac & car	15	15
1585	A594	60h black, sky bl & grn	15	15
1586	A594	1k black, brn & yel	28	15
1587	A594	1.20k black, dp car & vio	30	18
1588	A594	1.40k black, brn & dp org	*1.50*	*50*
		Nos. 1582-1588 (7)	*2.68*	
		Set value		*1.05*

Cultural personalities of the 20th cent. and UNESCO. See Nos. 1628-1633.

Painting Type of 1967

Czechoslovakian Art: 60h, Cleopatra II, by Jan Zrzavy (1890-1977). 80h, Black Lake (man and horse), by Jan Preisler (1872-1918). 1.20k, Giovanni Francisci as a Volunteer, by Peter Michal Bohun (1822-1879). 1.60k, Princess Hyacinth, by Alfons Mucha (1860-1939). 3k, Madonna and Child, woodcarving, 1518, by Master Paul of Levoca.

1968, Nov. 29 Engr. *Perf. 11½*

1589	A565	60h multi	38	24
1590	A565	80h multi	38	38
1591	A565	1.20k multi	1.10	60
1592	A565	1.60k multi	75	85
1593	A565	3k multi	*4.50*	*3.50*
		Nos. 1589-1593 (5)	*7.11*	*5.57*

Sheets of 4.

1968, Dec. 18 Engr. & Photo.

Slovak Fairy Tales: 60h, The Proud Lady. 80h, The Ruling Knight. 1k, Good Day, Little Bench. 1.20k, The Spellbound Castle. 1.80k, The Miraculous Hunter. The designs are from illustrations by Ludovit Fulla for "Slovak Stories."

1594	A595	30h multi	15	15
1595	A595	60h multi	16	15
1596	A595	80h multi	22	15
1597	A595	1k multi	30	15
1598	A595	1.20k multi	30	15
1599	A595	1.80k multi	*1.50*	*65*
		Nos. 1594-1599 (6)	*2.63*	
		Set value		*1.00*

Czechoslovakia Nos. 2 and 3 — A596

1968, Dec. 18

1600	A596	1k violet bl & gold	75	65

50th anniv. of Czechoslovakian postage stamps.

Crescent, Cross and Lion and Sun Emblems A597

ILO Emblem A598

Design: 60h, 12 crosses in circles forming large cross.

1969, Jan. 31 *Perf. 11½*

1601	A597	60h black, red & gold	20	15
1602	A597	1k black, ultra & red	35	15
		Set value		20

No. 1601: 50th anniv. of the Czechoslovak Red Cross. No. 1602: 50th anniv. of the League of Red Cross Societies.

1969, Jan. 31

1603	A598	1k black & gray	28	15

50th anniv. of the ILO.

Cheb Pistol — A599

Historical Firearms: 40h, Italian pistol with Dutch decorations, c. 1600. 60h, Wheellock rifle from Matej Kubik workshop c. 1720. 1k, Flintlock pistol, Devieuxe workshop, Liege, c. 1760. 1.40k, Duelling pistols, from Lebeda workshop, Prague, c. 1835. 1.60k, Derringer pistols, US, c. 1865.

1969, Feb. 18

1604	A599	30h black & multi	15	15
1605	A599	40h black & multi	16	15
1606	A599	60h black & multi	16	15
1607	A599	1k black & multi	24	15
1608	A599	1.40k black & multi	35	15
1609	A599	1.60k black & multi	*1.25*	*48*
		Nos. 1604-1609 (6)	*2.31*	
		Set value		*85*

Bratislava Castle, Muse and Book — A600

Designs: No. 1611, Science symbols and emblem (Brno University). No. 1612, Harp, laurel and musicians' names. No. 1613, Theatrical scene. No. 1614, Arms of Slovakia, banner and blossoms. No. 1615, School, outstretched hands and woman with linden leaves.

1969, Mar. 24 Engr. *Perf. 11½*

1610	A600	60h violet blue	20	15

Engraved and Photogravure

1611	A600	60h black, gold & slate	20	15
1612	A600	60h gold, blue, blk & red	20	15
1613	A600	60h black & rose red	20	15
1614	A600	60h rose red, sil & bl	20	15
1615	A600	60h black & gold	20	15
		Nos. 1610-1615 (6)	1.20	
		Set value		30

50th anniv. of: Komensky University in Bratislava (#1610); Brno University (#1611); Brno Conservatory of Music (#1612); Slovak Natl. Theater (#1613); Slovak Soviet Republic (#1614); cent. of the Zniev Gymnasium (academic high school) (#1615).

Baldachin-top Car and Four-seat Coupé of 1900-1905 — A601

Designs: 1.60k, Laurin & Klement Voiturette, 1907, and L & K touring car with American top, 1907. 1.80k, First Prague bus, 1907, and sectionalized Skoda bus, 1967.

1969, Mar. 25 Engr. & Photo.

1616	A601	30h blk, lil & lt grn	15	15
1617	A601	1.60k blk, org brn & lt bl	40	20
1618	A601	1.80k multi	*1.25*	*75*
		Nos. 1616-1618 (3)	*1.80*	*1.10*

Peace, by Ladislav Guderna — A602

1969, Apr. 21 *Perf. 11*

1619	A602	1.60k multi	50	35

20th anniv. of the Peace Movement. Issued in sheets of 15 stamps and 5 tabs.

Horse and Rider, by Vaclav Hollar — A603

Old Engravings of Horses: 30h, Prancing Stallion, by Hendrik Goltzius, horiz. 80h, Groom Leading Horse, by Matthäus Merian, horiz. 1.80k, Horse and Soldier, by Albrecht Dürer. 2.40k, Groom and Horse, by Johann E. Ridinger.

Perf. 11x11½, 11½x11

1969, Apr. 24

Yellowish Paper

1620	A603	30h dark brown	20	15
1621	A603	80h violet brown	20	15
1622	A603	1.60k slate	40	15
1623	A603	1.80k sepia	40	25
1624	A603	2.40k multi	*2.75*	*70*
		Nos. 1620-1624 (5)	*3.95*	*1.40*

M. R. Stefánik as Astronomy Professor and French General A604

1969, May 4 Engr. *Perf. 11½*

1625	A604	60h rose claret	20	15

Gen. Milan R. Stefánik, 50th death anniv.

St. Wenceslas Pressing Wine, Mural by the Master of Litomerice A605

Design: No. 1627, Coronation banner of the Estates, 1723, with St. Wenceslas and coats of arms of Bohemia and Czech Crown lands.

1969, May 9 Engr. *Perf. 11½*

1626	A605	3k multicolored	1.50	1.40
1627	A605	3k multicolored	1.50	1.40

Issued to publicize the art treasures of the Castle of Prague. See Nos. 1689-1690.

Caricature Type of 1968

Caricatures: 30h, Pavol Orszagh Hviezdoslav (1849-1921), Slovak writer. 40h, Gilbert K. Chesterton (1874-1936), English writer. 60h, Vladimir Mayakovski (1893-1930), Russian poet. 1k, Henri Matisse (1869-1954), French painter. 1.80k, Ales Hrdlicka (1869-1943), Czech-born American anthropologist. 2k, Franz Kafka (1883-1924), Austrian writer.

Engraved and Photogravure

1969, June 17 *Perf. 11½x12*

1628	A594	30h black, red & blue	15	15
1629	A594	40h black, blue & lt vio	15	15
1630	A594	60h black, rose & yel	15	15
1631	A594	1k black & multi	28	15
1632	A594	1.80k blk, ultra & ocher	35	18
1633	A594	2k blk, yel & brt grn	*1.50*	*50*
		Nos. 1628-1633 (6)	*2.58*	
		Set value		*95*

Issued to honor cultural personalities of the 20th century and UNESCO.

"Music," by Alfons Mucha — A606

Paintings by Mucha: 60h, "Painting." 1k, "Dance." 2.40k, "Ruby" and "Amethyst."

1969, July 14 *Perf. 11½x11*

Size: 30x49mm

1634	A606	30h black & multi	15	15
1635	A606	60h black & multi	15	15
1636	A606	1k black & multi	18	15

Size: 39x51mm

1637	A606	2.40k black & multi	*1.40*	*1.10*
		Nos. 1634-1637 (4)	*1.88*	
		Set value		*1.30*

Alfons Mucha (1860-1930), painter and stamp designer (Type A1).

Pres. Svoboda and Partisans A607

Design: No. 1639, Slovak fighters and mourners.

1969, Aug. 29 *Perf. 11*

1638	A607	30h ol grn & red, *yel*	15	15
1639	A607	30h vio bl & red, *yel*	15	15
		Set value	24	15

25th anniversary of the Slovak uprising and of the Battle of Dukla.

Tatra Mountain Stream and Gentians A608

Designs: 60h, Various views in Tatra Mountains. No. 1644, Mountain pass and gentians. No. 1645, Houses, Krivan Mountain and autumn crocuses.

1969, Sept. 8 Engr. *Perf. 11*

Size: 71x33mm

1640	A608	60h gray	22	15
1641	A608	60h dark blue	22	15
1642	A608	60h dull gray vio	22	15

Perf. 11½

Size: 40x23mm

1643	A608	1.60k multi	40	18
1644	A608	1.60k multi	*1.50*	*50*
1645	A608	1.60k multi	40	18
		Nos. 1640-1645 (6)	*2.96*	
		Set value		*1.05*

20th anniv. of the creation of the Tatra Mountains Natl. Park. Nos. 1640-1642 are printed in sheets of 15 (3x5) with 5 labels showing mountain plants. Nos. 1643-1645 issued in sheets of 10.

Bronze Belt Ornaments A609

Archaeological Treasures from Bohemia and Moravia: 30h, Gilt ornament with 6 masks. 1k, Jeweled earrings. 1.80k, Front and back of lead cross with Greek inscription. 2k, Gilt strap ornament with human figure.

Engraved and Photogravure

1969, Sept. 30 *Perf. 11½x11*

1646	A609	20h gold & multi	15	15
1647	A609	30h gold & multi	15	15
1648	A609	1k red & multi	20	15
1649	A609	1.80k dull org & multi	35	20
1650	A609	2k gold & multi	*1.75*	*40*
		Nos. 1646-1650 (5)	*2.60*	
		Set value		*80*

"Mail Circling the World" A610

1969, Oct. 1 Engr. *Perf. 12*

1651	A610	3.20k multi	1.40	90

16th UPU Cong., Tokyo, Oct. 1-Nov. 14. Issued in sheets of 4.

Coat of Arms Type of 1968

Engraved and Photogravure

1969, Oct. 25 *Perf. 11½*

1652	A590	50h Bardejov	16	15
1653	A590	50h Hranice	16	15
1654	A590	50h Kezmarok	16	15
1655	A590	50h Krnov	16	15
1656	A590	50h Litomerice	16	15
1657	A590	50h Manetin	16	15
		Nos. 1652-1657 (6)	96	
		Set value		30

Painting Type of 1968

Designs: 60h, Requiem, 1944, by Frantisek Muzika. 1k, Resurrection, 1380, by the Master of the Trebon Altar. 1.60k, Crucifixion, 1950, by Vincent Hloznik. 1.80k, Girl with Doll, 1863, by Julius Bencur. 2.20k, St. Jerome, 1357-67, by Master Theodorik.

1969, Nov. 25 *Perf. 11½*

1658	A565	60h multi	25	22
1659	A565	1k multi	25	22
1660	A565	1.60k multi	35	30
1661	A565	1.80k multi	65	55
1662	A565	2.20k multi	*2.50*	*2.25*
		Nos. 1658-1662 (5)	*4.00*	*3.54*

Sheets of 4.

Symbolic Sheet of Stamps — A611

1969, Dec. 18 *Perf. 11½x12*

1663	A611	1k dk brn, ultra & gold	40	40

Issued for Stamp Day 1969.

Ski Jump — A612

Designs: 60h, Long distance skier. 1k, Ski jump and slope. 1.60k, Woman skier.

1970, Jan. 6 *Perf. 11½*

1664	A612	50h multi	15	15
1665	A612	60h multi	15	15
1666	A612	1k multi	20	15
1667	A612	1.60k multi	*1.00*	*32*
		Nos. 1664-1667 (4)	*1.50*	
		Set value		*52*

Intl. Ski Championships "Tatra 1970."

Ludwig van Beethoven — A613

Portraits: No. 1669, Friedrich Engels (1820-95), German socialist. No. 1670, Maximilian Hell (1720-92), Slovakian Jesuit and astronomer. No. 1671, Lenin, Russian Communist leader. No. 1672, Josef Manes (1820-71), Czech painter. No. 1673, Comenius (1592-1670), theologian and educator.

1970, Feb. 17 Engr. *Perf. 11x11½*

1668	A613	40h black	15	15
1669	A613	40h dull red	15	15
1670	A613	40h yellow brn	15	15
1671	A613	40h dull red	15	15
1672	A613	40h brown	15	15
1673	A613	40h black	15	15
		Set value	65	30

Anniversaries of birth of Beethoven, Engels, Hell, Lenin and Manes, 300th anniv. of the death of Comenius, and to honor UNESCO.

Bells A614

Designs: 80h, Machine tools and lathe. 1k, Folklore masks. 1.60k, Angel and Three Wise Men, 17th century icon from Koniec. 2k, View of Orlik Castle, 1787, by F. K. Wolf. 3k, "Passing through Koshu down to Mishima" from Hokusai's 36 Views of Fuji.

Engraved and Photogravure

1970, Mar. 13 *Perf. 11½x11*

Size: 40x23mm

1674	A614	50h multi	15	15
1675	A614	80h multi	18	15
1676	A614	1k multi	25	15

Size: 50x40mm

Perf. 11½

1677	A614	1.60k multi	45	30
1678	A614	2k multi	60	35
1679	A614	3k multi	*1.65*	*1.00*
		Nos. 1674-1679 (6)	*3.28*	*2.10*

EXPO '70 Intl. Exhib., Osaka, Japan, Mar. 15-Sept. 13, 1970. Nos. 1674-1676 issued in sheets of 50, Nos. 1677-1679 in sheets of 4.

Kosice Townhall, Laurel and Czechoslovak Arms — A615

1970, Apr. 5 *Perf. 11*

1680	A615	60h slate, ver & gold	25	15

Government's Kosice Program, 25th anniv.

"The Remarkable Horse" by Josef Lada — A616

Lenin — A617

Paintings by Josef Lada: 60h, Autumn, 1955, horiz. 1.80k, "The Water Sprite." 2.40k, Children in Winter, 1943, horiz.

1970, Apr. 21 *Perf. 11½*

1681	A616	60h black & multi	18	15
1682	A616	1k black & multi	35	15
1683	A616	1.80k black & multi	45	20
1684	A616	2.40k black & multi	*1.50*	*65*
		Nos. 1681-1684 (4)	*2.48*	*1.15*

1970, Apr. 22

Design: 60h, Lenin without cap, facing left.

1685	A617	30h	dk red & gold	15	15
1686	A617	60h	black & gold	18	15
			Set value	33	15

Lenin (1870-1924), Russian communist leader.

Fighters on the Barricades — A618

Design: No. 1688, Lilac, Russian tank and castle.

1970, May 5 *Perf. 11x11½*

1687	A618	30h	dull pur, gold & bl	15	15
1688	A618	30h	dull grn, gold & red	15	15
			Set value	25	15

No. 1687: 25th anniv. of the Prague uprising. No. 1688: 25th anniv. of the liberation of Czechoslovakia from the Germans.

Prague Castle Art Type of 1969

Designs: No. 1689, Bust of St. Vitus, 1486. No. 1690, Hermes and Athena, by Bartholomy Springer (1546-1611), mural from White Tower.

1970, May 7 Engr. *Perf. 11½*

1689	A605	3k	maroon & multi	1.75	1.50
1690	A605	3k	lt blue & multi	1.75	1.50

Compass Rose, UN Headquarters and Famous Buildings of the World — A619

Engraved and Photogravure

1970, June 26 *Perf. 11*

1691	A619	1k	black & multi	25	20

25th anniv. of the UN. Issued in sheets of 15 (3x5) and 5 labels showing UN emblem.

Cannon from 30 Years' War and Baron Munchhausen — A620

Historical Cannons: 60h, Cannon from Hussite war and St. Barbara. 1.20k, Cannon from Prussian-Austrian war, and legendary cannoneer Javurek. 1.80k, Early 20th century cannon and spaceship "La Colombiad" (Jules Verne). 2.40k, World War I cannon and "Good Soldier Schweik."

1970, Aug. 31 *Perf. 11½*

1692	A620	30h	black & multi	15	15
1693	A620	60h	black & multi	15	15
1694	A620	1.20k	black & multi	35	15
1695	A620	1.80k	black & multi	35	18
1696	A620	2.40k	black & multi	*1.65*	*65*
			Nos. 1692-1696 (5)	*2.65*	
			Set value		*1.00*

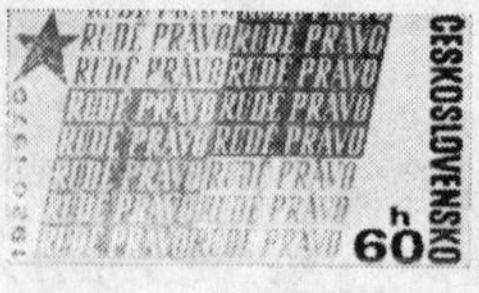

"Rude Pravo" (Red Truth) A621

1970, Sept. 21 *Perf. 11½x11*

1697	A621	60h	car, gold & blk	15	15

50th anniv. of the Rude Pravo newspaper.

"Great Sun" House Sign and Old Town Tower Bridge, Prague — A622

Designs: 60h, "Blue Lion" and Town Hall Tower, Brno. 1k, Gothic corner stone and Town Hall Tower, Bratislava. 1.40k, Coat of Arms and Gothic Tower, Bratislava, and medallion. 1.60k, Moravian Eagle and Gothic Town Hall Tower, Brno. 1.80k, "Black Sun" and "Green Frog" house signs and New Town Hall, Prague.

1970, Sept. 23 *Perf. 11x11½*

1698	A622	40h	black & multi	15	15
1699	A622	60h	black & multi	15	15
1700	A622	1k	black & multi	26	15
1701	A622	1.40k	black & multi	*1.75*	*52*
1702	A622	1.60k	black & multi	45	16
1703	A622	1.80k	black & multi	55	20
			Nos. 1698-1703 (6)	*3.31*	
			Set value		*1.10*

Germany-Uruguay Semifinal Soccer Match — A623

Designs: 20h, Sundisk Games' emblem and flags of participating nations. 60h, England-Czechoslovakia match and coats of arms. 1k, Romania-Czechoslovakia match and coats of arms. 1.20k, Brazil-Italy, final match and emblems. 1.80k, Brazil-Czechoslovakia match and emblems.

1970, Oct. 29 *Perf. 11½*

1704	A623	20h	blk & multi	15	15
1705	A623	40h	blk & multi	15	15
1706	A623	60h	blk & multi	16	15
1707	A623	1k	blk & multi	30	15
1708	A623	1.20k	blk & multi	35	15
1709	A623	1.80k	blk & multi	*1.75*	*45*
			Nos. 1704-1709 (6)	*2.86*	
			Set value		*75*

9th World Soccer Championships for the Jules Rimet Cup, Mexico City, May 30-June 21.

Congress Emblem — A624

1970, Nov. 9 Engr. & Photo.

1710	A624	30h	blk, gold, ultra & red	20	15

Congress of the Czechoslovak Socialist Youth Federation.

Painting Type of 1967

Paintings: 1k, Seated Mother, by Mikulas Galanda. 1.20k, Bridesmaid, by Karel Svolinsky. 1.40k, Walk by Night, 1944, by Frantisek Hudecek. 1.80k, Banska Bystrica Market, by Dominik Skutecky. 2.40k, Adoration of the Kings, from the Vysehrad Codex, 1085.

1970, Nov. 27 Engr. *Perf. 11½*

1711	A565	1k	multi	25	25
1712	A565	1.20k	multi	35	35
1713	A565	1.40k	multi	40	40
1714	A565	1.80k	multi	50	45
1715	A565	2.40k	multi	*2.25*	*2.25*
			Nos. 1711-1715 (5)	*3.75*	*3.70*

Sheets of 4.

Radar — A625

Designs: 40h, Interkosmos 3, geophysical satellite. 60h, Molniya meteorological satellite. 1k, Astronaut and Vostok satellite. No. 1720, Interkosmos 4, solar research satellite. No. 1720A, Space satellite (Sputnik) over city. 1.60k, Two-stage rocket on launching pad.

1970-71 Engr. & Photo. *Perf. 11*

1716	A625	20h	blk & multi	15	15
1717	A625	40h	blk & multi	15	15
1718	A625	60h	blk & multi	15	15
1719	A625	1k	blk & multi	25	15
1720	A625	1.20k	blk & multi	35	15
1720A	A625	1.20k	blk & multi ('71)	35	15
1721	A625	1.60k	blk & multi	*1.40*	*35*
			Nos. 1716-1721 (7)	*2.80*	
			Set value		*80*

Issued to publicize "Interkosmos," the collaboration of communist countries in various phases of space research. Issue dates: No. 1720A, Nov. 15, 1971; others, Nov. 30, 1970.

Face of Christ on Veronica's Veil — A626

Slovak Ikons, 16th-18th Centuries: 60h, Adam and Eve in the Garden, vert. 2k, St. George and the Dragon. 2.80k, St. Michael, vert.

1970, Dec. 17 Engr. *Perf. 11½*

Cream Paper

1722	A626	60h	multi	18	15
1723	A626	1k	multi	28	25
1724	A626	2k	multi	52	48
1725	A626	2.80k	multi	*1.65*	*1.65*
			Nos. 1722-1725 (4)	*2.63*	*2.53*

Sheets of 4.

Carrier Pigeon Type of 1920 — A627

Engraved and Photogravure

1970, Dec. 18 *Perf. 11x11½*

1726	A627	1k	red, blk & yel grn	50	50

Stamp Day.

Song of the Barricades, 1938, by Karel Stika — A628

Designs (Czech and Slovak Graphic Art): 50h, Fruit Grower's Barge, 1941, by Cyril Bouda. 60h, Moon (woman) Searching for Lilies of the Valley, 1913, by Jan Zrzavy. 1k, At the Edge of Town (working man and woman), 1931, by Koloman Sokol. 1.60k, Summer, 1641, by Vaclav Hollar. 2k, Gamekeeper and Shepherd of Orava Castle, 1847, by Peter M. Bohun.

Engr. & Photo.; Engr. (40h, 60h, 1k)

1971, Jan. 28 *Perf. 11½*

1727	A628	40h	brown	15	15
1728	A628	50h	black & multi	15	15
1729	A628	60h	slate	15	15
1730	A628	1k	black	30	15
1731	A628	1.60k	black & buff	48	16
1732	A628	2k	black & multi	*1.25*	*32*
			Nos. 1727-1732 (6)	*2.48*	
			Set value		*75*

Saris Church A629

Bell Tower, Hronsek A630

Designs: 1k, Roofs and folk art, Horácko. 2.40k, House, Jicin. 3k, House and folk art, Melnik. 3.60k, Church of St. Bartholomew, Chrudim. 5k, Watch Tower, Nachod. 5.40k, Baroque house, Posumavi. 6k, Cottage, Orava. 9k, Cottage, Turnov. 10k, Old houses, Liptov. 14k, House and wayside bell stand. 20k, Houses, Cicmany.

Engraved and Photogravure

1971-72 *Perf. 11½x11, 11x11½*

1733	A630	1k	multi	25	15
1734	A629	1.60k	multi	45	15
1735	A630	2k	multi	55	15
1736	A629	2.40k	multi	65	15
1736A	A630	3k	multi ('72)	85	15
1737	A629	3.60k	multi	1.00	15
1737A	A630	5k	multi ('72)	1.25	15
1738	A629	5.40k	multi	1.25	15
1739	A630	6k	multi	1.50	15
1740	A630	9k	multi	2.25	25
1740A	A629	10k	multi ('72)	2.75	25
1741	A629	14k	multi	3.25	22
1741A	A629	20k	multi ('72)	5.00	75
			Nos. 1733-1741A (13)	21.00	
			Set value		2.00

Nos. 1736A, 1738, 1740 are horizontal.

See No. 2870.

Coat of Arms Type of 1968

1971, Mar. 26 *Perf. 11½*

1742	A590	60h	Zilina	16	15
1743	A590	60h	Levoca	16	15
1744	A590	60h	Ceska Trebova	16	15
1745	A590	60h	Uhersky Brod	16	15
1746	A590	60h	Trutnov	16	15
1747	A590	60h	Karlovy Vary	16	15
			Nos. 1742-1747 (6)	96	
			Set value		30

"Fight of the Communards and Rise of the International" — A631

Design: No. 1749, World fight against racial discrimination, and "UNESCO."

1971, Mar. 18 *Perf. 11*

1748	A631	1k	multicolored	28	18
1749	A631	1k	multicolored	28	18

No. 1748 for cent. of the Paris Commune. No. 1749 for the Year against Racial Discrimination. Issued in sheets of 15 stamps and 5 labels.

A632

A633

Design: Edelweiss, mountaineering map and equipment.

1971, Apr. 27 *Perf. 11½x11*

1750 A632 30h multicolored 18 15

50th anniversary of Slovak Alpine Club.

1971, Apr. 27 *Perf. 11½*

1751 A633 30h Singer 18 15

50th anniversary of Slovak Teachers' Choir.

Abbess' Crosier, 16th Century A634

Design: No. 1753, Allegory of Music, 16th century mural.

1971, May 9

1752 A634 3k gold & multi 1.50 1.25
1753 A634 3k blk, dk brn & buff 1.50 1.25

See Nos. 1817-1818, 1884-1885, 1937-1938, 2040-2041, 2081-2082, 2114-2115, 2176-2177, 2238-2239, 2329-2330, 2384-2385, 2420-2421.

Lenin — A635

Designs: 40h, Hammer and sickle allegory. 60h, Raised fists. 1k, Star, hammer and sickle.

1971, May 14 *Perf. 11*

1754 A635 30h blk, red & gold 15 15
1755 A635 40h blk, ultra, red & gold 15 15
1756 A635 60h blk, ultra, red & gold 15 15
1757 A635 1k blk, ultra, red & gold 30 15
Set value 62 20

Czechoslovak Communist Party, 50th anniv.

Star, Hammer-Sickle Emblems — A636

Design: 60h, Hammer-sickle emblem, fist and people, vert.

Perf. 11½x11, 11x11½

1971, May 24 **Engr. & Photo.**

1758 A636 30h blk, red, gold & yel 15 15
1759 A636 60h blk, red, gold & bl 20 15
Set value 28 15

14th Congress of Communist Party of Czechoslovakia.

Ring-necked Pheasant — A637

Designs: 60h, Rainbow trout. 80h, Mouflon. 1k, Chamois. 2k, Stag. 2.60k, Wild boar.

1971, Aug. 17 *Perf. 11½x11*

1760 A637 20h orange & multi 15 15
1761 A637 60h lt blue & multi 15 15
1762 A637 80h yellow & multi 15 15
1763 A637 1k lt green & multi 18 15
1764 A637 2k lilac & multi 45 18
1765 A637 2.60k bister & multi *1.90* *65*
Nos. 1760-1765 (6) *2.98*
Set value *1.00*

World Hunting Exhib., Budapest, Aug. 27-30.

Diesel Locomotive A638

Gymnasts and Banners A639

1971, Sept. 2 *Perf. 11x11½*

1766 A638 30h lt bl, blk & red 15 15

Cent. of CKD, Prague Machine Foundry.

1971, Sept. 2 *Perf. 11½x11*

1767 A639 30h red brn, gold & ultra 15 15

50th anniversary of Workers' Physical Exercise Federation.

Road Intersections and Bridge — A640

1971, Sept. 2 **Engr. & Photo.**

1768 A640 1k blk, gold, red & bl 28 15

14th World Highways and Bridges Congress. Sheets of 25 stamps and 25 labels printed se-tenant with continuous design.

Chinese Fairytale, by Eva Bednarova — A641

Designs: 1k, Tiger and other animals, by Mirko Hanak. 1.60k, The Miraculous Bamboo Shoot, by Yasuo Segawa, horiz.

Perf. 11½x11, 11x11½

1971, Sept. 10

1769 A641 60h multi 20 15
1770 A641 1k multi 35 15
1771 A641 1.60k multi 85 25
Nos. 1769-1771 (3) 1.40
Set value 45

Bratislava BIB 71 biennial exhibition of illustrations for children's books.

Apothecary Jars and Coltsfoot A642

Intl. Pharmaceutical Cong.: 60h, Jars and dog rose. 1k, Scales and adonis vernalis. 1.20k, Mortars and valerian. 1.80k, Retorts and chicory. 2.40k, Mill, mortar and henbane.

1971, Sept. 20 *Perf. 11½x11*

Yellow Paper

1772 A642 30h multi 15 15
1773 A642 60h multi 15 15
1774 A642 1k multi 30 15
1775 A642 1.20k multi 42 15
1776 A642 1.80k multi 70 22
1777 A642 2.40k multi *1.50* *45*
Nos. 1772-1777 (6) *3.22*
Set value *1.00*

Painting Type of 1967

Paintings: 1k, "Waiting" (woman's head), 1967, by Imro Weiner-Král. 1.20k, Resurrection, by Master of Vyssi Brod, 14th century. 1.40k, Woman with Pitcher, by Milos Bazovsky. 1.80k, Veruna Cudova (in folk costume), by Josef Mánes. 2.40k, Detail from "Feast of the Rose Garlands," by Albrecht Dürer.

1971, Nov. 27 *Perf. 11½*

1779 A565 1k multi 32 32
1780 A565 1.20k multi 45 45
1781 A565 1.40k multi 55 55
1782 A565 1.80k multi 70 70
1783 A565 2.40k multi *2.25* *2.25*
Nos. 1779-1783 (5) *4.27* *4.27*

Sheets of 4.

Workers Revolt in Krompachy, by Julius Nemcik — A643

1971, Nov. 28 *Perf. 11x11½*

1784 A643 60h multi 20 15

History of the Czechoslovak Communist Party.

Wooden Dolls and Birds — A644

Folk Art and UNICEF Emblem: 80h, Jug handles, carved. 1k, Horseback rider. 1.60k, Shepherd carrying lamb. 2k, Easter eggs and rattle. 3k, "Zbojnik," folk hero.

1971, Dec. 11 *Perf. 11½*

1785 A644 60h multi 20 15
1786 A644 80h multi 28 15
1787 A644 1k multi 40 15
1788 A644 1.60k multi 60 15
1789 A644 2k multi 1.25 38
1790 A644 3k multi 2.25 55
Nos. 1785-1790 (6) 4.98
Set value 1.25

25th anniv. of UNICEF.

Runners, Parthenon, Czechoslovak Olympic Emblem A645

Designs: 40h, Women's high jump, Olympic emblem and plan for Prague Stadium. 1.60k, Cross-country skiers, Sapporo '72 emblem and ski jump in High Tatras. 2.60k, Discus thrower, Discobolus and St. Vitus Cathedral.

1971, Dec. 16 **Engr. & Photo.**

1791 A645 30h multi 15 15
1792 A645 40h multi 15 15
1793 A645 1.60k multi 45 20
1794 A645 2.60k multi 1.75 65
Nos. 1791-1794 (4) 2.50
Set value 85

75th anniversary of Czechoslovak Olympic Committee (30h, 2.60k); 20th Summer Olympic Games, Munich, Aug. 26-Sept. 10, 1972 (40h); 11th Winter Olympic Games, Sapporo, Japan, Feb. 3-13, 1972 (1.60k).

Post Horns and Lion — A646

1971, Dec. 17 *Perf. 11x11½*

1795 A646 1k blk, gold, car & bl 30 15

Stamp Day.

Figure Skating A647

"Lezáky" A648

Designs (Olympic Emblems and): 50h, Ski jump. 1k, Ice hockey. 1.60k, Sledding, women's.

1972, Jan. 13 *Perf. 11½*

1796 A647 40h pur, org & red 15 15
1797 A647 50h dk bl, org & red 16 15
1798 A647 1k mag, org & red 32 15
1799 A647 1.60k bl grn, org & red *1.25* *30*
Nos. 1796-1799 (4) *1.88*
Set value *50*

11th Winter Olympic Games, Sapporo, Japan, Feb. 3-13.

1972, Feb. 16

Designs: No. 1801, Boy's head behind barbed wire, horiz. No. 1802, Hand rising from ruins. No. 1803, Soldier and banner, horiz.

1800 A648 30h blk, dl org & red 15 15
1801 A648 30h blk & brn org 15 15
1802 A648 60h blk, yel & red 15 15
1803 A648 60h sl grn & multi 15 15
Set value 50 20

30th anniv. of: destruction of Lezáky (No. 1800) and Lidice (No. 1802); Terezin concentration camp (No. 1801); Czechoslovak Army unit in Russia (No. 1803).

Book Year Emblem A649

Steam and Diesel Locomotives A650

1972, Mar. 17 *Perf. 11½x11*

1804 A649 1k blk & org brn 30 15

International Book Year 1972.

1972, Mar. 17 *Perf. 11½x11*

1805 A650 30h multi 20 15

Centenary of the Kosice-Bohumin railroad.

"Pasture," by Vojtech Sedlacek — A651

Designs: 50h, Dressage, by Frantisek Tichy. 60th, Otakara Kubina, by Vaclav Fiala. 1k, The Three Kings, by Ernest Zmetak. 1.60k, Woman Dressing, by Ludovit Fulla.

1972, Mar. 27 *Perf. 11½x11*

1806 A651 40h multi 15 15
1807 A651 50h multi 15 15
1808 A651 60h multi 18 15
1809 A651 1k multi 30 18
1810 A651 1.60k multi *85 85*
Nos. 1806-1810 (5) *1.63*
Set value *1.45*

Czech and Slovak graphic art. 1.60k issued in sheets of 4. See #1859-1862, 1921-1924.

Ice Hockey A652

Design: 1k, Two players.

1972, Apr. 7 *Perf. 11*

1811 A652 60h blk & multi 18 15
1812 A652 1k blk & multi 35 15
Set value 20

World and European Ice Hockey Championships, Prague.

For overprint see Nos. 1845-1846.

Bicycling, Olympic Rings and Emblem — A653

1972, Apr. 7

1813 A653 50h shown 20 15
1814 A653 1.60k Diving 60 15
1815 A653 1.80k Canoeing 70 15
1816 A653 2k Gymnast *1.40 48*
Nos. 1813-1816 (4) *2.90*
Set value *76*

20th Olympic Games, Munich, Aug. 26-Sept. 11.

Prague Castle Art Type of 1971

Designs: No. 1817, Adam and Eve, column capital, St. Vitus Cathedral. No. 1818, Czech coat of arms (lion), c. 1500.

1972, May 9 *Perf. 11½*

1817 A634 3k blk & multi *2.25 1.75*
1818 A634 3k blk, red, sil & gold 1.25 75

Sheets of 4.

Andrej Sladkovic (1820-1872), Poet — A654

Portraits: No. 1820, Janko Kral (1822-1876), poet. No. 1821, Ludmilla Podjavorinska (1872-1951), writer. No. 1822, Antonin Hudecek (1872-1941), painter. No. 1823, Frantisek Bilek (1872-1941), sculptor. No. 1824, Jan Preisler (1872-1918), painter.

1972, June 14 *Perf. 11*

1819 A654 40h pur, ol & bl 15 15
1820 A654 40h dk grn, bl & yel 15 15
1821 A654 40h blk & multi 15 15
1822 A654 40h brn, grn & bl 15 15
1823 A654 40h choc, grn & org 15 15
1824 A654 40h grn, sl & dp org 15 15
Set value 72 30

Men with Banners — A655

1972, June 14 *Perf. 11x11½*

1825 A655 30h dk vio bl, red & yel 15 15

8th Trade Union Congress, Prague.

Art Forms of Wire A656

Ornamental Wirework: 60h, Plane and rosette. 80h, Four-headed dragon and ornament. 1k, Locomotive and loops. 2.60k, Tray and owl.

1972, Aug. 28 *Perf. 11½x11*

1826 A656 20h sal & multi 15 15
1827 A656 60h multi 20 15
1828 A656 80h pink & multi 28 15
1829 A656 1k multi 40 15
1830 A656 2.60k rose & multi *1.40 45*
Nos. 1826-1830 (5) *2.43*
Set value *75*

"Jiskra" A657

Engr. & Photo.

1972, Sept. 27 *Perf. 11½x11*

Size: 40x22mm

Multicolored Design on Blue Paper

1831 A657 50h shown 15 15
1832 A657 60h "Mir" 20 15
1833 A657 80h "Republika" 25 15

Size: 48x29mm

Perf. 11x11½

1834 A657 1k "Kosice" 30 15
1835 A657 1.60k "Dukla" 45 15
1836 A657 2k "Kladno" *1.75 55*
Nos. 1831-1836 (6) *3.10*
Set value 95

Czechoslovak sea-going vessels.

Hussar, 18th Century Tile — A658

1972, Oct. 24 *Perf. 11½x11*

1837 A658 30h shown 15 15
1838 A658 60h Janissary 15 15
1839 A658 80h St. Martin 20 15
1840 A658 1.60k St. George 45 15
1841 A658 1.80k Nobleman's guard 50 15
1842 A658 2.20k Slovakian horseman *1.75 60*
Nos. 1837-1842 (6) *3.20*
Set value *1.00*

Horsemen from 18th-19th century tiles or enamel paintings on glass.

Worker, Flag Hoisted on Bayonet A659

Star, Hammer and Sickle A660

1972, Nov. 7 *Perf. 11x11½*

1843 A659 30h gold & multi 15 15
1844 A660 60h rose car & gold 15 15
Set value 23 15

55th anniv. of the Russian October Revolution (30h); 50th anniv. of the Soviet Union (60h).

Nos. 1811-1812 Overprinted in Violet Blue or Black

CSSR
MAJSTROM
SVETA

1972 *Perf. 11*

1845 A652 60h multi (VBl) 5.25 4.50
1846 A652 1k multi (Bk) 5.25 4.50

Czechoslovakia's victorious ice hockey team. The overprint on the 60h is in Czech and reads CSSR/MISTREM/SVETA; the overprint on the 1k (shown) is in Slovak.

Painting Type of 1967

Designs: 1k, "Nosegay" (nudes and flowers), by Max Svabinsky. 1.20k, Struggle of St. Ladislas with Kuman nomad, anonymous, 14th century. 1.40k, Lady with Fur Hat, by Vaclav Hollar. 1.80k, Midsummer Night's Dream, 1962, by Josef Liesler. 2.40k, Pablo Picasso, self-portrait.

1972, Nov. 27 **Engr. & Photo.**

1847 A565 1k multi 55 35
1848 A565 1.20k multi 70 50
1849 A565 1.40k blk & cream 85 65
1850 A565 1.80k multi 1.10 1.00
1851 A565 2.40k multi *2.50 2.50*
Nos. 1847-1851 (5) *5.70 5.00*

Sheets of 4.

Goldfinch — A661

Songbirds: 60h, Warbler feeding young cuckoo. 80h, Cuckoo. 1k, Black-billed magpie. 1.60k, Bullfinch. 3k, Song thrush.

1972, Dec. 15

Size: 30x48½mm

1852 A661 60h yel & multi 16 15
1853 A661 80h multi 22 15
1854 A661 1k lt bl & multi 22 15

Engr.

Size: 30x23mm

1855 A661 1.60k multi 35 15
1856 A661 2k multi 45 20
1857 A661 3k multi *2.50 75*
Nos. 1852-1857 (6) *3.90*
Set value *1.35*

Post Horn and Allegory — A662

1972, Dec. 18 **Engr. & Photo.**

1858 A662 1k blk, red lil & gold 30 30

Stamp Day.

Art Type of 1972

1973, Jan. 25 *Perf. 11½x11*

Designs: 30h, Flowers in Window, by Jaroslav Grus. 60h, Quest for Happiness, by Josef Balaz. 1.60k, Balloon, by Kamil Lhotak. 1.80k, Woman with Viola, by Richard Wiesner.

1859 A651 30h multi 15 15
1860 A651 60h multi 15 15
1861 A651 1.60k multi 45 15
1862 A651 1.80k multi *1.25 60*
Nos. 1859-1862 (4) *2.00*
Set value *88*

Czech and Slovak graphic art.

Tennis Player — A663

Figure Skater — A664

Torch and Star — A665

1973, Feb. 22 *Perf. 11*

1863 A663 30h vio & multi 15 15
1864 A664 60h blk & multi 15 15
1865 A665 1k multi 30 15
Nos. 1863-1865 (3) 60
Set value 27

80th anniversary of the tennis organization in Czechoslovakia (30h); World figure skating championships, Bratislava (60h); 3rd summer army Spartakiad of socialist countries (1k).

Star and Factories — A666

Workers' Militia, Emblem and Flag — A667

1973, Feb. 23

1866 A666 30h multi			15	15
1867 A667 60h multi			15	15
Set value			22	15

25th anniversary of the Communist revolution in Czechoslovakia and of the Militia.

Capt. Jan Nalepka, Major Antonin Sochor and Laurel
A668

Designs (Torch and): 40h, Evzen Rosicky, Mirko Nespor and ivy leaves. 60h, Vlado Clementis, Karol Smidke and linden leaves. 80h, Jan Osoha, Josef Molak and oak leaves. 1k, Marie Kuderikova, Jozka Jaburkova and rose. 1.60k, Vaclav Sinkule, Eduard Urx and palm leaf.

1973, Mar. 20 *Perf. 11½x11*

Yellow Paper

1868 A668	30h	blk, ver & gold	15	15
1869 A668	40h	blk, ver & grn	15	15
1870 A668	60h	blk, ver & gold	15	15
1871 A668	80h	blk, ver & gold	20	15
1872 A668	1k	blk, ver & grn	28	15
1873 A668	1.60k	blk, ver & sil	*60*	*18*
Nos. 1868-1873 (6)			*1.53*	
Set value				*56*

Fighters against and victims of Fascism and Nazism during German Occupation.

Virgil I. Grissom, Edward H. White, Roger B. Chaffee — A669

Designs: 20h, Soviet planetary station "Venera." 30h, "Intercosmos" station. 40h, Lunokhod on moon. 3.60k, Vladimir M. Komarov, Georgi T. Dobrovolsky, Vladislav N. Volkov, Victor I. Patsayev. 5k, Yuri A. Gagarin.

1973, Apr. 12 *Perf. 11½x11*

Size: 40x22mm

1874 A669	20h	multi	15	15
1875 A669	30h	multi	15	15
1876 A669	40h	multi	15	15

Engr.

Perf. 11½

Size: 49x30mm

1877 A669	3k	multi	1.25	55
1878 A669	3.60k	multi	1.65	1.10
1879 A669	5k	multi	*3.75*	*3.50*
Nos. 1874-1879 (6)			*7.10*	*5.60*

In memory of American and Russian astronauts.

Radio — A670

Telephone and Map of Czechoslovakia
A671

Television — A672

1973, May 1 *Perf. 11½x11*

1880 A670	30h	blk & multi	15	15
1881 A671	30h	lt bl, pink & blk	15	15
1882 A672	30h	dp bl & multi	15	15
Set value			27	15

Czechoslovak anniversaries: 50 years of broadcasting (No. 1880); 20 years of telephone service to all communities (No. 1881); 20 years of television (No. 1882).

Coat of Arms and Linden Branch — A673

1973, May 9 *Perf. 11x11½*

1883 A673	60h	red & multi	20	15

25th anniv. of the Constitution of May 9.

Prague Castle Art Type of 1971

Designs: No. 1884, Royal Legate, 14th century. No. 1885, Seal of King Charles IV, 1351.

1973, May 9 *Perf. 11½*

1884 A634	3k	blue & multi	85	1.00
1885 A634	3k	gold, grn & dk brn	1.25	1.75

Sheets of 4.

Coat of Arms Type of 1968

1973, June 20

1886 A590	60h	Mikulov	15	15
1887 A590	60h	Zlutice	15	15
1888 A590	60h	Smolenice	15	15
Nos. 1886-1888 (3)			45	
Set value				24

Coats of arms of Czechoslovakian cities.

Heraldic Colors of Olomouc and Moravia
A674

Anthurium
A675

1973, Aug. 23 **Engr. & Photo.**

1889 A674	30h	multi	15	15

University of Olomouc, 400th anniv.

1973, Aug. 23 *Perf. 11½*

Sizes: 60h, 1k, 2k, 30x50mm.; 1.60k, 1.80k, 3.60k, 23x39mm.

1890 A675	60h	Tulips	75	75
1891 A675	1k	Rose	35	25
1892 A675	1.60k	shown	35	20
1893 A675	1.80k	Iris	35	20
1894 A675	2k	Chrysanthemum	*2.25*	*2.25*
1895 A675	3.60k	Cymbidium	75	35
Nos. 1890-1895 (6)			*4.80*	*4.00*

Flower Show, Olomouc, Aug. 18-Sept. 2. 60h, 1k, 2k issued in sheets of 4, others in sheets of 10.

Hunting Dogs
A676

1973, Sept. 5

1896 A676	20h	Irish setter	15	15
1897 A676	30h	Czech terrier	15	15
1898 A676	40h	Bavarian hunting dog	15	15
1899 A676	60h	German pointer	24	15
1900 A676	1k	Cocker spaniel	32	15
1901 A676	1.60k	Dachshund	*1.00*	*25*
Nos. 1896-1901 (6)			*2.01*	
Set value				*62*

50th anniversary of the Czechoslovak United Hunting Organization.

St. John, the Baptist, by Svabinsky — A677

Works by Max Svabinsky: 60h, "August Noon" (woman). 80h, "Marriage of True Minds" (artist and muse). 1k, "Paradise Sonata I" (Adam dreaming of Eve). 2.60k, Last Judgment, stained glass window, St. Vitus Cathedral.

1973, Sept. 17 **Litho. & Engr.**

1902 A677	20h	black & pale grn	15	15
1903 A677	60h	black & buff	15	15

Engr.

1904 A677	80h	black	25	18
1905 A677	1k	slate green	30	22
1906 A677	2.60k	multi	*1.50*	*1.25*
Nos. 1902-1906 (5)			*2.35*	*1.95*

Centenary of the birth of Max Svabinsky (1873-1962), artist and stamp designer. 20h and 60h issued in sheets of 25; 80h and 1k se-tenant in sheets of 4 checkerwise; 2.60k in sheets of 4.

Trade Union Emblem — A678

1973, Oct. 15 **Engr. & Photo.**

1907 A678	1k	red, bl & yel	25	15

8th Congress of the World Federation of Trade Unions, Varna, Bulgaria.

Painting Type of 1967

Designs: 1k, Boy from Martinique, by Antonin Pelc. 1.20k, "Fortitude" (mountaineer), by Martin Benka. 1.80k, Rembrandt, self-portrait. 2k, Pierrot, by Bohumil Kubista. 2.40k, Ilona Kubinyiova, by Peter M. Bohun. 3.60k, Virgin and Child (Veveri Madonna), c. 1350.

1973, Nov. 27 *Perf. 11½*

1908 A565	1k	multi, vio bl inscriptions	*1.75*	*1.10*
a.		1k multi, black inscriptions	*15.00*	*14.00*
1909 A565	1.20k	multi	*1.75*	*1.10*
1910 A565	1.80k	multi	48	30
1911 A565	2k	multi	75	45
1912 A565	2.40k	multi	75	45
1913 A565	3.60k	multi	1.00	60
Nos. 1908-1913 (6)			*6.48*	*4.00*

Sheets of 4. Nos. 1910-1913 printed se-tenant with gold and black inscription on gutter.

Central background bluish gray on No. 1908, light bluish green on No. 1908a.

Postilion — A679

1973, Dec. 18

1914 A679	1k	gold & multi	25	20

Stamp Day 1974 and 55th anniversary of Czechoslovak postage stamps. Printed with 2 labels showing telephone and telegraph.

Bedrich Smetana — A681

Pablo Neruda, Chilean Flag — A682

"CSSR" — A680

Comecon Building, Moscow — A683

1974, Jan. 1

1915 A680	30h	red, gold & ultra	15	15

5th anniversary of Federal Government in the Czechoslovak Socialist Republic.

1974, Jan. 4 *Perf. 11x11½*

1916 A681	60h	shown	16	15
1917 A681	60h	Josef Suk	16	15
1918 A682	60h	shown	16	15
Nos. 1916-1918 (3)			48	
Set value				24

Smetana (1824-84), composer; Suk (1874-1935), composer, and Pablo Neruda (Neftali Ricardo Reyes, 1904-73), Chilean poet.

1974, Jan. 23

1919 A683	1k	gold, red & vio bl	25	15

25th anniversary of the Council of Mutual Economic Assistance (COMECON).

Symbols of Postal Service — A684

1974, Feb. 20 *Perf. 11½*

1920 A684	3.60k	multi	95	45

BRNO '74 National Stamp Exhibition, Brno, June 8-23.

Art Type of 1972

Designs: 60h, Tulips 1973, by Josef Broz. 1k, Structures 1961 (poppy and building), by Orest Dubay. 1.60k, Bird and flowers (Golden Sun-Glowing Day), by Adolf Zabransky. 1.80k, Artificial flowers, by Frantisek Gross.

1974, Feb. 21 *Perf. 11½x11*

1921 A651	60h	multi	15	15
1922 A651	1k	multi	30	16
1923 A651	1.60k	multi	45	20
1924 A651	1.80k	multi	90	32
Nos. 1921-1924 (4)			1.80	83

Czech and Slovak graphic art.

Oskar Benes and Vaclav Prochazka
A685

Portraits: 40h, Milos Uher and Anton Sedlacek. 60h, Jan Hajecek and Marie Sedlackova. 80h, Jan Sverma and Albin Grznar. 1k, Jaroslav Neliba and Alois Hovorka. 1.60k, Ladislav Exnar and Ludovit Kukorelli.

1974, Mar. 21 *Perf. 11½x11*

1925	A685	30h	indigo & multi	15	15
1926	A685	40h	indigo & multi	15	15
1927	A685	60h	indigo & multi	15	15
1928	A685	80h	indigo & multi	20	15
1929	A685	1k	indigo & multi	26	15
1930	A685	1.60k	indigo & multi	75	22
			Nos. 1925-1930 (6)	1.66	
			Set value		54

Partisan commanders and fighters.

"Water, the Source of Energy"
A686

Symbolic Designs: 1k, Importance of water for agriculture. 1.20k, Study of the oceans. 1.60k, "Hydrological Decade." 2k, Struggle for unpolluted water.

1974, Apr. 25 **Engr.** *Perf. 11½*

1931	A686	60h	multi	15	15
1932	A686	1k	multi	22	20
1933	A686	1.20k	multi	35	30
1934	A686	1.60k	multi	45	40
1935	A686	2k	multi	1.50	1.50
			Nos. 1931-1935 (5)	2.67	2.55

Hydrological Decade (UNESCO), 1965-1974. Sheets of 4.

Allegory Holding "Molniya," and Ground Station
A687

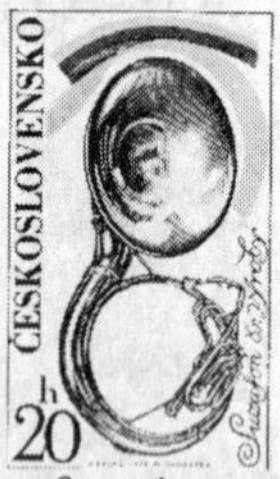

Sousaphone
A688

1974, Apr. 30 **Engr. & Photo.**

1936	A687	30h	vio bl & multi	15	15

"Intersputnik," first satellite communications ground station in Czechoslovakia.

Prague Castle Art Type of 1971

Designs: No. 1937, Golden Cock, 17th century locket. No. 1938, Glass monstrance, 1840.

1974, May 9 **Engr.** *Perf. 11½*

1937	A634	3k	gold & multi	1.40	1.25
1938	A634	3k	blk & multi	1.40	1.25

Sheets of 4.

Engraved and Photogravure

1974, May 12 *Perf. 11x11½*

1939	A688	20h	shown	15	15
1940	A688	30h	Bagpipe	15	15
1941	A688	40h	Violin, by Martin Benka	15	15
1942	A688	1k	Pyramid piano	30	15
1943	A688	1.60k	Tenor quinton, 1754	80	25
			Set value	1.30	55

Prague and Bratislava Music Festivals. The 1.60k also commemorates 25th anniversary of Slovak Philharmonic Orchestra.

Child — A689

1974, June 1 *Perf. 11½*

1944	A689	60h	multi	15	15

Children's Day. Design is from illustration for children's book by Adolf Zabransky.

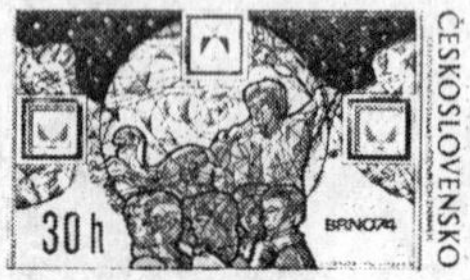

Globe, People and Exhibition Emblems
A690

Design: 6k, Rays and emblems symbolizing "Oneness and Mutuality."

1974, June 1

1945	A690	30h	multi	15	15
1946	A690	6k	multi	1.50	1.00

BRNO 74 Natl. Stamp Exhib., Brno, June 8-23. Sheets of 16 stamps and 14 labels.

Resistance Fighter — A691

Actress Holding Tragedy and Comedy Masks — A692

1974, Aug. 29 *Perf. 11½*

1947	A691	30h	multi	15	15

Slovak National Uprising, 30th anniversary.

1974, Aug. 29

1948	A692	30h	red, sil & blk	15	15

Bratislava Academy of Music and Drama, 25th anniversary.

Slovak Girl with Flower — A693

1974, Aug. 29

1949	A693	30h	multi	15	15

SLUK, Slovak folksong and dance ensemble, 25th anniversary.

Hero and Leander
A694

Design: 2.40k, Hero watching Leander swim the Hellespont. No. 1952, Leander reaching shore. No. 1953, Hero mourning over Leander's body. No. 1954, Hermione, Leander's sister. No. 1955, Mourning Cupid. Designs are from 17th century English tapestries in Bratislava Council Palace.

1974-76

1950	A694	2k	multi	1.65	1.25
1951	A694	2.40k	multi	1.75	1.25
1952	A694	3k	multi	2.25	1.75
1953	A694	3k	multi	75	65
1954	A694	3.60k	multi	2.50	2.00
1955	A694	3.60k	multi	1.00	90
			Nos. 1950-1955 (6)	9.90	7.80

Issue dates: Nos. 1950-1951, Sept. 25, 1974. Nos. 1952, 1954, Aug. 29, 1975. Nos. 1953, 1955, May 9, 1976.

Soldier Standing Guard, Target, 1840 — A695

Painted Folk-art Targets: 60h, Landscape with Pierrot and flags, 1828. 1k, Diana crowning champion marksman, 1832. 1.60k, Still life with guitar, 1839. 2.40k, Salvo and stag in flight, 1834. 3k, Turk and giraffe, 1831.

1974, Sept. 26 *Perf. 11½*

Size: 30x50mm

1956	A695	30h	black & multi	15	15
1957	A695	60h	black & multi	15	15
1958	A695	1k	black & multi	22	15

Engr.

Perf. 12

Size: 40x50mm

1959	A695	1.60k	green & multi	42	35
1960	A695	2.40k	sepia & multi	70	60
1961	A695	3k	multi	*2.25*	*2.25*
			Nos. 1956-1961 (6)	*3.89*	*3.65*

UPU Emblem and Postilion — A696

UPU Cent. (UPU Emblem and): 40h, Mail coach. 60h, Railroad mail coach, 1851. 80h, Early mail truck. 1k, Czechoslovak Airlines mail plane. 1.60k, Radar.

Engraved and Photogravure

1974, Oct. 9 *Perf. 11½*

1962	A696	30h	multi	15	15
1963	A696	40h	multi	15	15
1964	A696	60h	multi	15	15
1965	A696	80h	multi	20	15
1966	A696	1k	multi	28	15
1967	A696	1.60k	multi	1.00	22
			Nos. 1962-1967 (6)	1.93	
			Set value		67

Sealed Letter — A697

Post Rider — A699

Stylized Bird — A698

Postal Code Symbol — A698a

Designs: 20h, Post Horn, Old Town Bridge Tower. No. 1971, Carrier pigeon. No. 1979, Map of Czechoslovakia with postal code numbers.

1974, Oct. 31 *Perf. 11½x11*

1968	A699	20h	multi	15	15
1969	A697	30h	brn, bl & red	15	15
1970	A699	40h	multi	15	15
1971	A697	60h	bl, yel & red	16	15
			Set value	39	20

See No. 2675.

Coil Stamps

1975 **Photo.** *Perf. 14*

1976	A698	30h	brt bl	15	15
1977	A698	60h	carmine	18	15
			Set value		20

1976 *Perf. 11½*

1978	A698a	30h	emer	15	15
1979	A698a	60h	scar	15	15
			Set value	23	15

Nos. 1976-1979 have black control number on back of every fifth stamp.

Ludvik Kuba, Self-portrait, 1941
A700

Paintings: 1.20k, Violinist Frantisek Ondricek, by Vaclav Brozik. 1.60k, Vase with Flowers, by Otakar Kubin. 1.80k, Woman with Pitcher, by Janko Alexy. 2.40k, Bacchanalia, c. 1635, by Karel Skreta.

1974, Nov. 27 **Engr.** *Perf. 11½*

1980	A700	1k	multi	32	25
1981	A700	1.20k	multi	48	30
1982	A700	1.60k	multi	55	40
1983	A700	1.80k	multi	55	50
1984	A700	2.40k	multi	2.25	2.00
			Nos. 1980-1984 (5)	4.15	3.45

Czech and Slovak art. Sheets of 4.

See Nos. 2209-2211, 2678-2682, 2721-2723, 2743, 2766-2768.

Post Horn
A701

Engraved and Photogravure

1974, Dec. 18 *Perf. 11x11½*

1985	A701	1k	multicolored	30	20

Stamp Day.

Still-life with Hare, by Hollar — A702

Designs: 1k, The Lion and the Mouse, by Vaclav Hollar. 1.60k, Deer Hunt, by Philip Galle. 1.80k, Grand Hunt, by Jacques Callot.

1975, Feb. 26 *Perf. 11½x11*

1988	A702	60h	blk & buff	15	15
1989	A702	1k	blk & buff	24	15
1990	A702	1.60k	blk & yel	45	18
1991	A702	1.80k	blk & buff	1.00	50
			Nos. 1988-1991 (4)	1.84	
			Set value		80

Hunting scenes from old engravings.

Guns Pointing at Family — A703

Young Woman and Globe — A704

Designs: 1k, Women and building on fire. 1.20k, People and roses. All designs include names of destroyed villages.

1975, Feb. 26 *Perf. 11*

1992	A703	60h	multi	18	15
1993	A703	1k	multi	28	15
1994	A703	1.20k	multi	32	15
			Nos. 1992-1994 (3)	78	
			Set value		27

Destruction of 14 villages by the Nazis, 30th anniversary.

1975, Mar. 7 *Perf. 11½x11*

1995	A704	30h	red & multi	15	15

International Women's Year 1975.

Little Queens, Moravian Folk Custom A705

Folk Customs: 1k, Straw masks (animal heads and blackened faces), Slovak. 1.40k, The Tale of Maid Dorothea (executioner, girl, king and devil). 2k, Drowning of Morena, symbol of death and winter.

1975, Mar. 26 **Engr.** *Perf. 11½*

1996	A705	60h	blk & multi	20	20
1997	A705	1k	blk & multi	35	35
1998	A705	1.40k	blk & multi	50	50
1999	A705	2k	blk & multi	1.25	1.25
			Nos. 1996-1999 (4)	2.30	2.30

Sheets of four.

Coat of Arms Type of 1968

Engraved and Photogravure

1975, Apr. 17 *Perf. 11½*

2000	A590	60h	Nymburk	15	15
2001	A590	60h	Znojmo	15	15
			Set value		15

Coats of arms of Czechoslovakian cities.

Czech May Uprising — A706

Liberation by Soviet Army — A707

Czechoslovak-Russian Friendship — A708

Engr. & Photo.; Engr. (A707)

1975, May 9

2002	A706	1k	multi	25	15
2003	A707	1k	multi	25	15
2004	A708	1k	multi	25	15
			Nos. 2002-2004 (3)	75	
			Set value		36

30th anniv. of the May uprising of the Czech people and of liberation by the Soviet Army; 5th anniv. of the Czechoslovak-Soviet Treaty of Friendship, Cooperation and Mutual Aid.

Adolescents' Exercises — A709

Designs: 60th, Children's exercises. 1k, Men's and women's exercises.

Engraved and Photogravure

1975, June 15 *Perf. 12x11½*

2005	A709	30h	lil & multi	15	15
2006	A709	60h	multi	15	15
2007	A709	1k	vio & multi	25	15
			Nos. 2005-2007 (3)	55	
			Set value		27

Spartakiad 1975, Prague, June 26-29. Nos. 2005-2007 each issued in sheets of 30 stamps and 40 labels, showing different Spartakiad emblems.

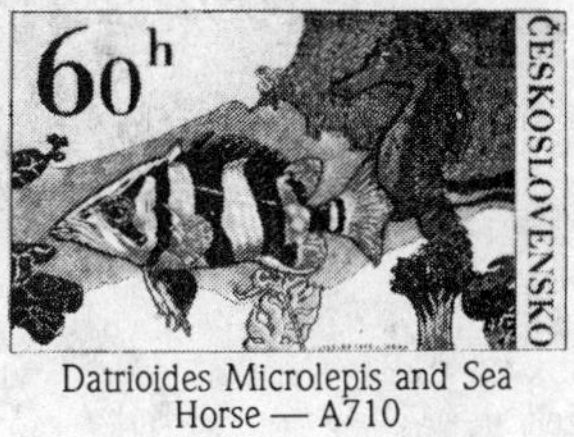

Datrioides Microlepis and Sea Horse — A710

Tropical Fish (Aquarium): 1k, Beta splendens regan and pterophyllum scalare. 1.20k, Carassius auratus. 1.60k, Amphiprion percula and chaetodon sp. 2k, Pomacanthodes semicirculatus, pomocanthus maculosus and paracanthorus hepatus.

1975, June 27 *Perf. 11½*

2008	A710	60h	multi	18	15
2009	A710	1k	multi	35	15
2010	A710	1.20k	multi	42	16
2011	A710	1.60k	multi	52	20
2012	A710	2k	multi	*1.75*	*50*
			Nos. 2008-2012 (5)	*3.22*	*1.16*

Pelicans, by Nikita Charushin — A711

Book Illustrations: 30h, The Dreamer, by Lieselotte Schwarz. 40h, Hero on horseback, by Val Muntenau. 60h, Peacock, by Klaus Ensikat. 80h, Man on horseback, by Robert Dubravec.

1975, Sept. 5

2013	A711	20h	multi	15	15
2014	A711	30h	multi	15	15
2015	A711	40h	multi	15	15
2016	A711	60h	multi	15	15
2017	A711	80h	multi	*40*	*20*
			Set value	*65*	*48*

Bratislava BIB 75 biennial exhibition of illustrations for children's books.

Nos. 2013-2017 issued in sheets of 25 stamps and 15 labels with designs and inscriptions in various languages.

Strakonice, 1951 A712

Designs: Motorcycles.

1975, Sept. 29 *Perf. 11½*

2018	A712	20h	shown	15	15
2019	A712	40h	Jawa 250, 1945	15	15
2020	A712	60h	Jawa 175, 1935	15	15
2021	A712	1k	ITAR, 1921	30	18
2022	A712	1.20k	ORION, 1903	35	20
2023	A712	1.80k	Laurin & Klement, 1898	1.65	40
			Nos. 2018-2023 (6)	2.75	
			Set value		95

Study of Shortwave Solar Radiation A713

Soyuz-Apollo Link-up in Space — A714

Designs: 60h, Study of aurora borealis and Oréol satellite. 1k, Study of ionosphere and cosmic radiation. 2k, Copernicus, radio map of the sun and satellite.

1975, Sept. 30

2024	A713	30h	multi	15	15
2025	A713	60h	yel, rose red & vio	18	15
2026	A713	1k	bl, yel & vio	30	18
2027	A713	2k	red, vio & yel	45	20

Engr.

2028	A714	5k	vio & multi	*2.50*	*2.50*
			Nos. 2024-2028 (5)	*3.58*	*3.18*

International cooperation in space research. No. 2028 issued in sheets of 4.

The design of No. 2026 appears to be inverted.

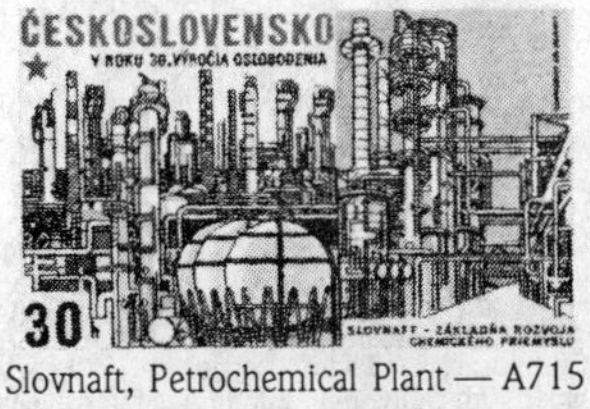

Slovnaft, Petrochemical Plant — A715

Designs: 60h, Atomic power station. 1k, Construction of Prague subway. 1.20k, Construction of Friendship pipeline. 1.40k, Combine harvesters. 1.60k, Apartment house construction.

Engraved and Photogravure

1975, Oct. 28

2029	A715	30h	multi	15	15
2030	A715	60h	multi	15	15
2031	A715	1k	multi	30	15
2032	A715	1.20k	multi	35	15
2033	A715	1.40k	multi	40	15
2034	A715	1.60k	multi	*75*	*40*
			Nos. 2029-2034 (6)	*2.10*	
			Set value		*88*

Socialist construction, 30th anniversary. Nos. 2029-2034 printed se-tenant with labels.

Pres. Gustav Husak — A716

1975, Oct. 28 **Engr.**

2035	A716	30h	ultra	15	15
2036	A716	60h	rose red	15	15
			Set value	21	15

Prague Castle Art Type of 1971

Designs: 3k, Gold earring, 9th century. 3.60k, Arms of Premysl Dynasty and Bohemia from lid of leather case containing Bohemian crown, 14th century.

1975, Oct. 29

2040	A634	3k	blk, grn, pur & gold	75	75
2041	A634	3.60k	red & multi	*2.00*	*2.00*

Sheets of 4.

Miniature Sheet

Ludvik Svoboda, Road Map, Buzuluk to Prague, Carnations — A717

1975, Nov. 25

2042	A717	10k	multi	12.00	12.00

Pres. Ludvik Svoboda, 80th birthday.

Exists imperf., value $55.

Art Type of 1967

Paintings: 1k, "May 1975" (Woman and doves for 30th anniv. of peace), by Zdenek Sklenar. 1.40k, Woman in national costume, by Eugen Nevan. 1.80k, "Liberation of Prague," by Alena Cermakova, horiz. 2.40k, "Fire 1938" (woman raising fist), by Josef Capek. 3.40k, Old Prague, 1828, by Vincenc Morstadt.

1975, Nov. 27 **Engr.** *Perf. 11½*

2043	A565	1k	blk, buff & brn	26	26
2044	A565	1.40k	multi	30	30
2045	A565	1.80k	multi	60	52
2046	A565	2.40k	multi	95	95
2047	A565	3.40k	multi	1.75	1.50
			Nos. 2043-2047 (5)	3.86	3.53

Sheets of 4.

Carrier Pigeon — A718

Engraved and Photogravure

1975, Dec. 18 *Perf. 11½*

2048	A718	1k	red & multi	28	15

Stamp Day 1975.

Frantisek Halas — A719

Wilhelm Pieck — A720

Frantisek Lexa — A721

Jindrich Jindrich — A722

Ivan Krasko — A723

1976, Feb. 25 *Perf. 11½*

2049	A719	60h multi	15	15
2050	A720	60h multi	15	15
2051	A721	60h multi	15	15
2052	A722	60h multi	15	15
2053	A723	60h multi	15	15
		Nos. 2049-2053 (5)	75	
		Set value		38

Halas (1901-49), poet; Pieck (1876-1960), pres. of German Democratic Republic; Lexa (1876-1960), professor of Egyptology; Jindrich (1876-1967), composer and writer; Krasko (1876-1958), Slovak poet. No. 2051 printed in sheets of 10, others in sheets of 50.

Ski Jump, Olympic Emblem A724

Designs (Winter Olympic Games Emblem and): 1.40k, Figure skating, women's. 1.60k, Ice hockey.

1976, Mar. 22 *Perf. 12x11½*

2054	A724	1k gold & multi	25	15
2055	A724	1.40k gold & multi	32	18
2056	A724	1.60k gold & multi	*42*	*25*
		Nos. 2054-2056 (3)	*99*	*58*

12th Winter Olympic Games, Innsbruck, Austria, Feb. 4-15.

Javelin and Olympic Rings — A725

Designs (Olympic Rings and): 3k, Relay race. 3.60k, Shot put.

1976, Mar. 22 *Perf. 11½*

2057	A725	2k multi	65	20
2058	A725	3k multi	95	32
2059	A725	3.60k multi	*1.40*	*65*
		Nos. 2057-2059 (3)	*3.00*	*1.17*

21st Olympic Games, Montreal, Canada, July 17-Aug. 1.

Table Tennis — A726

1976, Mar. 22 *Perf. 11x12*

2060	A726	1k multi	30	15

European Table Tennis Championship, Prague, Mar. 26-Apr. 4.

Symbolic of Communist Party A727

Worker, Derrick, Emblem A728

1976, Apr. 12 *Perf. 11x12*

2061	A727	30h gold & multi	15	15
2062	A728	60h gold & multi	15	15
		Set value	23	15

15th Congress of the Communist Party of Czechoslovakia.

Radio Prague Orchestra — A729

Dancer, Violin, Tragic Mask — A730

Actors — A731

Folk Dancers — A732

Film Festival — A733

1976, Apr. 26 *Perf. 11½*

2063	A729	20h gold & multi	15	15
2064	A730	20h pink & multi	15	15
2065	A731	20h lt bl & multi	15	15
2066	A732	30h blk & multi	15	15
2067	A733	30h vio bl, rose & grn	15	15
		Set value	30	25

Czechoslovak Radio Symphony Orchestra, Prague, 50th anniv. (No. 2063); Academy of Music and Dramatic Art, Prague, 50th anniv. (No. 2064); Nova Scena Theater Co., Bratislava, 30th anniv. (No. 2065); Intl. Folk Song and Dance Festival, Straznice, 30th anniv. (No. 2066); 20th Intl. Film Festival, Karlovy Vary (No. 2067).

Hammer and Sickle
A734 A735

Design: 6k, Hammer and sickle, horiz.

1976, May 14

2068	A734	30h gold, red & dk bl	15	15
2069	A735	60h gold, red & dp car	25	15
		Set value		17

Souvenir Sheet

2070	A735	6k red & multi	1.50	1.50

Czechoslovak Communist Party, 55th anniv. #2070 contains a 50x30mm stamp.

Ships in Storm, by Frans Huys (1522-1562) A736

Old Engravings of Ships: 60h, by Václav Hollar (1607-77). 1k, by Regnier Nooms Zeeman (1623-68). 2k, by Francois Chereau (1680-1729).

Engraved and Photogravure

1976, July 21 *Perf. 11x11½*

2071	A736	40h buff & blk	15	15
2072	A736	60h gray, buff & blk	15	15
2073	A736	1k lt grn, buff & blk	30	15
2074	A736	2k lt bl, buff & blk	*1.25*	*40*
		Nos. 2071-2074 (4)	*1.85*	
		Set value		*60*

"UNESCO" A737

1976, July 30 *Perf. 11½*

2075	A737	2k gray & multi	50	45

30th anniversary of UNESCO. Sheets of 10.

Souvenir Sheet

Hands Holding Infant, Globe and Dove A738

1976, July 30

2076		Sheet of 2	6.75	6.00
a.		A738 6k multi	3.00	2.50

European Security and Cooperation Conference, Helsinki, Finland, 2nd anniv.

Merino Ram — A739

Couple Smoking, WHO Emblem and Skull — A740

Designs: 40h, Bern-Hana milk cow. 1.60k, Kladruby stallion Generalissimus XXVII.

1976, Aug. 28 *Perf. 11½x12*

2077	A739	30h multi	15	15
2078	A739	40h multi	15	15
2079	A739	1.60k multi	35	18
		Set value	50	28

Bountiful Earth Exhibition, Ceske Budejovice, Aug. 28-Sept. 12.

1976, Sept. 7 *Perf. 12x11½*

2080	A740	2k multi	75	40

Fight against smoking, WHO drive against drug addiction. Printed in sheets of 10 (2x5) with WHO emblems and inscription in margin.

Prague Castle Art Type of 1971

Designs: 3k, View of Prague Castle, by F. Hoogenberghe, 1572. 3.60k, Faun and Satyr, sculptured panel, 16th century.

1976, Oct. 22 **Engr.** *Perf. 11½*

2081	A634	3k multi	2.00	2.00
2082	A634	3.60k multi	75	50

Sheets of 4.

Guernica 1937, by Imro Weiner-Kral A741

1976, Oct. 22

2083	A741	5k multi	1.25	60

40th anniv. of the Intl. Brigade in Spain.

Zebras A742

Designs: 20h, Elephants, vert. 30h, Cheetah. 40h, Giraffes, vert. 60h, Rhinoceros. 3k, Bongos, vert.

Engraved and Photogravure

1976, Nov. 3 *Perf. 11½x11, 11x11½*

2084	A742	10h multi	15	15
2085	A742	20h multi	15	15
2086	A742	30h multi	15	15
2087	A742	40h multi	15	15
2088	A742	60h multi	15	15
2089	A742	3k multi	1.25	50
		Set value	1.75	78

African animals in Dvur Kralove Zoo.

Art Type of 1967

Paintings of Flowers: 1k, by Peter Matejka. 1.40k, by Cyril Bouda. 2k, by Jan Breughel. 3.60k, J. Rudolf Bys.

1976, Nov. 27 **Engr.** *Perf. 11½*

2090	A565	1k multi	80	60
2091	A565	1.40k multi	1.00	80
2092	A565	2k multi	1.65	1.25
2093	A565	3.60k multi	90	75
		Nos. 2090-2093 (4)	4.35	3.40

Sheets of 4. Emblem and name of Praga 1978 on horizontal gutter.

Postrider, 17th Century, and Satellites — A743

1976, Dec. 18 **Engr. & Photo.**

2094 A743 1k multi		25	15

Stamp Day 1976.

Ice Hockey — A744

Arms of Vranov — A745

Designs: 1k, Biathlon. 1.60k, Ski jump. 2k, Downhill skiing.

1977, Feb. 11 ***Perf. 11½***

2095 A744	60h multi	15	15
2096 A744	1k multi	30	15
2097 A744	1.60k multi	*1.25*	*24*
2098 A744	2k multi	55	32
	Nos. 2095-2098 (4)	*2.25*	*86*

6th Winter Spartakiad of Socialist Countries' Armies.

1977, Feb. 20

Designs: Coats of Arms of Czechoslovak towns.

2099 A745	60h shown	15	15
2100 A745	60h Kralupy & Vltavou	15	15
2101 A745	60h Jicin	15	15
2102 A745	60h Valasske Mezirici	15	15
	Nos. 2099-2102 (4)	60	
	Set value		24

See Nos. 2297-2300.

Window, Michna Palace — A746

Prague Renaissance Windows: 30h, Michna Palace. 40h, Thun Palace. 60h, Archbishop's Palace, Hradcany. 5k, St. Nicholas Church.

1977, Mar. 10

2103 A746	20h multi	15	15
2104 A746	30h multi	15	15
2105 A746	40h multi	15	15
2106 A746	60h multi	15	15
2107 A746	5k multi	*1.75*	*75*
	Nos. 2103-2107 (5)	*2.35*	
	Set value		*98*

PRAGA 1978 International Philatelic Exhibition, Prague, Sept. 8-17, 1978.

Children, Auxiliary Police A747

1977, Apr. 21 ***Perf. 11½***

2108 A747 60h multi		15	15

Auxiliary Police, 25th anniversary.

Warsaw, Polish Flag, Bicyclists A748

Congress Emblem A749

Designs: 60h, Berlin, DDR flag, bicyclists. 1k, Prague, Czechoslovakian flag, victorious bicyclist. 1.40k, Bicyclists on highways, modern views of Berlin, Prague and Warsaw.

1977, May 7

2109 A748	30h multi	15	15
2110 A748	60h multi	16	15
2111 A748	1k multi	*48*	*25*
2112 A748	1.40k multi	35	20
	Nos. 2109-2112 (4)	*1.14*	
	Set value		*58*

30th International Bicycle Peace Race Warsaw-Prague-Berlin.

1977, May 25 ***Perf. 11½***

2113 A749 30h car, red & gold		15	15

9th Trade Union Congress, Prague 1977.

Prague Castle Art Type of 1971

Designs: 3k, Onyx footed bowl, 1350. 3.60k, Bronze horse, 1619.

1977, June 7 **Engr.**

2114 A634	3k multi	1.10	1.00
2115 A634	3.60k multi	1.65	1.50

Sheets of 4.

French Postrider, 19th Century, PRAGA '78 Emblem A750

Postal Uniforms: 1k, Austrian, 1838. 2k, Austrian, late 18th century. 3.60k, Germany, early 18th century.

1977, June 8 **Engr. & Photo.**

2116 A750	60h multi	15	15
2117 A750	1k multi	26	15
2118 A750	2k multi	45	18
2119 A750	3.60k multi	*1.90*	*75*
	Nos. 2116-2119 (4)	*2.76*	
	Set value		*1.05*

PRAGA 1978 International Philatelic Exhibition, Prague, Sept. 8-17, 1978.

Nos. 2116-2119 issued in sheets of 50 and sheets of 4 with 4 labels and horizontal gutter.

Coffeepots, Porcelain Mark A751

Mlada Boleslav Costume A752

Czechoslovak Porcelain and Porcelain Marks: 30h, Urn. 40h, Vase. 60h, Cup and saucer, jugs. 1k, Candlestick and plate. 3k, Cup and saucer, coffeepot.

1977, June 15

2120 A751	20h multi	15	15
2121 A751	30h multi	15	15
2122 A751	40h multi	15	15
2123 A751	60h multi	15	15
2124 A751	1k multi	25	15
2125 A751	3k multi	*1.10*	*65*
	Nos. 2120-2125 (6)	*1.95*	
	Set value		*1.00*

1977, Aug. 31 **Engr.** ***Perf. 11½***

PRAGA Emblem and Folk Costumes from: 1.60k, Vazek. 3.60k, Zavadka. 5k, Belkovice.

2126 A752	1k multi	25	25
2127 A752	1.60k multi	*2.00*	*2.00*
2128 A752	3.60k multi	75	70
2129 A752	5k multi	85	85
	Nos. 2126-2129 (4)	*3.85*	*3.80*

Issued in sheets of 10 and in sheets of 8 plus 2 labels showing PRAGA '78 emblem.

Old Woman, Devil and Spinner, by Viera Bombova A753

Book Illustrations: 60h, Bear and tiger, by Genadij Pavlisin. 1k, Coach drawn by 4 horses (Hans Christian Andersen), by Ulf Lovgren. 2k, Bear and flamingos (Lewis Carroll), by Nicole Claveloux. 3k, King with keys, and toys, by Jiri Trnka.

1977, Sept. 9 **Engr. & Photo.**

2130 A753	40h multi	15	15
2131 A753	60h multi	15	15
2132 A753	1k multi	25	15
2133 A753	2k multi	50	18
2134 A753	3k multi	*1.75*	*50*
	Nos. 2130-2134 (5)	*2.80*	
	Set value		*88*

Prize-winning designs, 6th biennial exhibition of illustrations for children's books, Bratislava.

Globe, Violin, Doves, View of Prague — A754

1977, Sept. 28 ***Perf. 11½***

2135 A754 60h multi		18	15

Congress of International Music Council of UNESCO, Prague and Bratislava.

Souvenir Sheets

"For a Europe of Peace" A755

Designs: 1.60k, "For a Europe of Cooperation." 2.40k, "For a Europe of Social Progress."

1977, Oct. 3

2136	Sheet of 2	75	60
a.	A755 60h multi	25	25
2137	Sheet of 2	1.75	1.25
a.	A755 1.60k multi	50	50
2138	Sheet of 2	2.50	2.00
a.	A755 2.40k multi	80	80

2nd European Security and Cooperation Conference, Belgrade. Nos. 2136-2138 each contain 2 stamps and 2 blue on buff inscriptions and ornaments.

S. P. Korolev, Sputnik I Emblem — A756

Sailors, Cruiser Aurora — A757

Designs: 30h, Yuri A. Gagarin and Vostok I. 40h, Alexei Leonov. 1k, Neil A. Armstrong and footprint on moon. 1.60k, Construction of orbital space station.

1977, Oct. 4

2139 A756	20h multi	15	15
2140 A756	30h multi	15	15
2141 A756	40h multi	15	15
2142 A756	1k multi	28	15
2143 A756	1.60k multi	80	25
	Set value	1.30	50

Space research, 20th anniv. of 1st earth satellite.

1977, Nov. 7

2144 A757 30h multi		15	15

60th anniv. of Russian October Revolution.

"Russia," Arms of USSR, Kremlin A758

"Science" A759

1977, Nov. 7

2145 A758 30h multi		15	15

55th anniversary of the USSR.

1977, Nov. 17

2146 A759 3k multi		75	35

Czechoslovak Academy of Science, 25th anniversary.

Art Type of 1967

Paintings: 2k, "Fear" (woman), by Jan Murdoch. 2.40k, Jan Francisci, portrait by Peter M. Bohun. 2.60k, Vaclav Hollar, self-portrait, 1647. 3k, Young Woman, 1528, by Lucas Cranach. 5k, Cleopatra, by Rubens.

1977, Nov. 27 **Engr.** ***Perf. 11½***

2147 A565	2k multi	40	35
2148 A565	2.40k multi	*2.50*	*2.25*
2149 A565	2.60k multi	1.75	1.50
2150 A565	3k multi	70	65
2151 A565	5k multi	1.10	1.00
	Nos. 2147-2151 (5)	*6.45*	*5.75*

Sheets of 4.

View of Bratislava, by Georg Hoefnagel — A760

Design: 3.60k, Arms of Bratislava, 1436.

1977, Dec. 6

2152 A760	3k multi	1.90	1.50
2153 A760	3.60k multi	90	65

Sheets of 4. See Nos. 2174-2175, 2270-2271, 2331-2332, 2364-2365, 2422-2423, 2478-2479, 2514-2515, 2570-2571, 2618-2619.

Stamp Pattern and Post Horn — A761

1977, Dec. 18 **Engr. & Photo.**

2154 A761 1k multi		25	15

Stamp Day.

Zdenek Nejedly — A762

Karl Marx — A763

1978, Feb. 10 ***Perf. 11½***

2155 A762 30h multi		15	15
2156 A763 40h multi		15	15
Set value		18	15

Zdenek Nejedly (1878-1962), musicologist and historian; Karl Marx (1818-1883), political philosopher.

Civilians Greeting Guardsmen — A764

Intellectual, Farm Woman and Steel Worker, Flag — A765

1978, Feb. 25

2157 A764 1k gold & multi		25	15
2158 A765 1k gold & multi		25	15
Set value			20

30th anniv. of "Victorious February" (No. 2157), and Natl. Front (No. 2158). See note after 2190.

Yuri A. Gagarin, Vostok I — A766

10k Coin, 1964, and 25k Coin, 1965 — A767

Design: 30h, 3.60k, like No. 2140.

Engraved; Overprint Photogravure (Blue and carmine on 30h, green and lilac rose on 3.60k)

1978, Mar. 2 ***Perf. 11½x12***

2159 A766 30h dk red		25	25
2160 A766 3.60k vio bl		*4.50*	*4.00*

Capt. V. Remek, 1st Czechoslovakian cosmonaut on Russian spaceship Soyuz 28, Mar. 2-9.

1978, Mar. 14 **Engr. & Photo.**

Designs: 40h, Medal for Culture, 1972. 1.40k, Charles University medal, 1948. 3k, Ferdinand I medal, 1568. 5k, Gold florin, 1335.

2161 A767 20h sil & multi		15	15
2162 A767 40h sil & multi		15	15
2163 A767 1.40k gold & multi		*2.00*	*30*
2164 A767 3k gold & multi		65	38
2165 A767 5k gold & multi		1.00	50
Nos. 2161-2165 (5)		*3.95*	
Set value			*1.30*

650th anniversary of Kremnica Mint.

Tire Tracks and Ball — A768

Congress Emblem — A769

1978, Mar. 15

2166 A768 60h multi		15	15

Road safety.

1978, Apr. 16 ***Perf. 11½***

2167 A769 1k multi		25	15

9th World Trade Union Cong., Prague 1978.

Shot Put and Praha '78 Emblem — A770

Designs: 1k, Pole vault. 3.60k, Women runners.

1978, Apr. 26

2168 A770 40h multi		15	15
2169 A770 1k multi		32	15
2170 A770 3.60k multi		1.25	75
Nos. 2168-2170 (3)		1.72	
Set value			90

5th European Athletic Championships, Prague 1978.

Ice Hockey — A771

Designs: 30h, Hockey. 2k, Ice hockey play.

1978, Apr. 26

2171 A771 30h multi		15	15
2172 A771 60h multi		15	15
2173 A771 2k multi		40	18
Nos. 2171-2173 (3)		70	
Set value			35

5th European Ice Hockey Championships and 70th anniversary of Bandy hockey.

Bratislava Type of 1977

Designs: 3k, Bratislava, 1955, by Orest Dubay. 3.60k, Fishpound Square, Bratislava, 1955, by Imro Weiner-Kral.

1978, May 9 **Engr.** ***Perf. 11½***

2174 A760 3k multi		1.10	1.00
2175 A760 3.60k multi		1.65	1.50

Sheets of 4.

Prague Castle Art Type of 1971

Designs: 3k, King Ottokar II, detail from tomb. 3.60k, Charles IV, detail from votive panel by Jan Ocka.

1978, May 9

2176 A634 3k multi		75	50
2177 A634 3.60k multi		2.00	2.00

Sheets of 4.

Ministry of Post, Prague A772

Engraved and Photogravure

1978, May 29 ***Perf. 12x11½***

2178 A772 60h multi		15	15

14th session of permanent COMECOM Commission (Ministers of Post and Telecommunications of Socialist Countries).

Palacky Bridge A773

Prague Bridges and PRAGA '78 Emblem: 40h, Railroad bridge. 1k, Bridge of May 1. 2k, Manes Bridge. 3k, Svatopluk Cech Bridge. 5.40k, Charles Bridge.

1978, May 30

2179 A773 20h blk & multi		15	15
2180 A773 40h blk & multi		15	15
2181 A773 1k blk & multi		25	15
2182 A773 2k blk & multi		50	25
2183 A773 3k blk & multi		70	35
2184 A773 5.40k blk & multi		3.00	1.00
Nos. 2179-2184 (6)		4.75	
Set value			1.80

PRAGA 1978 International Philatelic Exhibition, Prague, Sept. 8-17.

St. Peter and Apostles, Clock Tower, and Emblem — A774

Town Hall Clock, Prague, by Josef Manes, and PRAGA '78 Emblem: 1k, Astronomical clock. 2k, Prague's coat of arms. 3k, Grape harvest (September). 3.60k, Libra. 10k, Arms surrounded by zodiac signs and scenes symbolic of 12 months, horiz. 2k, 3k, 3.60k show details from design of 10k.

1978, June 20 ***Perf. 11½x11***

2185 A774 40h multi		15	15
2186 A774 1k multi		28	15
2187 A774 2k multi		50	20
2188 A774 3k multi		*2.00*	*75*
2189 A774 3.60k multi		75	25
Nos. 2185-2189 (5)		*3.68*	*1.50*

Souvenir Sheet

Perf. 12x12

2190 A774 10k multi		7.00	7.00

PRAGA'78 Intl. Philatelic Exhibition, Prague, Sept. 8-17. No. 2190 contains one 50x40mm stamp. Sheet exists imperf.

A non-valid souvenir sheet contains 4 imperf. copies of No. 2157. Sold only with PRAGA ticket.

Folk Dancers — A775

1978, July 7 ***Perf. 11½x12***

2191 A775 30h multi		15	15

25th Folklore Festival, Vychodna.

Overpass and PRAGA Emblem A776

Designs (PRAGA Emblem and): 1k, 2k, Modern office buildings (diff.). 6k, Old and new Prague. 20k, Charles Bridge and Old Town, by Vincent Morstadt, 1828.

1978 ***Perf. 12x11½***

2192 A776 60h blk & multi		15	15
2193 A776 1k blk & multi		26	15
2194 A776 2k blk & multi		52	25
2195 A776 6k blk & multi		2.75	1.10
Nos. 2192-2195 (4)		3.68	1.65

Souvenir Sheet

Engr.

2196 A776 20k multi		6.50	6.50

PRAGA 1978 Intl. Phil. Exhib., Prague, Sept. 8-17. No. 2196 also for 60th anniv. of Czechoslovak postage stamps. No. 2196 contains one 61x45mm stamp.

Issue dates: Nos. 2192-2195, Sept. 8; No. 2196, Sept. 10.

Souvenir Sheet

Apollo's Companion, by Titian A777

Design: No. 2197b, King Midas. Stamps show details from "Apollo Flaying Marsya" by Titian.

1978, Sept. 12 ***Perf. 11½***

2197 Sheet of 2		6.75	6.75
a. A777 10k multi		3.00	3.00
b. A777 10k multi		3.00	3.00

Titian (1488-1576), Venetian painter. No. 2197 with dark blue marginal inscription "FIP" was sold only with entrance ticket to PRAGA Philatelic Exhibition.

Exhibition Hall — A778

Engraved and Photogravure

1978, Sept. 13 ***Perf. 11½x11***

2198 A778 30h multi		15	15

22nd International Engineering Fair, Brno.

Postal Newspaper Service — A779

TV Screen, Headquarters and Logo — A780

Newspaper, Microphone A781

1978, Sept. 21 *Perf. 11½*

2199	A779	30h multi	15	15
2200	A780	30h multi	15	15
2201	A781	30h multi	15	15
		Set value	24	15

Postal News Service, 25th anniv.; Czechoslovakian television, 25th anniv.; Press, Broadcasting and Television Day.

Sulky Race A782

Pardubice Steeplechase: 10h, Falling horses and jockeys at fence. 30h, Race. 40h, Horses passing post. 1.60k, Hurdling. 4.40k, Winner.

1978, Oct. 6 *Perf. 12x11½*

2202	A782	10h multi	15	15
2203	A782	20h multi	15	15
2204	A782	30h multi	15	15
2205	A782	40h multi	15	15
2206	A782	1.60k multi	38	22
2207	A782	4.40k multi	1.75	80
		Nos. 2202-2207 (6)	2.73	
		Set value		1.25

Woman Holding Arms of Czechoslovakia A783

1978, Oct. 28 *Perf. 11½*

2208	A783	60h multi	15	15

60th anniversary of independence.

Art Type of 1974

Paintings: 2.40k, Flowers, by Jakub Bohdan (1660-1724). 3k, The Dream of Salas, by Ludovit Fulla, horiz. 3.60k, Apostle with Censer, Master of the Spissko Capitals (c. 1480-1490).

1978, Nov. 27 **Engr.**

2209	A700	2.40k multi	60	45
2210	A700	3k multi	70	65
2211	A700	3.60k multi	2.50	2.00
		Nos. 2209-2211 (3)	3.80	3.10

Slovak National Gallery, 30th anniversary.

Musicians, by Jan Könyves — A784

Slovak Ceramics: 30h, Janosik on Horseback, by Jozef Franko. 40h, Woman in Folk Costume by Michal Polasko. 1k, Three Girls Singing, by Ignac Bizmayer. 1.60k, Janosik Dancing, by Ferdis Kostka.

Engraved and Photogravure

1978, Dec. 5 *Perf. 11½x12*

2212	A784	20h multi	15	15
2213	A784	30h multi	15	15
2214	A784	40k multi	15	15
2215	A784	1k multi	30	15
2216	A784	1.60k multi	1.00	25
		Set value	1.50	48

Alfons Mucha and his Design for 1918 Issue — A785

1978, Dec. 18 *Perf. 11½*

2217	A785	1k multi	25	15

60th Stamp Day.

COMECON Building, Moscow — A786

1979, Jan. 1 *Perf. 11½*

2218	A786	1k multi	25	15

Council for Mutual Economic Aid (COMECON), 30th anniversary.

Woman's Head and Grain — A787

Woman, Workers, Child, Doves — A788

1979, Jan. 1

2219	A787	30h multi	15	15
2220	A788	60h multi	16	15
		Set value	24	15

United Agricultural Production Assoc., 30th anniv. (30h); Czechoslovakian Federation, 10th anniv. (60h).

Soyuz 28, Rockets and Capsule — A789

Designs: 60h, Astronauts Aleksei Gubarev and Vladimir Remek on launching pad, vert. 1.60k, Soviet astronauts J. Romanenko and G. Grecko, Salyut 6 and recovery ship. 2k, Salyut-Soyuz orbital complex, post office in space and Czechoslovakia No. 2153. 4k, Soyuz 28, crew after landing and trajectory map, vert. 10k, Gubarev and Remek, Intercosmos emblem, arms of Czechoslovakia and USSR.

1979, Mar. 2

2221	A789	30h multi	15	15
2222	A789	60h multi	20	15
2223	A789	1.60k multi	50	15
2224	A789	2k multi	1.90	50
2225	A789	4k multi	80	50
		Nos. 2221-2225 (5)	3.55	
		Set value		1.20

Souvenir Sheet

2226	A789	10k multi	4.00	4.00

1st anniv. of joint Czechoslovak-Soviet space flight. Size of No. 2226: 76x93mm (stamp 39x55mm). No. 2226 has Cyrillic inscription, No. 2455a does not. No. 2226 exists imperf.

Alpine Bellflowers A790

Stylized Satellite, Dial, Tape A791

Mountain Flowers: 20h, Crocus. 30h, Pinks. 40h, Alpine hawkweed. 3k, Larkspur.

1979, Mar. 23 *Perf. 11½*

2227	A790	10h multi	15	15
2228	A790	20h multi	15	15
2229	A790	30h multi	15	15
2230	A790	40h multi	15	15

Perf. 14

2231	A790	3k multi	1.40	75
		Nos. 2227-2231 (5)	2.00	
		Set value		1.00

Mountain Rescue Service, 25th anniversary. The 3k exists perf. 11½.

1979, Apr. 2

2232	A791	10h multi	15	15

Telecommunications research, 30th anniv.

Artist and Model, Dove, Bratislava Castle — A792

Cog Wheels, Transformer and Student — A793

Musical Instruments, Bratislava Castle — A794

Pioneer Scarf, IYC Emblem — A795

Red Star, Man, Child and Doves — A796

1979, Apr. 2

2233	A792	20h multi	15	15
2234	A793	20h multi	15	15
2235	A794	30h multi	15	15
2236	A795	30h multi	15	15
2237	A796	60h multi	16	15
		Set value	48	25

Fine Arts Academy, Bratislava, 30th anniv.; Slovak Technical University, 40th anniv.; Radio Symphony Orchestra, Bratislava, 30th anniv.; Young Pioneers, 30th anniv. and IYC; Peace Movement, 30th anniversary.

Prague Castle Art Type of 1971

Designs: 3k, Burial crown of King Ottokar II. 3.60k, Portrait of Mrs. Reitmayer, by Karel Purkyne.

1979, May 9 *Perf. 11½*

2238	A634	3k multi	1.75	1.65
2239	A634	3.60k multi	85	75

Sheets of 4.

Arms of Vlachovo Brezi, 1538 — A797

Animals in Heraldry: 60h, Jesenik, 1509 (bear and eagle). 1.20k, Vysoke Myto, 1471 (St. George slaying dragon). 1.80k, Martin, 1854 (St. Martin giving coat to beggar). 2k, Zebrak, 1674 (mythological beast).

1979, May 25 *Perf. 11½x12*

2240	A797	30h multi	15	15
2241	A797	60h multi	15	15
2242	A797	1.20k multi	28	15
2243	A797	1.80k multi	*1.00*	*30*
2244	A797	2k multi	40	18
		Nos. 2240-2244 (5)	*1.98*	
		Set value		*70*

Forest, Thriving and Destroyed A798

Designs: 1.80k, Water. 3.60k, City. 4k, Cattle. All designs show good and bad environment, separated by exclamation point; Man and Biosphere emblem.

1979, June 22 **Engr.** *Perf. 11½*

2245	A798	60h multi	15	15
2246	A798	1.80k multi	32	25
2247	A798	3.60k multi	*1.75*	*75*
2248	A798	4k multi	75	40
		Nos. 2245-2248 (4)	*2.97*	*1.55*

Man and Biosphere Program of UNESCO.

Blast Furnace — A799

Engraved and Photogravure

1979, Aug. 29 *Perf. 11x11½*

2249 A799 30h multi 15 15

Slovak National Uprising, 35th anniversary.

Frog and Goat A800

Book Illustrations (IYC Emblem and): 40h, Knight on horseback. 60h, Maidens. 1k, Boy with sled following rooster. 3k, King riding flying beast.

1979, Aug. 30 *Perf. 11½x11*

2250	A800	20h multi		15	15
2251	A800	40h multi		15	15
2252	A800	60h multi		16	15
2253	A800	1k multi		30	15
2254	A800	3k multi		*1.75*	*50*
		Nos. 2250-2254 (5)		*2.51*	
		Set value			*78*

Prize-winning designs, 7th biennial exhibition of illustrations for children's books, Bratislava; International Year of the Child. Printed with labels showing story characters.

"Bone Shaker" Bicycles, 1870 A801

Bicycles from: 20h, 1978. 40h, 1910. 60h, 1886. 3.60k, 1820.

1979, Sept. 14 *Perf. 12x11½*

2255	A801	20h multi	15	15
2256	A801	40h multi	15	15
2257	A801	60h multi	15	15
2258	A801	2k multi	50	20
2259	A801	3.60k multi	2.00	65
		Nos. 2255-2259 (5)	2.95	
		Set value		1.00

Bracket Clock, 18th Century — A802

Designs: 18th century clocks.

1979, Oct. 1 *Perf. 11½*

2260	A802	40h multi	15	15
2261	A802	60h multi	15	15
2262	A802	80h multi	85	25
2263	A802	1k multi	25	15
2264	A802	2k multi	50	20
		Nos. 2260-2264 (5)	1.90	
		Set value		70

Art Type of 1967

Paintings: 1.60k, Sunday by the River, by Alois Moravec. 2k, Self-portrait, by Gustav Mally. 3k, Self-portrait, by Ilia Yefimovic Repin. 3.60k, Horseback Rider, by Jan Bauch. 5k, Dancing Peasants, by Albrecht Dürer.

1979, Nov. 27 **Engr.** *Perf. 12*

2265	A565	1.60k multi	40	28
2266	A565	2k multi	45	42
2267	A565	3k multi	60	55
2268	A565	3.60k multi	3.25	3.25
2269	A565	5k multi	1.10	1.00
		Nos. 2265-2269 (5)	5.80	5.50

Bratislava Type of 1977

Designs: 3k, Bratislava Castle on the Danube, by L. Janscha, 1787. 3.60k, Bratislava Castle, stone engraving by Wolf, 1815.

1979, Dec. 5

2270	A760	3k multi	70	65
2271	A760	3.60k multi	1.90	1.90

Stamp Day — A803

Engraved and Photogravure

1979, Dec. 18 *Perf. 11½x12*

2272 A803 1k multi 25 15

Electronic Circuits — A804

Designs: 50h, Satellite dish. 2k, Airplane. 3k, Computer punch tape.

1979-80 **Photo.** *Perf. 11½x12*

Coil Stamps

2273	A804	50h red	15	15
2274	A804	1k brown	25	15
2275	A804	2k green ('80)	50	20
2276	A804	3k lake ('80)	70	25
		Nos. 2273-2276 (4)	1.60	
		Set value		60

The 1k comes in two shades.

Runners and Dove A805

Engraved and Photogravure

1980, Jan. 29 *Perf. 12x11½*

2289 A805 50h multi 15 15

50th Intl. Peace Marathon, Kosice, Oct. 4.

Downhill Skiing — A806

1980, Jan. 29 *Perf. 11½x12*

2290	A806	1k shown	24	15
2291	A806	2k Speed skating	80	30
2292	A806	3k Four-man bobsled	65	28
		Nos. 2290-2292 (3)	1.69	73

13th Winter Olympic Games, Lake Placid, NY, Feb. 12-24.

Basketball — A807

1980, Jan. 29 *Perf. 11½*

2293	A807	40h shown	15	15
2294	A807	1k Swimming	25	15
2295	A807	2k Hurdles	1.75	40
2296	A807	3.60k Fencing	75	35
		Nos. 2293-2296 (4)	2.90	1.05

22nd Olympic Games, Moscow, July 19-Aug. 3.

Arms Type of 1977

1980, Feb. 20 *Perf. 11½*

2297	A745	50h Bystrice Nad Pernstejnem	15	15
2298	A745	50h Kunstat	15	15
2299	A745	50h Rozmital Pod Tremsinem	15	15
2300	A745	50h Zlata Idka	15	15
		Set value	48	24

Theatrical Mask — A808

Slovak National Theater, Actors — A809

1980, Mar. 1

2301	A808	50h multi	15	15
2302	A809	1k multi	25	15
		Set value		15

50th Jiraskuv Hronov Theatrical Ensemble Review; Slovak National Theater, Bratislava, 60th anniversary.

Mouse in Space, Satellite — A810

Police Corps Banner, Emblem — A811

Intercosmos: 1k, Weather map, satellite. 1.60k, Intersputnik television transmission. 4k, Camera, satellite. 5k, Czech satellite station, 1978, horiz. 10k, Intercosmos emblem, horiz.

Perf. 11½x12, 12x11½

1980, Apr. 12

2303	A810	50h multi	15	15
2304	A810	1k multi	25	15
2305	A810	1.60k multi	1.75	20
2306	A810	4k multi	75	40
2307	A810	5k multi	1.00	50
		Nos. 2303-2307 (5)	3.90	1.40

Souvenir Sheet

2308 A810 10k multi 3.25 2.50

Intercosmos cooperative space program.

1980, Apr. 17 *Perf. 11½*

2309 A811 50h multi 15 15

National Police Corps, 35th anniversary.

Lenin's 110th Birth Anniversary — A812

Design: #2311, Engels's 160th birth anniv.

1980, Apr. 22

2310	A812	1k tan & brn	25	15
2311	A812	1k lt grn & brn	25	15
		Set value		20

Old and Modern Prague, Czech Flag, Bouquet A813

Boy Writing "Peace" A814

Pact Members' Flags, Dove A815

Czech and Soviet Arms, Prague and Moscow Views A816

1980, May 6 *Perf. 12x11½*

2312	A813	50h multi	15	15
2313	A814	1k multi	25	15
2314	A815	1k multi	25	15
2315	A816	1k multi	25	15
		Nos. 2312-2315 (4)	90	
		Set value		35

Liberation by Soviet army, 35th anniv.; Soviet victory in WWII, 35th anniv.; Signing of Warsaw Pact (Bulgaria, Czechoslovakia, German Democratic Rep., Hungary, Poland, Romania, USSR), 25th anniv.; Czechoslovak-Soviet Treaty of Friendship, Cooperation and Mutual Aid, 10th anniv.

Souvenir Sheet

UN, 35th Anniv. A817

1980, June 3 **Engr.** *Perf. 12*

2316 Sheet of 2 2.75 2.75

a. A817 4k multicolored 1.25 1.25

Athletes Parading Banners in Strahov Stadium, Prague, Spartakiad Emblem A818

Engraved and Photogravure

1980, June 3 *Perf. 12x11½*

2317	A818	50h shown	15	15
2318	A818	1k Gymnast, vert.	25	15
		Set value		15

Spartakiad 1980, Prague, June 26-29.

Aechmea Fasciata — A819

A820

1980, Aug. 13 *Perf. 12*

2319 A819 50h *Gerbera Jamesonii* 15 15
2320 A819 1k *Aechmea fasciata* *1.65* *25*
2321 A819 2k *Strelitzia reginae* 70 25
2322 A819 4k *Paphiopedilum* 1.40 50
Nos. 2319-2322 (4) *3.90* *1.15*

Olomouc and Bratislava Flower Shows.

1980, Sept. 24 *Perf. 11½x12*

Designs: Folktale character embroideries.

2323 A820 50h Chad girl 15 15
2324 A820 1k Punch and dog 25 15
2325 A820 2k Dandy and Posy 48 20
2326 A820 4k Lion and moon *2.50* *75*
2327 A820 5k Wallachian dance 1.00 40
Nos. 2323-2327 (5) *4.38* *1.65*

National Census A821

1980, Sept. 24 *Perf. 12x11½*

2328 A821 1k multi 25 15

Prague Castle Type of 1971

Designs: 3k, Old Palace gateway. 4k, Armorial lion, 16th century.

1980, Oct. 28 *Perf. 12*

2329 A634 3k multi 2.00 1.90
2330 A634 4k multi 75 65

Sheets of 4.

Bratislava Type of 1977

Designs: 3k, View across the Danube, by J. Eder, 1810. 4k, The Old Royal Bridge, by J.A. Lantz, 1820.

1980, Oct. 28

2331 A760 3k multi 2.00 1.90
2332 A760 4k multi 75 65

10th Anniversary of Socialist Youth Federation — A822

1980, Nov. 9 *Perf. 12x11½*

2333 A822 50h multi 15 15

No. 2137 Overprinted in Red: 3. / MEZINARODNI VELETRH ZNAMEK / ESSEN '80

1980, Nov. 18

2334 A755 1.60k multi *14.00* *14.00*

Czechoslovak Day/ ESSEN '80, 3rd International Stamp Exhibition, No. 2334 has overprinted red marginal inscription.

Art Type of 1967

Designs: 1k, Pavel Jozef Safarik, by Jozef B. Klemens. 2k, Peasant Revolt mosaic, Anna Podzemma. 3k, St. Lucia, 14th century statue. 4k, Waste Heaps, by Jan Zrzavy, horiz. 5k, Labor, sculpture by Jan Stursa.

1980, Nov. 27 **Engr.** *Perf. 12*

2335 A565 1k multi 1.10 1.10
2336 A565 2k multi 2.25 2.25
2337 A565 3k multi 50 50
2338 A565 4k multi 85 85
2339 A565 5k multi 1.00 1.00
Nos. 2335-2339 (5) 5.70 5.70

Stamp Day — A823

Engraved and Photogravure

1980, Dec. 18 *Perf. 11½x12*

2340 A823 1k multi 25 15

7th Five-year Plan, 1981-1985 A824

1981, Jan. 1 *Perf. 11½*

2341 A824 50h multi 15 15

International Year of the Disabled — A825

1981, Feb. 24

2342 A825 1k multi 25 15

Landau, 1800 A826

1981, Feb. 25 *Perf. 12x11½*

2343 A826 50h shown 15 15
2344 A826 1k Mail coach, 1830 26 25
2345 A826 3.60k Mail sled, 1840 *4.00* *1.75*
2346 A826 5k 4-horse mail coach, 1860 1.00 1.00
2347 A826 7k Open carriage, 1840 1.50 1.50
a. Sheet of 4 *15.00* *12.00*
Nos. 2343-2347 (5) *6.91* *4.65*

WIPA '81 Intl. Philatelic Exhibition, Vienna, Austria, May 22-31. No. 2347a issued May 10.

Wolfgang Amadeus Mozart — A827

Famous Men: No. 2348, Joesph Hlavka (1831-1908). No. 2349, Juraj Hronec (1881-1959). No. 2350, Jan Sverma (1901-44). No. 2351, Mikulas Schneider-Trnavsky (1881-1958). No. 2352, B. Bolzano (1781-1848). No. 2353, Dimitri Shostakovich, composer. No. 2354, George Bernard Shaw, playwright.

1981, Mar. 10 *Perf. 11½*

2348 A827 50h multi 18 15
2349 A827 50h multi 18 15
2350 A827 50h multi 18 15
2351 A827 50h multi 18 15
2352 A827 1k multi 80 25
2353 A827 1k multi 35 15
2354 A827 1k multi 35 15
2355 A827 1k multi 35 15
Nos. 2348-2355 (8) 2.57
Set value 79

Souvenir Sheet

Yuri Gagarin A828

1981, Apr. 5 *Perf. 12*

2356 Sheet of 2 5.50 4.00
a. A828 6k multicolored 2.25 2.00

20th anniv. of 1st manned space flight.

Workers and Banner A829

1981, Apr. 6 *Perf. 12x11½*

2357 A829 50h shown 15 15
2358 A829 1k Hands holding banner 26 15
2359 A829 4k Worker holding banner, vert. 1.00 35
Nos. 2357-2359 (3) 1.41
Set value 49

Czechoslovakian Communist Party, 60th anniv.

Congress Emblem, View of Prague A830

1981, Apr. 6

2360 A830 50h shown 15 15
2361 A830 1k Bratislava 25 15
Set value 15

16th Communist Party Congress.

Agriculture Museum, 90th Anniv. A831

Natl. Assembly Elections A832

1981, May 14 *Perf. 11½x12*

2362 A831 1k multi 25 15

1981, June 1

2363 A832 50h multi 15 15

Bratislava Type of 1977

Designs: 3k, Bratislava Castle, by G.B. Probst, 1760. 4k, Grassalkovic Palace, by C. Bschor, 1815.

1981, June 10 *Perf. 12*

2364 A760 3k multi 2.00 2.00
2365 A760 4k multi 75 50

Uran and Red October Hotels A833

Successes of Socialist Achievements Exhibition: 1k, Brno-Bratislava Highway, Jihlava. 2k, Nuclear power station, Jaslovske Bohunice.

1981, June 10 *Perf. 12x11½*

2366 A833 80h multi 20 15
2367 A833 1k multi 25 15
2368 A833 2k multi 50 20
Nos. 2366-2368 (3) 95
Set value 38

Border Defense Units, 30th Anniv. — A834

Civil Defense, 30th Anniv. — A835

Army Cooperation, 30th Anniv. — A836

Rysy Youth Mountain Climbing Contest A837

Engraved and Photogravure

1981, July 11 *Perf. 11½*

2369 A834 40h multi 15 15
2370 A835 50h multi 15 15
2371 A836 1k multi 25 15
2372 A837 3.60k multi 90 32
Nos. 2369-2372 (4) 1.45
Set value 52

30th Natl. Festival of Amateur Puppet Ensembles — A838

1981, July 2 *Perf. 11½*

2373 A838 2k Punch and Devil 48 20

Souvenir Sheet

Guernica, by Pablo Picasso — A839

1981, July 2 **Engr.** *Perf. 11½x12*

2374 A839 10k multi 3.75 3.25

Picasso's birth centenary; 45th anniv. of Intl. Brigades in Spain.

Cat Holding Flower, by Etienne Delessert — A840

8th Biennial Exhibition of Children's Book Illustrations (Designs by): 50h, Albin Brunovsky, vert. 1k, Adolf Born. 2k, Vive Tolli. 10k, Suekichi Akaba.

Engraved and Photogravure

1981, Sept. 5 *Perf. 11½*

2375 A840 50h multi 15 15
2376 A840 1k multi 24 15
2377 A840 2k multi 42 20
2378 A840 4k multi 95 45
2379 A840 10k multi 4.00 2.00
Nos. 2375-2379 (5) 5.76 2.95

Prague Zoo, 50th Anniv. — A841

1981, Sept. 28 *Perf. 11½x12*

2380 A841 50h Gorillas 15 15
2381 A841 1k Lions 25 15
2382 A841 7k Przewalski's horses 1.65 80
Nos. 2380-2382 (3) 2.05 1.10

Anti-smoking Campaign — A842

1981, Oct. 27 *Perf. 12*
2383 A842 4k multi 1.00 60

No. 2383 se-tenant with label.

Prague Castle Art Type of 1971

Designs: 3k, Carved dragon, Palais Lobkovitz, 16th cent. 4k, St. Vitus Cathedral, by J. Sember and G. Dobler, 19th cent.

1981, Oct. 28
2384 A634 3k multi 65 65
2385 A634 4k multi 2.00 2.00

Sheets of 4.

Art Type of 1967

Designs: 1k, View of Prague, by Vaclav Hollar (1607-1677). 2k, Czechoslovak Academy medallion, engraved by Otakar Spaniel (1881-1955). 3k, Jihoceska Vysivka, by Zdenek Sklenar (b. 1910). 4k, Still Life, by A.M. Gerasimov (1881-1963). 5k, Standing Woman, by Pablo Picasso (1881-1973).

1981, Nov. 27 **Engr.** *Perf. 12*
2386 A565 1k multi 2.25 2.25
2387 A565 2k multi 50 50
2388 A565 3k multi 75 75
2389 A565 4k multi 1.00 1.00
2390 A565 5k multi 1.25 1.25
Nos. 2386-2390 (5) 5.75 5.75

Sheets of 4. Sheets of No. 2390 exist with center gutter inscribed with Philexfrance 82 and FIP emblems. Value, $15.

Stamp Day — A843

Engraved and Photogravure

1981, Dec. 18 *Perf. 11½x12*
2391 A843 1k Engraver Edward Karel 25 15

Russian Workers' Party, Prague Congress, 70th Anniv. — A844

1982, Jan. 18 *Perf. 12*
2392 A844 2k Lenin 50 35
a. Sheet of 4 *5.50 5.00*

No. 2392 issued in sheet of 8.

1982 World Cup Soccer A845

Designs: Various soccer players.

1982, Jan. 29 *Perf. 12x11½*
2393 A845 1k multi 25 15
2394 A845 3.60k multi 70 35
2395 A845 4k multi 1.40 50
Nos. 2393-2395 (3) 2.35 1.00

10th World Trade Union Congress, Havana — A846

Arms of Hrob — A847

1982, Feb. 10 *Perf. 11½*
2396 A846 1k multi 25 15

1982, Feb. 10 *Perf. 12x11½*

Arms of various cities.

2397 A847 50h shown 15 15
2398 A847 50h Nove Mesto Nad Metuji 15 15
2399 A847 50h Trencin 15 15
2400 A847 50h Mlada Boleslav 15 15
Set value 48 20

See Nos. 2499-2502, 2542-2544, 2595-2597, 2783-2786.

50th Anniv. of the Great Strike at Most — A848

1982, Mar. 23 *Perf. 11½*
2401 A848 1k multi 25 15

60th Intl. Railway Union Congress A849

1982, Mar. 23 *Perf. 12x11½*
2402 A849 6k Steam locomotive, 1922, electric, 1982 1.50 75

10th Workers' Congress, Prague A850

George Dimitrov A851

1982, Apr. 15
2403 A850 1k multi 25 15

1982, May 1
2404 A851 50h multi 15 15

A852

10th Lidice Intl. Children's Drawing Contest — A853

Engravings: 40h, The Muse Euterpe Playing a Flute, by Crispin de Passe (1565-1637). 50h, The Lute Player, by Jacob de Gheyn (1565-1629). 1k, Woman Flautist, by Adriaen Collaert (1560-1618). 2k, Musicians in a Hostel, by Rembrandt (1606-1669). 3k, Hurdygurdy Player, by Jacques Callot (1594-1635).

1982, May 18 *Perf. 11½x12*
2405 A852 40h multi 15 15
2406 A852 50h multi 15 15
2407 A852 1k multi 25 15
2408 A852 2k multi 48 20
2409 A852 3k multi 90 60
Nos. 2405-2409 (5) 1.93 1.25

1982, May 18
2410 A853 2k multi 1.00 1.00

Issued in sheets of 6.

40th Anniv. of Destruction of Lidice and Lezaky — A854

1982, June 4 *Perf. 11½*
2411 A854 1k Girl, rose 25 15
2412 A854 1k Hands, barbed wire 25 15

Souvenir Sheet

UN Disarmament Conference — A855

1982, June 4 *Perf. 12*
2413 Sheet of 2 7.50 6.00
a. A855 6k Woman holding doves 3.50 2.75

Souvenir Sheet

2nd UN Conference on Peaceful Uses of Outer Space, Vienna, Aug. 9-21 — A856

1982, Aug. 9 **Engr. & Photo.**
2414 Sheet of 2 7.50 7.00
a. A856 5k multi 3.50 3.00

Krivoklat Castle A857

1982, Aug. 31 *Perf. 12x11½*
2415 A857 50h shown 15 15
2416 A857 1k Statues (Krivoklat) 26 15
2417 A857 2k Nitra Castle 52 24
2418 A857 3k Pottery, lock (Nitra) 75 35
a. Souv. sheet of 4, #2415-2418 2.50 2.00
Nos. 2415-2418 (4) 1.68
Set value 75

50th Anniv. of Zizkov Hill Natl. Monument — A858

1982, Sept. 16
2419 A858 1k multi 25 15

Prague Castle Art Type of 1971

Designs: 3k, St. George and the Dragon, 1373. 4k, Tomb of King Vratislav I, 10th cent.

1982, Sept. 28 *Perf. 12*
2420 A634 3k multi 2.00 65
2421 A634 4k multi 75 75

Sheets of 4.

Bratislava Type of 1977

Designs: 3k, Paddle steamer, Parnik, 1818. 4k, View from Bridge, 19th cent.

1982, Sept. 29
2422 A760 3k multi 2.00 65
2423 A760 4k multi 75 75

European Danube Commission — A859

1982, Sept. 29 *Perf. 11½x12*
2424 A859 3k Steamer, Bratislava Bridge 75 35
a. Souvenir sheet of 4 6.50 5.25
2425 A859 3.60k Ferry, Budapest 95 50
a. Souvenir sheet of 4 8.50 7.00

16th Communist Party Congress — A860

1982, Oct. 28 *Perf. 12x11½*
2426 A860 20h Agriculture 15 15
2427 A860 1k Industry 25 15
2428 A860 3k Engineering 75 35
Nos. 2426-2428 (3) 1.15
Set value 50

30th Anniv. of Academy of Sciences — A861

1982, Oct. 29 *Perf. 11½*
2429 A861 6k Emblem 1.50 75

65th Anniv. of October Revolution A862

Design: 1k, 60th anniv. of USSR.

1982, Nov. 7 *Perf. 12x11½*
2430 A862 50h multi 15 15
2431 A862 1k multi 25 15
Set value 20

Jaroslav Hasek, Writer, Sculpture by Josef Malejovsky — A863

Sculptures: 2k, Jan Zrzavy, freedom fighter, by Jan Simota. 4.40k, Leos Janacek, composer, by Milos Axman. 6k, Martin Kukucin, freedom fighter, by Jan Kulich. 7k, Peaceful Work, by Rudolf Pribis.

Engraved and Photogravure

1982, Nov. 26 *Perf. 11½x12*

2432 A863 1k multi 24 15
2433 A863 2k multi 48 20
2434 A863 4.40k multi 1.00 50
2435 A863 6k multi 1.25 70
2436 A863 7k multi 3.00 1.50
Nos. 2432-2436 (5) 5.97 3.05

Art Type of 1967

Paintings: 1k, Revolution in Spain, by Josef Sima (1891-1971). 2k, Woman Dressing, by Rudolf Kremlicka (1886-1932). 3k, The Girl Bride, by Dezider Milly (1906-1971). 4k, Performers, by Jan Zelibsky (b. 1907). 5k, The Complaint of the Birds, by Emil Filla (1882-1953).

1982, Nov. 27 *Perf. 12*

2437 A565 1k multi 1.00 25
2438 A565 2k multi 2.00 50
2439 A565 3k multi 75 75
2440 A565 4k multi 1.00 1.00
2441 A565 5k multi 1.25 1.00
Nos. 2437-2441 (5) 6.00 3.50

Stamp Day — A864

1982, Dec. 8 *Perf. 11½*

2442 A864 1k Engraver Jaroslav Goldschmied (1890-1977) 25 15

A865

A866

1983, Jan. 10 Engr. *Perf. 12x11½*

2443 A865 50h dark blue 15 15

Pres. Gustav Husak, 70th birthday. See No. 2686.

1983, Feb. 24 Engr. & Photo.

Designs: 50h, Jaroslav Hasek (1882-1923), writer. 1k, Julius Fucik (1903-1943), antifascist martyr. 2k, Martin Luther (1483-1546). 5k, Johannes Brahms (1833-1897), composer.

2444 A866 50h multi 15 15
2445 A866 1k multi 25 15
2446 A866 2k multi 45 18
a. Souvenir sheet of 4 *12.00 9.00*
2447 A866 5k multi 1.10 45
Nos. 2444-2447 (4) 1.95
Set value 78

Nordposta '83 Intl. Stamp Exhibition, Hamburg. No. 2446a issued Nov. 1.

Workers Marching — A867

Family — A868

1983, Feb. 25 *Perf. 11½*

2448 A867 50h multi 15 15
2449 A868 1k multi 26 15
Set value 15

35th anniv. of "Victorious February" (50h), and Natl. Front (1k).

World Communications Year — A869

Perf. 11½, 12x11½ (2k)

1983, Mar. 16

2450 A869 40h multi 15 15
2451 A869 1k multi 25 15
2452 A869 2k multi 45 20
2453 A869 3.60k multi 90 40
Nos. 2450-2453 (4) 1.75
Set value 75

Various wave patterns. 2k, 40x23mm; 3.60k, 49x19mm.

7th World Ski-jumping Championships A870

1983, Mar. 16 *Perf. 11½*

2454 A870 1k multi 25 15

Souvenir Sheet

5th Anniv. of Czechoslovak-USSR Intercosmos Cooperative Space Program — A871

1983, Apr. 12 *Perf. 12*

2455 Sheet of 2 14.00 7.00
a. A871 10k multi 6.00 3.00

See No. 2226.

Protected Species A872

1983, Apr. 28 *Perf. 12x11½*

2456 A872 50h Butterfly, violets 15 15
2457 A872 1k Water lilies, frog 25 15
2458 A872 2k Pine cones, crossbill 48 20
2459 A872 3.60k Herons 90 38
2460 A872 5k Gentians, lynx 1.00 38
2461 A872 7k Stag 5.25 1.50
Nos. 2456-2461 (6) 8.03 2.76

A873

A874

Soviet Marshals.

1983, May 5 *Perf. 11½*

2462 A873 50h Ivan S. Konev 15 15
2463 A873 1k Andrei I. Sheremenko 25 15
2464 A873 2k Rodion J. Malinovsky 48 20
Nos. 2462-2464 (3) 88
Set value 33

30th anniv. of Czechoslovak-Soviet defense treaty.

1983, July 13 *Perf. 12*

2465 A874 2k multi 50 20
a. Souvenir sheet of 4 5.00 4.00

World Peace and Life Congress, Prague. No. 2465 issued in sheets of 8.

Emperor Rudolf II by Adrian De Vries (1560-1626) A875

Art treasures of the Prague Castle: 5k, Kinetic relief, Timepiece, Rudolf Svoboda.

1983, Aug. 25 *Perf. 11½*

2466 A875 4k multi 1.00 40
2467 A875 5k multi 1.25 50

See Nos. 2518-2519, 2610-2611, 2654-2655, 2717-2718, 2744-2745, 2792-2793.

9th Biennial of Illustrations for Children and Youth — A876

Illustrators: 50h, Oleg K. Zotov, USSR. 1k, Zbigniew Rychlicki, Poland. 4k, Lisbeth Zwerger, Austria. 7k, Antonio Dominques, Angola.

1983, Sept. 9 Engr. & Photo.

2468 A876 50h multi 15 15
2469 A876 1k multi 26 15
2470 A876 4k multi 1.00 40
2471 A876 7k multi 1.75 70
a. Souv. sheet of 4, #2468-2471 3.50 2.50
Nos. 2468-2471 (4) 3.16 1.40

World Communications Year — A877

Emblems and aircraft.

1983, Sept. 30 *Perf. 11½*

2472 A877 50h red & black 15 15
2473 A877 1k red & black, vert. 25 15
2474 A877 4k red & black 1.00 75
Nos. 2472-2474 (3) 1.40
Set value 90

60th anniv. of the Czechoslovak Airlines.

16th Party Congress Achievements — A878

1983, Oct. 20 *Perf. 12x11½*

2475 A878 50h Civil engineering construction 15 15
2476 A878 1k Chemical industry 25 15
2477 A878 3k Health services 75 40
Nos. 2475-2477 (3) 1.15
Set value 55

Bratislava Type of 1977

Designs: 3k, Two sculptures, Viktor Tilgner (1844-96). 4k, Mirbachov Palace, 1939, by Julius Schubert (1888-1947).

1983, Oct. 28 *Perf. 12*

2478 A760 3k multi 2.00 65
2479 A760 4k multi 1.00 1.00

Natl. Theater, Prague, Centenary — A879

1983, Nov. 8 Engr. *Perf. 11½*

2480 A879 50h Natl. Theater building 15 15
2481 A879 2k State Theater, Natl. Theater 50 20
Set value 25

Messenger of Mourning, by Mikolas Ales — A880

Designs: 2k, Genius, theater curtain by Vojtech Hynais (1854-1925). 3k, Music, Lyric drawings by Frantisek Zenisek (1849-1916). 4k, Symbolic figure of Prague, by Vaclay Brozik (1851-1901). 5k, Hradcany Castle, by Julius Marak (1832-1899).

1983, Nov. 18 Engr.

2482 A880 1k multi 1.40 30
2483 A880 2k multi 2.75 60
2484 A880 3k multi 75 65
2485 A880 4k multi 1.00 85
2486 A880 5k multi 1.25 1.00
Nos. 2482-2486 (5) 7.15 3.40

Warrior with Sword and Shield, Engraving, 17th Cent. — A881

Engravings of Costumes: 50h, Bodyguard of Rudolf II, by Jacob de Gheyn (1565-1629). 1k, Lady with Lace Collar, by Jacques Callot (1592-1635). 4k, Lady, by Vaclav Hollar (1607-77). 5k, Man, by Antoine Watteau (1684-1721).

Engraved and Photogravure

1983, Dec. 2 *Perf. 11½x12*

2487 A881 40h multi 15 15
2488 A881 50h multi 15 15
2489 A881 1k multi 25 15
2490 A881 4k multi 75 40
2491 A881 5k multi 2.25 75
Nos. 2487-2491 (5) 3.55
Set value 1.35

Stamp Day — A882

1983, Dec. 18

2492 A882 1k Karl Seizinger (1889-1978), #114 25 15

Czechoslovak Federation, 15th Anniv. — A883

1984, Jan. 1 *Perf. 11½*
2493 A883 50h Bratislava, Prague Castles 20 15

35th Anniv. of COMECON A884

1984, Jan. 23
2494 A884 1k Headquarters, Moscow 25 15

1984 Winter Olympics A885

1984, Feb. 7 *Perf. 12x11½*
2495 A885 2k Cross-country skiing 50 25
2496 A885 3k Hockey 75 30
a. Souvenir sheet of 4 3.75 3.00
2497 A885 5k Biathlon 1.25 50
Nos. 2495-2497 (3) 2.50 1.05

Intl. Olympic Committee, 90th Anniv. — A886

1984, Feb. 7 *Perf. 11½x12*
2498 A886 7k Rings, runners, torch 1.75 70

City Arms Type of 1982

1984, Mar. 1 *Perf. 12x11½*
2499 A847 50h Kutna Hora 15 15
2500 A847 50h Turnov 15 15
2501 A847 1k Martin 25 15
2502 A847 1k Milevsko 25 15
Nos. 2499-2502 (4) 80
Set value 30

Intercosmos Space Program — A887

Resistance Heroes — A888

Various satellites. Nos. 2503-2507 se-tenant with labels showing flags.

1984, Apr. 12 *Perf. 11½x12*
2503 A887 50h multi 15 15
2504 A887 1k multi 16 15
2505 A887 2k multi 35 20
2506 A887 4k multi 75 40
2507 A887 5k multi 1.40 50
Nos. 2503-2507 (5) 2.81 1.40

1984, May 9 *Perf. 11x11½*

Designs: 50h, Vendelin Opatrny (1908-44). 1k, Ladislav Novomesky (1904-44). 2k, Rudolf Jasiok (1919-44). 4k, Jan Nalepka (1912-43).

2508 A888 50h multi 18 15
2509 A888 1k multi 25 15
2510 A888 2k multi 50 20
2511 A888 4k multi 1.00 35
Nos. 2508-2511 (4) 1.93
Set value 70

Music Year — A889

1984, May 11 *Perf. 11½*
2512 A889 50h Instruments 15 15
2513 A889 1k Organ pipes, vert. 25 15
Set value 15

Bratislava Type of 1977

Designs: 3k, Vintners' Guild arms, 19th cent. 4k, View of Bratislava (painting commemorating shooting competition, 1827).

1984, June 1 *Perf. 12*
2514 A760 3k multi 75 75
2515 A760 4k multi 1.00 1.00

Issued in sheet of 4.

Central Telecommunications Building, Bratislava — A890

1984, June 1 *Perf. 11½*
2516 A890 2k multi 45 15

A891

A893

1984, June 12 *Perf. 12*
2517 A891 5k UPU emblem, dove, globe 1.75 1.25

1984 UPU Congress. Issued in sheet of 4 with and without Philatelic Salon text.

Prague Castle Type of 1983

Designs: 3k, Crowing rooster, St. Vitus Cathedral, 19th cent. 4k, King David from the Roundnice, Book of Psalms illuminated manuscript, Bohemia, 15th cent.

1984, Aug. 9 **Engr. & Photo.**
2518 A875 3k multi 65 40
2519 A875 4k multi 90 65

1984, Aug. 28 *Perf. 11½x12*

Playing cards.

2520 A893 50h Jack of Spades, 16th cent. 15 15
2521 A893 1k Queen of spades, 17th cent. 25 15
2522 A893 2k 9 of hearts, 18th cent. 50 25
2523 A893 3k Jack of clubs, 18th cent. 75 35
2524 A893 5k King of hearts, 19th cent. 1.25 60
Nos. 2520-2524 (5) 2.90 1.50

Slovak Natl. Uprising, 40th Anniv. A894

1984, Aug. 29 *Perf. 12x11½*
2525 A894 50h Family, factories, flowers 15 15

Battle of Dukla Pass (Carpathians), 40th Anniv. — A895

1984, Sept. 8 *Perf. 11½x12*
2526 A895 2k Soldiers, flag 40 15

1984 Summer Olympics A896

1984, Sept. 9 *Perf. 12x11½*
2527 A896 1k Pole vault 20 15
2528 A896 2k Bicycling 40 20
2529 A896 3k Rowing 60 35
2530 A896 5k Weight lifting 1.00 45
a. Souv. sheet of 4, #2527-2530 2.00 1.75
Nos. 2527-2530 (4) 2.20 1.15

16th Party Congress Goals and Projects A897

1984, Oct. 28 *Perf. 12x11½*
2531 A897 1k Communications 16 15
2532 A897 2k Transportation 32 20
2533 A897 3k Transgas pipeline 50 30
a. Souvenir sheet of 3 2.50 2.00
Nos. 2531-2533 (3) 98 65

Art Type of 1967

Paintings: 1k, The Milevsky River, by Karel Stehlik (b. 1912). 2k, Under the Trees, by Viktor Barvitius (1834-1902). 3k, Landscape with Flowers, by Zolo Palugyay (1898-1935). 4k, King in Palace, Visehrad Codex miniature, 1085. 5k, View of Kokorin Castles, by Antonin Manes. Nos. 2534-2537 horiz.; issued in sheets of 4.

1984, Nov. 16 *Perf. 11½*
2534 A565 1k multi 85 25
2535 A565 2k multi 1.10 50
2536 A565 3k multi 65 65
2537 A565 4k multi 85 85
2538 A565 5k multi 1.10 1.00
Nos. 2534-2538 (5) 4.55 3.25

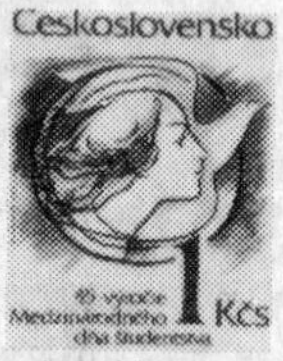

Students' Intl., 45th Anniv. — A898

Birth Cent., Antonin Zapotocky — A899

1984, Nov. 17
2539 A898 1k Head, dove 20 15

Engr. & Photo.

1984, Dec. 18 *Perf. 11½*
2540 A899 50h multi 15 15

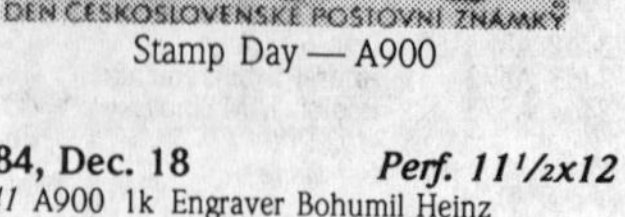

Stamp Day — A900

1984, Dec. 18 *Perf. 11½x12*
2541 A900 1k Engraver Bohumil Heinz (1894-1940) 20 15

City Arms Type of 1982

1985, Feb. 5 *Perf. 12x11½*
2542 A847 50h Kamyk nad Vltavou 15 15
2543 A847 50h Havirov 15 15
2544 A847 50h Trnava 15 15
Set value 24 15

University of Applied Arts, Prague, Centenary — A901

1985, Feb. 6 *Perf. 11½x12*
2545 A901 3k Art and Pleasure, sculpture 60 30

Trnava University, 350th Anniv. — A902

1985, Feb. 6 *Perf. 11½x12*
2546 A902 2k Town of Trnava 40 20

Military Museum Exposition A903

1985, Feb. 7 *Perf. 11½x12, 12x11½*
2547 A903 50h Armor, crossbow, vert. 15 15
2548 A903 1k Medals, vert. 20 15
2549 A903 2k Biplane, spacecraft 40 18
Nos. 2547-2549 (3) 75
Set value 33

Vladimir I. Lenin (1870-1924), 1st Chairman of Russia — A904

1985, Mar. 15 **Engr.** *Perf. 12*
2550 A904 2k multi 50 30

No. 2550 printed in sheets of 6.

UN 40th Anniv., Peace Year 1986 A905

1985, Mar. 15
2551 A905 6k UN, Peace Year emblems *1.75 1.50*

Issued in sheets of 4.

A906

A907

Engraved and Photogravure

1985, Apr. 5 *Perf. 11½*

2552 A906 4k Natl. arms, twig, crowd 80 40

Kosice govt. plan, Apr. 5, 1945.

1985, Apr. 5

2553 A907 50h Natl. arms, flag, soldiers 15 15

Natl. Security Forces, 40th anniv.

Halley's Comet, INTERCOSMOS Project Vega — A908

Design: Emblem, space platform, interstellar map, intercept data.

1985, Apr. 12 *Perf. 12x11½*

2554 Sheet of 2 *7.50 6.75*
a. A908 5k multicolored *1.75 1.50*

Project Vega, a joint effort of the USSR, France, German Democratic Republic, Austria, Poland, Bulgaria and CSSR, was for the geophysical study of Halley's Comet, Dec. 1984-Mar. 1986.

European Ice Hockey Championships, Prague, Apr. 17-May 3 — A909

1985, Apr. 13

2555 A909 1k Hockey players, emblem 20 15

No. 2555 Ovptd. "CSSR MISTREM SVETA" in Violet Blue

1985, May 31 *Perf. 12x11½*

2556 A909 1k multi *2.75 2.75*

Natl. Chess Org., 80th Anniv. — A910

1985, Apr. 13 *Perf. 11½*

2557 A910 6k Emblem, game board, chessmen 90 50

Anniversaries — A911

1985, May 5 *Perf. 11½x12*

2558 A911 1k May Uprising, 1945 15 15
2559 A911 1k Soviet Army in CSSR, 1945 15 15
2560 A911 1k Warsaw Treaty, 1950 15 15
2561 A911 1k Czech-Soviet Treaty, 1970 15 15
Nos. 2558-2561 (4) 60
Set value 45

Spartakiad '85, Strahov Stadium, Prague, June 27 — A912

Designs: 50h, Gymnasts warming up with rackets and balls. 1k, Rhythmic gymnastics floor exercise, Prague Castle.

1985, June 3 *Perf. 11½, 11½x12*

2562 A912 50h multi 15 15

Size: 53x22mm

2563 A912 1k multi 18 15
Set value 25 15

WWII Anti-Fascist Political Art A913

Drawings and caricatures: 50h, Fire, and From the Concentration Camp, by Joseph Capek (1887-1945). 2k, The Conference on Disarmament in Geneva, 1927 and The Prophecy of Three Parrots, 1933, by Frantisek Bidlo (1895-1945). 4k, The Unknown Warrior to Order, 1936, and The Almost Peaceful Dove, 1937, by Antonin Pelc (1895-1967).

1985, June 4 *Perf. 12x11½*

2564 A913 50h multi 15 15
2565 A913 2k multi 28 18
2566 A913 4k multi 60 40
Nos. 2564-2566 (3) 1.03 73

Helsinki Conference on European Security and Cooperation, 10th Anniv. — A914

1985, July 1 **Engr. & Photo.**

2567 A914 7k multi 1.50 1.00
a. Souvenir sheet of 4 7.00 7.00

An imperf. souv. sheet similar to No. 2567a was issued June 1, 1988 for FINLANDIA '88 and PRAGA '88.

12th World Youth Festival, Moscow A915

1985, July 2

2568 A915 1k Kremlin, youths 18 15

A916

A918

1985, Sept. 3 *Perf. 11½*

2569 A916 50h multi 15 15

Federation of World Trade Unions, 40th anniv.

Bratislava Type of 1977

Designs: 3k, Castle and river, lace embroidery by Elena Holeczyova (1906-1983). 4k, Pottery cups and mugs, 1600-1500 B.C.

1985, Sept. 4 **Engr.** *Perf. 12*

2570 A760 3k multi 55 45
2571 A760 4k multi 75 60

Issued in sheets of 4.

Engraved and Photogravure

1985, Sept. 5 *Perf. 11½*

Children's book illustrations: 1k, Rocking Horse, by Kveta Pacovska, USSR. 2k, Fairies, by Gennadij Spirin, USSR. 3k, Butterfly and Girl, by Kaarina Kaila, Finland. 4k, Boy and Animals, by Erick Ingraham, US.

2572 A918 1k multi 15 15
2573 A918 2k multi 28 18
2574 A918 3k multi 45 25
2575 A918 4k multi 60 35
a. Souv. sheet of 4, #2572-2575 3.50 2.75
Nos. 2572-2575 (4) 1.48 93

10th biennial of illustrations.

5-Year Development Plan — A919

1985, Oct. 28 *Perf. 12x11½*

2576 A919 50h Construction machinery 15 15
2577 A919 1k Prague subway, map 15 15
2578 A919 2k Modern textile spinning 28 22
Nos. 2576-2578 (3) 58
Set value 40

16th Communist Party Congress goals.

Prague Castle — A920

A921

Engr., Engr. & Photo. (3k)

1985, Oct. 28 *Perf. 12*

2579 A920 2k Presidential Palace Gate, 1768 30 22
2580 A920 3k St. Vitus' Cathedral 45 38

Sheets of 6.

Engraved and Photogravure

1985, Nov. 23 *Perf. 11½x12*

Glassware: 50h, Pitcher, Near East, 4th cent. 1k, Venetian pitcher, 16th cent. 2k, Bohemian goblet, c. 1720. 4k, Harrachov Bohemian vase, 18th cent. 6k, Jablonec Bohemian vase, c. 1900.

2581 A921 50h multi 15 15
2582 A921 1k multi 15 15
2583 A921 2k multi 28 22
2584 A921 4k multi 60 42
2585 A921 6k multi 90 70
Nos. 2581-2585 (5) 2.08 1.64

Arts and Crafts Museum, Prague, cent.

Art Type of 1967

Designs: 1k, Young Woman in a Blue Gown, by Jozef Ginovsky (1800-1857). 2k, Lenin on the Charles Bridge, Prague, 1952, by Martin Sladky (b. 1920). 3k, Avenue of Poplars, 1935, by Vaclav Rabas (1885-1954). 4k, The Martyrom of St. Dorothea, 1516, by Hans Baldung Grien (c. 1484-1545). 5k, Portrait of Jasper Schade van Westrum, 1645, by Frans Hals (c. 1581-1666).

1985, Nov. 27 **Engr.** *Perf. 12*

2586 A565 1k multi *1.25 1.00*
2587 A565 2k multi 35 35
2588 A565 3k multi 55 45
2589 A565 4k multi 75 60
2590 A565 5k multi 90 75
Nos. 2586-2590 (5) *3.80 3.15*

Sheets of 4.

Bohdan Roule (1921-1960), Engraver — A922

Engraved and Photogravure

1985, Dec. 18 *Perf. 11½x12*

2591 A922 1k multicolored 16 15

Stamp Day 1985.

Intl. Peace Year — A923

1986, Jan. 2

2592 A923 1k multi 16 15

Philharmonic Orchestra, 90th Anniv. — A924

EXPO '86, Vancouver — A925

1986, Jan. 2 *Perf. 11½*

2593 A924 1k Victory Statue, Prague 16 15

1986, Jan. 23 *Perf. 11½*

Design: Z 50 LS monoplane, Cenyerth Prague-Kladno locomotive, Sahara Desert rock drawing, 5th-6th cent. B.C.

2594 A925 4k multicolored 60 40

City Arms Type of 1982

1986, Feb. 10 *Perf. 12x11½*

Size: 42x54mm

2595 A847 50h Myjava 15 15
2596 A847 50h Vodnany 15 15
2597 A847 50h Zamberk 15 15
Set value 25 20

17th Natl. Communist Party Congress, Prague, Mar. 24 — A926

1986, Mar. 20 *Perf. 11½*

2598 A926 50h shown 15 15
2599 A926 1k Industry 18 15
Set value 25 15

Natl. Communist Party, 65th Anniv. — A927

1986, Mar. 20 *Perf. 12x11½*

2600 A927 50h Star, man, woman 15 15
2601 A927 1k Hammer, sickle, laborers 18 15
Set value 25 15

Natl. Front Election Program A928

1986, Mar. 28

2602 A928 50h multi 15 15

Karlovy Vary Intl. Film Festival, 25th Anniv. — A929

1986, Apr. 3 *Perf. 11½*
2603 A929 1k multi 18 15

A930

A931

1986, Apr. 8 **Engr. & Photo.**
2604 A930 1k multi 18 15

Spring of Prague Music Festival.

1986, Apr. 25
2605 A931 50h multi 15 15

Prague-Moscow air service, 50th anniv.

Intl. Olympic Committee, 90th Anniv. — A932

1986, May 12 *Perf. 11½x12*
2606 A932 2k multi 30 20

1986 World Cup Soccer Championships, Mexico — A933

1986, May 15 *Perf. 12x11½*
2607 A933 4k multi 60 40

Women's World Volleyball Championships, Prague — A934

1986, May 19
2608 A934 1k multi 18 15

Market value for a particular scarce stamp may remain relatively low if few collectors want it.

Souvenir Sheet

Intl. Philatelic Federation, FIP, 60th Anniv. — A935

1986, June 3 **Engr.** *Perf. 12*
2609 A935 20k multi 4.50 3.50

Exists imperf. and with perforations between stamps omitted.

Prague Castle Type of 1983

Designs: 2k, Jewelled funerary pendant, 9th cent. 3k, Allegory of Blossoms, sculpture by Jaroslav Horejc (1886-1983), St. Vitus' Cathedral.

1986, June 6 **Engr.** *Perf. 12*
2610 A875 2k multi 32 30
2611 A875 3k multi 70 45

UN Child Survival Campaign — A937

Toys.

Engraved and Photogravure

1986, Sept. 1 *Perf. 11½*
2612 A937 10h Rooster 15 15
2613 A937 20h Horse and rider 15 15
2614 A937 1k Doll 24 16
2615 A937 2k Doll, diff. 48 32
2616 A937 3k Tin omnibus, c. 1910 75 50
Nos. 2612-2616 (5) 1.77
Set value 1.05

UNICEF, 40th anniv.

Registration, Cent. — A938

1986, Sept. 2 *Perf. 11½x12*
2617 A938 4k Label, mail coach 60 45

Bratislava Type of 1977

1986, Sept. 11 **Engr.** *Perf. 12*
2618 A760 3k Sigismund Gate 55 38
2619 A760 4k St. Margaret, bas-relief 70 52

Sheets of four.

Owls — A939

Engraved and Photogravure

1986, Sept. 18 *Perf. 11½*
2620 A939 50h Bubo bubo 15 15
2621 A939 2k Asio otus 32 25
2622 A939 3k Strix aluco 50 35
2623 A939 4k Tyto alba 65 50
2624 A939 5k Asio flammeus 80 65
Nos. 2620-2624 (5) 2.42 1.90

Souvenir Sheet

Intl. Brigades in Spain — A940

Theater curtain: Woman Savaged by Horses, 1936, by Vladimir Sychra (1903-1963), Natl Gallery, Prague.

1986, Oct. 1 **Engr.** *Perf. 12*
2625 Sheet of 2 3.00 2.75
a. A940 5k multi 1.25 1.00

Locomotives and Streetcars — A941

Engraved and Photogravure

1986, Oct. 6 *Perf. 12x11½*
2626 A941 50h KT-8 15 15
2627 A941 1k E458.1 16 15
2628 A941 3k T466.2 48 30
2629 A941 5k M152.0 80 52
Nos. 2626-2629 (4) 1.59 1.12

Paintings in the Prague and Bratislava Natl. Galleries A942

Designs: 1k, The Circus Rider, 1980, by Jan Bauch (b. 1898). 2k, The Ventriloquist, 1954, by Frantisek Tichy (1896-1961). 3k, In the Circus, 1946, by Vincent Hloznik (b. 1919). 6k, Clown, 1985, by Karel Svolinsky (1896-1986).

1986, Oct. 13 **Engr.** *Perf. 12*
2630 A942 1k multi 18 15
2631 A942 2k multi 38 30
2632 A942 3k multi 52 42
2633 A942 6k multi 1.10 90
Nos. 2630-2633 (4) 2.18 1.77

Art Type of 1967

Designs: 1k, The Czech Lion, May 1918, by Vratislav H. Brunner (1886-1928). 2k, Boy with Mandolin, 1945, by Jozef Sturdik (b. 1920). 3k, Metra Building, 1984, by Frantisek Gross (1909-1985). 4k, Portrait of Maria Maximiliana at Sternberk, 1665, by Karel Skreta (1610-1674). 5k, Adam and Eve, 1538, by Lucas Cranach (1472-1553).

1986, Nov. 3 **Engr.** *Perf. 12*
2634 A565 1k multi *20 15*
2635 A565 2k multi *40 28*
2636 A565 3k multi *60 38*
2637 A565 4k multi *80 55*
2638 A565 5k multi *1.00 65*
Nos. 2634-2638 (5) *3.00 2.01*

Sheets of 4.

Stamp Day — A943

Design: V.H. Brunner (1886-1928), stamp designer, and No. 88.

Photo. & Engr.

1986, Dec. 18 *Perf. 11½x12*
2639 A943 1k multicolored 15 15

World Cyclocross Championships, Jan. 24-25, Central Bohemia — A944

1987, Jan. 22 *Perf. 11½*
2640 A944 6k multi 1.00 60

Czechoslovakian Bowling Union, 50th Anniv. — A945

1987, Jan. 22 *Perf. 11½*
2641 A945 2k multi 35 20

State Decorations — A946

Designs: 50h, Gold Stars of Socialist Labor and Czechoslovakia. 2k, Order of Klement Gottwald. 3k, Order of the Republic. 4k, Order of Victorious February. 5k, Order of Labor.

1987, Feb. 4 *Perf. 12x11½*
2642 A946 50h multi 15 15
2643 A946 2k multi 35 22
2644 A946 3k multi 50 45
2645 A946 4k multi 70 40
2646 A946 5k multi 85 50
Nos. 2642-2646 (5) 2.55 1.72

Butterflies A947

1987, Mar. 4
2647 A947 1k Limenitis populi 15 15
2648 A947 2k Smerinthus ocellatus 30 22
2649 A947 3k Pericallia matronula 45 30
2650 A947 4k Saturnia pyri 60 38
Nos. 2647-2650 (4) 1.50 1.05

Natl. Nuclear Power Industry A948

1987, Apr. 6
2651 A948 5k multi 75 50

11th Revolutionary Trade Union Movement Congress, Apr. 14-17, Prague — A949

1987, Apr. 7 *Perf. 11½*

2652 A949 1k multi 15 15

Souvenir Sheet

INTERCOSMOS, 10th Anniv. — A950

Design: Cosmonauts Alexei Gubarev of the USSR and Vladimir Remek of Czechoslovakia, rocket and emblem.

1987, Apr. 12 **Engr.** *Perf. 12*

2653 Sheet of 2 3.50 3.50
a. A950 10k multi 1.75 1.75
b. Souv. sheet of 4, litho. & engr., imperf. *7.00 7.00*

No. 2653b issued Nov. 15, 1987.

Prague Castle Art Treasures Type of 1983

Designs: 2k, Three Saints, stained-glass window detail, c. 1870, St. Vitus Cathedral, by Frantisek Sequens (1830-1896). 3k, Coat of Arms, New Land Rolls Hall, 1605.

1987, May 9 *Perf. 11½*

2654 A875 2k multi 30 20
2655 A875 3k dk red, slate gray & yel org 45 30

Nos. 2654-2655 each printed in sheets of 6.

PRAGA '88 A951

Photo. & Engr.

1987, May 12 *Perf. 12x11½*

2656 A951 3k Telephone, 1894 50 32
2657 A951 3k Postal van, 1924 50 32
2658 A951 4k Locomotive tender, 1907 75 42
2659 A951 4k Tram, 1900 75 42
2660 A951 5k Steam roller, 1936 85 52
Nos. 2656-2660 (5) 3.35 2.00

Printed in sheets of 8 + 2 labels picturing telephone or vehicles. Nos. 2657-2658 also printed in sheets of 4 + label picturing vehicles.

Destruction of Lidice and Lezaky, 45th Anniv. — A952

Drawings: No. 2661, When the Fighting Ended, 1945, by Pavel Simon. No. 2662, The End of the game, 1945, by Ludmila Jirincova.

1987, June *Perf. 11½*

2661 A952 1k blk, cerise & vio 15 15
2662 A952 1k blk, gold, pale lil & cerise 15 15
Set value 20

Union of Czechoslovakian Mathematicians and Physicists, 125th Anniv. — A953

Designs: No. 2663, Prague Town Hall mathematical clock, Theory of Functions diagram. No. 2664, J.M. Petzval (1807-1891), J. Strouhal (1850-1922) and V. Jarnik (1897-1970). No. 2665, Geographical measurement from A.M. Malletta's book, 1672, earth fold and Brownian motion diagrams.

1987, July 6 *Perf. 11½x12*

2663 A953 50h multi 15 15
2664 A953 50h multi 15 15
2665 A953 50h multi 15 15
Set value 30 25

A954

A955

Award-winning illustrations.

1987, Sept. 3 *Perf. 11½*

2666 A954 50h Asun Balzola, Spain 15 15
2667 A954 1k Frederic Clement, France 20 15
2668 A954 2k Elzbieta Gaudasinska, Poland 40 26
a. Souv. sheet of 2 + label 80 60
2669 A954 4k Marija Lucija Stupica, Yugoslavia 80 52
Nos. 2666-2669 (4) 1.55 1.08

11th Biennial of Children's Book Illustration, Sept. 11-Oct. 30, Bratislava.

1987, Sept. 23

2670 A955 50h Eternal flame, flower 15 15

Theresienstadt Memorial for the victims from 23 European countries who died in the Small Fortress, Terezin, a Nazi concentration camp.

Socialist Communications Organization, 30th Anniv. — A956

1987, Sept. 23

2671 A956 4k Emblem, satellite, dish receiver 65 40

Jan Evangelista Purkyne (1787-1869), Physiologist A957

1987, Sept. 30

2672 A957 7k multicolored 1.10 75

Views of Bratislava A958

Designs: 3k, Male and female figures supporting an oriel, Arkier Palace, c. 1552. 4k, View of Bratislava from Ware Conterfactur de Stadt Presburg, from an engraving by Hans Mayer, 1563.

1987, Oct. 1 **Engr.** *Perf. 12*

2673 A958 3k multicolored 52 35
2674 A958 4k multicolored 70 45

Printed in sheets of 4 with Bratislava Castle (from Mayer's engraving) between.
See Nos. 2719-2720, 2763-2764, 2800-2801.

Type of 1974

Photo. & Engr.

1987, Nov. 1 *Perf. 12x11½*

2675 A699 1k Post rider 15 15

PRAGA '88, Aug. 26-Sept. 4, 1988. No. 2675 printed se-tenant with label picturing exhibition emblem.

October Revolution, Russia, 70th Anniv. A959

Establishment of the Union of Soviet Socialist Republics, 65th Anniv. — A960

1987, Nov. 6 *Perf. 12x11½*

2676 A959 50h multicolored 15 15
2677 A960 50h multicolored 15 15
Set value 15 15

Art Type of 1974

Paintings in national galleries: 1k, Enclosure of Dreams, by Kamil Lhotak (b. 1912). 2k, Tulips, by Ester Simerova-Martincekova (b. 1909). 3k, Triptych with Bohemian Landscape, by Josef Lada (1887-1957). 4k, Accordion Player, by Josef Capek (1887-1945). 5k, Self-portrait, by Jiri Trnka (1912-1969).

1987, Nov. 18 **Engr.** *Perf. 12*

2678 A700 1k multi 18 15
2679 A700 2k multi 38 22
2680 A700 3k multi 55 32
2681 A700 4k multi 75 45
2682 A700 5k multi 95 60
Nos. 2678-2682 (5) 2.81 1.74

Czech and Slovak art. Issued in sheets of 4.

69th Stamp Day — A961

Portrait of Jacob Obrovsky (1882-1949), stamp designer, Bohemian Lion (Type SP1), sketch of a lion and PRAGA '88 emblem.

Photo. & Engr.

1987, Dec. 18 *Perf. 11½x12*

2683 A961 1k multicolored 15 15

No. 2683 printed in sheet of four with eight labels se-tenant with stamps, inscribed "100 Years of the National Philatelic Movement in Czechoslovakia" in Czech. The four labels between the "blocks of six" are blank.

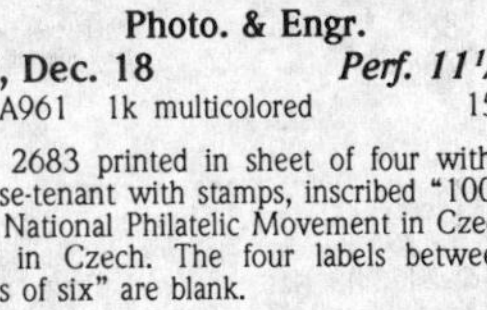

Czechoslovak Republic, 70th Anniv. — A962

1988, Jan. 1 *Perf. 12x11½*

2684 A962 1k Woman, natl. arms, linden branch 15 15

Natl. Front, 40th Anniv. — A963

1988, Feb. 25 *Perf. 11½*

2685 A963 50h multicolored 15 15

Husak Type of 1983

Photo. & Engr.

1988, Jan. 10 *Perf. 12x11½*

2686 A865 1k brt rose & dk carmine 15 15

Olympics — A965

1988, Feb. 1 *Perf. 11½x12*

2687 A965 50h Ski jumping, ice hockey 15 15
2688 A965 1k Basketball, soccer 18 15
2689 A965 6k Discus, weight lifting 1.00 85
Nos. 2687-2689 (3) 1.33 1.15

Exist in souv. sheets of 2, imperf. between and in souv. sheets of 2, imperf.

Victorious February, 40th Anniv. — A966

Design: Statue of Klement Gottwald by Rudolf Svoboda.

1988, Feb. 25 *Perf. 11½*

2690 A966 50h multicolored 15 15

No. 2690 exists in a souvenir sheet of two No. 2690 and two postally invalid copies of No. 637, imperf. Sheet exists imperf.

Classic Automobiles — A967

1988, Mar. 1 *Perf. 12x11½*

2691 A967 50h 1914 Laurin & Klement 15 15
2692 A967 1k 1902 Tatra NW Type B 28 18
2693 A967 2k 1905 Tatra NW Type E 55 35
2694 A967 3k 1929 Tatra 12 Normandie 85 55
2695 A967 4k 1899 Meteor 1.10 72
a. Bklt. pane, 2 3k, 3 4k + label
Nos. 2691-2695 (5) 2.93 1.95

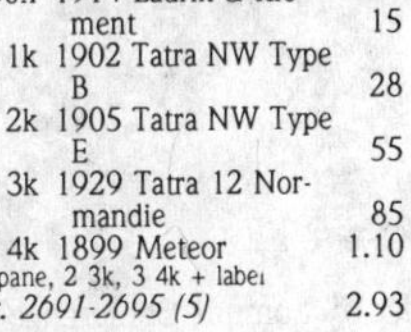

Postal Museum, 70th Anniv. A968

Praga '88 emblem and: 50h, Postman, Malostranske Namesti Square p.o., Prague, c. 1742, and Velka Javorina television transmitter, 1979. 1k, Telecommunications Center, Mlada Boleslav, 1986, and Carmelite Street p.o., Prague, c. 1792. 2k, Prague 1 (1873) and Bratislava 56 (1984) post offices. 4k, Communications Center, Prachatice (1982), postman and Maltetske Nameski Square p.o., Prague, c. 1622.

1988, Mar. 10

2696 A968 50h multi 15 15
2697 A968 1k multi 22 16
2698 A968 2k multi 42 28
2699 A968 4k multi 90 60
a. Souv. sheet, 2 each #2698-2699 3.75 2.00
Nos. 2696-2699 (4) 1.69 1.19

In No. 2699a the top pair of Nos. 2698-2699 is imperf. at top and sides.

A969

A970

1988, Mar. 29 ***Perf. 11½***

2700 A969 50h multicolored 15 15

Matice Slovenska Cultural Assoc., 125th anniv.

1988, May 12 **Photo. & Engr.**

PRAGA '88. (Exhibition emblem and aspects of the Museum of Natl. Literature, Prague): 1k, Gate and distant view of museum. 2k, Celestial globe, illuminated manuscript, bookshelves and ornately decorated ceiling. 5k, Illuminated "B" and decorated binder of a medieval Bible. 7k, Celestial globe, illuminated manuscript, Zodiacal signs (Aries and Leo), view of museum.

2701 A970 1k multicolored 25 15
a. Souvenir sheet of 4 1.25 60
2702 A970 2k multicolored 50 28
a. Souvenir sheet of 4 2.50 1.25
2703 A970 5k multicolored 1.25 75
a. Souvenir sheet of 4 6.50 3.00
2704 A970 7k multicolored 1.50 80
a. Souvenir sheet of 4 7.25 3.25
b. Souv. sheet of 4, imperf., #2701-2704 3.50 2.50
Nos. 2701-2704 (4) 3.50 1.98

PRAGA '88 — A971

Exhibition emblem and fountains, Prague.

1988, June 1 ***Perf. 11½x12***

2705 A971 1k Waldstein Palace 25 16
2706 A971 2k Old town square 52 25
2707 A971 3k Charles University 80 40
2708 A971 4k Prague Castle 1.10 52
a. Souv. sheet of 4, #2705-2708 2.75 1.75
Nos. 2705-2708 (4) 2.67 1.33

Souvenir Sheet

Soviet-US Summit Conference on Arms Reduction, Moscow — A972

Design: The capital, Washington, and the Kremlin, Moscow.

1988, June 1 ***Perf. 12x11½***

2709 A972 4k blue blk, dark red & gold 2.25 1.25

Exists imperf.

PRAGA '88 A973

Exhibition emblem and modern architecture, Prague: 50h, Trade Unions Central Recreation Center. 1k, Koospol foreign trade company. 2k, Motol Teaching Hospital. 4k, Culture Palace.

1988, July 1 ***Perf. 12x11½***

2710 A973 50h multicolored 15 15
2711 A973 1k blk, lt blue & bister 24 15
2712 A973 2k multicolored 45 26
a. Souv. sheet, 2 1k, 2 2k + 4 labels, imperf. 1.75
2713 A973 4k multicolored 95 52
a. Souv. sheet, 2 50h, 2 4k + 4 labels, imperf. 2.50
Nos. 2710-2713 (4) 1.79 1.08

Souvenir Sheet

PRAGA '88 — A974

Design: Exhibition emblem and Alfons Mucha (1860-1939), designer of first Czech postage stamp.

1988, Aug. 18 **Engr.** ***Perf. 12***

2714 A974 Sheet of 2 3.00 1.75
a. 5k multicolored 1.50 85

Czech postage stamps, 70th anniv.

Souvenir Sheets

PRAGA '88 A975

Paintings: 5k, *Turin, Monte Superga,* by Josef Navratil (1798-1865), Postal Museum, Prague. Details of *Bacchus and Ariadne,* by Sebastiano Ricci (1659-1734), Natl. Gallery, Prague: No. 2716a, Ariadne. No. 2716b, Bacchus and creatures.

1988

2715 Sheet of 2 2.75 1.50
a. A975 5k multi 1.50 85
2716 Sheet of 2 5.50 3.25
a.-b. A975 10k any single 2.75 1.50

Issue dates: 5k, Aug. 19. 10k, Aug. 26. No. 2716 exists with emblem and inscription "DEN F.I.P. JOURNEE DE LA FEDERATION INTERNATIONALE DE PHILATELIE."

Prague Castle Type of 1983

Painting: 2k, Pottery jug, 17th cent. 3k, *St. Catherine with Angel,* 1580, by Paolo Veronese.

1988, Sept. 28 **Engr.** ***Perf. 12***

2717 A875 2k shown 95 52
2718 A875 3k multi 1.25 70

Issued in sheets of 6.

Bratislava Views Type of 1987

Designs: 3k, *Hlavne Square, circa 1840* an etching by R. Alt-Sandman, 1840. 4k, *Ferdinand House, circa 1850,* a pen-and-ink drawing by V. Reim.

1988, Oct. 19

2719 A958 3k multicolored 95 52
2720 A958 4k multicolored 1.25 70

Issued in sheets of 4.

Art Type of 1974

Paintings in natl. galleries: 2k, *With Bundles,* 1931, by Martin Benka (1888-1971). 6k, *Blue Bird,* 1903, by Vojtech Preissig (1873-1944). 7k, *A Jaguar Attacking a Rider,* c. 1850, by Eugene Delacroix (1798-1863).

1988, Nov. 17 **Engr.** ***Perf. 12***

2721 A700 2k multicolored 30 15
2722 A700 6k multicolored 90 40
2723 A700 7k multicolored 1.05 45
Nos. 2721-2723 (3) 2.25 1.00

Czech and Slovak art. Issued in sheets of 4.

Stamp Day — A978

Design: 1k, Jaroslav Benda (1882-1970), illustrator and stamp designer.

Photo. & Engr.

1988, Dec. 18 ***Perf. 11½x12***

2724 A978 1k multicolored 15 15

Paris-Dakar Rally — A979

Trucks: 50h, Earth, Motokov Liaz. 1k, Liaz, globe. 2k, Earth, Motokov Tatra. No. 607. 4k, Map of racecourse, turban, Tatra.

1989, Jan. 2 ***Perf. 12x11½***

2725 A979 50h multicolored 15 15
2726 A979 1k multicolored 15 15
2727 A979 2k multicolored 26 15
2728 A979 4k multicolored 52 26
Nos. 2725-2728 (4) 1.08
Set value 50

Czechoslovakian Federation, 20th Anniv. — A980

1989, Jan. 1

2729 A980 50h multicolored 15 15

Jan Botto (1829-1881) A981

Taras Grigorievich Shevchenko (1814-1861) A982

Jean Cocteau (1889-1963) A983

Charlie Chaplin (1889-1977) A984

Jawaharlal Nehru (1889-1964) and "UNESCO" — A985

Famous men: No. 2732, Modest Petrovich Musorgsky (1839-1881).

Photo. & Engr.

1989, Mar. 9 ***Perf. 12x11½***

2730 A981 50h brn blk & lt blue green 15 15
2731 A982 50h shown 15 15
2732 A982 50h multicolored 15 15
2733 A983 50h red brn, grnh blk & org brn 15 15
2734 A984 50h blk, int blue & dark red 15 15
2735 A985 50h brn blk & lt yel green 15 15
Set value 45 30

Shipping Industry A986

1989, Mar. 27

2736 A986 50h *Republika* 15 15
2737 A986 1k *Pionyr,* flags 15 15
2738 A986 2k *Brno,* flags 22 15
2739 A986 3k *Trinec* 32 18
2740 A986 4k Flags, mast, *Orlik* 45 25
2741 A986 5k *Vltava,* communication hardware 55 32
Nos. 2736-2741 (6) 1.84 1.20

Pioneer Organization, 40th Anniv. — A987

Photo. & Engr.

1989, Apr. 20 ***Perf. 11½***

2742 A987 50h multi 15 15

Art Type of 1974

Details of *Feast of Rose Garlands,* 1506, by Albrecht Durer, Natl. Gallery, Prague: a, Virgin and Child. b, Angel playing mandolin.

1989, Apr. 21 **Engr.** ***Perf. 12***

Miniature Sheet

2743 Sheet of 2 4.75 2.50
a.-b. A700 10k any single 2.50 1.25

Prague Castle Art Type of 1983

Designs: 2k, Bas-relief picturing Kaiser Karl IV, from Kralovske tomb by Alexander Colin (c. 1527-1612). 3k, Self-portrait, by V.V. Reiner (1689-1743).

1989, May 9 **Photo. & Engr.**

2744 A875 2k dark red, sepia & buff 30 16
2745 A875 3k multi 45 24

Printed in sheets of 6.

Souvenir Sheet

PHILEXFRANCE '89, French Revolution Bicent. — A988

1989, July 14 **Engr.** ***Perf. 12***
2746 A988 5k brt blue, blk & dk red 75 35

Haliaeetus albicilla
A989

Photo. & Engr.
1989, July 17 ***Perf. 12x11½***
2747 A989 1k multicolored 15 15

World Wildlife Fund — A990

Toads and newts.

1989, July 18 ***Perf. 11½x12***
2748 A990 2k *Bombina bombina* 30 15
2749 A990 3k *Bombina variegata* 45 16
2750 A990 4k *Triturus alpestris* 60 22
2751 A990 5k *Triturus montandoni* 75 28
Nos. 2748-2751 (4) 2.10 81

Slovak Folk Art Collective, 40th Anniv. — A991

1989, Aug. 29 ***Perf. 12x11½***
2752 A991 50h multicolored 15 15

Slovak Uprising, 45th Anniv. — A992

Photo. & Engr.
1989, Aug. 29 ***Perf. 11½x12***
2753 A992 1k multicolored 15 15

A993

A994

Award-winning illustrations.

1989, Sept. 4 ***Perf. 11½***
2754 A993 50h Hannu Taina, Finland 15 15
2755 A993 1k Aleksander Aleksov, Bulgaria 15 15
2756 A993 2k Jurgen Spohn, West Berlin 25 15
2757 A993 4k Robert Brun, Czechoslovakia 50 25
a. Souvenir sheet of 2 1.20 60
Nos. 2754-2757 (4) 1.05
Set value 50

12th Biennial of Children's Book Illustration, Bratislava.

1989, Sept. 5 **Engr.** ***Perf. 11½x12***

Poisonous mushrooms.

2758 A994 50h *Nolanea verna* 15 15
2759 A994 1k *Amanita phalloides* 15 15
2760 A994 2k *Amanita virosa* 30 15
2761 A994 3k *Cortinarius orellanus* 45 22
2762 A994 5k *Galerina marginata* 75 38
Nos. 2758-2762 (5) 1.80
Set value 88

Bratislava Views Type of 1987

Views of Devin, a Slavic castle above the Danube, Bratislava.

1989, Oct. 16 **Engr.** ***Perf. 12***
2763 A958 3k Castle, flower 1.65 75
2764 A958 4k Castle, urn 2.25 1.25

Printed in sheets of 4.

Jan Opletal (1915-39) — A996

Photo. & Engr.
1989, Nov. 17 ***Perf. 12x11½***
2765 A996 1k multicolored 15 15

Intl. Student's Day. Funeral of Opletal, a Nazi victim, on Nov. 15, 1939, sparked student demonstrations that resulted in the closing of all universities in occupied Bohemia and Moravia.

Art Type of 1974

Paintings in Natl. Galleries: 2k, *Nirvana*, c. 1920, by Anton Jasusch (1882-1965). 4k, *Winter Evening in Town*, c. 1907, by Jakub Schikaneder (1855-1924), horiz. 5k, *The Bakers*, 1926, by Pravoslav Kotik (1889-1970), horiz.

1989, Nov. 27 **Engr.** ***Perf. 12***
2766 A700 2k multicolored 1.10 65
2767 A700 4k multicolored 2.25 1.25
2768 A700 5k multicolored 2.75 1.65
Nos. 2766-2768 (3) 6.10 3.55

Printed in sheets of 4.

Stamp Day — A997

Design: Portrait of Cyril Bouda, stamp designer, art tools and falcon.

Photo. & Engr.
1989, Dec. 18 ***Perf. 11½x12***
2769 A997 1k multicolored 15 15

A998

A999

Photo. & Engr.
1990, Jan. 8 ***Perf. 11½x12***
2770 A998 1k multicolored 15 15

UNESCO World Literacy Year. Printed se-tenant with inscribed label picturing UN and UNESCO emblems.

1990, Jan. 9 ***Perf. 11½***

Famous men: No. 2771, Karel Capek, writer. No. 2772, Thomas G. Masaryk. 1k, Lenin. 2k, Emile Zola, French writer. 3k, Jaroslav Heyrovsky (1890-1987), chemical physicist. 10k, Bohuslav Martinu (1890-1959), composer.

2771 A999 50h multicolored 15 15
2772 A999 50h multicolored 15 15
2773 A999 1k multicolored 16 15
2774 A999 2k multicolored 32 18
2775 A999 3k multicolored 48 25
2776 A999 10k multicolored 1.65 88
Nos. 2771-2776 (6) 2.91
Set value 1.50

Nos. 2771 and 2775-2776 inscribed "UNESCO."

Pres. Vaclav Havel
A1000

Handball Players
A1001

1990, Jan. 9 ***Perf. 12x11½***
2777 A1000 50h red, brt vio & blue 15 15

See No. 2879.

1990, Feb. 1 ***Perf. 11½***
2778 A1001 50h multicolored 15 15

1990 Men's World Handball Championships, Czechoslovakia.

Flora — A1002

A1003

Photo. & Engr.
1990, Mar. 1 ***Perf. 11½***
2779 A1002 50h *Antirrhinum majus* 15 15
2780 A1002 1k *Zinnia elegans* 16 15
2781 A1002 3k *Tigridia pavonia* 45 25

Perf. 12x12½

2782 A1002 5k *Lilium candidum* 80 45
Nos. 2779-2782 (4) 1.56
Set value 84

City Arms Type of 1982

Photo. & Engr.
1990, Mar. 28 ***Perf. 12x11½***
2783 A847 50h Prostejov 15 15
2784 A847 50h Bytca 15 15
2785 A847 50h Sobeslav 15 15
2786 A847 50h Podebrady 15 15
Set value 30 20

1990, Apr. 16 ***Perf. 11½x12***
2787 A1003 1k brn vio, rose & buff 20 15

Visit of Pope John Paul II.

World War II Liberation
A1004

Photo. & Engr.
1990, May 5 ***Perf. 11½***
2788 A1004 1k multicolored 20 15

Souvenir Sheet

150th Anniv. of the Postage Stamp — A1005

1990, May 6 **Engr.** ***Perf. 12***
2789 A1005 7k multicolored 1.25 65

Stamp World London 90.

World Cup Soccer Championships, Italy — A1006

Photo. & Engr.
1990, May 8 ***Perf. 11½***
2790 A1006 1k multicolored 15 15

Free Elections
A1007

1990, June 1
2791 A1007 1k multicolored 15 15

Prague Castle Type of 1983

1990, June 6, 1990 **Engr.**
2792 A875 2k Gold and jeweled hand 35 18
2793 A875 3k Medallion 52 26

Art treasures of Prague Castle. Printed in sheets of 6.

Helsinki Conference, 15th Anniv. — A1008

Perf. 12x11½
1990, June 21 **Photo & Engr.**
2794 A1008 7k multicolored 1.10 60

Dr. Milada Horakova A1009

1990, June 25 *Perf. 12x11½*
2795 A1009 1k multicolored 15 15

Intercanis Dog Show, Brno A1010

Designs: 50h, Poodles, 1k, Afghan hound, Irish wolfhound, greyhound. 4k, Czech terrier, bloodhound, Hannoverian hound. 7k, Cavalier King Charles Spaniel, cocker spaniel, American cocker spaniel.

1990, July 2
2796 A1010 50h multicolored 15 15
2797 A1010 1k multicolored 16 15
2798 A1010 4k multicolored 60 32
2799 A1010 7k multicolored 1.10 55
Nos. 2796-2799 (4) 2.01 1.17

Bratislava Art Type of 1987

1990 **Engr.** *Perf. 12*
2800 A958 3k Ancient Celtic coin 52 28
2801 A958 4k Gen. Milan Stefanik 70 32

Issue dates: 3k, Sept. 29. 4k, July 21.
Printed in sheets of 4.

Grand Pardubice Steeplechase, Cent. — A1011

Photo. & Engr.
1990, Sept. 7 *Perf. 12x11½*
2802 A1011 50h multicolored 15 15
2803 A1011 4k multi, diff. 70 36
Set value 41

Protected Animals A1012

Litho. & Engr.
1990, Oct. 1 *Perf. 12x11*
2804 A1012 50h Marmota marmota 15 15
2805 A1012 1k Felis silvestris 16 15
2806 A1012 4k Castor fiber 65 35
2807 A1012 5k Plecotus auritus 85 42
Nos. 2804-2807 (4) 1.81 1.07

Conf. of Civic Associations, Helsinki — A1013

Perf. 12x11½
1990, Oct. 15 **Litho. & Engr.**
2808 A1013 3k blue, gold & yel 50 30

Christmas — A1014

Photo. & Engr.
1990, Nov. 15 *Perf. 11½x12*
2809 A1014 50h multicolored 15 15

Art Type of 1967

Works of art: 2k, Krucemburk by Jan Zrzavy (1890-1977), horiz. 3k, St. Agnes of Bohemia from the St. Wenceslas Monument, Prague by Josef V. Myslbek (1848-1922). 4k, The Slavs in their Homeland by Alfons Mucha (1860-1939). 5k, St. John the Baptist by Auguste Rodin (1840-1917).

1990, Nov. 27 **Engr.** *Perf. 11½*
2810 A565 2k multicolored 32 18
2811 A565 3k multicolored 50 28
2812 A565 4k multicolored 60 32
2813 A565 5k multicolored 80 45
Nos. 2810-2813 (4) 2.22 1.23

Karel Svolinsky (1896-1986), Vignette from No. 1182 — A1016

1990, Dec. 18 **Photo. & Engr.**
2814 A1016 1k multicolored 15 15

Stamp Day.

A1017

A1018

1991, Jan. 10 *Perf. 11½*
2815 A1017 1k multicolored 15 15

European Judo Championships, Prague.

1991, Jan. 10

Design: A. B. Svojsik (1876-1938), Czech Scouting Founder.

2816 A1018 3k multicolored 30 15

Scouting in Czechoslovakia, 80th Anniv.

Bethlehem Chapel, Prague, 600th Anniv. — A1019

1991, Feb. 4 *Perf. 12x11½*
2817 A1019 50h multicolored 15 15

Wolfgang Amadeus Mozart (1756-1791), Old Theatre — A1020

1991, Feb. 4
2818 A1020 1k multicolored 15 15

Steamship Bohemia, 150th Anniv. — A1021

1991, Feb. 4 *Perf. 11½x12*
2819 A1021 5k multicolored 50 25

Famous Men — A1022

Designs: No. 2820, Antonin Dvorak (1841-1904), composer. No. 2821, Andrej Kmet (1841-1908), botanist. No. 2822, Jaroslav Seifert (1901-1986), poet, Nobel laureate for Literature. No. 2823, Jan Masaryk (1886-1948), diplomat. No. 2824, Alois Senefelder (1771-1834), lithographer.

1991, Feb. 18 *Perf. 12x11½*
2820 A1022 1k multicolored 18 15
2821 A1022 1k multicolored 18 15
2822 A1022 1k multicolored 18 15
2823 A1022 1k multicolored 18 15
2824 A1022 1k multicolored 18 15
Nos. 2820-2824 (5) 90
Set value 50

#2820-2824 printed with se-tenant labels.
See No. 2831.

Europa — A1023

A1024

Photo. & Engr.
1991, May 6 *Perf. 11½x12*
2825 A1023 6k blk, bl & red 60 30

Photo. & Engr.
1991, May 10 *Perf. 11½x12*
2826 A1024 1k multicolored 15 15

General Exhibition in Prague, cent.

Antarctic Treaty, 30th Anniv. A1025

1991, May 20 *Perf. 12x11½*
2827 A1025 8k multicolored 80 40

Castles — A1026

Scenic Views — A1027

1991, June 3 *Perf. 11½*
2828 A1026 50h Blatna 15 15
2829 A1026 1k Bouzov 15 15
2830 A1026 3k Kezmarok 30 15
Set value 45 22

Famous Men Type

Design: Jan Palach (1948-1969), Student.

Photo. & Engr.
1991, Aug. 9 *Perf. 12x11½*
2831 A1022 4k black 40 20

Printed se-tenant with label.

Photo. & Engr.
1991, Aug. 28 *Perf. 11½*
2832 A1027 4k Krivan mountains 40 20
2833 A1027 4k Rip mountain 40 20

A1028

A1029

Illustrations by: 1k, Binette Schroeder, Germany. 2k, Stasys Eidrigevicius, Poland.

Photo. & Engr.
1991, Sept. 2 *Perf. 11½*
2834 A1028 1k multicolored 15 15
2835 A1028 2k multicolored 15 15
Set value 25 15

13th Biennial Exhibition of Children's Book Illustrators, Bratislava.

1991, Sept. 27 **Engr.** *Perf. 11½*

Design: Father Andrej Hlinka (1864-1938), Slovak nationalist.

2836 A1029 10k blue black 1.15 55

Art of Prague and Bratislava — A1030

Designs: No. 2837, Holy Infant of Prague. No. 2838, Blue Church of Bratislava.

1991, Sept. 30
2837 A1030 3k multicolored 35 18
2838 A1030 3k multicolored 35 18

Flowers — A1031

Christmas — A1033

Photo. & Engr.
1991, Nov. 3 *Perf. 12x11½*
2839 A1031 1k Gagea bohemica 15 15
2840 A1031 2k Aster alpinus 20 15
2841 A1031 5k Fritillaria meleagris 50 25
2842 A1031 11k Daphne cneorum 1.10 55
Nos. 2839-2842 (4) 1.95 1.10

Art Type of 1967

Paintings: 2k, Everyday Homelife by Max Ernst. 3k, Lovers by Auguste Renoir. 4k, Head of Christ by El Greco. 5k, Coincidence by Ladislav Guderna. 7k, Two Maidens by Utamaro.

1991, Nov. 3 **Engr.** *Perf. 11½*
2843 A565 2k multicolored 22 15
2844 A565 3k multicolored 32 16
2845 A565 4k multicolored 45 22
2846 A565 5k multicolored 55 28
2847 A565 7k multicolored 78 40
Nos. 2843-2847 (5) 2.32 1.21

1991, Nov. 19
2848 A1033 50h multicolored 15 15

Stamp Day — A1034

Design: Martin Benka (1888-1971), stamp engraver.

Photo. & Engr.

1991, Dec. 18 *Perf. 11½x12*
2849 A1034 2k multicolored 20 15

1992 Winter Olympics, Albertville — A1035

1992, Jan. 6 *Perf. 11½*
2850 A1035 1k Biathlon 15 15

Photo. & Engr.

1992, May 21 *Perf. 11½*
2851 A1035 2k Tennis 22 15

1992 Summer Olympics, Barcelona.

Souvenir Sheet

Jan Amos Komensky (Comenius), Educator — A1036

1992, Mar. 5 **Engr.**
2852 A1036 10k multicolored 1.00 1.00

World Ice Hockey Championships, Prague and Bratislava — A1037

1992, Mar. 31 **Photo. & Engr.**
2853 A1037 3k multicolored 34 18

Traffic Safety A1038

1992, Apr. 2
2854 A1038 2k multicolored 22 15

Expo '92, Seville — A1039

1992, Apr. 2
2855 A1039 4k multicolored 45 22

Discovery of America, 500th Anniv. A1040

1992, May 5 **Engr.**
2856 A1040 22k multicolored 2.65 1.30

Europa. Printed in sheets of 8.

Czechoslovak Military Actions in WWII — A1041

Designs: 1k, J. Kubis and J. Gabcik, assassins of Reinhard Heydrich, 1942. 2k, Pilots flying for France and Great Britain. 3k, Defense of Tobruk. 6k, Capture of Dunkirk, 1944-45.

1992, May 21 **Engr.** *Perf. 12x11½*
2857 A1041 1k multicolored 15 15
2858 A1041 2k multicolored 22 15
2859 A1041 3k multicolored 32 16
2860 A1041 6k multicolored 65 32
Nos. 2857-2860 (4) 1.34
Set value 64

A1042

A1043

Photo. & Engr.

1992, June 10 *Perf. 11½*
2861 A1042 2k multicolored 22 15

Czechoslovakian Red Cross.

1992, June 30
2862 A1043 1k multicolored 15 15

Junior European Table Tennis Championships, Topolcany.

Beetles — A1044

1992, July 15
2863 A1044 1k Polyphylla fullo 15 15
2864 A1044 2k Ergates faber 22 15
2865 A1044 3k Meloe violaceus 32 16
2866 A1044 4k Dytiscus latissimus 42 20
Nos. 2863-2866 (4) 1.11
Set value 53

The 1k exists with denomination omitted.

Troja Castle A1045

1992, Aug. 28 **Engr.** *Perf. 11½*
2867 A1045 6k shown 65 32
2868 A1045 7k Statue of St. Martin, vert. 75 38
2869 A1045 8k Lednice Castle 90 45
Nos. 2867-2869 (3) 2.30 1.15

Chrudim Church Type of 1971

Photo. & Engr.

1992, Aug. 28 *Perf. 11½x11*
2870 A629 50h multicolored 15 15

> *Czech Republic and Slovakia stamps can be mounted in the Scott annual Czech Republic and Slovakia supplement.*

Postal Bank — A1045a

Photo. & Engr.

1992, Aug. 28 *Perf. 11½x12*
2870A A1045a 20k multicolored 2.25 1.10

Antonius Bernolak, Georgius Fandly A1046

Photo. & Engr.

1992, Oct. 6 *Perf. 12x11½*
2871 A1046 5k multicolored 55 28

Slovakian Educational Society, bicent.

Cesky Krumlov — A1046a

Photo. & Engr.

1992, Oct. 19 *Perf. 11½x12*
2871A A1046a 3k brick red & brown 35 18

See No. 2890.

Painting Type of 1967

Paintings: 6k Old Man on a Raft, by Koloman Sokol. 7k, Still Life of Grapes and Raisins, by Georges Braque, horiz. 8k, Abandoned Corset, by Toyen.

Perf. 11½x12, 12x11½

1992, Nov. 2 **Engr.**
2872 A565 6k multicolored 65 32
2873 A565 7k multicolored 75 38
2874 A565 8k multicolored 90 45
Nos. 2872-2874 (3) 2.30 1.15

Christmas — A1047

Photo. & Engr.

1992, Nov. 9 *Perf. 12x11½*
2875 A1047 2k multicolored 22 15

Jindra Schmidt (1897-1984), Graphic Artist and Engraver — A1048

Photo. & Engr.

1992, Dec. 18 *Perf. 11½x12*
2876 A1048 2k multicolored 22 15

Stamp Day.

On January 1, 1993, Czechoslovakia split into Czech Republic and Slovakia. Czech Republic listings continue here. Slovakia can be found in Volume 5.

CZECH REPUBLIC

AREA — 30,449 sq. mi.
POP. — 10,311,831 est. 1992

Natl. Arms — A1049

1993, Jan. 20 **Photo. & Engr.** *Perf. 11*
2877 A1049 3k multicolored 33 16

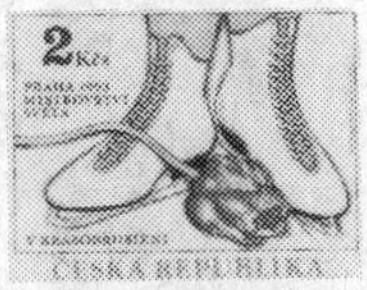

1993 World Figure Skating Championships, Prague — A1050

1993, Feb. 25 *Perf. 11½x11*
2878 A1050 2k multicolored 22 15

Havel Type of 1990 Inscribed "Ceska Republika"

Photo. & Engr.

1993, Mar. 2 *Perf. 12x11½*
2879 A1000 2k vio, vio brn & blue 22 15

St. John Nepomuk, Patron Saint of Czechs, 600th Death Anniv. A1051

1993, Mar. 11
2880 A1051 8k multicolored 90 45

See Germany No. 1776; Slovakia No. 158.

Holy Hunger, by Mikulas Medek — A1052

1993, Mar. 11 *Perf. 11½*
2881 A1052 14k multicolored 1.20 60

Europa.

Sacred Heart Church, Prague A1053

1993, Mar. 30 **Engr.** *Perf. 11½*
2882 A1053 5k multicolored 45 22

Brevnov Monastery, 1000th Anniv. — A1054

Perf. 12x11½

1993, Apr. 12 **Litho. & Engr.**

2883 A1054 4k multicolored 38 18

1993 Intl. Junior Weight Lifting Championships, Cheb — A1055

Photo. & Engr.

1993, May 12 *Perf. 11½*

2884 A1055 6k multicolored 55 28

Clock Tower and Church, Brno — A1056

1993, June 16 **Engr.** *Perf. 12x11½*

2885 A1056 8k multicolored 75 38

Brno, 750th anniv.

Arrival of St. Cyril and St. Methodius, 1130th Anniv. — A1057

1993, June 22 **Photo. & Engr.**

2886 A1057 8k multicolored 75 38

Souvenir Sheet

State Arms — A1058

1993, June 22 *Perf. 11½*

2887 A1058 8k Sheet of 2 1.45 75

Architecture Type of 1992 Inscribed "Ceska Republika" and

A1059

Cities: 1k, Ceske Budejovice. 2k, Usti Nad Labem. #2890, like #2871A. #2890A, Brno. 5k, Plzen. 6k, Slany. 7k, Ostrava. 8k, Olomouc. 10k, Hradec Kralove. 20k, Prague. 50k, Opava.

Perf. 12x11½, 11½x12

1993-94 **Photo. & Engr.**

2888	A1059	1k deep claret & org	15	15
2889	A1059	2k red violet & blue	18	15
2890	A1046a	3k gray blue & red	28	15
2890A	A1059	3k dark blue & red	25	15
2891	A1059	5k bluish green & brn	48	24
2891A	A1059	6k green & org yel	70	35
2891B	A1059	7k black brown & grn	75	38
2892	A1059	8k deep violet & yel	75	38
2893	A1059	10k olive gray & red	95	48
2894	A1059	20k red & blue	1.90	95
2895	A1059	50k brown & green	4.75	2.35
		Nos. 2888-2895 (11)	11.14	5.73

Issued: No. 2890A, 3/30/94; 6k, 10/1/94; 7k, 11/23/94; others, 7/1/93. This is an expanding set. Numbers may change.

World Rowing Championships, Racice — A1060

Photo. & Engr.

1993, Aug. 18 *Perf. 11½*

2901 A1060 3k multicolored 32 16

A1061

Trees — A1062

Famous men: 2k, August Sedlacek (1843-1926), historian. 3k, Eduard Cech (1893-1960), mathematician.

1993, Aug. 26 *Perf. 12x11½*

2902 A1061 2k multicolored 22 15
2903 A1061 3k multicolored 32 16

1993, Oct. 26 *Perf. 11½*

2904 A1062 5k Quercus robur	55	28
2905 A1062 7k Carpinus betulus	75	38
2906 A1062 9k Pinus silvestris	1.00	50
Nos. 2904-2906 (3)	2.30	1.16

Christmas — A1063

A1064

Photo. & Engr.

1993, Nov. 8 *Perf. 11½*

2907 A1063 2k multicolored 18 15

Art Type of 1967 Inscribed "CESKA REPUBLIKA"

Paintings: 9k, Strahovska Madonna, by Po Roce, 1350. 11k, Composition, by Miro, horiz. 14k, Field of Green, by Van Gogh, horiz.

1993 **Engr.** *Perf. 11½x12*

2908 A565 9k multicolored 55 28

Perf. 12x11½

2909 A565 11k multicolored	1.00	50
2910 A565 14k multicolored	1.25	65
Nos. 2908-2910 (3)	2.80	1.43

Issued: 11k, 14k, Nov. 8; 9k, Dec. 15.

Photo. & Engr.

1994, Jan. 19 *Perf. 11½*

2911 A1064 2k multicolored 20 15

Intl. Year of the Family.

Jan Kubelik (1880-1940), Composer A1065

Photo. & Engr.

1994, Jan. 19 *Perf. 11½*

2912 A1065 3k multicolored 25 15

UNESCO A1065a

Designs: 2k, Voltaire (1694-1778), philosopher. 6k, Georgius Agricola (1494-1555), mineralogist, humanist.

1994, Feb. 2 *Perf. 12x11½*

2913 A1065a 2k multicolored 16 15
2914 A1065a 6k multicolored 48 25

A1066

A1067

Photo. & Engr.

1994, Feb. 2 *Perf. 11½*

2915 A1066 5k multicolored 40 20

1994 Winter Olympics, Lillehammer.

Photo. & Engr.

1994, May 4 *Perf. 11½*

Europa (Marco Polo and): No. 2916, Stylized animals, Chinese woman. No. 2917, Stylized animals.

2916 A1067 14k multicolored	1.10	55
2917 A1067 14k multicolored	1.10	55
a. Pair, #2916-2917	2.25	1.10

A1068

A1070

Architectural Sights — A1069

1994, May 18

2918 A1068 5k Eduard Benes 40 20

1994, May 18

UNESCO: 8k, Houses at the square, Telc. 9k, Cubist house designed by Chochol, Prague.

2919 A1069 8k multicolored 65 32
2920 A1069 9k multicolored 75 35

Photo. & Engr.

1994, June 1 *Perf. 11½*

2921 A1070 2k Children's Day 18 15

Dinosaurs A1071

Perf. 11½x11, 11x11½

1994, June 1 **Litho.**

2922 A1071 2k Stegosaurus	18	15
2923 A1071 3k Apatosaurus	28	15
2924 A1071 5k Tarbosaurus, vert.	45	22
Nos. 2922-2924 (3)	91	52

A1072

A1073

Photo. & Engr.

1994, June 1 *Perf. 11½x11*

2925 A1072 8k multicolored 75 38

1994 World Cup Soccer Championships, US.

1994, June 15 *Perf. 11x11½*

2926 A1073 2k multicolored 18 15

12th Pan-Sokol Rally, Prague.

Intl. Olympic Committee, Cent. — A1074

1994, June 15

2927	A1074	7k multicolored	65	32

UPU, 120th Anniv. A1075

1994, Aug. 3 Engr. *Perf. 11½*

2928	A1075	11k multicolored	1.25	65

Songbirds — A1076

Designs: 3k, Saxicola torquata. 5k, Carpodacus erythrinus. 14k, Luscinia svecica.

Photo. & Engr.

1994, Aug. 24 *Perf. 11x11½*

2929	A1076	3k multicolored	32	16
2930	A1076	5k multicolored	55	28
2931	A1076	14k multicolored	1.65	80
		Nos. 2929-2931 (3)	2.52	1.24

Historic Race Cars — A1077

Photo. & Engr.

1994, Oct. 5 *Perf. 11½*

2932	A1077	2k 1900 NW	22	15
2933	A1077	3k 1908 L&K	35	18
2934	A1077	9k 1912 Praga	1.00	50
		Nos. 2932-2934 (3)	1.57	83

Christmas — A1078

Photo. & Engr.

1994, Nov. 9 *Perf. 11½*

2935	A1078	2k multicolored	22	15

Art Type of 1967 Inscribed "CESKA REPUBLIKA"

Engraving or paintings: 7k, Stary Posetilec A Zena, by Lucas Van Leyden. 10k, Moulin Rouge, by Henri de Toulouse-Lautrec. 14k, St. Vitus Madonna, St. Vitus Cathedral, Prague.

1994, Nov. 9 Engr. *Perf. 12*

2936	A565	7k multicolored	75	38
2937	A565	10k multicolored	1.00	50
2938	A565	14k multicolored	1.40	70
		Nos. 2936-2938 (3)	3.15	1.58

Nos. 2936-2938 printed in sheets of 4.

SEMI-POSTAL STAMPS

Nos. B1-B123 were sold, in sets only, at 1½ times face value at the Philatelists' Window of the Prague P.O. for charity benefit. They were available for ordinary postage.

The overprints of Nos. B1-B123 have been well forged.

Austrian Stamps of 1916-18 Overprinted in Black or Blue

a POŠTA ČESKOSLOVENSKÁ 1919

1919 *Perf. 12½*

B1	A37	3h brt vio	20	25
B2	A37	5h lt grn	20	25
B3	A37	6h dp org (Bl)	60	50
B4	A37	6h dp org (Bk)	*1,050.*	*1,050.*
B5	A37	10h magenta	60	75
B6	A37	12h lt bl	60	65
B7	A42	15h dl red	20	25
B8	A42	20h dk grn	20	25
a.		20h green	110.00	70.00
B9	A42	25h blue	30	40
B10	A42	30h dl vio	30	40
B11	A39	40h ol grn	30	40
B12	A39	50h dk grn	30	40
B13	A39	60h dp bl	30	40
B14	A39	80h org brn	30	40
B15	A39	90h red vio	70	75
B16	A39	1k car, *yel* (Bl)	50	60
B17	A39	1k car, *yel* (Bk)	125.00	100.00
B18	A40	2k light bl	1.90	1.90
a.		2k dark blue	2,250.	1,750.
B19	A40	3k car rose	50.00	27.50
a.		3k claret	850.00	775.00
B20	A40	4k yel grn	15.00	8.25
a.		4k dp grn	40.00	26.00
B21	A40	10k violet	200.00	110.00
a.		10k deep violet	225.00	125.00
b.		10k black violet	240.00	135.00

The used value of No. B18a is for copies which have only a Czechoslovakian cancellation. Some of the copies of Austria No. 160 which were officially overprinted with type "a" and sold by the post office, had previously been used and lightly canceled with Austrian cancellations. These canceled-before-overprinting copies, which were postally valid, sell for about one-fourth as much.

Granite Paper

B22	A40	2k lt bl	2.00	2.00
B23	A40	3k car rose	7.25	6.00

The 4k and 10k on granite paper with this overprint were not regularly issued.

Excellent counterfeits of Nos. B1-B23 exist.

Austrian Newspaper Stamps Overprinted

b POŠTA ČESKOSLOVENSKÁ 1919

Imperf

On Stamp of 1908

B26	N8	10h carmine	1,400.	1,400.

On Stamps of 1916

B27	N9	2h brown	15	15
B28	N9	4h green	22	22
B29	N9	6h deep blue	15	15
B30	N9	10h orange	2.75	2.75
B31	N9	30h claret	1.10	1.10
		Nos. B27-B31 (5)	4.37	4.37

Austrian Special Handling Stamps Overprinted in Blue or Black

Stamps of 1916 Overprinted

c POŠTA ČESKOSLOVENSKÁ 1919

Perf. 12½

B32	SH1	2h claret, *yel* (Bl)	27.50	25.00
B33	SH1	5h dp grn, *yel* (Bk)	*1,000.*	*750.00*

Stamps of 1917 Overprinted

d POŠTA ČESKOSLOVENSKÁ 1919

B34	SH2	2h cl, *yel* (Bl)	25	35
a.		Vert. pair, imperf. btwn.	*175.00*	
B35	SH2	2h cl, *yel* (Bk)	60.00	35.00
B36	SH2	5h grn, *yel* (Bk)	25	25

Austrian Air Post Stamps, #C1-C3, Overprinted Type "c" Diagonally

B37	A40	1.50k on 2k lil	190.00	140.00
B38	A40	2.50k on 3k ocher	190.00	140.00
B39	A40	4k gray	850.00	700.00

1919

Austrian Postage Due Stamps of 1908-13 Overprinted Type "b"

B40	D3	2h carmine	*3,000.*	*2,750.*
B41	D3	4h carmine	20.00	15.00
B42	D3	6h carmine	11.00	8.00
B43	D3	14h carmine	75.00	35.00
B44	D3	25h carmine	40.00	20.00
B45	D3	30h carmine	275.00	225.00
B46	D3	50h carmine	900.00	825.00

Austria Nos. J49-J56 Overprinted Type "b"

B47	D4	5h rose red	20	30
B48	D4	10h rose red	20	30
B49	D4	15h rose red	20	30
B50	D4	20h rose red	2.00	1.50
B51	D4	25h rose red	1.25	1.00
B52	D4	30h rose red	50	50
B53	D4	40h rose red	2.00	1.75
B54	D4	50h rose red	275.00	250.00

Austria Nos. J57-J59 Overprinted Type "a"

B55	D5	1k ultra	12.50	10.00
B56	D5	5k ultra	55.00	35.00
B57	D5	10k ultra	225.00	225.00

Austria Nos. J47-J48, J60-J63 Overprinted Type "c" Diagonally

B58	A22	1h gray	27.50	17.50
B59	A23	15h on 2h vio	140.00	110.00
B60	A38	10h on 24h bl	100.00	85.00
B61	A38	15h on 36h vio	1.00	1.00
B62	A38	20h on 54h org	100.00	85.00
B63	A38	50h on 42h choc	1.00	1.00

Hungarian Stamps Ovptd. Type "b"

1919 Wmk. 137 *Perf. 15*

On Stamps of 1913-16

B64	A4	1f slate	1,200.	1,050.
B65	A4	2f yellow	3.50	2.50
B66	A4	3f orange	45.00	25.00
B67	A4	6f olive grn	4.50	4.50
B68	A4	50f lake, *bl*	1.25	1.00
B69	A4	60f grn, *sal*	50.00	20.00
B70	A4	70f red brn, *grn*	1,300.	875.00

On Stamps of 1916

B71	A8	10f rose	275.00	190.00
B72	A8	15f violet	125.00	95.00

On Stamps of 1916-18

B73	A9	2f brn org	15	15
B74	A9	3f red lil	16	15
B75	A9	5f green	15	15
B76	A9	6f grnsh bl	60	60
B77	A9	10f rose red	1.40	2.25
B78	A9	15f violet	22	22
B79	A9	20f gray brn	5.50	5.00
B80	A9	25f dl bl	80	75
B81	A9	35f brown	6.75	6.75
B82	A9	40f ol grn	1.75	1.50

Overprinted Type "d"

B83	A10	50f red vio & lil	80	80
B84	A10	75f brt bl & pale bl	75	75
B85	A10	80f yel grn & pale grn	1.10	1.10
B86	A10	1k red brn & cl	1.40	1.40
B87	A10	2k ol brn & bis	5.50	5.50
B88	A10	3k dk vio & ind	37.50	37.50
B89	A10	5k dk brn & lt brn	140.00	90.00
B90	A10	10k vio brn & vio	950.00	750.00

Overprinted Type "b"

On Stamps of 1918

B91	A11	10f scarlet	22	22
B92	A11	20f dk brn	28	28
B93	A11	25f deep blue	1.40	1.25
B94	A12	40f olive grn	1.50	1.25
B95	A12	50f lilac	67.50	25.00

On Stamps of 1919

B96	A13	10f red	7.00	6.00
B97	A13	20f dk brn	*2,750.*	*2,750.*

Same Overprint On Hungarian Newspaper Stamp of 1914

Imperf

B98	N5	(2f) orange	20	30

Same Overprint On Hungarian Special Delivery Stamp

Perf. 15

B99	SD1	2f gray grn & red	25	35

Same Ovpt. On Hungarian Semi-Postal Stamps

B100	SP3	10f + 2f rose red	52	60
B101	SP4	15f + 2f violet	90	90
B102	SP5	40f + 2f brn car	7.00	3.50
		Nos. B98-B102 (5)	8.87	5.65

Hungarian Postage Due Stamps of 1903-18 Overprinted Type "b"

1919 Wmk. 135 *Perf. 11½, 12*

B103	D1	50f green & black	*525.00*	*525.00*

Wmk. Crown (136, 136a)

Perf. 11½x12, 15

B104	D1	1f green & black	*500.00*	*500.00*
B105	D1	2f green & black	*275.00*	*275.00*
B106	D1	12f green & black	*2,500.*	*2,500.*
B107	D1	50f green & black	150.00	150.00

Wmk. Double Cross (137)

Perf. 15

On Stamps of 1914

B110	D1	1f green & black	425.00	400.00
B111	D1	2f green & black	225.00	225.00
B112	D1	5f green & black	600.00	600.00
B113	D1	12f green & black	*1,750.*	*1,750.*
B114	D1	50f green & black	150.00	150.00

On Stamps of 1915-18

B115	D1	1f green & red	175.00	140.00
B116	D1	2f green & red	1.00	80
B117	D1	5f green & red	12.50	10.00
B118	D1	6f green & red	1.50	1.50
B119	D1	10f green & red	60	60
a.		Pair, one without overprint		
B120	D1	12f green & red	2.00	2.00
B121	D1	15f green & red	7.50	5.00
B122	D1	20f green & red	1.00	1.00
B123	D1	30f green & red	45.00	35.00
		Nos. B115-B123 (9)	246.10	195.90

Excellent counterfeits of Nos. B1-B123 exist.

Bohemian Lion Breaking its Chains — SP1

Mother and Child — SP2

Perf. 11½, 13½ and Compound

1919 Typo. Unwmk.

Pinkish Paper

B124	SP1	15h gray green	15	15
B125	SP1	25h dark brn	15	15
a.		25h light brown	*10.00*	
B126	SP1	50h dark blue	15	15

Photo.

Yellowish Paper

B127	SP2	75h slate	15	15
B128	SP2	100h brn vio	15	15
B129	SP2	120h vio, *yel*	15	15
		Set value	30	48

Nos. B124-B126 commemorate the 1st anniv. of Czechoslovak independence. Nos. B127-B129 were sold for the benefit of Legionnaires' orphans. Imperforates exist.

See No. 1581.

Regular Issues of Czechoslovakia Surcharged in Red:

a

+ 25 +

b

1920 *Perf. 13½*

B130	A1(a)	40h + 20h bister	70	1.10
B131	A2(a)	60h + 20h green	70	1.10
B132	A4(b)	125h + 25h gray bl	1.40	2.75
		Nos. B130-B132 (3)	2.80	4.95

President Masaryk — SP3

Wmk. Linden Leaves (107)

1923 Engr. *Perf. 13½x14½*

B133 SP3	50h gray green	75	65
B134 SP3	100h carmine	1.25	70
B135 SP3	200h blue	4.00	4.25
B136 SP3	300h dark brown	4.25	4.50
	Nos. B133-B136 (4)	10.25	10.10

5th anniv. of the Republic.

The gum was applied through a screen and shows the monogram "CSP" (Ceskoslovenska Posta). These stamps were sold at double their face values, the excess being given to the Red Cross and other charitable organizations.

International Olympic Congress Issue

Semi-Postal Stamps of 1923 Overprinted in Blue or Red

CONGRES OLYMP. INTERNAT.
PRAHA1925

1925

B137 SP3	50h gray green	5.00	5.00
B138 SP3	100h carmine	8.50	8.50
B139 SP3	200h blue (R)	57.50	57.50
	Nos. B137-B139 (3)	71.00	71.00

These stamps were sold at double their face values, the excess being divided between a fund for post office clerks and the Olympic Games Committee.

Sokol Issue

Semi-Postal Stamps of 1923 Overprinted in Blue or Red

VIII. SLET VŠESOKOLSKÝ
PRAHA 1926

1926

B140 SP3	50h gray green	3.75	4.25
B141 SP3	100h carmine	3.75	4.25
B142 SP3	200h blue (R)	17.00	18.00
a.	Double overprint		
B143 SP3	300h dk brn (R)	27.50	30.00
	Nos. B140-B143 (4)	52.00	56.50

These stamps were sold at double their face values, the excess being given to the Congress of Sokols, June, 1926.

Catalogue values for unused stamps in this section, from this point to the end of the section, are for Never Hinged items.

Midwife Presenting Newborn Child to its Father; after a Painting by Josef Manes

SP4 SP5

1936 Unwmk. Engr. *Perf. 12½*

B144 SP4	50h + 50h green	50	45
B145 SP5	1k + 50h claret	85	75
B146 SP4	2k + 50h blue	2.00	1.90
	Nos. B144-B146 (3)	3.35	3.10

"Lullaby" by Stanislav Sucharda

SP6 SP7

1937 *Perf. 12½*

B147 SP6	50h + 50h dull green	48	35
B148 SP6	1k + 50h rose lake	1.00	70
B149 SP7	2k + 1k dull blue	1.90	1.40
	Nos. B147-B149 (3)	3.38	2.45

President Masaryk and Little Girl in Native Costume — SP8

1938 *Perf. 12½*

B150 SP8	50h + 50h deep green	42	48
B151 SP8	1k + 50h rose lake	48	55

Souvenir Sheet

Imperf

B152 SP8	2k + 3k black	3.00	3.50

88th anniv. of the birth of Masaryk (1850-1937).

Allegory of the Republic Type Souvenir Sheet

1938 *Perf. 12½*

B153 A89	2k (+ 8k) dark blue	2.50	2.50

The surtax was devoted to national relief for refugees.

"Republic" and Congress Emblem — SP10

St. George Slaying the Dragon — SP11

1945 Engr.

B154 SP10	1.50k + 1.50k car rose	16	15
B155 SP10	2.50k + 2.50k blue	25	20

Students' World Cong., Prague, Nov. 17, 1945.

1946

B156 SP11	2.40k + 2.60k car rose	20	15
B157 SP11	4k + 6k blue	45	20

Souvenir Sheet

Imperf

B158 SP11	4k + 6k blue	75	75

1st anniv. of Czechoslovakia's liberation. The surtax aided WW II orphans.

Old Town Hall Type of 1946 Souvenir Sheet

1946, Aug. 3 *Imperf.*

B159 A114	2.40k rose brown	70	60

Brno Natl. Stamp Exhib., Aug., 1946.
The sheet was sold for 10k.

"You Went Away" — SP14

"You Remained Ours" — SP15

"You Came Back" — SP16

1946, Oct. 28 Photo. *Perf. 14*

B160 SP14	1.60k + 1.40k red brn	42	50
B161 SP15	2.40k + 2.60k scarlet	20	26
B162 SP16	4k + 4k deep blue	38	48
	Nos. B160-B162 (3)	1.00	1.24

The surtax was for repatriated Slovaks.

Barefoot Boy — SP17

Woman and Child — SP18

Designs: 2k+1k, Mother and child. 3k+1k, Little girl.

Perf. 12½

1948, Dec. 18 Unwmk. Engr.

B163 SP17	1.50k + 1k rose lilac	20	15
B164 SP17	2k + 1k dp blue	15	15
B165 SP17	3k + 1k rose car	18	22
	Nos. B163-B165 (3)	53	
	Set value		38

The surtax was for child welfare.
Labels alternate with stamps in sheets of Nos. B163-B165.

1949, Dec. 18 *Perf. 12½*

Design: 3k+1k, Man lifting child.

B166 SP18	1.50k + 50h gray	*2.50*	*1.25*
B167 SP18	3k + 1k claret	*4.50*	*1.75*

The surtax was for child welfare.

Dove Carrying Olive Branch

SP19 SP20

1949, Dec. 18

B168 SP19	1.50k + 50h claret	*3.25*	*1.25*
B169 SP20	3k + 1k rose red	*3.25*	*1.50*

The surtax was for the Red Cross.

AIR POST STAMPS

Nos. 9, 39-40, 20, and Types of 1919 Surcharged in Red, Blue or Green:

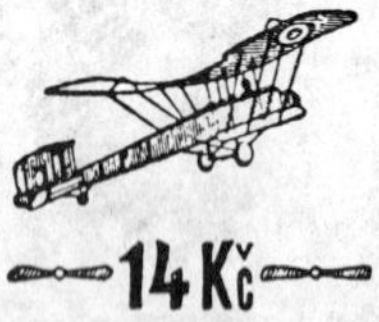

1920 Unwmk. *Imperf.*

C1 A1	14k on 200h (R)	7.75	15.00
a.	Inverted surcharge	52.50	
C2 A2	24k on 500h (Bl)	21.00	30.00
a.	Inverted surcharge	77.50	
C3 A2	28k on 1000h (G)	21.00	30.00
a.	Inverted surcharge	80.00	
b.	Double surcharge	87.50	
	Nos. C1-C3 (3)	49.75	75.00

Perf. 14, 14x13½

C4 A1	14k on 200h (R)	14.00	14.00
a.	Perf. 14x13½	55.00	52.50
C5 A2	24k on 500h (Bl)	32.50	32.50
a.	Perf. 14x13½	77.50	77.50
C6 A2	28k on 1000h (G)	25.00	25.00
a.	Inverted surcharge	110.00	110.00
b.	Perf. 14	425.00	350.00
	Nos. C4-C6 (3)	71.50	71.50
	Nos. C1-C6 (6)	121.25	146.50

Excellent counterfeits of the overprint are known.

Stamps of 1920 Surcharged in Black or Violet:

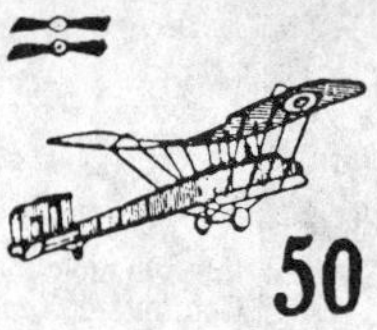

1922, June 15

C7 A8	50h on 100h dl grn	1.50	1.50
a.	Inverted surcharge	35.00	
b.	Double surcharge	32.50	
C8 A8	100h on 200h vio	2.00	3.25
a.	Inverted surcharge	35.00	
C9 A8	250h on 400h brn (V)	5.00	7.50
a.	Inverted surcharge	35.00	
	Nos. C7-C9 (3)	8.50	12.25

Fokker Monoplane AP3

Smolik S 19 AP4

Smolik S 19 — AP5

Fokker over Prague — AP6

1930, Dec. 16 Engr. *Perf. 13½*

C10 AP3	50h deep green	15	15
C11 AP3	1k deep red	24	24
C12 AP4	2k dark green	55	52
C13 AP4	3k red violet	1.25	95
C14 AP5	4k indigo	95	80
C15 AP5	5k red brown	1.40	1.50
C16 AP6	10k vio blue	3.50	3.50
a.	10k ultra	6.00	6.25
C17 AP6	20k gray violet	4.25	3.00
	Nos. C10-C17 (8)	12.29	10.66

Two types exist of the 50h, 1k and 2k, and three types of the 3k, differing chiefly in the size of the printed area. A "no hill at left" variety of the 3k exists.

Imperf. copies of Nos. C10-C17 are proofs.

Perf. 12

C10a AP3	50h deep green	1.90	1.90
C11a AP3	1k deep red	18.00	18.00
C12a AP4	2k dark green	14.00	14.00
C14a AP5	4k indigo	6.00	6.25
C15a AP5	5k red brown	525.00	
C17a AP6	20k gray violet	4.00	3.00

Perf. 12x13½, 13½x12

C11b AP3	1k deep red	2.75	2.75
C12b AP4	2k dark green	9.25	9.25
C17b AP6	20k gray violet	425.00	

Type of 1930 with hyphen in Cesko-Slovensko

1939, Apr. 22 *Perf. 13½*

C18 AP3	30h rose lilac	15	15

Catalogue values for unused stamps in this section, from this point to the end of the section, are for Never Hinged items.

Capt. Frantisek Novak — AP7

Plane over Bratislava Castle — AP8

Plane over Charles Bridge, Prague — AP9

1946-47 *Perf. 12½*

C19 AP7	1.50k rose red	16	15
C20 AP7	5.50k dk gray bl	38	15
C21 AP7	9k sepia ('47)	90	15
C22 AP8	10k dl grn	80	45
C23 AP7	16k violet	1.10	36
C24 AP8	20k light blue	1.25	35
C25 AP9	24k dk bl, *cr*	90	90
C26 AP9	24k rose lake	1.75	75
C27 AP9	50k dk gray bl	3.25	1.50
	Nos. C19-C27 (9)	10.49	4.76

No. C25 was issued June 12, 1946, for use on the first Prague-New York flight.

Nos. C19-C24, C26-C27 Surcharged with New Value and Bars in Various Colors

1949, Sept. 1 *Perf. 12½*

C28 AP7	1k on 1.50k (Bl)	15	15
C29 AP7	3k on 5.50k (C)	25	15
C30 AP7	6k on 9k (Br)	35	15
C31 AP7	7.50k on 16k (C)	50	18
C32 AP8	8k on 10k (G)	50	28
C33 AP8	12.50k on 20k (Bl)	75	30
C34 AP9	15k on 24k rose lake (Bl)	1.75	55
C35 AP9	30k on 50k (Bl)	1.25	60
	Nos. C28-C35 (8)	5.50	2.36

Karlovy Vary (Karlsbad) — AP10

1951, Apr. 2 **Engr.** *Perf. 13½*

C36 AP10	6k shown	2.00	52
C37 AP10	10k Piestany	2.00	75
C38 AP10	15k Marienbad	4.00	52
C39 AP10	20k Silac	*5.25*	*3.00*
	Nos. C36-C39 (4)	*13.25*	*4.79*

View of Cesky Krumlov — AP11

Views: 1.55k, Olomouc. 2.35k, Banska Bystrica. 2.75k, Bratislava. 10k, Prague.

1955 *Perf. 11½*

Cream Paper

C40 AP11	80h olive green	1.10	15
C41 AP11	1.55k violet brn	1.10	35
C42 AP11	2.35k violet blue	1.75	20
C43 AP11	2.75k rose brown	2.50	35
C44 AP11	10k indigo	3.50	1.50
	Nos. C40-C44 (5)	9.95	2.55

Issue dates: 10k, Feb. 20. Others, Mar. 28.

Airline: Moscow-Prague-Paris — AP12

Design: 2.35k, Airline: Prague-Cairo-Beirut-Damascus.

Engraved and Photogravure

1957, Oct. 15 **Unwmk.** *Perf. 11½*

C45 AP12	75h ultra & rose	50	15
C46 AP12	2.35k ultra & org yel	1.00	20

Planes at First Czech Aviation School, Pardubice AP13

Design: 1.80k, Jan Kaspar and flight of first Czech plane, 1909.

1959, Oct. 15

C47 AP13	1k gray & yel	20	15
C48 AP13	1.80k blk & pale bl	95	15
	Set value		20

50th anniv. of Jan Kaspar's 1st flight Aug. 25, 1909, at Pardubice.

Mail Coach, Plane and Arms of Bratislava — AP14

Design: 2.80k, Helicopter over Bratislava.

1960, Sept. 24 **Unwmk.** *Perf. 11½*

C49 AP14	1.60k dk bl & gray	*2.00*	95
C50 AP14	2.80k grn & buff	*3.00*	*1.50*

Issued to publicize the National Stamp Exhibition, Bratislava, Sept. 24-Oct. 9.

AP15

AP16

Designs: 60h, Prague hails Gagarin. 1.80k, Gagarin, rocket and dove.

1961, June 22

C51 AP15	60h gray & car	20	15
C52 AP15	1.80k gray & blue	55	20
	Set value		25

No. C51 commemorates Maj. Gagarin's visit to Prague, Apr. 28-29; No. C52 commemorates the first man in space, Yuri A. Gagarin, Apr. 12, 1961.

1962, May 14 **Engr.** *Perf. 14*

Designs ("PRAGA" emblem and): 80h, Dove and Nest of Eggs. 1.40k, Dove. 2.80k, Symbolic flower with five petals. 4.20k, Five leaves.

C53 AP16	80h multi	40	22
C54 AP16	1.40k blk, dk red & bl	1.25	1.00
C55 AP16	2.80k multi	2.00	1.75
C56 AP16	4.20k multi	3.00	2.50
	Nos. C53-C56 (4)	6.65	5.47

PRAGA 1962 World Exhibition of Postage Stamps, Aug. 18-Sept. 2, 1962.

Vostok 5 and Lt. Col. Valeri Bykovski AP17

Design: 2.80k, Vostok VI and Lt. Valentina Tereshkova.

1963, June 26

C57 AP17	80h slate bl & pink	38	15
C58 AP17	2.80k dl red brn & lt bl	85	25

Space flights of Valeri Bykovski, June 14-19, and Valentina Tereshkova, first woman astronaut, June 16-19, 1963.

PRAGA 1962 Emblem, View of Prague and Plane — AP18

Designs: 60h, Istanbul '63 (Hagia Sophia). 1k, Philatec Paris 1964 (Ile de la Cité). 1.40k, WIPA 1965 (Belvedere Palace, Vienna). 1.60k, SIPEX 1966 (Capitol, Washington). 2k, Amphilex '67 (harbor and old town, Amsterdam). 5k, PRAGA 1968 (View of Prague).

Engraved and Photogravure

1967, Oct. 30 *Perf. 11½*

Size: 30x50mm

C59 AP18	30h choc, yel & rose	15	15
C60 AP18	60h dk grn, yel & lil	16	15
C61 AP18	1k blk, brick red & lt bl	26	15
C62 AP18	1.40k vio, yel & dp org	38	16
C63 AP18	1.60k ind, tan & lil	42	26
C64 AP18	2k dk grn, org & red	60	35

Size: 40x50mm

C65 AP18	5k multi	*2.75*	*2.25*
	Nos. C59-C65 (7)	*4.72*	*3.47*

PRAGA 1968 World Stamp Exhibition, Prague, June 22-July 7, 1968. No. C59-C64 issued in sheets of 15 stamps and 15 bilingual labels. No. C65 issued in sheets of 4 stamps and one center label.

Glider L-13 — AP19

Airplanes: 60th, Sports plane L-40. 80h, Aero taxi L-200. 1k, Crop-spraying plane Z-37. 1.60k, Aerobatics trainer Z-526. 2k, Jet trainer L-29.

1967, Dec. 11

C66 AP19	30h multi	15	15
C67 AP19	60h multi	15	15
C68 AP19	80h multi	20	15
C69 AP19	1k multi	24	15
C70 AP19	1.60k multi	38	20
C71 AP19	2k multi	*1.25*	*55*
	Nos. C66-C71 (6)	*2.37*	
	Set value		*1.00*

Charles Bridge, Prague, and Balloon — AP20

Astronaut, Moon and Manhattan — AP21

Designs: 1k, Belvedere, fountain and early plane. 2k, Hradcany, Prague, and airship.

1968, Feb. 5 **Unwmk.** *Perf. 11½*

C72 AP20	60h multi	24	15
C73 AP20	1k multi	35	20
C74 AP20	2k multi	65	55
	Nos. C72-C74 (3)	1.24	90

PRAGA 1968 World Stamp Exhibition, Prague, June 22-July 7, 1968.

1969, July 21

Design: 3k, Lunar landing module and J. F. Kennedy Airport, New York.

C75 AP21	60h blk, vio, yel & sil	20	15
C76 AP21	3k blk, bl, ocher & sil	1.00	75

Man's 1st landing on the moon, July 20, 1969, US astronauts Neil A. Armstrong and Col. Edwin E. Aldrin, Jr., with Lieut. Col. Michael Collins piloting Apollo 11.

Nos. C75-C76 printed with label inscribed with names of astronauts and European date of moon landing.

TU-104A over Bitov Castle AP22

Designs: 60h, IL-62 over Bezdez Castle. 1.40k, TU-13A over Orava Castle. 1.90k, IL-18 over Veveri Castle. 2.40k, IL-14 over Pernstejn Castle. 3.60k, TU-154 over Trencin Castle.

1973, Oct. 24 **Engr.** *Perf. 11½*

C77 AP22	30h multi	15	15
C78 AP22	60h multi	15	15
C79 AP22	1.40k multi	26	15
C80 AP22	1.90k multi	38	20
C81 AP22	2.40k multi	*2.75*	*85*
C82 AP22	3.60k multi	52	30
	Nos. C77-C82 (6)	*4.21*	*1.80*

50 years of Czechoslovakian aviation.

Old Water Tower and Manes Hall — AP23

Designs (Praga 1978 Emblem, Plane Silhouette and): 1.60k, Congress Hall. 2k, Powder Tower, vert. 2.40k, Charles Bridge and Old Bridge Tower. 4k, Old Town Hall on Old Town Square, vert. 6k, Prague Castle and St. Vitus' Cathedral, vert.

Engraved and Photogravure

1976, June 23 *Perf. 11½*

C83 AP23	60h ind & multi	15	15
C84 AP23	1.60k ind & multi	35	15
C85 AP23	2k ind & multi	45	15
C86 AP23	2.40k ind & multi	50	25
C87 AP23	4k ind & multi	90	32
C88 AP23	6k ind & multi	3.25	85
	Nos. C83-C88 (6)	5.60	1.87

PRAGA 1978 International Philatelic Exhibition, Prague, Sept. 8-17, 1978.

Zeppelin, 1909 and 1928 — AP24

Designs (PRAGA '78 Emblem and): 1k, Ader, 1890, L'Eole and Dunn, 1914. 1.60k, Jeffries-Blanchard balloon, 1785. 2k, Otto Lilienthal's glider, 1896. 4.40k, Jan Kaspar's plane, Pardubice, 1911.

1977, Sept. 15 *Perf. 11½*

C89 AP24	60h multi	15	15
C90 AP24	1k multi	32	15
C91 AP24	1.60k multi	50	15
C92 AP24	2k multi	70	22
C93 AP24	4.40k multi	*2.25*	*75*
	Nos. C89-C93 (5)	*3.92*	*1.42*

History of aviation.

SPECIAL DELIVERY STAMPS

Doves — SD1

1919-20 Unwmk. Typo. *Imperf.*

E1	SD1	2h red vio, *yel*	15	15
E2	SD1	5h yel grn, *yel*	15	15
E3	SD1	10h red brn, *yel* ('20)	38	38
		Set value	50	50

For overprints and surcharge see Nos. P11-P13.

1921 White Paper

E1a	SD1	2h red violet	3.00	
E2a	SD1	5h yellow green	2.75	
E3a	SD1	10h red brown	52.50	
		Nos. E1a-E3a (3)	58.25	

It is doubted that Nos. E1a-E3a were regularly issued.

PERSONAL DELIVERY STAMPS

Catalogue values for unused stamps in this section are for Never Hinged items.

PD1

Design: No. EX2, "D" in each corner.

1937 Unwmk. Photo. *Perf. 13½*

EX1	PD1	50h blue	25	30
EX2	PD1	50h carmine	25	30

PD3

1946 *Perf. 13½*

EX3	PD3	2k deep blue	35	35

POSTAGE DUE STAMPS

D1

1918-20 Unwmk. Typo. *Imperf.*

J1	D1	5h deep bister	15	15
J2	D1	10h deep bister	15	15
J3	D1	15h deep bister	15	15
J4	D1	20h deep bister	15	15
J5	D1	25h deep bister	18	15
J6	D1	30h deep bister	30	15
J7	D1	40h deep bister	32	25
J8	D1	50h deep bister	32	15
J9	D1	100h blk brn	1.25	15
J10	D1	250h orange	4.75	1.40
J11	D1	400h scarlet	6.50	1.40
J12	D1	500h gray grn	2.50	20
J13	D1	1000h purple	3.50	25
J14	D1	2000h dark blue	15.00	60
		Nos. J1-J14 (14)	35.22	
		Set value		4.75

For surcharges see Nos. J32-J41, J57.

Nos. 1, 33-34, 10 Surcharged in Blue — **100 DOPLATIT**

1922

J15	A1	20h on 3h red vio	35	16
J16	A2	50h on 75h slate	95	20
J17	A2	60h on 80h olive grn	30	15
J18	A2	100h on 80h olive grn	50	15
J19	A1	200h on 400h purple	70	15
		Nos. J15-J19 (5)	2.80	81

Same Surcharge on Nos. 1, 10, 30-31, 33-34, 36, 40 in Violet

1923-26

J20	A1	10h on 3h red vio	15	15
J21	A1	20h on 3h red vio	15	15
J22	A1	30h on 3h red vio	15	15
J23	A1	40h on 3h red vio	22	15
J24	A2	50h on 75h slate	1.40	15
J25	A2	60h on 50h dk vio ('26)	2.75	1.25
J26	A2	60h on 50h dk bl ('26)	2.75	1.50
J27	A2	60h on 75h slate	1.25	15
J28	A2	100h on 80h ol grn	40.00	75
J29	A2	100h on 120h gray blk	1.40	15
J30	A1	100h on 400h pur ('26)	80	15
J31	A2	100h on 1000h dp vio ('26)	1.75	25
		Nos. J20-J31 (12)	52.77	4.95

Postage Due Stamp of 1918-20 Surcharged in Violet — **50**

1924

J32	D1	50h on 400h scar	1.00	15
J33	D1	60h on 400h scar	3.00	70
J34	D1	100h on 400h scar	2.00	20
		Nos. J32-J34 (3)	6.00	1.05

Postage Due Stamps of 1918-20 Surcharged with New Values in Violet as in 1924

1925

J35	D1	10h on 5h bister	15	15
J36	D1	20h on 5h bister	15	15
J37	D1	30h on 15h bister	25	15
J38	D1	40h on 15h bister	32	15
J39	D1	50h on 250h org	1.10	20
J40	D1	60h on 250h org	1.40	50
J41	D1	100h on 250h org	3.50	35
		Nos. J35-J41 (7)	6.87	
		Set value		1.28

Stamps of 1918-19 Surcharged with New Values in Violet as in 1922

1926 *Perf. 14, 11½*

J42	A2	30h on 15h red	70	35
J43	A2	40h on 15h red	52	15

DOPLATIT 30 — On #J44-J49

DOPLATIT — On #J50-J56

1926 Violet Surcharge *Perf. 14*

J44	A8	30h on 100h dk grn	15	15
J45	A8	40h on 200h violet	24	15
J46	A8	40h on 300h ver	95	26
a.		Perf. 14x13½		30.00
J47	A8	50h on 500h dp grn	50	15
a.		Perf. 14x13½	2.50	
J48	A8	60h on 400h brown	1.00	16
J49	A8	100h on 600h dp vio	2.50	35
a.		Perf. 14x13½	30.00	1.25
		Nos. J44-J49 (6)	5.34	1.22

1927 Violet Overprint

J50	A6	100h dark brown	65	15
a.		Perf. 13½	275.00	15.00

Surcharged with New Value in Violet

J51	A6	40h on 185h org	18	15
J52	A6	50h on 20h car	24	15
a.		50h on 50h carmine (error)		5,750.
J53	A6	50h on 150h rose	30	15
a.		Perf. 13½	12.50	2.00
J54	A6	60h on 25h brown	42	20
J55	A6	60h on 185h orange	55	15
J56	A6	100h on 25h brown	60	20
		Nos. J50-J56 (7)	2.94	
		Set value		77

No. J52a is known only used.

No. J12 Surcharged in Violet — **200**

1927 *Imperf.*

J57	D1	200h on 500h gray grn	3.25	2.50

Catalogue values for unused stamps in this section, from this point to the end of the section, are for Never Hinged items.

D5

D6

1928 *Perf. 14x13½*

J58	D5	5h dark red	15	15
J59	D5	10h dark red	15	15
J60	D5	20h dark red	15	15
J61	D5	30h dark red	15	15
J62	D5	40h dark red	15	15
J63	D5	50h dark red	15	15
J64	D5	60h dark red	15	15
J65	D5	1k ultra	22	15
J66	D5	2k ultra	65	15
J67	D5	5k ultra	1.10	15
J68	D5	10k ultra	2.00	15
J69	D5	20k ultra	4.50	15
		Nos. J58-J69 (12)	9.52	
		Set value		85

1946-48 Photo. *Perf. 14*

J70	D6	10h dark blue	15	15
J71	D6	20h dark blue	15	15
J72	D6	50h dark blue	15	15
J73	D6	1k carmine rose	15	15
J74	D6	1.20k carmine rose	28	15
J75	D6	1.50k carmine rose ('48)	35	15
J76	D6	1.60k carmine rose	40	15
J77	D6	2k carmine rose ('48)	40	15
J78	D6	2.40k carmine rose	75	15
J79	D6	3k carmine rose	1.00	15
J80	D6	5k carmine rose	1.65	15
J81	D6	6k carmine rose ('48)	2.00	15
		Nos. J70-J81 (12)	7.43	
		Set value		60

D7

D8

1954-55 Engr. *Perf. 12½, 11½*

J82	D7	5h gray green ('55)	15	15
J83	D7	10h gray green ('55)	15	15
J84	D7	30h gray green	15	15
J85	D7	50h gray green ('55)	15	15
J86	D7	60h gray green ('55)	18	15
J87	D7	95h gray green	35	15
J88	D8	1k violet	35	15
J89	D8	1.20k violet ('55)	35	15
J90	D8	1.50k violet	70	15
J91	D8	1.60k violet ('55)	45	15
J92	D8	2k violet	85	15
J93	D8	3k violet	1.10	15
J94	D8	5k violet ('55)	1.40	22
		Nos. J82-J94 (13)	6.33	
		Set value		82

Perf. 11½ stamps are from a 1963 printing which lacks the 95h, 1.60k, and 2k.

Stylized Flower — D9

Designs: Various stylized flowers.

Engraved and Photogravure

1971-72 *Perf. 11½*

J95	D9	10h vio bl & pink	15	15
J96	D9	20h vio & lt bl	15	15
J97	D9	30h emer & lil rose	15	15
J98	D9	60h pur & emer	15	15
J99	D9	80h org & vio bl	15	15
J100	D9	1k dk red & emer	25	15
J101	D9	1.20k grn & org	20	15
J102	D9	2k blue & red	42	15
J103	D9	3k blk & yel	48	15
J104	D9	4k brn & ultra	85	15
J105	D9	5.40k red & lilac	1.00	20
J106	D9	6k brick red & org	1.40	30
		Nos. J95-J106 (12)	5.35	
		Set value		1.00

All except 5.40k issued in 1972.

OFFICIAL STAMPS

Catalogue values for unused stamps in this section are for Never Hinged items.

Coat of Arms — O1

1945 Unwmk. Litho. *Perf. 10½x10*

O1	O1	50h dp slate grn	15	15
O2	O1	1k dp bl vio	15	15
O3	O1	1.20k plum	22	15
O4	O1	1.50k crimson rose	15	15
O5	O1	2.50k bright ultra	22	15
O6	O1	5k dk vio brn	28	22
O7	O1	8k rose pink	42	38
		Nos. O1-O7 (7)	1.59	
		Set value		85

Redrawn

1947 Photo. *Perf. 14*

O8	O1	60h red	15	15
O9	O1	80h dk olive grn	15	15
O10	O1	1k dk lilac gray	15	15
O11	O1	1.20k dp plum	15	15
O12	O1	2.40k dk car rose	15	15
O13	O1	4k brt ultra	15	15
O14	O1	5k dk vio brn	18	18
O15	O1	7.40k purple	32	28
		Set value	92	85

There are many minor changes in design, size of numerals, etc., of the redrawn stamps.

NEWSPAPER STAMPS

Windhover — N1

1918-20 Unwmk. Typo. *Imperf.*

P1	N1	2h gray green	15	15
P2	N1	5h green ('20)	15	15
a.		5h dark green	40	15
P3	N1	6h red	38	28
P4	N1	10h dull violet	15	15
P5	N1	20h blue	15	15
P6	N1	30h gray brown	15	15
P7	N1	50h orange ('20)	24	18
P8	N1	100h red brown ('20)	40	28
		Set value	1.30	1.00

Nos. P1-P8 exist privately perforated.

For surcharges and overprints see Nos. P9-P10, P14-P16.

Stamps of 1918-20 Surcharged in Violet — *** 5 ***

1925-26

P9	N1	5h on 2h gray green	60	38
P10	N1	5h on 6h red ('26)	42	38

Special Delivery Stamps of 1918-20 Overprinted in Violet — **NOVINY**

1926

P11	SD1	5h apple grn, *yel*	20	18
a.		5h dull green, *yellow*	50	40
P12	SD1	10h red brn, *yel*	15	15

With Additional Surcharge of New Value

P13 SD1	5h on 2h red vio, *yel*		35	60
	Nos. P11-P13 (3)		70	93

Catalogue values for unused stamps in this section, from this point to the end of the section, are for Never Hinged items.

Newspaper Stamps of 1918-20 Overprinted in Violet **O.T.**

1934

P14 N1	10h dull violet	15	15
P15 N1	20h blue	15	15
P16 N1	30h gray brown	18	22
	Set value	28	32

Overprinted for use by commercial firms only.

Carrier Pigeon — N2

1937 *Imperf.*

P17 N2	2h bister brown	15	15
P18 N2	5h dull blue	15	15
P19 N2	7h red orange	15	15
P20 N2	9h emerald	15	15
P21 N2	10h henna brown	15	15
P22 N2	12h ultra	15	15
P23 N2	20h dark green	15	15
P24 N2	50h dark brown	15	15
P25 N2	1k olive gray	15	15
	Set value	54	47

For overprint see Slovakia Nos. P1-P9.

Bratislava Philatelic Exhibition Issue
Souvenir Sheet

1937 *Imperf.*

P26 N2 10h henna brn, sheet of 25 4.00 4.50

Newspaper Delivery Boy — N4

1945 Unwmk. Typo. *Imperf.*

P27 N4	5h dull blue	15	15
P28 N4	10h red	15	15
P29 N4	15h emerald	15	15
P30 N4	20h dark slate green	15	15
P31 N4	25h bright red vio	15	15
P32 N4	30h ocher	15	15
P33 N4	40h red orange	15	15
P34 N4	50h brown red	15	15
P35 N4	1k slate gray	15	15
P36 N4	5k deep vio blue	15	15
	Set value	60	55

CZECHOSLOVAK LEGION POST

The Czechoslovak Legion in Siberia issued these stamps for use on its mail and that of local residents. Forgeries exist.

Urn and Cathedral at Irkutsk — A1

Armored Railroad Car — A2

Czechoslovak Legion Post stamps can be mounted in the Scott Czechoslovakia album.

Sentinel — A3

Lion of Bohemia — A4

1919 Litho. *Perf. 11½*

1	A1 25k carmine	14.00	
a.	Imperf.	14.00	
2	A2 50k yellow green	14.00	
a.	Imperf.	14.00	
3	A3 1r red brown	32.50	
a.	Imperf.	32.50	
	Nos. 1-3 (3)	60.50	
	Nos. 1a-3a (3)	60.50	

Originals of Nos. 1-3 and 1a-3a have yellowish gum. Ungummed remainders, which were given a white gum, exist imperforate and perforated 11½ and 14. Value per set, $3.

Embossed
Perce en Arc in Blue

4 A4 (25k) blue & rose 2.50

Two types: I- 6 points on star-like mace head at right of goblet; large saber handle; measures 19½x24¾mm. II- 5 points on mace head; small saber handle; measures 20x25mm.

No. 4 Overprinted **1920**

1920

5 A4 (25k) bl & rose 7.00

Both types of No. 4 received overprint.

No. 5 Surcharged with New Values in Green **2**

6	A4	2k bl & rose	25.00
7	A4	3k bl & rose	25.00
8	A4	5k bl & rose	25.00
9	A4	10k bl & rose	25.00
10	A4	15k bl & rose	25.00
11	A4	25k bl & rose	25.00
12	A4	35k bl & rose	25.00
13	A4	50k bl & rose	25.00
14	A4	1r bl & rose	25.00
		Nos. 6-14 (9)	225.00

BOHEMIA AND MORAVIA

Catalogue values for unused stamps in this country are for never hinged items, beginning with Scott 20 in the regular postage section, Scott B1 in the semi-postal section, Scott J1 in the postage due section, Scott O1 in the official section, and Scott P1 in the newspaper section.

German Protectorate

Stamps of Czechoslovakia, 1928-39, Overprinted in Black

BÖHMEN u. MÄHREN

ČECHY a MORAVA

Perf. 10, 12½, 12x12½

1939, July 15 Unwmk.

1	A29	5h dk ultra	15	*20*
2	A29	10h brown	15	*20*
3	A29	20h red	15	*20*
4	A29	25h green	15	*20*
5	A29	30h red vio	15	*20*
6	A61a	40h dk bl	2.50	*4.75*
7	A85	50h dp grn	15	*20*
8	A63	60h dl vio	2.50	*4.75*
9	A60	1k rose lake (212)	75	*1.75*
10	A60	1k rose lake (256)	30	*85*
11	A64	1.20k rose lilac	3.00	*6.25*
12	A65	1.50k carmine	2.50	*4.75*
13	A79	1.60k olive grn	2.50	*4.75*
a.		"Mähnen"	16.00	*27.50*
14	A66	2k dk bl grn	1.10	*1.75*
15	A67	2.50k dk bl	3.00	*4.50*
16	A68	3k brown	3.00	*4.75*
17	A70	4k dk vio	3.50	*5.00*
18	A71	5k green	3.50	*5.75*
19	A72	10k blue	4.75	*9.50*
		Nos. 1-19 (19)	33.80	*60.30*

The size of the overprint varies, Nos. 1-10 measure 17½x15½mm, Nos. 11-16 19x18mm, Nos. 17 and 19 28x17½mm and No. 18 23½x23mm.

Catalogue values for unused stamps in this section, from this point to the end of the section, are for never hinged items.

Linden Leaves and Closed Buds — A1

1939-41 Photo. *Perf. 14*

20	A1	5h dark blue	15	15
21	A1	10h blk brn	15	15
22	A1	20h crimson	15	15
23	A1	25h dk bl grn	15	15
24	A1	30h dp plum	15	15
24A	A1	30h golden brn ('41)	15	15
25	A1	40h orange ('40)	15	15
26	A1	50h slate grn ('40)	15	15
		Set value	50	50

See Nos. 49-51.

Castle at Zvikov — A2

Karlstein Castle — A3

St. Barbara's Church, Kutna Hora — A4

Cathedral at Prague — A5

Brno Cathedral — A6

Town Square, Olomouc — A7

1939 Engr. *Perf. 12½*

27	A2	40h dark blue	15	15
28	A3	50h dk bl grn	15	15
29	A4	60h dl vio	15	15
30	A5	1k dp rose	15	15
31	A6	1.20k rose lilac	40	*65*
32	A6	1.50k rose car	15	15
33	A7	2k dk bl grn	15	15
34	A7	2.50k dark blue	15	15
		Set value	1.10	*1.10*

No. 31 measures 23½x29½mm, No. 42 measures 18½x23mm.
See #52-53, 53B. For overprints see #60-61.

Zlin — A8

Iron Works at Moravská Ostrava — A9

Prague — A10

1939-40

35	A8	3k dl rose vio	18	15
36	A9	4k slate ('40)	15	15
37	A10	5k green	40	*38*
38	A10	10k lt ultra	30	*65*
39	A10	20k yel brn	90	*1.25*
		Nos. 35-39 (5)	1.93	*2.58*

Types of 1939 and

Neuhaus — A11

Lainsitz Bridge near Bechyne — A14

Pernstein Castle — A12

Samson Fountain, Budweis — A15

Pardubice Castle — A13

Kromeriz — A16

Wallenstein Palace, Prague — A17

1940 Engr. *Perf. 12½*

40	A11	50h dk bl grn	15	15
41	A12	80h dp bl	25	*40*
42	A6	1.20k vio brn	38	25
43	A13	2k gray grn	20	15
44	A14	5k dk bl grn	20	15
45	A15	6k brn vio	20	*25*
46	A16	8k slate grn	20	*35*
47	A17	10k blue	45	30
48	A10	20k sepia	1.10	*1.50*
		Nos. 40-48 (9)	3.13	*3.50*

No. 42 measures 18½x23mm; No. 31, 23½x29½mm.

Types of 1939-40

1941

49	A1	60h violet	15	15
50	A1	80h red org	15	15
51	A1	1k brown	15	15
52	A5	1.20k rose red	15	15
53	A4	1.50k lil rose	15	15
53A	A13	2k light blue	15	15
53B	A6	2.50k ultra	15	15
53C	A12	3k olive	20	15
		Set value	98	1.05

Nos. 49-51 show buds open. Nos. 52 and 53B measure 18¾x23½mm and have no inscriptions below design.
For overprints see Nos. 60-61.

Antonin Dvorák — A18

1941, Aug. 25 Engr. *Perf. 12½*

54	A18	60h	dull lilac	15	*15*
55	A18	1.20k	sepia	26	26

Antonin Dvorák (1841-1904), composer.
Labels alternate with stamps in sheets of #54-55.

Farming Scene A19

Factories A20

1941, Sept. 7 Photo. *Perf. 13½*

56	A19	30h	dk red brn	15	15
57	A19	60h	dark green	15	15
58	A20	1.20k	dk plum	20	*25*
59	A20	2.50k	sapphire	25	*40*
			Set value	65	

Issued to publicize the Prague Fair.

Nos. 52 and 53B Overprinted in Blue or Red

1942, Mar. 15 *Perf. 12½*

60	A5	1.20k	rose red (Bl)	30	*50*
61	A6	2.50k	ultra (R)	45	*50*

3rd anniv. of the Protectorate of Bohemia and Moravia.

Adolf Hitler A21

17th Century Messenger A22

1942 Photo. *Perf. 14*

Size: 17½x21½mm

62	A21	10(h)	gray blk	15	15
63	A21	30(h)	bister brn	15	15
64	A21	40(h)	slate blue	15	15
65	A21	50(h)	slate grn	15	15
66	A21	60(h)	purple	15	15
67	A21	80(h)	org ver	15	15

Perf. 12½

Engr.

Size: 18x21mm

68	A21	1k	dl brn	15	15
69	A21	1.20(k)	carmine	15	15
70	A21	1.50(k)	claret	15	20
71	A21	1.60(k)	Prus grn	15	*50*
72	A21	2k	light blue	15	25
73	A21	2.40(k)	fawn	15	*25*

Size: 18½x24mm

74	A21	2.50(k)	ultra	15	25
75	A21	3k	olive grn	15	25
76	A21	4k	brt red vio	15	25
77	A21	5k	myrtle grn	15	25
78	A21	6k	claret brn	15	25
79	A21	8k	indigo	15	25

Size: 23½x29¾mm

80	A21	10k	dk gray grn	15	*1.00*
81	A21	20k	gray vio	30	*1.00*
82	A21	30k	red	75	*1.50*
83	A21	50k	deep blue	1.50	*3.00*
			Set value	3.75	

1943, Jan. 10 Photo. *Perf. 13½*

84	A22	60h	dark rose violet	15	15

Stamp Day.

Scene from "Die Meistersinger" — A23

Richard Wagner — A24

Scene from "Siegfried" — A25

1943, May 22

85	A23	60h	violet	15	15
86	A24	1.20k	carmine rose	15	15
87	A25	2.50k	deep ultra	15	*20*
			Set value	26	*40*

Richard Wagner (1813-83).

St. Vitus' Cathedral, Prague — A26

Adolf Hitler — A27

1944, Nov. 21 Engr. *Perf. 12½*

88	A26	1.50k	dull rose brn	15	15
89	A26	2.50k	dull lilac blue	15	*25*
			Set value	22	

1944

90	A27	4.20k	green	20	*50*

SEMI-POSTAL STAMPS

Catalogue values for unused stamps in this section are for never hinged items.

Nurse and Wounded Soldier — SP1

Red Cross Nurse and Patient — SP2

Perf. 13½

1940, June 29 Photo. Unwmk.

B1	SP1	60h + 40h indigo	55	*60*
B2	SP1	1.20k + 80h deep plum	70	*65*

Surtax for German Red Cross.
Labels alternate with stamps in sheets of #B1-B2.

1941, Apr. 20

B3	SP2	60h + 40h indigo	38	*60*
B4	SP2	1.20k + 80h dp plum	38	*65*

Surtax for German Red Cross.
Labels alternate with stamps in sheets of #B3-B4.

Old Theater, Prague — SP3

Mozart — SP4

1941, Oct. 26

B5	SP3	30h + 30h brown	15	15
B6	SP3	60h + 60h Prus grn	15	15
B7	SP4	1.20k + 1.20k scar	24	*45*
B8	SP4	2.50k + 2.50k dk bl	45	*55*
		Nos. B5-B8 (4)	99	*1.30*

150th anniversary of Mozart's death.
Labels alternate with stamps in sheets of Nos. B5-B8. The labels with Nos. B5-B6 show two bars of Mozart's opera "Don Giovanni." Those with Nos. B7-B8 show Mozart's piano.

Adolf Hitler — SP5

Nurse and Soldier — SP6

1942, Apr. 20 Engr. *Perf. 12½*

B9	SP5	30h + 20h dl brn vio	15	15
B10	SP5	60h + 40h dl grn	15	15
B11	SP5	1.20k + 80h dp claret	15	15
B12	SP5	2.50k + 1.50k dl bl	15	*35*
		Set value	50	

Hitler's 53rd birthday.

1942, Sept. 4 *Perf. 13½*

B13	SP6	60h + 40h deep blue	15	15
B14	SP6	1.20(k) + 80(h) dp plum	15	15
		Set value	15	15

The surtax aided the German Red Cross.

Emperor Charles IV — SP7

Peter Parler — SP8

John the Blind, King of Bohemia — SP9

Adolf Hitler — SP10

1943, Jan. 29

B15	SP7	60h + 40h violet	15	15
B16	SP8	1.20k + 80h carmine	15	15
B17	SP9	2.50k + 1.50k vio bl	15	20
		Set value	20	42

The surtax was for the benefit of the German wartime winter relief.

1943, Apr. 20 Engr. *Perf. 12½*

B18	SP10	60h + 1.40k dl vio	15	*15*
B19	SP10	1.20k + 3.80k carmine	15	*25*
		Set value	20	

Hitler's 54th birthday.

Bohemia and Moravia stamps can be mounted in the Scott Czechoslovakia album or Germany album part 2.

Deathmask of Reinhard Heydrich — SP11

Eagle and Red Cross — SP12

1943, May 28 Photo. *Perf. 13½*

B20	SP11	60h + 4.40k black	30	*40*

No. B20 exists in a miniature sheet containing a single copy. It was given to officials attending Heydrich's funeral.

1943, Sept. 16 *Perf. 13*

B21	SP12	1.20k + 8.80k blk & car	15	15

The surtax aided the German Red Cross.

Native Costumes SP13

Nazi Emblem, Arms of Bohemia, Moravia SP14

1944, Mar. 15 *Perf. 13½*

B22	SP13	1.20(k) + 3.80(k) rose lake	15	15
B23	SP14	4.20(k) + 10.80(k) golden brn	15	15
B24	SP13	10k + 20k saph	16	*30*
		Set value	30	

Fifth anniversary of protectorate.

Adolf Hitler — SP15

Bedrich Smetana — SP16

1944, Apr. 20

B25	SP15	60h + 1.40k olive blk	15	15
B26	SP15	1.20k + 3.80k slate grn	15	20
		Set value	15	30

1944, May 12 Engr. *Perf. 12½*

B27	SP16	60h + 1.40k dk gray grn	15	15
B28	SP16	1.20k + 3.80k brn car	15	20
		Set value	15	30

Bedrich Smetana (1824-84), Czech composer and pianist.

PERSONAL DELIVERY STAMPS

PD1

1939-40 Unwmk. Photo. *Perf. 13½*

EX1	PD1	50h indigo & blue ('40)	45	*80*
EX2	PD1	50h carmine & rose	55	*1.10*

POSTAGE DUE STAMPS

Catalogue values for unused stamps in this section are for never hinged items.

D1

1939-40 Unwmk. Typo. *Perf. 14*

J1	D1	5h dark carmine	15	15
J2	D1	10h dark carmine	15	15
J3	D1	20h dark carmine	15	15
J4	D1	30h dark carmine	15	15
J5	D1	40h dark carmine	15	15
J6	D1	50h dark carmine	15	15
J7	D1	60h dark carmine	15	15
J8	D1	80h dark carmine	15	15
J9	D1	1k bright ultra	15	*30*
J10	D1	1.20k brt ultra ('40)	22	*32*
J11	D1	2k bright ultra	80	*90*
J12	D1	5k bright ultra	80	*1.00*
J13	D1	10k bright ultra	1.25	*1.65*
J14	D1	20k bright ultra	3.25	*4.25*
		Nos. J1-J14 (14)	7.67	*9.62*

OFFICIAL STAMPS

Catalogue values for unused stamps in this section are for never hinged items.

Numeral
O1

Eagle
O2

1941, Jan. 1 Unwmk. Typo. *Perf. 14*

O1	O1	30h ocher	15	15
O2	O1	40h indigo	15	15
O3	O1	50h emerald	15	15
O4	O1	60h slate grn	15	15
O5	O1	80h org red	65	20
O6	O1	1k red brn	25	15
O7	O1	1.20k carmine	25	15
O8	O1	1.50k dp plum	45	15
O9	O1	2k brt bl	45	15
O10	O1	3k olive	45	15
O11	O1	4k red vio	80	45
O12	O1	5k org yel	2.00	90
		Nos. O1-O12 (12)	5.90	
		Set value		2.00

1943, Feb. 15

O13	O2	30(h) bister	15	15
O14	O2	40(h) indigo	15	15
O15	O2	50(h) yel grn	15	15
O16	O2	60(h) dp vio	15	15
O17	O2	80(h) org red	15	15
O18	O2	1k chocolate	15	15
O19	O2	1.20(k) carmine	15	15
O20	O2	1.50(k) brn red	15	20
O21	O2	2k lt bl	15	20
O22	O2	3k olive	15	20
O23	O2	4k red vio	15	20
O24	O2	5k dk grn	15	*35*
		Set value	1.00	1.50

NEWSPAPER STAMPS

Catalogue values for unused stamps in this section are for never hinged items.

Carrier Pigeon
N1 N2

1939 Unwmk. Typo. *Imperf.*

P1	N1	2h ocher	15	15
P2	N1	5h ultra	15	15
P3	N1	7h red orange	15	15
P4	N1	9h emerald	15	15
P5	N1	10h henna brown	15	15
P6	N1	12h dark ultra	15	15
P7	N1	20h dark green	15	*25*
P8	N1	50h red brown	15	*35*
P9	N1	1k greenish gray	15	*35*
		Set value	95	*1.60*

No. P5 Overprinted in Black **GD-OT**

1940

P10	N1	10h henna brown	15	*30*

Overprinted for use by commercial firms.

1943, Feb. 15

P11	N2	2(h) ocher	15	15
P12	N2	5(h) light blue	15	15
P13	N2	7(h) red orange	15	15
P14	N2	9(h) emerald	15	15
P15	N2	10(h) henna brown	15	15
P16	N2	12(h) dark ultra	15	15
P17	N2	20(h) dark green	15	15
P18	N2	50(h) red brown	15	15
P19	N2	1k slate green	15	*25*
		Set value	50	81

Numerical Index of Volume 2 Watermark Illustrations

Watermark	Country
a-g	Chile
84-90	Argentina
91	Austria
96	Belgium
97-101	Brazil
103	China
104-105	Cuba
106	Cuba
107	Czechoslovakia
116	Colombia
125	Albania
127	Colombia
135-136, 136a	Czechoslovakia
140	Cyrenaica
145	Bulgaria
168	Bulgaria
171	Armenia
193	Brazil
194	Colombia
205	Argentina
206	Brazil
215	Chile
218	Brazil
220	Albania
221-222	Brazil
229	Colombia
232	Angola
236	Brazil
245	Brazil
249	Brazil
255	Colombia
256	Brazil
261	China
264	Brazil
267-268	Brazil
270-271	Brazil
275	Bulgaria
278	Croatia
281	Brazil
287	Argentina
288	Argentina
321	Cuba
323	China
331	Colombia
334	Costa Rica
341	Czechoslovakia
346	Colombia
365	Argentina
368	China
370	China
376	Cuba

1996 Vol. 2 Number Changes

Number in 1995 Catalogue	Number in 1996 Catalogue
Andorra, French	
380A-381	381-382
382-383	384-385
388-389	386-387
389B	388
Angola	
4b	deleted
90a, 93a	footnoted
181a, 182a, 183a-183b	footnoted
RAJ4-RAJ5	footnoted
Angra	
20a	deleted
Armenia	
433A	434
434-435A	435-437
436	438
440	439
Azores	
47a	deleted
94a	deleted
118a	deleted
Bolivia	
140c	footnoted
Brazil	
2259A-2259B	2260-2261
2260-2261	2262-2263
2269-2270	2266-2267
2273-2274A	2268-2270
2275-2277	2271-2273
Bulgaria	
3419A-3419B	3420-3421
3420-3433	3422-3435
3433A-3433C	3436-3438
3434-3437	3439-3441
3586	3585
3588-3588A	3586-3587
3589-3590	3588-3589
3593	3590
3596	3591
Central Africa	
C350	C351
C351	C350
China	
1a, 2a, 3a	footnoted
34a	deleted
Colombia	
Antioquia H3	Colombia H4
Costa Rica	
83	83d
83d	83
463	RA112
Cuba	
223	223a
223a	223

Index and Identifier

All page numbers shown are those in this Volume 2

Illustrated Identifier begins on page 966

Illustrated Identifier

This section pictures stamps or parts of stamp designs that will help identify postage stamps that do not have English words on them.

Many of the symbols that identify stamps of countries are shown here as well as typical examples of their stamps.

See the Index and Identifier on the previous pages for stamps with inscriptions such as "sen," "posta," "Baja Porto," "Helvetia," "K.S.A.", etc.

Linn's Stamp Identifier is now available. The 144 pages include more 2,000 inscriptions and over 500 large stamp illustrations. Available from Linn's Stamp News, P.O. Box 29, Sidney, OH 45365.

HEADS, PICTURES AND NUMERALS

GREAT BRITAIN

Great Britain stamps never show the country name, but, except for postage dues, show a picture of the reigning monarch.

Victoria

Edward VII George V Edward VIII

George VI

Elizabeth II

Silhouette (sometimes facing right, generally at the top of stamp)

The silhouette indicates this is a British stamp. It is not a U.S. stamp.

VICTORIA

Queen Victoria

INDIA

Other stamps of India show this portrait of Queen Victoria and the words "Service" and "Annas."

AUSTRIA

YUGOSLAVIA

(Also BOSNIA & HERZEGOVINA if imperf.)

BOSNIA & HERZEGOVINA

Denominations also appear in top corners instead of bottom corners.

HUNGARY

Another stamp has posthorn facing left

BRAZIL

AUSTRALIA

Kangaroo and Emu

NEW ZEALAND

GERMANY

Mecklenburg-Vorpommern

SWITZERLAND

ORIENTAL INSCRIPTIONS

CHINA

中 中 Any stamp with this one character is from China (Imperial, Republic or People's Republic).

Some Chinese stamps show the Sun

中華民國郵票

Most stamps of Republic of China show this series of characters.

Stamps with the China character and this character are from People's Republic of China. 人

Calligraphic form of People's Republic of China

Chinese stamps without China character

REPUBLIC OF CHINA

PEOPLE'S REPUBLIC OF CHINA

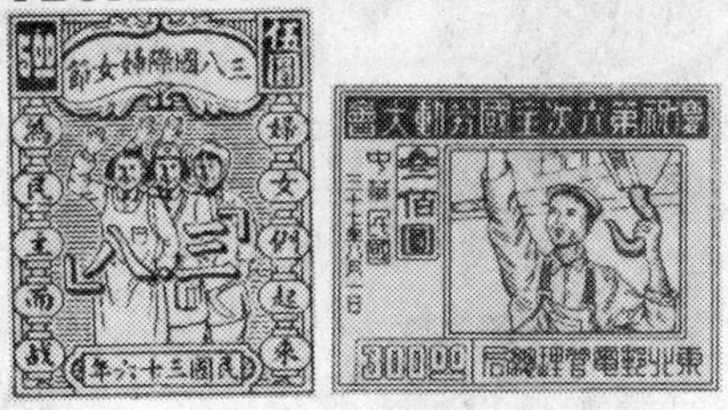

Mao Tse-tung

MANCHUKUO

Temple

The first 3 characters are common to many Manchukuo stamps.

Emperor Pu-Yi

The last 3 characters are common to other Manchukuo stamps

Orchid Crest

Manchukuo stamp without these elements

JAPAN

Chrysanthemum Crest

Country Name

Japanese stamps without these elements

RYUKYU ISLANDS

Country Name

PHILIPPINES (Japanese Occupation)

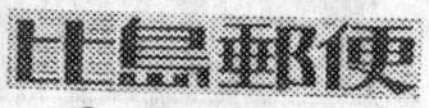
Country Name

NORTH BORNEO (Japanese Occupation)

Indicates Japanese Occupation

Country Name

MALAYA (Japanese Occupation)

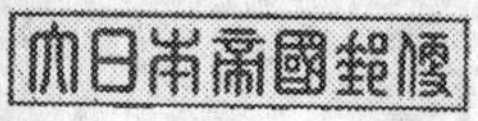
Indicates Japanese Occupation

Country Name

BURMA (Japanese Occupation)

Indicates Japanese Occupation

Country Name

Other Burma Japanese Occupation stamps without these elements

Burmese Script

KOREA

These two characters, in any order, are common to stamps from the Republic of Korea (South Korea) or the unlisted stamps of the People's Democratic Republic of Korea (North Korea)

This series of four characters can be found on the stamps of both Koreas.

Yin Yang appears on some stamps

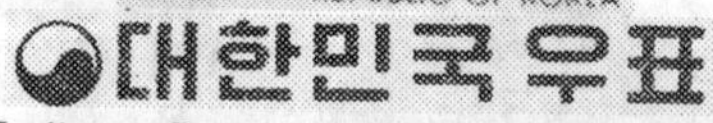
Indicates Republic of Korea (South Korea)

THAILAND

Country Name

King Prajadhipok and Chao P'ya Chakri

CENTRAL AND EASTERN ASIAN INSCRIPTIONS

INDIA - FEUDATORY STATES

Alwar

Bhor

Bundi

Similar stamps come with different designs in corners and differently drawn daggers (at center of circle)

Faridkot

Hyderabad

Similar stamps exist with straight line frame around stamp, and also with different central design which is inscribed "Postage" or "Post & Receipt."

Indore

Jammu & Kashmir

Jhalawar

Nowanuggur

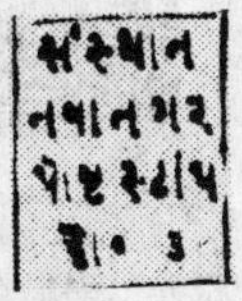

Rajpeepla

Soruth

BANGLADESH

NEPAL

Similar stamps are smaller, have squares in upper corners and have five or nine characters in central bottom panel

TANNU TUVA

ISRAEL

GEORGIA

ARMENIA

The four characters are found somewhere on pictorial stamps. On some stamps only the middle two are found.

ARABIC INSCRIPTIONS

AFGHANISTAN

Many early Afghanistan stamps show Tiger's head, many of these have ornaments protruding from outer ring, others show inscriptions in black

Arabic Script

Mosque Gate & Crossed Cannons

BAHRAIN

EGYPT

IRAN

Country Name

Note Crown

Lion with Sword

JORDAN

LEBANON

Similar types have denominations at top and slightly different design

LIBYA

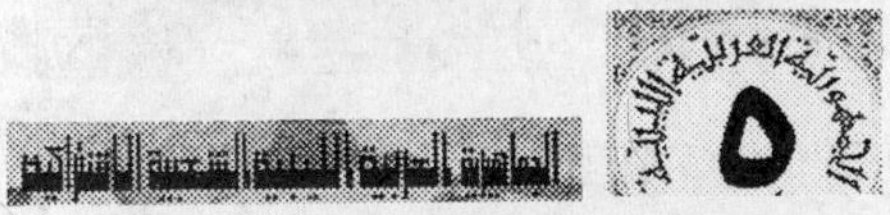

Country Name in various styles

Other Libya stamps show Eagle and Shield (head facing either direction) or Red, White and Black Shield (with or without eagle in center).

SAUDI ARABIA

Note Tughra (Central design)

Palm Tree and Swords

SYRIA

THRACE

YEMEN

PAKISTAN - Bahawalpur

Country Name in top panel, star and crescent

TURKEY

Star & Crescent

Tughra (similar tughras can be found on stamps of Afghanistan and Saudi Arabia)

Mohammed V

Mustafa Kemal

Plane, Star and Crescent

TURKEY IN ASIA

Other Turkey in Asia pictorials show star & crescent

GREEK INSCRIPTIONS

GREECE

Country Name in various styles
(Some Crete stamps overprinted with the Greece country name are listed in Crete.)

Lepta

ΔΡΑΧΜΗ ΔΡΑΧΜΑΙ ΛΕΠΤΟΝ

Drachma Drachmas Lepton

Abbreviated Country Name ΕΛΛ

Other forms of Country Name

No country name

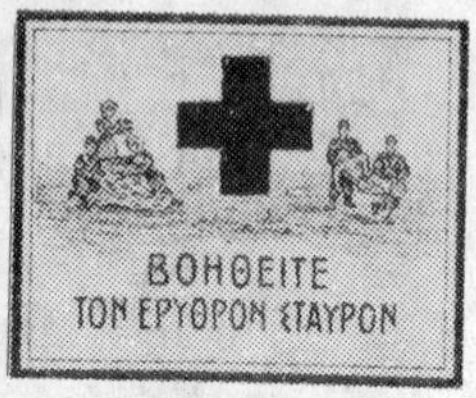

CRETE

Country Name

These words are on other stamps

Grosion

Crete stamps with a surcharge that have the year "1922" are listed under Greece.

EPIRUS

Country Name

IONIAN ISLANDS

CYRILLIC INSCRIPTIONS

RUSSIA

Postage Stamp

Imperial Eagle

Postage in various styles

Abbreviation for Kopeck 

 Abbreviation for Ruble

 Russia

Abbreviation for Russian Soviet Federated Socialist Republic

Abbreviation for Union of Soviet Socialist Republics

RUSSIA - Army of the North

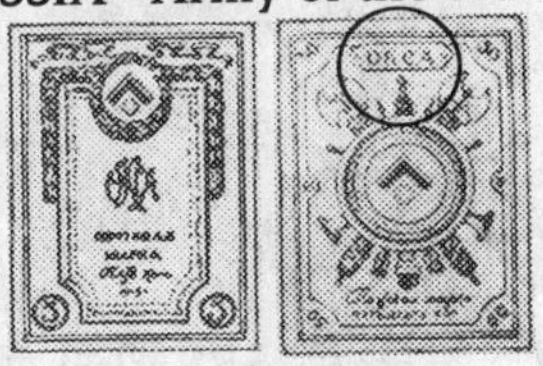

"OKCA"

RUSSIA - Wenden

RUSSIAN OFFICES IN THE TURKISH EMPIRE

These letters appear on other stamps of the Russian offices.

The unoverprinted version of this stamp and a similar stamp were overprinted by various countries (see below).

ARMENIA

FAR EASTERN REPUBLIC

Country Name

SOUTH RUSSIA

Country Name

FINLAND

Circles and Dots on stamps similar to Imperial Russia issues

BATUM

Forms of Country Name

TRANSCAUCASIAN FEDERATED REPUBLICS

Abbreviation for Country Name

KAZAKHSTAN

Country Name

KYRGYZSTAN

Counrty Name

ROMANIA

TADJIKISTAN

Counrty Name & Abbreviation

UKRAINE

Country Name in various forms

The trident appears on many stamps, usually as an overprint.

Abbreviation for Ukrainian Soviet Socialist Republic

WESTERN UKRAINE

Abbreviation for Country Name

AZERBAIJAN

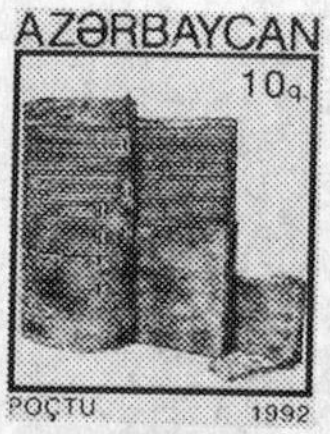

Country Name

Azerbaijan Soviet Socialist Republic

MONTENEGRO

Country Name in various forms

Abbreviation for country name

No country name (A similar Montenegro stamp without country name has same vignette.)

SERBIA

Country Name in various forms

Abbreviation for country name

YUGOSLAVIA

Showing country name

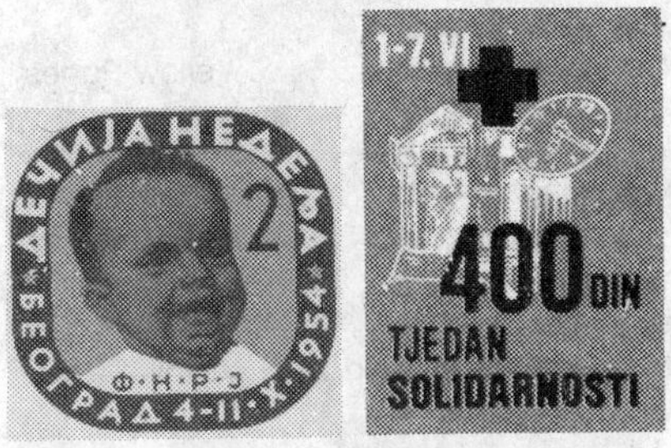

No Country Name

MACEDONIA

Country Name

BULGARIA

Country Name Postage

Stotinka Abbreviation for Stotinki

Stotinki (plural)

Country Name in various forms and styles

НР България

No country name

Abbreviation for Lev, leva

MONGOLIA

Country name in one word

Tugrik in Cyrillic

Country name in two words

Mung in Cyrillic

Mung in Mongolian

Tugrik in Mongolian

Arms

No Country Name

INDEX TO ADVERTISERS – 1996 VOLUME 2

MENTION SCOTT WHEN RESPONDING TO ADVERTISEMENTS!

1996
Volume 2
DEALER DIRECTORY YELLOW PAGE LISTINGS

This section of your Scott Catalogue contains advertisements to help you conveniently find what you need, when you need it...!

Accessories

H & S ROGG
P.O. Box 1076
Port Richey, FL 34673-1076
813-848-7697

FREEWAY STAMP SUPPLIES
635 S. Raymond Ave.
Suite D
Fullerton, CA 92631
714-447-8100 or 800-447-8105
714-447-8100 FAX

Aerophilately

HENRY GITNER PHILATELISTS INC.
P.O. Box 3077-S
Middletown, NY 10940
914-343-5151/800-947-8267
914-343-0068 FAX

Accessories

Albania

FRANK GEIGER PHILATELISTS
242 W. Saddle River Road
Suite 5
Upper Saddle River,
NJ 07458-2620
201-236-8122
201-236-8133 FAX

Albums

VIDIFORMS COMPANY INC.
Showgard House
110 Brenner Drive
Congers, NY 10920
914-268-4005
914-268-5324 FAX

Albums & Accessories

THE KEEPING ROOM
P.O. Box 257
Trumbull, CT 06611-0257
203-372-8436

Andorra

FRANK GEIGER PHILATELISTS
242 W. Saddle River Road
Suite 5
Upper Saddle River,
NJ 07458-2620
201-236-8122
201-236-8133 FAX

Andorra-French

JOE HARRIS
P.O. Box 13430
Baltimore, MD 21203
410-732-4791

Appraisals

APX
P.O. Box 952
Yakima, WA 98907
509-452-9517

FOUNTAIN SQUARE STAMP & COIN INC.
27 Fountain Square Plaza
Cincinnati, OH 45202
513-621-6696
513-621-3901 FAX

UNIQUE ESTATE APPRAISALS
1937 NE Broadway
Portland, OR 97232
503-287-4200

Approvals

THE STAMP ACT
Rt. 1 P.O. Box 93
East Orland, ME 04431
800-743-7832

Approvals - Personalized

THE KEEPING ROOM
P.O. Box 257
Trumbull, CT 06611-0257
203-372-8436

Approvals - Worldwide

Approvals - Topicals

STUART KATZ
P.O. Box 656 SM
Middleton, MA 01949
508-777-2327

Approvals - Worldwide

49ER STAMP CO.
P.O. Box 416
Lebanon, NH 03766

M & H DAVISON
Box 510 - T
South Sutton, NH 03273-0510

ROSS WETREICH INC.
P.O. Box 1300
Valley Stream, NY 11582-1300
516-825-8974

Argentina - Ducks

METROPOLITAN STAMP CO. of CHICAGO, INC.
P.O. Box 1133
Chicago, IL 60690-1133
815-439-0142
815-439-0143 FAX

Armenia

FRANK GEIGER PHILATELISTS
242 W. Saddle River Road
Suite 5
Upper Saddle River,
NJ 07458-2620
201-236-8122
201-236-8133 FAX

Approvals - Worldwide

Asia

ALLKOR STAMP COMPANY
Box 1346
Port Washington, NY 11050
516-883-3296 TELEPHONE & FAX

REGENCY STAMPS, LTD.
Le Chateau Village #106
10411 Clayton Road
St. Louis, MO 63131
800-782-0066
314-997-2231 FAX

MICHAEL ROGERS, INC.
199 E. Welbourne Ave.
Winter Park, FL 32789
407-644-2290
407-645-4434 FAX

Auction House

B TRADING CO.
114 Quail Street
Albany, NY 12206
518-465-3497 TELEPHONE & FAX

REGENCY PHILATELIC AUCTIONS, LTD.
LeChateau Village #106
10411 Clayton Road
St. Louis, MO 63131
800-782-0066
314-997-2231 FAX

Auctions

CEE-JAY STAMP AUCTIONS,INC.
P.O. Box 321
Waldorf, MD 20604
301-843-2022
301-705-7255 FAX

Auctions

CHARLES G. FIRBY AUCTIONS
6695 Highland Road Suite #107
Waterford, MI 48327
810-666-5333
810-666-5020 FAX

HARMER-SCHAU AUCTION GALLERIES INC.
617A Second Street
Petaluma, CA 94952
707-778-6454
707-763-6772 FAX

STAMP CENTER/DUTCH COUNTRY AUCTIONS
4115 Concord Pike
Wilmington, DE 19803
302-478-8740
302-478-8779 FAX

Austria

JOSEPH EDER
P.O. Box 5517
Hamden, CT 06518
203-281-0742
203-230-2410 FAX

FRANK GEIGER PHILATELISTS
242 W. Saddle River Road
Suite 5
Upper Saddle River,
NJ 07458-2620
201-236-8122
201-236-8133 FAX

HENRY GITNER PHILATELISTS INC.
P.O. Box 3077-S
Middletown, NY 10940
914-343-5151/800-947-8267
914-343-0068 FAX

Auctions

SCOTT®

CATALOGUE TABS

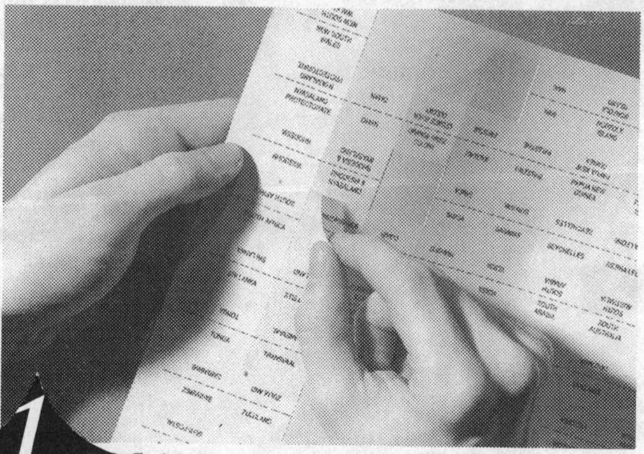

1 Select and peel tab off sheet.

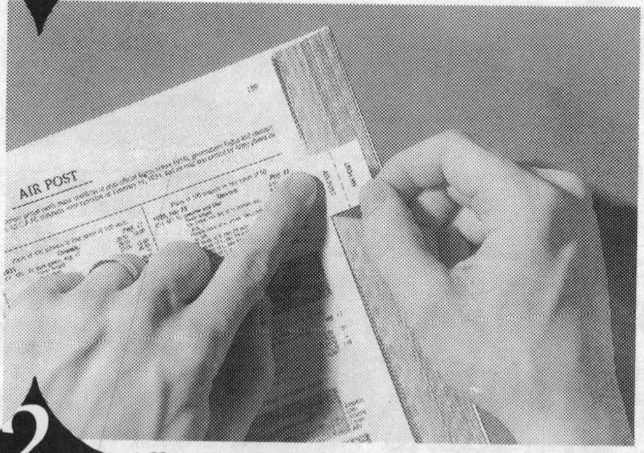

2 Affix a portion of the tab to the appropriate page. Fold tab in half at the dotted line.

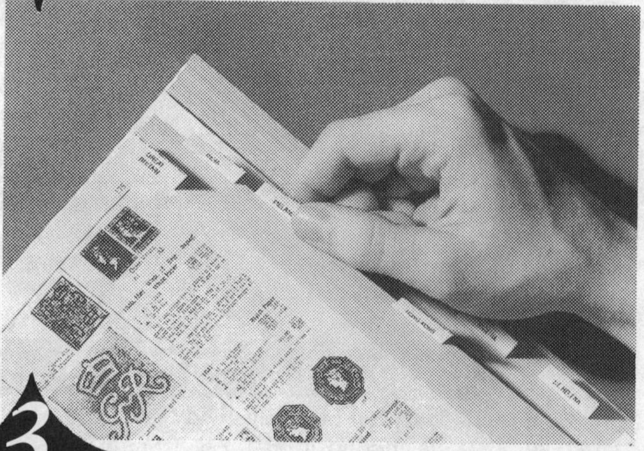

3 Use tabs to reference catalogue listings. Blank tabs also included.

Scott Catalogue Tabs make looking up listings as easy as 1-2-3!

Tabs are sold for each volume of the catalogue, plus the Specialized and the Classic.

Item No.		Price
CLGT1A	Volume 1A	$2.95
CLGT1B	Volume 1B	$2.95
CLGT2	Volume 2	$2.95
CLGT3	Volume 3	$2.95
CLGT4	Volume 4	$2.95
CLGT5	Volume 5	$2.95
CLGT6	U.S. Specialized	$2.95
CLGTC	Classic	$2.95

FOR PRODUCT AND ORDERING INFORMATION
CALL
1-800-572-6885

Available from your favorite dealer or direct from:

Scott Publishing Co.
P.O. Box 828
Sidney OH 45365

Austria

JOE HARRIS
P.O. Box 13430
Baltimore, MD 21203
410-732-4791

HUNGARIA STAMP EXCHANGE
P.O. Box 3024
Andover, MA 01810
508-682-0242
508-794-2567 FAX

R. SCHNEIDER
Box 23049
Belleville, IL 62223
618-277-8543
618-277-1050 FAX

PACIFIC CREST STAMPS
P.O. Box 960
Venice, CA 90294-0960
310-577-2076 TELEPHONE & FAX

Autographs

JAMES REEVES
P.O. Box 219SP
Huntingdon, PA 16652
814-643-5497 TELEPHONE & FAX

Automatic Album Update Service

DELAWARE VALLEY STAMP CO.
69 Strasburg Road
Atglen, PA 19310
610-593-6684

Azerbaijan

FRANK GEIGER PHILATELISTS
242 W. Saddle River Road
Suite 5
Upper Saddle River,
NJ 07458-2620
201-236-8122
201-236-8133 FAX

Baltic States

HENRY GITNER PHILATELISTS INC.
P.O. Box 3077-S
Middletown, NY 10940
914-343-5151/800-947-8267
914-343-0068 FAX

JOE HARRIS
P.O. Box 13430
Baltimore, MD 21203
410-732-4791

Belarus

FRANK GEIGER PHILATELISTS
242 W. Saddle River Road
Suite 5
Upper Saddle River,
NJ 07458-2620
201-236-8122
201-236-8133 FAX

Belgium

FRANK GEIGER PHILATELISTS
242 W. Saddle River Road
Suite 5
Upper Saddle River,
NJ 07458-2620
201-236-8122
201-236-8133 FAX

Belgium

HENRY GITNER PHILATELISTS INC.
P.O. Box 3077-S
Middletown, NY 10940
914-343-5151/800-947-8267
914-343-0068 FAX

JOE HARRIS
P.O. Box 13430
Baltimore, MD 21203
410-732-4791

Belgium-New Issues

BELGIUM STAMP AGENCY IN NORTH AMERICA
One Unicover Center
Cheyenne, WY 82008-0026
800-443-4225
800-628-3123 FAX

Booklets

GERSON'S INT'L INC.
520 SW Yamhill Street, Suite #402
Portland, OR 97204
503-228-5233
503-228-5288 FAX

Brazil

FRANK GEIGER PHILATELISTS
242 W. Saddle River Road
Suite 5
Upper Saddle River,
NJ 07458-2620
201-236-8122
201-236-8133 FAX

Bulgaria

FRANK GEIGER PHILATELISTS
242 W. Saddle River Road
Suite 5
Upper Saddle River,
NJ 07458-2620
201-236-8122
201-236-8133 FAX

HUNGARIA STAMP EXCHANGE
P.O. Box 3024
Andover, MA 01810
508-682-0242
508-794-2567 FAX

China

JUNO STAMPS
1765 Juno Avenue
St. Paul, MN 55116
800-714-3469
612-699-2510 FAX

China - All

FRANK GEIGER PHILATELISTS
242 W. Saddle River Road
Suite 5
Upper Saddle River,
NJ 07458-2620
201-236-8122
201-236-8133 FAX

China - Mainland

MICHAEL ROGERS, INC.
199 E. Welbourne Ave.
Winter Park, FL 32789
407-644-2290
407-645-4434 FAX

China - Taiwan

MICHAEL ROGERS, INC.
199 E. Welbourne Ave.
Winter Park, FL 32789
407-644-2290
407-645-4434 FAX

Chinese Literature

MICHAEL ROGERS, INC.
199 E. Welbourne Ave.
Winter Park, FL 32789
407-644-2290
407-645-4434 FAX

China,Peoples Republic-New Issues

CHINA STAMP AGENCY IN NORTH AMERICA
One Unicover Center
Cheyenne, WY 82008-0003
800-443-4225
800-628-3123 FAX

Collections

GAYLAND BIRD
Box 8073
Dept. S
Asheville, NC 28814
704-645-6949 TELEPHONE & FAX

HENRY GITNER PHILATELISTS INC.
P.O. Box 3077-S
Middletown, NY 10940
914-343-5151/800-947-8267
914-343-0068 FAX

Costa Rica - Ducks

METROPOLITAN STAMP CO. of CHICAGO, INC.
P.O. Box 1133
Chicago, IL 60690-1133
815-439-0142
815-439-0143 FAX

Covers - Asia

MICHAEL ROGERS, INC.
199 E. Welbourne Ave.
Winter Park, FL 32789
407-644-2290
407-645-4434 FAX

Covers - Worldwide

MICHAEL ROGERS, INC.
199 E. Welbourne Ave.
Winter Park, FL 32789
407-644-2290
407-645-4434 FAX

Covers - Zeppelins

MICHAEL ROGERS, INC.
199 E. Welbourne Ave.
Winter Park, FL 32789
407-644-2290
407-645-4434 FAX

Croatia

FRANK GEIGER PHILATELISTS
242 W. Saddle River Road
Suite 5
Upper Saddle River,
NJ 07458-2620
201-236-8122
201-236-8133 FAX

Czechoslovakia

FRANK GEIGER PHILATELISTS
242 W. Saddle River Road
Suite 5
Upper Saddle River,
NJ 07458-2620
201-236-8122
201-236-8133 FAX

HUNGARIA STAMP EXCHANGE
P.O. Box 3024
Andover, MA 01810
508-682-0242
508-794-2567 FAX

SOCIETY FOR CZECHOSLOVAK PHILATELY, INC.
Tom Cossaboom, SCP Secretary
Box 25332
Scott Air Force Base, IL 62225
(USA)

Czech - New Issues

CZECH REPUBLIC STAMP AGENCY IN NORTH AMERICA
One Unicover Center
Cheyenne, WY 82008-0024
800-443-4225
800-628-3123 FAX

Dead Countries

MICHAEL ROGERS, INC.
199 E. Welbourne Ave.
Winter Park, FL 32789
407-644-2290
407-645-4434 FAX

Collections

...OT GOING ON
...PAGES OF
...P MONTHLY

Private Viewing

A full-color, two page spread showcasing some of the world's most beautiful and intriguing stamps.

Catalogue Update

The most authoritative new issue listing of its kind, showing more stamps in more detail than other philatelic publications. Every month more than 800 stamps are catalogued and identified from hundreds of countries. The listings are presented in the same format as the Scott Catalogue, complete with Scott numbers and illustrations.

Just History

An entertaining glimpse of the people, places and events behind the stamps. In this age of high speed stamp production and computer generated images, Just History is a refreshing change of pace.

Amazing Stamp Stories

A full-color story page done in the classic illustrated style of Ripley's "Believe It or Not." There's a new story each month dealing with some of the world's greatest issues, remarkable stamp discoveries and the people associated with them.

SCOTT

FREE LOOK NO COST AND NO OBLIGATION

For a free look at Scott Stamp Monthly, call 1-800-488-5351. If you decide to subscribe you'll receive 11 more issues for the low rate of $17.95. If you decide not to subscribe, write cancel on the bill and return it and owe nothing. The free issue is yours to keep!

Discount Supplies

VERUS DISCOUNT STAMP CO.
P.O. Box 187
West Chicago, IL 60186
708-896-8938

Duck Stamps

TRENTON STAMP & COIN CO.
1804 RT. 33
Trenton, NJ 08690
800-446-8664
609-587-8664 FAX

Europa

GERSON'S INT'L INC.
520 SW Yamhill Street, Suite #402
Portland, OR 97204
503-228-5233
503-228-5288 FAX

Europe

REGENCY STAMPS, LTD.
Le Chateau Village #106
10411 Clayton Road
St. Louis, MO 63131
800-782-0066
314-997-2231 FAX

Europe-West

PACIFIC CREST STAMPS
P.O. Box 960
Venice, CA 90294-0960
310-577-2076 TELEPHONE & FAX

France

JOSEPH EDER
P.O. Box 5517
Hamden, CT 06518
203-281-0742
203-230-2410 FAX

German Area

R. SCHNEIDER
Box 23049
Belleville, IL 62223
618-277-8543
618-277-1050 FAX

Germany

JOSEPH EDER
P.O. Box 5517
Hamden, CT 06518
203-281-0742
203-230-2410 FAX

Inverted Centers - World

MARTIN SELLINGER
Box 47
White Plains, NY 10602
914-948-4246
914-682-7384 FAX

Latin America

BROOKSIDE STAMPS
P.O. Box 412
Worthington, OH 43085
614-436-0524

Lots & Collections

DAVE ALLEGO
P.O. Box 13
Ambridge, PA 15003-0013
412-266-4255

GAYLAND BIRD
Box 8073
Dept. S
Asheville, NC 28814
704-645-6949 TELEPHONE & FAX

Mail Bid Sales

CONNEXUS
P.O. Box 453
Guilford, CT 06437
203-453-4298
203-458-2220 FAX

JUNO STAMPS
1765 Juno Avenue
St. Paul, MN 55116
800-714-3469
612-699-2510 FAX

QUEST INTERNATIONAL
P.O. Box 139A,
Thames Ditton,
Surrey, KT7 OER,
UNITED KINGDOM
44-181-398-7740
44-181-398-4661 FAX

Mail Order

B & D HOBBIES
P.O. Box 4
Gladstone, OR 97027
503-656-3149

BOB BECK
Box 3209 Harbourtown Station
Hilton Head Island, SC 29928
803-671-3241

Mail Order

LOG HOUSE PHILATELIST
Box 267 Harju Road
Grand Marais, MI 49839

SHARI'S STAMPS
104-3 Old Highway 40 #130
O'Fallon, MO 63366
800-382-3597

Middle East - Arab

THE PERFECT PERF
P.O. Box 16127
Pittsburgh, PA 15242
412-429-1618
412-561-0660 FAX

Mounts

VIDIFORMS COMPANY INC.
Showgard House
110 Brenner Drive
Congers, NY 10920
914-268-4005
914-268-5324 FAX

New Issues

DAVIDSON'S STAMP SERVICE
P.O. Box 20502
Indianapolis, IN 46220
317-255-9408

New Issues - Retail

BOMBAY PHILATELIC CO., INC.
P.O. Box 7719
Delray Beach, FL 33484-7719
407-499-7990
407-499-7553 FAX

GERSON'S INT'L INC.
520 SW Yamhill Street, Suite #402
Portland, OR 97204
503-228-5233
503-228-5288 FAX

HERRICK STAMP CO.
P.O. Box 219
Lawrence, NY 11559
516-569-3959
516-569-7093 FAX

STANLEY M. PILLER
3351 Grand Ave.
Oakland, CA 94610
510-465-8290
510-465-7121 FAX

THE NEW ISSUE CLUB
P.O. Box 1926
Beaverton, OR 97075

New Issues - Scandinavia

NORDICA
P.O. Box 284
Old Bethpage, NY 11804
516-931-3485 TELEPHONE & FAX

Philatelic Societies

AMERICAN PHILATELIC SOCIETY
Dept TZ P.O. Box 8000
State College, PA 16803
814-237-3803
814-237-6128 FAX

SOCIETY FOR CZECHOSLOVAK PHILATELY, INC.
Tom Cossaboom, SCP Secretary
Box 25332
Scott Air Force Base, IL 62225
(USA)

Postcards

AURORA BOREALIS STAMP & SUPPLY
2273 S. 65th Street
Milwaukee, WI 53219
800-362-1010
414-543-0340 FAX

Proofs & Essays

HENRY GITNER PHILATELISTS INC.
P.O. Box 3077-S
Middletown, NY 10940
914-343-5151/800-947-8267
914-343-0068 FAX

E. JOSEPH MCCONNELL INC.
P.O. Box 683
Monroe, NY 10950
914-496-5916
914-782-0347 FAX

Publications - Collector

GLOBAL STAMP NEWS
P.O. Box 97
Sidney, OH 45365-0097
513-492-3183
513-492-6514 FAX

MEKEEL'S WEEKLY STAMP NEWS
Box 5050-sy
White Plains, NY 10602
800-MEKEEL-1
914-997-7261 FAX

Mail Bid Sales

New Issues

Romania

GEORGE ARGHIR
Detunata 17-27 P.O. Box 521
RO-3400 Cluj-Napoca 9
ROMANIA
+40-64-194410 TELEPHONE/FAX

Safes - Stamps

KINGSBERY MANUFACTURING CORP.
715 West Zavala Street
Crystal City, TX 78839
800-445-0763

Stamp Accessories

BROOKLYN GALLERY COIN & STAMP
8725 4th Avenue
Brooklyn, NY 11209
718-745-5701
718-745-2775 FAX

Stamp Packets

AURORA BOREALIS STAMP & SUPPLY
2273 S. 65th Street
Milwaukee, WI 53219
800-362-1010
414-543-0340 FAX

Stamp Shows

BEACH PHILATELICS
P.O. Box 150
Virginia Beach, VA 23458-0150
804-425-8566 TELEPHONE & FAX

CONNECTICUT STAMP SHOWS
Box 5050-sy
White Plains, NY 10602
800-MEKEEL-1
914-997-7261 FAX

HIGHTSTOWN SECOND SATURDAY BOURSE
Monmouth St.(RTE.633) opposite
Ramada Inn
Exit 8 New Jersey Turnpike
Hightstown, NJ 08520

AL SOTH
P.O. Box 22081
Milwaukie, OR 97269
503-794-0956

STAMP STORES

Arizona

B.J.'S STAMPS / BARBARA J. JOHNSON
6342 W. Bell Road
Glendale, AZ 85308
602-878-2080
602-412-3456 FAX

California

ASHTREE STAMP & COIN
2410 N. Blackstone
Fresno, CA 93703
209-227-7167

BROSIUS STAMP & COIN
2105 Main Street
Santa Monica, CA 90405
310-396-7480

FISCHER - WOLK PHILATELICS
24771 "G" Alicia Parkway
Laguna Hills, CA 92653
714-837-2932

HERB'S STAMP CENTER
11748 Washington Place
West Los Angeles, CA 90066
310-397-3883

KENRICH CO.
9418-A Las Tunas Drive
Temple City, CA 91780
818-286-3888
818-286-6035 FAX

NATICK STAMPS & HOBBIES
405 S. Myrtle Avenue
Monrovia, CA 91016
818-305-7333
818-305-7335 FAX

STANLEY M. PILLER
3351 Grand Ave.
Oakland, CA 94610
510-465-8290
510-465-7121 FAX

THE STAMP GALLERY
1515 Locust Street
Walnut Creek, CA 94596
510-944-9111

Colorado

ACKLEY'S ROCKS & STAMPS
3230 N. Stone Ave.
Colorado Springs, CO 80907
719-633-1153

SHOWCASE STAMPS
3865 Wadsworth Blvd.
Wheat Ridge, CO 80033
303-425-9252
303-425-7410 FAX

Connecticut

J&B STAMPS & COLLECTIBLES
41 Colony Street
Meriden, CT 06451
203-235-7634

MILLER'S STAMP SHOP
41 New London Turnpike
Uncasville, CT 06382
203-848-0468 TELEPHONE & FAX

Washington, D.C.

WOODWARD & LOTHROP STAMP DEPT.
11th & G St. NW
Washington, DC 20013
202-879-8028

Florida

BEACH STAMP & COIN
971 E. Eau Gallie Blvd.
and Highway A1A Suite G
Melbourne Beach, FL 32937
407-777-1666

ARLINGTON STAMP & COIN CO.
1350 University Blvd.,North
Jacksonville, FL 32211-5226
904-743-1776

HAUSER'S COIN & STAMP
3425 S. Florida Ave.
Lakeland, FL 33803
813-647-2052
813-644-5738 FAX

HUGO'S STAMP EMPORIUM
P.O. Box 5527
Lake Worth, FL 33466
407-966-7517

INTERCONTINENTAL/RICARDO DEL CAMPO
7379 Coral Way
Miami, FL 33155-1402
305-264-4983
305-262-2919 FAX

JACK'S COINS & STAMPS
801 Northlake Blvd.
North Palm Beach, FL 33408
407-844-7710

Florida

JERRY SIEGEL/STAMPS FOR COLLECTORS
1920 E. Hallandale Beach Blvd.
Suite 507
Hallandale, FL 33009
305-457-0422 TELEPHONE & FAX

NEW ENGLAND STAMP
4987 Tamiami Trail East
Village Falls Professional Ctr
Naples, Fl 33962
813-732-8000
813-732-7701 FAX

ST. JOHN'S STAMP SHOP
2 Aviles Street
St. Augustine, FL 32084
904-829-9673

SARASOTA STAMP DEPOT
1564 Main Street
Sarasota, FL 34236
813-365-5415

THE STAMP PLACE
576 First Avenue North
St. Petersburg, FL 33701
813-894-4082

WINTER PARK STAMP SHOP
199 E. Welbourne Ave.
Suite 201
Winter Park, FL 32789
800-845-1819
407-628-0091 FAX

Florida

WHEN VISITING CENTRAL FLORIDA BE SURE TO STOP BY...

Send 32¢ long SASE for our
MONTHLY NEWSLETTER of stamps for sale!

Michael Rogers - Alvin Hintz

WINTER PARK STAMP SHOP
199 E. Welbourne Ave., 2nd floor, Winter Park, FL 32789
Phone 407-628-1120 • FAX 407-628-0091
1-800-845-1819
Open Mon. through Fri. 10am-6pm • Sat. 10am-3pm (4 miles North of Orlando)

Georgia

BLUE RIDGE STAMP CO.

801 E. MAIN STREET
POST OFFICE BOX 2230
BLUE RIDGE, GA 30513
1-800-61-STAMP
FAX 706-632-3908

WE OFFER A FULL LINE OF STAMPS & SUPPLIES FOR THE BEGINNER AND THE ADVANCED COLLECTOR.

WE OFFER A NEW ISSUE SERVICE UNIQUE FROM OTHERS: NO MINIMUMS AND WE STOCK THE COUNTRIES WE SERVICE.

Our 4500 Sq. Ft. Store Is Located In The N. Georgia Mtns. Surrounded By Antique, Craft, and Specialty Shops.

B.I.A.
CSA

STAMP STORES

Georgia

STAMPS UNLIMITED OF GEORGIA
133 Carnegie Way
Room 250
Atlanta, GA 30303
404-688-9161

Illinois

THE COLLECTORS DEN / L.V. FISCHER
P.O. Box 88148
Carol Stream, IL 60188-0148
708-545-9930 TELEPHONE & FAX

DON CLARK'S STAMPS
937 1/2 W. Galena Blvd.
Aurora, IL 60506
708-896-4606

H.C. STAMP & COIN CO.
10 Crystal Lake Plaza
Crystal Lake, IL 60014
815-459-3940

MARSHALL FIELD'S STAMP DEPT.
111 N. State Street
Chicago, IL 60602
312-781-4237

STAMP KING / RICHARD E. DREWS AUCTIONS
7139 W. Higgins Road
Chicago, IL 60656
312-775-2100
312-792-9116 FAX

Indiana

J & J COINS & STAMPS
7019 Calumet Avenue
Hammond, IN 46324
219-932-5818

KNIGHT STAMP & COIN COMPANY
301 Main Street
Hobart, IN 46342
800-634-2646

VILLAGE STAMP AND COIN
40 E. Cedar
Zionsville, IN 46077
317-873-6762

Kentucky

COLLECTORS STAMPS LTD.
4012 DuPont Circle #313
Louisville, KY 40207
502-897-9045

TREASURE ISLAND COINS & STAMPS
232 W. Broadway
Louisville, KY 40202
502-583-1222

Louisiana

LIVINGSTON STAMP & RARE BOOK CO.
13595 Henry Drive
Denham Springs, LA 70726
504-665-7815

Maryland

BALTIMORE COIN & STAMP EXCHANGE INC.
10194 Baltimore National Pike
Unit 104
Ellicott City, MD 21042
410-418-8282
410-418-4813 FAX

BULLDOG STAMP CO.
4641 Montgomery Ave.
Bethesda, MD 20814
301-654-1138

DELMARVA STAMPS & COLLECTIBLES
23 Salisbury Mall
Civic Avenue
Salisbury, MD 21801
410-742-7077

STAMP & COIN WORLD
511-A Delaware Avenue
Towson, MD 21286
410-828-4465 or 800-452-4560

Massachusetts

BATTLE GREEN STAMP COMPANY
4 Muzzey Street
Lexington, MA 02173
617-862-2330

FALMOUTH STAMP & COIN
11 Town Hall Square
Falmouth, MA 02540
508-548-7075 or 800-341-3701

J & N FORTIER
484 Main Street
Worcester, MA 01608
508-757-3657

KAPPY'S COINS & STAMPS
534 Washington St.
Norwood, MA 02062
617-762-5552
617-762-3292 FAX

ARLINGTON WARREN COLLECTIBLES
89 Warren St.
Arlington, MA 02174
617-641-1640
617-641-0870 FAX

Michigan

AMERICA'S STAMP STOP
23333 Orchard Lake Rd.
Farmington, MI 48334
810-474-4460

BIRMINGHAM COIN AND JEWELRY
1287 S. Woodward
Birmingham, MI 48009
810-642-1234
810-642-4207 FAX

MEL COON STAMPS
3833 Twelve Mile
Berkley, MI 48072
810-398-6085
810-398-4549 FAX

LIBERTY COINS & STAMPS
300 Frandor Avenue
Lansing, MI 48912
517-351-4720

THE MOUSE AND SUCH
696 N. Mill Street
Plymouth, MI 48170
313-454-1515

Minnesota

CROSSROADS STAMP SHOP
2211 West 54th Street
Minneapolis, MN 55419-1515
612-928-0119

JW STAMP COMPANY
5300 250th Street
Saint Cloud, MN 56301
612-252-2996

Missouri

KNIGHT'S COINS & STAMPS
323 South Ave.
Springfield, MO 65806
417-862-3018

REGENCY STAMPS, LTD.
Le Chateau Village #106
10411 Clayton Road
St. Louis, MO 63131
800-782-0066
314-997-2231 FAX

Nebraska

TUVA ENTERPRISES
209 So. 72nd Street
Omaha, NE 68114
402-397-9937

New Hampshire

BRUNELLE STAMPS & COINS
25 East Broadway
Derry, NH 03038
603-432-2658
603-437-7279 FAX

New Jersey

A.D.A STAMP CO., INC.
910 Boyd Street
Toms River, NJ 08753
908-240-1131
908-240-2620 FAX

BERGEN STAMPS & COLLECTABLES
717 American Legion Dr.
Teaneck, NJ 07666
201-836-8987

CHARLES STAMP SHOP
47 Old Post Road
Edison, NJ 08817
908-985-1071
908-819-0549 FAX

COLONIAL COINS & STAMPS
1865 Rt. #35
Wall Township, NJ 07719
908-449-4549

FAIRIDGE STAMP INC.
447 Broadway
Westwood, NJ 07675
201-666-8869

RON RITZER STAMPS & COLLECTIBLES
Millburn Mall
2933 Vauxhall Road
Union, NJ 07088
908-687-0007 TELEPHONE & FAX

TRENTON STAMP & COIN CO.
1804 RT. 33
Trenton, NJ 08690
800-446-8664
609-587-8664 FAX

New Mexico

THE CLASSIC COLLECTOR
7102 Menaul Blvd. NE
Albuquerque, NM 87110
505-884-9516

New York

B.B.C. STAMP & COIN INC.
185 East Main St.
P.O. Box 2141
Setauket, NY 11733-0715
516-751-5662

JOHN'S COINS, CARDS & STAMPS INC.
36 West 34th Street
2nd Floor
New York, NY 10001
212-244-2646

LINCOL. COIN & STAMP
33 West Tupper Street
Buffalo, NY 14202
716-856-1884

SUBURBAN STAMPS, COINS AND COLLECTIBLES
120 Kreischer Road
North Syracuse, NY 13212
315-452-0593

VILLAGE STAMPS & COINS
22 Oriskany Blvd.
Yorkville Plaza
Yorkville, NY 13495
315-736-1007 or 800-490-1007

Ohio

CROWN & EAGLE
5303 N. High Street
Columbus, OH 43214
614-436-2042

HILLTOP STAMP SERVICE
P.O. Box 626
Wooster, OH 44691
216-262-5378

J L F STAMP STORE
3041 E. Waterloo Road
Akron, OH 44312
216-628-8343

LAZARUS STAMP DEPT.
141 S. High St.
5th Floor
Columbus, OH 43215
614-463-3214

THE LINK STAMP CO.
3461 E. Livingston Ave.
Columbus, OH 43227
614-237-4125 or 800-546-5726

NEWARK STAMP COMPANY
49 North Fourth Street
Newark, OH 43055
614-349-7900

Oregon

AL'S STAMP & COIN
2132 West 6th
Eugene, OR 97402
503-343-0091

D'S TOYS & HOBBIES
3312 N. Highway 97
Bend, OR 97701
503-389-1330

UNIQUE ESTATE APPRAISALS
1937 NE Broadway
Portland, OR 97232
503-287-4200

STAMP STORES

Pennsylvania

KAUFMANN'S STAMP DEPT.
400 Fifth Ave.
Pittsburgh, PA 15219
412-232-2598

LARRY LEE STAMPS
322 S. Front Street
Wormleysburg, PA 17043
717-763-7605

PENNSYLVANIA STAMP CO.
229 Sixth Street
McKeesport, PA 15132
800-545-6604

PHILLY STAMP & COIN CO. INC.
1804 Chestnut Street
Philadelphia, PA 19103
215-563-7341
215-563-7382 FAX

WORLD OF STAMPS & COINS
Route 611
Fountain Court Mall
Bartonsville, PA 18321
717-688-9829

Rhode Island

PODRAT COIN EXCHANGE INC.
769 Hope Street
Providence, RI 02906
401-861-7640
401-272-3032 FAX

South Carolina

THE STAMP OUTLET
Oakbrook Center #9
Summerville, SC 29484
803-873-4655

Tennessee

HERRON HILL, INC.
5007 Black Road
Suite 140
Memphis, TN 38117-4505
901-683-9644

Texas

ALAMO HEIGHTS STAMP SHOP
1201 Austin Hwy
Suite 128
San Antonio, TX 78209
210-826-4328

ARTEX STAMPS FOR COLLECTORS
3216 W. Park Row
Suite M
Arlington, TX 76013
817-265-8645

AUSTIN STAMP & COIN
13107 F M 969
Austin, TX 78724
512-276-7793

DALLAS STAMP GALLERY
1002 North Central Expressway
Suite 501
Richardson, TX 75080
800-759-9109
214-669-4742 FAX

METROPLEX STAMP CO.
11811 Preston Road At
Forest Lane
Dallas, TX 75230
214-490-1330

Utah

HIGHLAND STAMP SHOP
4835 S. Highland Dr. #1346
Salt Lake City, UT 84117
801-272-1141

Virginia

CENTURY STAMPS & COINS
6436 Brandon Ave.
Springfield, VA 22150
703-569-0739

KENNEDY'S STAMPS & COINS
7059 Brookfield Plaza
Springfield, VA 22150
703-569-7300

LATHEROW & CO. INC.
5054 Lee Highway
Arlington, VA 22207
703-538-2727

PRINCE WILLIAM STAMP & COIN CO.
14011-H St. Germain Dr.
Centreville, VA 22020
703-830-4669

Washington

HIDDEN TREASURES INC.
9960 N.W. Silverdale Way #11
Silverdale, WA 98383
360-692-1999

PEOPLE'S STAMP SERVICE
4132 F. Street
West Bremerton, WA 98312
360-377-1210

RAINIER PHILATELIC INC.
15405 First Avenue South
Burien, WA 98148
206-248-2367

TACOMA MALL BLVD. COIN & STAMP
5225 Tacoma Mall Blvd. E-101
Tacoma, WA 98409
206-472-9632

THE STAMP & COIN PLACE
1310 Commercial
Bellingham, WA 98225
360-676-8720
360-647-6947 FAX

THE STAMP GALLERY
10335 Main Street
Bellevue, WA 98004
206-455-3781 TELEPHONE & FAX

Wisconsin

AURORA BOREALIS STAMP & SUPPLY
2273 S. 65th Street
Milwaukee, WI 53219
800-362-1010
414-543-0340 FAX

HERITAGE STAMPS
11400 W. Bluemound Rd.
Milwaukee, WI 53226
800-231-6080
414-369-0741 FAX

JIM LUKES' STAMP & COIN
815 Jay Street
P.O. Box 1780
Manitowoc, WI 54221
414-682-2324

Supplies

FREEWAY STAMP SUPPLIES
635 S. Raymond Ave.
Suite D
Fullerton, CA 92631
714-447-8100 or 800-447-8105
714-447-8100 FAX

VIDIFORMS COMPANY INC.
Showgard House
110 Brenner Drive
Congers, NY 10920
914-268-4005
914-268-5324 FAX

Supplies & Accessories

BEACH PHILATELICS
P.O. Box 150
Virginia Beach, VA 23458-0150
804-425-8566 TELEPHONE & FAX

GLOBAL STAMP & COIN
460 Ridge Street
Lewiston, NY 14092
800-368-4328
715-754-8513 FAX

Supplies - Mail Order

GOPHER SUPPLY CO.
2499 Rice St. Suite 132
Roseville, MN 55113
612-486-8007
612-486-8441 FAX

STAMPCRAFT
P.O. Box 2425
Santa Clara, CA 95055
800-245-5389
408-241-4440 FAX

Supplies - Protective Sleeves

HOBBY HOUSE DISTRIBUTING
P.O. Box 18025
Indianapolis, IN 46218
317-547-1372

Supplies - Stamps & Coins

GOLD COAST COIN & STAMP SUPPLIES
1007 NE 43rd Street
Ft. Lauderdale, FL 33334
305-565-4688
305-565-4689 FAX

Supplies - Stamps & Coins

M.A. STORCK CO.
652 Congress Street
Portland, ME 04104
800-734-7271

Supplies - U.S. Stamps

CALUMET STAMPS
P.O. Box 83
Griffith, IN 46319
219-924-4836

Topicals

CHARLES P. SCHWARTZ
P.O. Box 165
Mora, MN 55051
612-679-4705

FRANK GEIGER PHILATELISTS
242 W. Saddle River Road
Suite 5
Upper Saddle River,
NJ 07458-2620
201-236-8122
201-236-8133 FAX

Topicals - Animals

BICK INTERNATIONAL
P.O. Box 854
Van Nuys, CA 91408
818-997-6496
818-988-4337 FAX

Topicals - Butterflies

HENRY GITNER PHILATELISTS INC.
P.O. Box 3077-S
Middletown, NY 10940
914-343-5151/800-947-8267
914-343-0068 FAX

Topicals - Churchill

BICK INTERNATIONAL
P.O. Box 854
Van Nuys, CA 91408
818-997-6496
818-988-4337 FAX

Topicals - Columbus

MR. COLUMBUS
Box 1492
Frankenmuth, MI 48734

Topicals - Miscellaneous

Topicals - France

E. JOSEPH MCCONNELL INC.
P.O. Box 683
Monroe, NY 10950
914-496-5916
914-782-0347 FAX

Topicals - Miscellaneous

AKSARBEN TOPICALS
P.O. Box 2033
Council Bluffs, IA 51502-2033
712-322-9061

AURORA BOREALIS STAMP & SUPPLY
2273 S. 65th Street
Milwaukee, WI 53219
800-362-1010
414-543-0340 FAX

DISCOUNT TOPICALS
P.O. Box 74-7435
Rego Park, NY 11374
212-726-8075

GERSON'S INT'L INC.
520 SW Yamhill Street, Suite #402
Portland, OR 97204
503-228-5233
503-228-5288 FAX

MEKEEL'S WEEKLY STAMP NEWS
Box 5050-sy
White Plains, NY 10602
800-MEKEEL-1
914-997-7261 FAX

MINI - ARTS
Estherville, IA 51334
712-362-4710

Topicals - Miscellaneous

THE NEW ISSUE CLUB
P.O. Box 1926
Beaverton, OR 97075

Topicals - Music

AKSARBEN TOPICALS
P.O. Box 2033
Council Bluffs, IA 51502-2033
712-322-9061

Topicals - Transportation

DISCOUNT TOPICALS
P.O. Box 74-7435
Rego Park, NY 11374
212-726-8075

United Nations

BEACH PHILATELICS
P.O. Box 150
Virginia Beach, VA 23458-0150
804-425-8566 TELEPHONE & FAX

United States

BEACH PHILATELICS
P.O. Box 150
Virginia Beach, VA 23458-0150
804-425-8566 TELEPHONE & FAX

Topicals - Miscellaneous

United States - Plate Blocks

BEACH PHILATELICS
P.O. Box 150
Virginia Beach, VA 23458-0150
804-425-8566 TELEPHONE & FAX

Vietnam - North

ALLKOR STAMP COMPANY
Box 1346
Port Washington, NY 11050
516-883-3296 TELEPHONE & FAX

Want Lists

GERSON - REITER INC.
520 SW Yamhill Street, Suite #402
Portland, OR 97204
503-228-5233
503-228-5288 FAX

PACIFIC CREST STAMPS
P.O. Box 960
Venice, CA 90294-0960
310-577-2076 TELEPHONE & FAX

Want Lists - Worldwide

ST. JOHN'S STAMP SHOP
2 Aviles Street
St. Augustine, FL 32084
904-829-9673

Wanted - Estates

TOWN & COUNTRY STAMPS LTD.
P.O. Box 13542-S
St. Louis, MO 63138
314-869-7063
314-869-7851 FAX

Wanted To Buy

FRANK GEIGER PHILATELISTS
242 W. Saddle River Road
Suite 5
Upper Saddle River,
NJ 07458-2620
201-236-8122
201-236-8133 FAX

Western Europe

EDWARD J. MCKIM
1373 Isabelle
Memphis, TN 38122

Wholesale

HENRY GITNER PHILATELISTS INC.
P.O. Box 3077-S
Middletown, NY 10940
914-343-5151/800-947-8267
914-343-0068 FAX

Wholesale - Accessories

SCOTT - EDELMAN SUPPLY CO.
1111 E. Truslow Avenue
Fullerton, CA 92631
714-680-6188
714-680-0962 FAX

Wholesale Collections

A.D.A STAMP CO., INC.
910 Boyd Street
Toms River, NJ 08753
908-240-1131
908-240-2620 FAX

Wholesale Philatelic & Numismatic Accessories

ECONOMICAL WHOLESALE CO.
6 King Philip Road
Worcester, MA 01606
508-853-3127

HARRY EDELMAN
111-37 Lefferts Blvd.
P.O.Box 20140
So. Ozone Park, NY 11420
718-641-2710
718-641-0737 FAX

M. C. CLAYTON
290 East Grand Avenue
S. San Francisco, CA 94080
415-873-7577
415-873-7573 FAX

GLASCOCK, INC.
P.O. Box 18888
San Antonio, TX 78218
210-655-2498
210-655-2585 FAX

GOLD COAST COIN & STAMP SUPPLIES
1007 NE 43rd Street
Ft. Lauderdale, FL 33334
305-565-4688
305-565-4689 FAX

CHARLES R. HEISLER INC.
500 Oak Grove Drive
Lancaster, PA 17601
800-784-6886
717-299-2366 FAX

LEDO SUPPLY CO.
P.O. Box 1749
Sandpoint, ID 83864
800-257-8331

M.A. STORCK CO.
652 Congress Street
Portland, ME 04104
800-734-7271

NORTHERN ILLINOIS COIN & STAMP INC.
122 S. Grove Ave.
Elgin, IL 60120
708-695-0110
708-695-1154 FAX

POLLARD COIN & STAMP SUPPLY CO., INC.
5220 E. 23rd Street
Indianapolis, IN 46218
317-547-1306
317-547-1311 FAX

SCOTT WESTERN
5670 Schaefer Ave. No. L
Chino, CA 91710
909-590-5030
909-465-6368 FAX

Wholesale Supplies

DOUBLE J. STAMPS
P.O. Box 1127
Arlington Heights, IL 60006
708-843-8700
708-843-2878 FAX

JOHN VAN ALSTYNE STAMPS & SUPPLIES
1787 Tribute Rd. Suite J
Sacramento, CA 95815
916-565-0600
916-565-0539 FAX

Worldwide

DAVE ALLEGO
P.O. Box 13
Ambridge, PA 15003-0013
412-266-4255

AMERICAN STAMP & COIN CO.
7225 N. Oracle Rd.
Suite #102
Tucson, AZ 85704
520-297-3456

ROBERT E. BARKER
P.O. Box 888063
Dunwoody, GA 30356
800-833-0217
404-671-8918 FAX

BLUE WATER STAMPS
P.O. Box 20074
Lambton Mall Postal Outlet
Sarnia, Ontario N7S 6J3
CANADA
519-869-8787

MEL COON STAMPS
3833 Twelve Mile
Berkley, MI 48072
810-398-6085
810-398-4549 FAX

GERSON - REITER INC.
520 SW Yamhill Street, Suite #402
Portland, OR 97204
503-228-5233
503-228-5288 FAX

HERITAGE STAMPS
11400 W. Bluemound Rd.
Milwaukee, WI 53226
800-231-6080
414-369-0741 FAX

MARLIN LARSON
217 Country Garden Lane
San Marcos, CA 92069
619-744-1435
619-744-5119 FAX

MCMILLAN & WIFE
2740 Sarver Lane
San Marcos, CA 92069
619-744-1435
619-744-5119 FAX

Worldwide

EDWARD J. MCKIM
1373 Isabelle
Memphis, TN 38122

DAVID TOMERAASEN
P.O. Box 178100
San Diego, CA 92177-8100
619-276-1288
619-274-1200 FAX

Worldwide - Approvals

M & H DAVISON
Box 510 - T
South Sutton, NH 03273-0510

Worldwide - Price Lists

HALL'S STAMPS (ITEX)
P.O. Box 8095
Spokane, WA 99203
509-536-9378 TELEPHONE & FAX

Worldwide - Year Sets

BOMBAY PHILATELIC CO., INC.
P.O. Box 7719
Delray Beach, FL 33484-7719
407-499-7990
407-499-7553 FAX

FRANK GEIGER PHILATELISTS
242 W. Saddle River Road
Suite 5
Upper Saddle River,
NJ 07458-2620
201-236-8122
201-236-8133 FAX

HENRY GITNER PHILATELISTS INC.
P.O. Box 3077-S
Middletown, NY 10940
914-343-5151/800-947-8267
914-343-0068 FAX

D.N. KENROD
6278 N. Federal Hwy. Suite 414
Ft. Lauderdale, FL 33308-1908

Worldwide